Who's Who of American Women

Biographical Reference Works
Published by Marquis Who's Who

Who's Who in America

Who Was Who in America

   Historical Volume (1607-1896)

   Volume I (1897-1942)

   Volume II (1943-1950)

   Volume III (1951-1960)

   Volume IV (1961-1968)

   Volume V (1969-1973)

   Volume VI (1974-1976)

   Volume VII (1977-1981)

Who Was Who in American History—Arts and Letters

Who Was Who in American History—The Military

Who Was Who in American History—Science and Technology

Who's Who in the Midwest

Who's Who in the East

Who's Who in the South and Southwest

Who's Who in the West

Who's Who of American Women

Who's Who in Government

Who's Who in Finance and Industry

Who's Who in Religion

Who's Who in American Law

Who's Who in the World

Who's Who Biographical Record—Child Development Professionals

Who's Who Biographical Record—School District Officials

World Who's Who in Science

Directory of Medical Specialists

Marquis Who's Who Publications/Index to All Books

Traveler's Guide to U.S. Certified Doctors Abroad

Who's Who
of American Women ®

13th edition
1983-1984

MARQUIS
Who's Who

Marquis Who's Who, Inc.
200 East Ohio Street
Chicago, Illinois 60611 U.S.A.

Library of Congress Catalog Card Number 58-13264
International Standard Book Number 0-8379-0413-7
Product Code Number 030282

Table of Contents

Preface

The thirteenth edition of *Who's Who of American Women* marks the twenty-fifth anniversary of publication of this reference book. As women have entered a variety of professions in greater numbers since 1958, when the first edition was published, there has been an increasing interest in and need for their biographical data.

In the first volume of *Who's Who of American Women,* volunteer workers in civic, religious, and club activities constituted almost 16 percent of the biographees. While the proportion of women in these areas has declined, increasing prominence has been achieved in many other fields. This directory includes women who are moving up in professional areas to which they are relatively new as well as those at high levels in fields traditionally accessible to women. For example, the volume contains considerable representation of women in all areas of government: federal officials, high-level state positions, mayors, judges, and military officers. Outstanding women are found in many sectors of business, such as advertising, banking, insurance, and publishing. In addition, women entrepreneurs who head their own businesses constitute an important segment of the biographees.

This volume includes a greater number of women physicians, lawyers, and engineers, as well as ordained ministers and rabbis. As always, women are important in the performing arts—dance, theater, opera—with increasing representation in music as, for example, players in symphony orchestras.

In preparing the contents of this edition—approximately 21,500 sketches—the Marquis researchers have drawn on a variety of contemporary sources: newspapers, periodicals, professional associations, and other information. The result has been coverage of personal and professional biographical information about women in virtually every important field of endeavor.

Selection of a name for inclusion in *Who's Who of American Women* is based on reference value; biographees are of current reference interest. Some women are eligible for listing because of position, while others have distinguished themselves by noteworthy achievements in their fields. Many listees qualify by virtue of both position and accomplishment.

In most sketches, the biographical data come from the best available sources—the individuals listed. This information is reviewed by Marquis staff before being written as sketches. After each biographee has verified and returned a prepublication proof, the sketch is put into final form for publication. Where reference-worthy individuals fail to submit biographical data, Marquis researchers compile the facts, drawing on a variety of sources to assure accuracy and currency of information. Sketches compiled in this manner are denoted by an asterisk.

In assembling this comprehensive reference source on outstanding American women, Marquis Who's Who editors and researchers have exercised diligent care in the preparation of each biographical sketch. Despite all precautions, however, errors may occasionally occur. Users of this directory are invited to draw the attention of the publisher to such errors so that corrections can be made in a later edition.

A number of the biographees in this volume also appear in *Who's Who in America*. However, in view of the complementary relationship between the two volumes, most women biographees in *Who's Who in America* do not have sketches in *Who's Who of American Women*. For reference use, this volume contains an index of all women listees in the forty-second edition of *Who's Who in America*.

As *Who's Who of American Women* observes a quarter century of publication, the thirteenth edition continues the tradition of excellence established in 1899 with publication of the first edition of *Who's Who in America*. The essence of that tradition is the continuing effort at Marquis Who's Who to produce reference works that are responsive to the needs of their users.

Adele Hast, Ph.D.
Editor-in-Chief

Standards of Admission

The major criterion for determining who will be included in *Who's Who of American Women* is the extent of a woman's reference value. Such reference interest is judged on either of two factors: (1) the position of responsibility held, or (2) the level of achievement attained by the individual.

Admission based on the factor of position includes the following examples:

High-level federal officials

High-ranking military officers

Specified elected and appointed state officials

Mayors of major cities

Principal officers of selected businesses

Outstanding educators from major universities and colleges

Principal figures of cultural and artistic institutions

Heads of major women's organizations

Recipients of major awards and honors

Members of selected honorary organizations

Other women chosen because of incumbency or membership

Admission based on individual achievement is based on objective qualitative criteria. To be selected, a woman must have attained conspicuous achievement. The biographee may scarcely be known in the local community but may be recognized in some field of endeavor for noteworthy accomplishment.

Key to Information in this Directory

❶ WATTS, JANE O'RILEY, ❷ home economist; **❸** b. Madison, Wis., Aug. 1, 1923; **❹** d. Daniel John and Bridget Kara (McCreary) O'Riley; **❺** B.S., Wooster Coll., 1944; M.S., Ohio State U., 1947, Ph.D., 1950; **❻** m. Benjamin Greene Watts, Nov. 7, 1948; **❼** children—Benjamin, Marie, Lisa. **❽** Tchr., River Forest (Ill.) High Sch., 1946-48; research asst. Ill. State Agrl. Expt. Sta., Lemont, 1948-50; consumer service rep. Eastern Ill. Gas Co., Chgo., 1955-61; dir. home economics Warden Packaging Co., Chgo., 1961—; cons. home economics, HEW, 1966—. **❾** Active Greater Chgo. United Fund; mem. Elmhurst (Ill.) Bd. Edn., 1970—; trustee Wooster Coll. **❿** Served to lt. WAC, 1944-46. **⓫** Named Bus. Woman of Yr., Elmhurst Women's Club, 1969. **⓬** Mem. Am. Home Economics Assn., Home Economists in Bus. (treas. Chgo. chpt. 1965-66), Alpha Xi Delta. **⓭** Democrat. **⓮** Lutheran. **⓯** Clubs: Order Eastern Star, Butterfield Country. **⓰** Author: The Working Woman's Cookbook, 1967. **⓱** Home: 542 Farwell Ave Elmhurst IL 60126 **⓲** Office: 1250 Eastern St Chicago IL 60606

Key

❶ Name
❷ Occupation
❸ Vital statistics
❹ Parents
❺ Education
❻ Marriage
❼ Children
❽ Career
❾ Civic and political activities
❿ Military record
⓫ Awards and certifications
⓬ Professional and
    association memberships
⓭ Political affiliation
⓮ Religion
⓯ Clubs (including lodges)
⓰ Writings and special achievements
⓱ Home address
⓲ Office address

The biographical listings in *Who's Who of American Women* are arranged in alphabetical order according to the first letter of the last name of the biographee. Each sketch is presented in a uniform order as in the sample sketch above. The many abbreviations used in the sketches are explained in the Table of Abbreviations.

Table of Abbreviations

The following abbreviations and symbols are frequently used in this Directory

* (An asterisk) following a sketch indicates that it was researched by the Marquis Who's Who editorial staff and has not been verified by the biographee.

A.A. Associate in Arts
AAAL American Academy of Arts and Letters
AAAS American Association for the Advancement of Science
AAHPER Alliance for Health, Physical Education and Recreation
A. and M. Agricultural and Mechanical
AAU Amateur Athletic Union
AAUP American Association of University Professors
AAUW American Association of University Women
A.B. Arts, Bachelor of
AB Alberta
ABC American Broadcasting Company
AC Air Corps
acad. academy, academic
acct. accountant
acctg. accounting
ACDA Arms Control and Disarmament Agency
ACLU American Civil Liberties Union
A.C.P. American College of Physicians
A.C.S. American College of Surgeons
ADA American Dental Association
a.d.c. aide-de-camp
adj. adjunct, adjutant
adj. gen. adjutant general
adm. admiral
adminstr. administrator
adminstrn. administration
adminstrv. administrative
adv. advocate, advisory, adviser
advt. advertising
A.E. Agricultural Engineeer
A.E. and P., AEP Ambassador Extraordinary and Plenipotentiary
AEC Atomic Energy Commission
aero. aeronautical, aeronautic
aerodyn. aerodynamic
AFB Air Force Base
AFL-CIO American Federation of Labor and Congress of Industrial Organizations
AFTRA American Federation TV and Radio Artists
agr. agriculture
agri. agricultural
agt. agent
AGVA American Guild of Variety Artists
agy. agency
A&I Agricultural and Industrial
AIA American Institute of Architects
AIAA American Institute of Aeronautics Astronautics
AID Agency for International Development
AIEE American Institute of Electrical Engineers
AIM American Institute of Management
AIME American Institute of Mining, Metallurgy, and Petroleum Engineers
AK Alaska
AL Alabama
ALA American Library Association
Ala. Alabama
alt. alternate
Alta. Alberta
A&M Agricultural and Mechanical
A.M. Arts, Master of
Am. American, America
AMA American Medical Association

A.M.E. African Methodist Episcopal
Amtrak National Railroad Passenger Corporation
AMVETS American Veterans of World War II, Korea, Vietnam
anat. anatomical
ann. annual
ANTA American National Theatre and Academy
anthrop. anthropological
AP Associated Press
APO Army Post Office
apptd. appointed
apt. apartment
AR Arkansas
ARC American Red Cross
archeol. archeological
archtl. architectural
Ariz. Arizona
Ark. Arkansas
Arts D. Arts, Doctor of
arty. artillery
ASCAP American Society of Composers, Authors and Publishers
ASCE American Society of Civil Engineers
ASHRAE American Society of Heating, Refrigeration, and Air Conditioning Engineers
ASME American Society of Mechanical Engineers
assn. association
asso. associate
asst. assistant
ASTM American Society for Testing and Materials
astron. astronomical
astrophys. astrophysical
ATSC Air Technical Service Command
AT&T American Telephone & Telegraph Company
atty. attorney
AUS Army of the United States
aux. auxiliary
Ave. Avenue
AVMA American Veterinary Medical Association
AZ Arizona

B. Bachelor
b. born
B.A. Bachelor of Arts
B. Agr. Bachelor of Agriculture
Balt. Baltimore
Bapt. Baptist
B.Arch. Bachelor of Architecture
B.A.S. Bachelor of Agricultural Science
B.B.A. Bachelor of Business Administration
BBC British Broadcasting Corporation
B.C.,BC British Columbia
B.C.E. Bachelor of Civil Engineering
B.Chir. Bachelor of Surgery
B.C.L. Bachelor of Civil Law
B.C.S. Bachelor of Commerical Science
B.D. Bachelor of Divinity
bd. board
B.E. Bachelor of Education
B.E.E. Bachelor of Electrical Engineering
B.F.A. Bachelor of Fine Arts
bibl. biblical
bibliog. bibliographical
biog. biographical
biol. biological
B.J. Bachelor of Journalism
Bklyn. Brooklyn
B.L. Bachelor of Letters
bldg. building
B.L.S. Bachelor of Library Science

Blvd. Boulevard
bn. battalion
B.&O.R.R. Baltimore & Ohio Railroad
bot. botanical
B.P.E. Bachelor of Physical Education
br. branch
B.R.E. Bachelor of Religious Education
brig. gen. brigadier general
Brit. British, Britannica
Bros. Brothers
B.S. Bachelor of Science
B.S.A. Bachelor of Agricultural Science
B.S.D. Bachelor of Didactic Science
B.S.T. Bachelor of Sacred Theology
B.Th. Bachelor of Theology
bull. bulletin
bur. bureau
bus. business
B.W.I. British West Indies

CA California
CAA Civil Aeronautics Administration
CAB Civil Aeronautics Board
Calif. California
C.Am. Central America
Can. Canada, Canadian
CAP Civil Air Patrol
capt. captain
CARE Cooperative American Relief Everywhere
Cath. Catholic
cav. cavalry
CBC Canadian Broadcasting Company
CBI China, Burma, India Theatre of Operations
CBS Columbia Broadcasting System
CCC Commodity Credit Corporation
CCNY City College of New York
CCU Cardiac Care Unit
CD Civil Defense
C.E. Corps of Engineers, Civil Engineer
CENTO Central Treaty Organization
CERN European Organization of Nuclear Research
cert. certificate, certification, certified
CETA Comprehensive Employment Training Act
CFL Canadian Football League
ch. church
Ch.D. Doctor of Chemistry
chem. chemical
Chem. E. Chemical Engineer
Chgo. Chicago
chirurg. chirurgical
chmn. chairman
chpt. chapter
CIA Central Intelligence Agency
CIC Counter Intelligence Corps
Cin. Cincinnati
Cleve. Cleveland
climatol. climatological
clin. clinical
clk. clerk
C.L.U. Chartered Life Underwriter
C.M. Master in Surgery
C.& N.W.Ry. Chicago & Northwestern Railway
CO Colorado
Co. Company
COF Catholic Order of Foresters
C. of C. Chamber of Commerce
col. colonel
coll. college
Colo. Colorado
com. committee
comd. commanded
comdg. commanding

comdr. commander
comdt. commandant
commd. commissioned
comml. commercial
commn. commission
commr. commissioner
condr. conductor
Conf. Conference
Congl. Congregational
Conglist. Congregationalist
Conn. Connecticut
cons. consultant, consulting
consol. consolidated
constl. constitutional
constn. constitution
constrn. construction
contbd. contributed
contbg. contributing
contbn. contribution
contbr. contributor
Conv. Convention
coop., co-op. cooperative
CORDS Civil Operations and Revolutionary Development Support
CORE Congress of Racial Equality
corp. corporation, corporate
corr. correspondent, corresponding, correspondence
C.&O.Ry. Chesapeake & Ohio Railway
C.P.A. Certified Public Accountant
C.P.C.U. Chartered property and casualty underwriter
C.P.H. Certificate of Public Health
cpl. corporal
CPR Cardiac Pulmonary Resuscitation
C.P.Ry. Canadian Pacific Railway
C.S. Christian Science
C.S.B. Bachelor of Christian Science
CSC Civil Service Commission
C.S.D. Doctor of Christian Science
CT Connecticut
ct. Court
CWS Chemical Warfare Service
C.Z. Canal Zone

d. daughter
D. Doctor
D.Agr. Doctor of Agriculture
DAR Daughters of the American Revolution
dau. daughter
DAV Disabled American Veterans
D.C., DC District of Columbia
D.C.L. Doctor of Civil Law
D.C.S. Doctor of Commercial Science
D.D. Doctor of Divinity
D.D.S. Doctor of Dental Surgery
DE Delaware
dec. deceased
def. defense
Del. Delaware
del. delegate, delegation
Dem. Democrat, Democratic
D.Eng. Doctor of Engineering
denom. denomination, denominational
dep. deputy
dept. department
dermatol. dermatological
desc. descendant
devel. development, developmental
D.F.A. Doctor of Fine Arts
D.F.C. Distinguished Flying Cross
D.H.L. Doctor of Hebrew Literature
dir. director
dist. district
distbg. distributing
distbn. distribution

distbr. distributor
disting. distinguished
div. division, divinity, divorce
D.Litt. Doctor of Literature
D.M.D. Doctor of Medical Dentistry
D.M.S. Doctor of Medical Science
D.O. Doctor of Osteopathy
D.P.H. Diploma in Public Health
D.R. Daughters of the Revolution
Dr. Drive
D.R.E. Doctor of Religious Education
Dr.P.H. Doctor of Public Health, Doctor of Public Hygiene
D.S.C. Distinguished Service Cross
D.Sc. Doctor of Science
D.S.M. Distinguished Service Medal
D.S.T. Doctor of Sacred Theology
D.T.M. Doctor of Tropical Medicine
D.V.M. Doctor of Veterinary Medicine
D.V.S. Doctor of Veterinary Surgery

E. East
E. and P. Extraordinary and Plenipotentiary
Eccles. Ecclesiastical
ecol. ecology, ecological
econ. economic
ECOSOC Economic and Social Council (of the UN)
E.D. Doctor of Engineering
ed. educated
Ed.B. Bachelor of Education
Ed.D. Doctor of Education
edit. edition
Ed.M. Master of Education
edn. education
ednl. educational
EDP electronic data processing
Ed.S. Specialist in Education
E.E. Electrical Engineer
E.E. and M.P. Envoy Extraordinary and Minister Plenipotentiary
EEC European Economic Community
EEG electroencephalogram
EEO Equal Employment Opportunity
EKG electrocardiogram
E.Ger. German Democratic Republic
elec. electrical
electrochem. electrochemical
electrophys. electrophysical
elem. elementary
E.M. Engineer of Mines
ency. encyclopedia
Eng. England
engr. engineer
engring. engineering
entomol. entomological
environ. environmental, environment
EPA Environmental Protection Agency
epidemiol. epidemiological
Episc. Episcopalian
ERA Equal Rights Amendment
ERDA Energy Research and Development Administration
ESEA Elementary and Secondary Education Act
ESSA Environmental Science Services Administration
ethnol. ethnological
ETO European Theatre of Operations
Evang. Evangelical
exam. examination, examining
exec. executive
exhbn. exhibition
expdn. expedition
expn. exposition
expt. experiment
exptl. experimental

F.A. Field Artillery
FAA Federal Aviation Administration
FAO Food and Agriculture Organization (of the UN)
FBI Federal Bureau of Investigation
FCA Farm Credit Administration
FCC Federal Communication Commission
FCDA Federal Civil Defense Administration
FDA Food and Drug Administration
FDIA Federal Deposit Insurance Administration
FDIC Federal Deposit Insurance Corporation
F.E. Forest Engineer
FEA Federal Energy Administration
fed. federal
fedn. federation
fgn. foreign
FHA Federal Housing Administration
fin. financial, finance
FL Florida
Fla. Florida
FMC Federal Maritime Commission
FOA Foreign Operations Administration
found. foundation
FPC Federal Power Commission
FPO Fleet Post Office
frat. fraternity
FRS Federal Reserve System
FSA Federal Security Agency
Ft. Fort
FTC Federal Trade Commission

G-1 (or other number) Division of General Staff
Ga., GA Georgia
GAO General Accounting Office
gastroent. gastroenterological
GATT General Agreement of Tariff and Trades
gen. general
geneal. genealogical
geod. geodetic
geog. geographic, geographical
geol. geological
geophys. geophysical
gerontol. gerontological
G.H.Q. General Headquarters
G.N.Ry. Great Northern Railway
gov. governor
govt. government
govtl. governmental
GPO Government Printing Office
grad. graduate, graduated
GSA General Services Administration
Gt. Great
GU Guam
gynecol. gynecological

hdqrs. headquarters
HEW Department of Health, Education and Welfare
H.H.D. Doctor of Humanities
HHFA Housing and Home Finance Agency
HI Hawaii
hist. historical, historic
H.M. Master of Humanics
homeo. homeopathic
hon. honorary, honorable
Ho. of Dels. House of Delegates
Ho. of Reps. House of Representatives
hort. horticultural
hosp. hospital
HUD Department of Housing and Urban Development
Hwy. Highway
hydrog. hydrographic

IA Iowa
IAEA International Atomic Energy Agency
IBM International Business Machines Corporation
IBRD International Bank for Reconstruction and Development
ICA International Cooperation Administration
ICC Interstate Commerce Commission
ICU Intensive Care Unit
ID Idaho
IEEE Institute of Electrical and Electronics Engineers
IFC International Finance Corporation
IGY International Geophysical Year
IL Illinois
Ill. Illinois
Illus. illustrated
ILO International Labor Organization
IMF International Monetary Fund
IN Indiana
Inc. Incorporated
ind. independent
Ind. Indiana
Indpls. Indianapolis
indsl. industrial
Inf. infantry
Info. information
ins. insurance
insp. inspector
insp. gen. inspector general
inst. institute
instl. institutional
instn. institution
instr. instructor
instrn. instruction
internat. international
intro. introduction
IRE Institute of Radio Engineers
IRS Internal Revenue Service
ITT International Telephone & Telegraph Corporation

J.B. Jurum Baccolaureus
J.C.B. Juris Canonici Bachelor
J.C.L. Juris Canonici Lector
J.D. Juris Doctor
j.g. junior grade
jour. journal
jr. junior
J.S.D. Jurum Scientiae Doctor
J.U.D. Juris Utriusque Doctor
Judge Adv. Gen. Judge Advocate General

Kans. Kansas
K.C. Knights of Columbus
K.P. Knights of Pythias
KS Kansas
K.T. Knight Templar
Ky., KY Kentucky

La., LA Louisiana
lab. laboratory
lang. language
laryngol. laryngological
LB Labrador
lectr. lecturer
legis. legislation, legislative
L.H.D. Doctor of Humane Letters
L.I. Long Island
lic. licensed, license
L.I.R.R. Long Island Railroad
lit. literary, literature
Litt. B. Bachelor of Letters

Litt. D. Doctor of Letters
LL.B. Bachelor of Laws
LL.D. Doctor of Laws
LL.M. Master of Laws
Ln. Lane
L.&N.R.R. Louisville & Nashville Railroad
L.S. Library Science (in degree)
lt. lieutenant
Ltd. Limited
Luth. Lutheran
LWV League of Women Voters

m. married
M. Master
M.A. Master of Arts
MA Massachusetts
mag. magazine
M.Agr. Master of Agriculture
maj. major
Man. Manitoba
M.Arch. Master in Architecture
Mass. Massachusetts
math. mathematics, mathematical
MATS Military Air Transport Service
M.B. Bachelor of Medicine
MB Manitoba
M.B.A. Master of Business Administration
MBS Mutual Broadcasting System
M.C. Medical Corps
M.C.E. Master of Civil Engineering
mcht. merchant
mcpl. municipal
M.C.S. Master of Commercial Science
M.D. Doctor of Medicine
Md., MD Maryland
M.Dip. Master in Diplomacy
mdse. merchandise
M.D.V. Doctor of Veterinary Medicine
M.E. Mechanical Engineer
ME Maine
M.E. Ch. Methodist Episcopal Church
mech. mechanical
M.Ed. Master of Education
med. medical
M.E.E. Master of Electrical Engineering
mem. member
meml. memorial
merc. mercantile
met. metropolitan
metall. metallurgical
Met. E. Metallurgical Engineer
meteorol. meteorological
Meth. Methodist
Mex. Mexico
M.F. Master of Forestry
M.F.A. Master of Fine Arts
mfg. manufacturing
mfr. manufacturer
mgmt. management
mgr. manager
M.H.A. Master of Hospital Administration
M.I. Military Intelligence
MI Michigan
Mich. Michigan
micros. microscopic, microscopical
mil. military
Milw. Milwaukee
mineral. mineralogical
Minn. Minnesota
Miss. Mississippi
M.I.T. Massachusetts Institute of Technology
mktg. marketing
M.L. Master of Laws
MLA Modern Language Association
M.L.D. Magister Legnum Diplomatic

M.Litt. Master of Literature
M.L.S. Master of Library Science
M.M.E. Master of Mechanical Engineering
MN Minnesota
mng. managing
Mo., MO Missouri
moblzn. mobilization
Mont. Montana
M.P. Member of Parliament
M.P.E. Master of Physical Education
M.P.H. Master of Public Health
M.P.L. Master of Patent Law
Mpls. Minneapolis
M.R.E. Master of Religious Education
M.S. Master of Science
MS Mississippi
M.Sc. Master of Science
M.S.F. Master of Science of Forestry
M.S.T. Master of Sacred Theology
M.S.W. Master of Social Work
MT Montana
Mt. Mount
MTO Mediterranean Theatre of Operations
mus. museum, musical
Mus.B. Bachelor of Music
Mus.D. Doctor of Music
Mus.M. Master of Music
mut. mutual
mycol. mycological

N. North
NAACP National Association for the Advancement of Colored People
NACA National Advisory Committee for Aeronautics
NAD National Academy of Design
N.Am. North America
NAM National Association of Manufacturers
NAPA National Association of Performing Artists
NAREB National Association of Real Estate Boards
NARS National Archives and Record Service
NASA National Aeronautics and Space Administration
nat. national
NATO North Atlantic Treaty Organization
NATOUSA North African Theatre of Operations
nav. navigation
N.B., NB New Brunswick
NBC National Broadcasting Company
N.C., NC North Carolina
NCCJ National Conference of Christians and Jews
N.D., ND North Dakota
NDEA National Defense Education Act
NE Nebraska
N.E. Northeast
NEA National Education Association
Nebr. Nebraska
neurol. neurological
Nev. Nevada
NF Newfoundland
NFL National Football League
Nfld. Newfoundland
N.G. National Guard
N.H., NH New Hampshire
NHL National Hockey League
NIH National Institutes of Health
NIMH National Institute of Mental Health
N.J., NJ New Jersey
NLRB National Labor Relations Board
NM New Mexico
N.Mex. New Mexico
No. Northern

NOAA National Oceanographic and Atmospheric Administration
NORAD North American Air Defense
NOW National Organization for Women
N.P. Ry. Northern Pacific Railway
nr. near
NRC National Research Council
N.S., NS Nova Scotia
NSC National Security Council
NSF National Science Foundation
N.T. New Testament
NT Northwest Territories
numis. numismatic
NV Nevada
NW Northwest
N.W.T. Northwest Territories
N.Y., NY New York
N.Y.C. New York City
N.Z. New Zealand

OAS Organization of American States
Ob-Gyn obstetrics-gynecology
obs. observatory
O.D. Doctor of Optometry
OECD Organization of European Cooperation and Development
OEEC Organization of European Economic Cooperation
OEO Office of Economic Opportunity
ofcl. official
OH Ohio
OK Oklahoma
Okla. Oklahoma
ON Ontario
Ont. Ontario
ophthal. ophthalmological
ops. operations
OR Oregon
orch. orchestra
Oreg. Oregon
orgn. organization
ornithol. ornithological
OSRD Office of Scientific Research and Development
OSS Office of Strategic Services
osteo. osteopathic
otol. otological
otolaryn. otolaryngological

Pa., PA Pennsylvania
P.A. Professional Association
paleontol. paleontological
path. pathological
P.C. Professional Corporation
PE Prince Edward Island
P.E. Professional Engineer
P.E.I. Prince Edward Island
PEN Poets, Playwrights, Editors, Essayists and Novelists (international association)
penol. penological
P.E.O. women's organization (full name not disclosed)
pfc. private first class
PHA Public Housing Administration
pharm. Pharmaceutical
Pharm.D. Doctor of Pharmacy
Pharm.M. Master of Pharmacy
Ph.B. Bachelor of Philosophy
Ph.D. Doctor of Philosophy
Phila. Philadelphia
philharm. philharmonic
philol. philological
philos. philosophical
photog. photographic

phys. physical
physiol. physiological
Pitts. Pittsburgh
Pkwy. Parkway
Pl. Place
P.&L.E.R.R. Pittsburgh & Lake Erie Railroad
P.O. Post Office
PO Box Post Office Box
polit. political
poly. polytechnic, polytechnical
P.Q. Province of Quebec
P.R., PR Puerto Rico
prep. preparatory
pres. president
Presbyn. Presbyterian
presdl. presidential
prin. principal
proc. proceedings
prod. produced (play production)
prof. professor
profl. professional
prog. progressive
propr. proprietor
pros. atty. prosecuting attorney
pro tem pro tempore
PSRO Professional Services Review Organization
psychiat. psychiatric
psychol. psychological
PTA Parent-Teachers Association
PTO Pacific Theatre of Operations
pub. publisher, publishing, published
publ. publication
pvt. private

quar. quarterly
q.m. quartermaster
Q.M.C. Quartermaster Corps
Que. Quebec

radiol. radiological
RAF Royal Air Force
RCA Radio Corporation of America
RCAF Royal Canadian Air Force
R.D. Rural Delivery
Rd. Road
REA Rural Electrification Administration
rec. recording
ref. reformed
regt. regiment
regtl. regimental
rehab. rehabilitation
rep. representative
Rep. Republican
Res. Reserve
ret. retired
rev. review, revised
RFC Reconstruction Finance Corporation
R.F.D. Rural Free Delivery
rhinol. rhinological
R.I., RI Rhode Island
R.N. Registered Nurse
roentgenol. roentgenological
ROTC Reserve Officers Training Corps
R.R. Railroad
Ry. Railway

s. son
S. South
SAC Strategic Air Command
SALT Strategic Arms Limitation Talks
S.Am. South America
san sanitary
SAR Sons of the American Revolution

Sask. Saskatchewan
savs. savings
S.B. Bachelor of Science
SBA Small Business Administration
S.C., SC South Carolina
SCAP Supreme Command Allies Pacific
Sc.B. Bachelor of Science
S.C.D. Doctor of Commercial Science
Sc.D. Doctor of Science
sch. school
sci. science, scientific
SCLC Southern Christian Leadership Conference
SCV Sons of Confederate Veterans
S.D., SD South Dakota
SE Southeast
SEATO Southeast Asia Treaty Organization
sec. secretary
SEC Securities and Exchange Commission
sect. section
seismol. seismological
sem. seminary
sgt. sergeant
SHAEF Supreme Headquarters Allied Expeditionary Forces
SHAPE Supreme Headquarters Allied Powers in Europe
S.I. Staten Island
S.J. Society of Jesus (Jesuit)
S.J.D. Scientiae Juridicae Doctor
SK Saskatchewan
S.M. Master of Science
So. Southern
soc. society
sociol. sociological
S.P. Co. Southern Pacific Company
spl. special
splty. specialty
Sq. Square
sr. senior
S.R. Sons of the Revolution
S.S. Steamship
SSS Selective Service System
St. Saint
St. Street
sta. station
statis. statistical
stats. statistics
S.T.B. Bachelor of Sacred Theology
stblzn. stabilization
S.T.D. Doctor of Sacred Theology
subs. subsidiary
SUNY State University of New York
supr. supervisor
supt. superintendent
surg. surgical
SW Southwest

TAPPI Technical Association of Pulp and Paper Industry
Tb Tuberculosis
tchr. teacher
tech. technical, technology
technol. technological
Tel.&Tel. Telephone & Telegraph
temp. temporary
Tenn. Tennessee
Ter. Territory
Terr. Terrace
TESL Teaching English as a Second Language
Tex. Texas
Th.D. Doctor of Theology
theol. theological
Th.M. Master of Theology
TN Tennessee
tng. training

topog. topographical
trans. transaction, transferred
transl. translation, translated
transp. transportation
treas. treasurer
TV television
TVA Tennessee Valley Authority
twp. township
TX Texas
typog. typographical

U. University
UAW United Auto Workers
UCLA University of California at Los Angeles
UDC United Daughters of the Confederacy
U.K. United Kingdom
UN United Nations
UNESCO United Nations Educational, Scientific and Cultural Organization
UNICEF United Nations International Children's Emergency Fund
univ. university
UNRRA United Nations Relief and Rehabilitation Administration
UPI United Press International
U.P.R.R. Union Pacific Railroad
urol. urological
U.S. United States
U.S.A. United States of America
USAAF United States Army Air Force
USAF United States Air Force

USAFR United States Air Force Reserve
USAR United States Army Reserve
USCG United States Coast Guard
USCGR United States Coast Guard Reserve
USES United States Employment Service
USIA United States Information Agency
USIS United States Information Service
USMC United States Marine Corps
USMCR United States Marine Corps Reserve
USN United States Navy
USNG United States National Guard
USNR United States Naval Reserve
USO United Service Organizations
USPHS United States Public Health Service
U.S.S. United States Ship
USSR Union of the Soviet Socialist Republics
USV United States Volunteers
UT Utah

VA Veterans' Administration
Va., VA Virginia
vet. veteran, veterinary
VFW Veterans of Foreign Wars
V.I., VI Virgin Islands
vice pres. vice president
vis. visiting
VISTA Volunteers in Service to America
VITA Volunteers in Technical Service
vocat. vocational
vol. volunteer, volume

v.p. vice president
vs. versus
VT., VT Vermont

W. West
WA Washington
WAC Women's Army Corps
Wash. Washington
WAVES Women's Reserve, U.S. Naval Reserve
WCTU Women's Christian Temperance Union
W. Ger. Germany, Federal Republic of
WHO World Health Organization
WI Wisconsin
Wis. Wisconsin
WSB Wage Stabilization Board
WV West Virginia
W. VA. West Virginia
WY Wyoming
Wyo. Wyoming

YK Yukon
YMCA Young Men's Christian Association
YMHA Young Men's Hebrew Association
YM & YWHA Young Men's and Young Women's Hebrew Association
YWCA Young Women's Christian Association
yr. year

zool. zoological

Alphabetical Practices

Names are arranged alphabetically according to the surnames, and under identical surnames according to the first given name. If both surname and first given name are identical, names are arranged alphabetically according to the second given name. Where full names are identical, they are arranged in order of age—with the elder listed first.

Surnames beginning with De, Des, Du, however capitalized or spaced, are recorded with the prefix preceding the surname and arranged alphabetically, under the letter D.

Surnames beginning with Mac and Mc are arranged alphabetically under M.

Surnames beginning with Saint or St. appear after names that would begin Sains, and are arranged according to the second part of the name, e.g., St. Clair before Saint Dennis.

Surnames beginning with prefix Van are arranged alphabetically under letter V. Surnames containing the prefix Von or von are usually arranged alphabetically under letter V; any exceptions are noted by cross references.

Compound hyphenated surnames are arranged according to the first member of the compound. Compound unhyphenated surnames are treated as hyphenated names.

Parentheses used in connection with a name indicate which part of the full name is usually deleted in common usage. Hence Abbott, W(illiam) Lewis indicates that the usual form of the given name is W. Lewis. In such a case, the parentheses are ignored in alphabetizing. However if the name is recorded Abbott, (William) Lewis, signifying that the entire name William is not commonly used, the alphabetizing would be arranged as though the name were Abbott, Lewis.

Who's Who of American Women

AAKRE, S. MAUREEN, social services adminstr.; b. Granite Falls, Minn., Dec. 30, 1945; d. Bernard S. and Marjorie (Skjefte) Aakre; B.A. magna cum laude, No. Ariz. U., 1973, M.A., 1977; m. Glenn E. Williams, July 31, 1979. Sr. cons. Social Dynamics, Inc., under contract to HEW, San Francisco, 1974-75; pres. AAKRE Cons.'s; coordinator Fairbanks (Alaska) Native Assn. Adult Learning Center, 1976-77; instr. Tanana Valley Coll., Fairbanks, 1976-77; founder, exec. dir. Women in Crisis-Counseling and Assistance (WIC-CA), Fairbanks, 1977-78; dir. dept. human resources Esca-Tech. Corp.; cons. Tanana Chiefs Conf. Land Claims Coll., 1975; del. Alaska conf. Internat. Women's Year, 1977; bd. dirs. Tanana Valley Citizen's Council on Work and Edn., 1977—, Abused Women's Aid In Crisis, 1979—, pres., 1980—; chairperson com. tng. and tech. assistance Alaska Network Domestic Violence and Sexual Assault, 1980—; exec. dir. Alaska Women's Resource Center, 1980—. Named Alaska Outstanding Young Woman of Yr., Gen. Fedn. Womens Clubs, 1977. Mem. NOW (task force coordinator 1976-77), Am., Pacific sociol. assns., Soc. for Study Social Problems, Alaska Adult Edn. Assn. (treas.), Am. Tae Kwon Do Assn. (6th deg. Green Belt), Am. Chung Do Kwon Assn. Clubs: Sons of Norway, Fairbanks Noon Jaycees (dir. 1977—). Author: Guide to Nonprofit Organizations in Alaska; Resource Directory for Alaska Network, also supplementary tng. programs. Home: 585 Dowling Rd Anchorage AK 99502

AARON, CHLOE WELLINGHAM, bus. exec.; b. Santa Monica, Calif., Oct. 9, 1938; d. John Rufus and Grace (Lloyd) Wellingham; B.A., Occidental Coll., 1961; M.A., George Washington U., 1966; m. David Laurence Aaron, Aug. 11, 1962; 1 son, Timothy Wellingham. Free-lance journalist, contbg. articles on TV to various publs. including N.Y. mag., Art in Am. and Washington Post, 1965-70; dir. public media program Nat. Endowment for Arts, Washington, 1970-76; sr. v.p. programming Public Broadcasting Service, Washington, 1976-81; pres. Chloe Aaron Assos., Inc., N.Y.C., 1981—; mem. trustee com. on film Mus. Modern Art, N.Y.C.; mem. film and video com. Whitney Mus. Am. Art, N.Y.C.; mem. nat. adv. bd. Center for Book. Mem. Nat. Acad. TV Arts and Scis., Internat. Radio and TV Soc., Am. Women in Radio and TV. Office: 609 Fifth Ave New York NY 10017 *

AARON, NORMA SCHILDER, psychol. cons.; b. N.Y.C., Sept. 17, 1924; d. Meyer and Tillie (Richman) Schilder; B.S. cum laude, N.Y.U., 1947; M.A., Hofstra U., 1966, Ph.D., 1982; m. Robert S. Aaron, Mar. 23, 1946; children—Andrew L., Daniel D. Former mem. psychol. staff hearing and speech L.I. Jewish Hillside Med. Center, New Hyde Park, N.Y.; now mem. staff Com. on Handicapped, N.Y.C. Sch. Dist. Mem. Mildred Werner League for Cancer Research (v.p.), Am. Psychol. Assn., Nassau County Psychol. Assn. Co-author: Somniquest: The five types of sleeplessness and how to overcome them, 1979.

ABARBANEL, KARIN, communications specialist, mag. editor, writer; b. N.Y.C., Feb. 23, 1950; d. Albert and Dorothy Irene (Fennell) A.; B.A. magna cum laude, Middlebury Coll., 1971; M.A., Columbia U., 1972, postgrad., 1972-73. Edn. coordinator Am. Film Theatre, N.Y.C., 1973-74; resume/career cons. Janice LaRouche Assos., N.Y.C., 1974—; asso. editor Foundation News, N.Y.C., 1976-79; editor The Exec. Female, N.Y.C., 1977—; mgr. corp. communications, editor Outlook mag. Booz, Allen & Hamilton, Inc., N.Y.C., 1979—; lectr., cons. in field. George W. Ellis fellow, 1971-72; Columbia U. fellow, 1972-73. Mem. Internat. Assn. Bus. Communicators, Advt. Women N.Y., Com. Small Mag. Editors and Pubs., Women's Inst. for Freedom of Press, Women in Founds./Corp. Philanthropy, Nat. Assn. Female Execs., Columbia U. Alumni Assn., Middlebury Met. Club, Phi Beta Kappa. Co-author: Woman's Work Book, 1977, The Art of Winning Foundation Grants, 1975; also articles on career and fin. advancement, women in founds., youth employment, tech. and mgmt., community devel., grants planning and proposal writing. Office: Booz Allen & Hamilton Inc 101 Park Ave New York NY 10178

ABARE, ARALYNN ANN, journalist; b. Ticonderoga, N.Y., June 13, 1951; d. George R. and Dorothy (Gould) A.; B.A. in Am. Studies, State U. N.Y., Albany, 1973; M.A. in Mass Communications, Syracuse U., 1975. News editor Skaneateles (N.Y.) Press, 1974; leisure sect. editor Watertown (N.Y.) Daily Times, 1975-77; asst. news editor Cocoa (Fla.) Today, 1977-79; instr. dept. communications U. Central Fla., Orlando, 1979—. Recipient Frank E. Gannett award for service in journalism, 1974. Mem. Women in Communications, Assn. Edn. in Journalism, Sigma Delta Chi. Home: 1301 Palmer St Apt 9 Orlando FL 32801 Office: U Central Fla Orlando FL 32816

ABBATE, RUTH RUDYS, librarian; b. Chgo., June 2, 1930; d. Joseph F. and Anna (Serbenta) Rudys; B.A., U. Chgo., 1950; M.A. in Library Sci., Rosary Coll., 1972; children—Keith A. Krisciunas, Kevin L. Krisciunas, Kenneth M. Krisciunas; stepchildren—Anita L. Abbate, Vincent A. Abbate. Tchr. elem. sch. Westmont, Ill., 1961-63; librarian Dist. 105 public schs., La Grange, Ill., 1972—, tchr. program for gifted children, 1979-81, 82—, coordinator gifted program, 1981-82. Mem. ALA, Ill. Library Assn., NEA, Ill. Edn. Assn., AAUW. Roman Catholic. Home: 5800 Doe Circle Westmont IL 60559 Office: 1001 Spring Ave La Grange IL 60525

ABBOTT, ANN AUGUSTINE, social worker, educator; b. Green Bay, Wis., July 6, 1943; d. Walter A. and Ethel D. Augustine; B.S. in Psychology, St. Norbert Coll., West DePere, Wis., 1965; M.S.S. in Social Work (U.S. Children's Bur. fellow), Bryn Mawr Coll., 1969, Ph.D. (NIMH fellow), 1977, postgrad. in higher edn. adminstrn. Higher Edn. Resource Services Summer Inst. for Women, 1978. Acad. tutor, counselor Devereux Schs., Devon, Pa., 1965-67; psychol. clinic coordinator Pa. State U., University Park, 1969-71; social worker Tidewater Mental Health Clinic, Williamsburg, Va., 1971-72; adj. prof. Pa. State U., King of Prussia, 1973-75; vis. lectr. Community Coll. of Phila., 1975-76; asst. prof. dir. social work, community psychology Widener U., Chester, Pa., 1976-81, project dir. Univ. Yr. for Action, 1976-81, project cons. Adult Competency Tng. Grant, 1976-80; asst. prof., dir. B.A. in Social Work, Rutgers U., Camden, N.J., 1981—. Tennis coach Nat. Jr. Tennis League, Phila., 1974-76; mem. adv. bd. Salvation Army; mem. adv. bd. mental health program Community Coll. Pa.; mem. budget rev. bd., vice chmn. allocations United Way. Vocation Rehab. Tng. grantee, 1964. Mem. Nat. Assn. Social Workers (del. assembly rep. 1978-82), Acad. Cert. Social Workers, Council on Social Work Edn., Nat. Council on Family Relations, Eastern, Pa. sociol. assns., Am. Orthopsychiat. Assn., Eastern Ednl. Research Assn. Home: 227 Arden Rd Gulph Mills PA 19428 Office: Rutgers U 327 Cooper St Camden NJ 08102

ABBOTT, LYNNE CLARK, clin. social worker, educator; b. Nashville, Apr. 21, 1943; d. Ernest Dwight and Hazel Marie (Martyn) Clark; student Meml. Hosp. Sch. Nursing, 1961-63; B.A., Sangamon State U., 1974; M.S. in Social Work, U. Tenn., 1976; D.S.W., U. Ala., 1982; m. Brent Johnston Morris, Dec. 3, 1977; children by previous marriage—Lance, Darren, Wendy, Brendan. Social worker Family Services Center, Springfield, Ill., 1974-75, Dede Wallace Community Mental Health Center, Nashville, 1976; instr. psychiatry U. Ala., Huntsville, 1976—; cons. in field; pvt. practice psychotherapy, Huntsville, 1976—. Lobbyist, Nat. Assn. Social Workers, 1978—; pres. PTA, Springfield, 1971-72, parent educator, 1973-74; treas. Ala. Polit. Action for Candidate Election, 1978—. Lic. cert. social worker, Ala.; named Social Worker of Yr., Nat. Assn. Social Workers, Huntsville, 1979, 80. Mem. Acad. Cert. Social Workers, Soc. Tchrs. Family Medicine, Nat. Assn. Social Workers, Ala. Soc. Clin. Social Workers, Ala. Soc. Hosp. Social Workers, Coalition for Social Work Legis. Home: 708 Versailles Dr Huntsville AL 35803 Office: 201 Governors Dr Huntsville AL 35801

ABBOTT, MARY ELLEN, educator; b. Parkton, Md., Jan. 12, 1932; d. Alvah M. and Grace V. (Carr) Hoffheiser; B.S., Towson State U., 1952; M. in Spl. Edn., U. Md., 1965; postgrad. Johns Hopkins U., 1966-70, Loyola Coll., 1971-78; m. David Carson Abbott, Dec. 22, 1956. Tchr. public schs., Balt., 1952-70; spl. edn. tchr. public schs., Baltimore County, Md., 1970-74; asst. prin. Chatsworth Sch., Reisterstown, Md., 1974-78, prin., 1978—. Mem. Nat. Assn. Elem. Sch. Prins., Md. Assn. Elem. Sch. Prins., Baltimore County Assn. Elem. Sch. Prins., Tchrs. Assn. Baltimore County, Nat. Assn. Tchrs., Met. Assn. Children with Learning Disabilities, Council for Exceptional Children, Council for Basic Edn., Amatur Radio Assn. Md. Contbr. articles in field to profl. jours. Home: 1342 Martin Dr Baltimore MD 21229 Office: 222 New Ave Reisterstown MD 21136

ABBOTT, VIRGINIA MILLER, speech pathologist, educator; b. Washington, Dec. 25, 1942; d. Edward Donald and Virginia Augusta (Grohs) Miller; B.A., George Washington U., 1964; M.Ed., Fitchburg State Coll., 1972; m. Henry L. Abbott, Jr., Aug. 30, 1966. Dir. speech and hearing clinic Burbank Hosp., Fitchburg, Mass., 1968-72; cons. tchr. Leominster (Mass.) Public Schs., 1972-76; chmn. evaluation team, spl. needs dept. Lunenburg (Mass.) Public Schs., 1977-81; dir. religious edn. Christ Ch., Fitchburg, Mass., 1980-82; speech-lang. pathologist Groton-Dunstable (Mass.) Public Schs., 1982—; pres., co-founder Christopher Learning Center, Fitchburg, Mass., 1982—. Sec. Mason (N.H.) Planning Bd., 1972-74, mem., 1975-76. Mem. Am. Speech and Hearing Assn. (cert. clin. competence in speech pathology), Mass. Speech and Hearing Assn., N.H. Speech and Hearing Assn., Soc. Family Therapy and Research, Council Exceptional Children, Quota Club, (treas.), NOW, Sigma Alpha Eta, Zeta Tau Alpha. Republican. Episcopalian. Home: 498 Valley Rd Mason NH 03048 Office: 569 Main St Fitchburg MA 01420

ABDULLAH, SAMELLA B. E. P., psychotherapist, educator; b. Chgo., Mar. 9, 1934; d. Samuel Richard and Addie Loraine (Jordan) Berry; B.S., Howard U., 1955, M.S.W. (NIMH grad. stipendee), 1959; Ph.D. in Psychology, Heed U., Fla., 1978; divorced; children—Tracey, Makola Mjasiri, Ghanima Kibibi. Legal aid social worker United Charities Chgo., 1962-64; instr. med. social work Northwestern U. Med. Sch. Clinic, Chgo., 1964-67; dir. social work Near N. Children's Center, Chgo., 1967-69; coordinator children's adolescent services Englewood Mental Health Center, Chgo., 1972-75; dir. Woodlawn Mental Health Center, Chgo., 1975-77; pvt. practice psychotherapy, 1979—; psychologist S. Central Community Services, 1982—; community prof. Governor's State U., Park Forest, Ill.; lectr. Jane Addams Coll. Social Work, U. Ill., Chgo.; instr. Central YMCA Community Coll., Chgo.; cons. Mau-Glo Sch. Mentally Retarded, Chgo. Mem. Ill. Mental Health Planning Bd., 1968-69; mem. service evaluation com. United Way of Chgo., 1977—; mem. Chgo. City-Wide Community Mental Health Bd., 1979—. Cert. clin. social worker, Ill. Mem. Acad. Cert. Social Workers, Assn. Black Psychologists, Am. Group Psychotherapy Assn., League of Black Women, Alpha Kappa Alpha. Columnist Chgo. Daily Defender, 1982. Home: 7204 S Paxton Ave Chicago IL 60649 Office: 111 N Wabash Ave Suite 1104 Chicago IL 60602

ABE, SUZANNE YVONNE, med. technologist; b. New Brunswick, N.J., Dec. 14, 1947; d. George Agustus and Florence (Roxbury) Abry; M.T., Perth Amboy (N.J.) Gen. Hosp., 1966; m. Osamu Abe, Feb. 14, 1976; 1 dau., Desha Yoko. Asst. supr. dept. microbiology Perth Amboy Gen. Hosp., 1966-71; supr. microbiology G.N. Wilcox Hosp., Lihue Kauai, Hawaii, 1971-76; med. technologist Kaiser Found. Hosp., Honolulu, 1976—. Mem. Am. soc. Clin. Pathologists. Home: 1716 Keeaumoku St 806 Honolulu HI 96822 Office: 1697 Ala Moana Blvd Honolulu HI 96822

ABEL, THEODORA MEAD, clin. psychologist; b. Newport, R.I., Sept. 9, 1899; d. Robert Gillespie and Elsie (Cleveland) Mead; A.B., Vassar Coll., 1921; M.A., Columbia U., 1924, Ph.D., 1925; diploma U. Paris, 1923; m. Theodore Abel, Nov. 9, 1924; children—Peter, Caroline, Zita. Researcher on emotions NRC, 1927-29; researcher on mental retardation Kaura Spellman Fund, 1935-36; Keith Fund researcher cultural variables Office Naval Research, 1947-49; dir. psychology Postgrad. Center Mental Health, N.Y.C., 1947-71; researcher on facial disfigurement NIMH, 1949-51; mem. faculty U. Ill., 1926-27, Sarah Lawrence Coll., 1929-35, L.I. U., 1951-62; ind. practice psychology, Alburquerque, 1971—; clin. prof. U. N.Mex., 1978—; chief family therapy Child Guidance Center Albuquerque, 1971—. Trustee Palisades (N.Y.) Sch. Bd., 1954-55, pres., 1956. Diplomate in clin. psychology Am. Bd. Profl. Psychology. Fellow Am. Psychol. Assn., Am. Orthopsychiat. Assn., Am. Group Psychotherapy Assn.; mem. Am. Assn. Marital and Family Therapy, World Assn. Social Psychiatry, Am. Psychopath. Assn., N.Y. State Psychol. Assn. (Psychologist of Yr. award 1972), N.Mex. Psychol. Assn. Democrat. Unitarian. Author: Psychological Testing in Cultural Contexts, 1973; co-author: The Subnormal Adolescent Girl, 1940; Facial Disfigurement, 1952; Culture and Psychotherapy, 1974; contbr. articles to profl. jours. Home: 4200 Sunningdale St NE Albuquerque NM 87110

ABEL, WILMA, civic worker, gift shop owner; b. Wayne County, Iowa, Mar. 29, 1909; d. Clarence Otto and Harriet Beatrice (Scales) Brown; student schs. Corydon, Iowa; m. Floyd Eugene Abel, Aug. 22, 1926; children—Wayne, Wretha, Louise. Owner gift shop, Chariton, Iowa, 1949—; tchr. ceramics, adult edn. high sch. Pres. Chariton Bus. and Profl. Women, 1976-77; pres. Daus. of Union Vets. of Civil War State of Iowa, 1978-79, pres. Chariton, 1963-73; pres. PTA, 1942-45; chmn. Rep. Women, Lincoln Twp. Lucas County, Iowa, 1963-66; 4-H leader, 1943-47; supt. Lucas County 4-H Fair Women's Bldg., 1965-80; sec. Chariton Geneal. Soc., 1970-72; asst. supt. floriculture Iowa State Fair, Des Moines, 1970-72; pres. Chariton Federated Garden Club, 1953, 54, 56, 65, 66, 70. Mem. Christian Church (Disciples of Christ). Took flower arrangements to State Fair, 1957-73. Home: 648 Osage St Chariton IA 50049

ABELES, LOISMAY CONN, ednl. adminstr.; b. Worcester, Mass., Sept. 1, 1931; d. Benjamin and Esther (Norris) Conn; student Goucher Coll., 1949-50, Wheelock Coll., 1950-51; B.A., magna cum laude, Clark U., 1968, M.A., 1971; Ed.D. (fellow), U. Mass., 1975; m. Robert Arent Abeles, June 24, 1972; children—Steven H., James C., Beth Ellen T. Hurowitz; stepchildren—Martha Abeles Lara, Laurie J., Betsy A. Tchr. and trainer Headstart, Kansas City, Mo., 1972-73; field agt. in edn. State Dept. Edn., Montpelier, Vt., 1973-74; grad. student adv. and instr. Anisa project, U. Mass., Amherst, 1974-76; dir. ednl. research Kodaly Mus. Tng. Inst., Watertown, Mass., 1976-79; instr. Wheelock Coll., Boston, 1979; dir. ednl. research Kodaly Center of Am., West Newton, Mass., 1979—; cons. corp. mgmt. and ednl. research, 1979—; ednl. systems cons. L.M. Ericsson, Inc., Framingham, Mass., 1979—. Mem. Worcester (Mass.) Human Rights Adv. Com., 1971-73; pres. Worcester Art Mus. Members' Council, 1972-73, mus. corporator, 1973—; bd. dirs. The Meml. Hosp., Worcester, 1976—, Public Radio Sta. WICN, Worcester, 1976-79, Jewish Home for Aged, Worcester, 1979—; trustee Kodaly Center Am., West Newton, Mass., 1979—. NIMH grantee, 1976-79. Mem. Am. Psychol. Assn., Nat. Assn. for Edn. of Young Children, Assn. for Advancement of Psychology, Am. Ednl. Research Assn. Jewish. Home: 2 Rollingwood Dr Worcester MA 01609 Office: Kodaly Center of America 1326 Washington St West Newton MA 02165

ABELL, ALICE VIRGINIA SIMS (MRS. NORMAN ABELL), civic worker; b. Elizabethtown, Ky., June 29, 1902; d. Francis Leroy and Antoinette (Freeman) Sims; student N.Y. Sch. Design, Otis Art Inst., Cal. Sch. Fine Arts; student U. Ariz., 1921-22; m. Norman Abell, Mar. 19, 1927; children—Norman, Virginia Frances (Mrs. James Langdon Blake), Arlene Alice (Mrs. Francis Bruce Robertson). Pres., Abell Enterprises, Long Beach, Calif., 1954—. Gray Lady A.R.C., Long Beach, 1942-45; chmn. arts and crafts, 1945; mem. Pan Hellenic Bd., Long Beach, 1961; vol. Meml. Hosp. Aux., Long Beach, 1960—, occupational therapy chmn., 1960-62; organizer minimal universal lang. project, 1958; mem. Regional Arts Council. Recipient first prize Santa Ana (Calif.) Art Exhibit, 1941. Mem. D.A.R., Art Mus. Assn., Los Angeles World Affairs Council, Internat. Platform Assn., Smithsonian Assos., Town Hall of Calif., Gamma Phi Beta. Episcopalian. Clubs: Otis Art Associates (Los Angeles); Queen Mary. Home: 4022 Pacific Ave Long Beach CA 90807

ABELL, LERON EVELYN, med. technologist; b. Tifton, Ga., Dec. 31, 1912; d. Elbert David and Mary Elvira (Willis) Paulk; student in med. tech. U. Houston, 1952-56; student continuing edn. U. Ga., 1960, Ga. State U., 1967; m. C. Stanley Abell, Oct. 6, 1935; 1 son, James Gerald. Chief Blood Bank, J.D. Hosp., Houston, 1950; chief med. technologist, Diagnostic Hosp. Houston, 1956; chief bacteriology and mycology Teaching Hosp., U. Fla., 1959; developed teaching program for clin. lab. assts. North Ga. Vocat. Sch., Clarkesville, 1960; developed Med. Diagnostic and Research Labs., Atlanta, 1962, chief, 1963; pub. health instr. Center for Disease Control, Atlanta, 1966-78; author: Simple Technique for Blood Cholesterol, 1959; (with Wallace and Woodcock) Medical Technology Retraining in Six Months, 1970; mem. steering com.; Listen, Look, and Learn, 1973; tchr., cons. editor; cons. home and field courses in various state health depts. U.S. and ters., 1974-78. Mem. Nat. Assn. Ret. Fed. Employees, Am. Legion Aux. Republican. Baptist. Clubs: Order Eastern Star, Am. Legion Aux. Home: 1209 Murray Ave Tifton GA 31794

ABELLA DE HERRERA, MARISELA, bus. exec.; b. Havana, Cuba, Feb. 5, 1943; d. Carlos and Angela (Acosta) Abella; B.S., Barry Coll., Miami, Fla., 1962; m. Alberto Herrera Nogueira, Apr. 6, 1968; 1 son, Carlos Alberto Herrera Abella. Asst. to v.p. and gen. mgr. bonding dept. Manuel San Juan (P.R.) Co. Inc., 1962-64; asst. corp. sec. and exec. sec. to pres. and stockholder Interstate Gen. Corp., Hato Rey, P.R., 1964-72, corp. sec. and pvt. sec. to corp. pres., 1972-79; sec.-treas., dir. A. H. Enterprises, Inc., Caparra Heights, P.R., 1979—; v.p., sec., dir. El Viajero, Inc. dir. A. H. Enterprises, Inc., San Juan. Roman Catholic. Clubs: Caribe Hilton Swimming and Tennis, Barry Coll. Alumnae Assn. Home: 909 Borinquen Towers 2 Caparra Heights PR 00920 Office: Calle Ensenada #412 Caparra Heights PR 00920

ABELLO, MONICA IRAO, social worker; b. Philippines, May 4, 1935; came to U.S., 1970, naturalized, 1975; d. Melecio Mabalon and Ceferina Rey (Irao) A.; B.S.E., Northwestern Visayan Colls., 1955; B.S.S.W., Centro Escolar U., 1958; M.S.W., San Francisco State U., 1974; m. Ger Igtanloc, May 5 1963 (div.); children—Gerrymon, Genevieve. Gray lady Philippine Nat. Red Cross, Manila, 1955-58; welfare aide Social Welfare Adminstrn., Aklan, Philippines, 1958-60; sch. counselor, tchr. Bur. Public Schs., Davao/Cotabato, Philippines, 1960-68; welfare officer Dept. Social Welfare, Gagayan de Oro City, Philippines, 1968-70; social worker Cath. Social Services, San Francisco, 1974-80; mental health counselor North County Mental Health Orgn., Daly City, Calif., 1980—; cons.; tchr. parents' effectiveness tng. Program coordinator Philippine Nat. Day, 1979; core group coordinator Filipino People's Far West Conv., 1979, Bay Area Task Force for Def. of Filipino Immigrant Rights, 1980—. Lic. social worker, Philippines. Mem. Nat. Assn. Social Workers, Filipino Christian Soc., Fayco, Filipino Mental Health Resources Group, Filipino-Am. Sr. Assn. of West Bay (cons., organizer), Filipino-Am. Involvement League of Daly Center (auditor). Mem. Cursillo Movement. Home: 181 Irvington St Daly City CA 94014 Office: 45 Southgate Ave Daly City CA 94015

ABESS, BERTHA UNGAR, investment co. exec.; b. Atlanta, Mar. 11, 1916; d. Arthur Arnold and Marcella (Marshall) Ungar; student Pine Manor Jr. Coll., Wellesly, Mass., 1932-33, Sophie Newcomb Coll., New Orleans, 1933-34; m. Leonard L. Abess, Mar. 25, 1936; children—Linda, Marcella, Leonard. Vice pres. Ungar Buick Co., Miami, Fla., 1965—; v.p. Ungar Marshall Co., Miami, 1965—; dir. Fed. Fire and Casualty Co.; trustee Ungar-Abess Found. Past pres. North Beach Elem. Sch. PTA, Miami Beach; past foreperson Dade County (Fla.) Grand Jury, bd. dirs. Grand Jury Assn.; trustee Greater Miami Opera Assn.; past bd. dirs. Lowe Gallery, Miami; founding mem. Mt. Sinai Hosp., Miami Beach, Fla.; chairperson, trustee Bertha Abess Children's Center, Inc., Miami; vol. Red Cross, Miami; mem. U. Miami Soc. Founders, Coral

Gables, Fla. Democrat. Jewish. Club: Palm Bay, Jockey, Westview, Ocean Reef; Harmonie (N.Y.). Home: 5255 Collins Ave PHB Miami Beach FL 33140

ABKEN, THELMA OREBAUGH, med. sec.; b. Glasco, Kans., Aug. 12, 1921; d. Fred Peter and Lilly May (Mathews) Orebaugh; student Rio Hondo Community Coll., 1971-72; children by previous marriage—Kathleen Marie, Alfred Lewis. Sec., asst. to bus. mgr. Fred C. Nelles Sch., Whittier, Calif., 1962-77; profl. sec., Met. State Hosp., Norwalk, Calif., 1977-80, clerical cons. to exec. dir., 1980—. Pres., PTA; v.p. Whittier council PTA; sec., v.p. Whittier Edn. Study Council, 1960—; mem. lay adv. com. Rancho Sch. Dist., Pico Rivera, Calif., mem. publicity staff Whittier Democratic Club, 1965—; sec. Pico Rivera Christian Ch. Mem. Whittier Profl. Womens Assn., Calif. State Employees Assn. (pres.). Office: 11400 Norwalk Blvd Norwalk CA 90650

ABLER, ELIZABETH E., writer; b. Chgo., Sept. 6, 1917; d. Arthur and Bertha (Chon) Engelman; student Oberlin Coll., 1934-35; B.A., U. Chgo., 1938, postgrad., 1938-39; m. Julius Abler, Oct. 21, 1942; children—William Lewis, Katherine Abler Harvey. Columnist, Movie-Radio Guide, Chgo., 1940-43; free-lance writer articles, stories, poetry, 1958—; judge Am. Rose Soc., 1977—; instr. writing Central Lake County Arts Council, Libertyville, Ill., 1978—; lectr. Garden Club Ill., 1974—. Exec. com. Chamber Music Soc. Chgo., 1956-65; exec. bd. Children's Home and Aid Soc., 1961-71; women's bd. dirs. Alliance Française of Chgo., 1959-79, Fine Arts Music Found., 1960-71, Ill. Opera Guild, 1961-69. Christian Scientist. Clubs: Arts of Chicago; The Quadrangle.

ABNER, DORIS MARIE, bus. exec.; b. Burdine, Ky., Sept. 22, 1935; d. Walter Theodore and Cora Beaman (Thompson) Hammock; student Sinclair Community Coll., 1974-77; m. John William Overley, July 31, 1954 (dec. 1957); children—John, Cheryl; m. 2d, George Herman Abner, Nov. 24, 1959; 1 dau., Kimberley. Sec., NCR, Dayton, Ohio, 1953-55, 58-60; office mgr. Bergstrom Paper Co., West Carrollton, Ohio, 1966-74; office mgr. Con/Steel Corp., Dayton, 1974-77; office mgr. Allcon Bldg. Co., West Carrollton, 1977—; tchr. Kettering Adult Night Sch. Youth dir. West Carrollton Baptist Ch., 1972-76; dir. Coop. Office Edn., West Carrollton High Sch., 1972-74. Republican. Home: 433 Gibbons Rd West Carrollton OH 45449 Office: PO Box 308 1170 E Central Ave West Carrollton OH 45449

ABRAHAMS, BETH, info. services co. exec.; b. Springfield, Mass., June 14, 1954; d. Kenneth Gordon and Rosalie (Saffer) A.; cert. in data processing Computer Processing Inst., 1974. Customer software rep. Olivetti Corp., Hartford, Conn., 1974-77; regional customer service rep. Harris Corp., Burlington, Mass., 1977-79; product mgr. of devel. Shear Devel. Co., Boston, 1979-81; mgr. integration and test NEC Info. Systems Inc., Lexington, Mass., 1981—. Home: 47A Beacon Village Burlington MA 01803 Office: 5 Militia Dr Lexington MA 02173

ABRAHAMSEN, CATHIE ELLEN, nurse; b. Chgo., July 28, 1950; d. Phillip Michael and Doris Catherine (Foster) Gearon; A.D.N., Mayfair Jr. Coll., Chgo., 1974; B.S. in Nursing, No. Ill. U., 1978, M.S. in Nursing, 1980; m. Paul Abrahamsen, Sept. 24, 1974; children— Jena, Kyra. Staff nurse U. Ill. Hosp., 1974-75; staff nurse Henry Horner Childrens Center, Chgo., 1976-77, head nurse, 1978-79, asst. dir. social skills program, 1978-79, after care coordinator, 1978-79; head nurse Chgo. Lakeshore Hosp., 1977-78; instr. Northwestern U., Chgo., 1980—; adj. instr. Ill. Sch. Dist. 211; pvt. practice nursing cons., Palatine, Ill., 1979—; instr. Elmhurst Coll., 1982—. Mem. Ill. Nurses Assn. Home: 102 E Gilbert St Palatine IL 60067 Office: 190 Prospect Ave Elmhurst IL 60126

ABRAHAMSON, SHIRLEY SCHLANGER, justice, lawyer; b. N.Y.C., 1933; d. Leo and Ceil (Sauerteig) Schlanger; A.B., N.Y.U., 1953; J.D., Ind. U., 1956; S.J.D., U. Wis., 1962; m. Seymour Abrahamson, 1953; 1 son, Daniel Nathan. Asst. dir. Legislative Drafting Research Fund, Columbia U. Law Sch., 1957-60; admitted to Wis. bar, 1962, since practiced in Madison; mem. firm Lafollette, Sinykin, Anderson & Abrahamson, 1962-76; justice Wis. Supreme Ct., 1976—; prof. U. Wis. Sch. Law, 1966—. Mem. Mayor's Adv. Com., Madison, 1968-70; mem. Gov.'s Study Com. on Jud. Orgn., 1970-73; mem. Wis. Bd. Bar Commrs., 1973-76; bd. visitors Ind. U. Law Sch., 1972—; adv. bd. Nat. Inst. Justice, Dept. Justice, 1980—; commr. ins. Consumers Adv. Council. Bd. dirs. LWV, Madison, 1963-65, Union council Wis. Union, U. Wis., 1970-71; bd. dirs. Wis. Civil Liberties Union, 1968—, chmn. Capital Area chpt., 1969. Mem. Am. (mem. council sect. legal edn. and admissions 1976—), Wis. Dane County bar assns., Am. Law Inst., Nat. Legal Aid and Defender Assn. (mem. appellate evaluation design adv. com. 1979-80), Wis. Jud. Council, Order of Coif, Phi Beta Kappa. Editor: Constitutions of the United States (National and State) 2 vols., 1962. Home: 2012 Waunona Way Madison WI 53713 Office: Wis Supreme Ct State Capitol Madison WI 53702

ABRAMOVITZ, RACHELLE S., audiologist; b. N.Y.C., Jan. 23, 1950; d. Abraham and Regina (Rosman) Schleifer; B.A. magna cum laude, Queens Coll., 1971, M.A. (teaching fellow), 1973; Ph.D., City U. N.Y., 1979; m. Asher Abramovitz, Oct. 20, 1974; children—Joshua, Shira Perla. Lectr., Queens Coll., N.Y.C., 1971-75, 79—, Hunter Coll., N.Y.C., 1977-79; audiologist Orthopedic and Rehab. Center, N.Y.C., 1975—, Beth Israel Hosp., N.Y.C., 1978-79. Mem. Am. Speech and Hearing Assn. Democrat. Jewish. Home: 105-27 65th Rd Forest Hills NY 11375 Office: 175-62 Hillside Ave Jamaica NY 11432

ABRAMOWICZ, JANET, painter; b. N.Y.C.; B.F.A., Accademia delle Belle Arti, Bologna, Italy, 1952, M.F.A., 1953; children—Alex, Anna. Instr. graphic techniques Accademia delle Belle Arti, 1952-55; instr. art and architecture U. Ill., 1955-56; sr. lectr. fine arts Harvard U., 1971—; painter; works exhibited one-person shows Nantenshi Gallery, Tokyo, Susan Caldwell, N.Y.C., Galleria del/Milione, Milan, Italy, La Strozzina di Palazzo Srozzi, Florence, Italy; lectr. Can., U.S. and Japan; corr. on art Asahi Evening News, Tokyo. Fulbright sr. fellow, 1978-80; fellow Japan Found., 1980, MacDowell Colony, 1975-76, Radcliffe Inst., 1962-64. Contbr. articles to profl. jours. Office: Fogg Art Museum Quincy St Cambridge MA 02138

ABRAMS, JEAN GARDNER, artist, educator; b. Braxton, Miss., Feb. 23, 1936; d. Ambros and Bonnie Catherine (Clark) Gardner; B.S. in Edn., Delta State U., Cleveland, Miss., 1964; M.A., U. Miss., 1968, M.F.A. in Painting, 1980; m. Joseph Robert Abrams, III, May 23, 1954; children—Catherine Jean, Robert Wade. Instr. art Miss. Delta Jr. Coll., Moorhead, 1968—, also art coordinator fine arts dept.; one-woman exhbns. include Miss. Delta Jr. Coll., 1963, Seymour Library, Indianola, Miss., 1964, Percy Library, Greenville, Miss., 1967, U. Miss., 1968, 80, Miss. Art Edn. Assn., 1968. Miss. Arts Festival, 1973, Greenwood Arts Festival, 1972, Central Delta Acad., 1973, Moorhead Library, 1974, Greenville First Fed. Savs. and Loan, 1974, Miss. Art Colony travel shows, 1964, 65, 69, 70, 77, U. Miss., 1964, Delta State U., Miss. Arts Festival, 1967, 68, 73, Cleveland Crosstie, 1970-71, 75, 76, Miss. Art Assn. Jr. Coll. Faculty Exhibit, 1972, Mainstream Mall Gallery, Greenville, 1973, 74, 75; also Faculty exhibits; exhibiting artist Gulf South Galleries; represented permanent collections U. Miss., Newborn Center, Miss. Med. Center, Miss. Delta Jr. Coll., also pvt. collections. Sunday sch. tchr., mem. choir, dir. children's choir Second Baptist Ch., Indianola, Miss. Recipient award Monroe (La.) Ann., 1968, Miss. Nat. Watercolor Show, 1967, 68; hon. mention Cleveland (Miss.) Crosstie Festival, 1971, Holiday Arts Festival, McComb, Miss., 1974; 1st place in oils So. Contemporary Arts Festival, Greenville, Miss., 1966, 2d place in oils, 2d place in watercolor, 1968. Mem. Nat. (past Miss. chmn. tchr of art in higher edn.; state del. 1974-75), Miss. (past pres.) art edn. assns., Miss. Jr. Coll. Art Tchrs. (past chmn.), Miss. Delta Jr. Coll. Faculty Assn. (past chmn.), Nat. Soc. Lit. and Arts, Miss. Art Assn., So. Watercolor Soc., Kappa Pi, Kappa Delta Pi, Delta Kappa Gamma (past membership chmn., past chpt. v.p.). Home: 500 Olive St Moorhead MS 38761 Office: Miss Delta Jr Coll Moorhead MS 38761

ABRAMS, MARJORIE DALE, educator; b. Chgo., Nov. 26, 1937; d. Allen and Audrey Rose A.; A.B., U. Fla., 1958; M.Ed., U. Miami, 1969, Ph.D., 1975. Tchr., Dade County, Fla., 1958-59; sr. personnel counselor James Pair Personnel, Atlanta, 1959-61; asst. to personnel mgr. Corn Products Internat., N.Y.C., 1961-64; personnel mgr. Burdines div. Federated Dept. Stores, Miami, Fla., 1964-67; placement counselor Miami Dade Community Coll., Miami, 1968-69; asst. dean of students U. Miami, 1969-75; asst. research scholar U. Fla., Gainesville, 1975-76; adj. prof. mgmt. Fla. Internat. U., Miami, 1976-79, asst. prof. higher edn. Sch. Edn. and Allied Professions, mem. grad. faculty, 1979-82; edn. and bus. cons., condr. workshops on leadership and mgmt. career devel., human relations and human resource develop. Nat. Endowment for Humanities fellow, 1976. Mem. Nat. Assn. Women Deans, Adminstrs. and Counselors, Soc. for Intercultural Edn., Tng., and Research. Democrat. Jewish. Author: Leadership Achievement Among Women, 1975; Men and Women Together: A New Challenge, 1981. Home: Route 3 Box 176 Chapel Hill NC 27514

ABRAMS, ROSALIE S., state legislator; b. Balt.; d. Isaac and Dora (Rodbell) Silber; R.N., Sinai Hosp., 1938; postgrad. Columbia U., 1939-40; B.S., Johns Hopkins U., 1963, M.A. in Polit. Sci., 1969; m. William Abrams; 1 dau., Elizabeth Joan. Public health nurse, 1941-43; bus. mgr. Sequoia Med. Group, Calif., 1946-47; asst. bus. mgr. Silber's Bakery, Balt., 1947-53; mem. Md. Ho. of Dels., 1967-70; mem. Md. Senate, 1970—, majority leader, 1978—; chmn. Dem. Party of Md., 1978—; guest lectr., witness before congl. coms. Platform com. on nat. health care Dem. Nat. Com., 1979—; chmn. Md. Humane Practices Commn., 1978—, mem., 1971-74; mem. New Coalition, 1979—, State-Fed. Assembly Com. on Human Resources, 1977—, Md. Comprehensive Health Planning Agency, 1972-75, Md. Commn. on Status of Women, 1968—, Am. Jewish Com.; bds. dirs. Sinai Hosp., Balt., 1973—, Balt. Jewish Council, Cross Country Improvement Assn., 1969—, Fifth Dist. Reform Democrats, 1967—; chmn. legis. com. Balt. Area Council on Alcoholism, 1973-75. Served with Nurse Corps USN, 1944-46. Recipient Louise Waterman Wise Community Service award, 1969, award Am. Acad. Comprehensive Health Planning, 1971, Balt. News Am. award, Women of Distinction in Medicine, 1971, traffic safety award, Safety First Club of Md., 1971, Ann London Scott Meml. award for legis. excellence, Md. Chpt. NOW, 1975, Md. Nurses Assn., 1975, service award Balt. Area Council on Alcoholism, 1975. Md. Order Women Legislators (pres., 1973-75), Nat. Conf. State Legislatures (human resources and urban affairs steering com. 1977—), Nat. Legis. Conf. (human resources task force, intergovt. relations com. 1975—). Jewish. Office: 216 Senate Office Bldg Annapolis MD 21401

ABRAMS, RUTH I., state justice; b. Boston, Dec. 26, 1930; d. Samuel and Matilda B. A.; B.A., Radcliffe Coll., 1953; LL.B., Harvard U., 1956; hon. degrees Mt. Holyoke Coll., 1977, Suffolk U., 1977, New Eng. Sch. Law, 1978. Admitted to Mass. bar, 1957; partner firm Abrams, Abrams & Abrams, Boston, 1957-60; asst. dist. atty. Middlesex County (Mass.), 1961-69; asst. atty. gen. Mass., chief appellate sect. criminal div., 1969-71; spl. counsel to Supreme Jud. Ct. Mass., 1971-72; asso. justice Superior Ct. Commonwealth of Mass., 1972-77; asso. justice Supreme Jud. Ct. Mass., Boston, 1977—. Mem. Gov.'s Commn. on Child Abuse, 1970-71, Mass. Law Revision Commn. Proposed Criminal Code for Mass., 1969-71. Recipient Radcliffe Coll. Achievement award, 1976, Radcliffe Grad. Soc. medal, 1977. Mem. Am. Bar Assn. (com. on Proposed fed. code 1977—), Mass. Bar Assn., Am. Law Inst., Am. Judicature Soc. (dir. 1978), Am. Judges Assn., Mass. Assn. Women Lawyers. Editor: Handbook for Law Enforcement Officers, 1969-71. Office: Supreme Judicial Ct 1300 New Courthouse Boston MA 02108 *

ABRAMS, WILLAMAE STEVENS, social gerontologist; b. Pineora, Ga., Feb. 8, 1924; d. Clarence and Viola (Holmes) Stevens; B.A., Eastern Coll., 1959; M.S.W., U. Pa., 1964; Ph.D., Union Grad. Sch., Cin., 1978; m. Watson Abrams, Nov. 25, 1945; children—Clarence W., Charles W., William D. Asst. dir. Assn. Greater Wilmington Neighborhood Centers, 1970-74; dir. edn. and tng. div. aging State of Del., 1974-80; dir. urban gerontology program Morgan State U., Balt., 1980—; mem. Summer Faculty Research and Devel. Workshop, Howard U., 1982. Dist. chmn. Del. Republican Com.; mem. Black Rep. Assn. Del.; founder Del. Caucus on the Black Aged (NAACP Pres.'s award 1978); mem. bd. Nat. Caucus Center on Black Aged. Mem. Acad. Cert. Social Workers, Nat. Assn. Social Workers (Del. pres. 1978-80), Nat. Caucus on the Black Aged. Presbyterian. Research on provision and utilization of social services, retirement and second careers, transp. mgmt. Office: Box 670 Morgan State University Baltimore MD 21239

ABRAMSON, JOAN, author, cons.; b. Los Angeles, Oct. 7, 1932; d. Roman and Katherine (Merkin) Freulich; B.A., UCLA, 1954, M.S., 1955; m. Norman Abramson, July 4, 1954; children—Mark, Carin. Reporter, Palo Alto (Calif.) Times, also Redwood City (Calif.) Tribune, 1955-59; editor Ravenswood Post, Menlo Park, Calif., 1959; freelance writer, editor, Calif., 1959-64; stringer Time mag., Boston, 1965-66; corr. Time-Life Books, Hawaii, 1966-72; instr. U. Hawaii, 1967-73, dir. New Coll., 1973; dir. fed. programs Hawaii Loa Coll., 1978-79; free lance, cons. communications, 1973—; author: The Invisible Woman: Discrimination in the Academic Profession, 1975; Mark Twain's Letters From the Sandwich Islands, 1976; Photographers of Old Hawaii, 1977; Old Boys, New Women: The Politics of Sex Discrimination, 1979; also numerous articles; co-author: The Hill of Life, 1968; Forty Years in Hollywood, 1971; The Faces of Israel, 1972. Grantee Women's Ednl. Equity Act, 1977-78, Fund for Investigative Journalism, 1977, Ford Found., 1982. Address: 3044 Kiele Ave Honolulu HI 96815

ABRAMSON, ROCHELLE SUSAN, violinist; b. Detroit, Jan. 1, 1953; d. Seymour I. and Mayme (Tureck) A.; B.Mus., U. Mich., 1973; M.Mus., Juilliard Sch. Music, 1975, Profl. Studies degree, 1976. Founding mem. Trio N.Y., 1975-78, Muse-Arts Ensemble, Los Angeles, 1978—; 1st violin N.Y.C. Ballet Orch., 1976-78, Los Angeles Philharmonic Orch., 1978—. Recipient awards Artists Internat. Young Musicians Auditions, 1977, Nat. Fedn. Music Clubs Biennial String Competition, 1973, Stillman-Kelly String Competition, 1968, Nat. Arts Club, 1976, Palm Beach Flagler-Matthews Competition, 1974, Charleston Symphony Competition, 1976, Kingsport Symphony Competition, 1975, Talman Prize, Soc. Am. Musicians, 1975, Young Artist award Music Study Club Detroit, 1978. Home: 1750 Camino Palmero Los Angeles CA 90046

ABRAMS-SMITH, PAULA SARA, psychologist; b. N.Y.C., Nov. 22, 1951; d. Arnold and Naomi Frances (Gettenberg) Abrams; cert. Institute Montesano, Switzerland, 1969; B.A., U. Wash., Seattle, 1972; M.S., Nat. Coll. Edn., 1974; Ph.D., Northwestern U., 1977; exec. tng. program Harvard Bus. Sch., Buffalo, 1980-81; m. James Theodore Smith, Nov. 23, 1979. Program coordinator spl. edn. programs Abraham Lincoln Center, Chgo., 1973-74; tchr., psychologist, program supr. Dysfunctioning Child Center, Michael Reese Hosp. and Med. Center, Chgo., 1974-78; research and child psychologist Fisher-Price Toys, East Aurora, N.Y., 1978—; asst. adj. prof. devel. psychology SUNY, Buffalo, 1980—. Mem. Amherst Players, 1978-79, Orchard Park Chorale Group, 1980-81. Mem. AAAS, N.Y. Acad. Scis., Am. Psychol. Assn., N.Y. Met. Assn. Applied Psychology, Nat. Assn. Underwater Instrs., Phi Delta Kappa. Asso. editor Sch. Psychology Internat. Jour., 1980—. Office: 4828 Bussendorfer Rd Hamburg NY 14075

ABREGO, SUSAN REED, educator; b. Denver, Nov, 10, 1946; d. Fred Denton and Frances Ellen (Youberg) Reed; B.S., Hardin-Simmons U., 1968; m. Russell Martin Abrego, Dec. 21, 1968; children—Russell Martin, Christopher Ryan. Tchr., dir. drama-speech McCullum High Sch., Harlandale Ind. Schs., San Antonio, 1968-70, Edison High Sch., San Antonio, 1970-72; tchr., dir. drama North Mesquite (Tex.) High Sch., 1972-74; tchr., dir. drama-speech, tournament dir. Wilson Middle Sch., Plano, Tex., 1974-76; drama dir., tchr. Grand Prairie (Tex.) High Sch., 1976-78; tchr. English, spelling dir., 1978-80, tchr., chmn. English dept., 1981—. Mem. St. Elizabeth Sch. Home and Sch. Orgn., 1976—; advent Montessori Parents Orgn., Dallas, 1981—. Mem. Dallas Shakespeare Soc., NEA, Tex. Tchrs. Assn., Tex. Classroom Tchrs. Assn., Nat. English Tchrs. Assn., Tex. Ednl. Theater Assn., Hardin-Simmons U. Alumni Assn. (v.p. 1972-73), DAR. Democrat. Roman Catholic. Home: 1608 Whitedove Dr Dallas TX 75224 Office: 101 High Sch Dr Grand Prairie TX 75050

ABSHIER, SHIRLEY ANN, geologist; b. Vernon Center, N.Y., Oct. 19, 1936; d. Harry E. and Anna (Cuomo) Sauerhafer; B.Sc., U. Tex., El Paso, 1969; m. Jon F. Abshier, Nov. 5, 1964; children—Debrah, Gerald, Thomas, Patricia. Social services welfare caseworker N.Mex. Health and Social Service Dept., Grants, 1969-72; petroleum geologist Mobil Oil Corp., Denver, 1973-80, editor Mobil Denver E & P Newspaper, 1979-80, mem. speakers' bur., 1979-80; sr. geologist Sunmark Oil Co., Denver, 1980-81; dist. geologist Trans-Tex. Energy, Inc., 1981—. Chmn., N.Mex. Crippled Childrens Assn., 1970-72; charter mem. Grants Boys Ranch, 1970-72; mem. N.Mex. Gov.'s Com. on Mental Health, 1970-72; Jefferson County rep. to Republican County Conv., 1976—. Mem. Am. Assn. Petroleum Geologists, Rocky Mountain Assn. Geologists, Profl. Geologist, Clear Creek County Mining and Metals Assn. Republican. Episcopalian. Editor: RMAG Guidebook, 1979; editor Mobil Messenger, 1979. Home: 19029 W 60th Pl Golden CO 80401 Office: Security Life Bldg Denver CO 80212

ABSHIRE, MARY YOUNG, dietitian, restaurateur; b. El Campo, Tex., Jan. 10, 1952; d. Robert Joshua and Virginia Bernice (Braden) Young; B.S. in Home Econs., U. Tex., Austin, 1973; postgrad. Tex. Woman's U., Houston, 1978—; m. Russell John Abshire, June 22, 1978. Dietetic trainee U. Tex. M.D. Anderson Hosp., Houston, 1974-75; regional dietary cons. Nat. Living Centers, Victoria, Tex., 1975-77; quality assurance dietitian Nat. Living Centers, Houston, 1977, chief corp. dietitian, dietary services coordinator, 1978-81; restaurant owner, El Campo, Tex., 1981—. Registered dietitian. Mem. Am. Dietetic Assn., Cons. Dietitians in Health Care Facilities Group, Dietitians in Bus. and Industry Practice Group, Nutrition Today Soc., Tex. Dietetic Assn., S. Tex. Dietetic Assn., Tex. Restaurant Assn., Omicron Nu. Roman Catholic. Home: 1301 Humphrey Ln El Campo TX 77437 Office: 1804 US Hwy 59 Bypass El Campo TX 77437

ABT, VICKI, sociologist; b. N.Y.C., Dec. 9, 1942; d. Harold and Sylvia (Marcus) A.; student (tuition scholar) Mich. State U., 1960-61; B.A., Hofstra U., 1963; M.A., Pa. State U., 1966; Ph.D. (Univ. fellow), Temple U., 1972; 1 dau., Andrea Abt Jones. Teaching asst., research fellow Temple U., 1967-71; instr. Pa. State U. Ogontz Campus, 1966-71, assoc. prof. sociology, advisor women's studies, 1971—; research cons. Phila. Dept. Mental Health and Retardation. Chmn. Bucks County Community Devel. Citizens Com., 1975—. Mem. Am. Sociol. Assn., Am. Psychol. Assn., Popular Culture Assn., Assn. Anthrop. Study of Play, Soc. Psychol. Study Social Issues, NOW. Jewish. Club: B'rith Sholom. Contbr. articles to profl. jours., chpts. in books. Home: 1617 Graham Rd Meadowbrook PA 19046 Office: Pennsylvania State University Ogontz Campus Sutherland Bldg Abington PA 19001

ABZUG, BELLA SAVITZKY, former congresswoman, lawyer; b. N.Y.C., July 24, 1920; d. Emanuel and Esther Savitzky; B.A., Hunter Coll., 1942; LL.B., Columbia U., 1945; m. Maurice M. Abzug, June 4, 1944; children—Eve Gail, Isobel Jo. Admitted to N.Y. bar, 1947; pvt. practice, N.Y.C., 1944-70, 80—; legis. dir. Women Strike for Peace, 1961-70; mem. 92-94th Congresses from 19th and 20th Dist. N.Y.; presiding officer Nat. Women's Conf., 1977, Nat. Commn. on Observance of Internat. Women's Year, 1977; co-chairperson Pres.'s Nat. Adv. Com. on Women, 1978; pres. Women U.S.A., Inc. Mem. Women Strike for Peace, Nat. Urban League, Women's Prison Assn., Members of Congress for Peace Through Law, Democratic Study Group, NOW, Nat. Women's Polit. Caucus, Women's Action Alliance, Hadassah, ACLU, UN Assn. U.S., B'nai B'rith. Office: 76 Beaver St New York NY 10005 *

ACACIO, CORAZON, pediatrician; b. Manila, June 12, 1942; naturalized, 19 d. Deo and Lily Arabejo; ed. U. St. Thomas, Manila; m. I. P. Acacio, Mar. 27, 1971; children—Gerald, Joyce. Intern, N.Y.C., 1965; resident in medicine Univ. Hosp., Cleve., after 1966, then in pediatrics Michael Reese Hosp., Chgo.; practice medicine specializing in pediatrics; mem. staff Michael Reese Hosp.; physician Nutri-system Weight Loss Centers. Mem. Am. Women's Med. Assn., Kane County Women's Aux., Ill. State Med. Soc. and Aux.

ACCAD, EVELYNE, linguist; b. Beirut, Lebanon, Oct. 6, 1943; d. Fuad Elias and Suzanne (Steudler) A.; came to U.S., 1965, naturalized, 1973; A.A., Beirut Coll. for Women, 1965; B.A., Anderson Coll., 1967; M.A., Ball State U., 1978; Ph.D., Ind. U., 1973; m. Jay Zerbe, June 13, 1969. Instr., Anderson Coll., part time 1967-68; tchr. French and English, counselor Internat. Coll., Beirut, 1968-70; asst. prof. French, U. Ill., Urbana, 1974-79, asso. prof., 1979—, mem. faculty Center Asian Studies, 1970—. Center for Advanced Study fellow, 1978-79; recipient Spl. Recognition award Ill. Arts Council, 1979. Mem. African Lit. Assn., Am. Assn. Tchrs. of French, African Studies Assn., Women's Caucus for MLA, Arab Am. U. Grads, MLA, Nat. Women's Studies Assn., Middle East Studies Assn. Author: Veil of Shame: The Role of Women in the Modern Fiction of North Africa and the Arab World (Delta Kappa Gamma Internat. Educators award), 1978; Montjoie Palestine! or Last Year in Jerusalem, 1980; (novel) L'Excisée, 1982; (monograph) The Long Life Struggle of the Arab and the North African Women, 1982; also film script on mutilated women, articles and revs. Office: Dept French U Ill Urbana IL 61801

ACHESON, ALICE BREWEN, publicist; b. Indiana, Pa., July 26, 1936; d. Stewart F. and Anna M.J. (Mohr) Brewen; A.B., Bucknell U., 1958; M.A., CUNY, 1963; m. Donald H. Acheson, Dec. 12, 1970 (dec.). Tchr. English and Spanish, Mt. Vernon (N.Y.) High Sch., 1958-69; exec. sec., then exec. asst. Media Medica, Inc., N.Y.C., 1969-71; with McGraw Hill Book Co., N.Y.C., 1971-78, asso. editor, 1971-76, publicity asso., 1977-78; asso. publicity dir. Simon & Schuster, N.Y.C., 1979-80, Crown Publishers Inc., N.Y.C., 1980-81; ind. publicist, prin. Alice B. Acheson, N.Y.C., 1981—. Recipient Partner-in-Edn. award N.Y.C. Bd. Edn., 1977, 78. Mem. Publishers Publicity Assn., Editorial Freelancers Assn., Nat. Assn. Female Execs., Am. Soc. Profl. Cons. Address: 144 E 84th St New York NY 10028

ACHOR, SHIRLEY, educator; b. Dallas, June 3, 1928; d. Donald Glenn and Mary (Chambers) Coolidge; B.A. with honors, So. Meth. U., 1969, M.A., 1971, Ph.D., 1974; m. William Benson Parker, Oct. 7, 1950 (div. 1957); 1 dau., Tracy; m. 2d. Hubert Eugene Achor, Nov. 28, 1958. Instr., Richland Coll., Dallas, 1973-74; lectr. Tex. Women's U., Denton, Tex., 1974; asst. prof. anthropology East Tex. State U., Commerce, 1975-81, asso. prof., 1981—. Sec., bd. dirs. Involvement of Mexican Ams. in Gainful Endeavors, 1973. NSF traineeship, 1969-73; Ford Found. fellow, 1973-74. Fellow Am. Anthropol. Assn., Soc. Applied Anthropology, Inst. for Study of Earth and Man; mem. Council on Anthropology and Edn., Soc. Med. Anthropology, Southwestern Social Sci. Assn., Nat. Assn., Bilingual Educators, Phi Beta Kappa. Author: Mexican Americans in a Dallas Barrio, 1978. Office: Dept Sociology and Anthropology East Tex State Univ Commerce TX 75428

ACHTEN, ESTHER (MRS. ALFRED FRIEDMAN), physician; b. Dchurin, Russia, Nov. 27, 1919; d. Jacob and Lifsa (Lernerman) Achten; M.S., Escuela Preparatoria de Mexico, 1937; M.D. cum laude, Nat. U. Mex., 1943; m. Alfred Friedman, Dec. 3, 1944: children—Jack, Frank, Stanley, Melvin. Came to U.S., 1944, naturalized, 1950. Intern, Orange County Gen. Hosp., Orange, Calif., 1947-49; mem. Ross-Loos Med. Group, Los Angeles, 1951—, partner, 1969—, historian, 1969—; gen. practice medicine, Los Angeles, 1951—. Active Pioneer Women for Israel. Fellow Am. Acad. Family Physicians; mem. AMA, Am. Israel, Calif., Los Angeles County med. assns. Home: 1222 S Genesee Ave Los Angeles CA 90019 Office: Ross-Loos Med Center 1711 W Temple St Los Angeles CA 90026

ACKALL, GAIL ARLINE, ednl. adminstr.; b. Chgo., Apr. 10, 1938; d. Fred L. and Lois M. (Dickinson) Wagoner; student Transylvania U., 1955-58; B.A., Valparaiso U., 1960; M.A., Western Mich. U., 1979; m. Edward Ackall, June 14, 1958; children—Diane, Denise, David. Lab. dir. for physician, 1961-68; tchr. Merrillville (Ind.) Jr. and Sr. High Sch., 1968-71; chemistry supr. Mercy Hosp., Benton Harbor, Mich., 1973-79; edn. coordinator Providence Meml. Hosp., El Paso, 1979-81; ednl. dir. med. tech. program U. Tex., El Paso, 1981—. Bd. dirs. El Paso Med. Arts Fed. Credit Union. Mem. Am. Soc. Clin. Pathologists, Am. Soc. Med. Technologists, Am. Soc. Allied Health Professions (dir.). Republican. Mem. Christian Ch. (Disciples of Christ). Home: 533 Redd Rd El Paso TX 77932 Office: 1101 N Campbell El Paso TX 79902

ACKEN, BRENDA THOMAS, corp. exec.; b. Princeton, W.Va., Mar. 16, 1947; d. Murl Price and Pauline Farmer (Woolwine) Thomas; B.S. in Bus. Adminstrn., Concord Coll., Athens, W.Va., 1968. Sr. acct. Higgins & Borman, attys. and C.P.A.s, Beckley, W.Va., 1968-74; sec.-treas., dir. S. Atlantic Coal Co., Inc., Permac, Inc., REP Aviation, Inc., Bakertown Coal Co., Inc., REP Sales, Inc., Tri-States Sales Co., Bluefield, W.Va., 1974—. Treas., bd. dirs. Bluefield Community Hosp., 1979-81, vice chmn. bd. dirs., 1981-82; adv. bd. Bluefield Salvation Army, 1979-82; mem. mus. subcom. Pocahontas Coalfield Centennial Celebration, 1981-82. C.P.A., W.Va. Mem. Am. Inst. C.P.A.s, Nat. Assn. Accts., W.Va. Soc. C.P.A.s (pres. So. chpt. 1976-77, state dir. 1978-81, v.p. 1981-82, Outstanding Chpt. Pres. award, 1977, Outstanding Com. Chmn. award 1979). Republican. Mem. Ch. of God. Clubs: Fincastle Country, Bluefield Quota (pres. 1978-79, dist. gov. 1980-81). Home: 628 Parkway Bluefield WV 24701 Office: 127 North St Bluefield WV 24701

ACKERMAN, DIANA FELICIA, philosophy educator; b. Bklyn., June 23, 1947; d. Arthur and Zelda (Sondack) A.; A.B. summa cum laude, Cornell U., 1968; Ph.D., U. Mich., 1976. Asst. prof. philosophy Brown U., Providence, 1974-79, assoc. prof., 1979—; vis. asst. prof. philosophy UCLA, 1976; fellow Center Advanced Study in Behavioral Scis., Stanford U. Mem. ACLU, Am. Philos. Assn., Author articles in field. Office: Brown U Providence RI 02912

ACKERMAN, DIANE LEIGHTON, author; b. N.Y.C., Sept. 2, 1945; d. Lewis Charles and Florence Marie (Nicholls) Leighton; B.A., Barnard Coll., 1966; m. Martin S. Ackerman, June 29, 1971; 1 dau., Kelly Leighton. Publicity asst., Renault, Inc., N.Y.C., 1966-67, Curtis Publ. Co., 1967-68; beauty editor Status Mag., N.Y.C., 1968-79; publicity mgr. Clinique Labs., Inc., N.Y.C., 1969-71; pres. R.N.B. Leasing Corp., N.Y.C., 1971—, Sovereign Am. Arts Corp., N.Y.C., 1971—; books include: Money, Ego, Power: A Manual for Would-Be Wheeler Dealers, 1976; Living Rich: A Manual for Would-Be Big Spenders, 1978; Getting Rich: The Smart Woman's Guide to Successful Money Management, 1980; The Only Guide You'll Ever Need to Marry Money, 1982; editor: Arthur B. Davies, Essays on His Art, 1973, The Drawings of Maurice Sterne, 1974. Mem. public relations com. Democrats Abroad, London, 1974-78; trustee Martin S. Ackerman Found., 1971—. Home and Office: 730 Park Ave New York NY 10021 Office: 50 Rockefeller Plaza New York NY 10020

ACKERMAN, DOREEN, TV costume designer; b. N.Y.C., Dec. 10; d. Milton Issac and Frieda (Stein) A.; B.S. in Edn., N.Y.U., 1951; M.F.A., Yale U., 1957; m. Frank Bernardo, Dec. 12, 1968; 1 dau., Gwendolyn. TV costume designer; prodns. include: Decoy, 1958; Deadline, 1959; The Arthur Murray Party, 1953; Sesame St., 1970; The Dick Cavett Show, 1970; Secret Storm, 1965-68; The Edge of Night, 1968—. Trustee exec. bd. United Scenic Artists, 1967-68, Beth Chaviruth, 1978—; bd. dirs. Haworth Home and Sch.; mem. cultural arts com. JCC on the Palisades. Nominated for Emmy award, 1979. Mem. Nat. Acad. TV Arts and Scis. Office: E U E Screen Gems 222 E 44th St New York NY 10017

ACKERMAN, FREDA STERN, investment research co. exec.; b. N.Y.C., Mar. 17, 1947; d. Alfred S. and Gertrude (Scher) Stern; B.A. in Polit. Sci., City U. N.Y., 1968; m. Kenneth Jay Ackerman, Nov. 4, 1972 (div. 1980). Analyst mcpl. bond research Dun & Bradstreet Inc., N.Y.C., 1968-71, sr. analyst mcpl. bond research, 1971-73; asst. v.p. mcpl. bond research Moody's Investors Service, Inc., N.Y.C., 1973-75, v.p., asso. dir., 1975-79, sr. v.p., dir. mcpl. bond dept., 1979-81, exec. v.p., dir. mcpl. bond dept., 1981—. Mem. Mcpl. Forum of N.Y., Soc. Mcpl. Analysts, Fin. Women's Assn., Women's Econ. Roundtable, Mcpl. Analysts Group of N.Y., Mcpl. Fin. Officers Assn. Democrat. Home: 315 E 86th St New York NY 10028 Office: 99 Church St New York NY 10007

ACKERMAN, LOUISE MAGAW, writer, civic worker; b. Topeka, July 9, 1904; d. William Glenn and Anna Mary (Shaler) Magaw; B.S., Kans. State U., 1926; M.A., U. Nebr., 1942; m. Grant Albert Ackerman, Dec. 27, 1926; children—Edward Shaler, Anita Louise. Free lance writer, 1930—. Mem. Lincoln Community Arts Council. Mem. Nat. Soc. Daus. Colonial Wars (nat. pres. 1977-80), DAR (past v.p. gen.), Americans of Armorial Ancestry (sec. 1976-82), Nat. Huguenot Soc. (2d v.p. 1977-81), Nebr. Writers Guild (past sec.-treas.), Nat. League Am. Pen Women, Lincoln C. of C., Phi Kappa Phi. Republican. Club: Nat. Writers, Order Eastern Star. Home: Eastmont Towers III Apt 428 6335 O St Lincoln NE 68510

ACKERMAN, SUSAN JANE, advt. co. exec.; b. Utica, N.Y., Oct. 10, 1941; d. Richard James and Annette Louise (Gardner) A.; B.A. cum laude, Harvard U., 1964, postgrad., 1963-64. Research project dir. Young and Rubicam Inc., N.Y.C., 1964-67; dir. of research Bresnick Co., Inc., Boston, 1967-69, Cambridge Mktg. Group Inc., N.Y.C., 1969-72; dir. mktg. Muir Cornelius Moore Inc., N.Y.C., 1973-75; asso. dir. mktg. and research Grey Advt. Inc., N.Y.C., 1975-77, v.p. and sr. assoc. dir. mktg. and research, internat. research coordinator, 1978—. Republican. Episcopalian. Office: Grey Advt Inc 777 3d Ave New York NY 10017

ACKERMANN, GRETCHEN LOUISE, editor; b. Mt. Clemens, Mich., Sept. 29, 1929; d. Harold F. and Norah Medora (Aldrich) Reinhardt; student Albion Coll., 1947-48; B.S., Mich. State U., 1951; m. Ralph C. Ackermann, Mar. 14, 1953 (dec.); children—Brian, Bradley, Jeffrey. Society editor South Macomb News, 1951-53; research writer City of Dearborn (Mich.), 1953-55; reporter, women's editor Dearborn Times-Herald, 1968-70; religious editor, Lifestyles editor, Dearborn Press & Guide, 1970-82, Lifestyles editor, 1982—. Pres., Dearborn Community Arts Council, 1977-79; mem. Mich. Gov.'s Council of Arts, Arts Promotion Adv. Panel. Recipient editorial awards Mich. Health Council, Mich. Press Assn. Mem. Women in Communication, Dearborn Writers' Guild, Pub. Relations Soc. Am., Dearborn C. of C., Woman's Nat. Farm and Garden Assn. Presbyterian. Home: 246 S York St Dearborn MI 48124 Office: 15340 Michigan St Dearborn MI 48126

ACRIDGE, DOROTHY MARIE, real estate exec.; b. St. Louis; ed. Lindenwood Coll., U. Mo.; m. Dec. 13, 1968; 1 son, Dean Richard. Real estate broker, 1960—; pres., chmn. bd. 100 Percenters Inc., franchisor of Realty Executives, Calif.; pres. United Realty Assos., Inc., San Diego; lectr. in field. Mem. Am. Soc. Profl. and Exec. Women. Republican. Home: 8286 Caminito Lacayo LaJolla CA 92037 Office: Realty Executives Nat Hdqrs 1277 Camino Del Rio S San Diego CA 92108

ACTON, ANN, hosp. adminstr.; b. Kankakee, Ill., June 7, 1942; d. Lawrence Donald and Yvonne Marie (Dionne) Boudreau; student Coll. St. Francis, Joliet, Ill., 1959-61; B.A. cum laude in Psychology, So. Ill. U., Carbondale, 1971, postgrad., 1980-82; m. William Arden Acton, Aug. 26, 1961; children—Cory Francis, Michael Arden, Gregory Lee. Asst. dir. human resources Shawnee Community Coll., Ullin, Ill., 1973-74; health planner, adminstrv. asst. Miss.-Ohio Valley Regional Planning Commn., Mounds, Ill., 1974-75; health planner, planning coordinator, field dir., asso. dir. Comprehensive Health Planning in So. Ill., Carbondale, 1975-81; dir. planning and devel. Franklin Hosp., Benton, Ill., 1981—. Adv. com. Lions of Ill. Hearing Services, Ill. Com. Definitional Study of Devel. Disabilities, Ill. Med. Soc.; policy adv. com. Coal Miners Respiratory Disease Program; mem. Regional 208 Water Quality Com., Comprehensive Health Planning in So. Ill.; chairperson Greater Egypt Health Council. Mem. Am. Public Health Assn., Am. Health Planning Assn., Nat. Rural Primary Care Assn., Am. Assn. Hosp. Planning, Ill. Hosp. Public Relations Soc., Phi Kappa Phi. Democrat. Roman Catholic. Club: Ladies Elks. Home: 108 N Horrell St West Frankfort IL 62896 Office: Franklin Hospital 201 Bailey Ln Benton IL 62812

ACZEL, SUSAN KENDE, mathematician; b. Budapest, Hungary, June 22, 1927; s. Lajos and Iren Kende; came to Can., 1965, naturalized, 1972; B.Sc., U. Budapest, 1948; M.Sc., U. Szeged, 1950; m. John D. Aczel, Dec. 14, 1946; children—Catherina Aczel Schulze, Julie Aczel More. Teaching asst. U. Szeged, 1949-50; asst. prof. Tech. U. Miskolc, 1950-52; head cultural dept. City of Debrecen, 1953-55; research asso. U. Waterloo (Ont., Can.), 1965-71. Mem. J. Bolyai Math. Soc. Author bibliographies on math. books in Hungary and on works on functional equations, 1964-75. Home: 97 McCarron Crescent Waterloo ON N2L 5M9 Canada

ADAIR, BURNETA, oil co. exec.; b. Cheney, Kans.; d. Franklin LeRoy and Massie May (Baldock) Young; student Kans. State Coll., 1937-40; m. John G. Austin (dec. 1944); 1 son, John David Austin; m. 2d, Edgar Harvey Adair (dec.); 1 son, Edgar Harvey Adair. Owner, operator Adair Oil Co., Wichita, Kans., 1964—. Bd. dirs. Wichita Collegiate Sch., 1958-62, Wichita Symphony Soc., 1961-64, Wichita Art Assn., 1960-70, Wichita Civic Ballet, 1979—, Wichita Art Mus. Found., 1960-70. Republican. Congregationalist. Clubs: Wichita, Wichita Country, Crestview Country (Wichita, Kans.); Springs, Sunrise (Rancho Mirage, Calif.). Office: 1005 E 2d St Box 2823 Wichita KS 67201

ADAIR, JACQUELINE WALLER, accountant, financial exec.; b. Birmingham, Ala., Aug. 3, 1933; d. Frank Lester and Treasure (Gupton) Waller; B.S., Auburn U., 1955; m. William Michael Adair, Nov. 19, 1955; children—Jennifer Ann, Lauri Lu. Service rep. Liberty Mut. Ins. Co., Birmingham, 1955-56; interior decorator Castner Knott Dept. Store, Nashville, 1956; dept. head sec. So. Baptist Home Mission Bd., Nashville, 1957; treas. Kesler-Klaxon, Inc., Atlanta, 1966-74; treas. Adair Advt., Inc., Atlanta, 1974—; financial cons. several corps. Mem. exec. bd. Riley Elem. Sch. PTA, 1966-70; Brownie troop leader N.W. Ga. council Girl Scouts U.S.A., 1964-65; mem. exec. bd. Riverwood High Sch. PTA, 1971-77, treas., 1975-77. Mem. Auburn U. Alumni Assn., AAUW, Delta Zeta. Republican. Baptist. Home: 3333 Sewell Mill Rd Marietta GA 30062 Office: 2 Northside 75 Suite 333 Atlanta GA 30318

ADAIR, JOAN, investment co. exec.; b. Spokane, Wash., Jan. 18, 1935; d. John Sherman and Laura Georgina (Barnes) Harris; student Santa Ana (Calif.) Coll., 1970-72; divorced; children—Laurie Gaye, Marcus Paul. Personnel asst. City of Tustin (Calif.), 1972-77; office mgr. Santa Ana Coll., 1977-78; agy. N.Y. Life Ins. Co., 1978-79; exec. sec. Tchrs. Mgmt. & Investment Co., Newport Beach, Calif., 1979-80, regional mgr., 1980—. Mem. Nat. Assn. Securities Dealers, Am. Soc. Profl. and Exec. Women, Nat. Assn. Bus. and Indsl. Saleswomen, Internat. Assn. Fin. Planners, Nat. Assn. Female Execs. Home: 5200 Irvine Blvd Sp 221 Irvine CA 92714 Office: 1911 S Commercenter E Suite 409 San Bernardino CA 92408

ADAMCZYK, PAULA MARCHEWKA, mfg. co. exec.; b. Salem, Mass., Feb. 13, 1949; d. Stanley J. and Mariba M. (Markwuith) Marchewka; B.A. in English, Suffolk U., 1971, M.B.A., 1975. Tchr., Peabody (Mass.) High Sch., 1971-72; chief accountant Industrial Cab Co., Essex, Mass., 1972-74, asst. controller, 1974-75; corporate controller, treas. Madico, Inc., a Van Leer corp., Woburn, Mass., 1975-82; v.p. fin. VanLeer Plastics, 1982—; asst. treas. Keyes Fibre Co., 1982—. Bd. dirs. Woburn Council of Social Concern, 1976—. Mem. Nat. Assn. Accountants, Assn. M.B.A. Execs., Woburn C. of C., Audubon Soc., Jacques Cousteau Soc., NOW. Home: 5 Connolly Pl Beverly Farms MA 01915 Office: 64 Industrial Parkway Woburn MA 01810

ADAMIAN, HELEN MARGARET, savs. and loan exec.; b. Reinbeck, Iowa, Jan. 26; d. Walter Magnus and Gertrude Effie (Hildebrand) Thompson; grad. Am. Savs. and Loan Inst., 1971; m. Parnag Gabriel Adamian, June 23, 1979. Bookkeeper, City Nat. Bank, Dixon, Ill., 1948-52; head teller Bank of Melbourne & Trust Co. (Fla.), 1952-56; mem. personnel dept. Boeing Airplane Co., Melbourne, 1956-57; with First Fed. Savs. & Loan of Brevard County, Melbourne, 1957—, now sr. v.p., corp. sec., mktg. mgr. Bd. dirs. ARC, Melbourne. Named Outstanding Woman Exec., Platinum Coast Career Women, 1970. Mem. Home Builders Assn. Brevard (asso.), S. Brevard Bd. Realtors (asso.), Nat. Assn. Home Builders (dir. Brevard chpt. 1973-78), Home Owners Warranty Council Mid Fla. (dir. 1976, 77), Inst. Fin. Edn. (chpt. dir. 1969-81), Melbourne C. of C. Republican. Episcopalian. Clubs: Pilot (charter mem., pres., dir.), Organ; Eau Gallie Yacht (Indian Harbour Beach, Fla.); Suntree Golf and Country (N. Melbourne, Fla.), Patrick Air Force Officer (Patrick AFB, Fla.). Office: PO Box 1000 Melbourne FL 32901

ADAMKO, SUSAN MARIE, mktg. exec.; b. Little Falls, N.Y., July 9, 1948; d. Michael and Frances (Dolezek) Adamko; A.A.S., SUNY, Alfred, 1968; B.S. in M.T., SUNY, 1972. Lab. technician Upstate Med. Center, Syracuse, 1968-71, tech. specialist, 1972-78; product specialist Beckman Instruments, Irvine, Calif., 1978-81; market planning adminstr. Beckman Instruments, Brea, Calif., 1981—; lectr. in field. Patron, Syracuse Symphony Pops Orch., 1973; volunteer Cerebral Palsy Found., 1982. Am. Soc. Clin. Pathologists Ednl. scholar, 1973. Mem. Am. Mgmt. Assn., Am. Soc. Clin. Pathologists, Am. Assn. Clin. Chemists. Contbr. articles to profl. jours. Office: 200 S Kraemer St Brea CA 92647

ADAMO, EVELYN FELEPPA (MRS. IDO ADAMO), psychologist; b. Mt. Vernon, N.Y., Aug. 18, 1936; d. Alfred E. and Anna E. (Foresti) Feleppa; B.S., Boston U., 1958; M.A., Fordham U., 1961, Ph.D., 1965; m. Ido Adamo, June 20, 1964; children—Sonya, Alisa. Research asst. Child Devel. Centre, N.Y.C., 1961-62; clin. intern Norwich (Conn.) Hosp., 1962-64; research psychologist Douglas Hosp., Montreal, Que., Can., 1964-65; cons. psychologist Clifton T. Perkins Hosp., Jessup, Md., 1967—, Mental Health, Cheverly, Md., 1968—; pvt. practice psychotherapy, Laurel, Md., 1971—, Bowie, Md., 1973—; mental health cons. Job Corps, 1981—. Fellow Md. Psychol. Assn.; mem. Am., Eastern, psychol. assns., Sigma Xi. Contbr. articles to profl. jours. Home: 10901 Balantre Ln Potomac MD 20854

ADAMS, ALICE PATRICIA, sculptor; b. N.Y.C., Nov. 16, 1930; d. Charles P. and Loretto G. (Tobin) Adams; student Adelphi Coll., 1948-50; B.F.A., Columbia U., 1953; postgrad. (French Govt. fellow 1953-54, Fulbright Travel grantee 1953-54) L'Ecole Nat d'Art Decoratif, Aubusson, France, 1953-54; m. William D. Gordy, Feb 7, 1969; 1 dau., Katherine Adams Gordy. One-man shows, N.Y.C., 1972, 74, 75, Hall Bromm Gallery, N.Y.C., 1979, 80; group shows include: Whitney Mus. Am. Art, N.Y.C., 1971, 73, Indpls. Mus. Art, 1974, Nassau County Mus. Fine Arts, Roslyn, N.Y., 1977, Wave Hill, Riverdale, N.Y., 1979; represented in permanent collections: Wilson Coll., Chambersburg, Pa., Weatherspoon Gallery U. N.C., Greensboro, U. Nebr., L'Ecole Nat d'Art Decoratif; lectr. Manhattanville Coll., Purchase, N.Y., 1960-79; instr. sculpture Sch. Visual Arts, 1980—. Creative Artists Pub. Service grantee, 1973-74, 76-77; Nat. Endowment for Arts Artists grantee, 1978-79; Guggenheim fellow, 1981-82. Home: 55 Walker St New York NY 10013 *

ADAMS, BETTY VIRGINIA, road constrn. co. exec.; b. Butler, Ga., Jan. 6, 1925; d. William Burton and Martha William (Duckworth) A.; B.A., U. N.C., 1946; B.A., Va. Intermont Coll., 1944. Ptnr., Adams Constrn. Co., Roanoke, Va., 1946—; asst. sec.-treas. Fuel Oil & Equipment Co., Inc., Roanoke, 1949—; chmn. Sailfish Marina Stuart, Inc., Stuart, Fla., 1973-81; partner Roanoke & Salem Trucking Co., Roanoke, 1949—. Mem. Va. Asphalt Assn., Va. Roadbuilders Assn. Methodist. Club: Roanoke Country. Office: PO Box 12627 Roanoke VA 24027

ADAMS, BEULAH GRACE JENKINS (MRS. ADDISON FRANK ADAMS), abstract co. exec.; b. Bastrop, Tex., Nov. 29, 1909; d. Hartford and Beulah Alice (Hemphill) Jenkins; B.A., Baylor U., 1930; postgrad. U. Tex., 1933, 39, U. Colo., 1934; m. Addison Frank Adams, Dec. 26, 1938; children—Forrest Jenkins, Alice Ann (Mrs. Charles Woodrow Miller). Tchr., Bastrop Pub. Schs., 1930-41; v.p., mgr. Bastrop County Abstract Co., Inc., 1942—. Mem. AAUW, Tex. Geneal. Soc., Am., Tex. land title assns., Am. Assn. Petroleum Landmen, Delta Kappa Gamma. Baptist. Home: 1707 Pecan St Bastrop TX 78602 Office: 901 Main St POB 550 Bastrop TX 78602

ADAMS, BROOKE, actress; b. N.Y.C.; attended High Sch. Performing Arts, Inst. Am. Ballet; studied with Lee Strasberg. Film appearances include: Car Wash, 1976, Days of Heaven, 1978, Invasion of the Body Snatchers, 1978, A Man, a Woman and a Bank, 1979, Cuba, 1979, Tell Me a Riddle, 1980; TV movies include: James Dean: Portrait of a Friend, The Last of the Belles, The Lords of Flatbush, The Daughters of Joshua Cabe, Murder on Flight 502; appearances on TV series include: The Bob Newhart Show, Police Woman. Office: care Writers and Arts Agency 450 N Roxbury Dr Beverly Hills CA 90210 *

ADAMS, CHRISTIE TEWKSBURY, public relations exec.; b. San Diego, Dec. 27, 1949; d. Henry Jackson and Lillian B. Adams, Jr.; student Am. Coll. Switzerland, Leysin, 1968-69; B.A. in Art History, Stanford U., 1972; postgrad. U. Hawaii, 1972-73. Advance publicist NBC Entertainment Corp., NBC TV/RCA, Burbank, Calif., 1974; advance rep. Ice Capades, Hollywood, Calif., 1974-76; asst. v.p. Pioneer Fed. Savs. and Loan, Honolulu, 1976-78; dir. public relations Kapiolani/Children's Med. Center, Honolulu, 1979—; site coordinator for Hawaii Health Fair '81. Judge, publicist Hawaii's Jr. Miss Scholarship Program, 1978; mem. Liberty House Consumer Bd., Honolulu, 1978; mem. working women panel Glamour mag., 1979; mem. cast Honolulu Press Club's Gridiron Shows, 1980, 81; TV hostess Friends of Hawaii Public TV's Festival Nights membership/fund-raising dr., 1981. Named to Mademoiselle mag. Coll. Bd., 1971; named 2d runner-up Miss Internat. Beauty Pageant, Honolulu, 1972; recipient awards including Gallery award Hawaii Communicators Assn., 1979, 80, 1st place award for instl. newspapers and mags. Hawaii Med. Assn., 1980, cert. of appreciation YWCA, 1980, citation for 1st place in internal publs. div. splty. hosps. Acad. Hosp. Pub. Relations' ann. MacEachern Awards Competition, 1981; named 1 of 5 winners Hosp. Forum jour. Photography Contest, 1980. Mem. Am. Mktg. Assn., Am. Soc. Hosp. Pub. Relations, Assn. Western Hosps., Hawaii Film Bd., Hosp. Pub. Relations Assn. Hawaii (charter), Internat. Assn. Bus. Communicators (2d v.p., dir. and program co-chairperson Hawaii chpt. 1982), Nat. Assn. Female Execs. (charter), Arts Council Hawaii (charter), Daus. Hawaii, Friends of Iolani Palace, Hawaii Geog. Soc., Hist. Hawaii Found. (charter), Honolulu Acad. Arts, Inventors Council Hawaii (charter; sec., dir. and publicist 1978-79, v.p., dir. 1979-80), Lovers of Arts (charter), Nat. Trust Hist. Preservation. Club: Stanford of Hawaii (sec. 1979-80, dir. 1979-81). Author various internal and external corp. publs., including ann. reports, brochures, fliers, greeting cards, invitations, newsletters. Office: 1319 Punahou St Honolulu HI 96826

ADAMS, CHRISTINE HANSON, pharm. co. exec.; b. Hackensack, N.J., May 24, 1950; d. Kenwood Alwin and Doris (Rogers Hanson; B.A. cum laude, Lafayette Coll., 1972; M.B.A., Duke U., 1979; m. L. Ashby Adams, June 1, 1974. Sales rep., mktg. research Hoffman LaRoche, Nutley, N.J., 1972-76; mktg. research, product mgmt. Burroughs Wellcome, Research Triangle Park, N.C., 1976-79; dir. mktg. research Winthrop Labs., N.Y.C., 1979-81; group product mgr. Pfizer-Pfipharmecs, N.Y.C., 1980—. Mem. Healthcare Bus. Women's Assn., Pharm. Mktg. Research Group, Fortune 500 Bus. and Profl. Women's Club, Am. Mktg. Assn. Republican. Episcopalian. Home: 105 W 55th St New York NY 10019 Office: 235 E 42d St New York NY 10017

ADAMS, DOROTHY BROOKS, city social service ofcl.; b. Gloucester, Va., Aug. 3, 1923; d. Reuben Crystal and Bessie Elizabeth (Davenport) Brooks; m. Alfred Westley Adams, Jr., Nov. 30, 1944; children—Joyce Adams Sanchez, Alfred Westley. With Maiden Form Brassiere Co., Bayonne, N.J., 1946-50, Exquisite Form Brassiere Co., Bayonne, 1950-53, Margon Doll Co., Bayonne, 1953-54, Pert Form Brassiere Co., Bayonne, 1967; with Bayonne Housing Authority, 1968—, social service worker, 1980—; adv. Bayonne Housing Authority Unity Council. Mem. Bayonne Mayor's Com., 1969, 70, 71, 72, 78; vol. Bayonne Hosp.,

1966-68; Central N.J. TB Clinic, 1967-70; mem. Liberty State Park Public Adv. Commn. Recipient Outstanding Citizen award Flournoy-Gethers post VFW, 1981, Dist. 3 and Ladies Aux. VFW, 1981, COM-BIN-ATIONS of Jersey City, 1981. Mem. NAACP (1st woman pres. Bayonne chpt. 1967-68, 1st v.p. 1979-80), NCCJ. Democrat. Baptist (deaconess 1957—). Club: Dorothy Adams Travel. Address: 71 W 44th St Bayonne NJ 07002

ADAMS, EENA J. CARLISLE, dietitian, educator; b. Mt. Hope, Kans.; d. Alfred George and Nora Agnes (Kissick) Carlisle; student Ohio U., 1954-61; B.S. in Home Econs., Kans. State U., 1960; M.S. in Foods and Nutrition, 1970; m. Lawrence D. Adams, Dec. 11, 1940: children—Karen Jean Adams McCarthy, Maureen Janet Adams Mitchell. Tchr., Leonardville, Kans., 1939-40, Jan'es Pvt. Sch., Front Royal, Va., 1949-52, Forestdale Sch., McCracken County, Ky., 1952-53, Jackson (Ohio) County and City Schs., 1953-68, Head Start, Jackson, 1965-68; grad. teaching asst. Kans. State U., Manhattan, 1969-70; asst. prof. home econs. Wayne (Nebr.) State Coll., 1970-76; asst. prof. home econs. and dietetics Morehead (Ky.) State U., 1976-82, coordinator energy mgmt. asst. program, 1979-80; cons. dietitian, 1980—. Mem. Front Royal (Va.) Recreation Council. Delta Kappa Gamma Annie Webb Blanton scholar, 1968. Mem. Am. Dietgtic Assn. (registered dietitian), Nutrition Today Soc., Soc. Nutrition Edn., Am. Home Econs. Assn., Inst. Food Tech., W.Va.-Ohio-Ky. Dietetic Assn., Ky. Dietetic Assn., Ohio Edn. Assn., Chi Omega, Delta Kappa Gamma (pres.), Alpha Lambda Delta. Home: Ka-Mel Farms Beaver OH 45613 also Crique Side Apt 4 Morehead KY 40351 Office: Morehead State U Morehead KY 40351

ADAMS, EVA B(ERTRAND), former dir. U.S. Mint, lawyer, cons.; b. Wonder, Nev.; d. Verner Lauer and Cora (Varble) Adams; B.A., U. Nev., LL.D., 1967; M.A., Columbia, 1937; J.D., Washington Coll. Law, 1968; LL.M., George Washington U., 1950; LL.D., U. Portland, 1966. Tchr., Las Vegas High Sch.; asst. dean women, instr. English, U. Nev., 1937-40; adminstrv. asst. to Senator Pat McCarran, 1940-54, Senator Ernest Brown, 1954, Senator Alan Bible, 1954-61; admitted to Nev. bar, 1950, D.C. bar, 1950; dir. Bur. Mint, Teasury Dept., 1961-66, 66-69; mgmt. cons., 1969—, atty., Washington. Dir. Tele-Trip Corp., Mut. of Omaha Fund Mgmt. Co., Interest Shares. Trustee Palm Beach, (Fla.) Acad.; bd. dirs. Med. Coll. Pa., Interlochen Center for Arts. Mem. adv. com. on rights and responsibilities of women (sec.), HEW, 1974-76. Mem. Reno C. of C., Senate Secs. Assn. (pres. 1943-44), Sales and Marketing Execs., Bus. and Profl. Women, Am. Newspaper Women's Assn., Am. Women in Radio and Television, Cap and Scroll, commn. on White House Fellows, 1970-73, Kappa Alpha Theta, Phi Kappa Phi, Kappa Delta Pi. Clubs: 1925 F Street, Soroptimist. Home: 701 Skyline Blvd Reno NV 89509 Office: Mutual of Omaha 1700 Pennsylvania Ave NW Washington DC 20006 *

ADAMS, FRANCES GRANT, club woman; b. Springfield, Ill.; d. Daniel Harmon and Adah (Morris) Grant; A.B., U. Ill., 1960; student Ill. Wesleyan U., 1938-39, U. Miami, (Fla.), 1945, Am. Inst. Banking, 1959-60; m. Jack R. Adams, Oct. 24, 1945 (dec. 1975); children—Jack Richard, Jr., Alexander Beall, Frances Grant II. Sec., Ill. Senate, 1936; sec., bus. mgr. Wesleyan U. Ill., 1938-39; sec. to chief staff Flying Tng. Command, USAAF, 1951, personnel supr. U.S. Army Air Base, Ephrata and Moses Lake, Wash., 1941-42; job classification and adminstrv. survey analyst Canal Zone, 1942-44; sec. to comdr. USAF Res. Wing, Pitts., 1951-55; sec. to mayor City of Wheeling (W.Va.), 1955-59; sec. W.Va. Ho. of Dels., 1965-66, 77-80, W. Va. Senate, 1981—; mem. D.A.R., 1949—, nat. vice chmn. service for vet. patients, 1968-71, editor W.Va. news, 1965-71, parliamentarian W.Va. soc., 1979, dir. No. dist. W.Va., 1980—; nat. chmn. public relations Nat. Soc. Women Descs. Ancient and Honorable Arty. Co., 1974-77; mem. Nat. League Am. Pen Women, 1949—, nat. 3d v.p., 1971-72, nat. rec. sec., 1966-68, nat. chmn. orgn., 1972-74, nat. chmn. commemorative endowment fund, 1976-80. Mem. AAUW, Magna Charta Dames, Colonial Order of the Crown, Order of Washington, Phi Beta Kappa. Democrat. Presbyterian. Home: Route 1 Box 63 Elkins WV 26241

ADAMS, HAZEL GREENLEE REDFEARN (MRS. PAYTON F. ADAMS II), educator; b. Monroe, N.C., Nov. 12, 1905; d. Ephraim Eugene and Rebecca (Laney) Redfearn; student Radford Coll., 1924; A.B., U. Ky., 1940, M.A., 1953; postgrad. U. Neb., 1955; m. Payton F. Adams II, July 11, 1928; children—Payton F. III, Juliette Greenlee (Mrs. J. B. Hawk). Elementary tchr. Larchmont Sch., Norfolk, Va., 1924-28, Winchester (Ky.) City Schs., 1943-53; supr. Clark County (Ky.) Schs., 1953-61; supr. student tchrs. Ky. Wesleyan Coll., 1945-48; instr. Wesleyan Coll., Macon, Ga., 1960; asst. and asso. prof. edn. Dakota Wesleyan U., Mitchell, S.D., 1961-69; asso. prof. early childhood edn. Pfeiffer Coll., Misenheimer, N.C., 1969—, supr. student tchrs., 1969-73. Chmn., Clark County Community Council, 1950-52, Clark County Recreation Bd., 1955-60; supr. Teen-Town Winchester, 1954-60; mem. adv. council Southeastern Christian Coll., Winchester, Ky., 1977—; active Clark County Hosp. Aux. Mem. AAUW, AAUP, NEA, S.D. Edn. Assn., DAR (treas. chpt. 1975-80), Assn. Supervision Curriculum Devel., Assn. for Childhood Edn., Assn. Childhood Edn. Internat. (adviser Pfeiffer Coll. chpt. 1972-73), N.C. Assn. Supervisory Educators. Mitchell Bus. and Profl. Women Club, Albemarle Bus. and Profl. Women (pres. 1972-73), Ky. Hist. Soc., Nat. Trust Hist. Preservation, Phi Kappa Phi (pres. 1964-66), Delta Kappa Gamma (pres. 1964-66), Pi Gamma Mu. Methodist. Clubs: Irvine (Ky.) Garden, Daniel Boone Music, Christian Women's, Order Eastern Star. Home: 136 College St Winchester KY 40391 Office: Pfeiffer Coll Misenheimer NC 28109

ADAMS, HELEN ALICE REIS, real estate broker; b. St. Louis, May 4, 1924; d. Edwin Joseph and Gladys Ellen (Hines) Reis; student public schs., St. Louis; children—Robert Harden Owen, David Alan Adams, Charles Michael Adams. Salesperson, Dolan Co., Realtors, Clayton, Mo., 1952-61; pres., broker Adams Realty Co., Pasadena Hills, Mo., 1961-62; owner, pres. Helena Co., Kansas City, Kans., 1962-65; v.p. Varnum/Armstrong/Deeter, Inc., Overland Park, Kans., 1965-79; Realtor-asso. Cummings Realty Inc., Ft. Lauderdale, Fla., after 1979, now Stockamore Realty, Inc., Ft. Lauderdale, Fla. Vice pres. bd. dirs. Breakthrough House; bd. dirs. Henderson Mental Health Center Aux. Mem. Nat. Assn. Realtors, Johnson County (Kans.) Bd. Realtors, Ft. Lauderdale Bd. Realtors, Women's C. of C. Kansas City, Internat. Transactional Analysis Assn., Kans. U. Alumni Assn. Republican. Editor: Stockamore Bull. Home: 5100 N Ocean Dr Apt 311 Fort Lauderdale FL 33308 Office: Stockamore Realty Inc 4727 N Ocean Blvd Fort Lauderdale FL 33308

ADAMS, HELEN FRANCES, metal works co. exec.; b. Louisville, Oct. 3, 1930; d. Morris E. and Sarah E. (Singer) Yates; student U. Cin., 1961-63, U. Louisville, 1970-72; m. Charles J. Haendel, Oct. 15, 1949 (div. 1964); children—Charles, Glen, Scott, Susan; m. 2d, Irvin Adams, June 19, 1969 (dec. Aug. 16, 1970). Office mgr. Joseph Zobay, Inc., Cin., 1963-65, Tru-Wall Inc., Cin., 1965-67, Chgo. Ornamental Iron Co., Melrose Park, Ill., 1974-76; field acct. Turner Constrn. Co., Cin., 1967-74; controller Reliable Sheet Metal Works, Inc., Elk Grove Village, Ill., 1976-80; corp. officer Allied Mech. Industries, Inc., Chgo.; adv. constrn. tech. Triton Coll., River Grove, Ill. Pres. St. James Sch. PTA, Cin., 1962. Mem. Nat. Assn. Women in Constrn. (past chpt. pres., nat. dir. Region 13, past nat. com. chmn., nat. treas.). Home: 5400 Astor Ln Rolling Meadows IL 60008 Office: 5210 N Otto Ave Chicago IL 60656

ADAMS, IRENE MANKE, mgmt. cons.; b. St. Peter, Minn., Jan. 5, 1944; d. George Edward and Margaret Jeanette (Katzenmeyer) Manke; B.S., Hamline U., 1965; postgrad. Mankato State U., 1969-72; m. Rex C. Adams, Apr. 8, 1978. Tchr. public schs., De Soto, Wis., 1966-69, Le Center, Minn., 1969-74; mgmt. cons. Profl. Budget Plan, Madison, Wis., 1974-76, WOFAC, Moorestown, N.J., 1976-78; instr. U. Alaska, Anchorage, 1978; mgr. No. Inst. of Anchorage, 1979; area rep. Sycom, Anchorage, 1980—; sales asso. Century 21 Northwind, Anchorage, 1981—. Bd. dirs. Eastern Conf., United Ch. of Christ, 1973-74. Named Anchorage Bus. Leader of Day, 1980. Mem. Am. Mgmt. Assn., Nat. Assn. Realtors, Alaska Assn. Realtors, Anchorage Bd. Realtors. Clubs: Anchorage Bus. and Profl. Women's (2nd v.p. 19 -), Order of Eastern Star (worthy matron 1974-75). Address: 3110 Draco Dr Anchorage AK 99502

ADAMS, JEAN RUTH, entomologist; b. Edgewater Park, N.J., Aug. 17, 1928; d. Herbert Raymond and Gertrude Gladys (Budd) A.; B.S., Rutgers U., 1950, Ph.D. (Trubeck fellow), 1962. Lab. technician Rohm & Haas Co., Bristol, Pa., 1951-57; postdoctoral fellow U. Pa., Phila., 1961-62; research entomologist U.S. Dept. Agr., Agr. Research Center, Beltville, Md., 1962—; cons. insect pathology, electron microscopy, 1958—. Mem. nominating com. D.C. Bapt. Conv., 1977-79, dir. Acteens, Mission Youth Orgn., D.C. Bapt. Conv., 1972—, Sunday sch. tchr. 1st Bapt. Ch., Hyattsville, Md., 1962—, chmn. Christian edn. bd., 1973-74, mem. nominating com., 1974-77, mem. bd. missions, 1977-80, ch. treas., 1973-74, mem. choir, 1979—, diaconate, 1980—, vice chmn., 1981-82; trustee Bapt. Home, 1982—. Registered profl. entomologist. Mem. Electron Microscopy Soc. Am. (chmn. sci. exhibits ann. meeting 1982), Entomol. Soc. Am., Am. Soc. for Cell Biology, Soc. for Invertebrate Pathology (sec. 1982-84), Washington Soc. for Electron Microscopy (council 1980—, sec. 1980-82), Washington Entomol. Soc., Md. Entomol. Soc., Washington Electron Microscopy Council (sec.-treas. 1976-78), Sigma Xi, Sigma Delta Epsilon. Contbr. articles to profl. jours. Home: 6004 41st Ave Hyattsville MD 20782 Office: US Dept Agr Agr Research Center-W Insect Pathology Lab Bldg 011A Room 214 Beltsville MD 20705

ADAMS, JEANNE MARIE, clin. social worker; b. Miami Beach, Fla., Apr. 4, 1951; d. John H. and Eula E. (Strickland) A.; A.A., Miami-Dade Community Coll., 1971; B.S., Fla. State U., 1973; grad. cert. in gerontology Rocky Mountain Gerontology Center, U. Utah, 1978; M.S.W., U. Kans., 1981. Outreach worker Steele Brooks Center, Tallahassee, Fla., 1971-72; social worker trainee Dade County (Fla.) Comprehensive Drug Program, Miami, 1973; counselor Steele Brooks Drug and Alcohol Info. Center, Tallahassee, 1974; social worker community services div. United Way, Miami, 1975; social worker Hallandale (Fla.) Social Services, 1975, North Central Mont. Community Mental Health Center, Great Falls, 1976-79; clin. social worker trainee The Menninger Found., Topeka, 1980-81; clin. social worker Miami Jewish Home and Hosp., Douglas Gardens Community Mental Health Center, Miami Beach, 1981—. Bd. dirs. ret. sr. vol. program, Great Falls, Mercy Home, Great Falls. Recipient Nat. Council on Mental Health Center award of excellence, 1976. Mem. Nat. Assn. Social Workers, Western Gerontology Soc. Address: 10 NE 132d St North Miami FL 33161

ADAMS, JO-ANN MARIE, computer systems analyst; b. Los Angeles, May 27, 1949; d. Joseph John and Georgia S. (Wein) A.; A.A., Pasadena City Coll., 1968; B.A., Pomona Coll., 1970; M.A., Calif. State U., Los Angeles, 1971. Secondary tchr. South Pasadena (Calif.) Unified Schs., 1970-71; appraiser Riverside County (Calif.) Assessor's Office, 1972-74; systems and procedures analyst Riverside County Data Processing Dept., 1974-76, supervising systems analyst, 1976-79; systems analyst computer Boeing Computer Services Co., Seattle, 1979-81; sr. systems analyst Thurston County, Olympia, Wash., 1981—; instr. Riverside City Coll., 1977-79. Chairperson legis. task force Riverside/San Bernardino chpt. NOW, 1975-76, chpt. co-chairperson, 1978; mem. ethics com. Calif. NOW Inc., 1978; alt. del. Calif Democratic Caucus, 1978. Mem. NOW, Nat. Abortion Rights Action League, Am. Mgmt. Assn., Nat. Assn. Female Execs., Nat. Assn. Computing Machinery, Pomona Coll. Alumni Assn. Home: 12313 98th Ave E Puyallup WA 98373 Office: 2000 Lake Ridge Dr SW Olympia WA 98502

ADAMS, KAREN GUNHILD, librarian; b. Eriksdale, Man., Can., May 3, 1946; d. Everet Harold and Margaret Anna (Goranson) Sidwall; B.A. with honors, U. Man., 1967; M.L.S., U. Western Ont., 1975; postgrad. U. Winnipeg; children—Karina Jarry, Richard Everet. Spl. projects dir. Evergreen Sch. Div., 1975-76; cataloger Man. Govt. Pub. Library Services, Winnipeg, 1977-78, cons., 1978-81, acting dir., 1979-81, dir. pub. library services br. dept. cultural affairs and hist. resources, 1981—; instr. evening program Red River Community Coll., 1978-79; cons. librarian Teshmont Cons., 1977-78. Dir., Ft. Rouge Child Care, 1977-79, chmn., 1979-81. Mem. Can. Library Assn., Inst. Pub. Adminstrn. Can., Provincial and Territorial Library Dirs. Council (sec. 1981—), Man. Library Assn. (dir. 1980-81). Office: 139 Hamelin St Winnipeg MB R3T 4H4 Canada

ADAMS, KATHERINE M. THOMAS, news anchor-reporter; b. Pitts., Oct. 16, 1952; d. Timothy L. and Gace (Mason) Thomas; student Malone Coll., 1970-72, Kent State U., 1974; m. Herman L. Adams; 1 son, H. Dean. Copywriter, WJKW-TV, Storer Broadcasting, Cleve., 1974-75, prodn. asst., 1975-76, reporter, 1976—, noon news anchor, 1976—, weekend anchor WJBK-TV, Storer Broadcasting Co., Detroit, 1982—. Mem. community adv. bd. Salvation Army; mem. Cleve. Mayor's Community Relations Bd., 1980. Mem. Am. Fedn. Television and Radio Artists. Salvationist. Office: 5800 S Marginal Rd Cleveland OH 44103

ADAMS, LAURIE MARIE, art historian, psychoanalyst, educator; b. N.Y.C., Sept. 29, 1941; d. Daniel Edward and Helen Louise (Nelson) Schneider; B.A., Newcomb Coll., 1962; M.A. in Psychology, Columbia U., 1963, Ph.D. in Art History, 1967; m. John Brett Adams, July 24, 1970; children—Alexa, Caroline. Prof. art history John Jay Coll., City U. N.Y., 1966—; vis. asst. prof. U. Fla., Gainesville, 1967, Sarah Lawrence Coll., Bronxville, N.Y., 1967, Mt. Holyoke Coll., 1972; lectr. Columbia U., N.Y.C., 1968, instr. Sch. of Visual Arts, N.Y.C., 1976; pvt. psychoanalytic practice N.Y.C., 1978—. Recipient CUNY summer travel grantee, 1967, 68; Columbia summer travel grantee, 1966. Mem. Am. Psychol. Assn. (asso.), Coll. Art Assn., N.Y. Center for Psychoanalytic Tng. (asso.). Editor: Giotto in Perspective, 1974; Art Cop, 1974; Art on Trial, 1976. contbr. articles to profl. jours. Office: 444 W 56th St New York NY 10019

ADAMS, MARCIA HOWE, lawyer; b. Pasadena, Calif., Apr. 2, 1948; d. Paul Henry and Dorothy Mae (Powell) Howe; B.A., Wellesley Coll., 1970; postgrad. Hastings Coll. Law, 1975-76; J.D., Stanford U., 1978; m. Jonathan E. Adams III, June 20, 1970; 1 dau., Natalie Marie. Tchr. social studies Bates Jr. High Sch., Sumter, S.C., 1970-72; med. sec. physiology dept. U. Pa., Phila., 1973; mem. paralegal staff Pepper, Hamilton & Scheetz, Phila., 1973-74, Petty, Andrews, Tufts and Jackson, San Francisco, 1974-75; admitted to Calif. bar, 1978, U.S. Dist. Ct. bar, 1978; asso. firm Ware, Fletcher & Freidenrich, Palo Alto, Calif., 1978-80; atty. Hewlett-Packard Co., Palo Alto, 1980—. Elder 1st Presbyn. Ch. of Palo Alto, 1981-83. Mem. Am. Bar Assn., State Bar Calif., Palo Alto Bar Assn. Club: West Bay Wellesley (v.p. 1980-81). Office: 3000 Hanover St Palo Alto CA 94304

ADAMS, MARGARET DIANE, assn. exec.; b. St. Paul, Oct. 31, 1937; d. William Frank and Margaret Mary (O'Donnell) Rudolph; B.A., Met. State U., 1976; m. Ronald Earl Adams, Feb. 25, 1976; children—Margaret, Michelle and Mark (triplets); children by previous marriage—Roberta, Barbara, William, John, Dana. Bookkeeper, Universal CIT Credit Corp., 1956-59; clk. U. Minn., 1963-65; sec. Granville House, St. Paul, 1965-67, adminstrv. asst., 1967-72; adminstrv. asst. Assn. of Halfway House Alcoholism Programs of N. Am., Inc., St. Paul, 1972, project coordinator, 1973-74, project dir., 1974-78, acting dir., 1978-79, exec. dir., 1979-81; pres. Adams Enterprises, 1981—; cons. Nat. Center for Alcohol Edn.; lectr., adviser Lakewood Community Coll. Mem. Nat. Assn. Female Execs. (network dir. 1979—), Nat. Assn. Alcoholism Counselors, Minn. Assn. Alcoholism Counselors, Minn. Assn. Alcoholism Counselors, Ind. Assn. Alcoholism and Drug Abuse Counselors (cert. alcoholism and drug counselor), Nat. Coalition for Adequate Alcoholism Programs, N. Am. Indian Women's Council on Chem. Dependency. Author: Women: On Women in Recovery, 1976; mem. editorial bd. Do It Now Found., 1978-79. Office: Adams Enterprises 996 Bush Ave Saint Paul MN 55106

ADAMS, MARGARET PATRICIA, accountant; b. Washington, Pa., Feb. 5, 1931; d. Michael and Mary Ann (Kerin) A.; B.S., Point Park Coll., Pitts., 1974. From office clk. to acctg. supr. Indsl. Enterprises Washington, Inc., 1949-72; acctg. supr. Reliance Electric Co. div. Exxon Corp., Washington, Pa., 1972-75, plant controller, 1975—. Bd. dirs. Pa. Assn. Blind, Washington, 1981—, fin. chmn., 1962. Mem. Acctg. Assn. Washington County (dir.), Bus. and Profl. Women's Club, Washington County History and Landmarks Found., Friends of Washington Library, Cath. Daus. Am. Roman Catholic. Club: Gaelic Arts (Pitts.). Home: 272 Crest Ave Washington PA 15301 Office: 320 Museum Rd Washington PA 15301

ADAMS, MARJORIE ELLEN, librarian; b. Salisbury, Md., Oct. 20, 1941; d. Harold Burl and Christine (Baker) Adams; B.S., U. Del., 1963; M.L.S., Ind. U., 1969. Tchr., Bridgeville (Del.) Consol. Schs., 1963-65, St. Charles Sch., Bloomington, Ind., 1965-67; reference librarian Undergrad. Library, Ind. U., Bloomington, 1969; asst. head circulation dept. Ohio State U. Libraries, Columbus, 1969-70, serial bibliographer, 1970-71, head serial div. acquisition dept., 1971—. Mem. ALA, Ohio Library Assn., Acad. Library Assn. Ohio, Ohio Valley Group Tech. Service Librarians. Democrat. Roman Catholic. Office: Ohio State Libraries 1858 Neil Ave Columbus OH 43210

ADAMS, MIRIAM (MRS. WILLIAM S. HOWLAND), communications specialist; b. N.Y.C., July 8, 1941; d. Joseph Vincent and Rose Sandra (Zeichner) Mazzola; B.A., Coll. City N.Y., 1963; m. William Stapleton Howland, Feb. 14, 1974. Account exec. Jay DeBow & Partners, Inc., N.Y.C., 1963-66; asst. dir. public affairs Meml. Sloan-Kettering Cancer Center, N.Y.C., 1966-75, dir. office of cancer communications, 1975—, dir. cancer communications internship program, 1977—, mem. cancer control steering com., 1979—; exec. news editor Oncology Times, 1979—; vis. lectr. Grad. Sch. Health Edn., Adelphi U., 1979—. Mem. exec. com. Coalition on Critical Health Issues N.Y. State; mem. adminstrv. bd. Soc. Meml. Sloan-Kettering Cancer Center, mem. citywide adv. council on sch. health N.Y.C. Mem. Am. Med. Writers Assn., Internat. Communication Assn., Hosp. Public Relations Soc. Greater N.Y., Community Agy. Public Relations Assn. Clubs: Sitzmark Golf and Tennis, Griffis Faculty, Cornell U., Publicity. Home: 345 E 68th St New York NY 10021 Office: 1275 York Ave New York NY 10021

ADAMS, ODESSA CHASTAIN, credit union exec.; b. Brownwood, Tex., Jan. 10, 1909; d. Homer Hardin and Dora Frances (Baugh) Chastain; B.S., Howard Payne Coll., Brownwood, 1949; diploma class credit union personnel, U. Houston, 1974; m. William Franklin Adams, Dec. 25, 1929; 1 son, Gene Darrell. Bookkeeper, 1927-29; tchr. math. Monahans (Tex.) High Sch., 1942-74; mgr. Ward County (Tex.) Tchrs. Credit Union, Monahans, 1957—; chpt. pres. Permian Credit Union, 1968-69. Mem. Fed. Dist. Jury, Pecos, Tex., 1976, Monahans City Com. for Beautification, 1956. Mem. NEA, Tex. Tchrs. Assn., S.W. CUNA Sch. Grad. Assn. Democrat. Baptist. Club: Order Eastern Star. Home: 902 S Dwight St Monahans TX 79756 Office: 810 S Betty St Monahans TX 79756

ADAMS, PATRICIA ANN, communications cons.; b. Kitchener, Ont., Can., July 11, 1937; d. Douglas Arthur and Eileen Ada (Baldock) Stuebing; student public schs., Ont.; m. Anthony S. Adams, Jan. 3, 1972; children—Michael, Kathy, Shari. Sports reporter Toronto Globe & Mail, 1953-55; reporter The Daily News, Hamilton, Ont., 1955; free lance public relations writer, Toronto, Ont., 1955-62; critic Telegram, Toronto, 1963, Toronto Daily Star, 1964-65; dir. communications at Microsystems and Bell Can., Ottawa, Toronto and Montreal, 1960-70, communications planner, 1971-72; mgr. ops., dir. info. services Govt. of Ont., Toronto, 1972-75; pres., owner Tri-Com Communications, Ltd., Toronto, 1977—; dir. Ont. Pl. Corp., 1979-81. Adv. bd. Ryerson Polytech. Inst., Toronto, 1977; mem. Internat. Indsl. TV Assn., 1970-71, sec., 1970-78. Mem. Assn. Women Execs. (pres. 1977—), Toronto Bd. Trade. Club: Empire. Address: 61 Berkeley St Toronto ON M5A 2W5 Canada

ADAMS, PEGGY HOFFMAN, govt. ofcl.; b. Mpls., July 21, 1936; d. Donald Brooks and Margaret Jane (Gruber) Hoffman; B.S., Cedar Crest Coll., 1958; m. Harry C. Adams, Dec. 26, 1968; children—Frank, Harry, Edward, Irene. Tchr., Allentown (Pa.) Sch. Dist., 1958-69; sales rep./reporter Quakertown (Pa.) Free Press, 1974-76; advt. cons. Media Dynamics, Bedminster, Pa., 1973-76; dir. Bucks County Consumer Protection and chief sealer weights and measures, Doylestown, Pa., 1976—; dir. Blue Cross Greater Phila. sec.-treas. Bedminster Bicentennial Com., 1976-78, Bedminster Hist. Commn., 1978-82; active Opera Guild of Opera of Phila., 1970—; committeewoman Pa. Republican Com., 1974—; alt. del. Rep. Nat. Conv., 1972; co-chmn. fin. Bucks County Rep. Com., 1975—. Mem. Upper Bucks C. of C. (dir. 1979—), Am. Standard Testing Materials, Soc. Consumer Affairs Profls. (treas. Delaware Valley chpt. 1981—), Pa. Assn. Weights and Measures (legis. chmn.), Nat. Conf. Weights and Measures (nat. chmn. W/M Week), N.E. Conf. Weights and Measures (chmn. consumer edn.), Nat. Assn. Consumer Agy. Adminstrs., Bucks County Fedn. Women's Clubs (legis. chmn.). Ch. of Christ. Club: Quakertown Women's (past pres.). Editor, co-pub. History of Bedminster, 1976; Richland, The Manor, The Township, Quakertown, 1978. Home: PO Box E Edge Hill Rd Bedminster PA 18910 Office: Court House Annex Broad and Union Sts Doylestown PA 18910

ADAMS, ROBYN GROPPER, courier co. exec.; b. Manhattan, N.Y., Oct. 15, 1952; d. Harold and Dee (Zwail) Gropper; student Bradley U., 1970-72, Ohio U., 1972-73; B.S. in Edn. magna cum laude, U. Cin., 1976. With World Courier, 1977—, mktg. rep., Dallas, 1978-80, mgr., San Francisco, 1980, regional mgr. for Calif., Oreg., Wash. State, Burlingame, 1980—. Active Big Sisters Am., Community Workshop, Hunger Project, Holiday Project, active EST Found. Mem. San Francisco C. of C., Air Cargo Assn., San Francisco World Trade Club, San Francisco Jr. C. of C. Home: 562 Vermont St San Francisco CA 94107 Office: 1633 Bayshore Hwy Burlingame CA 94010

ADAMS, SHIRLEY LILLIAN, nurse, educator; b. Ocala, Fla., Nov. 4, 1925; d. John Crosswhite and Martha Ruth (Comer) Bowman; R.N., Gordon Keller Sch. Nursing, 1947; student U. Tampa, 1947-49; B.S. in

Nursing Edn., Duke U., 1957; postgrad. in geriatrics U. South Fla., 1971-72; m. Lester Howe, Oct. 17, 1949 (dec.); m. 2d Bruce Waldo Adams, Oct. 24, 1959; children—Marguerite (dec.), Lori, Bruce Hubert. Sec. subdepot U.S. Army, Drew Field, Tampa, Fla., 1943-44; stewardess Nat. Airlines, 1947-48; pediatric nurse, head pediatric dept. Tampa Gen. Hosp., 1948-51, med. surg. nurse, head nurse Sch. Nursing, 1952-54, med.-surg. coordinator, 1957-59, dir. Gordon Keller Sch. Nursing, 1959-62; part-time tchr. health ARC, Hillsborough County, Tampa, 1963-80; cons. Fla. Bd. Nursing, 1960-61. Vol. sch. clinic nurse, 1981-82; mem. ARC, Nat. Heart Assn., Nat. Arthritis Assn., Multiple Sclerosis Soc., March of Dimes Assn., Easter Seal Guild, Am. Cancer Soc., Christian Women's Fellowship, Yale U. Parents Club, St. John's Parents Club, Christ the King Parents Club; tchr. Sun Coast council Girl Scouts U.S.A.; active Children's Home Aux., Republican Women, polit. campaigns. Recipient award Am. Legion, 1941. Mem. Nat. League of Nursing (cons.), Am. Nurses Assn., Dist. Nurses Assn., Gordon Keller Nursing Alumnae Assn. (adv. bd. 1958-59, reunion chmn. 1982), Duke U. Alumnae Assn. (area chmn. 1959, 65, 66), U. Tampa Alumnae Assn., Asthmatic and Gulf Coast Respiratory Soc., Nat. Hist. Soc., Nat. Smithsonian Assocs., Mem. Christian Ch. (Disciples of Christ) (Sunday sch. tchr.). Clubs: Aux. to Egypt Temple Shrine, Aux. to Masonic Lodge. Home: 74 Bahama Circle Tampa FL 33606

ADAMS, SUZANNE WYCKOFF, YWCA exec.; b. Chgo., May 8, 1947; d. James Berton and L. Lorraine (St. Pierre) Wyckoff; B.S., Iowa State U., Ames, 1970; m. Gerald Wayne Adams, Oct. 16, 1976. Community programs specialist OEO, Des Moines, 1970-73; asso. dir. Kidney Found. Iowa, Des Moines, 1973-75; dir. pub. relations Am. Cancer Soc., Jefferson City, Mo., 1975-76; outreach adminstr. Mid-Am. Cancer Center, Kansas City, Kans., 1977-79; exec. dir. Kansas City (Mo.) YWCA, 1979—; adv. bd. survival skills workshops. Bd. dirs. Dial A Ride. Mem. Nat. Assn. Female Execs., Mo. Assn. Social Welfare, Dimensions Unlimited (pres. 1979-80), Greater Kansas City C. of C., Greater Kansas City Women's C. of C. (bd. dirs.), United Way Agy. Execs. Assn. (treas. 1982). Mem. Christian Ch. (Disciples of Christ). Editor newsletters Am. Cancer Soc., 1975-76, Dimensions Unlimited, 1978-79. Office: 1000 Charlotte St Kansas City MO 64106

ADAMS (STIRLING), ANNE BUTLER, mktg. and public relations exec.; b. Shaw AFB, S.C., Mar. 7, 1944; d. John Adrian and Mary Margaret (Rogers) Butler; B.A. in Edn. and Bus. Edn., La. State U., 1965, M.B.A., 1970; postgrad. in journalism U. Nev., Reno, summer 1982; m. Evan M. Stirling, Dec. 9, 1977. Tchr. public high schs., La., Ga., N.C., 1965-69; loan officer City State Bank, Honolulu, 1969-72; asst. credit mgr. Trailmobile Inc., Dallas, 1972-74; credit and collections mgr. Lear Corp., Reno, 1974-75; gaming supr. Del Webb's, Reno, 1976-77; gaming supr. Summa Corp., Reno, 1977-80; editor Bus. Monitor/Vigen Publs., Sparks, Nev., 1980-81; founder Kamerus Labs., Reno, 1982; dir. Mansfield Bank & Trust Co. (La.). Mem. Public Relations Soc. Am., Internat. Assn. Bus. Communicators, Am. Mktg. Assn., Nat. Assn. Female Execs. Republican. Methodist. Club: Mansfield Country, Hidden Valley Country. Office: 604 Lander Reno NV 89503

ADAMSKY, CATHRYN, psychologist; b. Auburn, Mass., Dec. 18, 1933; d. John Stanley and Mary Ann A.; B.A., Clark U., 1955; Ph.D., U. Rochester, 1959; children—Deborah Levison, Lara Levison. USPHS fellow Yale U., New Haven, 1960-61; asst. prof. dept. psychiatry U. Chgo., 1968-71; asso. prof. dept. psychol. sci. Ind. U.-Purdue U., Ft. Wayne, 1971-81; coordinator women's studies U. N.H., Durham, 1981—; mem. Mayor's Adv. Com. on Status of Women, Ft. Wayne, 1974-75. Mem. Am. Psychol. Assn., Eastern Psychol. Assn., Assn. Women in Psychology (spokeswoman 1979—), Ind. Civil Liberties Union (chmn. women's rights com. N.E. chpt.), Nat. Abortion Rights Action League, Amnesty Internat. Home: 21A Lexington St Dover NH 03820 Office: U NH 307 A Dimond Library Durham NH 03824

ADAMSON, JEANNE ANNE, real estate exec.; b. Phoenix, Mar. 12, 1950; d. Raymond E. and Beverley Adams (Mordetzky) A.; student Phoenix Coll., 1968—. Legal sec./asst. Murphy & Posner, Phoenix, 1970-77; owner Profls., Ltd., Phoenix, 1977; sales asso. Tom Fannin & Assos., Phoenix, 1978; adminstrv. v.p. David R. Johns Real Estate Group, Phoenix, 1978—. Mem. Women Emerging, Nat. Assn. Female Execs., Network, Nat. Assn. Realtors, Real Estate Securities and Syndication Inst., Profl. Exchange, Ariz. Assn. Realtors, Phoenix Bd. Realtors. Club: La Posada Racquet. Office: 1414 E Indian School Rd Phoenix AZ 85014

ADAMSON, LUCILE FRANCES, consultant; b. Chetopa, Kans., Nov. 10, 1926; d. Truby Herbert and Anna Helen (Gail) A.; B.S., Kans. State U., 1948; M.S., State U. Iowa, 1950; Ph.D., U. Calif., Berkeley, 1956. Asst. prof. nutrition Hawaii Agrl. Expt. Sta., 1956-60; asst. prof. dept. pediatrics U. Mo., Med. Center, Columbia, 1960-64; research asso., dir. Core Lab., Harvard U. clin. research unit Thorndike Meml. Lab., 1964-70; sr. research assoc. dept. biochemistry Monash U., Melbourne, Australia, 1970-72; staff scientist Environ. Def. Fund, Washington, 1972-74; prof., program adminstr. program macroenviron. and population studies Howard U., Washington, 1974-81; propr. Biomed. Lit. Intelligence Services, Washington, 1981—; cons. environ. and occupational health, lab. safety, biomed. lit. revs., evaluations. Co-chmn. environ. task force Mayoral Transition Com., Washington, 1978. Mem. Am. Chem. Soc., Am. Inst. Nutrition, Am. Pub. Health Assn., Nat. Environ. Health Assn., Soc. Occupational and Environ. Health. Contbr. articles to profl. jours. Research on hormonal effects on amino acid transport and protein/mucopolysaccharide synthesis in vitro.

ADAMS-RYAN, DIANE, social worker; b. Chgo., Apr. 7, 1947; d. Louis Bernard and Fan (Firestone) Sklarewitz; A.B., San Diego State U., 1970, M.S. in Social Work, 1972; m. R. Michael Ryan, Dec. 18, 1980. Social worker Onslow County Dept. Social Services, Jacksonville, N.C., 1970-71; supr. social work services dept. mental health Mercy Hosp. and Med. Center, San Diego, 1972-77; pvt. practice, San Diego, 1975—; sr. psychiat. social worker Children's Inpatient Service Community Mental Health, San Diego, 1977-82, grad. field instr. San Diego State U., 1974-81. Cert. oral commr. Calif. Bd. Behavioral Scis. Mem. Soc. Clin. Social Work, Am. Public Health Assn., Nat. Assn. Social Workers, Acad. Cert. Social Workers. Contbr. articles to profl. jours. Address: 8950 Villa La Jolla Dr La Jolla CA 92037

ADAMS-SELICO, SHIRLEY LUCILE, nurse; b. Marshall, Tex., Feb. 22, 1941; d. Gerald Hugo and Ella Mary (Hodges) Adams; B.S., Howard U., 1962; grad. Los Angeles County Sch. Nursing, 1975; children—Sherilyn Marie Lum, E. Gerald Steven Lum, Michael J. Premmer. Staff nurse spl. care nurseries, newborn intensive care unit Los Angeles-U. So. Calif. Med. Center Women's Hosp., 1975-81, critical care nurse neonatalogy, 1976-81, clin. instr. nursing. Social vice chmn. Young Democrats Am., Washington, 1962. Mem. Nat. Assn. Negro Women, Nat. Assn. Female Execs., Philathias Soc., ACLU, Psi Chi. Roman Catholic. Office: Queen of Valley Hosp 1115 S Sunset Ave West Covina CA 91790

ADDELSON, KATHRYN PYNE, philosopher, educator; b. Providence, Apr. 22, 1932; d. Joseph Abraham and Catherine (Newton) Etchells; A.B., Ind. U., 1961; Ph.D., Staford U., 1968; m. Richard U. Addelson, Oct. 31, 1980; children—Catherine Casey, V. Shawn. Instr. philosophy Bryn Mawr Coll., 1965-66, CCNY, 1966-67; asst. prof. U. Chgo., 1967-72; prof. philosophy and sociology Smith Coll., 1972—; vis. prof. Northwestern U., 1969, 80, U. Calif., Berkeley, 1971, Loyola U., Chgo., 1974-75. Fellow Nat. Endowment Humanities, 1978-79, Mellon Found., 1978-81. Mem. Soc. Women in Philosophy, Am. Philos. Assn. Exec. editor Feminist Studies, 1976-80. Address: Dept Philosophy Smith Coll Northampton MA 01060

ADDINGTON, GEORGIA LOUISE, med. adminstr.; b. Phila., Sept. 4, 1933; d. George Zimlick and Irene Louise Layer; M.T., Franklin Sch. Sci. and Arts, 1956; m. Donald B. Addington, Aug. 15, 1959; children—David Shepherd, Jonathon Scott. Technologist, biochem. assay LaWall & Harrison Labs., Phila., 1953-56; med. asst., technologist S.G. Shepherd, M.D., Phila., 1957-62; med. technologist S.T. Wild, M.D., N.Y.C., 1963-66; adminstrv. asso., office mgr. Alaska Plastic Surgery Assos., Anchorage, 1968-79; clin. instr. Franklin Sch. Sci. and Arts, 1959-60. Pres., Curtain Raisers, Alaska Repertory Theatre, 1980, bd. dirs., 1980. Mem. Alaska Credit Women Internat., Plastic Surgery Adminstrv. Assos., Confrerie de la Chaine des Rotisseurs. Club: Soroptimists. Home: 15104 Sunset Dr NE Bainbridge Island WA 98110

ADDISON, ANNE SIMONE POMEX (MRS. JOHN ADDISON), television exec.; b. Antwerp, Belgium, Dec. 2, 1927; d. Eli and Mary Deborah (Rubinstein) Cleeman; B.A., Barnard Coll., 1947; M.A., Columbia U., 1952; m. Joseph B. Pomex, Mar. 6, 1947 (div. Apr. 1954); 1 son, Steven M.; m. 2d, John Addison, Sept. 1, 1966. Instr., Columbia U., 1947-48; circulation dir. Ford Found., N.Y.C., 1952-58; asso. dir. Broadcasting Found. Am., radio, N.Y.C., 1958-60; dir. NET (WNET-13) TV internat. dir., 1960—; pres. Communications Internat., 1980—; cons. cultural dept. Dept. State, Washington, 1961. Bd. dirs. Coll. Skills, Inc., N.Y.C. Recipient awards, medals for fostering understanding and cultural cooperation, Austria, Belgium, Holland, Israel, Italy, Brazil. Mem. Am. Women Radio and TV (1st v.p. 1972—), Advt. Club Am., Am. Women in Communications. Contbr. articles to profl. jours. Home: 1035 Fifth Ave New York NY 10028 Office: 767 Fifth Ave New York NY 10022

ADDISON, ARLENE NEWMAN, life ins. co. exec.; b. Phila., Sept. 28, 1946; d. Frederick Paul and Rita Newman; B.A., Temple U., 1969; M.A., Washington U., St. Louis, 1974. Edn. program specialist, public info. specialist Dept. HEW, Washington, 1969-71; advt. cons., Los Angeles, also instr. Antelope Valley Coll., Lancaster, Calif., 1974-78; mgr. advt. and promotions Beneficial Standard Life Ins. Co., Los Angeles, 1978—. Recipient Audio Visual award Internat. Assn. Bus. Communicators, 1978. Mem. Am. Mktg. Assn., Life Advertisers Assn., Am. Mgmt. Assn., Women in Communications, Internat. Assn. Bus. Communicators. Office: 3700 Wilshire Blvd Los Angeles CA 90010

ADDISON, MARY JANE, civic worker; b. Beaumont, Tex.; d. Henry Davis and Corinne (Carter) Pond; R.N., Jefferson Davis Sch. Nursing, 1945; student U. Houston; m. Eugene Morse Addison, Mar. 10, 1946; children—Eugene Morse, Paul Davis. Mem. choir First Bapt. Ch.; den mother Cub Scouts, 6 years, recipient Den Mothers award, 1961; pres. Huntsville (Tex.) PTA, 1955-56, v.p. dist. bd., 1956-57, state life mem. PTA, 1967; pres. Women's Missionary Union, First Bapt. Ch., 1965-68; chmn. heritage com. Mayor's Bicentennial Com., 1974-76; chmn. city beautification com. Tex. Sesquicentennial Celebration, 1982—; pres. Woman's Forum, Tex. Fedn. Womens Clubs, 1972-74, 80-81, named Woman of Year, 1974; charter and life mem. Hosp. Aux., pres., 1971-72; bd. dirs. Cultural Arts Center; active Sam Houston Meml. Mus., Walker County Hist. Commn., Tex. Hist. Found.; mem., dir., sponsor Community Choir. Decorated Grand Peiory of Am. Order St. John of Jerusalem, dame Knights Hospitaller. Mem. African Violet Soc. Am., Daus. Republic of Tex. (pres. Houston chpt. 1970-75, 79-81, registrar 1975—, state rec. sec. gen. 1973-75, state 1st v.p. gen. 1975-77, pres. gen. 1977-79), DAR (regent Mary Martin Elmore Scott chpt. 1972-74, 82-84), Daughters Am. Colonists (regent Capt. John Utie chpt., state corr. sec. 1977-79), UDC (dist. rec. sec. 1974-76, dist. gov. 1981-83), Colonial Dames Am., Dames of Ct. of Honor, Tex. Hist. Assn. (dir., cert. of commendation 1980, 81, mem. state heritage com.), Walker County Geneal. Soc., San Jacinto Mus. History Assn., Lone Star Drama Hist. Assn. (state adv. bd.), Victorian Soc. (charter mem. Tex. chpt.), Am., Tex. (pres. 38th Dist. 1977—) nurses assns., AMA, Spain and Tex. Soc., Tex., Tri-County (past pres.) med. auxs., Tex. Acad. Family Physicians (charter) Beautify Tex. Council. Clubs: Garden (past pres. chmn. city beautification com.); Univ. Women Sam Houston State U. (charter). Address: Huntsville TX 77340

ADDISS, SUSAN SILLIMAN, health planning agy. adminstr.; b. New Haven, Apr. 3, 1931; d. Thomas North and Susan Silliman (Bennett) Tracy; B.A., Smith Coll., 1951; M.P.H., Yale U., 1969, M.Ur.S., 1969; children—Justus Joseph, Susan Silliman. Health educator New Haven Health Dept., 1969-72; dir. Valley Health Dept., Ansonia, Conn., 1972-76; chief Bur. Health Planning and Resource Allocation, Conn. Dept. Health Services, Hartford, 1976—; lectr. dept. epidemiology and public health Yale U. Sch. Medicine, dept. Community Medicine U. Conn. Health Center. Recipient award for achievements enhancing status of women Conn. Fedn. Bus. and Profl. Womens Clubs, Inc., 1976; Smith Coll. medal for service to community, 1981. Mem. Am. Public Health Assn., Conn. Public Health Assn., Am. Health Planning Assn., Phi Beta Kappa. Office: Conn Dept Health Services 79 Elm St Hartford CT 06115

ADDY, JO ALISON PHEARS, economist; b. Ger., May 2, 1951; d. William and Paula (Lee) Phears; B.A., Smith Coll., 1973; M.B.A., Adelphi U., 1975; postgrad. Stanford U., 1975—; m. Tralance Obuama Addy, May 25, 1979; children—Mantse, Miishe. Economic analyst Morgan Guarenty, N.Y.C., 1973-75; econs. con. Nat. Planning Assn., Washington, 1976; Rand Corp., summer 1978; economist World Bank, San Francisco, 1982—; lectr. in field. NSF fellow, 1976-79. Mem. Am. Econ. Assn. Club: ILA. Home: 1904 Rockcliff Ct Arlington TX 76012 Office: Crocker Nat Bank 1 Montgomery St San Francisco CA 76012

ADELBERG, HELEN MIRIAM, physician; b. Bronx, N.Y., May 5, 1937; d. Nathan and Lillian (Pisnoy) K.; student CCNY, 1959, UCLA, 1959-60; M.D., U. So. Calif., 1964; m. Marvin Adelberg, Aug. 30, 1959; children—Diane, Kenneth. Intern, Los Angeles County-U. So. Calif. Med. Center, Los Angeles, 1964-65; resident Cedars-Sinai Med. Center, Los Angeles, 1965-68; fellow in endocrinology U. So. Calif., 1968-69; practice medicine specializing in internal medicine and endocrinology, Los Angeles, 1970—; mem. staff Cedars-Sinai Med. Center, Encino Hosp., Tarzana Med. Center, Sherman Oaks Community Hosp., Valley Presbyn. Hosp.; v.p. Adelberg Labs., Encino, Calif.; cons. on med. hosp. devices and procedures to industry. Diplomate Am. Bd. Internal Medicine. Mem. AMA, Calif. Med. Assn., Los Angeles Soc. Internal Medicine, Diabetes Assn. So. Calif., ACP, Women in Bus., Los Angeles County Women's Med. Assn., Phi Delta Epsilon. Contbr. articles to med. jours. Office: 16311 Ventura Blvd Suite 650 Encino CA 91436 *

ADELMAN, BETSY COLLEN, rehab. orgn. adminstr.; b. Chgo., Apr. 4, 1930; d. Harold I. and Florence (Grossman) Collen; B.A., Roosevelt U., 1970, M.A., 1976; children—Cary, Grant, Skyler. Mem. staff Chgo. Town News, 1969-70; tchr. Chgo. Lighthouse for the Blind, 1970-72, dir. office skills tng. programs, 1973—; tchr. visually handicapped Wright Jr. Coll., Chgo., 1974-75; pvt. practice counseling, Skokie, Ill. Den mother Boy Scouts Am., Skokie, 1962-68. Ill. Dept. Rehab. Services grantee, 1975, 77-82. Mem. Am. Personnel and Guidance Assn., Nat. Rehab. Assn., Nat. Rehab. Counselors Assn., Am. Assn. Workers for the Blind, Am. Rehab. Counselors Assn., Ill. Rehab. Assn., Ill. Fedn. of the Blind, Roosevelt U. Alumni Assn., Am. Council for the Blind. Home: 8930 N Kolmar Ave Skokie IL 60076 Office: 1850 W Roosevelt Rd Chicago IL 60608

ADELMAN, DOROTHY LEE MCCLINTOCK DELFS, artist, printmaker, educator; b. N.Y.C.; d. Erwin Lee and Phyllis (Slater) McClintock; student Art Students League, N.Y.C., Westchester Art Workshop, Hudson River Mus., Silvermine Guild for Artists, Sherman Bus. Sch., Mt. Vernon, N.Y.; m. Hamilton Delfs, Sept. 3, 1941; 1 son, David Hamilton; m. 2d, Emanuel L. Adelman, Sept. 16, 1961. Formerly sec. J. Walter Thompson, N.Y.C., with Saucy Susan Products, Inc., Briarcliff Manor, N.Y.; tchr. printmaking Westchester Art Workshop, White Plains, N.Y.; seminar lectr. in printmaking Elizabeth Seton Coll., Yonkers, N.Y.; one man shows include: Katonah (N.Y.) Gallery, 1972, Mari Gallery, Mamaroneck, N.Y., 1974, Greenwich (Conn.) Art Barn, 1973, 75; group shows include: Hudson River Mus., Yonkers, N.Y., Graphic Soc., N.H., 1974; represented in permanent collections including: Hudson River Mus., Sears, Roebuck & Co., N.Y.C., Beneficial Life Ins. Co., N.Y.C.; mem. council Katonah (N.Y.) Gallery; bd. dirs. White Plains Outdoor Art Festival; cons. printmaking Girl Scouts U.S.A., Chappaqua, N.Y., 1973, 75; mem. arts, humanities and media com. Ogden P. Reid for Gov., 1972. Recipient Dirs. and Purchase award Westchester Art Workshop, White Plains, 1969; purchase award Hudson River Mus., Yonkers, 1971; 1st and 3d award Larchmont Printmaking, 1972; 1st and best in show, printmaking St. Lukes Hosp. Benefit Exhbn., N.Y.C., 1971. Mem. Art Students League (life), Mamaroneck Artists Guild, Yonkers Art Assn., Westchester Art Soc., Council for Arts in Westchester (visual arts affiliates exec. bd.), Abraxas Artists Group (treas.). Home and Studio: Heritage Hills of Westchester 36A East Hill Dr Somers NY 10589

ADKINS, ELIZABETH ANNE, clin. social worker; b. Danville, Ill., Apr. 8, 1941; d. Albert William and Elizabeth Adele (Bahnke) A.; B.A., So. Ill. U., 1963; M.S.W., San Diego State U., 1969. Tchr., Clarence (N.Y.) Central Jr. High Sch., 1963-64; asst. adminstr. D'Youville Coll., 1964; caseworker Erie County Welfare Dept., Buffalo, N.Y., 1964-65; child welfare worker Los Angeles County Dept. Adoptions, 1965-72; public health social worker Los Angeles County Public Health Dept., 1972-74; corp. sec. Health Adv. Group, Inc., Los Angeles, 1978-80; social work supr. Los Angeles County-U. So. Calif. Med. Center, Los Angeles, 1974—. Mem. Los Angeles County Commn. on Life Support Policies, 1979-81; mem. adv. council bio-ethics NCCJ, 1977-78; mem. Santa Monica Symphony, 1970—. Lic. clin. social worker. Mem. Acad. Cert. Social Workers, Nat. Assn. Social Workers (chmn. public relations com.), Los Angeles County Bar Assn. Com. on Legal Aspects of Bioethics, Hastings Center of Soc. Ethics and the Life Scis., Mensa, DAR. Home: 2700 N Cahuenga Blvd E #2207 Los Angeles CA 90068 Office: 1200 N State St Room 6433 Los Angeles CA 90033

ADKINS, LINDA BERKLEY, banker; b. Richmond, Va., May 30, 1943; d. Berkley Benjamin and Mary Virginia (Vassar) Adkins; B.S., James Madison U., 1965. Tchr. English and theater Fairfax (Va.) County Schs., 1966-74; supr., asst. mgr., mgr., word processing officer United Va. Bank Richmond, 1978—; cons. word processing. Mem. Word Processing Assn. Richmond, Am. Mgmt. Soc., Internat. Word Processing Assn., NOW, Richmond Womensbooks/YWCA. Baptist. Office: United Va Bank 9th & Main Richmond VA 23219

ADKINS, LYNN FRANTZ, educator; b. Huntington, W.Va., Apr. 21, 1944; d. Lester Newton and Helen (Wartenberg) Frantz; A.B., Marshall U., 1966; M.S.W., W.Va. U., 1971; Ph.D., U. Pitts., 1975; m. Ryland W. Crary, Oct. 16, 1976; children—Todd Adkins, Toni Crary. Teaching fellow Founds. of Edn., U. Pitts., 1971-72; program dir. Durham (N.C.) Drug Rehab. Center, 1972-73; state tng. coordinator N.C. State Office of Child Devel., Raleigh, 1972-78; asst. prof., supr. field program dept. sociology and anthropology N.C. State U., 1973-78; asso. prof., head sociology and social work Bethany Coll., 1978—, dir. public edn. and tng., 1980—. Mem. council Clara Welty Hospice Council, 1979—; mem. W.Va. Dept. Welfare Area I Adv. Council, 1980. Mem. Acad. Cert. Social Workers, W.Va. Nat. Assn. Social Workers, W.Va. Health Systems Agy., Child Welfare League Am., Nat. Women's Studies Assn., Council on Social Work Edn., Wake County Mental Health Assn., Ohio Valley Philosophy Soc., History of Edn. Soc., Annual Conclave Found. Edn., N.Central Women's Studies Assn., AAUP, Bethany Book Club. Home: Box 147 Bethany WV 26032 Office: Bethany Coll Dept Sociology and Social Work Bethany WV 26032

ADKINS, PATRICIA GUYNES, educator; b. Paris, Tex., Aug. 23, 1925; d. James Tillman and Margaret Ann (Brady) Guynes; B.A., U. Tex., El Paso, 1960; M.A., Tex. Women's U., 1961; Ph.D., U. Colo., 1966; m. Fitzhugh Lee Adkins, May 24, 1944; children—Patricia Dean, Fitzhugh Lee. Asso. prof. U. Tex., El Paso, 1961-69; dir. early childhood edn. Region XIX Edn. Center, El Paso, 1970—; cons. spl. edn. for handicapped pre-schs. Mem. El Paso City Planning Commn., 1960-62; bd. dirs. El Paso YWCA, El Paso council Girl Scouts U.S.A. Mem. Council Exceptional Children, Assn. Children with Learning Disabilities. Republican. Episcopalian. Club: Jr. League (El Paso). Contbr. articles to profl. jours. Home: 609 La Cruz El Paso TX 79902 Office: 6611 Boeing St El Paso TX 79997

ADKINS, SHIRLEY CALDWELL, real estate broker; b. Nashville, Oct. 7, 1936; d. Albert Garner and Ruby E. (Lampley) Caldwell; student U. Tenn., Nashville, 1971-74; m. Robert D. Adkins, June 27, 1953; children—Melanie, Mitzi, Robby. With Kimbrough-Kavanaugh & Assos., Nashville, 1962-75, v.p. comml. loan dept., 1962-75; exec. v.p. Kimbrough-Adkins & Assos., Nashville, 1975—. Lic. real estate broker, Tenn. Real Estate Commn. Mem. Am. Inst. Real Estate Appraisers, Nashville Bd. Realtors, Nashville Apt. Assn. (v.p.), Nat. Secs. Assn. (cert. profl. sec., dir. Nashville chpt. 1976). Baptist. Clubs: Capitol (Nashville); Order of Eastern Star (Hendersonville, Tenn.). Home: Route 1 Box 317 Chapmansboro TN 37035 Office: Kimbrough-Adkins & Assos 18th Floor L&C Tower Nashville TN 37219

ADLER, ELIZABETH THOMPSON (MRS. MILTON P. ADLER), civic worker; b. South Bend, Ind., Sept. 16, 1914; d. David Headley and Emma (Crawford) Thompson; B.S. in Phys. Edn. and Psychology, U. Wis., 1937; postgrad. Purdue U., 1934-35; m. Milton Pokorny Adler, Dec. 28, 1938; children—Ruth Louise (Mrs. Phillip Ruder), Coleman E. II. Instr. phys. edn. Sophie Newcomb Coll., New Orleans, 1937-38, McMain High Sch., New Orleans, 1938-39; supr. Dr. Alton Ochsner Cancer Clinic, Charity Hosp., New Orleans, 1946-49; mem. Touro Infirmary Bd. Aux., 1947-48; mem. citizenship awards com. Orleans Parish Sch. Bd., 1947-57, chmn., 1950-56; mem. vol. adminstrv. bd. Charity Hosp., 1947-50; life mem. Sara Mayo Hosp. Guild, 1953—, bd. dirs., 1961-62; exec. com. Nat. Conf. Christians and Jews, 1950, bd. dirs., 1951-61; mem. House of Detention Bd., City of New Orleans, 1951-54; mem. health edn. com. New Orleans YWCA, 1939-41, bd. dirs., 1939-52, v.p., 1948 pres., 1949-52, chmn. reconstrn. fund dr., 1947, del. regional conf., Atlanta, 1948, chmn. Y-Teens com., 1947-48, del. nat. conv., San Francisco, 1949, mem. resolutions com., 1949, del. regional conf., Houston, 1950, mem. nat. conv. com., discussion leader, 1950, del. nat. conv., Chgo., 1952, mem. centennial planning com., 1952-55, del. Y-Teen planning conf., Jackson, Miss., 1950, dean discussion leadership tng. conf. Gulf Park (Miss.) Coll., 1951-53, mem. nat. support com., 1948-53, rep. from La. to nat. bd. for centennial, 1952-55; chmn. New Orleans Com. Race Relations, 1952-53; mem. Tulane-Lyceum Assn. Bd., 1951-61, financial sec., 1954-59, treas., 1960-61; chmn. speakers bur.

Mother's March on Polio, 1952; vice chmn. campaign United Fund, 1954; chmn. citizens com. services to children Dept. Pub. Welfare, 1954-61; mem. La. com. White House Conf. Children and Youth, 1959-60, La. del., 1960, exec. com., 1960; bd. dirs. Urban League, 1955-61; chmn. Eisenhower Birthday Dinner Celebration, 1956; chmn. women's div. pub. and pvt. schs. U.S. Treasury Bond Drive, 1957-58; hospitality chmn. Brandeis U. Area Conf., 1957; bd. dirs. inst. com. Community Vol. Service, 1952; hospitality chmn. Nat. and La. Conf. Social Work conv., New Orleans, 1953; v.p. bd. lay regents Xavier U., 1959, pres. 1960-61; bd. dirs. DePaul Hosp. Guild, 1961-69; mem. New Coll. Library Com., Sarasota, Fla.; mem. bd. Fed. Housing Authority, Ft. Myers, 1966-69, Girl Scouts U.S.A., 1965-67; pres. Blue Water Forest Assn., 1971-72; mem. Central Fla. Regional Library Bd., 1971-73; chmn. bd. trustees Context Industries Library Scholarship Fund, 1973-76. Free lance writer-photographer, 1973—. Recipient Merit certificate for distinguished service to City of New Orleans, from mayor of New Orleans. Mem. D.A.R., Needlework Guild Am., League Women Voters, Women's Auxiliary New Orleans C. of C. Presbyn. Author: Wakulla Springs, Its History, Legend, Birds and Wildlife, 1977; Wild Birds of Florida, 1981; Wild Bird Calendar, 1983. Contbr. poetry to Caravan of Verse, An Anthology, 1949; contbr. stories and photos Fla. Wildlife mag. Club: Sanibel-Captiva Shell Club (v.p. 1965-66). Home: The Landings Treehouse #49 1461 Landings Circle Sarasota FL 33581

ADLER, FREDA, educator; b. Phila., Nov. 21, 1934; d. David and Lucia Green (Wolfson) Schaffer; B.A., U. Pa., 1956, M.A., 1968, Ph.D., 1971; m. Gerhard O.W. Mueller, Feb. 29, 1976; children by previous marriage—Mark, Jill, Nanci. Teaching fellow U. Pa., 1967-68, research asst., 1968-69; instr. psychiatry Temple U., 1971-72; research coordinator Addiction Sci. Center, 1971-72; asst. prof. Med. Coll. Pa., 1972-74, research dir. Sect. on Drug and Alcohol Abuse, 1972-74; asso. prof. criminal justice Rutgers U., 1974-79, prof., 1979—; mem. faculty Nat. Judicial Coll. U. Nev., 1973—; rep. Internat. Prisoners Aid Assn., 1975; cons. in field. Mem. Am. Soc. Criminology (Herbert Block award 1972, Beccaria Gold Medal Deutsche Kriminologische Gesellschaft 1979), U. Pa. Alumni Assn. (dir. 1974-77, asso. editor LAE Jour. 1977—), Am. Sociol. Assn., Internat. Assn. Penal Law. Author: (with others) Medical Lollipop, 1974, A Systems Approach to Drug Treatment, 1974; Sisters in Crime, 1975; (with others) The Criminology of Deviant Women, 1979; editor (with others) Review Internationale de Droit Penal, 1974; Crime and the International Scene, 1972, The Incidence of Female Criminality in the Contemporary World, 1982. Home: 30 Waterside Plaza Apt 37J New York NY 10010 Office: 15 Washington St Newark NJ 07102

ADLER, JOAN ELLEN, speech pathologist, spl. edn. cons.; b. Newark, July 20, 1947; d. David and Belle (Brody) Yeselson; B.S., Emerson Coll., 1969; M.A., Hunter Coll., 1972; M.Ed. in Spl. Edn., Am. U., 1980; M.S.W., Cath. U. Am., 1981; children—Joshua, Deborah. Speech, lang. pathologist Christ Church Child Center, Bethesda, Md., 1973; speech pathologist Yonkers (N.Y.) Public Schs., 1969-72; lang. pathologist Christ Church Child Center, 1978-79; resource, diagnostic prescriptive tchr. elem. grades, assessment specialist dept. edn. Montgomery County Public Schs., Potomac, Md., 1979—; instr. U. D.C., summer 1979; freelance writer on social issues. Bd. dirs. Inverness Recreation Club, 1976-78; co-dir. women's week Jewish Community Center, 1976; vol. Arthritis Found.; mem. Montgomery County Bd. Social Services, 1982—. Am. Mem. Am. Speech and Hearing Assn., Council for Exceptional Children. Home: 10911 Deborah Dr Potomac MD 20854

ADLER, JOYCE SPARER, lit. critic, educator; b. N.Y.C., Dec. 2, 1915; d. Louis and Lillian (Solomon) Lifshutz; B.A. cum laude, Bklyn. Coll., City U. N.Y., 1935, M.A., 1951; m. Irving Adler, Sept. 16, 1968; children—Ellen, Laura. Tchr. English public high schs., N.Y.C., 1940-54, acting chmn. dept. English, 1950-52; editor Blood, Jour. Hematology, N.Y.C., 1954-55; tchr. English to fgn. dels. to UN, N.Y.C., 1956-63; tchr. English, Ramaz High Sch., N.Y.C., 1956-63; founding mem. U. Guyana, Georgetown, 1963-68, prof. lit., 1963-68, editor univ. newsletter, 1964-68; author books: Language and Man, 1970; War in Melville's Imagination, 1981; Attitudes Towards Race in Guyanese Literature, 1967; contbr. critical essays to anthologies, lit. jours.; occasional mem. coll. faculties, 1981—; lectr. in field; invited main speaker Internat. Conf. on Commonwealth Lit., Liège, Belgium, 1974, Nat. Conf. African and Caribbean Lit., U. Mo., 1973, ann. Melville Soc. Meeting, 1978, Bennington Coll. Conf. on Am. Indian, 1977. Recipient Nat. Second prize English Jour., 1953. Mem. MLA, Internat. Assn. Commonwealth Lit. and Lang. Studies, Vt. Acad. Arts and Scis. (trustee 1981—, sec. 1981—), Melville Soc. Free-lance writer song lyrics, short stories, plays, 1956-63. Home and Office: North Bennington VT 05257

ADRAIN, PATRICIA KELLUM, public info. specialist; b. Paterson, N.J., Sept. 29, 1945; d. Harold E. and Margaret (Sloan) Delaney; student Webber Coll., 1963-64, U. South Fla., 1973; m. Charles E. Adrain, June 6, 1981; children— Kenneth, Cheryl, Sean. Speech technician, adminstrv. asst. MacDonald Clinic, Tampa, Fla., 1973-77; dir. Cape Coral YMCA-Lee County YMCA, Ft. Myers, Fla., 1977-81; project dir. Community Care for the Elderly, Sr. Friendship Centers, Inc., Ft. Myers, 1982—. Bd. dirs. Lee County YMCA, Lee County Dance Council, Lee County Youth Soccer Assn., 1978-82; mem. Lee County Child Adv. Council, 1979. Mem. Community Coordinating Council, Assn. Profl. Dirs. YMCA, Fla. Assn. Health and Social Services. Clubs: Lee County Women's Tennis Assn., Fiddlesticks Country, Forrest Country. Office: PO Box 1774 Fort Myers FL 33908

ADREON, BEATRICE MARIE RICE, pharmacist; b. Huntington, W.Va., July 23, 1929; d. Lloyd Emerson and Beatrice (Odell) Rice; student Mary Washington Coll., 1947-49; B.S. in Pharmacy, Med. Coll. Va., 1952; M.A. in Spl. Studies and Women's Studies, George Washington U., 1976; m. Harry Barnes Adreon, Jr., Dec. 27, 1952. Summer vol. worker pharmacies De Paul Hosp., Norfolk, Va., 1949, U.S. Marine Hosp., Norfolk, 1950; pharmacist Washington Clinic, 1954-71; counselor George Washington U., 1976-77, cons. gerontology health scis. dept., 1977—; cons. medicine control traffic patterns nursing homes Cross & Adreon, Washington, 1962—; founder, pres. Pharmacy Counseling Services, Inc. Instr. advanced first aid ARC, 1952—, civil def. instr., 1952—; vol. Spanish Edn. Devel. Center, Washington, 1972; mem. Arlington (Va.) Community Services Bd., chmn. com. substance abuse. Recipient Arnold and Marie Schwartz award in pharmacy, 1980. Mem. Acad. Pharmacy Practice, Am. Pharm. Assn., Va. Pharm. Assn., Potomac Pharmacists Assn., AAAS, Am. Inst. History of Pharmacy, Panhellenic Assn., Kappa Epsilon. Episcopalian (mem. bishop's com. neighborhood services 1967-69, chmn. services for aged div. 1967-69). Contbr. articles in field to profl. jours. Home: 4524 N 19th Rd Arlington VA 22207

ADRIAN, PATRICIA LEE GRIMSHAW, assn. exec.; b. Reliance, S.D., July 20, 1938; d. Walter George and Dorthy Veronica (Zastrow) Grimshaw; student Sinte Gleska U., 1973; m. Robert Earl Adrian, Oct. 12, 1957; children—James Robert, Thomas Edward, Kevin Patrick, David Duane. Sec., Cherry Todd Electric, 1956-57; tchr. White River (S.D.) Ind. Sch. Dist., 1970-71; dir. S.D. Beef Industry Council, 1970-73, pres., 1972-73, exec. v.p., 1973—; exec. sec., lobbyist S.D. Livestock Assn., part-time 1977—; pres. Mktg. Internat., Inc., 1981—; partner Prairie Press; dir. Nat. Livestock and Meat Bd. Gov.'s rep. to nutrition symposium Old West Regional Commn., 1979-80; mem. S.D. Indsl. Devel. Commn., 1979—; mem. S.D. Agrl. Mktg. Commn., 1980—; mem. adv. com. S.D. Vocat. Tech. Edn. Commn. for Agr.; bd. dirs. S.D. Livestock Expansion Found., 1981—. Recipient Disting. Service award S.D. Stockgrowers Assn., 1974, S.D. State U., 1976. Mem. Nat. Fedn. Press Women, Am. Soc. Assn. Execs., Nat. Cattlemen's Assn., S.D. Livestock Assn., Am. Agri-Women, U.S. Meat Export Fedn. (dir. 1980—), S.D. Press Women's Assn., S.D. CowBelles (pres.). Republican. Roman Catholic. Home: Star Route Box 222 White River SD 57579 Office: 110 W Capitol St Pierre SD 57501

AESCHLIMAN, LEA HUTCHINSON, state ofcl.; b. Lynn, Mass., May 15, 1943; d. Albert Savage and Eleanor (Newhall) Hutchinson; B.A., Smith Coll., 1964; M.P.A., U. N.H., 1981; m. Nicholas R. Aeschliman, Oct. 9, 1965; children—Christopher, Matthew. Research analyst Joint Econ. Com., U.S. Congress, 1965-68; mem. N.H. Ho. of Reps., Concord, 1977-82; commr. N.H. Pub. Utilities Commn., 1982—. Mem. Nat. Conf. State Legislatures. Democrat. Unitarian. Club: Portsmouth Coll. Office: State House Concord NH 03301

AFFINITO, MONA GUSTAFSON, psychologist, educator; b. Bristol, Conn., Oct. 28, 1929; d. Carl Arthur and Jennie Alida (Anderson) Gustafson; B.A., Conn. Coll., 1951; M.A., Boston, U., 1952, Ph.D., 1964; m. Louis A. Affinito, Oct. 3, 1955 (div. Dec. 1976); children—Douglas Anthony, Lisa Marie. Instr., Johnson (Vt.) Tchrs. Coll., 1952-53, U. Vt., Burlington, 1953-55; mem. faculty So. Conn. State Coll., New Haven, 1958—, prof. psychology, 1970—, acting chmn. psychology dept., 1974-75, chmn. psychology dept., 1975-80, acting dean arts and scis., 1978; pvt. practice clin. psychology, Hamden, Conn. 1981—. Mem. Am. Psychol. Assn., Conn. Psychol. Assn., NOW. Democrat. Lutheran. Office: So Conn State Coll 501 Crescent St New Haven CT 06515 also 3074 Whitney Ave Hamden CT 06518

AFRIDI, PARVEEN NIAZ, psychiatrist; b. Farrukhabad, India, June 20, 1944; came to U.S., 1972; d. Niaz Mohammed and Zakia Sultana Khan-Afridi; M.D. magna cum laude (Merit scholar), S.M.S. Med. Coll., Japiur, India, 1968; m. Mohammed Kalimi, Apr. 26, 1970; 1 son, Omar. Rotating intern S.M.S. Med. Coll. Hosp., Jaipur, 1968-69; attending med. officer dept. ob-gyn, Kota and Meerut, India, 1969-72; postdoctoral research Inst. Cancer Research, Columbia U., N.Y.C., 1972-73; resident in psychiatry N.Y. U.-Bellevue Med. Center, N.Y.C., 1974-77; attending psychiatrist Manhattan Psychiat. Center, N.Y.C., 1977-80; clin. instr. psychiatry Albert Einstein Med. Center, N.Y.C. and attending psychiatrist Jacobi Hosp., 1980-81; clin. instr. psychiatry Downstate Med. Center, N.Y.C. and sr. attending psychiatrist Kings County Hosp., N.Y.C., 1981—. Active Fedn. Indian Assn. U.S.A. Named one of best psychiat. residents Manhattan Psychiat. Center, 1974-75; recipient Physicians Recognition award AMA, 1977. Mem. Am. Psychiat. Assn., Am. Psychiatrists from India (life), N.Y. U.-Bellevue Psychiat. Soc. Home: 510 2d Ave New York NY 10016 Office: 451 Clarkson Ave Brooklyn NY 11203

AFTERGOOD, LILLA, biochemist, nutritionist; b. Krakow, Poland, Jan. 10, 1925; came to U.S., 1949, naturalized, 1956; d. Jacob and Zofia (Selzer) Anisfeld; B.S., Sorbonne U., 1948; M.S., U. So. Calif., 1951, Ph.D., 1956; m. Edgar Aftergood, Aug. 17, 1949; children—David, Steven, Annette. Sr. research asso. dept. biochemistry U. So. Calif., 1956-59; asso. research biochemist Sch. Public Health, UCLA, 1959-80. Mem. Am. Inst. Nutrition, Am. Heart Assn., Council on Arteriosclerosis, AAAS, Sigma Xi. Co-author: Nutrition for Today, 1973; Nutrition and Motherhood, 1982; mem. editorial bd. M.D., Nutrition; contbr. numerous articles to sci. jours.

AGAR, EUNICE JANE, artist; b. Gt. Barrington, Mass., May 14, 1934; d. Charles William and Elinore Lillian (Warner) A.; B.A., Wellesley Coll., 1956; student Art Students League N.Y., 1957-60, 68-69, Jean Liberte, 1960-63, Robert B. Hale, 1968-69, Edmond Cassarella, 1968-69. With Am. Artist Mag., N.Y.C., 1957-63, asst. editor, 1958-60, mng. editor, 1960-63; painting and graphics instr. Simon's Rock Early Coll., Great Barrington, Mass., 1969-78, chmn. studio arts program, 1974-78, chmn. Div. Art, 1975-78; one woman shows at LeMoyne Art Center, Tallahassee, 1966, High Point Galleries, Lenox, Mass., 1967, Albany (N.Y.) Inst. History and Art, 1967, Newport (R.I.) Art Assn., 1968, Graphic Arts Gallery, Springfield, Mass., 1968, Gallery One, Hillsdale, N.Y., 1970, The Hall Sch., Pittsfield, 1976, Berkshire Sch., Sheffield, Mass., 1977, Westenhook Gallery, Sheffield, 1980; represented in pvt. collections. Mem. Art Students League N.Y. Contbr. articles to Am. Artist, Am. Art and Antiques. Address: Egremont Plain Rd Route 1 Box 18 Great Barrington MA 01230

AGEEL, MARYANN CATHERINE AL, nurse; b. Derby, Conn., Dec. 22, 1938; d. Herman Martin and Maryann Shumaker; R.N., St. Vincent's Hosp., Bridgeport, Conn., 1959; B.S. in Nursing, St. Louis U., 1964, M.S.N., 1974; 1 son. Staff nurse hosps. in Conn. and Mo., 1959-80; instr. Maryville Coll., St. Louis, 1978-80; asst. dir. nursing Valley Children's Hosp., Fresno, Calif., 1980—; past pres. Greater St. Louis Soc. Health Educators and Trainers; vice chmn. Nursing Adminstrs. Council San Joaquin Valley; mem. curriculum task force community mems. nursing dept. U. Calif., Fresno, 1981-82. Mem. Am. Soc. for Nursing Service Adminstrs., Calif. Soc. Nursing Service Adminstrs., Nursing Adminstrs. Council, Sigma Theta Tau. Roman Catholic. Office: 3151 Millbrook St Fresno CA 93703

AGER, JEAN BARRINGTON, clin. psychologist; b. Cin., Mar. 25, 1946; d. Robert Barrington and LaJean Florence (Flaherty) A.; B.A., Western Coll., 1967; Ph.D., Bryn Mawr Coll., 1977: postgrad. U. Cin., Dartmouth Coll., Miami U., Oxford, Ohio, Harvard U., Harvard Divinity Sch. Research asst. Social Sci. Research Council, Cambridge, Mass., summer 1966; residence hall counselor Miami U., 1967-68; counselor Bryn Mawr (Pa.) Hosp. Sch. Nursing, 1968-69; psychol. intern Bryn Mawr Coll., 1969-71, clin. psychologist Child Study Inst., 1971-80; Sch. psychologist, Upper Darby, Pa., 1981-82; clin. psychologist Daniel C. Wilson Hosp., Charlottesville, Va., 1982—; psychologist Ednl. Records Bur., Bryn Mawr, 1969-73; lectr. Cabrini Coll., 1973. Vol. worker geriatric centers, local mental instns. Cert. sch. psychologist, Va.; lic. clin. psychologist, Va. Mem. Am. Psychol. Assn., Pa. Psychol. Assn., Mensa. Presbyterian. Home: 2527 Hydraulic Rd Apt 20 Charlottesville VA 22901 Office: David C Wilson Hosp 2101 Arlington Blvd Charlottesville VA 22901

AGLIPAY, ELIZABETH ESQUIOJA, nurse; b. Manila, Philippines, Jan. 13, 1946; came to U.S., 1974; d. Juanito A. and Corazon (Esquioja) Aglipay; B.Nursing, Far Eastern U., 1967. Staff nurse Ottawa (Ont., Can.) Civic Hosp., 1968-69, Westminster Hosp., London, Ont., 1969-71, Victoria Hosp., London, 1971-72, Mt. Sinai Hosp., N.Y.C., 1974-77; staff nurse N.Y. Hosp. and Cornell Med. Center, N.Y.C., 1978—. Mem. Nat. Assn. Female Execs. Roman Catholic. Home: 423 E 70th St Apt 4F New York NY 10021 Office: 525 E 68th St New York NY 10021

AGOSTINO, NELLIE AGNES, educator; b. Hartford, Conn., Nov. 2, 1927; d. Paul and Lucy (Uccello) Agostino; B.A., St. Joseph Coll., 1949; M.A., Trinity Coll., 1952. Substitute tchr. Hartford High Schs., 1949-51; instr., chmn. fgn. lang. dept. East Hartford High Sch., 1951—, student-faculty basketball program chmn., coordinator advanced placement and coop. programs, chmn. graduating com., mem. discipline com., chmn. faculty social com., curriculum consol. com., 1982—; chmn. lang. sect. for evaluating com. New Eng. Secondary Sch. team Dorchester High Sch.; gen. membership chmn. Lang. Conv.; chmn. Town Lang. Articulation Com.; local chmn. arrangements Latin State Contest; participant seminar for teaching advanced Latin, Trinity Coll. Reader, mem. liturgy com., bldg. fund Ch. of St. Timothy; instr. CYO, mem. discipline com., dir. workshop com.; program chmn., treas. East Hartford High Sch. PTA; active Ann Uccello for Mayor campaign 1st Congl. Dist. Republican Party; trustee St. Joseph Coll., 1978-82, co-chmn. ann. sustaining fund, 1982-83. Mem. Classical Assn. Am., Classical Assn. New Eng., Jr. Classical League (state chmn.), Conn. Lang. Tchrs. Assn. (sec.), Conn. (com. chmn. Math. Conv.), East Hartford (bldg. rep., sec.) edn. assns., Conn. Lang. Tchrs. Assn. (sec.), Am., Conn. (v.p.) assns. Italian tchrs., St. Joseph Coll. Alumnae Assn. (pres. 1978-82), Trinity Alumni Assn., Delta Kappa Gamma (sec., co-chmn. publicity). Clubs: Hartford Council Cath. Women, Italian Hist. Soc. Co-adviser student sect. La Voce. Home: 228 King Philip Dr West Hartford CT 06117 Office: 777 Burnside Ave East Hartford CT 06108

AGRESTI, MIRIAM MONELL, psychologist; b. N.Y.C., Mar. 23, 1926; d. James McCloud and Marion Henrietta (Zippel) Monell; B.S. in Chemistry, Queens Coll., 1947; M.A. in Sci. Edn., Columbia U., 1949; Ph.D. in Clin. Psychology, Yeshiva U., 1976; postgrad. Ackerman Inst. Family Therapy, 1977-81, L.I. Jewish Hosp. Human Sexuality Center; children—Robert, Carol. Psychology intern Creedmoor Psychiat. Center, Queens, N.Y., 1963-64, family therapist, 1964-69; psychologist Northeast Nassau Psychiat. Center, Kings Park, N.Y., 1969-72; adminstrv. dir. Friendship House Day Hosp., Glen Cove, N.Y., 1972-74; psychologist and team leader Central Islip (N.Y.) Psychiat. Center, 1974-75; tchr., coordinator family therapy program Pilgrim Psychiat. Center, West Brentwood, N.Y., 1976-80; pvt. practice psychotherapy, 1977—; co-dir. L.I. Family Inst., 1976-79; cons. family therapy Cath. Charities, 1979, St. Vincent's Hall, 1979, Nassau County Mental Health Assn., 1980; adj. faculty Sch. Edn., C.W. Post Coll., L.I. U., 1972, CUNY, 1978-80. Lic. psychologist, N.Y. Diplomate Am. Bd. Family Psychology. Fellow Am. Orthopsychiat. Assn., Internat. Council Sex Edn. and Parenthood of Am. U.; mem. Am. Psychol. Assn., N.Y. State Psychol. Assn., Nassau County Psychol. Assn., Suffolk County Psychol. Assn., Am. Assn. for Marriage and Family Therapy (pres. L.I. chpt. 1981—), Acad. Family Mediators, Assn. Humanistic Psychologists, Am. Orthopsychiat. Assn., Pi Lambda Theta. Unitarian. Address: 11 Wren Dr Woodbury NY 11797

AGUILERA, DONNA CONANT, nurse educator; b. Kinmundy, Ill.; d. Charles E. and Daisy L. (Frost) Conant; R.N., Gordon Keller Sch. Nursing, 1947; B.S., UCLA, 1963, M.S., 1965; Ph.D., U. So. Calif., 1974; m. George Limon Aguilera, Feb. 17, 1948; children—Bruce Allen, Craig Steven. Teaching asst. UCLA, 1965, grad. research asst., 1965-66; assoc. prof. nursing edn. Calif. State U., Los Angeles, 1966-81; prof., chmn. grad. div. U. Md., Balt., 1981-82; vis. lectr. UCLA, 1982—; nurse-cons. crisis intervention Benjamin Rush Center, Los Angeles, 1967-82; originator, project dir. Project Link, Lab. for Ind. Nursing Knowledge, Calif. State U.; mem. select com. psychiat. care and evaluation NIMH; career tchr. appointee NIMH, 1965-66; mem. def. adv. com. Women in the Services, 1978-82; apptd. to Nat. Maternal-Child Health Research Grants Rev. Com., 1982-86. NIH fellow U. So. Calif., 1972-75. Fellow Am. Acad. Nursing (pres. 1977-78), Acad. Psychiat. Specialists (award for scholarship and research 1982); mem. Am. Nurses Assn., Nat. League Nursing, Faculty Women's Assn., AAUP, Alpha Tau Delta, Sigma Theta Tau. Author: Crisis Intervention: Theory and Methodology, 1978, 4th edit., 1982; Review of Psychiat. Nursing, 1977; Psychiat. Nursing, 7th edit., 1978; contbr. articles to profl. publs. Home: 3924 Dixie Canyon Ave Sherman Oaks CA 91423 Office: UCLA Center for Health Scis Los Angeles CA 90024

AGUIRRE, BARBARA JEAN, librarian; b. Corinne, W.Va., Feb. 4, 1935; d. Paul F. and Mary Phyllis (Chambers) Kirk; B.S., Concord Coll., 1965; m. Thomas J. Aguirre, Dec. 22, 1953; 1 son, Thomas Kirk. Asst. librarian Bluefield Coll., 1965-67; asst. librarian Logan Campus, So. W.Va. Community Coll., 1971-73, librarian, 1973—. Mem. W.Va. Library Assn., W.Va. Edn. Media Assn., W.Va. Community Coll. Assn., LWV, Beta Sigma Phi. Methodist. Clubs: Woman's of Logan (pres. 1978), Order Eastern Star, Logan Bus. and Profl. Women's. Home: PO Box 334 Logan WV 25601 Office: Library So W Va Community Coll Logan WV 25601

AGUIRRE, MARIA ELENA, constrn. co. exec.; b. Nuevo Laredo, Tamps., Mex., Mar. 14, 1948; came to U.S., 1966, naturalized, 1972; d. Jose and Tomasita A.; student Laredo (Tex.) Jr. Coll., 1967-68, St. Mary's U., 1969-74; B.A., U. Houston, 1975. Adminstrv. sec. Homecraft Corp., Houston, 1976, adminstrv. supr., dir. public relations, 1976-77, sales cons. new home sales, 1977-80; mgr. sales devel. U.S. Home Corp., Houston, 1980-81, dir. internat. mktg., 1981—. Mem. Nat. Assn. Female Execs., Houston Exec. Club. Republican. Baptist.

AGUR, CHRISTINE VALENTINE, social worker; b. Eng., Aug. 11, 1900; d. Francis and Marie Graham (Kinloch) Inman-Kane; elem. tchr's. cert. San Francisco State Tchrs. Coll., 1925; B.A., U. So. Calif., 1932, M.A., 1933, M.S.W., 1939; m. Robert Allen Agur, 1939 (dec. 1949); stepsons—Donald E. Agur, Patrick Graham Agur. Tchr., Riverside County, Calif., 1925, 26, 29-30, Orange County, 1927, 29; social worker, Los Angeles County, 1934-35, 36-43, San Diego County, 1934-36, State of Calif., 1936-37; clin. social worker VA, Van Nuys, Calif., 1945-50, Long Beach, Calif., 1950-70; med. social worker Thera Medics Home Health Agy., Orange, Calif., 1971-78. Sec., pres. Long Beach Council on Alcoholism; sec., then pres. Nat. Council on Alcoholism. Served with AUS, 1944-45. Recipient various awards. Mem. Nat. Assn. Social Workers (chmn. council on med. health services, chmn. recruitment com.) Acad. Cert. Social Workers (chmn. social service com.), Geriatric Health Care Council West Orange County, Jacques Cousteau Soc., Sierra Club, UN Assn., LWV, Common Cause. Democrat. Contbr. articles in field to profl. jours. Home: 132 Cottonwood Ln Seal Beach CA 90740

AHERN, ARLEEN FLEMING (MRS. GEORGE IRVING AHERN), librarian; b. Mt. Harris, Colo., Oct. 15, 1922; d. John R. and Josephine (Vidmar) Fleming; B.A., U. Utah, 1943; M.A., U. Denver, 1962; postgrad. U. Colo., 1967; m. George Irving Ahern, June 14, 1944; 1 son, George Irving. Library asst. Army Air Force Library, Salt Lake City, 1943-44; library asst. Colo. Women's Coll. Library (now U. Denver/CWC Campus), 1952-60, acquisitions librarian, 1960—, rep. Adult Edn. Council Denver, 1960—, asso. prof. librarianship. Committeewoman, Republican Com., Denver, 1958-59. Mem. ALA, Mountain Plains Library Assn., Colo. (1st v.p., pres. 1969-70, dir. 1971—), Library Assn., Altrusa Club of Denver (2d v.p. 1968-69, dir. 1971-74, 76, 78), Soc. Am. Archivists, Mountain Plains Adult Edn. Assn., AAUP. Home: 746 Monaco Pkwy Denver CO 80220 Office: 7055 E 18th Ave Denver CO 80220

AHERN, MARGARET ANN, nun, nurse, educator; b. Manchester, N.H., Nov. 23, 1931; d. Timothy Joseph and Helen Bridget (Kearns) Ahern; R.N., Sacred Heart Hosp. Sch. Nursing, 1952; B.S.N., Mt. St. Mary Coll., 1957; M.Nursing, Cath. U. Am., 1965. Entered Sisters of Mercy, Roman Catholic Ch., 1956; staff nurse Sacred Heart Hosp., Manchester, 1954-57, operating rm. supr., 1957-62, med.-surg. nursing instr., 1962-66, dir. Sch. Nursing, 1966-75; dir. Sch. Nursing, Cath. Med. Center, Manchester, N.H., 1975-79, dir. dept. edn. and mem. sr. mgmt., 1979—. Mem., sec. bd. dirs. Health Edn. Consortium, 1977—; bd. dirs. Vis. Nurse Assn., 1981—; adv. bd. Hesser Coll., 1980—, N.H. Voc-Tech. Coll., 1979—; mem. United Health Systems Agy., 1977—; mem. adv. council on continuing edn. St. Anselm Coll., 1978—; mem. gen. chpt.

Sisters of Mercy, 1968-70, 79-81, chmn. fin. bd., 1981—, chmn. Bd. Conciliation and Arbitration, 1982—. Mem. Am. Nurses Assn., N.H. Nurses Assn., Nat. League for Nursing, New Eng. Cath. Hosp. Assn., New Eng. Edn. and Research Orgn., N.H. Heart Assn., Sigma Theta Tau. Democrat. Roman Catholic. Contbr. articles to profl. jours. Home: 647 Canal St Manchester NH 03104 Office: 100 McGregor St Manchester NH 03102

AHERN, MARGARET MARY, television news editor; b. Chgo., Nov. 16, 1949; d. James Lott and Nora (McNelis) A.; B.A., Columbia Coll., 1971; M.A., Roosevelt U., 1982; m. Pierre deVise, Nov. 16, 1979. Editorial asst. Chicago Sun-Times, 1968-74; reporter, editor City News Bur. Chgo., 1974-77; news assignment editor Sta. WBBM-TV, Chgo., 1977—; cons. Chgo. Regional Inventory. Mem. Chgo. Symphony Orchestral Assn., Columbia Coll. Alumni Assn. Club: City (Chgo.). Office: 630 N McClurg Ct Chicago IL 60611

AHLERS, LINDA JOY, mortgage banker; b. Los Angeles, Feb. 10, 1951; d. George Livingston and Joyce Beverly (Sharpe) Lane; ed. jr. colls. So. Calif., Am. Inst. Banking, Chgo. Mercantile Exchange, Chgo. Bd. Trade, Nat. Inst. Econs.; 1 son, Link. Officer, head note dept. Bank of Am., Los Angeles, 1968-75; account exec. Am. Internat. Trading Co., Los Angeles, 1975-76; with Coldwell Banker Residential Mortgage Services, Los Angeles, 1976-79, Chgo., 1979-81, asst. v.p., br. mgr., Santa Ana, Calif., 1981—; dir. Advert Pub. Co.; tchr. financing classes. Mem. Republican Presdl. Task Force, 1981-82. Lic. real estate sales person, Calif., Ill. Mem. Nat. Assn. Female Execs., Women in Mgmt., Ill. Mortgage Bankers Assn., Assn. Profl. Mortgage Women (past officer). Home: 711 Ocean Ave Unit 428 Huntington Beach CA 92648 Office: 2132 N Main St Santa Ana CA 92706

AHLGREN, MILDRED CARLSON (MRS. OSCAR ALEXANDER AHLGREN), club woman, lectr., writer, public relations cons.; b. Chgo.; d. August John and Hilda Sophia (Peterson) Carlson; student Columbia Coll., U. Chgo.; m. Oscar Alexander Ahlgren, June 6, 1923; 1 dau., Adrienne Haeuser. Spl. corr. Hammond (Ind.) Times 1935-52. Pres. Ind. Fedn. Women's Club, 1941-44; dean of dirs., mem. exec. com. Gen. Fedn. Women's Clubs, 1943-44, rec. sec., 1944-47, 2d v.p., 1947-50, 1st v.p., 1950-52, pres., 1952-54; nat. sponsoring com. Allied Youth; nat. adv. com., public relations panel Savs. Bonds, U.S. Treasury; mem. Planning Commn. Ind. State, 1941-43, Personnel Bd., 1943-46; chmn. women's div. Ind. War Fin. Com., 1940-46; chmn. women's com. Ind. War History Commn., 1945-48; mem. Ind. com. George Foster Peabody radio awards; mem. Gov's. Com. of Children and Youth. Chmn. Women's Nat. Com. Savs. Bonds; mem. nat. planning com. White House Conf. on Edn., 1953-54; asst. to dir. U.S. Savs. Bonds Div., Treas. Dept., 1955-57; public relations cons.; observer food gift program FAO Austria, 1953; ruling elder Nat. Presbyn. Ch. Trustee, Ind. State Employes Retirement Fund, 1949-52, Ind. State Tchrs. Colls., 1952-58; bd. dirs. Ind. Inst. Psychiat. Research; trustee Radio Liberty Com.; v.p. All Am. Conf. Nat. co-chmn. Women for Nixon and Lodge, 1960. Recipient Royal Order of Vasa (Sweden), 1954; George Washington medal Freedoms Found., 1954, 70; Hoosier Halo, Hammond Newspaper Guild, 1953; numerous other honors and awards; named Ind. Woman of Yr., Theta Sigma Phi, 1952. Mem. Nat. Fedn. Press Women, Nat. League Am. Penwomen, Bus. and Profl. Women's Am. Legion Aux., Am. Women in Radio and Television, Women in Communications, Scandinavian Found. (hon.), LWV, PEO, Alpha Delta Pi, Phi Beta, Beta Gamma Epsilon. Republican. Presbyterian. Clubs: San Antonio Breakfast: Chautauqua (N.Y.) Woman's: Ind. Harbor (Ind.) Women's (hon.); Ind. Women's Press; Whiting (Ind.) Woman's (hon. life, dir.); Nat. Press (Washington); Lake Hills Country; Am. Newspaper Women's (Washington); Washington. Research on status of women, S.Am., 1950, W.I. and Alaska, 1953, Russia, 1956, 71. Home: Dupont East 1545 18th St NW Washington DC 20036 Office: 1734 N St NW Washington DC 20036

AHMANSON, CAROLINE LEONETTI, banker, civic worker; b. San Francisco, Apr. 12, 1918; student U. Calif., Berkeley, Calif. Sch. Design, San Francisco; m. Howard Ahmanson (dec.). With Fed. Res. Bank of San Francisco, chmn. bd. dirs., 1981—; chmn. bd. Caroline Leonetti Ltd. of Hollywood; dir. Walt Disney Prodns. Mem. adv. council County and City of Los Angeles; mem. Nat. Council on Humanities nat. adv. council Peace Corps; bd. trustees Calif. Mus. Sci. and Industry, Los Angeles County Mus. Art; bd. govs. Performing Arts Council of the Music Center; vice-chmn. Am. Assn. Mus. Trustees Coms.; bd. dirs. Los Angeles World Affairs Council; mem. nat. com. U.S.-China Relations; bd. dirs. Greater Los Angeles Visitors and Convention Bur.; bd. dirs., chmn. Los Angeles-Guangzhou (Canton) Sister City Assn. Mem. Los Angeles Area C. of C. (v.p.). Author: Twenty-Four Steps to Loveliness, 1950. Office: Fed Res Bank of San Francisco PO Box 7702 San Francisco CA 94120

AHRENS, WENDY JOAN, data processing exec.; b. Glen Cove, N.Y., Aug. 4, 1950; d. Thomas J. and Isabelle Taylor; student U. Md., Augsburg, W.Ger., 1969-71, SUNY, Farmingdale, 1972-74; m. Kent E. Ahrens, May 9, 1969; 1 son, Kenneth K. Sales rep. Met. Life Ins. Co., Huntington, N.Y., 1974-76, sales mgr., Flushing, N.Y., 1976-79; asst. dir. market devel. J. C. Penney Life Ins. Co., Dallas, 1979-81, dir. employment, 1981-82; mktg. cons. Informatics, Gen., Dallas, 1982—; instr. ins. mktg. S. La. U., Lafayette, 1980. Chmn. recruiting Industry Task Force on Women and Minorities, Washington, 1980—; chmn. United Way, L.I., N.Y., 1977; mem. telethon com. Easter Seals, N.Y.C., 1978. Recipient Pres.'s Conf. award Met. Life Ins. Co., 1974, 75; Nat. Quality award Nat. Assn. Underwriters, 1974, 75, Nat. Sales Achievement award, 1974, 75. Mem. Soc. Ins. Researchers, Nat. Assn. Life Underwriters, Gen. Agts. and Mgrs. Conf., Women's Life Underwriters Conf. Contbr. articles in field to profl. publs. Home: 4105 Early Morn Plano TX 75075 Office: 2425 N Central Expressway Richardson TX 75080

AHUJA, SAVITRI, choreographer, dancer; b. Bombay, India, Oct. 9, 1924; d. Sir Kishandas and Rukhmani (Bajaj) Menda; came to U.S., 1959, naturalized, 1974; student Govt. Acad. Dance, Drama and Music, Bombay, 1930-42, Nrityabitan Sch., Calcutta, India, 1942-49; 1 son, Narayan. Instr. Indian classical dances and Hatha Yoga, India, 1944-59; owner, dir. Savitri's Studio, Washington, 1960—; lectr. in field. Author: Savitri's Way: To Perfect Fitness Through Hatha Yoga, 1979. Address: 5180 34th St NW Washington DC 20008

AIELLO, BARBARA, puppeteer; b. Pitts., Nov. 6, 1947; d. Antonio and Helen (Kaupiek) A.; B.S. in Spl. Edn., Indiana U. of Pa., 1968; M.A., George Washington U., 1971; postgrad. Harvard U. Sch. Edn., 1973-74; m. Barr Andrew Forrest, Aug. 9, 1976; 1 dau., Rosanna. Tchr. public schs. Butler, Pa., 1968-69, Gaithersburg, Md., 1969-70; tchr. trainer Boston U., 1971-72; editor Teaching Exceptional Children, Reston, Va., 1974-76; pres. The Kids on the Block, Inc., puppets, 1977—; cons. to parent groups, 1976—. Recipient Media award One to One, N.Y.C., 1977. Mem. Council for Exceptional Children, Nat. Spina Bifida Assn. (profl. adv. council 1979—), Italian Sons and Daus. of Am., Washington Women in Bus., Internat. Soc. of Puppeteers, Kappa Delta Pi. Producer Invisible Children, TV program, also Kids on the Block; contbr. articles on disability to N.Y. Times edn. supplement.

AIKEN, JEANNE ELLEN, violinist; b. Portland, Oreg., May 20, 1925; d. Emory Allen and Helen Marie (Oakerman) Shephard; student public schs., Portland, Oreg.; m. Frederick Irwin Aiken, June 4, 1946; children—Patricia Nan, Judy Lynn, Lawrence William. Staff violinist, violist Radio Sta. KOIN, Portland, Oreg., 1943-55; 1st violinist, violist Portland Symphony, 1947-55; violinist Los Angeles Philharmonic Orch., 1956—, now asso. prin. 2d violin; chmn. Los Angeles Orch. Com., chmn., 1980-82, mem. pension com., 1979—, del. Internat. Conf. Symphony and Opera Musicians, 1980. Democrat. Presbyterian. Office: 135 N Grand St Los Angeles CA 90012

AIKENS, JOAN DEACON, govt. ofcl.; b. Lansdowne, Pa., May 1, 1928; d. Robert Wallace and Bessie (Crook) Deacon; B.A., Ursinus Coll., 1950, LL.D. (hon.), 1979; 1 son, Donald R. Fashion cons. Park Ave. Shop, Swarthmore, Pa., 1971-73; v.p. Lew Hodges Communications, Inc., Valley Forge, Pa., 1973-75; commr. Fed. Election Commn., Washington, 1975, vice chmn., 1977-78, chmn., 1978-79. Republican. Office: Fed Election Commn 1325 K St NW Washington DC 20463 *

AILLON, LUZ EUGENIA, psychiat. social worker; b. Potosi, Bolivia, Nov. 15, 1939; came to U.S., 1972; d. Enrique and Victoria A.; M.S. in Social Work, San Andres U. (Bolivia), 1964, Ph.D., 1970; M.A. in Social Psychology, Mo. U., 1969. Social worker Bolivian Inst. Studies and Social Action, 1964-67; prof. social psychology San Andres U., La Paz, Bolivia, 1970; social psychologist, psychiat. social worker Bolivian Inst. Studies and Social Action, LaPaz, 1970-71; asst. prof. U. Utrecht (Holland), 1971-72; pvt. practice as psychiat. social worker, Hartford, Conn., 1972—; psychiat. social worker supr. Child Guidance Clinic, Hartford, 1974—; mem. State Bd. Examiners for Spanish Speaking Social and Case Workers, 1979; clin. cons. dept. children and youth services Div Children and Protective Services and Div. Instns. and Facilities, 1981-82. Mem. Community Council, 1976. Mem. Nat. Assn. Social Workers. Club: Lioness. Office: 170 Sigourney St Hartford CT 06115

AIMEE, JOYCE, arts adminstr., theatrical agt.; b. Bklyn., May 4, 1930; d. David Joseph and Jessica Hollis (Ganz) Geronimus; student (scholar) Mus. Modern Art, N.Y.C., 1945-47; m. William McPeck Titchnell, Nov. 2, 1966; children—Matthew Bruce, David Langland. Musician, singer, painter, 1940-67; theatrical agt., Hollywood, Calif., 1967—; owner, pres. Aimée Entertainment, Van Nuys, Calif., 1969—; pres., exec. dir. Americana Dance Theater, Inc.; exec. dir. Americana/CAFCA, Los Angeles, 1979-81. Pres., San Fernando Valley Arts Council, 1977-79, 82—, v.p. exec. bd., 1979-82; exec. bd. dirs. San Fernando Valley Cultural Soc. Found. Named Accordionist of Yr., World Accordion Rev., 1960, 61, 62; recipient commendations from mayor Los Angeles, 1969, 79, Pres. U.S., 1979; St. Gauden's art medal. Mem. Musicians Union, AFTRA, Screen Actors Guild, Calif. Confedn. Arts, Los Angeles Area Dance Alliance, Internat. Orphans (charter). Address: 13743 Victory Blvd Van Nuys CA 91401

AINSBERG, EDITH GORDON, singer, tchr.; b. Canton, Ohio, July 11, 1924; d. Harry and Sarah (Axelrod) Gordon; diploma (Margaret McGill scholar) Juilliard Sch. Music, 1948; m. Louis M. Ainsberg, May 30, 1964; children—Mark Sherman, Sharon. Soloist, Tanglewood and Paris Opera Ballet's prodn. of Milhaud's Salade, 1948; leading role in Menotti's The Telephone and The Medium on Broadway also nat. tour, 1949-50, CBS-TV Omnibus, 1952; soloist Little Orch. Soc. in world premiere of Babar, The Elephant, 1954-61; leading soprano Goldovsky Opera Theatre in Barber of Seville, 1954; lead soprano Chautauqua Opera, 1961; soloist Cleve. Symphony, 1959-61, Boston Symphony, 1961, City Symphony of N.Y., 1964, Bronx Arts Ensemble Orch., 1974-76, 77, 78, 79-81; tchr. voice Riverdale Sch. of Music, 1964—, also 92d St. Y Music Sch.; concert tour in Israel, 1964; appeared at Hudson River Mus., Yonkers; recitals Carnegie Hall, 1974, Coll. Mt. St. Vincent, 1975-76; also TV appearances. Mem. selection panel Bronx Council on Arts, 1974-75. Recipient Alice M. Ditson award Juilliard Sch. Music. Recorded Mozart's Impresario for Mercury Records, Kurt Weill's Frauen Tanz for Leonarda Records; rec. artist Tikva Records. Mem. N.Y. Singing Tchrs. Assn., Am. Soc. Jewish. Club: Music (bd. govs.). Home: 4525 Henry Hudson Pkwy Riverdale NY 10471

AINSLIE, MARY EISEL, banker; b. San Antonio, Tex., Dec. 8, 1949; d. Harry Louis and Reta Delores (Maershbecker) E.; B.B.A., U. Houston, 1975, M. Fin., 1978; grad. Southwestern Grad. Sch. Banking, Dallas, 1982; m. Richard Clayton Ainslie, June 3, 1978. Ops. mgr. VISA center U.S. Nat. Bank, Galveston, Tex., 1968-73, sr. v.p. comml. loans 1979—, also sec. to bd. dirs.; asst. nat. bank examiner Office of the Comptroller of the Currency, Houston, 1974-79. Mem. Nat. Assn. Bank Women. Baptist. Office: PO Box 179 2201 Market St Galveston TX 77553

AINSWORTH, DORIS STEWART, mktg. and advt. cons. co. exec.; b. Dallas, June 13, 1932; d. James H. and Ruth Pearl (Knott) Stewart; B.S. in Journalism, So. Meth. U., 1953; M.A., North Tex. State U., 1976; m. Horace D. Ainsworth, Jr., Dec. 10, 1955; children—James Denton, Ann Louise, Public relations asst. Ayres Compton Assos., Dallas, 1953-54; asst. editor Dallas Mag., Dallas C. of C., 1954-55; dir. public relations Dallas Petroleum Center, 1975-78; mktg. asst. Murray Investment Co., Dallas, asst. to pres., 1978; dir. communications Cox Sch. Bus., So. Meth. U., Dallas, 1978-81, mem. adv. bd. women in mgmt. program, 1981-82; adminstrv. officer, mktg. dir. Citizens Bank, Richardson, Tex., 1981-82; pres. Ainsworth Assos., Dallas, 1982—. Treas. Frisco (Tex.) Youth Center, 1975; sec. Frisco PTA, 1974; mem. adminstrv. bd. Lovers Lane United Meth. Ch., 1970. Mem. Women in Communications, Nat. Assn. Bank Women, Bank Mktg. Assn., Zeta Tau Alpha (pres. 1956). Office: 8300 Douglas St Suite 729 Dallas TX 75225

AIRTH, MISKIT, TV programming exec.; b. Live Oak, Fla., May 29, 1939; d. George Edward and Dorothy A.; A.B., Randolph Macon Woman's Coll., 1961; M.A., Dallas Theater Center, Baylor U., 1963. Mem. repertory theater, tchr.-dir. Children's Theater, Dallas Theater Center, 1961-63; with Nat. Theater Co., touring children's theater, 1963-64, Phoenix Theater, Am. Place Theater, Shakespeare-in-the-Park, N.Y.C., 1964-69; producer Sta. WPIX-TV, N.Y.C., 1969-75; asso. producer Good Morning America, ABC-TV, N.Y.C., 1975-76; producer A Woman Is—With Bess Myerson, Sta. WCBS-TV, N.Y.C., 1976-77; exec. producer Sta. WABC-TV, N.Y.C., 1977-80; dir. program devel. for East Coast, Viacom Enterprises, N.Y.C., 1980-81; dir. programming and studio ops. Warner Annex Cable Communications, 1981—; vis. scholar Boston U. Communications Inst.; lectr. Womanschool, N.Y.C., Randolph-Macon Woman's Coll., Lynchburg, Va., New Sch. for Social Research, N.Y.C., Inst. New Cinema Artist, N.Y.C. Mem. adv. com. So. Ohio Coll.; mem. planning com. Nat. Cancer Communications Conf., Houston. Recipient 2 silver medals Internat. Film Festival N.Y., 1979, 80, EMMY awards: outstanding documentary, 1971, 72, 80, outstanding mag., 1980, outstanding entertainment, 1980, 2 awards of excellence, Communications Excellence for Black Audiences, 1979, 80, award Nat. Cable TV Assn., 1982. Mem. Nat. Acad. TV Arts and Scis. (gov. N.Y.C. chpt.), Am. Women in Radio and TV (dir. N.Y.C. chpt.), Women in Cable (founder, 1st pres. Cin. Tri State chpt.), Phi Beta Kappa. Prodns. include New York Closeup, weekly film documentary Sta. WPIX-TV, 1969-73 (8 N.Y. area Emmy awards, 2 personal awards), WABC Spl. Reports, documentary series, 1977-80, WABC YOU! show (Emmy for pilot show), WABC instant spl. Life Was Worth Living, N.Y.C.: You Can't Get There From Here (Emmy), The Town That Build N.Y., (Emmy), Elvis-Love Him Tender with Joel Siegel (Emmy), prodns. for QUBE Cable, Studio 30, on location, others. Office: Warner Amex Cable Communications 11252 Cornell Park Dr Cincinnati OH 45242

AITCHISON, BEATRICE, transp. economist; b. Portland, Oreg., July 18, 1908; d. Clyde Bruce and Bertha (Williams) Aitchison; A.B., Goucher Coll., 1928, Sc.D. (hon.), 1979; A.M., Johns Hopkins, 1931; Ph.D. in Math., 1933; M.A. with honors in Econs., U. Oreg., 1937. Asso. prof. math. U. Richmond, 1933-34; lectr. statistics Am. U., 1934-44; instr. econs. U. Oreg., 1939-41; jr. statistician advancing to sr. statistician ICC, 1938-48, prin. transport economist, 1948-51; dir. transport econs. div. Office Transp., Dept. Commerce, 1951-53; dir. transp. research Post Office Dept., Washington, 1953-58, dir. transp. research and statistics, 1958-67, dir. transp. rates and econs., 1967-71; transp. cons., 1971—. Cons. Traffic Analysis and Forecasting Office Def. Transp., 1942-45; cons. mil. traffic. service U.S. Dept. Def., 1950-53. Recipient Alumnae Achievement citation Goucher Coll., 1954; First Ann. Fed. Woman's award, 1961, Career Service award Nat. Civil Service League, 1970. Fellow Am. Statis. Assn., A.A.A.S.; mem. Am. Econ. Assn., Am. Soc. Traffic and Transp., Transp. Research Forum, Phi Beta Kappa, Sigma Xi, Pi Lambda Theta, Phi Delta Gamma. Episcopalian. Contbr. to numerous govt. publs. Home and office: 1929 S St NW Washington DC 20009

AJZEN, RACHEL KLOTZ, psychologist; b. Tel Aviv; came to U.S., 1966, naturalized, 1976; d. Aron and Joheved Klotz; B.A., Hebrew U. Jerusalem, 1967; M.A., U. Ill., 1968, Ph.D. in Ednl. Psychology, 1970; postgrad. in clin. psychology U. Mass., 1980-82; m. Icek Ajzen, June 5, 1966: children—Ron, Elie, Jonathan. Trainee in clin. psychology Northampton (Mass.) State Hosp., 1971; asst. prof. Tel Aviv U., 1972; sch. psychologist Amherst (Mass.) Schs., 1974—; pvt. practice psychology, Amherst, 1974—; cons. psychologist to various orgns. and agys. Served with Israeli Air Force, 1960-62. Cert. sch. psychologist, Mass.; cert. elem. tchr., Mass.; cert. sch. guidance counselor, Mass.; lic. psychologist, Mass. Mem. Am. Psychol. Assn., Israeli Psychol. Assn. Author: (with A. Klingman) Principles and Methods of Educational Counseling, 1978. Office: Amherst Schs Amherst MA 01002

AKERS, JEANNE ANNE, communications exec.; b. Olympia, Wash., Mar. 1, 1945; d. Stephen Elmer and Norma Jeanne (Bair) A.; student Radford Coll., 1963-64, U. Hawaii, 1965-66. Exec. asst. to Norman Vincent Peale, N.Y.C., 1971-73; assoc. dir. Guideposts Outreach Ministries, N.Y.C., 1973-75; dir. media services and planning Found. for Christian Living, Pawling, N.Y., 1982—; owner features syndication entitle Positive Thinking (Norman Vincent Peale), 1982—. Mem. Am. Women in Radio and TV. Mem. Dutch Reformed Ch. Home: 450 E 63d St New York NY 10021 Office: 1025 Fifth Ave New York NY 10028

AKERS, MURIEL EVA, educator; b. Flat River, Mo., Aug. 1, 1905; d. William Thomas and Bessie May (Richards) Furry; A.A., Flat River Jr. Coll., 1961; B.S. in Edn., Washington U., St. Louis, 1963; m. John Thomas Akers, July 29, 1923; children—Gracin Edward, Earl Lindell, Carl Ray. Tchr., Bismarck (Mo.) Elementary Sch., 1963-73, Leadwood Elementary Sch., Irondale, Mo., 1973-76; subsitute tchr. Potosi (Mo.) Elementary and Jr. High Sch., Belleview (Mo.) Elementary Sch., Desloge (Mo.) Elementary Sch., Valley Schs., Caledonia, Mo., 1976—. Chmn., Office Caledonia Community Betterment, 1965-74; pres. Mo. E. Conf. Archives and History Commn. Meth. Ch., 1978. Recipient ann. certificate for outstanding leadership Mo. Community Betterment, 1965-74, Gov.'s Leadership award, 1967, plaque Meramec Regional Planning Commn., 1978. Mem. Mo. Tchrs. Assn., Nat. Ret. Tchrs. Assn., Bellevue Valley Hist. Soc. (pres. 1975-78), Writers Guild Washington County (organizer, pres. 1978). Methodist (rec. sec., historian, organist). Clubs: Order Eastern Star; Home Extension. Composer: Beneath the Blue of Heaven, 1950; O, Prince of Peace, We Come, 1960; I've Been Looking for You, 1960; Ozark Pioneers, 1978. Home: Caledonia MO 63631

ALAUPOVIC, ALEXANDRA VRBANIC, artist, educator; b. Slatina, Yugoslavia, Dec. 21, 1921; d. Joseph and Elizabeta (Papp) Vrbanic; student Bus. Sch., Zagreb, Yugoslavia, 1940-41, Acad. Visual Arts, Zagreb, Yugoslavia, 1944-48; postgrad. Acad. Visual Arts, Prague, Czechoslovakia, 1949, Art Sch., U. Ill., 1959-60; M.F.A., U. Okla., 1966; m. Peter Alaupovic, Mar. 22, 1947; children—Betsy, H. Clark Hyde. Came to U.S., 1958, naturalized, 1964. Sec., Arko Liquer & Yeast Factory and Distillery, Zagreb, 1941-44; instr. U. Okla., Norman, 1964-66; instr. three dimensional design sculpture Oklahoma City U., 1969—, Okla. Sci. Found., Oklahoma City, 1969-75; one-woman shows at Okla. Art Center, Oklahoma City, U. Okla. Mus. Art, Norman, Extraordinary Usuals, Aspen, Colo., 1976; exhibited art in group shows Springfield (Mo.) Art Mus., Okla. U. Mus., Norman, 7th Ann. Temple Emanuel Brotherhood Arts Festival, Dallas; represented in permanent collections Okla. U. Art Mus., Okla. State Art Collection, Mercy Health Center. Recipient Jacobson award U. Okla., 1964; hon. mention in sculpture Philbrook Art Center, Tulsa, 1967; 1st sculpture award Philbrook Art Center, Tulsa, 1970. Mem. Okla. Sculpture Soc., Internat. Sculpture Center. Home: 11908 N Bryant St Oklahoma City OK 73111 Office: Route 1 Box 167A Oklahoma City OK 73111

ALBANESE, HELEN GARSHANIN, psychiatrist; b. Belgrade, Yugoslavia, Mar. 14, 1941; came to U.S., 1955, naturalized, 1961; d. Nikola and Katarina (Zrinski) Garshanin; B.A., N.Y. U., 1962; M.D., Columbia U., 1967; m. Richard A. Albanese, Jan. 18, 1963; children—Ilana, Lara. Intern, resident in internal medicine Mountainside Hosp., Montclair, N.J., 1967-70; staff psychiatrist San Antonio State Hosp., 1971-74, 77-79; resident in psychiatry U. Tex. Health Sci. Center, San Antonio, 1974-77; staff psychiatrist Audie Murphy VA Hosp., San Antonio, also asst. prof. U. Tex. Health Scis. Center, San Antonio, 1979—. Active Girl Scouts U.S.A. Diplomate Am. Bd. Psychiatry and Neurology. Mem. Am. Med. Women's Assn., AMA, Tex. Med. Assn., Am. Psychiat. Assn., Tex. Psychiat. Assn., Phi Beta Kappa. Democrat. Office: Audie Murphy Veterans Administration Hospital San Antonio TX 78284

ALBANESE, LICIA, operatic soprano; b. Bari, Italy, July 22, 1913; d. Michele and Maria (Rugusa) Albanese; studied voice under Giuseppina R. Baldassare Tedeschi, Milan, Italy, 1932-35; LL.D., Seton Hall U.; L.H.D., Manhattan Coll., Fairfield (Conn.) U., Caldwell (N.J.) Coll., Marymount Manhattan Coll.; Mus.D. cum laude, St. Peters U., Jersey City; D.F.A., Siena Coll., Loudonville, N.Y.; m. Joseph Gimma, Apr. 7, 1945. Won nat. singing contest, Italy, 1935; made an unexpected debut in role of Madame Butterfly in Milan, Italy, 1934, when the leading soprano became ill; formal debut at Royal Theater, Parma, Italy, in role of Madame Butterfly, Dec. 19, 1935; sang at inauguration of Vatican City radio sta. and was decorated by Pope Pius XI; made records of La Boheme with Beniamino Gigli, 1939; sang at concert in honor of Sir Neville Chamberlin and Lord Halifax, Rome, 1939; sang at Covent Garden for Festival of King George VI; made debut at Met. Opera House, N.Y.C., in Madame Butterfly and La Traviata, 1940. Adv. council 3d St. Music Sch. Settlement; trustee Bagby Music Lovers Found., N.Y.C.; chmn. Puccini Found., N.Y.C. Decorated lady grand cross Order Holy Sepulchre. Home: 800 Park Av New York NY 10021 *.

ALBANTIDES, MARGARET ELOISE, bus. exec.; b. N.Y.C., Oct. 14, 1942; d. Joseph and Hilda Bezares; student Bernard Baruch Sch. Bus., CCNY, 1960-65, LaSalle U. extension, 1978—; m. 1981; 1 son. Adminstrv. asst. London Records, Inc., N.Y.C., 1965-69; bus. mgr. dept. radiology Lenox Hill Hosp., N.Y.C., 1969-72; field supr. Activ div. Met. Tobacco Co., Long Island City, 1972-74; sales rep. Met. Life Ins. Co., N.Y.C., 1974-77; pres. Admar's Mdse. Co., Inc., New City, N.Y.,

1976-81; propr. The Button Factory, 1981—. Mem. New City C. of C., Soc. Advancement Mgmt. (sec. 1974). Office: Box 309 New City NY 10956

ALBEE, GRACE ARNOLD, artist; b. Scituate, R.I., July 28th, 1890 m. Percy F. Albee, May 10, 1913 (dec. 1959); children—Edward F. II, John F., Nathaniel E., William C., Percy F. Jr. Painter and engraver; represented in Bklyn. Mus. by purchase award, 1947; represented in mus. of R.I. Sch. Design, Library of Congress, Met. Mus., N.Y.C., Carnegie Inst. Mus., Pitts., Okla. A&M Coll., Stillwater, Nat. Mus. Art. Stockholm, Cleve. Mus. Art, Kansas City Mus., John Herron Art Mus., N.Y., Boston and Newark pub. libraries, Phila. Mus., Melrose (Mass.) Library, Pa. State Library, Harrisburg, Nat. Gallery Art, Washington, Bethlehem Library, Peacham (Vt.) Library, Lynchburg (Va.) Art Club, collection of King Victor Emmanuel of Italy (1940), Cayuga Mus. Hist. and Art, Auburn, N.Y., Albany (N.Y.) Print Club, Norton Mus. West Palm Beach, Fla., Portland (Maine) Mus. Art, Nat. Bezalel Mus., Jerusalem Culver Mil. Acad., Notre Dame U., Nat. Gallery, various pvt. collections; one-woman show wood engravings Bklyn. Mus., 1976. Nat. Academician, 1946; life fellow Met. Mus. Art, 1962. Recipient numerous awards including Eugenia F. Atwood Purchase prize at Phila. Print Club, 1949, print prizes N.A.D., Conn. Acad., Hunterdon County Art Center, 1959; Albany Purchase Prize, 1959, 60; Conn. Acad. Purchase prize, 1961; Trenton Mus. Purchase prize, N.A.D. prize, 1959, 62; gold medal for wood engraving Am. Artists Profl. League, 1961, first prize in graphics, 1974; Oakes-on-the-Hill prize Providence Water Color Club, 1964; Florence Kane prize Providence Art Club, 1964; prize Am. Artists Profl. League, 1965; medal and citation contbn. visual arts, painting and wood engraving, Providence Art Club, 1965, R.I. Sch. Design Alumni Assn., 1965; Best of Yr. award drawing, Non Profl. Inst. Pa., 1965; Bowen Purchase award Albany Print Club, 1967, Purchase award, 1976; Helen Gould Kennedy award Academic Artists, 1968; Samuel Finley Breese Meml. award N.A.D., 1962, 72, numerous others. Hon. vice chmn. R.I. Sch. Design Alumni Fund, 1960. Fellow Am. Artists Profl. League (prize 1961, chmn. jury of Selection and awards 1968); mem. NAD (chmn. graphic art membership com. 1953—, mem. jury 1974), Conn. Acad., Providence Water Color Club (life). Albany Print Club, Providence Art Club, Boston Printmakers, Academic Artists' Assn., Met. Mus. N.Y. (life). Reproductions in numerous publs. Home and studio: Apt 333 Bldg 2 1357 Wampanoag Trail East Providence RI 02914 *

ALBERGA, ALTA WHEAT, artist; b. Ala.; d. James Richard and Leila Savannah (Sullivan) Wheat; B.A., M.A., Wichita State U., 1954; B.F.A., Washington U., St. Louis, 1961; M.F.A., U. Ill., 1964; m. Alvyn Clyde Alberga, Dec. 3, 1930. Mem. faculty Wichita (Kans.) State U., 1955-56, Webster Coll., St. Louis, 1962, Presbyn. Coll., Clinton, S.C., 1969-74; pvt. art tchr., Greenville, S.C., 1974—; substitute tchr. Greenville County Schs.; tchr. painting Tempo Gallery Sch., Greenville, 1974—, Greenville County Mus. Sch., 1975—; one-woman shows: Greenville County Mus., 1979, Greenville Artists Guild Gallery, 1979, Wichita State U., 1954, St. Louis Artists Guild, 1956, N.C. State U., 1965; group shows include: Pickens County Mus., 1979, Inter/Art 81, Washington 1981, Guild Greenville Artists, 1982; represented in pvt. collections; bd. dirs. Greenville Artists Guild, 1977-79, Guild Gallery, 1978, Guild Greenville Symphony, 1982-83. Recipient Richard K. Weil award St. Louis Mus., 1957; Purchase prize S.C. Arts Commn., 1972. Mem. Artists Equity (pres. St. Louis chpt. 1962), Internat. Platform Assn., Art Students League, Guild Greenville Artists, S.C. Artists Guild, Southeastern Council Printmakers, Greenville Symphony Guild, Kappa Pi, Kappa Delta Pi. Democrat. Home: 11 Overton Dr Greenville SC 29609

ALBERGOTTI, LILA FRETWELL, civic worker, musician; b. Anderson, S.C., July 31, 1929; d. Raymond and Lila (Brownlee) Fretwell; B.Mus., Salem Coll., 1950; m. William Greer Albergotti, Mar. 31, 1951; children—Samuel Fretwell, Raymond Mackay, Lila Brownlee (dec.), Mary Argoe, Paul McAlpin. Choir dir. Good Hope Presbyn. Ch., Iva, S.C., 1967-82. Bd. dirs. Children's Bur. S.C., 1968-82, chmn., 1976-80; chmn. bd. dirs. Anderson County (S.C.) Meals on Wheels, 1976—; bd. dirs. Anderson-Oconee Council on Aging, 1973-82, chmn. bd., 1980; bd. dirs. Foothills United Way, 1982—; founder, chmn. steering com. Lifeline Ministry Soup Kitchen, Anderson, 1982—; mem. Mayor's Com. on Hiring the Handicapped, 1978—. Recipient local, dist., regional Sertoma Service to Mankind award, 1977; named Anderson (S.C.) Woman of Yr., Beta Sigma Phi, 1979. Mem. Presbyn. Music Assn. Episcopalian. Clubs: Anderson Women's, Anderson Garden, Anderson County. Home: 406 Shannon Way Anderson SC 29621

ALBERS, BEULAH MAXINE WHICKER, county ofcl.; b. Carthage, Mo., July 1, 1924; d. Benjamin A. and Beulah B. (King) Whicker; grad. Central Bus. Coll., 1942; postgrad. U. Denver, 1945-47, U. Colo., 1968-70; m. Theodore Earl Albers, Apr. 4, 1943; children—Ted Loren, Rhonda Gayle. With U. Denver, 1947-49; dep. county treas., 1952-54; State of Colo., City of Boulder, 1962-64; exec. sec. to bank v.p., 1966-68; commr. Mesa County, Colo., 1974—; chmn. Walker Field Public Airport Authority; chmn. Colo. West Area Council Govts.; bd. mem. Wand, Inc. Mem. Colo. Land Use Commn., 1979-82; mem. Colo. State Adv. Council for Title I Community Services and Continuing Edn. Programs, Colo. Commn. Higher Edn., 1976-79; mem. Mesa Coll. Citizens Adv. Council, 1975-76; chmn. Mesa County Heart Unit, 1975. Named Lioness of Yr., Grand Junction Lions Club, 1973, Woman of Achievement, Colo. Bus. and Profl. Women, 1974. Mem. Nat. Assn. Counties Ofcls. (mem. land use steering com. 1975—), Colo. Counties, Inc. (pres. 1982), P.E.O., C. of C., LWV. Republican. Clubs: Bookcliff Country, Greenbelt, Altrusa, Club 20. Office: PO Box 897 Grand Junction CO 81501

ALBERT, BEVERLY FOIT, architect; b. Buffalo, Apr. 28, 1938; d. Franklin and Ruth Marie (Fix) Foit; B.Arch., Cornell U., 1961; M.Arch., SUNY, Buffalo, 1975; Ph.D., Humanistic Psychology Inst., 1978; m. James T. Albert, Dec. 28, 1963; children—James T., Jeffrey J., Richard A. Partner firm Castle, Baschnagel, Maharan & Albert, Buffalo, 1966-69; asso. firm Castle, Hamilton, Houston & Lownie, Buffalo, 1970-71; prin. firm Foit-Albert and Assos., Buffalo, 1976—; asso. prof. Sch. Architecture and Environ. Design, Buffalo, 1969—. Recipient Research award Progressive Architecture mag., 1975. Mem. Soc. Archtl. Historians, Constrn. Specifications Inst., Assn. Bus. and Profl. Women in Constrn., Assn. Minority Enterprises N.Y. Contbr. articles to profl. publs. Home: 10 Maple Dr Orchard Park NY 14127 Office: 700 Main St Buffalo NY 14202

ALBIN, KAREN BETH, architect; b. N.Y.C., Aug. 22, 1952; d. Michael and Rose (Kopelson) A.; B.A., N.Y.U., 1973; M.Arch., U. Pa., 1977. Archtl. designer, draftsman Harrison & Abramovitz, N.Y.C., 1977-79; interior architect Skidmore, Owings & Merrill, N.Y.C., 1979-80; intermediate designer Richard B. Dempsey, Architect, N.Y.C., 1980-81; project designer Noel Jeffrey, Inc., N.Y.C., 1981—; guest mem. jury N.J. Sch. Architecture, 1979—. Mem., Manhattan Community Bd. 5, 1978—. Mem. AIA. Home: 21 W 58th St New York NY 10019 Office: 22 E 65th St New York NY 10021

ALBIN, MAJORIE ANN, banker; b. Tuscola, Ill., Aug. 8, 1930; d. George David and Mae L. (Perry) Martin; student Eastern Ill. U., 1948, 49, Wharton Sch., U. Ill., m. John S. Albin, Sept. 10, 1949; children—Perry S., Martin L., David A. Tax acct. Longview, Ill., 1963—; cashier, chief exec. officer Longview State Bank, 1978—, also dir.; dir. Newman Manor, Inc., Plant Pals, Inc., Longview Capitol Corp., Albi Pork Farm, Inc. Bd. dirs. Jarman Hosp., Tuscola, Continental Manor Nursing Home, Newman, Ill. Office: Longview State Bank Box 37 Longview IL 61852

ALBRECHT, CAROL LEE, human resources cons.; b. Cleve., June 28, 1947; d. Byron Joseph and Janet Carol (Ramsey) A.; B.A. cum laude, Milton Coll., 1970; M.S.W., U. Wis., 1972. Program dir. Nev. Div. Mental Health, Las Vegas, 1973-74; state planner Gov.'s Council on Devel. Disabilities, Phoenix, 1974-77; specialist for Persons with Handicaps for Gov.'s Office, Phoenix, 1977-79; human resources cons. United Mgmt. Systems, Inc. of Ariz., Phoenix, 1979-81; chief exec. officer Cactus Industries, Phoenix, 1981—; cons. Nat. Gov.'s Assn., 1979—; State of Ariz. rep. at White House Conf. on Handicapped Individuals, 1976, mem. Gov.'s Com. on Employment of Handicapped. HEW fellow, 1970-71; recipient Citation of Merit, Gov. of Ariz., 1977. Mem. Ariz. Affirmative Action Assn., Ariz. Congress for Action, Young Execs. Assn. Contbr. articles to profl. jours. Home: PO Box 1273 Carefree AZ 85377 Office: 4120 N 38th Dr Phoenix AZ 85019

ALBRIGHT, MADELEINE KORBEL, political scientist; b. Prague, Czechoslovakia, May 15, 1937; d. Josef and Anna (Speeglova) Korbel; B.A. with honors, Wellesey Coll., 1959; M.A., Columbia U., 1968, cert. Russian Inst., 1968, Ph.D., 1976; m. Joseph Medill Patterson Albright, June 11, 1959; children—Anne Korbel, Alice Patterson, Katharine Medill. Reporter, Rolla (Mo.) Daily News, 1959; with public relations dept. Ency. Brit., 1960; chief legis. asst. U.S. Senator Muskie, 1976-78; mem. staff NSC charge congressional liaison, 1978-81; fellow Woodrow Wilson Internat. Center for Scholars, Washington, 1980-81. William H. Donner prof. internat. affairs and dir. women in fgn. service Sch. Fgn. Service, Georgetown U., 1982—. Bd. dirs. Beauvoir Sch., Washington, 1968-76, chmn., 1972-76; mem. exec. com. Chpt. of Washington Cathedral, 1972-76, mem., 1978—; mem. Black Student Fund Bd. Trustees, 1969-78, chmn. scholarship com., 1976; mem. exec. com. D.C. Citizens Better Public Edn., 1975-76; mem. commn. study reorgn. P.E. Ch. Found. Washington, 1976-77; trustee Democratic Forum, 1976-78, Williams Coll., 1978-82; chmn. fgn. relations task force, polit. action com. Women's Nat. Dem. Club, 1975-76; Dem. campaign aide U.S. senators Mondale, 1972, Stevenson, 1974; Washington coordinator Maine for Muskie, 1975-76. Mem. Council Fgn. Relations, Am. Polit. Sci. Assn., Czeckoslovak Soc. Arts and Scis. Am., Women's Nat. Dem. Clubs, Am. Assn. Advancement Slavic Studies. Episcopalian. Office: Sch Fgn Service Georgetown Univ Washington DC 20007

ALBRITTON, BETTYE HATTER, social service agy. exec.; b. Ruston, La., Apr. 13, 1940; d. Elbert and Oneder (Williams) H.; B.A.B.A., Grambling Coll., 1962; m. Harold Albritton, Jan. 14, 1978; 1 son, Gerald Wayne. Adminstrv. asst. Grambling Coll., 1962-65; tchr. St. Martin de Porres Elem. Sch., Amarillo, Tex., 1965-66; editor I dept. psychology U. Tex., Austin, 1967-73; head fin. service sect. Drug Abuse Prevention div. Tex. Dept. Community Affairs, Austin, 1973-78; contract specialist San Diego Regional Employment and Tng. Consortium, 1978-81, program devel. specialist, 1981—; family counselor drug abuse prevention; vol. Upward Bound program Wiley Coll. Founder and pres. human relations com. Austin Public Sch. System PTA, 1970-71, v.p. PTA, 1971-72. Recipient award for human relations com. involvement Tex. PTA, 1971, appreciation award San Diego City Sch. Youth Employment and Tng. Program, 1979; cert. of appreciation Calif. Assn. Work Experience Educators, 1980, Sacred Heart Ch., Austin, 1972. Democrat. Roman Catholic. Home: 892 Kelton Rd San Diego CA 92114 Office: 861 6th Ave San Diego CA 92112

ALCOTT, SUSAN, writer, entertainment prodn. asst.; b. Los Angeles, June 7, 1940; d. William Kenneth and Hazel Stella (Pearson) Allin; student Los Angeles Harbor Coll., 1958-59, El Camino Coll., 1959-61, Calif. State U., 1961-64, Writers Guild Am. West, Inc., 1970-74, Arthur Alsberg's Advanced Screenwriting Workshop, 1980-81; div. Teaching asst., lab. technician Calif. State U., Los Angeles, 1963-64; with Musifon, Inc., Los Angeles, 1965-69; with Mickey Garrett & Assos., Public Relations, Los Angeles, 1967-68; freelance reader Screen Gems TV, Burbank, Calif., 1972; corp. sec.-treas., adminstrv. asst., dir. Don Perry Enterprises, Inc., Los Angeles, 1969-80; free-lance bus. and public relations writing service Susan Alcott's Scribe Services Ltd., Sherman Oaks, Calif., 1981—; personal asst. to Lelan Rogers, gen. mgr. Kenny Rogers Prodns. Inc., Los Angeles, 1981—; actress theatres So. Calif.; actress films, TV, commls.; poetry published Poetry Parade mag., Writers Guild Am. West Inc., newspapers; lyricist Nobody's Child. Recipient Writers Guild Found. award, 1972, cert., 1974. Mem. ASCAP, Screen Actors Guild, Am. Film Inst., Nat. Assn. Female Execs., Planetary Soc. Editor: Patterns, 1982. Office: 8255 Beverly Blvd Los Angeles CA 90048

ALDAPE, ALICIA CATALINA GONZALEZ (ALINA), lawyer; b. Mexico City, Sept. 21, 1952; d. John William Gonzalez Esparza and Alicia Hermelinda Aldape Cantu; B.A., Mexico City Prep. Sch., 1970; student Coll. Notre Dame, 1970-71; B.A. in Polit. Sci. with honors, Stanford U., 1974, J.D., 1977. Admitted to Calif. bar, 1977; asso. firm McCutchen, Doyle, et al, 1977-80, Lasky, Haas, Cohler & Munter, 1980—. Pres., mem. ct. Philip Jessup Internat. Law Moot Ct. Competition, 1978-79; sec., chmn. membership com., bd. dirs. Bay Area Profl. Women's Network, 1980—; bd. dirs. Stanford Bay Area Jrs. Mem. Am. Soc. Internat. Law, Am. Bar Assn. (sect. internat. law, antitrust sect.), State Bar Calif. (bus. law sect.). Democrat. Roman Catholic. Clubs: Bay, San Francisco Eastern (dir.). Office: 505 Sansome St 12th Floor San Francisco CA 94111

ALDAVE, BARBARA BADER, educator, lawyer; b. Tacoma, Dec. 28, 1938; d. Fred A. and Patricia W. (Burns) Bader; B.S. (Nat. Merit scholar), Stanford U., 1960; J.D., U. Calif., Berkeley, 1966; m. Ralph Theodore Aldave, Apr. 2, 1966; children—Anna Marie, Anthony John. Admitted to Oreg. bar, 1966, Tex. bar, 1982; assoc. law firm, firm Eugene, 1967-70; asst. prof. U. Oreg., 1970-73; vis. prof. U. Calif., Berkeley, 1973-74; vis. prof., asst. prof. to prof. U. Tex., Austin, 1974—, co-holder James R. Dougherty chair for faculty excellence, 1981-82, Piper prof., 1982. Del. Tex. Democratic Conv., 1980; mem. Austin Dem. Forum and women's com. Travis County Dem. Orgn.; chmn. bd. dirs. Women's Advocacy Project. Recipient Teaching Excellence award U. Tex. Student Bar Assn., 1976, 1st ann. appreciation award Thurgood Marshall Legal Soc. of U. Tex., 1980-81. Mem. Travis County Women Lawyers Assn., Stanford Alumni Assn., Bread for the World, Network, Campaign for Polit. Rights, Clergy and Laity Concerned, Lawyers Alliance for Nuclear Arms Control, Order of Coif, Phi Delta Phi, Omicron Delta Kappa. Roman Catholic. Club: Stanford (Austin). Home: 803 Cedar Park Dr Austin TX 78746 Office: 727 E 26th St Austin TX 78705

ALDEN, CAROLYN CARLTON, accountant, cons. econs. exec.; b. Tulsa, Feb. 27, 1941; d. Henry Ellis and Estelle Mildred (Baker) Carlton; student Tulane U., 1959-62; B.S. magna cum laude, Okla. State U., 1966; m. Richard J. Alden, Aug. 29, 1964. Supr., Coopers & Lybrand, Dallas, 1967-72, project mgr., N.Y.C., 1972-76, nat. dir. profl. edn., 1976-79; mng. partner Alden and Assos., N.Y.C. and Newport Beach, Calif., 1979—; v.p. The Network; mem. bus. adv. bd. U.S. Senate. Active, Girls Club N.Y., Madison Ave Presbyn. Ch. Named Outstanding Bus. Woman, Boston Coll., 1978; Price Waterhouse grad. fellow, 1965; Phillips Petroleum Co. scholar, 1959; C.P.A., Okla., Tex., N.Y. Mem. Am. Inst. C.P.A.s (ednl. materials and exchange com. 1976-79), Am. Women Soc. C.P.A.s (dir. 1976-77), N.Y. State Soc. C.P.A.s, Tex. Soc. C.P.A.s, Nat. Assn. Accts., Am. Soc. for Tng. and Devel., Phi Kappa Psi, Beta Alpha Psi. Republican. Circulation editor Acctg. Jour., 1977-78; mem. editorial bd. Woman C.P.A., 1976-77; contbr. articles to profl. jours. Home: 140 S Bay Front Newport Beach CA 92662 Office: 10 W 66th St Suite 8F New York NY 10023

ALDERMAN, ALICE MAE (MRS. DONALD C. ALDERMAN), librarian; b. Westby, Wis.; d. Hjalmar Otto and Agatha Hilda (Mortenson) Rudrud; A.A., North Park Coll., 1945; B.S. magna cum laude, U. Wis., 1965, M.S., 1966, postgrad., 1966—; m. Donald C. Alderman, Dec. 12, 1946; children—Deborah (Mrs. Cecil Rolfe), Andrew, Brent, Marsha. Lab. technician Leaf Brands, Chgo., 1945-46; teaching asst. U. Wis., Madison, 1965-66; with Wis. State Hist. Soc., Madison, 1966—, cataloger documents, 1967-74, asst. documents librarian, 1974—. Mem. ALA, Am. Scandinavian Found., Kappa Delta Phi, Beta Phi Mu. Mem. Modern Woodmen of Am. Author: Organizing Wisconsin Public Documents, 1974; contbr. articles to profl. jours.; co-editor, compiler: Wisconsin Public Documents. Home: 1715 Laurel Crest Madison WI 53705 Office: 816 State St Madison WI 53706

ALDERMAN, MINNIS AMELIA, psychologist, bus. exec.; b. Douglas, Ga., Oct. 14, 1928; d. Louis Cleveland and Minnis (Wooten) A.; A.B., Ga. Coll. at Milledgeville, 1949; M.A., Murray State U., 1960; fellow U. Utah, summers 1974, 75. Camp counselor Camp Sloan, Conn., summer 1949; music dir. Umatilla (Fla.) public sch., 1949-50, Campbell High Sch., Fairburn, Ga., 1950-54; music and drama dir., tchr. English and speech Wells (Nev.) High Sch., 1954-59; tchr. English and history Sinking Fork Sch., Hopkinsville, Ky., 1960; counselor White Pine High Sch., Ely, Nev., 1960-68; instr. psychology, guidance and counseling Murray (Ky.) State U., summers 1961, 62; instr. guidance and counseling U. Nev. Extension, 1963-68, mem. home econs. adv. bd., 1977—; psychologist Ely Mental Health Center, 1969-75, Nev. Job Service, 1975-79; owner Minisizer Exercising Salon, 1969-71, Minimimeo Mimeographing, 1969—, Knit Knook, 1969—, Gift Gamut, 1977—, City Service Sta.; pres. Creative Crafters Gift Shoppe; sec.-treas. Great Basin Enterprises Corp., 1969-71; pvt. tchr. piano, violin, voice, 1981—; band dir. Sacred Heart Sch., 1982—; test supt. Coll. Entrance Exam. Bd. and Am. Coll. Testing, 1960-68. Pres. White Pine County Mental Health Assn., 1960-63, 78—; mem. Gov.'s Mental Health State Commn., 1963-65; bd. dirs. White Pine County Sch. Employees Fed. Credit Union, 1961-68, pres., 1963-68; 2d v.p. White Pine Community Concert Assn., 1965-67, pres., 1967, treas., 1975—; dir. Community Choir, 1974—; mem. Gov.'s Commn. on Status Women, 1968-72; sec.-treas. White Pine Rehab. Tng. Center for Retarded Persons, 1973-75; dir. Ret. Sr. Vol. Program, 1973-74; vice chmn. Great Basin Health Council, 1973-75; sec.-treas. Great Basin chpt. Nev. Employees Assn.; vice chmn. White Pine Council on Alcoholism and Drug Abuse, 1975-76, chmn., 1976-77; bd. dirs. White Pine chpt. ARC, 1976—, Nev. Hwy. Safety Leaders, 1977—; grants author, originator Community Tng. Center for Retarded People, 1972, Ret. Sr. Vol. Program, 1974, Nutrition Program for Sr. Citizens, 1974, Sr. Citizens Center, 1974, Home Repairs for Sr. Citizens, 1974, Sr. Citizens Home Assistance Program, 1977, Creative Crafters Assos., 1976; mem. Nev. Gov.'s Commn. on Hwy. Safety, 1979—; reporter precinct ABC News, 1966; mem. adv. bd. U. Nev. Extension Service, 1977—; mem. adv. bd. for sr. citizens Lincoln and White Pine counties, 1982—; mem. Commn. on Status and Role of Women, Calif.-Nev. ann. conf. United Meth. Ch., 1981. Mem. NEA (life), Nev. Edn. Assn., Counselors on Alcoholism, Addictions and Related Dependencies, AAUW (pres. 1964-65, state area rep. in edn. 1965-67; state implementation chmn. edn. 1967-69, state area adviser 1969-73), Bus. and Profl. Women's Club (1st v.p. 1965-66, pres. 1966-68, asst. dist. dir. 1967-68, state civic participation chmn. 1967-68, dist. dir. 1968-70, state 2d v.p. 1969-70, state rec. sec. 1968-69, state 1st v.p. 1970-71, state pres.-elect 1971-72, state pres. 1972-73), DAR, Internat. Platform Assn., Mensa (test adminstr. 1966—), Am. Personnel and Guidance Assn. (state memberships chmn. 1962-65), Am. Sch. Counselors Assn., Nat. Vocat. Counselors Assn., Nat. Fedn. Ind. Bus. (dist. chmn. 1971—), Nat. Assn. Women Deans and Counselors, Nat. Assn. Female Execs., NOW, Delta Kappa Gamma (2d v.p. 1964-66, state program chmn. 1965-69, 1st v.p. 1966-68, state 1st v.p. 1967-69, chpt. pres. 1968-72, state pres. 1969-71), Gen. Fedn. Women's Clubs (dist. pres. 1970-75), Beta Sigma Phi (chpt. sponsor 1970-72). Clubs: White Pine Knife and Fork (2d v.p. 1968-69, 1st v.p. 1969-70, pres. 1970-71, sec.-treas. 1978—), Ely Woman's (pres. 1969-70). Methodist (lay speaker 1967—, lay leader to regional conf. 1977—, choir dir. 1960—). Author: Handbook for Counselors; Guidance Handbook for Teachers; Guidance Handbook for Administrators; Discipline Handbook; Handbook Workshop Career Development, also articles. Home: 945 Ave H PO Box 457 East Ely NV 89315 Office: Murry St PO Box 457 East Ely NV 89301 also 1113 Ave F PO Box 323 East Ely NV 89315

ALDERS, MAJORIE ANNETTE, electron microscopist; b. Denver, Feb. 11, 1940; d. Rudolph Joseph and Genwyth Annette (Wherry) Vrobel; B.A., U. Colo., 1962; postgrad. Western State Coll., 1963-65; M.S., U. Denver, 1977; m. Donald David Alders, Aug. 22, 1962; 1 dau., Misti Ann. Microbiology technician U. Colo. Med. Center, Denver, 1962-63, genetic research technician, 1965-66, radiation research technician, 1966-68; cellular ultrastructure research technician VA Hosp., Denver, 1968-70; electron microscopist U.S. Dept. Agr., Agriculture Research Service, Arthropodborne Animal Diseases Research, Denver, 1970—. Sec. Colo. Acad. Parent Council, 1980-81; tchr. St. Joan of Arc Cath. Church Elementary Sch. Tchrs. Assn., 1971-81; fed. women's program adviser U.S. Dept. Agr. Rocky Mountain Region, 1980—. Recipient Honor award for superior service U.S. Dept. Agriculture, 1972. Mem. AAAS, Am. Soc. Microbiology, Electron Microscopy Soc. Am., Federally Employeed Women, Contbr. articles to various publs. Office: US Dept Agriculture Research Service Denver Fed Center Box 25327 Denver CO 80225

ALDREDGE, THEONI VACHLIOTIS, costume designer; b. Athens, Greece, Aug. 22, 1932; d. Gen. Athanasios and Meropi (Gregoriades) Vachliotis; student Am. Sch., Athens, Goodman Theatre, Chgo., 1949-53; m. Thomas E. Aldredge, Dec. 10, 1953. Mem. design staff Goodman Theatre, 1951-53; head designer N.Y. Shakespeare Festival, 1962—; designer numerous Broadway shows, Off Broadway shows, ballet, opera, television spls.; films include Great Gatsby, Network, Cheap Detective, Fury, Eyes of Laura Mars, The Champ, The Rose, Semi-Tough, You're a Big Boy Now; Broadway shows include Sweet Bird of Youth, Mary Mary, Who's Afraid of Virginia Wolf, A Delicate Balance, Championship Season, Sticks and Bones, Two Gentlemen of Verona, Three Penny Opera, A Chorus Line (Theatre World award 1976), Annie, Ballroom, Grand Tour, Dream Girls. Recipient Brit. Motion Picture Acad. award for The Great Gatsby, 1976; Obie award for Disting. Service to Off Broadway Theatre, Village Voice, 1976; Antoinette Perry award for Annie, 1977, for Barnum, 1981; Maharam award for Peer Gynt; Drama Desk award for 42nd Street, 1981; numerous other Drama Desk and Critics awards. Mem. United Scenic Artists, Costume Designers Guild, Acad. Motion Picture Arts Scis. (Oscar award Great Gatsby 1975). Office: 890 Broadway New York NY 10006

ALDRICH, LYNNE MERRILL, ednl. adminstr.; b. Detroit, July 23, 1946; d. Claude E. and Irene (Suzanne) (Keil) Gardner; A.B. in Polit. Dvi., W. Va. U., 1969; postgrad. Wayne State U., 1980—. Asst., then acring area mgr. Fotomat Corp., Detroit, 1969-70; acad. service officer dept. biol. scis. Wayne State U., 1970—. Bd. dirs., sec. LaSalle Townhouse Coop. Assn., 1978-82. Recipient Humanitarian award

Wayne State U., 19—. Mem. Nat. Assn. Female Execs. Club: Wayne State U. Faculty. Office: Dept Biol Scis Wayne State U Detroit MI 48202

ALDRICH, STEPHANIE RAE, chemist; b. Akron, Ohio, June 26, 1944; d. Steven Paul and Fannie Alberta (Beck) Hegedus; student Purdue U., South Bend (Ind.) Campus, evenings 1972-73; children—Todd Clifton, Robert LeRoy. Tchr. reality therapy, activities dir. Rehab. Center, Michigan City, Ind., 1972-74; metallurgy, sand control apprentice Josam Mfg. Co., Michigan City, 1978-79; with Manley Bros. div. Brit. Indsl. Sands, Ltd., Chesterton, Ind., 1979—, analytical chemist, mgr. quality control, research and devel. labs., 1980—. Mem. AAAS. Democrat. Lutheran. Contbr. poetry to various publs. Home: 1215 Earl Rd Michigan City IN 46360 Office: Manley Bros 128 S 15th St Chesterton IN 46304

ALDRICH, WILLIE L. B., librarian; b. Cleve., Sept. 9, 1924; d. Alfred and Hattie Ross (Batts) Banks; B.S., Coll. of Livingston, Salisbury, N.C., 1945, C.R.E., 1949; M.S. in L.S., Atlanta U., 1964; m. Thomas N. Aldrich, Feb. 11, 1947. Bible tchr. Salisbury public schs., 1953-54; asst. librarian Rowan County Br. Library, 1955-58; tchr., librarian Cleveland High Sch., Shelby, N.C., 1957-58; librarian Dunbar High Sch., East Spencer, N.C., 1958-60: asst. librarian Carnegie Library, Coll. Livingston, 1960-62, head seminarian librarian W.J. Walls Center, 1962—; del. Gov. N.C. Conf. Libraries. Sec. edn. sect. Mayor Salisbury Commn. Status Women, 1970—; mem. Rowen Citizens for Better Libraries; bd. dirs. N.C. Easter Seals Soc., Bishop J.W. Walls Found.; v.p. Rowan-Salisbury unit Ch. Women United, 1978-80. Recipient Service award Coll. of Livingston Alumni Assn., 1980. Mem. ALA, Salisbury-Rowan Library Assn., Delta Sigma Theta.

ALDRIDGE, ALEXANDRA, educator; b. Chgo., July 23, 1940; B.A. in Sociology, (asst.), Millikin U., 1961; M.A. in English, Northwestern U., 1963; Ph.D. in Comparative Lit. (fellow 1967-68), U. Mich., 1978. Instr. English, Wayne State U., Detroit, 1968-72; lectr. Am. culture U. Mich., 1975, lectr. humanities, 1980, lectr. humanities/engring., 1975-81; assoc. prof., dir. grad. studies in interdisciplinary tech. Eastern Mich. U., Ypsilanti, 1982—; lectr. univs. throughout Europe; writer, cons. Westdeutscher Rundfunk, 1972-73; cons. Ctr. 20th Century Studies, U. Wis., Milw., Kent State Univ. Press, others. Hon. degree Instituto Politechnico National de Mex., 1981. Mem. U. Mich. Women's Research Club, Am. Comparative Lit. Assn., Conf. Utopian Studies, Sci. Fiction Research Assn., World Future Soc. Co-editor: Alternative Futures quar., 1978—; editor issue Extrapolation, 1977; contbr. articles to scholarly jours. Office: Sill Hall Coll Tech Eastern Mich U Ypsilanti MI 48197

ALDRIDGE, DELORES PATRICIA, educator, sociologist; b. Tampa, Fla., June 8, 1941; d. Willie Lee and Mary Ellen (Bennett) Aldridge; B.A., Clark Coll., 1963, M.S.W., Atlanta U., 1966; Ph.D., Purdue U., 1971; m. Kwame Essuon, June 17, 1972. Teaching asst. sociology dept. Purdue U., West Lafayette, Ind., 1968-69, research asso., 1969-70; exec. dir. Greater Lafayette Community Center, West Lafayette, 1970-71; faculty Emory U., Atlanta, 1971-75, asso. prof. Black studies and Inst. Liberal Arts, 1976-77; dir. Afro-Am. and African studies, asso. prof. sociology, sr. research asso. Center for Research and Social Change, Atlanta, 1977—; adj. asso. prof. social scis. Shaw U., Raleigh, N.C., 1972—; vis. lectr. sociology Spelman Coll., Atlanta, 1972-73; on leave as policy analyst Dept. Agr., 1980-81; cons. in field. Bd. dirs. So. Center for Studies Pub. Policy, 1972; v.p. Art Festival Atlanta, 1972-74. Emory U. research grantee, Am. Forum Internat. study fellow, NDEA fellow, NIMH grantee, Merrill fellow in fgn. studies, NEA fellow, 1979. Mem. Assn. Social and Behavioral Scientists (v.p., then pres., exec. bd.), Am. Sociol. Assn., So. Sociol. Soc., Assn. for Study Afro-Am. Life and History, Nat. Council Black Studies (regional coordinator), Am. Council Family Relations, Am. Studies Assn. Contbr. numerous articles to profl. publs.; editorial bd. Jour. Social and Behavioral Scis., Rev. of AfroAm. Issues and Culture, Umoja: Jour. Black Studies. Home: 2931 Yucca Dr Decatur GA 30032 Office: Candler Library Bldg Atlanta GA 30322

ALESCHUS, JUSTINE LAWRENCE, land broker; b. New Brunswick, N.J., Aug. 13, 1925; d. Walter and Mildred Lawrence; student Rutgers U.; m. John Aleschus, Jan. 23, 1949; children—Verdene Jan, Janine Kimberley, Joanna Lauren. Dept. sec. Am. Baptist Home Mission Soc., N.Y.C., 1941-49; claims examiner Republic Ins. Co., Dallas, 1950-52; broker Damon Homes, L.I., 1960-72; exclusive broker estate of Kenneth H. Leeds, L.I., 1980—. Pres. Nassau-Suffolk Council of Hosp. Aux., 1981-82; mem. com. hosp. auxs. of Hosp. Assn. of N.Y. State; bd. dirs. aux. of St. John's Episcopal Hosp., Smithtown, N.Y., also hon. mem., past pres., hosp. adv. bd. Mem. Suffolk County Real Estate Bd., L.I. Mid-Suffolk Businessmen's Assn., 110 Bus. Center for Women, Smithtown Bus. and Profl. Women's Network, L.I. Assn., JEI Com., West Suffolk Civic Assn. Republican. Lutheran. Club: Smithtown Women's. Office: 300 Hawkins Ave Lake Ronkonkoma NY 11779

ALEXA, NANCY ANN, orgn. exec.; b. Yonkers, N.Y., July 9, 1954; d. Harry and Mae (Poirier) Alexa; student Elizabeth Seton Jr. Coll., 1975, Rutgers U., 1984—. With Technicon Instruments Corp., Tarrytown, N.Y., 1974-80, asst. to gen. mgr., 1979-80; adminstrv. asst. to v.p. corp. communications Purolator, Inc., Piscataway, N.J., 1981; with NPO/Task Force Inc., N.Y.C., 1981—. Mem. Nat. Assn. Female Execs., Nat. Women's Polit. Caucus. Office: 124 E 40th St New York NY 10016

ALEXANDER, BARBARA LYNNE, film producer; b. Los Angeles, Jan. 6, 1942; d. Henry and Esther (Weiss) Alexander; student U. Calif., Berkeley, 1960-61; B.A., UCLA, 1963. Tchr., Culver City (Calif.) Unified Sch. Dist., 1963-67; producer, dir., writer Comprenetics, Inc., Los Angeles, 1970-74; asso. producer Sutherland Prodns., Los Angeles, 1974-75; partner/producer Snow Prodns., Los Angeles, 1976-81; v.p. theatrical devel. Odyssey Communication, Inc., Culver City, 1977-81; v.p. prodn. Inst. for Career and Vocat. Tng., Culver City, 1979-81; ind. producer, Los Angeles, 1981—; partner Owens & Alexander Prodns., Los Angeles Recipient Info. Film Producers of Am. Bronze award, 1972, 76, 79; Am. Indian Film Festival Spl. Achievement award, 1978, 80, Bronze and Silver award Internat. Film and TV Festival of N.Y., 1978, 80; Columbus Film Festival Bronze award, 1979; U.S. Indsl. Film Festival Gold Camera award, 1979; Film Adv. Bd. award of excellence, 1976, others. Mem. Acad. TV Arts and Scis., Women in Film (bd. dirs. 1978-80), Los Angeles Cinimatheque (founding mem., bd. dirs. 1976-78). Address: 12310 Dorothy St Los Angeles CA 90049

ALEXANDER, BARBARA SHAPIRO, psychiat. social worker; b. St. Louis, May 6, 1943; d. Harold Albert and Dorothy Miriam (Leifer) Shapiro; B.Mus. Edn., Washington U., St. Louis, 1964; postgrad. U. Ill., 1964-66; M.S.W., Smith Coll., 1970; postgrad. Inst. Psychoanalysis, Chgo., 1971-73; grad. Child Therapy Program, 1980; cert. therapist Sex Dysfunction Clinic, Loyola U., Chgo., 1975; m. Richard E. Alexander. Research asst., NIMH grantee Smith Coll., 1968-70; probation officer Juvenile Ct. Cook County, Chgo., 1966-68, 70; therapist Madden Mental Health Center, Hines, Ill., 1970-72; supr., therapist, field instr. U. Chgo., U. Ill. Grad. Schs. Social Work, also Pritzker Children's Hosp., Chgo., 1972-80; therapist, cons., also pvt. practice, 1973—; instr. tng. and advanced tng. Effectiveness Tng. Assos., Chgo., 1974; instr. psychology Northeastern U., Chgo., 1975; intern Divorce Conciliation Service, Circuit Ct. Cook County, 1976-77; mem. postgrad. curriculum devel. com. Loyola U., 1981. Bd. dirs. North Am. Found., Grant Park Concerts Soc. Recipient Sterling Achievement award Mu Phi Epsilon, 1964. Cert. social worker, Ill. Mem. Acad. Cert. Social Workers, Nat. Assn. Social Workers, Ill. Soc. Clin. Social Work (dir., chmn. services to mems. com., editor newsletter, dir. referral service), Am. Assn. Marriage and Family Counselors, Assn. Child Psychotherapists, Am. Assn. Sex Educators and Counselors, Nat. Rehab. Assn., Amateur Chamber Music Players Assn., Jewish Geneal. Soc., Smith Coll. Alumni Assn. (dir.). Democrat. Jewish. Contbr. to profl. publns. Home: 179 E Lake Shore Dr Chicago IL 60611 Office: 919 N Michigan Ave Suite 3012 Chicago IL 60611

ALEXANDER, BEATRICE WITTE, educator; b. Fredericksburg, Tex., Jan. 1, 1922; d. Oliver Bernard and Will Mignon (Whiting) Witte; B.A., Tex. Woman's U., 1942; M.A., U. Tex., Austin, 1946; m. Theodor Walter Alexander, Sept. 6, 1947; children—Richard Witte, Ronald Walter. Instr. fgn. langs. Tex. Tech. U., Lubbock, 1945-61, asst. prof. French, 1961-71, asso. prof., 1971—. Recipient first Pi Delta Phi Nat. award for chpt. moderators, 1969; Mortar Bd. award for excellence in teaching, 1978. Mem. Modern Lang. Assn. Am., Am. Assn. Tchrs. French, South Central Modern Lang. Assn., AAUW. Methodist. Contbr. articles to profl. jours. Home: 3405 25th St Lubbock TX 79410 Office: Box 4649 Dept Classical and Romance Langs Tex Tech U Lubbock TX 79409

ALEXANDER, CAROL GREENE (MRS. KENNETH ALEXANDER), librarian; b. Washington, Oct. 13, 1933; d. Lawrence William and Inez Ages (Browne) Greene; student Ohio Wesleyan U., 1950-51; A.B., Brown U., 1954; M.S., Case Western Res. U., 1957; m. Kenneth Alexander, Oct. 14, 1968; 1 dau., Donna. Reference librarian sci. div. N.Y. Public Library, 1957-58; sci. reference librarian Library of Congress, Washington, 1959-66; adminstrv. librarian AEC, Germantown, Md., 1966-70, Nat. Agrl. Library, Beltsville, Md., 1970-72; librarian John Jay Coll. Criminal Justice, City U. N.Y., 1972-74; tech. info. officer ERDA, Washington, 1974-77; dir. U.S. nat. focal point UN environment program's internat. referral system, dep. chief Library Systems br. EPA, Washington, 1977-79; dir. Office of Library Systems and Services, EPA, Washington, 1979—; chmn. exec. adv. com. Fed. Libraries Network, 1982-83; cons. environ. program UN, 1977—. Mem. Am. Soc. Info. Sci., Alumni Assn. Brown U. (dir. 1973-74). Office: PO Box 24131 Washington DC 20024

ALEXANDER, DORIS MAY, real estate broker, ins. agt., estate planner; b. Dryad, Wash., Aug. 22, 1914; d. Henry P. and Emma (Olson) Hanson; student Grays Harbor Bus. Coll., 1938-39, Yakima Valley Coll., 1968-69; grad. Dale Carnegie Course, 1969, Realtors Inst., 1978; m. Edwin J. Alexander, Nov. 26, 1972 (dec. 1981); 1 son, Jack M. Morehead; stepchildren—Gerry L. Alexander, Robert Alexander. Owner, mgr. Morehead's Grill, Chehalis, Wash., 1947-57; owner, mgr. Shurkold Refrigeration, Yakima, Wash., 1957-67; dist. mgr. Hamilton Mgmt. Co., Yakima, 1964-70, Spokane, Wash., 1970-72, ITT Hamilton Ins. Co., Yakima, 1964-70, Spokane, 1970-72; real estate broker, 1968—, owner, broker Palisades West Real Estate and Ins., Olympia, Wash., 1975—; office mgr., writer Food For Thought column Olympia News, weekly paper, 1972-75; condr. estate planning seminars. Mem. Republic Precinct Com., Olympia; sec. Christmas Island, Olympia, 1974-79; pres. Thurston County Women's Republican Club, 1980-81; active March of Dimes fund drs. Recipient Membership award Olympia C. of C., 1978; named to Million Dollar Club ITT Services Sales, 1968. Mem. Wash. Assn. Realtors, Greater Olympia C. of C. (dir. 1978-79, treas. 1979-80), Nat. Assn. Securities Dealers, Profl. Ins. Agts. Wash., Nat. Assn. Realtors, Farm and Land Inst., Realtors Nat. Mktg. Ins., Am. Bus. Women's Assn. (pres. Yakima chpt. 1970, named Woman of Yr. Olympia chpt. 1982). Baptist. Home: 621 S Plymouth St Olympia WA 98502 Office: 621 S Capitol Way Suite 704-706 Olympia WA 98501

ALEXANDER, ETHEL SKYLES, state legislator; b. Chgo.; student Wilson Jr. Coll., Loop Coll. With Clerk's Office Criminal Div., Circuit Ct. Cook County, dep. clk., 1973—; ward committeewoman 20th Ward Regular Democratic Orgn., precinct capt.; mem. Ill. Ho. Reps. Pres. First Ch. Deliverance 300 voice Radio and TV Adult Choir. Mem. Chgo. Urban League, NAACP, Parkway Community House. Office: Ill Ho of Reps State Capitol Springfield IL 62706 *

ALEXANDER, JANE, actress; b. Boston, Oct. 28, 1939; d. Thomas Bartlett and Ruth (Pearson) Quigley; student Sarah Lawrence Coll., 1957-59, U. Edinburgh, 1959-60; m. Robert Alexander, July 23, 1962 (div. 1969); 1 son, Jason; m. 2d, Edwin Sherin, Mar. 29, 1975. Appeared prodns. Charles Playhouse Boston, 1964-65, Arena Stage, Washington, 1965-68, 70—, Am. Shakespeare Festival including plays The Merry Wives of Windsor, Mourning Becomes Electra, Major Barbara, Stratford, Conn., summers 1971-72, Broadway prodns. Great White Hope, 1968-69, 6 Rms Riv Vu, 1972-73, Find Your Way Home, 1974, The Heiress, 1976, First Monday in October, 1978, Goodbye Fidel, 1980, Monday After the Miracle, 1982; appeared in The Time of Your Life, Plumstead Playhouse, Washington and Los Angeles; also appeared plays Present Laughter, 1975, Hamlet, 1975, The Master Builder, 1977, Losing Time, N.Y.C., 1979, Antony and Cleopatra, Atlanta, 1981, Hedda Gabler, Stamford, Conn., 1981; appeared in films Great White Hope, 1969, A Gunfight, 1970, The New Centurions, 1972, All the President's Men, 1976, The Betsy, 1978, Kramer vs. Kramer, 1979, Brubaker, 1980, Night Crossing, 1982; appeared in TV films Welcome Home Johny Bristol, 1971, Miracle on 34th St., 1973, Death Be Not Proud, 1974, Eleanor and Franklin, 1976, Eleanor and Franklin: The White House Years, 1977, A Question of Love, 1978, Lovely, 1978, Playing For Time, 1980, Dear Liar, 1981, Calamity Jane's Diary, 1981, In the Custody of Strangers, 1982; appeared in TV spl. A Circle of Children, 1977. Recipient Antoinette Perry award, 1969; Theatre World award; Drama Desk award; TV Critics Circle award, 1977; Emmy award, 1981.

ALEXANDER, JEANNE MERCHANT, sci. instrument mfg. co. exec.; b. Haskell, Tex., Dec. 2, 1942; d. Ralph W. Merchant and R. Helen (Kindley) Tanner; student Western Conn. State Coll., 1979-80; m. Charles H. Alexander, July 7, 1962; 1 son, Charles Bradley. Dental asst., office mgr. Dr. H. Gustavus, Abilene, Tex., 1961-63; credit interviewer Beterman's Furniture, St. Louis, 1965-66; accounts receivable specialist Kimball Wholesale Grocery, Abilene, 1963-65; asst. to market group coordinator Ridgefield (Conn.) Group, 1974-75; office mgr. Curken Sci. Inc., Danbury, Conn., 1975—, treas., 1978—, v.p., 1980—. Co-chmn. sch. fair PTA, Conn., PTA chmn., 1973-74; mem. fin. com. United Meth. Ch., Danbury, 1980—; caucus mem. def. U.S. Congressional Adv. Bd., 1982 Notary public, Conn., 1977—. Mem. LWV, Nat. Thespian Soc. Democrat. Methodist. Clubs: Rocking Roosters Sq. Dance (co-treas. 1977, co-pres. 1978). Home: East Hayestown Rd Danbury CT 06810 Office: PO Box 727 Hawleyville CT 06440

ALEXANDER, JUDITH ANN, bank cons.; b. Fort Sill, Okla., Oct. 14, 1940; d. James Buchanan and Gerry Lee (Gibbs) Permenter; student U. Okla., 1958-59; B.A. in English, U. Tulsa, 1962; M.B.A., U. Okla., 1969; postgrad. U. St. Thomas, 1975-78; m. Robert Miles Turner, Oct. 28, 1962 (div. 1972); m. 2d, Clarence Withers Alexander, Dec. 19, 1975. Asst. cashier So. Nat. Bank of Houston, 1971-73, asst. controller, 1973-74, asst. v.p. and asst. controller, 1974, v.p., controller, 1974-77, sr. v.p., controller, 1977-79, cons., 1979—. Mem. Houston Mus. Fine Arts, Houston Bot. Soc., NOW, Nat. Wildlife Fedn., Nat. Audubon Soc., Am. Soc. Women Accountants, Beta Gamma Sigma, Gamma Phi Beta. Republican. Office: 7715 Burning Hills Houston TX 77071

ALEXANDER, LENORA COLE, govt. ofcl.; b. Buffalo, Mar. 9, 1935; d. John L. and Susie L. (Stamper) Cole; B.S., SUNY Coll., Buffalo, 1957; M.Ed., SUNY, Buffalo, 1968, Ph.D., 1974; m. Theodore M. Alexander, June 22, 1975. Tchr. pub. schs., 1957-61; with Dept. Labor, now dir. Women's Bur., Washington. Former mem. D.C. Rental Accommodations Commn. Mem. Nat. Council Negro Women, Washington Opportunities for Women (past dir.), Legal Aid Soc. Washington (past trustee), Nat. Assn. Student Personnel Adminstrs. (past v.p.), Delta Sigma Theta. Office: Women's Bur Dept Labor Washington DC 20210

ALEXANDER, MARGO, hosp. food service adminstr.; b. Bklyn., May 10, 1952; d. Al and Ethel (Levinson) Isaacs; B.A., Bklyn. Coll., 1974; M.A., N.Y. U., 1977; postgrad. Pace U., 1980-81. Clin. dietitian Brookdale Med. Center, Bklyn., 1974-77; supervising dietitian Beth Israel med. Center, N.Y.C., 1977-78; asso. dir. food service L.I. Coll. Hosp., Bklyn., 1978-82, dir., 1982—; cons., lectr. in field. Mem. N.Y. State subcom. food, farm and nutrition. Registered dietitian. Mem. Greater N.Y. Dietetic Assn. (chmn. legis. and public policy com.), Am. Hosp. Assn.-Am. Soc. Hosp. Food Service Adminstrs., Hosp. Food Adminstrs. Assn. (dir., treas.), Am. Dietetic Assn. Editor: Nutrition for the 80's. Office: L I Coll Hosp Food Service 340 Henry St Brooklyn NY 11201 *

ALEXANDER, MARIE PHILLIPS, retail store exec.; b. Fairmont, W.Va., Apr. 25, 1944; d. Joseph D. and Florence J. (Lowery) Phillips; B.S. in Advt. Mgmt., W.Va. U., 1966; 1 dau., Cristen Marie. Copywriter, Pitts. Press, 1966-67; with Joseph Horne Co., Pitts., 1967-74, copywriter, 1967-74, advt. mgr. Gateway Budget Shops, 1969-72, suburban store advt. mgr., copy chief home store, 1972-74; exec. copy dir., asst. to advt. dir. Shillito's, Cin., 1974-76; advt. dir. Halle's, Cleve., 1976-78; sales promotion dir. Hengerer's Buffalo, 1978-79; v.p. sales promotion and mktg. Loveman's of Ala., Birmingham, 1979-80; v.p. sales promotion and advt. J. Byrons of Fla., Miami, 1980-82; v.p. Creative Decisions, Inc., N.Y.C., 1982—. Publicity com. Cleve. ARC; bd. dirs. Western N.Y. Retail Mchts. Assn., Birmingham Downtown Action Com.; fundraising com. City of Hope. Recipient awards of excellence Ad Clubs of Pitts. and Cin.; recipient award for one of best nat. ad campaigns Retail Ad Week, 1977, cert. of achievement in retail mktg. Nat. Research Bur., 1978, 1st place direct mail award Nat. Retail Mchts. Assn., 1979, award of excellence Retail Advt. Conf. S.E. Conf., 1981. Mem. Am. Advt. Fedn., Advt. Women of Buffalo, Fashion Group Miami and N.Y. Home: 5085 SW 89th Ave West Lauderdale FL 33328 Office: 1414 Ave of Americas New York NY 10019

ALEXANDER, MARY LOUISE, educator; b. Ennis, Tex., Jan. 15, 1926; d. Emmett F. and Florence (Hill) Alexander; B.A., U. Tex., 1947, M.A., 1949, Ph.D., 1951. Instr., research asst. Genetics Found., U. Tex., 1944-51; postdoctoral fellow biology div. AEC, Oak Ridge, 1951-52; postdoctoral research fellow U. Tex., 1952-55; research asso. U. Tex.-M.D. Anderson Hosp. and Tumor Inst., Houston, 1956-58, asst. biologist, 1959-62; research scientist Genetics Found. U. Tex., Austin, 1962-67; research cons. Brookhaven Nat. Lab., Upton, N.Y., 1955; research participant Oak Ridge Inst. Nuclear Studies, 1951-77; asso. prof. biology S.W. Tex. State U., San Marcos, 1966-69, prof., 1970—. Nat. Cancer Inst. fellow Inst. Animal Genetics, Edinburgh, Scotland, 1960-61. Mem. Genetics Soc. Am., Radiation Research Soc., Am. Soc. Human Genetics, Sigma Xi, Gamma Phi Beta, Phi Sigma, Alpha Epsilon Delta. Home: Hunter's Glen Route 2 Box 119 San Marcos TX 78666

ALEXANDER, MARY LOUISE, ins. broker; b. St. Cloud, Minn., Mar. 5, 1950; d. Thomas E. and Jean E. (Wichman) A.; B.F.A., Stephens Coll., 1972. Riding dir. Hidden Valley Farms, Newton, N.J., 1974, El Dorado Ranch, Westtown, N.Y., 1974; riding instr. Frances Reker Sch. of Horsemanship, Rockford, Minn., 1975; instr. Area Learning Center, Dist. 742, St. Cloud, 1976, asst. dean of boys, 1976; sales rep. N.W. Nat. Life Ins. Co., St. Cloud, 1977-78; prin. Mary Alexander Ins. Agy., Cold Spring, Minn., 1978—; pres. Mary Alexander Agy., Contempory Ins. Concepts, Maxi-Mktg. Inc., 1980—; owner mgr. Mary Alexander Sch. Horsemanship; distbr. nat. equine products; dealer Scranton Mfg. Co. Mem. Nat. Assn. Health Underwriters, Internat. Life Ins. Council, Life Ins. Leaders Minn., Minn. Assn. Health Underwriters, Minn. Assn. Farm Mut. Ins. Co., Forum Exec. Women St. Cloud, Minn. Horse Council. Lutheran. Club: Bus. and Profl. Women's. Home and Office: Route 2 Box 49 Cold Spring MN 56320

ALEXANDER, MYRTIS DALE PARSONS, county ofcl.; b. Chatham, La., June 15, 1921; d. James Thomas and EverLee Gertrude (Smith) Parsons; student La. State U., 1959, 1960; m. Landen Alexander, Sr., Feb. 3, 1940; 1 son, Landen. With Nat. Youth Assn., 1939-42; lab. technician Cinclair Sugar Mill, Brusly, La., 1942-46, 56—; with La. Dept. Employment Security, 1946-55, account clk II, 1952-55. Mem. West Baton Rouge Parish Police Jury, 1975—; mem. Port of Greater Baton Rouge Commn., 1976-80, pres., 1978-79; chmn. drainage com. West Baton Rouge Parish, 1975-80, mem. roads, fin., fire protection and solid waste disposal coms., 1975—. Mem. NOW, State Assn. Police Jurors, Nat. Assn. Counties, Bur. of Women East Baton Rouge Parish, Cath. Daus. Assn. Democrat. Roman Catholic. Home: 412 Hebert St Brusly LA 70719 Office: PO Box 496 Port Allen LA 70767

ALEXANDER, PATRICIA MULLINS, educator; b. Washington, Oct. 28, 1947; d. William C. and Rosina A. (Munari) Mullins; B.A. summa cum laude, Bethel Coll., McKenzie, Tenn., 1970; M.Ed., James Madison U., 1979; Ph.D., U. Md., 1981; 1 son, John Franklin. Elem. sch. tchr. Shenandoah County Public Schs., Woodstock, Va., 1973-77, instr. and developer exceptional students reading and math. lab., 1977-79; asst. prof. ednl. curriculum and instrn. Tex. A&M U., College Station, 1981—; cons. Mem. Am. Ednl. Research Assn., Internat. Reading Assn., Nat. Reading Conf., Coll. Reading Assn., Phi Delta Kappa, Phi Mu (life). Author: (with J. Muia) Gifted Education: A Comprehensive Roadmap, 1982; also articles. Office: Coll Edn Tex A&M U College Station TX 77843

ALEXANDER, SHANA, journalist, author, commentator; b. N.Y.C., Oct. 6, 1925; d. Milton and Cecelia (Rubenstein) Ager; student Vassar Coll., 1942-45; m. Stephen Alexander, 1951 (div.); 1 dau., Katherine. Feature writer PM newspaper, N.Y.C., 1944-47; with Harper's Bazaar, N.Y.C., 1946-47; entertainment editor Flair, N.Y.C., 1950; corr. Life mag., N.Y.C., 1951-59, columnist, 1961-64, writer monthly column The Feminine Eye, 1964-69; editor McCall's Mag., N.Y.C., 1969-71; commentator Sixty Minutes, CBS-TV, 1974-79; host What's Happening America, Sta. WOR-TV, 1980—. Founding mem. Nat. Women's Polit. Caucus; former dir. Am. Film Inst.; bd. dirs. N.Y. State Council on Arts. Author: The Feminine Eye, 1970; Shana Alexander's State-By-State Guide to Women's Legal Rights, 1975; Talking Woman, 1976; Anyone's Daughter, The Times and Trials of Patty Hearst, 1979; Very Much a Lady: The Untold Story of Jean Harris and Dr. Herman Tarnower, 1983. Office: 502 Park Ave New York NY 10022

ALEXANDER, SHARON GILES, advt. splty. exec.; b. Orange, N.J., Sept. 12, 1951; d. William R. and Althea B. Giles; B.S., Morgan State U., 1973; M.Ed., Rutgers U., 1975. Pres., EPC Internat., Inc., East Orange, N.J., 1977—. Recipient Kizzy award, 1980, Chad Sch. award, 1981; Sharon A. Giles Day proclaimed by Mayor of West Orange, 1981. Mem. Advt. Splty. Inst., Am. Mktg. Assn., Splty. Advt. Assn. Internat., Nat. Assn. Female Execs., NAACP, Urban League. Democrat. Baptist. Home: 4 Davidson St Belleville NJ 07109 Office: 141 S Harrison St East Orange NJ 07018

ALEXANDER, SHARON KAY, med. technologist; b. Marion, Ill., Aug. 10, 1953; d. Clyde William and Jewell (Gibbons) Campbell; A.S. with honors, John A. Logan Jr. Coll., 1973; B.S. in Microbiology, So. Ill. U., 1975, postgrad., 1975-76; m. Mitchell H. Alexander, June 7, 1980. Library asst. John A. Logan Jr. Coll., Carterville, Ill., 1973; med. asst., sec. Hugh D. McGowan, Carbondale, Ill., 1973-77; sec. Container Stapling Corp., 1977; co-asst. office mgr. Am. Investment, Carbondale, 1977; med. transcriptionist Marion Meml. Hosp., Herrin, Ill., 1978; med. technologist Herrin Hosp., 1978—. Ill State scholar, 1971-72. Mem. Am. Soc. Microbiology, So. Ill. Med. Tech. Edn. Group, South Central Assn. Clin. Microbiology, Notaries Assn. Ill. Democrat. Mem. Ch. Jesus Christ of Latter-day Saints. Home: 103 Blossom St Apt E Carterville IL 62918 Office: Herrin Hosp 201 S 14th St Herrin IL 62948

ALEXANDER, SHARON LEA, fin. planner; b. Sisseton, S.D., Feb. 4, 1944; s. Cecil Marion and Bernice Elaine (Skogen) Plant; student Edmond Community Coll., 1974-76, City U., 1982—. Tumor clinic coordinator U. Wash. Hosp., Seattle, 1964-66; exec. sec. Kenworth Motor Truck Co., Seattle, 1966-71; exec. sec. Donaldson, Hafer, Cassidy & Price, Attys., Seattle, 1971-72; mgr. purchasing and reprographics Blue Cross of Wash. and Alaska, Seattle, 1972-82; fin. planner, Seattle, 1982—. Advisor Jr. Achievement Am., 1980-81. Mem. Purchasing Mgmt. Assn. Wash., Pacific N.W. Regional Minority Purchasing Council (chmn.). Home: 4719 176th St SW #F-1 Lynnwood WA 98036 Office: Suite 900 Plaza 600 Bldg Seattle WA 98101

ALEXANDER, SHIRLEY BENIGSON, publisher; b. N.Y.C., Oct. 16, 1925; d. Benjamin and Pauline (Falk) Benigson; B.S., Western Conn. State Coll., 1947; M.A., Yale U., 1949; m. Laurence A. Alexander, Aug. 9, 1953; children—Jane, Margaret. Publisher, Alexander Research and Communications, Inc., N.Y.C., 1957—; chmn. Newsletter Clearing House, 1974; judge Ann. Newsletter Awards, 1972—. Mem. Newsletter Assn. Am. (Pub. of Year award 1980; pres. 1979-80; a founder), Fulfillment Mgmt. Assn., Direct Mktg. Creative Guild. Club: Yale (N.Y.C.). Author: An Inside Look at the Newsletter Field, Report on Survey of Newsletters, 1975. Home: 145 E 15th St New York NY 10003 Office: 270 Madison Ave Suite 1505 New York NY 10016

ALEXANDER, SUSAN REED, econ. analyst; b. Charleston, W.Va., Mar. 3, 1941; d. Andrew Stirling and Betsy Reed (Miller) A.; A.B. in Math., Sweet Briar Coll., 1963; postgrad. Golden Gate U., U. Houston, 1977—. Adminstrv. asst. Earl and Wright, Cons. Engrs., San Francisco, 1965-72; programmer/analyst Bechtel, Inc., San Francisco, 1972-79, econ. analyst Bechtel Petroleum, Inc., Houston, 1979—. Mem. Jr. League San Francisco, Am. Contract Bridge League (lifemaster 1974). Office: Bechtel Petroleum Inc PO Box 2166 Houston TX 77001

ALEXANDER, WILMA JEAN, educator; b. Columbus, Kans., May 25, 1938; d. Glen Burton and Wilma May (Jenner) Heavin; B.S., Kans. State Coll., Pittsburg, 1959, M.S., 1967; Ed.D., Okla. State U., Stillwater, 1973; m. Leslie W. Alexander, Dec. 20, 1958; 1 dau., Glenella Jean. Tchr. English, Baxter High Sch., Baxter Springs, Kans., 1959-61, bus. and English, Pineville (Mo.) High Sch., 1961-63, bus. and English, Netawaka, Kans., 1963-64, 2d grade and bus., Hillsboro, Mo., 1964-68; prof. bus. edn. and adminstrv. services Ill. State U., Normal, 1970—; project adminstr. microcomputer skills, curriculum devel. and dissemination. Recipient research grants. Mem. Assn. Records Mgrs. and Adminstrs. (past pres.), Central Ill. Word Processing Assn. (sec.), Ill. Bus. Edn. Assn. (past dir.), North Central Bus. Edn. Assn., Nat. Bus. Edn. Assn., Bloomington/Normal Personnel Council. Author: Student's Guide to Learning Experiences, rev. edit., 1979; editor Business Education into the Eighties, 1979. Office: 345 Williams Hall Ill State U Normal IL 61761

ALEXIOU, MARINA S., bus. mgmt. co. exec.; b. N.Y.C., Feb. 12, 1940; d. Stanley and Mary S. (Couloumbi) A.; bus. cert. in bus. mgmt. U. N.C., 1959. Legal sec. Jordan, Wright, Henson & Nichols, attys., Greensboro, N.C., 1959-60; with North Am. Philips Co., 1961— (co. mergered with Consol. Electronics 1969 then became North Am. Philips Corp.), 1969—, adminstrv. asst. to chmn., chief exec. officer and dir., 1977-82, adminstrv. asst. to chmn. bd., 1982—; adminstrv. asst. to chmn. governing com. U.S. Philips Trust; mem. U.S. Senatorial Bus. Adv. Bd. and Steering Com., Washington; mem. adv. bd. Am. Security Council, Washington; mem. Rep. Presdl. Task Force, Washington. Asst. chmn. fund raising Am. Cancer Soc., 1978—; dep. chmn. exec. Republican Com. of Bronxville (N.Y.), 1980—. Mem. Nat. Assn. Exec. Sec., Nat. Assn. Female Execs., Am. Soc. Profl. and Exec. Women, Internat. Platform Assn., UN We Believe (exec. planning com.), Smithsonian Nat. Assos., N.Y. Philharm. Soc. Republican. Greek Orthodox. Home: Northgate Alger Ct Bronxville NY 10708 Office: North American Philips Corp 100 E 42nd St New York NY 10017

ALFORD, BETTY JUNE, coll. adminstr.; b. St. Louis, June 9, 1932; d. Roland Johnson and Marie (Hord) Bohon; student Drury Coll., 1950-52; B.S., Tex. Woman's U., 1954, M.A., 1956, Ph.D., 1965; m. Joe G. Alford, Aug. 21, 1958; children—Mark Allan, Matthew. Tchr. public schs., Tex.; instr. Baylor U., 1956-57; mem. faculty Tex. Woman's U., Denton, 1958—, asso. prof. nutrition and research, 1976-79, prof., 1979—, chmn. dept. nutrition and food scis., 1976-79, dean Coll. Nutrition, Textiles and Human Devel., 1979—. Mem. AAAS, Am. Dietetic Assn., Am. Home Econs. Assn., Am. Inst. Nutrition, Tex. Dietetic Assn., Soc. Nutrition Edn., Tex. Home Econs. Assn. (pres. 1974-75). Baptist. Author: Nutrition in the Life Cycle, 1982; contbr. articles to profl. jours. Office: Box 23564 Tex Woman's Univ Denton TX 76204

ALFSEN, LOIS JEAN, home economist; b. Waupaca, Wis., Aug. 9, 1934; d. Allan William and Sara Margaret (Plowman) Schroeder; B.S., U. Wis., Stevens Point, 1956; m. George W. Alfsen, June 12, 1960; children—Geoffrey Wayne, Gregg Allan. Tchr. home econs. Hortonville (Wis.) High Sch., 1956-58, Preble High Sch., Green Bay, Wis., 1958-60, Waupaca High Sch., 1960-61; tchr. consumer edn. Gateway Tech. Inst., Kenosha and Racine, Wis., 1974-76; consumer info. coordinator consumer services Johnson Wax, Racine, 1975; mem. home econs. vocat. edn. adv. com. Racine Unified Sch. Dist., 1981—. Rep., Racine Women's Civic Council, 1967-68, 78-79; lay del. to state conf. Wis. United Meth. Conf., 1981—. Mem. Internat. Fedn. Home Econs., Am. Home Econs. Assn., AAUW, Home Economists in Bus. (nat. public relations com. 1981-82), NOW, Nat. Consumer League, Wis. Home Economists in Homemaking (chmn. 1967-68), Wis. Rural Homemaking Instrs., Wis. Home Econs. Assn. (newsletter asst. editor, dist. meeting reservations chmn., exec. com., state council, state v.p.), Wis. Home Economists in Bus. (ways and means chmn., mem. exec. bd.), Wis. Women's Network, Wis. PTA, Racine Home Econs. Assn. (pres. 1967-68, 78-79), Phi Upsilon Omicron. Home: 1128 Shorecrest Dr Racine WI 53402 Office: 1525 Howe St Racine WI 53403

ALGER, NELDA ELIZABETH, immunopathologist; b. Ithaca, N.Y., Dec. 14, 1923; d. Harry B. and Edna Alice (Underwood) A.; B.S., U. Mich., 1945, M.S., 1947; Ph.D., N.Y. U., 1962. Instr., Highland Park Jr. Coll., 1947-48; mem. faculty Hunter Coll., 1948-49, Columbia U. Med. Coll., 1949-52; instr. parasitology N.Y. U., N.Y.C., 1952-62, asst. prof., 1962-64; asso. prof. immunology U. Ill., Urbana, 1964—. Mem. sci. socs. Methodist. Contbr. articles to profl. jours. Home: 2206 Southmoor St Champaign IL 61820 Office: Dept Genetics U Ill Urbana IL 61801

ALGERMISSEN, VIRGINIA LANTZ-LUTTERBIE, med. librarian; n. Kearney, Nebr., June 30, 1929; d. Ray Jonathon and Effie Mabel (Johnston) Lantz; B.Mus., U. Colo., 1949; M.A., U. Denver, 1961; m. Robert W. Lutterbie, Aug. 22, 1949; children—Vincent Miles, Brian Robert. Med. library asst. Salt Lake Gen. Hosp. Library br. U. Utah, 1955-61; asst. prof. library sci. U. Utah, 1961-63; reference librarian, Medlars strategist NIH Library, HEW, 1964-76; acquisitions librarian, then asso. librarian U. N.Mex. Sch. Medicine, 1967-68; asst. prof. library sci. U. Mo., Columbia, 1969-73; head med. library, U. Mo., Kansas City, 1973-76; asso. prof., dir. med. scis. library Tex. A&M U., College Station, 1976—; guest prof. La. State U., U. Mo., Columbia. Mem. Assn. Am. Health Scis. Library Dirs., Am. Assn. Am. Med. Colls., Med. Library Assn., South Central Regional Library Group, Phi Kappa Phi, Sigma Alpha Iota. Presbyterian. Home: 2138 Kazmeier Pl Bryan TX 77801 Office: Med Library Tex A&M U College Station TX 77843

ALGOZINE, JANIS LYNN ACHESON, coll. ofcl.; b. Lafayette, Ind., May 18, 1946; d. Gerald W. and Evelyn Marie (Mugg) Acheson; B.A., Purdue U., 1968; M.S., 1976; children—Angela Jean, Joy Lynn. Tchr., Brookston (Ind.) Elem. Sch., 1968-69; art and music tchr. St. Lawrence Sch., Lafayette, 1972-73; spl. edn. substitute tchr. Isleta Sch. Corp., El Paso, Tex., 1975; tchr. educable mental retardation Tecumseh Jr. High Sch., Lafayette Sch. Corp., 1976; dir. Study Skills Center, Silver Lake Coll., Manitowoc, Wis., 1978, dir. student services, instr., 1978—. Advisor, Circle K Internat. Mem. Midwest Coll. Placement Assn., Assn. Sch. Coll. and Univ. Staffing, Wis. Career Planning and Placement Assn., Council for Exceptional Children, Nat. Clearing House for Computer Programs, Alpha Phi. Roman Catholic. Home: 4304 Columbus St Two Rivers WI 54241 Office: Silver Lake Coll 2406 S Alverno Rd Manitowoc WI 54220

ALI, FAIZUNISA AKBAR, psychologist, educator; b. Hyderabad, India; came to U.S., 1965, naturalized, 1967; d. Abdul R. and Samadunisa (Begum) Khan; B.A. in Psychology, Osmania U., India, 1962, M.A. in Child Psychology, 1964; M.A. in Ednl. Psychology, UCLA, 1967; postgrad. U. Ill., 1972-75; m. Mir Akbar Ali, Apr. 24, 1965; children—Ather, Arshad. Jr. research scientist and asso. Inst. for Juvenile Research, Chgo., 1967-72, research scientist, 1972-75; instr. ednl. psychology U. Ill., Chgo., 1972; staff psychologist Henry-Horner Children's Center, Chgo., 1975-76, acting dir. childhood devel. program, 1976-77; project dir. Children's Collective, Los Angeles, also research psychologist, 1977-79; founder, program dir. Systems for Integrated Society, Inc. (SIS), Lomita, Calif., 1978—. HEW grantee, 1977. Mem. Am. Psychol. Assn., Am. Ednl. Research Assn., Soc. for Research in Child Devel. Contbr. articles to jours. in psychology.

ALIPURIA, MARY HELTON, court reporter; b. Shreveport, La., Aug. 31, 1932; d. Luther and Mary (Davis) Helton; student Howard U., Chgo. Coll. Commerce, Roosevelt Coll.; 1 son, Hari Lee. Ct. reporter Alma Parker & Assos., Chgo., 1955, Parker & Helton, Ct. Reporters, Chgo., 1956-63, Mary Helton, Ct. Reporter, Chgo., 1963-67; ofcl. ct. reporter Circuit Ct. of Cook County, Chgo., 1967—. Active Operation Push, NAACP, Urban League, NOW. Certified shorthand reporter, Ill. Mem. Nat. Shorthand Reporters Assn., Ill. Ofcl. Ct. Reporters Assn. Republican. Roman Catholic. Office: 1340 S Michigan Ave Chicago IL 60615

ALKIRE, GINA KAY, credit union exec.; b. Jacksonville, N.C., Mar. 13, 1953; d. Sidney Hugh and Arlene A.A.; B.A. in Econs., U. Calif., San Diego, 1975. Br. mgr. Mission Fed. Credit Union, San Diego, 1975-78, asst. gen. mgr., 1979-80; loan mgr. Telephone Employees Credit Union, Los Angeles, 1978-79; gen. mgr., chief exec. officer Electricians Fed. Credit Union, San Diego, 1981—. Bd. dirs. Colony Homes Homeowners Assn., 1979—, treas., 1980—. Mem. San Diego Credit Union Mgr.'s Assn. (treas. 1981—, pres. 1982—), Credit Union Execs. Soc., Nat. Assn. Female Execs. Office: 9455 Ridgehaven Ct Suite 195 San Diego CA 92123

ALKIRE, SALLY ANN, real estate exec.; b. Springfield, Ill., Oct. 24, 1937; d. Harry Lee and Edith Louise (Day) Strain; A.A., Springfield Jr. Coll., 1957; B.S., Western Ill. U., 1960, M.S., 1965; children—Sheila Renee, Mark Edward. Tchr. social sci. Joliet (Ill.) West High Sch., 1967-70; faculty Joliet Jr. Coll., 1970-71; property mgr. residential mgmt., v.p., dir. condominium sales and mgmt. Vavrus & Assos., Joliet, 1972-78; property mgr. Residential div. Charles E. Smith Mgmt., Arlington, Va., 1978-80; dist. mgr. Nat. Corp. for Housing Partnerships, Washington, 1980-82, regional v.p., 1982—; lectr. in field. Mem. Property Mgmt. Assn., Nat. Inst. Real Estate Mgmt. Republican. Unitarian. Address: 9906 #6 Walker House Rd Gaithersburg MD 20879

ALLAN, MARGARET CATHERINE, psychologist; b. Edmonton, Alta., Can., Dec. 1, 1947; d. Edward Ainslie and Eileen Mary (Jones) A.; B.A., U. B.C., 1970; M.A., U. Iowa, 1975, m. George Allen Heimann, Oct. 21, 1970; 1 son, Matthew Wesley. Research asst. evaluation and exam. service U. Iowa, Iowa City, 1973-75; ednl. researcher Vancouver (B.C.) Bd. Edn., 1976-77; project dir. govt. evaluation U. B.C., Vancouver, 1977—. Mem. Am. Psychol. Assn., Am. Personnel and Guidance Assn., Nat. Council Measurement in Edn., Am. Ednl. Research Assn. Clubs: Daus. of the Nile, Order Jobs Daughters (past queen). Home: 2784 W 20th Ave Vancouver BC V6L 1H2 Canada Office: U British Colombia Vancouver BC V6T 1W5 Canada

ALLAN, VIRGINIA RACHEL, ednl. adminstr.; b. Wyandotte, Mich., Oct. 21, 1916; d. Clare Floyd and Leta (Benedict) Allan; student Olivet Coll., 1935-36, LL.D., 1974; A.B., U. Mich., 1939, M.A. (fellow), 1945; L.H.D. (hon.), Central Mich. U., 1976; D.P.A. (hon.), Eastern Mich. U., 1981. With Detroit Bd. Edn., 1939-55; pres., co-owner Cahalan Drug Stores, Wyandotte, Mich., 1955-72; pres. Cahalan Corp., 1972—; dep. asst. sec. state for public affairs, Washington, 1972-77; spl. asst. to dean Grad. Sch. Arts and Scis. for Women's Studies Program and Policy Center, George Washington U., 1977—; pres. I.W.D. Corp., 1977—. Public mem. fgn. service officer selection bd. State Dept., 1971; prin. observer U.S., UN Seminar on Participation of Women in Econ. Life, Gabon, Africa, 1971; del., UN Seminar on Women, Moscow, 1970; chmn. Pres. Nixon's Task Force Women's Rights and Responsibilities, 1969. Regent Emeritus Eastern Mich. U., Ypsilanti, alt. rep. World Conf. Observance Internat. Women's Year, 1975; del. at large Nat. Women's Conf., 1977—; del. World Conf. of UN Decade for Women, 1980; bd. dirs. Population Reference Bur.; nat. adv. council Girl Scouts U.S.A. Recipient Outstanding Achievement award U. Mich., 1964, Athena award Intercollegiate Assn. Women Students, 1971, Diamond award City Wyandotte, 1963; named one of Top Ten Working Women in Met. Detroit, 1963. Mem. Nat. Fedn. Bus. and Profl. Women's Clubs (nat. pres. 1963-64, chmn. strategy planning com. 1981-84), AAUW, Mortar Bd., Phi Beta Kappa, Phi Kappa Phi, Delta Kappa Gamma. Club: Zonta. Home: 3504 Stoney Brae Rd Falls Church VA 22044 Office: George Washington U Washington DC 20052

ALLARD, META KAY, librarian, mktg. services co. exec.; b. Bklyn., Jan. 2, 1916; d. Charles and Muriel (Wahrer) Kay; B.A. in Biology, Rice U., Houston, 1937; cert. med. tech., Harris County Hosp., Houston, 1938; M.L.S., SUNY, Geneseo; basic cert. Am. Inst. Banking, 1976; m. Albert Henry Allard, Dec. 7, 1941; children—Barbara Coe, David M. Allard. Research technologist Gorgas Hosp., Panama, C.Z., 1939-42; asso. prof. library sci. Rochester (N.Y.) Inst. Tech., 1962-68, librarian Grad. Chemistry Research Library, 1968-70; cons. library extension div. Ariz. State Library, 1970-71; dir. library services Lincoln First Bank, N.A., Rochester, 1972-81; chmn. bd., treas. Allard Mktg. Services, 1981—; coordinator seminars. Mem. Spl. Libraries Assn. (chpt. pres. 1979-80), Women's Polit. Caucus. Republican. Presbyterian. Clubs: Monroe County Library (pres. 1974-75), Altrusa. Home and office: 50 Bright Oaks Dr Rochester NY 14624

ALLARD, PATRICIA FRANCES, employment counselor; b. North Charleroi, Pa., Feb. 22, 1950; d. Edward Alexander and Matilda Frances (Sikora) Szymanske; student pvt. schs., Donora and Charleroi, Pa.; m. Gary Martin Allard, Jan. 2, 1969 (div. Apr. 1979); children—Gary Patrick, Eric Edward. Head delivery dept. Walkers Dept. Store, Long Beach, Calif., 1968; regional mgr. Tempo Personnel, Greensburg, Pa., 1976-79, regional mgr., office mgr., 1979, employment counselor, 1979—; temporary automotive clk. United Parcel Service, New Stanton, Pa., 1979-80.

ALLDREDGE, NOREEN SUNDERLAND, librarian, univ. ofcl.; b. Sacramento, Apr. 8, 1939; d. Harold and Cecelia (Doherty) Sunderland; B.A., Mount St. Mary's Coll., 1961; M.S., Columbia U., 1965; M.A., Tex. A&M U., 1980. Asst. reference librarian U. Nev., Reno, 1965-66; librarian Desert Research Inst., 1966-70, univ. bibliographer/circulation librarian, 1970-74, head collection devel., 1974-76; asst. dir. Tex. A&M Libraries, College Station, 1976-81; dir. libraries Mont. State U., Bozeman, 1981—. Mem. ALA, Mont. Library Assn., NOW. Home: 1615 S Black St Bozeman MT 59715 Office: Library Mont State U Bozeman MT 59717

ALLEGRA, MARISA IDA CALZOLARI, psychiatrist; b. Verbania, Torino, Italy; came to U.S., 1956, naturalized, 1962; d. Amilcare and Paola Bice (Alberizzi) Calzolari; M.D. summa cum laude, Bologna U., 1949; postgrad. Brown U., 1976; children—Ludwig Armand, David Paul, Christopher John. Pediatric and gen. practice medicine, Bologna, Italy, 1949-53; permanent staff physician Ospedale Maggiore, Bologna, 1953-56; resident in psychiatry Brown U., Providence, 1973-76; fellow in child psychiatry Bradley Hosp., Providence, 1976; practice medicine specializing in psychiatry, Providence, 1976—; cons. Family Service, 1976-80. Pres. R.I. Civic Choral and Orch., 1974-76, bd. dirs., hon. pres., life mem.; bd. dirs. R.I. Philharm. Orch.; active R.I. Sch. Design. Diplomate Am. Bd. Psychiatry and Neurology. Mem. AMA. Am. Psychiat. Assn., R.I. Med. Assn., Providence Med. Assn., Butler Hosp. Staff Assn., Am. Med. Womens Assn., Providence Preservation Soc., Newport Preservation Soc. Clubs: Conamicut Yacht (Jamestown, R.I.); Faculty, Brown (Providence). Home: 220 Blackstone Blvd Providence RI 02906

ALLEN, ANNE MONTEITH, realtor; b. Granite Falls, N.C., June 1, 1925; d. Nathan Young and Hattie Mae (Butler) Monteith; R.N., Watts Sch. Nursing, 1946; postgrad. U. N.C., 1961; m. Louis E. Allen, Apr. 2, 1949; children—Elizabeth Allen Buet-Saint Upery, Louis Eugene, James Morris. Real estate salesman Brown Realty Co. Inc., Greensboro, N.C., 1960-71; owner Anne Allen & Assos., Greensboro, 1974—; dir. Community Bank of N.C. Gen. vol. chmn. Cerebral Palsy Campaign, 1973. Named Greensboro Realtor of Yr., 1975. Mem. Greensboro Bd. Realtors (past pres., dir.), N.C. Assn. Realtors (pres. 1979-80), Better Bus. Bur., Sales and Mktg. Execs., Greensboro C. of C. (dir.), Nat. Assn. Realtors, Nat. Mktg. Inst., Watts Alumnae Assn. Republican. Home: 1220 Onslow Dr Greensboro NC 27408 Office: PO Box 10152 Greensboro NC 27404

ALLEN, ARCOLA JEANNE, anesthesia edn. cons., bus. exec.; b. Terre Haute, Ind., May 8, 1939; d. Monroe and Rosie E. (Bishop) Pickette; A.A., San Jose State Coll., 1960; B.S. in Nursing, U. Calif., Berkeley, 1963; B.A. in Psychology, Colombia Coll., 1977; postgrad. Wichita Clinic Sch. of Anesthesia, 1970-72, Wichita State U., 1980; M.Nursing Adminstrn., Columbia Pacific U., 1981, doctoral candidate, 1982; m. Robert Irving Allen, Feb. 19, 1959; children—Robert Irving, Michael, Brian, John, Mark, Jeffrey. Staff nurse surgery O'Connor Hosp., San Jose, Calif., 1962-64; mem. heart team St. Bernardines Hosp., Calif., 1964-65; mem. nursing staff surg. unit. St. Bernardette Hosp., Anchorage, 1965-67, St. Francis Hosp., Wichita, Kans., 1967-69; head nurse urology sect. Wichita Clinic, 1970-79, dir. Sch. of Anesthesia, 1974-79; inservice edn. staff St. Francis Hosp., Wichita, 1974-79; field underwriter Home Life Ins., of N.Y.C., Wichita, 1980-82; owner, chief exec. officer Dan'cer'cise of Wichita and Jenn-Arc Enterprises, 1982—; anesthesia edn. cons., 1978—; co-developer courses and programs in anesthesia Wichita State U. Pres. Wichita chpt. Jack and Jills of Am., 1978—; sec., treas. Wind Rows Home Owners Assn., 1980—. Recipient Cert. of Achievement, Chgo. Musical Coll., 1958. Mem. Am. Assn. Nurse Anesthetists (cert.), Kans. Assn. Nurse Anesthetists Am. Nurses Assn., Progressive Women of Wichita (Cert. of Appreciation 1979), Nat. Assn. Female Execs., Nat. Assn. Life Underwriters. Republican. Roman Catholic. Home: 305 Wind Row Lake Dr Goddard KS 67052

ALLEN, BARBARA (BARBARA ALLEN ROSSER), broadcast journalist; b. Detroit, Feb. 12, 1952; d. Perry E. and Dorothy A. (Craig) Allen; student St. Mary's Coll., Notre Dame, Ind., 1970-72, U. Fla., 1973; m. James Jeffery Rosser, Aug. 27, 1977. News reporter Stas.-WNOG-WNFM-Cablevision 2, Naples, Fla., 1972-73, talk show hostess, 1972, newscaster, 1972-73; anchorperson Sta.-WBBH-TV, Ft. Myers, Fla., 1974-76, dir. pub. affairs, 1975-76; newscaster, reporter Sta.-KTUL-TV, Tulsa, 1976-79; weekend anchor, reporter Sta. WRC-TV, Washington, 1979—; free-lance corr. NBC Network Radio, 1979—; cons. broadcast classes Lee County Schs., 1974-76. Recipient Best Newscast award Okla. AP Broadcaster, 1976, 77. Mem. Am. Women in Radio and TV, Sigma Delta Xi (dir. Ft. Myers chpt. 1976, Tulsa chpt. 1977-78, v.p. Tulsa chpt. 1978-79). Home: 20236 Grazing Way Gaithersburg MD 20879 Office: 4001 Nebraska Ave NW Washington DC 20016

ALLEN, BEATRICE, piano tchr.; b. N.Y.C., June 30, 1917; d. Samuel and Rose (Krell) Hyman; student N.Y. U., 1933-36; diploma (scholar), Inst. Musical Arts, N.Y.C., 1939, postgrad. (scholar), 1939-40; diploma (fellow, letter commendation), Juilliard Grad. Sch., N.Y.C., 1943; m. Eugene Murray Allen, Jan. 23, 1937; children—Marlene Allen Galzin, Julian Lewis. Mem. faculty prep. div. Juilliard Sch. Music, 1957-69, Moravian Coll., 1967-68, Northampton County Area Community Coll., 1968-70, Manhattan Sch. Music, 1969—, Community Music Sch., Allentown, Pa., 1982—; condr. Tchrs. Workshop, Antioch Coll., Yellow Springs, Ohio, 1965; Bach lectr., recitals various univs.; concert appearances Town Hall, N.Y.C., Chautauqua, N.Y., others. Winner N.J. Artists contest, 1936. Address: 2100 Main St Bethlehem PA 18017

ALLEN, BELLE (MRS. WILLIAM KARP), mgmt. cons. exec. and communications cons.; b. Chgo.; d. Isaac and Clara (Friedman) A.; U. Chgo.; Pres., Belle Allen Communications, Chgo., 1955—; pres., chmn. bd. William Karp Cons. Co., Inc., Chgo., 1979—; v.p., treas. Cultural Arts Surveys, Inc., Chgo., 1965-79; nominee consumer adv. council FRS, 1979—. Founding mem. womens Bd United Cerebral Palsy Assn. Chgo., 1954, bd. dirs., 1954-58; mem. Welfare Public Relations Forum, 1958-62; dir. personnel placement Indsl. Relations Research Assos., 1960-61; mem. exec. com., chmn. public relations com. Regional Ballet Ensemble Chgo., 1961-62; bd. dirs. Soc. for Chgo. Strings, 1963-64; mem. Ill. State C. of C., 1961-74, Chgo. Hist. Soc., 1962-63, Field Mus. Natural History, 1966-74; mem. campaign staff Adlai E. Stevenson II, 1952, 56, John F. Kennedy, 1960; press conf. staff Eleanor Roosevelt, 1960; pres. Democratic Fedn. Ill., 1958-61; mem. Independent Dem. Coalition, 1968-69; dir. Citizens for Polit. Change, 1969; campaign mgr. City Council Chgo. aldermanic election, 42d Ward, 1969; mem. Ill. Gov.'s Grievance Panel,

1979—; mem. adv. governing bd. Ill. Coalition on Employment of Women, 1980—. Recipient Outstanding Service award United Cerebral Palsy Assn. Chgo., 1954; Communications award The White House, 1961, Publicity Club Chgo. (chmn. inter-city relations com. 1960-61, Disting. Service award 1968), Amer. Bicentennial Research Inst., Library of Human Resources Award, 1973; Mem. Affirmative Action Assn. (dir. 1981—, chairperson membership com. 1981—), Indsl. Relations Research Assn., The Fashion Group (council 1981—), NOW, Nat. Assn. Inter-Group Relations Ofcls. (nat. conf. program com. 1959), Soc. Personnel Adminstrs., Women's Equity Action League, Chgo. Assn. Commerce and Industry (public relations com. 1961-63), Forum. Club: Chicago Press (chmn. women's activities 1969-71). Editor, contbr. to articles and papers in bus. and profl. jours., publs., manuals, book; editor The Bull., 1981—. Office: 900 N Michigan Ave Chicago IL 60611

ALLEN, BERTHA LEE, social worker, family counselor; b. Bexley, Miss., Mar. 28, 1908; d. Charles H. and Winnie (McLeod) A.; student Maryville Coll., 1928-29; B.A., Miss. U. for Women, 1932; postgrad. U. Ala., 1936, La. State U., 1937, Miss. State U., 1939, U. Miss., 1940; M.S.W., Tulane U., 1949. Tchr. high sch. English and Latin, Rocky Creek and Lucedale, Miss., 1932-33, Agricola, Miss., 1933-36, Tchula, Miss., 1936-44; child welfare worker Miss. Dept. Public Welfare, Jackson, Columbus, Pascagoula, 1944-48; caseworker Columbia (Miss.) Tng. Sch., 1949-50; case work supr., chief social worker Osawatomie (Kans.) State Hosp., 1950-51; dir. casework Miss. Children's Home Soc., Jackson, 1952-54; casework supr. Child and Family Service, Mobile, Ala., 1954-58; supr. casework practice Family Counseling Center, Mobile, 1958-65; caseworker ARC Disaster Services, Hurricane Betsy, New Orleans, 1965, Family Service Soc., New Orleans, 1965-66, Jewish Family and Children's Service, New Orleans, 1966-71, Willow Wood, New Orleans Home for Jewish Aged, 1971-73; pvt. practice individual, marital and family counseling, New Orleans, Mobile, Lucedale, 1969—; cons. Wilmer Hall Protestant Children's Home, YWCA, Mobile, 1954-65, Providence Nursing Home, New Orleans, 1972-77, Willow Wood, New Orleans Home for Jewish Aged, 1974-75. Bd. dirs. Mulherin Home for Spastic Children, Mobile, 1958-59; charter mem., sec. Miss. Mental Health Assn., 1953-54; mem. casework com. Mobile Council Social Agys., 1954-58, mem. inter-agy. planning com., 1958-62, mem. in-service tng. com., 1963-65; mem. program com. Southeastern Inst., Family Service Assn. Am., 1960; mem. planning com. Mobile County Mental Health Assn., 1964-65; sec. Assn. Maternity and Adoption Agys., New Orleans, 1969-70. Cert. first aid instr. ARC; life teaching cert., Miss.; social work cert., La., Ala. Mem. Nat. Assn. Social Workers, Acad. Cert. Social Workers, La. Soc. Clin. Social Work, Internat. Platform Assn., Eta Sigma Phi, Oakliegh Garden Soc. Presbyterian. Home and Office: Route 9 Box 796 Lucedale MS 39452 also 1050B Palmetto St Mobile AL 36604

ALLEN, BRENDA JOYCE, mgmt. cons.; b. Detroit, June 10; d. William Howard and Ottie Faye (Mills) A.; A.B. in Math. and Econs. (Nat. Merit scholar, Edn. Abroad fellow), U. Calif., Berkeley, 1976; M.S. in Ops. Research, George Washington U., 1981; m. Robert E. Lighthourne, Mar. 2, 1970; 1 dau., Shonja Diane. Profl. asst. Coll. of Alameda (Calif.), 1972; sci. data analyst Lawrence Berkeley Lab., 1972-74; actuarial student Met. Life Ins. Co., 1975; tutor Student Learning Center, U. Calif., Berkeley, 1975-76; lectr. urban studies Howard U., 1977; research fellow Logistics Mgmt. Inst., Washington, 1978—; lectr., cons. in field; freelance editor tech. papers. Mem. Nat. Assn. Female Execs. (network dir. 1981—), Ops. Research Soc. Am., Am. Econ. Assn., Nat. Contract Mgmt. Assn., Delta Sigma Theta (chpt. treas. 1978-80). Author articles in field. Home: PO Box 40052 Washington DC 20016 Office: 4701 Sangamore Rd PO Box 9489 Washington DC 20016

ALLEN, CHARLOTTE HALE, author, journalist; b. Jacksonville, Fla., Jan. 6, 1928; d. Anthony W. and Eleanor (Cunningham) Hale; student Armstrong Jr. Coll., 1947-48; m. Orman Cleveland Allen, Mar. 30, 1974; 1 son by previous marriage—Stanley R. Smith, Jr. Copy writer Sta. WSAV, Savannah, Ga., 1948-49, copy dir., 1949-51; copy dir. Sta. WSAV-TV, Savannah, 1955-57; with advt. dept. Savannah News-Press, 1957-59; staff writer Atlanta Jour.-Constitution Sunday Mag., 1960-70; free lance writer, 1969—; cons. for U.S. CSC, 1976-79; guest speaker various colls., high schs., clubs and churches, 1969—; founder Time of Your Life mgmt. seminar, 1978, Facing Forward motivational seminar and workshop on aging, 1982; speech writer for state polit. candidates, 1959-68; news writer U.S. Army, Ft. Stewart, Ga., 1951. Vol. worker Savannah Symphony, 1955-59; bd. dirs. Savannah Mental Health Assn., 1957-59; trustee Ga. Conservancy, Inc., 1968-70. Author: Full-Time Living, 1978; (with Layona Glenn) I Remember, I Remember, 1968; editor and writer for various books by Anita Bryant and Bob Green, 1970-77; contbr. book revs. to newspapers. Address: 6341 Vernon Woods Dr NE Atlanta GA 30328

ALLEN, CONSTANCE CHURCHYARD, state ofcl.; b. Tulsa, Aug. 12, 1924; d. Leonard S. and Elizabeth C. Allen; student U. Okla., 1942-43; B.A., U. Tulsa, 1948, postgrad. 1969-70; postgrad. U. Mich. extension, 1954-55, Lake Erie Coll., 1959. Adult program dir. YWCA, Tulsa, 1958-60; recreation supr. Tulsa Park and Recreation Dept., 1960-72; supr. Okla. Dept. Recreation, 1972-76, informational rep. services, 1976—; adj. clin. faculty Okla. Coll. Osteopathic Medicine, 1980—. Judge, Jr. Miss Pageant, 1975. Served with Army Service Clubs, Korea, 1956-58. Mem. Okla. Recreation and Parks Soc., U. Tulsa Alumni Assn., Chi Omega. Club: Diamond Head Country. Home: 28 Westwind Diamond Head Sand Springs OK 74063 Office: Route 4 Box 9 Sand Springs OK 74063

ALLEN, CONSTANCE OLLEEN WEBB, artist, designer; b. Camphill, Ala., June 10, 1923; d. Alonza Evans and Sara Alvesta (Jones) Adcock; student George Washington U., 1942-44; Instituto Allende, Mexico, 1970; m. Byron B. Webb, Oct. 12, 1947; children—Martha Ellen, Alan James, Deana Olleen; m. 2d, Walton Stanley Allen, Mar. 11, 1976. Instr. painting pvt. studio, 1969-72; instr. drawing and painting Univ. of Sci. and Arts of Okla., 1974; owner, mgr. The Studio Gallery, Chickasha, Okla., 1978—; exhibited one-woman shows: Upstairs Art Gallery, Chickasha, 1971, The Galleria, Norman, Okla., 1972, Gilcrease Art Gallery, Tulsa, 1973, 74; exhibited group shows: Upstairs Art Gallery, 1971, 72, Mus. of the Gt. Plains, Lawton, Okla., 1970, Arts Club, Washington, 1972, 74; represented Indian Hall of Fame, Duncan, Okla., Restauranteur Collection. Recipient over 50 awards in competitive art exhibits. Mem. Artists Equity Assn., Okla. Watercolor Assn., Okla. Art Guild. Democrat. Address: 2009 Carolina Ave Chickasha OK 73018

ALLEN, DEBRA HONEYCUTT, research chemist; b. Gastonia, N.C., Nov. 15, 1955; d. John Fred and Evelyn Eletha (Connell) Honeycutt; B.S. magna cum laude in Textile Chemistry, N.C. State U., 1979; A.A.S. in Chem. Engring. Tech., Central Piedmont Community Coll., 1976; m. John Andrew Allen, July 26, 1980. Research technician Collins & Aikman, Charlotte, N.C., 1976-77, corp. research chemist, 1980—. Mem. Am. Assn. Textile Chemists and Colorists, Nat. Assn. for Female Execs., Kappa Tau Beta, Sigma Tau Sigma, Phi Theta Kappa. Republican. Lutheran. Home: 330-5 Orchard Trace Ln Charlotte NC 28213 Office: PO Box 32665 Charlotte NC 28232

ALLEN, DORIS VIRGINIA, psychologist; b. Highland Park, Mich., Mar. 28, 1929; d. George Herman and Myrtle Johannah (Anderson) A.; B.S., U. Mich., 1950; M.A., Wayne State U., 1963, Ph.D., 1965; m. Wesley A. Grisdale, Apr. 29, 1968. Instr. to prof. dept. audiology Wayne State U., Detroit, 1965—. HEW research grantee, 1967-69; Nat. Inst. Neurol. and Communicative Disorders and Stroke research grantee, 1976-80. Mem. Am. Psychol. Assn., N.Y. Acad. Scis., Soc. Research in Child Devel., Am. Ednl. Research Assn., Midwestern Psychol. Assn., Psychonomic Soc., AAAS. Contbr. articles sci. jours. Office: 4201 Saint Antoine St 5E Detroit MI 48201

ALLEN, HELEN LOUISE, govt. ofcl.; b. Wildwood, N.J., Mar. 21, 1932; d. Thomas Alexander and Helen Levenia (Hazzard) Stonewall; cert. West Chester Bus. Sch., 1950; m. Robert Sidney Allen, June 20, 1953 (dec.); 1 son, Robert Sidney III. Supervisory procurement technician U.S. Army Electronics Command, Phila., 1968-71, mgmt. technician, 1971-74; personnel asst. Fed. Energy Adminstrn., Phila., 1974-78; personnel officer Region III, Dept. Energy, Phila., 1978-82; ret., 1982; counselor, tchr., trainer and cons. in field. Recipient Camp 20th Century, camping award Phila., 1970, Legion of Honor award Chapel of Four Chaplains, 1969, Superior Service award Fed. Energy Adminstrn., 1976; Outstanding Service award U.S. Army Electronics Command, 1972, 73, Sustained Superior Service award, 1962, 66; Outstanding Service award Dept. Energy, 1977, 81, Sustained Superior Service award, 1979, 81. Mem. Intergovtl. Personnel Mgmt. Assn., NAACP, Phila. Citizens in Action. Episcopalian. Home: 5536 Walton Ave Philadelphia PA 19143

ALLEN, HELGA, business exec.; b. Vienna, Austria, Jan. 12, 1935; came to U.S. 1940, naturalized 1967; d. Armin Gruber; B.S. in Zoology, U. R.I., 1956; B.S., Manhattan Coll., 1973; M.S., Adelphi U., Garden City, N.Y., 1980; children—Rona, Sheryl. Controller, Hampton Mgmt. Co., Bronx, N.Y., 1967-70; asst. controller Saxon Industries, L.I., 1970-79; group controller Litton Office Products Co., L.I., 1979-80; dir. ops. Executone, Inc., Jericho, N.Y., 1980—, now pres. Mem. Am. Mgmt. Assn., Nat. Assn. Female Execs. Home: 2 E Mill Dr Great Neck NY 11021 Office: 2 Jericho Turnpike Jericho NY 11753

ALLEN, ISABEL ELAINE, educator; b. N.Y.C., Oct. 18, 1948; d. John Thomas and Claire Isabel (Meldrum) Allen; B.A., Skidmore Coll., 1970; M.A., U. Evansville, 1975; Ph.D., Cornell U., 1979; m. Jeffrey Richard Seaman, Jan. 21, 1978; 1 son, Christopher Allen. Statis. cons. Historic New Harmony, Inc. (Ind.), 1975; research/teaching asst. dept. econs. and social stats. Cornell U., Ithaca, N.Y., 1976-78; asst. prof. stats. Wharton Sch., U. Pa., Phila., 1978—; cons. Dept. Revenue, Commonwealth of Pa., 1979-81, Def. Logistics Agy., U.S. Dept. Def., 1980-81. Bd. dirs. Parent-Infant Center, Phila., 1980-81, treas., 1980-81. Cornell fellow, 1977, research fellow in population, 1976; U. Pa. faculty summer fellow and grantee, 1979; Prudential fellow for inflation research, 1981-82. Mem. Am. Statis. Assn., Population Assn. Am., Biometric Soc., Classification Soc., Soc. for Computer Simulation, Internat. Assn. Statis. Computing, Phila. Fin. Assn. Contbr. articles to profl. jours. Home: 4717 Larchwood Ave Philadelphia PA 19143 Office: Dept Statistics Wharton Sch CC Univ of Pa Philadelphia PA 19104

ALLEN, JANET BURKE, engring. technician, product designer; b. Hopkinsville, Ky., July 30, 1945; d. Abner Lewis Burke and Rosemary (Miller) Burke Pace; student U. Ky., 1963-64; B.S. in Bus. Adminstrn., Austin Peay State U., 1971; m. William F. Allen, July 30, 1966; children—Juliet, Meredith (dec.). Draftsman, ITT-Grinnell, Princeton, Ky., 1966-69; draftsman Central Tool & Die, Hopkinsville, Ky., 1969-70; social worker Ky. Dept. Human Resources, Paducah, 1971-73; engring. draftsman Union Carbide Corp., Paducah, 1973-75, sr. engring. asst., 1975-76; engring. asst. Hunter Martin & Assocs., Paducah, 1976-79; project designer, safety coordinator Proform, Paducah, 1979—. Mem. legis. and regulatory com. Purchase Area Environ. Forum, Paducah, 1981—; mem. sanctuary choir, tchr. First Baptist Ch., Paducah. Named Duchess of Paducah, Mayor of Paducah, 1976; named to Outstanding Young Women Am., U.S. Jaycees, 1981. Mem. Am. Soc. Cert. Engring. Technicians, Inst. Cert. Engring. Technicians, Austin Peay State U. Alumni Assn., Beta Sigma Phi. Democrat. Home: 248 Ridgewood Ave Paducah KY 42001 Office: 700 Terr Ln Paducah KY 42001

ALLEN, JEANNE SUITOR, real estate agy. exec.; b. Perryton, Tex., Oct. 23, 1934; d. Lonnie and Anna M. Suitor; student Tex. Tech U., 1955; m. Norman C. Allen, June 8, 1952; children—Cynthia, Lex. Asst. mgr. Neiman Marcus, 1957-58; asst. to pres. Sanger Harris, 1958-63; partner Allen Zarcaro Realty, Houston, 1978—, now broker and v.p. Treas., Freeman Library Bd., 1967-72; mem. vestry St. Christopher Episcopal Ch.; chmn. United Way, Tex. Gulf Coast; bd. dirs. Coll. of Mainland real estate dept. Mem. Houston Bd. Realtors, Pasadena Bd. Realtors, Women's Council Realtors, Clear Lake C. of C., Houston Livestock Com. (life), Bay Civic Arts Mus. Home: 306 Crestwood St Seabrook TX 77586 Office: Allen Zarcaro Realty 1199 NASA One Houston TX 77058

ALLEN, JENNIFER JO, journalist; b. Hamilton, Ohio, June 1, 1951; d. William Joseph and Virginia Lee (Adkins) A.; B.A. in Journalism magna cum laude, Ball State U., 1972. Reporter, Brookville (Ind.) Democrat, 1972; asst. women's editor, police writer, youth coordinator, gen. reporter Anderson (Ind.) Herald, 1972-73; edn. editor Hamilton Jour.-News, 1973-74, nat. and internat. news editor, ch. editor, women's columnist, layout and design editor, 1974-79; exec. editor Daily Sun, Corsicana, Tex., 1979—; career clinic tchr. Anderson and Hamilton schs. Bd. dirs. Planned Parenthood of Butler County (Ohio), 1973-74; active in pub. relations Butler County Democratic Com.; bd. dirs. Navarro County chpt. ARC, 1979— Corsicana chpt. ARC; bd. dirs. Corsicana Community Playhouse, 1979—, sec., 1981; mem. deanery council, sec. Episcopal Diocese of Dallas, 1980—. Recipient Med. Reporting award Ind. Med. Assn., 1973. Mem. Women in Communications, Pub. Relations Soc. Am., Press Women Am., NOW (Butler County Woman of Yr. 1975, Butler County Spl. Achievement award 1977), Ball State Alumni Assn., Animal Protection Inst. Am., Am. Soc. Newspaper Editors, Nat. AP Mng. Editors Assn. (vice chmn. citations com. 1982), Tex. AP Mng. Editors Assn. Tex. (program chmn. 1980—, state contest chmn. 1981), Bus. and Profl. Women, Assn. Bus. Women Am., Corsicana C. of C. (dir.), Sigma Delta Chi, Kappa Tau Alpha. Episcopalian. Club: Altrusa (corr. sec. local chpt. 1975). Home: 508 Wesley Dr Corsicana TX 75110

ALLEN, JOAN RACHELLE, statistician; b. N.Y.C., June 24, 1947; d. Lester A. and Emma N. (Pinkofsky) Kraus; A.B., U. Mich., 1968; M.A., U. Calif., Berkeley, 1969; m. David Cary Allen, Oct. 19, 1969; children—Michael Zev, Lisa Arielle. Public health statistician Calif. Dept. Public Health, Berkeley, 1969-72; systems analyst Tex. Inst. Rehab. and Research, Houston, 1972-74; statistician Am. Optometric Assn., Washington, 1974-76, George Washington U., Washington, 1977-78; cons. statistician Nat. Center for Health Stats., Hyattsville, Md., 1976-79, mem. faculty Applied Statistics Tng. Inst., 1977-81; research analyst Health Care Agy., Orange County, Santa Ana, Calif., 1979—. Pres., Sierra Broadmoor Community Assn., 1982. Mem. Am. Statis. Assn., So. Calif. Statis. Soc.

ALLEN, JOANN LONG, real estate investment co. exec., artist; b. Laurens County, S.C., Nov. 25, 1932; d. Julius Vernon and Ruby Evelyn (Boland) Long; student Palmar Coll., 1964; B.A., Jacksonville U., 1970, M.A. in Math., 1974; m. Walter Gregory Allen, Jr., Oct. 12, 1952; 1 dau., Vivian JoAnn; 1 stepdau., Janet A. Henry. With Colonial Properties, Inc., Jacksonville, Fla., 1965—, dir., 1970—, sec., 1970-76, sec., treas., 1976-79, v.p., 1979—; group shows include: St. Augustine Art Assn., 1979—, Artists' Gallery, 1978—, Jacksonville U., 1980. Pres. Artists' Gallery, 1980; bd. dirs. Jr. Woman's Club Jacksonville, 1958-60, Garden Club Jacksonville, 1958, Duval County Hosp. Aux., 1960-61, Duval County Council Camp Fire Girls, 1973-75, Southside Women's Club, 1973-74, Empire Point Com. Council, 1976; mem. Mayor's Adv. Com. on Status of Women, 1978-79. Recipient various awards and hon. mentions for paintings and drawings. Mem. Jacksonville Symphony Guild, Jacksonville Art Mus., Arts Assembly, Jacksonville Watercolor Soc., Friends of Fine Arts, Friends Jacksonville U. Library, Jacksonville U. Alumni Assn., St. Augustine Art Assn., Art League Jacksonville. Republican. Episcopalian. Clubs: Ponte Vedra, River, Pilots (dir. 1974-75). Home: 1508 Campbell Ave Jacksonville FL 32207 Office: 3116 Atlantic Blvd Jacksonville FL 32207

ALLEN, LOUISE, writer, educator; b. Alliance, Ohio, Sept. 21, 1910; d. Earl Wayne and Ella Celesta (Goodall) A.; student Cleve. Coll. Western Res. U., 1963, Lakeland Community Coll., 1981-82; m. Benjamin Yukl, June 27, 1936; children—Katherine Anne Yukl Johnston, Kenneth Allen, Richard Lee, Margaret Louise Yukl Border. Co-founder, Sch. Writing, Cleve., 1961-62; founder, dir. Allen Writers' Agy., Wickliffe, Ohio, 1963—; editorial asso. criticism service Writer's Digest mag., 1967-69; instr. Lakeland Community Coll., Mentor, Ohio, 1973—, Cuyahoga Community Coll., 1975—. Mem. Mensa, Assn. Mundial de Mujures Periodistas y Escritoras, Women in Communications, Nat. League Am. Pen Women, DAR, Textile Arts Club of Cleve. Mus. Art. Republican. Congregationalist. Clubs: Shore Writers (founder), Euclid Three Arts; Women's City (Cleve.). Contbr. articles to mags. Address: 29308 Eddy Rd Wickliffe OH 44092

ALLEN, MARGARET DAY, newspaper reporter; b. Starkville, Miss., Oct. 30, 1951; d. Augustine and Willie Marzee (Myers) Day; B.A. in English, Miss. State U., 1973; M.A. IN Journalism, U. Miss., 1978; m. Robert John Allen, Aug. 23, 1975. Reporter, Tate County Democrat, Senatobia, Miss., 1976-77; editor Rankin County News, Brandon, Miss., 1977-80; instr. Miss. Valley State U., Itta Bena, 1980-81; reporter Greenwood (Miss.) Commonwealth, 1981—. Mem. Nat. Press Photographers Assn., Miss. Press Women, Sigma Delta Chi. Office: PO Box 549 Greenwood MS 38930

ALLEN, MARIA GEORGINA QUEVEDO, social worker; b. Camaguey, Cuba, Oct. 30; came to U.S., 1961, naturalized, 1970; d. Pedro Manuel and Dolores (Peralta) Quevedo; Doctora en Leyes, U. La Habana, Cuba, 1943; M.S.W., Fla. State U., 1969; m. Wilfredo O. Allen, Sept. 8, 1950; children—Wilfredo, Jorge A. Social worker Fla. State Dept. Welfare, Cuban refugee program, 1962-67; caseworker Health and Rehab. Services, 1969-71; supr. social services U. Miami Comprehensive Health Care Program, 1971-74; social worker, supr. evaluation unit. Goodwill Industries, Miami, 1974-79; regional social services supr. dept. youth and family devel. Met. Dade County, Fla., 1974—; asst. prof., field instr. Barry Coll., 1974—. Recipient Miami City Commn. for Vol. Services in Child Day Care award, 1977. Mem. Nat. Assn. Social Workers, Acad. Cert. Social Workers, Cuban Bar in Exile, Fla. State U. Alumni Assn., Coalition Spanish Am. Women. Roman Catholic. Club: Cuban Women's. Office: 11025 SW 84th St Miami FL 33173

ALLEN, MARILYN MYERS POOL, theatre dir.; b. Fresno, Calif., Nov. 2, 1934; d. Laurence B. and Asa (Griggs) Myers; B.A., Stanford U., 1955, postgrad., 1955-56; postgrad. U. Tex., 1957-60, W. Tex. State U. summers 1962, 63; m. Joseph Harold Pool, Dec. 28, 1955; children—Pamela Elizabeth, Victoria Anne, Catherine Marcia. Pvt. tchr. drama, speech, acting, directing, speech correction, Amarillo, Tex., 1960-82, Midland, Tex., 1982—; free-lance radio and TV actress; asst. mng. dir. Amarillo Little Theatre, 1964-66, mng. dir., 1966-68, play dir., 1980; mng. dir. Horsehoe Players, touring profl. theater, 1969-73; actress, multi-media prodn. Palo Duro Canyon, 1971; dir. touring children's theatre, 1978-79 guest actress in Medea, Amarillo Coll., 1981. Pres., Tex. Non-Profit Theatres, 1972-74, 75-77; 1st v.p. High Plains Center for Performing Arts, 1969-73; adv. mem. dept. fine arts Amarillo Coll., 1980-82. Adv. mem. Tex. Constnl. Revision Commn., 1973-75; mem. adv. council U. Tex. Coll. Fine Arts, 1969-72; community adv. com. for women Amarillo Coll., 1975-79; conv. program com. Am. Theatre Assn., 1978, program participant 1978-80, bd. dirs., 1980—; bd. dirs. Amarillo Found. Health and Sci. Edn., 1976-82, program v.p., 1979-81; bd. dirs. Domestic Violence Council, 1979-82, March of Dimes, 1979-81, YMCA Motivation of People, Tex. Panhandle Heritage Found., 1964—, Friends of Fine Arts, W. Tex. State U., 1980-82, Amarillo City Library, 1980-82, Amarillo Symphony, 1981-82. Recipient cert. of appreciation Woman of Year, Amarillo Bus. and Profl. Women's Club, 1966; Best Actress award for Hedda Gabler role Amarillo Little Theatre 1965, Best Dir. award for Rashomon, 1967; named woman of Yr., Beta Sigma Pi, 1980; Travel fellow AAUW, 1973, 78. Mem. Am. Community Theatre Assn. (dir. 1969-72, 82—), S.W. Theatre Conf. (dir. 1973-76, 82—, exec. com. 1982—), Tex. Theatre Council (dir. 1974—, exec. com., pres. 1975-76), AAUW (br. pres. 1973-75, state chmn. cultural interests 1975-77, state 1st v.p. 1977-79), DAR, (chpt. chaplain 1971-75, historian 1975-77), C. of C. (fine arts council), U.S. Judo Assn., Symphony Guild, Amarillo Art Assn., Midland Symphony Guild Amarillo Law Wives Club (pres. 1976-77). Disciples of Christ.

ALLEN, MARTI FERNALD, mktg. communications exec.; b. Glen Ridge, N.J., Oct. 16, 1949; d. Frank Louis and Elizabeth (Fernald) A.; student Rollins Coll., 1967-68; B.A., Drew U., 1971; M.A., N.Y.U., 1973; postgrad. Rutgers U., 1979—, Chobb Inst. Computer Tech., 1981-82. Media buyer Sussman & Sugar, N.Y.C., 1973-75; public relations coordinator Bozell & Jacobs, Union, N.J., 1975-77, public relations account exec., 1977-78; communications mgr. Engineers, Inc., Newark, 1978-79; mktg. communications cons. AT&T, Morris Plains, N.J., 1979—. Coordinator, Union County (N.J.) ERA Coalition, 1974; publicity chmn. Union County Women's Polit. Caucus, 1976-77; mem. Union County (N.J.) Freeholders Adv. Bd. on Status of Women, vice chmn., 1982-83. Mem. NOW (pres. Summit Area 1974-75, public relations chmn. 1975-76, N.J. coordinator ERA Com. 1978), Berkley Heights (N.J.) Bus. and Profl. Women's Club (chmn. personal devel. 1981-82), Phi Chi Theta. Republican. Home: 8 Edgar St Summit NJ 07901

ALLEN, MARY CATHERINE MITCHELL (MRS. WALTON ALBERT ALLEN), educator; b. Iva, S.C.; d. George Francis and Cinderella (Harris) Mitchell; A.A., Anderson Jr. Coll., 1946; B.S. in Edn., Central State Coll., Edmond, Okla., 1962; M.Ed., U. Ga., 1968; Ed.S., Atlanta U., 1974; m. Walton Albert Allen, Apr. 15, 1949; children—Susan Marie, Joel Walton, Barbara Ann. Tchr., prin. Anderson County (S.C.) Schs., 1946-52; tchr. West Clayton Sch., College Park, Ga., 1964-66, guidance counselor, 1966—. Active Girl Scouts U.S.A., 1946-68; bd. dirs. Cherokee Estates, Inc. Mem. NEA, Ga., Clayton County (public relations com. 1967-68, chmn. profl. devel. com. 1975-78) edn. assns., AAUW, Am. (state coordinator elem. counselors), Ga. personnel and guidance assns., Ga. Assn. Sch. Counselors, Alpha Delta Kappa (chpt. treas. 1970-72, dist. chaplain 1972—, chpt. pres. 1974-76), Kappa Delta Pi. Home: 2765 Jerome Rd College Park GA 30337 Office: 5580 Riverdale Rd College Park GA 30337

ALLEN, MAXINE HOKE, elec. distbn. co. ofcl.; b. Mooresville, N.C., Apr. 12, 1950; d. Elliott Earl and Euvena (Lineberger) Hoke; A.A.S., Central Piedmont Community Coll., 1971; m. Sept. 1, 1980. Sec., Am. Credit Corp., Charlotte, N.C., 1970-73; real estate broker, Charlotte,

1975; sec. Gen. Electric Co., Charlotte, 1978-79; adminstrv. asst. Gen. Electric Supply Co., Atlanta, 1979—. Recipient Quality Maker award Gen. Electric Co., 1981. Mem. Nat. Assn. Female Execs., Phi Beta Lambda. Democrat. Baptist. Office: 6540 Peachtree Industrial Blvd Norcross GA 30091

ALLEN, MURIEL HARRIET HERBITS, psychologist; b. Waltham, Mass., Apr. 11, 1925; d. William and Julia (Gluck) Herbits; B.S., U. Mass., 1946; M.Ed., Boston U., 1963, Ed.D. in Counseling Psychology, 1969; m. Max James Allen, Sept. 15, 1948; children—Peter Alexander, Richard Laurence. Co-dir. Stewart-Allen Assos., Andover, Mass., 1969—; cons. psychologist Wilmington (Mass.) Sch. System, 1969—; project initiator Town of Brookline (Mass.), 1969-71; lectr. Salem (Mass.) State Coll., 1973-79; psychologist Mass. Rehab. Commn. First v.p. Aid for Cancer Research Assn., 1962. Social and Rehab. Adminstrn. research fellow, 1968-69; lic. psychologist, Mass.; cert. Nat. Council Health Service Providers in Psychology. Fellow Nat. Rehab. Counseling Assn., Mass. Rehab. Assn. (pres. 1979, Disting. Service award); mem. Am. Psychol. Assn., Mass. Rehab. Counseling Assn. (dir. 1972-78), Am. Personnel and Guidance Assn., Phi Delta Kappa. Asso. editor Jour. of Rehab., 1980—. Home: 114 Clinton Rd Brookline MA 02146 Office: Wilmington Sch System Middlesex Ave Wilmington MA 01887

ALLEN, PAMELA KAY, nurse; b. Denton, Tex., June 4, 1949; d. Ruby Sauls Allen; L.V.N., Denton Sch. Vocat. Nursing, 1969; B.S. in Nursing, Tex. Woman's U., Denton, 1978. Hosp. and office nurse, 1973-76; dir. nurses Nat. Living Center, Sanger, Tex., 1980; health care planning coordinator Care Inn of Sanger, 1980; dir., tchr. vocat. nursing Irving (Tex.) Ind. Sch. Dist., 1979-80; nursing skills lab. asst. El Centro Coll., Dallas, 1979; student health care nurse Tex. Woman's U., 1981—. Mem. Denton Police Res., 1981—. Mem. Am. Nurses Assn., Nat. League Nursing, Tex. Assn. Vocat. Nurse Educators, Tex. Women's U. Alumni Assn., Bus. and Profl. Women's Club. Methodist.

ALLEN, PAULINE VIRGINIA, accountant; b. Guntown, Miss., Feb. 7, 1909; d. Henry James and Madia Jane (Kennedy) A.; student Southwestern U., Memphis, 1927-29, 32-33, U. Miss., 1933-34; A.B., Duke U., 1935. Math. tchr. high sch., Pleasant Grove, Miss., 1936-37; clk. ins. agy., Tunica, Miss., 1940-48; bookkeeper, Tunica, 1952-56; accountant Tunica County Hosp., 1956—. Mem. Hosp. Fin. Mgrs. Assn. Democrat. Methodist. Club: Order Eastern Star. Home: Box 96 Tunica MS 38676

ALLEN, RUTH, ret. orthodontist; b. Tampico, Ill.; d. Richard S. and Nora (Antisdel) Allen; A.A., Pasadena (Calif.) Jr. Coll., 1937; D.D.S., U. So. Calif., 1950, certificate orthodontics, 1951, M.Dental Surgery in orthodontics, 1953. Pres. Pasadena Dental Assts., 1941-42, So. Calif. Dental Assts., 1945; asso. Dr. Spencer R. Atkinson in pvt. practice and orthodontic research, 1950-67; practice orthodontics, Pasadena; ret.; guest lectr. Los Angeles City Coll., 1950-58; asst. prof. grad. orthodontics U. So. Calif., 1954-57. Mem. Am., So. Calif. dental assns., Am. Assn. Orthodontists, Pacific Coast Orthodontic Soc., Assn. Am. Women Dentists, Upsilon Alpha, Beta Sigma Phi. Club: Altrusa (pres. Pasadena 1956-57). Editor Pacific Coast Orthodontic Consultation Group Bull. Address: 3353 Rubio Crest Dr Altadena CA 91001

ALLEN, SAMUELELLA ELIZABETH, former payroll and tax exec.; b. N.Y.C., July 6, 1945; d. Samuel and Ruth Elizabeth (Sydes) Allen; A.A., Cambridge Bus. Sch., 1964. Sales auditor, acct. Robert Hall, 1963-67; payroll and tax acct. A.E. Schimmel, Inc., N.Y.C., 1967-72; payroll and asst. tax supt. Amax, Inc., N.Y.C., 1972-74; payroll and tax mgr. Brentano's, Inc., N.Y.C., 1975-81; bus. adv. Bellocchio Uomo Ltd., 1979—. Democrat. Roman Catholic.

ALLEN, SARAH FRANCES, contractor; b. Tampa, Fla., Sept. 2, 1943; d. Ralph Walter and Allie Rebecca (Stafford) Overman; ed. U. South Fla.; children—Wiliam Kennon, Heather. Founder, pres. Sarah Allen Homes, Inc., 1974—. Mem. Sarasota Com. of 100; bd. dirs. Asolo State Theater. Mem. Fla. Bd. Realtors, Sarasota-Manatee Contractors Assn., Nat. Assn. Home Builders, Fla. Assn. Home Builders, DAR. Republican. Episcopalian. Home and Office: Sarasota FL 33581

ALLEN, SHARON AMERINE, speech pathologist; b. Alexandria, La., Apr. 22, 1942; B.A. in Speech Therapy, Northwestern State U., Natchitoches, La., 1965, M.A. in Speech Pathology, 1968; children—Lisa, Brooke. Speech therapist public schs., La., 1965-71; speech and hearing cons. Nicholls State U., Thibodaux, La., 1973-78; prin. TARC-Wonderland Houma, La., 1978—. cert. tchr., La. Mem. Am. Speech, Lang. and Hearing Assn. (cert.), La. Speech and Hearing Assn., Am. Assn. Mental Deficiency, Devel. Disabilities Council La. Home: 202 Lynwood Houma LA 70360 Office: 1 McCord Rd Houma LA 70360

ALLEN, SUSAN BURDETTE, entrepreneur; b. Durham, N.C., Nov. 18, 1951; d. Malcolm Burdette and Louise (Lloyd) A.; B.S. in Interior Design, U. N.C., Greensboro, 1973. Mgr., designer Intra, Greensboro, 1973-75; designer Priba Interiors, W.Ger., 1976-78, Comml. Office Furniture, Washington, 1978-79; owner, mgr. Phasedesign, Greensboro, 1979—; creator, owner Funnybusiness, Greensboro and Winston-Salem, N.C., 1979—; owner Funny U., Greensboro, 1982—; speaker in field of downtown revitalization and historic preservation. Bd. dirs. Old Greensborough Preservation Soc. Mem. Women's Profl. Forum, Nat. Assn. Female Execs. Mem. editorial bd. Hamburger Sq. Post. Home: PO Box 5492 Greensboro NC 27403 Office: 231 N Greene St Greensboro NC 27401

ALLEN-TAYLOR, SHIRLEY JEANNE, educator; b. Tyler, Tex., Dec. 19, 1941; d. Ralph Carnell and Theressa Gunzell (Carter) Allen; B.A. in English and Lit., Gallaudet Coll., 1966; M.A. in Guidance and Counseling, Howard U., 1972; postgrad. U. Rochester; m. George Taylor, July 25, 1980. Classification clk. U.S. Peace Corps, Washington, 1965; distbn. clk. U.S. Post Office, Washington, 1966-67; editorial clk. IRS, Washington, 1967; residence hall supr./tchr. Gallaudet Coll., Washington, 1967-73; asso. prof. human devel. (curriculum devel. and teaching) Rochester (N.Y.) Inst. Tech., 1973—. Mem. Nat. Assn. Women Deans, Adminstrs. and Counselors, Nat. Assn. of the Deaf, Conf. of Am. Instrs. of the Deaf, Delta Epsilon. Democrat. Baptist. Home: 395 Ravenwood Ave Rochester NY 14619 Office: 1 Lomb Meml Dr Rochester NY 14623

ALLEN-WESTON, CAROL LOU, educator; b. Manhattan, Kans., June 12, 1946; d. Noah and Patricia Lorraine (Daylight) Allen; B.A., Wichita State U., 1969; M.S., Ariz. State U., 1970; m. Raymond R. Weston, July 25, 1975; 1 son, Chief. With Bur. Indian Affairs, Dept. Interior, 1973—, dean instrn. Haskell Indian Jr. Coll., Lawrence Kans., 1977-80, edn. program adminstr., Muskogee, Okla., 1980—. Sec., United Fund Lawrence, 1979-80; art commr. Douglas County (Kans.), 1977-80. Mem. Nat. Indian Edn. Assn., N.Am. Indian Tennis Assn. (pres. 1978-79). Home: PO Box 1376 Muskogee OK 74401 Office: Old Federal Bldg Muskogee OK 74401

ALLEY, BARBARA (MRS. JEROLD S. SIMON), fashion editor, actress; b. Trenton, June 15, 1936; d. John Hamlin and Grace (Brown) A.; B.S. cum laude with honors, U. N.C., Greensboro, 1957; cert. in fashion design Parsons' Sch. Design, N.Y.C., 1958; m. Jerold Stanton Simon, Dec. 25, 1970. Fashion design, ednl. and merchandising positions, 1958-62; TV actress in TV commls., commentator, 1962—; TV interviewer N.Y. World's Fair, RCA-TV, 1964; weather girl Sta. WPIX-TV, N.Y.C., 1966-67; fashion dir., narrator The Ski Show Expowinter shows, 1968—; fashion editor Skiing mag., N.Y.C., 1974—; color commentator, fashion narrator Women's Pro Ski Racing Championships, 1978; former ski instr., parachutist, mountain climber, Grand Teton, Wyo., Matterhorn, Switzerland. Mem. Screen Actors Guild, AFTRA, Omicron Nu. Office: Skiing Mag 1 Park Ave New York NY 10016

ALLIES, VICTORIA ROSSINI, chem. engr.; b. Southington, Conn., May 27, 1950; d. Leon and Lillian (Wanagus) Rossini; student Middlebury Coll., 1968-70; B.A. with honors, U. Conn., 1972, M.S., 1979; M.B.A., U. Phoenix, 1980—; m. James M. McCarron, June 18, 1980; stepchildren—James Roy, Delores, Lynn. Adhesive chemist Loctite Corp., Newington, Conn., 1972-76, adhesives engr., 1976-87; market devel. mgr. Gen. Electric, Laminated Materials Dept., Coshocton, Ohio, 1978-79; chem. process engr. ITT-Courier Terminal Systems, Inc., Tempe, Ariz., 1979-80; sr. chem. process engr., environ. engring. supr. Digital Equip. Corp., Tempe, 1980-82; pres./cons. Tng. 'n' Tech., Tempe, 1982—. instr. chemistry Maricopa Community Coll., Phoenix, 1981—; fin. backer Tng. in Tech., Tempe, 1981—. Mem. Am. Chem. Soc., Ariz. Printed Circuit Bd. Assn., Soc. Women Engrs. Patentee on temporary bonding adhesives. Home: 11455 S Half Moon Dr Phoenix AZ 85044 Office: 1901 W 14th St Tempe AZ 85281

ALLISON, ADELE MOYER, public relations cons., journalist, artist; b. Connellsville, Pa.; d. Enoch Edward and Flora (McKinley) Moyer; B.A., U. Pitts., 1934; postgrad. Shippensburg State Coll.; cert. Paris-Am. Acad., Paris, Inst. Allende, Mex.; m. William Francis Allison, Apr. 8, 1938 (div. 1965); 1 son, William Moyer. Society editor Pitts. Press, 1936-41; public relations dir. New Kensington (Pa.) plant Aluminum Co. Am., 1944-47; news reporter Ossining (N.Y.) Citizen Register, 1947-49; free-lance writer, publicist, public relations ofcl., 1950-54; public relations dir. Magee-Women's Hosp., Pitts., 1954-61; dir. public relations Met./Pitts. Ednl. TV Sta. WQED, 1961-66; publicity, public relations dir. Carnegie Inst. Mus. Art's 1967 exhbn. painting and sculpture; public relations cons. Community Coll. of Allegheny County, 1971-77. Mem. women's com. Pitts. Symphony Soc.; mem. nat. bd. Med. Coll. Pa., Phila. Recipient Freedoms Found. award, 1977. Mem. Pitts. Press Club, Women's Press Club Pitts. (1st award for public relations 1955, 59), Washington Press Club, English-Speaking Union, Kappa Kappa Gamma. Episcopalian. Home: 116 A Queen St Chestertown Eastern Shore MD 21620 also 773 N 27th St Philadelphia PA 19130

ALLISON, HOLLY A., bus. exec.; b. N.Y.C., July 3, 1946; d. Robert Paul and Freda Elizabeth (Klein) Allison; B.A., Rider Coll., 1968; student N.Y.U. Real Estate Inst., 1978—. Asst. to communications v.p. Chase Manhattan Bank, 1968-69; mgr. Allied Service, N.Y.C., 1969-72; v.p. Plaza Bus. Systems, Inc., N.Y.C., 1972-75; owner, pres. Sunshine Temporary Office Personnel Inc., 1975—; sec.-treas., dir., owner Holdee Assos., 1975—. Recipient White House award for successful women in bus. Mem. Internat. World Processing Assn., Am. Mgmt. Assn., Nat. Assn. Women Bus. Owners, Nat. Assn. Personnel Women, Sales Execs. Club, Nat. Assn. Bus. and Profl. Women., Assn. Personnel Cons., Adminstrv. Mgmt. Soc., Whitney Mus., Guggenheim Mus., Met. Mus. Art. Jewish. Contbr. articles to profl. jours., mags. Home: Suite 10B 342 E 67th St New York NY 10021

ALLISON, MYRA ANN, nurse; b. Shelbyville, Ind., Oct. 10, 1947; d. Max A. and Hilda May (Gosnell) Hungerford; grad. Indpls. Sch. Practical Nursing, 1968; m. Stephen K. Allison, July 12, 1969; children—Samuel Kenneth, Max Alan. Nurse, Coleman Hosp., Indpls., 1967-70, Med. Personnel Pool, Indpls., 1973-76; nurse in geriatrics Alteheim Community Retirement Home, Indpls., 1978—. Methodist.

ALLISON, PATRICIA ANNE, educator; b. Terre Haute, Ind., Aug. 28, 1934; d. Ernest and Leatha M. (Mace) Bailey; B.S. cum laude, Ind. State U., 1972, M.S., 1976; m. Harold E. Allison, June 28, 1953; children—Linda, Betty Jean, Janet, Terry, Michael. Tchr. educable mentally handicapped Crestwood Sch., Paris, Ill., 1972-77, tchr. learning disabilities, 1977-81, tchr. transition room for learning disabilities, 1981—. Leader-4-H. Mem. Internat. Reading Assn., Ill. Reading Assn., Assn. Retarded Citizens (bd. dirs. 1974-79, pres. 1978-79), Council for Exceptional Children, Assn. for Children with Learning Disabilities (founder Edgar County chpt., pres. 1979-80), Ill. Edn. Assn., NEA, Am. Assn. Mental Deficiency, Kappa Delta Pi, Delta Kappa Gamma, Lambda Psi Sigma. Republican. Methodist. Home: 1007 Douglas St Paris IL 61944 Office: Route 3 PO Box 160 Paris IL 61944

ALLMAN, MARGO HUTZ, sculptor, painter; b. N.Y.C., Feb. 23, 1933; d. Werner H. and Avis (Newcomb) Hutz; student Smith Coll., 1950-51, Moore Coll. Art, 1952-54, Hans Hofmann Sch. Art, 1953, U. Del., 1967-70; m. William B. Allman, Feb. 19, 1954; children—Avis Louise, David Drue. One-person shows include: Wallingford (Pa.) Art Center, 1964, Windham Coll., 1974, Bloomsburg State Coll., 1976, 77, Moore Coll. Art, 1979; group shows include: Phila. Art Alliance, 1954, Del. Art Museum, Wilmington, 1958 (Ann. Show Drawing prize), 65, 67, Print Club, Phila., 1959, U. Del., 1977, Del. State Arts Council, Wilmington, 1981; represented in permanent collections, including: Del. Mus., Phila. Mus.; works include: Ferro Cement Sculpture, Tidewater Pub. Co., Centerville, Md., 1975, Crocheted Sculpture of Herculon, Hercules Inc., Wilmington, 1975. Bd. dirs. Robert Small Dance Co., N.Y.C., 1979-80. Recipient Mildred Boericke prize Print Club, Phila., 1958, Landscape prize Wilmington Trust Bank, 1969. Mem. Moore Coll. Art Alumnae Assn., Del. Center Contemporary Arts, Del. Art Mus. Unitarian. Home: Rose Hill Manor RD 1 Box 45B West Grove PA 19390

ALLYSON, JUNE (BORN JAN ALLYSON), actress; b. Lucerne, N.Y.; d. Arthur and Clare Allyson; student pub. schs., N.Y.C. Actress, stage appearances include: Sing Out the News, Very Warm for May, Higher and Higher, Panama Hattie, Best Foot Forward; motion pictures include: Girl Crazy, 1943, Best Foot Forward, 1943, Thousands Cheer, 1943, Meet the People, 1943, Two Girls and a Sailor, 1944, Music for Millions, 1944, Her Highness and the Bellboy, 1945, The Sailor Takes a Wife, 1945, Two Sisters From Boston, 1945, Till the Clouds Roll By, 1946, The Secret Heart, 1946, High Barbaree, 1947, Good News, 1947, The Bride Goes Wild, 1947, Words and Music, 1948, The Three Musketeers, 1948, Little Women, 1948, The Stratton Story, 1948, The Reformer and the Redhead, 1949, Right Cross, 1950, Too Young to Kiss, 1951, The Girl in White, 1951, The Glenn Miller Story, 1954, Remains to be Seen, 1953, Executive Suite, 1954, Strategic Air Command, 1955, You Can't Run Away From It, The Opposite Sex, 1956, Interlude, 1957, My Man Godfrey, 1957, Stranger in My Arms, 1958, They Only Kill Their Masters, 1972, Letters from Three Lovers, 1973, Blackout, 1978; appeared in TV movie See the Man Run, 1972, Vegas, 1978; star June Allyson Show, 1960-61; TV appearances include Love Boat, Dick Powell Theatre, Zane Grey Theatre, Burke's Law, Sixth Sense. Address: care Contemporary Artists Ltd 132 Lasky Dr Beverly Hills CA 90212 *

ALMAN, EMILY ARNOW, sociologist, lawyer; b. N.Y.C., Jan. 20, 1922; d. Joseph Michael and Cecilia (Greenstone) Arnow; B.A., Hunter Coll., 1948; Ph.D., New Sch. for Social Research, 1963; J.D., Rutgers U., Newark, 1977; m. David Alman, Aug. 1, 1940; children—Michelle Alman Harrison, Jennifer Alman Michaels. Probation officer, N.Y.C., 1945-48; asso. prof. sociology Douglass Coll. Rutgers U., Newark, 1960—; admitted to N.J. bar, 1978; individual practice law, Highland Park, N.J., 1978—. Candidate for mayor, City of East Brunswick, 1972; chmn. Concerned Citizens of East Brunswick, 1970-78; pres. bd. trustees Concerned Citizens Environ. Fund., East Brunswick, 1977-78. Mem. Am., N.J. Middlesex County bar assns., Am. Sociol. Assn., Assn. Fed. Bar State of N.J., Assn. Trial Lawyers Am., Trial Lawyers Assn. Middlesex County, Law and Soc. Assn., Am. Judicature Soc., Nat. Assn. Women Lawyers, N.J. Assn. Women Lawyers, ACLU, AAUP, Women Helping Women. Author: Ride The Long Night, 1963; screenplay, The Ninety-First Day, 1963. Home: 611 S Park Ave Highland Park NJ 08904

ALMOND, PATRICIA ANNE, property mgmt. co. adminstr.; b. Riverhead, N.Y., Feb. 12, 1959; d. William Kenneth and Joan Patricia (Kirwan) A.; exec. sec. diploma Jefferson Shores Secretarial Sch., Port Jefferson, N.Y., 1978. Personnel sec., 1978-80; adminstr. Total Tech. Inst., Ft. Lauderdale, Fla., 1981-82; exec. asst. Otter Corp., Atlanta, 1982—. Mem. Nat. Assn. Female Execs. (network dir.), Internat. Travel/Trade Consumer Orgn. Home: 6670C Peachtree Industrial Blvd Atlanta GA 30360 Office: 3312 Piedmont Rd Atlanta GA 30305

ALONSO, MARTHA RITA, clin. psychologist; b. Havana, Cuba, Sept. 19, 1935; came to U.S., 1961, naturalized, 1969; d. Eustaquio Francisco and Regla Palacios A.; B.A., Fla. State U., 1967; M.S., U. Ga., 1970, Ph.D., 1973. Staff psychologist Community Mental Health Center of Escambia County, Pensacola, Fla., 1972-74; staff psychologist Mailman Center Child Devel., U. Miami (Fla.) Med. Sch., 1974-78, dept. child psychiatry, 1978-79, clin. asst. prof. pediatrics and psychiatry, 1974—; pvt. practice, Miami, 1976—; cons. Head Start program U. Miami, 1979—. Mem. Am. Psychol. Assn. (mem. bd. ethnic minority affairs 1981—), Southeastern Psychol. Assn., Fla. Psychol. Assn., Dade County Psychol. Assn. Nat. Hispanic Psychol. Assn. Office: 525 NW 27th Ave Suite 105 Miami FL 33125

ALPAUGH, PATRICIA KAY, clin. psychologist; b. Pomona, Calif., May 3, 1947; d. John William and Betty Beatrice (Rothrock) Haines; B.A., Occidental Coll., 1969; M.A., U. So. Calif., 1975, Ph.D., 1977. Juvenile probation officer Marion County Juvenile Ct., Indpls., 1970-71; mgr. Pacific Telephone Co., Pasadena, Calif., 1971; vol. coordinator Hathaway Home for Children, Highland Park, Calif., 1971-73; psychology tng. grantee U. So. Calif., Los Angeles, 1973-77; ednl. therapist, psychol. asst. Learning Center, Arcadia, Calif., 1973; dir. peer counseling program Adult Counseling Center, Andrus Gerontology Center, U. So. Calif., 1976-77; acting chief psychology Ingelside Mental Health Center, Rosemead, Calif., 1978, supr. psychology dept., 1978—; asst. prof. Grad. Sch. Psychology, Fuller Theol. Sem., Pasadena, 1978—; gerontol. cons., 1977—; pvt. practice clin. psychology, marriage, family and child counseling, 1977—. Lic. psychologist, Calif.; lic. marriage, family and child counselor, Calif. Mem. Am. Psychol. Assn., Calif. Psychol. Assn., Gerontol. Soc., Phi Beta Kappa, Phi Kappa Phi. Author: (with M. Haney) Counseling the Older Adult, 1978; contbr. articles to profl. jours. Office: 1730 Huntington Dr Suite 202A South Pasadena CA 91030

ALPERIN, GOLDIE GREEN, cons. librarian, lawyer; b. Des Moines, Aug. 16, 1905; d. Morris and Bessie (Miliwer) Green; LL.B., Drake U., 1927; m. Moses Alperin, Dec. 25, 1930 (dec. 1950); children—Herschel Burton, Judith Miriam. Admitted to Iowa bar, 1927, U.S. Supreme Ct. bar, 1959; practice in Des Moines, 1927-30; law librarian Chgo. Bar. Assn., 1951-63; dir. Def. Information Office, Chgo., 1963-65; librarian book selections Northwestern U. Law Sch. Library, 1966-72; ret., 1972. Named one of 20 rep. U.S. women lawyers of various phases practice Women's Adjustment Bd., London, Eng., 1957; One of Outstanding Women of Am. Bicentennial, Austin (Tex.) Bicentennial Com., 1976; cert. religious sch. tchr. Bd. Jewish Edn., Chgo., 1951. Mem. Am. (sec. 1960-65), Chgo. (past exec. bd., editor 1958-59) assns. law libraries, Nat. Assn. Women Lawyers (regional) dir. 1960-64). Jewish religion. Asst. editor Women Lawyers Jour., 1961-67, exec. bd., 1961-67. Home: 3100 Lake Shore Dr Chicago IL 60657

ALPERT, ANN SHARON, computer agt.; b. Indpls., Feb. 24, 1938; d. Oscar and Adele Alpert; B.S. in Edn., Ind. U., 1959. Tchr., Indpls. public schs., 1959-60; librarian George Fry & Assos., Chgo., 1960-62, DeLeuw, Cather & Co., Chgo., 1962-65, Arthur Young & Co., C.P.A.s, Chgo., 1965-74; statis. asst. Sargent & Lundy, Chgo., 1974-81, computer liaison agt., 1981—. Office: 55 E Monroe St Chicago IL 60603

ALPERT, LINDA M., nurse; b. Boston, Jan. 25, 1941; d. Sidney M. and Blanche (Kaplan) Omansky; B.S.N., U. Ariz., 1963; children—Sandra, Jeffrey. Staff nurse Handmaker Nursing Home, 1964; staff relief nurse Tucson Med. Center, 1967-68, nurse recruiter, 1968-70, head nurse cystic fibrosis center, 1970-76, head nurse, dir. chest clinic and allergy clinic, 1976-82; adminstr., dir. Pulmonary Care Center, Good Samaritan Med. Center, Phoenix, 1982—; program coordinator Ariz. Chest Symposium, 1971-82; mem. adv. com. Sch. Respiratory Therapy, Pima Community Coll., 1979—. Bd. dirs. Tucson chpt. Cystic Fibrosis Found., 1971-82. Mem. Ariz. Nurses in Mgmt., Am. Thoracic Soc., Ariz. Thoracic Soc., Sigma Theta Tau. Jewish. Club: Soroptimist. Home: 5900 E Thomas Rd Apt E225 Scottsdale AZ 85251 Office: 1111 E McDowell Rd Phoenix AZ 85006

ALPERT, ROSALIND ALICE, securities trader, trust co. exec.; b. Poughkeepsie, N.Y., Sept. 28, 1954; d. Norman and Adeline A.; B.A. in Stats., Princeton U., 1976. Vice pres., securities trade Bankers Trust Co., N.Y.C., 1976—. Bd. dirs. 750 Park Ave., N.Y.C. Office: 16 Wall St New York NY 10005

AL-QADI, CAROLYN ANN, police officer, archeologist; b. Chgo., Aug. 9, 1942; d. George Merton and Juanita Mary (Battistoni) Grant; B.A., U. Chgo., 1964; student Savannah Vocat. Tech. Law Enforcement Sch. (Ga.), 1976; vocat. cert. Armstrong State Coll. Managerial Sch., 1976; m. Ali Muhammad Al-Qadi, June 19, 1964; children—Umar Ali, Halimah Ali. Humane officer and shelter mgr. Chatham-Savannah Humane Soc., 1975-76; security mgr. Levy's of Savannah Dept. Store, 1976-77; sr. officer and investigator Ga. Ports Authority Police, Savannah, 1977-82; cons. Ga. Gov.'s Conf. on Edn. Pullman grantee, 1960-62; U. Chgo. grantee, 1960-63. Mem. Am. Bus. Women's Assn. (pres. chpt. 1978; del. nat. conv. 1978), Mensa, Ga. Archeol. Soc., Am. Anthrop. Assn. Mem. archeol. excavation team, Kampsville, Ill., 1962, Carlisle, Ill., 1963. Office: PO Box 2406 Savannah GA 31402

ALS, HEIDELISE, infant psychologist; b. Krumbach, West Germany, Nov. 8, 1940; came to U.S., 1964, naturalized, 1968; d. Heinrich Maria and Elizabeth (Broicher) Als; B.S., U. Wurzburg, 1963; M.S., U. Pa., 1968, Ph.D., 1975; m. Frank Hopkins Duffy, Jan. 1, 1978; 1 son by previous marriage, Christopher Markoe Rivinus; stepchildren—Lisa, Stephen Worcester, Victoria Cane. Research asso. pediatrics and psychiatry, child devel. unit Children's Hosp. Med. Center, Boston, 1973—, instr. pediatrics, 1973-78; research asso. pediatrics Harvard U. Med. Sch., Boston, 1975-77, asst. prof., 1977—. Mem. Am. Psychol. Assn., Am. Soc. Social Biology, AAAS, Soc. Research Child Devel., Soc. Human Ethology, Internat. Conf. Infant Studies, ACLU. Democrat. Home: 49 Harrison St Brookline MA 02146 Office: Child Development Unit Childrens Hospital Medical Center 300 Longwood Ave Boston MA 02115

ALSBERG, EVERYL PARKER, retail co. exec.; b. Springhill, Okla., Oct. 14, 1921; d. Airy Lasker and Pearl Ellen (Collinsworth) Snelson; student U. So. Calif., 1943; B.S., U. Tulsa, 1953; postgrad. UCLA, 1953-58, Occidental Coll., 1958-62; M.A. in Adminstrn., Calif. State U.,

Los Angeles, 1962, postgrad., 1962-74; Ph.D., Walden U., 1979; m. Willis Parker, Jr., 1942 (dec.); children—Richard, Pennye Ellen; m. 2d, Harold Alsberg, 1969. Tchr., Fairfax, Va., 1953-55, Los Angeles City Schs., 1956-57; tchr. La Canada (Calif.) Unified Sch. Dist., 1957-62, prin. Paradise Canyon Elem. Sch., 1962-76, dir. instrn. K-8, 1976-78; cons. ednl. adminstrn., 1978-81; mgr. Peck & Peck, Annapolis, Md., 1981—; dir. PDQ Bus. Services, 1979-81, v.p., 1980. Dir. jr. high fellowship Presbyterian Ch., 1960-62; pres. Annapolis Bon Haven Community Assn., 1981—. bd. dirs. Colonial Players Annapolis, 1979-82, sec., 1981-84. Mem. Assn. Supervision and Curriculum Devel., Elementary Sch. Sci. Assn. (past sec., v.p., pres.), Profl. Educators Group, NEA, PTA (life), Mortar Bd., Kappa Delta Pi, Delta Kappa Gamma (pres. 1980-82, 2d v.p. 1982—), Phi Mu (past chpt. adviser, pres. Glendale alumna club, nat. pub. relations dir., nat. membership dir., nat. pledge dir., dist. alumnae dir.), Republican. Club: Annapolis Panhellenic (scholarship chmn.). Home: 778 Bon Haven Dr Annapolis MD 21401 Office: 137 Annapolis Mall Annapolis MD 21401

ALSPACH, JOANN GRIF, nurse, educator; b. Waterbury, Conn., Dec. 7, 1947; d. Joseph Francis and Dora Estelle (Cote) Griffin; B.S.N., Cath. U. Am., 1969, M.S.N., 1976; m. Rodger L. Alspach, Aug. 14, 1971; 1 dau., Jennifer L. Staff nurse U.S. Navy Nurse Corps, Chelsea, Mass., 1969, Naval Hosp. Boston, 1969-73, charge nurse, 1969, staff/charge nurse, 1970-74; clin. specialist critical care nursing Suburban Hosp., Bethesda, Md., 1976-80, dir. critical care nursing internship program, 1976-80; clin. nurse expert Heart and Lung Nursing Service Clin. Center, NIH, Bethesda, 1980-81, staff nurse, Cardiac Surgery Unit, 1981, clin. nurse educator, Critical Care Nursing Service, 1981—; clin. preceptor Med.-Surg. Nursing, Clin. Specialist Practicum, Cath. U. Am., 1977, U. Md., 1977; adj. asst. prof. nursing, Cath. U. Am., Washington, 1980-81; lectr. in field; cons. in field. Active ARC, Washington, 1980—, Lung Assn. Mid-Md., Rockville, 1981—. Served with Nurse Corps, USN, 1969-74. Recipient Chi Iota Pi Acad. Award, 1969; U.S. Navy Women Officer Sch. Leadership award, 1969, Honor award, 1969. Mem. Am. Assn. Critical-Care Nurses (sec. bd. dirs. 1979-81), Am. Soc. Hosp. Pharmacists (mem. selection panel 1981—), Am. Nurses Assn., Md. Nurses Assn., Nat. League for Nursing, Md. League for Nursing, Am. Heart Assn., Montgomery County Heart Assn., Nat. Critical Care Inst. Edn., Met. D.C. Council for Critical Care Nursing, Am. Med. Writers Assn., Sigma Theta Tau, Kappa Gamma Pi. Author: Critical Care Nursing Internship Program: Program Syllabus, 1977; The Educational Process in Critical Care Nursing, 1982; manuscript reviewer Advanced Critical Care Nursing, 1980, Study Guide: Critical Care Nursing, 1980, Critical Care Nursing Practice Text, 1981; editor: Care Curriculum for Critical Care Nursing, 3d edit.; nurse editor Vitalines, 1982—; editorial bd. Heart and Lung, Jour. of Critical Care, 1979—; Dimensions of Critical Care Nursing, 1981—, others; also articles. Home: 2900 Southaven Dr Annapolis MD 21401 Office: NIH Bldg 10 Room 7C 416 9000 Rockville Pike Bethesda MD 20205

ALSPAUGH, JANE BRADNER (MRS. ROBERT ODO ALSPAUGH), civic worker; b. Cleve., Mar. 13, 1920; d. Hosea Townsend and Jessie (Morison) Bradner; student Smith Coll., 1941; m. Robert Odo Alspaugh, Dec. 6, 1941; 1 dau., Janet Bradner. Dir. Am. Commerce Corp., Cleve., Alspaugh & Co., Cleve. Chmn. garden club Cleve. Jr. League, 1954; chmn. jr. council Cleve. Mus. Art, 1957-59, mem. adv. bd., 1958-59; mem. Adult Edn. Council Greater Cleve.; mem. jr. bd. St. Luke's Hosp., Cleve.; mem. bd. of women's com. Cleve. Orch., 1963-66, membership chmn., 1965-66; mem. bd. women's com. Inst. Music Cleve., 1963-67; mem. women's Play House; mem. Careers in Social Work Scholarship com. Welfare Fedn.; exec. com. women's com. Natural Sci. Mus.; sec. women's com. Natural History Mus., 1972—; mem. women's adv. council Western Res. Hist. Soc., 1973—, sec. council, 1975—; corr. sec. Western Res. Women's Republican Club, 1955-57; trustee; mem. exec. com. Garden Center Greater Cleve., 1957-61; bd. women's com. Cleve. Inst. Art, chmn. membership com., 1962-64; bd. mem. Cleve. Orch., chmn. edn. com., 1964-65. Mem. Laurel Sch., Smith Coll. alumni assns. Episcopalian. Clubs: Town and Country Garden (v.p. 1966-68, pres. 1968-69), Smith College of Cleveland (pres. 1960-62, women's com. Cleve., scholarship chmn., 1965-67, nominating chmn. 1967-68), Intown. Home: 2952 Fairmount Blvd Cleveland Heights OH 44118

ALSTON, LELA, Ariz. state senator; b. Phoenix, June 26, 1942; d. Virgil Lee and Frances Mae Koonse Mulkey; B.S., U. Ariz., 1967; M.S., Ariz. State U., 1971; m. Gerald W. Alston, 1960; children—Brenda Susan, Charles William. Tchr. high sch., 1968—; mem. Ariz. State Senate, 1977—. Named Disting. Citizen, U. Ariz. Alumni Assn., 1978. Mem. NEA, Ariz. Edn. Assn., Am. Home Econs. Assn., Ariz. Home Econs. Assn., Am. Vocat. Assn. Methodist. Office: Capitol Bldg Senate Wing Phoenix AZ 85007 *

ALSTON, REBECCA BOONE, educator, artist; b. Poplarville, Miss., May 12, 1951; d. Daniel Travis and Dahlia (Penton) Boone; B.F.A., Auburn U., 1975; M.Arch., Kans. State U., 1981; 1 dau., T. Angela. Free-lance designer, graphic designer Miss. State Parks, 1975-76; designer planning dept. Clairon Ledger News Room, Jackson, Miss., 1976-78; prof. Coll. Architecture and Design Kans. State U., Manhattan, 1978—; cons. and free-lance designer, 1975—. Mem. Citizens Against Nuclear Disposal. Mem. Women in Design Internat., Kansas City Arts Coalition, Manhattan Art Council. Exhbns. include planial space and color variations exhbn., 1978. Home: 1835 Fairchild Ave Manhattan KS 66502 Office: Coll Architecture and Design Seaton Hall Kans State U Manhattan KS 66502

ALSTROM, MARGUERITE LURENE GRIFFITH (MRS. JOHN THOMAS ALSTROM), educator; b. Coffeyville, Kans., Feb. 15, 1915; d. Clyde Earl and Mary Lurene (Spear) Griffith; A.B., U. So. Calif., 1946; postgrad., 1957; M.A., Occidental Coll., 1948; m. John Thomas Alstrom, Feb. 23, 1952. Job analyst War Manpower Commn., Los Angeles, 1942-44; asst. dir. Vocat. Planning Service, Los Angeles, 1945-46; vocational and mgmt. cons., 1946-66; instr. psychology Occidental Coll., Los Angeles, 1946-47, dir. vocat. guidance, 1947-51; lectr. pub. adminstrn. U. So. Calif., Los Angeles, 1955-58; city clk. Monterey Park, Calif., 1956-65; vocat. cons. HEW, Los Angeles, 1962-66, Agana, Guam, 1966-73; asst. to pres. U. Guam, 1966-69, asst. v.p. acad. affairs, 1969-70, chmn. dept. pub. adminstrn., 1970-73; instr. Sun City Campus, Rio Salado Community Coll., Phoenix, 1975—. Served as capt. USAF, 1951-53. Mem. Am. Psychol. Assn. (emeritus), Nat. Vocat. Guidance Assn. (emeritus), Phi Kappa Phi, Pi Sigma Alpha, Psi Chi, Chi Omicron Gamma. Author: Administrative Analysis Techniques, 1968. Contbr. articles to profl. jours. Home: 17203 Foothills Dr Sun City AZ 85373

ALT, JANE FULTON, psychiat. social worker; b. Chgo., May 26, 1951; d. Maurice and Muriel (Fantus) Fulton; A.B. with distinction in Edn., U. Mich., 1973; M.A., U. Chgo., 1975; m. Howard Lang Alt, Nov. 27, 1976; 1 dau., Katie Jane. Inpatient psychiat. social worker Inst. Psychiatry, Northwestern Meml. Hosp., Chgo., 1975-76, outpatient psychiat. social worker, 1976-79; pvt. practice psychiat. social work, Chgo., 1979—; research cons. Ill. Gov.'s Commn. To Revise Mental Health Code, 1974; instr. dept. allied health and scis. Northwestern U. Med. Sch., Chgo., 1976—; mem. mastectomy counseling project Nat. Cancer Inst., Northwestern U. Med. Sch.-Northwestern Meml. Hosp., 1981—. Registered cert. social worker, Ill. Mem. Acad. Cert. Social Workers, Nat. Assn. Social Workers, Mortar Bd. Home: 2203 Orrington Ave Evanston IL 60201 Office: 645 N Michigan Ave Chicago IL 60611

ALT-AWOOD, SANDRA JEAN, social worker; b. Grand Rapids, Mich., July 30, 1942; d. Albert J. and Rosemarie Edna (Armock) A.; B.A. cum laude, Mercy Coll. of Detroit, 1968; M.S.W., U. Mich., 1970; m. John Anthony Awood, Dec. 20, 1975. Tchr., St. Brigid Elem. Sch., Midland, Mich., 1966-67; acad. counselor Mercy High Sch., Farmington, Mich., 1966-67; clin. social worker Hawthorn Center, Northville, Mich., 1970-73; dir. clin. services Barat Human Services, Detroit, 1973-78; pvt. practice clin. social work, 1978—; cons. to children's agys. Mich. Assn. Children's Agys., 1979-80; mem. adv. bd. social work program Mercy Coll. of Detroit, 1979—, part-time instr., 1080-81, editor study on social work program, 1980; mem. spl. edn. adv. com. to Ann Arbor (Mich.) Schs., 1971-72; mem. Foster Grandparent Adv. Council, Wayne County, Mich., 1975-79. Recipient award for children's services Detroit Free Press, 1978. Mem. Nat. Assn. Social Workers (sec.-treas. Oakland unit 1976-77), Acad. Cert. Social Workers, Nat. Assn. for Female Execs., Mich. Assn. for Emotionally Disturbed Children (pres. 1971-72), League Cath. Women, Kappa Gamma Pi, Kappa Delta Pi, Alpha Mu Gamma. Democrat. Home and office: 210 Fairfax St Birmingham MI 48009

ALTEKRUSE, JOAN MORRISSEY, physician; b. Cohoes, N.Y., Nov. 15, 1928; d. William T. Dee and Agnes Kay (Fitzgerald) Morrissey; A.B., Vassar Coll., 1949; M.D., Stanford U., 1960; M.P.H., Harvard U., 1965; D.P.H., U. Calif., Berkeley, 1973; m. Ernest Brenton Altekruse, Dec. 17, 1950; children—Michael, Philip, Clifford, Lisa, Janice, Charles, Sean, Sam, Patrick. Med. officer USPHS, San Francisco, Boston, 1960-64; asst. health officer Fla. Bd. Health, 1964-65; med. officer, cons. Calif. Dept. Pub. Health, 1966-69; with dept. community psychiatry U. Heidelberg (W. Ger.), 1970-72; med. dir. Fla. Dept. Health and Rehab. Services, 1972-75; chmn. health adminstrn. U. S.C. Sch. Pub. Health, Columbia, 1975-77, prof., chmn. dept. preventive medicine and community health, 1979—. Mem. bd. Vol. Health Agys., S.C. Heart Assn., S.C. March of Dimes, Democratic Leadership Conf. S.C.; mem. S.C.-Am. Council Edn. Council for Women in Health Edn. Adminstrn. Served with USMC, 1949-51; with USPHS, 1960-64. Recipient Disting. Vol. award March of Dimes, certificate of merit Heart Assn.; World Health fellow, 1974; USPHS fellow, 1964, 67-69. Mem. Am. Pub. Health Assn., Am. Coll. Preventive Medicine, Assn. Tchrs. Preventive Medicine (dir.), Pub. Health Polit. Action Com. Democrat. Roman Catholic. Home: 3918 W Buchanan Dr Columbia SC 29206 Office: Dept Preventive Medicine and Community Health Sch Medicine U SC Columbia SC 29208

ALTENHAUS, AMY LOUISE, psychologist; b. N.Y.C., July 7, 1950; d. Julian Leroi and Corrinne (Batlin) A.; B.A. with honors, U. Wis., Madison, 1972; M.S., Rutgers U., 1977, Ph.D., 1978. Therapist, researcher U. Wis. Superior Student Lab., Madison, Wis., 1972-73; clin. psychology intern Family Service and Child Guidance Center, Orange, N.J., 1975-76; grad. asst. Rutgers U. Coll. Counseling Center, New Brunswick, N.J., 1976-77, psychologist, dir. Crisis Center, supervising psychologist, 1977-80; dir. adolescent pregnancy project Jersey Shore Med. Center, Neptune, N.J., 1980—, chief psychologist, 1981—; pvt. practice, Freehold, N.J., 1980—; outpatient dept. psychologist Freehold Area Hosp., 1980—; mem. adv. bd. Acad. Rev., N.Y.C., 1980—; cons. dept. ob-gyn. Mt. Sinai Med. Sch., N.Y.C., 1978—; field supr., joint appointment Grad. Sch. Applied and Profl. Psychology, New Brunswick, 1978—. NSF fellow, 1974-75. Mem. Am. Psychol. Assn. (co-chmn. task force on clin. psychology and competent female behavior 1981—), Am. Women in Psychology (former mem. admissions com. Grad. Sch. Applied and Profl. Psychology), N.J. Psychol. Assn., N.Y. Acad. Sci. Nat. Register Health Service Providers in Psychology. Office: Jersey Shore Med Center Community Mental Health Center 1945 Corlies Ave Neptune NJ 07753

ALTENHAUS, CORRINNE BATLIN (MRS. JULIAN ALTENHAUS), psychologist; b. N.Y.C., July 27, 1926; d. Louis and Rose (Cuttler) Batlin; B.S., Purdue U., 1946; M.Ed., Rutgers U., 1955, Ed.D., 1964; postdoctorate certificate in child psychiatry and child guidance (postdoctorate fellow), Postgrad. Center Mental Health, N.Y.C., 1971; m. Julian Altenhaus, Nov. 27, 1947; 1 dau., Amy Louise. Sch. psychologist Orange (N.J.) Bd. Edn., 1951-64, Millburn (N.J.) Bd. Edn., 1964-67; pvt. practice as psychologist, Millburn, 1967—. Coadj. staff Rutgers U., 1964-65, Newark State Coll., 1965-68, Seton Hall U., 1969-70; psychologist Stevens Inst. Tech. Psychol. Lab., 1965-68; faculty Postgrad. Center Mental Health, N.Y.C., 1972-75. Mem. profl. adv. bd. Children's Inst., 1973—. Trustee Child Guidance Clinic Oranges and Maplewood, N.J., 1961-69. Diplomate Am. Bd. Psychol. Examiners in Sch. Psychology. Fellow Am. Orth-Psychiat. Assn.; mem. Am., N.J. (mem.-at-large exec. bd. 1977-79), Essex County (pres. 1976—, trustee) psychol. assns., Kappa Delta Pi, Phi Delta Kappa. Home: 49 Claremont Dr Maplewood NJ 07040 Office: 120 Millburn Ave Millburn NJ 07041

ALTER, ESTELLE, psychiat. social worker; b. Bklyn.; d. Morris and Mollie (Sturm) Scheinberg; B.A. magna cum laude, Bklyn. Coll., 1966; M.S.W., Yeshiva U., 1976; postgrad. Columbia U. Lectr., book reviewer, 1955—; psychiat. social worker Creedmoor Psychiat. Center, 1976-79, Rockland Psychiat. Center, Orangeburg, N.Y., 1979-81; social work supr. Manhattan Psychiat. Center, 1981—; TV host-producer program Stimulus—The Psychol. Aspects of—, 1978—. Chmn. young profls. com. United Jewish Appeal, 1978. Mem. Nat. Assn. Social Welfare, Nat. Acad. TV Arts and Scis., N.Y. Acad. Sci., Assn. Orthodox Jewish Scientists. Club: B'nai B'rith (v.p. programming). Office: Manhattan Psychiat Center Wards Island NY

ALTER, MARIA POSPISCHIL, educator; b. Vienna, Austria; d. Karl M. and Ludmilla (von Adamovic) Pospischil; came to U.S., 1947, naturalized, 1949; B.A., U. Okla., 1948, M.A., 1950; Ph.D., U. Md., 1961; m. 1956 (div. 1977); children—Assunta, Sylvia, Nora. Mem. faculty Howard U., Washington, 1955-66, Case Western Res. U., Cleve., 1966-69; academic cons. Am. Assn. Tchrs. German, Phila., 1969-73; asso. prof. German, Villanova (Pa.) U., 1974-82, prof., 1982—. Mem. Am. Assn. Tchrs. German, AAUP, MLA, Northeastern, Phila. Area modern lang. assns., Lessing Soc., Internat. Arthur Schnitzler Research Assn. (jour.). Author: The Role of the Physician in the Works of Arthur Schnitzler and Hans Carossa, 1971; contbr. articles to profl. jours. Office: Dept Modern Langs Villanova Univ Villanova PA 19085

ALTHAUS, BARBARA DONALSON, furniture co. owner, Realtor; b. Fort Worth, Mar. 20, 1937; d. Thomas Kyle and Lucille (Martin) Donalson; student U. Tex., 1955-57; m. Dudley Nolin Althaus, Dec. 25, 1969. Legal exec. sec. firm McCully & Christensen, Houston, 1959-64; office mgr. H.A. Bornefeld, Jr., Houston, 1964-69; owner, mgr. Althaus Acres Realtors and Auctioneers, Inc., Fredericksburg, Tex., 1969—, Althaus Acres Furniture, Fredericksburg, 1979—; asso. Nixon Real Estate Co., Fredericksburg, 1978-81. Chmn. Damenfest, 1977; pres. Tex. Auctioneers Assn. Aux., 1977, pres., 1981-82. Mem. Nat. Auctioneers Assn. Aux., Tex. Auctioneers Assn. Aux., Southwest Home Furnishing Assn., Tex. Assn. Realtors, Gillespie County Bd. Realtors, DAR (organizing regent 1974-76, state chmn. jr. Am. citizens 1976-79, registrar 1980-82), Daus. Am. Colonists (state chmn. colonial heritage 1981-83), Fredericksburg C. of C. (ambassador 1980—), Daus. of Republic Tex., Alpha Phi. Democrat. Methodist. Home: 319 Broadmoor St Fredericksburg TX 78624 Office: PO Box 312 1906 N Llano St Fredericksburg TX 78624

ALTHOLZ, MARIA CRISTINA, interior designer; b. Barranquilla, Colombia, Jan. 23, 1946; came to U.S., naturalized, 1969; d. Heriberto and Maria Cristina Pabon; Bachelor, U. Javeriana, Bogota, Colombia, 1967; student (Inst. scholar) Internat. Inst. Interior Designers, Washington, 1969-70; children—Andrew Kristian, Roxanna Marie. Draftsman, designer Muebles Flamingo, Barranquilla, 1967-69, Ray Bates Assos., Washington, 1969-70, Evelyn Mayer's Interiors, Chgo., 1970-71, Robert Kingsley Industries, Johannesburg, South Africa, 1971-74; partner, designer Ambiente Interiors, Houston, 1974-78; pres., designer, owner Pabon Designs, Dallas, 1978—. Recipient thesis merit award U. Javeriana, 1967. Mem. Am. Soc. Interior Designers (profl.). Roman Catholic. Home and office: 226 Woodcrest Richardson TX 75080

ALTHOUSE, MARTHA, savs. and loan assn. exec.; b. Orangeburg, S.C., Apr. 6, 1943; d. Woodrow Elie and Pearl (Wall) Rudd; student Patricia Stevens Finishing Coll., 1961-62, U. N.C., 1965-67, Foot Hill Coll., 1971-72; 1 dau., Robin Marie. With Chevy Chase Savs. and Loan, Inc. (Md.), 1972—, v.p., controller, 1977—; sec.-treas. Glade Drive Devel. Co., North Ode Street Devel. Co., 1981—; asst. sec. Manor Investment Co. Mem. Fin. Mgrs. Soc. Savs. Instns. (editor chpt. newsletters. chmn. chpt. coms., nat. award of excellence 1977-78, treas. 1981-82), Nat. Savs. and Loan League, Md. Savs. and Loan League, Women's Network, Republican. Club: Jr. Women's. Home: 5713 Magic Mountain Dr North Bethesda MD 20852 Office: 8401 Connecticut Ave Chevy Chase MD 20015

ALTIERI, JEANNETTE CORVINO, acct.; b. Bridgeport, Conn., May 8, 1937; d. Christopher C. and Julia Marie (Carbonara) Corvino; student U. New Haven, 1975, Air Traffic Cont. Sch., 1976; m. Mario Dominic Altieri, Mar. 29, 1954; children—Jeanmarie, Michael, Lisa Ann, John Christopher. Office mgr. Sportmen Accessories, Inc., Bridgeport, Conn., 1972-76; office mgr. New Haven Travel Service, Inc. (Conn.), 1976-79; sr. acct. Warnaco Outlet Stores, Inc., Bridgeport, 1979—. Exec. adviser Jr. Achievement, 1980—. Mem. Nat. Assn. Female Execs., Am. Soc. Profl. and Exec. Women. Home: 43 Bunting Rd Seymour CT 06483 Office: 325 Lafayette St Bridgeport CT 06602

ALTIZER, BARBARA FARMER, assn. exec.; b. Dickenson County, Va., Mar. 14; d. Clarence Edward and Helen Irene (Ratcliffe) Farmer; A.A.S., S.W. Va. Community Coll., 1970; 1 son, Richard B. With Richlands (Va.) Area C. of C., 1971—, exec. v.p., 1974—, exec. dir. Va. Coal Council, 1979—. Recipient gov.'s cert. of recognition Commonwealth of Va., 1980; Dist. Service award Cumberland Plateau Planning Commn., Lebanon, Va., 1980. Mem. Va. C. of C., Va. C. of C. Execs., U.S. C. of C. Presbyterian. Address: 2418 2d St Richlands VA 24641

ALTMAN, CYNTHIA BETCHEN, pharm. co. exec., psychiatrist; b. Bryn Mawr, Pa., May 19, 1954; d. Robert H. and Carole Joy (Betchen) Altman; research student Hahnemann Med. Coll., 1971-72; B.S. with distinction, Pa. State U.-Jefferson Med. Coll., 1975, M.D., 1977. Intern, internal medicine Crozer-Chester Med. Center, Upland, Pa., 1977-78; resident in psychiatry U. Pa., Phila., 1978-79; asso. dir. clin. investigation, research and devel. SmithKline Beckman Corp., Phila., 1979-82, dir. project mgmt. and strategic planning, 1982—; instr. dept. psychiatry and human behavior Jefferson Med. Coll., Phila., 1980—, vol. faculty, 1974—. Bd. Affiliates for doctoral tng. program in teratology. Recipient Smith Kline Research and Devel. award, 19 ; diplomate Nat. Bd. Med. Examiners. Mem. Am. Soc. for Clin. Pharm. and Therapeutics, Histamine Research Soc. of N. Am., Fed. of State Med. Bds., Am. Acad. Med. Dirs., AMA, Am. Med. Women's Assn., Am. Heart Assn. (council on clin. cardiology and laennec CV sound Soc.), Am. Psychol. Assn., Am. Assn. of Psychiat. Adminstrs., Am. Coll. Neuropsychopharm., Soc. for Clin. Trials, Drug Info. Assn., Project Mgmt. Internat., J. Marion Sims Ob-Gyn Soc., Hobart Amory Hare Honor Med. Soc., Fedn. of Jewish Agys. (LDC cabinet, Young Physicians, com. on health services, commn. on aging, co-chmn. LDC membership), Alumni Assn. of Jefferson Med. Coll. (exec. council). Contbr. articles in field of medicine to profl. jours. Office: Smith Kline Beckman Corp 1500 Spring Garden St Philadelphia PA 19101

ALTMAN, CYNTHIA CAROLINE, psychotherapist; b. Greensburg, Pa., Dec. 27, 1951; d. George W. and Amelia Marlene (Svesnik) A.; B.A. in Psychology, Carlow Coll., 1973; M.Ed., U. Pitts., 1974. Researcher, Vocat. Rehab. Center, Pitts., 1973; counselor Psychol. Assos., Greensburg, Pa., 1978-79; child psychotherapist Westmoreland Hosp. Community Mental Health Center, Greensburg, 1975—. Bd. dirs. Westmoreland County chpt. March of Dimes; adv. bd. Mt. Aloysius Jr. Coll. Mem. Am. Psychol. Assn., AAUW. Clubs: Westmoreland County Coll., Pilot Internat. Home: 1611 Clay Pike North Huntingdon PA 15642 Office: 532 W Pittsburgh St Greensburg PA 15601

ALTMAN, JEAN, jewelry mfg. co. exec.; b. N.Y.C., Mar. 24, 1928; d. Rubin and Molly (Itzkowitz) Weiner; student public schs., also specialized courses; m. A. Arthur Altman, June 24, 1950; children—Marlene Ann, Mitchell Kevin, Risa Faith. Co-founder, v.p., Ct. of King Arthur, N.Y.C., designer, 1961—. ORT scholar, 1977-81. Mem. Fashion Group, Jewelers Bd. Trade, Jewelry Industry Council, Mfg. Jewelers and Silversmith Am., Jewelry Inst., Jewelry Casters Assn., Jewelers Security Alliance, Fashion Group. Liberal. Jewish. Home: 65-41 Wetherole St Forest Hills NY 11374 Office: 15 W 28th St New York NY 10001

ALTMAN, MARY ANN, mgmt. cons.; b. Honesdale, Pa., May 31, 1930; d. James Thomas and Uvinza (Dailey) Spence; B.A., Dickinson Coll., 1951; J.D., Dickinson Sch. Law, 1954; 1 son, Thomas Knox. Admitted to Pa. bar, 1954; practiced in Harrisburg, Pa. and Phila., 1955-60; mgmt. cons. for attys. Daniel J. Cantor & Co., Phila., 1960-70; mgmt. cons. Altman & Weil, Inc., Ardmore, Pa., 1970-82, pres., 1970—. Pres., Narberth Civic Assn., 1974-75. Mem. Assn. Legal Adminstrs. (life), ABA, Pa. Bar Assn., Phila. Bar Assn., Mensa. Republican. Episcopalian. Author: (with Robert I. Weil) How To Manage Your Law Office, 1972; Managing Your Accounting and Consulting Practice, 1976; Introduction to Law Practice Management, 1981. Office: 600 Haverford Rd Haverford PA 19041

ALTON, ANN LESLIE, lawyer; b. Pipestone, Minn., Sept. 10, 1945; d. Howard Robert and Camilla Ann (DeMong) Alton, Jr.; B.A., Smith Coll., 1967; J.D., U. Minn., 1970; m. Gerald Russell Freeman. Admitted to Minn. bar, 1970; asst. county atty., Hennepin County, Mpls., 1970—, felony prosecutor, criminal div., 1970-75, acting chief citizens protection div., 1975-76, chief citizen protection, econ. crime div., 1976-79, chief econ. crime unit, 1979—; instr. Hamline U. Law Sch., St. Paul, 1973-76; adj. prof. law William Mitchell Coll. Law, St. Paul, 1977—; adj. prof. law U. Minn. Law Sch., Mpls., 1978—; lectr. in field, 1970—; vice. chmn. bd. dirs. Minn. Program on Victims of Sexual Assault, 1974-76; bd. dirs. Physician's Health Plan, Health Maintenance Orgn., 1976-80, exec. com. 1977-80; mem. legal drug abuse subcom. Gov. Minn. Adv. Com. Drug Abuse, 1972-74; chmn. corp. policy task force Hennepin County Med. Soc. Child Abuse Project Coordinating Com., 1982—. Mem. Am., Minn. (criminal law sect.), Hennepin County (ethics com. 1973-76, criminal law com. 1973—, co-vice chmn. 1979-81, unauthorized practice law com. 1977-78, individual rights and responsibilities com. 1977-78) bar assns., Nat. Dist. Attys. Assn., Minn. County Attys. Assn., Minn. Trial Lawyers Assn., Am. Judicature Soc., Minn. Women Lawyers, U. Minn. Law Sch. Law Alumni Assn. (dir. 1979—). Mem. Democratic-Farmer-Labor Party. Author articles, pamphlet, manual. Home: 2105 Xanthus Ln Plymouth MN 55447 Office: 2000 Hennepin County Govt Center Minneapolis MN 55487

ALTOPIEDI, ALICE E., social worker; b. Cairo; d. Mark Rembouli and Mary (Copsahili) Rembouli; came to U.S., 1962, naturalized, 1970, came to Can., 1971; M.S.W. (Fulbright scholar), U. Pa., 1964; m. Joseph Altopiedi, Jan. 16, 1965; 1 dau., Roxanne. Supr. social worker Spring Grove State Hosp., Balt., 1964-66, Prince George's County (Md.) Health Dept., 1968-70, Hosp. for Sick Children, Toronto, Ont., Can., 1971-72; sr. social worker Toronto Bd. Edn., Ont., 1972-73; chief social worker Peel Meml. Hosp., Brampton, Ont., 1973-81; pvt. practice social work, Etobicoke, Ont., 1981—; field instr. U. Toronto Sch. Social Work, U. Pa., U. N.C., U. W.Va., Carleton U. Sch. Social Work, 1979—. Mem. admissions com. U. Toronto. Mem. Nat. Assn. Social Workers, U.S. Acad. Cert. Social Workers, Ont. Assn. Profl. Social Workers, Assn. Field Practice Educators (exec. com.). Greek Orthodox. Home and Office: 296 Mill Rd Apt C16 Etobicoke ON M9C 4X8 Canada

ALTSCHULER, JOANNE, clin. social worker; b. London, Sept. 10, 1949; came to U.S., 1950, naturalized, 1966; d. Leo Altschuler and Deborah Potak; A.B. magna cum laude in French, Ind. U., 1971; M.S.W., U. So. Calif., 1975; M.Jewish Communal Studies, Hebrew Union Coll., 1975. Psychiat. social worker Jewish Home for Aged, San Francisco, 1971-73; community organizer/psychiat. social worker Jewish Family Service, Los Angeles, 1975-77; caseworker/psychiat. social worker Freda Mohr Multiservice Center for Sr. Citizens, Los Angeles, 1977-80, psychiat. social worker, 1981—; casework supr. HEW grant project Jewish Family Service, Los Angeles, 1980-81, staff cons. to Com. on Aging, 1978-80; social work preceptor Freda Mohr Health Clinic, Los Angeles, 1981—; pvt. practice social work, 1981—. Founding organizer Listening Line, Bloomington, Ind., 1970-71; founding mem. Fairfax Community Food Co-op, 1977—. Recipient Walter S. Hilborn award for social service, 1975; Gen. Motors scholar, 1968-71, others; lic. clin. social worker, Calif. Mem. Nat. Assn. Social Workers, Acad. Cert. Social Workers, Soc. Clin. Social Work, Jewish Resources Inc. (dir. 1975—), Amnesty Internat., Alliance for Survival, Natural Resources Def. Council, Hebrew Union Coll. Alumni Assn. (treas. 1979-80), Phi Beta Kappa. Author: The Jewish Family: Past, Present and Future, 1979. Home: 839 Palms Blvd Venice CA 90291 Office: 351 N Fairfax Ave Los Angeles CA 90036

ALVARADO, IRMA, educator, migrant counselor; b. TorreÓn, Mex., Dec. 17, 1946; came to U.S., 1957, naturalized, 1970; d. Ernesto and Socorro (García) Chapa; B.A. in Secondary Edn., Tex. A&M U., 1970; M.Ed., cert. in counseling, Pan Am. U., Edinburg, Tex., 1976, postgrad., 1973-74; m. Erasmo Alvarado, Jr., June 30, 1968; children—Yvette, Melissa, Erasmo Eli, Aaron John. Tchr. English as second lang. Donna (Tex.) Ind. Sch. Dist., 1970-72, migrant ednl. supr., 1978-79; dir. ednl. component Jobs for Progress, Inc., 1972-73, dir. ednl. and counseling component, 1973-74; home sch. counselor, community supr., 1974-77; office mgr., owner Idea Design Group, 1977-78; summer migrant recruiter, Mont., 1980; migrant elem. counselor, owner Alvarado's PreKinder-Day Care, Donna, 1979—. Counselor drug addicts, Vietnam vets. tchr. and reality therapy trainer; pres. Donna City Library Bd.; chmn. Mental Health Assn.; area vol. Cancer Soc.; del. Baptist Conv.; sec.-treas. dir. Women's Missionary Union; mem. parent adv. com. EESA; mem. task force Tex. Assessment Basic Skills. Named Disting. Student, Tex. A&M U., 1970; lic. cosmetologist, Tex.; cert. in teaching, counseling, bilingual occupational linguistic tng., essential mgmt. skills, Tex. Mem. Tex. Tchrs. Assn., Rio Grande Valley Personnel and Guidance Assn., Tex. Personnel and Guidance Assn., Valley Assn. Planning Evaluation and Research, Nat. Assn. Day Care Centers, Gideons Internat. (sec.-treas.). Founder, El Puente Sch. Newspaper, 1974. Home: 424 N 17th St Donna TX 78537 Office: 116 N 10th St Donna TX 78537

ALVARADO, VIOLET ELLEN, mfg. co. exec.; b. Midway, W.Va., Apr. 30, 1939; d. Ira Lee and Cassie Brooke (Cole) Garten; student No. Va. Community Coll., 1969-74, U. Md., 1970-73, El Camino Coll., 1977-78; B.S. in Mgmt., Pepperdine U., 1981; m. Archie R. Riley, Apr. 1, 1955 (dec. Nov. 1965); children—Mark R., Virginia E.; m. 2d, Gus Alvarado, Aug. 10, 1972 (div. May 1978). Lab aide Westinghouse Astro Electronics Co., Newberry Park, Calif., 1960-64; technician Tech. Mgmt. Corp., Burlingame, Calif., 1964-65, Hewlett Packard Co., Palo Alto, Calif., 1965-68, Microwave Assos., Sunnyvale, Calif., 1968-69; phys. sci. technician Naval Research Lab., Washington, 1969-76; electronics engr. TRW Semiconductors, Lawndale, Calif., 1976-78, mfg. mgr., 1978—. Pres., Women's Athletic Assn., Woodbridge, Va., 1972-75. Mem. Nat. Assn. Female Execs., Am. Vacuum Soc., Electronics Chem. Soc. Democrat. Contbr. articles to semiconductor jours. Office: 14520 Aviation Blvd Lawndale CA 90260

ALVARE, ANITA MARIE, public relations cons.; b. Phila., Dec. 31, 1952; d. Louis John and Rosemary Audrey (Cosgrove) A.; art student Rosemont Coll., 1970-71. With Certain Teed Corp., Valley Forge, Pa., 1972-81, asst. mgr. communications, 1976-78, public relations mgr., 1978-81; owner, pres. Alvare Assos., Wayne, Pa., 1981—. Republican. Roman Catholic. Club: Publicity. Home: 417 Strafford Ave Wayne PA 19087 Office: 322 E Lancaster Ave Wayne PA 19087

ALVAREZ, JOYE TOWNSEND, educator; b. Memphis, Nov. 28, 1938; d. Robert and Ehrma Townsend; B.A., Chgo. Conservatory Music, 1968; M.A. in Edn., Calif. State U., Los Angeles, 1977; M.S. in Edn., Calif. Lutheran Coll., 1980. Tchr. secondary edn. Los Angeles Unified Sch. Dist., 1970-74, 77-82; edn. specialist. Mem. Calif. State U. Sch. Edn. Alumni Assn., Alpha Delta Chi. Home: 8375 Fountain Ave Hollywood CA 90069

ALVAREZ, RAQUEL, physician; b. Sagua La Grande, Cuba, Nov. 23, 1928; d. Manuel E. and Adelaida (Santalis) Alvarez; came to U.S., 1970, naturalized, 1976; B.S. U. Havana, 1953, M.D., 1953; m. Orlando Arrom, Sept. 29, 1950; (div. Aug. 1966); children—Orlando, Carlos M., Raquel. Gen. practice medicine in Holquin ote, Cuba, 1953-70; intern Augustana Hosp., Chgo., 1972, resident in pathology, 1973; practice medicine specializing in family practice, Chgo., 1973—; mem. staffs Augustana, St. Mary of Nazareth, st. Elizabeth hosps., Chgo. Diplomate Am. Bd. Family Practice. Fellow Am. Acad. Family Physicians; mem. AMA, Ill., Chgo. med. socs., Am. Women's Med. Assn., Am. Acad. Family Practice, Cuban Med. Assn. in Exile. Presbyterian. Home: 9140 Keystone Skokie IL 60076 Office: St Elizabeth Profl Plaza 1431 N Western Suite 212 Chicago IL 60622

ALVAREZ, SYLVIA ELAINE, social worker; b. Atlanta, June 22; d. J.T. and Sylvia Hortense (Burdett) Freeman; B.A., Goddard Coll., 1962; M.S.W., N.Y. U., 1968. Staff psychotherapist Pacific Psychotherapy Assos., San Francisco, 1972-74, clin. dir., 1974-77; team leader Operation Outreach, VA, San Francisco, 1977—; cons. in field. Bd. dirs. Mental Health Bd. San Francisco, 1971, Suicide Prevention, 1974-75. Mem. Soc. Clin. Social Workers, Nat. Assn. Social Workers. Office: 616 16th St Oakland CA 94612

ALVAREZ-RIONDA, MERCEDES, advt. agy. exec.; b. Havana, Cuba, Sept. 24, 1942; came to U.S., 1960, naturalized, 1971; d. Jose Manuel and Teresita (Rionda) Alvarez; B.B.A., U. Miami (Fla.), 1963; postgrad. Manhattanville Coll., Purchase, N.Y., 1964. Sr. research exec. J. Walter Thompson Co., N.Y.C., 1966-78; v.p., research dir. Isidore, Lefkowitz, Elgort, N.Y.C., 1978-79, Bozell and Jacobs Inc., N.Y.C., 1979—. Mem. N.Y. Advt. Club. Republican. Roman Catholic. Address: 420 E 55th St New York NY 10022

ALVARIÑO DE LEIRA, ANGELES (ANGELES ALVARIÑO), biologist, oceanographer; b. El Ferrol, Spain, Oct. 3, 1916; came to U.S., 1958, naturalized, 1966; d. Antonio Alvariño-Grimaldos and Carmen Gonzalez Díaz-Saavedra; B.S. and Letters summa cum laude, U. Santiago de Compostela, Spain, 1933; M. Natural Scis., U. Madrid, 1941, cert. Doctorate, 1951, Ph.D. summa cum laude, 1967; Biologist-Oceanographer, Spanish Inst. Oceanography, 1952; m. Eugenio Leira-Manso, Mar. 16, 1940; 1 dau., Angeles. Prof. biology Coll. El Ferrol, Spain, 1941-48; fishery research biologist dept. Sea Fisheries Spain, 1948-52; histologist Superior Council Sci. Research, 1948-52; biologist, oceanographer Spanish Inst. Oceanography, 1950-57; biologist Scripps Inst. Oceanography, U. Calif., La Jolla, 1958-69; fishery research biologist Nat. Marine Fisheries Service Southwest Fisheries Center, NOAA, U.S. Dept. Commerce, La Jolla, 1970—; asso. prof. U. Nat. Autonomous Mexico; research asso. San Diego State U. Brit. Council fellow, 1953-54; Fulbright fellow, 1956-57; NSF grantee, 1961-69; U.S. Office Navy grantee; 1958-69, Calif. Coop. Oceanic Fishery Investigation grantee, 1958-69; UNESCO grantee, 1979. Fellow Am. Inst. Fishery Research Biologists, San Diego Soc. Natural History; mem. Assn. Natural History Soc., Western Naturalists Soc., Calif. Acad. Scis., Biol. Soc. Washington, Hispano-Am. Assn. Researchers on Marine Scis., Marine Biol. Assn. U.K., Sigma Xi. Contbr. articles to profl. jours., chpts. to sci. books. Discovered 14 new species of animals. Home: 7535 Cabrillo Ave La Jolla CA 92037 Office: PO Box 271 La Jolla CA 92038

ALVERS, LINDA KAY, nursing bus. exec.; b. Evansville, Ind., June 26, 1952; d. Henry N. and Marian H. (Clark) Alvers; B.S. in Nursing, U. Evansville, 1974, M. in Nursing Sci., 1979. Staff nurse Vanderbilt Med. Center, Nashville, 1974-75, St. Mary's Hosp., Evansville, 1975-77, dir. pediatric intravenous therapy, 1977-79; instr. U. Evansville Sch. Nursing, 1977-79; v.p. and dir. continuing med. edn. Audio Transcripts, N.Y.C., 1978-81; founder, pres. Nat. Nursing Network, Inc., N.Y.C., 1981—; adj. prof. U. Evansville, 1979—; instr. ARC, 1978—. Recipient Outstanding Instr. award U. Evansville Sch. Nursing, 1979, Nat. Alumni Achievement award U. Evansville, 1980. Mem. Am. Nurses Assn., N.Y. State Nurses Assn., Nat. Assn. Female Execs., NOW, N.Y. State Nurses for Polit. Action, Women Bus. Owners N.Y. Club: Fortune 500. Editorial bd. Infusion mag., 1978—. Home: 225 Central Park West New York NY 10024 Office: 250 W 57th St Suite 224 New York NY 10107

AMADEO, JOAN CHERIÉ, boxing safety products co. exec.; b. Waterloo, Iowa, Mar. 17, 1935; adopt dau. Eldo Ernest and Vera (Sullivan) Kluss; ed. San Jose State Coll., Am. Coll.; student pension adminstrn. Loyola U. Sch. Law; m. James Michael Amadeo, May 4, 1952; children—Maureen Michelle, Karen Kathleen, Jaime Joan, John James, Gerard Samuel. Legal asst. firm Owen Cunningham, 1962-67; dir. compliance Am. Republic Assurance Co., 1967-76; asst. v.p. claims, compliance dir. Guardsman Life Ins. Co., 1977-80; v.p. ins. ops. Meredith Corp., Des Moines, 1981—, also chmn. bd., chief exec. officer A-Plus Athletic Corp., 1981—. Team leader United Way Services, 1981; mem. Iowa Commn. for Women. Profl. legal sec.; registered prin. Nat. Assn. Securities Dealers; C.L.U. Mem. Am. Soc. C.L.U.s (chmn. Heubner edn. com. Des Moines chpt.), Nat. Assn. Legal Assts. (co-author Pub. Relations Handbook, seminar leader ann. meeting), Soc. Group Contract Analysts, U.S.A. Amateur Boxing Fedn. (mktg. com., safety edn. com.). Roman Catholic. Past editor Legal Affairs and Iowa LS Profile. Home: 821 23d St West Des Moines IA 50265

AMARA, LUCINE, opera and concert singer; b. Hartford, Conn., Mar. 1, 1927; d. George and Adrine (Kazanjian) Armaganian; student Music Acad. of West, 1947, U. So. Calif., 1949-50; m. Jan. 7, 1961 (div. June 1964). Appeared in Hollywood Bowl, 1948; soloist with San Francisco Symphony, 1949-50; with Met. Opera, N.Y.C., 1950—; recorded Pagliacci, 1951, 60; singer with Hartford, Pitts., Central City, New Orleans operas, 1952-54; appeared Glyndebourne Opera, 1954, 55, 57, 58, Edinburgh Festival, 1954; singer Aida, Terme Di Caracalla, Rome, 1954, also Stockholm Opera, N.Y. Philharm., St. Louis Civic Light Opera, 1955-56; has appeared in leading or title roles in several operas including Otello, Carmen, Don Giovanni, Il Trovatore, Tosca; appeared in title role of Turandot with Toledo and Dayton Opera Cos., 1979, with Stamford Opera Co., 1981; sang title role of Aida with Seattle Opera Co., 1980; sang role of Amelia in Un Ballo in Maschera, Met. Opera, N.Y.C., 1981; appeared with St. Petersburg (Fla.) Opera in title role of Tosca, 1981; appeared Vienna, Stuttgart Stattsopers; opera and concert tour, Russia, 1965; concert, Manila, 1968; tours, Paris, 1966, Mex., 1966, Far East, 1968; rec. artist Columbia, RCA Victor, Met. Opera Record Club, Angel. Recipient 1st prize Atwater-Kent Radio auditions, 1948. Mem. Sigma Alpha Iota. Home: 260 West End Ave New York NY 10023 Office: Metropolitan Opera New York NY 10023 *

AMATO, DOLORES ROSE, reading cons.; b. Newark, Nov. 7, 1941; d. Amelio and Carmela Amato; B.A., Caldwell Coll., 1963; M.A. in Reading, Keane State Coll., N.J., 1966; postgrad. Tex. So. U., 1976-78. Elem. sch. tchr., Parsippany, N.J., 1963-66; nat. reading cons. Harcourt Brace-Jovanovich, N.Y.C., 1966-72; dir. reading K-12, Houston Ind. Sch. Dist., 1972-79; nat. reading cons. and author, Houston, 1979—. Recipient Outstanding Educator award Nat. Soc. Creative Intelligence, 1975. Mem. Internat. Reading Assn., Am. Bus. Women's Assn., Assn. Supervision and Curriculum Devel. Author: Frost Reading and Math Program, 1979; Economy Spanish Reading Keys Basal Readers, 1978, 79; Enrich Comprehension Reading Series Books, 1981-82; contbg. author: Reading Basics Plus, 1976, 80. Address: 1 Wind Poppy Ct The Woodlands TX 77381

AMATO, ROSEMARY MARCELLA, electric co. exec.; b. Cleve., May 17, 1952; d. Sam Anthony and Elizabeth Barbara (Cherney) A.; B.S.B.A., John Carroll U., 1974; postgrad. Ga. State U., 1976, Samford U., 1981. Asst. to controller Mr. Coffee, Cleve., 1973-75; staff acct. Luria Bros., Cleve., 1975-76; capital acctg. mgr. Reliance Electric Co., Cleve., 1976-77, cost acct., Gainesville, Ga., 1977-79, modernization controller, Cleve., 1979-80, regional controller, Birmingham, Ala., 1980—. Mem. AAUW, Nat. Assn. Female Execs., Nat. Assn. Accts. Republican. Roman Catholic. Office: 3100 Pinson Valley Pkwy Birmingham AL 35217

AMBARDAR, VEENA, educator; b. Kashmir, India, June 23, 1950; came to U.S., 1979; d. Shankar Nath and Jay (Kishori) Kaul; B.S. with honors, U. Delhi, 1969, M.S., 1971; Ph.D., Indian Inst. Tech., 1975; m. Om P. Ambardar, Feb. 15, 1976; 1 child, Sheenie Ambardar. Lectr. dept. math. Indian Inst. Tech., Kharagpur, 1976-77; sr. sci. officer Heat Transfer & Fluid Flow Group, Research & Devel. Div., Bharat Heavy Elec. Ltd., India, 1977-79; sr. mem. tech. staff Computer Sci. Corp., Pitts., 1980; asst. prof. dept. math. U. South Fla., Tampa, 1980-81, asst. prof. of computer sci., dept. computer sci. div. natural sci., 1981—; lectr. in field; cons. in field. Council of Sci. and Indsl. Research postdoctoral fellow, 1975-76, sr. research fellow, 1974-75, jr. research fellow, 1972-74; Indian Inst. Tech. research fellow, 1971-72; Internat. Shankar's Painting award, 1966. Mem. IEEE, Assn. for Computing Machinery. Contbr. articles to profl. jours. Home: 8431 Wakulla Dr Tampa FL 33617 Office: Dept Computer Sci Div Natural Sci New Coll Univ S Fla Sarasota FL 33580

AMBERSON, MARGARET ELIZABETH, educator, dean; b. Rome, Ga., May 6, 1918; d. Hampton Brewster and Nancy (Miller) A.; A.B., Shorter Coll., 1939; postgrad. Emory U., 1952; M.Ed., U. Ga., 1956. Tchr. French and English, Rome City Schs., 1939-61; tchr. French, counselor, dean students Thornwood Sch., Rome, 1961-73; tchr. French, dean of women, counselor Darlington Sch., Rome, 1973—. Participant in local fund drives. Recipient Star Tchr. award Ga. C. of C., 1965. Cert. tchr., counselor, Ga. Mem. Am. Assn. Tchrs. French, Nat. Assn. Women Deans and Counselors, Ga. Assn. Counselors, AAUW, Shorter Coll. Alumnae Assn., Delta Kappa Gamma (chpt. pres. 1958-60, state welfare chmn. 1956-58). Presbyterian. Home: 329 E 11th St Rome GA 30161 Office: Darlington School Cave Spring Rd Rome GA 30161

AMBEWADIKAR, JAYMALA VILAS, physician; b. Bombay, India, July 29, 1945; came to U.S., 1973; d. Vasudeo Govind and Malattibai Vasudeo Joshi; I.Sc., Jai Hind Coll. Arts and Sci., Bombay; M.B., B.S., U. Bombay; m. Vilas Ganesh Ambenwadikar, Nov. 22, 1972; children—Samrat Vilas, Rashmi Vilas. Intern, resident in medicine Lohmanya Tilak Hosp., Bombay; house physician St. Barnabas Med. Center, Bronx, N.Y., 1974-75; resident in internal medicine Kingsbrook Jewish Med. Center, N.Y.C., 1975-76, Beekman Downtown Hosp., N.Y.C., 1977-78, Meth. Hosp., 1978-79; fellow in hematology Cabrini Med. Center, 1979-80; med. cons., inpatient coordinator Greenpoint Hosp., 1980; practice medicine specializing in internal medicine, S.I., N.Y., 1981—; assoc. physician N.Y. State Dept. Civil Services, 1981—; physician Bayley Seaton Hosp., 1981-82. Mem. N.Y. State Med. Soc., Richmond County Med. Soc., N.Y. Vets. Police Assn. Hindu. Home: 27 Victoria Rd Staten Island NY 10312 Office: 4056 Amboy Rd Staten Island NY 10308

AMBLER, ALDONNA RICKMERS, mgmt. cons. and trainer; b. Salamanca, N.Y.; d. Albert Donald and Zelda Ruth (Cutlip) Rickmers; B.S. summa cum laude in Elem. Edn., Trenton (N.J.) State Coll., 1974; M.S.W., U. Pa., 1976; m. Chester William Ambler, III, Aug. 21, 1971. Self-employed singer/songwriter, 1962-70; quality control reviewer N.J. Dept. Welfare, 1972-73; elem. sch. tchr., N.J., 1973-74; sch. social worker, Pine Hill, N.J., 1974-75; edn. specialist Family Maintenance Orgn., Phila., 1975-76; community cons. specialist, then mental health cons. N.E. Community Mental Health Center, Phila., 1976-78; dir. cons. and edn. services Family Service Assn. Atlantic County, N.J., 1978-79; co-owner, prin. Ambler and Overholt Cons., Inc., human resource devel., Riverton, N.J., 1979—. Bd. dirs. N.E. br. Phila. YWCA, 1978—, chmn. personnel com., 1979, v.p., 1980. Mem. Acad. Cert. Social Workers, Nat. Assn. Social Workers, Am. Soc. Tng. and Devel., AAUW, Assn. Mgmt. Cons., Greater Phila. C. of C. Home: 67 S Poplar Ave Maple Shade NJ 08052 Office: AOC Inc 414 Main St Riverton NJ 08077

AMICK, CAROL CAMPBELL, state legislator; b. Cleve., June 17, 1945; d. Charles Lorayne and Janet Robertson Gilchrist (Campbell) Amick; B.S., Iowa State U., 1968; M.P.A., Harvard U., 1981; m. William Stevenson Moonan. Reporter radio-TV news WOI-AM-FM-TV, Ames, Iowa, 1967-68; asst. editor Belmont (Mass.) Citizen, 1968-69; reporter-announcer WCAS Radio, Cambridge, Mass., 1968-69; editor Minute-Man, Bedford, Mass., 1969-74; mem. Mass. Ho. of Reps., Boston, 1974-77, Mass. Senate, 1977—. Journalism instr. night sch. Middlesex Community Coll., 1972, adviser student newspaper, 1973; project coordinator photography class Concord (Mass.) Prison, 1972-73; journalism lectr. Bedford public schs., 1969—. Mem. Charter Commn., Bedford, 1973-74; mem. Opportunities Industrialization Center, Inc., 1972, Friends of Bedford Library, 1973—; insp. wood, bark, and manure Town of Bedford, 1972-75, mem. publs. com., 1972-74; mem. Nat. Conf. State Legislatures, 1975—; community cabinet dir. United Way, 1973. Mem. Bedford Democratic Town Com., 1972—; trustee Bedford Public Library, 1976-78; bd. dirs. Mental Health Assn. Central Middlesex, 1976-78; chmn. Legis. Water Study Commn., 1977—, Legis. Com. on Natural Resources and Agr., 1978—; mem. Mass. Caucus Women Legislators, 1975—. Recipient Reporting award New Eng. Press Assn., 1970; Outstanding Woman in Govt. award Nat. Jaycee Women, 1981. Mem. Women in Communications, Bedford LWV, Alpha Lambda Delta, Sigma Kappa. Mem. Ch. of Christ. Home: 18 Crescent Ave Bedford MA 01730 Office: State House Boston MA 02133

AMIDON, ELIZABETH ANNE, med. device mfg. co. exec.; b. Somerville, Mass., Dec. 18, 1950; d. George Silas and Margaret (Falvey) A.; A.A., Santa Barbara City Coll., 1973; student (NSF grantee) Stanford U., summer 1974; B.A. in Biology, U. Calif., Santa Cruz, 1976. Research asst. U. Calif., Santa Cruz, 1973-75; teaching asst. in botany Santa Barbara City Coll., 1975-76; sterilization supr. McGhan Med. Corp., Santa Barbara, 1976-77, quality assurance auditor, 1977-78; mktg. supr. Cox-Uphoff Internat., Santa Barbara, 1979-80; procurement quality assurance supr. Am. Heyer-Schulte Corp., Goleta, Calif., 1980—, mem. pres.'s sci. and engrng. adv. council, 1981—. Mem. Am. Soc. Quality Control, Nat. Assn. Female Execs., South Coast Bus. Network. Home: 1618-B Chino St Santa Barbara CA 93101 Office: 600 Pine Ave Goleta CA 93017

AMIDZICH, GAIL M., legis. asst.; b. Milw., May 3, 1950; d. Lawrence and Rita Marie (St. Clair) Amidzich; B.A., Marquette U., 1972; M.A., Am. U., 1977; Press asst. Muskie for Pres. campaign, 1972; advt. copywriter Gimbels Midwest, 1973-74; corr. Women's Almanac, 1974; now legis. asst. to Rep. Zablocki (Wis.), Washington. Mem. Wis. State Soc., Marquette U. Alumni Assn., Capitol Hill Women's Polit. Caucus, Assn. House Democratic Press Assts. Club: Arlington County Women's Soccer League. Office: Room 2183 Rayburn House Office Bldg Washington DC 20515 *

AMINZADEH, LYNN THERESE, computer co. exec.; b. Washington, Jan. 5, 1953; d. Thomas Andrew and Margaret Mary (Dimond) Wilkinson; student public schs., Rockville, Md.; m. Mansour Aminzadeh, Jan. 5, 1973; 1 dau., Rana Christine. Adminstrv. asst. Best Products Co., Rockville, 1970-72; acctg. supr. Dreyfuss Brothers, Bethesda, Md., 1972-75, Iran, 1975-76; office mgr. Datacomp Corp., Washington, 1977-78, mgr. adminstrn., 1979—. Mem. Order of Carmelites Discalsed Secular, Roman Catholic Ch. Mem. Nat. Assn. Purchasing Mgmt., Purchasing Mgmt. Assn. Washington (dir.). Home: 15521 Germantown Rd Germantown MD 20874 Office: 5272 River Rd Washington DC 20016

AMMANN, LILLIAN ANN NICHOLSON, plant co. exec.; b. Pearsall, Tex., June 20, 1946; d. Harvey Franklin and Annie Laura (Matthews) Nicholson; B.A. magna cum laude, Southwestern U., 1968; m. Jack Jordan Ammann, Jr., May 31, 1967; 1 son, William Erik. Inventory mgr. Kelly AFB, San Antonio, 1967-70; employment counselor Tex. Employment Commn., San Antonio, 1970-75; owner, operator Lillie's Lovely Little Gardens, San Antonio, 1975-77, Lillie's Interior Landscapes, San Antonio, 1980—; pres. Cas Mann Inc. doing bus. as Lillie's & Sherry's Plants & Pottery, San Antonio, 1977-80. Mem. Magic Knight African Violet Soc. (pres. 1976-77, 78-79), Interior Plantscape Assn., Women in Bus., Nat. Assn. for Self-Employed, Greater San Antonio C. of C., North San Antonio C. of C. Episcopalian. Author: Lillie's Lovely Little Gardening Book, 1976. Home and office: 603 Mauze San Antonio TX 78216

AMMONS, CAROL HAMRICK, psychologist; b. Tampa, Fla., Feb. 22, 1929; d. Joe Fred and B. Carolyn (Patton) Hamrick; B.A., Harriette Sophie Coll., Tulane U., 1947, M.A., 1949; Ph.D. (M. Hagin fellow 1953-54), U. Ky., 1955; m. Robert Bruce Ammons, Aug. 1949; children—W. Carl F., Robert Bruce, S.M. Douglas, M.M. Elizabeth, Richard L.M., A. Stephanie J., Ailsa Glenyss E. Lectr. psychology U. Louisville, 1949-55; ind. practice psychology, Louisville, 1949-55, Grand Forks, N.D., 1955-56, Missoula, Mont., 1956—; faculty affiliate U.

Mont., 1966—; sec. Mont. Bd. Psychologist Examiners, 1970-72. Mem. AAAS, Am. Psychol. Assn., Internat. Council Psychologists, Mt. Psychol. Assn., AAUW, LWV. Author articles in field; editor Perceptual and Motor Skills, 1949—, Psychol. Reports, 1955—. Home: 411 Keith Ave Missoula MT 59801 Office: PO Box 9229 Missoula MT 59807

AMOS, LEIGH PERRY, genealogist, educator; b. Eugene, Oreg., Mar. 16, 1927; d. Jesse Lee and Alice Ellen (Cady) Perry; student World Conf. on Records, Salt Lake City, 1969; genealogy seminars Brigham Young U., 1969, 73, 77; m. Richard Louis Amos, June 22, 1948; children—Sherilyn Hahn, James Thomas, Ronald Steven, Vince Jeffrey. Pvt. practice genealogy teaching, Ketchikan, Alaska, 1969-73; instr. genealogy Umpqua Community Coll., Roseburg, Oreg., 1978—; instr. genealogy Ch. of Jesus Christ of Latter day Saints, Ketchikan, 1960-63, 67-73 speaker World Conf. on Records. Pres., Relief Soc. Ch. of Jesus Christ of Latter day Saints, Ketchikan, 1962-63; den mother S.E. Alaska council Boy Scouts Am., Ketchikan, chmn. annual scoutarama, 1964. Named Mother of Yr. in Ketchikan. Mem. Geneal. Soc. Douglas County, (pres. 1978—), D.A.R. (chpt. registrar 1980—), Geneal. Soc. S.E. Alaska (founder, pres. 1970-73, established Geneal. Library). Compiler, editor Happy Eating from Alaska, 1961, Our Day, 1965, The Harlan Newsletter, 1979. Home: 251 E 3570 S Salt Lake City UT 84115

AMOS, LOVIE LOUISE, pub. utility exec.; b. Manchester, Ga., Sept. 6, 1920; d. John McKinley and Ida Lavonia (Swearingen) Black; grad. Cassville (Mo.) pub. schs., 1938; m. Harry F. Amos, Dec. 13, 1938; children—Jane Cornelia, Catherine Ann. Clk., East Bay Municipal Utility Dist., Oakland, Calif., 1946-51, clerical supr., 1951-73, office supr., 1973-76, mgr. admnstrv. services, 1977—. Mem. Am. Records Mgrs. and Admnstrs. (chpt. pres.), Am. Congress Surveying and Mapping, Nat. Microfilm Assn., Internat. Word Processing Assn. (dirs. 1975-76, v.p. 1976-77, chmn. 1977—, chpt. pres. 1979-80). Address: 554 Tennent Ave Pinole CA 94564

AMOWITZ, GEORGETTE WEISZ, choreographer, educator; b. Paris, Oct. 26, 1929 (parents Am. citizens); d. Bela and Margaret (Goldman) Weisz; B.A., U. Wis., 1951; postgrad. Juilliard Sch., 1951-53; tchrs. cert. Labanotation, Dance Notation Bur., Inc., 1956, advanced cert. Labanotation, 1960; m. J. David Amowitz, Jan. 30, 1954 (dec. 1979); children—Michael Bennett, Steven Paul, Susan Lynn. Choreographer, Va. Grass Roots Opera Theatre, Lynchburg, 1955-58, Briar Patch Summer Theatre, Sweet Briar, Va., 1956, Lynchburg Little Theatre, 1955, 60, 67, 76, Lynchburg Coll. Opera Theatre, 1958, 63, Lynchburg Fine Arts Center, 1969, 74, Randolph-Macon Woman's Coll. Dance Concerts, Lynchburg, 1958-74; part-time instr. dance Randolph-Macon Woman's Coll., 1956, 58, 59-62, 63, 64-65, 70-71, lectr. dance 76-77, 78-79, 82; part-time lectr. dance Hollins Coll., 1977; reconstructor dance works Lynchburg Fine Arts Center, 1958, 59, 62, 70, 71, 75, Hollins (Va.) Coll., 1976, 77, 80, Sweet Briar Coll., 1963; Talent Trust instr. Lynchburg City Schs., 1974-75, Fine Arts Center, 1974-75; v.p. Dance div. Fine Arts Center, 1973-74, asso. dir., 1974-75, dir. Dance Players, 1969; dir. Jr. Dansnotators of Lynchburg, 1958-66, Little Dance Theatre, 1959-63, Lynchburg Dance Theatre Workshop, 1966-76; pvt. tchr. contemporary dance technique and Labanotation, Lynchburg, 1958-76; lectr. dance U. Wis., Milw., 1981-82; lectr. in field. Fellow Internat. Council Kinetography Laban; mem. Dance Notation Bur. (dir. 1956-57, 61-64), Va. (chmn. dance dept. 1967-75, 2d v.p. 1975-77), Nat. (chmn. dance dept. 1975-77) fedns. music clubs, Am. Dance Guild, U. Wis. Alumni Assn. (life), Hadassah (life). Choreography copyrighted for Amahl and the Night Visitors, 1959; And After the Journey, 1981. Office: Dance Dept Randolph-Macon Women's Coll Lynchburg VA 24503

AMPARAN, MARIA ELENA, personnel exec.; b. Los Angeles, Aug. 19, 1945; d. John S. and Concepcion (Mendez) A.; A.A., East Los Angeles Coll., 1967; B.A. in Journalism, Calif. State U., Los Angeles, 1969. Sec., coordinator press and publicity Sta. KNBC, 1969-70; prin. public relations rep. model cities program East N.E. neighborhood City of Los Angeles, 1970-72; public info. aide Housing Authority, Los Angeles, 1972; editor So. Calif. Rapid Transit Dist., 1972-73; coordinator dept. community services County of Los Angeles, 1973-76; employment specialist Kaiser Permanente Med. Care Program, Los Angeles, 1976-79; personnel supr. McDonald's Corp., San Diego, 1979—. Vol., coordinator Youth Motivation Task Force, 1976-79; mem. employer adv. com. Career Planning Center, Inc., 1978-79. recipient commendation award Los Angeles County Bd. Supervisors. Mem. Personnel Mgmt. Assn. San Diego, Personnel Mgmt. Assn. of Aztlan (chairperson ad hoc placement com., pres. San Diego chpt. 1982—, nat. publicity chmn. 1982—), Profl. Women's Journalism Soc., Beta Phi Gamma. Democrat. Roman Catholic. Office: 8840 Complex Dr Suite 300 San Diego CA 92123

AMSTUTZ, LEORA EDWARDS (MRS. MELVIN E. AMSTUTZ), former ch. assn. exec.; b. Marion, Ind., Sept. 12, 1909; d. Charles W. and Josephine (Bouvier) Edwards; student Sherwood Coll. Music and Dramatic Art, 1926-28; also pvt. study; m. Melvin E. Amstutz, Nov. 21, 1931 (dec. Jan. 1970); children—Carol Dawn Amstutz Kozma, Joy Diane Amstutz Caldwell. Exec. sec. Waukegan Area Council Chs., 1952-69; founder Waukegan Area Ch. Women United, 1952; producer, commentator own radio program Religion in the News, Sta. WKRS, 1958—, producer, narrator Songs of Faith, 1979—, also chmn. Radio Ministry; sec. organizing bd. mgmt. Lake County Mental Health Clinic, 1959-69; profl. dramatic reader, soloist, dir. plays, actress in amateur plays, platform and pulpit speaker, 1923—. Council mem. Girl Scouts U.S.A., 1937-45, pres., 1940-43, v.p., 1939, treas., 1943-45; bd. dirs. YWCA, 1945-52; sec. bd. dirs. North Lake County Mental Health Soc., 1953-70; bd. dirs. Lake County Welfare Council, Community Chest, USO; v.p. orgn. bd. 1st v.p. Civic Music Assn.; sec. orgn. bd. Lake County Council on Alcoholism, now mem. adv. bd.; organizer 1st Interfaith Women's Council, 1964—; co-founder, mem. exec. bd. Waukegan Area Interfaith Conf. Religion and Race, 1963—; treas. Lake County Welfare Council, 1961-67; organizing mem. bd. dirs. Lake County Music Center; mem. Am. Field Service Exchange Student Orgn.; charter bd. mem. OEO Vol. Adv. Council; bd. mem. Chgo. Home Missionary Soc.; mem. edn. com. Am. Cancer Soc.; mem. adv. council Lake County Health Dept.; mem. Lake County Urban League; bd. dirs., charter mem. Christian Ch. Supplies, Inc., 1972—; bd. dirs., pres. Victory Hosp. Aux., also mem. hosp. governing bd.; mem. Victory Hosp. Assn.; bd. dirs. Friends Library Waukegan, pres., 1981—; bd. dirs. Lake County Blumberg Meml. Blood Bank, 1976—, Happy Day Nursery Sch., 1979—; com. mem. Lake County Bd. Welfare Services, 1978—; bd. dirs. Waukegan Area Crimestoppers, 1982—; mem. Community Concert Assn., (founder), Waukegan Symphony Assn. (founder), LWV (radio chmn.), Family Service Agy., Nat. Assn. Council Secs. (nat. exec. bd. 1965-68), Planned Parenthood Aux. of Lake County, WCTU, Woman's Soc. of Christian Service (past pres.); mem. home service com. ARC; adv. com. Practical Nurse Program, 1955-70; religious coordinator, celebration producer Waukegan Bicentennial Commn.; mem. council of laity Garrett Theol. Sem., Evanston, Ill., 1981—; pres. adminstrv. bd. 1st United Meth. Ch., 1978—; voting mem. No. Ill. Conf. United Meth. Ch. Selected Community Woman of Achievement, 1956; recipient Brotherhood award NAACP, 1957; Brotherhood award B'nai B'rith, 1959; Ann. Lake County Mental Health award, 1969; Appreciation award Happy Day Sch., 1967; Community Service award Met. Council NAACP, 1968; House resolution Ill. Legislature, 1975; Valiant Woman award Waukegan Area and Nat. Ch. Women United, 1978; Spl. Achievement award Victory Hosp., 1978 Community Service award Lake County Urban League Guild, 1981. Mem. Internat. Platform Assn. Republican. Methodist (numerous offices and com. memberships in ch. orgns.). Clubs: Altrusa (dir.; Outstanding Woman in Lake County History award 1976), Woman's. Home: 2200 Hyde Park Ave Waukegan IL 60085

AMUNDSON, LORNA MAY, health ins. exec.; b. Manila, Mar. 24, 1938 (mother Am. citizens); d. Kwok Chun and Ruth Mabel (McCullough) Mack; student Park Coll., Mo., 1954-56; B.A., U. Kans., 1960; M.S., U. Tenn., 1968; Danforth fellow, Mountain Lake Biol. Sta., U. Va., 1972; postgrad. Bowling Green State U., 1973, U. Kans., 1974; m. John Carl Amundson, Feb. 14, 1975; 1 dau. by previous marriage, Kathryn Ann Cordonnier. Hostess, sci. illustrator Mus. Natural History, U. Kans., 1956-58; instr. biology S.E. Mo. State U., 1962-65, 69-74; asso. dir. Kern County PSRO, Calif., 1975, exec. dir. PSRO Area 21, Calif., 1975-80; exec. dir. Alliance Pvt. Physicians, Blue Cross of Calif., 1980—. Democratic chairwoman, Cape Girardeau, Mo., 1970; candidate for Cape Girardeau City Council, 1971, 72. Named Outstanding Tchr., S.E. Mo. State U. Div. Scis., 1973. Mem. AAAS, Sigma Xi. Contbr. articles to profl. jours.

ANABLE, ANNE CURRIER STEINERT, journalist; b. Boston, Feb. 18; d. Robert Shuman and Lucy Pettingill (Currier) Steinert; grad. West Hill Jr. Coll., Boston, 1951; m. Anthony Anable, Jr., 1962 (div. 1965). Reporter women's pages N.Y. Jour. Am., N.Y.C., 1961-66, World Jour. Tribune, N.Y.C., 1966-67; fashion editor Cleve. Plain Dealer, 1967-73; fashion and beauty editor New Woman mag., Ft. Lauderdale, Fla., 1973-75, 78-79; contbg. editor Conn. sect. N.Y. Times, 1977-81; beauty editor L'Officiel/USA, 1979. Recipient Fashion Reporting award N.Y., 1970. Mem. Fashion Group. Home: 7 Flower Hill Pl Port Washington NY 11050

ANAGNOST, CATHERINE COOK, lawyer; b. Tegea, Greece, Feb. 10, 1919; d. Peter and Athena (Reppas) C.; diploma Northwestern U., 1942; C.P.A., 1943; m. Themis Anagnost, Aug. 15, 1942; children—Maria, Alexander, James. Accountant, 1942-48; admitted to Ill. bar, 1948, U.S. Supreme Ct. bar, 1960, practiced law in Chgo., 1948—; mem. Anagnost & Anagnost. Former dir. Chgo. chpt. Girl Scouts U.S.A. Dir. Women's Adv. Council N.Y. World's Fair, 1964-65; v.p., dir. Beverly Farm Found.; chmn. 1966 Founders Day Program, Northwestern U. Mem. United Rep. Fund Ill.; Rep. candidate for judge Municipal Ct., Chgo., 1960, 62, for judge Circuit Ct. Cook County, 1964, 74-76; alternate del. to Rep. Nat. Conv., 1964. Recipient Merit award Northwestern U., 1964. Mem. Nat., Ill. fedns. bus. and profl. women's clubs, Nat., Ill., N.W. fedns. Republican women, Am. (ho. of dels. 1965-67), Ill., Chgo., West Suburban (past pres.), Hellenic (past pres.) bar assns., Women's Bar Assn. Ill. (past dir.), Hellenic Profl. Soc. Ill., Nat. Assn. Women Lawyers (pres. 1963-64), Am., Ill. trial lawyers assns., Internat. Fedn. Women Lawyers, Am. Assn. Attys.-C.P.A.'s, Internat. House Assn. (past treas. Chgo.), Northwestern U. Alumni Assn. Republican. Mem. Order Eastern Star, White Shrine. Clubs: Greek Women's University; Execs. Home: 2345 N Oak Park Ave Chicago IL 60635 Office: 11 S LaSalle St Chicago IL 60603 *

ANAGNOST, MARIA ATHENA, surgeon; b. Chgo., Oct. 21, 1943; d. Themis John and Catherine (Cook) A.; B.A., Northwestern U., 1965; M.D., U. Ill., 1973. Resident in surgery U. Chgo. Hosps. and Clinics, 1973-74; gen. surgery resident Michael Reese Med. Center, Chgo., 1975-79, chief resident, 1979-80; practice medicine specializing in surgery; surg. staff Oak Park (Ill.) Hosp., Westlake Community Hosp., Melrose Park, Ill., Gottlieb Meml. Hosp., Melrose Park, St. Anne's Hosp., Chgo., St. Anne's Hosp. West, Northlake, Ill., Good Samaritan Hosp., Downers Grove, Ill., Michael Reese Med. Center. Candidate for alderman, Chgo., 1964. Diplomate Am. Bd. Surgery, Nat. Bd. Med. Examiners. Recipient Physicians' Recognition award AMA. Fellow Internat. Coll. Surgeons; mem. AMA, Ill. Med. Soc., Chgo. Med. Soc., Hellenic Med. Soc., U. Ill. Alumni Assn., Northwestern U. Alumni Assn. Contbr. articles to profl. jours. Office: 150 N Oak Park Ave Oak Park IL 60301 also 2340 Highland Lombard IL 60148 also 11 S LaSalle St Chicago IL 60603 *

ANAGNOST, VIRGINIA STAMES, home economist, educator; b. N.Y.C., Oct. 1, 1935; d. Steve G. and Antiope D. (Papageorge) Stames; B.S. cum laude, Hunter Coll., 1957; M.S., U. Tenn., 1958; m. Constantine S. Anagnost, July 26, 1959; children—Christine, Stephanie Ann, Steven. Dietitian, N.Y. Hosp./Cornell U. Med. Center, N.Y.C., 1954-55; food technologist Gen. Foods Corp., N.Y.C., 1955-57; instr. food sci. U. Tenn., Knoxville, 1958-60, 66-68, asst. dean, asst. prof. home econs., 1969—; asst. dir. product devel. and quality control Wintergarden Corp., Knoxville, 1962-65. Cons. to Senator Howard Baker, 1979-80; mem. Knoxville bd. NCCJ, 1981—; youth commr. Diocese of Atlanta, Greek Orthodox Ch. North and S.Am., 1980-82, Carolina Conf., 1981-82; Knoxville advisor Greek Orthodox Youth Am., 1974-82, Greek Orthodox Young Adult League, 1980-82; tri-state area supr. Southeastern Fedn. Greek Orthodox Choirs, 1981-82; chmn. bd. auditors St. George Greek Orthodox Ch., Knoxville, 1975-80; mem. bylaws com. St. George Philoptochos Soc., 1981-82; Knoxville chmn. World Community Day, Ch. Women United, 1981. U. Tenn. grad. assistantship, 1957-58. Mem. Am. Home Econ. Assn., Assn. Adminstrs. Home Econ., Nat. Council Adminstrs. Home Econ., Inst. Food Technologists, Southeastern Council on Family Relations, So. Assn. Home Econ. Adminstrs., Tenn. Assn. Home Econ. Adminstrs., Tenn. Home Econ. Assn., AAUP, NEA, Tenn. Edn. Assn., Student Talent Edn. Assn. Knoxville, Phi Upsilon Omicron, Omicron Nu. Editor, U. Tenn. Coll. Home Econs. Ann. Report, 1968-77. Home: 7609 Twining Dr Knoxville TN 37919 Office: Coll Home Econ Univ of Tenn Knoxville TN 37916

ANAND, DOROTHEY PERRY, educator; b. Pittston, Pa., Nov. 3, 1935; d. Frank J. and Eugenia (Gudaitis) Perry; student Meadowbrook Music Sch., 1950-52, Parsons Sch. Design, 1955; B.A., Coll. Misericordia, 1957; postgrad. Am. U., 1961-62, Nassau Community Coll., 1963-80, N.Y.U., 1969, SUNY, Stonybrook, 1974, Whittier Coll., 1975, Huntington Art League, 1980—; M.A., Goddard Coll., 1978; m. Tilak R. Anand, Dec. 30, 1965. Chartist, A.C. Nielsen Co., N.Y.C., 1956; copywriter and librarian Sta. WPTS, Pittston, Pa., 1957-58; copywriter Sta. WPTV, Palm Beach, Fla., 1958; tchr. Annapolis (Md.) High Sch., 1958-59; instr. lit. Trinity Coll., Washington, 1959-60; tchr. art (part-time) Sacred Heart Sch., Bethesda, Md., 1959-60; instr. dept. English, Immaculata Jr. Coll., Washington, 1960-61; instr. English, Am. U., Washington, 1961; tchr. English, Deer Park (N.Y.) Sch. Dist., 1962-67, developmental reading tchr., 1967-77, reading lab. tchr., 1977—; ordained metaphysical minister, 1979. Cert. tchr., N.Y. Mem. Internat. Reading Assn., Deer Park Tchrs. Assn., N.Y. Edn. Assn., Assn. Supervision and Curriculum Devel., NOW, Assn. Research and Enlightment, Rosicrucian Order. Roman Catholic. Club: Bus. and Profl. Women's. Contbr. poems to lit. publs. Home: PO Box 101 Old Westbury NY 11568

ANARGYROS, NEDRA FLORENCE HARRISON, cytotechnologist; b. N.Y.C., Dec. 3, 1915; d. Leverette Roland and Florence Martha (Pickard) Harrison; student Emerson Coll., 1936; cert. in cytology U. Calif., San Francisco, 1957; m. Spero Drosos Anargyros, Oct. 21, 1940 (div. 1969). Supr. cytology San Francisco Gen. Hosp., 1957—. Mem. Am. Soc. Clin. Pathologists (affiliate mem.), Am. Soc. for Cytotech. (affiliate mem., cert. cytologist), Women Flyers of Am., DAR (1st regent La Puerta de Ora chpt., San Francisco), Nat. Soc. Colonial Dames of Am., Huguenot Soc. of Calif. Republican. Christian Scientist. Club: Presidents of Mercer U. (Macon, Ga.). Home: 2503 Clay St San Francisco CA 94115 Office: 22nd and Potrero Sts San Francisco CA 94110

ANASTOLE, DOROTHY JEAN, mfg. co. exec.; b. Akron, Ohio, Mar. 26, 1932; d. Leonard L. and Helen (Sagedy) Dice; student De Anza Jr. Coll., Cupertino, Calif., spring 1969; children—Kally, Dennis, Christopher. Various secretarial positions in mfg., 1969-75; office mgr. Sci. Devices Co., Mountain View, Calif., 1975-76; exec. adminstrv. sec. corp. office Cezar Industries, Palo Alto, Calif., 1976-77; office and personnel mgr. AM Bruning Co., Mountain View, 1977-81; dir. employee relations Consol. Micrographics, Mountain View, 1981—. Bd. dirs. Agnew State Hosp., San Jose, Calif., 1966-72, div. chmn. program mentally retarded, 1966-72, staff tutor, 1966-72. Recipient Service award Agnew State Hosp., 1972. Mem. Am. Soc. Profl. and Exec. Women, Adminstrv. Mgmt. Soc. Office: 303 Ravendale Dr Mountain View CA 94043

ANCKER-JOHNSON, BETSY, physicist, exec.; b. St. Louis, Apr. 29, 1927; d. Clinton James and Fern (Lalan) Ancker; B.A. in Physics with high honors (Pendleton scholar), Wellesley Coll., 1949; Ph.D. magna cum laude, U. Tuebingen (Germany), 1953; D.Sc. (hon.), Poly. Inst. N.Y., 1979; LL.D. (hon.), Bates Coll., 1980; m. Harold Hunt Johnson, Mar. 15, 1958; children—Ruth P. Johnson, David H. Johnson, Paul A. Johnson, Martha H. Johnson. Instr., jr. research physist U. Calif., 1953-54; physicist, Sylvania Microwave Physics Lab., 1956-58; mem. tech. staff RCA Labs., 1958-61; research specialist Boeing Co., 1961-70, exec., 1970-73; asst. sec. commerce for sci. and tech., 1973-77; dir. phys. research Argonne Nat. Lab. (Ill.), 1977-79; v.p. environ. activities staff Gen. Motors Tech. Center, Warren, Mich., 1979—; affiliate prof. elec. engring. U. Wash., 1964-73. Mem. staff Inter-Varsity Christian Fellowship, 1954-56. Trustee Wellesley Coll., 1972-77. AAUW fellow, 1950-51; Horton Hollowell fellow, 1951-52; NSF grantee, 1967-72. Fellow Am. Phys. Soc. (councillor-at-large 1973-76), IEEE; mem. Nat. Acad. Engring.; Phi Beta Kappa, Sigma Xi. Author, patentee in field. Office: Environmental Activities Staff GM Technical Center Warren MI 48090 *

ANDAMO, EVELYN MACHAN, occupational therapist; b. Laguna Province, Philippines, Apr. 22, 1944; came to U.S., 1970, naturalized, 1979; d. Nicholas Sichon and Genoveva Angeles (Jimenez) Machan; B.S. in Occupational Therapy, U. Philippines, 1966; M.P.A., Calif. State U., Long Beach, 1977; m. Emmanuel Andamo, Apr. 6, 1968; children—Evaleen Genevieve, Emmalyn Nativity, Emmanuel Nicholas III. Head occupational therapist Elks Cerebral Palsy Clinic, Rizal, Philippines, 1966-67, Parry Sound (Ont., Can.) Gen. Hosp., 1967; staff occupational therapist Toronto (Ont.) Gen. Hosp., 1967-69; dir. vocat. rehab. and therapy services McKinnon Philips Hosp., Owen Sound, 1969-70; occupational therapist-in-charge Nat. Therapy Assn., Van Nuys, Calif., 1970-71; dir. adjunctive therapy Edgemont Hosp., Hollywood, Calif., 1971-72; staff occupational therapist Spastic Children's Found., Los Angeles, 1972; clin. supr. Los Angeles County Crippled Children's Services, 1972-75; chief occupational therapist Los Angeles County-Long Beach Gen. Hosp., 1975—. Mem. Am. Soc. for Public Adminstrn., Am. Occupational Therapy Assn., Occupational Therapy Assn. Calif., M.P.A. Alumni Assn. Calif. State U.-Long Beach (sec. 1979-80), Pi Alpha Alpha, Phi Delta Gamma. Contbr. articles to profl. jours.

ANDERSEN, ALVERNA IDA, banker; b. Mankato, Minn., Feb. 12, 1929; d. Alfred Adolph and Ida Marie (Birk) Grieger; student public schs. Neligh, Nebr.; m. Robert Duaine Andersen, Nov. 23, 1960. Sec., Neligh Public Schs., 1946-48; salesperson S.S. Kresge Co., Sioux Falls, S.D., 1948-50; bookkeeper Gamble Skogmo Co., Sioux Falls, 1950-51; with Northwestern Nat. Bank, Sioux Falls, 1951—, ops. officer, 1971-76, auto bank mgr., 1976—. Mem. Nat. Assn. Bank Women. Republican. Lutheran. Home: 1704 S 9th Ave Sioux Falls SD 57105 Office: 108 South Dakota Ave Sioux Falls SD 57102

ANDERSEN, BONNIE JEAN, mfg. co. exec.; b. Chgo., May 15, 1929; d. George F. and Eleanor Evelyn (Moss) Masters Polack; student North Park Coll., 1946-47, Northwestern U., 1958-60; children—Jennifer, Jeffrey, Susan. Office mgr., Hollis Constrn. Co., Glenview, Ill., 1958-60; pres. Atlas Plastic Specialties, Inc., Chgo., 1960-78, Action Plastic Group, Inc., Northfield, Ill., 1979—; owner, pres., gen. mgr. A-1 Laminators, Northfield, 1978-79, B.J. Andersen & Assos., 1979—; chmn. bd. Atlas Plastic Specialties, Inc., Action Plastic Group Inc.; cons. plastic engring. Asst. to pres. Ill. Childrens Home and Aid Soc., 1977-78. Mem. Soc. Plastics Engrs., Nat. Assn. Female Execs., Ill. Burglar and Fire Alarm Assn. Episcopalian. Clubs: N. Glen Women's Assn. Ladies Oriental Shrine (officer 1975). Home: 338 Crooked Creek Northfield IL 60093 Office: 466 Central St Northfield IL 60093

ANDERSEN, GRETCHEN MANN, see Aona, Gretchen Mann

ANDERSEN, LOUISE STEVENSON, assn. exec.; b. Glastonbury, Conn., Apr. 1, 1919; d. Lewis William and Mabel Jane (Bidwell) Stevenson; B.A., Conn. Coll., 1941; M.Ed., U. Md., 1968; m. Henry Testman Andersen, July 5, 1941; children—Marcia (Mrs. David Wilder Welles), Susan (Mrs. Anthony Alexander Kossiakoff). Asst. social worker State of Conn., 1941-43; tchr. Lafayette Sch., Havana, Cuba, 1951-53; dir. Karachi (Pakistan) Am. High Sch., 1955-57; tchr. social studies Richard Montgomery High Sch., Rockville, Md., 1961-71; exec. dir. Conn. Coll. Alumni Assn., New London, 1971—. Home: 15 Church St Noank CT 06340 Office: Conn Coll Mohegan Ave New London CT 06320

ANDERSEN, MARIANNE SINGER, psychotherapist, ednl. adminstr.; b. Baden nr. Vienna, Austria, June 18, 1930; came to U.S., 1940, naturalized, 1946; d. Richard L. and Jolanthe (Garda) Singer; B.A., Hunter Coll., City U. N.Y., 1950, M.A., 1974; Ph.D., Fla. Inst. Tech., 1980; 1 son, Richard Esten. Book editor specializing in psychology and psychiatry various pub. firms including W.W. Norton Co., Sterling Pub. Co., E.P. Dutton Co., N.Y.C., 1950-71; research asso. Inst. for Research in Hypnosis, N.Y.C., 1974—, fellow in clin. hypnosis, 1976, dir. seminars, 1978—; psychotherapist specializing in hypnotherapy Morton Prince Center for Hypnotherapy, 1976—, dir. weight control clinic, 1980—, dir. clin. services, 1981—; dir. adminstrn. Internat. Grad. U., N.Y.C., 1974-77; adminstrv. coordinator Internat. Grad. Sch. Behavior Sci., Fla. Inst. Tech., 1978; lectr. hypnosis and hypnotherapy to mental and phys. health profls., 1977—; pvt. practice psychotherapy, 1977—. Mem. Soc. for Clin. and Exptl. Hypnosis, Internat. Soc. for Clin. and Exptl. Hypnosis, Am. Psychol. Assn. Author: (with Louis Savary) Passages: A Guide for Pilgrims of the Mind, 1972; research on treatment obesity with hypnotherapy. Home: 60 W 57th St New York NY 10019 Office: 10 W 66th St New York NY 10023

ANDERSEN, ROBERTA LAMONT, oil co. exec.; b. Superior, Nebr., Aug. 25, 1937; d. Virgil C. and Elizabeth M. (Fisher) Bartlett; B.A. in English with distinction, Colo. State U., 1959; M.A. in Journalism, U. Wyo., 1978; m. Robert D. Andersen, Aug. 25, 1978; children—Kelly, Diane, Susan. Legal sec. Fischer and Wilmarth, Ft. Collins, Colo., 1963-65; pvt. secretarial service, Laramie, Wyo., 1965-66; legal sec. Smith and Stanfield, Laramie, 1967-71; exec. sec. to pres. First Nat. Bank of Laramie, 1971-72; exec. sec., public relations asst. Edward Hines Lumber Co., Laramie, 1972-78, Aurora, Colo., 1978-81, public relations dir., 1976-81; public lands coordinator Amoco Prodn. Co., Denver, 1981—; chmn. Colo. Resources Consortium, 1978-81, RMOGA public lands com. Am. Petroleum Inst. Onshore Com., 1981—. Trustee Outdoors Unlimited, Inc., 1973—, nat. pres., 1977-79. Mem. Nat. Assn. Press Women, Colo. Timber Industry Assn., Am. Forestry Assn., Am. Forest Inst. (mem. Western communications com. 1972-81), Conservation Edn. Assn., Rocky Mountain Outdoor Writers and Photographers, Colo. Press Women, Nat. Forest Products Assn. (communications com. 1979-81), Soc. Profl. Journalists-Sigma Delta Chi, Phi Kappa Phi. Republican. Club: Zonta Internat. Author: Happiness is a Well Managed Forest (Conservation Edn. award 1974), 1973. Home: 1545 S Fraser Way Aurora CO 80012 Office: 2032 Amoco Bldg 1670 Broadway Denver CO 80202

ANDERSEN, SHARON BOROS, nurse; b. Cadillac, Mich., Apr. 22, 1940; d. James Eugene and Dorothy Louise (Laizure) Boros; R.N., Henry Ford Hosp., Detroit, 1961; B.S. in Nursing with honors, Mich. State U., 1969; divorced. Staff psychiat. nurse Henry Ford Hosp., 1961-63; head nurse Traverse City (Mich.) Regional Psychiat. Hosp., 1964-66, area supr. gerontology, then acting asst. dir. nursing, 1969-79, dir. nursing inservice edn., 1979-80, asst. dir. nursing, 1980—. Mem. Am. Nurses Assn., Mich. Nurses Assn., Traverse City Dist. Nurses Assn. (past dir.). Home: 4358 Five Mile Rd Route 1 Williamsburg MI 49690 Office: Box C Traverse City MI 49684

ANDERSON, AGNES M., counselor, banker; b. Beloit, Wis., May 2, 1900; d. Albert C. and Rose E. (Welter) Anderson; student Am. Inst. Banking, 1920-50, also various coll. and night sch. courses. With Beloit State Bank, 1918-28; with 1st Wis. Nat. Bank of Milw., 1928-65, secretarial asst., 1928-48, mgr. women's dept., 1949-65, asst. cashier, 1951-65; travel counsellor Bay Travel Mart, Inc., Milw., 1971—; asso. v.p. customer service Univ. Nat. Bank, Milw., 1971-73. Wis. women's chmn. U.S. Savs. Bonds Program, 1953-70. Sec. to bd. dirs. Bishop Haas Social Service Fund, 1958-69. Bd. dirs. Cerebral Palsy of Greater Milw., 1960-70; treas. bd. dirs., mem. exec. com. Eisenhower Meml. Cerebral Palsy Work Tng. Center, Milw., 1970-80. Recipient Eisenhower award U.S. Savs. Bonds Com., 1956, Cerebral Palsy award, 1963. Mem. Am. Inst. Banking (nat. women's com. 1949), Nat. Assn. Bank Women (chmn. Milw. group 1956, chmn. Wis. membership com. 1958), Lalumiere League (publicity chmn. Milw. 1970-72, chmn. auditing com. 1976-80). Roman Catholic (past pres. Altar Soc.). Clubs: Woman's of Wis., Milw. Tiffany (v.p., mem. bd. 1959-73); Quarter Century (1st Wis. Nat. Bank Milw.). Co-author: Stretching the Dollar, Budget Book, 1951, rev. edit., 1961. Home: 4001 N Prospect Ave Milwaukee WI 53211 Office: Bay Travel Mart Inc 517 E Silver Spring Dr Milwaukee WI 53217

ANDERSON, ALLAMAY EUDORIS, dietitian; b. N.Y.C., July 18, 1933; d. John Samuel and Charlotte Jane (Harrigan) Richardson; B.A., Queens Coll., City U. N.Y., 1975; profl. mgmt. cert. Adelphi U., 1978; m. Edgar Leopold Anderson, Jr., Apr. 14, 1957; 1 son, David Lancelot. Mem. staff sch. food service, dietitian Bd. Edn., N.Y.C., 1968—; profl. devel. cons., N.Y.C., 1978—; partner Masiba Bldg. Corp., Corona, N.Y., 1975-82. Devel. coordinator League for Better Community Life, Inc., 1977-82, treas. exec. bd., 1970-76; officer N.Y.C. Community Devel. Agy. Mem. N.Y. State Sch. Food Service Assn., Nat. Soc. Fund Raising Execs., Queens Coll. Home Econs. Alumni Assn. (v.p., chmn. bylaws com.). AAUW. Episcopalian. Home: 100-13 34th Ave Corona NY 11368 Office: 40 Irving Pl New York NY 10010

ANDERSEN, ANN HOWSER, fin. exec.; b. Tulsa, July 11, 1924; d. Benjamin Harrison and Addie Lou (Kelly) Howser; B.S., Sterling Coll., 1948; m. Kenneth Wesley Anderson, May 29, 1956; 1 son, Kenneth Wesley. Office mgr. Kentube Co., Tulsa, 1960-70, Houston & Klein, Inc., attys., Tulsa, 1975-79, Anesthesia Assos., Inc., Tulsa, 1979-80; owner, mgr. Andeaton Investment Co., Tulsa, 1976—. Officer bd. administrs. Esplanade Homeowners Assn., 1980—. Mem. Nat. Assn. Female Execs. Republican. Presbyterian. Address: 2421 E 73d Pl Tulsa OK 74136

ANDERSON, ANN MARIE CASSAGNE, microbiologist; b. New Orleans, Apr. 19, 1944; d. Charles Emile and Julie Marie (Sierra) Cassagne; B.S. magna cum laude, Loyola U. of South, 1966; M.S., La. State U., 1968, Ph.D., 1971; m. Robert B. Anderson, June 25, 1966. Med. technologist Touro Infirmary, New Orleans; instr. clin. hematology Tulane U. Sch. Pub. Health, New Orelans, 1969-72, instr. dept. environ. health scis., 1969-72, asst. prof., 1972-76, assoc. prof., 1976—, mem. grad. faculty and internat. health faculty, 1977—, adj. assoc. prof. Sch. Engring., 1974—. Pres. women's aux. New Orleans chpt. La. Engring. Soc.; bd. dirs. Children's Carnival. HEW grantee, 1974-82. Mem. Am. Pub. Health Assn. (sect. council environ. 1978-82), Am. Soc. Microbiology, Am. Soc. Med. Technologists, Soc. Environ. Geochemistry and Health, Soc. Exptl. Biology and Medicine, P.E.O., Biodeterioration Soc., Sigma Xi, Delta Omega. Democrat. Roman Catholic. Clubs: New Orleans Opera Guild, Orleans, Le Petit Theatre de Vieux Carre, Tulane Med. Internat. (pres.). Home: 5920 Memphis St New Orleans LA 70124 Office: 1430 Tulane Ave New Orleans LA 70112

ANDERSON, ANNETTE MCKENZIE, speech pathologist; b. Charleston, S.C., Aug. 20; d. Frank and Adele (Notis) McKenzie; B.S., Hampton Inst., 1963; M.S., Fed. City Coll., 1974. Tchr., speech clinician Charleston County (S.C.) public schs., 1963-73; univ. coordinator skills and curriculum devel. workshop Howard U., Washington, 1974; speech pathologist Cerebral Palsy Assn. Montgomery County, Rockville, Md., 1974-75; clin. supr. Speech and Hearing Clinic, Fed. City Coll., Washington, 1975-76; speech and lang. pathologist D.C. Public Schs., Washington, 1976—; cons. Dept. Edn. and Psychol. Founds., U. D.C., 1979, Inst. for Gifted and Talented, Washington, 1979—. Bd. dirs. YWCA, Charleston, S.C., 1973. Recipient cert. of clin. competence Am. Speech and Hearing Assn.; cert. tchr., D.C. Mem. Am. Speech and Hearing Assn., Council for Exceptional Children, Cerebral Palsy Assn., NEA, Nat. Hampton Alumni Assn. (chpt. v.p. 1970-73), Zeta Chi Omega chpt. Alpha Kappa Alpha. Democrat. Baptist. Clubs: Nat. Assn. Negro Bus. and Profl. Women's, Friday Morning Music. Home: 4850 Connecticut Ave Washington DC 20008 Office: 100 Gallatin St Washington DC 20011

ANDERSON, ANTOINETTE J(OSEPHINE), computer co. exec.; b. Kansas City, Kans., Nov. 28, 1943; d. Raymond and Margaret (McCabe) Burwell; B.S.Ed., Central Mo. State U., 1965; postgrad. in fin. Rockhurst Coll., 1979—; m. Joe Neill Watkins, June 12, 1969 (div.); children—Sherrie Lynn, Neil Jason. Exec. asst. to pres. Dimensional Mktg. Inc., Kansas City, Mo., 1975-76; dir. public relations Westgate State Bank, Kansas City, Kans., 1976; mgr. acctg. dept. Ozark Nat. Life Ins. Co., Kansas City, 1976-81; revenue acctg. mgr. United Telecom Computer Group, Overland Park, Kans., 1981—; fin. cons. City of Houston Lake, 1969—; aviation mktg. cons., 1975—. Platte County rep. Kansas City Met. Commn. on Status of Women, 1979-81. Mem. Nat. Assn. Exec. Females, Northland Women's Polit. Caucus, Sigma Kappa, Pi Omega Pi, Kappa Delta Pi, Alpha Phi Delta, Alpha Phi Sigma. Democrat. Club: Pilot Internat. (chmn. internal affairs 1978, 80). Home: 5484 NW Venetian Dr Kansas City MO 64151 Office: 5454 W 110th St Overland Park KS 66211

ANDERSON, BARBARA A., sociologist; b. Ames, Iowa, Aug. 10, 1948; d. A.I. and Carolyn Anna (Barnes) Snow; A.B. in Math., U. Chgo., 1970; Ph.D. in Sociology, Princeton U., 1974; M.A., Brown U., 1977; m. Michael P. Anderson, June 14, 1969. Research assoc. Office Population Research, Princeton U., 1973-76; research assoc. Econ. Growth Center, Yale U., 1974-75, asst. prof. sociology, 1975-76; assoc. prof. sociology Brown U., Providence, 1976—; vis. mem. Inst. Advanced Study, 1974. NIH grantee, 1976-77; Guggenheim fellow, 1982-83; NSF grantee, 1980-83; Ford-Rockefeller grantee, 1975-76. Mem. Am. Sociol. Assn., Am. Hist. Assn., Assn. Advancement Slavic Studies, Population Assn. Am. (dir. 1983-85), Social Sci. History Assn. Co-author: Human Fertility in Russia Since the Nineteenth Century, 1979; Internal Migration During the Modernization of Russia in the Late Nineteenth Century, 1980. Home: 32 Alfred Stone Rd Providence RI 02906 Office: Dept Sociology Brown U Providence RI 02912

ANDERSON, BARBARA ANN, educator; b. Atlanta, June 2, 1928; d. Roy and Mary Louise (McCormick) Boling: A.B. in Lang. Arts, Fla. State U., 1950; M.Ed. summa cum laude, Central State U., Edmond, Okla., 1972; m. Robert Lee Anderson, June 6, 1950; children—Michael Lee, Lynnda Louise, Robert Scott. Tchr. lang. arts schs. in Okla. and Kans., 1964—; tchr. Putnam City High Sch., Oklahoma City, 1966—; tchr. grammar for tchrs. Okla. State U. extension, 1978; mem. Okla. Profl. Practices Commn., 1974-81. Co-chmn. edn. project Okla. Bicentennial, 1975-76; Democratic precinct sec., 1976-77; del. Okla. Dem. Conv., 1979-80, active local Lyric Theatre, YMCA. Hilda Maehling fellow, NEA, 1976; named Tchr. of Yr., Putnam City Sch. Dist., 1978, 82. Mem. NEA (del. 1974-82), Nat. Fedn. Press Women, Okla. Edn. Assn. (dir. 1979-81, chmn. public relations com., del. 1975—), Putnam City Assn. Classroom Tchrs. (pres. 1974-75, editor publs. 1973—, exec. bd. 1972—), Okla. Press Women (sec. 1976-79, scholarship chmn. 1978-79), Sigma Kappa. Episcopalian. Author curriculum materials, articles in field. Office: 5300 NW 50th St Oklahoma City OK 73122

ANDERSON, BARBARA BROWN, educator; b. Birmingham, Ala., Aug. 9, 1947; d. Albert Owens and Elizabeth Dollie (Blevins) O.; B.A., Miles Coll., 1968; M.A., Atlanta U., 1972; student U. Ala., Tuscaloosa, 1978-81; m. Wayne A. Anderson, Nov. 21, 1970; children—Jocelyn Ayanna, Carice Elizabeth. Instr., Miles Coll., 1969-74, 76—; adminstrv. asst., drug counselor Birmingham Urban League, 1975; part-time instr. U. Ala., Birmingham, 1977-80. Mem. Ala.-Miss. Sociol. Soc., Alpha Kappa Delta. Baptist. Home: 315 Zeigler Ave Hueytown AL 35023 Office: Div Social and Behavioral Scis Miles Coll Birmingham AL 35208

ANDERSON, CARA LIANNE WRIGHT, speech pathologist; b. Bellingham, Wash., Nov. 12, 1941; d. Leland Clinton and Lillie Agnes (Stone) Wright; B.A., Ariz. State U., 1966; M.A., U. N.Mex., 1970; m. E. Paul Anderson, Sept. 7, 1967; 1 dau., Sarabeth. Speech therapist Albuquerque Public Schs., 1966-67; dir. Albuquerque Aphasia and Speech Cons., 1971—; chmn. N.Mex. Speech Pathology and Audiology Lic. Bd., 1981—; mem. N.Mex. PSRO, 1977-80, vice chmn., 1978, chmn., 1979; mem. profl. adv. bd. Hosp. Home Health Care Agy., 1973—; chmn. continuing edn. com. rehab. dept. St. Joseph Hosp., Albuquerque. CA grantee, 1968-71, fellow, 1967. Mem. Am. Speech and Hearing Assn., Am. Acad. Pvt. Practice in Speech Pathology and Audiology, Am. Congress Rehab. Medicine, Nat. Soc. Autistic Children, N.Mex. Speech and Hearing Assn. (chmn. govtl. affairs com. 1978-82), S.W. Soc. Aging, Albuquerque Speech and Audiology Profls., Albuquerque Assn. Children Learning Disabilities. Republican. Congregationalist. Office: 1401-A University Ave NE Albuquerque NM 87102

ANDERSON, CAROL ANN, ins. adjuster; b. Omaha, Oct. 18, 1946; d. Robert Thomas and Ethal Elizabeth (Sipple) Whelan; student (Ak-Sar-Ben scholar 1964-66), U. Omaha, 1964-66, U. Nebr., 1973—; m. Robert Dale Anderson, Sept. 17, 1973; children by previous marriage—Sheri Lynn Tasker, Maurice Francis Tasker. Ins. underwriter Nat. Indemnity Co., Omaha, 1970-73; ins. adjuster Assoc. Adjusters, Inc., Omaha, 1973-76, owner, 1976—; owner, mgr. Anderson Claim Service, Inc., Omaha, 1976—. Cast mem. Omaha Gridiron Rev., 1976—. Mem. Nat. Assn. Ind. Ins. Adjusters, Nebr. Claims Assn. of Omaha, Casualty and Surety Claims Assn. of Iowa, S.W. Iowa Claims Assn. (pres. 1980). Republican. Roman Catholic. Editor/pub. Accidently Speaking, 1977—; assoc. pub. Jour. Genealogy mag., 1976-80. Office: 150 S 38th St PO Box 31097 Omaha NE 68131

ANDERSON, CAROL ANN MEYERS, publishing co. exec.; b. Ypsilanti, Mich., June 13, 1950; d. James Henry and Mary Michele (DeLuca) Meyers; French student U. Montpelier (France), summer 1966; B.A. in French and Journalism, Mich. State U., 1972. Editorial research supr. Woman's Day mag., N.Y.C., 1974-75; advt. account mgr. McCall Pattern Co., N.Y.C., 1975; S.E. mgr. Interiors/Residential Interiors mag. Billboard Publs., N.Y.C., 1976-77; account mgr. Redbook mag., N.Y.C., 1977-80; sr. account supr. Food & Wine mag. Am. Express Pub. Corp., N.Y.C., 1980—; mem. Advt. Women N.Y., 1975-79, dir. public relations, 1978-79. Pres., Sisters of the Shield of Theta Delta Chi, 1970-72; v.p. Mich. State U. Panhellenic Council, 1970. Mem. N.Y. U. Med. Center Vol. Orgn. Mem. French Inst., Alliance Française. Office: 90 Park Ave New York NY 10016

ANDERSON, CAROLYN RUTH, billing service co. exec.; b. Harvey, Ill., Oct. 4, 1939; d. Owen Donald and Fannie (Westerberg) Kinsey; student So. Ill. U., 1957-60; children—David Kenneth, Kristin Lynn, Kathrin Lynn. Mgr., Brown Radiology Assos., Augusta, Ga., 1975-81; corp. treas., bus. adminstr. Med. Computer Billing Services, Inc., Augusta, 1981—; co-founder, co-pres. Med. Data Service Clients Group. Mem. Radiology Bus. Mgrs. Assn. (co-pres. Ga. 1977—, sec. So. region 1980-81, pres. So. region 1982-83, nat. dir. 1981-82), Central Savannah River Area-Med. Mgrs. Assn. (v.p. 1981-82), Micru Internat., Nat. Assn. Female Execs., Sigma Kappa. Methodist. Office: 810 13th St Augusta GA 30902

ANDERSON, CAROLYN RUTH, interior designer, writer; b. Evansville, Ind., Aug. 20, 1941; d. Maurice Osborn and Fairy Helen (Burnau) Hunt; B.A., Boston U., 1963; M.S., Columbia U., 1965; cert. in interior design N.Y. Sch. Interior Design, 1968; m. Gerald Lee Anderson, June 5, 1965; children—Clifford Blake, Gwendolyn Cheryl. Marriage counselor, child guidance counselor Family Agy. of N.Y. Community Service Soc., N.Y.C., 1966-67; pres. Carolyn Anderson Corp., Interior Design, Greenwich, Conn., 1968—. Bd. dirs. Round Hill Nursery Sch., Greenwich, Conn., 1975-76, PTA of North St. Sch., Greenwich, 1976—; den leader, coach Boy Scouts Am., Greenwich, 1978-80; Brownie leader Girl Scouts U.S.A., Greenwich, 1979-80, Jr. Girl Scout leader, 1981—; vol. Dept. Social Services, Greenwich, 1978—. Cert. social worker, N.Y. Congregationalist. Author: The Complete Book of Homemade Ice Cream, Milk Sherbet and Sherbet, 1972. Address: 138 Clapboard Ridge Rd Greenwich CT 06830

ANDERSON, CHERYL, internat. govt. affairs adviser; b. Camp Campbell, Ky.; d. Edward Gustav and Virginia Leona (Case) A.; B.A., U. Wash., 1969; m. Richard T. Ney, July 4, 1975; children— Alexander Case, Justin Anderson. Asst. press sec. Senator Warren G. Magnuson, Washington, 1969-71; parliamentarian officer Australian Senate, Canberra, Australia, 1971-72; adminstrv. asst. Richard Ney Asso., Inc., Washington, 1972-73, account rep., 1973-74, v.p., 1974-77; v.p., sec., dir. Advocacy Internat., Ltd., Washington, 1977—. Contbr. articles to profl. jours. Home: 702 Blueberry Hill Rd McLean VA 22101 Office: 600 New Hampshire Ave NW Washington DC 20037

ANDERSON, CLAIRE ANN, toy and hobby sales rep.; b. Seguin, Tex., July 31, 1940; d. Aaron George and Pearl Bertha Marie (Dornhoefer) Saegert; m. Billy Joe Anderson, Jan. 17, 1975; children—Dana Elaine, Toni Denise. Legal sec. firm Jacobson & Ludlum, Austin, Tex., 1959-62; office mgr., security specialist Hamilton Standard div. United Aircraft Corp., Houston, 1964-67; sales rep. Mattel Toymakers, Houston, 1967-76, Leisure Dynamics, Inc., Houston, 1977-80, Knickerbocker Toy Co., Conroe, Tex., 1981—. Mem. Southwestern Toy and Hobby Assn., Nat. Assn. Female Execs. Republican. Lutheran. Club: Order Eastern Star. Home and Office: 3140 White Oak Valley Conroe TX 77302

ANDERSON, DAUN ROBIN, systems engr.; b. Winchester, Mass., Oct. 15, 1950; d. Ernest Lawrence and Muryle Caroline (Sandgren) A.; B.A. in Modern Langs., Coll. William and Mary, 1972; M.A. in French, Pa. State U., 1975. Teaching asst. Pa. State U., 1972-73; info. analyst to tech. research analyst GTE Labs., Waltham, Mass., 1977-80; software specialist Comml. Union Assurance Cos., Boston, 1980-81; systems engr. Nixdorf Computer Corp., Waltham, Mass., 1981—. Mem. Assn. Systems Mgmt. Home: 30 Kilsyth Rd Unit 31 Brookline MA 02146 Office: 204 2d Ave Waltham MA 02154

ANDERSON, DORIS EHLINGER, lawyer, author, editor; b. Houston, Dec. 1; d. Joseph O. and Cornelia L. (Pagel) Ehlinger; B.A., Rice U., 1946; cert. Sam Houston Tchrs. Coll., 1947; LL.B., U. Tex., 1951, J.D., 1955; m. Wiley Newton Anderson, Jr., Aug. 26, 1946; children—Wiley Newton III, Joseph Ehlinger. Tchr., Houston Ind. Sch. Dist., 1946-48; admitted to Tex. bar, 1950, since practiced in Houston; mem. firm Ehlinger and Anderson, 1950-52, 55—; asso. firm Price, Guinn, Wheat and Veltmann, Houston, 1952-55. Founder, dir. Liberty Belles and Beaux, Houston, 1975—; mem. Gov.'s Com. on the Rights of Women, 1972; parliamentarian Harris County (Tex.) Flood Control Task Force, 1973—; bd. dirs. Friends of Fondren Library, Mus. Am. Architecture and Decorative Arts, Houston Bapt. U. Named staff Tex. Navy; recipient Woman of Yr. award YWCA, 1978, 80. Mem. Tex. Bar Assn., Am. Arbitration Assn. (panel of arbitrators), UDC, Coll. Women's Assn., Freedoms Found., Soc. Rice U. Women (pres. 1977-79), Am. Mus. Soc. (dir.), San Jacinto Descs., Daus. Republic of Tex., Sarah Lane Lit. Soc., Houston Edn. Excellence Program, Bayou Bend Docent, Kappa Beta Pi. Author: (with Roy Cullen and Louis Welch) Houston: City of Destiny, 1980; also articles and papers. Home: 5556 Cranbrook Dr Houston TX 77056

ANDERSON, DOROTHY KESSINGER, optometrist; b. Boise, Idaho, Mar. 31, 1947; d. Walter Ira Kessinger and Ruth Mildred (Giles) Kessinger McCullough; student So. Missionary Coll., 1966-67; O.D., So. Coll. Optometry, 1971; m. Frank S. Anderson, Jr., Aug. 20, 1972. Optometrist, Wesley-Jessen, Inc., Chgo., 1971-72; partner optometric practice, New Orleans, 1973-75, pvt. practice optometry specializing in contact lenses and vision devel., New Orleans, 1975—. Named Optometrist of Yr. for La., 1979; recipient appreciation award Lions Club, 1978, 80. Mem. Am. Optometric Assn., Optometric Extension Program, La. Assn. Optometrists (dir. 1975-78, exec. bd. 1979, v.p. 1980, pres.-elect 1981), New Orleans Optometric Soc. (pres. 1975-78), New Orleans Contact Lens Soc. (pres. 1978), Coll. Optometrists in Vision Devel. Office: 605 Lapalco Blvd Gretna LA 70054 also 435 Apple St Norco LA 70079

ANDERSON, EILEEN RUTH, mayor; b. Bell, Calif., Oct. 18, 1928; d. Elmer E. and Ellen S. (Martini) Pulling; B.A., U. Hawaii, 1950, postgrad., 1972-73; m. Clifford F. Anderson, Oct. 10, 1950; children—Mark Alexander, Patricia Manulani Anderson Dauterman, Lorita Ellen Anderson Naipo. Personnel technician dept. personnel services State of Hawaii, 1956-61, mgmt. analyst, dept. budget and fin., 1961-64, legis. analyst Office of Legis. Auditor, 1966-70, program evaluation analyst dept. budget and fin., 1970-73, chief budget, planning and mgmt. div., 1974, dir. fin., 1974-80; tech. cons. Public Employees Compensation Appeals Bd., 1964-65; personnel mgmt. services technician City and County of Honolulu Dept. Civil Service, 1965-66, mayor City and County of Honolulu, 1981—. Den mother Boy Scouts Am., 1961-62; sec. Kaneohe Little League, 1962-63; asst. leader Girl Scouts U.S.A., 1963-64; mem. Altar Guild, Calvary Episcopal Ch., 1970-73; mem. budget and allocations com. Aloha United Way, 1978-79, dir., 1980-82; adv. council Liliuokalani Trust, 1979-80. Mem. Am. Soc. Pub. Adminstrn., Public Personnel Assn. (pres. Hawaii chpt. 1965-66), Bus. and Profl. Women. Democrat. Office: 530 S King St Honolulu HI 96813

ANDERSON, ELEANOR, nurse; b. N.Y.C., Apr. 10, 1917; d. Einar Eric and Gerda Sophia (Rosèn) A.; diploma White Plains Hosp. Sch. Nursing, 1939; operating room postgrad. course Postgrad. Hosp., 1943; student St. John's U., 1954; B.S., Columbia U. Tchrs. Coll., 1960, M.A., 1966. Staff nurse White Plains (N.Y.) Hosp., 1939-43, asst. operating room supr., instr., 1943-53, supr. operating room, 1953-70, supr. operating room and recovery room, 1970-78. Mem. N.Y. State, Am. nurses assns., Assn. Operating Room Nurses, White Plains Hosp. Alumnae Assn. (corr. sec.). Republican. Lutheran. Contbr. articles to profl. jours.

ANDERSON, FRANCES JANE, religious denominational exec.; b. Freeport, Ill., Oct. 1, 1931; d. Lillian Rose A.; A.B., Millikin U., 1953; student Salvation Army Sch. for Officers Tng., 1953; M.S., Northwestern U., 1970. Ordained minister, Salvation Army, 1953; editor youth publs. Salvation Army, Chgo., 1956-75; asst. dir. public relations for central states, 1975-77; writer, editor bd. communications Bapt. Gen. Conf., Arlington Heights, Ill., 1977-81, editorial mgr., public affairs, 1981—; mem. faculty Olivet Coll., Kankakee, Ill., 1981—; prof. communications Salvation Army Sch., Chgo., 1981—. Mem. Salvation Army Com. for White House Conf. on Children and Youth, 1960, 70. Mem. Women in Communications (rec. sec. 1980, newsletter editor 1981, treas. 1982, pres.-elect North Shore chpt. 1982-83), Conf. Editors Ch. Mags. for Children and Youth, MacDowell Artists Assn. Contbr. articles to religious jours. Home: 2430 N Kennicott Dr Apt 2D Arlington Heights IL 60004 Office: 2002 S Arlington Heights Rd Arlington Heights IL 60005

ANDERSON, FRANCES SWEM, former nuclear med. technologist; b. Grand Rapids, Mich., Nov. 27, 1913; d. Frank Oscar and Carrie (Strang) Swem; student Muskegon Sch. Bus., 1959-60; certificate Muskegon Community Coll., 1964; m. Clarence A.F. Anderson, Apr. 9, 1934; children—Robert Curtis, Clarelyn Christine Anderson Schmelling, Stanley Herbert. X-ray file clk., film librarian Hackley Hosp., Muskegon, Mich., 1957-59; student refresher course in nuclear med. tech. Chgo. Soc. Nuclear Med. Techs., 1966; radioisotope technologist and sec. Hackley Hosp., 1959-65; nuclear med. technologist Butler Meml. Hosp., Muskegon Heights, Mich., 1966-70, Mercy Hosp., Muskegon, 1970-79; ret., 1979. Mem. Muskegon Civic A Capella choir, 1932-39; mem. Mother-Tch. Singers, PTA, Muskegon, 1941-48, treas., 1944-48; with Muskegon Civic Opera Assn., 1950-51; mem. choir Evang. Covenant Ch., Muskegon, 1953-79, choir sec., 1963-69, tchr. Sunday sch., 1954-75, supt. Sunday sch., 1975-78, treas. Sunday sch., 1980—, ch. sec., 1981—, chmn. master planning council, also coordinator centennial com. Cert. nuclear medicine technologist. Mem. Am. Registry Radiologic Technologists, Internat. Platform Assn. Home: 5757 E Sternberg Rd Fruitport MI 49415

ANDERSON, GEORGANNA KOCH, Realtor, broker; b. Lima, Ohio, Apr. 19, 1938; d. George Henry and Anna Louise (Fisher) Koch; student Ohio No. U., 1957; B.S., Ohio State U., 1960, postgrad., 1960-61; children—Anna Kristine, Christian Spencer, Brett Derek. Tchr., Lima (Ohio) Sch. Dist., 1960-61, Columbus (Ohio) Sch. Dist., 1961-63, Lamplighter Sch., Dallas, 1974-78; asso. Merrill Lynch Paula Stringer Realtors, Inc., Dallas, 1978-81; dir., treas. Consol. Bottling Co., Lima, Ohio and Corpus Christi, Tex., 1974-77. Mem. Nat. Congress Parents and Tchrs., Nat. Bottlers Assn., Greater Dallas Bd. Realtors, Tex. Edn. Assn., Nat. Assn. Female Execs., Delta Delta Delta, Delta Omicron. Methodist.

ANDERSON, GEORGIANA N., public relations specialist; b. St. Petersburg, Fla., Jan. 22, 1928; d. Charles Beverly and Georgiana Lowen (Foster) Neel; A.A., St. Petersburg Jr. Coll., 1948; B.A. with honors, U. South Fla., 1976. Adminstrv. asst. Sta. WPIN, St. Petersburg, 1954-68; partner advt. firm Anderson, Fisher & Morgan, Inc., St. Petersburg Beach, Fla., 1968-71; adminstrv. asst. Sta. WTOG-TV, St. Petersburg, 1971-72; public relations dir. So. Pinellas chpt. ARC, 1972-79; asst. dir. communications dept., public relations specialist Pinellas County Sch. Bd., Clearwater, Fla., 1979—. ARC grantee, 1974-76. Mem. Am. Bus. Women's Assn. (pres. Sunshine chpt. 1964, named Woman of Yr. 1965), Nat. Assn. Press Women, Nat. Sch. Bd. Public Relations, Fla. Public Relations Assn. Democrat. Episcopalian. Office: PO Box 4688 Clearwater FL 33518

ANDERSON, HELEN ELAINE, retail co. exec.; b. Barnesville, Ohio, June 10, 1952; d. Charles Edward and Wilma Imelda (Kemp) Anderson; B.A., Marietta Coll., 1974. Nat. advt. copywriter Sears Roebuck & Co., Chgo., 1975-77, asst. nat. catalog mktg. mgr., 1977-79, asst. nat. buyer accent furniture and wall decor, 1979-81, nat. retail mdse. sales coordinator home fashion accessories, 1981—. Mem. Nat. Assn. Female Execs., Intaglio, Pi Delta Epsilon, Chi Delta Phi. Alpha Sigma Tau. Home: 235 Spring Hill Dr Roselle IL 60172 Office: Sears Roebuck & Co D/621 Sears Tower Chicago IL 60684

ANDERSON, IONA LUCILLE, educator; b. Bklyn.; d. Oliver Cromwell and Clarine (Atwell) Ashby; B.A., Hunter Coll., 1942; M.A., N.Y.U., 1959; Ph.D., Heed U., 1978; m. Aeolus Anderson, Oct., 1943 (dec.); children—Wendie Anderson Peterson, Robert. Acting chmn. div. edn. U.S. Signal Corps, 1943-45; profl. asst. to engrs. Dept. Commerce, 1945-46; tchr. N.Y.C. Bd. Edn., 1946-69; asst. prof. Bd. Higher Edn. N.Y.C., Bklyn. Coll., 1969-74; asst. prof. English as 2d lang. Medgar Evers Coll., 1974—, acting chairperson div. tchr. edn., 1982—; field supr. Bank St. Coll., 1969-71; cons., evaluator Bd. Edn., Fordham U. Chairperson edn. com. Flatbush Devel. Corp., N.Y.C., 1973, N.E. Flatbush Community Council, 1975; mem. Community Bd. 17, N.Y.C. Ednl. Research Opportunity postdoctoral fellow, 1979-82. Mem. Tchrs. English to Speakers Other Langs., N.Y. State Tchrs. English to Speakers Other Langs. Bilingual Educators Assn., Nat. Assn. Remedial and Devel. Studies, Assn. Supervision and Curriculum Devel., Phi Lambda Theta, Phi Delta Kappa. Author: The Effectiveness of an Open Classroom Approach on Second Language Acquisition, 1976; author grant proposals. Home: 1116 Willmahr St Brooklyn NY 11212 Office: 1150 Carroll St Brooklyn NY 11225

ANDERSON, JACQUELINE JONES, educator; b. Hartford, Conn., July 13, 1935; d. Ella B. (Jones) Anderson; B.A., N.H. Coll., 1979; cert. Hartford U., 1971, Hartford Coll. for Women, 1971, U. Conn., 1978; children—Wilfred, Gregory, Kevin, Kyle. With Community Renewal Team, CAP Agy., Hartford, 1966-69; freelance tng. cons., Hartford, 1974—; dir. Health Care Dept., Hartford Hosp., 1969—. Bd. dirs. Ambulatory Health Care Planning, Inc., 1970-71, PIT I Drugs, 1972-75, YMCA, 1973—, Toward an Allied Health Career Today, 1973-77, Get the Lead Out, 1974—, Child Guidance Center, 1974-78, AMISTAD Group Home for Girls, 1977—, Upper Albany Community Orgn., 1977—, Health Systems Agy., 1977—, Bergdorf Health Planning Com., 1977-79, Black Coalition on Health Issues, 1978—, Elderly Crisis Intervention, 1979—; mem. Conn. Stroke Program, 1972, Blue Hills Clinic task force on drugs, 1972-73, Mayor's Health Services Com., 1973-77, Community Health Adv. Com., City of Hartford, 1978—; resource person Planned Parenthood, 1972-77; Justice of the Peace, Hartford County, 1972-75; mem. Republican Town Com., 1973—; councilwoman Hartford Ct. of Common Council, 1975-77, many others. Recipient Cert. of Merit, CRT of Greater Hartford, 1972; Outstanding Woman of Yr. award Conn. Women's Soc., 1979; Cert. of Appreciation, Health Systems Agy. of N.C. Conn., 1980; Upper Albany Community Orgn. Service to Community award, 1981; others. Mem. Am. Public Health Assn., Conn. Hosp. Assn., New Eng. Public Health Assn., Soc. for Patient Reps., Alliance of Black Social Workers. Republican. Methodist. Contbr. articles to profl. jours. Home: 101 Tower Ave Hartford CT 06120 Office: 80 Seymour St Hartford CT 06115

ANDERSON, JANE LOUISE BLAIR, librarian, horse breeder; b. Wilkinsburg, Pa., Nov. 6, 1948; d. Francis Preston and Mary Louise (Maxwell) Blair; B.S. in Edn., Clarion State Coll., 1971; M.S.L.S., Duquesne U., 1974; m. Russell Karl Anderson, Jr., Apr. 20, 1973; children—Christina Lynn, Melissa Jane. Substitute tchr. Wilkinsburg Schs., 1971, tchr. Head Start, 1971; librarian Franklin Regional Schs. Intermediate High Sch., Murrysville, Pa., 1971—; breeder quarter horses, Fenelton, Pa., 1978—. Vol. mem. Rescue 5 Ambulance, Murrysville, 1974-76, Medic I ambulance, 1976-78; sec. Franklin Area REACT, 1976-78; first aid instr. ARC, Murrysville, 1975-80; instr. CPR, Am. Heart Assn., Westmoreland County, 1976-80; vol. worker with deaf, 1978—; vol. United Cerebral Palsey, Butler, Pa., 1981—. Cert. public librarian, Pa. Mem. Westmoreland County Library Assn., Pa. Library Assn., Am. Quarter Horse Assn., Pa. Quarter Horse Assn., Ohio Quarter Horse Assn., Butler County Farmers Market Assn. Presbyterian. Home: Fern Valley Farm PO Box 12 Fenelton PA 16034 Office: 3220 School Rd Murrysville PA 15668

ANDERSON, JEAN, author, editor; b. Raleigh, N.C., Oct. 12, 1931; d. Donald Benton and Marian March (Johnson) Anderson; B.S., Cornell U., 1951; M.S. (Pulitzer Traveling scholar), Columbia, 1957. Women's editor N.C. Agrl. Extension Service, 1951-54, Raleigh Times, 1954-56; asst. editor Ladies' Home Jour., N.Y.C., 1957-59, editorial asso., 1959-62, mng. editor, 1963; sr. editor Venture Mag., 1964-71; contbg. editor Family Circle mag., 1975—. Recipient So. Women's Achievement award Reed & Barton, 1963, George Hedman Meml. award, 1971; R.T. French Tastemaker award, 1975, 80. Mem. Am. Home Econs. Assn., Home Economists in Bus., Les Dames d'Escoffier (v.p. 1981-83), N.Y. Women's Culinary Alliance, Author's League, N.Y. Travel Writers, Gamma Phi Beta, Phi Kappa Phi, Omicron Nu. Author: (with Yeffe Kimball) The Art of American Indian Cooking, 1965; Food Is More Than Cooking, 1968; Henry the Navigator, Prince of Portugal, 1969; The Family Circle 16-Volume Illustrated Library of Cooking, 1972; The Haunting of America, 1973; The Family Circle Cookbook, 1974; (with Elaine Hanna) The Doubleday Cookbook, 1975; Recipes from America's Restored Villages, 1975; The Green Thumb Preserving Guide, 1976; The Grass Roots Cookbook, 1977; Jean Anderson's Processor Cooking, 1978; (with Ruth Buchan) Half a Can of Tomato Paste and other Culinary Dilemmas, 1980; Jean Anderson Cooks, 1982; Unforbidden Sweets, 1982. Home: care McIntosh and Otis 475 Fifth Ave New York NY 10017

ANDERSON, JEAN FOSTER, home economist; b. Fort Worth, Mar. 23, 1952; d. P.A. and Myrtle (Tipton) Foster; B.S., Tex. Tech. U., 1973; M.S., N. Tex. State U., 1979; m. Randall Harold Anderson, Aug. 25, 1972; 1 son, Randall Clayton. Asst. county extension agt. Wichita County, Wichita Falls, Tex., 1973-74, county agt. 4-H, Parker County, Weatherford, Tex., 1974-80. Recipient Youth Appreciation award Weatherford Optimist Club, 1979. Mem. Tex. Assn. 4-H Agts. (dist. dir.), Nat. Assn. Extension 4-H Agts., Tex. Assn. Extension Home Economists, Nat. Assn. Extension Home Economists, Phi Upsilon Omicron. Mem. Ch. of Christ.

ANDERSON, JEAN VALERIE, chem. co. exec.; b. Cheshire, Eng., Jan. 25, 1944; came to U.S., 1969, naturalized, 1979; d. Harry Ewart and Audrey Constance (Reece) A.; student Lowther Coll., Eng., 1956-60, Foulkes Bus. Sch., 1960-62, Hunter Coll., N.Y.C., 1973-75, New Sch. Social Research, 1980-81. Adminstr., Sir. Hugh Casson & Partners, Architects, London, 1963-65, Stucke, Harrison, Ritchie & Partners, Architects, Johannesburg, South Africa, 1966-67; asst. to area comptroller Hilton Internat. Co., Montreal, Que., Can., 1967-69; asst. to comptroller Intercontinental Hotels, 1969-71; asst. to U.S. rep. to U.N., sr. partner Amen, Weisman & Butler, N.Y.C., 1973-76; asst. to pres. Nat. Econ. Research Assos., N.Y.C., 1976-78; mgr. Imperial Chem. Industries, Ltd., N.Y.C., 1978—. Coordinator, Expo '67, Montreal, 1969; vol. Mount Sinai Hosp., N.Y.C., 1976-77. Mem. Nat. Passenger Traffic Assn., Corp. Travel Assn. Clubs: Royal Liverpool (Eng.); Women's Nat. Republican. St. Barthalomews Ch. (N.Y.C.). Home: 1391 Madison Ave New York NY 10029 Office: 645 Fifth Ave New York NY 10022

ANDERSON, JOAN SCHEUERMANN, clin. psychologist, educator; b. New Orleans, Mar. 17, 1933; d. Leonhard Naef and Margaret Scheuermann; B.A., Sophie Newcomb Coll., 1954; Ph.D., U. Houston, 1969; m. Frank Clayton Anderson, Jr., Apr. 30, 1954; children—Frank Clayton III, Mollie Elise. Pvt. practice clin. psychology, Houston, 1969—; asst. prof. Baylor Coll. Medicine, Houston; chmn. Tex. Bd. Examiners of Psychologists, 1982. Bd. dirs. Living Bank, 1965—, Children's World, 1970-75, Homes of St. Mark, 1977—. Mem. Am. Psychol. Assn., Tex. Psychol. Assn. (pres. 1977), Houston Psychol. Assn. (pres. 1979). Episcopalian. Office: 1535 West Loop S Suite 222 Houston TX 77027

ANDERSON, JOANN MARIE, railroad ofcl.; b. Buffalo, Feb. 26, 1934; d. Francis and Mercedes (Halloran) Bronson; B.S., Annhurst Coll., 1955, M.A., 1956. Editor, columnist Hartford (Conn.) Courant, 1955-59; producer, hostess daily interview program Sta. ZBM-TV, Hamilton, Bermuda, 1959-64; editor/creator Trade Winds column Royal Gazette, Hamilton, 1959-64; public relations dir. Princess Hotels, Hamilton, 1962-64, Alcohol Safety Action Project, Fairfax, Va., 1970-75; mgr. employee assistance program Amtrak, Arlington, Va., 1975—; lectr. on employee assistance programs; cons. addictive disorders, Fairfax County. Bd. dirs. Women's Home, Arlington, 1973-74; chmn. No. Va. Intergroup, 1978-79; bd. dirs. Council on Alcoholism Fairfax County. Named to YMCA Acad. Women Achievers, 1981; recipient Amtrak Pres.'s achievement award, 1981, also named Employee of Year. Mem. Nat. Fedn. Press Women, Nat. Assn. Labor/Mgmt. Adminstrs. and Consultants on Alcoholism, Va. Press Women (six 1st place awards for writing 1977-79), Public Relations Soc. Am., Nat. Council on Alcoholism, Washington Area Council on Alcoholism and Drug Abuse, Alcohol and Drug Programs of N.Am., Nat. Assn. Alcoholism Counselors, Va. Assn. Alcoholism Counselors, R.R. Personnel Assn. (chmn. employee assistance program dirs. sect. 1980-81), Am. Council Railroad Women. Office: Amtrak 2009 14th St Arlington VA 22201

ANDERSON, JOLENE SULLIVAN, publisher; b. Tulare, Calif.; d. James P. Sr., and Helen B. (Walters) Slover; ed. Victor Valley Coll., Riverside City Coll.; m. Douglas R. Anderson, June 14, 1975; 1 dau. by previous marriage—Sabrina Jo. Model, Connor Sch. Modeling, Fresno, Calif., 1955-65; actress M. Kosloff Studios, Hollywood, Calif., 1965; nat. sales mgr. Armed Services Publs., 1966-68; pres., dir. Sullivan Publs., Inc., Riverside, Calif., 1970—. Mem. Riverside Tourist and Conv. Com., 1981, public relations com. YWCA, 1981; treas. DeAnza Verde Homeowners, 1978; active U.S. Ski Team, Rape Crisis Center. Mem. Riverside C. of C., San Bernardino C. of C., Ontario C. of C., Rancho Cucamonga C. of C., Printers Industries Am. Club: Soroptimists (chmn. 1981). Home: Riverside CA Office: 2904 Rubidoux Blvd Riverside CA 92509

ANDERSON, JUDITH ETHEL, nurse; b. Buffalo, Feb. 11, 1939; d. Ross Bartlet and Evelyn Grace (Lemke) McIntyre; R.N., Buffalo Gen. Hosp. Sch. Nursing, 1959; B.S., State U. N.Y. at Buffalo, 1965; m. James Edward Anderson, Nov. 23, 1961; children—Scott, Kirstin. Nurse, Buffalo State Hosp., 1959-61, Buffalo Gen. Hosp., part-time 1960, Buffalo VA Hosp., 1961-64; camp nurse, summer 1965; nurse Buffalo Children's Hosp., part-time 1965-68; pvt. duty nurse, part-time, evenings 1962-71; pub. health nurse Erie County Health Dept., 1966-67; clin. instr. pub. health nursing State U. N.Y., Buffalo, 1967-68, coordinator refresher nurse programs, 1968; cons. refresher nurse program Trocaire Coll., fall 1968; various ednl. positions Bd. Co-op. Ednl. Services, Erie 1 dist., 1968-70, instr. adult licensed practical nurse program, Lancaster, N.Y., 1977-78; instr. West Seneca (N.Y.) Children's Psychiat. Hosp., 1970; coordinator homemaker-home health aide program, pub. health nursing supr. Vis. Nursing Assn. Buffalo, 1971-77; instr., coordinator personal care services aide tng. program Child and Family Services Soc. Erie County, 1977, instr., coordinator personal care service and home health aide Genesee County program, 1978-79; lectr. grad. program SUNY, Buffalo, 1978-79, adj. clin. faculty Sch. Nursing; lectr. Genesee Community Coll., 1978-79; dir. nursing and patient services Genesee County Health Dept., 1978—; adj. clin. faculty Daemen Coll. Sch. Nursing. Active ARC, Developmental Disabilities Council Genesee County; bd. dirs. Genesee Family Counseling Center; vice chmn. Genesee County Vol. Hospice League; mem. Genesee County Youth Program; mem. Remove Intoxicated Drivers; mem. fund allocations com. Genesee United Fund. Mem. Am. Nurses Assn., N.Y. Nurse Assn., Am. Public Health Assn., N.Y. Public Health Assn., N.Y. State Council Home Health Agys., Buffalo Meml. Soc., Buffalo Gen. Hosp., SUNY at Buffalo Sch. Nursing alumni assns., Genesee Interagy. Council, Am. Cancer Soc., Genesee Womans Network. Unitarian-Universalist. Contbr. articles to profl. jours. Home: 10504 Gillate Rd Alexander NY 14005 Office: 3837 W Main St Rd Batavia NY 14020

ANDERSON, JUDITH WYCKOFF, securities co. exec.; b. Chgo., July 25, 1946; d. Carlyle E. and Elizabeth (Wyckoff) A.; B.A., Briarcliff Coll., 1968; postgrad. Keller Grad. Sch. Mgmt., 1979—. Cartographer, Rand McNally & Co., Chgo., 1966; with A.G. Becker & Co., Chgo., 1968—, asst. v.p., 1976-81, v.p., 1981—; Dir. vols. Fetridge for Congress, 1972. Mem. Nat. Assn. Securities Dealers (registered rep.), Commodities Future Trading Commn., N.Y. Stock Exchange (registered rep.). Republican. Methodist. Clubs: Woman's Athletic Club Chgo., Chgo. Fin. Exchange, Glen View, Jr. League of Chgo. (treas. Soupcon 1979—). Home: 21 W Goethe 9A Chicago IL 60610 Office: 1 First National Plaza Suite 2900 Chicago IL 60603

ANDERSON, JUNE BARBARA, designer; b. N.Y.C., Feb. 22, 1929; d. Jay and Anita B. Kroll; B.F.A., Columbia U., 1951; m. William Anderson, Nov. 16, 1962; children—Lincoln, Odile. Vice pres. design Soptra Fabrics, N.Y.C., 1962-76; dir. design Prints for TEXFI Industries, Inc., N.Y.C., 1976-81, Prints for Razor Mills, Scissor Prints div., 1981—. Recipient Tommy award, 1981. Mem. Fashion Group. Office: 1460 Broadway New York NY 10036

ANDERSON, KAREN ELIZABETH, ins. co. ofcl.; b. Brockton, Mass., Jan. 16, 1954; d. Lawrence Wellman and Emmaline Davis (Gillock) Anderson; B.S., Medaille Coll., 1981. Asst. mgr. Gurney Bros. Jewelers, Brockton, Mass., 1970-75; adminstrv. asst./asst. sports info. dir. Stonehill Coll., North Easton, Mass., 1975-77; tchr. public schs., Hodgdon, Maine, 1977-78; supr. Magrams, Glens Falls, N.Y., 1978-79; supr., unit head Exchange Mut. Ins. Co., Buffalo, 1979—. Bus. mgr. Brockton Community Sch. Playhouse, 1976-77; chmn. vols. Summerfest '77, Brockton Community Sch. Program; mem. adv. bd., bus. mgr. Div. for Youth-Employment Unit. Recipient cert. of commendation N.Y. Regional Data Ednl. Systems, 1981; cert. Am. Alliance Insurers, Am. Mgmt. Assn. Mem. Exec. Female, Inc., Nat. Assn. Female Execs. Lutheran. Clubs: Internat. Order Rainbow Girls (worthy adviser 1972). Home: 901 Elmwood Ave Buffalo NY 14222 Office: 741 Delaware Ave Buffalo NY 14201

ANDERSON, KATHLEEN SHAW, ornithologist; b. Livingston, Mont., June 15, 1923; d. Ernest Wakefield and Kathleen Mary (Arthur) Shaw; m. Paul Timothy Anderson, Nov. 7, 1947; children—Wakefield Timothy, Kathleen Mary. Ornithologist, Encephalitis Field Sta., Lakeville, Mass., 1957-68; exec. dir. Manomet (Mass.) Bird Obs., 1969—. Trustee, past pres. Plymouth County Wildlands Trust; past pres. Union Ch. Soc. South Carver, Mass.; mem. Mass. Trails Adv. Com., 1974—; mem. nongame adv. com. Div. Fisheries and Wildlife, Commonwealth of Mass., 1981—. Mem. Am. Ornithologists Union (elected), Wilson Ornithol. Soc., Cooper Ornithol. Soc., Brit. Ornithologists Union, Northeastern Bird-banding Assn. (past dir.), Eastern Bird-Banding Assn. (dir.), Nuttall Ornithol. Club, Ecol. Soc. Am., New Eng. Wildflower Soc. (dir. 1978—). Contbr. articles to profl. jours. Home: RFD 2 Winter St Middleboro MA 02346 Office: PO Box 936 Manomet MA 02345

ANDERSON, LEE BERGER (MRS. WILLIAM HOOKER RYLAND), lawyer; b. Holden, W.Va.; d. Arthur F. Berger; J.D. with highest honors, George Washington U., 1939, LL.M., 1941; m. Donald Brown Anderson (dec.); m. 2d, William Hooker Ryland. Admitted to D.C. bar, 1939, Idaho bar, 1949, Md. bar, 1973, U.S. Supreme Ct. bar, 1947, U.S. Ct. Claims, 1947; atty. Office Solicitor, U.S. Dept. Labor, 1942-43; individual practice law, Caldwell, Idaho, 1948-53; trial atty. U.S. Dept. Justice, Washington, 1943-48, 53-72; pvt. practice law Md. and D.C., 1972—. Lectr. D.C. YWCA, Washington, 1965-71; arbitrator arbitration panel Office Consumer Affairs, Montgomery County (Md.), 1973; speaker fed. women's program Speakers List, U.S. Civil Service Commn., 1976—. Chmn. legal sub-com. D.C. Commn. Status of Women, 1967-69; mem. jud. conf. U.S. Ct. Appeals, D.C. Circuit. Mem. Am. Arbitration Assn., Am. Judicature Soc., Am., Internat., D.C. (chmn. civil service law com. 1977—), Internat. (council 1976—), Fed., Md. State, Montgomery County bar assns., Women's Bar Assn. D.C. (pres. 1969-70), Nat. Assn. Women Lawyers (sec., chmn. com. women in public service, editor jour. 1973, v.p. 1974-75, pres. 1976-77, mem. exec. bd. 1977—, del. Internat. Bar Assn.), D.C. Fedn. Bus. and Profl. Women (sec. state fedn., chmn. state legislation com. 1969-71), Potomac Toastmistress Club (pres.), D.C. Quota Club (dir.), Caldwell Bus. and Profl. Women (pres.), LWV (pres. Caldwell), Phi Alpha Delta, Phi Delta Delta (pres. alumnae chpt. 1964, 71). Republican. Home: 3809 Montrose Driveway North Chevy Chase MD 20815

ANDERSON, LILLIE MAE, social worker; b. Columbia, S.C., Apr. 15, 1918; d. Julius and Lillie (Thompson) Hardy; B.A. magna cum laude, Benedict Coll., 1959; postgrad. Howard U., 1960-61; M.S.W., Atlanta U., 1969; postgrad., U. S.C., 1975, 78, So. Regional Inst., 1976, U. Ala., 1980; m. Calvin R. Goff, Aug. 1, 1981. Beautician, Columbia, S.C., 1938-45; file clk. Office Dependency Benefits, Newark, 1945-46; group leader Utility Electric Corp., East Newark, N.J., 1946-52; owner, propr. A & W Store, Columbia, 1952-56; group worker Bethlehem Community Center, Columbia, 1959-60; social worker S.C. Mental Health, Columbia, 1960-63, 66-68, Pilgrim State Hosp., West Brentwood, N.Y., 1963-66; supr. Columbia Housing Authority, 1969-71; social worker VA, Lyons, N.J., 1971, Dorn VA Hosp., Columbia, 1971—, coordinator visually impaired service, instr. cardiac rehab. program. Mental health grantee, 1960-61; VA grantee, 1968-69. Mem. Nat. Assn. Social Workers, State of S.C. Bd. Social Work Registration, Richland and Lexington Counties Social Work Assn., Social Work Club (pres. 1973), Zeta Phi Beta, Alpha Kappa Mu. Democrat. Roman Catholic. Home: Route 5 Box 166 Columbia SC 29203 Office: Dorn VA Hosp Garners Ferry Rd Columbia SC 29201

ANDERSON, LINDA MARIE, mfg. co. exec.; b. Berkeley, Calif., July 29, 1955; d. Michael and Rae (Kaitz) A.; B.C.E., U. Calif., Berkeley, 1977. Project engr. paper products Procter & Gamble, Modesto, Calif., 1977-78, prodn. supr., 1979-80, product tech. engr., Cin., 1980—. Home: 829 Clearfield Ln Cincinnati OH 45240 Office: 6105 Center Hill Rd Cincinnati OH 45224

ANDERSON, LINDA SUE, healthcare computer info. systems profl.; b. Columbus, Ohio, Aug. 13, 1947; d. Charles Robert and Arlene Faye (Wilhelm) Anderson; B.A. in Sociology, Pa. State U., 1969. Accounts receivable specialist Hahnemann Med. Coll. and Hosp., Phila., 1971-73, asst. patient accounts mgr., 1973-75; installation dir., account mgr. spl. projects Shared Med. Systems, Malvern, Pa., 1975-80, internat. installations dir., 1981, installation project support specialist, 1982—. Mem. Healthcare Fin. Mgmt. Assn. Home: 50 S Valley Rd Paoli PA 19301 Office: 51 Valley Stream Pkwy Malvern PA 19355

ANDERSON, LOIS MARILYN, psychologist; b. Cambridge, Minn., Mar. 19, 1934; d. Oliver F. and Marjorie C. (Strait) Ledin; B.S., Gustavus Adolphus Coll., 1956; Ph.D. (fellow), U. Minn., 1969; m. Malcolm Charles Anderson, July 9, 1960; 1 son, Andrew Ledin. Intern in counseling Student Counseling Bur. and U. Hosp., U. Minn., 1959-60; research psychologist InterStudy, Mpls., 1969-73; state program mgmt. coordinator for human services Minn. Dept. Adminstrn., St. Paul, 1973-77, asst. dir. mgmt. services div., 1977-79; staff psychologist Minn. State Services for the Blind, 1979-81, dir. psychol. services, 1981—; lectr. U. Minn. Grad. Schs. Public Affairs and Social Work, 1975, 76. Treas. Scout Mothers of Viking council troop 129, Boy Scouts Am., Mpls., 1979-81; chairperson facilities planning and space planning coms. N.W. YMCA Bd. Mgmt., 1971-73; mem. Twin Cities Met. Council Adv. Com. on Waste Mgmt. and Water Quality, 1976-78; Sunday sch. tchr., sec., mem. ch. council Salem Luth. Ch., 1979—; bd. dirs. Camden Community Theatre, 1981—. Mem. Am. Psychol. Assn., Minn. Psychol. Assn., Minn. Women Psychologists, Psi Chi, Pi Lambda Theta. Lutheran. Author: (with others) AFDC Employment and Referral Guidelines, 1973; Impact of Welfare Reform on the Elderly Poor, 1973; Medicaid Cost Containment and Long Term Care, 1976. Home: 4400 Victory Ave Minneapolis MN 55412 Office: 1745 University Ave Saint Paul MN 55104

ANDERSON, LONI, actress; b. St. Paul, Aug. 5; d. Klaydon and Maxine (Kalin) A.; student U. Minn.; m. Ross Bickell, Jan. 28, 1974; 1 dau. by previous marriage, Deidra. Stage debut in Born Yesterday, 1970; stage appearances include: Star Spangled Girl, Send Me No Flowers, Never Too Late, Paris Is Out, Any Wednesday, The Death and Life of Sneaky Fitch, Fashion, The Patrick Pearse Motel; musical appearances include: Fiddler On The Roof, Can-Can, The Threepenny Opera, The Secret Life of Walter Mitty; guest appearances on TV shows include: Three's Company, The Incredible Hulk, Love Boat, Three On A Date (film), Barnaby Jones, Phyllis; appeared on TV series WKRP in Cincinnati; TV film The Jayne Mansfield Story, 1980; film Vigilante Force, 1976. Mem. SAG. Address: care Kingsley Cotton & Associates 321 S Beverly Dr Beverly Hills CA 90212 *

ANDERSON, LYNN, singer; b. Grand Forks, N.D., Sept. 26, 1947; d. Casey and Elizabeth Jane (Haaby) Anderson; m. Glen Sutton; 1 dau., Lisa; m. 2d, H.H. Stream, III; children—Melissa, William Gray. Appeared on TV shows: Lawrence Welk, Ed Sullivan, Dean Martin,

Johnny Carson, Andy Williams; recording artist Permian Records; albums include Flower of Love, Games People Play, How Can I Unlove You?, It Makes You Happy, Keep Me in Mind, No Love at All, Rose Garden, Smile for Me, Top of the World, You're My Man, What a Man My Man Is, I've Never Loved Anyone More, Listen to a Country Song, All the King's Horses, Country Girl, I Love What Love is Doing to Me, He Ain't You, Outlaws, Even Cowgirls Get the Blues. Named Female Singer of Year, Country Music Assn., 1970; recipient Grammy award, 1970; 16 Gold records, 2 Platinum records. Office: 850 Overton Ln Nashville TN 37220

ANDERSON, MARCIA ANN, educator; b. Bloomfield, Nebr., Feb. 22, 1942; d. Frank H. and Minnie L. Peitzmeier; B.A., Midland Lutheran Coll., Fremont, Nebr., 1954; M.Ed., U. Nebr., 1969; Ph.D., So. Ill. U., 1975; 1 dau., Erika Brooke. Instr. Stromsburg (Nebr.) Sr. High Sch., 1964-66; instr. Adult High Sch., Lincoln, Nebr., 1966; instr. Millard Lefler Jr. High Sch., Lincoln, 1966-70; instr. Lincoln Sch. Commerce, 1966-70; instr. East High Sch., Lincoln, 1970; instr. bus. edn. program So. Ill. U., 1970-74, asst. prof., supr. secretarial and office specialties, 1975-81, asst. prof., program coordinator bus. edn., 1975-81, asso. prof. bus. edn., 1981—; corp. pres. Career Assos., Inc., 1981—. Mem. AAUW, Am. Ednl. Research Assn., Am. Vocat. Assn., Am. Vocat. Edn. Research Assn., Ill Bus. Edn. Assn., Ill. Vocat. Assn., Internat. Word Processing Assn., Nat. Assn. Bus. Tchr. Edn., Nat. Assn. Tchr. Educators for Bus. and Office Edn., Nat. Bus. Edn. Assn., Phi Delta Kappa, Delta Pi Epsilon, Iota Lambda Sigma. Lutheran. Contbr. in field. Home: RR 6 Heritage Hills Carbondale IL 62901 Office: Dept Vocat Edn Studies Bus Edn Program So Ill U Carbondale IL 62901

ANDERSON, MARCIA ELAINE, retail sales exec.; b. Evanston, Ill., Mar. 26, 1947; d. Franklin Wesley and Margaret Lois Helikson; student Tyler Sch. Art, 1966, Grossmont Coll., 1973-74; m. Andrew G. Anderson, Aug. 10, 1974; children—Daniel, Carey. Sales exec. Princess House Products Inc., North Dighton, Mass., 1973—, div. sales organizer San Diego area. Recipient numerous sales awards. Mem. Career Women's Assn. (pres.), Women in Sales, NOW, Nat. Mgmt. Assn., Nat. Assn. Female Execs. Home: 5929 Highplace Dr San Diego CA 92120

ANDERSON, MARGARET TAYLER, univ. guidance center adminstr.; b. Castle Rock, Wash., May 1, 1918; d. George Lawrence and Frances Tressie (Huntington) Tayler; A.B., Willamette U., Salem, Oreg., 1939, M.A., 1940; M.A., Columbia U., 1967, profl. cert. in student personnel, 1970; m. James Kress Anderson, Dec. 31, 1940; children—Bret Douglas, Blythe Rebecca, Beth Lynn, Burke Stuart. Asst. traveling Librarian Oreg. State Library, 1940; chemist Reynolds Metals Co., Longview, Wash., 1941; electronics technician Sperry Gyroscope Co., Lake Success, N.Y., 1942-43; adminstrv. asst. New Sch. Social Research, N.Y.C., 1944-49; self-employed real estate broker, Palisades, N.Y., 1952—; dir. Rockland County Guidance Center for Women, Rockland Community Coll., Nyack, N.Y., 1969—; adv. bd. Nyack Headstart, 1970-72; mem. adj. faculty Coll. New Rochelle, spring 1977; assoc. faculty Empire State Coll., 1982—. Democratic candidate for Rockland County clk., 1961; bd. visitors Rockland State Hosp., 1957-63, Haverstraw Ecumenical Project, 1969-77; mem. N.Y. State Displaced Homemakers Adv. Council, 1978-80. Mem. Nat. Assn. Women Deans, Adminstrs. and Counselors (adv. council continuing edn. 1973-74), Rockland County Mental Health Assn. (dir. 1954-70), Rockland County Bd. Realtors (pres. 1966-67), Profl. Women's Caucus (pres. 1972-73), Am. Personnel and Guidance Assn., Rockland County Manpower Council, Rockland County Child Devel. and Daycare Council, Rockland Bus. and Profl. Women, Pearl River Assn. Univ. Women. Home: Route 9W Palisades NY 10964 Office: Rockland County Guidance Center 83 Main St Nyack NY 10964

ANDERSON, MARIAN, contralto; b. Phila., Feb. 17, 1902; d. John Berkeley and Anna Anderson; ed. Phila. pub. schs.; mus. edn. pvt. study in Phila., N.Y. and abroad; hon. degrees 23 Am. ednl. instns., 1 Korean; m. Orpheus H. Fisher, July 24, 1943. As child sang in Union Bapt. Ch. choir, Phila.; a fund raised through a church concert enabled her to take singing lessons under an Italian instr.; won 1st prize in competition with 300 others at N.Y. Lewisohn Stadium, 1925; began singing career, 1924; debut in Un Ballo in Maschera, Met. Opera, 1955; has made many concert tours of the U.S. and Europe; one of the leading contraltos in world; appearances in all famous concert halls, stadia, now ret. U.S. del. to UN, 1955, also 13th Gen. Assembly. Recipient Bok Award, 1940, Congl. Medal of Honor, 1977; awarded Finnish decoration "probenignitate humana," 1940; decorations from Sweden, Philippines, Haiti, Liberia, France, numerous states and cities in U.S.; Yokus Lo medal (Japan). Mem. Alpha Kappa Alpha. Author: My Lord, What a Morning. Home: Danbury CT 06810 Office: care ICM Artists Ltd 40 W 57th St New York NY 10019

ANDERSON, MARIAN MARGARET, county extension agt.; b. Osage, Iowa, Aug. 15, 1946; d. Leo and Stella Marie (Heimermann) Smith; A.A., Austin Jr. Coll., 1966; B.S., Iowa State U., 1968; m. Arthur E. Anderson, Sept. 6, 1975. County extension agt., Big Stone County, Ortonville, Minn. Bd. dirs. United Fund, 1978-79. Mem. Minn. Assn. Extension Agts. (officer), Nat. Assn. Extension Home Economists. Am. Home Econs. Assn., Epsilon Sigma Phi. Roman Catholic. Home: Rt 2 Box 100 Ortonville MN 56278 Office: 342 NW 2d St Ortonville MN 56278

ANDERSON, MARIANE BEANE, clin. lab. mgr.; b. Lancaster, Pa., June 7, 1931; d. Paul Esbenshade, Sr. and Viola (Fisher) Beane; B.S. in Med. Tech., Elizabethtown Coll., 1954; m. W. Eugene Anderson, Aug. 21, 1954; children—Mary Lynne, Brent Eugene, Brian Keith. Med. technologist Lancaster Gen. Hosp., 1953, Hershey (Pa.) Hosp., 1953-55; successively med. technologist, quality control supr., tech. services mgr., regional lab. mgr. Consol. Biomed. Labs., Inc., Columbus, Ohio, 1971—. Mem. Central Ohio Soc. Med. Technologists (sec., pres.), Am. Soc. Clin. Pathologists (registered med. technologist, affiliate), Am. Soc. Med. Technologists, Ohio Soc. Med. Technologists, Assn. Women in Sci., Dublin Women in Bus. and Professions, Worthington Bus. and Profl. Women. Home: 323 Clover Ln Dublin OH 43017 Office: 6370 Wilcox Rd Dublin OH 43017

ANDERSON, MARIE, editor, former univ. adminstr.; b. Pensacola, Fla., May 15, 1916; d. Robert H. and Marie (Willard) A.; A.B., Duke U., 1937; postgrad. Katharine Gibbs Sch., 1939. Researcher Batten, Barton, Durstine & Osborne, N.Y.C., 1946; reporter, copy reader women's dept. Miami (Fla.) News, 1946-50; sub-editor Miami Herald, 1950-55, asst. women's editor, 1955-59, women's editor, 1959-71; dean univ. relations and devel. Fla. Internat. U., 1973-75, asst. to v.p. community affairs, 1975-76, alumni coordinator, 1976-78; editor Update mag. Hist. Assn. So. Fla., 1979—. Recipient Fla. Women's Press Club award, J.C. Penney U. Mo. award. Mem. Jr. League, Soc. Profl. Journalists, Women in Communications, Phi Beta Kappa, Delta Delta Delta, Theta Alpha Phi, Delta Kappa Gamma. Democrat. Episcopalian. Author: Julia's Daughters: Women in Dade's History, 1979. Home: 2840 SW 28 Terr Miami FL 33133

ANDERSON, MARIE LORETTA, univ. adminstr.; b. Waltham, Mass., Aug. 31, 1924; d. William E. and Loretta M. (Walsh) Foley; student Waltham public schs.; m. George L. Anderson, June 2, 1946; 1 son, Jeffrey G. Sec., Raytheon Mfg. Co., Waltham, 1943-46; sales sec. U.S. Gypsum Co., Boston, 1945-50; adminstr. dept. biology Brandeis U., Waltham, 1960—. Mem. Soc. Research Adminstrs., Common Cause. Club: Fairs n'Squares Sq. Dance (v.p.). Office: Dept Biology Brandeis Univ Waltham MA 02254

ANDERSON, MARILYS ANN, med. technologist; b. Balt., June 15, 1950; d. Harry Kenneth and Bonnie Bolt (O'Shields) Dicely; B.S. in Med. Tech., Coll. Charleston (S.C.), 1972; m. Allen Franklin, Mar. 25, 1972; children—Hillary Erin, Lyndsey Morgan. Med. technologist Med. U. S.C., Charleston, 1972-73, Ga. Baptist Hosp., Atlanta, 1973-75; med. technologist, then supr. St. Joseph Meml. Hosp., Murphysboro, Ill., 1975-81; med. technologist chemistry Richmond Meml. Hosp., Rockingham, N.C., 1981—; instr. hematology Med. U. S.C., 1972-73. Mem. Am. Soc. Clin. Pathologists (affiliate), So. Ill. Med. Tech. Ednl. Group (charter, past sec.). Democrat. Baptist. Office: Richmond Meml Hosp Lab Rockingham NC 28379

ANDERSON, MARJORIE E. A., mus. adminstr.; b. Providence, Jan. 30, 1939; d. Anthony and Marian Amado; A.B., Massasoit Community Coll., 1974; B.A., Southeastern Mass. U., 1976; 1 dau., Sherry Antonnette. Head start parent coordinator HEW, Plymouth South Shore Community Action Council, Plymouth, Mass., 1971-74, counselor Neighborhood Youth Corps, 1974-76; dir. Parting Ways, The Mus. of Afro-Am. Ethnohistory, Inc., Plymouth, Mass., 1974—; pres. Parting Ways Corp., 1975—, dir., 1976-80. Mem. Plymouth Bicentennial Commn., 1974-76; mem. Mass. Bicentennial Commn., 1975-80; mem. Plymouth Arts Council, 1980—, Plymouth Fair Housing Commn., 1980-81, Mass. Social Service Area Adv. Bd., 1980-81. Mem. African-Am. Museums Assn. (New Eng. counselor at large 1980—), Assn. for Study Afro-Am. Life and History, Am. Assn. Museums, Am. Assn. State and Local History, Nat. Trust for Hist. Preservation. Democrat. Office: 130 Court St Plymouth MA 02360

ANDERSON, MARLA BETH, educator; b. Indpls., Apr. 16, 1956; d. Donald James and Shirley Rae (Williams) A.; B.A., U. Mo., St. Louis, 1980; M.A., U. Kans., Lawrence, 1982, postgrad., 1982—. Adminstrv. asst. Patman Meat Co., Los Angeles, 1977-78; regional sales service rep. Esprit de Corps, San Francisco, 1978-79; mgr. parts dept. Schneider Service Co., St. Louis, 1979-80; instr. communication studies U. Kans., Lawrence, 1980-82. Mem. Big Brother-Big Sister Orgn., Columbia, Mo., 1975-76. Mem. Internat. Communication Assn., Phi Kappa Phi. Home: 1315 1/2 W 19th Terr Lawrence KS 66044 Office: U Kans 1034 Wescoe Hall Lawrence KS 66044

ANDERSON, MARLENE SUE, mgmt. cons.; b. Sterling, Ill., Mar. 8, 1931; d. Enos L. and Evelyn (Sundberg) Rohrer; B.S., No. Ill. U., 1956, M.Ed., 1956, M.S. in Counseling, 1971; m. Robert H. Anderson, Aug. 15, 1953; children—Cynthia Lynn, David Paul. Instr., William Rainey Harper Coll., Palatine, Ill., 1975, Triton Coll., River Grove, Ill., 1979-81; pres., owner Anderson & Assocs., Mgmt. Tng., Hinsdale, Ill., 1970—; speaker in field. Counselor, Wholistic Health Center, Hinsdale, 1971-73. Mem. Ill. Tng. and Devel. Assn., Am. Soc. Tng. and Devel., Women in Mgmt. (chpt. treas. 1979), Chgo. Assn. Commerce and Industry, Oak Brook (Ill.) Assn. Commerce and Industry, Oak Brook Execs. Club, Execs. Club Chgo., Nat. Assn. Female Execs. Mem. Union Ch. Author: Health Assertive Management, 1978; also articles, chpts. in book. Address: 5509 S Oak St Hinsdale IL 60521

ANDERSON, MARY CROW (MRS. JAMES ROBERT DICKIE ANDERSON), educator; b. Sumter, S.C., July 21, 1922; d. Orin Faison and Innis (Cuttino) Crow; student Winthrop Coll., 1938-39; A.B. magna cum laude, U. S.C., 1942, M.Ed., 1952, Ph.D., 1966; postdoctoral study Exeter Coll., Oxford U., 1971; m. James Robert Dickie Anderson, July 5, 1942; children—James Orin, Barbara Innis, Richard Cothonneau. Tchr. high sch., Bamberg, S.C., 1942, Dentsville, S.C., 1950-51, Columbia, S.C., 1951-56, 60-71; prin. Heathwood Hall Episcopal Sch., Columbia, 1956-60; tchr. English and humanities Dreher High Sch., Columbia, 1960-71, chmn. English dept., 1967-69; asst. prof. U. S.C., Columbia, 1971-75, asso. prof., 1975—, mem. faculty senate, 1973-76, 79—. Mem. creative writing, sch. participation coms. S.C. Tricentennial Commn.; mem. Workshop theatre; chmn. visitation ministry Trinity Cathedral Hosp., 1981—; lic. lay reader Episcopal Diocese Upper S.C., 1981—. Mem. Société de l'Histoire Protestantisme français, South Caroliniana Soc. (exec. council 1979—), S.C. Hist. Soc., Robert Burns Soc., Nat., S.C. (pres. 1967-68) councils tchrs. English, MLA, South Atlantic MLA, DAR (chpt. 1st vice regent 1960-62), Daus. Holy Cross (chmn. chpt. 1953, co-chmn. chpt. 1967-68), Huguenot Soc., Columbia Music Festival Assn., Columbia Stage Soc., Columbia Historic Found., Columbia Art Assn., English-Speaking Union (dir. Columbia br. 1971-73), Phi Beta Kappa (v.p. Alpha of S.C. chpt. 1976-77, pres. 1977-78), Delta Kappa Gamma (v.p. Alpha Eta of S.C. 1976-78, pres. 1978-80), Alpha Psi Omega, Chi Omega. Author: The Huguenot in the South Carolina Novel. Home: 727 Abelia Rd Columbia SC 29205

ANDERSON, MARY JANE, publisher, public relations specialist; b. Richmond, Va., May 27, 1930; d. Francis W. and Margaret G. (Esbrook) A.; B.A. in Journalism, Wayne State U., 1952. Staff writer Skyline mag. and Mich. Motor Carrier, Detroit, 1952-54; reporter Fairchild Publs., Detroit, 1954-57, Home Furnishings Daily/Footwear News, Chgo., 1957-67; food service editor Billboard Publs., N.Y.C., 1967-72; owner The Anderson Report/Catering Merchandiser, also MJA Pub. Relations, Chgo., 1979—. Active local Republican campaigns; broadcaster Chicagoland Radio Info. Services for blind and print handicapped; vol. Rec. for the Blind, N.Y.C. Named Food Editor of Yr., Nat. Assn. Coll. and Univ. Food Services. Mem. Women in Communications (past pres.), Internat. Food Editorial Council (past v.p.). Home and office: 211 E Delaware Apt 1504 Chicago IL 60611

ANDERSON, MARY JORGENSEN, mathematician; b. Winchester, Tex., Oct. 31, 1937; d. Roy Lewis and Nellie Joyce (Hart) Jorgensen; B.S., La. State U., 1965, M.S., 1968, Ph.D., 1979; m. Edmund Hughes Anderson, Oct. 10, 1975; children—Carolyne Gail, Gary Steven, Christopher Lewis. Engring. technician La. Dept. Hwys., Baton Rouge, 1957-60; grad. asst. La. State U., 1965-68, 76-78; instr. in math. Miss. State U., 1970-76, asst. prof. math., 1978-81; mathematician Superior Oil Co., Midland, Tex., 1981—. Mem. Am. Math. Soc., Assn. Women in Math., Miss. Acad. Scis., Pi Mu Epsilon, Phi Delta Kappa. Episcopalian. Contbr. research Papers to Profl. Jours. Home: Route 4 140 Barbara Ln Midland TX 79701 Office: Superior Oil Co PO Box 3901 Midland TX 79702

ANDERSON, MARY LOUISE, mktg. ofcl.; b. Marshall, Minn., June 30, 1942; d. Otto Sigurdur and Catherine (Feller) A.; B.S., U. Minn., 1964. Research analyst Nat. Security Agy., Ft. Meade, Md., 1964-67; with fin. dept. Air Am., 1967-68; conv. coordinator Am. Alumni Council, Washington, 1968-71; sales mgr. John A. Tetley Co., Inc., San Francisco, 1971-75, regional sales mgr., 1979—; sales mgr. Marriott Inn, Berkeley, Calif., 1975-79. Mem. Hotel Sales Mgrs. Assn., Animal Protection Inst., Sausalito Environ. Action Com. Club: Metropolitan. Home: 55 Rodeo Ave Sausalito CA 94965 Office: 450 Sansome St San Francisco CA 94111

ANDERSON, MILADA FILKO, mfg. co. exec.; b. Chgo., Nov. 17, 1922; d. John and Anna (Sianta) Filko; B.S., Northwestern U., 1944, M. Mgmt., 1979; m. George Anderson, Aug. 29, 1945 (div. 1974); children—Mark, Renee, Teri. Tchr. history, Evanston (Ill.) Twp. High Sch., 1946; tchr. social studies, Mt. Prospect (Ill.) Jr. High Sch., 1947-48; dir. F&B Mfg. Co., Chgo., 1965—, corp. sec., 1969-72, pres., 1972—, chmn. bd., 1972—. Mem. Northwestern U. Profl. Womens Assn., Nat. Assn. Investment Clubs, Execs. Club Chgo., Zeta Tau Alpha. Office: F&B Mfg Co 5480 Northwest Hwy Chicago IL 60630

ANDERSON, PATRICIA LACONSTANCE, radio exec.; b. Pavo, Ga., July 12, 1952; d. Richard Russell and Dahlia (Jenkins) A.; B.A. in Speech and Journalism, U. Mich., 1976. Editor, Minority Bull. office career planning and placement U. Mich., Ann Arbor, 1975; newscaster Sta. WJZZ-FM, Bell Broadcasting Co., Detroit, 1977; publicity liaison Detroit Citizens for Proposal "A", 1977; sales services dir. Pathfinder Communications Corp., Stas. WCUZ/WMLW, Grand Rapids, Mich., 1978—; cons. pub. relations and advt. to small bus. Mem. Women in Communications, Inc. (at large), Assn. Study Afro-Am. Life and History. Democrat. Address: 1 McKay Tower Grand Rapids MI 49503

ANDERSON, PEGGY JEAN, univ. adminstr., linguist; b. Fargo, N.D., Mar. 28, 1945; d. Walter Raymond and Elizabeth (Snider) A.; B.S. in Edn., Emporia State U., 1967; M.A. in Linguistics, U. Kans., 1979; m. Richard John Robinson, Apr. 18, 1981. Tchr. spl. edn., English, Kansas City (Kans.) Public Schs., 1967-68; tchr. Somerdale (N.J.) Public Schs., 1968-73; dir. fgn. staff, instr. YMCA Japan, Fukuoka, 1973-77; instr. Applied English Center, U. Kans., Lawrence, 1977-79; coordinator English as Second Lang. Programs, U. Iowa, 1979-81; curriculum coordinator Intensive English Lang. Center, Wichita State U., 1981-82, asso. dir. center, 1982—; reviewer Scott-Foresman Pub. Co.; cons. to community groups, public schs., internat. bus. Nat. Assn. Fgn. Student Affairs grantee, 1980—. Mem. Nat. Tchrs. English to Speakers Other Langs., Mid-Am. Tchrs. English to Speakers Other Langs., (pres. elect), Nat. Assn. Fgn. Student Affairs, Linguistic Soc. Am., Mid-Am. MLA. Democrat. Episcopalian. Research in second lang. acquisition, teaching methodology, curriculum design. Home: 3826 Meadowlane Wichita KS 67218 Office: Intensive English Lang Center Wichita State U Wichita KS 67208

ANDERSON, PENELOPE PENCE, advt. exec.; b. Salt Lake City, Jan. 23, 1943; d. Joseph Thomas and Carol Gretchen (Hofmann) Pence; B.A., U. Wash., 1963; M.A., Annenberg Sch. Communications, U. So. Calif., 1977. Asst. media buyer J. Walter Thompson Advt., Los Angeles, 1963-64; public relations dir. John Lithen Corp., Beverly Hills, Calif., 1964-65; public service dir. Metromedia KTTV, Los Angeles, 1965-66; asso. producer Winchell-Mahoney Show, Metromedia KTTV, Los Angeles, 1966-67; asso. editor Sterling Publs., Tarzana, Calif., 1967-74; spl. features corr. N.Y. Times, 1972-75; mgr. product promotion Informatics Inc., Canoga Park, Calif., 1975-79; mgr. mktg. communications Rexon Bus. Machines Corp., Culver City, Calif., 1979-80; account mgr. Keye-Donna Pearlstein Inc., Beverly Hills, Calif., 1980-81; account exec. Tycer-Fultz-Bellack, Palo Alto, Calif., 1981—. Mem. Women In Communications. Club: Hollywood (Calif.) Women's Press, Peninsula Women in Advt., Peninsula Mktg. Assn. Home: 3357 Brittan Ave #17 San Carlos CA 94070

ANDERSON, PENNY ELLIOTT, journalist; b. Fayetteville, Ark., Feb. 21, 1943; d. Dannie and Lolita (Mitchell) Elliott; student Northeastern State Coll., 1961-62; B.A., U. Okla, 1965; m. Roger A. Anderson, May 2, 1981. Public relations dir. United Appeal of Greater Oklahoma City area, 1970-72; public relations specialist Western Electric Co., Oklahoma City, 1973-74; hosp. relations officer Univ. Hosp. and Clinics, Oklahoma City, 1974-76; internal communications coordinator Resource Scis. Corp., Tulsa, 1976-78; communications specialist Wilson Foods, Oklahoma City, 1978; news editor Dental Econs. Mag., Pennwell Pub. Co., Tulsa, 1979—. Mem. Public Relations Soc. Am. (charter mem. health sect. 1976), Am. Assn. Dental Editors, Am. Bus. Press, Women in Communications, U. Okla. Alumni Assn., Oklahoma City Area Hosp. Council (v.p. public relations div. 1974-76), Alpha Phi Alumnae. Democrat. Mem. Christian Ch. Contbr. articles to profl. jours. Home: 2816 S 138th E Ave Tulsa OK 74134 Office: PO Box 3408 Tulsa OK 74401

ANDERSON, PHYLLIS REINHOLD, business exec., engr., cons.; b. Denver, July 29, 1936; d. Floyd Reinhold and Minerva Eva (Needham) A.; Metall. Engr., Colo. Sch. Mines, 1962; M.B.A., U. Chgo., 1968; children—Kristin Elizabeth, Michele Ann. Mill metallurgist, supr., U.S. Steel Corp., 1962-66; research and devel. sr. metallurgist, supr., research planner, Continental Can Co., 1966-73; mgr. corp. planning, B. F. Goodrich Co., 1973-76; mktg. cons., regional asso. Strategic Planning Inst., Cambridge, Mass., 1975-76; project mgr. corp. planning, sales engring. corp. research and devel. planning Signode Corp., Glenview, Ill., 1976-80; pres., prin. cons. Corp. Devel. Assos., Inc., Oak Brook, Ill., 1980—; asso. Strategic Planning Inst., initial exec. com., chmn. membership com., 1975-76; dir. Quest Assos. Mgmt. and Quality Consultants; instr. bus. analysis and planning methods. Active psychiat. support services, career counseling women's groups and individuals. Recipient leadership award Chgo. YWCA, 1977. Mem. N.Y. Acad. Scis., Am. Soc. Metals, Soc. Women Engrs., Am. Mktg. Assn., Nat. Assn. Women Bus. Owners, AAAS, Mensa. Clubs: Execs., Whitehall. Author: Corporate Strategic Planning: An Integrated System, 1981. Home: 2201 S Highland Ave Lombard IL 60148 Office: PO Box 946 Oak Brook IL 60521

ANDERSON, ROMELDA JEREOS, nurse; b. Manila, Philippines, Oct. 18, 1945; came to U.S., 1968, naturalized, 1976; d. Moises Gonzales and Maria (Capule) Jereos; B.S.N., Philippine Union Coll., 1968; M.S., Loma Linda U., 1971; m. Darryl A. Anderson, June 18, 1972; children—Jennifer Lynn, Trisha Jean. Float staff nurse/charge nurse Loma Linda (Calif.) U., 1968-71; asst. prof. Sch. Nursing, Philippine Union Coll., Caloocan, 1971-72; charge nurse Respiratory Care unit, Loma Linda U. Med. Center, 1972-74, critical care instr. for edn. and tng., 1974-75; surg. unit coordinator Glendale (Calif.) Adventist Med. Center, 1975-77; dir. Calif. Home Health Services, Port Hueneme, Calif., 1977-78; asso. dir. nursing Glendale Adventist Med. Center, 1978-80, dir. clin. practice, 1980—. Recipient Outstanding Student award, Loma Linda U., 1971; Altrusa grantee, 1970; Philippine Union Coll. grad. sch. scholar, 1968-71. Mem. Calif. Soc. Nursing Service Adminstrs. Seventh-day Adventist. Editorial adv. bd. Cumulative Index to Nursing and Allied Health Lit., 1981—. Home: 5300 Dahlia Dr Los Angeles CA 90041 Office: 1509 Wilson Ter Glendale CA 91206

ANDERSON, RUTH I., educator; b. Millerton, Pa., Apr. 17, 1919; B.S. in Commerce, Grove City (Pa.) Coll.; M.C.S., Ind. U., also Ed.D. Instr., U.S. Naval Tng. Sch., Bloomington, Ind., 1943-44; prof., head dept. bus. edn. and secretarial adminstrn. Tex. Christian U., Ft. Worth, 1946-53; prof. bus. adminstrn. Sch. Bus., N. Tex. State U., Denton, 1953—, Piper prof., 1973; vis. summer prof. U. Oreg., U. Colo., N.Y. U., U. Tenn., Ind. U. Bd. dirs. Denton County Heart Assn., 1962-63, Fairhaven, home sr. citizens, 1957-70; mem. Denton Bd. Adjustments, 1969-75. Recipient Mountain Plains Leadership award, 1970, Disting. Alumni award Grove City Coll., 1970, John Robert Gregg award, 1972, Disting. Tchr. award N. Tex. State U. Alumni Assn., 1972, Spl. Recognition award N. Tex. State U., 1977; named Bus. Tchr. of Year, Ft. Worth, 1955, Bus. Edn. Tchr. of Year, Tex., 1972. Mem. Nat Bus. Edn. Assn. (membership chmn. for Tex.), Nat. Assn. Bus. Tchrs. Edn. (dir., program chmn. 1964-65), Tex. Bus. Edn. Assn. (past v.p.), Denton Bus. and Profl. Women's Club (pres. 1962-64; Woman of Year award 1969, dist. winner 1971), Delta Pi Epsilon (pres. 1964-65). Author textbooks in field. Home: 810 Stanley St Denton TX 76201 Office: Coll Bus North Tex State U Denton TX 76203

ANDERSON, RUTH JUNE TRUNNELL, govt. ofcl.; b. Washington, Dec. 8, 1927; d. Walter J. and Ruth (Weber) Trunnell; student U. Md.,

1944-46; 1 dau., Susan. Adminstrv. asst. to chmn. FCC, Washington, 1956-57; chmn. ICC, Washington, 1957-60, Com. on Commerce, U.S. Senate, Washington, 1960-61; case worker Senator Richard B. Russell, Washington, 1961-62; adminstrv. aide to Sec., Dept. Commerce, Washington, 1962-64; adminstrv. asst. Judge Roy L. Morgan, Washington, 1966-69; asst. postmaster gen., Washington, 1969-71; asst. to dir. congressional relations OEO, Washington, 1971-72; dir. spl. projects AEC, Washington, 1972-75; mgr. Fed. Women's Program, U.S. Nuclear Regulatory Commn., Washington, 1972—; pres. Federally Employed Women, Inc., Bethesda, Md., 1979-82. Recipient Bronze medal U.S. Dept. Commerce, 1967; Silver medal Nuclear Regulatory Commn., 1978. Mem. Soc. Women Engrs., N.Y. Acad. Sci., Nat. Women's Polit. Caucus, NOW, Federally Employed Women (Outstanding Performance award 1980). Editor: NRC Fed. Women's Program News, 1978—. Office: US Nuclear Regulatory Commn Rm 7211 MNB Washington DC 20555

ANDERSON, RUTH NATHAN, columnist; b. N.Y.C., Jan. 28, 1934; d. Solomon and Anna (Cornick) Gans; student N.Y. U., George Washington U., evenings 1952-56; m. Arthur Aksel Anderson, Jr., Sept. 11, 1971; stepchildren—Jack Anderson, Barbara Anderson, Terri Anderson. Newsletter editor Washington Post, 1952-53; chief med. writer, press officer Nat. Multiple Sclerosis Soc., N.Y.C., 1953-55; feature editor Crusade for Freedom, Radio Free Europe, N.Y.C., 1955-58; editor jr. TV dept. TV Revue, N.Y.C., 1958-61; feature-series reporter N.Am. Newspaper Alliance, Women's News Service, N.Y.C., 1961-69; writer, originator Doctor's Grapevine column Nat. Features Syndicate, Chgo., 1969-73; author-owner syndicated column VIP Med. Grapevine, Round Lake, Ill., 1973—; women's editor N.Y. Murray Hill News, 1977—; feature news corr. United Feature Syndicate, 1979—; contbg. editor Nashville Entertainer, 1979—; celebrity health news editor, feature writer Consumer's Med. Reporter mag., Chgo., 1981—; tchr. journalism, creative writing, speech arts Fla. State Bd. Adult Edn., 1968-69; lectr. writing seminars for faculty U. Ill. at Chgo. Circle Campus, 1970—. Trustee, sec. bd. Round Lake Public Library, 1977—; Right-to-Read vol. tutor jr. high schs., Round Lake, 1977—; singer ARC entertainment com. Bedside Network, 1974—. Mem. Chgo. Women in Broadcasting, Lake County Assn. Journalists, Chgo. Unltd., Press Vets. Assn., Internat. Platform Assn., Future Physicians Am. (hon.), Am. Med. Writers Assn., Nat. Assn. Female Execs. Clubs: Chgo. Press, Chgo. Advt. Author booklet: How You Can Be a Part of Your United Nations, 1959; contbr. articles to various mags. including Parents, Pageant, Mademoiselle, Science Digest, Reader's Digest, TV Guide, TV Radio Mirror, This Week, Am. Weekly, Am. Home Am. Health, others; features on U.S. presidents in archives of Hoover, Truman, Eisenhower, Kennedy and Johnson presdl. libraries. Rec. artist mus. comedy songs, country pop for Am. Sound label. Home: 161 Nasa Circle Round Lake IL 60073

ANDERSON, SHARON ROE, coll. adminstr.; b. Trona, Calif., Nov. 3, 1944; d. Lawrence A. and Kathryn L. Roe; B.A., St. Olaf Coll., 1966; m. Roger Hartley Anderson, Aug. 28, 1965; 1 son, Colby Pierce. Asst. dir. vol. services Mt. Sinai Hosp., 1964; dir. inner city field services Greater Mpls. council Girl Scouts U.S.A., 1966-70; adminstr. and registrar Edina (Minn.) Montessori Schs., 1973-76; research specialist Hubert H. Humphrey Inst. Public Affairs, U. Minn., 1976-78, asst. to dir. 1977-80, adminstr., 1980-82, assoc. to dir., 1982—. Mem. com. on aging United Way Mpls., 1980—, mem. allocations com., 1982—; mem. Minn. Bd. on Aging, 1973-81; chmn. task force Minn. Long Term Care State Plan, 1981—; mem. sch. bd. Edina Montessori Sch., 1973-74; pres. Minn. unit bd. Am. Contract Bridge League, 1981—; trustee Sci. Mus. Minn., 1981—. Home: 5701 Bryant Ave S Minneapolis MN 55419 Office: 909 Social Sciences Bldg 267 19th Ave S Minneapolis MN 55455

ANDERSON, STEPHANIE MYKS, mfg. co. exec.; b. Hartford, Conn., Apr. 25, 1918; d. Michael Adam and Tekla (Korinyuik) Myks; student public schs., Scranton, Pa.; m. Charles Anderson, Nov. 7, 1937; children—Carla Janice, Stephen Henry, Linda June. With Sperry Gyroscope, New Hyde Park, N.Y., 1941-43, T.J. Long Plastics, L.I., N.Y., 1957-58; owner Standard Printed Circuits, Inc., Sherburne, N.Y., 1960—. Address: 44 S Main St PO Box 488 Sherburne NY 13460

ANDERSON, SUSAN LOU, lawyer; b. Washington, July 14, 1947; d. Howard Lester and Katherine (Anderson) Hershock; A.B. in Chemistry, Eastern Coll., 1969; J.D., Villanova U., 1972. Admitted to Pa. bar, 1972, U.S. Dist. Ct. and Circuit Ct. Appeals, 1973; dir. bail bond project Montgomery County Bar Assn., 1971-72; staff atty. Fidelcor, Inc. and The Fidelity Bank, Phila., 1972-75, asst. sec., assoc. counsel, 1973-75, asst. v.p., asst. sec., asst. counsel, 1975-76, acting head personnel, 1975, dep. head legal dept., v.p., asst. sec., asst. counsel, 1976-78; partner firm Littleton and Anderson, Phila., 1978-82; sole practice, 1982—; sec.-treas. Pa. Bd. Law Examiners, 1976—; lectr. Temple U., Pa. Bar Inst. Trustee Marriage Council of Phila., Inc., 1977—. Recipient certificate of leadership Phila. YWCA, 1976. Mem. Am., Pa. (vice chmn. corp., banking and bus. law sect., sec. legal edn. and bar admission), Phila. bar assns. Home: 3644 Darby Rd Bryn Mawr PA 19010 Office: The Sugar Refinery 225 Christ Ch Walkway Philadelphia PA 19106

ANDERSON, THELMA KAY, pharm. co. exec.; b. Sims, Ill., Nov. 2, 1938; d. Henry Audry and Leota Zelma (Wells) Linder; B.S., McKendree Coll., 1961; student Sch. Med. Tech., Meth. Hosp. of Central Ill., 1962; M.B.A., Rutgers U., 1975; m. Raymond Francis Anderson, Apr. 18, 1964. Lab. asst. McKendree Coll., 1959-61; med. technologist The Methodist Hosp. of Central Ill., 1962-63; hematology supr. and instr. USAF Hosp., Scott AFB, Ill., 1963-65; hematology supr. VA Hosp., East Orange, N.J., 1965-66; teaching supr. Perth Amboy (N.J.) Gen. Hosp., 1966-69, chief technologist, lab. mgr., 1969-72; adj. faculty Middlesex Coll., 1972-73; gen. supr., adminstrv. dir. lab. ops. Center for Lab. Medicine, Metuchen, N.J., 1972-73; med lab. supr., dir. tng. Schwarz-Mann div. Becton-Dickinson & Co., Orangeburg, N.Y., 1973-74; nat. ednl. coordinator, tech. cons. services specialist Roche Diagnostics, Nutley, N.J., 1974-76, product sales mgr., 1976-80, product mktg. mgr., 1980—; adj. faculty Middlesex County Coll., also med. tech. adviser council. Mem. N.J. Soc. Med. Tech. (dir., past pres. 1972-73, chmn. membership com. 1979-80), Am. Soc. Med. Tech. (asso. ed. Jour. 1979—), N.J. Blood Bank Assn., Am. Soc. Microbiologists. Home: 732 Van Nest Dr Martinsville NJ 08836 Office: 340 Kingsland St Nutley NJ 07110

ANDERSON, VERGIE LOUISE, real estate broker; b. Jackson, Tenn., Sept. 28, 1947; d. Calvin and Crystal Louise (Matthews) A.; B.A. in Polit. Sci., Loyola U., Chgo., 1977. With Anderson Real Estate, Evanston, Ill., 1973—, v.p., 1973—. Mem. ladies aux. St. Bernard Hosp., Chgo. Recipient various service and recognition awards. Mem. Nat. Assn. Realtors, Nat. Assn. Real Estate Brokers, N.Shore Bd. Realtors, Ill. Assn. Realtors, Operation Push, NAACP, League Black Women, Urban League, Nat. Assn. Negro Bus. and Profl. Women's Clubs, Internat. Orgn. Women Execs. Baptist. Home: 4250 N Marine Dr Chicago IL 60613 Office: 1610 Maple Ave Evanston IL 60201

ANDERSON, VICTORIA ELAINE, real estate mgmt. co. exec.; b. San Diego, Sept. 4, 1946; d. William Brigham and Helen Louise (East) Anderson; A.A. with honors, Hillsborough Community Coll., 1976; B.A., U. So. Fla., 1978; 1 dau., Kimberly Ann Miley. Property mgr. First Property Mgmt. Corp., St. Petersburg, Fla., 1974-76; property mgr. Flagship Bank of Tampa, 1977-78; pres. Regency Property Mgmt., Inc., Clearwater, Fla., 1978-80; asst. mgmt. v.p. First Property Mgmt. Corp., Tampa, Fla., 1980—. Mem. Am. Bus. Women's Assn., Community Assn. Inst., Contractors and Builders Assn., Nat. Assn. Female Execs., Nat. Fedn. Ind. Bus. Home: 13300 Indian Rocks Rd Apt 305 Largo FL 33540 Office: First Property Mgmt Corp Tampa FL

ANDERSON, VIVIENNE, educator; b. Phila.; B.S., Temple U., 1936, M.Ed., 1939; Ed.D., Columbia U., 1955. Tchr., Phila. Pub. Schools, 1936-47, exec. asst. to Phila. supt., 1947-50; acting chief bur. secondary curriculum devel. N.Y. State Dept. Edn., Albany, 1950-65, chief bur. continuing edn. curriculum devel., 1965-67, dir. div. humanities and arts, 1967-74, asst. commr. for gen. edn. and curriculum services, 1974-77, asso. commr. for instructional services, 1977—, exec. asst. to exec. dep. commr., 1979—; adj. prof. doctoral program Tchrs. Coll., Columbia U., 1961-64, coordinator paperback books in edn. project, 1964-66; adj. prof. doctoral program SUNY, Albany, 1961-64; cons. Columbia U., Kellogg Found., CBS, Phila. City Planning Commn.; edn. adviser U.S. Edn. Commr., Lincoln Center, Saratoga Performing Arts Center; pres. Albany League of Arts, 1968-70; v.p. N.Y. State Citizens Com., 1973—; chairperson N.Y. State Alliance for Arts in Edn., 1973—; co-chairperson N.Y. State Com. Arts for Handicapped; exec. bd. Ten-State Consortium on Arts in Edn.; hon. bd. dirs. N.Y. State Spl. Olympics; mem. nat. adv. bd. Kennedy Center; chmn. Nat. Com. Arts for the Handicapped; mem. task force Nat. Endowment for Arts; mem. nat. fine arts com. 1980 Internat. Olympics; chmn. Citizens Planning Com. Greater Albany; Recipient numerous awards including Freedoms Found. award, N.Y. State Woman of Yr. award N.Y. Nat. Humanities Assn. Club: City (pres.) (Albany). Author: Patterns of Educational Leadership, 1956; The School Administrator and the Press, 1956; The School Adminstrator and His Publications, 1957; Your America, 1965, rev. edit., 1968; Paperbacks in Education, 1966; contbr. numerous articles to profl. jours. and newspapers; author numerous safety booklets, tchr. guides. Office: Office Spl Asst to Exec Dep Commr New York Education Dept Albany NY 12234

ANDERSON, WILMA PRATHER, legal adminstr.; b. Elizabeth, W.Va., June 5, 1923; d. Hugh and Debba Lewis Prather; student W.Va. U., 1940-42, Wayne State U., 1945-46; cert. Nat. Surety Bond Sch.; m. Jack Anderson, Jan. 26, 1945. Clk., Ford Motor Co., Dearborn, Mich., 1942-45; office mgr., bookkeeper Mims & Stephens Ins., Midland, Tex., 1946-55; ins. underwriter Lee Durrell & Co., Midland, 1955-58; gen. ins. agt. Anderson Ins. Agy., Midland, 1958-71; adminstr. firm Turpin, Smith, Dyer & Saxe, Midland, 1971—. Bd. dirs. La Floreicita Day Nursery. Lic. ins. agt., Tex. Mem. Nat. Assn. Legal Adminstrs., Permian Basin Assn. Legal Adminstrs. (charter mem., v.p., pres. 1982), Am. Bar Assn. (asso.). Office: Turpin Smith Dyer and Saxe 1st Nat Bank 3d Floor Midland TX 79701

ANDERSON OLIVO, MARGARET ELLEN, physiologist, educator; b. Omaha, June 17, 1941; d. Clarence Lloyd and Anita Emma (Kruse) Anderson; B.A., Augustana Coll., Sioux Falls, S.D., 1963; Ph.D. (NSF predoctoral fellow), Stanford U., 1967; m. Richard F. Olivo, Sept. 4, 1971. NIH postdoctoral fellow Harvard U., 1968-70; research asso. Lab. of Neuro-biology U. P.R., 1970-71; vis. asst. prof. Clark U., 1972; asst. prof. Bennington (Vt.) Coll., spring 1973; asst. prof. Smith Coll., Northampton, Mass., 1973-79, asso. prof. dept. biol. scis., 1979—. NIH research grantee, 1974—. Mem. Soc. for Neuro-sci., Soc. Gen. Physiologists, Biophys. Soc., Soc. Am. Zoologists. Office: Smith College Northampton MA 01063

ANDRE, BABETTE YVONNE, bus. exec., pilot; b. San Francisco, Jan. 26, 1942; d. Leo Fred and Dorothy (Fisher) Andre; B.A. in Polit. Sci., U. Calif., Berkeley, 1963; postgrad. San Francisco State Coll., 1966, U. Colo., Denver, 1970. Peace Corps vol., Bafoussam, Cameroun, Africa, 1963-65; French tchr. Punahou Acad., Honolulu, 1966-68; pub. info. officer Commn. Community Relations City and County of Denver, 1970-71, info. writer, 1973-78; traffic reporter Sta. KOA-AM, Denver, 1978; pres. Baroness Royal Airways Services; mem. faculty dept. aerospace sci. Met. State Coll., Denver, 1975-80; gold seal flight instr.; public relations/advt. cons. Active various social agys. and programs, including Head Start. Cert. tchr., Calif., Hawaii, N.Y.; cert. flight and ground instr., FAA. Mem. Colo. Flight Instrs. Assn., Aircraft Owners and Pilots Assn., CAP, Colo. Pilots Assn., 99's, Alpha Eta Rho. Clubs: PC Flyers, Denver Press. Contbr. articles to Colo. Bus., Rocky Mountain News; author and photographer various informational city publs. Home: 89 Sherman St Denver CO 80203

ANDREAS, JOYCE KAY, musician, conductor; b. Cedar Rapids, Iowa, June 27, 1940; d. Louis Frederick and Leoma Bernice (Shellhammer) Pech; B.Mus.Ed. cum laude, Morningside Coll., 1962; M.A. magna cum laude, U. Iowa, 1968; m. Reuben Peter Andreas, June 21, 1963; children—David Glenn, Jonathan Peter, Marc Louis. Tchr. music, Pasadena (Calif.) City Schs., 1962-63; violinist, violist with orchs. including Pasadena, Oklahoma City, Wichita Falls, Tex., Cedar Rapids, Sioux City, Iowa, Ridgewood, N.J., San Gabriel, Calif., Irvine, Calif., Pacific Symphony, Calif., Long Beach, Calif.; tchr. music Eastern Christian Schs., North Haledon, N.J., 1970-77; music dir., conductor Saddleback Community Symphony Orch., Saddleback Community Coll., Mission Viejo, Calif., 1977—; Suzuki Festival coordinator N.J., 1971-77, Orange County, Calif., 1977—. Sioux City Symphony scholar, Aspen Music Festival, 1960. Mem. Am. String Tchrs. Assn. (founder chpt. Saddleback Coll. 1980), Music Tchrs. Assn. Calif. (state chmn. strings/cert. merit program), Music Educators Nat. Conf., Suzuki Assn. Americas, Suzuki Music Assn. Calif., Nat. Sch. Orch. Assn. Mem. Christian Reformed Ch. Address: 26572 Via Manolete Mission Viejo CA 92691

ANDREASEN, NANCY COOVER, psychiatrist; b. Lincoln, Nebr., Nov. 11, 1938; d. John A. and Pauline G. (Gaudreau) Coover; B.A. summa cum laude, U. Nebr., 1958, Ph.D., 1963; M.A., Radcliffe Coll., 1959; Fulbright fellow Oxford (Eng.) U., 1960; M.D., U. Iowa, 1970; divorced; children—Susan, Robin. Instr. English, Nebr. Wesleyan U., 1960-61, U. Nebr., 1962-63; asst. prof. U. Iowa, 1963-66; resident in psychiatry U. Iowa Med. Center, 1970-73, mem. faculty, 1973—, prof. psychiatry, 1981—. Recipient Menninger award psychiat. research, 1973; U. Iowa Faculty Scholar award, 1980—; Woodrow Wilson fellow, 1958-59. Mem. AMA, Am. Psychosomatic Soc., Am. Psychiat. Assn., Soc. Research Life History, Soc. Health and Human Values, Psychiat. Research Soc., Am. Coll. Psychiatrists, Am. Psychopath. Assn. (sec. 1981), N.Y. Acad. Scis., Johnson County Med. Soc., Phi Beta Kappa. Author: John Donne: Conservative Revolutionary, 1964; Understanding Mental Illness: A Layman's Guide, 1973; also articles. Asso. editor, book forum editor Am. Jour. Psychiatry. Home: 5 Lakeview-River Heights Iowa City IA 52249 Office: Psychiat Hosp 1-1189 U Iowa 500 Newton Rd Iowa City IA 52242

ANDRESKI, BETTY MAY, chem. co. exec.; b. Florida, N.Y., Mar. 28, 1931; d. Roy and Lela Alice (Sherman) Pixley; student public schs., Broadalbin, N.Y.; children—Michele, Phyllis, Robert. Bookkeeper, Mitchell Tile Co., Schenectady, 1949-60; bookkeeper, dir. Dur-A-Flex, Inc., Hartford, Conn., 1968—. Home: 32 Barbonsel Rd East Hartford CT 06118 Office: Dur-A-Flex Inc 100 Meadow St Hartford CT 06114

ANDRESS, CHARLOTTE FRANCES, emerita social work exec.; b. Birmingham, Ala., Apr. 22, 1910; d. Francis Samuel and Tommie (Daniel) Andress; B.S., Birmingham-So. Coll., 1932; A.M. in Social Service Adminstrn., U. Chgo., 1943. Asst. dir. Girl Scouts Am., Birmingham, 1932-35, exec. dir., Nashville, 1935-41; instr. Loyola U., Chgo., 1942-45; dir. U.S.O., Augusta, Ga., 1945-48; asst. dir. YWCA, Chgo., 1948-50, exec. dir., St. Louis, 1950-53; dir. group work, youth service Fedn. Protestant Welfare Agys., N.Y.C., 1953-59; exec. dir. Inwood House, N.Y.C., 1959-82, exec. dir. emerita, 1982—. Chmn. adv. bd. Jefferson Park Center, 1959-65; nat. camp com. Camp Fire Girls, 1959-68; bd. Social Work Vocat. Bur., 1961-66; dir. Trail Blazer Camps, 1957—, chmn. personnel com., 1982—; mem. Camp Sharparoon com. N.Y.C. Mission Soc., 1960-76, mem. personnel com., 1962-66; adv. bd. social welfare Meth. Ch., 1958-63; mem. United Meth. Bd. Missions, 1964-72; bd. Bethel Meth. Home, 1965-72, sec. bd., 1966-72; women's com. Japan Internat. Christian U. Found., 1969—; adv. bd. Isabella Thoburn Coll., 1967—; chmn. nat. com. Wesleyan Service Guild, 1970-72; trustee Christ United Meth. Ch., 1975—; trustee Martha Mertz Found., 1979—, sec., 1981—. Named Disting. Alumna Birmingham So. Coll., 1981. Cert. social worker, N.Y. Mem. Nat. Assn. Social Workers (sec. bd. N.Y.C. chpt. 1958-60, chmn. personnel standards and practices 1960-69, 73-74), Acad. Cert. Social Workers, Nat. Conf. on Social Welfare, Bethany Deaconess Soc. (dir. 1971—, sec. 1974-76, pres. 1976—), Internat. Conf. Social Welfare, N.Y. Deaconess Assn. (dir. 1969—, sec. 1971—), Gamma Phi Beta. Democrat. Club: Cosmopolitan. Home: 102 E 22d St New York NY 10010 Office: 320 E 82d St New York NY 10028

ANDREW, BONIETA MAE, nurse; b. Peoria, Ill., Dec. 10, 1951; d. Porter William and Yolanda Mae (Dasch) Polston; R.N., Lutheran Hosp., Ft. Wayne, Ind., 1970-73; m. Michael Andrew, Oct. 6, 1973; children—Barry Michael, Darrin Wesley, Ryan Alan. Staff nurse surg. dept. Luth. Hosp., Ft. Wayne, 1973-74; staff nurse Murphy Med. Center, Warsaw, Ind., 1974-76; asst. adminstrv. supr. Koskiusko Community Hosp., Warsaw, Ind., 1976—; coordinator Home Health Care Koskiusko County, 1st hospice team in county; part-time psychiat. nurse Otis R. Bowen Center for Human Services, Warsaw. Mem. Koskiusko Nurses Soc. (co-founder). Methodist. Home: 407 Oak Hill Dr Warsaw IN 46590 Office: 827 S Union Warsaw IN

ANDREW, JANE HAYES, ballet co. exec.; b. Phila., Jan. 1, 1947; d. David Powell and Vivian Muriel (Saeger) Hayes; A.B., Barnard Coll., 1968; cert. Harvard Arts Mgmt. Seminar, 1972; m. Brian David Andrew, June 14, 1977; 1 son, Kevin Hayes. Theatre mgr. Minor Latham Playhouse, Barnard Coll., N.Y.C., 1970-74; co. mgr. Houston Ballet, 1974-77; editor Cultural Directory, Greater Phila. Cultural Alliance, 1977; co. mgr. Ballet West, Salt Lake City, 1978—. Dorothy D. Spivack grantee, 1973. Club: Zonta. Office: PO Box 11336 Salt Lake City UT 84147

ANDREWS, ANN MARIE, psychologist; b. Phila., Nov. 9, 1931; d. Frank L. and Anna Marie (Malloy) Craver; R.N., Jefferson Sch. Nursing, 1952; B.S., U. Pa., 1955, M.S., 1962, Ed.D., 1971; postgrad., U. Pa., Pa. State U.; m. Robert F. Andrews, Dec. 1, 1956; children—Robert, Craig, Michael. Nurse, asst. head nurse Jefferson Hosp., Phila., 1952, nurse Community Nursing Service Public Health, Delaware County, Pa., 1954; sch. nurse Darby Twp. (Pa.) Sch. Dist., 1959-62; substitute tchr. Central Bucks (Pa.) Sch. Dist., 1964, sch. nurse, 1965, counselor, 1966-74; supr. spl. edn., spl. services Centennial Sch. Dist., Warminster, Pa., 1974—; mem. faculty Chestnut Hill Coll.; pvt. practice psychotherapy, 1975—. Mem. Am. Psychol. Assn., Pa. Psychol. Assn., Nat. Assn. of Pupil Personnel Adminstrs. (trustee, editor), Pa. Assn. Pupil Personnel Adminstrs., Bucks County Assn. for Children with Learning Disabilities, Bucks County Sch. Counselors Assn. Roman Catholic. Club: Soroptimist Internat. of Warminster (pres. 1981, dir. 1982). Home: 3362 Holicong Rd Mechanicsville PA 18934 Office: Centennial Sch Dist Centennial Rd Warminster PA 18974

ANDREWS, CAROL CORDER, polit. scientist, educator; b. Wilmington, Del.; d. Kenneth Wilson and Aurelia Moreland (Speer) Corder; B.A. (Gen. Motors nat. scholar), Duke, 1960; Certificat d'Etudes Politiques, Institut d'Etudes Politiques, U. Paris (France), 1961; M.A. (East Asian Inst. fellow), Columbia, 1964, Ph.D., 1978; postgrad. Inter-Univ. Program for Chinese Lang. Tng., Taipei, Taiwan, 1966-67; div.; 1 son, Ethan Andrews. Research contract for study Taiwanese-Mainlander polit. relations Brookings Instn., Washington, 1967; research Kuomintang Party Archives, Taichung, Taiwan, 1967-68; asst. prof. polit. sci. Holy Names Coll., Oakland, Calif., 1970-71, asso. prof., 1979—, chairperson dept. history and polit. sci., 1979-80. Bd. dirs. Alameda County chpt. UN Assn. U.S.A., World Without War Council, 1979—. Recipient Contemporary China Studies Com. award, 1967-70. Nat. Def. Fgn. Lang. fellow, 1962-64, 65-67. Mem. Am. Polit. Sci. Assn., Women's Caucus for Polit. Sci., Assn. for Asian Studies, AAUP, Internat. Platform Assn., Phi Beta Kappa. Democrat. Episcopalian. Club: Commonwealth of Calif. Contbr. articles to profl. jours. Home: 612 Vincente Ave Berkeley CA 94707

ANDREWS, CAROLYN, broadcasting co. sales exec.; b. Ticonderoga, N.Y., Aug. 30, 1948; d. Norman Bruce and Ruth (Adams) A.; student U. East Anglia, Norwich, Eng., 1968-69; A.B., Mt. Holyoke Coll., 1970; M.B.A., Simmons Coll., 1975; m. James Garrett Walley, May 17, 1980. Recruiting rep. Seven Coll. Conf., Northampton, Mass., 1970-71, co-dir. conf., 1971-72; asst. dir. admissions Emma Willard Sch., Troy, N.Y., 1972-74; spls. project analyst, Treasury, CBS, Inc., N.Y.C., 1975-77; account exec. trainee CBS TV Network, N.Y.C., 1977-78. account exec. nat. sales, 1978-80, account exec. eastern sales, 1980—. Vol. career counselor CBS, Mt. Holyoke Coll. Mem. Internat. Radio and TV Soc., Mus. Modern Art. Club: Mt. Holyoke, N.Y. Office: 51 W 52d St New York NY 10019

ANDREWS, EVELYN PATRICIA, social services adminstr.; b. Atlanta, Oct. 2, 1937; d. Leroy and Ola Andrews; B.A., Clark Coll., Atlanta, 1959; M.S.W. (N.Y. State scholar 1966), Howard U., 1968; M.P.A., Am. U., 1982. Caseworker, then supr. N.Y.C. Dept. Social Services, 1960-68; social worker Protective Services for Children, D.C. Dept. Human Resources, 1968-72, supr., 1972-77, br. chief Child Protective Services Div., 1977—; cons. Big Bros. Nat. Capital Area, 1976-78. Recipient meritorious service awards United Negro Coll. Fund, Progressive Nat. Bapt. Conv., Clark Coll. Alumni Assn., others. Mem. Nat. Assn. Female Execs., Zeta Phi Beta, Baptist. Home: 2100 Brooks Dr Apt 621 Forestville MD 20747 Office: 500 1st St NW Washington DC 20001

ANDREWS, JOAN PRENTICE, furniture mfg. co. exec.; b. N.Y.C., July 3, 1947; d. Paul Revere and Virginia Prentice A.; B.A., Briarcliff Coll., 1969; A.A.S. with highest honors, Fashion Inst. Tech., 1973; M.A. with honors, Pratt Inst., 1978. Tchr. art history Fashion Inst. Tech., 1975-77; v.p., gen. partner Charles Craig Furniture, N.Y.C., 1979—; chmn. bd. Finesse Furniture, High Point, N.C., 1980—. Recipient Nat. Portfolio award, 1973. Mem. SID. Club: Stanwich (Greenwich, Conn.). Office: 979 3d Ave New York NY 10021

ANDREWS, JOYCE ANDREA, TV and film scriptwriter; b. N.Y.C., Aug. 25, 1946; d. Michael Ralph and Dorothy Katherine (Kull) Andrews; B.A. in Communication Arts (N.Y. State Regents scholar), Fordham U., 1968; M.S. in Instructional Tech., U. So. Calif., 1975. Intern, Sta. WCBS-TV news, N.Y.C., 1967-68; copywriter, audio visual specialist Montgomery Ward, N.Y.C., 1968-70; dept. mgr. Saks Fifth Ave., White Plains, N.Y., 1970-72; public relations team leader air pollution project N.Y. and N.J., 1972-74; free lance audio visual writer Walt Disney Ednl. Media Co., Burbank, Calif., 1975-76; writer, production coordinator Pyramid Films, Santa Monica, Calif., 1976; TV and film scriptwriter Dept. Navy, San Diego, 1976—. Mem. Am. Film

Inst., Informational Film Producers Assn., Nat. Acad. TV Arts and Scis. (San Diego chpt.), Assn. Ednl. Communications and Tech. Democrat. Roman Catholic. Home: 6780 Friars Rd San Diego CA 92108 Office: Naval Education and Training Code N51 921 W Broadway San Diego CA 92132

ANDREWS, JUDITH LYNNE, maritime co. exec.; b. Chgo., July 7, 1948; d. Fred Woodrow and LaVerne Mildred (Johnson) Andrews; B.A. in Econs., So. Ill. U., 1971; M.B.A. in Fin. Mgmt., Ill. Benedictine Coll., 1979. Acctg. mgr. McDonald's Corp., Chgo., 1973-78, Wickes Corp., Chgo., 1978-79; dir. fin. Carte Blanche Corp., Los Angeles, 1979-82; mgr. fin. Crowley Maritime Corp., Long Beach, Calif., 1982—. Office: 19 Pine Ave Long Beach CA 90802

ANDREWS, JULIE, actress, singer; b. Walton-on-Thames, Eng., Oct. 1, 1935; d. Edward C. and Barbara Wells; studied with pvt. tutors; studied voice with Mme. Stiles-Allen; m. Tony Walton May 10, 1959 (div.); 1 dau., Emma; m. 2d, Blake Edwards, 1969. Debut as singer Hippodrome, London, 1947; appeared in pantomime Cinderella, London, 1953; appeared Broadway prodn. The Boy Friend, N.Y.C., 1954, My Fair Lady, 1956-60, Camelot, 1960-62; films include Mary Poppins (Acad. award for best actress, 1964), 1964. The Americanization of Emily, 1964, Torn Curtain, 1966. The Sound of Music, 1966, Hawaii, 1966. Thoroughly Modern Millie, 1967, Star!, 1968. Darling Lili, 1970. The Tamarind Seed, 1973, 10, 1979, Little Miss Marker, 1980. S.O.B., 1981. Made TV debut in High Tor, 1956; star TV series the Julie Andrews Hour, 1972-73, also spls. Recipient N.Y. Drama Critics award My Fair Lady, 1955-56; Golden Globe award Hollywood Fgn. Press Assn., 1964, 65; named World Film Favorite (female), 1967. Author: (as Julie Edwards) Mandy, 1971; The Last of the Really Great Whangdoodles, 1974. Office: care Creative Artists Agy 1888 Century Park E Suite 1400 Los Angeles CA 90067 *

ANDREWS, MARGARET ELIZABETH, rehab. counselor; b. Buffalo, Mar. 19, 1948; d. Arthur Carl and Grace Ellen Metzler; B.A. in Psychology, SUNY, Buffalo, 1970, Ed.M., 1972; m. William Edward Andrews, June 13, 1970; 1 son, Jonathan Luke. Rehab. counselor Niagara Frontier Vocat. Rehab. Center, Buffalo, 1972-73; clin. asso. pvt. psychiat. practice, Williamsville, N.Y., 1973-74; dir. intake DeVeaux Sch., Niagara Falls, N.Y., 1974-76; sr. rehab. counselor dept. child psychiatry and behavioral scis. Children's Hosp., Buffalo, 1976-78; dir. West Side Counseling Center, Buffalo, 1978-80; adj. faculty dept. community and social services SUNY, Buffalo, 1979—; asst. dir. family planning dept. Deaconess div. Buffalo Gen. Hosp., Corp., 1980—. Co-chmn. Niagara County Rape Task Force, 1973-74. Cert. rehab. counselor. Mem. Am. Personnel and Guidance Assn., Am. Rehab. Counselors Assn., Center for Women in Mgmt., Bus. and Profl. Women. Office: Deaconess Div Buffalo Gen Hosp Corp 1101 Humboldt Pkwy Buffalo NY 14208

ANDREWS, MARY ELLEN, public relations exec.; b. Corning, N.Y., Nov. 10, 1931; d. Edwin Hardy and Edith Marie (Lowe) Ober; B.A., Mt. Holyoke Coll., 1953; postgrad. Syracuse U., 1974-75; m. James A. Reynolds, Jan. 28, 1962; m. 2d, Richard Hale Andrews, July 14, 1970; 1 dau., Amy Elizabeth; stepchildren—R. Hale, D. Gage, Philadelphia M. French/English translator Les Ateliers de Construction Electrique de Charleroi, N.Y.C., 1954-55, French Nat. R.R., N.Y.C., 1955-56; public relations asst. Steuben Glass, N.Y.C., 1956-64; French/English translator Corning (N.Y.) Internat. Corp., 1964-67; research asst. Corning Glass Wks. Found., 1967-70; French/English translator Corning Internat. Corp., 1972-75; office mgr. Beak Assos., Ithaca, N.Y., 1975-77; corporate relations staff, devel. office, Cornell U., Ithaca, 1977-79; staff asst. evening programs, Elmira Coll., N.Y., 1979-80, dir. public relations, 1980—, advisor student newspaper, The Octagon, 1980—. Bd. dirs. Elmira Symphony and Choral Soc., 1982—. Mem. Public Relations Soc. Am., Council for Advancement and Support of Edn. Democrat. Presbyterian. Editor-in-chief Campus Mag., 1980—. Home: RD 2 Old Corning Rd Watkins Glen NY 14891 Office: Elmira Coll Park Pl Elmira NY 14901

ANDREWS, MINNA FEINBERG (MRS. NATHAN ANDREWS), artist; b. N.Y.C.; d. Joseph and Bessie (Atkin) Feinberg; student Parson's Sch. Design; grad. Pratt Inst. Fine Arts, 1920; studied with George Elmer Brown, Joseph Newman, Alex Redein, Umberto Romano; m. Nathan Andrews, July 3, 1952 (dec.). Partner, Twins Advt. Art Service, N.Y.C., 1923—; one-man shows Town House Gallery, Woodstock, N.Y., 1952, Charles Barzansky Galleries, N.Y.C., 1957; exhibited in group shows Ward Eggeleston Galleries, 1953, 54, 55, N.A.D., N.Y.C., 1957—, Tokyo (Japan) Municipal Art Mus., 1960, Riverside Mus., N.Y.C., 1960, Royal Acad. Galleries, Edinburgh, Scotland, 1963, Royal Soc. Birmingham Eng. Galleries, 1964, Nat. Acad. Design Annual, 1963, Allied Artists Annuals, 1961-63, Palazzo Vecchio, Naples at the Salvator Rosa in the Pub. Gardens, 1972, Norfolk (Va.) Mus. Arts and Scis., Lever House, N.Y.C., 1965, 67, 68, 72; represented in permanent collections Rose Art Mus., Brandeis U., Waltham, Mass., Yeshiva U., N.Y.C., Norfolk Mus. Arts and Scis. (Va.) Recipient cert. of award Woman Art Concept, Inc., 1978. Mem. Nat. Assn. Women Artists, Artists Equity Assn. N.Y., Woodstock Artists Assn. Home: 239 E 79th St New York NY 10021

ANDREWS, SALLY SPRATT, occupational health cons.; b. Charlotte, N.C., Mar. 5, 1942; d. Robert Gilroy and Jean Marie (Little) Spratt; A.B., Duke U., 1963; M.A.T. (Harvard fellow), Harvard U., 1967; M.A., U. N.C., Chapel Hill, 1979; postgrad. U. Tex. Houston Health Sci. Center, 1980-81; m. James Massengale Nelson, Aug. 5, 1979; 1 son by previous marriage, John Young Andrews II. Research asst. Rockefeller Bros. Fund, N.Y.C., 1963-64; vol. Peace Corps, 1964-66; tchr. social studies and psychology, Lexington, Mass. and Durham, N.C., 1967-73; mem. Peace Corps selection and tng. staff, Virgin Islands, 1968; mem. faculty, dir. admissions dept. health adminstrn. Duke Med. Center, Durham, 1975-78; faculty asso. behavioral sci. and health services orgn., asst. to dean continuing edn. U. Tex. Sch. Public Health, Houston, 1978-81; cons. occupationally-related health complaints, Houston, 1981—. Continuing edn. adv. bd. Houston Health Sci. Center, 1979-81; rep. continuing edn. dirs. nat. meeting Nat. Inst. Occupational Safety and Health, 1979, 81; bd. dirs. chpt. Parents Without Partners, 1975-78; adv. bd. Durham Mental Health Center-Durham City Schs. Program, 1976-78. USPHS fellow, 1974-75. Mem. Soc. Occupational and Environ. Health, Am. Public Health Assn., Tex. Soc. Public Health Educators, Tex. Public Health Assn. (cons., state recognition award 1981), Houston Patient Edn. Assn., Nat. Assn. Female Execs., Harvard-N.E. Combined Schs. Alumni Club, Phi Beta Kappa, Pi Sigma Alpha, Phi Kappa Delta. Presbyterian. Author: Which School for Me?, Educational Needs Analysis of Texas Public Health Personnel, 1982. Home: 7304 Staffordshire St Apt 3 Houston TX 77030 Office: PO Box 20186 Houston TX 77025

ANDREWS, SUSANNAH SMITH, psychologist; b. Jackson, Miss. Mar. 15, 1949; d. Sydney Allen and Frances Eager (Witty) Smith; grad. Vassar Coll., 1970; M.S., San Jose State U., 1973; postgrad. Calif. Sch. Profl. Psychology, 1972-75, Ph.D., 1975; m. Kent Andrews, Aug. 14, 1976; 1 son, Nathan. Dir., Drug Diversion Program for Adults Family Service Assn., San Diego, 1974; pre-and postdoctoral fellow Mercy Hosp., San Diego, 1974-76; dir. Adul Day Treatment Program, San Luis Obispo Community Mental Health Center, Calif., 1977-78, dir. research and program evals., 1977-78; pvt. practice clin. psychology San Luis Obispo, 1977-80, Gulfport, Miss., 1980—; faculty U. So. Miss., 1981—; staff Garden Park Hosp., Gulfport Meml. Hosp., Biloxi Bay Regional Hosp.; cons. organizational devel.; co-founder, dir. Anred and Anorexia Nervosa Related Eating Disorders, 1979—. Vice pres. local bd. Am. Cancer Soc.; del. People-to-People trip to China. Mem. Mem. Am. Psychol. Assn., Calif. Psychol. Assn., Miss. Psychol. Assn., Jacques Cousteau Soc., Save the Whales Found., Am. Forest Assn., Nat. Wildlife Assn., Sierra Club. Columnist: NE Miss. Daily Jour.; contbr. article to profl. jour.; composer: Talking to Myself, 1975; Shadows of Mind, 1975. Office: 3106 11th St Gulfport MS 39501

ANDREWS, THEODORA ANNE, librarian; b. Carroll County, Ind., Oct. 14, 1921; d. Harry Floyd and Margaret Grace (Walter) Ulrey; B.S. with distinction, Purdue U., 1953; M.S., U. Ill., 1955; m. Robert William Andrews, July 18, 1940 (div. 1946); 1 son, Martin Harry. Asst. reference librarian Purdue U., West Lafayette, Ind., 1955-56, pharmacy librarian, instr., 1956-60, pharmacy librarian, asst. prof., 1960-65, pharmacy librarian, assoc. prof. library sci., 1965-71, prof. library sci., pharmacy librarian, 1971-79, prof. library sci., pharmacy, nursing and health scis. librarian, 1979—. Mem. Purdue Women's Caucus, 1973—, v.p., 1975-76, pres., 1976-77; mem. Internat. Women's Yr. Regional Planning Com., 1977; del. Ind. Gov.'s Conf. Libraries and Info. Services, 1978. U. Ill. grad. fellow, 1954-55. Mem. Spl. Libraries Assn. (John H. Moriarty award Ind. chpt. 1972), ALA, Med. Library Assn., AAUP, Am. Assn. Colls. Pharmacy, Kappa Delta Pi, Delta Rho Kappa. Baptist. Author: A Bibliography of the Socioeconomic Aspects of Medicine, 1975; A Bibliography of Drug Abuse Including Alcohol and Tobacco, 1977; A Bibliography of Drug Abuse, Supplement 1977-1980, 1981; Bibliography on Herbs, Herbal Remedies and Natural Foods, 1982; sect. editor Advances in Alcohol and Substance Abuse, 1981—; contbr. articles to profl. jours. Office: Pharmacy Bldg Purdue U West Lafayette IN 47907

ANDROS, HELEN MARY, ins. exec.; b. Calexico, Calif.; d. Harry Dimitre and Marguerite Mandy (Shalhoob Oliver) A.; C.L.U., Am. Coll., Bryn Mawr, Pa., 1977. Sec., adminstrv. asst. Gen. Electric Co., Santa Barbara, Calif., 1956-61; agt., broker, registered rep. Pacific Mut. Life and Univ. Securities Corp., Santa Barbara, 1962—; founder County Savs. & Loan, 1978—. Mem. adv. bd. Am. Cancer Soc.; bd. dirs. Santa Barbara Futures Found., 1980. Mem. Am. Soc. Chartered Life Underwriters (bd. dirs. Ventura-Santa Barbara Counties chpt. 1978—, chpt. officer 1980-82), Nat. Assn. Life Underwriters, Women Leaders Round Table (bd. dirs., officer 1969-72), Women Life Underwriters Conf. NALU, Estate Planning Council Santa Barbara, Santa Barbara Assn. Life Underwriters (pres. 1980—), Channel City Womens Forum (bd. dirs.), Santa Barbara Hist. Soc. Republican. Roman Catholic. Office: 3820 State St Santa Barbara CA 93105

ANDUJAR, BETTY RICHARDS, state senator; b. Harrisburg, Pa., Nov. 6, 1912; d. Karl Elmer and Katherine M. (Beetem) Richards; B.A., Wilson Coll., Chambersburg, Pa., 1934; m. John Jose Andujar, Aug. 16, 1935; children—Betty Jo Andujar Mayberry, Linda. Mem. Tex. State Senate, 1972—. Mem. Tex. Republican Exec. Com., 1964-76, Rep. Nat. Com., 1976-80. Named Exec. Woman of Yr., Zonta Club Ft. Worth, 1977; recipient Founders' medal Tex. Coll. Osteo. Medicine, 1978, Good Neighbor of Yr. award, Internat. Good Neighbor Council, 1979. Address: 2630 West Freeway 233 Fort Worth TX 76102

ANGEL, VERA FAY, realty co. exec. b. Covington, Ky., Oct. 7, 1928; d. Loren Jerome and Clara Blaine (McNay) Rusk; grad. high sch.; m. James Bird Angel, June 20, 1947; children—Terry Lee, Daryl Jay, Paula Kay Angel Wing. Owner, Vera Angel Realty, Inc., Covington, 1957—; dir. Kenton-Boone Bd. Realtors, 1976—. Mem. Covington City Commn., 1968-71; vice chmn. No. Ky. chpt. Am. Cancer Soc., 1976-77, chmn., 1977-78, local chmn. and state dir., 1974; chmn. Kenton County Heart Fund, 1977. Mem. No. Ky. C. of C. (dir. 1975—, sec. 1979), Kenton-Boone Bd. Realtors (pres. 1979), Nat. Assn. Realtors, Ky. Assn. Realtors (sec. 1978), No. Ky. Homebuilders Assn., Latonia Bus. Assn. Democrat. Baptist. Home: 47 Madonna Ln Cold Spring KY 41076 Office: 3618 Caroline St Covington KY 41015

ANGELETTI, EVELYN MARIE, lawyer; b. Atlanta, July 27, 1947; d. Fred and Marie (Merck) Angeletti; B.A., Agnes Scott Coll., 1969; J.D., Emory U., 1972. Admitted to S.C. bar, 1972; asso. law firm Haynsworth, Perry, Bryant, Marion & Johnstone, Greenville, S.C., 1972-77; atty. The Liberty Corp., Greenville, 1978, asst. sec., 1979, asst. counsel, asst. sec., 1979—; asst. counsel, asst. sec. Liberty Life Ins. Co., 1979-82, asso. counsel, asst. sec., 1982—; asst. sec. Cosmos Broadcasting Corp., 1981—; instr. dept. continuing edn. Furman U., Greenville, 1979—. Legal adviser, bd. dirs. Old Ninety Six council Girl Scouts U.S., 1977—; legal adviser Greenville YWCA, 1976—, Greenville Humane Soc., 1974—. Mem. Am. Bar Assn., S.C. Bar. Assn., Mortar Bd. Roman Catholic. Club: Zonta (pres. 1976-77), Agnes Scott Alumnae (pres. 1979—). Office: 2000 Wade Hampton Blvd Greenville SC 29615

ANGELINO, DOLORES KEATING, mgmt. analyst; b. Hackensack, N.J., May 9, 1951; d. George Joseph and Catherine Margaret (Brady) Keating; B.A. in Math., William Paterson Coll., Wayne, N.J., 1973; postgrad. in acctg. LaSalle Coll., Phila., 1978—; m. Rudolph Peter Angelino, Apr. 24, 1976. Supply systems analyst U.S. Navy, Bayonne, N.J., 1973-76, fiscal acctg. asst., 1976-77, mgmt. analyst Navy Internat. Logistics Control Office, Phila., 1978—. Mem. Nat. Assn. Female Execs., Phila. Women's Network, Cath. Daus. Americas. Roman Catholic.

ANGELL, JEAN BLETTNER, lawyer; b. Washington, Sept. 21, 1944; d. Edward F. and Margaret L. (Maw) Blettner; B.A., Wellesley Coll., 1966; J.D., Harvard U., 1969; m. Christopher C. Angell, Jan. 16, 1971; children—Elizabeth M., Margaret B., Christopher E. Admitted to N.Y. bar, 1970; asso. firm Donovan, Leisure, Newton & Irvine, N.Y.C., 1969-78; partner firm Williamson & Hess, N.Y.C., 1978-79, Richards O'Neil & Allegaert N.Y.C., 1979—. Mem. Am. Bar Assn., N.Y. State Bar Assn., Assn. Bar City N.Y. Democrat. Episcopalian. Clubs: River, Cosmopolitan (N.Y.C.). Home: 156 E 66th St New York NY 10021 Office: 660 Madison Ave New York NY 10021

ANGELO, GAYLE-JEAN, research scientist, educator; b. Winchester, Mass., Nov. 27, 1951; d. John William and Josephine Marie (Tavano) A.; B.A. in Physics with honors, Northeastern U., 1975, M.Ed. in Curriculum and Instrn.-Sci. and Math., 1978; postgrad. Tchrs. Coll., Columbia U., 1982—. Asst. clin. chemist Boston Med. Lab., Inc., 1971-72; asst. exptl. physicist Northeastern U., 1975-76; head dept. sci. Girls Cath. High Sch., Malden, Mass., 1977-78; research and teaching asst. Columbia U., N.Y.C., 1978-79, research asso., 1982—; research scientist Air Force Rocket Propulsion Lab., Edwards AFB, Calif., 1980-81; instr. math. Golden Gate U., Cerro Coso Community Coll., 1981-82, Columbia U., N.Y.C., 1982—. Served with USAF, 1980-81; mem. Air N.G. Decorated Air Force Commendation; cert. secondary tchr., Mass.; cert. community coll. tchr., Calif. Mem. AAAS, Am. Assn. Physics Tchrs., Am. Phys. Soc., Assn. for Women in Sci., Nat. Council Tchrs. Math., Nat. Sci. Tchrs. Assn., Soc. for Coll. Tchrs., Sch. Sci. and Math. Assn., Soc. Physics Students, N.Y. Acad. Scis., Am. Mensa Ltd., Northeastern U. Alumni Assn., Kappa Delta Pi, Phi Delta Kappa, Sigma Delta Epsilon. Home: 113 Butler Ave Wakefield MA 01880 Office: Dept Math and Sci Edn Box 210 Tchrs Coll Columbia U New York NY 10027

ANGELOU, MAYA, author; b. St. Louis, Apr. 4, 1928; d. Bailey and Vivian (Baxter) Johnson; hon. degrees Smith Coll., 1975, Mills Coll., 1975; 1 son, Guy Johnson. Asso. editor Arab Observer, Cairo, Egypt, 1962-63; writer Ghanaian Times, Accra, 1963-65, Ghanaian Broadcasting Corp., 1963-66; asst. adminstr. Inst. African Studies, U. Ghana, 1963-65; feature editor African Rev., 1965-66; lectr. U. Calif., 1966; author: I Know Why the Caged Bird Sings, 1970; Just Give Me A Cool Drink of Water 'Fore I Die 1971; (screenplay) Georgia, Georgia, 1972; Gather Together in My Name, 1974; Oh Fray My Wings Are Gonna Fit Me Well, 1975; Singin' & Swingin' & Gettin' Merry Like Christmas, 1976, And Still I Rise, 1978. Mem. New Nat. Women's Year Commn. Home: PO Box N Hot Springs CA 95416 Office: care Random House 201 E 50th St New York NY 10017 *

ANGERMAN, EVELYN LOUISE, musician, edcuator; b. DeKalb, Ill., Mar. 30, 1927; d. Hugo F. and Gladys (Coudrey) Carlson; B.Music Edn., Northwestern U., 1948; postgrad. Western Mich. U., No. Ill. U.; m. Robert E. Angerman, Aug. 26, 1950; children—Alison, Robert Todd. Instrumental music cons. Kalamazoo Pub. Schs., 1949-60; music edn. tchr., applied clarinet tchr. Kalamazoo Coll., 1964—; bass clarinetist Kalamazoo Symphony, Grand Rapids (Mich.) Symphony; pres. players com.; leader Kalamazoo Symphony Woodwind Quintet. Pres., Kalamazoo Concert Band; sec. Community Concerts; v.p. Kalamazoo Concert Band. Mem. Kalamazoo Fedn. Musicians (dir.), Kalamazoo Golf Assn., Modern Music Masters, Pi Kappa Lambda, Sigma Alpha Iota. Methodist. Home: 1405 Baker Dr Kalamazoo MI 49001 Office: 700 Academy St Kalamazoo MI 49001

ANGLE, JUDY ARLENE, phys. therapist; b. Kensington, Md., July 8, 1949; d. Clarence Elden and Rheba Hanna A.; student Bowling Green U., 1967-68; B.S.P.T., Ohio State U., 1971, M.S. in Allied Med. Professions (HEW trainee), 1972. Clin. instr. U. Miami, 1973-74; home health phys. therapist and cons., Miami and Ft. Lauderdale, Fla., 1974-76; staff therapist Warren (Ohio) Gen. Hosp., 1977; therapist Naples (Fla.) Community Hosp., 1978; therapist Homemakers Upjohn, Naples, 1978—; prin. owner/adminstr. J.A. Angle & Assos. Inc., phys. therapy services, Naples, 1979—. Lic. phys. therapist, Ohio, Fla. Mem. Am. Phys. Therapy Assn. Office: 500 5th Ave S Suite 518 Naples FL 33940

ANGLE, MARGARET SUSAN, lawyer; b. Lincoln, Nebr., Feb. 20, 1948; d. John Charles and Catherine (Sellers) A.; B.A. in Polit. Sci. with distinction, U. Wis., Madison, 1970, M.A. in Scandinavian Studies (tuition scholar, NDEA fellow), 1972, J.D. cum laude, 1976. Law clk. in Madison and Mpls., then Chgo., 1974-76; admitted to Wis. bar, 1977, Minn. bar, 1978; law clk. U.S. Dist. Ct., Mpls., 1977-78; asso. firm Faegre & Bensen, Mpls., 1978—. Mem. Am. Bar Assn., Minn. Bar Assn., Wis. Bar Assn., Hennepin County Bar Assn; Order of Coif. Note and comment editor U. Wis. Law Rev.; contbr. articles to profl. publs. Home: 221 Loring Way 210 W Grant St Minneapolis MN 55403 Office: 1300 Northwestern Bank Bldg Minneapolis MN 55402

ANGLE, SHARON ANN, legal asst.; b. Fairland, Okla., Sept. 8, 1946; d. Bernie and Thelma Louise (Wilmoth) Pennington; cert. Paralegal Inst. Ariz., 1979; student N.E. Okla. A&M Coll., Miami, 1980-82; 1 son, David Scott. Service rep. Gen. Telephone Co., Belvidere, Ill., 1968-69, bus. office supr., 1969; sec. to dir. adult edn. Rock Valley Community Coll., Rockford, Ill., 1970-73; legal sec. Hall, Stockwell & Wooley, Miami, 1975; legal asst. law firm Garrette & Stockwell, Miami, 1976-79; sec. Ray Son, Inc., Miami, 1980—, Maverick Enterprises, 1980—. Mem. adv. bd. N.E. Okla. A&M Coll., 1980—. Club: Hi-Noon Bus. and Profl. Women's (pres. 1979-80). Home: 410 5th St SE Miami OK 74354 Office: PO Box 1245 Miami OK 74354

ANGLUND, JOAN WALSH, author, illustrator; b. Hinsdale, Ill., Jan. 3, 1926; d. Thomas F. and Mildren (Pfiefer) Walsh; student Art. Inst. Chgo., 1944, Am. Acad. Art, 1945; m. Robert Lee Anglund, Nov. 9, 1947; children—Joy Ann, Todd Emerson. Author, illustrator: A Friend is Someone Who Likes You (N.Y. Times selection as 1 of 10 best illus. books 1958), 1958; The Brave Cowboy, 1959; Look Out the Window, 1959; Love is a Special Way of Feeling, 1960; In a Pumpkin Shell, 1960; The Cowboy and His Friend, 1961; Christmas is a Time of Giving, 1961; Nibble Nibble Mousekin, 1962; Spring is a New Beginning, 1963; Cowboy's Secret Life, 1963; A Pocketful of Proverbs, 1964; Un Ami, C'est Quelqu'an qui t'aime; Childhood is a Time of Innocence, 1964; A Book of Good Tidings, 1965; What Color is Love, 1966; A Year is Round, 1966; A Cup of Sun, 1967; Amor Est Semsus Quidam Peculiaris, 1968; A is for Always, 1968; Morning is a Little Child, 1969; A Slice of Snow, 1970; Do You Love Someone?, 1971; Cowboy's Christmas, 1972; Old Nursery Rhymes, 1973; Goodbye Yesterday, 1974; A Birthday Book, 1975; Christmas Cookie Book, 1976; The Joan Walsh Anglund Story Book, 1978. Office: Atheneum Pubs Inc 122 E 42d St New York NY 10017 *

ANGOTTI, CATHERINE MARIE, nutritionist; b. Arlington, Va., Nov. 9, 1946; d. Frank William and Catherine Jeannette (Kolakoski) Poos; B.S., James Madison U., 1968; R.D., Med. Coll. Va., 1969; postgrad. Va. Poly. Inst. and State U., 1975; m. John Joseph Angotti, Sept. 15, 1973; 1 dau., Heather Jeannette. Home economist Washington Gas Light Co., 1968; clin. dietitian Fairfax Hosp., Fairfax, Va., 1969-73; pvt. practice as nutrition cons., Alexandria, Va., 1972—; nutrition cons. Manassas (Va.) Manor Nursing Home, 1973-74, Bio-Tech., Inc., Falls Church, Va., 1977-78; nutrition surveyor JWK Internat., Annandale, Va., 1980-81; nutrition cons. NASA, Washington, 1977—; pres. Nutrition Cons., Inc., 1980—. Del. for Va. Dietetic Assn. to Va. Council on State Legis., 1974-76; mem. Com. for Pub. of Regional Diet Manual, 1971-73. Food Service Execs. awards scholar, 1967; Mem. Am. Dietetic Assn. (named outstanding Young Dietitian of Yr. 1975), Va. Assn. Allied Health Profls. (del. 1974-79, bd. dirs. 1975-77), Cons. Nutritionists (Va. state coordinator 1976-79), D.C. Dietetic Assn., Va. Dietetic Assn. (exec. bd. 1974-76, 82—), No. Dist. Dietetic Assn. (exec. bd. 1970—, treas. 1980-82, pres. elect 1982-83), Fairfax County Nutrition Com., Nat. Assn. Female Execs., Soc. for Nutrition Edn. Democrat. Roman Catholic. Contbr. articles to profl. jours. Home: 2727 Oak Valley Dr Vienna VA 22180 Office: 5249 Duke St Alexandria VA 22304

ANGUIANO, LUPE, bus. exec.; b. La Junta, Colo., Mar. 12, 1929; d. Jose and Rosario (Gonzalez) A.; student Ventura (Calif.) Jr. Coll., 1948, Victory Noll Jr. Coll., Huntington, Ind., 1949-52, Marymount Coll., Palos Verdes, Calif., 1958-59, Calif. State U., Los Angeles, 1965-67; M.A., Antioch-Putney-Yellow Springs, Ohio, 1978. S.W. regional dir. NAACP Legal Def. and Ednl. Fund, Los Angeles, 1965-69; civil rights specialist HEW, Washington, 1969-73; S.W. regional dir. Nat. Council Catholic Bishops, Region X, San Antonio, 1973-77; pres. Nat. Women's Employment and Edn., Inc., San Antonio, 1978-81; pres. Lupe Anguiano & Assos., 1981—; cons. Tex. Dept. Human Resources, Dept. Labor, Women's Bur.; proposal reader U.S. Office Edn.-Women's Equity Act; mem. Tex. Adv. Council on Tech.-Vocat. Edn. Calif. del. White House Conf. on Status Mexican-Ams. in U.S., 1967; founding mem. policy council Nat. Women's Polit. Caucus, 1971—; Tex. and nat. del. Internat. Women's Year, 1976-77; chmn. Nat. Women's Polit. Caucus Welfare Reform Task Force, 1977—; co-chairperson Nat. Peace Acad. Campaign, 1977-81; founder, bd. dirs. Nat. Chicana Found., Inc., 1971-78; bd. dirs. Calif. Council Children and Youth, 1967, Rio Grande Fedn. Chicago Health Centers, S.W. Rural States, 1974-76, Women's Lobby, Washington, 1974-77, Rural Am. Women, Washington, 1978—, Small Bus. Council Greater San Antonio. Recipient Community award Coalition Mexican-Am. Orgns., 1967, Outstanding Service award Washington, 1968, Thanksgiving award Boys' Club, 1976, Outstanding

Service award Tex. Women's Polit. Caucus, 1977, Liberty Bell award San Antonio Young Lawyers, 1981, Vista award for exceptional service to end poverty, 1980, Headliner award San Antonio Women in Communications, 1978, Woman of Year award Tex. Women's Polit. Caucus, 1978; named Outstanding Woman of Yr., Los Angeles County, 1972; Woman of the 80s Ms. mag., 1980; Wonder Woman Found. award, 1982. Mem. Assn. Female Execs., Pres.'s Assn., Am. Mgmt. Assn. Democrat. Roman Catholic. Author: (with others) U.S. Bilingual Education Act, 1967, Texas A.F.D.C. Employment and Education Act, 1977; manuals Women's Employment and Education Model Program. Office: Lupe Anguino & Assos PO Box 28251 San Antonio TX 78228

ANIKEEFF, PAMELA TATIANA, psychologist; b. Detroit, Sept. 27, 1948; d. Alexis Michael and Josephine W. (Obroslinski) A.; A.B., U. Calif., Berkeley, 1970; M.A., U. Akron (Ohio), 1972; Ph.D. (grad. teaching asso. 1973-77), Ohio State U., 1977. Research psychologist, then program mgmt. analyst U.S. Dept. Transp., Washington, 1978-81, mem. evaluation team Nat. Task Force for Safety Belts and Child Restraint Devices, 1982—. Mem. Am. Psychol. Assn., Assn. Women in Sci., Nat. Assn. Female Execs., Soc. Psychol. Study Social Issues, Guild Natural Sci. Illustrators, Assn. Advancement Psychology, Women's Equity Action League, Sierra Club. Home: 3140 Wisconsin Ave NW Apt 614 Washington DC 20016

ANNABLE, BETTY KATHRYN, assn. exec.; b. Heppner, Oreg., May 16, 1915; d. George Irvin and Rosana Marguerite (Westfall) Burnside; B.A. in Edn., Western U., 1937; postgrad. Calif. State U., San Jose, 1955-59; m. Forrest J. Annable, Sept. 7, 1936; children—Roderic F., Meredith Kathryn, Vicki Ilene. Tchr., Mendon (Mich.) Public Schs., 1937-39, 41-43, Owosso (Mich.) Public Schs., 1943-45; exec. dir. Shiawassee (Mich.) Girl Scout Council, 1945-49, dist. dir., Oakland, Calif., 1949-51; tchr., adminstr. Castro Valley (Calif.) Unified Sch. Dist., 1951-60; founder, owner, mgr. Bus. Enterprise, Castro Valley, 1961-74; exec. v.p. Castro Valley (Calif.) C. of C., 1974—; dir., sec. bd. Centennial Bank, Hayward, Calif., 1976—; dir. Highland Place Coop., Inc., Castro Valley, 1979-81. Bd. dirs. San Francisco Area council Girl Scouts U.S.A. 1956; active Castro Valley Cancer League. Recipient various public service awards. Mem. NEA, Calif. Edn. Assn., Castro Valley C. of C. (dir. 1962-74, pres. 1974), Castro Valley Hist. Soc. (founder, pres. 1972-76), Delta Kappa Gamma. Democrat. Home: 19100 103 Crest Ave Castro Valley CA 94546 Office: 21096 Redwood Rd Castro Valley CA 94546

ANNIS, LINDA FERRILL, ednl. psychologist; b. South Bend, Ind., Sept. 10, 1943; d. Everett William and Mary Ruth (Chapman) Ferrill; B.S., Ball State U., 1964; M.Ed., U. Ill., Urbana, 1967; Ph.D., Purdue U., 1976; postdoctoral fellow Ednl. Testing Service, Princeton, 1976-77; m. David Boyden Annis, Aug. 22, 1964. Tchr., Public Schs. Champaign (Ill.), 1964-69; mem. faculty Ball State U., Muncie, Ind., 1969—, asso. prof. ednl. psychology, 1978-80, prof., 1980—; cons. Psychol. Corp., various pubs. Mem. Am. Fedn. Tchrs., Am. Ednl. Research Assn., Am. Psychol. Assn., Alpha Chi Omega. Democrat. Author: The Child Before Birth, 1978; Study Techniques, 1983. Home: RR 12 Box 192 Bayberry Ln Muncie IN 47302 Office: Dept Ednl Psychology Ball State U Muncie IN 47306

ANON, ELLEN LURIE, clin. psychologist; b. Cin., Aug. 30, 1954; d. Max Leonard and Miriam (Rudnick) Lurie; student Tulane U., 1971; B.A. summa cum laude, U. Cin., 1974, M.A., 1976, Ph.D., 1980; m. Jack Bryant Anon, Oct. 4, 1980; 1 son, Joshua David. Psychiat. emergency therapist, 1976-80; adj. asst. prof. Cin. Gen. Hosp., 1980—; lectr. psychology Xavier U., Cin., 1981—; pvt. practice clin. psychology, Cin., 1982—. Danforth fellow competition rep. U. Cin., 1974; lic. clin. psychologist, Ohio. Mem. Am. Psychol. Assn., Phi Beta Kappa, Psi Chi. Office: 3210 Burnet Ave Suite 301 Cincinnati OH 45229

ANSCHUETZ, ROBERTA COOK, orgn. exec., civic worker; b. Denver, May 30, 1918; d. Robert Carl and Meta Christene (Griep) Cook; B.M.E., U. Kans., 1939; m. Norbert Lee Anschuetz, Mar. 13, 1943; children—Carol Anschuetz Bosley, Ellen Anschuetz Lewis, Susan, Nancy Anschuetz Stahl. With Pa.-Central Airlines, 1941-43, Panama Canal Co., 1943-44; officer Am. Women's Clubs, Greece, Thailand, France, Egypt, Lebanon; chmn. Civilian Wives at Nat. War Coll., 1956-57; non-govtl. orgn. observer at UN, 1971-73; coordinator for vols. Hubert Humphrey presdl. campaign, Washington, 1972; bd. dirs. N.Y.C. Com. for UNICEF, 1979—; mem. Com. for Govt. Relations for the Independent Sector, 1980—; pres. Nat. Council of Women of U.S., Inc., 1978-80; mem. bd. Washington Home com. Am. Mus., Bath. . Mem. AAUW, Women United for UN, Mortar Bd., Mu Phi Epsilon. Office: Nat Council of Women of US Inc 777 United Nations Plaza New York NY 10017

ANSLEY, NIN MCCABE, fashion writer; b. Mineral Wells, Tex., July 26, 1918; d. Rex and Ruth (Hillsman) McCabe; ed. Mary-Hardin Baylor Coll.; also seminars and univ. extension courses; m. James Ansley, Nov. 15, 1941; 1 dau., Janis. Fashion copywriter Neiman-Marcus Co., Dallas, 1950-55; account supr. women's accounts Don L. Baxter Advt. Agy., Dallas, 1955-66; dir. public relations Security World Pub. Co., Los Angeles, 1967-70; fashion dir. Merle Norman Cosmetics, 1970—; lectr. in field. Mem. Dallas Advt. League, Fashion Group, Color Mktg. Group, Dallas Press Club, Nat. Writers Club. Republican. Episcopalian. Contbr. numerous articles to mags. Home: 13080 Dronfield Ave 55 Sylmar CA 91342 Office: 9130 Bellanca Ave Los Angeles CA 90045

ANSO, MARIKO HIRATA, army officer; b. Tokyo, Japan, May 10, 1954; came to U.S., 1961, naturalized, 1966; d. Susan Marie (Hirata) Benkert; student U. Hawaii, 1972-73, U. Md., European Br., 1975-77, Am. Technol. U., 1978—; m. Aavo Peeter Anso, Dec. 19, 1975. Teller receptionist Pacific Savs. and Loan Assn., Honolulu, 1973-74; enlisted U.S. Army, 1974, advanced through grades to 2d lt., 1980, gen. mechanic/operator, W. Ger., 1975-77; sr. personnel records specialist, Ft. Hood, Tex., 1978-79, noncommd. officer in charge evaluation reports sect., 1979—. Active Hawaii Upward Bound Program, 1969-72.

ANTENEN, ANN MARIE, gen. contractor; b. Richmond, Va., May 19, 1925; d. Henry Aubrey and Emily Burwell (Boggs) Doyle; B.S. in Arch., U. Cin., 1946; m. Jay F. Antenen, Dec. 26, 1951; children—Susan Doyle, Jay F. Market researcher Proctor & Gamble, Cin., 1946-48; archtl. designer, officer mgr. David Maxfield, Oxford, Ohio, 1949-51; tchr. art YWCA, Hamilton, Ohio, 1959-71; pres. Ann Antenen-Restoration, Inc., Hamilton, 1981—; tchr. program designer of creative program for youth 1st United Presbyn. Ch., Hamilton, 1965-75; internat. cons. Inst. Cultural Affairs, Chgo. Regional Office, Cin. local office, community renewal thru social and econ. devel. Mem. Hamilton City Council, 1976-82, mayor, 1978-80; exec. budget com. United Way, 1976-81; bd. dirs. Alcoholism Council, 1976—; founder, lst pres. Hamilton-Fairfield Arts Council, 1979—; mem., chmn. archtl./environ. review panel Ohio Arts Council, 1978-79. Mem. Nat. League Cities (pub. employer-employee relations task force), U.S. Conf. of Mayors Community Devel. and Urban Arts Task Force. Democrat. Presbyterian. Club: Hamilton Garden (pres. 1976-77). Home: 30 Pinecrest Ln Hamilton OH 45013

ANTHONY, ANNE, ins. agy. exec.; b. Dothan, Ala., Oct. 24, 1943; d. James Cleo and Annie (Arnold) A.; student Draughon's Bus. Coll., 1961-62. Sec., Travelers Ins. Co., Greenville, S.C., 1962-64; with Continental Assurance Co., Chgo., 1964-74, asst. mgr. Atlanta claims, 1968-69, adminstrv. asst. and office mgr., group mktg. dept., New Orleans, 1969-73; pres. Profl. Mass Mktg. Am., Inc., New Orleans, 1974-77; pres., owner Plan Adminstrs. U.S., Inc., New Orleans, 1977—. Mem. Mass Mktg. Ins. Inst. (dir.), Profl. Ind. Mass-Mktg. Adminstrs. Republican. Methodist. Office: 2515 Canal St New Orleans LA 70119

ANTHONY, ANNIE ARNOLD, research analyst; b. Headland, Ala., Apr. 19, 1911; d. Linus Ivey and Mattie Narcissus (Posey) Arnold; student U. Ala., 1942; Research Inst. Am., 1980; m. James C. Anthony, Aug. 6, 1933 (dec.); children—Jerry A., Anne. Owner, realtor Annie Arnold Real Estate, Dothan, Ala., 1932-33; agt. trust dept. Mchts. Nat. Bank, Mobile, Ala., 1932-36; now cons. research analysis, Greenville, S.C. Sec ward 4, precinct 16, Greenville, 1956-58; policewoman, City of Greenville, 1955-62. Mem. Nat. Hist. Soc. Democrat. Methodist. Clubs: Greenville Country Dem. Women's, Christian Women's, Nat. Travel. Home and Office: 309 Grove Rd Greenville SC 29605

ANTHONY, BONNIE RUBIN, physician; b. N.Y.C., Dec. 29, 1943; d. Milton J. and Gertrude R. (Pollack) Belasco; student Hunter Coll., City U.N.Y., 1961-64; Ph.D., Columbia U., 1969; M.D., Georgetown U., 1975; m. Robert N. Anthony Jr., June 7, 1965; children—Patricia, Michelle, Scott, Michael. Intern, Georgetown Univ. Washington D.C., 1975-76; resident Georgetown U. Hosp., Washington, 1975-77; chief resident VA Hosp., Washington D.C., 1977-78; practice medicine specializing in psychiatry; mem. staffs Montgomery Gen. Hosp. Shady Grove Adventist Hosp. Psy. Dir. Women Ctr. for Growth, Rockville 1982. Mem. Am. Psychoanalytic Assn., AAAS, Am. Psychiatric Assn., Am. Womans Med. Assn., Nat'l Academy Sci. Home: 11106 Ralston Rd Rockville MD 20852

ANTHONY, CHRISTINE HOLLAND, civic worker; b. Oklahoma City, Dec. 18, 1916; d. Albert Houston and Mable Lenora (Gordon) Holland; B.S. in Econs., Okla. U., 1938; L.H.D., Oklahoma City U., 1977; m. Guy Mauldin Anthony, Mar. 27, 1945; children—Charles Ross and Guy Mauldin (twins), Robert Holland, Roy Jay, Jack Holland, Tom Albert. Dir. home service dept. Okla. Gas & Electric Co., Enid and Muskogee, 1938-45, corp. dir., 1971—; chmn. Oklahoma City br. Fed. Res. of Kansas City, 1977—; bd. dirs. Allied Arts Oklahoma City. Bd. dirs. World Neighbors, Oklahoma City, Internat. Health and Devel. Trust, Eugene, Oreg.; active United Way, Oklahoma City; bd. dirs., former v.p. Okla. Symphony Soc.; bd. advisors Mercy Hosp., Oklahoma City, also chmn. involvement and devel. com.; bd. trustees United Way; bd. dirs. Meth. Ch. of Nichols Hills, Oklahoma City. Named to Okla. Hall of Fame, 1979. Mem. Oklahoma City C. of C., Phi Beta Kappa. Democrat. Clubs: Oklahoma City Golf and Country, Okla. Heritage Soc., Jr. League, Okla. Art Center, Rotary Ann. Home: 6707 N W Grand Blvd Oklahoma City OK 73116

ANTHONY, DAISY CHRISTINA, accountant; b. Ladysmith, Wis., Jan. 19, 1950; d. Richard Gail and Marie Christina (Hoppes) Goins; B.S., U. Wis., LaCrosse, 1971; m. Donald James Anthony, June 7, 1970; children—Richard Emory, Stacie Christina. Tchr., public schs., La Crosse, Wis., 1971-73; pres. Daisy's Acctg. and Fin. Adv., Holmen, Wis., 1974—, La Crosse Tax Center, 1979—; gen. partner Indianhead Tax Center, Bruce, Wis., 1981—; tchr. adult classes, seminar and guest speaker in field. Mem. Nat. Soc. Public Accts., Wis. Assn. Accts., Holmen Area Civic and Commerce Assn. Lutheran. Home: Rural Route 1 Holmen WI 54636 Office: Professional Plaza 510 Amy Dr Holmen WI 54636

ANTHONY, GERALDINE CECILIA, educator; b. Bklyn., Oct. 5, 1919; d. William and Agnes Josephine (Murphy) A.; B.A., Mt. St. Vincent U., 1951; M.A. in Philosophy, St. Johns U., N.Y.C., 1956, Ph.D. in English, 1963. Joined Congregation of Sisters of Charity of Halifax, Roman Cath. Ch., 1942; tchr. jr. and sr. high schs., Boston, N.Y., 1942-62; prof. English, Mt. St. Vincent U., Halifax, N.S., 1965—. Recipient cert. in 17th Century poetry Exeter Coll., Oxford U., Eng., 1964; fellow in journalism U. Minn., 1965. Mem. Assn. Can. Univs. Tchrs. English, Assn. Canadian Theatre History. Author: John Coulter, 1976; Gwen Pharis Ringwood, 1981; editor: (series) Profiles in Canadian Drama, 1977; Stage Voices, 1978. Home and Office: Mount St Vincent U Halifax NS B3M 2J6 Canada

ANTHONY-PEREZ, BOBBIE COTTON MURPHY, psychologist; b. Macon, Ga., Nov. 15, 1923; d. Solomon Richard and Maude Alice (Lockett) Cotton; B.S. in Math., DePaul U., 1953, M.S. in Math., 1954, M.A. in Gen./Exptl. Psychology, 1975; M.S. in Math. Edn., U. Ill., Urbana, 1959; Ph.D. in Measurement, Evaluation and Statis. Analysis (Univ. scholar 1964-65), U. Chgo., 1967; m. Andrew S. Perez, June 20, 1979; 1 dau., Freida Maude Chapman. Tchr., Chgo. Public Schs., 1954-68; asst. prof. psychology Chgo. State U., 1968-74, asso. prof., 1974-77, prof., 1977—; cons. math. U. Chgo., 1965; psychologist Worthington Hurst, 1971-72; research coordinator Howard U. Inst. Urban Affairs, 1977. Program chairperson Chatham Avalon Park Community Council, Chgo., 1976-80, v.p. subarea 2, 1977-79, chairperson bus. relations, 1981-82, exec. v.p., 1979-81; bd. dirs., v.p. community affairs Chatham Bus. Assn., Chgo.; bd. dirs., rec. sec. Community Mental Health Corp., Chgo.; bd. dirs. Chatham unit Am. Cancer Soc., Chgo.; coordinator Commn. on Higher Edn., Ingleside Whitfield Parish, Chgo. Recipient Merit award Chgo. State U., 1977, 79, 81, also various service and appreciation awards Ingleside Whitfield Parish, Chatham Bus. Assn., Chatham Park Community Council, and various student orgns.; NSF fellow, 1957, 58, 58-59. Mem. Internat. Assn. Applied Psychology, Am. Psychol. Assn., Midwestern Psychol. Assn., Internat. Assn. Ednl. and Vocat. Guidance, Am. Ednl. Research Assn., Midwestern Ednl. Research Assn., Nat. Assn. Black Psychologists, Nat. Assn. Women Deans, Adminstrs. and Counselors (editorial bd. jour. 1975-77), Kappa Gamma Pi, Pi Mu Epsilon, Psi Chi, Pi Lambda Theta. Methodist. Contbr. articles to profl. jours. Office: Psychology Dept 9500 S King Dr Chicago IL 60628

ANTICAGLIA, ELIZABETH AHLFORS, writer; b. N.Y.C., Sept. 14, 1939; d. Harold and Hilma Ahlfors; B.A., N.Y. U., 1961; m. J.R. Anticaglia, Sept. 21, 1962; children—Jeannine, Jason. Editorial asst. Glamour mag., 1959, House and Garden mag., 1960; asst. prodn. editor Living For Young Homemakers, 1961, Vogue mag., 1961-62; tchr. English, Brit. Sch., Bologna, Italy, 1962-66; author books: A Housewife's Guide To Women's Liberation, 1972; Twelve American Women, 1975; Heroines of '76, 1975; columnist Companion mag. and Today's Post newspaper, 1971-73; contbr. to mags. and textbooks. Mem. NOW, First State Authors, Authors Guild. Home: Hockessin DE

ANTILL, SUSAN ELLEN, woven label plant exec.; b. Fairmont, W.Va., Nov. 30, 1939; d. Marion Earsel and Bessie Evelyn Shaw; student W. Va. U., 1959, Hagerstown Jr. Coll., 1980—; m. Ronald Gelain, Apr. 4, 1958; children—Ronald Kelvin, Teresa Elaine, David Earsel, Michel Gelain. Office clk. Alkahn Labels, Inc., Williamsport, Md., 1968-69, prodn. coordinator, 1970-76, asst. plant mgr., 1976—. Mem. Internat. Mgmt. Council, 1979—; mem. State Md. Employment Adv. Com., 1979—. Republican. Home: 1036 The Terrace Hagerstown MD 21740 Office: South Conococheague Williamsport MD 21795

ANTON, CHERYL LYNN, business exec.; b. Toledo, Nov. 3, 1953; d. Ralph Herbert and Coletta Marie (Nickerson) Synder; student U. Toledo, 1971-73; m. John B. Eggleston, 1980; 1 son, John Daniel. With Kroger Co., Toledo, 1972-80, dept. supr. merchandising; sales dir. Growth Unltd., Toledo, 1979-80; owner CJ's Bar, Toledo, 1980—. Mem. Nat. Assn. Female Execs. (network dir. 1979—), Nat. Assn. for Women. Democrat.

ANTOUN, ANNETTE AGNES, newspaper editor-publisher; b. Franklin, Pa., Mar. 7, 1927; d. Adrien Uriel and Charlotte Mary (McMullen) Adelman; student Allegheny Coll., Meadville, Pa.; m. Frederic George Antoun, July 19, 1947; children—Frederic G., Gregory S., Lawrence J., Mark J. (dec.), Laurence A., Scott J., Jonathan M., Lisa A. Founder, editor-pub. Paxton Herald, Harrisburg, Pa., 1960—; founder, owner Graphic Services, advt. and graphics, Harrisburg, 1972—; owner Communications System Design, 1978—; pres. Susquehanna Valley Assos., Inc., 1978—; co-editor French Creek Patriot, community newspaper, Cochranton, Pa., 1972. Bd. dirs. Tb and Health Soc., 1967—, exec. bd., 1967—, sec., 1972—; mem. communications com. Tri-County United Fund, 1973, mem. com. children's services, 1975—; bd. dirs. Pa. sect. Am. Lung Assn., 1973—, treas., 1976, sec., 1979-80, v.p., 1980-81; sec. bd. Central Pa. Lung Assn., 1969-73; bd. dirs. Harris Commn., 1975—, Cath. Social Service Harrisburg, 1972-76; mem. extension planning com. YMCA, 1975—; bd. govs. Camp Curtin YMCA, 1980—; rep. dir. Pa. Lung Assn., 1973, treas., 1975-76, sec. bd., 1977—; exec. bd. Lower Paxton Coalition Community Groups, 1973—; mem. communications bd. Catholic Diocese Harrisburg, 1971—; co-chmn. Dauphin County Ethics Com., 1979-80; chmn. bldg. com. Juvenile Detention Home, 1976—; chmn. fund raising com. Greater Harrisburg Arts Council, 1977—; mem. Dauphin County bd. Com. Children and Youth, 1982—. Recipient Advocate award Paxton Area Jaycees, 1969, 73; citation Am. Legion Pa., 1971, CAP, 1972, medallion Am. Legion Pa., 1972; award Am. Cancer Soc., 1969-79; March of Dimes award, 1969-79; numerous others. Mem. Internat. Platform Assn., Associated Public Communication Officers. Club: Pleasant Hills Community. Home: 4910 Earl Dr Harrisburg PA 17112 Office: 101 Lincoln St Harrisburg PA 17112

ANTOUN, SISTER, M. LAWREACE, coll. pres.; b. Meadville, Pa., Dec. 30, 1927; d. George K. and Freda (Habib) Antoun; B.S. Villa Maria Coll., 1954; M.S., Notre Dame U., 1959, postgrad. (doctoral candidate). Instr. chemistry Villa Maria Coll., Erie, Pa., 1955-61, asst. prof. chemistry, 1965-66, pres. 1966—; planning cons. Middle States Assn./Commn. Higher Edn.; mem. edn. info. centers task force Pa. Enrollment Planning Project; mem. adv. com. to council higher edn. Pa. Bd. Edn.; bd. dirs. Sisters of St. Joseph. Second v.p. United Way of Erie County; mem. Commonwealth Jud. Council; chairperson adv. council McMannis Ednl. Trust Fund; past mem. Home Rule Charter Com.; adv. bd. human ecology Cornell U.; mem. com. on intra-instnl. planning Nat. Center for Higher Edn. Mgmt. Systems; past mem. exec. com. region 9/10 Northwestern Pa. Planning Council; past mem. bd. incorporators St. Vincent Health Center. Mem. Am. Chem. Soc., Am. Assn. Ind. Colls. and Univs., Pa. Assn. Coll. and Univs., Pa. Assn. Ind. Colls. and Univs., Sigma Xi. Home: Erie PA 16505

AONA, GRETCHEN MANN, educator; b. Omaha, June 25, 1933; d. Albert Paul and Gladys Louise (Mann) Andersen; A.B., San Jose State U., 1951, M.A. in Art, 1966; m. Daniel Kaleikoa Aona, Jr., June 16, 1979. Tchr. elem. schs., Sunnyvale, Calif., 1951-54; instr. art, tchr. elem. sch., Sister of the Holy Cross, South Bend, Ind., Idaho Falls, Idaho, 1954-60; textbook illustrator math. and stats. dept. Stanford U., 1960-63; grad. admissions clk. San Jose State U., 1966-67; sci. illustrator Melabs, Mountain View, Calif., 1967; instr. art, crafts, and photography Kapiolani Community Coll., Honolulu, 1967—, chairperson humanities dept., 1978-79; one-woman shows in photography include: Fantasy Images, Queen Emma Gallery, Honolulu, 1977, Foyer Gallery, Leeward Community Coll., Honolulu, 1980; group exhbns. include: Photo '70, '71, '72, Honolulu, Art Hawaii One, Honolulu Acad. Art, 1974, 75, Gt. Hawaiian Open Art Exhbn., 1981, Artists of Hawaii, Honolulu Acad. Arts, 1981. Recipient Purchase award Honolulu Acad. Art, 1981. Mem. Am. Crafts Council, World Crafts Council, Hawaii Craftsmen, Arts Council Hawaii, Internat. guild Craft Journalists, Authors and Photographers. Democrat. Roman Catholic. Author: Creative Exploration in Crafts, 1976. Home: 45-453 B Mokulele Dr Kaneohe HI 96744 Office: Kapiolani Community Coll 620 Pensacola St Honolulu HI 96814

APELMAN, MAJA, educator, cons.; b. Vienna, Austria, Sept. 3, 1922; came to U.S., 1940, naturalized, 1946; d. Sascha and Beate (Kolischer) Chernakov; student Barnard Coll., 1940-43; B.A., Black Mountain Coll., 1944; M.A., U. Minn., 1947; M.S., Bank Street Coll. Edn., N.Y.C., 1966; Ph.D., U. Colo., 1981; 1 son, Mark. Pre-sch. tchr. in pvt. schs., N.Y.C., 1957-67; instr. Headstart Leadership Devel. Program, N.Y.U., N.Y.C., 1967-71; part-time instr. in curriculum Bank Street Coll. Edn., N.Y.C., 1967-71; mem. staff Mountain View Center for Environ. Edn., Boulder, Colo., 1971-80, research asso. in sci. edn., 1980-82; cons. in edn., 1967—. Nursery teaching fellow, 1962-64. Mem. Nat. Assn. for Edn. Young Children. Contbr. articles to edn. jours.; translator (with Eric Bentley): The Good Woman of Setzuan (Bertolt Brecht), 1948; The Caucasian Chalk Circle (Bertolt Brecht), 1948. Home: 755 Lincoln Place Boulder CO 80302

APFELBAUM, DIANE KAHAN, philatelic co. exec.; b. Phila., Sept. 18, 1932; d. Frederic Ellis and Ceclia (Wolfe) Kahan; B.A., M.A., U. Pa., 1979; m. Martin Apfelbaum, Feb. 4, 1951; 4 children. With Internat. Philatelic Co., Phila., 1970—, exec. v.p., 1972—; auctioneer, seminar leader in field. Mem. Am. Stamp Dealers Assn., Am. Philatelic Assn., Philatelic Traders Soc., Internat. Fedn. Stamp Dealers, Phila. C. of C., Phila. Center City Proprs. Democrat. Jewish. Club: Phila. Art Alliance. Office: 2006 Walnut St Philadelphia PA 19103

APGAR, NANCY STEPLETON, musician, educator; b. Mercer, Pa., Dec. 22, 1928; d. Grover Adlai and Georgetta (Gibson) Stepleton; Mus.B. with distinction, U. Rochester, 1950; Mus.M., Northwestern U., 1951; m. Horace Vincent Apgar, Sept. 1, 1951; children—David Arthur, Georgann. Music faculty Oklahoma City U., 1951-76; pianist Oklahoma City Symphony Orch., 1953-73, bd. dirs., 1974-77; v.p. Oklahoma Pet Supply Co., Inc., 1976—. Republican committeewoman from 5th Dist., 1971-75; chmn. Oklahoma County Rep. Com., 1975-79; campaign coordinator Zink for U.S. Senate Com., 1980; mem. exec. com. Okla. State Rep. Com., 1975—, state chmn., 1982—; del. Rep. Nat. Conv., 1976, mem. credentials com.; mem. Nat. Rep. Com., 1982—. Mem. Oklahoma City Arts Commn., 1980—. Named Outstanding Okla. Educator, 1975. Mem. Nat. Coll. Musicians (piano adjudicator), Oklahoma City Obedience Tng. Club (charter mem.), Sportsmen's Club, Oklahoma City Figure Skating Club (pres. 1977-78), Okla. Heritage Assn., Sigma Alpha Iota, Pi Kappa Lambda. Presbyterian. Contbr. articles to profl. jours. Home: 4235 Bush Blvd Oklahoma City OK 73112

APPEL, ANTOINETTE RUTH, neuropsychologist; b. N.Y.C., Mar. 31, 1943; d. Leon S. and Augusta (Marienberg) A.; B.A., U. Vt., 1964; M.A., Mt. Holyoke Coll., 1965; postgrad. Yeshiva U., 1965-66, Hofstra U., 1966; Ph.D. (Univ. fellow, dissertation fellow), City U. N.Y., 1972. Instr., C.W. Post Coll., Greenvale, N.Y., 1968-69; lectr./instr. Queens Coll., Flushing, N.Y., 1970-71; fellow in neurology, instr. ophthalmology Mt. Sinai Sch. Medicine, N.Y.C., 1971-74; adj. asst. prof. St. Francis Coll., Bklyn., 1974; asst. prof. dept. psychology So. Ill. U. Sch. Medicine, Carbondale, 1974-76; USPHS intern Conn. Valley Hosp., Middletown, Conn., 1976-77; asst. prof., asst. project coordinator Nat. Alcohol Research Center, dept. psychiatry U. Conn. Health Center, Farmington, 1977-79; neuropsychologist/asst. prof. program in medicine Brown U., Providence, 1979-82; adj. asst. prof. psychology U. R.I., Kingston and Providence, 1979—; pvt. practice psychology, 1981—; invited speaker

NATO Neuropsychology Conf., 1980, Internat. Council Psychology, 1980, 22d Internat. Congress of Psychology, 1980; cons. Narco Bio-systems, 1974-75, commr. mental health State of Conn., 1978-79. Bd. dirs. Sojourner House, 1979—, Combined Hosp. Alcoholism Program, 1978, Hartford Interval House, 1978. Served with WAC, 1963. Recipient Hartford Salute award, 1979; USPHS tng. fellow, 1966-67; NIMH predoctoral fellow, 1967-70. Mem. Am. Psychol. Assn. (mem. exec. bd.), Assn. Women in Psychology (mem. steering com.), Eastern Psychol. Assn. (chmn. 1980 conv.), Conn. Psychol. Assn. (council 1978-79), R.I. Psychol. Assn., N.Y. Acad. Scis., Sigma Xi. Psi Chi. Home: 722 Manomet Ct Wethersfield Commons Warwick RI 02886 Office: 21 Planet St Providence RI 02903

APPEL, JUDITH, investment adv. co. exec.; b. Budapest, Hungary, Feb. 25, 1935; came to U.S., 1939, naturalized, 1945; d. Max and Margaret (Szusz) Kane; B.A., Bklyn. Coll., 1956; m. Gerald Appel, May 27, 1956; children—Marvin Laurence, Marion Fran. Tchr. public schs., 1956-60; with N.Y. State Employment Service, 1960-61; co-owner Marketability, Great Neck, N.Y., 1973-78; sec. Signalert Corp., Gt. Neck, 1973—, v.p., 1977—; gen. partner various investment partnerships. Home: 97 Myrtle Dr Great Neck NY 11021 Office: Signalert 185 Great Neck Rd Great Neck NY 11021

APPEL, TOSCA, rehab. counselor; b. Stuttgart, W.Ger., Mar. 16, 1948; came to U.S., 1949, naturalized, 1955; d. Morris and Rena (Zimmerman) A.; B.A., Northeastern U., Boston, 1970; M.S., Boston U., 1977. Group rehab. counselor Children's Hosp. Med. Center, Boston, 1975-76, Lemuel Shattuck Hosp., Boston, 1976-77, Circle Manor Nursing Home, Brighton, Mass., 1977-78, Brookline (Mass.) Multi-Service Sr. Center, 1978-79, Boston Center Ind. Living, 1979-81 lectr. Youville Hosp. Sch. Nursing; clin. asso. Boston U., 1981—. Mem. Nat. Rehab. Assn. (Rubin Margolin award Mass. chpt. 1977), Am. Personnel and Guidance Assn., Nat. Rehab. Counseling Assn. Home: 100 S Huntington Ave Apt 401 Jamaica Plain MA 02130

APPELBAUM, JUDITH PILPEL, editor, educator; b. N.Y.C., Sept. 26, 1939; d. Robert Cecil and Harriet Florence (Fleischl) Pilpel; B.A. with honors, Vassar Coll., 1960; m. Alan Appelbaum, Apr. 16, 1961; children—Lynn Stephanie, Alexander Eric. Editor, Harper's Mag., N.Y.C., 1960-74; mng. editor Harper's Weekly, 1974-76; sr. cons. Atlas World Press Rev., 1977; mng. editor Publishers Weekly, 1978-81; mng. dir. Sensible Solutions, Inc., 1979—; contbg. editor Publishers Weekly, 1981—; faculty N.Y.U. Center for Pub., 1981—, Pub. Inst. of U. Denver, 1981—, City U. N.Y. edn. in pub. program, 1982—; editorial adv. Book Industry Study Group Newsletter, 1980—; adv. bd. Coordinating Council of Lit. Mags., 1980—. Mem. Authors Guild, PEN, Com. Small Mag./Press Editors and Publishers, Soc. for Scholarly Pub., Women's Forum. Author: (with Nancy Evans) How to Get Happily Published, 1978, rev. edit., 1982; editor: (with Tony Jones and Gwyneth Cravens) The Big Picture: A Wraparound Book, 1976; The Question of Size in the Book Industry Today, 1978; Getting a Line on Backlist, 1979. Office: Sensible Solutions Inc 14E 75th St New York NY 10021

APPELL, CLARA TAUBMAN, psychologist, family therapist; b. N.Y.C., July 31, 1921; d. Max and Yetta (Schubert) Taubman; B.S., Ohio State U., 1942, M.A. (Grad. fellow 1945-46), 1946; Ed.D., Columbia U., 1959; m. Morey L. Appell, Sept. 16, 1942 (dec.); children—Laurie, Randy Johnson, Glenn, Jodie, Jonathan. Tchr., Centerburg (Ohio) High Sch., 1942-43, Nathan Hale High Sch., Moodus, Conn., 1943-44, Franklin D. Roosevelt High Sch., Hyde Park, N.Y., 1944-45, N.Y.C. schs., 1947-48; dir. Colony House Child Care Center, Bklyn., 1946-47; lectr. Bklyn. Coll., 1950-53, 1955-61; parent educator Child Guidance League, Bklyn., 1962-64; asso. prof. Ind. State U., Terre Haute, 1964-66, co-dir. Family Life Center, 1964-66; prof. child devel., family life, head start coordinator Menomonie U. Wis., Stout, 1966-67; dir. home day care tng. program, child devel. family life specialist Bank Street Coll., N.Y.C., 1967-68; cons. Conn. State Dept. Edn., Hartford, 1968-69; coordinator child devel., family life Greenwich (Conn.) Health Assn., 1969-71; adj. prof. child devel., family life, and TV and family Queens Coll., N.Y.C., 1975-79; pvt. practice marriage and family therapy, Greenwich; br. cons. U. Conn., Stamford, 1979-80, adj. lectr., 1982—; cons. human devel., 1971—; psychol. cons. Hospice of Stamford, 1981-82; cons. Greenwich Assn. Retarded Citizens, 1982—; program moderator Sta. WGCH, Greenwich, 1969-71, 74-80; pres. Morey L. Appell Human Relations Found., Greenwich, 1977—; cons. Butterick Pub. Co., N.Y.C., 1979-80. Bd. dirs. Mother Center, Inc., 1979—, Stamford Family Life Workshops, Inc., 1979—; mem. Conn. Media and Communications Task Force for White House Conf. on Families, 1979-80. Recipient Diamond Anniversary award Ohio State U., 1971. Fellow Am. Orthopsychiat. Assn., Internat. Council Sex Edn. and Parenthood; mem. Internat. Council Psychologists, Am. Assn. Marriage and Family Therapists, Am. Assn. Sex Edn., Counseling and Therapy, Am. Home Econs. Assn., Assn. Family Conciliation Cts., Am. Psychol. Assn., Assn. for Humanistic Psychology, Groves Conf. Marriage and the Family, Forum for Death Edn. and Counseling, Nat. Council Family Relations, Soc. for Research in Child Devel., Soc. for Psychol. Study Social Issues, Internat. Women's League for Peace and Freedom, Pi Lambda Theta, Kappa Delta Pi, Omicron Nu. Author: (with Morey L. Appell) We Are Six, 1959; Now I Have A Daddy Haircut, 1960; Glenn Learns to Read, 1964; contbr. numerous articles to profl. jours. Home and Office: 145 Old Church Rd Greenwich CT 06830

APPELT, JUDY PARKER, urban econ. devel. cons.; b. San Antonio, Mar. 27, 1938; d. D. Roy and Florence Mildred (Tedford) Parker; B.A., U. Tex., Austin, 1960, Ph.D. in Geography, 1975. Tchr., Clear Lake Jr. High Sch., Westminster, Colo., 1960-63; writer-editor high sch. geography project NSF, Boulder, Colo., 1968; asst. prof. geography Winona (Minn.) State U., 1977-80; cons. urban econ. devel. First Nat. Bank Boston, also Council N.E. Econ. Action, Boston, 1980—. Mem. econ. modeling subgroup Boulder Growth Study Commn., 1975; mem. Mayor Winona Truck Route Commn., 1980; vice chmn. Winona County Environ. Health Task Force, 1980. Grantee Dept. Labor, 1970, Winona State U., 1980. Mem. Assn. Women Geographers, LWV, Mensa. Democrat. Unitarian-Universalists.

APPENFELDT, LINDA LANDT, psychologist; b. Buffalo, Nov. 21, 1943; d. Edward and Alma G.; Ph.D. (NDEA fellow), U. Miami, Coral Gables, Fla., 1973; 1 dau., Deirdre. Clin. intern Winter Haven (Fla.) Hosp., 1974-75; pvt. practice clin. and forensic evaluation, adult and child psychotherapy, St. Petersburg, Fla., 1976—; ct. psychologist Pinellas County (Fla.). Diplomate Am. Bd. Forensic Psychology. Mem. Am. Psychol. Assn., Fla. Psychol. Assn., Pinellas Psychol. Assn. Office: 5800 49th St N Suite 208 S Saint Petersburg FL 33706

APPLEGATE, CAROL BARR, nurse; b. Decatur County, Ind., May 19, 1930; d. Arthur and Nelle Mae (Harrell) Wright; R.N., Marion County Sch. Nursing, Indpls., 1953; diploma Ind. U., 1953; m. Robert H. Applegate, Apr. 27, 1951; children—Debra, Douglas, Diana, Donna. Staff nurse Geneva (N.Y.) Gen. Hosp., 1954-55; mem. nursing staff Hancock Meml. Hosp., Greenfield, Ind., 1957—, dir. nursing service, 1964-74, dir. profl. service, 1974—; mem. adv. bd. Gallahue Mental Health Assn., 1980—. Mem. Nat. Assn. Female Execs., Central Ind. Emergency Med. Services Assn. (dir.), Ind. Assn. Quality Assurance Profls., Ind. Sheriffs Assn., Gen. Federated Club Women Am. (chpt. pres. 1965-66). Democrat. Methodist. Club: Order Eastern Star.

APPLEGATE, MINERVA IRONS, nursing educator; b. Lakewood, N.J., Mar. 8, 1941; d. Alfred Harold and Nancy Virginia (Webb) Irons; A.A.S. cum laude, Ocean County Coll., 1968; postgrad. U. Pa., 1968; B.S. in Nursing cum laude, U. Miami, 1971; M.Ed., Teachers Coll., Columbia U., 1974, Ed.D., 1980; postgrad. Georgetown U., 1976. Staff and charge nurse Point Pleasant (N.J.) Hosp., 1968-69, 70; family advisor, nurse Ocean Community Econ. Action Now (Head Start), Toms River, N.J., 1971-72; instr. Coll. Nursing, U. Miami, Coral Gables, Fla., 1974; asso. prof., co-dir. Kellogg Curriculum Project, Coll. Nursing, U. South Fla., Tampa, 1976—; cons. Vis. Nurses Assn., participant community workshops. United Way rep. U. S. Fla.; health planning bd. U. South Fla. Recipient med. award for excellence in nursing Paul Kimball Hosp., 1968; USPHS Profl. Nurse trainee, 1970-71, 72-74, 75; Vol. Service award Community Meml. Hosp., 1964, Outreach certificate N.J. Community Action Tng. Inst., 1971. Mem. Am. Nurses Assn., Nat. League Nursing, AAUP, U. South Fla. Coll. Nursing Honor Soc., Pi Lambda Theta, Sigma Theta Tau, Epsilon Tau Lambda. Republican. Collaborator videotape series, Rutgers U., 1973-74. Address: Dept Nursing Univ So Florida 4202 Flowler Ave Tampa FL 33620

APPLETON, CAROL SUZUMI, bus. services co. exec.; b. Whitefish, Mont., Dec. 30, 1940; d. Yoshikazu and Mariko (Shigeta) Sakahara; student Kinman Bus. U., 1958-60; m. Robert Appleton, Jan. 28, 1961; children—Robert, Susan Lynn. Clk.-typist Kinman Bus. U., Spokane, Wash., 1959-60; med. girl Friday, Robert A. Stier, M.D., Spokane, 1960-61; sec. Martin-Marietta Corp., Tucson, 1961-63, Tucson Clinic, 1964-66; office mgr. James T. Flanagan, M.D., Ontario, Oreg., 1966-78; owner, mgr. Appleton Secretarial Service, Treasure Valley Temporary Services, S & A Computer Services, Ontario, 1978—; mem. secretarial adv. com. Ontario High Sch., 1981—, chmn., 1981; mem. computer adv. com. Treasure Valley Community Coll., 1982—. Precinct person Malheur County Republican Com., 1972-78; local area pres. Babe Ruth Baseball, 1981—, state area commr., 1981—; treas. Ontario Little League Baseball, 1979—. Mem. Am. Entrepreneurs Assn., Nat. Assn. Female Execs., Ontario C. of C. (community action council), Beta Sigma Phi (past pres., v.p., sec.). Republican. Club: Ontario Jaycee Wives (pres. 1969-70). Home and office: PO Drawer J Ontario OR 97914

APPLEWHAITE, LOUISE JUNE, psychiat. nurse; b. Bryn Mawr, Pa., d. William James and Sarah Louise (Hill) Harley; A.A. in Nursing, SUNY, Farmingdale, 1973; B.S. in Community Health, SUNY Coll., Westbury, 1975; M.Profl. Studies in Human Service, N.Y. Inst. Tech., 1976; m. Leon B. Applewhaite, Dec. 19, 1959. Communication cons. N.Y. Telephone Co., Hempstead, 1960-1970; clin. specialist endocrinology-oncology research L.I. Jewish-Hillside Med. Center, New Hyde Park, N.Y., 1973-80, psychiat. research nurse, 1980—. Asst. fin. sec. Key Women Am., 1979-81; mem. Tanglewood Civic Assn., 1960—; corr. sec. Friends Lakeview Library, 1978-81. Mem. Am. Nurses Assn., Nat. Nurses Soc. Alcoholism, Alcohol and Drug Problem Assn. N.Am., Am. Public Health Assn., N.Y. State Nurses Assn., Bus. and Profl. Women's Club Central Nassau, Delta Sigma Theta. Republican. Presbyterian. Home: 7 Lawrence Ave Rockville Centre NY 11570

APPLEWHITE, ROBERTHA LILLIAN, librarian, educator; b. N.Y.C., Sept. 29, 1954; d. George and Lillian Holmes; B.A. magna cum laude, Bklyn. Coll., 1975; M.A., N.Y.U., 1979; M.L.S. (fellow), Queens Coll., 1981; m. Guy Sahadeo, June 20, 1975; children—Shlomo, Tzeporaw, Tzefereaw, Rawchayl. Instr. English, Washington Bus. Inst., N.Y.C., 1975-78; instr. English, librarian Royal Bus. Sch., N.Y.C., 1978—. Mem. Nat. Bus. Edn. Assn., ALA, Nat. Assn. Female Execs., N.Y.U. Alumni Assn. Democrat. Author: Bibliography of Career and Occupational Literature for Women 1970-80, 1980; Bio-bibliography of Ten Black Artists, 1980. Home: 570 New Jersey Ave Brooklyn NY 11212 Office: 250 W 18th St New York NY10011

APUNA, SANDI ROSENBERRY, ins. co. ofcl.; b. Ft. Wayne, Ind., Sept. 21, 1947; d. Raymond Ralph and Ruth Mildred Rosenberry; B.A., U. Wash., 1972; diploma in spl. early childhood Bellevue Community Coll., 1976; grad. Hawaii N.G. Mil. Acad., 1980, Life Underwriters Tng. Council Course, 1981; student Am. Coll. Life Underwriters, Hawaii, 1982—; m. Samuel K. Apuna, Jr., Sept. 26, 1980. Owner, dir. Small World Sch., 1976-78; instr. Infant Lab., Bellevue (Wash.) Community Coll., 1976-77 sales rep. Met. Life Ins. Co., 1979-80, sales mgr., Honolulu, 1980-82; mktg. assoc. John Hancock Life Ins. Co., Honolulu, 1982—. Served to 1st lt. USAR. Named Met. Rookie of Yr., Hawaiian Dist., 1979; recipient ins. sales awards; qualifying mem. Million Dollar Round Table. Nat. Quality award, Nat. Sales Achievement award. Registered ins. rep., Hawaii. Mem. Honolulu Assn. Life Underwriters (sec. 1981-82, pres. elect 1982-83), Nat. Women Life Underwriters Conf. (co-regional dir.), Gen. Agts. and Mgrs. Assn. (Met. Agt. of Yr., Hawaiian dist. 1981), Res. Officers Assn., Civil Affairs Assn. Club: Downtown Bus. and Profl. Women's (pres. 1981—, ways and means chmn. young careerist sect. 1982, state young careerist bd. 1982-83), state young careerist judge 1982. Home: 98-1764-D Kaahumanu St Pearl City HI 46782 Office: 1144 10th Ave Suite 300 Honolulu HI 96816

APYAN, ANGEL, retail carpet co. exec.; b. Worcester, Mass., Mar. 4, 1929; d. Hugas and Agnes (Bedrosian) Hovagimian; m. Sarkis Apyan, Oct. 11, 1947; children—Roseanna, Daniel, Paul, Carol. With Apyan Rug Co., Kenosha, Wis., 1947—, pres., 1977—. Mem. Nat. Assn. Female Execs. Congregationalist. Address: 6515 5th Ave Kenosha WI 53140

ARANT, PATRICIA M., educator; b. Mobile, Ala., Dec. 2, 1930; B.A., Ala. Coll., 1952; A.M., Radcliffe Coll., 1957; Ph.D., Harvard U., 1963. Researcher, U.S. Govt., Washington, 1952-56; asst. prof. Russian, Vanderbilt U., Nashville, Tenn., 1963-65; asst. prof. asso. prof., prof. Slavic langs. and lits. Brown U., Providence, 1965—, also assoc. dean Grad. Sch., Am. Council Learned Socs.-Social Scis. Research Council grantee, 1969, Internat. Research and Exchange grantee, 1973. Mem. Am. Assn. Tchrs. Slavic and East European Langs., Am. Folklore Soc. Author: Russian for Reading, 1982. Home: 7 Arnold St Providence RI 02906 Office: Box E Brown U Providence RI 02912

ARASTEH, JOSEPHINE DURKATZ, psychologist, health sci. adminstr.; b. Detroit, June 15, 1925; d. Joseph and Louise (Schwass) Durkatz; B.S., U. Mich., 1947; postgrad. Merrill-Palmer Inst., 1950-51; M.A., U. Mich., 1950; Ph.D., U. Chgo., 1960; m. A. Reza Arasteh, July 13, 1957; children—Dariush K., Roya L. Research asst. Fels Research Inst., Yellow Springs, Ohio, 1951-53; research psychologist NIMH, 1957-58, 61-69; research asso. prof. psychology U. Ill., 1969-71; program analyst USPHS, 1971-77; health scientist adminstr. Nat. Inst. Child Health and Human Devel., NIH, Bethesda, Md., 1977—. NIMH grantee, 1969-71. Mem. Am. Psychol. Assn., Soc. Research in Child Devel. Author: (with A. Reza Arasteh) Creativity in the Life Cycle, 2d edit., 1976, Man and Society in Iran, 1970; contbr. articles profl. jours. Office: Room 7C 18 Landow Bldg Bethesda MD 20205

ARBELBIDE, SYLVIA JEAN, geologist; b. Weiser, Idaho, June 7, 1951; d. Ollie Marion and Betty Lou (Kilpatrick) A.; student Boise State Coll., 1969-71; B.S. in Geol. Scis., U. Wash., 1973. Underground geologist Magma Copper Co., Superior, Ariz., 1973-75; area geologist Bur. Land Mgmt., Golden, Colo., 1975-77; dist. geologist Bur. Land Mgmt., Canon City, Colo., 1977-78, state office geologist, Denver, 1978-80; phys. scientist Bur. Mines, Denver, 1980—; govt. witness oil shale patent applications. Mem. Jefferson Symphony, 1977—. Recipient unit citation Foothills Environ. Statement, 1977. Mem. AIME, Rocky Mountain Assn. Geologists, Assn. Women Geoscientists, Colo. Scientific Soc., Nat. Assn. Female Execs., NOW. Clubs: Carter Lake Sailing, Internat. Class Laser Assn. Contbr. articles to profl. jours. Home: 364 Goldco Circle Golden CO 80403 Office: Bldg 20 Denver Fed Center Denver CO 80225

ARBUCKLE, DOROTHY FRY, civic worker, bus. exec., former librarian; b. Eldred, Ill., Jan. 23, 1910; d. William George and Sylvia (Mitchell) Fry; student Northwestern U., 1927-28, U. Ill., 1928-30; m. Lloyd Arbuckle, May 13, 1933 (dec. May 1960); children—Kathryn Diane, William Franklin. Free-lance reporter, Ind., Ill., 1931; librarian Lake Village, Ind. Meml. Twp. Library, 1946-62; petroleum jobber, distbr. Lake Village Shell Oil Co., 1960—; dir. Arbuckle Oil Co., Inc.; oil jobber rep. Internat. Oil Seminar, Monte Carlo-Monaco, 1977; dir. Lake View Retirement Home. Pres., Lake Village Sch. Corp., 1962—; twp. chmn. Multiple Sclerosis, Newton County, Ind., 1962-65, Cancer Soc., 1971—; mem. Heart Assn. Northwest Ind., George Ade Meml. Hosp. Aux., 1968-75; nat. oil industry chmn. Laymen's Nat. Bible Com., 1970, asso. chmn. Com., 1971-72; dir. exec. bd. N.W. Ind. Planning Commn. Area Library Services Authority; mem. exec. bd. Newton County Health Planning Commn., 1973-75; mem. natural resource div. Fish and Wildlife Commn., 1975—, key oil men's com. for 2d congressional dist., 1975. Bd. dirs. Newton County Hist. Soc. Corp. Mem. Ind. Library Assn., Ill. Woman's Press Assn., Nat. Fedn. Press Women, Midland Authors, Children's Reading Roundtable, DAR (poetry award 1979, nat. poetry award 1980 Ind. Am. Heritage award 1981), ASCAP, Ind., Ill., Newton County (vice pres., program chmn. 1966—) hist. socs., Am. Women Composers, Grange, Internat. Platform Assn. Presbyterian. (elder). Author: The After-Harvest Festival, 1955; Andy's Dan'l Boone Rifle, 1965; anthem: words and music The Church Wherein I Worship, 1955; The Hour Will Come, 1962; ballads: I Never Knew, 1960, By the Kankakee River, 1973. Address: Lake Village IN 46349

ARBUS, LOREEN JOY, cable TV exec.; b. white Plains, N.Y.; d. Leonard H. and Isabelle (Winstein) Golderson; student U. Pa., Harvard U., N.Y.U.; B.A., New Sch. Social Research, 1971; m. Norm Chandler Fox, Jan. 31, 1970. Profl. dancer Charles Weidman Co., N.Y.C., 1969-71; free-lance designer, N.Y.C., 1972—; editor Cosmopolitan Mag., N.Y.C., 1971-72; free lance prodn. asst., film editor, Los Angeles, 1972-73; film coordinator Imagivision, 1973-74; story analyst ABC Network, Los Angeles, 1974-75; program coordinator Late Night TV, Good Morning Am., ABC Network, Los Angeles, 1975, program exec. spls., Late Night TV, Good Morning Am., 1975-77, program exec., 1977-78, exec. producer Primetime Dramatic, Variety and Children's Spls., 1978-79; contbg. editor Los Angeles Mag., 1978—; v.p. in charge West Coast programming Showtime Entertainment, Los Angeles, 1979-82; v.p. programming Cable Health Network, Los Angeles, 1982—; bd. dirs. U. So. Calif. Cinema Circulus. Exec. dir. Media Office of Gov.'s Com. for Employment Handicapped; co-founder Los Angeles Com. to Implement Passage of ERA. Mem. Acad. TV Arts and Scis. (Showtime rep. pay cable adv. com.), Women in Film Found. (trustee), Writers Guild Am., Women in Communications, Women in Bus., Women in Radio and TV, Women in Cable, Hollywood Women's Press Assn. Co-creator comedy pilots, episodic writer Angie, Lou Grant, Tony Randall Show, Marcus Welby, M.D., Gen. Hosp., others, 1975—. Office: 9356 Santa Monica Blvd Beverly Hills CA 90210

ARCHBOLD, NORMA PEARL PARRISH, computer co. exec.; b. Portage de Sioux, Mo., Feb. 15, 1938; d. Henry Kimler and Ruth Watson (Fountain) Parrish; B.A., U. Mo., 1959; M.A., Loyola U., Chgo., 1975; m. Kenyon Allan Archbold, June 10, 1961 (dec. 1975); children—Cameron Allan, Jennifer Anne, Jeffrey Thomas, Christopher Michael. Dir. religion edn. St. Mary's Sch., Des Plaines, Ill., 1971-75, Our Lady Mother of Ch., Chgo., 1975-78; asso. engr. Western Electric Co., Rolling Meadows, Ill., 1978-82; pres. Appletree Systems, Inc., Elmwood Park, Ill., 1982—; speaker in field. Mem. Nat. Assn. Female Execs. Home: 451 N Winston St Palatine IL 60067 Office: 7912 W Grand Ave Elmwood Park IL 60635

ARCHER, LEOLA H., writer, educator; b. Vasper, Tenn., Jan. 30, 1901; d. Perry and Martha Belle (Hale) Huckaby; student Conservatory of Music, Lexington, Ky., 1924-25, U. Tenn., 1927-28; m. Jesse Oscar Archer, Dec. 17, 1919; 1 son, James Ormand. Editor, West Knoxville Press, 1954-57; columnist West Side Story, 1962-69; instr. creative writer U. Tenn., Knoxville, 1965—. Pres. East Tenn. Baptist Hosp., 1969-71; librarian West Hills Baptist Ch., 1973—. Mem. Nat. League Am. Pen Women, Tenn. Women's Press and Authors Club. Author: (poetry) Whiteship Sailing, 1936; Write This Way Folks, 1972; contbr. articles, short stories, poems to mags. Home: 825 Whitehall Rd Knoxville TN 37919

ARCHER, VIOLET BALESTRERI, composer, musician, educator; b. Montreal, Que., Can., Apr. 24, 1913; d. Cesare B. and Beatrice (Azzi) A.; Mus.B. McGill U., Can., 1936, Mus.D. (hon.), 1971; Mus.B. (Bradley Keiler Meml. scholar), Yale U., 1948, Mus.M. (Ditson fellow), 1949; diploma in organ Royal Can. Coll. Organists, 1938. Instr. music McGill U., Can., 1943-47; vis. music instr. U. Alta., summers 1948, 49; resident composer N. Tex. State U., 1950-53; vis. prof. music Cornell U., Ithaca, N.Y., summer 1952; asst. prof. music U. Okla., Norman, 1953-61; asso. prof. music U. Alta., Edmonton, Can., 1962-70, prof., 1970-78, prof. emeritus music, 1978—, chmn. div. theory and composition, 1962-78; resident composer Banff Sch. Fine Arts, summers 1978, dir. Can. Music Competitions, Inc., 1972-82; accompanist, chamber music performer; organist Westmount Park United Ch., Montreal, others. Recipient Queen's Silver Jubilee medal, 1978. Mem. Soc. Music Theory, Can. League Composers (selection com. 1972-76), Can. Music Council (dir. 1979-82), Coll. Music Soc., Alta. Composers Assn. (1st v.p. 1977-82), Am. Women Composers, Internat. Folk Music Council, Can. Fedn. Music Tchrs., Can. Folk Music Soc. exec. com. 1964-67), Can. Fedn. Music Tchrs., Can. Music Library Assn., Assn. Can. Women Composers, Soc. Artists (dir. 1972-74), Can. Assn. Univ. Schs. Music (com. theory 1957-70), Edmonton Musicians Assn., Edmonton Chamber Music Soc., Am. Assn. Univ. Composers, Royal Can. Coll. Organists Assn., Accademia Tiberina of Rome, Unione Della Legion D'oro, Latitude 53 Soc. Artists (dir. 1980—), Pi Kappa Lambda, Sigma Alpha Iota. Composer numerous instrumental works including: 3 Sonatinas for Piano, 1941, 48, 79, Eleven Short Pieces for Piano, 1964, Rondo for Piano, 1964, Theme and Variations for Piano, 1964, Sonatina for Organ, 1971, Sonata for Oboe and Piano, 1978, Four Bagatelles for Piano, 1979, Sonata for Horn and Piano, 1980, Brass Quintet, 1975, Fanfare and Passacaglia for Orch., 1964, Divertimento for Orch., 1968; numerous vocal compositions with instrumental accompaniment including anthems with organ, also a cappella for mixed voices. Home: 10805 85th Ave Edmonton AB T6E 2L2 Canada

ARCHIBALD, MARGARET CAMP, hosp. exec.; b. Buffalo, Feb. 7, 1926; s. Grover Cleveland and Marion (Gray) Camp; ed. Coll. Our Lady of Good Counsel (now Pace U.), 1943-47; m. John J. Archibald, June 7, 1947 (dec.); children—Deborah, Margaret, John. Vice pres., mfrs. rep. J.J. Archibald Co., 1975-82; spl. project coordinator Coca Cola Bottling Co. N.Y., 1982; sales Steinkamp & Britton Real Estate, 1971—; dir. vol. services St. Agnes Hosp. Mem. Westchester Assn. Vol. Adminstrs., N.Y. Assn. Dir. Vols. Health Facilities. Republican. Roman Catholic. Clubs: Oreinta Beach and Yacht, Am. Boxer, Westchester Kennel, Saw Mill River Kennel, Am. Kennel (dir.). Home: 5 Baraud Rd Scarsdale NY 10583 Office: 305 North St White Plains NY 10605

ARCHIPRETE, NANCY CAROLYN BAILEY, child care center adminstr.; b. Newton, Mass., May 5, 1937; d. Francis Lee and Grace Louise (Forster) Bailey; A.B., Tufts U., 1958; Ed.M., Harvard U., 1964; postgrad. Babson Coll., 1975, Bentley Coll., 1980; m. Joseph W. Archiprete, Nov. 27, 1974; children—Scott David Bergstrom, Andrew Olen Bergstrom. Tchr., Green Acres Day Sch., Waltham, Mass., 1958; spl. needs tutor Norwalk (Conn.) Public Schs., 1967; founder, dir. Saugatuck Nursery Sch., Westport, Conn., 1968; dir. Living and Learning Inst. for Tchrs. Young Children, Waltham, 1970—; v.p. personnel Living & Learning Centres, Inc., Waltham, 1970-73, exec. v.p., 1974—; pres. Child Care Mgmt., Inc., Needham, 1980—; cons. Child Care Services, Inc., Canton, Mass., 1979; mem. Mass. Office for Children Task Force, 1974-78; mem. adv. bd. Waltham br. Shawmut Community Bank, 1975-77. Bd. mem. YMCA, Waltham, 1977. Mem. Nat. Assn. Edn. Young Children, Nat. Assn. Child Devel. and Edn., Nat. Assn. Female Execs. Office: 764 Main St Waltham MA 02194

ARCILA, MARILYN WALSH, mfg. co. exec.; b. Bklyn., June 13, 1948; d. James Joseph and Wanda Josephine (Zelenski) Walsh; student U. Otaawa, 1977-79; m. Nonato Arcila, Aug. 12, 1967; 1 dau., Therese-Marie. Mem. staff purchasing dept. Simmonds Precision Co., N.Y.C., 1967-68; exec. sec. Bronson Imports, N.Y.C., 1968-75; reporter Ottawa Jour. and Emporium Echo, 1975-77; chief acct. Arcila and Assos., N.Y.C., 1973-75; pres., gen. mgr. Mich. Etching Inc., Grand Rapids 1979—. Dir. Confraternity of Christian Doctrine, Okla. and Pa. Roman Catholic Ch.; mayor, Borough of Driftwood, Cameron County, Pa., 1976; adviser N.Y. State Assembly, 1974. Mem. Nat. Assn. Female Execs., Nat. Fedn. Ind. Bus., Soc. Automotive Engs. (subcom. 1979—), Soc. Mfg. Engrs., Am. Soc. Women Accts. Republican. Office: 266 Front St SW Grand Rapids MI 49504

ARD, JULIE ANN, fin. exec.; b. Poplarville, Miss., May 8, 1941; d. Buford G. and Adie (Rawls) Ard; A.A., Pearl River Coll., 1961. Mgr. Supercheck Dept., Nat. Bank of Commerce, New Orleans, 1965-70; acct. Hiram Walker, New Orleans, 1970-74; controller Canteen Service of New Orleans, 1975—. Mem. Am. Soc. Women Accts. (chpt. officer 1979-80). Club: Profl. Woman's. Office: 110 W Airline Hwy Suite F Kenner LA 70062

ARDELT, BARBARA KRYSTYNA, biochemist; b. Warsaw, Poland, Jan. 2, 1938; came to U.S., 1972, 79; d. Wincenty and Teresa (Skopczynska) Broniszewski; biology student U. Warsaw, 1956-61; Ph.D., Polish Acad. Scis., Wroctaw, 1967; m. Wojciech Ardelt, Apr. 13, 1962; 2 children. Asst., Fibiger Lab., Copenhagen, 1965, Central Inst. Brain Research, Amsterdam, Holland, 1970; postdoctoral U. N.C. Med. Sch., Chapel Hill, 1972-73; biochemist Purdue U., West Lafayette, Ind., 1979—. Mem. Polish Biochem. Soc., Solidarity. Roman Catholic. Contbr. articles to profl. jours. Office: Purdue U West Lafayette IN 47907

ARECHAVALETA, CARMEN LATOUR, Realtor; b. Havana, Cuba, July 8, 1940; d. Eduardo and Carmen E. (Soto Padrera) Latour; B.A., Villanova U., Havana, 1960; m. Ramon Arechavaleta, July 6, 1963; children—Ramon E., Cristina, Lilian, Victor. Realtor asso., sales mgr. Latin Am. div. Rose Grodon Realty, Miami, Fla., 1964-73; pres. Realty Center Miami, Inc., 1973—. Mem. Nat. Assn. Realtors, Miami, Coral Gables bds. Realtors, Roman Catholic. Club: Big Five. Home: 2900 DeSoto Blvd Coral Gables FL 33134 Office: 351 Minoroa Coral Gables FL 33134

ARENDT, KATHERINE LOCKHART, economist; b. Washington, Sept. 23, 1952; d. Luther Bynum and Betty Jane (Brodnan) Lockhart; B.A., Duke U., 1974; M.A., Tufts U., 1975; postgrad. U. Va., 1976-78; m. Douglas M. Arendt, May 9, 1981. Economist developing nations U.S. Dept. Treasury, Washington, 1978-79, Export-Import Bank U.S., Washington, 1979—. U. Va. Gov.'s fellow, 1976-78. Office: 811 Vermont Ave NW Washington DC 20571

ARENSON, KAREN WATTEL, journalist; b. Long Beach, N.Y., Jan. 3, 1949; d. Harold Louis and Sara (Gordon) Wattel; S.B., M.I.T., 1970; M. in Public Policy, Harvard, 1972; m. Gregory Keith Arenson, Sept. 4, 1970. Russell Sage Found. fellow, 1972; asso. dir. Nat. Affiliation of Concerned Bus. Students, Chgo., 1972-73; corr., corr. Bus. Week Mag., N.Y.C., corr., 1973-79, editor, 1977-78; reporter N.Y. Times, 1978—; vis. com. dept. econs., M.I.T., ednl. counselor. Recipient Women in Communications Matrix award, 1982; recipient journalism award, Washington Monthly, 1981. Author: The New York Times Guide to Making the New Tax Law Work for You, 1981. Home: 125 W 76th St New York NY 10023 Office: 229 W 43d St New York NY 10036

ARENTSEN, ALICE ANN GRECUS, rubber co. exec.; b. Edgewater, N.J., June 28, 1933; d. Alexander and Margaret O. (Watson) Grecus; student U. Pitts., 1950-52; children—Lee Ann, Alan, David. Lab. technician Alcoa Aluminum Co., Edgewater, N.J., 1952-57; with Dunlop Tire & Rubber Co., Saddle Brook, N.J., 1966—, ter. mgr., 1974—. Mem. Bus. and Profl. Women's Club (N.J. legislation chmn.). Republican. Presbyterian. Office: Dunlop Tire & Rubber Co 299 Market St Saddlebrook NJ 07662

ARESTY, ESTHER BRADFORD, writer; b. Syracuse, N.Y.; d. Jacob and Bertha (Levin) Bradford; student De Paul U.; m. Jules Aresty, June 20, 1936; children—Robert Joseph, Jane A. Silverman. Radio commentator Sta. WJJD, Chgo., 1931-35; advt. mgr. Mandel Bros., Chgo., 1934-36; freelance writer, radio and TV scriptwriter, 1936—, also stories children mags., cons. history dealing with home, table, cookery and manners. Mem. assocs. bd. McCarter Theatre, Princeton, N.J. Mem. Authors League Am. Author: The Grand Venture, 1963; The Delectable Past (Cookbook Guild selection), 1964; The Best Behavior, 1970; The Exquisite Table, 1980; (as Elaine Arthur) Romance in Store, 1983; contbr. articles to Ency. Americana and nat. mags. Home: 41 Armour Rd Princeton NJ 08540

ARETSKY, DOLORES L., TV prodn. co. exec.; b. N.Y.C., Aug. 18, 1942; d. Theodore and Lillian (Marcus) Gromack; B.A. in Psychology, Hunter Coll., 1963; M.A. in Communication Arts, William Paterson Coll., 1979; m. Philip J. Aretsky, Feb. 2, 1964; children—Eric Jon, Lynne Alison. Tchr. N.Y.C. Public Sch. System, 1963-65; freelance public relations cons., 1967-73; reporter The Record, The Suburban News, 1973-76; TV news reporter U.S. Columbia Cablevision, Oakland, N.J., 1978; talent coordinator Midday WNEW-TV, N.Y.C., 1978-79; press sec. Rep. Andrew Maguire-N.J. Congressman, 1980; pres. Horizon Prodns., Ridgewood, N.J., 1980—; producer, moderator Women's Horizon, cable TV talk show, Teaneck, N.J. 1980—. Chmn, major fundraiser Valley Hosp., Ridgewood, N.J., 1980-81; vol. polit. campaigns and community orgns. Mem. Am. Women in Radio and TV, Women in Communications, N.J. Women's Press Club, LWV, NOW, Women's Polit. Caucus, Nat. Geographic Soc., Nat. Audubon Soc., Smithsonian Assos., Internat. Center Photography.

ARGIRIS, LEA ANNE, foundry exec.; b. Chgo., Oct. 13, 1935; d. Joseph John and Anna Mary (Kosiba) Gawlik; B.S., R.N., St. Theresa's Coll., 1957; M.B.A., Harvard U., 1979; m. Theodore C. Argiris, July 14, 1963; children—Lisa Alexandra, Dean Christopher. Treas., Hampden Investment Co., Chgo., 1964-70; sec. Barrett Mfg. Co., Chgo., 1966-71, v.p., 1971-79; treas. Alpha Cast Inc., Whitewater, Wis., 1971-73, v.p., treas., 1973-80, exec. v.p., 1980—, also dir.; dir. Indsl. Fin. Co., Chgo., Barrett Mfg. Co. Bd. visitors U. Wis., 1979—; bd. dirs. Sinnissippi Council Boy Scouts Am., 1981—; mem. fund raising com. Congressman Les Aspen, 1979—. Mem. Am. Foundry Soc. Greek Orthodox. Club: Annunciation Ch. Women's. Home: Route 2 McCabe Rd Whitewater WI 53190 Office: 520 N Jefferson St Whitewater WI 53190

ARGO, DOROTHY PECK (MRS. HARALSON BUTLER ARGO), chems. co. exec.; b. Cunningham, Ky.; d. Clifton Bolen and Dean (Brooks) Peck; student Union U., 1922-23, Memphis Acad. Arts, 1936-37, 44-45; m. Haralson Butler Argo, Apr. 28, 1937; 1 dau., Anne Evans (Mrs. Edward Lorraine Sanders). Dress designer, mfr., Memphis, 1935-37; inventor, pres. Argosheen Products Corp., Argo & Co., Inc., Memphis, Spartanburg, S.C., 1942—. Div. chmn. ARC, 1957; capt. United Fund, 1967; patron Music Found. Spartansburg, Little Theatre, Ballet Guild. Mem. Hotel Sales Mgmt. Assn., Am., Fla., S.C. hotel-motel assns., Internat. San. Supply Assn. Episcopalian. Clubs: Piedmont, Country of Spartanburg. Contbr. articles to profl. jours., consumer publs. Home: 705 DuPre Dr Spartanburg SC 29302 Office: 182-190 Ezell St Spartanburg SC 29304

ARGUELLES, LOUISE WATTS, banker; b. Turrell, Ark., Aug. 12, 1924; d. Arthur C. and Mary Evelyn (Greenhaw) Watts; student Iowa State Tchr.'s Coll., 1944, U. Md., 1948-49; basic cert. Am. Inst. Banking, 1977; children—Paul M., Robert A., Raymond A. Adminstrv. sec. Nat. Airlines, Miami, Fla., 1957-63; sec. 1st Nat. Bank of Maitland (Fla.), 1963-64; officer mgr. for neurosurgeons office, 1964-69; corp. sec. S.E. Nat. Bank of Orlando (Fla.), 1973—, sec. to bd. dirs., since 1975—; regional office adminstr. Central Fla. region IV, S.E. Banking Corp., Orlando, 1973—. Bd. dirs. Sheltered Community Residences, Inc., 1975-77; mem. Seminole County Republican Exec. Com., 1979-80, Orange County Rep. Exec. Com., 1981. Served with WAVES, USNR, 1944-48. Mem. Nat. Assn. Bank Women. Baptist. Office: SE Bank 222 N 2d St Jacksonville Beach FL 32250

ARIZA, SANDRA KAY, educator; b. Grand Rapids, Mich., Aug. 24, 1947; d. Phillip and Beverly Jane (Storz) Elve; A.A., Grand Rapids Jr. Coll., 1967; B.A., Mich. State U., 1973, M.A. in Spanish, 1974; postgrad. N.Y. U., 1976—; 1 dau., Tracy Jo. Grad. asst. Mich. State U., 1973-75; instr. Calvin Coll., Grand Rapids, 1975-81, asst. prof., 1981—. Mem. Am. Assn. Tchrs. Spanish and Portuguese. Home: 2641 Almont St SE Grand Rapids MI 49507 Office: Spanish Dept Calvin College Grand Rapids MI 49506

ARKIN, LUCILLE MAESE, interior plantscaping co. exec.; b. Bklyn., Feb. 18, 1951; d. Albert Joseph, Sr., and Grace Elizabeth (Addeo) Maese; student St. John's U., 1976-78; m. Stephen Robert Arkin, May 17, 1980. Sec., Hudson Pulp & Paper, N.Y.C., 1973-76; benefits coordinator Scali, McCabe, Sloves, N.Y.C., 1976-78; v.p., controller New Growth Plantscape, Ltd., N.Y.C., 1978—; dir. public relations Found. for Interior Plantscape Edn. and Research. Mem. Hort. Soc. N.Y., Adminstrv. Mgmt. Soc., Nat. Assn. Female Execs. Home: 785 West End Apt 2E New York NY 10025 Office: 129 W 28th St New York NY 10001

ARKUS, HELENA B., pianist, piano tchr.; b. N.Y.C.; d. Aaron and Esther (Munstock) Bankoff; student N.Y.U., 1925-27, Boston U., 1936; piano student Alberto Jonas, Arthur Friedheim, Edwin Hughes; composition student Percy Goetschius; m. James H. Arkus, Aug. 9, 1927 (dec. 1949); children—Albert, Deanne Arkus Klein, Edmund, Muriel Arkus Celkupa. Pvt. tchr. piano, 1925—; writer program notes N.Y. Orchestral Soc., Jamaica Symphony Orch., 1965—; lectr. Piano Tchrs. Congress, 1976; chmn. N.Y. State Nat. Music Week, 1976, 77, 78; N.Y. state chmn. Mason and Hamlin Competition, 1976-77, 78-80, Stillman Kelley Competition, 1977; internat. Bach Soc. rep. to Internat. Music Council, Prague and Bratislava, 1977; U.S. rep. European Piano Tchrs. Assn., 1978—. Recipient Presdl. citation, 1976. Mem. Nat. (dir. N.Y. div., pres. dist. X and II, chmn. Nat. Music Week 1973-77, N.Y. State Jr. Festival chmn. 1973-76, chmn. biennial young artists competition N.Y. State 1978), N.Y. (v.p. 1976-80, 1st v.p. N.Y. State 1980, acting pres. 1981—, chmn. Young Artists competition) fedns. music clubs, Music Tchrs. Nat. Assn. (N.Y. State and nat. cert. diplomas), Am. Coll. Musicians (faculty and judge mem.), Piano Tchrs. Congress N.Y. (past program chmn., rec. sec., hon. v.p., judge), Leschetizky Assn. (judge, ofcl. rep.), Internat. Bach Soc. (ofcl. rep.), Asso. Music Tchrs. League (rec. sec. 1968), Bklyn. Music Tchrs. Guild (judge, certification diploma), N.Y. Orchestral Soc. (exec. dir., hon. plaque 1965), Piano Tchrs. Congress (hon. v.p., bronze plaque 1973). Contbr. to Musicianship through Improvisation, 1966. Home: 141-17 72d Crescent Kew Gardens Hills NY 11367

ARLING, DONNA DICKSON, social worker; b. Jersey Shore, Pa., July 8, 1945; d. Eugene Robert and Helen Louise (Bardo) Dickson; B.S., Pa. State U., 1967; M.S.W., Smith Coll., 1969; m. Bryan Jeremy Arling, Aug. 28, 1969; children—Elissa Dickson, Jeremy Swenson. Psychiat. social worker North County Mental Health Center, Palo Alto, Calif., 1969-71, VA Hosp., Washington, 1971-77; pvt. practice psychiat. social worker, Washington, 1978—; field instr. social work Cath. U., 1974-76, Howard U., 1976-77. Cert. in group therapy Center for Group Studies, Washington; lic. clin. social worker, Md. Mem. Nat. Registry Health Care Providers in Clin. Social Work, Nat. Assn. Social Workers, Greater Washington Soc. Clin. Social Work, Acad. Cert. Social Workers, Smith Coll. Sch. Social Work Alumnae Assn. (mem. Washington steering com. 1974—, So. regional rep. alumnae exec. com. 1977-81, class sec. 1976-81). Democrat. Club: Columbia Country (Chevy Chase, Md.). Home: 3803 Taylor St Chevy Chase MD 20015 Office: 1015 33d St NW Washington DC 20007

ARMAGOST, ELSA GAFVERT, computer co. communication cons.; b. Duluth, Minn., Jan. 26, 1917; d. Axel Justus and Martina Emelia (Magnuson) Gafvert; grad. with honors Duluth Jr. Coll., 1936; B.J., U. Minn., 1938; postgrad. in Public Relations and Bus., 1977-78; m. Byron William Armagost, Dec. 8, 1945; children—David Byron, Laura Martina. Freelance editor, Duluth, 1939-42; procedure editor and analyst U.S. Steel, Duluth, 1942-45; fashion advt. staff Dayton Co., Mpls., 1945-48; systems applications and documentation mgr. Control Data Corp., Mpls., 1969-74, promotion specialist, mktg. editor, 1974-76, corp. staff coordinator info. on edn., 1976-78, instr. communications, publ. specialist, 1978-79, communication cons., 1979—. Bd. dirs. LWV; v.p. Sewickley Valley Hosp. Aux., Sewickley Valley Mental Health Council; dir. publicity Sacred Arts Expo, World Affairs Council radio program, Pitts., 1962-68. Mem. AAUW (1st v.p. Venezuela), Women in Communications (job mart dir.), Nat. Fedn. Press Women, Assn. Devel. Computer-Based Instr. Systems, Internat. Platform Assn., Friends of Mpls. Inst. of Arts, U.S. Senatorial Bus. Adv. Bd., Bus. Advs. Inc. (Mpls.), Phi Beta Music Soc. Home: 9500 Collegeview Rd Bloomington MN 55437 Office: PO Box 0 Minneapolis MN 55440

ARMBRECHT, CAROL ANN, nurse; b. Youngstown, Ohio, Mar. 4, 1950; d. Albert A. and Angeline M. (Ciarniello) Salata; B.S. in Nursing, Case Western Res. U., 1972; M.S., Tex. Woman's U., 1979; m. Karl James Armbrecht, May 26, 1972; children—Abby, Lyn. Staff nurse Univ. Hosps. Cleve., 1972-73, 74-75, St. Elizabeth Hosp. Med. Center, Youngstown, 1973-74, clin. coordinator, 1976-79; instr. nursing Youngstown State U., 1975-76, Pa. State U., Sharon and Monaca, Pa., 1980—; grad. asst. Kent (Ohio) State U., 1979-81, asst. prof. nursing, 1981—; psychology intern Towne Sq. Psychol. Services, Canfield, Ohio, 1981—. Recipient Cushing-Robb award Case Western Res. U., 1973; research grantee Case Western Res. U. Nursing Alumni Assn., 1979. Mem. Am. Nurses Assn., Nurses Assn. Am. Coll. Ob-Gyn, Ohio Nurses Assn., Tex. Woman's U. Alumni Assn., Phi Delta Kappa, Sigma Theta Tau. Roman Catholic. Author articles in field. Home: 58 Overhill Rd Youngstown OH 44512 Office: Sch Nursing Kent State U Summit St Kent OH 44242

ARMENTO, MARIANNE, state ofcl.; b. Hampton, Iowa, Mar. 21, 1948; d. Ervin John and Margaret Wilma Carolina (Bessman) Meyer; B.A., Kalamazoo Coll., 1970; m. Paul A. Armento, III, Aug. 16, 1975. Personnel asst. Central Nat. Bank, Chgo., 1970-71, personnel adminstr., 1971-74, human resources officer, 1974-75; personnel analyst Ill. Dept. Personnel, Springfield, 1975-76, lead personnel analyst, 1976-78, supr. reconsiderations and appeals, div. tech. services, 1978—. Asso. mem. and choir mem. 1st Congregational Ch., Springfield, 1977—. Mem. Nat. Assn. Female Execs. Mem. United Ch. Christ. Office: Ill Dept Central Mgmt Services 504 Stratton Bldg Springfield IL 62706

ARMIJO, MARGARET SUZZANE MAESTAS, ednl. adminstr.; b. Las Vegas, N.Mex., June 3, 1951; d. Frank M. and Agneda S. Maestas; cert. in library mgmt. U. Ariz., 1975; B.A. in L.S., N.Mex. Highlands U., 1976; M.L.S. equivalent, State N.Mex., 1976; m. John Paul Armijo, Nov. 27, 1982. Part time library work Donnelly Library, N.Mex. Highlands U., Las Vegas, 1973-76; library intern, Nat. Agrl. Library, Tech. Info. Systems, Library of Congress, Washington, 1975; learning resource ctr. dir. Luna Vocat. Tech. Inst., Las Vegas, 1977—; mem. coms. N.Mex. Learning Resource Center Council, pres., 1982-83. Mem. N.Mex. Library Assn., Consortium N.Mex. Acad. Libraries, SW Library Assn., Seminar on Aquisitions of Latin Am. Library Materials, ALA. Republican. Roman Catholic. Home: 2311 West Dr Las Vegas NM 87701 Office: PO Box 300 Las Vegas NM 87701

ARMISTEAD, CECYL MARTIN, utility co. exec.; b. Red Level, Ala., Feb. 24, 1927; d. Frank Gordon and Dell (Beasley) Martin; student Browning Bus. Sch., Albuquerque, 1954, U. N.Mex., 1954-77; m. Sydney E. Armistead, Jr., Jan. 19, 1946; 1 son, Sydney E. With Community Public Service Co., Silver City, N.Mex., 1950-54; with Gas Co. of N.Mex., Albuquerque, 1954—, mgr. personnel and safety, 1972—; bd. dirs. So. Union Employees Credit Union. Bd. dirs. Presbyterian Hosp. Found., 1980—; v.p., sec. Pilot Club of Albuquerque, 1973-74, pres., 1975; chmn. Pvt. Industry Council, 1981. Recipient Presdl. citation for work Pvt. Industry Council, 1982. Cert. profl. sec., 1971. Mem. Nat. Sec. Assn., Am. Soc. Personnel Adminstrs., N.Mex. Personnel Assn., Greater Albuquerque C. of C. Baptist.

ARMISTEAD, KATHERINE KELLY (MRS. THOMAS B. ARMISTEAD III), interior designer, travel cons., civic worker; b. Pitts., Apr. 14, 1926; d. Joseph Anthony and Katherine Arnold (Manning) Kelly; grad. Finch Jr. Coll., 1946; m. Thomas Boyd Armistead, III, Nov. 29, 1952; children—Katherine Kelly (Mrs. Donald P. Jacobs), Thomas Boyd IV. Editor news, sec. Sta. WOR, N.Y.C., 1946-51; with Dumont TV, 1951-52; editor Social Service Rev., 1956-57; interior designer, Los Angeles, 1963—; travel cons. Gilner Internat. Travels, Beverly Hills, Calif., 1980—; pres. Jrs. Social Service, Los Angeles, 1962-64; nat. chpt. chmn. Associated Alumnae of Sacred Heart, 1960-66; mem. Luminaires-Estelle Doheny Eye Found.; pres. La Floristas, 1967-68, Los Angeles Orphanage Guild, 1969-70; coordinator Jr. Mannequin Assisteens, Assistance League So. Calif., 1971-72; mem. patroness com. Hollywood Bowl; pres. docent council Los Angeles County Mus. Art, 1976-77 pres. decorative arts council, 1977-80, chmn. Am. antiques conf., 1979-81, mem. costume council, mem. past pres.' council, 1981—; bd. dirs. Los Angeles Orphanage Guild, 1970-82; trustee Neurol. Learning Center, Pasadena, Calif., 1978-80. Republican. Roman Catholic. Clubs: Beach (Santa Monica, Calif.); Bel Air Garden (treas. 1980—). Home: Los Angeles CA

ARMOR, GERALDINE K. (JERRY), property mgmt. exec.; b. Watertown, S.D., Mar. 26, 1945; d. Horace and Hazel Deloris (Sprouse) Tarbox; student Nettleton Bus. Coll., 1963. Gen. mgr. Western Mall Properties, Sioux Falls, S.D., 1969-78; gen. mgr. Western Mall div. Balcor Propoerty Mgmt. Inc., Sioux Falls, 1979-80; pres. Conception, Inc., Sioux Falls, 1979—. Pres., S.D. Animal Welfare League, 1978. Recipient Bus. Woman of Yr. award, 1976. Mem. Internat. Council Shopping Centers, Sioux Falls. C. of C., United Comml. Travelers Am. Office: PO Box 453 Sioux Falls SD 57101

ARMS, KAREN GARDNER, univ. adminstr.; b. Anita, Iowa, Oct. 5, 1934; d. Edwin L. and Dorothy D. (Phelps) Gardner; B.S., Northwest Mo. State U., 1957; M.S., U. Akron, 1971; Ph.D., Kent State U., 1974; m. Walter Eugene Arms, June 3, 1956; children—Deborah L., Denise L. Tchr. secondary public schs. in Iowa, 1957-66, Ohio, 1969; lectr. U. Akron (Ohio), 1970-72; grad. asst., instr. Sch. Home Econs., Kent (Ohio) State U., 1972-74, asst. prof., 1974-76, asst. dean Coll. Fine Arts, 1976-80, asso. prof., 1980—, dir. Sch. Home Econs., 1980—; Trustee First United Methodist Ch., Akron, 1979—. Mem. Am. Home Econs. Assn., Nat. Council Family Relations, Ohio Council Family Relations (pres. 1977-78), Ohio Home Econs. Assn., Am. Vocat. Assn., Ohio Vocat. Assn., Greater Akron Area Home Econs. Assn., Nat. Assn. Women Deans, Adminstrs. and Counselors, Ohio Assn. Women Deans, Adminstrs. and Counselors (pres.-elect 1982-83), Pi Omega Pi, Kappa Delta Pi, Pi Lambda Theta, Omicron Delta Kappa, Kappa Omicron Phi. Contbr. articles on home econs. to profl. publs. Office: 100 Nixson Hall Kent State Univ Kent OH 44242

ARMSTEAD, MARION, automotive co. ofcl.; A.S. in Commerce, Henry Ford Community Coll., 1977; grad. U. Mich., 1981; m. July 10, 1952 (div.); 1 dau., Karen A. Clk. typist Mich. dist. U.S. Army Ordnance, Detroit, 1955-56, U.S. Army Tank-Automotive Center, Detroit, 1956-62; control clk. Def. Automotive Supply Center, Detroit, 1962-63; with Ford Motor Co., Dearborn, 1963—, personnel rep. A, 1975-77, indsl. relations analyst, 1977—. Recipient Superior Performance Award cert. Def. Supply Agy., 1963, Suggestion award Ford Motor Co., 1967. Mem. Nat. Assn. Female Execs., Am. Soc. Personnel Adminstrn., Detroit Area Women's Network. Clubs: Greyfriars/Waring Block. Office: Ford Motor Co Dearborn Tool and Die Plant Indsl Relations Office 3001 Miller Rd Dearborn MI 48121

ARMSTRONG, ALEXANDRA, fin. planner; b. Washington, Sept. 26, 1939; d. William C. and Rhoda E. Armstrong; B.A., Newton Coll. of Sacred Heart, 1960. With Ferris & Co., Inc., Washington, 1961-77; rep. N.Y. Stock Exchange, Washington, 1967—; sr. v.p. Julia N. Walsh & Sons, 1977—; lectr. Immaculata Coll., 1977-78, Cath. U., 1978-79, Am. U., 1979-80; mem. Washington Bd. Trade; allied mem. N.Y. Stock Exchange; lic. ins. agt., 1977—; adv. bd. Women's Nat. Bank, Washington. Cert. fin. planner. Mem. Internat. Assn. Fin. Planners (treas., nat. dir. 1981-82, mem. exec. com.), Nat. Assn. Women Bus. Owners (dir., pres. chpt. 1980—), Inst. Cert. Fin. Planners (dir. 1980), Fin. Women's Assn. N.Y., Bus. and Profl. Women's Club (Businesswoman of Year 1978), Women's Forum of Washington (a founder), Sacred Heart Alumnae (past dir.), Am. Newspaper Women's Club, Nat. Speakers Assn. Club: Jr. League (Washington). Columnist for mags. and newspaper; nat. speaker. Home: 2555 Pennsylvania Ave NW #917 Washington DC 20037 Office: 910 17th St NW Suite 717 Washington DC 20006

ARMSTRONG, ALICE CATT, author, publisher; b. Ft. Scott, Kans., Feb. 7; d. Charles H. and Florence (Pakenham) Catt; student jr. coll., also specialized courses; Litt.D., St. Andrews U., Eng., 1969, St. Paul's Coll. and Sem., Italy, 1970; 6 hon. doctorates; 1 son, Gary Olyn. Actress

Little Theatre groups Pasadena Playhouse, 1942-48; tchr. dramatic arts, Hollywood, Calif., 1946-48; editor, pub. Hist. Research Publ., Los Angeles, 1949—; frequent appearances on radio, TV stas., So. Calif.; lectr. State dir., public relations Calif. Epilepsy Soc., 1956-57; co-chmn. Calif. com. Freedoms Found. Valley Forge, 1956; founder, organizing dir., v.p. Execs. Dinner Club of Beverly Hills and Bel Air, Calif., 1958; mem. Los Angeles County Mus., Blue Ribbon Com. Los Angeles Music Center, Internat. Student Center, Inc., U. Calif.; co-chmn. celebrities Norma Talmadge Meml., 1962; internat. chmn. Sibelius Centennial Celebration U.S., 1965; chmn. Hollywood Bowl Concert, 1965; mem. Opera Guild So. Calif. Decorated dame Grand Cross Royal and Sovereign Order St. Laurent, dame Grand Cross Order Piast by Count Leopold, dame of Grace Hosp. and Order St. John of Jerusalem; recipient Woman of Achievement award Calif. Women Golden West, 1951; Nat. Travel Guide award Nat. Writers Club, Denver, 1958; award Hollywood Mus. Assn., 1962; Am. Wisdom award of Honor, 1965; named Outstanding Citizen Calif., Ariz., Hawaii Sr. Citizens mag., 1966; Journalism and Lit. award Dictionary Internat. Biography, 1967; Americanism Edn. League award, 1966; numerous citations U.S. and Eng., other countries. Mem. Nat. Soc. Magna Charta Dames (chaplain), Los Angeles World Affairs Council, Nat. Writers Club, Historic Los Angeles Assn., Save-the-Redwoods League, Calif. C. of C., Internat. Platform Assn. (dir.), Art Patrons Assn., Inc., Roger Wagoner's So. Calif. Choral Assn., Bel-Air (Calif.) Fedn. Women's Club (pres. 1979-80), Soc. Descs. Knights of Garter, Town Hall Calif., Profl. Writers League, Soc. Children's Book Writers. Clubs: Celebrity Books and Authors, Order Eastern Star. Author: California Biographical and Historical Series, 1950—; Dining and Lodging on the North American Continent, 1958; And They Called It Society, 1961-62; editor 200th Anniversary of California Issue, 1968; also radio skits, travel guides, children's stories, poems. Address: Cordell Views 1331 Cordell Pl Los Angeles CA 90069

ARMSTRONG, ALMETTA, educator; b. Candor, N.C., Aug. 18, 1938; d. Andrew Chesley and Rushia Bell (Capel) Armstrong; A.B., Shaw U., 1938; M.S., A & T State U., 1959. Tchr. public schs. N.C., 1958—, Highland Sch., Mt. Gilead, 1981—. Del. Democratic Nat. Conv., N.Y.C., 1980; mem. N.C. Human Relations Council, Raleigh, 1978-81. N.C. Inmate Labor Commn., Raleigh, 1977-81; mem. alcohol-drug abuse adv. bd. Sandhill Mental Health Bd. Recipient award N.C. Council Status of Women, 1981, N.Y. State Black Leadership Caucus award, 1981, Outstanding Achievement award Shaw U., 1979, Outstanding Woman award NAACP, 1981. Mem. N.C. Assn. Educators, NEA, Internat. Platform Assn. Baptist. Home: Route 2 Box 128 Candor NC 27229 Office: Highland Sch Mount Gilead NC 27603

ARMSTRONG, ANNE LEGENDRE (MRS. TOBIN ARMSTRONG), corp. dir., educator; b. New Orleans, Dec. 27, 1927; d. Armant and Olive (Martindale) Legendre; grad. Vassar Coll., 1949; m. Tobin Armstrong, Apr. 12, 1950; children—John Barclay, Katharine A., Sarita S., Tobin and James L. (twins). Trustee Kenedy County (Tex.) Sch. Bd., 1968-74; mem. Rep. Nat. Com. from Tex., 1968-73, co-chmn., 1971-73; del. Rep. Nat. Conv., 1964, 68, 72; counsellor to Pres. U.S., 1973-74; U.S. ambassador to Gt. Britain and No. Ireland, 1976-77; dir. Gen. Motors Corp., Halliburton Co., Gen. Foods Corp., First City Bancorp. Tex. Inc., Boise Cascade Corp.; chmn. adv. bd., vice-chmn. exec. bd. Center for Strategic and Internat. Studies, Georgetown U., 1977-81 professorial lectr. in diplomacy, 1977—. Bd. dirs. Atlantic Council, 1977—; trustee So. Meth. U., 1977—; chmn. Pres.'s Fgn. Intelligence Adv. Bd., 1981—. Guggenheim Found., 1980—; mem. vis. com. Kennedy Sch. Govt., Harvard U., 1978—; mem. pres.'s council Tulane U., 1977-80; bd. regents Smithsonian Instn., 1978—; bd. overseers Hoover Instn., 1978—; mem. Congl. Awards Bd., 1980—; co-chmn. Reagan-Bush Campaign, 1980. Recipient Rep. Woman of Yr. award, 1979, Texan of Yr. award, 1981. Mem. English-Speaking Union (chmn. 1978-80), Council Fgn. Relations, Phi Beta Kappa. Club: Econ. N.Y. (trustee). Home: Armstrong Ranch Armstrong TX 78338 Office: Center For Strategic and Internat Studies Georgetown U 37th and O St NW Washington DC 20057 *

ARMSTRONG, BARBARA NOTTINGHAM, educator; b. Durbin, W.Va., May 23, 1936; d. Bruce Kerr and Mary Evelyn (Wilmoth) Nottingham; B.S. cum laude, W.Va. U., 1958, M.S., 1961; Ph.D., Ohio State U., 1969; m. John C. Armstrong, June 1, 1959; children—Deborah Clark, John Scott. 4-H Club agt. W.Va. U., 1958-61; nutrition cons. Nutrition Assn. Greater Cleve., 1961-62; instr. home. mgmt., dir. home mgmt. house W.Va. U., 1962-66; asst. prof. family and child devel. Sch. Home Econs., Ohio State U., 1968-72; mem. research faculty Ohio Agrl. Research and Devel. Center, 1968-72; asso. prof., dir. research and devel., prof. home econs. and family ecology U. Akron, 1972—, head dept., 1972-78; mem. Gov. Ohio Task Force on Aging, 1972-74, Nat. Task Force Child Abuse and Neglect, 1976—, Nat. Task Force Aging, 1976—; adv. bd. Program Older Adults, Akron, 1974—; cons., speaker in field. Recipient Outstanding Teaching award Sch. Home Econs., Ohio State U., 1971, Alumni award for distinguished teaching, 1972; Outstanding 4-H Alumna award W.Va., 1974. Mem. Nat., Ohio (pres. 1971-72; Presdl. award 1975) councils family relations, Am., Ohio home econs. assns., Gerontol. Soc., Nat. Extension 4-H Club Agts. Assn., W.Va. Alumnae Assn. (past v.p.), Mortar Bd., Chimes (hon.), Omicron Nu, Phi Upsilon Omicron, Phi Delta Kappa, Kappa Delta; asso. mem. Found. Thanatology, Assn. Study Afro-Am. Life and History, Kappa Omicron Phi. Methodist. Club: Order Eastern Star. Contbr. articles to profl. jours. Home: 437 Spring Grove Dr Tallmadge OH 44278 Office: 215 Schrank Hall Univ Akron Akron OH 44325

ARMSTRONG, BEVERLY ALVA, speech and lang. pathologist; b. N.Y.C., Sept. 16, 1951; d. John Henry and Elizabeth (Brown) A.; A.B., Brown U., 1973; M.S., Columbia U. Tchrs. Coll., 1976; m. Darryl Christian, July 12, 1980. Lang., speech and hearing clinician Presch. Center for Communication Devel., Bristol (Conn.) Public Schs., 1976-77; speech and lang. pathologist White Plains (N.Y.) Public Schs., 1977-81 mem. dist. staff devel. team, 1980-81; speech and lang. pathologist Savannah-Chatham County Public Schs., 1981—. Mem. White Plains Com. on Handicapped, 1978—; minority rep. Brown U. Nat. Alumni Schs. Program, 1977-79. Rehab. Services Adminstrn. trainee, 1974-75; lic. speech pathologist, Conn. Mem. Am. Speech and Hearing Assn. (cert.), Conn. Speech and Hearing Assn. Presbyterian. Home: 6 John Dory Ct Savannah GA 31410 Office: 208 Bull St Savannah GA 31401

ARMSTRONG, CHRISTINE, energy co. exec.; b. Los Angeles, June 23, 1952; d. Robert Pirr and Helen (Christian) A.; B.S., U. Ariz., 1974; M.A., Ohio State U., 1976; J.D., U. Puget Sound, 1982. With labor relations dept. Ford Motor Co., Lima, Ohio, 1976-78; with profl. relations dept. Rockwell Internat., Los Angeles, 1978-79; human resource adminstr. N.W. Energy Services, Co., Kirkland, Wash., 1980—. Mem. NOW, Women's Law Caucus, Wash. Women United. Office: PO Box 1090 Kirkland WA 98033

ARMSTRONG, CLARA JULIA EVERSHED, ret. coll. adminstr.; b. Murray, Utah, Aug. 25, 1911; d. Elmer B. and Lenora K. (Tripp) Evershed; student Henager Bus. Coll., 1936-37; m. Rollin S. Armstrong, Sept. 29, 1956; foster children—Maxwell Rollin, Ruth Elizabeth, Robert Neil, Philip Samuel. Office mgr., credit mgr. D.N. & E. Walter & Co., Salt Lake City, 1937-48; with Latter Day Saints Bus. Coll., Salt Lake City, 1948-76, sec., 1948-52, fgn. student adviser, 1952-55, vet. coordinator, 1952-55, rehab. counselor, 1952-55, registrar, 1955-62, sec.-treas., after 1962, then entrance counselor and employment dir., to 1976. Mem. Ch. of Jesus Christ of Latter-day Saints (pres. Ward Mut. Improvement Assn. 1941-45). Home: 35 F St Salt Lake City UT 84103

ARMSTRONG, DARLENE CAROLYN, court reporter; b. Wichita, Kans., Dec. 2, 1938; d. Edward and Grace G. Whalen; diploma McMahon Ct. Reporting Sch., 1978; student U. Colo., 1956, Quincy (Ill.) Coll., 1963; m. Carl Armstrong, Sept. 5, 1951 (div.); children—Todd Norman, Brian (dec.). Civilian aerospace sec., 1973-77; VA med. sec., 1977-78; ofcl. and freelance ct. reporter, 1978—; owner Action Ct. Reporting, Inc., Houston and Galveston, Tex., 1978—. Active local mental health assns.; pianist, 1963—. Recipient Presdl. citation; cert. ct. reporter. Mem. Nat. Shorthand Reporters Assn., Tex. Shorthand Reporters Assn. Club: Toastmistress Internat. (Outstanding Woman award). Address: 1021 US National Bank Galveston TX 77027

ARMSTRONG, DIANNE OWENS, educator; b. Atlanta, Jan. 6, 1935; d. James Hamilton and Kathleen Pollard (Keefe) Jones; student U. Calif., Berkeley, 1952-53, (Coll. scholar) Vassar Coll., 1955-56; B.A., U. Ill., 1957; M.A., St. John's U., 1976; m. David Armstrong, July 6, 1958 (div.); children—Sydney, David, Emily, Malcolm. Corr., Elizabeth Arden, N.Y.C., 1957; tchr. English, Martin Luther High Sch., Maspeth, N.Y., 1972-76, Naperville (Ill.) North High Sch., 1978—; instr. Coll. DuPage, 1978—. Bd. dirs. Child Study Assn. Am., 1958-60. Mem. Nat. Council Tchrs. English, Sierra Club. Democrat. Episcopalian. Home: 415 Dawes Ave Wheaton IL 60187 Office: Naperville North High Sch Naperville IL 60556

ARMSTRONG, GEORGETTA CLARKSTON, educator; b. Chgo., Dec. 10, 1919; d. Lucas Chauncy and Lyda Mae (Jones) Clarkston; B.A., Roosevelt U., 1956, M.A., 1960; m. Jewel Samuel Armstrong, Aug. 30, 1970. Requisition clk.-typist U.S. Air Force, Chgo., 1943-50; clk., pub. relations office Roosevelt U., Chgo., 1950-57; sec. Woodlawn A.M.E. Ch., Chgo., 1950-57; classroom tchr. Chgo. Bd. Edn., 1957-70, spl. reading tchr., 1970-72, instructional team leader, 1972-75, counselor Woodson North Elem. Sch. and Oakenwald South Elem. Sch., 1975—. Tchr. Sunday sch. Woodlawn A.M.E. Ch., 1938-68, dir. bd. Christian edn., 1957-69. Mem. Am. Personnel and Guidance Assn., Ill. Guidance and Personnel Assn., Assn. for Supervision and Curriculum Devel., Internat. Reading Assn., AAUW, Nat. Assn. U. Women (pres. 1968-72, treas. 1972-76, sec. N. Central sectional conf. 1971-76), Roosevelt U. Alumni Assn. (life), Phi Delta Kappa. Office: Woodson North Elem Sch also Oakenwald South Elem Sch Chicago IL

ARMSTRONG, HELEN ELIZABETH, violinist; b. Rockford, Ill., Mar. 16, 1943; d. Robert Bruce and Hannah Spencer Armstrong; student Am. Conservatory of Music, Chgo., 1955-60; Mus.B. (scholar), Juilliard Sch. Music, 1965, M.S., 1966; children—Deborah, David. Debut as concert violinist, Rockford, 1949; recitalist and orchestral soloist; soloist with orchs., including Boston Orch., Indpls. Orch.; soloist Martha Graham Dance Co.; judge various musical competitions; rec. artist; radio and TV appearances; affiliate artist-tchr. SUNY, Purchase; also pvt. tchr. Recipient award Soc. Am. Musicians, 1957; named Outstanding Artist of Ill., Rockford Symphony Orch., 1959; prize winner Tibor Varga inter-violin competition Nat. Fedn. Music Clubs, 1976; Mu Phi Epsilon Meml. Found. grantee, 1978. Mem. Am. Women Composers, Mu Phi Epsilon (v.p. N.Y.C. alumni chpt. 1977).

ARMSTRONG, JANE BOTSFORD, sculptor; b. Buffalo; d. Samuel Booth and Edith (Pursel) Botsford; student Middlebury Coll., 1939-40, Pratt Inst., 1940-41, Art Students League, 1962-64; m. Robert Thexton Armstrong, July 3, 1960. One-man shows: Frank Rehn Gallery, N.Y.C. 1971, 73, 75, 77, Columbus (Ohio) Gallery Fine Arts, 1972, Columbia (S.C.) Mus. Art, 1975, New Britain (Conn.) Mus. Am. Art, 1972, Johnson Gallery, Middlebury (Vt.) Coll., 1973, Mary Duke Biddle Gallery for Blind, N.C. Mus. Art, 1974, J.B. Speed Art Mus., Louisville, 1975, Buffalo State U., 1975, Marjorie Parr Gallery, London, 1976, Ark. Art Center, Little Rock, 1977, Columbus (Ga.) Mus. Arts and Crafts, 1977, Cummer Art Gallery, Jacksonville, Fla., 1977, spl. children's exhbn. Dallas Fine Arts Mus., 1978, Wichita Art Mus., 1978, 82, Wadsworth Atheneum, Hartford, Conn., 1979, Southeastern Center for Contemporary Art, 1980, Chautaqua Nat. Exhbn. Am. Art, 1980, Rollins Coll., Winter Park, Fla., 1981, others; exhibited in USIA group exhbn., Europe, 1975-76, Critics Choice, The Sculpture Center, N.Y.C., 1972, 81; group shows: Phila. Mus., 1972, Nat. Collection Fine Arts, 1971-72, Artists of Am., Colo. Heritage Center, Denver, 1981-82 represented in numerous acad., indsl., pub. and pvt. collections; now represented by Sid Deutsch Gallery, N.Y.C. Recipient Pauline Law Prize Allied Artists Am., 1969, 70, Gold medal, 1977; Ralph Fabri medal, 1978; Cert. of Merit, NAD, 1973; Council Am. Artists' Socs. prize Nat. Sculpture Soc., 1973, Anonymous Mem.'s award, 1975, 76, Bronze medal, 1976; Dr. Maurice B. Hexter prize, 1980; Charles N. Whinston Meml. prize Nat. Assn. Women Artists, 1973, C.D. Murphy Meml. prize, 1979, Elizabeth S. Blake prize, 1980; Chaim Gross Found. award, 1980; Porton award, 1981. Mem. Nat. Arts Club (gold medal for sculpture 1968, 69, 71, best in show 1973, Edith W. Macguire award 1975, plaque of honor 1977), Audubon Artists (medal of honor 1972), Knickerbocker Artists (Alice Standish Buell Meml. prize 1972, Elliot Liskin award 1979), Sculptors Guild, Allied Artists Am., Nat. Sculpture Soc. Home: 2909 S Ocean Blvd Highland Beach FL 33431 (summer) Spring Park Studio PO Box 38 Saluda NC 28773

ARMSTRONG, MARGARET GREEN, health care exec.; b. Nathalie, Va., Oct. 1, 1923; d. John Collins and Frances (Oliver) Green; B.S., Coll. William and Mary, 1944; M.S.W., Va. Commonwealth U., 1946; postgrad. Columbia U., 1950, U. Ga., 1969. Dir., Child Guidance Clinic, Clearwater, Fla., 1960-62; psychotherapist Karen Horney Psychoanalytic Inst., N.Y.C., 1964-66; HRS regional dir. social services, St. Petersburg, Fla., 1973-75, dist. program supr., Clearwater, Fla., 1975—; pvt. practice psychotherapy, Clearwater, 1960—. Mem. Am. Assn. Mental Deficiency, Fla. Soc. Clin. Social Workers, Am. Group Psychotherapy Assn., Acad. Cert. Social Workers, Nat. Assn. Social Workers, AAUW, Pilot Internat., English Speaking Union. Club: Bus. and Profl. Women's. Home: 400 Island Way Clearwater FL 33515 Office: 2255 E Bay Dr Clearwater FL 33516

ARMSTRONG, MINNIE OLIVER, supermarket chain exec.; b. Boise, Idaho, Sept. 3, 1927; d. Joseph and Minnie Belle (Houde) Oliver; grad. high sch.; m. Charles L. Armstrong, July 30, 1955. Stenographer, C.C. Anderson Co., Boise, 1945; with Ada County (Idaho) Assistance Dept., 1945-48; with Albertson's Inc., Boise, 1948—, sec., 1969—; asst. sec. Skaggs-Albertson's Properties Inc., 1971-75, sec., 1975—; asst. sec. Tex. Albertson's, Inc., 1970-75, sec., 1975—; asst. sec. AFC, Inc., 1974—; sec., dir. Albertson's Realty, Inc., 1960—, Monte Mart, Inc., 1975—. Bd. dirs., sec. J.A. and Kathryn Albertson Found.; trustee Joseph Buell Scott Trust. Mem. Am. Soc. Corporate Secs. Mem. Seventh-day Adventist Ch. Home: 2756 S Cloverdale Rd Boise ID 83709 Office: 250 Parkcenter Blvd Boise ID 83726 *

ARMSTRONG, SHARON ANNE JASMINE, govt. ofcl.; b. Vallejo, Calif., Dec. 1, 1943; d. Ignacio Andaya and Mavis Harriet (Luke) Jasmine; student Seattle U., 1962-65, San Francisco State U., 1969-76, U. San Francisco, 1978—: m. Thomas Doric Armstrong, May 9, 1964; Buyer, U.S. Navy Exchange Office, Kenitra, Morocco, 1965-66, supply mgmt. asst. comptrollers office, 1966-68; staff technician dining service office Pacific Telephone Co., San Francisco, 1969-69; purchasing agent Office Services sect. HEW, San Francisco, 1969-72, asst. office services mgr., 1972-75, div. dir. adminstrv. services, 1975-80; chief. resources mgmt. div. IRS, Seattle, 1980—; instr. CPR, USPHS Region IX, San Francisco, 1980; mem. facilities com. N.W. Fed. Credit Union, 1981—. Served with USCGR, 1972—. Lic. real estate salesman, Calif. Mem. Fed. Mgrs. Assn., Nat. Assn. Female Execs., Nat. Notary Assn., Assn. Fed. Women Execs., Profl. Mgrs. Assn., Reserve Officers Assn. (mem. exec. bd. 1980—), Toastmistresses. Democrat. Roman Catholic. Home: 25316 128th Ave SE Kent WA 98031 Office: 915 2d Ave Seattle WA 98174

ARMSTRONG, VICKIE LYNN, state legislator, educator; b. Collbran, Colo., Sept. 14, 1951; A.A., Mesa Coll., 1971; B.S., U. Colo., 1974. Tchr. Sch. Dist. 51, Grand Junction, Colo.; now mem. Colo. Ho. of Reps. Past chmn. Mesa County Young Republicans, Young Republicans Colo. Methodist. Office: Colorado Ho of Reps State Capitol Denver CO 80203 *

ARMSTRONG-POPPELBAUM, SYLVIA FINCH, social service agy. exec.; b. Jamestown, N.Y., Sept. 28, 1939; d. Charles Leslie and Josephine Van Vliet (Phillips) Finch; A.B. cum laude, Syracuse U., 1961; postgrad. U. Buffalo, 1962-64, Utica Coll., 1975; m. Thomas L. Poppelbaum, June 16, 1979; children by previous marriage—Ronald C. Armstrong, Andrew D.G. Armstrong. Tchr. secondary social studies, Williamsville, N.Y., 1961-64; dir. Oneida County Youth Bur., Utica, N.Y., 1976-77; asst. for contract mgmt. Oneida County CETA Program, Utica, 1977-79; exec. dir. Planned Parenthood of the Mohawk Valley, Utica, 1979—. Mem. Oneida County Youth Bd.; bd. dirs. Central N.Y. Health Systems Agy. Mem. Nat. Execs. Dirs. Council Planned Parenthood, LWV (dir. Utica-Rome area). Home: 30 Hamilton Pl Clinton NY 13323 Office: Planned Parenthood of the Mohawk Valley 1424 Genesee St Utica NY 13502

ARNAUDO, PATRICIA SUSAN ALEXANDER, govt. ofcl.; b. Peoria, Ill., Jan. 3, 1943; d. Barton and Marian Francis (Gordon) Alexander; B.A., U. Mich., 1964, M.P.A., 1965, doctoral student, 1970-71; m. David Lloyd Arnaudo, Apr. 30, 1966. Program analyst HEW, 1966-69; research assoc. cons. firm, 1969-70; program developer D.C. Mayor's Office, 1970-75; sr. program analyst HUD, Washington, 1975-76, dep. dir. project mgmt. div., chief sect. 8 mgmt. br., 1976-78, dir. existing housing div., 1979-81, dep. dir. Office of Indian Housing, 1981-82, acting dir. Office Indian Housing, 1982—. Active Hopkins House, Low-Income Housing Coalition, Olde Town Civic Assn. (all Alexandria, Va.). Recipient cert. of spl. achievement HUD, 1977, cert. of merit, 1979, cert. of superior service, 1980; recipient planning award City of Alexandria. Mem. Nat. Assn. Housing and Redevel. Officers, Am. Soc. Pub. Adminstrn. Episcopalian. Contbr. articles to profl. jours. Home: 413 S Fairfax St Alexandria VA 22314 Office: HUD 451 7th St SW Washington DC 20410

ARNDT, CYNTHIA, educator; b. N.Y.C., Sept. 27, 1947; d. Charles Joseph and Pura Maria (Rios) A.; B.A., Hunter Coll., M.A., 1975; profl. diploma in bilingual adminstrn. Fordham U., 1981. Adminstrv. asst. to asst. registrar Hunter Coll., N.Y.C., 1968-69; cataloguer asst. Finch Coll. Library, N.Y.C., 1974; tchr. N.Y.C. Bd. Edn., 1974-82, bilingual coordinator Jr. High Sch. 143 M, N.Y.C., 1982—. HEW scholar. Mem. Nat. Assn. for Bilingual Edn., Am. Art Soc., Center for Inter-Am. Relations, Puerto Rico Educators Assn., Nat. Travel Club, Pi Delta Kappa, Kappa Delta Pi. Democrat. Roman Catholic. Home: 50 W 97th St New York NY 10025 Office: 515 W 182d St New York NY 10033

ARNDT, DIANNE JOY, artist, photographer; b. Springfield, Mass., Dec. 20, 1939; d. Samuel Vincent and Carrie Lillian Annino; student Art Students League, 1965-71; B.F.A. with honors in Painting, Pratt Inst., 1974; student photojournalism, Columbia U., 1979-80; M.A., Hunter Coll., 1981; m. Joseph Vincent Bower, June 16, 1979; 1 dau. by previous marriage—Christabelle Nita Arndt. Photojournalist, photo cons. to mags. and bus., N.Y.C., 1978—; pub. relations assoc. McGraw-Hill Book Co., 1975-78; artist, filmmaker, 1962—; head art dept. Lower and Middle Sch., St. Hilda's and St. Hugh's Sch., 1980-81; instr. Women's Interart Center, 1972-73, painting McGraw-Hill, Inc., 1975-76; exhbns. include: Kenkeleba House, 1982, A.I.R. Gallery, 1982, Franklin Furnace, 1982, Just Above Midtown, 1978, Aldrich Mus. Contemporary Art, Ridgefield, Conn., 1976, Women's Interart Center, 1972-76; Unicorn, 1975, Artists Space, 1975, Pratt Inst., 1972-74, The Mus., N.Y.C., 1972, The Church, Stockbridge, Mass., 1972. Recipient Exptl. Writing award Columbia U., 1967, 1st prize in show Springfield (Mass.) Mus. Fine Art, 1967. Mem. Am. Soc. Mag. Photographers, Artists Talk on Art (bd. dirs.), Profl. Women Photographers, Publicity Club N.Y., Internat. Soc. Copier Artists, Found. for Community of Artists.

ARNDT, JOANNE LORAINE, retail exec.; b. Flint, Mich., Sept. 19, 1925; d. Oliver Orson and Blanche Edna (Grady) Valentine; student public schs., Flint; m. Edward Conrad Arndt, Dec. 22, 1944; children—Linda S., Susan L. Murphy, Michael E., Constance L. With Sears, Roebuck & Co., Flint, 1964—, div. mgr. lingerie shop, 1970—, budget shop, 1970-80, hosiery, handbags and luggage depts., 1980—. Mem. DAR. Republican. Presbyterian. Home: 420 Dale St Flushing MI 48433 Office: 3191 Linden Rd Flint MI 48507

ARNDT, MARY JO, nurse; b. La Porte, Ind., July 16, 1944; d. Edward Paul and Theresa Emily Frontczak; B.S.N., Loyola U. Chgo., 1966; M.A.Ed., Murray State U., 1975; Ed.D., Ball State U., 1981; m. Terry L. Arndt, Aug. 27, 1972; children—Karen Suzanne. Staff nurse Childrens Meml. Hosp., Chgo., 1966; instr. nursing, 1967; instr. nursing Murray (Ky.) State U., 1967-69, 73-75; staff nurse U. Ky. Med. Center, Lexington, 1969-70; instr. nursing U. Ark., Fayetteville, 1970-71; public health nurse Washington County, Ark., 1971-72; asst. prof. nursing Ball State U., Muncie, Ind., 1975—. Mem. Ind. Nurses Assn., Sigma Theta Tau, Phi Delta Kappa. Republican. Roman Catholic. Clubs: Univ. Wives. Home: 4405 N Redding Rd Muncie IN 47304 Office: Dept Nursing Ball State U Muncie IN 47306

ARNOLD, CAROLE MARIE, banker; b. Magnolia, Ark., Dec. 20, 1945; d. Meyer Loeb and Gladys Mae (Olive) Herndon; student U. Tex., Austin, 1963-65, also various courses Am. Inst. Banking, Intermediate Banking Sch. With Central Power & Light Co. Tex., Pearsall, 1966-68, jr. acctg. clk., Uvalde, 1968-70; with Frost Nat. Bank, San Antonio, 1970—, asst. v.p., mgr. account services, 1978-79, v.p., mgr. account services, 1979—; mem. indsl. adv. council Bexar County Opportunities Industrialization Center, 1977-78; adv. com. program planning, div. continuing edn. U. Tex., San Antonio, 1976-77. Bd. dirs. San Antonio YWCA, 1979-80. Mem. Am. Inst. Banking (chmn. coms. San Antonio chpt.), Nat. Assn. Bank Women (chpt. chmn. 1979-80, Southwestern regional scholar 1980). Office: 100 W Houston St San Antonio TX 78296

ARNOLD, DIANNE EKBERG, banker; b. Kenmare, N.D., Oct. 14, 1944; d. Gustave S. and Helen M. (Nelson) Ekberg; B.S. in Econs. and Stats., U. Minn., 1966; m. Robert A. Arnold, Dec. 19, 1964; children—Dawn, Jeffrey. With First Nat. Bank St. Paul, 1966—, v.p., div. head comml. lending dept., 1978-80, sr. v.p., mem. mgmt. com. consumer group, 1980—; dir. AHW Corp.; mem. steering com. U. Minn. Mgmt. Acad. Bd. dirs. Baptist. Hosp. Fund, St. Paul, 1982—; exec. bd. Indianhead council Boy Scouts Am., 1980—. Mem. Am. Bankers Assn., Robert Morris Assn., Minn. Women's Econ. Roundtable (dir.), St. Paul C. of C. (adv. com. Inst. Community Leadership). Clubs: Minnesota (sec.-treas., dir. 1981-82), St. Paul Athletic. Office: 332 Minnesota St Saint Paul MN 55101

ARNOLD, FLORENCE MILLNER, artist; b. Prescott, Ariz., Sept. 16, 1900; d. George Thomas and Cora Grace (Paxton) Millner; diploma Mills Coll., 1923; B.S. in Edn., U. So. Calif., 1937; postgrad. Claremont Coll., 1938-40; m. Archibald Adrian Arnold, Aug. 14, 1925; 1 dau., Adrienne (Mrs. Jonathon Chakerian). Supr. music Placentia (Calif.) schs., 1924-41; tchr. music Fullerton (Calif.) High Sch., 1941-48, Buena Park (Calif.) schs., 1948-66; one-women shows Long Beach Mus. Art, 1961, 69, 70, Calif. State U. at Fullerton, 1967; retrospective Fullerton Arts Commn., 1974; numerous group shows including Esther Robles Gallery, Los Angeles, 1965, Laguna Beach Mus. Art, 1966-68, Women U.S.A., 1973; represented in permanent collections at Long Beach Mus. Art, Laguna Beach Mus. Art, Fullerton Coll., Mills Coll. Art, U. Calif., Fullerton. Cons. program for gifted children Buena Park Schs., 1973-74. Mem. goals com. City Fullerton, 1970. Bd. dirs. Muckenthaler Cultural Center, 1964-78; pres. Art Alliance Calif. U. Calif., Fullerton, 1976-77; bd. trustees Fullerton Sci. Mus., 1971-74. Named Woman of Year Fullerton C. of C., 1973. Mem. Los Angeles County Mus. Art, Laguna Beach Mus. Art (dir. 1967-69), Orange County Art Assn. (pres. 1960-62, 1968-69), Smithsonian Inst. (Archives Am. Art), Delta Kappa Gamma. Address: 1136 Valencia Mesa Dr Fullerton CA 92633 *

ARNOLD, GAIL WALLACE, constrn. supt.; b. Oneida, N.Y., June 3, 1946; d. Earl Jay and Edith Evelyn (Allen) Devendorf; student Onondaga Community Coll., 1977-79; m. Claude Arnold, July 29, 1963 (div. Nov. 1969); children—Joseph Todd, Thomas Edwin. Restaurant owner, Chittenango, N.Y., 1974-76; asst. constrn. super Taylor Woodrow Blitman, Lowell, Mass., 1979; asst. contract adminstr. Cambridge (Mass.) Housing Authority, 1980-81; constrn. supt. Boston Housing Authority, 1981—; cons. Drug abuse counselor, Chittenango, 1976-79; mem. Millis Alcohol and Drug Abuse Assn.; chmn. Chittenango chpt. March of Dimes, 1974. Democrat. Roman Catholic. Clubs: Fin, Fur and Feather Hunt, Oak Tree Women's League (Millis, Mass.). Home: 143 Dover Rd Millis MA 02054

ARNOLD, HELEN, Okla. state legislator; b. June 17, 1927; B.S., Kans. State U. Mem. Okla. State Ho. of Reps., 1977—. Office: Okla Ho of Reps State Capitol Oklahoma City OK 73105 *

ARNOLD, HENRIETTA DOWS, corporate exec.; b. Cedar Rapids, Iowa, Oct. 19, 1921; d. Sutherland C. and Frances Daisy (Mills) Dows; student The Masters Sch., Dobbs Ferry, N.Y., 1936-37; student Greenwood Sch., Ruxton, Md., 1938-39, Coe Coll., 1939-41, Chgo. Art Inst., 1945-46; hon. degree Coe Coll., 1978; m. Duane Arnold, Apr. 27, 1946; children—Margaret, Helen, Duane, Elizabeth, Mary. Sec., Iowa Electric Light & Power, Cedar Rapids, 1942-43; with advt. dept. Sunkist Fruit Growers, Los Angeles, 1943-45; v.p., dir. Central Iowa Telephone Co., Cedar Rapids, 1960-66; v.p., corporate dir. Dows Real Estate Co., Cedar Rapids, 1969—; v.p., dir. Dows Maniti Dairy Farm, Inc., Cedar Rapids, 1969-77; v.p., dir. Dows Farms, Inc., Cedar Rapids, 1969—; dir. Sutherland Sq., Cedar Rapids. Bd. dirs. YWCA, Cedar Rapids Art Assn., Public Health Nursing Assn.; trustee, mem. exec. com., bldg. com. Coe Coll.; trustee, mem. fin. and edn. coms. Menninger Found., Topeka. Mem. Jr. League, Cedar Rapids Hist. Assn. Republican. Presbyn (mem. religious edn. com., instr., trustee). Home: 321 Crescent St Cedar Rapids IA 52403 Office: 212 Dows Bldg PO Box 409 Cedar Rapids IA 52406

ARNOLD, JANET NINA, hosp. adminstr.; b. Poughkeepsie, N.Y., Apr. 23, 1933; d. Paul Dudley and Pauline Katherine (Board) Bartram; A.B., Vassar Coll., 1955; postgrad. Sch. Med. Tech., Albany Med. Center, 1955-56; M.S., Vassar Coll., 1963; M.H.S.M., Webster Coll., 1981; m. Robert William Arnold, Dec. 19, 1954; children—Paul Dudley, Janet Elizabeth. Research asst., med. technologist H. Aird Boswell, M.D., Troy, N.Y., 1956-59; teaching supr., adminstrv. cons. Vassar Bros. Hosp., Poughkeepsie, N.Y., 1959-69; adv. to med. lab., lectr. med. mycology Vassar Coll., Poughkeepsie, 1961-66; asst. lab. mgr. Boulder (Colo.) Meml. Hosp., 1975-80; cons. hosp. planning Mercy Med. Center, Denver, 1981—; acad./adminstrv. cons. U. Guam, Vassar Coll., Boulder Community Hosp., others. Sec., bd. dirs. Sanitas Fed. Credit Union, 1977-78, pres., 1979—. Vassar Coll. teaching fellow, 1961-63; NSF research fellow, 1960-62. Mem. Am. Acad. Microbiology, Soc. for Gen. Microbiology, Am. Soc. Med. Technologists, Colo. Public Health Assn., Med. Mycological Soc. of the Ams. Republican. Episcopalian. Asso. editor Am. Jour. Med. Tech., 1980—; contbr. articles to profl. jours. Home: 4195 Chippewa Dr Boulder CO 80303

ARNOLD, JOANNE EASLEY (MRS. SANDERS GIBSON ARNOLD), educator, univ. ofcl.; b. Hutchinson, Kans., June 18, 1930; d. Orland Royce and Bernice Anna (Daugherty) Easley; B.A., U. Colo., 1952, M.A., 1965, Ph.D., 1971; m. Sanders Gibson Arnold, June 7, 1952; 1 son, Sanders Gibson. Reporter, mem. editorial staff Boulder (Colo.) Daily Camera, 1955-56; tchr. journalism, speech and English, Boulder High Sch., 1956-71, dir. publs., 1958-69, chmn. dept. English, 1967-69; asst. dir. Nat. Center for Higher Edn. Mgmt. Systems, Western Interstate Commn. for Higher Edn., Boulder, 1971-74; asso. prof. journalism U. Colo., Boulder, 1974—, asso. dean Sch. Journalism, 1974-75, 82—, asso. vice chancellor for acad. affairs, 1975-80; adviser Elem. and Secondary Edn. Act, Title III, Colo., 1972-75; cons. Bur. Communications, U. Colo., 1970-71; cons. elementary and secondary edn., organizational communication, lectr.; mem. Western Interstate Commn. for Higher Edn., 1975—. Commr., vice chmn. Boulder Public Libraries, 1973-76; mem. com. on fiscal policy City of Boulder, 1972-73; mem. Boulder Valley Sch. Dist. Re-2 Bd. Edn., 1975-79; mem. nat. adv. council Girl Scouts Am., 1977—; trustee Boulder Library Found., 1974-76, Boulder Meml. Hosp.; mem. Women's Rep. Club, Boulder, 1968-76. Newspaper Fund fellow Wall St. Jour., 1961; Nat. Woman of Achievement, Nat. Fedn. Press Women, 1979. Mem. Nat. Soc. for the Study of Communication, Speech Assn. Am., Kappa Tau Alpha, Theta Sigma Phi, Alpha Delta Kappa, Phi Kappa Delta, Pi Beta Phi. Club: U. Colo. Alumni (dir. 1954) (Boulder). Editor: Higher Edn. Mgmt., 1971-74. Contbr. articles to profl. jours. Home: 815 Park Ln Boulder CO 80302

ARNOLD, JUDITH ELLEN, hotel exec.; b. Sedalia, Mo., Nov. 30, 1949; d. Bert and Alice Florianne (Messier) Saunders; B.A., U. Mex., 1969; 1 son, Robert Lawrence. Dir. public relations Biloxi Hilton Resort Hotel and Conv. Center, 1975—, asst. mgr., 1978—; dir. advt. B & H Advt. Agy., Biloxi, 1976—; mgr. Biloxi Condominiums, 1980—; Named Hon. col., Gov. Cliff Finch, 1976-79. Mem. Biloxi C. of C., Nat. Fedn. Press Women. Episcopalian. Home: 2501 Gulf Ave 34 Gulfport MS 39501 Office: 3580 W Beach Blvd Biloxi MS 39531

ARNOLD, KATHLEEN HARDIMAN, public relations cons.; b. Chgo., Feb. 6, 1947; d. Kirkland James and Johnie Viola (Rand) Reed; B.A., San Francisco State U. Personnel cons. Careers Internat., Inc., Chgo., 1966-69; investigator, sales coordinator Ill. Inst. Continuing Legal Edn., Chgo. and Springfield, 1970; info. and research specialist ETA Public Relations, Inc., Chgo., 1970-72; public relations and promotion dir. Sta. WTVS, ednl. TV, Detroit, 1972; corp. asst. to gen. mgr. Sta. WJLB, Detroit, 1972-74; propr. K. H. Arnold, communications and public relations cons., San Francisco, 1974—. Mem. San Francisco Commn. on Status of Women, 1977-80. Mem. Am. Futurists for Edn. Women, AFTRA, Am. Women Radio and TV, Broadcast Music, Inc., Nat. Assn. Ednl. Broadcasters, Nat. Assn. Media Women, Nat. Women's Studies Assn., Public Relations Soc. Am., Women in Communications, NOW, Nat. Assn. Negro Bus. and Profl. Women's Clubs, Black Women Organized for Action, Nat. Council Negro Women, NAACP, San Francisco Black Leadership Forum, Mensa. Club: Commonwealth (San Francisco). Address: PO Box 6677 San Francisco CA 94101

ARNOLD, KATHLEEN SPELTS, state legislator; b. Miami, Fla., Oct. 25, 1941; d. John Keith and Mary Fay (Webber) Shay; B.A., U. Colo., 1963; m. Richard J. Spelts, Feb. 8, 1964; children—Melinda Kathleen, Meghan Shay, Richard John; m. Harold G. Arnold, Jan. 31, 1982. Tchr., Bear Creek High Sch., Jefferson County, Colo., 1963-64, 66-68; asst. to promotion control mgr. Ford Internat. Co., W.Ger., 1965; employee Colo. Legislature, 1976; dep. campaign mgr. for Colo., U.S. Senator Bill Armstrong, 1977; mem. Colo. Ho. of Reps., 1978—, vice chmn. judiciary com., 1978-79, chmn. judiciary com., 1980-82; Colo. rep. Nat. Council State Legislatures, Arts and Humanities, 1980-82. Mem. U. Colo. Alumni Bd., 1971-74; chmn. South Met. Denver Heart Fund, 1974; mem. Jefferson County Sch. Bd. Curriculum Council, 1975, Jefferson County (Colo.) Econ. Devel. Com., 1976; sec., bd. dirs. Littleton Fire Protection Bd., 1976-77. Mem. LWV, Delta Delta Delta. Republican. Presbyterian. Home: 6436 W Frost Dr Littleton CO 80123 Office: State Capitol Bldg Denver CO 80203

ARNOLD, LINDA JOYCE, ednl. adminstr.; b. N.Y.C., Jan. 18, 1950; d. Richard Arnold and Mildred Louise Roderick; student St. Clair County Community Coll., 1968-71; B.A., SUNY, Old Westbury, 1972; M.Ed., reading specialist C.W. Post Coll., L.I. U., 1976; project dir. mental retardation staff tng. project, Bklyn., 1977—, co-developer, implementor of program, adminstr. Testing Assessment Placement Ctr. No. 6, Bklyn., 1982—. Mem. AAUW, Internat. Reading Assn., One to One. Democrat. Office: 270 Flatbush Ave Extension Brooklyn NY 11201

ARNOLD, LYNN NEWMAN, telephone co. exec.; b. Santa Ana, Calif., July 31, 1951; d. John Harold and Francis Anne (Russell) Newman; student Fullerton Jr. Coll., 1973-74, Orange Coast Coll., 1972-73; m. David Lee Arnold, Sept. 29, 1979. With Pacific Telephone, Orange County, Calif., 1969-79, mktg. office supr., 1976-77, communications cons., 1977-79; account exec. C & P Telephone, Norfolk, Va., 1980—; owner Matagi Kennels, Grafton, Va., 1980—; v.p. Old Dominion Firearms, Yorktown, Va., 1981; guest lectr. Old Dominion U., Tidewater Regional Justice Tng. Center, 1981. Active Va. bd. of dirs., Peninsula Council Battered Women, 1981-82; mem. emergency services adv. com. York County Bd. Suprs., 1982—. Recipient C & P Telephone Spirit of Service award, 1981. Mem. Peninsula Women's Network, Nat. Assn. Female Execs., Associated Public Safety Communications Officers. Home: 130 Duff Dr Grafton VA 23692 Office: PO Box 1461 Military Circle Norfolk VA 23501

ARNOLD, MARY BERTUCIO, pediatric endocrinologist; b. Fitchburg, Mass., Sept. 29, 1924; d. George and Louise (Byrolly) Bertucio; A.B., Vassar Coll., 1945; M.D., U. Vt., 1950; M.A., Brown U., 1974; m. John Hampton Arnold, July 28, 1956 (dec. Apr. 1972); children—John, Mark, Matthew. Intern, resident Hartford (Conn.) Hosp., 1950-52; asst./sr. pediatric resident Babies' Hosp., Columbia-Presbyn. Med. Center, N.Y.C., 1952-54; pediatric endocrinology research fellow Mass. Gen. Hosp., Boston, 1954-57; asst. in pediatrics Harvard U. Sch. Medicine, Boston, 1955-57; instr. pediatrics/asst. prof. U. N.C. Sch. Medicine, Chapel Hill, 1959-65; lectr. med. sci./assoc. prof. pediatrics Brown U., Providence, 1966-74, assoc. prof., 1974—; chmn. dept. pediatrics, dir. pediatric endocrinology Roger Williams Gen. Hosp., Providence, 1971—. Chmn., Heart Health in the Young Com., Am. Heart Assn., R.I. Affiliate, Inc., 1979—; mem. adv. com. New Eng. Regional Hypothyroidism Screening Program, 1976—; mem. subcom. pediatric planning rev. guidelines Hosp. Assn. R.I., 1976—; mem. program com. R.I. Clin. Diabetes Assn., 1975—. Recipient Carrbee award U. Vt. Sch. Medicine, 1950, Excellence in Teaching award Brown U., 1978. Mem. Endocrine Soc., Lawson Wilkins Pediatric Endocrine Soc., Am. Fedn. Clin. Research, AAAS, Am. Med. Women's Assn., Am. Acad. Pediatrics, AMA, New Eng. Pediatric Soc., So. Soc. Pediatric Research, R.I. Clin. Diabetes Assn. (pres. 1975-77), Sigma Xi. Episcopalian. Contbr. articles to profl. jours. Office: 825 Chalkstone Ave Providence RI 02908

ARNOLD, NINA RAE, textile artist, designer, weaver; b. Chgo., June 22, 1940; d. Raymond Earl and Helen Lucille (Motsinger) Davidson; B.S., So. Ill. U., 1963; M.S., Ill. State U., 1975; textile study, Sweden, 1973; sculptural welding, Middlesborough Coll. Art, Eng., 1974; m. Dennis Lee Arnold, Mar. 20, 1960; 1 son, Anthony. Tchr., Herrin Jr. High Sch., 1963-64; asst. prof. weaving and art Black Hawk East Coll., 1970-75; owner, operator Nina's Weaving Studio, Kewanee, Ill., 1969—; freelance textile designer, 1975—; designer wall hangings and tapestries, 1975—; crafts dir. historic Swedish Bishop Hill, Ill., 1969-70; one woman shows: U. N.D., Grand Forks, 1966, U.S. Cultural Center, Kabul, Afghanistan, 1967, Ill. State U., 1975, Hundley House Gallery, Carbondale, Ill., 1979; group shows include: Mass. Nat. Art Shows, Fall River, 1965, 68, Civic Art Center, Galesburg, Ill., 1969, 72, Container Corp. Am. 10th Annual Fine Arts Exhbn., Rock Island, Ill., 1972, Ill. Craftsmen Ill. State Mus., Springfield, 1975, Grad. Student Beinnial Ill. State U., 1975, Mcpl. Gallery, Davenport, Iowa, 1976, Stanley Gallery, Muscatine, Iowa, 1977, 80, Scada Art shows, Springfield, 1977—, Yolanda Fine Arts Gallery, Winnetka, Ill., 1980, Lakeview Mus., Peoria, Ill., 1981, Fiber-Paper Show, Iowa City, Iowa, 1982; represented in permanent collections: Ill. State U., Parkland Coll., Champaign, Ill., Farmers State Bank, Knoxville, Ill. Mem. Peoria Art Guild. Democrat. Baptist. Author: Arts and Crafts Manual for Peace Corps Volunteers in Afghanistan, 1967. Home and Office: Rural Route 1 Box 55 Kewanee IL 61443

ARNOLD, RACHEL LOONEY, sec.; b. Paint Bank, Va., Feb. 26, 1916; d. George Crockett and Mabel Clara (Haynes) Looney; student Lynchburg (Va.) Coll., 1934-35; cert. in theory and organ Randolph-Macon Woman's Coll., Lynchburg, 1940; student Phillips Bus. Coll., Lynchburg, 1955; m. Clarence Bryan Arnold, Jr., Aug. 20, 1941 (div.), 1 dau., Merlyn Dawn Arnold Cloyd. Receptionist, bookkeeper Dr. G.C. Looney, Optometrist, Lynchburg, 1941-42; pianist Madison Heights (Va.) Christian Ch., 1930-40, organist, 1940-54; organist Meml. Christian Ch., Lynchburg, 1954-74; cashier dept. circulation Lynchburg News & Daily Advance, 1956; sec. to dean coll. and dean students Lynchburg Coll., 1956-61, sec. to dean student affairs, 1961—. Mem. Profl. Secs. Internat. Home: 204 E Cadbury Dr Lynchburg VA 24501 Office: Lynchburg College Lynchburg VA 24501

ARNOLD, SHEILA, state legislator; b. N.Y.C., Jan. 15, 1929; d. Michael and Eileen (Lynch) Keddy; coll. courses; m. George Longan Arnold, Nov. 12, 1960; 1 son, Peter; 1 son by previous marriage, Michael C. Young; stepchildren—Drew, George Longan, Joe. Mem. Wyo. Ho. of Reps., 1978—, mem. coms. mines, minerals and indsl. devel., hwys. and transp. Former mem., sec. Wyo. Land Use Adv. Com.; past pres. Democratic Women's Club, Laramie; past vice-chmn. Albany County Dem. Central Com.; past mem. Dem. State Com. Mem. Laramie Area C. of C. (Top Hand award 1977; pres.), LWV. Episcopalian. Clubs: Faculty Women's (past pres.), Zonta, Laramie Women's, Cowboy Joe. Office: Capitol Bldg Cheyenne WY 82001

ARNOLD, SUSAN BIRD, safety edn. products co. exec.; b. Reading, Pa., Feb. 28, 1951; d. Frank Edward and Esther (Savidge) Bird; B.A., Mercer U., Macon, Ga., 1972; m. Robert Melvin Arnold, Jr., Mar. 18, 1972; children—Jennifer Michelle, Amelia Michelle, Stephanie Michelle. Audio-video technician Internat. Safety Acad., 1971; with Internat. Loss Control Inst., 1974—, mgr. ednl. products div., 1978—, v.p. press div., Loganville, Ga., 1980—; mng. editor Internat. Risk Control Rev. Mem. adv. com. Inst. Safety, Health and Rehab. for the Exceptional, 1978-79. Methodist. Home: Route 4 Loganville GA 30249 Office: Internat Loss Control Inst Hwy 78 Loganville GA 30249

ARNOLD, SUSAN CAROL, psychologist; b. Louisville, Ga., Aug. 6, 1951; d. Fred Walton and Lily Hazel (Barker) A.; A.S., Middle Ga. Coll., 1971; B.S., U. Ga., 1973, M.S. (Zimmer scholar), 1975, Ph.D., 1977; m. David Jackson Waldrep, Aug. 21, 1976; 1 dau., Amy Catherine Waldrep. Psychology trainee VA Hosp., Augusta, Ga., 1973-74; teaching asst. dept. psychology U. Ga., Athens, 1974-75; clin. psychology intern Va. Treatment Center for Children, Med. Coll. Va., 1975-76; clin. psychologist child and adolescent services N.E. Ga. Community Mental Health Center, Athens, 1976-77; child services coordinator Johnston County (N.C.) Mental Health Center, Smithfield, 1977-78, clin. services dir., 1978—. Mem. Johnston County Youth Task Force, 1978—, sec., 1980-81, chair, 1981—; mem. Johnston County Title XX Planning Com., 1979. Lic. psychologist, N.C. Mem. Am. Psychol. Assn., Southeastern Psychol. Assn., N.C. Psychol. Assn., Assn. for Retarded Citizens, N.C. Juvenile Services Assn., Phi Beta Kappa, Phi Kappa Phi, Psi Chi. Democrat. Methodist. Contbr. articles, revs. to profl. jours. Office: PO Box 411 Smithfield NC 27577

ARNOTT, SHEARON TRUDE, computer co. ofcl.; b. Chgo., June 23, 1952; d. Alfred Samuel Trude and Carolyn (Shearon) Trude; B.S. in Mgmt., Purdue U., 1973; m. David S. Arnott, Sept. 14, 1979. Mktg. rep. data processing IBM, Indpls., 1973-76, fin. industry specialist, Miami, Fla., 1976-79; regional sales mgr. Citicorp., Orlando, Fla., 1979-81; mktg. projects mgr. Systeme Corp., Orlando, 1981—; treas. Arnone, Inc. Mem. Nat. Assn. Female Execs., Am. Mgmt. Assn., Nat. Assn. Bank Women. Republican. Episcopalian. Home: 424 Village View Ln Longwood FL 32750 Office: 3443 Parkway Center Ct Orlando FL 32804

ARONSON, LOIS MARIE HOGUE, home economist; b. New Rochelle, N.Y., June 3, 1935; d. Charles Henry and Isable Louise Hogue; B.S. in Home Econs., U. Vt., 1957; M.S. in Human Behavior and Devel., Drexel U., Phila., 1978; m. Karl Edward Aronson, Sept. 1, 1956; children—James Karl, Kirsten Marie. 4-H agt., Vt., 1957-58, Gloucester County, N.J., 1961-63; home economist Nestle's Co., White Plains, N.Y., 1959-60; extension home economist/4-H agt., Camden County, N.J., 1964-65; spl. assignments with N.J. Coop. Extension Service, 1966-68; extension home economist, Camden County, 1968—. Recipient Service Honor award Camden County Bd. Freeholders, 1979. Mem. Am. Home Econs. Assn., Nat. Assn. Extension Home Economists, N.J. Assn. Extension Home Economists, N.J. Home Econs. Assn., So. Counties Home Econs. Assn., Tri-County Nutrition Council, AAUP, Epsilon Sigma Phi. Club: Soroptimist Internat. Author: Nutrition for the Elderly, 1975; also newspaper column and radio program; hostess weekly TV program. Office: 152 Ohio Ave Clementon NJ 08021

ARRECHE, CANDY ANN, lawyer, blood bank exec.; b. Santurce, P.R., July 7, 1954; d. Candido C. and Olga (Holdun) A.; B.A. cum laude in History and Fgn. Langs., Fla. Technol. U., 1974; J.D. magna cum laude, Inter-Am. U., 1976. Donor recruiter P.R. Community Blood Center, Inc., Santurce, 1974-76; law clk. firm Calderon Rosa Silva y Vargas, San Juan, P.R., 1975-76; admitted to P.R. bar, 1977; atty. Coop. Devel. Corp., San Juan, 1977; law clk. San Juan Jud. Center, 1978; individual practice law, Santurce, P.R. 1978—; exec. dir. P.R. Community Blood Center, Hosp. Sagrado Corazon, Santurce, 1981—; treas. Hosp. Sagrado Corazon. Den mother Cub Scouts Miami council Boy Scouts Am., 1970-72; active gubernatorial election Fla., 1971; translator for Spanish-speaking voting population, presdl. election, 1972. Recipient Key to City Coral Gables (Fla.), 1971; notary public, P.R. Mem. P.R. Bar Assn., Am. Bar Assn., Internat. Bar. Assn., Fla. Assn. Blood Banks, Am. Assn. Blood Banks, Better Bus. Bur. of P.R., C. of P.R., Fla. Technol. U. Alumni. Roman Catholic. Club: Rosecrusian Order. Office: 1301 Jesus T. Piñero Ave Puerto Nuevo PR 00920

ARREDONDO, JOY GRACE, real estate broker; b. Roswell, N.Mex., Jan. 24, 1929; d. Jess Dewaco and Pauline (Lozano) Dominguez; student West Valley Jr. Coll., 1975-76; m. Chris Franco Arredondo, Apr. 3, 1949; children—Nancy Lynn, Christopher Anthony, Leslie Ann. Engring. asso. Raytheon Semi-Condr., 1963-74; office mgr., co-owner Jude Realty, Campbell, Calif., 1974—. Notary public, lic. real estate salesman and broker, Calif. Mem. San Jose Real Estate Bd., Nat. Assn. Realtors, Calif. Assn. Realtors, Alpha Gamma Sigma. Democrat. Roman Catholic. Home: 5186 Meridian Ave San Jose CA 95118 Office: 101 W Hamilton St Campbell CA 95008

ARROYO, MARTINA, soprano; b. N.Y.C.; pupil Marinka Gurevich Mo Martin Rich, Joseph Turnau, Rose Landver; student Kathryn Long Course Met. Opera. Debut Carnegie Hall, 1958; leading soprano Met. Opera, N.Y.C., in roles including Il Trovatore, Aida, Madama Butterfly, Un Ballo in Maschera, Cavalleria Rusticana, La Forza del Destino, Vespri Siciliani, Don Giovanni, La Gioconda, Macbeth, Andrea Chenier, Tosca; performed opening night Met. season, 1970-71, 71-72, 73-74; performed at La Scala, Milan, Munich Staatsoper, Berlin Deutsche Oper. Rome Opera, Vienna State Opera, Covent Garden, Teatro Colon, Buenos Aires, San Francisco, Chgo. and all major opera houses; soloist N.Y., Vienna, Berlin, Royal (London), Paris philharms., San Francisco, Pitts., Phila., Chgo., Cleve. symphonies, Concertgebouw, other major orchs.; frequent performer Saratoga, Ravinia, Tanglewood festivals and festivals Vienna, Berlin, Edinburgh, Helsinki; oratorios include Verdi and Dvorak Reguiems, Beethoven Missa Solemnis and Choral Fantasy, Judas Maccabaeus, others; recs. for Columbia, London, Angel, DGG, Philips records, RCA. Mem. Nat. Endowment of Arts, Washington; trustee Carnegie Hall, N.Y.C. Named Outstanding Alumna, Hunter Coll., N.Y.C. Address: care Thea Dispeker 59 E 54th St New York NY 10022 *

ARSHT, LESLYE ALENE, communications exec.; b. St. Louis, June 28, 1945; d. Raymond I. and Marjorie M. (Meyer) Arsht; A.A. Vernon Jr. Coll., 1965; B.A., U. Houston, 1968. Mem. White House staff President's Daily News Summary, Washington, 1969-71, nat. research coordinator Presdl. Election Campaign, 1972; info. specialist EPA, Washington, 1973-75; spl. asst. to asst. dir. of corp. communications Union Carbide Corp., Washington, 1975-77, mgr. public relations, Washington office, 1977-79; mgr. corp. communications Cabot Corp., Boston, 1979—. Precinct chmn. Harris County (Tex.), 1967-68. Recipient Communicator of Yr. award Yankee chpt. Internat. Assn. Bus. Communicators, 1981; Bronze award Northeast chpt. Assn. for Multi-Image Shows, 1982. Mem. Women in Communications (Matrix award 1981), Public Relations Soc. Am., Nat. Press Club. Jewish. Contbr. articles in field to profl. publs. Office: Cabot Corp 125 High St Boston MA 02110

ARTEMIS, JOHNNIE (JOHNETTA) MAE, freelance business cons.; b. Mt. Carmel, Ill., May 31, 1945; d. John Franklin and Thelma Mae (Dustman) Gore; student Fla. State U., 1963-65, U. N.H., 1981—; m. Nathan Alan Teichholtz, Feb. 10, 1980. Programmer/analyst Nat. Life and Accident Ins. Co., Inc., Nashville, 1969-71; systems analyst State of Tenn., Nashville, 1971-72; sr. programmer/analyst Stone & Webster Engring. Co., Boston, 1972-74, Genesco Inc., Nashville, 1974-75; sr. mktg. specialist Digital Equipment Corp., Merrimack, N.H., 1975-78; account mgr. telecommunications industry Data Gen. Corp., Westboro,

Mass., 1978-80; freelance cons., 1980—; lectr. on women in mgmt. and bus., women's rights. Asst. state coordinator NOW, N.H., 1977, state coordinator, 1977-78, state coordinator ex-officio, 1979-80; del. N.H. Democratic State Conv., 1978; town chmn. Anderson for Pres. Campaign, 1980. Cert. data processor; registered bus. programmer. Address: Pavillion Rd Amherst NH 03031

ARTER, MARGARET HELEN, coll. adminstr.; b. Indpls., July 7, 1929; d. William Andrew and Dorothy (Metzgar) Wade; B.S. with distinction, Ind. U., 1950; M.A., U. So. Calif., 1951; Ph.D., Ariz. State U., 1972; m. Glenn A. Arter, Aug. 20, 1954 (div. 1969); children—Brian D., Adrienne M., Bruce A. Tchr. speech Woodmere Acad., N.Y., 1952-53; tchr. English, Blue Island, Ill., 1955-56; reports controller/coordinator Comprehensive Youth Services Program, Cleve. Bd. Edn., 1966-69; research asso. and asst. Ariz. State U. Coll. Edn., Tempe, 1969-73; dir. spl. assistance and dir. grants planning and mgmt. Cuyahoga Community Coll., Cleve., 1974-78; dean instruction, asst. supt. Palo Verde Coll., Blythe, Calif., 1979—; lectr. in field. Chmn. bicentennial com. Cuyahoga Community Coll., 1975-76, pres. Women's Orgn. of Metro. campus, 1976-77. Butler U. scholar, 1946-48; Ariz. State U. scholar, 1969; NDEA fellow, 1971; Rockefeller Found. grantee, 1970. Mem. Am. Assn. Higher Edn., Assn. for Study of Higher Edn., Soc. Research Adminstrs., Nat. Council for Resource Devel., Nat. Council Univ. Research Adminstrs., Assn. for Instl. Research, Women's Equity Action League, So. Calif. Deans of Instrn., Calif. Women in Higher Edn., Calif. Assn. Instl. Research. Unitarian Universalist. Club: Parents Without Partners. Contbr. articles to profl. jours. Home: 760 W Ocotillo Rd Blythe CA 92225 Office: 811 W Chanslorway Blythe CA 92225

ARTERBERY, VIVIAN JUSTICE, corp. librarian; b. Houston, June 21, 1937; d. Henry Ernest and Frankie Burt (Mott) Justice; B.A., Howard U., 1958; M.S., U. So. Calif., 1965; m. Augustus C. Arterbery, Dec. 12, 1959; 1 dau., Elayne. Librarian, Space Tech. Labs., 1959-60; adminstrv. librarian Aerospace Corp., Los Angeles, 1960-79; library dir. Rand Corp., Santa Monica, Calif., 1979—; instr. U. So. Calif., 1976; cons. HEW grants rev. panel, 1974, 75, 76; mem. qualification panel for librarians exam., Calif., 1977. Active, Women for the Music Center, 1972-73; active JFK Democratic Club, 1963-67; active Los Angelenos, 1976. Named Woman of Yr., Santa Monica YWCA, 1981. Mem. Spl. Libraries Assn. (pres. so. Calif. chpt. 1973-74, instr. preconf. seminar 1969, bd. dirs. 1981-83), Calif. Library Assn. (councilor, chmn. nominating com. 1982), So. Calif. Interlibrary Loan (mem. adv. bd. 1974-76), Librarias Sodalitas (dir. 1978—, pres. 1981), Jack and Jill of Am., Inc., Links, Inc. (chpt. v.p.), U. So. Calif. Library Sch. Alumni Assn. (pres.), Alpha Kappa Alpha. Roman Catholic. Author: Directory of Special Libraries in Southern California, 1965; Mechanized Circulation Control System, 1967; The Use of Computer Terminals in the Library, 1976. Home: 16440 Sloan Dr Los Angeles CA 90049 Office: 1700 Main St Santa Monica CA 90406

ARTERS, LINDA BROMLEY, public relations cons.; b. Phila., Dec. 18, 1951; d. Edward Pollard and Rosalyn Irene (Bromley) A.; B.A., Thiel Coll., Greenville, Pa., 1973. Customer relations dir. Artmann Devel. Corp. Inc., Media, Pa., 1973-74; with Southeast Nat. Bank, Malvern, Pa., 1974-78, public relations coordinator, 1976-78; propr. Linda B. Arters Public Relations and Advt., Media, 1978—; past mem. pvt. industry council County Delaware (Pa.) CETA Program; past chmn. communications com. small bus. council Delaware County C. of C. Mem. Phila. Indoor Tennis Corp., 1977—; bd. dirs. United Cerebral Palsy of Delaware County. Mem. Internat. Assn. Bus. Communicators, Nat. Fedn. Ind. Bus., Nat. Assn. Female Execs., Public Relations Soc. Am., Phila. Public Relations Assn. U.S. Tennis Writers Assn. Republican. Presbyterian. Office: 1155 Baltimore Ave Media PA 19063

ARTHUR, JUDY LYNN, equal employment adminstr.; b. Memphis, Nov. 23, 1944; d. James Willard and Rubye Owen (Robinson) A.; B.S. in Journalism, Memphis State U., 1966; postgrad. Pepperdine U., 1977—; m. Thomas C. Findley, Jan. 26, 1979. Writer-editor U.S. Army, Ft. Knox, Ky. and Stuttgart, W.Ger., 1966-69; writer-editor U.S. Navy, Memphis, 1969-77, EEO specialist, 1977—; free-lance reporter Memphis Press Scimitar, 1969, 70, 72, UPI, 1970-73. Recipient Merit award U.S. Navy Dept. Chief of Info., 1970. Mem. Women in Communications, Federally Employed Women, Am. Mgmt. Assn., Nat. Press Club, Toastmasters Internat., Bus. and Profl. Women, Gamma Phi Beta. Home: 2665 Welchlawn Cove Memphis TN 38134 Office: EEO Office Naval Tech Tng Command Naval Air Sta Millington TN 38054

ARTHUR, NANCY SAGE, interior designer; b. Canton, Ohio, Nov. 24, 1941; d. Walter Fuller and E. Nadyne (Jackson) Sage; B.S. in Edn., Kent State U., 1963; m. James William Arthur, June 19, 1964; children—William, Walter, Jennifer. Elem. tchr., pub. schs., Akron, Ohio, 1963-66; sales agt. Currie Hall Investment Co., Kent, Ohio, 1973-76; partner Somethin Spl. Interiors, Kent, 1974-79; pres. Nancy Arthur Interiors, Inc., Kent, Ohio, 1980—; sec.-treas. Trans Ohio Bldg. Co., 1975-80. Mem. jr. bd. Akron City Hosp. 1964-67; dir. Mahoning River Valley Camp Grounds, Inc., 1979—. Mem. Am. Soc. Interior Designers (assoc.). Clubs: Jr. League, Chestnut Soc. of Kent. Address: 1515 Lake Martin St Kent OH 44240

ARTHURS, ALBERTA BEAN, found. exec.; b. Framingham, Mass., Dec. 20, 1932; d. Maurice and Eleanor Irene (Levenson) Bean; B.A., Wellesley Coll., 1954; Ph.D., Bryn Mawr Coll., 1972; m. Edward Arthurs, Dec. 20, 1960; children—Lee Michael, Daniel Jacob, Madeleine Hope. Editor, Liberty Mut. Ins. Co. Mag., Boston, 1954-56; dir. admissions Eliot-Pearson Sch., Tufts U., Medford, Mass., 1957-59, instr. English, 1958-62; instr., lectr. Rutgers U., New Brunswick, N.J., 1964-72, asst. prof., 1972-73; dean Radcliffe Coll., Cambridge, Mass., 1973-75, Harvard U., Cambridge, 1975-77; pres. coll., prof. English, Chatham Coll., Pitts., 1977-82; dir. humanities Rockefeller Found., N.Y.C., 1982—; dir. Culbro Corp., Salzburg Seminar in Am. Studies. Bd. dirs. Harbridge House, 1980-82, Presbyn.-Univ. Hosp. of Pitts., 1979-82, Pitts. Symphony Soc., 1980-82; trustee Hotchkiss Sch., 1975—, Ellis Sch., 1977-82. Clubs: Duquesne (Pitts.); Harvard (N.Y.C.). Office: Rockefeller Found 1133 Ave of Americas New York NY 10036

ARTIS, CAROLYN, employment agency exec.; b. Covington, Ky., Jan. 5, 1937; d. Carl E. and Marjorie G. Artis. Pres., dir. Lynn Carol, Inc., numerous cities, Calif., 1965—, also Zip Temporary Personnel Services, Encino, 1965—; owner, operator 4 resort hotels in Santa Barbara and 2 in Santa Monica, Calif., 1 in Palm Springs, Calif. Mem. Wage Bd. Indsl. Welfare Commn. State of Calif. Mem. Calif. Employment Assn. Author: Facts and Fables about Hiring Your Own Help Wanted Ads, 1974. Office: 16255 Ventura Blvd #1118 Encino CA 91436

ARTMAN, BARBARA DEATON, insurance agt.; b. Greenville, Miss., June 23, 1954; d. Lucian Kimbrough and Betty Aileen (Morgan) Deaton; B.A. in Social Work, Delta State U., 1974, postgrad., 1974; postgrad. Miss. State U., 1980—; m. Paul Compton Artman, Jr., Aug. 9, 1975; 1 son, Paul Compton. Out-reach worker Sixty-Plus Agy., South Delta, Miss., 1974; resource tchr. Bolivar County (Miss.) Schs., Cleve., 1974-75; employment interviewer Miss. Job Service, Greenville, 1975-78, employment counselor, 1978-81; gen. agt. Deaton and Assos., Greenville, 1981—; dir. women's affairs Sta. WBAQ; dir. Life-Line Counseling Services, State of Miss.; cons. Right-to-Life, Inc. Mem. Miss. Personnel and Guidance Assn., Delta Area Personnel and Guidance Assn., Delta Delta Delta (alumnae pres.). Clubs: Women of Catholic Ch., KC Aux. (pres.). Home: 729 Shattuck St Greenville MS 38701 Office: PO Box 656 Greenville MS 38701

ARTUD, LUISA BETZAIDA, govt. ofcl.; b. Guayama, P.R., Jan. 14, 1955; d. Julio and Sylvia (Corujo) A.; B.A. cum laude, U. P.R., 1977; cert. Am. Econ. Assn. Summer Program, Northwestern U., 1977. Survey statistician U.S. Bur. Census, N.Y.C., 1978-80, supervisory survey statistician, 1980—. Mem. Nat. Assn. Female Execs. Republican. Roman Catholic. Office: US Bur Census 26 Federal Plaza New York NY 10278

ARTY, MARY ANN, state legislator; b. Phila., Nov. 24, 1926; d. Henry J. and Pearl (VanDike) Scheid; R.N., Med. Coll. Pa., 1946; B.S., West Chester State Coll., 1965; m. Thomas B. Arty; children—James Scheid, Janis Arty Hamilton, John Thomas. Supr., staff nurse instr. nursing of children Med. Coll. Pa., 1951-54; nurse educator Adult Vocat. Sch. Nursing, 1960-65; dir. dept. health, Springfield Twp., Delaware County, Pa., 1965-76; dir. Office Intercommunity Health Coordinator, County of Delaware, Pa., 1976-79; mem. Pa. Ho. of Reps., 1979—; mem. adv. bd. Grad. Sch. Nursing Widener U., 1980—; bd. overseers Coll. Nursing, U. Pa., 1982—. Commr., Springfield Twp., 1977—; vice chmn. Delaware County Republican Exec. Com., 1976—; del. Rep. Nat. Conv., Miami, 1972; mem. Govt. Study Commn., Delaware County Home Rule Charter, 1973. Recipient Benjamin Rush award Delaware County Med. Soc., 1975, Award of Merit, Am. Acad. Pediatrics, 1981, Award of Merit, Delaware-Chester County Dental Soc., 1979. Mem. Am. Nurses Assn., Nat. Order Women Legislators, Bus. and Profl. Women, Pa. Nurses Assn., Springfield LWV. Lutheran. Office: 438 Baltimore Pike Springfield PA 19064

ARTZ, BONITA JUNE, educator; b. Trumbull, Nebr., Apr. 8, 1928; d. Doyle Verene and Mable (Hill) Kreutz; student Hastings Coll., 1946-47; B.A. in Elem. Edn. and L.S., Kearney State Coll., 1970, M.A. in Elem. Edn., 1979; m. Dean Burdell Artz, Aug. 22, 1948; children—Lynn Doyle, Julie Kay, Carol Anne. Tchr., Huntley Consol. Sch., 1947-48, 49-50, Ragan Consol. Sch., 1952-53; kindergarten Title I tchr. Alma (Nebr.) Public Sch., 1964—. Committeewoman Republican party, 1958-64; vol. Heart Fund, Cystic Fibrosis. Mem. NEA, Nebr. State Edn. Assn., Nebr. Assn. Edn. Young Children, Internat. Reading Assn., Alma Tchrs. Assn., Alma Bus. and Profl. Assn., Delta Kappa Gamma. Republican. Mem. Christian Ch. Clubs: Harlan County Barbershop Chorus, Order Eastern Star (worthy matron Excelsior chpt. 1973, 74, 80, 81, chmn. Rainbow adv. bd., past mother adviser Rainbow Girls), Prairie Shufflers, Lake Promenaders Sq. Dance. Home: 808 Division St Box 406 Alma NE 68920 Office: 515 N Jewel St Alma NE 68920

ARVEDON, MAELYN NORMA SIGAL, bank security ofcl.; b. Boston, Nov. 21, 1954; d. Samuel and Sandra (Levin) Sigal; A.B. magna cum laude, Boston Coll., 1976, M.B.A., 1981; m. David K. Arvedon, June 3, 1979. Successively teller, asst. head teller, research analyst, head teller, customer service rep., audit asst. Mut. Bank for Savs. and predecessor, Boston, 1976-81, loss prevention specialist, 1981—. Adv. Com. to Elect Frank Rich Gov. of Mass., 1981; adv. Jr. Achievement, 1982-83. Recipient ins. sales awards; cert. in life ins. Mass. Savs. Bank. Mem. Nat. Assn. Female Execs., Old Girls Network, Savs. Bank Women of Mass., Mass. Police Fraudulent Check Assn. Jewish. Office: 45 Franklin St Boston MA 02110

ASAI, JANINE MARCIA, public relations agy. exec., journalist; b. Phila., Aug. 12, 1954; d. Paul and Idelle Elaine Hoffman; B.S. in Chemistry, Calif. State U., Long Beach, 1978, M.S., 1979, B.A. in Journalism, 1980; m. Shinji Asai, Aug. 20, 1975; 1 dau., Michelle Mari. With Sun Rose U.S.A. Inc., 1975-80, dir. internat. sales and mktg., Huntington Beach, Calif., 1975-80; exec. dir. Pacific Hosp. of Long Beach Found., 1980-81; owner, prin. Janine Asai & Assos., Huntington Beach, Calif., 1981—; condr. seminars, cons. in field. Vol. historian Fountain Valley Community Hosp., 1977-79. Served as nurse USAF, 1973-75, Res., 1975-78. Mem. Nat. Assn. Female Execs. (network dir.), Internat. Sales and Mktg. Execs. (dir.), Women in Communications, Nat. Sporting Goods Assn., Public Relations Soc. Am., NOW, New Alliance for Gay Equality. Club: B'nai B'rith. Contbg. author, editor revs./opinions Lesbian News, 1978—.

ASAY, LINDA HAWLEY, lawyer, corp. exec.; b. Evanston, Ill., Dec. 9, 1938; d. Howard Hawley and Willa (Myers) Hawley Asay; B.A., Mills Coll., Oakland, Calif., 1960; J.D., Washburn U., 1965; postgrad. U. Okla., George Washington U. Law Sch., U. Kans. Law Sch.; m. Robert W. Spaeth, July 28, 1979. Admitted to Kans. bar, 1965, N.Y. bar, 1971; staff asst. U.S. Ho. of Reps., 1961-63, Kans. Senate, 1965; atty. Kans. Bd. Social Welfare, Topeka, 1965-67, Council of State Govts., Washington, 1967-69; exec. asst. atty. gen. State of N.Y., N.Y.C., 1969-75; legis. asst. to U.S. Senator Charles Percy of Ill., Washington, 1975-77; Washington rep. CPC N.Am., 1977-79, dir. govt. affairs and csl. CPC N.Am. div., Englewood Cliffs N.J., 1979-82, dir. corp. affairs CPC Internat., Englewood Cliffs, 1982—. Mem. Republican Women's Task Force; bd. dirs. New Leadership Fund, Public Affairs Council; trustee Found. Pub. Affairs. Mem. ABA, New York County Lawyers Assn., Women in Govt. Relations, Conf. Bd. (pub. affairs research council). Office: CPC Internat Inc Plaza Englewood Cliffs NJ 07632

ASBELL, RIVA LEE, univ. adminstr.; b. Camden, N.J., Sept. 15, 1940; d. Nathan and Irene (Kauffman) A.; A.B., U. Pa., 1962; cert. in orthoptics Columbia U. Coll. Physicians and Surgeons, 1963. Mem. adj. staff dept. ophthalmology Frankford Hosp., Phila., 1973-77; instr. dept. ophthalmology Hahnemann Med. Coll. and Hosp., Phila., 1975-77, adminstr. dept., 1975—; asst. prof., 1977—. Mem. Am. Assn. Cert. Orthoptists, Am. Assn. Cert. Allied Health Personnel in Ophthalmology, Assn. Univ. Profs. in Ophthalmology (adminstr.'s sect.). Assoc. editor: Management of Complications in Ophthalmic Plastic Surgery, 1976. Home: 1810 S Rittenhouse Sq Philadelphia PA 19103 Office: 5001 Frankford Ave Philadelphia PA 19124

ASBILL, PAULINE PORTER (MRS. DAVID ST. PIERRE ASBILL), office mgr.; b. Royston, Ga., Sept. 19, 1906; d. James Alexander and Ophelia Kathryn (Fowler) Porter; R.N., Med. Coll. S.C. Sch. Nursing, 1926; m. David St. Pierre Asbill, Feb. 9, 1928; 1 son, David St. Pierre. Nurse charge pediatrics dept. Roper Hosp., Charleston, S.C., 1926-28; nurse obstet. dept. N.Y. Polyclinic Med. Sch. and Hosp., N.Y.C., 1928-29; mgr. physician's office, Columbia, S.C., 1934—. State civil def. nurse Richland County Civil Def. Council, S.C., 1953—. Mem. Woman's Aux. Assn. Surgeons So. Ry. and Seaboard Air Line R.R. Systems; woman's aux. Columbia Med. Soc. (chmn. decorations 1948-55, v.p. 1942); S.C. Med. Assn. (charge decorations 1952-55). Mem. Columbia Art Assn. (art com. 1935-36), Delphian Soc., Internat. Platform Assn. Episcopalian. Clubs: Columbia Woman's (publicity chmn. 1940; decorations com. 1939), Forest Lake Country, Altrusa (Columbia). Home: Senate Plaza 1520 Senate St Columbia SC 29201 Office: 1417 Barnwell St Columbia SC 29201

ASBJORNSON, HELEN E. (LONGSTRETH), real estate investment co. exec.; b. N.Y.C., Dec. 8, 1935; d. Clyde Marion and Elizabeth (Rudolph) Longstreth; B.A., State U. Iowa, 1957, J.D., 1959, postgrad., 1960; M.Ed., Mont. State Coll., 1961; postgrad. U. Minn., 1961-62; m. Norman H. Asbjornson, March 1963; children—Elizabeth Erica, Scott Marion. Mem. bus. adminstrn. staff Northwestern Bell Telephone Co., Omaha, 1959-60; bus. adminstrn. mgr. Diversified Equities, Mpls., 1961; research asst. U. Nebr., 1962; instr. Elkhorn (Nebr.) public schs., 1963-64. Vol. worker Children's Hosp.; active Omaha Symphony Guild, Women's Assn. of Joslyn Art Mus., Omaha Civic Music Assn. Mem. Am. Council Christian Ch., Amvets Aux., C. of C., Am. Legion Aux., State U. Iowa Alumni Assn., AAUW (legis. chmn.), Soc. Liberal Arts, Nat. Vocat. Guidance Assn., Inc., Am. Personnel and Guidance Assn., Inc., Nat. socs. profl. engrs. auxs., Omaha Montessori Soc., Neb. Hist. Soc., Airplane Owners' and Pilots' Assns., Am. Citizens' Forum, Mont. Guidance Assn., DAR (bd. dirs.), Mensa (highest group, Intertel), NOW, Minn. Fencing Assn., Les Amis du Vin, Bacchus Wine Soc., Psi Chi, Kappa Beta Pi (pres. chpt. 1957-58, del. Province conv. 1958). Republican. Protestant. Address: 6442 Margaret's Ln Edina MN 55435

ASCHER, AMALIE ADLER, author, journalist, lectr.; b. Balt.; d. Charles and Alene (Steiger) Adler; B.A., Goucher Coll., 1949; m. Eduard Ascher, May 18, 1954; children—Kenneth Charles Weinberg, Cynthia Cecille. Garden columnist Balt. Sunday Sun, 1976—, feature writer, 1968—, contbr. Sunday Sun mag., 1968—; hostess, writer The Flower Show, Md. Center for Public Broadcasting, 1973—; lectr. numerous states and fgn. countries, 1965—. Recipient Quill and Trowel award Garden Writers Assn. Am., 1980; Cert. of Merit for hort. lit. Nat. Council State Garden Clubs, Inc., 1975, named Flower Arranger of Year, 1973. Mem. Garden Writers Assn. Am. (dir. 1975-76), Indoor Gardening Nat. Council State Garden Clubs, Inc (dir., chmn. 1977-79), Authors Guild, Authors League, Am. Soc. Hort. Sci., Am. Inst. Floral Designers, Am. Hort. Soc., English Ceramic Circle. Republican. Jewish. Author: The Complete Flower Arranger, 1974. Contbr. numerous articles to various mags. and newspapers. Home and Office: 610 W 40th St Baltimore MD 21211

ASCHER, MARCIA PATRICIA GETELMAN, oil co. exec.; b. Bronx, N.Y., Mar. 17, 1939; d. Joseph and Mildred Barbara (Simkin) Getelman; B.A., SUNY, New Paltz, 1960; postgrad. Fairleigh Dickinson U., 1977-78; m. Robert C. Ascher, July 10, 1960; children—Russell Scott, Daryl Ileen. Import mgr. Keystone Camera Co., Clifton, N.J., 1976-78, Yorx Electronics Co., Totowa, N.J., 1978-79; adminstrv. v.p. Williston Oil Corp., Clifton, 1979—, sec., 1979—. Recipient gold medal award Deborah Hosp., 1970. Mem. Orgn. Rehab. through Tng. Democrat. Jewish. Home: 19 Copley Ct Wayne NJ 07470 Office: Williston Oil Corp 62 Mount Prospect Ave Clifton NJ 07015

ASCHER-NASH, FRANZI, writer; b. Vienna, Austria, Nov. 28, 1910; came to U.S., 1938, naturalized, 1944; d. Luise Frankl and Leo Ascher; grad. cum laude, Humanistisches Maedchengymnasium, Vienna, 1928; student Vienna Acad. Music, 1929-31; m. Edgar R. Nash, Nov. 21, 1959. Freelance short story writer, Vienna, 1934-38; after arrival in U.S., lectr. women's clubs under auspices of N.Y. Herald Tribune; music reviewer Neue Volkszeitung weekly, N.Y.C.; monthly light essay Austro-Am. Tribune; writer radio playlets German-Am. Writers Assn.; host short German lang. radio programs Sta. WBNX; tchr. New Sch. Social Research, N.Y.C.: writer annotations for classical records; host radio program The Story of the Art Song, Sta. WFUV-FM; readings of poetry, essays, short stories Sta. WNYC, N.Y.C.; lectr. on the art song; contbr. essays and poems German-Am. Studies mag., Lyrik und Prosa mag., Lyrica Germanica mag., Schatzkammer; author: (novella) Das Zwoelftonwunder, 1952; (novella) Confession in the Twilight (1st prize The Villager mag.), 1948; (books) Bilderbuch aus der Fremde, 1948, Gedichte eines Lebens, 1976, Lauf, lauf, Lebenslauf (a memoir), 1982; others; (anthologies) Reisegepaeck Sprache (pub. in bilingual version In Her Mother's Tongue 1982), 1980, Album of International Poets, 1981; also poetry. Recipient citation Soc. German-Am. Studies, 1973. Mem. Assn. German Lang. Authors in Am., Soc. German-Am. Studies (participant symposia on aspects of Am. music, pub. in various compendia entitled Occasional Papers), Literarische Union (W. Ger.), Tagore Inst. of Creative Writing (India). Club: B'nai B'rith. Home: 40-25 Hampton St Elmhurst NY 11373

ASH, BARBARA ANNE, lawyer; b. Buffalo, June 27, 1942; d. Donald F. and Evelyn T. Ash; A.B., U. Rochester (N.Y.), 1964; J.D., U. Kans., 1969; 1 dau., Alexandra Sarah. Admitted to N.Y. bar, 1969, Pa. bar, 1977; asso. firms in N.Y.C., 1969-76; mem. faculty Rutgers U. Coll. Law, 1976-81, Ohio State U. Coll. Law, 1981—; cons., ind. practice law, 1976—. Mem. Am. Bar Assn. Home: 1504 Essex Rd Columbus OH 43221 Office: 1659 N High St Columbus OH 43210

ASH, LINDA LEE, librarian; b. Watseka, Ill., Apr. 5, 1946; d. Carl Martin and Engelina Johanna (Wienrank) Duis; M.L.S., U. Ill., 1971; m. Lyn Gale Ash, Dec. 23, 1968; children—Nancy, Cynthia, Ryan. Media specialist Tolono (Ill.) Public Schs., 1969-70; librarian Fairbury-Cropsey (Ill.) Schs., 1970-72; media specialist Univ. High Sch., Ill. State U., Normal, 1972-73, dir. Coll. Edn. Instrnl. Materials Lab., 1979—, also librarian Spl. Edn. Instrnl. Materials Lab.; cons. material selection, adaptation for handicapped learners. Dir. ch. libraries St. John's Lutheran Ch., Bloomington, Ill. Mem. Council Exceptional Children, Internat. Reading Assn., Assn. Supervision and Curriculum Devel., Alpha Lambda Delta, Beta Phi Mu, Delta Kappa Gamma. Democrat. Lutheran. Compiler: Research in Arts and the Handicapped; An Annotated Bibliography, 1981. Home: 1409 Heritage Rd W Normal IL 61761 Office: 324 Fairchild Hall Ill State U Normal IL 61761

ASH, MARIANNE YEAGER, veterinarian; b. Logansport, Ind., Sept. 22, 1948; d. Charles Leonard and Helen Louise (Martin) Yeager; B.Mus. Edn., Northwestern U., 1970; D.V.M., Purdue U., 1977; m. Stephen R. Ash, Aug. 24, 1969; children—Emily Louise, Sarah Elizabeth. Staff veterinarian, dir. Yeager & Sullivan, Inc., Camden, Ind., 1977—, Triangle Feeds, Inc., 1977—, Star Roller Mills, Inc., 1977—. Mem. Am. Assn. Swine Practitioners, AVMA, Purdue Alumni Assn. Home: 2500 N 400 E St Lafayette IN 47905 Office: PO Box 11 Camden IN 46917

ASH, MARY ELLEN (MRS. JAMES THEODORE ASH), lawyer; b. Wichita, Kans., Oct. 3, 1908; d. Loyd Inman and Nora (Martin) Aldrich; Brown's Bus. Coll., 1925, Western Ill. U., 1926-27; LL.B., Columbus U., 1940; m. James Theodore Ash, Oct. 4, 1941 (dec. June 1969); 1 dau., Mary Jo (Mrs. E.O. Farley). Admitted to U.S. Dist. Court, U.S. Ct. of Appeals, 1941, Ill. bar, 1949; adjudicator Social Security Bd., Washington, 1940-41, Chgo., 1942-43; pvt. law practice, Mendota, Ill., 1956—. Mem. Ill. Bar Assn., Sigma Delta Kappa. Club: Mendota Woman's. Home and office: 909 21st St Mendota IL 61342

ASH, MARY KAY, cosmetics co. exec.; b. Hotwells, Tex., May 12; d. Edward Alexander and Lula Vember (Hastings) Wagner; student U. Houston, 1943-44; m. Melville Jerome Ash, Jan. 6, 1966 (dec.); children—Marylyn Cates, Ben Rogers, Richard Rogers. Unit mgr. Stanley Home Products, Easthampton, Mass., 1938-52; officer World Gift Co., Dallas, 1952-63; chmn. bd. Mary Kay Cosmetics, Inc., Dallas, 1963—; TV appearances, including 60 Minutes, Today, Donahue Show, 700 Club; speaker in field. Mem. Tex. Gov.'s Commn. on Status of Women, 1970; mem. Chancellor's Council, U. Tex., 1974-75; vol. Dallas County Community Action Com., 1975. Recipient Mktg. Citizenship award Memphis chpt. Am. Mktg. Assn., 1973; Hall of Fame award Direct Sales Assn., 1976; Leadership award Dale Carnegie, 1978; Horatio Alger award, 1978; Cosmetic Career Woman of Yr. award Cosmetic Career Women, Inc., 1978; Golden Plate award Am. Acad. Achievement, 1980; named Outstanding Corp. Sales Exec., Gallagher's Report, 1981. Republican. Baptist. Office: 8787 Stemmons Dallas TX 75247

ASH, VIRGINIA MARIA, piano tchr.; b. Rigby, Idaho, Apr. 22, 1918; d. Hugh Hastings and LaVera Maria (Jensen) Judd; student Cdlo. Woman's Coll., Denver, 1936-37; m. Henry Woodrow Ash, June 1, 1938; children—Anthony Woodrow, Fredric Judd, Rosalie Marie, David Charles. High sch. tchr., Moore, Idaho, 1946-47, Richfield, Idaho, 1947-49; newspaper reporter Buhl (Idaho) Herald, 1955-56, Citizen Record, Filer, Idaho, 1957-60; pvt. piano tchr., 1947—. Candidate for Mayor of Buhl, 1979; bd. dirs. Twin Falls Community Concert Assn., 1962-72. Mem. Twin Falls Music Club, Magic Valley Chorale, Idaho Writers League. Democrat. Clubs: Christian Woman's, Order Eastern Star (past matron). Author various articles, poetry. Address: 809 11th St Buhl ID 83316

ASHBROOK, BEULAH MAE, career counselor; b. Murray, Ky., Sept. 28, 1934; d. Eneas Hall and Cozette (Glisson) A.; B.S., Murray State U., 1955; M.A., Duke U., 1964; M.Ed., Memphis State U., 1971; Ed.D., U. Tenn., Knoxville, 1973. Med. technologist hosps. in Tenn. and N.C., 1956-60; teaching supr. Duke U., 1964-66; asst. prof. U. Tenn. med. units, Memphis, 1967-71; research asso. AMA, 1972-73; dir. edn. Am. Soc. Allied Health Professions, Washington, 1973-79; owner, pres. Ashbrook Assos., career devel. cons., Annapolis, Md., 1979—; lectr. George Mason U., Fairfax, Va. Fellow USPHS, 1962-63, NDEA, 1972. Mem. Am. Psychol. Assn., Am. Personnel and Guidance Assn., Am. Soc. Tng. and Devel., AAUW, USCG Aux. Republican. Methodist. Club: Order Eastern Star. Office: PO Box 1621 Annapolis MD 21404

ASHBURN, SARAH JO, ednl. evaluator; b. Graham, Tex., Dec. 23, 1939; d. Harold and Hattie Jo (Bryson) Heard; B.S., W. Tex. State U., 1963, M.A., 1966; Ed.D., Am. U., 1976; m. Pat Ashburn; children—Stephen, Sarah Elizabeth, Robert, Shirley Denise. Tchr., Boulder (Colo.) Valley Sch. Dist., 1966-67; social worker Prince William County (Va.) Dept. Public Welfare, 1968-69; research analyst Am. U., Washington, 1972-73; support tchr., evaluator Public Schs., Ithaca, N.Y., 1973-75; sr. research scientist Nat. Public Services Research Inst., Alexandria, Va., 1975-76; research and evaluation cons., Houston, 1977-78; evaluator Galveston (Tex.) Ind. Sch. Dist., 1978-80, dir. research and evaluation, 1980-81, exec. dir. curriculum and instrn., 1981—. Bd. mgrs. Bapt. Home for Children, 1971-73; mem. Bd. Christian Edn., Washington, 1974-76. Mem. Am. Psychol. Assn., Am. Ednl. Research Assn., Nat. Council Measurement in Edn., Assn. Children with Learning Disabilities, Assn. Supervision and Curriculum Devel., Tex. Assn. Planning, Evaluation and Research. Republican. Methodist. Home: 4330 Long Grove Dr Seabrook TX 77586 Office: PO Drawer 660 Galveston TX 77550

ASHBY, JENNIFER DOROTHY, physician; b. Southampton, Eng., June 21, 1939; came to U.S., 1963, naturalized, 1967; d. George and Annemarie (Gross) MacGregor; student Cheltenham (Eng.) Ladies Coll., 1955-57; M.B.B.S., St. Thomas Hosp. Med. Sch., London, 1962; m. Robert Ashby, 1963 (dec.); children—Jeannette, Colin, Denys. Intern, St. Luke's Hosp., St. Louis, 1963-64; tng. in dermatology Washington U., St. Louis, 1964-66, St. John's Hosp. for Diseases of Skin, London, 1970-71; staff dermatologist Truman Med. Center, Kansas City, Mo., 1971-81; asst. prof., docent U. Mo. Sch. Medicine, Kansas City, 1972-76, asso. prof., docent, 1976-77, asso. prof. medicine, 1977-81, asso. clin. prof., 1981—; practice medicine specializing in dermatology, Kansas City, 1981—; mem. staffs St. Mary's Hosp., Trinity Lutheran Hosp. Co-founder, v.p. Psychic Studies Inst., Kansas City, 1975—. Mem. Am. Acad. Dermatology, AMA, Am. Med. Women's Assn., Soc. Philosophy and Medicine, S.W. Clin. Soc., Mo. Med. Assn., Jackson County Med. Soc., Psychic Research Soc. Kansas City (co-founder), Spiritual Frontiers Fellowship (life). Office: 2900 Baltimore Kansas City MO 64108

ASHCRAFT, JOY HILL, med. technologist; b. Jacksonville, Fla., Nov. 1, 1942; d. James Lloyd and Hazel (Miles) Hill; A.A., Central Fla. Jr. Coll., 1962; B.A., Fla. State U., 1964; m. Ronald Eugene Ashcraft, Dec. 29, 1974; 1 son, Brian Eugene. Med. technologist Piedmont Hosp., Atlanta, 1966-68; med. technologist Parkland Meml. Hosp., Dallas, 1968-78, teaching supr. hematology, 1968-70, Sch. Med. Tech., 1970-72, asst. supr. hematology lab., 1973-78. Sponsor, The 500 Inc., Dallas. Named Clin. Tchr. of Yr. in Hematology, Parkland Meml. Hosp., 1978. Mem. Dallas Symphony Assn., Dallas Mus. Fine Arts, Am. Soc. Clin. Pathologists, Phi Theta Kappa. Episcopalian. Clubs: Park Cities Women of Rotary (pres.), Dallas Knife and Fork.

ASHCRAFT, LAURIE CRAGG, consumer products co. mgr.; b. Washington, May 28, 1945; d. Richard Edwards and Dorothy (Shawhan) Cragg; B.A., Northwestern U., 1967; m. W. Dale Ashcraft, Sept. 3, 1977. Research analyst Allstate Ins. Co., Northbrook, Ill., 1968-70; project supr. Marsteller, Inc., Chgo., 1970-74; mktg. research mgr. corporate mktg. dept. Internat. Harvester, Chgo., 1974-76; asso. dir. mktg. research Libby, McNeill & Libby, Chgo., 1976-78; project mgr. mktg. research S.C. Johnson, Racine, Wis., 1978-80; mktg. research mgr. Softsoap div. Minnetonka, Inc. (Minn.), 1980—; guest lectr. market research various univs. and assns. Mem. Am. Mktg. Assn. (Meritorious Service award 1975; chmn. career conf. 1975, dir. chpt. 1975—), Jr. League Mpls., NOW, Alliance Française, Alpha Delta Pi. Club: Woman's Athletic. Research collaborator: The Coming Matriarchy, 1981. Home: 2721 W 47th St Minneapolis MN 55410 Office: PO Box 1A Minnetonka MN 55410

ASHCRAFT, VIRGINIA CARSON, fin. analyst; b. Tegucigalpa, Honduras, Mar. 12, 1949; came to U.S., 1952; d. Howard William and Nelda (Hoover) A.; B.A., Smith Coll., 1971; postgrad. N.Y. U., 1972-76, M.B.A., 1979; m. John Willard Everitt, Sept. 24, 1977. With Morgan Guaranty Trust Co. of N.Y., N.Y.C., 1971—, comml. bank mgmt. program, 1971-72, fin. analysis dept., non-ferrous metals industry, 1972-77, chem. industry, 1977, bus. devel. group, v.p., 1977—. Chartered fin. analyst. Mem. N.Y. Soc. Security Analysts, Inst. Chartered Fin. Analysts.

ASHCROFT, MARY CATHERINE, state legislator; b. Bellows Falls, Vt., June 26, 1953; B.S., U. Vt., 1974; J.D., Cath. U. Am., 1979; practice law, Bellows Falls, Vt.; mem. Vt. Ho. of Reps., 1980—. Vice-chairperson Rockingham Planning Commn.; vice-chairperson Rockingham Zoning Bd. Adjustment; chairperson Mcpl. Govt. Merger Study Com. of Rockingham; mem. Bellows Falls Crime Prevention Task Force; mem. Rockingham Democratic Com., Windham County Dem. Com.; past zoning adminstr., health officer Rockingham, Vt. Mem. Bellows Falls Hist. Soc., ABA, Vt. Bar Assn. Office: Vt Ho of Reps State House Montpelier VT 05602 *

ASHDOWN, MARIE MATRANGA (MRS. CECIL SPANTON ASHDOWN, JR.), writer, lectr.; b. Mobile, Ala.; d. Dominick and Ave (Mallon) Matranga; student Maryville Coll. Sacred Heart, Springhill Coll.; m. Cecil Spanton Ashdown, Jr.; children—John Stephen Gartman, Vivian Marie Gartman, Cecil Spanton III, Charles Coster. Feature star daily program Sta. WALA, also WALA-TV, Mobile; photographer, model for Louise Sheridan, Mobile; now instr. continuing edn. Marymount-Manhattan Coll. Mem. Am. Women in Radio and TV, Am. Businesswomen's Assn. Recipient cert. of merit for extraordinary service March of Dimes. Mem. Nat. Inst. Social Scis. Contbr. to Opera Mementos, Time-Life Collectibles Series. Home: 25 Sutton Pl S New York NY 10022

ASHE, AMELIA H., educator; b. Bklyn., Oct. 16, 1916; d. Isadore M. and Sophie (Yancovici) Haimowitz; B.A., Hunter Coll., 1938; M.A. in English, Bklyn. Coll., 1945, M.A. in Guidance and Counseling, 1955; Ph.D. in Guidance and Personnel, N.Y.U., 1966; m. Murray Wexler, June 20, 1937 (dec. 1961); children—Richard Mark, Susan Ellen (Mrs. Stuart Lahn); m. 2d, David I. Ashe, Dec. 26, 1962. Tchr. English, Far Rockaway High Sch., N.Y.C., 1948-59; guidance counselor Plainview (L.I.) High Sch., N.Y., 1959-63; supr. NDEA Inst. Counseling, Bklyn. Coll., summer 1963; instr. guidance and personnel dept. Sch. Edn., N.Y.U., 1963-67, supr. NDEA Inst., 1963-64; asst. prof., coordinator grad. program in guidance and counseling Richmond Coll., City U. N.Y., 1967-69, asso. prof., 1970-74, prof. emeritus, 1974—; chmn. com. coordinators grad. programs in guidance and counseling City U. N.Y., 1971-74; cons. Center Urban Edn., N.Y. State Dept. Edn.; dir. Consortium for Bilingual Counselor Edn., 1972-73, 74-75. Mem. N.Y.C. Bd. Edn., 1974—, v.p., 1981—, N.Y.C. Tchrs. Retirement Bd., 1978—. Mem. AAUP, N.Y. Acad. Public Edn., Kappa Delta Pi, Alpha Epsilon Phi. Home: 1020 Park Ave New York NY 10028 Office: Bd Edn 110 Livingston St Brooklyn NY 11201

ASHER, JANE FITZGERALD (MRS. JACK O'HAIR ASHER), lawyer; b. Little Rock, Dec. 3, 1929; d. Sam L. and Georgia Duffey (Hubbert) Fitzgerald; A.A., Los Angeles City Coll., 1951; student UCLA, 1951-52; J.D., Tulane U., 1957; m. Jack O'Hair Asher, Aug. 22, 1957; children—Duffey Ann, William Michael Fitzgerald, John Russell II (dec.). Admitted to La. bar, 1957, Alaska bar, 1959, U.S. Ct. of Appeals bar, 1960, Ill. bar, 1968; law clk. U.S. Dist. Ct. of Alaska, Juneau, 1957-58; atty. Vets. Affairs Commn., Juneau, 1958-59; asst. atty. gen. State of Alaska, Juneau, 1959-60, reviser of statutes, 1960-67; counsel judiciary coms. Alaska Senate, 1963-66, Alaska House, 1965-66; mem. firm Dillavou, Overaker, Asher and Smith, Paris, Ill. Chmn. Alaska Am. Cancer Soc. Crusade, 1959; sec. Juneau-Douglas Concert Assn., 1961-62, treas., 1962-66; dir. Gold Creek Summer Theatre, 1964-66; v.p., mgr. Edgar County Concert Assn., 1969-79; bd. dirs. Juneau-Douglas Little Theatre, 1961-62, 64-65, YMCA, Paris, Ill., 1969-71; bd. dirs. Edgar County Children's Home, 1968—, treas., 1981—; v.p. Hangar, Inc., teen-age center, 1972-81; mem. regional adv. com. Ill. Dept. Children and Family Services, 1980—; pres. bd. dirs. Paris Tiger Tots Nursery, 1969-73; del. Ill. Conf. on Children's Priorities for 80s, 1981. Mem. Alaska, Am., La., Ill. bar assns., Nat. Women Lawyers (state del. 1959-67), Nat. LWV, AAUW, Phi Delta Delta. Club: Quota (treas. Juneau chpt. 1961-62, dir. 1962-64). Home: Box 501 Chicago Rd Paris IL 61944 Office: 236 W Court St Paris IL 61944

ASHINOFF, SUSAN JANE, menswear mfg. co. exec.; b. N.Y.C., Dec. 7, 1949; d. Lawrence Lloyd and Thelma B. (Rubens) A.; A.A., Dean Jr. Coll., 1969; B.A., Finch Coll., 1971; M.P.A., N.Y.U., 1977. Advt. coordinator menswear advt. New Yorker mag., N.Y.C., 1971-72; asso. Staub, Warrmbold & Assos., exec. search co., N.Y.C., 1972-80; exec. v.p. Muhammad Ali Sportswear, Ltd., N.Y.C., 1980-81; pres. Forum Sportswear, Ltd., N.Y.C., 1981—; pres. Coronet Licensing Corp., N.Y.C., 1980—. Mem. Nat. Assn. Men's Sportswear Buyers, Sporting Goods Mfrs. Assn., Men's Apparel Guild Calif., Am. Mgmt. Assn. Office: 350 Fifth Ave New York NY 10118

ASHLAND, EMELYNE IDA ANDREA, educator; b. Chgo., Oct. 29, 1910; d. Gustav A. and Ida Frances (Alex) A.; B.S., U. Chgo., 1931, S.M., 1933; postgrad. U. Calif. at Berkeley, 1939, U. Colo., 1940. Silhouette artist Century of Progress World's Fair, Chgo., 1933; trade mark artist Colgate-Palmolive Peet Co., Chgo., 1933-34; artist non-verbal IQ Test I.J.R., 1934; med. social worker Unemployment Relief Services, Chgo., illustrator Hygeia mag., 1934-35; tchr. Sterling Twp. (Ill.) High Sch., 1936-37, Chgo. Pub. High Schs., 1937-76; pioneer in traffic safety edn., 1948-51; evaluator sci. materials representing Chgo. South Side schs., 1948-51. Recipient certificate of appreciation Lake County Health Dept., 1976. Mem. Chgo. Tchrs. Union (charter), Soc. Circumnavigators (mem. Marco Polo club). Baptist. Researcher tomato canker incitant: Aplanobactor Michiganese; author (with Tsu-kiang Yen) Devel. of Flower and Fruit of Myrica Rubra, pub. China, 1950. Home: 773 Marion Ave Highland Park IL 60035

ASHLEY, BETH MACVICAR, editor; b. Newton, Mass., May 21, 1926; d. Guy Mortimer and Marion Croft (Whyte) MacVicar; B.A. in Journalism and Polit. Sci., Stanford U., 1947; m. Ross Warren Ashley, July 8, 1959 (dec.); children—Kenneth, Jeffrey, Peter, Gilbert, Guy. Program dir. sta. KTIM, San Rafael, Calif., 1947; reporter, city editor Inglewood (Calif.) Daily News, 1948-49; editor, reporter Dept. State news mag., Frankfurt-Munich-Berlin, 1949-51; news editor San Rafael Ind.-Jour., 1952-59, Lifestyle editor, 1974—. Bd. dirs. Marin County chpt. ARC, 1974-81, Marin Sr. Coordinating Council, 1978—, Coll. Marin Found., 1978—, Marin Civic Ballet, 1979—, Internat. Center Marin, 1976—. Mem. AAUW (hon. life), Phi Beta Kappa, Sigma Delta Chi, Theta Sigma Phi. Republican. Episcopalian. Home: 348 Bretano Way Greenbrae CA 94904 Office: Box 330 San Rafael CA 94915 also Alameda Del Prado Novato CA 94947

ASHLEY, ELIZABETH, actress; b. Ocala, Fla., Aug. 30, 1941; d. Arthur Kingman and Lucille (Ayer) Cole; student ballet with Tatiana Semenova; student La. State U., 1957-58; grad. Neighborhood Playhouse, N.Y.C., 1961; m. George Peppard (div.); 1 son, Christian Moore; m. 3d, James Michael McCarthy. Appeared on Broadway in The Highest Tree, 1961; Take Her, She's Mine, 1962; Barefoot in the Park, 1963, Agnes of God, 1982; appeared movies The Carpet Baggers, 1963, Ship of Fools, 1964, The Third Day, 1965, Marriage of a Young Stockbroker, 1971, Paperback Hero, 1974, Golden Needles, 1974, Rancho Deluxe, 1975, 92 in the Shade, 1976, The Great Scout and Cathouse Thursday, 1976, Coma, 1978, Windows, 1980, Paternity, 1981; TV movies include Second Chance, 1972, The Heist, 1972, Your Money or Your Wife, 1972; stage appearances include The Enchanted, Washington, 1973, The Skin of Our Teeth, Washington, 1975, Broadway, 1975, Cat on a Hot Tin Roof, Stratford, Conn. and Broadway, 1974; appeared approximately 200 TV films. Apptd. Pres.'s council 1st Nat. Council on the Arts, 1965-69; dir. Am. Film Inst., 1968-72. Recipient Antoinette Perry award, 1962. Mem. Actors Equity, Screen Actors Guild, AFTRA. Author: Postcards from the Road, 1978. Office: care William Morris Agy Inc 1350 Ave of Americas New York NY 10019 *

ASHLEY, FREDDIE JEAN MARTIN, sales rep.; b. Tuscaloosa, Ala., Oct. 16, 1935; d. Fred Franklin and Bess Estelle (Langley) Martin; B.F.A., U. Ala., 1956; children—Ross T., Richard M., Robert F. Mgr. wallpaper, color cons. Cole Supply Co., Tuscaloosa, 1953-55; exec. sec. to pres. Chemoil Corp., New Orleans, 1957-59; account exec. Arrow Bus. Interiors, Memphis, 1974-76; exec. sales rep. Johns-Manville, Memphis, 1979—; partner ASP Partnership, real estate, 1980—. Bd. dirs. 19th Century Club, 1962-70; chmn. Germantown (Tenn.) Horse Show, 1964; youth coordinator Christ United Meth. Ch., 1971-73; bd. dirs. Republican Women's Club, 1972-73, state del., 1973; co-founder Germantown Community Theatre, 1973, bd. dirs., 1973-75. Mem. Bus. and Profl. Women's Club. Home: 1248 Faxon Ave Memphis TN 38104 Office: Ken-Caryl Ranch Denver CO

ASHLEY, LORYANA KIM, painter; b. N.Y.C., Oct. 10, 1949; d. John A. and Teresa (Kamienska) Rogers; student Royal Acad. Art, London, Mus. Modern Art, N.Y.C. One-woman exhbns. include Harkness House Gallery, N.Y.C., 1978, Royal Acad. Art, 1978, Studio 5, Milan, Italy, 1970.

ASHLEY, MERRILL, ballerina; b. St. Paul; attended Sch. Am. Ballet. With N.Y.C. Ballet, 1967—, prin. dancer, 1977—, leading roles in George Balanchine's Ballo della Regina and Ballade; has appeared in Flower Festival at Genzano, The Four Seasons, Jewels, Allegro Brillante, Vienna Waltzes, In the Night, In G Major, Goldberg Variations, Raymonda, Cortege Hongrois, Suite #3, Square Dance, Dances at a Gathering, Donizetti Variations; appeared in Public TV series Dance in America. Office: New York City Ballet Lincoln Center Plaza New York NY 10023 *

ASHMORE, BETTIE JANE, psychologist; b. Birmingham, Ala., Oct. 2, 1930; d. Henry Grady and Hazel Irene (Miller) A.; B.A., U. N. Ala., 1954; M.A. in Counseling and Clin. Psychology, U. Ala., 1957, Ph.D., 1968. Counselor, Miami Dade Jr. Coll. (Fla.), 1961-65; coordinator counseling Auburn (Ala.) U., 1967-68; field assessment officer (clin. psychologist) Peace Corps Brazil, U. Wis., Milw., 1968; clin. psychologist Mobile (Ala.) Mental Health Center, 1968-74, clin. dir. treatment services Gateway Drug Treatment Center, 1974-79, catchment area dir. Mobile County Community Mental Health Services, Inc., 1979—; staff cons., group therapy leader Crittenton Home; asst. prof. evening div. dept. psychology U. South Ala.; mem. allied profl. staff U. South Ala. Med. Center Hosp. and Clinics, Mobile; mem. Ala. Bd. Examiners in Psychology, 1974-79, vice chairperson, 1976-79; mem. adv. bd. Allied Health Occupations Program, Bishop State Jr. Coll.; mem. bd. profl. advisors Mastin Sch. Nursing, Mobile Gen. Hosp., 1973-74. Lic. clin., counseling, ednl. psychologist, Ala. Mem. Am. Psychol. Assn. (CHAMPUS reviewer 1978-81, peer trainer 1981—), Ala. Psychol. Assn., Mobile County Psychol. Assn. Contbr. articles to profl. jours. Home: 6159 Saint Gallen Ave S Mobile AL 33608 Office: 2400 Gordon Smith Dr Mobile AL 33617

ASHMORE, CARRIE MAE, educator; b. Springfield, Tenn., Mar. 5, 1923; d. James Dean and Vera Louvenia (Osborne) Barbee; student Tenn. State U., 1941-43; B.S., Wilberforce U., 1946; postgrad. Atlanta U., 1957-60, Chgo. State U., 1965, 70, 71, Roosevelt U., 1967, 68, 73; m. Edward Travis Ashmore, July 23, 1945; children—Travis Dean and Edward Lane (twins), Juanita Sherri, Angela Jean and Angelo Gene (twins), Andre Bernard. Tchr., Bransford High Sch., Springfield, Tenn., 1946-48; sec. Murrays Superior Products, Chgo., 1948-49; adminstrv. asst. Atlanta U., 1949-60; tchr. Atlanta Public Schs., 1960-62, Gary (Ind.) Public Schs., 1962-64, Wendell Phillips High Sch., Chgo., 1964-68; tchr. Hyde Park Career Acad., Chgo., 1969—; mem. tchr. corps project of Hyde Park Career Acad. and Roosevelt U. Recipient Am. Legion medal, 1941. Mem. Chgo. Assn. of Mentally Retarded, Lambda Eta Sigma, Zeta Sigma Pi. Methodist. Home: 422 W 98th St Chicago IL 60628 Office: 6220 S Stony Island Ave Chicago IL 60637

ASHTON, DORE, author, educator; b. Newark; d. Ralph N. and Sylvia (Ashton) Shapiro; B.A., U. Wis., 1949; M.A., Harvard, 1950; Ph.D. honoris causa, Moore Coll., 1975, Hamline U., 1982; m. Adja Yunkers, July 8, 1952; children—Alexandra Louise, Marina Svietlana. Asso. editor Art Digest, 1951-54; asso. critic N.Y. Times, 1955-60; lectr. Pratt Inst., 1962-63; head humanities dept. Sch. Visual Arts, 1965-68; prof. Cooper Union, 1968—; art critic, lectr., dir. exhbns. Bd. dirs. Found. for Edn. in Arts; adv. bd. John Simon Guggenheim Found.; chmn. Freedom to Write Com. of P.E.N. Recipient Mather award for art criticism Coll. Art Assn., 1963; Guggenheim fellow, 1964; Graham fellow, 1963; Ford Found. fellow, 1960; Nat. Endowment for Humanities grantee, 1980. Mem. Internat. Assn. Art Critics, Coll. Art Assn., Soc. Fellows N.Y.U., Phi Beta Kappa. Author: Abstract Art Before Columbus, 1957; Poets and the Past, 1959; Philip Guston, 1960; The Unknown Shore, 1962; Rauschenberg's Dante, 1964; Modern American Sculpture, 1968; Richard Lindner, 1969; A Reading of Modern Art, 1970; Pol Bury, 1971; New York (cultural guide), 1972; Picasso on Art, 1972; The New York School: A Cultural Reckoning, 1973; A Joseph Cornell Album, 1974; Yes, But, A Critical Biography of Philip Guston, 1976; A Fable of Modern Art, 1980; co-author: Rosa Bonheur, A Life and Legend, 1981; co-editor: Redon, Moreau, Bresdin, 1961; N.Y. contbg. editor Am. Art, 1945—, Studio Internat., 1961-74, Opus Internat., 1968-74, XXième Siècle, 1955-70, Arts, 1974—. Contbr. to Vision and Value series (Gyorgy Kepes), 1966, The New Art Anthology (Gregory Battcock), 1966. Home: 217 E 11th St New York NY 10003

ASHWORTH, PATRICIA LOU, educator; b. Moundsville, W.Va., May 5, 1926; d. Earl McCoy and Mabel Virginia (Pickett) Robinson; B.A., W.Va. U., 1948, M.A., 1950; m. John C. Ashworth, Sept. 2, 1950; children—Robin Ann Ashworth Tice, Melinda Lou. Instr., Waynesburg Coll., 1948-49, W.Va. U., 1950-51; instr. to prof. English, Beckley (W. Va.) Coll., 1964—, dean of women, 1966-78, chmn. English, chmn. div. fine arts, 1978—; mem. W.Va. Writing Project, 1980; adj. W.Va. Coll. Grad. Studies, 1980-81. Charter mem. Friends of Raleigh County Library, Community Concert Assn.; adv. bd. Woman's Resource Center, 1978-81; treas. Altar Guild, United Methodist Temple, 1978-82. Cert. life tchr., W.Va. Mem. W.Va. Coll. English Tchrs. (charter), W.Va. Speech Assn., W.Va. Writers (charter), Nat. Council Tchrs. of English, Southeastern Council Linguistics, Delta Kappa Gamma, Alpha Xi Delta. Clubs: Beckley Woman's (sec. 1980—), W.Va. U. Alumni (life), W.Va. Bar Aux. Home: 300 Glenn Ave Beckley WV 25801 Office: Beckley College S Kanawha St Beckley WV 25801

ASKEY, DELORES REGINA GILLUM, educator; b. Detroit, Nov. 12, 1948; d. Lloyd and Sallie (Whitsett) Gillum; B.S., Fisk U., 1970; M.S. (scholar), Syracuse U., 1971; 1 dau., Khalilah Maisha. Tchr. remedial and devel. reading Syracuse (N.Y.) Public Schs., 1970-71; tchr., counselor Upward Bound program Howard U., 1974; tchr. D.C. Public Schs., Washington, 1971-74; dir. health, edn. and service program Georgetown U. Med. Center, Washington, 1974-78; dir. health edn. Howard-Georgetown Comprehensive Cancer Center, Washington, 1978—; cons. in field; bd. advisors D.C. Citizens for Better Public Edn., D.C. Lung Assn., Operation PUSH Health com. Mem. Nat. Council Negro Women, AAHPER, D.C. Sci. Fair Assn., YWCA, NAACP, Alpha Kappa Alpha. Office: 2041 Georgia Ave NW Washington DC 20060

ASPINWALL, VALERIE GAY REICHMAN, broadcasting exec.; b. N.Y.C., Aug. 12, 1937; d. Gerson and Vivian Frances (Cohen) Reichman; B.A., Bennington Coll., 1959; postgrad. N.Y. U. Grad. Sch. Lit.; m. Everett H. Aspinwall, Jr., Apr. 18, 1964. Editorial asst. Bantam Books, N.Y.C., 1959-60; with program and news depts. ABC-TV, N.Y.C., 1960-65; editor Playboy Press, Chgo., 1965-66; public info. officer Am. Film Inst., Washington, 1968-69; public relations cons. Design Center, Inc., Washington, 1966-68, David Apter & Assos., Washington, 1969-73; co-owner, program dir. Sta. WPBR, Palm Beach, Fla., 1973—. Bd. dirs., public edn. and info. chmn. Palm Beach Area chpt. Leukemia Soc. Am., 1974—; dir.-at-large, public relations chmn., 2d v.p. Palm Glades council Girl Scouts U.S.A., 1976—; exec. bd., sec. Palm Beach Festival, Inc. Named Woman of Yr., Palm Beach County Commn. on Status of Women. Mem. Nat. Broadcast Editorial Assn., Women in Communications (v.p. Palm Beach chpt.), Am. Advt. Fedn., Advt. Club Palm Beaches (dir. 1975-76), Palm Beach Round Table (dir. 1974-76), Common Cause. Home: 3475 S Ocean Blvd Palm Beach FL 33480 Office: Sta WPBR 3000 S Ocean Blvd Palm Beach FL 33480

ASPREY, MARGARET SUSAN, computer co. mgr.; b. Los Alamos, June 25, 1952; d. Larned Brown and Margaret Elizabeth (Williams) A.; B.S., U. Calif., Davis, 1974; postgrad. Stanford U.; m. Richard F. Lyon, July 28, 1981. Software engr. GTE, Mountain View, Calif., 1974-76; mem. sci. staff Bell No. Research, Palo Alto, Calif., 1976-79; cons., Santa

Clara, Calif., 1979-80; vis. scientist Xerox Palo Alto Research Center, 1980-81; mgr. telephony software engring. D.A.V.I.D. Systems, Inc., Cupertino, Calif., 1981—; lectr. Stanford U., 1981-82. Mem. Assn. Computing Machinery, IEEE. Democrat. Office: 10062 Miller Ave Palo Alto CA *

ASPRIDY, CHRISOULA, educator; b. Rochester, May 9, 1926; d. John Louis and Eleny Dimitri (Misirlis) A.; B.A., U. Rochester, 1948, Ed.D., 1971; M.Ed., SUNY, Brockport, 1964. Tchr., Dundalk (Md.) Schs., 1949-51; exec. sec. Haloid Co., Rochester, N.Y., 1951-60; tchr. East Irondequoit (N.Y.) Schs., 1961—; founding dir. Rochester Montessori and Clover Montessori Schs.; dir. Rochester Children's House. Eastman Sch. Music scholar, 1935-41. Mem. Internat. Reading Assn., Delta Kappa Gamma. Greek Orthodox. Club: Garden Center of Rochester. Developer STICK-LES Alphabet Constrn. Kit, STICK-LES Alphabet Maps. Home: 2986 Lyell Rd Rochester NY 14606 Office: 95 Point Pleasant Rd Rochester NY 14622

ASTARITA, SUSAN GALLAGHER, communications co. exec.; b. Wilmington, Del., Oct. 6, 1941; d. Hugh Francis and Alice Clara (Pepper) Gallagher; A.B. in Polit Sci., Randolph-Macon Woman's Coll., 1963; M.A. in Comparative Govt., Georgetown U., 1973; postgrad. U. So. Calif., 1973-75; m. Bruce Thomas Astarita, May 24, 1969; 1 dau., Alice Catherine. Adminstrv. asst. George Washington U., Washington, 1964, Ford Found. grantee Nat. Assn. Edn. Broadcasters, Washington, 1965-66; asst. producer Youth Wants To Know, Theodore Granik Enterprises, Washington, 1966-68; community and public relations dir. Del. Tech. and Community Coll., Georgetown, 1968-72; writer-editor Inst. Indsl. Relations, UCLA, 1975-77; pres. Susan Astarita Communications, Rolling Hills Estates, Calif., 1977—; lectr. Harbor Coll. Bd. dirs. The Assos. (Palos Verdes Community Arts Assn.), 1977-79, Palos Verdes Symphony, 1978-79; mem. peninsula com. Calif. State U., Dominguez Hills. Mem. Women in Communications (dir. Los Angeles chpt. 1980—), Palos Verdes Peninsula C. of C. Democrat. Episcopalian. Office: 777 Silver Spur Rd Rolling Hills Estates CA 90274

ASTERITA, MARY FRANCES, physiologist; b. N.Y.C.; d. Martin A. and Mary L. (diPalma) A.; B.A., Marymount Coll., 1961; M.S., N.Y.U., 1969; Ph.D., Cornell U., 1973. Postdoctoral fellow Yale Univ. Sch. Medicine, New Haven, 1973-75; asst. prof. physiology Ind. U. Sch. Medicine, Gary, 1975—, dir. clin. biofeedback programs, 1980—; mem. research review com. Am. Heart Assn., 1979—. NIH fellow, 1974-75. Mem. Biofeedback Soc. Am., Biofeedback Soc. Ill. bd. of dir. 1980—, pres. 1982—), Am. Assn. Biofeedback Clinicians, Am. Physiol. Soc., Am. Heart Assn., Nat. Speakers Assn., Internat. Platform Assn. Contbr. articles to profl. jours. Office: 3400 Broadway Gary IN 46408

ASTIN, PATTY DUKE (ANNA MARIE DUKE), actress; b. N.Y.C., Dec. 14, 1946; d. John P. and Frances (McMahon) Duke; grad. Quintano's School for Young Profls.; m. 3d, John Astin, 1973. TV appearances include Armstrong Circle Theatre, 1955, The Prince and the Pauper, 1957, Wuthering Heights, 1958, U.S. Steel Hour, Meet Me in St. Louis, 1959, Swiss Family Robinson, 1958, The Power and the Glory, 1961, numerous others; theatrical appearances include The Miracle Worker, 1959-61, Isle of Children, 1962; motion picture appearance in The Miracle Worker (Acad. award as best supporting actress 1963), 1962, Valley of the Dolls, 1967, Me, Natalie (Golden Globe award as best actress 1970), 1969, My Sweet Charlie, 1970, appeared in TV series Patty Duke Show, 1963-64 (Emmy award as best actress 1964), TV film Before and After, 1979, Having Babies, The Women's Room, Captains and the Kings (Emmy award as best actress 1977). Corp. council Muscular Dystrophy Assns. Am. Address: care Kramer & Reiss 9100 Sunset Blvd Suite 240 Los Angeles CA 90069

ASTOR, MRS., VINCENT, found. exec., civic worker; b. Portsmouth, N.H.; d. John Henry and Mabel (Howard) Russell; LL.D. (hon.), Columbia U., 1971, Brown U., 1980; L.H.D. (hon.), Fordham U., 1980; m. Vincent Astor. Feature editor House and Garden, N.Y.C.; now pres., trustee Vincent Astor Found., N.Y.C.; v.p., trustee Astor Home for Children; trustee Marconi Internat. Fellowship, Sleepy Hollow Restorations; bd. overseers Cornell U. Med. Coll.; mem. bd. Library of Am.; trustee, chmn. Far Eastern art, com. mem. Met. Mus. Art, N.Y.C.; trustee and hon. chmn., mem. devel. com., mem. exec. com. N.Y. Public Library, N.Y.C.; trustee, mem. conservation com., mem. exec. com., hon. chmn. women's com. N.Y. Zool. Soc.; trustee, mem. exec. com., mem. council of fellows Pierpont Morgan Library; trustee, mem. exec. com. Rockefeller U.; mem. N.Y. State Park Commn., 1967-69; mem. Mrs. Lyndon Johnson's Beautification Com., Washington. Decorated dame Venerable Order of St. John of Jerusalem; recipient Anniversary medal N.Y. Public Library Astor, Lenox and Tilden Founds., 1961, award Sisters of Good Shepherd and Children of Madona Hts. Sch. for Girls, 1963, Client Award cert. N.Y. State Assn. Architects, 1964, Honor award HUD, 1966, cert. appreciation City N.Y., 1967, Michael Friedsam medal Archtl. League N.Y., 1968, award Brotherhood-In-Action, Inc., 1968, Outstanding Contbn. award Am. Soc. Landscape Architects, 1968, Spirit of Achievement award Albert Einstein Coll. Medicine, Yeshiva U., 1969, Good Samaritan award P. Ballentine & Sons, 1969, Prospect Block Civic Assn., 1969; Albert Gallatin medal N.Y. U., 1972, spl. citation AIA, 1973, Medal of Merit award Lotos Club, 1973. Pres.'s medal Mcpl. Art Soc., 1976, Gold Medal award N.Y. Zool. Soc., 1978, Elizabeth Seton Humanitarian award N.Y. Foundling Hosp., 1978, Little Apple award Met. Mus. Art, Morgan Library, N.Y. Public Library, N.Y. Zool. Soc. Rockefeller U., South St. Seaport and Sta.-WNET-TV/Channel 13, 1978, Albert S. Bard Merit award in urban landscape architecture City Club N.Y., 1967, Bishop's Cross, 1980; Forsythia award Bklyn. Bot. Garden, 1981, Women of Conscience award Appeal of Conscience Found., 1981, gold medal Nat. Inst. Social Sci., 1981, numerous others. Mem. Pilgrims of U.S., Mcpl. Art Soc., Navy League, Nat. Park Found. (asso.), Asia Soc., China Soc., Japan Soc. Clubs: Colony, Grolier, Sleepy Hollow, Coffee House, River, Knickerbocker. Author: Patchwork Child; The Bluebird is at Home; Footprints. Address: Astor (The Vincent) Found 405 Park Ave New York NY 10022

ASTUDILLO, MARY ELLEN, conv. bur. exec.; b. Weatherford, Tex., July 9, 1936; d. Escal Franklin and Nellie (Frantz) Duke; student Hardin Simmons U., 1954-57; B.A., U. Tex., 1959; m. Louis Astudillo, Sept. 6, 1959 (div.); children—Mariana, Louis. Account exec. Stas. Y95 FM and KIXY-AM, San Angelo, Tex., 1974-80, producer, hostess Sunday Concert, weekly radio program, 1974-80; account exec., producer and hostess classical music program Sta. KBIL-FM, San Angelo, 1980-82; dir. sales Conv. and Visitors Bur. San Angelo, 1982—. Mem. San Angelo Tourist and Conv. Bd., 1979-80, pres., 1980; bd. dirs. Concho Cadre, 1977-78, San Angelo Civic Theater. Mem. San Angelo Advt. Fedn. (dir.), San Angelo Press Club (dir.), AAUW. Democrat. Baptist. Home: 2606 Palo Duro Apt 177 San Angelo TX 76901 Office: 500 Rio Concho Dr San Angelo TX 76903

ASWAD, BETSY (BECKER), writer, educator; b. Binghamton, N.Y., Feb. 10, 1939; d. George Marrinan and Jane (Sprout) Becker; B.A. with high honors in English, Harpur Coll., Binghamton, 1961; M.A., SUNY, Binghamton, 1965, Ph.D. with distinction, 1973; m. Richard N. Aswad, Sept. 22, 1962; children—Richard, Kristin. Mem. film editing staff Sta. WNBF-TV, Binghamton, 1957; apprentice So. Tier Playhouse, summers 1957, 58; asst. editor Link Log, 1962-63; teaching asst., then instr. English, SUNY, Binghamton, 1963-74, mem. adj. faculty, 1974—, fellow Coll.-in-the Woods, 1973. Sec., Friends of Binghamton Public Library, 1977-78; co-program chmn. Tappan Circle, First Presbyn. Ch., Binghamton, 1979-80; vol. Probe, Binghamton Gen. Hosp., 1978-79, Meals on Wheels, 1979—. Author: Winds of the Old Days (Edgar Allan Poe spl. award Mystery Writers Am.), 1980. Home: 192 Deyo Hill Rd Binghamton NY 13905 Office: English Dept State Univ Binghamton NY 13901

ATCHINSON, BETTY MAY HAFER, sch. prin.; b. Mt. Pleasant, Mich., May 13, 1933; d. Bernard James and Elizabeth Rosella (Seibt) Hafer; A.A. with high honors, Delta Coll., 1966; B.S. cum laude, Central Mich. U., 1969; M.A., Ariz. State U., 1974; m. E. Roger Simon, June 23, 1951; children—Jeffrey, Janelle, Eric.; m. 2d, Glenn A. Atchinson, Aug. 6, 1972. Tchr., St. Johns Sch., Essexville, Mich., 1965-66, Essexville-Hampton Schs., Essexville, 1969-72; reading coordinator Apache Junction (Ariz.) Schs., 1972-74; dir. Right to Read program Ariz. Dept. Edn., 1974-78; prin. Indian Oasis Sch. Dist., Sells, Ariz., 1980-81; prin. Washington Elem. Sch. Dist., 1982—; pres. Options, Inc., ednl. research and cons., Phoenix, 1978—. Former chmn. Presbytery of Grand Canyon Task Force on Women; former co-chmn. Arizonans of Faith for ERA. Mem. Nat. Assn. Female Execs. Author manuals in field. Presbyterian. Office: Ocotillo Sch 3225 W Ocotillo Phoenix AZ 85017

ATHERTON, FLORA CAMERON, civic worker, former found. exec.; b. Waco, Tex.; d. William Waldo and Helen Emelyn (Miller) Cameron; A.B., Sweet Briar Coll., 1946; m. Holt Atherton; children—Ike Simpson Kampmann, III, Megan Cameron Kampmann. Dir., mem. exec. com. Certain-Teed Corp., 1971-78; exec. com. San Antonio World's Fair, 1968; mem. Pres.'s Mission to Latin Am., 1969; U.S. del. Inter-Am. Commn. Women, 1969-72; mem. citizens stamp adv. commn. U.S. Postal Service, 1969-71; cons. Bur. Inter-Am. Affairs, Dept. State, 1972-75; vice chmn. exec. com. Tex. Republican Party, 1958-60; del. Rep. Nat. Conv., 1960, 64, alt. del., 1968, sec. platform com., 1960; mem. Rep. Nat. Finance Com., 1965—, chmn. 1976-78; past pres. KAMKO Found.; trustee Trinity U., San Antonio, from 1965, chmn., 1976-78; trustee Sweet Briar Coll., 1969-78; mem. nat. council Met. Opera. Mem. San Antonio Jr. League, Colonial Dames Am. Home: 315 Westover Rd San Antonio TX 78209 Office: 4600 Broadway San Antonio TX 78209

ATKIN, EDITH, artist, poet; b. Washington, Nov. 12, 1921; d. Phillip and Sylvia Hirschel; student Md. Coll. Art and Design, 1973-79, Strayers Bus. Coll., Alice Kilbaum's Coll. Music; m. Irwin Symour; children—Sharon Welch, Joan Atkin Winewriter. Group exhbns. at Lynn Kottler Galleries, N.Y.C., Gudowsky Gallery, Silver Spring, Md., Akademia Raymond Duncan, Paris, Ligoa Duncan, N.Y.C., Salon Surindependants, Paris; represented in numerous pvt. collections. Mem. Nat. Tobacco Distbrs. Assn. Jewish.

ATKINS, CANDACE, property mgmt. exec.; b. Chgo., Aug. 19, 1946; d. Norman Randolph and Catherine Mary (Coughlin) Wolfe; A.A., Thornton Community Coll., 1966; student Inst. Real Estate Mgmt. Chgo., 1976, DuPage Sch. Real Estate, 1976; children—Amanda Kate, James N. Atkins. Resident mgr. Richton Sq. Apts., Richton Park, Ill., 1976, Cinnamon Creek Apts., Waukegan, Ill., 1976, Yorktown Apts. I, Lombard, Ill., 1977; property mgr. Center Ct. Gardens, Chgo., 1978, Cedarwood Coop., Park Forest, Ill., 1979; owner Hawthorne Property Mgmt. Co., Vernon Hills, Ill., 1980—. Named Accredited Resident Mgr. of Yr., Chgo., 1980; cert. property mgr. Mem. Inst. Real Estate Mgmt., Nat. Assn. Realtors, Chgo. Accredited Resident Mgrs. (chpt. pres., nat. chmn. recognition and services com.), Nat. Assn. Housing Coops., Nat. Assn. Profl. Resident Mgrs., Nat. Assn. Female Execs., Midwest Coop. Housing Assn., Cert. Property Mgrs. Assn. (exec. com. San Francisco chpt.). Republican. Roman Catholic. Address: 46 Addison San Francisco CA 94131

ATKINS, LEAH MARIE RAWLS, historian; b. Birmingham, Ala., Apr. 24, 1935; d. Jack and Lena Margaret (Jones) Rawls; B.S., Auburn (Ala.) U., 1958, M.A., 1960, Ph.D., 1974; m. George Arthur Atkins, June 7, 1954; children—George Timothy, Richard Brian, Laura Leigh, Jack Raymond. Instr. history Auburn U., 1960-69, U. Ala., Birmingham, 1972; asso. prof. history Samford U., Birmingham, 1972—; adv. com. Arlington Historic House, 1981—; cons. in field. Adv. bd. Ala. Public Library Service, 1979-81; mem. Gov. Ala. Com. Libraries, 1979-80. Named to Ala. Sports Hall of Fame, 1976; recipient award of merit Ala. Hist. Commn., 1977; Pi Gamma Mu scholar, 1981. Mem. Orgn. Am. Historians, So. Hist. Assn., Ala. Hist. Assn. (program chmn. 1977-78, exec. bd. 1980), Birmingham-Jefferson Hist. Soc. (Historian of Yr. award 1982), Birmingham Hist. Soc., Assn. Ala. Historians, DAR, Colonial Dames XVII Century, Daus. Am. Colonies, PEO, Phi Kappa Phi, Alpha Lambda Delta, Phi Alpha Theta, Pi Gamma Mu. Episcopalian. Author: The Valley and the Hills, 1981; also articles, manuals. Mem. editorial bds. profl. jours. Home: 2309 Ponderosa Circle Birmingham AL 35216 Office: SU Box 2261 Samford U Birmingham AL 35229

ATKINSON, ELIZABETH ANN, educator; b. Anderson, S.C., Dec. 3, 1946; d. Kermit Lee and Elizabeth Eber (Bailey) Atkinson; B.S., U. Ga., 1968, M.Ed., 1970, Ed.S., 1975, Ed.D., 1982. Vocat. office tng. and adult edn. coordinator Elbert County Comprehensive High Sch., Elberton, Ga., 1968-71, 1974—; vocat. office tng. coordinator Towers High Sch., Decatur, Ga., 1971-72; admissions dir. DeVry Inst. Tech., Atlanta, 1972-74; adult edn. coordinator evening div. Athens (Ga.) Tech. Sch., 1974—; adj. prof. Truett-McConnell Coll., 1982—; cons. Elberton Poultry Co., Nat. Leisure Enterprises, Inc.; speaker bus. and club groups; ins. specialist. Pres., Muscular Dystrophy Assn. Drive, 1976-77. Recipient award IRS, 1980; named Outstanding Bus. Tchr. Yr., Am. Mgmt. Assn. Mem. Am. Vocat. Assn., Ga. Vocat. Assn., Nat. Bus. Edn. Assn., Am. Mgmt. Assn., Nat. Assn. Educators, Ga. Bus. Edn. Assn., Phi Kappa Phi, Delta Pi Epsilon, Kappa Delta Pi. Baptist. Home: 23 Chestnut St Box 1057 Elberton GA 30635 Office: 600 Jones St Elberton GA 30635

ATKINSON, HARRIETTE SEELY, clin. psychologist; b. Norfolk, Va., Aug. 22, 1929; d. Charles S. and Virginia Ann (Boyce) Seely; B.A., Mary Washington Coll., 1951; M.A., U. Louisville, 1954; Ph.D., U. Colo., 1961. Asst. chief psychology service VA Hosp., Oakland, Calif., Martinez, Calif., 1961-69; chief psychologist Lake Cumberland Mental Health Center, Somerset, Ky., 1969; staff psychologist VA Hosp., Danville, Ill., 1969-70, VA Hosp., Boston, 1970-71; chief psychology service VA Med. Center, Martinsburg, W.Va., 1972-81; pvt. practice counseling psychology; 1981—. Mem. Am., W.Va. psychol. assns., AAAS. Roman Catholic. Home and Office: 919 Mary's Ln Martinsburg WV 25401

ATKINSON, JEANNE MARIE, clothing mfg. co. exec.; b. Chgo., Feb. 27, 1932; d. John William and Lempi Marie (Erickson) Pagnucco; B.A., Oberlin Coll., 1953; m. Bill Atkinson, Dec. 5, 1969; children by previous marriage—Robert J. Blinken, Jr., Rachel J. Blinken. Asst. designer Glen of Michigan, N.Y., 1953-55; head designer Pamela Martin Co., N.Y.C., 1960-62; designer Evan Picone Co., N.Y.C., 1963-65; partner Presentation Co., N.Y.C., 1966-73; v.p. Bill Atkinson Ltd., N.Y.C., 1973-80, Highland Queen Ltd., N.Y.C., 1981-82; exec. v.p. Anne French Fashions Ltd., N.Y.C., 1982—; mem. faculty Fashion Inst. Tech., 1981. Mem. Fashion Group, Phi Beta Kappa. Office: 32 W 40th St New York NY 10018

ATKINSON, JOAN LYON, educator; b. Memphis, Nov. 23, 1939; d. Robert Hershal and Otye Blanche (Kilpatrick) Lyon; B.A., Harding U., 1961; M.A., U. Tex., 1963; M.L.S., Pratt Inst., 1970; m. Jon Franklin Atkinson, June 19, 1964; children—Jon Christopher, Amy Frances. Instr. English, Abilene Christian U., Abilene, Tex., 1963-65; tchr. English, librarian Erasmus Hall High Sch., Bklyn., 1965-70; asst. prof. U. Ala., Tuscaloosa, 1973-80, asso. prof., 1980—; cons. in field; lectr. in field. Mem. Ala. Library Assn. (2nd v.p. 1981-82), ALA (dir.). Democrat. Mem. Ch. of Christ. Editor: Yarns, 1976-81, Ala. Librarian, 1981—. Home: 183 Woodland Hills Tuscaloosa AL 35405 Office: PO Box 6242 University AL 35486

ATKINSON, KATHLEEN JANE, educator; b. Kendallville, Ind., Mar. 9, 1947; d. Robert Martin and Barbra Helen (Surfus) Krippner; student Olympic Coll., Bremerton, Wash., 1965-67; B.S., Ind. U., Bloomington, 1969, M.S., 1973; m. Larry L. Atkinson, Aug. 5, 1971; 1 son, Kent Michael. Cashier Post Exchange, Bremerton, Wash., 1966-67; student tchr. New Haven (Ind.) High Sch., 1968-69; tchr. Village Woods Jr. High Sch., Ft. Wayne, Ind., 1969-71, Greenwood (Ind.) Community High Sch., 1972—. Mem. NEA, Ind. Tchrs. Assn., Greenwood Edn. Assn. (pres. 1979-80), Ind. U. Alumni Assn., Alpha Phi, Kappa Kappa Kappa. Republican. Methodist. Home: 730 Colonial Way Greenwood IN 46142 Office: 615 Smith Valley Rd Greenwood IN 46142

ATKINSON, LINDA MAE, chiropractor; b. Detroit, May 20, 1953; d. Ray and Mary (Paich) Elwart; D.C., Palmer Coll. Chiropractic, Davenport, Iowa, 1975; m. Warren Bernard Atkinson, Dec. 28, 1978; children—Devin Patrick, Derek Benjamin. Exec. coordinator Romulus (Mich.) Chiropractic Clinic, 1968-78; Exec. coordinator Arbor Vitae Chiropractic Centre, Chelsea, Mich., 1978-81, dir., chiropractor, v.p., sec.-treas., 1979—; speaker Parker Sch. Profl. Success. Mem. Internat. Chiropractic Assn., Women Doctors of Chiropractice, Mich. Chiropractic Council. Republican. Roman Catholic. Address: 7970 Clark Lake Rd Chelsea MI 48118

ATON, ANNA-LEE, mfr.'s rep.; b. Mpls., Apr. 11, 1945; d. Ren and Elva Anita (Bakken) A.; B.A., U. Minn., 1969; M.A., Lindenwood Coll., 1979. Life and health ins. agt. Acacia Mut. Life Ins. Co., Washington, 1970-71; sales rep. Pinehurst Textiles, Asheboro, N.C., 1971-72; job developer, counselor VISTA, Wilmington, Del., 1972-73; job developer, counselor Vocat. Exploration in Pvt. Sector, Neighborhood Youth Corps, Mpls., 1974; vocat. counselor Twin Cities Opportunities Industrialization Ctr., Mpls., 1974-76; guidance and placement counselor H.I.R.E.D., Mpls., 1976-80, devel. counselor, 1980-81; sales rep. Wendell's Inc., Mpls., 1982—; mem. community faculty Met. State U., St. Paul, 1982—; vol. counselor Walk-In Counseling Center, 1980—. Mem. Am. Personnel and Guidance Assn., Minn. Personnel and Guidance Assn., Nat. Assn. Counselor Educators and Suprs., Nat. Vocat. Guidance Assn., Minn. Vocat. Guidance Assn. (trustee, state coordinator Nat. Career Guidance Week 1978-81, Helping Hand award 1980). Club: Toastmasters (area gov.). Contbr. chpt. to book. Home: 911 22d Ave S 267 Minneapolis MN 55404

ATTAQUIN, HELEN AVIS, civic worker; b. Middleboro, Mass., Feb. 6, 1923; d. Benjamin Leslie and Helen Mitchell (Peters) A.; student Alma Coll., 1938-40, B.Sc.Ed., Lowell U., 1946; M.Ed., Boston U., 1966, Ed.D., 1975. Tchr., music supr., public schs., Mich., Ariz., Mass., 1946-73; dir. edn. Plimoth Plantation, Plymouth, Mass., 1973-74, Boston Indian Council, 1974; lectr. Southeastern Mass. U., 1976-77; developer Native Am. exhibits and programs, cons., research asst. Children's Mus., Boston, 1979-82. Bd. dirs. Plymouth Bay council Girl Scouts U.S.A., 1978—; bd. dirs. Greater Boston council Camp Fire Girls, 1974-77, cons., 1980—; bd. dirs. Wampanoag Tribal Council, Gay Head, Mass., Mass. Indian Assn.; trustee Intercultural Studies Group, Boston, 1973-81; mem. Mass. Indian Commn., 1981—pres. Coalition Eastern Native Ams., Washington, 1973-75; bd. dirs. Mass. Indian Assn.; mem. Mass. Indian Commn.; Pandist Mass. Council Arts and Humanities, 1980-81. Mem. Nat. Assn. Female Execs., Am. Soc. Notaries, South Shore Antique Auto Assn. Author: Brief History of Aquiniuh, 1970. Home: 74 E Grove St Middleboro MA 02346

ATTEE, JOYCE VALERIE JUNGCLAS, artist; b. Cin., Apr. 4, 1926; d. LeRoy Francis and Clara Marie (Becker) Jungclas; B.A., Rollins Coll., 1948; postgrad. U. Cin., 1952, 54, Art Acad. Cin., 1962-64, Edgecliff Coll., 1967; m. William Robert Attee III, Oct. 25, 1952; children—Robin Wilson, Wendy Ann. One-man shows: Loring Andrews Rattermann Gallery, 1964, Town Club, 1966, 69, 72, 75, 78, 81, Jr. League Office, 1975, Court Gallery, 1969, Bissingers', 1970, 76, Cin. Nature Center, 1974, 78, Cin. Country Day Sch., 1974; group shows include: Cin. Art Mus., 1962, Zoo Arts Festival, 1961, 62, 66, Town Club Cin., 1973-75, 77-79, 80-81, Palm Beach (Fla.) Galleries, 1974, Showcase of Arts, 1976, Ursuline Center, 1976, Court Galleries, 1977, Indian Hill Artists, 1957-76, 82, regional and local shows Nat. League Am. Pen Women, 77, 78, also nat. biennial art exhibit, 1970, Nat. Bicentennial Show, Washington, 1976, James H. Barker Gallery, Palm Beach, Fla., 1979, 80, 81, 82, Nantucket, 1982, Cin. Women's Club Show, 1979; represented in permanent collections: Bissingers, Cin.; Court Gallery, Cin. Recipient 1st prize in still life or flowers Cin. Womans Art Club, 1965, 69; Marjorie Ewell Meml. award, 1975. Mem. Nat. League Am. Pen Women (past pres. Cin. br., past state art chmn. 1st prize graphics 1975), Women's Art Club Cin. (past v.p.), Jr. League Cin., Jr. League Garden Circle (pres. 1974-75). Episcopalian. Clubs: Town, University, Camargo Racquet, Indian Hill. Author: Elbey Jay, 1964. Home: 8050 Indian Hill Rd Cincinnati OH 45243

ATTEL, ELIZABETH ANN, nurse; b. El Paso, Tex., July 19, 1947; d. Remus F. and Bernadine E. (McKay) Thomas; B.S.N., U. Colo., 1969; postgrad. U. Tex., El Paso; m. William Anthony Attel, Aug. 23, 1969; children—Timothy Louis, Theodore William. Asst. head nurse Med. Unit, Highland Hosp., Oakland, Calif., 1969-70; public health nurse Alameda, Calif., 1970-73; dir. childbirth edn. Parenthood Edn. Assn. El Paso, 1974—; exec. dir. Reproductive Services, Inc., El Paso, Tex., 1978-80; program coordinator Family Planning Services, R.E. Thomason Gen. Hosp., El Paso, 1980—, childbirth educator cons.; family planning mgmt. cons. James Bowman & Assocs., Nova Health Systems. Med. adv. bd. March of Dimes, El Paso; trustee Tex. Family Plannning Assn.; Named Outstanding Woman of El Paso, Internat. Yr. of Women, 1974. Mem. Am. Nurses Assn., Tex. Nurses Assn., Am. Soc. for Psychoprophylaxis in Obstetrics, Tex. Family Planning Assn., Nat. Family Planning and Reproductive Health Assn., Sigma Theta Tau. Contbr. articles to profl. jours. Home: 736 Westside Pl El Paso TX 79932 Office: 4824 Alberta St Suite 407 El Paso TX 79905

ATTERBERRY, JANICE ANN, accountant; b. Conway, Ark., Feb. 14, 1946; d. Thomas Dean and Winnie Faye (Robins) Clements; B.B.A., U. Central Ark., 1967; m. Travis Eward Atterberry, May 27, 1967; children—Ashley Elizabeth, Jennifer Kristin, Erica Anne. Auditor, E.L. Gaunt & Co., Little Rock, 1967-69; instr. acctg. and law Capital City Bus. Coll., Little Rock, 1969-71; v.p., controller Intermed, Inc., Little Rock, 1971-78; pvt. practice accounting, Little Rock. C.P.A., Ark. Active, Ark. Arts Center, Ark. Symphony Orch. Soc. Guild, Univ. Hosp. Aux., Ark. Children's Hosp. Aux. Mem. Am. Inst. C.P.A.s, Am. Woman's Soc. C.P.A.s (legis. com.), Ark. Soc. C.P.A.s, Am., Nat. acctg. assns., Ark. Orch. Soc. Guild, Ark. Arts Center, Little Rock Jaycettes (pres. 1977), Alpha Sigma Tau (v.p. local chpt. 1970). Democrat. Mem. Ch. Nazarene. Home: 3309 Doral Little Rock AR 72212 Office: 2 Financial Centre Suite 400 Little Rock AR 72211

ATTNEAVE, CAROLYN (ADAMS) LEWIS, psychologist; b. El Paso, Tex., July 2, 1920; d. James Irwin and Carrie Florence (Adams) Lewis; A.A., Yuba Jr. Coll., 1939; B.A., Chico State Coll., 1940; M.A., Stanford

U., 1947, Ph.D., 1952; Sc.D. (hon.), St. Vincent Coll., 1981; m. Fred Attneave, Oct. 7, 1949 (div. 1956); children—Dorothy Maude Attneave Jackson, Philip Henry. Dir. student personnel services Tex. State Coll. for Women, Denton, 1956-57; asst. prof. psychology Tex. Tech. U., Lubbock, 1957-60; coordinator Community Guidance Services Region V, Shawnee, Okla., 1961-67; sr. psychologist Phila. Child Guidance Clinic, 1967-69; coordinator public service careers Mass. Dept. Mental Health, Boston, 1969-72; lectr. Harvard Sch. Public Health, Cambridge, Mass., 1972-75; dir. Am. Indian studies U. Wash., Seattle, 1975-77, prof. psychology, adj. prof. psychiatry and behavioral scis., 1975—; cons. Indian Health Service, Ednl. Testing Service. Mem. Nat. Adv. Council on Women's Equity in Edn., 1978-82; dir. OHOYO (Am. Indian Women's Resource Center), 1981—; dir. Profl. Bd. Family Psychology, 1981; pres. Community Planning Assn., Shawnee, 1964-67. Served to lt. USCGR, 1942-47. Fellow Am. Psychol. Assn., Am. Orthopsychiat. Assn.; mem. Am. Family Therapy Assn. (dir. 1979—), Psychiat. Outpatient Centers Am. (pres. 1973). Author: (with Ross Speck) Family Networks, 1973; (with M. Beiser) Service Networks of IHS Mental Health Services, 1975; (with D. Kelso) Indexed Bibliography of American Indian Mental Health, 1981; contbr. articles to profl. jours. Home: 5206 Ivanhoe NE Seattle WA 98105 Office: Psychology NI-25 Univ Wash Seattle WA 98195

ATTWOOD, CYNTHIA LOU, lawyer; b. Chgo., Dec. 12, 1946; d. John Gordon and M. Louise (Crenshaw) A.; B.A., Oakland U., 1969; J.D., U. Minn., 1973. Admitted to D.C. bar, 1973; atty. employment sect. civil rights div. U.S. Dept. Justice, Washington, 1973-74; atty. appelate sect., civil rights div., 1974-79; counsel appellate litigation mine safety and health div. Office of Solicitor, U.S. Dept. Labor, Arlington, Va., 1979-80, dep. assoc. solicitor, 1980-81, assoc. solicitor, 1981—. Mem. Women's Equity Action League, D.C. Bar. Office: Office of Solicitor US Dept Labor 4015 Wilson Blvd Arlington VA 22203

ATTWOOD, MADGE LOUISE, nurse, educator; b. Watsonville, Calif., Feb. 24, 1928; d. Max Laverne and Estella Sara (Childers) Bellamy; B.S. in Nursing, U. Calif., Berkeley, 1949; M.S. in Public Health, UCLA, 1968; Ph.D., U. Mich., 1975; divorced; 1 son, Christopher. Staff nurse hosps. in Ohio and Calif., 1949-59; sch. nurse Los Angeles City Bd. Edn., 1959-68; tchr. high sch., 1968-71; USPHS trainee, 1966-67; post secondary health specialist Mich. Dept. Edn., 1971-72; dir. health projects, asst. prof. edn. U. Mich., 1972-78; asso. prof. edn., chmn. div. health occupations U. Ill., Urbana, 1978—; dir. edn. Washtenaw br. Am. Cancer Soc., 1976-77; cons. in field. Mem. Am. Vocat. Assn. (award of merit div. health occupations edn. 1978), Nat. League Nursing, Assn. Health Occupation Tchr. Educators, Phi Delta Kappa. Home: 2304 Sumac St Champaign IL 61820 Office: 1310 S 6th St Champaign IL 61820

ATWELL, CONSTANCE WOODRUFF, psychologist, govt. ofcl.; b. Phila., Jan. 27, 1942; d. Marston True and Viola Estelle (Habel) Woodruff; A.B. magna cum laude, Mt. Holyoke Coll., 1963; M.A., UCLA, 1965, Ph.D., 1968; m. Robert Herron Atwell, Sept. 4, 1972; stepchildren—Mary, Robert, John, Nancy, Carl; children—Catherine, Cynthia. Asst. prof. Pitzer Coll., Claremont, Calif., 1967-72, prof. asso. prof., 1972-77, prof. psychology, 1977-78; asst. prof. Claremont Grad. Sch., 1967-72, asso. prof., 1972-77, prof., 1977-78; research asso. faculty medicine, lectr. Univ. Coll., Nairobi, Kenya, 1968-69; grants asso. NIH, Bethesda, Md., 1978-79, chief office clin. applications of vision research Nat. Eye Inst., NIH, 1979—, chief strabismus, amblyopia and visual processing br., 1981—. Trustee, Claremont Collegiate Sch., 1975-77; chmn. guidance adv. com. Cabin John Jr. High Sch., Potomac, Md., 1980-81, pres. PTA, 1981-82; reader Recordings for the Blind, Claremont, 1973-78. USPHS grantee UCLA, 1964-67; Nat. Merit scholar, 1959-63. Mem. AAAS, Am. Psychol. Assn., Assn. Women in Sci., Assn. Research in Vision and Ophthalmology, Sigma Xi, Phi Beta Kappa. Contbr. book reviews and articles to profl. publs. Home: 8608 Timber Hill Ln Potomac MD 20854 Office: Nat Eye Inst Bldg 31/6A49 NIH Bethesda MD 20205

ATWOOD, MARGARET ELEANOR, author; b. Ottawa, Ont., Can., Nov. 18, 1939; d. Carl Edmund and Margaret Dorothy (Killam) Atwood; B.A., U. Toronto, 1961; A.M., Radcliffe Coll., 1962. Mem. faculty U. B.C., 1964-65, Sir George Williams U., 1967-68, U. Alta., 1969-70, York U., 1971-72; writer-in-residence U. Toronto, 1972-73, now Oxford U., Don Mills, Ont. Recipient E.J. Pratt medal, 1961; President's medal U. Western Ont., 1965; Gov. General's medal, 1966; Union Poetry prize Poetry mag., 1969; 1st place Centennial Commn. Poetry competition, 1967. Author: (poetry) Double Persephone, 1961, The Circle Game, 2d edit., 1967, The Animals in That Country, 1968, The Journals of Susanna Moodie, 1970, Procedures for Underground, 1970, Power Politics, 1971; You Are Happy, 1974; Selected Poems, 1976; Two-Headed Poems, 1978; True Stories, 1981; (fiction) The Edible Woman, 1969, Surfacing, 1972; Lady Oracle, 1976; Dancing Girls, 1977; Life Before Man, 1979; Bodily Harm, 1981; (non-fiction) Survival: A Thematic Guide to Canadian Literature, 1972; also short stories, TV scripts. Address: care Oxford U 70 Wynford Dr Don Mills ON Canada *

ATWOOD, MARY SANFORD, author; b. Mt. Pleasant, Mich., Jan. 27, 1935; d. Burton Jay and Lillian Belle (Sampson) Sanford; B.S., U. Miami, 1957; m. John C. Atwood, III, Mar. 23, 1957. Author: A Taste of India, 1969. Mem. San Francisco/N. Peninsula Opera Action, Hillsborough-Burlingame Newcomers, Suicide Prevention and Crisis Center, DeYoung Art Mus., Internat. Hospitality Center, Peninsula Symphony, San Francisco Art Mus., Mills Hosp. Assos. Mem. AAUW. Republican. Clubs: St. Francis Yacht, Commonwealth of Calif. Address: 40 Knightwood Ln Hillsborough CA 94010

AUBUCHON, SARAH RUTH, former state library ofcl., writer; b. Piedmont, Mo., Feb. 27, 1917; d. James I. and Blanche Geraldine (Over) Moon; student U. Wyo., 1937-39; m. Jack V. Aubuchon, May 31, 1953; 1 dau., Geraldine C. Aubuchon Adams. Writer/display sales Wyo. State Jour., Lander, 1946-48; salesman and broadcaster Sta. KOVE, Lander, 1948-50; salesman, writer Casper (Wyo.) Morning Star, 1950-53; sales mgr., asst. mgr., broadcaster Sta. KVWO, Cheyenne, Wyo., 1953-61; women's program dir. Sta. KFBC Radio and KFBC-TV, Cheyenne, 1962-71; editor, public relations officer Wyo. State Library, Cheyenne, 1972-80, State Archives, Museums and Hist. Dept., 1976-78, acting dir., 1978; book reviewer; participant workshops. Bd. dirs. Cystic Fibrosis Assn., 1968-71. Laramie County Mental Health Assn., 1965-68, 80—; chmn. Salvation Army Community Christmas Campaign, 1966, 67. Named Woman of Yr., Bus. and Profl. Women, 1967; recipient Golden Mike cert. for Wyo., Nat. Am. Legion Aux., 1967; spl. commendation State Library, Archives, Hist. Bd., 1980. Mem. Nat. Fedn. Press Women (various writing awards, 25 Yr. cert. 1980), Wyo. Press Women (state pres., 1973-75), Mountain Plains Library Assn., Wyo. Library Assn., Wyo. State Hist. Assn. Clubs: Zonta Internat. (pres. Cheyenne, 1969-70), Cheyenne Corral, Westerners. Methodist. Editor: Wyoming Library Roundup, 1972-80, State Library Outrider Newsletter, 1972-80; author TV documentaries, 1969, 77 (first place awards Nat. Fedn. Press Women); contbr. hist. articles to mags. and publs. Home: 4708 Greybull Ave Cheyenne WY 82009

AUCH MOEDY, NEDRA LOUISE, nursing home adminstr.; b. Berwyn, Nebr., Nov. 11, 1939; d. E. Ray and Dorothy Anne (Dinwiddie) Brown; student Kearney State Coll., 1957-58; m. Don E. Wilcox, Aug. 8, 1981; children by previous marriage—Amy Jeanne, Callie Anne. Sec., Nursing Home Builders, Inc., Broken Bow, Nebr., 1960-62, No. Natural Gas Co., Omaha, 1962-65; legal sec. firm Johnson, Kelly, Evans & Spencer, Broken Bow, 1965-66, 68-70; adminstr. Southview Manor, Cozad, Nebr., 1970-80, Hallmark Care Center, Omaha, 1980-82; bd. dirs. Crestview Home, Inc., Milford, Nebr., 1977-80. Emergency med. technician. Mem. Nebr. Health Care Assn. (dist. sec.-treas. 1974-75), Am. Coll. Nursing Home Adminstrs. (dist. sec.-treas. 1974-75, pres. 1979-80). Episcopalian. Club: Women's (community health dir. 1973-78). Home: 3302 Ernst St Omaha NE 68112 Office: Hallmark Care Center 5505 Grover St Omaha NE 68106

AUER, EMMA HENRIETTA, educator; b. Ancon, C.Z., July 14, 1913; d. George Harrison and Bertha Evelyn (Weiland) Auer; B.S., U. Ill., 1935, Ph.D., 1968; M.S., Washington U., St. Louis, 1958. Promotion dir., Boy'd, St. Louis, 1938-51; fashion advt. mgr., fashion dir. Famous-Barr, St. Louis, 1951-58; fashion dir., account liaison MacFarland, Aveyard & Co., Chgo., 1958-59; fashion dir., sales promotion cons. Ind. Retailers' Syndicate, N.Y.C., 1959-61; fashion dir. Carson Pirie Scott, Chgo., 1961-62; promotion dir. Harper's Bazaar, N.Y., 1962-64; asst. prof. bus. Washington U., St. Louis, 1945-58, No. Ill. U., DeKalb, 1967-68, Kans. U., Lawrence, 1968-69; asso. prof. Fla. State U., Tallahassee, 1969-76; chmn. dept. mktg. Suffolk U., Boston, 1976-77; prof. dept. consumer sci. Purdue U., West Lafayette, Ind., 1977, Cleve. State U., 1978, Boston State Coll., 1978-80, Babson Coll., 1980-81, U. Vt., 1981—. Am. Assn. Advt. Agencies grantee, 1969-70, 70-71. Mem. Am. Acad. Advt., Acad. Mktg. Sci., Am. Psychol. Assn., Assn. Consumer Research. Contbr. articles to profl. jours. Home: PO Box 225 Hanover St Station Boston MA 02113

AUERBACH, ANITA L., clin. psychologist; b. Flushing, N.Y., Dec. 23, 1946; d. Ben and Gussie (Zuckerman) Weiss; B.A. cum laude, SUNY, Buffalo, 1968, M.A., 1970; Ph.D. (N.Y. State Regents fellow 1970-72), George Washington U., 1977; m. Steven Miles Auerbach, May 25, 1969. Chief research youth crime control project D.C. Dept. Corrections, 1970-74; intern clin. psychology No. Va. Tng. Center, Fairfax, 1974-75, staff psychologist, then chief psychol. services, 1975-79; pvt. practice clin. psychology, McLean, Va., 1979—; lectr. Washington Tech. Inst., 1972-74, George Mason U., 1978—; cons. in field. Adv. bd. family edn. project Joseph P. Kennedy, Jr. Found., 1977-79; mem. regional appeals bd. No. Va. Public Sch. System, 1977-79. Recipient N.Y. State Scholar Incentive award, 1969; diplomate Am. Bd. Behavioral Medicine. Mem. Am. Psychol. Assn., Am. Soc. Clin. Hypnosis, Va. Acad. Clin. Psychologists, Va. Psychol. Assn., No. Va. Soc. Clin. Psychologists, Washington Soc. Study Clin. Hypnosis, Psi Chi, Alpha Lambda Delta. Author articles in field. Office: 1449 Dolly Madison Blvd McLean VA 22101

AUFDENKAMP, JO ANN, lawyer, banker; b. Springfield, Ill, Mar. 22, 1926; d. Erwin C. and Johanna (Ostermeier) A.; B.A., MacMurray Coll. for Women, 1945; B.L.S., U. Ill., 1946; postgrad. U. Chgo., 1964-66; J.D., John Marshall Law Sch., 1976. Asst. librarian Commerce Library U. Ill., 1946-48; librarian Fed. Res. Bank of Chgo., 1948-80; adminstr. info. services legal dept. Lincoln Nat. Life Ins. Co., Ft. Wayne, Ind., 1980-81; asst. trust officer Central Trust and Savs. Bank, Geneseo, Ill., 1981—; with Office Nat. Planning, Liberia, 1963. Mem. Am., Ill., Henry County bar assns. Republican. Lutheran. Office: Box 89 Geneseo IL 61254

AUFIERO, BARBARA MARIAN, educator; b. Brighton, Mass., Dec. 3, 1954; d. John and Gilda (Sateriale) Aufiero; B.A., Regis Coll., 1976; M.P.H., Yale U., 1981. Women's resource center coordinator Women's Occupational Health Resource Center, Columbia U., 1981—. Contbr. articles to profl. jours. Home: 870 Riverside Dr #6G New York NY 10032 Office: 60 Haven Rd B-1 New York NY 10032

AUGUST, KATHERINE, mortgage ins. co. exec.; b. Bridgeport, Conn., Feb. 13, 1948; d. Edward and Benita (Miller) Burstein; A.B., Goucher Coll., 1969; M.B.A., Stanford U., 1975. Legis and polit. sr. staff positions in Congress, Washington, 1969-73; cons. Dynapol, Palo Alto, Calif., 1974-75; mgmt. cons. McKinsey & Co., San Francisco and London, 1975-78; mgr. cash control Itel Corp., San Francisco, 1978, dir. fin., 1979; treas. PMI, San Francisco, 1979-82, v.p., 1980-82, sr. v.p., chief fin. officer, 1982—; lectr., cons. Fin. Execs. Inst., Corp. Planners Assn., No. Calif. Chief Fin. Officers Assn., Fin. Adv. Group Golden Gate U., Women's Forum. Mem. modern art council San Francisco Mus. Modern Art. Mem. Bay Area Profl. Women's Network (pres. 1978-79, dir. 1977-80), Stanford Bus. Sch. Alumni Assn. Office: PMI Mortgage Ins Co 601 Montgomery St San Francisco CA 94111

AUGUSTIN, ANN SUTHERLAND, author, realtor; b. Evergreen Park, Ill., Aug. 11, 1934; d. Donald A. and Helen E. (Dorsey) Sutherland; student Iowa State U., 1951-53; m. Edward J. Augustin Jr., Jan. 8, 1955 (div. 1974); children—Edward J. III, Kathryn, Donald J., Suzanne. Exec. sec. Standard Register Co., Chgo., 1953-55; tchr. adult edn. Maine Twp. Sch., Park Ridge, Ill., 1961-68; now realtor Century 21, Schaumburg, Ill., monthly columnist regional Century 21 newsletter; free lance writer. Republican. Roman Catholic. Author: Help! I Want to Remodel My Home, 1975; contbr. articles to Reader's Digest, MacFadden-Bartell, Playboy, Chgo. Daily News, Chgo. Tribune, Mt. Prospect Herald, others. Home: 1100 Randville Dr Palatine IL 60067 Office: Century 21 Country Squire 1050 S Roselle Rd Schaumburg IL 60193

AULD, JULIE ANNETTE, business exec.; b. Oak Park, Ill., July 30, 1949; d. Roger Martin and Evelyn Harriet (Strand) A.; student Valley City State Coll., 1967-68, De Anza Community Coll., 1968-70; B.A., U. Calif., Santa Barbara, 1971, postgrad. in edn.; postgrad. in bus. adminstrn. Santa Clara U., 1974-76; M.P.A., U. So. Calif., 1979. Prodn. control supr. Intel Corp., 1973-76; tchr. kindergarten, San Jose, Calif., 1976; tchr. elem. grades, Santa Barbara, 1972-73, Goleta, Calif., 1972-73, Shandon, Calif., 1976-77; instr. Cerritos Community Coll., Norwalk, Calif., 1977-78; coordinator vol. tutoring program Operation SHARE Found., Norwalk, 1977-78, vol. program cons., 1977-78; mgmt. cons. Williams & Co., Palo Alto, Calif., 1979-80; prodn. mgr. Rucker & Kolls, Mountain View, Calif., 1980-81; mfg. systems analyst Racal-Vadic Inc., Sunnyvale, Calif., 1982, prodn. planning mgr., 1982—. Mem. Calif. Tchrs. Assn., Native Am. Awareness, Am. Soc. Public Adminstrn., Mcpl. Mgmt. Assn., Am. Prodn. and Inventory Control Soc., Kappa Delta Pi.

AULD, SUSAN DANIELS, state legislator; b. Providence, May 22, 1940; d. James Bent and Anne Theresa (Primiano) Daniels; student Pembroke Coll., 1958-60; B.A., St. Anselm's Coll., 1968; postgrad. U. Vt.; m. John Hudson Auld, June 4, 1960; children—Julia, Bethany. Tchr., Goffstown (N.H.) High Sch., 1968-71; mgr. Central Vt. Area Office on Aging, Barre, 1973-76; tchr Twinfield High Sch., Plainfield, Vt., 1976-82; mem. Vt. Ho. of Reps., 1978—, asst. majority leader, 1980-82. Mem. Middlesex (Vt.) Sch. Bd., 1976-82. Named One of 10 Outstanding Republican Legislators in U.S., 1981. Mem. Delta Kappa Gamma. Episcopalian. Home: Wood Rd Middlesex VT 05682 Office: State Capitol Montpelier VT 05602

AULETTA, JOAN MIGLORISI, real estate broker; b. N.Y.C., July 23, 1940; d. Angelo George and Ann (Passa) Miglorisi; A.B.S., Bklyn. Community Coll., 1957; m. E.V. Auletta, Oct. 5, 1958; children—Ann, Vincent, George, Jeanne. Owner-mgr. Auletta Realty, also owner-mgr. E&J Pancake House, L.I., N.Y., 1974-76; office and fin. mgr. Larchwood Constrn. Co., Farmingville, N.Y., 1976-77; prodn. mgr. Lawlor Industries, Holtsville, N.Y., 1977-79; real estate and fin. adv. Family Home Improvement Corp., Queens Village, N.Y., 1979-81; co-owner Total Home Constrn. Co., N.Y.C., 1981—; assoc. broker Andor Group Realtors, Port Jefferson, N.Y., 1981—; owner-mgr. comml. property, 1970—. Roman Catholic. Home: 80 Smithtown Polk Blvd Centereach NY 11720 also 71-07 N 70th Ave Fort Lauderdale FL 33319 Office: 76 Nesconset Hwy Port Jefferson NY 11776 also 218-36 Hempstead Ave Queens Village NY 11429

AULL, FELICE, physiologist, educator; b. Vienna, Austria, Aug. 12, 1938; came to U.S., 1940, naturalized, 1946; d. Henry Benjamin and Gertrude Joan A.; B.A., Barnard Coll., 1960; Ph.D., Cornell U., 1964; m. Martin S. Nachbar, June 15, 1962; 1 dau. Physiologist, Radiobiol. Lab., Bur. Comml. Fisheries, Beaufort, N.C., 1964-65; instr. physiology N.Y. U. 1966-69, asst. prof., 1969-72, asso. prof., 1972—, dir. student-faculty liason program, 1981—; ad hoc reviewer study sects. NIH. NIH fellow, 1960-63, 65-66, grantee, 1968—. Mem. Am. Physiol. Soc., Biophys. Soc., Soc. Gen. Physiologists, N.Y. Acad. Sci., Harvey Soc., AAAS, Assn. Women in Sci. Contbr. articles in field. Office: Dept Physiology NY U Sch Medicine 550 1st Ave New York NY 10016

AUMOND-STRICK, SANDRA, diversified co. adminstrv. asst.; b. Holyoke, Mass., Sept. 1, 1937; d. George Raymond and Helen Mary (Shaker) Aumond; student Mt. Holyoke Coll., 1950; B.A. in History, Marymount Coll., Los Angeles, 1953; m. Benjamin T. Strick, Sept. 3, 1979; 1 dau., Joan. Various secretarial positions, 1954-70; with Swedlow, Inc., Garden Grove, Calif., 1970—, spl. asst. to chmn. bd., exec. asst. to pres. and chmn. bd., 1979—. Mem. vol. bd. Children's Hosp., Santa Ana, Calif., 1970-79; fund raiser City of Hope. Mem. Am. Mgmt. Assn., Women in Mgmt. Clubs: Balboa Bay, Coto de Caza, John Wayne Tennis. Home: 20 Crest Circle Corona Del Mar CA 92625 Office: 12122 Western Ave Garden Grove CA 92645

AUNE, JANET, univ. ofcl.; b. St. Louis; d. Lee P. and Betty Montgomery; B.S., St. Louis U., 1954, M.S., 1964, Ph.D., 1968; postgrad. Harvard U. Grad. Sch. Bus., 1977. Asst. prof. biology Harris Tchrs. Coll., St. Louis, 1964-66; asso. prof. biology Tex. Woman's U., Denton, 1968-75, prof., exec. dir., Houston Center, 1975-80; asst. vice chancellor health affairs U. Tex. System, Austin, 1980-81; v.p. acad. services U. Tex. Health Sci. Center, Dallas, 1981—; Tex. coordinator Office for Women, Am. Council on Edn., 1978. Pres. bd. Houston Acad. Medicine-Tex. Med. Center Library, 1979-80; chmn. profl. adv. com. Nat. Found.-March of Dimes, 1979-80. NSF scholar, 1967-68; named Outstanding Tchr., Tex. Woman's U., 1975. Mem. AAAS, Am. Assn. Higher Edn., Soc. Cell Biology, Sigma Xi. Address: 5323 Harry Hines Blvd Dallas TX 75235

AURELIAN, LAURE, educator; b. Bucharest, Romania, June 17, 1939; came to U.S., 1963, naturalized, 1971; d. George I. and Stella (Ben-Joseph) A.; M.S., Tel-Aviv U., 1962; Ph.D., Johns Hopkins U., 1966; m. I.I. Kessler, Nov. 24, 1970; 1 dau., Amalia D. Asst. prof. dept. lab. animal medicine and microbiology Johns Hopkins U. Sch. Medicine, Balt., 1969-74, asso. prof. dept. biophysics and biochemistry, 1975-82, asso. prof. dept. comparative medicine and biophysics, 1974-82; prof. dept. pharamacology U. Md., 1982—; mem. NIH study sects. internat. teaching, 1973. ACS grantee, 1970-74; NIH grantee, 1969—; others; named Disting. Young Scientist, Md. Acad. Sci., 1970. Mem. David Boyes Soc. Gynecol. Oncology, Brit. Coll. Can. (hon.) Am. Soc. Microbiology, AAAS, Am. Assn. Immunologists, Soc. Exptl. Biology and Medicine, Md. Acad. Sci., N.Y. Acad. Sci., Am. Assn. Cancer Research, Reticuloendothelial Soc. Editor Jour. Soviet Oncology, 1980—; contbr. articles to profl. jours. Home: 3404 Bancroft Rd Baltimore MD 21215

AUSTERMAN, VIRGINIA ILAINE, retail exec.; b. Waterville, Wash., July 5, 1946; d. Emil Edward and Hilda Jane (Sylvester) Vetter; student pub. schs., Waterville; m. Alan David Austerman, Dec. 3, 1966; children—Carol Lynn, Dawn Marie. Accounting clk. Kodiak (Alaska) Airways, 1965-66, O. Kraft & Son, Inc., Kodiak, 1966-68, City of Kodiak, 1969-75; owner, mgr. Kodiak Kwik Kopy, 1975—; pub. Kadiak Times, 1976-80; owner Austerman's Stationers, Kodiak, 1977—. Steering com. Kodiak State Parks Adv. Council, 1980, chair, 1981—. Mem. Beta Sigma Phi. Home: PO Box 2368 401 N Blvd Kodiak AK 99615 Office: 10th and Mill Bay Rd Kodiak AK 99615

AUSTIN, AURELIA, author; b. Decatur, Ga.; d. Herbert O. and Virgil Mary (Wells) A.; ed. So. Bus. U., Mpls. Sch. Art, Atlanta Conservatory of Music; pvt. organ studies. Pvt. sec. to pres. Ashcraft-Wilkinson, Atlanta, 1952-71, Duval Corp., Houston, 1972-77; author: Bright Feathers (award as best book of poems by a Georgian), 1958; Georgia Boys with Stonewall Jackson (award Ga. Writers Assn.), 1968; editor: Poetry Prisms, 1956; Leaves of Life, 1964; contbr. articles to mags.; columnist 13 Ga. newspapers. Mem. Nat. League Am. Pen Women (award 1970, pres. Atlanta br. 1980-82, state pres. Ga. 1982-84), Ga. Poetry Soc., Atlanta Writers Club (pres. 1967-68). Baptist. Home: 526 Hardondorf Ave Atlanta GA 30307

AUSTIN, DOROTHY WITTE, journalist; b. Necedah, Wis., Aug. 22, 1918; d. Emil Alfred and Marie (Wake) Witte; B.A. cum laude in Journalism, Marquette U., 1940; m. Harry Russell Austin, Oct. 3, 1953; children—Richard Kirk, Stephen Russell. With Cath. Herald Citizen, 1940-43; staff asst. A.R.C., Africa and Italy, 1943-45; advt. copy chief Gimbels, Milw., 1945-50; reporter Milw. Jour., 1950-67; asst. and asso. dir. Summerfest, 1967-69; reporter, feature writer Milw. Sentinel, 1970—; public speaker. Former pres. Women's Overseas Service League; former bd. dirs. Milw. County Hist. Soc. Recipient Women in Action award, U. Wis., Milw., 1964, award for women's interest features, Milw. Press Club, 1963, award for features, Wis. Press Women, 1976, staff award for excellence in reporting, Milw. Sentinel, 1977, Headliner award Southeastern Wis. chpt. Women in Communications, 1979, Faith and Humanities award, Nat. Council Jewish Women, Milw., 1979. Mem. Wis. Press Women (past pres.), Washington Press Club, Milw. Press Club (past sec.), Kappa Tau Alpha, Gamma Pi Epsilon. Unitarian. Home: 5858 N Lake Dr Milwaukee WI 53217 Office: 918 N 4th St Milwaukee WI 53201

AUSTIN, EILEEN KAY, educator; b. Chgo., Mar. 6, 1947; d. Richard James and Alice Antoinette (Holefelder) Austin; B.S.N., Spalding Coll., 1968; M.Ed., U. Fla., 1971, Ed.D., 1976. Nursing instr. Edison Community Coll., Ft. Myers, Fla., 1971-74; asso. coordinator Interinstl. Registered Nurse Program, Jacksonville, Fla., 1974-75; dir. nursing edn. U. No. Fla., Jacksonville 1975-80; adj. instr. div. continuing edn. U. Fla., Gainesville, 1980—; pres. Eileen K. Austin, Inc., Jacksonville, 1980—; adj. prof. Central Mich. U., Offcampus Grad. program, 1981—. Bd. dirs. Oak Psychiat. Center, Jacksonville, 1977—; treas. N.E. Fla. Nurses Council for Continuing Edn., 1981—. Mem. Fla. League for Nursing (chmn. public affairs and legis. com. 1981—), Fla. Nurses Assn., Dist. Nurses Assn. (2d v.p. 1978-79, dir. 1979-80), Phi Kappa Phi, Phi Delta Kappa, Phi Lambda Theta, Kappa Delta Pi. Democrat. Roman Catholic. Author: Guidelines for the Development of Continuing Education Offerings for Nurses, 1981. Home: 8924 Arcade Ave Jacksonville FL 32216 Office: 9926 Beach Blvd Suite 90 Jacksonville FL 32216

AUSTIN, GRACE BALIUNAS, periodontist; b. Vilnius, Lithuania, May 22, 1940; d. Adolph and Anna Catherine (Savage) Baliunas; B.S.,

U. Chgo., 1963; D.D.S., Northwestern U., 1967; cert. periodontics N.J. Dental Sch., 1976; m. Nov. 28, 1970. Asst. prof. Northwestern U. Dental Sch., Chgo., 1967-69; sr. clin. scientist Warner Lambert Co., Morris Plains, N.J., 1969-71; clin. asso. prof. periondontics N.J. Dental Sch., Newark, 1977—; pvt. practice periodontics, Berkeley Heights, N.J., 1978—; mem. staff Overlook Hosp., Summit, N.J., 1979—. Ill. State scholar, 1959; grantee Coll. Medicine and Dentistry N.J. Found., 1976; diplomate Am. Bd. Periodontology. Mem. Am. Acad. Periodontology, ADA, N.J. Dental Assn., Central Dental Soc., Internat. Assn. Dental Research, Psi Omega. Contbr. articles to profl. jours. Home: 420 Old Short Hills Rd Short Hills NJ 07078 Office: 576 Springfield Ave Berkeley Heights NJ 07922

AUSTIN, JOANN CLARK, lawyer; b. Balt., Oct. 15, 1939; d. Thomas Winder Young and Aurie Austin Clark; A.B., Earlham Coll., 1961; M.A.T., Johns Hopkins U., 1965; J.D. with honors, U. Md., 1978; 1 son, Lawan Tarn Petty. Research biologist Nat. Cancer Inst., Bethesda, Md., 1961-63; tchr. Brookline (Mass.) Public Schs., 1965-67; sr. computer programmer Computer Usage Co., Inc., Boston, Los Angeles, 1967-70; bookkeeper, bus. mgr. Koinonia Found., Balt., 1974-76; admitted to Maine bar, 1979; individual practice law, South China, Maine, 1979—; staff atty. Legal Services for the Elderly, Augusta, Maine, 1980-82. Bd. dirs. Sch. of Living, York, Pa., 1974-79, treas., 1975-79; trustee Balt. Monthly Meeting of Friends Homewood, 1976-79, clk. Vassalboro Quar. Meeting, 1981—; bd. dirs. Oak Grove-Coburn Sch., Vassalboro, 1982—; mem. exec. com. Am. Friends Service Com., 1977-78; bd. dirs. Sam Ely Community Land Trust, 1981—; bd. dirs. Maine Women's Lobby, 1981-82; selectman Town of China, 1981—; chmn. China Republican Town Com., 1982—; Mem. Am. Bar Assn., Maine State Bar Assn., China Area C. of C. (dir.), Vassalboro Grange, NOW, LWV, Natural Resources Council. Address: PO Box 115 Rt 32 N South China ME 04358

AUSTIN, LORA EVELYN, med. technologist; b. Grand Rapids, Mich., Sept. 6, 1926; d. Carlton and Florence Evelyn (Tyson) Austin; B.A., Olivet Coll., 1948; M.S., Calif. State U., Dominguez Hills, 1981. Intern in med. tech. Butterworth Hosp., Grand Rapids, Mich., 1948-49, staff med. technologist, 1949-52; staff So. Calif. Permanente Med. Group Lab., Los Angeles, 1952—, regional chief immuno-serologist, 1970—; mem. adj. faculty Calif. State U., Dominguez Hills, 1974—. Leader, Campfire Girls, Grand Rapids, Mich., 1949-52; asst. leader Girl Scouts U.S.A., Los Angeles, 1970-81. Recipient Disting. Alumni award Olivet Coll., 1978; lic. med. technologist, Calif., Nat. Cert. Agy. Mem. Am. Soc. Clin. Pathologists (assoc.), Calif. Assn. Med. Lab. Technologists, Am. Soc. Med. Technologists, Olivet Coll. Alumni Assn., Smithsonian Assos., Nat. Wildlife Fedn. Republican. Presbyterian. Home: 10707 Moorpark St Toluca Lake CA 91602

AUSTIN, MILDRED KELLER, educator; b. Chgo., Mar. 15, 1925; d. Raymond Lee and Mildred Elaine (Whitney) Keller; student Northwestern U., 1943-44; B.A., Randolph-Macon Women's Coll., 1947; M.S., U. Ill., 1950, postgrad. 1950-55; diploma Burnham Hosp. Sch. Med. Tech., 1972; m. James O. Austin, July 12, 1952; children—James O., David T., Richard D. Lab./teaching asst. Goucher Coll., Townsend, Md., 1947-48; research asst. dept. physiology U. Ill., Urbana, 1949-51, research assoc., 1951-55, dept. vet. physiology and pharmacology, 1964-71; coordinator spl. procedures Burnham Hosp. Lab., Champaign, Ill., 1972-73, instr. lab. inservice, asst. ednl. coordinator, 1973-74, assoc. edn. coordinator, 1975-77, edn. coordinator, 1977-80, program dir., 1980—; lectr. in field; cons. in field; site surveyor, team leader Nat. Accrediting Agy. for Clin. Lab. Scis., 1980-81, cons., 1981. Treas., Kindergarten PTA, 1959-60; den mother Boy Scouts Am., 1962-64. Mem. Am. Soc. Clin. Pathologists (cert.), Am. Soc. Med. Technologists, Ill. Soc. Med. Technologists, Midwest Assn. Clin. Resource Sharing, Sigma Xi, Sigma Delta Epsilon. Republican. Methodist. Contbr. articles to profl. jours. Home: 917 W Charles St Champaign IL 61820 Office: 407 S 4th St Champaign IL 61820

AUSTIN, PATRICIA ROSS, psychologist; b. Fort Benning, Ga., May 9, 1942; d. Walden Archibald and Priscilla (Ross) Chesley; B.A. magna cum laude, U. Minn., 1970, M.A. in Ednl. Psychology, 1972; m. John Atwood Austin, Jr., Aug. 12, 1978; children—Paul Gerhardt, Matthew Howe. Research asst. U. Minn., 1971-73, research fellow Med. Sch., 1973—. Episcopalian. Contbr. articles in field. Home: 1054 View Ln Mendota Heights MN 55118

AUSTIN, SHIRLEY JEAN BOYKIN, mgmt. cons.; b. Troy, Ala., Feb. 8, 1949; d. Robert D. and Lousie (Grider) Boykin; B.A. in Indsl. Psychology, U. Central Fla., Orlando, 1976; M.S. in Mgmt., Rollins Coll., Winter Park, Fla., 1981; m. William T. Austin, Feb. 25, 1967; children Stephen, Keith. Personnel asst. United Parcel Service, Atlanta, 1970; with mktg. dept. Am. Can Co., Cin., 1974; personal banker II, Sun 1st Nat. Bank, Orlando, 1977-79; asst. v.p., community reinvestment coordinator, loan officer AmeriFirst Fed. Savs. and Loan Assn., Orlando, 1979-81; sr. bus. devel. specialist North and Central Fla. Bus. Service Center, Minority Bus. Devel. Agy., Dept. Commerce, Orlando, 1981—; mem. adv. com. fin. program Valencia Community Coll. Pres. bd. dirs. Met. Orlando Urban League, 1981-83; bd. dirs. United Way Orange County, 1981, mem. budget rev. team, 1981-82; mem. Statewide Black Coalition, 1979-82; mem. community housing resource bd., fair housing div. HUD, 1980-81; regional sec. Nat. Urban League, 1981-83. Recipient Community Service award United Way Orange County, 1977-81, Citizen of Yr. award, 1981. Mem. Nat. Assn. Female Execs., Am. Bus. Women's Assn., NAACP, Orlando Area C. of C. Alpha Kappa Alpha. Office: 1310 W Colonial Dr Suite 27 Orlando FL 32804

AUSTIN, TRACY ANN, tennis player; b. Rolling Hills Estates, Calif., Dec. 12, 1962; d. George and Jeanne Austin; student public schs., Rolling Hills Estates; Profl. tennis player since age 15; winner Wimbledon Jr. Singles, 1978, 7 tournaments in 1979 including U.S. Open Tennis Championship and Italian Open Singles, Avon Tournament, 1980, Wimbledon Mixed Doubles, 1980, 7 tournaments in 1981 including Canadian Open, U.S. Open, Toyota Series, 1980. Named Most Impressive Newcomer, Women's Tennis Assn., 1977; Female Rookie of Yr., Tennis mag., 1977; Female Athlete of Yr., AP, 1979, 81; youngest person to win U.S. Open Tennis Championship, 1979. Office: care Dell Craighill Fentress and Benton 888 17th St NW Suite 1200 Washington DC 20006

AUSTIN-LETT, GENELLE, educator; b. Chgo.; d. Howard Joseph and Evelyn Gene (Reynolds) Blomquist; B.A., U. Ill., Chgo., 1969; M.A., No. Ill. U., 1972. Teaching and research asst. No. Ill. U., 1970-71; TV prodn. asst. Nat. Coll. Edn. High Sch. Workshop, 1972; prof. mass media and critical consumer Principia Coll., summer 1975; reviewer in interpersonal communication, media and behavioral scis. Houghton Mifflin, Harper & Row, William C. Brown, and Wadsworth Pub., 1972—, also asso. prof. speech communication and media Ill. Central Coll., East Peoria, 1971-79; editorial cons. Concordia Pub. House, 1978-82; program dir. Clayton (Mo.) U., 1978-82; instr. St. Louis Community Coll., 1980—; coordinator performing arts multimedia presentations, publicity and recruitment; lectr. media consumerism, psychopolitics and advt.; instr. communications, cons. crisis intervention Fed. Police Tng., 1974-75. Group leader Community Devel. Council, 1974; organizer 9th Ward Teenage Republicans, Chgo., 1963, coordinator, 1967-69; adviser to Ill. Central Coll. Young Reps., 1971-75; clk., dir. exec. bd., chmn. bd. 1st Ch. of Christ, Scientist, Peoria; nat. advisory bd. Am. Security Council; mem. Rep. Nat. Com. Recipient Honors Day recognition U. Ill., 1968, hon. mention Nat. Arts and Letters playwriting contest, 1972; lic. life ins. agt., Mo. Mem. Ill. Speech and Theatre Assn., Speech Communication Assn., Central States Speech Assn., Internat. Data Speak, Lakeview Center Arts and Scis. Clubs: U.S. Senatorial, Bible Investigation, Racquet. Author: (with others) Instructor's Manual for Mass Communication and Human Interaction, 1977; (with Jan Sprague) Talk to Yourself, 1976; contbr. articles to Christian Sci. periodicals.

AUTHIER, KAREN JANE, social worker; b. Omaha, Sept. 27, 1942; d. Forrest Lee and Gwendolyn Ann (Lawyer) Pflasterer; B.A., U. Nebr., Lincoln, 1964, M.S.W., 1969; m. Jerry Authier, Feb. 29, 1976; children—Sarah, Gabriel, Allison. Teen age dir. YWCA, Lincoln, Nebr., 1964-67, youth services dir., 1969-72; social service rep. Nebr. Dept. Pub. Welfare, Scottsbluff, 1973; psychiat. social worker Nebr. Psychiat. Inst., Omaha, 1974-77, instr., 1974-80, dir. social services, 1978—, asst. prof. psychiat. social work, 1980—; parent edn. cons. Region VII, HEW, Nebr. State Tech. Assistance Team; mem. adv. bd. Nebr. Council for Children With Behavior Disorders. Mem. Omaha Mayor's Commn. on Status Women, chmn. children's com., 1977; pres. Nebr. Adv. Com. on Child Abuse and Neglect, 1977-79, Omaha Council for Services to Children and Youth, 1979-80, Advocacy Office for Children and Youth, 1981-82. Mem. Acad. Cert. Social Workers, Nat. Assn. Social Workers (named Social Worker of Yr., Nebr. chpt. 1980), Nebr. Soc. Hosp. Social Work Dirs. Democrat. Lutheran. Home: 2000 Skyline Dr Elkhorn NE 68022 Office: Nebr Psychiat Inst 602 S 45th St Omaha NE 68106

AUTMAN, CAROL LYNNE, TV mgr. talent contracts; b. Wilmington, Del., Sept. 20, 1939; d. George Francis and Edythe (McClure) Autman; B.A. in Speech and Theatre and Psychology, Grinnell Coll., 1961; M.A. in Speech and Theatre, Ind. U., 1964; guardian of Molly Clogg. Actress, Alley Theatre, Houston, 1964-65; actress, mem. faculty Alley's Children's Theatre, Houston, 1964-65; artistic, bus. dir. The Children's Theatre Assn., Balt., 1965-68; co. mgr. Dames at Sea, N.Y.C., 1968-71; tour dir. Nat. Shakespeare Co., N.Y.C., 1971; mgr. talent contracts WNET/13 Public TV, N.Y.C., 1971—; cons. public TV stas., 1972-82. Block improvement capt., N.Y.C., 1971—; career counselor Grinnell (Iowa) Coll., 1978—; youth counselor Troubled Children and Families N.Y., 1970-82. Named Outstanding Contbr. to Ind. U., 1963. Ford Found. grantee, 1964. Mem. Nat. Acad. TV Arts and Scis., Nat. Assn. Ednl. Broadcasters, Am. Film Inst., Nat. Assn. Female Execs., Alumni Assn. Ind. Democrat. Methodist. Club: Swiss Ski. Home: 34 W 83d St New York NY 10024 Office: WNET/13 356 W 58th St New York NY 10019

AUTREY, AVIS KATHLYN, nursery and floral co. exec.; b. Easterly, Tex., Mar. 17, 1937; d. Albert Kelsey and Willie Mae (Scott) Autrey; student Sam Houston State U., 1957-60, U. Houston, 1964. Office mgr. McMahan Ins. Agy., Houston, 1960-63; office mgr., realtor Homes Jones Devel. and Ins. Agy., Houston, 1963-65; acct., office mgr. Office Services, Inc., Houston, 1966-69; mgr. acctg. Sam Proler Industries, Inc., Houston, 1969-74; with Raymond Internat., Inc., Houston, 1974-79, supr. corp. systems and procedures, 1976, hdqrs. fin. coordinator, 1976-77, adminstrv. fin. mgr., Ras Al Khaimah, Saudi Arabia, 1977-79; owner, mgr. AKA-Interiors/Exteriors, Houston and Plantersville, Tex., 1979-80, Bellfort Nursery and Florist, Inc., Houston, 1980—. Republican. Home: 4535 Elm St Bellaire TX 77401 Office: 6964 Bellfort St Houston TX 77087

AVANCENA, ROBERTA JEAN, mem. congressional staff; b. Washington, Nov. 26, 1950; d. Robert Theodore and Barbara Mae (Gaffney) A.; student Drew U., 1968-70; B.A. in English Lit. and Communications, Rutgers U., 1972; tchr. cert. Tufts U., 1973. Legis. asst. Rep. Gilbert Gude, 1973-76; sr. legis. asst. Rep. Newton Steers, 1977-78, Rep. Peter Peyser, 1979; co-chmn. Return Newton Steers for Congress Com., 1979-80; legis. dir. Rep. Jim Dunn, 1981—. Bd. dirs. House of Ruth for Homeless Women, 1977-78. Office: 1511 Longworth House Office Bldg Washington DC 20515

AVEDISIAN, MARGOT JEAN, instl. broker; b. Chgo., Aug. 24, 1954; d. Haig Aredis and Mary (Astorian) A.; student Randolph Macon Women's Coll., 1972-74; B.A., Miami U., Oxford, Ohio, 1976. Retail sales asst. Merrill Lynch, 1972-76; mcpl. bond sales E. F. Hutton Co., Cleve., 1976-78; govt. sales Kidder Peabody, Cleve., 1978-80, Smith Barney Co., Chgo., 1981—. Vol., Northwestern Hosp., 1981. Episcopalian. Office: 1 First Nat Plaza Chicago IL 60603

AVELAR, CARMEN MARIA, journalist, editor; b. San Francisco, Oct. 11, 1923; d. Miguel and Victoria Simon; grad. Merritt Bus. Coll., Oakland, Calif., 1943; m. Alfred J. Avelar, Jan. 19, 1946 (dec.); children—Richard M., Diana Avelar Kewell. Advt. copywriter Jackson Furniture Co., Oakland, Calif., 1942-46; women's feature writer Sparks Newspapers, Hayward, Calif., 1963-79, columnist, food editor, 1979—. Mem. Women in communications. Past mem. bd. dirs. Children's Hosp. Med. Center Aux., Oakland, Calif. Office: 116 W Winton Ave Hayward CA 94540

AVERELL, LOIS HATHAWAY, speech-lang. pathologist, audiologist; b. Boston, Apr. 8, 1917; d. Merle Leon and Mildred Hathaway (Allen) A.; diploma Wheelock Coll., 1941; B.S. in Edn., Boston U., 1942, Ed.M., 1953, postgrad., 1963-65. Kindergarten tchr. Dana Hall Schs., Wellesley, Mass., 1942-44; head tchr., pre-sch. program Brimmer and May Sch., Boston, 1944-52; speech therapist United Cerebral Palsy of South Shore, Inc., Quincy, Mass., 1952-53; dir. speech and hearing Meeting Street Sch. Children's Rehab. Center, Providence, 1953-57; head speech and hearing pathologist Children's Hosp. Med. Center, Boston, 1957-63; teaching fellow Boston U., 1963-64; dir. speech, hearing, and cleft palate clinic North Shore Children's Hosp., Salem, Mass., 1966-76; speech pathologist, audiologist South Shore Mental Health Assn., Quincy, 1977-78; speech-lang. pathologist, audiologist Mayflower House Child Care Center, Plymouth, Mass., 1978—. Cert. Mass. Dept. Edn. Mem. Am. Speech-Lang. and Hearing Assn. (dual cert. clin. competence), Mass. Speech and Hearing Assn., Am. Assn. Clin. Counselors (diplomate, sec. 1968-75), Nat. Alliance for Family Life (life mem.), Northeast Communication Enhancement Group, Pi Lambda Theta, Alpha Sigma Alpha. Republican. Baptist. Club: Zonta (1st v.p. 1975-77) (Salem). Home: 815 Washington St Whitman MA 02382 Office: 123 South St Plymouth MA 02360

AVERMAN, LINDA ANN, sales agt.; b. Miami, Fla., June 21, 1952; d. Edmund J. and Lee (Grell) A.; student Miami-Dade Jr. Coll., 1970-71; B.A. with honors, U. South Fla., 1975. Sales agt. Prudential Ins. Co., Santa Barbara, Calif., 1977-78, Ventura, Calif., 1978-81, Coelho Fin. Corp., Los Angeles, 1981—. Recipient nat. sales achievement award. Mem. Nat. Assn. Life Underwriters, Bus. and Profl. Women (legis. chair 1979). Office: 625 S Kingsley Dr Los Angeles CA 90005

AVERY, EDWINA AUSTIN, lawyer; b. Silver Creek, N.Y., Oct. 11, 1896; d. Llewellyn Philip and Harriet (Robinson) Austin; J.D., M.P.L., Nat. U. Law, 1927; student George Washington U., 1928-30, Dept. Agr. Grad. Sch., 1928-31, 41-42; m. Hastings Palmer Avery, June 11, 1924 (dec. June 13, 1973); children—Cecilia Ann (dec.), Barbara Ann (Mrs. Homer Dean Huffman). Admitted to D.C. bar, 1926, U.S. Supreme Ct. bar, 1938, with U.S. Govt., 1918-58, clk. with Office Adj. Gen., 1918-22, Dept. Interior, 1922-24, successively clk., asst. editor, asso. editor Bur. Plant Industry, Dept. Agr., 1924-43, editor, later naturalization examiner Immigration and Naturalization Service, Dept. Justice, 1943-58; practice law, 1958—; also cons. in immigration and nationality law. Chmn. Govt. Workers Council, 1929-37; only woman mem. Blue Ribbon Zoning Com.; only woman pres. Diston Heights Civic Assn., 1966-67. Trustee O. E. Howe Home for Unfortunate Girls, 1954—. Recipient citation D.C. State Fedn. Bus. and Profl. Women's Clubs, certificate City of St. Petersburg, Fla. Mem. Am., D.C., Fed., Women's (pres. 1933-35) bar assns., Am. Judicature Soc., Nat. Assn. Women Lawyers, League Women Voters, D.A.R., Bus. and Profl. Women's Club, West Coast (Fla.) George Washington U. Alumni Assn. (pres. 1973-74), Kappa Beta Pi (grand dean 1943-47). Christian Scientist. Author: A Welcome to U.S.A. Citizenship (Freedoms Found. award), 1951; (motion picture script) Twentieth Century Pilgrim (Freedom Found. award); It Did Happen Here, 1974; also TV scripts, articles. Editor and compiler: Laws and Regulations, Immigration and Naturalization Service, 1944; Laws Applicable to Immigration and Nationality, 1952. Address: 1991 42d St N St Petersburg FL 33713 *

AVERY, ELIZABETH ANNE, banker; b. Teaneck, N.J., June 29, 1933; d. Whitney Kent and Clara K.; B.A., Pace U., 1963. With Bankers Trust Co., N.Y.C., 1952—, mgr. benefits adminstrn. and planning, 1979—. Office: Bankers Trust Co 280 Park Ave New York NY 10017

AVERY, LYNN FAITH, nurse, adminstr., b. Malone, N.Y., Apr. 21, 1940; d. Evan Kirk and Geneva Cecilia (Boyea) Avery; A.A.S. in Nursing, Mohawk Valley Community Coll., 1975; B.A., Sacramento State U., 1981; children—Mark Pugh, Diane. Real estate broker Humphreys Real Estate, Whitesboro, N.Y., 1966-75; nurse C. Ozlu, M.D., Rome, N.Y., 1975-77; charge nurse Psychiatry Unit, New Hanover Meml. Hosp., Wilmington, N.C., 1977-78, Sutter Meml. Hosp., Sacramento, 1978-79; dir. nursing Crestwood Psychiat. Facility, Carmichael, Calif., 1979-82, adminstr. tng. program, 1981—; program cons. Nurses Aide Cert. Unit, Dept. Health Services, State of Calif,. 1982—. Active, Am. Cancer Soc., 1977-78; pres. PTA, Oriskany, N.Y., 1969. Cert. in vocat. edn. as nurse instr., Calif. Mem. Am. Nurses Assn. Republican. Presbyterian. Home: 6739 Will Rogers Dr Fair Oaks CA 95628 Office: 2422 Arden Way Sacramento CA 95825

AVILA, DAMIANA CORIA, social worker; b. Barugo, Leyte, Philippines, Aug. 19, 1942; came to U.S., 1972, naturalized, 1980; d. Juan A. and Maxima (Coria) A.; B.S. in Social Work, Centro Escolar U., Philippines, 1966; M.S.W., Jane Addams Sch. of Social Work, U. Ill., 1979. Social caseworker Child Caring Agy., Manila, Philippines, 1966-68, acting group living supr., 1968; field social worker Dept. Social Welfare, Philippines, 1969-71, sr. social worker, 1971, provincial social welfare officer, 1972; activity therapist Belden Manor Shelter Home, Chgo., 1972-73, social worker, 1973-74; social service cons. to various nursing homes and social service orgns., 1976—; social worker, patient care coordinator Pembridge House, Evanston, Ill., 1979-82; activity therapist cons. Wincrest Nursing Center, Chgo., 1980—; social worker (part-time) 3 Oaks Nursing Center, Evanston, 1979—; program coordinator Skokie (Ill.) Meadow II, 1982—; mem. staff services for work and rehab. Renaissance House, Chgo., 1976—. Named One of the Most Outstanding New Citizens for 1980, Citizenship Council of Met. Chgo. Mem. Nat. Assn. of Social Workers, Activity Dir. Soc. (dir. 1974—), U. Ill. Alumni Assn. Home: 6050 N California Ave Chicago IL 60659

AVRAM, HENRIETTE DAVIDSON, govt. info. systems exec.; b. N.Y.C., Oct. 7, 1919; d. Joseph and Rhea (Olsho) Davidson; student Hunter Coll., N.Y.C., George Washington U.; Sc.D. (hon.), So. Ill. U., 1977; m. Herbert Mois Avram, Aug. 23, 1941; children—Lloyd, Marcie, Jay. Systems analyst, methods analyst, programmer Nat. Security Agy., 1953-59; systems analyst Am. Research Bur., 1959-61, Datatrol Corp., 1961-65; supervisory info. systems specialist Library of Congress, Washington, 1965-67, asst. coordinator info. systems, 1967-70, chief MARC Devel. Office, 1970-76, dir. Network Devel. Office, 1976-80, dir. processing systems, network and automation planning, 1980—; lectr. dept. library sci. Cath. U. Am., 1973—. Chmn. subcom. 2 sectional com. Z39, Am. Nat. Standards Inst., 1966—; chmn. working group on content designators Internat. Fedn. Library Assns., 1972-77; chmn. subcom. 4 working group 1 on character sets Internat. Orgn. for Standardization, 1971—; mem. Com. for Coordination of Nat. Bibliog. Control, 1976-79; mem. steering com. MARC Internat. Network Study, 1975—; chmn. profl. bd. Internat. Fedn. Library Assns. and Instns., 1979—, chmn. info. tech. sect., 1978—, chmn. mgmt. and tech. div., 1979—; chmn. RECON Working Task Force, 1968-73. Recipient Superior Service award Library of Congress, 1968, Margaret Mann citation in cataloging and classification, 1971, Fed. Woman's award, 1974; award for achievement in library and info. tech. ALA-Library Info. Tech. Assn., 1980; co-recipient ACRL Acad./Research Librarian of Year award, 1979. Mem. ALA (dir., past pres. info. sci. and automation div.; Melvil Dewey award 1981), Am. Soc. Info. Sci., Assn. Computing Machinery. Bd. editors Jour. Library Automation, 1970-72; contbr. articles to profl. jours. Home: 1776 Elton Rd Silver Spring MD 20903 Office: Library of Congress Washington DC 20540

AWIS, VERONICA MARY, singer, nurse; b. Detroit, Sept. 9, 1926; d. Karl and Mary Ellen (Christoff) Lutz; R.N., St. Joseph Sch. Nursing, 1948; student profl. arts St. Joseph Coll.; vocal student Elio Gennari, 1950-65, Werner Singer, 1970-79, Goldschmidt, 1976- ; m. Edward Adam Awis, Feb. 18, 1950; children—JoEllen, Beth Ann, Brian Edward, Donald Alan, Karen Maureen. Staff nurse Mt. Carmel Hosp., Detroit, 1948-51, Lee Meml. Hosp., Ft. Myers, Fla., 1966-70, 75-80; in-service dir. Beacon-Donegan Nursing Home, Ft. Myers, 1980—; debut as concert singer in Detroit, 1951; lyric soprano singing leading roles in opera, oratorios S.W. Fla. Symphony Orch., 1967—; recitalist S.W. Fla., 1967—; instr. in field; vocat. instr. nursing Lee County Adult Edn., pres. bd. dirs. S.W. Symphony Orch., benefit performer Heart Fund, Easter Seal, chs. in S.W. Fla.; musical dir. St. Andrew's Cath. Ch., Cape Coral, Fla.; musical dir., soloist Temple Beth El, Cape Coral. R.N., Mich., Fla. Mem. Nat. Assn. Tchrs. of Singing, Soc. Symphony Women (founder, 1st pres.), Am. Bus. Women's Assn., Am. Nurses Assn. Lee County Alliance Arts. Republican. Roman Catholic. Home: 118 SW 57th St Cape Coral FL 33904

AWL, CHARLOTTE JANE, nurse, educator; b. St. Louis, Apr. 28, 1935; d. Herbert Vincent and Elizabeth Edwards (White) Pate; diploma, Presbyn. Hosp., Phila., 1956; B.S. in Gen. Nursing, Ind. U., 1960, M.S. in Nursing Edn., 1961; postgrad. (Ada Belle Clark Welsh scholar), Ill. State U., 1978—; m. Richard Allen Awl, Sept. 2, 1962; children—Deborah Jane, David Allen, Stephen Scott. Pvt. duty nurse, team leader women's surg. ward Presbyn. Hosp., 1956-57, head nurse, pvt. duty nurse, 1957-58; staff nurse Bloomington (Ind.) Hosp., 1958-60; pvt. duty nurse, 1960-62; instr. nursing DePauw U., 1961-63; instr., coordinator devel. sr. courses Meth. Med. Center, Peoria, Ill., 1963-64, staff nurse, 1964-66; cons. dept. nursing Bradley U., Peoria, 1966-67, asst. prof., 1967-72, asst. prof., asso. chmn. dept. nursing, 1972-74, asso. prof., asso. chmn. dept., 1974-78, asso. prof., asso. dir. div. nursing, 1978—. Cert. CPR instr. Ill. Heart Assn. Mem. Am. Assn. Critical Care Nurses, AAUP, Am. Nurses Assn., Assn. Operating Room Nurses, Council Baccalaureate and Higher Degree Programs of Nat. League Nursing, Am. Heart Assn., Ill. Assn. Maternal and Child Health, AAUW, Ind. U. Alumni Assn., Pi Lambda Theta, Sigma Theta Tau, Phi Kappa Phi, Kappa Delta Pi. Presbyterian. Home: 305 Dundee Rd East Peoria IL 61611 Office: Div Nursing Bradley U Peoria IL 61625

AWTRY, MARILYN (LYNNE) JOAN, research cons.; b. Amityville, N.Y., Feb. 11, 1933; d. William Arthur and Bertha Eliza (Wheland) Jackson; student N.Y. Inst. Applied Arts and Scis., 1950-51; m. Jack

Awtry, Apr. 27, 1952 (div. 1963); children—Jacalyn Susan, Nancy Jean Awtry Gustafson. Procurement asst. U.S. Air Force, Patrick AFB, Fla., 1963-66; contract negotiator/adminstr. NASA, 1966-72; contracting officer U.S. Coast Guard, Washington, 1972-82; ordained minister and medium Nat. Spiritualist Assn. of Chs., 1973—; pres. SAM, Inc., Arlington, Va., 1979—; lectr. in field; counsellor-medium in parapsychology, 1965—, monthly columnist The Nat. Spiritualist. Recipient Outstanding Performance awards U.S. Govt., 1961, 63, 65, 76, 81. Mem. South Cassadaga Spiritualist. Assn., Assn. for Research and Enlightenment, Nat. Contract Mgmt. Assn. Democrat. Clubs: Nat. Spiritualist Tchrs., Lily Dale Assembly. Author: (pamphlet) You and a Way, 1977; co-author: General Educational Course in Modern Spiritualism, 1981. Home: Three Lake St Cassadaga FL 32706 Office: Contracts NSC Jacksonville Naval Air Sta Jacksonville FL

AWTRY, NELL CATHERINE, former real estate exec.; b. Dallas, Sept. 29, 1900; d. Henry Hibbler and Laura Jane (Harris) Jacoby; B.A., So. Meth. U., 1935; postgrad. Columbia U., 1941-42; m. John Hix Awtry, Apr. 24, 1922; 1 dau., Nell Catherine Awtry Gilchrist (dec.). Real estate saleswoman Prince & Ripley, Scarsdale, N.Y., 1948, Midgeley Parks, Scarsdale, 1949, Cleveland E. Van Wert Inc., Scarsdale, 1954-60, Julia B. Fee, Inc., Scarsdale, 1960—. Mem. Scarsdale Realty Bd., Westchester Realty Bd., Zeta Tau Alpha. Republican. Baptist. Mem. Order Eastern Star (worthy matron 1961, 67), Am. Legion Aux., Am. Assn. Ret. Persons. Clubs: Scardale (N.Y.) Golf; Dallas Athletic; Laguna Hills Rep. Women's, Leisure World Rep. Author poems and lyrics. Home: PO Box 2833 3337-2A Punta Alta Rossmoor Leisure World Laguna Hills CA 92653

AXE, KATHLEEN ANN KENNEDY (MRS. ROGER DANIEL AXE), latex mfg. ofcl.; b. Ft. Monmouth, N.J., Dec. 11, 1952; d. Harold Quentin and Madeline Cecelia Kennedy; B.A. in Journalism (Hoosier scholar), Ind. State U., 1975, M.S. in Broadcasting, 1976. Staff writer Ind. Statesman, 1971-73, night editor and mem. editorial bd., 1973; asst. news dir. Sta. WISU, 1974, producer, 1975; co-chmn. Wabash Valley Press Conf., 1975; tech. writer Am. Latex Corp., Sullivan, Ind., 1977-78, specification writer/quality control analyst, 1978-80, quality control supr., 1980-82, quality assurance coordinator, 1982—. Active Sullivan County ARC; Sunday Sch. tchr. 1st Christian Ch. of Sullivan, 1978-80, children's ch. worker, 1979-80; participant Sullivan County Muscular Dystrophy Carnival, 1979. Recipient Creative Writing award Ind. State U., Alan C. Rankin Disting. Sr. award; Good Citizen award DAR; Scholastic Recognition award Erickson Hall, Pickeral Hall; lic. 3d class radiotelephone operator F.C.C. Mem. Am. Soc. Quality Control, Soc. Profl. Journalists, Nat. Geog. Soc., Sigma Delta Chi, Alpha Sigma Alpha, Alpha Phi Gamma, Pamarista Scholastic Hon., Delta Theta Tau, Alpha Lambda Delta. Club: Order Eastern Star (asso. conductress 1978, conductress 1979, Star Point Martha 1980, Star Point Adah 1981). Contbr. articles to publs. Home: 53 Nancy Ave PO Box 222 Bloomfield IN 47424 Office: 609 E Chaney St Sullivan IN 47882

AXELROOD, HELEN BLAU, actress, psychotherapist, weight loss mgmt. assn. exec.; b. Chgo., Feb. 13; d. Morris and Goldie (Bookstein) Blau; B.A., Roosevelt U., 1951, M.A., 1977; Ph.D., Marquette U., 1981; m. Jack Axelrood, June 27; children—Lisa, Barney, Larry, Michael. Appeared in: Caucasian Chalk Circle, 1952, Mooney's Kid Don't Cry, 1953, Round Dance, 1954, Dybuk, 1954, The Chicago Fire, 1971; actress, writer Bible Time, NBC-TV, 1960, The Artist Speaks, 1970; tchr. Chgo. Bd. Edn., 1958-62; art dir. Temple Emanuel, Chgo., 1957-58; primary supr. Temple Beth'el, Chgo., 1964-66; intern Drug and Alcohol Rehab. Center, Lutheran Gen. Hosp., Park Ridge, Ill., 1978; counselor Marquette U., Milw., 1979; pvt. practice psychotherapy, counseling, Evanston, Ill., 1976-82; counselor, psychotherapist Weight Care Inst. and counseling Clinic Inc., Evanston, 1981—; dir. 1982—. Mem. Speakers Bur., Oakton Community Coll.; mem. Winnetka Talent Pool. Recipient Dedicated Service award Temple Beth Emet, Evanston, 1960, Outstanding Service award Temple Beth El, 1970. Mem. Am. Psychol. Assn., Ill. Psychol. Assn., Am. Personnel and Guidance Assn., Ill. Guidance and Personnel Assn., Assn. Specialist in Group Work. Clubs: Variety of Ill. Contbr. articles to profl. publs. Office: 1601 Sherman Ave Suite 402 Evanston IL 60201

AXFORD, ETHEL IDELL, nurse; b. Dora, Ala., Mar. 6, 1913; d. William Claude and Mary Della (Skelton) McCoy; R.N., Sherman Hosp. Sch. Nursing, 1949; cert. in gerontology Sangamon State Coll., 1980; m. Harold Axford, Mar. 25, 1949. Surgery supr. El Monte (Calif.) Clinic, 1950-52; nurse Rosemead (Calif.) Sanitarium, 1953-57, West Covina (Calif.) Clinic, 1958-60; dir. nurses Monterey Sanitarium, San Gabriel, Calif., 1960-65; substitute indsl. nurse Decatur Industries (Ill.), 1965-72; dir. nurses Lake Shore Manor Extended Care Facility, Decatur, 1973-81; dir. Commn. of Aging, Decatur, 1977-79. Mem. Sherman Hosp. Alumni, Am. Bus. Womens Assn. Republican. Presbyterian. Home: 13 Northern Dr Decatur IL 62521

AYARES, LINDA JEANNE, public relations exec.; b. Camden, N.J., Apr. 1, 1953; d. Joseph Arthur and Elizabeth (Verrall) Ayares; B.A., Allegheny Coll., 1975; m. William R. Engel, Oct. 23, 1976. Asst. dir. public relations Spanish Nat. Tourist Office, N.Y.C., 1975-78; account exec. to sr. account exec. Cullen and Taylor Ltd., N.Y.C., 1978-81; v.p. Tromson Monroe Public Relations, N.Y.C., 1981—; v.p. Aerotours Internat., 1981—; narrator N.Y. Park Service and Internat. Year of Disabled programs Nat. Public Radio. Mem. Women in Communications. Office: 40 E 49th St New York NY 10017

AYDELOTTE, JUANITA LEE, mfg. co. exec.; b. Prairie City, Oreg., Oct. 18, 1944; d. Alva Guy and Ruth Anna (Holland) A.; student Blue Mountain Community Coll., 1962-64. With composing dept. East Oregonian Publ. Co., Pendleton, Oreg., 1963-74; applications engr. Tal-Star Computer Systems, Inc., Princeton Junction, N.J., 1974-75, supr. software distbn., 1975-77, mgr. software control, 1977-78, mgr. adminstrv. and library scis., 1978-80; configuration mgr. Logicon-Intercomp, Torrance, Calif., 1980-81; mgr. customer and system support Harris Composition Systems, Torrance, 1981—.

AYDELOTTE, MYRTLE E. KITCHELL, nursing cons.; b. Van Meter, Iowa, May 31, 1917; d. John and Lavara Josephine (Gutshall) Kitchell; B.S., U. Minn., 1939, M.A., 1947, Ph.D., 1955; m. William Osgood Aydelotte, June 22, 1956; children—Marie Elizabeth, Jeannette Farley. Head nurse Charles T. Miller Hosp., St. Paul, 1939-41; surg. teaching supr. St. Mary's Hosp. Sch. Nursing, 1941-42; instr. U. Minn., 1945-49; dir. dean-elect State U. Iowa, 1949, prof., dean, 1949-57, prof., acting chmn. psychiat. nursing dept., 1957-58; prof. Coll. Nursing, U. Iowa, 1949-62, 65-76, dir. dept. nursing U. Iowa Hosps. and Clinics, 1968-76; asso. chief nurse VA Hosp., Iowa City, 1963-64, chief of nursing research, 1964-65; exec. dir. Am. Nurses Assn., 1977-81; cons., 1982—. Served as capt. U.S. Army Nurse Corps, 1942-46; asst. chief nurse 26th Gen. Hosp., Eng., Africa, Italy, 1942-45; chief nurse 52d Sta. Hosp., Italy, 1945. Recipient Outstanding Achievement award U. Minn., 1959, Distinguished Service award U. Iowa. Mem. Am. Nurses Assn., Inst. Medicine, Psi Chi, Pi Lambda Theta, Sigma Theta Tau (nat. pres. 1955-57). Contbr. articles to profl. jours. Home: 201 N 1st Ave Iowa City IA 52240 also 149 Oswegatchie Rd Waterford CT 06385

AYERS, ANNE LOUISE, edn. specialist, psychologist; b. Albuquerque, Oct. 22, 1948; d. F. Ernest and Gladys M. (Miles) Ayers; B.A., U. Kans., 1970; M.Ed., Seattle Pacific U., 1971; postgrad. Hampton Inst., 1976-77, Coll. William and Mary, 1977-78, Va. Poly. Inst., 1978—. Co-counselor, Nutka Indian Migrant Camp, Seattle 1st United Methodist Ch., Vashion Island, 1967; counselor, interviewer, speech therapist Goodwill Industries, Seattle, 1970-71; cadet Pacific Sch. for Severely Mentally Retarded, Speech Handicapped and Emotionally Disturbed, Seattle, 1971; counselor intern Seattle Central Community Coll., 1971; staff cons. student devel. Central Wash. State U., Ellensburg, 1971-72; dir. Chapman Coll. Aerospace Def. Command/Residence Edn. Centers for Mont. and N.D., Orange, Calif., 1972-74; instr. psychology Hampton (Va.) Inst., 1976-77, also edn. service specialist, Ft. Monroe, Va., 1975-77 and edn. specialist Ft. Eustis (Va.) Transp. Sch., 1977-79; edn. specialist Nat. Mine Safety and Health Acad., Beckley, W.Va., 1979—. Hon. mem. Va. Sheriff's Assn. Mem. Nat. Assn. Student Personnel Adminstrs., Nat. Assn. Women Deans, Adminstrs. and Counselors, Am. Personnel and Guidance Assn., Assn. Federally Employed Women, Nat. Def. Transp. Assn. Office: Nat Mine Safety and Health Acad PO Box 1166 Beckley WV 25801

AYERS-ALLEN, VIVIAN ELIZABETH, poet, art center exec.; b. Chester, S.C., July 29, 1923; d. Robert Douglas and Vivian Myrtle (Graham) Ayers; grad. Barber-Scotia Coll., 1941; student Bennett Coll., 1942-43; m. Andrew A. Allen, Sept. 14, 1945; children—Andrew A., Phylicia Ayers, Deborah Kaye. Librarian, Rice U., Houston, 1964-67; organizer, editor Adept Quar., Houston, 1965-66; developer, dir. original Cultural Program for Community of Indigents of Houston-Harris County under aegis-alliance of Harris County Community Action Assn., The Parks Dept., Mcpl. Arts Commn. and Miller Outdoor Theater, Houston, 1967-74; founder, dir. The ADEPT New Am. Folk Center, Houston, 1970—. Recipient Plaques for Outstanding Service to Main St. Festival/Houston, 1971-74; Spl. Community Services award Alpha Kappa Alpha, 1980. Mem. ACLU, NAACP, Asso. Councils of Arts (exec. com. 1972-73), Afro-Am. Studies Alliance, Nat. Endowment, Women's Caucus for Art. Unitarian. Author: (poetry) Spice of Dawns, 1952; Hawk, 1957; (play) Bow Boly, 1962; The Marriage Ceremony, 1973. Home: 1615 Binz St Houston TX 77004 Office: 1617 Binz St Houston TX 77004

AYLWARD, JAYNE ANNE, Kans. state legislator; b. Salina, Kans., Aug. 28, 1956; d. Edward Michael and Norma (Schippel) Aylward; B.S., Kans. State U., 1978. Farmer, stockman, 1975—; mem. Kans. Ho. of Reps. from 73d Dist., 1979—. Mem. Kans. Livestock Assn., Kans. Farm Bur., Salina County Taxpayers Assn., Kans. State U. Alumni Assn. Roman Catholic. Office: Ho of Reps State Capitol Topeka KS 66612 *

AYOUB, CHRISTINE WILLIAMS, mathematician; b. Cin., Feb. 7, 1922; d. William Lloyd Garrison and Anne Christine (Sykes) Williams; A.B., Bryn Mawr Coll., 1942; A.M., Radcliffe Coll., 1943; M.A., McGill U., 1944; Ph.D., Yale U., 1947; m. Raymond G. Ayoub, July 1, 1950; children—Cynthia Anne, Daphne Nazeera. Instr. Cornell U., 1948-51; Office Naval Research fellow Inst. for Advanced Study, 1947-48; Sigma Delta Epsilon fellow, research assoc. Radcliffe Coll., 1951-52; mem. faculty Pa. State U., State College, 1953—, prof. math., 1967—; NSF Sci. Faculty fellow, vis. prof. U. Frankfurt (W.Ger.), 1966-67; vis. prof. U. Warwick (Eng.), 1979-80. Mem. Am. Math. Soc., Math. Assn. Am., Assn. for Women in Math., Sigma Xi. Quaker. Contbr. papers to profl. lit. Home: 120 Ridge Ave State College PA 16801 Office: Dept Math 303 McAllister Bldg Pa State U University Park PA 16802

AYRAULT, EVELYN WEST, psychologist, writer; b. Buffalo, Mar. 3, 1922; d. John and Evelyn (West) A.; B.S., Fla. State Coll. for Women, 1945; M.A., U. Chgo., 1947. Chief psychologist, asst. prin. Crippled Children's Sch., Jamestown, N.D., 1947-48; psychologist, tchr. spl. edn. dept. Sharon (Pa.) Public Schs., 1948-50; chief psychologist, instr. Med. Coll. Va., Richmond, 1950-52; pvt. practice, psychology N.Y.C., 1952-68; clin. psychologist, Erie, Pa., 1968—; dir. psychol. services United Cerebral Palsy Assn., Miami, Fla., 1952-54, Erie County (Pa.) Crippled Children's Soc., 1968-78; cons. NW Tri-County Intermediate Unit, Edinboro, Pa., 1978—. Mem. Am., N.Y. State, Pa. psychol. assns., Council for Exceptional Children, Psi Chi. Author: Take One Step, 1963; You Can Raise Your Handicapped Child, 1964; Helping the Handicapped Teenager Mature, 1971; Growing Up Handicapped, 1978; Sex, Love, and the Physically Handicapped, 1981. Home: 10054 W Law Rd North East PA 16428

AYSCUE, FREDA JEAN, investment/ins. co. exec.; b. Winston-Salem, N.C., June 13, 1950; d. Fred Jennings and Bessie Elizabeth Hauser; B.S. in Family Studies and Consumer Sci. (FS/CS scholar, Stokeley Van Camp Outstanding Achievement award 1974), San Diego State U., 1974; m. John H. Ayscue, Jr., Sept. 12, 1970. Sales coordinator Norris Industries, Los Angeles, 1974-75; ind. sales rep., So. Calif., 1975-78; regional mgr. Geno Designs, Atlanta, 1978-79; div. supt. Roosevelt Nat. Investment Co., New Orleans, 1979—; speaker in field. Mem. cons. council New Orleans/Bayou Health Systems Agy., 1981-82. Mem. Bus. and Profl. Women, Am. Soc. Profl. and Exec. Women, Nat. Assn. Female Execs., Home Economists in Bus., Womens Equity Action League, Women's Polit. Caucus, NOW (chpt. public relations chmn. 1979-81, del. nat. conv. 1980-81). Office: 3515 Melvil Dewey Dr Suite 203 Metairie LA 70002

AZZATO, JUDITH ANNE, social worker; b. Floral Park, N.Y., Dec. 23, 1946; d. John August and Eleanor (Buckley) Rissmeyer; B.A., Queens Coll., Flushing, N.Y., 1967; M.S.W., Fordham U., 1971; m. Michael J. Azzato, Jr., Aug. 19, 1967 (div. Aug. 1974). Caseworker, community organizer Suffolk County Dept. Social Services, Bay Shore, N.Y., 1967-73; field mentor Cornell U. Coll. Human Ecology, Ithaca, N.Y., 1974; social worker Northport-East Northport (N.Y.) Community Council, 1974-75; dir. YMCA Outreach Project, Bay Shore, 1976-77; therapist Luth. Community Services, 1978-79; social worker Suffolk Devel. Center, Melville, N.Y., 1978—; field instr. Adelphi U. Sch. Social Work. Bd. dirs. Econ. Opportunity Council of Suffolk, Inc., Patchogue, N.Y., 1974-77; mem. 2d Congressional Dist. Com. on Youth, 1976; bd. dirs. Suffolk County Youth Bd., 1974-75; mem. Suffolk County Conf. Juvenile and Criminal Justice, Inc., 1976-80; founding mem. Day Care Council of Suffolk, 1971-74, N.Y. State Assn. Child Day Care Councils, Inc., 1972-74; fundraiser Women's Polit. Caucus, 1973; mem. Youth Services Coordinating Council of Suffolk, 1975-77. Cert. social worker N.Y.; recipient award Suffolk County Community Service, 1977; N.Y. State-Suffolk County Dept. Social Services scholar, 1969-71. Mem. Nat. Assn. Social Workers (del. 1977, 79, 81, treas. Suffolk div. 1978-81, sec. N.Y. State council 1973-75; registry clin. social workers 1978, 82), Queens Coll. Alumni Orgn., Alpha Sigma Alpha. Contbg. author: First Directory of Child Day Care Centers in Suffolk County, 1972; newsletter editor Suffolk Nat. Assn. Social Workers, 1971-75; founding social worker Victims Info. Bur. of Suffolk, Inc., 1976-77.

BAACH, AMY JO, advt. agy. exec.; b. Louisville, Oct. 9, 1950; d. Jack E. and Shirley L. Baach; B.A., U. Louisville, 1972, postgrad., 1972-73. Tchr. English, Highland Jr. High Sch., Louisville, 1972-73; copywriter, traffic engr. Sta. WQHI, Louisville, 1973-74; owner, writer Baach Creative Services, Louisville, 1977—. Recipient 1st place award Ind. Art Dirs., 1977, merit award 5th Dist. Advt. Contest, 1978, 3 Silver Addy awards, 1981. Mem. Nat. Assn. Female Execs., Advt. Club Louisville. Office: Baach Creative Services 963 Baxter Ave Louisville KY 40204

BAAR, LILLIAN MARY, business exec.; b. Chgo.; d. James and Frances (Stanek) Shuss; student evening sch. J. Sterling Morton Jr. Coll., 1934-36; m. William D. Baar, July 25, 1942; 1 dau., Judith Barbara (Mrs. Joseph Topinka). Sec. to pres. Thordarson Mgr. Co., Chgo., 1935-37; sec. to ofcls. of Sears, Roebuck & Co., Chgo., 1937-43; broker, owner Baar Realty Co., Berwyn, 1944-69; real estate cons. Baar Realty, Inc., 1969-75; owner Baar & Baar Realtors, Berwyn, 1976—; ins. broker Lillian Baar Ins. Agy. Active ARC, Am. Heart Fund; v.p. Berwyn Community Chest, 1968-70, chmn., 1971-72, dir., 1973—; mem. Berwyn-Cicero Gov.'s Council Employment Handicapped, 1965-73; co-chmn. Berwyn Heart Fund, 1968-72; bd. dirs. Dialogue, 1st v.p., 1971-72, pres. (1st woman), 1972-74, trustee, 1973—; v.p. Ill. Council of Real Estate of City of Hope, 1976-77, chmn., 1978-79, hon. chmn., 1980—. Recipient Meritorious Service award Dialogue, 1971; Town of Cicero resolution as outstanding bus. and civic leader, 1972; Citizen of Yr. award Rotary Internat., 1976; Service award Grant Works Children's Center, 1981. Mem. Cermak Rd. Bus. Assn. (pres. 1961-64, dir. 1946—), West Towns Bd. Realtors (pres. 1965-66), Nat. (mem. women's council), Ill. assns. real estate bds., Nat. Inst. Real Estate Brokers, Ill. C. of C., Riverside C. of C., Berwyn C. of C. (treas. 1980—) Berwyn Bus. and Profl. Women's Club (pres. 1973-74), Czechoslovak Nat. Council Am. Clubs: Mothers of Alpha Gamma Delta, Ladies Aux. The Bohemian of Ceska Beseda, West Suburban Exec. Breakfast (dir. 1975—, treas. 1982—); Execs. (Chgo.). Home: Riverside IL 60546 Office: 6335 W Cermak Rd Berwyn IL 60402

BABB, MARION MCDOUGALL, journalist, soprano; b. Mayville, N.D., Dec. 1, 1918; d. Ole R. and Minnie (Johnson) Standahl; B.A. summa cum laude, Mayville State Coll., 1938; M.A., U. Wash., Seattle, 1970; voice pupil of William Pierce Herman and Coenraad Bos, N.Y.C., Fritz Lehmann, Vienna, Austria, Vittorio Ruffo, Milan, Italy; m. William James McDougall, Apr. 12, 1946 (div. 1963); children—Lawrence Dennis, Gwen King; m. 2d, Albert Leslie Babb, Aug. 27, 1972. Profl. opera singer, dramatic soprano, Europe and N.Y.C., 1946-63; debut Carnegie Hall, N.Y.C., 1958; 1st U.S. performance of Edgar, 1956; ch. soloist, Seattle and N.Y., 1958—; exec. asst. Seattle Trust & Savs. Bank, 1963-73; editor Nuclearscope, U. Wash., 1973—, Am. Nuclear Soc. Newsletter, 1973—; tchr. elocution, 1960—; freelance writer, 1960—; lectr. on artificial kidney, Japan and Korea, 1973, USSR, 1974. Mem. Women in Communications, Nat. Fedn. Press Women, Internat. Am. Bus. Communicators, Wash. Press Women. Presbyterian. Clubs: Musicians (Coral Gables, Fla.); Wash. Athletic (dir.). Home: 3237 Lakewood Ave S Seattle WA 98144

BABB, SANORA, writer; b. Leavenworth, Kans., Apr. 21, 1907; d. Walter Lacy and Jennie Anna (Parks) B.; student Kans. U., 1924; A.A., Garden City Jr. Coll., 1925; m. James Wong Howe, Sept. 18, 1949 (dec. 1976). Editor, The Clipper, 1940-41, Calif. Quar., 1951-52 (both Los Angeles); instr. short story UCLA Extension, 1959; novel; The Lost Traveler, 1958, Brit. edit., 1958; memoir: An Owl On Every Post, 1970, Brit. edit., 1971; contbr. short stories to anthologies (including Best American Short Stories 1950, 60), texts, mags., poems to mags. Mem. Authors Guild Am. Democrat. Office: care McIntosh & Otis 475 Fifth Ave New York NY 10017

BABBAGE, JOAN DOROTHY, journalist; b. Montclair, N.J., Jan. 10, 1926; d. Laurence Washburn and Dorothy A. (Davenport) B.; B.A. in English, Mt. Holyoke Coll., 1948; postgrad. Art Students League, New Sch. for Social Research; m. Vernon H. Ellsworth, Mar. 6, 1971. Publicist, Paramount Internat. Films, N.Y.C., 1952-58; reporter Newark News, 1960-67, food editor, 1967-72; feature writer, reporter Star-Ledger, Newark, 1972—. Vice pres. jr. group Women's Nat. Republican Club, N.Y.C., 1955. Recipient award N.J. br. Humane Soc., 1978; Outstanding Journalistic Achievement award North Jersey PICA Club, 1980. Contbr. restaurant revs., bus. articles to N.J. Bus. Mag., articles to Official Dog mag. Home: Washington Ave Montclair NJ 07042 Office: Star-Ledger Court St Newark NJ 07101

BABBIN, MONA JOY, mag. pub. co. ofcl.; b. Bronx, N.Y., Apr. 21, 1954; d. Jack and Shirley B.; B.A., U. Calif., Santa Barbara, 1976; M.B.A., Fordham U., 1981. Planning mgr. Four Winds Travel Co., N.Y.C., 1977-78; mktg., advt. mgr. Hertz Corp., N.Y.C., 1979-80; mgr. sales analysis Newsweek, N.Y.C., 1980—; career counselor Fordham U., 1980—. Mem. Nat. Assn. M.B.A.s, Nat. Assn. Female Execs., Women in Communications, NOW. Home: 209 E 25th St New York NY 10010 Office: Newsweek 444 Madison Ave New York NY 10022

BABBITT, BETTINA A., rehab. adminstr., educator; b. Seattle, May 25, 1940; d. Eugene Ainsley and Caroline Elizabeth (Mohr) B.; B.A., Calif. State U., Northridge, 1974, M.A., 1976; Ph.D., Claremont Grad. Sch., 1980; m. Donald J. Larson, Aug. 3, 1980; children—Steven Scott Brown, Caroline Elizabeth Marie Brown, David Douglas Brown. Curriculum specialist Acad. of Trades, Los Angeles, 1972-73; cons. indsl. relations Los Angeles area, 1974-75; rehab. mgr. Barrio Industries for the Handicapped, Los Angeles, 1975-77; rehab. coordinator Pomona Valley Workshop, Montclair, Calif., 1977-80; part time instr. Calif. Luth. Coll., 1980—; part time research asso. Exxon Edn. Found., 1980, Claremont Grad. Sch., 1980; cons. Chaffey Coll., 1980. Bd. dirs. Santa Monica Young Republicans, 1967-69. Grantee Erickson Found., 1974, Hoover Found., 1975. Mem. Am. Psychol. Assn., Assn. for Humanistic Psychology, Assn. for Advancement of Psychology, Nat. Rehab. Assn., Western Govtl. Research Assn., Pi Lambda Theta. Lutheran. Profl. speaker U. Hawaii, Hilo, 1978, U. Hawaii, Manoa, 1978; speaker profl. assn. confs. Home: 4211 Lorenzo Ln Stockton CA 95207

BABCOCK, BETTY THOMPSON, author; b. N.Y.C., Sept. 27, 1900; d. Lewis Steenrod and Geraldine Livingston (Morgan) Thompson; student Art Students League, N.Y.C., 6 yrs.; m. Richard Franklin Babcock, Feb. 7, 1920; children—Betsy Babcock Moulton, Geraldine Babcock Boone, Anne Babcock Bristow, Alice Babcock Lloyd (dec.). Author, illustrator Polo Horse and Horseman, The Sportsman, N.Y.C., 1931-40, Horse and Hound, The Field, London, 1932-39; assoc. editor Country Life, N.Y.C., 1940-42; illustrator Grolier Club, N.Y.C., 1938; Eastern rep. Bob & Betsy's Antique Nook. Active Arts and Skills Corps, ARC, 1942-45; dep. sr. warden CD, Woodbury, N.Y.; bd. dirs. Brearly Sch., Home Sch., Child Study Assn.; sec.-treas., mem. exec. com. Nassau-Suffolk Sch. Bd. Assn.; trustee Woodbury Bd. Edn.; mem. Central Sch. Dist. 2 Bd. Edn., Oyster Bay Twp., N.Y.; mem. Nat. Com. To Support Pub. Schs., N.Y. State Com. To Support Pub. Schs.; mem. adv. com. Nassau County Community Coll. Recipient N.Y. Pub. Library award, 1949, N.Y. State Tchrs. award, 1949; Disting. Service award Nassau-Suffolk Sch. Bds. Assn., 1967, N.Y. State Sch. Bds. Assn., 1969. Mem. Nat. Forest Assn., Am. Mus. Natural History, Nat. Audubon Soc. Quaker. Clubs: Colony (past gov.), Meadow Brook Hounds (hon. hunt sec. 1939-42). Author: The Expandable Pig, 1949; Betty Babcock's Illustrated Hunting Diary, 1948; illustrator: Just Hunting (H.T. Peters), 1935; Early American Sport (Robert Henderson), 1937. Home: Hark Away Woodbury NY 11797

BABCOCK, CATHERINE EVANS, artist, educator; b. Rydal, Pa., Feb. 23, 1924; d. William Wayne and Marion Catherine (Watters) Babcock; diploma Sarah Lawrence Coll., 1942; B.F.A., Tyler Sch. Fine Arts, Temple U., 1944, M.F.A., 1948; m. Douglas Paul Torre, May 28, 1977; adopted children—Eric Johannes, Elizabeth Jeanne. Tchr., Rudolf Steiner Sch., 1949; tchr. jr. high sch., Stratford, Conn., 1959-63; tchr. elem. art Locust Valley Primary and Elem. Schs., 1963-68; instr. Darien Community Center, 1975-81, Rowayton (Conn.) Arts Center, 1979—, also bd. mem., rec. sec. Portrait painter; artist to the Sea Services (USCG and USN); illustrator; Cutaneous Cryosurgery (Douglas Torre), 1978, rev., 1979, Undertow (Finn Havrevold), 1968; designer, painter mural for Babcock Surg. Wards, Temple U., Hosp., Phila., 1944; designer display Cryosurgery of Skin Cancer, Dallas, 1979; participant various art shows permanent collection U.S. Navy. Recipient awards including 6 awards, Am. Acad. Dermatology Art Shows, 2 awards Darien Art Shows, gold award, Dallas, 1979; certs. of appreciation USCG, 1971, 82, Naval Sta. of N.Y., 1981. Mem. Nat. Portrait Inst., Pastel Soc. Am. (cert. of merit), U.S. Navy League, Coast Guard Art Program, Navy Art Coop. and Liaison Com., Salmagundi Club. Congregationalist. Translator, illustrator: Atheneum, 1968 (library award). Home and Office: 122 Rowayton Ave Rowayton CT 06853

BABCOCK, JANICE BEATRICE, clin. lab. scientist; b. Milw., June 2, 1942; d. Delbert Martin and Constance Josephine (Dworschack) B.; B.S. in Med. Tech., Marquette U., 1964; M.A. in Mgmt. and Supervision, Central Mich. U., 1975, postgrad. in Edn. in Health Care, 1975—. Intern, St. Luke's Hosp., Milw., 1963-64; microbiologist St. Michael's Hosp., Milw., 1964-65; supr. clin. lab. service VA Regional Office, Milw., 1965-66; hosp. epidemiologist VA Center, Wood, Wis., 1966-74, supr. anaerobic microbiology and research lab, 1974-78, adminstrv. officer, chief med. tech., 1978—; research asso. dept. surgery Med. Coll. Wis.; tchr. in field Marquette U., U. Wis., Med. Coll. Wis.; lectr., cons. in field. Recipient Wood VA Fed. Woman's award, 1975; Profl. Achievement award Lab World jour., 1981. Registered med. technologist and microbiologist, clin. lab. scientist, Wis. Mem. Am. Soc. Microbiology, Am. Soc. Med. Tech. (Nat. Sci. Creativity award 1974; Nat. Microbiology Sci. Achievement 1978; Profl. Achievement Lectureship award 1981; Mem. of Yr. 1980), Wis. Assn. Med. Tech. (Mem. of Yr. 1979), Assn. Practitioners in Infection Control, Am. Public Health Assn., Clin. Lab. Mgmt. Assn., Am. Acad. Med. Adminstrs., Royal Soc. Health, Nat. Geog. Soc., Marquette U. Alumni Assn. (Merit award 1979), Alpha Mu Tau, Alpha Delta Theta, Sigma Iota Epsilon. Alpha Delta Pi (Alumni Honor award 1979). Club: Holiday Camera. Contbr. numerous articles to profl. jours. Home: 6839 Blanchard St Wauwatosa WI 53213 Office: VA Med Center 5000 W National Ave Wood WI 53193

BABCOCK, NELLIE JO, clin. social worker; b. Bozeman, Mont., Mar. 26, 1951; d. Harold Chester and Patricia Ann (Alexander) Babcock; student St. Andrews Presbyn. Coll., 1968-70; B.A. summa cum laude, U. Minn., 1972; M.S.W., U. Minn., 1974; m. Christopher J. Krenk, July 3, 1977. Psychiat. social worker Lane County Mental Health, Eugene, Oreg., 1974-75, Benton County Mental Health, Corvallis, Oreg., 1975-77, Clackamas County Mental Health, Marylhurst, Oreg., 1978; pvt. psychotherapist and cons. Lake Oswego (Oreg.) Counseling Assos., 1979—; dir. Family Growth Alternatives, Marylhurst, 1980—. NIMH trainee, 1972-74; registered clin. social worker, Oreg. Mem. Nat. Assn. Social Workers, Acad. Cert. Social Workers. Democrat. Home: 18585 SW Kristi Way Lake Oswego OR 97034 Office: 445 SW 2d St Lake Oswego OR 97034

BABCOCK, PATRICIA ANN, nurse; b. Shelbyville, Ind., Oct. 31, 1934; d. Laurence H. and Reba D. (Conway) Underwood; B.S. in Nursing, Ball State U., Muncie, Ind., 1957, M.A., 1975, Ed.D. (fellow), 1980; m. Robert A. Babcock, Mar. 30, 1958; children—Brett Alan, Richard Scott, Laura Ann. Office nurse, Muncie, 1957-60; staff nurse Porter Meml. Hosp., Valparaiso, Ind., 1961; head nurse St. Joseph Hosp., Logansport, Ind., 1963-65; sch. nurse, Gary, Ind., 1967-76; asso. prof. nursing Purdue U. North Central Campus, Westville, Ind., 1976—; cons. in field. Mem. AAUW (br. pres.), Am. Nurses Assn., AAUP, (chpt. pres.), Nat. Assn. Female Execs., Concern for Dying, Ind. Nurses Assn. (dist. pres.), Hospice of Porter County, Compassionate Friends, Eta Sigma Gamma, Sigma Theta Tau, Phi Delta Theta, Sigma Kappa. Republican. Methodist. Home: 115 Washington Ave Chesterton IN 46304 Office: Purdue U North Central Campus Westville IN 46391

BABEY, EVELYN RUTH, coll. ofcl.; b. N.Y.C.; d. Adam and Hedwig (Voigt) Babey; B.A., Queens Coll., 1967; M.S. in Edn. (intern) SUNY, Albany, 1969; Ph.D., N.Y.U., 1981. Asst. registrar N.Y.C. Community Coll., Bklyn., 1968-72, asso. registrar, 1972-74; registrar Kean Coll. of N.J., Union, 1974-82, adj. instr. dept. math., 1981—; dir. records Bklyn. Coll., City U. N.Y., 1982—; lectr. in field; mem. steering com. N.J./N.Y. Conf. Registrars and Admissions Officers, 1981-82, treas., 1981—. Patron mem. Newark Mus. Mem. Am. Assn. Higher Edn., Am. Assn. Collegiate Registrars and Admissions Officers, Middle State Assn. Collegiate Registrars and Officers of Admissions, N.J. Coll. and Univ., Registrars, Albany Student Personnel Alumni Assn. (treas. 1975-77, cert. of appreciation 1979), Am. Personnel and Guidance Assn., Am. Coll. Personnel Assn., AAUW, Nat. Assn. for Female Execs., Nat. Micrographics Assn. Presbyterian. Club: Elizabeth (N.J.) Town and Country. Contbr. articles to profl. jours. Office: Bklyn Coll City U NY Brooklyn NY 11210

BABIC, ANNE L(OUISE), educator; b. Glenshaw, Pa., Feb. 1, 1929; d. Frank J. and Anna K. (Hartz) B.; B.A., Antioch Coll., 1951; M.S.W. (HEW grantee), Syracuse U., 1969. Social service group worker, program dir. Brashear Assn., Pitts., 1952-61; exec. dir. Girls Club, Syracuse, N.Y., 1962-67; project coordinator, aging project Syracuse U., 1969-72, instr. and project coordinator Coll. for Human Devel., 1975—; exec. dir. Syracuse Met. Commn. on Aging, 1972-75; cons. to local offices for aging. Mem. steering com. Foster Grandparents, Syracuse, 1972-75, Ret. Sr. Vol. Program, Syracuse, 1972-75. Mem. Gerontol. Soc., N.Y. State Assn. Gerontology Educators. Office: Room 200 Slocum Hall Syracuse U Syracuse NY 13210

BABICH, BETH ELLEN, food co. exec.; b. Columbus, Ohio, Nov. 29, 1947; d. Robert and Marilyn (Barnett) B.; B.A. in Psychology, Ohio State U., 1969; M.Internat.Mgmt., Am. Grad. Sch. Internat. Mgmt., 1977. Counselor, cons. Ohio Bur. Employment Services, 1969-73; propr. retail art gallery, Toronto, Ont., Can., 1973-75; mktg. and advt. mgr. Ellio's Frozen Pizza div. Purex, Inc., 1977-78; mktg. mgr. The Drop Shop Ltd., cable TV installation parts, Roselle, N.J., 1978-80; product mgr. cheese and butter products mfg. div. Atlantic & Pacific Tea Co. Inc., Montvale, N.J., 1980-82; mktg. mgr. pies and pie shells Mrs. Smith's Frozen Foods Co., Pottstown, Pa., 1982—. Chmn. med. research com. Alzheimer's Disease Soc., 1980—; founding mem. singles div. United Jewish Appeal, Fort Lee, N.J., 1978—. Recipient Outstanding Creativity award Am. Dairy Assn., 1981. Mem. Nat. Assn. Female Execs., Am. Grad. Sch. Internat. Mgmt. Alumni Assn., Phi Alpha Theta. Office: PO Box 298 South and Charlotte Sts Pottstown PA 19406

BABICH, JOANNE MARIE, clin. psychologist; b. Sewickley, Pa., Oct. 9, 1951; d. John and Cookie Joanne B.; B.S. summa cum laude, U. Pitts., 1973; M.A., Ariz. State U., 1976, Ph.D. summa cum laude, 1980; m. Frederick W. Meister, June 12, 1982. Predoctoral intern in community medicine and clin. psychology Baylor Coll. Medicine, Houston, 1977-78; psychotherapist Terros Crisis Center, 1979-80; research fellow Tex. Research Inst. Mental Sci., Houston, 1978; mem. faculty Phoenix Coll., 1979—; cons. psychologist Family Villas, Inc. and clin. supr. New Ariz. Family, Inc., 1980—. Vol. gubernatorial campaign; planning com. Coronado Park Conservation Dist. Neighborhood. Mem. Am. Psychol. Assn., Assn. Women in Psychology, Maricopa Soc. Psychologists, Phoenix Soc. Clin. Hypnosis, Phoenix Psychoanalytic Study Group, Am. Assn. Suicidology, Phi Beta Kappa. Democrat. Office: 240 W Osborn Rd Suite 114 Phoenix AZ 85006

BABINGTON, JUDITH ANN, credit union exec.; b. Wendell, Idaho, May 24, 1941; d. Edward F. and Thelma (McLean) Mathison; cert. credit union exec. Credit Union Nat. Assn., 1979; grad. credit union personnel course U. Wis., 1981; m. Jack W. Babington, June 26, 1959; children—Jaylene, Cara. Optometric asst. Caldwell (Idaho) Vision Clinic, 1968-72; mgr. Canyon Med. Health Credit Union (Idaho), 1971—; sec. bd. dirs. Idaho Corp. Credit Union, 1977-80, pres., 1980—; mem. adv. bd. credit unions Idaho Dept. Fin. Mem. Caldwell Credit Women Internat. (treas. 1981—), Am. Bus. Women Assn. (sec. 1981—), Credit Union Exec. Soc. (sec.-treas. Idaho 1981—). Democrat. Roman Catholic. Home: 2105 Airport Caldwell ID 83605 Office: PO Box 158 Caldwell ID 83605

BABLANIAN, LILLIAN MURAD (MRS. ROSTOM H. BABLANIAN), textile co. exec.; b. Tiflis, USSR, May 29, 1917; d. Levon Murat and Veronica (Arvanian) Gondaktchian; diploma Conservatory Music, Nice, France, 1933; B.S. in Chem. Engring., Pratt Inst., 1947; postgrad. N.Y. U., 1958-60, Hofstra U., 1968-72; m. Rostom H. Bablanian, Oct. 29, 1955; children—Gregory Armen, Gayne Maria. Tracer, textile designer Rex Studios, N.Y.C., 1941-42; asst. to mgr. Pacific Food Products, Inc., Bklyn., 1947-48; with Murad Textile Print Works, Bklyn., 1948—, v.p., mgr., 1954-56, v.p., cons., 1956—; owner, mgr. Muratex Chems., Inc., N.Y.C., 1949-54; tchr. chemistry sch. dist., Oyster Bay, N.Y., 1958-82; lectr., demonstrator Armenian dance, Library Performing Arts, N.Y.C., Boston, Detroit, Washington, Hartford, Conn.; co-dir. Armenian Folk Dance Soc. N.Y. Recipient Adm. Richard L. Conolly Outstanding Tchrs. award C.W. Post Coll., 1968, Chem. Engring. Alumni award Pratt Inst., 1948. Mem. Soc. Women Engrs. (pres. 1952-53, trustee 1960-62), Nat. Sci. Tchrs. Assn. (life), N.Y. State Tchrs. Assn., Internat. Platform Assn. Tau Beta Pi. Contbr. to Enterprise Pilot, Oyster Bay; patentee water-base pigment binders. Home: 147 Anstice St Oyster Bay NY 11771 Office: 98 West St Brooklyn NY 11222

BABLER, MARCIA HERLACH, telecommunications corp. mgr.; b. Kansas City, Mo., Nov. 17, 1953; d. Arthur Dayton and Dorothy A. Herlach; student Mills Coll., 1971-72; B.A., Northwestern U., 1975; M.B.A., U. Wis., Madison, 1977; m. Scott David Babler, Dec. 27, 1979. Planner product mgmt. Hallmark Cards, Inc., Kansas City, Mo., 1978-79, sr. planner product mgmt., 1979-81; mgr. market and bus. plans United Telephone Systems Inc.-United Telecommunications, Inc., Fairway, Kans., 1981—. Mem. Blue Beret com. Am. Royal, 1979, breakfast com. 4-H Club, 1979, Night at Royal, nat. affairs coms. Women's C. of C. Club, 1979. Mem. Am. Mgmt. Assn., Kansas City Women's C. of C. Club: Northwestern U. Alumni of Greater Kansas City. Home: 5527 Roe Blvd Shawnee Mission KS 66205 Office: United Telephone Systems Inc Box 11315 Kansas City MO 64112

BABLES, MARILYN MARIE, lab. technician; b. Kans., Nov. 21, 1954; d. Leon B.; A.A., Kansas City (Kans.) Community Coll., 1976; B.A. in Biology, Park Coll., 1978. Quality control lab. technician Bayvet Labs., Shawnee Mission, Kans., 1979; microbiology lab. technician Bd. Public Utilities, Kansas City, Kans., 1979—. Mem. Kan Valley Med. Soc., Am. Water Works Assn., Nat. Assn. Female Execs., Women in Bus. (pres. 1980—), Urban League, Friends of Park Coll. Library. Republican. Mem. Christian Ch. (Disciples of Christ). Office: 3601 N 12th Kansas City KS 66104

BABRAJ, PATRICIA ANNE, assn. exec.; b. Chgo., Oct. 28, 1940; d. John M. and Frances (Cygan) Babraj. Sec. to lawyer, 1958-59; sec. to advt. space reps. Chilton Co., Chgo., 1959-63; exec. sec. Coop. Food Distbrs. Am., Park Ridge, Ill., 1963-67; meeting planner Fin. Mgrs. Soc. for Savs. Instns., Inc., Chgo., 1967-81; dir. convs. Am. Hardware Mfrs. Assn., Schaumburg, Ill., 1982—. Mem. Internat. Orgn. Women Execs., Nat. Assn. Female Execs., Am. Soc. Assn. Execs., Am. Soc. Profl. and Exec. Women, Chgo. Soc. Assn. Execs.

BABSON, EDITH YUNGBLUT, civic worker; b. Lincoln, Nebr., Oct. 7, 1896; d. Jacob and Marion (Logan) Yungblut; B.S. in Home Econs., U. Nebr., 1918; m. Paul Talbot Babson, Feb. 26, 1919; 1 son, Donald Paul. Vol. Wellesley (Mass.) Friendly Aid Bd., 1925-42; bd. dirs. Newton-Wellesley Hosp. Aid Assn., 1942-52, now hon. bd. dirs., pres., 1953-55; bd. dirs. Newton Wellesley Hosp., 1954-76; chmn. Entertainment for Soldiers and Sailors of Wellesley, 1942-45; mem. ladies com. Mus. Fine Arts, 1961-65; mem. corp. Mus. of Sci., Boston, Springfield (Mass.) Coll.; trustee U. Nebr. Found., Lincoln, 1976—, Crotched Mountain Rehab. Center for Handicapped Children, Greenfield, N.H., 1976—; hon. trustee Babson Coll., Babson Park, Mass. Named hon. admiral Nebr. Navy, 1971. Republican. Presbyterian. Club: Algonquin (Boston). Home: 330 Beacon St Boston MA 02116

BACA-BARRIGAN, POLLY, state senator, public relations specialist; b. La Salle, Colo., Feb. 13, 1941; B.A., Colo. State U., 1962; postgrad. Am. U. Editor trade union newspaper; public info. officer White House, Washington, 1962-68; public relations specialist; mem. Colo. Senate, 1978—, mem. agr. com., natural resources and energy com., bus. affairs and labor com., transp. com. Office: Colo Senate State Capitol Denver CO 80203 *

BACALL, LAUREN, actress; b. N.Y.C., Sept. 16, 1924; d. Natalie Bacall; student pub. schs., m. Humphrey Bogart, May 21, 1945 (dec. 1957); children—Stephen, Leslie; m. 2d, Jason Robards, July 1961 (div.); 1 son, Sam. Actress Broadway plays, Johnny 2x4, Franklin Street, 1942, Goodbye Charlie, 1959; motion picture actress, 1942—, pictures include To Have and Have Not, The Big Sleep, 1944, Confidential Agent, 1945, Dark Passage, 1947, Key Largo, 1948, Young Man With a Horn, 1949, Bright Leaf, 1950, How To Marry a Millionaire, 1953, Woman's World, 1954, The Cobweb, Blood Alley, 1955, Written on the Wind, Designing Woman, The Gift of Love, Flame Over India, 1959, Sex and the Single Girl, 1965, Harper, 1966, Murder on the Orient Express, 1974, The Shootist, 1976, Health, 1979, The Fan, 1980; appeared in Broadway play Cactus Flower, 1966-67, Woman of The Year, 1981-82; appeared in Broadway play Applause, 1969-71, also road co., 1971-72, London co., 1972-73; TV spl. The Paris Collections, 1968, Applause, 1973, Woman of the Year, 1981-82. Address: care Wallin Simon Black & Co 1350 Ave of Americas New York NY 10019

BACHER, CAROLYN SANDERS, social worker; b. N.Y.C., Feb. 16, 1938; d. Morris L. and Anne (Douglas) Sanders; B.S. in Edn., CCNY, 1959; M.S.W., Rutgers U., 1973; m. Joel Bacher, Dec. 24, 1957; children—Steven, Susan. Sch. social worker West Windsor-Plainsboro Schs., West Windsor, N.J., 1973—, affirmative action officer for handicapped, 1980—; parent effectiveness tng. instr. Rutgers Grad. Sch. of Social Work, New Brunswick, N.J., 1977-80, tchr. effectiveness tng. instr., 1979-80, co-adj. casework faculty, 1980, field instr., 1975-80, instr., cons., 1980; instr. Trenton State Coll. Pres. Greenbrook PTA, 1970-71; leader Girl Scouts U.S.A., 1974; mem. South Brunswick High Sch. Curriculum Com., 1978. Mem. N.J. Assn. Sch. Social Workers (corr. sec.), Nat. Assn. Social Workers, Acad. Cert. Social Workers, LWV. Home: 22 Dundee Rd Kendall Park NJ 08824 Office: West Windsor-Plainsboro Schs West Windsor NJ 08550

BACHER, JUDITH ST. GEORGE, exec. search cons. co. exec.; b. New Rochelle, N.Y., July 14, 1946; d. Thomas A. and Rose-Marie (Martocci) Baiocchi; B.S., Georgetown U., 1968; M.L.S., Columbia U., 1971; m. Albert Bacher, Jan. 2, 1972; 1 son, Alexander Michael. Researcher, Time Mag., N.Y.C. 1968-71; librarian Mus. of Modern Art. N.Y.C., 1971-72; cons. Informaco Inc., N.Y.C., 1972-74; cons. Booz-Allen & Hamilton, N.Y.C., 1974-79; research dir. Nordeman Grimm/MBA Resources Inc. N.Y.C., 1979—. Mem. White House Adv. Com. on Personnel, 1979—. Mem. The Research Roundtable (co-founder 1979), Phi Beta Kappa. Office: 717 5th Ave New York NY 10022

BACHER, ROSALIE WRIDE, ednl. adminstr., counselor; b. Los Angeles, May 25, 1925; d. Homer M. and Reine (Rogers) Wride; A.B., Occidental Coll., 1947, M.A., 1949; m. Archie O. Bacher, Jr., Mar. 30, 1963. Tchr., English, Latin, history David Starr Jordan High Sch., Long Beach, Calif., 1949-55, counselor, 1965; counselor Poly. High Sch., 1966; vocat. counselor Office Occupational Preparation, 1967-68; v.p. Washington Jr. High Sch., 1968-70; counselor Lakewood Sr. High Sch., Calif., 1965-66, asst. prin., 1970; vice prin. Jefferson Jr. High Sch., Long Beach, 1970-81, Marshall Jr. High Sch., Long Beach, 1981—. Chmn. vocat. guidance steering com Long Beach Unified Sch., Dist., 1963-68; mem. youth adv. com. Long Beach chpt. ARC. Mem. AAUW, Long Beach Personnel and Guidance Assn. (dir. 1958-60), Long Beach C. of C., Long Beach Sch. Counselors Assn. (sec. high sch. segment 1963-64), Phi Beta Kappa, Delta Kappa Gamma (chpt. pres. 1964-66, area dir. Calif., 1969-71, mem. state exec. bd. profl. affairs com. 1971-72, chmn. state profl. affairs com. 1972-74, Calif. needs assessment com. 1974-76), Phi Delta Gamma (pres. chpt. 1977-78, nat. by laws chmn. 1980-82), Pi Lambda Theta (pres. chpt. 1974-76, v.p. So. Calif. council 1975-77), Phi Delta Kappa (sec. chpt. 1977-78). Home: 265 Rocky Point Rd Palos Verdes Estates CA 90274 also 17721 Misty Ln Huntington Beach CA 92649 Office: 5870 E Wardlow Rd Long Beach CA 90808

BACHER-RACLYN, RENÉE MARGARET, travel co. exec.; b. Stamford, Conn., Feb. 4, 1944; d. Romeo and Rose (Killian) Bacher; student public schs.; m. Arnold Raclyn, June 16, 1979. Nat. dir. retail and bus. travel Thomas Cook Travel, N.Y.C., 1975-78; dir. cons. services AAA World Wide Travel, Falls Church, Va., 1978-79; v.p., gen. mgr. Gelco Travel Services, N.Y.C., 1980-82; dir. corp. travel Liberty Travel, Paramus, N.J., 1982—. Office: 50 A & S Dr Paramus NJ 07652

BACHI, NAOMI MABEL, guidance counselor; b. Weatherford, Okla., Mar. 26, 1916; d. Albert James and Maybell Rebecca (Patton) Baker; student Oklahoma City U., 1947-49, Rio Grande Coll., 1956-57; Chadron (Nebr.) State Tchrs. Coll., 1961-62, Central State U., 1965; m. Michael Mario Bachi, Apr. 5, 1947. Admissions and records clk. Central State U., Edmond, Okla., 1963-64, records asst., 1964-71, admissions and records counselor, 1971-72, admissions counselor for fgn. students, 1972-74, asso. internat. student advisor, 1974—. Mem. Edmond Democratic Women's Club, Nat. Assn. Fgn. Student Affairs, Central State U. Dames. Home: 3700 Mason Hills Dr Edmond OK 73034 Office: Internat Office Central State U Edmond OK 73034

BACHMAN, MARIE ROSALIE (MRS. EZRA DAVIS), dentist; b. Dorr, Mich., Aug. 18, 1907; d. Gustav Adolf and Bertha (Loew) Bachman; A.B., Calvin Coll., 1929; D.D.S., U. Mich., 1934, postgrad., 1959-60; postgrad. in oral surgery and anesthesia Northwestern U., 1935, Cook County Grad. Sch. Medicine, 1936, Ohio State U., 1954-56; m. Ezra Davis, Aug. 16, 1947. Pvt. practice dentistry, Grand Rapids, Mich., 1934—; mem. active staff Blodgett Meml. Hosp., 1944—. Fellow Acad. Gen. Practice; mem. Am. Dental Assn., Kent County Dental Soc. Home: 407 College Ave SE Grand Rapids MI 49503 Office: Med Arts Bldg Grand Rapids MI 49503

BACHMANN, MARGARET ALFREDA, ins. broker; b. Topeka, May 3, 1919; d. Ray Alfred and Mary Alice (Kilbride) Webb; student St. Louis U., 1946, 47; cert. med. records Kans. U., 1946; cert. Purdue U., 1976, cert. advanced bus. ins., 1975; grad. Life Underwriters Tng. Council, 1970; grad. Key Pact Inst. Advanced Studies, 1975; m. T. R. Bachmann, Aug. 31, 1940 (div.); children—Mark Theron, Kent Spencer, Monica Alice. Dep. county clk. Shawnee County (Kans.), 1937-40, auditor, 1943; med. record librarian Starmont Vail Hosp., Topeka, 1945-49; mgr. Trees Orthopedic Clinic, Topeka, 1949-59; owner, operator uniform shop, 1958-60, bridal shop, 1960-64; advt. rep. Consol. Enterprise, Kansas City and Marceline, Mo., 1964-67; ins. broker Woodman A&L, Kansas City, Kans., 1967-72; practice ins. and fin. brokerage, Kansas City, Kans., 1972—; owner, pres. Flock of Lambs, Christian supply mail order co., Overland Park, Kans., 1979—; founder, owner, operator Flock of Lambs To Make a Better Ewe (you), 1979—; producer feature films, cable TV shows, 1980-82; pres., chmn. bd. Alfreda's Fin. Devel.; exec. v.p., treas. Excelsius Prodns.; chmn. profl. seminars. Organizer, developer Cultural Art Center, Excelsior Springs, Mo., 1980. Named to Million Dollar Round Table, numerous times; recipient Disting. Salesman award Gov. Kans., 1968, 69; Nat. Quality award Nat. Life Underwriters, 1971, Nat. Sales Achievement award, 1971. Mem. Women's Leaders Round Table (life), Nat. Life Underwriters, Johnson County Wyandotte Life Underwriters, Women's C. of C. Republican. Roman Catholic. Clubs: Zonta Internat. (charter mem., organizer and 1st pres. Johnson County, Kans., club 1972-77), Charismatic Prayer Group. Contbr. articles to mags. Address: PO Box 12547 Shawnee KS 66212

BACIC, DIANA COPPOLA, advt. agy. exec.; b. Brooklyn Heights, N.Y., Oct. 23, 1946; d. Francis George and Josephine (Manco) Coppola; A.S., N.Y.C. Community Coll., 1966; B.A., Queens Coll., 1970; m. Peter Raymond Hinkle, Nov. 12, 1982. Media dir. Wesson & Warhaftig Advt., N.Y.C., 1972-77; advt. sales rep. Charles C. Cunningham, Inc. Park Ridge, N.J., 1977-78; dir. media/research MED Communications, Hopelawn, N.J., 1978—; mem. programs and seminars com. Pharm. Advt. Council, 1978—. Vol., Sports for the Handicapped Program, Garden State Rehab. Hosp., 1979—. Mem. Pharm. Advt. Council, Healthcare Bus. Woman Assn. Club: Irish Setter of Long Island. Home: B-12 Twinlights Terrace Highlands NJ 07732 Office: 655 Florida Grove Rd Hopelawn NJ 08861

BACK, JOYCE ANN, bank ofcl.; b. St. Peters, Ind., Nov. 25, 1931; d. Alphone William and Angela P. (Biltz) Wallpe; student public schs.; m. John Edward Back, Dec. 19, 1951; 1 son, Stephen John. Head quality control Sperry Rubber & Plastic Co., Brookville, Ind., 1949-52; 1st dep. auditor Franklin County, Brookville, 1955-60; cashier, asst. trust officer People's Trust Co., Brookville, 1960—. Sec., Adv. Com. Town of Brookville, 1961-65; precinct com. woman Democratic party, 1952-60. Named Outstanding Citizen, DAR, 1949; recipient Spl. Achievement award Boy Scouts Am., 1965. Mem. Am. Bankers Assn., Ind. Bankers Assn., Am. Legion Aux., Daus. Isabella, Franklin County Hist. Soc., Brookville Greyhound Booster Club, Delta Theta Tau. Roman Catholic. Club: Phohontas Order Red Men. Home: 1072 Fairfield Ave Brookville IN 47012 Office: People's Trust Co PO Box 7 Brookville IN 47012

BACK, KAREN LEE, film producer, dir.; b. Chgo., June 10, 1945; d. Joseph Charles and Zelda (Cole) Rutzky; B.A., U. Mich., 1967; M.F.A., N.Y.U., 1975. Producer, dir., writer, editor for films, including Cycle, 1975, Portrait of Paula (for AT&T), 1975; producer, dir. Inside Broadcasting for Post-Newsweek TV, Washington, 1977; Am. Film Inst. intern with Milos Forman on —Hair—, 1977-78; judge Am. Film Festival, N.Y.C., 1976, 77, 78; producer More Than Meets The Eye (for Xerox Corp.), N.Y.C., 1976; story analyst Orion Films, 1980; producer Walt Disney Prodns., 1981-82. Active vol. fund raiser for Cancer Research, 1960-64. Recipient Cine Golden Eagle award for Inside Broadcasting, Washington, 1977, intern Am. Film Inst. funded by Acad. Motion Picture Arts and Sci., 1977-78; recipient Dirs. Choice award Sinking Creek Film Festival, Nashville, 1976; films selected for showing at Mus. Contemporary Crafts, N.Y.C., 1974, Mus. Modern Art, N.Y.C., 1976, 77, Toronto Film Festival, 1977, Mus. Contemporary Art, Chgo., 1976, Internat. Center Photography, N.Y.C., 1979. Mem. Women in

Film. Contbr. numerous articles, pictures to profl. jours.; author: English as a Second Language Through Art, 1978; composer 5 songs. Address: 1881 Laurel Canyon Blvd Los Angeles CA 90046

BACKER, CLAIRE HAGGERTY, sch. librarian; b. Kingston, Pa., Dec. 2, 1932; d. Peter Edward and Travallyn Marie (Thompson) Haggerty; A.B., Susquehanna U., 1954; M.Sci.Ed., Temple U., 1971; postgrad. in library sci. Marywood Coll., 1979; M.L.S., Kutztown State Coll., 1981; m. George Bowes Backer, June 16, 1956 (dec.); children—Karen Patrice, Dianne Claire. Sci. instr. Nesbitt Meml. Hosp., Kingston, 1954-59, LuLac Environ. Council, Wilkes-Barre, Pa., 1973; tchr. earth space sci. Wyoming Valley West Sch. Dist., Plymouth, Pa., 1973-79, librarian, 1979—; mem. exec. bd. Friends of Hoyt Library. Sec., Woman's Aux. to Luzerne County (Pa.) Med. Soc., 1963-65, pres., 1971-72; sec. Woman's Aux., Wilkes-Barre Gen. Hosp., 1973; mem. exec. bd. Kidney Found., Wilkes-Barre. Mem. ALA, Pa. Sch. Library Assn., Pa. Library Assn., Kappa Delta. Club: Jr. League Wilkes-Barre. Home: 1 Turner St Forty-Fort PA 18704 Office: Wyoming Valley West High Sch Library Wadhams St Plymouth PA 18651

BACKMAN, ELIZABETH HELENA, editor; b. Saginaw, Mich., May 17, 1944; d. Frank Frederick and Reita St. Clair (Harris) Burman; B.A., Columbia U., 1968; m. Ian Jerome Sterling, Nov. 27, 1965 (div.); m. 2d, John William Backman, June 27, 1972 (div.); 1 son, Jonathan St. Clair Burman Potter. With Doubleday & Co., Inc., N.Y.C., 1968-69; editor Macmillian Co., 1969-70; sr. editor Hawthorn Books, 1970-80; owner Spirit of Bank Street and Co., antiques, paintings, rare books; owner Elizabeth H. Backman & Co., author's rep. and cons. editor, 1981—. Mem. Women in Publishing, Editors' Club. Address: 11 Bank St New York NY 10014

BACLESSE, MARJORIE P., interior designer; b. Jefferson City, Mo., June 21, 1923; d. Walter E. and Opal (Matthews) Butler; student Chgo. Sch. Interior Decorating, 1958-60; m. June 21, 1940; children—Arden Kay, Arla Gay. Owner, mgr. Marge Baclesse Interiors, Jefferson City, Mo., 1950—, Tiger Fashions, Jefferson City, 1976—. Chmn., Republican City Com., 1970-72. Mem. VFW Aux., Am. Legion Aux. (state pres. 1977-78, nat. exec. com. 1978-79), Am. Bus. Women's Assn. Republican. Methodist. Home: 1404 Karen Dr Jefferson City MO 65101 Office: 428 W Dunklin St Jefferson City MO 54101

BACON, CAROL ANN, nurse; b. Evergreen Park, Ill., Apr.2, 1941; d. Raymond Benjamin and Loretta Carolyn (Diimig) Hanson; R.N., St. Mary's Sch. Nursing, 1962; B.S., St. Francis Coll., 1979, postgrad., 1980—; div. Clin. charge nurse U. Ill. Hosp. and Clinics, 1962-71; supr. Oak Park (Ill.) Hosp., 1972-75; adminstr. Addison Med. Center, 1976-80; nurse, mktg. mgr., mgr. in charge occupational health program Doctors Emergency Officenter, Mt. Prospect, Ill., 1980—. Mem. Addison Indsl. Assn., Suburban Chgo. Assn. Occupational Health Nurses (v.p. 1981-82), Emergency Dept. Nurses Assn., Nat. Occupational Nurses Assn. Roman Catholic. Office: 830 E Rand Rd Mount Prospect IL 60056

BACON, CHARLOTTE ALZERA MEADE, educator; b. Alberta, Va.; d. Ollie and Pinkie Ann (Manson) Meade; B.S. with honors, Hampton Inst., 1946; M.Ed., U. Pitts., 1952; m. Edward D. Bacon, Jr., Aug. 11, 1962; children—Judith, Edward, Susan. Tchr., Downingtown (Pa.) Indsl. Sch., 1946-50; tchr. Aliquippa (Pa.) Pub. Schs., 1950—. Mem. program com. YMCA, Aliquippa, 1955-65; active Sewickley (Pa.) YMCA; vice chmn. Mayor's Commn. on Human Rights, 1972-76; mem. Citizens' Adv. Com., City of Aliquippa, 1975-77; mem. task force Beaver Castle council Girl Scouts Am., 1975—, also bd. dirs., leader Troop 77; bd. dirs. Sewickley Community Center; mem. long-range planning com. Aliquippa Sch. Dist.; pres. Willing Workers Missionary Soc.; mem. adv. bd. Aliquippa Better Community Assn.; mem. fund raising com. Women's Crisis Center, 1981—; vol. Adult Literacy Council of Beaver County, 1982; supr. Pa. State Fedn. Girls' Clubs, 1974-79. Recipient Woman of Yr. award Aliquippa Negro Bus. and Profl. Women's Club, 1970, Community Involvement award Delta Sigma Theta, 1972. Mem. AAUW (Aliquippa corr. sec. 1971-73, pres. 1977-79, Sojourner Truth award 1976), Pa. Fedn. Negro Women's Clubs (pres. 1969-73), Aliquippa Edn. Assn. (rec. sec. 1969-72), Negro Bus. and Profl. Women's Club (pres. 1960-62, 63-77), PTA (life), NAACP, N.W. Dist. Fedn. Women's Clubs (pres. 1974-77), Northeastern Fedn. Women's Clubs (exec. bd. 1973—), Nat. Assn. Colored Women's Clubs (exec. bd.), Nat. Assn. Negro Bus. and Profl. Women's Clubs (chmn. internat. relations N. Central dist. 1981—), Daniel B. Matthews Hist. Soc. of Sewickley, Three Rivers Reading Council, Keystone Reading Council, Leotta C. Hawthorne Reading Council, Black Women's Polit. Crusade, Hampton Inst. Alumni Assn., U. Pitts. Alumni Assn., World Affairs Council Pitts., Pa. Assn. Gifted Edn., Delta Sigma Theta. Baptist. Home: 311 Chadwick St Sewickley PA 15143 Office: New Sheffield Sch 21st St Aliquippa PA 15001

BACON, GERTRUDE MARDEN, judge; b. N.Y.C.; d. Ben and Eva (Spevak) Marden; B.S., Fordham U., 1939, LL.D. (only woman to receive sch. prize for highest grades), 1942; m. Lou Bacon, Jan. 21, 1943; children—Joy, Joel, James. Admitted to N.Y. bar, 1943. Vol. atty. Legal Aid Soc., 1954-68; pres. Joshua Orphan Aid, 1947-49; active Assn. for Mentally Retarded Children. Pres. bd. trustees Calhoun Sch., 1959-68; judge Family Ct., N.Y.C., 1968-72; pres., founder Parents Anonymous, N.Y.C., 1972—; mem. adv. bd. Filium, Internat. Orgn. to Re-evaluate our Treatment of Youth; mem. Nat. Task Force against Corporal Punishment of Children; advisory bd. Temple U. Nat. Center Study Corporal Punishment and Its Alternatives in Schs.; bd. dirs. Benjamin N. Cardozo Sch. Law. Recipient award Nat. Council Juvenile Ct. Judges, 1975; Mayor's award for vol. service to rehab. of family an children, 1979. Fellow Am. Acad. Matrimonial Lawyers, mem. Assn. Bar City N.Y. (mem. domestic relations ct. com.), N.Y. County Lawyers' Assn. (family ct. com.), Am. Bar Assn. Author: Who's Answering the Phone!, 1979. Home: Olympic Towers 641 5th Ave New York NY 10022 Office: Parents Anonymous 250 W 57th St New York NY 10019

BACON, JEAN GERLACH, orgn. exec.; b. Milw., Nov. 5, 1940; d. Lester August and Catherine Manson (Wilson) Gerlach; B.A. in History and Polit. Sci., Vassar Coll., 1962; postgrad. Columbia U. Tchrs. Coll., U. Mo., Kansas City, Kans. U., Central Mich. U.; m. Lyman C. Bacon, June 15, 1962; 1 dau., Elizabeth Anne. Elem. and secondary sch. tchr. schs. in Ga., N.Y., N.J., Kans. and Mo., 1962-72; mem. staff Mid-Am. Regional Council, 1974—, dir. dept. on aging, 1975—; asso. prof. U. Mo. Sch. Medicine; cons. in field. Chmn. grantsmanship com Kansas City (Mo.) Jr. League, 1973; found. chmn. Planned Parenthood Kansas City, 1972; chmn. women's com. Johnson County (Kans.) United Way, 1974-75; chpt. scholarship chmn. Am. Field Service, 1972, bd. dirs., 1972; bd dirs. Learning Exchange, 1972-73, Vol. Action Center, 1972-73, Kansas City Ballet, 1972-73, Renaissance West, 1974-75, Family and Children's Service Kansas City, 1978-82, Human Rescue, Inc., 1981-82, Kansas City YWCA, 1979-82. Mem. Nat. Assn. Area Agys. on Aging (charter), Gerontol. Soc., Western Gerontol. Soc. (editorial bd.), Am. Public Health Assn., Urban Elderly Coalition, Mo. Assn. Adminstrs. Area Agys. on Aging, Mid-Am. Congress on Aging, Am. Mgmt. Assn., Am. Acad. Polit. and Social Sci., Kansas City Jr. League, Kansas City Women's C. of C. Republican. Club: Kansas City Vassar (scholarship chmn. 1972-74). Home: 9119 Riggs Ln Overland Park KS 66212 Office: 20 W 9th St Kansas City MO 64105

BACON, SUSAN JEANNE, mech. engr.; b. Phila., Jan. 29, 1951; d. Robert Joseph and Elizabeth Grace B.; B.S. in Math., U. Pitts., 1971, B.S.M.E., 1974; postgrad. in bus. adminstrn. Calif. State U., Long Beach. Tech. writer Westinghouse Electric Co., Pitts., 1971; applications engr. Koppers Co., Balt., 1974-76; sales engr. U.S. Elec. Motors, Los Angeles, 1976-79, Foxboro Co., 1979—. Bd. dirs. Pitts. Free Clinic, 1973-74. Mem. Pacific Energy Assn. Home: 2206 S Shelton Santa Ana CA 92707

BACON, VICKY LEE, lighting services exec.; b. Oregon City, Oreg., Mar. 25, 1950; d. Herbert Kenneth and Lorean Betty (Boltz) Rushford; student Portland Community Coll., 1974-75, Mt. Hood Community Coll., 1976, Portland State Coll., 1979; m. Dennis M. Bacon, Aug. 7, 1971; 1 dau., Randene Tess. With All Electric Constrn., Milwaukie, Oreg., 1968-70; with Lighting Maintenance Co., Portland, Oreg., 1970-78; service mgr. GTE Sylvania Lighting Services, Portland, 1978-80, br. mgr., 1980—. Mem. Nat. Secs. Assn., Illuminating Engring. Soc., Nat. Assn. Lighting Maintenance Contractors. Office: 10775 SW Cascade Blvd Portland OR 97223

BACON-BERCEY, JUNE, meteorologist; b. Wichita, Kans., Oct. 23, 1932; B.A. in Math. and Meteorology (scholar), UCLA, 1954, M.A., 1955; M.A. in Pub. Adminstrn., U. So. Calif., 1979; postgrad. N.Y.U.; m. George W. Brewer; 2 children. Meteorologist, communicator Nat. Weather Service, Washington, 1956-62; engr. Sperry Rand Corp., 1962-64; cons. AEC, N.Y.C., 1964-65; TV meteorologist, news corr., morning hostess NBC stas., N.Y.C. and Buffalo, 1965-74; profl. lectr., 1974-75; ops. meteorologist, broadcaster Nat. Weather Service, 1975-79; pub. info. specialist, chief TV services NOAA, 1979—. Past bd. dirs. Black Profl. Devel., Women and Minorities. Mem. Am. Meteorol. Soc. (chpt. vice chmn. 1979), Women in Sci. and Engring., Am. Geophys. Union, Am. Assn. Pub. Adminstrn., N.Y. Acad. Scis., Nat. Tech. Assn., Alpha Kappa Alpha. Author articles in field. Endowed scholarship The June Bacon-Bercey Scholarship for Women in the Atmospheric Scis. Address: Bluebird's Hacienda Hinton Ranch Rd Pacifica CA 94044

BADDOUR, ANNE BRIDGE (MRS. RAYMOND F. BADDOUR), aviatrix; b. Royal Oak, Mich.; d. William George and Esther Rose (Pfiester) Bridge; student Detroit Bus. Sch., 1948-50; m. Raymond F. Baddour, Sept. 25, 1954; children—Cynthia Anne, Frederick Raymond, Jean Bridge. Stewardess, Eastern Airlines, Boston, 1952-54; instr. aeros. Powers Sch., Boston, 1958; co pilot, flight attendant Raytheon Co., Bedford, Mass., 1958-63; flight dispatcher, ferry pilot Comerford Flight Sch., Bedford, 1974-76; adminstrv. asst., ferry pilot, Jenney Beachcraft, Bedford, 1976; mgr., pilot Baltimore Airways, Inc., Bedford, 1976-77; pilot, flight facility M.I.T. Lincoln Lab. Flight Test Facility, Lexington, Mass., 1977—; aviation cons., corp. pilot Energy Resources, Inc., Cambridge, Mass., 1974—. Bd. dirs. Cambridge Opera, 1977-79; mem. campaign council Mus. Transp., Boston; mem. council assos. French Library in Boston; commr. Commonwealth of Mass., Mass. Aero. Commn., 1979—. Winner trophy Phila. Transcontinental Air Race, 1954, New Eng. Air Race, 1957. Mem. Fedn. Aeronautique International, Nat. Aero. Assn., Ninety-Nines, Aero Club New England (v.p., dir.), Aircraft Owners Pilots Assn., Nat. Pilots Assn., U.S. Sea Plane Pilots Assn., Assn. Women Transcontinental Air Race, Republican. Episcopalian. Clubs: Bostonian Soc., English Speaking Union, Friends of Switzerland, French Center Library, Belmont Hill, Aero of New Eng. (dir. 1978—), St. Botolph. Home: 96 Fletcher Rd Belmont MA 02178 Office: Draper Flight Test Facility Lincoln Lab MIT PO Box 98 Concord MA 01742

BADENHOP, SHARON LYNN, psychologist, educator; b. Roswell, N.Mex., Feb. 21, 1946; d. Charles Theodore and Anna (Burke) Badenhop; B.A. in Ednl. Psychology, SUNY, Oneonta, 1967, M.S., 1969, M.S. in Counselor Edn., 1971. Tchr., Gilbertsville (N.Y.) Central Sch., 1968-70; guidance counselor Delaware Acad., Delhi, N.Y., 1970-71; instr. SUNY, Oneonta, 1971-75; prof. SUNY, Delhi, 1974-75; psychol. case worker United Cerebral Palsy Assn., 1977-78; psychologist in psychogeratrics Rochester (N.Y.) Psychiat. Center, 1979, dir. edn. and tng. dept., 1979-81, psychologist, 1981—; instr. Rochester Inst. Tech., 1981—, U. Rochester, 1978—. Lic. guidance counselor, N.Y. State; cert. tchr. grades 1-6, N.Y. State. Mem. Am. Psychol. Assn., Am. Edn. Research Assn., N.Y. State Personnel and Guidance Assn., Clin. Sociology Assn. Home: 18 Hollingham Rise Fairport NY 14450 Office: Rochester Psychiat Center 1600 South Ave Rochester NY 14620

BADGETT, PATRICIA MCCLURE, chamber of commerce exec.; b. Frankfort, Ky., Oct. 4, 1939; d. John McClure and Evelyn Frances (Jones) Phythian; student Ky. Inst. Chamber Staff, Inst. Organizational Mgmt.; m. John Wesley Badgett, July 5, 1958; children—Kenny, Wesley, Tom, Jackie Sue. Adminstrv. asst. Frankfort chpt. ARC, 1970-74; exec. sec. Franklin County-Frankfort C. of C., 1974-78, exec. v.p., 1978—; mem. bd. Frankfort Tourist and Conv. Commn., 1978—. Named Citizen of Yr., Frankfort post Am. Legion, 1973; recipient Community Service award Frankfort Jaycees, 1981. Mem. Ky. Assn. C. of C. Execs. (pres. 1981-82), Am. Assn. Chamber Execs., So. Assn. Chamber Execs., Elkhorn Elem. PTA (dir. 1977-78), Beta Sigma Phi (pres. 1978). Baptist. Home: 520 Kickapoo Trail Frankfort KY 40601 Office: 210 W Main St Frankfort KY 40601

BAEHR, MELANY ERNA, psychologist; b. Kimberley, Republic South Africa, Oct. 25, 1920; came to U.S., 1948, naturalized, 1953; d. Ernest Horace and Hester Cecilia (Van Niekerk) White; B.S., U. Witwatersrand, Johannesburg, S. Africa, 1940, B.Ed., 1941, M.S., 1946, Ph.D., 1950; postgrad U. Chgo., 1948-49; m. George Otto Baehr, Sept. 9, 1949; children—Alexandra Elaine, Karen Estelle. Research officer South African Council for Sci. and Indsl. Research, 1946-49; project dir. Human Resources Center, U. Chgo., 1950-53, research asso., 1955-57, cons., 1957-62, div. dir., 1962-70, sr. research psychologist, asso. prof. social sci., 1970-78, asso. dir. research, 82, assoc. prof. social sci. div., 1982—, dir. human resources research and programs Office Continuing Edn., 1982—. Served with South African Air Force, 1939-45. Cert. psychologist, Ill. Fellow Am. Psychol. Assn.; mem. Ill. Psychol. Assn. (past pres. indsl. sect.), Sigma Xi, Psi Chi. Episcopalian. Author psychol. tests and measurement instruments; contbr. articles to profl. jours., chpts. to textbooks. Home: 5555 S Everett Av Chicago IL 60637 Office: 1225 E 60th St Chicago IL 60637

BAER, JEAN LOUISE (MRS. HERBERT FENSTERHEIM), editor, author; b. Chgo., May 17, 1926; d. Fred E. and Helen (Roth) Baer; B.A., Cornell U., 1945; m. Herbert Fensterheim, June 20, 1968. Writer press dept. MBC, N.Y.C., 1945-46; publicist Air Features, Inc., N.Y.C., 1946-49, Coll & Freedman Public Relations, N.Y.C., 1949-51; program info. editor Voice of Am., N.Y.C. and overseas, 1953; publicity dir. Seventeen mag., N.Y.C., 1953-68, spl. projects dir., sr. editor, 1968-74. Mem. Overseas Press Club Am. (sec. bd. govs.), Newswomen's Club N.Y. Club: Woman Pays (N.Y.C.). Author: Follow Me!, 1965; The Single Girl Goes to Town, 1968; The Second Wife, 1972; How To Be an Assertive (Not Aggressive) Woman, 1976; co-author: Don't Say Yes When You Want to Say No, 1975; Stop Running Scared!, 1977; The Self-Chosen, 1982. Home: 151 E 37th St New York NY 10016

BAER, JO WEBB, real estate exec.; b. Mt. Sterling, Ala., Feb. 28, 1936; d. John Henry and Annie Ellie (Southern) Webb; student U. Ala., Mobile, 1954-55, Northwestern U., Chgo., 1961-62, City Coll. N.Y., 1964-65; m. Peter Baer, Feb. 17, 1956; children—Barbara Ann, Kelly. Exec. dir. Fgn. Policy Council of N.Y. Democrats, 1967; Bronx campaign dir. for Eugene McCarthy, 1968; state campaign dir. for Morris Udall, 1976; sales mgr., Wright Brothers of Nyack, Inc. (N.Y.), 1972-79; pres. Baer & McIntosh Real Estate, Inc., Nyack, 1979—. Mem. Bd. Assessment and Rev., Town of Orangetown, N.Y., 1975-79; chairperson Friends of Nyacks, 1976-77; mem. Dem. Nat. Com., 1974-80. Named Citizen of Yr. Nyack, 1980. Mem. Nyack C. of C. (dir., pres. 1981-82), Rockland County Bd. Realtors (dir.). Home: 26 Terrace Dr South Nyack NY 10960 Office: 49 Burd St Nyack NY 10960

BAER, MARIANNE, advt. exec.; b. Elizabeth, N.J., July 5, 1932; d. Werner Kurt and Anne Sophie (Holzer) Baer; student Pratt Inst., 1950-52. Asso. creative dir., v.p. Ogilvy & Mather, Inc., N.Y.C., 1963-71; writer Botsford, Ketchum, Inc., San Francisco, 1971-74; asso. creative dir. Foote, Cone & Belding, Chgo., 1974-77; asso. creative dir., v.p. Conahay & Lyon, Inc., N.Y.C., 1977-79; writer Tracy-Locke, Inc., Dallas, 1979—. Recipient various nat. and internat. advt. awards, 1965—. Mem. Writers Guild Am. Moravian. Author: A Man's Woman, 1978. Home: 9833 Smokefeather Ln Dallas TX 75243 Office: Plaza of the Americas South Tower Dallas TX 75201

BAERGEN, VIOLET MARY, consumer services co. ofcl.; b. Arbor Vitas, Ont., Can., Apr. 11, 1925; d. William Charles and Ida Mae (Akkerman) Smith; student Western Coll. Commerce, Wenatchee, Wash., 1960, Wenatchee Valley Coll., 1962; m. David D. Baergen, Jan. 31, 1964; children—Gerald Hill, Linda Worley, Janet Van Horn, Robert Price. Office mgr. Darigold Dairy, Wenatchee, Wash., 1961; packing foreman Krispy K Fruit Co., Monitor, Wash., 1964-72; sr. acct. Eye and Ear Hosp., Wenatchee, 1972-75; self-employed restaurant owner, Kennewick, Wash., 1975-79; commn. agt. Greyhound Co., Pasco, Wash., 1979-82; owner, operator Tri Cities Consumer Services, chpt. People's Discount Club of Am., Pasco, 1982—; sec. Malaga (Wash.) Coop., 1963-69. Mem. Nat. Assn. Female Execs., Am. Dairy Goat Assn., Pacso C. of C. Republican. Methodist. Home: Route 2 Box 2828 Kennewick WA 99336 Office: 824 W Lewis St Pasco WA 99301

BAERM, PHYLLIS BARBARA SMITH, internist, hematologist; b. N.Y.C., Nov. 10, 1939; d. Joseph and Emma (Lawler) Smith; B.A., Pace U., 1958; M.A., Columbia U., 1965; M.D., Hahnemann Med. Sch., also M.P.H.; m. Stephen Daer, June 20, 1966; children—Jeniffer, Heidi, Jesse. Intern, Hahnemann Hosp., Phila., 1972-73; resident Carney Hosp., Boston, 1973-75; fellow in hematology Tufts U., 1975-78; internist, hematologist Neponset Health Center, Dorchester, Mass., 1978-81; staff Carney Hosp., St. Margaret Hosp., Parker Hill Hosp., Quincy City Hosp.; home care physician Vis. Nurs. Assn.; practice medicine, Wollaston, Mass., 1982—. Address: 115 Monroe Rd Quincy MA 02169

BAERWALDT, NANCY ANN, state ofcl.; b. N.Y.C., Jan. 11, 1940; d. Glenna G. Golladay; B.A., Bucknell U., 1961; M.A. in Econs., U. Mich., 1967. Research asst. U. Mich., Ann Arbor, to 1972; program analyst Mich. Dept. Social Services, Lansing, 1972-74; revenue and econ. analyst Mich. Dept. Mgmt. and Budget, Lansing, 1974-76; dir. research Mich. Dept. Labor, Lansing, 1976-77; dep. dir. Mich. Dept. Commerce, Lansing, 1978-80; commr. of ins. State of Mich., Lansing, 1980—. Mem. Nat. Assn. Ins. Commrs. Republican. Home: PO Box 1075 East Lansing MI 48823 Office: PO Box 30220 Lansing MI 48909

BAEZ, JOAN CHANDOS, activist, singer; b. Staten Island, N.Y., Jan. 9, 1941; d. Albert V. and Joan Chandos (Bridge) B.; H.H.D. (hon.), Rutgers U., 1980, Antioch Coll., 1980; m. David Victor Harris, Mar. 1968 (div. 1973); 1 son, Gabriel Earl. Appearances include: Ballad Room, Club 47, 1958-60, Gate of Horn, Chgo., 1958, Newport (R.I.) Folk Festival, 1959, 60; extended tour to colls. and concert halls, 1961—, Carnegie Hall, 1962, U.S. tour, 1975; rec. artist for Vanguard Records, 1960-72, A&M, 1972-75, Portrait Records, 1975—; concert tours Europe, 1965-66, 70, 72, 73, 80, Japan, 1966, U.S. and Europe, 1967-68; began refusing payment of war taxes, 1964; extensive TV appearances and speaking tours U.S. and Can. for anti-militarism, 1967-68; arrested for civil disobedience opposing draft, 1967; made trip to Hanoi, 1975. Founder, v.p. Inst. for Study of Nonviolence, Palo Alto, Calif. (now Resource Center for Nonviolence, Santa Cruz, Calif.), 1965; mem. nat. adv. council Amnesty Internat., 1974—; founder, pres. Humanitas Internat. Human Rights Com., 1979, attended Geneva Conf. on Cambodia as rep. of Humanitas, 1980. Author: Daybreak, 1968; (with David Harris) Coming Out, 1971; (songbook) And Then I Wrote. . . . , 1979. Office: Diamonds & Rust Prodns Inc PO Box 1026 Menlo Park CA 94025

BAGBY, FRANCES BOONE (MRS. WILLIAM HUGH BAGBY), realtor; b. Greensboro, N.C., Mar. 2, 1907; d. Robert Philemon and Effie (Geringer) Boone; student pub. schs. and bus. coll.; m. E. H. Young, Mar. 1, 1924 (div. 1941); children—Miriam Young Kvarnes, Richard Franklin; m. 2d, Edwin Russell Harrall, Apr. 25, 1943 (dec. Aug. 1978); m. 3d, William Hugh Bagby, Aug. 26, 1979. With Cone Mills, N.Y.C., 1927-42, Children's Home of Balt., 1943-46; dist. mgr. Beauty Counselors, Inc., 1956, nat. sect. mgr., 1957-61, div. mgr., 1961-63; realtor Russell T. Baker & Co., Inc., Lutherville, Md., 1963—. Mem. Md. Hist. Soc., English-Speaking Union, Women's Civic League, P.E.O., So. Dames Am. (nat. v.p.), Realtors Million Dollar Club (life), Internat. Platform Assn. Episcopalian. Clubs: Little Garden (pres.), Green Spring; Hunt Valley, Cosmopolitans, Center, Balt. Country, Mchts. Home: Halcyon House 6235 Fernway Baltimore MD 21212 Office: 1629 York Rd Lutherville MD 21093

BAGBY, SARAH-ANN, legal investigator; b. Portland, Oreg., Apr. 7, 1944; d. Frederick Augustus and Isabelle Armstrong (Diehl) Nitchy; student U. Calif., Santa Barbara 1961-64 Coll. Desert, 1965; 1 dau., Lisa Renee. Credit mgr. Axminster Med. Group, Los Angeles, 1970-73; staff investigator Searchers Investigating Co., Inc., Los Angeles, 1974-79; sr. investigator Teltec Investigations, Beverly Hills, Calif., 1979-80; founder, pres. Bagby Investigations, Los Angeles, 1980—. Recipient Outstanding Overall Musician award music dept. Coll of Desert, 1965. Mem. Nat. Assn. Female Execs., Calif. Assn. Lic. Investigators. Episcopalian. Home and Office: 5736 S Victoria Ave Los Angeles CA 90043

BAGGETT, ELEANOR RUTH, banker; b. Davidson County, Tenn., Nov. 1, 1943; d. Will and Sybil Eleanor (Vaughn) Ursery; grad. Tenn. Sch. Banking; m. Tommy Wayne Baggett, May 4, 1963; children—Donna Baggett Kessinger, Michael Wayne. Clk., Commerce Union Bank, Nashville, 61-63; with First Nat. Bank, Springfield, Tenn., 1963—, head savs. dept., now asst. v.p. Treas., Am. Cancer Soc., March of Dimes. Methodist. Home: Route 6 Box 163 Springfield TN 37172 Office: 2127 Memorial Blvd Springfield TN 37172

BAGGOTT, NANCY MARIE, real estate co. ofcl.; b. Highland Park, Mich., Nov. 3, 1949; d. Sydney and Julia Catherine (Schiftar) B.; B.S. in Bus. Adminstrn. with honors, Columbia Coll., 1978. Draftsman, Fed. Mogul Corp., Southfield, Mich., 1972-73; enlisted in U.S. Army, 1973, advanced through grades to staff sgt., 1977; intelligence analyst U.S. Army, Okinawa, 1973-74, guidance counselor/recruiter, San Francisco dist. recruiting command, 1974-77, profl. devel. and sales trainer, 1977-79, resigned, 1979; tng. and mktg. dir. TICKET Corp., San Jose, Calif., 1979-82; owner/prin. TICKET West, 1982—; public speaker. Decorated Army Commendation medal; lic. real estate agt. Mem. Nat. Assn. Female Execs., Real Estate Edn. Assn., Mil. Intelligence Assn. Office: 1419 Park St Suite D Alameda CA 94501

BAGGS, LEAH L. BATES, social leader; b. Franklinville, N.Y.; d. William Henry and Arlie Mae (Bozworth) Bates; A.B., Barnard Coll., 1922; student spl. courses various univs.; m. Linton Daniel Baggs, Jr., Oct. 1, 1926; children—Joan Bates (Mrs. Herbert A. McKenzie, Jr.), Linton Daniel III. Hon. bd. dirs. Macon Community Concert Assn., 1968—, pres., 1959-64; bd. dirs. Middle Ga. Camellia Soc.; v.p. Macon Grand Opera Assn., 1954—; vice regent Magna Charta Dames, 1968-70, regent Ga. div., 1970-72; hon. state regent Daus. Am. Colonists, 1962, nat. chmn. colonial heritage com., 1962-64, Bicentennial chmn. Ga. br., 1974-76; com. chmn. Ga. br. Sons and Daus. of Pilgrims Soc., 1954-55. Mem. AAUW, Ga. Soc. Mayflower Descs. (corr. sec. 1960-62), Pilgrim John Howland Soc., D.A.R., Middle Ga. Hist. Soc. (charter mem.). Am., S.C., Middle Ga. (dir.) camellia socs., Nat. Trust for Historic Preservation, Sigma Alpha Iota. Presbyterian. Clubs: Barnard College (Atlanta, v.p. 1967-72), Morning Music (pres. 1951-53), Atlanta Music, Capitol City Atlanta, Idle Hour Country (Macon, Ga.). Home: 1137 N Jackson Springs Rd Macon GA 31211

BAGLEY, EDYTHE SCOTT, educator; b. Marion, Ala.; B.S., Ohio State U., 1949; M.A., Columbia U., 1954; M.F.A., Boston U., 1965; m. Arthur M. Bagley, 1954; 1 son. Tchr. English, Westside High Sch., Talladega, Ala., 1949-52; instr. English, Elizabeth City (N.C.) State Coll., 1953-55; asst. prof. English, Albany (Ga.) State Coll., 1955-56, A&T Coll., Greensboro, N.C., 1956-57, Norfolk (Va.) State Coll., 1963-65; asso. prof. drama, head dept. Cheyney (Pa.) State Coll., 1971—. Bd. dirs. Martin Luther King, Jr. Center for Social Change, Atlanta. Mem. Am. Theatre Assn., Pa. Theatre Assn., Women's Internat. League for Peace and Freedom, Soc. for Lit. and Arts, NEA, Pa. Edn. Assn., NAACP, Nat. Council Negro Women, Links, Am. Acad. and Theatre, Alpha Psi Omega. Methodist. Home: 124 W Lafayette St West Chester PA 19380 Office: Cheyney State Coll Cheyney PA 19319

BAGLEY, LILLIAN ESTHER, sec., civic worker; b. Glenville, Ga., Sept. 21, 1908; d. William Stacey and Alma Virginia (Woodcock) Dubberly; grad. So. Bus. Coll., 1937; m. Lorne Bagley, Sept. 21, 1938; children—Loretta, Lynette and Lyneta (twins). Sec., So. Acceptance Corp., Orlando, Fla., 1934-38; sec. to Dr. John R. Keene, pres., bus. mgr. U. Central Fla. Symphony Orchestra, 1969—. Leader, Citrus council Girl Scouts U.S.A., 1951-52; recreation chmn. Fern Creek Sch., Orlando, 1950-51; fin. chmn. Howard Jr. High Sch., 1953; pres. Central Fla. Community Orchestra, 1961-68. Recipient recognition for work in fund raising for Lake Eola Bandshell. Democrat. Mem. Christian Ch. Office: U Central Fla Symphony Orchestra Box 25000 Orlando FL 32816

BAGLIORE, VIRGINIA, poet; b. Bklyn., Mar. 14, 1931; d. James and Josephine (Brunetti) Coglietta; student N.Y. U., Bklyn. Coll.; student of Kimon Friar; m. James Bagliore, Nov. 8, 1953; children—Rosanne, Lisa. Model, 1952-56; freelance promotional model, 1975-80; poet-tchr. creative poetry workshops, 1975—; condr. workshops Assn. Humanistic Psychology, 1978, 5th Am. Imagery Conf., 1981, Carroll St. Sch., 1981, Public Sch. No. 65, 1981, others; co-editor Eve's Legacy mag., 1980-82; lectr. workshop New Sch., 1982; sponsor, judge High Sch. Poetry Contest, 1977-82; contbr. poems various poetry mags.; poems represented anthologies; exhibited 5 poems at Cork Gallery, Lincoln Center, 1981; poems translated into Urdu; essays in The Study and Writing of Poetry; developed communication technique for improving lang. Recipient Cert. of Merit, Alan Foss Leukemia Found., 1975; Bill Burke award, 1976; Louise Bogan Meml. award, 1972; Louise Louis award, 1978. Mem. World Poets' Resource Center (Creative Service award 1979), Nat. League Am. Pen Women (v.p. letters 1978-82, pres. 1982—), N.Y. Poetry Forum, Avalon Soc., Eleanor Gaylee Found., Shelley Soc., Composers, Authors, and Artists of Am., Nat. Assn. Poetry Therapy.

BAGNALL, ELIZABETH ALICE, chem. engr.; b. Brighton, Mass., Dec. 4, 1952; d. James Joseph and Alice Lillian (Lidwin) B.; B.S. in Chem. Engring., M.I.T., 1975, M.S. in Chem. Engring., 1975. Devel. engr. Ciba-Geigy Corp., Cranston, R.I., 1975-77; research engr. FMC Corp., Princeton, N.J., 1977—; mem. Central Jersey Engring. Council, 1978-79. Mem. Am. Inst. Chem. Engrs., Soc. Women Engrs. (N.J. sect. treas. 1979—), Sigma Xi. Club: M.I.T. Alumni of Princeton (sec. 1979-80, v.p. programs 1980—). Patentee continuous process for manufacture of cyanoric acid. Office: PO Box 8 Princeton NJ 08540

BAHNER, SUE (FLORENCE SUZANNA BAHNER), broadcasting exec.; b. Phila., Feb. 10; d. William and Florence (Quinlivan) McElwee; diploma Columbia Bus. Sch., Phila.; m. David Stocking; children—Suzanna Elizabeth, Carol Aileen. Various exec. secretarial positions, 1954-74; office mgr. Sta. WYRD, Syracuse, N.Y., 1974, gen. mgr., 1974-80; gen. mgr. WWWG Radio, Rochester, N.Y., 1980—. Adv. bd. Home and Family Services of Rochester. Mem. Nat. Religious Broadcasters Assn. (sec. Eastern regional chpt. 1980-84), Greater Rochester (v.p. 1982-83), Greater Syracuse assns. evangels., Rochester Sales and Mktg. Execs., Syracuse Advt. Club, Onondaga Citizens League. Mem. Bible Ch. Club: Syracuse Press. Office: 1850 Winton Rd South Rochester NY 14618

BAILER, BONNIE LYNN, profl. fund raiser; b. N.Y.C., Oct. 11, 1946; d. Lloyd Harding and Marvelyne Amanda (Matthews) Bailer; B.A., Queens Coll., 1968, M.S., 1975; 1 son, Miles Bailer Armistead. Tchr. French, Intermediate Sch. 55, N.Y.C., 1968-75; acting chmn. fgn. lang. dept. N.Y.C. Public Sch. System, 1970-75; co-founder, v.p. Yellow Go-Rilla Prodns. Ltd., N.Y.C., 1975-78; nat. membership task force coordinator NAACP, N.Y.C., 1978-79, spl. contbn. fund corp. devel. officer, 1979—; asst. v.p. Gilbert Jones, Co., N.Y.C., 1979—; dir. Morningside Montessori Sch., N.Y.C., 1979-82. Adminstr., Manhattan Borough Pres. Campaign, 1977; press and info. cons. Annual Westside Community Conf., 1979-81. Mem. Nat. Assn. Female Execs., Council Concerned Black Execs., NAACP, NOW. Office: 150 E 58th St New York NY 10155

BAILEY, CAROLYN FAULKNER, computer programmer; b. Troy, Ala., Nov. 6, 1942; d. Martin C. and Sylvania (Knotts) Faulkner; B.S. in Computer Sci. and Mgmt., U. Ala., 1980; M.S. in Personnel Mgmt., Troy State U., 1982; postgrad. Auburn U., 1982—. Staff asst. Air War Coll., Maxwell AFB, Ala., 1970-74, editorial asst., asso. programmer, 1974-75; computer technician Air Force Data Systems Design Center, Gunter AFB, Ala., 1975—; planner, organizer, dir. ednl. seminars, workshops for women, 1979—; investment and fin. mgmt. cons., 1970—; data elements mgr., dir. Med. Systems, 1980—. Vol. counselor Montgomery Area Mental Health, 1979—. Mem. LWV, AAUW (dir.), Federally Employed Women (pres.), Cottage Hill Hist. Assn., U. Ala. Alumni Assn., Okaloosa Island Improvement Assn., Alpha Xi Delta, Beta Gamma Phi. Episcopalian. Contbr. articles to various publs. Home: 3503 Castle Ridge Rd Montgomery AL 36116 Office: Turner Bldg Gunter Air Force Station AL 36114

BAILEY, ELIZABETH ELLERY, govt. ofcl.; b. N.Y.C., Nov. 26, 1938; d. Irving W. and Henrietta (Dana) Raymond; B.A. in Econs. magna cum laude, Radcliffe Coll., 1960; M.S. in Computer Sci., Stevens Inst. Tech., Hoboken, N.J., 1966; Ph.D. in Econs., Princeton U., 1972; div.; children—James L., William E. From sr. tech. aid to mem. tech. staff, research head and supr. econ. analysis group Bell Telephone Labs., Holmdel, N.J., 1960-77; adj. asst., then adj. asso. prof. econs. N.Y. U., 1973-77; mem. CAB, Washington, 1977—, vice-chmn., 1981—; bd. editors Am. Econ. Rev., 1977-79. Vice pres. trustees, founding mem. Harbor Sch. Children with Learning Disabilities, Red Bank, N.J., 1969-72; mem. N.J.-Md. Assn. Children with Learning Disabilities, 1969—; trustee Princeton U., 1978-82; head parent action group St. Maurice Sch., Potomac, Md., 1979—. Program Design trainee Bell Telephone Labs., 1964-66, Doctoral support grantee, 1970-72. Mem. Am. Econ. Assn. (exec. com. 1981—; head com. status of women in econs. 1980-82). Author: Economic Theory of Regulatory Constraint, 1973; also articles. Editor: Selected Economics Papers of William J. Baumol, 1976. Home: 4601 N Park Ave Apt 1811 Chevy Chase MD 20015 Office: CAB 1825 Connecticut Ave NW Washington DC 20428

BAILEY, EXINE MARGARET, educator; b. Cottonwood, Minn., Jan. 4, 1922; d. Joseph Leonard and Exine Pearl (Robertson) Anderson; B.S., U. Minn., 1944; M.A., Columbia U., 1945, profl. diploma, 1951; m. Arthur Albert Bailey, May 5, 1956. Instr., Columbia U., N.Y.C., 1947-51; asst. prof. U. Oreg., Eugene, 1951-60, asso. prof., 1960-66, prof., 1966—, chmn. voice dept., 1969—, faculty dir. Europe, summers 1968, 76; vis. prof., head voice dept. Columbia U., summers 1952, 59; soloist Portland Symphony, 1969, Eugene Symphony, 1967, 71, 75; with Helmuth Rilling, 1973; guest appearances throughout U.S. Lobbyist, Oreg. State Bd. Higher Edn., 1977. Metro. Opera Assn. scholar, 1945; N.Y. Singing Tchrs. Singer of Yr., 1945. Mem. Nat Assn. Tchrs. Singing (N.W. region lt. gov. 1968-72), Music Tchrs. Nat. Assn. (state pres. 1974-76, nat. voice chmn. 1973-75, 81—). Republican. Contbr. articles to profl. jours. Home: 17 Westbrook Way Eugene OR 97405 Office: Sch Music Univ Oreg Eugene OR 97405

BAILEY, JANET DEE, pub. co. ofcl.; b. Newark, Aug. 23, 1946; d. Richard and Mary Louise (Dee) Shapiro; B.A. in English, U. Del., 1968; postgrad. in pub. N.Y. U., 1968-70; M.B.A. in Fin., Pace U., 1981; m. John Bailey, May 9, 1971. Prodn. editor bus. and profl. books dept. Prentice-Hall, Inc., Englewood Cliffs, N.J., 1968-70; editor Spl. Libraries Jour., Spl. Libraries Assn., N.Y.C., 1971-76, mgr. publs. dept., 1971-76; editorial cons., 1976-78; dir. mktg. services Knowledge Industry Publs., Inc., White Plains, N.Y., 1978-81; dir. inventory and contracts Macmillan Book Clubs, Inc., N.Y.C., 1981—. Mem. NOW (v.p. Central Westchester chpt. 1976-77), Westchester Ethical Humanist Soc. (newsletter editor 1977-78), Women of Westchester (asst. sec. 1979-80). Home: 1 Mansfield Rd White Plains NY 10605

BAILEY, JOLAN NAGY, speech pathologist; b. Hubo, Hungary, Aug. 25, 1948; came to U.S., 1951, naturalized, 1954; d. Louis Joseph and Elizabeth Marie (Ruszkay) N.; B.S. in Speech and Hearing, Ind. U. of Pa., 1971, M.Ed., 1972; m. Jim E. Bailey, May 31, 1980. Speech therapist Westmoreland County (Pa.) Intermediate Unit, 1972-73; speech and hearing specialist Ebensburg (Pa.) Center, 1974-77; speech and hearing specialist Exceptional Devel. Center, Torrance (Pa.) State Hosp., 1977-78, dir. developmental services, 1978—; pvt. practice for aphasics Latrobe (Pa.) Area Hosp. Cert. tchr., Pa. Mem. Am. Speech and Hearing Assn. (cert. clin. competence), Pa. Speech and Hearing Assn. Home: RD 2 Box 62AB Ligonier PA 15658 Office: PO Box 103 Exceptional Development Center Torrance PA 15779

BAILEY, JOSELYN ELIZABETH, physician; b. Pine Bluff, Ark.; d. Joseph Alexander and Angeline Elaine (Davis) B.; B.Mus., Manhattanville Coll., 1952; M.Music Edn., Manhattan Sch. Music, 1954; M.D., Howard U., 1971. Straight med. intern Huntington Meml. Hosp., Pasadena, Calif., 1971-72, resident, 1972-74; fell in nephrology Wadsworth VA Hosp., Los Angeles, 1975-77; practice medicine specializing in internal medicine and nephrology, Torrance, Calif.; mem. active staff Torrance Meml., South Bay, Little Company of Mary hosps.; cons. staff Del Amo Hosp.; attending staff Harbor Gen. Hosp.; courtesy staff San Pedro Peninsula Hosp.; active staff Bay Harbor Hosp., trustee, 1982—; dialysis unit rep. Renal Network Coordinating Council No. 4. Mem. Renal Physicians Assn., Am. Soc. Internal Medicine, Calif. Soc. Internal Medicine, So. Calif. Pvt. Practice Assn., Torrance Area C. of C. Roman Catholic.

BAILEY, LINDA JEAN (LYN), educator; b. Stoneham, Mass., Dec. 28, 1948; d. Chester G. and Alice M. (Moriarty) Bailey; B.S. with honors (spl. edn. sr. yr. fellow), Boston U., 1971; M.Ed. (spl. edn. grad. fellow), U. Ariz., 1972; postgrad. Ariz. State U., 1972—. Elem. tchr., 1972-75; learning disabilities specialist, Tolleson, Ariz., 1974-75; learning disabilities specialist Washington Elem. Dist., Phoenix, 1975-79, program specialist, 1979-82, instrnl. specialist, 1982—. Vol. worker St. Joseph's Hosp. Aux., 1976—, nat. Democratic campaigns, 1975-80; interviewer Planned Parenthood, 1980—. Mem. NEA, Ariz. Edn. Assn., Assn. for Children with Learning Disabilities, Council for Exceptional Children, Assn. for Supervision and Curriculum Devel., Washington Edn. Assn. Roman Catholic. Clubs: Scbba Diving, Ski. Office: Washington Elem Dist 3333 W Banff St Phoenix AZ 85021

BAILEY, MARY KATHRYN, ballet exec.; b. Louisville, Jan. 23, 1946; d. Carl Theodore and Adeline May (Campbell) Johnston; B.A. in Philosophy, Rice U., Houston, 1967; m. James Edwin Bailey, Aug. 20, 1966; 1 son, Michael Sean. Asst. dept. mgr. Foley's Dept. Store, Houston, 1967-68; sales mgr. Houston Ballet, 1974-75, mktg. dir., 1975-77, dir. adminstrn. and mktg., 1977—; bd. dirs. Assn. Am. Dance Companies; mem. Houston Conv. and Visitors Council. Mem. Primary Arts Confedn. Tex. (steering com.), Cultural Arts Council Houston, Houston C. of C. (cultural com.). Office: 615 Louisiana St Houston TX 77002

BAILEY, MONA HUMPHRIES, state ofcl.; b. Apalachicola, Fla., Dec. 14, 1932; d. Thornton G. and Minnie (Henry) Humphries; B.S. in chemistry Fla. A & M. U. 1954, postgrad. Am. U. 1959, U. Wash., 1959-60, M.S. in Sci., Oreg. State U. 1962; m. William Peter Bailey, Aug. 26, 1961; children—Peter, Christopher. Tchr. sci Live Oak & Panama City (Fla.) Schs. 1954-57; tchr., counselor Seattle Secondary Schs. 1959-67; personnel adminstrn. Seattle Schs. 1969-70; prin. Meany-Madrona Middle Sch., Seattle, 1970-73; asst. supt. Public Instrn. State of Wash., Tumwater 1974—. Bd. dirs. Totem council Girl Scouts U.S.A., Olympia, Wash. Recipient Meritorious Achievement award Fla. A & M U. 1981. Mem. Assn. Supervision and Curriculum Devel., Delta Sigma Theta (nat. pres.). Office: 7510 Armstrong St SW Tumwater WA 98504

BAILEY, MYRTLE ELIZABETH HOWELL, interior decorator; b. Landrum, S.C., Dec. 24, 1940; d. Miles Isom and Tessie Ella (Bowers) Howell; student interior decorating, LaSalle Extension U., 1976; m. Kendall T. Bailey, Nov. 26, 1959; children—Kenneth David, Steven Dwayne. Seamstress, Piedmont Industries, Fountain Inn, S.C., 1958-67; v.p. B & B Draperies, Inc., Mauldin, S.C., 1967; interior decorator, Mauldin, 1976—. Baptist. Clubs: Eastern Star (past matron), Golden Strip Shrinettes, Daus. of the Nile. Home: PO Box 502 310 Old Laurens Rd Mauldin SC 29662 Office: 202 N Main St Mauldin SC 29662

BAILEY, NANCY MARTIN, univ. adminstr.; b. Chgo., July 26, 1944; d. Ross J. and Marian (Shepherd) Martin; B.A., U. Wis., Madison, 1967; M.A., U. Ill., Champaign-Urbana, 1981; divorced; children—Ryan Martin Malmgren, Stuart Martin Bailey. Specialist botanist U. Wis., 1967-71; mem. faculty English dept. Univ. High Sch., Urbana, 1977-80; dir. Sch. Life Sci. Placement, U. Ill., 1980—. Chmn. adv. com. Urbana Park Dist., 1982-83. Mem. Assn. Interpretive Naturalists, Coll. Placement Council, Midwest Coll. Placement Assn., Am. Ednl. Studies Assn., Phi Delta Kappa, Kappa Delta Pi, Alpha Chi Omega. Episcopalian. Office: 390 Morrill Hall 505 S Goodwin St Urbana IL 61801

BAILEY, PAMELA GILES, govt. ofcl.; b. Reading, Pa., May 24, 1948; d. John S., Jr., and Nancy (Clymer) Giles; A.B., Mt. Holyoke Coll., 1970; m. William W. Bailey, Dec. 13, 1980; children—Suzanne, Robert, Nancy Needham. Mem. White House staff, Washington, 1970-75, research asst. to Vice Pres., 1970-71, research asst. to Pres., 1971-73, staff asst. to Pres., dir. research, 1973-74, staff asst. Domestic Council, 1974-75, asst. dir. Domestic Council, 1975; mgr. govt. consumer affairs Am. Hosp. Supply Corp., 1975-79, dir. govt. relations, 1980-81; asst. sec. for public affairs Dept. Health and Human Services, Washington, 1981—. Republican. Home: 7821 Wendy Ridge Ln Annandale VA 22003 Office: 200 Independence Ave SW Washington DC 20201

BAILEY, PATRICIA SUSAN, physician; b. N.Y.C., Dec. 18, 1943; d. Joel and Ethel (Miller) Salzburg; B.S. magna cum laude, Central Mich. U., 1970, M.A., 1972; M.D., Mich. State U., 1977; m. Del Whan, Mar. 27, 1981. Clin. instr. Mich. State U. Coll. Human Medicine, 1976-77; resident Los Angeles County-Harbor Gen. Hosp., UCLA Med. Center, Torrance, 1977-78; partner, physician in emergency medicine Kaiser-Permanente Hosp., Harbor City, Calif., 1978—; instr. Am. Heart Assn.; clin. instr. U. So. Calif. Coll. Medicine. Trustee, Delta Coll., 1972-74. Mem. Am. Coll. Emergency Medicine, Am. Physicians for Human Rights, Am. Physicians for Social Responsibility, So. Calif. Women for Understanding, NOW. Jewish. Author: (novel) The Summer of the Flea, 1980; contbr. to Echoes from the Heart (poetry anthology), 1982; contbr. articles to various publs. Home: 4016 Miraleste Dr Rancho Palos Verdes CA 90274 Office: 1050 W Pacific Coast Hwy Harbor City CA 90710

BAILEY, PEARL (MAE), singer; b. Newport News, Va., Mar. 29, 1918; d. Joseph James Bailey; student pub. schs., Phila.; m. John Randolph Pinkett, Jr., Aug. 31, 1948 (div. Mar. 1952); m. 2d, Louis Bellson, Jr., Nov. 19, 1952. Singer, 1933—; vocalist various popular bands; stage debut St. Louis Woman, N.Y.C., 1946, role Broadway musical House of Flowers, Hello Dolly, 1967-68, Arms and the Girl, Bless You All, Duey's Tale, Hurry Up America, and Spit; motion pictures include Variety Girl, Carmen Jones, St. Louis Blues, Porgy and Bess, Isn't It Romantic, That Certain Feeling, All the Fine Young Cannibals, The Landlord, Lost Generation, Norman, Is That You; contract artist Coral Records, Columbia Records, Decca; night club engagements N.Y.C., Boston, Hollywood, Las Vegas, Chgo., also London, 1950—; Star Pearl Bailey Show, ABC-TV, 1970-71, guest artist various TV programs; now spl. rep. U.S. del. to UN. Recipient Donaldson award, 1956; Spl. Tony award for Hello Dolly, 1967-68; Entertainer of Yr., Cue Magazine, 1967; March of Dimes award, 1968; U.S.O. Woman of Yr., 1969; citation from Mayor John V. Lindsay of N.Y.C. Author: Raw Pearl, 1969; Pearlie Mae; Talking to Myself, 1971; Pearl's Kitchen, 1973; Duey's Tale, 1975; Hurry Up, America and Spit, 1976. Address: care William Morris Agy Inc 1350 Ave of Americas New York NY 10019 *

BAILEY, RUTH HILL (MRS. A. PURNELL BAILEY), found. exec.; b. Roanoke, Va., Sept. 17, 1916; d. Henry Palmer and Carolyn Ruffin (Andrews) Hill; B.S. in Edn., Longwood Coll., Farmville, Va., 1939; postgrad. Ecumenical Inst., Jerusalem, 1979; m. Amos Purnell Bailey, Aug. 22, 1942; children—Eleanor Carol Bailey Harriman, Anne Ruth Bailey Page, Joyce Elizabeth Bailey Richardson, Jeanne Purnell Bailey Dodge. High sch. tchr. in Va., 1939-48; tour dir. to Europe and Middle East, 1963-73; syndicated columnist family newspaper, 1954-70; exec. sec. Nat. Methodist Found., Arlington, Va., 1979—; pres. Va. Conf. Bishop Cabinet Wives, United Meth. Ch., 1963-64; pres. Richmond (Va.) Ministers Wives, 1965-66; chmn. bd. missions Trinity United Meth. Ch., McLean, Va., 1975-79, adminstrv. bd., 1971—; sec. bd. dirs. Nat. Temple Ministries, Inc., 1981—; life mem. United Meth. Women. Div. sec. United Givers Fund, 1964-65. Recipient Staff award Bd. Higher Edn. and Ministry, United Meth. Ch., 1976. Clubs: Country of Va., Jefferson Woman's. Home: 7815 Falstaff Rd McLean VA 22102 Office: 1835 N Nash St Arlington VA 22209

BAILEY, SHARON LEE, energy co. mktg. exec.; b. Long Beach, Calif., Mar. 7, 1949; d. Marvin Lee and Wilma Ruth (Doll) B.; student L'Universite d'Aix-Marseille (France), 1970-71; B.A. in Cultural Anthropology cum laude, U. Calif., Santa Barbara, 1971; postgrad. in edn. Calif. State U., Long Beach, 1971-72; student of Dr. Moshe Feldenkrais, 1973-75; M.B.A. (Univ. fellow), UCLA, 1978; m. Curtis Bok, 1983. Owner, operator fitness and body movement bus., Calif., 1973-76; program coordinator Mktg. Mgmt. Program, UCLA, 1977; mktg. asst. Betty Crocker div. Gen. Mills, Inc., Mpls., 1978-79, asst. product mgr. Betty Crocker and Sperry divs., 1979-81, asst. mgr. promotion planning and devel. Big G div., 1981-82; mgr. div. mktg. Minnegasco div. Diversified Energies Inc., Mpls., 1982—; Gen. Mills rep., panelist U. Minn. Bus. Sch. Bus. Day, 1980; liaison with prospective M.B.A. students Revolving Around People. Gen. Mills Sperry coordinator United Way, 1981; precinct chairwoman Republican Party, Mpls., 1980-82, house dist. chairwoman, 1981-82, precinct, dist. and county del., 1980—, state del., 1982—, mem. Minn. Central Com., 1981—; photographer Bryn Mawr Bugle, Mpls.; active Minn. Internat. Center, Mpls., Bryn Mawr Neighborhood Assn., Mpls. Recipient award Gen. Mills Fitness Crusade, 1980. Mem. Assn. Nat. Advertisers, Am. Mktg. Assn., Promotion Mktg. Assn. Am., G.O.P. Feminist Caucus, Minn. Women's Polit. Caucus, Patty Berg 100 Women Club, Minn. Women's Network. Unitarian. Author: Acupressure, 1976; exhibited photographs in one-woman shows, Mpls., 1981, 82. Home: 212 Russell Ave S Minneapolis MN 55405 Office: 201 S 7th St Minneapolis MN 55440

BAIN, REBA JOYCE, nursing adminstr.; b. Pampa, Tex., June 9, 1930; d. Pink Oliver and Reba Faye (Ferrell) B.; diploma nursing U. Okla., 1953; B.S. in Nursing, Northwestern State U., 1957; M.S., N.E. Mo. State U., 1968; Ed.D., N.Mex. State U., 1974. Asso. dir. nursing Ariz. State Hosp., Phoenix, 1958-65; supr. (part-time) nursing Laughlin Hosp., Kirksville, Mo., 1965-67; adminstrv. asst. Hotel Dieu Hosp., El Paso, Tex., 1968-71; grad. asst. N.Mex. State U., 1971-72; dir. nursing R.E. Thomason Gen. Hosp., El Paso, 1972-73; asso. prof. dept. nursing Ind. U. Sch. Nursing, 1973-78, chmn. dept. nursing adminstrn., 1974-78; pres. Bain Systems, Inc., Nineveh, Ind., 1978—, cons. health care adminstrn., 1978—; asso. prof. nursing (part-time) Ball State U., Muncie, Ind., 1981-82; vis. prof. nursing U. Ala. Sch. Nursing, 1979; condr. nursing workshops, 1974—. Mem. Am. Nurses Assn., Ind. Citizens League for Nursing (dir. 1975-76), Nat. League for Nursing, Ind. State Nurses Assn. (mem. commn. nursing service 1981-83), Kappa Delta Pi, Sigma Theta Tau. Democrat. Baptist. Author: (with Doris J. Froebe) Quality Assurance Programs and Controls in Nursing, 1976; contbr. articles on nursing adminstrn. to profl. publs. Home: DF52B Dr5 Nineveh IN 46164 Office: PO Box 187 Nineveh IN 46164

BAINES, RUTH E., phys. therapist, educator, univ. adminstr.; b. Sept. 16, 1935; d. William Baines and Eula B.; B.A., Spelman Coll., Atlanta, 1957; cert. in phys. therapy U. Buffalo, 1959; M.A., N.Y.U., 1971, postgrad., 1974-77. Staff phys. therapist Public Health Dept., Rochester, N.Y., 1959-61; staff phys. therapist Meyer Hosp., Buffalo, 1961-63; unit supr. phys. therapy N.Y.U. Med. Center, 1967, asst. dir. postgrad. edn., 1967-72, research asso. phys. therapy dept., 1972-74; asst. prof. health services adminstrn. SUNY, Stony Brook, 1974-76, asst. prof. allied health resources, 1976-77, assoc. prof., 1978, clin. assoc. prof., 1980—, chmn. dept., 1977-80, asst. vice chancellor for health scis. SUNY Central Adminstrn., 1980—. Bd. dirs. Suffolk County Sickle Cell Project, 1980; cons. HEW, 1976-80; mem. N.Y. State. Bd. Phys. Therapy, 1976—; mem. youth panel appropriations and allocations com. United Way, Suffolk County, 1980. Mem. Am. Phys. Therapy Assn. (chmn. Greater N.Y. dist. 1970-74), Allied Health Assn. N.Y. (mem. policy adv. com.), Assn. Schs. Allied Health Professions, NAACP, Nat. Council Negro

Women. Office: Office of Research Grad Studies and Profl Programs SUNY State University Plaza Albany NY 12246

BAINS, LESLIE ELIZABETH, banker; b. Glen Ridge, N.J., July 28, 1943; d. Pliny Otto and Dorothy Ethel (Keeley) Tawney; B.A., Am. U., 1965; postgrad. N.Y.U., 1968; m. Harrison McKellar Bains, Jr., Mar. 7, 1970; children—Harrison McKellar III, Tawney Elizabeth. Asst. cashier Citibank, N.Y.C., 1965-73; asst. trust officer Mfrs. Hanover Trust Co., N.Y.C., 1973-74, asst. v.p., 1974-77, v.p., 1977-80; v.p., div. exec. Chase Manhattan Bank, N.A., N.Y.C., 1980—. Vice chmn., trustee Nat. Assn. Bank Women Ednl. Found., 1979-81; trustee Central Presbyn. Ch., Summit, N.J., 1979—, also chmn. fin. com. Mem. Nat. Assn. Bank Women (dir. Met. chpt. 1978—, nat. dir. 1979—, treas. 1981-83, v.p. 1983-84), Fin. Women's Assn., Bank Mktg. Assn., N.Y. Soc. Security Analysts, Women and Found. (fin. com.), Women's Econ. Roundtable. Clubs: Beacon Hill (Summit); Canoe Brook Country, Metropolitan. Office: 1211 Ave of Americas New York NY 10036

BAINUM, CHARLENE KUBO, psychologist; b. Takoma Park, Md., Dec. 18, 1953; d. Sakae and Hatsumi (Sakai) Kubo; B.A., Andrews U., 1975; Ph.D., U. Tenn., 1979; m. Bruce David Bainum, Nov. 25, 1979. Mem. faculty Pacific Union Coll., Angwin, Calif., 1979—, asst. prof. psychology, 1979—. Mem. Am. Psychol. Assn., Soc. Research in Child Devel., Phi Kappa Phi, Psi Chi. Democrat. Seventh Day Adventist. Office: Pacific Union Coll Angwin CA 94508

BAIR, MARY HELEN, radio program dir.; b. Marlow, Okla., Nov. 1, 1929; d. O. D. and Vera L. (Barrett) Griffin; grad. BMI Bus. Coll., 1948; m. Charles E. Bair, Dec. 22, 1951; 1 son, Michael Wayne. With Sta. KFRO, Longview, Tex., 1948—, sec. to mgr., 1948-62, program dir., 1962—, dir. ann. program Christmas Shopping with Mary Helen, 1952—. Co-founder Longview chpt. Muscular Dystrophy Assn. Am., 1962, N.E. Tex. chpt., 1975; dir. Gregg-North chpt. Am. Cancer Soc.; active Gregg County Assn. for Retarded Citizens; charter mem. St. Andrew Presbyn. Ch., deacon, 1968-71, elder, mem. of Session, 1972; mem. communications adv. bd. Pine Tree Ind. Sch. Dist., 1980-81; mem. Longview Womans Forum; team capt. membership dr. YMCA, 1982. Mem. Tex. Press Women (life, pres. dist. 9, 1972-73, treas. 1982-83, achievement award 1977, mem., chmn. coms.), Nat. Fedn. Press Women, Longview C. of C. (info. and public relations com.), Soc. Profl. Journalists, Epsilon Sigma Alpha (pres. local chpt. various terms, mem., chmn. coms.). Democrat. Home: 1105 W Garfield St Longview TX 75603 Office: Curtis Bldg PO Box 792 Longview TX 75606

BAIR, MYRNA LYNN, state senator; b. Huntington, W.Va., Oct. 26, 1940; d. Charles Thomas and Velma Elvera (Schoenlein) North; B.S. in Chemistry, U. Cin., 1962; Ph.D., U. Wis., 1968; m. Thomas Irvin Bair, Mar. 12, 1966; children—Thomas Irvin, Catherine Lynn. Asst. prof. chemistry Beaver Coll., Glenside, Pa., 1966-70; instr. chemistry U. Del., 1974-76, asst. prof. edn., 1977-79; asst. dir. pub. info. Del. Energy Office, Wilmington, 1978-79; mem. Del. Senate, 1981—. Bd. dirs. Del. Lung Assn.; trustee Wesley Coll.; mem. Nat. Republican Com., Brandywine Region Rep. Women's Club. Recipient Freshman award Chem. Rubber Co., 1959; DuPont Co. Teaching award, 1963; NSF fellow, 1964-66. Mem. AAUW, Delawareans for Energy Conservation, Phi Beta Kappa, Iota Sigma Pi, Alpha Lambda Delta. Author sci. articles. Home: 4 Little Leaf Ct Wilmington DE 19810 Office: Legislative Hall Dover DE 19901

BAIRD, EMILY NADINE BLACKWOOD, psychologist; b. Collingwood, Tenn., Oct. 18, 1921; d. John Henry and Flora Alice (Goff) Blackwood; B.A. in Journalism, U. Ala., 1946; M.A. in Psychology, U. West Fla., 1972; Ed.D., Nova U., 1976. Marital cons. Univ. West Fla., Pensacola, 1971-73; clin. counselor Community Mental Health Center, Pensacola, 1973-77; dir. Consultation and Edn., Lakeview Center, Pensacola Beach, Fla., 1977-82; first pres. Favor House, 1979; pres., dir., cons. Rape Crisis Center, Make Today Count, 1978-79; Fla. chmn. cons. and edn. Fla. Council Community Mental Health Ctrs. Chmn. service com. Am. Cancer Soc., 1978-81; chmn. woman's com. YWCA, 1978-80; chmn. Task Force Govt. Commn. on Status of Women, 1980—, commr., 1982-83; chmn. pub. relations com. Mental Health Assn., 1980-82; chmn. Reach to Recovery, Am. Cancer Soc., 1976-78; elder Gulf Breeze Presbyn. Ch., 1980-82. Recipient Citizenship award N.W. Fla. Social Workers, 1980. Mem. Am. Psychol. Assn., N.W. Fla. Psychol. Assn. (pres. 1980-81), Fla. Assn. Practicing Psychologists. Home: 904 Ariola Dr Pensacola Beach FL 32561

BAIRD, MARTHA ADRIENNE, hosp. adminstr.; b. Greenville, Pa., Nov. 23, 1951; d. James William and Marian Agnes (Oakes) B.; B.A., U. Pitts., 1972; teaching cert. Geneva Coll., 1973; M.H.A., Duke U., 1975. Adminstrv. asst. Wake County Med. Center, Raleigh, N.C., 1976-77, dir. outpatient clinics, 1977; quality assurance adminstr. Brookwood Health Services, Inc., Birmingham, Ala., 1977-78; dep. dir. Univ. Hosp., Stony Brook, N.Y., 1978-80; asso. exec. dir. Bellevue Hosp., N.Y.C., 1980—; guest lectr. Schs. Social Welfare and Allied Health, SUNY, Stony Brook; cons. Intercontinental Research, N.Y.C. Mem. steering com. South Fork Rural Health Initiative, 1979-80. Home: 212 E 47th St New York NY 10017 Office: Room MN-4 Bellevue Hosp New York NY 10016

BAIRD, MAURA, writer; b. Los Angeles, July 23, 1921; d. Frank E. and Louisa Eugenia (Wilson) Fensch; B.A., U. Calif., Berkeley, 1972; 1 dau., Lisa Lorena Baird-Evans. Editor/writer S. Pacific Studies Center, U. Calif., Santa Cruz, 1976-80; freelance writer, contbr. Ladies' Home Jour., The Lyric, The Ave Maria; contbr. travel columns to The Napa Register. Active Humane Soc., Napa, Calif., founding pres., 1972-73. Mem. AAUW, DAR., Phi Beta Kappa. Roman Catholic. Address: PO Box 415 Santa Cruz CA 95061

BAIRD, PATRICIA ANN, social worker; b. Hot Springs, Mont., Jan. 18, 1932; B.Sociology with highest honors, Ariz. State U., 1968; M.S.W., U. Mich., 1971; children—Darleen, Jeffrey. Maternal and child health supr. social services Maricopa County Dept. Health Services, Div. Public Health, Phoenix, 1971—; field instr. Ariz. State U., 1972—. Exec. bd. Ariz. Council on Sch.-age Parents, 1977—; mem. exec. bd. adv. council Ariz. Perinatal Program, 1974—; steering com. Teenage Pregnancy Coalition, 1979—; adv. bd. Planned Parenthood, 1977-79, Phoenix S. Community Mental Health, 1979—. Mem. Acad. Cert. Social Workers, Nat. Assn. Social Workers, U. Mich. Alumni Assn., Am. Public Health Assn., Phi Kappa Phi. Democrat. Club: U. Mich. Alumni of Phoenix. Editor Ariz. Perinatal News, 1975-77. Office: 1825 E Roosevelt St Phoenix AZ 85006

BAIRD, PAULA SQUETERI, broadcasting sales exec.; b. San Francisco, May 7, 1951; d. Emelio Louis and Alvera Coreen (Conti) Squeteri; B.S. in Public Relations, So. Ill. U., 1973; M.S. in Rehab. Counseling, 1976. Staff asst., dir. new student orientation So. Ill. U., 1973-75; sale rep. Bristol-Myers Corp., Chgo., 1976-78; account exec. Storer TV Sales div. Storer Broadcasting, Chgo., 1978-81; WMAQ-TV, NBC, Chgo., 1981—. Bd. dirs. profl. advisor Project SKIL, Youth service. Mem. Nat. Assn. Female Execs., Broadcast Advt. Club Chgo., NOW, Assn. Women in Radio and TV, Sigma Kappa. Home: 3238 Colfax St Evanston IL 60201 Office: WMAQ-TV NBC Merchandise Mart Plaza Chicago IL 60654

BAIRSTOW, FRANCES KANEVSKY (MRS. DAVID STEELE BAIRSTOW), educator, labor relations cons., arbitrator; b. Racine, Wis., Feb. 19, 1920; d. William and Minnie (DuBow) Kanevsky; student U. Wis., 1937-42; B.S., U. Louisville, 1949; student Oxford U. (Eng.), 1953-54; postgrad. McGill U., Montreal, Que., 1958-59; m. Irving P. Kaufman, Nov. 14, 1942 (div. 1949); m. 2d, David Steele Bairstow, Dec. 17, 1954; children—Dale Owen, David Anthony. Research economist U.S. Senate Labor-Mgmt. Subcom., Washington, 1950-51; labor edn. specialist U. P.R., San Juan, 1951-52; chief wage data unit WSB, Washington, 1952-53; labor research economist Canadian Pacific Ry. Co., Montreal, 1956-58; asst. dir. indsl. relations centre McGill U., 1960-66, asso. dir., 1966-71, dir., 1971—, lectr., indsl. relations dept. econs., 1960-72, asst. prof. faculty mgmt., 1972-74, asso. prof. faculty mgmt., 1974—; dep. commr. essential services Province of Que., 1976—; cons. on collective bargaining to OECD, Paris, 1979; cons., Nat. Film Bd. of Can., 1965-69; arbitrator Que. Consultative Council Panel of Arbitrators, 1968—, Ministry Labour and Manpower, 1971—; mediator Canadian Public Service Staff Relations Bd., 1973—; contbg. columnist Montreal Star, 1971—. Chmn. Nat. Inquiry Commn. Wider-Based Collective Bargaining, 1978. Fulbright fellow, 1953-54. Mem. Canadian Indsl. Relations Research Inst. (exec. bd. 1965-68), Indsl. Relations Research Assn. Am. (mem. exec. bd. 1965-68, chmn. nominating com. 1977), Nat. Acad. Arbitrators (bd. govs. 1977-80, program chmn. 1982-83), Soc. Profls. in Dispute Resolution (adv. council). Home: 3450 Redpath St Montreal PQ H3G 2G3 Canada Office: 1001 Sherbrooke St West Montreal PQ H3A 1G5 Canada

BAITSELL, WILMA WILLIAMSON, artist, educator; b. Palmyra, N.Y., July 5, 1918; d. Glen Hiram and Luetta (Newell) Williamson; B.S.E., SUNY, Oswego, 1957; M.S.E., Western State U., 1958; postgrad. Iowa State Tchrs. Coll., Syracuse U., Ind. State U., Cooper Union, McGill U. (Montreal); H.L.D., 1982; m. Victor Harry Baitsell, Oct. 29, 1941; children—Corin Victor, Coby Allan, Corrine Luetta. Tchr. rural sch., 1939-41, Phoenix Central Sch., 1957-71, SUNY, Oswego, 1971-77; ret., 1977; cons. area schs., Ford Found., 1965-68; art cons. N.Y. State Dept. Edn., summers 1968-70. Chmn. Republican Twp. Com.; pres. Oswego County Women's Rep. Club; chmn. Sch. Bldg. and Orgn. Com., 1954. Ford Found. sci. and math. grantee, 1958-59; recipient 1st prize Mid-States Art Show, 1981, hon. mention for painting, Yamiguchi, Japan, 1981, 1st prize Am. Craftsman's Show, 1973. Mem. N.Y. State Ret. Tchrs. Assn. (life), Internat. Soc. Edn. Through Art, Oswega Art Guild (life), Nat. Ret. Tchrs. Assn., Oswego County and Scriba Hist. Soc. (life), SUNY Oswego Alumni Assn. (life), N.Y. State Grange. Methodist. Club: Eastern Star. Author: Crafts for Children, 1976; Art for Campers, 1972; Nature Crafts, 1975; editor Summer Art, 1957-71. Home and Office: Route 4 Box 330 Oswego NY 13126

BAJAS, TERESITA YANEZ AWA, child psychiatrist; b. Cagayan de Oro City, Philippines, Jan. 12, 1942; d. Elpidio and Isidora (Yanez) Awa; student Xavier U., Philippines, 1961; M.D., U. Santo Thomas, Philippines, 1966; m. Edgardo P. Bajas, Nov. 25, 1967; 1 dau., Maria Theresa. Pediatric resident U. Santo Tomas, 1966-67; asst. instr. physiology Xavier U., 1967; practice medicine specializing in pediatrics, Philippines, 1967-68; intern Mt. St. Mary's Hosp., Niagara Falls, 1969; resident in pediatrics Bklyn. Jewish Hosp., 1970; resident in gen. psychiatry Kingboro Psychiat. Center, 1971-73; child psychiatry fellow S.I. Mental Health Soc., 1973-75; coordinator psychiatry Bushwick-Ridgewood Mental Health Clinic, 1976-77; supervising psychiatrist East Flatbush Mental Health Clinic, 1977-78; staff child psychiatrist S.I. Mental Health Children's Clinic, 1978-79; cons. child psychiatrist Children's Aid Soc. Goodhue Center; cons. psychiatrist Drs. Hosp. of S.I., Richmond Meml. Hosp., Golden Gate Nursing Home; assoc. staff psychiatrist St. Vincent's Hosp. of Richmond, Bayley Seton Hosp. Mem. Am. Psychiat. Assn., N.Y. Council Child Psychiatry, Am. Women's Med. Assn., Bklyn. Psychiat. Soc., Philippine Psychiatrists in Am., Philippine Med. Assn. in Am. (sec. 1975-76, dir. 1976-77). Home: 1 Wilson Terr Staten Island NY 10304 Office: 11 Ralph Pl Staten Island NY 10304

BAKAN, RITA, educator; b. N.Y.C., Nov. 7, 1930; d. Isaac and Fannie (Strom) Feierstein; B.A. cum laude, Bklyn. Coll., 1952; M.A., Mich. State U., 1955, Ph.D., 1968; m. Paul Bakan, Sept. 3, 1950; children—Laura, Joel, Michael. Tchr., Public Schs. Urbana (Ill.), 1952; sr. research investigator AIR, Palo Alto, Calif., 1968-69; asst. prof. Center Urban Affairs, Mich. State U., East Lansing, 1969-71; sr. psychologist Vancouver (B.C., Can.) Health Dept., 1971-73; prof. basic health scis. dept. B.C. Inst. Tech., Burnaby, 1973—; mem. sci. adv. com. B.C. Health Care Found., 1980—. Mem. B.C. Psychol. Assn., Can. Psychol. Assn., Am. Psychol. Assn., Phi Kappa Phi. Contbr. articles to profl. jours. Office: 3700 Willingdon Ave Burnaby BC V5G 3H2 Canada

BAKEMAN, CAROL ANN, architectural firm adminstr., singer; b. San Francisco, Oct. 27, 1934; d. Lars Hartvig and Gwendolyne Beatrice (Zimmer) Bergh; student UCLA, 1954-62; m. Delbert Clifton Bakeman, May 16, 1959; children—Laurie Ann, Deborah Ann. Singer, Roger Wagner Chorale, 1954—, Los Angeles Master Chorale, 1964—; librarian Hughes Aircraft Co., Culver City, Calif., 1954-61; head econs. library Planning Research Corp., Los Angeles, 1961-63; corp. librarian Econ. Cons., Inc., Los Angeles, 1963-68; head econs. library Daniel, Mann, Johnson & Mendenhall, architects and engrs., Los Angeles, 1969-71, corp. librarian, 1971-77, mgr. info. services, 1978—, mgr. office services, 1979—. Pres., Creative Library Systems, Los Angeles, 1974—; library cons. ArchiSystems, div. SUMMA Corp., Los Angeles, 1972—, Property Rehab. Corp., Bell Gardens, Calif., 1974-75, VTN Corp., Irvine, Calif., 1974, William Pereira & Assos., 1975. Mem. Assistance League, So. Calif., 1956—, mem. nat. auxiliaries com. 1968-72, 75-79, mem. nat. bylaws com. 1970-75, mem. asso. bd. dirs., 1966-76. Mem. Am. Guild Musical Artists, Am. Fedn. TV and Radio Artists, Screen Actors Guild, Spl. Libraries Assn. (mem. So. Calif. adv. council 1960-73), Council of Planning Librarians, Assn. Archtl. Librarians, Assn. Records Mgmt. Adminstrs., Nat. Micrographics Assn., Asso. Info. Mgrs., Los Angeles Master Chorale Assn. (dir. 1979—). Office: 3250 Wilshire Blvd Los Angeles CA 90010

BAKER, ALENE B., Okla. state legislator; b. Oct. 3, 1918. Mem. Okla. Ho. of Reps., Oklahoma City, 1981—. Office: Okla Ho of Reps State Capitol Oklahoma City OK 73105 *

BAKER, ALYSE OTVOS, speech pathologist; b. Hackensack, N.J., Feb. 2, 1950; d. Emery George and Maude (Vance) Otvos; B.A., magna cum laude with high honors in Psychology, Yale U., 1972; M.A.Ed., U. Mich., 1973, M.S. in Speech Pathology, 1974; m. Charles Manderville Baker, III, May 19, 1979. Speech pathologist Allegheny Gen. Hosp. and Allegheny County Assn. for Children with Learning Disabilities, Pitts., 1974-75; speech pathologist, remedial reading tchr., dept. learning and communication disorders West Penn Hosp., Pitts., 1975—; clin. instr. U. Pitts., part time, 1975—. Mem. Am. Speech Lang. and Hearing Assn. (cert. of clin. competence in speech pathology), Southwestern Pa. Speech and Hearing Assn., Internat. Reading Assn., Council Exceptional Children, Pitts. Yale Club (gov.). Home: 515 Glen Arden Dr Pittsburgh PA 15208 Office: West Penn Hosp Dept Learning and Communication Disorders Pittsburgh PA 15224

BAKER, AMY DEE, publisher; b. Calif., Aug. 31, 1941; d. Jack E. and Francis Z. Baker; B.A., Scripps Coll., 1963; M.L.S., U. Calif., Berkeley, 1964; M.F.A., Claremont Grad. Sch., 1966. Program coordinator Ford Found. Tamarind Workshop, 1966-68; v.p. Martha Jackson Gallery, N.Y.C., 1968-73; prodn. mgr. Petersburg Press, London, 1973-75; dir. John Weber Gallery, N.Y.C., 1975-77; pres. Lapp Princess Press, N.Y.C., 1976-79; exec. pub. Artforum mag., N.Y.C., 1970-79; adv. Mus. Modern Art, N.Y.C., 1977—; pres. Printed Matter Ltd. (non-profit); co-dir. Arts Communications (non-profit); lectr. in field. Contbr. articles to art jours. Office: 205 Mulberry St New York NY 10012

BAKER, ANITA LEA, bookkeeping service exec., accountant; b. Oklahoma City, Aug. 28, 1941; d. Leon M. and Juanita G. (Skaggs) Cottrell; student public schs.; m. John C. Baker, July 3, 1959; children—Rhonda Lynn, Dawn Rachelle, Darlene Dea, Danelle Lea. Bookkeeper Hurst, Thomas & Co., Oklahoma City, 1967-70; owner Baker's Bookkeeping, Del City, Okla., 1970-78; comptroller, acct., office mgr. Tom's Markets and Happy Foods, Oklahoma City, 1975-79; owner Acts Bookkeeping and Tax Service, Del City, 1980—. Mem. Bus. Women Am. (pres.). Republican. Baptist. Clubs: Moose; New Comers. Home: 4012 Prairie Lane Del City OK 73115 Office: 4541 SE 29th St Del City OK 73115

BAKER, ANNE E., state legislator; b. Washington, Oct. 20, 1951; student U. Md., Baltimore County, Goucher Coll.; m. William R. Stall. Organizational and polit. cons.; mem. Md. Ho. of Dels., 1979—; mem. Gov.'s Commn. on Adoption Laws. Treas. Md. Democratic Party, 1974-76; mem. Howard County Dem. Central Com., 1974-78; Dem. nat. committeewoman, 1976-80; vice chmn. East Coast Region Dem. Nat. Com., 1976-80; chmn. Md. Dem. Party Affirmative Action, 1974-78; mem. LWV, Common Cause, Md. Conf. Social Concern. Office: 226 Lowe Bldg Annapolis MD 21401 also Suite 205 Lakefront North Bldg 5550 Sterrett Pl Columbia MD 21044 *

BAKER, ARLENE MACHNIK, speech and lang. pathologist; b. Palmer, Mass., July 12, 1950; d. John Edward and Julia Ann Machnik; 1 son, Ethan John; B.A. in Psychology, Regis Coll., 1972; M.S. in Speech Pathology, U. Ariz., 1974; m. Robert Edward Baker, Aug. 11, 1973; 1 dau., Natasha Julie. Speech and lang. pathologist Portsmouth (N.H.) Rehab. Center, 1974-76, Cape Elizabeth (Maine) Public schs., 1976, Sch. Adminstrv. Dist. 57, Limerick, Maine, 1976-77, NE Hearing and Speech Center, Portland, Maine, 1977-78; pvt. practice speech and lang. pathology, Gorham, Maine, 1978—; cons. in field. Trustee, North Gorham Public Library, 1980-81, v.p., 1981-82. Rehab. Services Adminstrn. grantee, 1973-74. Mem. Am. Speech and Hearing Assn. (cert. clin. competence), N.H. Speech and Hearing Assn., Maine Speech and Hearing Assn., Maine State Soc. Aphasiologists (pres. 1978-79). Roman Catholic. Home and Office: RFD 2 N Gorham Rd Gorham ME 04038

BAKER, (BETTY) COLLEEN, promotion co. exec.; b. Aberdeen, S.D., Sept. 15, 1928; d. William Allen and Hazel Eugena Pratt; B.A., Iowa State U., 1978; m. Elmer Baker, Sept. 7, 1947; children—Allen, Claudia, Cathy. Dir. Iowa Authors; book broker; pub. Through Thin and Thin, Wooden Woman (poetry); owner, operator Collenn's Promotions, Slater, Iowa. Democrat. Office: PO Box 626 Slater IA 50244 *

BAKER, BETTY LOUISE, mathematician, educator; b. Chgo., Oct. 17, 1937; d. Russell James and Lucille Juanita (Timmons) B.; B.Ed. (PTA scholar), Chgo. Tchrs. Coll., 1961, M.A., 1964; Ph.D. (Univ. fellow), Northwestern U., 1971. Tchr. math. Harper High Sch., Chgo., 1961-69; tchr. math. Hubbard High Sch., Chgo., 1970—, chairperson dept., 1977—, mem. curriculum council, 1967; mem. Com. for Writing Criterion-Referenced Tests in Math., 1979-80; co-chmn. high sch. sect. Dist. 15 Math. Fair, 1982. Pres. Hubbard High Sch. P.T.S.A., 1979-81, 3d v.p., 1981-82, 1st v.p., 1982—; organist, Sunday Sch. tchr. Hope Luth. Ch., 1963—. Mem. Nat. Council Tchrs. of Math., Ill. Council Tchrs. of Math., Math. Assn. Am., Assn. Supervision and Curriculum Devel., Sch. Sci. and Math. Assn., Chgo. Tchrs. Union, Luth. Collegiate Assn., Kappa Delta Pi. Pi Lambda Theta, Phi Delta Kappa. Lutheran. Club: Walther League Hiking. Contbr. articles to math. jours. Home: 3214 W 85th St Chicago IL 60652 Office: Hubbard High School 6200 S Hamlin St Chicago IL 60629

BAKER, BONNIE TAYLOR, assn. exec.; b. Alma, Ga., Jan. 6, 1909; d. Walter Leon and Flora (Tuten) Taylor; student S. Ga. Coll., Douglas, 1925-26, Young Harris (Ga.) Coll., 1929-30, Southeastern U., Washington, 1939-40; m. Fred A. Baker, Oct. 26, 1940 (div. 1947). Sch. tchr., Pierce and Bacon Counties, Ga., 1925-28; with Fed. Govt. Services, Washington, 1930-56, systems analyst, sect. chief Dept. Commerce, SEC, Civil Service Commn., 1935-56; dir. Hist. Soc. Alma-Bacon County (Ga.), 1974—; historian, Bacon County, Ga., 1980—. Mem. John Floyd D.A.R. Soc., Huxford Genealogy Soc., Halifax Hist. Soc. Democrat. Methodist. Clubs: Pilot (sec.) (Washington); Pilot (bd. dirs.) (Alexandria, Va.); Pilot (Daytona Beach, Fla.); Am. Legion Women's Auxiliary, V.F.W. Women's Auxiliary (Alma, Ga.). Editor SEC Commn. Newsletter, 1939-40. Home: 201 Flora Ln Alma GA 31510 Office: Hist Soc Alma GA 31510

BAKER, CAROL ANN, city ofcl.; b. Charleston, S.C., May 13, 1952; d. Charles Lee and Mamie-Clara (Taylor) B.; B.A., Wake Forest U., 1973. Producer, announcer Sta. WFDD-FM, Winston-Salem, S.C., 1971-73; info. asst. City of Winston-Salem, 1973; info. coordinator Eugene (Oreg.) Parks and Recreation Dept., 1974-78; community relations dir. City of Eugene, 1978—. Mem. Met. Cable TV Commn., Eugene; bd. dirs. Sponsors, Inc. Mem. Women in Communications, League Oreg. Cities. Democrat. Presbyterian. Club: Oregon Track (dir.). Office: 777 Pearl St Eugene OR 97401 Home: 615 Princess St Eugene OR 97405

BAKER, CAROLYN PIERCE, lawyer; b. Memphis, Mar. 30, 1934; d. William Murray and Ethyle (January) Pierce; B.A., U. Ark., Little Rock, 1977, J.D., 1981; m. Thomas Harrison Baker, III, July 23, 1955; children—Catherine Baker Chatman, Jana Bess Baker Hunter. Human relations coordinator Little Rock Panel of Am. Women, 1972-75, dir., 1973-80; legal asst. Pulaski County Juvenile Ct., Little Rock, 1978-80; admitted to Ark. bar, 1981; dep. pub. defender Pulaski County, 1981—. Mem. AAUW, LWV, Ark. Women's Polit. Caucus (dir. 1973-79), Ark. Bar. Assn., Pulaski County Bar Assn., Phi Kappa Phi. Democrat. Home: 2 Arrow Brook Ct Little Rock AR 72207 Office: 312 Wallace Bldg Little Rock AR 72201

BAKER, CATHY MILES, lawyer; b. Baxley, Ga., Jan. 12, 1947; d. Thomas Peyton Jr. and Mary Jacqueline (Fennell) Miles; B.A., Mercer U., J.D., W.F. George Sch. of Law, 1971; m. James A. Baker, Nov. 17, 1979; 1 dau., Jacqueline Amelia. Admitted to Ga. bar, 1972; partner firm Miles & Baker, Baxley, 1971—; city atty. Surrency, Ga., 1973—. Treas. Appling County Assn. for Retarded Citizens, Baxley, 1973, 74. Mem. Am., Ga. bar assns., Phi Alpha Delta, Alpha Gamma Delta (treas. 1967). Baptist. Home: PO Box 484 Baxley GA 31513 Office: Fed Land Bank Office Highway #341 PO Box 412 Baxley GA 31513 *

BAKER, CONSTANCE MARIE, nurse, educator; b. Blossburg, Pa., June 29, 1937; d. John T. and Dorothy V. Baker; grad. Pa. Sch. Nursing, 1958; student Mansfield State Coll., 1960-62; B.S., U. Colo., 1964; M.S., U. Calif., San Francisco, 1967, D.Nursing Sci., 1975. Staff nurse Blossburg (Pa.) State Hosp., 1958-62, St. Joseph's Hosp., Fairbanks, Alaska, 1961-62; public health nurse Alameda County (Calif.) Health Dept., 1965-66; research asst. Sch. Nursing, U. Calif., San Francisco, 1968-69, lectr. grad. program in nursing, 1969-71; asso. prof. U. Okla. Coll. Nursing, Oklahoma City, 1972-78, prof., 1978—, dir. multi-media program, 1975—; cons. VA Hosp. Nursing Service, 1977—; nurse cons. to edn. and service on nursing/teaching strategies; mem. joint task force on practice Okla. Nurses Assn., Okla. Med. Assn., 1979—. Recipient cert. of appreciation, Surgeon Gen., SAC Med. Corps, 1977; Regents'

Superior Teaching award U. Okla., 1977. Mem. Am. Nurses Assn., Nat. League Nursing, Am. Assn. Higher Edn., Faculty Devel. and Evaluation Assn., Okla. Public Health Assn., Okla. League Nursing (pres.), Okla. Nurses Assn. (legis. com. 1979-81), Okla. Nurses Coalition for Action in Politics (pres. 1977-78, v.p. 1978-79), Sigma Theta Tau, Phi Delta Gamma. Contbr. articles to profl. jours. Home: 11609 Leaning Elm Oklahoma City OK 73120 Office: Box 26901 1100 N Stonewall St Oklahoma City OK 73190

BAKER, CORREAN MARRIE, speech pathologist; b. Crewe, Va., Aug. 26, 1949; d. Robert Leroy and Annie Lee (Jefferson) Lemaster; B.A., U. Md., 1972, M.A., 1973; m. Richard Lee Baker, June 4, 1972; children—Carissa Marrie, Terri Nicole. Speech pathologist Balt. City Public Schs., 1973-77, sr. tchr., 1980-81, sr. speech pathologist, 1981—; project dir. Children's Guild, Inc., Balt., 1977-80. Senatorial scholar, 1968-72; U. Md. fellow, 1972-73. Mem. Am. Speech, Lang., and Hearing Assn., Council Exceptional Children, NAACP. Democrat. Methodist. Home: 4651 Coleherne Rd Baltimore MD 21229 Office: 5921 Smith Ave Baltimore MD 21209

BAKER, COSETTE MARLYN, religious cons.; b. Miami, Fla., Sept. 22, 1933; d. Juel Marlyn and Corene Frances (Emery) Baker; B.B.A., U. Miami, Fla., 1955; M.R.E., So. Bapt. Theol. Sem., 1959. Dir. childhood edn. First Bapt. Ch., Knoxville, Tenn., 1959-63; minister to children South Main Bapt. Ch., Houston, 1964-73; asst. to minister of edn. Central Bapt. Ch., Miami, Fla., 1973-74; cons. in Sunday Sch. Dept., Bapt. Sunday Sch. Bd., Nashville, 1974—, cons. Children's Program sect., 1974—. Recipient YWCA award outstanding woman in religious work U. Miami, 1955. Mem. Tenn. Assn. for Edn. Young Children, Gamma Alpha Chi. Baptist. Author: God's Outdoors, 1967; writer Children's teaching tapes for Broadman Press, 1979-81. Home: 100 Longwood Pl Nashville TN 37215 Office: 127 9th Ave N Nashville TN 37234

BAKER, DIANE MCCARTER, real estate broker; b. LaGrange, Ga., Nov. 25, 1944; d. Tom L. and Edna Ruth (Camp) McCarter; student Auburn U., 1963-67; B.S., NE La. State U., 1975; student Am. Real Estate Inst., 1978—; m. David Ray Baker, May 12, 1967; children—James McCarter, Kandy Dy Ann. Ind. contractor, Omni Agy., real estate and ins., Monroeville, Ala., 1978-80, mgr. advt., 1980—, real estate broker, 1980—, also part-owner. Mem. Nat. Assn. Realtors, Nat. Home Econs. Assn., Community Concert Group, Alpha Omicron Nu. Republican. Methodist. Home: 401 Sunset Dr Monroeville AL 36460 Office: 1304 S Alabama Ave Monroeville AL 36460

BAKER, DIANE RHODES, communications co. exec.; b. Pitts., May 8, 1949; d. George Frederick and Betty Jane (Thatcher) Rhodes; grad. with honors Ellis Sch., Pitts., 1967; A.B. with honors, U. Chgo., 1971; postgrad. in bus. U. Chgo., 1975-76; M.B.A., Fairleigh-Dickinson U., Madison, N.J., 1982; m. Joseph Burrill Baker, Oct. 9, 1982. With Ill. Bell Telephone Co., 1971-78, mgr. operator services, Chgo., 1971-76, mktg. mgr. services/utilities, Chgo., 1977-78; mktg. strategist AT&T, Parsippany, N.J., 1979-81, mgr. exec. tng. and devel., 1982—. Mem. LWV, Am. Bus. Women's Assn., AAUW, Am., N.J. mktg. assns. Republican. Episcopalian. Home: 320 South St Morristown NJ 07960 Office: 99 Jefferson Rd Parsippany NJ 07054

BAKER, DOROTHEA ANNA, judge; b. Gilbertville, Mass., Feb. 11, 1927; d. Andrew and Ella (Gibbs) Baker; student Clark U., 1944-46; A.B., George Washington U., 1947, LL.B., 1948, LL.M., 1959; postgrad. Georgetown U., 1952-53. Admitted to D.C. bar, 1948; atty. Dept. of Def., 1948-51; atty. IRS; practice law, 1951—, also adminstrv. law judge Dept. Agr. Pres., Fed. Adminstrv. Law Judges Conf. Recipient D.A.R. award as outstanding youthful citizen, 1937. Mem. Am. Bar Assn., D.C. Bar Assn., Women's Bar Assn., Exec. Women in Govt., Order of Coif, Delta Theta Phi, Zeta Tau Alpha. Clubs: Capitol Hill, Congressional Country, Nat. Lawyers, Zonta Internat. Contbr. articles to profl. jours.; editor Newsletter, Fed. Adminstrv. Law Judges Conf. Home: 8007 Thornley Ct Bethesda MD 20034 Office: Dept Agriculture Washington DC 20250

BAKER, EDNA MAE, home economist; b. Guthrie, Okla., May 18, 1922; d. Robert Beecher and Lydia Mae (Guthrie) B.; B.S., Okla. State U., 1950; M.S., U. Wis., 1960. Tchr. elementary sch., Clark County Kans., 1943-48; county extension 4H agt., Okla. State U., El Reno, 1950-53; county extension home demonstration agt Okla. State U., Kingfisher, 1953-60; Northeast, Central and Northwest dist. supr. coop. extension Okla. State U., Stillwater, 1969-82, Co-dir. in-service tng. programs for coop. extension, 1967—. acting dist. dir. coop. extension service, 1973. Kellogg Found. fellow, 1960. Mem. Am. Home Econs. Assn., Okla. Home Econs. Assn. (dist. chmn. 1977-78), Extension Home Economists Assn. (sec. 1957, pres.-elect 1959), Okla. State U. Home Econs. Alumni Assn. (life), Okla. State U. Alumni Assn. (life), Epsilon Sigma Phi, Delta Kappa Gamma (2d v.p. 1981). Mem. Ch. of Nazarene (youth dir., Sunday sch. tchr., choir mem.).

BAKER, ELEANOR JEANETTE, investment co. exec.; b. Seattle, Aug. 1920; d. Crafton C. and Edith Elvira (Tidholm) Carroll; student Eugene (Oreg.) Bus. Coll., 1951, Marin Jr. Coll., Kentfield, Calif., 1967-68, 70-71; m. Wilson E. Baker, Aug. 24, 1962; children—Carroll Klingbile, Wayne D. McIntosh, Laurie A. Stitt. Legal sec., Oreg., 1957-62; asst. corp. sec. Life Ins. Co., San Francisco, 1963-68; v.p./corp. sec. Birr, Wilson & Co., Inc., San Francisco, 1968—; cons. broker/dealer and investment adv. start-up. Mem. council Emmanuel Lutheran Ch., Napa, Calif. Cert. profl. sec. Mem. Nat. Assn. Securities Dealers (CRD user com.). Republican. Club: Order of Amaranth (past honored matron). Home: 1067 Round Hill Circle Napa CA 94558 Office: 155 Sansome St San Francisco CA 94104

BAKER, ELEANOR MILDRED, personnel cons.; b. Passaic, N.J., July 18, 1924; d. Joseph and Minnie (Berzak) B.; B.A. in Edn., Montclair (N.J.) Coll., 1945; divorced; children—Janice, Pamela. Property Mgmt. mgr. Partroy Mgmt. Co., Clifton, N.J., 1960-70; tech. recruiter Snelling & Snelling, Ft. Lee, N.J., 1970-76; founder, 1976, since pres., owner Baker Personnel Ic., Clifton, also Baker Temps., Inc., Clifton; founder, 1981, since pres., owner Baker Personnel Morris Inc., also Baker Temps., Inc. Morris County. Mem. Nat. Assn. Personnel Cons., Nat. Assn. Accts., N.J. Assn. Personnel Cons., N.J. Assn. Women Bus. Owners, Hadassah. Clubs: Zonta, B'nai B'rith, Daus. Miriam. Home: 605 Grove St Clifton NJ 07013 Office: 48 State Hwy 46 Pine Brook NJ 07058 also 999 Clifton Ave Clifton NJ 07013

BAKER, ELIZABETH MARGARET LINE, sales exec.; b. Birmingham, Eng., Jan. 13, 1928; came to U.S., 1946, naturalized, 1958; d. William Russell Annesly and Mary (Edmunds) Line; student Syracuse U., 1948-49; m. Robert Elton Baker, July 21, 1956 (div. 1981); children—Elizabeth, Kimberly, William, Sara. Co-owner-operator Baker's Store & Motel, 1961-70; co-owner, gen. mgr. Baker's Motor Inn, Essex Junction, Vt., 1970-80; sales asso. Mountain View Properties, Morrisville, Vt., 1981—. Mem. Vt. Hotel Motel Assn. Republican. Episcopalian. Clubs: Altrusa (Burlington, Vt.); Order Eastern Star (Falls Church, Va.). Home: PO Box 119 Hyde Park VT 05655

BAKER, JANET ABBOTT, mezzo-soprano; b. Aug. 21, 1933; d. Robert Abbott and May (Pollard) Baker; student Coll. for Girls, York, Eng., Wintringham, Grimsby, Eng.; D.Mus. (hon.), Birmingham U., Leicester, Eng., 1973, London U., 1974, Oxford U., 1975, Hull U., 1975, U. Leeds, 1980; LL.D. (hon.), U. Aberdeen (Scotland), 1980; m. James Keith Shelley, 1957. Concert artist. Fellow St. Anne's Coll., Oxford U., 1975. Decorated dame Brit. Empire; recipient Daily Mail Kathleen Ferrier award, 1956; Queen's prize Royal Coll. Music, 1959; Shakespeare prize, Hamburg, 1971; Sonning prize, Copenhagen, 1979; Grammy award, 1975. Fellow Royal Soc. Arts; mem. Munster Trust. Office: care Ibbs & Tillett 450 Edgeware Rd London W2 England *

BAKER, JOSEPHINE L. REDENIUS, civic worker, ret. army officer; b. Oceanville, N.J., Aug. 31, 1920; d. Jacob and Josephine (Palmer) Redenius; student Columbia U., 1948-49, L.I.U., 1957-58, George Washington U., 1947-48; M.A. in Journalism, Am. U., 1963; L.H.D. (hon.), Temple U., 1964; postgrad. St. Charles Sem., 1978-81, Eastern Bapt. Theol. Sem., 1981—; m. Milton G. Baker (dec. 1976). Enlisted as pvt. WAAC, 1943, advanced through grades to lt. col. U.S. Army, 1963; intelligence officer atomic installations throughout U.S. and Can., 1943-53; asst. in Office Chief of Staff, Army Forces Far East, Japan, 1954-56; public info. officer Office Chief of Info., Washington, 1958-61; chief Women's Army Corps Recruiting, U.S. Army, 1962-66; info. liaison officer U.S. Army, 1966-67, ret., 1967; dir. public relations and devel. Valley Forge Mil. Acad. and Jr. Coll., Wayne, Pa., 1967-70, dir. found., 1970—; pres. Intercounty Trading Co., Inc., Surfside, Fla., 1976-80, Potential Gift Shop & Boutique, Ardmore, Pa., 1979-82; pres. bd. dirs. Surf Club Apts., Inc., 1977-79. Dir., Republican Women of Pa.; bd. dirs. Freedom Valley council Girl Scouts U.S.A., 1970—, Opera Guild Miami (Fla.); pres. found. bd. dirs. Chapel of St. Cornelius the Centurian, Wayne, Pa., 1976—; mem. aux. Miami Heart Inst. Decorated Legion of Merit, U.S. Army Commendation medal with 1st oak leaf; recipient Pa. Meritorious Service medal; Disting. Alumnus, Am. U., 1969. Mem. Public Relations Soc. Am., Am. Personnel and Guidance Assn., Am. Coll. Personnel Assn., Nat. Vocat. Guidance Assn., Am. Sch. Counselors Assn., Am. Legion Aux., Ret. Officers Assn., Assn. U.S. Army (Anthony J. Drexel Biddle medal 1968), Army-Navy Union, Assn. Measurement and Evaluation in Guidance, Emergency Aid of Pa., Am. Legion, Mil. Order World Wars, La Boutique des Huit Chapeaux et Quarante Femmes, Women in Communications, AAUW. Episcopalian. Clubs: Acorn, St. David's Golf, Surf. Address: Tower House 920 Eagle Rd Wayne PA 19087 also Surf Club Apts 9133 Collins Ave Surfside FL 33154

BAKER, JUSTINE CLARA, educator; b. Phila., Oct. 1, 1939; d. Michael Angelo and Justine Catherine (DeFlavia) Boni; A.B., Immaculata (Pa.) Coll., 1963; M.A.T.M., Villanova (Pa.) U., 1970; M.S. in Edn., U. Pa., Phila., 1973, Ph.D. candidate; m. Harold Jerome Baker, July 23, 1966. Tchr. math. and sci. pvt. and parochial schs., 1963-66; tchr. math. public secondary schs., Pa., 1967-69; tchr. math. and sci. parochial, pvt. and public schs., Pa. and N.J., 1973-80; instr. math., stats., and computer sci. Goldey Beacom Coll., Wilmington, Del., 1980—. Cert. tchr. math. and physics secondary schs., Pa.; cert. tchr. math. and comprehensive sci., N.J. Mem. Nat. Council Tchrs. of Math., Math. Assn. Am., World Future Soc., Am. Ednl. Research Assn., Assn. Computing Machinery, Phi Delta Kappa (pres. U. Pa. chpt. 1977-78, cert. of recognition 1976, 81, 82. Pres.'s award 1978, Service Key 1982). Republican. Roman Catholic. Author: The Computer in the School, 1975; Computers in the Curriculum, 1976; Microcomputers in the Classroom, 1982; contbr. articles to profl. jours. Home: 816 Eaton Rd Drexel Hill PA 19026 Office: 4701 Limestone Rd PO Box 5500 Wilmington DE 19808

BAKER, KATHLEEN MARY, state govt. ofcl.; b. Butte, Mont., Mar. 25, 1933; d. Hugh I. and Kathleen Mary (Harris) O'Keefe; B.A. in Communications, St. Mary Coll., Xavier, Kans., 1954; m. Nick B. Baker, Sept. 18, 1954 (div. 1970); children—Patrick, Susan, Michael, Cynthia, Hugh, Mardeen. Profl. singer, mem. Kathie Baker Quartet, 1962-72; research cons. Wash. Ho. of Reps., Olympia, 1972-73; info. officer Wash. Employment Security Commn., Seattle, 1973-81, dir. public affairs, 1981—; freelance writer, composer, producer, 1973—. Founder, pres. bd. Eden, Inc., visual and performing arts, 1975—; public relations chmn. Nat. Women's Democratic Conv., Seattle, 1979, Wash. Dem. Women, 1976—; bd. dirs., public relations chmn. Eastside Mental Health Center, Bellevue, Wash., 1979—. Recipient Black Community award for composition The Beaufort County Jail, Seattle, 1975, Silver medal Seattle Creative Awards Show for composing, directing and producing Rent A Kid, TV public service spot, 1979. Mem. Wash. Press Women. Democrat. Roman Catholic. Author handbook on TV prodn.; composer numerous songs, also producer Job Service spots. Home: 1485 168th Pl NE Bellevue WA 98008 Office: 212 Maple Park Olympia WA 98504

BAKER, LOIS JEAN, ins. co. exec.; b. Utica, N.Y., Jan. 8, 1942; d. John Adam and Gwendolyn (Davies) B.; student Am. Inst. Ins., 1960. Receptionist, Nat. Grange Mut. Ins. Co., Utica, 1959; with various ins. cos., 1960-70; with Combined Ins. Co. of Am., Albany, N.Y., 1972—, ter. mgr., 1972-76, asst. regional mgr., 1977-78, mgr. tng. instr., dist. mgr., 1979—. Named Combined Group of Cos. Divisional Ter. Mgr. of Yr., 1975. Mem. Nat. Assn. Female Execs., Beta Sigma Phi (extension officer 1975, city council rep. 1979, chmn. N.Y. state conv. 1980). Republican. Roman Catholic. Home: RD 3 Garfield Rd Jamestown NY 14701 Office: Computer Park Albany NY 12205

BAKER, LORRAINE, sch. adminstr.; b. Los Angeles, Aug. 20, 1935; d. Herbert McDowell and Izalia Lewena (Fee) Young; A.A., Los Angeles City Coll., 1955; B.A., Calif. State U., 1972; cert. sch. mgmt. (Rockefeller Found. fellow), Center for Ednl. Leadership, 1975-76; M.Ed., U. LaVerne, 1979; m. Rolland Alvin Baker, Mar. 16, 1955; children—Glenn, Eric. Tchr., La Canada (Calif.) Unified Sch. Dist., 1972-76, prin. Paradise Canyon Sch., 1976-79, bldg. adminstr. Foothill Intermediate Sch., 1979-80, coordinator curriculum K-12, 1980—. Mem. Assn. Supervision and Curriculum Devel., AAUW (chmn. profl. interest network), Assn. Calif. Sch. Adminstrs., Women in Mgmt., Affiliated Network Exec. Women, Assn. Calif. Sch. Adminstrs.

BAKER, MARGERY CLAIRE, broadcasting exec.; b. N.Y.C., May 5, 1948; d. Robert Charles and Elizabeth Madeline (Schiro) Baker; A.B., Barnard Coll., 1970; M.S., Columbia U., 1971. Asso. producer CBS News, N.Y.C., 1971-73, field producer, Los Angeles, 1973-76, broadcast producer, N.Y.C., 1976-78, v.p. public affairs broadcasts, 1978-81, sr. broadcast producer, 1982—. Officer alumni bd. Columbia U. Grad. Sch. Journalism. Mem. Nat. Acad. TV Arts and Scis., Internat. Radio and TV Soc., Sigma Delta Chi. Club: Quaker Ridge Golf (Scarsdale, N.Y.). Office: CBS News 524 W 57th St New York NY 10019 *

BAKER, MARGIE SPARKMAN, govt. ofcl.; b. Leon, Ky., Jan. 28, 1943; d. Frank and Lora Jane (Allen) Sparkman; student No. Va. Community Coll., 1975-77, George Washington U., 1977-79; B.A. in Sociology, Columbia Coll. Arts and Scis., 1979; m. Richard L. Baker, Nov. 21, 1962; 1 dau., Cheri Michelle. Various secretarial and adminstrv. positions U.S. Dept. Def. and U.S. Dept. Agr., Washington area, 1961-69; staff asst. to dep. for programs Am. Revolution Bicentennial Adminstrn., Washington, 1969-75; mgmt. analyst Office of Surface Mining and Reclamation Dept. Interior, Washington, 1978; adminstrv. asst. to legal counsel, Commn. on Accident at Three Mile Island, Washington, 1979; program analyst Mine Safety and Health Adminstrn., U.S. Dept. Labor, Arlington, Va., 1979—. Recipient Sustained Superior Performance award Commn. on Three Mile Island, Outstanding Achievement award Mine Safety and Health Adminstrn. Mem. Nat. Assn. Female Execs., Federally Employed Women, Am. Fedn. Govt. Employees (steward local 12). Home: 6826 Stoneybrooke Ln Alexandria VA 22306 Office: Wilson Blvd Arlington VA 22203

BAKER, MARGRETTA (GRETTA) HARDING, educator, ednl. broadcaster; b. Phila.; d. George Williamson and Sarah Martha (Kramer) B.; B.S. in Edn. with honors, U. Pa., 1929, postgrad., 1930-34. Tchr., Phila., 1930-36; asst. U. Pa., 1930-36; writer, creator radio quiz Sta. WMCA, N.Y.C., 1938-39; radio writer NCCJ, N.Y.C., 1944-45; instr. ednl. radio N.Y. U., 1944-47; creator, writer numerous radio dramas, 1948-56; creator, tchr. psychology course Inst. Arts and Scis., Columbia U., 1953-57; founder, dir. Vacation Coll., Daytona Beach, Fla., 1957-62; commentator programs on psychology St. KYW Westinghouse-NBC, Phila., 1966-67; tchr. psychology Rutgers U., Camden, N.J., 1965-69, 72-73; guest speaker ednl. TV. Bd. dirs. Am. Heart Assn., Daytona Beach, 1970-72. Recipient Arthritis Found. Journalism award, 1957. Mem. Nat. League Am. Pen Women, Inc. (TV editor and critic monthly mag. 1971-79; non-fiction article award 1979), U. Pa. Alumni Assn., Am. Movement for World Govt., World Federalists Assn.

BAKER, MARTENA KAY, govt. ofcl.; b. Mechanicsburg, Pa., Mar. 15, 1941; d. W. Penrose and Mary Elizabeth (McCurdy) Myers; student public schs.; m. David K. Baker, Aug. 20, 1968. Adminstrv. officer Internat. Decade of Ocean Exploration, NSF, Washington, 1972-75, div. ocean scis., 1975—. Sec. Occoquan Forest Civic Assn., 1978. Mem. Adminstrv. Mgmt. Soc. (chmn. membership records D.C. chpt. 1981), Nat. Mgmt. Assn. Home: 10849 Split Rail Dr Manassas VA 22111 Office: Div Ocean Scis NSF Washington DC 20550

BAKER, MARTHA ANN, nurse; b. Lee's Summit, Mo., Mar. 24, 1934; d. Chris Arthur and Lillie May (Harris) Ohmsieder; B.S., U. Kans., 1956; M.Ed., U. Nev., 1970; postgrad North Tex. State U., 1975—; postgrad. Tex. Women's U., 1974-77; m. Russell G. Baker, Apr. 5, 1958; 1 dau., Martha Lynn. Instr. nursing U. Kans., 1956-58; sch. nurse Neosho (Mo.) Pub. Schs., 1958-60; staff nurse Washoe Med. Center, 1963-64; asst. prof. instr. nursing Orvis Sch. Nursing, U. Nev., Reno, 1964-65, 70-71; asst. prof. nursing Baylor U., Dallas, 1971—. HEW fellow, 1968-69. Mem. AAUW, Am. Nurses Assn., Assn. Care of Children in Hosps. (ann. conf. planning com. 1980). Presbyterian. Club: Brookhaven Country. Home: 1408 Northridge Ct Carrollton TX 75006 Office: 3616 Worth St Dallas TX 75204

BAKER, NANCY ELLEN, social worker; b. Jamaica, N.Y., Nov. 1, 1945; d. Lewis George and Alice Elaine Holmes; B.A., Wells Coll., 1967; M.S.W., U. Mich., 1972; m. Kenneth Robert Baker, June 17, 1967; children—Matthew E., Alison N. Program mgr., inpatient services Wake County Mental Health Center, Raleigh, N.C., 1972-75; family therapist, parent educator Project Enlightenment, Raleigh, 1975-79; family therapist Polyclinic Rijks Psychiat. Inst., Eindhoven, Netherlands, 1979-80; outpatient clinician Community Counseling Service, Lebanon, N.H., 1980—. Mem. Acad. Cert. Social Workers, Nat. Assn. Social Workers, Am. Orthopsychiat. Assn., Address: Box 859 Hanover NH 03755

BAKER, OLEDA, beauty, diet and health products exec., writer; b. Miami, Fla., Aug. 12, 1934; d. Marvin and Thelma Freeman; m. Steven Baker, Dec. 9, 1967; 1 son, David Pettis. Model, N.Y.C. and Europe, 1960-73; pres. Oleda Unltd., beauty and health products, Inc., N.Y.C., 1976—; artist with solo exhbns. in primitive art; co-producer, writer, hostess Oleda's Beauty and Health Tips, TV, 1977—; author books including: The Model's Way to Beauty, Slenderness and Glowing Health, 1973; The I Hate to Makeup Book, 1975; Be a Woman, 1975; Oleda Baker's Age-Less Diet, 1976; How to Create the Illusion of a More Perfect Figure, 1976; Twenty-Nine Forever, 1977; How to Renovate Yourself from Head to Toe, 1980; Reluctant Goddess (novel), 1981; Women's Way to Riches; beauty editor Models' Circle Mag., 1975. Club: Knights of Malta (dame). Home: 5 Tudor City Pl New York NY 10017 Office: Oleda Unlimited Inc 1 E 44th St New York NY 10017

BAKER, PHYLLIS MARIE, state govt. adminstr.; b. Ponca City, Okla., Nov. 14, 1927; d. Ernest M. and Nelle (Babcock) Trout; B.A., Calif. State U., 1971; student Okla. State U., 1945-46; m. Ellis C. Baker, Sept. 7, 1946 (dec.); children—Robert Gordon (dec.), Phyllis Ann, Douglas Scott, Jeanne Elisabeth. Asso., Ruel Shumate Real Estate, Tampa, Fla., 1962-64; adminstr. state hosp. adminstrv. and support services Calif. Dept. Devel. Services, Sacramento, 1967—; v.p. Rancho Redwood Co., Inc., Sacramento, 1971—. Mem. Nat. Wildlife Soc., East African Wild Life Soc., Internat. Assn. Bus. Communicators, Phi Kappa Phi, Kappa Alpha Theta. Episcopalian. Editor: Calif. Mental Health Research Digest, 1969-72, exChange, 1972-75. Office: 744 P St Sacramento CA 95814

BAKER, RITA M., psychologist; b. Columbia, S.C., June 26, 1948; d. Lee C. and Ludie M. (Sanford) B.; B.S., U. S.C., 1971, M.A., 1973; postgrad. U. Tenn., 1975; M.P.A., U. Colo., 1980; doctoral candidate U. Denver, 1980—. Psychologist, S.C. Dept. Mental Health, Columbia, 1973-75, Dept. Vocat. Rehab., Columbia, 1975-76, Colo. Sch. for Deaf and Blind, Colorado Springs, 1976—; pvt. practice psychology, 1979—; bd. dirs. Mid-Colo. Commn. for Devel. Disabled. Mem. Am. Psychol. Assn., Assn. Women in Psychology. Contbr. articles to profl. jours. Home: 920 Red Mesa Dr Colorado Springs CO 80906 Office: Colorado Springs Counseling and Evaluation Center 625 N Cascade St Suite 330 Colorado Springs CO 80903 also PO Box 935 Colorado Springs CO 80901

BAKER, SANDRA FAYE, mktg. co. exec.; b. Del Rio, Tex., Aug. 1, 1949; d. Alonzo Roy and Erie Nell (Cloudt) Luce; A.S., S.W. Tex. Jr. Coll., 1969; B.S. in Edn., S.W. Tex. U., 1971; m. Tracy Baker, II, Aug. 5, 1972; children—Tracy III, Stuart. Elem. tchr. Killeen (Tex.) Ind. Sch. Dist., 1972-78; pres. Aquila Enterprises, Harker Heights, Tex., 1975—. Chmn. membership Harker Heights Elem. Sch. PTA, 1971-72; sch. supt. Heights Meth. Ch., 1979-80. Mem. Nat. Fedn. Ind. Bus. Republican. Methodist. Office: 851 Nola Ruth St Harker Heights TX 76543

BAKER, TONI, nursing home adminstr.; b. Beekman, N.Y., Dec. 29, 1922; d. Joseph James and Harriet Ann (Hadden) Dinka; A.A., Poughkeepsie (N.Y.) Bus. Coll., 1942; divorced; 1 son, Joseph H. Claims examiner N.Y. State Unemployment Commn., 1945-50; asst. advt. dir. Handy Andy Supermarkets, San Antonio, 1955-60; account exec. Notzon Advt., San Antonio, 1960-63; dir. pub. relations William W. Backus Hosp., Norwich, Conn., 1964-67; adminstr. Eliza Huntington Meml. Home, Norwich, 1967—; mem. rev. com. omnibus nursing home bill Dept. Aging Conn., 1976. Mem. Waterford (Conn.) Rep. Town Meeting, 1971-72, Waterford Bd. Fin., 1974. Served with USMCR, 1943-45. Recipient McCall's award, 1965, Pulse award, 1965; grantee Pub. Relations Council Am., 1967. Mem. Conn. Assn. Nonprofit Facilities for Aged, Norwich Women's Network, Norwich C. of C.

Democrat. Author, illustrator juvenile books, 1946-47. Home: 50 Surrey Ln Norwich CT 06360 Office: 99 Washington St Norwich CT 06360

BAKER, VERNA TOMLINSON (MRS. EARL M. BAKER), librarian; b. Phila., Apr. 14, 1915; d. Joseph Ullman and Mabel (Dolton) Tomlinson; student (scholar) Temple U., 1937-39, Phila. Coll. Bible, 1959-62; B.S., Bryan Coll., 1963; M.A., George Peabody Coll., 1964; M.A., Chgo. Grad. Sch. Theology, 1970; m. Earl M. Baker, Dec. 31, 1938 (dec. Nov. 1958); children—Earl M. III, B. Kimball. Asst. to expediter Brit. Admiralty Del., Naval Aviation Supply Depot, Phila., 1944-45; sec., manuscript reader Westminster Press, Phila., 1947-53; librarian Ben Lippen Sch., Asheville, N.C., 1953-58; gen. library work Nashville Pub. Library, 1963-64; with The King's Coll., Briarcliff Manor, N.Y., 1964—, reader services librarian, 1967—. Mem. N.Y., Westchester library assns. Christian Librarians fellow, 1965—. Author: Here in the Spring, 1968; editor: Poems Revisited, 1976; contbr. poems to anthologies, various mags. Office: The King's Coll Briarcliff Manor NY 10510

BAKER, VIRGINIA MARIE, county ofcl.; b. Tipton, Ind., Oct. 25, 1935; d. August G. and Berniece O. (Powell) Tebbe; student Ind. Acad. Public Service, 1976-81; m. James Arvil Baker, Nov. 4, 1954; children—Antoinette, Kathleen, Michael, Thomas, Sharon, Carol Ann. Office machine operator St. Francis Hosp., Miami Beach, Fla., 1953-54; with Levittown (N.Y.) Bank, 1954; staff St. Mary's Hosp., Knoxville, Tenn., 1954; office asst. A.G. Tebbe Farms, Tipton, Ind., 1955—; Tipton County assessor, 1975—. Mem. adv. com. Ind. Tax Bd., 1979—; Democratic precinct committeewoman, 1962—; vice chmn. Tipton County Dem. Party, 1974—, treas. 5th Dist., 1974-76; pres. Tipton County Women's Dem. Club, 1972-74, treas., 1979-81, sec., 1981-83. Mem. Ind. County Assessors Assn. (pres. 1978-80), Ind. Fedn. Dem. Women. Democrat. Roman Catholic. Clubs: Moose, St. Christopher Circle, Tipton Tractor Pull Assn., Daus. of Isabella. Home: 75 W Division Rd Tipton IN 46072 Office: Courthouse Tipton IN 46072

BAKER, WINDA LOUISE (WENDY), social worker; b. Suwannee County, Fla., July 16, 1952; d. Austin Sidney Baker and Jessie Mae (Williams) Baker Jones; B.A. in Theology, Berkshire Christian Coll., 1974. Clk.-typist State of Fla., Tallahassee, 1974-76; cashier Tallahassee-Eastern Theatres, 1975-76; field rep. Commn. Human Relations, 1976-77; asst. to dir. retirement living, sec., receptionist Advent Christian Village, Dowling Park, Fla., 1977-79, admissions counselor, social worker, after 1979, multi-purpose worker, 1980. Vol. ARC and Assn. Charities, 1977—; founder Suwannee County Overeaters Anonymous, Live Oak, Fla., 1982. Mem. Suwannee County Mental Assn., Assn. Informed Travelers, Christian Fin. Planning, Inc., Cheeks Sch. Gymnastics Alumni. Republican. Advent Christian. Home: 322 Pine Ave Live Oak FL 32060

BAKER-BRABAND, CLAIRE JOAN, nurse; b. Bklyn., Mar. 27, 1946; d. Herman Charles and Clara Marie (Plattner) Brown; R.N., Bklyn. Sch. Nursing, 1966; B.S. in Mgmt., St. Francis Coll., 1977; M.A. in Occupational Safety and Health, N.Y. U., 1982; m. Leonard A. Baker, Nov. 29, 1981. Head nurse Bklyn. Hosp., 1966-68; occupational health nurse Korvettes, N.Y.C., 1969-71, personnel mgr., 1971-75; mgr. occupational health services Royal Ins. Cos., N.Y.C., 1975-81; safety specialist Hoffmann-LaRoche, Inc., Nutley, N.J., 1982—; cons. seminars in occupational health. Cert. occupational health nurse, hosp. safety profl. Mem. Am. Mgmt. Assn., Am. Assn. Occupational Health Nurses, Nat. Safety Council, Am. Chem. Soc., Emergency Dept. Nurses Assn., Am. Soc. Safety Engrs., Am. Public Health Assn. Author publs. in field of occupational health. Home: 140 Parkside Dr Suffern NY 10901 Office: 340 Kingsland St Nutley NJ 07110

BAKIN, GLORIA WEISS, psychologist; b. Braddock, Pa., Nov. 21, 1928; d. Herman and Helen (Roddy) Weiss; B.A., Seton Hill Coll., 1962; M.Ed. in Counseling, Indiana U. Pa., 1966; cert. in psychology Duquesne U., 1970; postgrad. U. Pitts., 1979; m. 1948 (div. 1968); children—Thomas, Theresa, Kenneth, Joseph, Phillip. Tchr., chmn. social studies dept. Penn Trafford (Pa.) Schs., 1962-63; counselor, chmn. dept. Greensburg (Pa.) Salem Sch., 1966-70; psychologist, staff devel. specialist Allegheny Intermediate Unit, Pitts., 1970—; pvt. practice psychology, Greensburg, 1975—. Treas., Larimer Recreation Assn., 1956-66; vice chmn. N. Huntingdon Twp. Democratic Com., 1960-68. Mem. Am. Psychol. Assn., Nat. Assn. Sch. Psychologists, Pa. Psychol. Assn. (sec. 1978-82, editor state publ. 1978-79). Home: 421 N Maple Ave Greensburg PA 15601 Office: 1 Northgate Sq Greensburg PA 15601

BALANOFF, MIRIAM, lawyer, state legislator; b. N.Y.C., Mar. 4, 1926; J.D., U. Chgo., 1963; m. Clement Balanoff, May 4, 1952; children—Clement, Jane, Robert. Admitted to Ill. bar, 1963; individual practice law, Chgo., 1963—; mem. Ill. Ho. of Reps., 1979—. Mem. Chgo. Council of Lawyers (charter). Democrat. Office: 10607 Ewing Ave Chicago IL 60617

BALAZS, MARJORIE KARLENE, chemist; b. St. Louis, Nov. 9, 1932; d. Karl John and Marie Antoinette (Hoffman) Balazs; A.B., Washington U., St. Louis, 1954; M.A. (NSF grantee) Stanford U., 1963; M.S., U. San Francisco, 1968. Chemist, chief chem. lab, U.S. Geol. Survey, Denver, 1955-58; tchr. chemistry Jefferson County Schs., Lakewood, Colo., 1958-62; chemist life scis. Stanford (Calif.) Research Inst., 1963-68, chemist analytical physics and phys. scis., 1971-75; chemist semiconductor tech. Applied Materials, Santa Clara, Calif., 1968-71; pres. Balazs Analyt. Lab., Mountain View, Calif., 1975—. Mem. Electrochem. Soc., Filtration Soc., Am. Electronic Assn., ASTM, Peninsula Profl. Women's Network (pres. 1981-82). Contbr. articles to profl. jours. Office: 2284 Old Middlefield Way Suite 10 Mountain View CA 94043

BALCH, MARIAN LOUISE CARLSON, ednl. adminstr.; b. Milw., Feb. 20; d. Clifford Carl and Alta Marie (Diller) Carlson; B.A., U. Wis., M.A., 1976; m. Harold C. Balch (div.); children—Virginia Marie, Marilyn Elizabeth. Tchr., Madison (Wis.) Public Schs.; univ. supr. U. Wis., Madison, 1967-69, 74-76; reading specialist Middleton-Cross Plains Sch. Dist., Middleton, Wis., 1976-77; resident supr. Tchr. Tng. Center, U. Wis. Madison-Oregon Public Schs., 1977-79; Title I dir., cons. CESA 15, Madison, 1979—; ednl. cons. Pres., Nakoma Welfare League, 1971; dir. Manitowish Chain of Lakes Property Assn., 1971-72; mem. Council Mo. Synod Lutheran Ch.; state del. Dane County Republican Conv., 1970—. Mem. Internat. Reading Assn., Wis. Assn. Tchr. Educators, Madison Area Reading Council, Wis. State Reading Assn., Wis. Assn. Supervision and Curriculum Devel., Wis. Assn. State and Fed. Program Specialists, Nat. Council Tchrs. English, Nat. Assn. Female Execs., Pi Lambda Theta. Alpha Phi. Republican. Office: CESA 15 4201 Buckeye Rd Madison WI 53716

BALCOM, GLORIA DARLEEN, computer adminstrv. and mktg. cons.; b. Porterville, Calif., July 23, 1939; d. Orel A. and Eunice E. Stadtmiller; A.A., El Camino Coll., 1959; student computer sci. Harbor Coll., 1976-77; m. Orville R. Balcom, July 23, 1971; stepchildren—Cynthia Lou, Steven Raymond. Personnel trainee AiResearch div. Garrett Corp., Los Angeles, 1959-60, sales promotion adminstr., 1960-64; sales rep. Volt Temporary Services, El Segundo, Calif., 1965-69, mgr., Tarzana, Calif., 1969-71; co-owner, co-operator Brown Dog Engrng., Lomita, Calif., 1972-77; pres., owner, cons. MicroSly Mktg., Lomita, 1977—. Mem. Ind. Computer Cons. Assn. (nat. pub. relations com.), Nat. Assn. Female Execs., Am. Soc. Profl. and Exec. Women, NOW. Club: Torrence Athletic. Home and office: 24521 Walnut St Lomita CA 90717

BALDRIGE, LETITIA, public relations cons.; b. Miami Beach, Fla.; d. Howard Malcolm and Regina (Connell) Baldrige; B.A., Vassar Coll., postgrad. U. Geneva (Switzerland); D.H.L. (hon.), Creighton U., 1979, Mt. St. Mary's Coll., 1980; Robert Hollensteiner. Personal-social sec. to ambassador Am. Embassy, Paris, France, 1948-51, intelligence officer, 1951-53; asst. to ambassador Am. embassy, Rome, 1953-56; dir. public relations Tiffany & Co., 1956-61; social sec. to The White House, 1961-63; pres. Letitia Baldrige Enterprises, Chgo., 1964-69; dir. consumer affairs Burlington Industries, 1969-71; pres. Letitia Baldrige Enterprises, Inc., N.Y.C., 1972—; dir. The Outlet Co., Fed. Home Loan Bank N.Y.; mem. Com. of 200. Bd. dirs. Woodrow Wilson Found., Inst. Internat. Edn., Women's Forum Inc., Phoenix House; trustee Kenyon Coll., Gambier, Ohio, St. David's Sch., N.Y.C. Mem. Fashion Group, Am. Inst. Interior Designers (pub. relations assoc.). Republican. Author: Roman Candle, 1956; Tiffany Table Settings, 1958; Of Diamonds and Diplomats, 1968; Home, 1972; Juggling, 1976; revised Amy Vanderbilt's Book of Etiquette, 1978; The Entertainers, 1981. Syndicated columnist Los Angeles Times; contbr. to popular mags., also lectr. Office: Letitia Baldrige Enterprises Inc 151 E 80th St New York NY 10021

BALDUCCI, CAROLYN FELEPPA, author; b. Pelham, N.Y., Feb. 13, 1946; d. Ernest J. and Rosaria (Pignone) Feleppa; B.A., Manhattanville Coll., 1967; m. Gioacchino Balducci, Dec. 28, 1968; 1 dau., Sirad. Guest editor Mademoiselle mag., 1966; editorial asst. Ingenue mag., 1967-68; past copy editor Popular Culture Press, Bowling Green (Ohio) State U.; free-lance writer, 1969—; writer-in-residence, lectr. creative writing Residential Coll., U. Mich., Ann Arbor, 1976—; guest lectr. in field. Recipient Notable Book award ALA, 1970; grantee Ohio Pub. Program in Humanities, 1975, 77. Mem. Author's Guild, Soc. Children's Book Writers, Children's Lit. Coop., Mich. Writers in Schs. Author: Is There A Life after Graduation, Henry Birnbaum?, 1971; Earwax, 1972; play: Alucin, 1975; A Self-Made Woman: the Biography of Grazia Deledda, 1975; (filmscript) Margaret Fuller's Summer on the Lakes in 1843. Home: 624 5th St Ann Arbor MI 48103 Office: Residential Coll E Quad U Mich Ann Arbor MI 48109

BALDWIN, ANNA JEANELLE (JAN), interior decorator; b. Roscoe, Tex., June 18, 1939; d. Edward Luie and Norah Della (Walker); student Eastern N.Mex. U., 1964-67; m. Noland Baldwin, July 28, 1979; children—Jesse Lynn Dickens, Karen Jeannelle Dickens, Jeffery Steven Dickens. Saleswoman Dunlaps, Inc., Lubbock, Tex., 1967; asst. mgr., designer Fairmart Furniture Co., Odessa, Tex., 1967-70; designer, buyer Phillips Furniture, Odessa, 1970-75; gift mgr. Charlotte's Inc., El Paso, 1975-80; dir., interior decorator coordinator Parade of Homes, El Paso, 1977-79; owner Janelle's, design studio, Lovington, N.Mex., 1980—. Youth sponsor 1st Bapt. Ch., Odessa. Mem. El Paso Home Builders Assn., Las Cruces Home Builders Assn. Democrat. Baptist. Office: 5411 Mesa St N El Paso TX 79912

BALDWIN, ANNA JURTSCHENKO, clin. ednl. adminstr.; b. Villach, Austria, July 5, 1952; came to U.S., 1956, naturalized, 1970; d. Spiridon Platonovich and Zora (Anicic) Jurtschenko; B.S., George Washington U., 1973; postgrad. U. Md. Sch. Medicine, Balt., 1980—. Lab. technologist Washington Reference Lab., 1971; asst. to prof. George Washington U., 1972; med. technologist hematology, coagulation, urinalysis George Washington U. Med. Center, 1973-74, blood bank technologist, 1974-77; reference specialist blood reference lab. Washington Regional Blood Services, ARC, 1977-78; instr. program med. tech. U. Md. Sch. Medicine, Balt., 1978-82, clin. edn. coordinator, 1978-82; guest lectr. Towson State Coll./Union Meml. Hosp. program in med. tech., 1979, Balt. chpt. ARC, 1980; cons. Salisbury State Coll. program in med. tech., 1979. Mem. Am. Soc. Clin. Pathologists, Am. Soc. Med. Technologists, Am. Assn. Blood Banks, Am. Soc. Allied Health Professions, Mid-Atlantic Assn. Blood Banks. Author: (with Harmening and Sohmer) Modern Blood Banking and Transfusion Practices, 1982. Office: Dept Pathology U Md 10 S Pine St Baltimore MD 21201

BALDWIN, ELLEN JANE (MRS. HAL WEST), real estate co. exec.; b. N.Y.C.; d. Whitney and Edna Estelle (Bolles) Eckert; student N.Y. Sch. Design, 1956-58, New Sch. Coll. City N.Y., 1958-60; m. Hal West, Oct. 18, 1968; children (by previous marriage)—Richard A., Suzanne E. Real estate salesman, 1963-71; owner, broker Baldwin West and Assos., San Rafael, 1971—. Sec., Marin County (Calif.) Cerebral Palsy, 1962-64; bd. dirs. Santa Margarita Valley Homeowners Assn., 1972—, pres. 1976—. Cert. residential specialist. Mem. Grad. Realtors Inst. (cert.), Nat. Assn. Realtors, Calif. Assn. Realtors, Realtors Nat. Mktg. Inst., Marin County Bd. Realtors (dir. 1979—), Million Dollar Club (life). Home: 16 Galleon Way San Rafael CA 94903 Office: 200 Northgate One San Rafael CA 94903

BALDWIN, ESTHER EBERSTADT (MRS. ROBERT HOWE BALDWIN), personnel and ins. co. exec.; b. East Orange, N.J.; d. Edward Frederick and Elenita Contreras (Lembcke) Eberstadt; B.A., Notre Dame Coll. Md., 1919, M.A. (hon.), 1941, LL.D., 1958; Mus.B., Am. Inst. Applied Music, 1921; m. Robert Howe Baldwin, June 7, 1933. Pres., Mrs. E.E. Brooke, Inc., Personnel Cons., N.Y.C., 1923—, Robert H. Baldwin, Inc., Ins. Brokers, N.Y.C., 1955—; v.p. Davis, Dorland & Co., N.Y.C., 1955—; lectr. to colls., bus. and profl. groups. Mem. nat. council U.S. Com. for Refugees, 1963-64; mem. White House Conf. For World Refugee, 1963; mem. nat. council Am. Friends of Middle East, 1956-63, Pakistan-Am. Students Assn., 1957-62; mem. Greater N.Y. council Boy Scouts Am., 1956-58; Greater N.Y. chpt. ANTA. Pres. Robert H. Baldwin Found., 1956—. Mem. bd., exec. Com. Women's Nat. Republican Club, 1956-60, now life member. Bd. dirs., chmn., pres. Am. Com. to Befriend Arab Refugees, 1958—; bd. dirs. Council on Islamic Affairs, 1957-65, vice-chmn., 1958-63; bd. dirs. Near East Found., Notre Dame Coll. Md., Camp Fire Girls, Inc., Internat. Ednl. Devel.; mem. nat. council Met. Opera, 1967—; mem. Pres.'s Council Columbia U.; co-founder Arab and Am. Friendship Assn. Decorated Order Chevalier Ct. by Shah of Iran; recipient Pres.'s Medal Coll. Notre Dame; Esther Eberstadt Baldwin chair in Humanities established in honor by Notre Dame Coll. Md. Fellow Archeol. Inst. Am., Am. Geog. Soc.; founding mem. Jr. League of Oranges (Orange, N.J.); life mem. Acad. Polit. Sci., Am. Mus. Natural History, Assistance League So. Calif., Met. Mus. Art, N.Y. Zool. Soc.; mem. Nat. Inst. Social Scis., Pakistan-Am. C. of C., Soc. Women Geographers, AAUW, English Speaking Union, Columbia Assos., Soc. of Jesus (hon.), Delta Epsilon Sigma. Author: The Girl and Her Job, 1933; Career Clinic, 1940; The Right Job For You and How To Get It, 1944; Career Guide, 1943; Guide to Career Success, 1947; You and Your Personality, 1949. Contbr. articles to Cosmopolitan, Good Housekeeping, Mademoiselle, others. Home: 4 Pleasant St Woodstock VT 05091 Office: Davis Dorland & Co 2 World Trade Center New York NY 10048 also Near East Found 29 Broadway New York NY 10006

BALDWIN, JOAN (JODY) BOLLING, staff mem. U.S. Senate; b. Norton, Va., Aug. 31, 1930; d. Henry C. and Nelle E. (Mann) Bolling; A.B., Hollins (Va.) Coll., 1953; M.A., U. Va., 1955; m. Donald Winston Baldwin, Nov. 16, 1957; children—Winston Monroe, Elizabeth Bolling, Alan Henry. Sec. to asst. register of copyrights Library of Congress, Washington, 1955-59; mem. profl. staff U.S. Senate Republican Policy Com., 1959-62; press and research asst. to Senator Len B. Jordan of Idaho, 1962-64; research asst. Rep. Nat. Com., 1964; polit. researcher James N. Juliana Assocs., Washington, 1965-69; legis. asst. to Senator James B. Pearson of Kans., 1969-71; spl. asst. to asst. sec. HEW, 1971-73; dep. staff dir. and editor Legis. Notice, Senate Rep. Policy Com., 1973—. Del., Va. Rep. Conv., 1973—; pres. Alexandria (Va.) Rep. Women's Club, 1965-66; 2d v.p., 1st v.p. Alexandria Jr. Women's Club, 1963-64; treas. The Twig, 1968-69. Mem. Chi Omega. Anglican. Clubs: Capitol Hill; Senate Staff; Belle Haven Country (Alexandria). Office: 333 Russell Senate Office Bldg Washington DC 20510

BALDWIN, KAREN ARLENE, univ. food service exec.; b. Story City, Iowa, Mar. 2, 1953; d. Kermit L. and Wilma Arlene (Turner) Miskell; B.S., Iowa State U., 1975; m. Richard Baldwin, Dec. 16, 1978. Cook, Riverside Care Center, Ames, Iowa, 1972-73; with Iowa State U., Ames, 1973—, asst. mgr. food service, 1976-82, mgr. food service Linden Hall, 1982—. 4-H leader, Story City, 1971-73. Mem. Ames Jaycee-ettes. Republican. Methodist. Club: Altrusa. Home: 4125 Aplin Rd Ames IA 50010 Office: Linden Food Service Iowa State U Ames IA 50010

BALDWIN, MARGARET ANN, ins. and real estate agy. exec.; b. Brownwood, Tex., Oct. 30, 1933; d. Polk Ward and Juanita Maude (Jenkins) Lankford; student Brownwood Coll. Bus., 1951-52; student Vernon Regional Jr. Coll., 1978-79; m. Gene Baldwin, Sept. 10, 1953; children—Kathryn Elaine, Martha Jane. Ins. clk. T.E. Davis Agy., Vernon, Tex., 1952, jr. partner, 1969-72; owner, pres. Coffee Ins. & Real Estate Agy., Inc., Vernon, 1972—; owner Century 21 Real Estate Franchise, Vernon, 1976—. Mem. Vernon Bd. Realtors (pres. 1981-82), Tex. Assn. Realtors, Nat. Assn. Realtors, Ind. Ins. Agts. of Tex., Nat. Assn. Ins. Agts., Nat. Fedn. Ind. Bus., Vernon C. of C., Nat. Assn. Female Execs., Am. Soc. Profl. and Exec. Women. Baptist. Club: Vernon Art League. Home: 2130 Fannin St Vernon TX 76384 Office: 1701 Wilbarger St Vernon TX 76384

BALDWIN, MARY LEOLA, rural manpower and tng. co. exec.; b. Conway, S.C., Feb. 22, 1947; d. John Emily and Leoma Evelyn (Davis) Avant; B.S., S.C. State Coll., 1970; postgrad. George Washington U., 1972, Am. U., 1978-79; m. Jesse O. Baldwin, July 11, 1965 (dec.); children—Valeria Leoma, Emily Claroda. Tchr. secondary sci. Aiken County (S.C.) Public Schs., 1970-71; supply contract specialist Naval Security Sta., Washington, 1971-73; personnel cons. Associated Recruiters, Inc., Suitland, Md., 1973-75; personnel dir. NFU-Green Thumb, Arlington, Va., 1975-77, v.p. mgmt., budgets, program analysis, 1977-81, specialist methods mgmt., 1981—; cons. zero-based budgeting, grantsmanship; grants documentator Dept. Labor, 1977-81. Adv., Nat. Urban Coalition, 1979—; sgt.-at-arms White House Conf. on Aging, 1981; guidance adv. Montgomery County (Md.) PTA, 1981-82. Named Employee of Yr., NFU-Green Thumb, 1977; recipient Port of Jeffersonville award Jeffersonville, Ind., 1978. Mem. Am. Mgmt. Assn., Am. Soc. Personnel Dirs., S.C. State Coll. Alumni Assn., NEA. Democrat. Mormon. Club: Relief Soc. (dir.). Research on quality of work life of older people, 1979-80. Home: 3938 Tynewick Dr Silver Spring MD 20906 Office: 1401 Wilson Blvd Arlington VA 22209

BALDWIN, PATRICIA KAY, semicondr. co. personnel exec.; b. Mauston, Wis., Nov. 12, 1953; d. Arthur William and Ilo Jean (Crandall) B.; student Coll. Phys. Therapy, Marquette U., 1971-73; B.S. in Psychology cum laude, U. West Fla., 1974. Asst., AA Cons. Daum & Doll, Pensacola, Fla., 1977; personnel adminstr. DCA Reliability, Sunnyvale, Calif., 1978-79; acting personnel mgr. AVA-West div. Genrad, Santa Clara, Calif., 1979-80; human resources dir. Optoelectronics div. Gen. Instrument Corp., Palo Alto, Calif., 1980—. Mem. Santa Clara Valley Personnel Assn. Office: 3400 Hillview Ave Palo Alto CA 94304

BALDWIN, VELMA NEVILLE WILSON, cons.; b. Meade, Kans., Aug. 31, 1918; d. Charles Chester and Anna Velma (Neville) Wilson; A.B., U. Kans., 1940; m. Claude David Baldwin, Jan. 31, 1942 (dec. Nov. 1976). Placement working students U. Kans., 1940-41; personnel War Dept., Washington, 1942-45; research asst. Dr. A.C. Kinsey, Ind. U., 1946; with Carter Oil Co., Denver, 1948-50; personnel Bur. Budget, Washington, 1951-55; asst. to dir. personnel Treasury Dept., 1955-59; personnel officer, dir. adminstrn. Office Mgmt. and Budget, 1959-79; cons. in field. Mem. Am. Soc. Pub. Adminstrn. (past exec. bd.), Soc. Personnel Adminstrn. (exec. bd.). Home: 2234 49th St NW Washington DC 20007 Office: Office Mgmt and Budget Washington DC 20503

BALDWIN, WENDY HARMER, social demographer; b. Phila., Aug. 29, 1945; B.A. magna cum laude, Stetson U., DeLand, Fla., 1967; M.A., U. Ky., Lexington, 1970, Ph.D. (NDEA fellow, spl. grantee Population Council), 1973. Research asst. Columbian Assn. Med. Faculties, Bogatá, 1971; research asst. sociology U. Ky., 1971-72; health scientist adminstr. behavioral scis. br. Center Population Research, Nat. Inst. Child Health and Human Devel., NIH, 1972-79, chief social and behavioral scis. br., 1979—. Recipient Merit award NIH, 1978. Mem. Population Assn. Am. (dir. 1978-80), Am. Sociol. Assn. (sec. population sect. 1977-80), So. Sociol. Assn., Nat. Council Family Relations, Groves Conf. Marriage and Family. Author articles in field. Office: 7910 Woodmont Ave Rm 7C25 Bethesda MD 20205

BALES, DOROTHY LOUISE, violinist, artist, educator; b. Ketchikan, Alaska, Aug. 31, 1927; d. Harry and Lillian Mae (Pierce) Johnson; B.A., U. Oreg., 1948; B.Mus. with honors, New Eng. Conservatory, 1949; M.Mus., Boston U., 1950; postgrad. Marlboro Sch. Music, Acad. Internat. d'Ete; pupil of Ivan Galamian, Gabriel Bouillon; m. Robert Freed Bales, Sept. 14, 1951. Instr. violin New Eng. Conservatory, 1949-50; tchr. violin Longy Sch. Music, Cambridge, Mass., 1950-58; violin and chamber music tchr., orch. dir. Winsor Sch., Boston, 1950-55; lectr. music Emmanuel Coll., Boston, 1961-69, 1969—, asst. prof., 1969-74; lectr. Northeastern U., Boston, 1975-78, 82—; vis. asso. prof. U. Mass., Amherst, 1978; solo concert tours throughout U.S., 1964-68; concerts in Paris and Salzburg, 1952, 56, Vienna, 1964, 72, Geneva, 1964; contractor-concertmaster, 1962—; concertmaster Ch. of the Advent, Boston, 1964—. Asso. artist tchr. N.J. String Tchrs. Summer Conf., 1980—; founder, music dir. Chamber Music Soc. Cape Ann, 1960-62; workshop leader, cons. in field. Bd. dirs. Choral Art Soc., Scituate, Mass., 1978—. Grantee Ella Lyman Cabot Trust, 1956; winner N.W. Dist. Young Artists award Fedn. Music Clubs, 1938, Mus. Guild Boston Debut award, 1948. Mem. Am. String Tchrs. Assn. (pres. Mass. chpt. 1974—), Music Educators Nat. Conf., Am. Fedn. Musicians, Music Tchrs. Nat. Assn., Internat. League Women Composers, World Federalists. Sierra Club, Audubon Soc., Nature Conservancy, World Wildlife Fedn. Episcopalian. Author articles in field. Home: 61 Scotch Pine Rd Weston MA 02193

BALES, HAZEL LEONA, retail store exec.; b. Louisville, May 18, 1923; d. Alvie J. Albro and Bertie (Wilson) B.; grad. Ahrens Trade Sch., Louisville, 1940; m. Walter T. Bales, July 2, 1940. Bookkeeper, Parkland Supply Co., Louisville, 1943-45, pres., 1945—; pres. Bales Firestone #1 Inc., Louisville, 1950—, Bales Firestone #2 Inc., Louisville, 1956—, Bales Motors Acceptance Corp., Jeffersonville, Ind., 1966—. Mem. Nat. Tire Dealers and Retreaders Assn. Clubs: Pilot (Jeffersonville) (pres. 1972-73); Desk and Derrick (Louisville) (dir. 1977—). Home: 1515 Charlestown Jeff Rd Jeffersonville IN 47130 Office: 4313 Preston Hwy Louisville KY 40213

BALFOUR, JOAN POMS, social worker; b. N.Y.C., Mar. 17, 1941; d. Frank and Belle (Schwartz) Poms; B.S. cum laude, CCNY, 1962; M.S.W., Fordham U., 1977; children—Steven Paul, Michael Jay. Tchr. public schs., N.Y.C., Rockland County, 1962-70; dir. After Sch. Center,

Orangeburg, N.Y., 1966-70; med. social worker Good Samaritan Hosp., Suffern, N.Y., 1977-79; clin. supr. Vol. Counseling Service, New City, N.Y., 1977—; psychotherapist in pvt. practice, Pomona, N.Y., 1977—; clin. social worker, biofeedback therapist Rockland County Community Mental Health Clinic, Pomona, 1975—; faculty Rockland Community Coll., 1978-81. Founding mem. Women's Center Project, Nyack, N.Y., 1974; bd. dirs. Shire Village Camp, Cummington, Mass., 1980-81; employment compliance chair Rockland County chpt. NOW, 1974-75, founding mem., 1973; mem. N.Y. State Com. on Women's Issues, 1979-80, N.Y. State Com. on Nominations and Leadership Identification, 1980—. Cert. social worker, N.Y.; lic. tchr., N.Y. Mem. Mental Health Assn. Speaker's Bur., Rockland Community Coll. Speaker's Bur., Nat. Assn. Social Workers (exec. com. Hudson Valley div. 1979-81), NOW, Assn. for Humanistic Psychology, Am. Women in Psychology, N.Y. Assn. for Humanistic Psychology, Rockland Coalition for Free Choice, Rockland County Conservation Assn., People for the Am. Way, ACLU, Common Cause, Coalition to Keep Ramapo Green (treas.), Rockland Family Shelter. Address: 311 Parkside Dr Suffern NY 10901

BALFOUR, LINDA FRIER, univ. ofcl.; b. Houston, Mar. 29, 1944; d. Robert Henry and Ina Loyce (Riley) Frier; B.B.A., Southwestern U., 1966; postgrad. N.C. State U., 1968, U. N.C., Chapel Hill, 1980; m. Robert F. Hill, June 7,. 1978; 1 son, James Burton. Tchr., Franklin (Tex.) High Sch., 1966-67; sec. N.C. Bd. Higher Edn., Raleigh, 1967-68, statis. analyst, 1968-73; social research asst. gen. adminstrn. U. N.C. System, Chapel Hill, 1973-77, social research asso., 1977-78, dir. data collection and reporting, 1979—; cons. to instnl. researchers on coll. campuses; N.C. Higher Edn. Gen. Info. Survey coordinator Nat. Center Edn. Stats., Dept. Edn. Active Nat. Found. Ileitis and Colitis, Nat. Arbor Found. Mem. N.C. State Employees Assn., N.C. Assn. Instl. Research (exec. com. 1978—), So. Assn. Instl. Research. Author: Statistical Abstract of Higher Education in North Carolina, 1967—; Higher Educational Opportunities in North Carolina, 1967—. Office: U NC-Gen Adminstrn PO Box 2688 Chapel Hill NC 27514

BALICK, HELEN SHAFFER, bankruptcy judge; b. Bloomsburg, Pa.; d. Walter W. and Clarissa K. (Bennett) Shaffer; J.D., Dickinson Sch. Law, 1966; m. Bernard Balick, June 29, 1967; Admitted to Pa. bar, 1967, Del. bar, 1969; probate adminstr. Girard Trust Bank, Phila., 1966-68; pvt. practice law, Wilmington, Del., 1969-74; staff atty. Legal Aid Soc. Del., Wilmington, 1969-71; master Family Ct. Del., New Castle County, 1971-74; U.S. bankruptcy judge Dist. of Del., 1974—; U.S. magistrate, Wilmington, 1974-80. Pres. bd. trustees Community Legal Aid Soc., Inc., 1972-74; mem. Citizens Adv. Com. Wilmington, 1973-74, Wilmington Bd. Edn., 1974. Mem. ABA, Del. Bar Assn., Fed. Bar Assn., Nat. Conf. Bankruptcy Judges, Nat. Assn. Women Lawyers, Nat. Conf. Spl. Ct. Judges, Nat. Lawyers Club, Nat. Assn. Women Judges, Wilmington Women in Bus. (bd.), Dickinson Sch. Law Gen. Alumni Assn. (exec. bd. 1977-80, v.p. 1981—), Phi Alpha Delta. Office: US Courthouse 844 King St 6th Floor Wilmington DE 19801

BALL, BETTY J., psychiatric social worker; b. Sherman, Tex., Aug. 9, 1933; d. J. E. and Ethyl V. (Chesnut) B.; B.S., Okla. Bapt. U., 1954; M.R.E., Carver Sch. (Sem.), Louisville, 1958; M.S.W., Smith Coll., 1964. Phys. edn. instr., housemother Northeastern A&M Jr. Coll., Miami, Okla., 1954-56; phys. edn. tchr. Hamilton Jr. High Sch., Houston, 1956-57; with Lubbock County (Tex.) Child Welfare Dept., Lubbock, 1958-59; state casework supr. five counties Wyo. State Dept. Public Welfare, Cheyenne, 1959-62; casework supr. Natrona County Dept. Public Welfare, Casper, Wyo., 1962-63; psychiat. social worker Inst. for Juvenile Research, Chgo., 1964-66, Infant Welfare Soc. of Chgo., 1966-71; dir. Day Hosp. for Children, Madden Mental Health Center, Ill. Dept. Mental Health, Hines, 1971-78, children and adolescent coordinator subregion 10, 1978—; advisory bds. Triton Coll. and Better Boys Found. Active Lakeview Citizens' Council, pres. block club, 1979-80. Mem. Nat. Assn. Social Workers, Acad. Cert. Social Workers. Club: Lakeshore Center. Compiler, editor: Factors Influencing Child Development, 1969; dir., editor, contbr. to Children's Day Treatment - A Handbook, 1973; co-author: A Behavioral Deviancy Profile, 1975; contbr. to film New Beginnings - A Day Hospital for Children, 1975; contbr. articles in field to profl. publs., papers to profl. confs. Home: 1029 W Wolfram St Chicago IL 60657 Office: 1200 S 1st Ave Hines IL 60141

BALL, DIANE ALTMAN, librarian; b. Chattanooga, Sept. 4, 1932; d. William A. and Louise (Kendrick) Altman; B.S. in Edn., Miami U., Oxford, Ohio, 1968; M.Ed., Wright State U., Dayton, Ohio, 1977; m. Richard E. Ball, Oct. 10, 1953; children—David Allen, Anne Louise. Children's librarian Miamisburg (Ohio) Public Library, 1952-53; librarian W. Carrollton (Ohio) Jr.-Sr. High Sch., 1958-60; substitute tchr. Miamisburg, W. Carrollton and Oakwood City sch. dists., 1964-68; media specialist Oakwood Jr.-Sr. High Sch., Dayton, 1968—; mem. various assessment and evaluation teams for state and pvt. agys.; vice-chmn. Ohio Multitype Interlibrary Cooperation Com., 1975-81 Leader Monday Night circle, 1973-74, 76—. Mem. Ohio Assn. Sch. Librarians (dir. Western dist. 1971-73, state pres. 1975-76), Oakwood Tchrs. Assn. (com. chmn. 1973-74, 78—), Ednl. Media Council Ohio, NEA, Ohio, Western Ohio edn. assns., ALA, Ohio Library Assn., Am. Assn. Sch. Librarians (mem. standards com. 1976—; rep. to rev. com. Am. U. Press Services 1977—, chmn. AUPS 1982, chmn. Unit II, 1981-83; regional dir. 1978-81, chairperson 1982-83), Ohio Ednl. Library Media Assn. (1st past pres., co-chmn. consol. project), LWV, Delta Kappa Gamma. Contbr. profl. publs. Home: 2410 Fairmont Ave Dayton OH 45419 Office: 1200 Far Hills Ave Dayton OH 45419

BALL, EVE (KATHERINE EVELYN), author; b. Clarksville, Tenn., Mar. 14, 1890; d. Samuel Richard and Gazelle (Gibbs) Daly; B.S. in Edn., Kans. State Tchrs. Coll., Pittsburg, 1918; M.S. in Edn., Kans. U., 1928; H.H.D. (hon.), Coll. Artesia (N.Mex.), 1970. Tchr. elem., secondary schs. and colls., Independence, Kans., 1914-19, elem. and high schs., Tulsa, 1920-21, high sch., Dodge City, Kans., 1946-47; tchr. coll. English, spl. courses in Apache culture, 1968-70. Pres., N.Mex. Folklore Soc., 1947. Recipient Cert., Ruidoso (N.Mex.) C. of C., 1972. Mem. Western Writers Am. (Golden Spur 1975) NEA, N.Mex. Tchrs. Assn., DAR, Kappa Kappa Gamma, Pi Lambda Theta. Club: Order Eastern Star. Author: Ruidoso, the Last Frontier, 1963; Bob Crosby, World Champion Cowboy, 1965, Ma'am Jones of the Pecos, 1967; In the Days of Victorio, 1970; My Girlhood Among Outlaws, 1973; Indeh, An Odyssey of the Apaches, 1980; contbr. articles in field to profl. jours.

BALL, LINDA ANN, educator; b. Des Moines, Aug. 10, 1942; d. Vern Ray and Orletha Ann Carmichael; student Iowa State U., 1960-62; B.S. in Edn., Drake U., 1964; M.S. in Edn., Ill. State U., 1981; m. Robert Ray Ball, Aug. 15, 1964; children—Lindsay, Ryan, Justin. Tchr., Marshalltown, Iowa, 1964-68; TV tchr. Sta. WAND-TV, Decatur, Ill., 1969-71; tchr. Des Moines Public Schs., 1973-79; adv. Ill. State U. Panhellenic, Normal, 1979-80; tchr. Metcalf Lab. Sch., Ill. State U., Normal, 1980—; presenter workshops and confs. Active Jr. Women's Club, Assn. Advocacy and Edn. Disabled Citizens, Mid-Central Planning Commn. for Handicapped, Friends of the Arts; pres. JayceeEttes, Campfire Girls Council. Cert. reading specialist, early childhood tchr. Mem. Ill. Reading council, Early Childhood Edn. Assn., Ill. Edn. Assn., Delta Zeta (collegiate province dir.), Delta Kappa Gamma. Democrat. Home: 208 Robert Dr Normal IL 61761 Office: Metcalf Lab Sch Ill State U Normal IL 61761

BALL, LUCILLE, actress; b. Jamestown, N.Y., Aug. 6; d. Henry D. and Desiree (Hunt) Ball; ed. high sch., dramatic sch.; studied with John Murray Anderson; m. Desi Arnaz, Nov. 30, 1940 (div.); children—Lucie Desiree, Desiderio Alberto IV; m. 2d, Gary Morton, Nov. 19, 1961. Motion picture actress, 1934—; pictures include Roberta, Chatterbox, Follow the Fleet, Stage Door, Having Wonderful Time, Affairs of Annabell, Room Service, Valley of the Sun, Seven Days Leave, DuBarry Was a Lady, Best Foot Forward, Meet the People, Thousands Cheer, Without Love, Love from a Stranger, Her Husband's Affairs, Long, Long, Trailer, Forever Darling, Facts of Life, Critic's Choice, Yours, Mine and Ours, Mame; star TV shows I Love Lucy, The Lucy Show, Here's Lucy; starred on Broadway in Wildcat; pres. Desilu Prodns., Inc., 1962-67, Lucille Ball Prodns., 1967—. Recipient Emmy award for best comedienne, 1952, 55, 67, 68, Golden Apple Award, 1973, Ruby Award, 1974, Entertainer of the Yr., 1975. Presbyterian. Office: care Twentieth Century Fox PO Box 900 Beverly Hills CA 90213 *

BALL, MARGARET ANN, ins. co. exec.; b. Lorimor, Iowa, Feb. 23, 1938; d. Edmund Carl and Lola Mary (Edwards) Porter; student Drake U., 1963-70; m. Gary Ernest Ball, June 29, 1954; children—Monte, Marla, Mark. Rater, Farm Bur. Mut., Des Moines, 1957-60; rater Gt. Am. Ins. Co., Des Moines, 1963-66; underwriter The Atlantic Cos., Des Moines, 1966-71; asst. sec. Multiple Line Underwriters, Des Moines, 1971-80; asst. v.p. Employers Mut. Cos., Des Moines, 1980—; mem. faculty Drake U., 1973-78, Simpson Coll., 1974-75. C.P.C.U. Republican. Mem. Christian Ch. (Disciples of Christ). Mem. Order Eastern Star. Home: 579 Lake Panorama Panora IA 50216 Office: 717 Mulberry St Des Moines IA 50309

BALL, OTEKA ANN LITTLE, home economist; b. Madill, Okla., Feb. 2, 1939; d. Reuel Winfred and Oteka Delores (Wilson) Little; student Okla. U., 1957-59; B.S., So. Methodist U., 1962; postgrad. Rice U., 1962; M.S., Okla. State U., 1976; m. M. Gerald Ball, Sept. 5, 1959; children—Jeremy D., Oteka Lyn. Prin., broker Oteka Ball Real Estate Firm, Shawnee, Okla., 1970-76; instr. Seminole Jr. Coll., 1976-78; asst. prof. home econs. and edn., head home econs. Okla. Baptist U., 1978—; partner Land Oil Co., 1980—. Bd. dirs. Jack Little Found., Madill, 1970—; v.p. bd. dirs. Child's World, Shawnee, 1973-76; bd. dirs. YMCA, Shawnee, Okla., 1978—; mem. Hockaway Alumni Bd., Dallas, 1980-82; mem. Okla. Gov.'s Com. on Children and Youth, 1976-80. Mem. AAUP, Am. Home Econs. Assn., Assn. Couples for Marriage Enrichment, Nat. Council Adminstrs. Home Economists, PEO, Omicron Nu, Phi Kappa Phi. Democrat. Methodist. Home: 1320 N Broadway Shawnee OK 74801 Office: 500 W University Shawnee OK 74801

BALL, SHIRLEY DOUGLASS, ednl. adminstr.; b. McKees Rocks, Pa., Nov. 20, 1930; d. Clifford Stanley and Sarah Elizabeth (Poultney) Douglass; B.Music Edn., Grove City Coll., 1952; M.Music Edn., Duquesne U., 1968; Ph.D., U. Pitts., 1979; postgrad. Calif. Coll., 1978-79, St. Bonaventure U., 1982. Elem. sch. music tchr. Ringgold Sch. Dist., 1966; jr. high sch. music/choral dir. Elizabeth (Pa.) Forward, 1966-69, secondary sch. English tchr., 1969-78; prin. intern Norwin Sr. High Sch., Irwin, Pa., 1978-79; prin. No. Potter Jr.-Sr. High Sch., Ulysses, Pa., 1979-82; asst. supt. Springford Area Sch. Dist., Royersford, Pa., 1982—. Buhl Found. grantee, 1978-79. Mem. Am. Assn. Sch. Adminstrs., Assn. Supervision and Curriculum Devel., Nat. Ret. Tchrs. Assn., Pa. Assn. Secondary Sch. Prins., Theta Alpha Phi, Delta Kappa Gamma. Republican. Presbyterian. Clubs: Order Eastern Star. Home: 4099 Defford Pl Norristown PA 19403 Office: Collegeville PA 19403

BALLANCE, SHARON MARIE, nurse; b. Aurora, Ill., Feb. 2, 1942; d. Arthur E. and Virginia M. Kuhn; A.S. in Nursing, Long Beach (Calif.) City Coll., 1977; B.S. in Nursing, Calif. State U., Long Beach, 1980, M.S. in Nursing, 1982; m. Roderic O. Ballance, Feb. 11, 1961; children—Kelly Michelle, Britton Lewis, Ryan Kortney. Mem. nursing staff St. Mary's Hosp., Long Beach, 1975-78, pulmonary rehab. clinician, 1978-81, home health clinician, 1981—. Mem. Long Beach Lung Assn. (women's council, mem. med. adv., fund-raising, edn. coms.), Am. Nurses Assn., Nat. Rehab. Assn., Long Beach C. of C., Long Beach City Coll. Alumni Assn. (sec.), Calif. State U. at Long Beach Alumni Assn. (dir. 1981-82), Internat. Hostesses. Republican. Roman Catholic. Clubs: Alamitos Bay Garden; Long Beach Yacht; Cabrillo Beach Yacht. Home: 42 64th Pl Long Beach CA 90803 Office: 1050 Linden Ave Long Beach CA 90813

BALLANTINE, MARY KEITH, state legislator; b. Louisville, Aug. 30, 1926; d. Nicholas H. and Sallie Ewing (Marshall) Dosker; B.A., U. Ky.; M.A., Ind. U.; m. Robert W. Ballantine, 1954; children—Sallie, Frank. Commr. Jackson County, Mich., 1971-78; mem. Mich. Ho. of Reps., 1979—. Mem. Citizens Com. on Paperwork Reduction (exec. com. 1978), AAUW (dir. 1969-71), Farm Bur., Mortar Bd., Kappa Kappa Gamma. Home: 1809 Herkimer St Jackson MI 49203 Office: Room 104 1/2 State Capitol Bldg Lansing MI 48909 *

BALLANTINE, MORLEY COWLES, newspaper publisher; b. Des Moines, May 21, 1925; d. John and Elizabeth (Bates) Cowles; student Smith Coll., 1943-44, Stanford U., 1944-45, U. Minn., 1948-49; B.A., Ft. Lewis Coll., Colo., 1975; Litt.D., Simpson Coll., Indianola, Iowa, 1980; m. Arthur Ballantine, July 26, 1947 (dec. Nov. 1975); children—Richard, Elizabeth, William, Helen. Pub., Durango (Colo.) Herald, 1952—, Cortez (Colo.) Sentinel, 1958-60; dir. 1st Nat. Bank Durango, Des Moines Register & Tribune. Mem. Colo. Anti-Discrimination Commn., 1959-61, Colo. Com. on Ednl. Endeavor, 1959-63; mem. Colo. bd. LWV, 1954-57, mem. Durango bd., 1953-59; mem. Jud. Dist. Selection Com., 1967-72; pres. S.W. Colo. Mental Health Center, 1964-65; mem. State Welfare Adv. Com., 1967-71, Colo. Population Adv. Council, 1972-75; mem. Colo. Commn. Status Women, 1972-75, Colo. Land Use Commn., 1975-81; trustee Choate/Rosemary Hall, 1973-81, Fountain Valley Sch., Colorado Springs, 1976—, Simpson Coll., Indianola, Iowa, 1981—. Recipient 1st place award for editorial writing Nat. Fedn. Press Women, 1955, (with husband) Outstanding Journalist award U. Colo., 1967, Outstanding Alumna award Rosemary Hall, Wallingford, Conn., 1969, (with husband) Disting. Service award Ft. Lewis Coll., 1970. Mem. Colo. Press Assn. (dir. 1979-80). Clubs: Federated Woman's (Durango); Mill Reef (Antigua, W.I.); Colo. Press; Washington Press. Episcopalian. Home: 175 W Park Ave Durango CO 81301 Office: care Herald Drawer A Durango CO 81301

BALLARD, BETTY RUTH WESLEY, x-ray equipment co. exec.; b. Birmingham, Ala., Nov. 11, 1924; d. Henry Gaston and Ruth Lorine (Whitfield) Wesley; degree Glenn Tech. Inst., 1942-46; m. Douglas Hayden Ballard, Oct. 24, 1941; 1 son, Douglas Hayden. Mgr., Nbc Restaurant, 1960-68; corp. sec. X-Ray Service and Sales, Inc., 1960-68; pres. Ballard X-Ray Co., Birmingham, Ala., 1968—. Exec. com. Democratic Party; election law commr. State of Ala.; hon. dep. sheriff Shelby County, Ala.; mem. adminstrv. bd. 1st United Methodist Ch., Montevallo, Ala. Mem. Ala. Soc. Radiol. Technologists, Ala. Hosp. Assn., Inst. Hosp. Auxilians, Ala. Cattlemen's Assn., LWV, 20th Spl. Forces Group Aux. Methodist (adminstrv. bd., trustee ch.). Clubs: Downtown (Birmingham); The Club Inc. Home: Flying-X-Ranch Route 1 Box 29 Montevallo AL 35115 Office: 2701 4th Ave S Birmingham AL 35233

BALLARD, GLORIA BERNADETTE, fashion editor; b. Nashville, Nov. 15, 1951; d. William Bernard and Hazel Gloria (Blaine) Ballard; B.A. with honors, U. Tenn., Nashville, 1977; m. Henry Alan Martin, May 9, 1975; 1 son, Nathan. File clk. Nat. Life & Accident Ins. Co., Nashville, 1973-75; feature writer The Tennessean, Nashville, 1975-78, fashion editor, 1978—; cons. in field. Mem. Sigma Delta Chi. Office: 1100 Broadway Nashville TN 37202

BALLARD, KAYE, actress; b. Cleve., Nov. 1926; d. Vincent and Lena (Nacarata) Balotta. Broadway appearances include Three To Make Ready, Top Banana, The Golden Apple, Carnival, Molly, The Pirates of Penzance; starred in Touch and Go, 2 command performances, Brit. TV spl., London; toured in Annie Get Your Gun, Gypsy, Wonderful Town, Look Ma I'm Dancin', Out of This World, Minnie's Boys, also others; star Mothers-in-Law series NBC-TV; guest star appearances include Steve Allen, Johhny Carson, Perry Como, Dinah, Merv Griffin, Love American Style, Love Boat, Fantasy Island, Alice, Patty Duke Show, Jerry Lewis Show, Doris Day Show, Trapper John; movies include The Girl Most Likely, A House Is Not a Home, The Ritz, Freaky Friday, In Love Again; nightclub appearances include Blue Angel, Bon Soir, Plaza Hotel, Les Mouches (all N.Y.C.), Palmer House, Mr. Kelly's (Chgo.), Ciro's, Mocambo, Studio One, Coconut Grove, Hollywood, Calif. Recipient Italian-Am. award; Dallas State Fair award for Gypsy; Sarah Siddons award. Mem. Actors Equity Assn., AFTRA, Screen Actors Guild, Am. Guild Variety Artists. Address: Fred Amsel & Assocs Inc 215 S La Cienga Blvd Suite 200 Beverly Hills CA 90211

BALLARD, PATRICIA MAE, social worker; b. Berea, Ky., June 13, 1945; d. Alonzo Wilson and Fannie Louise (Martin) B.; B.A. in Sociology and Social Work, Berea Coll., 1967. Social worker Ky. Dept. Econ. Security, Louisville, Newport and Richmond, 1967, 68-74; social work supr. Ky. Dept. Human Resources, Berea, 1974—; mem. nat. adv. bd., Ky. adv. bd. Title XX Tng. for Social Workers; co-chmn. Madison County Interagy. Conf. Chmn. employment com. Greater Berea Area Human Relations Council, 1970-71; bd. dirs. Mountain Maternal Health League, 1979-81; vol. dir. Central Community Center, 1969-78; adv. bd. Prospect House Group, MEPCO Home Health Agy., 1981—; mem. Madison County Devel. Assn., 1970-71; instl. rep. Boy Scouts Am., 1971-76. Lic. social worker, Ky. Mem. Ky. Human Services Assn., Nat. Fedn. Bus. and Profl. Women's Clubs. Baptist. Home: Rt 1 Berea KY 40403 Office: PO Box 461 Berea KY 40403

BALLARD, TARY, editor, publisher, ednl. adminstr.; b. Griggsville, Ill., Mar. 14, 1916; d. Rexford De and Elysabeth Eugenia (Dunbar) Tompkins; B.A., Calif. State U., 1970; student North Central Coll., Naperville, Ill., 1938-39, Orange Coast Coll., 1965-66; A.A., Los Angeles City Coll., 1969; children by previous marriage—George C., James Ballard, Janice Suzanne Martinez. Pvt. instr. piano, Wash., 1953-63; reporter Mid Valley News, El Monte, Calif., 1971, editor, 1972-79, publisher, 1979—; pub. info. officer Mountain View Sch. Dist., El Monte, 1979—; dir. Mid Valley Pub. Co. Inc. Mem. Five Points Businessmens Assn. (v.p. 1975-77, pres. 1977-79), Women in Communications. Home: 4501 N Peck Rd Apt 78 El Monte CA 91732 Office: 2850 N Mountain View Rd El Monte CA 91732

BALLEISEN, CAROLYN KIMMELFIELD, lawyer; b. Bklyn., June 12, 1930; d. Isadore M. and Belle (Stern) Kimmelfield; A.B. cum laude, Barnard Coll., 1950; J.D. (Harlan Fiske Stone scholar), Columbia U., 1952; m. Donald H. Balleisen, Apr. 8, 1960; children—Ellen Margaret, Wendy Sue, Edward James. Admitted to N.Y. State bar, 1953, Ky. bar, 1971; research asst. income tax project Am. Law Inst., 1952-53; asso. firm Lord Day & Lord, N.Y.C., 1953-59; revision editor Rabkin & Johnson Fed. Income Gift & Estate Taxation Reporter, N.Y.C., 1959-60, 67-68; vis. asso. prof. law U. Louisville, 1969-70; tax cons., Louisville, 1970—; dir. Ky. Housing Corp., 1973-78. Vice pres. Ky. Dance Council, 1972-78, 79-80; v.p. Nat. Council Jewish Women, Louisville, 1973-77, chmn. state pub. affairs, 1977-81, recipient Hannah Solomon award, 1980; mem. citizens adv. group Jefferson County Office Housing and Community Devel., 1973—, vice chmn., 1979—; chmn. adv. com. Community for Ednl. Excellence, 1976-77; chmn. steering com. Louisville Area Coalition for Human Needs and Budget Priorities, 1977-78; pres. Louisville Ballet Co., 1978-79; bd. dirs. Metro United Way, 1977—; mem. task force on legis. and funding Jefferson County Bd. Edn., 1978—; mem. community adv. bd. Kentuckiana Public Broadcasting Corp., 1979—; chmn. Jefferson County Cable Communications Commn., 1982—. Mem. Am., Ky., Louisville bar assns. Democrat. Jewish. Club: Women's City. Editor Columbia Law Rev., 1951-52. Home: 3102 Runnymede Rd Louisville KY 40222

BALLENGER, GLORIA HANCE, psychologist; b. Indpls., Jan. 9, 1934; student Vassar Coll., 1951-53; Ph.D. in Clin. Psychology, Am. U., 1975; m. Carl Ballenger, July 27, 1976; children—Eliot, Lowell, Oliver, John. Psychology intern VA Hosp., Phoenix, 1974-75; clin. supr. Ariz. State Hosp., Phoenix, 1975-77; sr. psychologist Mid-Columbia Center, The Dalles, Oreg., 1977-78; cons., edn. coordinator San Luis Obispo County (Calif) Mental Health, 1978-81; sr. clin. psychologist Waikato Hosp., Hamilton, N.Z., 1981—. Chmn., San Luis Obispo Community Health Council, 1979-80; alt. mem. San Luis Obispo Health Commn., 1979-81; bd. dirs. Hospice, San Luis Obispo, 1979-81. Recipient service award Soroptomist Internat., 1979, Center for Law Edn., UCLA, 1979. Mem. Am. Psychol. Assn., Calif. Psychol. Assn., Ariz. Psychol. Assn., Oreg. Psychol. Assn., San Luis Obispo Psychol. Assn. (pres.), AAUP. Home: 18 Mahoe St Hamilton New Zealand Office: Waikato Hospital Hamilton New Zealand

BALLENTHIN, KATHLEEN ALICE, ednl. cons.; b. Cambridge, Minn., Feb. 23, 1942; d. Willi Ewald and Adeline Florence (Heyer) B.; B.S., Valparaiso U., 1964, M.A., 1968; postgrad. Va. Poly. Inst. and State U., Blacksburg, 1973-75. Elementary sch. tchr., Ill., Ind., 1964-69; administrv. asst. Luth. Human Relations, 1969-70; tchr. English as a second lang. pvt. elementary schs., Caracas, Venezuela, 1970-76; prof., coordinator English as a second lang. Met. U., Caracas, 1976-80; head ednl. counselor, asst. and acting dir. Am. Bur. Internat. Edn., Caracas, 1979-81; ednl. cons., counselor, dir. Am. Edn. Center, Caracas, Venezuela, 1981—. Mem. Nat. Assn. Fgn. Student Affairs, Venezuelan Am. Assn. U. Women. Lutheran. Home: 509 SW 8th St Faribault MN 55021 Office: Am Edn Center H-46 Care Jet Cargo Internat PO Box 520010 Miami FL 33152

BALLI, MAXINE SOWARDS, city ofcl.; b. Clintwood, Va., Dec. 19, 1929; d. Leonard Noel and Mary Martelia (Kelley) Sowards; A.A., George Washington U., 1949, B.A. in Polit. Sci. (Outstanding Sr. Woman award), 1951; m. Carl Eugene Balli, Aug. 9, 1952; children—Charles Leonard, Mary Elizabeth. Research analyst U.S. Govt., 1951-53; adminstrv. sec. Martin Aircraft Co., 1954-57. Mem. Econ. Devel. Bd., City of Coral Gables (Fla.), 1974—. Mem. Internat. Platform Assn., DAR, P.E.O., Alpha Delta Pi (Most Outstanding Regional Alumna award 1967). Republican. Methodist. Club: Cotillion (Miami). Home: 3301 Granada Blvd Coral Gables FL 33134

BALLMER, DORIS LOUISE, fin. planner; b. Bremen, Ohio, Nov. 23, 1928; d. Lawrence C. and Ruth D. (Bowen) Morris; diploma Lancaster (Ohio) Bus. Coll.; postgrad. various specialized courses; m. James E. Ballmer, Aug. 24, 1947; children—James David, Diana J. Lab. technician Benvenue Labs., Bedford, Ohio, 1943-45; various secretarial and office positions, 1945-46, 48-59; dir. recreation for suburbs City of Rochester (N.Y.), 1961-63; exec. sec. Camargo Ins. Agencies, Cin., 1969-72; head research and devel. Craft div. Fibre-Glass Evercoat, Inc., Cin., 1972-74; office mgr. Tamarin, Inc., Cin., 1974-77, v.p., 1977—; pres. Balco Internat., Loveland, Ohio, 1978-82; exec. sec. Oliver Cos.,

Fin. Planning and Ins. Assos. Mem. Nat. Assn. Female Execs., N.E. Women's Assn., Presbyn. Women's Soc., Amway Corp. Assn., Jaycees. Home: 9206 E Kemper Rd Loveland OH 45140

BALOS, KAREN, social worker, psychotherapist; b. Bklyn., July 12, 1942; d. Selig and Beatrice (Zirinsky) B.; B.A., Antioch U., 1964; M.S.W. (NIMH psychiat. fellow), Hunter Coll., CUNY, 1969. Research asst. Albert Einstein Coll. Medicine, N.Y.C., 1961, 64-67, U. Ala. Med. Center, Birmingham, 1962; lab. asst. Downstate Med. Center, Bklyn., 1963; psychiat. aide McLean Hosp., Belmont, Mass., 1963; research asst. Sloan Kettering Inst., N.Y.C., 1964; psychiat. social worker Community Services Sect., Calif. Dept. Health, Hayward, 1969-75; practice psychotherapy, Berkeley, Calif., 1976—; clin. dir. Downs Syndrome League, 1978—; program devel. cons. to residential facilities for mentally ill and mentally retarded adults, 1978-81; field work supr. genetic counseling program U. Calif., Berkeley, 1979—. Lic. clin. social worker, Calif., 1972—. Home: 1421 Kains Ave Berkeley CA 94702 Office: Center for Evaluation and Service 2020 N Broadway Suite 107 Walnut Creek CA 94596

BALSLEY, IROL WHITMORE (MRS. HOWARD L. BALSLEY), educator; b. Venus, Nebr., Aug. 22, 1912; d. Sylvanus Bertrand and Nanna (Carson) Whitmore; B.A., Nebr. State Tchrs. Coll., Wayne, 1933; M.S., U. Tenn., 1940; Ed.D., Ind. U., 1952; m. Howard Lloyd Balsley, Aug. 24, 1947. Tchr. high schs., Osmond and Walthill, Nebr., 1934-37, Van Sant Sch. Bus., Omaha, 1938; asst. prof. Ind. U., 1942-49; lectr. U. Utah, 1949-50, Russell Sage Coll., 1951-52; prof. office adminstrn. La. Tech. U., 1954-65, head dept., 1963-65; prof. bus. edn. and secretarial adminstrn. Tex. Tech U., Lubbock, 1965-72, prof. edn., chmn. bus. tchr. edn. program, 1972-75; prof. office adminstrn. and bus. edn. U. Ark., Little Rock, 1975-79, prof. emeritus, 1980—; adj. prof. office mgmt. Hardin-Simmons U., 1980-81; coordinator of USAF clk.-typist tng. program Pa. State, 1951, instr., head office tng. sect. TVA, 1941-42; editorial asst. Southwestern Pub. Co., 1940-41. Mem. Nat. (past pres. Research Found.), So. bus. edn. assns., Nat. Assn. Bus. Tchrs. Edn., Nat. Collegiate Assn. for Secs. (co-founder, past nat. pres., nat. exec. sec. 1976-81, nat. adv. com. 1981—), Phi Delta Kappa, Pi Lambda Theta, Delta Pi Epsilon (past nat. sec.), Beta Gamma Sigma, Pi Omega Pi, Sigma Tau Delta, Alpha Psi Omega, Delta Kappa Gamma. Author: (with Wanous) Shorthand Transcription Studies, 1968; (with Robinson) Integrated Secretarial Studies, 1963; (with Wood and Whitmore) Homestyle Baking, 1973; Century 21 Shorthand, Theory and Practice, 1974; (with Hoskinson) Century 21 Shorthand, Intensive Dictation and Transcription, 1974; Self Paced Learning Activities, Vol. I, Century 21 Shorthand Collegiate Series, 1977; Dictation: The Corporate View, 1980. Address: 6501 15th Ave W Bradenton FL 33529

BALTER, FRANCES SUNSTEIN, civic worker; b. Pitts.; d. Elias and Gertrude (Kingsbacher) Sunstein; student Sarah Lawrence Coll., 1939-41, New Sch. Social Research, 1941-43, Bennington Coll., summers 1941, 42; cert. Harvard Inst. Arts Adminstrn., 1973; m. James Stone Balter May 15, 1948; children—Katherine (Mrs. Ross Anthony), Julia Frances, Constance (Mrs. Owen Cantor), Daniel Elias; m. 2d, Harry Philip Blum, Mar. 1, 1982. Adminstrv. asst., asso. producer Ednl. Television WQED-TV, Pitts., 1963-67; producer, mng. dir. Freedom Readers, 1964-67; a founder, incorporator, sec. bd. dirs. Pitts. Council for Arts, 1967-70; cultural cons. Mayor's Office, Dir. of Office of Cultural Affairs, Pitts., 1968; a founder Three Rivers Arts Festival 1960; co-dir. Ohio and Miss. River Valley Art Festival, 1961-62; mem. Pa. Council on Arts, 1972-78, mem. exec. com., 1975-78; co-founder Pioneer Crafts Council Mill Run Pa., 1972; exec. dir. POETRY ON THE BUSES, 1974—. Recipient Woman of Year award in art Post Gazette, 1969. Mem. Asso. Councils on Arts, Nat. Soc. Arts and Letters. Home: 1021 Devonshire Rd Pittsburgh PA 15213

BALTHASER, LINDA IRENE, univ. adminstr.; b. Kokomo, Ind., Feb. 25, 1939; d. Earl Isaac and Evelyn Pauline (Troyer) Showalter; B.S. magna cum laude, Ind. Central U., 1961; M.S., Ind. U., 1962; m. Kenneth James Balthaser, June 1, 1963. Tchr. bus. edn. Southport High Sch., Indpls., 1962-63; sec., adminstrv. sec. Office of Pres., Ind. U., Bloomington, 1963-66; with Ind. U.-Purdue U., Fort Wayne, Ind., 1969—, asst. to dean Coll. of Arts and Letters, 1970—, founding co-dir. Weekend Coll., 1979-80. Bd. dirs. Associated Chs. Fort Wayne, 1980. Ind. Conf. N. Evang. United Brethren Ch. scholar, 1957-61. Mem. Fort Wayne-Allen County Hist. Assn., Embassy Theatre Found., Fort Wayne Mus. Art, Historic Fort Wayne, Fort Wayne Zool. Soc., Am. Assn. Univ. Adminstrs., Internat. Platform Assn., Delta Pi Epsilon, Phi Alpha Epsilon, Epsilon Sigma Alpha, Mensa. Lutheran. Club: Univ. Women's (pres. 1968-69). Home: 2917 Hazelwood Ave Fort Wayne IN 46805 Office: 2101 Coliseum Blvd E Fort Wayne IN 46805

BALTHROPE, JACQUELINE MOREHEAD, ednl. cons.; b. Phila.; d. Jack Walton and Minnie Jessie (Martin) Morehead; B.S. in Edn. with honors, Central State U., Wilberforce, Ohio, 1949; M.A. in Edn. with honors, Case-Western Res. U., 1959; m. Robert Granville Balthrope; children—Robert Granville, Yvonne Gertrude, Robin Bernice. Elem. master tchr. Cleve. Bd. Edn., 1950-65, leadership devel. tchr., 1965-69, asst. prin. elem. sch., 1969-77, prin. elem. sch., 1977-80; ednl. cons., Cleve., 1980—. Vol. religious and social orgns. Mem. Cleve. Council Adminstrs. and Suprs., Elem. Sch. Prins., Internat. Reading Assn., AAUW, LWV, Phi Delta Kappa, Delta Kappa Gamma, Alpha Kappa Mu, Zeta Sigma Pi, Pi Lambda Theta, Alpha Kappa Alpha, Phi Delta Kappa, Eta Phi Beta, Gamma Phi Delta. Methodist. Clubs: Top Ladies of Distinction (local founder, 1st pres.), Jr. League, Sen Mer Rekh. Author: African Boy Comes to America, 1960, also sequel; contbr. articles to profl. jours., mags., newspapers. Address: 16220 Delrey Ave Cleveland OH 44128

BALTIMORE, LINDA OWLETT, psychologist, educator; b. Middlebury Center, Pa., Apr. 13, 1937; d. John Quentin and Kathleen Alice (Davis) Owlett; B.S., Pa. State U., 1970; M.A., Marywood Coll., 1975; postgrad. Union Grad. Sch./West, 1979—; m. Richard Abe Baltimore, Oct. 9, 1970; children—Kelly, Kristina. Biology lab. asst., office asst. Pa. State U., University Park, 1966-68, research and teaching asst., 1968-70; instr. psychology Pa. State U., Wilkes-Barre, 1970-76, asst. prof., 1976-79; asso. dir. KNBC and ARC Health Fair Expo '80 for So. Calif., 1980-81; acting campaign dir. United Way of Riverside, 1980; community relations dir. CPC Alhambra Psychiat. Hosp., Rosemead, Calif., 1982—. Dist. trainer vols., counselor Am. Cancer Soc., Wilkes-Barre, 1972-79. Mem. Am. Psychol. Assn., N.E. Pa. Psychol. Assn. (pres. 1976-78). Presbyterian. Home: 3204 Pinefalls Dr West Covina CA 91792 Office: 4619 Rosemead Blvd Rosemead CA 91770

BANBURY, SHERA, electronics mfg. co. mktg. exec.; fin. planning cons.; b. St. Louis, Jan. 28, 1943; d. Harold Wellington Banbury and Dorothy Mary (LeVan) Banbury Kuper; student Mills Coll., 1960-62; B.A., Hanover Coll., 1964; M.A.Ed. (Ford Found. Project I scholar), U. Rochester, 1965; children—Sean Lachlan Connin, Lance Banbury Connin. Tchr. art, English, social studies, public and pvt. schs., Rochester, N.Y., 1964-74; substitute tchr., tutor, public schs., Naples and Churchville, N.Y., 1974-76; mktg. sec., receptionist Bristol Harbour Village, Canandaigua, N.Y., 1976-77; dir. advt. and promotions Sonnenberg Gardens, Canandaigua, 1977-79; mgr. advt. and sales promotion EDMAC Corp., Fishers, N.Y., 1979-80, mgr. internat. market devel., 1980—; fin. planning cons. Gradinger & Assos., Rochester, 1982—; adv. Canandaigua C. of C., 1978-79; reporter, co-editor Villager newspaper, Bristol Harbour Village, 1974-76. Founder, pres. Churchville-Chili Tchr. Aides, 1971-74. Recipient Gold Key, Nat. Scholastic Art Exhibit (2), 1959. Mem. Bus. Profl. Advt. Assn., Finger Lakes Assn., World Trade Council, Kappa Alpha Theta. Club: Churchville-Chili Garden. Contbr. articles to co. publs. Home: 461 Eastbrooke Ln Rochester NY 14618 Office: PO Box 750 Fishers NY 14453

BANCROFT, ANNE, actress; b. N.Y.C., Sept. 17, 1931; d. Michael and Mildred (DiNapoli) Italiano; grad. Christopher Columbus High Sch., N.Y.C.; m. Mel Brooks. Broadway debut in Two for the Seesaw, 1958; starred on Broadway as Annie Sullivan in The Miracle Worker, 1959-60, The Devils, Golda, 1977; films include: Don't Bother to Knock, 1952, Treasure of the Golden Condor, 1952, Tonight We Sing, 1953, The Kid from Left Field, 1953, A Life in the Balance, 1954, Demetrius and the Gladiators, 1954, Gorilla at Large, 1954, The Raid, 1954, The Girl in Black Stockings, 1955, The Last Frontier, 1955, New York Confidential, 1955, Naked Street, 1956, Walk the Proud Land, 1956, Nightfall, 1956, The Miracle Worker, 1962, The Pumpkin Eater, 1964, Seven Women, 1966, The Slender Thread, 1966, The Graduate, 1967, Young Winston, 1972, The Prisoner of 2d Avenue, 1975, The Hindenburg, 1975, Lipstick, 1976, Silent Movie, 1976, The Turning Point, 1977, The Elephant Man, 1980; dir., writer, actress Fatso, 1979; TV appearances include The Goldbergs, Danger, Suspense, Philco-Goodyear Playhouse; guest on Perry Como Show, Bob Hope-Chrysler Show; TV spl. Annie-The Woman in the Life of a Man, Tom Jones Show, Jesus of Nazareth. Recipient Tony award for Two for the Seesaw; Oscar award best actress of yr. for movie recreation of role in Miracle Worker, 1962, also Tony award for stage version; Emmy award for tv spl., 1970. Address: care 20th Century Fox Studios 10201 W Pico Los Angeles CA 90064

BANCROFT, ELIZABETH A(BERCROMBIE), analytical chemist; b. Washington, Mar. 2, 1947; d. John Chandler and Ruth Abercrombie (Robinson) B.; A.B., Harvard U./Radcliffe Coll., 1979; postgrad. in Forensic Scis., John Jay Coll. Criminal Justice, 1982. Asst. dir. research Bagley Fordyce Research Labs., N.Y.C., 1979—. Mem. Assn. Ofcl. Analytical Chemists, Am. Chem. Soc., AAAS, Am. Inst. Chemists, Forensic Sci. Soc., Am. Assn. Clin. Chemistry, Am. Acad. Forensic Scis. (affiliate), Internat. Reference Orgn. Forensic Medicine, Chemists Club, English Speaking Union. Republican. Episcopalian. Clubs: Harvard of N.Y.C.; Westside Rifle and Pistol. Home: 625 Park Ave New York NY 10021 Office: 22 E 49th St New York NY 10017

BANCROFT, MARTHA FOGG, systems engr., spectroscopist; b. Boston, Dec. 4, 1948; d. Oscar Marshall and Charlotte Lucille (Salisbury) Fogg; student Mackinac Coll., 1966-68, Broward Community Coll., 1968-69; B.S. in Chemistry with honors, U. Fla., 1972; m. Christopher Bancroft, June 30, 1973 (div. 1976). Scientist, product coordinator Instrumentation Lab. Inc., Lexington, Mass., 1972-76; sr. exec. partner Celdat Design Assos., N.H., N.Y., Minn., 1974—; sr. engr. avionics div. Honeywell, Mpls., 1977-82, prin. engr. corp. Honeywell, 1982—; tech. asso. U. Rochester Sch. Medicine, Rochester, N.Y., 1977; chmn. bd., officer N. Am. Dressage Inst., Hugo, Minn., 1980—. Bd. dirs. Coon Creek Watershed Property Owners' Assn., 1979-80. Recipient Honeywell Avionics spl. achievement award, 1979, IR-100 awards, 1975, 78, Honeywell Tech. awards, 1980, 82. Mem. Soc. for Applied Spectroscopy (officer 1975—), Phi Theta Kappa, Phi Kappa Phi. Invited lectr., patentee in field; contbr. writings to publs. Address: PO Box 73 Hugo MN 55038

BANDY, IRENE GESA, state ofcl.; b. Montgomery, W.Va., Aug. 30, 1940; d. Ernest and Gesa Wolff; B.S. in Edn., Ohio U., 1962; M.A., Eastern Ky. U., 1967; Ph.D., Ohio State U., 1979; 1 son, Nicholas E. Tchr. pub. schs., Gainesville, Fla., 1962-64, Cin., 1964-65; guidance supr. Eastern Ky. U., 1967-68; counselor Napoleon (Ohio) Schs., 1968-73; cons. div. guidance and testing Ohio Dept. Edn., Columbus, 1973-77, asst. dir., 1977-79, exec. dir. adminstrn., 1979-82, asst. supt., 1982—; instr. Bowling Green State U., 1973. Inst. Ednl. Leadership Edn. Policy fellow, 1981-82. Mem. Am. Personnel and Guidance Assn. (dir. 1979-82), Ohio Personnel and Guidance Assn. (You Done Good award 1980), Buckeye Assn. Sch. Adminstrs., Phi Delta Kappa. Contbr. articles in field. Office: 65 S Front St Columbus OH 43215

BANERJEE, MARIA NEMCOVA, educator; b. Prague, Czechoslovakia, Nov. 22, 1937; came to U.S., 1957, naturalized, 1966; d. Joseph and Marie (Karlikova) Nemec; Baccalaureat, Coll. Marie de France, 1955; M.A., U. Montreal, 1957; Ph.D., Harvard U., 1962; m. Dibyendu Kumar Banerjee, Nov. 18, 1961. Teaching fellow Harvard U., Cambridge, Mass., 1958-59; instr. Wellesley (Mass.) Coll., 1959-60; asst. prof. Brown U., Providence, 1962-64; asst. prof. Smith Coll., Northampton, Mass., 1966-72, asso. prof., 1972-79, prof., 1979—; sr. scholar IREX (Internat. Research and Exchange Bd.), Inst. Russian Lit., Leningrad, 1973. Mem. Am. Assn. Advancement Slavic Studies, Czechoslovak Soc. Arts and Scis. in Am. Democrat. Roman Catholic. Contbr. articles to profl. jours. Office: Russian Dept Smith Coll Northampton MA 01060

BANK, CHERIE LYNN, broadcast journalist; b. St. Louis, June 15, 1950; d. Preston and Celeste Bank; B.A. with honors, U. Wis., 1972; postgrad. Webster Coll. Successively newsroom sec., writer, film editor, reporter, producer, producer and anchor 6 and 10 pm news Sta. KTVI-TV, Channel 2, St. Louis, 1972-79; reporter, anchorwoman Sta. WCAU-TV, Phila., 1979—; lectr. to ednl. and civic groups; tchr. communications. Voted Outstanding Newscaster in St. Louis. FM radio poll, 1977; recipient Emmy nomination for Outstanding Local Anchorperson, St. Louis chpt. Nat. Acad. Television Arts and Scis., 1976, 77, 78; award for public service Pa. AP, 1979; 1st pl. award for news reporting Nat. Commn. for Working Women, also hon. mention for feature report; Odyssey award. Office: WCAU-TV Cityline and Monument Ave Philadelphia PA 19131

BANK, DENA CITRON, author, former social worker; b. Columbia, S.C., July 23, 1912; d. Max and Rose (Silber) Citron; B.A., U. S.C., 1934; M.S.W., Columbia U., 1936; 1 dau., Barbara Eileen Bank Frank. Social worker, N.Y.C., 1936-42; med. and psychiat. social worker, Ft. Jackson, S.C., 1954-58; chief social worker Vocat. Rehab. Dept., Columbia, 1959-61; exec. dir. Friendship Center, Columbia, 1961-65; research, adminstrv. asso. Jules Bank Assos., Greensboro, N.C., 1965-69; tchr. social casework, parliamentary procedure to various instns., clubs, 1948—. Bd. dirs. YWCA, USO, PTA; bd. dirs. Columbia LWV, 1947—, pres., 1962-64. Mem. Nat. Assn. Social Workers, Acad. Cert. Social Workers, S.C. Mental Health Assn., Phi Beta Kappa, Alpha Kappa Gamma. Club: Zonta Internat. Author: How Things Get Done—The Nitty-Gritty of Parliamentary Procedure, 1979. Home: Apt 1159 Quail Run Apts Quail Run Dr Columbia SC 29206

BANKS, BARBARA JOAN, med. technologist; b. Alton, Ill., Nov. 6, 1953; d. James Creighton and Patsy Keitra (Hulson) B.; B.A., So. Ill. U., 1975; B.S., Jewish Hosp. Med. Tech. Sch., 1977. Sec., lab. asst. Alton Meml. Hosp. Lab., 1969-76; med. technologist Jewish Hosp., St. Louis, 1977-81, asst. supr., 1981—. Mem. Am. Soc. Clin. Pathologists. Methodist. Home: 522 Nirk St Apt C Kirkwood MO 63122 Office: Jewish Hospital 216 S Kingshighway St Louis MO 63110

BANKS, BEATRICE, utility co. exec.; b. Uniontown, Ala., July 24, 1936; d. Robert and Lucy Mary (Warren) B.; B.S. in Family Life Edn., Wayne State U., 1963. Teletype and long distance operator AT&T, 1955-61; tchr. clothing and family living Detroit public schs., 1963; residential consumer services adviser Detroit Edison Co., 1963-71, asst. supr. residential consumer services, 1971-72, asst. mgr. Detroit Wayne customer and mktg. services, 1972-74, mgr. Detroit Wayne customer and mktg. services, 1974-75, dir. mktg. services Detroit div., 1975-79, dir. customer and mktg. services Macomb div., 1979-80, asst. mgr. Detroit div., 1980—. Bd. dirs. Operation PUSH Detroit; mem. Mich. Civil Rights Commn.; precinct del. Mich. Republican Party. Recipient Headliners award Women of Wayne, 1976. Mem. Am. Home Econs. Assn., Mich. Home Econs. Assn., NAACP (life mem., Appreciation award 1977, 78, 79). Methodist. Club: Women's Econ. (Detroit). Office: Detroit Edison Co 2000 2d Ave Room 404 GO Detroit MI 48226

BANKS, BETTIE SHEPPARD, psychologist; b. Birmingham, Ala., June 8, 1933; d. Francis Wilkerson and Bettie Pollard (Woodson) Sheppard; B.A., Ga. State U., 1966, M.A., 1968, Ph.D., 1970; m. Frazer Banks, Jr., Mar. 22, 1952; children—Bettie Woodson, Lee Frazer III. Clin. asso. Lab. for Psychol. Services, Ga. State U., 1968-70; intern Ga. Mental Health Inst., Atlanta, 1970-71, psychologist, 1971-72, chief psychologist, 1973; pvt. practice, Atlanta, 1972—. Diplomate in clin. psychology Am. Bd. Profl. Psychology. Fellow Ga. Psychol. Assn. (chmn. div. E 1980); mem. Am. Acad. Psychotherapists (exec. com. 1980-82), Am. Psychol. Assn., Am. Group Psychotherapy Assn., Atlanta Group Psychotherapy Soc. (exec. com. 1982), Southeastern Psychol. Assn. Episcopalian. Club: Jr. League. Cons. editor Voices, 1978—. Office: 2905 Peachtree Rd NE Atlanta GA 30363

BANKS, DORIS OWEN, hosp. exec.; b. Detroit, Mar. 13, 1928; d. John Lee and Eskaline (Gentry) Owen; student Cleary Coll., Ypsilanti, Mich., 1945, DePaul U., Chgo., 1956, Kellberg Inst., Chgo., 1958, Wayne State U., 1977; A.A., Wayne County Community Coll., 1976; B.B.A., Mercy Coll., Detroit, 1978; M.A., Central Mich. U., 81. Sr. sec. Wayne State U., Detroit, 1963-64; sec. to supt. Police/Fire Communications, City of Detroit, 1964-70; sec. Detroit Residential Manpower, 1971; contractor/specialist D.O. Banks Flexile Med. Secretarial Service, Detroit, 1972—; ops. mgr. oncology service Providence Hosp., Southfield, Mich., 1972—. Facilitator/organizer Mich. chpt. Children of Aging Parents. Lic. massage therapist; cert. instr. in therapeutic manipulation. Mem. Am. Med. Writers Assn., Mich. Holistic Health Assn., Nat. Assn. Female Execs., Am. Mgmt. Assn. Contbr. articles to profl. jours. Home: 24530 Old Orchard Rd Novi MI 48050 Office: 16001 W Nine Mile Rd Southfield MI 48075

BANKS, ELENA ADAMS, educator; b. Bloomington, Ind., Oct. 13; d. Henry Sherman and Myrtle Mae (Butcher) Adams; B.S., Ind. U., 1945; M.Ed., U. Md., 1964; postgrad. George Washington U., U. Md., Ind. State U.; 1 son, Jonathan Ray. Tchr. public schs., Ind. and Md.; adminstrv. and spl. asst. various depts. U.S. Govt., Washington; faculty Ind. State U., Terre Haute, 1968—, asso. prof. Sch. Bus., 1983—; lectr. Named Kappa Delta Pi Tchr. of Yr., 1976; recipient commendation for service U.S. Govt. Mem. Ind. Bus. Educators Club, Ind. Bus. Edn. Assn., N. Central Bus. Edn. Assn., Nat. Bus. Edn. Assn., Ind. Vocat. Assn., Am. Vocat. Assn., Profl. Secs. Internat., Alumni Assn. Ind. U., Beta Gamma Sigma, Delta Kappa Gamma, Phi Delta Kappa, Delta Pi Epsilon. Club: Faculty Women's of Ind. State U. Contbr. articles, poetry, stories to popular profl. jours. and mags. Home: 320 Robinwood Dr Terre Haute IN 47803 Office: Sch Bus Statesman Tower E Ind State Univ Terre Haute IN 47809

BANKS, MARGARET AMELIA, librarian; b. Quebec City, Que., Can., July 3, 1928; d. Thomas Herbert and Bessey (Collins) B.; B.A., Bishop's U., Lennoxville, Que., 1949; M.A., U. Toronto, 1950, Ph.D., 1953. Archivist Ont. Archives, Toronto, 1953-61; law librarian U. Western Ont., London, 1961—, asso. prof. faculty law, 1974—. Mem. Am. Assn. Law Libraries, Can. Assn. Law Libraries, Am. Inst. Parliamentarians, Nat. Assn. Parliamentarians, Osgoode Soc. Anglican. Author: Edward Blake, Irish Nationalist, 1957; Using a Law Library, 1st edit., 1971, 2d edit., 1974, 3d edit., 1980. Office: Faculty Law Library U Western Ont London ON N6A 3K7 Canada

BANNISTER, ELIZABETH THORNING, social worker, apple grower; b. Yakima, Wash., July 26, 1916; d. Edward Arthur and Emily Augusta (Thorning) B.; student Yakima Valley Jr. Coll., 1934-35; A.B., U. Wash., 1938; M.S.W., U. So. Calif., 1956. Public assistance and child welfare worker Kittitas and Clark County (Wash.) Welfare Depts., 1939-46; area supr. Children's Home Soc. Wash., Walla Walla, 1947-51, adminstrv. asst., Seattle, 1952-57, asst. state dir., 1957-64, exec. dir., 1964-80; pres. Pyramid Orchards, Inc., Yakima, 1970—. Gen. chmn. N.W. Regional Conf. Child Welfare League Am., Seattle, 1972; citizen mem. disciplinary bd. Wash. State Bar Assn., 1981—. Recipient Matrix Table Woman of Achievement award Theta Sigma Phi, 1970. Mem. Wash. Assn. Child Care Agys. (pres. 1967-69), Council Accreditation Services for Families and Children, Inc. (Western Service Council, 1979-80), Nat. Assn. Social Workers (1st v.p. 1963-65), Wash. Assn. Social Welfare (pres. 1957-59), Phi Beta Kappa, Delta Delta Delta. Episcopalian. Clubs: Soroptimist Internat., Seattle-N. Home: 10660 Sand Point Way NE Seattle WA 98125 Office: Pyramid Orchards Inc 5105 W Nob Hill Blvd Yakima WA 98908

BANNISTER, MARGARET ALICE TRIMBLE, public relations specialist; b. Oklahoma City, Okla., Dec. 15, 1924; d. Clyde Waldrop and Mary Melissa (Murray) Trimble; B.A. in Journalism, U. Okla., 1945; teaching cert. U. Mo., St. Louis, 1969, postgrad. extension, 1970-71; postgrad. U. Wash., 1973; m. Lawrence R. Bannister, Jan. 18, 1947 (div. 1968); children—Karen Bannister Torretta, Barbara Jean Bannister Jewett, Sally Ann. Reporter, Alva (Okla.) Review-Courier, 1945-46, Clinton (Okla.) Daily News, 1946-47; public relations asst. U. Okla., Norman, 1947-51; editorial asst. Consol.-Vultee Aircraft Corp., Ft. Worth, 1951-53; coordinator community relations Berkeley (Mo.) Sch. Dist. (merged with and name changed to Ferguson Sch. Dist. R-2 1975), 1968-72, dir. community relations, 1973-81; ednl. public relations and editorial cons. Mem. Women in Communication, Nat. Sch. public Relations Assn. (officer Greater St. Louis chpt. 1969-71, 73-74), Soroptimists Internat. (charter mem. N. St. Louis County chpt.). Methodist (past mem. bd. stewards, youth council). Home: 2040 Argo Dr Florissant MO 63031 Office: 655 January Ave Ferguson MO 63135

BANTA, NANCY JEANNE, petroleum geologist; b. Cookville, Tenn., Aug. 22, 1952; d. Lucas Voorhis and Louise Marian (Finn) B.; B.S. cum laude (N.Y. State Regents scholar), Beloit Coll., 1974. Exploration geologist Internat. Exploration and Prodn. div. Getty Oil Co., Los Angeles, 1974—. Vol., San Fernando Valley council Girl Scouts U.S.A. Mem. Am. Assn. Petroleum Geologists, Geol. Soc. Am., Los Angeles Basin Geol. Soc., Assn. Women In Sci., Assn. Women Geoscientists (nat. v.p.), NOW, Mortar Bd., Nat. Honor Soc. Republican. Presbyterian. Specialist in geology of Europe, S.Am. Home: 3311 Robinson Ave Austin TX 78722 Office: 3810 Wilshire Blvd Los Angeles CA 90010

BANTIVOGLIO, BARBARA MARIE, investment banking co. exec.; b. Camden, N.J., Feb. 19, 1944; d. Frank Andrew and Eleanor Josephine (DiBartolomeo) B.; B.A. cum laude, Rutgers U., 1965, M.L.S., 1973; m. William Wade Middleton, Nov. 9, 1974. Tchr. French and math. No. Burlington County Regional Sch. Dist., Columbus, N.J., 1965-76; asst. mgr. institutional sales Robinson-Humphrey Co., Inc., Atlanta, 1976—. Mem. Atlanta Assn. Women in Securities, (sec. 1980—), Nat. Assn. Female Execs., AAUW, Alliance Francaise d'Atlanta. Republican. Roman Catholic. Office: 2 Peachtree St NW Atlanta GA 30383

BARABASH, CLAIRE, psychologist, ednl. adminstr.; b. N.Y.C., Oct. 22, 1940; d. Maurice Isaac and Sarah (Libowsky) B.; B.A., Bklyn. Coll.,

1960, postgrad. (Ednl. Clinic fellow), 1962-63; M.S., CCNY, 1962; Ph.D., N.Y. U., 1978. Sch. psychologist Yonkers (N.Y.) Bd. Edn., 1963-65; sch. psychologist Bur. Child Guidance, N.Y.C., 1965-78, psychology supr., 1978-79; regional coordinator Office Student Support Services, N.Y.C. Bd. Edn., 1979-82, dep. asst. Supt. div. spl. edn., 1982—; adj. assoc. prof. psychology N.Y. U., 1979—; psychol. cons. Children's Aid Soc., 1978-82. Mem. Solomon Schecter Bd. Edn., 1979-80. Mem. Am. Psychol. Assn., Richmond County Psychol. Assn. (sec.), N.Y.C. Assn. Sch. Psychologists (pres.), Council Exceptional Children, Mensa, Psi Chi, Kappa Delta Pi. Home: 101 Clark St Brooklyn NY 11201 Office: 211 Daniel Low Terr Staten Island NY 10301

BARACKMAN, VICTORIA JEAN, health care, recruiting co. exec.; b. Wichita, Kans., Apr. 11, 1951; d. Wallace Eugene and Dorothy Lee Van Dorn; B.Med. Humanities, U. Kans., 1975; B.S. in Nursing, Wichita State U., 1978; postgrad. U. Kans.; m. Martin Lee, May 17, 1975. Research asst., asst. instr. U. Kans., 1973-76; research asst. Wichita State U., 1976-78; dir. community involvement and edn., legis. coordinator Health Systems Agy., Wichita, 1978-80; mktg. dir. family health plan Health Maintenance Orgn., Newton, Kans., 1980-81; dir. Health Care Recuiting Specialists, Wichita, 1981—; mem. faculty U. Kans.; grant writing cons., 1979—. Bd. dirs., sect. Furley Improvement Dist., 1980-82; committeewoman Lincoln Twp., 1980-82; pres. chpt. 24 EAA Ultralight Assn., 1981-82. Bus. and Profl. Women's scholar, 1976. Mem. Am. Nurses Assn., Kans. Nurses Assn., Involved Nurses Polit. Action, Kans. League Nursing, Nat. League Nursing, Kans. Public Health Assn., Kans. Press Women, Women's Polit. Caucus, Internat. Assn. Bus. Communicators, C. of C., Kans. Soc. Assn. Execs., Kans. Assn. Sch. Health, Sigma Theta Tau, Phi Kappa Phi, Omicron Delta Kappa. Club: Hobbie Sailing Fleet. Author articles in field. Home: Route 2 Valley Center KS 67147 Office: PO Box 1916 Wichita KS 67201

BARAN, JANE ANN, audiologist/speech pathologist; b. Taunton, Mass., Apr. 26, 1950; d. Stanley Francis and Helen Barbara (Slavick) Baran; B.A., U. Mass., 1972, M.A., 1974; Ph.D., Purdue U., 1979. Teaching/research asst. U. Mass., Amherst, 1972-74, Purdue U., W. Lafayette, Ind., 1974-77; dir. audiol. services Indpls. Speech and Hearing Center, 1977-79; asst. prof. audiology, speech pathology U. Mass., Amherst, 1979—; audiol. cons. Amherst and Turner Falls Public Schs., 1979—. Sigma Xi grantee, 1976-77. Mem. Mass. Speech-Lang.-Hearing Assn. (profl. com. 1979—, sec. 1981-82), Am. Speech-Lang.-Hearing Assn., Soc. for Research in Child Devel., Alexander Graham Bell Assn., Sigma Delta Epsilon. Contbr. articles to profl. jours. Home: 121A Brittany Manor Amherst MA 01002 Office: 18 Arnold House Amherst MA 01003

BARASCH, FRANCES KAREN, educator; b. N.Y.C., Apr. 10, 1928; d. Jacob Michael and Eva (Hochberg) Karen; B.A., Bklyn. Coll.; M.A., N.Y. U., Ph.D., 1964; m. Seymour Barasch, June 10, 1952; children—Paul Gerald, Elihu, Daniel. Mem. faculty N.Y. U., 1959-61, Pace U., 1961-69; mem. faculty Baruch Coll., CCNY, 1965—, prof. English, 1977—; pub. Resealse mag., 1979—; freelance writer, edn. and labor cons. Recipient Faculty Research award City U. N.Y., 1970, 71, 82, Baruch award Internat. Women's Year, 1976, Crystal award N.Y. U., 1982; fellow N.Y. U., 1957-59. Mem. N.Y. U. Grad. Sch. Arts and Scis. Alumni Assn. (pres. 1979-81), N.Y. U. Alumni Fedn. (dir.). Address: Box 23 Baruch Coll 17 Lexington Ave New York NY 10010

BARATZ, ADELE FLORA, nurse; b. Morristown, N.J., Aug. 11, 1926; d. Alexander and Rebecca (Leboff) Salton; grad. Sinai Hosp. Sch. Nursing, 1947; children—Alan Edward, Terri Sue. Staff nurse South Nev. Meml. Hosp., Las Vegas, 1948; office nurse in Los Angeles, 1949-53; staff nurse Sunrise Hosp., Las Vegas, 1974-76, relief charge nurse, 1976-78, charge nurse, 1978-80, house supr., 1980—, chmn. nursing quality assurance com., 1980, mem. nursing exec. com., 1981—, patient care evaluation com., 1981—, nurse-pharmacy com., 1982—; mem. adv. bd. Registered Nurse Refresher Program, Clark County Community Coll., 1974. Active Frontier council Girl Scouts U.S.A., dist. chmn., 1966-69, field v.p., 1969-71, pres., 1971-74, del. nat. council, 1973; nat. com. girl scouting Synagogue Council Am., 1976—; membership chmn. Las Vegas Area Council PTA, 1966; v.p. Crestwood PTA, 1967; rec. sec. John C. Freemont PTA, 1969, LWV, 1970—; S. Nev. Drug Abuse Council, 1973-75. Mem. Am. Nurses Assn. Jewish. Home: Las Vegas NV 89105

BARBER, BETTY OLETA, oil co. exec.; b. Pittsburg, Kans., June 11, 1928; d. Theodore Roosevelt and Juanita Marie (Luckey) Barber; B.A., Kans. State Tchrs. Coll., 1950. Clk., Spencer Chem. Co., (acquired by Gulf Oil Co. 1966), Pittsburg, 1950-53, acctg. clerk, 1953-60, jr. acct., Kansas City, Mo., 1960-67; acctg. clerk Gulf Oil Corp., Houston, 1967-70, acct. 1970-74, sect. supr., 1977-80, sr. supr., 1980—, mem. volumetric control com., 1980—. Office: PO Box 2063 Room 1150 Houston TX 77252

BARBER, KATHLEEN LUCAS, polit. scientist; b. Canton, Ohio, Apr. 9, 1924; d. Homer C. and Lela (Hay) Lucas; B.A., Wellesley Coll., 1944; M.A., Case Western Res. U., 1965, Ph.D., 1968; m. D. Robert Barber, June 1, 1946; children—Robert L., Ann H., John C., Charles A. Research asst. Democratic Nat. Com., 1946-47, NEA, 1947-49; mem. faculty John Carroll U., Cleve., 1968—, prof. polit. sci., 1978—, chmn. dept., 1977—; trustee George Gund Found., 1980—; public mem. bd. trustees Bar Assn. Greater Cleve., 1979-82. Mem. Shaker Heights (Ohio) City Council, 1973-79, vice mayor, 1979; vice chmn. Cuyahoga County Dem. Party, 1978-80, exec. com., 1978—; committeewoman Ohio Dem. Party, 1980-82; del. Dem. Nat. Conv., 1976, 80. Mem. Am. Polit. Sci. Assn., Midwest Polit. Sci. Assn., Ohio Assn. Economists and Polit. Scientists (pres. 1974-75), Pi Sigma Alpha. Unitarian. Author articles in field. Home: 3005 Kingsley Rd Shaker Heights OH 44122 Office: John Carroll U Cleveland OH 44118

BARBER, MARIAN LIN, accountant; b. Taiwan, Sept. 14, 1940; d. Hsui-ting and Yueh-O (Shih) Lin; came to U.S., 1969; B.A., Chung-hsing U., Taiwan, 1964; M.B.A., Ind. U., 1973; m. Dennis G. Barber. Tchr., Tou-wu Middle Sch., Taiwan, 1964-66; payroll clk. Mobil China Allied Chem. Indsl. Ltd., Taiwan, 1966-69; jr. acct. Abbott Labs., North Chicago, Ill., 1973-74; distbn. analyst dept. 291, 1974-76; sr. acct. Square D Co., Milw., 1976—. Taiwan Govt. research scholar Nat. Research Inst., Taipei, 1968. Mem. Orgn. Chinese Ams., Chinese-Am. Civic Club Milw. (treas. 1978-79, dir. 1979-82). Author: You Are What You Eat, 1978. Home: 4013 W College Ave Milwaukee WI 53221

BARBER, SUSAN A. MORSE, ednl. adminstr.; b. N.Y.C., Mar. 28, 1946; d. Henry H. and Marcella (Leifer) Morse; B.S., U. Mass., 1968; student Merrill-Palmer Inst. Human Devel. and Family Life, Detroit, 1967; M.Ed., U. Md., 1971; m. Robert E. Barber, Jr., June 21, 1975; children—Robert, Jon, Oran. Tchr., dir. Cloverdale Presch., Northampton, Mass., 1967-69; head tchr. Nat. Child Research Center, Washington, summer 1969; kindergarten tchr. Montgomery County Public Schs., Rockville, Md., 1969-71, child devel. tchr., chmn. dept. John F. Kennedy High Sch., 1971-73; dir. Child Devel. Center, Keene (N.H.) State Coll., 1974—, chmn. com. women in higher edn., 1979-80; mem. Cheshire County Child Abuse Help Team; adv. bd. N.H. Head Start; early childhood task force N.H. Dept. Edn. Mem. N.H. Commn. on Status of Women. Grantee Spaulding-Potter Found., 1973. Mem. N.H. Early Childhood Tchr. Educators, Nat. Assn. Edn. Young Children, N.H. Women Higher Edn. Democrat. Jewish. Home: 72 School St Keene NH 03431 Office: CDC Elliot Hall Keene State Coll Keene NH 03431

BARBER, WAYMAH NORRIS, psychologist; b. Portales, N.Mex., May 15, 1907; d. Elbert J. and Roxanne (Gates) Norris; B.A., Gt. Falls Coll. Edn., 1940; M.Ed., Temple U., 1946, Ed.D., 1949; student CUNY, U. So. Calif., U. Pitts.; m. Robert W. Barber, Mar. 12, 1949. Tchr. spl. edn., state and pvt. schs., 1930-41; tchr., research psychologist N.J. Sch. for Deaf, 1942-48; asso. prof. clin. psychology Fla. State U., 1948-49; dir. psychol. services Children Home Soc. N.J., Trenton, 1949-59, asst. exec. dir., 1959-63, exec. dir., 1963-74; cons. Montessori Sch., Princeton, N.J., 1971-73; pvt. practice psychologist, Washington, N.C., 1974—. Bd. dirs. Vis. Nurse Assn., YWCA, Beaufort County Mental Health Assn., 1982—; mem. N.J. Child Labor Laws Study Commn., 1970; chmn. bd. Mercer County Mental Health Bd., 1963-65. Mem. Council Agy. Execs., Child Welfare League Am. (chmn. Eastern regional conf. 1966), N.J. Pyschol. Assn. (sec. 1968-69), Eastern Psychol. Assn., N.C. Psychol. Assn., AAUP. Episcopalian. Fellow Am. Psychol. Assn. Clubs: Washington Garden, Yacht and Country. Contbr. articles to profl. jours. Address: 114 Fairway Dr Country Club Estates Washington NC 27889

BARBERA, EILEEN M., legislative aide; b. Sept. 22, 1955; d. Nathaniel and Anne (Repeti) Barbera; student St. Marys of Notre Dame, 1973-75; B.A. summa cum laude, Boston Coll., 1977; M.P.A., Am. U., 1980. Hosp. discharge planner-utilization rev. coordinator, 1977-79; research asst. Am. Enterprise Inst., 1979; legis. aide to Sen. Heinz (Pa.), Washington, 1980—. Office: Room 443 Russell Senate Office Bldg Washington DC 20510 *

BARBERENA, DORIS DAVIS, social services program adminstr.; b. Nauvoo, Ala., Mar. 29, 1923; d. Arlie Franklin and Lila Maude (Beasley) Davis; B.A., Anderson (Ind.) Coll., 1947, B.S., 1949; m. Guillermo Barberena, Feb. 17, 1951; children—Doris Maria, Guillermo, Ricardo, Mark, David. Missionary in Cuba, 1947-48; social worker county welfare, Anderson, 1949-50; social/religious worker Home Missions Council, Wis. and Tex., 1950-51; social worker, Leesburg, Fla., 1951-52, Family Service Assn., Ft. Worth, 1952-53; social worker, supr., program dir. Tex. Dept. Human Resources, Ft. Worth, 1962—; mem. Tex. Family Service Adv. Com., CETA Planning Council of Greater Ft. Worth, CETA Consortium; vice chmn. CETA Council, 1981-82. Mem. Tex. Public Employees Assn., Tex. Coalition for Juvenile Justice, Tarrant County Interagy. Council (chmn. services to deaf, chmn. services to youth 1981-82), Tarrant County Mental Health/Mental Assn. Mem. Church of God. Home: 6208 S Ridge Rd Fort Worth TX 76135 Office: 2526 Jacksboro Highway Fort Worth TX 76114

BARBIERI, ROSEMARY, real estate broker; b. N.Y.C.; d. Louis and Mary Perone; student New Haven-Hartford Bus. Sch., 1965, Lee Inst., 1972; m. Edmund Barbieri, Aug. 28, 1965; children—Edmund, Michael. IBM clk. billing dept. Town of Wallingford (Conn.) Water Div., 1965-66, payroll dept. G. O. Mfg. Co., New Haven, 1967-68; real estate agt. Combs & Lee Real Estate, 1972-76; prin. owner B & B Real Estate, Inc., Yalesville, Conn., 1976—. Named to Million Dollar Club, Achievement Circle; Grad. Realtors Inst., cert. residential specialist. Office: 322 Church St Yalesville CT 06492

BARBIS, JEAN WYATT, ins. and fin. exec.; b. Richlands, Va., Nov. 6, 1939; d. V.E. and Edith (Hunt) Wyatt; B.S. in Sociology, Miami U., Oxford, Ohio, 1961; M.S. in Human Resources (PEO fellow), SUNY, Binghamton, 1979; m. Elio M. Barbis, Sept. 3, 1960; children—Anthony, Susan, Margaret, Elizabeth. Editorial asst. Miami U., 1961; program dir. YWCA, 1964-70; adj. prof., cons., St. Louis, 1964—; ins. sales rep. Equitable Life Assurance Co., 1978-79, asst. dist. mgr., Rome, N.Y., 1979-81, ins. and fin. staff, Clayton, Mo., 1981—; cons. USAF, U.S. Govt. Active AAUW, YWCA, YMCA, Girl Scouts U.S.A. Mem. Nat. Assn. Life Underwriters (dir. local br.), N.Y. State Assn. Women's Studies, Am. Soc. Tng. Dirs., Nat. Assn. Security Dealers, Life Underwriting Tng. Council, Nat. Assn. Life Underwriters. Episcopalian. Office: 200 S Hanley Ste 1100 Clayton MO 63105

BARBOUR, CAROL GOODWIN, psychologist; b. Morganton, N.C., Sept. 15, 1946; d. Jesse Otho and Edith Adele (Goodwin) B.; A.B., Duke U., 1967; M.A., U. Mich., 1972, Ph.D., 1981. Research analyst State of Ill., Chgo., 1968-69; psychologist Med. Student Mental Health Service U. Mich., Ann Arbor, 1977-80, postdoctoral fellow in clin. psychology Adolescent Psychiatry, 1980-82, psychodiagnostic supr., 1973-77, supr. Psychol. Clinic, 1982—; pvt. practice in psychotherapy, Ann Arbor, 1980—. Fulbright grantee, U.S. Ednl. Found. in India, 1967-68. Mem. Am. Psychol. Assn., Psychologists Interested in Study of Psychoanalysis, Mich. Soc. Psychoanalytic Psychology, Mich. Psychol. Assn., Assn. Advancement of Psychology, Am. Civil Liberties Union, Mich. Oriental Art Assn. Home: 1113 Lincoln Ave Ann Arbor MI 48104 Office: 555 E William Ann Arbor MI 48109

BARBOUR, DELTA RAE, trade assn. exec.; b. Independence, Va., Apr. 28, 1937; d. Floyd McKinley an Nannie Ellen (Osborne) Boyer; student Strayer Bus. Coll., 1974-76, Prince Georges County Community Coll., 1976-77. Acct., Structural Clay Products Inst., Washington, 1962-66; office mgr. Joseph T. Hunt, D.D.S., Henderson, N.C., 1966-69, McGaughy, Marshall & McMillan, Washington, 1969-74; comptroller Sugar Assn., Inc., Washington, 1974—, asst. corp. sec., 1974—; realtor Century 21 Jack Justice Real Estate, Lanham, Md., 1978—. Mem. polit. action com. Prince Georges County Real Estate Bd., 1977-78. Mem. Nat. Soc. Notaries, Nat. Assn. Female Execs., Nat. Assn. Realtors, Prince Georges County Bd. Realtors, Am. Soc. Assn. Execs., Washington Soc. Assn. Execs. Democrat. Presbyterian. Club: Nat. Dem. Home: 9411 Van Buren St Lanham MD 20706 Office: 1511 K St Washington DC 20005

BARBOZA-CLARK, FRANCES E., med. technologist; b. Jersey City, June 22, 1938; d. Lawrence and Clementina Frances (Lopes) Barboza; diploma med. tech. Coll. Medicine and Dentistry N.J.-Rutgers U., 1970; div.; children—Donald, Renee, Edward. Chem. lab. technician, 1956-57; histology technician Coll. Medicine and Dentistry N.J.-Rutgers U. Med. Sch., 1969-72, research asst., 1972-75, med. technologist, 1975-81, sr. med. technologist, 1981—, also tchr., trainer students, supr. historology lab. Mem. Am. Soc. Clin. Pathologists (registered affiliate), Am. Soc. Med. Tech., Nat. Soc. Histotech., N.J. Soc. Histotech. (charter), NOW (chpt. coordinator 1979-81). Office: U Medicine and Dentistry NJ-Rutgers U Med Sch PO Box 101 Piscataway NJ 08854

BARCHAS, PATRICIA RUTH, sociologist; b. Chickasha, Okla., July 26, 1934; d. Bill Doherty and Jimmie Ione (Hendricks) Corbitt; B.A., Pomona Coll., 1956; postgrad. U. Chgo., 1961-62; Ph.D., Stanford U., 1971; m. Jack David Barchas, Feb. 9, 1957; 1 son, Isaac Doherty. Faculty, Stanford (Calif.) U., 1971—, dir. program in sociophysiology Lab. of Social Research, asst. prof. sociology and (courtesy) psychiatry and behavioral scis., 1975—; mem. Dept. Mental Health Research Panel, State of Ill., 1976-79; cons., co-author Nat. Inst. Neurol. Diseases report to Congress on biol. aspects of aggression, 1976; panel mem., co-author Inst. Medicine of Nat. Acad. Scis. report on psychobiol. research and mental health, 1978, biol. aspects of stress, 1980. Grantee, Harry Frank Guggenheim, 1972-73, Nat. Inst. Alcohol Research, 1972-73, Spencer Found., 1977-78; recipient Stanford U. research devel. award, 1971; spl. contract Office Naval Research, 1974, 79-82. Mem. Am. Sociol. Assn., AAAS, N.Y. Acad. Scis., Acad. Behavioral Medicine, Soc. Psychophysiol. Research, AAUP. Contbr. articles to profl. publs. Home: 669 Mirada Ave Stanford CA 94305 Office: Dept Sociology Stanford U Stanford CA 94305

BARCLAY, LISA KURCZ, psychologist, educator; b. Vienna, Austria, June 18, 1932; came to U.S., 1941, naturalized, 1947; d. Rudolf and Maria Elizabeth (Rixner) Kurcz; A.B. with honors, U. Mich., 1953, M.A., 1954; M.A.Ed., Idaho State U., 1964; Ph.D. (United Cerebral Palsy Assn. Am. fellow), Stanford U., 1969; m. James Ralph Barclay, Dec. 29, 1954; children—Anne, Robert, Gregory, Christopher. Instr., psychometrist Idaho State U., Pocatello, 1962-64; psychologist Pleasanton (Calif.) Schs., 1965-66, Castro Valley (Calif.) Schs., 1969; instr. Calif. State U., Hayward, 1966-67; asso. research scientist Am. Insts. for Research, Palo Alto, Calif., 1967-68; asst. prof. dept. human devel. and family relations U. Ky., Lexington, 1969-73, asso. prof. dept. family studies, 1973—; cons. in field. Bd. dirs. United Cerebral Palsy of the Bluegrass, 1970—; apptd. mem. Ky. Children's Adv. Council, 1972-74, Ky. Citizens Adv. Council to Bur. Social Services, 1974-79. Mem. Am. Psychol. Assn., Am. Ednl. Research Assn., Soc. Research in Child Devel., Ky. Psychol. Assn., Ky. Assn. Psychology in Schs., Ky. Citizens for Child Devel., Children's Def. Fund. Democrat. Episcopalian. Author: (with J.R. Barclay, et al) Appraising Individual Differences in the Elementary School Classroom: A Manual for the Barclay Classroom Climate Inventory, 1972; (with J.R. Barclay) The Barclay Early Childhood Assessment Guide, 1973; contbr. articles to profl. publs. Home: 1672 Linstead Dr Lexington KY 40504 Office: Dept Family Studies Univ Ky 315 Funkhouser Bldg Lexington KY 40506

BARD, ELIZABETH (ERZSEBET) MAZAK, psychologist, author; b. Akron, Ohio, June 25, 1947; d. Stephen George and Waldene B. (Williams) Mazak; B.A. in Fine Arts, U. Akron, 1968, M.S. in Reading Disabilities, 1972, M.A. in Sch. Psychology, 1976, Ph.D., 1980; postgrad. Kent State U., 1977-78, Gesell Inst., 1978; m. David Marshall Bard, Aug. 19, 1968. Tchr. public schs. Nantucket Island, Mass., 1968-70, Copley, Ohio, 1971-74; intern sch. psychologist Summit County, Ohio, 1975-76; psychologist Akron (Ohio) Public Schs., 1977—; guest lectr. U. Akron, 1977—; psychol. tester State Dept. Ohio, summer, 1980; pvt. practice psychoednl. assessment, Akron, 1980—; author: The Cat-IQ Test, 1980, The Pet Personality Test, 1981. Vol. All Am. Soap Box Derby, Akron, 1980-81, Children's Hosp., Akron, 1976-81. Recipient Cert. Appreciation Kiwanis Club, 1980. Mem. Nat. Assn. Sch. Psychology, Am. Psychol. Assn., Ohio Sch. Psychology Assn., Internat. Assn. Sch. Psychology, Kent/Akron Area Sch. Psychologist Assn., Tau Kappa Phi. Roman Catholic. Clubs: Akron Women's City, Univ., Turkeyfoot Island, Buchtells. Home: 4498 Lahm Dr Akron OH 44319 Office: 70 N Broadway St Akron OH 44308

BARDARSON, DOT EDNA, artist; b. Port Washington, N.Y., Dec. 27, 1932; d. Vernon Edwin and Blanche Ione Day; A.A., Lasell Jr. Coll., 1953; student U. Wash., 1954-56; m. Linne Rolf Bardarson, June 12, 1954; children—Dori Hollingsworth, Blaine, Rolf. Artist in residence Seward (Alaska) Schs., 1974, Petersburg and Point Hope (Alaska) Schs., 1977; exhibited one-person shows Kenai Mall, 1973, 76, Color Center, 1974, Artique, Anchorage, 1977, Old Church Gallery, Seward, Alaska, 1978, 79, The Frameworks, Anchorage, 1978, Limited Edition Gallery, Homer, Alaska, 1979, Rendezvous Gallery, Anchorage, 1979; exhibited group shows Seward Art Guild, 1971-72, Governor's Mansion, 1974-79, Art, Inc., Anchorage, 1977, 78, Advt. Fedn. Alaska, 1977; Alaska Watercolor Soc. Christmas Show, 1977, 78, 80, 81, also Ann. show, 1976-79, Rendezvous Gallery Statewide Watercolor Invitational, 1979, Frameworks, 1979, Artique, 1979, Breeze Inn, 1980, 81, Llubs Gallery, Edmonds, Wash., 1982, Lt. Gov.'s Office, 1980, 81, 82. commd. Fairbanks Public Safety Bldg., 1980; works on display Artique, Rendezvous Gallery, Frameworks, Faces, Places and Things, Juneau, Alaska, Alexander's, Sitka, Alaska, Limited Edition, Old Church Gallery, Rogue's Gallery, Moose Pass, Alaska, Art Inc., Anchorage, Bagoy Gallery, Anchorage, others. Bd. dirs. Alaska State Council on the Arts, 1976—; bd. dirs. Seward Concert Assn., Arts Seward. Recipient awards Beta Sigma Phi ann., 1973, 76, Alaska Contemporary Art Bank, 1978, 79, All Alaska Juried Show, 1977, 79, 82, Resurrection Bay Juried Show, 1978-81, Baca Juried Show, 1977, 79. Mem. Alaska Northwest watercolor socs., Ressurrection Bay Art Guild (pres. 1978-80), Port City Players, Seattle Classic Guitar Soc. Address: PO Box 636 Seward AK 99664

BARDIN, SARAH JEANETTE ZIEGLER, psychologist; b. East Cleveland, Ohio, Mar. 6, 1919; d. John Sherman and Mary White (Morton) Ziegler; B.F.A., Ohio U., Athens, 1943; student Boston Sch. Occupational Therapy, 1944; M.A. in Psychology, E. Carolina Coll., 1964; postgrad. N.C. State U., 1972—, doctoral candidate, 1975—; m. Benjamin Hume Bardin, Oct. 6, 1945; children—Jefferson Davis, Joan Lucille Bardin Lester, John Arthur. Occupational therapist hosps. in W.Va. and Va., 1945-46, 56-58; instr. Huntington (W.Va.) Galleries, 1953-56, Atlantic Christian Coll., Wilson, N.C., 1959-62, E. Carolina U., 1968, Lenoir Community Coll., Kinston, N.C., 1975-77; psychologist Wilson County and City Schs., 1966-68, Wilson-Greene Mental Health Center, 1968-70, Caswell Center, Kinston, 1970-72; self-employed psychol. examiner, Wilson, 1970—; dir. psychol. services Duplin County schs., Kenansville, N.C., 1976-77; cons. Howell's Child Care Center, Goldsboro, N.C., 1974-77; cons. Baptist Children's Homes of N.C., Kinston, 1974-81; co-founder, practitioner Wilson Psychol. Assos., P.A., 1977, owner, pres., 1981—. Lic. psychol. examiner, cert. sch. psychologist. Mem. Am., N.C. psychol. assns., Assn. Eastern N.C. Psychologists (sec.-treas. 1971-75, v.p., 1976-77, pres. 1978-79), Nat. Assn. Sch. Psychologists N.C. Sch. Psychology Assn., Am. Assn. Mental Deficiency, Nat. Acad. Neuropsychologists. Club: Altrusa. Home: 711 Trinity Dr Wilson NC 27893 Office: 601 W Nash St Wilson NC 27893

BARDO, PAMELA PIERREPONT, museum curator; b. Albany, N.Y., Feb. 4, 1947; d. August John and Beatrice (Varney) Bardo; B.A., Briarcliff Coll., 1969; M.A., U. Pitts., 1971. Teaching asst. U. Pitts., 1969-70; dir. Univ. Art Gallery U. Pitts., 1972-73; curator collections New Orleans Mus. Art, 1973-75, curator decorative arts, 1975—. Mem., sec. Save Venice, Inc., 1974—. Mem. Western Pa. Episcopal Bishop's Commn. Higher Edn., 1972-73. Bd. dirs., sec. Italian Art and Landscape Found., Pitts., 1972-73. Mem. Coll. Art Assn. Am., Am. Assn. Museums, Am. Assn. U. Profs., Brit. Nat. Trust. Democrat. Episcopalian. Home: 638 W Kemper Pl Chicago IL 60614

BARDON, JANE ELIAS, economist; b. Athens, Greece, Sept. 5, 1951; came to U.S., 1971, naturalized, 1977; d. Elias Theophanes and Apollonia (Jafetis) Bardouniotis; student (scholar) Bologna Center, Johns Hopkins U., 1974-75; B.A. (Pres.'s scholar), Temple U., 1974, M.A., 1977, Ph.D., 1982. Instr., Greek, German, English as fgn. lang., Athens, Greece, 1969; in charge deposits Nea Ionia br. Nat. Bank of Greece, 1970; research asst. econs. dept. Temple U., Phila., 1975-78, lectr. econs., 1979-80, supr. part-time faculty, econs. dept., 1979-80; economist div. internat. prices Bur. Labor Stats., Dept. Labor, Washington, 1980-81; economist internat. trade adminstrn. Dept. Commerce, Washington, 1981—. Mem. Am. Econ. Assn., NOW, Soc. Govt. Economists, Western Econ. Assn., Assn. Grad. Students in Econs. Temple U. (past pres.), Phi Beta Kappa, Omicron Delta Epsilon. Democrat. Home: 1420 N St NW Washington DC 20005 Office: Dept Commerce Washington DC 20230

BARDWICK, JUDITH MARCIA, educator; b. N.Y.C., Jan. 16, 1933; d. Abraham and Ethel (Krinsky) Hardis; B.S., Purdue U., 1954; M.S., Cornell U., 1955; Ph.D., U. Mich., 1964; m. John Bardwick, III, Dec. 18, 1954 (div.); children—Jennifer, Peter, Deborah. Lectr., U. Mich., Ann Arbor, 1964-67, asst. prof. psychology, 1967-71, asso. prof., 1971-75, prof., 1975—, asso. dean, 1977—; mem. population research study group NIH, 1971-75. Mem. social sci. adv. com. Planned Parenthood Am., 1973. Fellow Am. Psychol. Assn.; mem. Midwest Psychol. Assn., N.Y. Acad. Sci., Am. Psychosomatic Soc., Phi Beta Kappa. Author: Psychology of Women, 1971; In Transition, 1979; editor: Readings in the Psychology of Women, 1972; mem. editorial bd. Women's Studies, 1973—, Psychology of Women quar., 1975—; contbr. articles to profl. jours. Home: 2132 Spruceway Ln Ann Arbor MI 48103 Office: U Mich Ann Arbor MI 48109

BAREIS, BEVERLIE ELAINE, nurse; b. Rockland, Maine, July 22, 1925; d. Earle Raymond and Margaret Verrel (Long) Conant; R.N., New Eng. Deaconess Hosp., Boston, 1946; B.S. in Health Sci., Calif. State U., Northridge, 1976; M.A., Calif. State U., Los Angeles, 1981; m. David W. Bareis, Feb. 8, 1947; children—Ellen Ruth Bareis Scully, Karl Frederick, Paul Arthur, Kathilynn Bareis Marquette. Inservice supr. Motion Picture Country Hosp., Woodland Hills, Calif., 1960-66; nursing educator Los Angeles City Unified Schs., 1965—; staff devel. coordinator, then dir. community relations Brotman Meml. Hosp., Culver City, Calif., 1970-77; asst. dir. nursing and health programs ARC, 1978-80; asst. prof. Calif. State U., Los Angeles, part-time, 1981—; nursing educator paramed. br. Abram Friedman Occupational Center, Los Angeles 1980—. Recipient Gold medal Los Angeles County Heart Assn., 1966, Clara Barton medal ARC, 1972. Mem. Am. Public Health Assn., Nat. League Nursing, NEA, Los Angeles County Heart Assn., Am. Diabetic Assn., Sex. Edn. and Info. Council U.S., New Eng. Deaconness Hosp. Alumnae Assn., Phi Kappa Phi. Address: Santa Monica CA 90402

BARENHOLTZ, BARBARA LEE, furniture store exec.; b. St. Louis, Aug. 7, 1931; d. William Bertrand and Bernice (Susman) Lee; B.S., U. Mo., Columbia, 1953; m. Eugene S. Barenholtz, Jan. 3, 1954, (dec.); children—Robert, Betsy, Bill, Barbie. Mem. coll. bd. staff Mademoiselle Mag., Scruggs, Vandervoort, Barney, St. Louis, from 1952; pres. Barenholtz Furniture Co., Inc., Litchfield, Ill., 1977—. Pres., Madison Park PTA, Litchfield, Ill., 1964; pres. St. Francis Hosp. Aux., Litchfield, Ill., 1973. Mem. Retail Mktg. Guild. Jewish. Clubs: Litchfield Country, Missour Athletic. Home: 1217 E Union Ave Litchfield IL 62056 Office: Barenholtz Furniture Co 319 N State St Litchfield IL 62056

BARFOOT, SUSAN GRACE, social worker; b. Montgomery County, Ala., Aug. 24, 1946; d. Woodrow and Elma (Youngblood) B.; B.S., U. Ala., 1968, M.S.W., 1970, D.S.W., 1982. Psychiat. social worker N.Central Ala. Mental Health Center, Decatur, 1970-71; dir. social work, occupational/recreational therapy depts. Pineview Hosp., Hartselle, Ala., 1971-79; social worker VA Med. Center, Tuscaloosa, Ala., 1979—; field instr. U. Ala. Sch. Social Work, 1972-76, adj. instr. social work, 1975—, leader Foster Parent Specialized Care Workshop, 1978; field instr. Calhoun Community Coll., Decatur, 1972-76, Auburn (Ala.) U., 1976; cons. Falkville (Ala.) Nursing Home, 1976—. Vol. profl. backup N.Central Ala. Crisis Call Center, 1970-74; mem. home health services task force Pub. Health Dept., Birmingham, Ala., 1975-76; active Decatur Community Services Planning Council; bd. dirs. N.Central Ala. Regional Council, Ala. Council on Alcoholism; mem. profl. adv. bd. Morgan County Assn. for Mental Health, 1977; mem. profl. adv. council Home Health Agy., Tri-County Health Dept.; mem. adv. com. John C. Calhoun Jr. Coll. and Tech. Sch., Morgan County Dept. Pensions and Security; mem. adv. bd. Lakeshore Rehab. Hosp., Birmingham. First place winner Extendicare, Inc. Regional Achievement Contest, 1972. Mem. Nat. Assn. Social Workers (sec. Tenn. Valley unit. 1972-74, Social Worker of Year, Tenn. Valley unit 1974, chmn. state health com. 1972-75, state treas. 1976—), Nat. Therapeutic Recreation Soc., Ala. Soc. Hosp. Social Workers, Ala. Conf. Social Work (chmn. resolutions com.). Democrat. Baptist. Author: (with Mary Darner and Jack Sellers) Guidelines for Social Work Consultation to Medical Facilities, 1972; contbg. author: Where the Fun Is U.S.A., 1968. Home: 1030 53d Ave E Tuscaloosa AL 35404 Office: Social Work Dept VA Med Center Tuscaloosa AL 35401

BARHAM, NANCY WILDERMUTH, advt. account exec.; b. Bklyn., Aug. 2, 1956; d. George Frederick and Janet Neumann Wildermuth; student Centenary Coll., 1974-75; B.B.A. cum laude, Adelphi U., 1980; m. Blaine Michael Barham, June 6, 1981. Mktg. adminstr., permissions editor Holt, Rinehart and Winston, CBS, Inc., N.Y.C., 1976-78, 78-79; account exec. N.Y. Yellow Pages, Inc., N.Y.C., 1980-81; account exec. Ad Forum, Inc., N.Y.C., 1981, P.T.N. Pub. Corp., Woodbury, N.Y., 1982—. Mem. Am. Mktg. Assn., Mktg. and Advt. Club (pres.), Advt. Club N.Y., L.I. Advt. Club, Adelphi U. Alumni (dir.). Home: 620 Brooklyn Ave New Hyde Park NY 11040

BARHAM, PATTE, publisher, author, columnist; b. Los Angeles; d. Dr. Frank Barham (decd.) and Princess Jessica Meskhi Gleboff; student U. So. Calif., U. Ariz.; Litt.D., Trinity So. Bible Coll. war corr. Los Angeles Herald Express (Examiner), Korea; spl. features writer Hearst Predate-Ky. Features Syndicate. Former mem. U.S. Olympic Com.; life mem. AAU, former v.p. public relations; mem. costume council Los Angeles County Mus.; mem. internat. com. So. Calif. Philharmonic. Decorated dame Sovereign Order of Alfred the Great, grand cross, patron of honor; compagne de la Couronne d'Epines, Ancien Abbaye-Principaute de San Luigi. Mem. Nat. League Am. Pen Women, Muses-Alliance, Aviation Space Writers, English Speaking Union, DAR, St. Anne's Hosp. Guild, Social Service Aux., Delta Gamma. Clubs: Outrigger Canoe, Waikiki Yacht (Hawaii); Wilshire Country, Ebell (Los Angeles); Nat. Press (Washington, D.C.); Metropolitan (N.Y.C.); St. James (London); Tokyo Corrs.; Round the World; Gamble House (U. So. Calif.). Author: Pin up Poems; Rasputin: The Man behind the Myth. Address: 100 Fremont Pl Los Angeles CA 90005

BARI, RUTH AARONSON, mathematician, educator; b. Bklyn., Nov. 17, 1917; d. Israel and Becky (Gursky) Aaronson; B.A., Bklyn. Coll., 1939; M.A., Johns Hopkins U., 1943, Ph.D., 1966; m. Arthur Bari, Nov. 22, 1940; children—Gina, Judi, Martha. Jr. instr. Johns Hopkins U., 1941-43; tech. asst. Bell Telephone Lab., 1943-46; instr. U. Md., 1961-66; asst. prof., assoc. prof. math. George Washington U., Washington, 1966-76, prof., 1977—. Mem. Am. Math. Soc., Math. Soc. Am., AAAS, Assn. for Women in Math. Co-editor: Graphs and Combinatorics, 1973; contbr. tech. papers to publs.; invited lectr. profl. confs. Office: George Washington Univ Washington DC 20052

BARITOT, ELLEN EHLE, vision therapist; b. Phila., Dec. 6, 1944; d. Harry A. Ehle and Emily (Lewis) Jones; B.A., Goddard Coll., 1966; M.Ed. (Ford Found. grantee), George Washington U., 1967. Tchr., Md. and Pa., 1967-71; founding co-partner Optometric Vision Therapy Practice, Novato, Calif., dir. vision therapy, 1974-78; vision cons. to pvt. groups, 1974-79; vision therapist Arena Sch., San Rafael, Calif., 1979—; cons. in field; lectr. profl. and civic groups. Mem. Optometric Extension Program, Marin County Optometric Study Group. Designer, founder first vision therapy program in sch. for learning disabled children. Home: 117 E Richmond Ave Point Richmond CA 94801 Office: Arena School 1314 Lincoln Ave San Rafael CA 94903

BARKER, BARBARA ELIZABETH, cell biologist; b. Providence, Sept. 14, 1930; d. Gilbert H. and Margaret H. (Bloomfield) B.; B.S., U. R.I., 1952, Ph.D., 1965; M.S., Brown U., 1956. Cell biologist in pathology R.I. Hosp., Providence 1972—, co-dir. spl. hematology-immunology, 1972—, assoc. dir. hematology, 1978—; asst. prof. pathology Brown U., 1974-77, assoc. prof., 1977—; vis. specialist Care-Medico, Afghanistan, 1974-76, Algeria, 1962. Recipient 10-yr. service award Care Medico, 1972; 9 NIH and Am. Cancer Soc. grants, 1961-81. Mem. Am. Assn. Cell Biology, Sigma Xi. Contbr. articles on hematology to sci. jours. Co-discoverer pokeweed mitogen, 1964. Office: 593 Eddy St Providence RI 02902

BARKER, LAURA FAYE, nursing home adminstr.; b. Franklin Parish, La., Feb. 15, 1937; d. John Edward and Evielean (Welch) Russell; lic. practical nurse Alexandria Trade Sch., 1969; m. George Dilley, Oct. 13, 1953 (div.); children—John Dale, Billy Wayne; m. 2d, Eddie Wells, 1964; m. 3d, Columbus Barker, 1968. Aide, Riley's Nursing Home, Winnsboro, La., 1950-53, various nursing homes, La. and Calif., 1953-68; adminstr. Harrisonburg (La.) Nursing Home 1979—. Mem. La. Nursing Home Assn. Democrat. Mem. United Pentecostal Ch. Home: PO Box 308 Harrisonburg LA 71340

BARKER, MARTHA SMITH, nurse, educator; b. Columbia, S.C., Mar. 30, 1935; d. Lonnie Edward and Virginia (Faulkner) Smith; student Bob Jones U., 1953-54; R.N., Columbia (S.C.) Hosp. Sch. Nursing, 1957;; B.S. in Nursing, Med. U. S.C., 1980; div.; 1 dau., Michele de Calverhall. Instr., Columbia (S.C.) Hosp. Sch. Nursing, 1957-60; instr. Med. U. S.C. Sch. Nursing, 1960-67, dir. practical nurse program Coll. Allied Health Scis., 1967—, asst. prof., 1967—. Active, Isle of Palms Republican Com., 1965—. Federal grantee, 1967—. Mem. Am. Nurses Assn., Nat. League Nursing. Republican. Baptist. Home: 35 32d Ave Isle of Palms SC 29451 Office: Med U SC 171 Ashley Ave Charleston SC 29403

BARKER, NANCY NICHOLS, historian, educator; b. Mt. Vernon, N.Y., Dec. 26, 1925; B.A., Vassar Coll., 1946; M.A., U. Pa., 1947, Ph.D., 1955; m. 1950. Asst. instr. U. Pa., 1948-49; instr. U. Del., 1949-50; lectr. modern European history, 1955-67; asst. prof. to assoc. prof. history U. Tex., Austin, 1967-72, prof. history, 1972—. Tex. Research Inst. Research grantee, 1967-68; recipient Gilbert Chinard prize, 1972, Summerfield G. Roberts award, 1972. Mem. Am. History Assn., Soc. French Hist. Studies. Author: Distaff Diplomacy: The Empress Eugenie and the Foreign Policy of the Second Empire, 1967; editor (with others) Diplomacy in an Age of Nationalism: Essays in Honor of Lynn Marshall Case, Martinus Nijhoff, 1971; Recognition, Rupture and Reconciliation, Vol. I, 1971; Mission Miscarried, Vol. II, 1973; contbr. articles to profl. jours. Office: Dept of History University of Texas Austin TX 78712 *

BARKLEY, LINDA DOROTHY, reliability engr.; b. San Diego, Dec. 12, 1951; d. James Falls and Helen Patricia (Yoo) B.; B.A., U. San Diego, 1974; M.S., Loyola Marymount U., 1980. Project engr. Hughes Aircraft Co., El Segundo, Calif., 1978—; So. Calif. coordinator women and math. program, 1979—. Recipient Sci. award Bausch and Lomb, 1970. Mem. Soc. Women Engrs., Assn. Women in Math., Am. Math. Soc., Soc. Indsl. and Applied Math., Math./Sci. Interchange-Los Angeles, Women's Sports Found., Alumnae Assn. Acad. Our Lady of Peace, Alumni Assn. U. San Diego, Pi Mu Epsilon. Roman Catholic. Office: Hughes Aircraft Co PO Box 92919 Bldg S32/MS C314 Los Angeles CA 90009

BARKLEY, VADA LEE, educator; b. Union, Ark., Sept. 28, 1919; d. Robert Lee and Ada H. (Matheson) Beard; A.B., Bethany Nazarene Coll., 1942; M.A., U. Okla., 1950; m. Arthur E. Barkley, June 2, 1950. Tchr. pub. schs., Carnegie, Okla., 1942-43, Alden, Okla., 1943-44, Mustang, Okla., 1956-59, Hobart, Okla., 1962-69; instr. Bethany Nazarene Coll., 1946-50; exec. dir. S.W. Okla. Council Girl Scouts U.S., Hobart, 1959-61; instr. El Reno Jr. Coll., 1969—, chmn. communicative arts div., 1976-81; adj. faculty Bethany Nazarene Coll., 1982—. Republican. Mem. Ch. of Nazarene. Home: 2625 N Markwell Bethany OK 73008 Office: Bethany Nazarene Coll 6729 NW 39th Expressway Bethany OK 73008

BARKSDALE, AMELIA HOBBS, journalist; b. Blakely, Ga., July 9, 1912; d. Ralph Mortimer and Irene (Purifoy) Hobbs; edn. cert. Ga. State Coll. for Women, Milledgeville; diploma Perry Bus. Sch., extension br., Blakely, 1944; m. William Marcine Barksdale, Apr. 13, 1935; children—Bill, Thomas, Jimmy, Beverly (dec.). Corr., Albany (Ga.) Herald, 1946—, Dothan (Ala.) Eagle, 1946—, Columbus (Ga.) Enquirer, 1964—, Atlanta Constn., 1957—; soc. editor Early County News, Blakely, 1964-73; local news editor, newscaster, bookkeeper Sta. WBBK, Blakely, 1959-64; editor Early County Sch. Post, 1971-76. Pres., Blakely PTA, 1947; chmn. restoration and preservation com. Blakely Bicentennial Com., 1976. Recipient various service awards. Mem. DAR (past chpt. pres.), Early County Hist. Soc. (chmn. public relations 1968-82), Ga. PTA (life), Kolomoki Soc., Court Square Arts Council. Baptist. Clubs: Blakely Woman's (past trustee, public relations chmn.), Pilots (hon. mem., historian). Contbr. articles to hist. books and jours. Address: PO Box 48 Blakely GA 31723

BARKSDALE, DIXIE LEE BARKER, assn. exec.; b. Elsinore, Utah, May 25, 1930; d. Aaron Glen and Fawn Lenore (Braithwaite) Whitney; student Brigham Young U., Provo, Utah, 1956, Utah State U., 1957; m. Bruce W. Barksdale; children—Viviann Rose, Vicki Joan Barker, Whitney Dwain Barker. Pres., gen. mgr. Moab Broadcasting and TV Corp., 1969-77; dir. community devel. Grand County (Utah), Moab, 1976-81; exec. dir. Canyonlands Travel Region, 1976-81; econ. devel. cons. Mountainland Assn. Govts., 1981—. Bd. dirs. Utah Econ. and Indsl. Devel., 1969—, Utah Assn. Travel Regions, 1976-81; mem. Moab City Council, 1976-80; chmn. Grand County Democratic Com., 1968-69, Moab Drug and Alcohol Adv. Bd., 1973; mem. multiple-use adv. bd. Bur. Land Mgmt., 1980-82; mem. Provo City Planning Commn., 1982—, Provo City Site Plan Rev. Bd., 1982—. Named Woman of Yr., Epsilon Sigma Alpha, 1960, Friend of Utah, State of Utah, 1978. Mem. Moab C. of C. (pres. 1974-75), Provo C. of C. (indsl. devel. com. 1981—), Canyonlands Natural History Assn. (chmn. 1979-81), Utah Indsl. Devel. Execs. Assn. Democrat. Mormon. Club: Moab Women's Lit. (pres. 1959-60). Address: 110 West Pkwy Provo UT 84604

BARKSDALE, ELOISE EVANS, poet; b. Dardanelle, Ark., Aug. 1, 1906; d. Lewis Allen and Nelle (Goodman) Evans; student Central Bapt. Coll., 1924-25, U. Ark., 1925-26, Ark. Poly. Coll., 1929; m. William Donoho Barksdale, June 1, 1930; children—William Evans, Lewis Donoho. Tchr. music Dardanelle Public Schs., 1926-28; feature writer, reporter Ark. Democrat, Little Rock, 1929-30; organist chs. and temples, Ark., 1930-60; tchr. Fort Smith (Ark.) Public Schs., 1958-66; book reviewer S.W. Times Record, Fort Smith, 1965-68; author: (poetry) Remembering is Music, 1968 (Poets Roundtable award); poems in mags., newspapers and anthologies. Named Poet of the Present in Ark., 1968. Mem. Ark. State Pioneers Assn., (pres. chpt. 1972-77), Poets Roundtable Ark., Nat. League Am. Pen Women (pres. Fort Smith br. 1974-76), Roundtable Poets Fort Smith (pres. 1962-78), Haiku Soc. Am., DAR, PEO, Chi Omega Alumni Assn. Methodist. Home: 2515 S N St Fort Smith AR 72901

BARKSDALE, MILDRED WHITE, coll. dean; b. Kemper County, Miss., Dec. 27, 1922; d. James Rufus and Zellie (Riley) White; B.S. in Elem. Edn., Jackson (Miss.) State U., 1945; M.S. in Counseling Psychology, Ind. U., Bloomington, 1952, Ed.D. in Ednl. Psychology, 1958; m. Richard K. Barksdale, Apr. 15, 1960; children—James, Calvin, Adrienne. Mem. faculty spl. edn. N.C. Coll., Durham, 1952-60, Atlanta U., 1960-67, Ga. State U., Atlanta, 1967-71; asst. dean Coll. Liberal Arts, U. Ill., Champaign-Urbana, 1971—; cons. in field. Election judge Champaign County (Ill.), 1981-82. So. Edn. Found. fellow, 1958. Mem. Urban League, LWV, Pi Lambda Theta, Kappa Delta Epsilon, Alpha Lambda Delta. Democrat. Club: Zonta. Author articles in field. Home: 2207 Wyld Dr Urbana IL 61801 Office: 270 Lincoln Hall 702 S Wright St Urbana IL 61801

BARLIN, CAROLE ARLENE, ednl. adminstr.; b. Oakland, Calif., Nov. 7, 1935; d. Carl Christian and Leona Lillian (Vielhauer) Barlin; B.A., U. Calif., Berkeley, 1958; M.S., U. Redlands, 1971; 1 dau., Lizette Leona Swanson. Tchr., San Francisco Unified Sch. Dist., 1966-69, Los Angeles County Supt. Schs., 1971-74, asst. prin., 1974-76, prin., 1976, personnel coordinator, 1976—; lectr. —The Profl. Woman—. Mem. Assn. of Calif. Sch. Adminstrs. (officer 1976-82), Assn. of Los Angeles County Sch. Adminstrs. (pres. 1981-82), Women in Ednl. Leadership, Am. Speech and Hearing Assn. Office: 9300 E Imperial Hwy Downey CA 90242

BARLOW, ANNE LOUISE, pediatrician, med. research adminstr.; b. Skipton-in-Craven, Eng., Jan. 28, 1925; came to U.S., 1951, naturalized, 1954; grad. London (Royal Free Hosp.) Sch. of Medicine for Women, 1948; M.D., U. London, 1948; diploma in child health, Royal Colls. of Eng., 1950; M.P.H. with honors, Yale U., 1952; m. Howard Cadwell, May 19, 1951; children—Barbara Anne, John James Stewart; m. 2d, Alistair Ramsay, Dec. 19, 1969. House physician North Lonsdale Hosp., Barrow-in-Furness, Lancashire, Eng., 1948-49; house surgeon Royal Infirmary, Glasgow, Scotland, 1949; resident to profl. unit of child health Royal Hosp. for Sick Children, Glasgow, 1949-1950; jr. hosp. med. officer Knightswood Infectious Diseases Hosp., Glasgow, 1950; Rotary Found. Internat. fellow, U. Toronto (Ont., Can.) Med. Sch., 1950-51; research asst. Yale U. Sch. Public Health, New Haven, 1952-53; clinic physician in cancer prevention, Arlington, Va., part-time, 1953-54; resident, staff physician William H. Maybury Tb Sanatorium, Northville, Mich., 1954-56; research dir. Detroit Feeding Study with the Detroit City Health Dept., 1954-56; research asst., instr. sch. health U. Pitts. Grad. Sch. Public Health, 1957-62; pvt. practice specializing in pediatrics, Pitts., 1959-62, mem. courtesy staff St. Margaret's Hosp., Pitts., 1959-62; research asso. TiceLab. for Tb Research, Cook County Hosp., Chgo., 1962; med. writer product info. Abbott Labs., North Chicago, Ill., 1963-66, med. specialist antibiotic medicine, 1966-68, mgr. clin. devel. pharm. products div., 1968-71, asst. med. dir., 1971-72, mgr. parenteral nutrition hosp. products div., 1972-73, med. dir., 1973-80, v.p. med. affairs, hosp. products div., 1980—; cons. maternal, child and sch. health, dir. well baby clinics, Lake County (Ill.) Health Dept., 1963-76, pres. Tb Sanatorium Bd., 1976-79, dir., pres. Lake County bd. Health, 1979—; health officer Village of N. Barrington (Ill.), 1964-67; physician-adv. Head Start Lake County Community Action Project, 1970—; chmn. profl. adv. com. Lake County Health Dept., 1972—; preceptor Pediatric Nurse Asso. Program. Bd. dirs. Heart Assn. of Lake County, 1979—, chmn. nutrition com., 1980-82, v.p., 1982—; mem. sch. bd. Grant Twp. Community High Sch. (Ill. Dist. 124), 1973-79; sec. to governing bd. Spl. Edn. Dist. of Lake County, 1977-79; asso. Nat. Coll. of Edn., Evanston, Ill., 1976—. Lic. physician, Mich., Pa., Ill.; recipient award of merit for Outstanding Contbns. to Public Health, Ill. Public Health Assn., 1975, award of Merit for Outstanding Community Service to Lake County Community Action Project, 1976; award for Outstanding and Dedicated Service as Pres., Lake County Tb Sanatorium Bd., 1979. Mem. Am. Med. Women's Assn. (councilor for orgn. and mgmt. 1977-79, treas. 1980, 1st. v.p. 1981, pres.-elect 1982), Pharm. Mfrs. Assn. (med. sect.), Lake County Med. Assn., Ill. State Med. Soc., AMA, Chgo. Network, AAAS, Sigma Xi. Contbr. numerous articles on maternal and infant care, pediatrics and nutrition; patentee high calorie solutions of low molecular weight glucose polymer mixtures useful for intravenous adminstrn. Office: D-970 Abbott Park North Chicago IL 60164

BARLOW, PAULINE, educator; b. Pflugerville, Tex., Jan. 9, 1927; d. Wesley and Scottie Lee (Jones) B.; B.S., Samuel Huston Coll., 1950; M.Ed., Prairie View A&M U., 1964; cert. edn. of deaf Tex. Woman's U., 1973; postgrad. Miss. U., 1973. Clk., St. Joseph Grand Lodge, 1950-58; matron juvenile dept. Order Eastern Star, 1958-59; counselor Sunshine Day Camp for Underprivileged Children, 1959-60; tchr. Ebenezer Child Devel. Center, 1961-62; substitute tchr. Austin Ind. Sch. Dist., 1960-61; tchr. Tex. State Blind-Deaf and Orphan Sch., Austin, 1962-66, Tex. Sch. for Deaf, Austin, 1966—. Supr., Girl Scouts U.S.A., Girls' Club. Mem. NEA, Tex. State Tchrs. Assn., Tex. Soc. Interpreters for the Deaf, Austin Interpreters for the Deaf, Delta Sigma Theta. Mem. African Methodist Episcopal Ch. Home: 4911 Russett Hill Dr Austin TX 78723

BARMEN, VIRGINIA REPPERT, sch. psychologist; b. Philipsburg, Pa., Oct. 7, 1923; d. James Harold and Eleanor (Runk) Reppert; A.B., Wellesley Coll., 1945; M.S., Tchrs. Coll., Columbia U., 1956, profl. cert., 1965; m. Carl M. Barmen, July 27, 1963; children—John, James, Douglas Wilmerding. Intern, Kings Park (N.Y.) Hosp., 1956-58; sch. psychologist Lower Valley Schs., Locust Valley, N.Y., 1958-62, Barnard Sch. for Girls, N.Y.C., 1958-62, Commack (N.Y.) Schs., 1962—; lectr., 1962—. Bd. dirs. Freedom Center, L.I. Poetry Collective, 1979-80. Mem. Am. Psychol. Assn., N.Y. Assn. Sch. Psychologists, LWV, NOW. Contbr. poetry to lit. jours. and revs.; editor Xanadu, 1980-81. Office: Commack Schools Commack NY 11725

BARNA, LILLIAN CARATTINI, supt. schs.; b. N.Y.C., Jan. 18, 1929; d. Juan and Dolores Elsie Nieves (Alicea) Carattini; A.B. Hunter Coll. 1950; M.A. San Jose State U. 1970; m. Eugene Andrew Barna, July 1, 1951; children—Craig Andrew, Keith Andrew. Tchr., N.Y.C. Sch. Dist. 1950-52; tchr. Whittier (Calif.) Sch. Dist. 1952-54, tchr. high sch. 1954-56; tchr. presch. Long Beach and Los Gatos, Calif., 1958-67; supr. early childhood edn. San Jose (Calif.) Unified Sch. Dist. 1967-72, sch. adminstr., 1972-80, supt. schs., 1980—; cons. in field. Recipient Soroptimist Internat. Woman of Yr. award 1980, Western Region Puertorican Council Achievement award 1980, Assn. Puertorican Profls. Achievement award 1981, Calif. State U. Outstanding Achievement in Edn. award 1982. Mem. Nat. Assn. Edn. Young Children, Tchrs. English to Speakers of Other Langs., Women Leaders in Edn., Calif. Reading Assn., Calif. Assn. Women Adminstrs., Assn. Calif. Sch. Adminstrs., Phi Kappa Phi, Delta Zeta. Office: 1605 Park Ave San Jose CA 95126

BARNABY, JEAN MAE, city ofcl.; b. Worcester, Mass., Feb. 4, 1928; d. John and May W. (Pengalley) MacElroy; student Cerritos Jr. Coll., 1965-66, Orange Coast Coll., 1967-68, Mount San Antonio Jr. Coll., 1981; m. Robert Davis Barnaby, June 28, 1947; children—Kathleen Anne, Jane, Suzanne Elizabeth. Sec., claims adjuster State Mut. Life Ins. Co., Worcester, 1946-50; successively police dispatcher, police matron, communications supr. City of Brea (Calif.), 1966—. Mem. Brea Police Assn. (dir. 1971-72, pres. 1970, Assn. Mem. of Yr. 1971, 73), Asso. Public Safety Communications Officers, Inc. Republican. Roman Catholic. Home: 655 N Brea Blvd Brea CA 92621 Office: 1 Civic Center Circle Brea CA 92621

BARNARD, BARBARA UNGERLEIDER (MRS. RICHARD BARNARD), bus. exec.; b. Phila.; d. Harry Eduarde and Marian (Rice) U.; B.A., Smith Coll.; postgrad. Columbia U., U. Calif. at Los Angeles; m. Donald Rosenquest (dec.); children—Nils Christopher, Elin Jordis; m. 2d, Richard Barnard, Mar. 10, 1979. Asso. producer DuMont TV, N.Y.C.; dir. TV-motion picture dept. Mary Webb Davis, Inc., Los Angeles; v.p. Robert S. Howell Assos., Los Angeles; asso. merchandising editor Harper's Bazaar, Los Angeles; pres. The FMH Co., Studio City, Calif., 1966—; costume designer; dir. advt. and promotion Dr. Pepper Bottling Co. So. Calif.; lectr. U. Calif. at Los Angeles, Calif. State U., Long Beach. Exec. bd. Assn. Retail Mgmt. Info. Systems. Mem. Assistance League So. Calif. Mem. Fashion Group, Smith Coll. Alumnae

Assn., Smith Coll. Club So. Calif. (past pres.). Address: 3525 Berry Dr Studio City CA 91604

BARNARD, ELEANOR BETTY, public relations exec.; b. Chgo., Aug. 16, 1912; d. Harry S. and Lona Ruth (Brill) Spivak; Ph.B., U. Chgo., 1933, postgrad., 1936; m. Morton John Barnard, Aug. 16, 1936; 1 son, James W. Pres., Elbar Assos., public relations and advt., Winnetka, Ill., 1974—; vol., fundraiser law-related edn., 1974—; pres. Nat. Lawyers Wives and Husbands, 1976-77, chmn. law-related edn. com., 1977—; bd. dirs. Chgo. project Constl. Rights Found.; bd. dirs. sch. state law project Loyola U. Law Sch., Chgo.; mem. standing com. Law-Related Edn. for Public, Ill. State Bar Assn.; vol. spl. com. youth edn. for citizenship Am. Bar Assn. Mem. Coalition for Law-Related Edn., LWV (asso. editor county bull. 1972-74), Sigma Delta Tau. Author: Building Bridges to the Law, 1981; also articles, pamphlets in field. Address: 228 Woodlawn Ave Winnetka IL 60093

BARNARD, FRANCES FLYNN, civic worker; b. Fort Worth, Tex., Sept. 16, 1938; d. Elgate Daniel and Effie Danella (Ross) Hitch; B.S.R., Tex. Wesleyan U., 1975; postgrad. Tex. Christian U., 1975-77; m. Doyle Graves Flynn, June 12, 1958 (dec.); children—Stehlin, Shari, Shareese, Shawn; m. 2d, William Gene Barnard, Aug. 13, 1979. Employment developer City of Fort Worth, 1978-80; exec. dir. Am. Med. Consumers, Fort Worth, 1977-80; field dir. Circle T council Girl Scouts U.S.A., Fort Worth, 1980-81; cons. women's affairs; devel. specialist, Cassata Learning Center, 1981-82; bd. dirs. Widowed Persons Services, 1978-80; mem. task force Area 5 Health Systems Agy. Mem. Assn. Girl Scout Exec. Staff, AAUW, Am. Soc. Tng. and Devel., Widowed Persons Services, Hospice Assn., Alpha Kappa Delta. Roman Catholic. Democrat. Club: Order Eastern Star. Home: 6513 Armando St Fort Worth TX 76133

BARNARD, KATHLEEN RAINWATER, educator; b. Wayne City, Ill., Dec. 28, 1927; d. Roy and Nina (Edmison) Rainwater; B.S., So. Ill. U., 1949, M.S., 1953; postgrad. Ind. U., 1953; Ph.D., U. Tex., 1959; m. Donald L. Barnard, Aug. 17, 1947 (div. Mar. 1973); children—Kimberly, Jill. Tchr. public high sch. Wayne City, 1946-51; faculty asst. and lectr. Vocat. Tech. Inst., So. Ill. U., Carbondale, 1951-53; lectr. bus. edn. Northwestern U., Chgo., 1953-55; chmn. dept. bus. edn. San Antonio Coll., 1955-60; chmn. dept. bus., tchr. edn. DePaul U., Chgo., 1960-62; chmn. dept. bus. adminstrn. Chgo. City Coll., 1962-67, prof., 1968—. Cons. edn. and tng. div. Continental Ill. Nat. Bank & Trust Co., Chgo., 1967, Victor Corp., 1965—, First Nat. Bank Chgo., 1974; ednl. cons. Oak Park Pub. Schs., 1969-70. Exec. sec. bd. dirs. Coll. and Univ. Credit Union, 1975-78. Mem. Chgo. Assn. Commerce and Industry (edn., mgmt. coms.), Adminstrv. Mgmt. Soc. (edn., mgmt. coms.), Nat. Bus. Edn. Assn., Chgo. Bus. Edn. Assn., Small Bus. Opportunities Corp. (mgmt. devel. com.), Nat., North Central bus. edn. assns., Delta Kappa Gamma, Phi Lambda Theta, Pi Omega Pi, Alpha Delta Pi (sponsor), Sigma Phi (sponsor, pres. Alpha Theta chpt. 1958), Delta Pi Epsilon. Contbg. author: College Typewriting, 1960; Business Correspondence, 1962. Collaborator Ency. Brit., 1969—. Home: 920 Courtland Ave Park Ridge IL 60068 Office: 64 E Lake St Chicago IL 60601

BARNDT, JANE NILES, public sch. tchr.; b. Elkland, Pa., June 13, 1926; d. Homer Fred and Mamie E. (Spencer) Niles; B.S. in Bus. Edn., Bloomsburg (Pa.) State Coll., 1948; m. E. Ralph Barndt, Aug. 1956; 1 son, Fred S. Tchr. bus. Quakertown (Pa.) Community Sch. Dist., 1961—, coordinator dept. 1977—, area coordinator, 1980—; operator employment service for bus. students, Quakertown; mem. Pa. Adv. Council Bus. Edn., 1980—. Tchr. nursery sch. United Ch. of Christ, Perkasie, Pa., 8 yrs. Mem. Nat. Fedn. Bus. and Profl. Women's Clubs (pres. Pa. fedn. 1978-80), NEA, Nat. Bus. Edn. Assn., Pa. Ednl. Assn., Eastern Bus. Edn. Assn., Quakertown Community Ednl. Assn., Bucks County Bus. Edn. Assn. (past pres.). Republican. Nat. adv. bd. Today's Sec. mag. Home: 317 Market St Perkasie PA 18944 Office: Senior High Sch 600 Park Ave Quakertown PA 18951

BARNES, CAROLYN ELLEN, phys. therapist; b. Fairmont, W.Va., May 3, 1941; d. Hulett Gail and Pauline Ellen (Kuhn) B.; A.B., Fairmont State Coll., 1963; M.S., W.Va. U., 1966; cert. phys. therapy D.T. Watson Sch. Phys. Therapy, 1969; Ph.D., U. Pitts., 1976. Tchr., Bd. Edn. Baltimore County, 1963-65; asst. prof. phys. edn. James Madison U., Harrisonburg, Va., 1966-68; asst. prof. phys. therapy U. Pitts., 1969-76; asso. prof. phys. therapy W.Va. U., Morgantown 1977—. Trustee, Monongalia Riding for the Handicapped, 1980-81, med. adv. bd., 1981-82. Mem. Am. Phys. Therapy Assn., Democrat. Methodist. Office: Med Center WVa Univ Morgantown WV 26506

BARNES, CORINNE ANN, pediatric nurse, educator; b. Greenock Heights, Pa., July 3, 1928; d. George Julius and Elizabeth Sarah (Smythe) Meerhoff; R.N., Allegheny Gen. Hosp., Pitts., 1949; B.S.N., U. Pitts., 1960, M.N.Ed., 1963, Ph.D. in Nursing, 1974. Pediatric nurse adminstr. Allegheny Gen. Hosp., 1950-58; pediatric nurse specialist Children's Hosp., Pitts., and U. Pitts., 1966-70; undergrad. tchr. U. Pitts., 1965—, chmn. pediatric dept., 1970-72, program dir. grad. programs in nursing care of children, 1978—, cons. Mem. adv. com. Bright Beginnings; pres. Pitts. Women's Tennis Orgn., 1957. Nominee as Disting. Alumnus, U. Pitts. Sch. Nursing, 1982; recipient nursing grants. Fellow Am. Acad. Nursing; mem. Am. Nurses Assn., Pa. Nurses Assn., Allegheny Gen. Nurses Alumnae (pres. 1952), U. Pitts. Alumnae Assn., Assn. Child Care in Health, Soc. Research in Child Devel., Nat. League Nursing, Council Nurse Researchers, Sigma Theta Tau. Republican. Methodist. Clubs: Pitts. Tennis Assn., Fox Chapel Racquet, Zonta, Univ. Faculty. Co-editor Maternal-Child Nursing Jour., 1978—; mem. editorial bd. Jour. Am. Assn. Child Health, 1981-82; contbr. articles to pediatric and nursing jours. Office: 3500 Victoria Hall School of Nursing Pittsburgh PA 15261

BARNES, CYNTHIA ALEE, nurse; b. Chgo., July 8, 1952; d. John and Bobbie Jean Barnes; diploma Wesley Meml. Hosp., Chgo., 1973; B.S. in Nursing, U. Ill., 1975, M.S., 1979. Mem. nursing staff U. Ill. Hosps., Chgo., 1973-76, head nurse, 1977-78, asst. dir. nursing, 1980—; clin. nurse specialist critical care U. Chgo. Hosps., 1978; cons. Neonatal and Pediatric Services, Inc.; mem. faculty Symposia Medicus, U. Ill. Coll. Nursing. Recipient Bronze award Am. Acad. Pediatrics. Mem. Am. Assn. Critical Care Nurses, Assn. Care Children in Hosps., Sigma Theta Tau. Democrat. Lutheran. Author articles in field. Home: 1401 E 49th St Chicago IL 60615 Office: 1740 W Taylor St Suite 1500 Chicago IL 60620

BARNES, CYNTHIA LAVON, accountant; b. Seattle, Aug. 27, 1955; d. Porter Fields and Jacquelyn (Woodson) Banks; B.A. in Bus. Adminstrn. and Acctg., U. Wash., Seattle, 1976; m. Larry R. Barnes, July 6, 1973; children—Larry R., Simone Lavon. From intern, Seattle, to supervisory sr. auditor, Atlanta, Arthur Young & Co., C.P.A.s, 1976-81; dir. internal audit Nat. Data Corp., Atlanta, 1981—. Named Outstanding Alumnae Office Minority Affairs, U. Wash., 1978; C.P.A., Wash. Mem. Nat. Assn. Female Execs., Am. Inst. C.P.A.s, Am. Women's Soc. C.P.A.s, Beta Alpha Psi. Office: 1 Nat Data Plaza Atlanta GA 30329

BARNES, DALPHNA RUTH, nurse; b. Lamesa, Tex., May 11, 1933; d. Raymond Vernon and Hazel Blanche (Lemons) Boatright; A.A. in Nursing, Texarkana Coll., 1966; B.A. in Psychology, U. Houston, 1974; m. Alvin Burwell Barnes, Jan. 18, 1958; children—David Lynn, Jeanne Michele Barnes Boxley. Office nurse, 1966; staff nurse Little York Hosp., Houston, 1967-68, Belhaven Psychiat. Hosp., Houston, 1968; intensive care nurse Herman Hosp., Houston, 1968-69; office nurse, therapist, 1969; from staff nurse to infection control nurse Parkway Hosp., Houston, 1970-77; infection control coordinator Houston Northwest Med. Center, 1977—; adv. bd. Houston Hospice, 1980-82, bd. dirs., 1982—; meml. chmn. North Harris unit Am. Cancer Soc., 1979, v.p., 1980-81, founder, facilitator Cancer Interaction Group, 1980—; cons. death and dying. Served with USN, 1957-58. Recipient Sword of Hope award North Harris chpt. Am. Cancer Soc., 1979-80, 80-81. R.N. Mem. Assn. Practitioners Infection Control (pres. Houston chpt. 1980-81), Tex. Soc. Infection Control Practitioners (William L. Benson Meml. award 1980), Am. Soc. Profl. and Exec. Women, Audubon Soc., Giraffe Soc. Home: 20319 Belleau Wood Dr Humble TX 77338 Office: 710 FM 1960 West Houston TX 77090

BARNES, ELLEN E. KURTZ, educator; b. Claysburg, Pa., Jan. 7, 1941; d. Thomas William and Mary Ellen (Lingenfelter) Kurtz; B.S. with high honors in Elem. Edn., West Chester State Coll., 1962; m. Harold E. Barnes, Aug. 22, 1964; children—James P., Glenn M., R. Elizabeth, Margery E. Tchr., Coatesville (Pa.) Area Sch. Dist., 1962-65, 75; ednl. asst. Olivet Meth. Ch., Coatesville, 1968, supt. ch. study program, 1969-76, dir. nursery sch., 1973-76; pvt. practice, dir. ABC Nursery Sch., Coatesville, 1976—. Sec. lay activities com. Area Clergy Assn., Coatesville, 1973; exec. com. Coatesville Area Interfaith Council, 1973-74; bd. dirs. Coatesville YWCA, 1973; chmn. rural div. Coatesville dist. United Charities, 1974; E. Fallowfield Twp. chmn. Am. Cancer Soc., 1968, 73, 74; exec. bd. E. Fallowfield PTA, 1973-74; pres. Coatesville chpt. Ch. Women United. Mem. Nat. Assn. Female Execs. Republican. Clubs: Jr. Century Club of Coatesville (exec. bd. 1968-71, 72-78, treas. 1972-73, pres. 1976-77). Home and Office: R D 8 Box 458 Strasburg Rd Coatesville PA 19320

BARNES, GEORGENE O'DONNELL, public relations, mktg. exec.; b. Chgo., July 2; d. James George and Betty Frances (Schlundt) O'Donnell; student Northwestern U., 1947-49, U. Chgo., 1949-50; m. W. Wade Barnes, July 13, 1957, TV comml. supr. Benton & Bowles, Chgo., 1951-54; asso. producer films series, writer Laufman Prodns., Chgo., 1954-57; TV producer WNBC-TV, N.Y.C., 1957-63; TV writer Goodson-Todman, game show producers, N.Y.C., 1963-65; v.p. radio and TV spl. events MSEI, N.Y.C., 1965-70; pres. Barnes Assos., diversified public relations and advt. mktg., N.Y.C., 1970—; producer TV series Seen & Heard, cable, 1976—, Hearst/ABC Video, 1982; dir. Emerson Travel. Public relations dir. City Center Music and Drama Young People's Theater, 1970-73. Recipient award for Children's Center program WNYC-AM and FM, 1973. Mem. Am. Women in Radio and TV (dir., pres. elect 1968-69), Nat. Assn. TV Arts and Scis. (gov. N.Y. 1973—), Women Execs. in Public Relations, The Fashion Group, N.Y.C. Ballet Guild, N.Y.C. Opera Guild, Broadcast Industry Forums (nat. chmn. 1962-70). Author: Miniaturia, 1951; contbg. editor: Publicity Forum, Advice from 22 Experts, 1977. Home: 20 Beekman Pl New York NY 10022 Office: 1 Astor Plaza 4th Floor New York NY 10036

BARNES, HAZEL ESTELLA, educator; b. Wilkes-Barre, Pa., Dec. 16, 1915; d. Olin James and May Hannah (Petersen) B.; B.A., Wilson Coll., 1937; Ph.D., Yale U., 1941; D.Litt., Wilson Coll., 1965. Mem. faculty Woman's Coll. U. N.C., Greensboro, 1941-43, Queens Coll., Charlotte, N.C., 1943-45, Pierce Coll., Athens, Greece, 1945-48, U. Toledo, 1948-51, Ohio State U., Columbus, 1951-53; mem. faculty U. Colo., Boulder, 1953—, prof., 1961—, disting. prof. humanities Center Interdisciplinary Studies, from 1979; now philosophy prof.; dissting. vis. prof., dept. classic, State U. of San Diego; vis. lectr. Inst. Policy Studies, Washington, 1969. Guggenheim fellow, 1977-78; vis. prof. philosophy Yale U., 1974; Phi Beta Kappa vis. scholar, 1974-75, 77-78. Mem. Am. Philos. Assn., Am. Philol. Assn., Am. Soc. Aesthetics, Classical Assn. Middle West and South, Archeol. Inst. Am., Phi Beta Kappa (nat. senate 1979—). Author: The Literature of Possibility, 1959; An Existentialist Ethics, 1967; The University as the New Church, 1970; Sartre, 1973; The Meddling Gods, 1974; Sartre and Flaubert, 1981; translator: Being and Nothingness (Sartre), 1956; Search for a Method, 1963. Home: 896 17th St Boulder CO 80302 Office: Dept of Philosophy Campus Box 232 Univ Colo Boulder CO 80309

BARNES, HENRIETTA LEMMON, banker; b. Phila., Nov. 6, 1949; d. Emily Mamie Lemmon; A.A., Community Coll. Phila., 1970; student Sch. Bank Adminstrn., U. Wis.-Madison; m. Edward Earl Barnes, Apr. 30, 1977. With Provident Nat. Bank, Phila., 1972—, beginning as supr. money transfer dept., successively asst. ops. officer lockbox dept., asst. ops. officer, mgr. internal br. dept., ops. officer, mgr. money transfer dept., 1972-80, sr. ops. officer, mem. New System Implementation Project team, 1980-82, sr. ops. officer, asst. mgr. demand deposit acctg. dept., 1982—; ind. cons. Mary Kay Cosmetics. Asst. coordinator Young Adult Fellowship of Vine Meml. Baptist Ch. Home: Chestnut Hill Village 7740 A Stenton Ave Apt 103 Devon Philadelphia PA 19118 Office: Provident National Bank 17th and Sansom Sts Philadelphia PA 19103

BARNES, ISABEL JANET, microbiologist; b. Union City, N.J., Sept. 22, 1936; d. Carl Robert and Isabel Sarah (Cappelletti) B.; B.S., Pa. State U., 1958; M.S., Cornell U., 1960; Ph.D., Hahnemann Med. Coll., 1969; m. John D. Bowman, June 15, 1978. Asst. prof. Hershey Med. Center, Pa. State U., 1968-73; asst. prof., assoc. prof. Sangamon State U., Springfield, Ill., 1973-76; assoc. prof. microbiology U. Wis., Madison, 1976—, interim dean Sch. Allied Health Professions, 1981—. Mem. AAAS, AAUP, Am. Soc. for Microbiology, Am. Soc. Med. Technologists. Office: Room 1080 1300 University Ave Madison WI 53706

BARNES, JANE M., state legislator; b. Chgo., 1926; student St. Xavier Coll.; m. Warren S. Barnes; 2 children. Past asst. chief dep. sheriff of Cook County (Ill.); adminstrv. asst. Ill. Dept. Ins.; exec. sec. Worth Twp. (Ill.) Youth Commn.; mem. Ill. Ho. of Reps. Alt. del. 1972 Republican Conv.; committeewoman Worth Twp., 1966-74; pres. Worth Twp. Rep. Women's Orgn., 1964-66; mem. exec. bd. Ill. Fedn. Rep. Women, 1966-74, Rep. Women Power, Ill. Style and Women's Nat. Rep. Club; former chmn. March of Dimes; active PTA, Cubs Scouts, Brownie, Girl Scouts U.S.A.; bd. dirs. Oak Lawn Community Chest, Oak Lawn Bicentennial Commn.; mem. Christ Community Hosp. Women's Aux. Lic. real estate broker, Ill. Mem. LWV, Evergreen Park Bus. and Profl. Women's Orgn. Club: Beverly Law Women's (past pres.). Office: Ill Ho of Reps State Capitol Springfield IL 62706 *

BARNES, KAREN KINSEY, social worker, educator; b. Kansas City, Mo., July 1, 1930; d. Walter Washington and Anna Elizabeth (Moum) Kinsey; Asso. B.A. in Journalism, Colo. Woman's Coll., 1950; B.A. in English, Wash. State U., 1952; M.A. in English, U. Conn., 1955; M.S.W., U. Wash., 1964; children—Walter W., Jackie A. Instr. English, U. Conn., 1952-53, Wash. State U., 1961-62; social worker State of Maine, 1955, State of Wash., 1955-61, State of Vt., 1962-63, Vt. Children's Aid and Homefinding Soc., 1965-66, Luth. Family and Child Service, Spokane, Wash., 1966-70; Spokane area dir. Luth. Social Services of Wash., 1971-80; asst. prof. sociology Wash. State U., 1980—; asso. with psychiatrist in pvt. practice, 1980—. Mem. United Way Agy. Execs. of Spokane, 1971-80, chmn., 1975; bd. dirs. United Way of Pullman (Wash.), 1980—. Cert. social worker, Idaho. Mem. Nat. Assn. Social Workers, Assn. Clin. Social Workers, Acad. Cert. Social Workers, Wash. Assn. Child Caring Agys. (dir. 1975-79, sec. 1975-78).

BARNES, LINDA ERNESTINE ROBERTS, ins. agt.; b. Cleve., Jan. 18, 1951; d. Frank and Helen Ernestine (White) Roberts; student Fisk U., 1969-71, Cuyahoga Community Coll., 1971-73; m. W. Marvin Barnes, Aug. 14, 1976; 1 dau., Courtney Ernestine. Bus. mgr. W.M.B. Assos., L & M Auto Clinic, Cleve., 1975—; bus. mgr. Marco Assos. Architects/Engrs., Cleve., 1976-79; field underwriter N.Y. Life Ins. Co., Cleve., 1978-81; agt. Bus. Ins. Consultation, Protected Home Mutual, Cleve., 1981—. Vol., YWCA, 1978—. Recipient Vol. Pin, ARC, 1980, Mem. Life Underwriters Polit. Action Com., Delta Sigma Theta. Republican. Mem. Ch. of Religious Science. Club: Millionaires. Home: 3776 E 153d St Cleveland OH 44128 Office: 1900 Euclid Ave Suite 201 Cleveland OH 44115

BARNES, MARILYN ACKLEY (BARNES, PAT), ednl. audio-visual co. exec.; b. Bklyn., Mar. 17, 1932; d. Frederick Roberts and Hazel Delano (Downes) Ackley; A.S., Dean Jr. Coll., 1951; m. Cassius Bartlett Barnes, Oct. 10, 1953; children—Kathryn Parker Barnes Fenton, Thomas Gray. Sec. to editor coll. books Prentice-Hall, Inc., N.Y.C., 1951-53; sec. to prin. Archer St. Sch., Freeport (N.Y.) Public Schs., 1954-55; dir. purchasing Ednl. Activities, Inc., Baldwin, N.Y., 1969—. Third v.p. Central Council Aux., South Nassau Community Hosp., Oceanside, N.Y., 1968, 2d v.p., 1969; clk. of session United Ch., Rockville Centre (N.Y.), 1977-82. Mem. Purchasing Mgrs. Assn. N.Y. (sec. L.I. chpt. 1981—, dir. 1982—). Club: United Ch. Rockville Centre Mr. and Mrs. (pres. 1964-65). Home: 67 Pine St Rockville Centre NY 11570 Office: 1937 Grand Ave Baldwin NY 11510

BARNES, RAMONA LEETA, state legislator; b. Pikeville, Tenn., July 7, 1938; d. John Ellison and Pearlie Mae Wheeler; student Mich. State Coll., Waipahu Community Coll.; m. Larry Barnes, Apr. 11, 1960; children—Randall Lee, Michelle Annette, Michael Allen. Businesswomen, Anchorage; Alaska Ho. of Reps., 1978—, chmn. house judiciary com., mem. various coms.; mem. Alaska Rep. States Rights Coordinating Council, Western Lands Task Force, Citizens Adv. Commn. on Alaska Lands. Legis. affairs chmn. Elmendorf PTA Council, 1972-75; mem. Elmendorf Sch. Bd., 1973-76, chmn., 1975-76; adv. Anchorage Bd. Edn., 1975-76; trustee Blood Bank of Alaska, Anchorage Community Mental Health Center; del. Republican State Conv., 1976, 78, 80; bd. dirs. Anchorage Community Mental Health Center; past precinct committeewoman. Mem. Commonwealth North, Alaskan Outdoor Assn. (charter), Alaska Assn. Sch. Bds., Nat. Rifle Assn., Nat. Fedn. Republican Women, Am. Legis. Council, Council for Exceptional Children, Navy League, Profl. Businesswomen's Club. Mem. Churches of Christ. Club: Elmendorf Officer's Wives. Office: Pouch V Juneau AK 99811

BARNES, SHIRLEY MOORE, social worker, therapist, adminstr. mental health; b. Bedminster, N.J., Jan. 13, 1931; d. George and Marian Field (Van Nuys) Moore; student Tusculum Coll., 1948-50; B.A., Douglass Coll., 1952; M.S.W., U. Pa., 1954; m. William Edward Barnes, Sept. 13, 1952; children—John Leighton, Ellen Leigh, Kimberley Jean. Caseworker, Children's Aid Soc., Phila., 1952-55; psychiat. social worker West Jersey Hosp. Out-Patient Psychiat. and Alcoholic Clinic, Camden, N.J., 1960-61, VA Hosp., Brockton, Mass., 1972; psychiat. social worker, supr., aftercare coordinator, psychotherapist, adminstr. Mental Health Services Southeastern Vt., Springfield, 1973—; founder Beekman House, 1979. Mem. Acad. Cert. Social Workers, Nat. Assn. Social Workers, Psi Chi. Home: 3 Walnut Way Springfield VT 05156 Office: Mental Health Services Southeastern Vt 7 Main St Springfield VT 05156

BARNES, SONDRA ANICE, publisher; b. Clovis, N. Mex., Feb. 25, 1937; d. Victor Earl and Florence Aylene (Wyly) Grau; B.A., Calif. State U., Fullerton, 1967; M.S., Old Dominion U., Norfolk, Va., 1973; children—Gary Englestead, Brady Englestead. Reporter, broadcaster, advt. copy writer Sta. KTNM, Tucumcari, N.Mex., 1971-72; elem. sch. tchr., Placentia, Calif., 1967-72; counseling psychologist alcohol rehab., 1972-76; investment counselor A.A. Ajax Co., Inc., Anaheim, Calif., 1976-78; publisher BRASON-SARGAR Publs., Reseda, Calif., 1978—. Author: Life Is The Way It Is, 1978. Office: PO Box 842 Reseda CA 91335

BARNES, SYMIRIA PETERS, educator, soprano; b. Bolton, Miss., July 10; d. V.J. and Matilda J. (Buckley) Peters; B.Music Edn. in Voice, Jackson State U., 1959; M.A. in Adminstrn. and Supervision, Roosevelt U., 1982; student of Dora Lindgren and William Browning, Am. Conservatory Music, 1972-78, with Robert McFerrin, Roosevelt U., 1976-78; children—Stanford, Cedrick, Audwin. Choral dir. Tilden High Sch., Chgo., 1980—; tchr. voice and piano Mallette Music Sch., Chgo., 1980—; soprano opera and oratorio including performance in Aida premiere performance of Opera/South, Jackson, Miss., 1971: recitalist Young Artist Recital series, Chgo., 1973, Am. Conservatory of Music, 1975, Centennial Alumni Performers Series, Jackson State U., 1977; debut in concert Wigmore Hall, London, 1973; guest artist Nat. Talent Hunt Demonstration, Omega Psi Phi, Cleve., 1958; profl. mem. Chgo. Symphony Chorus. Winner ann. commencement solo audition Am. Conservatory Music, Chgo., 1972; recipient music scholarship award, Am. League Pen Women, 1972. Mem. Chgo. Tchrs. Union, Chgo. Musicians Assn., Nat. Assn. Negro Musicians (first place winner nat. voice contest U. Ill. 1957), Am. Guild Mus. Artists, Zeta Phi Beta. Baptist. Contbr. music sect. Handbook on Instructional Program of Chicago Public Schools, 3 vols., 1981. Office: 4747 S Union Chicago IL 60609

BARNES, VELMA ARDELL, real estate broker; b. Putnam, Okla., Aug. 20, 1910; d. Johnny and Lula (Bruce) Miller; B.A., Southwestern Coll., Weatherford, Okla., 1944; Ed.M., U. Okla., Norman, 1954, U. Calif., Berkeley, 1958; m. J.T. Bailey, Jan. 1, 1933; 1 son, Jay T.; m. 2d, Dewey Loyd Barnes, June 15, 1961 (dec.). Public sch. tchr., also artist, 1948-61; real estate broker, 1967—; asso. Velma A. Barnes Real Estate, Norman, Okla., 1967—. Recipient 1st pl. award Okla.-Tex. Water Color Show, 1960. Mem. Nat. Assn. Real Estate Bds., Western Art Assn., DAR. Home: 2602 Walnut Rd Norman OK 73069 Office: 2103 W Main St Norman OK 73069

BARNET, ELENA O., social worker; b. Lithuania, July 26, 1923; came to U.S., 1947, naturalized, 1952; d. Jurgis and Elena Ciurlys; B.A., New Sch. Social Research, N.Y.C., 1969; M.S.W., Hunter Coll., N.Y.C., 1972; m. Will Barnet, Mar. 4, 1953; 1 dau., Ona W. Social worker cancer center Meml.-Sloan-Kettering Hosp., N.Y.C., 1972—, now supr. social work dept. Mem. Nat. Assn. Social Workers. Roman Catholic. Office: 1275 York Ave New York NY 10021

BARNETT, BETTY JO, nurse; b. Mira, La., Dec. 4, 1929; d. Joe and Carrie Belle (Bundy) Martin; B.S.N., Northwestern U., 1957; children—Mary K., Janet M., Rebecca A., Cynthia D. Staff nurse Shreveport (La.) Charity Hosp., 1950-51, head nurse, 1952-54; supr. Confederate Meml. Med. Center, Shreveport, 1954-73, asst. dir. nursing, 1973-75; asso. dir. nursing La. State U. Hosp., Shreveport, 1975-81; asst. dir. nursing Bossier Med. Center, Bossier City, La., part time 1981—. Recipient Nurse of Yr. award La. State U., 1981. Mem. Shreveport Dist. Nurses Assn., La. Nurses Assn., Am. Nurses Assn., Sigma Theta Tau, Beta Chi, Lambda Alpha. Democrat. Mem. Ch. of Christ. Home: PO Box 411 Plain Dealing LA 71064 Office: Airline Dr Bossier City LA 71111

BARNETT, ELIZABETH, fgn. service officer; b. San Bernardino, Calif., May 26, 1954; d. John E., Sr., and Joan Olga (Connor) B.; B.A. summa cum laude, U. Mass., 1976; M.A. (fellow), Yale U., 1978. Fgn. service officer Dept. State, Washington, 1979—. Mem. Am. Fgn. Service Assn., Secs. Open Forum, AAUW, Consular Officers Assn., Phi Beta

Kappa. Clubs: Yale (N.Y.C.); Fgn. Service. Office: Dept of State Washington DC 20520

BARNETT, ELIZABETH RUTH, editor; b. Florence, S.C., Mar. 21, 1946; d. John Manley and Ruth (Gilland) B.; B.S. in Home Econs., Iowa State U., 1968; postgrad. Culinary Arts Inst., 1975. Home service rep. Orange & Rockland Utilities, Nyack, N.Y., 1967; editorial asst. House Beautiful mag., 1968-69; sr. engring. home economist Frigidaire div. Gen. Motors Corp., Dayton, Ohio, 1969-79, research devel. staff for publ. Microwave Cooking in 3 Speeds, 1977; tech. editor Frigidaire Co. of White Consol. Industries, Dayton, 1979—; mem. faculty Alumni Coll., U. Cin. Chmn., Oakwood Community Jaycee Aux., 1978. Mem. Am. Home Econs. Assn., Home Economists in Bus. Office: 3555 S Kettering Blvd Dayton OH 45449

BARNETT, JANE (SHELTON), market researcher; b. Hamilton, Ohio, Sept. 4, 1950; d. Fredrick Robert, II and Jewell (Wyatt) Shelton; B.A. in Communications and English, Bowling Green (Ohio) State U., 1971, M.A. in Interpersonal and Public Communication, 1977; m. Jeffrey Davis Barnett, Oct. 28, 1979. Account exec. Ohio div. So. Nat. Research Inst., Toledo, 1976-78; dir. market research and forecasting Elgin-Watham Watch Co., Chgo., 1978-79; account exec. Creative Promotions, Cin., 1979-80; dir. market research BCC div. Hillenbrand Indsutries, Batesville, Ind., 1980—; seminar leader, 1981. Rep., Educators Polit. Action Com., 1974-75; Democratic precinct capt., Chgo., 1978. Recipient Profl. Service award Ohio Edn. Assn., 1976; VA intern, 1978. Mem. Am. Mktg. Assn., Nat. Assn. Female Execs. Unitarian. Home: 404 Millville Ave Hamilton OH 45013 Office: BBC Div Hillenbrand Industries Hwy 46 Batesville IN 47006

BARNETT, LINDA RUTH, clin. psychologist; b. Yreka, Calif., Oct. 1, 1950; d. Chester Eugene and Ruth (Frields) B.; B.A., Stanford U., 1972; M.A., U. Ky., 1978, Ph.D., 1981. Staff psychologist Jessamine County Comprehensive Care Center, Nicholasville, Ky., 1975-76; coordinator clin. services Psychol. Services Center, U. Ky., Lexington, 1976-78; psychotherapist, cons. Cornelia B. Wilbur, M.D., P.S.C., Lexington, 1978-79; intern div. med. psychology dept. psychiatry Duke U. Med. Center, Durham, N.C., 1979-80, research asso., 1980-81; postdoctoral fellow dept. psychiatry and univ. health service U. Rochester (N.Y.), 1981—; invited lectr. women and psychology U. Ky., 1977—. Mem. Lexington Task Force on Battered Women, 1978-79. Mem. Am. Psychol. Assn., NOW, Assn. Advancement of Behavior Therapy, Assn. Women in Psychology. Democrat. Methodist. Home: 300 Hillside Ave Rochester NY 14610

BARNETT, OLA WILMA, educator; b. Los Angeles, Jan. 26, 1930; d. William and Ruth Carol (Phillips) King; B.A., UCLA, 1962, M.A., 1965, Ph.D., 1971; m. Donald Joseph Barnett, Nov. 27, 1941; children—Darlene Ola Blake, Donna Shirley Johnson. Research asst. UCLA, 1961-67; asst. prof. psychology Calif. State Poly. U., San Luis Obispo, 1967-70; asso. prof. psychology Pepperdine U., Malibu, Calif., 1970-79, prof. psychology, 1979—; sponsor Camp David Gonzales Tutorial Program, 1974-77. Recipient Vol. Service award Atascadero State Hosp., 1970; Action grantee, 1972-73. Mem. Am. Psychol. Assn., Nat. Council Crime and Delinquency, Am. Criminology Soc., Acad. Criminal Justice Soc., Am. Criminal Justice and Research Soc., Am. Psychology-Law Soc., AAUP, NOW, Western Psychol. Assn. Mem. Ch. of Christ. Mem. Nat. Coalition to Ban Handguns. Home: 24301 Sylvan Glen Rd Calabasas CA 91302 Office: Social Sci Div Pepperdine U Malibu CA 90265 *

BARNETT, PATRICIA RUTH, educator; b. Sioux Falls, S.D., Feb. 26, 1927; d. George Richard and Ruth Theresa (Bauch) B.; B.A. (Nat. Pepsi-Cola scholar), Coll. St. Catherine, St. Paul, 1949; M.A., Catholic U. Am., 1952; Ph.D., U. Denver, 1967. Mem. profl. touring co. Players, Inc., 1951-54, 55-56; prodn. asst., script girl NBC, Chgo., 1954-55; actress, prodn. asst. ABC and CBS, N.Y.C., 1956-58; exec. asst. Writers Guild Am.-East, N.Y.C., 1958-60; asst. prof. speech and drama St. Louis U., 1960-64; teaching fellow U. Denver, 1964-67; mem. faculty U. N.C., Chapel Hill, 1967—, asso. prof. drama, 1974—; actress Playmakers Repertory Co., Chapel Hill, 1980—; dir. community theatre prodn. Durham Theatre Guild, Carrboro Art Theatre, 1968-80; bd. dirs. Durham Theatre Guild, 1973-78. Mem. Actors Equity, Am. Theatre Assn., Children's Theatre Conf., Southeastern Theatre Conf., N.C. Theatre Conf., U. N.C. Faculty Assn., Phi Beta Kappa, Pi Kappa Delta, Pi Upsilon Delta, Delta Phi Lambda. Republican. Roman Catholic. Office: Dept Dramatic Arts U NC Chapel Hill NC 27514

BARNETT, SARA MARGARET, educator; b. Sikeston, Mo., Aug. 6, 1941; d. Grady Marvin and Mary Elizabeth (Love) Mills; B.S. in Med. Tech., U. Tex., Arlington, 1963; M.S. in Edn., U. Central Ark., 1968; postgrad. E. Tex. State U.; m. Herman Howard Barnett, Oct. 16, 1959; children—Gregory Lynn, Lori Elizabeth. Intern Baylor U. Med. Center, 1961-62; asst. supr. lab. Wadley Hosp., Texarkana, Tex., 1963-65, night lab. supr., 1976-77; public sch. tchr., Texarkana, 1965-69; med. technician Collom and Carney Clinic, Texarkana, 1969-72; tchr. biology Liberty-Eylau High Sch., Texarkana, 1972-76; tchr. biology, health occupations coordinator Tex. Sr. High Sch., Texarkana, 1977—; speaker in field. Martin-Lowrance scholar, 1981. Mem. NEA, Am. Soc. Clin. Pathologists, AAUW (chmn. edn. found. Tex. 1972-74), Tex. Tchrs. Assn., Tex. Classroom Tchrs. Assn., Tex. Soc. Med. Tech., Tex. Health Occupations Assn., Ark. Acad. Sci., Tex. PTA (life), Delta Kappa Gamma, Phi Delta Kappa. Democrat. Methodist. Author: Medical Laboratory Assistant, 1981. Home: 100 Pioneer St Texarkana TX 75501 Office: 2112 Kennedy Ln Texarkana TX 75503

BARNHARDT, HARRIET BOLGER, ednl. adminstr.; b. Charleston, S.C., Feb. 19, 1919; d. Thomas Thaddeus and Florence Lee (Burns) Bolger; cert. med. technologist Duke U., 1946; B.S., Elon Coll., 1975; M.Ed., Central Mich. U., 1979; children—Harriet Sandra Schiffley, Virginia Gail Barnhardt Kouchinsky. Chief med. technologist Tuomey Hosp., Sumter, S.C., 1947, Pryor Hosp., Chester, S.C., 1949, Simmons-Lupton Hosp., Burlington, N.C., 1949-55, Alamance County Hosp., Burlington, 1956-58, Kernodle Clinic, Burlington, 1959-61, Drs. Walker Blair and Williams, Burlington, 1962-63, Mebane (N.C.) Clinic, 1966-71, Biomed. Ref. Lab., Burlington, 1972-73; ednl. coordinator Elon Coll., N.C., 1974-76; ednl. coordinator, head dept. Florence Darlington Tech. Coll., Florence, S.C., 1976—. Mem. Am. Soc. for Med. Technologists, Am. Soc. Clin. Pathologists (affiliate mem., cert. med. technologist), S.C. Tech. Edn. Assn. Methodist. Author med. lab. tech. curriculum by competency based instrn. method. Home: 211 Wedgewood Dr Darlington SC 29532 Office: Florence Darlington Tech Coll PO Drawer 8000 Florence SC 29501

BARNHART, JANICE FAYE, welder; b. Ord, Nebr., Oct. 31, 1936; d. Charles Allen and Carla Marie (Larsen) B.; B.S., Central Wash. U., 1970; diploma welding tech., Columbia Basin Tech. Sch., Pasco, Wash., 1975; m. 2d, Gunars Albert Rieksts, Apr. 12, 1980; children—Derek, Tanya, Luke, Trina, Tracy, Timothy, Gunnar, Lisa, Laura. Engaged as welder and welding insp., 1974—; quality control welding insp. Hanford Nuclear Park, Richland, Wash., 1975-80; welder Uniflight, Bellingham, Wash., 1980—. Chmn. Richland Parks Bd., 1972. Mem. Women in Constrn., Women's Trade Center, Plumbers and Steam Fitters Union, Boilermakers Union. Home: 1703 Marie St Pasco WA 99301

BARNHILL, HELEN LUCILE, clin. chemist; b. Guysville, Ohio, June 27, 1927; d. Warren J. and Emma H. Barnhill; B.S. with honors, Ohio U., 1950, postgrad., 1956; diploma Springfield (Ohio) Hosp. Sch. Med. Tech., 1951. Supr. clin. chemistry City Hosp., Springfield, 1951-54, Mercy Hosp., Springfield, 1954-62, Community Hosp., Springfield, 1962—; adj. instr. Wittenberg U., Springfield; tchr., cons. in field. Past bd. dirs. Clark County Kidney Found. Mem. Am. Assn. Clin. Chemists, Am. Assn. Med. Technologists, Ohio Soc. Med. Technologists, Ohio Valley Soc. Clin. Chemists. Republican. Club: Springfield Altrusa (v.p. 1967-68, pres. 1969-71). Home: 702 N Burnett Rd Springfield OH 45503

BARNS, CAROLE SUSAN, telephone co. mgr.; b. Nome, Alaska, Nov. 21, 1944; d. Anton Raymond and Dorothy Virginia (Nelson) Johansen; B.A., U. Wash., 1967; m. Lee Miller, July 11, 1970; children—Jeffrey Miller, Anthony Nelson. Internal communications asst. Gen. Telephone Co. N.W., Everett, Wash., 1967-69, internal communications mgr., 1969-70, public affairs mgr., 1973-78, govtl. affairs mgr., 1978—; newswoman AP, 1970-73; free lance editor Washington Community Coll. Dist. 17, 1970-71. Recipient writing and editing awards Nat. Fedn. Press Women, Wash. Press Women. Mem. Women in Communications, Nat. Fedn. Press Women, Wash. Press Assn. Clubs: Spokane, Racquet (Spokane, Wash.). Home: S 1322 Grove St Spokane WA 99204 Office: PO Box 1179 Coeur d'Alene ID 83814

BARNS, DORETHA MAE CLAYTON, librarian, orgn. exec.; b. Fairmont, W.Va., Nov. 28, 1917; d. Sylvester Richard and Della Pearl (Morgan) Clayton; A.B., Fairmont State Coll., 1939; M.A., W.Va. U., 1940; B.S. in L.S., Western Res. U., 1947; m. William Derrick Barns, Sept. 3, 1947. Tchr., librarian Wetzel County (W.Va.) Schs., 1940-41, Preston County Schs., 1944-46; teaching fellow dept. English, W.Va. U., 1941-43, sec. to dean grad. sch., 1942-44, cataloguer library, 1947-48; dir., Internat. relations chmn. LWV W.Va., 1969—, 2d v.p., 1981—. Bd. dirs. W.Va. affiliate Council of Internat. Programs, 1975—. Mem. Women's Internat. League for Peace and Freedom, Kappa Delta Pi, Nu Alpha Phi. Republican. Mem. Soc. Friends. Club: Order Eastern Star. Author: An Outline of the West Virginia Merit System, 1957; West Virginia's Interest in Foreign Trade, 1971; International Services Available to West Virginia Businesses, 1980. Home: 512 Beverly Ave Morgantown WV 26505

BARNWELL, YSAYE MARIA, speech pathologist; b. N.Y.C., Feb. 28, 1946; d. Irving Frederick and Marcella (Robinson) B.; B.S., SUNY, Geneseo, 1967, M.S., 1968; Ph.D., U. Pitts., 1975; M.S.P.H., Howard U., 1981. Instr. speech Howard U., Washington, 1968, instr. Coll. Dentistry, 1969-72, asst. prof., 1972-78, asso. prof., 1978-80; tng. coordinator div. child protection Children's Hosp., Washington, 1982—; instr. dept. communicative arts Fed. City Coll., Washington, 1971-73. Founder, dir. All Souls Jubilee Singers, 1977-82; mem. Sweet Honey in the Rock, women's singing group. Mem. Am. Speech and Hearing Assn., Am. Cleft Palate Assn., Internat. Assn. Oral Myology asso. editor jour. 1977-81), D.C. Speech and Hearing Assn., Myofunctional Therapy Assn. Am., Soc. Craniofacial Genetics. Unitarian. Contbr. articles to profl. jours.; composer, arranger, music. Office: Div Child Protection Children's Hosp Nat Med Center 111 Michigan Ave NW Washington DC 20010

BARON, LILLIAN BRANSFORD, textile designer; b. Nashville, Dec. 14, 1935; d. Robert Sterling and Eula Vashtow (Waddy) Bransford; student Pratt Inst., 1953-55; grad. McDowell Sch. Fashion, 1956; student knit fabric design Fashion Inst. Tech., 1963; cert. N.Y. Sch. Interior Design, 1970; m. Laurence A. Baron, July 28, 1973. Asst. designer Donmoor, N.Y.C., 1963; designer Health-Tex, N.Y.C., 1963-68; chief designer, stylist Algro Knitting Mills, Milltown, N.J., 1968—; designs in profl. publs. including Calif. Apparel News, Men's Wear mag. Mem. The Fashion Group, Textile Stylist Guild, Nat. Assn. Female Execs. Democrat. Roman Catholic. Office: Algro Knitting Mills Ford Ave Milltown NJ 08850

BARON, LINDA ANN, cosmetic co. exec.; b. Flushing, N.Y., Nov. 9, 1943; d. Leonard Michael and Margaret Mary Cotone; grad. Gardner Sch. Bus., 1968; student George Washington U., 1970. Adminstrv. asst. U.S. Underseas Cable Corp., Washington, 1968-69; analyst programmer Friden div. Singer Co., Washington, 1969, programming mgr., 1970, systems sales exec., 1971; acct. exec. Clinique Labs., Inc., Washington and Balt., 1972, regional mktg. mgr. Md. and Va. markets, 1973-75, regional mktg. dir. Washington and Mid-Atlantic states, 1976-81, regional v.p., Southeast, 1982—; instr. merchandising, 1976—. Vol., ARC, Walter Reed and Bethesda Naval Hosp., Washington, 1969-71. Mem. Nat. Assn. Female Execs., U.S. Dressage Fedn., Potomac Valley Dressage Assn., Am. Horse Show Assn., Bass Anglers Sportsmen Soc., Washington Fashion Group. Roman Catholic. Home: 9224 Beech Hill Dr Bethesda MD 20817

BARON, NAOMI SUSAN, educator; b. N.Y.C., Sept. 27, 1946; d. Leonard and Ruth Joan (Josephson) B.; B.A., Brandeis U., 1968; Ph.D., Stanford U., 1972. Asst. prof. linguistics Brown U., 1972-79, assoc. prof., 1979—, assoc. dean, 1981—; vis. instr. R.I. Sch. Design, 1982—. Bur. Edn. Handicapped grantee, 1975—; Nat. Endowment for Humanities grantee, 1979-81. Mem. Linguistic Soc. Am., Semiotic Soc. Am., Am. Assn. Higher Edn., Am. Assn. Advancement of Humanities. Author: Language Acquisition and Historical Change, 1979; Speech, Writing and Sign, 1981. Office: PO Box 1865 University Hall Brown University Providence RI 02912

BARONIAN, MAUREEN MURPHY, securities dealer, state legislator; b. White Plains, N.Y., Aug. 5, 1934; d. Charles Thomas and Margaret M. Reed Murphy; A.S., Larson Coll., 1954; student U. Hartford, 1975-76; m. K. Albert Baronian, 1960; children—John Albert, Margaret Reed, James Andrew. Vice pres., sec., prin. Investors Services, Hartford, Conn., 1976—; mem. Conn. Ho. of Reps., 1981—. Sec. Chuck Matties Re-election to State Legislature, 1976-78; vice chmn. 10th Dist. Com., Republican Party, 1976—; mem. West Hartford Rep. Town Com., 1976—; mem. Charter Revision Commn., 1976-69, sec., 1976-77; chmn. West Hartford Fin. Adv. Bd., 1979; co-chmn., treas., dir. publicity Com. to Elect Robert T. Rowlson to Town Council, 1979; mem. Com. to Rev. and Revise West Hartford Rep. Party Rules, 1979-80; West Hartford chmn. primary day activities George Bush for Pres., 1980; corporator Inst. of Living, 1973—, aux. pres., 1973-75; chmn. Friends of Bushnell Meml., 1980—; bd. dirs. Hartford Symphony Soc., 1981—. Registered stock broker. Mem. Nat. Assn. Securities Dealers. Roman Catholic. Office: Conn Ho of Reps Hartford CT 06115

BAROODY, JUDITH RAINE, reporter, news anchorwoman; b. Richmond, Va., Nov. 28, 1953; d. Alfred Fred and Elizabeth (Irwin) B.; B.A., Coll. William and Mary, 1975. Reporter, Sta. WVEC-TV, Norfolk, Va., 1977—, producer, anchorwoman weekend news show, 1979—. Recipient Working Woman Broadcast award for news series Nat. Commn. for Working Women, 1981. Author articles for various mags. Home: 611 Raleigh Ave Norfolk VA 23507 Office: 110 3d St Norfolk VA 23510

BARR, ANNE ELIZABETH, educator; b. Iowa Falls, Iowa, Aug. 21, 1945; d. Robert Morgan and Jean Margaret (Good) Santee; B.A., U. Iowa, 1971; m. Jack Lewis Barr, June 27, 1965. Elem. sch. tchr., Iowa and Colo., 1966—; tchr. 3d grade Bear Creek Elem. Sch., Lakewood, Colo., 1979—. Mem. NEA, Internat. Reading Assn., Colo. Edn. Assn., Jefferson County Edn. Assn., PEO (chpt. pres. 1982), Alpha Xi Delta. Republican. Methodist. Office: 3125 S Kipling St Lakewood CO 80227

BARR, FRANCINE MARIE, communications co. ofcl.; b. Cleve., Jan. 21, 1947; d. Frank Andrew and Regina Mary (Kawalec) Wrobel; B.A. (Nat. Honor Soc. Scholar), Notre Dame Coll., 1969; postgrad. Royal Holloway Coll., London, 1969; M.A., Wayne State U., 1974; m. Robert F. Barr, May 30, 1970; 1 dau., Lisa Francine. Asso. editor Moving Out mag. Wayne State U., Detroit, 1971-74; editorial asst. Wilding div. Bell & Howell, Southfield, Mich., 1976, writer, 1977, account exec., 1978, sr. account exec., 1979-81; account supr. Maritz Communications Co., Southfield, 1982—. Mem. Nat. Assn. Female Execs. (network dir. 1979-80), Adcraft, Mich. Metaphys. Soc. Libertarian. Unitarian. Office: 18000 W Eight Mile Rd Southfield MI 48018

BARR, JEAN HOWARD, entrepreneur; b. Cambridge, Mass., Mar. 27, 1920; d. Charles Rudolf and Mildred Eleanor (Johnson) Howard; B.A., Brown U., 1942; m. Oliver James Barr, III, Apr. 24, 1943; children—Oliver James, Sandra Kay. Mfrs. rep. Holt-Howard Assos., Inc., Stamford, Conn., 1953-72; owner, pres., chmn. bd. JHB Internat., Inc. and JHB Imports, Inc., Denver, 1969—. Named Internat. Person of Year, 1975. Mem. Am. Home Sewing Assn. (dir. 1975—), Internat. Trade Assn. Colo., Jr. League Am. Republican. Club: Wiscasset (Maine) Yacht. Home: 6790 E Cedar St Apt 401 Denver CO 80024 Office: 1955 S Quince St Denver CO 80231

BARR, NORMA JEAN, nurse, educator; b. Alton, Ill., Oct. 18, 1950; d. Edward Brooks and Mildred (Bandy) Gause; diploma Barnes Hosp. Sch. Nursing, 1971; B.A., Webster Coll., 1976; M.Ed., U. Mo., 1980; m. Arnold Stanley Barr, Jr., Feb. 24, 1973; 1 son, David Stanley. Staff nurse Barnes Hosp., St. Louis, 1971-72, 1973-75, 78-79, instr. dept. edn. and tng., 1975-78; staff nurse St. John's Hosp., St. Louis County, Mo., 1972-73. instr., hosp. wide tng. specialist Christian Hosps., St. Louis, 1979—; primary instr. paramedic program St. Louis Community Coll. at Florissant Valley, St. Louis; CPR instr. Recipient Instr. Achievement award Barnes Hosp., 1977; cert. allied health tchr., Mo. Mem. Greater St. Louis Soc. Health Edn. and Tng., Am. Assn. Critical Care Nurses (CCRN bd. 1978—), Am. Soc. for Tng. and Devel., Mo. Assn. for Health Care Edn., Mo. Health Systems Agy., Nat. League for Nursing, Patient and Community Educators, Assn. To Advance Ethical Hypnosis. Republican. Methodist. Club: Order Eastern Star. Contbr. articles to profl. jours. Office: 11133 Dunn Rd Saint Louis MO 63136

BARRAGA, NATALIE CARTER, educator; b. Troy, Tex., Oct. 10, 1915; d. Bscom Debo and Grovie Wood (Harrison) Carter; B.S., N. Tex. State U., 1938; M.Ed., U. Tex., 1957; Ed.D., Peabody Coll. Tchrs., 1963; m. John Thomas Barraga, Aug. 9, 1943 (div. 1952); 1 dau., Karen Jeanne. Public sch. tchr., 1938-42; residential sch. tchr. N.Y. Inst. Edn. Blind, 1948-51, Tex. Sch. Blind, 1952-61; lectr., instr. U. Tex., 1952-61; mem. faculty Peabody Coll. Tchrs., 1961-63, asst. prof., 1963-66, asso. prof., 1966-70; prof. spl. edn. U. Tex., Austin, 1970—; mem. ofcl. bd. Austin Cerebral Palsy Center; lectr., speaker in field. Chmn. ofcl. bd. Univ. Christian Ch. (Disciples of Christ), Austin. Recipient Teaching Excellence award Tex. Mental Health Assn., Apollo award Am. Optometric Assn.; grantee U.S. Office Edn., 1965—. Mem. Assn. Edn. Visually Handicapped, Internat. Council Edn. Visually Handicapped, Council Exceptional Children, Pi Lambda Theta, Kappa Delta Pi, Phi Kappa Phi, Delta Kappa Gamma. Democrat. Author books, monographs, articles in field; editor: Education of Visually Handicapped. Home: 1215 Larkwood Dr Austin TX 78723 Office: EDB 306 U Tex Austin TX 78712

BARRAGAN, POLLY BACA, Democratic nat. committeewoman; b. LaSalle, Colo., Feb. 13, 1941; B.A., Colo. State U., 1962; postgrad. Colo. State U., Am. U. Editor, Washington Trade Union newspaper; public info. officer The White House; owner, cons. public relations firm, Thornton, Colo.; mem. Colo. Ho. Reps., 1974-78, chairwoman Democratic Caucus, 1977-78; mem. Colo. State Senate, 1978-80; vice-chairwoman Dem. Nat. Com., Washington, 1981—. Mem. Nat. Chicano Planning Council, Nat. Minority Legis. Edn. Program, Dem. Woman's Caucus. Office: The Democratic Party 1625 Massachusetts Ave NW Washington DC 20036 *

BARRAL, MYRLINDA VILLARIVERA, psychiatrist; b. Gumaca, Quezon, Philippines, Oct. 17, 1944; d. Victoriano V. and Teofila V. B.; M.D., U. Santo Tomas (Philippines), 1969. Intern, U. Santo Tomas; resident adult psychiatry Chgo. Med. Sch., 1974, Rush-Presbyn. St. Luke's Med. Center, Chgo., 1977; fellow child psychiatry Bradley Hosp., Riverside, R.I., 1977-79; staff psychiatrist St. Lawrence Psychiat. Center, Ogdensburg, N.Y., 1979—. Roman Catholic. Home: Station A Ogdensburg NY 13669

BARRETT, BETTY, sculptor; b. N.Y.C., Nov. 5, 1912; d. Charles and Jeanette (Kaufman) Palash; student N.Y.U., New Sch. Social Research, Art Students League, N.Y. Sch. Interior Design; m. Herbert Barrett, May 29, 1937; children—Nancy Jane, Katherine Louise. One-man shows include Library Performing Arts, Lincoln Center, 1973, The White House, 1976; exhibited in group shows Audubon Artists, 1970, Caravan House Gallery, N.Y.C., 1971, N.Y. Guild Sculptors, 1972; represented in pvt. collections, U.S. and Eng. Recipient sculpture award New Sch. Social Research show, 1968. Mem. English Speaking Union.

BARRETT, CLAIRE MIRIAM RONDEAU (MRS. CLIFFORD J. BARRETT), educator; b. Malden, Mass.; d. Charles E. and Gelia A. (Tessier) Rondeau; B.S., Tchrs. Coll. Providence, 1956; M.S., Fordham U., 1960, Ph.D., 1964; m. Clifford J. Barrett, Aug. 29, 1970. Guidance counselor Stella Viae Internat. Coll., Rome, 1964-65; asst. prof. Sch. Edn. Catholic U., Washington, 1966-68; prof. psychology Holy Trinity Mission Sem., Silver Spring, Md., 1965-69; asso. prof. Seton Hall U., Sch. Edn., South Orange, N.J., 1969—, chmn. dept. gen. profl. edn., 1972-75, asst. dean, 1977—; guidance dir. Regina High Sch., Hyattsville, Md., 1965-69; coll. supr. student teaching N.J. Pub. Schs., 1969—. Mem. N.J. Right to Life Com.; mem. N.J. Council for Ednl. Founds., 1970-72, Pro Ecclesia Com. Catholic Laymen, N.Y.C., 1971—. Mem. Am. Acad. Religion, AAUP, Internat. Platform Assn., Am. Profs. for Peace in Middle East, Am. Edn. Studies Assn., AAUW, Women in Religious Studies, Soc. for Arts, Religion and Contemporary Culture, Am.-Israel League, Am. Cath. Hist. Soc., N.J. Consortium Ind. Colls., Kappa Delta Pi. Roman Catholic. Author: Psychological Perspectives in Education, 1980. Home: 76 Lowell Ave West Orange NJ 07052 Office: Seton Hall U South Orange NJ 07079

BARRETT, ELIZABETH ANN MANHART, nurse researcher, educator, psychotherapist; b. Hume, Ill., July 11, 1934; d. Francis J. and Grace C. (Manhart) Fridy; B.S. summa cum laude in Nursing, U. Evansville, 1970, M.A., 1973, M.S. in Nursing, 1976; postgrad. in nursing N.Y. U.; grad. Gestalt Assocs. for Psychotherapy, 1982; children—Joseph B., Jeffrey F., Paula G., Pamela M. Shetler Carpino, Scott D. Inst. nursing u. Evansville (Ind.), 1970-73, asst. prof., 1973-76; staff nurse Welborn Baptist Hosp., Evansville, 1975-76; staff nurse Bellevue Psychiat. Hosp., N.Y.C., 1976-79; clin. tchr. CUNY, 1977-82; group practice Nurse Healers, 1979-82; pvt. practice psychotherapy, 1980—; nurse researcher Mt. Sinai Med. Center, N.Y.C., 1982—; asst. prof. Adelphi U., 1979-80. Mem. com. Regional Health Planning Council, Evansville, 1974-77. Mem. Am. Nurses Assn. (cert. psychiat.-mental health), Nat. League Nursing, Soc. Advancement in Nursing, Nurse Healers-Profl. Assos. Coop., East-West Acad. Healing Arts, NOW, Phi Kappa Phi, Sigma Theta Tau, Alpha Tau Delta. Home: 34-50 29th St Long Island City NY 11106 Office: 5 E 98th St New York NY 10029

BARRETT, MARY EL, govt. ofcl.; b. Chgo., July 3, 1948; d. Charles Joseph and Eleanor Bernadette (Lynch) Barrett; B.A., St. Xavier Coll., 1970; postgrad. Governors State U., 1976-77. Tchr. elem. grades Stony Creek Sch., Alsip, Ill., 1970-77; office mgr. Re-Election Campaign of Rep. Martin Russo, 1978, 80; legal asst. U.S. HEW, Chgo., 1979; dist. mgr. U.S. Dept. Commerce, Bur. of the Census, Tinley Park, Ill., 1980—. Intern, Ill. Gen. Assembly, 1976. Mem. Am. Fedn. Tchrs. Democrat. Roman Catholic. Office: 17728 Oak Park Ave Tinley Park IL 60477

BARRETT, NANCY SMITH, educator; b. Balt., Sept. 12, 1942; d. James Brady and Katherine Lee (Pollard) Smith; B.A. summa cum laude, Goucher Coll., 1963; M.A., Harvard U., 1965, Ph.D., 1968; children—Harold Clark, Christopher Ryland. Prof. econs. Am. U., 1966—; vis. prof. U. Gothenburg (Sweden), 1972-73; vis. scholar Inst. Econ. Studies, Belgrade, Yugoslavia, 1973; dep. asst. dir. Congressional Budget Office, 1975-76; sr. staff Council Econ. Advisers, 1977; dep. asst. sec. for policy, evaluation and research U.S. Dept. Labor, 1979-81. Woodrow Wilson fellow, 1963-64. Mem. Am. Econ. Assn., Phi Beta Kappa. Author: The Theory of Macroeconomic Policy, 1972, 75; Prices and Wages in U.S. Manufacturing, 1973; The Theory of Microeconomic Policy, 1974. Home: 2034 Hillyer Pl NW Washington DC 20009 Office: Dept Economics American U Washington DC 20016

BARRETT, PATRICIA LOUISE HESCH, educator; b. Fargo, N.D., Aug. 17, 1936; d. John Edward and Irene Marie (Sullivan) Yunker; A.A., San Joaquin Delta, Stockton, Calif., 1971; B.S. magna cum laude, Mankato State U., 1973, M.S., 1977; m. Robert T. Barrett, July 19, 1980; children—James P. Hesch, Janell Smith, John Hesch, Joel Hesch, Jerome Hesch. Mgr., Duebers Fabric Shop, Waseca, Minn., 1971; tchr. Waseca County Day Activity Center, 1973-74; spl. edn. tchr. Waseca Public Schs., 1974-77; dept. chmn. home and family services div. U. Minn., Waseca, 1977-79; specialist vocat. edn. for handicapped Riverside County Supt. Schs. Office, Riverside, Calif., 1979—. Precinct chmn. Democratic Farm Labor party, 1978; mem. adv. com. region 9 Council on Aging, 1979-80; mem. adv. com. Waseca County Group Home for Retarded, 1978-80; program coordinator Rural Family Life Center, Waseca, 1978-80; mem. Mayor's Com. Employment of Handicapped. Mem. NEA, Assn. Children with Learning Disabilities, Home Econs. Assn., Council Exceptional Children, Assn. Edn. Young Children, Phi Kappa Phi. Author: Prevocational Skills Checklist for Severely Handicapped, 1980; Career and Vocational Education for the Handicapped, 1981. Home: 5497 Inspiration Dr Riverside CA 92506 Office: Spl Schs and Services Riverside County Supt Schs PO Box 868 Riverside CA 92502

BARRINGTON, KATHERINE PETERSEN, retirement home adminstr.; b. Cedar Rapids, Iowa, Oct. 29, 1926; d. Walter Emil and Edna Katherine (House) Petersen; B.S. in Edn., U. Mo., 1949, postgrad. in health care mgmt., 1975; postgrad. in counseling U. Kans., 1974; children—Katherine A. Barrington Bagby, Douglas Steven. Tchr. bus. Univ. High Sch., Columbia, Mo., 1948-49; tchr. Pre-Sch. for Visually Handicapped, Kansas City, Mo., 1957-58; dir. George H. Nettleton Home, Kansas City, Mo., 1975—. Pres., Tomahawk Sch. PTA, Overland Park, Kans., 1959-60; v.p. PTA area council, Shawnee Mission, Kans., 1967-68; sec. to adminstrv. asst. to Senator James Pearson of Kans., 1971-72. Mem. Am. Coll. Nursing Home Adminstrs., Am., Mo. (v.p. 1977-78) assns. homes for aging, U. Mo. Alumni Assn., Delta Gamma (Nat. Cable award 1980). Republican. Methodist. Home: 9501 W 89th St Overland Park KS 66207 Office: 5125 Swope Pkwy Kansas City MO 64130

BARRON, CHARLOTTE, correctional instn. adminstr.; b. El Dorado, Ark., Nov. 6, 1941; d. Hugh and Margie (Everett) B.; B.A. with honors, N.E. La. State Coll., 1963; M.S.W., Tulane U., 1965. Psychiat. social worker S.E. La. State Hosp., Mandeville, 1965-67; social worker North County Mental Health Clinic, Daly City, Calif., 1967-68, NIMH Clin. Research Center, Ft. Worth, 1968-71; instr. Bur. Prisons Staff Tng. Center, Dallas, 1974-76; case mgr. Fed. Correctional Instn., Ft. Worth, 1971-72, unit mgr., 1972-74, case mgmt. coordinator, 1976-79, exec. asst., 1979—; adj. prof. criminal justice U. Tex., Arlington, 1977. Lic. social psychotherapist, Tex.; cert. Acad. Cert. Social Workers. Mem. Nat. Assn. Social Workers, Am. Correctional Assn. Episcopalian. Home: 4909 Emerald Lake Dr Fort Worth TX 76103 Office: 3150 Horton Rd Fort Worth TX 76119

BARRON, ERMA WILLIAMSON, statistician; b. Balt., June 10, 1940; d. Levi and Viola Williamson; B.S., Morgan State U., Balt., 1963; postgrad. Johns Hopkins U., George Washington U., U. Md.; m. James Barron; children—Michael, Jocelyn. Tchr. high sch. math., 1963-64; with Social Security Adminstrn., 1964-70, 73—, statistician, 1973-78, chief earnings and employment stats. br., 1978—, chmn. task force minority women, 1979—; with HEW, 1970-73, coordinator fed. women's program, 1972-73. Chmn. adv. com. women low-income Prince George's County Commn. Women, 1974-76; 2d v.p. Prince George's County Women's Polit. Caucus, 1975-76; bd. dirs. Project SAGA. Mem. Am. Statis. Assn., NAACP, Nat. Council Negro Women, Alpha Kappa Alpha. Democrat. Mem. United Ch. Christ. Author papers in field. Home: 8510 Nightingale Dr Lanham MD 20706 Office: 6401 Security Blvd Baltimore MD 21235

BARRON, GLORIA JOAN, historian, educator; b. Bklyn., May 19, 1933; d. Maurice Lee and Irene Barron; A.B., Wellesley Coll., 1954; M.A., Columbia U., 1956, postgrad., 1958-59; postgrad. U. Chgo., 1964-65; Ph.D. (AAUW fellow), Tufts U., 1971. Registrar, tchr. history Newton Jr. Coll., Newtonville, Mass., 1956-58; tchr. history upper sch. Brimmer and May Sch., Chestnut Hill, Mass., 1959-63; chmn. history dept. Winthrop (Mass.) High Sch., 1963-64; edn. specialist Office Edn., HEW, Washington, 1965-66; mem. faculty Framingham (Mass.) State Coll., 1970—, asso. prof. history, 1979—, chmn. dept., 1982—. Mem. Am. Hist. Assn., Orgn. Am. Historians, AAUW (area rep. cultural interests Boston br. 1974-76). Author: Leadership in Crisis: FDR and the Path to Intervention, 1973. Office: Framingham State Coll Framingham MA 01701

BARRON, ILONA ELEANOR, educator; b. Mass, Mich., Sept. 19, 1929; d. John and Nelma (Erickson) Makinen; state cert. No. Mich. U., 1951; B.S. in Elementary Edn., Central Mich. U., Mt. Pleasant, 1961; M.A. in Edn., U. Mich., Ann Arbor, 1966; postgrad. Mich. State U., East Lansing; m. George F. Barron; 1 son, Frederick Mark. Title I dir. Saginaw (Mich.) Twp. Community Schs., 1967-68, reading cons., 1971—; elementary internal cons. Mich. State U., 1968-71; elementary reading cons. Saginaw Twp. Public Schs., 1972—. Mem. NEA, Mich., Saginaw Twp. Edn. Assns., Saginaw Area Reading Council. Specialist in reading, methods of teaching developmental reading skills and enrichment. Home: 4891 Hillcrest Dr Saginaw MI 48603 Office: Plainfield Elementary Sch 2775 Shattuck Rd Saginaw MI 48603

BARRON, LAURA ROWE, fed. govt. elec. utility exec.; b. Albany, Ga., Oct. 3, 1950; d. Lester Harris and Harriette Elizabeth (Dozier) Rowe; B.S. magna cum laude, U. Tenn., 1972, M.B.A., 1982. Comml. interior designer T.H. Payne Co., Chattanooga, 1974-76; with TVA, Chattanooga, 1976-78, supr. Central travel sect., Knoxville, 1978—; mgmt. cons. Nolen Products Co., Knoxville, 1979-80. Mem. Nat. Mgmt. Assn., Federally Employed Women (sec. Knoxville chpt. 1978, mem. tng. com. 1980—), Nat. Passenger Traffic Assn., Inst. Bus. Designers, Embroiderers Guild Am., Zeta Tau Alpha Alumni Orgn., Phi Kappa Phi, Omicron Nu. Presbyterian. Home: 8316 Hunter Hill Dr Knoxville TN 37923 Office: Tenn Valley Authority 11 Liberty Bldg Knoxville TN 37902

BARRON, MABEL AMMONS, ret. hosp. adminstr.; b. Somerset, Pa., Dec. 28, 1906; d. Edward C. and Carrie M. (Berkey) B.; R.N., Western Pa. Hosp. Sch. Nursing, Pitts., 1928; student Tchrs. Coll., Columbia U., summers 1931-35; B.S., U. Pitts., 1943, M.A., 1944; D.H.L., Geneva Coll., 1962. Head nurse West Penn Hosp. Sch. Nursing, Pitts., 1928-30, med. supr., 1931-33, instr., 33-36, asst. prin., 1936-39; asst. adminstr. Magee Hosp., Pitts., 1939-52, dir. nursing, 1940-52; instr. U. Pitts. Sch. Nursing, 1940-43, asst. prof., 1944-53; adminstr. Ellwood City (Pa.) Hosps., 1952-73; spl. lectr. U. Pitts. Sch. Nursing, 1954-63. Bd. dirs. Ellwood City council Girl Scouts U.S.A., Lawrence County Mental Health Assn., Mental Health Clinic, Lawrence County Cancer Bd., Lawrence County Vis. Nurse Assn., 1966-73. Recipient Distinguished Service award, sr. citizen Jr. C. of C., Ellwood City, Pa., 1961; named Distinguished Dau. of Pa. Fellow Am. Coll. Hosp. Adminstrs.; mem. Hosp. Assn. Pa. (past pres.; chmn. council hosp. auxs.), Middle Atlantic Hosp. Assembly (pres.), Pa. Assn. Hosp. Auxs. (counsellor 1967-76), Sigma Theta Tau. Presbyterian (trustee). Clubs: Zonta, Bus. and Profl. Women's. Home: 110 2d St Ellwood City PA 16117

BARRON, NINA VIOLET, clin. psychologist; b. N.Y.C., Dec. 11, 1922; d. Jack and Blanche (Schecter) L.; B.A. magna cum laude, Fairleigh Dickinson U., 1973; M.A., St. John's U., 1975; Psy.D., Rutgers U., 1978; m. Jules Barron, July 9, 1944; children—Linda P. Mitchell, Jonathan. Intern, Bergen Pines County Hosp., Paramus, N.J., 1975-78; pvt. practice clin. psychology, Westwood, N.J., 1978—. Mem. Am., N.J. psychol. assns., AAUW. Address: 114 Honeysuckle Dr Westwood NJ 07675

BARRON, SANDRA COOGAN, accountant; b. Waltham, Mass., May 30, 1955; d. Patrick Arthur and Anne Marie (Schmidl) Coogan; B.B.A. with honors in Acctg., U. Tex., Austin, 1977; m. Claude Estes Barron, Sept. 30, 1978. Jr. acct. Elmer Fox, Westheimer & Co., El Paso, Tex., 1977-78; staff acct. Arthur Young & Co., San Diego, 1979, Seattle, 1979-80; state examiner Div. Mcpl. Corps., State of Wash., 1980-81; fin. analyst Mass. Mcpl. Wholesale Electric Co., 1982—. Mem. Am. Inst. C.P.A.s, Tex. Soc. C.P.A.s, Am. Women's Soc. C.P.A.s, Beta Gamma Sigma. Roman Catholic. Club: Tex. Exes. Address: 52 Stephens St Westover AFB MA 01022

BARROS, ANNAMARIE, mgmt. cons.; b. San Jose, Calif., Mar. 14, 1932; d. Anthony Clarence and Clara Magdalene Pacheco Vierra; B.A., Coll. Holy Names, Oakland, Calif., 1953; M.A., Central Mich. U., 1978; m. Richard L. Barros, June 11, 1960. Intern med. tech. O'Connor Hosp., San Jose, 1953-54; adminstrv. technologist Children's Hosp., San Francisco, 1958-65, Good Samaritan Hosp., San Jose, 1965-74; adminstrv. asst. public relations and mktg. Lab. Services, 1974-76; mgmt. devel. coordinator O'Connor Hosp., 1976-78; mgmt. cons., educator, propr. Health Mgmt. Analysts, Los Gatos, Calif., 1976—; adj. prof. grad. program clin. scis. San Francisco State U., 1976—; sec.-treas. Nat. Cert. Agy. Med. Lab. Personnel, 1977—. Bd. dirs. Santa Clara County chpt. ARC, 1980—; pres. Rinconada Hills Homeowners Assn., 1977-80. Named Med. Technologist of Yr. in Calif., 1969, 77. Mem. Am. Soc. Med. Tech. (pres. 1973-74, chmn. personnel relations com. 1981-82; named Adminstrv. Technologist of Yr. 1973, Mem. of Yr. 1978, recipient Profl. Achievement award 1979), Am. Soc. Allied Health Professions, Am. Mgmt. Assn., Calif. Soc. Med. Tech. Republican. Roman Catholic. Author articles, column in field. Address: 129 Callecita St Los Gatos CA 95030

BARRY, BESS SENTELL, banker; b. Germantown, Tenn., Dec. 22, 1926; d. Jack Williford and Bessie Agness (Coopwood) B.; student Tex. Women's U., 1945-46. With Union Planters Bank, Memphis, 1946—, investment ops. officer, 1973-75, asst. v.p., 1975-78, v.p. treasurer's div., 1978—. Mem. Germantown Hist. Preservation Com., 1975—, chmn., 1975-80, 82—; bd. dirs. Germantown Charity Horse Show, 1975—, exec. sec., 1952—; treas. Germantown Baptist Ch., 1954—, organist, pianist, 1941-81. Named Germantown Woman of Yr., 1977, Union Planters Woman Banker of Yr., 1976. Mem. Am. Inst. Banking, Nat. Assn. Bank Women, DAR (chpt. regent 1971-72, treas. 1976—). Club: Lamplighters Woman's (pres. 1975-76). Home: 2246 S Germantown Rd Germantown TN 38138 Office: 67 Madison Ave Memphis TN 38147

BARRY, JOAN LEBLANC, gerontologist, social service adminstr.; b. Providence, Oct. 28, 1937; d. Albert Richard and Elizabeth Rose (Edwards) LeBlanc; student U. R.I., 1957-58, R.I. Coll., 1955-56; B.A., Calif. State U., Sacramento, 1974, M.S.W., 1976; m. Edward Barry, Sr., May 26, 1958; children—Alexis, Leslie, Ted, Mark. Dir., Stanford Settlement Sr. Center, Sacramento, 1974-78; exec. dir. SOS, Inc., Orangevale, Calif., 1978—; chmn. bd. Eldercize, Inc., 1982—; cons. community agys., pvt. industry. Cert. community coll. tchr., Calif. Mem. Nat. Assn. Social Workers, Acad. Cert. Social Workers, Nat. Gerontol. Soc., Western Gerontol. Soc. Club: Soroptomist. Research on transp. for the elderly, exercise and aging. Home: 5110 Ruscal Way Fair Oaks CA 95628 Office: 6236 Main Ave Orangevale CA 95662

BARRY, JOYCE ALICE, dietitian; b. Chgo., Apr. 27, 1932; d. Walter Stephen and Ethel Myrtle (Paetow) Barry; student Iowa State Coll., 1950-52, Loyala U., 1952-58; B.S., Mundelein Coll., 1955; postgrad. Simmons Coll., 1963-64, U. Ga., 1979, Calif. Western U., 1980—. Prodn. supr. Marshall Field & Co., Chgo., 1955-59; dir. food services Women's Ednl. and Indsl. Union, Boston, 1959-62; dir. food services Wellesley (Mass.) Public Schs., 1962-70; cons. Stokes Food Services, Newton, Mass., 1960-70; regional dietitian Canteen Corp., Chgo., 1970—; vis. lectr.; restaurant cons. Mem. Nat. Consumer Panel; research adv. council Restaurant Bus. Mag.; career adv. council, treas. Dietitians in Bus. Mem. Am. Home Econs. Assn., Internat. Fedn. Home Economists, Home Economists in Bus., Am. Dietetics Assn., Soc. Nutrition Edn., Nat. Assn. Female Execs. Republican. Roman Catholic. Club: La Chaine des Rotisseurs. Home: PO Box 888244 Atlanta GA 30356 Office: 2951 Flowers Rd S Atlanta GA 30341

BARSANTI, JOANNE BARBARA, data processing cons.; b. Milw., Oct. 19, 1946; d. Bruce Julius and Barbara Ann (Banach) Walthers Von Alten; B.A. in English, Loyola U., 1969; m. John E. Barsanti, May 17, 1969; 1 son, Jason Eric. Programmer/analyst CNA Ins., Chgo., 1969-70; systems analyst 1st Fed. Savings & Loan, Milw., 1970-72; cons., account mgr., project mgr. Consumer Systems, Oakbrook, Ill., 1974-79; project mgr. CBM, Inc., Schaumburg, Ill., 1979—. Mem. Assn. Systems Mgmt. (pres. 1979-80, treas. 1980-81, publicity chmn. 1981-82). Roman Catholic. Author: Reflections in a Black Pond, 1973. Home: 230 Ashley Ct Roselle IL 60172 Office: 999 Plaza Dr Suite 100 Schaumburg IL 60195

BARSKY, MARILYN LEE, clin. psychologist; b. Detroit, Sept. 11, 1928; d. Lester Arthur and Helen Amy (Stein) Cannon; B.A., Smith Coll., 1950; B.Ed., U. Toledo, 1952; M.A., U. Mich., 1954; Ed.D., Rutgers U., 1966; m. James Barsky, June 30, 1957; children—Robert, Rosalind. Tchr., Public Schs. Evanston (Ill.), 1955-58; sch. psychologist, Livingston, N.J., 1965, Bloomfield, N.J., 1966-68; prof. Jersey City State Coll., 1968-69; sch. psychologist, East Orange, N.J., 1969-70; staff psychologist Family Service and Child Guidance Center of Oranges (N.J.), 1970-75, research asso., 1973-75; sr. research scientist Postgrad. Center for Mental Health, N.Y.C., 1976-78; pvt. practice clin. psychology, 1972—; cons. Montclair Acad., 1976-77, Rossi and Sperling Assos., 1978-80, N.J. Rehab. Cons., 1966—; adj. prof. Montclair State Coll., 1977—. Mem. Doe Vs. Klein Com., State of N.J.; trustee Temple Shomrei Emunah. Diplomate Am. Bd. Profl. Psychology; lic. psychologist, N.J.; cert. psychologist, N.Y.; lic. sch. psychologist, N.J. Mem. Am. Psychol. Assn., N.J. Psychol. Assn. (sec., com. profl. standards), N.J. Acad. Psychology, (continuing edn. com.), N.J. Mental Health Assn., Kappa Delta Pi; fellow Am. Orthopsychiat. Assn. Democrat. Contbr. articles to profl. jours. Home and office: 66 Oakridge Rd Verona NJ 07044

BARSNESS, WYLLA DECKER, psychologist; b. Denver, Oct. 21, 1924; d. Rutherford Losey and Gladys (Jarnagin) Decker; B.A., William Jewell Coll., 1949; M.S. in Psychology, Mont. State U., 1959; Ph.D. in Child Psychology (NIMH fellow), U. Minn., 1969; m. John Alton Barsness, June 9, 1951; children—John Alton, James David, Karen Elizabeth, Sarah Losey. Office mgr. Larimer County Hosp., Ft. Collins, Colo., 1942-45; instr. William Jewell Coll., 1949-53, Mont. State U., 1957-59; research dir. Bozeman (Mont.) Public Schs., 1966-69; asst. prof. psychology Boise State U., 1968-69, asso. prof., 1969-73, prof., 1973—; devel. cons. St. Lukes's Hosp., 1972-82. Bd. dirs. Info. and Referral Bd., United Fund, 1978—; regional dir., state del. Democratic Party; chpt. mem. St. Michael's Cathedral, 1972-75, dir. religions edn., 1972-75; dep. to gen. conv. Episcopal Ch., 1979, 82; chmn. social concerns com. Provincial Council, Episc. Diocese. Recipient Disting. Teaching award Boise State U. Alumni, 1980, 81; Danforth asso., 1973—. Mem. Soc. Research in Child Devel., Idaho Psychol. Assn. (pres. 1978-80), Rocky Mountain Psychol. Assn., HERS/West (chmn. Boise State U. chpt.). Democrat. Home: 1922 Mortimer Dr Boise ID 83702 Office: 1925 University Dr Boise ID 83725

BART, PAULINE BERNICE, sociologist; b. N.Y.C., Feb. 18, 1930; d. Emil and Mildred (Prozan) Lackow; B.A., UCLA, 1950, M.A., 1952, Ph.D., 1967; divorced; children—William Laurence, Melinda Bart Schlesinger. Vis. asst. prof. sociology U. So. Calif., Los Angeles, 1967-68; lectr. sociology U. Calif., Berkeley, 1968-70; asst. prof. sociology in psychiatry Sch. Medicine, U. Ill., Chgo., 1970-72, asso. prof., 1972-81, prof., 1981—; disting. vis. prof. women's studies San Diego State U., 1980; Roberts lectr. Grinnell (Iowa) Coll., 1975; Am. Psychol. Assn. lectr., 1977; vis. prof. sociology U. Calif., Santa Barbara, 1981; research person for com. on edn. Ill. Commn. on Status of Women; mem. subcom. Mayor's Commn. on Child Care, 1978-80. Mem. Am. Sociol. Assn. council; (chmn. sect. sociology of sex roles 1972-73), Soc. Study Social Problems (C. Wright Mills award com. 1972, elections com. 1978), Sociologists for Women in Soc. (steering com. 1970—), Nat. Assn. Women's Studies, Chgo. Women in Research, Assn. Women in Psychology. Co-author: The Students Sociologist's Handbook, 3d edit., 1981; author: (with Pat O'Brien) Stopping Rape: Women Who Did, 1980; asso. editor Jour. Health and Social Behavior, 1972-76, Psychology of Women Quar., 1978-81; editorial bd. Women and Health, 1976-81; editor spl. issues Jour. Marriage and the Family, 1971; contbg. editor Chrysalis, 1977-80; contbr. articles to profl. jours. Office: Dept Psychiatry Abraham Lincoln Sch Medicine Univ Ill PO Box 6998 Chicago IL 60680

BARTEK, BARBARA ANN, machinery buyer; b. Pitts., Aug. 7, 1953; d. Elmer and Victoria (Mroz) B.; student Westminster Coll., 1971-73; B.S. in Mgmt. magna cum laude, Boston U., 1975; postgrad. in bus. adminstrn. U. Mich. With Ford Motor Co., Dearborn, Mich., 1975—, now machinery buyer. Chmn. Community Ecology Club, Pitts., 1971; active Detroit Young Republicans. Mem. Beta Gamma Sigma, Psi Chi. Clubs: Ski, Ford Motor. Designer apparatus for tng. rats, 1972; composer clarinet solo, 1969. Home: 49011 I-94 Apt 302 Belleville MI 48111 Office: Room 2510 Ford Motor Co American Rd Dearborn MI 48121

BARTEL, ANN PELCOVITS, economist; b. N.Y.C., Sept. 15, 1949; d. Harry W. and Helen (Lassman) Pelcovits; B.A. summa cum laude, U. Pa., 1970; M.A., Columbia U., 1973, Ph.D., 1974; m. Charles H. Bartel, Aug. 30, 1970; children—Joseph, Sharon. Asst. prof. econs. U. Pa., Phila., 1974-76; asst. prof. bus. Columbia U., N.Y.C., 1976-78, asso. prof., 1978—; research asso. Nat. Bur. Econ. Research, N.Y.C., 1974—; cons. statis. and econ. analysis Title VII, 1977—. Herbert Lehman grad. fellow, 1970-74; Dept. Justice grantee, 1973-74; Dept. Labor grantee, 1979-80; Alfred Sloan Found. grantee, 1980-81; Found. Fund for Research in Psychiatry grantee, 1980-81. Mem. Am. Econ. Assn. Contbr. articles to profl. jours. Home: 1674 Buckingham Rd Teaneck NJ 07666 Office: 710 Uris Hall Columbia U New York NY 10027

BARTEL, JANIS CORCORAN, nurse; b. Ottawa, Ill., Apr. 7, 1953; d. John Joseph and Edith Marguerite (Read) Corcoran; B.S. in Nursing, No. Ill. U., 1975; M.S. in Nursing, Loyola U., Chgo., 1979; m. Aug. 19, 1978. Staff nurse, med. unit, coronary care unit Loyola U. Med. Center, Maywood, Ill., 1975-79; coordinator nursing edn. MacNeal Meml. Hosp., Berwyn, Ill., 1979-81; instr. nursing Moraine Valley Community Coll., Palos Hills, Ill., Triton Coll., River Grove, Ill. Cert. instr. CPR; R.N., Ill. Mem. Am. Nurses Assn., Ill. Nurses Assn., NOW, Sigma Theta Tau. Roman Catholic. Home: 4208 Blanchan Ave Brookfield IL 60513

BARTELL, ANGELA GINA BALDI, county ofcl.; b. Milw., Jan. 25, 1946; d. John B. and Marie (Rank) Baldi; B.A. in Psychology, German U. of Wis., 1969, J.D. magna cum laude, 1971; m. Jeffrey B. Bartell, Aug. 31, 1968; children—Jessica Marie, Carey Laurel, Chad Gerald, Dana Joyce, Nicholas John. Admitted to Wis. bar, 1972, Fed. Dist. Ct. bar, 1972; law trainee Wis. Dept. Justice, Madison, 1970; law clk. Hon. James E. Doyle, Fed. Dist. Judge for Western Dist. Wis., 1971-72; asso. firm LaFollette, Sinykin, Anderson & Munson, Madison, 1973-75, partner, 1976-77; circuit judge Dane County, Wis., 1978—; lectr. in field. Vice chairperson Com. on Child Advocacy, White House Conf. on Children and Youth, 1970; pres. Friends of Channel 21, 1978-79; bd. dirs. Community Dispute Settlement Center, 1980—. Recipient Delta Gamma shield award, 1980. Mem. Wis., Dane County, Am. bar assns., Nat. Assn. Women Lawyers, Nat. Assn. Women Trial Judges, Legal Assn. for Women, Bar Assn. Seventh Fed. Circuit, Order of Coif, Phi Beta Kappa. Mem. editorial bd. Wis. Law Review, 1969-71, articles editor, 1970-71. Office: Dane County Court House 313G City-County Bldg Madison WI 53709

BARTELL, SELMA DOROTHY CLASSEN, auto distbg. co. exec.; b. Fairview, Okla., Apr. 19, 1906; d. Dietrich John and Helena (Duerksen) Classen; grad. Kern County Jr. Coll., 1924; m. Henry Jacob Bartell, Mar. 1, 1925; children—Lula May, Ruben C., Florence Lucille, Clarence Henry, Lawson Wayne, Henry Lee. Owner, mgr. H.J. Bartell Bardahl Distbrs., Bakersfield, Calif., 1972—. Pres., PTA, 1932, 33, pres. Kern County Home Dept.; v.p. Calif. Farm Bur. Women; Calif. del. Asso. Country Women of the World, 1953; leader 4-H, 1936-; pres. Symphony Assos., 1967-68; pianist, Sunday sch. tchr. Mennonite Brethren Ch., 1920-60. Named Woman of Year, Valley Plaza Mchts. Assn., 1970. Mem. Rosedale Hwy. Bus. Assn. (pres. 1978), Desk and Derrick Bakersfield (pres. 1966-67). Republican. Home and office: 2001 Calloway Dr Bakersfield CA 93308

BARTER, RUBY SUNSHINE, Realtor; b. Omaha; d. Harry and Ruth (Gilman) Kolnick; B.S. in Med. Tech., Creighton U.; postgrad. Clarkson Meml. Hosp. Sch. Med. Tech., U. Colo. Sch. Continuing Edn.; m. Gerson Barter; children—Bruce, Mark, Sharon Sunshine Steinberg, Peggy Sunshine, Jeffrey, Randi Sunshine Simon, JoAnne Sunshine

Trombley, Ronald Sunshine. Med. technologist Creighton Meml. St. Joseph Hosp.; realtor Nat. Real Estate & Mgmt. Co., Heller-Mark & Co., Walpin & Co., Denver. Mem. Mayor's Adv. Com. on Denver's War on Poverty; project dir. Denver Citywide Headstart Vols.; mem. adv. com. Dialogue Regis Coll., Anti-Defamation League of B'nai B'rith; pres. B'nai B'rith Women Chpt. of Denver, B'nai B'rith Council of Denver; mem. Mountain States exec. com. Anti-Defamation League, Hillel Councils, B'nai B'rith Youth Council; mem. vol. staff Nat. Jewish Hosp., Jewish Community Center; mem. dist. exec. bd. B'nai B'rith Women; exec. chmn. B'nai B'rith Inst. Judaism; mem. exec. bd. Beth Joseph Congregation; active Adult Edn. Council Denver, Internat. House; Dolls for Democracy lady Denver Pub. Schs. Mem. Colo., Nat., Denver (liaison com. Real Estate Commn.; mem. edn. com.). bds. realtors, Real Estate Exchangers, Realtors Nat. Mktg. Inst., Real Estate Securities Syndication Inst. Cert. Comml.-Investment Mems. Home: 201 S Dexter St Denver CO 80222 Office: Suite 300 817 17th St Denver CO 80202

BARTHEL, CAROL ANN, govt. ofcl.; b. Valley Stream, N.Y., May 17, 1946; d. Henry Conrad and Lissette Catherine (Ehrmann) B.; B.A., Duke U., 1968; postgrad. Edinburgh (Scotland) U. 1968-69; M.Phil., Yale U., 1971, Ph.D., 1974; m. Dennis J. Gallagher, June 22, 1974. Teaching asst. Yale U., 1971-72; instr. Quinnipiac (Conn.) Coll., 1973; instr. U. Wis., Madison, 1974-75, asst. prof., 1975-78; legis. aide to Rep. Robert C. Krueger, Washington, 1978, Rep. William F. Clinger, Jr., Washington, 1979—. Fulbright scholar, 1968-69, Woodrow Wilson fellow, 1968, Danforth fellow, 1969-74. Mem. MLA, Soc. Values Higher Edn., Spenser Soc., Porlock Soc. Office: 1221 Longworth House Office Bldg Washington DC 20515

BARTHLEIN, ARLINE RUTH, tuba player, educator; b. Hartford, Conn., Feb. 4, 1931; d. Samuel and Bertha (Hunt) B.; B.Mus., Boston Conservatory of Music, 1961; postgrad. U. Vt., Burlington, 1977; scholar New Eng. Conservatory of Music, Boston. Music tchr. Gilbert Stuart Jr. High Sch., Providence, 1966-67, Cumberland (R.I.) Schs., 1967-70, Randolph Union High Sch., Randolph, Vt., 1970-73; band dir. Cumberland-Lincoln Boys' Club, 1970-73, Hopkington High Sch., Contoocook, N.H., 1977-79; music and fine arts librarian Attleboro (Mass.) Public Library; tuba player Portland (Maine) Symphony, 1955-70, Vt. Philharm., 1970—, Vt. Symphony, 1970—, Berkshire Symphony, 1974—, Williams Coll. Choral Soc. Orch., 1974—; tuba player, librarian Can. Opera Co. Orch., Ont., 1973; appearances with Leopold Stokowski, Bavarian Beer Garden Orch., Munich, Germany. Recipient R.I. Music Educators award (3); fellow Combs Coll. of Music, Phila., 1980-81. Mem. AAUW, Nat. Music Educators Assn., Mass. Geneal. Soc. Anglican Orthodox. Co-author: Project Prime, 1968. Home: 6 Elmwood Ave North Adams MA 01247

BARTHOLET, ELIZABETH IVES, art gallery exec.; b. N.Y.C.; d. Frederick M. and Edith (Wetherill) Ives; B.A., Bryn Mawr Coll., 1924; student U. Grenoble, summer 1922, Harvard U., summer 1926; m. Paul Bartholet, May 14, 1932; children—Paul Ives, Chauncey Ives, Elizabeth. Writer, art and music column Cambridge (Mass.) Tribune, 1925-28; contbr. articles to numerous mags., 1925-28; research reporter Fortune Mag., 1929-32; owner, dir. Bartholet Art Gallery, N.Y.C., 1957—. Mem. Appraisers Assn. Am. Club: Cosmopolitan. Home and Gallery: 55 E 76th St New York NY 10021

BARTHOLOME, ELAINE BLACK, banker; b. Hartford, Conn., Oct. 2, 1949; d. William T. and Constance L. Black, Jr.; student Central Conn. State Coll., New Britain, 1967-70, Pacific Coast Grad. Sch. Banking, U. Wash., 1981—. Sec. trust div. Hartford Nat. Bank & Trust Co., 1970-71; br. mgr., asst. treas. Charter Oak Bank & Trust Co., Hartford, 1971-76; v.p. charge corp. loan portfolio Bettendorf Bank & Trust Co. (Iowa), 1977—; speaker. Former tchr. Project Bus., Jr. Achievement, also cons. cert., 1979. Recipient Leadership award Wethersfield (Conn.) Recreation and Parks Dept., 1962. Mem. Nat. Assn. Bank Women, Bank Adminstrn. Inst. (dir.), Am. Inst. Banking (past dir.), Scott County Bankers Assn., Davenport C. of C., Bettendorf C. of C. Club: Outing (Davenport). Office: 1819 State St Bettendorf IA 52722

BARTHOLOMEW, LYNNE, pianist; b. Sellersville, Pa., Dec. 17, 1941; d. Charles G. and Wanda E. B.; B.Mus., U. Mich., 1963, M.Mus., 1965; postgrad. U. So. Calif., 1979-80. Teaching fellow U. Mich., 1963-65, instr., 1966-69, asst. prof. music, 1969-77, asso. prof., 1977—, mem. exec. com. Sch. Music, 1982-85; mem. piano faculty, mem. for All-State Sessions, Nat. Music Camp, Interlochen, Mich.; mem. adv. bd. for piano workshops Schoolcraft Coll., Livonia, Mich.; chmn. program com. Conf. on Women in Music, Ann Arbor, 1983. Fulbright scholar, Germany, 1965-66. Recipient Babcock award U. Mich., 1963, Wolaver award, 1965. Mem. Nat. Music Tchrs. Assn., Pi Kappa Lambda, Phi Kappa Phi. Home: 1327 Natalie #48 Ann Arbor MI 48105 Office: U Mich Sch Music Ann Arbor MI 48109

BARTHOLOMEW, RENE COOPER, nurse; b. Los Angeles, Oct. 30; d. Lee E. and Georgia M. (Washington) Cooper; B.S. in Biology (R. Cooper scholar 1966), Prairie View (Tex.) A&M Coll., 1970; R.N., Los Angeles Southwestern Coll., 1972; nurse practitioner cert. UCLA, 1973; m. Bertram R. Bartholomew, Jr., Aug. 25, 1978; children—Michael J., Michelle N. Mem. nursing staff West Adams Hosp., Los Angeles, 1972-74, Los Angeles County Sheriff's Dept., 1974-78, Daniel Freeman Hosp., Inglewood, Calif., 1978-79; head nurse telemetry and surg. care unit Calif. Hosp. Med. Center, Los Angeles, 1979-81; administrv. nurse cons. Western Park Hosp., Los Angeles, 1981—, critical care coordinator, 1982—; cons. in field. Mem. Black Nurses Assn., Calif. Nurses Assn., Delta Sigma Theta. Baptist. Home: 2433 Nadine St West Covina CA 91792 Office: 2231 S Western Los Angeles CA 90015

BARTLE, ANNETTE GRUBER (MRS THOMAS R BARTLE), artist, writer; b. Poland; came to U.S., 1940, naturalized, 1943; d. Henry and Maria (Harczyk) Gruber; Bacheliere, Sorbonne, Paris, 1940; B.A., Elmira Coll., 1943; student Ecole des Beaux Arts, Paris, 1940, Art Student League (scholar) 1949, 1947-50; m. Thomas R. Bartle, Dec. 5, 1957; 1 dau., Eve Marie. One woman shows include: Midtown Galleries, N.Y.C., 1957, 60, 63, 66, Feingarten, Chgo., 1957, Wickersham Gallery, 1970; exhibited in group shows; AAAL, 1963, Detroit Art Inst., 1958, 62, 65, 67, Pa. Acad., 1959, 60, 66, Butler Art Inst., 1960, 64, 65, Cin. Art. Mus., 1960, 62, 67; represented in permanent collections: Am. Internat. Underwriters, Union Carbide, Conn. Mut. Life, Mural Port Authority Heliport, N.Y. Worlds Fair; contbr. articles to mags., newspapers, jours. including: N.Y. Times, Christian Sci. Monitor, Phila. Inquirer, Los Angeles Times, Palm Beach Life, Travel Weekly, Diversion. Active various community drives. Recipient citation for outstanding achievements 90th U.S. Congress, 1968; Pan Am. Travelling fellow, 1950. Mem. Am. Fedn. Arts, Artists Equity. Address: 231 E 76th St New York NY 10021

BARTLETT, DAPHNE JOAN, actuary; b. Edinburgh, Scotland, June 27, 1936; came to U.S., 1953, naturalized, 1967; d. Robert Graham and Margaret (Welburn) Deas; A.B., Vassar Coll., 1957; m. David Bartlett, June 29, 1963 (div. 1973); 1 dau., Melinda. Research asst. Inst. Life Ins., N.Y.C., 1957-61; actuarial student John Hancock Mutual Life Ins. Co., Boston, 1961-63; v.p., actuary Transamerica Occidental Life Ins. Co., Los Angeles, 1963—. Youth soccer coach, 1977-80. Fellow Soc. Actuaries (v.p. 1980-81); mem. Am. Acad. Actuaries, Los Angeles Actuarial Club (pres. 1975-76). Office: 1150 S Olive St Los Angeles CA 90015

BARTLETT, ELIZABETH, poet; b. N.Y.C.; d. Lewis and Charlotte (Rosefield) Winters; B.S. in Edn., N.Y. Tchrs. Coll., 1931; postgrad. Columbia U., 1934-36; m. Paul Alexander Bartlett, Apr. 19, 1943; 1 son, Steven James. Instr. dept. speech and theatre So. Methodist U., 1945-47; dir. Creative Writers Assn., New Sch. Social Research, 1955; asst. prof. English, San Jose State U., 1960-61; asso. prof. U. Calif., Santa Barbara, 1962-64; poetry editor ETC: A Review of General Semantics, 1963-76; vis. lectr. San Diego State U., 1979, others; books of poetry include: Poems of Yes and No, 1952; Behold This Dreamer, 1959, Poetry Concerto, 1961, It Takes Practice Not to Die, 1964, Twelve-Tone Poems, 1968, Threads, 1968, Selected Poems, 1970, The House of Sleep, 1975, In Search of Identity, 1977, Address in Time, 1979, A Zodiac of Poems, 1979, Memory Is No Stranger, 1981; (one-act verse play) Dialogue of Dust, 1977; contbr. poems, short stories, essays to numerous publs.; book reviewer Los Angeles Times; one-woman show of graphics Athenaeum Library, La Jolla, Calif. Huntington Hartford Found. fellow, 1959-60; Montalvoa Assn. fellow, 1960-61; Yaddo and MacDowell fellow, 1970; Dorland Mountain Colony fellow, 1980; grantee in field. Mem. Poetry Soc. Am., Internat. Soc. Gen. Semantics.

BARTLETT, NATALIE DOBSON, lab. supplies and equipment co. exec.; b. Dedham, Mass., Sept. 27, 1931; d. Donald Findley and Alice (White) Dobson; A.A., Mt. Ida Jr. Coll., 1951; postgrad. U. Colo., 1963, Salem State Coll., 1967, Middlesex Community Coll., 1980-81; m. Harold D. Bartlett, Dec. 3, 1951; children—Brian D., Bradford. Sr. underwriter Slavic Vis. Bur., UN, 1951-52; stewardness United Airlines, 1953-54, instr., 1954, supr., 1955; partner Burt Agy., Golden, Colo., 1957-65; tchr. Billerica (Mass.) Public Schs., 1966-69; customer service rep. Addison Wesley Pub. Co., Reading, Mass., 1969-70, customer service mgr., 1970-76; customer service supr. Curtin Matheson Sci. Inc., Woburn, Mass., 1976-78, ops. mgr., 1978—; dir. Coastal States Marine, 1981. Chmn. publicity LWV, Billerica, 1970-71. Mem. Clipped Wings (pres. 1955-56), Nat. Assn. Bus. and Profl. Women, North Surburban C. of C. Republican. Episcopalian. Clubs: Rolling Green Health & Tennis, Duplicate Bridge League of Merrimack Valley. Home: 34 Royal Crest Dr North Andover MA 01845 Office: Curtin Matheson Scientific Inc 110a Commerce Way Woburn MA 01888

BARTLEY, DIANA ESTHER RIVERA, educator; b. N.Y.C., May 18, 1940; d. Manuel Peláez Rivera and Lila Esther Camacho; cert. proficiciency in French, U. Fribourg (Switzerland), 1960; B.A., Rosemont Coll., 1961; cert. proficiency in Italian, U. Florence, 1962; M.A., Middlebury Coll., 1963; A.M., Stanford U., 1964, Ph.D., Stanford 1970; research scholar U. Leningrad (USSR), Hertzen Padagogical Institute, Leningrad 1967-68, U. Moscow and First Moscow State Pedagogical Inst. Fgn. Langs., 1968, U. Helsinki, 1967; 1 son. Tchr., USIA Bi-Nat. Center, Madrid, 1961-62; tchr. French and Spanish, Fairfield (Conn.) Sch. Dist., 1963, Palo Alto (Calif.) Unified Sch. Dist., 1964-66; research asst. Center for Research and Devel. in Teaching, Stanford U., 1966-69; instr. dept. Spanish and Portuguese, U. Wis.-Milw., 1969-70, asst. prof. dept. curriculum and instrn., 1970-73, asso. prof., 1973-78, 80—, fed. project dir., 1970-78; cons., lectr. in field; mem. nat. rev. panels U.S. Office Edn. and U.S. Dept. Edn., 1975, 77, 80, 81; mem. scholar diplomat seminar U.S. Dept. State, 1981. Bd. dirs. Florentine Opera Aux., Milw., 1973-76, Literacy Services of Wis., 1974-76, Centro del Nino, Inc., Milw., 1982—; past mem. Jr. League, Milw.; mem. bd. Mequon PTA, 1981-82, also other civic activities. Fulbright Hays Sr. Fellow U. Warsaw (Poland), 1978-80, Ministry, Edn., Sofia, Bulgaria, 1980. Past Mem. Am. Council Teaching Fgn. Langs., Am. Assn. Tchrs. French, Am. Assn. Tchrs. Spanish and Portuguese, MLA, Nat. Assn. Bilingual Edn., Am. Ednl. Research Assn., AAUW, Teaching of English to Speakers Other Langs., Wis. TESOL Assn., Author numerous books and monographs, latest including: The Latin Child Goes Forth, Bilingual Early Education Experience Based Lessons, 1975; The Adult Basic Education TESOL Handbooks, 1979; contbr. numberous articles to profl. jours. Pi Lambda Theta (education) 1964; Sigma Delta Pi (Spanish) 1964; Phi Delta Kappa (education) 197 ; Certificate of Leadership Adult Education Association 1974; Outstanding Young Woman of America 1972; Outstanding Young Woman of America for State of Wisconsin 1975. Third place Helen H. Hanover Scholarship 1966 State of California. Home: 203 W Highview Dr Mequon WI 53092 Office: Sch Edn U Wis PO Box 413 Milwaukee WI 53201

BARTLEY, LEANN MARIE, microbiologist; b. Portland, Ore., Aug. 30, 1951; d. Allen Arthur and Sharon LaBelle (Wirth) Walters; B.S. in Microbiology, Oreg. State U., 1973; m. Dale William Bartley, July 8, 1972; 1 son, Chad William. Microbiologist, Rogue Valley Meml. Hosp., Medford, Oreg., 1974, sr. microbiologist, 1977, chief microbiology dept., 1981—. Mem. Am. Soc. Clin. Pathologists, Am. Soc. Microbiology, Am. Soc. Med. Tech., Assn. Oreg. Med. Tech. (dist. pres. 1981-82). Club: Emblem (Medford). Home: 1524 Stardust St Medford OR 97501 Office: 2825 Barnett Rd Medford OR 97501

BARTOK, MARGARET RIVA, psychologist; b. Pitts., Dec. 5, 1942; d. Victor E. and Helen M. (McShane) Riva; B.A., Carnegie-Mellon U., 1964; M.Ed., U. Pitts., 1968, M.Ed., 1968, Ph.D., 1975; postgrad. Duquesne U., 1976; m. Frederick F. Bartok, Apr. 12, 1969 (div. Jan. 1978); children—Rory Elizabeth, Keri Helene. Tchr., Los Angeles City Schs., 1964-65; research asst. U. Pitts., 1966-68; counselor Gateway Schs., Monroeville, Pa., 1968-73; instr. psychology Community Coll., Allegheny County, Pa., 1970—, Pa. State U., 1971-75, Duquesne U., 1976—; pvt. practice psychology, Greensburg, Pa., 1975—; psychologist Woodland Hills Sch. Dist., 1980—, inter-mediate unit 1, 1981—; cons. Hempfield Sch. Dist., Greensburg. Mem. Pa. Psychol. Assn., Nat. Assn. Sch. Psychologists, Am. Personnel and Guidance Assn. Democrat. Roman Catholic. Home: 3050 Williamsburg Dr Apt 7 Latrobe PA 15650 Office: Villawood Profl Center Pellis Rd Greensburg PA 15601

BARTOL, GENEVIEVE MARIE, nurse; b. Allentown, Pa., Apr. 14, 1936; d. Aloysius Stephen and Margaret Agnes (Pavlick) B.; R.N., Phila. Gen. Hosp., 1956; B.S. in Nursing, Villanova (Pa.) U., 1960; B.A. in Child Study, Maryknoll Coll., Quezon City, Philippines, 1968; Ed.D., Columbia U., 1976. Staff nurse, instr. Phila. Gen. Hosp., 1956-61, Maryknoll Sisters Center, Maryknoll, N.Y., 1961-66, St. Joseph's Hosp., Manapla, Philippines, 1967; mem. staff Maryknoll Coll. Child Study Center, 1967-72; assoc. prof. nursing La. State U., 1976-78, Duke U., 1978—; advocate for battered women. Grantee Sigma Theta Tau, 1980, Duke U., 1980. Mem. Am. Nurses Assn., Nat. League Nursing, Am. Orthopsychiatry Assn., Sigma Theta Tau. Democrat. Roman Catholic. Editorial bd. Jour. Psychiatry Nursing and Mental Health Services, 1979-81; referee Western Jour. Nursing Research, 1979—. Office: Sch Nursing Duke U Trent Dr Durham NC 27710

BARTOLET, SARA SUE, banker; b. Canton, Ohio, Aug. 7, 1924; d. Charles Arlington and Margaretta (McAbee) Stolberg; student public schs., Canton, Ohio; m. John Carl Bartolet, July 3, 1965. With Harter Bank & Trust Co., Canton, 1942—, asst. sec., 1956, asst. cashier, 1959, comptroller, 1961—; treas. Harter BanCorp, 1975-79; comptroller Second St. Community Urban Redevel. Corp., 1977—. Mem. Bank Adminstrn. Inst. (bd. dirs. 1974-75). Methodist. Clubs: Canton Women's, Order Eastern Star, Order of White Shrine of Jerusalem, Order of the Amaranth, Quota Internat. Home: 3500 Cockleburr Ridge NW Canton OH 44709 Office: 126 Central Plaza N Canton OH 44702

BARTON, ANN ELIZABETH, fin. exec.; b. Long Lake, Mich., Sept. 8, 1923; d. John and Inez Mabel (Morse) Seaton; student Mt. San Antonio Coll., 1969-71, Adrian Coll., 1943, Citrus Coll., 1967, Golden Gate U., 1976, Coll. Fin. Planning, 1980-82; m. H. Kenneth Barton, Apr. 3, 1948; children—Michael, John, Nancy. Tax cons., real estate broker, Claremont, Calif., 1967-72, Newport Beach, Calif., 1972-74; v.p., officer Putney, Barton, Assos., Inc., Walnut Creek, Calif., 1975—; dir., officer Century Fin. Enterprises, Inc., F.F.A. Inc. Cert. fin. planner. Mem. Internat. Assn. Fin. Planners, Calif. Soc. Enrolled Agts., Nat. Assn. Enrolled Agts., Nat. Soc. Public Accts., Inst. Cert. Fin. Planners. Office: 1705 N California Blvd Walnut Creek CA 94596

BARTON, BRIGID S., educator; b. Honolulu, June 1, 1943; d. William M. and Ellen C. Shanahan; B.A., Columbia U., 1965; M.A., U. Calif., Berkeley, 1968, Ph.D., 1976. Instr. art history Coll. Marin, 1968-71; lectr. U. Santa Clara (Calif.), 1974-76, asst. prof., 1976—, assoc. prof., 1982—, dir. DeSaisset Mus., 1978—. Mem. Coll. Art. Assn., Assn. Am. Museums. Office: DeSaisset Mus U Santa Clara Santa Clara CA 95053

BARTON, DOROTHY BRITTON, home economist; b. Calhoun, La., Dec. 31, 1934; d. Claude and Mary Alice (Gaulden) Britton; student So. U., 1953-54; postgrad., 1957, cert. in elem. edn., 1964; B.S. in Home Econs., Grambling State U., 1957; postgrad. Prairie View Coll., 1958, La. State U., 1972-73, La. Tech. U., 1976-78; m. George L. Tillman, Jan., 1951; 1 son, Frederick G.; m. 2d., LeRoy Barton, Aug. 16, 1958; 1 son, LeRoy. Asst. home economist La. Coop. Extension Service, Vidila, 1957-59, asso. area agt. in nutrition, Ruston, 1972—; tchr. home econs. Sunshine (La.) High Sch., Iberville Parish, 1960; tchr. Seymourville Elem. Sch., Plaquemine, La., 1961-69, Lenwil Elem. Sch., Ouachita Parish, West Monroe, La., 1969-72. Mem. Nat. Assn. Extension Home Economists, La. Assn. Extension Home Economists, Am. Home Econs. Assn., La. Assn. Home Economists, Epsilon Sigma Phi. Democrat. Baptist. Home: Route 2 Box 56 Calhoun LA 71225 Office: Lincoln Parish Courthouse Ruston LA 71270

BARTON, GLADYS HOLLANDER, advt. agy. exec.; b. Bklyn., Dec. 9, 1938; d. Abraham H. and Miriam (Reiman) Hollander; B.F.A. (Sch. Art League scholar 1956), Pratt Inst., 1960; m. Lawrence A. Barton, Dec. 16, 1958; children—Hugh, Ann, Jamie, Laura. Art dir. Clairol Inc., N.Y.C., 1961-63; pres., design cons. Gladys Barton Design, N.Y.C., 1966-73; art dir. Salisbury & Salisbury Inc., N.Y.C., 1973-74; sr. art dir. Wunderman, Ricotta & Kline Inc., N.Y.C., 1974-80, v.p., creative supr., 1980; v.p., creative supr. B&B Direct Inc. div. Benton & Bowles, N.Y.C., 1980—. Recipient Silver Echo award, 1979, 1st prize Franklin Mint Bicentennial Competition, 1976, Type Dirs. Club N.Y.C. award, 1978, Effie award, 1979. Mem. Nat. Assn. Female Execs., Art Dirs. Club N.Y. (v.p., Creativity award 1973, 77). Home: 245 Everit Ave Hewlett Harbor NY 11557

BARTON, NELDA ANN LAMBERT, nursing home adminstr.; b. Providence, Ky.; d. Eulis Grant and Rubie Lois (West) Lambert; student Western Ky. U., 1947-49; cert. med. tech. Norton Meml. Infirmary Sch. Med. Tech., 1950; student Cumberland Coll., 1978; m. Harold Bryan Barton, May 11, 1951 (dec. Nov. 6, 1977); children—William Grant (dec.), Barbara Lynn, Harold Bryan, Stephen Lambert, Suzanne. Pres., chmn. bd. Health Systems, Inc., Corbin, Ky., 1980—, Barton and Assos., Inc., Corbin, 1977—, Hazard Nursing Home, Inc., Ky., 1977—, Williamsburg (Ky.) Nursing Home, Inc., 1978—, Corbin Nursing Home, Inc., 1980—, Barbourville Nursing Home, Inc., 1981—; lic. nursing home adminstr. Mountain Laurel Manor, Corbin, 1980—; v.p. Southeastern Ky. Rehab. Com., 1981—. Pres. Corbin Central Elem. PTA, 1963-65; vice chmn. 9th dist. PTA, 1958-59, life mem.; Den mother Cub Scouts Am., 1965-67, recipient Bluegrass Council Boy Scouts Am. Thank You award, 1974; mem. Christian Women's Fellowship First Christian Ch., Corbin, circle chmn.; dir. Corbin Deposit Bank Bd., 1980—, exec. com., 1982—; mem. Corbin Community Devel., Com., 1970—, mem. Fair Housing Task Force, 1980—; mem. devel. bd. Cumberland Coll., 1981—; charter mem. Ky. Mansions Preservation Found. Inc., 1978; mem. adv. com. to City of Corbin, 1969-72; Republican nat. committeewoman for Ky., 1968—, mem. Nat. Conv. Site Selection Com., 1982—, Ambassador Club, 1981—, exec. com., 1976-80; co-chmn. Ky. Reagan-Bush Campaign, 1980; speaker 1980 Rep. Nat. Conv.; presidential Inaugural coordinator for Ky., 1981; mem. numerous coms. nat. convs., 1976-80; mem. Ky. Fed. Adv. Com., 1981; del; Rep. Nat. Conv., 1976; chmn. Ky. delegation Nat. Rep. Women's Conf., 1972; chmn. Whitley (Ky.) County Rep. Party, 1968-72, campaign chairwoman, 1968-72; regent Nat. Fedn. of Rep. Women; gov. 5th dist. Ky. Fedn. of Rep. Women, 1968-70, 1st v.p., 1968-70, chmn. state conv., 1970; pres. Corbin Rep. Women's Club, 1968; 5th dist. campaign chairwoman for Nunn, 1967, Lincoln Club Adv. Com., 1970—; mem. Ky. Fedn. Rep. Women Exec. Com., 1963—; named woman of yr., 1968-69; recipient Dwight David Eisenhower award, 1970; Recognition award Join Rep. Leadership of U.S. Congress, 1979; Mayor of Corbin proclaimed — Nelda Barton Day —, 1973. Mem. Fed. Council on Aging, White House Conf. on Aging (del. 1981), Am. Health Care Assn., Ky. Assn. Health Care Facilities (recipient Better Life award 1981, legis. com. 1980—), Ky. Peer Rev. Orgn. (long-term care adv. com. 1978—), Ky. Assn. Nursing Homes Adminstrs. (dir. polit. action com. 1979—), Cumberland Coll. Assn. Degree Nursing (chmn. adv. com. 1973-80), Ky. Med. Aux. Health Careers (chmn. 1965-68, 1973-75), Women's Aux. to So. Med. Assn. (Ky. councilor 1965-68, southeastern region councilor, 1966-67), Ky. Commn. on Women, Am. Med. Polit. Action Com., Ky. Ednl., Med. Polit. Action Com., Whitley County Med. Aux. (pres. 1959-60, Aux. to Ky. Med. Assn., Beta Omega Chi (pres. Western Ky. U. 1948-49). Clubs: 9th Dist. Ky. Fedn. Women's (vice-gov. 1960), Corbin Ossoli Women's (pres. 1961-62), Ky. Mothers Assn. (parliamentarian 1970—), Bus. and Profl. Women's. Address: 1311 7th St Rd Corbin KY 40701

BARTON, PHYLLIS JOAN LOSEKE, home economist, secondary sch. tchr.; b. Gem, Kans., Apr. 18, 1936; d. Fred William and Yelva (Knudson) Loseke; B.S. in Home Econs., Kans. State U., 1957; M.Ed. in Vocat.-Tech. Edn., Va. Poly. Inst. and State U., 1974; m. Benny Eugene Barton, June 6, 1960. Tchr. home econs. schs. in Kans. and Va., 1957-69; tchr. home econs. Hayfield Secondary Sch., Alexandria, Va., 1970-75, child care services coop. edn. coordinator, 1975—. Vice pres., sec. Williamsburg Manor Citizens Assn., 1975, 76. Recipient Outstanding Leadership award Nat. Capital Area March of Dimes, 1979, 80, 81; named hon. Ky. col., 1979. Mem. Nat. Future Homemakers Am. Assn. (dir. 1981—), Nat. Assn. Vocat. Home Econs. Tchrs. (sec. 1977-79, pres. elect 1980-81, pres. 1981-82, Service award 1978, 81), Va. Vocat. Assn. (Outstanding Citation award 1976), Am. Vocat. Assn., Am. Home Econs. Assn., Home Econs. Edn. Assn., NEA, Va. Edn. Assn., Fairfax Edn. Assn., Va. Home Econs. Tchrs. Assn. Babtist. Club: Alexandria Jr. Woman's (past pres.). Author: (cookbook) Hush Puppies and Other Stories, 1977; also consumer edn. teaching units; adv. bd. Favorite Recipes Press, 1982—. Home: 2232 Candlewood Dr Alexandria VA 22308 Office: 7630 Telegraph Rd Alexandria VA 22310

BARTOS, KAREN JEAN, chem. engr.; b. Cedar Rapids, Iowa, Sept. 6, 1956; d. Frank Russell and Beverly Jean (Carlson) B.; B.S.Ch.E., U. Iowa, 1978; M.B.A., Govs. State U., 1982; m. Bruce A. Boyd, Sept. 4, 1982. Constrn. engr. Amoco Chems. Corp., Chocolate Bayou, Tex., 1979; regional project/process engr. Mobil Chem. Co., Kankakee, Ill., 1979—; mem. Chem. EN Engring. Product Research Panel, 1980-81. Mem. Am. Inst. Chem. Engrs., Scholastic All-Am. Soc., U. Iowa Alumni Assn., Tau Beta Pi, Alpha Chi Sigma, Omicron Delta Kappa, Beta Sigma

Phi. Author: Iowa and You, 1977. Home: 21071 Gary Dr #206 Castro Valley CA 94546

BARTUSKA, DORIS GORKA, physician; b. student Bucknell Jr. Coll., 1946-48; B.S. in Biology, Bucknell U., 1949; M.D. (Kosciuszko Found. fellow), Woman's Med. Coll. Pa., 1954; m. Anthony John Bartuska; 6 children. Rotating intern Hosp. of Woman's Med. Coll., 1954-55, Kate Hurd Mead fellow in medicine, 1955-56, resident in medicine, 1956-57; NIH trainee in endocrinology Jefferson Med. Coll., 1957-58; NIH spl. fellow molecular medicine Hosp. of U. Pa., 1966-68; asst. dean, asso. in medicine Woman's Med. Coll. of Pa., 1958-66, asst. prof. medicine, asst. prof. clin. pathology, 1966-71; asso. prof. medicine, asso. prof. clin. pathology Med. Coll. Pa., 1971—, dir. sect. endocrinology and metabolism, 1973—, asso. dean for curriculum, 1974-76, acting dir. Center for Women in Medicine, 1976-78, prof. medicine, 1977—, mem. exec. com., 1970-71, pres. staff, 1973-74; cons. medicine VA Hosp., Phila., 1970—. Recipient Christian R. and Mary F. Lindback Distinguished Teaching award, 1974, Commonwealth Bd. award, 1981, Pa. Commonwealth Bd. award, 1981, Shaffrey award St. Joseph's U., 1982. Diplomate Am. Bd. Internal Medicine, Am. Bd. Endocrinology and Metabolism. Fellow ACP; mem. Med. Womens Internat. Assn. (del. 1976), Am. Soc. Human Genetics, Endocrine Soc., Am. Fedn. Clin. Research, AAAS, Assn. Women in Sci., Am. Thyroid Assn., Am. Med. Womens Assn. (chmn. publs. com. 1976-78, del. 1976), Assn. Am. Med. Colls. (womens liaison officer 1976—1st v.p. 1981), Pa. (del. 1977), Phila. County (chmn. N.W. br. 1976-79) med. socs., Phila. Endocrine Soc. (past pres.), Am. Diabetes Assn. Physiol. Soc. Phila., Phila. Coll. Physicians, Lawson Wilkins Soc. Pediatric Endocrinology, Alumni Assn. Womans Med. Coll. Pa. (pres. 1965-66, Alumni Achievement award 1975), Phi Sigma, Alpha Omega Alpha. Book rev. editor Jour. Am. Med. Women's Assn. contbr. articles to med. jours. Home: 3227 W Penn St Philadelphia PA 19129 Office: 3300 Henry Ave Philadelphia PA 19129

BARUCH, ROBERTA SARA, lawyer; b. Brookline, Mass., Jan. 3, 1949; d. Jordan J. and Rhoda (Wasserman) B.; A.B., U. Chgo., 1970; J.D., Harvard U., 1975; m. Jerome Ostrov, Sept. 3, 1978. Admitted to Mass. bar, D.C. bar; asso. firm Sherin & Lodgen, Boston, 1975-77; atty. Office Gen. Counsel, EPA, Washington, 1977-78; atty. Bur. of Competition, FTC, Washington, 1978-82, dep. asst. dir. for eval., 1982—. Office: Bur Competition FTC 6th and Pennsylvania Aves NW Washington DC 20580

BARZ, DIANE GAY (MRS. DANIEL J. BARZ), judge; b. Bozeman, Mont., Aug. 18, 1943; d. John G. and E. Bernice (Johnson) MacDonald; student U. Heidelberg (Germany), 1964; B.A. magna cum laude, Whitworth Coll., 1965; J.D. (Bur. Nat. Affairs scholar), U. Mont., 1968; m. Daniel J. Barz, Nov. 28, 1970. Admitted to Mont. bar, 1968; law clk., research asst. Mont. Supreme Ct., Mont. Criminal Commn., Helena, 1968-70; dep. county atty. Yellowstone County, Mont., 1970-75; partner firm Poppler & Barz, Billings, Mont., 1973-79; public adminstr. Yellowstone County, 1974-78; judge Dist. Ct. Mont., Billings, 1980—. Account exec. United Way, Billings, 1973; sec. Yellowstone County Republican Central Com., Billings, 1973-75; bd. dirs. S. Central Mont. Regional Mental Health Center, Billings, Yellowstone County Civic Center Commn., 1975-81; bd. dirs. Deaconess Hosp., 1980—, 4-H Mont., Salvation Army, 1982—. Mem. Young Lawyers Assn. (v.p., sec. 1970), Mont. Judges Assn., Am. Judges Assn., Nat. Assn. Women Judges, Bus. and Profl. Women's Club (named Mont. Young Career Woman 1970), Mont., Yellowstone County bar assns., Jr. League Billings, Billings Jr. C. of C., Phi Delta (named Woman of Year 1970). Home: 3425 Laredo Pl Billings MT 59102 Office: Yellowstone County Courthouse Billings MT 59107

BASILE, ABIGAIL JULIA ELLEN HERRON (MRS. JOSEPH BASILE), employment counselor, state ofcl.; b. St. Louis, June 15, 1915; d. Charles Arthur and Abigail (Edwards) Herron; student Kansas City Jr. Coll., 1948-50, U. Kans., 1959; B.S. in Bus. Adminstrn., Rockhurst Coll., 1965; M.Ed., U. Mo., 1967; m. Joseph Basile, Aug. 15, 1939. Employment security dep. Mo. Div. Employment Security, Kansas City, 1945-59, youth coordinator, employment counselor, 1959-65, counselor, supr., 1965-81. Mem. Mo. Assn. Social Welfare. Mem. Am. Personnel and Guidance Assn., Nat. Vocat. Guidance Assn., Am. Vocat. Assn., Internat. Assn. Personnel in Employment Security (pres. Mo. 1966-67, internat. sec. 1968), Nat. Rehab. Assn., Nat. Employment Counselors Assn., Urban League, Am. Legion Aux., Personnel Research Forum, Profl. Counselors Assn. Democrat. Episcopalian. Home: 228 Haines PO Box 13884 Edwardsville KS 66113

BASILI, ANNAMARIA GERMAINE, speech pathologist; b. Bklyn., Oct. 13, 1944; d. Basil Lucien and Marie Grace (Tesoriero) Basili; B.A., St. Joseph's Coll., 1965; M.A., Columbia U. Tchrs. Coll., 1967; Ph.D., Purdue U., 1971; m. John B. Zonak, Sept. 28, 1973; children—Christina Germaine Basili Zonak, Stephanie Germaine Basili Zonak. Speech pathologist and audiologist VA, Asheville, N.C., 1971-72, chief audiology and speech pathology VA Med. Center, Ft. Howard, Md., 1972—; cons. edn. service VA Central Office, Washington; cons. VA Med. Center, Birmingham, Ala. Lic. speech pathologist, Md. Mem. Am. Speech, Lang. and Hearing Assn., Internat. Neuropsychol. Soc., Md. Speech, Lang. and Hearing Assn. Home: 210 Oak Dr Pasadena MD 21122 Office: VA Med Center Fort Howard MD 21052

BASKERVILLE, E. YVONNE, social worker; b. Riverhead, N.Y., Oct. 22, 1952; d. John Edward and Jessie (Spruill) Durham; B.A. in Sociology, Rider Coll., 1974; M.S.W., Howard U., 1975; m. Lewis Raymond Baskerville, Aug. 28, 1976; 1 dau., Janel LeVon. Psychiat. social worker Pilgrim Psychiat. Center, Brentwood, N.Y., 1976; foster care social worker Family and Child Services, Washington, 1977-78; social worker dept. social services County of Montgomery, Wheaton, Md., 1978—. Pres. Shades of Gospel Choir Trinity A.M.E. Zion Methodist Ch., Washington, 1977-79, dir. children's choir, 1977-78. Mem. Nat. Assn. Social Workers, Nat. Council Negro Women (affiliate), Acad. Cert. Social Workers, Delta Sigma Theta. Office: 2424 Reedie Dr Wheaton MD 20902

BASKETT, ANNE HELEN, travel agy. exec.; b. Kalamazoo, Jan. 22, 1941; d. Robert Elton and Helen Gertrude (Menten) Serfling; B.A., Emory U., 1962. Vol., Peace Corps, Philippines, 1962-64; sales rep., mgr. Smith Bell Travel, Manila, 1964-70; mgr., owner Daly Travel Services, San Francisco, 1970—. Mem. Am. Soc. Travel Agts., Pacific Area Travel Assn. Pub., editor The Daly News. Office: Daly Travel Service 391 Sutter St San Francisco CA 94108

BASKIN, BARBARA HOLLAND, educator; b. Detroit, Aug. 27, 1929; d. C. F. and Ruth (Herman) Harriman; B.A., Wayne State U., 1951; M.A., U. Mich., 1957; Ed.D., Wayne State U., 1968; m. Alex Baskin, Aug. 15, 1954; children—Julie Susan, Amy Shael. Tchr., Detroit Public Schs., 1951-53, 55-57; instr. U.S. Army, 1953-54, Office Spl. Edn., Wayne State U., Detroit, 1964-68; ednl. dir. Sagamore Psychiatric Hosp., Melville, N.Y., 1970; cons. gifted BOCES #3, Suffolk County, N.Y., 1971; asst. prof. SUNY, Stony Brook, 1971-76, dir. Office Spl. Edn., 1977, asso. prof., 1981—; cons. First co-pres. Suffolk County chpt. Council for Exceptional Children, 1978-79; impartial hearing officer in sch. dists. resolving sch./parent conflicts about handicapped children. P.L. 85-926 fellow, 1966-68; SUNY grantee, 1975-76; ALA award for Outstanding Reference Book, 1978, 80; BOCES minigrantee, 1978-79. Mem. Am. Assn. Mental Deficiency, Univ. Assn. SUNY Stony Brook. Author: (with Karen Harris) The Special Child in the Library, 1976, Books for Gifted Child, 1980, The Mainstreamed Library, 1982, Notes From a Different Drummer: A Guide to Juvenile Literature Protraying the Handicapped (awards, Am. Library Asso. and Pres.'s com. on Employment of Handicapped). Home: 32 Seville Ln Stony Brook NY 11790 Office: Office Spl Edn S 101 SUNY Stony Brook NY 11794

BASKIN, JUNE ELIZABETH, ednl. adminstr.; b. Williamsport, Pa., June 1, 1921; B.S., Kutztown State Coll., 1949; M.F.A., Syracuse U., 1954; Ed.D., Pa. State U., 1964. Art tchr. public schs., 1949-59; art supr. Williamsport (Pa.) Area Sch. Dist., 1959—; command crafts dir. U.S. Army (Ger.) Spl. Services, 1955-57; part-time lectr. art edn. Lycoming (Pa.) Coll., 1962-66, continuing edn. program Pa. State U., 1966-70 lectr. history of architecture. Williamsport Area Community Coll., 1965-70, calligraphy instr., 1971-82; calligraphy instr. Bloomsburg (Pa.) State Coll.; 1978-79; demonstrator, juried craftsman Pa. Guild Craftsmen. Recipient citation U.S. Army, 1956; Delta Kappa Gamma Pa. fellow, 1962-63. Outstanding Woman award Pa. div. AAUW, 1980; Community Service award Am. Legion, 1980; Woman of Yr. award Williamsport br. AAUW, 1962; Gold award Pa. Sch. Press Assn., 1970; Gold Key award Columbia U. Press Assn., 1966; Outstanding Art Educator award Pa. Art Edn. Assn., 1980-81; Excellence in Edn. award Pa. State U., 1982. Mem. Pa. Art Edn. Assn. (exec. bd.), Nat. Art Edn. Assn., Assn. Supervision and Curriculum Devel., Pa. Assn. Elem. and Secondary Sch. Prins., Nat. Assn. Secondary Sch. Prins., Soc. Italic Handwriting (Eng.), Soc. Scribes and Illuminators (Eng.), Soc. Scribes (N.Y.), Calligraphic Soc. Pa., Pa. Guild Craftsmen (chmn. standards com. Williamsport chpt.), Greater Williamsport Community Arts Council (past pres.), Bald Eagle Art League, AAUW (life), Delta Kappa Gamma. Office: 605 W 4th St Williamsport PA 17701 also 502 Main St Williamsport PA 17701

BASKIN, ROBERTA, investigative reporter; b. Atlanta, Jan. 16, 1952; d. Allan Michael and Suzanne June (Pallister) B.; ed. Elmira Coll.; m. William C. Nigut, Jr., May 21, 1982. Dir., Accent Neighborhood City of Syracuse (N.Y.), 1972-74, dir. consumer affairs dept., 1974-77; consumer reporter Sta. WMAQ-TV, Chgo. 1977-79; investigative reporter Sta. WLS-TV, Chgo. 1979—; speaker in field. Recipient Peabody award, 3 Nat. Press Club awards for consumer journalism, Emmy award, 3 UPI awards, Jacob Scher Investigative Reporting award, Peter Lisagor award, Internat. Radio TV News Dirs. award for Investigative Reporting, Abe Lincoln award for Disting. Journalism. Mem. AFTRA (dir. Chgo. chpt.), Chgo. Press Club. Office: 190 N State St Chicago IL 60601

BASLOCK, GAYLE PINCOSKI, nurse; b. Bad Axe, Mich., Oct. 21, 1939; d. John and Amelia (Gregurash) Pincoski; A.Nursing, Flint Community Coll., 1960; B.S., U. Ala., 1975, M.Adminstrv. Sci., 1979; m. Ronald William Baslock, June 18, 1960; children—Elizabeth Ann, Anita Louise. Staff nurse Baraga County Hosp., L'Anse, Mich., 1962-64; staff nurse Huntsville (Ala.) Hosp., 1964-69, instr. tech. tng./staff devel., 1975-79, infection control nurse, 1979-80, clin. coordinator, 1980—; office nurse Pediatric Assos., Huntsville, 1969-74; asso. faculty Madison County CPR Assn., 1975—. Leader, Girl Scouts U.S.A., 1972-80; beautification chmn. Rolling Hills Sch., 1972-81. U. Ala. honor scholar, 1974-75; lic. nurse, Mich., Ala. Mem. Am. Nurses Assn., Madison County Nurses Soc., Alumni Assn. U. Ala., Assn. for Practitioners in Infection Control, Oncology Nurses Assn., Nat. Lupus Assn., Am. Heart Assn., Am. Cancer Soc., Sigma Theta Tau. Roman Catholic. Clubs: Cedars Garden (pres. 1979, 82). Home: 6505 Creighton Ave NW Huntsville AL 35810 Office: 101 Sivley Rd Huntsville AL 35801

BASS, BETTY ZOE PASSMORE (MRS. ERIC BASS), artist; b. Burlington, Wis., Mar. 26, 1926; d. Dempster Stewart and Bettina (Rakow) Passmore; student U. Ariz., 1943, U. Miami, 1944-47; B.A., UCLA, 1955; M.A., Stanford U., 1963; m. Eric Bass, Oct. 10, 1948. Designer, partner haute couture firm Eric Bass, Beverly Hills, Calif., 1949-53; fine art painting, Lakeside and Los Angeles, Calif., 1953—; exhibited UCLA Art Gallery, 1955, Art Center, LaJolla, Calif., 1957, So. Calif. Exposition, 1961; Oriental art research travel to Japan, Thailand, India, 1959-60. Chmn. opening night dinners San Diego Opera Guild, also chmn. LaJolla Assos.; mem. Asian arts com. Fine Arts Soc.; v.p. San Diego com. Los Angeles Philharmonic; v.p. Women's Assn. Salk Inst.; chmn. benefit ball San Diego Symphony, 1971; chmn. dinners Civic Light Opera. Bd. dirs. U. Calif. at San Diego Hosps. Aux.; bd. dirs. women's com. San Diego Symphony Assn. Named a San Diego Woman of Elegance, 1972; chmn. Social Service League benefit for Darlington House, 1976; chmn. benefit fashion show for U. San Diego, 1979. Mem. Soc. Mayflower Descs., DAR, Social Service League, La Jolla Civic Orch. Assn., Old Globe Theater 400, Klee Wyk Soc. Mus. Man, La Jolla Mus. Contemporary Art, World Affairs Council, Country Friends, Starlight Women's Assn. (v.p.), U. San Diego Aux. (v.p.), Delta Gamma. Club: Stanford (San Diego). Home: PO Box 2064 La Jolla CA 92037

BASS, RUTH, educator; b. Boston, Oct. 11, 1938; d. Samuel and Beatrice (Wexler) Gilbert; B.A. magna cum laude, Radcliffe Coll., 1960; M.A., N.Y. U., 1962, Ph.D., 1978; m. Harvey Bass, Apr. 15, 1967; 1 son, Michael. Lectr., U. Bridgeport (Conn.), 1963-64; lectr. Queens Coll., N.Y.C., 1965-66; instr. N.Y. U., N.Y.C., 1980-81; faculty Bronx Community Coll., City U. N.Y., 1965-69, asst. prof., 1970-78, asso. prof., 1978-81, prof. art, 1981—; art critic Art News, 1979—; art writer Arts mag., Art World, Art in Am., McGraw-Hill Dictionary of Art, Dictionary of 20th Century Art, others. Bd. advisors Artists Choice Mus., 1980; mem. Bronx Council on Arts, 1970—, Art Students League N.Y., 1973—; moderator Panel on Realist Art sponsored Bklyn. Mus. and Louis Abrons Arts for Living Center, 1980—. Arts and Soc. fellow, 1981; SUNY Research Found. grantee, 1975-76; Bronx Community Coll. fellow, 1979-80. Mem. Coll. Art Assn., AAUP, Women in the Arts, Artists Equity Assn. N.Y., Am. Soc. Aesthetics. Contbr. articles to profl. jours.

BASSETT, BETTY ANNE, librarian; b. Beaver Falls, Pa., May 26, 1943; d. Robert Bliss and Clarissa Antoinette (Persing) B.; B.A., Grove City Coll., 1965; M.L.S., Case Western Res. U., 1966; m. Roy E. Metcalfe. Librarian, Berkshire Sch. Dist., Burton, Ohio, 1966-69; tech. librarian Xerox Corp., Webster, N.Y., 1970-74; mgr. tech. info. centre Xerox Research Centre Can., Mississauga, Ont., 1974—; mem. library techniques adv. com. Sheridan Coll., 1979—. Mem. Spl. Libraries Assn. (dir. Toronto chpt. 1979-80, pres.-elect 1980-81, pres. 1981-82), Can. Library Assn., Sheridan Park Assn. (editor Union List of Serials, 4th edit., 1975-76, chmn. library and info. sci. com. 1977-79), Can. Assn. Info. Sci. Contbr. articles to profl. jours. Home: 2680 Canberra Rd Mississauga ON L5N 1M7 Canada Office: 2480 Dunwin Dr Mississauga ON L5L 1J9 Canada

BASSETT, CALLA MARIE, physician; b. Glens Falls, N.Y., Dec. 28, 1954; d. Elmer Howard and Laura Gertrude (Malark) B.; B.S., St. Lawrence U., 1976; M.D., SUNY, Syracuse, 1980; m. Robert Constantine, May 20, 1978; children—Sara Ann, John Maxwell. Intern, St. Joseph Hosp. Health Center, Syracuse, 1981; physician Appalachian Regional Hosp., Nat. Health Service Corps Med. Office, Hazard, Ky., 1981—. Mem. AMA, Am. Acad. Family Physicians, Mortar Bd., Phi Beta Kappa, Beta Beta Beta. Home and office: Home Place Ary KY 41712

BASSETT, DOROTHY RICHARDS, artist; b. Cambridge, Mass., Aug. 4, 1918; d. George and Evangeline Booth (Richards) Richards; grad. Boston Art Inst., 1949; children—Jon Eric, Marc Alan, Dana Kimball. Draftsman, United Shoe Machinery Co., 1937-42; blueprinter, advt. artist A.C. Lawrence Leather Co., Peabody, Mass., 1949-51; propr. Studio Shop and Studio Potters, Beverly, Mass., 1951-53; tchr. ceramics and art, Kingston, N.H., 1953—; two-man exhbn. Topsfield (Mass.) Library, 1960; owner, operator Ceramics Shop, West Stewartstown, N.H. Served with USNR, 1942-44. Recipient Profl. award New Eng. Ceramic Show, 1975; also numerous certificates in ceramics. Home: Route 2 Box 92D Colebrook NH 03576 Office: Bishop Brook Rd West Stewartstown NH 03597

BASSETT, MARJORY HELEN JESSUP, public relations cons.; b. Hutchinson, Kans.; d. Barclay Leander and Alma Belle (Curnutt) Jessup; B.A., U. Iowa. Dir. pub. relations, pub. service and spl. programming KFH-AM, Wichita, 1951-53; mgr. radio and TV, Brit. Tourist Authority, N.Y.C., 1954-74; pub. relations cons., N.Y.C., 1975—; adj. asso. prof. journalism L.I. U., 1977. Hon. life mem. Kans. Congress Parents and Tchrs. Sta. received 1st pl. Pub. Service award Billboard Mag. Mem. Women in Communications, Nat. Acad. TV Arts and Scis., Am. Women in Radio and TV, Nat. Arts Club. Home and Office: 81 Irving Pl New York NY 10003

BASTEDO, HELEN WILMERDING, civic worker; b. N.Y.C., Jan. 5, 1917; d. Lucius and Helen (Cutting) Wilmerding; ed. pvt. sch.; m. Philip Bastedo, Feb. 4, 1937; children—Russell, Bayard, Cecily, Christopher. Active Planned Parenthood of Manhattan, Bronx, 1937-66, chmn. 1952-55; active Planned Parenthood N.Y.C., 1966—; chmn. fund raising com. Planned Parenthood Fedn. Am., 1952-53, vice chmn., 1968-71; mem. Women's Aux. Union Settlement, 1939-58; mem. Women's bd. Women's Hosp., 1954-58; vice chmn. Women's com. Lincoln Center for Performing Arts, 1958-63, co-chmn. seat endowment com. 1960-63; mem. Assn. Vol. Sterilization, 1951-73. Episcopalian. Clubs: River, Cosmopolitan. Home: 925 Park Ave New York NY 10028

BASTIAN, (ROSE) MARIE, banker; b. Belmont, Ohio, Apr. 27, 1940; d. Montraville Sharp and Doris Avanell (Young) Hollingsworth; student Ohio State U., 1959; grad. Ohio Sch. Banking, 1974, Stonier Grad. Sch., Rutgers U., 1980. With Bancohio Ohio Nat. Bank, Columbus, 1965—, exec. sec., 1968-71, salary adminstr., 1971-76, asst. v.p., mgr. personnel dept., 1976, v.p., chief personnel officer, 1976—; instr. Columbus Tech. Inst., 1978—. Mem. Friends of WOSU Devel. Com.; mem. bus. adv. council Franklin U.; trustee Met. Learning Community, United Cerebral Palsy of Columbus and Franklin County; bd. dirs. Met. Women's Center; sr. v.p. Human Resource Group, 1979—. Nat. Assn. Bank Women scholar, 1972. Mem. Am. Soc. Personnel Adminstrs., Personnel Soc. Columbus, Am. Inst. Banking, Am. Bankers Assn. (employee relations com.), Nat. Assn. Bank Women, Assn. Bank Women, Adminstrv. Mgmt. Soc. (survey com.), Columbus Area C. of C. (public affairs com.). Home: 5141 Pebble Ln Columbus OH 43220 Office: 155 Broad St E Columbus OH 43265

BATAILLE, GRETCHEN MARIE, educator; b. Mishawaka, Ind., Sept. 28, 1944; d. George H. and Adrienne (VanderHeyden) Mueller; student Purdue U., 1962-65; B.S., Calif. Poly. U., 1966, M.A., 1967; D.Arts, Drake U., 1977; children—Marc David, Erin Marie. Instr., Iowa State U., 1967-77, asst. prof. English, 1977-81, asso. prof., 1981—, chmn. Am. Indian studies program, 1976-81; mem. adv. com. Indian edn. Iowa Dept. Public Instrn. Chmn. Iowa Civil Rights Commn., 1977-79; mem. Iowa Humanities Bd., 1981—. Mem. Nat. Assn. Interdisciplinary Ethnic Studies (exec. council 1980-84), MLA, Assn. Study Am. Indian Lit. (exec. bd.), NOW. Author: The Pretend Indians: Images of Native Americans in the Movies, 1980; The Worlds Between Two Rivers, 1978; contbr. articles to profl. jours. Home: 1602 Grand St Ames IA 50010 Office: Dept English Iowa State U Ames IA 50011

BATCHELOR, GLADYS P., financial planner; b. Plainfield, N.J., Sept. 19, 1932; d. Joseph Frank and Mabel (Kellerman) Purchess; A.A. in Bus. Mgmt./Acctg., Rutgers U., 1956; B.Gen. Studies summa cum laude, Ohio U., 1974, M.Ed., 1978; m. Andrew Jackson Batchelor, June 8, 1957; children—Allison Jay, Andrew Jackson. Adminstr., Public Service Electric & Gas Co., Plainfield, 1950-57; adminstr. Internat. Tel. & Tel. Corp., Nutley, N.J., 1957-59; coordinator, cons. women's programs Ohio State U., Newark, 1975; counselor and program coordinator Ohio U., Lancaster, 1976-77, asst. to dir. exec. MBA program, 1977-79; sr. fin. cons. Forward Planning Assos., Columbus, Ohio, 1979—; pvt. practice fin. planning and cons., specializing in fin. needs of women, 1980—. Treas., trustee, mem. organizing com. Ohio Women, Inc.; vice-pres. Ohio Commn. on Status of Women, 1976; vice-pres. bd. dirs. Lancaster-Fairfield County YWCA; coordinator Internat. Women's Yr. Fairfield County, 1975. Mem. Internat. Assn. Fin. Planners (v.p., dir. Central Ohio chpt.), World Future Soc., AAUW, Nat. Assn. Women's Studies. Methodist. Home: 1260 Ridgewood Way NE Lancaster OH 43130

BATDORF, ANNETTE NORDINE, home economist; b. Burlington, Wash., Feb. 17, 1940; d. C. Harold and Violet E. (Roseland) Nordine; B.S. in Home Econs. Edn., Wash. State U., Pullman, 1972; children—Kurt R., Kraig L. Tchr. home econs. Yelm (Wash.) High Sch., 1962; presch. tchr. Newport Hills Coop. Presch., Bellevue Community Coll., 1972-73; adminstr. Nave Pierson Winery, Los Angeles, 1973-74; gen. office worker Mida Metal Products Co., Pasadena, Calif., 1974-76; demonstrator Sunbeam appliances, Tacoma, 1976; saleswoman Continental Distbn. Co., Tacoma, 1977; home economist Tacoma Public Utilities Dept., 1977-79, energy conservation educator, 1979—; guest lectr., adv. bd. home and family life Tacoma Community Coll.; guest lectr. Clover Park Community Schs. Mem. Elec. Women's Round Table (nat. newsletter award 1979, chmn. Puget Sound chpt. 1980, 81), Am. Home Econs. Assn., Home Economists in Bus., Home Economists in Home Making, Tacoma Home Econs. Assn. Office: City of Tacoma Dept Public Utilities PO Box 11007 Tacoma WA 98411

BATDORF, TERRIE LEE, banker; b. Toledo, June 7, 1949; d. Lawrence Edward and Alta F. (Segrist) B.; B.B.A. in Acctg., Ohio U., 1972; M.S. in Mgmt., Rensselaer Poly. Inst., 1975. Fin. trainee Pratt & Whitney Aircraft, 1972-74; acct. Medicare head office Aetna Life & Casualty Co., 1974-75; successively fin. analyst, ops. mgr., project mgr. asst. v.p., ops. head Citicorp processing treasury div. Citibank, N.A., N.Y.C., 1975—, also funds mgr. Citicorp, parent co. Mem. Nat. Assn. Accts. (dir. chpt.), Phi Gamma Mu (regional dir.). Methodist. Club: Citibank Bridge. Office: 20 Exchange Pl 42d Floor New York NY 10043

BATE, MARJORIE ELISE DUNLAP, educator; b. Berkeley, Calif., Apr. 4, 1913; d. Luther Albert and Elsa Marie (Miller) Dunlap; B.S., U. Calif., Berkeley, 1934, M.S. (Flood fellow), 1936; postgrad. Fresno State Coll., 1948-60; adminstrv. credential Hayward State U., 1969; m. Lyal Harry Bate, June 15, 1941; children—George Edward, Stephen Dunlap. Tchr., dept. chmn. Watsonville (Calif.) High Sch., 1936-42, Porterville (Calif.) High Sch., 1952-61; mem. faculty Porterville Coll., 1961-64; mem. faculty Contra Costa Coll., San Pablo, Calif., 1964—, dean instrn., 1969-76. Sec., Cella Vinyards, Fresno, Calif., 1949-51. Mem. AAUW, Calif. Ret. Tchrs. Assn., Phi Beta Kappa, Beta Gamma Sigma, Phi Chi Theta, Kappa Phi. Democrat. Co-author: Legal Office Procedures, 2d edit., 1981.

BATES, BARBARA J. NEUNER, town ofcl.; b. Mt. Vernon, N.Y., Apr. 8, 1927; d. John Joseph William and Elsie May (Flint) Neuner; B.A., Barnard Coll., 1947; m. Herman Martin Bates, Jr., Mar. 25, 1950; children—Roberta Jean Bates Jamin, Herman Martin III, Jon Neuner. Confidential clk. to supr. town Ossining (N.Y.), 1960-63; pres. BNB Assos., Briarcliff Manor, N.Y., 1963—, Upper Nyack Realty Co., Inc.,

Briarcliff Manor, 1966-71; receiver taxes Town of Ossining (N.Y.), 1971—. Vice pres. Ossining (N.Y.) Young Republican Club, 1958; pres. Young Womens Rep. Club Westchester County (N.Y.), 1959-61; regional committeewoman N.Y. State Assn. Young Rep. Clubs, 1960-62; mem. Westchester County Rep. Com., 1963—; mem. Ossining Womens Rep. Club, 1960—, Westchester County Womens Rep. Club, 1957—. Mem. Jr. League Westchester-on-Hudson, DAR, N.Y. State Assn. Tax Receivers and Collectors, Receivers of Taxes Assn. of Westchester County, (legis. liaison, v.p.), Hackley Sch. Mothers Assn. (pres. 1966-68), R.I. Hist. Soc., Ossining Bus. and Profl. Women's Club, Am. Soc. Notaries, Westchester County Hist. Soc., Briarcliff-Scarborough Hist. Soc. Congregationalist. Club: Ossining Emblem. Home: 78 Holbrook Ln Briarcliff Manor NY 10510 also RFD 2 Chepachet RI 02814

BATES, BETSEY, artist; b. Dobbs Ferry, N.Y., Nov. 29, 1924; d. Homer Morgan and Dorothy (Graef) Smith; B.F.A. magna cum laude, Beaver Coll., 1946; m. Guy C. Bates, Aug. 30, 1947 (div. 1965); children—Carleton Jane, Leslie Collins; m. 2d, Joseph M. Gerhart, June 13, 1978. Designer, painter, illustrator, printmaker for advt. agys., corps. and pubs.; works include: Christmas card Easter Seal Soc., 1974, mural for RCA TV Studio, Switzerland, 1977; represented in collections: Washington Hilton Hotel, Houston Marriott, Syracuse Marriott, Chgo. Marriott, Texaco, World Book, Lynell, Grad. Hosp. of Phila, Butler Inst. Am. Art, Danskin, Inc., Episcopal Acad., Hahnemann Hosp., Friends Central Sch., Continental Bank, Fed. Res. Bank, Free Library Phila., Germantown Hosp., Montgomery Hosp., Smith Kline Pharm., McNeil Pharm. Recipient cert. of merit Nat. Consumer Fin. Assn., 1963; cert. of excellence Phila. Art Dirs. Club, 1964; award Nat. Community Arts Program, Golden Disc, Beaver Coll., 1975; Best of Show award Norristown Borough (Pa.) Council of Arts, 1980. Mem. Artists Equity Assn., Phila. Art Alliance, Nat. Trust Hist. Preservation, Artists Guild Delaware Valley (Golden Plum award 1977). Home and Office: 1330 Valley Forge Rd RD 1 Norristown PA 19401

BATES, BEULAH MAY (BILLIE), educator; b. Aldrich, Mo., Jan. 13, 1912; d. Oliver Worden and Flora May (Saylor) Mitchell; B.S., S.W. Mo. State U., 1933; student U. Nev., Las Vegas, 1965-67; m. Russell Elliot Bates, July 26, 1936; children—Cornelia May, Laurel Jeanne. Tchr., high sch. Advance, Mo., 1934-35, Holland, Mo., 1935-36; personnel clk. Bur. Reclamation, Dept. Interior, Boulder City, Nev., 1945-46, sec., 1947-66, adminstrv. asst., tng. officer, 1967-75; instr. leadership devel., communications and parliamentary law Clark County Community Coll., Henderson, Nev., 1978—. Recipient Spl. award Gov. N.Mex., 1973, Meritorious award Dept. Interior, 1975. Cert. profl. sec.; registered profl. parliamentarian. Mem. Nat. Assn. Parliamentarians, Nev. Assn. Parliamentarians (pres. 1980-82), Am. Soc. Tng. and Devel., Nat. Assn. Female Execs., AAUW, Am. Inst. Parliamentarians, LWV, Common Cause, Nat. Assn. Ret. Fed. Employees. Mormon. Club: Toastmistresses (div. v.p. 1976-77). Address: 641 5th St Boulder City NV 89005

BATES, LURA WHEELER, trade assn. exec.; b. Inboden, Ark., Aug. 28, 1932; d. Carl Clifton and Hester Ray (Pace) Wheeler; B.S. in Bus. Adminstrn., U. Ark., 1954; m. Allen Carl Bates, Sept. 12, 1954; 1 dau., Carla Allene. Sec.-bookkeeper, then officer mgr. Asso. Gen. Contractors Miss., Inc., Jackson, 1958-77, dir. adminstrv. services, 1977—, asst. exec. dir., 1980—; adminstr. Miss. Constrn. Found., 1977—; sec. AIA-Asso. Gen. Contractors Liaisonship Coms., 1977—; sec. Carpenters Joint Apprenticeship Coms., Jackson and Vicksburg, 1977—. Sec., Marshall Elem. Sch. PTA, Jackson, 1962-64, v.p., 1965; sec.-treas. Inter-Club Council Jackson, 1963-64; tchr. adult Sunday sch. dept. Hillcrest Bapt. Ch., Jackson, 1975—; mem. exec. com. Jackson Christian Bus. and Profl. Women's Council, 1976-80, sec., 1978-79, pres., 1979-80. Named Outstanding Woman in Constrn. Miss., 1962-63; Outstanding Mem. Nat. Assn. Women in Constrn., various times. Fellow Internat. Platform Assn.; mem. Nat. Assn. Women in Constrn. (chpt. pres. 1963-64, 76-77, nat. v.p. 1965-66, 77-78, nat. dir. Region 5, 1967-68, nat. sec. 1970-71, 71-72, pres. 1980-81, coordinator cert. constrn. asso. program 1973-78, guardian-controller Edn. Found. 1981-82), Nat. Assn. Parliamentarians, Delta Delta Delta. Editor NAWIC Image, 1968-69, Procedures Manual, 1965-66, Public Relations Handbook, 1967-68, Profl. Edn. Guide, 1972-73; author digests in field. Home: 3673 Meadow Ln Jackson MS 39212 Office: Suite 866 I-55 Pl 866 Foley St Jackson MS 39202

BATES, MARGARET LOUISE, polit. scientist; b. Grand Rapids, Mich., June 28, 1924; d. Albert H. and Marion L. (Powers) B.; B.A., Rockford (Ill.) Coll., 1945; M.A., Fletcher Sch. Law and Diplomacy, Medford, Mass., 1946; Fulbright scholar Bristol (Eng.) U., 1950-51, Makerere (Uganda) Coll., 1951-52; D.Phil. (Ford Found. fellow 1954-56), Oxford (Eng.) U., 1958; LL.D. (hon.), Ohio Wesleyan U., 1974. Editorial asso. World Peace Found., 1946-50; instr. Rockford Coll., 1952-54, Goddard Coll., Plainfield, Vt., 1958-64; asso. prof. govt. Smith Coll., 1964-71; prof. polit. sci. New Coll., Sarasota, Fla., 1971-75, New Coll., U. South Fla., 1975—; lectr. Peace Corps, others. Mem. African Studies Assn., Am. Polit. Sci. Assn., Internat. Studies Assn., UN Assn. Author articles in field, chpts. in books; editorial bds. profl. jours. Address: 5700 N Tamiami Trail Sarasota FL 33580

BATES, MARTHA PEARL, guidance counselor; b. Abilene, Tex., Dec. 22, 1933; d. Robert Madison and Mildred Alene (Manton) Copenhaver; B.S. in Psychology, Coll. William and Mary, 1956; M.Ed. in Guidance and Counseling, Loyola Coll., Balt., 1974; m. Charles Benjamin Bates, Apr. 9, 1960; children—Benjamin Madison, Lelia Ann, William Andrew. tchr., Montgomery County (Md.) schs., 1956-57, Balt. County schs., 1959-61, 62-64; with customer service and enrollment dept. Group Hospitalization, Inc., Washington, 1957-59; elem. sch. guidance counselor Baltimore County schs., 1973—; leader workshops, cons. in field, 1976—. Pres. Women's Soc. Christian Service, Salem United Methodist Ch., Joppa, Md., 1969-70, co-founder ch. library, 1965, Sunday sch. tchr., 1975-77, Sunday sch. sec., 1967-68; active local Cub Scouts, Brownies, Girls Softball Teams. Mem. NEA, Am. Personnel and Guidance Assn., Am. Sch. Counselors Assn., Md. Tchrs. Assn., Md. Personnel and Guidance Assn., Md. Sch. Counselors Assn., Tchrs. Assn. Baltimore County, Baltimore County Counselors Assn. Democrat. Office: 1717 Weyburn Rd Baltimore MD 21237

BATES, MARY LEE, librarian; b. Ordway, Colo., Aug. 28, 1926; d. James Milton and Grace Bernice Bennett; B.A., Linfield Coll., McMinnville, Oreg., 1948; M. in Librarianship, U. Wash., Seattle, 1968; m. Melvin Lane Bates, Aug. 23, 1947; children—Richard Lane, Katherine Lee, Ronald Martin, Marjorie Ellen. Tchr. schs. in Oreg., 1948-53; librarian Arlington (Oreg.) High Sch., 1962-64, Blue Mountain Community Coll., Pendleton, Oreg., 1963—; vis. prof. U. Oreg. Sch. Librarianship, summers 1971-73; evaluator N.W. Assn. Schs. and Colls., 1970—; cons. in field. Mem. Task Force for Battered Women, Rootseller Food Coop. Named Pendleton's First Woman Citizen, 1971. Mem. ALA, Pacific N.W. Library Assn. (pres. 1977-78), Oreg. Library Assn. (pres. 1974-75), AAUW (pres. Pendleton br. 1971-72), Common Cause, Oreg. Consumer League, Oreg. Women's Polit. Caucus, Umatilla County Hist. Soc., Pendleton C. of C., Freedom To Read Found., LWV. Democrat. Clubs: Pendleton Women's (pres. 1971-72), Altrusa, Soroptomists of Pendleton (Women Helping Women award). Home: PO Box 1091 Pendleton OR 97801 Office: PO Box 100 Pendleton OR 97801

BATES, MARY MARTHA, nurse; b. Georgetown, Tenn., Aug. 23, 1932; d. Ray Cuthbert and Charlie Pearl (Snodgrass) Marler; B.A., Carson Newman Coll., 1954; diploma Bapt. Meml. Hosp. Sch. Nursing, Memphis, 1957; student Southwestern Bapt. Theol. Sem., 1980—; m. Stanley R. Bates, Sept. 21, 1957; children—Elizabeth Ann. Staff nurse, Bapt. Hosp., Jacksonville, Fla, 1957-58, Mrytle Beach AFB Hosp., S.C., 1958-60; office nurse Dr. A.B. Russell, Ft. Walton Beach, Fla., 1964-65; nurse ARC, 1966; substitute tchr. Glasgow, Mont., 1966-68, Dover, Del., 1969-71; ednl. counselor Glasgow AFB, Mont., 1968; sch. health nurse Merced (Calif.) City Schs., 1968-69; asst. night supr. Del. Home and Hosp., Smyrna, 1971-72; staff nurse Eisenhower Hosp., Colorado Springs, Colo., 1975-78; asst. dir. nursing and staff devel. dir. Highland (Calif.) House Health Care, 1975-76; staff nurse Plymouth Village Convalescent Hosp., Redlands, Calif., 1976-78, Harris Hosp. Meth., Ft. Worth, 1978-79; preadmissions nursing coordinator, quality assurance coordinator Huguley Meml. Hosp., Ft. Worth, 1979—. Dir., Del. Girls in Action, 1971-72; mem. exec. com. Md. Womens Missionary Union, 1972. Mem. Nat. Assn. Quality Assurance Profls., Metro Area Quality Assurance Profls., So. Bapt. Social Workers Assn., So. Bapt. Assn. Ministries with Aging. Republican. Baptist. Home: 6517 Arthur Dr Fort Worth TX 76134

BATES, MAYOLYN H., state legislator; b. Jamaica, Vt., Apr. 8, 1913; grad. pub. schs.; widowed; 1 son. Owner, mgr. Flamstead of Vt.; mem. Vt. Ho. of Reps., 1979-80, 81—. Bd. dirs. Mental Health Services Southeastern Vt., Council on Aging for Southeastern Vt.; bd. dirs., chmn. Springfield Meal Site Adv. Bd. Mem. VFW Aux. Baptist. Office: Vt Ho of Reps State Ho Montpelier VT 05602 *

BATES, MERCEDES A., food co. exec.; b. 1915; grad. Oreg. State U., 1936. Supr. home service So. Calif. Gas Co., 1939-46; owner, mgr. food cons. firm Calif., 1948-60; sr. editor food dept. McCall's Mag., 1960-64; with Gen. Mills, Inc., dir. Betty Crocker Kitchens, 1964—, v.p., 1966—, v.p., dir. Betty Crocker Food and Nutrition Center, 1977—; dir. Minn. Gas Co., 1977—. Mem. Pres.'s Commn. White House Fellows, 1971-76. Mem. Am. Home Econs. Assn. (pres. 1970-71), Minn. Better Bus. Bur. (chmn. 1981—). Office: General Mills Inc 9200 Wayzata Blvd Minneapolis MN 55426

BATES-NISBET, (CLARA) ELISABETH, piano tchr., poet, lawyer; b. Houston, Dec. 4, 1902; d. William David and Kate Broocks (Arnall) Bates; B.A., U. Tex., 1938; M.A., U. Houston, 1941; LL.B., S. Tex. Sch. Law, 1937. Tchr. public schs., Houston, 1923-49, prin., 1950-73, prin. Longfellow Elem. Sch., 1950-52, Mamie Sue Bastian Elem. Sch., 1952-60, James Arlie Montgomery Elem. Sch., 1960-73; admitted to Tex. bar, 1937; tchr. piano, Houston, 1928—. Life mem. chancellor's council U. Tex., Tex. Congress Parents and Tchrs. Mem. State Bar Tex., Houston Bar Assn., Tex. Tchrs. Assn. (life), Ex-Students Assn. U. Tex. Austin (life), Tex. Geneal. Soc., Magna Charta Dames (organizing charter mem. E. Tex. Colony, 3d vice regent courier Round Table Tex. div. 1962-66), Tex. Hist. Assn. (patron, life), Colonial Dames XVII Century (registrar Col. John Alston chpt. 1966-68, mem. nat. com. on Am. history 1966-68), Alston-Willems-Boddie-Hillard Soc. N.C., Colonial Order Crown, San Augustine County Hist. Soc. (charter), San Jacinto Descs., Daus. Republic Tex. (organizing charter mem. Ezekial Cullen chpt. 1953, rec. sec. gen. 1963-65, compiler, editor anns. 1963-65, 2d v.p. gen., chmn. orgn. 1965-67), Soc. Descs. Charlemagne, DAR (Tejas chpt. regent 1966-68, mem. nat. coms.), Soc. Descs. Knights of Most Noble Order of Garter, Daus. Am. Colonists (organizer charter mem. LaSalle chpt.), UDC, Sovereign Colonial Soc. Ams. Royal Descent, Plantagenet Soc., Dames of Ct. of Honor, Daus. of Founders and Patriots of Am., Freedoms. Found. Valley Forge, Internat. Platform Assn., Smithsonian Instn., Bates Family of Old Va. Assn., Jamestowne Soc. (organizing gov. First Tex. Co. 1982), Delta Kappa Gamma (life, 1st v.p. Eta Delta chpt. 1966-68), Nat. Soc. Poets. Co-founder Perpetual Endowment Fund Daus. Republic Tex., also perpetually endowed Presdl. scholarship in law, history, govt. or music U. Tex. at Austin, and Kate Broocks Bates award for research in Tex. history Daus. Republic Tex.; founder Kate Harding Bates Parker Award Fund for Jr. Historians Orgns. of Tex. Hist. Assn., Kate Harding Bates Parker Fund for Library of Daus. Republic Tex., Emma Broocks Arnall perpetually endowed Geology Scholarship Fund at U. Okla. at Norman, perpetual endowment U. Tex. at Austin Fine Arts Center, Kate Broocks Bates Recital Hall named in honor of mother. Address: 2305 Woodhead St Houston TX 77019

BATESON, MARY CATHERINE, anthropologist; b. N.Y.C., Dec. 8, 1939; d. Gregory and Margaret (Mead) B.; B.A., Radcliffe Coll., 1960; Ph.D., Harvard U., 1963; m. J. Barkev Kassarjian, June 4, 1960; 1 dau., Sevanne Margaret. Mem. faculty Harvard U., 1963-66, Ateneo de Manila, 1966-68, Northeastern U., Boston, 1969-71; ednl. cons., Tehran, 1972-74; mem. faculty Damavand Coll., Tehran, 1975-77, U. No. Iran, Babolsar, 1977-79; dean of faculty, prof. anthropology Amherst Coll., 1980—; vis. scholar anthropology Harvard U., 1979-80; pres. Inst. Intercultural Studies, N.Y.C., 1979—. Grantee NSF, 1968-69, Wenner-Gren Found., 1972-73. Mem. Am. Anthrop. Assn., Soc. Iranian Studies, Lindisfarne Assn., World Soc. Ekistics. Author: Structural Continuity in Poetry: A Linguistic Study of Five Early Arabic Odes, 1970, Our Own Metaphor: A Personal Account of a Conference on Consciousness and Human Adaptation, 1972; co-editor: Approaches to Semiotics, 1964. *

BATISTE, PEARL THERESA, educator; b. Jeanerette, La., Dec. 9, 1930; d. Erris and Pearl (Armelin) Edgerly; B.A., Calif. State U., San Francisco, 1975; M.A. in Edn., U. San Francisco, 1978; M.S. in Pepperdine U., 1979; m. Berwick Batiste, Sept. 12, 1950; children—Michael, Keith, Ronald, Elissa, Ingrid, Patrick. Dir. counseling tng. dept. Amrick Advt., Oakland, Calif., 1976-77; public relations dir. San Francisco Ednl. Found., Oakland, 1977-78; fashion model, instr., substitute tchr. Barbizon Modeling Sch., 1975-76; program and project coordinator Oakland Public Schs., 1976—. Mem. Amway Exec. Women Assts., Profl. Woman Exec. Corp. Am., Black Profl. Bus. Women Assts., Nat. Alliance Black Edn. Democrat. Roman Catholic. Club: Fashionnete Social. Author: The Influence of African on American Fashion, 1980. Home: 2509 Tulare Ave El Cerrito CA 94530

BATSON, LEONORA L., retail co. exec.; b. Asbury Park, N.J., July 14, 1936; d. William and Elizabeth (Labagh) Little; student Ind. U., 1953-56; B.S. in Mus., Julliard Sch. Music, 1958; M.B.A., N.Y. U., 1978; m. Robert G. Batson, Jan. 13, 1962; 1 son, James A. Mgmt. cons. Booz Allen & Hamilton, N.Y.C., 1972-76; personnel mgr. DHJ Industries, Inc., N.Y.C., 1976-77, dir. personnel and indsl. relations, 1977-79; dir. corp. human resources Stop & Shop Cos. Inc., Boston, 1979—. Adv. bd. middle mgmt. continuing edn. program Babson Coll., Wellesley, Mass. Mem. Am. Soc. Tng. and Devel., Am. Soc. Personnel Adminstrn., Am. Compensation Assn., Beta Gamma Sigma, Pi Kappa Lambda, Pi Lambda Theta. Episcopalian. Home: 8 Wilshire Dr Scituate MA 02066 Office: Corp Human Resources Stop & Shop Companies Inc PO Box 369 Boston MA 02101

BATTEN, ANNE, state legislator, real estate broker; b. Flushing, N.Y., July 24, 1932; d. Francis and Jeanne N. Kelly; student Goddard Coll., 1979-80; m. James C. Batten, Aug. 16, 1952; children—Robert, Barbara. Real estate broker, East Hardwick, Vt., 1964—; mem. Vt. Ho. of Reps., 1980-81, 82—. Mem. Hardwick Planning Commn., 1972-73, Republican Town Com., 1970-82; treas. Hardwick Hist. Soc., 1981-82; mem. Northeastern Vt. Devel. Assn., 1981-82; mem. Vt. Gov.'s Commn. on Status of Women, 1981—. Mem. Hardwick C. of C., Vt. Women's Polit. Caucus (vice chmn.). Address: RD 1 Box 249 East Hardwick VT 05836

BATTEN, KRISTINE WITMER, cardiologist, naval officer; b. West Reading, Pa., June 21, 1951; d. Cameron T. and Julianne (Haas) Witmer; B.A., Bucknell U., 1973; M.D. (scholar) Med. Coll. Pa., 1977; m. George B. Batten, June 11, 1977. Commd. ensign U.S. Navy, 1977, advanced through grades to lt. comdr., intern Naval Regional Med. Center, Oakland, Calif., 1977-78; resident in internal medicine, 1978-80, staff cardiologist, dir. CCU, 1982—; cardiology fellow Letterman Army Med. Center, San Francisco, 1980-82. Mem. Am. Med. Women's Assn., Am. Heart Assn., Am. Coll. Cardiology (affiliate), Alpha Omega Alpha. Research in rheumatic heart disease in Micronesian Islands. Office: Box 5806 Naval Regional Medical Center Oakland CA 94627

BATTIN, MARGERY MILNE, business exec.; b. Toronto, Ont., Can., Mar. 25, 1927 (parents Am. citizens); d. Cecil Paton and Mildred Conboy (Smith) Milne; B.A. in Econs., Wellesley Coll., 1948; m. Richard Horace Battin, Aug. 25, 1947; children—Thomas, Pamela, Jeffrey. Mem. staff Mcpl. Cons., Inc., 1968; dir. resource survey project Mass. Dept. Mental Health, 1969-74; dir. community affairs Mass. Resdl. Programs, Inc., 1974-76; prin. Strategy Devel. Assos., 1980—. Mem Lexington Town Meeting, 1960-74; mem. Lexington Bd. Selectmen, 1974—, chmn., 1977-79; chmn. Lexington Structure of Town Govt. Com., 1966-69; chmn. Lexington Center Rivitalization Com., 1980—; mem. Gov.'s Local Govt. Adv. Com., 1976-80; mem. adv. council dept. public mgmt. and adminstrn. Suffolk U., 1977—, chmn., 1981-82; mcpl. rep. State Social Policy Com., 1978; bd. dirs. Mass. Assn. for Mental Health, 1977—, Lexington Vis. Nurse Assn., 1974, Lexington Interfaith Corp., 1972-74; trustee Cary Meml. Library, 1974—, Re-Place Inc., 1970-74; mem. N.W. Met. Health Council, Health Planning Council Greater Boston, 1976-79; mem. steering com. New Eng. Human Services Coalition, 1976-77, Mass. Council of Human Service Providers, 1975-77; lectr. Radcliffe seminars, 1976. Mem. Nat. League of Cities (public safety policy com. 1977-78), Women in Mcpl. Govt., Boston Network for Women in Politics and Govt., Women Elected Mcpl. Ofcls. (chmn. 1975-77), Middlesex County Selectmen's Assn. (pres. 1977), Mass. Selectmen's Assn. (pres. 1979-80), Mass. Mcpl. Assn. (trustee, chmn. tax policy com. 1979-80), Lexington LWV (v.p. 1958-60), Lexington Hist. Soc., Citizens for Lexington Conservation, Citizens for Lexington Public Schs., M.I.T. Women's League. Club: Wellesley (Boston). Home: 15 Paul Revere Rd Lexington MA 02173 Office: Town Office Bldg Massachusetts Ave Lexington MA 02173

BATTIN-DUPREE, BARBARA ELLEN, found. exec.; b. N.Y.C., Mar. 5, 1949; d. Milton A. and Katherine A. Lessler; B.S.C. cum laude, Ohio U., 1972; m. H.E. Dupree, Oct. 25, 1980; children—Leigh, Donna. Traffic dir., exec. sec. Sta. WRFD, Columbus, Ohio, 1972-73; public relations dir. Central Ohio Lung Assn., Columbus, 1973-74; free lance voice work Sta. WSAZ-TV, Huntington, W.Va., 1974-77; writer, client liaison, voice talent John McCormack Advt. Co., Huntington, 1974; bldg. fund raising dir., asst. chpt. mgr. Tri-State Red Cross Blood Center and Huntington-Cabell County Red Cross chpt., Huntington, 1974-77; exec. dir. Huntsville Hosp. Found. and dir. devel. Huntsville (Ala.) Hosp., 1977—. Bd. dirs. Madison County chpt. ARC, 1977-80; bd. dirs. Huntsville Interfaith Vol. Transp. Service, 1979-80; pres. bd. dirs. Huntsville Women's Center, 1979-80; bd. dirs. Pathfinders, 1979-81, Girls Scouts of No. Ala., 1972, Hospice of Huntsville, 1982. Recipient 1st pl. Public Relations Council Ala., 1980, 1st pl. Lantern award So. Public Relations Fedn., 1981; 1st pla. award for spl. public relations program Public Relations Council Ala., 1981. Mem. Nat. Assn. Hosp. Devel. (fellow; regional research chairperson, dir. edn. fund, mem. nat. edn. com. 1977-82), Nat. Soc. Fund Raising Execs., Madison County C. of C. and Indsl. Devel. Assn., AAUW, Public Relations Council Ala. (dir. N.Ala. chpt., v.p. programs 1981-82, v.p. membership 1983-84). So. Public Relations Fedn. Club: Temple Bnai Sholom Sisterhood Hadassah. Office: 101 Sively Rd Huntsville AL 35801

BATTLE, JIMMIE LORENE NELSON, educator; b. Waurika, Okla., Oct. 9; d. James Searcy and Mary Elizabeth (Ellis) Nelson; B.S., Langston U., 1944; M.S., Okla. State U., Stillwater, 1953; Ph.D., U. Md., 1976; m. Huey Jefferson Battle, Sept. 14, 1942; children—Sandra Elizabeth, Huey James, Michael Brent. Educator, Okla., 1946-50; dir. Nursery Sch. Lab. Center, Langston (Okla.) U., 1954, 57-59; kindergarten tchr. Oklahoma City Public Schs., 1960-62; demonstration tchr. Lab. Sch., Virginia State U., Petersburg, 1962-73, asso. prof. edn., 1962-81, prof., 1981—, dir. Center for Young Children, 1973—, coordinator dept. early childhood edn., 1980—; cons. in field; coordinator workshops in field. Bd. dirs. Day Nursery, Richmond, Va., 1974—, Child Care Center, Gillfield Baptist Ch., Petersburg, 1969-73. Mem. NEA, Va., Chesterfield edn. assns., AAUP, Nat. Assn. Edn. Young Children, Va. Assn. Early Childhood Edn., Assn. Childhood Edn. Internat., So. Assn. Children Under Six, Jack and Jill of Am. (Disting. Jill award, 1975, Internat. Yr. of Child award 1979), Alpha Kappa Alpha, Kappa Omicron Phi, Kappa Delta Pi Phi Delta Kappa, Alpha Kappa Mu. Democrat. Baptist. Club: Order Eastern Star. Home: 20316 Loyal Ave Ettrick VA 23803 Office: Box 77 Va State Coll Petersburg VA 23803

BATTLE, KATHLEEN, opera singer, soprano; b. Portsmouth, Ohio; B.M., M.M., U. Cin. Debut in Brahms Requiem, Festival of Two Worlds, Spolito, Italy; sang in The Magic Flute, Barber of Seville, Abduction from Sergalio, for Met. Opera, 1981-82, Arabella, 1983; appears frequently with San Francisco Opera; regular guest N.Y., Chgo., Boston, Cleve., Phila. orchs.; appears regularly at Ravinia and Cin. May festivals; solo recitalist Lincoln Center, N.Y.C., 1981-82, San Francisco, 1982; soloist Berlin Philharm., 1982; has recorded for Decca, RCA, CBS Records. Recipient Martha Baird Rockefeller Fund award; winner WGN-Ill. Opera Guild Audition of the Air. Office: Care Columbia Artists Management Inc 1965 W 57th St New York NY 10019 *

BATTLE, LOIS, writer, actress; b. Subiaco, Australia, Oct. 6, 1941; came to U.S., 1946, naturalized, 1962; d. John Henry and Doreen Mary (White) B.; student Fullerton Jr. Coll., 1956-58; B.A., UCLA, 1962. Author books: Season of Change, 1980; War Brides, 1982; actress. Mem. Writers Guild, Actors Equity Assn., Screen Actors Guild, AFTRA. Office: care St Martin's Press 175 5th Ave New York NY 10010

BATTLE, LUCY TROXELL (MRS. J.A. BATTLE), educator; b. Bridgeport, Ala., June 28, 1916; d. John Price and Emily Florence (Williams) Troxell; student U. Ala., Montevallo, 1934-35; B.S. Fla. So. Coll., 1949; postgrad. U. South Fla., 1950, 52, Fla. State U., 1963, Oxford (Eng.) U., 1979; m. Jean Allen Battle, Aug. 25, 1940; 1 dau., Helen Carol. Asst. postmaster, Bridgeport, Ala., 1936-40; asst. dir. personnel office Sebring (Fla.) AFB, 1942-44; tchr. Cleveland Court Sch., Lakeland, Fla., also Forest Hill Sch., Carrollwood Sch., Tampa, Fla., 1949-64; dean of girls Greco Jr. High Sch., Tampa, 1964-68. Bd. dirs. Tampa Oral Sch. for Deaf. Recipient Outstanding Service award Fla. So. Coll. Woman's Club, 1942. Mem. NEA, Am. Childhood Edn. Internat., AAUW, Delta Kappa Gamma, Kappa Delta Pi, Phi Mu. Methodist. Club: Carrollwood Village Golf and Tennis. Author: (with J.A. Battle) The New Idea in Education, 1968. Home and office: 11011 Carrollwood Dr Tampa FL 33618

BATTREALL, CAROLYN MAY, design engr.; b. Indpls., Apr. 18, 1931; d. Paul Joseph and Hester Mildred (Harsin) B.; B.S. in Elem. Edn., Ind. U., 1983. With Ind. Bell Telephone Co., 1950—, beginning as long distance operator, successively clerical asst., DDD coordinator, Muncie, Ind., 1966-69, state trunk coordinator, 1969-71, trunk forecaster, 1971-78, transmission engr., 1977-78, electronic switching system design engr., Indpls., 1978—. Vice pres. Ind. chpt. U.S. Assn. Blind Athletes;

communication chmn. 1982 World Goal Ball Championship, Butler U., Indpls. Cert in spl. edn., Ind. Mem. Telephone Pioneers Am. (community service chmn. 1971-76, 2d v.p. Hoosier State chpt. 1976-77). Democrat. Roman Catholic. Home: 4305 Greenway Dr Indianapolis IN 46220 Office: 220 N Meridian St VP 610 Indianapolis IN 46204

BAUCHMOYER, MADELEINE ANNE, nurse; b. Los Angeles, Feb. 19, 1945; d. William Frederick and Dorothy Rose (Dalton) Muller; B.S. in Nursing, Catholic U. Am., 1966; M.Ed., U. Miami (Fla.), 1973; M.Nursing, La. State U., 1980; m. A.J. Bauchmoyer, Jan. 14, 1978; children—Regina Louise, Karl Celby. Nurse clinician Miami VA Hosp., 1970; mem. faculty Miami-Dade Community Coll., 1970-73, U. Miami Med. Sch., 1973-75; dir. nursing, coordinator health care program U. Miami, 1973-75; mem. faculty Nicholls State U., Thibideaux, La., 1976-78, La. State U. Sch. Nursing, New Orleans, 1978-80; asst. prof. nursing U. Southwestern La. Coll. Nursing, Lafayette, 1980—, dir. ednl. mobility track 1982—; symposia participant. Reader mass St. Jules Roman Catholic Ch., Lafayette, 1982—. Served as officer Nurse Corps, USNR, 1964-69; comdr. Res. Navy scholar, 1964-66. Mem. Am. Council Nurse Researchers, Am. Nurses Assn., Nat. League Nursing, AAUP, Mental Health Assn. Lafayette, Res. Officer Assn. (past chpt. v.p.), Naval Res. Assn., Southwestern La. Arts Council, Spring Fiesta Hist. Assn., Sigma Theta Tau. Republican. Club: Univ. Women's. Office: Coll Nursing U Southwestern La PO Box 42490 Lafayette LA 70504

BAUER, BARBARA TOYNE, physicist; b. Columbia, Mo., Oct. 19, 1944; d. Guy Edwin and Bertha Happy Toyne; B.S. in Physics, St. Louis U., 1966; M.S. in Physics, U. Kans., 1968. Systems engr. IBM, 1969; researcher U. Kans., 1970; software systems devel. mgr. Bell Telephone Labs., Piscataway, N.J., 1972—. Mem. IEEE, Bell Labs. Women Mgrs. Network (chmn.). Author: Computer Assisted Instruction Evaluation Guidelines. Office: 6 Corporate Pl Piscataway NJ 08854

BAUER, CAROL ANN, dental office adminstr.; b. Milw., May 4, 1934; d. Cyril Severn and Ruth Marie (Bonnett) Zalewski; student Lakeshore Tech. Inst., 1968-78; m. Lyle Henry Bauer, June 27, 1953; children—Robert, Barbara, Mary, Lynn, Timothy, Anne, Eric, William, Peter. Clk., S.S. Kresge Co., Manitowoc, Wis., 1951; cashier Gt. Atlantic & Pacific Tea Co., Manitowoc, 1952; bookkeeper Manitowoc Savs. Bank, 1952-53; psychiat. technician Holy Family Hosp., Manitowoc, 1969; co-mgr. Jellystone Campgrounds Ltd., Sturgeon Bay, Wis., 1969; bus. mgr., receptionist for dental surgeons, Manitowoc, 1971-79; bookkeeping dept. Manitowoc County Bank, 1979-79; dental receptionist, office mgr., Manitowoc, 1979—. Notary public, Wis. Mem. Nat. Assn. Dental Assts. Roman Catholic. Home: 1602 S 15th St Manitowoc WI 54220 Office: 3322 Menasha Ave Manitowoc WI 54220

BAUER, ELIZABETH KELLEY (MRS. FREDERICK WILLIAM BAUER), policy analyst, assn. exec.; b. Berkeley, Calif., Aug. 7, 1920; d. Leslie Constant and Elizabeth Jeanette (Worley) Kelley; A.B., U. Calif. at Berkeley, 1941, M.A., 1943; Ph.D. (fellow), Columbia U., 1947; m. Frederick William Bauer, July 5, 1944; children—Elizabeth Katherine Bauer Berg, Frederick Nicholas. Instr. U.S. history and studies Barnard Coll., N.Y.C., 1944-45; lectr. history U. Calif. at Berkeley, 1949-50, 56-57; research asst. Giannini Found., 1946-49, asst. research agrl. economist, 1957-60; exec. sec. Internat. Conf. on Agrl. and Coop. Credit, U. Calif. at Berkeley, 1952-53, exec. sec. South Asia Project, 1955-56; registrar Holy Names Coll., Oakland, Calif., 1971-72; research asso. Brookings Instn. and Nat. Acad. Public Adminstrn., Washington, 1973; fgn. affairs officer Internat. Energy Affairs, Fed. Energy Adminstrn. Washington, 1974-77; fgn. affairs officer Office of Current Reporting, Internat. Affairs, Dept. Energy, Washington, 1977-81; dir. policy analysis and evaluation Nat. Coal Assn., Washington, 1981—. Mem. Calif. Com. to Revise the Tchrs. Credential, 1961; trustee Grad. Theol. Union, Berkeley, 1972-74; bd. dirs. St. Paul's Towers and Episcopal Homes Found, Oakland, 1971-72. Recipient Superior Achievement award Dept. Energy, 1980. Mem. AAUW (Calif. chmn. for higher edn. 1960-62), Internat. Assn. Energy Economists, Prytanean Honor Soc., AAAS, P.E.O., Mortar Bd., Phi Beta Kappa, Pi Lambda Theta, Sigma Kappa Alpha, Phi Alpha Theta, Pi Sigma Alpha. Democrat. Episcopalian. Author: Commentaries on the Constitution, 1790-1860, 1952; (with Murray R. Benedict) Farm Surpluses: U.S Burden or World Asset?, 1960; (with Florence Noyce Wertz) The Graduate Theological Union, 1970. Co-author, editor: The Role of Foreign Governments in the Energy Industries, 1977. Home: 7805 Radnor Rd Bethesda MD 20817 Office: 1130 17th St NW Washington DC 20036

BAUER, FRANCES BRAND, research scientist; b. N.Y.C., July 5, 1923; d. Benjamin and Gussie (Fuchs) Brand; A.B., Bklyn. Coll., 1943; M.S., Brown U., 1945, Ph.D. in Applied Math., 1948; m. Louis Bauer, Oct. 1, 1948 (dec. 1978). Research asso. applied math. Brown U., 1945-48; research asso. aero. engring. structures Poly. Inst. Bklyn., 1949-50; sr. mathematician Reeves Instrument, N.Y.C., 1950-51, 52-61; sr. research scientist elasticity, fluid dynamics and computing Courant Inst. Math. Scis., N.Y. U., 1961—; mathematician Bur. Standards, 1951-52. Recipient Pub. Service award NASA, 1976, certificate recognition, 1977, 80; Rockefeller Found. fellow, 1945. Mem. Math. Soc., Assn. Computing Machinery, Sigma Xi. Democrat. Jewish. Club: Zonta (treas.) (N.Y.C.). Co-author: Supercritical Wing Sections I, 1972, Sections II, 1975, Sections III, 1977; A Computational Method in Plasma Physics, 1978. Home: 200 East End Ave New York NY 10028 Office: Courant Inst 251 Mercer St New York NY 10003

BAUER, KATHRYN ANN, comml. credit co. mgr.; b. Chagaramas, Trinidad, Feb. 24, 1951; d. John F. and Helen C. Bauer; student Highline Coll., 1969-70, Delta Coll., Stockton, Calif., 1974-76, Calif. State U., San Jose, 1976-78; B.A. in Social Sci. (Bank of Am. scholar), Calif. State U., Sacramento, 1982. File clk. Dun & Bradstreet, Seattle, 1969-70, exec. sec., Los Angeles, 1970-74, bus. analyst, San Jose, Calif., 1976-78, divisional ops. mgr., Sacramento, 1978-79, ops. mgr., 1979—; seminar leader small bus. classes. Active YMCA and camp programs, 1965-81. Mem. Sacramento C. of C., Small Bus. Council, Women in Bus. Council. Republican. Roman Catholic.

BAUER, MARCIA THOMPSON, educator; b. Buffalo, Jan. 14, 1932; d. Leslie Philip and Emma Margaret (Elsheimer) Thompson; B.S. in Edn., SUNY, Buffalo, 1953; M.Ed., Coll. William and Mary, Williamsburg, Va., 1974, Ed.S., 1975, Ed.D., 1977; children—Janet, Diana, Paul R., David, Leslie. Tchr. schs., N.Y. State, N.C. and Va., 1953-73; mem. staff Christopher Newport Coll., Newport News, Va., 1976; asst. prof. guidance and counseling Valdosta (Ga.) State Coll., 1977—; ind. practice counseling, 1979—. Mem. Am. Personnel and Guidance Assn., Assn. Sex Therapists and Counselors, Ga. Assn. Counselor Educators. Unitarian-Universalist. Home: 248 Hammock Trail E Lake Park GA 31636 Office: Sch Edn Valdosta State Coll Valdosta GA 31698

BAUER, NANCY HELEN, ins. co. exec.; b. San Angelo, Tex., Sept. 6, 1940; d. Charles Frank and Thelma Leone (Gordon) Hemphill; student Abilene Christian U., 1962, Richland Coll., 1976-77, U. Tex., Dallas, 1978; m. Clarence Gerald Bauer, Aug. 15, 1968; children—Lucinda Cheryne Watson, Charles Scott Watson, John Robert Watson, Sally Ann Bauer. Owner, Hemphill Office, Albany, Tex., 1962-70; owner acctg. service, Richardson, Tex., 1970-75; mgr. bus. office Plano (Tex.) Gen. Hosp., 1975-76; controller Alpha Oil & Gas, Inc., Dallas, 1977-78; asst. v.p., systems mgr. Internat. Underwriters, Inc., Richardson, 1978-82, v.p., 1982—. Enrolled agt. IRS. Mem. MICRU Internat., AMORS User Assn. (dir., chmn. liaison com.), Phi Theta Kappa. Republican. Baptist. Club: Order Eastern Star. Home: 2409 Coleshire Plano TX 75075 Office: Penthouse Suite 100 N Central Expressway Richardson TX 75080

BAUER, SUSAN CAROL, educator; b. N.Y.C., June 28, 1949; d. Ernest Benjamin and Helene Michalene (Siergiej) Bauer; B.S. in Bus. Edn., Baruch Coll., 1974; M.A. in Secondary Edn.-Bus., Adelphi U., 1976; profl. diploma in sch. adminstrn. C.W. Post Center, L.I.U., 1978. Exec. sec. Union Carbide Corp., N.Y.C., 1967-72; tchr bus. Sewanhaka High Sch., Floral Park, N.Y., 1974-76; asst. prof. secretarial sci. and word processing SUNY, Farmingdale, 1976—; condr. word processing seminars. Cert. profl. sec. Mem. Internat. Info. Word Processing Assn. (pres. L.I. chpt. 1981-83), Profl. Secs. Internat. (chairperson cert. profl. sec. and edn. com. L.I. chpt. 1980-82, pres.-elect 1982-83 Nat. Assn. Female Execs., Nat. Bus. Edn. Assn. Republican. Roman Catholic. Office: SUNY Whitman Hall Farmingdale NY 11735

BAUER-BURKE, JUDITH ANN, social worker; b. Mpls., May 28, 1947; d. Francis C. and Marion G. Bauer; B.S., U. Minn., 1973; M.S.W., U. Denver, 1975; M.S. in Ednl. Psychology, U. Utah, 1979; m. Frank E. Burke, Dec. 10, 1977. Child psychiat. technician Glenwood Hills Hosp., Golden Valley, Minn., 1970-73; program coordinator Alcohol-driving countermeasures program, Denver, 1975-77; job coach Salt Lake County Employment and Tng. Adminstrn., 1978; psychology intern U. Utah Med. Center, 1977-79; clin. dir. chem. dependency center West Park Hosp., Cody, Wyo., 1979-80; pvt. practice clin. social work, Cody, 1980—. Mem. AAUW, Nat. Assn. Social Workers, Acad. Cert. Social Workers, Phi Kappa Phi. Club: Soroptomists. Home and Office: 2119 23d St Cody WY 82414

BAUGH, MARLENA DOROTHY, nursing adminstr.; b. Montreal, Que., Can., July 18, 1944; d. Horace Grenville and Dorothy Eleanor (McCubbin) B.; R.N., Hotel Dieu Hosp., 1965; B.S.N., Windsor U., 1971; M.A., Tchrs. Coll. Columbia U., 1975. Staff nurse Hotel Dieu, St. Jerome, Que., 1965-66; charge nurse Doctors Hosp., Detroit, 1968-72; staff nurse Phelps Meml. Hosp., Tarrytown, N.Y., 1973; dir. nursing Elmhurst (Ill.) Extended Care Center, Inc., 1975-76; nursing adminstr. Loretto Hosp., Chgo., 1977—. Mem. Am. Nurses Assn. (cert. adminstr.), Council Nursing Adminstrn. Episcopalian. Home: 120 E George St Bensenville IL 60106

BAUM, HELEN RYBA, public relations exec.; b. Darien, Conn., Jan. 11, 1932; d. Michael A. and Helen (Wissman) Ryba; student in public relations and mktg. Northwestern U., 1963-64, U. Wis., Madison, 1977; m. Arthur H. Baum, Oct. 10, 1977. With Union Trust Co., Stamford, Conn., 1950—, asst. v.p., 1969-77, v.p. community relations, public relations and legis. affairs, 1977—; justice of peace, State of Conn., 1974—; public relations coordinator for two legislators State of Conn., 1970-75; instr. Am. Inst. Banking, 1965-70; public relations chmn. for state rep. from Darien, Conn., 1974; public relations chmn. Stamford Hosp. Women's Aux., 1970-74. Mem. public relations com. Stamford United Way, 1962-74; mem. Darien Town Meeting, 1970-74; chmn. publicity 1968 campaign, Stamford Republican Party. Mem. Stamford Area Commerce and Industry Assn. (Sacian award 1976), Conn. Bankers Assn. (mem. legis. com.), Conn. Bus. and Industry Assn., Stamford-Norwalk Jr. League (dir. 1976—). Republican. Club: Landmark. Office: Union Trust Co 300 Main St Stamford CT 06904

BAUM, INGEBORG RUTH, librarian; b. Berlin, Sept. 20, 1916; d. Ella Koch; Oberlyceum (scholar), Kassel, Germany, 1926-33; postgrad. Georgetown U., 1963-70; m. Albert Otto Baum, Feb. 16, 1938 (div. 1960); children—Harro Siegward, Helma Sigrun (Mrs. George Meadows). Came to U.S., 1951, naturalized, 1957. Export corr. Bitter-Polar, Germany, 1933-35, Henschel Locs, Germany, 1936; exec. sec. Fieseler Airplane Mfrs., Germany, 1936-38; interpreter, sec. UNRRA, Germany, 1946-48; payroll supr., civilian dept. U.S. Army, Wetzlar PX, Germany, 1948-51; asst. librarian Supreme Council, Ancient and Accepted Scottish Rite, Washington, 1951-70, acting librarian and museums curator, 1970—; appraiser rare books and documents; v.p. Merical Elec. Contractors, Inc., Forestville, Md., 1974—. Mem. Am. Soc. Appraisers, Calligraphers Guild. Mem. Ch. Jesus Christ of Latter-day Saints. Free-lance contbr. to Pabelverlag, Rastatt, Germany, Harle, Ofcl. Publs., Inc., others. Home: 2480 16th St NW Apt 416 Washington DC 20009 Office: 1733 16th St NW Washington DC 20009

BAUM, NEHAMA TCHIA, ednl. adminstr., psychologist; b. Israel, July 3, 1937; came to U.S., 1976, naturalized, 1979; d. Eliezer and Shoshana Israeli; diploma Sch. Social Work, U. Tel Aviv (Israel), 1958; student Bezalel Acad. Art, Jerusalem, 1966-67; B.A. in Art History, Hebrew U. of Jerusalem, 1971, B.A. in Spl. Edn., 1970, M.A. cum laude, 1972; Ph.D. in Applied Psychology, U. Toronto, 1980; m. Moshe Baum, 1956; children—Michael, Karni. Social worker family therapy Ministry of Welfare, Israel, 1958-59; dir. social work dept., Dimona, Israel, 1961; research asso. Sch. Social Work, U. Tel Aviv, 1962-66, guest prof. spl. edn., 1972-76; guest prof. spl. edn. Haifa (Israel) U., 1972-76, Sch. for Occupational Therapy, Hebrew U. of Jerusalem, 1972-76; dir. profl. devel. program for tchrs. Ministry of Edn., Israel, 1974-75; cons. counseling and sex edn. regional high schs. in Israel, 1975-76; supr. learning potential project Ont. Inst. for Studies in Edn., U. Toronto, 1979-80; founder, dir. Thera-Studies Inc., sch. for multi-handicapped, Toronto, 1978—. Exhibited sculpture and paintings in various galleries in Israel, 1968-72, Can., 1975-79, U.S., 1975-76; actress with Nat. Radio of Israel, Army Theatre, Ohel Theatre, Tel Aviv, 1946-59. Served with Israeli Army, 1955-56. Mem. Am. Psychol. Assn., Council Exceptional Children, Am. Assn. Study of Mental Imagery, C.G. Jung Found., Israeli Assn. Creative Therapies. Jewish. Office: 95 Faywood Blvd Downsview ON M3H 2X5 Canada

BAUM, SELMA, consumer affairs specialist; b. Bklyn., Jan. 15, 1924; d. Samuel and Tillie (Bayer) Goldman; ed. N.Y. U., New Sch. for Social Research; m. Milton W. Baum, Jan. 19, 1947; children—Victor C., Cynthia Baum-Baicker. Communications mgr. Sobel & Goldman, Inc., N.Y.C., 1941-48; public relations cons., 1948-65; comparison shopper Gimbels, Valley Stream, N.Y., 1965-67, mgr. comparison shopping office, N.Y.C., 1967-75, dir. consumer affairs, 1975—; lectr. in field. Mem. Am. Mgmt. Assn., Nat. Retail Mchts. Assn. (consumer affairs com.), Nat. Assn. Female Execs., Fashion Group, Am. Council on Consumer Interests, Soc. Consumer Affairs Profls. in Bus. (chpt. pres. 1981-82), Soc. Consumer Affairs Profls. in Bus. (pres. adv. council 1981-82), Greater N.Y. WINS (cons. regional affairs com.). Home: 843 Longview Ave North Woodmere NY 11581 Office: Gimbels 33 and Broadway New York City NY 10001

BAUMAN, GLORIA DARK, coll. ofcl.; b. Winston-Salem, N.C., May 29, 1939; d. Arthur Odell and Martha Mae (Penn) Dark; B.S. in Home Econs., N.C. Central U., 1962; postgrad. Nat. Program Edn. Leaders fellow) Ohio State U., Columbus, 1973-74; m. Darryl D. Bauman, July 2, 1976; 1 dau., Christie D. Pearson. Dir. urban devel./consumer edn. Expt. in Self-Reliance, Winston-Salem, 1966-72; field placement/supt. intern N.C. Dept. Edn., Raleigh, 1972-74; studied innovation in edn., Norway, Denmark, London; regional field rep. Nat. Council Aging, Kansas City, Mo., 1974-77; dir. adminstrn., edn. and personnel Black Econ. Union, Kansas City, Mo., 1978-81; mem. part-time faculty Pioneer Community Coll., Kansas City, Mo., 1979—, job placement specialist, 1981—; cons. in field. Mem. Nat. Assn. Female Execs., Mo. Assn. Jr. Colls. Baptist. Home: 12417 Ewing Circle Grandview MO 64030 Office: 1710 The Paseo Kansas City MO 64108

BAUMAN, SANDRA SPIEGEL, nurse; b. N.Y.C., June 30, 1949; d. Siegmund and Ruth (Josias) S.; student Boston U., 1967-70; B.S. in Nursing, Adelphi U., 1971, postgrad., 1973-74; M.S. in Community Counseling, Barry Coll., 1981; postgrad. Fla. Atlantic U./Fla. Internat. U., 1982—, Gestalt Inst. Miami, 1982—; m. H. Lee Bauman, Nov. 3, 1978. Staff nurse educator obstetrics Albert Einstein Hosp., N.Y.C., 1971-72, head nurse newborn nurseries, 1973-74; asst. instr. maternity nursing St. Johns Riverside Hosp., 1972-73; head nurse obstetrics and nurseries, high risk nursery Mt. Sinai Hosp., Miami Beach, Fla., 1974-78; clin. nursing supr., div. pediatrics Jackson Meml. Hosp., Miami, 1978, coordinator div. clin. edn., 1978-81, quality assurance coordinator Maternal-Child Hosp. Center, 1979-81, perinatal coordinator, 1980-81, also core nursing mem. child protection team, 1979-81, asst. adminstr. ob-gyn, 1981-82; adminstr. Meadowbrook Med. Center, Inc., Dania, Fla., 1982—; instr. Sch. Nursing, Fla. Internat. U., North Miami, 1982—, coordinator child bearing and child rearing courses, 1982—; mem. Fla. Bd. Nursing, 1979—, vice chmn., 1981-82, chmn., 1982—; CPR instr., 1978. Mem. Am. Nurses Assn. (regional editor 1980—), Council High Risk Perinatal Nurses, Am. Personnel and Guidance Assn., Am. Pub. Health Assn., Sigma Theta Tau. Contbr. articles to RN mag. Office: Fla Internat U Sch Nursing Bay Vista Campus North Miami FL 33181

BAUMANN, CAROL EDLER, educator; b. Plymouth, Wis., Aug. 11, 1932; d. Clarence H. and Beulah (Weinhold) Edler; B.A. in Internat. Relations, U. Wis., 1954; Ph.D. (Marshall scholar, hon. Woodrow Wilson fellow), U. London, 1957; m. Richard J. Baumann, Feb. 28, 1959; children—Dawn, Wendy. Instr. dept. polit. sci. U. Wis., Madison, 1957-61; project assoc. Nat. Security Studies Group, 1958-61; lectr. U. Wis., Milw., 1961-62, asst. prof., 1962-67, assoc. prof., 1967-72, prof., 1972—; dep. asst. sec. assessments and research Bur. Intelligence and Research, U.S. Dept. State, Washington, 1979-81; vis. prof. Grad. Sch. Internat. Service, Am. U., Washington, 1981. Mem. Pres.'s Commn. on Fgn. Lang. and Internat. Studies, 1978-79, Wis. Gov.'s Commn. on UN, 1964-79. Mem. Am. Polit. Sci. Assn., Council Fgn. Relations, Internat. Studies Assn., Atlantic Council U.S. (com. Atlantic studies), Nat. Council Community World Affairs Orgns., Phi Beta Kappa, Phi Eta Sigma, Phi Kappa Phi. Democrat. Lutheran. Author: The Diplomatic Kidnappings, 1973; Western Europe: What Path to Integration?, 1967; contbr. articles on contemporary European polit. affairs to scholarly jours. Home: 2296 Sherman Rd Jackson WI 53037 Office: Office Internat Studies and Programs U Wis-Milw PO Box 340 Milwaukee WI 53201

BAUMANN, CECILIA LOUISE CLOUGHLY, coll. adminstr.; b. Albuquerque, Feb. 18, 1943; d. Cecil Pershing and Mary Louise (Bezemek) Cloughly; B.A. magna cum laude, Oberlin Coll., 1965; postgrad. (Fulbright scholar) U. Munich, Germany, 1965-66; M.A., Northwestern U., 1967, Ph.D., 1970. French hornist Graunke Orch., Munich, 1965-66; asso. prof. German, chmn. dept. Elmhurst (Ill.) Coll., 1968-73; Fulbright and study abroad advisor Inst. Internat. Edn., Chgo., 1973-74; dir. Oldenborg Center for Modern Langs. and Internat. Relations, Pomona, Calif., 1974—; French hornist, community orchs., 1966—. Recipient Merit cert. Goethe House N.Y. and Am. Assn. Tchr. German, 1978; sr. Fulbright fellow, W.Ger., 1979. Mem. MLA, Am. Assn. Tchrs. German (co-founder, co-dir. placement info. centers, 1973-77), Am. Council Teaching Fgn. Langs., Calif. Fgn. Lang. Tchrs. Assn., Nat. Assn. Fgn. Student Affairs, Modern and Classical Lang. Assn. So. Calif., Philol. Assn. Pacific Coast, Western Assn. German Studies, Phi Beta Kappa. Author: Advisor's Guide to Study Abroad, 1975; Wilhelm Mueller, The Poet of the Schubert Song Cycles: His Life and Works, 1981; translator: A Pictorial History of the Horn, 1975; asso. editor Schatzkammer der deutschen Sprachlehre, Dichtung und Geschichte, 1978—; contbr. articles to profl. jours. Home: Oldenborg Center Dirs Residence Pomona College Claremont CA 91711

BAUMANN, MARLYS ANN, nurse, ednl. adminstr.; b. Grafton, N.D., Sept. 1, 1946; d. Gilfred Duane and Pauline (Oline) Moen; diploma St. Andrew's Sch. Nursing, Bottineau, N.D., 1967; B.S.N., Moorhead State U., 1982; m. Michael Baumann, Sept. 2, 1967; children—Michelle Ann, Mark Duane. Staff nurse St. Joseph Hosp., Grafton, N.D., 1967-68; staff nurse, asst. head nurse Dakota Hosp., Fargo, N.D., 1968-69, clin. instr. practical nursing, 1971-74; charge nurse Scott and White Hosp., Temple, Tex., 1969-70; staff nurse St. Joseph Hosp., Grafton, 1970-71; practical nursing faculty N.D. State Sch. Sci., Wahpeton, 1974-81, chmn. dept., 1981—; mem. N.D. Nursing Needs and Resources Com., 1969, Clay Cancer Bd., 1974-77, N.D. Nursing Edn. Consortium, 1979—. Vol., Riveredge Hospice, 1979—; mem. ch. council, bd. edn. Bethel Luth. Ch., 1979-81. Named Outstanding Mrs. Jaycee, Barnesville, Minn., 1975-76. Mem. Nat. League Nursing (council practical nurse programs), LWV. Club: Homemakers. Home: 1010 Richland Wahpeton ND 58075 Office: 706 Dakota Ave Wahpeton ND 58075

BAUMANN, MARY JANE, lawyer; b. Teaneck, N.J., Mar. 19, 1944; d. Roland Smith and Mary Jane (Roberts) Tremble; B.A. with honors, Ramapo Coll. of N.J., 1974; M.A. (fellow), Eagleton Inst., Rutgers U., 1978, J.D., 1978; m. Ulrich A. Baumann, Feb. 4, 1963; children—Kristin, U. Roberts, Jeffrey. Legis. asst. to N.J. Assemblyman, 1974-75; chmn. Bergen County (N.J.) Mental Health Bd., 1975-77; dir. consumer affairs Bergen County, 1980; realtor asso., Franklin Lakes, N.J., 1980—; admitted to N.J. bar, 1981; dir. adminstrv. services N.H. Bettigole, Design Engrs., Paramus, N.J., 1981-82; pvt. practice law, Hasbrouck Heights, N.J., 1982—. Mem. Wyckoff Fed. Grants Com., 1976; dir. Friends of Ramapo Coll., 1977—; bd. dirs. Ramapo Coll. Alumni, 1980—; Wyckoff Community Devel. rep., 1979; Dem. candidate N.J. State Assembly, 1979; mem. Bergen County Energy adv. bd., 1980. Recipient Am. Legion award, 1957. Mem. N.J. Realtors Assn., NOW. Episcopalian. Club: Altrusa (pres. elect). Home: 550 Lee Ct Wyckoff NJ 07481 Office: Heights Plaza 777 Terrace Ave Hasbrouck Heights NJ 07604

BAUMEISTER, ELEANOR H., club woman; b. Lake Linden, Mich., Oct. 2, 1909; d. Thomas and Sarah (Madigan) Hoskins; B. Music Edn., U. Minn., 1930; m. Carl Frederick Baumeister, Apr. 19, 1930; 1 son, Richard. Co-founder, advt. mgr. The Corn Belt Livestock Feeder, trade mag., 1948-51. Publicity dir. Patron's Council, Riverside-Brookfield High Sch., 1951-53; pres. MacNeal Meml. Hosp. Women's Aux., 1956, mem. adv. bd., 1957; sec. High Sch. Dist., 208 Caucus, 1965-67. Dir., rec. sec. S.W. suburban chpt. Am. Cancer Soc., pres. central suburban unit, 1969-71, treas., 1972—; mem. citizens adv. com. Morton Coll. Sch. Nursing. Bd. dirs. Riverside Pub. Library, 1960-72, pres. bd., 1967-71, sec. bd., 1971-72. Mem. Gen. Fedn. Women's Clubs, P.E.O. (pres. Riverside chpt. 1955-56, Ill. corr. sec. 1956, rec. sec. 1957-58, fin. officer Ill. home 1958-63, dir.). Republican. Presbyterian. Clubs: Riverside Woman's (pres. 1954-56); Chicago Farmers. Home: 120 S Delaplaine Rd Riverside IL 60546

BAUMER, BEVERLY BELLE, journalist; b. Hays, Kans., Sept. 23, 1926; d. Charles Arthur and Mayme Mae (Lord) B.; B.S., U. Kans., 1948. Summer intern reporter Hutchinson (Kans.) News, 1946-47; continuity writer, dir. women's program Sta. KWBW, Hutchinson, 1948-49; dist. editor Salina (Kans.) Jour., 1950-57; commd. writer State of Kans. Centennial Yr., 1961; contbr. Popular Mechanics, Travel, bus. publs., 1958—; owner, mgr. apts. Hutchinson, 1967—; freelance genealogist, 1970—. Hon. fellow Anglo-Am. Acad. (Cambridge, Eng.); mem. New Eng. Historic Geneal. Soc., Nat. Soc. Magna Carta Dames, Nat. Soc. Sons and Daus. Pilgrims (chaplain Kans. br.), Nat. Soc. Daus. Founders and Patriots Am., Nat. Soc. Daus. Am. Colonists (chpt. organizing regent 1979, state resolutions com.), DAR, Colonial Dames of 17th Century (chpt. chaplain), Plantagenet Soc., Internat. Platform Assn. Home and Office: 204 Curtis St Hutchinson KS 67501

BAUMGARTNER, EILEEN MARY, govt. ofcl.; b. St. Cloud, Minn.; d. Florian H. and Kathleen (Keefe) B.; B.A., Coll. St. Catherine, St. Paul, 1964; M.P.A., U. Minn., Mpls., 1970. Tchr., U.S. Peace Corps, Ethiopia, 1964-66; researcher N.Y. Med. Coll., N.Y.C., 1967-68, Minn. State Planning Agy., St. Paul, 1970-73; legis. analyst tax com. Minn. Ho. of Reps., St. Paul, 1973-78; legis. asst. to Congressman Sabo, U.S. Ho. of Reps., Washington, 1979—. Bd. dirs. Alumni Assn., Hubert H. Humphrey Inst. Public Affairs, U. Minn., 1982—. Mem. Am. Soc. Pub. Adminstrn. Democrat. Roman Catholic. Office: 426 Cannon Office Bldg Washington DC 20515

BAUML, BETTY JEAN, educator; b. N.Y.C., Aug. 6, 1930; d. Walter and Rose (Siegel) Zeidner; B.A., Ohio State U., 1951, M.A., 1953; Ph.D., U. Calif., Berkeley, 1957; m. Franz Heinrich Bauml, Aug. 27, 1958; children—Mark, Deborah. Instr., Immaculate Heart Coll., Los Angeles, 1958-61; prof. dept. fgn. langs. and lits. Calif. State U., Northridge, 1961—. Mem. Modern Lang. Assn., Phi Beta Kappa. Author: A Dictionary of Gestures, 1975. Office: Dept Fgn Langs and Lits Calif State U 18111 Nordhoff St Northridge CA 91330

BAUMLER, JEAN IDA, nurse; b. West Union, Iowa, Apr. 22, 1951; d. Melvin John and Rita Theresa (Lansing) Baumler; B.S., Viterbo Coll., LaCrosse, Wis., 1973; M.S., San Jose (Calif.) State U., 1980. Health supr. Camp Ehawee Scout Camp, LaCrosse, 1973; staff nurse, then asst. head nurse Letterman Army Med. Center, San Francisco, 1972-75; staff nurse Palo Alto (Calif.) VA Hosp., 1975—. Treas. Fair Oaks 90 Homeowners Assn., 1980—. Served with Nurse Corps, U.S. Army, 1972-75. Mem. Geront. Soc. Am. (rep. biol. scis. sect.), Internat. Assn. Gerontology, Nurses Orgn. VA, Western Geront. Soc. Contbr. articles to profl. jours. Home: 781-5 N Fair Oaks Ave Sunnyvale CA 94086 Office: 3801 Miranda Ave Palo Alto CA 94304

BAUMRIND, ROSALYN MURIEL, psychologist; b. Bronx, Aug. 3, 1933; d. Samuel Howard and Rose (Halpern) Greenwald; B.A. magna cum laude, Brooklyn Coll., CUNY, 1950, M.A., 1954; Ph.D. (NIMH fellow), Adelphi U., 1967; children—Martin, Lydia, Sandra. Tchr., N.Y.C. Bd. Edn., 1950-62, Hebrew Inst. L.I. (N.Y.), 1957-62; psychologist phys. medicine and rehab. dept. Elmhurst Gen. Hosp., Queens, N.Y., 1964; asst. prof. Sch. Edn. Bklyn. Coll., CUNY 1967—; pvt. practice clin. psychology, N.Y.C., 1967—. Author TV tapes, articles in field. Home and Office: 141 E 37th St New York NY 10016

BAUNACH, PHYLLIS JO, corrections researcher; b. Amityville, N.Y., July 29, 1947; d. Edward Lincoln and Josephine Caroline (Dayton) B.; B.A. (scholar), U. Rochester, 1969; Ph.D., U. Minn., 1974; m. July 17, 1976. Instr., U. Minn., 1974; vis. asst. prof., 1975; mem. Gov.'s Com. on Crime Prevention and Control, 1974-76; asso. professorial lectr. George Washington U., Washington, 1977; instr. Univ. Coll., U. Md., College Park, 1980—, lectr., 1981; correctional research specialist Nat. Inst. Justice, Washington, 1976—; cons. Calif. Youth Authority, Murton Found. Criminal Justice. Treas., Evang. Lutheran Mission, 1975; mem. choir, substitute dir., worship and music com. Our Saviors Luth. Ch. Nat. Inst. Justice fellow, 1978-79; AAUW Young scholar, 1982-83; recipient Outstanding Performance award Dept. Justice, 1979, 81. Mem. Am. Soc. Criminology, Am. Correctional Assn., Am. Psychology Assn., Assn. Programs on Female Offenders, Resource Network Female Offenders, Nat. Trust Historic Preservation, Smithsonian Assos., Am. Mus. Natural History, Phi Beta Kappa. Research on mothers in prison; contbr. articles to profl. jours. Office: 633 Indiana Ave NW Room 867 Washington DC 20531

BAUR, ANN ELIZABETH, wholesale dairy exec.; b. Jackson, Calif., June 17, 1952; d. A.D. and Eleanor (Welch) LeBel; student pub. schs. Amador County, Calif.; m. David L. Baur, Sept. 4, 1976; children—Jason Burk, Dawn Marie Burk. Asst. to editor Nat. Bottle Gazette, Amador City, 1970-71; mgr. Douglas Oil Co., Lodi, Calif., 1973-74, FHA Housing, Jackson, 1973-74; asst. to v.p. Knapp Mobile Homes, Hermiston, Oreg., 1974-75; bookkeeper Guy Cook, C.P.A., Jackson, 1977-79; pres. Jackson Amador Creamery Inc. (Calif.), 1979—. Mem. council Amador Tuolumne Community Action Agy.; mem. Amador County Mental Health Adv. Bd.; bd. dirs. Amador County Crisis Line. Mem. Jackson Bus. Assn., Amador County C. of C., Amador County Bd. Trade, Nat. Fedn. Ind. Businesses. Democrat. Office: 605 Broadway Jackson CA 95642

BAURER, JOAN RUTH, investment co. exec., fin. counsellor; b. N.Y.C., July 10, 1934; d. Jack Maurice and Elsie Frank (Galkin) Lawson; B.A., Queens Coll., 1955; postgrad. Hunter Coll., 1955-57, Fresno State Coll., 1966-67; postgrad. in fin. Calif. State Coll., Bakersfield, 1973-76; m. Martin E. Baurer, Sept. 23, 1953 (div. May 1979); children—Benjamin Zachary, Valery Suzanne. Tchr. home econs., Astoria, N.Y., 1957-59, New Rochelle, N.Y., 1958-60; tchr. gen. sci., Liverpool, N.Y., 1960; account exec. Internat. Securities Co., Bakersfield, 1975-77, Blunt, Ellis & Loewi Co., Inc., Waukegan, Ill., 1977-79; with All Am. Mgmt., Des Plaines, Ill., 1979—; pres. Joan Baurer & Co. Inc., registered investment adv., Crystal Lake, 1981—. Vol. dir. menu planning Guild House, restaurant for benefit Child Guidance Clinic, Bakersfield, 1964-66; pres. McHenry County Estate Planning Council. Mem. Internat. Assn. Fin. Planners, AAUW, Crystal Lake C. of C., Women's Network of Crystal Lake (head steering com.). Club: Ski. Office: 451 Coventry Green Suite 100 Crystal Lake IL 60014

BAUTISTA-MYERS, LILIAN, community coll. adminstr.; b. San Diego; d. Jose Delos Angeles and Juanita (Perez) Bautista; B.A. in English, Calif. State U., Northridge, 1970; M.S. in Edn., SUNY, Albany, 1972; Ed.D. in Ednl. Adminstrn., Okla. State U., 1980; m. Donald Allen Myers, Oct. 28, 1966; 1 son, David Allen; children by previous marriage—Sherri Lynn, Johnny Martin. Adminstrv. officer, writer Capitol Hill Educator, Albany, 1972-73; asst. to dir., tech. editor/writer, coordinator grant and contract activities, contracts and grants mgmt. officer Okla. State U., 1973-79; co-owner/writer The Last Word, writing and graphic arts, Omaha, 1979-81; freelance writer, copywriter, editor, 1972-82; coordinator grants mgmt. and devel., found. dir. Met. Tech. Community Coll., Omaha, 1981—. Mem. Nat. Council Resource Devel., Regional NOW, ACLU, LWV (chpt. exec. bd. 1974-75). Democrat. Author, editor in field. Home: 406 N 94th St Omaha NE 68114 Office: PO Box 3777 Omaha NE 68103

BAUTZ, LAURA PATRICIA, astronomer; b. Washington, Sept. 3, 1940; d. Charles Kothe and Laura (Stauverman) B.; B.A. in Physics, Vanderbilt U., 1961; Ph.D. in Astronomy, U. Wis., Madison, 1967. From instr. to assoc. prof. astronomy Northwestern U., Evanston, Ill., 1965-75; sr. staff assoc. NSF, Washington, 1975-79, dep. dir. physics div., 1979-81, dir. astronomy div., 1982—. Mem. Am. Astron. Soc., AAAS, Internat. Astron. Union, Phi Beta Kappa. Home: 1325 18th St NW Apt 506 Washington DC 20036 Office: 1800 G St NW Washington DC 20550

BAXT, SAIDA HEYMAN, dermatologist; b. Lakewood, N.J., Mar. 23, 1943; d. Phillip and Charlotte Heyman; B.A., Bennington Coll., 1962; M.D., N.Y. U., 1966; m. Sherwood Baxt, Dec. 20, 1964; children—Rebecca, Chiara. Intern, Kings County Hosp., 1966-67, resident in dermatology, 1967-69, chief resident in dermatology, 1969-70, asst. clin. instr., 1970-72; asst. instr. dermatology Beth Israel Hosp., 1972-74; practice medicine specializing in dermatology, Bergen County, N.J. Diplomate Am. Bd. Dermatology. Office: Medical Plaza 351 Evelyn St Paramus NJ 07452

BAXTER, ANNE, actress; b. Michigan City, Ind., May 7, 1923; d. Kenneth Stuart and Catherine (Wright) B.; ed. pub. schs. White Plains, Chappaqua and Bronxville, N.Y., Theodora Irvine's Sch. of Theater, 1934-36, The Lenox Sch., 1937, The Brearley Sch., 1938-39, Studio Sch. Twentieth Century Fox, 1940; m. John Hodiak, July 7, 1946; 1 dau., Katrina Baxter; m. 2d, Randolph Galt, Feb. 18, 1960; children—Melissa, Maginel; m. 3d Daniel Klee, Jan. 30, 1977. Studied with Ouspenskava for 3 years; played in Seen But Not Heard, 1936, There's Always A Breeze, Madame Capet, 1937, Susan and God, Summer Playhouse, Dennis, Mass., 1938, Spring Meeting Cape Playhouse, 1939, (Broadway play) Square Root of Wonderful, The Joshua Tree, London; appeared in motion pictures 20 Mule Team; Great Profile; Charley's Aunt, Swampwater, Magnificent Ambersons; Pied Piper; Crash Dive; Five Graves to Cairo, North Star; The Sullivans, Guest in the House, Angel on My Shoulder, Royal Scandal, Outcasts of Poker Flat, My Wife's Best Friend, Sunday Dinner for a Soldier, Blue Gardenia, I Confess, Carnival, All About Eve, Yellow Sky, You're My Everything, Fool's Parade, Stranger on the Run, The Glass Hammer, Lapin 360, The Late Liz, Ten Commandments, One Desire, The Spoilers, Three Violent People, Chase a Crooked Shadow, Summer of the 17th Doll, Cimarron, 1960, Walk on the Wild Side, 1961; Mix Me a Person, 1962, The Tall Women, The Busy Body, Jane Austen in Manhattan, 1980; 5 mos. tour John Browns Body, 1955-56, Noel Coward in Two Keys, 1975; appeared on Broadway in Applause; appeared in Theatre Group prodn. of Cause Celebre, 1979-80. Received Acad. Award and Fgn. Press award as best supporting actress in The Razor's Edge, 1947. Presbyterian. Author: Intermission, 1976. Office: care Chasin-Park-Citron Agy 9255 Sunset Blvd Los Angeles CA 90069 *

BAXTER, HEDWIG GERDA, histologist; b. Kellenhusen, Germany, Mar. 6, 1945; came to U.S., 1950, naturalized, 1964; d. Otto and Ane Kalvaitis; A.A., Clinton Community Coll., 1981; postgrad. SUNY, Plattsburgh; 1 dau., Marta Ane. With CV/PH Med. Center, Plattsburgh, N.Y., 1964-70; with hematology sect., animal health div. Ayerst Labs., Chazy, N.Y., 1970-71, histologist, 1972—. Mem. Nat. Soc. Histotechnology, N.Y. Histotechnological Soc., Am. Soc. Clin. Pathologists. Home: PO Box 223 West Chazy NY 12992 Office: Ayerst Research Labs Animal Health Division Chazy NY 12921

BAXTER, PATRICIA JAMES, psychologist, educator; b. Oklahoma City, Feb. 7, 1940; d. Ralph H. and Edria V. (McMurry) James; B.A. in Psychology, Tulsa U., 1961; M.A. in Clin. Psychology, North Tex. State U., 1963; postgrad. U.S. Internat. U., 1973—; m. Tom R. Baxter, June 9, 1961; 1 dau., Susan Reese. Psychologist, Denton (Tex.) State Sch. for Mentally Retarded, 1963-66, Calif. Dept. Rehab., Los Angeles, 1969-75; rehab. counselor Tex. Dept. Rehab., Sherman, 1966-69; pvt. practice clin. psychology, Russellville, Ark., 1975—; instr. psychology Coll. of Ozarks, Clarksville, Ark., 1976—; cons. psychol. aspects for deaf, 1971—. Mem. Am. Psychol. Assn., Ark. Psychol. Assn., Ark. Assn. Human Services. Episcopalian. Author: A Manual of Psychological Testing for Counselors, 1973. Home: Route 1 Box 193A London AR 72847 Office: Hurie Hall College of Ozarks Clarksville AR 72830

BAXTER, VERONICA ANN, ednl. adminstr.; b. Portland, Oreg.; B.A. in Edn., Holy Names Coll., 1956; M.Ed., Seattle U., 1964; postgrad. U. Oreg., 1967, Portland State U., 1972, Internat. Inst. of Psychology of Learning, Prague, Czechoslovakia, 1972, Lifelong Learning Centers, Scandinavia, 1977. Joined Order of Sisters of Holy Names, Roman Catholic Church, 1948; elem. tchr., 1949-62, prin., 1962-68; provincial asst. Sisters of Holy Names, Portland, 1968-71; exec. dir. Christie Sch., Marylhurst, Oreg., 1968-74; instr. Marylhurst Coll., 1973, pres. Marylhurst Coll. for Lifelong Learning, 1974—; mem. task force on child care Dept. Human Resources, State of Oreg., 1971; staff Am. Mgmt. Assn., 1972; adv. com. Oreg. Ednl. Coordinating Commn., 1978; speaker profl. confs. in field. Named Woman of Yr., Portland Women's Forum of C. of C., 1979, one of Oreg.'s 100 Most Powerful Women Oregon Mag., 1981; recipient medal U. Portland, 1981. Mem. Oreg. Ind. Colls. Assn. (trustee, pres. exec. com., 1979). Office: Marylhurst Coll for Lifelong Learning Marylhurst OR 97036

BAYARD, ANNA CHERNOFF, lawyer; b. Bklyn., Nov. 6, 1916; d. Joseph and Sarah Chernoff; B.S. in Edn., Bklyn. Coll., 1936; read for law; m. Edward Bayard, Sept. 24, 1939. Legal office mgr., N.Y.C., 1937-61; assoc. Samuel Pivar, 1937-65; admitted to N.Y. bar, 1961; partner firm Caponi & Bayard, Bklyn., 1965—. Active Cancer Care, Inc., Kingsway Jewish Center. Mem. N.Y. County Lawyers Assn., Bklyn. Bar Assn. Clubs: B'nai B'rith; KP Aux. (past lodge pres., life mem.).

BAYAZES, GEORGIA, real estate and fin. cons.; b. N.Y.C., Jan. 29, 1920; d. Prokop and Sappho (Galetsa) B.; B.A. in Bus. Adminstrn., Bklyn. Coll., 1941; postgrad. N.Y. U., 1958. Asst. to treas. Hubschman Factors Corp., N.Y.C., 1942-52; office mgr. Koeppel & Koeppel, N.Y.C., 1952-57; real estate mgr. Ramapo Estates, Inc., N.Y.C., 1957-77; real estate and fin. cons. Seth Evans & Aronson, Inc., N.Y.C., 1977—, also sec.; dir. Hardware Designers, Inc., Mt. Kisco, N.Y. Co-chairperson benefit luncheons Assn. for Help to Retarded Children, N.Y.C., 1976, Cooley's Anemia Found., N.Y.C., 1977, N.Y. Hosp. Cardiac Children's Fund, N.Y.C., 1978, St. Michaels Home, Yonkers, N.Y., 1975, Holy Cross Sem. of Brookline, Mass., 1973, St. Basils Acad. of Garrison, N.Y., 1974; pres. Ladies Philoptochos Soc., Greek Orthodox Ch. of Assumption, Bklyn., 1972-77, Sunday sch. tchr., 1954-82, sec. Archdiocesan Dist. Bd., 1980-81; pres. Hellenic Soc. Bklyn. Coll. Mem. Stats. Soc. and Bur. Econ. Research Bklyn. Coll. Club: Hellenic Univ. (sec., treas.). Home: 639-80th St Brooklyn NY 11209 Office: 866 UN Plaza Suite 575 New York NY 10017

BAYER, MARGRET HELENE JANSSEN, plant biologist; b. Hamburg, Ger., July 8, 1931; permanent U.S. resident, 1962; d. Ernst and Hildegard (Sens) Janssen; diploma biology U. Hamburg, 1958, Dr.rer.nat., 1961, Dr.rer.nat. habil., 1976; m. Manfred E. Bayer, Aug. 26, 1958; children—Ada, Thora. Research asst. and instr. Inst. Botany, U. Hamburg, 1958-61; research asso. Inst. Cancer Research, Phila., 1961-77, sr. research asso., 1977—; vis. prof. U. Hamburg, 1975, 76; lectr. U. Pa., 1980. Grantee NSF; Damon Runyon fellow. Fellow Deutsche Forschungsgemeinschaft; mem. Am. Soc. Microbiology, Am. Soc. Plant Physiology, Internat. Assn. Plant Tissue Culture, N.Y. Acad. Sci. Contbr. articles to profl. jours. Office: Inst Cancer Research/Fox Chase Cancer Center Philadelphia PA 19111

BAYER, PATRICIA LAURIE, securities trader; b. N.Y.C., Oct. 27, 1955; d. Abba and Eileen Bayer; student Lake Forest Coll., 1973-75, Fordham U. Sec., First Boston Corp., N.Y.C., 1975-76, trading asst., 1976-77, Euro-dollar cert. of deposit trader, London, 1977-78, bankers acceptance and money market swing trader, head Yankee certs. of deposit and bankers acceptances, asst. v.p., N.Y.C., 1981—; Euro-dollar cert. of deposit trader asst. treas., mgr. Amex Bank Ltd., London, 1978-79; domestic cert. of deposit trader, 2d. v.p. Smith Barney Harris Upham, N.Y.C., 1979-81. Chmn. fundraising telethon Manhattan Theatre Club, 1980. Finalist Am. Song Festival Lyric Competition II, 1977. Mem. Certificate of Deposit Dealers Assn., Am. Guild Authors and Composers. Jewish. Clubs: Tennisport Inc. (N.Y.C.), Green Hollow Tennis (E. Hampton, N.Y.). Office: Park Ave Plaza New York NY 10055

BAYLIS MALLIA, LINDA MERYL, credit co. exec.; b. Lynbrook, N.Y., Sept. 9, 1946; d. Jack and Sylvia (Brodsky) Baylis; B.A. in Psychology, CCNY, 1967, M.S. in Sch. Psychology, 1971; m. Anthony P. Mallia, Sept. 2, 1979. Personnel mgr. Citibank, N.Y.C., 1975-76, mgr. manpower planning and devel., internat. services div., 1976-77; mgr. evaluation processes Internat. Paper Co., N.Y.C., 1977-78, mgr. human resources planning, 1978-80; dir. orgn. and mgmt. resources Am. Express Co., N.Y.C., 1980—. Lic. sch. psychologist, N.Y. State. Mem. Exec. Study Conf. (past dir.), Human Resources Planning Soc., Am. Psychol. Assn., Met. Assn. Applied Psychologists. Office: American Express Plaza New York NY 10004

BAYLISS-ALLEN, MADELINE THERESE, mktg. co. exec.; b. N.Y.C., Oct. 11, 1954; d. Eugene R. and Madeline D. Bayliss; B.A. with honors in Human Communication, Colgate U., 1975; postgrad. in bus. N.Y. U., 1978—; m. Jeffrey Thomas Allen, June 20, 1981. Unit dir. United Way N.Y.C., 1976-77, indsl. div. dir., 1977-79; mgr. area communications, United Way Tri-State, N.Y.C., 1979; sr. cons. Urban Bus. Assistance Corp., 1979-80; mgr. corp. mktg. Mfrs. Hanover Leasing Corp., N.Y.C., 1980—. Bd. dirs. Colgate U. Mem. Nat. Assn. Female Execs., Am. Mktg. Assn., Phi Beta Kappa. Office: 270 Park Ave New York NY 10017

BAYLY, PATRICIA ANNE, psychologist; b. Troy, N.Y., Dec. 4, 1952; d. Richard Yeilding and Martha (Coffey) Bayly; B.A. cum laude with honors in Psychology (Kellas scholar), Russell Sage Coll., 1974; M.S. in Ednl. Psychology and Statistics, SUNY, Albany, 1975, Ed.S. in Sch. Psychology, 1976, doctoral studies in ednl. psychology, 1978—. Psychologist, North Colonic Central Schs., Loudonville, N.Y., 1976-77, Enlarged City Sch. Dist. of Troy, 1977—; adj. instr. psychology Russell Sage Coll., Troy, 1978—. Bd. dirs. Drug Abuse and Prevention Council Troy, 1979-80, sec., 1980—; bd. dirs., edn. chmn. Jr. League Troy, 1978-79, adv. planning chmn., 1980-81, tng. chmn., 1982-83; bd. dirs. Am. Cancer Soc., 1982—. Mem. Am. Psychol. Assn., N.Y. State Psychol. Assn., Psychol. Assn. Northeastern N.Y., Nat. Assn. Sch. Psychologists, N.Y. Assn. Sch. Psychologists, Sch. Psychologists Upstate N.Y., Sch. Psychology Educators Council of N.Y. State, Russell Sage Coll. Alumnae Assn. (exec. bd. 1974-78, sec. 1978-82, 1st v.p. 1982—), Athenian Honor Soc., Psi Chi. Roman Catholic. Club: Russell Sage Troy Alumni (pres. 1976-83). Home: 19 Brentwood Ave Troy NY 12180 Office: 1976 Burdett Ave Troy NY 12180

BAYM, NINA, educator, univ. ofcl.; b. Princeton, N.J., June 14, 1936; d. Leo and Frances (Levinson) Zippin; B.A., Cornell U., Ithaca, N.Y., 1957; M.A., Harvard U., 1958, Ph.D., 1963; m. Gordon Baym, June 1, 1958; children—Nancy, Geoffrey; m. 2d, Jack Stillinger, May 21, 1971. Asst., U. Calif., Berkeley, 1962-63; instr. U. Ill., Urbana, 1963-67, asst. prof. English, 1967-69, assoc. prof., 1969-72, prof., 1972—, dir. Sch. Humanities, 1976—. Guggenheim fellow, 1975-76; AAUW hon. fellow, 1975-76; Nat. Endowment Humanities fellow, 1982-83. Mem. Robert Frost Soc. (adv. bd.), Am. Studies Assn. (exec. council 1982—), MLA (exec. com. 19th century Am. lit. div., adv. council Am. lit. sect.). Author: The Shape of Hawthorne's Career, 1976; Woman's Fiction: A Guide to Novels by and about Women in America, 1978; also essays; mem. editorial bd. Am. Quar., Jour. Aesthetic Edn., Am. Lit. Office: 608 S Wright St Urbana IL 61801

BAYMILLER, LYNDA DOERN, social services supr.; b. Milw., July 6, 1943; d. Ronald Oliver and Marian Elizabeth (Doern) B.; student U. Hawaii, 1962, Mich. State U., 1965; B.A., U. Wis., 1965, M.S.W., 1969. Peace Corps vol., Chile, 1965-67; social worker Luth. Social Services of Wis. and Upper Mich., Milw., 1969-77, contract social worker, 1978-79; dist. supr. Children's Service Soc. Wis., Kenosha, 1977-78; social services supr. Sauk County Dept. Social Services, Baraboo, Wis., 1979—. Bd. dirs. Zoo Pride, 1975-77, life mem.; life mem. Zool. Soc. Milw. County; bd. dirs. Sauk County Mental Health Assn., 1979—; pres. bd. dirs. Growing Pl. Day Care Center, Kenosha, 1977-78. Mem. Nat. Assn. Social Workers, Acad. Cert. Social Workers, Wis. Social Services Assn., AAUW (br. sec. 1982—), U. Wis. Alumni Assn. (life), Am. Legion Aux., DAR, Nat. Soc. Magna Charta Dames, Eddy Family Assn. (life mem.), Nat. Soc. Ancient and Hon. Arty. Co. of Mass., Daus. Colonial Wars, Morris Pratt Inst., Internat. Crane Found. (patron), Alpha Xi Delta (Theta chpt.). Clubs: Sweet Adelines (chpt. pres. 1971), Order Eastern Star. Author: (with Clara Amelia Hess) Now-Won, A Collection of Feeling (poetry and prose), 1973. Home: 332 4th Ave Baraboo WI 53913

BAYUS, LENORE WEATHERLY, librarian, public relations exec.; b. N.Y.C., Apr. 11, 1923; d. John Bruce and Lena Catherine (Ferguson) Weatherly; B.S., Indiana U. of Pa., 1944; postgrad. in Library Sci. and Communications, Case-Western Res. U., 1945, 47; M.L.S., U. Pitts., 1966; m. J. Daniel Bayus, Aug. 14, 1948. Sch. librarian, 1944-48; reference librarian Carnegie Library of Pitts., 1969-71, young adult specialist, 1972-73, public relations dir., 1973—; tchr. communications Point Park Coll., 1977-78, Community Coll. Allegheny County, 1980—; public relations cons. Mem. ALA (Library Public Relations Council award 1976; Nat. Library Week com. 1980); Pa. Library Assn. (public relations task force 1975-79, public relations chmn. 1979), Women in Communications, Inc. (v.p. 1979), AAUW, Beta Phi Mu (chpt. pres. 1979-80). Clubs: Churchill Valley Country, Pitts. Press., Zonta of Pitts. (dir. 1981-83). Editor SYNC, 1972-73; editorial adv. PLA Bull., 1976-77, GSLIS Alumni Bull., 1976-77; media reviewer Previews, 1972-80, Library Jour., 1980—; book reviewer Pitts. Press, 1978—; contbr. articles to profl. jours.; freelance writer. Home: 203 Shackelford Dr Monroeville PA 15146 Office: 4400 Forbes Ave Pittsburgh PA 15213

BAZIK, EDNA FRANCES, mathematician; b. Streator, Ill., Dec. 26, 1946; d. Andrew and Anna Frances B.; B.S. in Edn., Ill. State U., Normal, 1969; M.Ed., U. Ill., Champaign, 1972; Ph.D., So. Ill. U., Carbondale, 1976. Tchr. math. jr. high sch. Northlawn Sch., Streator, 1969-74; instr. math. edn. So. Ill. U., 1974-76; asst. prof. math. Concordia Coll., River Forest, Ill., 1976-78, Ill. State U., Normal, 1978—; math. cons. to sch. dists., pubs.; dir. NSF grant, 1980-82; speaker, workshop leader 175 meetings. Mem. Nat. Council Tchrs. of Math., Ill. Council Tchrs. of Math. (dir.), Sch. Sci. and Math. Assn. (reviewer), Math. Assn. Am., Ill. Council Maths. Edn., Nat. Council Suprs. Math., NEA, Ill. Edn. Assn., U.S. Metric Assn., Ill. Curriculum Council (exec. bd. 1982-84), Assn. Tchr. Educators, Am. Ednl. Research Assn., Assn. Supervision and Curriculum Devel., Assn. Childhood Edn. Internat., Council Exceptional Children, Research Council Diagnostic and Prescriptive Math., Phi Delta Kappa (pres. 1982-83), Pi Mu Epsilon, Phi Kappa Phi, Delta Kappa Gamma. Republican. Lutheran. Clubs: Bloomington-Normal Christian Women's (fin. sec. 1982-83). Woman's Profl. Author: (with Paige Budreck, Thiessen and Wild) Elementary Mathematical Methods, 1978; Channeling Helpful Ideas for Learning Difficulties in Mathematics, 1979; (with Wilmot) Mind Over Math, 1980; (with Thornton, Dossey and Tucker) Teaching Mathematics to Children with Special Needs, 1982; (with Lovell, Piland, McCarthy, Janes and Decker) A Collective Bargaining Contract Analyzer for Community Colleges, 1982; author Ideas sect. Arithmetic Tchr.,

1982-83. Home: 202 Riss Dr Normal IL 61761 Office: Mathematics Dept Illinois State University Normal IL 61761

BAZLEY, ANGELA ROSARIO, educator; b. N.Y.C., May 25; d. Marcelino and Rosa Maria (Colon) Rosario; B.A., Hunter Coll., N.Y.C., 1957; M.A. (grad. asst. 1957-59), Pa. State U., 1959; m. Russell Stuart Bazley, Aug. 25, 1962; 1 son, John Robert. Non-English coordinator Bd. Edn., Jr. High Sch. 44, N.Y.C., 1959-60, cons. Mayor's Office, 1960, 61; instr. Pa. State U., 1960-61; instr. Spanish, Clinton-Walton Adult Center, Bronx, N.Y., 1961, Jr. High Sch. 123, Bronx, N.Y., 1961-65; dist. coordinator Office Dist. 10, Bronx, 1969-71, dir. Bilingual Mini Sch., 1971-72; dir. Bilingual Pupil Services Bd. Edn., Bklyn., 1973-79; dir. Center Staff Devel., Instructional and Supportive Services, Bklyn., 1979—; chmn. adv. council bilingual edn. N.Y. State, 1979-81. Recipient various leadership awards for bilingual edn. Mem. Nat. Assn. Bilingual Edn., N.Y. State Assn. Bilingual Edn. Author proposals in field. Home: 18 Alexander Ln Croton-on-Hudson NY 10520 Office: 131 Livingston St Brooklyn NY 11201

BEACH, ELIZABETH CAROLINE, psychiatrist; b. Spartanburg, S.C., Dec. 3, 1910; d. Henry and Ella Martha (Zaloudek) Kreisinger; A.B., Cornell U., 1931; M.D., Albany Med. Coll., 1943; certified in psychoanalysis New Orleans Psychoanalytic Inst., 1956; m. Kenneth Harold Beach, Sept. 17, 1948; children—Pamla Laura, Jennifer Lynn. Intern, L.I. Coll. Hosp., Bklyn., 1944; resident in psychiatry Psychiat. Inst. Presbyn. Hosp., 1945, Bellevue Hosp., N.Y.C., 1946; practice medicine specializing in psychiatry and psychoanalysis, Houston, 1960—; instr. New Orleans Psychoanalytic Inst., 1958-59; asst. clin. prof. psychiatry Baylor U. Mem. Am. Med. Women's Assn., Houston Psychiat. Assn., Am. Psychiat. Assn., AMA, Harris County Med. Soc., Houston Soc. Psychiatry and Neurology. Episcopalian. Home: 10 S Briar Hollow Ln Houston TX 77027 Office: 2121 Sage Rd Suite 320 Houston TX 77056

BEACH, MARGARET GASTALDI (MRS. EDWARD WOODBRIDGE BEACH), found. exec., nurse; b. Placerville, Calif., Aug. 10, 1915; d. Giovanni Batista and Josephine (Bisagno) Gastaldi; student Sacramento City Coll., 1934; grad. Mercy Coll. Nursing, 1938; m. Edward Woodbridge Beach, Feb. 15, 1946 (dec. Aug. 1968); children—Laura G. (Mrs. Robert L. Phillips), Edward Woodbridge, Margaret J. In charge urol. dept. Mercy Hosp., Sacramento, 1938-42; tchr. urology to student nurses, 1943-45. Treas., Germana M. Wilson Meml. Scholarship Found., 1967—. Mem. Woman's Aux. AMA, Sacramento County Women Med. Soc., Am. Legion Aux., Italian Cultural Soc. Clubs: Carriage Trade, Women of the Moose, Hon. Guild St. Patrick's Day Mummurs. Home: 6255 14th Ave Sacramento CA 95820

BEAHLER, ELECTRA CATSONIS, lawyer; b. Washington, Aug. 6, 1933; d. Achilles and Anastasia (Carzis) Catsonis; B.A. with honors, Pa. State U., 1955; J.D. with honors, George Washington U., 1969; m. John Leroy Beahler, Feb. 7, 1973. Asst. editor Aero Digest, Washington, 1955-56, Fairchild Engine & Airplane Co., Washington, 1956-57; exec. asst. internat. pub. relations dept. Kaiser Industries Corp., Washington, 1957-60; sec. to pres. George Washington U., Washington, 1960-62; legis. asst. to Congressman Donald D. Clancy, Washington, 1962-67; adminstrv. asst. to Congressman John M. Ashbrook, Washington, 1968-73; minority csl. edn. House Com. Edn. and Labor, U.S. Ho. of Reps., Washington, 1981—; admitted to D.C. bar, 1970, U.S. sup. Ct. bar, 1974. Recipient Schaeffer award Phi Delta Delta, 1962. Mem. ABA, Lawyer-Pilots Bar Assn., Internat. Orgn. Women Pilots, Ninety-Nines, Airplane Owners and Pilots Assn., D.C. Bar, Women's Bar Assn. D.C., George Washington U. Law Assn. Office: 2100 Rayburn House Office Bldg Washington DC 20515

BEAL, MARJORIE JANET, bookstore owner; b. Mpls., Apr. 21, 1929; d. Arnold Edward and Helen Scott Schwarz; B.A., Keuka Coll., 1950. Account exec. Smith, Hagel & Knudsen Advt., N.Y.C., 1955-59; v.p. Guilie, Smith & Beal Advt., Sunnyvale, Calif., 1963-65; advt./community relations dir. Bell Savs., San Mateo, Calif., 1974-76; coordinator/lectr. Lowry R.E. Investment Seminars, Reno, 1976-82; owner ESP Bookstore, Phoenix, 1982—; pres. Esoteric Speakers Platform, Phoenix. Recipient Bronze Mailbox, Direct Mail Advt. Assn., 1965, Cert. of Honor, Western Advt. Assn., 1965. Mem. Nat. Assn. Female Execs., Am. Soc. Profl. and Exec. Women, Nat. Speakers Assn. Address: CREACOM Communication Co PO Box 7636 Phoenix AZ 85011

BEALE, GEORGIA ROBISON, historian; b. Chgo., Mar. 14, 1905; d. Henry Barton and Dora Belle (Sledd) Robison; A.B., U. Chgo., 1926, A.M., 1928; Ph.D., Columbia U., 1938; student Sorbonne and Coll. de France, 1930-34; m. Howard Kennedy Beale, Jan. 2, 1942; children—Howard Kennedy, Henry Barton Robison, Thomas Wight. Reader in history U. Chgo., 1927-29; lectr. Barnard Coll., 1937-38; instr. Bklyn. Coll., 1937-39; asst. prof. Hollins (Va.) Coll., 1939-41, Wellesley Coll., 1941-42, Castleton (Vt.) State Coll., 1968-70; vis. asso. prof. U. Ky., Lexington, 1970-72. Mem. Madison (Wis.) Civic Music Assn. and Madison Symphony Orch. League, 1958—; hon. trustee Culver-Stockton Coll., 1974—. Univ. fellow Columbia U., 1929-30. Mem. AAUW (European fellow 1930-31), Am., So. hist. assns., Soc. French Hist. Studies, Western Soc. French History, Am., Brit. socs. 18th century studies, Phi Beta Kappa, Pi Lambda Theta, Phi Alpha Theta, Pi Kappa Delta. Clubs: Reid Hall (Paris); Brit. Univ. Women's (London). Author: Revelliere-lépeaux, peaux, Citizen Director, 1938, 72; Academies to Institut, 1973; Bosc and the Exequatur, 1978, also articles. Address: The Ridge Orford NH 03777 also 2816 Columbia Rd Madison WI 53705

BEALL, JOANNA MAY, painter; b. Chgo., Aug. 17, 1935; d. Lester Thomas and Dorothy Welles (Miller) B.; student Yale U. Sch. Fine Arts, 1953-57, Art Inst. Chgo., 1957; m. H.C. Westermann, Mar. 31, 1959. One-man shows include: Great Bldg. Crack-Up Gallery, N.Y.C., 1973, James Corcoran Gallery, Los Angeles, 1974, Gallery Rebecca Cooper, Washington, 1975; group shows: Allan Frumkin, Chgo., 1960, 61, Whitney Mus., N.Y.C., 1973, Art Inst. Chgo., 1976, Univ. Galleries, Los Angeles, 1979, Xavier Fourcade, N.Y.C., 1980; vis. artist U. Colo., Boulder, 1979. Mem. Artists Equity Assn., Visual Artists and Galleries Assn. Article The World of Joanna Beall (Melinda Wortz) appeared in Art Week mag., 1974. Home: Box 28 Brookfield Center CT 06805

BEAMAN, MARGARINE GAYNELL, scrap metal co. exec.; b. Mason, Tex., Feb. 26; d. Ryland and Margaret Lena (Anderegg) Geistweidt; student Tex. Lutheran Coll., Seguin; diploma hotel-motel acctg. with distinction, U. Mich., 1964; m. Robert W. Beaman, May 18, 1974; 2 stepchildren. Sec., Nixon-Clay Comml. Coll., Austin, Tex., 1959-62, dir. night sch., 1966-71, dir. tech. trade and bus. coll. day sch., 1971-75; various clerical and adminstrv. asst. positions, 1959-72; owner Beaman Metal Co., Inc., Austin, 1974—; pvt. practice acctg. and bus. cons., 1975—. Mem. housing com. Austin Resource Center for Ind. Living; originator Braille signs and directories in Austin and State of Tex. Named Woman of Year in Austin, Austin Bus. and Profl. Women, 1964. Mem. Bus. and Profl. Women's Club (dist. pres. 1978-80), Hotel-Motel Greeters Internat. (past chpt. pres.), Cert. Consumer Credit Execs. (past chpt. pres.), Credit Women Austin (past pres.), Austin Jr. Women's Fedn. (past pres.), Tex. Assn. Pvt. Schs. (sec.-treas.), Tex. Florists Assn., Sigma Phi Epsilon. Lutheran. Home: 1406 Wilshire Blvd Austin TX 78722 Office: 3409 E 5th St Austin TX 78702

BEAN, ELIZABETH HARRIMAN, county legislator; b. Buffalo, Sept. 23, 1923; d. Lewis Gildersleeve and Grace (Bastine) Harriman; B.A. in History, Smith Coll., 1945; cert. social welfare adminstrn. U. Ill., 1948; m. Charles Palmer Bean, Sept. 13, 1947; children—Katherine Bean Yancey, Bruce P., Margaret E., Sarah H., Gordon T. Claims adjuster Liberty Mut. Ins. Co., Washington, 1945; instr. U.S. Armed Forces Inst., Philippines and Okinawa, 1946; social caseworker Family Services Agy., Champaign, Ill., 1949-50; county rep. Schenectady County (N.Y.) Bd. Reps., 1976—; lectr. Robert A. Taft Inst., SUNY, Albany. Chmn. N.Y. State Legis. Forum, Albany, 1966-68; chmn. N.Y. State Citizens' Info. Service, 1968-72; trustee Russell Sage Coll., 1972—; mem. Capital Dist. Regional Planning Commn. of N.Y. State, Albany, 1976-80; bd. dirs. Albany Med. Center Hosp., 1976—, Sunnyview Hosp. and Rehab. Center, Schenectady, 1978—. Recipient Public Service Recognition award YWCA of Schenectady, 1979, Susan B. Anthony award LWV, Schenectady, 1980. Mem. Suprs. and County Legislators of N.Y. State, N.Y. State Assn. Counties. Republican. Episcopalian. Clubs: Fortnightly of Schenectady, Torch, Zonta (Schenectady). Home and Office: 2221 Stone Ridge Rd Schenectady NY 12309

BEAN, RUTHANN, probation officer; b. Grand Rapids, Mich., May 17, 1949; d. Roland Dale and Maria Hanna (Way) Miller; student Western Mich. U., 1967; B.S. with honors, Mich. State U., 1970; M.S.W., U. Kan., 1974. Work Incentive Program counselor Kan. Div. Employment, Topeka, 1971; juvenile probation officer Douglas County, Lawrence, Kan., 1971-72, chief juvenile probation officer, 1972-75; U.S. probation officer Western Dist. Mo., Kansas City, 1975—; faculty U. Kan. Sch. Social Welfare, 1977, Fed. Judicial Center, 1979—. Mem. adv. council Lawrence Sch. Dist., 1971-74; mem. youth diversion program Overland Park, Kan., 1979—. Mem. Nat. Assn. Social Workers, Fed. Probation Officers Assn., Am. Probation and Parole Assn., Kan. Assn. Social Workers, Phi Mu. Home: 9218 Mastin St Overland Park KS 66212 Office: 253 US Courthouse 811 Grand Ave Kansas City MO 64106

BEANE, JEANNINE WILMA DUBE, fin. exec.; b. Fitchburg, Mass., Mar. 5, 1949; d. Louis Amedee and Gertrude Virginia (Richards) Dube; student public schs., Fitchburg; m. Alden G. Beane, 1981. Asst. to pres. Elena Dress Mfg. Co., Leominster, Mass., 1967-73; office mgr., buyer Technology Diversified Inc., Columbia, S.C., 1973-76; bus. mgr. Nat. Entertainment & Campus Activities Assn., 1976-79; comptroller Fanny's Inc., Columbia, 1979-80; sec.-treas., dir. Fanny's Biscuits of Wilmington, Inc., 1979-80; budget analyst U.S. Capital Corp., Columbia, 1980-81; office mgr., acct. Fuller Comml. Brokerage Co., Atlanta, 1981—; moderator, panelist various bus. related workshops. Mem. NOW, Am. Mgmt. Assn., Am. Soc. Assn. Execs. Republican. Contbr. to poetry anthologies, mags. Home: 760 Piedmont Way NE Atlanta GA 30324 Office: 3340 Peachtree Rd NE Atlanta GA 30026

BEARCE, JEANA DALE, painter, educator; b. St. Louis, Oct. 3, 1929; d. Clarence Russell and Maria Emily Dale; B.F.A. (McMillian scholar), Washington U., St. Louis, 1951; M.A., N.Mex. Highlands U., 1954; m. Lawrence F. Rakovan, June 7, 1969; children—Barbara Emily, Luke, Francesca. Vis. artist, various lectureships, India, Pakistan, 1961-62; founder art dept. U. Maine, Portland, 1965, chmn. and dept. rep., 1965-70, asst. prof. art, 1967-70, asso. prof., 1970-81, prof., 1981—; exhibited works in one-woman shows: Portland (Maine) Mus. Art, 1958, U. Maine, Orono, 1958, 65, 69, 77, 80, Madras (India) Govt. Mus., 1962, Gallery 65, Paris, 1964, Bristol (R.I.) Mus. Art, 1965, Center Gallery, N.Y.C., 1974, Benbow Gallery, Newport, R.I., 1979, others; exhibited in group shows, including: Boston Mus. Art, Library of Congress, Phila. Print Club, Springfield (Mo.) Mus., Birmingham (Ala.) Mus. Art, others; represented in permanent collections: St. Louis Art Mus., U.S. Edn. Found. in India, New Delhi, U. Maine, Orono and Portland, Sarasota (Fla.) Art Assn., Bowdoin Coll., Brunswick, Maine; works include: murals N.Mex. Highlands U., mural Bowdoin Longfellow-Hawthorn Library, Brunswick, sculpture reliefs St. Bartholomew, Cape Elizabeth, Maine, St. Charles Ch., Brunswick; mem. artists' com. Maine Art Gallery, 1957-75; mem. Maine com. Skowhegan Sch. Painting and Sculpture, 1972—. Recipient various awards, including Fannie Cook award People's Art Center, St. Louis, Prix de Paris, N.Y. Nat. Competition, 1958, 59. Mem. Bowdoin Coll. Mus. Assos. Home: 327 Maine St Brunswick ME 04011 Office: U So Maine College Ave Gorham ME 04038

BEARD, BARBARA SUE, communications cons.; b. Logansport, Ind., Nov. 24, 1940; d. Orma C. and G. Lucille (Williams) Handy; B.A., Franklin Coll., 1962; M.A., Butler U., 1971; m. John A. Beard, Aug. 26, 1961; children—Kent Alan, Tracy Lynne. Lectr., Ind. U., 1971-79, Ind. Central U., 1973-76; instr. Ind. Vocat. Tech., Coll., Indpls., 1971-79, dir. extended services, 1980-82; communications cons., 1982—. Mem. selection com. Lawrence Twp. Sch. Bd. Mem. Women in Communications, Am. Bus. Communicators, Am. Vocat. Assn., Am. Soc. Tng. and Devel., Ind. Bus. Communicators, Ind. Vocat. Assn., Delta Delta Delta. Republican. Baptist. Club: Women's Department. Author: The Counselor's Handbook, 1976; editor: the Haas Review, 1979. Home: 7222 Brompton Ct Indianapolis IN 46250

BEARD, VICTORIA NANCY, mktg. sales rep.; b. Seattle, Mar. 19, 1945; d. Walter A. and Nancy (Paksis) Vane; A.A., Coll. San Mateo, 1965; B.A. in Sociology and Psychology, Chico (Calif.) State Coll., 1969. Sales mgr. The Emporium, Palo Alto, Calif., 1963-66; mgr., bus. rep. rehab., Chico, 1969-73; dir. Janet Rea Modeling Sch., Fresno, Calif., 1973-77; Realtor, 1976-77; account mgr., sr. sales exec. specializing in comml. and indsl. sales Fresno Title Ins. & Trust, 1977—; designer women's sportswear. Policewoman, Chico Police Dept., 1969-71. Lic. Realtor, Calif. Mem. Fresno C. of C., Homebuilders Assn. Fresno, Fresno Bd. Realtors (affiliate), Assn. Women in Mgmt., Nat. Assn. Female Execs., Internat. Platform Assn., Profl. Sales Women Fresno. Republican. Home: 3392 W Wrenwood Ave Fresno CA 93711 Office: 5100 N 6th St Fresno CA 93710

BEARD, VIRGINIA HARRISON, psychologist; b. St. Louis, Sept. 9, 1941; d. Monroe Colemon and Lula Lucille (Spicer) Harrison; B.A.Ed., Harris Tchrs. Coll., 1964; M.S., So. Ill. U., 1968; Ph.D., St. Louis U., 1976; m. Otis Charles Beard, Aug. 21, 1965; children—Bostic Charles, Bonji Lucille. Counselor, jr. high sch., University City, Mo., 1969-71; psychologist King Fanon Community Mental Health Center, Center for Human Concerns, St. Louis Juvenile Ct., 1973-75; community staff coordinator Med. Sch. St. Louis U., 1976-78, also instr.; exec. dir. Center for Family Mental Health, St. Louis, 1978-80; dir. psychol. services Yeatman-Union Sarah Mental Health Center, 1980—; instr. George Warren Brown Sch. Social Work, 1978-79, Fontbonne Coll., 1979; cons. Job Corps, Head Start, Salvation Army. Chmn., Gov.'s Adv. Council on Aging, 1976-78; mem. planning com. Regional White House Conf. on Families; sec. Regional Adv. Council for Psychiat. Services; 1st v.p. Annie Malone Children's Home; mem. Div. Family Service Child Consultative Treatment Team; 1st v.p. Conf. on Edn. Ford Found. fellow, 1971-72; Inst. Applied Gerontology fellow, 1973-75. Mem. Am. Psychol. Assn., Mo. Psychol. Assn., Chums, Inc., Alpha Kappa Alpha. Baptist. Home: 4114 W Kossuth St Saint Louis MO 63115 Office: 4731 Delmar Blvd Saint Louis MO 63108

BEARDEN, MILDRED KING, educator; b. Jackson, Miss.; d. Leonard Decatur and Sue (King) B.; student Piedmont Coll., 1916-17; A.B. cum laude, Anderson Coll., 1921; student U. Va., 1923, Clemson U., summer 1945; M.A., U. S.C., 1936. Tchr. English and history Fruitland Inst., Hendersonville, N.C., 1921-22, and S.C. high schs. at Piedmont, 1922-24, Westminster, 1924-38, 58-63, public speaking coach, 1958-63, advisor high sch. newspapers and coll. mag., 1955-69; tchr. English and history, Walhalla, 1938-58; asst. prof. English, Lander Coll., Greenwood, S.C., 1963-65; prof. English, Anderson (S.C.) Coll., 1965-69, Toccoa Falls (Ga.) Bible Coll., 1969-70; corr. Greenville (S.C.) News, 1945—; column writer Jour.-Tribune, Seneca, S.C., 1962—. Mem., sec. bd. women visitors U. S.C., 1940-50; adviser, sec. S.C. Scholastic Press Assn., 1960-63. Recipient DAR medal, 1921. Mem. Nat. Coll. English Assn. (nominating com. 1980), Ga.-S.C. Coll. English Assn., Nat. Council Tchrs. English (S.C. judge achievement awards contest 1969, dir. 1957-59), S.C. Speech Assn., South Atlantic Modern Lang. Assn., Internat. Platform Assn., AAUW, NEA, S.C. Edn. Assn. (council of dels. 1937), Beta Sigma Phi (hon.). Democrat. Baptist. Clubs: Anderson Coll. Campus; As You Like It (pres. 1932, sec. 1958-60). Home: 201 N Broad St Westminster SC 29693

BEARMAN, THERESA ELLEN, lawyer; b. N.Y.C., Nov. 18, 1953; d. Edward E. and Alma Bearman; student U. Pa., 1971-73; B.A., U. Ariz., 1975; J.D., U.N.C., 1978; postgrad. Georgetown U., 1980-82. Admitted to Calif. bar, 1980; tax mgmt. asso. Silverstein & Mullens, Washington, 1979-80; tax counsel to Rep. Marty Russo, 3rd Dist. of Ill., Washington, 1980-82; legis. rep. Hayes Edison Electric Inst., Washington, 1982—. Mem. ABA, Phi Beta Kappa, Phi Kappa Phi, Phi Alpha Delta. Jewish.

BEARN, MARGARET SLOCUM, lawyer, educator; b. Fanwood, N.J., June 20, 1924; d. Clarence W. and Emma (Elliot) Slocum; B.A. with honors, Swarthmore Coll., 1945; LL.B., Yale U., 1948; m. Alexander G. Bearn, Dec. 20, 1952; children—Helen Bearn Pennoyer, Gordon. Admitted to N.Y. bar, 1950; asso. firm Grossman & Grossman, N.Y.C., 1948-50, Lewinson, Lewinson & Fieland, 1950-54; dir. admissions, then dean Lab. Inst., Mdsg., N.Y.C., 1954-73; asst. prof., asst. dean N.Y. Law Sch., 1973-74, asso. prof., asso. dean, 1974-81, acting dean, spring 1980; mem. N.Y.C. Mayor's Com. Judiciary, 1980; mem. jud. screening panels, 1974—. Mem. N.Y.C. Community Bd. 1, 1979—, chmn. police and fire com., 1979—; sec., bd. dirs. Chambers-Canal Civic Assn., 1977—. Woodrow Wilson fellow, 1979, 80. Mem. Am. Bar Assn. (law schs. insp. team 1978—), Assn. Am. Law Schs. (chmn. sect. on teaching law outside law sch. 1980-81), N.Y. County Lawyers Assn. (chmn. com. on legal edn. and admission to bar 1980—). Presbyterian. Club: Cosmopolitan. Office: NY Law Sch 57 Worth St New York NY 10028

BEARSS, JOYCE CLARKE, telephone co. mgr.; b. Jamestown, N.Y., July 7, 1930; d. Garnet Garfield and Margaret Alberta (Mooney) Clarke; m. William S. Bearss, May 28, 1955. Sec., N.Y. Telephone Co., Buffalo, 1955-65, asst. dial service supr., 1965-66, dial service supr., 1966-80, community affairs mgr., 1980—. Bd. dirs. D'Youville Coll., Center for Women in Mgmt.; exec. bd. dirs., asst. sec. bd. Niagara Frontier Industry Edn. Council; bd. dirs. Bry-Lin Hosp., Jr. Achievement; bd. dirs., chmn. nominating com. Am. Lung Assn. Western N.Y.; bd. dirs., treas. Coordinated Care Mgmt. Corp.; mem. examiners N.Y. State Nursing Home Adminstrs.; del. White House Conf. on Aging; mem. Victim-Witness Task Force County Erie; bd. dirs. U.S. Ski Team, Buffalo Support Group; mem. Soc. Community Affairs Profl.; mem. adv. bd. Erie County Dept. Sr. Services; mem. Senator Javitz Bd.; mem. exec. bd. Erie County Republican Com.; mem. Buffalo Susquicentenial Media Com.; active various community drives. Recipient Service awards Am. Lung Assn., 1981, Erie County Dept. Sr. Services, 1980. Mem. Telephone Pioneers Am., Women for Downtown, Buffalo Area C. of C. Clubs: Wanakah Country; Capitol Hill; Zonta (dir.) (Buffalo). Home: S-4934 Clifton Pkwy Hamburg NY 14075 Office: 1 M & T Plaza Buffalo NY 14203

BEASLEY, EDWINA JOYCE, dentist; b. Nashville, Dec. 11, 1942; d. James Edward and Ruby O. (Smith) Finley; B.A., Calif. State U., Long Beach, 1966, M.A., 1968; D.D.S., UCLA, 1977. Tchr. public schs., Long Beach and Anaheim, Calif., also Saddleback Coll., Mission Viejo, Calif., 1967-73; gen. practice dentistry, Long Beach, 1977-79; dir. Harbor Dental Soc. Outpatient Service, St. Mary Med. Center, Long Beach. Mem. ADA, Calif. Dental Assn., Los Angeles Dental Soc., Am. Assn. Women Dentists, Harbor Dental Soc., Orange County Dental Soc. Republican. Presbyterian. Home: 6541 Rugby St Huntington Park CA 90255 Office: 6438 Rita Ave Huntington Park CA 90255

BEATON-SIMMONS, KAREN, coll. adminstr.; b. Providence, Mar. 9, 1944; d. Allan and Arlene Beaton; B.A., U. R.I., 1965; M.Ed., U. Ga., 1974; postgrad. in bus. adminstrn. Bryant Coll.; m. 1965 (div.); children—Laura, Andrew. Speech pathologist, 1965-79; part-time faculty U. R.I., 1978-79; dir. ann. giving Bryant Coll., Smithfield, R.I., 1979-81, dir. devel., 1981—; pvt. practice speech pathology, Cranston, R.I., 1979—. Mem. State Advs. for Gifted Edn., 1980—, pres., 1980-81. Mem. Council Advancement and Support of Edn., R.I. Assn. Women Deans, Adminstrs. and Counselors, Am. Speech and Hearing Assn., R.I. Speech and Hearing Assn., Greater Providence C. of C. (ambassador), Alpha Chi Omega, Kappa Delta Pi. Baptist (choir, deaconess). Office: Bryant Coll Box 40 Smithfield RI 02917

BEATTIE, DIANA SCOTT, biochemist, educator; b. Cranston, R.I., Aug. 11, 1934; d. Kenneth Allen and Lillian Francis (Barton) Scott; B.A., Swarthmore Coll., 1956; M.S., U. Pitts., 1958, Ph.D., 1961; m. Benjamin Howard Beattie, June 30, 1956 (div. 1975); children—Elizabeth, Sara, Rachel, Ruth; m. 2d, Robert Nathan Stuchell, Feb. 6, 1976. Research asso. U. Pitts., 1961-67, VA Hosp., Pitts., 1967-68; asst. prof. Mt. Sinai Sch. Medicine, N.Y.C., 1968-70, asso. prof., 1970-75, prof., 1976—; mem. grad. faculty biomed. scis. City U. N.Y., 1968—, biochemistry, 1971—, biology, 1974—; mem. biochemistry ad hoc study sect. NIH, 1978-79, phys. biochemistry rev. group, 1980—; mem. faculty research award panel City U. N.Y., 1978-80. Recipient award Am. Women in Sci., 1979; NIH grantee, 1966—, NSF grantee, 1970—. Mem. Am. Soc. Biol. Chemists, Am. Soc. Cell Biology, Biophysics Soc., Gerontol. Soc. Contbr. articles to profl. jours. Mem. editorial bd. Archives of Biochemistry and Biophysics, 1975-78, Jour. Bioenergehis, 1975—. Research subcellular biochemistry, mitochondrial metabolism and biogenesis. Office: Dept Biochemistry Mount Sinai Sch Medicine Fifth Ave and 100th St New York City NY 10029 *

BEATTIE, NORA MAUREEN, ins. co. exec.; b. Bklyn., July 10, 1925; d. Robert Gamble and Eileen Benedict (Geaney) B.; B.A. summa cum laude, St. John's U., 1947, M.S., 1949, D. Comml. Sci. (hon.), 1980. With N.Y. Life Ins. Co., N.Y.C., 1948—, v.p., actuary 1974—; actuary, dir. N.Y. Life Ins. and Annuity Corp.; treas., dir. N.Y. Guarantee Corp. Mem. Soc. Actuaries, Am. Acad. Actuaries, Bus. and Profl. Women's Club. Republican. Roman Catholic. Office: NY Life Ins Co 51 Madison Ave New York NY 10010

BEATTIE, TEODOZJA KUREK, typographic co. exec.; b. Poreba-Zawiercie, Poland, Mar. 27, 1922; came to U.S., 1946, naturalized, 1950; d. Piotr and Marianna (Wronski-Makowka) Kurek; student U. Hartford, 1957-60; children—Sylvia Teodozja, Christopher Andrew. Supr. internat. banking Hartford Nat. Bank & Trust Co., 1962-64; econ. research asst. Fed. Res. Bank Mpls., 1966-67; internat. banking officer, internat. econ./polit. analyst Wachovia Bank & Trust Co., Winston-Salem, N.C., 1967-75; pres., founder T.K.B. Internat. Corp., Winston-Salem, 1976, pres. Hendricks Miller Typog. Co. div., Washington, 1977—, Global Trading Corp., Washington, 1977—. Mem. Printing Industries Am., Printing Industry Met. Washington (dir.), Internat. Typographers Assn., Small Bus. Assn. Home: 500 23d St NW B-1106

Washington DC 20037 also 2870 Robinhood Rd Winston-Salem NC 27106 Office: 2363 Champlain St NW Washington DC 20009

BEATTY, LEONA EVELYN, banker; b. Jeannette, Pa.; d. Darwin Ansley and Eva Evelyn (Franke) Fennell; B.A. in English, U. Pitts., 1975; 1 son, Thomas Richard. Advt. dept. asst., sec. NBC, Pitts., 1958-59; asst. sec.-treas. Babcock Fla. Co., Pitts., 1959-68, exec. sec. to chmn. bd. Babcock Lumber Co., Pitts., 1959-68; with Fed. Home Loan Bank of Pitts., 1968—, asst. v.p., 1975-82, corp. sec., 1981-82, sec., 1982—. Mem. adv. com. Vocat. Rehab. Ctr. Allegheny County. Mem. Am. Soc. Personnel Adminstrn., Exec. Women Internat. (bd. dirs. 1983—), Nat. Assn. Female Execs., Nat. Forum Exec. Women, Pitts. Personnel Assn., Pa. Assn. Notaries. Office: Eleven Stanwix St Gateway Center Pittsburgh PA 15222

BEATTY, PATRICIA M., dance theatre ofcl., choreographer; b. Toronto, Ont., Can., May 13, 1936; d. Clifford G. and Jean G. (Brown) B.; student Havergal Coll., Toronto; B.A. in Dance, Bennington (Vt.) Coll., 1959. Founder, tchr., choreographer New Dance Group of Can., 1965-68; co-founder Toronto Dance Theatre Sch. and Performing Co., 1968, now dir., tchr., choreographer; dance tchr., Can., 1965-75; choreographer 14 original dance works for Toronto Dance Theatre. Can. Council grantee. Address: 80 Winchester St Toronto ON M4X 1B2 Canada

BEATTY, (RUTH) OPAL (MRS. E. EVERETT BEATTY), corp. exec.; b. Martelle, Iowa, Nov. 6, 1906; d. Dana Logan and Nellie Olin (Wood) Stearns; B.A., Cornell Coll., 1929, B.S.M., 1932; postgrad. Northwestern U., summer 1931, U. Iowa, summer 1936; m. (Edward) Everett Beatty, Feb. 1, 1938; children—Dennis, Jerry, Delight, Larry. Tchr. secondary schs. Ill. and Iowa, 1929-37; instr. Cornell Coll., Mt. Vernon, Iowa, summers 1934, 35; state news reporter Cedar Rapids (Iowa) Gazette, 1939-47; part time bookkeeper Newhall Grain Co. (Iowa), also Atkins Grain Co. (Iowa), 1945-59; part time bookkeeper Shellsburg (Iowa) Grain and Lumber Co., 1959—, dir., corp. treas., 1958—. First woman on Shellsburg Community Sch. Bd., 1954-57; den mother Cub Scouts Hawkeye Area Council Boy Scouts Am., 1947-59; guardian Iowana Council Camp Fire Girls, 1956-64, bd. dirs., 1958-62; vice chmn. Benton County Dem. party, 1962-64, alt. del. Dem. nat. conv., 1964; sec. Library Bd., 1974-75; mem. women's com. Cedar Rapids Symphony; pres. Presbyn. Ch. Circle, 1952-53. Recipient Den Mother award, Boy Scouts Am., 1957, service award, 1959; cert., appointee Iowa Commn. for Sr. Citizens, 1960. Corp. mem. Iowa Lumber Dealer's Assn., Wood Products Co., Iowa Grain and Feed Assn. Clubs: Beethoven, Woman's (pres. 1966-67), Order Eastern Star (organist White Lily chpt. 1949-54). Violinist; author Centennial History of Shellsburg, Iowa, 1954; writer, dir. pageant, 1954; co-author supplement for celebration, 1979. Home: 409 Grand Ave Shellsburg IA 52332 Office: 207 Commercial St Shellsburg IA 52332

BEATTY-MCCAA, JANICE MARIE, banner and flag mfg. co. exec.; b. New Orleans, Sept. 25, 1953; d. Gerald Francis and Janice Marie (McCartt) Beatty; B.S., La. State U., 1980; m. Adrian L. McCaa, June 9, 1971 (div.); 1 dau., Shirley Janicé. Seamstress for banners and sports La. State U., Baton Rouge, 1979—, Nat. Coll. Athletic Assn. track sec., 1979—; owner, operator Wings-The Initial Corp., Baton Rouge, 1981—. Roman Catholic. Home: 9895 Florida Blvd Baton Rouge LA 70815 Office: 2043 Dallas Dr Baton Rouge LA 70806

BEAUCHAMP, DANIELLE MARIE, energy cons; b. Paris, May 30, 1950; d. William Ellsworth and Veronica Ellen (Klimek) Beauchamp; B.A., Vassar Coll., 1972; M.P.A., Harvard U., 1979. Editor, Library of Congress, Washington, 1972; legis. asst. to Jaime Benitez, Resident Commr. from P.R., U.S. Ho. of Reps., Washington, 1973; research analyst energy and power subcom. U.S. Ho. of Reps., Washington, 1975; energy cons. McKinsey & Co., Washington, 1981—. Mem. job discrimination study Capitol Hill Womens Polit. Caucus, 1975. Matthew Vassar scholar, 1968, 69. Mem. AAAS, Am. Soc. Public Adminstrn., Washington Assn. Profl. Anthropologists, Women's Council on Energy and the Environment, Kennedy Sch. Alumni Assn. (exec. council 1980—), Phi Beta Kappa. Clubs: Mensa, Vassar, Harvard. Home: 4100 W St NW Washington DC 20007 Office: 1700 Pennsylvania Ave NW Washington DC 20006

BEAUDETTE, MARCELLA RAYMONDE, nurse; b. Woonsocket, R.I., Nov. 23, 1925; d. Raoul and Elianne G. (Girouard) B.; diploma St. Joseph's Hosp. Sch. Nursing, Providence, 1947; B.S. in Nursing, Boston Coll., 1955; postgrad. Boston U., 1958-59. Staff nurse St. Joseph's Hosp., Providence, 1947-52, Notre Dame Hosp., Central Falls, R.I., 1952-55, Providence VA Hosp., 1955; med. and surg. supr. Malden (Mass.) Hosp.. 1955-59, asst. dir. nurses, 1959-62; asst. dir. nurses Robert B. Brigham Hosp., Boston, 1962-70, dir. nursing, 1970-80; dir. surg./rheumatology/orthopedic nursing Brigham and Women's Hosp., Boston, 1980—. Mem. St. Joseph's Hosp., Boston Coll. sch. nursing alumnae assns., Nat. League Nursing, Am., Mass. socs. nursing service adminstrs., Boston Mus. Fine Arts, French Library in Boston, Smithsonian Assocs., Appalachian Mountain Club. Roman Catholic. Office: 75 Francis St Boston MA 02115

BEAUDOIN, CAROL ANN, psychologist; b. Lowell, Mass., Mar. 30, 1949; d. Adrien P. and Rita J. (LeBlanc) B.; B.A. with honors, U. Fla., 1971; M.Ed. in Counseling, Boston U., 1973, Ed.D. in Counseling Psychology, 1979. Psychiat. aide U. Fla.-Shands Teaching Hosp., Gainesville, 1970-71; trainee VA Hosp., Gainesville, 1971-72; attendant Boston State Hosp., 1972, intern, 1973; intern Univ. Hosp., also Counseling Center, Northeastern U., Boston, 1973-74, Dorchester Mental Health Center, also Carney Hosp., 1974-75; staff psychologist Human Resource Inst., Boston, 1974-80, treatment team leader, 1975-80; pvt. practice psychology, Brookline, Mass., 1980—. Mem. Am. Psychol. Assn. Office: 1101 Beacon St Brookline MA 02146

BEAUDRY, AGNES PORTER, educator; b. Charleston, W.Va., Dec. 9, 1932; d. Walter C. and Grace Elizabeth (Hemmings) Porter; B.A., Marshall U., 1954; M.A., Case Western Res. U., 1958; Ph.D., U. Ill., Urbana, 1968; m. James George Beaudry, June 2, 1973. Tchr., Kanawha County (W.Va.) Public Schs., 1954, Fairfax Hall Jr. Coll., Waynesboro, Va., 1955-57, Mansfield (Ohio) High Sch., 1958-59, Ft. Hays (Kans.) State Coll., 1959-60; asst. U. Ill., 1962-65, instr., 1965-67; asst. prof. Romance langs. DePauw U., Greencastle, Ind., 1967-72, asso. prof., 1972-80, prof., 1980—. Fulbright grantee, 1954-55. Mem. Am. Assn. Tchrs. French, MLA, Women's Caucus for Modern Langs., Phi Kappa Phi, Pi Delta Phi. Contbr. articles to scholarly jours. Home: 1503 Sheri Circle Plainfield IN 46168 Office: Dept Romance Langs DePauw U Greencastle IN 46135

BEAUFAIT, DORIS ELAINE O'DONNELL, reporter; b. Cleve., June 21, 1921; d. John Laurence and Stella Agnes O'Donnell; student Case Western Res. U., 1940-44, John Carroll U., 1944-47; m. Howard Beaufait, Sept. 1957. With Cleve. News, 1944-58, Cleve. Plain Dealer, 1958-59; with Cleve. Zool. Soc., 1959-62; staff Univ. Hosps., Cleve., 1961-63; reporter Cleve. Plain Dealer, 1963-70; with News-Herald, Willoughby, Ohio, 1970-71, Office of the Mayor, Cleve., 1972-73; investigative reporter/writer Tribune Rev., Greensburg, Pa., 1973—. Mem. Pa. Jud. Merit Selection Commn., Westmoreland County, 1980-81. Mem. Ligionier Valley Hist. Soc., Women in Communications, Pa. Newspaper Women's Assn., Theta Sigma Phi, Sigma Delta Chi. Roman Catholic. Club: Press. Contbr. articles to profl. jours. Home: RD 3 PO Box 71D Ligonier PA 15658 Office: Cabin Hill Dr Greensburg PA 15601

BEAULIEU, EDITH AGNES, state legislator; b. Millenocket, Maine, Feb. 23, 1937; d. Wilfred and Rose (Madore) Saucier; student schools Eaglelake and Portland, Maine; m. Edgar R. Beaulieu, Nov. 10, 1956; children—Cynthia, Susan, Edgar R., Kathleen. Columnist, Parent-Tchrs. in Action, Portland Evening Express, 1968-74; mem. Maine Ho. of Reps., 1976—, mem. joint standing com. on edn., 1976—, mem. joint standing com. on labor, 1976—, chmn., 1981—, sec. labor com., 1976—; chmn. Maine firefighters edn. and tng. adv. com.; shop steward Am. Newspaper Guild, AFL-CIO, 1974—. Bldg. com. Portland Library, Munjoy Hill Sch., Vocat. Sch.; pres. Munjoy Hill PTA, 1966-80; life mem. Maine Congress of PTA; mem. Portland Sch. Com., 1974-77, chmn. citizens' adv. com. to Sch. Com., 1972-75; mem. Save the Promenade Com., Portland Bicentennial Com.; asso. mem. Italian Heritage Center; chmn. Portland Sch. Safety Com., 1973-80; co-chmn. bicentennial coin project, Portland; bd. dirs. Munjoy Hill Neighborhood Orgn., 1976-80; active United Way. Mem. Nat. Conf. of Legislators (edn. rep. for Maine), Maine Assn. Women Hwy. Safety Leaders. Democrat. Roman Catholic. Office: 79 State House Augusta ME 04330

BEAUMONT, C(LARA) ESTELLE, editor, nurse; b. Cook County, Ill., May 10, 1937; d. Carl Franklin and Clara Pearline (Smith) Roberts; grad. Silver Cross Hosp. Sch. Nursing, Joliet, Ill., 1958; R.N., U. Ill., 1959; postgrad. Case Western Res. U., 1960; B.A. in Mag. Journalism, Bowling Green State U., 1982; m. Perry Mills Beaumont, Jan. 1, 1960; children—Perry H., Tamara C. Staff nurse Meth. Hosp., Peoria, Ill., 1958-59; emergency room nurse MacNeal Meml. Hosp., Berwyn, Ill., 1959; asst. clin. instr. St. Francis Hosp., Peoria, 1960; student health dir. St. John Hosp., Cleve., 1961; nurse rehab. unit, research unit Highland View Hosp., Cleve., 1965-66; inhalation therapy nurse Sturdy Meml. Hosp., Attleboro, Mass., 1968; vis. nurse Foxboro (Mass.) Vis. Nurse Assn., 1969-70; asso. editor Nursing, Intermed. Communications, Inc., Horsham, Pa., 1972-80; prodn. editor RN mag., 1980—; editor, cons. Curtis Pub. Co., ECRI, Infusion, Jour. Emergency Nursing, JORRI, Med. Communications, Ross Labs., S-N Publs.; instr. writing Cleve. State U., 1978-79; coordinator workshops on writing and documentation; judge writing contests. Mem. Am. Med. Writers Assn., Am. Pub. Health Assn., Am. Soc. Bus. Press Editors, Cleve. Area League Nursing. Methodist. Address: 591 Harley Dr Columbus OH 43210

BEAUMONT, MONA MAGDELEINE, artist; b. Paris, Jan. 1, 1927; came to U.S., 1942, naturalized, 1945; d. Jacques Hippolyte and Elsie M. (Didisheim) Marx; B.A., U. Calif., Berkeley, 1945, M.A., 1946; postgrad. Harvard U., 1945-46, Fogg Mus., Cambridge, 1945-46, Hans Hoffman Studios, N.Y.C., 1946; m. William G. Beaumont, Dec. 20, 1946; children—Garrett, Kevin. One-woman shows at Galeria Proteo, Mexico City, 1960, Gumps Gallery, San Francisco, 1962, 64, 65, Palace of Legion of Honor, San Francisco, 1964, L'Armitiere Gallery, Rouen, France, 1966, Hoover Gallery, San Francisco, 1967, San Francisco Mus. Modern Art, 1968, Galeria Van der Voort, San Francisco, 1969, William Sawyer Gallery, San Francisco, 1972, Palo Alto (Calif.) Cultural Center, 1975, Galerie Alexandre Monnet, Brussels, 1974, Honolulu Acad. Arts, 1980; exhibited in group shows at San Francisco Mus. Modern Art, 1954, 57, 68, San Francisco Art Inst., 1958-74, DeYoung Meml. Mus., San Francisco, 1960-62, Grey Found. Tour of Asia, 1963, Bell Telephone Invitational, Chgo., 1968, Richmond Art Center, 1968, Los Angeles County Mus. Art, 1973, Galerie Zodiaque, Geneva, 1974, others; represented in permanent collections: Oakland (Calif.) Mus. Art, City and County of San Francisco, Hoover Found., San Francisco, Grey Found., Washington, Bulart Found., San Francisco; also numerous pvt. collections. Recipient Jack London Sq. Ann. Painting award, 1965; Purchase award Grey Found., 1963; Ann. award San Francisco Women Artists, 1966, 68; Purchase award San Francisco Art Festival, 1966; One-Man Show award San Francisco Art Festival, 1975. Mem. Soc. for Encouragement of Contemporary Art, Bay Area Graphic Arts Council, San Francisco Art Inst., Archives of Am. Art, San Francisco Mus. Modern Art, Delta Epsilon, Delta Chi Alpha. Address: 1087 Upper Happy Valley Rd Lafayette CA 94549

BEAUPRE, LINDA JOANNE LYLE, librarian; b. Oakland, Calif., Aug. 5, 1943; d. John Gunnar and Virginia Helen (Johnson) Lyle; A.B. in History, U. Calif., Berkeley, 1965; A.M.L.S., U. Mich., 1967; m. Dean Albert Beaupre, Aug. 12, 1967 (div.). Supr. microform reading room, periodicals reading room, interlibrary loan unit at grad. library U. Mich., 1967-69; mem. library staff U. Calif., Berkeley, 1969-78, reference, coll. devel. librarian Moffitt Undergrad. Library, 1969-72, coordinator public services, 1972-75, adminstrv. asst. to asso. univ. librarian for public services, 1977-78, instr. bibliography I, 1971, 74-75; head librarian reference services dept. gen. libraries, then acting asst. dir. public services U. Tex., Austin, 1978-80, asso. dir. public services, 1980—. Council Library Resources acad. library mgmt. intern, 1975-76. Mem. ALA, Tex. Library Assn., Tex. Assn. Coll. Tchrs., NOW, AAUW, ACLU, Sierra Club. Author articles in field. Editorial bd. Jour. Acad. Librarianship, 1980-83. Office: Gen Libraries PCL 3 200 U Tex Austin TX 78712

BEAUSOLEIL, DORIS MAE, housing specialist, govt. agy. ofcl.; b. Chelmsford, Mass., Jan. 9, 1932; d. Joseph Honorius and Beatrice Pearl (Smith) B.; student State Tchrs. Coll., Lowell, Mass., 1949-51; B.A. in Sociology and Psychology, Goddard Coll., Plainfield, Vt., 1954; M.A. in Human Relations, N.Y. U., 1957. With div. human rights N.Y. State, N.Y.C., 1960-69, housing dir., 1966-68; housing cons. Nat. Com. Against Discrimination in Housing, N.Y.C., 1969-70; housing cons. Edwin Gould Found., N.Y.C., 1970-71; human resources cons. interfaith housing strategy com., housing cons. Fedn. Prot. Welfare Agencies, Inc., N.Y.C., 1971-72; self-employed housing cons., 1972-74; equal opportunity compliance specialist Region II HUD, N.Y.C., 1975-78, Fed. women's program coordinator, 1975-79; br. chief Title VI Sect. 109 Compliance div. fair housing and equal opportunity Region II, HUD, N.Y.C., 1979—; founding mem. N.Y. State HUD Com.; adv. panel Housing Mag., 1979; cons., examiner N.Y. State Civil Service Commn., 1970—. Mem. Nat. Assn. Human Rights Workers (Outstanding Service award 1974), Citizens Housing and Planning Council, Federally Employed Women, Nat. Assn. Housing and Devel. Ofcls. Republican. Unitarian. Clubs: Women's City N.Y., Rep. Bus. Women's (N.Y.C.). Home: 392 Central Park W New York NY 10025 Office: 26 Federal Plaza Room 3502 New York NY 10278

BEAVER, BONNIE VERYLE, veterinarian, educator; b. Mpls., Oct. 26, 1944; d. Crawford F. and Gladys I. Gustafson; B.S., U. Minn., 1966, D.V.M., 1968; M.S., Tex. A&M U., 1972; m. Larry J. Beaver, Nov. 25, 1972. Instr. vet. surgery and radiology U. Minn., 1968-69; instr. vet. anatomy Tex. A&M U., College Station, 1969-72, asst. prof., 1972-76, asso. prof., 1976-82, prof., 1982—. Vice pres. Brazos Valley Regional Sci. and Engring. Fair, 1974—; bd. dirs. Am. Cancer Soc., Brazos Valley unit, 1976—, v.p., 1977—. Named Citizen of Week, The Press, 1981. Mem. AVMA, Tex. Vet. Med. Assn., Women's Vet. Med. Assn., Brazos Valley Vet. Med. Assn., Am. Animal Hosp. Assn., Animal Behavior Soc., Am. Soc. Vet. Ethology, Am. Assn. Vet. Clinicians, Vet. Computer Soc., Assn. Am. Vet. Med. Colls., Phi Sigma, Sigma Epsilon Sigma, Phi Zeta, Phi Delta Gamma. Contbr. numerous articles on vet. medicine to profl. jours.; editorial bd. Applied Animal Ethology, 1981-82. Home: RFD 3 Box 354 College Station TX 77840 Office: College of Vet Medicine Dept of Vet Anatomy Texas A&M College Station TX 77843

BEAVER, JEANNE ENGEL, ballet dir.; b. Los Angeles, June 4, 1954; d. William N. and Joy A. Engel; B.S. with honors in Ballet, Ind. U., Bloomington, 1975; m. Jeffry W. Beaver, Nov. 1, 1975. Dancer, Indpls. Ballet Theatre, 1975-76, dir. wardrobe, 1977-79; co-artistic and adminstrv. dir. Met. Ballet St. Louis, 1979—; mem. teaching staff LeVine Acad. Ballet; costumer Bob Kramer's Marionnettes, 1981—. Co. mem. Dance Concert Soc., Arts and Edn. Council Greater St. Louis. Home: 561 Town Hall Ct Saint Louis MO 63141 Office: 11607 Olive Blvd Saint Louis MO 63141

BEAVER, PATRICIA LEE, art dealer; b. St. Joseph, Mo., Nov. 9, 1938; d. Charles Weck and Ruby (Babbitt) Dunlap B.F.A., Washburn U., 1961; m. Harold R. Beaver, June 17, 1962; children—Christopher, Laura. Art dir. Geeco, Inc., St. Joseph, 1961-63; art dir. Central Sign Co., Kansas City, Mo., 1963-67; owner, mgr. Gallery III, Hendersonville, Tenn., 1969—; instr. pottery Vol. State Community Coll., 1975; chmn. bd. Tenn. Crafts Fair, Inc., 1975-79. Mem. crafts adv. panel Tenn. Arts Commn., 1973—, chmn., 1976-79. Named Friend of the Arts, City of Hendersonville, 1976. Mem. Tenn. Artist Craftsmen Assn. (hon.), Hendersonville Arts Council (chmn. 1976), Profl. Picture Framers Am., Am. Crafts Council. Episcopalian. Home: Forest Harbor Dr Hendersonville TN 37075 Office: 122 Stadium Dr Hendersonville TN 37075

BEAVERS, IRENE, home economist; b. Hopkinsville, Ky., June 4, 1926; d. James Claudius and Mary Loula (Graham) B.; B.S., Peabody Coll., 1948; M.S., Iowa State U., 1953; Ph.D. U. Wis., 1962. Asst. and home demonstration agt. U.S. Dept. Agr., Russellville and Frankfort, Ky., 1948-52, 54-55; extension asst. Iowa State U., 1952-53; dist. home econs. supr. Iowa State U., 1955-60; program leader home econs. Fed. Extension Service, U.S. Dept. Agr., Washington, 1963-65; prof. home econs. edn. Iowa State U., Ames, 1965—; home econs. edn. cons. Kasetsart U., Bangkok, 1977; external examiner U. Pertainian (Malaysia), 1982. Recipient Iowa Adult Edn. Achievement award, 1973; fgn. travel grantee Iowa State U., 1972, 79. Mem. Adult Edn. Assn. (chmn. family life sect. 1981), Nat. Assn. Tchr. Educators Home Econs., Am. Vocat. Assn. (treas. 1975-76), Iowa Adult Edn. Assn. (pres. 1970), Internat. Fedn. Home Econs., Am. Home Econs. Assn., AAUW, Phi Delta Kappa, Phi Delta Gamma, Phi Kappa Phi. Editor in brief Jour. Extension, 1974-77; contbr. articles to profl. jours. Home: 2707 Luther St Ames IA 50010 Office: Dept Econs Iowa State U Ames IA 50011

BEAVERS, JESSIE MAE (MRS. LEROY A. BEAVERS), journalist; b. Los Angeles; d. Albert and Arnette Marie (Hoyt) Brown; m. LeRoy A. Beavers, Jr., June 27, 1948; children—Deborah Elaine, LeRoy Albert, Kimberly Arnetta. Social columnist Calif. Eagle, Los Angeles, 1940-48; social editor family sect. Los Angeles Sentinel, 1949—; cons. So. Calif. Gas Co., 1959-61, Calif. Turkey Adv. Bd., 1962-64. Mem. Los Angeles Human Relations Commn., 1972—, pres., 1973-77; mem. Los Angeles County Music and Performing Arts Commn., 1976; bd. dirs. Stovall Found., Los Angeles School Vols. and Doves. Recipient Arch Angel award Los Angeles Bus. Assn., 1967; Ida B. Wells award Nat. Assn. Media Women, 1968; Mary McLeod Bethune award Nat. Council Negro Women, 1973; Ambassador of Goodwill award Women for Good Govt., 1973; Vol. Activist award Germaine Monteil, 1972; Human Relations award Soodo Women's U., Seoul, Korea, 1977. Mem. Nat. Assn. Media Women (founder Los Angeles chpt., 1965, Founder's Cup award, 1975), Women in Communications, Calif. Human Relations Assn., Links, Alpha Kappa Alpha, Iota Phi Lambda. Baptist. Office: 1112 E 43d St Los Angeles CA 90011

BEAVERS, MARY EISELE, clin. psychologist; b. Chgo., Oct. 3, 1939; d. Charles Wesley and Blanche Mae (Kennell) Eisele; B.A., Radcliffe Coll., 1962; M.A. (NIMH fellow), U. Ariz., 1970, Ph.D. in Psychology, 1973; 1 son, John Miller Adam. High sch. tchr. Valley Sch. Girls, Tucson, 1963-66; clin. psychologist student counseling service U. Ariz., 1972-76, asst. dir., 1976—, acting dir., 1980, dir. univ.-wide honors program, 1980—, lectr. psychology, 1974-76. Co-founder Tucson Gilbert and Sullivan Theatre, 1966, bd. dirs., 1966-71; alumni interviewer Harvard-Radcliffe Admissions Office, 1976—; admistrv. bd. St. Francis in the Foothills Meth. Ch., 1978-81; mem. Ariz. Opera Co. Cert. psychologist, Ariz.; cert. Nat. Register Health Care providers in Psychology. Mem. Am. Psychol. Assn., Ariz. Psychol. Assn., So. Ariz. Psychol. Assn., Internat. Transactional Analysis Assn., Nat. Collegiate Honors Council, Catalyst Network Nat. Women's Info. Democrat. Methodist. Office: Math Bldg 507 University of Arizona Tucson AZ 85721

BECCARI, NANCY JUDITH HALL (MRS. ARMANO A. BECCARI), educator; b. Marietta, Ohio; d. Robert Earl and Bernice (Underwood) Hall; B.A. cum laude, U. Miami, 1958, M.Ed., 1961, postgrad., 1970—; m. Turner M. Hiers, Oct. 29, 1942; m. 2d, Armano A. Beccari, Aug. 31, 1974. Tchr. pub. schs., Ga., Fla.; dir. Reading Center, Nova High Sch., Ft. Lauderdale, Fla., 1963—, Lauderdale Reading Clinic, 1965—. Mem. Internat. Reading Assn., Am. Ednl. Research Assn., AAUW, Nat. Soc. for Study Edn., Kappa Delta Pi, Alpha Delta Kappa, Kappa Kappa Iota, Epsilon Tau Lambda, Phi Lambda Pi. Clubs: Le Club Internationale, Rolls Royce Owners. Home: 1479 NE 174th St North Miami Beach FL 33162

BECHER, BARBARA ANN, clin. psychologist; b. Jamaica, N.Y., Mar. 11, 1931; d. Peter A. and Ruth (Gannon) B.; B.A., Coll. of New Rochelle, 1953; M.A., Fordham U., 1956; Ph.D., 1965; postgrad. (post-doctoral fellow 1966-67), U. Wis. Med. Sch., 1966-67. Pvt. practice psychology, Jamaica Estates, N.Y., 1956—; staff psychologist Fordham U., N.Y.C., 1956-66, Am. Mgmt. Psychologists, N.Y.C., 1967-68; chief psychologist Cath. Charities, Mineola, N.Y., 1967—; chief psychologist Jewish Guild for the Blind, N.Y.C., 1968-79; adj. faculty St. Johns U., Jamaica, N.Y., 1975-77, 79-80, N.Y. Inst. Tech., Commack, N.Y., 1976-78, Fordham U., Bronx, 1958-61, Seton Hall U., Newark and South Orange, N.J., 1965-66; cons. Passionist Seminary, Jamaica Estates, 1968—. Mem. Am. Psychol. Assn., N.Y. State Psychol. Assn., Eastern Psychol. Assn., Psychologists Interested in Religious Issues (exec. bd.), Sigma Xi. Roman Catholic. Home: 171-30 Mayfield Rd Jamaica Estates NY 11432 Office: Cath Charities 110 Main St Mineola NY 11501

BECK, ARIADNE PLUMIS, psychologist; b. Orange, N.J., Jan. 24, 1933; d. George Nicholas and Panagiota Beatrice (Drevas) Plumis; A.B.A., Fashion Inst. Tech., 1952; B.S., Cornell U., 1954; M.A., U. Chgo., 1969, Ph.D. candidate; m. Robert Nason Beck, Feb. 16, 1958. Teaching and research asst. U. Chgo., 1955-60, instr., 1960-71, staff counselor Counseling and Psychotherapy Research Center, 1959-66; dir. Ill. Inst. Tech. Counseling Center, 1971-77; pvt. practice psychology, Chgo., 1977—. Mem. Am. Psychol. Assn., Ill. Psychol. Assn., Am. Personnel and Guidance Assn., Ill. Group Psychotherapy Soc., Am. Group Psychotherapy Assn., Internat. Soc. Psychotherapy Research. Contbr. in field. Home: 6357 Blackhawk Trail Indian Head Park IL 60525

BECK, AUDREY PHILLIPS, state senator; b. Bklyn., Aug. 6, 1931; d. Gilbert Wesley and Mary (Reilly) Phillips; B.A. with high honors, U. Conn., 1953, M.A. with distinction in Econs., 1955; m. Curt Frederick Beck, 1951; children—Ronald Pierson, Meredith Wayne. Mem. faculty dept. econs. U. Conn., Storrs, 1960-67; planning economist Windham Regional Planning Agy., 1967-68; vis.prof. practical politics Center for Am. Women in Politics, Rutgers U., 1975-76; mem. Conn. Ho. of Reps., 1969-75, asst. minority leader, 1973-75; mem. Conn. Senate, 1975—, chmn. fin. com., 1977—, asst. majority leader, 1977—. Mem. Bd. Fin., Mansfield, Conn., 1965-71; mem. Mansfield-Univ. Liaison Com., 1967-68, Conn. Housing Commn., 1969-71; del. Democratic Nat. Conv., 1972; chmn. Dem. State Platform Com., 1974, 76, 78; mem. com. on campaign financing and legis. ethics Nat. Legis. Conf., 1974-76, mem. com. on sci. and tech., 1977—; mem. Conn. State Govts. Regional Tax Com., 1975—; mem. Northeastern U.S. Legis. Task Force. Mem. LWV, Conn. Fedn. Dem. Women's Clubs (newsletter editor 1969-71), Bus. and Profl. Women, AAUW, Am. Soc. Planning Ofcls. (pres. 1977), Phi Beta Kappa, Phi Kappa Phi, Artus, Gamma Chi Epsilon, Delta Sigma Rho. Office: Conn State Senate Hartford CT 06115 *

BECK, DOROTHY FAHS, social researcher; b. N.Y.C.; d. Charles Harvey and Sophia (Lyon) Fahs; A.B., U. N.C., 1928; M.A., U. Chgo., 1932; Ph.D. (Gilder fellow), Columbia U., 1944, postdoctoral study, 1955-56; Am.-German Student Exchange fellow, Germany, 1928-29; m. Hubert Park Beck, Aug. 20, 1930; 1 dau., Brenda E.F. Dir. econ. research ADA, 1929-32; social worker Emergency Relief Adminstrn. N.J., 1933-34; statistician N.Y. State Emergency Relief Adminstrn., 1934-35, U.S. Office Edn., 1935-36; asso. social economist U.S. Central Statis. Bd., 1936-38; research supr., author Am. Coll. Dentists, 1940-42; statistician Am. Heart Assn., 1947-53, Cornell U. Med. Coll., part-time 1951-53; asst. prof. biostats. Am. U. Beirut, part-time 1954: dir. research Family Service Assn. Am., N.Y.C., 1956-81, dir. study counselor attitudes and feelings, 1982—, counselor, research cons., 1982—. Fellow Am. Sociol. Assn.; mem. Acad. Cert. Social Workers, Am. Assn. Marriage and Family Counselors (affiliate), Nat. Conf. Family Relations, Groves Conf., Am. Statis. Assn., Nat. Assn. Social Workers, Soc. Study Social Problems, Am. Pub. Health Assn., Phi Beta Kappa. Liberal. Unitarian-Universalist. Author: Patterns in Use of Family Agency Service, 1962; Marriage and the Family Under Challenge, 1976; New Treatment Modalities, 1978; co-author: Costs of Dental Care Under Specific Clinical Conditions, 1943; Myocardial Infarction, 1954; Clients Progress within Five Interviews, 1970; How to Conduct a Client Follow-Up Study, 1974, 2d enlarged edit., 1980; Progress on Family Problems, 1973. Home: 523 W 121st St New York NY 10027 Office: Family Service Assn Am 44 E 23d St New York NY 10010

BECK, FLORENCE VIOLA WALTON, social worker; b. Montrose, Pa., Oct. 9, 1907; d. Herbert E. and Mae C. (Porter) Walton; tchr.'s cert. Mansfield State Tchrs. Coll., 1929; M.S.W., U. Pitts., 1954; m. Ralph C. Beck, Aug. 22, 1931 (dec. June 1973); 1 dau., Mary (Mrs. David Hart). Caseworker, supr., exec. dir. Susquehanna County Bd. Assistance, Pa. Dept. Welfare, Montrose, 1934-54, exec. dir., 1962-71; psychiat. social work supr., chief psychiat. social worker Binghamton (N.Y.) Psychiat. Center, N.Y. State Dept. Mental Hygiene, 1971-82; clin. social worker, social work supr., acting chief social service VA Hosp., Wilkes-Barre, Pa., 1954-57; chief psychiat. social worker Broome County Mental Health Clinic, Binghamton, 1957-60, Elmira (N.Y.) Psychiat. Clinic, 1960-61; social doctor George Jr. Republic, Freeville, N.Y., 1961-62; part-time social work cons. Montrose Gen. Hosp., Asa Park Nursing Center, Montrose Bd. dirs. Susquehanna County Mental Health Assn.; bd. dirs. Am. Cancer Soc., treas., 1963—, pres. Susquehanna County unit, sec. Pa. div., 1973—; bd. dirs., sec. Binghamton Psychiat. Center Aux. Mem. Nat. Assn. Social Workers (charter, dir., treas. So. Tier (N.Y.) chpt. 1972-74, Social Worker of Yr. So. Tier chpt. 1976), Acad. Cert. Social Workers, Am. Pub. Welfare Assn., Community Services of Pa. (trustee), Bus. and Profl. Women's Clubs, Inc. (charter mem. Montrose, pres. 1951-53, Woman of Yr. 1975, dist. dir. 1955-57). Home: 3 Mitchell Hill Montrose PA 18801

BECK, FRANCES JOSEPHINE MOTTEY (MRS. JOHN MATTHEW BECK), educator; b. Eleanora, Pa., July 12, 1918; d. George F. and Mary (Wisnieski) Mottey; B.S., Ind. State Tchrs. Coll., 1939; M.A., U. Chgo., 1955; m. John Matthew Beck, Aug. 23, 1941. Jr. visitor Pa. Dept. Pub. Assistance, 1940-41; asst. to the sec. Dept. Edn., U. Chgo., 1952-58, asst. dean of students Grad. Sch. Edn., 1958-75; asst. to dean Sch. Edn., DePaul U., Chgo., 1975—, asst. prof., 1979—; dir. MST Reading Cons. Program, 1968-70; reading instr. Central YWCA, Chgo., 1958-61. Mem. Nat., Ill. assns. women deans and counselors, Internat. Reading Assn., Am. Ednl. Research Assn., Pi Lambda Theta (nat. v.p. 1966-70, nat. 1st v.p. 1971-74), Sigma Sigma Sigma, Delta Kappa Gamma. Author: (with others) Extending Reading Skills, Levels 1,2,3, 1976. Contbr. articles to profl. jours. Office: 2323 N Seminary St Chicago IL 60614

BECK, HELEN J., artist; b. Chgo., July 13, 1908; d. Irwin E. and Anna (Lion) Weil; grad. Prague Art Inst., 1923, Chgo. Inst. Fine Arts, 1927; m. Hugo Beck, Oct. 11, 1931; children—Dolores Ann (dec. 1976), Sandra L. Beck Sabul. Staff advt. artist Wieboldt Stores, Chgo., 1928-31; Chgo. USO; creator Sunshine Rag Doll; lectr. civic, sch. and art groups. Comdr. Emergency and Disaster Corps, Chgo. ARC, 1940-49; nurses' instr. first aid Ill. Masonic Hosp., 1941-46; speaker Am. Cancer Soc.; coordinator Chgo. Tb mobile units, 1940-45. Recipient Meritorious Service medal U.K. War Relief, 1944, Presdl. awards ARC, 1945, 46, meritorious service award Kiwanis, 1965. Mem. Am. Assn. Ret. Persons, West Suburban Ostomy Assn. (visitor's program), Chgo. Ostomy Assn. Author travelogues.

BECK, KAREN LYNN, interior designer; b. N.Y.C., Dec. 3, 1941; d. Edward and Lillian Marker; student N.Y.C. Community Coll., 1959-61, N.Y.U., 1961-62, New Sch., 1963-64, Ramapo Coll., 1976-77; m. Sanford E. Beck, Oct. 24, 1965; children—Marni Jill, Julia Dawn. Owner antique bus., Vt. and N.Y., 1965-68; interior design-antique bus. woman, 1968-78; owner Interiors Group, Tenafly, N.J., 1978—. Active community art projects N.J. Artists, Visual Artists and Galleries Assn. Mem. Nat. Assn. Female Execs., N.J. Women Bus. Owners Assn., C. of C. Bergen County (ambassador group). Jewish. Home: 40 Dawn Ln Suffern NY 10901 Office: 120 County Rd Tenafly NJ 07670

BECK, MARGIT, artist; b. Tokay, Hungary; d. Samuel and Johanna (Blau) Beck; student Art Inst. of Oradeamare (Rumania), 1929-32, Art Student League, N.Y.C., 1945-46; m. Sidney Schwartz; children—Joan, John. Came to U.S., 1932, naturalized, 1938. Theatrical scenic designer, 1934-36; formerly mem. art faculty Hofstra U.; now asst. prof. art faculty N.Y. U., Empire State Coll., N.Y. State U.; exhibited works in one-man shows Contemporary Arts, N.Y.C., 1955, 58, 59, San Joaquin Mus., Stockton, Calif., 1956, Hofstra Coll., L.I., 1958, Lincoln High Sch., N.Y.C., 1959, Mus. Fine Arts, Greenville, S.C., 1959, Babcock Gallery, N.Y.C., 1962, 64, 66, 68, 71, 72, 75, Phila. Art Alliance, 1968, Mansfield (Pa.) State Coll., 1965, Queens Coll., N.Y.C., 1973, Port Washington (N.Y.) Library, 1978; Mus. Fin. Art, Wichita, Kans., 1980, U. Wyo., 1980; exhibited in group shows Whitney Mus. Ann., Corcoran Biennial, Chgo. Art Inst. Ann., Pa. Acad. Ann., Allentown (Pa.) Mus. Fine Arts, Lehigh U., Bethlehem, Pa., Bklyn. Mus. Internat. W.C. Biennial NAD Ann., Butler Inst. Ann., U. Nebr. Ann., Springfield (Mass.) Mus., Akron Art Inst., Am. Acad. Arts and Letters, N.Y.C., Am. Soc. Contemporary Artists, Riverside Mus., N.Y.C., Southeby Parke Bernet, N.Y.C., Art U.S.A., Ringling Mus., Davenport (Iowa) Municipal Gallery, São Paulo Mus., N.Y. World's Fair, Am. Fedn. Arts Internat.; travelling exhbns. include State Dept. sponsored exhbns., Am. embassies and mus. abroad; represented in permanent collections Peabody Mus., Cambridge, Mass., Speed Mus., Louisville, Morse Mus., Rawlins Coll., Hofstra Coll., Hunter Coll., Herbert Lehman Coll., N.Y.C., Miami U., Oxford, Ohio, Norfolk (Va.) Mus., Sheldon Meml. Mus., Lincoln, Nebr., Glichtenstein Mus., Safaad, Israel, Lyman Allen Mus., New London, Conn., Mansfield (Pa.) State Coll., Whitney Mus., others; also many pvt. collections and pub. bldgs. Recipient Gold medal oil Hofstra Coll., 1954; Purchase prize watercolor, 1955, Silver medal, 1956, Gold medal, 1957; Medal of Honor, Nat. Assn. Women Artists, 1956, watercolor award, 1957, 63, oil award, 1958, 64; Winsor and Newton oil award, 1959, others; MacDowell Found. Residence fellow, 1957, 59, 60, 75; Walker award oil Audubon Artists, 1965, Medal Honor, 1968, 71, Henry Ward Ranger Fund Purchase award NAD, 1965, 73, Andrew Carnegie award, 1973; Child Hassam award Am. Acad. Arts and Letters, 1968, 69, 72. Mem. Artists Equity Assn. (past mem. exec. bd.), Audubon Artists (v.p. 1968-71, Stephen Hirsch award 1975, James D.H. Meml. award 1982), NAD (full academician, Edwin Palmer award 1975), Coll. Art Assn. Am., Women in Arts. Address: 22 Florence St Great Neck NY 11023

BECK, MARILYN MOHR, columnist; b. Chgo., Dec. 17, 1928; d. Max Mohr and Rose (Lieberman) Mohr; A.A., U. So. Calif., 1948; m. Roger Beck, Jan. 8, 1949 (div. 1975); children—Mark Elliott, Andrea; m. 2d, Arthur Levine, Oct. 12, 1980. Free-lance writer nat. mags., newspapers, Hollywood, Calif., 1959-63; featured Hollywood columnist Valley Times, Citizen News, Hollywood, 1963-65; West Coast editor Sterling Mags., Hollywood, 1963-74; featured free-lance entertainment writer Los Angeles Times, 1965-67; Hollywood columnist Bell-McClure Syndicate, 1967-72, also chief West Coast bur.; Hollywood columnist NANA Syndicate, 1967-72; syndicated Hollywood columnist N.Y. Times Spl. Features, 1972-78, United Features Syndicate, 1978-79, Chgo. Tribune-N.Y. News Syndicate, 1979—; radio personality Marilyn Beck's Hollywood News Reports, KFT Radio, 1974-76, Marilyn Beck's Hollywood Out-Takes Spl., NBC, 1977, 78; Hollywood corr. KABC-TV, 1981. Recipient Citation of Merit, Los Angeles City Council, 1973; press award Publicists Guild Am., 1974. Club: Hollywood Women's Press. Author: Marilyn Beck's Hollywood, 1973. Address: PO Box 11079 Beverly Hills CA 90213

BECK, NANCY MANN MCCONNICO (MRS. EARL C. BECK, JR.), civic worker; b. Memphis, Aug. 31, 1931; d. John Davis and Pauline (Hilton) McConnico; grad. So. Sem. and Jr. Coll., 1949; m. Dean Carlton DuBois, Aug. 19, 1950 (div. Nov. 1963); children—Denise Hilton, Dean Carlton; m. 2d, Earl C. Beck, Jr.; 1 son, John Harrington. Asst. buyer, sportswear John Gerber Co., Memphis, 1949-50; fashion coordinator J. Hilton McConnico, Designer, Paris, 1963-65; buyer, mgr. Bridal Salon, Goldsmiths, Memphis, 1965-70, French Room, 1970-72. Press relations Hunter Lane for mayor, 1967; v.p. West Memphis Fine Arts Center, 1977-79; chmn. Crittenden County-Mmephis, regional chmn. Mid-South Billy Graham Crusade for May 1978; chmn. Children's Art Day, Memphis, 1976-78, Memphis Symphony Ball, 1981; co-chmn. Crittenden County Jim Guy Tucker for U.S. Senate; bd. dirs. Crittenden Fine Arts Center, 1979—, Memphis Orchestral Soc., 1981—, Am. Symphony Orch. League; bd. dirs. Memphis Symphony League, 1977-78, pres., 1980—; trustee So. Sem. Jr. Coll., Buena Vista, Va., 1982—. Mem. Internat. Platform Assn., Memphis Arts Council, Josephine Circle (pres. 1963-64), Woman's Exchange. Episcopalian. Club: Town and Country Garden (pres. 1975-77). Home: Casa Lorraine Plantation Hughes AR 72348 Office: Route 1 Box 50 Hughes AR 72348

BECK, PATRICIA (LOU), ednl. adminstr.; b. Oakdale, Nebr., Dec. 6, 1923; d. Elmer C. and Theo J. (Burner) Malm; student Dallas Secretarial Inst., 1940-41; student various univ. courses, 1968-80; m. Jack G. Elam, July 26, 1974; children—Karlyn Beck Edwards, Thomas A. Beck. Christine L. Beck, Susan P. Beck. Sec., Anderson & Johnson, Midland, Tex., 1958-63; office mgr. C.C. Thomas, Midland, 1963-68; registrar Permian Basin Grad. Center, Midland, 1968-69, dir. adminstrn. 1969-71, exec. dir., 1971-79, pres., 1979—; cons., tchr. office mgmt. and procedures, acctg.; dir. Permian Basin Grad. Center; v.p., dir. 2501 Corp. Mem. Nat. Secs. Assn., Bus. and Profl. Women, MENSA. Home: 2501 Princeton Midland TX 79701 Office: PO Box 1518 Midland TX 79702

BECK, PATRICIA (MCDERMOTT), photographer; b. Detroit, July 18, 1953; d. George Edward and Eileen Mary (Rinke) B.; student Oakland U., 1971-73; B.S.J. in Photojournalism with honors (Paul Schutzer Meml. fellow), Ohio U., 1975; m. Bruce Charles McDermott, May 4, 1979. Photographer, Observer and Eccentric newspapers, Troy, Mich., 1975-76; photographer's asst., darkroom technician D.G.M. Studios, Bloomfield Hills, Mich., 1976-77; staff photographer Detroit Free Press, 1977—. Recipient 2d Pl. News Picture of Yr. award Mich. AP, 1978; News Photography award Detroit Press Club, 1977; 1st Pl. Picture Story award UPI, 1981; News Photography award Detroit Press Club Found., 1982; Overall Community Media award Awareness Communication Team for Developmentally Disabled, 1982; Disting. Service award Oakland County Assn. Retarded Citizens, 1981; ARC of Excellence award for Mich., 1981, Nat., 1981. Mem. Women in Communications, Nat., Mich. (1st Pl. award Category X, 2d Pl. award fashion 1979) press photographers assns., Sigma Delta Chi, Kappa Tau Alpha. Home: 29135 Westbrook Pkwy Southfield MI 48075 Office: 321 W Lafayette Detroit MI 48321

BECK, SHARON ELIZABETH, business ofcl.; b. San Bernardino, Calif., June 27, 1946; d. Leroy James and Elizabeth Eileen (Shaughnessy) Bruce; B.A., U. Okla., 1968. Adminstr. govt. affairs Crystal Oil Co., Shreveport, La., 1974-77; mgr. govtl. regulations Charter Oil Co., Jacksonville, Fla., 1977-79; sr. cons. energy regulatory group Peat, Marwick, Mitchell & Co., Dallas, 1979-80, mgr., Los Angeles, 1980; asso. Wheat, Luke & Hahn, Houston, 1980-81; mgr. govtl. regulations Tex. Energy, Houston, 1981—. Mem. NOW, Ind. Petroleum Assn. Am., Am. Petroleum Inst., Calif. Ind. Producers Assn., Town Hall Assn., Mensa. Club: Petroleum (Los Angeles). Office: 12600 N Borough Suite 260 Houston TX 77067

BECK, TONI, choreographer, educator; b. N.Y.C., Oct. 4, 1925; d. Samuel and Margaret (Wise) B.; B.A., Oberlin Coll., 1946; M.A., Columbia U., 1949; postgrad. Harvard U., 1972; m. Bob Glatter, Dec., 1952 (div. 1965); 1 dau., Lesli; m. 2d, Paul Bosner, 1969. Asst. prof. dance Washington U., St. Louis, 1949-51; lectr. So. Meth. U., Dallas, 1959-60, asst. prof., 1960-63, asso. prof., 1963-65, prof. dance, 1965—, chmn. dance div., 1965—; tchr. Modern Ballet Studio, Dallas, 1954-68, Rubin Acad. Music, Jerusalem, 1971, Bat Dor Studios, Tel Aviv, 1972, Internat. Ballet Center, Copenhagen, 1976; tchr. Utah Repertory Co., 1974; tchr./choreographer Scapino Ballet, Amsterdam, Netherlands, 1976, choreographer, 1977; choreographer Bat Dor Dance Co., Tel Aviv, 1972, 74, 77, Irish Ballet Co., Cork; choreographer mus. piece Konstellationen, Graz, Austria, 1975; artistic dir. Repertory Dance Co. S.W., 1977-79; co-founder Beck & Cury Co., beauty and health concepts, 1979; mem. adv. bd. to the arts Dallas Ind. Sch. Dist., 1974—, chmn. com. for arts magnet sch. evaluation; exec. dir. Greenhouse, 1982—. Named One of Most Outstanding Profs., So. Meth. U., 1976-77; Ford Found. grantee, 1951-52; So. Meth. U. grantee, 1964, Danforth grantee, 1964-65. Mem. Actor's Equity, AFTRA, Nat. Dance Tchrs. Guild, AAUP. Author: Fashion Your Figure, 1971; Focus Your Figure, 1973; contbr. articles to mags. including Vogue, Harper's Bazaar, Cosmopolitan. Home: 3327 Mockingbird Ln Dallas TX 75205 Office: The Greenhouse PO Box 1144 Arlington TX 76010

BECKER, ANN WATTERS, civic worker; b. N.Y.C.; d. William G. and Lucile (Miller) Watters; student pvt. schs., Harcum Jr. Coll., Child Edn. Found.; mem. Ralph E. Becker; children—William Watters, Donald Lee, Pamela Rose, Ralph E. Chmn. spl. events D.C. chpt. Am. Cancer Soc., 1957-59, dir., 1959—, sec. exec. bd., 1962-64, 72—; bd. trustees Washington Community Sch. Music, Washington Choral Arts Soc.; mem. women's com. Nat. Symphony Orch., 1950—, bd. dirs., 1970—; bd. dirs. Mother's Club of St. Albans Sch., 1958-59, sec., 1962-63, pres., 1963-64; bd. govs. St. Albans Sch., 1969-75; pres. Women St. Alban's Ch., 1965-66; founder, pres. Met. Washington chpt. Achievement Rewards for Coll. Scientists, 1969-72, bd. dirs., 1972-76; organizing mem. Friends John F. Kennedy Center Performing Arts; exec. com. D.C. Commn. on Aging; rec. sec. League Republican Women, 1955-57, exec. bd., 1955-59, pres., 1981-83; women's com. Corcoran Art Gallery; women's bd. George Washington U. Hosp., 1954—; bd. dirs. women's com. George Washington U. Hosp.; bd. dirs. Washington Ballet; chmn. Washington com. Frontier Nursing Service, Wendover, Ky.; 1st pres. D.C. Fedn. Rep. Women, 1982—; pres., League Rep. Women of D.C.; regent Nat. Fedn. Rep. Women; co-chmn. cultural events com. Presdl. Inaugurals, 1953, 57, 69, 73, 81; mem. Nat. Com. Sponsors for Margaret Sanger Inst. Human Reprodn. and Devel.; exec. com. All Hallows Guild, Washington Cathedral; chmn. flower mart Textile Mus., 1972, chmn. distaff com. Recipient St. George's medal and cert. Ann. Nat. Divisional award Am. Cancer Soc., 1975; decorated Order Stella Della Solidarieta Italiana 1st class, 1970. Mem. Salvation Army Aux. (1st v.p. 1959-61, dir. 1959-66, 74-75), Soc. Assocs. Smithsonian Instn., World Affairs Forum, sec. 1960-79), YWCA, LWV, Daus. Utah Pioneers, Women's Aux. Soc. Calif. Pioneers. Episcopalian (vestry 1966-69). Clubs: Capitol Hill, Am. News Women's (asso. mem., dir.), Capital Speakers.

BECKER, BARBARA KELLER, librarian; b. Findlay, Ohio, Nov. 21, 1923; d. Louis Conrad and Margaret Belle (Holcombe) Keller; A.B., Oberlin Coll., 1945; A.B., U. Mich., 1948, postgrad., 1966-67; postgrad. Hillsdale Coll., 1970, Wayne State U., 1972; m. Jack Becker, Dec. 27, 1947 (div. Oct. 12, 1962); children—Nancy (Mrs. Kenneth Lee Johnson), Anne (Mrs. Frederick Kenneth Warneke), John. Librarian, Jones, Day, Cockley & Reavis, attys., Cleve., 1945-47; fgn. and internat. law acquisitions librarian U. Mich. Law Library, Ann Arbor, 1947-48; asst. librarian Findlay (Ohio) Pub. Library, 1951-52; librarian Mich. Municipal League, Ann Arbor, 1959-63; asst. librarian Parke, Davis & Co., Ann Arbor, 1963-69, research librarian, 1969-79; supr. library services Warner-Lambert Co., Ann Arbor, 1979—; cons. Beth Israel Library, Ann Arbor, 1965-67, Planned Parenthood Clinic, Ann Arbor, 1965-66. Pres. Washtenaw County (Mich.) chpt. Muscular Dystrophy Assns. of Am., 1958-59; mem. adv. council Ann Arbor Pub. Library, 1958-63; cookie chmn. Huron Valley Girl Scout Council, Ann Arbor, 1963-74. Washtenaw County (Mich.) del. Dem. State Conv., 1948; registered voters file chmn. Ann Arbor (Mich.) Rep. City Com., 1955-57. Mem. Spl. Libraries Assn. (pres. Mich. chpt. 1971-72, treas. pharm. div. 1972-75, dir. 1976-77, chmn. 1977-78), Med., Washtenaw County (v.p. 1960-61) library assns., Friends of the Ann Arbor Pub. Library (dir. 1963-68, pres. 1967), Women's Aux. Washtenaw County Bar Assn. (dir., treas. 1960-65), Met. Detroit Med. Library Group. Republican. Episcopalian (mem. vestry 1970-73). Mem. Order Eastern Star. Clubs: Huron Valley Swim, Liberty Racquet (Ann Arbor). Home: 645 East Shore Dr Whitmore Lake MI 48189 Office: 2800 Plymouth Rd Ann Arbor MI 48106

BECKER, BETTIE GERALDINE, artist; b. Peoria, Ill., Sept. 22, 1918; d. Harry Seymour and Magdalene Matilda (Hiller) Becker; B.F.A. cum laude, U. Ill., Urbana, 1940; postgrad. Art Inst. Chgo., 1942-45, Art Student's League, 1946, Ill. Inst. tech., 1948; m. Lionel William Wathall, Nov. 10, 1945; children—Heather Lynn (dec.), Jeffrey Lee. Dept. artist Liberty Mut. Ins. Co., Chgo., 1941-43; with Palenskie-Young Studio, 1943-46; free lance illustrator N.Y. Times, Chgo. Tribune, Saturday Rev. Lit., 1948-50; pvt. tutor, tchr. studio classes. Exhibited one-man show Crossroads Gallery, Art Inst. Chgo., 1973; exhibited group shows including Critics' Choice show Art Rental Sales Gallery Art Inst. Chgo., 1972, Evanston-North Shore exhbns., 1964, 65, Chgo. Soc. Artists, 1967, 71, Union League, 1967, 72; represented in permanent collection Witte Meml. Mus., San Antonio; executed mural (with F. Wiater) Talbot Lab. U. Ill., Urbana, 1940. Active Campfire Girls, Chgo., 1968, 70; art chmn., mem. exec. bd. local PTA, 1959-60; active various art festivals, 1967—. Recipient Newcomb award U. Ill., 1940. Mem. Chgo. Soc. Artists (rec. sec. 1968-77), Soc. Illustrators, Northeastern Wis. Arts Council (2d v.p.), Alumni Assn. Art Inst. Chgo. Contbr. poetry to various publs. Home: Juddville Rd Fish Creek WI 54212

BECKER, CAROL ANN, liquor co. exec.; b. Bronx, N.Y., Nov. 20, 1954; d. Isidore A. and Adele S. B.; B.S., Syracuse U., 1976; postgrad. N.Y. U., 1979. Staff writer public relations Schenley Industries, Inc., N.Y.C., 1976-77, exec. trainee, 1977-78, asst. brand mgr. Schenley Distillers Co. div., 1978-80, product mgr., 1980—; dir. Lerner Shops, Inc. Jewish. Home: 178 E 80th St New York NY 10021 Office: 888 7th Ave New York NY 10106

BECKER, DIANE LOUISE, auditor; b. Chgo., June 4, 1950; d. Dolores L. (Wessel) Marcinek; A.A., Coll. of DuPage, 1972; B.S., Elmhurst Coll., 1977. With Sunbeam Holdings, Wilmington, Del., 1978—, internat. corp. auditor, 1980—. Mem. Nat. Assn. Female Execs. Office: Sunbeam Holdings Inc Wilmington DE 19810

BECKER, DONA TURPIN, educator; b. St. Louis, Apr. 30, 1935; d. Paul Penn and Frances Geraldine (Fitzwater) Turpin; A.B. (honor scholar), Washington U., St. Louis, 1956; M.A., U. Mo., St. Louis, 1978; children from previous marriage—Dawn, Daniel. Tchr., public schs., Jennings, Mo., 1956, Warrensburg, Mo., 1958, KnobNoster, Mo., 1959, Normandy, Mo., 1957, 60-62; tchr. math. sr. high sch., Normandy Schs., St. Louis, 1973—. Bd. dirs. Campus Y, Washington U.; pres. Neighborhood Assn.; tchr. Sunday Sch., 3d Bapt. Ch.; v.p. Ladue Schs. PTA; com. chmn. Mo. Bapt. Hosp. Aux.; leader Girl Scouts. Mem. NEA, Mo. Edn. Assn., Normandy Tchrs. Assn. (treas.), Phi Delta Kappa, Washington U. Alumni Assn., U. Mo. at St. Louis Alumni Assn., Mortar Bd. Alumnae Assn. (pres.). Baptist. Home: 49 Stoneleigh Towers St Louis MO 63132 Office: 6701 St Charles Rock Rd St Louis MO 63133

BECKER, EDNA R., automobile dealer; b. Snow Twp., N.D., Mar. 16, 1932; d. Eduard and Christina (Henne) Rivinius; grad. high sch.; m. Robert John Becker, July 4, 1954 (dec. May 1980); children—Marsha, Brenda, Pamela. Bookkeeper, Gambles, Bismarck, N.D., 1949-51; typist Safety Responsibility div. State of N.D., Bismarck, 1951-52; billing clk. Quandrud, Brink & Reibold, Inc., Bismarck, 1952-54; sec.-treas. West River Motors, Inc., Hettinger, N.D., 1961-80, gen. mgr., 1980-81, pres., treas., mgr., 1981—; counselor high sch. distributive edn. class. Chmn., Adams County Easter Seals, 1962-66, Hettinger chpt. Am. Heart Assn., 1969-70; clk. election bds.; ABC reporter for nat. election LWV, Bismarck. Mem. Hettinger C. of C., N.D. Automobile Dealers Assn., Nat. Automobile Dealers Assn., Hettinger Community Hosp. Aux. Republican. Lutheran. Clubs: Hettinger Bus. and Profl. Women, Eagles Aux., Elks, Hettinger Luth. Ch. Ladies Circles. Address: PO Box 832 Hettinger ND 58639

BECKER, GAIL LYNN, mktg. cons., dietitian; b. East Orange, N.J., May 14, 1943; d. Max and Ree (Forman) B.; B.S., Drexel U., 1965. Dietitian, Peter Bent Brigham Hosp., Boston, 1965-68; dir. dietetics St. Vincent's Hosp., Bridgeport, Conn., 1968-69; dir. dietetic services Best Foods div. CPC Internat., Englewood Cliffs, N.J., 1969-73; nutrition mgr. Weight Watchers Internat., Inc., Manhasset, N.Y., 1973-75; mktg. communications cons. Gail Becker Assos., Inc., Fort Lee, N.J., 1975—. Mem. Am. Dietetic Assn., Am. Home Econs. Assn., Am. Women in Radio and TV, Soc. Nutrition Edn., Inst. Food Technologists, Instl. Food Service Editors Council, Soc. Consumer Affairs Profls., Women in Communications, Home Economists in Bus. Contbr. articles to profl. jours. Home and Office: 2357 Linwood Ave Fort Lee NJ 07024

BECKER, JANET ARLENE, med. technologist; b. Wheeling, W.Va., Dec. 1, 1940; d. Ralph Charles and Clara Elizabeth (Bock) B.; B.S. in Med. Tech., West Liberty State Coll., 1963; cert. med. technologist Ohio Valley Med. Ctr., 1963; M.A. in Health Edn., W.Va. U., 1978. Edn. coordinator Ohio Valley Med. Center, Wheeling, W.Va., 1964-65, 1974, med. tech. edn. coordinator, 1965-68, hematology supr., 1968-82; with St. Margaret Meml. Hosp., Pitts., 1982—; ; instr. Wheeling Coll. Clin. Hematology, 1982—; instr. Ohio Valley Med. Center, West Liberty State Coll., W.Va. No. Community Coll., Wheeling. Mem. Am. Soc. Clin. Pathologists (cert. med. technologist, specialist in hematology, clin. lab. scientist). Republican. Methodist. Home: RD 2 PO Box 319 W Alexander PA 15376 Office: 815 Freeport Rd Pittsburgh PA 15215

BECKER, JAQUELINE HOPE, psychotherapist; b. Staten Island, N.Y., Dec. 12, 1943; d. Benjamin J. Becker and Estelle Lillian (Fox) Becker Mendel; B.S., Wagner Coll., 1966; M.S., Yeshiva U., 1975, Ph.D., 1979. Social group worker, supr. Jewish Community Center, Staten Island, 1962-69, CUNY, 1970-72, Bernard Baruch Student Personnel, Staten Island, 1970-72; tchr. emotionally disturbed N.Y.C. Bd. Edn., 1966-73; evaluation specialist Research and Devel. Center, Yeshiva U., N.Y.C., 1973-75; asst. dir. Pvt. Sch. Emotionally Disturbed, N.Y.C., 1975-76; pvt. practice psychotherapy, N.Y.C., 1976—. Cert., Ethical Hypnosis Tng. Center, 1981. Mem. Am. Psychol. Assn., Assn. Transpersonal Psychology, Assn. for Advance Ethical Hypnosis, Dream Community. Office: 1 University Pl New York NY 10003

BECKER, JOHANNA LUCILLE, educator; b. Denver, Dec. 17, 1921; d. Arthur John and Irene Elizabeth Becker; B.F.A., U. Colo., 1943; M.A., Ohio State U., 1945; M.A., U. Mich., 1969, Ph.D., 1975. Joined Sisters of St. Benedict, Roman Cath. Ch., 1950; chmn. art dept. Maryville Coll., St. Louis, 1945-47; instr. Ill. State U., Bloomington, 1948-49; assoc. prof. St. John's U., Collegeville, Minn., 1952-60; mem. faculty Coll. St. Benedict, St. Joseph, Mo., 1952—, prof. art, 1975—, acad. dean, 1954-60; speaker on ceramics, cons. in field. Bd. dirs. World Affairs Center, U. Minn. Fulbright fellow, 1963; Rackham fellow, 1969; C.L. Freer fellow, 1967-68. Mem. World Affairs Council (dir.), Assn. Asian Studies, Oriental Ceramic Soc., Asiatic Soc. Japan, AAUW (fellow 1969-70). Author: Karatsu Ceramics of Japan: Origins, Fabrication and Types, Vol. I-II, 1974; also articles. Address: Convent St Benedict St Joseph MN 56374

BECKER, MARCIA ROSE, psychologist; b. Phila., Mar. 19, 1937; d. David Joshua and Naomi (Carner) Rose; B.A. in Psychology, Adelphi U., Garden City, N.Y., 1958; M.S. in Clin. Psychology, CCNY, 1960; M.A. in Social Psychology, New Sch. Social Research, 1964, Ph.D., 1968; m. Gordon M. Becker, 1970 (div.); m. 2d, James D. Emery, 1982. Research asst. Office Instl. Research, Hunter Coll., N.Y.C., 1959-62, Community Service Soc., N.Y.C., 1962-65; lectr. psychology Hunter Coll., 1965-67; asso. prof. psychology, chmn. M.A. program in community psychology Fed. City Coll., Washington, 1968-74; ind. practice psychology and astrological counseling, Hollywood, Fla., 1981—; psychologist Renaissance Revitalization Center, Nassau, Bahamas, 1975; lectr., coordinator counseling Coll. Bahamas, 1976-80; condr. workshops in parapsychology throughout U.S. Grantee NIMH, 1972. Mem. Am. Psychol. Assn., Assn. Humanistic Psychology, Parapsychol. Assn., Spiritual Frontiers Fellowship, Fla. Psychol. Assn., Am. Soc. Psychical Research, Fla. Soc. Psychol. Research, S. Fla. Astrological Assn. Mem. Unity Ch. Address: PO Box 827 Hollywood FL 33022

BECKER, MARY ANNE, banker; b. Chgo., May 14, 1937; d. Eugene Bunte and Kathryn (Byrne) Reiner; student Mundelein Coll., Chgo.; married; children—Kathryn, Richard, Teresa. With No. Trust Co., Chgo., 1963—, head securities custody div., 1976—, 2d v.p., 1981—. Mem. Nat. Assn. Bank Women, Corp. Fiduciaries Assn. Home: 4000 Cleveland St Skokie IL 60076 Office: 50 S La Salle St Chicago IL 60675

BECKER, MARY ELIZABETH BUNTIN, retail chain exec.; b. Washington Mills, N.Y., June 14, 1925; d. Allen McMurtry and Vera (Attleberger) Thompson; student Bowling Green (Ohio) State U., 1943-44; diploma Lab. Inst. Fashion Mdsg., N.Y.C., 1947; m. Charles Olah, May 1945; 1 dau., Katherine Louise; m. 2d, Thomas Austin Buntin, Dec. 24, 1950; children—Thomas Austin, Richard Franklin; m. 3d, John Jacob Becker. Dept. mgr. Mosleys, Detroit and Miami Beach, Fla., 1947-53; buyers Blumbergs Dept. Store, Dothan, Ala., 1954-59; with Sears, Roebuck & Co., 1959—, asst. retails sales mgr., N.Y.C., 1965-67, buyer, N.Y.C. and Chgo., 1967—; tchr. classes on labeling. Served with WAC, 1944-46. Mem. Bus. and Profl. Women's Club. Republican. Club: Altrusa. Home: 814 E Hackberry Dr Arlington Heights IL 60004 Office: Sears Tower BSC (2-15) D/627 2 N LaSalle St Chicago IL 60018

BECKER, MARY LOUISE, polit. scientist; b. St. Louis; d. W. R. and Evelyn (Thompson) B.; B.S., Washington U., St. Louis, 1949, M.A. (Blewett fellow), 1951; Ph.D. (resident fellow 1952-56), Radcliffe Coll., 1957; postgrad. (Fulbright scholar) U. Karachi (Pakistan), 1953-54; m. 1966 (div.); children—James, John. Intelligence research analyst Dept. State, Washington, 1957-59; internat. relations officer AID, Washington, 1959-64, community relations officer, 1964-66, sci. research officer, 1966-71, UN relations officer, 1971—; adviser U.S. dels. 19th, 21st, 23d, 26th governing council sessions UN Devel. Program; adv. U.S. del. 3d prep. com. meeting World Conf. UN Decade for Women; lectr. internat. relations civic orgns., student groups, 1954—. Mem. adv. bd., chmn. student placement Washington Citizenship Seminar, Nat. YMCA-YWCA, Washington, 1961-71. Mem. Am. Polit. Sci. Assn., Soc. Internat. Devel., Assn. Asian Studies, Asia Soc., Am. Soc. Public Adminstrn., Am. Friends Middle East, AAUW, Mo. Soc. Washington (sec. 1959-60), Mortar Bd., Chimes, Alpha Lambda Delta, Beta Gamma Sigma, Eta Mu Phi, Pi Sigma Alpha. Presbyterian. Club: International (Washington). Author: Muhammed Iqbal, 1965. Contbg. editor: Concise Ency. of Middle East, 1973. Contbr. articles to govt. publs. Office: AID Washington DC 20523

BECKER, MILLIE BELBER, found. exec.; b. Atlantic City, Apr. 2, 1941; d. Leon H. and Florence (Grossman) Belber; student Am. U., 1959-62; m. Marvin S. Becker, Feb. 10, 1962; children—Carrie Susan, Anne Raquel. Office mgr. urology practice, Somers Point, N.J., 1975-80; pres. Ruth Newman Shapiro Cancer and Heart Meml. Fund, Margate, N.J., 1979—. Home: 6 Princeton Ln Linwood NJ 08221 Office: 620 Shore Rd Somers Point NJ 08244

BECKER, SALLY, real estate developer; b. Chgo., Apr. 12, 1931; d. Albert and Shirley (Wittenberg) Cohen; B.A. in English, U. Ill., 1952; m. Robert Becker, Apr. 5, 1952; children—Robin, Stephan. Real estate developer, prin. Sally Becker Real Estate, Chgo., 1967—. Election judge; active Ill. Forum, Nat. Fedn. Republican Women, Nat. Gallery Women's Art, Washington; sustaining fellow Art Inst. Chgo. Jewish. Clubs: Carlton, Yale of Chgo. Office: PO Box 286 Kenilworth IL 60043

BECKER, SAMUELLA REBECCA, communications exec.; b. Akron, Ohio, Sept. 23, 1954; d. Samuel and Mary Julia (Lengyel) Becker; B.S.J., Ohio U., 1975. Editorial asst. Talk Mag., N.Y.C., 1976; mng. editor Argosy Mag., N.Y.C., 1976-78; media cons./writer Union Carbide Corp., N.Y.C., 1978-80; mgr. internal communications SCM Corp., N.Y.C., 1980—. Asst. in Mario Cuomo's campaign for Mayor of N.Y.C., 1976. Mem. Women in Communications, Public Relations Soc. Am., Internat. Assn. Bus. Communicators, Soc. Profl. Journalists, Women's Econ. Roundtable, Sigma Delta Chi, Alpha Delta Pi. Democrat. Presbyterian. Contbr. articles to profl. jours. Home: 420 E 72d St New York NY 10021 Office: 299 Park Ave New York NY 10171

BECKER PEARCE, ANNE MARIE, nurse; b. Phila., Nov. 1, 1927; d. George and Anna Veronica (Hughes) Becker; R.N., St. Joseph's Hosp., Phila., 1948; cert. Jefferson U. Hosp. Sch. Anesthesia, 1954; divorced; children—Mary, Kristin, Theresa Angela, Anthony. Eve. supr. St. Joseph's Hosp., 1952-53, anesthetist, 1954—; sr. staff nurse anesthetist Fitzgerald Mercy Hosp., Darby, Pa., 1979—; cons., tchr., lectr., hypnotist, 1970—. Mem. Am. Assn. Nurse Anesthetists, Assn. Advancement Ethical Hypnosis (chpt. pres. 1977-82), Am. Nurses Assn., Am. Guild Hypnotherapists, ASTM, Pa. Assn. Nurse Anesthetists (pres. 1979), Ramblewood Civic Assn. Roman Catholic. Author chpts. in book on hypnosis. Office: 3182 S 17th St Philadelphia PA 19145

BECKET, FLORA GRACE, acct., mgmt. systems cons.; b. Calhoun, Ga., Dec. 20, 1943; d. Claude Huckabee and Jimmie Mae (Merritt) Rogers; student San Jose State U., 1975—; m. Michael P. Becket, Jan. 26, 1974; children—Roni Root, Lori Falk, Christi Wagner. Customer service mgr. Gen. Electric Credit Corp., Oklahoma City, 1964-65; office mgr. HLS Inc., Sunnyvale, Calif., 1970-72; personnel/office adminstr. Arthur Andersen & Co., San Jose, Calif., 1971-73; office mgr. Phifer & Schink, C.P.A.s, Mountain View, Calif., 1973-76; mgmt. cons., San Jose, 1976—; mgmt. cons., acting chief fin. officer Allstate Investment Corp., San Jose, 1978-82; mgmt. cons., v.p., chief fin. officer Becket & Co., Inc., 1982—. Mem. Nat. Assn. Female Execs., Am. Soc. Profl. and Exec. Women. Republican. Baptist.

BECKETT, ADELE CECILIA MAAS STEVENS (MRS. GARNER A. BECKETT), civic worker; b. Chgo., May 8, 1900; d. Louis Herman and Mamie (Mayrhofer) Maas; student U. Wash., 1917-18, Washington U., St. Louis, 1922-23; m. Dillon Stevens, Apr. 11, 1918 (dec. Dec. 1953); 1 dau., Barbara (Mrs. John Albert Arnett); m. 2d, Garner A. Beckett, Oct. 28, 1967 (dec. Apr. 1974). Partner, Dillon Stevens & Co. Publicity chmn. John Burroughs Jr. High Sch. PTA, 1934, Los Angeles High Sch. PTA, 1936-37, Euterpe Opera Reading Club, 1937-38; pres. Glaides, 1946, v.p., 1963; finance chmn. Ebell of Los Angeles, 1955-57, sec. creative writing dept., 1962-63, asst. curator dept., 1971-72, chmn., 1973-81, chmn. writer's workshop, 1972-81; mem. Calif. Club, Friends of Claremont Colls., Calif. Inst. Tech. Assos., Postscripts. Recipient award for blood bank work ARC, 1943, various awards for fiction. Mem. English-Speaking Union, Around the World Club. Author: Relatively Speaking, 1981. Home: 621 San Vicente Blvd Apt 209 Santa Monica CA 90402

BECKETT, GRACE, educator; b. Smithfield, Ohio, Oct. 7, 1912; d. Roy Martin and Mary (Hammond) Beckett; A.B., Oberlin Coll., 1934, A.M., 1935; Ph.D., Ohio State U., 1939. Music supr. pub. schs., Kelleys Island, Ohio, 1935-36; grad. asst. econs. Ohio State U., 1936-39; asso. prof. econs. and music Ind. Central Coll., 1939-41; with U. Ill., Champaign-Urbana, 1941—, asst. prof. econs., 1945-51, asso. prof. econs., 1951-73, asso. prof. emerita, 1973—. Mem. Am., Midwest econ. assns., Music Educators Nat. Conf., Econ. History Assn., Music Tchrs. Nat. Assn., Am. Fin. Assn., AAAS, N.Y. Acad. Scis., Ill. Music Educators Assn., Ill. Music Tchrs. Assn., Nat. Sch. Orch. Assn., Oberlin Friends of Art, Am. Hist. Assn., Ohio Acad. History, Ohio, Md. geneal. socs., Ohio, Md. hist. socs., Met. Mus. Art (nat. asso.), Krannert Art Mus. Assos. (U. Ill.), Interlochen (Mich.) Alumni Assn., (life), Winchester-Frederick County (Va.) Hist. Soc., Phi Beta Kappa, Pi Lambda Theta, Phi Chi Theta, Alpha Lambda Delta. Methodist. Club: University of Illinois Women's. Author: Reciprocal Trade Agreements Program, 1941, 2d edit., 1972. Contbr. articles to profl. publs. Address: PO Box 386 Urbana IL 61801

BECKETT, MILDRED LOUISE, educator; b. Leslie, Ark., Feb. 15, 1927; d. Benjamin Frank and Floy Myrtle (West) Holsted; B.A., Okla. Coll. Liberal Arts, 1948; B.A. in Math., Okla. Coll. Liberal Arts, 1949; postgrad. Okla. A. and M. U., summer 1949, St. Mary of the Plains Coll., summer 1968; m. Ralph Beckett, June 10, 1951; children—Connie, Joanne, David, James. Tchr. public schs., Holcomb, Kan., 1948-51, 67, Garden City (Kan.) public schs., 1968-70, Jennie Wilson Grad Sch., 1970-76, 79—. Exhibit chmn. for local artists for show during Bee Empire Days, Garden City, 1977-79; pres. Sand Hills Art Assn., 1977-78, chmn. Art in Park, 1976. Mem. Kan. Edn. Assn., NEA, Garden City Area Ednl. Assn. Republican. Methodist. Home: 1106 Harding St Garden City KS 67846 Office: 1401 Harding St Garden City KS 67846

BECKMAN, PATRICIA ANN, systems analyst; b. Clearwater, Nebr., Feb. 28, 1931; d. Rudolph Frank and Margaret Mary (McCarthy) Funk; A.A., Black Hawk Coll., 1975; B.A., Western Ill. U., 1977; m. Duane George Beckman, June 28, 1952 (dec. 1965); children—Douglas Duane, Annette Marie, Jeffrey Thomas, Debra Lynn, Timothy Joseph. Programmer-analyst, auditing asst., acctg. and personnel asst. First Nat. Bank of Moline (Ill.), 1967-77; programmer-analyst Tex. Eastern Transmission Corp., Houston, 1978-80; systems analyst Cabot Corp., Houston, 1980—. Roman Catholic. Office: 921 Main St Suite 900 Houston TX 77002

BECKNER, MARY KATHRYN, accountant; b. Mendota, Ill., Dec. 5, 1904; d. Edward J. and Mary (Hoerner) Cannon; student pub. schs.; m. Lester W. Beckner, Dec. 5, 1931. Pvt. sec., 1922-41; treas. Wayside Press, Inc., 1941—, also dir.; sec.-treas., dir. Kenneth B. Butler & Asso., 1944—; treas. Butler Typo-Design Research Center, 1951—, Surrey Hill Arabians, Inc.; dir., treas. Packaging Digest Inc., 1964-70. Mem. Red Cross Canteen, Mendota Community Hosp. Aux.; bd. dirs. LaSalle County unit Am. Cancer Soc. Mem. Ill., Mendota chambers commerce, Nat. Council Catholic Women, Nat. Secs. Assn. (Sec. of Yr. Aishi chpt., treas. 1977—), Internat. Arabian Horse Assn. Roman Catholic. Elk. Clubs: Woman's (treas. pub. affairs dept.); Antique Automobile of America (sec.-treas. Mendota). Home: 1312 Burlington St Mendota IL 61342 Office: 700 14th Ave Mendota IL 61342

BEDDINGFIELD, FLORENCE BUICE, assn. exec.; b. Atlanta, Feb. 16, 1918; d. Oscar Jesse and Lillie Viola (Campbell) Buice; A.A. in Liberal Arts, Monroe A&M U., 1939; student in counseling West Ga. Coll., 1974, in bus. adminstrn. and counseling Ga. State U., 1970-74; m. William C. Beddingfield, May 6, 1939; children—Susan B., William C., Cheryl B. Personnel chief USAAF, Warner Robbins, Ga., Sheppard AFB, Tex., 1942-44; auditor, gen. accountant, Atlanta, 1944; personnel counselor U.S. C.E., Sacramento, 1945; Civil Service examiner and trainer, job placement counselor VA, Atlanta, 1945-48; exec. dir. Cobb County Emergency Aid Assn., Inc., Marietta, Ga., 1959—; condr. various seminars; fin. counselor workshops Ridgeview Hosp., Smyrna, Ga., 1978—. Chmn. bd. commrs. Marietta Housing Authority, 1977—; mem. humanities com. Atlanta Regional Commn.; mem. Ga. Bd. Mental Health, Cobb County Bd. Mental Health, Manpower Commrs.; mem. adv. com. Cobb County Adjustment Center; mem. CETA Bd. Commrs. Recipient citation Ga. State Crime Commn., 1975; Recognition award So. Bell, 1976; Service award Superior Ct. Judges of Cobb County, 1976; Outstanding Service award Atlanta Regional Commn., 1978; Citizenship award Smyrna Civitans, 1979; Cobb County gen. assistance grantee, 1973—. Mem. Nat. Conf. Social Workers, Vocat. Rehab. Assn., Nat. Mental Health Assn., Ga. Mental Health Assn., Nat. Assn. Retardation, Smyrna Jr. C. of C., Cobb County Community Council (organizer, sec. 1961, pres. 1972). Republican. Episcopalian. Clubs: K.C., Marietta Optimist, Executive Women's. Contbr. articles to various publs. Home: 619 Serramonte Marietta GA 30067 Office: 737 Church St Suite #360 Marietta GA 30060

BEDELL, CATHERINE BARNES, govt. ofcl.; b. Yakima, Wash., May 18, 1914; d. Charles H. and Pauline (Von Loon) Barnes; M.Ed., U. Wash., 1936; m. Donald W. Bedell, 1970; children—Melinda Ellen, James Collins, May Sullivan. Mem. Wash. Ho. of Reps., 1952-58; mem. Congress from 4th Wash. Dist., 1959-70; presdl. appointee, bd. dirs. Bd. Incorporators, Nat. R.R. Passenger Corp., 1971; chmn. U.S. Internat. Trade Commn., 1971-75, commr., 1975—. Mem. Bus. and Profl. Women, Young Republican Fedn., Exec. Women in Govt., AAUW. Episcopalian. Clubs: Altrusa, Soroptimist. Office: US Internat Trade Commn 701 E St NW Washington DC 20436 *

BEDELL, GAYNELL PACK (MRS. F. KEITH BEDELL), Christian Sci. practitioner; b. Paintsville, Ky.; d. William Reaves and Iuka D. (Welch) Pack; grad. W.Va. Bus. Coll.; m. Charles T. Skeer, 1931 (dec. 1949); children—William Thom, Zoe (Mrs. A. G. Vecchione); m. 2d, Frederick Haller, July 25, 1953 (dec. Apr. 1957); m. 3d, F. Keith Bedell, Nov. 21, 1966. Mgr. fashion shops, 1942-46; star Claire Angrist radio fashion show, Huntington, W.Va., 1942-46; fashion cons., resident rep. Goode-Bridgeman, Inc., N.Y.C., 1946-54; mem. Christian Sci. Ch., practitioner, N.Y.C., 1931—. Pres., 1st Ch. of Christ Scientist, Huntington, W.Va., reader, Flushing, N.Y., 1951-53. Mem. Nat. Fedn. Bus. and Profl. Women's Clubs (pres. Huntington). Home: 25 Sutton Pl S New York NY 10022 Office: 342 Madison Ave New York NY 10017

BEDFORD, MADELEINE ALANN PECKHAM, civic worker; b. Ontario, Calif., Jan. 25, 1910; d. Allen Lewis and Madeleine (Elliott) Peckham; A.B., U. Calif., Berkeley, 1930, M.A., 1937; LL.D., Tex. Christian U., 1973; m. Charles Francis Bedford, Dec. 30, 1930; children—Madeleine Alann, Frances Ellen, Charlotte Jean. Supr. tchr. tng. and counseling, in charge testing Univ. High Sch., U. Calif., Berkeley, 1931-38; tchr. English to fgn. born San Leandro (Calif.) Evening Schs., 1931-38; treas. Tarrant County Day Care Assn., 1953-54; pres. Ft. Worth and Tarrant County council Camp Fire Girls, 1961-63, mem. Nat. council, 1968-75, pres. Nat. council, 1965-68, NGO rep. to UN, 1968-69, nat. bd. dirs., 1960-68, bd. dirs. Houston council, 1971-72, mem. congress of Nat. Camp Fire Girls, 1975—; pres. Ft. Worth Lit. Council, 1963-65; v.p. Tarrant County United Fund and Community Council, 1963-66, mem. exec. com. bd. dirs., 1963—; pres. Ft. Worth chpt. Am. Field Service, 1964-66; chmn. budget sub-com. United Fund, 1959-68, chmn. met. div. Tarrant County, 1970; chmn. speakers tours, films div., United Way Tarrant County Campaign, 1973, chmn. planning and research div., 1973-75; v.p. United Way Met. Tarrant County, 1973-75; mem. exec. com. United Way Tex., 1979—; sec. Tex. United Community Services, 1968-70, v.p., 1970-73, pres., 1973-75; mem. Mid-Am. Regional Vol. Task group United Way Am., mem. nat. com. agy. support, 1975—; Tex. state rep. for UNICEF, 1969—, mem. coordinating bd. for U.S. Com. of UN Childrens Fund, 1981—; chmn. Mayor's Council on Youth Opportunity, 1972-73; del. White House Conf. on Children and Youth, 1970; sec. social services adv. com. Tex. Dept. Human Resources, 1975-76, chmn., 1976-77; mem. nat. bd. Nat. Conf. Social Welfare, 1976—; colleague nat. assembly Nat. Vol. Health and social welfare orgns., 1978—; bd. dirs. Tarrant County chpt. ARC; bd. dirs. United Cerebral Palsy, pres. elect, 1975, pres. Tarrant County Br., 1976—, mem. nat. corp., 1976—, v.p., Tex., 1977—; bd. dirs. Tarrant County Community Action Agy., Tarrant County Community Council, Tex. Social Welfare Assn.; trustee Assn. Grad. Edn. and Research, 1971—; trustee Tex. Christian U., also bd. visitors; trustee Tex. Coll. Osteo. Medicine Found., 1980—; mem. adv. council Sch. Social Work, U. Tex., Austin, 1980—; mem. adv. council for fin. assistance Tex. Dept. Human Resources, 1980—; pres. Womens Haven Tarrant County, 1979-81, bd. dirs., 1979—; mem. exec. com. Community Trust Tarrant County, 1981—; bd. dirs. Family and Individual Services Tarrant County, 1981—, Ft. Worth Girls Club, 1979—; mem. adv. council for adult basic edn. Ft. Worth Ind. Sch. Dist., 1976—; fellow Forum of Ft. Worth, 1981—. Recipient Gulick award, 1961, Wo-he-lo award, 1968 Camp Fire Girls; award of Excellence for Outstanding Leadership and Service Tarrant County Community Council, 1964, Civic award First Lady Ft. Worth Altrusa, 1966, Hercules award for Outstanding Vol. Leadership in Social Welfare United Way, 1977. Mem. Ft. Worth Lecture Found., DAR, Mortar Board, Family Service Assn. (bd. dirs.), Phi Beta Kappa (pres. Ft. Worth 1958-59), Alpha Chi Omega, Pi Sigma Alpha. Episcopalian. Club: Ft. Worth Woman's (past pres. history sect.). Home: 7 Westover Rd Fort Worth TX 76107

BEDFORD, RUTH ALICE HAEDIKE (MRS. EDWIN GARRARD BEDFORD), librarian; b. Chgo.; d. William Henry and Alice (Lohr) Haedike; student Beloit Coll., 1932-33; B.S., U. Ill., 1936, M.S., 1954, postgrad.; m. Edwin Garrard Bedford, June 6, 1942; children—David Edwin, Ellen Louise. Instr. U. Ill. Library, Urbana, 1954-64; asst. prof. library sci. U. Utah Libraries, Salt Lake City, 1964-68; asso. librarian Butler Library, State U. Coll., Buffalo, 1968-79, mem. personnel com. tech. services div., 1972-75, chmn., 1974-75, mem. faculty advisory council instructional resources, 1971-73. Mem. tech. services com. Western N.Y. Library Resources Council, 1968-73. Mem. State U. N.Y. Librarians' Assn., Am. Assn. U. Profs., ALA, Kenan Center (charter mem.), Delta Phi Alpha. Club: Order Eastern Star. Home: 905 Charlesgate Circle East Amherst NY 14051

BEDNORZ, MILDRED WEBER, nurse; b. Victoria, Tex., Aug. 9, 1932; d. Victor Henry and Leona Annie (Wieland) Weber; diploma St. Josephs Sch. Nursing, Houston, 1952; B.S. in Nursing, Dominican Coll., Houston, 1953; m. Edward Julius Bednorz, Sept. 2, 1955; children—Edward Michael, Nick Alan, John Vincent, Joseph Victor, Robert Wayne, Douglas Patrick. Pediatric staff nurse St. Josephs Hosp., Houston, 1952-54; staff, head nurse Victoria (Tex.) Hosp., 1954-60, 63; office nurse, Victoria, 1960-62; staff and head nurse Detar Hosp., Victoria, 1965-75, asst. dir. nursing, 1975-79; asst. dir., head nurse Crossroads Surg. Center, Victoria, 1981—; nursing cons.; Doctors Hosp., Victoria. Chmn. com. 100, Victoria Ind. Sch. Dist., 1979, mem. adv. bd. vocat. sch., 1977-79. Mem. Victoria C. of C., Associated Nursing Alumni Houston, Tex. Assn. Post Anesthesia Nurses, Am. Soc. Post Anesthesia Nurses, VFW Aux. Roman Catholic. Home: 701 Northgate Rd Victoria TX 77904 Office: Crossroads Surg Center 1903 E Sabine St Victoria TX 77901

BEE, ANNA COWDEN, educator; b. Birmingham, Ala., Feb. 17, 1922; d. Porter Guthrie and Marion Irene (McCurry) Cowden; A.B., Samford U., 1944; student Chalif Sch. Dance, N.Y.C., 1950-54; m. Alon Wilton Bee, Oct. 21, 1942; children—Anna Margaret Bee Foote, Alon Wilton. Mem. faculty Byram High Sch., Jackson, 1945-52; mem. faculty Hinds Jr. Coll., Raymond, Miss., 1952—, dir. Hi-Steppers, girls' precision dance group; chaperone Miss Mississippi to Miss Am. Pageant; condr. charm clinics for teenagers; judge beauty pageants. Bd. dirs. Multiple Sclerosis Soc., Jackson, 1966-72; state chmn. Miss. Easter Seal Soc. campaign, 1966, 79; chmn. women's div. United Way, Jackson, 1973. Named Woman of Achievement, Jackson Bus. and Profl. Women's Club, 1967-78; disting. faculty of the yr. award Hinds Jr. Coll., 1981; Miss. Legislature commendation for contbn. to youth, 1981. Mem. Nat. Faculty Dance Educators Am., Dance Masters Am., Miss. Edn. Assn., Miss. Assn. Health and Phys. Edn., Beta Sigma Omicron. Democrat. Baptist. Producer halftime shows Gator Bowl, 1958, 64, 81, Sugar Bowl, 1960, Hall of Fame Bowl, 1977, 79. Home: 304 Alta Woods Blvd Jackson MS 39154 Office: Hinds Jr Coll Raymond MS 39154

BEE, HELEN LUCILLE, psychologist; b. Tacoma, Apr. 27, 1939; d. Austin Edward and Susan Lee (Emmons) Bee; B.A. magna cum laude, Radcliffe Coll., 1960; Ph.D. in Psychology, Stanford U., 1964; m. George Chase Douglas, Mar. 19, 1972; children—Rex, Arwen. Asst. prof. psychology Clark U., Worcester, Mass., 1964-65; asst. prof., then asso. prof. U. Wash., Seattle, 1965-72, sr. research asso. dept. psychology and Sch. Nursing, 1979; cons. United Cerebral Palsy, Rand Corp., Danforth Found. Chmn. Sch. Bd. Orcas Sch. Dist., Eastsound, Wash., 1974-77, Happy Valley Sch. Bd., 1980—. Mem. Soc. Research in Child Devel., Am. Psychol. Assn., Nat. Council Family Relations, Theosophical Soc. Seattle, Happy Valley Found. (dir. 1979—), Orcas Island Found. (dir. 1972-78). Author: The Developing Child, 1975, 78, 81; (with Sandra K. Mitchell) The Developing Person, 1979; (with John Houston and David Rimm) Invitation to Psychology, 1979, 83. Home: 4535 NE 94th St Seattle WA 98115 Office: CDMRC Residence WJ-10 Univ Wash Seattle WA 98195

BEE, MARY RICE, advt. agy. exec.; b. Homer, N.Y., Aug. 11, 1933; d. John Moak and Isabella A. (Gilkerson) Rice; student Cortland (N.Y.) State Tchrs. Coll., 1951-54, Russell Sage Coll., 1968; children—Heather Jo Bee Chestnut, Edward R., Jr. Co-founder, v.p. Bee Bus. Forms, Schenectady, 1964-68; sales mgr. Gideon Putnam Hotel, Saratoga Springs, N.Y., 1968-71; founder, 1971, since pres. Madison North Mktg. Communications Agy.; dir. Flah's; mem. adj. faculty Union Coll., Schenectady. Former mem. bd. United Cerebral Palsy Schenectady County, Ind. Living of Capital Dist., United Way Schenectady County, Jr. Achievement Capital Dist.; past trustee Schenectady Mus.; bd. dirs. Schenectady chpt. ARC, Hospice of Schenectady County, Salvation Army of Schenectady County, Freedom Forum of Schenectady, Albany League Arts adv. council to Bd. Regents N.Y. State, Pvt. Industry Council. Recipient Crystal Prism award 2d dist. Am. Advertisers Fedn., 1975. Mem. Northeastern Fedn. Profl. Communicators (Silver medal 1975), Schenectady County C. of C. (pres. 1979). Democrat. Mem. Dutch Reformed Ch. Home: Synder Rd Alplaus NY 12008 Office: 6 Union St Schenectady NY 12305

BEE, SARAH ANN, rehab. adminstr.; b. N.Y.C., Oct. 4, 1947; d. Edward F. and Toby Palasz; B.S., Boston U., 1969, M.S., 1975; m. David W. Bee, Aug. 2, 1970. Intern, VA Hosp., Boston, 1974-75; counselor Mass. Rehab. Commn., Boston, 1975-77; rehab. specialist Internat. Rehab. Assos., Inc., Boston, 1977-78, service unit adminstr., 1978—; attended Pres. Com. on Employment of the Handicapped, Washington, 1981. Cert. rehab. counselor. Mem. Nat. Rehab. Assn., Nat. Rehab. Counseling Assn., Mass. Rehab. Assn. (pres. elect), Nat. Assn. Rehab. Profls. in Pvt. Sector. Home: 61 Royal St Allston MA 02134 Office: 200 Unicorn Park Dr Woburn MA 01801

BEECH, OLIVE ANN MELLOR, aircraft co. exec.; b. Waverly, Kans., Sept. 25, 1903; d. Frank B. and Suzannah (Miller) Mellor; ed. public schs., Paola; student pvt. schs. and night courses; D.Sc. in Bus. Adminstrn. (hon.), Southwestern Coll., 1954; m. Walter H. Beech, Feb. 24, 1930; children—Suzanne Mellor (Mrs. Thomas N. Warner), Mary Lynn (Mrs. William L. Oliver, Jr.). Office mgr., bookkeeper Staley Elec. Co., Augusta, Kans., 1921-24; office mgr. and sec. to Walter H. Beech, pres. Travel Air Co., Wichita, Kans., 1924-29; founder with husband Beech Aircraft Corp., Wichita, 1932, sec., treas., dir., 1932-50, pres., chief exec. officer, chmn. bd., dir., 1950-68, chmn. bd., chief exec. officer, 1968—, also chmn. bd., chief exec. officer subs. orgns.; dir. Fourth Nat. Bank and Trust Co., Wichita; dir., mem. exec. com. Raytheon Co., 1980—. Adv. bd. Nat. Air and Space Found. of Smithsonian Instn.; mem. adv. bds. other aero. museums; bd. dirs. Nat. 4-H Found., United Fund Wichita and Sedgwick County, Wichita Symphony Soc., Nat. Jr. Achievement, Met. Wichita Council, Wichita Area Devel. Council; trustee Southwestern Coll., Winfield, Kans., Wichita State U. Endowment Assn., St. Francis Sch. Nursing Council; trustee Wesley Med. Center, 18 years, now trustee emeritus; chmn. bd. trustees Wichita Art Assn.; nat. trustee Nat. Symphony, 1973-75; bd. dirs., mem. exec. com. Music Theatre Wichita. Participated in Am. Bankers Assn. Forum in panel discussion on Women's Part in War Effort, N.Y.C. 1943. Chosen by N.Y. Times as one of 12 most disting. women U.S., 1943; recipient Lady Hay Drummond-Hay Trophy for 1952, as woman having done most for aviation; Wright Bros. Civilian award, 1980; Sands of Time Kitty Hawk Civilian award, 1980; inducted into Internat. Forest of Friendship Memory Ln., 1978, Aviation Hall of Fame, 1981; named Kansan of Year by Native Sons and Daus. of Kans., 1958; Dirs.' medal Freedoms Found. Valley Forge, 1953; Over the Years award Wichita C. of C., 1963; Nat. Angel Flight award, 1968; Meritorious award Nat. Bus. Aircraft Assn., 1969; named one of Am.'s ten most successful bus. women by nation's bus. and fin. editors, 1970; one of nation's most outstanding women Am. Mothers Com., 1970; Disting. Service award Bus. Aviation, 1971; one of ten highest-ranking women in big bus. Fortune mag., 1973, 78; recipient Disting. Service citation U. Kans., 1974; elected Elder Statesman of Aviation, Nat. Aero. Assn., 1974. Mem. Women's Aero. Assn., Nat. Aero. Assn. (Wright Bros. Meml. trophy 1980), U.S., Kans., Wichita chambers commerce, AIAA, Nat. Aviation Hall of Fame (bd. nominations), Nat. Fedn. Bus. and Profl. Women (dir.). Methodist (trustee). Clubs: Soroptimist (hon. life dir. Wichita), Wichita Country, Wichita, Wings (Disting. Achievement award 1981). Home: 48 Mission Rd Eastborough Wichita KS 67207 Office: Beech Aircraft Corp Wichita KS 67201

BEECHER, RUTH DOWNTON, assn. exec.; b. Manchester, N.H., Dec. 26, 1936; d. Ray Eugene and Dorothy (Muir) Downton; student Keene State Coll., 1954-57, N.H. Coll., 1979-81, Inst. for Orgnl. Mgmt., U. Del., 1981; m. Floyd Beecher, May 10, 1958; children—Deborah, Thomas, David, Robert. With Amoskeng Nat. Bank, Manchester, N.H., 1957-59; with Waumbec Mills, Inc., Manchester, 1972-79; dir. membership services, v.p. small bus. devel. Greater Manchester C. of C., 1979—; bus. cons. SBA, 1980—, active core exec., 1980—, mem. Small Bus. Adv. Bd. State of N.H. Trainer leaders Girl Scouts U.S.A., 1972-80; mem exec. bd. Service Corp. Ret. Execs. (SCORE), 1980—; bd. dirs. WON, Inc., Manchester, 1981—; active United Way, 1979-81; chmn. Heart Fund, 1979; key person Manchester Federated Arts, 1980-81. Recipient SBA Outstanding Service award, 1980, United Way Appreciation award, 1980, 81. Mem. Am., New Eng., N.H. C. of C. execs., Am. Bus. Women's Assn., Nat. Assn. Female Execs., Inst. Organizational Mgmt., Nat. Notary Assn. Club: N.H. Opera League, Concord Luncheon Group. Home: 5 Woodlawn Ave Bedford NH 03102 Office: 57 Market St Manchester NH 03101

BEEDLE, LYNN SIMPSON, educator; b. Orland, Calif., Dec. 7, 1917; s. Graville L. and Carol (Simpson) B.; B.S., U. Calif., 1941; M.S., Lehigh U., 1949, Ph.D., 1952; m. Ella Marie Grimes, Oct. 20, 1946; children—Lynn, Helen, Jonathan, David, Edward. With Todd-Calif. Shipbldg. Corp., Richmond, Calif., 1941; instr. Postgrad. Sch., U.S. Naval Acad., officer-in-charge Underwater Explosions Research div. Norfolk (Va.) Naval Shipyard, 1941-47; dir. Lehigh U. Fritz Engring. Lab., Bethlehem, Pa., 1960—, prof. civil engring., 1958-77, Univ. Disting. prof., 1978—. Served with USNR, 1941-47. Recipient Robinson award Lehigh U., 1952, Hillman award, 1973; E.E. Howard award ASCE, 1963, Research prize, 1956; Silver medal Am. Welding Soc., 1957; Constrn. award Engring. News Record, 1965, 73; Regional Tech. Meeting award Am. Iron and Steel Inst., 1958; T.R. Higgins award Am. Inst. Steel Constrn., 1973; Engr. of Year award Lehigh Valley sect. Nat. Soc. Profl. Engrs., 1977. Fellow ASCE (hon. mem.; dir. 1974-77; dir. Lehigh Valley sect. 1977—, past chmn. structural div. exec. com., past mem. research com.); mem. Structural Stability Research Council (life mem., chmn. 1966-70, dir. 1970—), Welding Research Council, Am. Inst. Steel Constrn., Nat. Acad. Engring., Council on Tall Bldgs. and Urban Habitat (chmn. 1970-76, dir. 1976—), Internat. Assn. Bridge and Structural Engring. (hon.). Presbyn. (elder 1957—). Author: Plastic Design of Steel Frames, 1958; (with others) Structural Steel Design, 2d edit., 1974; editor-in-chief: Planning and Design of Tall Buildings, 5 vols., 1978-81; contbr. articles to profl. jours. Home: 102 Cedar Rd Hellertown PA 18055 Office: Fritz Engring Lab Lehigh Univ Bethlehem PA 18015 *

BEEMAN, NANCY LEE, mfg. co. exec.; b. Fairview, W.Va., Dec. 15, 1936; d. Ord Milburn and Nellie Ermel (Tennant) Billingslea; student public schs. Ambridge, Pa.; m. June 29, 1954; children—Lawrence W., Richard Allen, Diana Lynn. Promotion supr. Beaver (Pa.) County Times, 1967-74; office mgr., bookkeeper Easter Seal Soc. Crippled Children and Adults, Beaver, 1974-75; controller, corp. sec. Internat. Titanium Corp., New Brighton, Pa., 1975—. Dir. deaf dept. Bible Bapt. Ch., Mars, Pa., 1978—, mem. budget com. Home: 125 Springer Plan Freedom PA 15042 Office: PO Box 192 New Brighton PA 15066

BEEMER, MARLAYNE, engring. and constrn. co. ofcl.; b. Sedalia, Mo.; d. Fordyce Carlton and Fannie Ethel (Williams) Close; A.A., Orange Coast Coll., 1973; m. Richard L. Beemer, Feb. 2, 1962; children—Carla Henderson, Marla Franklin, Lauren Beemer, Richard A. Salesperson, instr. The Real Estaters, Costa Mesa, Calif., 1964-67; instr., artist Marlayne's, Costa Mesa, 1967-71; sec. to controller Santa Fe Engring. & Constrn. Co., Orange, Calif., 1971-74, exec. sec. to pres., 1974-78, asst. to pres., 1978—; lectr. in field. Cert. in real estate, Calif. Mem. Costa Mesa Art League, Desk & Derrick Profl. Orgn. Office: 505 S Main St PO Box 1401 Orange CA 92668

BEER, ALICE STEWART (MRS. JACK ENGEMAN), musician, educator; b. Redwood Falls, Minn., Sept. 29, 1912; d. Robert and Isabel (Montgomery) Stewart; Mus.B., Northwestern U., 1934, Mus.M., 1952; postgrad. Johns Hopkins U., 1954, 60, Mexico City Coll., 1956 U. Md., 1957; m. Jack Engeman, Dec. 14, 1974; children by previous marriage—W. Robert, Jane K. Beer Mosher, Elizabeth S. Beer-Stevens. Tchr. public schs., Lawton, Mich., 1934-39, Battle Creek, Mich., 1949-51; tchr. Balt. Public Schs., 1951-53, supr. music, 1953-77; tchr. summer sessions various colls. and univs., 1957—; adj. faculty, prof. Peabody Inst., John's Hopkins U., Balt., 1981—. Mem. Nat. Fedn. Press Women, Music Educators Nat. Conf., Md. Music Educators Assn., Md. Fedn. Press Women, Trust Historic Preservation, Soc. Preservation Md. Antiquities, Md. Hist. Soc., Balt. Mus. Art, Balt. Symphony Assn., Phi Beta. Democrat. Presbyterian. Clubs: Towson Univ., Women's (Johns Hopkins U.). Author: Teaching Suggestions, Birchard Music Series II and III, 1962; Teaching Music: What, How and Why, 1973; Teaching Music to the Exceptional Child: A Handbook for Mainstreaming, 1980; Teaching Music, 1982; Patriotic Color Sound Filmstrips, 1967-69. contbr. articles to profl. jours. Home: 611 Debaugh Ave Towson MD 21204 Office: Music Edn Dept Peabody Inst Johns Hopkins U Baltimore MD 21202

BEER, JEANETTE MARY AYRES, educator; b. Wellington, N.Z.; d. Alexander Samuel and Una Doreen (Castle) Scott; B.A., Victoria U., N.Z., 1954, M.A. 1st class, 1955; B.A. 1st class, Oxford U., Eng., 1958, M.A., 1962; Ph.D. (fellow), Columbia U., 1967; m. Colin Gordon Beer, June 27, 1959; children—Stephen James Colin, Jeremy Michael Alexander. Asst. lectr. French, Victoria U., Wellington, 1956; lectrice French and English, U. Montpellier (France), 1958-59; instr. French, Otago U., Dunedin, N.Z., 1963-64, Barnard Coll., Columbia U., N.Y.C., 1966-68; asst. prof. French, Fordham U., Bronx, N.Y., 1968-69, asso. prof., 1969-76, prof., 1976-80, acting asso. dean Thomas More Coll., 1972-73, dir. medieval studies, 1972-80; prof. French, head dept. fgn. langs. and lits. Purdue U., West Lafayette, Ind., 1980—; mem. nat. bd. cons. Nat. Endowment for Humanities, 1977—. Nat. Endowment for Humanities grantee, 1975; AATF research fellow, 1979. Mem. MLA, Medieval Acad., Internat. Arthurian Soc., Soc. Rencesvals, Comparative Lit. Assn., Am. Assn. Tchrs. French. Anglican. Author: Villehardouin—Epic Historian, 1968; A Medieval Caesar, 1976; Medieval Fables-Marie de France, 1981; Narrative Conventions of Truth in the Middle Ages, 1981; gen. editor Teaching Language through Literature, 1971—; contbr. articles to profl. jours. Mem. adv. bd. Dictionary of the Middle Ages, 1981—. Office: Dept Fgn Langs and Lits Purdue Univ West Lafayette IN 47907

BEERBOHM, CYNTHIA JENNIFER, advt. ofcl.; b. Detroit, Sept. 6, 1940; d. Marvin and Regina Cynthia (Barfknecht) B.; B.A. in Speech (Ford Fund scholar), U. Mich., 1962; postgrad. Sch. of Drama, Yale U., 1963-64, Northwood Inst. Extension, 1969. Media buyer Young and Rubicam Internat., Detroit, 1968-73; sr. media buyer Marschalk Advt., Cleve., 1973-75; sales account exec. Sta. WUAB-TV, Cleve., and Sta. KDKA-TV, Pitts., 1975-76; v.p., asso. media dir. Griswold-Eshleman Co., Cleve., 1976—. Public relations com. Greater Cleve. council Boy Scouts Am. Mem. Cleve. Assn. Broadcasters (bd. dirs.), Cleve. Advt. Club, Am. Soc. Profl. and Exec. Women, AFTRA (N.Y. chpt.), Actors Equity, Zeta Phi Eta. Clubs: Advt., Broadcast. Office: 55 Public Sq Cleveland OH 44113

BEERS, DORIS CREIGHTON, realtor; b. Enfield, N.H., Aug. 6, 1908; d. Harris Edgar and Ada (French) Creighton; grad. public schs.; m. Robert Clayton Beers, Sept. 22, 1934 (dec. Sept. 1965); children—Diane Elaine (Mrs. Edward C. Schmults), Bradford B. Head sec. to chmn. Democratic State Com. N.H., 1929-30; sec. Gen. Motors Acceptance Corp., 1930-32, J.R. Poole, Boston, 1932-36; saleswoman Town & Country Homes, Boston, 1956-58; founder Cedar Realty, Wellesley Hills, Mass., 1958, owner, 1958-81. Sec., Wellesley (Mass.) ARC Fund Drive, 1955; pres. Melrose (Mass.) Jr. High Sch. PTA, 1953; chmn. bus. Wellesley United Fund Drive, 1974. Mem. Greater Boston Real Estate Bd., Nat. Assn. Realtors, West of Boston Realtors (sec. Council 1966), Nat. Assn. Women Realtors, Wellesley C. of C. Congregationalist. (past sec. guild Melrose Highlands). Clubs: Wellesley Republican, Wellesley Women's. Home: 27 Livermore Rd Wellesley Hills MA 02181 Office: 33 Washington St Wellesley MA 02181

BEERS, HELEN BOYCE LAUGHLIN, service co. exec.; b. Simms, Tex., June 24, 1935; d. Harvey O'Dell and Mamie Pearl (Jackson) Tidwell; student Massey Sch. of Real Estate, 1968; m. Cecil Laughlin, Dec. 24, 1961 (dec. 1967); children—Grant Hunter, Lowry Ashe; m. 2d, Carl Keith Beers, Mar. 21, 1972. Personnel clk. Tex. Agrl. Extension Agy., College Station, 1953-55, Sun Oil Co., Dallas, 1955-56; personnel GAO, Washington, 1956-57; sec. to pres. Stekoll Petroleum Co., Dallas, 1957-58; personnel clk. HEW, Dallas, 1958-59; co-founder, pres. Apt. Selector, Inc., Dallas, 1959—; instr. So. Methodist U., 1969-75. Mem. Nat. (dir. 1977-78), Tex. (dir. 1969-72), Tarrant County (treas. 1976-77, exec. v.p. 1977-78, Mem. of Year, 1975, 76, Spl. award for outstanding contbns. 1978), Dallas (sec. 1969-71, treas. 1971-72, Service award, lectr. 1968), Houston, San Diego, Atlanta, Austin, San Antonio apt. assns., Sales and Mktg. Execs. Republican. Methodist. Office: 4123 N Central Expressway Dallas TX 75204

BEERS, SANDRA DARIA, internat. banker; b. Niskayuna, N.Y., Aug. 4, 1952; d. Milford Charles and Alma Bernadette (Gaynor) Beers; A.B., Mt. Holyoke Coll., 1974. Global creit trainee Chase Manhattan Bank N.A., N.Y.C., 1974-75, fin. analyst Banco del Comercio, Bogota, Colombia, 1975; asst. treas., relationship mgr. East European Lending, 1975-77, 2d v.p., dep. rep., Moscow, 1977-79, team mgr. credit devel. program, 1979-82, v.p., mgr. mktg. devel., London, 1982—. Home: 35 Kensington Pl London W8 7PR England Office: Woolgate House Coleman St London Ec 2P 2HD London England

BEESON, BETTY SPILLERS, educator; b. Muncie, Ind., Sept. 30, 1930; d. George W. and Gladys Elizabeth (Mills) Spillers; B.S., Ball State Tchrs. Coll., 1954; M.S., U. Omaha, 1963; Ed.D., U. Nebr., 1975; m. John D. Beeson, Feb. 1, 1952. Tchr., Salina (Kans.) Public Schs., 1954-59; instr. edn. U. Omaha, 1963-66; instr. edn. Ball State U., Muncie, Ind., 1969-70, asso. prof., 1975—; founder Muncie Children's Mus.; workshop presenter. Pres. bd. dirs. United Day Care Center, Muncie; bd. dirs. Home Learning Center, Muncie. Mem. Muncie Assn. Edn. Young Children (past v.p.), Nat. Assn. Edn. Young Children, Ind. Assn. Edn. Young Children (regional rep.), Assn. Childhood Edn., Assn. Tchr. Educators, Kappa Delta Pi, Phi Delta Kappa, Alpha Chi Omega, Kappa Kappa Kappa. Republican. Methodist. Club: USAF Officers Wives (dir.). Contbr. articles to profl. jours. Home: 3204 Twickingham Dr Muncie IN 47304 Office: Tchrs Coll Ball State U Muncie IN 47306

BEESON, MARY RUTH (PETE), personnel mgmt. cons.; b. Glen Rose, Tex., Nov. 15, 1913; d. Quentin Orestes and Maude Elma (Embree) Gaither; student Wright's Law Sch., 1931, U. Tex., 1934, San Antonio Coll., 1937, St. Mary's U., 1937-39, Am. U., 1952-53; m. Charles Edward Beeson, Nov. 15, 1940; children—Peter Gaither Embree, Caroline Jane. Exec. asst. to state dir. of ops., Works Progress Adminstrn., San Antonio, 1935-40; certifying officer, adminstrv. asst. Civilian Personnel Office, Army Air Force, San Antonio Aviation Cadet Center, 1941-46; personnel officer IRS, Washington, 1957-63, employment officer, Austin Service Center, 1963-74, chmn. Fed. Women's Program Planning Com., 1963-68, chmn. Equal Employment Opportunity Planning Com., Austin Service Center, 1963-73, mem. regional commr.'s adv. com. on Fed. Women's Program, IRS, Dallas, Tex., 1972-74; cons. in personnel mgmt., Austin, 1976—; cons. on curriculum, Camp Gary Job Corps, 1965. Chmn. Parent Edn. Com., Falls Church Schs., 1952-54; mem. exec. com. Community Coordinated Child Care Com., Austin, 1968-72; mem. adv. commn. to Tex. Legis. Council's study on the handicapped, Austin, 1970-73; mem. adv. com. on vocat. office edn. to Austin Ind. Sch. Dist., 1965-69; chmn. mayor's Com. on Devel. Child Care, Austin, 1970-75; chmn. Austin Mayor's Commn. on Status of Women, 1970-75, mem., 1975—; mem. citizens adv. bd. Travis County Juvenile Bd., 1981—. Recipient Outstanding Service to the Deaf award Tex. Edn. Agy., 1967, Fed. Woman's Award Bd. citation, Disting. IRS Worker for the Handicapped award IRS Commr., 1972, Pres.'s Com. on Employment Handicapped award, 1974. Mem. Internat. Personnel Mgmt. Assn., Austin Personnel Assn., Am. Mgmt. Assn. Unitarian. Inventor: Hycab, insulated coaster, car wastebasket. Home and Office: 2700 Valley Springs Rd Austin TX 78746

BEFAME, JEANNETTE, reporter, writer; b. Wahpeton, N.D., July 15, 1919; d. Frederick and Sykea (Ashton) Befame; A.B., Stanford, 1941; m. John Allen Sontheimer, Aug. 10, 1968 (dec.); m. 2d, W. Gordon Eustice, May 7, 1976. Reporter, San Francisco News, 1941, Sacramento Union, 1942; now newspaper feature writer-reporter San Jose (Calif.) Mercury-News; radio work, news reporter, interviews, San Francisco, 1947; TV guest appearances, 1956; during World War II wrote newscasts for overseas. Del. Asian-Am. Journalists Conf. at East-West Center in Hawaii, 1965. Sec. Santa Clara County unit Am. Cancer Soc. Recipient (1st woman) Edward McQuade Meml. award for outstanding pub. service in journalism, 1955, Top Story award, met. dailies div. Calif. State Fair, 1956, Theta Sigma Phi Matrix award, 1964. Mem. Am. Assn. U. Women, Calif. Press Women (chartering pres. peninsula dist.), Stanford Alumni Assn. (sec. San Jose area 1962-63), Women in Communications (chpt. organizer, 1st pres. 1960, pres. Palo Alto chpt. 1975-76), Sigma Delta Chi (dir. No. Calif. chpt.). Club: San Francisco Press. Home: 1560 Plateau Ave Los Altos CA 94022 Office: San Jose Mercury-News San Jose CA 95125

BEGELMAN, HEDDA JOAN, psychotherapist; b. Bronx, N.Y., June 5, 1939; d. Reuben and Edith (Fink) B.; B.S., Adelphi U., 1960; M.S.W., Columbia U., 1965. Social worker Sheltering Arms Children's Services, N.Y.C., 1965-67; psychiat. social worker, Girls Town, N.Y.C., 1967-69, Mid-Nassau Guidance Center, Hicksville, N.Y., 1969-76, Hempstead (N.Y.) Consultation Ctr., 1969-74, Mid-Nassau Family Counseling Ctr., Hicksville, 1969-76; pvt. practice psychotherapy, Farmingdale, N.Y., 1975—; speaker on sexuality various univs. Vol., Am. Cancer Soc. Cert. in psychotherapy Ind. Bronx Consultation Center; cert. in hypnosis, L.I. Soc. Clin. Hypnosis; lic. cert. social worker, N.Y. Mem. Nat. Assn. Social Workers, Acad. Cert. Social Workers. Home and Office: 3 Dolphin Dr Farmingdale NY 11735

BEGG, DEBBIE ANN, nurse; b. Pitts., June 20, 1951; d. Miles G. and Margaret Ann Bawden; R.N., Pitts. Hosp., 1972; B.S. in Health Services, Point Park Coll., Pitts., 1982; m. Peter R. Begg, Oct. 16, 1971; children—Peter, Brian, Allison. Staff nurse Middlesex Gen. Hosp., New Brunswick, N.J., 1972-73; charge nurse Forbes Health System, Pitts., 1973-78; coordinator med. div. ICM Bus. Sch., Pitts., 1978—; CPR and first aid instr., 1978—. Sec., Newmyer Sch. PTA, Pitts., 1980-82. Recipient Vol. Service award ARC, 1981. Mem. Am. Assn. Med. Assts. (chmn. continuing edn. com. Allegheny County 1981-82, pres.-elect 1982—, surveyor curriculum rev. bd.), Pitts. Hosp. Alumni Assn. Roman Catholic. Home: 8104 St Lawrence St Pittsburgh PA 15218 Office: 10 Wood St Pittsburgh PA 15222

BÉGIN, MONIQUE, Canadian minister nat. health and welfare b. Rome Mar. 1, 1936 (parents Canadian citizens); d. Lucien and Maria Ludovica (Van Havre) B.; M.A. in Sociology, U. Montreal; postgrad. U. Paris, McGill U.; Ph.D. in Law (hon.), St. Thomas U. (N.B., Can.), 1976. Exec. sec. Royal Commn. Status of Women; adminstrv. research br. CRTC; mem. Ho. of Commons from Montreal-St.-Michel, 1972-79, Saint-Léonard-Anjou, 1979—; minister nat. revenue, 1976-77; minister nat. health and welfare, 1977-79, 80—; del. Commonwealth Conf., 1973, UN Gen. Assembly; head Canadian del. Colombo Plan. Co-chmn. nat. conv. Liberal Party, 1973; v.p. Nat. Liberal Caucus, 1975—; founding mem. Fedn. Que. Women; bd. dirs. Canadian Human Rights Fedn. Address: House of Commons 443-S Ottawa ON K1A 0A6 Canada also Dept Nat Health And Welfare Brooke Claxton Bldg Ottawa ON K1A 0K9 Canada

BEHL, MARJORIE, painter; b. Pocahontas, Ark.; ed. Collins Sch. Art, Layton Art Inst., Calif. Coll. Arts and Crafts, Coll. William and Mary. Exhibited in shows at Gibbes Gallery, Charleston, S.C., also juried shows, 1958, Norfolk Mus. Art, 1959, 66, de Young Mus., San Francisco, 1957, Little Rock Art Mus., 1958, Va. Mus. Fine Arts, 1957, 59, 60, Winston-Salem Mus. Fine Arts, Fla. State Water Color Show, 1971, Hermitage Mus., numerous others; one-man shows include: Norfolk Mus., Va. State Mus.; works represented in permanent collections: Borden Co., U. Va., Charlottesville, Valentine Mus. Art, Richmond, Va. State Mus., Va. Nat. Bank, Walter Chrysler Mus., City of Norfolk, Norfolk Public Sch. Collection, Va. Nat. Bank, also other public and pvt. collections; tchr. Norfolk Collegiate Sch.; judge Venice (Fla.) Art Center W. Coast Watercolor Show, 1980. Recipient 1st watercolor prize Ark. State Mus., 1957, awards Virginia Beach Boardwalk Exhbn., 1963, 64, Tidewater ann. Norfolk Mus., 1957, 65. Mem. Soc. Western Art, Virginia Beach Art Assn., Tidewater Art Assn., Sarasota Art Assn. Address: Apt 809 Westminster-Canterbury 3100 Shore Dr Virginia Beach VA 23451

BEHME, GERALDINE CAMILLERI, retail exec.; b. Ogden, Utah, Dec. 22, 1919; d. Gerald Miller and Catherine Elizabeth (Pottiger) Steed; grad. high sch.; m. Robert Lee Behme, July 16, 1982; children by previous marriage—Jean Kay Crawford, Joan Faye, William Gi-more, Pauline Ross, Cheri Foley, Bruce Camilleri. With Los Gatos Aviaries (Calif.), 1944-50; presented bird shows, 1950-52; owner Andy's Pet Shop, San Jose, Calif., 1952—; mng. dir. Am. Pet Shows, Los Angeles and San Francisco, 1980—; bd. dirs. Pet Industry Joint Adv. Council, Washington, 1976—; mem. Animal Adv. Com. Santa Clara County, 1982—; bd. dirs. United Cerebral Palsy; mem. Calif. Pet Bird Adv. Com., 1974—; mem. Santa Clara County Task Force Humane Treatment of Animals, 1979-80; Named Woman of Yr., Am. Bus. Women's Assn., Palo Alto, Calif., 1980; recipient Edward B. Price award Western World Pet Supply Assn., 1981. Mem. San Jose Hist. Soc., San Jose Symphony Assn. Club: Soroptimists. Office: 1280 The Alameda San Jose CA 95126

BEHR, MARION RAY, artist, author; b. Rochester, N.Y., Sept. 12, 1939; d. Justin Max and Sophie Gusta (Koffler) Rosenfeld; B.Art Edn., Syracuse U., 1961, M.F.A., 1962; m. Omri Marc Behr, June 24, 1962; children—Dawn Marcy Yael, Darrin Justin Mason, Dana Marisa Jana. Freelance contbr. illustrations for stories, crafts, mag. covers and toy designs to nat. mags. including McCall's, Good Housekeeping, Lady's Circle, 1962-77; artist; works exhibited Contemporary Am. Artists, Scarsdale, N.Y., 1964, Am. Women Artists, Douglass Coll., 1977; creator survey Women Working Home—the Invisible Workforce, 1978; pres. Women Working Home, Inc., Edison, N.J., 1980—; condr. workshops; books include: (with others) Women Working Home: the Homebased Business Guide and Directory, 1981; illustrator: Jewish Holiday Book, 1977; extensive radio and TV appearances rep. Nat. Alliance Homebased Businesswomen. Mem. Kean for Gov. campaign, 1981; mem. White House Conf. on Free Enterprise Zones, 1982. Syracuse U. alumni grantee, 1957. Mem. Nat. Alliance Homebased Businesswomen (pres. 1980-82, originator, founder), Women's Caucus for Art. Jewish. Home and office: 24 Fishel Rd Edison NJ 08820

BEHR, TINA, speech pathologist; b. Newark, Nov. 10, 1949; d. William Morris and Edith (Geffner) B.; B.S., Trenton State Coll., 1971; postgrad. Emerson Coll., 1971-72; M.A., Montclair State Coll., 1974; m. David Levy, Sept. 24, 1978. Dir. speech and hearing dept. Hamburg (Pa.) Center, 1974-77; speech and lang. program supr. Children's Psychiat. Center, Eatontown, N.J., 1978—, also chmn. edn. dept. Mem. Am. (cert. clin. competence), Monmouth County (charter, corr. sec. 1979-80), sec. 1979-80), N.J. speech and hearing assns. Home: 246 Albert Pl Elberon NJ 07740 Office: 59 Broad St Eatontown NJ 07724

BEHRMANN, POLLY (MRS. JOHN BEHRMANN), educator; b. Framingham, Mass., Nov. 24, 1925; B.S. in Edn. and Recreational Leadership, U. Mass., 1947; grad. various spl. edn. courses; married; children—James, Judith, Charles, Roland. Camp dir. YMCA, 1948-50; reading tutor emotionally disturbed, mentally retarded and physically handicapped, 1947-65; kindergarten dir., tchr., Framingham, Mass., 1960-65; supr. learning disabilities Reading Research Inst., Wellesley, Mass., 1966; master tchr. Summer Inst. Learning Disabilities, Am. Internat. Coll., 1968-69; remedial reading and learning disabilities tchr., Framingham, 1966-71; tchr., diagnostician Liberty Council Schs., Sudbury, Mass., 1970-71; master tchr. Summer Inst. Learning Disabilities, Framingham State Coll., 1971; coordinator learning disabilities Framingham Middle Schs., 1971-73; mem. faculty Clark U., Worcester, Mass., 1973; spl. educator Resource Center, Wellesley (Mass.) Coll., 1972—; treas. Mass. Council Exceptional Children, 1974-75, bd. dirs., 1968-72, adv. bd., 1973—; condr. workshops, lectr., cons. in field. Recipient award Mass. Assn. Children with Learning Disabilities, 1970; named Mass. Mother of Yr., 1979. Mem. Phi Kappa Phi. Author: Number-Letter Dice, 1978; Read It-Make It, 1976; Activities for Developing Visual Perception, 1974; Activities for Developing Auditory Perception, 1975; How Many Spoons Make a Family, 1974; Why Is It Always Me, 1980; co-author: Excel I, Excel II: Parents as Playmates; 1981; dept. editor Day Care Mag., Highlights Mag.; also activitity and curriculum materials, articles. Address: 115 Lake Rd Framingham MA 01701

BEIL, KAREN MAGNUSON, editor, writer; b. Boston, Feb. 15, 1950; d. Victor Berger and Dorothy (Hall) Magnuson; student Upsala Coll., 1967-68; B.A. Cum laude, Syracuse U., 1971; m. James A. Beil, Feb. 24, 1973; 1 dau., Kimberly Erika. News reporter City News Bur. of Chgo., 1971-72; environ. research editor N.Y. State Dept. Environ. Conservation, Albany, 1973-75; asst. editor N.Y. State Environ., Albany, 1975-76, editor, 1976-78; assoc. dir. info. services The Conservationist Mag., N.Y. State Environ. and Environ. Notice Bull. of N.Y. State Dept. Environ. Conservation, Albany, 1978-81; freelance editor and writer, 1981—; cons. in field. Mem. Nat. Audubon Soc., Lit. Advocacy Pals Soc., Soc. Children's Book Writers. Contbr. articles to profl. jours.

BEIRNE, HELEN D., state agy. adminstr.; B.S., U. Idaho; postgrad. Stanford U., Syracuse U., Northwestern U.; Ph.D., U. Denver. Adminstr. and clin. dir. Alaska Crippled Children's Assn., 1956-68; mem. Alaska Ho. of Reps., 1969-70, 73-77; commr. Alaska Dept. Health and Social Services, 1978—. Served as women's med. specialist U.S. Army, Korea and Japan. Office: Dept Health and Social Services Alaska Office Bldg Pouch H-01 Juneau AK 99811 *

BEISLER, SALLY JEAN, chem. co. exec.; b. Pitts., Aug. 14, 1945; d. Rexford C. and Sue (Hopta) Arnold; B.S., U. Pitts., 1971, M.B.A., 1978; m. Joseph L. Beisler, Feb. 5, 1977; children—Susan Marie, Michael Anthony. With nuclear fuel mgmt. and sales staff Westinghouse Electric Co., Pitts., 1969-74; mgr. mfg. and internat. mktg. Borg Warner Chem. Co., Parkersburg, W.Va., 1974-78; mem. mktg. staff St. Joe Zinc Co., Pitts., 1978-79; market devel. specialist Mobay Chem. Co., Pitts., 1980—; dir. Med. Planning & Cons., Pitts., 1979—. Mem. Exec. Womens Council Pitts., Soc. Plastics Engrs., Flexible Packaging Assn. Home: 4320 Centre Ave Pittsburgh PA 15213 Office: Mobay Rd Pittsburgh PA 15205

BELAGA, JULIE DOREN, state legislator; b. Boston, July 12, 1930; d. David and Laka L. Doren; B.S. in Edn., Syracuse (N.Y.) U., 1951; m. Myron W. Belaga, July 4, 1952; children—Debra, David, Heather. Mem. Planning and Zoning Commn., Westport, Conn., 1972-75, chmn., 1973-75; rep. Westport (Conn.) Town Meeting, 1975-77; chmn. employee compensation com. Conn. Coastal Area Mgmt. Advisory Bd., 1975; mem. Conn. Ho. of Reps. from 136th Dist., 1977—, asst. minority leader, 1979; mem. steering com. Conn. Acad. Sci. and Engring., 1978—. Mem. AAUW, League Women Voters (past chpt. pres.), Westport/Weston Arts Council, Community Council Westport/Weston, Republican Women Westport. Office: House Representative The Capitol Hartford CT 06115 *

BELCHER, JENNIFER ASHLEY, c. of c. exec.; b. Aurora, Ill., Sept. 7, 1950; d. Walter Martin, Jr. and Mignon Julia (Ohm) Ashley; student W.Va. Tech. U., 1968-70; children—Amy Lisabeth, Jeffrey Matthew. Adminstrv. asst. Princeton (W.Va.)-Mercer County C. of C., 1977, exec. dir., 1977—; bd. dirs. New River Travel Council, 1979—, Mercer County Econ. Opportunity Council, 1978—; sec. Princeton Area Aus. Devel. Corp., 1977—, New River Travel Council, 1980, 81. Asst. treas. Princeton-Athens United Fund, 1977—. Mem. Am. C. of C. Execs., U.S. C. of C., W.Va. Indsl. Devel. Assn., W.Va. C. of C. Execs. Assn. (sec.-treas. 1978-80, pres.-elect 1981), W.Va. C. of C. Club: Princeton Civitans (dir. 1979-80, pres.-elect 1980). Office: Princeton C of C Mercer at Center St Princeton WV 24740

BELETZ, ELAINEETHEL, nurse; b. N.Y.C., Jan. 5, 1944; d. Harry and Rose (Friedman) B.; R.N., Mt. Sinai Hosp., N.Y.C., 1968; B.S. in Nursing, Fairleigh Dickinson U., 1970; M.A., N.Y.U., 1974; M.Ed., Columbia U., 1978, Ed.D., 1979. Staff nurse ICU Mt. Sinai Hosp., 1968-70, asst. head nurse, 1970; adminstrv. supervisory relief nurse, 1973-74, 77-78; clin. instr. Roosevelt Hosp. Sch. Nursing, N.Y.C., 1970-73; nurse gerontologist St. Luke's Hosp. Center, N.Y.C., 1974; asst. dir. nursing Bklyn. Hosp., N.Y.C., 1975-77; asst. prof. nursing Hunter Coll., CUNY, 1978-81; v.p. nursing Mt. Sinai Hosp., Med. Center, Chgo., 1982—; lectr.; cons. nursing adminstrn., labor relations in health care; mem. tax force on block grants. Ill. Dept. Health. Fellow Am. Acad. Nursing; mem. Am. Nurses Assn. (dir. 1982—; pres. 1979-81), N.Y. State Nurses Assn. (dir. 1975-78, cert. of appreciation 1981), Ill. Nurses Assn., Chgo. Nurses Assn., Indsl. Relations Research Assn., Am. Hosp. Assn., Am. Soc. Nursing Service Adminstrs., N.Y. Counties Registered Nurses Assn. (Amanda Silvers award 1981), Shershower Benevolent Assn. Jewish. Contbr. articles to profl. jours. Office: Mount Sinai Hospital Medical Center California at 15th St Chicago IL 60608

BEL GEDDES, BARBARA, actress; b. N.Y.C., Oct. 31, 1922; d. Norman and Helen Belle (Sneider) Bel Geddes; student Buxton Sch., Putney; Andrebrook; m. Carl Schreuer, Jan. 24, 1944 (div. 1951); 1 dau., Susan; m. 2d. Windsor Lewis, Apr. 15, 1951 (dec.); 1 dau., Betsy. First stage role in School for Scandal, Clinton (Conn.) Playhouse, 1939; made Broadway debut in Out of The Frying Pan, 1940; appeared in Little Darling, 1942; Nine Girls, 1943; Mrs. January and Mr. X., 1944; Deep Are the Roots (Clarence Derwent award), 1945; The Moon is Blue, 1952; The Living Room, 1954; Cat on a Hot Tin Roof, 1955; The Sleeping Prince, 1956; Silent Night, Lonely Night, 1959; Mary, Mary, 1961; The Porcelain Year, 1965; Everything in the Garden, 1967; Finishing Touches, 1973; Ah, Wilderness, 1975; motion pictures include: The Long Night, 1946, I Remember Mama, 1948, Blood on the Moon, 1948, Caught, 1949, Panic in the Streets, 1950, Fourteen Hours, 1951, The Five Pennies, 1959, Five Branded Women, 1960, By Love Possessed, 1961, The Todd Killings, 1970, Summertree, 1971; appears regulary as Eleanor Southward Ewing on TV show Dallas, 1978—. Recipient Theatre World award, 1946. Author, illustrator: (children's books) I Like to Be Me, 1963, So Do I, 1972; designer greeting cards for George Caspari Co. Office: care Press Relations WCBS-TV 51 W 52d St New York NY 10019 *

BELGRAVE, DOLORES JEAN, govt. ofcl.; b. Jersey City, Oct. 23, 1933; B.S., Empire Labor Coll., N.Y.C., 1976; M.S.S., L.I. U., 1978; postgrad. in law; 1 son, David. With N.Y. Telephone Co., 1952-69; self-employed saleswoman, 1969-70; counselor EEO, U.S. Postal Service, 1970-79, labor relations exec., Bklyn., 1979—; cons. in field. Mem. Am. Soc. Tng. and Devel., Council Concerned Black Execs. Office: 271 Cadman Plaza E Brooklyn NY 11201

BELKE, GENEVIEVE O., bus. exec.; b. Chgo., Oct. 13, 1923; d. Samuel and Rella Irene (Grappy) Ortaggio; m. Arnold H. Belke, Sept. 29, 1956; children—Denise, John. Mgr. billing dept. Gen. Electric Co., Cleve., 1942-46; bookkeeper Am. Tool & Die, Kalamazoo, Mich., 1946-49; office mgr. Castro Mfg. Co., Chgo., 1949-52; public acct. Harris Kerr Forster & Co. Chgo., 1953-55; internal auditor Edgewater Golf Club, Chgo., 1955-56; acct., office mgr. Boodell Sears Sugrue & Crowley, Chgo., 1956-62; controller Allied Leasing Co., Alco Fin. Services, Northfield, Ill., 1968-75; controller, corp. sec. Lake Communications, Inc., Niles, Ill., 1977-80; acctg. mgr. R.J. Macdonald Internat. Corp., Elk Grove Village, Ill., 1980-81. Bd. dirs. Wheeling High Sch. Scholarship Found. Mem. Nat. Assn. Accts. (dir. Ill. N.E. chpt., pres. 1979-80, mem. nat. com. on chpt. ops. 1980—). Home: 2634 Forrest Ln Arlington Heights IL 60004

BELKIN, JANET E., lawyer; b. N.Y.C.; d. Irving and Pauline H. Ehrenreich; B.A., Vasser Coll., 1958; Ph.D., St. Johns U., 1975; J.D., Hofstra U.; m. Myron Belkin, June 29, 1958; children—Lisa, Gary, Kira. Tchr. spl. edn., N.Y.C., 1958-60; adj. faculty St. Johns U., 1970-75, Nassau Community Coll., 1971-75; pvt. counselor, 1971-75; admitted to N.Y. bar; atty. govt. relations Equitable Life Ins. Co., N.Y.C., 1978—. Chmn. Hudson group Democratic Nat. Com. Task Force, 1981—; mem. legis. com. N.Y.C. Commn. Status Women; bd. dirs. Merrick (N.Y.) Sr. Citizens Center. Mem. ABA (vice chmn. adminstrv. law com.), Assn. Calif. Life Ins. Cos. (dir.), N.Y. State Bar Assn., Assn. Bar City N.Y., Women in Housing and Fin., Women in Govtl. Relations. Clubs: City (N.Y.C.), B'nai Brith. Home: 3014 Hewlett Ave Merrick NY 11566 Office: 1285 Ave of Americas New York NY 11566

BELL, ANITA IRIS, psychometrician; b. Lubbock, Tex., Mar. 6, 1949; d. Vernon Ellis and Ivean (Iler) B.; B.A., Tex. Tech. U., 1971; M.S., Carnegie Mellon U., 1972; Ph.D., U. Ga., 1977. Asst. dir. dept. psychometrics Nat. Bd. Med. Examiners, Phila., 1975-78, asso. dir. dept. psychometrics, 1979-81, sr. psychometrician, 1981—. Elder, Old Pine St. Ch., Phila. Mem. Am. Ednl. Research Assn., Assn. Am. Med. Colls., Am. Psychol. Assn., Carnegie Mellon Alumni Clan, Tex. Tech Ex-Students Assn. (dist. rep.), Phi Mu. Democrat. Home: 1500 Locust St Apt 3220 Philadelphia PA 19102 Office: 3930 Chestnut St Philadelphia PA 19104

BELL, BARBARA ELLEN, chemist, mfg. co. exec.; b. Cabell County, Huntington, W.Va., Oct. 7, 1938; d. Arvil Reed and Vivian D. (Davis) Bell; B.S. in Chemistry cum laude, Marshall U., 1965, postgrad., 1970—. Clin. chemistry supr. Cabell Huntington Hosp., 1965-76; instr. dept. medicine Marshall U., Huntington, 1972-77, Nat. Mgmt. Assn., Huntington, 1979—; chemist Chemetron Corp., Huntington, 1976-77; sr. chemist C-Amine dept. BASF-Wyandotte Corp., Huntington, 1977-78, operation supr., 1978—. Mem. Am. Chem. Soc. (pres. Central Ohio Valley sect.), Nat. Mgmt. Assn. (dir. 1982—), Am. Soc. Clin. Pathologist, Chi Beta Phi. Mem. Apostolic Ch. Contbr. articles to profl. jours. Home: 222 Norway Ave Huntington WV 25705 Office: PO Box 2166 Huntington WV 25722

BELL, BRITTON, mgmt. cons.; b. Louisville, June 18, 1948; d. Elbert Pinckley and Betsy Ann (Gordon) Watts; B.A. in Bus. Mgmt. and Profl. Communications, Alverno Coll., Milw., 1981; m. James H. Bell, Jr., Mar. 15, 1969 (div. Dec. 1972); 1 son, Scott Elbert. Acct., Am. Mut. Reins. Co., Chgo., 1967-69; office services Shell Oil Co., Detroit, 1969-71; personnel asst. RTE Corp., Waukesha, Wis., 1973-74; law office adminstr. John W. Cusack, S.C., Waukesha, 1974-77; dist. rep. Reynolds and Reynolds Co., Milw., 1977-79; founder, pres. Profl. Mgmt. Services, Brookfield, Wis., 1979—; speaker, cons., seminar leader in field. Active local election com., NOW. Served with USN, 1966-67. Mem. Am. Mgmt. Assn., Nat. Assn. Female Execs., Acad. Mgmt., Nat. Assn. Accts., Alverno Coll. Alumnae Profls. Assn. Republican. Roman Catholic. Home: 1569 S Carriage Ln New Berlin WI 53151

BELL, CAROLYN SHAW, educator, economist; b. Framingham, Mass., June 21, 1920; d. Clarence Edward and Grace (Wellington) Shaw; A.B. magna cum laude, Mt. Holyoke Coll., 1941; Ph.D., London (Eng.) Sch. Econs., 1949; m. Nelson S. Bell, Aug. 26, 1953; 1 dau. by previous marriage, Tova Marie. Economist, OPA, 1941-45; research economist London Sch. Econs., 1946-47, Social Sci. Research Council, Harvard, 1950-53; mem. faculty Wellesley Coll., 1950—, prof. econs., 1962—, chmn. dept., 1962-65, 79-82, Katharine Coman prof. econs., 1970—. Pub. mem. Fed. Adv. Council on Unemployment Ins., 1974-77, chairwoman, 1975-77; bd. econ. advisers Pub. Interest Econ. Center; bd. overseers Amos Tuck Grad. Sch. Bus. Adminstrn., Dartmouth, 1973-79; mem. econ. policy council UN Assn., 1976—; trustee Joint Council Econ. Edn., 1975—, Tchrs. Ins. and Annuity Assn., 1977—; mem. NRC Commn. on Behavioral Scis. and Edn., 1977—. Mem. Am. Econs. Assn. (chmn. com. on status of women in econs. profession 1972-74, mem. exec. com. 1975-77), AAUP (pres. Wellesley chpt. 1965-66), AAUW (Shirley Farr fellow 1961-62), ACLU, Assn. Evolutionary Econs. (dir. 1973-75), Eastern Econ. Assn., UN Assn. (dir. 1980—), Boston Econ. Club, Phi Beta Kappa (pres. chpt. 1978-80). Author: (with W.W. Cochrane) Economics of Consumption, 1956; Consumer Choice in the U.S. Economy, 1967; The Economics of the Ghetto, 1970; (with others) Coping in a Troubled Society, 1974; also articles. Radio and television commentator, cons. Mem. bd. editors Challenge, Jour. Econ. Edn. Home: 167 Clay Brook Rd Dover MA 02030 Office: Wellesley Coll Wellesley MA 02181

BELL, DONNA, retail exec.; b. Hemingford, Nebr., Sept. 21, 1932; d. Henry and Louella (DeVoss) Steil; student Lincoln Law Sch., Sacramento; m. Larry Bell, Dec. 9, 1951; children—Barbara, Charles, Sandra, Michael. Musician, Alliance, Nebr., 1946-50; various secretarial positions, 1950-57; traveling lectr. Stanley Home Products Co., Topeka, 1958-62, Design for Learning System for Women, 1970-74; adminstrv. sec. McBell Industries, Oshkosh, Nebr., 1971; owner restaurant, Oshkosh, 1972-74, Tahoe Gift Shop, Sacramento, 1974—; exec. sec. to dep. dir. for legislation Calif. Employment Dept., 1979-81; staff employment and tng. specialist Gov.'s Adv. Council, Calif. Employment Devel. Dept., 1981—. Dist. chmn., pres. bd. dirs. Guiding Star council Girl Scouts, Ogallala, Nebr., 1964-73, mem. merger and affirmative action nat. task force, 1973-74; pres. Garden County Fedn. Women's Clubs, 1972, dist. chmn. music contests, 1972-74. Mem. Nat. Assn. Female Execs. Republican. Lutheran. Home: 2613 Warrego Way Sacramento CA 95826 Office: 800 Capitol Mall Sacramento CA 95814

BELL, EVELYN LORENTZEN, dept. store ofcl.; b. Oslo, Norway, Mar. 30, 1948; came to U.S., 1952, naturalized, 1980; d. Øivind and Evelyn Byrd (LaPrade) L.; B.A., Marymount Coll., N.Y.C., 1978; m. Theodore A. Bell, Sept. 9, 1978. Asso. editor fabrics Harper's Bazaar, N.Y.C., 1973-76, fashion editor, 1979; creative service coordinator Hoechst Fibers Co., 1976-78; fashion coordinator Am. Silk Mills, N.Y.C., 1979-82; coordinator fashion and spl. events Marshall Field & Co., Chgo., 1982—. Mem. Fashion Group. Club: Colony (N.Y.C.).

BELL, JAYNELLE KHAMILLAH, pharm. mfg. co. mgr.; b. Oakland, Calif., Feb. 26, 1953; d. William Hayes and Genieve Cartwright (Hilton) Jenkins; B.A., U. Calif., Berkeley, 1976; M.B.A. (Basic Edn. Opportunity grantee, Consortium fellow), U. So. Calif., 1979; m. James M. Bell, June 28, 1980; children—Robert, Semaj. Bus. mgr. U. Calif.-Berkeley publ. Blue and Gold, 1975-76; mktg. analyst Oakland Tribune/Gannett Publs., 1976-77; sales rep. Procter & Gamble Co., San Francisco dist., 1979-81; dist. mgr. Drackett Products div. Bristol Myers Corp., Dublin, Calif., 1981—. Participant Big Sister Program, San Francisco, 1974—; voter registrar for Congressional campaign, 1971—. Mem. Nat. Assn. Female Execs., Women in Advt., Nat. Council Negro Women (publicity dir. asst. 1979), LWV. Republican. Methodist. Club: Profl. and Bus. Women's. Editor United Meth. Women newsletter, 1982. Home: 345 Goheen Circle Vallejo CA 94590 Office: Drackett Products div Bristol Myers Corp 11875 Dublin Blvd Suite A-160 Dublin CA 94566

BELL, JOANNE IRENE, educator; b. Huntington, Pa., Aug. 1, 1928; s. George C. and Alma (Love) B.; B.A., Juanita Coll., Huntington, 1949; M.S.W., U. Pa., 1954; postgrad. U. Md., 1967-70. Social worker, acting dir. Child Welfare Service, Lewistown, Md., 1949-52; supr. Balt. Dept. Social Services, 1954-61; div. supr. San Francisco Dept. Social Services, 1961-66; instr. social welfare extension U. Calif., Berkeley, 1961-66; specialist HEW, Washington, 1966-67; asso. prof. social work U. Ky., Lexington, 1970—; cons. in field; chmn. Exceptional Children Adv. Com., 1972-75; adv. bd. Bluegrass Employment and Tng. Program, 1976; mem. Children's Services Com., 1960-70, Regional Crime Commn. Juvenile Delinquency, 1975-76; mem. exec. bd. Bluegrass Assn. Retarded Citizens, 1980—. Mem. adv. com. Bluegrass Area Devel. Dist., 1979—; mem. exec. bd. Growth and Research for Women, 1979—. Fellow Pa. Dept. Social Welfare, 1952-53, U.S. Children's Bur., 1967-69; grantee Ky. Research Found., NIMH, 1976. Mem. Council Social Work Edn., Nat. Assn. Social Work, AAUP. Roman Catholic. Author in field. Home: Shalcey Farm Route 1 Box 282 Wilmore KY 40390 Office: 629 Patterson Office Tower Univ Ky Lexington KY 40506

BELL, KATHLEEN ANNE, export agt.; b. Evanston, Ill., Apr. 7, 1941; d. William Bryan and Agnes Patricia (Diederich) Healy; B.S., Northwestern U., 1965; M.B.A., Golden Gate U.; children—Dennis Bell, Amy Bell, Stefanie Bell. Tchr. public schs., Elk Grove, Ill., 1966-73; internat. export agt. Emery Air Freight Corp., Chgo., 1977—. Mem. UNICEF, Republican Nat. Com. Mem. Internat. Visitors, English Speaking Union, Brookfield Zool. Soc., Lincoln Park Zool. Soc., Northwestern U. Library Council, Art Inst. Chgo., NEA, Council Exceptional Children, Council Fgn. Relations, Adler Planetarium, Chgo. Hist. Soc., Shedd Aquarium, Field Mus. Natural History, Nat. Assn. Female Execs., AAUW, Council Cath. Women, Oriental Inst., Delta Gamma. Air Cargo Assn., Internat. Bus. Club, Am. Mgmt. Assn., N.W. Trade Club, Northwestern U. Alumni Assn. Republican. Roman Catholic. Home: 936 Wilshire Court Vernon Hills IL 60061

BELL, KONSLYNNIETTA HUTCHINSON, business exec.; b. Bklyn., Nov. 27, 1943; d. Stanley George and Lennie D. (Baker) Hutchinson; student Howard U., 1960-63, Cinderella Career Coll., 1963-65; B.A., U. D.C., 1980; 1 son, Armone Anthoni H. Editorial asst. AAAS, Washington, 1963-68; research asst. Nat. Med. Assn. Found., Washington, 1968-69; office mgr. Washington Area Bus. Service, 1969-70; proofreader Digital Photographics, Washington, 1971-72; asst. to info. dir. Interracial Council for Bus. Opportunities, Washington, 1972; sec. U.S. Ho. of Reps., 1972-73; asst. adminstrv. officer Opportunity Funding Corp., Washington, 1980; sales rep. Xerox Reprodn. Center, Xerox Corp., Arlington, Va., 1980—; v.p. Universal Mktg. Inc. Acting sec. Ft. Totten Civic Assn., Washington. Named Miss U. D.C., 1978; recipient acad. award Alpha Kappa Alpha, 1960. Mem. Am. Soc. Profl. and Exec. Women, Nat. Assn. Female Execs. (mem. ward IV council), Assn. Ednl. Communication and Tech., Assn. Childhood Edn., Home Econs. Edn. Assn., Zeta Phi Beta, Phi Gamma Nu. Republican. Episcopalian. Club: Internat. Boutique. Research in field. Home: 4828 Ft Totten Dr NE Washington DC 20011 Office: 1900 Wilson Blvd Arlington VA 22201

BELL, LINDA CRAWFORD, mag. editor; b. Harrisburg, Pa., Jan. 13, 1948; d. Elwood F. and Reba J. (Stakley) Crawford; student Pa. State U., 1965-68; m. Daniel Locke Bell II, July 18, 1970; children—Daniel Locke III, Ian Spencer. With Soviet Life Mag., Washington, 1969—, sr. editor, 1976—. Bd. dirs., public relations adv. Emerson Gallery Art, McLean, Va., 1976—. Democrat. Episcopalian. Office: Soviet Life Mag 1706 18th St NW Washington DC 20009

BELL, LUCILLE ELIZABETH, nurse; b. San Pierre, Ind., June 5, 1924; d. Joseph Frank and Anna Sophie (Badenhoop) Fenzel; R.N. Evang. Hosp., Chgo., 1948; B.S. in Health Scis., Coll. St. Francis, Joliet, Ill., 1978; m. Howard R. Bell, July 5, 1952; children—Rae Anne Bell

Simpson, Howard, Jan Marie, Scott, Craig, Brian. Staff nurse Evang. Hosp., 1948-52; mem. nursing staff St. Margaret Hosp., Hammond, Ind., 1960—, night supr., 1970-79, dir. nights, 1979—. Mem. Am. Nurses Assn., Coll. St. Francis Alumnae Assn., Evang. Hosp. Nurses Alumnae Assn. (hon. life). Mem. United Ch. Christ. Home: 5214 Howard Ave Hammond IN 46320 Office: 5454 Hohman Ave Hammond IN 46320

BELL, LUCILLE LOWERY, nurse-anesthetist; b. Jacksonville, Fla., Apr. 6, 1924; d. Benjamin and Mary Lowery; student Edward Waters Coll., 1939-41; diploma Brewster Hosp. Sch. Nursing, 1942; grad. anesthesia Cook County Hosp., 1947. Sec., treas. Fed. Duval Enterprises, Inc., Jacksonville, 1957; founder Nightengale Home Nursing Care Class, Inc., Jacksonville, 1975; nurse, counselor Greater Jacksonville Econ. Opportunity Program. Bd. dirs., trustee Mt. Ararat Convalescent Home. Certified in psychiat. nursing Fla. Bd. Health; recipient Distinguished Service citation Fla. div. Am. Cancer Soc., 1966. Mem. Am. Nurses Assn., Chi Eta Phi (charter). Baptist.

BELL, MARVA JO, bank exec.; b. Thomas, Okla., Mar. 22, 1940; d. John William and Edith Isola (Osteen) Dillmon; student public schs., Fay, Okla., Rome and South Haven, Kans.; m. Jerry Dean Bell, Nov. 25, 1959; children—Jerry Dean, Sonya Ann. With Alexander State Bank (Kans.), 1973—, asst. v.p., 1978-80, exec. v.p., cashier, 1980—. Club: Order Eastern Star.

BELL, MARY, real estate and investment cons.; b. Bklyn., June 5, 1907; d. Alonzo Chandler and Emily (Cox) B.; student Skidmore Coll., 1924-25, Pratt Inst., 1925-28, Hunter Coll., 1926, Berlitz Sch., 1927, U. Fla., 1947; children—Chandler Rogers Dann, Diana Dann Smelser. Photographer, Thomas Cook Co., 1927, Mary Bell Studio, Westfield, N.J., 1928-31, Aero. Art and Advt. Surveys, Ayer, N.Y., 1932; silver designer for Tiffany, Reed & Barton; advt. work for Timken Detroit Axle Co., 1935-41; with Bell Electric Motor Co., Garwood, N.J., 1920, mgr. Bell Factory Terminal, Garwood, 1939-41, sec. treas., 1941-45, pres., 1945-52; sec. Bell Haven Inc., Miami, Fla., 1945-51, v.p., 1951-82, also dir.; v.p. Bell Bros. Co., Miami, 1945-82, also dir.; sec. Noren Estates Co., Pt. Reyes, 1975-80, also dir.; founding mem. Central Valley Savs. and Loan (Calif.). Mem. Republican Nat. Com., Rep. Congressional Com.; founding mem. Marin Cultural Center, 1980. Mem. Ariz. State Horsemen, Calif. State Horsemen, Calif. Equestrian Patrol, Pratt Alumni Assn. Contbr. articles to New Yorker, N.Y. Herald Tribune, N.Y. Times, Country Life, Popular Aviation, Sportsman Pilot, others. Episcopalian.

BELL, MARY CATLETT (COCABELL), artist; b. Weleetka, Okla., Sept. 26, 1924; d. Stanley Bowlware and Alma Bertha (Cagle) Catlett; B.A. in Lang., U. Okla., 1946; m. J. Stewart Bell, Sept. 15, 1951; 1 son, William Catlett. One woman shows at R.S. Barnwell Art Center, Shreveport, La., 1980, Exhibit in Gov.'s Gallery, State Capitol, 1981; exhibited in group shows at 61st ann. exhbn. Allied Artists of Am., N.Y.C., 1974, Watercolor U.S.A., Springfield, Mo., 1975, 150th, 153d exhbns. Nat. Acad. Design, N.Y.C., 1975, 78, Okla. Bicentennial Art Exhbn., 1976, Living Women Living Art, Okla. Art Center, Kerr Conf. Center, others; represented in permanent collections at Okla. Hist. Soc., Oklahoma City. Mem. Okla. Art Center, Okla. Watercolor Assn., Okla. Mus. Art, Jr. League of Oklahoma City, Delta Delta Delta. Republican. Methodist. Address: 2 Colony Ln Oklahoma City OK 73116

BELL, MARY ELIZABETH, accountant; b. San Antonio, Dec. 20, 1937; d. Thomas Alfred and Mary Elizabeth (McMurrain) Beniteau; B.B.A., Baylor U., 1959; M.B.A., U. Tex., 1960; m. William Woodward Bell, May 31, 1969; children—Susan Elizabeth, Carol Ann. Teaching asst. U. Tex., Austin, 1959-60; prin. Deloitte, Haskins & Sells, C.P.A.'s, Dallas, 1960-69; county auditor Brown County (Tex.), 1972-78; pvt. practice acctg., Brownwood, Tex., 1969—; acct. Brownwood Regional Hosp. Women's Aux., 1969—. Named Outstanding Com. Chmn., Dallas chpt. C.P.A.s, 1968-69; C.P.A., Tex. Mem. Brownwood C. of C. (dir. 1979-82, sec.-treas. 1981-82), Tex. Soc. C.P.A.s (dir. 1979-82, trustee Ednl. Found. 1981—, sec.-treas. Found. 1982-83), Am. Inst. C.P.A.s, Am. Soc. Women Accts., Am. Woman's Soc. C.P.A.s, AAUW, Pi Beta Phi, Baylor U. Alumni Assn. (dir. 1979-82). Baptist. Clubs: Brownwood Woman's (pres. 1980-81), Rotary Ann (v.p. 1982-83), Baylor U. Hankamer Sch. Bus. Alumni Bd. Home: PO Box 1564 Brownwood TX 76801 Office: 109 N Fisk St Brownwood TX 76801

BELL, MARY KATHERINE, mathematician; b. Pensacola, Fla., Apr. 14, 1909; d. Charles Henry and Mary Elizabeth (Sellers) Walker; B.S., Fla. State U., 1931; M.A. in Math. (Laws fellow), U. Cin., 1932; m. Clarence Russell Bell, Aug. 11, 1937; 1 dau., Charlotte Ann Bell Layman. Tchr., P.K. Young Sch., 1931-32, Pensacola High Sch., 1932-37, Wilbanks Elem. Sch., 1952-57, Austin Jr. High Sch., 1957-62; prof. math. Lamar U., Beaumont Tex., 1962—, Regents prof., 1976—, Piper prof., 1978, prof. emeritus, 1979—, assoc. prof. math., 1979—, acting head math. dept., 1982-83. Former pres., bd. dirs. YMCA; v.p. AAUW, 1942; leader United Appeals, 1978-81; mem. Rothwell Student Center Bd., 1979—; pres. United Meth. Women, 1952-54; chmn. council ministries 1st United Meth. Ch., 1981—, chmn. com. on edn., 1978-81. Mem. Tex. Assn. Coll. Tchrs., Math. Assn. Am., Nat. Council Tchrs. of Math., Sabine Area Council Math. (pres. elect 1982-83), Tex. Council Tchrs. Math., Alethea Lit. Soc., Hist. Soc. S.E. Tex., Beaumont Art Mus., AAUW, Delta Kappa Gamma, Phi Kappa Phi, Pi Mu Epsilon, Beta Pi Theta. Democrat. Author: Computational Skills, 1975; Manual of Computational Skills, 1975. Home: 1900 Central Dr Beaumont TX 77706 Office: Box 10047 Lamar University Beaumont TX 77710

BELL, MAUD MELINDA (MRS. WESLEY FAGAN, JR.), former educator, realtor; b. Portsmouth, Va., June 24; d. Charles Edward and Lucy H. (Barnes) Bell; A.B. cum laude, Shaw U., 1932; postgrad. CCNY; M.A., Columbia U., 1964, postgrad.; m. Wesley Lee Fagan, June 24, 1944 (div.). Tchr., French and English Robeson County Tng. Sch., Maxton, N.C., 1932-35; tchr. English, guidance counselor, chmn. English dept., dir. dramatics public schs., Norfolk, Va., 1935-55; tchr. English Alexander Hamilton High Sch., Bklyn., 1956-57, Andrew Jackson High Sch., Queens, L.I., N.Y., 1957-72; guidance counselor, tchr. English, reading specialist John F. Kennedy High Sch., Riverdale, N.Y.C., 1972-77, ret., 1977; lic. real estate saleswoman, N.Y. State, 1955—. Sponsor YWCA; leader Girl Scouts U.S.A.; past supr. ch. sch., adult Bible class tchr. United Meth. Ch.; campaign mgr. Democratic Gubernatorial election Horace Edwards, Va.; pres. NAACP, No. Westchester. Named Woman of Yr., Norfolk, 1950. Mem. Friends of Westchester Community Coll., Am. Assn. Ret. Tchrs., Am. Assn. Ret. Persons, United Fedn. Tchrs., Bus. and Profl Women's Club of Westchester (chairperson internat. affairs com. 1978-80), Alpha Kappa Alpha. Clubs: Social (charter mem. Norfolk), Elks. Contbr. articles on lit. to profl. jours. Home: Hudsonview Old Post Rd N Croton-on-Hudson NY 10520 Office: Real Estate Sales Mgmt 115-05 178 Pl St Albans LI NY 11434

BELL, MILDRED LENORE, writer, graphoanalyst; b. Wibaux, Mont., Jan. 26, 1920; d. Louis J. and Beryl Lenore (Snyder) Crawford; student U. Calif., Los Angeles, 1964-65, Orange Coast Coll., 1974-75, Famous Writers Sch., 1969-72, Internat. Graphoanalysis Soc., Chgo., 1974-78; children—Joseph E., Stephen C. With Procurement and Contract Adminstrn., Dept. Def., 1953-74, contract adminstr., Pasadena, Calif., 1961-65, Los Angeles, 1965-74; ret., 1974; tchr. graphoanalysis, Newport Harbor, Calif., 1977. Recipient Snoopy award NASA, 1968. Mem. Am. Legion Aux. (pres. Newport Beach, Calif. unit 1976-77, mem. exec. com.). Author: Single Servings; contbr. articles to popular publs.; columnist Orange County Daily Pilot, San Diego Union, 1974-76; painting: Magnificent Solitude (Def. Supply Agency, Alexandria, Va., First Pl. and Nat. Hon. Mention 1966), Serenity (2d pl. award Ebasco, N.Y.C., 1978). Home: 160 E 21st St Apt E Costa Mesa CA 92627

BELL, PHYLLIS RUTH, editor; b. Smith Center, Kans., Aug. 5, 1929; d. Oscar Lawrence and Bonnie Lenora (Schroeder) Bloomer; student public schs. Lebanon, Kans.; m. Lennie Dale Bell, Apr. 3, 1948; children—Risë Dale, Vicky Sue, Gloria Jeanne. With The Lebanon Times, 1962—, mng. editor, 1968—, bus. mgr., 1968—. Election bd. clk. Smith County Democrats, 1958-60; leader 4-H Club, 1957-71, 81-82. sec. Lebanon PRIDE, 1972, pres., 1973-75. Recipient awards Kans. Press Assn., 1970, 71. Mem. Lebanon Hub C. of C. (sec.-treas. 1970—), Kans. Press Women (dir. 1975-76), North Central Kans. Geneal. Soc., DAR, Am. Legion Aux., VFW Aux. Mem. Christian Ch. (Disciples of Christ). Clubs: Music Study, Christian Womens Fellowship, Kans. Farmers Union, Publicity. Author: History of William Slater Family, 1972; researcher genealogy, 1970—. Home: Route 1 Lebanon KS 66952 Office: 413 Main St Lebanon KS 66952

BELL, REGINA JEAN, steel co. exec.; b. Lebanon, Mo., July 27, 1927; d. Stephen S. and Ida M. (Reaves) B.; B.A., Draughens U., 1948; postgrad. Butler U., Ind.-Purdue U., Indpls. Prodn. mgr. Howe Mfg. Co., Inc., Indpls., 1958-64; v.p. budgetary control Howe Engrng. Co., Inc., Indpls., 1964-67; mgr. material control Nat. Aluminum Div., Indpls., 1968—. Mem. Purchasing Mgmt. Assn. Office: PO Box 18272 5800 Massachusetts Ave Indianapolis IN 46218

BELL, ROXANNE BEAIR, carwash mfg. co. exec.; b. Coffeyville, Kans., Sept. 9, 1942; d. Clarence A. and Gravette Beair; student Coffeyville Coll., 1960-61, Kans. State Coll., 1963, Toledo U., 1968, Aurora Coll., 1969; 1 dau., Shelly. Sec. to athletic dept. Kans. State Coll., 1962-65; adminstrv. asst. The Rooney Co., Tulsa, 1965-67; supr. Sch. Sales div. Indsl. Arts Equipment, Toledo, 1967-69; with Indsl. Sales, Cedar Rapids, Iowa, 1969-72; v.p. Southern Pride, Inc., Burlington, N.C., 1975-80, pres., 1980—. Sec., NAACP, Aurora, 1968; sec. Bd. Local Improvements, Aurora, 1969; adminstrv. asst. Commn. Public Property, Aurora, Ill., 1970-72; campaign mgr. U.S. Ho. of Reps., Ill., 1972. Mem. Nat. Carwash Council, Internat. Carwash Assn. Republican. Home: 37-C Fountain Manor Dr Greensboro NC 27405 Office: 1312 Whitsett St Burlington NC 27215

BELL, RUBY TATE, educator; b. Phila., Aug. 8, 1931; d. Clevester Virgil and Ruby (Robinson) Tate; B.Ed., Cheyney State Coll., 1953; M.Ed., Antioch U., 1973; Ed.D. candidate Temple U., 1978—; m. Rudolph L. Bratcher, Mar. 7, 1953; children—David A., Stephen A.; m. 2d, William H. Bell Jr., Aug. 24, 1980. Tchr., William Dick Sch., Phila., 1954-69; chairperson, team leader, assembly coordinator R. R. Wright Sch., 1969-71, tchr., lead tchr., team leader E. W. Rhodes Middle Sch., 1971—, reading specialist, coordinator reading program, acting vice-prin., reading dept. chairperson; ednl. cons.; pres., Vel Bell, Inc., Ednl. Services Corp.; editor Learn At Home Pubis. Named to Cheyney State Coll. Athletic Hall of Fame. Mem. Phila. Fedn. Tchrs., Internat. Reading Assn., Black Women's Ednl. Alliance, Kappa Delta Pi. Baptist. Address: 6 Northgate Ct Willingboro NJ 08046

BELL, SHARON ELAINE, nursing adminstr.; b. Dayton, Ohio, Apr. 25, 1942; d. Jack and Sara (Sabo) Matusoff; B.S. in Nursing, Ohio State U., 1964, M.A. in Edn., 1975; m. George Michael Bell, Jan. 5, 1969; 1 son, Chad Michael. Camp nurse Boston YMCA Camp, N.H., 1964, 65; staff nurse Ohio Tb Hosp., Columbus, 1964-66, Columbus Public Health Dept., 1966-68; instr. Sch. Practical Nursing Columbus Public Schs., 1968-77, tchr. coordinator, 1977-78, supr. sch., 1978-80, supr. health occupation programs, 1978—; vice chmn. Tri-Rivers Sch. of Practical Nursing Adv. Bd.; ex-ofcl. mem. Ohio Commn. on Nursing. Mem. Ohio State Nurses Assn., Columbus Adminstrs. Assn., Ohio Orgn. Practical Nurse Educators, Central Office Adminstrs. Assn., Ohio Assn. for Adult Educators, Am. Vocat. Assn. Jewish. Office: 100 Arcadia Ave Columbus OH 43202

BELL, SHARON JOYCE, state legislator; b. Birmingham, Ala., June 30, 1944; B.S., Auburn U.; J.D., U. Tenn. Mem. Tenn. Ho. of Reps. Bd. dirs. Child and Family Services, Consumer Credit Counseling Services; hon. trustee Juvenile Home, Knox County. Mem. Tenn. Bar Assn. Office: Tenn Ho of Reps State Capitol Nashville TN 37219 *

BELL, SUSAN JANE, state legislator; b. Houlton, Maine, Dec. 19, 1948; d. Leighton H. and Geraldine G. (Grant) B.; B.S., U. Maine, Orono, 1970, M.A., 1971. Tchr., Houlton (Maine) High Sch., 1970-73; tchr., coach Oxford Hills High Sch., South Paris, Maine, 1973-77; health edn. coordinator Oxford Hills Sch. Dist., South Paris, 1977-80; mem. Maine Ho. of Reps., 1980—, mem. joint standing com. on state govt., 1980-82, joint select com. on alcoholism, 1981-82. Bd. dirs. Androscoggin Home Health, 1977-78, Oxford County unit Am. Cancer Soc., 1977-80; coordinator drug alcohol team Oxford Hills, 1979-80. Republican. Episcopalian. Club: Nordic Ski.

BELL, VIOLET MABEL, adminstr., artist; b. Elmhurst, N.Y., Nov. 8, 1924; d. Charles H. and Violet (Reinhart) Bell; B.S., Columbia U., 1948. Writer, Yearbook, UN, N.Y.C., 1948-53; editor-writer photographs and exhibits sect. Office Public Info., 1953-73, acting chief, 1973-74, chief, 1974-80; free-lance portrait artist, 1980—; dir. UN Fed. Credit Union, 1977—, New Options Tng., Inc., N.Y.C., 1977—; cons. Family Forum Staten Island, 1978—; editorial and graphics cons. Socio-Systems, Inc., Washington, 1975-79. Mem. Am. Soc. Picture Profls., Art Students' League (life). Clubs: Forsgate Country (Jamesburg, N.J.); Smithsonian Inst. (Washington).

BELLAMY, CAROL, city ofcl.; b. Plainfield, N.J., 1942; B.A. with honors, Gettysburg Coll., 1963; J.D., N.Y. U. Vol., Peace Corps, Guatemala; asso. firm Cravath, Swaine and Moore, N.Y.C.; past asst. commr. Dept. Mental Health and Mental Retardation Services, N.Y.C.; mem. N.Y. State Senate, 1972; pres. N.Y.C. City Council, 1978—. Bd. dirs. Met. Transp. Authority. Mem. Nat. League Cities (chmn. human devel. com.). Office: The New York City Council City Hall 250 E Broadway New York NY 10007 *

BELLE, SHIRLEY DORIS, social services adminstr.; b. Jersey City; d. Willis Howard and Emma W. (Daye) Watkins; student Rutgers U., 1971; m. Lester J. Belle (dec.); 12 children. Asst. dir. CETA Tng. Program, Bayonne, N.J., 1980—. Chairperson, Hudson County Family Planning Program, 1973-74. Mem. NAACP (exec. bd. Bayonne). Mem. A.M.E. Ch. Office: 409 Ave C Bayonne NJ 07002

BELLER, LUANNE E(VELYN), accountant; b. Fort Dodge, Iowa, Feb. 5, 1950; d. Gerald L. and Evelyn (Liston) Heyl; B.A., Oreg. State U., 1977; M.B.A., Rochester Inst. Tech., 1981; m. Stephen M. Beller, June 28, 1970; children—Clancy Dee, Corby Lu. Accountant, Meml. Union, Oreg. State U., Corvallis, 1976-77; plant accountant Dubois Plastics Products, Avon, N.Y., 1977-79; coll. acct. SUNY Coll. Arts and Scis., Geneseo, 1979-81; gen. acctg. supr. M&M/Mars, Cleveland, Tenn., 1981—. Mem. Nat. Assn. Accts., AAUW, Phi Kappa Phi, Beta Gamma Sigma, Beta Alpha Psi, Phi Chi Theta. Democrat. Methodist. Home: 315 N Jackson Athens TN 37303 Office: 3500 Peerless Rd Cleveland TN 37311

BELL-KING, BARBARA ANNE, educator; b. Montgomery, Ala., Apr. 18, 1924; d. Robert M. and Lilli B. (Howard) Mosley; B.A., Spelman Coll., Atlanta, 1944; M.S., Pepperdine U., Los Angeles, 1973, M.P.A., 1974, M.B.A., 1980; Ph.D, U.S. Internat. U., San Diego, 1978; m. Michael Sebastian King, Jan. 22, 1975; children—Barbara, Sandra and Andra (twins), Richard. Housing adv. City of Berkeley (Calif.), 1960-68; regional relocation dir. HUD, San Francisco, 1968-70, area dep. dir., Los Angeles, 1970-72; asst. dir. Los Angeles Office Urban Devel., 1973-75; asso. prof. public adminstrn. Pepperdine U., 1975-80; vis. assoc. prof. Sch. Public Adminstrn., U. So. Calif., 1980-82, disting. vis. practitioner applied behavioral sci., 1982—; also mgmt. cons. Bd. dirs. region IV, United Way Los Angeles, 1980-82. Recipient various service awards. Mem. Am. Soc. Public Adminstrn., Nat. Assn. Housing and Redevel. Ofcls., Soc. Study Symbolic Interaction, Am. Soc. Tng. and Devel. (bd. dirs. Los Angeles chpt.), Nat. Assn. Female Execs., Negro Bus. and Profl. Women's Club. Unitarian. Home: 4631 S Mullen St Los Angeles CA 90043 Office: VKC 377 U So Calif Los Angeles CA 90007

BELLMAN, BARBARA JOAN, occupational therapist; b. Richmond, Va., Sept. 28, 1930; d. William Henry and Avis Hillsman (Daprato) B.; student U. Md., 1949-51; B.S., Va. Commonwealth U., 1953, cert. in occupational therapy, 1954. Staff therapist Handicapped and Crippled Children's Clinic, Washington, 1954-56; asst. chief therapist C. Melvin Sharpe Health Sch., Washington, 1956-59; clin. dir. D.C. Gen. Hosp., Washington, 1959-69, chief therapist, 1969—; assoc. clin. prof. Howard U., Temple U., Boston U., 1978—; mem. admissions com. dept. occupational therapy Howard U., 1975—. Recipient Outstanding Performance award D.C. Govt., 1961, 66, Excellent Performance award, 1979, 81. Mem. Am. (cert. com. 1968-78), D.C. (pres. 1958-60, dir. 1960-61, 65-66, 68-69) occupational therapy assns., Alpha Gamma Delta. Club: Prince George's County (Md.) Quota (1st v.p. 1972-74, 2d v.p. 1974-75, membership chmn. 1975-76, dir. 1976, sec. 1977-78). Mem. editorial bd. Am. Jour. Occupational Therapy, 1973-76. Home: 12202 Whitehall Dr Bowie MD 20715

BELLO-REUSS, ELSA NOEMI, physician; b. Buenos Aires, Argentina, May 1, 1939; came to U.S., 1972; d. Jose F. and Julia M. (Hiriart) Bello; B.S., U. Chile, 1957, M.D., 1964; m. Luis Reuss, Apr. 15, 1965; children—Luis F., Alejandro E. Intern J.J. Aguirre Hosp., Chile, 1963-64; resident in internal medicine U. Chile, Santiago, 1964-66; practice medicine specializing in nephrology Santiago, 1967-72; Internat. NIH fellow U. N.C., Chapel Hill, 1972-74; vis. asst. prof. physiology U. N.C., Chapel Hill, 1974-75; Louis Welt fellow U. N.C.-Duke U. Med. Center, 1975-76; asst. prof. medicine, physiology and biophysics Washington U. Sch. Medicine, St. Louis, 1976—, Jewish Hosp. St. Louis, 1976—. Mem. Internat., Am. socs. nephrology, Am. Fedn. Clin. Research. Contbr. articles on nephrology and epithelial electrophysiology to med. and physiology jours., chpt. to nephrology text.

BELLOVICS, DONNA MAE, nurse, educator; b. Rock Island, Ill., June 24, 1932; d. Harry John and Mabel Anna (Krueger) Ohms; R.N. (Annie Yates scholar), Los Angeles County Gen. Hosp., 1954; B.S. in Nursing, Marycrest Coll., 1965; M.A., U. Iowa, 1969; Ed.D., Walden U., 1975; m. Stephen M. Bellovics, June 24, 1955; children—Michael, Anne, George. Staff nurse, asst. head nurse Moline (Ill.) Public Hosp., 1956-58; pvt. duty nursing, 1960-64; instr. lic. practical nursing, Davenport, Iowa, 1964-65; instr. Moline Pub. Diploma Nursing, 1965-67; asst. prof. Marycrest Coll., 1969-70; assoc. prof. assoc. degree nursing program, chmn. dept. Black Hawk Coll., 1970—. Chmn. nursing scholarship com. Henry County March of Dimes, 1974—. Mem. Am. Nurses Assn., Sigma Theta Tau. Republican. Presbyn. Club: Spring Creek Grange. Home: Rural Route 1 Box 46B Geneseo IL 61254 Office: 6600 34th Ave Moline IL 61265

BELLOWS, CAROLE KAMIN, lawyer; b. Chgo., May 24, 1935; d. Alfred and Sara (Liebenson) Kamin; B.A., U. Ill., 1957; J.D., Northwestern U., 1960; m. Jason E. Bellows, June 28, 1958 (dec. June 1980); children—Marcia, Douglas, Daniel. Admitted to Ill. bar, 1960; law clk. Chief Justice Ill. Ct. of Claims, Chgo., 1962-72; partner Bellows & Bellows, Chgo., 1970-79, Reuben & Proctor, Chgo., 1979—. Bd. dirs. Uptown Poverty Law Center, 1982—. Recipient Maurice Weigle award for outstanding service to organized bar, 1970, U. Ill. Mothers Assn. medallion of honor, 1975, Northwestern U. Alumnae award, 1978. Fellow Am. Bar Found. (sec. 1982-83); mem. Am. Bar Assn. (sec. 1967-73, chmn. sect. individual rights and responsibilities 1975—, mem. ho. of dels. 1975—, com. on bar activities and services 1978—), Ill. Bar Assn. (chmn. Bill of Rights com. 1965-67, bd. govs. 1969-79, mem. assembly 1972-79, chmn. budget com. 1976-77, chmn. legis. com. 1978-79, pres. 1977-78), Chgo. Bar Assn. (chmn. constl. revision com. 1973-74), Am. Law Inst., League Women Voters of Ill., Womens Bar Assn. Ill., Decalogue Soc., Nat. Conf. Bar Presidents (exec. council 1977—), Northwestern U. Sch. Law Alumni Assn. (pres. 1982-83). Club: Law (Chgo.). Editor: Your Bill of Rights, 1967, 69. Home: 725 LaPorte Ave Wilmette IL 60091 Office: 11 S LaSalle St Suite 2001 Chicago IL 60603

BELLOWS, VIRGINIA LOUISE, tel. co. exec.; b. Fort Wayne, Ind., July 25, 1951; d. Raymond Francis and Abigail Ann (Vaughan) B.; B.S., U. Miami (Fla.), 1972, M.B.A., 1979; m. Michael Ross, Aug. 16, 1975. With So. Bell Tel. Co., Miami, 1972-79, staff mgr., Atlanta, 1979—. Pres., Acanthus of Fla., Inc. Mem. Arts and Scis. Alumni Assn. U. Miami (dir. 1979), Nat. Assn. Female Execs., Am. Soc. Profl. and Exec. Women, Nat. Assn. M.B.A. Execs. Republican. Episcopalian. Club: Toastmasters. Home: 6036 Millstone Run Stone Mountain GA 30087 Office: 675 W Peachtree St NE Room 34159 Atlanta GA 30375

BELLUGI, URSULA HERZBERGER, educator; b. Jena, Germany, Feb. 21, 1931; came to U.S., 1935, naturalized, 1940; d. Max and Edith (Kaufmann) Herzberger; B.A., Antioch Coll., 1952; Ed.D., Harvard U., 1967; m. Edward S. Klima; children—David, Robin. Sr. research asst. Harvard U., Boston, 1964-67, asst. prof. dept. social relations, 1967-68, vis. lectr. Linguistics Inst., 1968; vis. asst. prof. dept. psychology Rockefeller U., N.Y.C., 1969; adj. asst. prof. dept. psychology U. Calif., San Diego, 1969-70, adj. asso. prof., 1970-76, adj. prof., 1977—; dir. Lab. Lang. and Cognitive Studies, Salk Inst. Biol. Studies, San Diego, 1970—, research prof., 1981—; vis. prof. Consiglio Nationale delle Ricerche, Rome, 1981; adj. prof. dept. communicative disorders San Diego State U., 1982—; mem. nat. adv. com. edn. of deaf HEW; mem. adv. bd. Nat. Inst. Neurol. and Communicative Disorders. Trustee Salk Inst., 1982—. NSF grantee, 1974—, NIH grantee, 1970—. Mem. Am. Psychol. Assn., Internat. Linguistic Assn., Linguistic Soc. Am., Soc. Neurosci., Psychonomic Soc., Soc. Research in Child Devel., Internat. Assn. Study of Child Lang., European Brain and Behavior Soc., Am. Assn. Applied Linguistics, Brit. Brain Research Assn. Author: (with E.S. Klima) The Signs of Language (Assn. Am. Pubs. award), 1979; Signed and Spoken Language, 1980; contbr. numerous articles on founds. of lang. to profl. jours.; editorial bd. Jour. Child Lang., Jour. Applied Linguistics, Jour. Speech and Hearing Disorders, Sign Lang. Studies, Jour. Human Communication, Contemporary Psychology; contbr. chpts. to books. Home: 6649 Michaeljohn Dr La Jolla CA 92037 Office: Salk Inst PO Box 85800 San Diego CA 92138

BELLWARD, GAIL DIANNE, pharmacologist, educator; b. Brock, Can., May 27, 1939; d. Eric H. and Mildred E. (Cyr) B.; B.Sc. (Pharm.), U. B.C. (Can.), 1960, M.Sc., 1963, Ph.D., 1966. Asst. prof. pharm. scis. U. B.C., Vancouver, 1967-73, asso. prof., 1973-79, prof., 1979—, chmn. div. pharmacology and toxicology, 1981—; fellow dept. medicine Emory

U., Atlanta, 1968-69; vis. prof. Royal Postgrad. Med. Sch., London, 1975; cons. various health and govt. agys., 1970—; vis. prof. U. Toronto, 1971-72, U. Sask., Dalhousie U., 1975-76. Recipient award of Merit, Lambda Kappa Sigma, 1980. mem. Am. Soc. Pharmacology and Exptl. Therapeutics, Can. Fedn. Biol. Scis. (dir. 1977-80), Pharmacol. Soc. Can. (sec. 1977-80), Soc. Toxicology Can., Fedn. Am. Socs. Exptl. Biology. Contbr. articles on drug metabolism, toxicology and pharmacology to profl. jours. Office: Faculty of Pharm Sciences Univ BC Vancouver BC V6T 1W5 Canada

BELMER, BARBARA JANE, hosp. research adminstr.; b. West Chester, Pa., Feb. 22, 1931; d. Charles William and Eleanor Munger (Steele) B.; B.A., Elmira (N.Y.) Coll., 1952. Pvt. bus. and law and acctg., 1952-57; asst. for spl. projects, exec. sec. to mem. bd. trustees Meml. Sloan-Kettering Cancer Center, N.Y.C., 1957-63, asst. dir. grants and contracts, 1963-65, grants mgmt. supr., 1965-69, grants mgmt. asst., 1969-74; research adminstr. St. Luke's Hosp. Center, N.Y.C., 1974-79; adminstr. St. Luke's Inst. Health Scis., N.Y.C., 1978-79; research adminstr. St. Luke's-Roosevelt Hosp. Center, 1979—; adminstr. St. Luke's-Roosevelt Inst. Health Scis., 1979—; mem. hospice com. St. Luke's Hosp. Center, 1975—. Pres., 400 E. 88th St. Block Assn., 1973-75. Mem. Soc. Research Adminstrs., Public Responsibility in Medicine and Research, Smithsonian Assos., Met. Mus. Art (asso.). Home: 436 E 88th St New York NY 10028 Office: St Luke's Roosevelt Inst Health Sciences Amsterdam Ave at 114th St New York NY 10025

BELOVITCH, JEANNE ANN, public relations writer; b. Cin., June 7, 1945; d. Charles and Mildred Jane (Flinchpaugh) Belovitch; B.S., Boston U., 1967. Asst. v.p. sales promotion Putnam Fund Distbrs., Boston, 1971-74; prin. Jeanne Belovitch & Assos., Boston, 1974-75; account exec., creator, producer, moderator arts program Sta. WWEL, Medford, Mass., 1975-78; writer public affairs United Way of Mass. Bay, Boston, 1978-82; pres. Boston Firsts, Inc., 1980—; mgr. G&R Publs., Inc., Boston, 1982—; cons. fund raising Cambridge (Mass.) YWCA, 1979; instr. Fenway Free U., Boston; adv. creative writer's Workshop Walpole Prison. Mem. Boston U. Alumni Assn. (dir. Coll. Basic Studies). Jewish. Contbr. articles to newspapers and mags. Home: 24 Appleton St Boston MA 02116 Office: 648 Beacon St Boston MA

BELOW, NANCY LYNN, banker; b. Toledo, June 3, 1938; d. William George and Marjorie (Mundhenk) Yeagle; student U. Toledo, 1956-57; m. Kenneth W. Below, Feb. 20, 1965 (dec. Mar. 1981). Bookkeeper, West Central Med. Group, Toledo, 1957-59; sec. Prudential Ins. Co. Am., Toledo, 1959-64, office mgr., 1965-70; loan originator Ohio Citizens Trust Co., Toledo, 1970-75, asst. v.p. mortgage loans, 1975-76, v.p. mortgage loans, 1976-81, v.p. community relations, 1981—. Treas. bd. trustees Toledo Neighborhood Housing Services, Inc., Toledo YWCA, Downtown Toledo Community Trust Bd., Women Involved in Toledo, Inc.; chmn. urban homesteading lotter com. City of Toledo, 1978—; mem. Downtown Housing Task Force, 1977-78; trustee N.W. Ohio Chpt. Nat. Kidney Found. Mem. Nat. Assn. Bank Women, Am. Inst. Banking (gov. 1972-76), Beta Sigma Phi. Congregationalist. Clubs: Zonta, Cooley Canal Yacht Club Ladies Aux. (treas. 1980—). Office: Ohio Citizens Bank PO Box 1688 Toledo OH 43603

BELTON, LINDA WEBER, nurse, adminstr.; b. Erie, Pa., Jan. 26, 1950; d. James E. and Mildred E. (Dougherty) Weber; R.N., Jameson Sch. Nursing, 1970; student Westminster Coll., 1967-68, Mercyhurst Coll., 1976-77; B.S. in Nursing Adminstrn., Columbia Pacific U., 1981, M.S. in Nursing Adminstrn., 1982; B.S. in Psychology, SUNY, 1982; m. Lawrence Winfield Belton, June 27, 1969; children—Marshall LeMaster, Adrienne Elizabeth. Nursing supr. Chatham (Pa.) Extended Care Facility, 1973-75; clin. coordinator rehab. services St. Vincent Health Center, Erie, Pa., 1975-77; dir. nursing Shady Acres Nursing Home, Madison, Ohio, 1977-79; nurse adminstr. Meml. Hosp. of Carbon County, Rawlins, Wyo., 1979-81, asst. hosp. adminstr., 1981—; cons. Rawlins Health Occupations Center. Mem. Wyo. State Continuing Edn. com., 1981-83; bd. dirs. Am. Cancer Soc., 1980—; mem. Child Protection Team, Rawlins, 1979-80, Family Life Ministry team, 1981—. Recipient Am. Cancer Soc. Participation award, 1981. Mem. Nat. League for Nursing, Am. Nurses Assn. (cert. in nursing adminstrn.), Wyo. Nurses Assn. (dir. 1980—). Club: Bus. and Profl. Women's. Contbr. articles to profl jours.

BELY, JEANETTE LOBACH, educator; b. Bklyn., Jan. 15, 1916; d. John M. and Antonina M. Lobach; B.B.A., St. John's U., 1938, Ph.D., 1961; M.A., Tchrs. Coll., Columbia U., 1939; children by previous marriage—Jeanette Zinaida Bely, Leone Bely Keeler. Instr. secretarial studies and accountancy Lamb's Bus. Tng. Sch., 1940; tchr.-in-charge sch. adminstrn. Miller Schs., Inc., N.Y.C., 1941-48; lectr. Hunter Coll., N.Y.C., 1954; part-time instr. secretarial studies Pace Coll., 1951-54; prof. edn. and lectr. Baruch Coll., City U. N.Y., N.Y., 1954—, asst. to sec. gen. faculty, 1973-78. Mem. Presdl. Task Force, 1982. Mem. Nat. Bus. Edn. Assn. (Meritorious Service award 1978), Adminstrv. Mgmt. Soc. (Merit award 1969), Bus. Edn. Assn. Met. N.Y. (pres. 1975-76, exec. com. 1963—), Bus. Tchrs. Assn. N.Y. State, Eastern Bus. Edn. Assn., Eastern Bus. Tchrs. Assn., Delta Pi Epsilon. Mem. Eastern Orthodox Ch. Author: (with R. Landroth) Pitman Secretarial Shorthand for Colleges, 1978, Instructor's Handbook, 1978; contbr. articles on bus. edn. to profl. jours.; editorial bd. McGraw Hill, 1978; co-editor Bus. Edn. Assn. Yearbook, 1965-66. Home: 1024 E 93d St Brooklyn NY 11236 Office: Bernard M Baruch College 17 Lexington Ave New York NY 10010

BELYEA, HELEN REYNOLDS, geologist; b. St. John, N.B., Can., Feb. 11, 1913; d. Arthur Sefton and Eleanor (Reynolds) B.; B.A., Dalhousie U., 1934, M.A., 1936, LL.D., 1977; Ph.D., Northwestern U., 1939; D.Sc., Windsor U., 1976. Geologist, Geol. Survey Can., 1945-74, sr. geologist, 1960-74. Served as It. Women's Royal Can. Naval Service, 1943-45. Decorated officer Order of Can. Fellow Royal Soc. Can.; mem. Can. Soc. Petroleum Geologists (hon.; Barlow award medal, Alta. Achievement award 1976), Geol. Assn. Can., Soc. Econ. Paleontologists and Mineralogists, Internat. Assn. Sedimentologists, Alpha Gamma Delta. Clubs: Glencor, Calgary Golf and Country. Home: Apt 14 230 21st Ave SW Calgary AB T2S 0G6 Canada Office: Inst Sedimentary and Petroleum Geology 3303 33d St NW Calgary AB T2L 2A7 Canada *

BELYEA, MARLOU, twp. ofcl., mayor; b. Burbank, Calif., Sept. 11, 1926; d. Allan Francis and Louise (La Rue) Rau; B.A., Scripps Coll., 1947; m. Robert C. Belyea, June 15, 1947; children—Marlou, Wendy Lee, Carolyn Anne. Legis. aide to assemblywoman Ann Klein, Morristown, N.J., 1973; mem. Pequannock Twp. Planning Bd., 1975-77, Pequannock Twp. Council, Pompton Plains, N.J., 1977-81, mayor Pequannock Twp., 1979-80. Mem. N.J. Fedn. Elected Women Ofcls., N.J. Fedn. Republican Women, AAUW, LWV (N.J. dir. 1969-71). Home: 134 Mountain Ave Pompton Plains NJ 07444

BEMAN, NAN O'BRIEN, social worker; b. Milw., Jan. 17, 1948; d. Robert Ward O'Brien and Harriett (Price) Stockanes; B.A., Beloit Coll., 1970; M.S.W., U. Minn., 1976; m. David C. Beman, Nov. 28, 1970; children—Cameron, Sarah. Correctional counselor Minn. Dept. Corrections Mpls., 1971-73; family counselor for ct. services Hennepin County Domestic Relations Dept., Mpls., 1975-76; sr. social worker Hennepin County Child Services Dept., 1976-82, prin. social worker, 1982—; clin. field instr. U. Minn., 1976—; guest lectr. Coll. St. Katherine, St. Paul, 1978—. Mem. U. Minn. Grad. Sch. Social Work Alumni Assn. (sec.-treas., dir. 1977-81). Home: 319 W 50th St Minneapolis MN 55419 Office: 300 S 6th St Room 16-A Minneapolis MN 55487

BENAMY, ROSLYN HEIDECORN, educator; b. N.Y.C., May 24, 1929; d. Philip and Sarah (Krauss) Heidecorn; B.S., N.Y. U., 1954, M.B.A., 1957; m. Daniel A. Benamy, June 6, 1952; children—Philip, Leonard, David, Leah. Lectr., Bklyn. Coll., 1954-55; instr. Fairleigh Dickinson U., Rutherford, N.J., 1955-60, Bronx Community Coll., 1960-62; prof. bus. edn. Rockland Community Coll., Suffern, N.Y., 1966—; tng. cons. Am. Cyanimide Corp., Pearl River, N.Y., 1980-81, Rockland County Social Services Agy., Pomona, N.Y., 1979-80, Rockland County Office of Aging, New City, N.Y., 1977-82. Trustee, Temple Emeth, Teaneck, N.J., 1978-81; exec. bd. Teaneck Citizens for Public Schs., 1972-73; water resource chmn. Teaneck LWV, 1969-70; Democratic dist. committeewoman Bergen County Dist. 13, 1963-69. Recipient Chancellor's award for excellence in teaching SUNY, 1981. Mem. Nat. Bus. Edn. Assn. (exec. bd. 1980-81), Eastern Bus. Edn. Assn. (pres. 1980-81), Am. Vocat. Assn., Internat. Info./Word Processing Assn. (chpt. pres. 1981-82). Contbr. articles to profl. jours. Home: 295 Churchill Rd Teaneck NJ 07666 Office: 145 College Rd Suffern NY 10901

BENBROOK, CONNIE LOUISE SKAGGS, petroleum co. ofcl.; b. Miami, Okla., Dec. 30, 1946; d. Everett Gene and Doloris Nadine (Foreman) Skaggs; A.A., N.E. Okla. A&M U., 1967; B.S. in Bus. Adminstrn., Kans. State Coll., Pittsburg, 1969; m. W.D. Benbrook, June 6, 1969; children— Brian Patrick, Sean Michael. Student advisor data processing dept. N.E. Okla. A&M U., Miami, 1965-67; programmer Sinclair Oil Co., Independence, Kans., 1967-69; with data processing dept. Cities Service, Bartlesville, Okla., 1969-71; data processing sales and tech. services Phillips Petroleum Co., Bartlesville, 1971-75, tng. coordinator comml. system devel., 1975-79, supr. tng. and internal systems, 1979-80, supr. personnel benefits, 1980-81, supr. other corp. systems, 1981—; instr. Tri-County Tech., Bartlesville, 1980—; instr. data processing Coffeeville (Kans.) Jr. Coll. Mem. Am. Soc. Tng. and Devel. Democrat. Baptist. Office: 424 IC Bldg Phillips Petroleum Co Bartlesville OK 74003

BENBROOK, FAY FAXON, psychiatrist; b. Los Angeles, Mar. 1, 1931; d. Floyd Harold and Thelma Rose (Adamson) Faxon; B.S., UCLA, 1953; M.D., Stanford U., 1957; m. Samuel Parker Benbrook, Sept. 21, 1956; children—Carol Ann, Diana Fay. Intern, VA, Los Angeles, 1958-59; resident U. Calif., Irvine, 1968-70; resident Neuropsychiat. Inst.-UCLA, 1970-72, asst. clin. prof. child psychiatry, 1972—; practice medicine specializing in psychiatry and child psychiatry, Los Angeles, 1972—. Mem. Am. Med. Women's Assn. Club: Sierra. Office: 10921 Wilshire Blvd 507 Los Angeles CA 90024-3976

BENDER, BETTY WION, librarian; b. Mt. Ayr, Iowa, Feb. 26, 1925; d. John F. and Sadie Augusta (Guess) Wion; student Drake U., 1942-44; B.S., N. Tex. U., 1946; M.A., U. Denver, 1957; m. Robert F. Bender, Aug. 24, 1946. Asst. cataloger N. Tex. State Coll., Denton, 1946-49; cataloger So. Meth. U., Dallas, 1949-51; reference asst. Ind. State Library, Indpls., 1951-52; periodicals librarian So. Meth. U., Dallas, 1952-53, head of acquisitions, 1953-56; grad. asst. U. Denver, 1956-57; acting head librarian Ark. State Coll., 1958, librarian, 1958-59; cataloger St. Louis Public Library, 1966-67; librarian Eastern Wash. State Hist. Soc., Spokane, 1960-66, 67; reference librarian Spokane Public Library, 1968, circulation librarian, 1968-73, library dir., 1973—; mem. Wash. State Library Commn., 1979—. Bd. dirs. Inland Empire Goodwill Industries, 1975-77, NW Regional Found., 1975-77. Mem. ALA, AAUW (Betty W. Bender fellowship named in her honor 1972), Pacific NW Library Assn., Washington Library Assn. Lutheran. Club: Zonta. Office: Spokane Public Library W 906 Main Ave Spokane WA 99201

BENDER, SANDRA DIANE BROWN, cosmetics co. exec.; b. Evansville, Ind., Oct. 5, 1943; d. James A. and Marye (Miller) Brown; A.B., Ind. U., 1965, M.S., 1970; M.B.A., N.Y.U., 1979. Tchr. schs., Pine Bluff, Ark., Louisville, 1965-71; talk show co-host Sta. WHAS-TV, Louisville, 1971-72; grants adminstr., program specialist Girl Scouts U.S.A., N.Y.C., 1973-75; with Burlington Industries, 1975-78; div. sales mgr. Avon Products, Rye, N.Y., 1978—. Mem. Assn. M.B.A. Execs., Nat. Assn. Female Execs., Ind. U. Alumni Assn. Home: 170 W 23d St Apt 5A New York NY 10011 Office: Avon Products Division St Suffern NY 10901

BENDHEIM, LEONORE CAROLINE, social worker; b. Amsterdam, Holland, Oct. 26, 1921; came to U.S., 1943, naturalized, 1949; d. Martin and Alice S. (Mayer) B.; student Traphagen Sch. Design, N.Y.C., 1943-46; B.A. in Art Edn., Kans. U., 1970; B.A. in Social Work, Washburn U., 1972; M.S. in Clin. Counseling, Emporia State Coll., 1974; postgrad. Kans. State U., 1980—. Interior designer, Mehagian's Home Furnishings, Phoenix, Ariz., 1951-59; prin. Leonore C. Bendheim, interior designer, Phoenix, 1959-63; research asst. Menninger Research Clinic, Topeka, Kans., 1963-64; art therapist Topeka State Hosp., 1966; vol. Vocat. Rehab. Center for the Blind, Topeka, 1967; social worker Kans. Psychiat. Reception and Diagnostic Center, Topeka, 1970-73; social worker VA Hosp. and Med. Center, Topeka, 1973—. Pres., Unitarian Universalist Fellowship, Topeka, 1976-77; active Unitarian Universalist Women's Fedn. and Service Com., coordinator for aged in Kans. Recipient various design awards, 1947-63; lic. social worker, Kans. Mem. Counseling and Guidance Soc., NE Kans. Assn. Social Welfare, Nat. Assn. Humanists, Am. Inst. Interior Designers, Am. Art Therapy Assn., Nat. Assn. Social Workers, Mid-West Weavers Assn., Ashram Soc. Unitarian. Home: 2601 SW James St Topeka KS 66614 Office: 2200 Gage Blvd Topeka KS 66622

BENEDETTO, LOIS LEONARD, civic worker; b. N.Y.C., Dec. 12, 1944; d. John James and Lillian Marie (Gramer) Leonard; B.A., Marymount Manhattan Coll., 1966; M.A., Fordham U., 1967; postgrad. in bus. U. Chgo.; m. William Benedetto, Apr. 20, 1968; children—Michael, William. Instr. mathematics CCNY, 1967-68, Marymount Manhattan Coll., N.Y.C., 1968-71; bd. dirs. Northwestern Meml. Hosp., Chgo., 1977—, pres. Service Bd., 1976—; exec. leader Spl. Gifts Div., Crusade of Mercy, Chgo., 1976—; mem. Women's Bd., Lincoln Park Zool. Soc., Chgo., 1976—; jr. governing bd. Chgo. Symphony Orch, 1975-76; mem. bd. govs. Chgo. Heart Assn., 1978—. Roman Catholic. Clubs: Woman's Athletic, Jr. League, Saddle and Cycle. Address: 1105 Park Ave New York NY 10028

BENEDICT, REBECCA CRAIG, accountant; b. Bellevue, Ohio, Mar. 27, 1946; d. Walter Leroy and Frances Klavora Craig; B.S. with honors in Gen. Bus., Eastern Mont. Coll., 1980; m. George A. Benedict, Jan. 7, 1977; 1 son, Craig Charles. Supt., Kathleen-Louise Mfg. Co., Spokane, Wash., 1970-72; with Deluxe Check Printers, Billings, Mont., 1972-76; owner, mgr. Benedict's Tax Service, Billings, 1976—. Mem. Am. Soc. Women Accts., Nat. Assn. Enrolled Agts., Alpha Psi Kappa. Republican. Mem. Assemblies of God Ch. Clubs: Eastern Mont. Coll. Faculty Women's (treas. 1978, 79). State editor: State Tax Coordinator, Research Inst. Am., 1981-82. Home and Office: 1011 N 32d St Billings MT 59101

BENEKE, MILLIE STONG, civic worker, city ofcl., author; b. Prairie City, Iowa; d. Rueben Ira and Lillian (Garber) Stong; student Washington U., 1942-43, Mankato State Coll., 1951, 67; m. Arnold W. Beneke, Aug. 10, 1939; children—Bruce Arnold, Paula Rae, Bradford Kent, Cynthia Jane, Lisa Patrice. Exec. sec. chmn. Vol. Services, ARC, St. Paul, 1940-41; v.p. Pi House, St. Paul, 1972-77; founder, bd. dirs., chmn. Project Interaction Boutique, Minn. Correctional Instn. for Women, Shakopee, 1971—, supervising vol., 1970—. Chmn. McLeod County Diversion Program, 1974-81. Republican chairwoman McLeod County (Minn.), 1969-73; mem. Rep. Minn. Platform com., 1970; McLeod County del. Rep. Minn. Central Com., 1969—; mem. Rep. Feminist Caucus; alderman Glencoe City Council, 1974-80; v.p. Friends of Library, 1975—; bd. dirs. Buffalo Creek Players, 1976—, v.p., 1980—; bd. dirs. Mpls. Children's Theatre Co. Housing for elderly named in her honor. Mem. Glencoe Bus. and Profl. Women (Woman of Year 1975). Lutheran. Author: (play) The Garage Sale, 1978; Politics Unusual, 1979; The Househusband and the Working Wife, 1982, also children's plays. Home: 330 Scout Hill Dr Box 215 Glenview Woods Glencoe MN 55336

BENENSON, ESTHER SIEV (MRS. WILLIAM BENENSON), gerontologist, educator, nursing home adminstr.; b. Jerusalem, Aug. 16, 1925; d. Joshua and Anna (Sanders) Siev; A.A.S., Queens Coll., 1957; B.S., Hunter Coll., 1972, M.S., 1974; Ed.M., Columbia U. Tchrs. Coll., 1976, Ed.D. in Gerontology, 1981; m. William Benenson, Sept. 15, 1957; children—Michael J., Sharon G., Amy L., Blanche S. Exec. dir. Flushing (N.Y.) Manor Nursing Home, 1959—, Flushing Manor Care Center, 1974—. Registered nurse; licensed X-ray technician. Mem. N.Y. State Bd. Examiners for Licensing Nursing Home Adminstrs., 1970-74; mem. adv. council N.Y. State Health Planning Commn., 1974; adj. asso. prof. dept. health care and public adminstrn. C.W. Post Center, L.I. U., 1972-77. Fellow Am. Coll. Nursing Home Adminstrs., Am. Assn. Med. Adminstrs., Royal Soc. Health; mem. N.Y. State Nursing Home Assn., Am. Public Health Assn., Soc. Public Health Educators, Gerontol. Soc., Bus. and Profl. Women's Club Greater Flushing, Women's Aux. Med. Soc. State N.Y., Women's Aux. AMA, Doctors Wives Aux. Flushing Hosp. and Med. Center. Office: 35-15 Parsons Blvd Flushing NY 11354

BENGTSON, ESTHER G., state legislator; b. Froid, Mont., Oct. 30, 1927; d. Goodwin and Elizabeth (Jorgensen) Bergh; student U. Mont., 1945-47, Eastern Mont. Coll., 1964-67; m. Lawrence E. Bengtson; children—Kristianne Bengtson Wilson, Monica Bengtson Holland, Jennifer. Mem. Mont. Ho. of Reps. 1975—; alt. del. Democratic Nat. Conv. 1976. Mem. Mont. Edn. Assn., Shepherd Edn. Assn., Sigma Kappa. Lutheran. Office: Montana Ho of Reps Capitol Station Helena MT 59620 *

BENHAM, CAROLINE MARGARET (SZVETECZ), social worker, lawyer; b. Oklahoma City, July 30, 1941; d. Webster Lance, Jr., and Catherine (Collier) B.; B.A., Colo. Coll., 1963; M.S.W. (NIMH fellow), U. Denver, 1965; J.D., U. Colo., 1975; m. Frank C. Szvetecz, Mar. 21, 1975; children—Jason, Tynan; stepchildren—Charles, Anne, Matthew. Social worker, prin. social worker Ft. Logan Mental Health Center, Denver, 1965-69; pvt. practice social work, 1969-71; admitted to Colo. bar, 1975; individual practice law, Colorado Springs, Colo., 1975-76; juvenile ct. referee 4th Jud. Dist., State of Colo., Colorado Springs, 1976-79, juvenile ct. commr., 1979—, dist. ct. referee, 1981—. Vice chmn., acting chmn. El Paso County Placement Alternatives Commn., 1979—; bd. dirs. Chins Up Youth Care Homes, chmn. task force/planning com.; Jr. League community adv. bd., 1978-80; Colorado Springs Citizens Goals conferee; mem. Pikes Peak Children's Advocates. Lic. social worker, Colo. Mem. Am. Bar Assn., Colo. Bar Assn., El Paso County Bar Assn., Colo. Women's Bar Assn., Women Lawyers of Fourth Jud. Dist., Am. Trial Lawyers Assn., Colo. Trial Lawyers Assn., Nat. Assn. Social Workers, Acad. Cert. Social Workers, Nat. Assn. Counsel for Children, Nat. Council Juvenile and Family Ct. Judges, Profl. Women's Assembly, Delta Gamma. Democrat. Participant, lectr. seminars in field; contbr. to juvenile sect. District Court Judges Benchbook, 1981. Home: 2115 Payton Circle Colorado Springs CO 80915 Office: Judicial Bldg 20 E Vermijo Ave Colorado Springs CO 80903

BENINSON, ELLEN LYNN, bus. mfg. co. exec.; b. Detroit, Dec. 4, 1953; d. Joseph and Eleanor (Stolmach) B.; B.A. in Communications, Mich. State U., 1976. Advt. account exec. Mich. State News, East Lansing, 1974-76; adminstrv. mgmt. trainee Pitney Bowes, Trenton, N.J., 1976, asst. adminstrv. mgr., Orange, N.J., 1976-77, asst. adminstrv. mgr. II, Cleve., 1977, adminstrv. mgr. V, Wichita, Kans., 1977-79; adminstrv. mgr. III, Phoenix, 1979—; student instr. communication dept. Mich. State U., 1975-76. Social action chmn. Temple Emanu-El, Wichita, 1979. Recipient Gen. Mgrs. award Mich. State News, 1975, Adminstrv. achievement award Pitney Bowes, 1978, 79. Mem. Adminstrv. Mgmt. Soc., The Exec. Female, Jewish Profl. and Bus. Women Am., Mich. State U. Alumni Assn., Sigma Alpha Mu Little Sisters (pres. 1974-75). Jewish. Home: 925 W Peoria Ave 15 Phoenix AZ 85029 Office: 9424 N 25th Ave Phoenix AZ 85021

BENJAMIN, LORNA SMITH, psychologist; b. Rochester, N.Y., Jan. 7, 1934; d. Lloyd Albert and Esther (Tack) Smith; A.B., Oberlin Coll., 1955; Ph.D., U. Wis., 1960; children—Laureen, Linda. NIMH fellow dept. psychiatry U. Wis., 1958-62, clin. psychology intern, 1960-64, asst. prof., 1966-71, asso. prof., 1971-77, prof. psychiatry, 1977—; research asso. Wis. Psychol. Inst., Madison, 1962-66. Mem. Am. Psychol. Assn., AAAS, Soc. Psychotherapy Research, Phi Beta Kappa. Contbr. articles to profl. jours. Office: Dept Psychiatry U Wis 600 Highland Ave Madison WI 53792

BENJAMIN, PAMELA SOUTHWORTH, interior designer; b. Hartford, Conn., Oct. 20, 1952; d. James Rollins and Jeanne Marthe (Bouvier) Southworth; B.S., U. Conn., 1975; m. Thomas Gerard Benjamin, July 29, 1972. Interior designer Continental Ill. Nat. Bank, Chgo., 1979-81; dir. design OFP Total Design Cons., Stamford, Conn., 1981; space planner Midwest Stock Exchange, Chgo., 1981; office planner, interior designer Abbott Labs., North Chicago, Ill., 1982—; regional sec. Inst. Bus. Designers, 1979-81, v.p., 1981—. Mem. social com. Lake Hinsdale Tower Assn., 1978-81; mem. congressional campaign com. Midwest Communications Assn., 1981-82. Recipient cert. of recognition for Outstanding Contbn., Inst. Bus. Designers, 1981; First prize Design-A-Toy Contest, Mansfield (Conn.) Tng. Sch., 1975. Mem. Am. Soc. Interior Designers, Inst. Bus. Designers, Midwest Communications Assn., Lake Hinsdale Tower Assn. Home: 6340C Americana 218 Clarendon Hills IL 60514 Office: 1400 Sheridan Rd Abbott Park North Chicago IL 60064

BENN, INGRID ILEANA, publishing co. exec.; b. Arroyo, P.R., May 1, 1953; came to U.S., 1955; d. Roberto and Virginia (Cancel) B.; A.B. magna cum laude, Wilmington (Ohio) Coll., 1975; M.B.A. cum laude, Ohio State U., Columbus, 1977. With Charles E. Merrill Pub. Co., Columbus, 1977—, product mgr., 1979-81, mktg. mgr. trade pub., 1982, also dir. internat. sch. div. Mem. Assn. M.B.A. Execs., Am. Booksellers Assn., Nat. Assn. Female Execs., ALA. Roman Catholic. Home: 4215 E Broad St Columbus OH 43213 Office: 1300 Alum Creek Dr Columbus OH 43216

BENN, PHYLISS ASHMUN, lawyer; b. Washburn, Wis., Aug. 26, 1924; d. Van Sanford and Margaret Fiege Ashmun; B.A., U. Wis.-Madison, 1946; J.D., Valparaiso U., 1975; m. Donald W. Benn, Aug. 30, 1947; children—David W., Martha Ann, Ruth L., Robert Samuel. City editor Niles (Mich.) Daily Star, 1946-47; editorial asst. Towndan Pub. Co., LaPorte, Ind., 1964-71; admitted to Ind. bar, 1975; asso. firm Smith and Smith, LaPorte, 1975-79; individual practice law, LaPorte, 1979—. Chmn. City of LaPorte Human Rights Commn., 1980-82; precinct committeewoman Democratic County Com., 1974-82, del. Dem. Nat. Conv., 1976; vol. Girl Scouts U.S.A., No. Ind. Council, 1948-70, v.p.,

1964-67. Mem. LaPorte City Bar Assn. (sec. 1981-82), Family Service Assn. (dir. 1979—), AAUW (LaPorte br. grantee 1973, pres. 1958-59, state dir. 1960-63), Am. Bar Assn., Ind. Bar Assn., County Bar Assn., Family Mediation Service, LaPorte County Child Protection Team, Phi Beta Kappa. Home and Office: 1001 Maple Ave LaPorte IN 46350

BENNER, ANN WRIGLEY, sales exec.; b. Brevard, N.C., Oct. 30, 1943; d. George and Edith Charlotte (Patton) Wrigley; student Converse Coll., 1961-62; children—Arthur, Paige. Store mgr. Heskett's Carpets DBA Gen. Floors, Inc., Oakland, Calif., 1972-76; Pacific Flooring distbr. Burlington House Carpets, Emeryville, Calif., 1976-78; ter. sales mgr. J.P. Stevens & Co., Inc., Gulistan Div., San Francisco, 1978-82; regional sales mgr. Cambray Mills, Inc., Garden Grove, Calif., 1982—. Patron, Performing Artists Group, San Francisco, 1981—. Recipient Outstanding Sales award Pres.'s Council, Burlington House Carpets, 1977; named to Laurel Soc. and Million Dollar Club, J.P. Stevens & Co. Mem. San Francisco Floor Covering Assn. Club: USMC Wives' (pres. 1968). Home: 8061 Peppertree Rd Dublin CA 94568 Office: 7397 Doig Dr Garden Grove CA 92641

BENNETT, BETTY BESSE, librarian; b. Omaha, Feb. 18, 1921; d. Gordon Stanley and Besse Harriet (Amos) B.; B.A., Mcpl. U. Omaha, 1942; B.S. in L.S., U. Ill., 1943; M.A., U. Iowa, 1948; M.L.S., Tex. Woman's U., 1960. Asst. documents librarian U. Iowa Library, Iowa City, 1943-50; reference and documents librarian Kans. State Tchrs. Coll. Library, Pittsburg, 1950-57, reference librarian, archivist, 1957-67; reference and research librarian Stephen F. Austin State U. Library, Nacogdoches, Tex., 1967-72, govt. documents librarian, 1972—; resource cons. Gov.'s Conf. on Libraries, Austin, Tex., 1974. Clk. session Presbyterian Ch., 1967-80, ruling elder, 1975—; exec. dir. Telephone Reassurance Program for Elderly Shut-Ins, 1977-80. Mem. AAUW, AAUP, ALA (state document classifcation com. 1974-80, state documents task force) Tex. (chmn. govt. documents round table 1975-76), Southwestern library assns., Tex. Assn. Coll. Tchrs., Nacogdoches Friends of the Library, Alpha Xi Delta. Presbyterian. Office: Stephen F Austin State U Library Nacogdoches TX 75962

BENNETT, BETTY T., edni. adminstr.; b. N.J.; B.A., Bklyn. Coll., 1962; M.A., N.Y. U., 1963; Ph.D., 1970; children—Peter, Matthew. Asst. prof. (adj.) English dept. and comparative lit. SUNY, Stony Brook, 1970-75, asst. chmn. comparative lit., 1971-72, asst. to dean Grad. Sch., 1970-79, adj. asso. prof., 1975-79; asso. prof. English and humanities Pratt Inst., Bklyn., 1979-81, prof., 1981—, dean Sch. Liberal Arts and Scis., 1979—; Danforth Found. fellowship reader, 1978-79, edn. liaison officer N.Y. State, 1977-80. Nat. Endowment Humanities fellow, 1974-75; Henry E. Huntington Library fellow, 1976; Am. Council Learned Socs. fellow, 1977-78; Am. Philos. Soc. grantee, 1979-80. Mem. AAUP, AAUW, Bklyn. Coll. Alumni, Byron Assn., Keats-Shelley Assn., MLA, N.Y. U. Alumni Assn., Phi Beta Kappa. Author: British War Poetry in the Age of Romanticism: 1793-1815, 1976; The Evidence of the Imagination, 1978; The Letters of Mary Wollstonecraft Shelley, Vol. I, 1980. Home: 181 Steuben St Brooklyn NY 11205 Office: 200 Willoughby Ave Brooklyn NY 11205

BENNETT, BEVERLEY LOREE, educator; b. Dallas, Oreg., Nov. 19, 1926; d. Albert John and Myrtle Clara (Chase) Bennett; B.S., U. Oreg., 1948, M.S., 1950; postgrad. U. Calif., Berkeley, 1956. Tchr. summer programs Portland Park Bur., Eugene, Oreg., 1949, Portland, Oreg., 1946, 47, 48, Ashland, Oreg., 1950; instr. phys. edn. So. Oreg. State Coll., Ashland, 1950-53, asst. prof., 1953-65, asso. prof., 1965-81, prof., 1981—; tchr. phys. edn. Lincoln Elem. Sch., Ashland, 1953-57; organizer spl. olympics track, basketball and swimming meets for retardates, 1976-80; evaluator Willamette U. dept. of phys. edn., Salem, Oreg., 1975; sec. Oreg. State Phys. Fitness Com., 1955-59. Mem. Gov.'s Commn. for Women, State of Oreg., 1972-78, sec., 1975; mem. Jackson County Commn. on Status of Women, 1981-82. Mem. Am. Coll. Sports Medicine, AAUW, AAHPER (chmn. scholarship com. 1968, sec., mem. exec. council N.W. dist. 1968-70), Oreg. Assn. for Health, Phys. Edn. and Recreation (pres. 1965-66), Delta Kappa Gamma, Kappa Delta Pi. Democrat. Methodist. Home: 740 Pennsylvania St Ashland OR 97520 Office: Southern Oregon State College Ashland OR 97520

BENNETT, BOBBIE JEAN, state ofcl.; b. Gwinnett County, Ga., July 13, 1940; d. William Claude and Clara Maude (Nichols) Holcome; B.B.A. magna cum laude, Ga. State U., 1973; 1 dau., Terri Lynne. With Ga. State Merit System, Atlanta, 1960—, sr. acct., 1967, asst. div. dir., 1968-70, fiscal officer, 1970-74, div. dir., 1975-78, asst. dep. commr., 1978—. Mem. Ga. Fiscal Mgmt. Council, Ga. Council Personnel Adminstrn., Nat. Assn. Deferred Compensation Adminstrs. (sec.), Beta Gamma Sigma, Phi Kappa Phi, Beta Alpha Psi. Democrat. Home: 2072 Malabar Dr NE Atlanta GA 30345 Office: 244 Washington St SW Atlanta GA 30334

BENNETT, CORRINTHA REBECCA, dance and movement therapist; b. Lansing, Mich., June 22, 1948; d. Jack Chase and Katherine Louise (Kraft) Krause; B.A., DePauw U., 1970; M.S. (grantee) Hunter Coll., 1973; m. Thomas P. Bennett, Oct. 4, 1975 (div.). Guest therapist Exec. Inn for Alcoholics, Fla., 1974; therapist, tng. supr. St. Elizabeth's Hosp., Washington, 1974-79, chief dance therapy sect., dir. internship program, 1979-80; mem. adj. faculty Goucher Coll. Grad. Sch., Towson, Md., also pvt. practice psychotherapy, Washington and Europe, 1980—; guest lectr., cons. in Europe. Mem. Nat. Assn. Female Execs., Am. Dance Therapy Assn. (nat. dir. 1977-80), Am. Assn. Sex Educators, Counselors and Therapists. Home: 1110 S Carolina Ave SE Washington DC 20003 Office: 1062 Thomas Jefferson St NW Washington DC 20007

BENNETT, DOLORES B., orgn. adminstr.; b. Clarkston, Utah, Oct. 26, 1920; d. Golden L. and Sarah P. Buttars; student Utah State U., 1938-40; m. James Austin Bennett, Sept. 18, 1940; children—James R., Carl R., Calleen, Marilyn, Marvin C. Vice chmn. Republican Party, Cache County, Utah, 1962-68, 1st congressional dist. vice chmn., 1963-66, 69-72; bd. dirs. Utah State Fair, 1964-69, vice chmn., 1967-69; v.p. Utah Fedn. Republican Women, 1971-73, pres., 1973-77, bd. dirs. nat. fedn. 1973-80, co-chmn. fund raising com., 1978-80; v.p. Utah Womens Legislative Council, 1976-77; del. Internat. Women's Year Conf., 1977; mem. City of Logan Zoning and Planning Commn., 1974—, chmn. 1976-78; mem. City of Logan Bd. Adjustments, 1978—. Vice pres. Utah Freedom Found. of Valley Forge. Mormon. Office: 714 N 150th St W Logan UT 84321

BENNETT, DOROTHY KEMLER, ednl. adminstr., psychologist; b. Cambridge, Mass., June 1, 1935; d. Joseph Aaron and Rae (Shapiro) Kemler; B.S. magna cum laude, Tufts U., 1956; Ed.M. (fellow), Harvard U., 1957, Ed.D., 1970; m. Edward Martin Bennett, Apr. 1, 1959; children—James, Robert. Sch. psychologist Westwood (Mass.) Public Schs., 1969-73, dir. psychol. services, 1973-74; dir. spl. needs Winthrop (Mass.) Public Schs., 1974-77; dir., Multiple Careers Magnet Center, Dallas Public Schs., 1978—; cons. religious edn. dept. Unitarian-Universalist Assn., Boston, 1971-73. Mem. bd. dirs. Lexington (Mass.) Counseling Service, 1970-72. USPHS fellow Judge Baker Guidance Center, Boston, 1957-58. Mem. Am. Psychol. Assn., Council for Exceptional Children, Am. Vocat. Assn., Sigma Xi, Pi Lambda Theta, Pi Delta Kappa. Home: 6930 Wildglen Dr Dallas TX 75230 Office: 4528 Rusk Ave Dallas TX 75204

BENNETT, EUDORA SMITH, hosp. adminstr.; b. W. Franklin, Pa., July 16, 1924; d. Merton Henry and Ruby-Estelle Grace (Allen) Smith; R.N., Robert Packer Hosp. Tng. Sch. Nurses, Sayre, Pa., 1945; m. Raymond Leslie Bennett, Dec. 21, 1946 (div. Jan. 1967); children—Ann Marie, Donald Hasbrouck, Stanley Douglas. Gen. duty nurse Robert Packer Hosp., 1945-46, supr. pediatrics, 1947-48; pvt. duty nurse Carbondale (Pa.) Gen. Hosp., 1948-49; supr. Monmouth Meml. Hosp., Long Branch, N.J., 1950-51; adminstr. Montrose (Pa.) Med. Center, 1951—, also dir.; dir. Med. Arts Nursing Center, Montrose; a founder Med. Arts Clinic, Montrose, 1952; mem. exec. com. Pa. Statewide Health Coordinating Council, 1976—. Bd. dirs., mem. exec. com. N.Y.-Pa. Health Planning Council, 1969—, chmn. Susquehanna County chpt., 1971-72; mem. bd. Northeastern Human Parts Assn., 1971—; mem. Susquehanna County Ambulance and Emergency Services Assn., 1971—. Named Spirit of Nursing, Robert Packer Hosp., 1945. Mem. Am., Pa. (dir. 1982-83, planning and devel. com. 1978—, small and rural hosp. com.) hosp. assns., Hosp. Council N.E. Pa. (chmn. 1982-83), Health Care Facilities Assn. Pa. Republican. Presbyterian. Club: Y-Gradale (Montrose). Home: 42 Maple St Montrose PA 18801 Office: 3 Grow St Montrose PA 18801

BENNETT, GENEVIEVE, artist; b. Chgo., Feb. 11, 1927; d. Joseph and Mary (Szuba) Sieczka; B.A., Calif. State U., Fullerton, 1974, Long Beach, M.A., 1978; student Art Inst. Chgo., 1942, Am. Acad. Art, Chgo., 1949; m. William A. Bennett, Jan. 31, 1953; children—William G., J. Daniel, Gordon Dean. One woman shows: Hunt Library, Fullerton, Calif., 1971, 79, Fullerton Library, 1976, 78, Calif. State U., Long Beach, 1978; group shows include: Laguna Beach Mus. Art, 1969, Springville Mus. Art, Utah, 1975, Chapman Coll., Orange, 1974, Mus. of San Bernardino, Redlands, 1979, Mus. N. Orange County, Fullerton, 1980, Woodrose Gallery, Huntington Beach, 1977, Wesler and Weis Gallery, Encino, 1979; Collectors Choice Gallery, Laguna Beach, 1967, Design Recycle Gallery, Fullerton, 1977, Common Ground Gallery, Fullerton, 1975, 76, 77, 78, 79. Chmn. symposium on healing arts of Am. Indians, Calif. State U., Fullerton, 1975. Mem. Orange County Art Assn. (pres. 1979-80), Muckenthaler Cultural Center (dir. 1979—), Laguna Beach Art Mus., Toranna Art League, Internat. Platform Assn., Am. Film Inst. Christian Ch. Address: 2026 W Judith Ln Anaheim CA 92804

BENNETT, GLORIA KNIGHT, life ins. co. exec.; b. Eddie and Ruby (Buckner) Knight; A.A., Loop City Coll., 1970; B.A., Roosevelt U., 1972, M.A., 1974; m. James Bennett, Apr. 4, 1968; 1 dau., Monique Jene. Counselor Model Cities, Chgo. Commn. on Urban Opportunity, 1975; supr., counselor manpower div. Chgo. Dept. Human Services, 1978; dist. agt. Lutheran Mut. Life Ins. Co., Homewood, Ill., 1980-81, supr., 1981—; pres. Bennett's Ins. & Fin. Service, Chgo., 1980—; gen. agt. Paul Revere Life, Chgo., Union Fidelity, Trevose, Pa., 1980—, Am. Ins. Cons., Los Angeles, 1981—. Mem. Campaign Assocs. for Wilinski for Alderman Com., 1978; community organizer United Neighborhood Orgn.; bd. dirs. St. Felicitious Home-Sch. Assn. Ford Found. fellow, 1970. Mem. Nat. Assn. Life Underwriters. Democrat. Roman Catholic. Club: Million Dollar. Home: 9806 S Hoxie St Chicago IL 60617 Office: 900 Ridge Rd 3N Homewood IL 60630

BENNETT, GWENDOLYN, mgmt. cons., govt. ofcl.; b. N.Y.C., July 24, 1949; d. Fred J. and Luvelna (Leake) B.; B.S. in Mktg., Fordham U., 1973; postgrad. in Bus. Adminstrn., St. John's U.; m. Daniel Harris, Oct. 21, 1972 (annulled 1974). Sr. employment security clk. N.Y. State Employment Office, Bronx, 1969-73; payroll-accounting clk. Western Pacific R.R. Co., San Francisco, 1973-74; asst. store mgr. S.S. Kresge Co., Troy, Mich., 1974-75; bus. devel. counselor Lower East Side Econ. Devel., N.Y.C., 1975-77; mktg./procurement specialist Capital Formation, Inc., N.Y.C., 1977-79; pres. Bennett Internat., Inc., N.Y.C., 1979-82; sr. procurement analyst/chief small and disadvantaged bus. utilization office Dept. Def., N.Y.C., 1982—, mgr. fed. women's program, 1981—; del., chmn. procurement com. N.Y. del. White House Conf. on Small Bus., 1980; advisor After Sch. Workshop Grant Program, Abyssinian Bapt. Ch.; bd. dirs. PCCS Corp., Minority Women's Task Force, N.Y.C. Mgmt. com. to elect Pres. Carter; Sunday Sch. tchr. Abyssinian Bapt. Ch., chmn. Afro-Am. Com., 1978; task force Luth. Ch. Am., 1978; mem. Nat. Council Negro Women, NAACP, YWCA. Mem. Am. Mgmt. Assn., Nat. Assn. Black Mfrs., Minority Bus. Opportunity Com. of Fed. Exec. Bd., Nat. Women's Conf., N.Y./N.J. Purchasing Council. Baptist.

BENNETT, HARRIET, painter; b. N.Y.C.; d. John and Henrietta (Jantzen) Bultman; student Art Students League N.Y., Bklyn. Mus., New Sch. for Social Research, Pratt Graphic Art Center. One-woman shows at Marino Gallery, N.Y.C., 1958, Condon Riley Gallery, N.Y.C., 1959, Cichi Gallery, Rome, Italy, 1962, Galerie de l'Université, Paris, France, 1962, Woodstock Gallery, London, Eng., 1965; group shows Women's Internat. Center, N.Y.C., 1976, Long Beach Art Gallery, N.Y.C., 1978, N.Y. Artists Equity Assn., N.Y.C., 1979, Murray Hill Art Assn., N.Y.C., 1979. Recipient Falmouth Artists Guild award, 1962, Internat. Women's Yr. award Internat. Women Artists Slide Exhbn., 1976. Mem. Artists Equity Assn. N.Y., Women in Arts Found., Women's Interart Center, Eleanor Gay Lee Gallery Found. Address: PO Box 839 Grand Central Station New York NY 10017

BENNETT, HELEN BENTON, extension agt.; b. Colbert, Ga., May 12, 1927; d. Samuel Nathaniel and Bertha (Whitworth) Benton; student Tift Coll., 1944-46; B.S. in Home Econs., U. Ga., 1948; m. Osee Venson Bennett, Apr. 15, 1950; children—Carolyn Bennett Severson, Mary Cathryn. Extension agt. Coop. Extension Service of Hall County, Gainesville, Ga., 1948-50, 54-61; tchr. Lyman Hall Sch., 1953-54, 65-66, Lanier Sch., 1964-65; Hall County extension agt., 1966—. Mem. N.E. Ga. Med. Center Aux.; former chairperson Hall County Nutrition Com. Mem. Am. Home Econs. Assn., Ga. Home Econs. Assn., Ga. Assn. Extension Home Economists (Disting. Service award 1969), Nat. Assn. Extension Home Economists (Outstanding Extension Home Economist, Disting. Service award 1973), Ga. Home Econs. Assn. (past chairperson Area L), Women's Missionary Union (dir.), Epsilon Sigma Phi. Clubs: Pilot (Pilot of Yr. 1979-80), Eastern Star. Home: Route 10 Box 26 1 Gainesville GA 30501 Office: Hall County Courthouse Gainesville GA 30501

BENNETT, JOAN, actress; b. Palisades, N.J., Feb. 27, 1910; d. Richard and Adrienne (Morrison) Bennett; ed. pvt. schs.-Miss Chandor's and Miss Hopkins' (N.Y.C.), St. Margaret's (Waterbury, Conn.), L'Ermitage (Versailles, France); m. John Marion Fox, 1926 (div. Aug. 1928); 1 dau., Diana; m. 2d, Gene Markey, writer, Mar. 16, 1932 (div. 1937); 1 dau., Melinda; m. 3d, Walter Wanger, 1940 (div. 1965); children—Stephanie, Shelley; m. 4th, David Wilde, Feb. 14, 1978. Made stage debut in Jarnegan with father, 1928; appeared in films Bull Dog Drummond, Three Live Ghosts, Disraeli, Maybe It's Love, Moby Dick, Putting on the Ritz, Many a Slip, Doctors' Wives, She Wanted a Millionaire, Careless Lady, The Trial of Vivienne Ware, Week Ends Only, Wild Girl, Me and My Gal, Arizona to Broadway, Little Women, Pursuit of Happiness, Man Who Reclaimed His Head, Mississippi, Private Worlds, She Couldn't Take It, 13 Hours By Air, Big Brown Eyes, Wedding Present, Vogues of 1938, The Texans, Artists and Models, Trade Winds, The Man in the Iron Mask, Housekeeper's Daughter, Green Hell, House Across the Bay, The Man I Married, Son of Monte Christo, I Married A Nazi, She Knew All the Answers, Man Hunt, Wild Geese Calling, Confirm or Deny, Twin Beds, The Wife Takes a Flyer, Girl Trouble, Margin for Error, The Woman in the Window, Nob Hill, Colonel Effingham's Raid, Scarlet Street, Woman on the Beach, The Macomber Affair, The Secret Beyond The Door, Hollow Triumph, Reckless Moment, Father of the Bride, For Heaven's Sake, Father's Little Dividend, Love that Brute, We're No Angels, 1955, There's Always Tomorrow, Desire in the Dust, Suspiria, 1976; TV movies Suddenly Love, 1978, A House Possessed, 1980; Divorce Wars, 1981; stage plays Stage Door, 1938, Love Me Little, Janus, Pleasure of His Company, Fallen Angels, Jane, The Man Who Came to Dinner, The Boy Friend, Butterflies are Free; TV series. Too Young to Go Steady, Dark Shadows; also Never Too Late (London), 1963-64. Lectr. The Bennett Playbill, 1971-73. Author: (with Lois Kibbee) The Bennett Playbill, 1970.

BENNETT, KATHERINE ANN, cosmetics co. exec.; b. Alexandria, La., Dec. 12, 1939; d. Charles D. and Esther V. (Whaley) Ward; student Cambridge U., 1960, Mercer U., 1976-77; m. Preston G. Bennett; children—Kerry D. Wolfe, Michael W. Wolfe. Sec. treas. Yellow-Cab Co., Inc., Alexandria, 1962-70; dist. sales mgr. Avon Products, Inc., Atlanta, 1970-75, mgmt. asso., 1975-77, div. sales mgr., 1977—. Loaned exec. United Way Campaign, Atlanta. Mem. Nat. Assn. Female Execs. Republican. Roman Catholic. Office: 2200 Cotillion Dr Atlanta GA 30338

BENNETT, LEANNA LOIS, life ins. agt.; b. Kennett, Mo., May 5, 1943; d. Thomas William and Wanda Louise (McMahon) B.; student U. Ill., 1961-63, Washington U., 1965-70; M.S. in Fin. Services, Am. Coll., 1978; postgrad. Calif. Western Sch. Law, 1981—. Sec. with Northwestern Mut. Life Ins. Co., Champaign, Ill., 1963-68; agy. cashier Home Life of N.Y., St. Louis, 1969; ins. sales William K. Halliburton Assos., St. Louis, 1970-75; adminstrv. asst. James R. Maddux, Camarillo, Calif., 1976; asst. dir. agy. tng. Occidental Life, Los Angeles, 1977-81; agt. Northwestern Mut. Life Ins. Co., 1981—; bd. St. Louis Life Underwriters Assn., 1974-75; moderator Life Underwriters Tng. Council, 1971-79, 81-82, nat. content and techniques com., 1980-82; sec. Council of Field Underwriters, 1973-74, pres., 1974-75, C.L.U. instr., 1982; Chmn. music com. First Bapt. Ch., 1966-68; vol. Homer G. Phillips Hosp., 1970-75; mem. Los Angeles Jaycees, 1978-79. C.L.U. Mem. Nat. Assn. Life Underwriters, Am. Soc. C.L.U.'s, Nat. Assn. Female Execs. (dir. 1979-80), Fedn. Bus. and Profl. Women (com. chmn. 1974-75), Women Life Underwriters Conf. (state rep.), Women Leaders Round Table (chmn. nat. cross-country seminars 1978-79). Republican. Home: 1943 5th Ave San Diego CA 92101 Office: 233 A St Suite 800 San Diego CA 92101

BENNETT, MELBA JUNE, vocal scientist, mezzo soprano, educator; b. Salt Lake City, Mar. 5, 1930; d. Heber Charles and Ruth Christine (Ernstrom) Egbert; A.A., Westminster Coll., Salt Lake City, 1948; B.F.A., U. Utah, 1953, M.S., 1963; m. Stanley Evan Bennett, July 27, 1966; children—Dean Stanley, Lisa Ann. Appeared in mezzo soprano roles, Utah Opera Theater, in concert with Utah Symphony Orch., Regina, Sask., Can., Symphony, Santa Barbara Fiesta Days, 1953-64; instr. bus. edn., human relations, English, self improvement, Stevens Henager Coll., Salt Lake City, 1957-62; instr., U. Utah, Salt Lake City, 1962-63; tchr. bus., music Carl Hayden High Sch., Phoenix, 1963-65, Phoenix Union High Sch., 1965-68; instr. bus., music, Glendale (Ariz.) Community Coll., 1966—; computer edn. Deer Valley High Sch., Glendale, 1981—. Dir. choir, musical performances, tchr. trainer Sunday Sch. tchr. Mormon Church; active fund-raising, Arthritis, Am. Cancer Soc. campaigns. Recipient Stevens Meml. award for scholastic achievement, Westminster Coll., 1948, scholarship, Music Acad. of the West, U. Utah, 1953, 54, Pa. Coll. for Women Summer Opera Workshop, 1951. Mem. Nat. Assn. Tchrs. of Singing, Delta Kappa Gamma. Republican. Home: 4429 W Las Palmaritas Dr Glendale AZ 85302 Office: Glendale Coll 6000 W Olive St Glendale AZ 85302

BENNETT, MIRIAM FRANCES, biologist; b. Milw., May 17, 1928; d. Stanley Edward and Dorothy (Wheeler) B.; A.B., Carleton Coll., 1950; A.M., Mt. Holyoke Coll., 1952; Ph.D. (Univ. fellow), Northwestern U., 1954; A.M. (hon.), Colby Coll., 1973. Instr. to prof., chmn. biology dept. Sweet Briar Coll., 1954-73; chmn., Dana prof. biology Colby Coll., Waterville, Maine, 1973-80, William R. Kenan, Jr., prof. biology, 1980—; vis. investigator Inst. Zoology, U. Munich (W.Ger.), 1960-61, 62, 68, 76. Trustee, Kents Hill Sch.; mem. corp. Marine Biol. Lab. NSF fellow, 1960-61. Fellow AAAS; mem. Am. Inst. Biol. Scis., Am. Soc. Zoologists, Crustacean Soc., Ecol. Soc. Am., N.Y. Acad. Scis., Internat. Soc. Chronobiology, Sigma Xi. Republican. Episcopalian. Author: Living Clocks in the Animal World, 1974; papers on chronobiology and amphibian endocrinology. Home: Ten Lots Rd Fairfield ME 04937 Office: Dept Biology Colby Coll Waterville ME 04901

BENNETT, PHYLLIS HAMILTON, pipeline contracting co. exec.; b. Bonham, Tex., Apr. 14, 1947; d. Joseph Thurman and Anne Alene (Seals) Hamilton; student Draughon's Bus. Sch., 1965; m. Robert Dwain Bennett, May 31, 1969; children—Benjamin Dwain, Robert Joseph. Sec., Sheraton-Dallas Hotel, 1965; sec. client service dept. Praetorian Mutual Life Ins. Co., Dallas, 1965-67; mgr. advt. sales aids, editor Compans mag. Life Ins. Co. S.W., Dallas, 1967-69; sales agt. Arlington (Tex.) Real Estate, 1972-73; sec.-treas. Becco, Inc., Arlington, 1973—. Mem. Am. Bus. Women's Assn. (Woman of Year 1979).

BENNETT, SARAH ISABEL NEFF (SALLY), author, composer; b. Fountain Springs, Pa.; d. Franklin Daniel and Jennie Catherine (Bright) Neff; student Banks Bus. Coll., 1940-41, Gwen Shock Modeling and Dramatic Sch., 1941-42, U. Pa., 1942; m. Paul H. Bennett, Nov. 1, 1947. Model, John Wanamaker's, Phila., 1942; legal sec. Dept. Justice, Phila., 1945-46; writer, performer, disc jockey Radio and TV Sta. WLWA, Atlanta, 1954-56; playwright, actress Karamu Little Theater and Lakewood Little Theater, Cleve., 1957-59; founder, pres., owner Solar Record Co., Cleve., 1959—; composer Broadcast Music Co., Cleve., 1958—; founder, pres. Composers Showcase, Inc., Cleve., 1965—, Music Pub. Co., Cleve., 1966, First Big Band Hall of Fame, Cleve., 1975—; contbr. to Palm Beach (Fla.) Life, Palm Beacher Daily. Mem. nat. council Met. Opera, N.Y.C., 1967—; mem. John F. Kennedy Center, 1967—; founder, pres. Animal Welfare Vols., Inc., Cleve., 1969—; founding bd. dirs. Great Lakes Shakespeare Festival, Cleve., Cleve. Indian Basebelles. Mem. Nat. League Am. Pen Women (pres. 1962-63, music chmn. Palm Beach chpt., pres. br. 1982-83), Am. Guild Authors and Composers, Am. Women in Radio and TV, Am. Guild Variety Artists, Broadcast Music, Palm Beach Quills, Palm Beach Opera, Preservation Found. Palm Beach, Palm Beach Hist. Soc., DAR. Clubs: Cleve. Yachting, Racquet Internat., Women's City (Cleve.). Author: Sugar and Spice, 1972; composer: Magic Moments.

BENNETT, SHARON KATHLEEN, coloratura, educator; b. West Jefferson, Ohio; d. Harold Stewart and Dorothy Eleanor (McKinley) B.; B.Mus., M.Mus., Eastman Sch. Music. Operatic appearances Met. Opera Studio, 1967-69, Israel Festival, 1974, Nuremberg Opera, 1970-73, NAPAC, S. Africa, 1974, 76, Vigo, Seville and Cadiz, Spain, 1976, Hamburg State Opera, 1973-76, Scottish Opera, 1976-77, Chautauqua Opera Assn., 1968, Dublin Grand Opera, 1977, Columbus (Ohio) Symphony, 1978, Heidelberg (W. Ger.) Opera, 1978, Seattle Opera Co., 1978, Brevard Performing Arts Festival (Fla.), 1978, Welsh Nat. Opera, 1979, Santa Fe Opera, 1979, Friends of French Opera, Carnegie Hall, 1981; orch. appearances Hamburg State Philharm., 1974, Balt. Symphony, 1980, Hudson Valley Philharm., 1980, Milw. Symphony, 1977, Nat. Symphony, 1969, Cleve. Orch., 1964, 65, Southeast Iowa Symphony, 1981, Basically Bach Festival, Anchorage, 1982; solo recitals Schroon Lake Festival, N.Y., 1968, Carnegie Recital Hall, 1969, Nuremberg, W. Ger., 1973, Hamburg, W. Ger., 1974, Phillips Gallery, Washington, 1966, Town Hall, N.Y.C., 1974; asst. prof. U. Iowa, 1980—. Martha

Baird Rockefeller grantee, 1966, 68; Corbett Found. grantee, 1969; Iowa Council of Arts grantee, 1981-83. Mem. Nat. Assn. Tchrs. Singing, AAUP, AAUW, Music Tchrs. Nat. Assn., Sigma Alpha Iota.

BENNETT, SOJA PARK, physician; b. Suwon, Korea, Apr. 17, 1943; d. Yong Joon and Ok Hyun (Kim) Park; B.S., Whitworth Coll., 1965; M.D., Vanderbilt U., 1968; m. Thomas W. Bennett, June 10, 1969; children—Drake Park, Jason Park. Cons. in endocrinology Harlem Hosp., N.Y.C., 1974-78; asst. prof. pediatrics Columbia U., 1976-78, clin. asst. prof., 1979; practice medicine specializing in endocrinology; clin. asst. prof. pediatrics Ind. U., Ft. Wayne, 1981—. Fellow in pediatric endocrinology Columbia U., 1970-72, Cornell U., 1972-73. Diplomate Nat. Bd. Med. Examiners, Am. Bd. Pediatrics with subsplty. in endocrinology. Mem. Environ. Mutagen Soc. Home: 2404 Forest Park Blvd Fort Wayne IN 46802 Office: 347 W Berry St Fort Wayne IN 46802

BENNINGTON, ANNA LAURA, educator; b. Hot Springs, S.D., July 13, 1932; d. Thomas Henry and Myrtle Christine (Christianson) Callan; B.S.B.A., U. Denver, 1954; M.Ed., U. Ariz., 1978; m. J.T. Bennington, Dec. 19, 1954; 1 son, J.T. Tchr. public schs., Tuolumne, Calif., 1954-55, bus. coll., 1958-62; sec. to dir. purchasing State of Kans., 1962-64, to state senator, Kans., 1965; tchr. Dept. of Def., Eng., 1965-68; tchr. coordinator Tucson Unified Sch. Dist., 1970-73, tchr. counselor, 1976-77; tchr., dept. head Dept. Def., W. Ger., 1973-76; tchr. educator, vocat. office edn., dept. bus. and career edn. U. Ariz., Tucson, 1978—; Specialist in word/info. processing; cons. in acctg. Mem. Tucson Bus. Educators (pres.), Am. Vocat. Assn., Nat. Assn. Tchr. Educators Bus. and Office (pres.-elect), Ariz. Vocat. Assn. (v.p.), Nat. Assn. Spl. Needs Personnel, Internat. Soc. Bus. Educators, Internat. Word Processing Assn. (treas. So. Ariz. chpt.), Assn. Tchr. Educators Kappa Delta, Beta Alpha Psi, Phi Delta Kappa, Pi Omega Pi, Alpha Lambda Delta. Democrat. Episcopalian. Home: 4121 N Larrea Ln Tucson AZ 85715 Office: Box 308 Coll of Education Univ of Ariz Tucson AZ 85721

BENNINGTON, MARCY MARIE, psychologist; b. South Bend, Ind., Feb. 1, 1949; d. John William, Jr. and Constance Dorothy (Weingartner) Truemper; A.B., Ind. U., Bloomington, 1971; M.Ed., U. Mo., St. Louis, 1976; Ph.D. (teaching asst./instr.), St. Louis U., 1981; m. Mark Ian Bennington, Sept. 7, 1968. Adminstrv. asst. Psychol. Service Center, St. Louis, 1974-75; personnel asst. Orchard Corp. Am., St. Louis, 1975-77; sch. psychology intern Pattonville Schs., Maryland Heights, Mo., 1978-79; diagnostician, evaluation coordinator Wentzville (Mo.) Schs., 1979-80, dir. spl. edn., 1980—. Speaker to community groups. Phi Beta Kappa scholar. Mem. Am. Psychol. Assn., Nat. Assn. Sch. Psychologists, Am. Personnel and Guidance Assn., Council Exceptional children. Home: 1470 Shagbark Ct Chesterfield MO 63017 Office: Wentzville Schs 1 Campus Dr Wentzville MO 63385

BENOIT, SHARON BARIE, state legislator; b. Midland, Tex., Nov. 28, 1944; d. Robert Benoit and Inez F. (Sutherland) B.; A.A., Westbrook Coll., 1965; B.S., U. So. Maine, 1973; 1 dau., Nicole Frances. Dir. devel. and public relations Mercy Hosp., Portland, Maine; mem. Maine Ho. of Reps., 1976—, mem. judiciary com. and pub. utility com. Mem. Am. Bus. Women's Assn. Democrat. Roman Catholic. Office: Box 67 State House Augusta ME 04333

BENSCH, MARLENE CLARA, psychologist; b. Sun Prairie, Wis., Sept. 28, 1940; d. Fred James and Clotilda (Weber) Broome; student Schoolcraft Coll., 1970-72; B.A., Oakland U., 1975, M.A. in Clin. Psychology, 1979; m. Paul Bensch, Nov. 7, 1959; children—David, Elizabeth, Timothy, Christopher. Psychologist Oakland County Juvenile Ct., Pontiac, Mich., 1979—. Mem. Am. Psychol. Assn., Mich. Assn. Profl. Psychologists. Co-author articles in profl. jours. Home: 15024 Susanna Livonia MI 48154 Office: 1200 N Telegraph Pontiac MI 48053

BENSEL, CAROLYN KIRKBRIDE, psychologist; b. Orange, N.J., Sept. 21, 1941; d. William Everitt and Margaret Mary (McGlynn) B.; A.B. with honors in Psychology, Chestnut Hill Coll., 1963; M.S., U. Mass., 1964, Ph.D. (Univ. fellow), 1967. Teaching asst. U. Mass., Amherst, 1963-64, research asst., 1964-66; human factors psychologist Grumman Aerospace Corp., Bethpage, N.Y., 1967-71; chief human factors group U.S. Army Natick (Mass.) Research and Devel. Labs., 1971—. Lic. psychologist, Mass. Mem. Am. Psychol. Assn., Human Factors Soc., Ergonomics Soc., Soc. Engring. Psychologists, Internat. Ergonomics Assn., AAAS, Sigma Xi. Editor: Proc. 23d Ann. Meeting of Human Factors Soc., 1979. Office: Individual Protection Lab US Army Natick Research and Devel Labs Kansas St Natick MA 01760

BENSEN, ANNETTE WOLF, graphic art co. exec.; b. Bklyn., Aug. 7, 1938; d. Isidor and Sylvia Wolf; A.A.S., N.Y.C. Community Coll., 1958; postgrad. Pratt Inst., 1974-75; m. Gene Bensen, Oct. 14, 1979. With Wagner-Ellsberg, Inc., N.Y.C., 1958-62; art dir. Island Pen Mfg. Inc., Stacie Pen, Curtis Rand Industries, Inc., N.Y.C., 1962-68; with G.S. Lithographers, Inc., 1968-70; partner, pres. Rembrandt's Mother, Inc., 1970-72; co-owner, pres. Film Comp, Inc., 1972-75; plant mgr. Expertype, Inc., 1975—; adj. lectr. N.Y.C. Community Coll., 1971-75. Mem. Nat. Assn. Female Execs., Am. Printing History Assn., Printing Industries Met. N.Y., N.Y. Composition Assn., Club Printing Women N.Y., Women in Design, Typographers Assn. N.Y., Women in Prodn. Inc., Aircraft Owner and Pilots Assn., Nat. Pilots Assn. Office: Expertype Inc 300 Park Ave S New York NY 10010

BENSKINA, MARGARITA O. (PRINCESS ORELIA), dancer, singer, musician; b. Colon, Panama, Mar. 16; naturalized U.S. citizen, 1956; d. Jose and Amelia Benskina; student parochial schs., Havana, Cuba, and Colon, Panama, Harren High Sch., N.Y.C.; diploma for instrs. in modeling, N.Y. Acad. Theatrical Arts, 1962; grad. N.Y. Sch. Floral Designing, 1971; postgrad. Queens Coll., 1982; 1 dau., Pearl A. Quintyne. Has appeared in theatres, night clubs in various cities U.S., including Connie's Inn Broadway Night Club, Broadway Cotton Club, Leon and Eddie's; in Dance with Your Gods, Calling All Stars, Broadway Parade, N.Y.C., after 1935; mem. Afro-Cuban dance team, Orelia and Pete, 1942; toured with Asadata Dofara Dance Opera, Kykunkor, 1947; now appearing with own ensemble; toured Can. with own dance co., Bacanal, 1950; starred in UN program Stars of the West Indies, also TV program Tropical Holiday, CBS; toured with Sam Manning Calypso Concert Co., 1954; personal mgr. for modern jazz group Rouse-Watkins-Les Modes Quintet, 1956, also dance and mus. groups; prod., dir. concerts, N.Y.C., 1959; produced, directed, starred in concert program Princess Orelia's Pot Puree, Town Hall, N.Y.C., 1964; appeared on Ghana radio, 1971-77; owner, mgr. retail religious mdse. store, N.Y.C.; ordained to ministry Internat. Spiritual Healers Fellowship, 1956. Vol., Bellevue Hosp., N.Y.C. Recipient J.F. Kennedy Library for Minorities Heritage award, Am. Honorarium award, 1966. Mem. Broadcast Music, Inc., Synanon, Negro Women's Guild, Washington, Council Negro Am. Women (life), Media Women. Author: (poetry) No Longer Defeated and Other Poems, 1972; The Inflammable Desire to Rebel, 1973; I Have Loved You Already, 1974; I Thank You, Father, 1975; Library To Whom It May Concern, 1978. Contbr. to New Voices in American Poetry, 1972-73. Home: 192-22 100th Ave Hollis NY 11423

BENSON, DOROTHY ANN DURICK (MRS. ROBERT BRONAUGH BENSON), psychologist, bus. exec.; b. Grand Forks, N.D.; d. William James and Grace (Johnson) Durick; B.S. with distinction, U. N.Mex., 1950; M.A. in Psychology, U. Minn., 1952; m. Robert Bronaugh Benson, May 8, 1954. Research asst. psychology dept. U. Minn., 1950-52; instr., counselor Student Counseling Service, Kans. State Coll., 1952-54; psychometrist, counselor Stephens Coll., 1957-58; dir. Benson Bldg. Materials Inc., Columbia, Mo., 1958—; partner Koti Krafts from Finland. Mem. exec. bd. U. Mo. YWCA, 1961-64; mem. Columbia Friends of Library; active LWV Columbia, 1955—, bd. dirs., 1955-61, pres., 1958-59. Mem. King's Daus., Phi Kappa Phi, Psi Chi Phi Sigma. Home: PO Box 3 Columbia MO 65205 Office: Benson Lumber Gen Office 710 Business Loop 70 W Columbia MO 65201

BENSON, KAREN MCCARTHY, state legislator; b. Haverhill, Mass., Mar. 18, 1947; d. Lawrence A. and Barbara V. McCarthy; B.S., U. Kans., 1969, postgrad. in bus. adminstrn., 1978—; M.A., U. Mo., Kansas City, 1975; m. Arthur A. Benson II, Sept. 20, 1969. Tchr. English, Shawnee Mission South High Sch., Overland Park, Kans., 1969-75; tchr. upper sch. humanities Sunset Hill Sch. for Girls, Kansas City, Mo., 1975-76; mem. Mo. Ho. of Reps., 1976—, acting chmn. energy com., chmn. sub-com. fin., vice chmn. consumer protection com. English Speaking Union grantee, Stratford-upon-Avon, Eng., 1974. Mem. del. Am. Council Young Polit. Leaders to Yugoslavia, 1978, to People's Republic of China, 1979; bd. dirs. Com. for County Progress, Jackson County, Mo., Citizens Assn., Kansas City, Mo. Named to Outstanding Young Woman Am., U.S. Jaycees, 1979; recipient Mo. award Phi Chi Theta, 1979; European Community Visitors grantee alternative energy research, 1982; Harvard U. Inst. Politics fellow, 1982. Mem. Nat. Conf. State Legislatures, Nat. Order Women Legislators, LWV, Phi Delta Kappa. Democrat. Office: House PO Jefferson City MO 65101

BENSON, LUCY PETERS WILSON, cons., former govt. ofcl.; b. N.Y.C., Aug. 25, 1927; d. Willard Oliver and Helen (Peters) Wilson; B.A., Smith Coll., 1949, M.A., 1955; L.H.D. (hon.), Wheaton Coll., Norton, Mass., 1965, Carleton Coll., 1973, Bucknell U., 1972; LL.D. (hon.), U. Mass., 1969, U. Md., 1972, Amherst Coll., 1974, Clark U., 1975; H.H.D., Springfield Coll., 1981, Bates Coll., 1982; m. Bruce Buzzell Benson, Mar. 30, 1950. with jr. exec. tng. program Bloomingdale's, N.Y.C., 1949-50; engaged in pub. relations Smith Coll., 1950-53, Mt. Holyoke Coll., 1955; research asst. dept. Am. studies Amherst Coll., 1956-57; pres. League Women Voters, Amherst, Mass., 1957-58, 59-61, dir. Mass., 1957-61, pres. Mass., 1961-63, 63-65, nat. bd. dirs., 1965-66, 2d v.p., 1966-68, nat. pres., 1968-74; sec. human services Commonwealth of Mass., 1975-77; mem. Spl. Commn. on Adminstrv. Rev., U.S. Ho. of Reps., 1976-77; undersec. state for security assistance, sci. and tech., Washington, 1977-80; former trustee Northeast Utilities; dir. Dreyfus Fund, Dreyfus Liquid Assets, Dreyfus Spl. Income Fund, Continental Group, Inc., Grumman Corp., Sci. Applications, Inc. Mem. steering com. Urban Coalition, 1968, exec. com., 1970-75, 80—, co-chmn., 1973-75; mem. Gov. Mass. Spl. Com. Rev. Sunday Closing Laws, 1961; mem. spl. commn. Mass. Legislature to Study Budgetary Powers of Trustees U. Mass., 1961-62; mem. Gov. Mass. Com. Rev. Salaries State Employees, 1963, Mass. Adv. Bd. Higher Ednl. Policy, 1962-65, Mass. Bd. Edn. Adv. Com. Racial Imbalance and Edn., 1964-65, Mass. adv. com. U.S. Commn. Civil Rights, 1964-73; vice chmn. Mass. Adv. Council Edn., 1965-68; mem. Mass. Com. Children and Youth Com. to Study Report by U.S. Children's Bur., Mass. Youth Service Div., 1967; mem. pub. adv. com. U.S. Trade Policy, 1968; mem. vis. com. John F. Kennedy Sch. Govt.; mem. Trilateral Commn.; mem. Town Meeting, Amherst, 1957-74, fin. com., 1960-66; mem. Nat. News Council, 1980—, chmn., 1982—; trustee Edn. Devel. Center, Newton, Mass., 1967-72, Nat. Urban League, 1974-77, Smith Coll., 1975-80, Brookings Instn., 1974-77 Alfred P. Sloan Found., 1975-77, 81—; bd. dirs. Catalyst; former bd. govs. Am. Nat. Red Cross, Common Cause, Women's Action Alliance. Recipient Achievement award Bur. Govt. Research, U. Mass., 1963; Distinguished Service award Boston Coll., 1965; Smith Coll. medal, 1969; Distinguished Civic Leadership award Tufts U., 1965; Distinguished Service award Northfield Mount Hermon Sch., 1976; Radcliffe fellow Radcliffe Inst., 1965-66, 66-67. Mem. Nat. Acad. Pub. Adminstrn., ACLU, UN Assn., Urban League, NAACP, Council Fgn. Relations, Assn. Am. Indian Affairs, East African Wildlife Soc., Jersey Wildlife Preservation Trust Channel Islands. Home: 46 Sunset Ave Amherst MA 01002 Office: Benson & Assos Inc Suite 511 1611 N Kent St Arlington VA 22209 also 46 Sunset Ave Amherst MA 01002

BENSON, MABLE ANNIE MAE RANSAW, clin. social worker; b. Pitts., Nov. 23, 1926; d. Romie Ransaw and Adellar (Edison) Ransaw Yarbourgh; B.A., U. Pitts., 1948; M.S.W., 1960; Ph.D. (hon.), Colo. State Christian Coll., 1972; postgrad. in Bus. Adminstrn., Carlow Coll., 1979—, in Social Work, U. Pitts., 1981; m. Earlee Benson, May 25, 1946; children—Dexter Earlee, Terrilena Elizabeth. Saleswoman, N.C. Life Mut. Ins. Co., Pitts., 1952-53; clk. Carnegie Inst. Tech. Engring. Library, Pitts., 1954-56; child care worker Western Psychiat. Inst. and Clinic, Pitts., 1956-58; social worker Dept. Public Welfare and Children's Hosp., Pitts., 1957-59; outpatient supr. Mayview State Hosp., Pitts., 1960-63, psychiat. social worker Council House, 1963-64; med. and psychiat. social worker St. Margaret's Hosp., Pitts., 1964-67; med. social worker cons., rodent control adminstr. Allegheny County Health Dept., Pitts., 1967-72, asst. chief community service, 1972, acting chief, 1972-81, chief bur. community service devel., 1973—, chief social service Allegheny County Health Dept., 1981-82, ret., 1982; pvt. practice clin. social work cons. to med., psychol., and bus. profls. and employees, Pitts., 1982—; co-founder Homewood-Brushton Citizens Improvement Assn., co-chmn. subcom. social services, com. home-delivered services Area Wide Commn. on Services to Aged; cons. Multiple Purpose Program for Older Citizens; mem. community relations com. South Hill Council for Aged, mem. Pa. Gov.'s Boarding Home Task Force; adv. com. for Sr. Companions; adv. com. Sch. of Social Work, Northside Geriatric Council. Bd. dirs. Family Planning Council Southwestern Pa.; task force for Internat. Yr. of Developmentally Disabled; city planning com. on Personal Care Boarding Homes. Mem. Nat. Assn. Social Workers. Assn. Black Social Workers, NAACP, Internat. Platform Assn., Delta Sigma Theta. Baptist. Home: 7221 Kedron St Pittsburgh PA 15208

BENSON, ROSEANN, educator; b. Bloomington, Ill., Oct. 9, 1948; d. Walter Latham and Rose Isabelle (Schlosser) B.; B.A., Brigham Young U., 1970, M.S. (scholar, Dean's fellow), 1979. Instr. water safety, spl. courses and confs., Brigham Young U., Provo, Utah, 1969-71, asst. women's swimming coach, research asst., 1976-77, grad. intern in kinesiology, 1978; coach swimming Notre Dame Acad., St. Petersburg, Fla., 1971-73; coach swimming and volleyball, tchr. St. Petersburg Cath. High Sch., 1973-76; asst. coach men and women's swimming, part-time tchr. San Diego State U., 1977-78; coach boys swimming Serra High Sch., San Diego, 1978; instr. phys. edn., head coach women's swimming and diving James Madison U., Harrisonburg, Va., 1979—. Mem. AAHPER, Am. Swim Coaches Assn., Nat. Coll. Swimming Coaches Assn., Nat. Collegiate Women's Swimming Coaches Assn. (dir.), U.S. Swimming Coaches Assn., Va. Swimming Coaches Assn., Am. Water Skiing Assn., U.S. Volleyball Assn. Mormon. Home: 2024 Belleair Rd Clearwater FL 33516 Office: James Madison U Godwin Box 40 Harrisonburg VA 22807

BENTH, HELEN FRANCES, hosp. ofcl.; b. Brockton, Mass., Feb. 27, 1919; d. Charles F. and Mabel E. (Holmer) Hartford; student Boston U., 1938-40, Sheridan Coll., 1965—; m. Emil Ellsworth Bud Benth, Feb. 22, 1946; children—Emil E., Steven Charles, Barry Hartford, Joel David. Legal sec. to various attys., Williston, N.D., 1946-51; public stenographer, Williston, 1951-52; exec. sec. The Wood Co., Sheridan, Wyo., 1952-57; clk.-stenographer U.S. Dept. Agr., Farmers Home Adminstrn., 1961-63; sec. to mgr. Elks, Sheridan, 1963-72; exec. sec. All Am. Indian Days, Inc., Sheridan, 1960-63; vol. N. Am. Indian Found., Wyo., 1960-74, sec., treas., 1966-67; clk.-stenographer VA Hosp., Sheridan, 1972-73; staff asst. to chief of vol. service VA Med. Center, Sheridan, 1973-79, chief vol. service, 1980—. Vice pres. Sheridan Civic Theatre Guild, 1956-58; trustee First Congregational Ch., Sheridan, 1978-79. Served with WAC, 1945-46. Recipient Commendation VA Hosp., 1973; Ford Found. fellow, 1956. Mem. DAR (chpt. treas. 1976-78), Am. Legion Aux. (unit pres. 1979-80), Wyo. Am. Legion (dept. chaplain 1976-82, dept. vice-comdr. 1982—), Soc. Mayflower Descs. Wyo. (gov. 1968-69). Republican. Columnist Wyoming Cowboy Legionnaire, 1976—; editor Post 7 Am. Legion newsletter, 1969—. Home: 21 S Vale Sheridan WY 82801 Office: VA Med Center Sheridan WY 82801

BENTLEY, ANTOINETTE COZELL, lawyer; b. N.Y.C., Oct. 17, 1937; d. Joseph Richard and Rose (LaFata) Cozell; B.A. with distinction, U. Mich., 1960; LL.B., U. Va., 1961; m. Robert D. Bentley, Aug. 28, 1960; children—Robert S., Anne W. Admitted to N.Y. bar, 1962, N.J. bar, 1971; asso. Sage Gray, Todd & Sims, N.Y.C., 1961-65; counsel Farrell, Curtis, Carlin & Davidson, Morristown, N.J., 1970-73; asst. sec. Crum and Forster, N.Y.C., 1973, sec., 1975-75, v.p., sec., csl., 1975—; trustee Crum and Forster Found., N.Y.C. Vice-pres. Mendham (N.J.) Bd. Edn., 1976-79; trustee N.J. Conservation Found., 1981—, Morris Mus. Arts and Scis., 1981—. Mem. Womens Econ. Roundtable, League Women Voters, Am. Bar Assn., Am. Soc. Corporate Secs., Assn. Corporate Csl. N.J. (2d v.p., mem. exec. com.), N.J. State Bar Assn. Home: 16 Prospect St Mendham NJ 07945 Office: 305 Madison Ave Morristown NJ 07960

BENTLEY, BETTY JANE, civic worker; b. Grundy Center, Iowa, Nov. 18, 1922; d. Raymond Foster and Lella B. (Bates) Schneider; student schs. Grundy Center; m. Leland Elmer Bentley, Sept. 23, 1951; 1 dau., Linda Jane Juncker Clapsaddle. Telephone operator Iowa State Telephone Co., Grundy Center, 1940-44; sec. Grundy County Courthouse, Grundy Center, 1944-45, Hardin County (Iowa) County Courthouse, 1949-51, USDA, Grundy Center, 1951-53. Women's chmn. Grundy County Farm Bur., 1968, various offices, 1963—; Rep. precinct chmn. Palermo Twp.; registrar, chmn. Women's Day, Grundy Center Centennial, 1977; twp. election chmn. ofcl., 1960—; officer Grundy County Hist. Soc., pres., 1977, pub. book chmn., 1981; active Grundy Center Sr. Housing, Iowa Farm Bur. Fedn., Grundy County Republicans. Methodist. Clubs: Iowa Fedn. Women's Clubs (Grundy County pres. 1966-68, yearbook judge 3rd dist.), Palermo Twp. Woman's Club (all offices), Farm Bur. Women. Contbr. writings, pub. chmn. Grundy County Hist. Soc. publ., 1977. Home and Office: RFD 1 Box 110 Grundy Center IA 50638

BENTLEY, GAIL ELIZABETH, mfg. co. exec.; b. San Francisco, Apr. 22, 1954; d. Donald Homer and Margaret Kathryn (Abbett) Outsen; B.B.A., Tex. Tech. U., 1975; m. David O. Bentley, Aug. 31, 1980; 1 son, Christopher Allen. Owner, operator The Hayrick, Lubbock, Tex., 1973—, Bookkeeping & Bus. Adv. Service, Lubbock, 1976—; treas. bd. dirs., mgr. Johnson Mfg. Fed. Credit Union, 1978—. Mem. Phi Gamma Nu. Republican. Home: 2218 32nd St Lubbock TX 79411 Office: Route 10 PO Box 5A Lubbock TX 79411

BENTLEY, HELEN DELICH, internat. cons., journalist; b. Ruth, Nev.; d. Michael and Mary (Kovich) Delich; B.J., U. Mo., 1944; LL.D. (hon.), U. Md., 1970, U. Alaska, 1973, U. Mich., 1974; D.H.L. (hon.), Bryant Coll., 1971, U. Portland, 1972, L.I.U., 1976, Goucher Coll., 1979; m. William Roy Bentley, June 7, 1959. Reporter, Ely (Nev.) Record, 1940-42; polit. campaign mgr. for Senator James G. Scrugham, White Pine County, Nev., 1942; bur. mgr. UP, Ft. Wayne, Ind., 1944-45; reporter Balt. Sun, 1945-53, maritime editor, 1953-69; chmn. FMC, Washington, 1969-75, Am. Bicentennial Fleet, Inc., 1973-76; pres. Internat. Resources & Devel. Corp., Washington, 1976—, HDB Internat., Inc., 1977—; TV and film producer world trade and maritime shows, 1950-64; pub. relations adv. Am. Assn. Port Authorities, 1958-62, 64-67. Bd. dirs., mem. council Ch. Home and Hosp.; bd. dirs. United Seamen's Service, Oceanic Ednl. Found.; mem. council Md. Hist. Soc., Ville Julie Coll., Stevenson, Md., Montessori Soc. Central Md., Slavic-Am. Nat. Assn. Recipient numerous honors including awards from AFL-CIO Maritime Port Council Greater N.Y., 1965, Ironworkers and Shipbuilders Council, AFL-CIO, 1966, AOTOS award United Seamen's Service, 1971; N.Y. Freight Forwarders and Brokers Assn., 1972, Am. Legion, 1973, Navy League U.S., 1973, Jerry Land medal Soc. Naval Architects and Marine Engrs., 1974, George Washington Honor medal Valley Forge Freedoms Found., 1971, 76; named Republican Woman of Yr., 1972; honored by U.K. Chamber Shipping, 1973. Mem. Greater Balt. Com. (chmn. rail com. 1976—). Mem. Greek Orthodox Ch. Editor: Seaport Histories, Ports of Americas, 1961. Home: 408 Chapelwood Ln Lutherville MD 21093 Office: PO Box 10619 Towson MD 21204

BENTLEY, NANCY WUCINICK, ednl. adminstrs.; b. Massillon, Ohio, Dec. 7, 1951; d. Mike Eli and Anna Wucinick; B.A. cum laude, Kent State U. (Ohio), 1973, M.Ed., 1977; postgrad. Ohio U., 1982—; m. E. Ross Bentley, Oct. 20, 1973. Residence staff adv. Kent State U. residence halls, 1971-73; social worker Trumbull County Children Services Bd., Warren, Ohio, 1973-75; resident mgr., counselor Trenton (N.J.) State Coll., 1975-76, adv. Coll. Arts and Scis., 1976-77; dir. student services Ohio U., Zanesville, 1977—; cons. career/life planning, coll. admissions, child abuse. Trustee, Central Presbyterian Ch., 1981-85, mem. worship com., 1980-82, sec., 1982; co-sponsor Zanesville chpt. Parents Anonymous, 1979-81; mem. Big Brother/Big Sister Program Zanesville, 1982. Mem. Nat. Assn. Student Personnel Adminstrs., Nat. Assn. Women Deans, Adminstrs., and Counselors, Ohio Assn. Women Deans, Adminstrs. and Counselors, Ohio Coll. Personnel Assn., Ohio Fedn. Bus. and Profl. Women's Clubs, Alpha Delta Kappa, Alpha Phi Omega. Club: Pilot (dir. Zanesville 1981-83, dist. compass area leader 1981-82). Author: The Changes of Manpower Utilization in Stark County (Ohio), 1972. Home: 1317 Lake Dr Zanesville OH 43701 Office: 1425 Newark Rd Zanesville OH 43701

BENTON, BARBI, actress, singer, entertainer; b. N.Y.C.; student U. Barcelona (Spain), 1964, Sacramento State U., 1965-68, vet. medicine, UCLA, 1968-70; m. George Gradow. Actress various TV commls., 1968-71; active TV shows including regular on Hee Haw, 1970-76, featured dancer on Laugh-In, 1968-70, guest star Love Boat, Fantasy Island, Vegas, When the Whistle Blows, Charlie's Angels, McCloud series, co-star network series Sugartime, 1978, actress movies of the week: Love on the Run, The Great American Beauty Pageant, Murder at the Mardi Gras; star syndicated spl. A Barbi Doll for Christmas, 1977, Country Christmas, 1979; presenter various music awards shows; guest TV talk shows; singer, starring shows including The Big Show, Sonny and Cher Show, Sha Na Na, The Palace, The Monte Carlo Show, The Midnight Special, recording artist including albums: Barbi Doll, Barbi Benton, Something New, Brass Buckles, also single recordings, concert appearances, fairs, festivals, hotels; hostess Playboy After Dark TV series, 1969-70; model three covers Playboy Mag., 1969-70; stage debut in play I Love My Wife, 1982, Oklahoma, 1982; appeared Circus of the Stars TV spls., 1980, 81, John Denver Celebrity Ski Tournament, 1981, ABC TV's Wide World of Sports, various telethons including Easter Seals and Jerry Lewis. Active Muscular Dystrophy Assn., Am. Cancer Soc. (receives all proceeds from Barbi Benton Invitational Backgammon Tournament). Voted top female singer, Scandinavia, 1978. Owner antique shop, Aspen, Colo., 1976. Address: care Shefrin Co PO Box 48559 Los Angeles CA 90048

BENTON, BEATRICE HOPE, ednl. cons.; b. San Antonio, Nov. 7, 1946; d. Donald Francis and Beatrice Hope (Peche) Benton; A.B. in Chemistry, North Adams State Coll., 1968; M.Secondary Edn., Boston U., 1972; m. Peter T. Borghi, Aug. 12, 1980; 1 dau., Kathryn Benton. Tchr. chemistry Cathedral High Sch., Springfield, Mass., 1968-69; tchr. sci. and history Munich (W.Ger.) Am. High Sch., 1969-70; tchr. English, Tokyo, Japan, 1970-71; tchr. chemistry and sci. Marlborough (Mass.) High Sch., 1971-80; project dir., adminstr. ESEA, Marlborough Pub. Schs., 1976-77; project dir., proposal writer Title III, Title IX, U.S. Dept. Edn., 1975-76, 76-77; evaluation team New Eng. Assn. Schs. and Colls., 1974, 78; mem. regional dept. edn. com., 1977-78; ednl. cons., lectr., 1978—. Energy conservation rep. Marlborough's Overall Econ. Devel. Com., 1976; chmn. Marlborough's Energy Conservation Task Force, 1975; dir. Walk for Mankind, 1972; sec. Group Action for Marlborough Environment, 1975-76; bd. dirs. Girls Club, Marlborough, 1979; pres. Sisters, Inc., 1979—. Mem. NOW, Women's Polit. Caucus, NEA, Mass. Teachers Assn., Mass. Sci. Teachers Assn. Home and office: 2675 York Rd Columbus OH 43221

BENTON, DEBRA ANN, mgmt. cons.; b. Quinter, Kans., Dec. 16, 1953; d. Fred Herman and Teresa Catherine (Feldt) B.; B.S. in Econs. and Fin., Colo. State U., 1974; m. Alan Lovejoy, May 10, 1981. Account rep. Control Data Corp., Denver, 1974-76; v.p. Exec. Mktg. Cons., Denver, 1976-78; mng. partner Benton Mgmt. Resources, outplacement cons., Denver, 1978—; dir. spl. opportunities women Colo. Women Bus. Enterprises Directory. Mem. Nat. Assn. Bus. and Indsl. Saleswomen (founder, exec. dir. 1979). Mem. Mgmt. Adv. Service, Soc., Mktg. Profl. Services. Republican. Roman Catholic. Author articles in field. Office: 90 Corona St Suite 1407 Denver CO 80218

BENTON, EVELYN FLEMING, librarian; b. Ponchatoula, La., Aug. 10, 1921; d. Walter Raleigh and Mabel Magdalene (Varnado) Fleming; B.F.A. with high distinction and spl. mention in music, Okla. State U., 1943; student U. Tex. Grad. Sch. Library Sci., 1959-60; m. Douglas C. Benton, Aug. 25, 1942; children—Walter Bradford, Christopher Paul. Circulation asst. Tulsa Public Library, 1944, 1st asst. tech. dept., 1945; reference asst. Okla. State U., Stillwater, 1946-48, jr. reference librarian, 1948-50; piano tchr., Baytown, Tex., 1958-60; asst. librarian Lee Coll., Baytown, 1960-66; library dir. Deer Park (Tex.) Public Library, 1967—; mem. automation com. Houston Area Library System Long Range Planning Com.; mem. Library Services and Constrn. Act adv. council Tex. State Library, 1981—. Pres., San Jacinto Music Tchrs. Assn., 1960, Baytown Unitarian Fellowship, 1965; chmn. Heritage '76 Com., Deer Park Bicentennial Commn.; mem. Public Library Adv. Council, Sam Houston State U. Sch. L.S. Mem. Am., Tex. (chmn. nominating com. 1971-72, chmn. reference roundtable 1972-73, sec. dist. V, 1969, treas. dist. VIII, 1971, dist vice chmn., chmn. elect 1980—), Southwestern (conf. program com., Tex. (dist. chmn.), Public (editorial com.) library assns., Tex. Mcpl. Library Dirs. Assn. (pres. 1981-82), Phi Kappa Phi, Sigma Alpha Iota (treas. Iota Alpha chpt. 1942-43). Unitarian. Co-author: An Introduction to the Houston Area Library System Computer Access Network, 1979; contbr. articles to profl. jours. Home: 5874 Doliver Houston TX 77057 Office: 3009 Center St Deer Park TX 77536

BENTON, KATHRYN M. BRADLEY, escrow co. exec.; b. Carnegie, Pa.; d. Charles A. and Mary (Halpin) Bradley; student U. Calif. at Los Angeles, 1929-35; m. Robert E. Benton, Sept. 14, 1935 (dec. Sept. 1965); 1 dau., Barbara A. (Mrs. Bernard P. Drachlis). Co-founder, pres. Eagle Rock Escrow Co., Los Angeles, 1962—. Charter exec. sec. United Orgns., 1966-68, N.E. Taxpayers Assn., 1966—; bd. dirs., founder, sec. Robert E. Benton Meml. Found. Mem. Eagle Rock Bus. and Profl. Womens Club, Eagle Rock C. of C. Club: Womens Twentieth Century. Home: 5320 Vincent Ave Los Angeles CA 90021 Office: 5012 Eagle Rock Blvd Los Angeles CA 90041

BENTON, LINDA SUE, human resources co. exec.; b. Crockett, Tex., Sept. 20, 1953; d. Clell L. and Carolyn Sue (Bolch) Benton; B.A. in Home Econs., Ambassador Coll., 1975. Adminstrv. asst. Ambassador Coll. Student Info. Center, Big Sandy, Tex., 1975-76; with Diversified Human Resources Group, Inc., Dallas, 1976—, agy. mgr., 1978-80, trainer, 1980, remote br. mgr., 1980-81, sr. mgr., 1981-82, human resources tng. coordinator, 1982—. Mem. Nat. Assn. Personnel Cons., Assn. Personnel Cons., Nat. Assn. Female Execs., Metroplex Assn. Personnel Cons. Republican. Mem. Ch. of God. Office: 15400 Knoll Trail Suite 212 Dallas TX 75248

BENTON, MARJORIE CRAIG, civic worker; b. Phila., July 26, 1933; d. James Henry and Edith K. (Kinhead) Craig; student Conn. Coll. for Women, 1951-53; B.A., Nat. Coll. Edn., 1967; m. Charles William Benton, June 13, 1953; children—Adrianne, Craig, Scott. Chmn., Save the Children Fedn., N.Y.C.; mem. adv. bd. Northwestern Inst. Psychiatry, Chgo.; U.S. commr. Internat. Year Child; vice-chmn., trustee Better Govt. Assn., Chgo.; co-chmn. Ams. for SALT; mem. exec. bd. Films, Inc., Wilmette, Ill., Alliance to Save Energy, Washington, Democratic House and Senate Council, Washington; bd. dirs. Inst. Policy Studies, Washington, Internat. League Human Rights, N.Y.C.; mem. adv. bd. Cook County Welfare Services Com., Chgo., Nat. Women's Polit. Caucus, Washington, Women's Campaign Fund, Washington; hon. trustee Nat. Symphony Orch., Washington, UN Assn. Chgo.; public del. U.S. Mission to UN; del. U.S. Mission to UN, 1978; mem. UN Assn. Commn., 1978-79; U.S. rep. to UNICEF; mem. adv. com. AID, 1979; del. Democratic Nat. Conv., 1972, 76; mem. Dem. Nat. Com. Commn. on Del. Selection, 1973; mem. Ill. Dem. Platform Com., 1975; mem. Ill. Dem. Affirmative Action Council, 1975; mem. Credentials Com., Carter floor leader Dem. Conv., 1976; 51.3 Com. chmn. for Ill., 1976; Ill. co-chmn. Inaugural Com., 1977; del. Dem. Mid-Term Conv.; mem. Procedures Com. for Dem. Mid-Term Conv., 1978. Recipient Public Service award UNICEF, 1978; Alumni Service award Nat. Coll. Edn., 1979. Clubs: Arts (Chgo.); River (N.Y.C.). Democrat. Unitarian.

BENTON, NELKANE OLGA, broadcasting co. exec.; b. N.Y.C., June 15, 1935; d. Ruben and Olga Marie (Catchings) B.; m. Thomas J. Hill, June 1, 1979; children—Donna, Marie. Press and record promoter Bing Crosby; now dir. community relations KABC/KIOS Am. Broadcasting, Inc., Los Angeles. Former mem. Gov. Reagan's Consumer Task Force. Recipient cert. achievement ABC, Inc., 1977, 79, 80. Mem. Women in Communications, Public Interest Radio and TV Ednl. Soc. (v.p.), Consumer Credit Counselors (dir.). Democrat. Office: 3321 S La Cienega Los Angeles CA 90016

BENTON, PATRICIA, poet, musician, playwright; b. Westchester County, N.Y.; d. Louis and Pearl (Ascher) Rosenstein; B.A., Miss Mason's Sch. and Jr. Coll., 1925; Diploma in Music and Advanced Music, Westchester Conservatory Music, 1928; m. May 27, 1928; 1 dau., Barbara Benton Wgbster. Author: The Whispering Earth, 1950; Signature in Sand, 1953; The Young Corn Rises, 1954; Medallion South West, 1956; Cradle of the Sun, 1958; Manhattan Mosaic, 1964; author hist. bicentennial pageant; numerous other books; producer, author miracle play of SW, Miracle of Roses, 1953-72; cons. poetry. Nominated for Pulitzer prize, 1960; complete collection of works in Boston U. Library. Fellow Royal Soc. Arts (London); mem. Nat. Soc. Arts and Letters (founder, pres. N.Y. chpt. 1960-62, nat. lit. chmn., Ariz. chpt., 1964-66; chmn. Festival of Fine Arts 1982), Nat. Arts Council, Poetry Soc. Am., N.Y. Women's Press Club, ASCAP, Dramatists Guild, Authors Guild. Republican. Home: 7849 E Glen Rosa Scottsdale AZ 85251 Office: care Frederick Fell Inc 386 Park Ave S New York City NY 10016

BENTON, SUZANNE, sculptor, mask ritualist; b. N.Y.C., Jan. 21, 1936; d. Alex and Florence (Matkoff) Elkins; B.A. in Fine Arts, Queens Coll., 1956; children—Daniel, Janet. Creator, Mask Ritual Theatre, over 140 mask ritual performances throughout U.S. and world; one woman-shows of sculpture include: Wadsworth Atheneum, Hartford, Conn., 1975, Internat. Christian Coll., Tokyo, 1976, Chemould Gallery, Bombay, 1977, Hellenic Am. Union, Athens, 1977, Internat. House, New Orleans, 1978, BITEF Internat. Theatre Festival, Belgrade, Yugoslavia, 1978, Condon Gallery, N.Y.C., 1981, Korean Cultural Service Galleries, N.Y.C., 1982; group shows include: USIS, Eastern Europe, 1971-75, Stamford (Conn.) Mus., 1976, Expo '74, Seattle, Nat. Sculpture Conf., Kans. U., 1974; convenor Conn. Feminists in the Arts, 1970-72; nat. coordinator NOW Women in the Arts, 1973-76. Grantee Conn. Commn. on Arts, 1973, 74, United Methodist World and Women's Div., 1976. United Presbyn. Program Agency, 1976, United Ch. Bd. Homeland Ministries, 1976. Mem. Artists Equity N.Y.C., Nat. Press Women, Nat. Korean Women's Sculpture Assn. (hon.), Am. Crafts Council, Participation Project Found., Nat. Assn. Women Artists (Amelia Peabody award 1979). Author: The Art of Welded Sculpture, 1975. Address: 22 Donnelly Dr Ridgefield CT 06877

BENYO, JUDITH ANNE, mktg. adminstr.; b. Conrad, Mont., Jan. 23, 1941; d. Julius and Mildred Clara (Fetting) Mozer; B.A., Colo. Women's Coll., 1964; postgrad. U. No. Colo., 1975-76. Field dir. Cleve. council Camp Fire Girls, 1964-66; dist. dir. Denver Area council Camp Fire Girls, 1967-72; asso. dir. admissions and coll. relations Colo. Women's Coll., 1973-76; asst. dir. admissions and records U. Mont., 1976-79; market adminstr. Mountain Bell, Helena, Mont., 1979—. Past pres. Region VII Camp Fire Girls Profls.; active Jr. Achievement. Named an Outstanding Young Woman Am., 1970. Mem. Mont. Assn. Collegiate Registrars and Admissions Officers, Nat. Assn. Women Deans, Adminstrs. and Counselors. Democrat. Lutheran. Home: 1314 Shirley Rd Helena MT 59601 Office: 1805 Prospect Helena MT 59601

BERARD, MARJORIE NELSON, health care adminstr.; b. Chippewa Falls, Wis., Aug. 15, 1918; d. Eli William and Emily Picotte Nelson; B.A., Coll. St. Benedict, St. Joseph, Minn., 1940; M.S.S.W., St. Louis U., 1942; m. Celse A. Berard, Oct. 5, 1943; children—Maryann, Michele B. Reardon, Suzanne B. Parks, Renee, Celse A., Elise, Jeanne. Social worker dept. children Cath. Charities St. Louis, 1941-69; psychiat. social worker community mental health clinic St. Louis State Hosp., also outpatient clinic St. Francis Mercy Hosp., 1966-74; founder, exec. dir. Profl. Counseling Center, Inc., New Haven, Mo., 1972-78; founder, adminstr. Profl. Home Health Services, Inc., New Haven, 1974—; cons. med. social work to community orgns. Mo. Div. Health grantee, 1974, Mid-East Area Agy. on Aging grantee, 1975—. Mem. Acad. Cert. Social Workers, Nat. Assn. Social Workers (Mo. Social Worker of Yr. 1981), Nat. Assn. Home Health Agys., Soc. Hosp. Social Work Dirs., Am. Hosp. Assn. (dir.), Mo. Hosp. Assn. Social Workers, Mo. Assn. Home Health Agys., Mo. Hosp. Assn. Roman Catholic. Home: 1508 First Pkwy Washington MO 63090 Office: 101 Arizona St New Haven MO 63068

BERBRICH, JOAN DOLORES, educator, writer; b. Richmond Hill, N.Y., May 12, 1925; d. John A. and Dorothy (Scharen) B.; B.A., SUNY, Albany, 1946; M.A., Columbia U., 1949; Ph.D., N.Y. U., 1964. Tchr. English, Mineola (N.Y.) High Sch., 1949-75, supr., 1959-75; books include: Three Voices from Paumanok: The Influence of Long Island on Cooper, Bryant, and Whitman, 1969; 101 Ways to Learn Vocabulary, 1971; Wide World of Words, 1975; Writing Practically, 1976; Writing Creatively, 1977; Writing Logically, 1978; Writing About People, 1979; Writing About Fascinating Things, 1980; Writing About Curious Things, 1981, Writing About Amusing Things, 1981; editor: The Heritage of Long Island, 1970; lectr. in field. Roman Catholic. Home: 5 Owen Ave Glens Falls NY 12801

BERBYNUK, STELLA RADLIN, former ednl. adminstr.; b. Creighton Mine, Ont., Can., Apr. 18, 1916; d. George and Raifta (Bordeianu) Radlin; m. 1936 (div.); 1 son, Gregory Peter. Sec.-treas. Johnstel Metal Products Ltd., Windsor, Ont., 1948-57, v.p., 1957-62, co-owner, dir., 1948-62; adminstrv. asst. Luria Bros., N.Y.C., 1962; internat. research analyst Mfrs. Nat. Bank of Detroit, 1963-65; with Detroit Bank & Trust, 1965-67; owner, operator The Place of the Thames, 1971—; former mem. faculty econs. dept. St. Clair Coll. Applied Arts and Tech., Windsor, 1967—, devel. officer, 1976-81. Bus. edn. coordinator Ministry Edn. Kenya under auspices Can. Internat. Devel. Agy., 1974-75. Mem. planning bd. Twp. of Tilbury North, 1980—. World U. Scholar, 1959. Mem. Soc. Women Engrs. (chmn. 1962-63), Can. Inst. Internat. Affairs (sec.-treas. Windsor br.), Ont. Film Soc. (treas. Windsor br.). Club: Women's Econ. (Detroit). Home: Rural Route 5 Lighthouse Cove Tilbury ON N0P 2L0 Canada

BERENDS, JOAN CLAIRE, educator, nurse; b. Grand Rapids, Mich., Sept. 23, 1926; d. Claude and Clara (Bultman) Zandstra; R.N., Sch. Nursing Blodgett Meml. Hosp., 1948; B.S., Calvin Coll., 1949; M.A., Mich. State U., 1968; Ph.D. in Occupational Edn., U. Mich., 1981; m. Warren Herman Berends, Oct. 7, 1948; children—David Warren, Barbara Joan. Head nurse obstetrics Blodgett Meml. Hosp., Grand Rapids, 1948-51, nursing arts instr., 1951-54; instr. nutrition Calvin Coll., Grand Rapids, 1957-61; instr. nutrition and physiology Grand Rapids Jr. Coll., 1961-71, dir. asso. degree nursing program, 1971-74, instr. fundamentals of nursing, 1974—. Recipient Good Citizenship award DAR, 1943. Mem. Am., Mich. (continuing edn. com. 1973-76) nurses assns., Nat., Mich. leagues nursing, Am. Vocat. Assn. Marian Louise Withey Guild (pres. 1956), Grand Rapids Jr. Coll. Faculty Assn. (sec. 1981—). Mem. Reformed Ch. Am. Club: Jr. League (community adv. council 1982—). Home: 2425 Okemos Dr SE Grand Rapids MI 49506 Office: 143 Bostwick Ave NE Grand Rapids MI 49502

BERESFORD-HOWE, CONSTANCE ELIZABETH, novelist, educator; b. Montreal, Que., Can.; d. Russell and Marjory (Moore) Beresford-H.; B.A., McGill U., Montreal, 1945, M.A., 1946; Ph.D., Brown U., 1950; m. Christopher W. Pressnell, Dec. 30, 1961; 1 son, Jeremy. From lectr. to asso. prof. English, McGill U., 1949-69; prof. English, Ryerson Poly. Inst., Toronto, 1971—; author: The Unreasoning Heart, 1945; Of This Day's Journey, 1947; The Invisible Gate, 1949; My Lady Greensleeves, 1955; The Book of Eve, 1973; A Population of One, 1976; The Marriage Bed, 1981; The Cuckoo's Nest, 1982. Recipient Can. Booksellers award, 1976; Dodd, Mead Intercollegiate Lit. fellow, 1945; grantee Can. Council, 1975, Ont. Arts Council, 1976. Mem. PEN, Writers Union Can. Home: 16 Cameron Crescent Toronto ON M4G 1Z8 Canada Office: Ryerson Inst 50 Gould St Toronto ON Canada

BERG, ADRIANE GILDA, lawyer, fin. planner; b. Bklyn., Sept. 15, 1948; d. Arthur and Gertrude (Horowitz) B.; B.A., Bklyn. Coll., 1968; J.D., N.Y.U., 1971. Admitted to N.Y. bar, 1972, U.S. Supreme Ct. bar, 1978, N.J. bar, 1980; asso. firm Kaye, Scholer, Fierman, Hays & Handler, N.Y.C., 1971-72, firm Phillips, Nizer, Benjamin, Krim & Ballon, N.Y.C., 1972-74; asst. gen. counsel Community Service Soc. N.Y., N.Y.C., 1974-77; individual practice law, N.Y.C., 1974—; instr. New Sch. Social Research, 1974—; lectr. in field of family law and fin. planning. Mem. adv. com. Child Support Project HEW, 1977; condr. family law clinics NOW; bd. dirs. Law for Laymen; cons. N.Y. Post Grad. Center, N.Y. Divorce Counseling Center. Mem. N.Y. State Bar Assn. (chmn. trust and estate com. gen. practice sect. 1982), Am. Arbitration Assn., Internat. Assn. Fin. Planners, Phi Beta Kappa, Kappa Delta Pi. Author: Moneythink: Financial Planning Finally Made Easy, 1982; contbr. articles to legal jours. Address: 2 Pennsylvania Plaza New York NY 10021

BERG, CAROL SUE, assn. exec.; b. Newark, June 17, 1946; d. James and Emma Suzanna (Bodner) Hutchison; B.S., Newark State Coll., Union, N.J., 1970; M.A., Montclair State Coll., Upper Montclair, N.J., 1972; m. Kenneth J. Berg, June 14, 1980; 1 son, Frederick James. Tchr., coach schs. in N.J., 1967-74; field rep. N.H. Edn. Assn., 1975-76; asst. exec. dir. Pinellas Classroom Tchrs. Assn., 1976-78; field rep. Minn. Edn. Assn., 1978-81, organizational specialist membership and field services, Mpls., 1981—. Scottish Rite scholar, 1964; grad. fellow Montclair State Coll., 1970. Mem. Nat. Staff Assn., Nat. Assn. Female Execs., Profl. Staff Assn. of Minn. Edn. Assn., Montclair State Coll. Alumni Assn. Mem. Democrat-Farm-Labor Party. Presbyterian. Club: Order Eastern Star. Office: 41 Sherburne Ave Saint Paul MN 55103

BERG, GAYLE ROCKMORE, psychologist; b. Bklyn., Sept. 20, 1951; d. Henry H. and Ruth (Frankel) Rockmore; B.S., Syracuse U., 1973; M.S., Boston U., 1974; postgrad. N.Y.U., 1976—; m. Alfred Kit Berg, May 22, 1976. Program coordinator Vocat. Adjustment Center, Boston, 1973-74, coordinator client programming and placement, 1975; asst. chief rehab. counselor Mt. Sinai Hosp., N.Y.C., 1976-78, asst. clin. program dir. Day Treatment Center, 1978—; project dir. vocat. study Mt. Sinai Med. Coll., N.Y.C., 1982—; vocat. cons. Mem. Sen. Oliver's spl. com. to propose rehab. legis. State of Mass., 1975. Dept. Rehab. Counseling teaching asst., 1973-74. Cert. rehab. counselor, Mass.; cert. spl. edn. tchr. Mem. Mass. Rehab. Counseling Assn. (exec. bd. 1975), Am. Psychol. Assn., Nat. Rehab. Assn., Nat. Rehab. Counseling Assn., Phi Kappa Phi, Eta Phi Upsilon. Home: 150 Westwood Circle Easthills NY 11577 Office: 1 Gustav Levy Pl KCC-9 New York NY 10029

BERG, JEAN HORTON LUTZ, author; b. Clairton, Pa.; d. Harry Heber and Daisy (Horton) Lutz; B.S., U. Pa., in 1935, M.A., 1937; m. John Joseph Berg, July 2, 1938; children—Jean Horton, Julie Joanne, John Joel. Tchr. English and Latin, Bridgeville (Del.) High Sch., 1936-38; tchr. creative writing Radnor Twp. Adult Edn. lectr. in field; author: Three Mice and A Cat, 1950, The Jolly Jumping Man, 1950, The Noisy Clock Shop, 1950, The Playful Little Dog, 1951, Baby Susan's Chicken, 1951, The Big Jump-up Book of Farm Animals, 1952, Christmas In Song and Story, 1953, The Traveling Twins, 1953, It's Fun to Peek, 1955, The Big Jump-up Book of Trains, Trucks and Planes, 1955, Tuggy the Tugboat, 1958, Pierre, The Young Watchmaker, 1961, The O'Learys and Friends 1961, Baby Raccoon, 1963, The Little Red Hen, 1963, The Wee Little Man, 1963, Big Bug, Little Bug, 1964, Bright Candle Light, 1966, There's Nothing to Do, So Let Me Be You, 1966, Miss Kirby's Room, 1966, Miss Tessie Tate, 1967, Nobody Scares a Porcupine, 1968, What Harry Found When He Lost Archie, 1970, Mr. Koonan's Bargain, 1971, numerous others, latest being I Cry When The Sun Goes Down, 1976, The Story of Jesus, 1977, The Story of Peter, 1979. Mem. exec. bd. Friends' Central Sch. Home and School Assn., 1965-67; bd. dirs. Wayne Art Center, 1950-57; bd. vols. Health and Welfare Council Phila., 1970-71; exec. bd. Infant Day Care Center of Young Great Soc., Phila., 1971-74; bd. dirs. St. Davids Christian Writers Conf. Recipient Medallion of Phila. award, 1963, Follett award, 1961, Alumni Merit award U. Pa., 1969. Mem. Nat. League Am. Pen Women (pres. Chester County br. 1967-68), Parents Council Suburban Phila. (pres. 1966-67, exec. bd.), Radnor Hist. Soc., Gen. Alumni Soc. U. Pa., LWV, ASCAP, Authors League, Phila. Childrens Reading Round Table, Authors Guild, Assn. Alumnae U. Pa. (officer, exec. bd.), Kappa Alpha Theta, Eta Sigma Phi, Pi Lambda Theta. Christian Scientist. Home: 207 Walnut Ave Wayne PA 19087

BERG, JUDITH SANDRA, social worker; b. Boston, Dec. 25, 1935; d. Maurice and Matilda B. (Seskin) Davis; B.S. (scholar), Simmons Coll., 1957; M.A. (scholar). Sch. Social Service Adminstrn., U. Chgo., 1959; M.F.T. cert. Family Inst. Chgo., Northwestern U., 1982; m. Harold Berg, July 27, 1969; children—Jerrold, Melanie, Larry, Julie, Salli. Social worker Family Service Bur., United Charities, Chgo., 1958-61; U. Chgo. researcher at Ill. Home and Aid Soc. and La Rabida San., 1963-65; social worker Sch. Dist. 71, Niles, Ill., 1967-69; social worker Sch. Dist. 68, Skokie, Ill., 1969-80; co-founder AIM Unltd., diagnostic and treatment facility, Skokie, Ill., 1979—; cons. various sch. dists., 1970—. Mem. commn. on growth and planning, bd. dirs. religious sch. Temple Judea-Mizpah, Skokie. Mem. Nat. Assn. Social Workers, Acad. Cert. Social Workers, Ill. Assn. Sch. Social Workers, Ill. Assn. Cert. Social Workers, North Shore Assn. Retarded Citizens. Home: 9012 Kenneth St Skokie IL 60076 Office: 9012 Kenneth St Skokie IL 60076

BERG, MARIE MAJELLA, coll. pres.; b. Bklyn., July 7, 1916; d. Gustav Peter and Mary Josephine (McAuliff) Berg; B.A., Marymount Coll., Tarrytown, N.Y., 1938; M.A., Fordham U., 1948; D.H.L. (hon.), Georgetown U., 1970. Joined Sisters of The Sacred Heart of Mary, Roman Catholic Ch., 1934; tchr., registrar Marymount Coll., 1948-57; registrar Marymount Coll. Va., Arlington, 1957-58, pres., 1960—; registrar Marymount Coll., Tarrytown, 1958-60; cons. in field. Mem. adv. com. ednl. TV, Va. Council Higher Edn., mem. exec. com. pvt. coll. adv. com., 1974—; mem. evaluation teams So. Assn. Colls. and Schs.; exec. com. Va. Coll. Fund, 1972-73, sec., 1973, 75-76. Charter bd. dirs. Arlington chpt. Reading is Fundamental, 1975—; mem. exec. com. Sisters' Council, Diocese of Arlington, 1978—, mem. Evangelization Commn., 1979—, Bishop's Pastoral Council, 1979—. Kellogg Found. grantee 1961, U.S. Office Edn. grantee, 1962. Mem. Nat. Catholic Edn. Assn., Am. Council Edn., Am. Assn. Higher Edn., Assn. Va. Colls. (exec. com. 1968—), Council Ind. Colls. Va. (v.p. 1972-73, exec. com. 1973-74), Nat. Council Ind. Jr. Coll. (sec. 1969-72), So. Assn. Colls. Women (sec.-treas. 1969-72, pres.-elect 1975-76, pres. 1976-77), Ch. Related Colls. South (pres. 1971-72), Arlington Citizens Participation Council, Arlington Chorus, Arlington Com. 100, LWV, AAUW, Arlington, Va. chambers commerce. Author articles, biographies. Address: 2807 N Glebe Rd Arlington VA 22207

BERG, SYLVIA LOUISE, educator; b. N.Y.C., Dec. 29, 1939; d. Joe and Fay (Streim) Maydeck; B.S., Oswego Coll., 1958; M.S., Hofstra U., 1959; postgrad. N.Y. U., 1960-65; children—Mitchell Ian, Nancy Patricia. Tchr., Public Sch. 198, N.Y.C. Bd. Edn., 1965—; adj. prof. edn. N.Y. U., 1965—; pvt. tutor, 1965—; cons. in field; job presentations; adv. skills in speed reading; condr. sci. seminars Fordham U., Sci. Council; cons. Elaine Goldhill Travel Cons. Bd. dirs. 301 E. 78th St. Corp., N.Y.C., sec., 1979-81; treas. Singles Coordinating Com., N.Y.C. Mem. SUNY Assn., Nat. Assn. Female Execs., Audubon Assn., United Fedn. Tchrs. Home: 301 E 78th St New York NY 10021 Office: Public Sch 158 1458 York Ave New York NY 10021 also 330 E 33d St Suite 8G New York NY 10016

BERGEMANN, MARJORIE ANN, nurse anesthetist; b. Staten Island, N.Y., Nov. 24, 1930; d. David Archer and Anna Hilda (Bloch) Stamler; R.N., Fordham Hosp., 1953; B.A. in Edn., Ottawa U., 1979; doctoral candidate Nova U., 1979—; cert. R.N. anesthetist Prince Georges County Gen. Hosp., 1974; m. Till Bergemann, Mar. 22, 1953; children—Jill Susan, Carol Sarah, Eve Louise. Head nurse Fordham Hosp., 1953-54, Montefiore Hosp., 1954-55; head nurse Prince Georges Gen. Hosp., 1955-57, staff nurse, 1969-72, staff anesthetist, clin. instr., 1974-80; staff anesthetist, clin. instr. Johns Hopkins Hosp., 1980; staff anesthetist Georgetown U. Hosp., Washington, 1981—; pres. Ednl. Assos., Inc.; edn. cons.; instr. critical care nursing Prince Georges Community Coll.; nurse anesthetist adv. council Md. Bd. Examiners of Nurses, 1982. Mem. Am. Nurses Assn., Md. Nurses Assn., Am. Assn. Nurse Anesthetists,

Md. Assn. Nurse Anesthetists (pres. 1982-83), Nat. Center Nursing Ethics, Am. Soc. Regional Anesthesia, Am. Pain Soc., Eastern Pain Assn. Writer poetry. Office: Box 346 Greenbelt MD 20770

BERGEN, CANDICE, actress, photojournalist; b. Beverly Hills, Calif., May 9, 1946; d. Edgar and Frances (Westerman) B.; ed. U. Pa.; m. Louis Malle, Sept. 27, 1980. Model during Coll.; films include: The Group, The Sand Pebbles, The Day the Fish Came Out, Live for Life, The Magus, Soldier Blue, Getting Straight, The Hunting Party, Carnal Knowledge, T.R. Baskin, The Adventurers, 11 Harrowhouse, Bite the Bullet, The Wind and the Lion, The Domino Principle, The End of the World in our Usual Bed in a Night Full of Rain, Oliver's Story, Starting Over, Rich and Famous, 1981; photojournalist credits include articles for Vogue, Esquire, Cosmopolitan, Playboy, Life; dramatist (play) The Freezer included in Best Short Plays of 1968. Address: care Creative Artists Agy Inc 1888 Century Park E Suite 1400 Los Angeles CA 90067 *

BERGENE, EUNICE RUTH, state legislator; b. Ashley, N.D., Mar. 24, 1931; d. Gottlieb and Freda (Haerter) Walz; R.N., 1953; m. James Dale, Dec. 27, 1954; children—Jill Meredith, Janies Theodore. Clin. nurse, Jamestown, N.D.; staff nurse San Diego County Hosp., Haoke, Mont.; now mem. Mont. Ho. of Reps. Mem. central com. Republican party, 1974-75; pres., bd. mem. Ch. Women, Am. Lutheran Ch., 1976-79. Mem. League Women Voters (chmn. voter service). Lutheran.

BERGER, BONNIE GROSS, educator; b. Champaign, Ill., May 20, 1941; d. Bernard G. and Mildred G. Berger; B.S., Wittenberg U., 1962; M.A., Columbia U., 1965; Ed.D., 1972; 1 son, Stephen Casher. Tchr., George Rogers Clark Jr. High Sch., Springfield, Ohio, 1962-64; supr. phys. edn. Agnes Russell Elem. Sch., N.Y.C., 1964-65; asst. prof. N.Y. State U., Geneseo, 1965-66; asst. prof. Dalhousie U., Halifax, N.S., Can., 1969-71; asst. prof. dept. phys. edn. Bklyn. Coll., 1971-77, assoc. prof., 1978-81, prof., 1982—; cons. in field of sport psychology. Mem. N.Am. Soc. Psychology of Sport and Phys. Activity (outstanding dissertation of yr. award 1971), Am. Psychol. Assn., AAHPERD Internat. Soc. Sports Psychology, Can. Soc. Psychomotor Learning and Sport Psychology. Contbr. chpts. to The Psychology of Running, 1981, Running Therapy and Psychology, 1981; contbr. articles to profl. jours. Home: 20 Waterside Plaza New York NY 10010 Office: Department of Physical Education Brooklyn College Brooklyn NY 11210

BERGER, JANE MAULDIN, psychologist; b. Atlanta, July 28, 1945; d. John Frank and Lilly Belle (Casey) Mauldin; B.A., U. Ga., 1966; M.S. (NDEA fellow), U. Ga., 1967; Ph.D. in Psychology, U. Miami, 1971; M.B.A., Nova U., 1982; m. Michael L. Berger, Jan. 8, 1966; children—Louis Jefferson Mauldin, James Ivan Mauldin, Sarah Elizabeth Mauldin. Instr. psychology Miami-Dade Community Coll., 1968-71, asst. prof., 1971-73, asso. prof., 1976-79, prof., 1979—; pvt. practice psychology, Miami, 1971—; guest lectr. U. Miami; cons. Dade County Rape Treatment Center; guest speaker civic groups. Cert. psychologist, Fla. Mem. Am. Psychol. Assn., Fla. Psychol. Assn., Dade County Psychol. Assn., Mental Health Assn. Dade County, S. Fla. Forum Death Edn. and Counseling, Phi Beta Kappa, Phi Kappa Phi. Office: Suite 310 7400 N Kendall Dr Miami FL 33156

BERGER, JULIE ANN, social worker; b. Newark, Sept. 18, 1950; d. Murray M. and Estelle C. (Sperber) Monestersky; student U. Wis., 1968-70; B.A., Tufts U., 1972; M.S.W., Rutgers U., 1973; m. Richard G. Berger, Jan. 5, 1974. Med. social worker dialysis unit VA Hosp., East Orange, N.J., 1974-76, med. social worker hosp.-based home-care program and outpatient clinic, 1976-77; med. social worker dialysis unit Morristown (N.J.) Meml. Hosp., 1977-81; field instr. casework sequence Rutgers U. Grad. Sch. Social Work, 1978; social work rep. to N.J. Renal Network Council, Inc., 1979-81, mem. subcom. on allied health profl. practice, 1978-81, mem. by-laws com., 1978-79, sec. to full council, 1980-81. Mem. Acad. Cert. Social Workers, Nat. Assn. Social Workers, Nat. Assn. Patients on Hemodialysis and Transplant, Council Nephrology Social Workers, N.J. Dialysis and Transplant Assn. (sec. 1976-78, pres. 1978-80). Home: 49 Hillside Ave Caldwell NJ 07006

BERGER, SHIRLEY JUNE, corporate exec.; b. Washington, June 28, 1932; d. Milton Chapel and Lillian (Davis) Kurland; student public schs., Washington; m. Kalvin Berger, May 19, 1957 (dec.); children—Andrew, Charles, Marilyn. Exec. sec. Mayer & Co., Washington, 195056, H.L. Merin Co., N.Y.C., 1957-58; owner, operator Custom Color Lab., Palo Alto, Calif., 1959—, pres., chmn. bd., 1978—; pres. Cutzpah, Inc., 1976-79. Bd. Dirs. Tmpel Beth David, Cupertini, Calif., 1973. Recipient Public Service award USO, 1952. Mem. Nat. Fedn. Ind. Bus., Assn. Profl. Color Labs., Assn. Bay Area Profl. Labs., Photo-Mktg. Assn. Contbr. articles to profl. jours. Office: 947 Industrial Ave Palo Alto CA 94303

BERGERE, ANN L., ins. co. exec.; b. Middletown, Conn., Dec. 27; A.S., Middlesex Community Coll., Middletown, 1977. Office mgr. Arthur A. Watson & Co., Hartford, Conn., 1942-60; with Middlesex Mut. Assurance Co., Middletown, 1960—, asst. sec., 1975-77, corp. sec., personnel mgr., 1977—. Deaconess Rocky Hill Congregational Ch. Club: Middletown Soroptomists (treas. 1977-79, corr. sec. 1979-80). Office: 200 Court St Middletown CT 06457

BERGERON, MARY ELLEN, fed. agy. ofcl.; b. Tooele, Utah, Oct. 29, 1945; d. Russell Edmund and Mary Alice (Papish) B.; B.A. summa cum laude, North Adams (Mass.) State Coll., 1967; M.P.A. with honors (Maxwell scholar, Maxwell fellow), Syracuse U., 1969; postgrad. Northwestern U., 1976. With HUD, 1969—, beginning as urban intern, Chgo., successively spl. asst., dir. prodn., chief processing br., Columbus, Ohio, program analyst, Chgo., dep. dir. housing mgmt. div., dep. dir. housing div., 1969-80, dir. housing div., Columbus, 1980—. Mem. program devel. com. YWCA. Recipient Disting. Alumni award North Adams State Coll., 1981. Mem. Am. Soc. Public Adminstrn. (council Central Ohio chpt. 1972, 82), Nat. Assn. Female Execs., Met. Women's Center, Columbus Women's Network. Club: Metropolitan (Columbus). Home: 1236 Ashland Ave Columbus OH 43212 Office: 200 N High St Columbus OH 43215

BERGIN, KAY VOLLERS, writer, lectr.; b. Waterbury, Conn., Nov. 29, 1921; d. Henry Herman and May Catherine (Hartman) Vollers; B.S., Central Conn. State Coll., 1943; M.A.L.S., Wesleyan U., Middletown, Conn., 1957; m. Francis X. Bergin, Dec. 2, 1944; 1 dau., Sandy. Tchr., dept. chmn. Naugatuck (Conn.) High Sch., 1951-67; prof. Mattatuck Community Coll., 1967-74; exec. dir. Conn. Permanent Commn. Status Women, 1974-75; dep. bank commnr. State of Conn., 1975-78; N.Y. dist. mgr. Nat. Neighborhood Reinvestment Corp., N.Y.C., 1978-82; mem. faculty Nat. Assn. Mut. Savs. Banks. Del., Nat. Women's Conf., Houston, 1977; examining faculty Charter Oak Coll.; bd. dirs. Conn. Public TV, 1978—; mem. Conn. Regional Mktg. Authority, 1979. Bd. dirs. Conn. Preservation, Action, Waterbury Action to Preserve Our Heritage; mem. adv. council Profl. Devel. Center, Mattatuck Community Coll. Named Disting. Woman of Conn., 1976; recipient award Conn. chpt. Bus. and Profl. Women, 1976. Mem. AAUW, NOW, Nat. Women's Polit. Caucus, Nat. Abortion Rights Action League, Women in Housing and Fin. (dir.). Democrat. Episcopalian.

BERGLAND, MARY JO, home economist; b. Batavia, Iowa, Sept. 12, 1940; d. Charles Edward and Dorothy Isabel (Hull) Newland; B.S. in Home Econs., Auburn (Ala.) U., 1963; postgrad. No. Ill. U.; diploma Acad. de Cuisine, 1979; m. Gary Clark Bergland, Mar. 4, 1962; 1 dau., Malia Joan. Supr. home demonstration dept. Govt. Am. Samoa, Pago Pago, 1963-65; tchr. home econs. high schs. in Ill., 1970-77; pres. Microcookery Center Inc., Glen Ellyn, Ill., 1976—; cons., tchr. in field, also newspaper columnist. Recipient Processed Prepared Food award, 1979. Mem. Internat. Assn. Cooking Schs. (charter). Microwave Power Inst., Am. Home Econs. Assn., Chgo. Home Economists in Bus., Lake Shore Home Econs. Assn. (past pres.), AAUW. Presbyterian. Author: The Best of Microcookery, 1978; Best of Microcookery-Quiches, 1978; Best of Microcookery-Cookies, 1979; Hors d'Oeuvres for Each Season, 1980; also feature articles in mags. Home and office: 681 N Park St Glen Ellyn IL 60137

BERGLIN, LINDA LEE, state legislator; b. Oakland, Calif., Oct. 19, 1944; d. Freeman B. and Norma P. (Lund) Waterman; B.F.A., Mpls. Coll. Art and Design, 1968. Mem. Minn. Ho. of Reps., 1973—, asst. majority leader, 1976, chmn. council econ. status women, 1975, chmn. health subcom., 1980, chmn. div. I taxes, 1980. Recipient Leadership in Govt. award Mpls. YWCA, 1980. Mem. Nat. Conf. State Legislators, Urban League, Americans for Democratic Action, Minn. Women's Polit. Caucus. Mem. Democrat-Farmer-Labor Party. Methodist. Office: Room 230 State Office Bldg Saint Paul MN 55101 *

BERGMAN, JANICE JOAN, nurse; b. Axtell, Kans., Jan. 6, 1938; d. Alban Matthias and Angela Philomena (Karnowski) Haug; R.N., Marymount Coll., 1959; m. Paul Harold Bergman, Nov. 28, 1959; children—Janel, Jolene, Jennifer. Staff nurse Seneca (Kans.) Hosp., 1959; charge nurse St. Mary's Hosp., Kansas City, Mo., 1960-62; asst. dir. nursing services N. Kans. Meml. Hosp., North Kansas City, Mo., 1963-67; dir. health occupations program Kans. Dept Edn., 1967; co-owner, dir. nursing Cresview Manor, Seneca, 1968—; gerontol. nurse cons. Kans. State Dept. Vocat. Edn., 1977; Am. Nurses Assn. rep. Nat. Task Force on Credentialing in Nursing, 1980—; gerontol. nurse cons. NE Kans. Area Agy. on Aging; ad hoc adv. 1981 White House Conf. on Aging, Nat. Observer. Mem. Am. Nurses Assn. (exec. Com. div. gerontol. nursing practice), ANA Council of Nursing Home Nurses, Kans. Coalition on Aging, Kans. Public Health Assn., Kans. State Nurses Assn., NE Kans. Regional Adv. Com. for Nurses, Bus. & Profl. Women's Club (pres. 1973-75), Nemaha County Mental Health Assn. (pres. 1976-78), Nemaha County Hist. Soc., Dist. 13 Nurses Assn. (pres. 1976-78), Nemaha Valley Community Hosp. Guild, Jaycee Jaynes (pres. 1971), C. of C. Mem. editorial adv. bd. Geriatric Nursing, 1982—; contbr. articles in field to profl. jours. Home: 713 Castle St Seneca KS 66538 Office: 808 N 8th St Seneca KS 66538

BERGMAN, NORMA WOLK, lawyer; b. Rochester, N.Y., July 10, 1946; d. Robert and Miriam (Waltuck) Wolk; A.B., U. Rochester, 1968; J.D. with distinction (Am. Jurisprudence awards criminal law, remedies), Emory U., 1976; m. Frank E. Jenkins, III, Sept. 1, 1979; children by previous marriage—Jeffrey Allen, Daniel Robert. Teaching and research asst. Emory U. Law Sch., 1974-76; admitted to Ga. bar, 1976; atty. firm Greene, Buckley, De Rieux & Jones, Atlanta, 1976-79, Sci.-Atlanta, Inc., 1979—. Co-chmn. legis. com. Henderson Mill Elem. Sch. PTA, 1981-82, v.p., 1982-83; sec. Henderson Mill Civic Club, Inc., 1981-82; bd. dirs. Planned Parenthood Atlanta, 1978; mem. Emory U. Law Sch. Fund Com., 1978. Mem. Am. Bar Assn., State Bar Ga. (chmn. intrastate moot ct. com. 1978-79, co-chmn. orgn. younger lawyers sect. 1981-82, chmn. legal edn. and admissions to bar com. 1982-83, co-chmn. corp. counsel com. young lawyers sect. 1982-83, exec. council young lawyers sect. 1980-83), Ga. Assn. Women Lawyers, Atlanta Bar Assn., Corporate Counsel Assn. Greater Atlanta (dir. 1981-83), Order of Coif, Phi Delta Phi. Book revs. editor Emory U. Law Jour., 1975-76. Office: 1 Technology Pkwy Box 105600 Atlanta GA 30348

BERGMANN, ELIZABETH WEIL, educator; b. Evansville, Ind., June 22, 1937; d. Ervin Isaac and Frances (Winfield) Weil; B.S., Juilliard Sch., 1960; M.A., U. Mich., 1963; m. Klaus Bergmann, July 7, 1965; children—Michelle Julie, Christopher Klaus. Mem. faculty Jose Limon Dance Studio, N.Y.C., 1959-61; founder, dir. Ann Arbor (Mich.) Dance Theatre, 1963-74; vis. asso. prof. U. Calif., San Diego, 1981; asso. prof. dance, chmn. dept. U. Mich., 1961—; guest lectr., tchr., dancer, choreographer N.Y., Mich., Ohio, Ind., Ill., Calif. Recipient Disting. Faculty award U. Mich., 1979; grantee Nat. Endowment Arts, 1975, 80; Rackham Faculty grantee, 1978. Mem. Nat. Dance Guild, Council Dance Adminstrs. Choreographer: Tikal, 1981; Carmina Burana, 1980; The Unicorn, The Gorgon and The Manticore, 1979; Beacon, 1978; The Planets, 1976. Home: 1157 Aberdeen St Ann Arbor MI 48104 Office: 1310 N University Ct Ann Arbor MI 48109

BERGSTEIN, DOROTHY INA, clin. social worker; b. Jersey City, Apr. 10, 1940; d. Melvin Louis and Marjorie (Knaster) Kramer; A.A., Centenary Coll. for Women, 1960; B.A. magna cum laude, Upsala Coll., 1973; M.S.W., Rutgers U., 1975; m. Melvyn H. Bergstein, Aug. 28, 1960; children—Merri Lee, Jodi. Clin. social worker Newark Family Service, 1974-75; mem. staff, clin. social worker Essex County Guidance Center, East Orange, N.J., 1975-76; adminstr. Jewish Family Service, Ledgewood, N.J., 1976-77; clin. social worker emergency psychiat. service Morristown (N.J.) Meml. Hosp., 1977—; owner, dir. Counseling and Consultation Services, Morristown, N.J. bd. dirs. Jersey Battered Women's Services, 1976-77; lectr.; cons. family life sect. N.J. Bar, 1977-79, correction reform com., 1976-77. Lic. marriage counselor. Mem. Nat. Assn. Social Workers, N.J. Assn. Women Therapists, Acad. Cert. Social Workers (cert. family therapist), Psi Chi. Jewish. Office: 66 Maple Ave Morristown NJ 07960

BERGSTROM, ERICA JUNE, psychologist; b. Los Angeles, June 30, 1951; d. Evert and Annette Bergstrom; B.A. with honors in psychology, Stanford U., 1973; Ph.D., U. Pa., 1981; m. Sidney Edward Croul, Dec. 29, 1979. Instr., U. Pa., Phila., 1975, 76; research psychologist Carrier Found., Belle Mead, N.J., 1980—; head Stanford in France Program for Emotionally Disturbed Children, 1970-71. Head Swedish lang. program Seamen's Ch., 1980—; active Am.-Swedish Mus. Fulbright fellow, 1974. Mem. Am. Psychol. Assn., Assn. of Labor-Mgmt. Adminstrs. and Cons. on Alcoholism (research com.), World Affairs Council of Phila., AAAS, Alcohol and Drug Problems Assn. N. Am., Phi Beta Kappa. Contbr. articles in field to profl. jours. Home: 4557 Boone St Philadelphia PA 19128 Office: Carrier Found Research Div Belle Mead NJ 08502

BERGSTROM, TRUDY SONDEREGGER, educator; b. N.Y.C., July 10, 1937; d. Ernest and Gunda (Seidle) Sonderegger; student Baldwin-Wallace Coll., 1954-57; A.B., Rollins Coll., 1960, M.A.T., 1964, postgrad. in adminstrn. and supervision, 1973-76; m. James Edward Bergstrom, Jan. 2, 1970; 1 dau., Carin Sue. Sec. to pres. Rollins Coll., 1958-59; elem. tchr. Orlando (Fla.) Public Schs., 1960-74, early childhood resource tchr., 1974-76, basic skills resource tchr., 1977-80, curriculum resource tchr., primary edn. specialist, 1980—; cons., workshop presenter. Mem. Orange County Classroom Tchrs. Assn., Fla. Teaching Profession, NEA, Zeta Tau Alpha, Pi Gamma Mu, Pi Kappa Delta, Delta Phi Alpha, Phi Delta Kappa, Delta Kappa Gamma. Contbr. articles to local publs. Home: 6342 Meadow Ridge L Orlando FL 32810 Office: 8101 Benrus Orlando FL 32812

BERK, KAREN MAE, state govt. adminstr.; b. Bklyn., Mar 29, 1943; d. Harry and Minerva G. Sternberg; B.A., UCLA, 1964. With Dept. Employment Devel., State of Calif., Sacramento, adminstr. evaluation and mgmt. analysis div.; cons. in field. Mem. Sacramento Women's Network, Sacramento Jewish Bus. and Profl. Women, Internat. Assn. Personnel in Employment Security. Office: 800 Capitol Mall Sacramento CA 95814

BERKA, MARIANNE GUTHRIE, educator; b. Queens, N.Y., Dec. 25, 1944; d. Frank Joseph and Mary (DePaul) Guthrie; B.S., Ithaca (N.Y.) Coll., 1966, M.S. (grad. asst.), 1968; doctoral candidate N.Y.U.; m. Jerry George Berka, June 1, 1968; children—Katie, Keri. High sch. tchr., 1966-67; asso. prof. health, phys. edn. and recreation Nassau Community Coll., Garden City, N.Y., 1968—. Mem. Assn. Women Phys. Educators N.Y. State (chpt. chmn. 1973-74, chpt. treas. 1980-82), AAHPER, N.Y. State Assn. Health, Phys. Edn. and Recreation, Nat. Council Family Relations, Am. Assn. Sex Educators, Counselors and Therapists (cert. sex educator), Sex Info. and Edn. Council U.S. Roman Catholic. Home: 90 Bay Way Ave Brightwaters NY 11718 Office: P226 HPER Nassau Community Coll Garden City NY 11530

BERKE, JUDIE, artist, writer, prodn. co. exec.; b. Mpls., Apr. 15, 1938; d. Maurice M. and Sue (Supak) Kleyman; student U. Minn., 1956-60, Mpls. Sch. Art, 1945-59. Free lance illustrator and designer, 1959—; pres. Berke-Wood, Inc., N.Y.C., 1971—, Manhattan Rainbow & Lollipop Co., subs. of Berke-Wood, Inc., 1971—, pres. Get Your Act Together, club act staging, N.Y.C., 1971—; owner The Coordinator, Judie Berke Pub.; co-pres. JAM Entertainment, Embassy Records; guest lectr. at various colls. and univs. in Calif. and N.Y., 1973—; writer, illustrator, dir. numerous ednl. filmstrips, 1972—, latest being Focus on Professions, 1974, Focus on the Performing Arts, 1974, Focus on the Creative Arts, 1974, Workstyles, 1976, Wonderworm, 1976, Supernut, 1977; author, illustrator film Fat Black Mack (San Francisco Ednl. Film Festival award, Mus. Modern Art permanent film collection), 1970; designer posters and brochures for various entertainment groups, 1963—; head prodn. Advanced Audio Visual Systems, 1979—; writer, producer Holidays, read along films for United Learning Corp., 1979; cons. to numerous film and ednl. cos.; composer numerous songs, latest being Time is Relative, 1976, Love Will Live On in My Mind, 1976, My Blue Walk, 1976, Let Me Sing a Love Song, 1982, Best Friends Baby Sister, 1982, Let's Go Around Once More, 1982; composer/author off-Broadway musical Street Corner Time, 1978; contbr. children's short stories to various publs., articles to mags. and jours. Trustee The Happy Spot Sch., N.Y.C., 1972—. Mem. Am. Acad. Polit. and Social Sci., Broadcast Music Inc., Nat. Writers Club. Address: 11417 Vanowen St North Hollywood CA 91605

BERKE, VIRGINIA VETTA, pub. co. advt. promotion staff; b. N.Y.C., May 8, 1926; d. Morris and Sadye (Weiss) Luckower; B.A., Syracuse U., 1947; m. Joseph Berke, July 20, 1956 (dec. Aug. 1, 1973); children—Dawn, Adam, Bill. Mem. advt. promotion staff Vogue Pattern Book, Conde-Nast Publs., N.Y.C., 1948-51; advt. mgr. Print mag., N.Y.C., 1952-56, R.C. Publs., N.Y.C., 1968—, now advt. dir. Home: 2100 Linwood Ave Apt 16-0 Fort Lee NJ 07024 Office: 355 Lexington Ave New York NY 10017

BERKELMAN, ANNIE, cosmetics mfg. co. exec.; b. 1935; B.A., Bates Coll., 1957. Advt. copy writer Harold Cabot & Co., Inc., 1958-60; advt. copywriter Hoag & Provandie Inc., 1960-62; group head, advt. copy Norman, Craig & Kummel Inc., 1962-66; with Avon Products Inc., 1966—, group dir. field support, 1978-79, v.p. field communications, 1979-81, v.p. prodn. and quality, 1981—; dir. Great Oaks Ins. Co., Springfield, Mass. Office: Avon Products Inc 9 W 57th St New York NY 10019 *

BERKEN, LINDA MAE, motion picture co. exec.; b. N.Y.C., July 16; d. Israel and Frieda Ruth Lusskin; B.S., Hofstra Coll. Sec., ABC-TV, N.Y.C., 1970-74, supr. talent, 1974-77, dir. artist relations, 1977-81, talent coordinator A.M. America, 1973-74; v.p. talent relations Columbia Pictures, Burbank, Calif., 1981—. Office: Columbia Pictures Columbia Plaza South Burbank CA 91505

BERKEY, MARILYN ROCHELLE, jeweler; b. Tacoma, Mar. 6, 1944; d. William Norman and Mary Lucille (LaPine) Rochelle; student Famous Artist's Sch., 1967-69, Buresch Fine Arts Sch., 1969-71, Art Students League, N.Y.C., 1971-72; m. James Howard Berkey, Jr., Aug. 18, 1962 (div. 1973); 1 dau., Jamie Lucille. Mgr. fine jewelry Weisfield's Inc. City Store, Orange, Calif., 1972-76, J.E. Caldwell & Co., Phila., 1976-78, Marcus Jewelers div. Kay Corp., King of Prussia, Pa., 1978-80; owner, pres. Creative Challenge Assos., retail cons., Wayne, Pa., 1980—. Com. mem. Notre Dame de Namur, Villanova, Pa., 1981—; active Multiple Sclerosis Soc. Mem. Gemological Inst. Am. (student asso.), Democrat. Roman Catholic. Home and Office: 219 Sugartown Rd K303 Strafford Wayne PA 19087

BERKMAN, CLAIRE FLEET, psychologist; b. New Orleans, Dec. 5, 1942; d. Joel and Margaret Grace (Fishler) Fleet; B.A., Boston U., 1964; M.Ed., Harvard U., 1966; Ed.D., Boston U., 1970; m. Arnold Stephen Berkman, Apr. 27, 1975; children—Janna Samantha, Micah Seth Siegel. Asst. prof. Counseling Center, Mich. State U., East Lansing, 1971-75, asso. prof., 1975-78, asso. prof. dept. psychiatry, 1975—; pvt. clin. practice, 1975—; cons. Cath. Family Social Service, Lansing, 1979—. Vice pres. Kehillat Israel Synagogue, 1975-76; bd. dirs. Jewish Welfare Fedn., Lansing, 1974-75. NDEA fellow, 1968-70. Mem. Am. Psychol. Assn., Mich. Psychol. Assn., Am. Mental Health Assn. of Israel. Office: 1812 Michigan National Tower Lansing MI 48933

BERKO, SHIRLEY SUE, civic worker; b. St. Louis, Feb. 27, 1934; d. Burton and Sylvia Ruth (Sheinbein) Bierman; lab. x-ray technician cert. Calif. Inst. Med. Tech., 1954; m. Perry J. Hasson, Mar. 27, 1955; m. 2d, Stanley F. Berko, Mar. 13, 1966; children—Grace Hasson Rodman, Brenda Hasson Factor, Holly Hasson, Joseph Hasson; stepchildren—Bonnie Bann, Renee Shoemaker, Dean Berko. Youth commr. Temple Beth Emet, Anaheim, Calif., 1970-73, pres. Sisterhood, 1977-78, temple exec. v.p., 1979-80, pres., 1980-82; chmn. adult edn. Pacific SW br. Women's League for Conservative Judaism, 1978-80, v.p., 1980-82, chmn. Israel affairs, 1982-84. Recipient Woman of Achievement award Temple Beth Emet Sisterhood, 1979, Woman of Yr., 1980; Merit award U. Judaism, 1981. Mem. PTA (hon. life). Address: 2220 Della Ln Anaheim CA 92802

BERKOWITZ, ALICE BETH, editor; b. Bklyn., May 15, 1952; d. Murray and Shirley Ruth (Levinson) B.; B.A. magna cum laude in Art and English, Bklyn. Coll., 1973. Asst. to art dir. Cosmopolitan mag., N.Y.C., 1973-74, copy editor, 1974-76; mng. editor Young Pres.'s Orgn., N.Y.C., 1976-78, editor, 1978—; photographer, freelance copy editor. Home: 333 E 34th St New York NY 10016 Office: 52 Vanderbilt Ave New York NY 10017

BERL, ETHEL GARFUNKEL, psychologist; b. Jersey City, May 1, 1906; d. Samson and Rose Garfunkel; B.A. cum laude, Hunter Coll., 1927; M.A., Columbia U., 1928; Ph.D., N.Y. U., 1940; m. Alexander Berl, July 31, 1932. Mem. faculty Hunter Coll., City U. N.Y., 1927-74, prof. psychol. founds. of edn. and mental health, 1928-74, prof. emeritus, 1974—; pvt. practice counseling and cons. psychology, N.Y.C., 1958—; cons. Coll. and Career Cons., Inc., 1960-74, Sch. Nursing, L.I. U., 1965, Hunter Coll.-Bellevue Sch. Nursing, 1974, Brookdale Center on Aging, Hunter Coll., 1976-78. Mem. edn., tng. and recruiting coms. Greater N.Y. council Girl Scouts U.S.A., 1945-51; dir. Scholarship and Welfare Fund, Hunter Coll., 1951—. Named to Hunter Coll. Hall of Fame; cert. psychologist, N.Y. Mem. Am. Psychol. Assn., N.Y. State Psychol.

Assn., Hunter Coll. Alumni Assn. (past v.p., past dir., past bus. mgr.), Phi Beta Kappa, Pi Mu Epsilon, Kappa Delta Pi.

BERLAGE, GAI INGHAM, educator; b. Washington, Feb. 9, 1943; d. Paul Bowen and Grace (Artz) Ingham; B.A., Smith Coll., 1965; M.A., So. Meth. U., 1968; Ph.D., N.Y. U., 1979; m.; 2 children. Tchr., Nelson High Sch., Lovingston, Va., 1965-66, Ridgefield (Conn.) Public Sch., 1966-67, Piner Jr. High, Sherman, Tex., 1968-69; faculty Southeastern Coll., Durant, Okla., 1968, Norwalk (Conn.) Community Coll., 1971-77; instr. sociology Iona Coll., New Rochelle, N.Y., 1971-74, asst. prof. sociology, 1974—, chmn. dept. sociology, 1981—; research cons. Health Studies Inst., New Rochelle, 1980—; lectr. in field; reviewer articles in field. Mem. Wilton Task Force Com. on Public Health Nursing Assn., 1981-82; commr. Wilton Commn. on Aging & Social Services, 1980—, chmn., 1982—; advisor Wilton Assn. Gifted Edn., 1981-82, pres., 1980-81. Iona Coll. grantee, 1981, summer 1981, 80-81; NSF grantee, 1980-81, 79-80, traineeship award, 1967-68; Iona Coll. dissertation fellow, 1975. Mem. Am. Sociol. Assn., Nat. Council on Crime and Delinquency, Nat. Inst. for Sport and Social Analysis, N.Am. Youth Sport Inst., N.Am. Soc. Sociology of Sport, So. Sociol. Soc., N.Y. Sociol. Assn., Mid-South Sociol. Assn. Contbr. articles to profl. jours.

BERLEEN, JEANETTE RUTH, Wash. state legislator; b. Dickenson, N.D., Nov. 2, 1952; d. Edward Louis and Jean (Flowers) Fatton; A.A., Highline Community Coll., 1972; B.A., U. Wash., 1976; div. Acct. Puget Sound Hosp., 1976-77, Wash. State Hosp. Commn., 1977-78; budget analyst West Seattle Gen. Hosp., 1978-81, Orgnl. Cons., 1981-82; mem. Wash. Ho. Reps., 1981—. Mem. Hosp. Fin. Mgmt. Assn., Beta Alpha Psi. Contbr. article to hosp. publ. Methodist. Club: Toastmasters. Office: Wash State Ho Reps State Capitol Olympia WA 98504

BERLINCOURT, MARJORIE ALKINS, govt. ofcl.; b. Toronto, Ont., Can., June 2, 1928; came to U.S., 1950, naturalized, 1956; d. Herbert John and Ellen Florence (Barker) Alkins; B.A., U. Toronto, 1950; M.A., Yale U., 1951, Ph.D., 1954; m. Ted Gibbs Berlincourt, Feb. 28, 1953; 1 dau., Leslie Ellen Berlincourt Yale. Editorial dir. Tech. Publs., Rocketdyne, 1956-59; lectr. classics U. So. Calif., 1959-61; assoc. prof. classical history Calif. Luth. Coll., 1961-67, Calif. State U., Northridge, 1967-71; prof. Met. State Coll., Denver, 1971-72; program dir. div. fellowships Nat. Endowment Humanities, for summer seminars and fellowships Washington, 1972-78, dep. dir. div. research programs, 1978—; vis. lectr. Georgetown U., 1972. Recipient Calif. Faculty Research award, 1970; Sterling fellow Yale U., 1950-53. Mem. Am. Assn. Ancient Historians, Am. Assn. Advancement Humanities. Episcopalian. Author: De Surprise en Surprise, 1953; Entrez Petits Amis, 1954; Victory as a Coin Type, 1973; contbr. articles to profl. jours. Office: 806 15th St NW Washington DC 20506

BERMAN, ARIANE R., painter; b. Freeport Danzig, Poland, Mar. 27, 1937; B.F.A., Hunter Coll., 1959; M.F.A. (scholar), Yale U., 1962; postgrad. (AAUW fellow, Fondation des Etats-Unis fellow) Ecole des Beaux Arts and Atelier William Hayter, Paris, 1962-63. One-woman shows: Galleria d'Arte Helioart, Rome, 1974, Center Gallery, Conn., 1963, Brentano's Gallery, N.Y.C., 1973, Graphic Art Gallery, Tel Aviv, 1973, Public Mus., Oshkosh, Wis., 1974, Ward-Nasse Gallery, N.Y.C., 1974, 77, 80, Phila. Art Alliance, 1980, Kornblee Gallery, N.Y.C., 1982; group shows include: Cité Internationale de l'Université de Paris, Purdue U., Print Club of Albany (N.Y.), De Andries Gallery, St. Johns U., Sarah Lawrence Coll. Gallery, Aames Gallery, N.Y.C., Boston Printmakers, Phila. Art Alliance, Nat. Arts Club, N.Y.C., Butler Inst. Am. Art; represented in permanent collections: Met. Mus. Art, Wustum Mus. Fine Arts, Phila. Mus. Art, Purdue U., Russ Togs Corp., Am. Petroleum Inst., Westport Restaurants, Inc., Charles E. Ellis Coll., Am. Color Print Soc., Athena Gallery, Readers Digest, Inc., Litton Industries; numerous commns.; mem. nat. screening com. for Fulbright grants in painting, juror, 1976, 77, chairperson, 1977, 78. Recipient Stella Drabkin Meml. Gold medal, 1973; Catherine Lorillard Wolfe Arts Club Gold medal, 1973; Yale U. Printing prize, 1960; Purdue U. Purchase prize, 1964; Am. Color Print Soc. Purchase prize, 1973; Dorothy Ferriss award, 1982; Sheffield Art League award, 1982; named to Hunter Coll. Alumni Assn. Hall of Fame, 1974. Mem. Silvermine Guild Artists, Am. Color Print Soc., Nat. Assn. Women Artists, N.Y. Soc. Women Artists (corr. sec. 1980-81), Yonkers Art Assn., Artists Equity, Pen and Brush, Inc. Address: 161 W 54th St New York NY 10019

BERMAN, CAROL, state senator; b. Bklyn., Sept. 21, 1923; d. Hyman and Sarah (Levy) B.; A.B., U. Mich., Ann Arbor, 1943; m. Seymour Jerome Berman, May 19, 1944; children—Elizabeth Berry, Charles E. Congressional aide, then aide to N.Y. State assemblyman; mem. Bd. Edn. Lawrence (N.Y.), 1972-76; mem. N.Y. Senate, 1978—. Mem. Commn. Water Resource Needs L.I., 1980; chmn. Emergency Coalition to Stop SST, 1977; former pres. Lawrence High Sch. PTA; former vice chmn. Nassau County Democratic Com.; del. Dem. Nat. Conv., 1976, 80. Recipient award merit N.Y. State Sch. Bds. Assn., 1976; Hannah G. Solom award Nat. Council Jewish Women, 1978; Women of Year award Nassau Herald, 1978. Mem. Nassau County Women's Polit. Caucus (vice chmn. 1972-75), Lawrence Assn. (gov. 1977), LWV, Hadassah, Nat. Council Jewish Women, ARMDI, Common Cause, NOW, Am. Jewish Congress, NAACP. Office: Room 306 Legis Office Bldg Albany NY 12247

BERMAN, CLAIRE GALLANT, writer; b. N.Y.C., July 4, 1936; d. Max and Rebecca (Yarus) Gallant; A.B., Barnard Coll., 1957; m. Noel Berman, July 19, 1959; children—Eric, Mitchell, Orin. Sr. editor Cosmopolitan mag., N.Y.C., 1958-63; contbg. editor New York mag., 1971-77; books include: A Great City for Kids, 1969; We Take This Child: A Candid Look at Modern Adoption, 1974; Making It As a Stepparent, 1980, What Am I Doing in a Stepfamily, 1982; contbr. articles to newspapers and mags. including N.Y. Times, Ladies Home Jour., Redbook; dir. public edn. Permanent Families for Children Child Welfare League, N.Y.C., 1975—; editor: Adoption Report, 1975—. Mem. Stepfamily Assn. Am. (dir. 1980—), Am. Soc. Journalists and Authors (exec. council 1981—), Authors League Am. Home: 52 Riverside Dr New York NY 10024 Office: 67 Irving Pl New York NY 10003

BERMAN, DIANA LEONORA, social worker; b. N.Y.C., July 14, 1932; d. Benjamin and Betty (Schwartz) Styler; B.A. (scholar), U. Mich., 1953, M.S.W. (scholar), 1955; postgrad. Columbia U. Sch. Social Work, spring 1970; m. Irwin Berman, 1956; children—Kenneth, Benjamin. Caseworker, Jewish Social Service Bur., Detroit, 1955-56, Jewish Child Care Assn., N.Y.C., 1956-59, Play Sch. Assn., N.Y.C., summer 1966, Neurol. Service, Montefiore Hosp., Bronx, 1967-70; pediatric caseworker Jewish Meml. Hosp., N.Y.C., 1970-71; pediatric social worker, child abuse coordinator Mountainside Hosp., Montclair, N.J., 1972-81, mem. speakers bur.; with Daus. of Israel, West Orange, N.J., 1982—; cons. Assn. for Children of N.J.; Pres., Inter-agy. Council Bloomfield (N.J.), 1979—, v.p., 1977-79. Cert. social worker, N.Y. Mem. Nat. Assn. Social Workers, Assn. for Children of N.J., Child Study Assn. Am. (book rev. com. 1970, 71), Planned Parenthood, LWV. Editor newspaper Alumni Assn. Sch. Social Work, 1956; contbr. articles to profl. jours. Home: 530 Valley Rd Montclair NJ 07043 Office: Daughters of Israel West Orange NJ

BERMAN, ELEANOR, writer, public relations cons.; b. Birmingham, Ala., May 7, 1934; d. Abraham and Bertha (Sirote) Greenwald; B.A., Smith Coll., 1955; m. Robert S. Berman, June 16, 1956; children—Thomas Jonathan, Eric Lee, Terry Ellen. Dir. public info. Stamford (Conn.) Mus., 1970-73; publicity mgr. Macmillan Pub. Co., N.Y.C., 1973-75; asso. dir. corp. news bur. Macmillan Inc., N.Y.C., 1975-76; free-lance writer, public relations cons., 1976—; author books: The Cooperating Family, 1977; Re-Entering, 1980; The New Fashioned Parent, 1980; Away for the Weekend, 1982; contbg. author: KLM's Guide to the U.S.A., 1979; Ian Keown's Caribbean Hideaways, 1979; Ian Keown's European Hideaways, 1980; Very Special Places, 1981; contbr. articles to nat. mags.; travel corr. Mem. Am. Soc. Journalists and Authors, Authors Guild.

BERMAN, EVA, food broker; b. Havana, Cuba, Oct. 17, 1942; came to U.S., 1960, naturalized, 1965; d. Sender and Taiba (Dworin) Golman; student U. Mich., 1964, N.Y.U., 1967; 1 dau., Raquel. Asst. to intensive English coordinator U. Mich., Ann Arbor, 1964; asst. to univ. plaza residents coordinator N.Y.U., 1966-68; food broker John G. Martin, San Francisco, 1969-74; pres. Sunshine Food Sales, Inc., Miami, Fla., 1974-81; pres., owner E & R Internat. Seafood, Inc., Miami Beach, Fla., 1981—. Treas., Steve Fraser City Council, Sausalito, Calif., 1971. Mem. Nat. Oceanographic Found., Nat. Fisheries Inst., Southeastern Fisheries Assn., Organized Fisherman of Fla., Nat. Assn. Female Execs., Miami Food Brokers Assn., Miami Food Trade Assn. Address: 7640 Bayside Ln Miami Beach FL 33141

BERMAN, MIRA, advt.-public relations agy. exec.; b. Danzig, Germany, June 1, 1928; d. Max and Riva (Gutman) Berman; ed. Julliard Sch. Music, David Mannes Coll., N.Y.U., Columbia U.; m. Richard D. Freedman, Jan. 23, 1972. Mem. advt. staff Bamberger's Newark, 1951-52; promotion dir. Bond Clothes, N.Y.C., 1952-55, Robert Hall, N.Y.C., 1955-56; copy dir. Gimbels Dept. Store, N.Y.C., 1956-57; public relations and fashion dir. Snellenburgs, Phila., 1957-59; sr. v.p. Lavenson Bur. Advt., Phila., 1959-66; founder, pres. Allerton Berman & Dean, Inc., N.Y.C., 1966-76; chmn., chief operating officer, creative dir. Gemini Images, Inc., N.Y.C., 1976—; producer Waif Ball div. Internat. Social Services, 1970-73, Amita Ball, 1970-78, Mishekenot Shaananim, Cultural Center, Jerusalem, 1973-75, Fashion Week, Tel Aviv, 1972-74, Bicen-Crystal Research; faculty tourism and travel adminstrn. dept. New Sch. Social Research, 1976—; lectr. in field; mem. Nat. Advt. Rev. Bd., 1975-77. Named Advt. Woman of Yr., Am. Advt. Fedn., 1971; recipient TV's. Gold medal Internat. Film & TV Festival, 1971, 72. Mem. Am. Mgmt. Assn. (co-chmn. Conf. on Mktg. Through Retailers 1967, transl. work into Japanese, Spanish and German; co-chmn. Conf. on Mng. Profit and Growth in World Travel and Tourism 1973, lectr.), Nat. Council of Women of U.S. (mem. exec. com. 1982—). Producer films, including: Israel 25—A Celebration, 1973 (Internat. Film & TV Festival's Grand award 1973); editor: (with Malcolm P. McNair) Marketing Through Retailers, 1967. Office: Gemini Images Inc 1790 Broadway Suite 711 New York NY 10019

BERMAN, MONA S. (MRS. CARROLL Z. BERMAN), theatrical dir., producer; b. Jersey City; d. Edward and Mary (Auster) Solomon; B.A., Beaver Coll.; postgrad. Columbia U.; M.F.A., Boston U.; m. Carroll Z. Berman; children—Marcie S. Berman Ries, Laura Jane. Tchr. English, drama Jersey City High Schs.; actress Mass. Valley Players, Holyoke; owner, dir. The Theatre Sch. and Producing Co., Maplewood, N.J.; chmn. drama edn. YM-MWHA of Met. N.J. Cons., Clark Center for Performing Arts, N.Y.C., 1965-66; instr. South Orange, Maplewood Adult Sch., 1967; artistic dir. Children's Theatre Co. Inc., Maplewood, 1968-70; cons. The Whole Theater Co., 1974—; dir. pub. relations Co. 3 by 2. Active Boston United Fund, 1955-59, chmn. Boston residential area, 1957; bd. dirs. Greater Boston Girl Scouts Am., 1956-58, Tufts Med. Faculty Wives, 1956-58. Mem. Am. Theater Assn. Playwright: Hello Joe, 1967; That Ring in the Center, 1968; The Big Show, 1970; Interim, 1974; Who Can Belong?, 1979; producer, dir. A Night of Stars; guest theatre reviewer El Paso Herald Post, 1980-82. Address: 5803 Mira Serena El Paso TX 79912

BERMAN, MURIEL MALLIN, bus. exec., civic worker; student Cedar Crest Coll., D.F.A. (hon.); O.D., Pa. Coll. Optometry; student U. Pitts., Carnegie Tech. U., Muhlenberg Coll.; hon. degree Wilson Coll.; Ph.D. (hon.), Hebrew U. Jerusalem, 1982; m. Philip I. Berman; children—Nancy, Nina, Steven. Underwriting mem. Lloyd's of London, 1974—; v.p. Hess's Dept. Stores, Inc.; sec., treas. Philip and Muriel Berman Found.; v.p., dir. Hamilton at Ninth Corp.; sec., dir. Fleetways, Inc., lectr. on world travel and art various sch., clubs and community orgns.; founder and donor Art Slide Library Exchange, Carnegie-Berman Coll., Pa.; del. to UNICEF; mem. ad hoc com. UNICEF Bd. on Latin Am. and Africa; mem. council Pa. Council on Arts; mem. Pa. Commn. for Women; mem. council Pa. Humanities Council; 1979—; producer Guest Spot TV program; mem. adv. council Cedar Crest Coll.; del. to Democratic Nat. Conv., 1972, 76, mem. platform com.; U.S. State Dept. del. to UN Internat. Women's Yr., Mexico City, 1975; mem. adv. com. to U.S. Center for Internat. Women's Yr., Washington; trustee, chmn. bd. Lehigh County Community Coll.; trustee Kutztown State Coll., vice chmn., 1960-66; trustee Pa. Ballet, Phila., Allentown (Pa.) Art Mus. Aux., Baum Art Sch., Bonds for Israel, United Fund, Lehigh Valley; trustee, chmn. Lehigh Valley Ednl. TV, trustee, vice chmn. Allentown Symphony; bd. dirs. Heart Assn. of Pa. Hon. fellow Hebrew U., 1975; recipient Myrtle Wreath award Pa. region Hadassah, Outstanding Woman award YWCA, 1973, Henrietta Szold award Hadassah, Disting. Citizen award Boy Scouts Am., 1982, Hazlett award Pa. Council for Arts, 1982; named Woman of Valor, Bonds for Israel. Mem. Jewish Publ. Soc. (pres.), Fgn. Policy Assn., LWV, Am. Fedn. Art, NOW, Lehigh County Hist. Soc., Lehigh Art Alliance, Phila. Art Alliance, Pa. Acad. Arts, Met. Mus., Mus. of Modern Art, Mus. of Primitive Art, Jewish Mus. (N.Y.), Met. Opera Guild. Clubs: Wellesley (N.Y.), Woman's (fine arts chmn.). Address: 20 100 Nottingham Rd Allentown PA 18103

BERMAN, PHYLLIS WALDMAN, psychologist; b. Bklyn., Apr. 19, 1938; d. Abraham and Sarah Waldman; M.A., U. Wis., 1960, Ph.D., 1963; m. Mark Berman, Feb. 3, 1957; 1 son, Marc A. Asst. prof. ednl. psychology U. Wis., 1963-65; asst. prof. Pa. State U., University Park, 1968-69, assoc. prof. psychology, 1969-73; assoc. prof. psychology Fla. State U., Tallahassee, 1974-79; health scientist adminstr. Human Learning and Behavior br. Nat. Inst. Child Health and Human Devel., Bethesda, Md., 1979—. Southeastern Psychol. Assn. vis. woman scholar 1974-79; NIMH fellow, 1965, 66; U.S. Office Edn. grantee. Fellow Am. Psychol. Assn.; mem. Soc. for Research in Child Devel., Nat. Council on Family Relations. Co-editor: Women: A Developmental Perspective, 1982; contbr. articles to profl. jours. Home: 10631 Montrose Ave Apt 203 Bethesda MD 20814 Office: Human Learning and Behavior Br Nat Inst Child Health and Human Devel 7C18 Landow Bldg 7910 Woodmont Ave Bethesda MD 20205

BERMAN, RITA, editor, author; b. London, June 2, 1932; came to U.S., 1954, naturalized, 1976; d. Louis and Sophie (Mishkin) Castleman; student Pitman's Bus. Coll., London, 1947-49; spl. student Mich. State U., Colo. State U.; m. Ezra Berman, Aug. 30, 1959; children—Jessica, Rebecca. Reporter, Va. Metro News, Reston, 1972-73; various office positions and med. sec. positions, 1967-53; freelance writer, Chapel Hill, N.C., 1973—; columnist Durham Morning Herald, 1981—; part-time editorial asst. Vitamins and Hormones, 1976-81, Pharm. Revs., 1976-81; condr. seminars, author numerous book revs., articles in bus. and trade jours. Recipient 1st pl. feature article contest Tar Heel Writers Roundtable, Raleigh, N.C., 1973; Achievement award mag. article Carolina chpt. Soc. Tech. Communications, 1977, Merit award, 1975, 80. Mem. Nat. Writers Club, Durham/Chapel Hill Pub. Relations Soc., Women in Communications (sec.-treas. Triangle chpt. 1977-78, membership chmn. 1979-80, membership com. So. region 1979-80, pres. 1980-81). Address: 316 Estes Dr Chapel Hill NC 27514

BERMAN, ROSALIND, state legislator; b. N.Y.C., Apr. 3, 1925; d. Bernard Israel and Ida (Minsky) Schub; B.A., U. Conn., 1946; m. Arnold Wilson Berman, Nov. 9, 1947; children—Barry, Kenneth, Mark. Social worker, Bridgeport, Conn., 1946-47; sch. counselor Hillhouse and Lee high schs., New Haven, 1966-70; alderman City of New Haven, 1969-77, park commr., New Haven, 1971-74, Coliseum commr., 1970-72; mem. Conn. Ho. of Reps., 1976—. Mem.-adv. com. Sacred Heart U.; bd. advisers S. Central Community Coll Recipient Editors award Lee High Sch., 1976, State of Conn. Resolution of Honor, 1977, Outstanding Legislator award Conn. Citizens' Action Group, 1981; Spl. Honor award Women's Issues Network. Fellow, Timothy Dwight Coll., Yale U., 1975—. Mem. Order Women Legislators. Republican. Jewish. Office: State Capitol Hartford CT 06115

BERMAN, SIEGRID VISCONTI, interior designer; b. Bremen, Germany, May 22, 1944; came to U.S., 1951, naturalized, 1956; d. Walter L. and Annegrete M. (Wolf) Knapp; self-educated. Designer, Shepard Martin Assos., N.Y.C., 1968-76; facilities mgr. Unifert, USA, N.Y.C., 1976-78; owner Siegrid Visconti Berman Interiors, N.Y.C., 1978—; dir. interiors DAT Cons., N.Y.C., 1980—; dir. Ten Park Ave Corp., 1979-81. Bd. dirs. Temple Spiritual Research and Learning, 1981-82; reader Lighthouse for Blind. Colo. State Coll. scholar, 1962. Mem. AFTRA, Screen Actors Guild. Composer songs, illustrator book. Office: 118 W 16th St New York NY 10011

BERN, FLORENCE, artist; b. Milw.; d. Nathan and Bessie (Sherman) Schapiro; B.F.A., U. Wis., Milw., 1974, M.F.A., 1977; student Layton Art Sch., Milw., 1965-69; m. Leslie S. Bern, Jan. 29, 1950; children—Ross Hillel, Jay Scott, Eric Mitchell, Cindy Chaya Eliefja. Comml. illustrator Gimbels, Milw., 1943-49; artist Rhea Mfg. Co., Milw., 1949, The Grand and Bitkers, Supreme Mfg. Co., 1950-54; art dir., coordinator Cong. Beth El Ner Tamid Religious Sch., Milw., 1972-74; art coordinator tchr. Cong. Emanuel Bn'e Jeshurun, Milw., 1977-81, chmn. inter religious affairs com., 1978-80; designer covers and mass media pubs. for community orgns.; one woman shows: Bresler Galleries, Milw., 1970, Milw. Jewish Community Center, 1973, 78, Wis. Center, Madison, 1979, Concordia Coll., Milw., 1981; group shows include: Monroe Gallery, Chgo., 1970, Ozaukee Art Center, Cedarburg, Wis., 1972, U. Wis. Alumnae Shows, 1974, 75, 77, 79-82, Wustum Mus., Racine, Wis., 1977-82, Milw. Pub. Library (purchase award League Milw. Artists 1968), Nat. League Am. Pen Women (1st place woodcut 1969, hon. mention 1976); traveling exhbn. Watercolor Wis., 1977, 78, 80, 81, 82; represented in permanent collections Milw. Public Library, N. United Presbyn. Ch., Milw., Congregation Bn'e Jeshurum, Milw., Milw. Jewish Home Aged. Mem. Cath.-Jewish Dialogue Com. Milw., 1978—; vol. Rogers Meml. Hospice, 1978-79; block capt. March of Dimes, 1977; mem. public relations com. Congregation Emanuel Bn'e Jeshurun, v.p. Community Involvement Sisterhood, 1980—, initiator —Women: One in Spirit, women's interfaith network, 1980—, steering com., 1982-84; mem. Milw. sponsoring com. 6th Nat. Workshop on Christian Jewish Relations, chmn. culture and the arts com. Mem. Wis. Painters and Sculptors Bd., Wis. Fine Arts Assn., U. Wis. Milw. Alumni Assn., Wis. Arts Council, Milw. Art Center, Orgn. for Rehab. and Tng., Wis. Soc. for Jewish Learning, Hadassah, Am. Jewish Com. (v.p.), Milw. Jewish Fedn., Wis. Interreligious Task Force on Soviet Jewry, Nat. Council Jewish Women (co-pres. Milw. sect.), Milw. Jewish Council, Milw. Assn. Interfaith Relations (steering com., social concerns subcom.), Milw. Bibl. Archeology Soc., Nat. Mortar Bd. Designer logo for Nat. Workshop on Christian-Jewish Relations. Studio: 2341 W Green Tree Rd Milwaukee WI 53209

BERNAL, VIOLA ELENA, nurse; b. Barstow, Calif., Sept. 20, 1956; d. Nicolas and Terecita (Garcia) B.; B.S. in Nursing, Calif. State U., Los Angeles, 1978. Nurse, ARC, Camp Pendleton, Calif., 1975-76; caseworker supr., disaster nurse reservist Calif. State U., 1976-78; nurse Garfield Med. Center, Monterey Park, Calif., 1979-80; critical care nurse Kaiser Med. Center, Honolulu, 1980—. Mem. Am., Hawaii nurses assns., Critical Care Nurses Assn., Alpha Tau Delta. Roman Catholic. Home: 1676 Ala Moana #203 Honolulu HI 96815 Office: 1697 Ala Moana Honolulu HI 96815

BERNARD, CATHY SUE, real estate co. exec.; b. Bronx, N.Y., Nov. 13, 1949; d. Burton and Norma (Ebb) B.; B.B.A., George Washington U., 1971, M.B.A., 1978; M.A., U. Miami, 1972. Staff coordinator Newman Report on Higher Edn., HEW, Washington, 1971-74; evaluation specialist Office of Econ. Opportunity, Washington, 1974; asst. prof. bus. No. Va. Community Coll., 1974-76; owner, partner CSB Assocs. Ltd., Silver Spring, Md., 1976—; dir. Oublier Corp., Beverly Hills, Calif.; mem., author Montgomery County (Md.) Task Force on Moderate Priced Housing; mem. Montgomery County Housing Opportunities Commn., Community Housing Resources Bd.; mem. New Horizons Task Force, Ad Hoc Housing Task Force; speaker housing needs and devel. seminars. Mem. staff Democratic Nat. Convs., 1972, 76. Mem. Apt. and Office Bldg. Assn. (dir.), Bd. Realtors, Inst. Real Estate Mgmt. (cert. property mgr.; Hughes award 1980), Women's Polit. Caucus, Hadassah, LWV, B'nai B'rith Women, NOW, Montgomery County C. of C. (dir., v.p. housing). Club: Suburban Women's Dem. Jewish. Office: 515 Thayer Ave Silver Spring MD 20910

BERNARD, MARCELLE THOMASINE, physician; b. N.Y.C., Aug. 11, 1920; d. René Jules and Antoinette (Byrnes) B.; A.B. magna cum laude, Coll. of St. Elizabeth, 1941; M.D., N.Y. Med. Coll., 1944; M.A. in Corp. and Polit. Communications, Fairfield U., 1982; m. Edmund D. Marinucci, Mar. 30, 1967. Intern, Flower and Fifth Ave Hosps., 1944-45; family practice medicine and geriatrics, N.Y.C., 1947-79, Norwalk, Conn., 1974—; attending physician St. Francis Hosp., Bronx, 1950-65, Union Hosp., N.Y.C., 1957-79; attending staff Frances Schervier Home and Hosp., N.Y.C., 1952-76, pres. med. bd., 1959-60, v.p., 1965; attending staff St. Patrick's Home, N.Y.C., 1954-79, pres. med. bd., 1962; med. dir. St. Joseph's Heritage House, Danbury, Conn., 1972-75, Overlook Manor, Norwalk, 1981—; mem. med. bd. Notre Dame Convalescent Home, Norwalk, 1974—; asso. attending physician Norwalk Hosp., 1977—; mem. N.Y. State Dept. Health Bd. Examiners of Nursing Home Adminstrs., 1973-77; bd. dirs. Blue Cross-Blue Shield, 1975-79; bd. dirs., vice chmn. long-term care com. Fairfield County PSRO, 1979. Mem. exec. com. Bronx Tb and Health Assn., 1956-60; hon. surgeon Life Sav. Service N.Y.C., 1959-70; v.p. Bronxboro Commn. on Aging, 1961-63; chmn. profl. edn. com. Bronx chpt. Am. Cancer Soc., 1966-68, vice chmn. adv. bd., 1969-75, bd. dirs. So. Fairfield Unit, mem. med. affairs com., 1974—; mem. Ladies of Charity; mem. adv. bd. Bronx div. Salvation Army, 1964-79, Norwalk div., 1977—; mem. Conn. Region IV Area Agy. Aging, 1976—; mem. long term health care com. Commn. Aging, 1976-78; bd. dirs. Conn. Community Care, Childrens and Family Services. Named Lady Equestrian Order Holy Sepulchre Jerusalem. Served as lt. M.C. Women's Res., USN, 1945-47. Diplomate Nat. Bd. Med. Examiners. Fellow Am. Acad. Family Physicians (charter; pres. Bronx chpt., 1969-72), Am. Geriatrics Soc.; mem. N.Y. State Med. Soc. (chmn. public med. care com. 1963-65, chmn. aging and nursing homes com. 1973-78), Bronx County (pres. 1965-66, mem. bd. censors 1966-68), Conn. (pub. relations com.), Norwalk (sec. 1974-79, v.p. 1979-81, pres. 1981-82), Fairfield County (chmn. pub. relations com.) med. socs. Asst. editor Jour. Am. Med. Women's Assn., 1949-55.

Contbr. articles on geriatrics to med. jours. Home: Pine Hill Rd East Norwalk CT 06855 Office: 83 East Ave Norwalk CT 06851

BERNARD, THELMA RENE, constrn. co. adminstr., author; b. Phila., May 2, 1940; d. Michael John and Louise Thelma (Hoffman) Campione; grad. high sch.; m. Gene Bernard, Feb. 17, 1962. Sec., Penn Mut. Life Ins. Co., Phila., 1958-64, Suffolk Franklin Savs. Bank, Boston, 1964-66, Holmes & Narver, Inc., Las Vegas, Nev., 1968-71; constrn. site office mgr. Miles R. Nay, Inc., Las Vegas, 1972-74; adminstrv. asst. to pres. N.W.S. Constrn. Corp., Inc., Las Vegas, 1974—. Mem. Nat. League Am. Pen Women (pres. Red Rock Canyon br. 1976-78), Internat. Platform Assn., Nat. Assn. Women in Constrn. (corr. sec. Las Vegas chpt. 1975-77, rec. sec. 1977-78), Humanitarian Soc. Quakertown (Pa.), Antique Valentine Assn. Author: Blue Marsh, 1972; Winds of Wakefield, 1972; Moonshadow Mansion, 1973, 2d edit., 1976, Spanish transl., 1974, German transl., 1977; also song lyrics. Editor: Cactus Courier. Office: 305 W St Louis Ave Las Vegas NV 89102

BERNARDEZ, TERESA, psychiatrist; b. Buenos Aires, Argentina, June 11, 1931; B.A., Liceo No. 1 de Senoritas, U. Buenos Aires, 1948, M.D., 1956; cert. psychiatry Menninger Sch. Psychiatry, 1960; 1 son, Diego Bonesatti. Intern, Hosp. de Clinicas, U. Buenos Aires, 1955-56; resident Topeka State Hosp.-Menninger Sch. Psychiatry, 1957-60; postgrad. fellow C. F. Menninger Meml. Hosp., Topeka, 1960-62, staff psychiatrist, 1962-65; staff psychiatrist Menninger Found. Dept. Psychotherapy and Preventive Psychiatry, 1965-71; asst. prof. dept. psychiatry Mich. State U., East Lansing, 1971-74, asso. prof., 1974-79, prof. Coll. Human Medicine, 1979—; fellow Masters & Johnson Inst. Fellow Am. Psychiat. Assn.; mem. Am. Group Psychotherapy Assn., Amnesty Internat. (med. capacity com. 1981—), NOW. Club: Zonta. Contbr. articles to profl. jours. Home: 835 Westlawn St East Lansing MI 48823 Office: A236 E Fee Hall Dept Psychiatry Mich State U East Lansing MI 48824

BERNARDINO, EVELINA ABUEL, dermatologist; b. Manila, Philippines, Jan. 21, 1937; came to U.S., 1965; d. Jose I. and Josefina (Ibanez) Abuel; A.A., U. Phillipines, 1956, B.S. cum laude in Medicine, 1957, M.D., 1961; m. Vitaliano B. Bernardino, Jr., May 24, 1964; children—Vitaliano P. III, Jose Victor, Carlo Roberto, Vittorio. Rotating intern Phillipine Gen. Hosp., Manila, 1960-61, resident in medicine, 1962-65, instr., 1968-72; resident in dermatology Temple U. Health Scis. Center, Phila., 1965-66, 73; fellow in dermal pathology Mass. Gen. Hosp., Boston, 1966-67; practice medicine specializing in clin. dermatology and dermal pathology, Philippines; tchr. U. Phillipines and dermatologist Chinese Gen. Hosp., Ospital ng Maynila and Capitol Med. Center, Manila, 1968-72; practice medicine specializing in dermatology, Langhorne, Pa.; mem. staff St. Mary, Lower Bucks and Am. Oncol. hosps., 1972—; speaker profl. meetings; clin. research instr. Temple U. Health Scis. Center, 1975-76, research asst. prof., 1976-77. Lic. physician, Philippines; diplomate Am. Bd. Dermatology. Fellow Phila. Dermatol. Soc., Am. Acad. Dermatology, Am. Acad. Dermal Pathology; mem. Bucks County Med. Soc., Pa. Med. Soc., Phi Kappa Phi. Roman Catholic. Contbr. articles profl. jours. Home: RD 1 Shannon Ln Newton PA 18940 Office: Saint Mary Medical Bldg Suite 211 Langhorne PA 19047

BERNAY, BETTI (MRS. J. BERNARD GOLDFARB), artist; b. N.Y.C., Sept. 21, 1926; d. David Michael and Anna Gaynia (Bernay) Woolin; grad. costume design Pratt Inst., 1946; student Nat. Acad., N.Y.C., 1947-49, Art Students League, N.Y.C., 1950-51; m. J. Bernard Goldfarb, Apr. 19, 1947; children—Manette Deitsch, Karen Lynn. One-man shows at Galerie Raymond Duncan, Paris, France, Salas Municipales, San Sebastian, Spain, Circulo de Bellas Artes, Madrid, Spain, Bacardi Gallery, Miami, Fla., Columbia (S.C.) Mus., Columbus (Ga.) Mus., Galerie Andre Weil, Paris, France, Galerie Hermitage, Montecarlo, Monaco, Casino de San Remo (Italy), Galerie de Arte de la Caja de Ahorros de Ronda, Malaga, Spain, Centro Artistico, Granada, Spain, Circulo de la Amistad, Cordoba, Spain, Galerie Andre Weil, Paris, France, Studio Gallery H, N.Y.C., Walter Wallace Gallery, Palm Beach, Fla., Museo Bellas Artes, Malaga, Spain, Harbor House Gallery, Miami Beach, Fla., Crystal House Gallery, Miami Beach, Fla., Internat. Gallery, Jordan Marsh, Miami, Fontainebleau Gallery, Miami Beach, Fla., Carriage House Gallery, Miami Beach; exhibited in group shows at Painters and Sculptors Soc., Jersey City (N.J.) Mus., Salon de Invierno, Museo Malaga, Spain, Salon des Beaux Arts, Cannes, France, Nat. Acad. Gallery, N.Y.C., Salon des Artistes Independants, Paris, Salon des Artistes Francais, Paris, Salon Populiste, Paris, Salon de Otono, Madrid, Spain, Salamagundi Club, N.Y.C., Nat. Assn. Painters and Sculptors Spain, Madrid, Phipps Gallery, Palm Beach, Fla., Lever House, N.Y.C., Knickerbocker Artists, N.Y.C., Artists Equity, Hollywood (Fla.) Mus., Nat. Arts Gallery, N.Y.C., Springfield (Mass.) Mus., ACA Gallery, N.Y.C., Argent Gallery, N.Y.C., Nat. Acad. Gallery, N.Y.C., Gables Art Gallery, Miami, Gibralter Internat. Art Exhbn., Gault Gallery Cheltenham, Phila., Century Gallery, Miami, Fla., Met. Mus. and Art Center, Miami, Lord & Taylor Gallery, N.Y.C., Pageant Gallery, Galerie 99 (both Miami), Rosenbaum Gallery, Palm Beach, Fla., Planet Ocean, Miami; represented in permanent collections at Museo de Malaga, Circulo de la Amistad, Cordoba, Spain, I.O.S. Found., Geneva, Switzerland, Columbia (S.C.) Mus., others. Recipient Medal for artistic merit City of N.Y., Sch. Art Leagues, N.Y.C.; Prix de Paris, Raymond Duncan, 1958; others. Mem. Nat. Assn. Painters and Sculptors Spain, Nat. Assn. Women Artists, Societe des Artistes Francais, Societe des Artistes Ind., Fedn. Francais des Societes d'Art Graphique et Plastique, Artists Equity, Am. Artists Profl. League, Women's Caucus for Art, Profl. Artists Guild, Nat. Soc. Lit. and the Arts, Am. Fedn. Art, South Fla. Shell Club. Address: 10155 Collins Ave Bal Harbour FL 33154

BERNAY, ELAYN K., market researcher, educator; b. Paterson, N.J., July 29, 1928; d. Max and Leah (Rosen) Katz; M.B.A., Coll. City N.Y., 1965, Ph.D., 1973; m. Paul Bernay, Feb. 1, 1948; 1 dau., Laura. Dir. research Harper-Atlantic (Harper's Mag., Atlantic Monthly), N.Y.C., 1958-76; dir. research Ms. Mag., N.Y.C., 1976—; asso. prof. Baruch Coll., City U. N.Y., 1970-78; prof. dir. Center for Applied Research, Pace U. Grad. Sch. of Bus., 1978—. Bd. dir. A.P.A. cons. research div., 1978—. Recipient IOWE Leadership Award, 1980. Mem. AAAS, Am. Assn. Pub. Opinion Research, Am. Mktg. Assn. (pres. N.Y. chpt. 1976—, nat. dir. 1975—), Media Research Dirs. Assn., Advt. Research Found., Travel Research Assn. (pres. N.Y. chpt. 1976), Am. Psychol. Assn., Assn. for Consumer Research, Advt. Women N.Y., Am. Council Consumer Interests, Am. Statis. Assn., Beta Gamma Sigma. Contbr. articles in field to profl. jours. Home: 201 E 17th St New York City NY 10003 Office: 41 Park Row New York City NY 10038

BERNDT, JOYCE NADINE TARLEN, health care exec.; b. Wichita, Kans., Feb. 23, 1937; d. Clevelon Jacob and Edna Lucile Dempsey; B.A., U. Calif., San Jose, 1969; divorced; children—Jame Lynne Tarlen, Daren Jane Tarlen. Front office mgr. Pennsula Mortgage Co., San Jose, 1962-64; tchr. vocat. edn. to mentally retarded Joseph McKinnon Sch., San Jose, 1967-78; owner adminstr. Victoria House and Victoria House Ranch, facility for developmentally disabled adults, Forestville, Calif., 1978—, Victoria House Transp., Forestville, 1979—; pres. bd. dirs. Sonoma County Orgn. Retarded, 1979-81, Becoming Independent, Santa Rosa, Calif., 1979-82; mem. Santa Clara County Com. Sexuality and Devel. Disabilities, 1976-79, exec. com., area coordinator Santa Clara County Spl. Olympics, 1969-81. Mem. Nat. Assn. Women Execs., Calif. Tchrs. Assn., Calif. Assn. Retarded. Democrat. Roman Catholic. Address: 6871 Covey Rd Forestville CA 95436

BERNER, BEVERLY ANN, advt. exec.; b. Indpls., Dec. 11, 1948; d. Donald R. and Esther D. Berner; B.S. in Communications with honors, Ithaca Coll., 1970. Traffic coordinator J.Walter Thompson Co., Chgo., 1972-73, asst. to producer radio and commls., 1973-75; traffic mgr. Biddle Advt., Chgo., 1975-76; from account group coordinator to account exec. Clinton E. Frank Advt., Chgo., 1976-78; account exec. Gardner Advt., St. Louis, 1978—. Mem. Alpha Epsilon Rhp. Office: Gardner Advt 10 Broadway St Louis MO 63102

BERNHARDT, JO-ANN MARIE, union ofcl.; b. Phila., June 11, 1940; d. Joseph D. and Connie T. (Tesauro) Amatelli; student Holy Family Coll., Phila., 1970-71; m. Charles Bernhardt, Jr., Nov. 7, 1959; children—Charles III, Joseph S. Mem. exec. bd.-at-large Sch. Employees Local 1201, Phila., 1973-75, rec. sec., 1976-79, sec.-treas., 1980—, also editor newsletter; mem. council AFL-CIO; legis. aide Maritime Port Council, 1981—; v.p. Pa. Labor Press, 1977—. Mem. Nat. Assn. Female Execs., Del. Valley Coalition for Jobs. Roman Catholic. Office: 33 S 17th St Suite 500 Philadelphia PA 19103

BERNHEIM, HEATHER STANCHFIELD PETERSON (MRS. CHARLES BERNHEIM), civic worker; b. Houston; d. Weed and Mylla (Stanchfield) Peterson; student U. Tex., 1938-42; m. Charles A. Bernheim, July 18, 1973. Docent chmn. Harris County Heritage Soc., 1969-70, v.p., after 1970; vol. worker Hermann Hosp., 1968-69; team capt. Mus. Fine Arts Ball, Houston, 1969; maintenance fund drive worker Mus. Fine Arts, 1970; docent Costume Inst., Met. Mus. Art, N.Y.C., 1978, co-chmn., 1979-80, chmn., 1981-82, mus. guide, 1978—; bd. dirs. Planned Parenthood N.Y.C. Mem. N.Y. Jr. League, Kappa Alpha Theta Alumni Assn. Club: Houston. Home: 33 E 70th St Apt S-E New York NY 10021 also 173 Sage Rd Houston TX 77056

BERNKOPF, JEANNE FRANK, book editor; b. N.Y.C.; d. Louis J. and Rayner (Parver) Frank; A.B. magna cum laude, Smith Coll.; m. Michael Bernkopf, Sept. 5, 1965. Asst. to sci. editor, then asst. editor trade dept. Macmillan Co.; editor E.P. Dutton & Co., 1956-69; sr. editor Delacorte Press, 1969—; book doctor for other pubs. Mem. Phi Beta Kappa, PEN. Compiler: (anthology) Boucher's Choicest, 1969. Home and Office: 876 Park Ave New York NY 10021 Office: Delacorte Press 245 E 47th St New York NY 10017

BERNS, ELLEN MARSHA SCHIMMEL, designer, artist; b. Bklyn., Oct. 3, 1948; d. Milton O. and Ruth Mildred (Mall) Schimmel; student U. Okla., Norman, 1966-68; B.A. in Art History and Art, U. Tex., Austin, 1970; cert. in interior design, El Centro Coll., Dallas, 1978; postgrad. Parsons Sch. Design, N.Y.C., 1978-79, NAD, 1980-81, Am. Watercolor scholar, 1982. Fashion coordinator Neiman Marcus, 1971-73, exec. trainee 1973-74; display designer Apparel Mart and Trade Mart, 1972; owner, operator Ellen S. Berns Interiors, Dallas, 1974-78; artist, interior designer LCL Design Assos., Inc., N.Y.C., 1980-81, Swanke Hayden Connell Architects, N.Y.C., 1981—; commns. include: art for conf. area Judi S. Hall Interiors, San Francisco, 1981, Nursery wall mural Marble Collegiate Ch., 1980, editorial and conceptual illustrations Nat. Assn. Credit Mgmt., 1981; works exhibited Temple Emanuel, Dallas, 1978, Parsons Sch. Design, 1979, 82, Suzanne's Gallery, N.Y.C., 1980; freelance artist, designer rugs Sylvan-Garret Showroom, 1978, Peter Wolf & Assos., 1975; lectr. Parsons Sch. Design. Mem. Am. Soc. Interior Designers, Women in Design (asso.). Office: 400 Park Ave New York NY 10028

BERNSTEIN, ANNE CAROLYN, psychotherapist, psychologist, educator; b. N.Y.C., Apr. 8, 1944; d. Alfred J. and Clara (Handelman) B.; B.A. magna cum laude, Brandeis U., 1965; Ph.D. (USPHS grantee), U. Calif., Berkeley, 1973; m. Conn M. Hallinan, Jan. 16, 1982; stepsons—Sean, Antonio, Brian; 1 son, David Alexander. Psychologist, Family Therapy Inst. of Marin, San Rafael, Calif., 1972-73; psychologist, lectr. Cowell Coll., U. Calif., Santa Cruz, 1973-75; clin. lectr. family practice residency program, U. Calif., San Francisco, 1974-76; contract instr. John F. Kennedy U., Orinda, Calif., 1975, Calif. Sch. for Profl. Psychology, San Francisco, 1975-77, Calif. State U., Hayward, 1977; program dir. M.A. in Psychology and Family Reunification, San Francisco Dept. Social Services, Lone Mountain Coll., and U. San Francisco, 1977-81; prof. Wright Inst., Berkeley, 1981—; psychologist Rockridge Health Plan, Oakland, Calif., 1979—; pvt. practice clin. psychology and psychotherapy, Berkeley, 1974—. Treas., bd. dirs. Children's Rights Group, San Francisco, 1976—. Mem. Psychotherapy Inst. (mem. coordinating council 1981-82), Am. Family Therapy Assn., Am. Psychol. Assn., No. Calif. Family Therapy Assn., Sex Info. and Edn. Council of U.S., Am. Assn. Sex Educators, Counselors and Therapists, Am. Orthopsychiat. Assn., Soc. for Psychol. Study of Social Issues, Phi Beta Kappa. Author: The Flight of the Stork, 1978, 2d edition, 1980; contbr. articles to profl. publs., including Parents Mag. Home: 3033 Dana St Berkeley CA 94705 Office: 2728 Durant St Berkeley CA 94704

BERNSTEIN, CAROL, molecular biologist; b. Paterson, N.J., March 20, 1941; d. Benjamin and Mina (Regenbogen) Adelberg; B.S. in Physics, U. Chgo., 1961; M.S. in Biophysics, Yale U., 1963; Ph.D. in Genetics, U. Calif., Davis, 1967; m. Harris Bernstein, June 7, 1962; children—Beryl, Golda, Benjamin. Postdoctoral fellow U. Calif., Davis, 1967-68; research asso. U. Ariz., Tucson, 1968-75, adj. asst. prof., 1975-81, adj. asso. prof., 1981—. Prin. investigator Nat. Found. grant, 1975-76; co-prin. investigator grants NSF and NIH, 1975—. Mem. Genetics Soc., Am. Soc. Microbiology, AAUP (chpt. pres.), Fedn. Am. Scientists, Biophys. Soc. Democrat. Jewish. Contbr. articles profl. jours. Home: 2639 E 4th St Tucson AZ 85716 Office: Dept Molecular and Medical Microbiology Coll Medicine U Ariz Tucson AZ 85724

BERNSTEIN, DIANE ARDITH, audiologist, speech therapist, designer; b. Bridgeport, Conn., Feb. 1, 1939; d. Joseph and Augusta Popkin; B.S., Adelphi U., Garden City, N.Y., 1960, M.S., 1973; children—David, Stefanie. Speech therapist Bd. Coop. Extension Services, Westbury, N.Y., 1960-61, Carle Place (L.I.) Sch. System, 1961-62, Cerebral Palsy Center, Jamaica, N.Y., 1963-64; audiologist Suffolk Hearing and Speech Center, Bayshore, N.Y., 1973-82, N.Y.C. Bd. Edn., 1982—; pres. Adornments by Denny, fashion accessories. Mem. Am. Speech and Hearing Assn., N.Y. State Speech and Hearing Assn., L.I. Speech and Hearing Assn. Democrat. Jewish. Home: 6 Shore Park Rd Great Neck NY 11023 Office: 500 E 78th St New York NY

BERNSTEIN, FLORENCE HENDERSON, singer, actress; b. Dale, Ind., Feb. 14; d. Joseph and Elizabeth (Elder) Henderson; student Am. Acad. Dramatic Arts, 1951-52; m. Ira Bernstein, Jan. 9, 1956; children—Barbara, Joseph, Robert, Elizabeth. Stage debut in Wish You Were Here, N.Y.C., 1952; stage appearances include: Oklahoma, 1952-53, 53, 54, The Great Waltz, 1953, Fanny, 1954, The Sound of Music, 1960-61, 78, The Girl Who Came to Supper, 1963, South Pacific, 1967, 80, Annie Get Your Gun, 1974, Bells Are Ringing, 1978; also numerous cabaret appearances, including MGM Grand Hotel, Las Vegas; TV appearances include: host Bell Telephone Hour, The Brady Bunch series, 1969-74, Brady Bunch spls., 1976-77, also and variety shows; appeared in movie Song of Norway, 1970. Office: care William Morris Agy Ltd 151 El Camino Beverly Hills CA 90212 *

BERNSTEIN, JOAN CAROL KOSTA, speech pathologist; b. Bronx, N.Y., Jan. 2, 1941; B.F.A., Ithaca Coll., 1962; M.A., Columbia U., 1965, Ed.D. (Office Edn. fellow 1968-70), 1972; m. Joel S. Bernstein, Aug. 27, 1961; children—Mark, Fran, Eric. Instr., supr. hearing and speech Tchrs. Coll., Columbia U., N.Y.C., 1965-70; instr. communications dept. Fairleigh Dickinson U., Teaneck, N.J., 1972-76; supr. CCNY, 1977; dir. speech and hearing center Bergen Pines County Hosp., Paramus, N.J., 1977; pvt. practice speech and lang. pathology, Dumont, N.J., 1965—. Bd. dirs. Good Neighbor Fund, Dumont, 1975—. Recipient Disting. Service award N.J. Internat. Yr. of Disabled Persons, 1981. Mem. Am. Speech, Lang. and Hearing Assn., Internat. Assn. Logopedics and Phoniatrics, N.J. Speech and Hearing Assn. Kappa Delta Pi, Theta Alpha Phi. Club: B'nai B'rith. Contbr. articles to profl. jours. Home: 91 White Beeches Dr Dumont NJ 07628 Office: Bergen Pines County Speech and Hearing Center E Ridgewood Ave Paramus NJ 07652

BERNSTEIN, JOSEPHINE HELENA, clin. psychologist; b. Chgo., July 5, 1929; d. Emmanuel Bernard and Bessie Birdie (Kaplan) Fink; B.A., UCLA, 1952, M.A., 1956, Ph.D., 1961; m. Joseph C. Bernstein, Dec. 18, 1965 (dec.); 1 son, Allen Emanuel. Intern, UCLA Clinic, 1953; clin. psychology trainee VA, Los Angeles, 1953-56, 58-60; caseworker Jewish Com. for Personal Service, Los Angeles, 1957-58; clin. psychologist VA Outpatient Clinic, Los Angeles, 1960-61; clin. psychologist Rancho Los Amigos Hosp., Los Angeles, 1962-63, Brentwood VA Hosp., Los Angeles, 1963-65, Gateways Hosp., Los Angeles, 1965-69, chief psychologist, 1966-69; asst. chief psychologist Westwood Meth. Ch. Clinic, Los Angeles, 1964-66; clin. psychologist Los Angeles County Mental Health Clinic, Juvenile Hall, 1972—; tchr. Calif. Grad. Inst., 1971—, pres. bd. trustees, 1979-81. Mem. Los Angeles County Psychol. Assn., Calif. State Psychol. Assn., Am. Psychol. Assn., Internat. Transactional Assn., Psi Chi, Pi Gamma Mu. Home: 2345 Longden Dr San Marino CA 91108 Office: 1605 Eastlake Los Angeles CA 90033

BERNSTEIN, STELLA MAINE, silk flower wholesaler, civic worker; b. Balt., Oct. 3, 1936; d. Benjamin L. and Isabella (Maine) Striner; A.A. cum laude, Marjorie Webster Jr. Coll., 1954; m. Paul Bernstein, Aug. 18, 1957; children—Julie, Mark, Ellen, Jeffrey. Co-owner P & S Assos., Inc., Kensington, Md., 1980—. Rec. sec. N.W. Br. Citizens Assn.; del. Allied Civic Assn.; precinct treas. Democratic Nat. Com.; mem. Women's Nat. Dem. Club, Women's Nat. Symphony; former pres. Jewish Home for Retarded Children, Shaare Tefila Parents Tchrs. Assn., Brandeis Nat. Women's Com., Service Guild Greater Washington; past pres. Am. Soc. Technion Women's Div.; bd. dirs. Jewish Social Service Agy., Jewish Council for Aging, women's div. United Jewish Appeal, Jewish Community Center; v.p. chpt. Am.-Israel Cultural Found.; life mem. Hadassah, Nat. Children's Center, Zionist Orgn. Am., Brandeis Nat. Women's Com., Hebrew Home for Aged; life mem., bd. dirs. Nat. Council Jewish Women; mem. ORT, Jewish Hist. Soc., Cultural Alliance, Md. Com. for Arts. Recipient Achievement award Service Guild, 1974-75, 80-81. Mem. Nat. Fedn. Bus. and Profl. Women's Clubs, Zionist Orgn. Am. (v.p. Brandeis dist.). Home: 717 McCeney Ave Silver Spring MD 20901 Office: 10417 Metropolitan Ave Kensington MD 20895

BERO, MARILYN PROCINO, civic worker; b. Auburn, N.Y., Sept. 12, 1937; d. Jack Anthony and Mary Louise (Cefaratti) Procino; B.A. in Elem. Edn., Marywood Coll., 1959; postgrad. Syracuse U., 1961; m. James Donald Bero, Feb. 10, 1962; children—Mark D., Michael A., Matthew R. Tchr. 3d grade Auburn Sch. System, 1959-61. Mem. Seneca Falls (N.Y.) Sch. Dist. Bd., 1976—, v.p., 1978, pres., 1980—, dir., 1978—; co-chmn. bldg. fund drive Nat. Women's Hall of Fame, Inc., Seneca Falls, 1978-79, pres., 1980—; bd. dirs. Seneca County Child Care Ctr., 1975—, pres., 1976-79; bd. dirs. Alpha Day Sch., Seneca Falls, 1972-75, Happiness House, Geneva, N.Y., 1968-72; adv. commn. Women's Rights Nat. Hist. Park. Mem. AAUW, Women's League Seneca Falls (pres. 1978-79). Republican. Roman Catholic. Home: 2934 Route 89 Seneca Falls NY 13148 Office: PO Box 335 Seneca Falls NY 13148

BERO-GIUDICE, ANDREA CELESTE, mfg. co. exec.; b. Gardena, Calif., Sept. 24, 1954; d. Andy Ernest and Loretta Victoria (Seidel) Bero; student UCLA, 1974-76; m. Joseph John Giudice, Sept. 23, 1978. Dept. mgr. Grodin's of Calif., 1970-72; salesperson, dir. window display Charleston's of Calif., 1972-74; with Confidence Golf Co., Gardena, Calif., 1974—, asst. nat. sales mgr., 1978-80, ops. mgr., 1980—. Mem. Nat. Assn. Female Execs. Democrat. Roman Catholic. Office: 13402 Estrella Ave Gardena CA 90248

BERRY, BARBARA LUCILE, mental health clinic exec.; b. Roanoke, Va., Jan. 3, 1945; d. Edward and Doris (Jefferies) B.; B.A., Rutgers U., 1972, M.S.W., 1974; m. James Zarka, June 24, 1975. Social worker Riverdale Children Assn., 1974-76, Janet Meml. Home, 1976; founder Woodwind Family Assn., mental health facility, Paterson, N.J., 1977—, also adminstr. profl. services Janet Meml. Home, 1976-79; exec. dir. Willia Hardgrow Mental Health Clinic, 1980—. Cert. social worker, N.Y. Mem. Register Clin. Social Workers, Acad. Cert. Social Workers, Bergen County Health and Welfare Assn., Biofeedback Soc. Am., Mental Health Assn. N.J., Ednl. Legis. Action Network. Home: 103 Maryland Ave Paterson NJ 07503 Office: Box 2563 Paterson NJ 07509

BERRY, ERMA JEAN, data processing cons.; b. Chgo., Dec. 8, 1948; d. Odell and Rosalie (Moore) Gray; B.G.S., Roosevelt U., 1978; m. Ronald Berry, Aug. 28, 1971. Computer operator, Bell Lab., Naperville, Ill., 1968-69; computer operator, programmer VA, Hines, Ill., 1969-72; computer programmer Morton Salt Co., Chgo., 1972-73; sr. programmer Ill. Central R.R., Chgo., 1973-75; sr. programmer CNA Ins. Co., Chgo., 1975-79; sr. systems cons. CBM Systems Cons., Chgo., 1979-80, project leader, Trailer Train, 1980—. Recipient Outstanding Performance award VA, 1970. Mem. Am. Mgmt. Assn., Nat. Assn. Female Execs., Black Female Forum. Mem. Christ Universal Temple. Office: Trailer Train 101 N Wacker Dr Chicago IL 60606

BERRY, EVELYN MARIE, orgn. devel. exec.; b. Austin, Tex., July 21, 1950; d. Jim Smither and Helen (Kirby) B.; B.A. in French and Comparative Lit., Ind. U., 1972, M.A. in Comparative Lit., 1977; m. Anthony Smokovich, Sept. 16, 1979. Dir. drug edn. Ind. U., Bloomington, 1971-73; program coordinator human resources dept. City of Bloomington, 1973-77, dep. controller, grantsperson, 1977; trainer, sr. asso. Grantsmanship Center, Los Angeles, 1977-78; pres., treas. Berry Assos.; adj. instr. Ind. U. Sch. Public and Environ. Affairs; cons. U.S. Office of Edn., U. Ga., Dept. Energy, Equitable Life Assurance Soc., Chase Manhattan Bank, Del. Dept. Econ. Opportunity, Children's Hosp. Med. Center, Cin. Mem. Am. Soc. Public Adminstrn., Am. Soc. Planning Ofcls., Nat. Assn. Female Execs., Phi Beta Kappa. Author: The Influence and Reception of Madame de Stael in America, 1977; co-author: Grantsmanship in Academia, 1979. Home: 2948 Lexington Ave Mohegan Lake NY 10547

BERRY, IRMGARD BEINHOFF, psychologist; b. Trais-Horloff, Germany, Feb. 15, 1935; came to U.S., 1968, naturalized, 1981; d. Wilhelm and Else (Bley) Beinhoff; B.A., St. Edward's U., Austin, 1973; M.A., U. Tex., Austin, 1976, Ph.D., 1981; m. Peter F. Berry, Jan. 20, 1968; children—Christopher, Michael. Mem. German Fgn. Service, various locations, 1958-64; adminstrv. asst. Nat. Research Council of Can., 1964-68; mem. faculty St. Edward's U., 1976—, mgmt. tng. cons., 1981—; planner Tex. State Library, 1982—. Career devel. action team dir. Lone Star council Girl Scouts U.S.A., Austin. Mem. Nat. Assn.

Female Execs., Am. Psychol. Assn., Am. Soc. Tng. and Devel., Phi Kappa Phi. Democrat. Lutheran. Home: 9003 Blue Quail Austin TX 78758 Office: 3001 S Congress St Austin TX 78704

BERRY, KATHRLYN BALLARD, educator; b. Plaquemine, La., Jan. 15, 1926; d. Elisha and Florence Louise (Smith) Ballard; B.A., Leland Coll., 1957; M.Ed., So. U., 1971; divorced; children—Donald Greg, Van Clayton, Joeirthel Almenia, Edryie Joe. Public sch. tchr., La., 1944—, 2d grade tchr. Bains (La.) Elem. Sch., 1978—. Vol. fund drives Easter Seal, ARC; supt. Sunday Sch., tchr. young adult boys' class, fin. sec. usher bd. Plymouth Rock Baptist Ch.; mem. La. Bapt. State Conv.; active Boy Scouts Am., Girl Scouts U.S.A. Named Woman of Yr., Macedonia Bapt. Ch., Plaquemine, 1976; Tchr. of Yr., City of Bains, 1978. Mem. NEA, La. Educators Assn., West Feliciana Tchrs. Assn., Iberville Parish Voters League, Nat. Congress Christian Educators, West Feliciania Parish Women's Aux. Democrat. Clubs: Eastern Star, Ct. of Calanthe, Daus. of Elks, Amarhant, Happillanders Civic (hon.). Home: PO Box 481 Plaquemine LA 70764 Office: Bains Elem Sch Bains LA 70713

BERRY, LENORA ANNE, law firm fin. exec.; b. Laredo, Tex., Sept. 18, 1944; d. Tom Neal and Lora Ruth (Lindholm) Terry; student Tex. Womens' U., 1962; children—Cassandra Elisabeth, Laura Anne. Personnel and acctg. supr. Tex. Dept. Human Resources, Austin, 1964-69; controller firm Hutcheson & Grundy, Houston, 1969—; cons. firm Creel Abogados, Mexico City, 1978. Mem. staff, fin. div. George Bush Presdl. Campaign; mem. Republican Presdl. Task Force. Recipient cert. of appreciation Office Edn. Assn. Tex., 1979. Mem. Assn. Legal Adminstrs., Houston Bar Assn. (asso.). Republican. Episcopalian. Home: 6437 Creekbend Houston TX 77096 Office: 3300 Two Allen Center Houston TX 77002

BERRY, LUCILLE MARIE, educator; b. Nameoki, Ill., June 2, 1936; d. P. Louis and Frieda Catherine (Feltman) B.; B.S., St. Louis U., 1958, M.S. in Commerce, 1963, postgrad. in edn., 1963—. Supr. cashiers St. Louis U., 1958-64, supr. grants and contracts, 1964-66, chief funds acct., 1966-71; fin. asst. to provincial treas. Religious of Sacred Heart, St. Louis, 1971-74, provincial treas., 1974-75; controller Maryville Coll., St. Louis, 1975-76, dir. bus. and fin., 1976-79, adj. instr., 1972-76, adj. asst. prof., 1976-79, asso. prof., 1979—, acting div. chmn. mgmt., 1979-80, chmn., 1980—. Mem. Am. Soc. Women Accts., Mo. Assn. Acctg. Educators, Midwest Bus. Adminstrs. Assn., Am. Assn. Accts., Pi Lambda Theta. Office: 13550 Conway Rd Saint Louis MO 63141

BERRY, MARGARET C., ret. coll. adminstr.; b. Dawson, Tex., Aug. 8, 1915; d. Winfred and Lillian (McCluney) Berry; B.A., U. Tex., 1937; M.A., Columbia U., 1943, Ed.D., 1965. Tchr., El Campo (Tex.) High Sch., 1937-41, Freeport (Tex.) High Sch., 1941-42, Ball High Sch., Galveston, Tex., 1942-47; asst. dean-registrar Navarro Jr. Coll., Corsicana, Tex., 1947-50; dean of women East Tex. State U., Commerce, 1950-62; asso. dean of women U. Tex., Austin, 1962-68, asst. dean of students, 1968-69, asso. dean of students, 1969-71, dir. research and devel. programs, office of v.p. for student affairs, 1970-76, dir. univ. writings collections, 1976-80. Mem. exec. bd. Austin Drug Central, 1971-73. Mem. Nat. Assn. Women Deans, Adminstrs. and Counselors (chmn. research com. 1969-71, editor jour. 1972-80), Tex. Assn. Women Deans, Adminstrs. and Counselors (pres. 1953-55), Am. Coll. Personnel Assn., Am. Personnel and Guidance Assn., Nat. Assn. Student Personnel Adminstrs., Tex. Assn. Student Personnel Adminstrs. (v.p. 1971-73), Mortar Board, Alpha Lambda Delta (pres. nat. exec. council 1976-79), Golden Key (hon.), Kappa Delta Pi, Pi Lambda Theta, Omicron Delta Kappa, Phi Eta Sigma, Delta Kappa Gamma (chpt. pres. 1957-59). Methodist (chmn. local adminstrv. bd. 1975-77). Author: U.T. Austin Traditions and Nostalgia, 1975; Women in Educational Administration, 1979; The University of Texas: A Pictorial Account of Its First Century, 1980; contbr. hist. materials Cook'ern Horns, 1981. Home: 8502 Greenflint Ln Austin TX 78759

BERRY, MARY FRANCES, govt. ofcl., educator; b. Nashville, Feb. 17, 1938; d. George Ford and Frances Southall (Wiggins) B.; B.A., Howard U., 1961, M.A., 1962; Ph.D. (Civil War Round Table fellow), U. Mich., 1966, J.D., 1970; 9 hon. degrees. Admitted to D.C. bar, 1972; asst. prof. history Central Mich. U., Mt. Pleasant, 1966-68; asst. prof. Eastern Mich. U., Ypsilanti, 1968-69, assoc. prof., 1969-70; assoc. prof. U. Md. College Park, 1969-76, acting dir. Afro-Am. studies, 1970-72, dir., 1972-74, acting chmn. div. behavioral and social scis., 1973-74, provost, div. behavioral and social scis., 1973-76; prof. history and law U. Colo., Boulder, 1976-80, chancellor, 1976-77; prof. history, law, sr. fellow Inst. for Study Ednl. Policy, Howard U., Washington, 1980—; asst. sec. for edn. HEW, Washington, 1977-80; mem. U.S. Commn. on Civil Rights, 1980—, vice chmn., 1980-82; adj. assoc. prof. U. Mich., Ann Arbor, 1970-71. Chmn., Md. Commn. on Afro-Am. and Indian History and Culture, 1974-76; mem. com. visitors U. Mich. Law Sch., 1976-80; mem. nat. com. Careers for Older Ams., 1979—; trustee Tuskegee Inst., 1980—; adv. bd. Feminist Press, 1980—; mem. editorial adv. com. Marcus Garvey Papers, 1981—; mem. research adv. com. Joint Center for Polit. Studies, 1981. Mem. Nat. Acad. Pub. Adminstrn., Orgn. Am. Historians (exec. bd. 1974-77), Assn. for Study Afro-Am. Life and History (exec. bd. 1973-76), Am. Hist. Assn. (v.p. profl. div. 1980-83), Am. Soc. Legal Historians, ABA, Nat. Bar Assn., D.C. Bar Assn. Author: Black Resistance/White Law, 1971, Military Necessity and Civil Rights Policy, 1977, Stability, Security and Continuity-Mr. Justice Burton and Decision-Making in the Supreme Court, 1945-58, 1978, (with John W. Blassingame) Long Memory-The Black Experience in America, 1982; contbr. articles, revs. to profl. jours.; assoc. editor: Jour. Negro History, 1974-78. Office: US Commn on Civil Rights 1121 Vermont Ave NW Washington DC 20425

BERRY, ROSE BRIGID, social worker; b. McBride Canyon, N.M., Mar. 5, 1926; d. Patrick James and Bertha Cecilia (MacDonald) Berry; B.A., Mount St. Scholastica Coll., 1947; M.S.W., St. Louis U., 1950. Med. social worker Colo. State Hosp., Pueblo, 1948-49; asst. dir. social service VA Hosp., Phoenix, 1951-55; dir., clin. social work cons. social service dept. Phoenix Indian Med. Center, 1956-82; individual practice clin. social worker, 1982—. Mem. Internat. Med. Soc. Paraplegia (asso.), Nat. Assn. Social Workers, Clin. Social Workers Soc., St. Louis U. Alumni Assn. Republican. Roman Catholic. Home: 3894 N 30th St Phoenix AZ 85016

BERRYMAN, ALICE DAVIS (MRS. CECIL WELLS BERRYMAN), concert pianist, composer, educator; b. North Platte, Nebr.; d. George Warren and Alice (Clark) Davis; studied piano with August Borglum, Omaha, Wager Swayne, Paris, Rudolph Ganz, Switzerland, Maine, Denver, N.Y.; mus. analysis Cecil Berryman; theory, harmony, composition and orchestration with Emile Schwartz, Paris Conservatoire; music course New Coll., Oxford, 1969; m. Cecil Wells Berryman, Dec. 19, 1916 (dec. 1960); children—Edward Davis, Warren Leigh, Rudolph Barton. Concert pianist, numerous concerts alone and jointly with husband and three sons, Paris, N.Y. and Midwest, 1912—; debut Princess Theatre, N.Y., 1915; accredited tchr. piano Berryman Piano Conservatory, 1916-60, U. Omaha, 1930-56; work shop tchrs. and players courses Presbyn. U., 1929; nat. judge of piano, Tex., Iowa, Ohio, Va., Tenn., Wis., Alaska, Kans., 1939—; judge internat. record contests, 1954—. Mem. Hall of Fame, Piano Guild U.S.A. Mem. Am. Coll. Musicians (nat. membership com.; recipient award 1982), Nat., Nebr. (exec. com.; cert. chmn.), Omaha (pres. 1977-78), music tchrs. assns., Nat. Guild Piano Tchrs. (faculty mem.), PEO. Presbyterian. Composer 13 pub. pieces. Home: 5018 Izard St Omaha NE 68132

BERSAK, CAROLYN BETH, social worker; b. Bronx, N.Y., Feb. 15, 1949; d. Sidney Irwin and Shirley Belle (Greenstein) Love; B.A., Carnegie Mellon U., 1971; M.S., Columbia U., 1973; postgrad. Center for Modern Psychoanalytic Studies, 1974—, Adelphi U., 1978—. Social worker Mosholu Montefiore Community Center, Bronx, 1973-74; coll. program coordinator, supr. Kings County Hosp., Bklyn., 1974-77; supr. Beth Israel Outpatient Alcohol Clinic, N.Y.C., 1977-79; pvt. practice psychotherapy, N.Y.C., Poughkeepsie, N.Y., 1977—; instr. social work Marist Coll., Poughkeepsie, 1980—, Hudson Valley program Adelphi U. Fellow N.Y. State Soc. Clin. Social Work Psychotherapists (chpt. v.p.); mem. Nat. Assn. Social Workers, Nat. Accreditation Assn. Psychoanalysis (affiliate), Registry Clin. Social Workers, Acad. Cert. Social Workers. Home: 30 Garfield Pl Poughkeepsie NY 12601 Office: 30 Garfield Pl Poughkeepsie NY

BERSHEN, AUDREY L'HOMMEDIEU HARBUR, psychotherapist; b. New Haven, Oct. 12, 1931; d. Curtiss Lovell and Alice Elizabeth (Beecher) L'Hommedieu; student Mt. Holyoke Coll., 1949-51; B.S. in Art Edn., N.Y. U., 1955, M.S.W., 1968; m. James Albert Harbur, Sept. 18, 1954 (div. Oct. 1967); children—Edward Curtiss, Elizabeth L'Hommedieu; m. 2d, Louis Sanvil Bershen, July 5, 1973 (dec. Nov. 1974). Chief psychiat. social worker Center for Preventive Psychiatry, White Plains, N.Y., 1968-73; pvt. practice psychotherapy, 1970—; chief psychiat. social worker North Nassau Mental Health Center, Manhasset, N.Y., 1976-79; profl. cons. L.I. Schizophrenia Assn., 1976-79; chief psychiat. social worker Bio-Behavioral Psychiatry, Gt. Neck, N.Y., 1979—; adv. bd. Soc. of Obsessive Compulsive Disorders. Fellow Soc. of Clin. Social Work Psychotherapists; mem. Nat. Assn. Social Workers, Found. of Thanatology (charter mem. Westchester chpt.). Office: 560 Northern Blvd Suite 209 Great Neck NY 11021

BERTINO, MARIANNE ROSE, constrn. cons. co. exec.; b. Bklyn., Sept. 8, 1940; d. Salvatore and Mary (Ospitale) B.; student bus. adminstrn. Adelphi U., 1962; student constrn. mgmt., UCLA, 1980. With Levitt & Sons, Inc., N.Y.C., 1963-71; owner, mgr. Bertino Communications, N.Y.C., 1971-77; owner, pres. Marianne Bertino & Assos., Los Angeles, 1977—. Mem. Nat. Assn. Women in Constrn. (dir. 1979-80), Women in Mgmt. (pres. 1979-82), Women Constrn. Execs. Council (founder), Comml./Indsl. Council, Bldg. Industry Assn. Home and Office: 6916 N Muscatel Ave San Gabriel CA 91775

BERTON, DENISE MEDVED, advt. agy. exec.; b. Knoxville, Tenn., May 21, 1952; d. Martin D. and Doris (Williams) Medved; student Wesleyan Coll., 1970-72; B.S. in Communications with honors, U. Tenn., 1974; m. Joseph F. Berton, III, Dec. 27, 1975; children—Jill, Joseph. Promotion coordinator Direct Mail Mktg. Assn., N.Y.C., 1974-75, ednl. speaker, 1980—; copy supr. Direct Mktg. Agy., Stamford, Conn., 1975-76, asso. creative dir., 1976-78, creative dir., 1978—, v.p., 1981—; founder, editor spokeswoman Businesswoman, 1976—; also actress. Nat. Kleid Collegiate Scholarship Judge, 1979-80; freelance writer maj. N.Y. firms, 1978-82; publicity coordinator Sue Bailey for Senate, 1980. Recipient Creative Excellence awards Direct Mail Mktg. Assn. Mem. Nat. Assn. Female Execs., Women Communications, Assn. Bus. and Profl. Women, Phi Kappa Phi. Baptist. Clubs: Democratic Women's, River Hills Ski. Office: 733 Summer St Stamford CT 06901

BERTRAM, PHYLLIS ANN, athletic ofcl., educator; b. Long Beach, Calif., July 30, 1954; d. William J. and Ruth A. (Hoge) Bertram; A.A., Long Beach City Coll., 1975, B.S. in Accounting, U. So. Calif., 1977; M.B.A., Calif. State U., Long Beach, 1978; J.D., Western State U., 1982. Instr., lifeguard City of Long Beach, Calif., 1972-78; sports ofcl. swimming, softball, volleyball, and basketball, 1972—; asst. commr. Metro. Conf. Community and Jr. Colls., Long Beach, 1978—; instr. seamanship, fire sci. and bus. adminstrn. Long Beach City Coll., 1977—; mgmt. cons., 1978—. Instr. CPR, water safety, small craft, first aid Am. Red Cross, 1972—; mem. Republican Nat. Com. Recipient resolutions Calif. Senate and Assembly, Long Beach City Council; numerous service awards Am. Red Cross; Ednl. research grantee, City of Long Beach, 1972. Mem. U. So. Calif. Alumni Assn., U. So. Calif. Commerce Assos., Assn. of MBA Execs., So. Calif. Volleyball Ofcls. Assn., So. Calif. Basketball Ofcls. Assn., Women's Basketball Ofcls. Assn., Women's Swim Ofcls. Assn. (pres.), So. Calif. Softball Umpires Assn., Calif. State U. at Long Beach Alumni Assn., Delta Theta Phi. Republican. Club: Seal Beach Yacht. Home: 2237 Albury Ave Long Beach CA 90815 Office: 4901 E Carson St Long Beach CA 90808

BERTSCH, CAROL ANN, advt. exec.; b. Mpls., July 22, 1936; d. Joseph Andrew and June Louise (Knop) Biegal; student U. Minn., 1954-55, 77; m. Richard Frank Bertsch, Dec. 1, 1956 (div.); children—Becky Ann, Steven Patrick. Asst. advt. mgr. Young-Quinlan Rothschild, Mpls., 1963-68; free-lance advt. writer, Mpls., 1968-71, 74-75, Scottsdale, Ariz., 1975-76; asst., advt. and sales promotion Donaldsons Mpls., 1972-74; asst. v.p. adv./corp. communications mgr. Piper, Jaffray & Hopwood, Inc., Mpls., 1977—; creative and mktg. cons. Office: 800 Multifoods Bldg Minneapolis MN 55402

BERTSCH, MURIEL MILLER ALLEN, state ofcl.; b. Fayetteville, Ohio, Apr. 3, 1905; d. Joseph Lowry and Beulah Elizabeth (Davis) Miller; student public schs.; m. Verne S. Allen, July 26, 1923 (dec. 1939); children—Phillip M., Dorcas Elizabeth; m. 2d, Roth U. Bertsch, Nov. 15, 1967. With Champion Paper & Fibre Co., 1943-54, supr. office clerical pool, 1947-54; 1st exec. dir. Sr. Citizens Ctr., Hamilton, Ohio, 1954-70; lectr. Miami U., U. Cin., 1960-70; mem., vice chmn. Ohio Commn. on Aging, Columbus, 1975—. Mem. planning com. Nat. Council on Aging, 1964; mem. tech. rev. com. Ohio Adminstrn. on Aging, Ohio Dept. Mental Health, Hygiene and Correction, 1965-70; chmn. planning com. Ohio Gov.'s Conf., 1976, mem., 1958-76; chmn. adminstrn. on aging. State Fair Com., 1968; mem. Ohio task force White House Conf. on Aging, 1971. Recipient various awards including: 1st Lady of Hamilton (Ohio) award Beta Sigma Phi, 1963, Muriel M. Allen Bertsch Day recognition Hamilton City Council, 1970, Hamilton's Outstanding Sr. Citizen award, 1977; named to Ohio Sr. Citizens Hall of Fame, 1978. Mem. Nat. Inst. for Sr. Centers, Ohio Assn. Centers for Sr. Citizens (founder, pres. 1958-67, 1st Muriel M. Allen Bertsch award 1976), Nat. Council on Aging (mem. ad hoc com. which developed Nat. Inst. for Sr. Ctrs.), Butler County Council on Aging, Women's Personnel Assn. Cin. (pres. 1954-55). Republican. Episcopalian. Club: Hamilton Altrusa (pres. 1953-55), Bridge. Contbr. articles, pamphlets to profl. lit. Home: 550 Emerson Ave Hamilton OH 45013 Office: Ohio Commn on Aging State Capitol Bldg Columbus OH 43204

BERZINS, ERNA MARIJA, physician; b. Latvia, Nov. 27, 1914; d. Arturs and Anna (Steckenbergs) Meilands; came to U.S., 1951, naturalized, 1956; M.D., Latvian State U., 1940; m. Verners Berzins, Aug. 24, 1935; children—Valdis, Andis. Mem. pediatric faculty Latvian State U., 1940-44; intern Good Samaritan Hosp., Dayton, Ohio, 1951-52; resident in pediatrics Children's Hosp. of Mich., Detroit, 1953-55; practice medicine specialising in pediatrics, Detroit, 1956-60; with ARC, Cleve., 1961-63; physician pediatric outpatient dept. Cleve. Met. Gen. Hosp., 1963—; asst. prof. Case-Western Res. U., Cleve., trustee Women's Gen. Hosp., Cleve. Mem. Am., Ohio med. assns., Acad. Medicine, No. Ohio Pediatric Soc., Am. Women's Med. Assn., Am. Med. Polit. Action Com. Lutheran. Address: 5460 Friar Circle Cleveland OH 44126

BERZON, BETTY, psychologist; b. St. Louis; d. Irvin and Eve B.; student Stanford U., 1946-48; B.A., UCLA, 1957; M.S., Calif. State U., 1962; Ph.D., Internat. Coll., Los Angeles, 1978. Caseworker, ARC, Mil. Hosp. Service, Pacific Area, 1955-57; asst. probation officer San Diego County, 1957-59; staff asso. Western Behavioral Scis. Inst., La Jolla, Calif., 1959-62, research asso., 1962-68; project dir., prin. investigator Vocat. Rehab. Adminstrn., 1965-67; tng. cons. U. Calif., Riverside, 1965-66; tng. cons. Calif. Dept. Rehab., Los Angeles, 1966-67; dir. group program devel. Human Devel. Inst., Inc., Los Angeles, 1968-70; project dir., program developer Research for Better Schs., Inc., Phila., 1973-76; pvt. practice psychotherpay, Los Angeles, 1972—; tng. cons. Gay Community Services Center, 1971—; bd. dirs. Whitman-Radclyffe Found., 1976-77, exec. v.p., 1976; nat. pres. Gay Acad. Union, 1977-79; hon. trustee Whitman-Brooks Found.; mem. council of overseers Mariposa Edn. and Research Found. Mem. Assn. Gay Psychologists, Am. Psychol. Assn. Co-editor: New Perspectives on Encounter Groups, 1972; Positively Gay, 1979; editorial bd. Jour. Humanistic Psychology. Office: 8235 Santa Monica Blvd Suite 218 Los Angeles CA 90046

BESEN, JANE PHYLLIS TRIPTOW, civic worker; b. Chgo., Aug. 6, 1921; d. Richard Herman and Rose (Krips) Triptow; student Northwestern U., 1946-47, East Los Angeles Coll., 1967-68; B.A. in English, Calif. State U., Los Angeles, 1978, postgrad. in English; m. Irving Besen, Mar. 25, 1951 (div. 1978); children—Glenn, Allen. Exec. sec. Chgo. Ordance Dist., War Dept., 1941-46, Aubrey, Moore & Wallace, Advt. Agy., Chgo., 1946; exec. sec. sales office McGraw-Hill Pub. Co., Chgo., 1947-51; exec. sec. Security Pacific Nat. Bank, Los Angeles, 1978—. Publicity chmn. Am Field Service, 1967-68; sec. Citizens Com for Good Govt., 1961; capt. United Crusade, Monterey Park, Calif., 1967—; publicity chmn. Monterey Park Art Assn., 1966-67, coor. sec., 1968, dir., 1965—, past pres., dir. newsletter, 1970—; chmn. Monterey Park Arts and Culture Com.; dir. in charge Bruggemeyer Library Shows, 1973-74; dep. registrar voters Calif. State U., Los Angeles, 1971-74; 3d v.p. in charge publicity Community Concerts Monterey Park. Recipient Top award Alhambra Open Show, 1972. Mem. Nat. League Am. Pen Women (rec. sec., treas. 1961-65), LWV (sec. Alhambra chpt. 1971-73 pres. chpt. 1973-74, action chmn., publicity chmn. 1977-78, hospitality chmn. 1980—), Residents Assn. Monterey Park. Club: Northwestern U. Alumni So. Calif. (corr. sec. 1979-80). Home: 1540 Arriba Dr Monterey Park CA 91754

BESHAR, CHRISTINE, lawyer; b. Paetzig, Germany, Nov. 6, 1929; d. Hans and Ruth (vonKleist-Retzow) vonWedemeyer; student U. Hamburg, 1950-51, U. Tuebingen, 1951-52; B.A., Smith Coll., 1953; m. Robert P. Beshar, Dec. 20, 1953; children—Cornelia, Jacqueline, Frederica, Peter. Admitted to N.Y. Bar, 1960; asso. mem. firm Casey, Lane & Mittendorf, N.Y.C., 1960-63; asso. mem. firm Cravath, Swaine & Moore, N.Y.C., 1964-70, partner, 1971—. Bd. dirs. UN Assn., 1975—, Catalyst for Women Inc., 1977—, N.Y. State Bar and Am. Bar founds., 1977—; trustee Colgate U., 1978—. Inst. Internat. Edn. fellow, 1952-53; recipient Disting. Alumnae medal Smith Coll., 1974. Fellow Am. Coll. Probate Counsel; mem. Assn. Bar City N.Y. (exec. com., 1973-75), N.Y. State Bar Assn. (ho. of dels. 1971-80, v.p. 1978-80), Fgn. Policy Assn. (dir.). Presbyn. Clubs: Wall St., Cosmopolitan, Gipsy Trail. Home: 120 East End Ave New York NY 10028 Office: 1 Chase Manhattan Plaza New York NY 10005

BESNER, HILDA FAYE, clin. psychologist; b. Lima, Peru, Oct. 30, 1950; came to U.S., 1951, naturalized, 1956; d. Jacob M. and Hanna (Silverman) Besner; student Duke U., 1968-69; B.S. in Chemistry, U. Miami, 1971; M.S. in Psychology (fellow), Nova U., 1972, Ph.D. in Psychology (fellow), 1975. Guidance counselor Univ. Sch., Ft. Lauderdale, Fla., 1972-73; psychometrist Inst. Human Devel., Nova U., 1974, research asst. Biofeedback Lab., 1973-75; adj. prof., 1979—; clin. psychology intern Malcolm Bliss Mental Health Center, St. Louis, 1975-76; clin. psychologist Harbor House, St. Louis, 76; co-instr. U. Mo., St. Louis, 1976; biofeedback therapy and research cons., St. Louis, 1976; clin. psychologist Dade County (Fla.) Dept. Youth and Family Devel., Miami, 1977-78, Bessette, Farinacci and Assocs., Inc., Ft. Lauderdale, 1976-81; pvt. practice clin. psychology, 1981—; adj. prof. Fla. Sch. Profl. Psychology, Miami, 1979—; mem. Nat. Task Force Biofeedback as Adj. to Psychotherapy, 1978—. Pres., bd. dirs. Crisis Intervention Center, Ft. Lauderdale. Named Outstanding Young Career Woman, Nat. Bus. and Profl. Women, dist. 5, 1979; lic. psychologist, Fla. Mem. Am. Psychol. Assn., Fla. Psychol. Assn., Broward County Psychol. Assn., Biofeedback Soc. Am., Biofeedback Soc. Fla. (exec. bd.), Biofeedback Soc. Southeastern Fla. (pres. 1977-78), Ft. Lauderdale Bus. and Profl. Women's Assn. Contbr. articles to profl. jours.; guest reviewer Jour. Behavior Therapy and Exptl. Psychiatry, 1977—. Office: 1040 Bayview Dr Fort Lauderdale FL 33304

BEST, BARBARA BELLE, food corp. exec.; b. Granite, Okla., Aug. 23, 1942; d. Bert Allen and Minerva Belle (Leonard) Williams; B.S., Okla. State U., 1964; grad. bus. exec. program Stanford U., 1978; m. Douglas Diedrich. Adminstrv. intern Eastman Kodak Co., 1964-65; product supr. Pillsbury Co., Mpls., 1965-67; asst. dir. Food and Nutrition Council Minn., 1967-72; mgr. nutrition and quality assurance, consumer affairs rep. Gen. Mills, Inc., Mpls., 1972-76; product mgr. spl. projects, dir. spl. dietary products Henkel Corp., Mpls., 1976—; mgmt. and public relations cons. Adv. bd. mgmt. devel. program Coll. of St. Catherine, St. Paul. Mem. Sales and Mktg. Execs., Am. Dietetic Assn., Soc. Nutrition Edn., Phi Kappa Phi, Omicron Nu. Office: Henkel Corp 4620 W 77th St Minneapolis MN 55435

BEST, NANCY DOUGHERTY, educator; b. New Holland, Pa., May 18, 1931; d. Frank Harold and Kathryn (Ebersol) Dougherty; B.S., Drexel U., 1953; M.A., Millersville State Coll., 1972; M.S., Central Conn. State Coll., 1981; Ph.D., Pa. State U., 1978; children—Randolph, Kathryn Best Thomas, John, James. Tchr., Upper Darby, Pa., 1953-55; faculty Flathead County Community Coll., Kalispell, Mont., 1968-73; curriculum writer/tchr., Lancaster, Pa., 1973-76; intern Western Interstate Commn. Higher Edn., Boulder Valley, Colo., 1977-78; adj. instr. Pa. State U., State College, 1978; asso. prof. edn. Central Conn. State Coll., 1978-81; asst. prof. Oral Roberts U., Tulsa, 1981—; cons. in field. Vol., Mental Health Hotline, 1980-81, City of Faith, 1982-83. Pa. State U. grantee, 1975-78; recipient Phonetics award Millersville Summer Lang. Inst., 1971; Borden award Drexel U., 1952. Mem. Single Ministries AAUW, Am. Ednl. Research Assn., Am. Personnel and Guidance Assn., Phi Kappa Phi, Phi Delta Kappa. Christian Ch. Club: Women's Aglow. Contbr. articles to profl. jours. Office: 7777 S Lewis St Tulsa OK 74171

BETENSKY, ROSE HART, painter; b. N.Y.C., Sept. 6, 1923; d. Jacob and Clara Shainess; pupil of Josef Presser; m. Seymour Betensky, July 11, 1943; children—Joel, Richard. One-woman exhbns. include abstract, geometric forms in acrylic on canvas, acrylic on paper; group exhbns. include Nat. Acad. Galleries, 1960-77, Royal Acad., Edinburgh, Scotland, 1963, Norfolk (Va.) Mus. Arts and Sci., 1964, Cultural Inst. Tolsa, Guadalajara, Mex., 1965, Palazzo Vecchio, Florence, Italy, 1972, Union Carbide Corp., Citicorp Hdqrs., N.Y.C., Lever Bros. Fed. Bldg., N.Y.C. Mem. Nat. Assn. Women Artists (pres. 1970-72; Robert Simmons award 1960, Lillian Cotton prize 1970, Charlotte Orndorf prize 1972, Marion de Sola Mendes prize 1978), Am. Soc. Contemporary Artists (Windsor & Newton award 1976, Dorothy L. Feigan award 1978, Samuel Mann award 1979, Bee Paper Co. award 1980), N.Y. Soc. Women Artists (pres. 1969-70), Audubon Artists. Address: 66 Hayloft Ln Roslyn Heights NY 11577

BETSILL, MAYZELL KNIGHTON, chem. co. ofcl; b. Enoree, S.C., Dec. 7, 1941; d. Benjamin Levi and Annie (Grubbs) Knighton; student Limestone Coll., 1981—; m. Johnny Thomas Betsill, July 2, 1961; 1 son, Johnny Darrell. Sec., receptionist Reeves Bros., Inc., Woodruff, S.C., 1960-62; sec. to art dir. Cryovac div. W.R. Grace & Co., Duncan, S.C., 1963-64, supervising sec. tech. dept., 1974-78, word processing mgr., 1978—; sec., asst. personnel dir. Appleton plant J.P. Stevens Co., Anderson, S.C., 1965-74. Active Parent-Tchr.-Student Assn., James F. Byrnes High Sch., officer, 1977-78; mem. adv. com., sec. Cryovac United Way, 1977, capt., 1981; officer Westside Bapt. Ch., Spartanburg, S.C., 1976—; instr. ARC, 1972-76. Notary public, S.C. Mem. Internat. Info. Word Processing Assn. (bd. dirs.). Home: Route 1 PO Box 485 Moore SC 29369 Office: PO Box 464 Duncan SC 29334

BETTS, DAHNA MAY, bank exec.; b. Oak Park, Ill., Oct. 24, 1940; d. Henry Christian and Mildred Henrietta (Vlach) Dubs; student Triton Coll., 1973-76; student, North Central Coll., 1979-81; student Am. Inst. Banking, 1982—; m. Ralph Edward Fischer, Feb. 15, 1957, (div. 1974); children—Judith, Wally, Ralph, Dyhana; m. 2d Donald E. Betts, Aug. 24, 1974. Supr., Bresnahan Computer Service, Addison, Ill., 1967-70; operator, programmer, analyst various cos., 1970-76; programmer, analyst Loyola U. Med. Center, Maywood, Ill., 1976-77; sr. systems analyst, programmer Long Range Systems Planning div. Blue Cross Blue Shield Assn., Chgo., 1977-78; systems mgr. First Nat. Bank of Chgo., 1979—; exec. bd. officer Midwest Mark IV User Group, 1980—; mem. system evaluation com. Nat. IV League Inc. Mem. Nat. Assn. Female Execs. Home: 44 Bunting Ln Naperville IL 60565 Office: One First Nat Plaza Chicago IL 60670

BETTY, NORMA FRANCES, social worker; b. Saratoga, N.Y., Aug. 3, 1931; d. Ivanhoe Ralph and Nancy Rosetta (Carnegie) Carter; A.B. in Social Work, Ind. U., 1953, M.A. in Social Work, 1958; m. Warren R. Betty, July 25, 1953; children—Lisa Cheryl, Michael Warren. Producer, broadcaster radio program It's A Woman's World, Sta. WRMA, Montgomery, Ala., 1954-55; psychiat. social worker LaRue Carter Psychiat. Hosp., Ind. U. Med. Center, Indpls., 1957, Riley Child Guidance Clinic of Ind. U. Med. Center, 1958-59, Madelaine Borg Child Guidance Inst., Jewish Bd. Guardians, N.Y.C., 1959-61; psychiat. social worker S.I. Children's Mental Health Clinic, 1967-69; pvt. practice parent-child and adolescent therapy, S.I., 1975—; bd. dirs. S.I. Mental Health Soc., 1965-70; trainee Am. Inst. Psychoanalysis, 1981—. cons., lectr. in field. Fund raiser Girls Parents Sports Club S.I., 1976-79, N.Y. Urban League, 1980—; coordinator Police Athletic League, McDonalds Boys Basketball Team, Action for Children's TV, Save the Children Fedn., N.Y. Urban League, 1980—. Cert. clin. social work psychotherapist, N.Y. State; NIMH fellow, 1956-58. Fellow Soc. Clin. Social Work Psychotherapists, Am. Orthopsychiat. Assn.; mem. Nat. Assn. Social Workers, Assn. Parent-Child and Adolescent Therapists, Family Mediation Assn., Nat. Assn. Female Execs., Ind. U. Alumni Assn. (life; Cert. of Merit. 1982, Disting. Service award 1982, Mortar Bd. (sec.), Psi Chi, Alpha Kappa Alpha (2d nat. v.p. 1952-54, life). Clubs: Ind. U. Alumni of met. N.Y. (exec. com., Ind. U. Found. Com. 1951—). Address: 28 Madera St Staten Island NY 10309

BETZ, JEAN, investment securities co. exec.; b. Utica, N.Y., Mar. 1, 1927; d. Walter John and Anna (Pomichowska) Hapanowicz; student Utica Free Acad., 1941-45; B.S., Rider Coll., 1949; postgrad. Beaver Coll., 1964-65; m. Frank Theodore Betz, Apr. 18, 1949; children—Frank, Eleanor Jean, Richard Walter. Editorial writer Book Publishers Projects, Inc., N.Y.C., 1967-68; sec., dir. Frank T. Betz & Co., Inc., investment securities, Phila., 1966—. Editor: The First Book of Magic, 1968. Home: 1554 Hower Rd Abington PA 19001 Office: Philadelphia National Bank Bldg Philadelphia PA 19107

BEUF, ANN HILL, sociologist, educator; b. Phila., Oct. 1, 1938; d. Erle Gladstone and Helen Elizabeth (Harper) Hill; A.B., Bryn Mawr Coll., 1969, M.A., 1971, Ph.D. (Ford Found. grantee), 1972; children—Helen Beatrice, Carlo Gallatin, Peter Gallatin Penrose. Asst. prof. sociology U. Pa., 1972-77, dir. women's studies program, 1977—. Mem. UN Com. on Stigmatized Children, Indian Rights Assn.; bd. dirs. Little People's Day Care, Paoli, Pa. Grantee, Spencer Found., 1977, Nat. Endowment Humanities, 1978, NIH, 1979. Mem. Am. Sociol. Assn. (chairperson com. racial and ethnic minorities), Nat. Women's Studies Assn., Humanist Sociol. Soc., Pa. Soc., Mid-Atlantic Regional Women's Studies Assn. Author: Red Children in White America, 1977, Biting Off The Bracelet, 1979; co-editor: Childhood: A Social Construct, 1978; editorial bd. Feminist Press. Address: 140 Valley St Ardmore PA 19003

BEUGEN, JOAN BETH, communications co. exec.; b. Chgo., Mar. 9, 1943; d. Leslie and Janet (Glick) Caplan; B.S. in Speech, Northwestern U., 1965; m. Sheldon Howard Beugen, July 16, 1967. Founder, prin., pres. The Creative Establishment, Inc., Chgo., N.Y.C., 1969—. Del., White House Conf. on Small Bus., 1979; vice-chmn. Ill. Del. to White House Conf., 1979. Mem. Nat. Assn. Women Bus. Owners (pres. Chgo. chpt. 1979), Ill. Women's Agenda, Chgo. Assn. Commerce and Industry, Chgo. Audio-Visual Producers Assn., Chgo. Film Council. Contbr. articles in field to profl. jours. Office: 1421 N Wells St Chicago IL 60610

BEVERIDGE, LYNN RUTH, speech pathologist; b. Hartford, Conn., Jan. 9, 1953; d. Russell David and Ruth Julia (Seagren) Beveridge; B.S. in Edn., U. Hartford, 1974; postgrad. So. Conn. State Coll. Aide in learning disabilities class, substitute tchr. West Hartford (Conn.) public schs., 1975; speech, hearing, lang. pathologist New Britain (Conn.) public schs., 1978—. Lic. speech pathologist, Conn.; cert. speech and hearing specialist, Conn.; cert. elem. sch. tchr., Conn. Mem. Conn. Fedn. Tchrs., Am. Speech and Hearing Assn. (cert. clin. competence), Conn. Speech and Hearing Assn. Republican. Lutheran. Clubs: New Britain Tchrs., Order of Rainbow (worthy advisor 1970, state rep. 1971, recipient Grand Cross of Color 1972). Home: 47 Broadview St Newington CT 06111 Office: 27 Hillside Pl New Britain CT 06050

BEVERLY, TREVIA WOOSTER, pump co. exec., genealogist; b. Baytown, Tex., Nov. 7, 1931; d. Ray Brown and Annie Mae (Barrilleaux) Wooster; student public schs., Baytown, U. Houston; m. Murphy Travis Beverly, Aug. 30, 1950; 1 dau., Linda Diane Beverly McCumber. Various secretarial and clerical positions Prudential Ins. Co., Manpower, Inc., Aquatrol, Inc., Hercules Inc., Houston, 1952-72; sec.-treas., adminstrv. asst. A & M Pump Co., Houston 1974—. Bd. dirs. Houston Geneal. Inst. Mem. Nat. Water Well Assn., Tex. Water Well Assn., Tex. Geneal. Soc. (1st v.p., editor Stirpes), Baptist. Contbr. articles to geneal. quars. Home: 2507 Tannehill St Houston TX 77008 Office: A & M Pump Co 10612-F Hempstead Rd Houston TX 77092

BEVILACQUA, LINDA MARIE, univ. adminstr.; b. Jamaica, N.Y., Mar. 7, 1941; d. Michael and Eleanor B.; B.S. magna cum laude, Barry Coll., Miami, Fla., 1962; M.Ed., Siena Heights Coll., Adrian, Mich., 1969; Ph.D. (Outstanding Grad. Student 1980; Julius E. Barbour scholar 1980), Mich. State U., 1980. Joined Sisters of St. Dominic, Roman Catholic Ch., 1962; 1st grade tchr., Mich., 1964-69; asst. dean students, then dean students Barry U., 1969-78, dir. alternative programs, 1981-82, asso. v.p. acad. affair, 1982—; trustee Siena Heights Coll., 1978-80. Mem. Am. Assn. Higher Edn., Am. Assn. Univ. Adminstrs., Kappa Gamma Pi, Kappa Delta Pi, Phi Delta Kappa. Office: 11300 NE 2d Ave Miami FL 33161

BEVIS, PATRICIA ANN, banker; b. Florence, Ala., May 9, 1955; d. G. Joe and Billie (Grisham) B.; ed. U. Ala., 1977; cert. Sorbonne, Paris, summer 1977. Cosmetics buyer, br. store coordinator R. H. Macy's, N.Y.C., 1981-82; bank officer mktg. dept. Citibank, N.Y.C., 1982—. Recipient Outstanding Young Alumni award U. Ala., 1982. Mem. Panhellenic (sec. 1980), U. Ala. Alumni Assn., Alpha Delta Pi. *

BEWLEY, GEORGIA KAY, musician, educator; b. Tulsa, Oct. 26, 1940; d. Verlin George and Bernice Edna (Stonebraker) Brown; B.S., Okla. State U., 1961; m. George Franklin, Dec. 23, 1962 (div.); 1 son, Mark William Bewley. Elementary Music tchr. Ponca City Pub. Schs., 1961-64, instrumental music supervision sec., flag corps sponsor, 1975-82; elem. music tchr. Bartlesville (Okla.) Pub. Schs., 1982—; pvt. tchr. voice and piano, Ponca City, 1965—; soloist on gospel music rec., 1973; performer in sacred music concerts; substitute music tchr. local pub. schs. Mem. exec. bd. Garfield PTA, 1972—, pres., 1974-76: Bible tchr. Falls Creek Baptist Assembly, 1980. Recipient Danforth Found. award, 1958. Mem. Community Concert Assn., Nat., Okla., Ponca City music tchrs. assns., Nat. Federated Music Clubs, Ponca City Music Club (pres. 1973), Orange Quill, Sigma Alpha Iota, Phi Kappa Phi. Democrat. Home: 1559 Kings Dr Apt 1214 Bartlesville OK 74003 Office: 1100 S Jennings St Bartlesville OK 74005

BEY, JOAN S., public relations cons.; b. Boston, Ind., Nov. 30, 1927; d. Frank J. and Lestra Josephine (Turner) Schoemaker; B.S., St. Mary-of-the-Woods Coll., 1949; m. John Joseph Bey, May 8, 1954 (dec. 1968); children—Anna Marie, Joseph Michael, John Charles. Women's page reporter Indpls. Times, 1950-58; public relations dir. Weight Watchers of Central & Northeastern Ind. Inc., 1971-75; public relations dir. Am. Diabetes Assn. Ind. Affiliate, Indpls., 1975-76; freelance public relations cons., Indpls., 1977—. Mem. Woman's Press Club Ind. (pres. 1982—), Nat. Fedn. Press Women, Women in Communications Inc., Indpls. Press Club, St. Mary-of-the-Woods Coll. Alumni Assn. Roman Catholic. Address: 5872 N Keystone St Indianapolis IN 46220

BEYER, CHARLOTTE BISHOP, research and cons. co. ofcl.; b. N.Y.C., Oct. 16, 1947; d. Edward Morton and Charlotte Reid (Handy) Beyer; B.A., Hunter Coll., 1969; m. Warren P. Weitman, Jr., July 28, 1967; children—Catherine Scott, Michael Benjamin. With Bankers Trust Co., N.Y.C., 1970-81, v.p. trust services and securities ops., 1979-81; dir. Can. mktg. Technimetrics, Inc., N.Y.C., 1981—. Head Sunday sch. Grace Ch., Brooklyn Heights, N.Y. Mem. N.Y. State Bankers Assn. (trust ops. com.). Episcopalian. Office: Technimetrics Inc Citicorp Center 153 E 53d St New York NY 10021

BEYER, JACQUELYN L., geographer; b. Mitchell, S.D., July 11, 1924; d. Hayes Rutherford and Olive Grace (Garver) B.; B.A. in Journalism, U. Colo., Boulder, 1944, M.A. in Geography, 1954; Ph.D. in Geography, U. Chgo., 1957. Asst. prof. geography U. Mont., 1957-58, 59-60; vis. lectr. U. Tex., 1958-59; lectr. U. Cape Town (South Africa), 1960-64; asst. prof. Rutgers U., 1964-69; asso. prof. U. Colo., Colorado Springs, 1970-73, prof., 1973—, chmn. dept. geography and environ. studies. Served with WAC, U.S. Army, 1944-48, 52. Water Resources Research Inst. grantee, 1968-69. Mem. Assn. Am. Geographers, Nat. Council Geog. Edn. (exec. bd.), AAAS, Am. Assn. Higher Edn., African Studies Assn., Consortium on Peace Research, Edn. and Devel., Western African Studies Assn., Colo. Women Studies Assn., Soc. Women Geographers. Contbr. chpts., articles to profl. publs. Office: Dept Geog and Environ Studies U Colo Box 7150 Colorado Springs CO 80933

BEYER, KAREN ANN, social worker; b. Cleve., Jan. 30, 1942; d. William Pryor and Evelyn Ann Haynes; B.A., Ohio State U., 1965; M.S.W., Loyola U., Chgo., 1969; cert. Family Inst., Northwestern U., 1979; 1 dau., Jennifer. With Cuyahoga County Div. Child Welfare, Cleve., 1965, Dallas County Child Welfare Unit, Dallas, 1966, Luth. Welfare Services Ill., Chgo., 1967-73; pvt. practice clin. social work, Schaumburg, Ill., 1975—; therapist Family Service Assn. Greater Elgin (Ill.), 1973-77, dir. profl. services, 1977—; fieldwork social work instr. for Loyola U., U. Ill., 1977-80; pvt. practice family mediation, 1981—. Mem. Mediation Council Ill., Acad. Cert. Social Workers, Am. Assn. Marriage and Family Therapists. Unitarian. Home: 1809 Dumont Ln Schaumburg IL 60194 Office: 164 Division St Elgin IL 60120

BEYER, MARILYN, educator; b. Bronx, N.Y., Mar. 28, 1940; d. James I. and Anne B. (Wasserman) Goldstein; B.A., Queens Coll., 1961; M.S., Bklyn. Coll., 1964; m. Gerald Beyer, Aug. 19, 1961; children—Lauren, Russell, Kimberly. Tchr., N.Y.C. Public Schs., 1961-65; substitute tchr. Washington Public Schs., 1968-69, Dade County (Fla.) Schs., 1970-72; dir. early childhood edn. Harry Levin Pre-Sch. Center, Temple Beth Israel, Ft. Lauderdale, Fla., 1972—. Recording sec. Woodlands Sect. 2 Homeowners Assn., 1972—. Mem. S. Fla. Central Agy. Jewish Educators. Club: Woodlands Country. Home: 5912 Blue Beech Ct Tamarac FL 33319 Office: 7100 W Oakland Park Blvd Fort Lauderdale FL 33313

BEYER, SUZANNE, advt. agy. exec.; b. N.Y.C.; d. Harry and Jennie Hillman; grad. Conservatory of Musical Art, 1943-47, Nassau Community Coll., 1963-65; m. Isadore Beyer, Oct. 19, 1947; children—Pamela Claire, Hillary Jay. Singer, tchr. piano, N.Y.C., 1947-66; asst. to v.p. media dir. Robert E. Wilson, Advt., N.Y.C., 1967-72; media planner, media buyer Frank J. Corbett div. BBDO Advt., N.Y.C., 1972-77; media planner, media buyer Lavey/Wolff/Swift div. BBDO Advt., N.Y.C., 1977-80, sr. media planner, 1980—; soprano Opera Assn. Nassau, 1976—, United Choral Soc., Woodmere, L.I., N.Y., 1970—, Armand Sodero Chorale, Baldwin, L.I., 1980—. Mem. Pharm. Advt. Council, L.I. Advt. Club, Healthcare Businesswomen's Assn. Home: 66 Fonda Rd Rockville Centre NY 11570 Office: 488 Madison Ave New York NY 10022

BEYER-MEARS, ANNETTE, physiologist; b. Madison, Wis., May 26, 1941; d. Karl and Annette (Weiss) Beyer; B.A., Vassar Coll., 1963; M.S., Fairleigh Dickinson U., 1973; Ph.D., Coll. Medicine and Dentistry N.J., 1977; m. William H. Mears, Jr.; 1 son, Karl. NIH fellow Cornell U. Med. Sch., 1963-65; instr. physiology Springside Coll., Phila., 1967-71; teaching asst. dept. physiology Coll. Medicine and Dentistry N.J., N.J. Med. Sch., 1974-77, NIH fellow dept. ophthalmology, 1978-80; asst. prof. dept. ophthalmology U. Medicine and Dentistry N.J., N.J. Med. Sch., Newark, 1979—, asst. prof. dept. physiology, 1980—; cons. Alcon Labs. Chmn. admissions No. N.J., Vassar Coll., 1974-79; mem. minister search com. St. Bartholomew Episcopal Ch., Ridgewood, N.J., 1978, fund-raising chmn., 1978, 79; del. Epis. Diocesian Conv., 1977, 78. NIH Nat. Research Service award, 1978-80; NIH Research awardee, 1980—; Found. CMDNJ Research award, 1980. Mem. Am. Physiol. Soc., N.Y. Acad. Scis., Soc. for Neurosci., Assn. for Research in Vision and Ophthalmology, Internat. Soc. for Eye Research, AAAS, Sigma Xi, Aircraft Owners and Pilots Assn. Contbr. articles in field of diabetic lens and kidney therapy to profl. jours. Office: U Medicine and Dentistry NJ-NJ Med Sch Dept Physiology 100 Bergen St Newark NJ 07103

BEYRER, MARY KATHERINE, educator; b. South Bend, Ind., Mar. 3, 1922; d. Charles H. and L. Marie (Brickell) B.; B.A., Macalester Coll., 1944; M.S., MacMurray Coll., 1950; Ph.D., Ohio State U., 1959. Tchr. health and phys. edn. Buffalo (Minn.) High Sch., 1944-47, Harrisonburg (Va.) High Sch., 1948-51; teaching asst. MacMurray Coll., 1947-48; asst. prof. health and phys. edn. Madison Coll., Harrisonburg, 1951-56; teaching assoc. Ohio State U., Columbus, 1956-57, instr. health edn., 1957-59, asst. prof., 1959-61, assoc. prof., 1961-64, prof., 1964—, dir. Sch. Health, Phys. Edn., and Recreation, 1977-81. Bd. dirs. Epilepsy Assn. Central Ohio, 1961-82. Recipient Alumni citation Macalester Coll. 1964. AAHPER and Dance scholar, 1978-79. Mem. AAHPER and Dance (Honor Fellow award 1969, pres. 1982-83), Am. Acad. Phys. Edn., Am. Pub. Health Assn., Am. Sch. Health Assn., Assn. Supervision and Curriculum Devel., Ohio Assn. Health, Phys. Edn., Recreation and Dance (cert. of merit 1967), Am. Assn. Advancement Health Edn. (Profl. Service to Health Edn. award 1976, Scholar award 1978), Eta Sigma Gamma, Phi Delta Kappa. Republican. Presbyterian. Author: (with D. Oberteuffer) School Health Education, 1966; (with M.K. Solleder) Directory of Selected References and Resources for Health Education, 1969, 2d edit., 1981; editor: Health Education Completed Research, 1974, 2d edit., 1979. Home: 4012 Lyon Dr Columbus OH 43220 Office: 1760 Neil Ave Columbus OH 43210

BIAGINI, ESTHER PIER, interior designer; b. Chgo.; d. Silvio and Ilia (Paganelli) Nannini; student U. Ill., 1951-52; grad. Harrington Inst. Interior Design, 1981; m. Giulio J. Biagini, Oct. 5, 1952; children—Marc, Nannette, Lisa. Graphoanalyst; personal cons. in field; public relations cons. Bevmar Co., 1976. Active PTA; pres. Brookfield (Ill.) Library Bd., 1969-70, 72-73, treas., 1970-71, sec., 1967-68, 73-74. Recipient Am. Legion award, 1950. Mem. Am. Soc. Interior Designers, ALA, Ill. Library Assn., Ill. Dirs. Library Assn., Brookfield Woman's Club. Home: 4421 S Arthur Ave Brookfield IL 60513

BIANCO, DOLORES IRENE, med. technologist; b. New Haven, Jan. 10, 1932; d. Theodore Joseph and Coraline Rose (Poulen) Goergen; A.A. cum laude, Quinnipiac Coll., 1951; M.T., St. Raphael's Sch. Med. Tech., 1952; m. Pasquale A. Bianco, July 7, 1956; children—Nancy Jean, James Michael, Theodore Joseph, Catherine Rose. Med. technologist St. Raphael's Hosp., New Haven, 1952-54, Karl Hanson, M.D., Jacksonville, Fla., 1954-56, Alachua County Hosp., Gainesville, Fla., 1956-57, J. Hillis Miller Health Center, Gainesville, 1958-59; med. biology research technician VA Hosp., West Haven, Conn., 1960-61; relief, part-time technologist Borland-Hancock Clinic, McIver Clinic, Karl Hanson, M.D., Romaine and Root Lab., Jacksonville, 1963-68; technologist Karl Hanson, M.D., Jacksonville, 1969—; participant workshops in field; lectr. Jones Coll. Med. Arts, 1982—. Bd. dirs. Civic Music Assn., 1981—; active Jacksonville Symphony Guild, Delius Assn. Fla.; mem. adv. bd. Opera-a-la-Carte, Inc., 1982—; pres. Garden Club, 1982—, others. Mem. Am. Soc. Clin. Pathologists, Am. Soc. Med. Technologists, Fla. Soc. Med. Technologists. Roman Catholic. Clubs: Altrusa, Alliance Francaise. Fine arts reporter The River City News, 1981—. Home: 5423 Santa Rosa Way Jacksonville FL 32211 Office: 1661 Riverside Ave Suite C Jacksonville FL 32204

BIBBS, ARLENE MARIE, advt. agy. exec.; b. Chgo., Jan. 10, 1941; d. Mario and Vita (Carnesi) Arnone; B.F.A., Mundelein Coll., Chgo., 1960; diploma drama Cleve. Playhouse, 1961; m. John A. Bibbs, June 8, 1963 (div. 1972); 1 dau., Samantha Lynne. Internat. account mgr. Van Brunt & Co., Chgo., 1972-76; v.p. internat. HBC/Van Brunt, Chgo., 1976-77; internat. dir. Tatham-Laird & Kudner, Chgo., 1977-81; pres. AMB Internat. Inc., Chgo., 1981—. Mem. Internat. Advt. Assn. (pres. Mid-Am. chpt. 1982-84), Bus. and Profl. Advt. Assn. Democrat. Roman Catholic. Office: 3 E Huron St Chicago IL 60611

BIBEN, BARBARA RUBINSTEIN, public relations exec.; b. Seneca Falls, N.Y., Feb. 26, 1943; d. David Hugh and Hilda (Zeitlin) Rubinstein; student Eastman Sch. Dental Hygiene, 1961-63; m. James Harvey Biben, Feb. 9, 1964; children—Matthew Lee, Douglas Ross. Dir. Germanow Art Gallery, Rochester, N.Y., 1973-75; free-lance artist, Rochester, 1972-80; producer-host Pub. TV Arts Show, Rochester, 1977; pub. service mgr. Gannett Rochester Newspapers, 1978, dir. public service and promotion, 1979—; mem. N.Y. State Pubs. Newspaper in Edn. Commn., 1979-82. Bd. dirs. United Way, 1980-84, Rochester Bus. Opportunities, 1979—, GEVA Theatre, 1979—; v.p. Lend-A-Hand Charity; mem. Monroe Community Coll. Advisory Com., for Community Services, 1980—; dir. Ad Council, 1980—; bd. dirs. Jr. League, 1976-78; campaign mgr. Robert L. Dey for N.Y. State Senate, 1978; bd. dirs. Bus. Commn. Arts Greater Rochester, 1980—; commr. Brighton Cable Commn. Mem. Internat. Newspaper Promotion Assn. (dir. Ea. region), Women in Communication (dir.). Club: University. Home: 110 Runnymede Rd Rochester NY 14618 Office: Gannett Rochester Newspapers 55 Exchange St Rochester NY 14614

BICKERS, CONSTANCE RADCLIFFE, ins. co. exec.; b. Lorain, Ohio, Aug. 11, 1933; d. Howard Hugh and Harriet Alice (Lipple) Radcliffe; student LaSalle U., Lorain Community Coll.; m. Herbert Bennett Bickers, Nov. 24, 1955. Bookkeeper, McGeachie Plumbing and Heating Co., Lorain, 1950-51, Penn Rubber Co., Lorain, 1951-52, office mgr. Packard Motor Co., Lorain, 1952-54, Bay View Hosp., Bay Village, Ohio, 1954-57, acct., 1957-65, asst. adminstr., 1965-76; dir. provider affairs Blue Cross N.E. Ohio, Cleve., 1976-81, v.p. benefits adminstrn., 1982—. Mem. Hosp. Fin. Mgmt. Assn. (recipient Frederick T. Muncie award 1973, Dale L. Reed award 1969, 70, 71, 73, William G. Follmer award; nat. dir. 1973-74), Am. Coll. Osteo. Hosp. Adminstrs. (bd. examiners), Am. Soc. Women Accts., Am. Coll. Hosp. Adminstrs., Ohio Hosp. Assn., Health Care Adminstrs. N.E. Ohio, Fedn. Community Planning, Citizens League Greater Cleve., Am. Coll. Nursing Home Adminstrs., Am. Hosp. Assn., Nat. Council for Prescription Drug Program, Am. Med. Record Assn. Club: Women's City (Cleve.). Contbr. articles to profl. jours. Home: 315 Harris Rd Sheffield Lake OH 44054 Office: 2066 9th St E Cleveland OH 44115

BICKFORD, CLARA LOUISE GEHRING (MRS. GEORGE P. BICKFORD), educator; b. Cleve.; d. Frederick William and Emma (Motz) Gehring; B.A. cum laude, Bryn Mawr Coll., 1925; m. George P. Bickford, Apr. 6, 1933; 1 dau., Louise (Mrs. Douglas K. Boyd). Tchr. piano Cleve. Inst. Music, 1929-33, founder women's com., 1933, tchr. adult classes in music appreciation, 1934—, trustee, 1934—, pres. bd., 1949-52. Pres. women's com. Cleve. Orch., 1939-41, trustee, 1944—; mem. jr. council Cleve. Mus. Art; pres. Women's City Club Found., 1960-62; mem. vis. com. Western Res. Coll., 1979. Mem. Mu Phi Epsilon. Clubs: Bryn Mawr, Shaker Lakes Garden, Intown (Cleve.); Sulgrave (Washington). Home: 2247 Chestnut Hills Dr Cleveland OH 44106

BICKFORD, DRUCILLA ROBERTS, state legislator; b. East Lebanon, Maine, Oct. 4, 1925; d. Lester Hanscom and Doris Evelyn (Covey) Roberts; A.S., Lasell Jr. Coll., 1945; m. Everett Bickford, July 12, 1947; children—Thomas, Tara, Timothy, Tad. Legal sec. Putnam, Bell, Dutch & Santry, Boston, 1946-48; real estate salesman Old Colony Real Estate, Rochester, N.H., 1976-81; mem. N.H. Ho. of Reps., 1980—. Mem. Order Women Legislators, DAR (past regent Mary Torr chpt.). Republican. Congregationalist.

BICKLEY, TANYA ANNE, broadcasting exec.; b. N.Y.C., Dec. 11, 1941; d. Samuel Felton and Anna Kohler (Clark) B.; B.A., U. Bridgeport (Conn.), 1972, M.S., 1973. Sec. public affairs dept. Nat. Ednl. TV, 1964-65; with ticket and promotion dept. St. Louis Symphony, 1965-66; pres. Classical Radio for Conn, New Canaan, 1974—; adv. bd. Sta. WNCN; pres. Ad Hoc Com. Orgns. for Unique Radio. Mem. Town Players New Canaan; mem. Centennial Campaign com. Dana Hall Sch.; tchr. Sunday Sch., coordinator edn. curriculum 250th Anniversary, New Canaan Congl. Ch. Address: 671 West Rd New Canaan CT 06840

BICKNELL-JOHNSON, MARJORIE RUTH, mathematician; b. Santa Rosa, Calif., Mar. 22, 1938; d. Evan William and Clara Elizabeth (Mattson) Thomas; B.A. in Math., San Jose State Coll., 1962, M.A. in Math., 1964; m. Frank Emmett Johnson, Oct. 1, 1976; children—

Jeannette, Steven, Christopher, Ami. Tchr. math. Wilcox High Sch., Santa Clara, Calif., 1964, chmn. dept. math., 1974—; instr. math. De Anza Coll., 1978-81. Mem. Nat. Council Tchrs. Math., Fibonacci Assn. (dir. 1967—), Santa Clara Valley Math. Assn. (newsletter editor 1970-74), Calif. Math. Council. Contbr. numerous articles on number theory, matrix theory, combinatorics to profl. jours.; co-editor: A Primer for the Fibonacci Numbers, 1972; editorial bd. Fibonacci Quar. Jour., 1965—. Home: 1667 Calabazas Blvd Santa Clara CA 95051 Office: Wilcox High Sch 3250 Monroe St Santa Clara CA 95051

BICKNESE, EVELYN HOLLISTER, advt. co. exec.; b. Gary, Ind., Nov. 14, 1934; d. Ross R. and Leona Colburn (Metzker) Hollister; B.S., Clayton U., St. Louis, 1980; m. Donald Dale Bicknese, June 29, 1952; children—Ross, Leona, Ralph, Kent, Eileen, Susan. Owner, mgr. Bick Outdoor Advt. Co., Gary, Ind., 1957-80, Valparaiso, Ind., 1963-73, LaPorte, Ind., 1963—, St. Louis, 1981—. Leader Singing Sands council Girl Scouts U.S.A., 1972-75, Potawattomi council Boy Scouts Am., 1963-72; pres. Principia Patrons of Northwestern Ind., 1977-79; treas., exec. bd. Principia Mothers Club, 1981-82. Mem. Eight Sheet Outdoor Advt. Assn. (dir. 1975-83, pres. 1982—), Ind. Sign and Display Assn. (editor newsletter 1979, dir. 1978-80), Michiana Advt. Exec. Club, C. of C. Republican. Christian Scientist. Author: Mostly Manners and Survival Manners for Teenagers. Office: 0353 E 900 N LaPorte IN 46350 also 2122 S Mason Rd Saint Louis MO 63131

BIDDLE, ANA, business exec.; b. Pitts., Feb. 25, 1945; d. Roland Delmar and Lula Louise (Antonoplos) Borgersen; A.A., Bradford Jr. Coll., 1964; B.A., Northwestern U., 1966; postgrad. Radcliffe Coll., 1966; m. Ernest L. Biddle, Jr., Sept. 19, 1981. Asst. editor Oxford U. Press, N.Y.C., 1967-68; freelance arts reader Warner Brothers, N.Y.C., 1967-68; mng. editor Pure Bred Dogs mag., N.Y.C., 1968-72; dir. publicity and public relations Grosset & Dunlap Inc., N.Y.C., 1972-76; dir. publicity and public relations gen. books Harcourt Brace Jovanovich, Inc., N.Y.C., 1976-78; cons. Human Nature, Inc., 1977, Johnson Reprint, 1978, The Body Glove, Inc., 1978, London Daily Telegraph, 1979; with Daniel J. Edelman, Public Relations, N.Y.C., 1979-80; treas. King Tester Corp., King of Prussia, Pa., 1980-81, pres., 1981—. Mem. Publishers Publicity Assn., Public Relations Soc. N.Y., Women in Communications, English Speaking Union, Asia Soc., Pi Beta Phi. Republican. Clubs: N.Y. Jr. League (public relations chmn., bd. mgrs.), Doubles, Nat. Arts. Home: 929 Rock Creek Rd Bryn Mawr PA 19016

BIDDLE, MARY GERALDINE STATON, nurse; b. Camden, N.J., May 16, 1943; d. Maurice Glen and Mary Dolores (McNamara) Staton; diploma in nursing, Pa. Hosp., Phila., 1964; m. Theodore Long Biddle, June 6, 1970; children—Katherine Mary and Margaret Ann (twins). Staff nurse hosps. in Phila. and Denver, 1964-70; mem. adminstrv. staff nephrology U. Rochester (N.Y.) Med. Center, 1970—, nephrology nurse cons.; faculty mem. Sch. Nursing, U. Rochester, 1975—. Named Profl. Person of Yr., Genessee Valley Kidney Found., 1976. Cert. hemodialysis nurse Bd. Nephrology Examiners. Mem. Am. Assn. Nephrology Nurses and Technicians (dir. 1976-81), Nat. Kidney Found. (nat. program chmn., nursing 1982), Am. Heart Assn., End Stage Renal Disease Network Coordinating Council (exec. com. 1979—). Author papers in field. Home: 282 Hollywood Ave Rochester NY 14618 Office: Nephrology Unit Monroe Community Hosp 435 E Henrietta Rd Rochester NY 14603

BIDEZ, THELMA CALHOUN (MRS. EARLE FELTON BIDEZ), club woman; b. Rockmart, Ga.; d. William Alexander and Eudora (Davitte) Calhoun; student pvt. schs.; m. Earle Felton Bidez, Sept. 4, 1916; children—Earle Calhoun (dec.), Miriam Elizabeth (Mrs. Lloyd E. Clark), William Alexander. Vice pres. Froebel Circle, 1953-54, pres., 1954-56; awards chmn. Garden Club of Savannah, 1954-57; sec., 1957-58, 1st v.p., 1958-60; librarian Savannah chpt. D.A.R., 1957-58; adv. mem. M.B.L.S.; mem. Am. Bicentennial Research Inst. Mem. Ga., Polk County (charter) hist. socs., Nat. Geneal. Soc., Daus. Am. Colonists (regent 1970), Magna Charta Dames, Plantagenet Soc., N.W. Ga. Hist. and Geneal. Soc., Ga. Geneal. Soc., Clan Colquhoun Soc. N.Am. Episcopalian (edited early marriage records of St. John's Ch.). Home: 116 E 53d St Savannah GA 31405

BIDLEMAN, MARY JOSEPHINE, home economist; b. Cin., Nov. 5, 1935; d. August Louis and Wilma Gertrude (Mette) Juniet; B.S., Ariz. State U., 1979; m. William Ellsworth Bidleman, May 30, 1956; children—Marie Angela, Francis Leo, Mary Colette, Donald Valery. Decorator cons. Creative World, Scottsdale, Ariz., 1977; sales coordinator Gen. Semicondr. Industries, Tempe, Ariz., 1978; substitute tchr., Phoenix, 1979; freelance cons., counselor, Tempe, 1979—; hosp. chaplain aide, 1980—; crisis line counselor, 1981—. Mem. Phoenix Com. against Pornography, 1969; del. White House Conf. Handicapped, 1976; sec. Ariz. Congress for Action, 1977-78; adv. Governor's Conf. Energy, 1979. Recipient nat. award for women returning to edn. PEO, 1975. Mem. Am. Home Econs. Assn., Ariz. Home Econs. Assn., Nat. Assn. Cath. Chaplains, Ariz. Solar Energy Assn., N.Mex. Solar Energy Assn. Republican. Address: 1737 E Manhattan Dr Tempe AZ 85282

BIEGEL, EILEEN MAE, hosp. exec.; b. Eau Claire, Wis., Nov. 13, 1937; d. Ewald Frederic and Emma Antonia (Conrad) Weggen; student Dist. One Tech. Inst., 1974, also part time, corr. student U. Wis., Madison; grad. mgmt. seminars; m. James O. Biegel, Oct. 6, 1956; children—Jeffrey Alan, John William. Exec. sec. to pres. Broadcaster Services, Inc., Eau Claire, Wis., 1969-74; exec. sec. to exec. v.p. Am. Nat. Bank, Eau Claire, 1975-77; exec. asst. to pres. Luther Hosp., Eau Claire, 1977—; mem. secretarial adv. council Dist. One Tech. Sch. 1975—. State pres. Future Homemakers Am., 1955. Cert. profl. sec., 1980. Mem. Eau Claire Womens Network (founder, mem. steering com.), Profl. Secs. Internat. (chmn. goals and priorities com., pres. Eau Claire chpt. 1982-83), Chippewa Valley Hist. Mus. Lutheran. Home: 4707 Tower Dr Eau Claire WI 54701 Office: 310 Chestnut St Eau Claire WI 54701

BIENEN, KAY GUMBINNER, state legislator; b. N.Y.C., Jan. 1, 1938; d. Paul Gerald and Ruth (Gumpert) Gumbinner; B.A., Skidmore Coll., 1959; postgrad. U. Md., 1959-61; m. Sanford M. Bienen, Aug. 28, 1960; children—Laura Jeanne, Janet Susan. Summer intern Gumbinner Advt. Agy., N.Y.C., 1957-58; legis. aide to Arthur Dorman, Md. Ho. of Dels., 1972-74; mem. Md. Ho. of Dels., 1974-78, 78—. Mem. profl. adv. com. Mental Health Assn. Prince George's County, 1976—; mem., chmn. abuse adv. com. Prince George's Child and Adolescent Abuse, 1975-79; mem. Prince George's County Goals Adv. Com., 1971-72; mem. ad hoc com. Montpelier Cultural Arts Ctr.; mem. adv. com. Coll. Park Youth Services Bur.; mem. Md. Coalition Gifted and Talented Edn.; mem. exec. com. NCCJ; bd. dirs. Prince George's Coalition Handicapped Children; mem. Prince George's Office for Coordination Services to Handicapped; chief judge Democratic party, 1968-74. Recipient awards NOW Md., 1974, Laurel C. of C., 1977, Soroptimist Internat., 1979, Rosewood Parents Assn., 1979, Md. Planning Council Devel. Disabilities, 1980, College Park Bus. and Profl. Women's Club. Mem. LWV, NOW, Order Women Legislators, Women's Polit. Caucus, Laurel Bus. and Profl. Women's Club.

BIENENSTOCK, RANDEE H., ednl. and devel. psychologist, behavior analyst; b. N.Y.C., Dec. 18, 1952; d. Solomon and Julia (Reiss) B.; B.A., N.Y.U., 1973; M.S., U. Wis., Madison, 1976, Ph.D., 1979. Nat. Inst. on Aging scholar and research fellow U. Wis., Madison, 1977-79; research psychologist Fordham U., N.Y.C., 1979-80; behavior psychologist to Dr. H. Hartman, White Plains, N.Y., 1980-82; adminstr., psychologist Behavior Research Inst., Northridge, Calif., 1981—; psychol. cons. Mem. Am. Psychol. Assn., Am. Ednl. Research Assn., Soc. Research in Child Devel., Gerontol. Soc., Assn. for Behavior Analysis, Pi Lambda Theta. Office: Behavior Research Inst Calif 9342 Zelzah Ave Northridge CA 91325

BIER, CYNTHIA, systems engr.; b. Washington, Apr. 26, 1953; d. David Lawrence and Eleanor (Venglosky) B.; A.S., No. Va. Community Coll., 1973; B.A., Averett Coll., 1975. Sales, W. Bell & Co., Falls Church, Va., 1975-76; customer rep. Nat. Cash Register Corp., Columbia, Md., 1976-77, systems analyst, 1977-78; systems engr., instr. Four Phase Systems, Inc., Washington, 1979—. Chmn., Coll. Republicans, 1971-74; rep. 8th Dist. Central Rep. Com., 1971-73. Mem. Nat. Assn. Female Execs. Roman Catholic. Home: 8706 Parliament Dr Springfield VA 22151 Office: 1850 K St Suite 1000 Washington DC 20006

BIERCE, CAROL ANNE HOOVER, computer software specialist; b. Pensacola, Fla., Jan. 30, 1954; d. Ralph Alwin Hoover, Jr. and Hazel Floyce (Warren) Roberts; B.A. in Math. with highest distinction, U. North Fla., 1975, B.A.E. with highest distinction, 1976, M.B.A., 1979; m. Daniel Ambrose Bierce, Oct. 17, 1975; 1 son, Adam Anthony. Programmer, Sav-A-Stop, Inc., Orange Park, Fla., 1975-76; with City of Jacksonville (Fla.), 1976—, sr. application analyst, 1980-82, asst. info. systems officer, 1982—; project leader water and electric computer services, tech. support; cons. for Jacksonville Software Devel. Corp. Mem. Assn. M.B.A. Execs., Nat. Assn. Female Execs., Riverside-Avondale Preservation Soc., Fla. Epilepsy Found., Phi Theta Kappa, Pi Mu Epsilon. Democrat. Episcopalian. Home: 1624 Cherry St Jacksonville FL 32205 Office: City Hall Bay St Jacksonville FL 32202

BIERI, CHRISTEL DORIS HESSELSCHWERDT, mfg. co. exec.; b. Karlsruhe, W. Ger., Apr. 29, 1938; came to U.S., 1962, naturalized; d. Emil and Karolina Hesselschwerdt; B.S. in Langs., U. Geneva, Switzerland; M.A., U. Calif., Berkeley, 1966; m. Jurg H. Bieri, Apr. 21, 1962. Teaching asst. U. Calif., Berkeley, 1964-66; property mgr., Berkeley, 1966-73; bus. co-owner, gen. mgr. Vouvry, Switzerland, 1974-76; co-founder Heliodyne Inc., Richmond, Calif., 1976—, v.p. mktg., 1978—. Mem. No. Calif. Solar Energy Assn. (officer 1978-80), Internat. Solar Energy Soc. (Am. chpt.), Calif. Solar Energy Industries Assn. Home: 2350 Alva Ave El Cerrito CA 94530 Office: 700 S 4th St Richmond CA 94804

BIERNAT, LILLIAN M. NAHUMENUK, interior designer; b. Phila., Apr. 27, 1931; d. Peter and Anna (Wolonick) Nahumenuk; student pub. schs.; m. Joseph Anthony Biernat, July 22, 1951; children—Joseph A., Daria Ann, Karen Marie, Mark Allen, Brent Hilary. Receptionist, sec. Mayer, Magaziner & Brunswick, lawyers, Phila., 1950-53; owner Town House Interiors, Columbia, Conn., also Newton Square, Pa., 1956—, Lillian Biernat Interiors, Avon and Columbia, Conn. Mem. fund raising com. Girl Scouts U.S.A., 1968; exec. bd. Conn. Opera Guild, Hartford Ballet; pres. Friends of Hartford Ballet. Clubs: Womens, Garden (Newtown Square); Villagers Womens (Columbia). Address: 30 Hurdle Fence Dr Avon CT 06001

BIGBEE, NANCY PEARL, lawyer; b. Santa Fe, N.Mex., Feb. 12, 1947; d. Harry L. and Betty (Roe) Bigbee; B.A., Pomona Coll., 1969; J.D., U. Denver, 1976; 1 dau., Anne Marie Calvin. With Lentz, Evans & King, Denver, 1975; admitted to Colo. bar, 1976, asso. law firm Jones, Meiklejohn, Kehl & Lyons, Denver, 1976-80; pvt. practice law, Denver, 1980—; practitioner/tutor freshman legal writing course, U. Denver Coll. of Law, 1979—. Mem. U. Denver Nat. Law Alumni Council, 1977—, vice chmn., 1979-81; participant Transp. Task Force for Public Utilities Commn. Sunset Rev., Colo. Dept. Regulatory Affairs, 1982; Dem. precinct committeewoman 1980-82; fund raiser Metro Denver YMCA Youth Partnership campaign, 1980. Mem. Am., Colo. (mem. pub. utilities rules of practice com.), Denver bar assns., Motor Carrier Lawyers Assn., Assn. Interstate Commerce Commn. Practitioners, others. Quaker. Editor-in-chief Denver Law Jour., 1975-76; editor Proceedings, 1981 Transp. Law Inst. Office: 745 E 18th Ave Suite 101 Denver CO 80203

BIGELOW, MARY (MRS. RUDY GRAY BURTON), elec. co. exec., civic worker; b. Perry, N.Y.; d. Albert E. and Rebecca Ann (Miller) Davis; student Rochester Bus. Inst., Am. Inst. Banking, 1938, Woodbury Coll., 1944, UCLA, 1945; m. Richard Harned Bates, Oct. 4, 1940 (div. Sept. 1947); m. 2d, Floyd Burget Bigelow, 1948 (div. May 1952); 1 dau., Judith Lynne (Mrs. Daniel McMullen); m. 3d, Rudy Gray Burton, Nov. 17, 1962. Various positions, 1931-36; banking, 1936-41, advt., oil bus., 1944-50; sec.-treas. Emerald Bay Community Assn., Laguna Beach, Calif., 1950-52, Tel-I-Clear Systems, Inc., Laguna Beach, 1952-54; owner, operator Bigelow Bus. Services, Laguna Beach, 1954—; co-owner, mgr. Burton Electric, Laguna Beach, 1963—; owner Meri-Bee Originals Photography. Bd. dirs. Laguna Moulton Playhouse 1st Nighters, 1974—, Girls Clubs Laguna Beach, Laguna Beach Hist. Soc.; asst., bd. dirs. Three Arch Bay Dist., South Laguna, 1957-73; com. mem. Opera League and Lyric Opera Laguna Beach, 1968—; mem. U. Calif. at Irvine and Laguna Beach Friends of Library. Bd. dirs. Joe Thurston Found., 1957-64. Recipient various civic awards; named leading lady in bus. Laguna News-Post, 1971. Mem. Nat. Soc. Public Accts., Soc. Calif. Accts., Balboa, Dana Point power squadrons, World Affairs Council Los Angeles and Orange County, Laguna Beach C. of C. Mermaids (information chmn. Festival of Arts 1966, 67, 68), Smithsonian Instn., Inland Soc. Tax Cons., Internat. Photog. Soc., Anchorettes, Women in Chambers Commerce (congresswoman). Clubs: Altrusa Internat. (Laguna Beach) (treas., dir.), West Coast Yacht, Riviera. Home and office: 697 Catalina St Laguna Beach CA 92651

BIGLER, MARY GLENN, educator; b. Stevens Point, Wis., May 5, 1944; d. Ernest Dean and Maxine (Dermody) Glenn; B.A. in History, Aquinas Coll., 1965; M.A. in History, Eastern Mich. U., 1968, M.A. in Reading, 1971; Ph.D. in Curriculum and Instruction, U. Mich., 1974; m. William Wayne Bigler, Aug. 20, 1965; 1 dau., Beth Ann. Tchr., St. John's High Sch., Ypsilanti, Mich., 1965-69; reading cons., tchr. Ann Arbor (Mich.) Public Schs., 1969-75; field cons. Ednl. Cons. Assos., Englewood, Colo., 1975-77; asso. prof. tchr. edn. Eastern Mich. U., 1977—; keynote speaker at numerous confs.; honors convocation and grad. speaker, various high schs.; banquet speaker Reading '82 Conf., York U.; cons., workshop presenter in field. Mem. Assn. Supervision and Curriculum Devel., Internat. Reading Assn., Nat. Council Tchrs. English, Mich. Reading Assn. (pres. 1982-83), Internat. Platform Assn., Delta Kappa Gamma. Author: Reading and the Language Arts, 1974; contbr. articles to profl. jours. Home: 1332 King George Blvd Ann Arbor MI 48104 Office: 338 Pierce Hall Eastern Mich U Ypsilanti MI 48197

BIGLEY, NANCY JANE, microbiologist, immunologist; b. Sewickley, Pa., Feb. 1, 1932; d. William Howard, Sr. and Frances Jane (Engle) B.; B.S., Pa. State U., 1953; M.Sc., Ohio State U., 1955, Ph.D., 1957. Asst. prof. microbiology Ohio State U., 1965-68, asso. prof., 1968-69; asso. prof. Chgo. Med. Sch., 1969-72, prof. microbiology, 1972-76; prof., chmn. dept. microbiology and immunology Wright State U., Dayton, Ohio, 1976—; cons. Dayton VA Hosp., U.S. Army; Am. Soc. Microbiology Founds. lectr., 1975. Nat. Inst. Allergy and Infectious Disease research grantee, 1970-76; NSF grantee, 1978-79. Mem. Am. Assn. Immunologists, Am. Soc. Microbiology, Reticuloendothial Soc., Sigma Xi. Presbyterian. Author: Immunologic Fundamentals, 1975; editorial bd. Infection and Immunity, 1978-81. Home: 1427 Ticonderoga Ct Xenia OH 45385 Office: Wright State U Colonel Glenn Hwy Dayton OH 45435

BIKALES, GERDA V., assn. adminstr.; b. Breslau, Germany, May 14, 1931; came to U.S., 1946, naturalized, 1952; d. Victor and Blanche (Lefkowitz) Bierzonski; A.B., Upsala Coll., 1965; M.S.W., Rutgers U., 1971; m. Norbert M. Bikales, Apr. 28, 1951; children—Marguerite, Edward. Social worker United Hosps. Med. Center, Newark, 1971-74; asso. Center for Analysis of Public Issues, Princeton, N.J., 1975-78; program dir. population/immigration Nat. Parks and Conservation Assn., Washington, 1977-80; dir. membership/field ops. Fedn. Am. Immigration Reform, 1980—. Recipient Cert. of Appreciation Nat. U.S. Border Patrol Council, 1979. Mem. Acad. Cert. Social Workers, Population Soc. Club: Woman's Nat. Democratic. Author: Day Care: A Program in Search of a Policy, 1978; contbr. articles in field to profl. jours. Office: 2028 P St NW Washington DC 20036

BIKOWSKI, VERA ELLEN, speech pathologist; b. Cold Spring Harbor, N.J., Aug. 15, 1948; d. Anthony Joseph and Martha (Rugala) Polakas; B.A. cum laude, Bklyn. Coll., 1970, M.Ed., 1975; m. Dec. 20, 1969; 2 sons. Center tchr., tchr. trainer N.Y.C. Bur. for Speech Improvement, 1970-78; speech pathologist upgrade ednl. service Cold Spring Harbor (N.Y.) Schs., 1979-81, Speech Services, Inc., Sumter, S.C., 1981-82. Lic. speech pathologist, N.Y., S.C., Tenn.; cert. tchr. speech and hearing handicapped, N.Y., Tenn. Mem. Am. Speech and Hearing Assn. (cert. clin. competence in speech). Address: Route 2 Parkway Rd Tullahoma TN 37388

BILDERBACK, HELEN LAVONNE, constrn. co. exec.; b. Kinmundy, Ill., Feb. 17, 1936; d. James Avery and Vera May (Hoyt) Boughers; student public schs., Redondo Beach, Calif.; m. Paul Joseph Bilderback, July 20, 1963; children—Terri LaVonne, Cheryl Ann, Carol Lee. Electronics inspector quality assurance dept. Internat. Rectifier, Inc., El Segundo, Calif., 1960-63; sec.-treas. Bilderback Constrn. Co., Columbus, Ohio, 1971—. Mem. Nat. Assn. Female Execs., Inc. Roman Catholic. Home: 984 W Main St Westerville OH 43081 Office: 1966 Morse Rd Suite B Columbus OH 43229

BILDSTEIN, CAROLE ANNE, social worker; b. Colorado Springs, Colo., Feb. 3, 1950; d. Merle Vincent and Mildred Elaine (Worley) Woolley; B.A. in Social Work, Valparaiso (Ind.) U., 1972; M.S.W. (HEW grantee), SUNY, Albany, 1977; m. Ronald M. Bildstein, July 28, 1973. Residence dir. Emerson Coll., Boston, 1974-75; caseworker, team leader Benjamin Rose Inst., Cleve., 1977-79; social work planning asso. Fedn. Cath. Community Service, Cleve., 1979; exec. dir. Heart of Ohio council Girl Scouts U.S.A., Zanesville, Ohio, 1979-81. Vice chmn. cancer task force Luth. Met. Ministry, Cleve., 1978-79. Mem. Nat. Assn. Social Workers, Acad. Cert. Social Workers. Club: Valparaiso U. Women's. Home: 22790 TR 1193 Coshocton OH 43812 Office: 1215 Newark Rd Zanesville OH 43701

BILICH, MARION YELLIN, psychotherapist; b. Bklyn., Feb. 14, 1949; d. Bernard Perry and Sylvia Pierce (Spector) Yellin; B.A. in Humanities, Hofstra U., 1970; M.S., Sch. Social Work, Columbia U., 1975; m. Charles Bilich, Aug. 23, 1970; 1 dau., Karin. Pvt. practice psychotherapy dealing with eating disorders in women, Hewlett, N.Y., 1975—; condr. nat. workshops, 1979—. Mem. Soc. Clin. S.W. Psychotherapists, N.Y. Acad. Scis., Internat. Imagery Assn. Author: An Inner Journey: Weight Loss from the Inside Out; contbr. articles to profl. jours. Home and office: 406 Daub Ave Hewlett NY 11557

BILL, LUCY, employment agy. exec.; b. Prague, Czechoslovakia, May 25, 1928; came to U.S., 1951, naturalized, 1955; d. Friedrich and Greta (Desensy) Bill; student CCNY, 1951-54; m. Michael Berlin, Dec. 25, 1960 (dec. 1969). With Exptl. Sta., U.S. Dept. Agr., Quito, Ecuador, 1948-51; personnel supr. Grancolombiana S.S. Line, N.Y.C., 1951-60; personnel counselor Busher Agy., N.Y.C., 1960-62; owner Bil-Lu Personnel Agy., N.Y.C., 1962—. Office: 415 Lexington Ave New York NY 10017

BILLAUER, BARBARA PFEFFER, lawyer; b. Aug. 9, 1951; d. Harry George and Evelyn (Newman) Pfeffer; B.S. with honors, Cornell U., 1972; J.D., Hofstra U., 1975; M.A., N.Y. U., 1982; m. David Love, Feb. 14, 1982. Admitted to N.Y. bar, 1976, Fed. Dist. Ct. N.Y., 1977, U.S. Ct. Appeals for 2d circuit, 1978; asso. firm Bower & Garnder, N.Y.C., 1974-78; sr. trial atty. Joseph W. Conklin, N.Y.C., 1978-80; asso. dept. head firm. Curtis, Mallet-Prevost, Colt & Mosle, N.Y.C., 1980-82; partner firm Anderson, Russell, Kill & Olich, N.Y.C., 1982—; adj. asso. prof. N.Y.U. Grad. Sch., 1982; adminstrv. law judge N.Y.C. Dept. Transp. Mem. Met. Women's Bar Assn. (v.p. 1981—), ABA, Health Law Forum, N.Y. Bar Assn., Am. Soc. Law and Medicine, Am. Soc. Microbiology, AAUW. Office: 666 3d Ave New York NY 10017

BILLHARZ, CONSTANCE ELLEN CLARK, speech and lang. pathologist, ednl. diagnostician; b. Golden City, Mo., July 29, 1921; d. Harley B. and Flossie J. (Mitchell) Clark; B.A., Pace U., 1971; M.A., N.Y.U., 1975; M.P.S., Manhattanville Coll., 1978; m. Roger William Billharz, Jan. 12, 1946; 1 son, Roger Clark. Speech pathologist St. Joseph's Mental Health Clinic, Peekskill, N.Y., 1978-79; speech and lang. pathologist Rye (N.Y.) City Sch. Dist., 1980—; pvt. practice as ednl. diagnostician, North Tarrytown, N.Y., 1979—. Cert. spl. edn. tchr., tchr. speech and hearing handicapped, N.Y. State. Mem. Am. Speech Lang. and Hearing Assn. (cert. clin. competence in speech), N.Y. State Speech Lang. and Hearing Assn., Westchester Speech Lang. and Hearing Assn., Westchester Assn. Children with Learning Disabilities, Am. Arbitration Assn. Republican. Address: 467 Munroe Ave North Tarrytown NY 10591

BILLIE, ANNETTE CYNTHIA, mathematician; b. Orangeburg, S.C., July 25, 1934; d. Samuel and Bertha (Goldberg) B.; B.S., S.C. State Coll., 1956, M.S., 1963; Ph.D., U. Pitts., 1976. Tchr. schs. in S.C., 1956-63; mem. faculty Fayetteville (N.C.) State U., 1972—, prof. math., 1976—. Mem. Nat. Council Tchrs. Math., Math. Assn. Am., Nat. Assn. Mathematicians, AAUP, S.C. State Coll. Alumni Assn., Phi Delta Gamma, Phi Delta Kappa, Alpha Kappa Alpha. Democrat. Methodist. Club: Order Eastern Star. Address: 749 Edgehill Rd Chestnut Hills Fayetteville NC 28304

BILLINGSLEA, RUBY, social worker; b. Albany, Ga., Sept. 8, 1914; d. John Simmons and Hattie Billingslea; A.B. in Journalism, U. Ga., 1935; M.S.W., Tulane U., 1947. Social worker Dougherty County Dept. Public Welfare, Albany, 1938, Orleans Parish (La.) Dept. Public Welfare, 1939-44, Charity Hosp., New Orleans, 1951-52, Children's Bur., New Orleans, 1953-65; caseworker USO-Travelers Aid, 1945-47; supr. clin. social work Kingsley House Nursery Sch., New Orleans, 1966-77; social service researcher for psychologist, New Orleans, 1979—; lectr. La. State U. Sch. Social Welfare, 1959-60. Sec. speakers' bur. New Orleans Community Chest, 1949-50. Cert. social worker, La. Mem. Acad. Cert. Social Workers, Nat. Assn. Social Workers, La. Conf. Social Workers, Theta Sigma Phi.

BILLINGSLEA, WILLIE DEAN, assn. exec.; b. Atlanta, Nov. 25, 1937; d. Willie Lee and Emma Lou (Montgomery) Moore; student Blayton Sch. Acctg., 1956-58, Ga. State U., 1967, 74, 77; m. Grady Lee Billingslea, June 28, 1958; children—Grady Lee, Dynite Darlene, Willie DeMoore. Sec., Met. Atlanta Assn. for the Blind, 1958-69; clerical mgr.

Phyllis Wheatley br. YWCA, Atlanta, 1969-70; adminstrv. services supr. Community Council of Atlanta Area, 1970-75; bus. mgr. Gate City Day Nursery Assn., Atlanta, 1975—; field office mgr. Westat Research Inc., Rockville, Md., 1975; field staff coordinator Belden Asso., Dallas, 1972, 73, 76. Chmn. human relations com., Atlanta chpt. Continental Socs., 1979-80; troop membership chmn. Boy Scouts Am., Atlanta, 1976; sec. Benjamin E. Mays High Sch. PTA, 1981-82. Mem. NAACP (dir. 1974), Atlanta LWV, Am. Bus. Women Assn., Nat. Soc. Pub. Accts., Chi Mu Epsilon. Baptist. Address: 884 Rodney Dr SW Atlanta GA 30311

BILLINGTON, BETTY GERTRUDE, banker; b. Ingolstadt, Germany, July 3, 1948; came to U.S., 1948, naturalized, 1948; d. William G. and Getrude A. Moore; A.A., Mt. Wachusett Community Coll., Gardner, Mass., 1968. With Rochdale Store, Leominster, Mass., 1965-68; clk. Independent Lock Co., Fitchburg, Mass., 1968-69; with Fidelity Coop. Bank, Leominster, 1969—, br. mgr., asst. treas., 1970—. Sec. bd. dirs. ARC, Leominster; trustee Mt. Wachusett Community Coll. Mem. Mt. Wachusett Community Coll. Alumni Assn. (sec. 1980—). Methodist. Office: 29 Main St Leominster MA 01453

BILLMAN, SHARON LYNN, fin. exec.; b. Erie, Kans., Oct. 14, 1946; d. Edward Milton and Irene Loucille (Hines) Bowman; student schs., Erie; m. David R. Billman, Sr., June 4, 1966; 1 dau., Shanna Kay. Sales rep. Kans. Mobile Homes Inc., 1969-73; sec.-treas. Billmans Mobile Home Service Inc., Parsons, Kans., 1974—, Associated Transfer & Storage Inc., Parsons, 1979—. Gold cup chmn. S.E. Kans. Dist. Music Festival, 1979—. Mem. Parsons Women's Bowling Assn. (pres. 1972—), Kans. Women's Bowling Assn. (dir. 1979—). Democrat. Episcopalian. Home and Office: Route 4 East Hwy 160 Parsons KS 67357

BILLMEYER, DORIS MILDRED, librarian; b. Irvington, N.J., Sept. 27, 1915; d. George and Emma Louise (Karge) Schnibbe; student Newark Normal Sch., 1935-37; m. Bromley Harry, Sept. 4, 1937; children—Bromley Harry. Asst. librarian Maplewood (N.J.) Public Library, 1934-43; librarian Spring Lake (N.J.) Public Library, 1969-74, library dir., 1974—. Mem. Spring Lake Library Soc. (sponsor, advisor), Monmouth County Librarian's Assn. Lutheran. Clubs: Woman's (past pres., edn. com.); Order of Eastern Star. Office: Spring Lake Library 1501 3rd Ave Spring Lake NJ 07762

BILLOW, SANDRA JEAN, corp. ins. exec.; b. Columbus, Ohio, July 9, 1948; d. Lawrence R. and Carol L. (Edwards) B.; B.A. in Psychology with honors, Hollins (Va.) Coll., 1970; m. Leland E. Teschler, Oct. 20, 1979. Research asst. Hollins Coll., 1968, 69; ins. adminstr. Motel Mgmt. Corp., Arlington, Va., 1972-77; corp. ins. mgr. Stouffer Corp., Solon, Ohio, 1978-80; adminstr. property-liability ins. Sherwin-Williams Co., Cleve., 1980—. Recipient Pres. award for cost reduction Sherwin-Williams Co., 1981. Mem. Risk and Ins. Mgmt. Soc. (officer). Unitarian. Author articles in field.

BILLS, MARSHA RUTH, business ofcl.; b. Walters, Okla., Aug. 23, 1949; d. Raymond Lee and Ruth Ellen (McCord) Bills; B.A., Austin State U., 1971,; M.B.A., N.Y.U., U. Instr. Peace Corps, Thailand, 1971-72; tchr. English, history and French, mem. spl. community relations com. Dallas Ind. Sch. Dist., 1972-76; orgnl. asst. U.S. Senate Campaign, Dallas, 1976; public relations asst. Sta. KERA-TV, Dallas, 1976-78, Norton Simon, Inc., N.Y.C., 1978-80; account exec. Georgeson & Co., N.Y.C., 1980-81; mgr. investor relations Revlon, Inc., N.Y.C., 1982—; instr. Bayview Correctional Facility for Women, N.Y.C., 1981-82. Mem. Women in Communications, Fin. Soc. Communicators. Home: 120 E 89th St Apt 6F New York NY 10028 Office: 767 Fifth Ave New York NY 10152

BILLS, SHERYL JEAN, newspaper editor; b. Rushville, Ind., Aug. 4, 1945; d. Robert Jackson and Mary Elizabeth (Kehl) B.; B.A., Ind. U., 1968. Mem. staff Cin. Enquirer, 1967-82, asst. mng. editor features, 1979-80, mng. editor, 1980-82; planning editor USA Today, Gannett Newspapers, 1982—; speaker in field. Mem. adminstrv. bd. Hyde Park Community United Methodist Ch., Cin., 1981. Recipient Writing award Ohio Newspaper Women's Assn., 1971, 74; Ohio AP award for enterprise in journalism, 1974; award mag. covers Outdoor Writers Ohio-Ohio Press Photographers Assn., 1976; Penney-Mo. award newspaper Lifestyle sect., 1978, Outstanding Career Woman award Cin. YWCA, 1981. Mem. Women in Communications, AP Mng. Editors Assn., Am. Soc. Newspaper Editors, Sigma Delta Chi. Office: USA Today PO Box 500 Washington DC 20004

BILLUPS, P. ANTOINETTE, govt. ofcl.; b. Portsmouth, Va., Nov. 22, 1941; d. Linon Eugene and Sarah (Sensabaugh) Vann; B.S. in Math., Howard U., 1962; postgrad. Cath. U. Am.; m. Gregory Vincent Billups, May 6, 1978. Computer programmer Dept. Agr., Washington, 1964-69, systems analyst, 1969-75, supervisory systems analyst, 1975-79, chief systems analysis and programming br., 1979—, dept. mgr. fed. women's program. Sec. bd. dirs. Seward Sq. Assn. Mem. Nat. Assn. Female Execs., Washington Jr. C. of C., Alpha Kappa Alpha. Office: Dept Agr 14th and Independence Ave SW Washington DC 20250

BILODEAU, MARYPATRICIA, personnel dir.; b. Denver, Oct. 18, 1942; d. Leonard Francis and Eleanor Marie (Horan) Mitchell; B.S., Marywood Coll., 1964; m. Michel Bilodeau, Sept. 14, 1974; 1 son, Sean Patrick. Tchr. public schs., N.Y. and N.J., 1964-67; social services adminstr. Herkimer County (N.Y.) Dept. Social Services, 1967-74; program developer Merrimack (N.H.) Home Health Care; program dir. Cerebral Palsy Assn., Manchester, N.H., 1974-77; community services dir. Community Action Program, Concord, N.H., 1977-78; dir. personnel N.H. Ins. Co., Manchester, 1978—. Pres. bd. dirs. Internat. Center, Manchester, 1980—. Mem. Manchester Personnel Assn., Am. Bus. Women's Assn. Republican. Roman Catholic. Club: Zonta Internat. (pres. Manchester). Home: 939 Union St Manchester NH 03104 Office: 1750 Elm St Manchester NH 03104

BILSEL, ZELIHA, pediatrician; b. Kirklarel, Turkey, Apr. 24, 1924; d. Ismet and Emine (Tanriover) M.D., Med. Sch., 1947; m. Yilmaz C. Bilsel, Oct. 29, 1960; children—Deniz, Kurt. Dir. orphanage in Turkey, 1947-49; resident in pediatrics, Turkey, 1949-52; dir. orphanage, practice medicine specializing in pediatrics, Kirklarel, 1952-57; resident in pediatrics Homer Phillips Hosp., St. Louis, 1957-61, chief resident newborn premature nursery, 1959-61; fellow in cardiology, Augusta, Ga., 1961-63; practice medicine specializing in pediatrics, Kirklarel, 1963-66, Fairview Heights, Ill., 1970—; pediatrician outpatient clinic St. Louis Children's Hosp., 1966-70; pediatrics cons. for Pediatrics Clinic; cons. staff mem.; mem. staff Cardinal Glennon, St. Louis, Meml. Hosp., Belleville, Ill.; attending physician to high risk newborns and premature for So. Ill. Christian Welfare Hosp., East St. Louis, Ill. Mem. AMA, St. Clair Med. Soc., So. Ill. Med. Soc.

BINCER, WANDA LAWENDEL, psychiatrist; b. Warsaw, Poland, Oct. 4, 1930; came to U.S., 1950, naturalized, 1961; d. Leonard and Evelyn (Glocer) Lawendel; M.D., Royal Coll. Surgeons, Ireland, 1956; m. Adam M. Bincer, Apr. 2, 1972; children—Yvonne, Brian, Michael. Rotating intern St. Mary's Hosp., Rochester, N.Y., 1957-58; resident in psychiatry City Hosp., Elmhurst, N.Y., 1958-59, 61-63; house officer Princess Margaret Hosp., Nassau, Bahamas, 1959-60; staff psychiatrist Pontiac (Mich.) State Hosp., 1965-66; cons. psychiatrist Bur. Social Services, Grand Forks, N.D., 1966-68, Community Mental Health Center, Grand Forks, 1966-68; staff psychiatrist VA Hosp., Atlanta, 1968-70, Center for Interpersonal Study, Smyrna, Ga. and Brawner Hosp., 1970-72; practice medicine specializing in psychiatry, Madison, Wis., 1972—. Mem. City-County Com. on Sexual Assault, Madison, 1978-80; cons. Parental Stress Center, 1978—. Served with Polish Underground, 1944. Decorated Bronze Cross of Merit. Mem. Am. Psychiat. Assn., Wis. Psychiat. Assn. (com. on women), Am. Acad. Psychotherapists. Cons. editor Voices, 1978-80; contbr. to Problem Solver (ed. Zastro et al), 1976. Office: 217 S Hamilton Bldg Madison WI 53703

BINDER, LUCY SIMPSON, utility exec.; b. Phila., May 12, 1937; d. James G. and C. Lucy (Underwood) Simpson; B.S. in Bus. Adminstrn., Drexel U., Phila., 1959; m. Robert A. Binder, Aug. 12, 1967. With Phila. Electric Co., 1959—, asst. corp. sec., 1977-78, sec., 1978—. Mem. Am. Soc. Corp. Secs. Address: 2301 Market St Philadelphia PA 19101 *

BINDER, MILDRED KATHERINE, county public welfare agy. exec.; b. York, Pa., Jan. 5, 1918; d. Jemie Irving and Emma Jane (Billet) Binder; B.A. magna cum laude in Sociology, Hood Coll., 1940. Sec., mgr. Stock's Appliances, York, 1940-42; caseworker York County Bd. Assistance, Pa. Dept. Public Welfare, 1942-49, 1953-58, supr., 1949-53, 1958-59, exec. dir., 1959—. Mem. exec. com. York County Employment and Tng. Com.; mem. dept. task forces Social Service Delivery to Client Info. System, also mem. ops. rev. bd.; mem. bd. York County Council Alcoholism, 1959-62, Community Progress Council, 1965-67; co-chmn. Community Dialogue Com., 1968-69; mem. bd. Pre-Paid Health York, Inc., 1979; mem. human services planning coalition United Way, 1978—, chmn. council agy. execs., 1967-71, 1976-78; mem. consumer adv. councils Gen. Telephone, Met. Edison. Named Boss of Yr., Am. Bus. Women, 1973. Mem. Am. Public Welfare Assn., Exec. Dirs. Assn. Pa. (exec. com. 1979—, sec. 1980—), York Area C. of C., United Way of Pa. Clubs: Coll. of York, Hood Coll. (York). Home: 1611 W Market St York PA 17404 Office: PO Box M-41 130 N Duke St York PA 17405

BINDMAN, ANN, social services assn. adminstr.; b. Havana, Cuba, Mar. 11, 1944; came to U.S., 1951, naturalized, 1956; d. Alexander and Sybil (Rogow) Langer; B.A., CCNY, 1965; M.S.W., Columbia U., 1967; m. Ira Bindman, June 25, 1966. After-sch. supr. Children's Aid Soc., Frederick Douglas Community Center, N.Y.C., 1967-71; sr. social worker Wiltwyck Sch. Boys, Inc., N.Y.C., 1971-72; program dir. Children's Aid Soc., East Harlem Center, N.Y.C., 1972-73, dir., 1973-77; asst. exec. dir. Bklyn. Soc. Prevention Cruelty to Children, 1977-81, asso. exec. dir., 1981—. Mem. Nat. Assn. Social Workers, Acad. Cert. Social Workers, Nat. Conf. Social Welfare. Home: 166 E 96th St New York NY 10028 Office: PO Box 423 Brooklyn NY 11217

BINEGAR, GWENDOLYN ANN, social worker; b. Phoenix, Sept. 23, 1924; d. Glenn Marvin and Mary Lenore (Cartwright) Redington; B.S. in Sociology, Iowa State U., 1948; M.S.S., Bryn Mawr Coll., 1967; m. Lewis Albert Binegar, Nov. 2, 1951; children—Glen Albert, Birne Thomas, William Lewis, Alan Martin. Coordinator vols. Santa Barbara Mental Health Services, Lompoc, Calif., 1964; psychiat. social worker Child Study Inst., Bryn Mawr (Pa.) Coll., 1967-71; sr. social worker Ruth Sch. for Girls, Seattle, 1972; med. social worker Casa Colina Hosp., Pomona, Calif., 1973-74; supervising counselor San Gabriel Valley Regional Center, Pomona, 1974-79; asst. chief counselor San Diego Regional Center, 1979-80, chief counselor, 1980—; mem. regional adv. com. on devel. disabilities Health Tng. Center, Los Angeles, 1976-78; sec. Devel. Disabilities Council of San Gabriel Valley, 1976-77, Nat. Com. on Peace and Social Welfare, 1973-74. Lic. clin. social worker, Calif. Mem. Acad. Cert. Social Workers, Am. Assn. Mental Deficiency, Nat. Assn. Social Workers. Presbyterian. Home: 28809 Lilac Valley Center CA 92082 Office: 4355 Ruffin Rd San Diego CA 92123

BINGHAM, JINSIE SCOTT, broadcasting co. exec.; b. Greencastle, Ind., Dec. 28, 1935; d. Roscoe Gibson and Alpha Edith (Robinson) Scott; student DePauw U., 1952-53, Northwestern U., 1953, Coe Coll., 1953-54; m. Richard Innes Bingham, June 24, 1964; children by previous marriage—Douglas Scott Wokoun, Richard Frank Wokoun. Receptionist, Ind. House of Reps., Indpls., 1959; saleslady Avon Products, Greencastle, Ind., 1961-64; sales mgr. WJNZ Radio, Greencastle, Ind., 1969-77, owner, pres., gen. mgr., 1977—. Exec. sec. Ind. Young Democrats, 1958-60. Mem. Am. Women in Radio and TV (pres. Hoosier chpt. 1979-82), Indpls. Network Women in Bus., Women in Communications, Am. Legion, Ind. Broadcasters Assn. (v.p. 1981-82), Greencastle Bus. and Profl. Women's Club (pres. 1976-77, 79-80), Ind. Dem. Editorial Assn., Ind. C. of C., Greencastle C. of C. (dir. 1980-83, pres. 1982), VFW (past pres. aux.), Daus. of 1812 (pres. chpt. 1979-80); DAR, Delta Theta Tau. Protestant. Clubs: Job's Daus. (life); Women of Moose; Women's Press of Ind., Order Eastern Star. Office: PO Box 494 Greencastle IN 46135

BINGHAM, MARJORIE JEAN WALL, educator; b. St. Paul, Nebr., May 27, 1936; d. George Richard and Fay Maugerite Wall; B.A., Grinnell Coll., 1958; M.A., U. Minn., 1959, Ph.D., 1969; m. Thomas Egan, Feb. 28, 1975. Tchr. public schs., Davenport, Iowa, 1959-62, St. Louis Park, Minn., 1963-77; dir. women in world area studies St. Louis Park and Robbinsdale (Minn.) Schs., 1977—. Woodrow Wilson fellow, 1958-59. Mem. Wpmen Historians of Midwest (pres. 1980—, exec. bd. 1978—), Minn. Hist. Soc. (edn. bd. 1979—), Minn. Council of Social Studies (mem. exec. bd. 1977—), Phi Beta Kappa. Co-author: Women in World Cultures Series, Women in Israel, Islam, China, India, and USSR, 1980. Home: 5732 Lake Rose Dr Minnetonka MN 55343 Office: 6425 W 33d St Saint Louis Park MN 55426

BINNIE, MYRNA LORRAINE, med. technologist, microbiologist; b. Cheyenne, Wyo., Sept. 18, 1941; d. John William and Estella Christina (Stewart) Hart; B.S. with honors in Med. Tech., U. Wyo., 1964; M.S. in Microbiology, Ariz. State U., 1972; m. Ronald C. Bugh, Dec. 29, 1964 (div. Aug., 1972); 1 son, Robert Hart; m. 2d, Thomas G. Binnie, Apr. 18, 1980. Med. technologist Laramie County Meml. Hosp., Cheyenne, 1964; med. technologist Mesa (Ariz.) Luth. Hosp., 1965-73, supr. bacteriology dept., 1973-76, co-ordinator microbiology, 1976-81, lab. coordinator, 1981—; instr. microbiology Maricopa Tech. Coll., 1980. Mem. Am. Soc. Microbiology, Am. Soc. Clin. Pathologists (registered mem.), DAR, Sigma Xi, Sigma Pi Sigma, Beta Beta Beta. Republican. Club: Samoyed Am. Home: 617 N Ash St Mesa AZ 85201 Office: 525 W Brown Rd Mesa AZ 85201

BINSFELD, CONNIE BERUBE, state legislator; b. Munising, Mich., Apr. 18, 1924; d. Omer J. and Elsie (Constance) Berube; B.S., Siena Heights Coll., 1945, D.H.L. (hon.), 1977; postgrad. Wayne State U., 1966-67; m. John E. Binsfeld, July 19, 1947; children—John T., Gregory, Susan, Paul, Michael. County commr., Leelanau County, Mich., 1970-74; mem. Mich. Ho. of Reps., 1974-82. Del., Republican Nat. Conv., 1980. Named Mich. Mother of Year, Mich. Mothers Com., 1977; Northwestern Mich. Coll. fellow. Mem. Nat. Council State Legislators, LWV, Siena Heights Coll. Alumnae Assn. Republican. Roman Catholic. Home: Rural Route 2 Maple City MI 49664 Office: Ho of Reps State Capitol Lansing MI 48909

BINSTOCK, PENNY SCHWARTZ, psychologist, educator; b. N.Y.C.; d. William M. and Hattie (Spitz) Schwartz; B.A. with honors, N.Y. U.; M.A., Queens Coll., 1966; postgrad. New Sch. for Social Research, 1974-76; M.Phil., City U.N.Y., 1979, Ph.D., 1979; m. Morton I. Binstock, Nov. 23, 1960; children—Jeffrey, Jonathan, Jason. Therapist, intake worker L.I. Consultation Center, Rego Park, N.Y., 1973-74; adj. prof., grad. teaching fellow psychology dept. Bklyn. Coll., 1978-79, adj. lectr., 1979, adj. asst. prof., 1980—; adj. asst. prof. psychology Queens Coll., Flushing, N.Y., 1979—; co-dir. Collaborative Counseling Service, Port Washington, N.Y., 1981—; mem. exec. com. soc.-personality program Grad. Center, City U.N.Y., 1978—. Treas., Roslyn Creative Arts Workshop, 1972-73. Mem. Am. Psychol. Assn., N.Y. Acad. Scis., Eastern Psychol. Assn., Am. Horse Show Assn., Nassau-Suffolk Horsemen's Assn., Nat. Psychology Honor Soc., Sigma Xi. Clubs: Shelter Rock Tennis, Turf and Field. Home: 55 Montrose Ct Roslyn NY 11576 Office: Psychology Dept William James Hall Bklyn Coll Bedford and Ave H Brooklyn NY 11210 also Psychology Dept Queens Coll Flushing NY 11367

BIRCH, TERRIE HOLLOWED, hosp. ofcl.; b. Berwyn, Ill., Aug. 7, 1930; d. James Aloysius and Marie (Nohava) Hollowed; B.A. cum laude in Psychology, Rosary Coll., 1974; M.S. in Counseling Psychology, George Williams Coll., 1976; m. John E. Birch, Nov. 4, 1950 (div. Apr. 1969); children—John Edward, Christopher James, Terrie Johnice Birch Kallal, Laurence Patrick. Sec.-treas. John Birch & Co., Lombard, Ill., 1953-66, Terrie Birch & Co., Lombard, 1953-66, Alert Carpentry, Lombard, 1953-66, Durable Masonry, Inc., Lombard, 1953-66, Cherrywood Homes, Lombard, 1953-66; travel counselor, 1969-71; vocat. testing and counselor Women's Inc., Hinsdale, Ill., 1975-78, Office Manpower Planning, DuPage County (Ill.) Center, Wheaton, 1975-78; dir. vol. services Holy Family Hosp., Des Plaines, Ill., 1978—, also mem. aux.; mem. adv. com. Bensenville Home Soc. Ret. Sr. Vol. Program. Meml. and honor chmn., dir. Infant Welfare Soc., Chgo., 1963-65, pres. Western Springs Center, 1967; mem. career adv. council Wheeling (Ill.) High Sch. Mem. Ill. Soc. for Dirs. Vol. Services, Am. Soc. Dirs. Vol. Services, Chgo. Council Dirs. Vol. Services (edn. chmn.), U. Ill. Alumni Assn., AAUW Chgo. Drama League, Mensa, Pi Gamma Mu. Address: 2820 Brindle Ct Northbrook IL 60062

BIRCHETT, JO ANN, govt. ofcl.; b. Emporia, Kans., Feb. 19, 1944; d. Clarence Othel and Wilma Jane (Young) Birchett; B.S., Tex. A&I U., Kingsville, 1967. Cooperative edn. student NASA-Johnson Space Center, Houston, 1963-67, computer programmer, data analyst, 1967—. Mem. Fed. Women's Program com., 1979-81. Mem. AIAA, Am. Fedn. Govt. Employees (women's coordinator 1980-81, treas. 1981—). Democrat. Mem. Christian Ch. Home: Route 2 Box 2222 7510 Sunflower St Pearland TX 77584 Office: NASA Johnson Space Center Houston TX 77058

BIRD, MATHILDE GOODWIN, educator, writer; b. El Dorado, Ark., Sept. 14, 1925; d. Edwin Mark and Annye Franzine (Goodwin) Honan; student Manhattanville Coll., 1943-44; B.S. in Fgn. Service, Georgetown U., 1947; diplomas in French and Russian, U. Paris, 1952; postgrad. in anthropology U. Hawaii, 1958-59, Brandeis U., 1965-70; m. Christopher Bird, Mar. 7, 1954 (div.); children—Kristina Helena Mathilde, Julianne Puakalehuanani, Diana Appleton, Zvia Noelle. Mail clk. and cryptographer Dept. State, 1944-46; jr. accountant, 1946-47; mil. govt. intern, State Dept., Germany, 1947-49; pioneer tchr. French to young children Hanahauoli Sch., Honolulu, 1955-59, Wellesley (Mass.) Sch. System, 1964-67; journalist, arts critic Honolu Advertiser, 1956-57, Wellesley Townsman, 1974-76; tchr., lectr. Old Religion. Named Boston fashion pacesetter, 1968. Mother Grace Ryan scholar Manhattanville Coll., 1943-44; piano student Paul Wittgenstein; Fulbright scholar, 1949-51. Mem. Internat. Folk Music Conf., LWV. Clubs: Country (Wellesley); Pamet Harbor (Truro, Mass.). Contbr. articles to newspapers. Home: 529 Armijo St Santa Fe NM 87501

BIRD, NANCY BRAGG, communications co. exec.; b. Morgan County, Ala., May 27, 1939; d. Ray Donald and Mattie Lou Bragg; B.S., U. Tenn., 1965; m. Robert Lewis Bird, July 1, 1979. Accounting mgr. Ram Broadcasting of Tex., Inc., Dallas, 1970-74, gen. mgr., 1974-81, v.p. Western region, 1981—. Mem. Exec. Women Dallas, Dallas C. of C., Sales and Mktg. Execs. Dallas, Tex. Assn. Radio Systems (exec. sec. 1976-80). Republican. Baptist. Home: PO Box 10373 Dallas TX 75207 Office: Ram Broadcasting of Texas Inc 1330 N Industrial Blvd Dallas TX 75207

BIRD, ROSE ELIZABETH, state chief justice; b. Tucson, Nov. 2, 1936; B.A. magna cum laude, L.I. U., 1958; J.D., U. Calif. at Berkeley, 1965. Admitted to Calif. bar, 1966; clk. to chief justice Nev. Supreme Ct., 1965-66; dep. pub. defender, sr. trial dep., chief appellate div. Santa Clara (Calif.) County, 1966-74; tchr. Stanford U. Law Sch., 1972-74; sec. Calif. Agr. and Services Agy., also mem. governor's cabinet, 1975-77; chief justice Calif. Supreme Ct., 1977—. Chmn. Calif. Jud. Council, Commn. Jud. Appointments Calif.; pres. bd. dirs. Hastings Coll. Law, U. Calif., San Francisco; bd. councilors U. So. Calif. Law Center, 1975-77. Past bd. assos. San Fernando Valley Youth Found.; mem. Western regional selection panel President's Commn. White House Fellows, 1976-77. Ford Found. fellow, 1960. Democrat. Address: 350 McAllister St San Francisco CA 94102 *

BIRD, SUZANNE CRAFTS, interior design co. exec.; b. Darien, Conn., May 27, 1940; d. John Andrew and Lucretia (Bunel) Crafts; B.F.A., R.I. Sch. Design, 1962; m. Malcolm T. Bird, Jan. 5, 1963; children—Elizabeth, Melinda. Staff designer Rablen-West Co., Vero Beach, Fla., 1970-71, Ted von Hemert, Newport Beach, Calif., 1972-73; gen. mgr. Herndon Furniture (Va.), 1973-74; founder, owner Suzanne Bird Interiors Inc., Delray Beach, Fla., 1974—, Fashion Floors, Inc., Delray Beach. Mem. Am. Soc. Interior Designers. Republican. Methodist. Clubs: Womens Exec (pres. 1982-83), Womens Republican (v.p. 1978-79). Home: 724 Sunshine Dr Delray Beach FL 33444 Office: 1122 E Atlantic Ave Delray Beach FL 33444

BIRDSALL, NATALIE AUDIBERT, writer; b. Washington, Jan. 31, 1919; d. Xavier Marie and Natalie (Whiting) Audibert; student Rockland Community Coll., 1967-68, New Sch. for Social Research, 1968-71; m. Gregg C. Birdsall, Oct. 24, 1945; children—Marie, Isabelle. Research worker Newsweek, 1944-45, Film Counselors, Inc., 1945-46. Bd. govs. Warner House Assn. (nat. hist. landmark), treas., 1973-77. Mem. Seacoast, Dover writers. Ballad author: New Hampshire Profiles, 1975; also articles in various mags. Home: Portsmouth Ave New Castle NH 03854

BIRDWHISTELL, MIRIAM COLEMAN, social work adminstr., educator; b. Hancock County, Ohio, Oct. 1, 1919; d. Gale Talmadge and Ruth (Eckleberry) Coleman; B.A., Miami U., Oxford, Ohio, 1941; postgrad. (scholar), Sch. Social Service Adminstrn., U. Chgo., 1941-44; M.S.S.W., U. Louisville, 1954; Ed.D., U. Va., 1969; m. Ray L. Birdwhistell, Nov. 21, 1941; children—Jill Read, Nan Mead; m. 2d, Thomas Azumbrado, June 19, 1976. Clin. social worker Children's Meml. Hosp., Chgo., 1943-45, U. Louisville Gen. Hosp., 1949-51; dir. social work King's Daus. Hosp., Louisville, 1951-56; asst. prof. grad. dept. social work Bryn Mawr (Pa.) U., 1964-65; assoc. prof. social work Med. Sch., Temple U., Phila., 1964-65; prof., chmn. div. med. center social work U. Va., Charlottesville, 1965—, professorial lectr. dept. sociology, 1970—, cons. to Nat. Found., 1970-73; vis. prof. dept. social work, Plymouth, Eng., 1981. Founder 1st chpt. Zero Population Growth in Va., 1970; mem. adv. com. Charlottesville Shelter for Abused Women, 1977-81; advocate for reform child abuse legislation, Va. Gen. Assembly, 1975; mem. PTA, Loyal Temperance League. Grantee, Va. regional Med. Program, 1975-76, Va. Dept. Welfare and Instns., 1975-80. Mem. AAUP, Nat. Assn. Social Workers (nat. sec., 1976-78, pres. Va. chpt., 1976-77, named Social Worker of Yr., Va. chpt., 1977, rep. of orgn. trip to China, 1977), Soc. Hosp. Social Work Dirs. (nat. nominating com.,

1972-73), Acad. Cert. Social Workers (charter), Council on Social Work Edn., Phi Beta Kappa. Clubs: Va. Women's Polit. Caucus, Altrusa. Author: The Natural History of a Medical Social Work Administrator, 1981. Office: Univ Virginia Medical Center Box 223 Charlottesville VA 22901

BIRK, SUSAN ARNOLD, mktg. rep.; b. N.Y.C., Apr. 16, 1952; d. John Henry and Urania Marie (Bernadas) A.; B.A., Kirkland Coll., 1974; m. John Richard Birk; 1 son, John Richard. Systems engr. IBM Corp., 1974-75, mktg. rep., Syracuse, N.Y., 1975-78, nat. account mgr., N.Y.C., 1978-80, mktg. adminstr., Palo Alto, Calif., 1980-82, large system mktg. NAD div., San Francisco, 1982—. Republican. Roman Catholic. Home: 730 Spring Dr Walnut Creek CA 94598 Office: 425 Market St San Francisco CA

BIRKENSTEIN, LILLIAN RAY (MRS. GEORGE ULMAN BIRKENSTEIN), ornithologist; b. Phila., Oct. 9, 1900; d. Morris and Stella (Schloss) Rosenzweig; B.A. (coll. scholar), Wellesley Coll., 1922; student U. Pa., 1920-21, Northwestern U., 1936-37, Instituto Allende (Mexico), 1951-55, Academia Hispana-Americana (Mexico), 1960-68; m. George Ulman Birkenstein, Sept. 2, 1922; children—Dorothy (Mrs. Jose Vidargas), Jean (Mrs. Atlee Washington). Pres., Anker-Holth Mfg. Co., Port Huron, Mich., 1944-51; researcher local Spanish and tribal Indian names of Mexican birds, 1952—; vol. librarian, San Miguel Allende, 1954-64, tchr. ornithology Institute Allende, San Miguel Allende, 1973. Bd. dirs. Public Library San Miguel Allende, 1954-67, Hot Breakfasts for Sch. Children, San Miguel, 1957-61. Mem. San Miguel Allende Audubon Soc. (founder 1967, pres. 1967-71, dir. 1971—), Am. Soc. Mfg. Engrs. (hon. life), Am. Ornithologists Union, Cooper Ornithol. Soc., Linnaean Soc., Wilson Ornithol. Soc., Cornell Lab. Ornithology, Mexican Natural History Soc. (dir. 1972—), Mexican Ornitholog. Soc. (dir.), Internat. Com. for Bird Preservation (treas. Mexican sect. 1968—), Women's Aux. AIME (hon.). Clubs: San Miguel Allende Garden (1st v.p. 1971—); Golf Malanquin. Author: Native Names of Mexican Birds, 1981. Contbr. articles to various publs. Home: Tenerias 45 San Miguel Allende Guanajuato Mexico

BIRKHOLZ, GABRIELLA SONJA, speechwriter; b. Chgo., Apr. 11, 1938; d. Ladislav E. and Sonja (Kosner) Becvar; student Northwestern U., U. Wis., Alverno Coll., 1977—. Editor, owner Fox Lake (Wis.) Republican, 1962-65, MacFarland (Wis.) Community Life and Monona (Wis.) Community Herald, 1965-69; reporter Waukesha (Wis.) Daily Freeman, 1969-71; community relations Waukesha County Tech. Inst., 1971-73; publs. editor J. I. Case Co., Racine, Wis., 1973-80; v.p. Image Mgmt., Milw., 1980-82; speechwriter Miller Brewing Co., Milw., 1982—; guest lectr., resource person Alverno Coll., Milw., U. Wis., Parkside. Bd. dirs. Girl Scouts U.S.A., Racine, Big Sisters of Racine. Mem. Internat. Assn. Bus. Communicators (accredited), Women in Communications, Sigma Delta Chi. Contbr. articles to profl. jours. Home: 4405 Kennedy Dr Racine WI 53404 Office: 3939 W Highland Blvd Milwaukee WI 53208

BIRKITT, LINDA ANN AYLMER, phys. therapist; b. Oakland, Calif., Feb. 8, 1946; d. William Stanley and Phyllis Jane (King) Aylmer; student U. Md. at Munich, W.Ger., 1967-68; B.S., Calif. State Poly. U., 1963-69; M.A. (HEW scholar), U. So. Calif., 1973; m. John C. Birkitt, Sept. 13, 1980; children—Andra, Robert, Lowell, Daniélle. Staff phys. therapist Valley Presbyn. Hosp., Van Nuys, Calif., 1973-75; chief therapist Ingleside Mental Health Center, Rosemead, Calif., 1975-79, mem. Speakers Bur., 1976-79; lectr. Santa Monica City Coll., 1976-79; asst. chief phys. therapist Alhambra (Calif.) Community Hosp., 1979-81; pvt. practice phys. therapy, San Juan Capistrano, Calif., 1981—. Vol. fire fighter, El Cariso Village, Calif., 1979—; organizer village home owners El Cariso Village, Lake Elsinore, Calif., 1981. Mem. AAUW, Nat. Assn. Female Execs., St. Margaret's PTA. Episcopalian. Research in motivation as a factor in performance of phys. skill, verticality perception distortion in hemiplegic patients. Home: 32536 Ortega Hwy El Cariso Village Lake Elsinore CA 92330 Office: PO Box 1593 San Juan Capistrano CA 92693

BIRKLE, LYDIA SCHRACK BLOEDORN, audiologist; b. Orleans, Nebr.; d. Charles F. and Zoe (Schrack) Bloedorn; B.A., U. Denver, 1927, M.A., 1959; m. David L. Birkle, July 2, 1932 (dec. 1957). Tchr. high sch., Platteville, Colo., 1927-31; mgr. clin. audiology Colo. Hearing and Speech Center, Denver, 1959—. Mem. Acad. Rehabilitative Audiology, Am., Colo. speech and hearing assns., Am. Audiology Soc., Am. Tinnitus Assn., Pi Beta Phi. Congregationalist. Club: Centurion of Deafness Research Found. Home: 1901 Leyden St Denver CO 80220 Office: 4280 Hale Pkwy Denver CO 80220

BISAGNO, IRENE DRUCILLE, retail store owner; b. Sioux Falls, S.D., Aug. 2, 1934; d. Marshall Alexander and Edna Marie (Smith) Frank; student public schs., Santa Rosa, Calif.; m. Salvatore Bisagno, Nov. 8, 1952; children—Salvatore D., Robert L., Charles M., George H. Co-owner, Bisagno's Carrousel of Collectibles, Bisagno Enterprises, Santa Rosa, Calif. Active 4-H Club. Mem. Citizens for Law and Order, Air Craft Owners and Pilots Assn. Republican. Office: 1509 Willowside Rd Santa Rosa CA 95401

BISBEE, JOYCE EVELYN, home economist, cons.; b. Portage, Wis., May 15, 1941; d. Orris Dean and Helen Paulina (Golz) B.; B.S. in Home Econs. Edn., U. Wis., Stout, 1963; M.Ed., U. N.C., Greensboro, 1971. Tchr. home econs. Oshkosh (Wis.) Area Public Schs., 1963-64, coordinator home econs., 1968-74; extension home economist U. Wis. Coop. Extension, Racine County, 1964-68; mgr. ednl. relations J.C. Penney Co. Inc., N.Y.C., 1974-78; v.p., dir. Consumer Affairs Group, Creamer Dickson Basford, Inc., N.Y.C., 1978-81; pres. JE Bisbee, Creative Resources, N.Y.C., 1981—. Recipient Alumni Disting. Service award U. Wis., Stout, 1978. Mem. Am. Home Econs. Assn. (v.p. coop. relations, 1977-79), Home Economists in Bus., Soc. Consumer Affairs Profls. in Bus., Am. Soc. Profl. Cons., Advt. Women N.Y. Lutheran. Club: Altrusa. Office: 245 E 63d St New York NY 10021

BISCHOFF, MONICA, electron microscopist; b. Elizabeth, N.J., Mar. 2, 1944; d. Edward Benedict and Veronica (Kryszczuk) Zacharczyk; student Union Coll., Cranford, N.J., 1963-67. Lab. technician IPI Interchemical Corp., Elizabeth, 1962; sr. research technician Bristol-Myers Co., Hillside, N.J., 1963-75; tech. adminstr., electron microscopist Inst. Neurotoxicology Albert Einstein Coll. Medicine, Bronx, N.Y., 1975—; presenter papers profl. confs.; cons. in field. Mem. N.Y. Soc. Electron Microscopy. Contbr. articles to profl. jours. Home: 114 Madison Ave Apt 2 Englewood NJ 07631 Office: 1410 Pelham Pkwy Rm 518 Kennedy Center Albert Einstein Coll Medicine Bronx NY 10461

BISHOP, BLANCHE ELKINS, banker; b. Rogersville, Tenn., July 12, 1932; d. Hersle Etter and Virginia Ruth (Pearson) Elkins; student Whitney Bus., 1951-52; cert. Am. Inst. Banking, 1981; m. Paul Wess Bishop, July 6, 1952. Asst. trust officer First Eastern Nat. Bank, Kingsport, Tenn., 1973-78, trust officer, 1978—. Mem. planned giving com. Tusculum Coll., Greenville, Tenn. Mem. Tri-Cities Estate Planning Council (sec., v.p.), Nat. Assn. Bank Women (treas., vice chmn., nominating com. chmn., chmn. East Tenn. State Group, 1977-78, chmn. public affairs Tenn. State Council 1981-82, mem. exec. bd., module leader, Memphis 1979). Clubs: Altrusa, Women of Moose. Home: 201 Bloomington Dr Kingsport TN 27660 Office: First Eastern Nat Bank PO Box 1981 Kingsport TN 37662

BISHOP, DORIS JACKSON, govt. ofcl.; b. Rahway, N.J., June 26, 1927; d. Alfred Charles and Ella Mae (Snyder) Jackson; student Parsons Sch. Design, 1945, U. Nev., 1949, Coll. Charleston, 1971-72; m. Frank Davis Bishop (dec.). Statis. officer, mgmt. analyst Naval Supply Center, Charleston, S.C., 1958-73; dep. command EEO officer, Fed. Women's Program coordinator Naval Supply Systems Command, Washington, 1973-75; coordinator, dep. dir. EEO/Fed. Women's Program, Mil. Dist. Washington, U.S. Army, 1975-79; internal EEO program mgr. FHWA, Denver, 1979-80; regional EEO officer Nat. Park Service, Denver, 1980—. Bd. dirs. Amberwick Homeowners Assn., 1980-82, Greenhouse Condominium, Alexandria, Va., 1977-79. Served with USAF, 1951-53. Named Career Woman of Yr., Bus. and Profl. Women, Charleston, 1967; recipient Outstanding Performance awards, U.S. Navy, U.S. Army. Mem. Federally Employed Women, Am. Bus. Women's Assn., Women's Equity Action League, Am. Soc. Public Adminstrn., Navy League U.S. Clubs: Ports of Call Travel, Order Eastern Star. Columnist, Alex Port Packet, weekly, 1977-79. Home: 128 S Holman Way Golden CO 80401 Office: 655 Parfet St Denver CO 80225

BISHOP, FRANCES BLACKBURN, civic worker; b. West Palm Beach, Fla., Mar. 3, 1925; d. Julius Magath and Adele Eleanor (Berg) Blackburn; B.Mus.Ed., Fla. State U., 1945; postgrad. Columbia, 1959-62; M.A. in Musicology, U. Mo., 1958; m. Ben Bishop, May 20, 1946 (div. 1952); 1 dau., Jewel. Music tchr., Joiner, Ark., 1946-47, Franklin Square, N.Y., 1957-69; asst. placement dir. of internat. counselor exchange program. Assn. for World Travel Exchange, N.Y.C., 1970-74; exec. sec. Army Relief Soc., N.Y.C., 1975-76; adminstrv. sec. Am. Music Center, 1977-78; editorial asst. Sci. Digest, 1978—; violinist Bloomingdale Chamber Orch.; tchr. English adult evening classes, N.Y.C., 1972-75; mem. Met. Greek Chorale. Vol. Internat. Center. Mem. Soc. Asian Music. Home: 36 W 84 St New York NY 10024

BISHOP, ISABEL (MRS. HAROLD G. WOLFF), artist; b. Cin., Mar. 3, 1902; d. John Remsen and Anna Bartram (Newbold) Bishop; ed. Wicker Art Sch., Detroit, 1917-18, N.Y. Sch. Applied Design for Women, 1918-20, Art Students League N.Y., 1920-22, 1927-30; A.F.D. (hon.), Moore Inst., Phila., Bates Coll., Maine, Syracuse U., 1982; m. Harold George Wolff, Aug. 9, 1934. Instr. life painting and composition Art Students League, N.Y.C., 1936-37; instr. Snowhegan Sch. Painting and Sculpture, 1957, lectr., 1957, 60, 62, 64, 66; represented in Mus. Bibliotheque Nationale, Paris, Victoria and Albert Mus., London, Des Moines Art Center, Brit. Mus., Met. Mus., Whitney Mus., others, also art galleries, collections Paul Sachs, Johnson Collection, others; exhibited expns.; 12 one-man shows in N.Y.C., one-man show Berkshire Mus., Pittsfield, Mass., 1957; retrospective exhbns. Whitney Mus. Art, 1975, U. Ariz., 1974, Wichita (Kans.) State U., 1974. Recipient awards including W.A. Clark Prize, Bronze medal, Corcoran Gallery, Washington, 1945; Mrs. H. S. Noyes and Am. Artists Group prizes, 1947; Benjamin Franklin fellow Royal Soc. Art, 1965; first Altman prize NAD, 1967; Asso. mem. NAD, 1940; elected Nat. Academician, 1941. Fellow Royal Soc. Arts London; mem. Nat. Inst. Arts and Letters, Am. Acad. Arts and Letters, Am. Soc. Painters, Sculptors and Gravers, Soc. Am. Etchers, Nat. Arts Club, Phila. Water Color Club, Am. Group Cosmopolitan Club. Studio: 41 Union Sq W New York NY 10003

BISHOP, JOYCE ANN, coll. counselor, educator; b. West Mansfield, Ohio, June 16, 1935; d. Frederic J. and Marjorie Vere (Stephens) Armentrout; A.B., Albion Coll., 1956; M.A., Western Mich. U., 1969, postgrad., 1972-82; children—Belinda Lee, Thomas James. Tchr. phys. edn., health and cheerleading Walled Lake (Mich.) Jr. High Sch., 1956-58; instr. slimnastics adult edn. Milw. Public Schs., 1959-65; demonstrator, co. rep. Polaroid Corp., Cambridge, Mass., 1960-81; research asst. fetal electrocardiography Marquette U., Milw., 1962-64; tchr. phys. edn., health and cheerleading Brown Deer (Wis.) High Sch., 1963-65; instr. slimnastics adult edn., instr. volleyball Lakeview High Sch., Battle Creek, Mich., 1966—; dir. student activities, counselor, asst. prof. Kellogg Community Coll., Battle Creek, 1971—, now transfer counselor. Sec. adult bd. Teens, Inc., 1965-68. Cert. social worker. Recipient Master Teaching award Lakeview Schs., 1969; mem. Battle Creek Leadership Acad. Mem. Mich. Assn. Collegiate Registrars and Admissions Officers (pres. 1979-80), Am. Assn. Collegiate Registrars and Admissions Officers, Am. Personnel and Guidance Assn., Am. Coll. Personnel Assn., Mich. Personnel and Guidance Assn., Mich. Coll. Personnel Assn., Mich. Assn. Women Deans, Adminstrs. and Counselors, Mich. Assn. Coll. Admissions Counselors, AAUW, Alpha Chi Omega, Beta Beta Beta. Club: Battle Creek Altrusa. Home: 721 Eastfield Dr Battle Creek MI 49015 Office: 450 North Ave Battle Creek MI 49016

BISHOP, MARY LUCILLE, theater restoration cons.; b. Sapulpa, Okla., Mar. 18, 1918; d. Charles George and Lizzie Pearl (Little) York; A.A., Kansas City Jr. Coll., 1934-36; m. Kenneth Lawrence Bishop, June 5, 1937; 1 dau., Robin Bishop Allen. Office mgr. Am. Mut. Liability Ins. Co., Kansas City, Mo., 1939-42; sec. to pres. Devonian Oil Co., Midland, Tex., 1942-44; adminstrv. asst. to pres. Shawan & Assos., Columbus, Ohio, 1966-76; chmn. bldg. and restoration com. bd. trustees Historic Ohio Theatre, 1969-79; dir. bldg., restoration and grants Columbus Assn. for the Performing Arts, Columbus, 1979—; theater restoration and preservation cons. Mem. exec. com., bd. dirs. Columbus Symphony Orch., 1974-80; v.p. Columbus Assn. for the Performing Arts, 1971-74. Republican. Clubs: Columbus Metropolitan, Scioto Country. Home: 1380 La Rochelle Dr Columbus OH 43221 Office: 29 E State St Columbus OH 43215

BISHOP, WILLALMA BROWN, banker; b. Whiteside, Mo., Sept. 29, 1926; d. William Joseph and Alma Fay (Horton) Brown; student public schs.; m. Glen G. Bishop, June 26, 1964; 1 son, Kevin Lail. With Boatmens Bank of Troy (Mo.), 1945—, v.p., 1977—. Treas., Lincoln County Youth Fair, 1956—, Lincoln County Heart Assn., 1956—; mem. adv. com. sch. dist. bus. dept. Lincoln County, 1979—. Mem. Am. Inst. Banking, Troy C. of C. (treas. 1952—; Woman of Yr. award 1964), Troy Bus. and Profl. Women's Club (pres. 1956; Woman of Yr. award 1962). Democrat. Presbyterian. Clubs: Martha Dyer Federated (past pres.), Order Eastern Star. Home: 411 W College St Troy MO 63379 Office: 200 Main St Troy MO 63379

BISORDI, EILEEN MARY, ednl. adminstr.; b. Jamaica, N.Y., Nov. 29, 1945; d. William J. and Florence (Smith) Quinn; B.A., SUNY, Potsdam, 1968; M.A., Columbia U., 1969, M.Ed., 1976; m. Richard Bisordi, May 31, 1969; children—Anthony, Lisa. Tchr. spl. edn. Soundview Sch., Yorktown Heights, N.Y., 1968-71; dir. spl. edn. Margaret Chapman Sch., Hawthorne, N.Y., 1971-76, co-dir., 1976-78, exec. dir., 1979—; adj. instr. Westchester Community Coll., 1976—; cons. in field. Bd. dirs. N.Y. State Poets in the Schs., 1977—; mem. exec. com. N.Y. Spl. Olympics, 1977-79, bd. dirs., 1977-79, area 3 coordinator, 1971-78, regional coordinator N.E., 1978-79. Mem. N.Y. Assn. Pvt. Residential Facilities, Council for Exceptional Children, Council Adminstrn. Spl. Edn., Am. Assn. for Mental Deficiency, Kappa Delta Pi. Roman Catholic. Home: 48 Gurley Rd Stamford CT 06902 Office: 5 Bradhurst Ave Hawthorne NY 10532

BISOULIS, BECKY, fashion designer; b. Chgo.; d. Christ A. and Catherine (Marlas) B.; B.A., Northwestern U. Fashion coordinator Marshall Field & Co., 1966-68; creative advt. ofcl. Adrisin-Toni Co., 1969-72; fashion editor Sphere Mag., 1972-75; fashion designer B.B. Designs, Chgo., 1975—. Recipient Prix de Cachet, 1979. Office: Becky Bisoulis Inc 215 W Superior St Chicago IL 60611

BISSELL, BETTY DICKSON, stockbroker; b. Salina, Kans., Sept. 9, 1932; d. Henry Shields and Alta May Dickson; student U. Kans., 1949-52; cert. fin. planner, Coll. Fin. Planning, 1976; m. Buford Lyle Bissell, Jr., Nov. 1, 1952; 1 son, Bradford Dickson. With Dean Witter Reynolds Inc., Menlo Park, Calif., 1975—, asst. br. mgr., 1978—, asso. v.p. investments, 1980—. Pres. Jr. League San Jose (Calif.), 1963-64. Mem. Internat. Assn. Fin. Planners, Peninsula Stock and Bond Club, Pi Beta Phi. Republican. Episcopalian. Clubs: Commonwealth Calif., Summit League (Saratoga-Los Gatos), Jr. League (San Jose, Calif.). Office: 720 Santa Cruz Ave Menlo Park CA 94025

BISSELL, LECLAIR, physician; b. Ft. Monroe, Va., May 18, 1928; d. Clayton L. and LeClair (Gaillard) B.; B.A., U. Colo., 1950; M.S., Columbia U., 1952, M.D., 1963. Intern, then resident in medicine Roosevelt Hosp., N.Y.C., 1963-66, fellow endocrinology and metabolism, 1966-68; student Yale U. Sch. Alcohol Studies, 1970; faculty, School of Alcohol Studies, Rutgers U., School of Alcohol Studies, Salt Lake City; mem. staff Roosevelt Hosp., 1968—, attending physician depts. medicine and psychiatry, 1975—; asst. prof. clin. medicine Columbia U. Med. Sch., 1972-82; freelance writer, cons., 1982—; coordinator, then chief Smithers Alcoholism Treatment and Tng. Center, Roosevelt Hosp., 1968-79; cons., researcher, Edgehill Newport Inc., Beacon Hill Rd., Newport, R.I., alcoholism treatment, 1981-82 (pres. 1979-81); adv. council Nat. Inst. Alcohol Abuse and Alcoholism, 1978—; adv. comn. Status of Women, state of R.I., 1981—; mem. Com. Women and Alcoholism N.Y. State, Regional Coalition Spl. Needs Women Who Have Alcohol and Drug Problems; mem. task force alcoholism Carter Mental Health Commn.; radio and TV appearances. Recipient Merit award Public Health Assn. N.Y.C., 1976; R.I. Women of Year award, R.I. Bus. & Prfnl. Women's Club, 1981; Mel Shulstad award, Nat. Assn. Alcoholism Counselors, 1981. Mem. Assn. Labor-Mgmt. Adminstrs. and Cons. Alcoholism, Alcohol and Drug Problems Assn. N.Am., AAAS, Am. Assn. Suicidology, Am. Med. Soc. Alcoholism (v.p., pres. 1981—); AMA panel on alcoholism; Research Soc. on Alcoholism; Columbia U. Seminar Drugs and Soc., Harvey Soc., N.Y. State Assn. Councils Alcoholism, The Other Victims of Alcoholism, Women's Med. Assn. N.Y.C., N.Y. State Med. Soc. (past chmn. physicians com.). Club: Women's City (N.Y.C.). Author, co-author handbooks, audio-visual materials on alcoholism, contbr. articles to profl. jours. Address: Edgehill Newport Inc Beacon Hill Rd Newport RI 02840

BISSETT, LESLEY DRUCILLA, fin. co. exec.; b. Winnipeg, Man., Can., May 26, 1935; came to U.S., 1957, naturalized, 1962; d. R.R. and Maybelle (Poucher) Goodwin; cert. fin. planning Coll. Fin. Planning, 1977; children—John W., Richard L., Tom. J. Profl. ice skater, 1953-61, Western Can. champion, 1951; featured skater Shipstads & Johnson Ice Follies, 1957-61; mgr. mktg. adminstrn. Univ. Group, Long Beach, Calif., 1975-79; regional v.p. Keystone Massachusetts, Inc., Los Angeles, 1979-81; regional v.p. Integrated Resources Equity Corp., 1981—. Mem. Long Beach Bus. and Profl. Women's Assn. (pres. 1978-79, Woman of Yr. 1978), Los Angeles Fin. Planners Assn. (v.p. 1980—), Internat. Assn. Fin. Planners (nat. conv. speaker 1979, 82), Inst. Cert. Fin. Planners, Internat. Platform Assn. Presbyterian. Contbr. articles on fin. planning Women in Life Ins. Selling, The Nat. Businesswoman, The Grad. Woman. Office: 5347 S Valentia Way Englewood CO 80111

BISSONNETTE, KATHLEEN KUK, energy cons.; b. Claremont, N.H., Oct. 9, 1950; d. Stanley Joseph and Elizabeth (Boncarosky) Kuk; student Chatham Coll., 1968-70; B.A., Clark U., 1972; M.S., Mont. State U., 1973; Ph.D., W.Va. U., 1977; m. Gary K. Bissonnette, June 10, 1972. Instr. psychology W.Va. U., Morgantown, 1974-75; research asst. office research and devel. W.Va. U., 1974-78; extension specialist-energy W.Va. Energy Extension Service, Morgantown, 1978—; cons. dept. civil engring., 1977—. Mem. Am. Psychol. Assn., Soc. Psychol. Study Social Issues, W.Va. Extension Women's Assn., W.Va. County Agts. Assn., W.Va. Assn. Extension 4-H Agts. Democrat. Roman Catholic. Home: 472 Lawnview Dr Morgantown WV 26505 Office: B-3 Knapp Hall WVa Univ Morgantown WV 26506

BITA, LILI, author, actress; b. Zante, Greece, Dec. 23, 1935; came to U.S., 1959, naturalized, 1969; d. George and Eleni (Makri) Bitas; fine arts degree in music, Greek Conservatory of Music, 1954, in drama, Athens Sch. Drama, 1956; M.A. in Drama, U. Miami, 1978; m. Robert Zaller, Jan. 19, 1968; children—Philip, Kimon. Performer in Greek repertory Art Theatre, Civic Theatre and Royal Palace Garden Theatre, 1955-57; instr. Emporia (Kans.) Coll., 1960-62, U. Toledo, 1963-65, Bklyn. Conservatory of Music, 1967-68; guest lectr., condr. master classes, performer classic theatre various univs., U.S. and Europe, 1970—; actress radio, TV and stage; writer; books include: Steps on the Earth, 1955; Lightning in the Flesh, 1968; Furies, 1969; Zero Hour, 1971; Blood Sketches, 1973; Sacrifice, Exile, Night, 1976; Fleshfire: New and Selected Love Poems, 1980; translator: Anais Nin, A Spy in the House of Love, 1974, Delta of Venus, 1983; anthologies include: City Lights Anthology, 1974; Contemporary Greek Women Poets, 1979; guest dir. Fla. Internat. U., Aegean Inst. Women's Studies; cons. Dade County Poetry in the Schs. Program; charitable performances include ACLU, Ethical Culture Soc., Nat. Women's Week, Poetry Therapy Program, Odyssey House, Jackson Meml. Hosp. Italian Inst. Study fellow, 1956-57; Circle in the Sq. Theatre fellow, 1967-68; recipient group performance award Austin Theatre, 1978. Mem. Southeastern Theatre Conf., Alpha Psi Omega. Greek Orthodox. Club: Order of Knights of St. Dennis of Zante. Home and Office: 5901 SW 51st St Miami FL 33155

BITKER, MARJORIE MARKS (MRS. BRUNO VOLTAIRE BITKER), writer, editor; b. N.Y.C., Feb. 9, 1901; d. Cecil Alexander and Rachel (Fox) Marks; A.B. magna cum laude (Caroline Duror Meml. fellow), Barnard Coll., 1921; M.A., Columbia U., 1922; m. James C. Jacobson, 1922 (div. 1942); children—Emilie J. Jacobi, Margaret J. Strange, Elizabeth J. Hahn; m. 2d, John C. Mayer, Oct. 24, 1942 (dec. June 1945); m. 3d, Bruno Voltaire Bitker, Oct. 10, 1957. Free lance writer, 1922—; editor Farrar Straus, N.Y.C., 1946-47, G.P. Putnam's Sons, N.Y.C., 1947-53, David McKay Co., N.Y.C., 1953-55; now editorial cons., book reviewer, feature writer. Lectr., Hunter Coll., Coll. City N.Y., 1949-53; Women's Chair for Humanistic Studies, Marquette U., 1972-73. Mem. pres.'s council Alverno Coll., 1975-77; bd. visitors U. Wis., 1962-68; alumnae trustee Barnard Coll., 1964-68, Barnard-in-Milw.; bd. dirs. Friends Wis. Libraries. Recipient Barnard Alumnae Recognition award, 1978. Mem. AAUW, Women's Nat. Book Assn., Nat. Critics Circle, Women in Communications, Bookfellows Milw. (pres. 1971-73, dir.), Council Wis. Writers (dir. 1971-77), Phi Beta Kappa. Author: (novels) Gold of Evening, 1975, A Different Flame, 1976; contbr. articles and book revs. to mags. and newspapers. Address: 2330 E Back Bay St Milwaukee WI 53202

BITTERMAN, JOAN ASELTINE, coll. adminstr.; b. Evanston, Ill., Mar. 25, 1954; d. James Merrill and Lorraine Elizabeth (Hinks) A.; B.A., Aurora Coll., 1976; M.S.Ed., No. Ill. U., 1982, now postgrad. Asst. to registrar Ill. Benedictine Coll., Lisle, Ill., 1976-77; asst. registrar George Williams Coll., Downers Grove, Ill., 1977-79; dir. acad. advisement Aurora (Ill.) Coll., 1979—. Mem. Nat. Acad. Advisement Assn., Ill. Assn. Coll. Registrars and Admissions Officers, Adult Edn. Assn. Home: 872 Hill St Glen Ellyn IL 60137 Office: 347 Gladstone Ave Aurora IL 60507

BITTERMAN, MARY GAYLE FOLEY, state exec.; b. San Jose, Calif., May 29, 1944; d. John Dennis and Zoe Joyce (Hames) Foley; student

Dominican Coll. San Rafael, Calif., 1962-64, Georgetown U. Sch. Fgn. Service, 1965-66; B.A., U. Santa Clara, 1966; M.A., Bryn Mawr Coll., 1968, Ph.D., 1971; m. Morton Edward Bitterman, June 26, 1967; 1 dau., Sarah Fleming. Research assoc., project mgr. Environ. Simulation Lab., U. Hawaii, Honolulu, 1971-72, project mgr., 1972-74; gen. mgr. Hawaii Pub. Broadcasting Authority, Honolulu, 1974-80; dir. Voice of Am., Washington, 1980-81; dir. Hawaii Dept. Commerce and Consumer Affairs, Honolulu, 1981—; bd. dirs. East-West Center, Honolulu, 1975-80, Dillingham Corp., Honolulu, 1979-80; dir. Japan-U.S. TV Execs. Commn., 1976-80. Historian, Hawaii Democratic Com., 1971-72, vice chmn., 1972-74; U.S. del. UN Mid-Decade Conf. on Women, Copenhagen, 1979; trustee St. Andrew's Priory, Honolulu, 1982—. Recipient Outstanding Young Women of Am. award Hawaii C. of C., 1976. Mem. Nat. Acad. Pub. Adminstrn., Honolulu Community Media Council, Nat. Assn. Ins. Commrs., Conf. State Banking Suprs., Hawaii Jud. Council. Home: 229 Kaalawai Pl Honolulu HI 96816 Office: PO Box 541 Honolulu HI 96809

BITTERS, BARBARA AUDREY, women's issues advisor; b. Madison, Wis., Jan. 28, 1950; d. Eugene Arthur and Constance Winnefred (Denison) B.; B.A., U. Wis., 1972, M.S.W., 1975. Lectr., U. Wis. Women's Studies Program, 1976—; sex equity coordinator Dept. Public Instrn., State of Wis., 1978-79, asst. program dir. equal edn. programs, 1978; spl. advisor on women's issues Office Vocat. and Adult Edn., U.S. Dept. Edn., Washington, 1979—. Mem. Am. Vocat. Assn., Wis. Assn. for Vocat. and Adult Edn., Vocat. Edn. Equity Council, NOW, Nat. Women's Studies Assn., Nat. Assn. Advancement Black Americans in Vocat. Edn. Office: 7th and D Sts SW Room 5128 Washington DC 20202

BITTINGER, DOROTHY ROBERTA, nurse; b. Baltimore, Nov. 9, 1949; d. William Edward and Helen Roberta (Kirkpatrick) Drechsler; B.A., U. Md., 1971, B.S.N., 1974, postgrad 1979—. Nurse, ICU, U. Md., Balt., 1974-77; staff nurse ICU, CCU, Johns Hopkins Hosp., Balt., 1978; nurse clinician CCU, Balt. City Hosps., 1978-79; cardiac rehab. specialist Greater Balt. Med. Center, Balt., 1980—. Mem. Am. Assn. Critical Care Nurses, Am. Nurses Assn., Am. Heart Assn. Office: 6701 N Charles St Baltimore MD 21204

BITTNER, BARBARA NEWMAN, ednl. adminstr.; b. Pitts., May 4, 1931; d. Daniel Stephen and Hallie Harper (Wager) Newman; B.A., U. Pitts., 1953; M.Ed., Fla. Atlantic U., 1966; 1 son, Benjamin J. Lectr. dept. speech U. Pitts., 1951-53; sec. to v.p. Farmers Bank of Pompano, Pompano Beach, Fla., 1956-57; tchr. Hillsboro Country Day Sch., Pompano Beach, 1957-68; tchr., div. chmn. A.D. Henderson U. Sch., 1968-73, dir., 1973—. Mem. Am. Assn. Sch. Adminstrs., Assn. Supervision and Curriculum Devel., Nat. Assn. Lab. Schs., Nat., Fla. assns. gifted children, Phi Delta Kappa. Clubs: Pilot (Ft. Lauderdale, Fla.); Torch (Boca Raton, Fla.). Home: 4420 W Tradewinds Ave Lauderdale by the Sea FL 33308 Office: 500 NW 20th St Boca Raton FL 33431

BITTNER, JENNIE KATHRYN, counselor; b. Uniontown, Pa., Apr. 17, 1930; d. August Fritz Ernest Bittner and Kathryn Blanche (Shaw) Bittner Gavorchik; B.S. in Edn., Calif. State Tchrs. Coll., 1953; postgrad. U. Pitts., 1952-53; M.A. in Edn., W.Va. U., 1957. Lab. technician dept. research medicine U. Pitts., 1951-53; math. tchr. West Deer Twp. Sch. Dist., 1953-56; with Albert Gallatin Area Sch. Dist., Uniontown, Pa., 1956—, math. tchr. Fairchance Boro High Sch., 1956-58, Fairchance-Georges Joint High Sch., 1958-60, counselor Fairchance-Georges Sr. High Sch., Uniontown, 1960—; mem. Fayette County Com. on Teenage Pregnancy. Gen. Electric guidance fellow Syracuse U., 1961. Mem. Pa. Sch. Counselors Assn., Pa. Personnel and Guidance Assn., AAUW, DAR, Dames XVII Century, Nat. Ret. Tchrs. Assn., VFW Ladies Aux. Presbyterian. Clubs: Soroptimist, Rainbow Girls. Home: 44 Barton Mill Rd Uniontown PA 15401 Office: RD 5 Box 175 Uniontown PA 15401

BIVIN, JULIE KAY, nurse; b. Sallisaw, Okla., Nov. 29, 1950; d. O. R. and Beatrice Marie (Jones) VanDeLinder; Bible Found. cert. Ozark Bible Coll., 1971; Asso. Nursing, Westark Community Coll., 1973; m. Steve K. Bivin, Nov. 17, 1973; children—Jeremy Keeth, Ryan William. Grad. nurse pediatrics Sparks Regional Med. Center, Fort Smith, Ark., 1973; nurse, supr. Drumright (Okla.) Meml. Hosp., 1974-76; dir. nursing Drumright Nursing Home, 1976-77; mgr. nurse Ward Nursing Home, Tahlequah, Okla., 1977-82; nursing cons. Eufaula (Okla.) Manor, Inc., 1979-82, Honor Heights Nursing Center, Muskogee, Okla., 1981-82, Ward Manor Inc., 1982—. Area coordinator Leukemia drive, 1979, 80. Mem. Okla. Nursing Home Assn. Mem. Christian Ch. Club: Lioness (pres. 1976) (Drumright, Okla.). Office: 124 E Chickasaw St Tahlequah OK 74464

BIVINS, CAROLYN EARLINE FOSTER, home economist; b. Tuskegee Institute, Ala., Nov. 12, 1946; d. James Earl and Elinor (Hastings) Foster; B.S. in Home Econs. Edn., Tuskegee Inst., 1969; postgrad. Auburn (Ala.) U.; divorced; 1 dau., Adrienne Michelle. Home economist Atlanta Gas Light Co., 1969-71; extension home economist Escambia County, Brewton, Ala., 1974—; cons. in field. Recipient award outstanding leadership and service 4-H Women, 1979. Mem. NEA, Ala. Assn. Extension Home Economists, Ala. Coop. Extension Service Employees Orgn., NAACP, Phi Delta Kappa. Roman Catholic. Home: 110 Mason St Brewton AL 36426 Office: PO Box 768 Brewton AL 36427

BIXBY, KATHERINE COSTLOW (MRS. E. REW BIXBY), civic worker; b. Lusk, Wyo., Feb. 8, 1920; d. Jesse Patrick and Anna (Thompson) Costlow; student Cottey Coll., 1937-38; B.A., Doane Coll., 1941; m. E. Rew Bixby, May 30, 1942; children—Patrick William, Jean (Mrs. Hennessy). Tchr. elem. schs., Lusk, Wyo., 1941-42; exec. dir. Vol. Bur. Voluntary Center, Los Angeles, 1971-82; tchr. vol. mgmt. U. So. Calif., Marymount Coll., Valley Coll. Bd. dirs. Welfare Planning Council 1962-72, USO, 1965-71, Comprehensive Health Planning Los Angeles County, 1969-72, United Crusades Calif., 1968-72, Mayor's Com. on Aging, 1970-72, Los Angeles Mental Health Commn., 1967-72, Planned Protective Services, 1969-71, Camp Fire Girls, 1950-59. Bd. dirs. United Way, Inc., 1963-71. Recipient Gold Key United Way, 1963, Armed Forces Vol. award, 1966, Luther Gulick award Camp Fire Girls, 1959, Gold Medallion award USO, 1970, Koshland Found. award, 1977. Mem. Nat. Conf. Social Welfare (dir. 1976-78), Assn. Vol. Adminstrs. (regional chmn. 1981-82). Home: 920 Crestview Ave Glendale CA 91202 Office: 621 S Virgil St Los Angeles CA 90005

BIXLER, GLENDA ANN, univ. adminstr.; b. Morgantown, W.Va., Mar. 8, 1945; d. Glenn and Dorothy Lorraine (Ellenberger) B.; student W.Va. U., 1977—. With W.Va. U., Morgantown, 1963—, class scheduling analyst Office of Facilities Analysis and Utilization, 1975-77, facilities analyst Office of Facilities Analysis and Utilization, 1979-80, mgr. facilities info. systems, 1980—. Mem. Performing Arts Council, W.Va. U., 1972-76, mem. faculty devel. adv. council, 1979-81, now chairwoman Council for Women's Concerns, mem. women's studies adv. com. Mem. W.Va. U. Community Choir; premier sec. Worldwide Pictures Film, 1973, publicity dir., 1978; chmn. Council Women's Concerns Conf., 1980; bd. dirs. Morgantown chpt. ARC, sec., 1980-82, planning coordinator, 1982—; mem. Regional Facilities Planning Consortium. lay witness missioner Ch. Self-Renewal Seminars, 1975—. Named Morgantown Sec. of Yr., 1967. Mem. Nat. Assn. Female Execs, Am. Mgmt. Assn., Am. Soc. Profl. and Exec. Women. Republican. Home: C32 La Mesa Village Morgantown WV 26505 Office: 4 Oglebay Hall Annex WVa U Morgantown WV 26506

BIXLER, SUSAN ELIZABETH, seminar and cons. co. exec.; b. Cleve., Mar. 23, 1950; d. Bruce Melvin and Elizabeth (English) B.; B.A. in English and Edn., Baldwin-Wallace Coll., Berea, Ohio, 1972; m. Jose Vicente Porto, Mar. 27, 1982. Asst. dir. March of Dimes, Cleve., 1973-75; promotional dir. Bonne Bell Cosmetics, Atlanta, 1975-80; pres., owner Profl. Image, Inc., Atlanta, 1980—; instr. Fashion Inst. Atlanta; lectr. in field. Bd. dirs. City Center Dance Theatre, Atlanta. Mem. Cobb C. of C., Women Bus. Owners, Sales and Mktg. Execs., Atlanta Women's Commerce Club (charter). Author column You and Beauty, 1979—; contbr. articles to mags. Home: 1700 Ironwood Rd Marietta GA 30067 Office: 1905 Powers Ferry Rd Suite 205 Marietta GA 30067

BJUSTROM, REBECCA CHRISTINE, energy systems engr.; b. Moscow, Idaho, Jan. 1, 1954; d. Fred Victor and Frances Elizabeth (Plum) B.; B.S. in Chem. Engring., U. Idaho, 1976. Solar program coordinator Dept. of Energy, Oakland, Calif., 1976-78; tech. staff solar, mcpl. waste and geothermal energy systems The MITRE Corp., McLean, Va., 1978-80; coal liquefaction research and devel. coordinator Solvent Refined Coal Internat., Inc., 1981; petroleum engr. Amoco Prodn. Co., Denver, 1982—. Vol. in high sch. career guidance and counseling; chemistry and math tutor; mem. peace and social concerns com. Religious Soc. of Friends; active AMC Cancer Research Center and Hosp., Denver Art Mus. Mem. Soc. Women Engrs., Soc. Petroleum Engrs., English-Speaking Union, Internat. Sister Cities Program, People to People Corp. Denver, Mortar Bd., Tau Beta Pi, Alpha Lambda Delta. Home: 19563 E Milan Circle Aurora CO 80013 Office: 12005 E 45th Ave Denver CO 80239

BLACK, BRENDA CLEM, greenhouse owner; b. Paris, Ark., Feb. 12, 1947; d. Lewis Ray and Myrtle Eunice (Yancey) Clem; m. Russell Owen Black, June 4, 1966; children—John Stephen, Jeffrey Richard. Peace Corps vol., Uttar Pradesh, India, 1966; asst. acct. Donrey Media Group, Inc., Ft. Smith, Ark., 1966-67; various secretarial positions Manpower, Inc., Ft. Smith, 1967-68; exec. sec. Conn. Mut. Ins. Co., Gainesville, Ga., 1972; founder, owner, mgr. Blackland Farms, Inc., Prairie Grove, Ark., 1974—; owner Blackland Florist, 1980—; speaker to garden clubs. Bd. govs. Washington Regional Med. Center, Fayetteville, Ark., 1979—, chmn. community relations com., 1980-81, chmn. fin. com., 1982—, vice chmn., 1982—. Mem. Fla. Foliage Assn. (charter), Nat. Fedn. Ind. Businesses, Prairie Grove C. of C. (dir. 1979-80). Clubs: Jr. Civic League, Alpha Chi Omega. First woman appointee bd. govs. Washington Regional Med. Center. Home and Office: Route 2 Prairie Grove AR 72753

BLACK, CATHLEEN PRUNTY, publisher; b. Chgo., Apr. 26, 1944; d. James and Margaret (Hamilton) Black; B.A., Trinity Coll., Washington, 1966; m. Thomas Harvey, May 20, 1982. Adj. sales Holiday, 1966-68, Time and Leisure, 1968-70; sales adj. N.Y. mag., N.Y.C., 1970-72, pub., 1977—; adv. dir. Ms. mag., N.Y.C., 1972-77. Recipient Matrix award Women in Communication, 1982. Mem. Mag. Pubs. Assn. (dir.), Women in Communication, Women's Forum, Advt. Women N.Y. Office: NY Mag 755 2d Ave New York NY 10017

BLACK, CECELIA WHIDDEN, dental hygienist, educator; b. Bartow, Fla., May 15, 1944; d. Henry Pasco and Madelyn May (Owens) Whidden; B.S., Columbia U., 1966; M.A., Adelphi U., Garden City, N.Y., 1971; m. Louis Engleman Black, Sept. 5, 1966; 1 son, Kerrison Todd. Tchr. dental hygiene Franklin Square (N.Y.) Sch. Dist., 1967-70; clin. supr., asst. prof. dental hygiene de Hostos Community Coll., Bronx, N.Y., 1970-76; dir. dental hygiene U. Medicine and Dentistry N.J., Newark, 1976—, clin. asso. prof., chmn. dental aux. edn., 1979—; leader workshops, radio broadcaster. Recipient Excellence in Teaching award U. Medicine and Dentistry N.J., 1977. Founding mem. Bedford Barrow Commerce Block Assn, 1974, treas., 1974-76; Mem. Steering com. Around the Square: 150th Anniversary of Washington Square Park, 1982. Mem. Am. Dental Hygienists Assn., Am. Assn. Dental Schs., Am. Soc. Allied Health Professions, Nat. Assn. Female Execs., N.Y. State Dental Hygienists Assn. (pres. 1975-76), N.Y. State Dental Soc. (liaison 1976-80), N.Y.C. Dental Hygienists Assn. (pres. 1971-72), Am. Mgmt. Assn., AAUW, Columbia U. Dental Hygiene Alumnae Assn. (pres. 1972-73), Sigma Phi Alpha. Co-author textbook on dental mgmt., 1982. Producer ednl. video tapes. Home: 41 Commerce St New York NY 10014 Office: 100 Bergen St Newark NJ 07103

BLACK, COBEY, journalist; b. Washington, June 15, 1922; d. Elwood Alexander and Margaret (Beall) Cobey; B.A., Wellesley Coll. 1944; postgrad. U. Hawaii; m. Edwin Black, Nov. 30, 1945; children—Star, Christopher, Noel, Nicholas, Brian, Bruce. Exec. sec. to Irene, designer, Metro-Goldwin-Mayer, 1944; actress in W. Ger., 1945-46; women's editor Washington Daily News, 1947-50; columnist Honolulu Star Bull., 1954-65; cons. HEW, Peace Corps, 1960-61; travel editor Bangkok (Thailand) World, 1968-69; columnist Honolulu Advertiser, 1972—; publicist CBS-TV show Hawaii Five-O, 1978. Active LWV, Hawaii Commn. on Status of Women. Democrat. Episcopalian. Clubs: Nat. Press, Honolulu Press, Royal Bangkok Sports, Outrigger Canoe. Author: Birth of a Princess, 1964. Home: 4910 Kahala Ave Honolulu HI 96816 Office: Honolulu Advertiser Honolulu HI 96802

BLACK, DORIS ANN, nurse; b. Bedford, Va., Apr. 15, 1941; d. William Louis and Cora Mae (Farley) Rakes; R.N., Grace Hosp., Richmond, Va., 1962; m. Henry Peter Black, II, May 15, 1976; children—Roger, Robin, Henry. Dir. nursing Eastview Lodge, Richmond, Va., 1974; cert. officer Va. Dept. Health, 1974-78; adminstr., preceptor for adminstr.-in-tng. Richmond City, 1980; troubleshooter, now nursing home adminstr. Eastern div. Beverly Enterprises, 1980—; cons. in field. Mem. Va. Health Care Assn., Assn. Practitioners in Infection Control. Republican. Episcopalian. Author manuals. Home: 8400 Chelmford Rd Richmond VA 23235 Office: 3284 Virginia Beach Blvd Suite 200 Virginia Beach VA 23452

BLACK, EMILIE ANNABELLE, med. adminstr.; b. New Haven, Apr. 14, 1919; d. Louis Albert and Margaret Anne (Knopf) B.; B.S., George Washington U., 1942, M.D., 1945; m. Samuel James Solt, July 19, 1946; 1 dau., Margaret Solt Manoogian. Intern, Garfield Meml. Hosp., Washington, 1945-46, resident internal medicine, 1946-47; resident in pediatrics Children's Hosp. D.C., 1947-49; practice medicine specializing in pediatrics, Bethesda, Md., 1949-66; dir. S.W. Health Center, Washington, 1966-68; med. officer NIH, Bethesda, 1968—, asst. dir. clin. research NIGMS; clin. instr. pediatrics George Washington U. Fellow Am. Assn. Surgery of Trauma; mem. AAAS, Am. Burn Assn. (hon.; Harvey Stuart Allen Disting. Service award 1982), Internat. Soc. Burn Injuries, Am. Trauma Soc., Sigma Kappa. Republican. Lutheran. Club: Kenwood Country. Contbr. articles to profl. jours. Home: 5201 Watson St NW Washington DC 20016 Office: NIH-Nat Inst Gen Med Scis 5333 Westbard Ave Room 925 Bethesda MD 20205

BLACK, EVELYN GOLDEN, educator; b. Bangor, Maine; d. Samuel H. and Helen (Rybier) Golden; student Vassar Coll.; B.A. in Sociology, U. Maine; M.A. in English Edn., Ariz. State U.; postgrad. Nat. Art Sch., Washington, Vesper George Sch. Art, Boston, Boston U., Phoenix Coll., No. Ariz. U., Flagstaff, U. Ariz., Tucson; m. Bernard E. Black; children—Barry Golden, Brian Allan; 1 stepdau., Barbara (Mrs. Mark J. Beran). Interviewer, office mgr. Maine Employment Service, Biddeford and Old Orchard Beach; personnel adminstr. Vocat. Service, Boston; tchr. Good Shepherd Sch. for Girls, Phoenix; tchr., dept. chmn., work coordinator, spl. edn. Phoenix Union High Sch. and South Mountain High Sch., Phoenix; panelist KPHO-TV, Phoenix; Valley High Sch. spl. edn. rep. to Valley Coop. Council; participant in evaluation Ariz. High Sch. Work Edn. Programs. Asso. editor Westhils Neighborhood News; chmn. New Haven Mayor Candidates Meeting; chmn. Phoenix League Women Voters summer workshop on elementary sch. problems; pianist Israeli song-dance group, Phoenix; writer, dir., choreographer 10 plays and musicals for 6 civic orgns.; bd. dirs. Internat. Interest Club, Westville, Conn., Alexander Sch. for Girls, Phoenix; bd. dirs. League Women Voters of New Haven, sec., 1958; bd. dirs. Brandeis U. Women's Com., sec. Recipient certificate of achievement Dept. Labor Inst. on Disadvantaged Youth and Programmed Instrn., Nat. Counselor of Yr. award Nat. Assn. for Retarded Citizens. Mem. Sigma Mu Sigma, Kappa Delta Pi. Home: 2105 N 12th Ave Phoenix AZ 85007 Office: South Mountain High Sch 5401 S 7th St Phoenix AZ 85040

BLACK, JOANNE, fin. co. exec.; b. Balt., Dec. 28, 1942; d. Joseph and Mildred Winkes; student McCoy Coll., 1960-61, Harvard U., 1981. Advt. mgr. Celanese Fibers Co., N.Y.C., 1974-76; v.p. Am. Express Co., N.Y.C., 1974-78, sr. v.p. mktg. travelers cheques, N.Y.C., 1978—. Recipient Hall of Women Achievers award YMCA, 1981. Mem. Advt. Women N.Y., Am. Mgmt. Assn. Home: 865 First Ave New York NY 10017 Office: 125 Broad St New York NY 10004

BLACK, JOYCE MACWATTY, civic worker; b. Englewood, N.J., Nov. 27, 1928; d. Frank Lamont and Gladys Jeannette (Harkness) MacWatty; B.S., Skidmore Coll., 1948; m. Hiram Day Black, Mar. 5, 1949; 1 dau., Suzanne. Expert cons. ACTION, fed. agy., 1975-76; v.p. Volunteer: Nat. Center for Citizens Involvement, Washington, 1974—, League of Cities, U.S. Conf. Mayors, 1970; cons. to study future of voluntarism Office Policy Research, Washington, 1976-77; pres. Day Care Council, 1972—; v.p. Cancer Care, Inc. of Nat. Cancer Found., 1965—, v.p. Big Bros./Big Sisters Am., 1970—; chmn. N.Y. State Adv. Com. on Day Care, 1973-76; mem. N.Y. State Dept. Social Services Adv. Council, 1973—; co-chmn. Nat. Congress on Volunteerism and Citizenship '76, 1975-76; sect. chmn. Nat. Conf. Social Welfare, 1976—; bd. dirs. N.Y. State Assn. Human Services, 1971-76, N.Y. State Banking Bd., 1973-77, N.Y. State Council Humanities, 1973—, N.Y. State Council Voluntary Child Care Agys., Inc., 1974—, N.Y. State Temp. Commn. on Child Welfare, 1974-81, Welfare Research, Inc., 1974—; mem. women's exec. com. United Hosp. Fund, N.Y.C., 1954—; treas., v.p. N.Y. Jr. League, 1962-66; v.p. Hudson Guild Neighborhood House, N.Y.C., 1963—; v.p., treas. Planned Parenthood of N.Y., 1956-74; co-chmn. N.Y.C. Mayor's Voluntary Action Council, 1966—; v.p. Plays for Living, N.Y.C., 1966—, Fedn. Protestant Welfare Agys., N.Y.C., 1973—; pres. Voluntary Action Corp., N.Y.C., 1966—; v.p. YWCA, N.Y.C., 1968-76, YM/YWCA Day Care Corp., N.Y.C., 1973—; chmn. Resources Rev. Bd. of N.Y.C., 1973—; adv. bd. Sch. Spl. Studies Columbia U., 1975—; bd. dirs. Counseling and Human Devel. Center, 1977—; trustee Cultural Instns. Retirement Fund, 1973—; mem. adv. com. Agy. Child Devel., 1977—; v.p. Nat. Conf. Social Welfare, 1978; cons. HEW, 1978, Greater N.Y. Fund; mem. N.Y. State Bd. Social Welfare, 1979—; pres. Big Bros. N.Y., Inc., 1977; chmn. Internat. Yr. of Child, N.Y.C., 1979, Joint Action for Children, 1978; mem. Gov.'s adv. com. N.Y. State Conf. Children and Youth; vice-chmn. Hosp. Trustees N.Y. State; chmn. Trustees N.Y.C. Hosps; trustee N.Y. U. Med. Center, 1967; mem. other N.Y.C. bds. Recipient Outstanding Citizen award N.Y. Med. Soc., 1969, Mayoral award Mayor N.Y.C., 1969, 72, Outstanding Alumnae award Skidmore Coll., 1972, Lizette Sarnoff award Albert Einstein Med. Sch., 1975. Mem. Nat. Conf. Social Welfare, N.Y. State Assn. Human Services, Nat. Soc. Arts and Letters, Nat. Council Orgns. for Children, Youth, Jr. League, Child Welfare League Am. (pres.), Council on Accreditation on Services for Families and Children, Hosp. Assn. N.Y. State, Nat. Soc. Colonial Dames. Episcopalian. Clubs: Univ., Englewood Field; Siasconset Casino (Nantucket). Home: 520 E 86th St New York NY 10028 Office: Day Care Council of NY Inc 22 W 38th St New York NY 10018

BLACK, KAREN, actress; b. Park Ridge, Ill., July 1, 1942; d. Norman A. and Elsie (Reif) Zeigler; ed. Northwestern U.; studied with Lee Strasberg; m. Charles Black (div.); m. 2d, Robert Burton, 1973 (div. 1974); m. 3d, L. Minor Carson, July 4, 1975; 1 son, Hunter. Appeared on Broadway in The Playroom, 1965, Keep it in the Family, 1968; films include: A Gunfight, 1961, You're A Big Boy Now, 1967, Hard Contract, 1969, Easy Rider, 1969, Five Easy Pieces, 1970, Portnoy's Complaint, 1972, Rhinoceros, 1974, The Outfit, 1974 The Great Gatsby, 1974, The Day of the Locust, 1975, Nashville, 1975, Family Plot, 1976, Crime and Passion, 1976, Burnt Offerings, 1976, Capricorn One, 1978, In Praise of Older Women, 1979, Killer Fish, 1979, The Last Word, 1979, Valentine, 1979, Miss Right, 1980; TV film The Strange Possession of Mrs. Oliver, 1977, others. Recipient N.Y. Film Critics award for best supporting actress, 1970. Address: care Kimble-Parseghian Inc 9255 Sunset Blvd Suite 509 Los Angeles 90069 *

BLACK, KRISTINE MARY, biomaterials engr.; b. St. Paul, July 11, 1953; d. Jaurd Oliver and Dorothy Helen (Amos) B.; B.Physics, U. Minn., 1975, M.S. in Cell Biology, 1978, M.S. Metallurgy and Materials Sci., 1981. Analytical physicist Cardiac Pacemakers, St. Paul, 1978, qualifications engr., to 1981; biomaterials engr. St. Jude Med., Inc., St. Paul, 1981—. Mem. ASTM, Am. Soc. Metals, Nat. Assn. Female Execs., U. Minn. Inst. Tech. Alumni Soc. (dir. 1980-84). Contbr. articles to profl. jours. Office: Saint Jude Med Inc One Lillehei Plaza Saint Paul MN 55117

BLACK, MARTHA SUSAN LOWE, lawyer; b. Maryville, Tenn., Sept. 18, 1945; d. Ernest Broyles and Esther Charlotte (Carlson) Lowe; B.A. with honors, Mount Holyoke Coll., 1967; postgrad. (NDEA fellow), Rice U., 1967-69; J.D. (Green scholar), U. Tenn., 1973; m. David T. Black, June 7, 1975; children—Charlotte Carlson, Elizabeth Cannon. Admitted to Tenn. bar, 1974; asst., then asso. prof. U. Tenn. Coll. Law, Knoxville, 1973-81; mem. firm Kizer & Black, P.C., Maryville, Tenn., 1981—; chmn. U. Tenn. Commn. Women, 1979-80. Chmn., Blount County Foster Care Review Bd.; bd. dirs., vice chmn. Blount County Children's Home; mem. community adv. council Maryville Coll.; mem. Blount County Hist. Trust. Recipient Am. Jurisprudence and Corpus Juris Secundum awards, 1972; named Grad. of Yr., U. Tenn., 1973. Mem. Am. Bar Assn., Tenn. Bar Assn., Order Coif. Home: 329 Cates St Maryville TN 37801 Office: PO Box 395 303 Blount Nat Bank Bldg Maryville TN 37801

BLACK, MAUREEN, realty co. exec.; b. Manchester, Eng., Feb. 4, 1937; came to U.S., 1957, naturalized, 1962; d. William Henry and Kathleen Mary (Cleaver) Jackson; grad. Felt and Tarrant Comptometer Sch., Eng., 1953; student Alamogordo br. N.Mex. State U., 1959-60, 62-63; m. Charles J. Dugan, Nov. 1979; 1 dau., Karen Elizabeth Black. Office mgr., personnel dir. J.C. Penney Co., Alamogordo, 1958-66; exec. sec. to project mgr. Re-entry System div. Gen. Electric Co., Holloman AFB, 1967-68; soc. editor, columnist Alamogordo Daily News, 1968-73; regional corr. El Paso (Tex.) Times, 1968-75; free lance writer and photographer; script writer Film Unit 505, Alamogordo, 1971; realtor asso. Shyne Realty, Alamogordo, 1975-77, West Source Realtors, 1977-80; owner, broker Hyde Park West Realty Co., 1980—. Pres.,

Alamogordo Music Theatre, 1971-72. Mem. planning com. tourism, recreation, convs. Gov. of N.Mex., 1965; mem. N.Mex. State Film Commn., 1973-74; life mem. Aux. of Zia Sch. for Handicapped Children, pres. Aux., 1975-76, 80-82, mem. sch. bd., 1982-83. Recipient service award Nat. Found., March of Dimes, 1971; Americanism medal DAR, 1972; named Career Woman of Yr., Alamogordo chpt. Am. Bus. Women's Assn., 1971. Mem. Alamogordo C. of C. (chmn. convs. and motion picture com. 1965—), Nat. Assn. Realtors, Realtors Assn. N.Mex., Alamogordo Bd. Realtors (chmn. public relations com., v.p. 1981-82, pres.-elect 1982-83), N.Mex. Opera Guild. Home: 1206 Desert Eve Dr Alamogordo NM 88310 Office: PO Box 2021 Alamogordo NM 88310

BLACK, PAGE MORTON, civic worker; b. Chgo.; d. Alexander and Rose Morton; student Chgo. Mus. Coll.; m. William Black, Mar. 27, 1962. Singer, pianist, Pierre Hotel, N.Y.C., Warwick Hotel, One Fifth Ave. Sherry Netherland Hotel; singer Chock Full o' Nuts Radio Show; singer comml. Chock Full o' Nuts; dir. Chock Full o' Nuts Corp.; rec. artist MGM, Audio Fidelity Records; co-founder Page and William Black Post Grad. Sch. Medicine, Mt. Sinai Med. Sch., 1965—; sec., mem. exec. bd. Parkinsons Disease Found., Columbia U. Med. Center. Home: Premium Point New Rochelle NY 10801

BLACK, PEGGIE ARRECHE STODIECK, nurse; b. Alturas, Calif., Sept. 9, 1955; d. Frank and Janice Jeanette (Westervelt) Arreche; B.S. in Nursing, U. Nev., 1977; cardiovascular nurse specialist degree Ariz. Heart Inst., 1981; m. July 25, 1981. Staff nurse CCU and ICU, St. Mary's Hosp., Reno, 1977-80, cardiovascular nurse specialist cardiac care unit, 1981—; instr. Sedlock & Assos., Reno, 1982—. Bd. dirs. Washoe County chpt. Am. Heart Assn. Mem. Am. Assn. Critical Care Nurses (v.p. 1979). Democrat. Home: 1135 Nixon Ave Reno NV 89509 Office: 235 W 6th St Reno NV 89502

BLACK, ROSIE, state legislator; b. Springfield, Ohio, Jan. 23, 1954; d. Suzanne Kime; m. Ted W. Black, Oct. 9, 1970; children—Angela, Wyatt, Samuel. Salesperson Hansen Ford, Grand Forks, N.D., 1979—; dir. N.D. Blue Shield; mem. N.D. Ho. of Reps., 1977—. Bd. dirs. Quad County Community Action Agy., 1981—. Named Outstanding Young North Dakotan, N.D. Jr. C. of C., 1980, Grand Forks Jr. C. of C., 1980. Republican. Lutheran. Clubs: Lioness, Jayceettes (Grand Forks, N.D.). Home: 1615 Rider Rd Grand Forks ND 58201 Office: 3401 Gateway Dr Grand Forks ND 58201 also State House Capitol Bldg Bismarck ND 58505

BLACK, SANDRA, adminstrv. cons.; b. N.Y.C., Apr. 5, 1951; d. David Eastern and Norma (Springer) B.; B.A., Cornell U., 1975; student N.Y. U. Sch. Law, 1977-78. Adminstrv. asst. Center for Mgmt. Tech., Inc., N.Y.C., 1975-77; legal asst., paralegal Queens Legal Services Corp., Jamaica, N.Y., 1978-79; legal asst., paralegal Singer, Hutner, Levine & Seeman, N.Y.C., 1980; legal asst. Corbin, Silverman, Sanseverino & Taylor, N.Y.C., 1980-82; adminstrv. cons. N.Y. Cons. Group Ltd., N.Y.C., 1982—. Resource person Cornell Alumni Career Resource File, 1978—; mem. steering com. Network of Black Career Women, 1982—; Mem. publicity dir. South African Liberation Com., 1972-74. N.Y. State Regents Scholar, 1969-74; Cornell U. grantee, 1969-74. Mem. Cornell Black Alumni Assn. (pres., dir.), Cornell Alumni Assn. N.Y.C. (council), NAACP. Democrat. Episcopalian. Home: 266 Washington Ave Brooklyn NY 11205 Office: 56 Pine St New York NY 10022

BLACK, SHELIA LOUISE, edn. programs specialist; b. Hobart, Okla., Dec. 11, 1949; d. John Houston and Claris Geneva (Quick) Knight; student U. Okla., 1981—; m. Tommy Royce Black, Sept. 11, 1967; children—Jennifer, Jason. Sec. to program dir. Sta. KLBK-TV, Lubbock, Tex., 1974; mem. advt. dept. Dallas Morning News, 1976-77; mgr. secretarial pool U. Okla., 1980, edn. professions asst., 1981, edn. programs specialist, 1982—. Republican. Ch. Christ. Home: 1506 Lakecrest Dr Norman OK 73071 Office: 820 Van Vleet Oval Okla U Norman OK 73019

BLACK, SHIRLEY TEMPLE (MRS. CHARLES A. BLACK), former ambassador, former actress; b. Santa Monica, Calif., Apr. 23, 1928; d. George Francis and Gertrude Temple; ed. under pvt. tutelage; grad. Westlake Sch. Girls, 1945; m. John Agar, Jr., Sept. 19, 1945 (div. 1949); 1 dau., Linda Susan; m. 2d. Charles A. Black, Dec. 16, 1950; children—Charles Alden, Lori Alden. Began film career at age 3 1/2; played leading roles from the start; first full-length film was Stand Up and Cheer; made pictures for Paramount Studios and Twentieth Century-Fox Film Corp., including Little Miss Marker, Baby Take a Bow, Bright Eyes, Our Little Girl, The Little Colonel, Curly Top, The Littlest Rebel, Captain January, Poor Little Rich Girl, Dimples, Stowaway, Wee Willie Winkie, Heidi, Rebecca of Sunnybrook Farm, Little Miss Broadway, Just Around the Corner, The Little Princess, Susannah of the Mounties, The Blue Bird, Kathleen, Miss Annie Rooney, Since You Went Away, Kiss and Tell, 1945, That Hagen Girl, War Party, The Bachelor and the Bobby-Soxer, Honeymoon, 1947; narrator, actress TV series Shirley Temple Storybook, NBC, 1958, Shirley Temple Show, NBC, 1960; rep. to 24th Gen. Assembly of UN, 1969-70; U.S. Ambassador to Ghana, 1974-76; chief of protocol, White House, 1976-77; mem. U.S. del. on African Refugee Problems, Geneva, 1981; mem. pub. adv. com. UN Conf. on Law of the Sea; dep. chmn. U.S. del. UN Conf. on Human Environ., Stockholm, 1970-72; spl. asst. to chmn. Pres.'s Council on Environ. Quality, 1972-74; del. treaty on environ. USSR-USA Joint Commn., Moscow, 1972; mem. U.S. Commn. for UNESCO, 1973—; dir. Bank of Calif., Fireman's Fund Ins. Co., BANCAL Tri-State Corp., Del Monte Corp. Mem. Calif. Adv. Hosp. Council, 1969, San Francisco Health Facilities Planning Assn., 1965-69; Republican candidate for U.S. Ho. of Reps. from Calif., 1967; bd. dirs. Nat. Wildlife Fedn., Nat. Multiple Sclerosis Soc., UN Assn. U.S.A.; bd. dirs. exec. com. Internat. Fedn. Multiple Sclerosis Socs. Appointed col. on staff of Gov. Ross of Idaho, 1935; commd. col. Hawaiian N.G.; hon. col. 108th Reg., N.G. Ill.; dame Order Knights Malta (Paris), 1968; recipient Ceres medal FAO, Rome, 1975, numerous other state decorations. Mem. World Affairs Council No. Calif. (dir.), Council Fgn. Relations, Nat. Com. for U.S./China Relations. Club: Commonwealth of Calif. Address: Woodside CA *

BLACK, SUSAN HARRELL, fed. judge; b. Valdosta, Ga., Oct. 20, 1943; d. William H. and Ruth Elizabeth (Phillips) Harrell; B.A., Fla. State U., 1964; J.D., U. Fla., 1967; m. Louis Eckert Black, Dec. 28, 1966. Admitted to Fla. bar, 1967; asst. state's atty. 4th Jud. Circuit Fla.; asst. gen. counsel City of Jacksonville (Fla.); judge County Ct. Duval County, Fla.; judge 4th Jud. Circuit Ct. Fla.; U.S. dist. judge Middle Dist. Fla., Jacksonville, 1979—; former mem. faculty Nat. Jud. Coll., Reno. Mem. adv. bd., former trustee Jacksonville Hosp. Ednl. Program; mem. Jacksonville Council Citizen Involvement; trustee U. Fla. Law Sch. Mem. ABA, Fla. Bar Assn., Jacksonville Bar Assn., Conf. Circuit Judges (past chmn. edn. com., dean New Judges Coll.). Episcopalian. Office: 311 W Monroe St Jacksonville FL 32202 *

BLACKBURN, JOAN FRENCH, elec. wholesale co. exec.; b. Queen City, Tex., Feb. 16, 1935; d. DeWitt H. and Myrtle Lee (Latham) French; student LDL Inst., Boston, 1978-79, San Antonio Coll., 1979—; m. Don M. Blackburn, Sr., Sept. 27, 1969; childreSteven, Susan, Don, Jeff. Exec. sec. to regional mgr. Am. Petrofina Co. Tex., San Antonio, 1964-74; sec.-treas., Blackburn Drives & Controls, Inc., San Antonio, 1974—, dir., 1974—. Chmn. adv. bd. vocat. office edn. Churchill High Sch., 1976-78. Mem. Profl. and Bus. Women's Club San Antonio, Greater San Antonio C. of C., N.E. San Antonio C. of C. Republican. Methodist (chmn. Acolytes group). Home: 13307 Lobelia St San Antonio TX 78232 Office: 11926 Warfield Dr San Antonio TX 78216

BLACKBURN, SARA A., clin. nutritionist, educator; b. Dayton, Ohio, July 28, 1950; d. Mack Owen and Helen Comstock (Morris) B.; B.S., Purdue U., 1972, M.S., 1973; Sc.D., Boston U., 1980; m. Stephen T. Rose, 1974. Grad. instr. foods and nutrition Purdue U., 1972-73; nutrition cons. Bay State Mgmt. Corp., Quincy, Mass., 1973-76; instr. nutrition Brockton (Mass.) Hosp. Sch. Nursing, 1974-76; chief therapeutic dietitian Malden (Mass.) Hosp., 1976-77; clin. research nutritionist clin. nutrition unit Med. Center, Boston U., 1977-81, instr. nutrition Schs. Grad. Dentistry and Medicine, Sargent Coll. Allied Health, 1977-81; nutrition cons. for med. care affiliated, 1979-81; nutrition cons. cardiovascular fitness program Northeastern U., Boston, 1979; asst. prof. nutrition Fla. Internat. U., Miami, 1981—. Mem. Am. Dietetic Assn. Mass. Dietetic Assn., Am. Home Econs. Assn., Mass Home Econs. Assn., Am. Soc. for Parenteral and Enteral Nutrition, Soc. for Nutrition Edn. Contbr. articles to profl. jours. Office: Dept Dietetics and Nutrition Fla Internat U Tamiami Trail Miami FL 33199

BLACKMAN, JESSICA LYNN, lawyer; b. Bklyn., June 1, 1954; d. Norman Sidney and Sylvia (Bader) B.; B.A., Syracuse U., 1975; J.D., Western New Eng. Coll., 1978; m. Richard Andrew Schwabacher, Sept. 16, 1978. Admitted to Mass. bar, 1978; legis. asst. Senator John Tower, 1978-79, D.C. Mayor's Office, 1979-80, Congressman Alvin Baldus, Washington, 1980-81, Congressman Gus Savage, Washington, 1981—; teaching fellow Northfield/Mt. Hermon Sch., 1974. Reginald Heber Smith fellow, 1978. Mem. ABA, Mass. Bar Assn., Mass. Women's Bar Assn., D.C. Women's Bar Assn., Phi Alpha Delta, Delta Delta Delta. Democrat. Office: 1233 Longworth House Office Bldg Washington DC 20515

BLACKMAN, JOAN SARA, mktg. exec.; b. N.Y.C., May 25, 1948; d. Samuel William and Clara (Gershunoff) B.; B.A., Case Western Res. U., 1968. Research trainee Grudin Appel Research Corp., N.Y.C., 1968-69; research analyst BBDO Advt., N.Y.C., 1969-70; research analyst, mgr. mktg. research new products Nabisco Inc., N.Y.C., 1970-74, mgr. consumer research, Biscuit div., 1974-76, product mgr., East Hanover, N.J., 1976-82; asst. v.p., dir. mktg. Equitable Life Assurance Soc., N.Y.C., 1982—; lectr. in field; condr. seminars. Mem. Am. Mktg. Assn., Nat. Assn. Female Execs., Am. Soc. Profl. and Exec. Women. Home: 1590 Anderson Ave Fort Lee NJ 07024 Office: Equitable Life Assurance Soc 1285 Ave of Americas New York NY 10019

BLACKMAN, LISA ANDREA, audiologist; b. Boston, Dec. 10, 1952; d. Benjamin Alexander and Rebecca W.; B.A. cum laude, Queens Coll., 1973, M.A., 1975. Dir., adminstr. dept audiology Albert Einstein Med. Center, Phila., 1975-79; audiologic cons. Moss Rehab. Hosp., Phila., 1975-79; pvt. practice audiology, Phila., 1978—; N.E. rep. Widex Hearing Aid Co., also Hal-Hen Hearing Aid Accessory Co., 1980-81; 1980-81; dir. audiological research Cooper Med. Center, Camden, N.J., 1982—; course dir. Council of Accreditation for Occupational Hearing Conservation; lectr., cons. and program coordinator in field; pres. Better Hearing Inst. Pa. cert. hearing aid specialist. Mem. Am. Speech Lang. and Hearing Assn., Deafness Research Found., N.Y. Audiology Study Group, Am. Auditory Soc., Alexander Graham Bell Assn., Indsl. Audiology Soc., Am. Tinnitus Assn., Acoustical Soc. Am., Pa. Speech and Hearing Assn. Democrat. Jewish. Author: A Hearing Aid Handbook, 1979; contbr. article to profl. jour.

BLACKSTEN, ANNA MARIE, fire prevention technician, investigator; b. Fargo, N.D., Dec. 23, 1948; d. Ove Harold and Florence Mildred (Holsinger) Anderson; student Lane Community Coll., 1972-74; Criminology Cert. of Competancy, Inst. Applied Sci., 1978; children—David, Angela. Crime prevention officer, lab. technician Eugene (Oreg.) Police Dept., 1974-79; fire prevention technician, investigator Seaside Fire Dept., Seaside, Oreg., 1980—. Bus. and Profl. Women's Club scholar, 1976-77; cert. radiol. monitoring Nat. Emergency Tng. Center, 1982. Mem. Oreg. Fire Marshal's, Bus. and Profl. Women, Internat. Assn. Arson Investigators, Exec. Females, Inc., Oreg. Fire Edn. Assn., Oreg. Peace Officers Assn. Home: PO Box 89 Seaside OR 97138 Office: Seaside Fire Dept 851 Broadway Seaside OR 97138

BLACKSTOCK, DOROTHY EVELYN LYONS, artist; b. Tacoma, Aug. 4, 1914; d. Frank and Mildred Aubrey (Potts) Lyons; student Whitman Coll., 1931, Coll. Puget Sound, 1932, U. Wash., 1933; m. Carl Mims Blackstock, July 12, 1942; children—Carl Lyons, Gregory Lee. One-man shows State Hist. Mus., Olympia, Wash., Handforth Gallery, Tacoma; exhibited art in group shows at Seattle Art Mus., Woessner Gallery, Kittredge Gallery, U. Puget Sound, Frye Art Mus., Frederick and Nelson Little Gallery and Exhbn. Hall, Puget Sound Area Shows, NW Watercolor Show, Nat. League Am. Pen Women Biennials, Wash. State Hist. Mus.; represented in permanent collections Wash. State Hist. Mus. at Tacoma, Wash. State U. at Pullman; illustrator two covers Tacoma News Tribune Mag. Sect., five covers Seattle Times Mag. Sect. Art chmn. Music and Art Found., Seattle, 1962-64, bd. trustees, 1958-64; mem. Seattle hospitality com. Allied Arts. Named Woman of Year in art, 1959. Mem. Nat. League Am. Pen Women (br. pres. 1966-68, v.p. Seattle br. 1979-80), Seattle Co-arts and Quad-A Art Club, Fedn. Women's Club, Women's Edn!. Club (pres. 1960-61), Women Painters Wash. (pres. 1972-74), Artist's Equity, Seattle Art Mus. Clubs: Seattle Golf; Sand Point Golf and Country; Wash. Athletic. Home: 5520 Coniston Rd NE Seattle WA 98105

BLACKSTONE, SANDRA LEE, natural resources ofcl., govt. ofcl.; b. Washington; d. Fred J. and Madeline S. Blackstone; B.A., U. Vt., 1969; J.D., U. Denver, 1977; Ph.D., Colo. Sch. Mines, 1979. Systems analyst Martin Marietta Aerospace, Denver, 1969-74; cons. legal, econ. and regulatory matters W.R. Grace & Co., Colo. Energy Research Inst., Colo. Sch. Mines, Dowson, Nagel, Sherman & Howard, Denver, 1976-79; mgr. bus. devel. for synthetic fuels Rocky Mountain Energy subs. Union Pacific Corp., Denver, 1979-81; dep. dir. energy and mineral resources Bur. Land Mgmt., Dept. Interior, Washington, 1982—; lectr. U. Denver Coll. Law, 1981; mem. Colo. Adv. Council on Energy and Energy-Related Mineral Research, 1980-82. Republican precinct committeewoman, 1970-74; del. Denver County Rep. Conv., 1971, 74, Colo. State Rep. Conv., 1972. Colo. Energy Research Inst. fellow, 1974-76; Mobil Oil Co. natural resources fellow, 1975-76; Kennecott Corp. fellow, 1976-77. Mem. Am. Bar Assn., Colo. Bar Assn., Denver Bar Assn., Rocky Mountail Mineral Law Inst. (coal sect. subcom. 1979—). Republican. Contbr. articles to profl. jours. Office: 18th and C Sts NW Washington DC 20240

BLACKWELDER, LYNETTE BROWN, ins. exec.; b. Soperton, Ga., Mar. 12, 1939; d. Herbert J. and Bert Brown; student public schs. Treutlen County, Ga.; m. Oct. 6, 1976; children by previous marriage—Paula, Pamela. With Citizens & So. Nat. Bank, Macon, Ga., 1958-61; sec. City of Dublin (Ga.), 1962-65; sec., dispatcher Robert H. Hart & Assos., Inc., Fernandina Beach, Fla., 1971-73; mgr. Carswell of Fla., Inc., Fernandina Beach, 1973—. Bd. dirs. Fernandina Beach United Way; mem. Nassau County Democratic Exec. Com., 1978-80. Mem. Am. Bus. Women Assn. (Boss of Yr. award 1976), Amelia Island-Fernandina Beach C. of C. (pres. 1979, 80), Fla. Ind. Agts. Assn., Jacksonville Ind. Agts. Assn. Baptist. Clubs: Fernandina Beach Womans, Fernandina Beach Ladies Golf Assn. Home: PO Box 1204 Fernandina Beach FL 32034 Office: PO Box 890 Fernandina Beach FL 32034

BLACKWELL, ANNA CLARA GEE, musician, educator; b. Springfield, Ohio, Dec. 24, 1928; d. Barrett Newton and Letha (Cowen) Gee; student Wilberforce U., 1947-48, Wittenberg U., 1963-64, Wright State U., 1970-73, Sinclair Community Coll., 1977-79, Park Coll., 1981—; nominated D.H.L., Antioch Coll., 1977; m. Harold Blackwell, June 19, 1949; children—Harold, Barrett, Mary, Valerie, Cynthia. Budget analyst Wright-Patterson AFB, 1948—; tchr. Kincaid Music Studio, Springfield, Ohio, 1970-73, Keifer Jr. High Sch., Springfield, 1973-74; music dir., organist St. John Bapt. Ch., Springfield, 1946-71, Central Chapel A.M.E. Ch., Yellow Springs, Ohio, 1972—. Recipient numerous outstanding efficiency awards Wright-Patterson AFB, Outstanding Citizenship award Clark County Council Chs., 1971. Mem. Nat. Guild Piano Tchrs., Am. Coll. Musicians (tour to Europe 1976), Ohio Music Educators Conf., Am. Fedn. Musicians, NAACP. Democrat. Methodist. Club: In Towner Social (Yellow Springs). Composer songs; author: Twenty Two Days of Music in Europe; I Looked at Europe. Home: 244 Northwood Dr Yellow Springs OH 45387 Office: Wright Patterson AFB OH 45433

BLACKWELL, LUCY WHITE, ret. govt. ofcl.; b. Jackson, Tenn., Apr. 22, 1912; d. William Francis and Ethel (White) Blackwell; A.B., Lambuth Coll., 1933; postgrad. West Tenn. Bus. Coll., 1934-35. Stenographer, Tenn. Emergency Relief Adminstrn., Jackson, 1935; accounting clk. FSA, Jackson, Brownsville, Tenn., 1936-39; stenographer Tenn. Dept. Pub. Welfare, Jackson, 1939-40; clk., interviewer, local office mgr. Tenn. Dept. Employment Security, Jackson, 1940-73. Comdr. Am. Cancer Soc., Madison County, Tenn., 1943-54, dist. comdr. W. Tenn., 1947-48, rec. sec. Tenn. div., 1954-56, bd. dirs., 1945—, organizer Madison County unit, 1954, pres., 1954-55; bd. dirs. Jackson Community Chest, 1955-57; pres. League Women Voters, 1951. Treas., chmn. bd. trustees Jackson Free Library, 1948-57. Recipient R.E. Womack Alumni Achievement award Lambuth Coll. Alumni Assn., 1956; named Jackson-Madison Woman of Year, 1955. Mem. Internat. Assn. Personnel Employment Security (pres. Jackson chpt. 1956), Lambuth Coll. Alumni Assn. (pres. 1962-63). Presbyterian. Clubs: Pilot Internat. (past pres. Jackson, dist. gov. Tenn., internat. dir. exec. com.). Altrusa Internat. (chmn.). Home: 45 Belle Haven Dr Jackson IN 38301

BLAESE, LOIS PATIENCE, mfg. co. exec.; b. Atlantic City, Jan. 23, 1937; d. Louis Frank and Erma (Mott) Lamp'l; student public schs.; m. Donald Frank Blaese, Feb. 14, 1959; children—Monique, Donald Frank, Niccole. Div. mgr. Beeline Fashions, Bensenville, Ill., 1963-73; sec.-treas. Accurate Screw Machine Products Co. div. Blaese Enterprises, Columbus, N.J., 1973—. Coordinator Miss Columbus contest, 1981—; mem. Mansfield Twp. Bd. Edn., 1976-81, v.p., 1979-81. Mem. N.J. Sch. Bds. Assn., Columbus Civic Assn., Columbus Hist. Soc., Columbus Ladies Fire Co. Aux. Republican. Home: Mill Ln Columbus NJ 08022 Office: 12 Atlantic Ave Columbus NJ 08022

BLAGER, FLORENCE BERMAN, speech pathologist, educator; b. Wheeling, W.Va., July 2, 1928; B.A., Ohio U., 1950; postgrad. Hunter Coll., 1961-62; M.A., U. Denver, 1966, Ph.D. (Fed. Rehab. Services Adminstrn. fellow), 1970; m. Morton B. Blager. Editorial trainee dept. fashion Woman's Day, Inc., N.Y.C., 1950-51; pvt. sec. to media dir. Transp. Advt., Inc., Cleve., 1952-54; pvt. sec. to adminstrv. dir. dept. metall. engring. Case Inst. Tech., 1954-55; editorial asst. dept. articles Woman's Home Companion, N.Y.C., 1955-57; free lance theatre writing, producing and directing, N.Y.C., 1957-61; tchr. English, speech N.Y.C. Bd. Edn., 1962-65; chief speech pathology and audiology John F. Kennedy Child Devel. Center, U. Colo. Med. Center, Denver 1970—, asso. prof. dept. otolaryngology and psychiatry; adj. asso. prof. dept. speech pathology and audiology U. No. Colo., Greeley, 1971—, U. Denver, 1971—; project dir. videotape tng. series for speech pathologists. Mem. Am., Colo. speech and hearing assns., Soc. for Research in Child Devel., N.Y. Acad. Scis., Am. Assn. on Mental Deficiency, Broadcast Music, Theta Sigma Phi, Alpha Kappa Delta. Club: Soroptimists (service chmn.). Contbr. articles on speech and lang. of abused children, Down's infants and emotionally disturbed children to profl. jours. Address: 1894 S Ivy St Denver CO 80224

BLAGG-MILLER, PENNY JEAN, clin. psychologist; b. London, Nov. 7, 1944; came to U.S., 1970, naturalized, 1974; d. John Henry and Elizabeth Ivy (Dell) Tondeur; B.A., U. San Diego, 1974; M.A., U. of Ams., Mexico City, 1976; Ph.D., Union Grad. Sch., Ohio, 1982; m. Howard Miller, Apr. 11, 1980; 1 son, Sacha Alexander. Staff psychologist Floresta and Falcon Psychiat. Hosps., Mexico City, 1972-76, Reading (Pa.) Hosp., 1976-79; pvt. practice Psychiat. Assocs., Lancaster, Pa., 1979—; cons. Lancaster Osteo., Lancaster Gen. hosps. Mem. Am. Psychol. Assn., Pa. Psychol. Assn., Mexican Psychol. Assn., Benevolent Soc. Mex., Soc. Behavioural Medicine. Jewish. Research on multinat. execs. overseas, children's unconscious fantasies living near Three Mile Island, Pa. Home and office: 442 Ringneck Ln Lancaster PA 17601

BLAI, BERTHA, educator; b. Balt., May 24, 1915; d. Abraham and Mollie (Davis) Rosenberg; B.F.A., Tyler Sch. Art, Temple U., 1965; m. Boris Blai, Apr. 24, 1965; children—Anita Simon, Ruth Leventhal. Instr. ceramics, artist-in-residence Glassboro (N.J.) State Coll., 1973-76; head ceramics dept. DuCret Sch. Art, Plainfield, N.J., 1969-73; ceramicist, instr., adminstr. Blai Sch. Art, Melrose Park, Pa., 1976—; one-woman exhbns. include Widener Coll., Chester, Pa., 1977, Glassboro State Coll., 1973; group exhbns. include Civic Center, Phila., 1972, Art Alliance Phila., 1974. Mem. Nat. League Am. Pen Women, Pa. Guild Craftsmen (hon. life mem. Del. Valley chpt.). Address: 4th and High Aves Melrose Park PA 19126

BLAIN, CHARLOTTE MARIE, internist; b. Meadeville, Pa., July 18, 1941; d. Frank Andrew and Valerie Marie (Serafin) B.; student Coll. St. Francis, 1958-60, DePaul U., 1961-62; M.D., U. Ill., 1965; m. John G. Hamby, June 12, 1971 (dec. 1976); 1 son, Charles John. Intern, U. Ill. Hosp., 1965-66, resident in internal medicine, 1966-68, fellow in infectious diseases, 1968-69, chief resident in internal medicine, 1969-70; practice medicine specializing in internal medicine and family practice CMBY Clinic, Ltd., Elmhurst, Ill., 1970—; staff Elmhurst Meml. Hosp., chmn. pharmacology com., 1974-76, med. audit com., 1979-80; instr. internal medicine U. Ill. Hosp., 1969-72; asst. prof. medicine Loyola U., 1970-71, Chgo. Med. Sch., 1979—. Diplomate Am. Bd. Internal Medicine, Am. Bd. Family Practice. Fellow ACP, Am. Acad. Family Practice; mem. AMA, Ill., DuPage County med. socs., Am. Profl. Practice Assn., Am. Soc. Internal Medicine, Am. Soc. Contemporary Medicine and Surgery, Am. Med. Women's Assn., Am. Assn. Clin. Research, AAAS, Lyric Opera Chgo. Republican. Roman Catholic. Clubs: Univ. (Chgo.); Regis; Century (Meml. Hosp.), Courts (Elmhurst). Contbr. articles profl. jours. Research on shock, psychosomatic medicine. Home: 320 Cottage Hill St Elmhurst IL 60126 Office: 135 Cottage Hill St Elmhurst IL 60126

BLAIN, JACQUELYN ALICE GRIPPIN, cosmotologist; b. Springfield, Mass., Sept. 21, 1928; d. Roger Warren and Kathleen Alice (Proctor) Nash; student Springfield Conservatory Music, 1944-47, Hartford Conservatory Music, 1971-72, with concertmaster Bill Dalton, 1963-78; children—Diana Grippin, Lea Grippin, Lyn Grippin. With Watkins Bros., Inc., Hartford, Conn., 1964-79, asst. to owner, 1974-79; cosmotologist, Longmeadow, Mass., 1982—. Mem. Hammond Organ

Assn., Springfield Cosmotology Assn. (treas.). Home: 80 Kenmore Dr Longmeadow MA 01106

BLAIN, JACQUELYN SHIRES, writer, educator; b. Dallas, Aug. 14, 1950; d. George Thomas and Robbie Jo (Martin) Shires; B.A., U. Tex., 1972; M.A., U. Houston, 1981; 1 dau., Jennifer Ellen. Teaching asst, U. Houston, 1977-78, teaching fellow in English, 1978-79; graphics supr. Brown & Root, 1979-80; med. editor U. Tex. Med. Sch. at Houston, 1980-81; partner Bergin, Blain & Wilkinson, Corporate Communications and Creative Services, 1981—; adj. faculty U. Houston System, 1980—; free-lance writer. Mem. Soc. Tech. Communications (v.p. chpt. 1981-82), Communications Mgmt., Am. Med. Writers Assn., Tech. Communications Conf. Office: 2715 Bissonnet #404 Houston TX 77005 *

BLAIR, BILLIE GOODE, psychologist; b. Plainview, Tex., June 11, 1940; d. William McKinley and Mary Lara (Collis) Goode; B.S., Tex. Tech. U., 1962; M.S., San Diego State U., 1970; m. William David Blair, Dec. 21, 1958; 1 dau., Whitney Brete. Social worker Monterey County Welfare Dept., Monterey, Calif., 1966-67; instr. San Diego Jr. Coll., 1967-71; pvt. practice psychology, San Diego, 1969-71, 75—; psychologist Beaver Lodge Treatment Centre, Oliver, B.C., Can., 1974-76, exec. dir., 1976—; researcher San Diego State U., 1979—, asso. dir. Center Ethnographic Research, 1982—. Bd. dirs. South Okanagan Children's Services, Aid to Handicapped, Assn. for Mentally Retarded; pres. S. Okanagan Community Arts Council, 1978-79; bd. dirs. Okanagan Mainline Regional Arts Council, 1978-79; local campaign coordinator Trudeau for Prime Minister, 1979. Mem. Am. Psychol. Assn., Can. Psychol. Assn., Am. Personnel and Guidance Assn., B.C. Psychol. Assn., B.C. Assn. for Mentally Retarded, Calif. Council for Social Studies. Republican. Home: PO Box 2921 El Cajon CA 92021 Office: San Diego State U San Diego CA 92128

BLAIR, DIANE KINCAID, polit. scientist; b. Washington, Oct. 28, 1938; d. William Keeveny and Minna Bea (Rosenbaum) Divers; B.A., Cornell U., 1959; M.A., U. Ark., 1967; m. James B. Blair, Sept. 1, 1979; children by previous marriage—William Reid Kincaid, Kathryn Lea Kincaid. Contract analyst Pres.'s Commn. on Govt. Contracts, Washington, 1959-60; research asst. Spl. Com. on Unemployment Problems, U.S. Senate, 1960; legis. sec. to U.S. Sen. Stuart Symington, 1960-63; asst. prof. polit. sci. U. Ark., 1968—; cons. Sex Equality in Edn. Project, Am. Assn. Sch. Adminstrs., 1974-75. Chair Ark. Gov.'s Commn. Status of Women, 1971-73, mem., 1973-78; chair Gov.'s Commn. on Public Employees' Rights, 1975; commr. Ark. Ednl. TV Network, 1980—; mem. Democratic State Com., 1971—; Ark. del. Dem. Nat. Conv., 1972, also vice chair delegation; Ark. del. Nat. Women's Conf., 1977. Named Outstanding Faculty Mem., U. Ark., 1976, 78. Mem. Am. Polit. Sci. Assn., So. Polit. Sci. Assn., S.W. Polit. Sci. Assn., Midwest Polit. Sci. Assn., Western Polit. Sci. Assn., Ark. Polit. Sci. Assn., Phi Beta Kappa. Author: Silent Hattie Speaks: The Personal Journal of Sen. Hattie Caraway, 1979. Home: 1011 Tanglebriar St Fayetteville AR 72701 Office: Political Science Dept University of Arkansas Fayetteville AR 72701

BLAIR, JOAN, corp. exec.; b. N.Y.C., May 15, 1946; d. Adrian and Gladys (Sobel) B.; A.B., Conn. Coll., 1967; M.L.S., Simmons Coll., 1968; m. Donald Schuler, Oct. 6, 1974. Dir. sch. library Taipei (Taiwan) Am. Sch., 1968-69; mem. tech. staff Arthur D. Little, Inc., Cambridge, Mass., 1969-73; readers services librarian N.Y. U., N.Y.C., 1973-74; v.p., dir. mktg. C L Systems, Inc., Newtonville, Mass., 1974-80; product mgr. Digital Equipment Corp., Bedford, Mass., 1980—. Trustee Wayland (Mass.) Pub. Library, 1977-78.

BLAIR, LINDA, interior designer; b. N.Y.C., May 25, 1939; d. Samuel and Magda (Vogel) Bierman; student Ohio State U., 1957-60; B.A. cum laude, Goucher Coll., 1963; M.A., U. Bridgeport, 1968; postgrad. N.Y. Sch. Interior Design, 1972-74, Parsons Sch. Design, 1980-81; m. William F. Doescher, Nov. 25, 1977; children—Michelle, Marc Blair, Doug and Cinda Doescher. With mktg., advt. dept. James W. Rouse Co., Balt., 1963; v.p. purchasing and sales Treasure Chest Antiques and Interior Design, N.Y.C., 1968-74; dir. Linda Blair Assos., N.Y.C. and Scarsdale, N.Y., 1975—. Pres. ZRW Cancer fund N.Y. Jr. League, 1965; vol. Easter Seals Soc., 1980—. Mem. Am. Soc. Interior Designers (asso.), Nat. Home Furnishings League. Democrat. Office: 11A Fox Meadow Rd Scarsdale NY 10583

BLAIR, MARIE LENORE, educator; b. Maramec, Okla., Jan. 9, 1931; d. Virgil Clement and Ella Catherine (Leen) Strode; B.S., Okla. A. and M. Coll., 1956; M.S., Okla. State U., 1961, postgrad., 1965-68; m. Freeman Joe Blair, Aug. 26, 1950; children—Elizabeth Ann Blair Stone, Roger Joe. Reading specialist Pub. Schs. Stillwater (Okla.), 1966—. Bd. dirs. Okla. Reading Council. Mem. Internat., Okla., Cimarron (past pres.) reading assns., NEA, Okla. Edn. Assn., Stillwater Edn. Assn., Kappa Kappa Iota. Democrat. Mem. Christian Ch. (Disciples of Christ). Clubs: DeMoley Mothers, Rainbow Mothers, Lahoma, White Shrine Jerusalem (past grand master). Order Eastern Star (Grand Martha of Okla.), Order White Shrine Jerusalem (supreme queen's attendant), Internat. Order of Rainbow for Girls (Okla. exec. com.). Contbr. Okla. Reader. Home: Route 1 Maramec OK 74045

BLAIR, PRUDENCE WADDOCK, public relations dir., editor; b. St. Louis, Oct. 23, 1925; d. Joseph Patrick and Annie Laurie (Page) Waddock; B.J., U. Mo., Columbia, 1947; postgrad. Northwestern U., Chgo. campus, 1953-54; m. Giles Allen Blair, Jr., June 6, 1959; children—Annie-Laurie, Giles Allen, Rebecca Ralls. With news dept. KXOK Radio, St. Louis, 1947-48; agrl. editor Pet, Inc., St. Louis, 1949-52; asst. dir. public relations Am. Angus Assn., Chgo., 1953-56, St. Joseph, Mo., 1956-57; editor Bank-Trust News, Centerre Bank, Inc., St. Louis, 1957-62; substitute tchr./tchr. aide Webster Groves (Mo.) Sch. Dist., 1971-78; dir. public relations Edgewood Children's Center, Webster Groves, 1979—; notary public, 1978-82. Active Chgo. Young Democrats, 1953-56; asst. Brownie leader Girl Scouts U.S.A., 1965-66, 69-70, asst. scout leader St. Louis council, 1970-71, troop cookie chmn., 1974-78; active PTA, 1965—; active United Fund campaigns, 1958-62, 78—, loaned exec. United Way, 1981, recipient Grand award to indsl. publs. editor, 1959, certs. of excellence, 1960, 61; mem. planning com. local history project Community Sch., Webster Groves, 1978. Mem. Women in Communications, Nat. Assn. Mental Health Info. Officers (1st Place newsletters and spl. projects communications contest 1982), Community Service Public Relations Council Greater St. Louis (dir. 1980—, 1st v.p. 1982), Alpha Chi Omega. Episcopalian. Contbr. articles to nat. press. Home: 44 Sylvester Ave Webster Groves MO 63119 Office: Edgewood Children's Center 330 N Gore Ave Webster Groves MO 63119

BLAIR, VERA SWANS, office equipment co. exec.; b. Buffalo, Aug. 7, 1944; d. Bennie J. and Bernice M. Swans; Asso. Bus., Levitan Bus. Sch., 1965; B.A. in Human Services, Antioch U., 1975, M.A. in Adminstrn., 1978. Clerical adminstrv. asst. YWCA, Phila., 1965-67; pvt. sec. Rentex Corp., Phila., 1967-68; vocat. counselor Jewish Employment and Vocat. Service, Phila., 1968-70; union organizer Nat. Union of Hosp. and Nursing Home Employees, Phila., 1970-71; research and adminstrv. asst. N.C. State Dept. Correction, Raleigh, 1971-72; office operational mgr. O.I.C., Phila., 1972-73; career edn. specialist Phila. Bd. Edn., 1973-74; outreach office mgr. City of Phila., 1974-76, personnel adminstrn., 1976-79; internal control mgr. Xerox Corp., Wilmington, Del., 1979—. Bd. dirs. Apprenticeship Info. Center, 1975, 76; asst. sec. bd. dirs. Phila. Alternatives for Rehab., Inc., 1976, sec., 1977, 78, chmn. personnel com., 1976-78; chmn. United Negro Coll. Fund Campaign Dr., 1976-77; chmn. ann. banquet com. Crisis Intervention Network, 1980. Recipient award of appreciation U.S. Navy, 1976; cert. of appreciation Joint Action in Community Services, 1977. Mem. Nat. Assn. Female Execs., Am. Assn. Personnel Adminstrs., NAACP, People United to Save Humanity, Urban League, Organizational Devel. Network Phila. Democrat. Mem. Unity Ch. Home: 9 West Ct Beacon Hill Wilmington DE 19810

BLAIR, WINK DOROTHY, public relations exec.; b. Little Rock, Aug. 17, 1931; d. Charles I. and Ethel (Claiborne) Dameron; B.A., La. State U., 1952; postgrad. U. Havana, Cuba, 1953. Interviewer, Am. Embassy, Havana, 1952-53; adminstrv. asst. to Congressman Hale Boggs, Washington, 1954-57; adminstrv. asst. Hall Bartlett Prodns., Beverly Hills, Calif., 1958-64; owner Wink Blair & Assos., Scottsdale, Ariz., 1969—; free lance writer, photographer to nat., local publs., 1967—; exec. dir. Phoenix Arts Council, 1977-79, bd. dirs., 1980—; dir. publicity Bullock's Stores, Scottsdale, Ariz., 1979-81; pres. Wink, Inc., public relations. Bd. dirs. Phoenix Sister Cities Commn. Mem. Nat. Fedn. Press Women (v.p. Phoenix chpt.), Nat. Assn. Female Execs., Women in Communications. Club: Phoenix Press. Home: PO Box 2326 Scottsdale AZ 85252 Office: 7134 Main St Scottsdale AZ 85251

BLAKE, BARBARA LOUISE, educator: b. Mangum, Okla., Oct. 20, 1929; d. Joe Boyd and Mayme Cornelius (Patterson) Thompson; A.A., Altus Jr. Coll., 1968; B.S., Southwestern State U., 1970; M.S., Oklahoma City U., 1980; m. Lester Shields Blake, June 22, 1947; children—Larry Vance, Celia Luree Blake Nippert. Various retail positions, 1949-52, 57-76; tchr. math. Moore (Okla.) Public Sch., 1970-81; tchr., dir. gifted/talented math. program Moore High Sch., 1977—; mem. adv. council Moore-Norman Vocat.-Tech. Sch., 1981-82; adj. prof. Oklahoma City U., 1981-82; cons. gifted/talented programs; sec. Okla. Tchrs. Retirement Bd., 1979-83; pres. Okla. Assn. Gifted, Creative and Talented, 1980-81. Chmn. Greer County council Girl Scouts U.S.A., 1960-62; Democratic precinct chmn. Cleve. County (Okla.), 1977-81; mem. Moore Planning Commn., 1977-83. Named Tchr. of Yr., Moore High Sch., 1978. Mem. Nat. Assn. Gifted Children, NEA, Nat. Council Tchrs. Math., Okla. Council Tchrs. Math. (dist. dir. 1976-80, v.p. secondary sch. 1981—), Okla. Edn. Assn. (dist. pres. math. council 1973, del. assembly 1975-80), Assn. Classroom Tchrs. (bd. rep. 1971-77), Moore Edn. Assn., Women in Math., Magnum High Sch. Alumni Assn. (pres. 1957—). Democrat. Methodist. Home: 2505 Ridgewood St Moore OK 73160 Office: 300 N Eastern St Moore OK 73160

BLAKE, DONNA LINDSTRAND, social worker; b. Oak Park, Ill., Nov. 7, 1938; d. George Albert and Esther Gladys (Newberg) Lindstrand; student U. Ill., 1956-59; B.A., Northwestern U., 1960; M.S.W., UCLA, 1963; m. J. Bernard Blake, Aug. 20, 1960; children—Susan Esther, John Bernard. Caseworker, Family Service of Assistance League, Hollywood, Calif., 1963-66; marriage, family and child counselor/supr. Cath. Social Service, Santa Monica, Calif., 1974-82; pvt. practice psychiat. social work, Santa Monica; instr. Santa Monica Coll., 1978-79; field instr. UCLA, 1980-82. Bd. dirs. parents guild St. Augustine Episcopal Sch., 1973-75. NIMH fellow, 1961-62. Mem. Nat. Assn. Social Workers, So. Calif. Psychotherapy Assn., AAUW (chpt. dir. 1973-74). Office: 1247 Lincoln Blvd Santa Monica CA 90401

BLAKE, EVELYN RUTH, banker; b. Liberty, Mo., Nov. 7, 1920; d. Sterling Orbie and Bertha May (Stockham) Britton; student Allen County Community Coll., Am. Inst. Banking, Mo. Secretarial Sch., Internat. Sch. Graphoanalysis, Chgo.; m. Harold Lee Blake, Mar. 9, 1944 (dec.); children—Penny Lee Blake Kafka, Harold Lee II, Larry Gene. Exec. sec., Iola C. of C., 1951-55; v.p., asst. trust officer Iola State Bank, 1956—. Mem. adv. com. office edn. dept. Allen County Community Coll., Iola. Mem. Nat. Assn. Bank Women, Iola Bus. and Profl. Womens Club. Mem. Christian Ch. Office: Iola State Bank Box 650 Iola KS 66749

BLAKE, ILENE MILLS, county govt. exec.; b. Kegley, W.Va., Aug. 31, 1932; d. Ile Sheron and Okley Fay (Reid) Mills; student Concord Coll., 1950-51; B.B.A., George Washington U., 1967; m. Warren Porter Blake, May 24, 1951; children—Ile Wayne, Edward Dean. Adminstrv. asst. Arlington County, Arlington, Va., 1959-67; adminstrv. asst. Fairfax County, Fairfax, Va., 1967-71, budget analyst, 1971-72, budget officer, 1972-73, dir. Office Mgmt. and Budget, 1973—; treas. Blake-Mills Ltd.; v.p., chmn. bd. Energy Sav Center, Inc. Trustee, Sterling (Va.) Pub. Library, 1973—, treas., 1977; founder, bd. dirs. Blake Pvt. Sch. Mem. Municipal Fin. Officers Assn. Home: 125 Evergreen St Sterling VA 22170

BLAKE, JEAN ALESTINE, educator; b. Jamaica, Nov. 6, 1934; came to U.S., 1959, naturalized, 1974; m. Astley Constantine Lloyd and Zetilda Elizabeth (Gause) Henry; diploma edn. West Indies Coll., Jamaica, 1956; B.A. in Math., Union Coll., Lincoln, Nebr., 1961; M.A. in Math., Howard U., 1963; Ph.D. in Adminstrn., George Peabody Coll., 1978; m. John A. Blake, Dec. 16, 1961; children—Robert Alden Lloyd, Johnia Jean. Tchr., Carvalho's High Sch., Claremont, St. Ann, Jamaica, 1950-53; instr. math. West Indies Coll., 1954-58, Dupont Park Jr. Acad., Washington, 1963-64, Oakwood Coll. Acad. and Oakwood Coll., Huntsville, Ala., 1964-67; prof. math. Ala. A&M U., Normal, 1967—. Sabbath sch. asst. supr., div. leader, Sabbath sch. sec. Oakwood Coll. Seventh-day Adventist Ch., Huntsville. Mem. Ala. Assn. Coll. Tchrs. Math., Nat. Council Tchrs. Math., Pi Mu Epsilon. Contbr. articles in field. Home: 2628 Brookline Dr NW Huntsville AL 35810 Office: PO Box 116 Alabama A&M Univ Normal AL 35762

BLAKE, JULIE KIENAST, banker; b. West Germany, Feb. 25, 1948; came to U.S., 1960, naturalized, 1965; d. Guenter W. and Margaret H. (Fischer) Kienast; B.A., Wellesley Coll., 1970; postgrad. in program mgmt. devel. Harvard U., 1981; m. Jeffrey W. Blake, June 28, 1970. Analyst investment dept. Morgan Guaranty Trust Co., N.Y.C., 1971-77, mem. internat. fin. mgmt. dept., 1977-81, v.p., head German Desk Banking div., 1981—. Cert. fin. analyst. Home: Route 2 Hemlock Hollow Rd Mount Kisco NY 10549 Office: 23 Wall St New York NY 10015

BLAKE, KAY ANN, nurse; b. Wellington, Tex., Feb. 1, 1950; d. John Ruskin and Elizabeth (Green) Porter; student Amarillo Coll. Vocat. Nursing, 1971; m. Kenneth Noel Blake, Nov. 28, 1980. Nurse's aide Shamrock Gen. Hosp., 1968-69; nurse labor and delivery N.W. Tex. Hosp., 1970-76; pvt. scrub nurse Tex. Tech. U. Med. Sch., Amarillo, 1972-73; dir. nurses Leisure Lodge, Inc., Midland, Tex., 1977—; labor and delivery charge nurse Midland Meml. Hosp., 1977—. Mem. Nurses Assn. of Am. Coll. Obstetricians and Gynecologists. Mem. Ch. of Christ. Office: 2200 W Illinois St Midland TX 79701

BLAKE, ROBERTA SHARON SAVAGE, nurse; b. Scott County, Ill., Jan. 14, 1941; d. Carl Alvin Wesley and Helen Margaret (Price) Savage; R.N., Passavant Meml. Area Hosp., Jacksonville, Ill., 1961; m. Daniel H. Blake, Dec. 27, 1960; children—Heather Anne, Amber Noelle. Staff nurse White Hall (Ill.) Hosp., 1961-75, utilization rev. coordinator, 1976-79, inservice dir., 1979—, acting dir. nurses, 1979-80, dir. nurses, 1980—. Mem. North Greene Adv. Council, 1976-82; bd. dirs. Two Rivers council Girl Scouts U.S.A., 1978—, troop leader, 1976—. Mem. Ill. Soc. Nurse Adminstrs. Republican. Methodist. Club: Royal Neighbors Lodge. Home: 217 S Carrollton St White Hall IL 62092 Office: 407 N Main St White Hall IL 62092

BLAKE, TERRI (THERESA LANDS BLALACK), author; b. N.Y.C., Sept. 10, 1903; d. Fran and Anna Lands; student Orange Coast Coll., 1963-64, Los Angeles City Coll., 1965; m. Russell E. Blalack, July 1, 1920 (dec. 1976); children—Russell E., David E., Ronald R. Real estate owner, developer, Hollywood, Calif., 1953-62; actress appearing in various motion pictures, 1955-62; hostess TV program Take a Break with Terri Blake, Dayton, Ohio, 1966; speaker to various groups and orgns., 1966-78. Producer shows USO, 1955-56, VA, 1955-59; started campaign to promote Nat. Grandparents Day, 1968 (signed into law Sept. 5, 1979), campaign to prohibit mandatory retirement; mem. Republican Nat. Com.; bd. dirs., in charge publicity Hollywood Wilshire Symphony Assn. Recipient Mayor's Community Service award, Los Angeles, 1972; Community Service award New Neighbor Club, Dayton, Ohio, 1971; named World's Most Glamorous Grandmother, Hollywood C. of C., 1957; Ever Youthful Sr. Inspiration of Yr., Greater N.Y. Citizens Soc., 1972; Woman of Yr., Internat. Authors Guild, Oceanside, Calif., 1973; named Pin-Up Grandmother, Am. Legion of Oceanside (Calif.), 1979; White House honoree as founder Nat. Grandparents Day, Sept. 7, 1979; plaque for entertaining vets. Calif. Legislature, 1981; recipient awards Congl. Record, 1978, 79. Mem. Nat. League Am. Pen Women (pres. Los Angeles br. 1974-76, pres.'s citation, Woman of Achievement award 1981), Internat. Poetry Soc. (1st prize Houston 1969, 77). Clubs: Order of Eastern Star; Thursday Morning (Newport Beach, Calif.). Author: You Too Can Do It, 1970, 2d edit., 1979; guest appearance Tom Snyder Show, Sept. 6, 1979. Office: 570 N Rossmore Ave Hollywood CA 90004

BLAKELY, CARRELL RAE, metal products co. exec.; b. Hemingford, Nebr., July 27, 1936; d. Ray Willard and Marjorie Darlene (Carrell) Stull; A.A. in Bus. Adminstrn. and Acctg., Trinidad State Coll., 1974; m. Herbert S. Blakely, Aug. 31, 1972; children by previous marriage—Mickey F. Pugh, Rickey K. Pugh. Various secretarial and bookkeeping positions, 1953-65; legal sec. Wright & Kastler, Raton, N.Mex., 1965-68; pres. Elco Metal Products Corp., Harper, Kans., 1970—. Mem. Nat. Assn. Archtl. Mfrs. Republican. Roman Catholic. Author: True Marriage Vows, 1974. Home: 1005 Jenkins Rd Clayton NM 88415 Office: Elco Metal Products Corp Box 100 Burns Flat OK 73624

BLAKELY, MARTHA MARELLEN, publisher; b. Bklyn., Sept. 28, 1943; d. Ira Canfield, III, and Florence (Holmes) Mitchell; B.S., Cedar Crest Coll., 1966; m. James R. Blakely, Aug. 31, 1968; children—Karen Holmes, Thomas Howard. Chemistry technologist Valley Hosp., Ridgewood, N.J., 1966-68, Eastman Kodak Co., Rochester, N.Y., 1968-70; circulation mgr. Precious Metals Report, Inc., Newtown, Conn., 1976-78, chief exec. officer, 1978—. Bd. dirs. LWV; sec. AAUW, 1975, membership chmn., 1976. Mem. Fin. Mailers Assn. Office: PO Drawer A Sandy Hook CT 06482

BLAKENEY, ANNE BACON, occupational therapist; b. Morristown, Tenn., Mar. 16, 1947; d. David Ray and Ruth Anne (Speck) Bacon; B.S. with honors, U. Tenn., 1969; M.S. in Occupational Therapy (trainee HEW), Boston U., 1974; m. Michael Louis Blakeney, Apr. 13, 1974; children—Ruth Ellen, Kathleen. Unit dir. overseas recreation program ARC, Korea, 1969-70, recreation specialist U.S. Army Hosp., Ft. Polk, La., 1971; staff occupational therapist USPHS Hosp., Carville, La., 1975-78; mem. faculty U. N.C., Chapel Hill, 1978—, asst. prof. occupational therapy, 1981—; cons. in field. Vol., FISH Orgn., Morristown, Tenn., 1972, Ft. Saunders Community Project, Knoxville, Tenn., 1968-69. Served as officer USPHS, 1976-77. Mem. Am. Occupational Therapy Assn., World Fedn. Occupational Therapists, Soc. Behavioral Kinesiology, Center Neurodevel. Studies, Assn. Women Faculty, La. Occupational Therapy Assn. (pres. 1976-77), N.C. Occupational Therapy Assn. Democrat. Author articles in field. Office: Medical Sch Wing B207 H U NC Chapel Hill NC 27514

BLAKER, GERTRUDE GENEIEVE, food service mgmt. educator, dietitian; b. Barneston, Nebr., Nov. 10, 1917; d. Frank and Bessie (Kubicek) B.; B.S. (Regents scholar), U. Nebr., 1940; M.S., Cornell U., 1950; Ph.D. (fellow), U. Wis., 1967. Adminstrv. dietitian Univ. Hosps. Cleve., 1941-46; with Sky Chef's, Phoenix, 1946-48; asst. prof., asso. prof. Hotel and Restaurant Sch., Mich. State U., East Lansing, 1951-63; dietary cons. U. Wis. Med. Center, Madison, 1963-68; prof. food service mgmt., food sci. and nutrition Colo. State U., Fort Collins, 1968—; nat. cons. dietetics Surgeon Gen. USAF. Mary Swartz Rose fellow Am. Dietetic Assn., 1961-62, Medallion award, 1982. Mem. Am. Dietetic Assn., Am. Mgmt. Assn., Inst. Food Technologists, Nat. Restaurant Assn., Soc. Hosp. Foodservice Adminstrn., Foodservice Mgmt. Edn. Council, Soc. Advancement Foodservice Research, Am. Sch. Foodservice, Colo. Dietetic Assn., Colo. Restaurant Assn., Wyo. Restaurant Assn. Author: (with Karla Longree) Sanitary Techniques in Food Service, 2d edit., 1982. Office: Dept Food Sci and Nutrition Colo State U Fort Collins CO 80523

BLAKESLEE, DIANE PUSEY, fin. exec.; b. W. Chester, Pa., Apr. 12, 1933; d. Norman Solomon and Leona (Ruth) Pusey; student Hood Coll., 1951-54, Calif. Poly. State U., 1966; m. Earle Bevington Blakeslee, June 11, 1954; children—Samuel, Barbara, David, Ruth. With Nat. Bank of Avondale (Pa.), 1952-53, Bank of Am., Chino, Calif., 1954-55; registered rep. TMI Equities, San Luis Obispo, Calif, 1971-73, registered prin., br. mgr., 1973-78; registered prin., br. mgr. Walt Becker and Assos., San Luis Obispo, 1978-80; registered prin., owner Blakeslee & Blakeslee, San Luis Obispo, 1980—. Bd. dirs. San Luis Obispo Child Devel. Center, 1978—, Pvt. Industry Council, 1980—; bd. regents Coll. Fin. Planning, Denver, 1980—; counselor Family Services; active fund raiser for ch., symphony, PTA. Mem. Inst. Cert. Fin. Planners (dir), San Luis Obispo Life Underwriters, Internat. Assn. Fin. Planners, Nat. Assn. Life Underwriters. Republican. Quaker. Clubs: Symphony Guild, Women's Network, Quota. Home: 88 Country Club Dr San Luis Obispo CA 93401 Office: 1540 Marsh St San Luis Obispo CA 93401

BLANCHARD, D(IXIE) CAROLINE HUTCHENS, psychobiologist, b. Martinsville, Va., Nov. 10, 1941; d. Ralph Waldo and Dixie Hutchens; B.A., Hollins Coll., 1961; M.A., U. Iowa, 1963; Ph.D., U. Hawaii, 1972; m. Robert J. Blanchard, June 8, 1962; 1 son, Matthew. Research asso., asso researcher Bekesey Lab. Neurobiology, U. Hawaii, Honolulu, 1964—; instr., chmn. social sci. div. Honolulu Community Coll., 1971-73; instr. psychology U. Hawaii, 1971—, mem. grad. affiliate faculty, 1973—; NATO fellow U. Bergen (Norway), 1978-82; NIH grantee, 1971—. Mem. Animal Behavior Soc., Am. Psychol. Assn., Internat. Soc. for Research on Aggression. Democrat. Editor: Bull. of Internat. Soc. for Research on Aggression, 1972—; co-editor: Advances in the Study of Aggression; contbr. articles to profl. jours. Home: 43

Nawiliwili St Honolulu HI 96825 Office: U Hawaii 2430 Campus Rd Honolulu HI 96822

BLANCHETTE, PATTI, lawyer, state legislator; b. Exeter, N.H., Mar. 6, 1952; d. Thomas P. and F. Jean Jennings; B.A., U. N.H., 1974; J.D., Franklin Pierce Law Center, 1980; m. Michael R. Cornelius, May 6, 1978. Social worker Rockingham County Family Planning, Exeter; admitted to N.H. bar; asso. firm Boynton, Waldron, Doleac, Woodman & Scott, P.A., Portsmouth; mem. N.H. Ho. of Reps., 1974—, asst. dep. minority leader. Chmn. Newmarket (N.H.) Budget Com.; mem. N.H. Democratic Exec. Com. Home: New Rd Newmarket NH 03857 Office: Box 418 Portsmouth NH 03801

BLANCHFIELD, GEORGETTE LYNN, univ. adminstr.; b. Pitts., Oct. 10, 1954; d. George Lewis and Emilia Mary (Lubich) B.; B.A. in Journalism, Duquesne U., 1976. Free-lance writer, 1976—; reporter, prodn. asst. Pitts. Suburban Community Newspapers, Homestead, Pa., 1977-78; asst. dir. news and publs. Duquesne U., Pitts., 1978—. Vol., Action Center's Public Service Talent Pool Com., Pitts., 1979—. Named Outstanding Woman Journalism Grad., Duquesne U., 1976. Mem. Women In Communications (v.p. Pitts. chpt.), Council for Advancement and Support Higher Edn. Roman Catholic. Editor: Inside Duquesne. Home: 823 Mifflin Ave Pittsburgh PA 15221 Office: Univ Relations Duquesne U Pittsburgh PA 15282

BLANCO, AMANDA, photographer; b. San Salvador, El Salvador, Oct. 23, 1933; d. Felix and Julia Isabel (Raimundo) Blanco; M.F.A., Calif. Inst. Arts, 1981; B. Profl. Arts, Inst. Photography, Santa Barbara, Calif., 1971; m. Mario Escobar (div. 1966); children—Maurice, César-E., Rosa Eugenia, and Rocio E. Blanco. Instr., Calif. State U., Northridge, 1977-79; asst. course organizer Calif. Inst. Arts, Valencia, 1980-81; free lance photographer, Santa Barbara, 1981—. Ahmanson Found. scholar, 1980; Lew and Eddie Wasserman scholar, 1979. Mem. Calif. Women Higher Edn. (exec. bd. 1975-78), AAUW, Profl. Photographers Am. Author: The Many Faces of Jake Zeitlin, 1978; About Norman Corwin, 1980; Richard Hoffman at Seventy, 1982.

BLAND, LAUREL LEMIEUX, ednl. and sociol. research co. exec., author; b. Spokane, Wash., Feb. 23, 1926; d. Alfred T. and Bernice K. (Lawrence) LeMieux; A.A., Anchorage Community Coll., 1966; Ed.B. cum laude, U. Alaska, 1968, M.A., 1969; Ph.D., U. N.Mex., 1974; m. Frank H. Schricker, Mar. 30, 1976; children—Daniel Matthew Bland, Laurel Kathleen Bland Eisinger. Tech. asst. Alaska Human Rights Commn., Anchorage, 1967; liaison 2d Jud. Dist., Alaska Legal Services, Nome, 1968; instr. Alaska Meth. U., Anchorage, 1969-73; project dir. spl. hist. and cultural inventory of Imuruk Basin, Alaska, 1969-73; asst. prof. edn. U. Alaska, Fairbanks, 1974; prof. cross cultural edn. Sheldon Jackson Coll., Sitka, Alaska, 1974-79, now life appointment; exec. dir. Human Environ. Resources Services, Inc., Anchorage and Kennewick, Wash., 1970—; cons. to state and fed. govt. agys., Indian communities and orgns., 1964—. Mem. Soc. Intercultural Edn., Alaska Hist. Soc., Nat. Indian Edn. Assn., Soc. Indian and No. Edn., Arctic Inst. N.Am. Club: Altrusa. Author: (with William Oquilluk) People of Kauwerak, 1973; Northern Eskimos of Alaska, 1972; Alaska Legal Services Field Operation Manual, 1968; Manpower Needs to Construct the Trans-Alaska Pipeline, 1970; Alaska Native Population and Manpower Vol. 1, 1975, Vols. 2, 3, 1978; contbr. numerous articles on social anthropology to profl. publs.; specialist in EEO research; developed field techniques for Eskimo cultural heritage preservation. Home and Office: 1921 W 17th St Kennewick WA 99336

BLAND, MARY GROVES, community cons., state legislator; b. Kansas City; student Ottawa U., Penn Valley Coll., Pioneer Coll.; 4 children. Community cons.; mem. Mo. Ho. of Reps., 1980—. Active Vols. Against Hunger, Town Fork Creek Neighborhood Assn., Indiana Block Council. Recipient service award Mo. Black Leadership Assn.; Jefferson Community Service award. Democrat. Office: Mo Ho of Reps Jefferson City MO 65101 *

BLANDIN, NANETTE MARIE, govt. ofcl.; b. Seattle, May 10, 1948; d. J. Julien and Evelyn B. Baget; B.A. in Polit. Sci. and French with honors, U. Calif., Davis, 1970; M.P.A., Washington Public Affairs Center U. So. Calif., 1976; m. Don Michael Blandin, Sept. 2, 1972. Hdqrs. personnel officer Calif. Dept. Mental Hygiene, Sacramento, 1970-72; program dir. Calif. Adv. Coordinating Council Public Personnel Mgmt., Sacramento, 1972; budget examiner, mgmt. analyst Exec. Office President, Office Mgmt. and Budget, Washington, 1973-79; spl. asst. to insp. gen. Dept. Labor, 1979-80, chief div. assessment and tech. Office of Insp. Gen., 1980—; founder, co-chmn. Washington Young Profls. Forum, 1974-76; bd. dirs. Nat. Center Public Services Internship Programs, 1972-73; prof. adv. bd. George Mason U., 1978-79. Mem. Am. Soc. Public Adminstrn. (chmn. fin. and adminstrn. com. 1979-80, nat. council 1978-81, v.p. Nat. Capital Area chpt., Leadership award Nat. Capital Area chpt. 1978), Am. Assn. Budget and Program Analysts, Washington Women's Network, Pi Sigma Alpha (life). Author articles in field; bd. editors Public Adminstr. Rev.; bd. dirs., series editor The Bureaucrat. Home: 1913 Shepherd St NW Washington DC 20011 Office: 200 Constitution Ave NW Room S5030 Washington DC 20210

BLANK, MARJORIE KING, coll. dean; b. Kansas City, Mo., June 13, 1925; d. John Charles and Margaret Louise (Huling) King; student U. Mo., Kansas City, 1942-44; B.A., U. Mo., Columbia, 1947, M.Ed., 1951; Ed.D., U. Kans., 1978; m. Donald E. Blank, Aug. 22, 1947; children—Lawrence Dean, Douglas Eugene, Raymond Wayne. Counselor, U. Mo., Columbia, 1949-51; tchr. Kansas City (Kans.) schs., 1956-57; tchr., counselor Kansas City (Kans.) Community Coll., 1957-65, counselor, 1966-68, dir. admissions, 1968-72, asst. dean student services, 1972-77, asso. dean student services, 1977-81, dean student services, 1981—. Chairperson career devel. com. Kansas City Union Presbytery, 1978—; scholarship chmn., exec. bd. Kaw Valley chpt. March of Dimes, 1979-81, sec., 1981—. Mem. Nat. Assn. Student Personnel Adminstrs. (exec. bd. region IV West), Am. Personnel and Guidance Assn., Am. Coll. Personnel Assn., Nat. Vocat. Guidance Assn., Nat. Assn. Women Deans, Adminstrs. and Counselors, Am. Assn. Collegiate Registrars and Admissions Officers, Kans. Assn. Women Deans, Adminstrs. and Counselors, Kans. Assn. Student Personnel Adminstrs. (pres. 1980), Kans. Assn. Collegiate Registrars and Admissions Officers, Kansas City (Kans.) Women's C. of C. (exec. bd. 1980, 82-83), Phi Delta Kappa. Home: 8728 Mackey St Overland Park KS 66212 Office: 7250 State Ave Kansas City KS 66112

BLANK, RENEE MARION, mgmt. and tng. cons.; b. Jersey City; d. Paul and Mollie Horowitz; B.A. magna cum laude, Rutgers U., 1950; M.A., N.Y.U., 1971; m. Robert E. Blank; children—Marc, Paula. Program coordinator N.Y.U. Coop. Extension, 1965-68; program dir. Rutgers U. Coop. Extension, 1968-72; dir. tng. and orgn. devel. Bergen County council Girl Scouts U.S.A., 1972-78; prin. OPT Assos., Inc., Teaneck, N.J., 1978—. Trustee, N.J. Cultural Council, 1974-76; edn. chmn. Green Circle Human Relations Task Force, 1978—. Ford Found. grantee, 1981; Nat. Inst. Corrections grantee, 1980. Mem. Am. Soc. Tng. and Devel. (v.p. programs 1980), Phi Beta Kappa. Club: Altrusa. Office: 506 Maitland Ave Teaneck NJ 07666

BLANK, RUTH, Realtor; b. Chester, Pa.; d. Maurice Burt and Lillian (Federman) Burston; student Swarthmore Coll., 1936, Coll. of Desert, 1969; grad. Realtor's Inst., 1973; m. Ben Blank, Aug. 25, 1938; children—Diane, Jerry, Philip. Head property mgmt. dept. Ben Blank Co., Chester, Pa., 1945-60, gen. mgr., 1960—, exec. v.p., Palm Springs, Calif., 1969—. Adv. com. Coll. of Desert. Mem. Inst. Real Estate Mgmt. (cert. property mgr.), Internat. Real Estate Fedn. (del. Am. chpt. to congress Spain 1974, France 1975), Palm Springs Bd. Realtors (edn. com. 1975-76, chmn. ethics and profl. standards com. 1976-79, v.p. 1977-78, chmn. spl. awards com. 1979, chmn. multiple listing com. 1980; Realtor of Yr. 1981), Women's Council Realtors, Nat., Calif. (state chmn. profl. standards com., mem. interboard arbitration com., state dir. 1977, 78, 80, 81, 82) assns. Realtors, Realtors Nat. Mktg. Inst. (cert. residential broker, cert. residential specialist), Am. Arbitration Assn. (comml. panelist). Republican. Jewish. Club: Tamarisk Country (pres. women's golf aux. 1965-66). Contbr. articles to real estate publs. Office: 1478 N Palm Canyon Dr Palm Springs CA 92262

BLANKENSHIP, COLLEEN SUSAN, educator; b. Port Angeles, Wash., Oct. 28, 1949; d. Charles A. Kennedy and Lorraine E. Kennedy-Inman; B.A. in Sociology, U. Wash., 1971, M.Ed., 1973, Ph.D. in Edn., 1976; m. Timothy E. Blankenship, Mar. 20, 1971. Asst. prof. dept. spl. edn. U. Ill., Urbana, 1976-82, asso. prof., 1982—; cons. Ill. Office Edn., 1976-77, Guam Dept. Edn., 1980, 82; co-project dir. Coll. of Edn. Dean's grant, awarded by Bur. Edn. for the Handicapped, 1978-80; prin. investigator research project U. Ill. Research Bd., 1978-80. Recipient Excellence in Undergrad. Teaching award Coll. Edn., U. Ill., 1979, 82. Mem. Council Exceptional Children, Nat. Council Tchrs. of Math., Assn. Children with Learning Disabilities, Pi Lambda Theta. Co-author book sect.; contbr. articles to profl. publs. Home: 310 Arbours Dr Savoy IL 61874 Office: Dept Spl Edn 288 Education Bldg U Ill 1310 S 6th St Champaign IL 61820

BLANKS, WINNIE SMITH, nurse; b. Buffalo Junction, Va., July 14, 1931; d. Wimbish Wilson and Kathryn (Forlines) Smith; R.N., Meml. Hosp., Danville, Va., 1952; B.S. in Sociology, Averett Coll., Danville, 1978; m. Richard Harrison Blanks, Jr., Nov. 18, 1951; children—Robert Kevin, William Kyle. Office and hosp. nurse, Va., 1952, 54-59; dir., instr. Halifax Sch. Practical Nursing, South Boston, Va., 1963—; mem. Va. Vocat. Evaluation Team, 1981; mem. scholarship com. Halifax S. Boston Community Hosp., 1981; adv. com. Central Va. Health Systems Agy., 1982; med. adv. Mecklenburg County Life Savs. and Rescue Squad, 1981. Mem. Nat. League Nursing, Va. Vocat. Assn. Baptist. Club: Order Eastern Star. Home: PO Box 302 Clarksville VA 23927 Office: 2204 Wilborn Ave South Boston VA 24592

BLANKSTEIN, MARY FREEMAN, violinist; b. Rutherfordton, N.C., Oct. 26; d. Spurgeon Lee and Dexter (Forney) Freeman; diploma (Sch. scholar) Juilliard Sch. Music, 1955, B.S., 1958; student (Fulbright fellow) Brussels Conservatoire, 1958-59; Mus.M., U. Maine, 1975; student Emmett Gore, Christine and Edouard Dethier, Arthur Grumiaux, Joseph Fuchs, Erica Morini, others; m. Joseph Blankstein, Mar. 6, 1958; children—Margot, Philip. Violin soloist Little Orch. Soc. in Town Hall, 1955; asst. concertmaster Am. Symphony, N.Y.C., 1965-68, concertmaster, 1968-72; tchr. violin. prep. div. Juilliard Sch. Music, 1968-69; tchr. violin Manhattan Sch. Music, 1969—; pvt. tchr. violin and chamber music, 1970—; head instrumental dept. Chapin Sch., N.Y.C., 1973—; co-founder, mem. N.Y. Lyric Arts Trio, 1974—; solo recitals, U.S. and Europe; co-founder Downeast Chamber Music Center, Castine, Maine, 1977, also mem. faculty; rec. artists Musical Heritage Soc. Rec., also recs. with Am. Symphony under Leopold Stokowski. Mem. Am. String Tchrs. Assn., Music Tchrs. Nat. Assn.

BLANTON, SHIRLEY ANN, mfg. ofcl.; b. Connersville, Ind., Nov. 6, 1949; d. Lawrence Michael and Catherine Ann (Pflum) Risch; B.S. in Prodn. Mgmt. (Hoosier scholar), Ball State U., Muncie, Ind., 1982; m. Randell Blanton, Apr. 20, 1968; children—James Randell, Angela Marie. Sec. purchasing Stant Mfg., Connersville, 1968-72; sec. customer service H.H. Robertson, Connersville, 1974-77, prodn. control coordinator, supr., 1977-81, mgr. prodn. control, 1981—. Supr. Fayette County Girls Club; com. Fayette County blood drives, Fayette County Investment Club. Mem. Golden Key, Beta Gamma Sigma. Roman Catholic. Club: K.C. Aux. Home: Route 1 Box 108 Connersville IN 47331 Office: 800 W 18th St Connersville IN 47331

BLASER, PEG ROOS, state ofcl.; b. Ft. Dodge, Iowa, Jan. 19, 1925; d. Carlisle K. and Louise Anna (Klinger) Roos; B.S. in Sociology, Northwestern U., 1945; m. William L. Blaser, June 27, 1945; children—Glenn, Steven, Joan. Owner, Art Mart, Park Forest, Ill., 1952-63; research asso., acting exec. dir. Planning Consortium for Children's Services, 1976-77; dir. bds. and commns., Office of Gov. Ill., 1977-78; spl. asst. on women to Gov. Ill., Springfield, 1978-79; dir. Ill. Dept. Aging, Springfield, 1979—; adj. asso. prof. Sangamon State U., Springfield. Village trustee Park Forest, 1968-69; chmn. Ill. ERA Coalition, 1974-76. Mem. LWV lobbyist Ill. Gen. Assembly 1973-76, mem. state bd. Ill.). Unitarian. Home: 24 Bay Ridge St Springfield IL 62707 Office: Dept on Aging 421 E Capitol Ave Springfield IL 62706

BLASIER, MARTHA HIETT, speech pathologist; b. De Land, Ill., June 13, 1923; d. Jesse Earl and Edna Blanche (McMillen); H.; B.A., U. Ill., 1945; postgrad. U. Mexico, 1947; M.S. in Speech Pathology, U. Pitts., 1969; m. Cole Blasier, Sept. 20, 1947; children—Peter Cole, Martha Hamilton. Speech pathologist, Ill., N.Y. State, Washington and N.Y.C., 1945-66; instr. speech pathology Indiana U. of Pa. and Carlow Coll., 1969-70; speech pathologist Head Start Program, Pitts., 1970-74; instrl. adv. speech pathology Pitts. Bd. Public Edn., 1974—; clin. instr. dept. speech/theatre arts U. Pitts., 1979—; mem. spl. edn. adv. council Duquesne U., 1980—; bd. dirs. Eye and Ear Hosp., 1971—. Mem. Am. Speech, Lang. and Hearing Assn. (cert. clin. competence), Pa. Speech and Hearing Assn., S.W. Pa. Speech and Hearing Assn. (pres. 1980). Presbyterian. Clubs: Cosmopolitan (N.Y.C.); Pitts. Golf. Home: 5306 Westminster Pl Pittsburgh PA 15232 Office: 341 Bellefield St Pittsburgh PA 15213

BLASOR, JUNE GORDON, real estate exec.; b. Hillsboro, Tex., Dec. 28, 1940; d. Goyie T. and Neta (Sheffield) Gordon; student Baylor U., 1964-65; B.B.A. with honors, A&M U., 1976, M.B.A. with honors, 1977. Pres., NMP Machinery, Cuyahoga Falls, Ohio, 1977; adminstrv. asst. Can-Tex Industries, Mineral Wells, Tex., 1967-73; realtor Tarver & Eppes, Arlington, Tex., 1977-79; instr. Weatherford (Tex.) Coll., 1976-78; pres., owner Century 21 Centroplex Realty, Inc., Waco, Tex., 1979—; dir. NPM Machinery; cons. in field. Named Sec. of Yr., Nat. Sec. Assn., 1970. Mem. Women's Council of Realtors, Nat. Bd. Realtors, Arlington Bd. Realtors, Tex. Bd. Realtors, Waco Bd. Realtors, Am. Coll. Assn. for Women, C. of C. Clubs: 99, Century 21 Million Dollar. Contbr. articles to profl. jours. Office: 714 N Valley Mills Dr Waco TX 76710

BLASS, ROSANNE JOHNSON, educator; b. Mpls., Aug. 15, 1937; d. Eart Emmanuel and Rosella (Schanberger) Johnson; B.S., U. Minn., 1958; M.S., U. Tenn., 1972, Ed.D., 1975; m. William Errol Blass, June 6, 1959; children—Stephen William, Susan Kathryn, Julia Anne. Tchr., Wayzata (Minn.) Schs., 1958-59, Lansing (Mich.) Schs., 1959-63; co-founder, dir. Winona (Minn.) Nursery Sch., 1965-67; coordinator religious edn. John XXIII Student Center, Knoxville, Tenn., 1967-71; grad. asst. Reading Center, U. Tenn., 1971-73; examiner Tenn. Dept. Edn., 1972-73; reading clinician Bacon Miller & Assos., Knoxville, 1973-74; asst. prof. edn. Allegheny Coll., Meadville, Pa., 1974-81, asso. prof., 1981—, coordinator Instrn. Center, Cleveland Heights, Ohio, 1976—; cons. Mem. Am. Edn. Research Assn., Assn. Supervision and Curriculum Devel., Assn. Tchr. Edn., Internat. Reading Assn., Phi Delta Kappa, Pi Lambda Theta. Contbr. in field. Home: 1413 Grantleigh Rd South Euclid OH 44121 Office: The Alcazar Surrey & Derbyshire Cleveland Heights OH 44106

BLASSINGAME, SANDRA LOU, nurse, educator, univ. dean; b. Dallas, Nov. 8, 1937; d. James and Jessie (Leonard) Sears; B.S.N., Baylor U., 1960; M.S., Tex. Women's U., 1970; Ed.D., Nova U., 1980; m. Kenneth E. Blassingame, Sept. 27, 1963. Instr., Meth. Hosp. Sch. Nursing, Dallas, 1960-71; asst. prof. Dallas Bapt. Coll. Sch. Nursing, 1970-74, assoc. prof., 1974-81, prof., 1981—, dean Sch. Nursing, 1970—, assoc. dean acad. programs, 1981-82, dean acad. affairs, 1982—. Mem. Dist. 4 Tex. Nurses Assn. (dir. 1980—), Tex. Nurses Assn. (dir., sec. 1982—), Am. Nurses Assn., Nat. League for Nursing, Sigma Theta Tau. Democrat. Baptist. Club: Altrusa. Home: 6227 Highgate Ln Dallas TX 75214 Office: 7777 W Kiest St Dallas TX 75211

BLATT, GENEVIEVE, judge; b. East Brady, Pa., June 19, 1913; s. George F. and Clara M. (Laurent) B.; A.B., U. Pitts., 1933, M.A., 1934, J.D., 1937; LL.D. (hon.), St. Francis Coll., 1959, Villanova U., 1960, St. Joseph's Coll., 1964, Barry Coll., 1966, Seton Hill Coll., 1968, LaSalle Coll., 1970, Elizabethtown Coll., 1974, Dickinson Coll. Law, 1974, York Coll., 1975, St. Charles Sem., 1975, Cedarcrest Coll., 1976, Allentown Coll. of St. Francis de Sales, 1976. Mem. faculty U. Pitts., 1934-38; admitted to Pa. bar, 1938; sec., chief examiner Pitts. Civil Service Commn., 1938-42; asst. solicitor City of Pitts., 1941-45; dep. treas., exec. dir. Pa. State Dept. Treasury, 1945-49, sec. internal affairs, 1955-67, dir. departmental audits Auditor Gen., 1969; asst. dir. Pres.'s Office Econ. Opportunity, 1967-68; counsel Morgan, Lewis & Bockius, 1970-72; judge Commonwealth Ct. Pa., 1972—; mem. Pa. Bd. Pardons, 1955-67; sec. Pa. Indsl. Devel. Authority Bd. and Gen. State Authority Bd., 1956-67; Pa. del. to Interstate Oil Compact Commn., 1955-67, vice chmn., 1959-60; mem. weights and measures adv. com. Nat. Bur. Standards, 1960-67; mem. Pres.'s Commn. on Law Enforcement and Adminstrn. of Justice, 1965-67. Founder, exec. dir. Pa. Intercollegiate Conf. on Govt., 1934-72; founder, v.p. James A. Finnegan Fellowship Found., 1960—; bd. dirs. Center for Research in Apostolate, 1966-75, 80—; vice chmn. adv. council Nat. Conf. of Cath. Bishops, 1972-75; chmn. Harrisburg Cath. Diocesan Bicentennial Com., 1974-76; mem. exec. bd. Pa. Fedn. Democratic Women, 1940-72; del. Dem. Nat. Convs., 1936-68; Pa. Dem. Nat. Committeewoman, 1970-72; bd. mgrs. 41st Internat. Eucharistic Congress, 1975-76. Recipient Disting. Dau. Pa. award, 1956; Outstanding Citizenship award LWV, 1964; Pro Ecclesia et Pontifice medal, 1966; Phila. Fame award, Greater Phila. Women's Clubs, 1978; Bene Merenti medal Pope John Paul II, 1979. Mem. Am. Bar Found., ABA, Pa. Bar Assn., Dauphin County Bar Assn., Am. Judicature Soc., Nat. Assn. Women Judges, Nat. Assn. Women Lawyers, Nat. Bus. and Profl. Women's Clubs, Phi Beta Kappa, Delta Sigma Rho, Pi Tau Phi, Pi Sigma Alpha, Beta Sigma Phi, Delta Kappa Gamma. Clubs: Nat. Cath. War Veterans Aux., Nat. Cath. Women's Union, Eagles Aux., Soroptimists Internat. Office: 517 S Office Bldg Harrisburg PA 17120

BLATTSTEIN, DEBORAH MARIE SUKMAN, psychologist; b. St. Paul, Jan. 26, 1953; d. Robert and Millicent (Levin) Sukman; B.A. magna cum laude, Tulane U., 1975; M.A., U. Tex., 1977, Ph.D., 1978; postgrad. Baylor Med. Sch., 1980—; m. Abraham Blattstein, Aug. 5, 1974; 1 dau., Ayelet. Research asst. Sch. Nursing, U. Tex., Austin, 1976; research psychologist Research and Devel. Center for Tchr. Edn., U. Tex., Austin, 1977-80; cons. St. John's Devel. Center for the Mentally Retarded, Austin, 1975-76. Active CAP, 1976—. Mem. Am. Psychol. Assn., Am. Ednl. Research Assn., Southwestern Psychol. Assn., Phi Beta Kappa, Phi Kappa Phi, Pi Sigma Alpha, Alpha Lambda Delta. Jewish. Contbr. articles to jours. in psychology. Home: 7915 Deermeadow Dr Houston TX 77071

BLATZ, KATHLEEN ANN, state legislator; B.A., U. Notre Dame, 1976; M.S.W., U. Minn., 1978. Psychiat. social worker, 1981—; mem. Minn. Ho. of Reps., St. Paul, 1978—, mem. tax, health and welfare, gen. legis. and vets. affairs coms. Mem. LWV, Minn. Mental Health Assn. Independent Republican. Office: 357 State Office Bldg Saint Paul MN 55155

BLAUVELT, MELINDA, photographer, educator; b. Northampton, Mass., Sept. 15, 1949; d. Theodore Orlando and Melba Alice (Miller) B.; student Mt. Holyoke Coll., 1967-69; B.A., Yale U., 1971, M.F.A., 1973; m. Edwin E. Wells, Jr., July 3, 1982. One person shows: Harvard U., 1977, 78, Bayly Mus. U. Va., 1980, Wright Art Center Beloit (Wis.) Coll., 1981, Southeastern Center Contemporary Art, Winston-Salem, 1981, Mattingly-Baker Gallery, Dallas, 1982; group shows include: Yale Art Gallery, 1973, Addison Gallery of Am. Art, 1975, Harvard U., 1975, Va. Mus., Richmond, 1980, Nexus, Atlanta, 1980, Corcoran Gallery Art, Washington, 1981, 82, The Photography Gallery, La Jolla, Calif., 1982; Mus. Fine Arts, Houston, 1982; represented in permanent collections: Mus. Fine Arts, Houston, Dallas Mus. Fine Arts, Bayly Mus. U. Va., Corcoran Gallery of Art; lectr. art Smith Coll., 1974; teaching asst. Harvard U., 1974-75, lectr. visual and environ. studies, 1975-76, research fellow Carpenter Center for the Visual Arts, 1977-78; asst. prof. art U. Va., 1978—. Contbr. articles in field to profl. jours. Office: McIntire Department of Art Fayerweather Hall University of Virginia Charlottesville VA 22903

BLAYTON, DORIS, lawyer, educator; b. Atlanta; d. Jesse Bee and Willa May Blayton; A.B., Spelman Coll.; postgrad. U. Chgo., 1943-44; J.D., John Marshall Law Sch., 1949; M.B.A., Atlanta U., 1962, M.Ed., 1977. Mem. staff Jesse B. Blayton, C.P.A., Atlanta, 1943-77; admitted to Ill. bar, 1950, Ga. bar, 1951; mem. firm Daugherty & Combs, Atlanta, W.M. Mathews and D.A. Blayton, Atlanta; mem. faculty Ga. State Indsl. Coll., 1944-45, Ark. A.M.&N. Coll., 1966-67; supply tchr., Atlanta, 1974—. Mem. Nat. Bar Assn., State Bar Ga., Atlanta Bar Assn., Gate City Bar Assn., Black Women's Coalition of Atlanta, Nat. Council Negro Women, N.E.A., Ga. Edn. Assn., Atlanta Consumers Clubs, Delta Sigma Theta. Home and office: 1235 ML King Jr Dr SW Atlanta GA 30314

BLAZEY, CAREN WILCOX, food corp. exec.; b. Evanston, Ill., Dec. 4, 1942; d. Homer Bowen and Edna (Robinson) Wilcox, Jr.; B.A. in History, Wellesley Coll., 1964; M.A. in Internat. Relations, U. Pa., 1970. With internat. div. Girard Bank, Phila., 1969-71; asst. dean Coll. Liberal Arts for Women, U. Pa., Phila., 1971-73; ednl. cons., Harrisburg, Pa., 1973-75; mgr. govt. relations Hershey Foods Corp. (Pa.), 1975-80, dir. govt. relations, 1980—; mem. corp. Blue Shield of Pa., Camp Hill. Contract Compliance Adv. Bd. mem. Pa. Human Relations Commn., 1974-76. Mem. Public Affairs Council Washington (bd.), Chocolate Mfrs. Am. (chmn. public affairs com.), Grocery Mfrs. Assn. (chmn. public policy forum, 1977-80). Episcopalian. Club: Wellesley Alumnae Assn. Office: Hershey Foods Corp Hershey PA 17033

BLECK, PHYLLIS CLAIRE, physician and surgeon, musician; b. Oak Park, Ill., Mar. 10, 1936; d. William Fred and Mildred A. (Jones) B.; B.S., U. Ill., 1958; M.M., Northwestern U., 1968; D.M.A., U. So. Calif., 1970; postgrad. Autonoma U. of Guadalajara, Mex., 1973-76; M.D., Rush Med. Coll., 1979; M.S. in Surgery, U. Ill., 1983. Prin. trumpet Fla. Symphony Orch., 1960-66, Orch. Sinfonica Nat. de Peru, 1965; instr. Thornton Jr. Coll., 1966-68; lectr. U. So. Calif., 1969-73; asst. prof. Whittier Coll., 1973; asst. in gen. surgery Rush Presbyn. St. Luke's Med. Center, Chgo., 1979-82, instr. gen. surgery, 1982—. Mem. Kappa Delta

Pi, Pi Kappa Lambda, Sigma Alpha Iota. Editor: Mozart Divertimento for Winds; research on vascular ischemia.

BLED, RORY NORTON, tchr., restaurant owner; b. Berkeley, Calif., Oct. 10, 1945; d. Harold Clough and Audrey Leah (Neaman) Norton; B.A., tchrs. credential, U. Calif., Berkeley, 1967; M.A., Middlebury (Vt.) Coll., 1972; m. Serge François Bled, Mar. 9, 1975; children—Jeremy, Thierry. Tchr., Hayward, Calif., 1967-68; tchr. French and English, project coordinator Berkeley (Calif.) Public Schs., 1968—; co-owner Metropol Restaurant, Berkeley, 1981—; cons. Bay Area Writing Project. Bd. dirs., adv. council Berkeley Conservatory Ballet, 1975—. Recipient Lang. award Middlebury Coll., 1971; named Outstanding Tchr., Berkeley, 1975. Mem. Nat. Council Tchrs. English, Bay Area Curriculum Council, San Francisco Profl. Food Soc., Phi Beta Kappa. Office: 2271 Shattuck Ave Berkeley CA 94704

BLEDSOE, (ELLEN) ALENE, physician; b. Linden, Tex., May 5, 1914; d. Joseph Sidney and Clyde (Harkey) Bledsoe; B.A., Columbia Union Coll., 1941, postgrad; M.D., Loma Linda U., 1950. Intern, Bridgeport (Conn.) Hosp., 1949-50; resident home obstetrics Chgo. Maternity Center, 1950, Jacksonville (Ill.) State Psychiatry Hosp., 1951-52; resident in pathology St. Joseph's Hosp., Marshfield, Wis., 1952-53, Ill. Masonic Hosp., Chgo., 1954, Jewish Hosp., Cin., 1955, Kern County Hosp., Bakersfield, Calif., 1956, Gorgas Hosp., Calif., 1957, Sacramento Hosp., 1960; gen. practice medicine Skagway, Alaska, 1951; pathologist Mendocino, Calif., 1961-69; regional Cumberland, N.S., Can., 1970-72; quality control physician Cutter's Intake Labs., Stockton and Oakland, Calif., 1974-75; med. dir. Clinica de Salud para Familias, Hollister, Calif., 1975-76; practice medicine specializing in family medicine, Ft. Bragg, Calif., 1978—. Diplomate Am. Bd. Anat. and Clin. Pathology. Fellow Coll. Am. Pathologists, Am. Soc. Clin. Pathologists (emeritus fellow); mem. N.Y. Acad. Scis. (life mem.), Pan-Am. Med. Assn. (diplomate), World Med. Assn. (asso. mem.), Am. Cancer Soc., Am. Heart Assn., Am. Lung Assn., Calif. Acad. Scis. (sr. mem.). Republican. Adventist. Contbr. articles on pathology to profl. jours. Office: 684 S Main PO Box 729 Ft Bragg CA 95437

BLEDSOE, EVELYN JUNE, state legislator; b. Prudence, W.Va., Jan. 3, 1920; d. William Fanning and Alma Mae (Wilkerson) Cheek; grad. high sch.; m. Everett Bledsoe, Mar. 10, 1948; children—Bill, Charlotte, Walter, Charlie, Joey, Johnny. Mem. W. Va. Ho. of Dels. Mem. VFW Aux., Am. Legion (post pres. 9 1974), Upper Kanawha Valley Democratic Women's Club. Methodist. Address: 5630 Staunton Ave Charleston WV 25304

BLEGEN, JUDITH EYER, opera singer; b. Missoula, Mont., Apr. 27, 1941; d. Halward Martin and Dorothy Mae (Anderson) B.; student Music Acad. of West, 1962; B.M., Curtis Inst. Music, 1964; m. Raymond Gniewek, 1977; 1 son by previous marriage, Thomas Christopher Singher. Appeared with Met. Opera, N.Y.C., Vienna State Opera, Royal Opera House Covent Garden, Paris Opera, Chgo. Lyric Opera, San Francisco Opera, Miami Opera; worldwide concert tours. Address: care Thea Dispeker Artists Rep 59 E 54th St New York NY 10022 *

BLETHEN, SANDRA LEE, physician; b. San Mateo, Calif., May 16, 1942; d. Howard A. and Laura K. (Wolf) B.; S.B., U. Chgo., 1961; Ph.D. (NSF fellow), U. Calif., Berkeley, 1965; M.D., Albert Einstein Coll. Medicine, 1975; m. Fred I. Chasalow, Nov. 26, 1966. Instr. chemistry U. Calif., San Diego, 1968-69; asst. prof. San Francisco State U., 1969-71; resident Babies Hosp., N.Y.C., 1975-77; fellow N.C. Meml. Hosp., 1977-79; practice medicine specializing in pediatric endocrinology, 1979—; asst. prof. pediatrics Washington U. Sch. Medicine, St. Louis, 1979—; mem. staff St. Louis Children's Hosp., Barnes Hosp., St. Louis County Hosp.; med. adv. Human Growth Found., St. Louis, 1981—. USPHS fellow, 1965-67; diplomate Am. Bd. Pediatrics. Mem. Endocrine Soc., Lawson Wilkins Pediatric Endocrine Soc., Soc. Pediatric Research, Am. Chem. Soc. Contbr. articles on endocrinology to profl. jours. Home: 780 Hawthicket St Saint Louis MO 63131 Office: 500 S Kingshighway Saint Louis MO 63110

BLEVINS, ANNE HELEN, microbiologist; b. Kankakee, Ill.; d. George and Mary Anne (Hoffman) B.; R.N., Wausau Meml. Hosp. Sch. Nursing, 1927; student Columbia U., 1929-36, Marquette U., 1941, N.Y. U., postgrad. Med. Sch., Columbia U., 1936. Research asso. Post Grad. Hosp., Columbia U., N.Y.C., 1940-47; chief bacteriologist Univ. Hosp., N.Y.U. Bellevue Med. Center, 1948-53; chief supervising bacteriology Meml. Hosp., Meml. Sloan-Kettering Cancer Center, N.Y.C., 1953-68, asst. to dir., 1968—; cons. hosp. epidemiology. Recipient Elizabeth O. King award in clin. microbiology Am. Soc. Microbiology, 1970. Fellow Am. Acad. Microbiology; mem. Am. Soc. Microbiology, Am. Pub. Health Assn. (life), N.Y. Acad. Scis. (life). Republican. Roman Catholic. Club: Soroptimist International of New York. Home: 501 W 123d St New York NY 10027 Office: Memorial Hosp 1275 York Ave New York NY 10021

BLEVINS, MARY FRANCES DOBBS (MRS. J. CLARENCE BLEVINS), banker; b. Wilmore, Ky.; d. Charles Alvin and Rosa Lee (Bishop) Dobbs; grad. high sch.; m. J. Clarence Blevins, July 11, 1950. With 1st Nat. Bank, Nicholasville, Ky., 1942-80, asst. cashier, 1963-66, asst. v.p., 1966-80, auditor, 1964-66; collection agt. Gen. Telephone Co. Ky., 1960-65; bookkeeper Blevins Paint & Wallpaper Store, Lexington, Ky., 1956-74. Treas., Jessamine County Bd. Edn., Nicholasville, 1945-49; treas. Withers Meml. Public Library, 1961-80, also mem. adv. bd.; treas. Jessamine County Salvation Army Fund Drive, 1960; solicitor Jessamine County chpt. ARC, 1951, Arthritis Drive, 1967. Named Ky. col., 1963. Mem. Nat. Assn. Bank Women, Lena Madesin Phillips Bus. and Profl. Women's Club (treas. 1962), Nat. Audubon Soc. Mem. Christian Ch. (treas. Christian Women's Fellowship 1953, deaconess 1971-74, chmn. deaconess 1971). Home: 312 Hickory Hill Rd Nicolasville KY 40356 Office: 307 N Main St Nicholasville KY 40356

BLEY, CARLA BORG (MRS. MICHAEL MANTLER), composer, musician; b. Oakland, Calif., May 11, 1938; d. Emil Carl and Arlene (Anderson) Borg; student pub. schs. Oakland; m. Paul Bley, Jan. 27, 1959 (div. Sept. 1967); m. 2d, Michael Mantler, Sept. 29, 1967; 1 dau., Karen. Freelance jazz composer, 1956—; pianist Jazz Composers Orch., N.Y.C., 1964—; pianist European concert tours Jazz Realities, 1965-66; founder WATT, 1973—; toured Europe with Jack Bruce Band, 1975; mem. adv. bd. Jazz Composers Orch. Assn. Named winner internat. jazz critics poll Down Beat mag., 1966, 71, 72, 78, 79, 80; Guggenheim fellow 1972; Cultural Council Found. grantee, 1971, 79; Nat. Endowment for Arts grantee, 1973. Composed, recorded: A Genuine Tong Funeral, 1967; (with Charlie Haden) Liberation Music Orch., 1969; (opera) Escalator Over the Hill, 1970-71 (Oscar Du Disque De Jazz 1973); Tropic Appetites, 1973; composed: 3/4 (chamber orch.), 1974-75; recorded: Dinner Music, 1976; The Carla Bley Band-European Tour, 1977; Musique Mecanique, 1979; Social Studies, 1981; Carla Bley Live!, 1982. Office: 500 Broadway New York NY 10012

BLICKSILVER, EDITH, educator: b. N.Y.C., Jan. 6, 1926; d. Simon and Fanny Stettner; B.A., Queens Coll., 1947; M.A., Smith Coll., 1948; m. Jack Blicksliver, June 27, 1948; children—Paul, Diane, Robert. Lectr. history, English, Smith Coll., Northampton, Mass., 1947-48; prof. English, So. State Tchrs. Coll., Springfield, S.D., 1953-54; instr. English, Northeastern U., Boston, 1962-63; prof. Ga. Inst. Tech., Atlanta, 1961-62, 1963—. Grantee Ga. Inst. of Tech., AAUW. Mem. Multi-Ethnic Lit. Soc. U.S. (sec.), Coll. Eng. Assn. (pres. Ga.-S.C. regional br.), AAUW (corporate rep. from Ga. Inst. Tech.), Modern Lang. Assn. Am. Author anthology: The Ethnic American Woman: Problems, Protests, Lifestyle, 1978. Home: 1800 Timothy Dr NE Atlanta GA 30329 Office: Ga Inst Technology English Dept Atlanta GA 30332

BLISS, JOSEPHINE LESLEY, mag. cons.; b. Bradford, Yorkshire, Eng., May 9, 1930; came to U.S., 1975, naturalized, 1978; d. Lesley Charles and Edna (Bradley) Bell; student Penrhos Coll., N. Wales, 1935-46; Dipl., London Webber Douglas Coll. of Opera and Drama, London, 1946-49; m. D.J. O'Gorman, 1954 (dec. 1964); children—John Nicholas, Mark Charles, Sara Louise; m. 2d, Col. W.H. Bliss, Aug. 16, 1975. Mem. repertory theater, Swansea, S. Wales, 1949, West End, London, 1950, Royal Performance, 1950, Theatre Royal Drury Lane, London Palladium, 1952-53; entertainer Brit. Troops in Egypt, Malta, Far East, 1953-54, U.S. Troops in Eng., 1953-54; solo performance BBC-TV, 1958-59; adv., cons. Arlington Woman mag., 1979—; chmn. bd. dirs. Creative Arts Theatre and Sch., Arlington, Tex. Republican. Mem. Ch. England. Clubs: Arlington Newcomers (pres. 1978-79), Arlington Womans, Encore. Home: 2806 Augusta Ln Arlington TX 76012

BLISS, KAREN K., educator; b. Price, Utah, Nov. 22, 1938; d. Vennie and Sue (Erkkila) Kraync; B.S., U. Utah, 1962; M.S., Brigham Young U., 1973; 1 dau., Heidi Ann. Tchr. secondary schs., Utah, 1962-69; mem. faculty Snow Coll., Ephraim, Utah, 1969-79, dir. grants and projects, 1979-81; dir. devel., 1981—, asso. prof. family life, advisory com. for family life/family edn., 1978—; camp dir. Youth Conservation Corp., 1976-77, project dir., 1977-80. Dir. Snow Coll. USOE Minigrant Team for Drug Use Prevention, 1974-77; mem. Sanpete County Alcohol and Drug Adv. Council, 1975-77. Mem. NEA (life), Nat. Council Resource Devel. (dir. 1981-82), Snow Coll. Faculty Assn. (pres., 1976-77). Office: Snow College Ephraim UT 84627

BLISS, SALLY BRAYLEY, ballet dancer, educator, dir.; b. London, Eng., Sept. 18, 1937; d. John Wilfred and Zeversa Lorraine (Gibbon) Brayley; came to U.S., 1962; student Nat. Ballet Sch. Can., Toronto, 1950-62, Am. Sch. Ballet, summer 1953, 62-70, Am. Ballet Theatre Sch., 1962-70, Met. Opera Ballet Sch., 1962-66, Am. Ballet Center, 1966-70; m. Anthony A. Bliss, July 24, 1967; children—Mark Brayley, Timothy Newton. Ballet dancer Canadian Nat. Exhbn. Grandstand Show, 1951, television, Montreal, Que., 1953-54, Television Ballet Co. under direction Brian McDonald, 1955-62, Melody Fair Summer Stock, North Tonawanda, N.Y., 1959; soloist Nat. Ballet Can., 1956-62; summer stock Lenny Debin Circuit, 1961-62; prin. dancer Met. Opera Ballet, 1962-66, Jacob's Pillow with James Clouser, summer 1967; guest artist Am. Ballet Theatre, 1967; prin. dancer City Center Joffrey Ballet, 1968, N.Y.C. Opera, 1969; formed Joffrey II Co. with Jonathan Watts, 1969, asso. dir., 1969-75, dir., 1975—; adjudicator N.E. Regional Ballet Festival, 1974, S.E. Regional Ballet Festival, Pacific Regional Ballet Assn., 1975; owner Portledge Sch. Classical Ballet, Locust Valley, N.Y., 1973—; guest tchr. throughout U.S., 1970—. Mem. Nat. Assn. for Regional Ballet (dir.). Mem. Ch. of Eng. Office: Found for Joffrey Ballet 130 W 56th St New York NY 10019 *

BLITZ, CAROLYN JEANNETTE, c. of c. exec.; b. Jacksonville, Fla., May 21, 1952; d. Phillip L. and Marjorie H. Blitz; B.A., Ball State U., Muncie, Ind., 1975. Asst. dir. Soc. Ret. Execs., 1975-77; with Indpls. C. of C., 1977—, gen. mgr. community affairs, 1978-79, v.p. community affairs, 1979—; pres. Indpls. Alliance Jobs, 1980; chmn. bd. dirs. Indpls. Urban League, 1980; bd. dirs. Indpls. Bus. Devel. Found., 1978-81. Mem. Bus. and Profl. Women's Assn., Ind. Human Resources Devel. Group, Alpha Chi Omega (pres. 1977-79). Office: 320 N Meridian St Suite 928 Indianapolis IN 46204

BLITZ, JEANNETTE, furniture co. exec.; b. Poland, May 8, 1927; came to U.S., 1949, naturalized, 1954; d. Moses and Tsylia (Katz) Sobol; student public schs., Europe; m. John P. Pollak, Nov. 18, 1973; children by previous marriage—Regina, Mark, Helen. With Original Arts Mfg. Corp., Linden, N.J., 1956—; chmn. bd., pres. Andre Originals, Linden, 1969—; cons. on furniture design. Office: 2301 E Edgar Rd Linden NJ 07036

BLITZER, BARBARA JOAN SNYDER, publishing and video cons.; b. N.Y.C.; d. William and Gilda Snyder; B.F.A., Cooper Union; postgrad. New Sch., N.Y.U.; m. Fred J. Blitzer; 1 son, Charles William. Art dir. Carl Fischer, Inc., N.Y.C., Scholastic Mags., Inc., N.Y.C.; promotion dir. R.R. Bowker Co., N.Y.C., Associated Mag. Contbrs.; exec. v.p., creative dir., prin. Smith, Hagel & Snyder, Inc.; cons. book and periodical pubs., also book clubs; creative adv. Macmillan, Inc., asso. pub. Macmillan gen. books div., also v.p. Macmillan Pub. Co., Inc., 1968-78; creative and mktg. strategy cons. Macmillan, Inc., from 1978; now pres. Barbara Blitzer, Inc. Mem. Cooper Union Alumni Assn. (past gov.), Women In Cable, Am. Inst. Graphic Arts. Address: 2 Holly Tree Ln Rumson NJ 07760

BLITZER, PATRICIA VOLK, advt. agy. exec., writer; b. N.Y.C., July 16, 1943; d. Cecil Sussman and Audrey Elaine (Morgen) Volk; B.F.A. cum laude, Syracuse U., 1964; postgrad. Academie de la Grande Chaumiere, 1965, Sch. Visual Arts, 1969, New Sch. for Social Research, 1975, Columbia U., 1977—; Andrew Blitzer, Dec. 21, 1969; children—Peter Morgen, Polly Volk. Art dir. Seventeen Mag., N.Y.C., 1967-69, Harper's Bazaar, 1969; with Doyle Dane Bernbach, 1969—, v.p., copy supr., 1978—. Contbr. fiction and non-fiction to popular mags. Home: 1136 Fifth Ave New York NY 10028 Office: Doyle Dane Bernbach 437 Madison Ave New York NY 10022

BLIZNAKOV, MILKA TCHERNEVA, architect; b. Varna, Bulgaria, Sept. 20, 1927; d. Ivan Dimitrov and Maria Kesarova (Khorozova) Tchernev; came to U.S., 1961, naturalized, 1966; architect-engr. diploma, State Tech. U., Sofia, 1951; Ph.D., Engring.-Structural Inst., Sofia, 1955-59; Ph.D. in Architecture, Columbia U., 1971; m. Emile G. Bliznakov, Oct. 23, 1954 (div. Apr. 1974). Sr. researcher Ministry Heavy Industry, Sofia, 1950-53; practice architecture, Sofia, 1954-59; asso. architect Noel Combrisson, architect, Paris, 1959-61; designer Perkins & Will Partnership, White Plains, N.Y., 1963-67; project architect Lathrop Douglass, architect, N.Y.C., 1967-71; asso. prof. architecture and planning Sch. Architecture, U. Tex., Austin, 1972-74; prof. architecture and planning Coll. Architecture, Va. Poly. Inst. and State U., Blacksburg, 1972—; prin. works include Speedwell Ave. Urban Renewal, Morristown, N.J., 1967-69, Wilmington (Del.) Urban Renewal, 1968-70, Springfield (Ill.) Central Area Devel., 1969-71, Arlington County (Va.) Redevel., 1975-77. William Kinne scholar, summer 1970; NEA grantee, 1973-74, Am. Beautiful Found., 1973. Mem. Am. Assn. Tchrs. Slavic and E. European Langs., Soc. Archtl. Historians, Nat. Trust Historic Preservation, Am. Assn. Advancement of Slavic Studies, Assn. Collegiate Schs. Planning, Assn. Collegiate Schs. Architecture. Home: 219 Pine Dr Blacksburg VA 24060 Office: DEUS Coll Architecture Va Poly Inst and State Univ Blacksburg VA 24060

BLOCH, JUDITH SIMON, social worker; b. N.Y.C., Sept. 10, 1928; d. Solomon and Lena Simon; B.A., Bklyn. Coll., 1951; M.S.W., Columbia U., 1953; m. Milton Bloch; children—Deena, Natalie, Susan. Caseworker, Hillside Hosp., Glen Oaks, N.Y., 1951-54; lectr., group leader parent edn. groups, seminars Queens (N.Y.) Mental Health Soc., 1954-58; caseworker, family therapist Jewish Family Service, Bronx, N.Y., 1959-63; group leader, parent edn. lectr. Lifeline Center, Jamaica, N.Y., 1964-66; dir./founder community model demonstration program for young impaired children Pre-Schoolers Workshop, Syosset, N.Y., 1966—; asst. clin. prof. Adelphi U., Garden City, N.Y., 1976-77; lectr. in field. Mem. Nat. Assn. Social Workers, Am. Orthopsychiat. Assn. Contbr. articles to profl. jours.; producer, dir., writer 3 ednl. films. Home: 5 Diamond Ct Huntington NY 11743 Office: 47 Humphrey Dr Syosset NY 11791

BLOCH, JULIA CHANG, govt. agy. adminstr.; b. Chefoo, China, Mar. 2, 1942; came to U.S., 1951, naturalized, 1962; d. Fu-yun and Eva Chang; B.A., U. Calif., Berkeley, 1964; M.A., Harvard U., 1967; m. Stuart Marshall Bloch, Dec. 21, 1968. With Peace Corps, Sabah, Malaysia, 1964-66, tng. officer, Washington, 1967-68, evaluation officer, 1968-70; staff mem. minority staff Senate Select Com. Nutrition & Human Needs, 1971-76, chief minority counsel, 1976-77; dep. dir. Office African Affairs, U.S. Internat. Communication Agy., 1977-80; Inst. of Politics fellow Harvard U., Cambridge, Mass., 1980-81; asst. adminstr. Bur. for Food for Peace and Voluntary Assistance, AID, 1981—. Mem. adv. bd. Nat. Women's Polit. Caucus, 1978—; mem. adv. council World Human Needs Inst., 1981—. Mem. Orgn. Chinese Am. Women (chmn. bd. dirs.). Republican. Office: Agy for Internat Devel Dept of State Rm 3938 Washington DC 20523

BLOCK, BARBARA ANN, real estate co. exec.; b. Cle Elum, Wash., Sept. 25, 1936; d. Patrick M. and Mildred M. (Ashman) McLean; student Seattle U., 1955-56, U. Wash., 1956-58; m. Philip A. Block, Nov. 22, 1958; children—Philip A. (dec.), Patricia Coan, Robert, Teresa. With Ashman's Cafe, 1947-58, King County Central Blood Bank, 1955-58; sec.-treas. Alaska Transport Sales, Inc., 1965-70; edn. dir. Marston Real Estate Co., Anchorage, 1979-82; cons. Nat. PTA, 1965-82, Commn. on Individual Devel., 1981-82. Voter registrar, 1976-81; hon. mem. life Alaska PTA, 1976—, pres., 1979-81, regional v.p. nat., 1982—, hon. life mem. nat., 1979—; sec.-treas. Rural Alaska Community Action Program, 1980-81; mem. Exceptional Child Task Force on Alternative Financing, 1981, Co-op. Extension State Family Leadership Bd., 1981-82, Gov.'s Council for Handicapped and Gifted, 1981-82; parent seminar trainer PTA/March of Dimes, 1980-82. Recipient Outstanding Service award Anchorage Sch. Dist., 1977, Silver Clover award Anchorage 4-H Council, 1978. Mem. Nat. Bd. Realtors, Alaska Bd. Realtors (condominium chmn. 1981-82), Anchorage Bd. Realtors (Community Service award 1980). Republican. Roman Catholic. Club: Tower. Home: Star Route A Box 1738-K Anchorage AK 99507 Office: Marston Real Estate Co 2804 W Northern Lights Blvd Anchorage AK 99503

BLOCK, JANET LEVEN (MRS. ALBERT WILLIAM BLOCK), public relations exec.; b. Chgo.; d. Benjamin J. and Rosebud (Goldsmith) Leven; student Brenau Coll. for Women, Gainesville, Ga., Northwestern U.; m. Albert William Block, Sept. 27, 1947; children—Mitchell, Stephanie. Reporter, Chgo. Am. Newspaper, 1939-40; catalog advt. Alden's Chgo. Mail Order Co., N.Y.C., Chgo., 1940-42; stylist and public relations dir. Fashion Advt. Co., N.Y.C., 1942-44; asst. account exec., stylist Buchanan & Co., Advt. Agy., N.Y.C., 1944-46; advt. agy account exec. Abbott Kimball Co., Chgo., 1946-47; free-lance merchandising and public relations rep., Cin., 1960-64; v.p. public relations Shillito's, Cin., 1964—. Bd. dirs. Children's Heart Assn., 1975—; bd. dirs. Friends of City Parks, 1979-80, treas., 1982; bd. dirs. Great Rivers council Girl Scouts U.S.A., 1980—. Named YWCA Career Woman of Achievement, 1982. Mem. Fashion Group Cin. (past regional dir.), Downtown Council (promotion chmn. 1975-76, 80-81), Public Relations Soc. Am. (dir. 1974-75, sec. 1976, treas. 1977), TV Soc. Am., Bus. and Profl. Women's Club, Advt. Club Cin. (dir. 1967—, v.p. 1972, Advt. Woman of Yr. 1972, mem. Speakers Bur. 1973—, pres. 1973-74, AAF Silver medal 1976), Women in Communications. Home: 5300 Hamilton Ave Cincinnati OH 45224 Office: 7th and Race Sts Cincinnati OH 45202

BLOCK, JOYCE LUCHT, telephone co. exec.; b. Chgo., July 29, 1927; d. George Raymond and Florence (Lindemann) Lucht; A.A., N. Park Coll., Chgo., 1946; m. May 1, 1948 (dec.); 1 dau., Judith Florence. With Ill. Bell Telephone Co., Chgo., 1946-56, asst. engr., 1954-56; with Ind. Bell Telephone Co., Indpls., 1970—, personnel mgr., 1978—, equal employment opportunity coordinator, 1978—. Mem. Internat. Assn. for Personnel Women (pres. 1982—), Econ. Club Indpls., Bell Mgmt., Network Bus. Women. Lutheran. Office: 240 N Meridian St Indianapolis IN 46204

BLOCK, RITA LEE, fin. exec.; b. Utica, N.Y., Mar. 27, 1942; d. Robert Heine and Anne (Polivan) Block; student U. Miami, 1959-62, Syracuse U., 1962-64. Vice pres. corp. bonds Muller & Co., N.Y.C., 1973-81; agt. Barry J. Levien, Real Estate Broker, N.Y.C., 1975—; corp. bond, fixed income salesperson Wertheim & Co., N.Y.C., 1981—. Home: 245 E 87 St Apt 3A New York NY 10028 Office: 200 Park Ave New York NY 10166

BLOCK, RUTH, ins. co. exec.; b. N.Y.C., Nov. 7, 1930; d. Albert and Celia (Shapiro) Smolensky; B.A., Adelphi U., 1952; m. Norman Block, 1952. With Equitable Life Assurance Soc., 1952—, v.p., planning officer, 1973-77, sr. v.p. in charge individual life ins., 1977—, exec. v.p. individual ins. businesses, 1980—; chmn., chief exec. officer Equitable Variable Life Ins. Co., 1981—; dir. Informatics, Inc., 1973-76, Equitable Gen. Ins. Co., 1977-80, Med. Info. Bur., Equitable Money Market Fund; Mobil vis. exec. U. Iowa, 1978. Bd. dirs. Stamford (Conn.) YWCA, 1977-80; nat. chmn. Equitable United Way, 1978. Recipient Disting. Alumni award Adelphi U., 1979. Office: 1285 Ave of Americas New York NY 10019

BLOCK, WENDY, ins. co. ofcl.; b. Amityville, N.Y., Jan. 16, 1952; d. Herbert and Frances (Schaffel) B.; B.B.A., Adelphi U., Garden City, N.Y., 1975, M.B.A., 1977. Data mgmt. supr. Ins. Co. N.Am., Garden City, 1976-78, mgr. adminstrv. ops., White Plains, N.Y., 1978-80, field support mgr., Garden City, N.Y., 1980-81, Houston, 1982—; sr. project mgr. Mass. Mut., Springfield, 1982. Mem. Am. Mgmt. Assn. M.B.A. Execs., Westchester Women's Ins. Assn., Nat. Assn. Female Execs., Adminstrv. Mgmt. Soc. INA 1775 St James Pl Houston TX 77001

BLODGETT, ANNE WASHINGTON, artist; b. N.Y.C., Apr. 17, 1940; d. Thomas Peabody and Martha (Allen) Blagden; student Smith Coll., 1961, Sch. Mus. Fine Arts, Boston, 1962-63; m. Thomas Noyes Blodgett, Sept. 15, 1962; children—Joanne Washington, Laura Landon, Thomas Noyes. One-woman shows Caravan Gallery, N.Y.C., 1971, Berkshire Mus., Pittsfield, Mass., 1971, N.E. Harbor Library, Maine, 1973, 75, Caravan Gallery, N.Y.C., 1974, Bodley Gallery, N.Y.C., 1976-82, Medici Gallery, London, 1973, Carspecken-Scott Gallery, Wilmington, Del., 1978; exhibited in group shows New Grafton Gallery, London, 1972, Red Barn, Fishers Island, N.Y., 1974, 76, Grist Mill, Farmington, Conn., 1975, Bull Hill Falls (Pa.) Art Assn., 1976, Pioneer Gallery, Cooperstown, N.Y., 1976, 78, Wingspread Gallery, Northeast Harbor, 1979, Ferguson Gallery, Hartford, Conn., 1980, Erikson Gallery, N.Y.C., 1981, Tomlyn Gallery, Jupiter, Fla., 1982; represented in permanent collections: Fitzwilliam Coll., Cambridge, Eng., Berkshire Mus., Competence Assurances Systems, Cambridge, Mass., Energy Absorptions Systems, Inc., Chgo., Charles River Partnership II, Boston, Research Media, Inc., Cambridge, Mass., Wilson Learning Co., Mpls., Mancom Co., Princeton, N.J., Quixote Co., Inc., Chgo., United Mining Co., N.Y.C., Respuestos Automotrices, Mexico City, Davis, Polk & Wardwell, Inc., N.Y.C., Ins. Co. N.Am., Phila., also numerous pvt. collections. Democrat. Episcopalian. Club: River (N.Y.C.). Home: 55 E 72d St New York NY 10021

BLODGETT, VIRGINIA JUNE BALLARD (MRS. RALPH WESLEY BLODGETT), ednl. adminstr.; b. Detroit; d. William King and Marie (Crossley) Ballard; A.B., Asbury Coll., 1935; M.S., Butler U., 1962; postgrad. U. Louisville, Ind. State U., Ball State U., Ohio State U., San Francisco State U.; Ph.D. (hon.), Colo. State Christian Coll.; m. Ralph Wesley Blodgett, Sept. 25, 1935; children—Vivian Sue Shields, Rebecca June Downing, Judith Elaine (Mrs. David Purvis). Tchr. Dependent Schs., Europe, 1951-54, English various high schs., Ind., Va., Fla., 1942-61; tchr., chmn. English dept. Woodview Sch., Indpls., 1961—, dean girls, 1964—; instr. evening div. Ind. Central Coll., Indpls., 1964-69, adult counselor, 1965—. Active various community drives. Gen. Electric Co. fellow, 1967. Mem. Am., Ind. (sec. 1969) assns. women deans and counselors, NEA, Ind. State Tchrs. Assn., Warren Twp. Classroom Tchrs., Central Ind., Ind. personnel and guidance assns., Alpha Delta Kappa. Methodist (tchr. ch. schs. 1935—). Home: 468 Brown St Noblesville IN 46060

BLOEDE, ELLEN LOUISE MILLER, social worker; b. Honolulu, Dec. 21, 1922; d. Ralph W. and Phoebe Miller; B.A., U. Hawaii, 1947, M.S.W., 1975; m. Victor C. Bloede, May 9, 1947; children—Karl A., Pamela E. Social worker, Md. Dept. Social Services, 1948-54, 58-61; social worker Hawaii Dept. Social Services, 1956-58, 1969-72; sr. social worker Hawaii Dept. Social Services and Housing, Kapiolani Children's Med. Center, Honolulu, 1974—; spl. cons. Native Hawaiian Study Commn., 1981—. Founder, 1st chmn. Leasehold Reform Assn., 1974—. Mem. Nat. Assn. Social Workers, Aboriginal Lands Hawaii Assn., Bishop Mus. Assn., Docent Bishop Mus. Co-founder, 1st Unitarian Ch. Honolulu, 1957. Club: Woman's Campus U. Hawaii. Home: 635 Onaha St Honolulu HI 96816

BLOEDE, MERLE HUIE, club woman; b. Brady, Tex., May 4, 1921; d. Hulon William and Anna (Lohn) Huie; student San Angelo Bus. Coll., 1944; m. Victor G. Bloede III, Mar. 11, 1945; children—Dee Anna Smith (Mrs. Gene Donald Bratton), Victor G. IV, Susan Lohn. Asst. supr. Office Censorship, San Antonio, 1942-43. Patroness North Shore Hosp., Manhasset, N.Y., 1954-56, 67-68; vol. Waldorf Sch. Scholarship Fund, Garden City, N.Y., 1957; asst. treas., exec. bd., mem. art com. Meml. Sloan-Kettering Cancer Center Soc., N.Y.C., chmn. pub. relations com., 1982-83 Mem. North Shore So. Soc. (pres. 1963-65). Republican. Mem. Community Reformed Ch. Clubs: Coral Beach and Tennis (Bermuda); Sands Point (N.Y.) Golf; Flower Hill Garden (chmn. community service com. 1967); Manhasset Bay Yacht; Quail Ridge Golf (Delray Beach, Fla.). Home: 400 E 54th St New York NY 10022 also 3612 Royal Tern Circle Quail Ridge Boynton Beach FL 33436 also 19 Duke of Gloucester Manhasset NY 11030

BLOMQUIST, KAREN LOIS, cons. criminal justice planning and policy; b. Cambridge, Mass., July 5, 1951; d. Robert Charles and Marjorie Isabel (Hamilton) B.; B.A., Bates Coll., 1973; M.S., So. Ill. U., 1975. Planner, Mass. Dept. Correction, Boston, 1975-77, Mass. Supreme Jud. Ct., 1977-79; dir. crime prevention City of Boston, 1979-80; dir. devel. Boston Pvt. Industry Council, 1980-81; cons. Cruz Blomquist Assos., criminal justice planning, policy, architecture, Boston, 1981—; vis. lectr. Lowell U., 1976—. Campaign mgr., state senator, 1980; bd. dirs. Allston Civic Assn. Recipient Bates Key. Mem. Am. Soc. Criminology, Am. Correctional Assn., NOW, Phi Kappa Phi. Address: 12 Bradbury St Allston Station Boston MA 02134

BLOMQUIST, LAURA LOUISE, librarian; b. Medford, Mass., July 18, 1930; d. Evriviades Nicholas and Elisabeth Marie Josef (Prevenier) Gavrelis; B.A., Tufts U., 1952; postgrad. Purdue U., 1952-53; M.L.S., Syracuse U., 1971; m. Robert Blomquist, Sept. 12, 1953 (div. Sept. 1979); children—Jefferson Lee, Eric Lee. Advt. researcher Aluminum Co. Am., Pitts., 1954-56; mktg. analyst Westinghouse Corp., Pitts., 1956-57; research asso. NSF project Syracuse (N.Y.) U., 1972; dir. Learning Resource Center, Cazenovia (N.Y.) Coll., 1972-77; librarian Mills Coll., Oakland, Calif., 1977-79; head edn. psychology library Ohio State U., Columbus, 1979—. Trustee Manlius (N.Y.) Public Library, 1970-73, Onondaga Library System, Syracuse, 1969-73; trustee, v.p. Rittenhouse Sq. Condominium Assn., 1980—. Mem. ALA, Spl. Library Assn., Ohio Library Assn. Office: Edn/Psychology Library Ohio State U Columbus OH 43210

BLOMSTRAND, CAROL ELAINE, communications co. exec., writer; b. St. Paul, June 28, 1938; d. Carl Oscar and Vernie Wilhelmina (Rosenbaum) B.; B.A. in English, Valparaiso U., 1960; postgrad. U. Minn., 1958, 59, Northwestern U., 1964, 65. Editorial asst. The Hotel Monthly, Chgo., 1961-62; feature writer Chgo. Market Daily, 1962-64; writer, photo editor Robert Snyder Assos., Chgo., 1964-68; asso. editor Chicago Mag., 1968-70, Sphere Mag., Chgo., 1971-73; editorial cons., writer Spare Time mag., Chgo., 1973-74; editor Commodity Trading Manual (textbook), Chgo. Bd. of Trade, 1974-76; dir. communications The Whittle Group, Chgo., 1976-78; creative dir., v.p. advt. Whittle Raddon Motley & Hanks, Inc., Chgo., 1979-81; pres. Blomstrand Communications, Inc., Chgo., 1981—; owner, pub. Money & You newsletter, 1981—; editorial cons. Pricing Newsletter. Membership chmn. 42nd Ward Young Republicans, 1963-64; asst. to chmn. Ill. Young Republicans, 1965-66. Recipient copywriting awards Art Direction Mag., 1979, Communications Collaborative, Inc., 1979, Art Directors Club, N.Y., 1979. Mem. Chgo. Women in Advt., Chgo. Soc. Communicating Arts. Home and office: 155 N Harbor Dr Apt 3008 Chicago IL 60601

BLOOD, ELIZABETH REID, ecologist, sci. found. adminstr.; b. Glasgow, Scotland, Apr. 1, 1951; came to U.S., 1955, naturalized, 1963; d. Campbell Reid and Cecilia (Gibb) Reid; B.S., Va. Commonwealth U., 1974, M.S., 1975; Ph.D., U. Ga., 1981. Research assoc. Va. Commonwealth U., Richmond, 1974-75; cons. J.R. Reed, Assocs., Newport News, Va., 1975-76; asst. program dir. NSF, Washington, 1981—; cons. in field. Named Outstanding Young Woman in Am., 1976. Mem. Am. Chem. Soc., Soc. for Applied Spectroscopy, Inst. of Ecology, Sigma Xi. Contbr. articles on ecology and chemistry to profl. jours. Office: 1800 6 St NW Washington DC 20556

BLOOM, CLAIRE, actress; b. London, Feb. 15, 1931; d. Edward Max and Elizabeth (Grew) Blume; student Badminton Sch., Bristol, Eng., Fern Hill Manor, New Milton, Eng.; pub. schs., Fla., N.Y.; m. Rod Steiger, Sept. 19, 1959 (div.); 1 dau. Anna. Appeared as Ophelia, Stratford-Upon-Avon, 1948; plays include Lady's Not for Burning, also Ring Around the Moon, London, 1949-51; in Romeo and Juliet, others, for Old Vic, also as Juliet in Old Vic tour of U.S.; film roles in Limelight, The Man Between, Richard III, Alexander the Great, Brothers Karamazov, Buccaneer, Look Back in Anger, Three Steps to Freedom, 1960, The Brothers Grimm, The Chapman Report, 1962, The Haunting, 1963, 80,000 Suspects, 1963, Alta Infidelita, 1963, Il Maestro di Vigeuono, 1963, The Outrage, 1964, The Spy Who Came in from the Cold, 1965, A Doll's House, 1973, Islands in the Stream, 1976, Clash of the Titans, 1981, Brideshead Revisted, 1982; appeared Broadway in Rashomon, 1959, at Royal Court Theatre, London, in Altona, 1960, A Doll's House, Hedda Gabler, 1971, Vivat! Vivat Reginal, 1972; New York appearance The Innocents, 1976; London appearances A Doll's House, 1973, A Streetcar Named Desire, 1974, Rosmersholm, 1977, The Cherry Orchard, 1981; also various roles Brit. and U.S. TV. Address: care Michael Linnit Globe Theatre Shaftesbury Ave London W1 England *

BLOOM, JANE MANSFIELD MAGINNIS, physician; b. Ithaca, N.Y., June 22, 1924; d. Ernest Victor and Miriam Rebecca (Mansfield) Maginnis; student Cath. Coll. Okla., 1942, Okla. State U., 1943; B.S., U. Mich., 1968, M.D., 1974; m. William Lee Bloom, Mar. 31, 1944; children—David, Jan, Carolyn, Eric, Joseph, Robert, Mary, Thomas, Patrick, Arthur. Intern, Wayne County Gen. Hosp., Detroit, 1974-75; resident in internal medicine St. Mary's Hosp., Rochester, N.Y., 1975-77; staff internal medicine Met. Hosp., Detroit, 1977-78. Diplomate Am. Bd. Internal Medicine. Mem. AMA, A.C.P., Am. Coll. Emergency Physicians, Am. Med. Women's Assn., Alpha Epsilon Iota. Home: PO Box 8288 Ann Arbor MI 48107

BLOOM, JEAN LOUISE, ednl. adminstr.; b. Balt., Apr. 24, 1923; d. Charles Antis and Louise B.; B.S. in Nursing Sci., U. Md., 1946, M.Ed. in Guidance and Counseling, 1949; diploma in counseling psychology Columbia U., 1958; Ph.D., N.Y. U., 1968. Dir. sch. programs Fedn. Handicapped, N.Y.C., 1958-67; asst. research prof., dir. innovative services U. Pitts., 1967-69; ednl. dir. Englewood (N.J.) Hosp. Sch. Nursing, 1949-51; rehab. counselor Queensboro (N.Y.) Tb and Health Assn., 1951-53, personnel mgr. Queens Workshop, 1953-54, dir. rehab. dept., 1954-57; prof., coordinator rehab. counselor edn. program Edinboro (Pa.) State Coll., 1969—; cons. Bd. dirs. Catholic Social Services, Erie, Pa., 1980—, Family Crisis Intervention, Erie, 1978—, Planned Parenthood, Erie, 1971-73; bd. dirs. Florence Crittendon Services, Erie, 1971-74, pres., 1973-74; mem. adv. bd. Young Adult Inst. Workshop, N.Y.C., 1964-67, Counseling Center, Corry, Pa., 1974-77. Mem. Pa. Rehab. Assn. (dir. 1981—), Am. Psychol. Assn., Nat. Rehab. Counseling Assn. (charter mem.), Nat. Rehab. Assn., Am. Personnel and Guidance Assn. Episcopalian. Contbr. articles to profl. publs. Home: RD 2 Cambridge Springs PA 16403 Office: Edinboro State Coll Dept Psychology and Counseling Edinboro PA 16444

BLOOM, JUDI LYNN, TV reporter; b. N.Y.C., July 30, 1950; d. Willard Earnest and Ann Felice (Lyons) Bloom; B.S., Cornell U., 1971; student film courses, Hunter Coll., N.Y.C. Asso. producer, undercover investigative reporter Sta. WNEW-TV, N.Y.C., 1971-73; producer, reporter Sta. WPLG-TV, Miami, Fla., 1973-74; anchor, host, producer Sta. WPBT-TV, Miami, 1974-75; reporter, anchor Sta. WINZ-AM, Miami, 1975-76; reporter Sta. WPVI-TV, Phila., 1976-78; reporter, anchor Sta. KTTV-TV, Los Angeles, 1978—; guest lectr. Fla. Internat. U., Dade Community Coll.; instr. Sta. KIIS broadcasting workshop; producer documentary film Grandpeople, 1975. Mem. Nat. Assn. Female Execs., AFTRA, Women in Radio and TV, Nat. Acad. TV Arts and Scis. Club: Los Angeles Press. Office: KTTV-TV 5746 Sunset Blvd Los Angeles CA 90028

BLOOM, LYNN MARIE ZIMMERMAN, educator; b. Ann Arbor, Mich., July 11, 1934; d. Oswald T. and Mildred (Kisling) Zimmerman; B.A., U. Mich., 1956, M.A., 1957, Ph.D., 1963; m. Martin Bloom, July 11, 1958; children—Bard, Laird. Teaching fellow English, Ohio State U., 1957-58, U. Mich., 1958-61; from lectr. to asso. Case Western Res. U., 1962-67; asst. prof., then asso. prof. Butler U., Indpls., 1970-74; asso. prof. English, U. N.Mex., 1975-78, Coll. William and Mary, Williamsburg, Va., 1978—; prof. English, chmn. dept. Va. Commonwealth U., Richmond, 1982—. Grantee Nat. Endowment Humanities, 1979-81, U.S. Office Edn., 1979-81, George Mason U. Writing Center, 1981. Mem. MLA, Nat. Council Tchrs. English (life), Coll. Conf. Composition and Communication (exec. com.), Women's Caucus Modern Langs., Am. Studies Assn., LWV, ACLU, Phi Beta Kappa, Phi Kappa Phi. Author: Doctor Spock: Biography of a Conservative Radical, 1972; Strategic Writing, 1982; also articles, poetry, revs.; co-author: The New Assertive Woman, 1975; asso. editor: American Autobiography: A Bibliography, 1945-80, 1982; co-editor: Bear, Man and God, 1964, 71, editor: Symposium, 1969; editor Forbidden Diary, 1980; editorial bd. Jour. English Teaching Techniques, 1976—, Writing Program Adminstrn., 1981—. Home: 302 Mill Neck Rd Williamsburg VA 23185

BLOOM, SHIRLEY GORDON, ins. co. exec.; b. Portland, Maine, June 4, 1944; d. Robert Woodman and Eleanor Russell (Thomas) Gordon; B.S. in Edn., U. So. Maine 1966, M.A. in Math. 1968; m. Carl Bloom, II, June 12, 1965; children—Timothy Scott, Brian Thomas, Debra. Actuarial student Union Mut. Life Ins. Co., Portland, Maine, 1970-72, supr. group pension services, 1972-74, mgr. group actuarial services, 1974-76, dir. pension actuarial services, 1976-78, 2d v.p. pensions, 1978-80, v.p. full service pensions 1980—. Bd. dirs. Raymond Recreation Assn., also treas.; trustee Unionmut. Charitable Found. Mem. Am. Acad. Actuaries, Pi Mu Epsilon, Beta Sigma Phi. Office: 2211 Congress St Portland ME 04122

BLOOMER, LINDA STONE, former TV broadcaster, writer; b. Atlanta, Nov. 11; d. Russell T. Wray; student Forrell Sch. Entertainment Arts, 1960-61, Phoenix Coll., 1960-61, Ga. State U., 1962-63; m. Howard Corbett Bloomer, July 1, 1978. Owner, Acad. Playhouse of Entertainment Arts, Charleston, S.C., 1969-70; promotion mgr. Sta. WUSN-TV, Charleston, 1967-69; promotion mgr., broadcaster Sta. KPHO-TV, Phoenix, 1970-78; dir. creative services Stas. KJJJ and KXTC, Phoenix, 1979-80; promotion dir. Stas. KTAR/KBBC-FM Radio, 1980-81; free lance writer, lectr.; dir. advt. and promotion for Short Excursions in Arizona, 1977—; lectr. on Ariz.; contbr. articles to various jours. and publications including: Phoenix mag., Ariz. Sports News Weekly, Ariz. Host; instr. communication Ariz. State U., 1977. Mem. Broadcast Promotion Assn., Acad. TV Arts and Scis., Am. Women in Radio and TV (past dir.), Phoenix Press Club, LWV, Mu Rho Sigma (life). Editor: Ad-Libber, Phoenix Ad Club, 1975-76. Address: PO Box 2313 Phoenix AZ 85002

BLOOMFIELD, CATHERINE SANDRA, psychologist; b. Louisville, Oct. 24, 1950; d. Coleman and Shirley R. B.; B.S. with distinction, U. Minn., 1972, M.A. in Psychology, 1977; m. Brock Siegel, Dec. 19, 1978; 1 son, Justin. Stagiere, EEC, Brussels, 1973; coordinator student community involvement project Center for Youth Devel. and Research, U. Minn., Mpls., 1974-75, pre-med. adv., 1975-77, mem. jr. staff, student counseling bur., 1977-78; counselor Coll. St. Catherine, St. Paul, 1978—; instr. continuing edn. for women U. Minn., 1977—. Vol. counselor Walk-In Counseling Center, Mpls., 1977—. Recipient Innovative Programs in Career Devel. award Gen Electric Career Edn. and Guidance Program, 1975; lic. psychologist. Mem. Am. Psychol. Assn., Minn. Women Psychologists, Minn. Lic. Psychologists, Psyche. Home: 459 Tarrymore Ave Minneapolis MN 55419 Office: Coll St Catherine 2004 Randolph Ave Saint Paul MN 55105

BLOOMFIELD, SALLY WARD, lawyer; b. Columbus, July 20, 1943; d. Paul F. and Anita (Smith) Ward; student Ohio Wesleyan U., 1963-64; B.A., St. Louis U., 1965; J.D., Ohio State U., 1969; m. David S. Bloomfield, June 4, 1969; children—David, Paul. Admitted to Ohio bar, 1969, N.Y. bar, 1970, U.S. Tax Ct. bar, 1969; tax analyst Price Waterhouse & Co., N.Y.C., 1969-70; asst. atty. gen. Public Utilities Commn. Ohio, 1970-71, asst. to commr., 1971-73, commr., 1973-77; partner firm Bricker & Eckler, Columbus, 1977—. Pres., trustee Columbus Met. Club, Inc., 1978-82; pres. CALL, Columbus, 1981; trustee United Way of Franklin County, Ohio; mem. Ohio Public Defender Commn., 1981—, Mayor's Econ. and Adv. Council, 1980—. Mem. Columbus Bar Assn., Nat. Council Coll. Law, Ohio State Bar Found., Am. Bar Assn. Democrat. Office: 100 E Broad St Columbus OH 43215

BLOSSER, PATRICIA ELLEN, educator; b. Paint Twp., Ohio, Apr. 17, 1931; d. Russell Ford and Mabel Ellen (Kastor) B.; B.A., Coll. Wooster, 1953; M.A., U. No. Colo., 1956, Wesleyan U., Middletown, Conn., 1962; Ph.D., Ohio State U., 1970. Tchr. secondary schs., Ohio, Ill., 1953-67; mem. faculty, research asso. Faculty Sci. and Math. Edn., Ohio State U., Columbus, 1967-70, asst. prof., 1970-74, asso. prof., 1974-79, prof. edn., 1979—, asso. dir. user services ERIC Clearinghouse Sci., Math. and Environ. Edn., 1979—. Margaret L. White fellow Delta Kappa Gamma, 1967, 69; grantee U.S. Office Edn., 1969, 72. Mem. Nat. Assn. Research in Sci. Teaching, Assn. Edn. Tchrs. in Sci. (pres. 1975-76), Nat. Sci. Tchrs. Assn. (dir. 1965-67, 76-77, 78-80), Am. Ednl. Research Assn., Assn. Supervision and Curriculum Devel., Sci. Edn. Council Ohio, Delta Kappa Gamma, Phi Delta Kappa, Pi Lambda Theta. Presbyterian. Editorial bd. Sci. Edn. jour., 1978—; editor: Investigation in Science Education, 1978; contbr. articles to profl. jours. Home: 2606 Brandon Rd Columbus OH 43221 Office: Coll Edn Ohio State U Columbus OH 43210

BLOUGH, CAROLYN JANE, reading dir.; b. Grandville, Mich., May 30, 1931; B.S., Western Mich. U., 1969, M.S. in Reading; married, 4 children. Tchr., Lowell (Mich.) Area Schs., 1961-70, reading cons., 1970-75, dir. reading, 1975—, coordinator basic skills K-12, 1977—. Mem. adminstrv. bd., tchr. Sunday sch. United Meth. Ch. Mem. Mich., Internat. reading assns., Kent County (Mich.) Reading Council, AAUW, Am. Ednl. Sci. Assn., Assn. Supervision and Curriculum Devel. Club: Order Eastern Star. Home: 623 N Jefferson St Lowell MI 49331 Office: Lowell Area Schs 700 Elizabeth St Lowell MI 49331

BLOUT, JOAN DREYFUS, designer, civic worker; b. Montgomery, Ala., Jan. 29, 1920; d. Jack Jonas and Ida (Lewis) Dreyfus; B.A., Finch Coll., 1940; m. Elkan R.B. Blout, Aug. 28, 1939; children—James E., Susan L. Blout Merry, William L. Treas., CHON Corp., Cambridge, Mass., 1974—; pres. Ya Ya Designs, Cambridge, 1977—. Bd. dirs. Cambridge Community Center, 1952—. Mem. Am. Acad. Polit. and Social Sci., Euthanasia Edn. Council. Home: 1010 Memorial Dr Cambridge MA 02138 Office: 3 Hingham St Cambridge MA 02138

BLOXOM, SHARON DEE, banker; b. El Paso, Tex., Aug. 31, 1948; d. Ennis and Virginia (Johnson) Brokks; ed. U. Tex., Nat. Bankers Assns. courses. Various acctg., banking positions, to 1975; with Continental Nat. Bank-El Paso, 1975—, now asst. v.p. Episcopalian. Office: 601 N Mesa El Paso TX 79901

BLUCHER, VICKI, advt. agy. exec.; b. N.Y.C., May 17, 1946; d. Philip and Jean (Cohen) B.; A.A., Bklyn. Coll., 1966. Producer, Steve Horn Prodns., 1972-74; freelance film producer, prodn. mgr. for film cos., N.Y.C., 1974-78; producer Wells, Rich, Greene/West, advt., Los Angeles, 1978-80; v.p., exec. producer TV commls. Benton & Bowles, advt., Los Angeles, 1980—. Recipient Clio awards, Internat. Broadcasting award, Arts Dirs. Club N.Y. award, Internat. Film Festival awards. Mem. Am. Film Inst., Film Soc. Lincoln Center, Women in Film, Western Region Assn. Producers, ACLU, Nat. Women's Polit. Caucus. Address: 22677 Pacific Coast Hwy Malibu CA 90265

BLUE, EDNA JENKINS GOSSAGE, civic worker; b. Emory Gap, Tenn., Aug. 7, 1909; d. Arthur A. and Lennie Belle (Bailey) Jenkins; student Tenn. Poly. U., 1926, U. Tenn., 1940-48, Tenn. Tech. U., 1950-60, Mars Hill Coll., 1965, Roane State Community Coll., 1977; m. Roy Lee Gossage, Jan. 17, 1927; children—Dorothy, Daniel Arthur; stepchildren—Roy Lee, Margaret; foster dau., Helen Kendall; m. 2d, William F. Blue, Sept. 20, 1978. With Tenn. Dept. Human Services, Clinton and Crossville, 1949-77, sr. counselor, 1970-77. Chmn., The New Eyes for the Needy program, Cumberland County, Tenn., 1960-77; pres. Anderson County (Tenn.) Parents Council for Cerebral Palsy, 1949-51; founder The Daniel Arthur Center for Cerebral Palsy, 1950, Daniel Arthur Rehab. Center, Oak Ridge, 1951—; pres. bd. dirs., co-founder Cumberland County Girls Club, 1976-77; mem. steering com., founder Hilltoppers, Inc., Cumberland, 1975, bd. dirs., 1975—, sec. bd., 1976-79; pres. Cumberland County Assn. for Retarded Citizens, 1978-79; pres. Janet Clark Meml. Group Home, Inc., 1977—; bd. dirs. United Fund, Cumberland, 1978—, Four C's cultural found., 1978; vol. Local Group Homes for the Developmentally Disabled, 1976-78; chmn. Santa for all Yr. Fund for Needy Children in Foster Care, 1975-78; charter mem. The Homesteds United Meth. Ch., 1946—, ch. treas., 1964-78, ch. historian, 1978—. Named Anderson County's Mother of Yr., 1951; Cumberland County's Woman of Achievement, 1963, Bicentennial Woman of History, 1976, others. Clubs: Homesteads United Meth. Women (pres. 1960-78), Cumberland County Bus. and Profl. Women's (pres. 1960-77). Columnist Cumberland Homesteader, 1935-39; author: Cumberland Homestead 1933-1955, 1956; A Church is Born, 1961; contbr. articles to profl. jours., poems to anthologies. Address: 12 Grassy Cove Rd Route 3 PO Box 202 Crossville TN 38555

BLUE, FRIEDL MARIE, window mfg. co. exec.; b. Wurzburg, Germany, Dec. 19, 1934; came to U.S., 1958, naturalized, 1967; d. Friedrick Wilhelm and Katharina Ida (Thiel) Schuster; A.B., Maria Hoh Coll., Simbach, W. Ger., 1954; m. Louis D. Blue, Sept. 26, 1969; children—Robert Benedict Fleming, Jacquelyn Kerry Blue. Cons., Diener Knitting Co., 1965-67; pres. Abalone Printing Co., Reading, Pa., 1967-75, Penn-Gen. Inc., Myerstown, Pa., 1980—; cons. Pennex Plastics, Inc. Mem. Exec. Female Assn. Republican. Lutheran. Clubs: Lebanon (Pa.) Country, Lebanon Ski; Quentin Riding. Home: 199 W McKinley Ave Myerstown PA 17067

BLUE, MARGARET AURELL, psychologist; b. Cushing, Okla., Sept. 20, 1939; d. Herbert M. and Olive M. (Starkey) Aurell; A.B. in Social Work, Ind. U., 1961; postgrad. Patna U., Bihar, India, 1961-62; M.A. in Guidance and Counseling, Ill. State U., 1972; Ph.D. candidate U. Ill.; m. H. Darrell Blue, Jan. 11, 1981; children by previous marriage—Robert W. Porter, Sharon M. Porter. Caseworker, Cook County Dept. Public Aid, Chgo., 1963; referral worker Chgo. Council on Alcoholism, 1972; rehab. counselor Ill. Div. Vocat. Rehab., Decatur and Champaign, 1973-79; teaching asst. ednl. psychology U. Ill., 1979-81; psychometrist Center Children's Services, Danville, Ill., 1981—; mem stroke task force Ill. Heart Assn., 1977-79. Mem. Nat. Rehab. Assn., Ill. Rehab. Assn. (past chpt. pres., dir.). Democrat. Home: 307 Fairview Dr Champaign IL 61820 Office: Center for Children's Services 702 N Logan St Danville IL 61832

BLUE, MARY MARGARET SHEEHAN, real estate broker; b. Jacksonville, Fla., Jan. 9, 1945; d. Francis Patrick and Kathryn Charlotte (Dunkerburger) Sheehan; student N. Fla. Jr. Coll., Fla. State U.; m. Warren Coleman Blue, Feb. 3, 1963; children—William W., Michael Christie. Bookkeeper, 1st Fed. Bank of Stuart (Fla.), 1964-69; bookkeeper, teller Fla. Nat. Bank, Perry, 1969-71; mem. loan dept. 1st Fed. Bank of Perry, 1971-77; owner, pres. Taylor County Realty, Perry, Fla., 1977—. Sec., Citizens Com. for Econ. Devel., Taylor County, Fla., 1980—. Mem. Taylor County C. of C. (dir. 1981—), Fla. Assn. Realtors. Democrat. Methodist. Clubs: Garden, Womens. Home: Boyd Rd Perry FL 32347 Office: 115 W Green St Suite 215 Perry FL 32347

BLUE, ROSE, author, educator; b. N.Y.C.; d. Irving and Frieda (Rosenberg) Bluestone; B.A., Bklyn. Coll.; postgrad. Bank St. Coll. Edn. Tchr., N.Y.C. Public Schs.; writing cons. Bklyn. Coll. Sch. Edn. Mem. Authors Guild Am., Authors League Am., MENSA, Profl. Women's Caucus, Broadcast Music, Inc. Author: A Quiet Place, 1969; Black, Black Beautiful Black, 1969; How Many Blocks in The World, 1970; Bed-Stuy Beat, 1970; I Am Here (Yo Estoy Aqui), 1971; A Month of Sundays, 1972; Grandma Didn't Wave Back, 1972; Nikki 108, 1973; We Are Chicano, 1973; The Preacher's Kid, 1975; Seven Years From Home,

1976; The YoYo Kid, 1976; The Thirteenth Year, 1977; Cold Rain on the Water, 1979; My Mother the Witch, 1981; Drama of Love, 1964; Let's Face It, 1961; My Heartstrings Keep Me Tied To You, 1963; Give Me A Break, 1962; Homecoming Party, 1966. Contbg. editor, contbr. Teacher mag., Day Care mag. Home and Office: 1320 51st St Brooklyn NY 11219

BLUESTEIN, JUDITH ANN, diversified industry exec.; b. Cin., Apr. 2, 1949; d. Paul Harold and Joan Ruth (Straus) Bluestein; B.A., U. Pa., 1969; postgrad. Am. Sch. Classical Studies, Athens, Greece, 1968, Vergilian Soc., 1970, 76, 77, 78, Hebrew Union Coll., Jewish Inst. Religion, Jerusalem, 1971, 1979-80, Hebrew Union Coll., Jewish Inst. Religion, Cin., 1980—, Am. Acad. in Rome, 1975; M.A. in Religion (Univ. fellow), Case Western Res. U., 1973, M.A. in Latin, 1973. Sec., Paul H. Bluestein & Co., Cin., 1964—; v.p. Panel Machine Co., 1966—, Blujay Corp., 1966—, Ermet Products Corp., 1966—; partner Companhia Engenheiros Industrial Bluestein do Brasil, Cin., 1971—; tchr. Latin, Cin. Public Schs., 1973-79. Mem. Archeol. Inst. Am., Classical Assn. Middle West and South (v.p. Ohio 1976-79), Am. Classical League, Ohio Classical Conf. (council 1976-79), Vergilian Soc., Soc. Bibl. Lit., Cin. Assn. Tchrs. Classics (pres. 1976-78), Am. Philol. Assn. Address: 3420 Section Rd Cincinnati OH 45237

BLUESTEIN, VENUS WELLER, psychologist; b. Milw., July 16, 1933; d. Richard T. and Hazel (Beard) Weller; B.S., U. Cin., 1956, M.Ed., 1959, Ed.D., 1966; m. Marvin Bluestein, Mar. 7, 1954. Psychologist in tng. Longview State Hosp., Cin., 1956-58; sch. psychologist Cin. Pub. Schs., 1958-65; asst. prof. psychology U. Cin., 1965-70, asso. prof., 1970-79, prof., 1979—, dir. undergrad. studies, 1976—, coordinator sch. psychology program, 1965-70, co-coordinator, 1970-75; cons. child psychologist. Sec., U.S. exec. com. research Children's Internat. Summer Villages, 1964-68; chmn. Ohio Interuniv. Council on Sch. Psychology, 1967-68. Diplomate Am. Bd. Examiners in Profl. Psychology. Mem. Am. Cin. (sec. 1961-62), Ohio (editor Ohio Psychologist 1961-68, citation 1972, Disting. Service award 1968) psychol. assns., Sch. Psychologists Ohio, AAUP, Forum for Death Edn. and Counseling, Kappa Delta Pi, Sigma Delta Pi, Psi Chi. Contbr. articles to profl. publs. Co-editor Ohio Psychologist, 1972-79. Office: U Cin Dept Psychology Cincinnati OH 45221

BLUITT, KAREN, systems engr.; b. N.Y.C., Oct. 25, 1957; d. James Bertrand and Beatrice Bluitt; B.S., Fordham U., 1979; M.B.A., Calif. State Poly. U., 1982; m. Kenneth Mark Curry, Nov. 24, 1979. Software engr. Hughes Aircraft Co., Fullerton, Calif., 1979-81, microprocessor engr. Beckman Instruments Co., Fullerton, 1981-82, Singer Co., Glendale, Calif., 1982-83; systems engr. Mitre Corp., Bedford, Mass., 1983—. Served to 1st lt. USAR, 1979—. Scholarship Gov. N.Y. Scholarship Com., 1975-79; Beta Gamma Sigma scholar, 1978—. Served to lt. USAR, 1979—. Mem. Nat. Assn. Female Execs., Assn. M.B.A. Execs., Res. Officers Assn., Civil Affairs Assn., LWV. Home: 19 Royal Crest Dr Nashua NH 03060 Office: Burlington Rd Bedford MA 01730

BLUM, BARBARA BENNETT, state ofcl.; b. Beaver, Pa., Jan. 18, 1930; d. Virgil Eudell and Ethel M. (Fink) Bennett; B.A., Vassar Coll., 1951; m. Robert M. Blum, June 21, 1951; children—Stephen B., Jonathan R., Thomas L., Jennifer. Dep. commr. N.Y.C. Dept. Mental Health and Mental Retardation, 1967-70; commr. spl. services for children N.Y.C. Human Resources Adminstrn., 1970-73; met. dir. N.Y. State Bd. Social Welfare, 1973-76; dir. Willowbrook project N.Y. State Dept. Mental Hygiene, 1976-77; commr. N.Y. State Dept. Social Services, Albany, 1977-82; former chairperson Council Public Welfare Adminstrs.; pres. Manpower Demonstration Research Corp., N.Y.C., 1982—. Founder, bd. dirs. Assn. Mentally Ill Children, 171-76. Office: 3 Park Ave New York NY 10016

BLUM, ELEANOR GOODFRIEND, educator; b. Detroit, July 16, 1940; d. William Henry and Dorothy Elaine (Oslander) Goodfriend; B.S. in Edn., Wayne State U., 1962, postgrad. Coll. Edn., 1979—; m. Jerome B. Blum, Aug. 18, 1963; children—Beth Goodfriend, Sara Caroline. Kindergarten tchr. Livonia, Mich., 1962-63, Montgomery County, Md., 1963-64; tchr. Detroit Public Schs., 1977—, also reading coordinator King High Sch.; mem. edn. com. New Detroit Inc., 1981—. Vol. Detroit office of Senator Robert Griffin, 1972-74, asst. to appointments sec. to Pres. Nixon, Washington, 1972-74; chmn. March of Dimes Drive, Farmington, Mich., 1975; pres. Potomac Village Homeowners Assn., 1975; mem. 19th dist. Republican Com., 1975—, precinct del. 20th precinct, West Bloomfield, Mich.; alt. del. to Nat. Rep. conv., 1976; mem. exec. com. Oakland County Rep. Com., 1977-78; mem. Bloomfield Women's Rep. Club, West Bloomfield Rep. Women's Club; chmn. health com. Doherty Elem. Sch., 1975—; mem. library com. Temple Beth El, Birmingham, Mich., 1976, mem. library and arts coms., 1977-78; mem. urban affairs com. Jewish Community Council, 1977-78, community relations com., 1978-80, chmn. met. concerns com., 1979; mem. adv. bd. Oakland County March of Dimes, 1977-78, mem. bd., 1979; mem. Friends of West Bloomfield Library, 1975—, NAACP, 1979—; mem. com. on sheltered workshops, dept. mgmt. and budget State of Mich., 1978-80. Address: 5123 Chestershire Dr West Bloomfield MI 48033

BLUM, JOAN KURLEY, fund raising exec.; b. Palm Beach, Fla., July 27, 1926; d. Nehad Daniel and Eva (Milos) Kurley; B.A., U. Wash., 1948; m. Robert C. Blum, Apr. 15, 1967; children—Christopher Alexander, Martha Jane, Louisa Joan, Danna Carolyn, Paul Helmuth. U.S. dir. Inst. Mediterranean Studies, Berkeley, Calif., 1962-65; devel. officer U. Calif. at Berkeley Alumni Assn., 1965-67; pres. Blum Assos., Fund-Raising Cons., San Anselmo, Calif., 1967—; faculty U. Calif. extension, Inst. Fund Raising, SW Inst. Fund-Raising U. Tex., U. San Francisco, U.K. Vol. Movement Group, London, Australasian Inst. Fund Raising. Recipient Golden Addy award Am. Advt. Fedn.; Silver Mailbox award Direct Mail Mktg. Assn., Best Ann. Giving Program award, others. Mem. Nat. Soc. Fund-Raising Execs. (dir.), Nat. Advt. of Hosp. Devel., Women Emerging. Club: Tamalpa Running. Contbr. numerous articles to profl. jours. Home: Kentfield CA 94903 Office: 292 Red Hill San Anselmo CA 94960

BLUMBERG, BARBARA SALMANSON (MRS. ARNOLD G. BLUMBERG), civic worker; b. Bklyn., Oct. 2, 1927; d. Sam and Mollie (Greenberg) Salmanson; B.A., DePauw U., 1948; postgrad. New Sch. for Social Reserach, N.Y.C.; m. Arnold G. Blumberg, June 19, 1949; children—Florence Ellen (Mrs. Schwartz), Martin Jay, Emily Anne. With pub. relations dept. Nate Fein & Co., N.Y.C., 1948-51; free lance, 1960—. Pres., UN Assn. Great Neck, N.Y., 1967—, chmn. China Study Workshop, 1966-67; leader Fertile Crescent Study Group; pres. Shalom chpt. Hadassah, 1955-57; exec. v.p. Lakeville P.T.A., Great Neck, 1963-65; exec. v.p. Great Neck South Jr. High Sch., 1965-66; co-chmn. Great Neck com. for UNICEF. Area co-chmn. Nassau County McGovern for Pres., 1972; v.p. Reform Democratic Assn. Great Neck; bd. dirs. New Dem. Coalition of Nassau; councilwoman North Hempstead Town Council, 1975-81; issues com. Nassau County Dem. Com.; bd. dirs. Citizen's Sch. Com., Great Neck; mem. council Great Neck Sr. Citizens Center; mem. adv. com. on pub. policy N.Y. State Assembly. Recipient award Anti-Defamation League, 1975; Alumni certificate DePauw U., 1977; award 3 dist. U.S. Coast Guard Aux., 1979; Israel Bonds award, 1980—. Mem. N.Y. Alumni Club DePauw U. (trustee), North Shore Archeal. Soc., Alpha Lambda Delta, Theta Sigma Phi. Club: L.I. Women's Network (gov. 1979). Home: 12 Birch Hill Rd Great Neck NY 11020

BLUMBERG, GRACE GANZ, educator, lawyer; b. N.Y.C., Feb. 16, 1940; d. Samuel and Beatrice (Finkelstein) Ganz; B.A. cum laude, U. Colo., 1960; J.D. summa cum laude, SUNY, 1971; LL.M., Harvard U., 1974; m. Donald R. Blumberg, Sept. 9, 1959. Admitted to N.Y. bar, 1971; confidential law clk. Appellate Div., N.Y. Supreme Ct., 4th Dept., Rochester, 1971-72; teaching fellow Harvard Law Sch., Cambridge, Mass., 1972-74; prof. law SUNY, Buffalo, 1974-81; prof. UCLA Law Sch., 1979—; cooperating atty. ACLU. Baldy Summer Research fellow in law and social policy, 1977, 78; SUNY research Found. summer faculty fellow, 1975. Mem. Am. Soc. Comparative Law, Am. Assn. Law Schs., ACLU. Editorial bd. Am. Jour. Comparative Law, 1977-81; contbr. articles in field to profl. jours. Address: Law Sch UCLA 405 Hilgard Ave Los Angeles CA 90024

BLUMBERG, JANE WEINERT (MRS. ROLAND K. BLUMBERG), banker, ind. oil producer; b. Seguin, Tex., Sept. 24; d. Hilmar Herman and Hilda (Blumberg) Weinert; B.A., U. Tex., 1937; M.A., Northwestern U., 1938; m. Roland K. Blumberg, Apr. 20, 1940; children—Carla Ann, Hilmar Daniel, Edward Austin. Chmn. bd., dir. Seguin State Bank & Trust Co. Sec., Seguin Sch. Bd., 1957-65; mem. Tex. Hosp. Adv. Commn., 1960-64; bd. dirs. Seguin United Fund, 1959, 67—; bd. regents Tex. Lutheran Coll., 1965—, U. Tex. System, 1977—. Mem. Dem. Nat. Com. from Tex., 1972-80. Mem. Phi Beta Kappa, Kappa Kappa Gamma. Democrat. Lutheran. Club: Seguin Shakespeare. Home: RFD 2 Box 236 Seguin TX 78155 Office: PO Drawer 231 Seguin TX 78155

BLUMBERG, JULIA BAUM, club woman, educator; b. Hazleton, Pa.; d. Benjamin and Ida Ruth (Lurie) Baum; Ph.B. summa cum laude, Muhlenberg Coll., Allentown, Pa., 1937; postgrad. N.Y. U., Columbia U.; m. Dr. Leo Blumberg, Aug. Columbia U.; 1938. Mem. faculty Bethleham (Pa.) Sr. High Sch., dir. placement comml. grads., 1938-46. Life mem. B'nai B'rith Women, organized Bethlehem group, 1938, pres. Bethlehem, 1938-39, pres. Dist. 3, 1945-46, mem. nat. exec. bd., 1957-59, rep. nat. orgn., 1957-59, chmn. nat. vocat. guidance, 1957-59, chmn. dist. 3 Klutznick scholarship award, 1966-69, mem. bd. B'nai B'rith Women of Wilmington, pres. vocational service bd., 1962-64; life mem. Temple Beth Emeth Sisterhood, mem. bd., 1949-59, 70-82; treas. Dist 8, Nat. Fedn. Temple Sisterhoods, 1952-56; mem. nat. exec. bd. nat. fedn., 1953-57; gen. chmn. Dist. 8 conv., Wilmington, 1957; pres. community adv. bd. Hillel Counselorship, U. Del., 1979-82; mem. bd. Wilmington City Fedn. Women's Clubs and Allied Orgns., 1951—, 1st v.p., 1961-63, pres., 1963-65; mem. bd. mgrs. Florence Crittendon Home of Del., 1955-61; mem. Women's div. Brandeis U.; life life mem. Aux. Kutz Home for Aged, also bd. dirs. aux., v.p., 1972-82; mem. Nat. Commn. Vocational Service, 1957-59, Mayor's Com. for Christmas, Mayor's Com. for UN; mem. bd. UNICEF, 1972—; mem. steering com. CARE, Inc., 1971—; mem. Del. Nature Edn. Center, Inc., Del. Council on Crime and Justice; bd. dirs. Hillel Found. Bldg. Fund Corp. Pa.; chmn. bldg. and furniture com., dedication com. Hillel Found. at U. Del., 1963-64, hon. life chmn. community adv. bd. univ. B'nai B'rith Hillel Counselorship; mem. women's div. Jewish Fedn. Del.; mem. bldg. fund com. St. Francis Hosp., 1973; v.p. bd. dirs. Kutz Home Aux. Mem. Nat. Council Jewish Women, Greater Wilmington Fedn. Women's Orgns. (dir. 1965-69, 69-73, 73-77, 77-82, pres. Past Officers Club 1965-67, historian 1973-75, dir. 1975—), Del. Mental Health Assn., Crippled Children and Adults Soc. Del., Hadassah (life), B'nai B'rith Women (life), Phi Sigma Iota. Jewish (life mem., pres. Sisterhood 1952-53, mem. bd. 1971—, dir. temple 1952-55). Clubs: Widener U. Faculty Wives (hon. life), New Century (internat. relations com. 1978-82, edn. com. 1978-82). Home: 1401 Pennsylvania Ave Wilmington DE 19806

BLUMBERG, RENA JOY, radio sta. exec.; b. Cleve., Oct. 31, 1934; d. Ezra Z. and Sylvia L. (Lamport) Shapiro; B.A. cum laude, Brandeis U., 1956; m. Michael S. Blumberg, Mar. 6, 1964; children—Cathy, David, Stuart. Tchr., book reviewer, lectr., 1957—; community relations dir. WIXY-AM and WDOK-FM, Cleve., 1972-80; community relations dir. WWWE/AM/WDOK/FM Combined Communications Corp., Gannett Co., Inc., 1980—; radio interviewer; co-host TV interview show, 1976-77. Chairperson Channel 25 TV Auction 1974-75; mem. exec. com. Cleve. Congress Internat. Women's Yr., 1975; v.p. Cleve. Area Arts Council, 1974—; mem. budget com., exec. com., endowment com. Jewish Community Fedn. Cleve., 1972—; hon. life mem. nat. bd. of women's com. Brandeis U., trustee, 1978—; exec. bd. Nat. U.S. Commn. for Women; founder Women Space; media adv. Jr. League Cleve.; bd. dirs. Bur. Jewish Edn., Med. Mut., Ohio Sch. Broadcast Technique, Am. Cancer Soc., Fedn. for Community Planning, Greater Cleve. Growth Assn., Coll. Jewish Studies, Jewish Community Fedn., Playhouse Sq. Found., Sch. on Magnolia, The Housing Advocates, Cleve. City Club Found., Council Human Relations, Cleve. Com. for Econ. Growth of Israel; mem. adv. bd. Friends of Shaker Sq., Arthritis Found.; vis. com. of bd. overseers Sch Mgmt., Case Western Res. U.; mem. Shaker Heights Citizens Com. Recipient Marvin and Milton Kane Young Leadership award, 1968; Bus. Woman Leader award YWCA, 1977; Outstanding Service award Womenspace Coalition for Service by a Woman in Behalf of Women, 1978; Twyla M. Conway award Radio-TV Council Greater Cleve., 1978, 79, 81, 82; Ohio State Media award Am. Cancer Soc., 1979, 80, 81, 82, Courage award Ohio div., 1982; Abe Lincoln award, 1978; award Radio TV Council, 1980; Generations award State of Israel Bonds, 1980; Matrix award Women in Communications, 1981; ORT Man of Yr. award, 1982; 1st ann. Lighthouse award Cleve. chpt. Pub. Relations Soc. Am., 1981; Women in Bus. Adv. of Yr. for Cleve. dist. award SBA, 1982; Newsleader award UPI, 1982; named to 1st ann. Cleveland Heights High Sch. Disting. Alumni Hall of Fame, 1981, numerous others. Clubs: Cleve. City (dir. 1973, v.p. 1975); Oakwood. Author: Headstrong—A Story of Conquests and Celebrations, Living through Chemotherapy, 1982. Home: 18910 S Woodland Rd Shaker Heights OH 44122 Office: 1250 Superior Ave Cleveland OH 44114

BLUMBERG, RHODA, author; b. N.Y.C., Dec. 14, 1917; d. Abraham and Irena (Fromberg) Shapiro; B.A. magna cum laude, Adelphi Coll., 1938; m. Gerald Blumberg, Jan. 7, 1945; children—Lawrence, Rena, Alice, Leda. Freelance writer, 1940—; researcher, writer CBS Radio, 1940-44; talent scout NBC Radio, 1945-46; researcher, writer for various mags., 1940-51; exec. editor Travel Guides, Simon Schuster, 1973-74. Trustee, Westchester Jewish Community Services, 1976—. Mem. Authors League, Authors Guild. Author: Firefighters, 1975, Sharks, 1975, UFO, 1976, First Ladies, 1977, Famine, 1978, Witches, 1979, Backyard Bestiary, 1979, The Truth About Dragons, 1980; First Travel Guide to the Moon, 1980; Southern Africa, 1981; Freaky Facts, 1981; Devils and Demons, 1982; many other teenage and juvenile books. Home: Baptist Church Rd Yorktown Heights NY 10598 Office: 1 Rockefeller Plaza Suite 1510 New York City NY 10020

BLUME, GINGER (ELAINE), psychologist; b. Lock Haven, Pa., Apr. 8, 1948; d. Martin Luther and Virginia Ruth (Rudy) B.; B.A., U. Fla., 1970, M.A., 1975, Ph.D., 1979. Predoctoral intern in psychology VA Hosp., West Haven, Conn., 1976-77; postdoctoral intern in psychology Elmcrest Psychiat. Inst., Portland, Conn., 1977-78; pvt. practice clin. psychology, Middletown, Conn., 1978—; mem. adj. psychology faculty Middlesex Community Coll.; bd. dirs. Gilead House halfway facility, SAFE sexual assault clinic, Family Resource Center; cons. in field. Mem. Am. Psychol. Assn., Conn. Psychol. Assn., Orthopsychiatry Assn., Internat. Imagery Assn., AAUW (chairperson local edn. found. program), Phi Kappa Phi, Kappa Delta. Club: Soroptomists. Home: 748 Long Hill Rd Middletown CT 06457 Office: 717 Newfield St Middletown CT 06457

BLUME, JUDY SUSSMAN, author; b. Elizabeth, N.J., Feb. 12, 1938; d. Rudolph and Esther (Rosefeld) Sussman; B.S. in Edn., N.Y. U., 1960; m. John M. Blume, Aug. 15, 1959 (div. Jan. 1976); children—Randy Lee, Lawrence Andrew. Author juvenile fiction books including: Are You There God It's Me, Margaret (selected as outstanding children's book 1970); Then Again, Maybe I Won't, 1971; It's Not the End of the World, 1972; Tales of a 4th Grade Nothing, 1972; Deenie, 1973; Blubber, 1974; Otherwise Known as Sheila the Great, 1976; Forever, 1976; Tiger Eyes (outstanding book for young adults 1981); others. Mem. Authors League and Guild, Soc. Children's Book Writers. Office: care Harold Ober Assos 40 E 49th St New York NY 10017

BLUME, SHEILA BIERMAN, psychiatrist, state ofcl.; b. Bklyn., June 21, 1934; d. Benjamin and Rose (Lazar) Bierman; student Cornell U., 1951-54; M.D. cum laude, Harvard U., 1958; m. Martin Blume, June 12, 1955; children—Frederick, Janet. Intern, Children's Hosp. Med. Center, Boston, 1958-59; Fulbright fellow to Tokyo U., 1959-60; resident in psychiatry Central Islip Psychiat. Center, 1962-65; dir. Charles K. Post Alcoholism Rehab. Center, Central Islip Psychiat. Center, 1964-79; dir. N.Y. State Div. Alcoholism and Alcohol Abuse, 1979—; clin. asso. prof. psychiatry Albany Med. Center, 1979—; apptd. to Nat. Commn. Alcoholism and Other Alcohol Related Problems, 1980; mem. Nat. Commn. Confidentiality of Health Records, 1976-80, Nat. Council on Compulsive Gambling, adv. bd., 1972—. Recipient Dr. Milton Helpern Disting. Physicians award for contbn. field of alcoholism, 1980. Mem. L.I. Council Alcoholism (dir. 1972-79), Am. Med. Soc. Alcoholism (pres. 1979-80), Nat. Council Alcoholism, (dir.). Editor: (with S. Zimberg and J. Wallace) Practical Approaches to Alcoholism Psychotherapy, 1978; editor Bull. Suffolk County Med. Soc., 1969-76; contbr. articles profl. jours., chpts. in books. Home: 284 Greene Ave Sayville NY 11782 Office: New York State Div of Alcoholism and Alcohol Abuse 194 Washington Ave Albany NY 12210

BLUMENTHAL, EILEEN POLLEY, psychologist; b. Santa Barbara, Calif., July 17, 1929; d. Rudolph Arthur and Frances O. (Holcombe) Polley; B.A., U. Calif., Berkeley, 1951; M.A., Rutgers U., 1964; Ph.D., U. Mich., 1976; m. W. Michael Blumenthal, Sept. 8, 1951; children—Ann Margaret, Gillian, Jane Eileen. Asst. prof. edn. Mercy Coll., Detroit, 1976-77; research asso. Nat. Acad. Scis., Washington, 1977-78; Washington liaison Soc. Research in Child Devel., 1978-79; asso. dir. U. Mich. Bush Found. Program in Child Devel. and Social Policy, Ann Arbor, 1979—; adv. council Nat. Inst. Child Health and Human Devel., Bethesda, Md., 1979-81. Bd. trustees Detroit Symphony Orch., 1981—, Hands-on Mus., Ann Arbor, 1980—. Mem. Soc. Research in Child Devel., Am. Psychol. Assn., Nat. Assn. Edn. of Young Children. Democrat. Research on children's lit. and edn. in China. Home: 2211 Devonshire Rd Ann Arbor MI 48104 Office: 3433 Mason Hall University of Michigan Ann Arbor MI 48109

BLUMENTHAL, GERDA RENEE, educator; b. Berlin, July 26, 1923; came to U.S., 1939, naturalized, 1947; d. Adolf and Olga (Posin) B.; B.A. magna cum laude, Hunter Coll., 1945; M.A., Columbia U., 1947, Ph.D., 1955. Lectr. French, Columbia U., 1946-52; instr. dept. modern langs. Washington Coll., 1955, asst. prof., 1955-58, asso. prof., 1958-61, prof., 1961-68, chmn., 1964-68; prof. French and comparative lit. Catholic U. Am., 1968—; lectr. French Govt. research grantee, 1948-49. Mem. AAUP, MLA, Am. Comparative Lit. Assn., Am. Assn. Tchrs. of French. Author: André Malraux: The Conquest of Dread, 1960; The Poetic Imagination of Georges Bernanos, 1965. Home: 4530 Connecticut Ave Washington DC 20008 Office: Dept Modern Languages Catholic Univ Washington DC 20064

BLUNT, BONNIE JANE, legal asst.; b. Ft. Dodge, Iowa, May 30, 1933; d. James Boyd and Edith Mae (Barton) Cox; A.A., Ft. Dodge Jr. Coll., 1953; postgrad. Drake U., 1954; student paralegal courses U. So. Calif., 1975-79; m. Fred E. Blunt, June 23, 1953; children—James Michael, Connie Mae. Sec., office mgr. Judge Dwight Rider, Fort Dodge, 1955-63; legal asst., office mgr. Rouse & Hamilton, Palos Verdes Estates, Calif., 1963-76; legal asst., sec. firm William A. Finer, Torrance, Calif., 1976—; sec. Preferred Estates Realty. Sec., South Bay Youth Service Center; vol. South Bay Hosp.; mem. South Bay Homeowners Assn.; sec., bd. dirs. Adelle David Found., 1970-76. Mem. Legal Secs. Assn. Long Beach. Lectr. in field. Home: 21301 Anza Ave Torrance CA 90503 Office: 21515 Hawthorne Blvd Suite 1250 Torrance CA 90503

BLUNT, DEROSETTE YVONNE HENDRICKS, constrn. corp. exec.; b. N.Y.C., July 6, 1934; d. Ernest and Velma Mae (Alexander) Hendricks; A.B. magna cum laude, Wheaton Coll., 1956; postgrad. Georgetown U. Law Center, 1970; m. Roger Reckling Blunt, June 9, 1956; children—Roger Reckling, Jennifer Mari, Amy Elizabeth, Jonathan Hendricks. Instr. English and history USAF Inst., Frankfurt, W. Ger., 1957-60; asst. reference librarian John F. Kennedy Sch. Public Adminstrn., Harvard U., Cambridge, Mass., 1960-61; social worker Boston Chpt. ARC, 1961-62; case worker Eastern Area ARC, Alexandria, Va., 1962-63; cons. NCCJ, Alexandria, Va. and Washington, 1971-74; pres. D. and R, Inc., Landscape Constrn., Washington, 1974—; v.p. Blunt Enterprises, Washington, 1979—; pres. Blunt Broadcasting, Inc., Washington, 1980—; dir. D. and R, Inc., Tyroc Constrn. Corp., Tyroc Mgmt. Services, Inc. Sec. 8th Dist. Democratic Com., 1971-74, Va. State Dem. Com., 1972-74; mem. Washington Suburban Dem. Women's Club; pres. Met. D.C. Ministry with Women, 1979; treas. Cabin John Jr. High Sch. PTA, 1979-80, v.p., 1980-82; v.p. Montgomery County NCCJ, 1979-80; active Nat. Urban League, ACLU (Md.), Montgomery (Md.) chpt. NAACP. Mem. Met. Washington Bd. of Trade, Am. Subcontractors Assn., Phi Beta Kappa. Presbyterian. Clubs: Links, Inc., Kiwanis-Wives. Office: 2018 5th St NE Washington DC 20002

BLUTH, ELIZABETH JEAN CATHERINE (B. J.), sociologist, educator; b. Phila., Dec. 5, 1934; d. Robert Thomas and Catherine Cecelia (Boxman) Gowland; B.A. in Sociology (Washington Semster fellow), Bucknell U., 1953; M.A., Fordham U., 1960; Ph.D., UCLA, 1970; m. Thomas Del Bluth, Aug. 20, 1960; children—Robert Thomas Del, Richard Del. Teaching fellow in methods social research Fordham U., 1957-58; reading instr. St. Margarets High Sch., Tappahannock, Va., 1958-59; instr. history, civics and English, Rosary High Sch., San Diego, 1959-60; instr., asst. prof. sociology Immaculate Heart Coll., Los Angeles, 1960-65; prof. sociology Calif. State U., Northridge, 1965—; cons. Immaculate Heart Community, Los Angeles, 1967-69. Mem. Citizens Adv. Council on Nat. Space Policy. Recipient Disting. Teaching award Calif. State U., Northridge, 1968, Alpha Omega Faculty awards, 1966, 74. Fellow Inst. for Advancement in Teaching and Learning, Calif. State U., 1974. Mem. Am. Sociol. Assn., AIAA (nat. com. on soc. and aerospace tech.), Am. Astronautical Soc., Space Studies Inst., Internat. Acad. Astronautics (com. on space econs. and benefits), Inst. for Social Sci. Study of Space (acad. adv. bd.), L5 Soc., Phi Beta Kappa. Republican. Author: Parsons General Theory of Action: A Summary of the Basic Theory, 1982; editor: (with others) Search for Identity Reader, Vol. I and II, 1973; (with S.R. McNeal) Update on Space, Vol. I, 1981; contbr. chpts. to books on space; contbr. articles to profl. jours. Office: Dept Sociology Calif State U Northridge CA 91330

BLUTTER, JOAN, interior designer; b. London, July 6, 1928; came to U.S., 1947, naturalized, 1952; d. Samuel and Bertha Wernick; m. Melvyn

Blutter, Oct. 29, 1948; children—Janet, Steven. Partner, Joslyn Interiors, Chgo., 1958-68; owner Joan Blutter/Designs, Chgo., 1968-81; pres. Blutter Design Group, Chgo., 1981—; cons. Wool Bur. Inc., N.Y.C. Vice pres. womens bd. United Cerebral Palsy. Fellow Am. Soc. Interior Designers (Presdl. citation 1975, 80, named Designer of Yr. 1979); mem. Home Fashion League. Clubs: Ravislo Country (Homewood, Ill.); Mchts. and Mfrs. (bd. govs.) (Chgo.). Contbr. articles in field. Home: 2801 N Sheridan Rd Chicago IL 60657 Office: 13-124 Merchandise Mart Chicago IL 60654

BLYTH, MYRNA GREENSTEIN, editor, author; b. N.Y.C., Mar. 22, 1940; d. Benjamin and Betty (Austin) Greenstein; B.A., Bennington (Vt.) Coll., 1960; m. Jeffrey Blyth, Nov. 25, 1962; children—Jonathan, Graham. Sr. editor Datebook mag., N.Y.C., 1960-62; Ingenue mag., N.Y.C., 1962-70; book editor Family Health mag., 1972-73; book and fiction editor, then asso. editor Family Circle mag., N.Y.C., 1974-78, exec. editor, 1978-81; editor-in-chief Ladies' Home Jour., N.Y.C., 1981—; freelance writer, contbr. mags., 1965—; author: (novels) Cousin Suzanne, 1975, For Better and For Worse, 1978. Office: 641 Lexington Ave New York NY 10022

BLYTHE, SHARLA PAULINE, transcribing and typing service co. exec.; b. Attica, Ind., Feb. 23, 1934; d. Homer Russell and Stella Jane Kirby; student Home Hosp. Sch. Nursing and Purdue U., 1952-63; m. Howard Donald Blythe, May 11, 1955; children—Howard Donald, Larry Alan. Pres., Profl. Transcribing and Typing Service, Inc., Stockton, Calif., 1977—; tchr. Mktg. Tng. Inst. Bus. Coll., 1971-73. Recipient award AAUW, 1952. Mem. Adminstrv. Mgmt. Soc. (v.p. edn.), Am. Med. Record Assn., Am. Assn. Med. Transcriptionists, Calif. Med. Record Assn., C. of C. (legis. com.). Republican. Baptist. Home: 3809 Marine Ave Stockton CA 95204 Office: 645 W Harding Way Suite 8 Stockton CA 95204

BOARD, MARY ANN, med. social worker; b. Mineola, Tex., Mar. 16, 1950; d. Ben Hardin and Mary Catherine (Lindley) Board; student Kilgore Jr. Coll., 1968-69; B.A. in Psychology, U. Houston, 1972, M.S.W., 1975. Coordinator handicapped student services U. Houston, 1975-76; coordinator vol. services Houston Lighthouse for Blind, 1976-77; new options social worker Inst. for Rehab. and Research, Houston, 1977—; cons. community workshops on disability, 1975—; mem. bd., sec. council on spl. populations Houston Parks and Recreation Dept., 1978—; del. White House Conf. on Handicapped Individuals, 1977. Bd. dirs. Houston Area Rehab. Assn., 1978—; bd. dirs., chmn. edn. com. Coalition for Barrier-Free Living, 1979—; mem. com. on handicapped scouting Sam Houston Area council Boy Scouts Am., 1976—. Named Handicapped Profl. Woman of Yr. for Tex., Pilot Club Internat., 1978. Mem. Acad. Cert. Social Workers, Nat. Assn. Social Workers, AAUW, Quilt Guild Greater Houston, Phi Theta Kappa. Methodist. Author: (with others) New Options, 1979, New Options Training Manual, 1979; (booklets) Independent Living with Attendant Care, 1980. Office: Inst for Rehab and Research 1333 Moursund Ave Houston TX 77030

BOARDMAN, SHIRLEY MARIE, univ. adminstr.; b. Kettle River, Minn., June 13, 1946; d. Joseph John and Marie (Woroniecki) Milczarek; student Coll. St. Scholastica, 1964-68; B.A., Ind. U., 1969, M.S., 1972. Resident counselor Coll. St. Scholastica, Duluth, 1964-66: fin. aids counselor Ind. U., Bloomington, 1966-69, regional campus coordinator, system fin. aids, 1969-72; dir. fin. aids Ind. U.-Purdue U., Indpls., 1972—. Mem. Nat. Assn. Student Fin. Aid Adminstrs., Nat. Urban League, Am. Mgmt. Assn., AAUW, Midwest Assn. Student Fin. Aid Adminstrs., Indpls. Urban League (treas. 1976—). Roman Catholic. Home: 537 Plymouth Rd Bloomington IN 47401 Office: The Berkey Bldg 920 W Michigan St Indianapolis IN 46202

BOARMAN, ANTHEA MARY, lawyer; b. London, Nov. 26, 1944; came to U.S., 1961, naturalized, 1967; d. Lewis W. and Ruth (Croley) Barnes; A.B., Newcomb Coll., 1964; J.D., U. Ky., 1967; children—Thanh Nhung Bishop, Cherise Elise Bishop, Colin Luke Simmons. Admitted to Ky. bar, 1968; mem. firm Gilliam, Bush & Boarman, 1968-70; Fayette County Juvenile judge, 1970; dir. Ky. Child Advocacy Council, Lexington, 1970-73; trial atty. Ky. Pub. Advocate and Defender, Frankfort, 1973; asst. to dir. children's programs Spindletop Research, then Council State Govts., Lexington, 1973-74; exec. dir. Lexington Fayette Urban County Human Rights Commn., Lexington, Ky., 1975—. Mem. Internat. Assn. Ofcl. Human Rights Agys. (bd. dirs. 1979—), Nat. Assn. Human Rights Workers (gen. counsel 1979—), Nat. Bar Assn., Ky. Bar. Assn., Fayette County Bar Assn., Agy. Exec. Forum. Democrat. Episcopalian. Home: 194 Castlewood Dr Lexington KY 40505 Office: 207 N Upper St Lexington KY 40507

BOATNER, MAXINE TULL (MRS. EDMUND BURKE BOATNER), writer, lectr.; b. Kentwood, La., Feb. 23, 1903; d. James Porter and Mai (Bailey) Tull; B.A., Millsaps Coll., 1924; M.A., Gallaudet Coll., 1926, L.H.D., 1960; M.A., Yale, 1951, Ph.D., 1952; m. Edmund Burke Boatner, July 19, 1928; 1 dau., Emma Barbara. Tchr. public schs., Belzoni, Miss., 1925-26, Miss. Sch. for Deaf, Jackson, 1926-28; writer Cleve. Plain Dealer, Cleve. News, 1928-31; tchr. Kendall Sch. for Deaf, Washington, 1932-33, N.Y. Sch. for Deaf, N.Y.C., 1933-35, Am. Sch. for Deaf, Hartford, Conn., 1935-49; writer, lectr., 1935—. Project dir. V.R.A., Dept. Health, Edn., Welfare, 1962-66. Dir. Hartford Symphony Soc. Hartt Opera-Theater Guild U. Hartford, Mark Twain Library and Meml. Commn., Hartley-Salmon Child Guidance Clinic; mem. corp. Hartford Public Library; mem. woman's bd. Hartford Sem. Found.; dir. Conn. Opera Guild. Dir. hist. research Conf. Execs. of Am. Schs. for the Deaf, hon. mem. Recipient Amelia Earhart Medal for Service to Humanity, N.Y. br. Am. Pen Women, 1960; Edward Allen Fay award Conf. Execs. Am. Schs. for Deaf Centennial, 1968.; named Woman of Yr., Gallaudet Coll. Women's Recreation Com., 1970. Mem. Trinity Coll. Library Assos., Yale U. Library Assos., West Hartford League Women Voters, AAUW (1st v.p. Greater Hartford), Nat. Soc. Arts and Letters, Nat. League Am. Pen Women (pres. Greater Hartford br.), Alumni assns. Millsaps Coll., Gallaudet Coll., Yale, Wadsworth Atheneum, Chi Delta Phi, Kappa Delta. Clubs: Town and County (Hartford), Yale of Hartford, Thursday (Lit.) of Hartford, Pilot; Woman's Press (N.Y.C.). Author: Voice of the Deaf, A Biography of Edward Miner Gallaudet, 1959; Dictionary of Idioms for the Deaf, 1966; also articles in profl. mags. and book reviews in newspaper. Home: 2 Linbrook Rd West Hartford CT 06107

BOATWRIGHT, ELAINE GREMILLION, educator; b. Alexandria, La., Feb. 25, 1942; d. Louis F. and Hallie Mable (White) Gremillion; student public schs.; m. Jimmy Elwyn Boatwright, Jan. 17, 1960; children—Sabrina, Richard, Stephanie. Religious edn. tchr. Holy Guardian Angels Roman Catholic Ch., Bridge City, La., 1969—, religious edn. coordinator, 1975—; sec., public relations adv. Gumbo Festival, Bridge City, 1973—; adult adv. Cath. Youth Orgn., 1969—. Named Woman of Yr., Holy Guardian Angels Ch., 1972, 73, Mother of Yr., 1975; Outstanding Cath. Woman, Archdiocese New Orleans, 1971. Mem. La. Assn. Fairs and Festivals, Council Cath. Women Archdiocese New Orleans. Club: Holy Guardian Angels Women's (pres. 1971-73, 77-79).

BOATWRIGHT, MARY HOWARD, mem. Republican Nat. Com.; b. Houston, Apr. 8, 1920; d. Arch Franklin and Dorothy (Bennett) Howard; A.B., Trinity Coll., Washington, 1941; m. Victor Taliaferro Boatwright, Aug. 29, 1945; children—Mary Dorsey, John Lord, William Howard, Mary Taliaferro. Mem. Bd. Wardens and Burgesses Stonington (Conn.) Borough, 1960-64; mem. Conn. Ho. of Reps. from 43d Dist., 1962-66; mem. Rep. Nat. Com. for Conn., 1972—. Roman Catholic. Address: 16 Denison Ave Stonington CT 06378

BOAZ, MARTHA TEAROSSE, educator; b. Stuart, Va.; d. James Robert and Kate Leslie (Gilley) B.; B.S., Madison Coll., 1935; B.S. in L.S., George Peabody Coll., 1937; M.S. in L.S., U. Mich., 1950, Ph.D., 1955. Tchr., librarian public schs., Va., Ky., 1935-40; asst. librarian Madison Coll., 1940-49; asso. prof. library sci. U. Tenn., 1951-52; asso. prof. U. So. Calif., 1953-55, prof. Sch. Library Sci., 1955-79, dean, 1955-79, dean emeritus, 1979—; research asso. Center for Study of Am. Experience, 1979-81; AID rep., Pakistan, 1962; U.S. State Dept. rep., Vietnam, 1962. Mem. ALA (pres. library edn. div. 1968-69, chmn. intellectual freedom com. 1964-66), Calif. Library Assn. (pres. 1962), Assn. Am. Library Schs. (pres. 1962-63), Beta Phi Mu (nat. pres. 1962). Author: Fervent and Full of Gifts, 1961; Current Concepts in Library Management, 1979; Issues in Higher Education and the Professions in the 1980s, 1981; Strategies for Meeting the Information Needs of Society in the Year 2000, 1981; compiler: The Quest for Truth, vol. 1, 1961, vol. 2, 1967; editor: Modern Trends in Documentation, 1959; Toward the Improvement of Library Education, 1973; contbr. numerous articles to profl. jours. Address: 1849 Campus Rd Los Angeles CA 90041

BOBRICK, GLADIS SMITH-WALDMAN, speech pathologist; b. N.Y.C., Mar. 10, 1907; d. Max and Henrietta (Smith) Waldman; A.B. cum laude, Hunter Coll., 1952; M.A., N.Y. U., 1954; m. William H. Bobrick, Nov. 9, 1924; 1 son, Arthur D. Bus. mgr. The Contemporary Jewish Record, N.Y.C., 1938-45; writer, synopsizer Story Dept. MGM Picture Co., N.Y.C., 1949; speech therapist cerebral palsy N.Y.C. Dept. Health, 1952; chief speech and hearing Goldwater Meml. Hosp., N.Y.C., 1952; spl. speech tchr., cons. for handicapped, tchr. creative drama N.Y.C. Bd. Edn., 1952-72; pvt. practice speech pathology, N.Y.C., 1950—; lectr., panelist at convs. Mem. fund raising com. N.Y. U. Alumni Sch. Edn., 1966-74; mem. Community Chorus, Temple Rodeph Sholom, N.Y.C., 1974-77; bd. dirs. Bus. and Profl. Club Temple Rodeph Sholom, 1975-79. Hunter Coll. teaching fellow, 1952. Mem. Am. Speech, Lang. and Hearing Assn. (cert. clin. competence), N.Y. State Speech, Lang. and Hearing Assn. (founding mem.), Speech Assn. Am., Internat. Council for Exceptional Children. Contbr. articles to profl. jours. Address: 185 E 85th St New York NY 10028

BOCARD, KAREN LAVINIA, univ. adminstr.; b. Versailles, Ky., Feb. 16, 1945; d. Henry Clefford and Irene Vivian (Ford) Shipp; student Orange Coast Coll., 1970-75; A.A., Saddleback Coll., 1977; student Calif. State U., Fullerton, 1977—; m. Kendall Edward Bocard. Stats. clk. Blood-Horse Mag., Lexington, Ky. 1963-66; enrollment supr. Registrar's Office, U. Calif., Irvine, 1966-68, mgr. central campus calendar, 1968-74, mgr. campus aux. services, 1974-78, dir. aux. services, asso. bus. mgr. student affairs, 1978—, coordinator U. Calif. at Irvine Women in Mgmt. Conf., 1979; leader staff devel. Recipient achievement citation AID, 1973; Staff Achievement cert. U. Calif., Irvine, 1973, Staff Service award, 1981. Mem. Irvine Bus. and Profl. Women's Club (charter mem., officer 1978—), San Orco Dist. Bus. and Profl. Women's Clubs (co-chairperson public relations 1980-81, chair Young Careerist 1982—), Women in Mgmt., Calif. Women in Higher Edn. (officer chpt. 1975-76), U. Calif. at Irvine Staff Assn. (rep. 1973-75). Office: 148 Administration Bldg U Calif Irvine CA 92717

BODANZA, MARY F., nurse, educator; b. Mt. Kisco, N.Y., Apr. 15, 1932; d. Carl and Margaret (Foudy) Feigenhauer; R.N., Westchester Sch. Nursing, 1953; B.S., SUNY, New Paltz, 1970; M.S. in Health Edn., Russell Sage Coll., 1979; children—Philip, Nora, Lucy, Christia. Staff nurse hosp., 1953-55; med. asst., 1955-57; prof. health tech., chmn. med. assisting Dutchess Community Coll., Poughkeepsie, 1970—; cons. N.J. State Bd. Higher Edn.; program surveyor Am. Assn. Med. Assts. AMA. Mem. Am. Assn. Med. Assts. (program surveyor), Kappa Delta Pi. Democrat. Author: Clinical and Laboratory Procedures in the Physician's Office, 1981. Office: Dutchess Community College Pendell Rd Poughkeepsie NY 12801

BODE, BARBARA, found. exec.; b. Evanston, Ill., Aug. 4, 1940; d. Carl and Margaret Emilie (Lutze) B; B.A. magna cum laude, U. Md., 1962, M.A. (Woodrow Wilson Nat. Found. fellow 1963-64), 1966; scholar Ludwig-Maximilians-Universitat, Munich, W.Ger., 1960-61; English Speaking Union scholar London U., summer 1964; Bundesrepublik scholar Goethe Institut, Lübeck, W. Ger., summer 1965; postgrad. (NDEA fellow) UCLA, 1966-67. Woodrow Wilson teaching fellow N.C. Central U., Durham, 1965-66; community developer Community Devel. Dept. Prince George's County (Md.), 1967-68; field dir. Nat. Council Hunger and Malnutrition in U.S., Washington, 1968-70; pres. Children's Found., Washington, 1970—; mem. food industry adv. commn. Fed. Energy Adminstrn., 1975-76. Mem. Citizens Bd. of Inquiry into Brookside Miners' Strike, Harlan, Ky., 1974; mem. nat. adv. com. Food Day, 1975, 76, 77, Rural Am. Women, 1978-80; dir., exec. com. Human Services Inst. for Children and Families, 1973-75; bd. dirs., v.p. Am. Freedom From Hunger Found., 1973-78, U.S. Com. on Refugees, 1976-78; dir., co-founder RAINBOW TV Works, 1976—, Nat. Council Women, Work and Welfare, 1976-77, Nat. Com. Responsive Philanthropy, 1975—; bd. dirs. Am. Parents Com., 1974-78, Rural America, Inc., 1975-79, Coalition for Children and Youth, 1975-79; cons., mem. steering and adv. coms. commns. and orgns. in field. Convenor Nat. Women's Polit. Caucus, 1971; nat. adv. bd. Women's Campaign Fund, 1975-77; active in press. bur. Poor People's Campaign, 1968; planning com. Women's Leadership Conf. Dem. Nat. Com., 1972, vice chmn. com. on regional conf. planning and strategy, 1969-70; active voting and civil rights campaigns, 1961—. Named one of Ten Outstanding Young Women of Am., various women's orgns., 1977. Mem. Rural Coalition, Washington Women's Network, Woman's Nat. Dem. Club, Rural Health Coalition. Episcopalian. Author: School Lunch Bag, 1971; Barriers to School Breakfast, 1979; contbr. numerous articles to profl. jours. Office: 1420 New York Ave NW Washington DC 20005

BODE, FRANCES MURPHY, dietitian; b. Hinton, Okla., Sept. 22, 1926; d. John Edward and Margaret Jane (Riley) Murphy; B.S. cum laude, Our Lady of the Lake U., 1948; cert. registered dietitian St. Mary's Hosp. and Mayo Clinic, 1950; M.S., U. Okla., 1978; m. Carl James Bode, Apr. 7, 1951; children—John, James, Jeffrey, Jane. Therapeutic dietitian St. Mary's Hosp., Rochester, Minn.; adminstrv. dietitian St. Anthony Hosp., Oklahoma City; tchr., Nichols Hill, Okla., Oklahoma City, Geary, Okla.; dir. day care center, also multipurpose centers Blaine County, Okla.; cons. dietitian, West Okla., 1968—; public relations Sugar Assn., Washington, 1976-79; real estate sales asso., 1979—. Pres., Blaine County Democratic Women, 1979-80; v.p. Blaine County History, 1980—. Mem. Am. Dietetic Assn., Am. Home Econs. Assn., Okla. Geneal. Soc., Okla. Hist. Soc., Oklahoma City Met. Bd. Realtors, Am. Legion Aux. Roman Catholic. Author: Weddings in the Oklahoma Territory, 1892-1907. Contbr. articles to profl. jours. Home: 114 N Galena St Geary OK 73040 Office: PO Box 2 Geary OK 73040

BODE, JANET, writer; b. Penn Yan, N.Y., July 14, 1943; d. Carl J. and Margaret E. (Lutze) B.; B.A., U. Md., 1965. Editor, tchr., personnel ofcl., Heidelberg, Munich and Augsburg, W. Ger., 1965-67; tchr., Tampa, Fla., 1967-68; program dir., community organizer Kaw Valley council Girl Scouts U.S.A., Topeka, 1968-69, public relations and program dir. Crossroads council, Edison, N.J., 1969-70; tchr. Am. Sch., Guadalajara, Mex., 1970-72; community organizer The Children's Found., Washington, 1972-73; writer, San Francisco and N.Y.C., 1973—; books include: View from Another Closet: Exploring Bisexuality in Women, (book club selection), 1976; Fighting Back: How to Cope with the Medical, Emotional and Legal Consequences of Rape (book club selection), 1978; Rape: Preventing It, Coping with the Legal, Medical and Emotional Aftermath (named outstanding social studies book Nat. Council Social Studies), 1979; Kids Having Kids: The Unwed Teenage Parent, 1980. Mem. San Francisco Women's Center, Bi-Center, Authors Guild, Feminist Writers Guild.

BODE, MARY KATHLEEN, sales and mktg. telecommunications exec.; b. Washington, Aug. 6, 1944; d. William A. and Catherine E. (Everett) Kelly; student Calif. State U., Northridge, 1964; m. Carl F. Bode, Feb. 8, 1964; children—Kelly Ann, Brian Allan. Editor newspaper Ramey AFB, P.R., 1966-69; engaged in polit. campaign mgmt., Calif., 1973-80; asst. dir. mktg. and sales ACRO Inc., Irvine, Calif., 1980—. Mem. Calif. Democratic Central Com., 1978—, Orange County Dem. Central Com., 1978—; bd. dirs. South Coast Repertory Theater. Mem. Nat. Soc. Women Execs. Roman Catholic. Home: 17302 Gurney Ln Huntington Beach CA 92714 Office: 2515 McCabe St Irvine CA 92714

BODEN, EVE RUTH HERZ, social worker; b. Germany, June 25, 1935; came to U.S., 1942, naturalized, 1954; d. Arthur and Flora (Ullman) Herz; B.S., N.Y. U., 1972; M.S.W., Yeshiva U., 1977; m. Ronald M. Boden, Dec. 25, 1954; children—Leslie, Scott, David. Dental hygienist, N.Y., 1954-69; instr. dental hygiene SUNY, Farmingdale, 1973-75; social worker Tempo Group, Woodmere, N.Y., 1977-78; pvt. practice psychotherapist, Syosset, N.Y., 1978—; social worker South Nassau Communities Hosp., 1978-79; social work coordinator LI. div. Am. Cancer Soc., Melville, N.Y., 1979-81. Bd. dirs. Profl. Adv. Bd., Community Youth Agy., Syosset, 1971—. Mem. Nat. Assn. Social Workers, Am. Soc. Group Psychotherapy and Psychodrama, Soc. Clin. Social Work Psychotherapists. Jewish. Home: 32 Sexton Rd Syosset NY 11791 Office: 175 Jericho Turnpike Syosset NY 11791

BODOIN, PAMELA JONES, real estate investment co. exec.; b. Orlando, Fla., Mar. 5, 1944; d. Rex Haden and Alys Ruth (Jones) B.; student Tex. Tech. U., 1962-66; B.S., U. Tex., Austin, 1977, postgrad., 1977—; children—Randal, Shannon. Tchr., team leader Austin (Tex.) Ind. Sch. Dist., 1967-69; writer, developer Southwest Ednl. Devel. Lab., Austin, Tex., 1969-71, Dallas Ind. Sch. Dist., 1971-72; pres. Ednl. Design Systems, Austin, Tex., 1972-78; pres. Bodoin Investments, Austin, 1978—; vis. prof. univs. Del. Democratic State Conv., 1972; patron La Guna Gloria Art Mus., 1977—; mem. We Care Austin, 1971. Mem. Austin Classroom Tchrs., Assn. Supervision and Curriculum Devel., NEA, Assn. Children with Learning Disabilities, Heritage Soc., LWV, Phi Delta Kappa. Home: 5003 Fairview Austin TX 78731 Office: 97 W Bee Cave Austin TX 78746

BOE, BEVERLY HOSKINS, mental health board adminstr.; b. Akron, Ohio, Oct. 4, 1931; d. Kenneth A. and Jeanette (Hudson) H.; R.N., St. Thomas Sch. Nursing, 1952; M.A., U. S. Fla., 1981; children—Eric N., Christopher K., Alex N. Staff nurse Massillon (Ohio) State Hosp., 1952-53; head nurse St. Thomas Hosp., Akron, 1953-58; nursing supr. Summit County Receiving Hosp., Cuyahoga Falls, Ohio, 1958-61; dir. nursing Bethesda Hosp., Denver, 1964-69; nurse supr. Med. Clinic, Marathon, Fla., 1971-73; program dir. Guidance Clinic Middle Keys, Marathon, 1973-75; program dir. Hillsborough Community Mental Health Center, Northside Community Mental Health Center, Tampa, Fla., from 1975; now exec. dir. Dist. III Mental Health Bd., Gainesville, Fla.; asso. U. S. Fla. Sch. Medicine, 1977—; cons. Fla. State Health and Rehab. Service, 1977—, Fla. State U., Tallahassee, 1977—, Fed. Action Agy., 1976—, Social Action Research Center, 1980—. Named Outstanding Dir. of Gerontology Program, Fla. Council Community Mental Health, 1978; apptd. dir. model program gerontology NIMH, 1979; HEW grantee, 1979. Mem. Nat. Assn. Social Workers, Bus. and Profl. Women, Exec. Females, Fla. State Bd. Nursing. Home: 5305 NW 57th Ln Gainesville FL 32601 Office: 1441 NW 6th St Gainesville FL 32601

BOEHM, ALICE E(VELYN), research psychologist; b. Prague, Czechoslovakia; came to U.S., 1941, naturalized, 1946; d. Leopold and Bertha Boehm; Ph.D., German U. in Prague, 1938; postdoctoral study Oxford (Eng.) U., 1940-41. Research asst. N.J. State Hosp., Trenton, 1941-42; ind. psychol. research, N.Y.C., 1947—. Fellow AAAS, Internat. Council Psychologists; mem. Am., Eastern, N.Y. State psychol. assns., N.Y. Acad. Scis., World Fedn. Mental Health (asso.). Contbr. articles to profl. jours. Home: 30 E 81st St New York NY 10028

BOEHM, ANN E., psychologist, educator; b. Newark, June 27, 1938; d. George and Josephine (Jacoby) B.; B.A., Wheaton Coll., 1960; M.A., Columbia U., 1963, Ph.D., 1966; m. Neville Kaplan, Aug. 2, 1973. Tchr. S. Plainfield (N.J.) Public Schs., 1960-62; clin.-sch. intern Devereaux Schs., Devon, Pa., 1964-65; research psychologist New Rochelle (N.Y.) Prekindergarten 1966-70; research asst. Tchr.'s Coll., Columbia U., N.Y.C., 1965-66, research asso., 1966-69, asst. prof., 1968-70, asso. prof., 1970-81, prof. psychology and edn., 1981—. Mem. Am. Psychol. Assn., Am. Ednl. Research Assn., Nat. Council on Measurement in Edn. Cons. editor Am. Jour. Mental Deficiency, 1980-81; contbr. numerous articles to profl. publs. Home: 4455 Douglas Ave Bronx NY 10471 Office: Tchr's Coll Columbia Univ New York NY 10027

BOEHM, PEGGY SUSAN, market research corp. ofcl.; b. Lake Charles, La., Apr. 28, 1954; d. Elmer Lee and Janeth Helene (Brinkman) B.; B.S. in Agrl. Sci., Purdue U., 1976, postgrad., 1976-77. Grad. counseling asst. Purdue U., West Lafayette, Ind., 1976-77; sr. project analyst Doane Agrl. Service, St. Louis, 1978-79; research mgr. Maritz Market Research, Inc., St. Louis, 1979-81; account exec. Maritz Market Research, Inc., St. Louis, 1981—. Mem. Nat. Agri-Mktg. Assn. (dir. 1979-80, com. chmn., 1979-80, sec. 1980-81), Am. Mktg. Assn. Clubs: Purdue Alumni Assn., Chi Omega Alumnae Assn. (corr. sec. 1978-79, com. chmn. 1979-80, rec. sec. 1980-81). Home: 24 Brookwood Acres Saint Louis MO 63131 Office: 1355 N Highway Dr Fenton MO 63026

BOEHM, SIDONIA H. VON KESSEL MCDANIEL, civic worker; b. Shrewsbury Park, Mo., Mar. 15, 1919; d. Charles H. and Ethelynn CoVan (Davis) von Kessel; student Northwestern U., 1942-44; m. Charles Byron McDaniel, May 5, 1939 (dec. 1970); m. 2d, Thomas J. Boehm, Jr., Nov. 19, 1975; stepchildren—Thomas J., III, Debbie Lee. Corp. sec., mgr. Liberty Sales System, Chgo., 1939-44; media dir. Hollywood Bread, Nat. Bakers, Chgo., 1944-53. Founder, pres. Bay Bouquet Garden Club, 1962-65; pres. Dunedin Youth Guild, 1965; founder Santa Claus Workshop, 1967; chmn. citizens beautification com. City of Dunedin (Fla.), 1967-70; founder chmn. Dunedin Hist. Soc., 1969, pres., 1973-74; charter sec. Mease Hosp. Devel. Bd., 1970-72; chmn. Toast-to-Life charity gala Mease Hosp., 1975, co-chmn., 1981-82; pres. Mease Hosp. Aux., 1977-80; pres. Episc. Churchwomen, Ch. of Good Shepherd, Dunedin, 1959-61, 70-72; aide to pres. Episcopal Churchwomen, Diocese of S.W. Fla., 1971-74; pres. Clearwater Garden Club, 1956, Clearwater Lions Aux., 1958; active Dunedin Fine Arts and Cultural Soc., Trident Soc. Recipient cert. of service Morton Plant Hosp., 1959; cert. of appreciation Fla. Fedn. Garden Clubs, 1971, Dunedin Lions Club, 1969, Dunedin Hist. Soc., 1976; award of appreciation, key to city, City of Dunedin, 1971. Home: PO Box 321 Dunedin FL 33528 Office: Mease Hosp Aux 833 Milwaukee Ave Dunedin FL 33528

BOELENS, DENISE MARIE, psychologist; b. Wichita, Kans., May 6, 1953; d. Clyde Donald and Wilma Ruth (Espenshade) B.; Ph.D., U. Wash., 1980. Chief alcohol dependence treatment unit VA Med. Center, Salt Lake City; mem. clin. faculty dept. psychiatry, dept. family medicine U. Utah Med. Center. Mem. Am. Psychol. Assn., Utah Psychol. Assn. Home: PO Box 8561 Salt Lake City UT 84108 Office: 500 Foothill Dr 116A Salt Lake City UT 84148

BOEPPLE, ELIZABETH DELAPP, psychologist; b. Syracuse, July 12, 1950; d. Howard W. and Irene (Gratien) DeLapp; B.A. cum laude, SUNY, Buffalo, 1971, M.Ed., 1974, Ph.D., 1977; m. Harwig Otto Boepple, June 6, 1970; children—Karen Anne, Kathryn Marie. Instr., SUNY, Geneseo, 1974-75; research coordinator Research and Devel. Complex, State U. Coll., Buffalo, 1976; psychologist West Seneca Devel. Center, 1977-79; psychologist N.Y. State Div. for Youth, Masten Park Secure Center, Buffalo, 1979—; instr. Erie Community Coll., 1973-75, Bryant & Stratten Bus. Inst., 1976. Cert. psychologist, N.Y. Mem. Am. Psychol. Assn., Phi Beta Kappa. Roman Catholic. Home: 190 Audubon Dr Snyder NY 14226 Office: 485 Best St Buffalo NY 14208

BOFILL, ANGELA, singer, rec. artist; b. Bronx, N.Y., 1955; student Hartt Coll. Music, U. Hartford, 19 - ; degree in Voice, Manhattan Sch. Music. Singer in night clubs, cabarets; rec. artist, 1979—. Office: care Arista Records Inc 6 W 57th St New York NY 10019 *

BOGAD, ALICE ROSE, beverage mfg. co. exec.; b. Waterbury, Conn., July 26, 1922; d. Edward A. and Catherine A. (Wood) Rose; student Hunter Coll., 1943, U. Okla., 1944, Am. U., 1945; m. Alfred J. Bogad, Sept. 30, 1971; children by previous marriage—Nancy, Karen, Eric. Propr., dir. Mid-Hudson Floor & Wall Co., Poughkeepsie, N.Y., 1948-51, Hudson Valley Welding and Supply, Poughkeepsie, 1951-55; propr. Colonial Knolls Devel. Co., 1955-65; asst. mgr. Dutchess County (N.Y.) Airport, 1965-68; propr. and mgr. Queen's Ransom Gallery, Poughkeepsie, 1967-71; sec., treas., dir. G.H. Ford Tea Co., Inc., Poughkeepsie, 1974—; guest lectr. on tea various schs. and community orgns., 1974—. Pres., Arlington High Sch. PTA, 1963-64; chmn. scholarship com. Arlington Sch. Dist., 1960-64; sec. to zoning bd. Town of Poughkeepsie, 1965-60, dep. zoning adminstr., 1971-73, chmn. Zoning Bd. Appeals, 1976-78; trustee Vassar Temple, 1979—, chmn. membership, 1978—; bd. dirs. Dutchess County (N.Y.) Arts Council, 1979—, chmn. public funding com., 1979-80. Served with WAVES, 1942-45. Recipient Life Member award PTA, N.Y. State, 1964, Outstanding Citizen award Dutchess County Bd. Legislators, 1981. Mem. Tea Assn. U.S. (asso. bd. dirs. 1977-78, chmn. 1979). Culinary Inst. Am. (cons. 1975—, mem. corp. 1980—, chmn. fellows com.) Bus. and Profl. Women's Assn. Republican. Jewish. Club: Zonta (sec. 1978-79). Contbr. articles on tea industry to bus. and trade jours. Home: 7 Wilbur Ct PO Box 3373 Poughkeepsie NY 12603 Office: 110 Dutchess Turnpike PO Box 3407 Poughkeepsie NY 12603

BOGAN, ELIZABETH CHAPIN, economist; b. Morristown, N.J., Aug. 22, 1944; d. Daryl Muscott and Tirzah (Walker) Chapin; A.B., Wellesley Coll., 1966; M.A., U. N.H., 1967; Ph.D. (Earhart, U. Pres.'s, NSF fellow), Columbia U., 1971; m. Thomas Rockwood Bogan, June 5, 1965; children—Nathaniel Rockwood, Andrew Allerton. Mem. faculty Fairleigh Dickinson U., Madison, N.J., 1971—, now asso. prof. econs., coordinator econs. and finance, arts, scis. and bus., 1979—, chmn. dept. econs. and fin., 1981—, reviewer U. Press. Sec., Lakes Adminstrn. com. The Hideout, Lake Ariel, Pa., 1978-80. Recipient Outstanding Tchr. award Fairleigh Dickinson U. Student Senate, 1979. Mem. Am. Econs. Assn., Women's Econs. Round Table, AAUP. Congregationalist. Club: Wellesley. Established Elizabeth Bogan award for acad. excellence in grad. econs., U. N.H. Office: Fairleigh Dickinson U 285 Madison Ave Madison NJ 07940

BOGAN, ELIZABETH JANETTE, accountant; b. Boaz, Ala., June 19, 1933; d. James Archie and Willie Myrtle (Anderson) Cook; B.B.A., West Ga. Coll., 1975, M.B.A., 1976; postgrad. Miss. State U., 1980; m. Herbert Elias Bogan, Mar. 30, 1967; 1 son, Gary Stephen. Acct., Saltmarsh, Cleaveland & Gund, C.P.A.s, Pensacola, Fla., 1961-64; instr. West Ga. Coll., Carrollton, 1976-77; asst. prof. acctg. Winthrop Coll., Rock Hill, S.C., 1978—. C.P.A., S.C. Mem. Am. Acctg. Assn., Nat. Assn. Accts. (dir. ednl. activities Gaston-Carolinas Area chpt.), S.C. Assn. C.P.A.s, S.C. Assn. Acctg. Instrs. Baptist. Home: Fox Fire Apt 1843-D Rock Hill SC 29730 Office: Sch Bus Winthrop Coll Rock Hill SC 29733

BOGARDUS, ETHEL KENRICK, civic worker, former health assn. exec.; b. Bklyn., Apr. 11, 1905; d. John Kenrick and Alicia (Riches) Samson; grad. Maxwell Tchr.'s Coll., 1925; postgrad. Cornell U., summer 1946, Columbia U. Sch. Adminstrv. Medicine, winter 1962; m. Emory Arthur Bogardus, Nov. 23, 1925. Social service case worker Town of Clarkstown (N.Y.), 1938-41, chief clk. War Price and Rationing Bd., 1941-45; social service case worker Rockland County (N.Y.) Bd. Child Welfare, 1945-46; exec. dir. Rockland County Tb, Heart and Public Health Assn., 1946-70, ret., 1970; active in planning and promotion of public health, mass x-ray surveys for schs., industry and gen. public, health edn., recruiting and tng. vols.; lectr. in field; asst. for naturalization cts. Rockland County Clk., 1968-79; mem. nat. adv. bd. Am. Security Council, 1971—; mem. U.S. Congressional Adv. Bd., U.S. Presdl. Task Force. Recipient citation for disting. service in eradication Tb, N.Y. Conf. Tb and Respiratory Disease Workers, 1970, Silver Tray for services to bd. dirs. Rockland County Tb and Public Health Assn., 1970. Mem. Daus. Am. Colonists (nat. chmn. flag U.S.A. com., chaplain and vet. service chmn. local chpt.), DAR (Continental Congress award 1977; state chmn. resolution coms., nat. vice chmn. NE flag U.S.A. com., past chpt. regent, past rec. sec., chpt. chaplain, state dir. 1978-79), Daus. Colonial Wars (nat. vice-chmn. program), Daus. Founders and Patriots (v.p. and program dir. N.Y. State), New Eng. Women (v.p. Poughkeepsie Colony 1974-75), Sons and Daus. of Pilgrims (councillor 1973-76), Soc. Old Plymouth Colony Descs., Hereditary Order Descs. Colonial Govs., Women Descs., Ancient and Hon. Arty. Co., Soc. Descs. Colonial Clergy, Order Ams. Armorial Ancestry, Nat. Huguenot Soc., Huguenot Soc. New Paltz (N.Y.), Dames Ct. of Honor. Vt. Soc. Colonial Dames, Flagon and Trencher, Daus. Union 1861-1865, U.S. Daus. of 1812, Washington Hdqrs. Assn., DAR N.Y. State Officers Club, DAR Ex-Regents Club N.Y. State, Hereditary Register. Contbr. articles to DAR Empire State News, 1974-79; author DAR news releases, 1976-77.

BOGER, GAIL PARSONS GREEN, educator; b. Worthington, Ind., June 8, 1914; d. Byron Tennison and Bula (Taylor) Green; B.S., Ind. U., 1950, M.S. (DuPont fellow), 1959; student Universidad International, Santandar, Spain, 1968; Ph.D., U. Utah, 1969; m. Alva B. Parsons, June 8, 1935; children—Donald Alva, Robert Bradley, Gail Marie Parsons Michel, Helen Jean Parsons Czuba. Instr., Fresno (Calif.) State Jr. Coll., 1948-54; asst. prof. Purdue U. Extension, Michigan City, Ind., 1955-58; tchr. jr.-sr. high sch., Michigan City, Ind., 1954-59; instr. Ind. U., Bloomington, Ind., 1959-64; prof. dept. edn. and Sch. Engring. Ohio No. U., Ada, 1964—; participant profl. confs.; chmn. nat. research com. Children's Internat. Summer Villages, Inc., now internat. chmn., chmn. research com., Newcastle, Eng., also trustee. Dupont fellow, 1957; NSF fellow, 1961, 63, NSF-AEC fellow, 1960. Mem. Am. Assn. Supervision and Curriculum Devel., Am. Assn. Coll. Tchrs. of Edn., AAUP, Nat. Assn. Edn. of Gifted (dir., past v.p.), Nat. Assn. Creative Children and Adults (trustee) Ohio Assn. Gifted Children, NEA, Ohio, N.W. Ohio edn. assns., Ohio Acad. Sci., Kappa Delta Pi, Kappa Sigma Pi, Kappa Phi. Democrat. Methodist. Club: Gifted Children's Study, Federated Women's. Contbr. articles to profl. jours. Home: 1703 Wonderlick Rd Lima OH 45805 Office: Dept Edn Ohio No U Ada OH 45810

BOGERTY, MARGARET ANN, assn. ofcl.; b. Newport News, Va., Sept. 21, 1952; d. Kenneth Miles and Clara (Bronson) B.; B.A., cum laude, U. New Haven, 1975; M.B.A., 1979; children—Beverly Ann Bogerty, Darnley Richmond Hodge. Asso. dir. Lovell Community Center of New Haven, 1975-76; tchr. Richard Lee High Sch., Hillhouse High Sch., New Haven, 1976-77; mgmt. and claims edn. instr. Hartford Ins. Group, Fairfield, Conn., 1977-79; asst. chief Adminstrv. Office to Mayor Biagio DiLieto, New Haven, 80; mgr. tng. and procedures United Services Automobile Assn., Washington, 1980—; cons. in mgmt. and human resource devel. Mem. 12th Ward Democratic Com.; former mem. bd. dirs. Greater New Haven Urban League; chmn. New Haven Mayor's Youthfest '80; public relations coordinator New Haven Downtown Council. Methodist. Home: 2651 Arlington Apt 301 Alexandria VA 22306

BOGGERO, JOHANNA DAGRADI, chemist; b. N.Y.C., Dec. 4, 1924; d. Louis Achille and Anna Maria (Raffa) Dagradi; A.B., City U. N.Y., 1944; m. Joseph Andrew Boggero, June 9, 1946; 1 dau., Anne Virginia. Analytical vitamin chemist Hoffman-La Roche, Inc., Nutley, N.J., 1944-46; analytical wine chemist Roma Winery, Fresno, Calif., 1952; petroleum chemist Twining Labs., Fresno, 1952-57, dir. petroleum dept., chemist, 1957-62; agrl. chemist U. Calif. Coop. Extension, Fresno County Farm Advisors Office, 1962—. Contbr. articles in field to profl. jours. Home: 3816 N Angus St Fresno CA 93726 Office: 1720 S Maple Ave Fresno CA 93702

BOGGS, ANNIE HAPPE, educator; b. Elsinore, Calif., Sept. 24, 1916; d. Henry Happe; B.A. in History, UCLA, 1938; m. Eugene W. Boggs; children—Steven Eugene, Michael Walter, Kathryn Anne Boggs Gilliland. Tchr., librarian Elsinore Joint Union High Sch. Dist., 1939-41; adminstrv. asst. admissions office U. Calif., Los Angeles, 1944-49; tchr. Los Angeles Unified Sch. Dist., 1958-61; tchr. Santa Maria (Calif.) Sch. Dist., 1961-69, Miller-Unruh reading specialist, 1969-79, reading cons., 1979-82. Mem. NEA, Calif. Tchrs. Assn., Santa Maria Elementary Educators Assn., Internat., Calif., Santa Barbara County (pres. 1973-74) reading assns., Delta Kappa Gamma (charter mem. chpt.). Co-author Santa Maria Reading Readiness Tests; dist. rep. for lang. skills devel. kindergarten-12th grades for No. Santa Barbara County; ran pilot programs in lang., lit., math. Certified in gen. secondary and elementary teaching, reading, early childhood edn., Calif.; specialist in lang. arts.

BOGGS, CORINNE CLAIBORNE (LINDY), congresswoman; b. Brunswick Plantation, La., Mar. 13, 1916; d. Roland and Corinne (Morrison) Claiborne; B.A., Sophie Newcomb Coll., Tulane U., 1935; D.Pub. Service (hon.), Trinity Coll., Washington, 1975; hon. degree St. Mary of Woods; LL.D. (hon.), Loyola U.; m. Thomas Hale Boggs, Jan. 22, 1938 (dec.); children—Barbara (Mrs. Paul E. Sigmund, Jr.), Thomas Hale, Corinne (Mrs. Steven V. Roberts). Tchr. history and English, St. James Parish, La., 1936-37; elected to 93d Congress to fill vacancy caused by death of husband, 1973; re-elected to 93d-98th Congresses from 2d La. Dist., mem. appropriations com. majority mem. from Ho. of Reps., Am. Revolution Bicentennial Adminstrn. Bd.; mem. campaign com. Democratic Nat. Com., 1974; chairwoman Dem. Nat. Conv., 1976. Pres., Dem. Congl. Wives Forum, 1955-56, Womans Nat. Democratic Club, 1957-58, Congl. Club, 1970-72; co-chmn. Inaugural Balls for Presidents John F. Kennedy, Lyndon Johnson, 1961-65. Bd. dirs. La. Council for Music and Performing Arts; hon. bd. dirs. Met. New Orleans chpt. Nat. Found. March of Dimes; bd. advisers. CLOSE-UP and Presdl. Classroom; bd. regents Smithsonian Instn.; mem. president's council Tulane U. Recipient Weiss Meml. award NCCJ, 1974; Distinguished Service medal Saint Mary's Dominican Coll., 1976; Humanitarian award AMVETS Nat. Aux.; Torch of Liberty award B'nai B'rith, 1976; Gala IV award Birmingham So. U., 1976, Eleanor Roosevelt award, 1977. Mem. Nat. Soc. Colonial Dames, League Women Voters, Internat. Fedn. Catholic Alumni. Office: Rayburn House Office Bldg Room 2353 Washington DC 20515 *

BOHAN, DORIS KAY, counselor; b. River Rouge, Mich., July 19, 1934; d. Leonard H.J.C. and Doris Blanche (Kirchstein) Feldmeyer; B.A., George Mason U., 1972, M.A., 1974; Ed.D., Va. Inst. Tech., 1983; m. John P. Bohan, Nov. 4, 1967; children—Thomas L., J. Michael, Richard B., Kaythrine J. Pvt. practice psychology, Hollidaysburg, Pa., 1976-77; instr. St. Francis Coll., Loretto, Pa., 1975-76; cons. Hollidaysburg State Hosp., 1975-77; chief psychologist Altoona (Pa.) Community Mental Health Center, 1974-77; psychologist Charles County Mental Health Clinic, LaPlata, Md., 1978; instr. George Mason U., 1978; psychologist St. Elizabeth's Hosp., Washington, 1978-81; pvt. practice counseling, Annandale, Va., 1981—; cons. mental health facilities; tchr. adolescent psychology and exptl. psychology. Bd. dirs. Altoona Head Start, 1975-77; public speaker, civic groups. Mem. Am. Psychol. Assn. (asso.), Am. Personnel and Guidance Assn., Va. Counselors Assn., Nat. Acad. Cert. Clin. Mental Health Counselors. Democrat. Roman Catholic. Home and Office: 5150 Piedmont Pl Annandale VA 22003

BOHANNON, KATHRYN T., environ. scientist; b. Seneca, Kans., Aug. 24, 1951; d. Robert Arthur and Vera Jeanne (Waugh) B.; B.A. in Chemistry and Modern Langs., Kans. State U., 1973. Chemist photog. tech. div. Eastman Kodak Co., Rochester, N.Y., 1974-75, environ. engr. synthetic chems. div., 1975-77, environ. scientist Colo. div., Windsor, 1978—; chemist Midwest Research Inst., Kansas City, Mo., 1977-78. 4-H project leader for tailoring Larimer County (Colo.). NSF summer grantee, 1971-72. Mem. Am. Chem. Soc., Phi Beta Kappa, Phi Kappa Phi, Alpha Lambda Delta, Phi Lambda Upsilon. Club: Toastmistress. Author papers in field. Home: 513 Pluto Ct Fort Collins CO 80526 Office: Eastman Kodak Co Kodak Colo Div Windsor CO 80551

BOHEN, BARBARA ELIZABETH, museum adminstr.; b. Bradford on Avon, Wiltshire, Eng., Apr. 24, 1941; came to U.S., 1960, naturalized, 1969; d. Charles Henry and Rhoda Victoria (Chenery) Jones; B.A. in Latin summa cum laude, Queens Coll., 1969; M.A., Inst. Fine Arts, N.Y. U., 1973, Ph.D. in Classical Art, 1979; m. Robert Bohen, Dec. 6, 1963; 1 dau., Leonora Roberta. Lectr. archeology N.Y. U., 1972-73; lectr. art history City U. N.Y., 1973; asst. to dir. Kerameikos Mus., Athens, Greece, 1977-78, ind. research asso., 1979-81; dir. World Heritage Mus., U. Ill., Urbana, 1981—, instr. Greek art, 1982—. NDEA fellow, 1969-73, Fulbright fellow, 1973-74, Danforth Women's fellow, 1974-77, Deutsche Forschung/schaft fellow, 1979-81. Mem. Midwest Mus. Assn., Am. Assn. Mus., Archaeol. Inst. Am., Am. Sch. Classical Studies. Author articles in field. Home: 1605 Sandpiper Ln Champaign IL 61820 Office: World Heritage Museum 484 Lincoln Hall 702 S Wright St Urbana IL 61801

BOHLE, SUE (MRS. JOHN BERNARD BOHLE), public relations exec.; b. Austin, Minn., June 23, 1943; d. Harold Raymond and Mary Theresa (Swanson) Hastings; B.S. in Journalism (Univ. scholar 1961-64, Panhellenic scholar 1964-65), Northwestern U., 1965, M.S. in Journalism, 1969; m. John Bernard Bohle, June 22, 1974; children—Jason John, Katie Christine. Tchr. public high Schs., Englewood, Colo., 1965-68; account exec. Burson-Marsteller Public Relations, Los Angeles, 1969-73; v.p., mgr. public relations J. Walter Thompson Co., Los Angeles, 1973-79; pres. The Bohle Co., Los Angeles, 1979—; free-lance writer; instr. communications Calif. State U. at Fullerton, 1972-73; instr. writing Los Angeles City Coll., 1975-76; lectr. U. So. Calif., 1979—. Dir. public relations Los Angeles Jr. Ballet, 1971-72; pres. Panhellenic Advisers Council, UCLA, 1972-73; mem. adv. bd. Los Angeles Valley Coll., 1974-75, Coll. Communications Pepperdine U., 1981—. Mem. Public Relations Soc. Am., Women in Communications, Shi-ai, Delta Zeta (editor The Lamp 1966-68), Kappa Alpha Tau. Contbr. articles to trade mags. Home: 3605 Longridge Ave Sherman Oaks CA 91413 Office: 1901 Ave of the Stars Los Angeles CA 90067

BOHLER, GLORIA ANN, educator; b. Eastman, Ga., Sept. 5, 1935; d. John Clancy and Monteen (Nutt) Bohler; B.S., Fla. State U., 1957; M.A., Appalachian State U., 1964; Ed.D., U. Ga., 1973. Pub. sch. tchr., Broward County, Fla., Ft. Lauderdale, 1957-63, tchr. jr. high sch., head social studies dept., 1965-67; grad. teaching asst. U. Ga., Athens, 1968-70; instr. social sci. U. Ga. Extension Center, Waycross, 1970-71; asst. prof. history Ball State U., Muncie, Ind., 1971-77, asso. prof., 1977— (on leave); tchr., Palm Beach County, Fla., 1979-80; social studies cons. and In-service Programs, Ohio and Ind. Schs. Mem. Nat. (mem. tchr. certification com.), Ind. (exec. bd., editor newsletter Viewpoints, chmn. publicity com. 1975-79) councils for social studies, AAUP, Kappa Delta Pi, Phi Delta Kappa, Phi Alpha Theta. Club: Alpha Chi Omega Alumnae (pres. 1961-63). Author: (with Claudia Crump and Maxine Dunfee) George Rogers Clark State Curriculum Guide and Filmstrips, 1975; (with Michael L. Hawkins) Graphic Skills in Social Science Education, rev. edit., 1970, others; editor children's books; also articles in profl. jours.

BOHN, JEANNE ZEMEK, TV exec.; b. Chgo., Nov. 23, 1928; d. Arthur Joseph and Esther (Kettleson) Zemek; B.A. cum laude, Knox Coll., 1950; m. Ralph Paul Bohn, Sept. 5, 1951; children—Sara Jeanne, Nathan Paul. Sec., Time Inc., Chgo., 1950-51; asst. Wieboldt's, Chgo., 1950-51; sec. to Dr. F. Grant, Union Theol. Sem., 1952; lectr. English, Bloomfield Coll., 1960-64; dir. community affairs sta. WSOC-TV, Charlotte, N.C., 1974—. Mem. program com. sta. WTVI, Inc. Bds. dirs. Charlotte-Mecklenburg Hosp. Authority, 1975; Charlotte Community Hosp., 1975; Planned Parenthood of Greater Charlotte, 1975; Charlotte Area Fund, 1979; Mecklenburg Literacy Com., 1978. Mem. Women in Communications Inc. (chpt. pres. 1979-80). Quaker. Office: WSOC Box 34665 Charlotte NC 28234

BOHNING, ELIZABETH EDROP, educator; b. Bklyn., June 26, 1915; d. Percy Tom and Marion Lothrop (Stafford) Edrop; B.A., Wellesley Coll., 1936; M.A., Bryn Mawr Coll., 1938, Ph.D., 1943; postgrad. Middlebury Coll., summer 1936, U. Cologne, 1936-37, U. Munich, summer 1955; m. William H. Bohning, Aug. 18, 1943; children—Barbara Bohning Young, Margaret Bohning Anderson. Faculty, Bryn Mawr Coll., 1938-39, Middlebury Coll. Summer Sch. German, 1956, 58, Grinnell Coll., 1940-41, Stanford U., 1939-40; prof. U. Del., Newark, 1967—, chmn. dept. langs. and lit., 1971-78; mem. exec. com. Del. Humanities Council. Pres., Del. Council Internat. Visitors. Recipient Lindback award for excellence in teaching, 1962. Mem. Am. Assn. Tchrs. German, East Central Soc. 18th Century Studies, Am. Council Study of Austrian Lit., Middle State Assn. Colls. and Schs. (trustee 1974-80), Phi Beta Kappa, Delta Phi Alpha, Phi Kappa Phi, Alpha Chi Omega. Episcopalian. Clubs: Wellesley Alumnae, Bryn Mawr Alumnae. Author: The Concept "Sage" in Nibelungen Criticism, 1944; contbr. articles on lit. to profl. jours. Home: Box 574 Newark DE 19711 Office: Dept Lang and Lit U Del Newark DE 19711

BOHNY, BARBARA JEAN, nursing educator; b. Paterson, N.J., Dec. 27, 1939; d. Eugene E. and Eleanor A. (Smith) B.; B.S. cum laude, Cath. U. Am., 1963; M.A., Columbia U., 1964; D.Nursing Sci., Cath. U. Am., 1973. Staff nurse St. Lukes Hosp., Newburgh, N.Y., summer 1965; instr. dept. nursing Mount Saint Mary Coll., Newburgh, 1965-68, asst. prof., 1968-73; clin. lectr. Sch. Nursing, Cath. U. Am., Washington, 1972; staff nurse St. Joseph's Med. Center, Paterson, summer, 1973; asso. prof. and curriculum coordinator William Paterson Coll. of N.J., Wayne, 1973-75; cons. dept. nursing Jersey City (N.J.) State Coll., 1975; acting chairperson dept. theoretical bases of nursing sci. N.Y. U., 1979, asso. prof. Sch. Edn., Health, Nursing and Arts Professions, 1980—; cons. Boy Scouts Am., Wayne, N.J., 1975, William Paterson Coll., 1974. Mem. Am. Nurses Assn., N.Y. State Nurses Assn. (v.p. 1966, dir. 1967-68), Nat. League Nursing, Soc. Advancement in Nursing, AAUP, AAUW, N.J. Nurses Assn., Sigma Theta Tau, Kappa Delta Pi, Pi Lambda Theta. Contbr. articles on nursing edn. to profl. publs. Home: 8 Summit Ave Haledon NJ 07508 Office: New York Univ Div Nursing Washington Sq New York NY 10003

BOHORFOUSH, BLISS PAGE, civic worker; b. Fairmont, N.C., Sept. 10, 1912; d. Matthew Eli and Leatie Patry (Horne) Page; R.N., N.C. Sanatorium Sch. Nursing, 1933; postgrad. Teachers Coll., Columbia U., 1945, Jr. Coll., 1954; B.S. in Nursing Edn., Med. Coll. Ga. Sch. of Nursing, 1957; m. W.E. Hoffman, Feb. 18, 1934; 1 dau., Paige Hoffman Sayers; m. 2d. Joseph G. Bohorfoush, Feb. 17, 1960; stepsons, David, William. Pvt. duty nurse, Augusta, Ga., 1934-36; supr., instr. U.S. govt. project, housekeeping aides, Augusts, 1941; dir. Wilhenford Hosp., Augusta, 1942-46; med. and surg. staff nurse Oliver Gen. Army Hosp., Augusta, 1947-48; supr., instr. contagious diseases Univ. Hosp., Augusta, 1948-49; gen. duty nurse, head nurse, supr., asst. chief nurse VA Hosp., Augusta, 1951-60. Pres. Page Meml. Assn., Fairmont, N.C., 1978-79, dir., 1979-80; treas. United Daus. of the Confederacy, 1974-79; pres. Aux. to Baldwin County Med. Soc., 1961-63, mental health chmn. to state Aux., 1962-64; chmn. nursing service com. ARC, 1957-60; mem. Am. Nurses Assn., dist. and nat., 1936-60; bd. dirs. Am. League for Nurses, 1950's; mem. AAUW, Daus. of the King (Episcopal Ch.). Recipient service certificates ARC, Baldwin County Med. Soc. Aux., So. Med. Aux. Episcopalian. Clubs: D.A.R., Ft. Wilkinson Garden (charter mem., pres., 1963-65), Carrington Woods Garden. Author: Mental Health in Georgia 1837-1965; researcher, writer Page family history; coordinator, chief researcher Biography of Physicians in Baldwin County since 1803; author: History of the Auxiliary to the Baldwin County Medical Society, 1979; contbr. articles, news items, letters to publs. Home: 1661 Stone Meadow Rd Milledgeville GA 31061

BOIKESS, OLGA SHNIPER, lawyer; b. Jamaica, N.Y., Dec. 25, 1938; d. Robert and Bella (Jarus) Shniper; B.A., Barnard Coll., 1960; J.D., UCLA, 1964. Admitted to Calif. bar, 1964, D.C. bar, 1969; law clk. U.S. Dist. Ct. for So. Dist. Calif., 1964-65; atty. gen. counsel's office, Office Econ. Opportunity, Exec. Office President, Washington, 1965-68; assoc. firm Galland, Kharasch, Calkins & Brown, Washington, 1968-75, mem. firm Galland, Karasch, Calkins & Morse, Washington, 1975—. Mem. ABA (vice chmn. transp. com.). Contbr. articles to profl. jours. Office: 1054 31st St NW Washington DC 20007

BOISVERT, BARBARA SUE KIRKPATRICK, bus. exec.; b. Moultrie, Ga., June 6, 1943; d. Dale Croft and Edna Elizabeth (Gordon) Kirkpatrick; student La. State U., New Orleans, 1962-63, Memphis State U., 1969-70, Draughon Bus. Coll., 1970 Humboldt State U., Arcata, Calif.; m. William Francis Boisvert, May 19, 1972; 1 son by previous marriage, Russell Lloyd Patterson. Asst. municipal bond trader U.M-.I.C., Memphis, 1968-70; asst. municipal bond underwriter Nat. Bank of Commerce, Memphis, 1970-72; household goods coordinator U.S. Naval Air Sta., Sigonella, Sicily, 1972-74; order coordinator Hewlett-Packard Co., New Orleans, 1974; exec. sec., trust dept. Bank of Am., Eureka, Calif., 1975-77, trust adminstr., trust dept., 1977-82; co-owner Custom Gems, 1982—; lectr. Coll. of Redwoods, Eureka, Calif.; lectr. seminar/workshop on estate planning for women. Leader 4-H Club, 1976-77. Mem. Am. Bus. Women's Assn. Club: Quota. Home: 1819 I St Eureka CA 95501 Office: PO Box 4100 Eureka CA 95501

BOKAN, PATRICIA ANNE, speech and lang. pathologist; b. Bethlehem, Pa., Feb. 5, 1954; d. Joseph Rudolf and Patricia Anne (Danner) B.; B.A., Douglass Coll., Rutgers U., 1976; M.Ed., U. Va., 1977. Speech and lang. pathologist The Med. Center at Princeton (N.J.), 1977—. Mem. Am. Speech and Hearing Assn. Home: A-20 Avon Dr Hightstown NJ 08520 Office: The Medical Center at Princeton Princeton NJ 08540

BOKROSS, AGNES HELEN, documentalist; b. Budapest, Hungary, Jan. 9, 1922; came to Can., 1957, naturalized, 1962; d. Lajos Ferenc and Andrea (Tómóry) Szakonyi; B.A. with honors in English, Sir George Williams U., Montreal, Que., Can., 1970; Ph.D. in Comparative Lit. (Woodrow Wilson fellow 1970-71, Ford fellow 1970-71, Can. Council doctoral awards 1972-74), McGill U., Montreal, 1974; m. Bela E. Bokross, 1943 (div. 1945); 1 dau., Apollonia Elizabeth Bokross Schofield. Indexer and archivist Internat. Civil Aviation Orgn., Montreal, 1957-72; lectr. in English lit. Concordia U., Montreal, 1974-80; multilingual annotator Nat. Library Can., Ottawa, Ont., 1975-81; documentalist Public Service Commn. Can., Ottawa, 1981—; tchr., cons. in field; interpreter Supreme Ct. Can. Recipient Gold medal Gov. Gen. Can., 1970; McGill U. travel research grantee, 1973. Mem. MLA, Can. Soc. Comparative Study Civilizations, Nat. Geog. Soc. Roman Catholic. Author Nat. Library of Can. Annotations Manual, 1979; contbr. essays to lit. jours.; papers to confs. Office: Public Service Commn L'Esplanade Laurier West Tower 930 300 Laurier W Ottawa ON K1A 0M7 Canada

BOLAND, DIANE MARIE, nurse; b. Bklyn., Sept. 10, 1947; d. John and Carmela (Marsala) Bertges; grad. Central Islip (N.Y.) Sch. Nursing, 1968; student C.W. Post Coll., 1965-68; B.S. in Behavioral Sci., N.Y. Inst. Tech., 1981. Staff nurse Central Islip Psychiat. Center, 1968-69, head nurse female surg. unit, 1976-78, nurse epidemiologist, 1978—; head nurse Central Islip Med. Surg. Bldg., 1969-74; instr. nursing Central Islip Sch. Nursing, 1974-76. Bd. dirs., v.p. Brentwood (N.Y.) Legion Vol. Ambulance. Cert. instr. CPR, Am. Heart Assn.; cert. emergency med. technician, pre-hosp. coronary care technician, N.Y. State. Mem. Am., N.Y. State nurses assns., Nat. Assn. Practitioners in Infection Control (treas. local chpt.), Profl. Nurses Assn., Profl. Nurses Assn. Central Islip P.C. (pres.), Central Islip Sch. Nursing Alumni. Roman Catholic. Home: 6 Willoughby St Brentwood NY 11717 Office: Office of Infection Control Central Islip NY 11722

BOLAND, JANET LANG, judge; b. Kitchener, Ont., Can., Dec. 6, 1924; d. George William and Miriam Janet (Geraghty) Lang; B.A., Waterloo Coll., 1946; law degree Osgoode Hall, 1950; m. John Brown Boland, Oct. 1, 1949; children—Michael, Christopher, Nicholas. Called to Ont. bar, 1950; mem. firm White, Bristol, Beck & Phipps, Toronto, Ont., 1959-69; partner firm Lang Michener, Toronto, 1969-72; county ct. judge, Toronto, 1972-76; judge Supreme Ct. of Ont., Toronto, 1976—; named Queen's counsel, 1965; co-chmn. Penal Reform for Women Joint Com., 1956-58. Mem. Jr. League Toronto. Roman Catholic. Home: 164 Inglewood Dr Toronto ON Canada Office: Osgoode Hall Queen St Toronto ON Canada

BOLDEN, HELEN ELAINE, social welfare exec.; b. Kansas City, Kans., May 28, 1934; d. Labrum Arthur and Retha (Norman) Fells; student Ohio State U., 1963; m. James L. Bolden, Sr. (div.); children—Leroy, David, Michael, James, Nugene, Rachelle. With Post Office Dept., Lima, Ohio, 1963-64; dir. Garfield Opportunity Center, Lima, 1965-74; founder Tot Lot, Inc., Garfield Sch., 1972; founder, exec. dir. Friendly Sr. Citizens and Disabled Persons Center, Inc., Lima, 1974—, Garfield Breakfast Program. Active, Black Elected Democrats, Ohio, Mem. Nat. Assn. of Black Aged, Social Workers Council Allen County, Nat. Urban Coalition, Regional Planning Commn. Baptist. Club: Order Eastern Star (Ct. of Colanthe). Home: 312 N Pine St Lima OH 45801 Office: 213 S Pine St Lima OH 45801

BOLEN, LANORA LUKE, educator; b. Oklahoma City, Mar. 12, 1934; d. Elmer Werthon and Nellie Lois (Owensby) Luke; student Okla. Bapt. U., 1952-55, Baylor U., 1953, Okla. Central State U., 1957, S.W. Mo. State U., 1960-61, St. Louis Inst. Music, 1964, So. Ill. U., 1968-70; B.Mus. Edn., So. Ill. U., 1970; postgrad. N. Tex. State U., 1975, Tex. Christian U., 1977; children by previous marriage—Paul Anthony DeOgny, Frederick Ronald DeOgny, Terri Sue DeOgny. Pvt. piano tchr., 1956-68; elem. music tchr. Clayton (Mo.) Sch. Dist., 1969-74; profl. musician TV comml. artist, 1967-75; exec. dir. Youth Orch. of Greater Ft. Worth, 1979-80; dir. founder Kinderplatz of Fine Arts, Inc., Ft. Worth, 1979—. Fin. chmn. LWV, St. Louis, 1966; pres. Republican Women's Club, Lewisville, Tex., 1976; vice chmn. Rep. Party, Tarrant County, Tex., 1977; bd. dirs. Youth Orch. Greater Ft. Worth, 1976-81, pres., 1979-81; chmn. Oktoberfest Symphony League, Ft. Worth, 1978; bd. dirs. Ft. Worth Symphony, 1980—; mem. exec. com. Youth Orch. div. Am. Symphony Orch. League, 1980—. Mem. Am. Orff-Schulwerk Assn., Nat. Music Educators Conf., Nat. Assn. for Edn. Young Children, Youth Orch. Assn., Nat. Fedn. Rep. Women, Am. Symphony Orch. League, Delta Kappa Gamma, Sigma Alpha Iota. Presbyterian. Clubs: Women's, Petroleum (Ft. Worth). Contbr. articles to profl. jours. Home: 3104 Spanish Oak Fort Worth TX 76109 Office: 4401 Trail Lake Dr Forth Worth TX 76109

BOLENE, MARGARET ROSALIE STEELE (MRS. ROBERT V. BOLENE), bacteriologist, civic worker; b. Kingfisher, Okla., July 11, 1923; d. Clarence R. and Harriet (White) Steele; student Oreg. State U., 1943-44; B.S., U. Okla., 1946; m. Robert V. Bolene, Feb. 6, 1948; children—Judith Kay, John Eric, Sally Sue, Janice Lynn, Daniel William. Technician bacteriology dept. Okla. Dept. Health, Oklahoma City, 1946-48; asst. bacteriologist Henry Ford Hosp., Detroit, 1948-49; bacteriol. cons., also asst. bus. mgr. Ponce Gynecology and Obstetrics, Inc., 1956—. Organizing dir. Bi-Racial Council, 1963; lay adviser Home Nursing Service, 1967-68; mem. exec. bd. PTA, 1956-71; active various community drives; sponsor Am. Field Service; patron Ponce Playhouse; bloodmobile vol. ARC; vol. Helpline. Republican precinct organizer, 1960. Mem. AAUW (treas. 1964-66), DAR (sec.-treas. 1961-67, 1st vice regent 1972-73, chpt. treas. 1974—), Kay-Noble County Med. Aux. (treas. 1957-58, 66-67), Ponca City Art Assn., Pioneer Hist. Soc., Okla. Heritage Assn., Daus. Founders and Patriots (state pres. 1981—), Nat. Huguenot Soc., Daus. Am. Colonists (chpt. pres. 1982—), Magna Charta Dames, Ancient and Honorable Arty. Co., Colonial Dames of 17th Century, U. Okla. Assn. (life), Lambda Tau, Phi Sigma, Alpha Lambda Delta. Presbyterian. Clubs: Ponca City Country, Ponca City Music, Red Rose Garden (pres. 1983), Twentieth Century. Home: 2116 Juanito Ave Ponca City OK 74601

BOLES, IDA DOKES, contractor, bus. exec.; b. Alexandria, La., Dec. 31, 1943; d. William, Jr., and Mary Lee Withers; certificate, Capitol City Bus. Coll., 1964; student Shorter Jr. Coll., 1965-67; cert. A-1 Sch. Real Estate, 1981; cert. Corp. Edn. Center, Princeton, 1980; Student U. Ark., Little Rock, 1980—; m. Earnest Leon Boles, June 20, 1979; children by previous marriage—Debbie Denise Dokes, Darrell Darnell Dokes, Derrell Donnell Dokes. Bricklayer, 1960-76; receptionist, copywriter Sta. KOKY, 1964-66; instr. office practices Shorter Jr. Coll., 1965-67; founder constrn. co. Bo-Dak Enterprises, Little Rock, 1970, pres., 1970—; with Teletype Corp. (Western Electric, AT&T subs.), 1966—, chief of controller large scale integrated display sect., 1976—; notary public; 8-A contractor SBA. Brain trust mem. Black Congressional Caucus, 1980—; mem. Ark. Arts Center; Little Rock Safety Commn., Little Rock Pvt. Industry Council, 1980—; NAACP. Recipient Recognition of Achievement award Nat. Small Bus., Cert. of Appreciation, City of Little Rock. Mem. Ark. Minority Contractors (sec. bd.), Nat. Bus. League Of Ark., Nat. Assn. Female Execs. Democrat. Baptist. Condr. survey moped and bicycle safety, results of which used by Ark. Legislature in preparation of moped safety legislation. Home: 2724 S Ringo Little Rock AR 72206 Office: 8200 Interstate Dr Little Rock AR 72209

BOLESKY, KAREN LUISE, retail health food co. exec.; b. Mansfield, Ohio, Mar. 9, 1941; d. Harold Francis and Lillian Amelia (Wilging) B.; B.A., U. S.Fla., Tampa, 1971, M.A., 1974. Pvt. practice family counseling, Tampa, 1975—; owner K.G. Real Food Co., Clearwater, Fla., 1976—; organizer, producer Fla. Feminist Festival, 1976. Cert. Gestalt therapist. Mem. Nat. Assn. Rehab. Counseling, Nat. Nutritional Foods Assn., Nat. Assn. Female Execs., Nat. Food Assn., Clearwater C. of C., Hunger Project, World Runners. Author papers in field. Home: 1441 Jungle Ave N Saint Petersburg FL 33710 Office: 6572 54th Ave N Saint Petersburg FL 33709

BOLEY BOLAFFIO, RITA, artist; b. Trieste, Italy; d. Angelo and Olga Senigaglia; came to U.S., 1939, naturalized, 1944; studied with Joseph Hoffmann, Kunstgewerbe Schule, Vienna, Austria; diploma violin Music Conservatory, Vienna; m. Orville F. Boley; children—Lucius R., Bruno A. Fashion and textile designer Wiener Werkstatte, Vienna and Milan, Italy; murals and displays throughout U.S., maj. exhns. collage and assemblage include Mus. of Art, Columbia, S.C., Am. House, N.Y.C., J.L. Hudson Gallery, Detroit, Pen and Brush Club, N.Y.C., Richard Kollmar's Gallery, N.Y.C., Guild Hall Mus., East Hampton, N.Y., James Pendleton Gallery, N.Y.C. Washington Art Assn. Conn. Mem. arts group ARC, 1942-44. Mem. Composer, Author and Artists Am. Home and Studio: 310 W 106th St New York NY 10025

BOLIN, SUSAN BECK, fin. co. exec.; b. Evanston, Ill., Nov. 24, 1944; d. H. Rodney and Muriel E. (Kirkman) Bolin; B.A., U. Ariz., 1966; postgrad. N.Y. Inst. Fin., 1978; children—Frederic Charles, Michael Gordon. Salesman, Robert Barker & Assos., Chgo., 1973-75; sec. to v.p. L.F. Rothschild, Chgo., 1976-78; stock broker Dean Witter Reynolds, 1978-79; market maker, stock options trader Chgo. Bd. Options Exchange, 1980—. Home: 472 E Westleigh Rd Lake Forest IL 60045 Office: Chicago Board Options Exchange 141 W Jackson Blvd Chicago IL 60604

BOLING, JEWELL, ret. govt. ofcl.; b. Randleman, N.C., Sept. 26, 1907; d. John Emmitt and Carrie (Ballard) Boling; student Women's Coll., U. N.C., 1926, Am. U., 1942, 51-52. Interviewer, N.C. Employment Service, Winston-Salem, Asheboro, 1937-41; occupational analyst U.S. Dept. Labor, Washington, 1943-57, placement officer, 1957-58, employment service adviser, 1959-61, occupational analyst, 1962, employment service specialist counseling and testing, 1963-69, manpower devel. specialist, from 1969. Recipient Meritorious Achievement award U.S. Dept. Labor, 1972. Mem. AAAS, N.Y. Acad. Scis., Am. Personnel and Guidance Assn. (profl. mem. nat. vocat. guidance assn.), Am. Rehab. Counseling Assn. (archivist 1964-68), Assn. Measurement and Evaluation in Guidance, Assn. Humanistic Psychology, Planetary Soc., Smithsonians, Sierra Club, Internat. Platform Assn., Audubon Naturalist Soc., Nat. Capital Astronomers (editor Star Dust 1949-58). Author: Counselor's Handbook, 1967; Counselor's Desk Aid, Eighteen Basic Vocational Directions, 1967; Handbook for New Careerists in Employment Security, 1971; contbr. articles to profl. publs. Address: Route 2 Box 141 Randleman NC 27317

BOLING, JUDY ATWOOD, civic worker; b. Madras, India, June 19, 1921 (parents Am. citizens); d. Carroll Eugene and Marion Frances (Ayrer) Atwood; A.A., San Antonio Jr. Coll., 1940; student Rogue Community Coll., Grants Pass, Oreg., 1978-79; m. Jack Leroy Boling, Apr. 8, 1941; children—Joseph Edward, Jean Ann, James Michael, John Charles. First aid instr. ARC, various locations, 1940-65, chmn. vols., Calif., 1961-62, Eng., 1964-65; den mother cub scouts Boy Scouts Am., Monterey, Calif., 1951-52; active Girl Scouts U.S.A., 1953—, council pres., Winema (Oreg.) Council, 1971-73, 79—, del. to nat. council, 1966, 72, 81, cons. for nat. pubs., 1971, 79; Sunday sch. tchr. Base Chapel, Pyote, Tex., 1949-51, choir dir., 1951; Sunday sch. adminstr. Base Chapel, Morocco, 1954-55; Sunday sch. tchr. Hermon Free Meth. Ch., Los Angeles, 1956-57; former liaison with local people in Japanese-Am., Franco-Am., Anglo-Am. orgns.; mem. Rogue Craftsmen Bd., Grants Pass, sec., 1972-78, v.p., 1978—; bd. dirs. Rogue Valley Opera Assn., 1978—, Community Concert, 1979—; public speaker. Recipient Thanks badge Girl Scouts U.S.A., 1957, 60, 73, Girl Scouts Japan, 1959, others; cert. of appreciation USAF, 1959, City of Hagi, City of Fukuoka (Japan), Gov. of Fukuoka Prefecture; citation Internat. Book Project. Mem. Josephine County Hist. Soc., So. Oreg. Resources Alliance, Am. Host Found. Republican. Club: Knife and Fork. Contbr. articles to profl. jours. Address: 3016 Jumpoff Joe Creek Rd Grants Pass OR 97526

BOLINGER, CAROL DARLENE, med. technologist; b. Brazil, Ind., Jan. 2, 1950; d. Arthur Clyde and Minnie Mildred (Sampson) B.; B.S., Ind. State U., 1971. Staff med. technologist Hematology Dept., Terre Haute (Ind.) Med. Lab., 1971-81, edn. coordinator, 1981—. Mem. Am. Soc. Med. Tech., Ind. Soc. Med. Tech. (dist. dir.), Am. Soc. Clin. Pathologists. Office: PO Box 1468 Terre Haute IN 47808

BOLINGER, SHIRLEY GOODWIN (MRS. JOHN RANDOLPH BOLINGER), former librarian; b. Seattle, July 11, 1907; d. Ervin Shirley and Eda (Hague) Goodwin; B.S. in Library Sci., U. Wash., 1931; m. John Randolph, Feb. 20, 1932; 1 son, Ervin Michael. Librarian elementary schs., Arlington, Va. until 1972. Mem. bd., v.p., Seattle YWCA, 1947-49; bd. mem. Travelers Aid Soc. of Tacoma, 1940-41, Travelers Aid Soc. of D.C., 1958-59; mem. bd. Washington Home for Incurables, 1952-59, Rock Spring Garden Club of Arlington, 1952-58. Mem. Jr. League of Washington, Nat. Symphony Orch. (women's com.), English Ceramic Circle, Antique Porcelain Soc. of Washington (founder), Smithsonian Assos., Nat. Trust for Historic Preservation, Friends of Kennedy Center, Am. Ceramic Circle, Kappa Kappa Gamma. Episcopalian. Clubs: Farmington Country (Charlottesville, Va.); Neighbors (Arlington). Home: 3224 N George Mason Dr Arlington VA 22207

BOLITHO, LOUISE GREER, ednl. adminstr.; b. Wenatchee, Wash., Aug. 13, 1927; d. Lon Glenn and Edna Gertrude (Dunlap) Greer; B.A., Wash. State U., 1949; m. Douglas Stuart Bolitho, June 17, 1950 (div. Dec. 1975); children—Rebecca Louise, Brian Douglas. Adminstrv. aide dept. geology Stanford (Calif.) U., 1967-70, adminstrv. asst. med. microbiology dept., 1970-74, adminstrv. asst. W.W. Hansen Labs. Physics, 1974-77, adminstrv. services mgr. Center for Research in Internat. Studies, 1977—. Mem. AAUW, Nat. Assn. Female Execs. Home: 3128 David Ave Palo Alto CA 94303 Office: Center for Research in Internat Studies Stanford U Stanford CA 94305

BOLLAR, MARJORIE ODESSA, nurse; b. N.Y.C., July 25, 1923; d. Charles Whitmore and Glenfield Ernesta (Griffith) Heath; grad. Central Islip Sch. Nursing, 1948; B.S. Edn. and Health, Coll. Oneonta, 1973; M.A., SUNY, Stony Brook, 1977; m. Wilbur B. Bollar, July 11, 1944; children—Diane Seaman, Ronald. Head nurse Central Islip (N.Y.) State Hosp., 1949-70; acting nurse adminstr. Central Islip Psychiat. Center, 1970-77, nurse adminstr., 1977-81, dir. nursing services, 1981—, coordinator for geriatrics, 1974—, overtime coordinator, 1980—, mem. instl. rev. com. on research proposals, 1975—, supr. research programs, tng. activities, tchr. affiliating nursing students and therapy aides div. research, chmn. unit med. records rev. com.; examiner N.Y. State Civil Service, 1982. Recipient 8th ann. Community Service award Eastern Suffolk Fed. Credit Union, 1980; cert. sch. nurse tchr., in-service edn. medication trainer and lectr., N.Y. Mem. Am. Public Health Assn., L.I. Minority Educators Assn., Internat. Platform Assn., Nat. Council Negro Women, N.Y. State Nurses Assn., Am. Film Industry Assn., Central Islip, Stony Brook alumnae, Centereach (N.Y.) C. of C., NAACP, Delta Sigma Theta (chmn. social actions com. Nassau alumni chpt.). Methodist. Research on follow up of geriatric subjects, discharged alcoholics and disturbed children, on geriatric hyperbaric oxygen therapy. Home: 218 N Washington Ave Centereach NY 11720 Office: Central Islip Psychiat Center Central Islip NY 11722

BOLLING, CHARLOTTE LEA, secretarial service co. exec.; b. Kurthwood, La., Aug. 25, 1926; d. David Stephen and Mae Josephine (James) Lea; student Stevens Coll., Baton Rouge, La., 1943-45; m. Paul Allen Bolling, Jan. 18, 1947; children—Patricia Lea, Peggy Lea Bolling Page, Paulette Ann Bolling Cosden. Sec., La. Hwy. Dept., Baton Rouge, 1944-46, VA, Washington, 1946, CAP, Washington, 1947; data technician Gen. Electric Co., Vanderberg AFB, Calif., 1962-65, engaged in computer sales and adminstrv. sec., 1965-67; owner, operator Exec. Services, Orlando, Fla., 1969—. Active various civic and polit. orgns. Mem. Orlando C. of C., Nat. Word Processing Assn., Nat. Assn. Secretarial Services, Fla. Answering Service Assn. Republican. Baptist. Home: 683 Blairshire Circle Winter Park FL 32792 Office: Exec Services 999 Woodcock Rd Suite 311 Orlando FL 32803

BOLLING, GLADYS V., social worker; b. Marion, Ala., Feb. 14, 1925; d. Wells and Florence (Foster) B.; A.B., Lake Forest (Ill.) Coll., 1948; M.S. in Social Scis. Adminstrn., Western Res. U., 1951. Social worker VA Hosp., North Chicago, Ill., 1952-55, supervisory social worker, 1955-62, asst. chief social work service, 1962-64, chief, 1976—; chief social work service VA Hosp., Pitts., 1964-73; chief social work service VA Westside Hosp., Chgo., 1973-76, VA Hosp. Med. Center, North Chicago, 1976—, VA leadership trainee, 1979; social worker Ill. Children's Home and Aid Soc., 1960-63; social work cons. Booth Meml. Hosp., 1961-64; adj. asso. prof. social work U. Pitts., 1970-73, Chgo. Med. Sch., 1976—; chmn. Tri-State Hosp. Assembly Social Work Conf. program, 1976. Bd. dirs. Eleanor Assn., Chgo., 1976—, exec. v.p. personnel, 1980—; alumni bd. govs. Lake Forest Coll., 1978—, exec. com., 1979—. Recipient VA Regional Dirs. commendation, 1973. Fellow Am. Orthopsychiat. Assn.; mem. Nat. Conf. Social Welfare, Nat. Assn. Social Workers (chmn. Soc. Hosp. Social Work Dirs. joint profl. standards rev. orgn. com. 1977-81), Internat. Council Social Welfare, Council on Social Work Edn. Methodist. Club: Altrusa Internat. (chmn. dist. 6 conf. 1980, dir. dist. 6 1979-81, 2d vice gov. 1981—, past pres. Chgo. club). Home: 3410 N Lake Shore Dr Chicago IL 60657 Office. VA Med Center North Chicago IL 60064

BOLLINGER, SHIRLEY ANN, accountant; b. Kansas City, Mo., Sept. 1, 1949; d. Charley L. and Eunice L. (Swinney) B.; student Central Meth. Coll., Fayette, Mo., 1967-68, U. Dijon, 1968; B.S. in Bus. Adminstrn., U. Mo., Columbia, 1971; M.S. in Taxation, Golden Gate U., 1981; m. James C. Harris, Dec. 14, 1974. Staff acct. Q.C. Murphy & Co., C.P.A.'s, Longview, Tex., 1971-72; tax sr. Touche, Ross & Co., Kansas City, Mo., 1973-74; tax supr. Moss, Adams & Co., San Francisco, 1974-78; pres. Shirley A. Bollinger Accountancy Corp., San Francisco, 1978-82. Treas. 101 States St. Homeowners Assn. C.P.A., Tex., Mo., Calif. Mem. Am. Women's Soc. C.P.A.s (nat. dir., treas., v.p. 1978-80), Am. Soc. Women Accts. (dir., sec.-treas. San Francisco chpt.), Women Entrepreneurs (treas. 1980-81), Am. Inst. C.P.A.s, Calif. Soc. C.P.A.s, San Francisco C.P.A. Soc. (tax com.), Hayes Valley Arts and Bus. Assn. (treas. 1981-82). Clubs: San Francisco Bay, Order of Eastern Star. Office: 387 Ivy St San Francisco CA 94102

BOLSTER, JACQUELINE NEBEN, communications exec.; b. Woodhaven, N.Y.; d. Ernest W. B. and Emily (Guck) Neben; student Pratt Inst., Columbia U.; m. John A. Bolster, May 8, 1954. Promotion mgr. Photoplay mag., 1949-53; merchandising mgr. McCall's, 1953-64; dir. promotion and merchandising Harper's Bazaar, N.Y.C., 1964-71; dir. advt. and promotion Elizabeth Arden Salons, N.Y.C., 1971-77, dir. communications, 1977—. Recipient Art Dir.'s award 1961, 66. Mem. Fashion Group, Inner Circle, Advt. Women N.Y. (life), Fashion Execs. Round Table. Home: 8531 88th St Woodhaven NY 11421 also Halsey Neck Ln Southampton NY Office: Elizabeth Arden Inc 55 E 52d St New York NY 10022

BOLTON-SMITH, PRUDENCE LEWIS, mgmt. cons.; b. Boston, Mar. 9, 1946; d. Wolfram L. and Elsie (Cole) Lewis; student U. Madrid (Spain), 1966; m. Carlile Bolton-Smith, Jr., Jan. 15, 1977. Corr., John P. Maguire Co., N.Y.C., 1968-71; asst. to pres. Cromwell Corp., N.Y.C., 1971-72, also corp. sec.; adminstrv. asst. to the exec. v.p. Rinfret Assos., N.Y.C., 1973-76; adminstrv. asst to chmn. Friedlich, Fearon & Strohmeier, N.Y.C., 1976-77; v.p. mgmt., sec.-treas. Morgan Newman Assos., Inc., Washington, 1977—. Cert. CPR. Mem. Smithsonian Assos., Nat. Assn. Female Execs. Republican. Episcopalian. Clubs: Sandbar Beach, The Waltz Group, Jr. League Washington. Office: 2121 K St NW Washington DC 20037

BOLTUCK, MARY ADAMS, psychologist; b. Yellow Springs, Ohio, Nov. 2, 1924; d. Clyde Stewart and Sarah (Walker) Adams; B.A. in Psychology, Miami U., Oxford, Ohio, 1946; M.A. in Clin. Psychology, State U. Iowa, 1948; postgrad. Wichita Guidance Center, 1949; m. Charles Joseph Boltuck, July 16, 1950; children—Richard Dale, Jane Ellen. Intern, mem. staff Wichita (Kans.) Guidance Center, 1948-50; probation psychologist Monroe County, Bloomington, Ind., 1950-53; clin. psychologist Galesburg (Ill.) State Research Hosp., 1953-55; clin. psychologist, instr. Kent State U., Ohio, 1957-64; instr., asst. prof., asso. prof., St. Cloud State U., Minn., 1964—; cons. Minn. Dept. Public Welfare, Campus, Lab. Sch., Headstart, Speech Clinic. Lic. cons. psychologist, Minn. Mem. Am. Psychol. Assn., Midwestern Psychol. Assn., Minn. Psychol. Assn., Central Minn. Psychol. Assn., NEA, AAUW, Internat. Assn. for Prevention of Child Abuse and Neglect, Nat. Assn. for Prevention of Child Abuse and Neglect, Assn. of Women Psychologists, St. Cloud Women's Center, Minn. Women Psychologists, Gray Panthers, Minn. Gerontol. Assn., NOW. Home: 2830 Edward Dr Saint Cloud MN 56301 Office: Dept Psychology St Cloud State U Saint Cloud MN 56301

BOLWELL, SUZANNE POLJACIK, civic worker; b. Pittsford, Vt., Aug. 14, 1927; d. Andrew P. and Helen (Suchan) Poljacik; B.S., U. Vt., 1949; R.N., U. Vt. Sch. Nursing, 1949; M.A., U. Toledo, 1967; m. Harry James Bolwell, Sept. 24, 1949; children—Brian James, Suzanne Carr. Instr. med. and surg. nursing Presbyn. Hosp., Newark, 1949-51; instr. ARC, S.C., 1952; clin. instr. East Tenn. Bapt. Hosp., Knoxville, 1953, White Plains Hosp. (N.Y.), 1954; instr. psychology and psychiat. nursing Kirkman Tech. High Sch., Chattanooga, 1961; part time instr. psychology Cuyahoga Community Coll., Cleve. 1969-74. Bd. mem. Vis. Nurse Assn., Cleve., Beech Brook Facility; bd. examiners United Fund, Chattanooga, 1959-61; mem. bd. Women's Orch. League Toledo, 1962-67, Health Hill Hosp., Cleve., 1968; mem. bd. Toledo Orch. Assn., 1965-67; past pres. women's com. Cleve. Orch.; mem. nat. com. sponsors Margaret Sanger Inst. Human Reprodn. and Devel., 1967-80; Sunday Sch. leader Episcopalian Ch. Mem. Tenn. (past treas.), Chattanooga (past pres.), Greater Toledo leagues of women voters. Clubs: Country, Intown, Clevelander, Kirtland Country; Garden. Home: Roundwood Rd Hunting Valley Chagrin Falls OH 44022

BOMAR, PORTIA HAMILTON, psychoanalyst, clin. psychologist; b. Cleve., July 19; d. Charles Brooks and Marion (Clements) Goulder; B.A., U. Mich., 1923; postgrad. Oxford (Eng.) U., 1923-25; M.A., Columbia U., 1932, Ph.D., 1940; m. William P. Bomar, July 1, 1966. Pvt. practice psychoanalysis and psychotherapy, N.Y.C., 1930-58; dir. teaching clinic Columbia-Presbyterian Med. Center, N.Y.C., 1942-50; asso. prof. psychology U. Richmond (Va.), 1964-66; lectr. psychology U. Tex., Austin, 1968-71; mem. faculty Southwestern Grad. Sch. Banking, So. Meth. U., Dallas, 1975-78. Vice chmn. Human Relations Commn., Ft. Worth, 1968-71; bd. dirs. Tarrant County (Tex.) Hist. Soc., 1968—, Child Study Center, Ft. Worth, 1972-78, Tarrant County Mental Health Assn., 1974-76, Casa Manana, Ft. Worth, 1974-76. Fellow Am. Psychol. Assn.; mem. Psychical Research Found., Parapsychology Assn., Chi Omega. Clubs: Rivercrest Country, Ft. Worth. Author: When 'Mid This Glory I Was Young, 1980; contbr. articles to profl. jours. Home: 1503 Hillcrest Fort Worth TX 76107

BOMBA, MARGARET ANN, mfg. co. exec., lawyer; b. Bklyn., July 1, 1947; d. Fred S. and Mary (Alban) Bomba; B.S., St. Francis Coll., 1975; postgrad. Columbia U., 1977; J.D., Bklyn. Law Sch., 1982; m. John N. Pizzuto, May 27, 1978. Sec., adminstrv. asst. Fieldcrest Mills, Inc., N.Y.C., 1966-71, product mgr. textiles for the home 1973—; sales and product mgmt. Wamsutta Mills Inc., N.Y.C., 1972-73. Office: 60 W 40th St New York NY 10018

BOMBA, ROSALIE, ins. broker; b. Providence, Sept. 3, 1928; d. Samuel and Sylvia (Reuter) Jacobs; student in bus., ins. U. R.I., 1968; m. Boruch Bomba, Mar. 9, 1952; children—Irwin Lee, Kenneth Marc, Steven Si. Bookkeeper, Westminster Jewelry Co., Providence, 1946-51, comml. Refrigeration, Providence, 1960-65; ins. broker, sec., treas. Bomba Ins. Agy., Inc., Leucadia, Calif., 1973—. Treas., N. County Shores chpt. Women's Am. Orgn. Rehab. Through Tng., 1979—. Mem. Am. Assn. Ins. Women, Profl. Ins. Agts. Am., Ind. Ins. Agts. Am., Am. Agt.'s Alliance. Jewish. Home: 1709 Greentree Rd Encinitas CA 92024 Office: 1410 N Hwy 101 Leucadia CA 92024

BOMBECK, ERMA LOUISE, author, columnist; b. Dayton, Ohio, Feb. 21, 1927; d. Cassius Edwin and Erma (Haines) Fiste; B.A., U. Dayton, 1949; m. William Lawrence Bombeck, Aug. 13, 1949; children—Betsy, Andrew, Matthew. Syndicated columnist Newsday Syndicate, 1965-70, Pubs.-Hall Syndicate, 1970, now Fields Newspaper Syndicate; contbg. editor Good Housekeeping Mag., 1969—. Mem. Theta Sigma Phi (Headline award 1969). Author: At Wit's End, 1967; Just Wait Till You Have Children of Your Own, 1971. Address: care Field Newspaper Syndicate 1703 Kaiser Ave Irvine CA 92714 *

BOMBERGER, AUDREY SHELLEY, nurse, adminstr.; b. Lebanon, Pa., June 12, 1942; d. Allen Aunspach and Ruth Mae (Arnold) Shelley; R.N., Reading (Pa.) Med. Center, 1963; B.S. in Edn., Millersville Coll., 1974; M.S. in Edn., Temple U., 1979; Ph.D., Columbia-Pacific U., Calif.; m. Edward K. Bomberger, Sept. 29, 1963; children—Beth-Ann, Gary Allen. Nurse, Hershey Hosp., Pa., 1963-64, Good Samaritan Hosp., Lebanon, 1964-65; charge nurse VA Hosp., Lebanon, 1965-70; charge nurse CCU, Lebanon Valley Gen. Hosp., Lebanon, 1970-74, dir. edn., 1975-79; dir. edn. St. Mary's Hosp., Reno, Nev., 1979—; speaker to health educators. Bd. dirs. Am. Heart Assn., Am. Cancer Soc. Served to maj. Nurses Corps, U.S. Army, 1977—. Cert. nurse adminstr. Mem. Nat. Critical Care Inst. Edn., Am. Assn. Critical Care Nurses, Res. Officers Assn. U.S., Am. Hosp. Assn., Health Edn. Media Assn. Am. Soc. Health Manpower Edn. and Tng. (Cert. of Appreciation 1981), Nev. Nurses Assn. (dir. Dist. 1), Am. Nurses Assn., Nat. League Nursing. Republican. Lutheran. Club: U.S. Officers. Author: Medical Review Text/Course in Pharmacology for Nurses, 1978; Radiation for Health Care Providers, 1983; contbg. author: Basic Nursing Skills; contbr. articles to profl. jours. Home: 1590 Zolezzi Ln Reno NV 89511 Office: St Mary's Hosp 235 6th St Reno NV 89520

BOMGARDNER, MARTHA-ANN, librarian; b. Ft. Knox, Ky., July 31, 1953; d. Bobby Gene and Barbara-Ann (Auwaerter) B.; student Rutgers U. in France, 1973-74; B.A., U. Ky., 1975, M.S.L.S., 1977. Research asst. Info. for Bus., N.Y.C., 1977; reference librarian Neptune (N.J.) Public Library, 1977-79; librarian U.S. Atty. for Dist. N.J., Newark, 1979-82; head reference Main Library, Dept. Justice, Washington, 1982—. Mem. Am. Assn. Law Librarians, Law Librarians' Soc. of Washington, Law Library Assn. Greater N.Y. Club: Scrabble Players. Office: Main Library Dept Justice 9th and Pennsylvania Ave Washington DC 20530

BOMKAMP, LORAINE MARY, educator; b. Cedar Rapids, Iowa, July 9, 1930; d. Frank William and Kathryn (Seifert) B.; student Clarke Coll., 1948-49; A.A. with distinction, Mt. Mercy Coll., 1950; B.A., U. Iowa, 1958, M.A. in Bus. Edn. and Office Mgmt., 1965. Sec., Simmons, Perrine, Albright, Ellwood and Neff, attys., Cedar Rapids, 1950-51, Century Engrng. Corp., Cedar Rapids, 1951-56; tchr. Wausau (Wis.) Tech. Inst., 1958-63; tchr. Cedar Rapids Community Sch. Dist., 1964—, coordinator data processing edn., 1964-65. Co-chmn. Donnelly Nursing Edn. Center, Mt. Mercy Coll., Cedar Rapids, 1975; chmn. Sister Immaculata Meml., 1972. Recipient Disting. Alumni award Mt. Mercy Coll., 1972; Women's Equality Day award Cedar Rapids Civic Groups, 1978. Mem. NEA, Nat. Secs. Assn. (award 1967), Am., Iowa (award 1970) vocat. assns., Bus. and Profl. Women's Club (dir. 1967-70, Woman of Year award 1977), AAUW, Cath. Daus. Am., Iowa State, Cedar Rapids edn. assns., Nat., Iowa (award 1969) bus. edn. assns., Iowa Office Edn. Assn., Internat. Fedn. Catholic Alumnae (regent 1968-69), Mt. Mercy, Clarke Coll., U. Iowa alumni assns., Data Processing Mgmt. Assn. (bd. dirs., sec. 1968-71, internat. dir. 1971-73, individual performance award 1978), Delta Kappa Gamma (pres. 1976-78). Roman Catholic. Contbr. articles on bus. edn. to profl. jours. Home: 1352 Hinkley Ave NW Cedar Rapids IA 52405 Office: 1243 20th St SW Cedar Rapids IA 52404

BOND, ALMA HALBERT, psychoanalyst; b. Phila., Feb. 6, 1923; d. Louis and Bertha Halbert; B.A., Temple U., 1944; M.A., N.Y. U., 1950; student Nat. Psychol. Assn. for Psychoanalysis, 1950-57, Ph.D., Columbia U., 1961; m. Rudy Bond, Feb. 1, 1948; children—Zane Philip, Janet, Jonathan. Mem. faculty Inst. Psychoanalytic Tng. and Research, N.Y.C.; pvt. practice psychoanalysis, N.Y.C. Served with USNR, 1944-46. Mem. Am. Psychol. Assn., Inst. Psychoanalytic Tng. and Research, Acad. Advancement Psychotherapy. Contbr. articles to profl. jours. Home: 11 E 87th St New York NY 10028

BOND, BEVERLY JEAN, communications specialist; b. Chgo., Aug. 29, 1952; d. E. Monte and Betty Jane (McCollister) B.; B.A., Tex. Tech U., 1974. Exec. mgmt. trainee Sears Roebuck & Co., Lubbock, Tex., 1973-75; chief assigner Southwestern Bell Telephone Co., Houston, 1976, chief deskman, 1976-77, repair foreman, 1977-78, installation foreman, 1978, chief deskman, 1978-79, PBX foreman, 1979-80; staff specialist bus. transition task force AT&T, Basking Ridge, N.J., 1981-82, staff mgr., 1982—. Fin. dir. Jr. Achievement, 1977-78. Mem. Nat. Assn. Female Execs. Republican. Roman Catholic. Home: 8D Dorado Dr Morristown NJ 07960 Office: 295 N Maple Ave Room 1216K2 Basking Ridge NJ 07920

BOND, CATHERINE MARY, communications analyst and counselor; b. N.Y.C., Feb. 17, 1939; d. John Herbert and Catherine (Kelly) Degen; A.B., Coll. New Rochelle, 1960; M.A., U. So. Calif., 1963; M.A., Azusa Pacific Coll., 1972; 1 son, James Kevin. Instr. English, Glendale (Calif.) Coll., 1964-66, U. Redlands, Calif., 1966-67, Calif. State U., Los Angeles, 1967-71; dist. tng. officer Calif. Dept. Corrections, Long Beach, 1972; dir. programs Calif. Family Study Center, Burbank, 1973-75; dir. Action Seminars for Progress, Santa Monica, Calif., 1975—; pvt. marriage, family and child counselor, 1974—; charter mem. profl. adv. bd. So. Calif. region Parents Without Partners. N.Y. State scholar, 1956-60; NDEA fellow, 1960-63. Mem. N.Y. Council Family Relations, Am., Calif. assns. marriage and family counselors. Home: 17020 Sunset Bl Pacific Palisades CA 90272 Office: Center Counseling and Psychotherapy 3017 Santa Monica Blvd Santa Monica CA 90404

BOND, CHARLENE ELLIS, anthropologist; b. Terrell, Tex., Dec. 2, 1950; d. Charles Thomas and Edith LaNell (Stephens) Ellis; B.S., Eastfield Coll., 1980; student So. Methodist U., 1980—; m. Robert Lee Bond, Aug. 16, 1969; 1 dau., Charity Katherine. Shipwreck mapper Tex. Hist. Commn., Austin, 1983—; lectr. marine archaeology. Mem. Am. Anthrop. Soc. Republican. Roman Catholic. Home: 2441 Materhorn St Dallas TX 75228 Office: So Methodist Univ Sch Law Dallas TX 75275

BOND, WILMA MCCRARY, educator; b. Madison, Tenn., Sept. 17, 1938; d. Keller Brit and Lee (Reid) McCrary; B.S. in Bus. Edn., Peabody Coll. Edn., Vanderbilt U., 1959; M.A. in Adminstrn. and Supervision, Va. Poly. Inst. and State U., 1974; m. Thomas Jefferson Bond, Jr., Mar. 14, 1959; children—Thomas Jefferson III, Julia Anne Bond Franklin. Legal sec. firm Witt, Gaither et al, Chattanooga, 1961-62; sec. trust dept. Hamilton Nat. Bank (now 1st Tenn. Nat. Bank), Chattanooga, 1959; real estate sales rep., Albuquerque, 1970-72; tchr., Va., Ky. and N.Mex., 1963-72; tchr. social studies and bus. edn. Herndon (Va.) High Sch., 1972—; sec. public relations AAA, 1981. Docent Museum History and Tech., Smithsonian Inst., Washington, 1972-77, co-chmn. weekend edn. program, 1975-77; arbiter Fairfax County Consumer Affairs Office, 1975—. Mem. Phi Delta Kappa. Clubs: Potomac Corral of the Westerners, Clans of Scotland, U.S.A. Author Fish and Wildlife Service publs., 1968, 70; co-author Va. curriculum guide for teaching law in public schs., 1978; book reviewer Chattanooga Times, 1960-75. Home: Box 1301 Vienna VA 22180 Office: 700 Bennett St Herndon VA 22070

BONDS, DUANE ROBINA, obstetrician-gynecologist; b. Washington, Sept. 23, 1947; d. Robert and Helen B.; B.S. in Biology, Rensselaer Poly. Inst., 1971; M.D., Albany Med. Coll., 1971. Jr. asst. resident in ob-gyn Albany Med. Center Hosp., 1971-72; resident in ob-gyn Johns Hopkins U. Hosp., 1972-76; cons. gynecology E. Balt. Med. Plan, 1976-77; perinatal research fellow U. Colo. Med. Center, 1977-79; asst. prof. ob-gyn Div. Maternal-Fetal Medicine, U. Pa., Phila., 1979—; presenter papers profl. confs. Mem. adv. bd. Nat. Women's Law Center, Washington. Recipient Kenneth M. Archibald prize in obstetrics, 1971; diplomate Am. Bd. Ob-Gyn. Fellow Am. Coll. Ob-Gyn; mem. Am. Med. Women's Assn. Contbr. articles to med. jours. Office: Jerrold Golding Div Maternal-Fetal Medicine Dept Ob-Gyn U Pa Hosp Box 619 3400 Spruce St Philadelphia PA 19104

BONDS, NADINE CELESTE, tng. specialist; b. East Chicago, Ind., Nov. 20, 1950; d. Thomas Jefferson and Mable Nanette (Hines) Perry; B.A., Purdue U., 1983; m. Richard Thomas Bonds, July 11, 1970; children—Marcel Tyrone, Rodney Darnell. Adminstrv. sales mgr. Allstate Ins. Co., Indpls., 1974-78; curriculum developer Midwestern telephone ops. GTE Westfield, Ind., 1978—. Exec. adviser Jr. Achievement, 1974-80. Fellow, Pryor Mgmt. Inst., 1979. Mem. NAACP, Urban League, Am. Soc. Personnel Adminstrs., Am. Soc. Profl. and Exec. Women, Am. Soc. Tng. and Devel., Internat. Assn. Personnel Women (treas., editor Carousel), Nat. Assn. Female Execs. (network dir.), Statonians, Inc., Alpha Kappa Alpha. Democrat. Methodist. Home: 6120 Foxwood Ln Indianapolis IN 46208

BONDS, RUTH DIANE (WAGONER), cellist, educator; b. Greensboro, N.C., May 24, 1954; Mus.B., U. N.C., Chapel Hill, 1976; Mus.M., U. Tex., Austin, 1980; m. Michael Scott Bonds, Apr. 5, 1980. Cellist, Greensboro (N.C.) Symphony Orch., 1974-78, Winston Salem (N.C.) Symphony Orch., 1976-78, Austin (Tex.) Symphony Orch., 1978-79; instr. U. Tex. String Project, 1978-80; instr. cello Parker Music Acad., Houston, 1980—, Canon Music Camp, 1978, Brazos Talent Edn., 1979-80. Eastern Music Festival scholar, 1971, Brevard Music Festival scholar, 1976, 77, Aspen Music Festival scholar, 1975. Mem. Suzuki: Assn. Ams. Home: 2818 S Bartell #11 Houston TX 77054

BONDS-WHITE, FRANCES ELIZABETH, psychotherapist, mgmt. cons.; b. Fairfield, Ala., Nov. 29, 1939; d. Erskine Webster and Lois Elizabeth (Graham) Bonds; B.A. with honors, Birmingham So. Coll., 1960; M.Ed., Temple U., 1973. Asso. sales mgr. 3D Advt. Corp., 1964; asst. stage mgr. Theater of the Living Arts, Phila., 1965; public relations writer, tchr. public schs., Phila., 1966-68, demonstration tchr., 1968-71, supr., tng. coordinator Head Start Pre-Sch. Program, 1971-72; ednl. cons. Research for Better Schs., 1972-73; instr., lectr. Temple U., Antioch Coll., Phila. Coll. Art, Community Coll. Phila., 1973-79; psychologist N.E. Community Mental Health Center, 1973-77; dir. parent edn. Hahnemann Hosp. Mental Health Center, Phila., 1975-76; chief clin. asso. Eastern Inst. for TA and Gestalt, 1976-77, clin. dir., owner, 1977—; cons. Ednl. Resource Services, 1973-79. Mem. Am. Group Psychotherapy Assn., Am. Orthopsychiat. Assn., Assn. Humanistic Psychology, Pa. Personnel and Guidance Assn., Delaware Valley Group Psychotherapy Soc., Am. Psychol. Assn., Delaware Valley Assn. Edn. of Young Children, Internat. Transactional Analysis Assn. (clin. teaching mem.), Internat. Group Psychotherapy Assn., Jean Piaget Soc., Nat. Assn. Edn. Young Children, Pa. Psychol. Assn. Clubs: Art Alliance, Plays & Players. Address: 1713 Pine St Philadelphia PA 19103

BONDURANT, AMY LAURA, lawyer, senatorial exec.; b. Union City, Tenn., Apr. 20, 1951; d. John Jay Crittenden and Doris Marie (Bell) B.; B.A. in Communications with distinction and honors, U. Ky., 1973; J.D., Wasington Coll. Law, Am. U., 1978. Admitted to Ky. bar, 1978; legis. asst. Office Senator Wendell Ford, Washington, 1975-78; counsel consumer affairs and trade regulation U.S. Senate Com. on Commerce, Sci. and Transp., Washington, 1978-80, minority counsel consumer affairs and trade regulation, 1980—; guest lectr. George Washington U. Law Sch., 1980-81, Georgetown U. Law Center, 1981. Mem. Ky. Bar Assn., Am. Bar Assn. Contbr. to reports of U.S. Senate Com. on Commerce, Sci., and Transp. Office: 5202 Dirksen Senate Office Bldg Washington DC 20510

BONE, JANET WITMEYER, author; b. Shamokin, Pa., Dec. 19, 1930; d. Paul Eugene and Kathryn (Bender) Witmeyer; B.A., Cornell U., 1951; m. David P. Bone, Oct. 27, 1951; children—Jonathan, Christopher, Robert, Daniel. Newspaper and trade mag. writer, freelance writer, 1962—; co-author: Understanding the Film, rev. edit., 1981; author: Opportunities in Film Production, 1983, Opportunities in Cable Television, 1983; tchr. creative writing adult edn. Sch. Dist. 211, Palatine, Ill., 1974—. Trustee William Rainey Harper Community Coll., Palatine, 1977—, sec. bd. trustees, 1979-82. Recipient Chgo. Working Newsman's award, 1968, Sch. Bell award Ill. Edn. Assn., 1968, Am. Polit. Sci. Assn. award disting. reporting public affairs, 1970. Mem. Phi Theta Kappa, Alpha Omicron Pi. Address: 353 N Morris Dr Palatine IL 60067

BONELLO, KATHLEEN PATRICIA, computer co. exec.; b. N.Y.C., Jan. 29, 1938; d. Vincent and Mary (Jones Wilson) O'Reilly; children—Philip Joseph, Susan Patricia. Programmer, IBM, 1960-61; analyst Shell Oil Co., 1962-63; founder, pres. Info. Systems Inc., Teaneck, N.J., 1964—. Pres. Paramus Coop Nursery Sch., 1971-72, bd. dirs., 1972-75; pres. Teaneck Little League, 1977-78, team mgr., 1974-77; pres. Bryant Sch. PTA, Mem. Assn. Computing Machinery, N.J. Network Bus. and Profl. Women (dir. 1980-82). Home: 843 Belle Ave Teaneck NJ 07666 Office: 322 Cedar Ln Teaneck NJ 07666

BONELLO, MARIE ANTOINETTE, educator; b. Boston, Aug. 17, 1918; d. Peter and Catherine (Schiaffino) Marchi; A.B. in Math. and Physics, Emmanuel Coll., Boston, 1941; M.Ed. (asst. 1965), Boston Coll., 1965; m. Edward L. Bonello, June 26, 1943; children—Lawrence, Vincent, Joanne. Public sch. tchr. Belmont, Mass. area, 1968-70; edn. coordinator Roxbury (Mass.) Action Program, 1975; exec. dir. New Eng. Sch. Career Tng., Boston, 1973—; pres. Bonello Enterprises, Inc., materials for learning to read through career tng., Cambridge, Mass., 1973—; ednl. and assessment coordinator community residences for mentally retarded Nexus Inc., Malden, Mass.; dir. tchrs. sci. course Boston Coll., 1964-65; ednl. dir. Columbia Point Alcoholism Program, 1976; cons. adult edn. programs. Mem. Mass. Commn. on Adult Edn., 1979; grantee, ednl. and assessment coordinator Solid State Tech. programs. Acad. Year Inst. fellow, Harvard U., 1960. Mem. NEA, Adult Edn. Assn., Nat. Sci. Tchrs. Assn., Soc. Women Engrs., Am. Soc. Tng. and Devel., Adult Edn. Assn. Author papers in field, career tng. manuals. Home: 15 Day St Arlington MA 02174 Office: 100 Pleasant St Malden MA 02148

BONEM, RENA MAE, geologist; b. Tucumari, N.Mex., May 6, 1948; d. David S. and Lorraine K. Bonem; B.S., N.Mex. Inst. Mining and Tech., 1970, M.S., 1971; Ph.D., U. Okla., 1975. Asst. prof. geology Hope Coll., Holland, Mich., 1975-79, Tex. Christian U., Ft. Worth, 1979-81, Baylor U., Waco, Tex., 1981—; cons. in field. Nat. chmn. coral reef splty. YMCA, 1977—, chmn. tech. papers nat. underwater activities conv., 1980, 82; dir. tng. Scuba instrs. Mich. area YMCA, 1978-79. Grantee Petroleum Research Fund, 1979-81, Tex. Christian U., 1980, Mellan Found., 1976, 78; Penrose grantee, 1975; Sigma Xi grantee, 1972, 75. Mem. Soc. Econ. Paleontologists and Mineralogists (sec. Gt. Lakes region 1978-80), Paleontol. Soc., Am. Assn. Petroleum Geologists, Geol. Soc. Am. (sec. mgmt. bd. 1982—), Internat. Paleontol. Assn., AAAS, Soc. Women Geoscientists, AAUW, AAUP, Sigma Xi, Sigma Gamma Epsilon. Presbyterian. Club: Order Eastern Star. Author articles in field. Office: Geology Dept Baylor U Waco TX 76798

BONFANTE, LARISSA, educator; b. Naples, Italy; came to U.S., 1939, naturalized, 1951; d. Giuliano and Vittoria (Dompé) B.; student Radcliffe U., 1950, U. Rome, 1954; B.A., Barnard Coll., 1954; M.A., U. Cin., 1957; Ph.D., Columbia U., 1966; m. Leo Raditsa, May 2, 1973; 1 dau. by previous marriage, Alexandra Bonfante-Warren. Instr., Rutgers U., 1963; with N.Y. U., 1963—, prof., chmn. dept. classics, 1978—; cons. in field. Mem. Archaeol. Inst. Am. (exec. com. 1982—), Assn. Mems. Inst. Advanced Study, Istituto di Studi Etruschi. Author: Etruscan Dress, 1975; Out of Etruria, 1981; translator: Chronology of the Ancient World (E.J. Bicherman), 1968; The Plays of Hrotswitha of Gandersheim, 1979; contbr. articles in field. Office: 25 Waverly Pl New York NY 10003

BONFIELD, BARBARA JEAN, educator; b. Auburn, Ind., Feb. 8, 1936; d. Paul and Jennie (Coscarelli) B.; B.S., Ball State U., Muncie, Ind., 1958; M.S., Ind. U., 1963. Tchr., Ft. Wayne (Ind.) Community Schs., 1958—, tchr. 4th grade Franke Park Sch., 1969—; mem. Community Career Edn. Council; participant Cultural Deprived Inst., NDEA, 1967. Mem. Internat. Reading Assn., NEA, Assn. Childhood Edn., Ind. Tchrs. Assn., Ft. Wayne Tchrs. Assn. (past pres.), AAUW, Auburn Bus. and Profl. Women's Club, Delta Kappa Gamma (chmn. numerous profl. coms.). Home: 331 W 2d St Auburn IN 46706 Office: 828 Mildred Ave Fort Wayne IN 46808

BONI, MIKI, advt. agy. exec.; b. Bklyn., Nov. 10, 1938; B.A., U. Guanajuato, 1974; m. Lawrence Boni, Nov. 16, 1956; children—Andrew, Viki. Dir. advt. and pub. relations Kebo, Inc., Natick, Mass., 1965-74; tchr. painting and drawing U. Guanajuato (Mex.), 1974-76; exec. dir. Kreativ Assos., Watertown, Mass., 1976—; cons. pub. relations and advt. Recipient spl. painting award Lincoln Center, 1978. Mem. Women Art Profls. (founder, v.p.). Clubs: Art Dirs., Advt. (Boston). Editor: Woman's World Gazette, 1976—.

BONIFACE, WENDY JANINE, nurse, educator; b. Syracuse, N.Y., Dec. 20, 1946; d. Theodore and Elizabeth (Rolli) Fibison; B.S., Russell Sage Coll., 1969; cert. U. Va., 1971; M. in Health Sci., McMaster U., Ont., Can., 1978; m. James Henry Boniface, July 5, 1969. Staff nurse U. Va. Hosp., Charlottesville, 1969-70; instr. asso. degree program Jefferson Community Coll., Watertown, N.Y., 1970-71; program coordinator dept. pediatrics U. Va., Charlottesville, 1971; pediatric nurse practitioner Covenant House Health Services, Phila., 1972-74, Children's Hosp. of Phila., 1974-76; lectr. primary care program for nurses faculty of health scis. McMaster U., Hamilton, Ont., Can., 1976-77; data gathering technician Montreal (Que.) Research Associates, 1977; instr. pediatric nursing program Yale U. Sch. Nursing, New Haven, 1978-80, research affiliate dept. human genetics, 1981—; instr. grad. faculty Sch. Nursing, U. Conn., Storrs, 1980—; cons. WHO, 1980. Mem. profl. adv. com. Nat. Found., March of Dimes, 1980—. Cert. pediatric nurse practitioner. Mem. Am. Nurses Assn., Inst. of Soc., Ethics and the Life Scis., Nurse Practitioner Assn. of Ont., Am. Soc. Human Genetics, Sigma Theta Tau. Presbyterian. Contbg. author: Interpersonal Skills for Health Professionals, 1980; guest editor: Issues in Health Care of Women. contbr. articles to jours. in nursing. Home: 352 Greene St New Haven CT 06511 Office: Sch Nursing Univ Conn Storrs CT 06268

BONN, BARBARA A., cosmetics industry cons., writer; b. Phila., Oct. 13, 1937; d. Harry and Lillian S. B.; B.A., Temple U., 1960. Asst. publicity dir. Phila. YMCA, 1960-63; publicist Ingenue Mag., 1963-65, sr. editor, 1965-68; sr. copywriter Revlon, Inc., 1968-73; creative dir. worldwide Helena Rubinstein, Inc., N.Y.C., 1973-80; pres. Barbara Bonn: Communication, Inc., N.Y.C., 1980—; writer numerous mag. articles, short stories, newspaper columns; series editor Helena Rubinstein Library of Beauty. Mem. Cosmetic Career Women, Fashion Group. Office: 25 W 81st St New York NY 10024 *

BONNEFIL, MARGARET CARSON, clin. social worker; b. Los Angeles, July 27, 1934; d. Allan MacDonald and Phyllis Josephine Carson; B.A., UCLA, 1957, M.S.W., 1959; m. Henri Bonnefil, July 14, 1962; children—Anne Marie, Rachel Elizabeth. Caseworker, Council Jewish Women of Los Angeles, 1959-63; clin. social worker Didi Hirsch Community Mental Health Center, Culver City, Calif., 1964-77, coordinator social work edn. and inservice tng., 1977—; pvt. practice clin. social work, Los Angeles, 1968—; lectr. UCLA Sch. Social Welfare, 1979—. Bd. dirs. Los Angeles chpt. Nat. Soc. Autistic Children, 1974-76. Fellow Soc. Clin. Social Work; mem. Nat. Assn. Social Workers, Am. Orthopsychiat. Assn. Contbg. editor: Journal of Clinical Social Work. Office: 11980 San Vicente Blvd Suite 612 Los Angeles CA 90049

BONNER, JEAN VANSTEENBERG, state govt. ofcl.; b. Denver, June 21, 1926; d. Harley and Mary Francis (Richert) Vansteenberg; R.N., Mercy Hosp., Denver, 1950; A.A. in Adminstrn., Regis Coll., Denver, 1952; m. John Wylie Bonner, Aug. 30, 1962; children—John Wylie, II, Patricia G. McRay, Michalene McRay. With Colo. Dept. Labor and Tng., 1957—, liability tax specialist, 1972—; tchr., trainer in field. Chmn. CAPE Polit. Action Com., Denver, 1975—. Home: 7542 S Holland St Littleton CO 80123 Office: 1210 Sherman St Denver CO 80203

BONNER, LILLY ANNELLE, educator; b. Toxey, Ala., Jan. 17, 1919; d. Martin C. and Lilly (Moseley) B.; B.S., U. So. Miss., 1946, M.A., 1954; Ed.D., Ind. U., 1964. Tchr. various high schs., Miss. and Ala., 1942-44, 48-58; instr. dept. bus. edn. U. So. Miss. 1958, asst. prof., 1959-65, acting chmn., 1963-64, asso. prof., acting chmn., 1965-68, prof., chmn., 1968—. Mem. Miss. Bus. Edn. Assn., Nat. Assn. Tchr. Educators in Bus. and Office Edn., Nat. Assn. Distributive Edn. Tchrs., So. Bus. Edn., Nat. Bus. Edn. Assn., Am. Bus. Communication Assn., Am. Vocat. Assn., Miss. Vocat. Assn., U. So. Miss. Alumni Assn., Phi Kappa Phi, Delta Pi Epsilon, Pi Omega Pi, Delta Kappa Gamma. Home: 1115 Adeline St Hattiesburg MS 39401 Office: 5083 Southern Station Hattiesburg MS 39401

BONNER, MARY WINSTEAD, educator; b. Nash County, N.C., Apr. 20, 1924; d. Charlie Edward and Mason Ann (Whitted) Winstead; B.S. cum laude, St. Paul's Coll., Lawrenceville, Va., 1946, L.H.D. (hon.), 1979; M.S., Va. State Coll., 1952; Ed.D., Okla. State U., 1968; cert. in Spanish, Emporia State U., 1979, postgrad., 1982; m. Thomas Edison Bonner, Aug. 9, 1956. Tchr. pub. sch. Greensville County, Va., 1946-52; supr. student tchrs., demonstration tchr. Lab. Sch., So. U., Baton Rouge, La., 1952-57; tchr. pub. schs. St. Louis, 1957-64; asst. prof. edn. Emporia (Kans.) State U., 1964-75, asso. prof., 1975-80, prof., 1980—; vis. prof. U. So. Calif., Los Angeles, summer 1968, Norfolk (Va.) State Coll., summers 1970, 72. Named Outstanding Alumna St. Paul's Coll., 1975; postdoctoral fellow in spl. edn. U. Kans., 1974. Mem. AAUW, Council for Exceptional Children, Internat. Reading Assn., Kans., Emporia reading councils, Nat. Assn. for Retarded Citizens, Nat. Council Negro Women, Caribbean Assn. on Mental Retardation, Sigma Gamma Rho (nat. edn. chmn. 1969-74, Hall of Fame), Sigma Delta Pi. Episcopalian. Club: Eastern Star. Author: Bonner Dominance Checklist; Educators' Diagnostic Guidebook and Reference Manual for Problems in Reading. Home: 1008 Watson St Emporia KS 66801 Office: Emporia State Coll Emporia KS 66801

BONNER, NATALIE ANN, banker; b. Parks, La., Feb. 20, 1939; d. Gaston Joseph and Mable Mary (Solari) Broussard; student Am. Inst. Banking, of U. Southwestern La., 1957-64; m. Roy Stanley Bonner, Nov. 25, 1963; children—Oliver Young, Roy Stanley. File clk. First Nat. Bank, Lafayette, La., 1957, bookkeeper, 1958, paying and receiving teller, 1960-62, collection teller, 1962-64; collection teller Am. Bank and Trust Co. of Houma, La., 1966, head teller, 1967-69, note teller, 1969-71, mgr. note dept., 1971-74, asst. cashier, consumer loan officer, 1974, asst. v.p., comml. loan officer, 1975-77, v.p., comml. loan officer in charge of note dept. functions, 1977—. Mem. Nat. Assn. Bank Women (group chmn. Bayou Group of La.). Home: 801 Barrow St Houma LA 70361 Office: 801 Barrow St Houma LA 70361

BONNEY, JANE LAMOINE, hosp. adminstr.; b. Riverside, Calif., Aug. 19, 1933; d. Hulbert Maitland and Merrian Jane (Huddleston) Baird; student Chaffey Community Coll., 1966-68; B.A., San Bernardino State Coll., 1970; M.S.W., Sacramento State U., 1975; children—Scott Towle, McKevitt Towle, Jennifer Towle. Rehab./neurology social worker Loma Linda (Calif.) Med. Center, 1975-76; dir. social service San Bernardino (Calif.) Community Hosp., 1976-79; mgr. social service dept. Desert Hosp., Palm Springs, Calif., 1979—. Chmn. quality of care com. Inland Counties Health Systems Agy., Riverside, 1977; bd. dirs. Hospice of Desert Communities, 1980—; bd. dirs. Am. Cancer Soc., Riverside, 1978—, chmn. service, 1978-80. Lic. social worker, Calif. Mem. Nat. Assn. Social Workers, Acad. Cert. Social Workers, Hosp. Social Worker Dirs. Assn. So. Calif. Unitarian. Home: 529 E County Line Rd Calimesa CA 92320 Office: 1151 N Via Miraleste St Palm Springs CA 92262

BONNICK, MARY ALAN, broadcasting exec.; b. Dallas, Apr. 1, 1954; d. Sydney Osdahl and Margery (Winston) B.; B.F.A., So. Meth. U., 1975. Asst. to film producer Jim Gable Film Service, Dallas, 1976-77; asst. public service dir. KDFW-TV, Dallas., 1978-80, public service dir., 1980—. Mem. public relations info. coms. Dallas Ballet, Dallas Assn. Retarded Citizens, United Way, March of Dimes, Am. Cancer Soc.; mem. 500, Inc., Dallas, 1981—. Recipient Beneficiary Service award Health Care Fin. Adminstrn., 1981; VA Commendation for public services, 1981; Easter Seals Communications award, 1981; others. Mem. Women in Communications, Am. Women in Radio and TV, Assn. Broadcast Execs. Tex., Kappa Delta (Dallas Alumnae Assn.). Episcopalian. Home: 3834 Regent Dr Dallas TX 75229 Office: 400 N Griffin St Dallas TX 75202

BONSNESS, JOAN DOREEN, educator; b. Noonan, N.D., Feb. 3, 1928; d. Alma C. (Wick) Brenno; student Concordia Coll., Moorhead, Minn., 1946-47; B.S., Minot State Coll., 1965; M.Ed., U. N.D., Grand Forks, 1968; m. Byron Bonsness, Jan. 3, 1948; children—Vicky, Rebecca. Tchr. pub. elem. schs., Columbus, N.D., 1948-61, Crosby, N.D., 1962-67; tng. fellow in mental retardation Minot State Coll., 1965; cons. in learning problems Title III Upper Des Lacs Elem. Guidance, Kenmare, N.D., 1968-71; project dir. N.W. spl. edn. model Title III ESEA Burke Central Sch., Lignite, N.D., 1971-75, project dir., developer/demonstrator in nat. diffusion network of Office of Edn., 1975—; cons. Recipient excellence in edn. award Nat. Assn. State Adv. Council Chairmen, 1974; Ednl. Pacesetter award Pres.'s Nat. Adv. Council Title III ESEA, 1974. Mem. Council for Exceptional Children, Found. for Exceptional Children, Assn. for Retarded Citizens. Lutheran. Home: Rural Route Columbus ND 58727 Office: Box 585 Lignite ND 58752

BONTRAGER, CHARLOTTE YVONNE, steel and plastic co. exec.; b. Buffalo, Dec. 9, 1939; d. Eli J. and Sarah (Roth) B.; A.S., Erie Community Coll., 1979; student Daemen Coll., Amherst, N.Y., 1981—. Billing clk., sec. Fredonia Seed Co. (N.Y.), 1960-61; bookkeeper Town Line Lumber Co., Inc. also Bontrager Constrn. Co., Inc., Alden, N.Y., 1964-67; bookkeeper Fabritron Inc., Alden, 1967-71; treas. R.A. Baker Affiliates, Inc., also Johnson Precision Works, Inc., Kenmore, N.Y., 1971—, also dir. Mem. Buffalo and Erie County Pvt. Industry Council, 1980—, mem. evaluation com. 1981—; bd. mgrs. Stoneledge Condominium Bd. Mgrs. Inc., v.p., 1981—. Notary public. Mem. Nat. Fedn. Female Execs., Nat. Tooling and Machining Assn. (exec. sec. Buffalo chpt.). Republican. Presbyterian (elder). Office: 1516 Military Rd Kenmore NY 14217

BOOK, ANITA-BAKER (MRS. WILLIAM S. BOOK), bus. exec., designer; b. Essex, Ill.; d. John Benjamin and Dora (Greenwald) Baker; student Chgo. Bus. Coll.; B.A., Columbia Conservatory, 1923, Grace Hickox Studios, 1926; student Chgo. Acad. Fine Arts; grad. Herzl Jr. Coll., 1936; grad. U. Chgo., 1941, U. Nebr., 1941; m. William Ship Book, Mar. 14, 1941. Tchr., owner dramatic art studio, Chgo., 1926-32; receptionist radio shows, 1927-32; sec. William Lemle Studios, 1930-34; mgr. N.Y. import office S.S. Sarna, 1933-34; creator, designer Bells of Sarna, 1935, specialist in Balinese art, lectr. throughout U.S. with exhbn. wood carvings and handicrafts from Dutch East Indies, 1934-41; sec. Consairways, Fairfield, Calif., 1945; owner, exec. dir. Binita Fruit & Gift Wares, Skokie, Ill., 1945—, exhbns. major gift and trade shows throughout U.S.; past treas. Natural Hygiene Press; original radio player Sta. WMAQ, Chgo., 1924; appeared with KYW Book Theatre, Old Vic Theatre Nat. Theatre, 1928, Chgo. Playwrights Theatre, Billy Bryant's Show Boat, Cort Theatre, Hollywood Players, Chgo. Century Progress, 1933-34; 1st mem.-player original Jack & Jill Players; with original prodn. When Chicago Was Young, Goodman Theatre and revival Studebaker Theatre, 1937. Mem. Skokie Beautification and Improvement Commn., Skokie Bicentennial Commn.; mem. nat. women's com. Brandeis U. Hon. fellow Harry S. Truman Library Inst. Mem. Am. Natural Hygiene Assn., Gift and Decorative Art Assn. (charter), Natural Food Assns., Organic Growers Ill., LWV (dir., historian Internat. Assn. Cancer Victims and Friends Skokie-Lincolnwood chpt., chmn. pub. relations, chmn. observation program publs.), Nat. Health Fedn., Skokie C. of C. (chmn. beautification com. 1968), U. Chgo. Alumni Assn. (life), Art Inst. Chgo. (life), Skokie Valley Symphony Orch., Skokie Valley Bus. and Profl. Women's Club, Nat. Fedn. Ind. Bus., AAUW, Poets and Patrons, Nat. Geog. Soc., Smithsonian Assos., North Shore Pub. Relations, Chgo. Hist. Soc., Actors Equity, Skokie Hist. Soc., Pioneer Women, Hadassah (life), Golden Key (chmn.), Field Mus. Club: Quarter Century (hon.). Editor: (with others) Early Skokie. Created and designed Bells of Serna, 1935. Home and office: 3811 Wright Terr Skokie IL 60076

BOOK, JEANNE MALLICOTT, psychologist; b. Concord, Ill., July 11, 1929; d. Raymond Mallicott and Louise (Becker) Mallicott Sooy; A.B. cum laude, MacMurray Coll., 1957; M.A., 1962; Ph.D., U. So. Calif., 1977; m. Kenneth Book, Apr. 27, 1946; children—Gary Kenneth, Susan Kay. Tchr., Northwestern (Ill.) High Sch., 1957-59, Ashland High Sch., 1959, 60; instr. MacMurray Coll., 1960-61; psychology intern Jacksonville (Ill.) State Hosp., 1961-62, staff psychologist, 1962-67; pvt. practice psychology, Ill., 1956-67; staff psychologist, asst. supt. Fresno County (Calif.) Youth Center, 1967-74; supr. program evaluation Fresno County (Calif.) Dept. Health, 1974-79, asso. dir. for mental health, 1979—; mem. faculty Chapman Coll., 1970-80; pvt. cons. program evaluation, 1978-79; adv. bd. Pinedale (Calif.) Edn. Project, 1977—; exec. bd. Jacksonville Area Assn. for Retarded Children, 1966, pres., 1967. Lic. psychologist, Calif. Mem. Am., Ill., Central Calif. (sec. treas. 1976) psychol. assns., Nat. Register for Health Service Providers. Home: 515 W Escalon St Fresno CA 93704 Office: PO Box 11867 1221 Fulton Mall Fresno CA 93775

BOOKER, CLAUDIA MAE, county ofcl.; b. Hempstead, Tex., June 26, 1948; d. Almater C. and Pauline Doris (Payne) Watson; B.Mus., Corpus Christi (Tex.) State U., 1975, M.A., 1977, now postgrad.; children—Charnella, Cherilyn. Activity therapist Nueces County Mental Health/Mental Retardation, Corpus Christi, 1975-77; parole caseworker II, State Bd. Pardons & Paroles, Corpus Christi, 1977-79; adult probation officer Nueces County Adult Probation, Corpus Christi, 1979—; lectr. in field. Bd. dirs. March of Dimes, 1976-80; pianist, dir. choirs St. John Bapt. Ch., 1979—; mem. allocations com. United Way of Coastal Bend, 1981—; v.p. Personal & Estate Guardianship Program of Corpus Christi, 1981—. Recipient Mental Health/Mental Retardation Service award, 1977; Leadership Corpus Christi speaker, 1979, 80, 81. Mem. Tex. Corrections Assn., Leadership Corpus Christi Alumni, Zeta Phi Beta. Democrat. Clubs: Black History-Cultural Com. Office: 901 Leopard St Rm 207 Corpus Christi TX 78401

BOOKSTAVER, LILLIAN ROSE, camp dir.; b. N.Y.C., May 4, 1916; d. Louis and Louetta (Swiger) Lerner; A.B., N.Y.U., 1939, M.Ed., 1959; m. Julian B. Bookstaver, Oct. 9, 1969 (dec. Mar. 1976); children by previous marriage—Elicia (Mrs. Seymour Faitell), Andrew Rose, Eliot Ian Rose. Dir. Camp Allegro, 1946—; pres. Allegro in the Berkshires, Inc., 1956—; dir. Camp Realty Corp. Adminstrv. officer ARC, 1942-44; active fund com. Nat. Found. Infantile Paralysis, Orgn. for Rehab. Tng. Mem. Assn. Pvt. Camps, Mu Sigma, Kappa Delta Pi. Jewish. Club: Hadassah (dir.). Home: 371 Audubon Rd Englewood NJ 07631 Office: Camp Allegro Pittsfield MA 01210

BOONE, CATHERINE ELIZABETH, nurse; b. Durban, S.Africa, Feb. 26, 1953; came to U.S., 1976; d. Graham Hugh and Elizabeth (Willemse) McMorland; B.S. in Nursing, Walla Walla (Wash.) Coll., 1975; M.S. in Nursing Adminstrn., Loma Linda (Calif.) U., 1981; m. Stephen Gregory Boone, June 12, 1981. Staff nurse hosps. in B.C., Can., Oreg. and Calif., 1975-77, 79-81; cons. Care Mgmt. Corp., Portland, Oreg., 1977-79; nursing project coordinator Corona (Calif.) Community Hosp., 1981-82; adult edn. tchr., Corona, 1981—; staff devel. educator, Hemet, Calif., 1982—. Seventh-day Adventist. Home: 117 Tiger Ln San Jacinto CA 92383 Office: 1116 E Latham Ave Hemet CA 92343

BOONE, DEBORAH ANN, recording artist; b. Hackensack, N.J., Sept. 22, 1956; d. Charles Eugene and Shirley Lee (Foley) B.; student parochial schs.; m. Gabriel Ferrer, Sept. 1, 1979; 1 son, Jordan Alexander. Recorded hit song You Light Up My Life, 1977; debut album You Light Up My Life, including selections End of the World and He's a Rebel, 1977; other albums include Midstream, 1978, Debby Boone, 1979, Love Has No Reason, 1980, With My Song, 1980, Savin' It Up, 1980; appeared on numerous TV shows, 1977—, including Tonight Show, Merv Griffin, Dinah, Good Morning America (with Rona Barrett), American Bandstand, The Midnight Special, John Denver Special, A Tribute to Elizabeth Taylor, The Billboards Awards, The Today Show, Gift of the Magi, 1978, 4 Pat Boone Family Specials, 1978-79, Jack Jones Hosts the Palace, Bob Hope Special, 1980, Cambodian relief special, 1980; star Debby Boone Special, 1980; star stage prodn. Seven Brides for Seven Brothers, 1981-82; toured U.S., S. Africa, Japan with father Pat. Recipient Am. Music award for song of year, 1977, Grammy award for best new artist, 1977, Nat. Assn. Theatre Owners award for best new personality, 1977, Gold and Platinum records for You Light Up My Life, 1977, Country Music award for best new country artist, 1977, Golden Plate award, 1978, Grammy award, 1980, Dove award, 1980; named Singing Star of Yr., AGVA, 1978. Author: (autobiography) (with Dennis Baker) Debby Boone—So Far, 1981. Office: 9255 Sunset Blvd Suite 519 Los Angeles CA 90069

BOONE, LESLIE SPEARMAN, educator; b. W. Palm Beach, Fla., July 18, 1930; d. Robert Ewell and Zonise (Wood) Spearman; B.A., U.S. Fla., Tampa, 1975, M.Ed., 1981; m. Floyd E. Boone, June 3, 1950; children—Zonise Jeanette Boone Swanson, Robert Edward, William Gordon. Head Start tchr. Manatee County (Fla.), 1967-75, head tchr. Bradenton (Fla.) Center, 1973-75; kindergarten tchr. Orange Ridge Elementary Sch., Bradenton, 1975—. Sunday sch. tchr. Trinity United Methodist Ch., Bradenton, 1958-78; instr. swimming, social worker ARC; active local PTA, Girl Scouts, Heart Fund. Mem. UDC, Alpha Delta Kappa. Democrat. Club: Sons of Norway. Home: 2611 26th Ave Dr W Bradenton FL 33505 Office: 400 30th Ave W Bradenton FL 33505

BOONE, LILLIAN RUTH, psychiatrist; b. Beverly, N.J., Aug. 25, 1945; d. Dwight Thurkill and Fannie Belle (Cobbs) B.; student U. Tex., El Paso, summer 1964; student Rutgers U., 1965-70; M.D. (Samuel F. Goldwyn fellow), Meharry Med. Coll., 1974. Resident in psychiatry SUNY Downstate Med. Center, Bklyn., 1974-77; practice medicine specializing in psychiatry, Bklyn., 1977—; mem. staffs Bklyn. Jewish Hosp., Meth. Hosp. Bd. suprs. Concord Nursing Home Inc., Bklyn. Recipient Achievement award Nat. Assn. Negro Bus. and Profl. Women's Clubs, Inc., Bklyn., 1982; Menninger Found. fellow, 1974. Mem. Nat. Med. Assn., Provident Med. Soc. Democrat. Baptist. Office: 163 Joralemon St Suite 1100 Brooklyn NY 11201

BOONSHAFT, HOPE JUDITH, fund raiser; b. Phila., May 3, 1949; d. Barry and Lorelei Gail (Rienzi) B.; B.A., Pa. State U., 1972; postgrad. Del. Law Sch., Kellogg Inst. Mgmt. Tng. Program writer Youth Edn., N.Y.C., 1972; legal aide to judge, Phila., 1973; dir. spl. projects Guiffre Med. Center, Phila., 1975; Arlen Specter senatorial campaign fin. dir., Phila., 1975; fin. dir. Jimmy Carter Presdl. Campaign, Atlanta, 1976; nat. fin. dir. Democratic Nat. Com., 1977-78; dir. devel. World Jewish Congress, N.Y.C., 1978; dir. devel. Yeshiva U., Los Angeles, 1979; dir. communications Nat. Easter Seal Soc., Chgo., 1979—; spl. adv. community relations The White House, 1977-80; guest lectr. U. Ill., 1982. Mem. Nat. Soc. Fundraisers, Women's Nat. Dem. Club, Alpha Chi Omega. Home: 3730 N Lake Shore Dr Apt 11A Chicago IL 60613 Office: 2023 W Ogden Ave Chicago IL 60612

BOOTH, ANNE MOTT, social worker; b. Nagpur, India, Mar. 3, 1931; d. John Livingstone and Celestine (Goddard) Mott (parents Am. citizens); B.A. cum laude, Swarthmore Coll., 1953; M.S.W., Columbia U., 1956; m. John Thomas Booth, Feb. 26, 1960; children—Alison, Miven, Roxanna. Asst. to program dir. UN program, Am. Friends Service Com., N.Y.C., 1953-54; psychiat. social worker Bur. Mental Health Services, Manhattan Children's Ct., N.Y.C., 1956-58; psychiat. social worker James Weldon Johnson Community Center, child guidance clinic, N.Y.C., 1958-60; psychiat. social worker, asst. dir. homemaker services in crisis situations Childrens Aid Soc., N.Y.C., 1960-63; remedial reading program N.Y.C. Public Schs. and Manhattan Country Sch., 1971-74; mem. profl. adv. bd. James Weldon Johnson Community Centers Inc., 1964-67. Active McGovern for President Campaign, Ramsay Clark for U.S. Senate; bd. dirs. Protestant Big Sisters. Mem. Nat. Assn. Social Workers, Phi Beta Kappa. Democrat. Unitarian. Club: Cosmopolitan. Home: Whites Wood Rd Litchfield CT 06759

BOOTH, BARBARA R., civic worker; b. N.Y.C., May 2, 1928; d. Benjamin C. and Ceclia (Lowe) Ribman; A.A., Centenary Jr. Coll., Hackettstown, N.Y., 1948; B.A., Barnard Coll., 1950; m. Mitchell B. Booth, July 13, 1952; 1 son, Brian S. Pres. women's alliance, chmn., Christmas fair 1st Congl. Ch. of City of N.Y., 1959-63; mem. vol. com. Sheltering Arms Children's Service, N.Y.C.; vol., coordinator high sch. visits N.Y. Hosp.; trustee Florence K. Griswold Meml. Fund. Com., All Souls Unitarian Ch., N.Y.C.; dir. women's div. Jefferson Dem. Club. N.Y.C.; committeewoman N.Y. County Dem. Com.; bd. govs., v.p. N.Y. Fruit and Flower Mission, Inc.; del. city conv., chmn. East Manhattan br. LWV; mem. spl. events com. N.Y. Assn. for Blind. Home: 75 East End Ave New York NY 10028

BOOTH, BEATRICE CROSBY, biol. oceanographer; b. Mpls., Aug. 29, 1938; d. George Christian and Beatrice (Goodrich) Crosby; B.A., Radcliffe Coll., 1960; M.A.T., Harvard U., 1962; M.S., U. Wash., 1969; m. Theodore William Booth, Dec. 23, 1960; children—Marguerite Morse, Kristina Wells, George Crosby. Teaching asst. U. Wash., Seattle, 1974, instr., 1975-78, research oceanographer, 1975-80, sr. oceanographer, 1980—; oceanographer NOAA, Seattle, 1978-79. NSF grantee, 1978-80, 80-82. Mem. Am. Soc. Limnology and Oceanography, AAAS, Phycological Soc. Am. Democrat. Contbr. articles to profl. jours. Home: 5521 17th Ave NE Seattle WA 98105 Office: Sch Oceanography Univ of Wash Seattle WA 98195

BOOTH, CAROL ANN, psychologist; b. Canton, Ohio, Nov. 20, 1952; d. Richard and Frances (Pacenza) LaMenza; B.A., Allegheny Coll., 1974; M.A., U. Pitts., 1976, Ph.D., 1977; m. Kenneth C. Booth, Aug. 20, 1977. Psychologist, Assn. Children with Learning Disabilities, Pitts., 1977; sch. psychologist Galena Park (Tex.) Schs., 1977-78; lectr. U. Houston, Clear Lake City, Tex., 1978-79; dir. infant devel. centers Gulf Coast Regional Mental Health and Mental Retardation Center, Galveston, Tex., 1978-80; sr. research asso. dept. pediatrics U. Tex. Med. Br., Galveston, 1981—; cons. Center for Human Devel., Dickinson (Tex.) Ind. Sch. Dist., 1980-82. Mem. Assn. Children with Learning Disabiltiies, Am. Psychol. Assn., Tex. Psychol. Assn., Galveston Psychol. Assn., Council Exceptional Children, Nat. Assn. Sch. Psychologist, East End Hist. Dist. Assn. Home: 1217 Church Galveston TX 77550 Office: One Shearn Moody Plaza Suite 7020 Galveston TX 77550

BOOTH, SHIRLEY, actress; b. N.Y.C., Aug. 30, 1909; d. Albert James and Virginia (Wright) Ford; ed. pub. schs., N.Y.C.; m. Edward F. Gardner, 1929 (div. 1941); m. 2d, William H. Baker, 1943 (dec. 1951). Played stock in several large cos. throughout U.S.; first major prodn. was Three Men on a Horse; appeared in Philadelphia Story, My Sister Eileen, Goodby My Fancy, A Tree Grows in Brooklyn; had leading roles Broadway prodns. Come Back Little Sheba, 1949-50, Time of The Cuckoo, 1952-53, By the Beautiful Sea, 1954, Desk Set, 1956, Miss Isobel, 1957, Juno, 1959, Nina, 1959, A Second String, 1960; movies include Come Back, Little Sheba, 1952, Main Street to Broadway, About Mrs. Leslie, 1954, Hot Spell, Matchmaker, 1958; TV series Hazel (as Hazel), 1961, A Touch of Grace, 1972-73. Recipient Academy award for Come Back, Little Sheba, 1952; Perry award for role in Time of the Cuckoo, 1953; named World's Best Actress, 6th Internat. Film Festival, Cannes, France, 1953; Sarah Siddons award as Actress of Yr., 1957; 1963 Emmy award for best actress Hazel series. *

BOOTHE, JOAN GILLIAM, editor; b. Aliceville, Ala., Oct. 2, 1954; d. Cleland Ray and Doris Eugenia (Hale) G.; B.S. cum laude, Miss. U. for Women, 1977; m. Bobby Boothe, Aug. 3, 1973; 1 dau., Heather. Sec., Gilliam Ins. Agency, Carrollton, Ala., 1972, First Nat. Bank of Aliceville, 1973; feature writer, corr. Pickens County (Ala.) Advertiser, 1974-77, editor, 1977; asso. editor Pickens County Herald, Aliceville, 1977-80, editor, 1980—; stringer Comml. Dispatch, Columbus, Miss., 1976-77. Chmn. Pickens County Cancer Crusade, 1978; chmn. public info. and public edn. Am. Cancer Soc., Pickens County, 1979-80; youth counselor Pickens County, United Methodist Ch. of Carrollton, 1973, youth dir., 1974; v.p. United Meth. Women, 1977, sec. Ina Hill Circle, 1975, mem. council on ministries, 1973, mem. adminstrv. bd., 1973, pres., 1979. Mem. Women in Communications, Sigma Delta Chi. Club: Carrollton Jr. Women (pres. 1979-80). Contbr. articles to Ala. Wheel Mag., newspapers. Home: PO Box 381 Carrollton AL 35447 Office: Pickens County Herald Aliceville AL 35442

BOOTHE, ROSALIE JOHNSON, mental health therapist; b. St. Thomas, V.I., June 15, 1938; d. Abraham and Edna Adelle (Berry) Johnson; B.S., Bklyn. Coll., 1960; M.S., Johnsom Sch. Profl. Arts, Jamaica, N.Y., 1963; m. Thomas Boothe, Sept. 17, 1958; children—Mrytice Linda, Saundra Adelle. Instr. bacteriology Portland (Oreg.) State U., 1973-74; family therapist Yaun Youth Care Center, Portland, 1971-73; adminstr. Alcohol Counseling and Recovery Program, Portland, 1974-76; pres., exec. dir. Exodus Programs, Portland, 1977—; cons. mental health Oreg. State Penitentary Women's Center. Mem. Nat. Edn. for Tchrs., Nat. Assn. Broadcasters, Alcohol Tng. Council, LWV, Portland C. of C. Office: 1639 NE Alberta St Portland OR 97211

BOOZER, VELMA ARLENE, lawyer, state ofcl.; b. June 9, 1954; d. Henry H. and Cornelia (Easley) B.; B.A. in Music, Princeton U., 1975; J.D., Villanova U., 1978. Faculty research asst. Princeton U., 1973-75; resident women's adv. Villanova U., 1975-78; admitted to Pa. bar, 1978; legal asst. to gen. counsel Region III, HEW, Phila., 1977-78; asst. atty. gen. Pa. Dept. State, Harrisburg, 1978-80; asst. counsel Pa. Public Utility Commn., Harrisburg, 1980-82, exec. asst. to commr., 1982—. Bd. dirs. Harrisburg YWCA. Recipient Naumberg award Princeton U., 1975. Mem. Pa. Bar Assn., Harrisburg Black Attys. Assn., Barristers Assn. Phila., Monday Club of Women's Network of Central Pa. (coordinating com., joint pres. 1980-82), Delta Sigma Theta.

BORCHERDT, WENDY HAWLEY (MRS. EDWARD RAHR BORCHERDT, JR.), spl. asst. to Pres.; civic worker; b. Oakland, Calif., Apr. 12, 1936; d. Stuart Meek and Lois (Weinmann) Hawley; B.A., Stanford, 1958; m. Edward Rahr Borcherdt, Jr., July 5, 1958; children—Kimberley, Edward Rahr III. asso. dir. Presdl. personnel The White House, Washington, 1981, spl. asst. to Pres. for public liaison, 1981—. Div. chmn. Community Chest, Los Angeles, 1960-61; active various community drives; Blue Bird leader Camp Fire Girls, 1966-68; tchr. leadership and mgmt. Teren & Co., 1976-77; pres. Tng. for Effective Mgmt., 1977-81; bd. dirs. Jr. League of Los Angeles, rec. sec., 1965-81, treas., 1969-70, pres., 1972-73; area rep. Assn. Jr. Leagues, 1973-75; vice chmn. Citizens for Law Enforcement, 1975-78; mem. subcom. on indsl. and comml. firm retention City of Los Angeles Econ. Adv. Council, 1976; bd. dirs., pres. Symphonians, 1961-66, Jr. Philharmonic com., 1971-81; bd. overseers Hoover Instn. War, Revolution and Peace, 1974-81; bd. govs. Town Hall, 1980-81; bd. dirs. Harvard Sch. Boys, 1975-78, Hancock Homes Owners Assn., 1975-77, Good Samaritan Hosp. Aux., 1975-81, Pacific Legal Found., 1980-81; vice chmn. Ind. Colls. So. Calif., 1975-81; div. chmn. Nixon, 1960, 62; area chmn. Goldwater, 1964, Reagan, 1966; asst. co-chmn. Women for Nixon, Los Angeles, 1968; area chmn. Samuel Yorty, 1969; campaign worker Ronald Reagan for Pres., 1976-81, regional fin. dir., 1979-81; vice chmn. adv. bd. Alcoholism Info. Center, Los Angeles; mem. exec. com. Ed Davis for Gov., 1978. Episcopalian (tchr. Sunday sch.). Clubs: Los Angeles Country, Beach, Stanford Women's (dirs., pres. 1965-69) (Los Angeles); Larchmont Republican (dir., v.p. 1975-80). Home: 2828 Wisconsin Ave NW Apt 108 Washington DC 20007 Office: The White House Washington DC 20500

BORCHERS, SISTER, JEANNETTE FRANCES, social worker; b. Dayton, Ohio, Jan. 8, 1914; d. Bernard John and Eleanor (Schenk) B.; student Sister of Charity Coll. Mt. St. Joseph, Ohio, 1932, B.S., 1936; M. Ed., U. St. Louis, 1956; postgrad. Xavier U., So. Colo. State Coll.; M.S.W., Ohio State U., 1971. Dietetic intern Good Samaritan Hosp., 1936-37, dietitian, 1937-38, St. Joseph Hosp., Mt. Clemens, Mich., 1938-41; instr. chemistry, home econs. Acad. Mt. St. Joseph, Ohio, 1941-46: instr. biology, home econs. St. James High Sch., Bay City, Mich., 1947-55; edn. dir. dietetic internship Good Samaritan Hosp., 1955-57, dir. dept. nutrition, 1957-64; dir. dietary dept. St. Mary-Corwin Hosp., 1964-65, coordinator hosp. in service edn., 1965-66; adminstr. El Pomar Retreat Center, Colorado Springs, 1966-69; social work adminstrv. resident U. Cin. Med. Center, 1971; social counselor St. Joseph Hosp., Mt. Clemens, Mich., 1972-74, dir. patient and family counseling services, 1974—. Exec. sec. Nat. Cath. Council on Home Econs., 1957-59, regional chmn., 1959-61; mem. project rev. com. Comprehensive Health Planning Council S.E. Mich., 1976—; chief nutrition services Med. and Health Div. Ohio Valley CD Authority, 1959-61; former mem. nutrition council Cin. Pub. Health Fedn. Bd. dirs. Sister Romuald Merit award Meml. Fund, 1957-64. Recipient Social Worker of Year award Macomb County, 1979. Mem. Am. Home Econs. Assn., Am. (chmn. corr. course for food service suprs. Colo.), Cin. (life mem., pres. 1963-64), Colorado Springs (pres.), Detroit dietetic assns., Am. Hosp. Assn., Soc. Hosp. Social Work Dirs. (sec. 1978), Nat. Cath. Council on Home Econs., Nat. Assn. Social Workers (pres. Mich. chpt. 1980—), LWV, Clin. Social Workers Soc., Contbr. articles to profl. jours. Address: St Joseph Hosp Mount Clemens MI 48043

BORDEN, BEATRICE JOY, resort devel. exec.; b. New Rochelle, N.Y., Apr. 7, 1942; d. George S. and Mary E. (Lenac) Polancic; student U. Md. in S.E. Asia, 1968-69, U. Hawaii, 1972-75. Adminstr., Pacific Architects & Engrs., Bangkok, Thailand, 1967-68, Control Data Corp., Bangkok, Thailand, and Saigon, South Vietnam, 1968-69; v.p. Makai Range Inc., Engring., Honolulu, 1971-73; exec. v.p. Lahaina Kaanapali & Pacific R.R., Honolulu, 1972; project coordinator Kaluakoi Devel. Corp., Honolulu, 1974-76; v.p. Pacific Dynamics Corp., Honolulu, 1974—, also dir.; sales mgr. Sunriver Devel. Corp., Portland, Oreg., 1976-78; v.p. mktg. and sales Sunriver Mgmt. Corp., 1978—. Mem. Sales and Mktg. Execs., Realtors Mktg. Inst., Inst. Managerial and Profl. Women, Oreg. Execs. Assn. (dir., 1978-79), United Land Inst., Am. Land Developers Assn. (dir. 1982—), Portland Advt. Fedn., Public Relations Roundtable. Office: 4800 SW Macadam Ave Suite 206 Portland OR 97201

BORDEN, FRANCES (MCCONVILLE, FRANCES), public relations agy. exec.; b. Boston, B.A. cum laude, Radcliffe Coll., Harvard U.; m. Daniel J. McConville. Mgr. consumer public relations Pfizer, Inc., N.Y.C., 1964-70; account exec. Howard Rubenstein, public relations agy., N.Y.C., 1976-77, Niki Singer Assos., public relations agy., N.Y.C., 1977-78; public relations dir. Waldorf-Astoria Hotel, N.Y.C., 1978-82; account exec. Jody Donohue Assos., N.Y.C., 1982—; cons. ethical programs and mktg., 1970-76; co-owner standardbred racing horses. Mem. U.S. Trotting Assn., Can. Trotting Assn., Am. Women in Radio and TV. Club: North River Power Squadron. 415 E 52d St New York NY 10022 Office: 32 E 57th St New York NY 10022

BORDER, LAURA LEA BAKER, educator; b. Steamboat Springs, Colo., Nov. 25, 1945; d. Claude A. and Mary (Chivington) Baker; B.A. sum laude, U. Colo., 1967, M.A., 1971; m. William Border, June 28, 1975; 1 dau., Alison Anne. Instr., U. Denver, spring, 1972; faculty U. Colo., Boulder, 1977—; lectrice d'Anglais, Université de Bordeaux, France, 1969-70. U. Colo. teaching associateship, 1967-69, 70-72. Mem. Colo. Assn. for Internat. Edn., Colo. Congress Fgn. Lang. Tchrs., Am. Assn. Tchrs. French. Author: Collage: Revision de Grammaire, 1981; Collage: Conparsations/Activites, Collage: Lectures Litteráires, Collage: Variétés Culturelles, 1981; (with others) Collage: Cashier d'exercices oraux et ecrits. Office: Dept French and Italian Univ of Colo Boulder CO 80309

BORDNER, MARJORIE RICH, educator, civic worker; b. McDonough County, Ill., Dec. 1, 1914; d. Harry R. and Merle (Turner) Rich; B.Ed., Western Ill. U., 1936; Ed.M., U. Mo., Columbia, 1940; m. Lawrence Inman Bordner, Apr. 21, 1946; children—Larry Richard, Larrilyn Louise. Tchr. various elem. and secondary schs., Ill.; instr. Western Ill. U. and Spoon River Coll.; acct., receptionist Bordner Air Conditioning-Refrigeration Co. Sec., Ill. orgn. DAR, mem. state bd. dirs., 1977, div. dir., regent, 1971—; pres. New Eng. Women Ill. Prairie Colony, 1974-76; sec. found. bd., exec. com. Western Ill. U., 1972—; mem. Western Ill. U. Alumni Council, 1972—, sec., 1981—; pres. Fulton County Hist. and Geneal. Soc., 1974-75, 80—, Spoon River Scenic Drive Assn., 1971-74; mem. Fulton County Planning Commn., 1971—; chmn. Fulton County Bicentennial, 1973-76; sec. Community Resource Devel. Exec. Council of Fulton County, 1979—; life mem. Ill. Hist. Soc., Ill. Geneal. Soc. Recipient Disting. Alumni award Western Ill. U., 1971, Achievement award, 1980. hon. parade marshal Canton Friendship Festival Parade, 1976. Contbr. articles to periodicals.

BORENSTEIN, EMILY RUTH, poet; b. Elizabeth, N.J., May 6, 1923; d. Louis and Jennie (Molowitz) Schwartz; student Julliard Sch., 1941-42; B.S. in Comparative Lit., Columbia U., 1964; M.A. in English, N.Y. U., 1972; m. Morris Borenstein, June 27, 1942; children—Rachel, Sandra, Marc. Author: Woman Chopping, 1978; Finding My Face, 1979; Cancer Queen, 1979; Night of the Broken Glass, 1981; contbr. numerous poems to poetry and lit. mags., anthologies, including Voices Within the Ark, The Modern Jewish Poets, 1980, Phoenix Rising, An Anthology of Contemporary Jewish Voices, 1981; Anthology of Mag. Verse, 1981; lectr. poetry workshops, poetry readings. Recipient Ann. Poetry award, Jewish Currents, 1978. Mem. Poets and Writers, Inc., Poetry Soc. Am., Columbia U. Alumni Assn., N.Y. U. Alumni Assn. Jewish. Club: Women's Univ. Home: 189 Highland Ave Middletown NY 10940

BORENSTINE, ROULA ALAKIOTOU, architect; b. Pireaus, Greece, 1945; came to U.S., 1968, naturalized, 1976; student architecture Athens Technol. Inst., 1963-66; B.Arch. with honors, U. Ill., Chgo., 1975; M.Arch. with honors, U. Ill., Urbana, 1978. With prodn. and research dept. Doxiadis Assos., Athens, Greece, 1963-64; with Lipasmata Co., Piraeus, 1964-68; with design and prodn. dept. Bur. Architecture, City of Chgo., 1976-80; founder, mgr. Roula Assos., Chgo., 1980—. Mem. AIA, Chgo. Women Architects, Hellenic Profl. Soc. Office: 14 W Erie St Chicago IL 60610

BORG, JACQUELINE DIANE, purchasing exec.; b. South Bend, Ind., Feb. 28, 1934; d. Dean Delbert and Mary Louise (Johnson) Clemmons; student U. Calif., Santa Barbara; children—Derek Frank, Karen Louise, Darren John, Andrew Dean. Sec. material Rockwell Internat., Thousand Oaks, Calif., 1977-78, expeditor, 1978-79, buyer, 1979-81, sr. buyer, 1981—. Mem. Nat. Mgmt. Assn., Nat. Assn. Female Execs., Republican. Office: 1049 Camino dos Rios Thousand Oaks CA 91360

BORGER, LINDA A. ANDERSON, speech and lang. pathologist; b. Newburgh, N.Y., Jan. 25, 1948; d. Frederick Raymond and Mary Frances (Bivona) Anderson; B.A., SUNY, Geneseo, 1971; M.S., So. Conn. Coll., 1973; m. Andrew Walling Borger, Apr. 2, 1977; 1 son, Erik; stepchildren—Christian, Kirsten. Speech and lang. pathologist Norwalk (Conn.) Public Sch. System, 1973-75, Highland Falls (N.Y.) Central Schs., 1975—; pvt. practice speech and lang. pathology, Garrison, N.Y.; mem. Planning and Placement Team Conn., 1973-75; asso. mem. Com. on Handicapped N.Y. State, 1975—. Lic. speech-lang. pathologist, N.Y. State, Conn. Mem. Am. (cert. clin. competence), N.Y., Conn. speech and hearing assns. Club: Sons of Norway. Home: Manitou Rd Garrison NY 10524 Office: Mountain Ave Highland Falls NY 10928

BORGESE, ELISABETH MANN, author; b. Munich, Germany, Apr. 24, 1918 d. Thomas and Katia (Pringheim) Mann; came to U.S., 1938, naturalized, 1941; diploma Conservatory of Music, Zurich, 1937; m. Giuseppe Antonio Borgese, Nov. 23, 1939; children—Angelica, Dominica. Research assoc., editor Common Cause, U. Chgo., 1945-51; editor Perspective USA, Diogenes Intercultural Publs., 1952-57; exec. sec. bd. editors Ency. Brit., Chgo., 1964-66; sr. fellow, assoc. Center for Study Democratic Instns., Santa Barbara, Calif., 1965—; Killam sr. fellow Dalhousie U., Halifax, N.S., Can., 1978-79, prof. dept. polit. sci., 1980—; author: To Whom It May Concern, 1962; Ascent of Woman, 1963; The Language Barrier, 1965; The Ocean Regime, 1968; The Drama of the Oceans, 1976; Seafarm: The Story of Aquaculture, 1980: The Mines of Neptune, 1983; contbr. short stories, essays to mags. Chmn. planning council Internat. Ocean Inst.; advisor Austrian del. 3d UN Conf. on Law of Sea, 1976—. Mem. Acad. Polit. Sci. AAAS, Am. Soc. Internat. Law, Author's Guild. Home: Sambro Head Halifax NS Canada Office: Dept Polit Sci Dalhousie U Halifax NS B3H 4H6 Canada

BORIS, RUTHANNA, dancer, choreographer, dance therapist, tchr.; b. Bklyn., Mar. 17, 1918; d. Joseph Jay and Frances (Weiss) Boris; student Profl. Children's Sch., N.Y.C. Prin. dancer Am. Ballet, N.Y.C., 1934, Ballet Caravan, N.Y.C., 1936; prima ballerina Met. Opera Co., N.Y.C., 1939, Ballet Russe de Monte Carlo, N.Y.C., 1942-49; prima ballerina, choreographer-in-residence Royal Winnipeg Ballet of Can., 1957, dir., 1957—; choreographer N.Y.C. Ballet, 1951, Joffrey Ballet, N.Y.C., 1966; prof. dance U. Wash., Seattle, 1965-82, adj. prof. dept. psychiatry Sch. Medicine, 1982—; dir. Boris-Hobi Concert Co., 1955—. Mem. adv. bd. Seattle Psychoanalytic Inst., 1975—. Registered dance therapist. Mem. AAUP, Am. Guild Mus. Artists (award 1964, bd. govs. 1942-64), Am. Dance Therapy Assn. (charter, bd. govs. 1963). Choreographer: Cirque de Deux, 1946; Quelques Fleurs, 1947; Cakewalk, 1951; Kaleidoscope, 1951, Will O' The Wisp, 1951, Wanderling, 1957, Pasticcio, 1955, Ragtime, 1975. Home: 4733 17th Ave NE Seattle WA 98105 Office: HCMHC 2MH12 ZA-31 U Washington 326 9th St Seattle WA 98105

BORISOFF, RISA POLGAR, social worker; b. Bklyn., Feb. 3, 1947; d. Franz J. and Lillian (Sherman) Polgar; B.A. (Univ. honors scholar 1969), N.Y.U., 1969; M.S.W., Adelphi U., Garden City, N.Y., 1977; m. Richard Stuart Borisoff, Aug. 17, 1967; children—Mindy J., Dara Fran. Sr. caseworker Westchester Children's Assn., White Plains, N.Y., 1978-79; social worker in youth residences Family Services of Westchester, White Plains, 1979—. Bd. dirs., sec. Pinebrook Homes Neighborhood Assn. Cert. social worker, N.Y. Mem. Nat. Assn. Social Workers. Home: 7 Adrian Circle Scarsdale NY 10583 Office: 470 Mamaroneck Ave White Plains NY 10605

BORKE, LOUISE ILENE, banker; b. Chgo., May 22, 1955; d. Mitchell Louis and Helene Myra (Finke) B.; student Vanderbilt U., 1972-73, Duquesne U., 1973-74; B.S., U. Pa., 1976; Trainee comml. lending program Bankers Trust Co., N.Y.C., 1976-77, account officer, Hong Kong desk, N.Y.C., 1977-78, sr. desk officer Hong Kong and People's Republic China, N.Y.C., 1978, asst. treas., dep. rep., Hong Kong, 1978-80, asst. v.p., mgr. Fin. Instns. Group, Hong Kong, 1980-82, v.p., project mgr. Product Devel. Group, N.Y.C., 1982—. Mem. Wharton Club N.Y., Fin. Women's Assn., Fin. Women's Assn., Bus. and Profl. Women's Assn. Democrat. Jewish. Club: Wharton of N.Y. Home: care 5459 Covode St Pittsburgh PA 15217 Office: 280 Park Ave New York NY 10017

BORKENHAGEN, CONSTANCE KATSON, lawyer; b. Albuquerque, June 30, 1942; d. Robert Virgil and Penelope (Papafrangos) Katson; B.A., Duke, 1964; J.D., U. N.Mex., 1975; m. Robert H. Borkenhagen, Apr. 23, 1965; children—Holly Gabrielle, Lea Monique. Legis. asst. U.S. Ho. of Reps., 1965-71; lobbyist Albuquerque Consumer Fedn., N.Mex. Legislature, 1971-75; admitted to D.C. bar, N.Mex. bar; with Dist. Atty.'s Office, 1974, County Pub. Defender's Office, 1975; legal journalist Doing Business in Europe; internat. law practice, London, Eng., 1976—; dir., gen. counsel Equator Petroleum Co., 1981—; lobbyist Criminal Sexual Conduct Act, 1974-75. Publicity dir. N.Mex. Arts and Crafts Fair, 1971-72; counsel Am. C. of C., London. Bd. dirs. Democrats Abroad. Mem. Am. Bar Assn. (ho. of dels. 1974-75; Disting. Service award 1974, 75), Internat. Bar Assn. (bus. law sect.), Internat. Assn. Women Lawyers, City Women's Network, Brit. Assn. Women Execs., Inst. Dirs., Internat. Platform Assn., Delta Theta Phi (sec. 1974-75). Episcopalian. Author profl. articles. Home: 29 Cambridge St London SW1 England Office: BCM Box 4700 London WC1V 6XX England

BORN, BROOKSLEY ELIZABETH, lawyer; b. San Francisco, Aug. 27, 1940; d. Ronald Henry and Mary Ellen (Bortner) Born; A.B., Stanford U., 1961, J.D., 1964; children—Nicholas Jacob Landau, Ariel Elizabeth Landau. Admitted to Calif. bar, 1965, D.C. bar, 1966; law clk. U.S. Ct. Appeals, Washington, 1964-65; legal researcher Harvard U. Law Sch., 1967-68; asso. firm Arnold and Porter, Washington, 1965-67, 68-73, partner, 1974—; lectr. law Columbus U. Sch. Law, Cath. U. Am., 1972-74; adj. prof. Georgetown U. Law Center, Washington, 1972-73. Bd. visitors Stanford U. Law Sch., 1977-79; bd. dirs. Nat. Legal Aid and Defenders Assn., 1972-79; trustee Center for Law and Social Policy, Washington, 1977—. Named Woman Lawyer of Yr., Women's Bar Assn. D.C., 1981. Mem. Am. Bar Assn. (chairperson sect. individual rights and responsibilities 1977-78, chairperson fed. judiciary com. 1980—), D.C. Bar (sec. 1975-76, bd. govs. 1976-79), Am. Law Inst., Lawyers' Com. for Civil Rights Under Law (trustee 1978—), Order of Coif. Pres. Stanford Law Rev., 1963-64. Office: 1200 New Hampshire Ave NW Washington DC 20036

BORNHOLDT, LAURA ANNA, found. exec.; b. Peoria, Ill., Feb. 11, 1919; d. John and Barbara (Kohl) Bornholdt; A.B., Smith Coll., 1940, M.A., 1942; Ph.D., Yale U., 1945. Asst. prof. history Smith Coll., Northampton, Mass., 1945-52; internat. relations asso. AAUW, Washington, 1952-57; dean Sarah Lawrence Coll., Bronxville, N.Y., 1957-59; dean women, adj. prof. history U. Pa., Phila., 1959-61; dean coll., prof. history Wellesley (Mass.) Coll., 1961-64; v.p. Danforth Found., St. Louis, 1964-73; sr. program officer Lilly Endowment Inc., Indpls., 1973-76. v.p. for edn., 1976—. Nat. adv. com. on black higher edn. and black colls. and univs. Dept. Edn., 1977—; mem. Yale U. Council, 1977—; emerita life trustee Coll. of Wooster (Ohio), 1977—; trustee St. Louis U., 1971-75. Recipient Yale U. Wilbur Cross medal, 1976. Mem. Am. Assn. Higher Edn., Phi Beta Kappa. Editorial bd. Jour. Higher Edn., 1970-76; adv. bd. Change Mag., 1980—. Home: 5521 Roxbury Terr Indianapolis IN 46228 Office: 2801 N Meridian St Box 88068 Indianapolis IN 46208 *

BORNSTEIN, CHRISTINE VERZAR, art historian; b. Basel, Switzerland, Sept. 5, 1940; d. Fritz and Edith Jean (McDougall) Verzar; came to U.S., 1966, naturalized, 1972; Ph.D., Basel U., 1966; postgrad. Florence U., 1963-64, London U., 1963; 1 son from previous marriage, Benjamin. Asst. prof. art history Boston U., 1966-69; lectr. Princeton (N.J.) U., 1969-70; asst. prof. U. Mich., Ann Arbor, 1973—, acting dir. Medieval and Renaissance Collegium, 1977-78. U. Mich. fellow, grantee, 1976-77; Boston U. Faculty grantee, 1967-68; Am. Philos. Soc. grantee, 1976; Nat. Endowment Humanities sr. research fellow, 1981-82. Mem. Coll. Art. Assn., Medieval Acad. Am., Internat. Center Medieval Art, Archeol. Assn. Am. Author: Die Romanischen Skulpturen der Abtei Sagra di San Michele, 1968; (with P.P. Soucek) The Meeting of Two Worlds: The Crusades and the Mediterranean Context, 1981; contbr. articles to profl. jours. Home: 1302 Horman Ct Ann Arbor MI 48104 Office: Dept Art History U Mich Ann Arbor MI 48109

BORNSTEIN, SHIRLEY DEMBOW, univ. adminstr.; b. Phila., Mar. 9, 1922; d. Harry L. and Fanny A. (Abramson) Dembow; student New Sch. for Social Research, 1964-67; B.A., U. Pa., 1971; M.Ed., Temple U., 1976; m. N. Herman Bornstein, May 22, 1939; children—Barry A., Steven J. Counselor career/job Jewish Employment & Vocat. Services, Phila., 1975-76; counselor Temple U., Phila., 1976-78, acting dir., 1978-79, dir., 1979—, asso. dir. Russell Conwell Services Center, 1979—. Bd dirs. Eldercraftsman, 1974-76, Moss Rehab. Hosp., 1971-74, Southeastern Pa. Mental Health, 1968-70; curriculum adv. Inst. Awareness, YM-YWHA, 1963-70; v.p. Sisterhood Beth Sholom Synagogue, 1962-63; active Children's Hosp. Aux., 1964-68. Mem. Am. Personnel and Guidance Assn., Nat. Assn. Women Deans, Adminstrs. and Counselors, Adult Edn. Council, Regional Network for Adult Students, Common Cause. Address: 1619 Walnut St Philadelphia PA 19103

BOROCHOFF, IDA SLOAN (MRS. CHARLES Z. BOROCHOFF), real estate exec., artist; b. July 29, 1922; d. Louis and Eva (Bistrick) Sloan; ed. U. Ga., 1939-40, Ga. State U., 1940, Chgo. Sch. Interior Decorating, 1966, Allegro Sch. Ballet, Chgo., Atlanta Ballet, 1948-54, Emory U., 1971-72; m. Charles Zachary Borochoff, Jan. 11, 1942; children—Lynn Borochoff Gould, Jean Sue Borochoff Shapiro, Toby Ann Borochoff Bernstein, Lance Mark. Investor and owner real estate, 1941—; v.p. Designs Unltd., Inc., Atlanta, 1964—; pres. Sloan Borochoff Gallery, Atlanta, 1970—; art lectr. Met. Ednl. Service; tchr. Ga. Inst. Tech.-Free U.; exhibited several one-woman shows, 1961-71, including Lovett Sch., 1972, 75, Ga. Inst. Tech., 1972, 75, Atlanta Mdse. Mart; art rev. columnist Northside Neighbor Newspapers. Bd. dirs. Atlanta Ballet, 1950-57; bd. dirs. Atlanta Music Club, also co-editor Newsletter; hostess Atlanta Arts Festival; capt. Heart Fund, 1968-76, area chmn. dr.; active various multi-media groups; artistic dir. Atlanta Playhouse Theatre; active Dogwood Festival; chmn., trustee Atlanta Playhouse Theatre. Recipient several art awards; named hon. alumnus Atlanta Art Inst., 1968, One of Ten Leading Ladies of Atlanta, J.C. Singles, 1976. Mem. Atlanta Press Club, Atlanta Writers Club (membership com.), Atlanta Artists Club, Atlanta Women's C. of C. (chmn. fine arts 1977-78), LWV, High Mus. Art, Ga. Writers Assn. Mem. B'nai B'rith Women (pres. chpt. 1975, mem. SE regional bd.). Clubs: Jockey, Progressive. Home: 3450 Old Plantation Rd NW Atlanta GA 30327 Office: 3451 Church St Scottdale GA 30079

BORON, MARION, musician, educator; M.A., Smith Coll.; Mus.B., Boston U.; doctoral studies Harvard U. Asst. prof. music Boston State Coll., 1966-82; past head music dept. Oxford Sch., Hartford (Conn.) Coll., Hartford Sem. Found.; with Scholarship Office, Mass. Bd. Higher Edn., Boston, 1982—. Mem. Am. Guild Organists (past dean Boston chpt.), Smithsonian Instn., AAUP, Am. Assn. Higher Edn. Composer organ concerto, also vocal, piano, and chamber music; author: Study Guide for Music Theory, 1974; Music Appreciation: Competency-Based Approach, 1976. Office: Scholarship Office Mass Bd Higher Edn Boston MA 02116

BOROS, CAROLYN MAY, banker; b. Burlington, Vt., July 14, 1941; d. Joseph Wilfred and Helen Constance (Fleury) LeClair; student Trinity Coll., 1959-61, U. Vt., 1977-80; m. Simon Boros, Sept. 30, 1961; children—Cynthia, Katalin, Matthew. Programmer, Chittenden Trust, Burlington, 1961-69; programming mgr. Howard Bank, Burlington, 1971-77; sr. programmer, analyst Digital Equipment Corp., S. Burlington, Vt., 1977-78; asso. programmer IBM, Essex Junction, Vt., 1978-79; EDP mgr., v.p., chief ops. officer Burlington Savs. Bank, 1979—; instr. Computer Environment Inst., 1969-70. Mem. Nat. Assn. Bank Women, Vt. Computer Users Group, Burlington Bus. and Profl. Women's Club. Roman Catholic. Home: 23 Shore Acres Dr Colchester VT 05446 Office: 146 College St Burlington VT 05401

BORRELL, BARBARA SUSAN, data processing exec.; b. Beacon, N.Y., Mar. 26, 1942; d. Francis Anthony and Helen Marie (Simpson) B.; B.S., Marywood Coll., 1963; M.S., Hunter Coll., 1969; M.B.A., Roosevelt U., 1980. Field sales cons. Nabisco Co. Inc., Elk Grove Village, Ill., 1975-78; product mgr. Douwe Egberts Superior Co., Bensenville, Ill., 1978-80; data processing system specialist NCR Corp., Phoenix, 1979—. Mem. Am. Dietetic Assn., Am. Diabetes Assn., Am. Home Econs. Assn., Central Ariz. Dist. Dietetic Assn., Ariz. Home Economists In Bus., Dietitians in Bus. and Industry, Data Processing Mgmt. Assn., Nat. Assn. Female Execs., Omicron Nu. Roman Catholic. Clubs: Phoenix Ski, Ski of Ariz., Casa Liturgy Rev. Address: 1605 E Borghese Pl Phoenix AZ 85016

BORST, BEATRICE, ret. real estate agt.; b. Pawling, N.Y.; d. Charles Austin and Grace Maria (Olmstead) B.; B.A. (Campbell scholar), UCLA, 1932; grad. Sawyer's Sch. Bus., 1934; M.A., U. Mich., 1940; profl. diploma Columbia Tchrs. Coll., 1952; postgrad. U. So. Calif., 1958, Lumbleau's Real Estate Sch., 1959, 65. Sec. to asst. dean Columbia U. Sch. Journalism, 1935-36; sec. advt. dept. Fortune Mag., N.Y.C., 1936-37; with research dept. CBS, N.Y.C., 1943; sec., asst. to dir. publicity Research Inst. Am., 1944; with sales dept. Doubleday Book Shops, N.Y.C., 1945-47; freelance writer, 1947; real estate saleswoman, 1959; realtor, asso. Culver Nichols, Realtor, Palm Springs, Calif., from 1965, now ret. Recipient Avery Hopwood award U. Mich., 1941. Mem. Calif. Real Estate Assn., Nat. Assn. Real Estate Bds., Palm Springs Bd. Real Estate (dir., 1966-68), DAR (Cahvilla chpt.), Colonial Dames 17th Century (Cape Ann chpt.), Phi Beta Kappa (1st prize essay contest, 1931). Republican. Presbyterian. Club: Palm Springs Woman's. Author: Nearer the Earth, 1941. Home: 643 Thornhill Rd Palm Springs CA 92262

BORTEL, GLADYS ELLA, nurse; b. Davison County, S.D., Apr. 13, 1922; d. Leo Brown and Nettie Olive (Leake) Rowley; R.N., Methodist

Hosp., Mitchell, S.D., 1943; m. Harry Virgil Bortel, Feb. 23, 1944 (dec.); children—Betty Lou Bortel, Griffith, Linda Kaye Bortel Shaneyfelt. Nurse, Sioux Valley Hosp., Sioux Falls, S.D., 1943-44, St. Joseph's Hosp., Mitchell, 1964; nurse Meth. Hosp., Mitchell, 1964-79, dir. nursing, 1979—. Sunday sch. tchr., 1960-80; foster parent, 1961-69. Mem. S.D. Soc. Nursing Service Adminstrs., Nat. Soc. Nursing Service Adminstrs., Meth. Hosp. Alumni Assn. (v.p.). Methodist. Home: 519 N Montana St Mitchell SD 57301 Office: 909 S Miller St Mitchell SD 57301

BORTIN, VIRGINIA LUNDGREN (MRS. GEORGE BORTIN), writer; b. Phila., June 19, 1936; d. William Francis and Vivian Florence (Smith) Lundgren; B.A., U. Pa., 1958; m. George Bortin, Feb. 18, 1967. Asst. producer WCAU-TV, Phila., 1954-58, dir. publicity, 1960-67, writer of TV documentaries and series, 1964-67; freelance writer and poet, 1967—; guest lectr. journalism dept. U. Pa., Phila., 1963-64. Mem. Pa. Hist. Soc., Egypt Exploration Soc. (London), Women in Communications. Episcopalian. Author: Publicity for Volunteers: A Handbook, 1981. Contbr. poetry and articles to various journals and anthologies.

BORTOLOTTI, NORMA MAY, investment exec.; b. Omaha, Apr. 8, 1931; d. Isidoro and Michelina (Cominoli) B.; Dickinson Secretarial Sch., Omaha, 1958; B.A., Duchesne Coll., 1954; postgrad. Creighton U., 1957, 58, 77, 78; Typist, W.O.W. Life Ins. Co., Omaha, 1948; with Universal Terrazzo & Tile Co., Omaha, 1949-77, sec., receptionist and acct., 1954-70, v.p., 1964-77; acct., hostess 7301 Corp., night club, Omaha, 1964-69, also dir.; v.p. NND Investment Co., Omaha, 1957—; mgmt. v.p. NND Investment Corp., Omaha, 1957—. Active local ward and precinct work Republican Party, 1975. Recipient Outstanding Service award Republican Party, 1975. Mem. E de M, Cath. Soc. Sacred Heart, Nat. Assn. Female Execs. Home: 9904 Florence Heights Blvd Omaha NE 68112

BORTON, MARILYN MILLER, recreation therapist; b. Paterson, N.J., Oct. 3, 1930; d. Calvin Henry and Lillian (Bennett) Miller; B.A. in Recreation, Syracuse (N.Y.) U., 1951; B.S. in Edn., Paterson State Tchrs. Coll., 1953; postgrad. Fairleigh Dickinson U.; m. Lee John Borton, June 9, 1951; children—Lee John, Nancy Lee, James Christopher, Susan Elizabeth. Dir., Village Sch. Retarded Children, Ridgewood, N.J., 1951-53; elementary sch. tchr., Wyckoff, N.J., 1953-56; tchr. Abbott Nursery Sch., Prospect Park, N.J., 1956-59; dir. Robin's Nest Nursery Sch., Bernardsville, N.J., 1964-66; dir. recreation Birchwood Convalescent Center, Edison, N.J., 1975—; sec.-treas. Borton Bus. Forms, Inc., 1968—. Bd. dirs. St. David's Kindergarten, Peters Twp., Pa., 1961-62, Passaic Twp. Youth Center, 1971-74, Watchung Hills Pop Warner Football, 1972-74; chmn. Helping Hand program Passaic Twp. Jaycees Wives, 1970-72; mem. Millington First Aid Squad, 1966—; charter mem., bd. dirs. Passaic Twp. First Aid Squad, 1974—, pres., 1976-77; instr. CPR and 1st aid ARC, 1974—; sec. Bicentennial Commn. Passaic Twp., 1974-76. Named Chmn. of Year, Passaic Twp. Jaycees Wives, 1970-71. Mem. Nat. Therapeutic Recreation Soc. Republican. Episcopalian. Home: 151 Division Ave PO Box 406 Millington NJ 07946 Office: 1350 Inman Ave Edison NJ 08820

BORYSEWICZ, MARY LOUISE, editor; b. Chgo., Aug. 3, 1934; d. Thomas J. and Mabel E. (Zeien) O'Farrell; B.A., Mundelein Coll., 1970; postgrad. in English lit. U. Ill, 1970-71; grad. exec. program U. Chgo., 1982; m. Daniel S. Borysewicz, June 11, 1955; children—Mary Adele, Stephen Francis, Paul Barnabas. Tchr. advanced level English for fgn.-speaking adults Evanston Twp. (Ill.) High Sch., 1969-71; editor sci. publs. AMA, Chgo., 1971-73; exec. mng. editor Am. Jour. Ophthalmology, Chgo., 1973—; guest lectr. U. Chgo. Med. Sch., 1979, Harvard U. Med. Sch., 1978, Northwestern U. Med. Sch., 1979, Am. Acad. Ophthalmology, 1976, 81. Mem. Am. Soc. Bus. Press Editors, Am. Soc. Profl. and Exec. Women, Council Biology Editors, Internat. Fedn. Sci. Editors Assns., Soc. Scholarly Pub. Contbr. articles to sci. publs.; editor: Ophthalmology Principles and Concepts, 4th edit., 1978, 5th edit., 1982. Office: 435 N Michigan Ave Chicago IL 60611

BORZI, PHYLLIS CORINNE, lawyer, govt. ofcl.; b. Port Jefferson, N.Y., Aug. 10, 1946; d. Phillip Louis and Marie Roberta (Mirabelli) B.; B.A., Ladycliff Coll., 1968; M.A., Syracuse U., 1970; J.D., Cath. U., 1978. High sch. English tchr., Bayport, N.Y., 1969-75; research assoc. Schanes Assocs., Washington, 1975-77; asso. Hogan & Hartson, Washington, 1978-79; majority legislative assoc. U.S. Ho. of Reps. Pension Task Force, Washington, 1979-80; pension csl. U.S. Ho. of Reps., Subcom. on Labor-Mgmt. Relations, Washington, 1981—. Mem. Am. Bar Assn., Women's Bar Assn., Bar Assn. D.C., D.C. Bar Assn. Democrat. Roman Catholic. Home: 5309 Riverdale Rd Apt 312 Riverdale MD 20737 Office: 2451 Rayburn House Office Bldg Washington DC 20515

BOSCHEN, LINDA BRAEDER, securities trader; b. Richmond, Va., Apr. 5, 1954; d. Robert Reynold and Janice (Ward) Braeder; grad. Montclair Kimberley Acad., 1971; student Dickenson Coll., 1971-72, Bloomfield Coll., 1980-82; m. Richard Edward Boschen, Jr., Sept. 29, 1979. Sales/Sec. G. A. Thompson, Inc., N.Y.C., 1973-75; head ops. Jesup and Lamont, Inc., N.Y.C., 1975-76; trader/stock options Sogen Swiss Internat., N.Y.C., 1976-77; instl. sales corporate bonds Moseley Hallgarten Estabrook, N.Y.C., 1977-78; govt. bond trader, Thomson McKinnon Securities, N.Y.C., 1978—. Class sec. Montclair Kimberley Acad. Alumni Assn., 1971-81. Mem. Montclair Hist. Soc., N.J. Hist. Soc., Nat. Assn. Female Execs, Nat. Assn. Security Dealers and Securities Exchange Commn. Republican. Episcopalian. Club: Totowa Racquet (Totowa, N.J.). Home: 764 Bloomfield Ave Montclair NJ 07042 Office: Thomson McKinnon Securities Inc One New York Plaza New York NY 10004

BOSEKER, BARBARA JEAN, educator; b. Milw., Dec. 2, 1944; d. Edward Herbert and Alice Margaret (Maas) B.; student U. Nigeria, Nsukka, 1966; B.S. (hon.) in Secondary Edn. (Elks Nat. and State Youth scholar), U. Wis., Milw., 1968; M.A. in Anthropology (Ford Found. fellow 1968-69, NDEA fellow 1970-71), U. Wis., Madison, 1971, Ph.D. in Edn. (NDEA fellow), 1978; m. Dale Leslie Sutcliffe, Aug. 8, 1975. Chemistry lab. technician Allen-Bradley Corp., Milw., 1963; coordinator Neighborhood Youth Corps, Madison, 1970; program devel. specialist Tchr. Corps, Madison, 1976-77; asst. prof. edn. Occidental Coll., 1978-80, Moorhead State U., 1980—; cons. Inst. Latin Am. Studies, U. Tex., Austin, 1980. Grant writer Fargo-Moorhead (N.D.) Indian Center, 1980. Cert. English tchr. grades 7 through 12, Wis. Mem. NEA, Am. Assn. Colls. Tchr. Edn., Mortar Bd., Phi Kappa Phi, Pi Lambda Theta, Kappa Delta Pi, Sigma Tau Delta, Sigma Epsilon Sigma. Democrat. Christian Scientist. Contbr. articles to Profl. Jours. Home: 3601 11th St S Apt 308 Fargo ND 58103 Office: Moorhead State U Moorhead MN 56560

BOSMA, BARBARA J., psychiat. social worker; b. Grand Rapids, Mich., Apr. 21, 1947; d. Gelmer A. and Cornelia (Van Wyke) Van Noord; B.A. with honors, U. Mich., 1968; M.S.W., Smith Coll., 1975; m. Peter A. Bosma, Mar. 29, 1969; 1 dau., Julia Kelly. Psychiat. social worker Franklin County (Mass.) Public Hosp., Greenfield, 1975-77; clin. supr. Northampton (Mass.) State Hosp., 1977-79; pvt. practice psychotherapy, also cons., 1978-79; psychotherapist Amherst (Mass.) Med. Assos., 1979—; mem. task force on adolescents Mass. Dept. Mental Health; adv. bd. Mass. State Hosp. Edn. Program. Mem. Nat. Assn. Social Workers, Acad. Cert. Social Workers, Amherst Area Feminist Counseling Collective. Mem. Christian Reformed Ch. Author papers in field. Office: 170 University Dr Amherst MA 01002

BOSNER, MARY CATHERINE ANNE, county ofcl.; b. N.Y.C., Aug. 29, 1951; d. Richard John and Mary Catherine (Murray) Cleary; B.A. in Econs. and English, Le Moyne Coll., Syracuse, N.Y., 1973; M.B.A., Rochester (N.Y.) Inst. Tech., 1977; m. Kevin Charles Bosner, Oct. 27, 1973. From budget technician to sr. mgmt. analyst Monroe County (N.Y.), 1974-79; asst. dir. adminstrn. Monroe County Dept. Probation, 1979—. Mem. Penfield Players Community Theatre.

BOSS, ANNA MARIE, color printer-processor; b. Indpls., Feb. 22, 1928; d. Albert Edward and Emma (Hofmann) Bergman; m. Bernard Alden Boss, Apr. 14, 1945; children—Danny Lee, Tylene Ann. Interviewing sec. Puget Sound Naval Shipyard, Bremerton, Wash., 1945-46; partner Bernie Alden Photography Studio, Costa Mesa, Calif., 1951-72; dir., cameraperson Teleprompter, Channel 7, Largo, Fla., 1974; mgr. color labs., Pinellas Park and Clearwater, Fla., 1975-77; color printer-processor Phil Graham, Master Photographer, St. Petersburg, Fla., 1977—. Lic. real estate, Fla. Mem. Am. Hibiscus Soc. Mem. Ch. of Christ. Home: 2524 12th Ave SW Largo FL 33540 Office: 3941 5th Ave N Saint Petersburg FL 33713

BOSSA, DIMPLE GERALDINE, trucking co. exec.; b. Loco, Okla., Dec. 1, 1927; d. David Jeff and Ida Leona Baker; m. Calvin Albert Bossa, Dec. 1, 1946; children—Calvin Alan, Micah Dean. Acct., Baker Constrn. Co., Ratliff City, Okla., 1972-74; owner, mgr. Ratliff City Trucking Co., 1974—. Tchr. Sunday sch. Assembly of God Ch., Ratliff City, 1960-70, supt., 1970-72; tchr. Sunday sch. Velma (Okla.) Assembly of God, 1972-79. Mem. Nat. Fedn. Independent Bus. Clubs: Ratliff City Home Extension (v.p. 1968-69), Ardmore Home Extension (v.p. 1970-71). Home: 1406 N 10th St Duncan OK 73533 Office: PO Drawer 100 Ratliff City OK 73081

BOSSART, WILMA IDA, ins. co. exec.; b. Saline, Mich., Feb. 5, 1933; d. Edward C. and Ida C. (Stahl) B.; student public schs., Saginaw, Mich. Sec., John Hancock Life Ins. Co., San Francisco, 1963-70, office mgr., London, Eng., 1970-73, adminstrv. asst., San Mateo, Calif., 1973-74; regional dir. agencies N. Am. Co. for Life & Health, Seattle, 1974-82. Republican. Lutheran. Home: 2301 S Jefferson Davis Hwy #1206 Arlington VA 22202

BOSSEN, DORIS STEPHENS, electronic co. exec.; b. Glendale, Calif., Oct. 21, 1928; d. William Harrison and Esther Alice (Teachworth) Stephens; B.A., Vassar Coll., 1950; M.A., Ohio State U., 1965, Ph.D., 1968; m. David A. Bossen, Sept. 1, 1950; children—Alison, Amy, Julie, Laura. Tchr., Los Angeles City Schs., 1953-55; asst. to dean of women Ohio State U., Columbus, 1966-67; dir. personnel Measurex Corp., Cupertino, Calif., 1968-72, v.p. personnel, 1972-78, v.p. corp. communications, 1978—. Bd. dirs. Commn. on Status of Women, San Jose, League of Friends, San Jose Friends Outside, San Jose. Mem. Public Relations Soc. Am., Peninsula Profl. Women's Network. Republican. Mem. Christian Ch. Contbr. articles to profl. jours. Home: 780 Mount Home Rd Woodside CA 94062 Office: 1 Results Way Cupertino CA 95014

BOSSETT, ANN JOYCE, hosp. adminstr.; b. LaFayette, La., Mar. 25, 1933; d. Norman Joseph and Mabel Ann (Catalon) Mouton; B.B.A., Tex. So. U., 1979; postgrad. St. Thomas U.Bus., Houston, 1983—; m. Webster D. Bossett; children—Jennifer Louise, Mark Bernard, Greta Michelle. Med. technologist Baylor Coll. Medicine, Houston, 1963-65; Tex. program dir. Xerox Corp., Houston, 1969-74; asst. adminstr. Houston Internat. Hosp. for Hosp. Affiliates, Inc., Nashville, 1977-78, asso. adminstr., Houston, 1978-79; hosp. adminstr. Houston Internat. Hosp., 1979—; cons. Gardner Lab., 1974-77. Chmn., Mental Health-Mental Retardation Adult Adv. Bd., 1982; trustee, rep. Greater Houston Hosp. Council, Mental Health Needs Council; mem. by laws com. Tex. Rehab. Commn., 1981-82. Mem. Am. Mgmt. Assn., Houston C. of C., AAUP, Tex. Hosp. Assn., Nat. Assn. Pvt. Psychiat. Hosps. (state legis. rep.; chmn. manpower com.), Am. Soc. Med. Technology, Tex. Soc. Med. Technology, Washington Bus. Group on Health, Fedn. Am. Hosps., Nat. Assn. Female Execs. Roman Catholic. Home: 6903 Vinewood Circle Houston TX 77088 Office: 6441 Main St Houston TX 77030

BOST, CECILE ROWE, journalist; b. Newton, N.C., Nov. 28, 1924; d. Marcus Marion and Myrtle Cidy (Gross) Rowe; A.B. cum laude, Catawba Coll., 1946; m. Robert Preston Bost, Apr. 28, 1946; 1 son, William Stephen. Tchr. English, Rock Springs High Sch., Denver, N.C., 1947-48; women's editor, producer, newscaster Sta. WNNC, Newton, N.C., 1948-53; editor, producer, air personality Sta. WIRC, Hickory, N.C., 1953-63; free-lance broadcaster, writer, producer Cecile Bost Reporting, 1963—; spl. corr. WBTV News, Charlotte, N.C., 1970—; reporter-producer documentary Cherokee Child (awards), 1977; chosen for Broadcast Pioneers Library, Washington, 1982; lectr. in field; columnist. Recipient N.C. Sch. Bell award, 1966; N.C. AP 1st pl. awards women's news, 1966, 68, 70, state news, 1968, documentary-pub. affairs, 1970; named Catawba County's Leading Citizen in Communications, Catawba News-Enterprise, Newton's Woman of Yr., 1953; recipient Disting. Service award Catawba Coll., 1975, award for bicentennial TV show Freedoms Found., 1976. Mem. Catawba Coll. Alumni Assn. (1st woman pres. 1964-66), Am. Women in Radio and TV (pres. N.C. chpt. 1964-66), N.C. Lit. and Hist. Soc., Internat. Platform Assn., N.C. Art Soc., Hist. Preservation Soc. N.C. Author short stories, one-act plays; contbr. articles to mags. and newspapers. Home: 503 E Herman St Newton NC 28658 Office: 503 E Herman St Newton NC 28658

BOSTIC, JACQUELINE WHITING, post office ofcl.; b. Houston, Jan. 3, 1938; d. Samuel and Martha (Countee) Whiting; student Fisk U., 1955-57, Hofstra Coll., 1958-59; B.S. in Psychology, Tex. So. U., 1977; m. Joseph W. Bostic, July 15, 1960; children—Shelby Lance, Ursula Denise, Kirksten Sinclair, Jacqueline Francelle. With U.S. Postal Service, 1961—, EEO investigator, Memphis, 1974-78, asst. to postmaster, South Houston, Tex., 1978, officer in charge, Highlands, Tex., 1978-79, EEO investigator, Memphis and Houston, 1979-81; EEO investigator, coordinator, Houston, 1981—; clk. craft pres. Am. Postal Workers Union, 1972-74; legis. council Tex. AFL-CIO, 1972-74; del. Harris County Central Labor Council, 1970-74. Bd. dirs. Met. Houston YWCA, 1970-78, 81—, exec. v.p., 1982—, sec., bd. dirs., 1974-76; active Houston Mental Health Assn., 1974; pres. Jack and Jill of Am., Inc., Houston, 1979-81, exec. bd., 1968-81, nat. v.p., 1982—; active Ben Taub Vol. Assn., 1970-72, ARC Vols., 1965-68; sec. Houston Citizens Area Constl. Revision Com., 1973; bd. dirs. W. McGregor Civic Assn., 1978-81; treas. 4th Ward Community Council, 1980—. Recipient Superior Accomplishment award U.S. Postal Service, 1969; Civic award Blue Triangle br. YWCA, 1975; Scholastic Achievement award Tex. So. U. Coll. Arts and Scis., 1977. Mem. Fisk Alumni Assn., Nat. Assn. Postal Suprs., Delta Sigma Theta. Democrat. Baptist. Home: 4410 Roseneath Dr Houston TX 77021

BOSTIC, STEPHANIE EVON, public relations exec.; b. Jamaica, N.Y., Mar. 22, 1953; d. Joseph Edward and Maud Gertrude (Wilson) B.; B.S. in Public Communications, Boston U., 1975. Public relations asst. U.S. Tennis Assn., N.Y.C., 1975-77, asst. dir. public relations, 1977-80, editorial asst. U.S. Tennis Assn. Player Records, 1975, 76, stats. coordinator U.S. Tennis Assn. Tennis Yearbook, 1976, project editor U.S. Tennis Assn. Player Records, 1977, 78, 79, U.S. Open Tennis Championships Media Guides, 1976, 77, 78, 79; dir. public relations Women's Tennis Assn., 1980, D. Parke Gibson Assocs., Inc., N.Y.C., 1981—; feature writer Queens Tribune, 1981. Chmn. public relations com., gen. vol. com. 4th Ann. United Negro Coll. Fund/Arthur Ashe Tennis Benefit, 1978. Mem. Nat. Assn. Media Women (dir. publicity Met. N.Y. chpt. 1979), Nat. Coalition 100 Black Women, Public Relations Soc. Am. (com. on minorities), Boston U. Sch. Public Relations Alumni Assn., (CEBA awards judge), Delta Sigma Theta. Home: 147-15 46th Ave Flushing NY 11355

BOSTON, LEONA, orgn. exec.; b. Joliet, Ill., Aug. 4, 1914; d. Dorie Philip and Margaret (Mitchell) B.; student LaSalle Extension U., 1936-67, 1946, U. Chgo., 1944-45. Tchr., Nat. Stenotype Sch., Chgo., 1937; stenotypist Rotary Internat., Evanston, Ill., 1937-44, sec. to comptroller, 1944-50, head personnel dept., 1950-65, exec. asst. to gen. sec., 1965-77; mem. exec. com. North Shore Festival of Faith, Northfield, Ill., 1978—. Bd. dirs. YWCA, Evanston, 1961-63. Mem. Bus. Profl. Women's Club Evanston (chmn. fin. com. 1977-78). Evangelical (fin. sec. Bible Ch., Winnetka 1965-68, treas. 1979-80). Club: Zonta (v.p., chmn. program com. 1969-70, pres. 1970-71, chmn. membership com. 1976-78, historian 1979-83) (Evanston). Home and Office: 350 W Schaumburg Rd Schaumburg IL 60194

BOSWELL, KATHERINE ANN SMITH, nurse; b. Mineral Wells, Tex., Mar. 31, 1951; d. Samuel Thomas and Frances (Logsdon) Smith; B.S.N., Tex. Woman's U., 1975; m. David Boswell, May 30, 1980; children—Wendy Lee, Joe Neil. Charge nurse Parkland Hosp., Dallas, 1975-76; dir. nursing Resort Lodge Nursing Home, Mineral Wells, Tex., 1977-80; charge nurse Palo Pinto Gen. Hosp., Mineral Wells, 1980; dir. LVN program Weatherford Coll., Mineral Wells, 1980—. Mem. policy council Head Star Program, 1980-83; leader Girl Scouts U.S.A., 1979—; Sun. sch. tchr. St. Luke's Episcopal Ch., 1980—, Episcopal Women's Orgn. Mem. Tex. Assn. Vocational Nurse Educators, Tex. Jr. Coll. Tchrs. Assn. Home: 610 SW 6th St Mineral Wells TX 76067 Office: Route 2 Mineral Wells TX 76067

BOSWELL, WINTHROP PALMER, writer; b. Bklyn., Dec. 17, 1922; d. Carleton Humphries and Winthrop (Bushnell) Palmer; B.A., Smith Coll., 1943; postgrad. U.S.C., 1956-58; M.A., San Francisco State Coll., 1969; m. James Orr Boswell, Oct. 26, 1946; children—James Lowell, Rosalind Palmer, John Winthrop. Research asst. G-2 Spl. Br., U.S. Army, 1943-46; research asst. Hoover Instn., Stanford, Calif., 1976; docent Filoli, 1979-80; writer; books include: Irish Wizards in the Woods of Ethiopia, 1971; The Snake in the Grove, 1972; The Killing of the Snake King in Abyssinia, 1973; Hisperica Famina or The Garden of God, 1974. Mem. Assn. Former Intelligence Officers Am., Soc. History of Discoveries, Medieval Assn. of Pacific. Club: Peninsula Country (San Mateo, Calif.), Francisca (San Francisco).

BOTCHIS, GLORIA SEBASTIANA, speech pathologist; b. Torrington, Conn., Mar. 7, 1932; d. Salvatore and Marianna (Cataluccio) Corpaci; A.A., Hillyer Coll., 1953; B.A., U. Hartford, 1954; M.S., Boston U., 1957; m. Stephen Joseph Botchis, June 21, 1959; children—Paul, Marianne. Tchr. English and social studies, drama dir. Torrington High Sch., 1954-56; speech pathologist Torrington Public Schs., 1957-63, Groton (Conn.) Public Schs., 1963-64, Waterford (Conn.) Public Schs., 1966-68, 70—. Second v.p., pres. bd. dirs. YWCA of Southeastern Conn., 1979-81; pres. Greek Orthodox Ladies Philoptochos Soc., 1974-78, 80—. Recipient cert. appreciation Southeastern Conn. C. of C., 1979. Mem. Am. Speech and Hearing Assn. (cert. clin. competence-speech), Conn. Speech and Hearing Assn., Waterford Fedn. Tchrs. Democrat. Home: 41 Beacon Hill Dr Waterford CT 06385 Office: Waterford Public Schs 48 Dayton Rd Waterford CT 06385

BOTELLE, SHARON KAY, educator; b. Schuyler, Nebr., Feb. 10, 1941; d. John Raymond and Margaret Mathilda (Weber) Swanda; B.A., Midland Coll., 1962; M.S., Bemidji (Minn.) State U., 1974; m. Warren E. Botelle, Jr., June 9, 1962 (div.); 1 dau., Katharine Margaret; stepchildren—Douglas Andrew, Leslie Ann. Tchr., Sch. Dist. #4, Fremont, Nebr., 1962-63; tchr. Fremont Sr. High Sch., 1963-65; substitute tchr. Branford (Conn.) Public Schs., 1965-69; tchr. English, reading Leigh (Nebr.) Public Schs., 1969-72; reading resource tchr. Schuyler (Nebr.) Public Schs., 1972-75; reading dir., title I adminstr. Faribault (Minn.) Area Schs., 1975—; chmn. Faribault Literacy Project. Treas., Luth. Ch. Women, Schuyler, 1974-75. Mem. Internat. Reading Assn., Minn. Reading Assn., Assn. Supervision and Curriculum Devel., Nat. Assn. Adminstrs. State and Fed. Edn. Programs, Minn. Assn. of Adminstrs. State and Fed. Edn. Programs (pres.), Nat Council Tchrs. English, Minn. Council Tchrs. English, Nat. Literacy Assn., Minn. Literacy Council, Delta Kappa Gamma. Home: 125 Evergreen Estetes Faribault MN 55021 Office: 2855 NW 1st Ave Faribault MN 55021

BOTHWELL, CHUNG THI NGUYEN, ins. co. exec.; b. Saigon, Vietnam, Nov. 19, 1949; came to U.S., 1969, naturalized, 1978; d. Tang Van and Nghi Thi (Tran) Nguyen; B.B.A., U. Miami (Fla.), 1974, M.B.A., 1980; m. Anthony Peirson Xavier Bothwell, Dec. 22, 1973; children—Anthony Peirson Xavier II, Thomas Theodore Nguyen. Budget analyst Fla. Power & Light Co., Miami, 1973-78; asst. to asso. dean grad. program Sch. Nursing, U. Wis., Madison, 1978-79; mgr. budgets and costs Central Life Assurance Co., Madison, 1980—. Project chmn. Madison chpt. ARC, 1978-79; human services commr., City of Madison, 1982—. Internat. student scholar, 1973. Mem. Nat. Assn. Accts., Am. Soc. Personnel Adminstrn., Am. Soc. Public Adminstrn., Acad. Mgmt. Republican. Roman Catholic. Club: Madison Quota. Home: 6301 Romford Rd Madison WI 53711 Office: 709 N Segoe Rd Madison WI 53705

BOTINE, KAREN ELIZABETH, educator, state ofcl.; b. Pocahontas County, Iowa, Mar. 21, 1942; d. Lester Ferdinand and Eleanor Barbara (Wiese) B.; B.S. in Home Econs. Edn., Iowa State U., 1963, M.S., 1970. Home econs. instr. Clarion (Iowa) Pub. Schs., 1963-68; dorm housemother Iowa State U., Ames, 1968-69, 69-70; asst. supr. home econs. edn. N.D. Bd. Vocat. Edn., Bismarck, 1970-76, state supr. home econs. edn., 1976—; cons. FHA/HERO, 1980, workshop instr., 1971, 76; mem. steering com. project on parenting edn. Bush Found., 1979-81; part-time adult edn. instr. Bismarck home econs. program, 1978-80; presenter Nat. Vocat. Home Econs. Conf., 1981. Mem. exec. com. to reactivate N.D. Commn. on Status of Women, 1972, Bismarck-Mandan Am. Lutheran Ch. Coordinating Council, 1978-80; mem. N.D. Safety Council, 1979-80, sec., 1979. Mem. NEA, N.D. Edn. Assn., Home Econs. Edn. Assn., Am. Vocat. Assn., N.D. Vocat. Assn., Nat. Assn. State Suprs. Vocat. Home Econs., Internat. Fedn. Home Econs., Am. Home Econs. Assn., N.D. Home Econs. Assn., Bismarck-Mandan Home Econs. Assn., N.D. Nutrition Council, Bismarck-Mandan Nutrition Council, Missouri Valley Adult Edn. Assn., N.D. Adult Edn. Assn., AAUW, Omicron Nu, Phi Kappa Phi, Delta Kappa Gamma. Office: State Capitol 15th Floor Bismarck ND 58505

BOTSCH, REBECCA JEAN, jewelry co. sales rep.; b. Hamilton, Ohio, Nov. 12, 1950; d. Raymond Martin and Ramona JoAnn (Arndt) B.; student Kent State U., 1969-71 (exchange student U. of Ams., Mexico City, 1970, 71); A.S., Fashion Inst. Tech., 1972. Asst. buyer, gen. sales mgr. Foley's, Houston, 1973-74; area sales mgr. Lazarus, Columbus, Ohio, 1974-75; nat. fashion coordinator, N.J. sales rep., S.E. region dist. sales mgr., N.Y.C., N.E. regional sales mgr. Ciani/Monet Jewelers div. Gen. Mills, 1976-81; southeastern regional sales rep. Arrowhead Jewelers, Atlanta, 1981—. PTA scholar, 1968. Mem. Nat. Assn. Female Execs. Methodist. Office: PO Box 7496 Marietta GA 30062

BOTSKO, LINDA LOUISE, property mgr.; b. Ambridge, Pa., June 7, 1948; d. Hugo Richard and Geraldine Louise (Saylor) Iorfido; B.S. in Edn., Slippery Rock State Coll., 1970; m. George John Botsko, June 27, 1970; children—Bryan Richard, Cristin Lee. Tchr. health and phys. edn. Apex (N.C.) High Sch., 1970-71; real estate agt. Thomas Realty, St. Louis, 1973-75; property mgr. Cameron Brown Co., Raleigh, N.C., 1975-78, Forest Glen Apts., Pitts., after 1978; public relations dir. Sawyer Bus. Sch., Pitts., 1978. Democrat. Roman Catholic. Club: Racquetball. Home: T10 Forest Green Dr Coraopolis PA 15108 Office: Forest Glen Apts 1112 Forest Green Dr Coraopolis PA 15108

BOTT, MARCELINE LOUISE, nurse; b. Craig, Colo., Feb. 9, 1929; d. Harmon January and Eva Irene (Miller) Bordeaux; R.N., St. Luke's Hosp. Sch. Nursing, 1950; B.A., U. Redlands, 1977; m. Thomas Albert Bott, Jan. 20, 1951; children—Kelly, Kim, Tracy, Nannette. Staff nurse Natrona County Hosp., Casper, Wyo., 1950-52, Washakie Meml. Hosp., Worland, Wyo., 1953-54; office nurse/scrub nurse Dr. Anderson, Worland, 1955-56; office nurse for County Health Dir., Casper, 1959-60; charge nurse/respiratory ward Rancho Los Amigos Hosp., Downey, Calif., 1964-67; critical care nurse Kaiser Found. Hosp., Bellflower, Calif., 1967-73, asst. dir. nursing service, 1973-80, adminstrv. asst. nurse recruiter, 1980—. Active, PTA, 1957-81; leader Bluebird Campfire Girls, 1959-60; leader Brownie troop, Girl Scouts U.S.A., 1957-59. Mem. Nat. Nurse Recruiter Assn., So. Calif. Assn. Nurse Recruiters. Democrat. Congregationalist. Clubs: Royal Neighbors of Am., Rainbow Girls. Home: 7631 Hershey Dr Buena Park CA 90620 Office: 9400 E Rosecrans Ave Bellflower CA 90706

BOTT, MARGARET DEATS, banker; b. Houston, May 27, 1942; d. Wayne Lawton and Margaret (Brown) Deats; student English, U. Houston, 1961-64; m. H.J. Bott, May 27, 1970. Owner, dir. Loft-on-Strand Gallery, Galveston, Tex., 1971-78; staff writer Galveston Daily News, 1972-75; asst. v.p. communications and tng. Land Bank Tex., Houston, 1979—. Past bd. dirs. Galveston YWCA, Galveston Conv. and Visitors Bur., Galveston County Cultural Arts Council, Galveston Hist. Found. Recipient Anson Jones award med. writing, 1973, 75, Am. Psychol. Assn. award social service writing, 1974. Mem. Houston C. of C. Office: PO Box 2649 Houston TX 77001

BOTTARI, MARIANNA TERESA, public relations exec.; b. Phila., Nov. 17, 1941; d. Guido and Malvina Rose (Seccia) Bottari; student U. Pa., 1962-64; cert. Charles Morris Price Sch. Journalism and Advt., 1965-66; student Temple U., 1966; grad. The Fund Raising Sch., 1980; m. Marc Lee Rubin, Jan. 2, 1982. News relations asst. Smith Kline & French Labs., Phila., 1962-64; public relations asst. St. Luke's and Children's Med. Center, Phila., 1964-66; adminstrv. asst. Goodway Printing & Pub. Co., Phila., 1966-69; public relation asst. Thomas Jefferson U. Hosp., Phila., 1969-71; public relations dir. Albert Einstein Med. Center, Phila., 1971-74, John Muir Meml. Hosp., Walnut Creek, Calif., 1974-77, Peralta Hosp., Oakland, Calif., 1977-80; community info. dir. Sequoia Hosp. Dist., Redwood City, Calif., 1980-82; public info. dir. Valley Meml. Hosp., Livermore, Calif., 1982—; career advisor Charles Morris Price Sch. of Journalism & Advt., 1966-73. Bd. dirs. Coop Center Council, 1977-78; v.p. Sun Country Homeowners Assn., 1977-79. Served with USNR, 1979-81. Recipient MacEachern Award citation Acad. Hosp. Public Relations, 1973, Cert. of Merit, 1976. Mem. Nat. Assn. Female Execs., Nat. Assn. Hosp. Devel., Hosp. Public Relations Assn. No. Calif., Internat. Assn. Bus. Communicators, Acad. Hosp. Public Relations. Home: 315 Gil Blas Rd Danville CA 94526 Office: 1111 E Stanley Blvd Livermore CA 94550

BOTTI, ELAINE MARY, psychologist; b. Bklyn., Apr. 19, 1947; d. Thomas Carmine and Mary (Senzino) B.; B.A., Hofstra U., 1969, Ph.D. (fellow), 1981; M.A. (fellow), New Sch. for Social Research, 1971. Research asst. William Alanson White Inst., 1971; research analyst Addiction Services Agy., N.Y.C., 1972; research scientist N.Y. State Dept. Mental Hygiene, 1972-74, sr. research scientist, 1974-76; clin. instr. psychiatry SUNY Downstate Med. Center, 1975—; research scientist Westchester County Dept. Social Services, 1977-79; asso. dir. research Addiction Research and Treatment Corp., 1980—. NIMH fellow, 1976. Mem. Am. Psychol. Assn., Assn. Women in Sci. Contbr. articles to profl. jours. Home: 69 1st Pl Brooklyn NY 11231

BOTTO, STEPHANIE ANN, investment exec.; b. Memphis, Aug. 5, 1949; d. Vincent Mitchell and Jeanne Abbott (Nicoll) B.; student Nova U., 1981—. With trust dept. ops. and investments Barnett Bank, Hollywood, Fla., 1973-74; ops. mgr. Kidder Peabody, Ft. Lauderdale, Fla., 1974-75; investment exec. Shearson Am. Express, Hallandale, Fla., 1975-81, Bache Halsey Stuart Shields, Hallandale, 1981—. Pres. Tallwood West Condo Assn.; dir. Big Bros./Big Sisters of Broward, 1976-80; Confraternity Christian Doctrine; tchr. Nativity Catholic Ch. Club: Miramar Lioness (2d v.p.). Office: 2100 E Hallandale Beach Blvd Hallandale FL 33009

BOTTOM, DONNA LOUISE, med. technician; b. Henderson, Ky., June 17, 1953; d. Charles Lee and Anna Rebecca (Benham) Dillehay; A.A.S., Henderson Community Coll., 1973; m. Brent E. Bottom, Dec. 6, 1975; 1 dau., Melissa Gayle. Staff, Meml. Hosp., Jasper, Ind., 1973-76, St. Joseph's Hosp., Huntingburg, Ind., 1977; med. lab. technician Community Meth. Hosp., Henderson, 1977—. Mickey Rabye Meml. scholar, 1973. Mem. Am. Soc. Clin. Pathologists. Address: 25 Kennedy Circle Henderson KY 42420

BOUCHER, ALFHEIDUR, communications exec.; b. Saud'arkrokur, Iceland, May 12, 1934; came to U.S., 1954, naturalized, 1962; d. Valgard Jean and Johanna (Arnadottir) Blondal; ed. Icelandic schs., Inst. Orgn. Mgmt. at Mills Coll.; children—John, Johanna, Jamie, Jacqueline, Jennifer. Owner, operator sporting goods store, Fairbanks, Alaska, 1962-70; field rep. to U.S. Sen., Juneau, Alaska, 1974-76; exec. v.p. Juneau C. of C., 1976-77; adminstrv. asst. to U.S. Sen. Mike Gravel, Washington, 1977-81; dir. govt. relations Ely, Guess & Rudd, Washington, 1981-82; dir. media services Rothstein/Buckley Inc., Washington, 1982—. Treas. Juneau Bicentennial Com., 1976; mem. Alaska Centennial Com., 1970, Juneau Little Theater; bd. dirs. Alaska Goldpanners Baseball Team. Recipient award City of White Horse (Can.), 1977; named Bus. Woman of Month, recipient certs. of appreciation City and Borough of Juneau. Mem. Nat. Assn. Female Execs., Washington Woman's Network. Democrat. Lutheran. Clubs: Kenwood Golf and Country (Bethesda, Md.), Quota. Contbr. Washington Report to Alaska Jour. Commerce and Industry. Home 5403 Cromwell Dr Bethesda MD 20816 Office: 2900 M St NW Washington DC 20007

BOUCHER, BETTY JANE, corp. sec.; b. Tampa, Fla., Oct. 16, 1944; d. Cecil Raymond and Bessie (Dean) B.; grad. Draughon's Bus. Sch., 1964. Clk., Philco Fin. Co., Memphis, 1964-65; with C.R. Boucher Constrn. Co., Memphis, 1965—, corp. sec., bookkeeper, 1975—. Bd. dirs. WAGES, Inc., 1979-82, treas., 1980-82; mem. Women's Exec. Council Memphis, 1980—, bd. dirs., 1981-82, rec. sec., 1982-83, nominee for bus. woman of yr., 1982; del. Memphis Jobs Conf., 1981; chmn. Pub. Affairs Council of Memphis, 1982-83. Named hon. mem. Memphis City Council, 1981. Mem. Nat. Assn. Women in Constrn. (pres. Memphis chpt. 13 1975-76, 78-79, Woman of Yr. in Constrn., Memphis chpt. 13 1981), Nat. Assn. Female Execs. Baptist. Club: Quota of Memphis (past pres.). Home: 3008 Joyce Ln Memphis TN 38116 Office: 2469 Frisco Memphis TN 38114

BOUCOT, KATHARINE ROSENBAUM (MRS. SAMUEL B. STURGIS), physician; b. Phila., Sept. 6, 1903; d. Morris and Hannah (Rottenberg) Rosenbaum; student U. Pa., 1922-23, Pa. State U., 1934-36; M.D., Woman's Med. Coll. Pa., 1942; M.P.H., Johns Hopkins U., 1954; L.H.D. (hon.), Keuka Coll., 1960; D.Sc. (hon.), Beaver Coll., 1967; D.M.Sc. (hon.), Woman's Med. Coll., 1968, Hahnemann Med. Coll., 1978; Litt.D. (hon.), Thomas Jefferson U., 1978; m. Joseph R. Boucot, Mar. 23, 1944 (dec. May 5, 1962); children—Arthur J., Nancy (Mrs. Milton Curtis Cummings, Jr.); m. 2d, Samuel Booth Sturgis, Nov. 18, 1964. Intern, Woman's Coll. Hosp., Phila., 1942-43; resident Herman Kiefer Hosp., Detroit, 1944; chest specialist, Phila., 1945—; cons. Woman's Coll. Hosp., Nat. Cancer Inst., Phila. Gen., Vets, Landis State hosps. (all Phila.); prof., chmn. dept. preventive medicine, 1952-68, clin. prof. medicine Woman's Med. Coll. Pa., 1952-68, emeritus prof. preventive medicine, 1968—; asso. medicine U. Pa. Grad. Sch. Medicine, 1951-63. Vice pres. William B. Lake Found., 1959-77; bd. dirs., hon. life mem. Phila. div. Am. Cancer Soc.; pres. Phila.—Montgomery Lung Assn., 1963-65; hon. trustee Beaver Coll. Recipient Elizabeth Blackwell award, 1956; Disting. Dau. Pa. award, 1964; Golden Plate award Am. Acad. Achievement, 1965; award Albert Einstein Woman's Aux., 1967; Phila. Gimbel award, 1968; named Woman of Year, Pa. State U., 1967; Trudeau medal Nat. Tb and Respiratory Disease Assn., 1969; Alumnae Achievement award Women's Med. Coll. Alumnae Assn., 1970; Penn Club award, 1972; Hall of Fame honoree Am. Lung Assn., 1980. Fellow Am. Pub. Health Assn., Am. Coll. Preventive Medicine (pres. 1969-70, Disting. Service award 1973; Katharine Boucot Sturgis ann. lectr. 1979), A.C.P., Phila. Coll. Physicians (v.p. 1970-72, pres. 1972-74); mem. Am., Pa. (ho. of dels. 1961-72), Phila. County (pres. 1968, Strittmatter award 1972) med. assns., Am. Thoracic Soc. (v.p. 1960-61, hon. mem., past pres. Eastern sect.), Pa. Trudeau Soc. (pres. 1958), Acad. Occupational Medicine, Pa. Public Health Assn. (exec. com. 1963), Am. Med. Women's Assn. (hon.), Laennec Soc. (past pres.), Am. Epidemiol. Soc., Woman's Med. Coll. Alumnae Assn. (past pres.), Alpha Omega Alpha. Episcopalian. Club: Cosmopolitan. Contbr. articles to profl. jours. Chief editor AMA Archives of Environmental Health, 1960-71. Address: 600 E Cathedral Rd A417 Philadelphia PA 19128

BOUDREAU, LORRAINE JEANETTE, nursing adminstr.; b. W. Warwick, R.I., Aug. 24, 1943; d. Joseph Onesime and Beatrice Violet (Lecuivre) Boudreau; Diploma in Nursing, Roger Williams Gen. Hosp., 1964; B.S. in Nursing, U. Va., 1974; M.Nursing, UCLA, 1977. Nurse specialist in alcohol rehab. VA Med. Center, Sepulveda, Calif., 1974-78, coordinator community psychiatry program, 1978-80; asst. chief nurse VA Med. Center, Kerrville, Tex., 1980—; asst. clin. prof. UCLA, 1978-79. Served with Nurse Corps, U.S. Army, 1965-71. Recipient Sustained Performance award, VA, 1979; Comdr.'s Spl. Recognition, 6222d USAR Sch., 1980. Mem. Res. Officers Assn., Assn. Mil. Surgeons of U.S., Tex. Soc. Hosp. Nursing Adminstrs., Tex. Hosp. Assn., Nat. League for Nursing, others. Republican. Roman Catholic. Office: Memorial Blvd Kerrville TX 78028

BOUGHTON, MAUREEN ELLA, mktg. exec.; b. Sydney, Australia, Feb. 11, 1944; came to U.S., 1965, naturalized, 1973; d. Patrick Yelverton and Joan Patricia (Heath) Williams; student Australian schs.; divorced; children—Edward, III, Tracy Yelverton. Account exec. Sta. KKOP-FM, Redondo Beach, Calif., 1976-77; pres. MAV Enterprises, Ventura, Calif., 1977—, Boughton Enterprises Inc., Ventura, 1980—; fashion and beauty editor South Bay mag., Calif. Good Life mag., Big Valley mag., also Skin Care mag., 1977-80. Mem. Nat. Assn. Female Execs., Am. Soc. Profl. and Exec. Women. Republican. Christian Scientist. Office: 2611 Ruhland Suite 4 Redondo Beach CA 90278

BOULANGER, CAROL SEABROOK, lawyer; b. N.Y.C., Sept. 14, 1942; d. John M. and Anne S. (Schlaudecker) Seabrook; B.A., Swarthmore Coll., 1964; LL.B., U. Pa., 1969; m. Jacques P. Boulanger, June 1, 1974; 1 son, Rodolphe. Admitted to N.Y. bar, 1970, U.S. Tax Ct., 1970; asso. firm Baker & McKenzie, N.Y.C., 1969-71; asso. Wender, Murase & White, N.Y.C., 1971-75, partner, 1975-82; partner firm Boulanger, Finley & Hicks, N.Y.C., 1982—. Founding mem. ARCS Found., Inc., N.Y. chpt., 1973-80, sec., 1973-75, v.p., 1975—; bd. mgrs. Swarthmore Coll., 1977-81. Mem. Am. Bar Assn., Assn. Bar City N.Y. (com. on internat. law 1980—). Office: 405 Park Ave New York NY 10022

BOULDING, ELISE MARIE, sociologist, educator; b. Oslo, July 6, 1920; came to U.S., 1923, naturalized, 1929; d. Joseph and Birgit (Johnsen) Biorn-Hansen; B.A., Douglass Coll., 1940; M.S., Iowa State Coll., 1949; Ph.D., U. Mich., 1969; m. Kenneth Boulding, Aug. 31, 1941; children—John Russell, Mark David, Christine Ann, Philip Daniel, William Frederic. Research asso. Survey Research Inst., U. Mich., 1957-58, Mental Health Research Inst., 1959-60, research devel. sec. Center for Research on Conflict Resolution, 1960-63; prof. sociology, project dir. Inst. Behavioral Sci., U. Colo., Boulder, 1967-78; prof., chmn. dept. sociology Dartmouth Coll., Hanover, N.H., 1978—, Montgomery vis. prof., 1978-79; mem. program adv. council Human and Social Devel. Program, UN U., 1977-80, v.p. UN U. council, 1980—. Internat. chairperson Women's Internat. League for Peace and Freedom, 1967-70; bd. dirs. Inst. for World Order. Recipient Disting. Achievement award Douglass Coll., 1973, Ted Lentz Peace prize, 1977; named Woman of Conscience, Nat. Council of Women, 1980; Danforth fellow, 1965-67; Faculty fellow U. Colo., 1974; Lindisfarne fellow, 1976-80; recipient Jesse Bernard award Am. Sociol. Assn., 1981. Mem. AAAS, AAUP, Am. Sociol. Assn., Internat. Sociol. Assn., Internat. Peace Research Assn., Internat. Studies Assn., Nat. Council Family Relations, World Future Studies Fedn., World Future Soc., Colo. Women's Forum. Quaker. Author: Image of the Future (transl. from Dutch), 1961; From a Monastery Kitchen, 1976; (with Nuss, Carson and Greenstein) Handbook of International Data on Women, 1976; The Underside of History: A View of Women Through Time, 1976; Women in Twentieth Century World, 1977; (with Burgess and K. Boulding) Social System of Planet Earth, 1980; Children's Rights and the Wheel of Life, 1979; Bibliography for World Conflict and Peace, 1979; (with others) Women and the Social Costs of Economic Development: Two Colorado Case Studies. Home: 890 Willowbrook Rd Boulder CO 80302 Office: Dept Sociology Dartmouth Coll Hanover NH 03755

BOUNDS, SARAH ETHELINE, historian; b. Huntsville, Ala., Nov. 5, 1942; d. Leo Deltis and Alice Etheline (Boone) Bounds; A.B., Birmingham-So. Coll., 1963; M.A., U. Ala., Tuscaloosa, 1965, Ed.S. in History, 1971, Ph.D., 1977. Tchr. social studies Huntsville City Schs., 1963, 65-66, 71-74; residence hall adv., dir. univ. housing U. Ala., Tuscaloosa, 1963-65, 68-71; instr. history N.E. State Jr. Coll., Rainsville, Ala., 1966-68; instr. history U. Ala., Huntsville, 1975, 78-80, dir. Weeden House Mus., 1981—; asst. prof. edn., supr. student tchrs. U. North Ala., Florence, 1978. Mem. AAUW, Assn. Tchrs. Educators, Nat. Council Tchrs. Social Studies, NEA, Ala. Hist. Assn., Ala. Assn. Historians, Ala. Assn. Tchrs. Educators, Huntsville Hist. Soc., Historic Huntsville Found., Alpha Delta Kappa, Kappa Delta Pi, Phi Alpha Theta. Methodist. Club: Huntsville Pilot. Home: 1100 Bob Wallace Ave SE Huntsville AL 35801

BOUQUARD, MARILYN LLOYD, congresswoman; b. Ft. Smith, Ark., Jan. 3; d. James Edgar and Iva Mae (Higginbotham) Laird; grad. Shorter Coll., 1963; m. Joseph P. Bouquard; children—Nancy Lloyd Smithson, Mari, Mort II, Deborah Lloyd Riley. Mem. 94-98th Congresses from 3d Tenn. Dist. Democrat. Office: Room 2334 Rayburn House Office Bldg Washington DC 20515 *

BOURG, BONNIE JEAN, univ. adminstr.; b. New Orleans, Feb. 17, 1927; d. Francis Floyd and Malvin Marguerite (Boudreaux) Bourg; B.A., Sophie Newcomb Coll., Tulane U., 1947; M.S., La. State U., 1948, Ph.D., 1979. Instr. in health and phys. edn. F. T. Nicholls Jr. Coll., La. State U. (name later changed to Nicholls State U.), 1947-50, head dept. women's health and phys. edn., 1950-63, dean women, 1963-77, dean student devel., 1977, asst. v.p. student affairs, 1977—; ednl. cons.; dir. Intra-coastal Co.; adv. bd. 1st Nat. Bank, Houma; mem. manpower planning adv. council Dist. III, La. Dept. Labor. Mem. City of Thibodaux (La.) Planning Commn., 1967-75; bd. dirs. Le Petit Theatre de Terrebonne, 1952-64, pres., 1957. Recipient Pres's. award Nicholls State U., 1975, named Hon. Alumna, 1975, Disting. Service award, 1980; Delta Kappa Gamma Soc. Internat. Epsilon State scholar, 1975-76; Berneta Minkwitz scholar, 1979-80; cert. tchr., counselor, La. Mem. Nat., La. assns. women deans, adminstrs. and counselors, Am., La. personnel and guidance assns., Am. Coll. Personnel Assn., Am. Assn. Higher Edn., Assn. for Psychol. Type, La. Sch. Counselors Assn., La. Folklore Soc., Terrebonne Hist. Soc., Delta Kappa Gamma, Phi Delta Kappa, Phi Mu. Democrat. Roman Catholic. Club: Thibodaux Music. Home: 306 Cherokee Ave Thibodaux LA 70301 Office: Nicholls State U Thibodaux LA 70301

BOURG, THERETHER ANDRUS, registered nurse; b. New Orleans, May 5, 1932; d. Earl and Agnes (Deville) A.; asso. degree nursing La. State U., Alexandria, 1971; m. Malcolm Bourg, Sept. 1950 (div.); children—Trudy, Malcolm (dec.), Conrad, Jacquelyn; m. 2d, Billy Max Nosler, Mar. 6, 1982 (dec. June 1982). Staff nurse Bunkie (La.) Gen. Hosp., 1971-73; VA Hosp., Pineville, La., 1976; dir. nurses Hessmer (La.) Nursing Home, 1973-75; dir. nursing Bayou Chateau Nursing Center, Simmesport, La., 1976-81; nurse Savoy Meml. Hosp., Mamou, La., 1981-82; dir. nursing Oakwood Village Nursing Care Center, Lafayette, La., 1982—; chmn. geriatrics continuing edn. La. State U., Alexandria, 1975—. Mem. Am. Bus. Women's Assn., Am. Nurses Assn., Nursing in Action (regional chmn.), La. Health Care Assn. (chmn. 1976-78). Democrat. Baptist.

BOURGAULT, CLODAUGH MARIE, nurse; b. Mt. Hope, Kans., Apr. 1, 1940; d. Julius John and Ellen Marie (Preisser) Blasi; R.N., St. Francis Hosp., Wichita, Kans., 1961; m. Francis Adelard Bourgault, Apr. 27, 1963; children—Kimberly Ann, James Michael, John Scott. Emergency room nurse St. Francis and St. Joseph hosps., Wichita and Phoenix, 1961-64, med. nurse, 1964-66, surg. nurse, 1966-68, head nurse med. surg. floor, 1969, emergency room nurse, 1970-72, 74-76; office nurse, office mgr., X-ray technician for osteo. physician, Pittsburg, Kans., 1977—. Active PTA St. Mary's Sch.; mem. altar soc. St. Mary's Ch. Mem. Am. Nurses Assn., Wives Aux. Kans. Assn. Osteo. Medicine (public relations). Home: 2103 Colonial Dr Pittsburg KS 66762 Office: 409 N Walnut Pittsburg KS 66762

BOURGAULT, KATHLEEN CROWLEY, librarian; b. Portland, Maine, Feb. 7, 1955; d. Clarence Basil and Edna Mae (Hadakin) Crowley; student U. Maine, 1973-77, U. N.H., 1979-80; m. Keith Ray Bourgault, Nov. 23, 1973. Asst. children's librarian Auburn (Maine) Public Library, 1971-73; children's librarian Alvan Bolster Ricker Meml. Library, Poland, Maine, 1973-78, head librarian, 1978—. Mem. Maine Library Assn., Small Public Libraries Assn. (exec. bd.). Roman Catholic. Home: 79 Bennett Ave Auburn ME 04210 Office: Box 98 Route 26 Poland ME 04273

BOURNE, AVIS COTTRELL (MRS. C. FRED BOURNE), educator; b. Boston, Sept. 1, 1905; d. Charles T. and Carolyn (Frink) Cottrell; A.B., Boston U., 1927, A.M., 1931; cert. U. Grenoble, 1927; m. Charles Fred Bourne, Aug. 14, 1932; 1 son, Richard Cottrell. Tchr., Sterling, Mass., 1927-28, 34-48, asst. prin., 1948-62, dir. guidance, 1962-71, certified psychometrist, 1962—; tchr., Walpole, Mass., 1928-31, Norwood, Mass., 1931-32. Adv. council women's div. Mass. Dept. Commerce. Mem. Wachusett Regional Sch. Dist. Com., 1955-67, chmn., 1958-59; mem. Sterling Hist. Commn., 1968—. Mem. AAUW (pres. No. Mass. br. 1957-61), Mass. Fedn. Bus. and Profl. Women's Clubs (various com. chairmanships and offices, state pres. 1957-59, dist. chmn. 1965-67, state parliamentarian 1969-71), Daus. Colonial Wars, Daus. Am. Colonists (Mass. regent 1973-76, hon. state regent 1976—, nat. historian 1976-79, nat. chmn. nat. def. 1979— nat. officers club 1980—), Daus. 1812 (v.p. Mass. 1977-78, pres. 1978—), Am. Mcht. Marine Library Assn. (nat. com. chmn.), Colonial Dames XVII Century (state rec. sec.; chpt. 1st v.p.), DAR, Mass. Tchrs. Assn., NEA (legis. agt. for Worcester County), New Eng. Women (v.p. Augusta Colony 1978-81, pres. 1981), Sterling (founder, trustee, charter pres.), Waterville hist. socs., Belgrade Heritage and Mus. Soc. (a founder), Mass. Sch. Counselors Assn. (trustee), Am. Personnel and Guidance Assn. (sec. Worcester County chpt.), New Eng. Guidance and Personnel Conf. (rep.), Mass. North Central Guidance Assn. (hon. life, pres. 1967-68, dir. 1968—), Piscataqua Pioneers, Belgrade Lakes C. of C., Pi Lambda Theta, Phi Sigma Pi, Theta Upsilon, Delta Kappa Gamma (state com. on personal growth and services). Clubs: Waterville Community Garden (v.p.), Oakland Garden. State Fedn. Garden (chmn. protocol com.). Home: Clinton Rd Sterling MA 01564 also PO Box 167 Belgrade Lakes ME

BOURNE, LUCIE JEAN WHITEHEAD, social worker; b. San Antonio, Jan. 15, 1928; d. Laurence Conner and Lucie Amelia (Keblinger) Whitehead; B.A., Wellesley Coll., 1950; M.S.W., Worden Sch. Social Service, San Antonio, 1970; m. Francis Stanley Bourne, Sept. 21, 1954; children—Laurence Nicholas Keblinger, Peter Stanley Whitehead, Elizabeth Amelia Keblinger. Tchr. social studies Burbank Sch., San Antonio, 1953-54; regional rep. Pre-Sch. Council, Washington, 1959-61, dir. summer pre-sch. program Am. Internat. Sch., New Delhi, India, 1962-63, bd. govs., chmn. cultural and social work liaison com., 1965-66; med. social worker Bexar County (Tex.) Hosp., 1968-70; substitute tchr. Sidwell Friends Sch., Washington, 1972-78; coordinator apprentice program Sidwell Friends Middle Sch., 1978—. Dir., Dumbarton Sr. Center, 1980-81; bd. dirs. Washington Modern Dance Soc., 1980—, Manipal Edn. and Med. Found. Mem. Nat. Assn. Social Workers, Am. Fgn. Service Women's Assn., AAUW. Democrat. Presbyterian. Clubs: Wellesley (v.p. Washington, 1978-80), Cleveland Park. Home: 3303 Highland Pl NW Washington DC 20008

BOUSLEY, GLORIA DIANE PARRISH, educator; b. Evansville, Ind., Dec. 3, 1932; d. Thomas Clifford Parrish and Cecelia Elizabeth (Graul) Parrish Armstrong; B.A. in Bus. Edn., Evansville Coll., 19S3; M.S. in Bus. Edn., Ind. U., Bloomington, 1958; Ph.D. in Occupational Edn., So. Ill. U., Carbondale, 1977; m. Donald R. Bousley, Aug. 2, 1958 (dec.). Guidance counselor, bus. tchr. Bridgeport (Ill.) Twp. High Sch., 1953-71; bus. tchr., chmn. bus. and human devel. div. Olney (Ill.) Central Coll., 1971—; adj. asst. prof. vocat. studies So. Ill. U., Carbondale, 1979—; mem. Ill. State Adv. Panel for Coop. Edn. at Post Secondary Level, 1979; mem. U. Ill./Ill. State Bd. of Edn. Staff Devel. adv. com., 1977-79; active in Ill. State Competency Based Edn. project, 1977—. Sec., 1st v.p. N.W. Territory Art Guild, 1968-71; chmn. found. com. Bus. and Profl. Women's Orgn., 1978, 79; vol. counselor Ill. State Dept. Vocat. Rehab., 1972—, Southeastern Ill. Mental Health Center, 1976-77. Recipient Nat. Office Mgmt. award, 1953, State Ill. grantee, 1979. Mem. Ill. Bus. Edn. Assn. (1st v.p. 1980, pres. 1981), Ill. Vocat. Assn. (dir. 1980), Am. Vocat. Assn. (state membership chmn. 1979), Nat. Bus. Edn. Assn. (state membership chmn. 1979), Nat. Secs. Assn., Internat. Soc., Eastern Ill. Bus. Edn. Assn., So. Ill. Bus. Edn. Assn., Phi Kappa Phi, Delta Kappa Gamma, Delta Pi Epsilon, Iota Lambda Sigma, Phi Mu (life). Contbr. articles to profl. publs.; co-author chpt. Business Education into the Eighties, 1979. Home: 13 Brian Dr Olney IL 62450 Office: Olney Central Coll Route 3 Olney IL 62450

BOUTILIER, BARBARA ELIZABETH, banker; b. Cranston, R.I., June 13, 1924; d. Albert William and Anna Deakin Amelia (Ross) Ash; diploma Edgewood Secretarial Sch., 1944; children—Linda Ann, Edward Laird. With Providence Inst. for Savs. (now Old Stone Bank), 1944-52, 65—, employee benefits mgr., 1976—. Advisor, Jr. Achievement, Providence, 1976-77; collector various fund drives; mem. troop com. Girl Scouts U.S.A., Cranston, 1968-70; adv. 4-H, Scituate, R.I., 1945-47. Mem. Nat. Assn. Bank Women (award, scholarship chmn. 1982-83), Am. Legion (pres. chpt. 1948), Am. Soc. Women Accts. (treas. 1977-78, pres. R.I. chpt. 1979-81), Personnel Club R.I. Home: 51 Friendly Rd Cranston RI 02910 Office: Old Stone Bank 150 S Main St Providence RI 02901

BOVARD, FAITH JEAN, economist; b. N.Y.C. Dec. 13, 1938; d. Martin and Grace vom Lehn; student CCNY, 1956-60; B.A., Hofstra U., 1969; M.B.A., U. Houston, 1980; children—Victoria, Jacqueline, Tracy. Staff mgr. Rayburn Country, Houston, 1973; exec. sec. Gulf Oil Corp., Houston, 1974-76, fin. analyst, 1976-80, sr. econ. analyst, 1980—. Mem. jr. bd. Kent County Hosp., Dover, Del., 1973; bd. dirs. Dover Newcomers Club, 1973. Mem. Beta Gamma Sigma. Republican. Club: Forum (Houston). Office: PO Box 2100 Houston TX 77001

BOVINGDON, MARGARET ELIZABETH GARDNER (MRS. GEORGE G. BOVINGDON), educator, civic worker; b. Tacoma, Sept. 11, 1937; d. Hilton B. Gardner and Isabelle (Anderson) G.; grad. Annie Wright Seminary, 1955; B.A., Stanford U., 1959, M.A., 1960; Orton-Gillingham Cert. in lang. disability instrn., 1978; m. George G. Bovingdon, Aug. 24, 1963; children—Gardner, Margaret, Peter Geil. Tchr., Los Altos (Calif.) Sch. Dist., 1961-62, The Helen Bush Sch., Seattle, 1962-64; lang. disability tutor, Seattle, 1977—. Mem. Jr. League Seattle, chmn. comm. resource bur.; mem. Helen Morrison Orthopedic Guild; sec. Arts for Youth Council; mem. bd. Seattle Jr. Programs; mem. Laurelhurst Sch. Adv. Council. Mem. N.W. Gifted Child Assn., The Orton Soc., Inc. Republican. Episcopalian. Clubs: Seattle Tennis, Sunset (Seattle). Home: 4104 50th Ave NE Seattle WA 98105 Office: The Villa Acad 5001 NE 50th St Seattle WA 98105

BOWATER, MARIAN LARSON, art gallery dir.; b. Emmons, Minn., Sept. 5, 1924; d. James Melvin and Hannah Elvira (Olson) Larson; student Gustavus Adolphus Coll., 1941-42; m. John J. Bowater, Jan. 22, 1945; children—Christine, Julianna, John James. Owner, dir. Bowater Gallery of Fine Art, Los Angeles, 1975—; active mus. shows; lectr. art clubs. Mem. Art Dealers Assn. So. Calif. Home: 12300 Kenny Dr Granada Hills CA 91344 Office: PO Box 648 Los Angeles CA 90048

BOWDEN, BARBARA MORGAN CUNNINGHAM, educator; b. Piedmont, Ala., June 20, 1933; d. Earl Sparks and Ilah Velma (McCord) Morgan; B.A., Auburn U., 1955; M.A., U. So. Miss., 1968; Ph.D., U. Ala., 1981; m. Carol C. Cunningham, Mar. 19, 1955 (dec.); children—Carolee Cunningham, Andrew Reed Cunningham, Miles McCord Cunningham; m. 2d, William A. Bowden, Jr., Dec. 19, 1976. Tchr. schs., Ala. and Miss., 1956-71; counselor Bayview Jr. High Sch., Gulfport, Miss., 1972-74; drug abuse counselor Gulfport City Schs., Gulf Coast Drug Abuse Center and Gulf Coast Mental Health Center, 1974-76; bilingual edn. specialist Birmingham (Ala.) City Schs., 1976-77; drug edn. specialist Ala. Dept. Edn., U. Ala., Birmingham, 1978-80; Title I instructional specialist Ala. State Dept. Edn., Montgomery, 1980-81, testing coordinator, 1981—; ednl. cons. State of Miss., 1972-74. Bd. dirs. Gulf Coast Symphony Guild, 1973-76, chmn., 1974; bd. dirs. Little Theatre, Gulfport, 1970-76; sec. Gulf Coast Drug Abuse Center, 1973-76. Recipient Gulf Coast Outstanding Citizen award Sta. WGCM-AM-FM, 1974. Mem. Am. Psychol. Assn., Nat. Assn. Alcoholism Counselors, AAUW, Ala. Personnel and Guidance Assn., Ala. Reading Assn., Ala. Assn. Suprs. and Dirs., Delta Kappa Gamma, Kappa Delta Pi. Democrat. Methodist. Clubs: Vestavia Country, Silhouettes, Crescent. Author: Experimental Careers, 1982; contbr. articles in field to profl. publs. Home: 2509 Beaumont Circle Birmingham AL 35216 Office: 601 State Office Bldg Dexter Ave Montgomery AL 36104

BOWDEN, MARGARET WILLIAMS, day care center adminstr.; b. Fordyce, Ark., Sept. 10, 1909; d. Handy and Allie Elizabeth (Moore) Williams; B.S.E., U. Pine Bluff, 1948; M.S., U. So. Calif., 1955; postgrad Tuskegee Inst., U. Ark., Monticello, U. Ark., Little Rock; m. George Simpson, July 7, 1928; 1 dau., Betty Ruth Simpson. Tchr. public schs., Ashley County, Ark., 1925-47; supr. Jeanes Co., Hamburg, Ark., 1947-48; prin. high sch. Wilmot, Ark., 1948-71; asst. supt. schs., Wilmot, 1971-73; adminstr. Williams Day Care Center, Crossett, Ark., 1974—; instr. nursing Crossett extension Winthrop Sch. Nursing; notary public, 1966—. Pianist, Bapt. Ch., also dir. vacation Bible Sch. Mem. Ashley County Tchrs. Assn. (past pres.), Ark. Tchrs. Assn., Alumni Assn. U. Ark. (Pine Bluff), S.E. Dist. Women's Assn. Ark. (2d v.p.), Alumni Assn. U. So. Calif. Clubs: Better Tng. of Wilmot and Crossett (dir.), Order Eastern Star, Amaranth (state dir. music). Home: 309 N Arksansas St Crossett AR 71635 Office: 107 N Florida St Crossett AR 71635

BOWDEN, MARY-LUCAS WILLIAMS, piano tchr.; b. Montgomery, Ala., Jan. 26, 1928; d. Thomas Bascom and Maude Bell (Graham) Williams; B.S. in Edn., U. Ala., 1948, postgrad., 1948-49; m. Warren Franklin Bowden, June 9, 1949; 1 dau., Pamela Victoria. Tchr. Decatur (Ga.) High Sch., 1954-55; pvt. tchr. piano, Alexandria, Va., 1967—; performer piano, dulcimer, organ, harmonica-melodica. Mem. NEA, Nat. Hon. Soc., Alpha Xi Delta. Republican. Methodist. Club: Hollin Hall Pool Assn. Author: The Key Signature Study, 1974; The Major Chinese Mode, 1979; One Family of Musical Modes Consisting of Three Sub-Family Modes, 1981. Home and office: 1609 Baltimore Rd Alexandria VA 22308

BOWE, CHARLEEN BERNICE, mech. equipment distbg. co. exec.; b. Peoria, Ill., Aug. 1, 1944; d. Charles E. and Colleen Esther (Cartwright) Bartholomew; student Ill. Central Coll.; children by previous marriage—Cynthia Lynn White, Thomas Page White. Various secretarial positions, West Palm Beach, Fla., 1964-68, Washington, Ill., 1968-69; sec. to pres. Linden & Co., Inc., Peoria, Ill., 1969-71, Yeomans Distbg. Co., Peoria, 1971-73; exec. adminstrv. sec. to br. mgr. Pitney Bowes, 1973-74; sec., treas. Bowe & Associates, Inc. (name changed to Water Power Inc. 1980), Peoria, 1974-78, pres., 1978—; mem. Constrn. Action Com. of Peoria, 1977—; mem. State of Ill. Plumbing Code Adv. Council. Leader, Kickapoo council Girl Scouts U.S., 1968-73. Mem. Peoria Econ. Devel. Assn. (dir.), Pvt. Industry Council (dir.), Nat. Assn. Female Execs., Nat. Assn. Women in Constrn. (past pres. Peoria chpt. 1977-78), Central Ill. Indsl. Assn., Nat. Assn. Women Bus. Owners (pres. chpt.), Peoria C. of C., Greater Peoria Contractors and Builders Assn. Presbyterian. Home: Rural Route 2 PO Box 273D Chillicothe IL 61523 Office: 8811 N Pioneer Rd Peoria IL 61615

BOWEN, BRENDA MAE, lab. technician; b. Lee County, Pennington Gap, Va., Aug. 20, 1949; d. James Howard and Inez Belle (Stanley) Wells; cert. Appalachian Regional Hosp. Sch. Cert. Lab. Assts., 1968; m. Dennis F. Bowen, Apr. 12, 1969; 1 dau., Ashley Denise. Lab. technician Harlan Appalachian Regional Hosp., Harlan, Ky., 1968-74, Lee County Community Hosp., Pennington Gap, 1974-75, 76; chief lab. technician Pennington Med. and Surg. Group, 1976—. Mem. Am. Soc. Clin. Pathologists, Nat. Cert. Agy. for Med. Lab. Personnel. Home: 848 Burgan Rd Pennington Gap VA 24277 Office: 132 Maple Ave Pennington Gap VA 24277

BOWEN, LINDA CAROLYN, educator; b. Graceville, Fla., Sept. 1, 1944; d. James Olon and Lottie Myrl (Woodham) Polston; B.B.A., Ga. State U., 1967, M.S. in Profl. Accountancy, 1971, Ph.D., 1972; m. Chester Edward Bowen, Oct. 20, 1962; children—Stephen Todd, Bradley Scott, Geoffrey Edward. Sr. asst., auditor Peat, Marwick, Mitchell & Co., C.P.A.s, Atlanta, 1967-69; asst. prof. acctg. Oglethorpe U., 1972-74; asst. prof. acctg. U. N.C., Chapel Hill, 1974-78, asso. prof., 1978—. Bd. dirs. Wesley Found., also chmn. fin. com., 1978-81. Recipient Tanner award as outstanding tchr. U. N.C., 1979; C.P.A., N.C., Ga. Mem. Am. Acctg. Assn., Am. Inst. C.P.A.s, N.C. Assn. C.P.A.s, Beta Alpha Psi, Beta Gamma Sigma. Methodist. Home: 815 Churchill Dr Chapel Hill NC 27514 Office: Sch Bus Adminstrn U NC New Carroll Hall Chapel Hill NC 27514

BOWEN, NANCY LEE, cosmetics distbr.; b. Marion, Kans., Apr. 20, 1936; d. Bernard Edward and Mildred Genevieve (Bailey) Broadstreet; B.A. in Home Econs. Edn. (tuition scholar), Sterling (Kans.) Coll., 1958; m. Rodney Mason Bowen, June 27, 1959; children—David Lane, Brent Edward (adopted), Cynthia Lynne, Amy Janelle. Tchr. home econs. Sterling High Sch., 1958-60; clothing instr. Junction City (Kans.) Jr. High Sch., 1963-64; owner, operator Fashion Two Twenty Cosmetics Distbn. and Tng. Center (name changed to Lady Finelle 1981), Manhattan, Kans., 1965—; cosmetics cons. Jaycees Pageant, 1968—. Republican precinct committeewoman, 1971, 80—; chaperone Miss Manhattan-K-State to Miss Kans. Pageant, 1969-74. Recipient Outstanding Jaycee Jayne pin, 1972; named Jayne of Month, 1973, 74. Mem. Home Economists in Homemaking (pres. 1967-68), Am. Home Econs. Assn., Kans. Home Econs. Assn., Beta Sigma Phi (chpt. pres. 1976-77). Republican. Baptist. Clubs: Couples Dinner Bridge, Pilot (pres. local club 1978-79, treas. Kans.-Mo. dist. 1981-82, dist. lt. gov. 1982-83, dist. gov. 1983—). Home: 751 Elling Dr Manhattan KS 66502 Office: 2312 Anderson Ave Manhattan KS 66502

BOWENS, GLORIA FURR, ednl. adminstr.; b. Detroit, Apr. 15, 1927; d. Leon Lewis and Iva Rose (Talbot) Furr; B.S., Tufts Coll., 1947; Ed.M., State Coll. Boston, 1968; Ed.D., Harvard U., 1975; 1 dau., Stephanie T. Sci. tchr. Boston Public Schs., 1961-71, asst. to the dir. orientation for integration, 1971-73; asst. supt. schs. Roosevelt (L.I., N.Y.) Sch. Dist., 1974-77; asst. dir. urban schs. collaborative Northeastern U., Boston, 1977-79, dist. IX coordinator curriculum and competency resources, 1979-81; acting dir. dept. mgmt. Boston Public Schs., 1981—; ptnr. antique shop, Newburyport, Mass., 1982—. Mem. Nat. Council Adminstrv. Women Edn. (exec. bd. 1970-73), Am. Assn. Sch. Adminstrs., North Shore Antiques Assn., Phi Delta Kappa. Office: Boston Public Schs 26 Court St Boston MA 02121

BOWER, FAY LOUISE, nurse educator, univ. dean; b. San Francisco, Sept. 10, 1929; d. James Joseph and Emily Clare (Andrews) Saitta; B.S., San Jose State Coll., 1965; M.S. in Nursing, U. Calif., San Francisco, 1966, D.Nursing Sci., 1978; m. Robert Davis Bower, July 2, 1949; children—R. David, Carol Jean Tomei, Dennis James, Thomas John. Office nurse, Palo Alto, Calif., 1950-55; staff nurse Stanford (Calif.) Hosp., 1964-66; charge nurse newborn nursery, summers 1966-67, staff nurse premature research center, 1967-73; asst. prof. nursing San Jose (Calif.) State Coll., 1965-70, asso. prof., 1970-75, prof., 1975-81, chairperson, 1978-81; dean U. San Francisco, 1981—; lectr. U. Calif., San Francisco, 1975. Mem. AAUP, Health Edn. Media Assn., Public Health Assn. Calif., Santa Clara Health Edn. Council, Commonwealth Club San Francisco, Calif. Nurses Assn., Calif. Tchrs. Assn., Sigma Theta Tau, Phi Kappa Phi. Author: Theoretical Foundations of Nursing, 3 vols., 1972, The Process of Planning Nursing Care, 1972, 77, 82; Fundamentals of Nursing Practice, 1978. Contbr. articles to profl. jours. Home: 1820 Portola Rd Woodside CA 94062 Office: U San Francisco 2130 Fulton St San Francisco CA 94117

BOWER, JANIS ELAINE, mfg. co. exec.; b. Berwyn, Ill., Oct. 21, 1940; d. Verne Franklin and Elaine (Swangren) B.; A.A., Coll. DuPage, 1979; student Elmhurst Coll., 1979—. Service rep., supr. service unit, supr. service and copy sect. R.H. Donnelley Telephone Directory Co., Chgo., 1960-67; products mgr. M.W. Riedel & Co., Alhambra, Calif., 1968-70; with Gen. Electric Co., Plastics div., Pittsfield, Mass., 1970—, sec., 1970-72, sales corr., 1972-73, sales service specialist, 1973-74, sales rep., 1975-78, nat. account mgr., 1978—. Mem. Soc. Plastics Engrs., Soc. Plastics Industry. Office: 1 Plastics Ave Pittsfield MA 01201

BOWER, MARGE EMILY, guidance counselor; b. Chgo., June 8, 1941; d. Elmore Arthur and Elsie Ruth (Sauer) B.; B.A., U. Mich., 1963; M.A., Loyola U., Chgo., 1967; postgrad. Loyola U., DePaul U., Bradley U., Western Mich. U., U. Mich. Tchr. English, sch. newspaper advisor South Shore High Sch., Chgo., 1963-67; guidance counselor Elmwood Park (Ill.) High Sch., 1967—. Chmn. com. out-of-state admissions and scholarships U. Mich. Nat. Alumnae Council, 1972-75, governing bd., 1972-75. Wall St. Jour. Newspaper Fund fellow, 1967. Mem. Nat. Assn. Women Deans, Adminstrs. and Counselors (exec. bd. 1979-81), Ill. Assn. Women Deans, Adminstrs. and Counselors, Am. Personnel and Guidance Assn., Ill. Guidance and Personnel Assn., Am. Sch. Counselors Assn., Ill. Sch. Counselors Assn., NEA, Ill. Edn. Assn., U. Mich. Alumni Assn. Club: North Shore U. Mich. Alumni. Editorial bd. Ill. Guidance and Personnel Assn. Quar., 1981-84, NAWDAC Jour., 1981-83. Home: 555 W Cornelia Ave Apt 707 Chicago IL 60657 Office: Elmwood Park High School 8201 W Fullerton Ave Elmwood Park IL 60635

BOWER, MARY MARGARET, library adminstr.; b. Detroit, Mar. 15, 1932; d. Raymond Gladstone and Mary Elizabeth (Carothers) B.; A.B., Wayne State U., 1956; M.A., U. Mich., 1965; m. Michael O. Braun, May 10, 1954 (div. 1963); children—Kolya Marie, Deor Elizabeth. Librarian, Detroit Public Library, 1965-67; asst. librarian Ferris State Coll., Big Rapids, Mich., 1968-72, head reference librarian, 1972-75, head info. services, 1976-78, head public services dept., 1978-79, acting dir., 1979, dir. library, 1980—; trustee Mich. Library Consortium. Mem. AAAS, Am. Soc. Info. Sci., ALA, Spl. Libraries Assn., Assn. Mich. State Coll. and Univ. Library Dirs. Author: Black History: A Bibliography, 1970; Black Literature, 1972, 73. Home: PO Box 1181 15848 157th Ave Big Rapids MI 49307 Office: Ferris State College Library Big Rapids MI 49307

BOWERS, HELEN SCHLANGEL, research co. tech. rep.; b. N.Y.C., Oct. 5, 1947; d. S. Mark David Schlangel and Gerta (Felsenburg) Schlangel Kahn; B.A., N.Y. U., 1969; M.A., Fairleigh Dickinson U., 1972; M.B.A. in Mktg. Mgmt.; Pace U., 1981; m. David Alan Bowers, Dec. 20, 1970. Research technician Ciba Geigy Corp., Ardsley, N.Y., 1969-73; sales rep. Hoyt Labs. div. Colgate Co., Needham, Mass., 1973-74; sales rep. BioQuest div. Becton Dickinson Corp., Cockeysville, Md., 1974-77; tech. rep. New Eng. Nuclear Co. div. E.I. duPont de Nemours, Boston, 1977—. Mem. Assn. Women in Sci., Health Physics Soc. Jewish. Club: Sheldrake Yacht. One woman show Jewish Mus., N.Y.C., 1961. Home: The Bowerie RFD 6 Crest & Hilltop Lake Mahopac NY 10541

BOWERS, JANETTE LAWHON, univ. adminstr.; b. Conroe, Tex., Nov. 13, 1933; d. Tot and Leslie Mae (Watkins) Lawhon; B.S., Sam Houston State U., 1954; M.A., Sul Ross State U., 1970; m. Richard Bowers, June 3, 1967; children—Connie, Clay, Cole, Kelly, Casey, George. Tchr. phys. edn. public schs., Pasadena, Cypress-Fairbanks, Tex., 1955-66; with health and phys. edn. dept. Sul Ross State U., Alpine, Tex., 1968-75, dir. adult and continuing edn., 1975—. Pres. chpt. Am. Cancer Soc., 1981, bd. dirs. Tex. div., 1981; sec. bd. trustees Alpine Ind. Sch. Dist., 1974-80; founder, chmn. bd. Sunshine House, 1977-82. Mem. Tex. Assn. Community Service and Continuing Edn. (pres. 1980), Tex. Assn. Health, Phys. Edn. and Recreation, Tex. Public Employees Assn., Am. Legion Aux., Delta Kappa Gamma. Presbyterian. Club: Pilot (gov. Tex. Dist. 1981-82). Home: Drawer 1440 Alpine TX 79830 Office: Sul Ross State University Box C 141 Alpine TX 79830

BOWERS, LAURA BODDIE JONES, librarian; b. Canton, Miss., June 24, 1915; d. Ben Hamlet and Laura Boddie (West) Jones; B.A., Newcomb Coll., New Orleans, 1936; B.S. in L.S., La. State U., Baton Rouge, 1937, M.S. in L.S., 1940; student Nat. Park Service Guide Sch., 1969; m. Earle Cooper Bowers, Jr., May 9, 1943; 1 son, Earle Cooper III. Librarian, Tulane U., 1937-40, Northwestern State U., 1940-42; army librarian Camp McCain, Miss., 1942-43; asst. mgr. Jones Drug Store, Canton, 1950-63; park guide Nat. Park Service, Manassas, Natchez Trace, Vicksburg, Miss., 1963-70; librarian Miss. Coll., 1970-71; dir. library services U. So. Miss., Natchez, 1972—; extra in TV spls. Freedom Road, Beulah Land, others. Bd. dirs. Canton Public Library, Old Capitol Mus. (Vicksburg); docent Jefferson Coll. Hist. Site (Washington, Miss.); active Natchez Guides Assn. (lic. guide), Natchez Hist. Soc., Friends of Jefferson Coll., ARC. Mem. ALA, Assn. La. Librarians, AAUW, DAR, Phi Mu. Episcopalian. Club: Natchez Garden. Compiler indexes: Silhouettes of Settlers, 1973; Education in the Old Southwest, 1975. Home: 415 Cherry St Natchez MS 39120 Office: Duncan Park University of Southern Mississippi Natchez MS 39120

BOWERS, PATRICIA ELEANOR FRITZ, economist; b. N.Y.C., Mar. 21, 1928; d. Edward and Eleanor (Ring) Fritz; student (scholar) Goucher Coll., 1946-48; B.A., Cornell U., 1950; M.A., N.Y.U., 1953, Ph.D., 1965. Statis. asst. Fed. Res. Bank N.Y., N.Y.C., 1950-53; lectr. Upsala Coll., East Orange, N.J., 1953-59; researcher Fortune Mag., N.Y.C., 1959-60; teaching fellow N.Y.U., N.Y.C., 1960-62, instr., 1962-64; economist Bklyn. Coll., CUNY, 1964—. Mem. Am. Econ. Assn., Econometric Soc., Met. Econ. Assn. (sec. 1963-68, pres. 1974-75), Am. Statis. Assn. (univs. chmn. ann. forecasting confs. 1970-71, 71-72). Club: Talbot Country (Easton, Md.). Author: Private Choice and Public Welfare, 1974. Home: 145 E 16th St New York NY 10003 Office: Dept Econs Brooklyn Coll CUNY Brooklyn NY 11210

BOWERSOCK, LINDA CHERYL, hosp. exec.; b. Nashville, Mar. 24, 1947; d. Ira Lafayette and Vera Lucile (Walker) Smith; B.A., Towson (Md.) State U., 1970, M.B.A., Loyola Coll., 1983; m. Chiles V.A. Bowersock, June 8, 1967 (dec.); 1 son, Justin. Office mgr. Bremer, Connolly, Hawfield, P.C., Washington, 1972-76; dept. adminstr. Children's Hosp., Washington, 1976-79; adminstrv. dir. Washington Hosp. Center, 1979—. Trustee, Nat. Presbyn. Sch., Washington, 1977-79. Mem. Am. Mgmt. Assn., Am. Coll. Hosp. Adminstrs., Am. Hosp. Assn., Bus. and Profl. Women's Club, Assn. Health Care Adminstrs. Nat. Capital Area. Office: 110 Irving St Washington DC 20010

BOWLES, FRANCES MARIE, personnel exec.; b. Paducah, Ky., Feb. 5, 1938; d. Jesse Raymond and Anna Lou (Varnell) Walker; student Murray State U., 1955-57; m. James Everette Bowles, July 9, 1973; children—Robert Wayne, Michael Ray, Benjamin Earl. Collection correspondent, office supr. Sears Roebuck & Co., Paducah, 1957-65; credit mgr. Jeans Dept. Store, Paducah, 1965-67; mgr., estimator Slay Plumbing & Heating, Paducah, 1967-72; office mgr. Amick & Helm C.P.A., Madisonville, Ky., 1972-74; mgr. Arch Mgmt. Corp., Madisonville, 1974—, exec. asst. to pres. of affilated cos., 1974—. Vol. United Way, Madisonville, Cancer Soc., Madisonville. Mem. Nat. Sec. Assn. (v.p. Madisonville chpt. 1974, pres. elect 1975, pres. 1976—), Nat. Assn. Exec. Secs., Nat. Assn. Female Execs. Democrat. Baptist. Home: 1061 Parkwood St Madisonville KY 42431 Office: PO Box 88 38 W Arch St Madisonville KY 42431

BOWMAN, GEORGIANA HOOD, mgmt. cons.; b. Middletown, Ohio, Jan. 19, 1937; d. George Simpson and Corinne Lula (Hunter) Hood; B.S. in Edn., Wilberforce U., 1965; M.A. in Adult Edn., Ohio State U., 1973, Ph.D. in Humanities Edn., 1976; m. Harris C. Bowman, Sept. 10, 1961. Tchr., Columbus (Ohio) Public Schs., 1965-72, ethnic studies planner, 1972-73, research planning and auditing specialist Title III project, 1973-74; coordinator black student programs and devel. Ohio State U., 1974-80; pres. G.H. Bowman Co., Mgmt. Consultants, Columbus, 1980—; human relations cons. Columbus Public Schs. Sec., bd. dirs. YWCA; bd. dirs. Columbus Urban League; 2d v.p., sec., bd. dirs. North Central Mental Health Center; bd. dirs., exec. bd. South Side Settlement House; 2d v.p. Columbus chpt. NAACP.; charter mem. Columbus Assn. Performing Arts Colleagues. Recipient cert. of appreciation Ohio Ho. of Reps., 1980, public service awards Delta Sigma Theta, Sertoma Club, Alpha Kappa Alpha, Big Bros./Big Sisters Assn. Mem. Youth Service Guild, Nat. Council Negro Women (Columbus pres., Public Service award), Phi Delta Kappa (nat. pres.), Pi Lambda Theta. Club: Circle Lets, Inc. Home: 2671 Cleveland Ave Columbus OH 43211 Office: 2671 Cleveland Ave Columbus OH 43211

BOWMAN, GLADYS WHEAT, candle co. exec.; b. Chillicothe, Ohio, Oct. 16, 1915; d. Martin and Lucy Marcella (Sower) Bower; student U. Cin., 1955-60; cert. in advt. So. Ohio Bus. Coll., 1960; m. Harry P. Bowman, July 27, 1953; children—Patricia L. Wheat, Kathryn. Advt. mgr. Fenton Dry Cleaners, 1947-53; exec. sec. mng. dir. public relations Steelcraft Mfg. Co., 1954-61; mgr. Colonial Village, 1961-68; dir. public relations Sta. WCMI, Ashland, Ky., 1968-69; mgr., dir. Candles 'n Such, Cin., 1970-75; product devel. mgr. Candle-Lite, Inc., Loveland, Ohio, 1975—, asst. gen. mgr., 1980—. Active Gen. Protestant Orphans Home. Mem. Nat. Candle Assn. (public relations chmn. Washington, nat. pres. 1981-82), Nat. Candle Mfrs. Assn. (dir.), Color Mktg. Group, Nat. Assn. Ret. People, Gold Star Wives Am., Smithsonian Inst., Huntington Advt. Club (hon., award), Cin. Advt. Club (hon.). Republican. Methodist. Contbr. articles to women's mags.; patentee in field. Home: 8430 Burns Ave Cincinnati OH 45216 Office: 301 W Loveland Ave Loveland OH 45140

BOWMAN, HAZEL LOIS, educator; b. Plant City, Fla., Feb. 18, 1917; d. Joseph Monroe and Annie (Thoman) B.; A.B., Fla. State Coll. for Women, 1937; M.A., U. Fla., 1948; postgrad. U. Md., 1961-65. Tchr., Lakeview High Sch., Winter Garden, Fla., 1939-40, Eagle Lake Sch., Fla., 1940-41; welfare visitor Fla. Welfare Bd., 1941-42; specialist U.S. Army Signal Corps, Arlington Hall, Va., 1942-43; recreation worker, asst. procurement officer ARC, CBI Theater, 1943-46; lab. technician Am. Cyanamid Corp., Brewster, Fla., 1946-47; instr., asst. prof. gen. extension div. U. Fla., Fla. State U., 1948-51; free-lance writer, editor, indexer, N.Y., Fla., 1951-55; staff writer Tampa (Fla.) Morning Tribune, 1956; staff writer, telegraph editor Winter Haven (Fla.) News-Chief, 1956-57; registrar/admissions officer U. Tampa, 1957-59; coll. counselor, Atlantic states, 1959-60; registrar/freshman adviser Towson State Tchrs. Coll., Balt., 1960-62; dir. student personnel, guidance, admissions Harford Jr. Coll., Bel Air, Md., 1962-64; instr. York (Pa.) Coll., 1965-66, asst. prof. English, journalism, 1966-69; tchr. S.W. Jr. High Sch., Lakeland, Fla., 1969-70; tchr. learning disabled Vanguard Sch., Lake Wales, Fla., 1970-82. Mem. AAUW, Assn. Supervision and Curriculum Devel., Internat. Reading Assn., Nat. Council Tchrs. English, Mortar Bd., Common Cause, NOW, Alpha Chi Alpha, Chi Delta Phi. Club:

Altrusa. Editor: Tampa Altrusan, 1958-60. Home: 511 NE 9th Ave Mulberry FL 33860 also 2549 S George St York PA 17403

BOWMAN, JEAN LOUISE, civic worker; b. Albuquerque, Apr. 3, 1938; d. David Livingstone and Charlotte Louise (Smith) McArthur; student U. N.Mex., 1956-57, U. Pa., 1957-58, Rocky Mountain Coll., 1972-74; B.S. with high honors, U. Mont., 1982, postgrad. in law, 1982—; children—Carolyn Louise, Joan Emily, Amy Elizabeth, Eric Daniel. Dir. Christian edn. St. Luke's Episcopal Ch., 1979-80; dir. 1st Bank West; bd. trustees Rocky Mountain Coll., 1972-80; bd. dirs. Billings (Mont.) Area C. of C., 1977-80; mem. City-County Air Pollution Control Bd., 1969-74, chmn., 1970-71; del. Mont. State Constnl. Conv., 1971-72, sec. conv., 1971-72; chmn. County Local Govt. Study Commn., 1973-76; mem. Billings Sch. Dist. Long Range Planning Com., 1978-79; former pres. Billings LWV, Silver Run Ski Club. Named one of Billings' most influential citizens, Billings Gazette, 1977. Republican. Home: 301 Northview Dr Missoula MT 59803

BOWMAN, KAREN, jazzercise instr.; b. Fall River, Mass., July 21, 1949; d. Albert F. and Kathleen C. (Lavigne) Doucette; A.S., Johnson & Wales Coll., 1970; m. Michael Allen Bowman, July 18, 1974. Sec., Dept. Army, Pentagon, Washington, 1970-71, AID, Vientiane, Laos, 1972-74, Am. embassy, Vienna, Austria, 1974-75, Beckman Microbics, Carlsbad, Calif., 1976-79, Am. embassy, Ankara, Turkey, 1979-81; jazzercise instr. Am. ambassador's residence, Ankara, 1979-81, Mem. Nat. Assn. Scuba Diving Schs. Office: Bank of Am 73700 Gorgonio Dr Twentynine Palms CA 92277

BOWNS, BEVERLY HENRY, coll. adminstr.; b. Ontario, Cal.; d. Glenn Alby and Irene Beatrice (Rygymyr) Henry; B.S. in Nursing, Columbia U., 1959; M.P.H., U. Minn., 1960; Dr.P.H., Johns Hopkins Sch. Hygiene and Public Health, 1968; m. Aug. 30, 1947. Indsl. nurse Sausalido (Calif.) Shipyards, 1945; public health nurse, dist. supr., Pocatello, Idaho, 1953; instr., adminstrv. asso. undergrad. program U. Calif. Coll. Nursing, San Francisco, 1960-63; asst. prof. grad. program Coll. Nursing, U. Md., Balt., 1968; asso. prof., chmn. community health nursing Coll. Nursing, Vanderbilt U., Nashville, 1970-72; prof., chmn. community health family nursing, grad. program Coll. Nursing, U. Tenn., Center for Health Sci., Memphis, 1972-77; dean Coll. Nursing, Rutgers, State U. N.J., Newark, 1977-81, prof. II, 1981—. Bd. dirs. Comprehensive Rape Crisis Center, Memphis, Mid-south Home Health Services. Frances Payne Bolton scholar; HEW Community Health Services grantee. Fellow Am. Public Health Assn., Am. Acad. Nursing; mem. Am. Nurses Assn., Nat. League Nursing, Council Nurse Researchers, Sigma Theta Tau, Pi Lambda Theta. Contbr. articles to various publs. Office: Rutgers Univ Coll Nursing University Ave Newark NJ 07102 *

BOWZER, LOREE, banker; b. Alliance, Nebr., Jan. 17, 1934; d. George Delbert and Minnie Alma (Haney) Gardner; student public schs., Hyannis; m. Merton M. Bowzer, Nov. 23, 1952; children—Creta, James, Kara. Sec., American Nat. Bank, Sidney, Nebr., 1954-74, asst. cashier, 1974-82, loan officer, 1977—, asst. v.p., 1982—. Pres. PTA Central Sch., 1974-76; sponsor Episcopal Youth Group. Mem. Nat. Assn. Bank Women, DAR, Ladies C. of C. Republican. Home: 2360 Maple St Sidney NE 69162 Office: 901 Tenth Ave Sidney NE 69192

BOX, JULIA CONSTANCE HART, anesthesiologist; b. Chgo., Oct. 24, 1927; d. Harry Gilbert and Mary Ann (Mikshunas) Hart; B.S., U. Ala., 1948; M.D., Tulane U., 1952; m. William Arthur Box, June 4, 1949; children—Michael Edward, Mary Catherine, James William. Intern, U. Miss. Med. Center, Jackson, 1952-53, resident in anesthesiology, 1959-61; pvt. practice gen. medicine, Newton, Miss., 1953-58; partner Anesthesia Services, Mobile, Ala., 1961-62, Drs. Johnson, Lane, Box, Bryant & Eubanks, Mobile, 1962-67, Drs. Johnson & Box, P.A., Mobile, 1967-74; officer Anesthesia Assos., Mobile, 1974-82, Anesthesia Assos. Mobile, P.C., 1982—; co-dir. respiratory therapy dept. Mobile Gen. Hosp., 1970-79, dir. Sch. Anesthesia for Nurses, 1970-78. Mem. Med. Soc. Mobile County, Am. Soc. Anesthesiologists Mobile Area Anesthesiologists, Am. Thoracic Soc., Am. Coll. Chest Physicians, Internat. Anesthesiology Research Soc., AMA, Soc. Cardiovascular Anesthesiologists, Soc. Neurol. Anesthesia and Neurologic Supportive Care, Am. Soc. Regional Anesthesia. Roman Catholic. Address: 133 Louiselle St Mobile AL 36690

BOXX, RITA MCCORD, banker; b. Greenwood, S.C., Aug. 10, 1930; d. John Thomas Logan and Dempsie (Dixon) McCord; student public schs.; m. John Douglas Boxx, Apr. 17, 1949; children—John Stephen, Eric Wesley, Merry Christine. Asst. mgr. Greenwood Ins. Agy., 1951-65, mgr., 1967-80; with Bankers Trust S.C., Greenwood, 1951—, asst. v.p. charge ins. dept., 1980—; tchr. ins. seminars. Mem. Nat. Assn. Ins. Women, Ind. Ins. Agts. Greenwood, Ind. Ins. Agts. S.C., Ind. Ins. Agts. Am., Greenwood Assn. Ins. Women, Greenwood C. of C. (dir. 1974-76, chmn. environ., energy and conservation com. 1974, chmn. edn. com. 1977). Baptist. Club: Greenwood Country. Home: 434 Dogwood Dr Greenwood SC 29646 Office: PO Box 1058 Greenwood SC 29648

BOYARSKY, ROSE EISMAN, psychologist; b. Jersey City, Mar. 16, 1924; d. Isadore and Clara (Klingenstein) Eisman; B.S. in Chemistry, U. Vt., 1944; M.A., Columbia U., 1946; Ph.D., Duke U., 1969; m. Saul Boyarsky, June 17, 1946; children—Myer William, Terry Linda, Hannah Gail. Psychologist, Durham (N.C.) County Mental Health Clinic, 1969-70; counselor U. Mo. Counseling Center, St. Louis, 1971-72; research asso. Masters and Johnson Inst., St. Louis, 1972-75; pvt. practice psychology, Boyhill Center, St. Louis, 1975—; research asso. Washington U. Med. Center depts. surgery, urology, St. Louis, 1977—; mem. asso. staff Jewish Hosp. of St. Louis, 1971—; dir. Archway Community for Drug Rehab., 1973—; mem. Eastern Mo. Regional Adv. Council for Psychiat. Services, 1975-81. Trustee Judea Reform Congregation of Durham-Chapel Hill, N.C., 1967-69. Mem. Psychologists in Pvt. Practice, Mo. Psychol. Assn. (pres. 1977-78), Am. Psychol. Assn., AAAS, Am. Women in Psychology, Soc. of Columbia Chemists, Phi Beta Kappa, Iota Sigma Pi. Contbr. articles in field to profl. jours. Home: 45 Portland Pl St Louis MO 63108 Office: 4625 Lindell Blvd St Louis MO 63108

BOYCE, DOREEN ELIZABETH, ednl. found. exec.; b. Antofagasta, Chile, Apr. 20, 1934; d. George Edgar and Elsie Winnifred Vaughan; B.A. with honors, Oxford (Eng.) U., 1956, M.A. with honors, 1960; m. Alfred Warne Boyce, Aug. 11, 1956; children—Caroline Elizabeth, John Trevor Warne. Lectr. and tutor in econs. U. Witwatersrand, South Africa, 1960-62; provost and dean of faculty, prof. econs. Chatham Coll., Pitts., 1963-79; prof. econs., chmn. dept. econs. and mgmt. Hood Coll., Frederick, Md., 1979-82; exec. dir. Buhl Found., Pitts., 1982—; dir. Duquesne Light Co., Dollar Savs. Bank, Microbac Labs., Inc. Mem. Frick Edn. Commn., Buhl Sci. Center, Fed. Jud. Nominating Commn., 1979-81, Gov.'s Council on Small Bus., 1979-82; del. White House Conf. on Small Bus., 1980; trustee Franklin and Marshall Coll., 1982—. Mem. Am. Econs. Assn., Exec. Women's Council, Am. Assn. Higher Edn. Office: Four Gateway Center Room 1522 Pittsburgh PA 15222

BOYCE, JEAN BRADSHAW, writer; b. Magrath, Alta., Can., May 19, 1917; d. Floyd Samuel and Jennie (Chipman) Bradshaw; B.S., U. Utah, 1939; m. Alma Houston Boyce, Sept. 2, 1942; children—Carolyn Boyce Johnes, David B., Barbara Boyce Timothy, Steven B. Lyricist I Love America pub. to Peter J. Wilhousky's musical arrangement of the Battle Hymn of the Republic, 1974; author collection of light verse, 1983; light vers pub. in N.Y. Times, Wall St. Jour., McCall's, Sat. Evening Post, Quote, Good Housekeeping, Family Weekly, Grit, Luth. Digest, Sunshine Mag., Cath. Digest, Good Reading, Mature Years, others. Pres., Relief Soc., 1976-78; active various charitable orgns. Recipient Utah Arts Council award, 1980; Utah Poetry Soc. award, 1974; League Utah Writers awards, 1972, 79; cert. of merit Am. Song Festival, 1977. Mem. Ch. of Jesus Christ of Latter Day Saints. Clubs: Salt Lake Swimming and Tennis, Windsor, Women's Aux. of Utah Bar Assn., Delta Gamma Sorority Mother's, Beta Theta Pi Frat. Mother's. Address: 2313 Berkeley St Salt Lake City UT 84109

BOYD, ALENE FOUNTAIN, social worker; b. Savannah, Ga., July 10, 1919; d. Andrew A. and Theola (Hurst) Fountain; student Ga. State Coll. for Women, 1937-39; A.B., U. Ga., 1941; M.S.W., Washington U., St. Louis, 1959. Caseworker, Savannah Children's Center; 1959-61, casework supr., 1964-69, adoptions supr., 1969-71; clin. social worker VA Regional Office, Macon, Ga., 1961-64; social worker VA Med. Center, Dublin, Ga., 1971-80. Bd. dirs. Ga. Conf. on Social Welfare, 1963-64. Mem. Nat. Assn. Social Workers, Acad. Cert. Social Workers, DAR, Audubon Soc., Alpha Gamma Delta. Episcopalian. Club: Altrusa Internat. Home: Route 3 Box 171 Pinpoint Savannah GA 31406

BOYD, ANN FISHER, marine exec.; b. Corpus Christi, Tex., Oct. 2, 1937; d. King and Jewel T. Fisher; diploma Durham's Bus. Coll., Victoria, Tex., 1956; m. Waymon L. Boyd, July 8, 1956; children—Wayne Allen, Randy Lynn. With King Fisher Marine Service, Inc., Port Lavaca, Tex., 1956-57, 61—, asst. sec.-treas., 1967—. Active local 4-H Club, Future Farmers Am. Baptist. Home: 2304 Larry St Port Lavaca TX 77979 Office: King Fisher Marine Service Magnolia Beach Rd Port Lavaca TX 77979

BOYD, CATHERINE ROBERTSON, home economist; b. Shawnee, Okla., June 10, 1938; d. James Marvin and Cleo Rebecca (Snyder) Robertson; B.S., U. Ky., 1959, M.S., 1962; Ph.D., U. Ala., 1982; m. Leroy H. Boyd, Jan. 28, 1958; children—Susanne, Diane. Tchr. jr. and sr. high sch., Versailles, Ky., 1959-62; med. research asst. U. Ky. Med. Center, Lexington, 1962-63; prof. home econs. Miss. State U., 1969—; dir. for Miss., Make it Yourself with Wool Contest, 1972—. Mem. adv. council Oktibbeha County 4-H; vol. 4-H leader. Recipient Teaching award Miss. State U. Coll. Agr., 1981. Mem. Am. Home Econs. Assn., Assn. Coll. Profs. Textiles and Clothing, Mid-South Ednl. Research Assn., Miss. Home Econs. Assn., Phi Upsilon Omicron, Omicron Nu, Kappa Delta Pi, Gamma Sigma Delta, Kappa Omicron Phi, Phi Delta Kappa. Baptist. Club: Miss. State U. Women's. Author 4-H bulletins. Home: 9 Oriole Dr Starkville MS 39759 Office: Drawer HE Miss State U Mississippi State MS 39762

BOYD, CHARLENE BENNETT, retail exec.; b. Bowling Green, Mo., Nov. 19, 1913; d. A.M. and Kathryn Pearl (Brown) Bennett; student U. Wis., Green Bay, St. Norbert Coll., DePere, Wis.; divorced; children—Walter, John, Rick. Organizer, dir. Mayflower Nursery Sch., Green Bay, 1954-60; dir. ch. edn. Union Congregational Ch., Green Bay, 1955-60, First Presbyn. Ch., Green Bay, 1960-65; mgr. Clarksville (Mo.) Skyloft, 1965-71; owner-mgr. The Pirates Cove, imports and antiques, Clarksville, 1965—. Organizer, Raintree Arts Council, 1971; pres. steering com. Miss. River Parkway Center, 1978-80; pres. Illiamo Travel Council, 1979; chmn. Clarksville Community Betterment Com., 1979-82. Recipient various service citations. Mem. Clarksville C. of C. (pres. 1978-80; Citizen of Year award 1976, Gov.'s Leadership award 1978). Episcopalian. Address: Box 265 Clarksville MO 63336

BOYD, DOROTHY ARLINE, former pub. relations exec.; b. Gt. Falls, Mont., June 3, 1922; d. Harry Oliver and Dora Amelia (Hexom) Thompson; student Eastern Mont. State Normal Sch., 1947-48; m. John B. Larimer, June 10, 1955 (dec. 1977); children—Judi Larimer Lund, Nancy Larimer Nelson, Susan, Lisa; m. 2d, Carroll W. Boyd, Mar. 6, 1981. Reporter-photographer Independent Record, Helena, Mont., 1949-55, Bloomington (Ill.) Pantagraph, 1956-58; editor Albany (Calif.) Times, 1961-71; dir. pub. relations Children's Hosp. Med. Center, Oakland, Calif., 1971-81; tchr. creative writing Albany Adult Sch. Former mem. Albany Planning and Zoning Commn.; past mem. Calif. Republican Central Com. Recipient 1st prize writing contest Nat. Press Women, 1957; 1st prize for best hosp. publ. S.M. Edison Chem. Co., 1972. Mem. Women in Communications, East Bay Press Club (past pres.), East Bay Women's Press Club (pres.), Am. Soc. Hosp. Public Relations Dirs., Acad. Hosp. Public Relations. Hosp. Public Relations Assn. No. Calif. (past pres.), Bay Area Soc. Indsl. Communicators, Albany C. of C. (past dir.). Lutheran. Club: Soroptimists (past pres. Albany chpt.). Home: 951 Euclid Ave Berkeley CA 94708

BOYD, DOROTHY RUTH, musician, educator; b. Atlantic City, Oct. 20, 1907; d. Herbert C. and Alice Frambes (Boice) Doughty; pvt. student of music, 1923-25; student Progressive Series Piano Inst., Jenkintown, Pa., 1924, Muskingum Coll., summers 1926-30; m. Merton Greer Boyd, June 24, 1930; children—Alys J. Boyd Carpenter, Merilyn J. Boyd Drumm, Merton Greer, Mildred K. Boyd Hibbard. Propr. pvt. music studios in N.J. and Ohio, 1924—, Mansfield, Ohio, 1957—; adjudicator, condr. music workshops; pres. Coshocton (Ohio) Music Club, 1944-45; organist, choir dir. Cambridge (Ohio) First Bapt. Ch., 1930-37; organist Newcomerstown (Ohio) Methodist Ch., 1938-41, Coshocton Evang. and Reformed Ch., 1942-46, St. Paul Luth. Ch., Mansfield, 1958—; choir dir. Bucyrus (Ohio) First Meth. Ch., 1947-57. Active local Camp Fire Girls, Girl Scouts, 4-H Club; mem. bd. Mansfield YWCA, 1960-62, 74-76; mem. women's com. Mansfield Symphony Soc.; chmn. Nat. Guild auditions Richland County, 1980—. Mem. Nat. Guild Piano Tchrs., Nat. Organ and Piano Guild, Music Tchrs. Nat. Assn., Ohio Music Tchrs. Assn. (county chmn. 1957-60, county sec.-treas. 1980-82, vice chmn. N. Central dist. 1976-80, chmn. 1961-67, state sec. treas. 1981—), Nat. Fedn. Music Clubs, Independent Music Tchrs. Forum (state chmn. 1977-78), Am. Coll. Musicians, Mansfield Music Study Club (sec. 1972-77). Republican. Lutheran. Club: Order Eastern Star. Address: 30 Darby Dr Lexington OH 44904

BOYD, ELLA LEE, civic worker; b. Way, Miss., Dec. 6, 1912; d. Willie Lee and Christine Geneva (Baker) Johnson; student schs., Canton, Miss. and Indpls.; m. Makies Boyd, Dec. 25, 1943. Active Baptist Ch., Decatur, Ill., Sunday sch. tchr., sec., dept. supt., pres. missionary group, 1944-71, 2d v.p. Young Women of Bapt. State Conv., 1955-57, supt. young people, 1952-71, sec. young peoples' dept. Gen. Bapt. Conv. Ill., 1961-62; local pres. Church Women United, 1969-70, area chmn. Woodriver Dist. Assn., 1965-71, com. mem., area chmn. Central East of Church Women United of Ill., 1970-73, publicity com.; publicity com., sec. Christian Found., 1976-79, sec. ind. fins. of chs.; active Community Hunger Appeal of Ch. World Service. Precinct 45 election judge, 1967-74; exec. bd. NAACP, 1945-50, Green Thumb Operation, 1974-80; mem. Sr. Citizens Adv. Bd. Recipient award Home Makers Ednl. Service, 1930. Clubs: Order Eastern Star (matron St. Mary's chpt. 65, 56-57, award 1958), Afro-Am. Sons and Daus. Home: 1994 Evandale Dr Decatur IL 62526

BOYD, JEAN K., psychiatrist; b. Wellesley, Mass., Sept. 7, 1944; d. James G. and Marie K. (Pfeifer) B.; B.A., Boston U., 1966; M.D., Med. Coll. Pa., 1971. Intern, resident in psychiatry Hahnemann Med. Coll. and Hosp., Phila., 1971-74; staff psychiatrist Med. Center Western Mass., 1974-75; cons. Mass. Rehab. Com., 1976—; mem. faculty U. Mass. and Tufts U., 1974-78; practice medicine specializing in psychiatry, Milford, Mass., 1975—; mem. staff Milford-Whitinsville Regional Hosp.; mem. courtesy staff Marlboro (Mass.) Hosp. Mem. Mass. Med. Soc., Mass. Psychiat. Soc., Am. Med. Women's Assn., Am. Psychiat. Assn., Thurber Med. Soc. Office: PO Box 298 215 West St Milford MA 01757

BOYD, JULIA MARGARET TART, youth ministries coordinator; b. Newton Grove, N.C., Mar. 7, 1921; d. Isaiah and Mary Lela (Blackman) Tart; B.S., E. Carolina U., 1942; m. Shelton Bickett Boyd, Feb. 21, 1944; children—Mary Bevan Boyd Berdine, Deborah Elizabeth Boyd Pearson. Adjudicator, Office Dependency Benefits, U.S. War Dept., Washington, 1942, Newark, 1942-45; mgr. Hallmark Card dept. Boyd Drugs, Mt. Olive, N.C., 1976-81. Pres., Goldsboro (N.C.) Dist. United Meth. Women, 1955-59, Goldsboro dist. coordinator Youth Ministries, United Meth. Ch., 1964—, mem. N.C. Conf. Bd. Edn., 1964-72, Goldsboro Dist. Council on Ministries, 1970—, mem. N.C. Conf. Council Youth Ministries, 1964—, chmn., 1972-76, named Lay Person of Yr., N.C. Conf. United Meth. Ch., 1979; corr. sec. Woman's Aux. N.C. Pharm. Assn., 1976-77, rec. sec., 1977-78, 2d v.p., 1978-79, 1st v.p., 1979-80, pres., 1980-81; pres. Mt. Olive High Sch. PTA, 1955-56, Sch. Band Patron's Club, 1964-65. Democrat. Club: So. Wayne Country. Home: PO Box 455 400 W Main St Mount Olive NC 28365

BOYD, LEONA JOHNSTON POTTER, former county welfare dir.; b, Creekside, Pa., Aug. 31, 1907; d. Joseph M. and Belle (McHenry) Johnston; grad. Ind. Normal Sch., 1927; student Las Vegas Normal U., summer 1933; courses Carnegie Inst. Tech. Sch. Social Work, summer 1945, U. Pitts. Grad. Sch. Social Work, 1956-57; m. Edgar D. Potter, July 16, 1932 (div.); m. 2d, Harold L. Boyd, Oct. 9, 1972. Tchr., Creekside Pub. Schs., 1927-30, Papago Indian Reservation, Sells, Ariz., 1931-33; caseworker, supr. Indiana County (Pa.) Bd. Assistance, 1934-54, exec. dir., 1954-68; ret., 1968; cons. assoc. Community Research Assocs., St. Paul; mem. bd. Lake Havasu Counseling Center Aux. Recipient Ind. Jaycees award for Disting. Service, 1966. Mem. Daus. Am. Colonists, Indiana County Tourist Promotion Bur. (hon. life), Am. Assn. Ret. Persons (chpt. historian), Sierra County (N.Mex.) Hist. Soc. Methodist. Club: Hot Springs Women's. Home: 507 N Foch St Truth or Consequences NM 87901

BOYD, MARY OLERT, lawyer; b. Holland, Mich., Aug. 28, 1930; d. Frederick H. and Sarah (Klooster) Olert; B.A., Hope Coll., 1952; postgrad. Johns Hopkins Med. Sch., 1952-53, Am. U., 1953-54, Vanderbilt Law Sch., 1955; J.D., Memphis State Law Sch., 1977; m. Joseph M. Boyd, Jr., Dec. 29, 1953; children—Andrew Martin, David Alexander, Martha Lucile. Tchr., Nashville City Schs., Dyer County Schs., Dyersburg (Tenn.) City Schs., 1954-62; free-lance journalist, Dyersburg, 1962-76; admitted to Tenn. bar, 1977; paralegal asst. J. M. Boyd, Jr., atty., Dyersburg, 1965-74; partner firm Boyd & Boyd, Dyersburg, 1977—; asst. dist. atty. 31st Jud. Dist. Tenn., 1980—; tchr. Dyersburg State Community Coll., 1977-80. Sec. exec. com. Democratic Party Dyer County, 1972-80, chmn., 1980—; chmn. W. Tenn. Dem. Caucus, 1982—; del. Dem. Nat. Conv., 1982—. NSF scholar Mich. Tech. U., 1960; recipient Labor Prize, Memphis State U. Sch. Law, 1977. Mem. Am., Tenn., Dyer County (v.p. 1980—) bar assns., Tenn. Trial Lawyers Assn., Tenn. Jaycettes (state pres. 1961-62). Democrat. Methodist. Clubs: Woman's (pres. 1963-65) (Dyersburg); Ninety-Nines (chmn. 1973-74) (Cape Girardeau, Mo.). Home: 607 Troy Ave Dyersburg TN 38024 Office: 403 Masonic St Dyersburg TN 38024

BOYD, MARY RUTH, univ. adminstr.; b. Clinton, Tenn., June 5, 1939; d. Hence Hicks and Georgia Belle (Rhyne) Henderson; student U. Tenn., Knoxville, 1957-58, Carson Newman Coll., Jefferson City, Tenn., 1959-60; m. James Wesley Boyd, June 19, 1965; children—Susan, Eddie. File clk. Union Peoples Bank, Clinton, 1956-57; mem. adminstrv. staff U. Tenn., Knoxville, 1960—, asst. dir. Career Planning and Placement Office, 1978—. Mem. So. Coll. Placement Assn. Baptist. Home: 7729 Maida Vale Circle Powell TN 37849 Office: 1534 W Cumberland St Knoxville TN 37996

BOYD, RUTH JOYCE, educator; b. Connersville, Ind., Mar. 12, 1934; d. Charles Merrill and Isabelle (Blackiston) Dickerson; student Ind. U., 1962; B.S., Ball State U., 1966; M.A., Ohio State U., 1974; children—Carolyn Rene, Teresa Lynn. Office mgr. Harry L. Parsons, Inc., 1958-63; tchr. visually impaired Akron (Ohio) Public Schs., 1966—; dir. adult sch. Summit County Soc. for Blind, 1974—. Mem. State of Ohio Mgmt. Bd. for Low Incident Project, 1975—; mem. local adv. com. Major Cities Project, 1975—; mem. adminstrv. bd. Meth. Ch. Recipient County DAR award, 1952, Comml. award, 1952, Akron Tchr. of Year award Akron Public Schs., 1976. Mem. Akron Edn. Assn., Council for Exceptional Children (pres. 1979), Delta Kappa Gamma (v.p. 1980), Pi Lambda Theta. Home: 55 Waldorf Dr Akron OH 44313 Office: 785 Carnegie Ave Akron OH 44314

BOYD, VIVIAN STALLWORTH, psychologist, educator; b. Cleve., May 6, 1939; d. Thomas and Ann (Dorel) Stallworth; B.A., Antioch Coll., 1961; M.A., U. Colo., 1967; M.A., U. Md., Sukiran, Okinawa, 1972; Ph.D., U. Md., 1975; m. Henry C. Boyd, Jr., Apr. 30, 1960; children—Henry C., III, Keith Thomas. Group tchr. Walden Pvt. Sch., N.Y.C., 1960-61; tchr. Am. Dependent Sch., Poiters, France, 1962-63, Norristown (Pa.) Public Schs., 1965-66; psychometrist, ofcl. tester U.S. Air Force Inst., 1969-70; tchr. Am. Dependent Sch., Sukiran, 1970-72; psychologist U. Md., College Park, 1975—, asst. prof. counseling, 1975—, also acting asst. dir. counseling services; founder, coordinator Nat. Data Bank Minority Mental Health Profls. in Coll., Univ. and Mental Health Centers, 1975—. Lic. psychologist, Md., Ohio, D.C.; lic. tchr., Ohio, Colo., Pa. Mem. Am. Psychol. Assn., Am. Coll. Counseling Assn., Am. Personnel and Guidance Assn., Phi Kappa. Contbr. articles to profl. jours. Office: Shoemaker Hall Counseling Center U Md College Park MD 20742

BOYER, ALTA ESSOM, preservationist, med. librarian; b. Lodi, N.Y., Oct. 18; d. Lewis Tunison and Emma Edith (Lott) Essom; B.A., William Smith Coll., 1936; student Syracuse U., 1960; M.L.S., SUNY, Geneseo, 1963; m. Charles H. Boyer, May 8, 1940; children—Charles C., Elizabeth A.; m. 2d, Charles A. Blohm, July 9, 1980. Chief library services Willard (N.Y.) Psychiat. Center, 1957-78; cons. S. Central Research Library Council, Ithaca, N.Y., 1974-78; pres. 20th Century Club, Ovid, N.Y., 1980—; preservationist documents Pa. Hosp., Phila., 1980—; cons. med. library archives materials. Trustee Finger Lakes Library System, 1978—; exec. com. Seneca County chpt. ARC, 1973-79; bd. dirs. Seneca County Community Services, 1981—, Regional Conf. Hist. Agys., 1982—. Mem. Lodi Hist. Soc. (pres. 1977-78), Med. Library Assn. N.Y. and Canada (mem. exec. bd. 1972-75), N.Y. Library Assn. (mem. exec. bd. 1969-71), William Smith Alumnae Assn. (mem. exec. council 1969-71), DeWitt Hist. Soc., Geneva Hist. Soc., N.Y. Preservation League, Historic Ithaca. Home: 8678 Watkins Glen Rd Lodi NY 14860 Office: 11514 Briar Forest Houston TX 77077

BOYER, BARBARA VIOLA, constrn. co. exec.; b. Lincoln, Nebr., Sept. 15, 1917; d. Claris Byron and May Blossom (Morris) Morey; student Nebr. Weslyan, 1935-36; m. Robert W. Boyer, May 11, 1937. Sec., treas. Carl W. Linder Co., Aurora, Ill., 1953—, co-owner, 1972-76; pres. B.B. Boyer Co., 1977—; pres. Ill. Constrn. Industry Com., 1981. Mem. Nat. Assn. of Women in Constrn. (chpt. pres. 1969-70), Fox Valley Contractors Assn. (dir. 1973-75), Asso. Gen. Contractors, Fox Valley Gen. Contractors (sec.-treas. 1976, v.p. 1978, pres. 1980), Aurora C. of C., Altrusa. Home: Rural Route 2 Maple Park IL 60151 Office: Elburn IL 60119

BOYER, GENE THELMA, feminist leader, retail exec.; b. Milw., July 11, 1925; d. Nathan and Rene (Hiller) Cohen; student U. Wis., Madison, 1946; m. Burton L. Boyer, Mar. 25, 1945; 1 dau., Bari Lynn. Various positions in journalism, sales, clerical and adminstrv. work, 1940-51; v.p. Matlin's Furniture Stores, Inc., Beaver Dam, Wis., 1951—; pres. Gene Boyer & Assocs., Inc., cons., 1981—. Vice chmn. Beaver Dam Housing Authority, 1968—; mem. Beaver Dam Planning Commn., 1968—; pres. Wis. Women's Edn. Fund; founder, 1979, since chmn. Wis. Women's Network; pres. Nat. Women's Conf. Center, 1981—. Named Woman Activist of Yr., Wis. Zero Population Growth, 1973, Woman of Yr. in Bus., Wis. State Jour., 1976, Outstanding Community Leader, Beaver Dam Kiwanis Club, 1976, Woman Bus. Leader, Women's Equity Action League, 1978. Mem. Nat. Home Fashions League, Nat. Assn. Women Bus. Owners, Midwest Home Furnishings Assn. (dir. 1980—), NOW (a founder 1966, nat. treas. 1970-71, v.p. fin. 1971-74, v.p. Legal Def. and Edn. Fund 1974—, Woman of Yr. award Wis. chpt. 1979), Beaver Dam C. of C. (founder women's div.). Club: Spectrum. Home: 1012 Lakeshore Dr Beaver Dam WI 53916 Office: 218 Front St Beaver Dam WI 53916

BOYER, JUELLE ANN, fin. exec.; b. Vallejo, Calif., Oct. 29, 1946; d. Herman and Christena Elizabeth (Buck) Rupkalvis; B.A., San Francisco State Coll., 1968; M.B.A., Golden Gate U., 1981; m. Ford S. Boyer, May 2, 1970. With Swiss Bank, St. Gallen, Switzerland, 1968, Getz Bros. & Co., Inc., San Francisco, 1969-70; cost analyst States Steamship Co., San Francisco, 1970-73; with City of Petaluma (Calif.), 1973—, now fin. officer, treas. Mem Regional Office Occupations adv. bd., 1980-81; vol. FISH; mem. ad hoc com. to form the Sonoma County Commn. on Status of Women, 1975. Calif. Fedn. Bus. and Profl. Women scholar, 1979-81. Mem. Nat. Fedn. Bus. and Profl. Women, Calif. Women in Govt., Mcpl. Fin. Officers Assn., Tips Network. Club: Internat. Order Foresters. Office: 11 English St Petaluma CA 94952

BOYER, MARY ELIZABETH, nurse; b. Covington, Va., Sept. 1, 1946; d. Phillip Lee and Mary Catherine (Bell) Rucker; L.P.N., A.C. Vocat. Sch., 1970; R.N., Atlantic Community Coll., 1973; B.A. in Psychology, Stockton State Coll., 1976; postgrad. Fairleigh Dickinson U., 1980; m. Joseph W. Boyer, Mar. 2, 1966; children—Joseph W., Josette A. Nurses aide Golden Crest Nursing Home, Atlantic City, N.J., 1968-71; charge nurse Senator Convalescent Center, Atlantic City, 1971-75; charge nurse, relief supr. Hebrew Old Age Center, Atlantic City, 1975-78; dir. nursing Westside Convalescent Center, Atlantic City, 1978—, inservice coordinator, 1978—; cons. in field. Pres., PTA, Pleasantville, N.J., 1972-73. Mem. Am. Nurses Assn., L.P.N. Assn., N.J. Nursing Home Adminstrs., Stockton State Coll. Alumni Assn., Atlantic Community Coll. Alumni Assn., NAACP. Republican. Methodist. Club: Elks (chaplain 1980). Home: 907 W Washington Pl Pleasantville NJ 08232 Office: 2153 Venice Ave Atlantic City NJ 08401

BOYER, MILDRED VINSON, educator; b. Newport, Tenn., June 1, 1926; d. Creed McNabb and Mildred Lucile (Vinson) B.; B.A., Baylor U., 1947, M.A., 1949; Ph.D. in Romance Langs., U. Tex., 1956. Asst. in Spanish, Baylor U., 1947-49, instr., 1950-51; teaching fellow in Spanish, U. Tex., 1949-50, 51-53, instr., 1953-54, asst. prof. Spanish and Italian, 1958-59, asso. prof. Spanish, 1962-66, prof., Spanish and edn., 1966—; instr. English, U. P.R., summer 1950; instr. Spanish and Italian, U. Ill., 1955-58; asst. prof. Spanish and Italian, U. Ark., 1958-59; asso. dir. Foggy Bottom Conf., Washington, 1960; cons. to schs., corps., pubs., Ednl. Testing Service, profl. jours. Inst. Internat. Edn. scholar to Cuba, 1947; Fulbright scholar to Italy, 1954-55; recipient research grants. Mem. Am. Assn. Tchrs. Spanish and Portuguese (nat. exec. council 1968-70), Tex. Fgn. Lang. Assn. (hon.), South Central Modern Lang. Assn., MLA (ERIC nat. adv. bd. 1971-73). Author: (with Andersson, Kaplan and Haden) An Experimental Study of Bilingual-Affective Education for Mexican-American Children in Grades K and 1: A Proposal, 1970; (with Theodore Andersson) Bilingual Schooling in the United States, 2 vols., 1970; The Texas Collection of Comedias Sueltas: A Descriptive Bibliography, 1978; translator: (with Harold Morland) (Dreamtigers Jorge Luis Borges), 1964; contbr. articles to profl. jours. Home: 902 Lund St Austin TX 78704 Office: Dept of Spanish and Portuguese University of Texas Austin TX 78712

BOYHAN, CYNTHIA MCCALLA, photojournalist; b. Elbert County, Ga., June 23, 1934; d. John Wayne and Flo (Haynes) McCalla; B.A. in Govt., Coll. William and Mary, 1956; children—Wayne, Leslie. Staff writer Wyo. Eagle, Cheyenne, 1956; with Laramie County Social Services, Cheyenne, 1956-57; social worker Fremont County Social Services, 1957-60; justice of the peace, Dubois, Wyo., 1961-72; editor Dubois Frontier, 1977-80; office mgr. Diamond D Ranches, Dubois, 1975-77; freelance photojournalist, 1977—; mem. Wyo. State Bd. C.P.A.s, 1975-80. Democratic state committeewoman, 1960-72; precinct committeewoman, 1960—; trustee Fremont County Library, 1964-70; mem. Wyo. Jud. Supervisory Com., 1981—; del. Dem. Nat. Conv., 1972. Quaker. Home and Office: Box 571 Dubois WY 82513

BOYKIN, DONNA BROWN, educator; b. Helena, Mont., Feb. 2, 1934; d. George Clarence and Leah Fiona (Hay) Brown; diploma No. Mont. Coll., 1954, B.A. in Elementary Edn., 1969; M.S. in Spl. Edn., Eastern Mont. Coll., 1971; doctoral candidate U. Mont., 1978-82; children—Elizabeth Lea, Laura Jean, Jonathan Matthews, Susan Louise. Tchr., Great Falls (Mont.) Pub. Schs., 1954-57, Stanton (Calif.) Pub. Schs., 1957-58; dir. Village Presch., Anaheim, Calif., 1960-64; tchr. Houston Illiteracy Council, 1965-67; master tchr. emotionally disturbed children Ednl. Adjustment Classes, Great Falls, 1968-73, precision tchr. Resource Room Children with Learning Disabilities, Lewis and Clark Sch., 1973-74, curriculum cons. spl. edn., 1974-78; mem. extension faculty Eastern Mont. Coll., 1975-78, Coll. Great Falls, 1975-78; asst. prof. spl. edn. U. Mont., Missoula, 1978-80; prin. elem. sch., Lolo, Mont., 1980—; lectr., cons. in field. Mem. Council Exceptional Children, Council Adminstrs. Spl. Edn., Council Children Behavior Disorders, Council Children Learning Disabilities, NEA, Assn. Supervision and Curriculum Devel., Assn. Children with Learning Disabilities, Phi Delta Kappa, Delta Kappa Gamma, Alpha Phi. Republican. Methodist. Home: 3219 Eldora Ln Missoula MT 59803 Office: Lolo Elem Sch Lolo MT 59847

BOYKIN, FRANCES LEWIS, social worker; b. Boston; d. Joel Randolph and Frances Virginia (Kenney) Lewis; B.S., Simmons Coll., 1945, M.S., 1946; m. Herbert Charles Boykin, Jr., Dec. 23, 1951 (div. 1958). Caseworker, Family Service of Orange, Maplewood, N.J., 1946-47; child welfare worker Riverdale Children's Assn., N.Y.C., 1946-51; supr., casework coordinator Asso. Day Care Services of Greater Boston, 1952-53; caseworker, advancing to sr. caseworker Salvation Army-Family Service, N.Y.C., 1955-74; psychiat. research, 1957-62; field supr. for student unit Salvation Army Corps and Community Centers, N.Y.C., 1974-79; adj. asst. prof. N.Y. U. Sch. Social Work, 1977-79. Bd. dirs. Assn. Bronx Community Orgns., 1964-73, v.p., 1968-69, treas., 1970-73; bd. dirs. N.Y.C. region NCCJ, 1976—, mem. exec. com., 1977—; mem. Bronx advisory com. Urban League, 1966-69. Cert. social worker, N.Y. State. Mem. Nat. Assn. Social Workers, Register Clin. Social Workers, Acad. Cert. Social Workers, Internat. Conf. Social Work (unofcl. agy. del. 1964—). Home: 2235 Fifth Ave New York NY 10037 Office: 361 W 125th St New York NY 10027

BOYKO, CARRIE JOHNSON, personnel exec.; nutrition cons.; b. Milw., Dec. 21, 1956; d. Roger H. and Joan L. Johnson; B.S., U. S. Fla., 1978; m. Alan J. Boyko, June 24, 1978. Tchr. bus. Hillsborough County Schs., Tampa, Fla., 1978-79; adminstrv. asst. Livingston & Haven, Inc., Charlotte, N.C., 1979-81, personnel adminstr., 1981—; nutrition cons., 1981—. Active United Way. Mem. Nat. Assn. Female Execs., Am. Soc. Personnel Adminstrs., N.C. Placement Assn., Charlotte Area Personnel Assn. Home and office: 7926 Oak Bark Ln Pineville NC 28134

BOYLAN, MARIAN LEESE, TV film dir.; b. Oakland, Calif., Dec. 8, 1926, d. Alexander Michael and Vera A. Leese; B.A., U. Wash., 1948; m. Bernard L. Boylan, Sept. 1, 1950. Pub. relations asst. Stephens Coll., Columbia, Mo., 1950-53; reporter Advertiser Jour., Montgomery, Ala., 1953-54, Columbia Tribune, 1954-55; film dir. Sta. KVOS-TV, Bellingham, Wash., 1957—. Mem. Whatcom Mental Health Bd., 1958-63; mem. Whatcom Mus. History and Art, Bellingham, 1968—, found. bd. dirs., 1974—, sec., 1976-78, treas., 1980-82, bd. dirs., 1982—; chmn. Bellingham Arts Commn., 1975-77; bd. dirs. Arts Alliance Wash., 1977-78; trustee Washington Commn. for Humanities, 1978—, mem. exec. com., 1980. Mem. AAUW (dir. Wash. div. 1975—, chmn. cultural interests, 1976-79, pres. Bellingham br. 1975-77, del. Pacific Basin conf. 1977, nat. cultural interests area rep. 1978-80, ednl. found. 1978-80, program devel. com., legis. program com. 1978-80, resolutions com. 1980-81, research and projects com. 1982—). Democrat. Clubs: Soroptimist, YWCA. Home: 413 Ridgeway Dr Bellingham WA 98225 Office: 1151 Ellis St Bellingham WA 98225

BOYLAN, VIRGINIA WALKER, lawyer; b. Washington, Dec. 29, 1941; d. Robert D. and Dorothy Elizabeth (Compton) Walker; B.A., Am. U., 1964; J.D., Cath. U. Am., 1979; m. James George Boylan, May 28, 1966; 1 dau., Kaithlin Janine. Admitted to Va. bar, 1979; resource specialist LWV of U.S., 1968-71; legis. asst. to Rep. John Melcher, 1971-76; staff atty. Select Com. on Indian Affairs, U.S. Senate, Washington, 1979—. Trustee, Nat. Reyes Syndrome Found., 1980—. Democrat. Office: 6317 Dirksen Senate Office Bldg Washington DC 20510

BOYLE, BARBARA ANNE, respiratory therapist; b. Newark, Aug. 28, 1937; d. Angelo Joseph and Florence Mary (Smith) Pecci; B.A., Kean Coll., 1969; diploma N.J. Univ. Medicine and Dentistry, Grad. Sch. Biomed. Scis., Sch. Respiratory Therapy, Newark, 1978; m. Owen Joseph Boyle, Oct. 17, 1971; stepchildren—Kevin, Anne. Tchr. of deaf and hearing impaired, Newark, 1969-70; tchr. deaf and multiply handicapped, Hackensack, N.J., 1970-73, Bergen County Bd. Spl. Services, 1973-74; mem. staff Caldwell (N.J.) Sch. System, 1974—; mem. faculty Essex County Vocat. Sch. System, 1979—; mem. staff St. Barnabas Med. Center, 1978-79, Montclair Community Hosp., 1980—. Spokesperson, Hanford Place Residents Assn. Mem. N.J. Assn. Children with Hearing Impairments, AAUW, West Caldwell Hist. Soc. Home: 22 Hanford Pl Caldwell NJ 07006

BOYLE, BARBARA DORMAN (MRS. KEVIN BOYLE), lawyer; b. N.Y.C., Aug. 11, 1935; d. William and Edith Dorman (Kleiman) Dorman; B.A. with honors, U. Calif., Berkeley, 1957; J.D., UCLA, 1960; m. Kevin Boyle, Nov. 26, 1960; children—David Eric, Paul Coleman. Admitted to Calif. bar, 1961, N.Y. bar, 1964, U.S. Supreme Ct. bar, 1973; atty. Am. Internat. Pictures, Los Angeles, N.Y.C., 1960-65, corp. asst. sec., 1962-65; partner Calif., Cohen & Boyle, Hollywood, 1967-74; exec. v.p. New World Pictures, Inc., 1974-82, Orion Pictures Corp., 1982—; dir. Murakami-Wolf Prodns., Inc., Fafinta, Inc., Los Angeles. Mem. vol. com. Marquez Elem. Sch., Pacific Palisades, Calif., 1970-73, chmn. resource com., 1972-73; legal adv. Park Century Sch., Santa Monica, Calif., 1973-74; mem. entertainment adv. com. UCLA Law Sch., 1976—, co-chairperson, 1979-81. Mem. N.Y., Calif., Hollywood, Los Angeles bar assns., Women in Film (charter mem., pres. 1977-78), Acad. Motion Picture Arts and Scis. Contbr. articles to profl. jours. Home: 557 Spoleto Dr Pacific Palisades CA 90272 Office: 1875 Century Park E Los Angeles CA 90067

BOYLE, JUNE OTT, state senator; b. Greeley, Colo., Sept. 30, 1917; d. Walter John and Millicent Williamson Ott; B.F.A., U. Colo., 1939; m. James M. Boyle, Sept. 2, 1939; children—Kathleen Boyle Champlain, Michael John. Mem. Wyo. Ho. of Reps., 1963-73; mem. Wyo. Senate, 1973—; instr. Wyo. Girl's State, 1965-81. Chmn., Democratic Central Com., Albany County, Wyo., 1960-61, Dem. nat. committeewoman, 1964-76; mem. S.E. Wyo. Mental Health Center Bd., 1964-70. Mem. Nat. Council State Legislators, Wyo. Commn. Women, LWV. Roman Catholic. Clubs: Federated Woman's, U. Wyo. Faculty. Women's. Home: 706 S 14th St Laramie WY 82070

BOYLE, KAYE, writer; b. St. Paul, Feb. 19, 1902; d. Howard Peterson and Katherine (Evans) Boyle; student Ohio Mechanics Inst., 1917-19; Litt.D. (hon.), Columbia U., 1971, So. Ill. U., 1982; L.H.D. (hon.), Skidmore Coll., 1977; m. Richard Brault, June 24, 1923 (div.); m. 2d, Laurence Vail, Apr. 2, 1931 (div.); children—Sharon Walsh, Apple-Joan, Kathe, Clover, Faith Carson, Ian Savin; m. 3d, Baron Joseph von Franckenstein (dec. 1963). Mem. faculty San Francisco State U. Recipient O. Henry Meml. prize, 1936, 1941; San Francisco Art Commn. award, 1978. Guggenheim fellow 1934, 61; Nat. Endowment for Arts sr. citizen grantee, 1980. Mem. Am. Acad. Arts and Letters. Author: A Glad Day (poems), 1930; Wedding Day (short stories), 1930; Plagued by the Nightingale (novel), 1931; Year Before Last (novel), 1932; Gentlemen, I Address You Privately, 1933; My Next Bride, 1934; Death of a Man, 1936; The White Horses of Vienna (short stories), 1937; Monday Night (novel), 1938; The Crazy Hunter (short novels), 1940; Primer for Combat, 1942; Avalanche, 1943, American Citizen (poems), 1944; A Frenchman Must Die, 1945; Thirty Stories, 1946; 1939 (novel), 1947; His Human Majesty, 1949; The Smoking Mountain, 1951; The Seagull on the Step, 1955; Three Short Novels, 1958; The Youngest Camel, 1959; Generation without Farewell, 1960; Collected Poems, 1962; Breaking the Silence, 1962; Nothing Ever Breaks Except the Heart, 1966; Pinky, the Cat, 1967; The Autobiography of Emanuel Carnevali, 1967; Being Geniuses Together, 1968; Pinky in Persia, 1968; Testament For My Students (poems), 1970; The Long Walk at San Francisco State (essays), 1970; The Underground Woman (novel), 1975; Fifty Stories, 1980. Contbr. short stories to mags. Address: care Watkins/Loomis Agy 150 E 35th St New York NY 10016

BOYLE, MARY O., state legislator; b. Cleve., Dec. 23, 1941; d. James and Catherine (Keane) O'Boyle; B.S. in Chemistry, St. Mary's Coll., Ind., 1962; postgrad. John Carroll U., Cleve., 1970; m. John J. Boyle, III, July 28, 1962; children—Catherine, John, James, Peter. Research chemist Sohio Research Co., Cleve., 1962-63; mem. Ohio Ho. of Reps., 1979—. Mem. Ohio coordinating com. Internat. Women's Yr., 1977; founding mem., trustee Heights Community Congress, 1977-78; pres. Cuyahoga Women's Polit. Caucus, 1976-78; mem. Commn. on Children and Families, legal com. and childcare issues com. Fedn. Community Planning, 1979—; mem. exec. com. Cuyahoga County and Ohio Democratic parties, 1974—. Recipient Rookie of the Term award, 1979-80; Public Service award Fedn. Community Planning, 1981; resolution of appreciation Coalition of Ednl. Orgns., 1982; award for Outstanding Legis. Service Jewish Community Center, 1982; Josephine Irwin award Women Space, 1982. Mem. Federated Democratic Women Ohio. Roman Catholic. Office: Ohio Ho of Reps State House Columbus OH 43215

BOYLE, NANCY REYNOLDS, home health agy. adminstr.; b. Rochester, N.H., Dec. 11, 1932; d. Robert Hodgkins and Helen Lee (Estey) Reynolds; R.N., New Eng. Baptist Hosp. Sch. Nursing, 1953; B.A., New Eng. Coll., 1977; m. John Emmanuel Boyle, Dec. 29, 1956. Pvt. duty nurse, Boston, 1953; neurosurg. nurse Lahey Clinic, Boston, 1953-56; staff nurse various hosps., N.H., Ky., 1956-58; staff nurse Dover Dist. Nursing Assn., 1959-62, supervising nurse, 1962-70, exec. dir., 1970—; trustee Stafford Savs. Bank, 1975—. Home nursing instr. Dover Girl Scouts and Campfire Girls, 1960-70; dir. N.H. Soap Box Derby, 1962-72; mem. City Adv. Com. on Urban Renewal, 1964-70, chmn., 1967; dir. Dover United Way, 1962-74; dir. Dover 350th Anniversary Celebration, 1973; dir. Dover Tomorrow, Inc., 1975—; mem. adv. com. Dover Adult Edn., 1962-76; bd. dirs. Strofford City unit Am. Cancer Soc., 1980—. Mem. Nat., N.H. (dir. 1981—) leagues for nursing, Am. Public Health Assn., Mass. Diploma Nurses Assn., Community Health Care Assn. N.H. (dir. 1981—). Clubs: Business and Profl. Women's (past pres.), Dover Quota Club (sec. 1977-78). Republican. Roman Catholic. Home: 4 Bellamy Rd Dover NH 03820 Office: 803 Central Ave Dover NH 03820

BOYLE, PATRICIA JEAN, judge; student U. Mich., 1955-57; B.A., Wayne State U., 1963, J.D., 1963. Admitted to Mich. bar; practice law with Kenneth Davies, Detroit, 1963; law clk. to U.S. Dist. judge, 1963-64; asst. U.S. atty., Detroit, 1964-68; asst. pros. atty. Wayne County, dir. research, tng. and appeals, Detroit, 1969-74; judge Recorders Ct. Detroit, 1976-78; judge U.S. Dist. Ct. Eastern Dist. Mich., Detroit, 1978—. Active Women's Rape Crisis Task Force, Vols. of Am. Named Feminist of Year, Detroit chpt. NOW, 1978; recipient Outstanding Achievement award Pros. Attys. Assn. Mich., 1978; Spirit of Detroit award Detroit City Council, 1978. Mem. Women Lawyers Assn. Mich., Fed. Bar Assn., Mich. Bar Assn., Detroit Bar Assn., Wayne State U. Law Alumni Assn. (Disting. Alumni award 1979). Office: US Dist Ct 251 Federal Bldg Detroit MI 48226

BOYLES, PATRICIA ANN, real estate exec.; b. Cleve., Mar. 7, 1951; d. Charles William and Ann Marie (Galla) B.; student Douglass Coll., 1969-72, Camden County Coll., 1976-77, Temple U., 1978. Advt. mgr., public relations dir. W.T. Grant Co., Somerset, N.J., 1972-73; staff announcer Sta. WGAY, Washington, 1973; freelance in broadcast prodn., Phila., 1973-75; adminstrv. dir. Houser Demolition Inc., Camden, N.J., 1975-76; exec. coordinator Capp Realty Co., Lindenwold, N.J., 1977-80; sales rep. Ryland Group, Inc., Cherry Hill, N.J., 1980—; corp. sec. Security Mortgage and Investment Co., 1977-80. Mem. Nat. Assn. Female Execs., Nat. Assn. Realtors, N.J. Assn. Realtors, Camden County Bd. Realtors, Am. Soc. Notaries, Am. Soc. Profl. and Exec. Women, Kings Grant Civic Assn. Home: 48 Queen Anne Ct Marlton NJ 08053 Office: Ryland Group Inc Delaware Valley Div 2D E Ridge Plaza Beverly-Rancocas Rd Willingboro NJ 08046

BOYLES, RUTH LINKENHOKER, educator; b. Princeton, W.Va., Dec. 18, 1951; d. George William, Jr. and Patricia (Lilly) Linkenhoker; B.S. in Elem. Edn., Concord Coll., 1973; M.A. in Elem. Edn., W.Va. Coll. Grad. Studies, 1978; m. Jackie Eugene Boyles, May 23, 1972 (dec.). Tchr., Thorn Elem. Sch., Princeton, 1973—. Mem. NEA, W.Va. Edn. Assn., Mercer County Edn. Assn. (sec. 1978), Delta Kappa Gamma (corr. sec. 1980, 2d v.p. 1982), Phi Delta Kappa. Republican. Methodist. Club: Civitan (pres. 1980). Office: 205 Thorn St Princeton WV 24740

BOYLLS, DIANA KAY, auditor; b. Evansville, Ind., Feb. 1, 1947; d. William Edward and Aura Katherine (Pfettscher) B.; B.S. in B.A., U. Evansville, 1969. With Shane Uniform Co., Evansville, Ind., 1969-70, Pearison Music Co., Poseyville, Ind., 1971-72; advt. rep., writer, editor weekly paper Mt. Vernon (Ind.) Pub. Co., Inc., 1972-75; auditor Posey County, Mt. Vernon, Ind., 1976—; cons. on County Ofcls. Handbook, 1978—. Sec., Posey County Assn. for Retarded Citizens, 1974-75; vice precinct committeeman Dem. Party, 1970-78, precinct committeemen, 1978-80. Mem. Ind. County Auditors Assn., Assn. Ind. Counties (pres. S.W. dist. 1982), Ind. Fedn. Bus. and Profl. Women's Clubs (dist. dir. 1979-81, state conv. chmn. 1982, state public relations chmn. 1982-83). Democrat. Ch. of Christ. Clubs: Mt. Vernon Bus. and Profl. Women's (pres. 1975-76), Order Eastern Star (matron 1976-77), Fraternal Order Police. Home: Rural Route 2 Box 256 Mount Vernon IN 47620 Office: Auditors Office Court House Mount Vernon IN 47620

BOZZO, JOANNE DEHAVEN, psychometrist, counselor; b. East Hampton, N.Y., Nov. 28, 1937; d. William David and Mary Ann (Benfield) DeHaven; B.A. in Psychology, U. Dayton, 1960; M.S. in Clin. Psychology, Marquette U., 1962; m. Paul Douglas Bozzo, Aug. 25, 1962 (div., 1977); children—Andrea, John William. Psychologist, DePaul Rehab. Center, Milw., 1962-64; diagnostician Child Study Service, Wayne State U., Detroit, 1964-69; pvt. practice psychol. examiner, Detroit, 1964-69; pvt. practice psychometrist-counselor, Tucson, 1973—; cons. Project Head Start, Ft. Worth; dir. Brewster Home, Inc.; chmn. personnel com., cons. burn unit St. Mary's Hosp., Tucson. Mem. Am. Psychol. Assn. (asso.), Ariz. Psychol. Assn. (asso.), Tucson C. of C. (membership relations com., 1979), Psi Chi. Democrat. Unitarian Universalist. Author: Personnel Policies and Practices Manual, Brewster Home, 1977; proposal for psychol. care of burn patients, St. Mary's Hosp. Home: 6041 Camino Esquina Tucson AZ 85718 Office: 3129 E 2d St Tucson AZ 85716

BRAASCH, CATHERINE IRENE HOPKINS, public relations dir.; b. Palo Alto, Calif., Aug. 15, 1948; d. Robert Hanchett Hopkins and Donna Ethel (Anderson) Hopkins Deebach; A.A. with honors, Cabrillo Coll., 1969; B.S.Ed. summa cum laude in Journalism, U. Wis., Whitewater, 1974; m. Leroy Raymond Thomas Braasch, Dec. 16, 1966; 1 dau., Sara Jill. Pres relations writer, Mont. Coll. Mineral Sci. and Tech., Butte, 1974-78; community relations dir. St. James Community Hosp., Butte, 1978—; lectr. workshops and classes in field; cert. facilitator Emerging Woman in Mgmt. Workshop. Asso./cons. for media relations Mont. (Gov's.) Adv. Council on Children and Youth, 1976-77; bd. dirs. Montanans for Children, Youth and Families, Inc., 1977-78, media cons., 1978—; mem. dist. bd. edn. Luth. Ch.-Mo. Synod, 1978—, Congregation Bd. of Stewardship and Ch. Properties, 1979—, lay voting del. to Mont. Dist. Convs., 1976-78, to Internat. Synodical Conv., St. Louis, 1979. Recipient nat. awards for excellence in football programs Nat. Assn. Intercollegiate Athletics, 1974-76; named Montana's Outstanding Young Woman of 1978. Mem. Am. Soc. Hosp. Public Relations, Nat. Assn. Hosp. Devel. (membership chmn. Mont.), Butte Press Club (pres., 1978-79), Sigma Delta Chi, Phi Kappa Phi. Democrat. Home: PO Box 154 Whitehall MT 59759 Office: St James Community Hosp 400 S Clark Butte MT 59701

BRABANT, SARAH CALLAWAY, sociologist, educator; b. LaGrange, Ga., Nov. 18, 1932; d. Enoch and Jennie Louisa (Crowell) Callaway; student Newcomb Coll., 1950-52, Auburn U., 1952-53; B.S., Memphis State U., 1967, M.A., 1968; Ph.D., U. Ga., 1973; m. Wilmer Everett Mac Nair, Aug. 14, 1973; children by previous marriage—Jennie Crowell, Enoch Callaway, Anne Delebart. Instr. sociology Memphis State U., 1968-70; vis. asst. prof. anthropology La. State U., summers 1973, 74; asst. prof. sociology U. Southwestern La., Lafayette, 1973-77, asso. prof., 1977—. Pres. Lafayette Mayor's Commn. on Needs of Women, 1977-79; bd. dirs. La. Council Human Relations, Faith House, United Christian Outreach, Half-Way House. Recipient Am. Personnel and Guidance Assn. Research award, 1977; Martin Luther King Humanitarian Service award Lafayette Council on Human Relations, 1978; Disting. Prof. award U. Southwestern La. Found., 1980. Mem. Mid-South Sociol. Assn. (v.p. 1976-77), So. Sociol. Soc., Southwestern Sociol. Assn., Am. Sociol. Assn., AAUP, AAUW. Democrat. Episcopalian. Club: Jr. League of Lafayette. Contbr. articles to profl. jours. Home: 149 Memory Ln Lafayette LA 70506 Office: PO Box 40198 University Southwestern Louisiana Lafayette LA 70504

BRABBLE, ELIZABETH WILLIAMS, home economist; b. Phila., Nov. 11; d. Judge and Clorine Williams; B.S. magna cum laude, Va. State Coll., 1960; M.S., Pa. State U., 1966, Ed.D., 1969; divorced; children—Cordelia, Celestine, William. Tchr., Norfolk (Va.) Public Schs., 1960-65; research asst. Pa. State U., 1965-68; asso. prof. home econs. U. Md., 1969-77, interim dean, 1973-75; vis. prof. Ahmadu Bello U., Zaria, Nigeria, 1975-76; dir. internat. family planning project Am. Home Econs. Assn., Washington, 1977-81; adminstr. and asso. prof. program internat. studies Howard U., Washington, 1981—; bd. dirs. Nat. Council Homemakers Health Aide Services, 1972-78. Recipient Mamie Seabrook award, 1960; Disting. Teaching award A. Lincoln Sch.; Norfolk, 1962; Public Service award Dept. Agr., 1971; Disting. Service award U. Md. Alumni, 1975. Mem. Am. Home Econs. Assn., Assn. Female Execs., Delta Sigma Theta, Phi Upsilon Omicron. Unitarian. Club: Wake Robin Golf (pres. 1980). Home: 8830 Piney Branch St Apt 712 Silver Spring MD 20903 Office: Howard U Washington DC 20059

BRACE, SHAE R., brokerage firm exec.; b. Flat River, Mo., June 25, 1930; d. Walter H. and Ruth (McClenahan) Adkins; B.S., Wayne State U., 1975; children—Michael Allen, Kevin James, Mark William. X-ray technician, Warren, Mich., 1959-60; asst. to purchasing agt. Rexair, Inc., 1960-62; with programming dept. WWJ-AM/FM/TV, Detroit, 1963-71; tech. writer/office mgr. Communico, Inc., Warren, Mich., 1971-75; asst. to mgmt. research cons. Wayne County Intermediate Sch. Dist., Wayne, Mich., 1975-77; sales asst. Mandey, Bennett, McDonald & Co., Detroit, 1977-79; account exec. First of Mich. Corp., Grosse Pointe, 1979-82; regional mgr. Mass. Fin. Services of Boston, 1982—. Vol., James Brickley's campaign for Detroit council, 1965, Roman S. Gribbs campaign for Detroit mayor, 1970, Ronald Reagan's campaign for Pres., 1979-80. Recipient Service award Channel 56 Auction, 1980, 81. Mem. Women's Ad Club, Women's Econ. Club, Econ. Club Detroit. Republican. Roman Catholic. Clubs: Boat (Detroit); Parapsychology Soc. Internat. Feature writer Update Mag., 1974-76; producer, writer, hostess Mich. Money Monitors, Grosse Pointe Cable TV, 1981-82. Home: 453 Saint Clair St Grosse Pointe MI 48230 Office: 200 Berkeley St Boston MA 02116

BRACEWELL, MARGARET ANN WILLIAMS, occupational therapist; b. Greenwich, Conn., July 23, 1944; d. James Horace and Lillian Anna (Carlock) Williams; B.S., Coll. St. Catherine, St. Paul, 1966; postgrad. N.Y. U., 1968; m. William Ray Bracewell, Jan. 16, 1971; children—Christina, Michael, James. HEW grantee for occupational therapy internships, 1966; staff occupational therapist Woodrow Wilson Rehab. Center, Fisherville, Va., 1967-69, supr. clin. affiliations, 1969-71; founder, dir. occupational therapy dept. Comanche County Meml. Hosp., Lawton, Okla., 1971-73, Southwestern Hosp., Lawton, 1973; occupational therapist Reha Westpfalz E.V., Ramstein, W.Ger., 1975-76; pvt. practice occupational therapy, Ukiah, Calif., 1979—. Mem. Am. Occupational Therapy Assn., Profl. Assn. Diving Instrs., AAUW. Roman Catholic. Club: College (Ridgewood, N.J.). Home: 356 George Pl Ukiah CA 95482 Office: 846 S Dora St Ukiah CA 95482

BRACIALE, VIVIAN LAM, immunologist; b. N.Y.C., June 5, 1948; d. Wing Ching and Wai Ching (Li) Lam; A.B. (N.Y. State Regent scholar), Cornell U., 1969; Ph.D., U. Pa., 1973; m. Thomas J. Braciale Jr., Aug. 5, 1972; children—Kara, Michael Stephen. Postdoctoral fellow U. Pa., Phila., 1974-75, Washington U. Med. Sch., St. Louis, 1975-76, research instr. immunology, 1978—; Nat. Research awardee, vis. fellow Australian Nat. U., Canberra, 1976-78. Mem. Am. Assn. Immunologists. Lutheran. Contbr. articles in immunology to profl. jours. Office: Washington University Medical School Dept Pathology 660 S Euclid St Louis MO 63110

BRACK, RITA MACDONALD, state legislator, educator, counselor; b. Roxbury, Mass., May 15, 1918; d. Daniel Joseph Edn., 1980—; Mary Ellen (O'Brian) MacDonald; B.S. in Edn., Boston State Coll., 1939; M.Ed., Rivier Coll., Nashua, N.H., 1966; m. John Joseph Brack, Oct. 4, 1942; children—Joan R. Brack Laberge, Lynda M., Susan T., John J., Judith A. (dec.), Lisa Brack Dougherty, Anne M., Martha, Maura. Asso. prof. N.H. Coll. Accounting and Commerce, Manchester, 1963-68; prof. edn., dir. counseling and placement Notre Dame Coll., Manchester, 1968—; mem. N.H. Ho. of Reps., 1976—; chmn. N.H. Coll. and Univ. Council Placement Dirs. Com., 1973-75; v.p. New Eng. Assn. Sch., Coll. and Univ. Staffing; vice chmn. New Eng. Bd. Higher Edn., 1980—; mem. profl. standards bd. N.H. Dept. Edn.; mem. 50th ann. com. Eastern Coll. Personnel Officers. N.H. coordinator Women in Community Service; organizer, adviser Manchester Hot Line; rep. to N.H. Gen. Ct.; mem. Stop and Shop Consumer Bd.; bd. Incorporators, trustee Cath. Med. Center, Manchester, Mental Health Center; pres. Sacred Heart Hosp. Assos., 1972-75; vice-chmn. bd. trustees Community Correctional Center, Manchester; mem. Gov. N.H. Commn. Pub. Edn.; del. N.H. Dem. Com., 1972, gen. chmn. conv., 1974; mem. Manchester Sch. Bd., 1976—; mem. Manchester Charter Revision Commn., 1981. Recipient various certificates of recognition; Woman of Achievement award Manchester chpt. Bus. and Profl. Women, 1979. Mem. Am. Personnel and Guidance Assn., AAUP, Women in Community Service. Address: 60 Hubbard St Manchester NH 03104 Office: 2321 Elm St Manchester NH 03104

BRACKEEN, EDITH HAYWOOD, TV sales exec.; b. Huntingdon, Tenn., Mar. 18, 1947; d. William Alton and Mattie Frances (Roberts) Haywood; B.S. in Bus. Edn., U. Tenn., Martin, 1969; m. William Scott Brackeen, II, Nov. 15, 1970; children—Kevin, Colin. Sec. to gen. mgr. Sta.-WLOK, Memphis, 1969-71; with Sta.-WPTV, West Palm Beach, Fla., 1971—, nat. sales mgr., 1976-78, gen. sales mgr., 1979—. Bd. dirs. Planned Parenthood, West Palm Beach, Family Services, Inc., West Palm Beach; mem. human rights com. Community Action Council, West Palm Beach. Mem. Am. Women in Radio and TV. Club: Advt. of Palm Beaches. Home: 315 Granada Rd West Palm Beach FL 33401 Office: 622 N Flagler Dr West Palm Beach FL 33401

BRACKEEN, JOANNE MARIE, bandleader, jazz pianist, composer; b. Ventura, Calif., July 26, 1938; d. Arthur Herbert and Marie Elizabeth (Langdon) Grogan; m. Apr. 15, 1960; children—Deryl, Susan, Marcus, Roselle. On tour and recorded with Art Blakey, 1969-72, Joe Henderson, 1972-78, Stan Getz, 1975-77; played Berlin Festival with own trio, 1977, 78; toured Europe, playing maj. jazz festivals, with own trio, 1977-78, 79; toured Midwest and Calif., 1979, 80, 7th Ave. S., N.Y.C., 1979, Bottom Line, N.Y.C., 1980, Women's Jazz Festivals, 1979-80, Fat Tuesdays, 1980; appeared in J.E. Berendt Calender Jazz '80, Monterey Jazz Fest, 1980, Newport Festival, 1981; solo pianist Carnegie Recital Hall, 1981; leader Joanne Brackeen Trio, touring U.S. and Europe, 1978, 79, 80; rec. artist, now with Columbia Tappan-Zee; latest of 10 albums: Aft, 1977, Prism, 1978, Mythical Magic, 1978, Keyed In, 1979, Snooze (Downbeat 5-star album), 1975, Ancient Dynasty, 1980, Special Identity, 1982; compositions include: Ancient Dynasty, Remembering, Beagles Boogie, El Mayorazgo, Haitt-B, Golden Garden, Lost or Found, Habitat, Einstein, Friday the 13th, Special Identity, Mystic Touch, others. Named Top Pianist for composition and performance, deserving wider recognition Jazz Critics Poll, Downbeat Mag., 1979, 80, 81; Nat. Endowment for Arts grantee, 1977, 79, 82. Office: care Helen Keane Artists Mgmt 49 E 96th St New York NY 10028

BRACKEN, HARRIET MARIE, ret. banker; b. Columbus, Ohio, May 20, 1919; d. Joseph F. and Ida E. (Kauderer) Oelgoetz; B.Sc. in Journalism, Ohio State U., 1941; children—Carol Lee, Drew Joseph. Advt. dir. F.&R. Lazarus and Co., Columbus, Ohio, 1942-46, 50-57; with Huntington Nat. Bank, Columbus, 1966—, v.p. public relations, 1974-82. Charter mem. Ohio Women's Hall of Fame, 1978. Mem. Public Relations Soc. Am. (Disting. Service award 1972), Nat. Assn. Bank Women. Club: Zonta.

BRACKEN, KATHLEEN ANN, nurse; b. Chgo., Mar. 14, 1947; d. Thomas James and Catherine Anastasia (Cowal) B.; R.N., CCRN, Little Company of Mary Hosp., Evergreen Park, Ill., 1968. Mem. staff Little Company of Mary Hosp., Evergreen Park, 1968-69, 71—, supr. intensive care units, 1976-79, dir. spl. care units, 1979—; staff nurse coronary care unit Little Co. of Mary Hosp., Torrence, Calif., 1969-70; staff nurse Chgo. Lying-In Clinic, U. Chgo., 1970-71; instr.-trainer cardiopulmonary resuscitation; bd. dirs., mem. CPR tng. com., chmn. nursing cardiovascular com. South Cook Heart Assn. Mem. Am. Nurses Assn., Am. Nurses Found., Chgo. Heart Assn., Assn. for Advancement Med. Instrumentation, Am. Assn. Critical Care Nurses (pres. Southside Chgo. Area chpt.), Chgo. Lung Assn. Home: 10321 S Campbell Ave Chicago IL 60655 Office: 2800 W 95th St Evergreen Park IL 60642

BRACKEN, PEG, author; b. Filer, Idaho, Feb. 25, 1918; d. John Lewis and Ruth (McQuesten) Bracken; A.B., Antioch Coll., 1940; m. Parker Edwards. Mar. 17, 1966; 1 dau., Johanna Kathleen. Author: The I Hate to Cook Book, 1960; The I Hate to Housekeep Book, 1962; I Try to Behave Myself, 1963; Peg Bracken's Appendix to The I Hate to Cook Book, 1966; I Didn't Come Here to Argue, 1969; But I Wouldn't Have Missed It for the World, 1973; The I Hate to Cook Almanack-A Book of Days, 1976; A Window Over the Sink, 1981. Mem. AFTRA, Screen Actors Guild, Authors Guild, PEN. Address: 66 Kanhana Pl Lahaina HI 96761

BRACKUP, ELLEN SUE, clin. psychologist; b. N.Y.C., June 10, 1952; d. Alvin Harold and Elaine (Rubin) B.; B.A. cum laude, Cornell U., 1973; M.A., Emory U., 1977, Ph.D., 1979. Psychol. trainee Grady Meml. Hosp., Atlanta, 1976-77; staff psychologist Emory Psychol. Center, Atlanta, 1974-78; psychiat. asst. Peachtree-Parkwood Hosp., Atlanta, 1977-78; clin. psychology intern Psychiat. Inst., Columbia U., N.Y.C., 1978-79; clin. psychologist Devereux Center in Ga., Kennesaw, 1979-80; pvt. practice clin. psychology, Smyrna, Ga., 1980-81, Marietta, Ga., 1982—. NIMH fellow, 1976-77. Mem. Am. Orthopsychiat. Assn., Soc. Research in Child Devel., Am. Psychol. Assn., Ga. Psychol. Assn., Phi Beta Kappa, Sigma Xi (asso.). Home: 1165 LaVista Rd NE #314 Atlanta GA 30324 Office: 1903 Powers Ferry Rd Suite 120 Marietta GA 30067

BRADDOCK, CAROL TIPTON, banker; b. Hamilton, Ohio, Sept. 7, 1942; d. Carlace Alpheus and Jimmie Louise Tipton; B.A., U. Cin., 1965, M.A., 1976; grad. Sch. Savs. and Loans, Ind. U., 1980; m. Robert L. Braddock, Aug. 1, 1964; children—Ryan Lawrence, Lauren Patricia Tipton. Buyer, The McAlpin Co., Cin., 1964-69; instr., placement coordinator Vogue Career Coll., 1971; exec. asst. Fed. Home Loan Bank Cin., 1973-76, asst. v.p., 1976-78, v.p., community investment officer, 1978—; cons. Neighborhood Reinvestment Corp., 1973-77. Vice pres. Zoning Bd. Appeals, City of Cin., 1976; mem. exec. com., trustee Sta. WCET-TV, 1974-78, sec., trustee, 1982—; pres. Minority Bus. Devel. Coalition, 1980-82; mem. Ohio State Hist. Preservation Adv. Bd.; trustee U. Cin. Found., 1982—, Boys' Clubs Greater Cin., Cin. Met. Exchange Club, Cin. Visitors and Conv. Bd. Recipient Outstanding Service award Urban Reinvestment Task Force, 1975; Achievement award YMCA, 1979. Mem. Women's Alliance (pres. 1971-73), Joint Underwriting Assn. (gov.), Jr. League, Nat. Trust Historic Preservation (adv. bd.). Delta Sigma Theta. Office: 2500 DuBois Tower Cincinnati OH 45202

BRADFORD, ANN LIDDELL, educator; b. San Leandro, Calif., Nov. 9, 1917; d. Charles Andrew and Emma Beauvard (De Camp) Liddell; B.A. in Edn. and Speech, Calif. State U., Fresno, 1952; M.A. in Speech Arts, Therapy and Edn., 1957; Ed.D. in Human Devel., Supervision and Adminstrn., U. Md., College Park, 1964; m. Gene Waukenas Bradford; children—Charles Churchill O'Neil, Margaret Ann O'Neil Gale. Tchr. primary grades, 1946-49; spl. therapist, 1952-54; gen. edn. cons. Supt. Kern County Edn., Bakersfield, Calif., 1954-64; supr.-cons. early childhood, primary edn., jr. high math.-sci. Santa Maria (Calif.) Unified Sch. Dist., 1964-66; asso. prof. edn. Calif. State U., San Francisco, 1966-69; prof. edn. Calif. State U., Sacramento, 1969—, chmn. dept. tchr. edn., 1981-82; cons. Commn. Tchr. Preparation and Licensing; mem. Network for Citizens Participation in Edn., 1982. Pres. bd. dirs. Community Child Care Programs, 1971-81. Mem. Nat. Assn. for Edn. Young Children, Calif. Profs. Early Childhood Edn. (newsletter editor, pub. 1973-80, v.p. 1979-82, pres. 1982—), Nat., Sacramento Valley (pres. 1974-76) assns. for edn. young children, Calif. Tchrs. Assn. Author: (with Kal Gezi) Children's Books; (with Harold Murai) Supplementary Reader. Specialist on human devel., elem. curriculum devel., early childhood edn., day care for children. Home: 686 Riverlake Way Sacramento CA 95831 Office: Calif State U Sch Edn 6000 Jay St Sacramento CA 95819

BRADFORD, BARBARA TAYLOR (MRS. ROBERT BRADFORD), journalist, author; b. Leeds, Eng., May 10, 1933; d. Winston and Freda (Walker) Taylor; student pvt. schs., Eng.; m. Robert Bradford, Dec. 24, 1963. Came to U.S., 1964. Women's editor Yorkshire (Eng.) Evening Post, 1951-53, reporter, 1949-51; editor Woman's Own, 1953-54; columnist London Evening News, 1955-57; exec. editor London Am., 1959-62; editor Nat. Design Center Mag., 1965-69; syndicated columnist Newsday Specials, L.I., 1968-70; nationally syndicated columnist Chgo. Tribune/N.Y. News Syndicate, N.Y.C., 1970-75, Los Angeles Times Syndicate, 1975—. Recipient Dorothy Dawe award Am. Furniture Mart, 1970, 71. Mem. Authors Guild, Nat. Home Fashions League, Nat. Soc. Interior Designers (Distinguished Editorial award 1969, Nat. Press award 1971), Am. Soc. Interior Designers. Author: The Innocent Are Wise, 1963; Complete Encyclopedia of Homemaking Ideas, 1968; A Garland of Children's Verse, 1968; How to Be the Perfect Wife, 1969; Easy Steps to Successful Decorating, 1971; Decorating Ideas for Casual Living, 1977; How to Solve Your Decorating Problems, 1976; (novels) A Woman of Substance, 1980; Voice of the Heart, 1982. Office: Suite 1101 Empire State Bldg 350 Fifth Ave New York NY 10118

BRADFORD, LOUISE MATHILDE, social worker; b. Alexandria, La., Aug. 3, 1925; d. Henry Aaron and Ruby (Pearson) Bradford; B.S., La. Poly. Inst., 1945; cert. in social work La. State U., 1949; M.S., Columbia U., 1953; postgrad. Tulane U., 1962, 64, La. State U., 1967; cert. U. Pa., 1966. With La. Dept. Public Welfare, Alexandria, 1945-78, welfare caseworker, 1950-53, children's caseworker, 1957-59, child welfare cons., 1959-73, social services cons., 1973-78, state cons. day care, 1963-66; dir. social services St. Mary's Tng. Sch., Alexandria, La., 1978—; del. Nat. Day Care Conf., Washington, 1964; mem. early childhood edn. com. So. States Work Conf., Daytona Beach, Fla., 1968; mem. La. adv. com. 1970 White House Conf. on Children, also del.; mem. So. region planning com. Child Welfare League Am., 1970-73; mem. profl. adv. com. Cenla chpt. Parents Without Partners, 1970; adj. faculty La. Coll., Pineville, lectr. Kindergarten workshop, 1970-72; mem. La. 4-C Day Care Licensing Rev. Com., Central La. 4-C Steering Com.; del. Internat. Conf. on Social Welfare, Nairobi, 1974, Jerusalem, 1978, Hong Kong, 1980. Pres., Les Soignees, Alexandria, 1947-48. Bd. dirs. Cenla Community Action Com., Alexandria, 1966-68. Mem. Acad. Cert. Social Workers, Nat. Assn. Social Workers, La. Bd. Cert. Social Work Examiners, So., La. assns. children under six, La. Conf. Social Welfare, Internat. Council on Social Welfare, Am. Pub. Welfare Assn. (S.W. region planning com. 1965), Am. Assn. on Mental Deficiency, DAR, Central La. Pre-Sch. Assn. (dir. 1967-70), Marquis Biog. Library Assn. (adv.). Methodist (kindergarten bd. 1967—, ofcl. bd. 1974-75, 77-81). Clubs: Rapides Golf and Country, Pilot (Alexandria). Home: 5807 Joyce St Alexandria LA 71301 Office: PO Box 7768 Alexandria LA 71306

BRADLEY, BESSIE LOUISE, banker; b. Lincoln, Nebr., Feb. 11, 1920; d. Buford Irving and Rachel Icel (Reynolds) Dickinson; B.S. in Edn., U. Nebr., 1943; m. Dale Bradley, Mar. 24, 1945. Tchr. bus. and English Mason City (Nebr.) High Sch., 1943-44, Mullen (Nebr.) High Sch., 1944-45; asst. cashier Bank of Mullen, 1969—. Bd. dirs. Guiding Star Girl Scout U.S.A. Council, 1963, neighborhood chmn., leader, trainer; sec. Cedarview Cemetery, 1970-81. Mem. Hooker County Geneal. Soc., Hooker County Hist. Soc. (sec. 1957-81). Methodist. Office: Bank of Mullen PO Box F Mullen NE 69152

BRADLEY, BONNIE, mezzo soprano; b. Wilmington, Del., Mar. 7, 1951; d. Archie Merill, and Blanche Ruth B.; Certs. in Oratorio, Song, Opera, Britten-Pears Sch. Advanced Musical Studies, Snape-on-Maltings, Eng., 1978; cert. in Opera, Inst. Musical Studies, Graz, Austria, 1977, Mozarteum Sommerakadamie, Salzburg, Austria, 1974; B.Mus. in Voice, Westminster Choir Coll., 1972; M.Mus. in Opera Performance, Manhattan Sch. Music, N.Y.C., 1975; m. Nicholas Nicosia, June 28, 1975; 1 dau., Francesca Maria Aida. Operatic and concert artist performing with opera cos. and maj. symphony orchs., recitalist U.S., Eng., Germany, Austria, the Caribbean, 1975—; instr. master classes colls. and univs.; adjudicater maj. vocal competitions. Helene Rubenstein Found. grantee, 1972-74; winner Artists Internat. Competition, 1976, Liederkranz Found. competition, 1978, Oratorio solo competition, 1977; recipient Minna Kauffman Ruud Found. competition award, 1976. Mem. Am. Guild Musical Artists, Nat. Assn. Tchrs. of Singing, Coll. Music Soc., N.Y. Arts Group. Office: Care Perrotta Mgmt 160 W 73rd St New York NY 10023

BRADLEY, CAROLYN A., clin. social worker; b. Newark, Mar. 27, 1953; d. Joseph John and Dolores Carolyn (Bersey) Bradley; B.A. in Sociology, Coll. of St. Elizabeth, Convent, N.J., 1974; M.S.W., Fordham U., 1978. Staff clinician St. Clare's Community Mental Health Center, Denville, N.J., 1974-79; med. social worker Jersey Shore Med. Center, Neptune, N.J., 1979-80, Jersey City, Med. Center, 1980—; social worker Middletown Twp. (N.J.) Child Study Team, 1980—; cons. social worker Somerset Med. Center Child Study Team, 1979—; pvt. practice clin. social work Mendham (N.J.) Child Devel. Center, 1979—. Vol. battered women's group, 1977-78, Neptune City First Aid Squad, 1979. Aldrin grantee, 1973-74. Mem. Nat. Assn. Social Workers, Acad. Cert. Social Workers, Nat. Feminist Therapists Assn., Smithsonian Assos., Mus. Natural History, NOW, Nat. Women's Polit. Caucus. Roman Catholic. Office: Belford School Belford NJ

BRADLEY, FLORENE JORDAN, librarian; b. Magnolia, Ark., Aug. 18, 1917; d. Thomas Scott and Nellie (Nipper) Jordan; student So. State Coll., Ark., 1935-37; B.A., Henderson State Tchrs. Coll., 1939; B.S. in L.S., Peabody Coll., 1947; m. Steve Bradley, Nov. 23, 1966. Librarian, tchr. Burdette High Sch., 1939-42, Calhoun High Sch., 1942-43, Magnolia High Sch., 1943-51; regional librarian Columbia-Lafayette-Ouachita-Calhoun Regional Library, Magnolia, 1951—. Pres., United Way Columbia County, 1979; sec. City Planning Commn., Columbia County Fair Bd. Named Magnolia Woman of Year service and civic clubs, 1963; Citizen of Yr., 1968. Mem. Magnolia Bus. and Profl. Women's Club (Woman of Year 1979), AAUW, Magnolia LWV, Ark. (past pres.), Southwestern (past chmn. pub. library div.) library assns., ALA (mem. notable books council adult services div. 1962-64), C. of C. (dir.), Delta Kappa Gamma. Methodist. Club: Quota. Home: 405 W Calhoun St Magnolia AR 71753 Office: 220 E Main St Magnolia AR 71753

BRADLEY, G. RUTH, real estate co. exec.; b. Pasadena, Tex., Dec. 10, 1937; d. Guy R. and Naomi B. (Agee) Thomas; children—Michael Wayne, Ronald Duane, Diana Lynn. With Escambia Council Advt., Pensacola, Fla., 1972; dist. sales mgr. Keyes Realtors, Miami, Fla., 1972-79; pres. Bradley Assocs. Realtors, Inc., Miami, 1979—; owner, pres. Ruth Bradley Real Estate Sch., Inc.; also mortgage broker. Mem. Nat. Assn. Realtors, Mortgage Brokers Assn., Womens Council Realtors, Sales Mktg. Execs., Am. Bus. Women Assn., Miami C. of C. Democrat. Clubs: Soroptimist (charter mem. Flamingo chpt.); Civitan, Order of Eastern Star. Office: Bradley Assos 18852 S Dixie Hwy Miami FL 33157

BRADLEY, GWENDOLYN, opera singer, soprano; b. N.Y.C.; degree N.C. Sch. Arts, Curtis Inst., Acad. Vocal Arts. Debut with Lake George Opera as Nanette in Falstaff, 1976; debut with Met. Opera as Le Rossignol in Ravel's L'Enfant et les Sortileges, 1981; Met. Opera performances include Tales of Hoffman, Le Rossignol, Siegfried, 1981; internat. operatic debut Corfu Festival, Greece, summer 1981; has appeared with Phila., Cleve., Central City Operas, Mich. Opera Theater; recitalist, concert performer; soloist Phila. Orch., Nat., Seattle, Honolulu Symphonies, Kansas City Philharm., Aspen Festival Chamber Orch.; recitals include Carnegie Hall, Phillips Gallery, Washington, community concerts. Nat. finalist Met. Opera Guild auditions; winner 26 competitions and awards. Office: care Columbia Artists Management Inc 165 W 57th St New York NY 10019 *

BRADLEY, JEAN SHIRLEY, social worker; b. Augusta, Ga.; d. Hyman Beryl and Celia (Levin) Lichtenstein; B.S.B.A., Ohio State U., 1947; directress cert. Montessori Tchrs. Tng., Drayton Falls, Mich., 1972; m. Philip R. Bradley, Dec. 25, 1947 (div.); children—Adam Joseph, Lisa Mirrell, Jordan Seth. Asst. editor Jour. Bus. Research, Ohio State U., 1947-48; acting dir. U.S. Bus. Census, Columbus, Ohio, 1948-50; kindergarten tchr., guidance counselor Groveport-Madison Local Sch., Groveport, Ohio, 1966-70; co-directress Montessori Sch., Dominican Coll., Columbus, 1973-74; counselor, newsletter editor Columbus Met. Community Action Orgn., 1974-80; CETA placement and job developer Columbus Dept. Community Services, 1980—; participant grantee Columbus Area Leadership Program, 1979-80. Mem. Ohio Edn. Assn., NEA, Columbus Women's Polit. Caucus, LWV. Unitarian. Clubs: Columbus Met., Leadership Columbus. Office: 60 E Main St Columbus OH 43215

BRADLEY, PEARLE ELIZABETH, historian; b. Melrose Highlands, Mass., Dec. 7, 1904; d. Edward John and Nettie May (Scovill) Quinn; A.B., Mt. Holyoke Coll., 1926; M.Ed., Boston U., 1934; M.A, Columbia U., 1941; Ph.D. (Royall Victor fellow), Stanford U., 1947; m. Harold Whitman Bradley, Dec. 5, 1947; children—Anne, David. Tchr. history Bloomfield (Conn.) High Sch., 1927-30, Chicopee (Mass.) High Sch., 1930-42; instr. history Stanford (Calif.) U., 1943-45; cons. internat. relations Mills Coll., Oakland, Calif., 1945-47; lectr. history LaVerne (Calif.) Coll., 1950-51; lectr. U. Tenn., Nashville, 1956-60; asst. prof. Fisk U., Nashville, 1960-67, asso. prof., 1967-72, asso. prof. emeritus, 1972—; research asst. UN Conf. on Internat. Orgn., 1945. Mem. Calif. Democratic State Exec. Com., 1950-54, Los Angeles County Dem. Com., 1953-54; chmn. 49th Assembly Dist. Council, Calif., 1952-53; co-chmn. Stevenson for Pres. campaign, Davidson County, Tenn., 1956; mem. women's com. Brandeis U., 1972—; pres. Davidson County Dem. Women's Club, 1968. Named Woman of Year, Nashville Bus. and Profl. Women's Club, 1968. Mem. League Women Voters, AAUW (pres. Nashville br. 1960-62, Tenn. div. 1969-71, state legis. chmn. 1977-81), Women's Civic Forum (pres. 1974-76, rec. sec. 1977-79), UN Assn. (pres. Nashville chpt. 1974-76, Outstanding Achievement award 1977).

Methodist. Club: Vanderbilt Women's. Home: 212 Craighead Ave Nashville TN 37205

BRADLEY, RAMONA KAISER, curator; b. Hamilton County, Ohio, Aug. 9, 1909; d. Oliver Barnard and Grace Lytle (Edwards) Kaiser; student Oakhurst Coll., Cin., 1926-28, Schuster-Martin Sch. Drama, 1931-33; m. Judson M. Bradley, Sept. 4, 1954. Sec. to patent atty., Cin., 1939-54; curator Sherman Indian Mus., Riverside, Calif., 1970—; cons. Title IV Project, Indian edn. Riverside Sch. Dist. Bd. dirs. Riverside Library, 1966-74, Riverside Cultural Heritage, 1974-80. Recipient Appreciation award Sherman Indian High Sch., 1977, honored for civic service City and Council Riverside, 1980, honor award D.A.R., 1981. Mem. Nat. League Am. Pen Women, D.A.R., Daus. Am. Colonists, Printing House Craftsmen, Inland Empire Mus. Consortium. Republican. Methodist. Club: Citrus Belt (hon.). Author: Glimpses Into the Past, 1940, Weavers of Tales, 1965. Home: 9130 Andrew St Riverside CA 92503 Office: 9010 Magnolia Ave Riverside CA 92503

BRADLEY, ROSALEE, psychologist; b. Calhoun, Mo., Sept. 20, 1939; d. Wayne Beecher and Alice Maureen (Shrout) B.; B.S., U. Mo., Kansas City, 1961; M.A., Hollins Coll., 1962; Ph.D., Wash. State U., 1969. Clin. psychologist No. State Hosp., Sedro-Wooley, Wash., 1968-73; psychologist, adminstrv. asst. Calif. Correctional Center, Susanville, Calif., 1974-78; pvt. practice, Susanville, Calif., 1978—; adj. faculty U. San Francisco. Bd. dirs. Conbela Assn. Seattle, 1972-74. Womens liaison rep. Calif. Dept. Corrections, 1975-78. Mem. Am. Psychol. Assn. Democrat. Home: Box 88 Janesville CA 96114 Office: 617 Main St Suite 204 Susanville CA 96130

BRADLEY, SUZANNE MCCUISTON, chemist; b. Evansville, Ind., Jan. 25, 1946; d. Forrest Thomas and Rosalie (Smith) McCuiston; B.S., Western Ky. U., Bowling Green, 1970; 1 dau., Lisa Fort. Plant Chemist Lenk Co., Franklin, Ky., 1968-70; with Kendall Co., 1972—, tech. editor, Walpole, Mass., 1978, plant supt. Fuquay-Varina, N.C., 1978—. Pres. Village Green Homeowners Assn., Cary, N.C., 1981-82; bd. dirs. Friends of Wake County Library; vol. narrator N.C. Dept. for Blind and Physically Handicapped. Mem. LWV (publicity chmn. Wake County and Cary unit). Republican. Methodist. Home: PO Box 465 Cary NC 27511 Office: Kendall Co PO Box 1058 Fuquay-Varina NC 27526

BRADLEY, SYLVIA DAWN, accountant; b. Blossburg, Pa., Dec. 25, 1937; d. Clifford Q. and Josephine M. (Baker) Root; grad. Lockyear's Bus. Coll., 1956; m. Sept. 14, 1956 (husband dec.); children—Dawn Denise, Heath Jason. Bookkeeper, Corum & Co., Inc., Madisonville, Ky., 1956-66; acct. Amick & Helm, C.P.A.'s, Madisonville, 1966-72; acct., sec.-treas. Margarita Fuels, Inc., Madisonville, 1972—, also dir.; pvt. practice acctg., Madisonville, 1966—. Pres., Hopkins County (Ky.) unit Am. Cancer Soc., 1975—. Mem. Bus. and Profl. Women's Clubs (Woman of Achievement 1977), Nat. Assn. Female Execs., West Ky. Coal Operators Assn., Beta Sigma Phi. Democrat. Baptist. Club: Daus. of Nile-Rizpah Temple. Home: 765 Homewood Dr Madisonville KY 42431 Office: PO Box 325 Madisonville KY 42431

BRADOW, FRANCES VANDIVER, program analyst; b. Columbus, Miss., Feb. 6, 1943; d. Chalmers Lofton and Ida Frances (Cook) Parr; student Mt. Holyoke Coll., 1960-61; A.B., U. Mich., 1964, M.A., 1965; m. Edward Hunt Duffield, Sept. 18, 1965; 1 dau., Amanda Marie; m. 2d Ronald Leslie Bradow, Jan. 6, 1980. Adminstrv. intern Maritime Adminstrn., Dept. Commerce, Washington, 1965-66, public info. specialist, 1966-68, mgmt. info. specialist, 1968-70, spl. asst., 1970-71; adminstrv. officer EPA, Research Triangle Park, N.C., 1971-73, program analyst, 1972—, chief tech. services sect. environmental criteria and assessment office, 1978—; EEO counselor, 1970—. Mem. North Carolinians United for ERA, 1972-79. Mem. Internat. Word Processing Assn., Air Pollution Control Assn., Federally Employed Women Inc., DAR, United Daus. of Confederacy, Chapel Hill Council Women's Orgns. Democrat. Unitarian-Universalist. Home: 4233 Laurel Ridge Dr Raleigh NC 27612 Office: MD-52 TSS ECAO EPA Research Triangle Park NC 27711

BRADSHAW, LILLIAN MOORE, librarian; b. Hagerstown, Md., Jan. 10, 1915; d. Harry M. and Mabel E. (Kretzer) Moore; B.A., Western Md. Coll., 1937; B.L.S., Drexel U., 1938, D.Litt. (hon.), 1978; m. William Theodore Bradshaw, May 19, 1946. Asst. adult circulation dept. Utica (N.Y.) Public Library, 1938-41, asst. head, 1941-43; adult librarian Enoch Pratt Free Library, Balt., 1943-44, asst. coordinator work with young adults, 1944-46; br. librarian Dallas Public Library 1946-47, readers adviser, 1947-52, head dept. circulation, 1952-55, coordinator work with adults, 1955-58, asst. dir., 1958-62, dir., 1962—. Mem. adv. group libraries Library of Congress, 1976-77; del. White House Conf. on Library and Info. Services, Washington, 1979; mem. bd. publs. So. Meth. U., 1970-78; mem. Tex. Gov.'s Commn. on Status of Women, 1970-72; Tex. del. to ad hoc com. for planning and monitoring White House Conf. follow up activities Nat. Commn. on Libraries and Info. Service, 1980; mem. Nat. Reading Council, Washington, 1970-73; Goals for Dallas, conferee, asst. task force leader, 1966-69, vice chmn. Goals Achievement Com. for Continuing Edn., 1971, chmn., 1972; mem. Com. to Plan the Future Goals for Dallas, 1973-74; chmn. Citizen Info. and Participation com. Goals for Dallas, 1976-77, trustee, exec. com., sec., 1977 treas., 1979—; mem. curriculum com. Leadership Dallas, 1978-79, adv. com., 1978-80; mem. Charter 100 of Dallas; mem. Tex. Com. for Humanities, 1980-84, treas., 1982. Bd. dirs. Hoblitzelle Found., 1971—; trustee Lamplighter Sch., 1974—. Named Tex. Librarian of Year, 1961 Public Adminstr. of Yr., 1981; recipient Disting. Alumnus award Drexel U. Library Sch., 1970, Titche's Arete award for epitome of excellence in chosen field, 1970; Disting. Service in a Profession award Dallas Hist. Soc., 1981. Mem. ALA (v.p. adult services div. 1966-67, pres. adult services div. 1967-68, council 1968-69, pres. 1970-71), Tex. Public Library Assn. (pres. 1964-65, chmn. public libraries div. 1955-56, chmn. awards com. 1973-74, 79-80, Disting. Service award 1975). Club: Zonta (pres. chpt. I, Dallas, 1976-77). Home: 6318 E Lovers Ln Dallas TX 75214 Office: 1515 Young St Dallas TX 75201

BRADSHAW, LOIS MASON, govt. ofcl.; b. Baytown, Tex., Nov. 16, 1931; d. Frank Barnes and Leona Elizabeth (Dunaway) Mason; A.A., Lee Coll., 1952; B.A. with honors, U. Houston/Clear Lake, 1982; m. William Benjamin Bradshaw, Sept. 5, 1953; 1 dau., Sandra Leigh. Sec., Exxon Refinery, Baytown, Tex., 1952-56, Shell Oil Refinery, Deer Park, Tex., 1958-60; with NASA-Johnson Space Center, Houston, 1962—, chief adminstrv. fin., fin. mgmt. div., 1974-79, mgr. program adminstrv. office, program ops. directorate, 1979—; mem. NASA Exchange Council, 1980—; mem. credit com. Johnson Space Center Fed. Credit Union, 1981—. Mem. personnel adv. com. First Baptist Ch., Deer Park, 1978-81. Recipient Superior Performance award NASA 1966, 69, Outstanding Performance Rating award, 1968-75-82, Apollo 17 Flag cert., 1981. Mem. Am. Bus. Women's Assn., Assn. Govt. Accts. Baptist. Home: 4202 Iris Ln Deer Park TX 77536 Office: NASA Johnson Space Center Houston TX 77058

BRADSHAW, ROXANNE ELIZABETH, educator; b. Pueblo, Colo., Oct. 31, 1943; d. Foster Costin and Martha M. (Moore) Moore; B.A., Western State Coll., 1965, M.A., 1969; m. David Lee Reinke, Dec. 15, 1974; stepchildren—Lisa Ann, Alison Lee. Advisor, Dean of Women's office Western State Coll., Gunnison, Colo., 1963-64; tchr., Pueblo, Colo., 1965-68; kindergarten tchr., Monument, Colo., 1968-69; women's counselor Rangely (Colo.) Coll., 1969-70; instr./coordinator tchr. aid program Pikes Peak Community Coll., Colorado Springs, 1970-74, instr. psychology, 1974—; developer grad. level tchr. aide course and workshop So. Colo. State Coll., 1970-73. Named Outstanding Woman in Edn., Beta chpt. Alpha Delta Kappa, 1981-82; W. G. Carr Profl. Study scholar, 1981. Mem. NEA (dir. 1976—, chmn. higher edn. com. 1981-82), Pikes Peak Community Coll. Faculty Assn., Colo. Edn. Assn., NOW, Alpha Delta Kappa. Democrat. Presbyterian. Office: 5675 S Academy Blvd Colorado Springs CO 80906

BRADT, DONA MARY SONTAG, info. center adminstr.; b. Hastings, Minn., Oct. 18, 1930; d. Edwin Gervase and Maude Marie (Hatten) S.; student Mt. St. Marys Coll., 1948, Library Sch. U. Minn., 1968-70; B.A., Met. State U., 1975; m. Arnold L. Bradt (div.); children—Michael Edwin, Robert Dana, Jeffrey Arnold, Peter Matthew, Andrew Hatten. Legal sec. Langevin & Langlais, 1964-65; librarian Econs. Lab., Inc., St. Paul, 1965—, head librarian, 1972-79, mgr. corp. info. center, 1980—. Mem. Am. Soc. Info. Sci., Spl. Libraries Assn., ALA, Minn. Library Assn., AAAS. Republican. Roman Catholic. Home: 7981 115th St S Cottage Grove MN 55016 Office: Econs Lab Inc Osborn Bldg Wabasha St Saint Paul MN 55102

BRADT, NORMA LESENE GIBBS, educator, adminstr.; b. Riverton, Minn., June 7, 1923; d. Paul C. and Bertha (Adams) Gibbs; A.A. in Psychology San Diego State U., 1949; B.S. in Psychology and Edn., Whittier (Calif.) Coll., 1960; M.S. in Edn. Adminstrn., Pepperdine U., 1974; m. Robert Davidson Bradt, 1949; 1 son, David Roy. Instr. parent edn. Whittier Schs., 1950-57, resource tchr., 1957-67, primary tchr., 1967-76, lang. specialist, 1976—. Chpt. pres., dist. officer PTA; bd. dirs. Long Beach (Calif.) Urban Redevel. Council. Cert. in gen. adminstrn., Calif. Mem. Nat. Congress Parents and Tchrs. (hon. life), Am. Family Service Assn., AAUW, Nat. Assn. Women, Women in Ednl. Leadership (officer), Beta Gamma Sigma. Ednl. research in Europe, Asia, Africa, Orient and Middle East; author curriculum materials. Office: 5020 Tierra Antigua Whittier CA 90601

BRADY, ADELAIDE BURKS, public relations agy. exec.; b. N.Y.C., June 27, 1926; d. Earl Victor and Audrey (Calvert) Burks; B.S., Boston U., 1946; m. James Francis Brady, Jr., June 22, 1946 (div. 1953); 1 son, James Francis III. Exec. v.p. Media Enterprises, 1952-55; dir. group relations Save the Children Fedn., N.Y.C., 1955-59; dir. public affairs div. Girl Scouts U.S.A., N.Y.C., 1959-69; pres. Communication Internat., Inc., Washington, 1969-73; pres. Burks Brady Communications, N.Y.C., Wilton, Conn., 1972—, Angel Shopper Catalog, Inc., Wilton, 1976—; exec. v.p. Arts in the Parks, Inc., Washington, 1971—. Mem. Women's Nat. Republican Club, 1968—; active Girl Scouts U.S.A.; bd. dirs. ARCS Found. Inc., Lenox Hill Hosp., N.Y.C.; chmn. bd. dirs., pres. Animal Lovers, Inc. Recipient Silver Reel award for film The Children of Now, Save the Children Fedn., 1968; decorated Order St. John of Jerusalem (Eng.), 1974. Mem. Public Relations Soc. Am., AAUW, NEA, Am. Women in Radio and TV, Nat. Ednl. Broadcasters Assn., Women Execs. in Public Relations, N.Y. Press Women (pres.), First Families Va., D.A.R., Daus. Am. Confederacy, Women in Communication, Internat. Platform Assn., Women's Polit. Caucus. Episcopalian. Club: Capitol Hill (Washington). Home: 267 Westport Rd Wilton CT 06897 Office: 785 Park Ave New York NY 10021

BRADY, BENNETT MANNING, mathematician, govt. ofcl.; b. Orangeburg, S.C., Apr. 11, 1943; d. William Ellis and Elizabeth (Mays) Manning; student Agnes Scott Coll., 1961-62; A.B., Vassar Coll., 1965; Fulbright fellow Cambridge U., 1965-66; M.A. (NSF fellow), U. Calif., Berkeley, 1968; postgrad. George Washington U., 1969-72; m. Roscoe Owen Brady, June 10, 1972; children—Roscoe Owen, Randolph Owen. Sr. mgmt. cons. Ernst & Ernst, Washington, 1968-70; research asso. Pres.'s Commn. Fed. Statistics, Washington, 1970-71; U.S. internat. statis. liaison OMB, Washington, 1971-78; spl. asst. to commr. labor statistics Bur. Labor Statistics, Washington, 1978-79, dir. Office Program Coordination and Evaluation, 1979—; cons. ops. research USAF, 1967-68; mem. faculty U. Calif., Berkeley, 1968; mem. U.S. delegation UN Statis. Commn., 1972. NASA fellow, 1964. Mem. Am. Math. Soc., Am. Statis. Assn., Inst. Mgmt. Sci., Ops. Research Soc. Am., Washington Ops. Research Council, Washington Statis. Soc., Phi Beta Kappa. Republican. Presbyterian. Club: Vassar (Washington). Author: (with J.S. Duncan) Statistical Services in Ten Years' Time, 1978; (with E. Robins and K.S. Tippet) Going Places with Children in Washington, 9th ed., 1979; editor OSD Statis. Notes, 1980—; contbr. articles on statis. devels. and research to profl. jours. Home: 9501 Kingsley Ave Bethesda MD 20814 Office: 441 G St NW Washington DC 20212

BRADY, DESSIE MARIE, pharmacist; b. Roslyn, Wash., Jan. 9, 1924; d. Frank Andrew and Jessie Addriana (Rouse) Brady; student Central Wash. Coll., 1942-43; B.S. in Pharmacy, Wash. State U., 1947. Pharmacist, Luddie's Pharmacy. Prosser, Wash., 1947-50; chief pharmacist Yakima Valley Meml. Hosp., 1950-80, staff pharmacist, 1980—. Mem. AAAS, Am. Pharm. Assn., Am. Soc. Hosp. Pharmacists, Wash. State Pharmacy Assn., Wash. State Alumni Assn. Lambda Kappa Sigma. Contbr. to Am. Inst. History of Pharmacy. Home: Route 3 Box 3746 Sunnyside WA 98944 Office: 2811 Tieton Dr Yakima WA 98902

BRADY, JEAN MARIE, microbiologist; b. Lockport, N.Y., Mar. 3, 1933; d. William Aloysius and Agnes Alice (Perkins) B.; B.S., Siena Heights Coll., Adrian, Mich., 1953; M.S., L.I.U., 1967; Ph.D., N.Y.U., 1974. Med. technologist Lockport Meml. Hosp., 1953-64, Niagara Falls (N.Y.) Meml. Hosp., 1964-65; research asso. St. Luke's, also St. Vincent's hosps., N.Y.C., 1965-75; asso. prof. biology Alphonsus Coll., Woodcliffe Lake, N.J., 1970-74, Felician Coll., Lodi, N.J., 1974; sr. microbiologist Becton-Dickinson Co., E. Rutherford, N.J., 1979—; mem. edn. com. Bergen County Adv. Council Aging, 1977. Fellow Royal Soc. Health; mem. AAUP, Am. Soc. Med. Tech., N.Y. Acad. Scis., N.J. Coll. and Univ. Coalition on Women's Edn. Roman Catholic. Author articles in field. Home: 39 Chestnut St Hillsdale NJ 07642 Office: Stanley St East Rutherford NJ 07070

BRADY, LINDA CAROL, architect; b. N.Y.C., May 18, 1949; d. John Joseph and Irene H. (Olawska) B.; B.Arch., Pratt Inst., 1971. Staff technician, draftsperson Gruzen & Partners, 1970-72; staff designer Warner, Burns, Toan, Lunde, 1973-75; archtl. cons. Citibank N.A., N.Y.C., 1976-77, staff architect, 1977—, asst. v.p., 1981—; corp. sec. Citidel, Inc., 1982- . Registered architect, N.Y. Mem. Am. Legion Aux., Pratt Alumni Assn., Nat. Classical Soc. Designer hotels, tourist lodges, schs.; planner courthouse annex, office interiors, libraries. Office: One Citicorp Center New York NY 10043

BRADY, MAUREEN ELIZABETH, educator; b. Chgo., Mar. 15, 1945; d. William James and Gertrude (Hunter) B.; B.S. in Edn., Ill. State U., Normal, 1967, M.S. in Ednl. Media, 1971; postgrad. Nat. Coll. Edn. Librarian, Sch. Dist. 47, Crystal Lake, Ill., 1967-69, Sch. Dist. 155, Crystal Lake, 1969-70; learning center tchr. Rugen Elem. Sch., Glenview, Ill., 1971-73, Sunny Hill Elem. Sch. Dist. 220, Barrington, Ill., 1974—. Mem. media com. Presbytery of Chgo.; mem. aux. Good Shepherd Hosp., Barrington. Mem. ALA, Ill. Library Assn., Assn. Ednl. Communications and Tech., Ill. Assn. Ednl. Communications and Tech., NEA, Ill., Barrington (bd. dirs.) edn. assns., Chgo. Suburban Audiovisual Roundtable (dir., sec.), Ill. Assn. Media in Edn., No. Ill. Media Assn., AAUW (dir. Barrington area br.), Friends of Minocqua (Wis.) Library, Friends of Barrington Area Library, Elgin Scottish Soc. (pres.), Alpha Beta Alpha, Kappa Delta Pi (dir.), Phi Delta Kappa. Cert. in geography, library sci., ednl. media, Ill. Home: 25955 W Cuba Rd Barrington IL 60010 Office: 2500 Helm Rd Carpentersville IL 60110

BRADY, PATRICIA ELLIS, fin. exec.; b. Wake Forest, N.C., Aug. 12, 1935; d. Fred Day and Pauline Clarice (Hagwood) Rogers; student Strayer Secretarial Sch., 1965-66; children—Michael, Timothy, Darlene. Bookkeeper Union Trust Co., Washington, 1952-55; with B.F. Saul Co., Chevy Chase, Md., 1957—, corporate sec., asst. v.p., 1976—, trustee profit sharing plan, 1979—; dir. Franklin Property Co., B.F. Saul Co. of Md., B.F. Saul Co. of Va., Columbia Credit Co. Mem. Am. Soc. Corporate Secs., Nat. Assn. Exec. Secs., Nat. Assn. Female Execs., Women of the Ch. of God. Home: 552 Bruce Ave Odenton MD 21113 Office: 8401 Connecticut Ave Chevy Chase MD 20815

BRADY, PATSY FAE, nursing adminstr.; b. King, N.C., Aug. 31, 1940; d. Esker Ray and Mildred Olivia (Tuttle) Smith; student U. N.C., Greensboro, 1958-60; R.N., Watts Hosp. Sch. Nursing, 1963; B.S. in Nursing, U. N.C., Chapel Hill, 1970; M.S. in Nursing, Duke U., 1977; m. Michael Wayne Brady, Nov. 30, 1963. Head nurse, supr. operating room Duke U. Hosp., Durham, N.C., 1963-66; instr. Sch. Nursing, Watts Hosp. Sch. Nursing, Durham, 1966-69, asst. dir. nursing, 1973-77; coordinator policy, procedures and materials Duke U. Hosp., Durham, 1978—. Instr. home health nursing ARC, 1977-78. Mem. Watts Alumni Assn. (bd. dirs., co-chmn. membership com. 1979—). Democrat. Baptist. Home: 1709 Cole Mill Rd Durham NC 27712

BRAGG, EMMA WHITE, psychologist, educator; b. Nashville, Tenn., Oct. 6, 1911; d. George Richardson and Hortense (Stone) White; B.A. cum laude, Fisk U., 1932, M.A., 1933; Ph.D., U. Chgo., 1952; m. Jubie Barton Bragg, Jr., Mar. 24, 1945. Registrar, Meharry Med. Coll., Nashville, 1939-48; mem. faculty W.Va. State Coll., Institute, 1952-53, Langston (Okla.) U., 1953-54, Tex. So. U., Houston, 1954-55, Phoenix Union High Sch. and Jr. Coll. System (Ariz.), 1956-57, Fisk U., Nashville, 1955-56, 57-59, N.C. State Coll., Durham, 1959-60, U. Wichita (Kans.), summer 1954; prof. edn. and psychology Ala. State Coll., Montgomery, 1961-65, head dept. psychology, 1963-65; prof. counseling psychology Tuskegee (Ala.) Inst., 1965-67; prof. psychology Tenn. State U., Nashville, 1967-78; pvt. practice counseling psychology, 1978—; vocat. expert Nashville Bd. Hearings and Appeals, 1968-76; cons. various govt. agys. and schs., 1968—; condr. workshops vocat. adjustment, 1978—. Lic. psychologist, Tenn.; diplomate Am. Bd. Examiners in Profl. Psychology; recipient Leadership Service award Ala. Leadership Study Program, 1965; Appreciation award Ala. Dept. Public Health, 1965; Achievement Scroll, Columbus (Ohio) chpt. Kappa Psi, 1965; Outstanding award Psychology Colloquium, Ala. State Coll., 1965; plaque S.C. State Coll. Psychic Probers, 1970; Profl. Achievement award U. Chgo. Alumni Assn., 1982. Mem. Am. Psychol. Assn., Tenn. Psychol. Assn., Southeastern Psychol. Assn., Nat. Assn. Disability Examiners, Nat. Vocat. Guidance Assn., Nashville Opera Guild, Nashville Symphony Guild, Delta Sigma Theta, Psi Chi. Democrat. Clubs: Fisk, U. Chgo., Book Lovers. Contbr. numerous articles on vocat. psychology to profl. jours. Address: 707 Ringgold Dr Nashville TN 37207

BRAGINSKY, DOROTHEA DORIAN, psychologist, educator; b. N.Y.C., July 31, 1939; d. Herman and Anna (Flaumenbaum) B.; B.A., Queens Coll., 1959; M.A., U. Conn., 1960, Ph.D., 1966. Research asso. VA Hosp., West Haven, Conn., 1966-68; research prof. Fairfield (Conn.) U., 1968—, prof., chmn. dept. psychology; cons. HUD, HEW. Mem. Am. Psychol. Assn., AAAS, Amateur Fencing League Am. Jewish. Club: Rolls Royce Owners. Author: Methods of Madness: The Mental Hospital as a Last Resort, 1969; Hansels and Gretels: Studies of Children in Institutions for the Mentally Retarded, 1971; Mainstream Psychology: A Critique, 1974; contbr. articles to profl. jours. Office: Psychology Dept Fairfield U Fairfield CT 06430

BRAGMAN, RUTH SUSAN, educator; b. Bklyn., Dec. 9, 1947; d. Benjamin and Miriam (Brown) Bragman; B.S., U. Wis., 1969; M.Ed., U. Tex., 1973; Ph.D., U. Md., 1980. Tchr./vol. Sherut La'Am, Tel Aviv, Israel, summer 1969-71; recreational therapist Austin (Tex.) State Sch., 1972; acad. asst. in phys. edn. for handicapped U. Tex., Austin, 1971-73, intern in adaptive phys. edn., 1972-73; head motility tchr. Diagnostic Edn. Sch., Tidewater Rehab. Inst., Norfolk, Va., 1973-76; water safety instr. for handicapped, ARC, Norfolk, 1975-76; grad. asst. in recreation U. Md., College Park, 1976; adaptive phys. edn. tchr. Alternative Sch., Washington, 1977; grad. asst. spl. edn. U. Md., 1977-79, intern in arts for handicapped, 1979-80; project coordinator Nat. Com. Arts for Handicapped, Washington, summer 1980; asst. prof. dept. spl. edn. and rehab. Memphis State U., 1980—; cons. in field; condr. workshops in field. Asst. in cardiac prevention and rehab. program Jewish Community Center, Norfolk, 1974-75; founder, leader handicapped Girls Scouts U.S.A., Norfolk, 1974-75; com. mem. exec. com. Spl. Olympics, Norfolk, 1974-76; com. mem. ad hoc com. on arts for handicapped children State of Tenn., 1981; mem. state monitoring team spl. edn. Dept. Edn., State of Tenn., 1981; steering com. spl. edn. alliance Memphis, 1982—. Memphis State U. faculty research grantee, 1982; U. Md. fellow, 1979-80, grad. assistantship in spl. edn., 1977-78, 78-79, in recreation, 1976-77; U. Tex. grad. study grantee, 1971-72, 72-73. Mem. Am. Ednl. Research Assn., Am. Psychol. Assn., Am. Vocat. Assn., Council for Exceptional Children, Evaluation Network, Nat. Council on Measurement in Edn., Mid-South Ednl. Research Assn., Phi Kappa Phi, Phi Lambda Theta. Contbr. articles to profl. jours. Home: 1429 Oak Manor #9 Memphis TN 38119 Office: Dept Spl Edn and Rehab Memphis State Univ Memphis TN 38152

BRAHLER, ELEANOR, pub. co. mgr.; b. Louisville, Ohio, June 28, 1941; d. Norbert J. and Orilla Marie (Kress) B.; B.S. in Elem. Edn., Duquesne U., 1971; M.S., Purdue U., 1978. Tchr. elem. grades Immaculate Conception Sch., Pitts., 1959-60, 61-63, St. Teresa Sch., Koppel, Pa., 1960-61, 63-66, St. Alexis Sch., Wexford, Conn., 1969-72, St. Paul Sch., North Canton, Ohio, 1966-69, 72-75; prin. St. Mary's Sch., Van Wert, Ohio, 1975-81; dist. mgr. World Book-Childcraft Internat., Inc., 1981—. Bd. dirs. Campfire Girls for Van Wert County, 1955, St. Mary's Sch., 1955-81; past bd. dirs. Council on Alcoholism. Democrat. Roman Catholic. Home: 722 George St Van Wert OH 45891

BRAIDEN, ROSE MARGARET, artist; b. Los Angeles, Nov. 25, 1923; d. Sylvester and Margaret Mary (Hines) B.; B.A., Mt. St. Mary's Coll., 1949; M.F.A., Calif. Coll. Arts and Crafts, 1958. Tchr. elem. schs., Los Angeles, 1945-58; art chmn. Bishop Montgomery High Sch., Redondo Beach, Calif., 1958-68; instr. art history and painting Mt. St. Mary's Coll., 1968-70; chmn. photo design dept. Brooks Inst. Photography, Santa Barbara, Calif., 1970-82; co-dir. Keystone Photog. Gallery, Santa Barbara, 1982—; works include: triptych wall mural Mt. St. Mary's Coll., mosaic St. Lawrence's Ch., stained glass windows St. Bernard's Ch. Mem. AIA, Guild of Religious Architects, Los Angeles County Art Mus., Soc. Photog. Educators. Democrat. Roman Catholic. Home: 2929 Paseo Tranquillo Santa Barbara CA 93105

BRAIKER, HARRIET BERYL, psychologist; b. Los Angeles, Nov. 22, 1948; d. Samuel R. and Lillian E. (Weinberger) B.; A.B. summa cum laude, UCLA, 1970, M.A., 1971, Ph.D., 1975. Teaching asst., research asst. dept. psychology UCLA, 1970-75; clin. intern San Fernando Valley Child Guidance Clinic, 1972-74; cons. Rand Corp., 1974-75; asso. social scientist, 1975—; instr. dept. human devel. UCLA; cons. Stanford Research Inst. NSF scholar, 1968. Mem. Am. Psychol. Assn., Western Psychol. Assn., Phi Beta Kappa. Author: (with others) Alcoholism and Treatment, 1978; The Course of Alcoholism; Who Commits Crime. Office: 1700 Main St Santa Monica CA 90406

BRAINARD, EDITH MAE, ret. librarian; b. Guthrie County, Iowa; d. Charles W. and Henrietta (Martin) Brainard; B.A., U. Iowa, 1927, M.A., 1928; B.S., U. Minn., 1932; student U. Chgo. Library Sch., 1944-45. Tchr. high sch. and jr. coll., St. Johns, Ariz., Waukon, Iowa, 1928-31; librarian Eldora (Iowa) Public Library, 1933-36, Southwestern Coll., 1936-42, Itasca Jr. Coll., 1942-43, Gustavus Adolphus Coll., 1943-44, Ill. Wesleyan U., 1945-47, James Millikin U., 1947-51; asst. librarian Portland (Oreg.) State Extension Center, 1951-52; head circulation and reference John McIntire Library, Zanesville, Ohio, 1952-53; head librarian McKinley Meml. Library, Niles, Ohio, 1953-69; lectr. U. Minn. Library Sch., summers 1937-42. Mem. Niles Mayor's Com. on Comic Books; mem. Niles council Girl Scouts U.S.A., 1964. Mem. Am., Ohio, Kans. (past pres.) library assns., Bus. and Profl. Women's Club (past pres. Eldora, Niles 1959-60). Club: Trumbull Toastmistress (v.p.). Contbr. articles profl. and ednl. jours. Home: Adair IA

BRAINARD, JAYNE DAWSON (MRS. ERNEST SCOTT BRAINARD), civic worker; b. Amarillo, Tex., Nov. 1; d. Bill Cross and Evelyn (McLane) Dawson; A.B., Oklahoma City U., 1950; m. Ernest Scott Brainard, Nov. 26, 1950; children—Sydney Jane, Bill Dawson. Sec.-treas. E.S. Brainard Inc., 1980—; v.p. J. Thornton Cattle Co., 1981—. Guardian, Camp Fire Assn., 1960-65; vol. N.W. Tex. Hosp. Aux., 1960-63; state chmn. Am. Heritage, DAR, 1963-67, regent chpt., 1966-67, parliamentarian chpt., 1975-79, state historian, state chmn. marshalls, 1967-70, 73-76, mem. state organizing com., 1967-70, nat. vice chmn. marshalls, 1969-79, state rec. sec., 1970-73, editor cookbook, 1972, nat. vice chmn. motion picture com., 1971-73, mem. nat. bd. mgmt., nat. chmn. state regent's dinner, 1980-81, mem. Nat. Officers Club, 1979—, Nat. Chmn.'s Assn., 1981—, mem. Tex. speakers staff, 1972-76, 76-79, Tex. vice-regent, 1976-79, pres. nat. vice-regents club 1977-78, vice chmn. state fin. com., 1976-79, Tex. DAR Gen. Conf. chmn., 1975, 78, state chmn. state regents project, 1973-76, area rep. nat. speakers staff, 1977-80, 82-83, editor Tex. Roster, 1976, mem. state by law com., 1973-76, pres. chpt. regents Club, 1973-74, pres. vice-regents club, 1977-78, Tex. state regent, 1979-82, pres. Tex. DAR State Officers Club, 1980-81, state parliamentarian, 1982-85; organizing pres. Children Am. Revolution, 1963-65, state chmn. mag. sustaining fund; organizing regent Daus. Am. Colonies, 1972, chmn., 1974-76; bd. dirs. Tamassee DAR Sch., Kate Duncan Smith Sch.; pub. relations Amarillo Little Theater, 1965-69, pres., 1968-69, dir., 1966-69; bd. mem., program com. chmn. Amarillo Camp Fire Council, 1965-67, 75—, vice chmn. council, 1976—, pres., 1977-78; chmn. Camp Fire Leaders Assn., 1964-65, bd. dirs., 1974-79, pres. Amarillo council, 1977-78; br. pres. AAUW, 1963-65, pub. relations, 1965-67, world affairs rep., 1965-67; sec.-treas. group League Democratic Women, 1964; pres. Panhandle Geol. Soc. Aux., 1959, Starlighters Dance Club, 1963-64; pres. Speaking of Living Study Club, 1962-63, sec., 1973-74, parliamentarian, 1976-77, pres., 1977-78; pres. Republican Woman's Club, 1968, 73, v.p., 1972; steering com. Nat. Library Week, 1966, 67, 68, Amarillo Chischom Trail Centennial, 1967; mem. Revitalize Amarillo Com., 1972, Amarillo Heart Bd., 1972-73, Historic Markers Task Force. Mem. Internat. Platform Assn., U.D.C. (rep. to Amarillo Geneal. Adv. Bd. 1973-74, 75-76, 76-77, pres. Amarillo Geneal. Adv. Bd. 1982-84), Nat. Assn. Parliamentarians (registered, pres. Hazel Crowley unit 1980—), United Daus. 1812 (organizing regent), Daus. Colonial Wars, Nat. Soc. So. Dames. Mem. Christian Ch. (bd. parliament 1965-66). Home: 2119 S Lipscomb St Amarillo TX 79109 Office: Box 1101 Amarillo TX 79105

BRAINARD, SUZANNE GAGE, psychologist, computer co. exec.; b. Jacksonville, Fla., Mar. 12, 1945; d. Fred Harrison and Dorothy Jeanne (Beck) Gage; A.A., Am. Coll., Paris, 1965; B.A., U. Fla., 1966; M.A., Ohio State U., 1969, Ph.D., 1972. Psychologist, Battelle Meml. Inst., Columbus, Ohio, 1967-70; fellow Ohio State U., 1970-71; head handicapped and human devel. research programs Nat. Inst. Edn., Washington, 1971-75; sr. research asso. Minn. Systems, Inc., Mpls., 1975-76; psychologist, mktg. exec. Control Data Corp., Arlington, Va., 1975-80; pres. Brainard Assos., Inc., 1980—; cons. in field. Mem. Am. Psychol. Assn., Am. Edn. Research Assn., Am. Soc. Tng. and Devel., Am. Mgmt. Assn. Episcopalian. Contbr. articles to profl. jours. Office: 1640 Beekman Pl NW Washington DC 20009 Office: 3717 Columbia Pike Arlington VA 22204

BRAITINGER-GOEHRING, MARLIESE URSULA, educator; b. Stuttgart, Ger., Jan. 27, 1938; d. Raymond and Anna (Weber) Braitinger; B.A.; Thiel Coll., 1960; M.A., Syracuse U., 1962; m. Walter G. Goehring II, June 16, 1962; children—Heidi U., Marliese O. Test adminstr. Thiel Coll., 1959-60; staff dean of women Syracuse U., 1960-62; prof. German and Spanish, Endicott Coll., Beverly, Mass., 1962—, also acting acad. dean, asso. dean women, dir. advanced studies, supervisory dept. head dept. fgn. langs. Bd. dirs Danvers YMCA, 1980—; mem. Am. Security Council, 1979—, Republican Nat. Com., 1979—. Named Most Distinguished Advisor Phi Theta Kappa, 1982. Mem. Women for Constl. Govt. Congregationalist Home: 5 Puritan Rd Wenham MA 01984 Office: Hale St Beverly MA 01915

BRAKAS, GUNDA MARIA, educator; b. Kleipeda, Lithuania, Sept. 18, 1935; came to U.S., 1952, naturalized, 1958; d. Martin and Gunhild Hoegh (Bryoe) B.; student Gettysburg Coll., 1954-56; B.S., Columbia U., 1958, M.S., 1971, postgrad., 1977—; postgrad. Rutgers U., 1977—. Dental hygienist in charge dental hygiene dept. Continental Ins. Co., 1958-65; supervising dental hygienist, periodontology dept. U. Zurich Dental Sch., 1965-68; dir. dental health edn. in pub. schs. Centre de Medicine Dentaire, Rabat, Morocco, 1968-70; instr. Columbia U., 1971-73; chief supr., instr. Dental Hygiene Sch., Zurich, 1973-75; asst. prof., clin. coordinator, past acting chmn. Bergen Community Coll., Paramus, N.J., 1976—. Mem. Am. Dental Hygienists Assn., Dental Hygienists Assn., Columbia U. Dental Hygiene Alumnae Assn., NEA, N.J. Edn. Assn., Am. Assn. Dental Schs., Nat. Asst. Female Execs., Danish Am. Soc., Am. Scandinavian Found., Delta Gamma, Delta Phi Alpha. Republican. Lutheran. Home: 70 Polifly Rd Hackensack NJ 07601

BRAKE, DOROTHY ZERYKIER, psychologist; b. Katowice, Poland, Jan. 11, 1950; came to U.S., 1969, naturalized, 1975; d. Michael and Helena (Stahl) Zerykier; B.A., Queens Coll., 1973; M.A., New Sch. Social Research, 1975; m. Jesse Copper Brake, May 27, 1978. Translator, 1969-70; adminstrv. asst. Internat. Univ. Booksellers, 1970-75; psychology intern Bergen Pines County Hosp., 1975-76; psychologist Caswell Center, Kinston, N.C., 1977-78; psychologist mental retardation services Dorothea Dix Hosp., Raleigh, N.C., 1978—. Mem. Am. Psychol. Assn., Assn. Retarded Citizens, Wake County Mental Health Assn.

BRAKONECKE, HELEN ELIZABETH, city ofcl.; b. Niles, Ohio, Mar. 2, 1931; s. Joseph and Elizabeth (Kovacs) Kuhn; cert. assessing, U. Mich., 1978; m. Edward S. Brakonecke, Nov. 15, 1949; children—Patricia Ed Brakonecke Thompson, Sandra Marie Brakonecke Babcock. Asst. adminstr. C. of C. So. Wayne County (Mich.), 1966-67; credit analyst Security Bank, Southgate, Mich., 1976-77; prodn. analyst Repub. Finishing Corp., 1967-70; assessor City of Trenton (Mich.), 1977—. Mem. Mich. Crippled Children's Com., 1967-73, Trenton Bd. Canvassers, 1964-77. Named Mrs. Mich., 1965-66. Mem. Internat. Assn. Assessing Officers, Mich. Assessors Assn., Wayne Assessors Assn., Trent Bus. and Profl. Women. Republican. Address: 5037 Argonne Blvd Trenton MI 48183

BRAM, ISABELLE MARY RICKEY MCDONOUGH, clubwoman; b. Oskaloosa, Iowa, Apr. 4; d. Lindsey Vinton and Heddy (Lundee) Rickey; B.A. in Govt., George Washington U., 1947, postgrad., 1947-49; m. Dayle C. McDonough, Jan. 20, 1949. Dep. tax assessor and collector Aransas Pass Ind. Sch. Dist., 1939-41; sec. to city atty., Aransas Pass, Tex., 1939-41; info. specialist U.S. State Dept., Washington, 1942-48. Treas., Mo. Fedn. Women's Clubs, 1964-66, 2d v.p., 1966-68, 1st v.p., 1968-70, pres., 1970-72, exec. com., dir., 1972—; exec. com. Missourians for Clean Water. Bd. dirs. Gen. Fedn. Women's Clubs; bd. dirs. DeKalb County Public Library, pres., 1966; bd. dirs. Mo. Girls Town Found.; bd. advs. Legal Aid Western Mo. Mem. Mo. Fedn. Woman's Clubs (parliamentarian), Am. Soc. in Glasgow (Scotland), DeKalb County Hist. Soc., Internat. Platform Assn., AAUW, Nat. League Am. Pen Women, Epsilon Sigma Omicron, Zeta Tau Alpha, Phi Delta Delta, Phi Delta Gamma. Democrat. Episcopalian. Clubs: Tri Arts, Wimodausis, Gavel, Ledgers (pres.), Isabelle McDonough Girls Town, DeKalb County Women's Democratic (pres. 1964), Shakespeare, Mo. Democratic, Fifty Year. Editor Mo. Clubwoman Mag. Home: Sloan and Cherry Maysville MO 64469

BRAMHALL, MARTHA FREIS, mgmt. cons., educator; b. Lincoln, Nebr. Mar. 8, 1943; d. Edward David and Willa (Hussey) Freis; A.A., Montgomery Coll., 1974; B.A., Cath. U., 1978, M.S.W., 1979; children—Laura Elizabeth, Katheryn Susan. Family services worker Montgomery County Assn. Retarded Citizens, Kensington, Md., 1972-74; community program specialist Anne Arundel County Community Action Agy., Annapolis, Md., 1974-75; psychiatric technician Suburban Hosp., Bethesda, Md., 1975-76; instr. mental health program Montgomery Coll., Takoma Park, Md., 1979—; pres. Bramhall Assocs., Silver Spring, Md.; cons. Montgomery Presch. Achievement Center, Silver Spring, Md., 1979-81, Montgomery County Assn. for Retarded Citizens, Kensington, 1979-80, Montgomery County Commn. for Handicapped Individuals, Rockville, Md., 1981, State of Md. Dept. Health & Mental Hygiene, Baltimore, 1980-81, Nat. Wildlife Fedn., 1981, Resource Applications, 1981-82, Am. Heart Assn., 1982. Vice pres. bd. dirs. Montgomery County Mental Health Assn., 1979-80, dir. case mgmt. program, 1982—. Mem. Assn. Humanistic Psychology, Ind. Psychology Assn., Am. Pub. Welfare Assn., Am. Orthopsychiat. Assn., Nat. Assn. Social Workers, Nat. Assn. Female Execs., Assn. Part-Time Profls., Am. Soc. for Tng. and Devel., Montgomery Mental Health Assn., Phi Beta Kappa. Contbr. articles to profl. jours.

BRAMLETT, MARY LYNNETTE HARRIS, banker; b. Corona, Calif., Sept. 18, 1953; d. Kenneth Frank and Kathy Lee (Hill) Harris; student U. Md., 1974-77, Southwestern Grad. Sch. Banking. Bookkeeper, First State Bank & Trust, Houston, 1972; successively teller, sec., relief supr., mgr., br. mgr. Peoples Nat. Bank of Md., Suitland, 1972-77; with Post Oak Bank, Houston, 1977-82, asst. v.p. ops. mgmt., 1980-82; asst. v.p. comml. loan ops. First City Nat. Bank Houston, 1982—. Bd. dirs. Big Sisters-Big Bros. of Houston, 1981; vol., Spl. Olympics, 1981; mediator Neighborhood Justice Center, 1981; speaker Speakers Bur., Houston Bar Assn., 1981. Mem. Nat. Assn. Bank Women, Am. Soc. Indsl. Security, NOW, Alpha Sigma Lambda. Mem. Christian Ch. Clubs: Bank Women's, Forum. Contbr. articles to profl. jours. Office: 1001 Main St Houston TX 77001

BRAMLETT, PATRICIA RUTH GOLDSWORTHY, educator; b. Colville, Wash., Nov. 29, 1940; d. Fred Mickelwait and Ruth Marion (Brock) Goldsworthy; B.A., U. N.Mex., 1962, M.A., 1977. Tchr. Spanish, N.Mex. and Ariz., 1963-68; adult edn. instr Project SER, Albuquerque, 1968-73; part-time instr. adult edn. Albuquerque Tech.-Vocat. Inst., 1973-77; instr. secondary and adult tchr. edn. U.N.Mex., 1976-77; adult edn. coordinator Dona Ana br. N.Mex. State U., Las Cruces, 1977—; mem. adv. bd. adult basic edn. U. N.Mex., 1980—, chmn., 1981-82; cons. in field. Named N.Mex. Outstanding Adult Educator, 1974-75, Hidalgo de Educación, N.Mex., 1973. Mem. Mountain Plains Adult Edn. Assn. (dir. 1978-80, editor newsletter 1979—), N.Mex. Adult and Continuing Edn. Assn. (pres. 1971-72), LWV (chpt. treas. 1978-80), Somerset Villa Townhouse Assn. (dir. 1979—). Home: Box 3035 UPB Las Cruces NM 88003 Office: Box 3DA Las Cruces NM 88003

BRAMSEN, JOELLEN MAY, savs. assn. ofcl.; b. Boone, Iowa, May 6, 1938; d. Virgil Albert and Alberta May (Petrie) Clabaugh; student sch., Klemme, Iowa; m. Gene L. Groves, June 20, 1956; children—Patricia, Perry, Danny; m. 2d Duane A. Bramsen, May 23, 1979. Bookkeeper, computer comml. account specialist, public relations officer, teller, receptionist, personal sec. to cashier and auditor, loan verification specialist United Home Bank, Mason City, Iowa, 1963-68; head teller, sec. to exec. v.p., receptionist, loan sec., public relations officer Mut. Fed. Savs. and Loan, Mason City, 1968-73; exec. sec., comml. ins. agt., life ins. agt., Mason City, 1973-78; asst. v.p. br. mgr. Home Fed. Savs. & Loan, Mason City, 1978—. Corp. bd. dirs., sec. Door Opener; chmn. Retail Devel. City, Moose Haven Retirement Center; mem. budget com. United Way; pres. Diabetic Assn., 1970, 71; mem. YWCA. Lic. real estate agt., Iowa. Mem. Savs. and Loan League (legis. com.), Mason City C. of C. (retail chmn., newsletter writer), Exec. Women, Ins. Women (pres. county 1974-75, treas. 1976), Women's C. of C. (treas. 1980-81), VFW, VFW Women's Aux., Am. Legion Aux., Future Women Am. Lutheran. Clubs: Women of Moose, Cooties. Mistress of ceremonies Mason City Bridal Shows for retailers, for various style shows, model for hair styling contests. Home: 310 N Taylor Mason City IA 50401 Office: 1825 4th St SW Mason City IA 50401

BRAMWELL, KATHARINE HONE EMMET, civic worker; b. N.Y.C., Oct. 19, 1914; d. Herman Le Roy and Helen (Dunscomb) Emmet; student Smith Coll.; m. Gerald Ames Bramwell, Sept. 22, 1934; children—Heidi Bramwell Humes, Katharine Bramwell Hamilton. Vol. worker for numerous charitable orgns., including Community Chest; operator gift shop Brit. War Relief, World War II, later for Community Chest; head fund raising drive St. Timothy's Sch., dist. dir. nat. auditions Met. Opera, N.J. dist. Trustee, St. Timothy's Sch., North Country Sch., Lake Placid, N.Y. Republican. Episcopalian. Home: Box 551 77 Bayard Ln Princeton NJ 08540

BRANCA, INEZ OLGA, constrn. co. exec.; b. N.Y.C., Feb. 7, 1915; d. Charles and Charlotte (Vernocchi) Monza; student Columbia U., 1938-39, CCNY, 1936-37; m. Barney Joseph Branca, Oct. 6, 1940; children—Joseph, Charles, Richard, Bernard. Sec., Jay Hormel & Co., N.Y.C., 1934-42; treas., corp. sec., office mgr. Bergen Engring. Co., East Rutherford N.J., 1943—. Roman Catholic. Mem. Glen Ridge (N.J.), Lodi (N.J.) (past pres.) women's clubs. Home: 2432 Harmon Cove Towers Secaucus NJ 07094 Office: Bergen Engring Co 375 Murray Hill Pkwy East Rutherford NJ 07073

BRANCATO, CAROLYN K., economist, energy specialist; b. St. Louis, Sept. 20, 1945; A.B., Barnard Coll., 1966; Ph.D., N.Y.U., 1974; m. Jerome Congress, Apr. 10, 1976. Securities analyst Dominick & Dominick, 1966-69; staff economist EPA, N.Y.C., 1970-73; expert witness N.Y. State Atty. Gen.'s Office, 1973-74; dir. econ. research service N.Y. State Legis. Inst., 1974-77; asst. prof. econs. Herbert Lehman Coll., 1974-78; staff dir. N.Y.C. Blackout Investigation, 1977-78; econ. cons. to pres. N.Y.C. Council, 1978-79; specialist in commerce and energy Congl. Research Service, Library of Congress, Washington, 1979—. Trustee, N.Y. Coll. Environ. Sci. and Forestry, 1974—. Office: Room 324 James Madison Bldg 101 Independence Ave SE Washington DC 20559 •

BRANCH, COATNEY ANN, nursing adminstr.; b. Breaux Bridge, La., Sept. 5, 1945; d. George W. and Irma T. Sibley; B.S., U. Southwestern La., 1968; m. Hershal R. Branch, June 24, 1967; children—Bridget, Barrett, Byron, Beau. Nurse, Am. Legion Hosp., Crowley, La., 1968-69; dir. nursing service Gary Meml. Hosp., Breaux Bridge, 1969—; sec.-treas., bd. dirs. Breaux Bridge Dozer Service, Inc. Vice-chmn. Home Health Services Adv. Bd., St. Martin Parish; mem. health manpower com. Acadiana Health Planning Council; mem. Acadiana Emergency Med. Service Council, 1980—, treas., 1980-81; chmn. St. Martin Parish CPR Awareness Com., 1979-81; den mother Cub Scouts Am., 1979-80; mem. Mid La. Health Agy. Systems, 1980-81; mem. cardiac care task force, 1980; mem. adv. bd. continuing edn. U. Southwestern La. Named Supr. of Year, Coop. Edn. Office, 1977-78. Mem. Am. Nurses Assn., Nurses Assn. of Am. Coll. Obstetricians and Gynecologists, Am. Heart Assn. (instr.-trainer CPR), La. Soc. Nursing Service Adminstrs. (bd. dirs. 1974-76), La. Nurses Assn., Lafayette Dist. Nurse Assn. Baptist. Home: 1017 E Bridge St Breaux Bridge LA 70517 Office PO Box 357 Breaux Bridge LA 70517

BRANCH, JEANNETTE DAVIS, psychiat. social worker; b. Montgomery, Ala., Feb. 9, 1923; d. Fred Tuggle and Eleanor Neucie Davis; B.S., Ala. State Tchrs. Coll., 1942; M.A., U. Chgo., 1949; postgrad. Ill. Inst. Tech., 1978—; children—James, Elliott, Eleanor. Social cons. Nat. Coll. Edn., Evanston, Ill. 1960-64; chief Children's Mental Health Services, Woodlawn Mental Health Center, Chgo. 1964-70, dir. 1970-75; asst. prof. psychiatry U. Chgo., 1967-70, assoc. prof., 1979—; dir. Southside Youth Program, Chgo., 1975-77; v.p. Human Services The Woodlawn Orgn., Chgo. 1981—; mem. peer rev. com. exptl. and spl. tng. programs NIMH, 1974-77, chmn., 1977. Cert. social worker, Ill. Mem. Am. Orthopsychiatric Assn., AAAS, AAUP. Roman Catholic. Author (with others) Mental Health and Going to School. Office: 5811 S Kenwood Ave Chicago IL 60637

BRAND, ELAINE, educator; b. N.Y.C.; d. Leon and Hannah Brownstein; B.A., Hofstra U., 1968; M.A., C.W. Post Coll., 1975; postgrad. SUNY, Stony Brook, 1976—; children— Holly, Sherry. Showroom sales mgr. Cohler Co., N.Y.C.; adj. prof. English dept. C.W. Post Coll., Brookville, L.I., N.Y., 1975-77, coordinator lectr. series, 1975-81; adj. prof. English dept. SUNY, Farmingdale, 1973-77; asst. prof. Sch. Bus., Adelphi U., Garden City, N.Y., 1977—. C.W. Post fellow, 1968-70; recipient Disting. Coordinator award, 1978. Mem. MLA, Mensa, Am. Soc. Tng. and Devel., L.I. Poetry Collective, Delta Sigma Pi. Home: 169 Syracuse Ave North Massapaqua NY 11758 Office: Sch Bus Adelphi U Garden City LI 11430

BRANDENBERG, ALIKI, author, illustrator; b. Wildwood Crest, N.J., Sept. 3, 1929; d. James Peter and Stella (Lagakos) Liacouras; grad. Phila. Mus. Coll. Art, 1951; m. Franz Brandenberg, Mar. 15, 1957; children—Jason, Alexa. Author, illustrator over 50 children's books including: My Hands, 1962; My Five Senses, 1962; The Story of Johnny Appleseed, 1963; A Weed is a Flower, 1965; Keep Your Mouth Closed, Dear, 1966; Three Gold Pieces, 1967; Hush Little Baby, 1968; My Visit to the Dinosaurs, 1969; Fossils Tell of Long Ago, 1972; Go Tell Aunt Rhody, 1974; At Mary Bloom's, 1976; The Two of Them, 1979, Mummies Made in Egypt, 1979 (Silver Slate Pencil from Dutch Children's Book Council 1981); Digging Up Dinosaurs, 1981; We Are Best Friends, 1982. Recipient 1st prize children's book award N.Y. Acad. Scis., 1977; jr. book award Boys' Club of Am., 1968. Address: 17 Regents Park Terr London NW1 7ED England

BRANDES, ILA ANN, indsl. engr.; b. Charlotte, N.C., Apr. 3, 1954; d. Roddy Arthur and Marguerite (Johnson) B.; B.A. in Psychology and Religion, U. N.C., Greensboro, 1977; cert. Maynard Mgmt. Inst., Charlotte, N.C., 1981. Quality assurance supr. Ball Corp., Asheville, N.C., 1977-79, indsl. engr., Muncie, Ind., 1979-80, methods and standards engr., 1980-82, indsl. engr. materials handling, 1982—; counselor Muncie Jr. Achievement, 1979-80. Mem. Nat. Assn. Female Execs. Presbyterian. Office: 345 S High St Muncie IN 47302

BRANDES, KAREN ANN, real estate broker; b. St. Louis, Aug. 15, 1941; d. William S. Kenner and Mary Lorayne (Tarpley) Hancock; student U. Tex., Arlington, Tex. Tech. U., So. Meth. U.; grad. Realtors Inst., 1974; m. William Heaton Brandes, Aug. 24, 1963; children—Kimberly Ann, William Hancock. Engaged in real estate bus., 1970—, pres., broker Brandes Real Estate, Inc., Irving, Tex., 1976—. Chmn., Irving Sch. Tax Equalization Bd., 1980; mem. adv. bd. Helping Hand Sch. Mem. Nat. Assn. Ind. Free Appraisers, Nat. Assn. Rev. Appraisers, Irving Bd. Realtors (dir. 1978-80, sec. bd., mem. exec. com. 1980—, v.p.), Greater Dallas Bd. Realtors, Irving C. of C. (dir. 1979-83). Presbyterian. Home: 800 Hillcrest Ct Irving TX 75062 Office: 2001 W Airport Freeway Irving TX 75062

BRANDNER, MARGARET ANNE SHAW, polygraph examiner; b. Denver, Sept. 4, 1937; d. Bertram and Bessie (Syme) Shaw; A.B., Loretto Heights Coll., 1959; grad. polygraph examiner Rocky Mountain Security Inst., 1978; diplomate forensic hypnotist Inst. Forensic and Investigative Hypnosis, 1980; m. Kenneth LeRoy Brandner, Dec. 26, 1970; children—Michele Marya, Micah Laird. Accountant, Denver Children's Home, 1970, Keny's Equipment, Inc., Green River, Wyo., 1971-78; polygraph examiner, sec., treas. Brandner Corp., Green River, 1978—. Mem. Am. Acad. Forensic Hypnotists, Am., Utah polygraph assns., Colo. Assn. Polygraph Examiners, Nat. Acad. Lady Polygraphists, World Congress Profl. Hypnotists, Nat. Fedn. Bus. and Profl. Women, Mensa. Roman Catholic. Home and Office: PO Box 1147 Green River WY 82935

BRANDON, CELIA, mail order catalog exec.; b. Methuen, Mass., July 18, 1939; d. Frederick G. and Mary L. (Feroce) Bodge; B.A., U. N.H., 1961; M.A. with honors, N.Y.U., 1972. English/drama tchr. high schs., Mystic, Conn., Rockport, Mass., Clarkstown, N.Y., 1961-69; edn. dir. N.Y. State Office Drug Abuse Services, N.Y.C., 1969-76; co-owner, bus. mgr., mail order dir. Body Sense, Newburyport, Mass., 1972-77; personal fin. mgr./counselor for individuals in pvt. practice, N.Y.C., 1976-79; pres., founder Rainbow's End Catalog Co., N.Y.C., 1979—; cons. in field. Grantee HEW, 1967. Mem. Assn. of Humanistic Psychology, Smithsonian Inst., Nat. Mail Order Assn., Nat. Assn. Women Bus. Owners, Am. Craft Council. Home: 122 W 74th St New York NY 10023 Office: PO Box 997 New York NY 10023

BRANDON, HELGA W., banker; b. Germany, Sept. 18, 1932; d. Gustaw and Irmgard (Fitsche) Willers; m. Richard Brandon, Jan. 19, 1980; 1 dau., Karen Ingeborg. With Bremer Bank, 1950-51; ops. supr. So. Ariz. Bank, Tucson, 1960; with Valley Nat. Bank, Phoenix, 1961—, now v.p. applications, mgmt. and improved services. Mem. Nat. Assn. Banking Women, Am. Bankers Assn. Republican. Lutheran. Club: Track (Phoenix). Home: 8212 N 1st Ave Phoenix AZ 85021 Office: 3620 N Black Canyon Phoenix AZ

BRANDON, LESLIE, social scientist; b. San Antonio, Sept. 19, 1945; d. Earl and Gloria (Grant) B.; B.A., U. Pitts., 1969, M.S.W., 1972; M.P.H., Columbia U., 1980. Research asst. Verve Research Corp., 1974-75; dir. counselors Women's Clinic, Washington, 1973-75; asso. public adminstrn. officer UN, 1975-77; asst. prof. dentistry Sch. Dental and Oral Surgery, Columbia U., 1977—. Mem. Am. Public Health Assn., Am. Acad. Polit. and Social Sci., AAAS, Soc. Internat. Devel., Am. Assn. Dental Schs., Internat. Assn. Schs. Social Work. Home: 245 E 63d St Apt 915 New York NY 10021 Office: 630 W 168th St New York NY 10032

BRANDON, LIANE, filmmaker, educator; b. Newark, July 7, 1939; d. Philip and Nita (Poster) B.; student St. Lawrence U., N.Y., 1957-59, U. Edinburgh (Scotland), 1959-60; exchange student U. Moscow, summer 1960; A.B., Boston U., 1962, M.Ed., 1967. Ski instr., Mt. Tremblant, Que., Can., 1960-62; actress Children's Theatre, Cambridge, Mass., 1960-62; film project dir., media studies English dept. coordinator Quincy (Mass.) Public Schs., 1964-73; asso. prof. film prodn. and media studies Sch. Edn., U. Mass., Amherst, 1973—; co-founder, mem. New Day Films, 1971—; media cons. N.Y. State Dept. Edn., 1968; film cons. Mass. Gov.'s Commn. on Status of Women, 1974; media cons. Mass. Dept. Edn., 1970-74; coordinator Mass. Young Filmmakers Festival, 1974-75; cons. Mass. Artists Found., 1975, 82; mem. adv. bd. Allston-Brighton 350, Inc., 1979-80; judge New Eng. Film Festival, 1980; trustee Theaterworks, 1981—; films exhibited Mus. Modern Art, Whitney Mus. Am. Art, Chgo. Art Inst., Nat. Film Theatre, London, Internat. Women's Film Festivals, Paris, Iran, N.Y., John F. Kennedy Center Performing Arts, Washington, also on TV; guest lectr. at various confs. on edn. and film, colls. and art schools in U.S. Recipient blue ribbon Am. Film Festival, 1972; Creative Artist award AAUW, 1975; Boston Coll. Film grantee, 1971-72; U. Mass. grantee, 1974; Mass. Found. for Humanities and Pub. Policy grantee, 1975. Mem. New Eng. Screen Edn. Assn. (v.p. 1971—), Assn. Ind. Video and Filmmakers. Contbr. articles on film prodn. to profl. jours.; dir., producer films including: Anything You Want to Be (The Ribbon, Am. Film Festival award), 1971; Betty Tells Her Story (Internat. Festival of Women's Films award), 1972; Not So Young Now as Then (Athens Film Festival award), 1974; Once Upon a Choice (Silver medal Houston Internat. Film Festival), 1980. Won lawsuit protecting film titles, 1978. Office: Sch Edn U Mass Amherst MA 01003

BRANDON, MARY JANE HOWARD, lawyer, social worker; b. New Orleans, Sept. 19, 1944; d. Victor Charles and Mildred Eileen (Neal) Howard; B.A., Southwestern at Memphis, 1966; M.S.W., U. Tenn., 1968; J.D., Loyola U., New Orleans, 1982. Social worker Head Start program City of Memphis, 1965; dir. adoptions St. Peter Home for Children, Memphis, 1968-71; dir. social services Ednl. Research & Treatment Center, New Orleans, 1971-77; social worker in pvt. practice, 1975-77; chief social worker Hope Haven-Madonna Manor, New Orleans, 1977-80; practice law, New Orleans, 1982—. Trustee, fin. sec. First Unitarian Ch., New Orleans; pres. adv. bd. ACC Adult Group Home, 1982—; mem. children's com. Mental Health Assn. NIMH fellow, 1966-68. Mem. Nat. Assn. Social Workers, Acad. Cert. Social Workers, La. Assn. Bd. Cert. Social Workers, Nat. Soc. Autistic Children, Am. Orthopsychiat. Assn., Am. Group Psychiat. Assn. Am. Soc. Internat. Law, ABA, Interam. Bar Assn., Internat. Bar Assn., La. Hist. Assn., Preservation Resource Center, La. Landmarks Soc. Republican. Roman Catholic. Home: 1418 8th St New Orleans LA 70115 Office: 2929 S Carrollton Ave New Orleans LA 70118

BRANDS, ALVIRA BERNICE, govt. health program exec.; b. Hader, Minn., July 9, 1922; d. Benjamin Christian and Alma Josephine (Linder) Moe; certificate St. Lucas Hosp. Sch. Nursing, Fairbault, Minn., 1943; B.S. with distinction in Nursing, U. Minn., 1958, M.Nursing Adminstrn., 1960; D.Sc. in Psychiat. Nursing, Catholic U. Am., 1975; m. Allen J. Brands, Nov. 27, 1971; children—David, Richard. Head nurse Anoka (Minn.) State Hosp., 1954-56, nursing supr., 1959-60, instr. nursing, 1960-63; chief nursing services med. services div. Minn. State Dept. Pub. Welfare, St. Paul, 1963-69; program analyst mental health care and services financing br. NIMH, HEW, Washington, 1975—; guest lectr. U. Md., 1972-73; cons. in field; mem. numerous health care adv. coms., Minn. and Washington, 1964—. Recipient Outstanding Service award Alcohol, Drug Abuse and Mental Health Adminstrn., Pub. Health Service HEW, 1976. Mem. AAUW, Am. Pub. Health Assn., Am. Assn. Mental Deficiency, Am. Assn. Retarded Children, Nat. League Nursing, Am. Nurses Assn. (council advanced practitioners psychiat. and mental health nursing), Am. Coll. Clin. Pharmacologists, Nat. Council on Drugs, Assn. Mil. Surgeons U.S. Author several NIMH pamphlets; producer film and video tape on mental retardation care. Home: 3024 Tilden St NW Washington DC 20008 Office: 5600 Fishers Ln Rockville MD 20852

BRANDT, ARLENE M., savs. and loan assn. exec.; b. Barron, Wis., Mar. 28, 1928; d. John Joseph and Hannah Sophie (Foss) Doonan; student public schs.; m. Floyd Brandt, Sept. 8, 1945 (div. 1973); children—Dennis, Bruce, Kevin. With West Allis (Wis.) Savs. & Loan Assn., 1958-81, controller, 1969-79, treas., 1979-81. Mem. Fin. Mgrs. Soc. for Savs. Instns., Inc. Home: 1029 N Jackson St Milwaukee WI 53202

BRANDT, AVRENE LAURA, clin. psychologist; b. N.Y.C., July 3, 1942; d. Max Bernard and Pauline (Slatin) Brandt; B.A., Hunter Coll., 1964; M.S. (NIMH fellow), U. Mass., 1968, Ph.D., 1971; m. William Hall, June 24, 1973; children—Wiley, Gabhriel, Elissa. Staff psychologist Ashbourne Sch., Elkins Park, Pa., 1969-71; chief psychologist Pottstown (Pa.) Area Mental Health Clinic, 1971-74; clin. service dir. Devereux Found., Devon, Pa., 1975—; cert. instr. Assertive Relations with Children, Phila. Bd. dirs. Resources for Human Devel. Mem. Phila. Clin. Neuropsychol. Group, Am. Psychol. Assn. Office: Devereux Found 19 S Waterloo Rd Devon PA 19333

BRANDT, DIANE L., state legislator; b. Estherville, Iowa, Aug. 28, 1938; d. Charles Marvin and Lorna I. (Burkhead) Robinson; B.S., Iowa State U., 1961. Mem. Iowa Ho. of Reps., 1975—. Bd. dirs. LWV Iowa, 1965-69, 72-74; mem. Cedar Falls Planning and Zoning Commn., 1972-74; v.p. Iowa Civil Liberties Union, 1973-74; mem. NAACP, AAUW (pres. Waterloo br. 1973-74). Democrat. Presbyterian. Office: State Capitol Des Moines IA 50319

BRANDT, JOE ANN MARIE, clin. psychologist; b. Mpls., Jan. 8, 1952; d. Henry Aimar and Estelle Ann (Smith) B.; B.A. cum laude, U. Ga., 1974; M.A., U. Ark., 1977, Ph.D., 1980; postgrad. U. Ala. Med. Center, 1981; m. William Arthur Dickinson, Apr. 4, 1981. Mem. interdisciplinary team in adolescent medicine U. Ala., 1978-79, intern, 1978-79, instr. psychology, 1979-80; pvt. practice clin. psychology Savannah Psychol. Cons. (Ga.), 1981—; cons. St. Joseph's Hosp., Candler Gen. Hosp., Broad Oaks Hosp., Midway Nursing Home. Mem. Ga. Conservancy, Hist. Savannah Assn., Am. Soc. Clin. Hypnosis, Assn. Advancement Psychology, Coastal Assn. Lic. Psychologists, Am. Psychol. Assn., Assn. Women Psychologists, Ga. Psychol. Assn., NOW, Sierra Club, Citizens for Clean Air. Roman Catholic. Research on predictors of effective family functioning, neuropsychol. correlates of degenerative brain disorders, effects of sexual misconceptions on marital happiness and satisfaction. Home: 520 E 44th St Savannah GA 31405 Office: 5105 Paulsen St Suite 145 Savannah GA 31405

BRANDT, KATHLEEN COLE, social worker, advt. agy. exec.; b. Cin., Nov. 22, 1946; d. James Scott and Kathryn Gertrude (Borisch) Cole; B.A., Miami U., 1968; M.S.W., U. Mich., 1972; M.M., Northwestern U., 1978; m. Brian Brandt, Mar. 21, 1970. Social worker Hamilton County Welfare Dept., Cin., 1969-70, Lucas County Children Services Bd., Toledo, 1970-74, East Maine Sch. Dist., Niles, Ill., 1974-77; account exec. Leo Burnett Advt. Agy., Chgo., 1978—; field instr. Loyola U., Chgo., 1976-77. Mem. Acad. Cert. Social Workers, Nat. Assn. Social Workers, Miami U. Alumni Assn. (dir. 1976—), Northwestern U. Profl. Women's Assn. Home: 414 Kelling Ln Glencoe IL 60022 Office: Leo Burnett Advt Agy Prudential Plaza Chicago IL 60601

BRANDT, RUTH ANNE WAGNER (MRS. HERBERT W. BRANDT), bus. exec., civic worker; b. Sandusky, Ohio, June 6, 1923; d. Clarence E. and Anna (Kopp) Wagner; B.S., Seton Hill Coll., 1945; M.S., Case Western Res. U., 1970. Clin. dietitian Univ. Hosps., Cleve., 1946-49, Henry Ford Hosp., Detroit, 1949-51; chief nutrition clinic VA Regional Office, Cleve., 1951-53; owner Branlon Studio, Shaker Heights, Ohio, 1974—; dir. nutrition services Univ. Suburban Health Center, South Euclid, Ohio; adj. instr. Case Western Res. U., 1970-74; dir. Wagner Realty Co., Sandusky, Mayfair Mgmt., Inc., Sandusky; sec., dir. Stellen, Inc., Sandusky. Mem. Cleve. Inst. Music, Mus. Natural History, Shaker Lakes Regional Nature Center, 1970-74; chmn. adv. bd. Community Nutrition Service, 1973-76; trustee Cleve. Health Edn. Mus. Mem. Am., Cleve. (pres. 1954-55) dietetic assns., Soc. Nutrition Edn., Recreation League Cleve. Clubs: Cleve. Skating, Cleve. Playhouse, Jr. League (Cleve.). Home: 2626 West Park Blvd Shaker Heights OH 44120 Office: Nutrition Services 1611 S Green Rd South Euclid OH 44121

BRANDVOLD, EVELYN HANSON, fin. exec.; b. Hansford County, Tex., Dec. 9, 1918; d. Thomas Emil and Julia (Walker) Hanson; grad. Pearcerian Bus. Coll., 1937; student (grantee) St. Olaf Coll., 1941-42; m. John A. Brandvold, May 9, 1942; children—Joan, Joyce, Larry, Carol, Nancy, Karen. Tchr., Pearcerian Bus. Coll., 1937; sec. to atty., Minot, N.D., 1937; asst. sec.-treas. Minot Prodn. Credit Assn., 1938-41; student asst. to dean of women St. Olaf Coll., Northfield, Minn., 1941-42; sec. Cook-Reynolds Co., Lewistown, Mont., 1942, Hill County Abstract Co., 1943; asst. to v.p. Citizens State Bank, Choteau, Mont., 1964-82; fin. cons. Ch. pianist, Carpio, N.D., 1929-36, Sunday sch. tchr., 1928-36, 42-50; mem., sec. bd. parish edn. Zion Lutheran Ch., Lewistown, Mont., 1950-53; sr. organist Faith Luth. Ch., Great Falls, Mont., 1954-64. Recipient Balfour medal, 1936. Republican. Lutheran. Address: 1000 Adobe Great Falls MT 59404

BRANDWENE, PHYLLIS NEUMAN, sales and mktg. agy. exec.; b. Duryea, Pa., Aug. 3, 1929; d. David and Sara D. (Levy) Neuman; student West Hampton Coll. Women, Richmond, Va., 1947, Luzerne County Community Coll., Nanticoke, Pa., 1967, King's Coll., Wilkes Barre, Pa., 1970-71, 78-80; m. Harold Brandwene, Mar. 3, 1957; children—Deborah, David. Acct. exec. Ward Radio, Pittston, Pa., 1972-76; sales mgr. Greenspon Advt. Agy., also Luzerne County Transp. Authority, Wilkes Barre, 1977-78; advt. mgr. Jewish Community Center Digest, Wilkes Barre, 1977—; owner, sales cons. Phyllis Brandwene Sales Agy., Kingston, Pa., 1978—. Sec. citizens adv. com. Luzerne-Lackawanna Transp. Authority; past vice chmn. Kingston's Home Rule Charter Commn., Mayor's Youth Council; bd. dirs. Econ. Devel. Council N.E. Pa.; organizer, past vice chmn. Jr. Great Books Study Program; past 1st vice chmn. Wilkes Barre chpt. Am. Jewish Com.; mem. adult edn. com. Jewish Community Center; past vice chmn. Northeastern Pa. Constl. Conv. Com., Bell Ringing Soc. Luzerne County Bicentennial Com.; past sec. Kingston Citizen's Adv. Com.; past West side chmn. Am. Heart Assn.; past v.p. LWV, Wilkes Barre; past bd. dirs. Wyoming Valley Ballet Soc., Jewish Welfare Agy. Mem. Am. Soc. Profl. cons., Internat. Assn. Bus. Communicators, West Side Bus. and Profl. Women, Greater Wilkes Barre C. of C., N.E. Pa. Advt. Club (dir.), Wyoming Valley Mgmt. Club, Nesbitt Hosp. Aux., Friends of Hoyt Library, Nat. Council Jewish Women, Luzerne County Mental Health Assn., Queen Esther Hebrew Ladies Aid Soc. (past treas.). Jewish (chmn. adult edn., Sunday Sch. tchr.). Clubs: Hadassah (past dir.), Order Eastern Star (past matron, past chmn. youth com.). Home: 637 Gibson Ave Kingston PA 18704 Office: 18 Pierce St Kingston PA 18704

BRANDWYNNE-COTSEN, JACQUELINE, strategic planning cons.; b. Bienne, Switzerland, 1937; came to U.S., 1959; diploma Hoehere Toechterschule, Zurich, 1957; postgrad. in philosophy and lit. Columbia U., New Sch. Social Research. UN corr., 1959-61; mktg. exec. Helena Rubinstein, Inc., N.Y.C., 1959-62; exec. v.p., mem. exec. bd., creative dir. Yardley of London, Inc., N.Y.C., 1964-69; propr. Brandywynne Assos. Inc., mktg. bus. strategy and advt., N.Y.C., 1969-76; strategic planning and devel. Citicorp, N.Y.C., 1976-81; cons. strategic planning Geosource, Inc., 1981—; dir. Monogram Industries, Neutrogena Corp.; advisor U.S. Council Econ. Advisors, 1975-76.

BRANGAN, SANDRA RAE, bus. services co. exec.; b. Milw., July 7, 1948; d. Raymond John and Sherlie May (Beason) Weeks; student various jr. colls., U. Evansville; B.A. in Bus. summa cum laude, San Francisco State U., 1976, M.B.A. in Mktg., 1978; m. William Lee Brangan, July 8, 1964. Sec., City of Garden Grove (Calif.), 1966-71; asst. Guidance Center, U. Evansville, 1971-72; asst. to dean Sch. Bus., San Francisco State U., 1973-76; mktg. asst. Clemco Industries, San Francisco, 1976-77; v.p., corp. sec. Acctex Corp., San Francisco, 1977—; speaker on small bus. mktg. to women entrepreneurs; participant San Francisco State U. Alumni Assn. seminars for undergrads. on various careers. Recipient award for vocat. arts Bank of Am., 1966. Mem. Assn. M.B.A. Execs., Nat. Assn. Female Execs., Am. Soc. Personnel Cons., Am. Soc. Profl. and Exec. Women, Internat. Assn. for Personnel Women, Bay Area Personnel Assn., No. Calif. Indsl. Relations Council, Calif. Employment Assn., Beta Gamma Sigma. Club: Schoeber's Racquetball. Office: 601 Montgomery #2025 San Francisco CA 94111

BRANNAN, ETHEL FORD, social scientist; b. New Castle, Del., May 27; d. Thomas Drennen and Helen Virginia (Gooding) Ford; B.S., Johns Hopkins U., 1951, M.Ed. with honors, 1956; profl. diploma Columbia U., 1964, Ed.D. cum laude, 1965; widow. Mem. staff Balt. Pub. Schs., 1930-42, 46-62, 65-66, adminstr., 1958-62, 1965-66; prof. social psychology and sociology U. Buffalo, 1966-67; prof. social studies edn. Glassboro (N.J.) State Coll., 1967-82, chmn. social studies edn. curriculum com., 1972-81, dir. Global Edn. Ctr., 1977-79, pres. World Edn. Council, 1977-82; curriculum cons., bd. dirs. N.J. Council Social Studies; mem. President's Commn. Global Edn., N.J. Consortium Global Edn. Served with WAVES, 1942-46. Recipient various service awards; research fellow U. Nairobi and Olduvai Gorge, Africa, 1975-76; named Outstanding Coll. Social Studies Educator of Yr., 1981. Mem. NEA (mem. ednl. leadership team to china 1979), Nat. Council Social Studies (pres. inter-nation exchange council 1981-82), Social Studies Suprs. Assn., AAUP, N.J. Edn. Assn., N.J. Council Social Studies, UN Assn., Phi Delta Gamma (pres. 1980-82), Pi Lambda Theta, Kappa Delta Pi, Phi Delta Kappa. Republican. Methodist. Clubs: Town and Country Women's, Johns Hopkins, Columbia U. Author: Cultural Unity and Curriculum, 1966; Improving Educational Programs for Disadvantaged Children, 1968; A Philosophy of Education for the 1970's, 1970; Creativity—What Is It, 1971; Individualized Reading and Social Studies, 1972; editor, contbr. to The Irregular Verb: To Teach, 1972; author curriculum materials, articles in field. Home: 34 Holly Ct West Apts Pitman NJ 08071 Office: Robinson Hall Glassboro State Coll Glassboro NJ 08028

BRANNOCK, JUANITA LEWIS, nursing home adminstr.; b. Rockingham, N.C., June 29, 1924; d. Goley Burkemore and Mary Ann (Hancock) Lewis; R.N., James Walker Meml. Hosp., Wilmington, N.C., 1945; student Henry Ford Community Coll., Detroit, 1976-79; m. James Edward Brannock, Apr. 11, 1964. Pvt. duty and gen. hosp. duty nurse, 1945-46; nursing supr. Moses H. Cone Meml. Hosp., Greensboro, N.C., 1962-64; clin. nursing supr. Wayne County Gen. Hosp., Westland, Mich., 1966-79; dir. nursing Park Nursing Center, Taylor, Mich., 1979-81, adminstr., 1981—; pres. Continuing Health Edn. S.E. Mich., 1980-82; sec. Dirs. Nurses Wayne-Oakland Counties. Mem. Am. Nurses Assn., Am. Coll. Nursing Home Adminstrs., Am. Bus. Women's Assn. Home: 14860 McLain St Allen Park MI 48101 Office: 12575 S Telegraph Rd Taylor MI 48180

BRANNON, EMMA COLLINS, writer, essayist, poet, speaker; b. Elbert County, Ga.; d. Oscar L. and Hannah M. (Bell) Collins; grad. Sam Houston Normal Inst., 1913, Washington Sch. Art, 1922; B.S., Stephen F. Austin U., 1957, M.A., 1959; m. Jameston R. Brannon, Nov. 25, 1915 (dec. 1965); 1 foster son, James; 1 son, Jameston R. Tchr. public schs., Carthage, Tex., 1911-12, 15-16, 33-35, Gary, Tex., 1913-15, 16-24; bus. mgr. Brannon's Farms and Grocery Store, Carthage, 1929-40; postmaster U.S. Post Office, Carthage, 1940-55; religious, patriotic, inspirational, humorous and historic poems, ch. and prison ministry tracts writer, 1913—. Active Blue Bird council Girl Scouts U.S.A., 1957-59; sponsor Camp Fire Girls, 1959-68; Sunday sch. tchr. 1st Bapt. Ch., Gary, 1913-34, Carthage, 1936-70, Rose Park Bapt. Ch., Shreveport, La., 1970-78. Recipient Silver Tray award Carthage Postal Service Rural/City Carrier-Clk. group, 1955, plaque U.S. Postal Service. Mem. Acad. Am. Poets, Poetry Soc. Tex., Panola Hist. Soc., Panola C. of C., Tex. Geneal. Soc., La. Geneal. Soc., DAR, Internat. Platform Assn., Am. Security Council, Nat. Fedn. Republican Women, Sam Houston Alumni Assn., Stephen F. Austin State U. Alumni Assn. Baptist. Clubs: Altrua (dir. 1950-52), Carthage Garden (pres. 1967-69). Author: These Passed Our Way, 1972; Wayside Blossoms (collection of poems), 1979. Home: Carthage TX 75633

BRANSCOM, MARTHA ANNE, civic worker; b. Batavia, N.Y., Dec. 6, 1932; d. Everett Edward and Francys Mary (Decker) Heye; m. James A. Reed Oct. 3, 1949; children—J. Michael, Alan B., Paul K., William K., Jeffrey S.; m. 2d, James K. Branscom, June 25, 1977. Communications operator, Riverside County sheriff, Indio, Calif., 1957-63; dispatcher, matron Palm Springs (Calif.) Police Dept., 1963-68; rental rep. Hertz Corp., Palm Springs, 1968-70; sec., acct. staff mem. Sunrise Corp., Palm Springs Healthcare, Riverside County Mental Health, all So. Calif., 1970-74; cook McGrath (Alaska) Roadhouse, 1974; native student counselor McGrath Schs., 1974-75; oiler Green Assos. Pipelines, 1975-76; social worker Dept. Health and Social Services, McGrath, 1976-77; station mgr. Polar Airlines, McGrath, 1977-80; asst. city adminstr. City of McGrath, 1980; sec./bookkeeper Sta. KSKO, 1980—. Mem. founding com. mental health local program, McGrath, 1976-78, sec.-treas., 1976-78; founding, sec. treas. Kuskokwin Valley Rescue Squad, 1979—; mem. Tanana Chiefs Mental Health Bd., Fairbanks, 1976-78; mem. McGrath Health Com., 1978—; chmn. Community Sch. Com.; mem. Alaska Adv. Council on Emergency Med. Services, Statewide Health Coordinating Council. Mem. Alaska Paramedical Assn., Nat. Registry EMT, Internat. Platform Assn. Republican. Presbyterian. Club: Crosswinds Ceramic. Home: 20J St PO Box 151 McGrath AK 99627 Office: City of McGrath McGrath AK 99627

BRANSCOMB, ANNE WELLS (MRS. LEWIS MCADORY BRANSCOMB), lawyer, cons.; b. Statesboro, Ga., Nov. 22, 1928; d. Guy Herbert and Ruby (Hammond) Wells; B.A., Ga. Coll., 1949, U. N.C., 1949; M.A., Harvard U., 1951; J.D. with honors, George Washington U., 1962; m. Lewis McAdory Branscomb, Oct. 13, 1951; children—Harvie Hammond, Katharine Capers. Admitted to D.C. bar, 1962, Colo. bar, 1963, U.S. Supreme Ct. bar, 1972, N.Y. bar, 1973; research asso. Pierson, Ball and Dowd, Washington, 1962; law clk. U.S. Dist. Ct. Judge William E. Doyle, Denver, 1962-63; atty. Williams and Zook, Boulder, Colo., 1963-66; individual practice law, Boulder, 1966-69; mem. firm Arnold and Porter, Washington, 1969-72; communications counsel TelePrompTer Corp., N.Y.C., 1973; chmn. bd. Kalba Bowen Assos., Inc., communications cons., Cambridge, Mass., 1977-80, v.p., 1974-77, sr. asso., dir., 1980-82; mem. organizing com. Telecommunications Policy Research Conf., 1976; pres. Moneyscan, Inc., fin. planning computer services, 1980—; vis. scholar Yale U. Law Sch., 1981-82. Public relations dir. Montgomery County (Md.) LWV, 1954-57; mass media chmn. AAUW, Chevy Chase, Md., 1959-62; del. Nat. Conf. on Crime, 1967; adv. bd. communications law program UCLA; co-chmn. Coordinating Com. for Low Income Housing for Boulder, 1966-68; bd. dirs. HELP for Boulder, Inc., 1968-69; commr. Public Housing Authority, Boulder, 1969-70; bd. dirs. Nat. Public Radio, 1975-78; trustee EDUCOM, Interuniv. Communications Council, Inc., 1976-78; Colo. chmn. Nat. Democratic Women's Conf., 1966; vice chmn. Colo. Dem. State Central Com., 1967-69; del. Dem. Nat. Conv., 1968, hearing officer credentials com., 1972; spl. asst. to nat. campaign dir. McGovern-Shriver campaign, 1972; policy planning Carter campaign, 1976; trustee Rensselaer Poly. Inst., 1980—; vis. com. Harvard U. Office Info. Tech., 1977—; mem. Carnegie Corp. Task Force on Public Broadcasting, 1976-77; adv. panel on public understanding of sci. NSF, 1977-78; vis. com. Inst. Computer Scis. and Tech., Nat. Acad. Scis., 1977-80; mem. Aspen Inst. Task Force on Telecommunications Policy, 1977; mem. tech. adv. bd. Dept. Commerce, 1978-81, WARC adv. com. Dept. State, 1978-79; pres. Soc. for Protection of First Wives. Recipient Alumni Achievement award Ga. Coll., 1980. Mem. Am. (chmn. communications div. and mem. council of sci. and tech. sect.), N.Y., D.C., Colo. bar assns., Fed. Communications Bar Assn., Am. Polit. Sci. Assn., Computer Law Assn. (dir.), Am. Arbitration Assn., Pacific Telecommunication Council (trustee), Internat. Inst. Communications, Order of Coif, Valkyries, Phi Beta Kappa. Contbr. articles to profl. jours.; editorial bd. Info. and Soc., 1980—; contbg. editor Jour. Communication, 1980—.

BRANSCOME, ZADA MAE, govt. program analyst; b. Seaman, Ohio, Oct. 19, 1938; d. Robert Acquilla and Eva Mae Jamison; student Wright State U., 1970-74; m. Robert Eugene Branscome, Jan. 19, 1957; children—Susan Gail, Sharon Lynn. Mgmt. technician U.S. Air Force, Wright Patterson AFB, Ohio, 1967-72, adminstrv. officer, 1972-74, chief mgmt. systems group, 1974-79, chief program integration br., 1979-81, comptroller, staff plans and integration officer Aero. Systems div., 1981—. Recipient Ann. Outstanding Performance Rating, U.S. Air Force, 1967-81. Mem. Women's Assn. (pres. chpt. 19 - , chpt. Woman of Yr. 1978-79), Nat. Assn. Female Execs., Am. Soc. Mil. Comptrollers. Clubs: Toastmistress (v.p. club 1980-81, pres. club 1981-82); Order Eastern Star (Vandalia, Ohio). Home: 41 Dahlia Dr Medway OH 45341

BRANSON, MARGARET ABER, businesswoman, former state legislator; b. Sheridan, Wyo., May 12, 1927; d. Seth Perry and Fannie Mary (Hults) Aber; B.A., U. Denver, 1949; postgrad. U. Oreg., 1972; m. Ralph B. Branson, July 16, 1959; children—Melissa, Malcolm, Seth, Alec. Columnist, Seward (Alaska) Phoenix Log, 1966-78; manpower specialist Alaska Skill Center, Seward, 1969-74; owner, mgr. Turquoise Barrabora, Cooper Landing, 1974—; mem. Alaska Ho. of Reps., Juneau, 1979-81. Pres., Cooper Landing Adv. Sch. Bd., 1975-76; v.p. Kenai Peninsula Borough Assembly, 1976-77; mem. Alaska Regional Manpower Tng. Bd., 1977-78, Kenai Peninsula Arbitration Bd., 1977—, Alaska Vocat.-Tech. Center Adv. Bd., 1981—; chmn. New Capitol Site Planning Commn., State of Alaska, 1981—. Recipient President's award Alaska Jaycees, 1964. Mem. Alaska Press Women, Nat. Fedn. Press Women, Nat. Order Women Legislators, Anchorage Republican Women. Club: Cooper Landing Community (pres. 1977-79).

BRANT, SHARON GAYNELL, constrn. co. ofcl.; b. Elkton, Md., Oct. 23, 1946; d. Roscoe Ellis and Nola Marie (Bocock) Wiles; student Milw. Tech. Coll., 1966-68, Concordia Coll., 1978; m. Jake Homer Brant, Nov. 27, 1973; children—Linda Christine, James William Melvin. Cashier, Morrison Cafeterias, Inc., Mobile, Ala., 1964-66; field acct. Ford, Bacon and Davis Constrn. Co., Pt. Allen, La., 1970-76; office mgr. Dunn and Day Constrn. Co., Bluefield, W.Va., 1976-78; subcontract adminstr. Pullman Kellogg Constrn. Co., Norca, La., 1978-80; buyer II, Daniel

Constrn. Co., Crystal River, Fla., 1981—. Vice chairperson Neighborhood React Group, Norca; treas. Community Action, Norca. Mem. Fla. West Coast Purchasing Mgmt. Assn., Bus. and Profl. Women's Assn., Data Processing Mgmt. Assn., Nat. Assn. Women in Constrn. Lutheran. Clubs: N.W. Fla. Photography, Dolls Collectors Am. Home: Star Route 6 Box 124 Dunnellon FL 32630

BRANTLEY, ANDREA KAY, ins. agt.; b. Lubbock, Tex., Oct. 12, 1947; d. Ray Travis and Patsy Ruth (Rutherford) Patterson; student Tex. Christian U., 1965-66, U. Tex., Austin, 1976-77, Tarrant County Jr. Coll., intermittently, 1968-77; children—Jason, Nicole, Justin. Ins. underwriter World Service Life Ins. Co., Ft. Worth, 1967-70; head instr. Shelton's New Image Modeling Sch., Ft. Worth, 1976-77, asst. dir., 1977-78; sales cons. New Eng. Life Ins. Co., Ft. Worth, 1979-80; agt. Northwestern Nat. Life Ins. Co., Ft. Worth, 1980—. Mem. Ft. Worth Life Underwriters. Club: Jr. Women's (Ft. Worth). Home: 3805 Van Denman Fort Worth TX 76116 Office: Finger Furniture 7917 Weatherford Hwy Fort Worth TX 76116

BRANTLEY, HELEN THOMAS, clin. psychologist; b. Palmerton, Pa., Jan. 29, 1942; d. Francis Clyde and Elizabeth (Jennings) Thomas; B.A., Duke U., 1963, Ph.D., 1973; m. John Croft Brantley, June 15, 1963; children—Elizabeth Ann, John Thomas. Psychologist pub. schs., Boothwyn, Pa., 1967; pvt. practice psychol. cons., Chapel Hill, N.C., 1971-77, 81—; research asso. Duke U., Durham, N.C., 1975-78; postdoctoral fellow in child psychology U. N.C. Sch. Medicine, Chapel Hill, 1977-78, research asst. prof., 1978-79, asst. prof. psychology, 1979-81. NIMH fellow, 1980-81. Mem. Am. Psychol. Assn., N.C. Psychol. Assn. Contbr. articles to profl. publs. Home: 104 Saratoga Trail Chapel Hill NC 27514 Office: 109 Conner Dr Suite 2206 Chapel Hill NC 27514

BRANT-MCCOY, ROBYN, comml. interior designer; b. Santa Monica, Calif., July 4, 1953; d. Robert William and Marilyn Ann (Van Atta) Brant; design designation, UCLA, 1980; m. James C. McCoy, Apr. 14, 1979. Prodn./inventory control mgr. Golden Oak, Los Angeles, 1975-77; sales asso. Scholar-Gillette Assocs., Los Angeles, 1978-79; owner Environ. Assocs., Inc., Los Angeles, 1979—; pres. New Era Interiors, Los Angeles, 1980—. Mem. Women in Mgmt., Women in Bus., Nat. Assn. Female Execs. Office: 1758 S La Cienega St Suite 4 Los Angeles CA 90035

BRANTON, MARILYN SUE BURDINSKY, biology educator; b. Springfield, Ill., May 25, 1944; d. Henry and Ruth E. (Watts) Burdinsky; B.S. in Zoology, U. Ill., 1966, M.S., 1972, Ph.D., 1978; m. James C. Branton, May 19, 1964; children—Colin, Jon, Aaron. Asst. prof. biology Olivet Nazarene Coll., Kankakee, Ill., 1978—. Chairperson, Kankakee Area Assn. Children with Learning Disabilities; mem. Orton Dyslexii Soc. Mem. N.Y. Acad. Sci., AAAS, Sigma Xi. Mem. Ch. of Nazarene. Club: Ladies in Fellowship Together. Home: 702 Burns Ct Bourbonnais IL 60914 Office: Box 56 Olivet Nazarene College Kankakee IL 60901

BRANWELL, LINDA MARIE, civic worker; b. Hanover County, Germany, Dec. 19, 1950; came to U.S., 1956, naturalized, 1960; d. Lester Michael and Helen Elizabeth (Podach) Nye; student Baldwin-Wallace Coll., 1969-70; grad. Humboldt Inst., 1971; m. Alan Jon Branwell, Aug. 18, 1973; children—Jason, Tisha. Sec. to agt. document sect. FBI, Washington, 1971-73; sec. Madison County Extension Service, London, Ohio, 1974-75. Vice pres. Welcome Wagon, 1977-78, pres., 1978-79; co-chmn. March of Dimes, 1979; capt. Community Concert Series, 1979; sec. Fostoria Hosp. Aux., 1981-82, v.p., 1982-83; corr. sec. Altrusa, 1982-83; capt. Community Concert Series, 1980-82; mem. Rosary Altar Soc. and Circle of Mercy, Roman Cath. Ch.; bd. dirs. Hosp. Assn. Club: Emblem #213. Home: 423 Glenview Dr Fostoria OH 44830

BRASHEAR, WANDA SUE, nursing adminstr.; b. Prairie Grove, Ark., June 19, 1939; d. Virgil and Walsie (Cone) Brashear; R.N., Hillcrest Med. Center, Tulsa, 1960; B.S., Coll. St. Francis, 1982. Pediatric staff nurse Hillcrest Med. Center, Tulsa, 1960-62; supr., asst. dir., dir. nursing service St. Anthony Hosp., Oklahoma City, 1962-67; staff nurse surgery St. Anthony Hosp., Denver, 1967-72, supr. surgery, 1972—. Registered nurse, Colo., Okla. Mem. Assn. Operating Room Nurses. Republican. Home: 8025 W Calhoun Pl Littleton CO 80123 Office: 4231 W 16th St Denver CO 80204

BRASHERS, ROSE MARY, telephone co. ofcl.; b. Little Rock, Apr. 17, 1952; d. George Phillip and Mae (Bradley) Rollman; student (scholar) Claremore Jr. Coll., 1974-76, Tulsa U., 1982—; m. Charles Brashers, Aug. 23, 1969; children—Charles W., Michael E. Asst. city clk. City of Chelsea (Okla.), 1971-73; sales rep. Reynolds Aluminum Supply Co., 1976-79; communications cons. Southwestern Bell Telephone Co., Tulsa, 1979-80, customer service supr., 1980-81, account exec., 1981—; speaker career edn. Mem. Nat. Assn. Legal Adminstrs. (asso.), Green Country Soccer Assn., Phi Theta Kappa. Democrat. Roman Catholic. Club: Amethyst Rev. Home: 13309 E 40th Pl Tulsa OK 74134 Office: 510 S Elgin St Room G118 Tulsa OK 74120

BRASSIER, ANN M(ARY), govt. human resources exec.; b. Los Angeles, Dec. 1, 1945; d. Daniel and Rose Mary (Marciano) Lucey; B.A., Benedictine Coll., 1967; postgrad. in mgmt. edn. Fed. Exec. Inst., 1978, Harvard U., 1979; m. Thomas Brassier, Jan. 20, 1968. Mgr. Los Angeles area office U.S. Office Personnel Mgmt., 1976-79, dir. office mgmt., Washington, 1979-82, dep. asso. dir. workforce effectiveness and devel., Washington, 1982—; instr. U. So. Calif. Sch. Public Adminstrn., 1980—. Recipient award for disting. service Commrs. CSC, 1978, Spl. commendation Los Angeles Fed. Exec. Bd., 1979. Mem. Am. Soc. Public Adminstrn. Office: 1900 E St NW Washington DC 20415

BRASWELL, FRANCES POSTEL, human relations counselor; b. St. Louis, Aug. 18, 1917; d. Philip Henry and Bessie Holnback Postel; B.A., Wellesley Coll., 1939; postgrad. Bowie State Grad. Sch., Austria, 1976, Amsterdam, 1977; M.A., Webster Coll., 1979; m. David M. Braswell, Dec. 7, 1942; children—Joan, David III, Philip, Carol. With world hdqrs. IBM, 1939-41; program dir. USO, Ft. Dix, N.J., 1941-42; with YMCA, Wilmington, Del., 1942-43; intern Met. Ch. Fedn. St. Louis Area, 1964-76; TV producer Journey Through Darkness, 1965-67; human relations counselor, Belleville, Ill., 1980—; v.p. Braswell and Assos. Ltd., Belleville, 1964; pres. Braswell-Postel Farm Ltd., Belleville, 1978—. Pres. St. Clair County Health and Welfare Council; bd. dirs. McKendree Coll., Belleville High Sch.-Jr. Coll., 1959-62; mem. Sesquicentennial Commn.; mem. adv. council Sta. KETC-TV, St. Louis. Recipient citation of honor Ch. Women United in Ill., 1967; named Outstanding Citizen, St. Clair County Health and Welfare Council, 1970; Woman of Yr., St. Louis Wellesley Club, 1969; profl. counselor N.Am. Soc. Adlerian Psychology. Mem. LWV, Urban League St. Clair County-Madison County, St. Clair County Hist. Soc., P.E.O. (pres. local chpt. 1977-79), Delta Kappa Gamma (hon.). Independent Republican. Methodist. Club: Wellesley (St. Louis). Home and Office: 12 Woodland Ct Belleville IL 62221

BRASWELL, SYLVIA PATRICIA, social worker; b. Quincy, Fla., Sept. 26, 1946; d. Ferris and Lillian Augusta (Wilson) Goldwire; B.S., N.C. A. and T. State U., 1969; M.S.W., Rutgers U., 1974; divorced. Social worker Essex County Welfare Bd., Newark, 1969-74; social services specialist Day Care Coordinating Council, Newark, 1974-76; clin. dir. United Community Corp., Newark, 1976-79; med. social worker Los Angeles County-U. So. Calif. Med. Center, 1979-80; psychiat. social worker S.E. Mental Health Services, Los Angeles County Dept. Mental Health, 1980—; cons. Nat. Council Negro Women, Calif. Assn. Health Services at Home. Mem. Assn. Black Social Workers, Nat. Assn. Social Workers, NAACP. Democrat. Baptist. Club: Four Seasons West Ski. Home: 4091 8th Ave Los Angeles CA 90008 Office: 1720 E 120th St Los Angeles CA 90059

BRATAAS, NANCY, state senator, mgmt. cons.; b. Mpls., Jan. 19, 1928; student U. Minn.; m. Mark Gerard Brataas; children—Mark, Anne. Pres., Nancy Brataas Assocs., Inc., mgmt. cons.; mem. Minn. Senate, St. Paul, 1975—, mem. commerce, employment, health, welfare, and corrections coms. State chairwoman Minn. Republican Party, 1963-69, Minn. Rep. Fin. Com., 1969-71. Mem. AAUW. Episcopalian. Club: Zonta Internat. Office: 139 State Office Bldg Saint Paul MN 55155 *

BRATT, HELEN IRENE JENKINS, artist; b. Charleston, W.Va., Nov. 29, 1920; d. George W. and Elsa Irene (Riley) Jenkins; student Kanawha Coll., 1938, 39, Morris Harvey Coll., 1939, 42, Mason Coll. of Music and Fine Arts, 1949, 55; m. John Lynn Bratt, Jan. 26, 1943; children—Mary Helen, George Michael, John Lynn. Art instr. Charleston (W.Va.) YWCA, 1965-72, Children's Mus. at Sunrise, 1966-70, Charleston Art Gallery, 1970-78; painter, exhibitor various shows and festivals. Brownie leader, 1954-58; pres. PTA, 1966-68. Recipient awards Rhododendron Festivals, 1968, 70, 75; selected for Art in the Embassies, 1967. Mem. Allied Artist of W.Va. (awards, 1959, 63), Nat. League Am. Pen Women (Charleston br.), W.Va Artists and Craftsmen's Guild and Gallery Eleven. Republican. Contbr. to book, Inklings, to Pen Woman mag. Home: 2522 Kanawha Blvd Charleston WV 25311

BRATTON, MARY JANE, editor; b. Seattle, Mar. 12, 1953; d. Dale Benjamin and Lilliam Ruth (Swanson) B.; B.A. Communications, Wash. State U., 1975. Reporter Bellevue Am. Newspaper, Bellevue, Wash., 1975-76, Mercer Island (Wash.) Reporter Newspaper, 1976; editor The Outlook Newspaper, weekly, Seattle, 1976-78, Univ. Herald, Seattle, 1978—. Mem. Women in Communications, Washington Press Women, Soc. Profl. Journalists. Home: PO Box 293 Olympia WA 98507 Office: 4710 University Way NE Seattle WA 98105

BRAUN, BARBARA ILENE, advt. agy. exec.; b. Charleston, W.Va., May 8, 1944; d. Arthur Goodman and Charlotte C. Braun; B.S., Northwestern U., 1966; M.B.A., Pepperdine U., 1982. Supr., Leo Burnett Advt., Chgo., 1966-67; account coordinator Lake Public Relations, London, Eng., 1967-68; account exec. Beneficial Standard Corp., Los Angeles, 1968-70; asso. Argosy Group, Los Angeles, 1970-73; owner Braun & Assos., Los Angeles, 1973—; lectr., cons. in field. Mem. Nat. Assn. Female Execs., Phi Beta. Democrat. Office: 6010 Wilshire Blvd Los Angeles CA 90036

BRAUN, EUNICE HOCKSPEIER, author, religious exec., lectr.; b. Alta Vista, Iowa; d. George Phillip and Lydia (Reinhart) Hockspeier; student Coe Coll., 1937-39, Northwestern U., 1944-47; m. Leonard James Braun, May 29, 1937. Freelance writer for mags., newspapers, 1947-52; bus. mgr. Baha'i Publishing Trust, Wilmette, Ill., 1952-55, mng. dir., 1955-71; internat. news editor Baha'i News, 1952-70; tchr. Baha'i schs., Alaska, Can. and U.S., 1958—; lectr. Baha'i Faith in U.S., Central Am., Europe, Africa, Asia, 1953—; cons. Baha'i Pub. Trust, New Delhi, India, 1972; mem. aux. bd. Continental Bd. Counselors, Baha'i Faith in the Ams., 1972—. Mem. Nat. League Am. Pen Women, Internat. Platform Assn., Women's Nat. Book Assn., Chgo. Book Clinic, Baha'i Faith, Iota Sigma Epsilon (Short Story prize Northwestern U.). Author: Know Your Baha'i Literature, 1959; The Dawn of World Peace, 1963; Baha'u'llah: His Call to the Nations, 1967; From Strength to Strength, Half Century of the Formative Age of the Baha'i Faith, 1978; A Crown of Beauty, 1982; contbr. essays to Baha'i World, Internat. Record. Home: 1025 Forestview Ln Glenview IL 60025

BRAUN, LENORE MARIE (MUSIELSKI), writer, psychologist; b. Bridgeport, Conn., Mar. 12, 1955; d. Joseph Stanislaus and Dolores Marie (Palumbo) Musielski; B.S. in Psychology (Silverstone grantee), U. Bridgeport, 1979, M.S. in Psychology, 1979; m. John Richard Braun, Mar. 9, 1979; 1 stepson, John Richard. Interviewer for unemployment compensation claims, security div. State of Conn., New Haven, 1976; fin. cons., rep. Investors Diversified Services, Fairfield, Conn., 1976-77; asst. supr. dept. customer service Bank Americard, Fairfield, 1977; mental health therapist Hall-Brooke Psychiat. Hosp./Found., Westport, Conn., 1977-79; lectr. in psychology U. Bridgeport, 1980—, Albertus Magnus Coll., 1980—, Western Conn. State Coll., 1982—; free-lance writer in psychology, 1980—; co-therapist area sch. system. Mem. Am. Psychol. Assn. (assoc.), Eastern Psychol. Assn., (assoc.), Conn. Psychol. Assn. (assoc.), Internat. Women's Writing Guild, Nat. Writers Club. Democrat. Roman Catholic. Research on creativity, child abuse. Home and Office: Bridgeport CT 06606

BRAUN, ROSLYN ROTKIN, psychologist; b. N.Y.C., Aug. 27, 1921; d. Meyer M. and Emma (Honigman) Rotkin; M.A., N.Y. U. Sch. Edn., 1947; m. Monroe Jacob Braun, Mar. 29, 1942; 1 son, Simon David. Intern, Mt. Sinai Hosp., N.Y.C., 1947; sch. psychologist N.Y.C. Bd. Edn., 1947-52; pvt. practice clin. psychology, Jamaica Estates, N.Y., 1952—; parent-edn. cons. various nursery schs., 1952—. Mem. Am. Orthopsychiat. Assn. (life), Am. Psychol. Assn., N.Y. Soc. Clin. Psychologists, Soc. Projective Techniques, Soc. Pediatric Psychology. Asst. editor Jamaica Estates Civic Assn. Bull., 1980—. Home and Office: 81-10 Haddon St Jamaica Estates NY 11432

BRAUNSCHWEIGER, HELEN REBECCA RAYMOND, artist; b. Norwich, Conn.; d. George Clark and Helen (Smith) Raymond; student Boston U. Art Sch., 1927-29, also pvt. study; m. John S. Lapp, Apr. 12, 1933 (dec. May 1953); 1 son, Sumner Philip; m. 2d, Walter J. Braunschweiger, Apr. 19, 1955 (dec. Nov. 1974). One man shows at DeBreaux Gallery, N.Y.C., 1957, La Fontanella Gallery, Rome, Italy, 1959, Iolas Gallery, N.Y.C., 1959, Scorpio Gallery, Los Angeles, 1961, Desert Art Center, Palm Springs, Calif., 1966, Zulch Gallery, Costa Mesa, Calif., 1968, San Gabriel Fine Arts Soc., 1974, Brentwood Savs. and Loan, 1974; exhibited in group shows at Calif. Art Club, Greek Theater, 1961, Valley Artists Guild, Los Angeles, 1964, Glendale Fed. Savs. (Calif.), 1964, Artists of S.W., Greek Theater, 1964, Waldorf Astoria, N.Y.C., 1964, Calif. Festival, 1964; represented in permanent collections City of Los Angeles City Hall, Occidental Life Ins. Co., Los Angeles, also numerous others. Mem. costume council Los Angeles County Mus.; mem. womens bd. Calif. Inst. Arts. Recipient two 2d prizes Nat. Assn. Am. Pen Women, 1960, 1st prize, 1976. Fellow Am. Profl. Artists League, Am. Inst. Fine Arts; mem. Calif. Council Traditional Artists (v.p., dir.), Valley Artists Guild, Artists of S.W., Palm Springs Civic Art Assn., Palm Springs Pathfinders, Calif. Art Club (dir.), San Gabriel Fine Arts Assn., Los Angeles Opera Guild, Mus. Assos., Pasadena Arts Council, Fine Arts Club Pasadena, Muses. Address: 720 S Orange Grove Blvd Apt 4 Pasadena CA 91105

BRAUNSTEIN, MARYA KALUZYNSKI, logistician, mgmt. cons.; b. Trani, Italy, Aug. 9, 1946; d. Marian and Kazimiera (Porankiewicz) Kaluzynski; came to U.S., 1950, naturalized, 1956; B.A., Emmanuel Coll., 1969; postgrad. Suffolk Law Sch., 1970; M.B.A., Boston U., 1976; m. Robert H. Anderson, Jan. 13, 1982. Editorial and adminstrv. asst. Orion Research Inc., Cambridge, Mass., 1970-72; exec. legal sec. PVH Retail, Boston, 1973-75; asso. C.A.C.I., Inc., Arlington, Va., 1976-77; sr. systems analyst Advanced Technology, Inc., McLean, Va., 1977-79; project mgr. EG& G Washington Analytical Services Center, Inc., Arlington, 1979; exec. v.p., treas., co-founder ANA-LOG Inc., McLean, 1979-81; mgmt. cons., Arlington, 1981—. Mem. Soc. Logistics Engrs. (editor Oracle 1980-81, cert. profl. logistician, nat. dir., treas. D.C. chpt.), Nat. Assn. Women Bus. Owners, Nat. Small Bus. Assn., Fairfax County C. of C., Emmanuel Coll. Alumni Assn. (past pres., treas.), Assn. Old Crows, Boston U. Alumni Assn. Home: 3472 S Utah St Apt B-2 Arlington VA 22206 Office: 1725 Jefferson Davis Hwy Arlington VA 22202

BRAWER, PATRICIA ELAINE, securities brokerage exec.; b. N.Y.C., July 3, 1945; d. Oscar I. and Iris (Pashman) Brawer; student U. Edinburgh (Scotland), 1965; B.A., Smith Coll., 1966; postgrad. N.Y. Inst. Fin., 1968. Prodn. asst. Merrill Lynch, N.Y.C., 1967-69; asst. to br. mgr. Shearson Hammill, N.Y.C., 1969-71; with Thomson McKinnon Securities, N.Y.C., 1971—, now asst. v.p. Bd. dirs. Village Light Opera Group Ltd., N.Y.C.; trustee Pop Warner Little Scholars; program dir. Regional Emergency Med. Services Council of N.Y.C. Mem. Meeting Planners Internat., English Speaking Union, Internat. Mensa Soc. Club: N.Y. Smith Coll. Address: 250 E 73d St New York NY 10021

BRAXTON, PATSY MALLARD, ednl. adminstr.; b. Wallace, N.C., May 17, 1943; d. Steven Hodges and Mary Elizabeth (Keith) Mallard; A.B., Guilford Coll., 1965; M.S., Old Dominion U., 1970; postgrad. Appalachian State U., East Carolina U., U. N.C., Greensboro; m. Howard M. Braxton Jr., Dec. 22, 1963; 1 son, Robert Steven. Tchr., Drewry Mason High Sch., Ridgeway, Va., 1965, Watauga High Sch., Boone, N.C., 1965-66; guidance counselor Elizabeth City (N.C.) Schs., 1966-71; asst. dir. student aid U. N.C., Greensboro, 1971-79; dir. student aid N.C. Sch. of the Arts, Winston-Salem, 1979—. Mem. N.C. Guidance Personnel Assn., N.C. Assn. Student Fin. Aid Officers (pres. 1978-79), So. Assn. Student Fin. Aid Officers, Nat. Assn. Student Fin. Adminstrs. Democrat. Presbyterian. Home: 109 Erskine Dr W Greensboro NC 27410 Office: North Carolina School of the Arts 200 Waughtown St Winston-Salem NC 27107

BRAY, CAROL PIPPIN, social worker; b. Wilmington, Del., Apr. 8, 1942; d. Leslie Larzelere and Mary (Desmond) Pippin; B.A., Coll. Misericordia, Dallas, Pa., 1964; M.S.W., Catholic U. Am., 1970; m. William John Bray, Jr., Mar. 15, 1975; children—Mary Christine, William John, III. Social worker Cecil County (Md.) Dept. Social Services, Elkton, 1964-68, Prince George's County (Md.), Hyattsville, 1970-72; social work supr. Gt. Oaks Center, Silver Spring, Md., 1972-77, dir. social work dept., 1977-78, acting adminstr. on rotation, facility for mentally retarded, 1977-78, social work team, 1980-81, mem. Outreach Team, 1981—. Mem. Nat. Assn. Social Workers, Acad. Cert. Social Workers. Democrat. Roman Catholic. Home: 900 Dennis Ave Silver Spring MD 21901 Office: 12001 Cherry Hill Rd Silver Spring MD 20904

BRAY, JACQUELINE HELEN, graphic designer; b. Mpls., Apr. 20, 1932; d. Irving Charles and Margaret May (Norris) Langlois; student art Mpls. Coll. Art and Design, U. Minn., U. Copenhagen, Cornell U., George Mason U., Fairfax, Va.; divorced; children—Leslee Marie, Judith Mae, David Edward, Laura Ann. Med. illustrator textbooks U. Minn., also univ. comml. artist, 1953-55; tech. illustrator Battelle Inst. N.W., Richland, Wash., 1966-68; artist Richland City Planning Dept., 1968-70; propr. studio, Aiken, S.C., also tchr. art Mead Hall, Aiken, 1970-75; sr. illustrator, designer Potomac Research Inc., 1977-78; graphic arts cons. Xerox Co., Leesburg, Va., 1978-79; art dir. CENTEC Corp., Reston, Va., 1979—; one-woman exhbn., Richland, 1968 art cons. Internat. Assn. Satellite Users: Martha Gould scholar, 1952. Mem. Indsl. Graphics Internat., Exec. Women's Assn. Illustrator: The Magic Machine, 1978. Home: 10721 Oldfield Dr Reston VA 22091 Office: 11260 Roger Bacon Dr Reston VA 22090

BRAY, PENELOPE ADAMS, aircraft accident investigation and reconstruction cons.; b. Reno, June 30, 1941; d. Frank and Billie (Stephens) Gunther; ed. Orange Coast Jr. Coll., 1962; m. Paul Bray, Jr., Mar. 29, 1975. Chief flight instr. Torbert Airways and Newport Skyways, 1968-73; real estate sales, Calif., 1973-76; nat. sales mgr. Palmas del Mar, Huumacao, P.R., 1976; real estate sales, N.Y., 1977-79; sec.-treas. Bray Studios, Inc., N.Y.C., 1979; now owner Aviation Tech. Cons., N.Y.C. Mem. Aircraft Owners and Pilots Assn., Nat. Assn. Flight Instrs. Home: 5 Rumpenmile Westport CT 06880 Office: 630 9th Ave New York NY 10036

BRAZELTON, A. RUTH HICKS, nurse; b. Upson County, Ga.; d. Lowell L. and Oddie M. Hicks; R.N., Cook County Hosp., Chgo., 1974; B.S., Coll. St. Francis, Joliet, Ill., 1978; M.S., DePaul U., Chgo., 1981. Staff nurse hosps. in Ill. and Calif., to 1980; nurse recruiter Jackson Park Hosp., Chgo., 1980—, pres. elect nursing service adminstrn. group, 1982—; condr. career counseling seminars. Mem. Nat. Black Nurses Assn. (chmn. scholarship com. chpt.), Am. Soc. Public Adminstrn., Nat. Assn. Female Execs., Chgo. Area Nurse Recruiters Assn., Alumni Assn. Coll. St. Francis. Office: 7531 S Stony Island Ave Chicago IL 60649

BRAZELTON, ERNESTINE CROSS (NINA), educator; b. nr. Braselton, Ga., Feb. 20, 1926; d. Jiley Mark and Pearl Brockett Cross; student UCLA, Calif. State U., Long Beach, Pepperdine U., U. Beirut (Lebanon); B.A. in Social Sci., 1964; M.A. in Edn., 1961; H.H.D. (hon.); m. Russell Worth Brazelton, Sept. 15, 1945 (div. 1973); children—Jeffrey, Karenina, Russ, Christopher Lee. Tchr., Bolsa Grande High Sch., Garden Grove, Calif., 1961—. Mem. Garden Grove Polit. Action Com.; exec. v.p. Newport Harbor City of Hope; active various polit. campaigns. Fulbright scholar, Middle East. Mem. Assn. Overseas Educators, LWV, AAUW, Hist. Soc., Consumer Pamel Am. (life), Mensa, Alpha Gamma Sigma, Alpha Delta Kappa. Contbr. articles to profl. publs. Home: Versilles on the Bluff 102 Scholz Plaza Apt 138 Newport Beach CA 92663 Office: 9401 Westminster Blvd Garden Citv CA 92642

BRAZER, WYNONA MARIE, acct.; b. Seattle, Mar. 6, 1937; d. Perry Henry and Katherine Emma Moler; A.A. in Tech. Arts, Olympic Community Coll., 1971; m. Henry Brazer, Dec. 1, 1955; children—Ronald, Kenneth, Gregory, Jeffory, Samuel, Nancy. Clk., Gt. No. and No. Pacific R.R., Laurel and Billings, Mont., 1955-63; office mgr., bookkeeper Denny's Music Co., Portland, Oreg., 1971-72; bookkeeper Acme Signs Inc., Portland, 1973-74; acct. The Old Spaghetti Factory Internat., Portland, 1974-75; close down mgr., lead acct. Portland Met. Steering Com.-EOA Inc., Portland, 1975-78; asst. controller Harsh Investment Corp., Portland, 1979; acctg. mgr. United Cerebral Palsy Assn., Portland, 1980—. Mem. Am. Bus. Women Assn. Home: 2855 Tibbetts St Portland OR 97202 Office: 7117 SE Harold St Portland OR 97206

BREAKFIELD, MARY ANN, lawyer; b. Atlantic City, Apr. 6, 1944; d. John and Margaret (McClintock) Greenwood; B.A. in English, New

Sch. for Social Research, 1967; M.A. in English, U. So. Calif., 1968; J.D., Calif. Western Sch. Law, 1971; postgrad. in labor law George Washington U., 1976-78; m. Robert H. Breakfield, May 25, 1971; 1 son, John Gage. Instr. English, Pasadena (Calif.) City Coll., 1968-69, El Camino Coll., Los Angeles, 1969-70; office mgr. Profl. Tax Co., Baily Crossroads, Va., 1972; admitted to S.C. bar, 1973, Mass. bar, 1975; asso. firm Harvey, Battey, Macloskie & Bethea, Beaufort, S.C., 1972-74; instr. law and English, U. S.C., Beaufort, 1973-74; affirmative action cons. Betsy Hogan Assos., Brookline, Mass., 1974-75; coll. atty. and exec. asst. to pres., asst. prof. bus. adminstrn. Winthrop Coll., Rock Hill, S.C., 1975—; program chair Internat. Women's Year Conf., S.C.; S.C. del. to Internat. Women's Year Conf., Houston; atty. Boston chpt. NOW; lectr. field women's rights. Mem. citizens adv. bd. Mass. Commn. Against Discrimination. Mem. Am. (equal opportunity liaison com.), Fed. (labor relations com.), Mass., S.C. (chmn. high sch. law program) bar assns., Mass. Assn. Women Lawyers, Nat. Assn. Women Attys., Nat. Assn. Coll. and Univ. Attys., Am. Arbitration Assn. (arbitrator), Women Execs. Home: 621 University Dr Rock Hill SC 29730 Office: Winthrop Coll Rock Hill SC 29733 *

BREAKSTONE, KAY LOUISE, public relations exec.; b. Allentown, Pa., Sept. 9, 1936; d. Morris H. and Mabel (Gruber) Senderowitz; B.S., N.Y. U., 1967; m. Jules L. Breakstone, Dec. 3, 1960; children—Enid, Jessica. With N.Y. Conf. Bd., 1967-69, Bache, Halsey Stuart, N.Y.C., 1969-70; securities analyst Dean Witter, N.Y.C., 1970-71; vice-pres. Burson Marsteller, Inc., N.Y.C., 1971-79, 81—; dir. investor relations Kennecott Corp., Stamford, Conn., 1979-81; dir. First Woman's Bank. Mem. Nat. Investor Relations Inst. (pres. 1980-81). Home: 7 E 74th St New York NY 10021 Office: 866 3d Ave New York NY 10022

BRECHAN, LINDA LEE LAUESEN, mgmt. cons.; b. Chgo., Feb. 1, 1939; d. Elstun Wilbur and Ella Cecilia (Boadry) Lauesen; student public schs., Mich. and Alaska; m. Robert L. Brechan, Sept. 20, 1963; children—Perri Lynn, Sheri Alyse, Michael Robert; stepchildren—Beverly, Kenneth, Curtis, Hollis, Scott, Donna, Lory, Kelly. Adminstrv. asst. North Pole Refining (Alaska), 1976-77; sec.-treas. PMS, Inc., Fairbanks, Alaska, 1977-79; owner, accountant Linda's Bus. Services, Fairbanks, 1979-81; owner, decorator Decorating Den/Alaska, Fairbanks, 1979-81; mgmt. cons., 1977—. sec.-treas. B & B Auto, Inc., 1976-78. Mem. Nat. Assn. Exec. Women, Nat. Assn. Women in Bus., Nat. Fedn. Bus. and Profl. Women's Clubs, Inc., Golden Heart Bus. and Profl. Women's Club, Alaska Fedn. Bus. and Profl. Women's Clubs (Alaska state young careerist chmn. 1979-80, 2d v.p. 1982-83). Democrat. Home: 1506 10th Ave Fairbanks AK 99701 Office: PO Box 60753 Fairbanks AK 99706

BRECHBIEL, PENNIE JO, enterostomal therapist, nurse; b. Wabash, Ind., Dec. 20, 1956; d. Rupert Otho and Donnabell Ruth (Hileman) B.; B.S. in Nursing, Ind. Central U., 1980, Asso. Degree in Sci., 1977. Staff nurse Hook Rehab. Center, Community Hosp. Indpls., 1977-81, enterostomal therapy coordinator, 1981—; continuing edn. instr. small hosps. and nursing homes. Mem. Internat. Assn. Enterostomal Therapists, Assn. Rehab. Nurses, NOW. Office: Community Hosp of Indianapolis 1500 N Ritter Ave Indianapolis IN 46219

BRECHBILL, SUSAN REYNOLDS, govt. ofcl.; b. Washington, Aug. 22, 1943; d. Irving and Isabell Doyle (Reynolds) Levine; B.A., Coll. William and Mary, 1965; J.D., Marshall-Wythe Sch. Law, 1968; m. Raymond A. Brechbill, June 29, 1973; children—Jennifer Rae, Heather Lea. Admitted to Va. bar, 1969, Fed. bar, 1970; atty. AEC, Berkeley, Calif., 1968-73, indsl. relations specialist AEC, Las Vegas, Nev., 1974-75; atty. ERDA, Oakland, Calif., 1976-77; atty. Dept. Energy, Oakland, 1977-78, dir. procurement div. San Francisco Ops. Office, 1978—; mem. faculty U. Calif. Extension; speaker Nat. Contract Mgmt. Assn. Ann. Symposiums, 1980, 81; speaker on doing bus. with govt. Named Outstanding Young Woman Nev., 1974. Mem. Va. State Bar Assn., Fed. Bar Assn., Nat. Contract Mgmt. Assn., Nat. Assn. Female Execs. Republican. Christian Scientist. Contbr. articles to profl. jours. Home: 67 Scenic Dr Orinda CA 94563 Office: 1333 Broadway Oakland CA 94612

BRECHEEN, DORIS WILKINSON, state ofcl.; b. Liberty, Miss., Feb. 1, 1927; d. Horace Eugene and Nora O'Neal (Foreman) Wilkinson; m. Leslie Eldred Brecheen, Sept. 3, 1953; children—Latitia Lanel, Bonness Orland, Leslie Doris, William Eldred. Credit investigator Joys Dept. Store, Baton Rouge, 1945-52; head bookkeeper Family Fin. Co., Baton Rouge, Houston, New Orleans, 1952-58; asst. bookkeeper Welfare Dept., Baton Rouge, 1958-59; credit investigator Montgomery Wards, Baton Rouge, 1960-63; revenue supr. petroleum products sect. La. State Dept. Revenue and Taxation, Baton Rouge, 1959—. Counselor, Crisis Intervention Center. Mem. Am. Soc. Profl. and Exec. Women, Nat. Assn. Female Execs. Baptist. Home: 8017 Sholar Dr Baton Rouge LA 70809 Office: 330 N Ardenwood Baton Rouge LA 70806

BRECHNER, ANA-MARÍ FERNÁNDEZ, advt./public relations exec.; b. Oriente Province, Cuba, Mar. 25, 1951; came to U.S., 1960, naturalized, 1970; d. Gilberto and Esmeralda Emiliana (Díaz) Fernández; grad. Miami Dade Community Coll., 1971; student Barry Coll., 1972-78. Adminstrv. asst. thru asst. v.p. nat. accounts Flagship Bank, Miami Beach, Fla., 1971-77; v.p. comml. lending Jefferson Nat. Bank, Miami Beach, 1977-78; pres. Inter-Am. Communications, Inc., Miami, 1978—; instr. Miami Dade Community Coll. Women in Mgmt. Program, 1980-81. Mem. Dade County Commn. on Status of Women, 1979—; chmn. Econ. Devel. Task Force of Commn. on Status of Women, 1979—; bd. dirs. Downtown Miami Bus. Assn., 1979—. Recipient Gran Orden Martiana of Cuban Lyceum for excellence in community service, 1976. Mem. Advt. Fedn. Greater Miami, Miami Beach C. of C. (hon. life), Greater Miami C. of C. (Hispanic Heritage Festival Com., New World Center Action Com.), Leadership Miami Alumni Assn., Coalition Hispanic Am. Women, Bus. and Profl. Women's Club. Home: 15105 NE 6 Ave North Miami Beach FL 33162 Office: 3050 Biscayne Blvd Suite 505 Miami FL 33137

BRECHT, FLORENCE MARIE, fashion counselor; b. Lexington, Mo., June 24, 1933; d. Ernest and Ellen Julie Belle (Key) Crider; student Jackson (Calif.) Public Schs.; m. Charles Fredrick Brecht, June 16, 1964 (dec. Oct. 1979); children—Jack Edward, Don Ray Arthur. 1 dau. by previous marriage, Beverly Ann Martin Brecht. Saleswoman, Stanley Home Products, Torrance, Calif., 1970-74; fashion counselor Fashion Frocks (merged with Queen's Way to Fashion), Niles, Ill., 1974—; songwriter, singer, musician. Recipient Gold cup for High Sales, Stanley Home Products, 1972; mem. Talent & Assoc. Cos., El Dorado-Amador Grange Credit Union, Pine Grove Civic Improvement Club. Democrat. Baptist. Clubs: Eagles. Home: 27239 Tiger Creek Rd Pioneer CA 95666

BRECK, JULIA NORTH, civic worker; b. El Paso, Tex., Oct. 2, 1910; d. Clarence L. and Ruth (Spaulding) North; B.S., Northwestern U., 1932; m. Louis William Breck, June 11, 1932; children—Louis William, Julia Ann, Alan N., Susan B. Designer-builder home, 1949, doctors office bldgs., 1947, 57, 72, 76; home redesigner, remodeler, El Paso, Tex., 1965—; bus. mgr. L. W. Breck M.D. Corp., El Paso, 1971—, adminstr. pension trust, 1971—; W. Tex.-N.M. sales mgr. Ortho Kinetics, Inc., 1976-79; chmn. W. Tex. Women for Johnson, 1947-48, El Paso Citizens for Ike, 1952, El Paso Citizens for Goldwater, 1964; sec. bd. mgrs. County Hosp., 1954; sec. El Paso Charter Commn., 1955; unsuccessful candidate for mayor of El Paso, 1961; pres. Amigos Mag., Inc., 1972, Profls. Fin. Group, Inc., 1972, Plaza Theater Corp., 1974; pres. El Paso Med. Aux., 1950; mem. El Paso Citizens Adv. Com., Tex. Hwy. Dept., 1964-70; chmn. women's div. Community Chest, 1974. Recipient First Lady of El Paso award Beta Sigma Phi, 1949, E award El Paso High Sch. 1964. Mem. Nat. Press Women, AAUW (pres. 1949), Tex. Press Women, DAR, El Paso Hist. Soc., C. of C. Women (dir. 1953), Alpha Chi Omega, Beta Sigma Phi. Presbyterian. Club: Woman's (El Paso). Asst. editor Amigos Mag. for Tourists, 1973-76; contbr. articles to profl. jours. and newspapers.

BREECE, JENANNE NELSON, lawyer; b. Evanston, Ill., Dec. 30, 1941; d. Oscar William and Anne L. (Moll) Nelson; B.S. magna cum laude, U. So. Calif., 1967, J.D., 1976; M.B.A., N.Y. U., 1972. Admitted to D.C. bar, 1977; sec., corporate officer Sta. KUPD-AM-FM, Phoenix, 1959-61; media dir. West, Weir & Bartel, Los Angeles, 1962-65; asso. media dir. Eisaman, Johns & Laws, Los Angeles, 1966-68; media supr. Ogilvy & Mathers, N.Y.C., 1968-69; v.p. media and mktg. services Smith-Gent Advt. Co., N.Y.C., 1969-71; media supr. The Media Dept., N.Y.C., 1971-72; v.p. media Perkal Advt. Co., Los Angeles, 1972-74; research asst. U. So. Calif. Law Center, 1975-76; atty. adv. FCC, Washington, 1977-80; gen. atty. U.S. Dept. Energy, Las Vegas, 1980—; pro bono atty. Friends of Animals, N.Y.C. Mem. D.C. Bar, Fed. Bar Assn., Bar Assn. D.C., Am. Bar Assn., Los Angeles Advt. Women, U. So. Calif. Alumni, Mensa, Cactus and Succulent Soc., North Shore Animal League, Friends of Animals, Defenders Wildlife. Phi Beta Kappa, Beta Gamma Sigma. Presbyterian. Office: US Dept Energy PO Box 14100 Las Vegas NV 89114

BREED, BARBARA ANN, coffee co. exec.; b. Coatsville, Pa., May 14, 1935; d. Francis E. and Bertha D. (Doan) Soule; student public schs., Fairfax, Va.; m. Harold Allen Breed, Feb. 3, 1952; children—Denice D., Allen Randolph. Sec., Atlantic Research, Gainesville, Va., 1960-63; sec. Ralston Purina Co., Alexandria, Va., 1963-65, asst. dir. ops., Manchester, N.H., 1965-70; guest relations mgr. Dunfey Family Hotels, Manchester, 1971-73; office mgr. and dir. adminstrn. Elkin Coffee Inc., Concord, N.H., 1974—. Exec. dir. N.Atlantic Youth Team Olympics, 1980—; account exec. United Way of Greater Concord, 1980; state public relations dir. Bicentennial Wagon Train, 1976. Free lance animal portrait painter, 1965—; breeder Appaloosa horses, Pembroke Farm, N.H., 1969—. Recipient Presdl. Sports award, Concord, 1974; named Woman of Achievement of Year, Concord Federated Bus. and Profl. Women, 1979. Mem. New Eng. Horsemen's Council, N.H. Granite State Appaloosa Assn. (dir. public relations 1973-82), Federated Bus. and Profl. Woman's Club (pres., chmn. public relations N.H. State 1980-81), Greater Concord C. of C. (dir. 1979-81), N.H. Horse and Trail Soc., Appaloosa Horse Club of Am. (nat. dir. 1982—). Contbr. articles to equine pubs. Home: 305 Pembroke St Concord NH 03301 Office: PO Box 1294 Concord NH 03301

BREED, FRANCES, assn. exec.; b. N.Y.C., Feb. 21, 1918; d. Henry Elbridge and Ethel (Burns) B.; artist's diploma Juilliard Sch. Music, 1936; A.B. cum laude, Barnard Coll., 1940; postgrad. Berkshire Music Center, 1940, Ind. U. Grad. Sch. Bus. Adminstrn., 1965, New Sch. Social Research, 1966, Brookings Instn., 1968, Columbia Grad. Sch. Bus., 1969; 1 dau., Ann. Concert violinist, soloist, U.S. and Europe, 1940-55; dir. St. Batholomew's Community Club, N.Y.C., 1956-60; dir. adminstrn. Planned Parenthood-World Population, N.Y.C., 1960-66; asso. dir. community services Sex Info. and Edn. Council of U.S., N.Y.C., 1966-69; exec. Harold L. Oram, Inc., N.Y.C., 1969-70; dir. devel. and public relations Nat. Audubon Soc., N.Y.C., 1971-77, v.p., 1977—, mgr. population program, 1979—; rep. UN Conf. on Human Environment, Stockholm, 1972, Nat. Council Philanthropy, 1974-75, Internat. Conf. Family Planning, Indonesia, 1981. Mem. Nat. Inst. Social Scis., Nat. Soc. Fund Raising Execs. (dir. N.Y.C. chpt.), Conf. UN Reps., UN Assn. of U.S. (exec. com. 1982). Office: 950 3d Ave New York NY 10022

BREEN, SISTER, ANNA MARY ROMUALDA, coll. adminstr.; b. Smiths Falls, Ont., Can., Feb. 7, 1920; d. Thomas Vincent and Lucy Agnes (Cauley) B.; B.A., U. Ottawa, 1939, M.A. in English, 1942, Ph.D. in English, 1960; postgrad. Fordham U., 1953-56. Joined Sisters of Congregation of Notre Dame, 1942; lectr. to prof. English, Marianopolis Coll., Montreal, Que., Can., 1944-65, prof. English, dir. student services, 1965-70, dir. gen., 1974—; adminstr. Congregation of Notre Dame, 1970-74. Active Positive Action, Alliance Que. Mem. Que. Coll. Assn., Assn. Can. Community Colls. Home and office: 3880 Cote des Neiges Montreal PQ H3H 1W1 Canada

BREEN, CAROLE RAMBACH, found. exec.; b. Kittanning, Pa., July 24, 1936; d. Benjamin and Lillian (Strug) Rambach; B.A., Tulane U., 1957; M.S.W., Washington U., St. Louis, 1976; m. Marvin Golden Breen, Dec. 23, 1956; children—Robin, Neff. Asso. dir. women's div. Jewish Welfare Fedn., St. Louis, 1971-74; dir. family life edn. dept. Jewish Community Centers Assn. St. Louis, 1976-77; dir. Jewish Community Endowment Fund of Jewish Welfare Fedn. of San Francisco, Marin County and the Peninsula, San Francisco, 1978—. Pres. New Orleans div. Brandeis U. Nat. Women's Com., 1966-68; co-chmn. New Orleans Tax Initiative, 1967. Mem. Nat. Assn. Social Workers, Nat. Women's Polit. Caucus, Council Jewish Women, Bay Area Exec. Women's Com., LWV. Jewish. Home: 18 Noche Vista Tiburon CA 94920 Office: Jewish Community Endowment Fund of Jewish Community Fedn San Francisco Marin County and the Peninsula 254 Sutter St San Francisco CA 94108

BREIHAN, EDNA MARIA THIES, ret. educator; b. Flossmoor, Ill., Jan. 22, 1911; d. Henry Frederick and Anna (Cohrs) Thies; student Valparaiso U., 1928-30; A.B., Coll. of St. Francis, 1953; M.Ed., De Paul U., 1957; certificate advanced study in reading U. Chgo., 1966; m. Armin Henry Breihan, June 26, 1937; children—Joanne, James. Tchr., Lutheran Parochial Schs., Detroit, Chgo., 1930-37; pvt. tchr. remedial reading, Homewood, Ill., Flossmoor, 1945-51; tchr. Culbertson Sch., Joliet, Ill., 1953-57, Central Sch., Lockport, Ill., 1955-58; reading cons. Lockport Twp. High Sch. 1958-66; reading coordinator Lockport Twp. Sch. Dist. 205, 1966-71, chmn. reading dept., 1971-75. Mem. Lockport Woman's Club (hon.), N.E.A., Internat. Reading Assn. (past pres. Will County council), Ill. Edn. Assn., Internat. Platform Assn., Lockport Bus. and Profl. Women's Assn., Am. Inst. Mgmt., Assn. Supervision and Curriculum Devel., AAUW, Delta Kappa Gamma, Chi Sigma Xi. Lutheran. Home: 1512 Briggs St Lockport IL 60441

BREITINGER, CAROL ANNE, newspaper mgr.; b. Audubon, N.J., Jan. 27, 1945; d. Alfred Marvin and Caroline Jean (Tait) Duus; student St. Joseph's U., 1982—; m. Carl Alexander Breitinger, Aug. 24, 1974. Classified adv. Courier-Post, Camden, N.J., 1963-73, classified outside salesman, 1973-74, pub. service mgr., 1974-80, promotion mgr., 1980—. Recipient Career Achievement Recognition award Camden County YWCA, 1981. Mem. Internat. Newspaper Promotion Assn. Presbyterian. Office: 301 Cuthbert Blvd Cherry Hill NJ 08002

BREKKE, JOANNE JUDITH, state legislator; b. North Bend, Wash., Apr. 18, 1935; d. Emil and Thelma (Mueller) Sorensen; B.A. in Sociology, U. Wash., Seattle, 1957; children—Melene, Marshall, Alison. Mem. Wash. Ho. of Reps., 1978—; mem. Wash. State Jail Commn. Bd. dirs. Norwest Found., Seattle Mental Health Inst., Scandinavia Today in Seattle; mem. King County Health Facilities Rev. Com. Mem. NOW, Women's Polit. Caucus, LWV. Democrat. Home: 6525 Sycamore Ave NW Seattle WA 98117 Office: House Office Bldg 427 Olympia WA 98504

BRELAND, JOY ANN BURT, ins. co. exec.; b. Crystal Springs, Miss., May 20, 1934; d. Vernon Ramsey and Nannie Lee (Furlow) Burt; B.S., Miss. Coll., 1956; 1 son, Loren Dewey. Agt., N.Y. Life Ins., Jackson, Miss., 1974-75; agt. Mutual of N.Y., Jackson, 1975-80, asst. to regional v.p., regional dir. mktg. services, 1980—. Mem. adv. bd. div. drug misuse Miss. Dept. Mental Health, 1972-77; bd. dirs. Jackson Mental Health Center, 1974-77. Mem. Jackson Assn. Life Underwriters (dir. 1979-80), Nat. Assn. Life Underwriters (state chairperson women life underwriters conf. 1979-80), Million Dollar Round Table, Women Leaders Round Table, AAUW. Republican. Baptist. Club: Nat. Assn. Jr. Auxs. Office: Suite 714 One Piedmont Center 3565 Piedmont Rd NE Atlanta GA 30305

BREMER, KENDA POWELL, health care exec.; b. Versailles, Mo., Sept. 27, 1942; d. Kenneth Lee and Mildred Marie (Rasa) Spalding; R.N., Mo. Baptist Sch. Nursing, St. Louis, 1963; student health systems mgmt. U. Mo., neuro nurse specialist Methodist Hosp., Houston, 1970; m. William Darrell Bremer, Aug. 5, 1972; 1 son, John Sanford Powell, III. Infirmary dir. U. Corpus Christi (Tex.), 1964; staff nurse Thomas Spann Clinic, Corpus Christi, 1964-65, Meth. Hosp., 1965-70; unit coordinator Tex. Inst. Rehab. and Research, 1970-71; dir. nursing Westwood Nursing Center, Clinton, Mo., 1972; exec. v.p. ops. new projects and planning Brooking Park Geriatrics Inc., Sedalia, Mo., 1972—. Mem. Am. Nurses Assn., Mo. Nurses Assn., Am. Coll. Nursing Home Adminstrs., Am. Health Care Assn., Mo. League Nursing Home Adminstrs., Nat. Assn. Female Execs. (network dir. 1980—). Republican. Lutheran. Club: Sedalia Altrusa (dir., treas. 1978-82). Home: Route 6 Box 148 A Sedalia MO 65301 Office: PO Box 1567 Sedalia MO 65301

BREMYER, JAYNE DICKEY, author; b. Charleston, W.Va., Nov. 12, 1924; d. George Henry and Nida (Dickey) Willianson; B.S., McPherson (Kans.) Coll., 1965; m. John K. Bremyer, Dec. 8, 1945; children—John K., Jr., Jeffrey W., Jill. Pres., Ability to Love Seminars, McPherson; leader seminars talks and workshops; author: Let's Fact It: What a Man Really Wants From a Woman and a Woman Really Wants From a Man, 1982; Journey to a Mountain Top, 1969; Dear God, 1979; Success Secrets, 1981; Dear God, Am I Important?, 1980. Mem. Nat. Speakers Assn., Profl. Hypnotists Am., Salespersons Am., AAUW, PEO, Fedn. Women's Clubs. Republican. Methodist. Office: PO Box 1242 McPherson KS 67460

BRENNAN, ADELINA CALABRO, confectionery co. ofcl.; b. Italy, Nov. 16, 1952; came to U.S., 1961, naturalized, 1970; d. John and Serafina Calabro; B.A., St. Peter's Coll., 1975; postgrad. Fairleigh Dickinson U., 1980-81; m. Robert F. Brennan, Sept 3, 1977. Acct., asst. to dep. controller Ferrero U.S.A., Inc., N.Y.C., 1975-76, traffic mgr., 1976-78, inventory and traffic and warehousing mgr., 1978-80, ops. mgr., 1980-82, dir. mgmt. services, 1982—. Office: 295 Madison Ave 14th Floor New York NY 10017

BRENNAN, DEBORAH ANN, nursing home adminstr.; b. Phila., July 31, 1947; d. Harry Clay and Margaret Ann (McConnel) Ward; B.A., Pa. State U., 1971; children—James Robert, Timothy Alexander. Dir. adminstrn. Pine Run Community, subs. Life Care Soc. Am., Doylestown, Pa., 1977-78, dir. mem. services, 1979-81, dir. mktg., 1980-81, spl. asst. to pres. Life Care Soc. Am., Doylestown, 1978-81; dir. resident and vol. services Evang. Manor, Phila., 1981—; corp. sec. Wardco Systems U.S.A. Mem. Nat. Assn. Female Execs., Social Service Workers Assn. (nursing homes sect.), Coalition of Advocates for Rights of Infirm Elderly. Mennonite. Home: 69 Providence Ave Doylestown PA 18901 Office: 8401 Roosevelt Blvd Philadelphia PA 19152

BRENNAN, DOROTHEA ELIZABETH, banker; b. Bridgeport, Conn., Mar. 14, 1950; d. Daniel Edward and Emily (Tabor) Brennan; B.A cum laude, Loyola U., New Orleans, 1972; M.A., Fairfield U. Grad. Sch. Communications, 1981. Asst. comptroller First Bank, New Haven, 1976-79, asst. v.p. mktg., 1979; comml. loan officer First Bank, Hartford, Conn., 1980-81, corp. banking officer, 1981—. Asst. treas. New Haven Preservation Trust, 1980—; chmn. communications com. Big Bro. Big Sister, New Haven, 1980-81; mem. citizens adv. com. U.S. Dept. Transp.; bd. mgrs. New Haven Boys Club, 1982—. Mem. Conn. Bankers Assn. (vice chmn. polit. action com., mem. legis. steering com.), Women Dirs. Inc. Republican. Roman Catholic. Office: First Bank PO Box 502 New Haven CT 06502

BRENNAN, LOUISE SMITH, state legislator; b. Chester, S.C., Nov. 11, 1922; d. Tom and Kate Varnadore Smith; B.A., U. N.C., Charlotte, 1970; M.A., U. N.C., Chapel Hill; m. Stanley L. Brennan, Sept. 25, 1965; children—Susan S. Mitchell, Jane S. Coleman, Robert T. Sutton, Jr. Lectr. polit. sci. dept. U. N.C., Chapel Hill, 1976-80; cons. Fairington Properties, 1974; v.p. Charlotte Sporting Goods Co., Inc., 1949-63; mem. N.C. Ho. of Reps., 1969, 77-78, 79-80, 81—, mem. local govt. liaison com. of govtl. bodies, 1978-80, mem. select com. on govtl. ethics, 1979-80, dist. chmn. 9th Dist. Democrats, 1970-77, vice-chmn. appropriations base budget com. on human resources. Mem. Legis. Study Commn. on Sch. Food Programs, 1980; bd. dirs. Eckerd Wilderness Camps, 1979—; mem. Gov.'s Commn. Party Reform, 1969-71; bd. dirs. (hon.) Juvenile Diabetes Assn., 1978-80; bd. dirs. Women's Forum, 1977-80. Mem. Exec. Women of Charlotte, AAUW, YWCA, Nat. Orgn. Women Legislators, Charlotte C. of C. Presbyterian. Office: NC Ho of Reps State Capitol Raleigh NC 27602 *

BRENNAN, MILDRED JOAN, ednl. adminstr.; b. Jersey City, Sept. 19, 1936; d. Charles and Maria Rose (Liquori) Pettinato; B.S., Seton Hall U., 1967; postgrad. St. Peter's Coll., 1972, Bryn Mawr Coll., 1976. With Lehigh Valley R.R., Bethlehem, Pa., 1954-71; sec. St. Peter'S Coll., Jersey City, 1972-73, asst. dir. devel., 1973-80, dir. devel. research and govt. grants, 1980—; v.p. Benmore Corp., Jersey City, 1977—. Mem. bd. trustees Heckman Found. Office: St Peter's Coll 2641 Kennedy Blvd Jersey City NJ 07306

BRENNAN, NANCY STERRETT, artist, designer; b. Cin., Dec. 25, 1933; d. Chester Korn and Bessie Helen (Coulter) Sterrett; B.A., Stanford U., 1955; secondary tchrs. credential San Francisco State U., 1956; m. Edwin Plank Brennan, Sept. 10, 1955; children—Frederick, Jean, Susanne, Nancy. Freelance artist and designer, 1955-78; designer San Francisco Designs, San Rafael, Calif., 1978-79; owner, operator Nancy Brennan Interiors, Napa, Calif., 1979—; carpet muralist for Scomas Restaurant, Marin County, Calif., Marin Gen. Hosp., Greenbrae, Calif., also many pvt. commns. Pres. Terra Linda Guild, Marin Mus. Sci., 1962. Recipient awards for assemblages and collages, Nat. League Am. Pen Women, 1976, 78, 82, Marin County Fair Show, 1978. Mem. Terra Linda Art Assn. (founder, dir. 1963-64, 73-74), Marin Soc. Artists, Nat. League Am. Penwomen. Presbyterian.

BRENNEKE, JUDITH STALEY, ednl. adminstr.; b. St. Louis, Aug. 24, 1945; d. Calvin Curtis and Coral Genelle (Keithley) Staley; B.S. in Bus. Edn., N.E. Mo. State U., 1969; M.S. in Bus. Edn., Western Ill. U., 1969; Ed.D. in Bus., No. Ill. U., 1978; m. John Charles Soper, Oct. 23, 1978; 1 dau., Michelle Kristine. Tchr., Macomb (Ill.) High Sch., 1972-76; asso. dir. Ill. Council Econ. Edn., instr. bus. edn. No. Ill. U., DeKalb, 1975-78, dir. Office Econ. Edn., 1979—; dir. Center Econ. Edn., asst. prof. econs. and mgmt. R.I. Coll., Providence, 1978-79; project dir. Consumer Edn. and Econ. Edn. in Public Schs., U.S. Office Edn./Joint Council Econ. Edn., Office for Consumers Edn., Washington, 1979-81; cons. ednl. agys. Mem. Ill. Consumer Edn. Assn., Am. Council Consumer Interests, Nat. Bus. Edn. Assn., Midwest Bus. Edn. Assn., Ill.

Bus. Edn. Assn., Am. Econs. Assn., Western Econs. Assn., Ill. Econ. Assn., Nat. Council Social Studies, Nat. Assn. Affiliated Econ. Edn. Dirs., Assn. Supervision and Curriculum Devel., Ill. Assn. Supervision and Curriculum Devel., Delta Pi Epsilon. Author: The Mochans: A Mythical Economic Society, 1976; Consumer Educations and Economic Educations in the Public Schools, 1981; Integrating Consumer Education and Economic Education into the School Curriculum, 1981; The Big Brown Bag: The Economics of the American Food Systems, 1981. Home: 1801 Raintree Ct Sycamore IL 60178 Office: Office for Econ Edn No Ill U DeKalb IL 60115

BRENNER, ARLEEN PASVANIS, nurse; b. Youngstown, Ohio, Oct. 8, 1947; d. Peter Alexander and Kathleen (Kefalos) Pasvanis; diploma Sch. Nursing Ohio Valley Hosp., 1968; m. Gary Rogers Brenner, June 19, 1976. Staff nurse Presbyn. U. Hosp., Pitts., 1968-69; asst. head nurse Ohio State U. Hosp., Columbus, 1969-72; staff nurse Dameron Hosp., Stockton, Calif., 1972-73; asst. clin. nursing coordinator, staff nurse Stanford (Calif.) U. Hosp., 1974—. Mem. Assn. Operating Rm. Nurses, Am. Women's Vol. Soc., Friends of Nursing Stanford U. Med Center. Greek Orthodox. Home: 1523 Altura Way Belmont CA 94002

BRENNER, BETTY BILGRAY, psychiat. social worker; b. Providence, Feb. 13, 1943; d. Albert Theodore and Clara (Simon) Bilgray; student U. Ariz., 1961-63; B.A., U. Mich., 1965, M.S.W., 1967; m. Douglas Brenner, Sept. 1, 1968; children—Steven, Michael, Deborah. Research asst. U. Mich. Sch. Social Work, summer, 1966; social worker Peter Bent Brigham Hosp., Boston, 1967-69; psychiat. social worker Union County Psychiat. Clinic, Summit, N.J., 1969-71; psychiat. social worker Montclair (N.J.) West Essex Guidance Center, 1977—; past cons. Springfield and New Providence (N.J.) Sch. Systems. Mem. Acad. Cert. Social Workers, Nat. Assn. Social Workers. Jewish. Home: 61 E Sherbrooke Pkwy Livingston NJ 07039 Office: 60 S Fullerton Ave Montclair NJ 07042

BRENNER, BEULAH LORRAINE CHATFIELD, savs. and loan officer; b. Oconomowoc, Wis., Mar. 29, 1922; d. Frank Silas and Theresa Margurite (O'Connor) Chatfield; student Schauffler Coll., 1941-43, Olivet Nazarene Coll., 1943-44; degree of distinction Inst. Fin. Edn., 1980; m. Gilbert Ellis Brenner, June 1, 1946 (dec. Dec. 1977); children—Barbara Jean Brenner Nolan, Richard Joseph. Girls and woman's dir. Kankakee (Ill.) YMCA, 1943-45; sec. to supt. Kankakee County (Ill.) Schs., 1945-49, adminstrv. asst. to supt., 1961-67; sec. to pres. Kankakee Community Coll., 1967-69, dir. public relations dept., 1969-72; student loan officer, mktg.-public relations assn. Kankakee Fed. Savs. & Loan Assn., 1972—, exec. dir. Kankakee Fed. Savers Club, 1972—; speaker public relations; cons. savers clubs. Treas., violinist Kankakee Symphony Orch., 1949-56; pres. woman's assn. Presbyterian Ch., 1959-60, mem. choir, 1941-72, 80-82; bd. dirs. Kankakee County Mental Health Center, 1969-81, v.p., 1973-75; mem. community relations com. Riverside Hosp. Found., 1974—, chmn. com., 1982; Kankakee County crusade chmn. Am. Cancer Soc., 1978, vice chmn., 1979, bd. dirs., 1979-82. Mem. Savs. Instns. Mktg. Soc. Am. Clubs: Zonta Internat., Round Table (Kankakee). Home: Kankakee IL 60901 Office: 310 S Schuyler Ave Kankakee IL 60901

BRENNER, CANDIS KAY, veterinarian; b. Houston, Sept. 7, 1954; d. Lawrence and Louise (Oberpriller) B.; student U. Houston, 1972-73; B.S. in Nursing cum laude, U. Tex., 1976; B.S. in Vet. Sci. cum laude Tex. A&M U., 1980, D.V.M., 1981. Sales corres. Brenner Elec. Sales, Houston, 1971-73; nurse John Sealy Hosp., Galveston, Tex., 1975; vet. technician Beechnut Animal Emergency Clinic, Houston, 1977-78; nurse Meth. Hosp., Houston, 1977-78; vet. technician Westbury Animal Hosp., Houston, 1979; veterinarian Golden Triangle Animal Hosp., 1981—. Registered nurse. Mem. Tex. Vet. Med. Assn., AVMA, Tarrant County Vet. Assn., Phi Zeta. *

BRENNER, JANET MAYBIN WALKER, lawyer; b. Arkansas City, Kans.; d. D. Arthur and Maybin (Gardner) Walker; A.B., U. So. Calif.; J.D., George Washington U., 1978; m. Edgar H. Brenner, Aug. 4, 1979; children—Margaret Maybin Jonas, Theodore Kimball Jonas, Amanda Nash Jonas. Admitted to D.C. bar, 1978; staff Tax Notes mag., Washington, 1978-79; practice tax law, Washington, 1979—. Trustee, No. Va. Fine Arts Assn., 1973-75; mem. women's com. Corcoran Gallery Art, 1969—, mem. Corcoran Art Sch. com., 1975—. Mem. D.C. Bar Assn., Women's Bar of D.C., Women's Legal Def. Fund. Club: Sulgrave (Washington). Home: 3325 R St NW Washington DC 20007 also Shadow Ridge Farm Washington VA 22747

BRENNER, JETTA S., hotel exec.; b. Providence, Feb. 27, 1926; d. Jules and Florence Sorgman; hon community prof. Fla. Internat. U., 1979; children—Kathy, Robert. Meeting planner Am. Math. Soc., Providence, 1965-68; sales staff Sheraton-Biltmore Hotel, Providence, 1968-71; conv. coordinator Sheraton-Boston Hotel, 1972-73; gen. mgr. Sheraton Russell Hotel, N.Y.C., 1973—; mem. adv. bd. Bus. Sch. Hotel Soc. Fairleigh-Dickinsen U. Chairperson hotel restaurant div. United Way of Tri State, 1978-79. Recipient Acad. Women Achievers award YWCA N.Y., 1980. Mem. Am. Hotel and Motel Assn., Hotel Assn. N.Y.C., Hotel Sales Mgmt. Assn., Hotel Execs. Club. Home and Office: 45 Park Ave New York NY 10016

BRENNER, LORY LEBOWITZ, audiologist; b. Phila., Dec. 31, 1948; d. William Bernard and Eva (Seligson) Lebowitz; A.B., Temple U., 1969, M.A., 1971; m. Maury M. Brenner, Jan. 21, 1973; children—Chaney Candice, Alison Joy. Clin. audiologist VA Outpatient Clinic, Phila., 1971-74, 76-78; pvt. practice audiology, Harrisburg, Pa., 1979—. Sec. bd. dirs. Dauphin Residences, Inc., 1977—; reader to the blind Nat. Council Jewish Women, 1975—; religious sch. tchr. Beth El Temple, Harrisburg, 1974—. Mem. Am. Speech, Lang. and Hearing Assn., Pa. Speech and Hearing Assn., Nat. Council Jewish Women. Home: 2955 Green St Harrisburg PA 17110

BRENNER-TOURTELOT, ELIZABETH FORD, geologist; b. Butte, Mont., Oct. 8, 1941; d. John Skoning and Frances Marshall (Ford) Brenner; A.B., Wellesley Coll., 1962; m. Harry A. Tourtelot, 1964 (div.); children—John Brenner, Frances Grace. From editorial clk. to geologist U.S. Geol. Survey, Denver, 1962-78; pres. X-Un-10 Co., Dillon, Mont., 1978—. Mem. Am. Geol. Inst., Tobacco Root Geol. Soc. (pres. 1980—), Am. Inst. Profl. Geologists, Geol. Soc. Am., Soc. Econ. Geologists, Rocky Mountain Assn. Geologists, AAAS, Assn. Women Geoscientists, NW Mining Assn., Mont. Mining Assn. (chpt. pres. 1981—), Mont. Geol. Soc., Colo. Sci. Soc., Wyo. Geol. Soc., N.Mex. Geol. Soc., Mont. Stockgrowers Assn., Beaverhead C. of C. Republican. Episcopalian. Club: Dillon Toastmistresses. Author papers in field. Home: 734 Morse St Dillon MT 59725 Office: PO Box 470 Dillon MT 59725

BRENNY, MARY CLARE, med. technologist/tech. cons.; b. Carroll, Iowa, Oct. 23, 1950; d. Clarence R. and Irene M. (Reicks) B.; B.S. in Med. Tech., Coll. Mt. Mercy, 1972. Staff technologist Mercy Hosp., Cedar Rapids, Iowa, 1972; supr. dept. hematology Redlands (Calif.) Community Hosp., 1972-75; tech. specialist/cons. coagulation Ortho Diagnostics, Inc., Raritan, N.J., 1975-80, area sales rep., Houston, 1980-81; med. technologist Houston N.W. Med. Center, 1981—; lectr., cons. hemodialysis. Mem. Am. Soc. Med. Tech., others. Roman Catholic. Contbr. articles to The Clotting Times newsletter, 1975-79. Address: 14555 Wunderlich St Apt 2604 Houston TX 77069

BRENZEL, NAN ELIZABETH, rehab. adminstr.; b. Peckville, Pa., Sept. 23, 1952; d. Frank J. and Dorothy A. (Williams) B.; B.S. in Psychology, Pa. State U., 1973; M.S. in Rehab. Counseling, U. Scranton, 1976; Ed.D., W.Va. U., 1979. Rehab. counselor Allied Services for the Handicapped, Inc., Scranton, Pa., 1973-76, Scranton Mental Health Center, 1976-77, also supr., 1978-79; admissions dir. dept. counseling and guidance W.Va. U., Morgantown, 1977-78, ednl. research asso. dept. ednl. research and field services, 1978-79; exec. dir. Hawaii Services on Deafness, Honolulu, 1979-80; asso. prof. rehab. research and tng. W.Va. U., Dunbar, 1980-81; dir. program evaluation W.Va. Vocat. Rehab. Research and Tng. Center, Dunbar, 1981—; cons. to U. Hawaii, 1979-80, Hawaii Assn. for Retarded Citizens, 1979-80, Easter Seals of Hawaii, 1979-80. Chmn. fin. mgmt. YWCA, Charleston, W.Va., 1981—. State of Hawaii grantee, 1979-80; HUD grantee, 1980. Mem. Am. Personnel and Guidance Assn., Am. Rehab. Counseling Assn., Evaluation Research Soc., Am. Psychol. Assn., Nat. Rehab. Assn., Evaluation Network Assn., Assn. for Measurement and Evaluation, AAUW, Phi Delta Kappa. Author: Manual for Sex Education, 1979; Human Sexuality Attitude Survey for Mentally Retarded Adults, 1979. Home: 844 Somerset Dr Charleston WV 25302 Office: One Dunbar Plaza Suite E Dunbar WV 25064

BRESLAWSKI, DONNA, mfg. engr.; b. Brockport, N.Y., Dec. 2, 1958; d. Daniel and Nancy Lee Breslawski; A.A.S. in Drafting and Design, SUNY at Morrisville, 1979; B.Tech. in Mech. Design Tech., SUNY at Utica, 1981. Asst. engr. Utica Screw Products, Inc. (N.Y.), 1980-81, engr., 1981-82; mfg. engr. O.P. Held, Inc., Utica, 1982—. Mem. Nat. Screw Machine Products Assn., Soc. Mfg. Engrs. (student chpt). Home: 1704 Pierrepont St Utica NY 13502 Office: 1303 Rutger St Utica NY 13504

BRESLIN, JANET ELLEN, mem. senatorial staff; b. St. Louis, Nov. 16, 1945; d. John A. and Priscilla M. Hoel; B.A., U. So. Calif., 1967; M.A., UCLA, 1970, Ph.D. (AAUW dissertation fellow), 1976; m. Patrick Breslin, Dec. 10, 1972; 1 dau., Cathleen Ann. Profl. staff mem. Commn. on Operation of the Senate, 1975; exec. asst. Office of Sen. Lloyd Bentsen, Washington, 1976-78; legis. dir. Office of Sen. Donald Stewart, Washington, 1978-81; sr. legis. asst. Office of Sen. Patrick Leahy, Washington, 1981—. Mem. Phi Beta Kappa. Democrat. Office: 427 Russell Bldg Washington DC 20510

BRESLIN, NETTIE SHLESER, psychologist; b. Toronto, Ont., Can.; d. Jacob and Anne Shirley (Ginsberg) Shleser; B.A., Roosevelt U., 1965; M.S., Ill. Inst. Tech., 1966; Ph.D., U. Chgo., 1973; m. Winston I. Breslin, June 20, 1939 (dec.); children—Paul R., Joanna R. Conf. sec. Grad. Sch. Bus., U. Chgo., 1958-60, adminstrv. asst. to dean, 1960-62; community orgn. rep. S.E. Chgo. Commn., 1962-63; counselor, instr. Chgo. City Coll., 1966-68; field supr., research asst. Grad. Sch. Edn., U. Chgo., 1969-70; lower sch. counselor U. Chgo. Lab. Schs., 1970-73, 75-78; public adminstrn. analyst IV UCLA Sch. Public Health, 1973-74; ednl. and psychotherapy cons., Chgo., 1968—; divorce mediator, 1982—. Registered psychologist, Ill. Fellow Am. Orthopsychiat. Assn.; mem. Am. Psychol. Assn., Ill. Psychol. Assn., Council Exceptional Children, Acad. Family Mediators, Mediation Council Ill., Pi Lambda Theta. Jewish. Home: 900 Lake Shore Dr Chicago IL 60611 Office: 111 N Wabash Ave Chicago IL 60602

BRESLIN, PEG MCDONNELL, state legislator; b. Ottawa, Ill., July 11, 1946; d. John Robert and Margaret Mary (Hanley) McDonnell; B.S., Loyola U., Chgo., 1969, J.D., 1970; m. John X. Breslin, May 18, 1974; 1 dau., Molly. Admitted to Ill. bar; atty. Chgo. Comm. Criminal Justice, 1970-71, Liberty Mut. Ins. Co., 1971-74, Ill. Bd. Edn., 1974-76; mem. Ill. Ho. of Reps. from 38th Dist. Democrat. Roman Catholic. Office: Ill House of Reps State Capitol Springfield IL 62706 *

BRESLIN-GILMARTIN, JANET, fin. co. exec.; b. Cambridge, Mass., Apr. 24, 1954; d. Paul Anthony and Esther (Drehs) Breslin; B.A. with distinction in Econs., Colby Coll., Waterville, Maine, 1976; M.B.A. (Most Outstanding Student award 1978), IMEDE, Lausanne, Switzerland, 1978; m. Richard John Gilmartin, Sept. 19, 1981. Comml. underwriting analyst Aetna Life and Casualty Co., Portland, Maine and Louisville, Ky., 1976-77; comml. package underwriter Fireman's Fund Ins. Co., Boston, 1977; sr. corp. auditor Am. Express Co., 1979-80, mgr. strategic planning travelers cheque div., 1980—, spl. assignment Consumer Fin. Services Group, Europe, 1982-83. Mem. Am. Mgmt. Assn., Nat. Assn. Corp. Strategic Planning, Sigma Kappa. Roman Catholic. Home: care IMEDE PO Box 1059 Lausanne CH-1001 Switzerland Office: Am Express Mgmt Services Am Express Plaza 125 Broad St New York NY 10004

BRETSCHNEIDER, ANN MARGERY, histotechnologist; b. Newton, Mass., May 11, 1934; d. Herman Frederick and Elizabeth Louise (Brady) B.; B.S., Northeastern U., Boston, 1957; M.S., Rutgers U., 1979. Histopathologic technician NIH, Bethesda, Md., 1957-58; chief histologic technician U. Ala. Med. Center, Birmingham, 1958-61; chief med. technologist in histology, instr. Muhlenberg Hosp., Plainfield, N.J., 1961-67; instr. anatomy Northeastern U., 1967-68; research-teaching specialist U. Medicine and Dentistry-Rutgers U. Med. Sch., 1968—; workshop leader, cons. in field. Mem. Am. Soc. Clin. Pathologists (affiliate), Nat. Soc. Histotech., Electron Microscopy Soc. Am., N.J. Soc. Histotech. Co-author: Thin Is In: Plastic Embedding of Tissue for Light Microscopy, 1981. Office: Dept Pathology Rutgers U Med Sch Piscataway NJ 08854

BRETT, CHARLOTTE MAE, genealogist; b. Westport Twp., Dickinson County, Iowa, Nov. 30, 1904; d. John Franklin and Jessie Clara (Cummings) B.; cert. U. No. Iowa, 1927, B.A., 1933; M.A., Columbia U., 1946; postgrad. Columbia U., 1951, 53, Western Ill. U., Macomb, 1958, Northwestern U., Evanston, Ill., 1964. Rural sch. tchr., 1924-25; elem. tchr., Guttenberg, Iowa, 1927-30, Mitchell, S.D., 1930-31, Smithland, Iowa, 1933-35, Western Springs, Ill., 1935-40, Hancock, Mich., 1941-44, Blue Island, Ill., 1944-70; ret., 1970; librarian Iowa Lakes Geneal. Soc., 1975—; family genealogist; former del. NEA convs.; chmn. cemetery canvass Clay County, Iowa, 1972—; regent Lydia Alden chpt. DAR, 1974-76; state corr. sec. Iowa Soc. Dames of the Ct. of Honor, 1974-78; regent Lakes chpt. Daus. of Am. Colonists, 1978-80, state chaplain Iowa affiliate, 1980-82. Recipient Buffalo Robe, Camp Fire Girls, 1925; life membership Ill. PTA, 1969, cert. Clay County Hist. Soc., 1979. Mem. NEA (life), Art Inst. Chgo. (life), 1st Families of Ohio, Daus. War of 1812, Huguenot Soc., U. No. Iowa Alumni Assn. (life), numerous hist. and geneal. socs. Clubs: Chgo. Doll Collectors, Cherrio Post Card. Author: (with others) Northwest Iowans Share Their Memories, 1978. Home: 218 E 4th St Apt 4A Spencer IA 51301

BRETZ, (ALMA) LINDA, library adminstr.; b. Far Rockaway, N.Y., Sept. 22, 1934; d. Rocco Joseph and Linda Alma (Ley) Mazza; B.S. in L.S., SUNY, Geneseo, 1956; M.F.A. in Dramatic Arts, Columbia U., 1959; m. Robert Lawrence Bretz, June 10, 1961; children—Erika Katharine, John Michael, David Reinhard. Librarian, N.Y.C. Public Library, 1956-59; asst. prof. library edn. SUNY Coll., Geneseo, 1959-66; librarian Lincoln br. Rochester (N.Y.) Public Library, 1966-67, head br., 1967-72; inservice tng. cons. Monroe County (N.Y.) Library System, Rochester, 1972-73, children's services cons., 1973-75, asst. dir. system, 1976-78, dir. Rochester Public Library and Monroe County Library System, 1978—; del. N.Y. Gov.'s Conf. Libraries, 1978, White House Conf. on Library and Info. Scis., 1979; trustee Reynolds Library; mem. adv. com. Main Office, Community Savs. Bank, 1981—. Bd. dirs. Opera Theatre of Rochester, Rochester Health Network, 1982—; mem. N.Y. State Profl. Librarians Cert. Exam. Com., 1973-78, chmn. 1977; registrar Rochester Bach Festival, 1975—. Mem. N.Y. Library Assn. (councilor-at-large 1976-80, pres. 1982), ALA Am. Soc. Public Administrn. (pres. Rochester-Monroe County chpt. 1979-80). Home: 32 Audubon St Rochester NY 14610 Office: 15 South Ave Rochester NY 14604

BRETZFELDER, DEBORAH MAY, mus. exhibit designer; b. Hazleton, Pa., Sept. 21, 1932; d. Joseph and Rose (Smulyan) Hirsh; student Syracuse U., 1950-53; m. Robert Bretzfelder, Dec. 24, 1955; children—Karl, Marc. Textile colorist, designer Cohn-Hall-Marx, N.Y.C., 1954-55; fashion coordinator Hecht's Dept. Store, Washington, 1956; free-lance artist, Washington, 1956-58; exhibits technician Smithsonian Mus., Washington, 1958-59, exhibits prodn. supr., 1959-63, exhibits specialist Smithsonian Mus., Nat. Mus. Am. History, 1963-75, visual info. specialist, project mgmt. officer, 1975—; cons. various firms, orgns., mus. personnel. Mem. violin sect. George Washington U. Orch. Mem. Am. Assn. Mus., Internat. Com. Mus., Nat. Soc. Historic Preservation, Tau Sigma Delta. Jewish. Club: Potomac Appalachian Trail. Home: 2748 Woodley Pl NW Washington DC 20008 Office: Smithsonian Nat Mus Am History 14th and Constitution NW Room 4210 Washington DC 20560

BREWER, JANE LYNN, plant scientist; b. Mount Pleasant, Mich., June 1, 1944; d. Charles Francis and Ruby Eileen (Grandon) Whitcomb; student Central Mich. U., 1962-64; B.A. with high distinction, Colo. State U., 1980; m. Jesse Wayne Brewer, Dec. 26, 1964 (div. 1978); children—Laura Elizabeth, Matthew Whitcomb. Technician, Potato Virus Lab., Colo. State U., Fort Collins, 1972, lab. asst. Colo. Seed Lab., 1976-78, seed analyst, mem. botany dept., 1978—, supr. germinator dept., 1982—. Mem. Phi Kappa Phi. Democrat. Home: 1916 Osage St Fort Collins CO 80525 Office: E-10 Plant Scis Colo State U Fort Collins CO 80521

BREWER, RUTH RUSSELL (MRS. JOHN I. BREWER), civic worker; b. Great Bend, Kans., June 21, 1904; d. Francis Vernon and Jettie (McBride) Russell; B.A., U. Wis., 1921; M.A., Columbia U., 1923; m. John I. Brewer, June 2, 1928; 1 son, John V. Instr., Bradley U., Peoria, Ill., 1923-26; service rep. Thrift Inc., Oak Park, Ill., 1927. Head surg. dressing unit ARC, Denver, 1943-44; chmn. women's div. Joint Appeal, Chgo., 1957, mem. woman's planning bd., 1957-61; treas. Kenwood Social Service Club, Chgo., 1953, 1st v.p., 1954, pres., 1955; corr. sec., 3d v.p. woman's aux. Infant Welfare Soc., Chgo., 1960-61, 1st v.p., 1963-64, pres., 1965-66, bd. adviser, 1967-68, bd. dirs.; bd. dirs. Infant Welfare Soc. of Chgo., 1966-71, Met. Chgo. YWCA, 1968—; mem. planning bd. Crusade of Mercy, 1957-70; treas. women's aux. Goodwill Industries. Mem. Kappa Alpha Theta. Club: Woman's Athletic (Chgo.). Home: 860 Lake Shore Dr Chicago IL 60611

BREWER, SUSAN CATHERINE (KITTY), printing co. exec.; b. Covington, Tenn., July 30, 1942; d. Daniel Fredrick and Mary (Lindsey) Jennings; student Memphis State U., 1960-61, 74—; 1 dau., Elizabeth Paige. Family lifestyles editor Covington Pub. Co., 1961-77; group mktg. rep. Equitable Life Assurance Soc., Memphis, 1977-82; consumer service rep. Mercury Printing Co., Memphis, 1982—. Publicity dir. St. Jude Children's Research Hosp., 1976-77, Covington Little Theatre, 1970-77, Tipton County Bus. and Profl. Women's Club, 1974-77, Covington Jaycettes, 1970-72, Rev. Book Club, 1972-74; bd. dirs. Memphis Area Newcomers. Recipient 1st and 2d press awards Tenn. Press Assn., annually 1969-77, 1st place award Tenn. Women's Press and Author Club, 1976-77, hon. mention U. Mo. Women's Editor contest, 1976; recipient 1st place art award in oils Tipton Art Assn., 1967; Nat. Sales Leader, 1979, 80, 81, 82. Mem. Nat. Fedn. Press Women (regional dir.), Women in Communications, Tenn. Press Assn., Memphis Pen Women, DAR, Tipton County Art Assn., Women of 1812, Am. Soc. Profl. and Exec. Women, Sales and Mktg. Execs. Memphis. Baptist. Home: 3128 Court St Bartlett TN 38134 Office: 2929 Convair Rd Memphis TN 38116

BREWSTER, ELIZABETH WINIFRED, educator, poet, novelist; b. Chipman, N.B., Can., Aug. 26, 1922; d. Frederick John and Ethel May (Day) Brewster; B.A., U. New Brunswick, 1946; M.A., Radcliffe U., 1947; B.L.S., U. Toronto, 1954; Ph.D., Ind. U., 1962; D. Litt., U. N.B., 1982. Cataloger Carleton U., Ottawa, Ont., Can., 1953-57, Ind. U. Library, Bloomington, 1957-58, N.B. Legis. Library, 1965-68, U. Alta. (Can.) Library, Edmonton, 1968-70; mem. English dept. Victoria (B.C., Can.) U., 1960-61; reference librarian Mt. Allison U. Library, Sackville, N.B., 1961-65; vis. asst. prof. English, U. Alta., 1970-71; mem. faculty U. Sask., Saskatoon, 1972—, asst. prof. English, 1972-75, assoc. prof., 1975-80, prof., 1980—. Recipient E. J. Pratt award for poetry U. Toronto, 1953; President's medal for poetry U. Western Ont., 1980. Mem. League Can. Poets, Writers' Union Can., Assn. Can. Univ. Tchrs. English. Author: East Coast, 1951; Lilloot, 1954; Roads, 1957; Passage of Summer, 1969; Sunrise North, 1972; In Search of Eros, 1974; Sometimes I Think of Moving, 1977; The Way Home, 1982; The Sisters, 1974; It's Easy To Fall on the Ice, 1977. Office: Dept of English Univ of Saskatchewan Saskatoon SK S7N 0W0 Canada

BREWSTER, EVELYN MACHUM, nurse; b. Wolfeboro, N.H., Mar. 19, 1924; d. Nathaniel Blair and Annie Irene (Machum) B.; R.N., Mass. Gen. Hosp., Boston, 1945. Staff nurse, pvt. surg. nurse, Boston and Denver, 1945-57; staff nurse to head nurse operating room Mass. Eye and Ear Infirmary, Boston, 1957-77, operating room dir., 1975—. Mem. Am. Assn. Operating Room Nurses, Am. Soc. Head and Neck Nurses, Am. Soc. Ophthalmic R.N.s. Office: Mass Eye and Ear Infirmary 243 Charles St Boston MA 02114

BREWSTER, OLIVE NESBITT, librarian; b. San Antonio, July 19, 1924; d. Charles Henry and Olive Agatha (Nesbitt) B.; B.A., Our Lady of the Lake Coll., 1945, B.S. in Library Sci., 1946. Asst. librarian aeromed. library U.S. Air Force Sch. Aviation Medicine, Randolph AFB, Tex., 1946-60, chief cataloger aeromed. library Sch. Aerospace Medicine, Brooks AFB, Tex., 1960—. Mem. ALA, Am. Soc. Indexers, Mensa. Anglican. Home: 1906 Schley Ave San Antonio TX 78210 Office: Aeromed Library USAF Sch Aerospace Medicine Brooks AFB TX 78235

BREY, VIRGINIA RUTH, cons. indsl. designer; b. Long Beach, Calif., Nov. 11.; d. Rufus Edward and Ruth Ella (Steen) Mayfield; student Del Mar Jr. Coll., Corpus Christi, Tex., 1956; children—Ann, Susan, Judith, Pamela, Rebecca. Geol. draftsman Standard Oil of Tex., other cos., 1956-73; cons. indsl. designer engring. firms, Houston, 1973—; prin. Virginia Brey Designs. Registered indsl. designer. Republican. Club: Who's Who Internat. Social for Charity. Home: 8299 Kingsbrook St Apt 181 Houston TX 77024 Office: 8554 Katy Freeway Suite 300 Houston TX 77024

BRICE-JOHNSON, JUANITA CHARLESTINE, educator; b. Bessemer, Ala., Aug. 16, 1928; d. Luther G. and Annie Louise (Craig) Brice; B.S., Ala. State U., 1943; M.S., N.Y. U., 1953; postgrad. Miles Coll., Birmingham, Ala., 1962, U. So. Calif., Los Angeles, 1964, U. Ala., 1970; m. Jeff Johnson, May 2, 1981. Tchr., Cobb Ave. High Sch., Anniston, Ala., 1943-53, Wenonah Jr. High Sch., Birmingham, 1953-60, Wenonah High Sch., Birmingham, 1960-68, No. High Sch., Flint, Mich., 1968—; sales clk. J. L. Hudson's Dept. Store, Flint, 1970—. Del., Democratic Precinct, Flint, 1977—, conv. del., 1977—. Recipient Civus Optimus, Mich. State U., 1977. Mem. United Tchrs. of Flint (treas. 1973-75),

Mich. Edn. Assn., Am. Fedn. Tchrs., NEA, NAACP, Phi Delta Kappa, Alpha Kappa Alpha. Baptist. Clubs: Negro Bus. Women Profl., Order Eastern Star, Elks, Dunbar High Sch. Alumni (internat. v.p.). Office: No High Sch G-3284 Mackin Rd Flint MI 48504

BRICK, LENORE MARIE, antique jewelry dealer, real estate broker; b. N.Y.C., Mar., 1924; d. Thomas and Marie (Schlossman) Greenberg; B.A., UCLA, 1945; m. Irving Feintech, June 24, 1945; children—Lisa Ann Marie Feintech, Wendy Lou Feintech; m. 2d, Murray Brick, July, 1968. Decorator, L.B. Interiors, 1947; dealer antique jewelry, The Family Jewels, Beverly Hills, Calif., 1972—; real estate broker S&S Industries Porter Ranch Devel. Co., Beverly Hills, 1976—. Designer, supplier jewelry for films Lombard and Gable, W.C. Fields and Me, China Town, 1972-74. Home: PO Box 1987 Beverly Hills CA 90213 Office: 18320 Hampton Ct Northridge CA 91326

BRICKER, RUTH BAKER, real estate co. exec.; b. Oak Park, Ill., Mar. 23, 1930; d. James Jasper and Mary (Finerman) Lippin; B.A., Antioch Coll., 1974, M.A., 1976; m. David Saul Baker, May 9, 1955; 1 son, Daniel Martin; m. 2d, Neal S. Bricker, Dec. 28, 1980. Western dir. Expts. in Art and Tech. (EAT), Los Angeles, 1969-75; owner Empire Real Estate and property Mgmt., Los Angeles, 1975—; cons. Security Pacific Bank Trust Dept., UCLA Chancellor's Office-Innovations in Faculty Housing; mem. City of Los Angeles Housing Task Force; exec. com. SPACES: Saving and Preserving Archtl. and Cultural Environments. Mem. bd. councillors Internat. Inst. Kidney Diseases UCLA; mem. Am. Found. for Pompidou Mus., Paris, France, 1980-81. Mem. Women in Bus., Western Los Angeles Regional Author: Getting Rich-Investing in Real Estate Partnerships, 1982; contbr. articles in field to profl. jours.; editor Experiments in Art and Tech., 1974-79.

BRICKER, VICTORIA REIFLER, educator; b. Hong Kong, China, June 15, 1940; came to U.S. 1947, naturalized 1953; d. Erwin and Henrietta (Brown) Reifler; A.B., Stanford U., 1962, A.M., Harvard U., 1963, Ph.D., 1968; m. Harvey Miller Bricker, Dec. 27, 1964. Vis. lectr. anthropology Tulane U., 1969-70, asst. prof., 1970-73, asso. prof., 1973-78, prof. 1978—. Guggenheim fellow, 1982; Wenner-Gren Found. Anthropl. Research grantee, 1971, Social Sci. Research Council grantee, 1972. Fellow Am. Anthrop. Assn. (mem. exec. bd. 1980—); mem. Am. Soc. Ethnohistory, Linguistic Soc. Am., Seminario de Cultura Maya, Societe des Americanistes, N.Y. Acad. Sci. Author: Ritual Humor in Highland Chiapas 1973, The Indian Christ, The Indian King: The Historical Substrate of Maya Myth and Ritual 1981; book rev. editor Am. Anthropologist 1971-73; editor: Am. Ethnologist 1973-76; gen. editor: Supplement to Handbook of Middle American Indians 1977—. Office: Department Anthropology Tulane University New Orleans LA 70118

BRICKNER, ESTELLE H., home care agy. exec.; b. East Meadow, L.I., N.Y., Apr. 21, 1954; d. Solomon and Marlene B.; B.A., SUNY, Binghamton, 1975; M.S.W., SUNY, Buffalo, 1977; m. Robert Schwartz, June 5, 1976. Cons. program devel. Erie County Dept. Sr. Services, Buffalo, 1977-79; dir. orgn. devel. In-Home Support Services (now U.S. Ethicare), Buffalo, 1979-80, v.p. ops., 1980—. Mem. Women in Mgmt., N.Y. State Assn. Propietary Home Care Agys., Phi Beta Kappa. Office: 590 Ellicott Square Bldg Buffalo NY 14203

BRIDGE, SHIRLEY GERALDINE, pharmacist; b. Seattle, May 24, 1922; d. Samuel and Hannah (Drucker) Selesnick; B.S. magna cum laude, U. Wash., 1945; m. Herbert M. Bridge, Jan. 25, 1948; children—Jonathan, Daniel. Pharmacist, Swedish Hosp., 1941-42, Peterson's Pharmacy, 1945-57, Snow's Pharmacy, 1957-64, Bon Marche Pharmacy, 1966-72, Pay 'n Save Pharmacy, Seattle, 1972—; part owner, dir. Ben Bridge Jeweler Inc. Pres., Seattle Women's Commn., 1971-74; bd. dirs., treas. Seattle Opportunities Industrialization Center, 1968-72; mem. steering com. U. Wash. Inst. on Aging; devel. council U. Wash., mem. Devel. Bd.; advisor to Seattle Speech and Hearing Center, 1978; past treas. 43d Dist., and committeewoman Democratic party. Recipient Wash. Pharm. Aux. scholarship, 1944, Lehn & Fink Pharm. medal, 1945; McKesson-Robbins scholar, 1945; a Jewish Nat. Fund Forest in Israel dedicated to Shirley and Herb Bridge, 1977. Mem. Wash. Pharm. Assn., NOW, Rho Chi (past pres.). Jewish. Clubs: Hadassah, Women's Univ., Wash. Athletic, U. Wash. Pres.'s (sec.-treas. 1981). Home: 2100 3d Ave #2003 Seattle WA 98121

BRIDGES, ANITA HAYGOOD, musician; b. Tuskegee, Ala., Feb. 16, 1938; d. Claude Martin and Alexina (Boyle) Haygood; B.Mus., Samford U., Birmingham, Ala., 1958; M.S. in Music, So. Baptist Theol. Sem., Louisville, 1960; postgrad. Fla. State U., U. S.C.; m. W.M. Bridges, Dec. 26, 1959; children—Teresa Joy, Brian Stuart. Prof. organ N. Greenville (S.C.) Coll., 1969-64; prof. organ, chorus, theory and harpsichord Anderson (S.C.) Coll., 1965—; organist-dir. St. John's United Methodist Ch., Anderson, 1967-81, Ch. of Holy Trinity, Clemson, S.C., 1981—; soloist opera and oratoria. Mem. Am. Guild Organists (chpt. charter mem.), Nat. Fedn. Music Clubs, Music Tchrs. Nat. Assn., AAUW, Nat. Guild Piano Tchrs., Keyboard Soc., Southwestern Hist. Soc., Anderson Music Club, Am. Choral Dirs. Assn. Recipient numerous workshop awards Birmingham Music Club. Home: 602 Wildwood Dr Anderson SC 29621 Office: 316 Boulevard Anderson SC 29621

BRIDGES, DORIS CROUCH, social work adminstr.; b. Goldsboro, N.C., May 20, 1909; d. Henry Leland and Ethel Jeraldine (Perkins) Crouch; B.A., Winthrop Coll., 1932; postgrad. Furman U., 1934; M.S. in Social Work, Columbia U., 1938; m. John Herold Bridges, July 7, 1950. Vocat. guidance dir., tchr. Greenville (S.C.) Jr. High Sch., 1935-43; methods engr. Sears, Roebuck & Co., Atlanta, 1943-49; with Dept. Human Resources, Atlanta, 1950-53; exec. dir. Atlanta Council Camp Fire Girls, Inc., 1953-65; personnel dir. Economic Opportunity Atlanta, Inc., 1965-74; exec. dir. Ga. chpt. Nat. Assn. Social Workers, Inc., Atlanta, 1974-80; personnel officer Sr. Citizens Services Met. Atlanta, Inc., 1980—. Moderator Atlanta Presbytery, Presbyn. Ch. U.S., 1979, mem. council, 1972-78, commr. to Gen. Assembly, Kansas City, 1979. Mem. Nat. Assn. Social Workers (Ga. pres. 1965-67), Ga. Conf. Social Welfare (pres. 1977-78, mem. bd. 1972-80), Dial Heights Civic Assn. (historian 1980), AAUW (chpt. pres. 1942), Ga. Gerontology Assn. Democrat. Clubs: Altrusa (Atlanta); Sun Dial Garden; Dial Heights Bridge; Stone Mountain Women's. Home: 412 Dial Way Stone Mountain GA 30083 Office: 34 10th St NE Atlanta GA 30309

BRIDGES, ELEUTHERIA (ELTRIA), artist, sculptor, interior designer; b. Adrianople, Turkey, Nov. 28, 1905; came to U.S., 1917, naturalized, 1943; d. Constantine Nicolaides and Aikaterine (Constantinou) Bezas; A.A., Cooper Union, 1926; student Art Students League, N.Y.C., 1925-26, Indsl. Sch. Art, N.Y.C., 1926-28, Grand Central Sch. Art, N.Y.C., 1928-29, William O. Forrest Summer Art Sch., Brooklin, Maine, 1932; m. Robert Wallace Bridges, June 22, 1933; children—Constance Louise (Mrs. Phillip Bodley), Rosalind Ellen. Stylist, Dennison Mfg. Co., N.Y.C., 1922; artist W.W. Brown, Engravers, N.Y.C., 1922-24; interior designer Darling Studios, N.Y.C., 1924-27; asst. to credit mgr. Mallinkrot Chems., N.Y.C., 1927; specialist for subscriber services dept. Moody's Investors Service, N.Y.C., 1928; asst. to sales devel. mgr. Fred F. French Investing Co., N.Y.C., 1928-29; free-lance artist, sculptor, interior designer, poet, author, 1947—; exhibited one-woman show, Blue Hill, Maine, 1968; mem. traveling art exhibit, Proctor & Gamble, 1932-34; exhibited group shows: Indsl. Sch.-Art, N.Y.C., 1927, Art League, Huntington, N.Y., 1963, 64, 65, Artists Group, East Meadow, N.Y., 1967, Solon Soc., Hempstead, N.Y., 1968, 69, 70. Mem. Solon Soc., Carman Ave. Artists Group, Huntington Twp. Art League, Sedgwick Hist. Soc., Daus. Penelope. Club: The Maine. Author: What Now, Iphigenia, 1971. Address: 2825 NE 21st Ave Fort Lauderdale FL 33306 also Fairhill Sedgwick ME 04676

BRIDGES, EMMA LOU, cytotechnologist; b. Indpls., Mar. 25, 1924; d. James Alverson and Helen Carolyn (Baldock) B.; student DePauw U., Ind. U., Cornell U. Med. Coll. Research asst., instr. Papanicolaou Research Lab., Cornell U. Med. Coll., 1956-60; chief cytotechnologist Papanicolaou Cancer Research Inst., Miami, Fla., 1961-66; chief cytotechnologist, instr., research asst., teaching coordinator Hahnemann Med. Coll. and Hosp., Phila., 1966-70; chief cytotechnologist, instr. Temple U. Med. Coll. and Hosp., Phila., 1970-73; owner, supr. Mary G. Papanicolaou Lab. Diagnostic Cytology, Plainfield, Ind., 1979—; past chmn. tech. adv. com. Dade County (Fla.) Community Cervical Cytology Program; cons. in field. Mem. Am. Soc. Clin. Pathologists, Inter-Soc. Cytology Council, Am. Soc. Cytology (1st sec. cytotechnologists adv. com. 1957-59), Am. Soc. Cytotech., Delta Alpha Gamma. Democrat. Author research papers in field. Address: 1407 Miami Ct N Plainfield IN 46168

BRIDGES, RAMONDA KUMP, psychotherapist; b. Fresno, Calif., Mar. 11, 1940; d. Ernest Joseph and Josephine (Miller) Kump; B.A., Pembroke Coll., 1962; M.S.W., U. Calif., Berkeley, 1973; m. William E. Bridges, Dec. 27, 1959; children—Anne Ramonda, Sarah Lyn, Margaret Kump. Social worker Oakland Family Service Agy., 1971-72; social worker Santa Clara (Calif.) Mental Health Agy., 1972-73; psychol. asst. Dr. James F.T. Bugental, Santa Rosa, Calif., 1973-75; pvt. practice psychotherapy, Santa Rosa, 1975—. Founder Primetimers, Forestville, Calif., 1975. Lic. social worker, marriage, family and child counselor, Calif. Mem. Assn. Humanistic Psychology, Nat. Assn. Social Workers, Calif. Assn. Marriage, Family and Child Counselors. Co-author: M.A.T.I.N.G. for Life, A New Look at Long Term Relationships, 1982. Home: 6773 Giovanetti Rd Forestville CA 95436 Office: 818 Cherry St Santa Rosa CA 95404

BRIEDE, BETTY MARIE, investment co. exec.; b. Jesup, Iowa, Apr. 17, 1926; d. Clyde and Marie Elizabeth (Casey) Cavitt; student U. Chgo., 1942-49; B.S., Western Mich. U., 1953; m. Robert Paul Briede, Aug. 21, 1946. Lab. technician Ill. Central. R.R. Hosp., Chgo., 1942-49, Borgess Hosp., Kalamazoo, 1949-53; with Briede Ent., Battle Creek, Mich., 1978—, pres., 1978-81. Dir. provisional training Jr. League, 1964-69; budget dir., exec. com., bd. dir., United Fund, 1964-69; asst. dir. Am. Cancer Soc. (asst. dir. Battle Creek Cancer Edn. Com.), 1964-69. Recipient Citation, United Fund, 1968. Mem. AAUW (treas. 1964-69), AM. Soc. Clin. Pathologists, Kappa Rho Sigma. Roman Catholic. Club: Battle Creek Country, Minges Creek Racket. Address: 249 Honey Ln Battle Creek MI 49015

BRIGGAMAN, JOAN SLIVA, bus. and office edn. cons.; b. New Britain, Conn., July 2, 1939; d. John and Adele (Smolenski) Sliva; B.S. in Bus. Edn., Central Conn. State U., 1961, also postgrad.; postgrad. U. Hartford, 1972-74; Ph.D., U. Conn., 1983; m. Donald E. Briggaman, Jr., June 15, 1963. Bus. tchr. O. H. Platt High Sch., Meriden, Conn., 1961-65; bus. tchr., dept. head Lewis S. Mills High Sch., Burlington, Conn., 1965-75; bus. and office edn. cons. Conn. Dept. Edn., Hartford, 1975—; cons. South-Western Pub. Co.; faculty Greater Hartford Community Coll., 1976-77. Mem. Conn. Bus. Educators Assn. (Tchr. of Year 1973), Eastern Bus. Educators Assn. (Tchr. of Year 1974), Adminstrv. Mgmt. Soc. (editor Hartford chpt. 1975—), Nat. Bus. Edn. Assn., Am. Vocat. Assn., Nat. Assn. State Suprs. Bus. and Office Edn., Delta Pi Epsilon. Author: Minding Your Own Business, 1978; Small Business Management-Record Keeping Procedures, 1980; also articles. Home: 63 N Mountain Rd Canton CT 06019 Office: PO Box 2219 Hartford CT 06115

BRIGGS, BARBARA, weight control therapist; b. Concord, N.H., June 4, 1927; d. Ernest and Thelma Alice (Twardoks) Briggs; L.P.N., Collier County Practical Nursing Sch., 1971-72; student Fullerton Jr. Coll., 1968-69, UCLA, 1969-70, Gesell Inst., 1951; children—Karen, Kathi, Paul. Optometric asst. Dr. Beale, Cocoa Beach, Fla., 1966-67, Dr. Berke, Santa Monica, Calif., 1968-69; exercise, weight therapist Slimmin' Women, Fullerton, Calif., 1969-70; sec. to plant mgr. United Telephone, Naples, Fla., 1970-71; hostess, dining room mgr. Hospitality Buffet, Hilton Inn, Naples, 1970-71; nurse Naples Community Hosp., 1971-72; pvt. nurse, 1972-75; owner Diet & Weight Control Clinic, Ft. Myers, Fla., 1975-79; owner, cons., Naples Weight Control Clinic, 1979—; speaker to local orgns., 1979—; various appearances TV talk shows. Developer weight control by mind control program. Home: 1212 Ridge St Naples FL 33940

BRIGGS, MARGARET A., coll. dean; b. Broken Bow, Nebr., July 29, 1929; d. George E. and Mae L. (Livingston) B.; B.S., Kearney (Nebr.) State Coll., 1954; M.S., Iowa State U., 1960; Ed.D., Columbia U., 1972. High sch. tchr., Nebr., 1954-59; asst. supr. Iowa Dept. Public Instrn., 1960-65; asst. prof. home econs. U. Nebr., 1966-67, U. Md., 1967-69; chmn. dept. home econs. N.W. Mo. State U., Maryville, 1971-78, acting asst. provost, 1976-78; head dept. home econs., asst. dean Coll. Edn. Mont. State U., Bozeman, 1978—. Mem. Am. Home Econs. Assn., Am. Vocat. Assn., Nat. Council Adminstrs. Home Econs., Mont. Home Econs. Assn. (pres. 1982), Mont. Vocat. Assn., Mont. Nutrition Council, Montanans for Children, Youth and Families, AAUW. Office: Herrick Hall Mont State U Bozeman MT 59717

BRIGGS, NANCY ERICKSON, educator, bus. cons.; b. Huron, S.D., July 28, 1944; d. Otto Palmer and Clara Marie (Schwartz) Erickson; B.A., Augustana Coll., 1966; M.A., U. So. Calif., 1968, Ph.D. (NDEA fellow), 1970; m. Rod Briggs, Dec. 27, 1966; children—Eric, Nicole. Prof. speech communication Calif. State U., Long Beach, 1970—; ednl. cons. to Newport Sch. Dist., Fountain Valley Sch. Dist., Los Angeles Free Public Theatre. Pres. Am. Luth. Ch. Women, Palos Verdes, 1981; mem. Chadwick Mothers Assn., Joy Bible Study. Named Outstanding Woman South Bay Area, 1981, Outstanding Prof., Sr. Citizen Club Calif. State U. Long Beach, 1981. Mem. Internat. Communication Assn., Speech Communication Assn. Am., Western States Speech Communication Assn., Am. Oratorical Assn. Author: Children's Literature through Storytelling and Drama, 1977; contbr. article to profl. jour.; speaker profl. convs. Office: 1250 Bellflower Blvd Long Beach CA 90840

BRIGGS, TRUDY HANKINSON, ednl. adminstr.; b. Poughkeepsie, N.Y., July 3, 1935; d. Arthur C. and Caroline G. (Mesler) Hankinson; B.S., Skidmore Coll., 1957; M.A. in Edn., SUNY, New Paltz, 1960, C.A.S. in Ednl. Adminstrn., 1974; m. Kenneth R. Briggs, June 2, 1957; children—Jeffrey, Kenneth R. III. Tchr., Poughkeepsie City Schs., 1958-72; asst. prin. Sheafe Rd. Elem. Sch., Wappingers Central Sch. Dist., Wappingers Falls, N.Y., 1973—. Chmn. State wide Adv. Com. on Equal Opportunity for Women in Edn.; bd. dirs. Dutchess County Hist. Soc., Community Children's Theatre, Community Exptl. Repertory Theatre;s Bardavon 1869 Opera House, Jr. League. Mem. Sch. Adminstrs. Assn., Wappingers Falls Adminstrs. Assn., N.Y. State Sch. Adminstrs. Assn. (treas. region IV), Dutchess County Adminstrs. Assn., AAUW (past pres.), Phi Delta Kappa. Home: 90 Beechwood Ave Poughkeepsie NY 12603 Office: Sheafe Road Elementary School Sheafe Rd Wappingers Falls NY 12590

BRIGHT, BARBARA WILSON, multimedia designer, producer; b. St. Louis, Nov. 18, 1935; d. Charles C. and Elizabeth (Brown) Wilson; A.B. in History, Antioch Coll., 1958; postgrad. Sch. Fine Arts, Columbia U., 1959-60, Sch. Edn., Bklyn. Coll., 1960; m. George W. Bright, Aug. 30, 1961 (div. 1977). Prodn. asst., copy supr. Basic Systems, Inc., N.Y.C., 1964-70; graphics mgr. Xerox Learning Systems, Xerox Corp., Greenwich, Conn., 1970-74, mgr. prodn. and mfg., 1974-77; pres. Highland Stewart, Inc., Ridgefield, Conn., 1977—; condr. numerous design and prodn. seminars. Coordinator 1982 campaign Senator Lowell Weicker. Recipient Graphic Design award, Design Mag., 1968, Design award, Printing Industries of Met. N.Y., 1967. Mem. Graphic Arts Tech. Found., Conn. Women's Polit. Caucus (chmn.). Republican. Episcopalian. Creator new method of mech. simulation; contbr. articles on human engrng. in ednl. packaging to publs. Home and Office: 30 Silver Spring Ln Ridgefield CT 06877

BRIGHT, JERLENE ANN, info. systems programs dir.; b. Norman, Okla., July 4, 1942; d. Hoyt David and Pearl Jerlene Little; Asso. in Bus., Okla. Sch. Banking and Bus., 1964; student U. Okla., 1974-76; m. James Bright, July 25, 1959; children—Bridget, Michelle, Erika. Project coordinator U. Okla. Computing Center, 1965-68, U. Okla. Research Inst./Oil Info. Center, 1968-74; dir. info. systems programs U. Okla., Norman, 1974—. Mem. Soc. Petroleum Engrs.; major presentations annually before large profl. energy oriented orgns. Home: 1511 Greenbriar Dr Norman OK 73069 Office: PO Box 3030 Norman OK 73070

BRIGHT, MARY KATHERINE, univ. ofcl.; b. Waukegan, Ill., Oct. 30, 1925; d. William Lincoln and Edna Belle (Wardlow) Manny; B.A. in English with honors, Calif. State U., Northridge, 1965; M.A. in English, U. So. Calif., 1968, postgrad. in lingustics and higher edn.; m. William Herbert Bright, Dec. 22, 1978; children—Marianne, Kurtina, Kristina. Instr., sr. lectr. English, English as second lang. Calif. State U., Northridge, and U. So. Calif., 1965-68, asst. dean summer session, exec. dir. summer session evening coll., 1969-74; dir. continuing edn. Calif. State U., Long Beach, 1974-78; assoc. dir. urban extension and non-credit programs Ohio State U., 1978-80; dir. office mgmt. devel. U. Ill. Coll. Bus. Adminstrn., Chgo., 1980—; conf. presenter; pres. Council Non-Traditional Studies, 1972-78; cons. W.Va. Bd. Regents, 1978. Mem. Nat. Univ. Continuing Edn. Assn., Sigma Alpha Alpha. Presbyterian. Office: 2426 UH Box 4348 University of Illinois Chicago IL 60680

BRIGHT, VIVIAN YVETTE, labor cons.; b. Bklyn., Dec. 4, 1938; d. Booker T. and Remisha (Gill) Sanders; A.A.S. in Acctg., Bklyn. Coll., 1960; computer program cert. L.I.U., 1967; postgrad. St. Francis Coll., 1977; B.S., New Sch. for Social Research, 1980, M.S., 1982; m. Lonnie M. Bright, Aug. 29, 1959; children—James M., Garry Harris, Marvin Sanders. Bookkeeper, Tela-Time Watch Co., N.Y.C., 1956-62, A & T Importers, Inc., Bklyn., 1962-72, comptroller, 1973, corp. sec./comptroller, 1973-82; local devel. corp. labor cons., Bklyn., 1982—. Bd. dirs. Harlem Children's Theatre Co., 1973—; pres. leadership council Open Communities of Bklyn. Inc., 1976—; trustee Addiction Research Treatment Corp., 1981—; treas. J.F.K. Dem. Club, 1980—, Ed Towns for Congress, 1982; bd. dirs. E. N.Y. Local Devel. Corp., 1980—, E. N.Y. Econ. Devel. Com., 1981—; Kings County committeewoman Dem. Party, 1978; leader Girl Scouts U.S.A., 1958—. Recipient N.Y. State Internat. Yr. of Child award, 1979; E. N.Y. Skill Center award, 1981; J.F.K. Woman of Yr. award, 1979; Zeta Phi Beta Zeta of Yr., 1966; Woman of Yr. award, 1982; Service award, City Council N.Y., 1979, State of N.Y., 1979, others. Mem. Bklyn. C. of C., German Am. C. of C., Am. Soc. Profl. and Exec. Women, Fgn. Trade Assn., Am. Mgmt. Assn., Zeta Phi Beta, NAACP (dir. 1982—). Democrat. Baptist. Clubs: Bus. and Profl. Women's, Nat. Council Negro Women, Coalition of 100 Black Women, Black Women Agenda, E. N.Y. Civic Assn., Order of Golden Circle. Address: 591 Pennsylvania Ave Brooklyn NY 11207

BRIGMAN, CONSTANCE MORGAN, broadcasting exec.; b. Winston-Salem, N.C., July 9, 1952; d. Otis Caston and Carol (Penrose) B.; A.A., Stephens Coll., 1972; B.A., U. Mo., Kansas City, 1974. Disc jockey sta. KCUR-FM, Kansas City, Mo., 1974; with Quastler Advt., Fairway, Kans., 1975; account exec. sta. KAYQ-AM, Kansas City, Mo., 1976-77, KBEQ-FM, Kansas City, Mo., 1977-78, KMBC-TV, Kansas City, Mo., 1978-80; nat. sales rep. Metro TV Sales (Metromedia), Chgo., 1980—. Mem. Am. Women in Radio and TV (chpt. affirmative action chmn. 1979), Advt. Club Kansas City, Alpha Epsilon Rho. Republican. Presbyterian. Home: 1419 N State Pkwy Apt 404 Chicago IL 60610 Office: Wrigley Bldg 410 N Michigan Ave Chicago IL 60611

BRILES, JUDITH, fin. planning co. exec.; b. Pasadena, Calif., Feb. 20, 1946; d. James and Mary (McKnight) Tuthill; student Coll. Fin. Planning, Denver, 1977-78; M.B.A., Pepperdine U., 1980; m. John Maling, Dec. 18, 1973; children—Shelley, Frank, Sheryl. Account exec. E.F. Hutton, Palo Alto, Calif., 1972-78; pres. Judith Briles & Co., Palo Alto, 1978—; pres. Briles & Assos., Palo Alto, 1980—; instr. DeAnza Coll., Canada Coll., Bd. dirs. Scholar Opera, Palo Alto, Foothill-DeAnza Colls. Found., Los Altos Hills, Calif. Mem. Commonwealth Club, Internat. Assn. Fin. Planners, Inst. Cert. Fin. Planners, Nat. Assn. Female Execs., Beta Sigma Phi. Republican. Author: The Woman's Guide to Financial Savvy, 1981. Office: 2345 Yale St Palo Alto CA 94306

BRILEY, MARGARET ELIZABETH WILLIS, nutritionist; b. Abilene, Tex., Aug. 5, 1929; d. Charles Grant, Sr., and Ivie May (Rape) Willis; B.S., U. Tex., Austin, 1950; M.S., Tex. Tech. U., 1968, Ph.D. (fellow), 1973; m. Clyde Briley, Jr., Aug. 19, 1950; children—Kathryn Ann Briley Riddles, Kimberly Susanne. Tchr. public schs., Lockney, Tex. and Tahoka, Tex., 1950-68; research asst. Coll. Animal Sci., Tex. Tech. U., 1968-73; asst. prof. Tex. Christian U., Ft. Worth, 1973-74; asso. prof. nutrition U. Tex., Austin, 1974—; cons. hosps., convalescent homes, Edn. Service Center. Research grantee. Mem. Tex. Nutrition Council (pres.), Am. Inst. Nutrition, Am. Dietetic Assn., Tex. Dietetic Assn., Austin Dietetic Assn., Soc. Nutrition Edn., Inst. Food Technologists. Methodist. Contbr. articles to profl. jours. Office: GEA 115 University of Texas Austin TX 78712

BRILEY, WANDA MARIE, basketball coach; b. Charleston, S.C., June 7, 1952; d. Alvin Joseph and Sarah Lou (Byrd) B.; B.S., U. S.C., 1974; M.A., Appalachian State U., 1977. Asst. volleyball and basketball coach, teaching asst. Appalachian State U., Boone, N.C., 1975-77; mem. faculty, head basketball and volleyball coach High Point (N.C.) Coll., 1977-79; head basketball coach Wake Forest U., Winston Salem, N.C., 1979—; dir. Lady Deacon Basketball Sch., 1981—, Wanda Briley Basketball Camp, 1979—. Mem. exec. com. Wade Trophy Com., 1977—; mem. N.C. Ethics and Eligibility Com., 1980-82. Named Carolinas Conf. Coach of Yr. in volleyball and basketball, 1978-79, Nat. Coach of Yr. Assn. Intercollegiate Athletics for Women, 1979; recipient Key to City, High Point City Council, 1978, Letter of Resolution for outstanding service High Point Council and Mayor, 1979; named to Basketball Hall of Fame, 1979. Mem. Nat. Coaches Assn. Democrat. Roman Catholic. Home: 1630 Village Pl Winston-Salem NC 27107 Office: Box 7265 Reynolda Sta Wake Forest U Winston-Salem NC 27109

BRILL, MARIAN M., retailing exec.; b. Kansas City, Mo., Oct. 18, 1930; d. Reuben and Carrie (Lebrecht) Melcher; student U. Mo., 1947-48, UCLA, 1948-49; m. Robert S. Brill, Nov. 6, 1949; children—Barbara Brill Gustin, Peggy A., Ruth Brill Desmond. With Brill's, Inc., Milw., 1965—, buyer jewelry and giftware, 1965-69, asst. buyer sportswear, furhishings, young men's dept., 1969-75, buyer young men's sportswear and outerwear, supr. Below the Belt Store, 1975—, dir.,

1969—, v.p., 1972—. Vice pres. Congregation Sinai Sisterhood, 1962-66; bd. dirs., program coordinator Friends of Milw. Public Mus., 1977—; past v.p., past dir. Muses, women's orgn. of Milw. Public Mus. Mem. Menswear Retailers Am. (regional v.p.). Office: Brills Inc 5900 N Port Washington Rd Milwaukee WI 53217

BRILL, NORA KENDALL, journalist; b. Worcestershire, Eng., Jan. 28, 1931; d. Kenneth William and Sibyl Winnifred (Brown) Kendall; B.A., Queens U., Kingston, Ont., 1971; m. Lawrence Brill Mar. 8, 1957 (dec.); children—Dianne, Jonathan, Troy, Michael. Tchr., Arthur Murray Studios, Toronto and Havana, 1950-52; reservation agt. United Airlines, Chgo., 1953-54; society columnist Tampa Times, 1975—. Del., Fla. Democratic Conv., 1981; mem. Arts Watch Task Force, 1981; pres. Las Damas De Arte, 1972; bd. dirs. Tampa Symphony Guild, Guilders of Tampa Bay Art Center, Easter Seal Guild. Named Outstanding Vol., Tampa Bay Art Center, 1975; recipient Diana award NOW, 1979. Mem. Athena Soc. (dir.), PEN, Tampa Bay Press Club, Women in Communications. Democrat. Home: 10604 Ilex St Tampa FL 33618 Office: PO Box 191 Tampa FL 33601

BRILLHART, MAXINE T., physician; b. Coffeyville, Kans., Nov. 11, 1915; d. Forest C. and Rena H. (Huffman) Thornton; M.D., U. Kans., 1950; m. Roy William Brillhart, Nov. 15, 1935; children—Robert Allen, Roy William. Intern Providence Hosp., Kansas City, Kans., 1950-51, now staff; pvt. practice medicine, Kansas City, 1951—; staff Bethany, St. Margaret, Providence hosps.; dir., sec. Allied Investors, Inc. Bd. dirs., v.p., sec. Med. Offices Lab.; past bd. dirs. Kansas City Med. and Dental Assts. Sch.; mem. Kans. Commn. on Status of Women, 1966. Recipient Matrix award Theta Sigma Phi, 1969. Fellow Am. Acad. Family Physicians; mem. AMA, Kans., Wyandotte County med. socs., Kans., Wyandotte County (sec.-treas. 1957-58) acads. family physicians, World, Am. Women's med. socs., S.W. Clin. Soc., English-Speaking Union, Internat. Personnel Research Soc., Am. Biog. Inst., Fellows Nelson Gallery, Friends of Art, Philharmonic Women's Com., Lyric Opera Guild, Univ. Assos. U. Mo. at Kansas City. Methodist. Clubs: Women's City, Soroptimist (pres. Kansas City 1965-66, Woman of Year 1962). Home: 4540 County Line Rd Kansas City KS 66106 Office: 1610 Washington Blvd Kansas City KS 66102

BRIM, ERMA L., nurse; b. Birmingham, Ala.; d. Norman and Gladys Hill; student Galileo Vocat. Nursing Sch., 1954; cert. in English, U. Calif. Extension, 1960, in Social Service, 1961; A.A. in Nursing, Community Coll. San Francisco, 1974; children—Emelda J. Atkins, Jon Brim Yasin. Lic. vocat. nurse Mt. Zion Hosp., San Francisco, 1954, San Francisco Gen. Hosp., 1954-70, R.N., 1970-77; nurse venereal disease clinic Dept. Public Health, San Francisco, 1977—; mem. Council on Continuing Edn. for Health Occupations, State of Calif., 1974. Rec. sec. Nat. Council Negro Women, San Francisco, 1963; mem. Rep. county and state central com., 1960-69; active parent aux. Recreation Center for Handicapped, nursing and health services ARC, Council of Rep. Women, PTA, NAACP; trustee Aid to Retarded Citizens; mem. spl. edn. commn. San Francisco Unified Sch. Dist.; mem. State of Calif. Maternal Child and Adolescent Health Bd., 1982; rec. sec. Woman's Soc. Christian Service Meth. Ch., 1965, Commn. on Christian Social Concerns, 1961-68, chmn., 1978; mem. State of Calif. Maternal, Child and Adolescent Health Bd., State of Calif. Council Developmental Disabilities. active Black Meth. Ch. Renewal, 1972. Recipient Disting. Citizens Service Citation, State of Calif., 1974. Mem. West Bay Health Systems Agy., Lic. Vocat. Nurses League, Civil Service Assn., Health Care Coordinating Council, Devel. Disabilities Council of San Francisco, Coalition of Black Trade Unionists, Service Employees Internat. Union (locals 250 and 400), Black Am. Polit. Assn. Calif., State Council Developmental Disabilities, Black Women Organized for Action, Black Women Organized for Polit. Action, Nat. Fedn. Rep. Women (San Francisco council), LWV. Address: 635 Spruce St San Francisco CA 94118

BRIMACOMBE, DOROTHY DARTMOUTH REDENBAUGH (MRS. ALFRED JOHN BRIMACOMBE), printing, stationery co. exec.; b. Quincy, Ill., Oct. 30, 1901; d. William Alfred and Mary Louise (Farr) Redenbaugh; tchrs. diploma Ellensburg (Wash.) Normal Sch., 1922; B.S. in Edn., Oreg. State U., 1926; m. Alfred John Brimacombe, Aug. 2, 1935. Tchr. pub. schs., Wapato, Wash., 1922-23, Seattle, 1923-25, 26-28; instr. journalism Ellensburg Normal Sch., 1928-31; receptionist Six Cos., Inc., Boulder City, Nev., 1931; co-owner, asso. editor Las Vegas Age, Nev., 1933-44; co-owner Brimmies Comml. Printing & Stationery, Las Vegas, 1944—. Sec., Nev. Safety Council, 1968—. Bd. dirs., exec. com. Nev. Safety Council, 1967—; Nev. mem. Nat. Assn. Women Hwy. Safety Leaders, 1969-71; bd. dirs. So. Nev. Drug Abuse Council, 1972—; founder Nike House, home for girls, 1972, pres. bd. dirs., 1972—. Pres., Nev. Fedn. Republican Women, 1952-53. Mem. AAUW (pres. Las Vegas sect. 1940-42, Nev. div. 1946-47), Las Vegas Bus. and Profl. Womens (pres. 1940-42), Nev. (pres. 1943-44), Nat. (treas. 1956-60) fedns. bus. and profl. women, Nat. Fedn. Press Women (regional v.p. 1946), Alpha Gamma Delta. Clubs: Mesquite (pres. Las Vegas 1940), Las Vegas Altrusa. Home: 2812 Mason Ave Las Vegas NV 89102 Office: PO Box 150 Las Vegas NV 89101

BRIMMER, PAULINE FRANCES, nurse, assn. exec.; b. Bradford, Pa., May 26; d. Anthony and Mary Onuffer; R.N., St. Vincent Hosp., Erie, Pa., 1949; B.S. in Nursing, U. Ariz., 1969, M.A. in Sociology, 1971, Ph.D., 1977. Staff nurse emergency room St. Vincent Hosp., Erie, 1949-52; staff nurse surg. unit Meml. Hosp. for Cancer and Allied Diseases, N.Y.C., 1952-53; office nurse, Erie, 1953-65; staff nurse med. unit VA Hosp., Tucson, 1966-68; dir. specific projects and cons. Pima Health Systems, Tucson, 1974-76; instr. Nursing Care and Consultation Ltd., Tucson, 1975-76; dir. dept. research and policy analysis Am. Nurses Assn., Kansas City, Mo., 1977—, also project officer Am. Nurses Found. and adj. prof. U. Mo., Kansas City. NIH fellow, 1969. Mem. Am. Nurses Assn., Council Nurse Researchers, Am. Sociol. Assn., Soc. Research Adminstrs. (editorial adv. bd.), Mo. Soc. for Sociology and Anthropology, Nat. Action Forum for Older Women, Gerontol. Soc. Nursing. Contbr. articles in field. Home: 4405 Rockhill Rd Kansas City MO 64110 Office: Am Nurses Assn 2420 Pershing Rd Kansas City MO 64108

BRINDAMOUR, MARY ELLEN, librarian; b. Lynn, Mass., Mar. 31, 1920; d. Roscoe Joseph and Gertrude Helen (Sheehan) Cowan; diploma Becker Bus. Coll., Worcester, Mass., 1939; librarian's cert. Northeastern U., Boston, 1968; cert. indsl. security mgmt. Def. Indsl. Security Inst., Richmond, Va., 1978; m. Andrew Lavigne Brindamour, Oct. 11, 1941; children—Lois Ann Brindamour Belliveau, Paul Edward, Claire Marie Brindamour Bravo. From payroll clk. to librarian Gen. Electric Co., Lynn, 1940-72; librarian, security supr. Dynamics Research Corp., Wilmington, Mass., 1974-78, mgr. corp. security, also corp. librarian, 1978-82. Mem. Spl. Librarians Assn., Route 128 Librarians, Am. Soc. Indsl. Security, Nat. Classification Mgmt. Soc., Nat. Assn. Female Execs., Am. Def. Preparedness Assn., U.S. Naval Inst. Roman Catholic. Home: 41 Thorpe Rd Lynn MA 01905

BRINDEL, JILL RACHUY, cellist; b. Chgo., Jan. 17, 1950; d. Bernard A. and June (Rachuy) B.; student Ind. U., 1968-70; B.M. (Tanglewood scholar), Roosevelt U., 1974; m. William Louis Klingelhoffer, July 30, 1972; children—Sarah Brindel, Louis Brindel. Asst. prin. cellist Chgo. Lyric Opera, 1974-76; mem. Chgo. Grant Park Orch., 1974-78; prin. cellist Chgo. Contemporary Chamber Players, 1974-77, Chgo. performances Joffrey Ballet, Am. Ballet Theater, N.Y.C. Ballet and Internat. Ballet Festival, 1975-79; mem. Houston Symphony, 1979-80; prin. cellist Joffrey Ballet, San Francisco, 1981; cellist San Francisco Symphony, 1981—; appeared on 5 nationally broadcast chamber concerts Chamber Music Sundaes, 1982; recitalist Chgo. Musical Coll., ann. 1972-75, 78, North Shore Music Center, 1971, Houston, 1978, 79, Old First Series, San Francisco, 1982. Recipient prizes Union Civic League, 1978, William C. Byrd competition, 1976, Chgo. Musical Coll. Concerto competition, 1972, 73, Dumas String award, 1972, Evansville competition, 1972, Crescendo Music Club, 1972, Farwell award, 1972. Mem. Am. Fedn. Musicians. Office: Davies Symphony Hall Van Ness and Hayes Sts San Francisco CA 94102

BRINEY, NANCY WELLS, publisher; b. Louisville; d. Edmond Daniel and Elsie Mae (Bald) Wells; student U. Louisville, 1932-33, William Rainey Harper Community Coll., 1965; B.A. with honors, N.Y.U., 1979; m. Paul Wallace Briney, Mar. 31, 1936; 1 son, Timothy Paul. With Jenny Lind Shop, Louisville, 1933-36; co-founder The Fireside Theatre Book Club, N.Y.C., 1948, editor Curtain Time, 1949-50; founder Barrington (Ill.) Town Hall Series, 1962—, Brownstone Press, Barrington, 1968—; lectr. William Rainey Harper Coll., Palatine, Ill., 1974—. Mem. Pub. Relations Soc. Am., Am. Mgmt. Assn., Costume Soc. Am. Episcopalian. Clubs: Chgo. Publicity, Suburban Press, Yale of N.Y., Jr. League of N.Y., Garden of Am., Louisville Country. Home: PO Box 375 Barrington IL 60010 Office: Brownstone Press PO Box 375 Barrington IL 60010

BRINK, JUDITH MARY, nurse; b. Milw., Jan. 14, 1934; d. Richard Cornelius and Marian Katherine (DeYoung) Oudersluys; student Hope Coll., Holland, Mich., 1952-53; R.N., Butterworth Sch. Nursing, Grand Rapids, Mich., 1956; divorced; children—Kathleen, Kirk. Instr., Butterworth Hosp. Sch. Nursing, 1956-59; dir. inservice edn. Lockwood McDonald Hosp., Petoskey, Mich., 1969-79; asst. dir. nursing No. Mich. Hosps., Inc., Petoskey, 1979-80, asso. dir. nursing, 1980—; bd. dirs. Emmet County chpt. Am. Heart Assn., 1978—; mem. interim bd. Petoskey Area Hospice, 1981—; cons., adv. in field. Mem. Women's Resource Center. Presbyterian. Home: 318 1/2 Petoskey St Petoskey MI 49770 Office: 416 Connable St Petoskey MI 49770

BRINKER, MARLENE ANN, health care exec.; b. Greene, Iowa, Apr. 12, 1934; d. Bernard Charles and Marian Bertha (Crimmings) Dailey; R.N., St. Mary's Hosp., Rochester, Minn., 1955; B.A. in Geology, Rutgers U., 1975; m. Ray Brinker, Jan. 12, 1957; children—Sally Jean, Marc Henry, Sheri Louise, Sara Jane, Lisa Ann, Wendy Renee. Staff med.-surg. nurse VA Hosp., Iowa City, Iowa, 1955-57; nurse radiology dept. Mason Clinic, Seattle, 1957-58; staff nurse USPHS Hosp., Staten Island, N.Y., 1958-63; instr. nursing Holy Name Hosp., Teaneck, N.J., 1963-64, St. Luke's Hosp., St. Louis, 1967-69; supr. Kelly Services, Ann Arbor, Mich., 1979-80; service dir. Kelly Health Care, Ann Arbor, 1980-81, dist. mgr. for Mich. and Ind., 1981—; mem. program and sub area coms. Comprehensive Health Planning. Mem. Pres.'s community relations bd. Rutgers U., 1975. Mem. N.Y. Acad. Scis. Democrat. Roman Catholic. Home: 2775 Tessmer Rd Ann Arbor MI 48103 Office: Office Suite 1001 Wolverine Tower 3001 S State Rd Ann Arbor MI 48104

BRINKLEY, ELISE HOFFMAN, nurse, educator; b. Barry, Tex., Mar. 10, 1922; d. James Edward and Laura Jack (Foster) Gay; R.N., Hermann Hosp., Houston, 1966; B.A. in Psychology, U. Houston, 1971; M.Ed., Prairie View U., Tex., 1973; postgrad. U. Tex., Austin, 1975-76; Ed.D. in Coll. Adminstrn., Nova U., Ft. Lauderdale, Fla., 1976; B.S. in Nursing, Tex. Womans U., Houston, 1982; postgrad. U. Tex., Galveston, 1978—; m. Billy Clarence Hoffman, June 20, 1941 (div. July 1980); children—Rosilyn Gay, Billy May; m. 2d, Roger M. Brinkley, Nov. 26, 1981. Staff nurse labor, delivery and emergency room, supr. operating room Polly Ryon Meml. Hosp., Richmond, Tex., 1960-63, dir. Sch. Vocat. Nursing, 1966-71; campus nurse supr. Tex. Dept. Mental Health and Mental Retardation, Richmond State Sch., 1971-72; dir. asso. degree nursing program Alvin (Tex.) Community Coll., 1972-79, chmn. Bicentennial Show Case, 1976, also mem. pres.'s merit award com. for faculty, fin. and scholarship com., fin. affairs com.; instr. San Jacinto Coll., Pasadena, Tex., 1982—; mem. Red Cross Nursing and Health Programs Adv. Com., 1974—; mem. Council Deans and Dirs. Nursing Schs. in Tex., 1975—; instr. cardio-pulmonary resuscitation Am. Heart Assn., 1976—; mem., conv. speaker Statewide Com. on Competencies, 1977—. Pres., Rosenberg PTA, 1953-55, Ft. Bend County PTA, 1956-57, Band Boosters, 1957-59; Rosenberg city chmn. Mothers March on Polio, 1954-58; mem. Gov.'s Com. on Drug Use and Drug Abuse, 1971-72; leader 4-H Club, 1952-54, Girl Scouts U.S.A., 1953-56; sponsor Alvin Nursing Students Assn., 1974-76; parliamentarian Democratic Party Ft. Bend County, 1970-71; bd. dirs. Salvation Army, 1958-60. Life mem. Nat. PTA, Tex. PTA; mem. AAUP, Tex. Jr. Coll., Alvin Community Coll. tchrs. assns., Am., Tex. nurses assns., Nat., Houston Area leagues for nursing, R.N.s of Ft. Bend County. Methodist. Club: Rosenberg Rebekah Lodge (past dist. dep. pres.). Author: Neurological Conditions of the Newborn, 1975; works listed in ERIC Clearinghouse for Jr. Colls., 1975, 76, 78. Home: 5114 Hwy 3 Dickinson TX 77539 Office: San Jacinto Coll Pasadena TX

BRINKLEY, PHYLLIS, speaker and program artist, stained glass artisan; b. Madison, Wis., May 28, 1926; d. Reynale R. and Florence (Jarvis) Crosby; B.A. in Speech and English, U. Wis., 1948, postgrad. in speech and oral interpretation of lit., 1949; m. William Malry, Jr., Aug. 5, 1949. Speaker, program artist, 1958—, current programs include First Ladies of our Land, Portrait of the Lincolns, Mary and Abraham, Stained Glass: Gift of Light; radio artist Focus on Books, Sta. WHA, 1967-72; tchr. speech, 1951-56; interpretative reader, 1950-58. Vol. hosp. aux.; public affairs chmn. Madison Civics Club; pres. Madison Women's Mcpl. Golf League, 1959; chmn. Little Sisters of Sisters of St. Benedict, 1968-69. Recipient award of excellence Wis. Fedn. Women's Clubs; named hon. cannoneer St. Louis Civil War Roundtable. Mem. Internat. Platform Assn., Nat. League Am. Pen Women, Phi Beta. Author: Abraham Lincoln and His Wife, Mary: Two Human Beings, 1975. Home: 6115 Imperial Dr Route 2 Waunakee WI 53597

BRINKLEY, RUTH ELIZABETH, ret. librarian; b. Lincoln, Nebr., Dec. 8, 1890; d. L. Robert and Ellen Carolyn (Nichols) Wilhelm; A.B., U. Kans., 1911; m. Joseph Arthur Brinkley, Oct. 31, 1912 (dec. 1968); children—Joseph Wilhelm, Robert Alexander, Ellen Rebecca Swenson, Ruth Kathleen Richards. Tchr. sci. Lawrence (Kans.) High Sch.; librarian Anacortes (Wash.) Pub. Library, now ret.; writer children's books. Named Anacortes Woman of Yr. Mem. AAUW. Methodist. Mem. Order Eastern Star. Clubs: Federated Women's, Soroptimist. Author articles and lectr.; initiated hobby exhbns., adult edn. and craft classes in library. Home: 5918 Sunset Dr Anacortes WA 98221

BRINSKO, ANN MARY, credit union ofcl.; b. Mahanoy City, Pa., Jan. 11, 1932; d. Joseph Edward and Sarah Janetta (Bernstel) Wahalec; ed. Internat. Corr. Schs., McCann Sch. Bus., spl. courses Pa. State U., U. Wis.; m. Robert Brinsko, Feb. 9, 1952; 1 dau., Cheryl Ann. Payroll clk. City Shirt Co., 1951-63; asst. postmaster U.S. Post Office, 1963-65; mem. trust dept. Pa. Nat. Bank & Trust Co., 1965-73; mgr. adminstrn. CTCE Fed. Credit Union, Reading, Pa., 1973—; fin. counselor. Vol., United Way, Mayor's office; sec. Com. for Policies for Effective Govt., 1981-82. Notary public. Mem. Credit Union Execs. Soc., CUNA Sch. Alumni Assn., Nat. Assn. Female Execs., Pa. Assn. Notaries, Reading C. of C. Republican. Mem. Reformed Ch. Club: Eastern Star (past matron, pres. Mahanoy City Past Matrons). Home: 17 Crestview Dr Forest Hills Pottsville PA 17901 Office: 125 Exeter St Reading PA 19601

BRINSON, MONICA MEAGHER, educator; b. Bklyn., July 18, 1932; d. Peter William and Julia (Sullivan) Meagher; B.S., State Coll. N.Y., Plattsburg, 1954; M.S., Purdue U., 1959; postgrad. U. Vt., U. Colo., U. Wis., SUNY, Buffalo; m. Paul J. Brinson, Aug. 6, 1966; 1 son, Colin Meagher Brinson. Instr., Vt. Coll., 1955-57; teaching asst. Purdue U., West Lafayette, Ind., 1957-59; prof. consumer and family studies, SUNY, Buffalo, 1959—, dir. consumer action, 1975-80; consumer rep. local Autocap, 1979-81. Mem. nat. adv. com. for flammable fabrics act, Consumer Product Safety Commn. 1976-78; cons. to sch. bds., bus.; arbitrator Buffalo Better Bus. Bur., 1974-82. Montgomery Ward/Quaker Oats grantee, 1976-78; CETA awardee, 1975-79. Mem. Am. Home Econs. Assn., ASTM, Am. Assn. Textile Tech., Assn. of Coll. Profs. Textiles and Clothing, Soc. Consumer Affairs Profls., Niagara Frontier Consumers Assn. (founder), Am. Council on Consumer Interests, Sigma Delta Upsilon, LWV. Contbr. articles to profl. jours. Home: 43 Dorset Dr Buffalo NY 14223 Office: CH 308 1300 Elmwood Ave Buffalo NY 14222

BRISCOE, ANNE M., scientist, educator; b. N.Y.C., Dec. 1, 1918; M.A., Vassar Coll., 1945; Ph.D. (Sterling jr. fellow, USPHS fellow), Yale U., 1949; m. William A. Briscoe, Aug. 20, 1955. From research asso. to asst. prof. Cornell U. Med. Coll., 1950-56; faculty Columbia Coll. Physicians and Surgeons, N.Y.C., 1956—, now asst. prof. medicine; lectr. Harlem Hosp. Center Sch. Nursing, 1968-77; adj. asst. prof. Hunter Coll., 1951-64, 73-75. Mem. N.Y.C. Commn. on Status of Women, 1979—; non-govtl. orgn. del. to UN; mem. adv. bd. WOMANSPACE; mem. adv. council Inst. Nuclear Power Ops., 1979—. Fellow Am. Inst. Chemists (sec. N.Y. chpt. 1981—), N.Y. Acad. Scis. (chairperson women in sci. com. 1978—bd. govs. 1981); mem. AAAS (mem. council), Am. Chem. Soc., Am. Soc. Clin. Nutrition, Am. Fedn. Clin. Research, Harvey Soc., Fedn. Orgns. for Profl. Women (treas. 1978-80), Assn. Women in Sci. Ednl. Founds. (pres. 1978-82), Assn. Women in Sci. (editor newsletter 1971-74, nat. pres. 1974-76), Assn. Yale Alumni (assembly rep. 1978—), Yale Grad. Sch. Alumni Assn. (pres. 1981—). Contbr. articles to profl. jours. Home: 2 Peter Cooper Rd New York NY 10010 Office: Dept Medicine Harlem Hosp Center New York NY 10037

BRISCOE, DIANE-FROST ASBURY, aviation co. exec.; b. Upper Montclair, N.J., Jan. 8, 1945; d. Philip and Mary Louise (Asbury) B.; B.S. cum laude, U. Ga., 1971. Adminstrv. asst. to pres. Airclaims, Inc., Washington, 1966-68, 71-72; admistrv. asst. to claims mgr. Rowedder Aviation Adjustment Service, Inc., Atlanta, 1972-75, claims rep., office mgr., 1975-79, asst. v.p., 1979-81, v.p., 1981—. Pres. Dana Marie Condominium Assn., 1979-81, comptroller, 1981; active Jr. League of Atlanta, 1972—. Recipient edn. award Nat. Assn. Ins. Women, 1978; asso. in mgmt. Ins. Inst. Am.; cert. profl. ins. woman, asso. in mgmt. Nat. Assn. Ins. Women, 1980; lic. pvt. pilot. Mem. Atlanta Claims Assn., Atlanta Assn. Ins. Women (corr. sec. 1978-79), Nat. Soc. Colonial Dames Am., Phi Kappa Phi. Republican. Episcopalian. Home: 408 Sycamore Dr Decatur GA 30030 Office: 1705 Commerce Dr NW Atlanta GA 30318

BRISCOE, GRETCHEN MARIE, nurse; b. Lake Placid, N.Y., Dec. 30, 1947; d. Robert Orville and Shirley Jean (MacDonald) Boevin; R.N., Meml. Sch. Nursing, Albany, N.Y., 1969; m. Michael A. Briscoe, Nov. 19, 1976; 1 son, Christopher Thomas. Floating head nurse Ireland Army Hosp., Ft. Knox, Ky., 1969; operating staff nurse, inservice of new personnel Meml. Hosp., Albany, N.Y., 1969-73; operating room and recovery room staff nurse Saratoga Hosp., Saratoga Springs, N.Y., 1973-75, asst. utilization rev. coordinator PSRO, 1975-79, supr. patient's services, 1979-80; asst. dir. nursing Fairview Healthcare Center, Bowling Green, Ky., 1980—; CPR instr.; mem. adminstrv. com. Bowling Green Hospice. Vol. instr. and nurse ARC. Mem. Am. Heart Assn., Ky. Nurses Assn. Dirs. Nursing and Asst. Dir. Nursing. Roman Catholic. Address: Dewey Lake Rd Route 9 Box 396 Bowling Green KY 42101

BRISCOE, MARY LOUISE, educator; b. Hutchinson, Kans., May 24, 1937; d. Arthur D. and Charlotte B. B.; B.A., Kans. State U., 1959; M.A., Bowling Green State U., 1961; Ph.D., U. Wis., 1968; 1 dau., Brenna. Asst. prof. U. Wis., Whitewater, 1967-72; coordinator women's studies program U. Pitts., 1972-77, assoc. prof., chmn. dept. English, 1977—. Mem. MLA. Author: Up Against the Wall, Mother, 1971; American Autobiography: A Bibliography, 1945-1980, 1982; assoc. editor: First Person Female American, 1980. Office: Dept of English University of Pittsburgh Pittsburgh PA 15213

BRISKIN, JACQUELINE ELIZABETH, author; b. London; came to U.S., 1938, naturalized, 1944; d. Spencer and Marjorie Orgell; m. Bert Briskin, May 9, 1948; children—Ralph, Elizabeth, Richard. Author: (novels) California Generation, 1970; Afterlove, 1974; Rich Friends, 1976; Paloverde, 1978; The Onyx, 1982. Mem. Authors Guild, PEN.

BRISSENDEN, PRISCILLA (SALLY) ARTHUR, psychotherapist; b. Wollaston, Mass., Mar. 3, 1925; d. William Glen and Elsie Catherine (Thompson) Arthur; B.A., Smith Coll., 1946, M.S.S., 1954; m. Arik Brissenden, Sept. 5, 1954; children—Mark, Kira, Noel. Personnel asst. Peter Bent Brigham Hosp., Boston, 1946-48; adminstrv. asst. Fletcher Sch. Law and Diplomacy, Tufts U., Medford, Mass., 1948-50; secretarial asst. Am. embassy, Paris, 1950-52; caseworker Family Services Cin., 1954-56; staff therapist Geraldine Pederson-Krag Clinic, Huntington, N.Y., 1968—; pvt. practice psychotherapy, 1970—; student supr., field adv. Adelphi U. Sch. Social Work. Fellow Clin. Social Work Psychotherapists; mem. Nat. Assn. Social Workers, Acad. Cert. Social Workers, Smith Coll. Alumni Assn. (past chpt. pres.). Home: RD Box 1328 Syosset NY 11791 Office: 7 High St Huntington NY 11743

BRISTOL, LINDA JANE, med. technologist; b. Houston, June 5, 1947; d. Carl Robert and Hattie (McKinney) Carlson; B.S., Lewis and Clark Coll., 1969; m. Thomas L. Bristol, Dec. 27, 1968; children—Robert, John, Elizabeth. Intern, Good Samaritan Hosp., Portland, Oreg., 1968-69; researcher U. Oreg. Med. Sch., 1969-70; staff microbiology Kaiser Hosp., Portland, Oreg., 1971; staff med. technologist ARC Lab., Portland, 1971-72. Mem. Am. Soc. Clin. Pathologists, Alpha Gamma. Republican. Mem. Ch. of Christ.

BRISTOL, MARIE MAHONEY, educator; b. Buffalo, Feb. 25, 1942; d. Joseph F. and Gertrude Ann (Shannon) Mahoney; B.A. Nazareth Coll. of Rochester (N.Y.), 1963; M.A., U. Utah, 1971; Ph.D. (fellow), U. N.C., 1979; m. Douglas W. Bristol, July 11, 1964; children—Douglas W., David W. Acad. adv. SUNY, Buffalo, 1963-64; asst. to dir. public relations Upstate Med. Center, Syracuse, N.Y., 1964-65; research asst. U. Utah, 1969-71; coordinator programs for emotionally disturbed children Fargo (N.D.) public schs., 1971-73; dir. services for infants and young children Southeast Mental Health and Retardation Center, Fargo, 1973-76; clin. asso. dept. psychiatry U. N.D. Sch. of Medicine, 1974-76; program dir. Joseph P. Kennedy Jr. Found., Washington, 1978-80, cons., 1980—, mem. nat. adv. bd. Let's Play to Grow, 1980—; research asst. prof. psychiatry U. N.C. Sch. Medicine, Chapel Hill, 1980—, also asso. dir. family studies Frank Porter Graham Child Devel. Center, U. N.C.; cons. Judevine Center for Autistic Children, 1977-78, Wahpeton Residential Indian Sch., 1975-76, grant rev. panels Bur. of Edn. for the Handicapped, 1978. Mem. policy council Southeast N.D. Community Action Agy., Fargo, 1974-76. N.Y. Regents scholar, 1959-63; Bush

Leadership summer fellow, 1976; spl. summer fellow Center Creative Leadership, Greensboro, N.C., 1976; research tng. program fellow U. N.C., 1977-78; lic. psychologist, Minn. Mem. Am. Psychol. Assn. (asso.), Council for Exceptional Children, Am. Assn. of Mental Deficiency. Author: (with E. Schopler) Autistic Children in Public School; also chpt. in book Finding and Educating the High Risk Infant; contbr. articles to psychol. jours. Office: 300 NCNB Plaza Chapel Hill NC 27514 *

BRISTOL, WANDA (JUNE) MASON, nurse, therapist; b. Ft. Cobb, Okla., Jan. 26, 1931; d. Alva Albert and Clara Belle (Bowman) Mason; A.A. diploma of nursing San Bernardino Valley Coll., 1951; B.S. (Polio Fund scholar), Calif. State U., Los Angeles, 1961, M.A., 1968; M.S. (USPHS grantee), Loma Linda U., 1964; M.S.Ed., U. So. Calif., 1976, postgrad., 1976—; m. Carl Eugene Bristol, Nov. 18, 1951 (div.); children—Bruce Edward, Brian Keith. Staff nurse San Bernardino County Hosp., 1951-52, head nurse, 1952-59; staff nurse San Bernardino Community Hosp., 1954; spl. staff nurse Riverside (Calif.) Health Nurse, 1959-60; instr. Mt. San Antonio Coll., 1961-62; sch. nurse Bloomington (Calif.) Sch. Dist. unified with Colton Joint Unified Sch. Dist., 1963—; pvt. practice marriage, family, and child counseling, Rialto, Calif., 1979—; also pvt. practice hypnotherapy; psychodrama practitioner; vol. counselor. Health chmn. Bloomington Community Services Council, including establishment dental clinic, 1964-67; mem. Colton Children's Services Council, 1967—; mem. mental health task force Los Angeles chpt. Calif. NOW. Mem. Am. Nurses Assn., Calif. Nurses Assn., Calif. Sch. Nurse Orgn., Assn. Colton Educators, Calif. Tchrs. Assn., Nat. Tchrs. Assn., Am. Assn. Marriage and Family Therapists, Calif. Assn. Marriage and Family Therapists, Am. Psychol. Assn., Calif. State Psychol. Assn., Inland Psychol. Assn., San Bernardino Mental Health Assn., Am. Soc. Group Psychotherapy and Psychodrama. Republican. Methodist. Contbr. articles to profl. jours. Home: 1485 N Mulberry Rialto CA 92376 Office: Ednl Services Center 10435 Cedar Ave Bloomington CA 92316

BRITT, RUTH EVANGELINE BURGIN, civic worker; b. Fayette, Mo., Mar. 15, 1907; d. Samuel Herschel and Lora (Miller) Burgin; student Wesleyan Woman's Coll., 1926-27; A.B., Tallahassee Woman's Coll., 1928; m. James T. Britt, Sept. 18, 1930; children—Thomas Burgin, Robert McCammon. Bd. dirs. Spofford Home for Children, 1937-38, Della Lamb Neighborhood House, 1937-38, YMCA, 1938-39; mem. Woman's City Club, Kansas City, Mo., 1931—, chmn. hosp. com., 1931-35; mem. Guild Friends Art at William Rockhill Nelson Gallery, 1961—; mem. fireside com. Kansas City Art Inst., 1948-49; mem. women's div. Kansas City Philharmonic Assn., 1966—, Kansas City Mus. Assn., 1966—; bd. mgrs. George H. Nettleton Home for Aged Women, 1968-73. Chmn. Christian-social relations Women's Soc. Christian Service, 1946-48, pres., 1937-38, chmn. missions, 1961-63; chmn. St. Francis Aux. of St. Francis Home for Boys, Salina and Ellsworth, Kan., 1946-48, supplies com. Community Chest Dr., 1951; vol. visitor for aged Mattie Rhodes Settlement House, 1948; Hosp. Gray Lady, 1948-50. Pres., Young Women's Democratic Club, 1931-33. Mem. UDC, D.A.R. (regent 1942-43). Methodist (mem. adminstrv. bd.). Address: 409 W 58th Terr Kansas City MO 64113

BRITTAIN, LAURA READING, dancer, educator; b. Longmont, Colo., July 25, 1945; d. David R. and Jeanne (McKibbin) Reading; A.A. in Theatre, Bakersfield Jr. Coll., 1965; B.A. in Theatre Arts, UCLA, 1968, M.A. in Dance, 1971; m. Darryl A. Brittain, June 28, 1969 (div.). Dancer, Gus Solomon's Dance Co., N.Y.C., 1971-73; asso. prof. dance and dance edn., artist-in-residence N.Y.U., 1973—, dir. N.Y. U. Washington Sq. Repertory Dance Co.; performer Michelle Berne Dance Co., Marjorie Gamso & Dancers, Linda Diamond Dance Co.; choreographer; regional co-dir. Am. Coll. Dance Festival, N.Y.C., 1978; guest lectr. Jerusalem Rubin Acad. Music and Dance, 1982. mem. Am. Dance Guild, N.Y. State Dance Assn., Dance Theatre Workshop. Democrat. Choreographer: Disengage, 1975; Summer Canon: Dreams & Episodes, 1977; Chinook, 1979. Office: 35 W 4th St New York NY 10003

BRITTAIN, PATSY JEAN, med. care adminstr.; b. Belton, Tex., Aug. 20, 1924; d. Andrew Jackson and Ruby Eugenia (Durham) Brittain. B.S., U. Puget Sound, 1950; M.A., Pacific Lutheran U., 1973. Dir. occupational therapy Alaska Territorial Health Dept., 1950-52; supr. occupational therapy H.T. Buckner Rehab. Center, Seattle, 1953-67; med. care adminstr. Wash. Dept. Social and Health Services, Olympia, 1967-82; cons. occupational therapy, 1967—; clin. lectr. U. Puget Sound, 1956-63, mem. alumni bd. dirs., 1977-80; mem. occupational therapy asst. adv. bd. Green River Community Coll. Served with USNR, 1945-46, 64-82. Named Alumna cum Laude, U. Puget Sound, 1975. Mem. Am., Wash. (pres. 1957-58) occupational therapy assns., AAUW, Am. Pub. Health Assn., U.S. Naval Inst., Naval Res. Assn. Clubs: Order Eastern Star; Wash. Athletic. Contbr. profl. jours. Home: 1406 Rolling Hills Terr Olympia WA 98502 Office: Dept Social and Health Services Olympia WA 98504

BRITTIN, DOROTHY HELEN CLARK, food scientist, nutritionist; b. Gadsden County, Fla., June 27, 1938; d. Herbert Hampton and Lucy Virginia (Stokes) Clark; B.S. cum laude, Fla. State U., 1960; M.S. (Jonnie McCerie Michie grad. fellow 1964-65), Tex. Tech U., 1965, Ph.D. (Faculty Research fellow 1972), 1974; m. Anthony Norman Brittin, Jan. 23, 1960; children—Ruth Virginia, Clark Norman, Carol Jeanette. Tchr., Mobile (Ala.) Public Schs., 1960; asst. county home demonstration agt. Nassau County (N.Y.), 1961-63; research and teaching asst. Tex. Tech U., Lubbock, 1963-65, instr., 1965-70, asst. prof., 1970-78, asso. prof. food and nutrition, 1978—; cons., speaker in field. Named Woman of Yr., Tex. Tech U., 1978. Mem. Am. Inst. Nutrition, Am. Home Econs. Assn., Am. Meat Sci. Assn., Am. Dietetic Assn. (registered dietitian), Tex. Dietetic Assn. (pres. 1978-79), Am. Soc. Animal Sci., Inst. Food Technologists, Soc. Nutrition Edn., Sigma Xi, Phi Kappa Phi, Omicron Nu, Kappa Delta Pi, Phi Upsilon Omicron, Tau Beta Sigma. Presbyterian. Author research papers in field. Home: 5220 15th St Lubbock TX 79416 Office: Dept Food and Nutrition Tex Tech Univ Lubbock TX 79409

BRITTINGHAM, JOYCE MARIE, accountant; b. St. Louis, Jan. 4, 1941; d. William Joyce and Mary Josephine (Van Straat) Sturgis; A.B. (Scholar 1959-61), Fontbonne Coll., 1963; M.A., St. Louis U., 1970; m. Dec. 27, 1969 (div.); 1 dau., Paula Therese. Instr., English, history St. Joseph's Acad., St. Louis, 1963-69; writer Vol. Action Center, Davenport, Iowa, 1974-75; bus. mgr. Quad City Montessori Assn., Davenport, 1975-78; office mgr. Frank Foundries, Corp., Moline, Ill., 1978-80, adminstrv. asst. to chmn. bd., from 1980; now supr. gen. acctg. Normoyle-Berg & Assos., Inc. Alt. del. Scott County Dem. Conv., 1972; bd. dirs. Quad City Montessori Assn., 1975-76. Mem. AAUW (exec. bd., budget dir. 1979-80), Quad City Personnel Assn., Am. Foundrymens Soc., Career Women's Network. Nat. Assn. Female Execs. Roman Catholic. Club: Pilot. Home: 1307 Hillside Dr Bettendorf IA 52722 Office: 701 26th Ave Rock Island IL 61201

BRITTON, CARMELITA VIOLA, physician; b. Kansas City, Mo., Nov. 26, 1949; d. Daniel Lavelle and Lucinda Marie (Barnes) B.; B.S., Rensselaer Poly. Inst., Troy, N.Y., 1973; M.D., Albany (N.Y.) Med. Coll., 1973. Intern, then resident in pediatrics St. Louis Children's Hosp., 1973-75, fellow in pediatric cardiology, 1975-77; dir. pediatric services St. Luke's Med. Bldg., St. Louis, 1979—; asst. pediatrician Washington U. Med. Sch., St. Louis, 1979—; co-dir. dept. pediatrics St. Louis City Hosp., 1978-80, dir. house-staff edn., 1980—; mem. Mo. Profl. Liability Rev. Bd.; bd. dirs. St. Louis Heart Assn., also mem. speakers bd. Mem. friends bd. St. Louis Art Mus.; mem. phys. edn. com. St. Louis YMCA; mem. adv. bd. Cardinal Ritter Coll. Prep. Sch., St. Louis. Fellow Am. Acad. Pediatrics. Author articles in field. Home: 1091 Purcell Ave Saint Louis MO 63130 Office: 1515 Lafayette Ave Saint Louis MO 63104

BRITTON, DOROTHEA SPRAGUE, hosp. public relations adminstr.; b. Cleve., Oct. 30, 1922; d. Paul Epworth and Ruth Emily (Horrocks) Sprague; A.B., U. Mich., 1948, M.A., 1949; postgrad. Columbia U., 1975; m. Alan B. Britton, Sept. 27, 1952; children—Dana Sprague Chabina, Deborah Beckwith Tracy Tuttle. Personnel mgr. George Worthington Co., Cleve., 1951-52; pres. Tacydot Products, Scarsdale, N.Y., 1964-70; adminstr. program devel. Nellie J. Crocker Health Center, Ossining, N.Y., 1971-72; adminstrv. dir. vol. services Roosevelt Hosp., N.Y.C., 1973-77; dir. community and public relations Peoples Bank for Savs., New Rochelle, N.Y., 1977-80; dir. public relations St. John's Riverside Hosp., Yonkers, N.Y., 1980—; lectr. women and mgmt., handicrafts, community banking. Mem. Am. Assn. Vol. Services Coordinators (cert.), N.Y. Assn. Dirs. Vols., Am. Soc. Hosp. Public Relations, Am. Soc. Dirs. Vol. Services, Am. Hosp. Assn., Savs. Bank Women N.Y., Pi Beta Phi. Clubs: Scarsdale Golf, Scarsdale Woman's. Author: An Op-Art Easter Bazaar, 1959; Dot Britton's 1969 Bazaar Book; Dot Britton's 1970 Christmas Bazaar Book; The Complete Book of Bazaars, 1973; The New Volunteer, 1976; The Legends of Christmas, 1978; 30 Years of Christmas Nonsense, 1981. Home: 4 Rock Hill Ln Scarsdale NY 10583

BRITTON, MORRENE HUGHES, farmer, cattle feeder, comml. pilot; b. Kansas City, Mo., June 24, 1941; d. Morrison and Irene (Arnold) Hughes; student Carleton Coll., 1959-60; B.S. cum laude in Agriculture, U. Mo., 1963; diploma Wilson Flight Tng. Center, 1966; m. Robert Lynn Britton, Jan. 21, 1967; 1 dau., Alison. Co-mgr., Hughes Farms (became Hughes Farms, Inc. 1971), Fayette, Mo., 1963-65, co-mgr., 1969-72, gen. mgr., pres., 1972—; flight instr. Boonville (Mo.) Airport, 1965-66, Wilson Flight Tng. Center, Kansas City, Kans., 1966-69; mem. various agrl. coms. Cert. comml., single and multi-engine aircraft flight instr. Bd. dirs. 1st Christian Ch., Fayette. Mem. Nat. Assn. Ind. Bus., Am. Farm. Bur. Assn., Nat. Cattlemen's Assn., Gamma Sigma Delta. Club: LTS. Home and Office: Route 3 Fayette MO 65248

BRITTON, RUTH STEIN, social worker; b. Chgo., Dec. 16, 1923; d. David Alex and Fannie Norma Stein; B.A., Calif. State U. at Long Beach, 1964; M.A., Goddard Coll., 1977; m. Alexander Leonard Britton, Aug. 26, 1948; children—Michele Diane, Sanford Alan. Dir. family welfare services Toberman Settlement House, San Pedro, Calif., 1964-69; med. social worker Long Beach (Calif.) Children's Clinic, 1970—. Bd. dirs. Long Beach Jewish Community Center. Lic. marriage, family and child counselor, Calif. Mem. Nat. Assn. Social Workers, Calif. Assn. Marriage and Family Counselors, Nat. Council Jewish Women, Calif. State U. Alumni Assn., Goddard Coll. Alumni Assn. Club: Hadassah. Home: 2821 Brimhall Dr Los Alamitos CA 90720 Office: c/o Long Beach Children's Clinic 2801 Atlantic St Long Beach CA 90801

BROADHURST, VIRGINIA VIEMEISTER, social worker, family therapist; b. Bklyn., May 7, 1935; d. Frederick H. and Ruth M. (Crossland) Viemeister; B.A., U. Md., 1970, M.S.W., 1973; children—David M., Steven G. Therapist, Family Services of Prince Georges County, Hyattsville, Md., part-time 1973; family therapist Karma Acad. for Boys, Rockville, Md., part-time 1974-75; facilitator-group leader Family Awareness Program, Rockville, 1974-76, 79-87; child mental health specialist Montgomery County Dept. Social Services, Rockville, 1976-78, foster care worker, 1979; primary therapist Regional Inst. for Children and Adolescents, Rockville, 1980—; facilitator, coordinator, trainer, mem. steering com. Discovery, singles discussion group Unitarian Ch. Rockville, 1975-78. Mem. Rockville Alt. Community Service Commn., 1980. Lic. cert. social worker, Md. Mem. Nat. Assn. Social Workers, Acad. Cert. Social Workers, Unitarian. Home: 501 Meadow Hall Dr Rockville MD 20851 Office: 15000 Broschart Rd Rockville MD 20850

BROBSTON, MARIE LOUISE, nurse; b. Davenport, Iowa, Jan. 23, 1939; d. Herman John and Margaret (Mourisse) Tank; R.N., Moline Public Hosp. Sch. Nursing, 1960; postgrad. St. Joseph's Coll., 1982—; m. James Merle Brobston, Dec. 2, 1967; children—Douglas Lee, Ronald Merle, Christopher James. Staff nurse, nursing supr. Moline (Ill.) Public Hosp., 1960-75; clin. instr. health occupations United Twp. High Sch., E. Moline, Ill. 1975-77; health service supr. E. Moline Care Center, 1977-79; dir. nursing Friendship Manor, Rock Island, Ill., 1979—; rep. nursing home Am. Cancer Soc. Mem. St. Anne's Circle, Altar and Rosary Soc., St. Patrick's Catholic Ch., Coloma, Ill., 1977—. R.N., Ill. Mem. Ill. Nurses Assn. (legis. com.), Moline Public Hosp. Nurses Alumnae, Whiteway Bowling League (v.p. 1979—). Home: RR 3 PO Box 207 Geneseo IL 61254 Office: 1209 21st Ave Rock Island IL 61201

BROCK, LORENA ROWAN, exploration co. exec.; b. Wharton, Tex., July 18, 1921; d. Spencer Ford and Susie O. (Moore) Rowan; B.B.A., Tex. U., 1938, U. Tex., 1939-42; m. Lawrence E. Brock, Feb. 18, 1950; children—(by previous marriage) Stephen H. Philbin, Susan Rowan Philbin; stepchildren—Lawrence E., Lee Monnett Brock Frahlich. Corporate sec. Offshore Exploration Corp., Precise Exploration Corp. and Brock Exploration Corp., New Orleans, 1967—, dir. Brock Exploration Corp. Tchr. Sun. sch., Daus. of the King Episcopal Ch., 1963—. Mem. DAR, Pi Beta Phi. Democrat. Home: 2704 Whitney Pl Apt 715 Metairie LA 70002 Office: 231 Carondelet St 5th Floor New Orleans LA 70130

BRODAHL, BETSEY ANN, educator; b. Wahoo, Nebr., Aug. 28, 1922; d. Alfred Joseph and Ruth (Erickson) Brodahl; B.A., Augustana Coll., 1944; M.A., Syracuse U., 1948; postgrad. Stanford U. Instr., Augustana Coll., Rock Island, Ill., 1947-48, asst. prof., dean women, 1948, asso. prof., asso. dean students, 1959—. Vice pres. bd. dirs. Found. for Crippled Children and Adults, Rock Island and Mercer Counties, 1956-57, 1970-71, 1975-77, sec., 1958-59, pres., 1977-79; v.p. bd. dirs. Tri-City Symphony Orch., 1970, 71, 72; pres. Friends of Art, 1977-79; bd. dirs. Deaconess Community of the Lutheran Ch. Am., sec., 1974; bd. dirs. Bethphage Mission 1968-74, sec., 1972-74. Recipient Vasa Medal, King of Sweden, 1975. Mem. Am. Scandinavian Found. (pres. Augustana chpt. 1969-71, sec. 1971, 72, 73), Augustana Hist. Soc. (pres. 1963-65; v.p. 1971, sec. 1971-73), Ill State Easter Seal Soc. (dir. 1973-76), Nat. Assn. Women Deans and Counselors, Ill. Deans of Women, AAUW, Am. Hist. Soc., Phi Beta Kappa. Republican. Home: 3052 10th Ave Rock Island IL 61201 Office: Augustana Coll Rock Island IL 61201

BRODER, PATRICIA JANIS, art historian; b. N.Y.C., Nov. 22, 1935; d. Milton W. and Rheba (Mantell) Janis; student Smith Coll., 1953-54; B.A., Barnard Coll., 1957; postgrad. Rutgers U., 1962-64; m. Stanley H. Broder, Jan. 22, 1959; children—Clifford James, Peter Howard, Helen Anna. Stock brokerage trainee A.M. Kidder & Co., N.Y.C., 1958; registered rep. Thomson & McKinnon Co., N.Y.C., 1959-61; ind. registered investment adviser, 1962-64; research, writing on art history Bronzes of American West, 1964-74, book pub., 1974 (Herbert Adams Meml. medal Nat. Sculpture Soc. 1975, Gold medal Nat. Acad. Western Art 1975); lectr., author on art of Am. West, 1970—. Recipient Wrangler award for best article Western Heritage, 1976, best art book award, 1981; Border Regional Library Assn. award, 1981. Mem. Western History Assn., AAUW. Author: Bronzes of the American West; The World of the Hopis; Hopi Painting Today; Dean Cornwell, Dean of Illustrators; Great Paintings of the Old American West; Taos: A Painter's Dream; American Indian Painting and Sculpture. Address: 488 Long Hill Dr Short Hills NJ 07078

BRODMAN, ESTELLE, librarian, educator; b. N.Y.C., June 1, 1914; d. Henry and Nettie (Sameth) Brodman; A.B., Cornell U., 1935; B.S., Columbia U., 1936, M.S., 1943, Ph.D., 1954; D.Sc. (hon.), U. Ill., 1974; postdoctoral study UCLA, 1959, U. N.Mex., 1960. Asst. librarian Cornell U. Sch. Nursing Library, N.Y.C., 1936-37; asst. to acting med. librarian Columbia U. Libraries, N.Y.C., 1937-49; asst. librarian for reference services Nat. Library Medicine, Washington, 1949-61; librarian, asso. prof. med. history Washington U. Sch. Medicine, St. Louis, 1961-64, librarian, prof. med. history, 1964-81; instr., Columbia U., 1946-52, Cath. U. Am., 1957; vis. prof. Keio U., Tokyo, Japan, 1962, U. Mo., 1971, 73; cons. Am. Hosp. Assn., NIH, AID, others. Documentation expert UN Tech. Assistance Program, New Delhi, 1967-68; expert tech. assistance program S.E. regional office WHO, New Delhi, 1970, UN Econ. Agy. for Asia and Far East, Bangkok, 1973, UN Fund for Population Affairs, 1976-77. Mem. Pres.'s Commn. Libraries, 1966-68. Mem. Am., Med. (spl. award 1957, Noyes award 1971; pres. 1964-65), library assns., Spl. Libraries Assn. (dir. 1949-52, John Cotton Dana award 1981), Bibliog. Soc. Am., Am. Assn. History Medicine (council 1967-68). Author: Development of Medical Bibliography, 1954; Bibliographical Lists for Medical Libraries, 1950. Editor: Bull. Med. Library Assn., 1947-57. Home: 19-09 Meadow Lakes Hightstown NJ 08520

BRODSKY, GERALDINE FRANCES, speech pathologist; b. South Hackensack, N.J., Mar. 16, 1939; d. Louis and Frances (Kaplan) Riggillo; B.A. cum laude, Bklyn. Coll., 1960; M.A., Stanford U., 1966; m. Marshall Brodsky, Jan. 23, 1960; 1 son, Daniel Louis Marc; m. 2d, Donald Longobardi, July 9, 1977. Speech improvement tchr. N.Y.C. Bd. Edn., 1960; speech therapist Poughkeepsie (N.Y.) Sch. Dist., 1962-65; speech pathologist St. Francis Hosp., Poughkeepsie, 1966-69; instr., clin. supr. SUNY, New Paltz, 1971-76; pvt. practice speech pathology, Poughkeepsie and Fishkill, N.Y., 1971-76; dir. Hudson Valley Speech Center, Rhinebeck, N.Y., 1976—; cons. Vassar Bros. Hosp., St. Luke's Hosp., various nursing homes. Sec., Earth Recovery Action, 1973; co-chairwoman Stewart Jetport Coalition, 1974; area coordinator Heart Fund drive, 1980. Mem. Mid-Hudson Speech and Hearing Assn., NAACP (mem. edn. com. 1964), N.Y. State Speech and Hearing Assn., Am. Speech and Lang. Hearing Assn., Am. Acad. Pvt. Practice, N.Y. Neuropsychology Group, Assn. for Children with Learning Disorders. Democrat. Jewish. Home: 9 Cedar Dr Rhinebeck NY 12572 Office: 91-93 Montgomery St Rhinebeck NY 12572 also 12 Broad St Fishkill NY 12524

BRODY, HELEN TANDLER, banker; b. N.Y.C., Sept. 11, 1947; d. Stephen Martin and Hannah K. (Korda) Tandler; B.A., Skidmore Coll., 1968; M.B.A., Columbia U., 1971. Ops. adminstr. ITT, N.Y.C., 1973-76; caseworker, budget dir. Am. Express Co., N.Y.C., 1976-78; v.p. Citcorp. Citicorp Services, N.Y.C., 1978-80; v.p. Citibank, N.A., N.Y.C., 1980—. Recipient New York Regents scholarship, 1964. Club: West Side Tennis (Forest Hills, N.Y.).

BRODY, LYNNE MAUREEN, librarian; b. Los Angeles, Apr. 9, 1941; d. Alec and Marian (Greffrath) Kirschner; A.B. (tuition scholar), Douglass Coll. of Rutgers U., 1962; M.L.S., Simmons Coll., 1966; postgrad. Columbia U., 1968-72; m. Robert Brody, Sept. 3, 1961; children—Dana, Gillian. Library intern M.I.T., 1965-66; asst. ref. librarian Brandeis U. Library, 1966-67; ref. librarian Roth Library, M.I.T., 1967-68; res. book librarian Barnard Coll., Columbia U., 1968-74; ref. librarian, collection devel. librarian U. Tex., Austin, 1974-79, head undergrad. library, 1979—. Mem. ALA, Soc. U. Tex. Librarians (pres. 1976-77). Home: 1610 West Ave Austin TX 78701 Office: ACA 101 University of Texas Austin TX 78712

BROECKING, ARDEN VIRGINIA ANDERSON, singer, music critic, educator, lectr.; b. New Rochelle, N.Y., Feb. 8; d. Gotthard Erland and Charlotte Virginia (Kitt) Anderson; student Neighborhood Playhouse Sch. of Theatre, 1954-56; B.Mus. magna cum laude, New Eng. Conservatory Music, 1954; student Carnegie-Mellon U., 1950-52; m. Wilfrid Broecking, July 14, 1962 (div.); children—Heidi Charlotte, Johannes D.E. Singer with Am. Savoyards, Conn. Grand Opera and others, 1957—; tchr. singing, lectr. on opera, 1978—; ednl. coordinator Conn. Grand Opera, Bridgeport, 1979—, stage dir., 1981—; ednl. coordinator Opera New Eng., 1979—; studio tchr. of singing; music critic Brooks Newspapers; artist-in-residence St. Luke's Chamber Music Center, Opera Camera. Youth coordinator, Darien Women's Republican Assn.; advisor Darien Teenage Reps. Mem. Actors Equity Assn., Am. Guild Musical Artists, Nat. Assn. Tchrs. of Singing, Nat. Writers Club (asso.), N.Y. State Sch. Music Assn. (Arion medal), Sigma Alpha Iota, Sigma Kappa. Club: Women's Nat. Rep. Founder Darien Consortium, 1971. Home: Darien CT 06820

BROERING, NAOMI CORDERO, librarian; b. N.Y.C., Nov. 24, 1929; d. Julius and Emily (Perez) Cordero; B.A., Calif. State U., 1961, M.A. in history, 1963; postgrad. UCLA, 1964, M.L.S. in Library Sci., 1966, postgrad. (NIH fellow), 1967; postgrad. U. West Los Angeles, 1970; m. Arthur J. Broering, 1971. Acquisitions and reference librarian U. So. Calif., 1967-68; chief librarian Children's Hosp., Los Angeles, 1968-71; asst. librarian Walter Reed Gen. Hosp., Washington, 1972; chief reader services, grant officer VA, Washington, 1972-75; assoc. librarian Med. Ctr., Georgetown U., Washington, 1975-78, librarian, 1978—; mem. adj. faculty Cath. U. Mem. Med. Library Assn. (dir. 1979-82), ALA, Am. Soc. Info. Sci., AAAS, Assn. Acad. Health Sci. Library Dirs., Spl. Library Assn. Club: Gulf and Country of Reston. Contbr. in field. Office: Georgetown University Med Ctr Library 3900 Reservoir Rd NW Washington DC 20007

BROGAN, MARY ROSE, psychologist; b. Peckville, Pa., Apr. 7, 1948; d. John F. and Sally E. (O'Connor) B.; A.B., Marywood Coll., 1970; M.S., SUNY, Cortland, 1975; Ph.D., U. S.D., 1977. Sch. psychologist Flandreau (S.D.) Indian High Sch., 1975-76; clin. psychology intern Conn. Valley Hosp., Middletown, Conn., 1976-77, clin. psychologist, 1977—, asst. dir. psychiat. residency tng. program, 1981—; pvt. practice psychology, Wethersfield, Conn., 1979-80, Middletown, 1980—; clin. cons. Gilead Halfway House, Middletown, 1980—. Mem. adv. bd. St. Agnes Home, Wethersfield, 1981—. Lic. clin. psychologist, Conn. Mem. Am. Psychol. Assn., Conn. Psychol. Assn. Office: Dept Psychology Conn Valley Hosp Middletown CT 06457 also 46 Washington St Middletown CT 06457

BROKENBOUGH, WILLA MAE, caterer; b. Clio, S.C., Dec. 5, 1921; d. Joseph and Rebecca (Ales) Burch; student Va. State U., 1940-41; m. John Robert Brokenbough, Feb. 4, 1942; children—Jack, Russell Allen, Diane Elaine Brokenbough Laws. Caterer, Elk's Lodge, Vineland, N.J., 1939-40; cafeteria mgr. Gen. Floor Co., Los Angeles, 1960-63, Schick Safety Razar Co., Culver City, Calif., 1963-66; owner, pres. Willa Brokenbough Parties, Los Angeles, 1963—. Recipient award SBA, 1978, 79. Mem. Calif. Restaurant Assn., Internat. Food Service Execs. Assn. Lutheran. Clubs: Eastern Star, Heroines of Jericho. Office: 4853 Crenshaw Blvd Los Angeles CA 90042

BROMBERG, PAULETTE, clin. social worker; b. Paterson, N.J., Jan. 13, 1941; d. Oscar and Ruth (Baker) B.; B.S., Fairleigh Dickinson U.,

1962; M.A., Paterson State Coll., 1965; M.S.W., U. Mich., 1971; postgrad. Case Western Res. U.; Classroom tchr. in N.J., 1962-69; youth leader, program dir. Paterson YM-YWHA, 1956-69; clin. social worker Huron Valley Child Guidance Clinic, Ypsilanti, Mich., 1971-73; sr. social worker U. Mich. child devel. project, 1973-75; vis. lectr. Eastern Mich. U., Ypsilanti, summers 1972-74; clin. social worker Ann Arbor VA Med. Center, 1975—; adj. lectr. U. Mich. Extension Service Social Work, 1978-80; pvt. practice psychotherapy, 1974—. Chmn. Soviet Jewry com. Washtenaw County (Mich.) Jewish Community Council, 1971, treas. council, 1972-73; bd. dirs. Temple Beth Emeth, Ann Arbor, 1973-75, chmn. gift com., 1979-82. Mem. Acad. Cert. Social Workers, Nat. Assn. Social Workers (chpt. treas. 1974-75, editor newsletter 1975-76), Mich. Assn. Infant Mental Health (chmn. cons., tng. and resources com. 1978-81), Mich. Soc. Clin. Social Work, Mich. Assn. Emotionally Disturbed Children, Am. Assn. Psychiat. Services Children. Home: 3720 Greenbrier Blvd Ann Arbor MI 48105 Office: 2215 Fuller Rd Ann Arbor MI 48105

BROMBERG, RACHEL BEREZOW, writer, artist, educator; b. Bklyn., July 24, 1917; d. Samuel and Lena (Jacobson) Berezow; B.A., N.Y. U., 1940; M.A., U. Wis., 1942; postgrad. (univ. fellow) Bryn Mawr Coll., 1942-44; m. Benjamin Bromberg, Dec. 24, 1964. Instr. advanced Spanish lit., French lit. U. Md., College Park, 1945-50; instr. English as 2d lang. Spanish-Am. Inst., N.Y.C., 1966—; dir. Vestibule Gallery, 1958—; pres. Rachel Frank Pub. Corp., 1958—; exhibited one-woman shows at Argent Gallery, Lynn Kottler Galleries. Recipient Gold medal Accademia Italia delle Arti e del Lavoro. Fellow Royal Soc. Arts; mem. MLA, AAUP, Artists Equity, Bryn Mawr Grad. Alumnae Soc. Club: Bryn Mawr (N.Y.C.). Author: Three Pastoral Novels, 1970; Selected Poems; also translations; poems included in anthologies; guest editor Poetry mag., 1953. Contbr. articles to profl. jours., Spanish-Am. newspapers. Home: 137-57 228th St Laurelton NY 11413 Office: 215 W 43d St New York NY 10036

BROMLEY, CATHERINE REED, rancher; b. Bradford, Ark., June 7, 1940; d. Claude Brewer and Lena Lucille (Rains) Reed; student Iowa Wesleyan Coll., 1958-60, Brigham Young U., 1963-65; m. Michael Fredrick Bromley, Apr. 1, 1965; children—Michael, Reed, Jess, Lori, Trisha, John, James. Partner, Bromley Farms, Inc., American Fork, Utah, 1965—, auditor, 1965—, v.p., 1968—. City coordinator March of Dimes Mother's March, 1979-80; mem. Miss American Fork Pageant com., 1977; sec.-treas. American Fork Jr. High Parent-Tchrs.-Students Assn. Recipient Latter Day Saints Golden Gleaner award, 1970. Mem. Pacific Egg & Poultry Assn., Farm Bur., Utah Egg Council, United Egg Producers, N.W. Egg Producers, Outstanding Farmers of Am. Fraternity, Pi Beta Phi (Iowa chpt.). Republican. Mem. Ch. of Jesus Christ of Latter-Day Saints. Clubs: Young Homemakers, Rotary. Home and Office: RFD 1 Box 265 American Fork UT 84003

BRONK, PAMELA ANN, mgmt. cons.; b. Los Angeles, July 30, 1945; d. Bill Richmond and Dolores Ann Trerise; A.B., U. Calif., Berkeley, 1976; M. Public and Pvt. Mgmt., Yale U., 1978; children—Tamara Sue, Brian Scott. Portfolio asso. Donaldson, Lufkis & Jenrette, N.Y.C., 1970-72; asso. securities analyst Rosenburg Capital Mgmt., San Francisco, 1972-76; mgmt. cons. McKinsey & Co., 1978—. Chmn. bd. dirs. Nat. Dance Inst., 1981—; trustee Found. Extension and Devel. Am. Profl. Theater, 1982. Mem. Fin. Women's Club, Phi Beta Kappa. Home: 201 Barnard Rd New Rochelle NY 10801 Office: 55 E 52d St New York NY 10022

BRONKIE, LYNN FERN, jeweler; b. New Haven, July 18, 1949; d. Willis Fredrick and Fern Elizabeth (Seeberg) B.; cert. Gemological Inst. Am., 1976; m. Wayne Bertram Kight, Aug. 25, 1979; children by previous marriage—Melissa Lynn Bronkie, Peter D. Bronkie. Apprentice, Willis F. Bronkie & Cia Ltda., Bogotá, Colombia, 1967-69, personal mgr., designer of jewelry, emerald buyer, gold jewelry buyer, Bogotá, 1972-77, v.p., 1979—; v.p., gen. mgr., dir., buyer Greenfire Emeralds of Colombia Ltd., Atlanta, -82, pres., gen. mgr., Hollywood, Fla., 1982—. Office: PO Box 6585 Hollywood FL 33021

BRONSON, GWENDOLYN TIBBITS, state legislator; b. Hartford, Conn., Apr. 19, 1937; student U. Conn., U. Vt.; m. Leman F. Bronson; 1 son, 2 daus. Mem. Vt. Ho. of Reps., 1981—. Bd. dirs. Shelburne Coop Nursery Sch., Onion River Food Coop.; mem. Shelburne Republican Com., Chittenden County Rep. Com., Vt. State Rep. Com.; active Girl Scouts U.S.A.; vol. Planned Parenthood Assn. Mem. John Clough Genealogy Soc., DAR. Club: Charlotte Pony (treas.). Methodist. Office: Vt Ho of Reps State House Montpelier VT 05602 *

BRONSON, PATRICIA ANN, educator; b. Leesville, La., Mar. 15, 1931; d. Glenn Cecil and Allie Lee (Copeland) Packer; student Northwestern State U., 1948-51; B.A., George Peabody Coll., 1960, M.A., 1962; m. John Orville Bronson, Jr., June 11, 1966; children—Richard Wayne McCoy, Victoria Patricia Elizabeth, Glenn Charles Stephen. Tchr., Nashville Met. Schs., 1962-65, Calhoun Tech. Jr. Coll., Decatur, Ala., 1965-67; asst. prof. math. Chesapeake Coll., Wye Mills, Md., 1967—. Mem. Math. Assn. Am., Nat. Council Tchrs. Math., AAUP, Miss., S.C. hist. socs., La. Hist. Assn., Theta Sigma Upsilon, Delta Kappa Gamma. Democrat. Episcopalian. Club: Order Eastern Star. Author: Index of the Census of 1850, Orangeburg and Pickens Districts, S.C., 1974. Home: Hopkins Hall Box 81 Wye Mills MD 21679

BRONSON, SHIRLEY GERENE, govt. agy. ofcl.; b. Grape Vine, Ark., Oct. 15, 1936; d. Dee Lawrence and Velma Geneva (Smith) Green; B.A. cum laude in Mgmt., Golden Gate U., 1975, M.B.A., 1977; m. Bobby Ed Bronson, Sept. 29, 1953; children—Richard Ed, David Dee, Daniel Lee, Robert Edward. Fed. women's program mgr. Air Force Flight Test Center, Edwards, Calif., 1973-74, budget/acctg. asst., 1973-74, asst. to comptroller, 1974-76, records mgmt. officer, 1976-77, program/budget analyst, 1977—; fed. women's program mgr. Air Force Space Div., Los Angeles, 1979—; contract tchr. Pacific Christian Coll. Calif. del. Nat. Women's Conf., 1977; mem. Fed. Task Force UN Decade for Women, 1977-79. Recipient Cert. of Merit, Air Force Systems Command, 1972, Outstanding Performance award, 1971, 72, 75, 76; Sustained Superior Performance award Dept. Air Force, 1971, 76, Cert. of Appreciation, 1976, Spl. Achievement award, 1971, 76; Spl. Recognition award Air Force Flight Test Center Fed. Women's Program, 1976; named Air Force Systems Command Fed. Women's Program Mgr. of Yr., 1979; Air Force Fed. Women's Program Mgr. of Yr., 1980. Mem. Nat. Assn. Female Execs., Am. Soc. Mil. Comptrollers, Federally Employed Women, Fed. Women's Program Com., Los Angeles Fed. Exec. Bd. Office: SD/ACB PO Box 92960 Worldway Postal Center Los Angeles CA 90009

BRONSON, SHIRLEY PAT, nurse; b. Shelbyville, Tenn., Dec. 23, 1935; d. Allen Clark and Willie Rose (Sutton) Melson; A.A. in Nursing, Middle Tenn. State U., 1972; student U. Tenn., 1973; m. Donald E. Bronson, Sept. 24, 1976; children by previous marriage—Jim Stubblefield, Pat Stubblefield (dec.), Lisa S. Christie. Staff nurse Bedford County Gen. Hosp., Shelbyville, 1965-70, shift supr., 1972, dir. nursing service, 1973-77; tchr. licensed practical nurses Tenn. Area Vocat. Sch., Shelbyville, 1972-73; dir. nursing service Glen Oaks Convalescent Center, Shelbyville, 1978—; nurse cons. Blvd. Ter., Murfreesboro, Tenn., 1979-82, Smyrna (Tenn.) Nursing Center, 1979-82. Active ARC; mem. adv. council for Allied Health Careers at Motlow State Coll. and U. Ala., Birmingham, 1980-82. Lic. profl. nurse, Tenn., La.; lic. nursing home adminstr. Mem. Tenn. Dir. Nursing Assn., Tenn. Health Care Assn. Republican. Mem. Ch. of Christ. Club: Murfreesboro Women Bowling Assn. Home: 324 Chestnut Dr Shelbyville TN 37160 Office: 1101 Glenoak Rd Shelbyville TN 37160

BRONZ, LOIS GOUGIS, educator, city ofcl.; b. New Orleans, Aug. 20, 1927; d. Alex and Elise (Cousin) Gougis; B.A., Xavier U., 1948; M.Ed., Wayne State U., 1952; m. Charles Bronz, Nov. 23, 1966; children—Edgar Taplin, Francine Taplin, Shelly Rita Talpin. Tchr., Orleans Parish Sch., New Orleans, 1948-61; dir. placement and recruitment Xavier U., New Orleans, 1961-66; mem. faculty Manhattanville Coll., Purchase, N.Y., 1968-75; tchr. Greenburgh Central 7 Sch. Dist., Hartsdale, N.Y., 1975—; cons. in field. Councilwoman Town of Greenburgh, N.Y., 1975—; pres. bd. dirs. Westchester Coop. Opportunity Program; founder Westchester Black Women's Polit. Caucus. Recipient Profl. award Nat. Assn. Negro Bus. and Profl. Womens Clubs, Inc., Westchester chpt., 1979; Polit. Awareness award Black Democrats of Westchester County 1979. Mem. Xavier U. Nat. Alumni Assn., (pres. 1976-80), Nat. Council Tchrs. Math., Women of Westchester, Greenburgh Tchrs. Assn. Democrat. Roman Catholic. Home: 282 Old Tarrytown Rd White Plains NY 10603 Office: PO Box 205 Elmsford NY 10523

BROOK, JUDITH SUZANNE, psychologist; b. N.Y.C., Dec. 31, 1939; d. Robert Edward and Helen (Zimmerman) Muser; B.A., Hunter Coll., 1961; M.A., Columbia U., 1962, Ed.D., 1967; m. David Brook, Dec. 15, 1962; children—Adam, Jonathan. Asst. prof. Queens Coll., Flushing, N.Y., 1967-69; research asso. Inst. for Developmental Studies, N.Y. U., 1969-71; research asso. Columbia U., 1971-73, sr. research asso., 1973—; spl. cons. dept. psychiatry Mt. Sinai Sch. Medicine, N.Y.C., 1979-80, asso. prof. psychiatry, 1980—. Lic. psychologist, N.Y. State. Mem. Am., Eastern, N.Y. State psychol. assns., Am. Ednl. Research Assn., Psi Chi, Kappa Delta Pi. Author: Study of Relationships Between Formal Organizational Structure and Organizational Climate in Selected Schools, 1972; (with others) The Psychology of Adolescence. Research and publs. in child devel. Office: Mt Sinai Sch Medicine 1 Gustave Levy Pl Annenberg 2274 New York NY 10029

BROOKE, LYNNE MADDOX, social worker, coal co. exec.; b. Las Cruces, N.Mex., June 11, 1947; d. Sidney M. and Dorothy M. (McKinley) Maddox; B.A., Baylor U., 1969; M.S.S.W., U. Tenn., 1971, postgrad., 1971-76; m. Telfair Brooke, III, June 8, 1974. Social worker East Tenn. Chest Disease Hosp., Knoxville, 1971-72; social worker Birth Defects Evaluation Center, U. Tenn. Center for Health Scis., Knoxville, 1972-79; mktg. rep. Nat. Energy Resources, Knoxville, 1979-80; v.p. Mountain States Coal Sales, 1980—; field instr. U. Tenn., 1974-79, guest lectr., 1975-79. Chmn. telarama patients Nat. Found. March of Dimes, 1973-79; bd. dirs. East Tenn. Spina Bifida Assn., 1973-77. Mem. Acad. Cert. Social Workers, Nat. Assn. Social Workers, N.C. Coal Inst., AAUW (dir. Knoxville br. 1976—, 1st v.p. 1979—), Symphony Women's Guild. Club: Village Green Garden. Home: 11509 N Monticello St Knoxville TN 37922

BROOKS, CAROLINE VOGEL (MRS. KENNETH LEE BROOKS), public relations exec., journalist; b. Wichita Falls, Tex., June 10, 1938; d. Irvin John and Mary Caroline (Meredith) Vogel; student Midwestern U., 1956-58; B.J., U. Tex., 1960; m. Kenneth Lee Brooks, Mar. 31, 1961; children—Amelia Louise, Mary Caroline. Reporter, Wichita Falls (Tex.) Times, 1960-61; editorial asst. U. Denver, 1961-62; dir. public relations William Jewell Coll., Liberty, Mo., 1962-65, 70-71; interim editor Liberty (Mo.) Tribune, 1969; instr. journalism Maple Woods Community Coll., Kansas City, Mo., 1971, asst. to pres. for info. services, 1971-77; public relations exec H & R Block, Inc., 1977-79; mgmt. info. analyst Argonne (Ill.) Nat. Lab., 1979—; public relations cons., 1971-79. Recipient 1st pl. award Mo. Press Women, 1970, 71, 72, 73. Mem. Women in Communications (chpt. pres. 1978), Nat. Fedn. Press Women (1st pl. award 1971, 72), Ill. Press Women. Editor Progress Edit. Townsend Communications, 1971—. Home: 988 Creekside Circle Naperville IL 60540 Office: Energy and Environ Systems Argonne Nat Lab Argonne IL 60439

BROOKS, DEBORAH DEE, systems analyst; b. Kingman, Kans., Jan. 18, 1951; d. Delbert Dexter and Ella Mae (Linscheid) B.; B.A. in Computer Sci., Kans. State U., 1973; M.L., Emporia (Kans.) State U., 1974. Asst. librarian Northwestern U., 1974-77; programmer, analyst Mgmt. Systems Tech., Inc., Chgo., 1977-78; tech. dir., systems analyst CALS project Elgin (Ill.) Community Coll., 1978-80; product mgr. Advanced Systems Inc., Elk Grove Village, Ill., 1980-81; data base adminstr. Wilson Jones Co., Chgo., 1981—; dir. CALS Services Group Ltd.; cons. in field. Mem. Assn. Computing Machinery, ALA, Am. Soc. Info. Sci. (chmn. Chgo. chpt. 1979). Presbyterian. Office: 6150 Touhy Ave Chicago IL 60648

BROOKS, GALE DOREEN, TV producer; b. Christiansburg, Va., May 23, 1941; d. Wilbert Earl and Edith Marie (Kammerdiener) B.; student Buffalo Bible Inst., 1959-60, Clarion State Coll., 1960-62; legis. asst. to congressmen Durwood Hall, Garry Brown and J. Herbert Burke, Washington, 1970-73; dist. rep. to Congressman John P. Murtha from 12th Pa. Dist., 1974-75; adminstrv. asst. to network program dir. Christian Broadcasting Network, Virginia Beach, Va., 1975-77, asso. producer The 700 Club, Virginia Beach and producer shows Practical Christian Living and Charisma, 1977-78; exec. producer Sta. WPCB-TV, Pitts., 1978-79; pres. Powerhouse Prodns., Inc., 1980—; cons. on TV equipment and prodn. to religious groups. Mem. Nat. Republican Women's Forum. Mem. Nat. Assn. Religious Broadcasters, Am. Film Inst. Home and Office: 2533 W Evans Dr Phoenix AZ 85023

BROOKS, GWENDOLYN, poet, author; b. Topeka, June 7, 1917; d. David Anderson and Keziah Corinne (Wims) B.; grad. Wilson Jr. Coll., Chgo., 1936; 10 hon. doctorates; m. Henry L. Blakely, Sept. 17, 1939; children—Henry L., Nora. Named One of 10 Women of Year, Mademoiselle mag., 1945; recipient award for creative writing Am. Acad. Arts and Letters, 1946; Pulitzer prize for poetry, 1950; Friends of Lit. award for poetry, 1964; Thormod Monsen award for lit., 1964; others; named Poet Laureate of Ill., 1968; Guggenheim fellow in creative poetry, 1946-47. Mem. Soc. Midland Authors. Author: Harper: A Street in Bronzeville, 1945; Annie Allen (poetry), 1949; Maud Martha (novel), 1953; Bronzeville Boys and Girls (book for children), 1956; (poetry) The Bean Eaters, 1960, Selected Poems, 1963, In the Mecca, Riot, 1969, Family Pictures, 1970, Aloneness, 1971, To Disembark, 1981; Report from Part One, 1972, Beckonings, 1975; Primer for Blacks, 1980; Young Poets Primer, 1980. Address: 7428 S Evans Chicago IL 60619

BROOKS, HINDI, television writer, story cons.; b. Detroit; d. Joseph and Fay (Kejsman) Bookstein; student Wayne State U., Detroit, 1944-46, UCLA, U. Judaism, Los Angeles City Coll., 1946-55; m. Manny Kleinmuntz, Oct. 6, 1951; children—Josh, Nomi. Freelance writer for television, movies, newspapers and mags., 1946—; drama critic, columnist Places mag., 1973-78; lectr. various univs. and secondary schs.; panelist Nat. Endowment Humanities. Recipient One-Act Play awards UN, 1950's, Jewish Centers Assn., 1950's, Second Place awards Back Stage mag., 1960's, Office Advanced Dramatic Research, 1970's, Humanitas award, 1975. Mem. Writers Guild Am. (bd. dirs.), Dramatists Guild, Women in Film (past 1st v.p., dir., past membership chairperson), Women in Theatre, Nat. Acad. TV Arts and Sci. Author: (plays) That's No Lady, 1962; What's His Name Gets All the Good Musicians, 1974; A Minor Incident, 1975; An Appointment with the Principal, 1976. Contbr. stories to Knowing, 1969, Le Sphinx mag., 1960. Office: care William Morris Agy 151 El Camino Dr Beverly Hills CA 90212

BROOKS, JAN LEEMAN, social worker; b. Cullman, Ala., Feb. 7, 1942; d. Walter Edward and Vivolene (Rushing) Leeman; B.A., David Lipscomb Coll., 1964; M.S.W., U. Ala., 1974. Dir. social work services The Retreat Mental Health Hosp., Decatur, Ala., 1974-76; tng. coordinator, instr. social work and gerontology Center for Study Aging, Sch. Social Work, Univ. Ala., Tuscaloosa, 1976-79, asst. prof., dir. undergrad. field edn., 1979-81, cons. Ala. developmental disabilities advocacy program, The Law Sch., 1981-82, research, teaching asst., 1982—. Named Social Worker of Year Ala. chpt. Nat. Assn. Social Workers, 1982. Mem. Nat. Assn. Social Workers, NAACP, League Women Voters, Wilderness Soc. Home: PO Box 313 University AL 35486

BROOKS, JANE BEAVER, clin. psychologist; b. Orange, N.J., Sept. 27, 1933; d. Charles Coleman and Henrietta Cecilia (Fear) Beaver; B.A. with honors, Vassar Coll., 1955; Ph.D. in Psychology (USPHS fellow 1956, 60-61), U. Calif., Berkeley, 1963; m. Bancroft Morgan Brooks, Sept. 23, 1960 (div., 1976); children—Bradley Taylor, Margo Pollard. Clin. psychologist Herrick Hosp., Berkeley, 1962-64; research psychologist Inst. Human Devel., U. Calif., Berkeley, 1965-78, lectr. psychology and health and med. scis., 1972-73, 77-78; clin. psychologist Kaiser Med. Center, Hayward, Calif., 1978—; cons. research projects Stanford U., U. Calif., San Francisco, fed. agys. Mem. Commn. on Aging City of Berkeley, 1978; cons. prisoner-oriented program San Quentin and Susanville; trustee Ch. Div. Sch. of Pacific, 1978. Mem. Am. Psychol. Assn., Calif. Psychol. Assn., Western Psychol. Assn., Soc. for Research in Child Devel., AAAS. Democrat. Episcopalian. Club: East Way Vassar (pres. 1971-74). Author: The Process of Parenting, 1981; contbr. articles to profl. publs. Home: 2810 Oak Noll Terr Berkeley CA 94705 Office: 27400 Hesperian Blvd Hayward CA 94545

BROOKS, JANET DELORES, coll. adminstr.; b. Sarasota, Fla., Mar. 12, 1947; d. Allen and Janie (Bentley) B.; B.S., Fla. A&M U., 1968; postgrad. in bus. adminstrn. U. Mich. Community services coordinator YMCA of Met. Detroit, 1970-73; public info. coordinator/editor dept. newsletter Wayne County Dept. Substance Abuse Services, Detroit, 1973-76; facility coordinator Wayne County Community Coll., Detroit, 1976—; pres. Brooks Diversified Cons. Services, Detroit, 1978—. Active, Black United Fund, Detroit, 1970—. Recipient United Way Communication Workshop award, 1976; named Outstanding Young Woman of Am., 1979. Mem. Nat. Assn. Black Journalists, NAACP, Better Bus. Bur., Detroit C. of C., Detroit Personnel Adminstrs. Assn., Am. Assn. Women in Community and Jr. Colls., Nat. Assn. Women Bus. Owners, Internat. Bus. Communicators, Nat. Assn. Media Women. Baptist. Clubs: Black Women Entrepreneurs (co-founder), Detroit Area Bus. Women's Network. Contbr. articles to profl. jours. Office: 660 Edison Plaza Suite 2350 Detroit MI 48226

BROOKS, JOANN, hosp. adminstr.; b. Roodhouse, Ill., Feb. 24, 1930; d. Howard H. and Leah Y. (Peters) Whitney; student Ill. State U., 1948-50, Western Ill. U., 1950-52; m. William D. Brooks, Apr. 27, 1951; children—Michael, Carol, Cathy. Tchr. schs. in Ill. and Mo., 1955-56, 60-63; unit clk., then unit mgr. Mo. Baptist Hosp., St. Louis, 1972-75, dir. unit mgmt., 1975—. Republican. Office: 3015 N Ballas Rd St Louis MO 63131

BROOKS, JOYCE ELAINE, ednl. adminstr.; b. Youngstown, Ohio, Oct. 1, 1939; d. Carl R. and Marie Hoyt; B.S. in Elementary Edn., Youngstown State U., 1961, M.S. in Elem. Edn., 1969, Ed.S., 1979; postgrad. in reading Bowling Green State U., Ohio State U.; m. Loran W. Brooks; children—Loran David, Cheryl Lynn, Cynthia Marie. Tchr., Greenford (Ohio) Sch., 1958-60; reading specialist C.H. Campbell Elementary Sch., Canfield, Ohio, 1967-77, Canfield High Sch., 1973-80; instrnl. supr. Mahoning County Office Edn., Youngstown, 1977—, dir. personnel services, 1980—; dist. chmn. dept. lang. arts Canfield Local Schs., 1973-77. Chmn., Mahoning County adv. council, local dir. Right-To-Read; lay mem. bd. Christian edn. Austintown Community Ch., 1973-74, deaconess, chmn. Christian edn. com. Mem. Internat. Reading Assn., Tri-County Reading Improvement Personnel, Assn. Supervision and Curriculum Devel., Ohio Assn. Supervision and Curriculum Devel., Mahoning County Elementary Prins. and Suprs. Assn., Ohio Suprs. Assn., Assn. Tchr. Educators, Assn. Early Childhood Edn., Canfield Ruritan Aux., Delta Kappa Gamma, Phi Delta Kappa. Cert. in elementary teaching, supervision of curriculum and adminstrn., reading specialty and supervision, Ohio; specialist in reading edn. and curriculum devel. Office: Mahoning County Office Edn Ohio One Bldg 25 E Boardman St Youngstown OH 44503 *

BROOKS, JOYCE HOLDER, educator; b. Chattanooga; d. Archie H. and Janie (Spain) Holder; B.S., U. Tenn., 1973, M.Ed., 1976, postgrad, 1976—; 1 son, Jonathan Timothy. Adjunctive therapist Moccasin Bend Hosp., Chattanooga, 1961—; dir. and pianist childrens choir Brainerd Baptist Ch., Chattanooga, 1973—; tchr. Henry L. Barger Sch., Chattanooga, 1980—. Vice pres. Freedom's Found., Chattanooga, local PTA. Recipient Freedom Found. Edn. award, 1977. Mem. AAUW, NEA, Tenn. Edn. Assn., Chattanooga Edn. Assn., Chattanooga Assn. Young Children (pres. 1973-78), U. Tenn. Alumni Assn., Kappa Delta Pi. Home: 940 Nason St Rossville GA 30741 Office: 4808 Brainerd Rd Chattanooga TN 37411

BROOKS, LORRAINE HELEN, constrn. co. exec.; b. Klamath Falls, Oreg., Oct. 11, 1935; d. Bernard M. and Helen (Edgerton) Bekker; student So. Oreg. Coll., 1953-55; m. William E. Brooks, Mar. 18, 1972. Bookkeeper, then office mgr. Nye Logging Co., Prospect, Oreg., 1955-58; office mgr., then sec.-treas., gen. mgr. Rogue River Valley Irrigation Dist., Medford, Oreg., 1958-70; sec.-treas., office mgr., dir. Arctic Bee Constrn., Inc., Anchorage, 1970—; sec.-treas., dir. B & R Properties, Inc., Anchorage, 1974—; partner William E. Brooks Co., Anchorage, 1970—. Hostess Miss Alaska Pageant, 1977-80. Mem. Bus. and Profl. Women's Club (v.p. Medford 1967), Air Force Assn. (life mem., treas. Anchorage chpt. 1976—), Campbell Lake Owners Assn. (treas. 1976-80), Porsche Club Am., Alaska Airman's Assn. Republican. Club: Rotary Wives (pres. 1978). Address: PO Box 6807 Anchorage AK 99502

BROOKS, LUCY ELIZABETH, blood bank technologist; b. New Castle, Pa., July 22, 1921; d. Francis Karl and Hannah Rose (Marshall) Brooks; A.B., Elmira Coll., 1943; M.T., Huntington Meml. Hosp., 1948. Lab. technologist Huntington Meml. Hosp., Pasadena, Calif., 1947-52, King County Central Blood Bank, Seattle, 1952-71; blood bank ref. lab. technologist ARC, Los Angeles and Orange County region, Santa Ana, Calif., 1971—; cons. technologist St. Mary's Hosp., London, 1964, Case Western Res. U., Cleve., 1966, Stanford U., Palo Alto, Calif., 1962. Served with WAC, 1943-46. Mem. Am. Assn. Blood Banks, Wash. Assn. Blood Banks (v.p. 1962), Am. Soc. Clin. Pathologists, Am. Soc. Med. Technologists, Calif. Blood Bank System, Calif. Assn. Med. Lab. Technologists. Republican. Presbyterian. Club: Elmira Coll. of So. Calif. Contbr. articles to profl. jours. Home: 1905 N Laird St Santa Ana CA 92706 Office: 600 Park Center Santa Ana CA 92705

BROOKS, MILA WILLIAMS, internat. devel. planning cons.; b. Topeka, May 30, 1927; d. John McConnell and Lola (Curry) Williams; A.B. in Polit. Sci., U. Kans., 1949; postgrad. U. Morelos (Mex.), 1964-66, CIDOC, Cuernavaca, Mex., 1966, Coll. Public Affairs, Am. U.,

1979-80; m. William Kenneth Brooks, Apr. 15, 1950 (div. 1961); children—Trenton McConnell, Bradford Wasson, Mila, Holly. Asso. exec. Country Club YMCA, Kansas City, Mo., 1950-61; dir. women's health club Jewish Community Center, Kansas City, 1961-64; newspaper columnist, radio talk show interviewer, dir. Centro de Salud Infantil, Cuernavaca, 1964-68; with office of vol. placement, dep. dir. Chile, U.S. Peace Corps, 1969-74; ind. cons. internat. devel. planning, Santiago, Chile, cons. Latin Am. Confedn. of YMCA, U.S. AID, Chile and Nicarague, 1974-77; cons. internatl. devel. planning, World Edn., Overseas Edn. Fund LWV, AID, Washington, 1977—; founder, owner cert. YMCA profl. program dir., recipient award for phys. fitness leadership, 1964. Mem. Soc. Internat. Devel., Am. Mgmt. Assn., Bed 'n' Breakfast Ltd., Washington, 1981—; Alpha Chi Omega. Unitarian. Home: 1307 Rhode Island Ave NW Washington DC 20005 Office: PO Box 12011 Washington DC 20005

BROOKS, (PATRICIA) SUANNE, govt. ofcl.; b. Syracuse, N.Y., Jan. 23, 1945; d. Roger Burton and Patricia Louise (Deady) B.; student U. Madrid, 1965-66; B.A., Salem Coll., 1967; M.P.A., U. Ga., 1980. Counselor, Neighborhood Youth Corps., Raleigh, N.C., 1967-68; vocat. rehab. specialist, Washington, 1968-69; spl. asst. to dir. Head Start, HEW, Washington, 1969-71, pub. affairs specialist, Atlanta, 1971-73, tech. assistance specialist, 1973-75, planning and evaluation specialist, 1975—; sr. program analyst Delivery Assessment, HHS, Atlanta, 1976-80, regional dir. Office of Refugee Resettlement, 1980—; transport rep. Hartsfield Internat. Airport Elderly and Handicapped Accessability Adv. Bd., 1977—; co-chmn. Southeastern Fed. Regional Council Task Force on Rural Transp., 1975-76; resource asso. Met. Atlanta Rapid Transit Authority, 1977—; mgmt. intern program selection com. U.S. CSC, Atlanta, 1973-75. Recipient HEW Superior Performance awards, 1969, 76. Mem. Nat. Acad. Sci., Transp. Research Bd., Am. Pub. Transp. Assn. (adv. elderly and handicapped transp. com. 1976—), New Eng. Antivivisection Soc., Animal Protection Inst. Am., Phi Kappa Phi, Pi Alpha Alpha. Republican. Presbyterian. Author: Transportation Authorities in Federal Human Services Programs, 1976; contbr. articles on pub. transp. to profl. jours. Home: 2083 Golf View Dr NW Atlanta GA 30309 Office: 101 Marietta Tower Suite 1403 Atlanta GA 30323

BROOKS, ROBIN DRAKE, social worker; b. Corpus Christi, Tex., Feb. 27, 1939; d. Alex and Paula Hybert (Conolly) Weil; B.A., Vassar Coll., 1961; M.S.W., U. Tex., Austin, 1965; m. Richard Lowell Brooks, Oct. 7, 1977; children by previous marriage—William Augustus Drake, Catherine Conolly Drake. Social worker Family Service Assocs., Houston, 1965-68, Kelsey Seybold Clinic, Houston, 1970-71, Ben Taub Hosp., Houston, 1973-74; chief social service dept. psychiatry Tex. Childrens Hosp., Houston, 1974-77; postgrad. extern in family therapy Georgetown U. Med. Sch., Washington, 1977-79; pvt. practice individual, family and group psychotherapy, Houston, 1978—; cons. Jewish Family Service, Houston, 1979-81; mem. faculty Baylor Coll. Medicine, Houston, 1973—, Houston-Galveston Family Therapy Consortium, 1978—. Mem. Houston Group Psychotherapy Assn. (dir. 1980—), Internat. Council for Advancement Pvt. Practitioners, Am. Group Psychotherapy Assn., Jr. League Houston. Episcopalian. Office: 5620 Greenbriar St Suite 100 Houston TX 77005

BROOKS, RUTH CLAUDIA HUTCHINS, educator; b. Pasadena, Md., Sept. 27, 1934; d. Francis Aldelbert and Catherine Claudia (Wigley) Hutchins; student U. Alaska, 1962-64, New Haven Coll., 1964-65, U. Bridgeport, 1965, Anne Arundel Coll., 1967-68; B.S., So. Conn. U., 1968; postgrad. Hood Coll., 1973, U. Md., 1974-75, Bowie State Coll., 1975-77; M.Ed., NEA, State Coll., 1975, Loyola Coll., 1977; Ph.D., Nova U., 1979; m. Joe Felix Brooks, Mar. 4, 1951; children—Joe Francis, Catherine Claudia. Tchr. trainable children Anne Arundel County Bd. Edn., Annapolis, Md., 1967-70, 1970-73, resource tchr. in continuum spl. edn., 1973-75; community liaison tchr. Emotionally Impaired Centers, 1975-77, pupil personnel worker, 1977—; lectr., Assn. for Retarded Children, 1966-67. Active Boy Scouts Am., 1961-63, Girl Scouts Am., 1965-67, Pioneer Girls Am., 1968-72; tchr. Sunday Sch., 1948-73. Recipient Den Mother's award, Boy Scouts Am., 1963, Certificate Appreciation Girl Scouts U.S., 1967, Pioneer Girls Am., 1972; award Outstanding Citizenship, 1975. Mem. NEA, Md. State Tchr. Assn., Council for Exceptional Children (chmn. membership 1971-72), Am. Assn. on Mental Deficiency, Tchrs. Assn. Anne Arundel County, Royal Soc. Health, Am. Assn. Spl. Educators, Internat. Platform Assn., Alpha Delta Kappa (program chmn. 1972-73, parliamentarian 1974-75), Epsilon Delta Chi. Club: Job's Daus. Home: 800 Stewart Ave Glen Burnie MD 21061 Office: Bd Edn Riva Rd Annapolis MD 21401

BROOKS, SHARON KAYE, lawyer; b. Springfield, Ill., Dec. 2, 1947; d. Robert Eugene and Shirley Mae (Kunkel) B.; B.A. in Social Scis., U. Calif., Berkeley, 1970, LL.B., 1974. Admitted to N.C. bar, 1975, D.C. bar, 1978; csl. to N.C. Commn. on Women and Human Relations Commn., 1974-77; So. field officer Democratic Nat. Com., 1977-78; assoc. chief csl. FAA, 1978-81; Coast Guard csl. to Mcht. Marine and Fisheries Com., U.S. Ho. of Reps., Washington, 1981—. Mem. Easter Seal Charity Ball Com., Washington, 1979—, N.C. ERA Com., 1974-77; exec. dir. Carter campaign in N.C., 1976; co-chair Boise (Idaho) ACLU, 1972; vol. VISTA, Boise, 1971-72, Greensboro, N.C., 1966-67. Recipient NAACP award for voter registration, 1967, award for minorities and women hiring FAA, 1981; lic. pilot. Mem. ABA, Women's Equity Action League, Phi Beta Kappa. Democrat. Author: Before and After the ERA in North Carolina, 1975; The Status of Women in North Carolina, 1975. Office: 1334 Longworth House Office Bldg Washington DC 20515

BROOKS, SUSAN WHITMORE, social worker; b. Cleve., Nov. 17, 1941; d. Robert Amsden and Betty Jane (Fast) Whitmore; A.B., Wilson Coll., 1963; M.Ed., Boston U., 1966; M.S. in Social Work, Simmons Coll., 1973; m. Benjamin Rix Brooks, May 31, 1970; children—Nathaniel Phillips, Alexander Whitmore, Joshua Cushing. Research asst. Mass. Gen. Hosp., Boston, 1963-64; tchr. presch. emotionally disturbed children James Jackson Putnam Children's Center, Roxbury, Mass., 1965-67; tchr./therapist Met. Gen. Hosp., Cleve., 1967-68; activity therapist Children's Hosp. Med. Center, Boston, 1968-71; psychiat. social worker Psychiat. Assos. of Silver Spring (Md.), 1974—; group therapist Family Life Center, Columbia, Md., 1979—; pvt. practice group therapy for children with learning disabilities, 1980—; cons. Mem. com. to study human sexuality Episcopal Diocese of Md., 1977-79; Sunday sch. tchr., mem. adv. bd. St. Peter's Ch., Ellicott City, Md., 1977—, vestry mem., 1978—. Cert. clin. social worker, Md. Mem. Nat. Assn. Social Workers, Am. Orthopsychiat. Assn., Acad. Cert. Social Workers, Wilson Coll. Club Greater Balt. Home: 9909 Ferndale Ave Columbia MD 21046 Office: Suite 604 8830 Cameron St Silver Spring MD 20910

BROOKS, YVONNE EVERETT, clin. social worker; b. Lakeland, Fla., July 18, 1945; d. Thomas and Emma Mae (Smith) Everett; B.A. (WCTU scholar), Paine Coll., 1968; M.S.W. (State of Ga. fellow), Atlanta U., 1972; 1 dau., Candice Yvette. Social work technician Central State Hosp., Milledgeville, Ga., 1968-70, chief social worker, 1972-73, sr. social worker, 1976-79, mental health-mental retardation in-patient unit dir., 1979—, social work cons. for lic. skilled nursing home, 1978-81; mental health specialist, mem. faculty Ga. Coll., Milledgeville, 1973-77; part-time therapist Oconee Alcohol Problem Center, Milledgeville, 1974-77; field instr. U. Ga. Sch. Social Work, 1972—. Pres., sec., bd. dirs. Baldwin County Students Clothes Bank Supporters, Inc.; sec.-treas. Baldwin County Democratic Adv. Com., 1973-76; troop leader Girl Scouts U.S.A., 1974-76. Mem. Nat. Assn. Social Workers (chmn. human rights issues com., exec. com. Ga. chpt.), Acad. Cert. Social Workers, Nat. Orgn. Human Service Educators, Am. Legion Aux. (1st v.p. 1974-76). Baptist. Home: 231 E Baldwin St Milledgeville GA 31061 Office: Unit 3 Extended Care Adult Psychiat Dir Central State Hosp Milledgeville GA 31062

BROOKS-GUNN, JEANNE, educator, research scientist; b. Bethesda, Md., Dec. 9, 1946; d. Richard Deyo and Mary Jean (Wood) Brooks; B.A., Conn. Coll., 1969; M.A., Harvard U., 1970; Ph.D., U. Pa., 1975; m. Robert Ward Gunn, 1970. Lectr., teaching fellow, adj. asst. prof. U. Pa., 1971-77, adj. faculty Penn Women Studies program, 1978—; asso. research scientist Inst. for Research in Human Devel., Ednl. Testing Service, Princeton, N.J., 1974-77, asso. dir. Inst. for Study of Exceptional Children, 1977—, research scientist, 1978—; research scientist pediatric service Roosevelt Hosp., N.Y.C., 1977—; asst. prof. clin. pediatric psychology Columbia U., 1978—; adj. faculty Princeton U., 1981—. Trustee, N.J. Neuropsychiat. Inst. Mem. Am. Ednl. Research Assn., Am. Psychol. Assn., Eastern Psychol. Assn., N.Y. Acad. Scis., Soc. Research in Child Devel., AAAS, Phi Delta Kappa, Phi Lambda Theta. Author: (with H. Matthews) He and She: How Children Develop Their Sex Role Identity, 1979; (with M. Lewis) Social Cognition and the Acquisition of Self, 1979; (with A. Petersen) Girls at Puberty, 1982; contbr. articles in field to profl. jours. Home: 29 E Delaware Ave Pennington NJ 08534 Office: Inst for Exceptional Children Educational Testing Service Princeton NJ 08541

BROOKSHIER, PEGGY ANN, mech. engr.; b. Idaho Falls, Idaho, Mar. 14, 1955; d. Yutaka and Miyoko (Konishi) Morishita; B.S., Calif. State U., 1977; m. Alan L. Brookshier, Nov. 18, 1978. Mech. engr., project mgr. U.S. Dept. Energy, Idaho Falls, 1977—. Mem. ASME. Office: 550 2d St Idaho Falls ID 83401

BROOME, MELODY, health agy. adminstr.; b. Calif., Nov. 22, 1947; d. Thomas and Henrietta Dunham; cert. in sickle cell counseling King-Drew Sickle Cell Center, Los Angeles, 1979; m. Edward C. Broome, Dec. 4, 1976; stepchildren—Kurtis, Tanyen, Deanna. Sec., Hughes Aircraft Co., Los Angeles, 1966-68, Control Data Corp., Los Angeles, 1968-70; office mgr. Stender & Lapides, Attys., San Francisco, 1970-73; program coordinator Sickle Cell Anemia Research and Edn., Inc., Oakland, Calif., 1973—; mem. community adv. bd. No. Calif. Comprehensive Sickle Cell Center, 1978—; coordinator Oakland Concours d'Elegance, 1979—. Budget panelist United Way Bay Area, 1979—, mem. speakers bur., 1977; mem. San Francisco High Blood Pressure Coordinating Council, 1976-78; Alameda County coordinator Maureen Reagan for U.S. Senate, 1982. Recipient King Football Conf. award, 1967; Outstanding Service award Oakland Public Schs., 1978. Republican. Mem. Christian Ch. Co-editor: Sickle Cell Patient-Perceived Needs Assessment, 1980. Office: 330 41st St Oakland CA 94609

BROOME, OLIVIA COE, horticulturist; b. Winston-Salem, N.C., July 13, 1941; d. Donald Bain and Rachel Helen (Rufty) (dec.) Coe; B.S., U. Ga., 1971; m. Frederick Roland Broome, Mar. 15, 1961; children—Fred, Jr., Rowena. Cons., U. Md. Co-op Extension Service, Annapolis, 1972; horticulturist Fruit Lab., U.S. Dept. Agr., Beltsville, Md., 1972—. Mem. Am. Soc. Hort. Sci., Tissue Culture Assn., Internat. Soc. Hort. Sci., Internat. Photography Soc. Contbr. articles to various publs. Home: 12605 Whiteholm Dr Upper Marlboro MD 20772 Office: US Dept Agriculture Room 118 Bldg 004 Beltsville MD 20705

BROSE, PHYLLIS MARIE, nurse; b. Stewartsville, Pa., Sept. 20, 1925; d. George Allan and Roberta Fern (Lintner) Magill; R.N., Columbia Hosp. Sch. Nursing, Wilkinsburg, Pa., 1946; cert. Sch. Anesthesia St. Francis Hosp., Pitts., 1948; m. Merle LaVerne Brose, Jan. 10, 1948; children—Linda Brose Kleinsteiber, Cheryl Brose Kleinheinz, Pamela Brose Zembal, Sandra Brose Jackson, William. Nurse, Columbia Hosp., 1946-47, anesthetist, 1948, staff nurse, 1949-50; nursing supr., coordinator dialysis U. Wis. Hosp., Madison, 1966—. Mem. med. and sci. bd. Kidney Found. Wis., 1970—, exec. bd. S. Central chpt., 1981; mem. planning com. Nat. Center Health Care Tech., 1980-81; mem. Network 13 Coordinating Council End-Stage Renal Disease, Inc. Recipient Exceptional Performance award in nursing U. Wis., 1977. Mem. Am. Assn. Nephrology Nurses and Technicians (pres. Wis. chpt. 1978-79). Club: Four Lakes Yacht. Home: 4517 Gregg Rd Madison WI 53705 Office: 600 Highland Ave Madison WI 53706

BROSIOUS, EFFIE MALOUF, med. research technologist; b. Niagara Falls, N.Y., Nov. 13, 1943; d. Jubert George and Samantha Elizabeth (Gunzelmann) Malouf; B.A., Fla. State U., 1965; M.A., Central Mich. U., 1975; m. John Walter Brosious, June 11, 1965; children—Melodie Darleen, John Matthew. Med. technologist Center for Disease Control, Atlanta, 1966-68, microbiologist, 1968-72, adminstrv. research technologist, 1972-78; asso. dir. Internat. Health Resource Center, Lihue, Hawaii, 1978-80; lab. supr. Joan Glancy Meml. Hosp., Duluth, Ga., 1980—. Mem. Am. Public Health Assn., Am. Soc. Med. Tech., N.Y. Acad. Scis., Nat. Assn. Exec. Women, Sigma Xi. Clubs: Zonta Internat. Author lab. manuals. Office: Joan Glancy Meml Hosp Duluth GA 30136

BROSNAN, CAROL RAPHAEL SARAH, musician, arts reports specialist; b. Paterson, N.J., July 19, 1931; d. Basil Roger Warnock and Mary Ellen Carroll (McDonald) Brosnan; student Montclair State Tchrs. Coll., 1948-49, George Washington U., Washington, 1956-61, U. Va., 1975, U. Oxford (Eng.), 1975, U. Calif., Berkeley, 1975; B.A., George Washington U., 1981; pupil Iris Brussels, Helen Yakobson. Adminstrv. clk. depts. Army and Def., Pentagon, Office Asst. Chief Staff Intelligence, Washington, 1955-58; clk. fgn. sci. info. program NSF, Washington, 1958-60, adminstrv. clk., 1960-65, adminstrv. fellowship clk. grad. fellowship program, 1965-72; reports specialist Nat. Endowment for Arts, Washington, 1972—; tchr. piano, Paterson, N.J., 1945-53; piano recitalist U.S., Heidelberg, W. Ger. Served with WAC, 1953-55. Recipient Young People's Concerts award, 1945. Hon. fellow Harry S. Truman Library Inst. Nat. and Internat. Affairs, 1975. Fellow Internat. Biog. Assn.; mem. Am. Assn. Advancement Slavic Studies, Am. Hist. Assn., Am. Philol. Assn., Acad. Polit. Sci. (contbg.), Am. Classical League, Phi Alpha Theta. Home: 4201 Massachusetts Ave NW Apt 3030C Washington DC 20016 Office: Nat Endowment for Arts Nat Found on Arts and Humanities 2401 E St NW Washington DC 20506

BROSOFF, ROSALYN JUDITH, broadcasting co. sales mgr.; b. Bronx, N.Y., Feb. 3, 1946; d. Louis and Esther (Zucker) B.; ed. Hunter Coll. Acctg. clk. Columbia Pictures Industries, N.Y.C., 1963-68, sr. acct., 1968-78, mgr. accounts receivable TV, 1978-80; mgr. fin. controls ABC-TV Spot Sales, N.Y.C., 1980—. Mem. Broadcasting Fin. Mgmt. Assn., Internat. Radio and TV Soc. Clubs: Tennis, N.Y. Health and Racquet. Office: 1345 Ave of Americas New York NY 10019

BROSSEAU, IRMA FINN, assn. exec.; b. Boston, Sept. 4, 1930; d. Harry and Alfreda (Zimmerman) Miller; B.S., Simmons Coll., 1952; m. George Brosseau, Jan. 14, 1978; children by previous marriage—Hester, Jonathan, Sarah. Asst. to prodn. mgr. Houghton Mifflin Pub. Co., Boston, 1952-56; desk editor, women's editor Quincy (Mass.) Patriot Ledger, 1956-58; desk editor, reporter, feature writer, women's editor Anchorage Times, 1958-60, 66-71; desk editor Anchorage News, 1965-66; program dir. Nat. Fedn. Bus. and Profl. Women's Clubs, Washington, 1972-78, exec. dir., 1978—. Mem. rev. panel Women's Ednl. Equity Act grants HEW; mem. scholarship rev. panel Girl's Clubs of Am.; mem. bd. advisors Ten Outstanding Young Women of Am.; bd. dirs. Nat. Motorcycle Commuter Assn.; mem. nat. steering com. Nat. Women's Agenda; speaker, panelist on women's issues. Mem. Am. Soc. Assn. Execs., Washington Soc. Assn. Execs., AAUW, ACLU, Va. Citizens Consumer Council, Women's Ednl. Action League, Potomac Bus. and Profl. Women's Club. Democrat. Office: Nat Fedn Bus and Profl Women's Clubs 2012 Massachusetts Ave NW Washington DC 20036

BROTHERS, BRENDA ALICE, govt. ofcl.; b. Massena, N.Y., Feb. 2, 1950; d. William James and Beverly Alice (Durant) Michaud; student public schs., Massena; m. Leslie Edward Brothers, Dec. 7, 1968; children—Timothy, Thomas. Telephone operator St. Lawrence Seaway Devel. Corp., Massena, 1971-74, clk.-steno, 1974-75, motor vehicle operator, 1975; air traffic control specialist FAA, Massena, 1976—. Served with USAF, 1968-69. Home: Star Route Massena NY 13662 Office: Federal Aviation Administration Route 2 Massena NY 13662

BROTHERS, JOYCE DIANE BAUER (MRS. MILTON BROTHERS), psychologist; b. N.Y.C.; d. Morris K. and Estelle (Rapoport) Bauer; B.S., Cornell U., 1947; M.A., Columbia U., 1949, Ph.D., 1953; L.H.D. (hon.), Franklin Pierce Coll., 1969; m. Milton Brothers, July 4, 1949; 1 dau., Lisa Robin. Mem. faculty Hunter Coll., 1948-53, Columbia U., 1948-53; research fellow UNESCO, 1949-50; host TV program Dr. Joyce Brothers, Sta. WNBC, 1958-63, Consult Dr. Brothers syndicated by ABC, 1961-66, Tell Me, Dr. Brothers syndicated by Triangle Films, 1964-70; syndicated on TV by Gen. Foods Co., Kohner Bros., 1972-77; Living Easy with Dr. Joyce Brothers syndicated by Trevira, 1972-75; radio program ABC, 1963-68; program Call Dr. Brothers, WNBC Radio, 1966-69, WMCA, 1969-71, NBC Radio Emphasis, 1966-75, NBC Monitor, 1966-75, NBC Radio Network Newsline, 1975—; newspaper column N.Am. Newspaper Alliance, 1961-72; columnist Good Housekeeping mag., 1964—, King Features Syndicate, 1972—; Cable News network corr., 1980—; cons. Magee Carpet Co., Sperry and Hutchins Co., ABC Films, Greyhound Corp., Hoechst Fibers, Inc., Armstrong-Cork Co., Reading Devel. Center. Recipient wisdom award of honor, 1965; named Woman of Achievement, Fedn. Jewish Women's Orgn., 1964; Justice Lodge citation for unselfish devotion and inspired leadership and service to community, 1963; named Profl. Woman of Yr. dist. 1 Bus. and Profl. Womens Clubs, 1968; Merit award Bar-Ilan U., Ramat, Israel, 1968, award Parkinson Disease Found., 1971, Deadline award for excellence in broadcasting radio news Sigma Delta Chi, 1971. Mem. Sigma Xi. Author: Ten Days to a Successful Memory, 1960; Woman, 1962; The Brothers System for Liberated Love and Marriage, 1972; Better Than Ever, 1976; How to Get Whatever You Want Out of Life, 1979; What Every Woman Should Know About Men. Office: NBC 30 Rockefeller Plaza New York NY 10020

BROTHERTON, NAOMI, artist; b. Galveston, Tex., Apr. 8, 1920; d. Hunter Smith and Vernon (Smart) Macon; B.A., Baylor U., 1941; m. Lem Brotherton, Nov. 20, 1941; children—Betty Brotherton Crudden, Robert James. Tchr. watercolor painting various workshops, 1962—; partner Artisan's Studio-Gallery, Dallas; 38 one woman shows since 1955, including: Oak Cliff Soc. Fine Arts, Dallas, 1961, Western N.Mex. U., Silver City, 1967, Baylor U., 1967, S. Ark. Art Center, El Dorado, 1969, Irving (Tex.) Art Center, 1972, Artisans Studio-Gallery, Dallas, 1981; group shows include: Panhandle Plains Hist. Mus., Canyon, Tex., 1968, Laguna Gloria Gallery of Tex. Fine Arts Assn., Austin, 1969, Barnwell Art Center, Shreveport, La., 1974, Galleria de Arte de Saltillo (Mex.), 1978, Artisans Studio-Gallery, Dallas, 1981, 82, Dallas Public Library, 1980; award-winning group shows include: Tex. Watercolor Soc., 1954, 66, 81, Tex. Fine Arts Assn., Dallas, 1963, 65, 67, 69, 70, 73, 74, Tex. Fine Arts Assn. State-wide, Austin, 1965, 67, 70, 73, 74, Southwestern Watercolor Soc., Dallas, 1964, 66, 67, 68, 69, 71, 72, 79, Gulf Coast Art Exhbn., Mobile, Ala., 1970, numerous others; represented in permanent collections: Baylor U., Ft. Worth Public Schs., S. Ark. Art Center, Brownsville (Tex.) Art Center, Pecos (Tex.) Art Center. Mem. Tex. Watercolor Assn., Southwestern Watercolor Soc., Tex. Fine Arts Assn., Artists and Craftsmen Assn. Dallas, Coppini Art Assn. of San Antonio, Beta Sigma Phi. Episcopalian. Author: Variations in Watercolor, 1981. Home: 4808 Oak Trail Dallas TX 75232 Office: Artisan's Studio Gallery 228 Walnut Hill Village Dallas TX 75220

BROTMAN, ARLENE SANDRA, social worker; b. N.Y.C., June 7, 1948; d. Sam and Sylvia Brotman; B.A. magna cum laude (NDEA fellow), SUNY, Albany, 1970; M.A., U. Pa., 1971; M.S.W., Adelphi U., 1977. Dir., Young Travelers Day Camp Plainview, Levittown, N.Y., 1971-72; social work asst. Big Bros./Big Sisters of Suffolk County, Catholic Charities, Diocese of Rockville Centre (N.Y.), 1973-76; social work asst. Westbury (N.Y.) Community Life Center, 1976-77; sch. social worker Oceanside (N.Y.) Public Schs., 1977—; psychotherapist Rockville Cons. Center, Rockville Centre, 1980—. Cert. social worker, N.Y. Mem. Acad. Cert. Social Workers, Nat. Assn. Social Workers, N.Y. Assn. Sch. Social Workers, Adelphi U. Alumni Assn. (dir.-at-large), Adelphi U. Sch. Social Work Alumni Assn. (exec. mem.), Signum Laudis, Nat. Slavic Honor Soc., Mu Lambda Alpha. Home: 55 Windsor Ave Apt 212 E Rockville Centre NY 11570 Office: Oceanside Schs Merle Ave Oceanside NY 11572

BROUDE, JOSEPHINE RACHEL, univ. exec.; b. N.Y.C., May 25, 1927; d. Emanuel and Eva (Lieberson) Rosen; A.B., Antioch Coll., 1949; m. Henry W. Broude, June 29, 1947. With Shepley, Bulfinch, Richardson & Abbott, Boston, 1950-54; interior designer, adminstrv. asst. Douglas Orr, AIA, New Haven, 1954-65; exec. asst. to provost, cons. for interior planning Yale U., New Haven, 1965—. Bd. govs. Mory's Assn., 1974—. Guest editor Mademoiselle mag., 1948. Office: Provost's Office Yale U New Haven CT 06520

BROUILLETTE, BARBARA JEAN, bank mktg. exec.; b. Derby, Conn., Mar. 26, 1945; d. Theodore and Josephine (Tramontano) Osiecki; student So. Conn. State Coll., 1975-79; grad. U. Colo. Sch. Bank Mktg., 1980; m. Robert Brouillette, Jan. 30, 1976; children—Kevin, Jolynn. Advt. mgr. Colonial Bank, Waterbury, Conn., 1975-77; v.p. mktg. Savs. Bank Ansonia (Conn.), 1977-79; v.p. mktg. Banking Center, Waterbury, Conn., 1979—; adv. Waterbury Area Schs. Distributive Edn. Program, 1981. Chmn. public relations Valley United Way, Ansonia, 1980; bd. dirs. Waterbury chpt. ARC, 1981; bd. dirs. Conn. Trails Council of Girl Scouts; corporator Hewett Meml. Hosp., Shelton, Conn., 1982. Mem. New Eng. Bank Mktg. Assn. (dir.), Nat. Bank Mktg. Assn. (adv. council 1981), Savs. Instns. Mktg. Soc. Am., Sales and Mktg. Execs. Western Conn. (dir. 1981), Hartford Ad Club, Nat. Assn. Bank Women, Savs. Bank Women Conn., New Haven Ad Club. Office: 60 N Main St Waterbury CT 06702

BROUSSARD, NORMAJ, artist, journalist, businesswoman; b. Lake Providence, La., Aug. 28, 1931; d. C. Thomas and Hazel Valli (Ainsworth) Edwards; student Stephen F. Austin State Coll., 1951-52, U. Tex., 1973—; mem. Internat. Workshop Danish Sch. Design, Copenhagen, 1973; m. Lee R. Broussard, Dec. 31, 1958; 1 dau., Cherie Antoinette; children from previous marriage—Bonnie Greening (Mrs. Allen P. Bennett), Billy E. Greening. Owner, The Chateau, Port Arthur, Tex., 1968—, Broussard's Mobile Villages, Port Arthur, 1960—, Studio Normaj, 1972—; journalist column Art Happenings, Port Arthur News, 1971-76; owner Normaj Broussard Assos., pub. relations, 1977—; pres., owner Travel Magic Corp.; organizer, sponsor Gulf Coast Arts and Crafts Festival, 1970, Jefferson County (Tex.) Arts and Crafts

Festival, 1972, Diamond Jubilee Fine Arts Show, 1973; tchr., lectr. in field. Founder, Tex. Artists Mus. Soc., 1972, pres., 1973-74; mem. com. Tex. Constl. Rev. Commn., 1973—; mem. Bicentennial Commn. Port Arthur; pres. Port Arthur chpt. Am. Cancer Soc., 1979; sec.-treas. Port Arthur Ministerial Alliance. Recipient numerous awards local and state art competitions including La. Art and Folk Festival, 1970-73, Sabine Area Art Show, 1972. Mem. Port Arthur Art Assn. Fine Arts Guild (pres. 1971), Diocesan Council Cath. Women (pres. 1965), Noon Bus. and Profl. Women's Club, Internat. Platform Assn., Tex. Fedn. Women's Clubs, Credit Mgmt. Assn. (pres. 1980), Tex. Poetry South and Major Poets Club, S.E. Area Arts Council (treas.), Port Arthur C. of C., Zeta Phi Delphians (pres. 1967), Beta Sigma Phi. Roman Catholic (pres. altar soc. 1965, 66). Club: Heritage Antique Study (pres. 1973-74). Address: 101 Dryden Pl Port Arthur TX 77640

BROWER, ANN M., newspaper exec.; b. Stowe, Pa., Nov. 26, 1924; d. Ralph J. and Mary A. (St. Cross) Capaldi; student Pottstown Sch. Bus., 1942-43; m. Francis T. Brower, Oct. 22, 1949; children—Patricia A., Karen L., Richard A. Bookkeeper, sec. Levin's Dept. Store, 1943-48; payroll clk., bookkeeper Pottstown (Pa.) Mercury, 1948-52, 66-73, office mgr., 1974-79, comptroller, 1979—; teller 1st Fed. Savs. and Loan, 1952-53. Active fundraiser Cub Scouts Am., Boy Scouts Am., 1969-79. Mem. Nat. Assn. Female Execs., North Coventry Fire Co. Aux. Office: 24 N Hanover St Pottstown PA 19464

BROWER, MARGARET MERCEDES, real estate exec., state ofcl.; b. Sault Ste. Marie, Mich.; d. Robert F. and Helen L. (Houlihan) Wagner; B.A., U. Chgo.; postgrad. Nat. Coll. Physiotherapy, 1931-33; diploma Edison Tech. U., 1948; postgrad. U. Wash., 1969, Portland State U., 1973; 1 son, Scott Gerald. Salesperson Ewing & Clark Realty, Seattle, 1950-51; sales mgr. Junction Realty, Seattle, 1951-53; salesperson McQuaid & Pickart Realty, Seattle, 1953-56; asso. broker, appraiser Admiral Realty, Seattle, 1956-81; real estate commr. State of Wash., Olympia, 1978—; lectr. in field. Real Estate Salesman of the Yr. award, City of Seattle, 1958; Woman of the Yr., Wash. State Women's Council, 1979; Award for outstanding service to handicapped children, Variety Clubs of Am., 1979; Citizen of the Yr., W. Seattle Bus. and Profl. Women's Club, 1980; Award of Merit, Seattle-King County Bd. Realtors, 1980. Mem. Wash. Assn. Realtors (dir.), Women's Council of Realtors, King County Bd. Realtors, (dir.), W. Seattle C. of C. (dir.), Nat. Assn. Women's Councils, Nat. Assn. Real Estate Appraisers, Am. Inst. Real Estate Appraisers, W. Seattle Bus. and Profl. Women's, V.F.W., Delphian Soc., Omega Tau Rho. Democrat. Roman Catholic. Clubs: Variety, Swedish, Washington Athletic, Glen Acres Golf, 34th Dist. Dem., Children's Orthopedic Hosp. Guild, Alki Community. Contbr. articles to profl. jours.; author: How You Can Go From Broke to Broker in Real Estate, 1981. Home: 2510 Alki Ave SW Seattle WA 98116 Office: 3222 California Ave SW Seattle WA 98116

BROWN, ADA KATHERINE, state legislator; b. South Windham, Maine, Jan. 2, 1927; d. Carl and Carrie (Grass) Magnusson; student Golden Sch. Beauty Culture; m. Willis James Brown, 1950; children—Kathryn Brown Deering, Brian. Owner, mgr. Ada's Beauty Shop, South Windham, Maine, 1949—; mem. Maine Ho. of Reps., 1979—. Mem. Nat. Hairdressers Assn., Maine Cosmotology Assn. Baptist. Office: Main Ho of Reps State Capitol Augusta ME 04330 *

BROWN, ALBERTA MAE, respiratory therapy nurse; b. Columbus, Ohio, Nov. 11, 1932; d. Sylvester Clarence and Malinda (Mason) Angel; grad. Antelope Valley Coll., 1961; A.A., Los Angeles Valley Coll., 1975; B.S., Calif. State U., Dominguez Hills, 1981; m. Norman Brown, Dec. 29, 1967; children—Charon, Stevan, Carole. Nurses aid, vocat. nurse, respiratory therapist St. Bernardines Hosp., 1965-69, Good Samaritan Hosp., Los Angeles, 1969-70, Midway Hosp., Los Angeles, 1973-81; allergy nurse, instr. respiratory therapy VA Hosp., Los Angeles, 1970—, also acting dept. head; instr. Los Angeles Valley Med. Technologists Sch., Compton Coll. seminar instr., 1979. Active Arrowhead Allied Arts Council of San Bernardino; CPR instr. Am. Heart Assn. Lic. vocat. nurse; R.N. Mem. Am. Assn. Respiratory Therapy, Nat. Honor Soc. Democrat. Baptist. Clubs: Social-Lites, Inc. of San Bernardino, Order Eastern Star. Patentee disposable/replacable tubing for stethoscope. also 1545 N Hancock St Orangewood Estates San Bernardino CA 92411 Office: VA Hospital Wilshire and Sawtelle Blvd Los Angeles CA 90073

BROWN, ANN CARLSON, psychiatrist; b. Lorain, Ohio, June 19, 1930; d. Benjamin and Edna (Dellinger) Carlson; B.S., Otterbein Coll., Westerville, Ohio, 1948; M.D., Case-Western Res. U., 1956; children—Catherine, Elizabeth, Robert, Andrew. Intern, St. Luke's Hosp., Cleve., 1956-57, resident in pediatrics, 1957-58; resident in psychiatry Hall Inst., Columbia, S.C., 1976-80; practice medicine specializing in psychiatry, Charlotte, N.C., 1980—. Recipient Ohio Gov.'s award for community action, 1974, Service to Mankind award Sertoma, Zanesville, Ohio, 1976. Office: 1900 Randolph Rd Charlotte NC 28207

BROWN, ANN NICHOLS, genealogist; b. N.Y.C., Jan. 22, 1942; d. Winfred Joslin and Lillian Russell (Mason) Nichols; student Western Coll. for Women, 1959-60; A.A., Endicott Jr. Coll., 1963; m. Jesse Brown, Jr., Nov. 30, 1963. Genealogist, DAR, Washington, 1975—. Mem. Bowie (Md.) Bicentennial Com., 1974-77. Mem. DAR (nat. vice chmn. geneal. records com. 1978-82, chmn. geneal. records com. Md. 1976-79, outstanding jr. mem. Eastern div. 1978), Prince George's County (Md.) Geneal. Soc., N.H., Hist. Soc., N.H. Old Graveyard Assn., Lyndeborough (N.H.) Hist. Soc. Episcopalian. Editor: History of Bowie, 1976; co-author: New Hampshire Genealogical Research Guide, 1982. Home: 3719 Irongate Ln Bowie MD 20715

BROWN, ANNA CAROLINE BAKER, educator; b. Lethbridge, Alta., Can., July 24, 1921; d. Alva Abraham and Lona (Eastman) Baker; B.A., U. Mont., 1943; M.A., U. Mich., 1948, Ph.D., 1963; m. Donald Frederick MacKenzie Brown, Oct. 16, 1945. Tchr., McGuffey (Ohio) High Sch., 1943-44; county extension agent home econs. Mich. State U. Coop. Extension Service, Washtenaw County, 1948-60; research asso. Dept. community and adult edn. U. Mich., 1964, research asso. Sch. Public Health, 1965-68, asst. dir. Community Health Services Study, 1968, research asso., lectr., Sch. Public Health, 1969-70, asst. prof. public health adminstrn., 1970-74, lectr., 1974—, dir. continuing edn. and alumni relations, 1974—. Served with U.S. Navy, 1944-46. Charles Pfizer Co., Inc. fellow, 1959. Mem. Mich. Public Health Assn. (1st v.p. 1981-82, 2d v.p. 1977-79), Am. Public Health Assn., Adult Edn. Assn. USA, Adult Edn. Assn. Mich., Phi Delta Kappa, Epsilon Sigma Phi. Office: University of Michigan School of Public Health 109 S Observatory Ann Arbor MI 48109

BROWN, ARLENE PATRICIA THERESA, artist; b. Elizabeth, N.J., Jan. 3, 1953; d. William J. and Adelaide Elizabeth (Von Krasa) B.; student Union Coll., 1971; B.A., Kean Coll., 1980. Owner, pres. Reni Co., Roselle, N.J., 1979—; pvt. tchr. art, Roselle, 1979—. Mem. Am. Women's Econ. Devel. Assn., 1979-83. Recipient 3d Place award Custom Car and Van Show, Meadowlands, N.J., 1981, 2d place award Custom Car and Van Show, Asbury Park, N.J., 19 . Mem. Graphic Artists Guild, Artists' Equity Assn., Somerset Art Assn., Summit Art Assn., Artist's Touring Assn., Alumni Assn. Kean Coll. Club: Morris County Ski. Patentee in field. Mailing Address: PO Box 186 Roselle Park NJ 07204

BROWN, BARBARA JURIST, chemist; b. Burbank, Calif., Oct. 3, 1954; d. John Michael and Belle Jane (Logan) Jurist; B.S. in Chemistry cum laude and with chemistry departmental honors, UCLA, 1975; m. Robert Edward Brown Apr. 8, 1978. Research chemist biochemistry research group Research and Devel. Labs., Carnation Co., Van Nuys, Calif., 1975—. Mem. Am. Chem. Soc., Inst. Food Technologists. Office: 8015 Van Nuys Blvd Van Nuys CA 91412

BROWN, BARBARA MAXINE, lawyer; b. St. John, Kans., June 29, 1936; d. Charles Robert and Oneida M. (Dawson) Garvin; student Phillips U., Enid, Okla., 1954-56; B.S. in Acctg. cum laude, U. Cin., 1976; J.D., No. Ky. U., 1980; m. Benjamin S. Brown, Apr. 21, 1955 (div. Jan. 1970); children—Candace M., Cynthia A. Acct., Cinderella Cleaners, Forest Park, Ohio, 1970-71; office mgr. High Voltage Systems, Inc., Sharonville, Ohio, 1971-73, Kanter Corp., Forest Park, 1974-75; mgr. corp. acctg. Silco, Inc., Norwood, Ohio, 1976-78; pension account exec. Union Centra Life Ins. Co., Forest Park, 1978-81; admitted to Ohio bar, 1980; individual practice law, Cin., 1980—; mem. part-time faculty U. Cin., Mt. St. Joseph Coll., Mt. St. Joe, Ohio. C.P.A., Ohio. Fellow Life Mgmt. Inst.; mem. Am. Bar Assn., Ohio Bar Assn., Cin. Bar Assn., Ohio Soc. C.P.A.s, Delta Mu Delta. Mem. Christian Ch. (Disciples of Christ). Home: 692 Fairborn Rd Cincinnati OH 45240 Office: 230 Northland Blvd Suite 237 Cincinnati OH 45246

BROWN, BARBARA STEIN, environ. scientist; b. Newark, Aug. 5, 1951; d. Louis and Louise (Mumper) Stein; student Am. U., 1969-71; B.S. in Biology, U. Miami, 1976, postgrad.; s. Ralph David Brown, Sept. 9, 1978. Sr. asso. scientist Environ. Sci. and Engring., Inc., Miami, 1978—. Mem. Ecol. Soc. Am., Am. Inst. Biol. Scis., Assn. Women in Environ. Professions. Office: 7600 SW Red Rd Suite 128 Miami FL 33143

BROWN, BEATRICE, symphony condr.; b. Leeds, Eng., May 17, 1917; came to U.S., 1921, naturalized, 1927; d. Abraham and Sarah (Levinson) B.; B.A., Hunter Coll., 1937; M.A., N.Y.U., 1939; Berkshire Music Center scholar, 1948-49; m. Morris Rothenberg, Jan. 29, 1961. Condr., Chamber Music Assocs., N.Y.C., 1950-53; music dir., condr. Scranton (Pa.) Philharm. Orch., 1963-72, Ridgefield (Conn.) Orch., 1969—, Western Conn. Symphony Orch., Danbury, 1981—, Housatonic Chamber Orch., 1982—; condr. N.Y., N.J., Conn. opera cos.; TV appearances; lectr.; violist symphony orchs., 1944—, Chamber Music Group, Musique Vivante, Am. Symphony Orch., Latvian Choir Orch., 1979—; instr. music Hunter Coll., 1937-43; tchr. music N.Y.C. Pub. Schs., 1944-61; adj. asst. prof. Lehman Coll., 1972-74; tchr. music Bronx High Sch. Sci., N.Y.C., 1970-79. Recipient Fulbright grant in conducting, 1953-55, Martha Baird Rockefeller grant in conducting, 1957-59, Peace award UN, 1980, Wellington award, 1981; named to Hunter Coll. Hall of Fame, 1972; named One of 100 Disting. Women in Conn., 1976, One of 5 outstanding Women in Ridgefield, Conn., 1979. Mem. Am. Symphony Orch. League, Condrs. Guild, Phi Beta Kappa.

BROWN, BETTE DAWN, nurse; b. St. John, N.B., Can., Mar. 8, 1933; d. George Bertrand and Greta Mae (McCurdy) Patterson; grad. Central Maine Gen. Hosp. Sch. Nursing, Lewiston, 1954; B. Nursing, McGill U., 1965, diploma/cert. teaching and supervision, 1959; m. Glendon E. Brown, Apr. 22, 1967 (dec.). With Province of N.B. Provincial Hosp. (name now Centracare, Inc.), St. John, 1955—, coordinator inservice edn., 1965-69, dir. ednl. programs, 1969-78, infection control officer, 1978—. Murial Archibald Nursing scholar, 1964-65. Mem. N.B. Assn. Region Nurses, Can. Hosp. Infection Control Assn., N.B. Infection Control Practitioner Group, Can. Mental Health Assn., Can. Nurses Assn., Internat. Council Nursing, Edgehill Old Girls Assn., McGill U. Grad. Soc. Mem. Woman's Baptist Soc. Atlantic Province of Canada. Home: 561 Lancaster Ave Saint John NB E2M 2L9 Canada Office: PO Box 3220 Postal Sta B Centracare Saint John NB Canada

BROWN, BETTY ANN, counselor; b. What Cheer, Iowa; d. William F. and Anna (Kelley) Tinsley; B.A., Iowa Wesleyan Coll., 1943; M.A., Ill. State U., 1971, postgrad., 1971—; m. Forrest Edwin "Dick" Brown, Nov. 19, 1943; children—Joanne Kelley, Thomas Edwin, Kenneth Scott (dec.), Richard Scott (dec.). Placement counselor Ill. State U. Placement Service, Normal, 1966-67; employment interviewer Ill. State Employment Service, 1967-68; fin. aid adv. Ill. State U., Normal, 1968—. Bd. dirs. Family Services of McLean County, 1979—; mem. Ill. N.G. Scholarship Bd., 1979—. Mem. Midwest Assn. Student Employment Adminstrs. (service award 1980), Am. Personnel and Guidance Assn., Nat. Vocat. Guidance Assn., Ill. Guidance and Personnel Assn., Am. Coll. Personnel Assn., Nat. Assn. Women Deans, Adminstrs. and Counselors, Nat. Assn. Work and the Coll. Student, Ill. Assn. Fin. Aid Adminstrs., Ill. State Univ. Adminstrs. Club, Kappa Delta Pi (pres. Mu chpt. 1979-81). Presbyterian. Club: Altrusa (chpt. pres. 1979). Home: 1907 Owens Dr Bloomington IL 61701 Office: Hovey 211 Ill State Univ Normal IL 61761

BROWN, BETTY JEAN, oil co. exec.; b. Chgo., Sept. 20, 1946; d. Richard David and Helen (Cicero) Baikie; student U. Okla., 1964-65, Central State U., Edmond, Okla., 1965-67; m. William George Brown III, Mar. 9, 1968; children—Bryan Joseph, David Wayne. Supr. Natural Gas Policy Act analysis Cities Service Gas Co., 1973-80; mgr. contracts adminstrn. Rambler Oil Co., 1980-81, Artesian Oil & Gas Corp., Oklahoma City, 1981—, also corp. asst. sec. Mem. Nat. Assn. Div. Order Analysts, Oklahoma City Bd. Realtors, Alpha Chi. Episcopalian. Home: 11120 Ashford Dr Yukon OK 73099 Office: 770 NE 63d St Oklahoma City OK 73105

BROWN, BILLIE AUGUSTINE, pub. sch. tchr.; b. Pangburn, Ark., Aug. 1, 1924; d. Prince Colombus and Icy May Wood; B.S. in Edn., Harding Coll., Searcy, Ark., 1962, M.S., 1966; M.A. in Guidance and Counseling, U. Central Ark., 1974; m. James A. Brown, Nov. 26, 1969; children by previous marriage—Terry Wood, Dawn Elizabeth, Benjamin McLove, Laura Delphine. Librarian, White County, Ark. 1947-52; U.S. postal clk., 1954; pub. sch. tchr., 1959—; art specialist Pulaski County (Ark.) Spl. Sch. Dist., 1978-79, instructional coordinator art, 1979—; co-founder, bd. advisers Ark. Young Artists Assn. Democratic committeewoman, 1978-82. Recipient 1st pl. award in pastel White County Art Show, 1957, 1st pl. in illus. poetry Ark. Festival Arts, 1973. Mem. Nat. Art Edn. Assn., Ark. Art Educators, Mid-So. Watercolorists, Ark. for Arts, Pulaski Assn. Classroom Tchrs., AAUW, Delta Kappa Gamma. Democrat. Baptist. Home: 5302 Dreher Ln Little Rock AR 72209 Office: 1500 Dixon Rd Little Rock AR 72216

BROWN, BONITA STARLIPER, nursing home adminstr.; b. Winchester, Va., May 26, 1942; d. Howard P. and Margaret E. Starliper; R.N., Winchester Meml. Hosp., 1963; postgrad. Lord Fairfax Community Coll., Middletown, Va.; m. Richard F. Brown, Mar. 10, 1962; children—Elizabeth, Christopher. Office nurse, 1963-66; mem. staff Shawnee Springs Nursing Home, Winchester, 1973—, orientation coordinator, shift supr., 1978-81, dir. nursing, asst. adminstr., 1978—; mem. nursing craft adv. com. health occupations Dowell J. Howard Vocat. Sch., Winchester, 1977-79; adj. faculty nursing program Shenandoah Coll., 1980-82; adv. craft com. James Rumsey nursing asst. program Martinsburg (W.Va.) Vocat. Sch., 1978-81; mem. edn. and tng. com. Va. Health Care Assn., 1980-81; employee adv. com. Va. Employment Commn., 1980-82. Mem. Nat. League Nursing, Am. Coll. Nursing Home Adminstrs., Winchester-Frederick County C. of C., Winchester Women's Civic League. Baptist. Address: Route 1 Box 181 Stephenson VA 22656

BROWN, BRENDA LEE LAWSON, univ. adminstr.; b. Louisville, Sept. 3, 1938; d. LaMont Harris and Charlotte Jeannette (Hughes) Lawson; B.A., Howard U., 1960; postgrad. U. Md., 1960, D.C. Tchrs. Coll., 1960-63; m. John Scott Brown, June 17, 1961; children—Courtney Hughes, Leigh Melle. Speech therapist, tchr. D.C. pub. schs., 1960-64; program asst. Community Relations Service, U.S. Dept. Justice, 1964-66, program devel. officer, 1970-71; dir. alumni affairs Howard U., Washington, 1967—; vis. lectr. D.C. Tchrs. Coll., 1962-64. Bd. dirs. Regional NCCJ, 1969-79, Met. YWCA, 1970-71. Mem. Am. Coll. Pub. Relations Assn., Nat. Soc. Fund Raisers, Nat. Soc. Fund Raising Execs., Council for Advancement and Support to Edn., Washington Urban League (dir. 1970-73). Alumni editor Howard U. mag., 1966-68. Home: 4225 17th St NW Washington DC 20011 Office: 2900 Van Ness St NW Washington DC 20008

BROWN, CAROL ANNE, mfrs. rep.; b. Detroit, Feb. 26, 1947; d. Bruno Walter and Irene Sabina (Derengowski) Siedlarz; student Los Angeles City Coll., 1971, DeAnza Community Coll., 1973; m. Leonard Brown, Apr. 24, 1976; 1 son, David. Sec., Fairchild Semicondrs., Detroit, 1965-69, inside sales rep., Mountain View, Calif., 1969-74; sales rep. Calif. Circuit Engring., Sunnyvale, 1974-76; owner, operator Brown Sales Co., Mission Viejo, Calif., 1976-79; pres., gen. mgr. S.W. Contemporary Sales, Inc., Scottsdale, Ariz., 1979—. Mem. Bus. and Profl. Women Am., Network Female Execs. Democrat. Roman Catholic. Home and Office: 12580 N 84th Pl Scottsdale AZ 85260

BROWN, CAROL OSMAN, writer, photographer, public relations cons.; b. Schenectady, Sept. 28, 1941; d. Sidney A. and Natalie (Charipper) Osman; B.A. in Mass. Communications, Ariz. State U., 1963; m. James Carrington Brown III, Nov. 3, 1961; children—James Carrington IV, Bryan Lee. Reporter, Prescott Evening Courier, Ariz. Republic, summer 1960; reporter, photographer Phoenix Gazette, 1961-65; public relations account exec. John S. Turner & Assos., Phoenix, 1965-66, Patton Agy., Phoenix, 1966-68; free-lance writer, 1961—, free-lance photographer, public relations cons., 1968—. Public relations exec. Childbirth Edn. Assn., Phoenix; den mother Cub Scouts, Theodore Roosevelt council Boy Scouts Am., 1978, 80; publicity chmn. Friendship Force, Phoenix; legis. rep. Balsz Sch. Dist., Phoenix, 1980. Named Outstanding Woman Journalist, Ariz. State U., 1962; recipient numerous awards for writing, photography and public relations, including Lulu, Los Angeles Advt. Women, 1968 (2); Writing competition winner Reader's Digest, 1979; Ariz. Edn. Assn. writing award, 1980. Mem. Ariz. Press Women (1st Pl. Writing award 1974, 75, 76), Nat. Fedn. Press Women (1st Pl. Photography award 1968), Ariz. Authors's Assn., Soc. Children's Book Writers. Republican. Presbyterian. Club: Phoenix Press. Home and Office: 4228 E Cambridge Phoenix AZ 85008

BROWN, CAROL WYNN, civic worker; b. Fort Worth, Aug. 17, 1937; d. Sproesser and Mildred Frances (Patton) Wynn; B.A. magna cum laude, Tex. Christian U., 1957; m. C. Harold Brown, June 14, 1957; children—Tracey, Terry, Allison, Harold. Bd. dirs. Camp Carter YMCA, 1974—; mem. Ft. Worth Jr. League, 1961-78, bd. dirs., 1964-68, sustaining mem., 1978—; mem. Ft. Worth Opera Bd., 1970-74, Ft. Worth Library Bd., 1973-79; mem. vol. center com. Tarrant County United Way, past chmn., 1972—, mem. planning and research council, 1975—, now mem. steering com., chmn. camping com.; chmn. ch. circle Univ. Christian Ch., Ft. Worth, 1975-77, study chmn., 1977-79, worship chmn. Christian Women's Fellowship, 1978—, mem. choir, 1978—; city camping chmn. 1st Tex. council Camp Fire Girls, 1968, vol. day camp counselor, 1966-72, leader, 1965-72; mem. Tex. Hist. Survey Commn., 1969-73; vol. Planned Parenthood, 1966-68, Blind Children's Service Center, 1964-66; pres. Ft. Worth Brittany Club, 1979—; trustee Tarrant County Youth Collaboration, 1982. Recipient Carnegie Hero cert., 1972; Distaff Handlers award Am. Brittany Club, 1977; Charlotte Joy Farnsworth award 1st Tex. council Camp Fire Girls, 1970. Mem. Ft. Worth C. of C. (ladies div.), Zi Eta Pi, Kappa Kappa Gamma (pres. Ft. Worth alumni 1965, pres. Epsilon Alpha House bd. 1967, chpt. adv. 1968-72). Republican. Club: Ft. Worth Pi Beta Phi Mothers (pres. 1980). Columnist: Am. Brittany Mag. Home: 2711 Park Hill Dr Fort Worth TX 76109

BROWN, CAROLE CHRISTINE, dietitian; b. Sioux City, Iowa, July 7, 1947; d. Vernon Earl and Esther Christine (Laursen) B.; B.S., Iowa State U., 1970. Intern, then dietitian, Cook County Hosp., Chgo., 1971-72; theapeutic dietitian Eugene C. Eppley Complex, Omaha, 1973-77, Children's Meml. Hosp., Omaha, 1973-74; dietitian Nebr. Meth. Hosp., Omaha, 1972—. Mem. Am. Dietetic Assn., Am. Soc. Hosp. Food Service Adminstrs., Nebr. Dietetic Assn. Methodist. Home: 2403 N 92nd Av #10 Omaha NE 68134 Office: 8303 W Dodge Omaha NE 68114

BROWN, CAROLYN JEAN, lawyer; b. Peoria, Ill., Aug. 23, 1936; d. Thurman Clifford and Clarina (Dentino) B.; B.S.B.A. with highest honors, Bradley U., 1964; J.D. cum laude, Northwestern U., 1968. Admitted to Ill. bar, 1968; asso. firm McDermott, Will & Emery, Chgo., 1968-71; asso. firm Pope, Ballard, Shepard & Fowle, Chgo., 1971-74, partner, 1975-78; partner firm Gardner, Carton & Douglas, Chgo., 1978-80; founder, prin. Carolyn J. Brown, P.C., Chgo., 1980—. C.P.A., Ill. Mem. Am., Ill., Chgo. bar assns., Chgo. Estate Planning Council, Order of Coif, Phi Kappa Phi, Zeta Pi. Clubs: Law, Monroe, Plaza. Home: 155 Harbor Dr Unit 2112 Chicago IL 60601 Office: Suite 4870 Three First National Plaza Chicago IL 60602

BROWN, CAROLYN SCURRY, biochemist; b. Greenwood, S.C., June 13, 1942; B.A., Winthrop Coll., Rock Hill, S.C., 1964; Ph.D., Vanderbilt U., 1969; married; 2 children. Predoctoral fellow biochemistry Vanderbilt U. Med. Sch., 1964-69, USPHS postdoctoral fellow, 1969-71; postdoctoral research asso. biol. scis. Purdue U., 1971-74, 74-75, vis. asst. prof., summer 1973; vis. asst. prof. biochemistry Clemson (S.C.) U., 1975-77, asst. prof., 1977—. Mem. Am. Soc. Microbiology, AAAS, S.C. Acad. Scis., Sigma Xi, Sigma Delta Epsilon. Contbr. articles to profl. jours. Address: Dept Biochemistry Clemson Univ Clemson SC 29631

BROWN, CHARLOTTE KATHERINE BRINSONT, social worker; b. Fort Worth, Tex., Dec. 29, 1942; d. Nathaniel and Lois Ren (Moore) Brinsont; B.A., Stanford U., 1965; M.S.W., U. Calif., Berkeley, 1967; m. Cecil L. Brown, Sept. 18, 1976. Social worker Children's Home Soc. of Calif., San Francisco, 1967-72, San Mateo County Dept. Public Health and Welfare (Calif.), 1972—. Lic. clin. social worker. Mem. Nat. Assn. Social Workers, Acad. Certified Social Workers, Am. Fedn. State County Mcpl. Employees, Stanford U. Alumni Assn., Phi Beta Kappa. Democrat. Office: 225-37th Ave San Mateo CA 94403

BROWN, CORNELIA ANITA, state ofcl.; b. Ottumwa, Iowa, July 31, 1944; d. Cornett and Pansy B. (Parker) Allen; B.A., Calumet Coll., 1982; m. Ralph Parkhurst Brown, Dec. 22, 1962; children—Karen Anita, Ralph Parkhurst. News reporter Sta. WJOB, Hammond, Ind., 1978-80; coordinator public relations Northwestern Ind. Regional Planning Commn., Highland, 1980—. Mem. Women in Communications, Inc., Alpha Kappa Alpha. Clubs: No. Ind. Links, Inc. (chmn. publicity 1980—), Jack & Jill Am., Inc., Siesta Bridge. Editor-in-chief monthly newsletter on regional planning. Home: 7425 Harold St Gary IN 46403 Office: 8149 Kennedy Ave Highland IN 46322

BROWN, DIANE ELENA, oil service co. exec.; b. New Orleans, Feb. 5, 1943; d. Henry T. and Carmen M. (Rodriguez) B.; B.A., U. Dallas,

1969. Instr. lang., dept. head Nolan High Sch., Ft. Worth, Tex., 1967-72; employment coordinator Collins Radio, Dallas, 1973; coordinator human resources register Dresser Industries, Inc., Dallas, 1974, adminstr. EEO, Houston, 1977, mgr. EEO, 1977, employee services mgr., 1981—; speaker bus. and profl. groups. Recipient award Pre-Release Center for Tex. Dept. Corrections, 1979. Mem. Am. Mgmt. Assn., Am. Soc. Personnel Adminstrn., Houston C. of C., Houston Personnel Assn. (pres. elect 1981, pres. 1982-83). Home: 800 Post Oak Blvd Houston TX 77056 Office: Dresser Industries Inc PO Box 6504 Magcobar Group Houston TX 77005

BROWN, DIANE KAY, nursing adminstr.; b. Parkersburg, W.Va., Sept. 26, 1952; d. Ray Harold and Lorraine Marie (Gwynn) Brown; R.N., St. Mary's Sch. Nursing, Huntington, W.Va., 1974; student W.Va. U., 1970-71, Marshall U., 1971-72, Parkersburg Community Coll., 1980-81. Office nurse M. H. Cummings, M.D., Huntington, W.Va., 1973-74; staff nurse Timken Mercy Hosp., Canton, Ohio, 1974-75; staff nurse St. Joseph's Hosp., Parkersburg, W.Va., 1975; ICU staff nurse Hershey (Pa.) Med. Center, 1975-78; asst. dir. nursing emergency services St. Joseph's Hosp., Parkersburg, W.Va., 1978—. Bd. dirs. Mid-Ohio Valley Emergency Services, Inc. Mem. Am. Assn. Critical Care Nurses, Nat. Assn. Female Execs. Inc., Emergency Dept. Nurses Assn. Republican. Methodist (mem. adminstrv. bd., chmn. health and welfare com., mem. ch. choir). Home: 7 Wildwood Dr Apt C Parkersburg WV 26101 Office: 19th St and Murdoch Ave Parkersburg WV 26101

BROWN, DOREEN LEAH HURWITZ, constrn. co. exec.; b. Marseille, France, June 11, 1927; came to U.S., 1939, naturalized, 1941; d. Nathan and Anne (Silverstone) Hurwitz; B.A. cum laude, Bryn Mawr Coll., 1947; m. Donald L. Brown, Dec. 30, 1951 (dec.); children—Claudia Geraldine, Nicole Deborah. Adminstrv. asst., interpreter, translator FAO, Washington, 1949-51; with Aldon Constrn. & Mgmt. Corp., Washington, 1951—, v.p., exec. officer, 1977—; consumer liaison Nat. Acad. Scis., 1973. Nat. chmn. nat. affairs Nat. Council Jewish Women, N.Y.C., 1971-75; pres. Consumer Edn. Council on World Trade, 1973-78, Consumers for World Trade, Washington, 1977—; mem. Women's Nat. Democratic Club, 1960—; mem. Internat. Trade Importers and Retailers Textile Adv. Com., Dept. Commerce. Mem. Bryn Mawr Coll. Alumnae Assn., Women in Community Service. Club: Woodmont Country. Office: Consumers for World Trade 1346 Connecticut Ave NW Washington DC 20036

BROWN, EDNA BARBARA, genealogist; b. Atlanta, Mo., June 18, 1921; d. Paul Lewis and Lena Alice (Newmyer) Jones; A.B., William Jewell Coll., 1943; postgrad. U. Colo., Boulder, summer 1945, Tchrs. Coll., Columbia U., summers 1947-49; cert. Eighteenth Inst. Geneal. Research, Am. U., 1968, Geneal. Inst., Houston, 1979; m. Eldon Hamilton Brown, June 18, 1950; 1 adopted son, Norman Lewis. Tchr. English, Concordia (Mo.) High Sch., 1943-45, Burley (Idaho) Jr. High Sch., 1945-47, Eugene Field Sch., Hannibal, Mo., 1947-48, Keating Jr. High Sch., Pueblo, Colo., 1948-51; genealogy librarian Pueblo Regional Library, 1966-71; pvt. practice genealogy, Littleton, Colo., 1971—. Chmn. First Media Center, Arapahoe Rd. Bapt. Ch., Littleton, 1971-73, chmn. 1st hist. com., 1974-76; organizing v.p. Columbine Geneal. and Hist. Soc., Littleton, 1973. Recipient Edward Eubank award William Jewell Coll., 1943. Mem. Colo. Geneal. Soc. (rec. sec. 1972-73, 1st v.p. 1981), Columbine Geneal. and Hist. Soc., State Hist. Soc. Mo., Colo. Hist. Soc., Nat. Geneal. Soc., Central N.Y. Geneal. Soc., Jacksonville (Ill.) Area Geneal. and Hist. Soc., DAR (chmn. lineage research com. Colo. State Soc. 1973-80, chmn. for publ. Colo. DAR Mem. and Ancestor Index 1980-81, vice regent Mt. Rosa chpt. 1981-83), Daus. Colonial Wars (historian 1980-83), Soc. Mayflower Descs. (bd. assts. 1979). Mortar Bd. Republican. Home and Office: 6583 S Downing St Littleton CO 80121

BROWN, ELIZABETH ANN, govt. agy. ofcl.; b. Toledo, Dec. 26, 1927; d. Samuel and Anna (McLaughlin) Brown; student Scott Community Coll., 1974-75, Black Hawk U., 1981—. With Rossford Ordnance Depot, Toledo, 1950-61, U.S. Army Armament Materiel Readiness Command, Rock Island, Ill., 1961-73; acctg. technician U.S. Army Materiel Readiness Command, Rock Island, 1974-81, chem. publs. writer, 1981—. Recipient various local awards for poetry. Mem. Equal Employment Working Group, Nat. League Am. Pen Women. Roman Catholic. Poetry pub. Driftwood East, 1976, Speak Out, 1975, Nat. Poetry Anthology, Best in Poetry, 1976, Jean's Jour., 1975, N.Am. Mentor, Lyrical Iowa, Iowa Day Brochure of Poems; contbr. poetry to Poet's Podium column Quad-City Times, 1972-75. Home: 1803 North St Bettendorf IA 52722 Office: US Army Armament Materiel Readiness Command Rock Island IL 61299

BROWN, ELIZABETH MARY, educator, nutritionist, entrepreneur; b. N.Y.C., Mar. 23, 1940; d. William Earl and Maria Mazariegos (Sagastume) Smith; B.A., N.Y.U., 1963; M.A. in Social Scis., Hunter Coll., 1968; postgrad. Columbia U. Tchr., N.Y.C. public schs., 1961-71; nutritionist, 1974; sr. supr. Shaklee Products, 1974—; partner Smith-Brown Assos., N.Y.C., 1974—; cons. in field. Mem. Nat. Assn. Female Execs., Am. Soc. Profl. and Exec. Women, Internat. Platform Assn., Exec. Woman, Women's Econ. Roundtable, Networks Unltd., Am. Mgmt. Assn., Theatre Devel. Fund, Am. Assn. Humanistic Psychology, Internat. Acad. Nutritional Cons., Nat. Health Fedn., Alt. Cancer Therapies, Assn. Research and Enlightenments, Hunter Coll. Alumni Assn. Address: 245 W 107th St #2E New York NY 10025

BROWN, ELIZABETH MYERS, publishing co. exec.; b. Bklyn., Dec. 31, 1915; d. Garry Cleveland and Caroline (Clark) Myers; B.S., Cornell U., 1937; M.A., Case Western Res. U., 1960; m. Kent Louis Brown, June 26, 1940; children—Karen Elizabeth (Mrs. Lyman Anders Johnson), Kent Louis, David Stuart, Garry Myers. Tchr., Walden, N.Y., 1937-38, Auburn, N.Y., 1938-39, Cleveland Heights, Ohio, 1939-40; asst. Erie County (N.Y.) home demonstration agt. govt. extension service Cornell U., Ithaca, N.Y., 1940-42; editorial asst. Highlights for Children, Columbus, Ohio, 1962-64, asst. editor, 1964-66, asso. editor, 1966—, asst. sec., 1968—, dir., 1960—; dir. Zaner-Bloser Co., 1972—; dir. Skillcorp Pubs., Inc. Mem. Metro Writers Workshop, 1970—; trustee New Day Press, 1972-79 (both Cleve.). Bd. dirs. Fedn. Cornell Women's Clubs, 1955-57, pres. Cornell Women's Club Cleve., 1953-55; bd. dirs. Nutrition Assn. Greater Cleve., 1964-68. Mem. Women's Assn. for Continuing Edn. (treas. 1959-61, pres. 1961-63), Women's Aux. Acad. Med. of Cleve. (pres. 1969-70), Ohio Med. Assn. Aux. (chmn. mems.-at-large com. 1970-71, mem. state bd. 1970-71, 75-77, dist. dir. 1975-77), Women's Nat. Book Assn. (dir. Cleve. chpt. 1978-82), Am. Soc. Mag. Editors. Home: 2861 Kersdale Rd Cleveland OH 44124 Office: 803 Church St Honesdale PA 18431

BROWN, EMMA VERNAL, nursing asst.; b. Roanoke, Va., Feb. 21, 1924; d. Ernest and Mary Jane (Richardson) Calloway; student public schs.; m. Joseph Whelton Brown, II, Nov. 4, 1943 (div.); children—Joseph Whelton III (dec.), James Ellven, Theodore, Enid, Kevin, Emily, Edwin, Stephanie, Douglas Lee. Mem. VA nursing staff, 1942—; nursing asst. VA Med. Center, Salem, Va., 1963—. Recipient Performance award VA, 1976, 81. Mem. Am. Fed. Employees Union, Gold Star Mothers. Baptist. Address: 2430 Staunton Ave NW Roanoke VA 24017

BROWN, ETHEL LULA MAE, educator; b. Seneca, S.C., Feb. 17, 1930; d. Enoch and Monicho Rebecca (Johnson) Brown; A.A., Friendship Jr. Coll., 1949; B.S. in Edn., S.C. State Coll., 1952. Tchr. sci. and math. Macedonia High Sch., Blackville, S.C., 1952-62; tchr. math. Seneca (S.C.) Jr. High Sch., 1964—, adult edn. tchr., 1968—. Bd. dirs. ARC, Seneca, 1968-69, v.p., 1968-70; bd. dirs. United Way, Seneca, 1970-76, sec., 1971-72. Recipient Appreciation Plaque for services rendered, United Way, 1977; Plaque for 25 yrs. service Oconee County Sch. System, 1977. Mem. Oconee Edn. Assn., S.C. Edn. Assn., NEA, Nat. Assn. Colored Women's Clubs. Baptist. Club: Mary McLeod Bethune Federated (pres. 1971-75). Address: Route 3 PO Box 120 Seneca SC 29678

BROWN, EVELYN ANN, counselor, therapist; b. Grant, Nebr., Jan. 20, 1945; d. Thomas Cartwright and Mildred Carrie (Wilkinson) Brown; B.A. summa cum laude, Nebr. Wesleyan U., 1968; M.A. (Vocat. Rehab. Adminstrn. fellow, 1968-69), U. Nebr., 1970. Coordinator residential services Bexar County Mental Health/Mental Retardation, (Tex.), 1973-74; cons. to orgns., San Antonio, 1974-80; vocat. rehab. counselor Mental Health Mental Retardation, Tex. Commn. for Blind, San Antonio, 1975-77; exec. dir. San Antonio Assn. Retarded Citizens, 1978-79; pvt. practice counselor, therapist, massage therapist, Austin, 1979—. Co-founder, facilitator Crystal Chalice, 1980—; mem. adv. bd. Tex. Assn. Child Care Workers, 1975—, adv. council Vol. Action Com., 1978-79. Mem. Austin Area Holistic Health Assn. (pres. 1980—), Assn. Humanistic Psychology, Found. Universal Unity, Human Unity Found., Health Freedom Council, Friends in Human Potential, Human Potential Inst., Tex. Assn. Child Care Workers, In-Ter Action Assos. Columnist, HOLOS, 1980—. Address: 914 Blanco St Austin TX 78703

BROWN, FRANCES GOLD, former health care adminstr.; b. Alameda, Calif., Apr. 24, 1913; d. Judel and Sadie (Pivnik) Gold; R.N., Mt. Zion Hosp., San Francisco, 1935; B.S., U. Calif., 1954, M.S., 1956; student Langley Porter Neuopsychiat. Inst., 1954-55; m. Robert Lee Brown, Nov. 27, 1941 (dec. July 1949); 1 son, Robert Lee. Gen. duty and pvt. nurse Alameda County, Calif., 1935-40, gen. duty, pvt. duty nurse, clin. nurse, 1949-56; gen. duty and head nurse Gorgas Hosp., Ancon, C.Z., 1940-42; supervisory nurse Fairmont Hosp., San Leandro, Calif., 1956-59; dir. nursing edn. Oreg. State Hosp., Salem, 1959-62; instr. psychiat. nursing U. Calif. Sch. Nursing, San Francisco, 1962-63; coordinator nursing services H. Douglas Singer Zone Center, Rockford, Ill., 1966-69; nursing adminstr. East Moline (Ill.) Mental Health Center, 1969-80; health care unit adminstr. East Moline Correctional Center, 1980-81; sec. Calif. Nurses Assn., 1953-59. Mem. adv. com. Black Hawk Coll., Moline. Mem. Am. Nurses Assn. (vice chmn. inter-group relations com. 1960-62), Ill. Conf. Women Leaders in Traffic Safety (pres.), AAUS, LWV, Rock Island County Mental Health Assn., ORT, Pi Lambda Theta. Jewish. Club: Zonta. Author articles in field. Home: care Heskin 317 Vassar Ave Kensington CA 94708

BROWN, GAYLIA DIANNE, clin. psychologist; b. Shenandoah, Iowa, Oct. 25, 1942; d. Vernon E. and Mariea Jeanne Brown; B.S., Western Mich. U., 1964, M.A., 1965; Ph.D., Purdue U., 1969. Clinic adminstr. Mental Health Center, San Diego, 1970-71; exec. dir. Out Patient Clinic, San Diego, 1971-72; clin. psychologist San Diego County Mental Health Services, 1972-76; pvt. practice clin. psychology, La Jolla, 1977—; instr. U. LaVerne, San Diego, 1972—; mem. La Jolla City Council, 1970—; cons. on mental health, 1972—. Mem. adv. bd. San Diego County Bd. Suprs., 1971-75. Mem. Am. Psychol. Assn., Calif. State Psychol. Assn., San Diego County Psychol. Assn., Soc. Clin. Psychologists, San Diego Soc. Clin. Hypnosis, Am. Soc. Clin. Hypnosis, Nat. Forum for Death Edn. and Counseling, Assn. for Past Life Research and Therapy, Sigma Kappa. Republican. Methodist. Home: 3525 Lebon Dr La Jolla CA 92037 Office: 5580 La Jolla Blvd Suite 178 La Jolla CA 92037 also 5333 Mission Center Rd Suite 338 San Diego CA 92108

BROWN, GEORGIA LYNN, govt. adminstr.; b. Gunnison, Colo., Oct. 18, 1940; d. George Scott and Florence Josephine (Lewis) Gorsuch; B.A., U. Colo., 1968; M.P.A., U. So. Calif., 1977; 1 dau., Wendy Roma. Intelligence specialist U.S. Dept. Army, Washington, 1968-69; personnel specialist, Washington, 1969, Corpus Christi, 1969-70; urban intern HUD, Denver, 1970-71, equal opportunity specialist, 1971-75, housing specialist, 1975-77; regional adminstr. Women's Bur., U.S. Dept. Labor, Denver, 1977—; mem. Colo. State Personnel Affirmative Action Adv. Bd., Colo. Commn. on Status of Women, Colo. Civil Rights Commn. Recipient Cert. of Achievement, HUD, 1977; Assn. Fed. Profl. and Adminstrv. Women Upward Mobility award, 1974. Mem. Am. Soc. Public Adminstrn., World Future Soc., Women's Polit. Caucus, Women's Forum, NOW (sec. Colo. orgn. 1974, pres. Denver chpt. 1975), Federally Employed Women. Office: 1961 Stout St Denver CO 80294

BROWN, HAZEL NIXON, nurse; b. Columbus County, N.C., June 30, 1940; d. Roy A. and Lela W. Nixon; B.S. in Nursing, Berea Coll., 1962; M.A.Ed., Wake Forest U., 1971; Ed.D., U. N.C., Greensboro, 1981; m. Leonard L. Brown, May 3, 1964; children—Charles Jacob, Mona Lee, Nadja Sue, David Leonard. Staff nurse Lula Conrad Hoots Meml. Hosp., Yadkinville, N.C., 1962-66; tchr. 4th grade Yadkinville Elem. Sch., 1966-67; instr. Sch. Nursing, Forsyth Meml. Hosp., Winston Salem, N.C., 1967-70, dir. Sch. Nursing, 1970-74; asst. prof. nursing U. N.C., Greensboro, 1974—; cons. Forsyth Meml. Hosp. Mem. Am. Nurses' Assn., Nurses' Assn. of Am. Coll. Obstetricians and Gynecologists (cert. inpatient obstetric nurse). Baptist. Clubs: Bus. and Profl. Women's, U. N.C. at Grennsboro Women's. Home: Route 2 Box 577 Yadkinville NC 27055 Office: U NC Spring Garden St Greensboro NC 27412

BROWN, HAZEL PEARL, educator, author; b. N.Y.C.; d. Edward Cameron and Edith May (Bradley) B.; B.S., Columbia U., 1944; M.A., N.Y. U., 1947; m. Harold Morgan Clough, June 29, 1928 (div. 1931). Supervising prin., Conn., 1927-36; dir. Gardner Grammar Sch., N.Y.C., 1936-42; prof. ednl. methods, speech, English, City Coll., City U. N.Y., 1942-47; prof. ednl. methods, voice and diction N.Y. U., 1947-60; dir. Speechphone Studio, N.Y.C., 1951—. Mem. Speech Assn. Am., N.Y. State Speech Assn., Internat. Platform Assn., Tchrs. English to Speakers Other Langs. Author: American Speech Sounds and Rhythm, 1950; Speechphone Method - 4 Courses on Speech Improvement, 1951. Home: 300 E 40th St New York City NY 10016 Studio: 525 Lexington Ave New York City NY 10017

BROWN, HELEN, state ofcl.; b. Winnfield, La., June 16, 1921; d. George Franklin and Lovie Rosalie (Fenall) B.; B.A., La. State U., M.A., Ed.D.; postdoctoral So. U. Exec. dir. Baton Rouge Girl Scout Council; classroom tchr. English and social studies, guidance counselor East Baton Rouge Parish Schs., then supr. English and humanities, dir. curriculum devel., supr. English, social studies and humanities, classroom tchr. English and social studies; instr. La. State U.; dir. bur. curriculum, inservice and staff devel. Office of Acad. Programs, La. Dept. Edn., Baton Rouge; mem. Nat. Humanities faculty; English and social studies cons. Exec. bd. Baton Rouge Speech and Hearing Found.; bd. dirs. Parents of Children with Cleft Palates; mem. Commn. on Needs of Women; adv. com. Jr. Service League Baton Rouge; program com. Baton Rouge Arts and Humanities Council; mem. Baton Rouge Task Force for Battered Wives and Abused Children. Recipient commendations Women's Leadership Inst., Am. Legion Instrn. Suprs. Assn., East Baton Rouge Council Tchrs. of English, Zeta Phi Beta. Mem. La. Assn. Sch. Execs. (commendation for leadership), La. Council Tchrs. of English, La. Ednl. Research Assn., Am. Assn. Sch. Adminstrs., Phi Delta Kappa, Phi Kappa Phi, Kappa Delta Phi, Delta Kappa Gamma. Democrat. Baptist. Club: Baton Rouge Quota (exec. bd.). Author numerous curriculum guides; contbr. articles profl. jours. Office: Louisiana Dept of Education PO Box 44064 Baton Rouge LA 70804

BROWN, HELEN GURLEY, author, editor; b. Green Forest, Ark., Feb. 18, 1922; d. Ira M. and Cleo (Sisco) Gurley; student Tex. State Coll. for Women, 1939-41, Woodbury Coll., 1942; m. David Brown, Sept. 25, 1959. Exec. sec. Music Corp. Am., 1942-45, William Morris Agy., 1945-47; copywriter Foote, Cone & Belding, Los Angeles, 1948-58; advt. writer, account exec. Kenyon & Eckhardt, Hollywood, Calif., 1958-62; editor-in-chief Cosmopolitan mag., 1965—, editorial dir. Brit. edit., 1972—, also 13 other overseas edits.; supervising editor EYE mag., 1967-68. Recipient Francis Holmes Achievement award for outstanding work in advt., 1956-59, Disting. Achievement award U. So. Calif. Sch. Journalism, 1971, ann. awards Am. Newspaperwomen's Assn., 1972, Am. Soc. Journalism Sch. Adminstrs., 1972, Disting. Achievement award in journalism, hon. alumnus Stanford U., 1977. Mem. Authors League Am., AFTRA, Am. Soc. Mag. Editors, Eta Upsilon Gamma. Author: Sex and the Single Girl, 1962; Sex and the Office, 1965; The Outrageous Opinions of Helen Gurley Brown, 1967; Helen Gurley Brown's Single Girl Cookbook, 1969; Sex and the New Single Girl, 1970; Having It All, 1982. Home: 1 W 81st St New York NY 10024 Office: Hearst Corp 224 W 57th St New York NY 10019

BROWN, JACQUELINE WILLIAMS, mental health adminstr.; b. N.Y.C., Oct. 17, 1930; d. James and Virture (Cooper) Williams; B.A., Hunter Coll., 1952; M.S.W., Columbia U., 1954; m. Clarence Lewis Brown, June 30, 1957; children—Lynda M., Judy S. Social worker Mt. Sinai Hosp. at Elmhurst (N.Y.), 1965-70; pre-kindergarten social worker Bur. Child Guidance, Bd. of Edn., N.Y.C., 1974-75; supr. psychotherapist East Harlem Mental Health Clinic, Children's Aid Soc., N.Y.C., 1976-79, coordinator clinic, 1979—; field instr. N.Y. U. Sch. Social Work, Hunter Coll. Sch. Social Work. Cert. social worker, N.Y. State. Mem. Nat. Assn. Social Workers, NAACP, Phi Beta Kappa. Home: 100 W 94th St Apt 18A New York NY 10025 Office: East Harlem Mental Health Clinic Children's Aid Soc 130 E 101st St New York NY 10029

BROWN, JEAN BUSH, educator; b. Springfield, Mo., Jan. 22, 1947; d. Denzil Lee and Betty Jean (Smith) Bush; B.A., Memphis State U., 1973, M.A., 1974, Ph.D., 1981; 1 son, Larry Garland. Proctor, Dept. Psychology, Memphis State U., 1972; research asst. NASA, Memphis State U., 1973-74, 74-75; grad. asst. Memphis State U., 1975, audiologist Audiol. Testing Services and grad. asst., 1975, Hearing Impaired program, 1977, Learning Center, 1977; Headstart Programs, Marshall & Fayette Counties (Miss.) grad. asst., 1977-78; grad. asst., audiologist Audiol. Testing Services, Memphis, 1978, 79-80; instr., coordinator audiol. services Dept. Communicative Disorders, U. Minn., Duluth, 1979-80, instr., dir. audiology programs, 1980-81, asst. prof., dir. audiology programs, 1981—; audiol. cons. Dept. Otolaryngology and Maxillo-Facial Surgery, U. Tenn., Memphis, 1975; audiol. supr. Memphis Oral Sch., 1976-77; audiol./speech cons. United Cerebral Palsy, 1979—, Duluth pub. schs., 1980—; lectr. in field. Cabrillo Coll. scholar, 1971, others. Mem. Am. Speech/Lang./Hearing Assn., Minn. Speech/Lang./Hearing Assn., Alexander Graham Bell Assn. for Deaf, Acad. Rehab. Audiology, Council for Exceptional Children, Nat. Hearing Assn., Am. Tinitus Assn., Council Univ. Suprs. of Practicum in Speech/Lang. Pathology, others. Home: 248 W Redwing St Duluth MN 55804 Office: 2400 Oakland Ave Duluth MN 55812

BROWN, JOANN KARREN, state ofcl.; b. American Fork, Utah, July 3, 1931; d. Alex Vaughn and Inez (Jones) Karren; student Utah Tech. Coll., Provo, 1976—; m. Leo J. Brown, Apr. 21, 1950; children—Karry James, Susan Kay, William Alex. Mem. Lehi City Council, 1969-82, mayor pro-tem, 1977-82; adminstrv. asst. Office of Lt. Gov., State of Utah, 1982—. Mem. Gov.'s Air Conservation Com.; fire sci. tng. adv. com. Utah Tech. Coll.; pres. Help, Inc.; mem. Utah Handicapped Awareness Com.; bd. dirs. Utah Valley Indsl. Devel. Assn.; former bd. dirs. United Way. Named Outstanding Utah County Citizen, 1977-78. Mem. Utah League Cities and Towns (pres. 1978-79, mem. various coms.), Lehi C. of C. Democrat. Mormon. Home: 793 E 760 N Lehi UT 84043

BROWN, JUDITH BABCOCK, civic worker; b. Washington, Nov. 5, 1948; d. Elden Reed and Ruth Marie (Harkcom) Babcock; student Louisburg Jr. Coll., 1967-68; B.A., U. N.C., 1971; m. Ronald Shelton Brown, Dec. 28, 1968; children—Seth Carson, Jeb Matthew. Social worker Onslow County Dept. Social Services, Jacksonville, N.C., 1971-75; real estate broker Strickland Realty, Jacksonville, 1977-78. Treas. Onslow Meml. Hosp. Aux., 1976-77, v.p., 1977-78, pres., 1978-79, bd. dirs. 1979—. Democrat. Baptist. Home: 1003 Summerbrook Pl Jacksonville NC 28540

BROWN, JUDITH OLANS, lawyer, educator; b. Boston, May 29, 1941; d. Sidney and Evelyn R. (Lefkovitz) Olans; A.B. magna cum laude with distinction, Mt. Holyoke Coll., 1962; LL.B. cum laude, Boston Coll., 1965; m. James K. Brown, Oct. 5, 1969. Admitted to Mass. bar, 1965; law clk. Supreme Jud. Ct., 1965-66; asso. firm Foley, Hoag and Eliot, Boston, 1966-69; chief counsel Mass. Dept. Community Affairs, Boston, 1969-70; atty. adv. Office of the Regional Counsel, HUD, Boston, 1970, asst. regional counsel, 1971, asso. regional counsel, 1971-72; instr. Boston U. Law Sch., 1971; instr. Northeastern U. Sch. Law, Boston, 1972, asso. prof., 1972-75, prof., 1975—; corporator Arlington Five Cents Savings Bank, 1974—. Loeb fellow, 1972-73. Mem. steering com., Lawyers Com. for Civil Rights under Law. Mem. Order of the Coif, Phi Beta Kappa. Contbr. articles to legal jours.; book rev. editor Boston Coll. Indsl. and Commercial Law Rev., 1964-65. Home: 336 North Ave Weston MA 02193 Office: 400 Huntington Ave Boston MA 02115

BROWN, JUDITH READER, nurse; b. Williamsport, Pa., Apr. 2, 1953; d. Orville Eugene and Mary Hennrietta (Trometter) Reader; R.N., York Hosp. Sch. Nursing, 1974; m. Harold Victor Brown, Sept. 13, 1975. Staff nurse/relief supr. Sunbury (Pa.) Community Hosp., 1974-77; evening supr. All Saints Hosp., Wyndmoor, Pa., 1977-78, clin. educator, 1978-80; dir. nursing services Greystone on the Greene, Inc., Phila., 1980-82; dir. nursing Services Millcroft Newark, lectr. in field. Recipient Cert. Randolph Skills Center, Phila., 1981. Mem. Pa. Nurses Assn., Am. Nurses Assn. Republican. Methodist. Home: 10 Upland Court Newark DE 19713 Office: 255 Possum Park Rd Newark DE 19711

BROWN, JUNE EVELYN, librarian; b. Ipswich, Eng., June 29, 1925; came to U.S., 1946, naturalized, 1954; d. Frederick George and Evelyn Claudia (Barker) Laws; nat. diploma in design Leicester (Eng.) Coll. Art and Tech., 1946; B.A. magna cum laude, Alfred (N.Y.) U., 1969; M.L.S., SUNY, Geneseo, 1970; m. Ronald Martin Brown, Apr. 14, 1945; children—Erica Karen, Diane Rosemary. Mem. library staff Alfred U., 1959—, asso. librarian, 1976-77, univ. librarian, 1977—. Title VI fellow, 1969-70. Mem. ALA, N.Y. Library Assn., Nat. Librarians Assn., Beta Phi Mu, Phi Kappa Phi, Phi Sigma Iota. Author articles in field. Home: 30 Sayles St Alfred NY 14802 Office: Herrick Meml Library Alfred Univ Alfred NY 14802

BROWN, JUNE GIBBS, govt. ofcl.; b. Cleve., Oct. 5, 1933; d. Thomas D. and Lorna M. Gibbs; B.B.A. summa cum laude, Cleve. State U., 1971, M.B.A., 1972; postgrad. Cleve. Marshall Law Sch., 1973-74; J.D., U. Denver, 1978; m. Ray L. Brown, Jan. 1, 1975; children—Ellen, Sheryl, Linda, Victor, Gregory, Carol. Real estate broker, office mgr. N.E. Realty, Cleve., 1963-68; staff acct. Frank T. Cicirelli, C.P.A., Cleve., 1970-71; asst. to comptroller S.M. Hexter Co., Cleve., 1971; grad.

teaching fellow Cleve. State U., 1971-72; dir. internal audit Navy Fin. Center, Cleve., 1972-75; mgr. fin. systems design burs. in Dept. Interior, Denver, 1975-79, insp. gen., Washington, 1979-81; insp. gen. NASA, Washington, 1981—. Recipient award Am. Soc. Women Accts., 1969, 70, 71; Raulston award Cleve. State U., 1971, Pres.'s award, 1971; Outstanding Achievement award U.S. Navy, 1973; Career Service award Chgo. region Fed. Exec. Bd., 1974, Outstanding Contbn. to Fin. Mgmt. award, Denver Region, 1977; Fin. Mgmt. Improvement award Joint Fin. Mgmt. Improvement Program, 1980; Outstanding Service award Nat. Assn. Minority C.P.A. Firms, 1980; named Woman of Yr., Bur. Land Mgmt., Dept. Interior, 1975. Mem. Assn. Govt. Accts. (nat. exec. com. 1977-80, vice chmn. nat. ethics com. 1978-80), Service award 1973, 76, Outstanding Achievement award, 1979). Am. Inst. C.P.A.s, Am. Accts. Assn., Assn. Fed. Investigators, Beta Alpha Psi. Office: Office Insp Gen NASA 400 Maryland Ave SW Washington DC 20546

BROWN, JUNE WILCOXON, writer; b. W. Lafayette, Ohio, Aug. 14, 1914; d. Ralph Foster and Pearl Almeda (Marx) Wilcoxon; B.A., U. Md., 1935; m. Albert W. Brown, Nov. 3, 1938; 1 son, Peter Wilcoxon. Freelance writer, 1945-60, 81—; editor Select mag., Madison, Wis., 1959-65; radio script writer Beverly Stark Radio Show, 1963-68, John Doremus Show, 1971-72; sit-in hostess Mary Brooks Jackson radio show, St. Thomas, V.I., 1966-75, Louise Noble Radio Show, St. Thomas, 1975-81; author monthly column Caribbean Corner, 1977-78; author fiction and articles in nat. magazines. Mem. Nat. League Am. Pen Women (pres. Madison 1954), St. Thomas Community Music Assn. (v.p. 1970-71), Women in Communications (Writers cup Madison 1951), Kappa Kappa Gamma. Republican. Address: Box 7396 Saint Thomas VI 00801

BROWN, KAREN KAY, microbiologist; b. Manhattan, Kans., July 25, 1944; d. Clarence Christian and Edna Dorothy (Spiecker) Kilker; B.S. in Biology and Chemistry, Washburn U., Topeka, 1966; Ph.D. in Molecular Biology (USPHS fellow 1967-71), Okla. State U., 1972; m. Harold Glendon Brown, June 18, 1966. Quality assurance microbiologist Cutter-Haver-Lockhart Corp., Shawnee, Kans., 1972, research microbiologist Bayvet div. Cutter Labs., 1972-75, sr. research scientist microbiology, 1975-82, prin. sci. immunology, 1982—, bio-hazards control officer, 1974—. Mem. Am. Assn. Lab. Animal Scientists (dir. Kansas City br. 1981-83, mem. regional exam. bd. 1981—, Am. Soc. Microbiology, AAAS, Am. Tissue Culture Assn., Am. Bus. Women's Assn., Sigma Xi, Phi Kappa Phi. Republican. Mem. Ch. of Christ. Author, patentee in field. Office: PO Box 390 Shawnee Mission KS 66201

BROWN, KAREN LEE, state legislator; b. Rumford, Maine, Apr. 14, 1953; d. Leland Richard and Barbara May (Dougherty) B.; B.A. in Psychology, U. Mass., 1975. Mem. Maine Ho. of Reps., 1976—; public relations cons. Boise Cascade, 1981; orgnl. cons. Citizens for Congresswoman Olympia Snowe; cons. George Bush for Pres., 1980; mem. Oxford County Republican Com., 1975-80; vice chmn. 2d Congressional Dist. Conv., 1978-80; chmn. Sen. William Cohen's U.S. Mil. Acad. selection com. Home: Box 32 Elm St Bethel ME 94217 Office: Box 20 State House Augusta ME 04333

BROWN, KAREN VANESSA, environ. scientist; b. Washington, Mar. 17, 1952; d. Herbert Lee and Faith Dunbar (Scott) Brown; B.S. in Biology, U. D.C., 1975. Ins. Agt. Aetna Life Ins. Co., Washington, 1974; chemist, sanitarian, environ. health specialist Environ. Health Adminstrn., Washington, 1977-81; spl. asst. to adminstr. EPA, Washington, 1981—. Chairperson Town Center Coop., 1981. Mem. Nat. Assn. for Female Execs., U. D.C. Alumni Assn. Republican. Roman Catholic. Club: Monday.

BROWN, KATHARINE EISENHART, artist; b. Princeton, N.J., Mar. 21, 1921; d. Luther P. and Katharine S. (Schmidt) Eisenhart; B.A., Vassar Coll., 1942; M.S. in Journalism, Columbia U., 1944; m. W. Danforth Compton, June 13, 1942 (dec.); children—John, Christina; m. 2d, Robert P. Brown, Apr. 3, 1959. Exhbns. include: Main Gallery Boston City Hall, 1978, Copley Art Assn., Boston, 1980, Clark Gallery, Lincoln, Mass., Cambridge (Mass.) Art Assn., 1981, Currier Art Gallery, Manchester, N.H., 1981, various art assns.; one person shows include: Cambridge Art Assn., 1976, Episcopal Theol. Sch. Library, Cambridge, 1973, Hilles Library of Radcliffe Coll., 1975, 82, Frameworks Gallery, Cambridge, 1977, Johnson (Vt.) State Coll., 1977, Vassar Coll., 1977, Harvard Law Sch. Library, 1978, Stonehill Coll., Easton, Mass., 1979. Recipient 1st prize Cambridge Art Assn., 1976, Quincy Coop. Bank award South Shore Art Center, 1977, hon. mention Sudbury Art Assn., 1979, hon. mention Concord Art Assn., 1979, juror's choice award, 1980, juror's award Cambridge Art Assn., 1981. Mem. Boston Visual Artists Union, Cambridge Art Assn., Copley Soc. Boston, Craftsman's Council, Concord Art Assn., Sharon Art Center, N.H. Art Assn., Phi Beta Kappa. Democrat. Episcopalian. Home: 16 Avon St Cambridge MA 02138

BROWN, KATHERINE SKINNER, property mgmt. exec.; b. Ruston, La., Sept. 30, 1944; d. John Willie and Verna Howelene (Shirey) Skinner; B.A., La. Tech. U., 1967; M.S. in Library Sci., La. State U., 1969; m. Tom S. Brown, Jan. 5, 1974; children—Megan Elizabeth, Alexander John. Librarian, Vidalia (La.) Elem. Sch., 1967-68, Children's Library, Houston Public Library, 1969-71; field cons. Tex. State Library, Austin, 1971-73; dir. Harris County Library, Houston, 1974-79; regional ops. coordinator First Internat. Service Corp., Houston, 1979-80; small bus. mgr. Houston C. of C., 1980-81; pres. Johnson Brown Inc., 1981—. Mem. Am. Bus. Women's Assn., Tex. Library Assn., Southwest Library Assn.

BROWN, KATHIE HAYS, nurse; b. Wheeling, W.Va., June 16, 1953; d. Harold MacElroy and Bernice Laura (Brown) Hays; R.N., Alderson Broaddus Coll., 1975, B.S.N., 1975; m. Richard Samuel Brown, June 5, 1976; children—Richard Samuel, Kyle Andrew. Staff nurse Vis. Nurse Assn., Wheeling, 1975-79; dir. nursing service Florence Crittenton Home, Wheeling, 1979—; cons. instr., supr. Wheeling Coll. Nursing Sch. and W. Va. U. postgrad. externs in community health, edn., 1979—; tchr. Lamaze classes; tchr. health Ohio County Schs. alt. sch. program. Recipient Nursing Writing award, 1975; Presdl. Award of Honor, Wheeling Jaycee-ettes, 1981. Mem. Nurses Assn. of Am. Coll. Obstetricians and Gynecologists, W.Va. Pub. Health Assn., Wheeling Jaycee-ettes (internal v.p. 1980-81), Ohio Valley Jaycee-ettes. Baptist. Clubs: Daus. of the Nile, Order Eastern Star. Home: 131 Grant Ave Wheeling WV 26003 Office: 2606 National Rd Wheeling WV 26003

BROWN, KATHLEEN E., utility exec.; b. Chgo., Feb. 17, 1949; d. David Jenkins and Shirley Lois (Kaltneger) Brown; B.S., U. Wis.-Madison, 1972; postgrad. Nova U., 1980—. Project specialist U. Wis., 1972-73, research asst., 1968-72; water quality control technician City of Ft. Lauderdale, Fla., 1974-75; treatment plant operator II Broward County (Fla.) Utilities Dept., Lauderdale Lakes, 1975-80, treatment plant mgr., 1980—. Mem. Am. Water Works Assn., Fla. Water and Pollution Control Operators Assn., Fla. Renaissance Guild, Nat. Assn. Female Execs. Club: Eastern Star. Contbr. articles in field to profl. publs. Office: 3701 N State Rd #7 Lauderdale Lakes FL 33319

BROWN, LAURA VENTRESCA, arts commr.; b. Washington, Oct. 2, 1915; d. Francesco and Florence Vendla Elizabeth (Olson) Ventresca; B.A., U. Ill., 1936, B.S. in L.S., 1941; postgrad. U. Md., 1961-62; m. George Berdine Brown, July 17, 1938; children—David Alan, Donald Kent, Douglas Scott. Librarian, Falls Church, Va., 1952-53; arts coordinator Anne Arundel County Dept. Recreation and Parks, Annapolis, Md., 1972-76; mem. Anne Arundel County Commn. Culture and Arts, 1976-81, chmn., 1980; mem. Commn. of Md. Hall for Creative Arts, Annapolis, 1978—; dir. Cultural-Edn. Centre, Inc., Annapolis. Membership chmn. Arlington County Women's Com. for Nat. Symphony, 1953-54; fine arts chmn. Marshall Sch. PTA, 1953-54; membership chmn. Anne Arundel County Concert Assn., 1959; chmn. symphony com. Anne Arundel Gen. Hosp. Aux., 1970-72; trustee Balt. Mus. Art, 1978—; patron Ballet Theatre of Annapolis, Annapolis Symphony Orch., Annapolis Colonial Players, Md. Fedn. Arts, Annapolis Summer Garden Theatre, Annapolis Children's Theatre, Annapolis Opera Soc., Hist. Annapolis, Balt. Mus. Recipient Vol. Service award Severna Park Jaycees, 1981, Anne Arundel County Exec., 1981, Md. Hall for Creative Arts, 1982, Gov. Md., 1982. Mem. Order Sons of Italy in Am., Sumi-E Soc. Am., Inc. (chmn. D.C. chpt. 1980; dir. 1980—; asso. editor Quar. 1982—), Ikebana Internat. (chpt. dir.; chmn. Annapolis workshop 1981-82), Pi Delta Phi. Home: 200 Riggs Ave Severna Park MD 21146

BROWN, LEANNA, state legislator; b. Providence, 1935; d. Harold and Esther Young; B.A. with honors, Smith Coll., 1956; m. W. Stanley Brown; children—William, Stephen. Mem. profl. staff govt. dept. Ednl. Testing Service, Princeton, 1956-60; councilwoman, Chatham Borough, 1969-72; mem. taxation and fin. com. Nat. Assn. Counties, 1976-79; dir. Morris County Bd. Chosen Freeholders, 1976, dep. dir., 1975, chmn. fin. com., 1975; freeholder, 1972-81; pres. N.J. Assn. Counties, 1978; chmn. N.E. N.J. Transp. Coordinating Com., 1979-80; mem. N.J. Assembly, 1980—; mem. adv. com. N.J. Public Broadcasting, 1979—; mem. corp. United Way of Morris County, 1978—; trustee Morris Mus. Arts and Sci., 1975—; trustee Arts Council of Morris Area, 1973—; del. White Ho. Conf. on Children, 1970; merit badge counselor Loantaka council Boy Scouts Am., 1975—; Morris County coordinator Millicent Fenwick for Senate, 1982; 76; mem. N.J. Republican Fin. Com., 1979-81. Mem. N.J. Assn. Elected Women (pres. 1982). Home: 7 Dellwood Ave Chatham NJ 07928

BROWN, LENA BOYD, educator; b. New Orleans, July 3, 1937; d. Eugene Alcus and Rose Mary (Lewis) B.; B.A., Xavier U., New Orleans, 1958; M.A., Howard U., 1960; Ed.D., Rutgers U., 1979. Mem. faculty So. U., New Orleans, 1960-61; tchr. Eastern High Sch., Washington, 1961-62; mem. faculty So. U., Baton Rouge, 1962-63, N.C. Central U., Durham, 1963-64, Howard U., Washington, 1964-65, Grambling (La.) State U., 1965-68, Tuskegee (Ala.) Inst., 1968-70; asso. examiner history and social studies Ednl. Testing Service, Princeton, N.J., 1970-79; asso. prof. edn. and social sci. Dillard U., New Orleans, 1979—; vis. fellow history Carnegie-Mellon U., 1967; Martin Luther King fellow Rutgers U., New Brunswick, N.J., 1977-78; cons. on social studies curriculum, tests and measurement. Mem. Nat. Council Social Studies, Orgn. Am. Historians, Assn. for Study Afro-Am. Life and Culture, Phi Delta Kappa, Kappa Delta Pi, Phi Alpha Theta. Roman Catholic. Guest editor, contbr. to Social Education, 1976. Office: Dillard U Gentilly Blvd New Orleans LA 70126

BROWN, LINDA JENKINS, govt. EEO specialist; b. Balt., Nov. 8, 1946; d. Bennie Richard and Naomi (Harris) Jenkins; B.S. in Edn. Morgan State U., 1971; M.P.A. (Fed. Hwy. Adminstrn. scholar), cert. mgmt., U. Balt., 1981; m. Charles E. Brown, II, July 3, 1965; 1 son, Charles E. III. Elem. tchr. Balt. County Bd. Edn., 1971-73; EEO specialist Dept. Def., Ft. Holabird, Md., 1973-75; EEO specialist Fed. Hwy. Adminstrn., Balt., 1975-78, regional contracts compliance officer, 1978-80, dep. chief internal EEO div., fed. women's program mgr., 1980—. Recipient Superior Performance award Fed. Hwy. Admistrn., 1980, Spl. Achievement award, 1982. Mem. Am. Soc. Public Adminstrn., Internat. Personnel Mgmt. Assn., Nat. Assn. Female Execs., Exec. Women's Network, Am. Bus. Women's Assn., Nat. Council Negro Women, Balt. Working Women, Zeta Phi Beta (Meritorious award, Cert. of Appreciation), Alpha Kappa Mu (Cert. of Merit). Home: 2401 Poplar Dr Baltimore MD 21207 Office: 400 7th St SW Washington DC 20590

BROWN, LINDA LEE, graphic designer; b. Raton, N.Mex., Oct. 29, 1955; d. John Tom and Anna Helen (Willett) Brown; A.S., Amarillo Coll., 1975; student W. Tex. State U., 1975-77. Teaching asst. Amarillo (Tex.) Coll., 1974-75; drafter natural gas div. Pioneer Corp., Amarillo, 1975-76, sr. drafter exploration div. Amarillo Oil Co. 1976-77; drafting supr. Thunder Basin Coal Co., Atlantic Richfield Co., Wright, Wyo., 1977—. Named Most Outstanding Woman, Beta Sigma Phi, 1980, 81; recipient Woman in the Industry recognition Internat. Reprographics Assn., 1980; grand prize winner Wyo. Art Show with painting titled Energy, 1976. Mem. Am. Inst. for Design and Drafting (dir. 1982-83, asst. editor Design and Drafting News 1982-83), Am. Legion Aux. Clubs: Wright Writers, 4-H. Author (poetry): God was Here, but He Left Early, 1976, Gift of Wings, 1980. Home: PO Box 114 Wright WY 82732

BROWN, LINDA WILEY, sch. prin.; b. Denver, Nov. 25, 1940; d. Philip Thomson and Bonnie Jean (Davidson) Wiley; student Temple U., 1961, B.A., Pa. State U., 1962; postgrad. Fla. Atlantic U., 1971; M.S., Nova U., 1975; m. John Harry Brown, Aug. 6, 1960; children—Bonnie Laura, Scott Randall. Pvt. instr. piano, Phila., Kansas City, Fairfax, Va., Fort Lauderdale, Fla., 1961-75; chmn. sch. bd. St. Peters Day Sch., Kansas City, Mo., 1964-68; tchr. music Fairfax Christian Sch., 1968-69; substitute tchr. Broward County, Fla., 1969-70; tchr. math. Margate (Fla.) Middle Sch., 1970-75; asst. adminstr. Hallandale High Sch. (Fla.), 1975-79, prin., 1979—; adj. prof. Nova U., 1975—. Coach, team mother Plantation Police Athletic League; mem. choir Plantation United Presbyterian Ch., also Broward County Community Chorus. Recipient Adminstr. of Yr. award Fla. Sch. Counselors Assn., 1981-82. Mem. Broward Prins. and Assts. Assn., Broward County Athletic Assn., Fla. Assn. Sch. Adminstrs., Nat. Assn. Secondary Sch. Prins., AAUW, Assn. Supervision and Curriculum Devel., Mensa, Hallandale C. of C., Mu Phi Epsilon, Phi Delta Kappa, Alpha Zi Delta. Democrat. Episcopalian. Office: 720 NW 9th Ave Hallandale FL 33009

BROWN, MABEL ETHEL, tax accountant; b. Norwich, N.D., Dec. 2, 1910; d. Edward and Augusta (Schwab) Simmons; student Fosters Tax Sch., San Leandro, Calif., 1952-53, Del Mar Coll., 1954, Bancroft Adult Sch., 1955-56, Alameda Adult Sch., 1955-62, U. Calif., 1961-62, Chabot Coll., 1963, Sunset Hi Adult Sch., 1967-68, Tech. Adult Sch., Oakland, Calif., 1965-73; m. George Victor Brown, Feb. 25, 1954; children—Arthur Ralph, Edward James (dec.), Jerry Lee Larsen. Prin., Mabel's Tax Service, Oakland, 1943-54; owner Gilroy Motel (Calif.), 1945-47; owner, operator Chatterbox, Avoca, Iowa, 1947-49; owner, mgr. Brown's Bus. Service, Flour Bluff, Tex., 1954-55, Hayward, Calif., 1954-80; owner Rocks Rough & Ready, jewelry shop; real estate saleswoman, notary public. Mem. VFW Aux. Democrat. Lutheran. Address: 28105 Mission Blvd Hayward CA 94544

BROWN, MABEL WELTON, lawyer; b. Geneseo, Ill., Dec. 7, 1916; d. Harry E. and Mabel (Welton) Brown; B.A., Oberlin Coll., 1938; J.D., U. Chgo., 1941. Partnership with father, Harry E. Brown, atty., 1941-44, sole owner, 1944-81; sr. partner firm Brown & Ray, 1981—; atty. for Green River Spl. Drainage Dist., Henry and Bureau counties (Ill.) Chmn. Geneseo Planning Commn., 1961-68. Mem. Am., Ill., Henry County (pres. 1973-76) bar assns., Am. Judicature Soc., Kappa Beta Phi. Republican. Methodist. Home: 115 E North St Geneseo IL 61254 Office: 115 N State St Geneseo IL 61254

BROWN, MAREL, writer; b. Carroll County, Ga., Dec. 17, 1899; d. George Britt and Olive (Summers) Snow; student Atlanta public schs.; m. Alex B. Brown, Oct. 8, 1919 (dec. Dec. 1975). Sec., asst. to editor Christian Index, Atlanta, 1924-30; sec., asst. to Baptist pastor, 1930-37; freelance writer, 1938—; books include: Red Hills, 1941; Hearth-Fire, 1943; Fence Corners, 1952; The Shape of a Song (Writer of Yr. award Atlanta Writers Club 1968-69, Poet of Yr. for Ga. award Dixie Council 1968), 1968; Lily May and Dan, 1946; The Greshams of Greenway, 1950; The Cherry Children, 1956; Three Wise Women of the East, 1970; Presenting Georgia Poets, 1979; instr. writing workshops; chmn. Ga. Poetry Day, 1957-59. Ga. chmn. Books for Russia, World War II; public relations coms. Atlanta Bond Drive, High Mus. Art. Recipient Ann. Spl. award Dixie Council Authors and Journalists, 1980. Mem. Nat. League Am. Pen Women, Poetry Soc. Am., Poetry Soc. Ga., Ga. State Poetry Soc., Ladies Burns Club Atlanta, Dixie Council Authors and Journalists, Rader Poetry Group Miami, Atlanta Hist. Soc., DeKalb County His. Soc., Am. Acad. Poets, Internat. Acad. Poets. Baptist. Home: 1938 N Decatur Rd NE Atlanta GA 30307

BROWN, MARGARET CANNON BOYCE, civic worker; b. Amarillo, Tex., Dec. 13, 1922; d. John Kirkpatrick and Margaret Owen (Curtis) Boyce; B.S., Tex. U., Austin, 1944; M.A., Columbia U., 1945; m. Shepherd Spencer Neville Brown, Mar. 31, 1951; children—Spencer, Margaret, Maria Stanton, Boyce. Instr. home econs. U. Tex., Austin, 1946-51; founder St. Paul's Episcopal Day Sch., Waco, Tex., 1956—, pres. sch. bd., 1960-61; pres. Waco Jr. League, 1959; pres. Waco Symphony Women's Assn., 1964; mem. youth protection com. Waco PTA City Council, 1968; pres. Crestview Sch. PTA, Waco, 1968; pres. St. Paul's Assn. Women, Waco, 1968-70; pres. corp. bd. Waco Cotton Palace, 1970—, founding chmn. pageant, 1971-74; pres. Tex. Women's Assn. Symphony Orch., 1972-73, Tex. Soc. Nat. Soc. Colonial Dames Am., 1974-78, corr. sec. nat. bd.; mem. natural scis. adv. council U. Tex., Austin; mem. Tex. Commn. on Arts, 1981—; trustee Hockaday Sch., Dallas, 1977-83. Recipient Liberty Bell award Waco Jr. Bar, 1972; named Woman of Yr., Baylor U. Mortar Bd., 1974, Altrusa Club, 1981. Mem. Daus. Republic Tex., Dallas Woman's Club, Waco Woman's Club, Thursday Lit. Club, Kappa Alpha Theta Alumnae Club (pres. 1972-74; Theta of Year award 1978), Pi Lambda Theta, Omicron Nu. Republican. Episcopalian. Club: Ridgewood Country. Home: Stanton Hall 2620 MacArthur Dr Waco TX 76708

BROWN, MARGARET MARY, psychologist; b. Albany, Calif., Dec. 6, 1943; d. Daniel Francis and Ethel Lucille (Cliff) B.; B.A., U. Calif., 1965; M.A., U. Kans., 1968; Ph.D., N.Y. U., 1982; m. Wayne A. Gordon, Nov. 9, 1979. Evaluator, dir. project devel. Kans. Regional Med. Program, Kansas City, 1969-73; health planner Mid-Am. Comprehensive Health Planning Agy., Kansas City, Mo., 1973-74; project coordinator Rehab. Indicators project Inst. Rehab. Medicine, N.Y.C., 1974—; cons. United Cerebral Palsy of N.Y., 1978—. USPHS fellow, 1965-68. Mem. Nat. Rehab. Assn., Evaluation Research Soc., Am. Psychol. Assn., Am. Assn. Women in Sci., Phi Beta Kappa. Office: 400 E 34th St New York NY 10016

BROWN, MARIAN RAYBURN, psychologist, writer; b. Clarkson, N.Y., Dec. 10, 1911; d. George Henry and Laura Belle (Mathewson) Rayburn; B.S., SUNY, Buffalo, 1935; M.A., U. Rochester, 1939; Ed.D., Columbia U., 1950; m. Ralph Adams Brown, Feb. 8, 1947; children—Richard Adams, Linda Viola Brown Kerr. Tchr. jr. high, public schs., Brockport, N.Y., 1931-37; guidance dir., public schs., Huntington, N.Y., 1937-45; research asst. Bur. Adminstrv. Research, Columbia U., 1946-47; vocat. counselor, asst. dean of women Cornell U., 1948-50; dean of women SUNY, Cortland, 1956-59, psychologist, 1969; psychologist Bd. Coop. Ednl. Services, Cortland, 1965-68; psychologist public schs., Homer, N.Y., 1972-74; pvt. practice psychology, counseling, Cortland, 1975—; author books: Impressions of America, 2 vols., 1966; American History Book List for High Schools, 1967; Europeans Observe the American Revolution 1976; contbr. revs. to various publs.; bd. dirs. Vol. Counseling; chmn. youth com. YWCA. Pres. bd. dirs. YWCA Ladies Lit. Club, Cortland, 1954—; chmn. Faculty Wives, SUNY, Cortland. Cert. counselor, sch. psychologist, N.Y. State. Mem. Nat. Assn. Sch. Psychologists, Sch. Psychologists Upstate N.Y., N.Y. State Psychologists. Republican. Presbyterian. Book rev. editor Social Edn., 1961-64. Home: 44 W Court St Cortland NY 13045

BROWN, MARIE ELIZABETH DUTTON, editor; b. Phila., Oct. 4, 1940; d. Benson Leroy and Josephine (Brown) Dutton; B.S. in Psychology, Pa. State U., 1962; m. Ken Brown, Sept 6, 1969; 1 dau., Laini Anise. Tchr., coordinator intergroup relations Sch. Dist. Phila., 1962-67; editor Doubleday & Co., N.Y.C., 1972-80, editor in chief Elan Mag., N.Y.C., 1980-82; editorial cons., 1982—. Home: 51 Saint Nicholas Pl New York NY 10031

BROWN, MARILYN LORETTA, mortgage banker; b. Bklyn., Nov. 13, 1931; d. John Francis and Annette (Martin) Brown; student Baker Bus. Sch., 1950; m. Ralph P. Iannone, Sept. 13, 1952; 1 son, John Patrick. Sec., Pringle, Hurd & Co., N.Y.C., 1952-56; corp. sec. Eleford & Rutgers, Inc., N.Y.C., 1956-59; corp. sec., v.p. Eleford & Counihan, Inc., N.Y.C., 1959-65; exec. v.p., sec., co-owner Eleford & Co., Inc., N.Y.C., 1965—; dir., officer Bartels & Eleford, real estate, S.I., N.Y.; dir. DeRand Investment Corp. Am.; trustee DeRand Real Estate and Investment Trust. Mem. Mortgage Bankers Assn. Am. (legis. com., nat. M.B.A. liaison), Mortgage Bankers Assn. N.Y. (pres., bd. govs.). Republican. Roman Catholic. Club: Richmond County Country (S.I.). Home: 684 Harris Ave Staten Island NY 10314 Office: Eleford & Co Inc 15 Beach St Staten Island NY 10304

BROWN, MARTHA ANNETTE ANGLIN, tax preparer; b. Sylvester, Ga., June 12, 1937; d. Perry C. and Lois O. (Calhoun) Anglin; student public schs., Chgo.; m. James E. Brown, Oct. 2, 1955; children—Gerald, Sandra, Lorrie. PBX operator Ill. Central Bell Telephone Co., 1957-60; sec. Sta. KRIH, Rayville, La., 1973-74, sta. mgr., 1974-80; tax preparer H & R Bloch, 1980—. Bd. dirs. Richland Parish Council on Aging. Democrat. Baptist. Club: Moose (Rayville). Home and Office: PO Box 169 Rayville LA 71269

BROWN, MARY CARNEY, state legislator; b. Midland, Mich., Aug. 18, 1935; d. Sheldon George and Wilma (Frith) Carney; A.B., M.A., Syracuse U.; m. Donald John Brown, 1956; children—Linda Brown Cook, Jeffrey, James. Former asst. prof. phys. edn. for women Western Mich. U.; mem. Mich. Ho. of Reps., 1976—, chmn. com. constnl. revision and women's rights, mem. coms. taxation, mental health, ins. and civil rights. Mem. Kalamazoo LWV (pres. 1969-73), Alpha Lambda Delta, Pi Lambda Theta. Home: 1624 Grand Ave Kalamazoo MI 49007 Office: Michigan House of Representatives State Capitol Bldg Lansing MI 48909 *

BROWN, MARY ELEANOR, physical therapist, educator; b. Williamsport, Pa., Jan. 1, 1906; d. Sumner Locher and Mary Kate (Eagles) Brown; student U. Wis. at Madison, 1927-28; B.A., Barnard Coll., 1931; M.A., N.Y.U., 1941; student N.Y.U., 1942-45, Western Reserve U., 1960-61; postgrad. U. Miami, Miami-Dade Jr. Coll., 1971-72, Cuesta Community Coll., 1977—. Supervising phys. therapist, research asst. Inst. for Crippled and Disabled, N.Y.C., 1941-46; instr. edn. N.Y.U., 1942-46; phys. therapist Childrens Rehab. Inst., Cockeysville, Md., 1946; organizing dir. phys. edn. State Rehab. Hosp., West Haverstraw, N.Y., 1946-47; phys. therapy cons. Nat. Soc. for Crippled Children and Adults, Chgo., 1947-49; physical therapy cons., dir. prof. services, dir. cerebral palsy sch. N.Y. State Dept. Health, Albany, N.Y. and Eastern N.Y. Orthopedic Hosp. Sch., Schenectady, N.Y., 1949-53; chief phys. therapist Bird S. Coler Hosp. for Chronic Diseases, N.Y.C., 1953-54; chief phys. therapist, instr. edn. St. Vincents Hosp. and N.Y.U., 1954-58; chief research asso. hand research Highland View Hosp., Cleve., 1958-64, cons. on kinesiology, hand research, 1964-65; supr. continuing edn. for phys. therapists, asst. prof. phys. therapy Case Western Res. U., Cleve., 1964-68; dir. phys. therapy Margaret Wagner House of Benjamin Rose Inst., Cleve., 1968-70; free lance writer, 1970—; 1st Mary Eleanor

Brown lectr. clin. phys. therapy research Inst. Rehab. and Research, Tex. Med. Center, Houston, 1979; active Planetary Initiative for the World We Choose. Adv. bd. Community Services Dept. Cuesta Community Coll., San Luis Obispo, Calif., 1977—. Recipient Award of Merit, Case-Western Res. U., 1970; award for clin. research Inst. Rehab. and Research, Tex. Med. Center, Houston. Mem. Inst. Gen. Semantics, World Confedn. Phys. Therapy, Am. Phys. Therapy Assn., Soc. for Behavioral Kinesiology (charter, treas. 1975-77). Contbr. articles in field to profl. jours. Home: 1337 Santa Ynez Ave Los Osos CA 93402

BROWN, MARY HELEN, nurse; b. Que. Can., Feb. 23, 1924; came to U.S., 1947, naturalized, 1954; d. Leo and Margaret (Noonan) Brown; R.N., St. Mary's Hosp. Sch. Nursing, 1947; B.S.E., Hunter Coll., 1958; M.A., Columbia U., 1961. Charge nurse Lempert Inst. of Otology, N.Y.C., 1947-54, head nurse, 1954-56, supr., instr., 1956-58; field supr. Tchrs. Coll., Columbia U., N.Y.C., 1958-61; asst. dir. nurses Meml. Sloan-Kettering Cancer Center, N.Y.C., 1961-69, assoc. dir. nurses, 1969-73, acting dir., 1973-74; dir. nursing practice, 1975—. Mem. Am. Nurses Assn., Nat. League for Nursing, Nursing Edn. Alumni Assn. of Tchrs. Coll., Am. Soc. Nursing Service Adminstrs. Democrat. Roman Catholic. Feature editor Cancer Nursing an Internat. Jour., 1978—. Home: 345 E 68th St New York NY 10021 Office: 1275 York Ave Room 1929E New York NY 10021

BROWN, MARY JOANNE SKIDMORE, speech/lang. pathologist; b. Detroit; d. Wesley LeRoy and Inez Elizabeth (Sackett) Skidmore; student Ohio Wesleyan U., 1949-50, Wayne State U., 1951-53; B.A., U. Mich., 1955; postgrad. U. Rochester, 1970, Nazareth Coll. of Rochester, 1971-74; M.S., SUNY, Geneseo, 1977; m. Irwin Brown, Nov. 11, 1956; children—Jennifer Elizabeth, Jason LeRoy. Speech correctionist Dearborn Twp. (Mich.) schs., 1955-56; speech therapist City Sch. Dist. of Rochester (N.Y.), 1956-58, Bd. Coop. Ednl. Services #2, Monroe County, N.Y., 1958-60; speech and lang. pathologist Bd. Coop. Ednl. Services, Wayne-Finger Lakes, Wayne Spl. Edn. Center, Williamson, N.Y., 1970—. Lic. speech pathologist, N.Y. State; cert. tchr. speech and hearing handicapped, N.Y. State. Mem. Wayne-Finger Lakes Speech and Hearing Assn. (pres. 1978-79), Am. Speech-Lang. and Hearing Assn. (cert. clin. competence), N.Y. Speech and Hearing Assn., Genesee Valley Speech and Hearing Assn., Golden Link Folk Singing Soc., Alpha Gamma Delta, Sigma Alpha Eta. Home: 3 Shellwood Dr Rochester NY 14618 Office: Wayne Spl Edn Center Wayne Finger Lakes Bd Coop Ednl Services Williamson NY 14589

BROWN, MAUDE OPAL NORRIS, pharm. co. mgr.; b. Benson, N.C., June 17, 1927; d. Ernest Hubert and Alma (Moore) Norris; student King's Bus. Coll., Raleigh, N.C., 1944-45; m. Robert William Brown, Sept. 26, 1948; children—Donna Rose, Robert William. Sec. to pres. Raleigh Bonded Warehouse, Inc., 1946-58; acting office mgr. Fed. Crop. Ins., Raleigh, 1958-61; dist. office mgr. Allied Chem. Corp., Raleigh, 1961-69; with Burroughs Wellcome Co., 1970—, adminstrv. secretarial mgr., Research Triangle Park, N.C., 1973-77, grants and projects costs adminstr., 1977—; sec., bd. dirs. Employees Credit Union, 1975-78. Mem. Am. Mgmt. Assn. Home: 310 Tiffany Circle Garner NC 27529 Office: Burroughs Wellcome Co 3030 Cornwallis Rd Research Triangle Park NC 27709

BROWN, MAUREEN CATHERINE, nurse; b. Los Angeles, Apr. 3, 1941; d. Elmer Patrick and Marjorie Cecilia (Flaherty) McAuliffe; A.A. in Nursing, E. Los Angeles Coll., 1967; B.S. in Nursing, U. Mo., Columbia, 1981; B.S. in Health Edn. with highest honors, U. Ill., Urbana, 1973, M.S., 1976; m. James David Brown, Apr. 30, 1976; 1 dau., Katie; children by previous marriage—Darcy, Nathan, Keven; stepchildren—Kreg, Mark, Dan. Staff nurse, evening supr. Carle Found. Hosp., Urbana, 1967-72; transfer project coordinator Champaign-Urbana Public Health Dist., 1973-75; developer Preventive Medicine Clinic, Carle Clinic, Urbana, 1975-76; Kellogg grantee dept. family and community medicine U. Mo., Columbia, 1976-81, instr. family nurse practitioner masters program, 1982—; guest lectr. Western Ill. U., 1982. Nurse practitioner Planned Parenthood-Fedn. Am.; mem. Rape Task Force Com., 1981—; mem. family service evaluation com., Champaign, 1975; mem. Com. on Aging Champaign County, 1973; mem. Telecare Adv. Bd. Champaign County, 1973. Am. Med. Students Assn. grantee, 1978. Mem. Am. Nurses Assn. (cert. family nurse practitioner), Mo. Nurses Assn., Sigma Theta Tau. Democrat. Roman Catholic. Club: U. Mo. Fortnightly. Contbr. articles to profl. jours. Home: 2507 Mallard Ct Columbia MO 65201 Office: U Mo S313 Sch Nursing Columbia MO 65211

BROWN, MAY ANNA, coll. adminstr.; b. Shawnee, Okla., Sept. 23, 1926; d. John Garland and Thelma (Penny) Lane; M.B.E., U. Okla., 1964; M.L.S., U. Okla., 1969; m. O.D. Brown, Jr., Aug. 30, 1945; 1 son, O.D., III. Instr. bus. and English Milano (Tex.) Public Sch., 1962-63; librarian, instr. bus. and English, Prague (Okla.) Public Sch., 1963-65; tchr. bus. English Hominy (Okla.) Public Sch., 1965-68; dir. Learning Resource Center Seward County Community Coll., Liberal, Kans., 1969—. Mem. AAUW (pres. 1976-78), ALA, Kans. Library Assn., Mt. Plains Library Assn., Kans. Assn. Ednl. Communications and Tech., Kans. Assn. Sch. Librarians, Delta Kappa Gamma. Methodist. Home: PO Box 1243 Liberal KS 67901 Office: PO Box 1137 Liberal KS 67901

BROWN, MILDRED, service station owner; b. San Antonio, Apr. 4, 1930; d. Thomas D. and Lena (Anderson) Sattiewhite; student St. Philip Coll., 1979; B.S., Southwest Tex. State U., 1981; m. Herman Brown, Jr., June 28, 1959 (dec., 1968); children—Jacqueline Taylor-Brown Henderson, Hermine Elyse. Aide, So. Jewelry Co., San Antonio, 1953-58; barber Delux Barber Shop, San Antonio, 1958-59; real estate sales, 1967-78; owner, mgr. Brown's Motors and Texaco Service Sta., San Antonio, 1960—. Sec., Project Free, 1976—; vice-chairperson San Antonio Black Women Polit. Caucus, 1977-79. Mem. Am. Bus. Women's Assn. Baptist (fin. sec., Sunday sch. tchr., mem. sr. choir, fin. sec.). Home: 1218 Fontaine Dr San Antonio TX 78219 Office: 1526 N New Braunfels Ave San Antonio TX 78208

BROWN, MILDRED AUGUSTA, mental health cons.; b. Waconia, Minn., Sept. 20, 1923; d. Walter Carl and Esther Vivian (Schmidt) Burandt; B.A. in Bus./Human Service Adminstrn., Met. State U., St. Paul, 1978; m. Clyde Furqueron, Nov. 5, 1944 (dec. 1957); children—Mary Jane Furqueron Mathews, Gene C.; m. 2d, Karl H. Brown, June 9, 1971 (dec. 1971). Exec. asst., regional dir. Browndale Ont., 1968-73; program developer Browndale Netherlands, Amsterdam, 1974; program developer, adminstr. Browndale Minn., St. Paul, 1975-76; U.S. asst. dir. Browndale Internat., 1975; residential facilities devel. coordinator St. Paul Assn. Retarded Citizens, 1977-78; planner Zoning Dept. St. Paul, 1979-80; cons. group homes, St. Paul, 1975-82; mem. ad hoc licensing com. Minn. Dept. Public Welfare, 1975-76; mem. Minn. Health Planning Bd., 1977-78. Leader, trainer Girl Scouts U.S.A., 1953-55; leader Cub Scouts, 1956-59. Recipient award Toastmasters Club, 1980; real estate lic., Minn. Mem. AAUW, Minn. Women's Network, Minn. Social Service Assn., Highland Park Bus. and Profl. Women, Am. Legion Aux. (chaplain Lester Tjernlund post 1975-82). Lutheran. Club: Quota. Author: Children's Residential Treatment Center, 1976; Development of Residential Facilities for Mentally Retarded Citizens, 1978. Home and Office: 714 Woodlawn Ave Saint Paul MN 55116

BROWN, MILDRED KATHERINE, data processing co. exec.; b. St. Croix Falls, Wis., June 24, 1911; B.A., Met. U., Mpls., 1978; M.A. in Edn., Villanova U., 1983. Local dir. Camden and Union Counties (N.J.), Girl Scouts U.S.A., regional trainer, Minn., S.D., N.D., 1932-42; retail buyer Hahne & Co., Newark, 1942-47; occupations adv. Pa. Hosp., Phila., 1947-52, coordinator devel., 1966-67; mgr. Frigate Book Shops, Phila., 1952-53; prin. sec. dept. phys. medicine U. Minn., Mpls., 1954-55; dir. exec. placement Lit Brothers Co., Phila., 1955-65; dir. manpower edn. and tng. Twin City Hosp. Assn., Mpls., 1967-72; coordinator Richmond Area (Va.) Va. Regional Med. Program, 1972-74; ednl. developer Control Data Corp., Arden Hills, Minn., 1974-77, adminstr. tng. human resources div., 1977-78, adminstr. field ops. div., 1978-79, mgr. courseware implementation U.S. Learning Center Network, 1979-82, cons., 1981-82; resource lectr. Community Coll., Temple U., Phila., 1955-60. Water safety instr. ARC, 1937-47; capt., Cancer Assn. Campaign, 1950-60; mem. task force clin. service for health manpower Health Manpower Commn., Washington, 1972-73. Mem. Am. Soc. Tng. and Devel., Am. Soc. Health, Manpower, Tng. and Edn. Club: Tarpon (Control Data Pres.'s award 1978). Editor, chief scriptwriter Taped Health Info. Service, 1970-72. Mpls. city champion women's archery. Home: 3326 Chicago Ave S Minneapolis MN 55407 Office: 8100 34th Ave S Minneapolis MN 55440

BROWN, MILDRED SCHAER, law office adminstr.; b. Little Rock, Dec. 16, 1921; d. Karl Arthur and Ruth Othelia (Hailey) Schaer; student U. Ark., Fayetteville, 1955-57; m. Harold Paul Brown, Jan. 26, 1946; 1 dau., Bonnie Katharine Brown Wiggins. Sec., Retail Credit Bur., Little Rock, 1941-44; sec. to sr. partner firm Wright, Lindsey & Jennings, Little Rock, 1944-46, 57-77, adminstrv. asst., 1978—; Ark. state dir. Nat. Assn. Legal Secs., 1957; pres. Greater Little Rock Legal Secs. Assn., 1958. Vol. nurses aide ARC, 1940-45. Mem. Ark. Archaeol. Assn. Democrat. Methodist. Home: 11 Narragansett Pl North Little Rock AR 72116 Office: 2200 Worthen Bank Bldg Little Rock AR 72201

BROWN, NANCI BOOTHE, bus. exec.; b. Longview, Tex., Aug. 7, 1935; d. Robert E. and Smith (Robinson) Boothe; student U. Okla., 1953-56; m. Bob D. Brown, July 13, 1956. Exec. sec. Williams Bros. Co., Amarillo, Tex., 1960-61, Producers Grain Corp., Amarillo, 1961-65; office mgr. Plains Nutrition Co., Guymon, Okla., 1967-69; sr. sec. Turpin, Smith, Dyer & Saxe, Midland, Tex., 1969-81; sec.-treas., dir. DST Exploration Corp., Midland, 1969—. Asst. sec. Permian Charitable Found., Inc., 1969-74. Mem. Tex. Assn. Legal Secs., Midland Legal Secs. Assn. (treas. 1974-75), Kappa Alpha Theta. Methodist. Home: 4600 Sandra Ln Odessa TX 79762 Office: 2220 E 8th St Odessa TX 79761

BROWN, NANCY JONES, social worker; b. Pitts., Jan. 27, 1943; d. Oliver Woodford and Alma (Wesley) Jones; B.A., Mt. Holyoke Coll., 1965; M.S.W., Smith Coll., 1967; m. George Dixon Brown, May 20, 1972; children—George Oliver Robinson, Janice Marileine. Caseworker 1, Child and Family Service, Norfolk, Va., 1967-68; sch. social worker, spl. services project Middletown (R.I.) Sch. System, 1969; sr. psychiat. social worker Newport County Mental Health Clinic, Newport, R.I., 1969-72; sch. social worker Wayne (Mich.)-Westland Community Schs., 1972-73; staff social worker Child Evaluation and Treatment Center, Barnert Hosp., Patterson, N.J., 1973-74; sr. social worker Community Center for Mental Health, Dumont, N.J., 1974-75; unit supr. Catholic Children's Aid Soc. Met. Toronto (Ont., Can.), 1975-76; exec. dir. Hamilton (Ont.) Family Services, 1976—. Mem. Nat. Assn. Social Workers, Acad. Cert. Social Workers, Ont. Assn. Profl. Social Workers, Ont. Coll. Cert. Social Workers, Ont. Assn. Family Mediation. Republican. Methodist. Home: 129 All Saints Crescent Oakville ON L6J 5Y6 Canada Office: 168 Lakeshore Rd E Oakville ON L6J 5C1 Canada

BROWN, NANCY LEE, educator, mathematician; b. St. Louis, May 17, 1925; d. Charles Alonzo and Leno Rosie (Squires) Roberts; B.A., Harris Stowe State Coll., 1946; M.Ed., St. Louis U., 1955; M.Ed., Washington U., St. Louis, 1968; m. Major Charles Brown, Dec. 23, 1946; children—Major Charles, Victor Ivy. Tchr. elem. schs. St. Louis Bd. Edn., 1951-67, counselor, 1967—; owner, mgr. Human Services Cons., St. Louis, 1967—; owner, mgr. Dial Tchr. Assistance, 1980—. Chmn. suprs. unit, young peoples div. St. James A.M.E. Ch., 1976—. NSF fellow, 1963-66. Mem. Nat. Assn. Univ. Women (pres. St. Louis, 1975-79), Mo. Guidance Assn., AAUW, Am. Personnel and Guidance Assn., St. Louis Public Sch. Guidance Assn., Mo. Tchrs. Assn., Delta Sigma Theta. Author: Easy Mathematics Review-Elementary Through College, 1980; contbr. Profiles in Silhouettes: The Contributions of Black Women in Missouri, 1980. Home: 955 Jeanerette Dr University City MO 63130 Office: PO Box 3143 University City MO 62130

BROWN, NATALIA TAYLOR, contract specialist; b. St. Louis, Mar. 3, 1928; d. Gentry and Olivia (Webb) Taylor; diploma with honors, Hubbard Bus. Coll., St. Louis, 1949; student Sch. Bus. Adminstrn., St. Louis U., 1983; m. Edward Brown, Sept. 30, 1951. Civilian with U.S. Army, St. Louis, 1964—, contract specialist Troop Support and Aviation Material Command, 1973—. Recipient Sustained Superior Performance award U.S. Army, 1970. Mem. NAACP, YWCA, Knights of St. Peter Claver, Ladies Aux., Urban League Met. St. Louis, Gamma Phi Delta (Elizabeth Garner Meml. award 1966). Roman Catholic. Home: 5160 Campfire Trail Apt J Florissant MO 63066 Office: 4300 Goodfellow St St Louis MO 63120

BROWN, NORMA ELAINE, air force officer; b. Valdosta, Ga., Feb. 11, 1926; d. Charles L. and Earlene B. (Burroughs) B.; B.S. in Phys. Edn., Fla. State U., 1949; adopted children—Bunny, Tim. Commd. 2d lt. U.S. Air Force, 1951, advanced through grades to maj. gen.; served in personnel and command positions in Washington, St. John's Nfld., Can., Brampton, Eng., Kelly AFB, Tex., Shu Lin Kou Air Sta., Taiwan, Ft. George G. Mead, Md., Goodfellow AFB, Tex., Wright-Patterson AFB, Ohio; now comdr. Chanute Tech. Tng. Center, Chanute AFB, Ill. Decorated Legion of Merit, Meritorious Service medal with oak leaf cluster, Air Force Commendation medal with 2 oak leaf clusters, Army Commendation medal. Mem. Air Force Assn. Presbyterian. Address: Chanute Tech Tng Center Chanute AFB IL 61868 *

BROWN, ORIL IRENE, psychologist; b. Maumee, Ohio, Sept. 16, 1908; d. Edwin Joseph and L. Irene (Remelsbecker) B.; student U. Toledo, 1926-28; B.S., Northwestern U., 1930; M.S., George Washington U., 1951, Ph.D., 1965. Asst., Medill Sch. Journalism, Northwestern U., 1930-36; copyreader Chgo. Tribune, 1933-36, European edition N.Y. Herald Tribune, 1936-37; editor Federal Writers Project, 1938-40, Northwestern U., 1940-41, Fgn. Broadcast Intelligence Service, 1942-51; research asst. Human Resources Research Office, 1952-53; sch. psychologist Portsmouth (Va.) Schs., 1953-54; staff psychologist N.D. State Hosp., 1955-56; instr. psychology Med. Coll. Va., 1957-60; staff psychologist Danville (Pa.) State Hosp., 1960-64; staff psychologist to dir. psychology Mental Hygiene Clinic, Toledo, 1964-77; pvt. practice psychology, Toledo, 1977—. Lic. psychologist, Ohio. Mem. Am. Psychol. Assn., Southeastern Psychol. Assn., Midwestern Psychol. Assn., Ohio Psychology Assn., N.W. Ohio Psychol. Assn., Am. Soc. Clin. Hypnosis, AAUW, Ohio Hist. Soc., Maumee Valley Hist. Soc., Nat. Trust for Historic Preservation, Sigma Xi. Episcopalian. Author: Youth under Dictatorship, 1940; contbr. articles in field. Home: 2270 Townley Rd Toledo OH 43614 Office: 2500 W Central Ave Toledo OH 43624

BROWN, PATRICIA ANN, mining co. exec.; b. Coal County, Okla., Jan. 15, 1938; d. Albert Scott and Clydia Renee (Baughman) Eddings; student public schs.; divorced; children—Pamela Renee, Leisa Kay. With Delta Mining Corp., 1961—, v.p., controller, Dallas. Mem. Women in Mining, Nat. Assn. Female Execs., Am. Entrepreneurs Assn. Republican. Baptist. Office: 1535 W Mockingbird St Suite 401 Dallas TX 75235 *

BROWN, PATRICIA BUFORD, travel agt.; b. Jacksonville, Fla., May 3, 1938; d. Herman and Mildred Wainwright (Newsome) Buford; B.A., Nat. U., San Diego, 1976, M.B.A., 1978; divorced; children—Andrew James, Allison Paige. Mem. Faculty Foothill Community Coll., San Diego, 1978-79; dir. admissions and records, registrar Western State U. Coll. Law, San Diego, 1969-79; dist. mgr. Victor Temp. Services, San Jose, Calif., 1979-81; v.p. sales Freedom Travel Service, San Jose, 1981—. Mem. Peninsula Profl. Women's Network, Women in Bus. (chmn. 1981), San Jose C. of C. (dir.). Address: 10895 Northview Sq Cupertino CA 95014

BROWN, PATRICIA IRENE MACDONALD, psychologist; b. Sendai, Japan, Sept. 10, 1947 (parents Am. citizens); d. Aleck Francis and Elizabeth Allen (Ruda) MacDonald; B.A., U. Tex., 1969; Ph.D. in Clin.-Community Psychology, 1974; m. Tod Gipson Brown, May 5, 1973; children— Keegan, Amiya. Research asst. U. Hawaii, 1970-71; counselor Los Alamos (N.Mex.) public schs., also facilitator Los Alamos 1st Offender Program, 1974-75; pvt. practice clin. psychology, 1974—; instr. No. br. U. N.Mex., 1974; chief mental health service Santa Fe service unit Indian Health Service, 1975—. Mem. Am. Psychol. Assn., N.Mex. Council Crime and Delinquency, N.Mex. Council Community Mental Health Services, Phi Beta Kappa, Sigma Xi, Psi Chi. Author papers in field. Home: Route 1 Box 191 Santa Fe NM 87501 Office: USPHS Indian Hosp Cerrillos Rd Santa Fe NM 87501

BROWN, PATRICIA LYNN, info. scientist; b. Lafayette, La., Oct. 1, 1928; d. William Madison and Maude Juanita (Thomas) B.; B.S. in Chem. Engring., U. Southwestern La., 1947; M.A. in Chemistry, U. Tex., 1949. Instr. analytical chemistry Smith Coll., Northampton, Mass., 1949-50; chemist R&M Labs., Peabody, Mass., 1950; research asso. in indsl. toxicology Albany (N.Y.) Med. Coll., 1950-51; lit. searcher Ethyl Corp., Ferndale, Mich., 1951-55; sr. tech. writer-editor Atomic Power div. Westinghouse Co., Pitts., 1955-57; mgr. info. services Tex. Instruments, Dallas, 1957-66; sr. researcher-info. sci. Battelle Meml. Inst., Columbus, Ohio, 1966-76; asso. dir. Travenol Labs., Inc., Morton Grove, Ill., 1976—. Mem. Engring. Socs. Library Bd., 1961-63, 66-71; loaned exec. United Way, 1973, 74, 75. Mem. Soc. Women Engrs. (pres. 1961-63), Am. Chem. Soc., Spl. Libraries Assn., Soc. for Tech. Communication, Associated Info. Mgrs., Am. Soc. for Info. Sci. Contbr. articles to profl. jours. Home: 1109 Skylark Dr Palatine IL 60067 Office: 6301 Lincoln Ave Morton Grove IL 60053

BROWN, PHYLLIS JANE, trucking and rental co. exec.; b. Middleport, Ohio, Mar. 26, 1931; d. Robert L. and Juanita J. (Wolfe) Mason; student public schs., also seminars and bus. courses; m. John Edward Brown, July 11, 1949; children—Diane Lynn Brown Ludwig, Donna Rae Brown Klinka, Phyllis Ann Brown Kampel, John Paul, Linda Lee Brown Roche, Kimberly Dawn. A founder, sec.-treas. J & P Properties, Inc., Apopka, Fla., 1958—. Mem. Am., Fla. trucking assns., Fla. Nurserymen and Growers Assn. Republican. Baptist. Home: 10300 Charles Limpus Rd Orlando FL 32811 Office: 1350 Sheeler Rd Apopka FL 32703

BROWN, REBECCA FERREE, indsl. chem. exec.; b. Randleman, N.C., May 14, 1926; d. John Joseph and Kyvel (Gray) Ferree; ed. Kings Bus. Coll., U. N.C., Greensboro; m. Robert E. Brown, Oct. 27, 1945. With S.T. Wyrick & Co., 1949-69; exec. v.p., comptroller indsl. chem. and leasing Mark Mfg. Corp., Greensboro, N.C., 1969—. Bd. dirs., corp. sec. Masonic and Eastern Star Home of N.C., 1978-82; sec., bd. dirs. Young Democratic Com., 1948-55; sec. Women of the Ch., chmn. Missionary Circle, Meth. Ch. Clubs: Garden, Eastern Star (worthy grand matron N.C. 1975-76), Women's Bus., Garden, Order Amaranth. Address: 921 Greenwood Dr Greensboro NC 27410

BROWN, RITA MAE, author; b. Hanover, Pa., Nov. 28, 1944; B.A., N.Y.U., 1968; Ph.D., Inst. for Policy Studies, 1976. Works include: The Hand That Cradles the Rock, 1971; Rubyfruit Jungle, 1973; Songs to a Handsome Woman, 1973; A Plain Brown Rapper, 1976; Six of One, 1978; (novel) Southern Discomfort, 1982; Sleepless Nights, 1982; (TV show) I Love Liberty, prod. ABC, 1982; lectr. Fed. City Coll., 1970-71; mem. faculty Goddard Coll., 1973—. Office: care Julian Bach Lit Agy 747 3d Ave New York NY 10017 *

BROWN, ROSALIE LEDBETTER, agrl. co. exec.; b. Sinton, Tex., May 4, 1919; d. Leander Madison and Dora Eva (Moses) Ledbetter; student Port Arthur (Tex.) Bus. Coll., 1937; m. Lawrence Ray Brown, Dec. 4, 1937; children—Patricia Brown Kelly, Jerry Ray, Carol Brown Moore. Legal sec., then bookkeeper, Sinton, 1937, 42-52; self-employed in bookkeeping service, 1953-75; adminstrv. asst. to exec. dir. San Patricio County Community Action Agy., Sinton, 1975-76; office mgr. Jackson-Stripling Co., Sinton, 1977—; freelance reporter San Patricio County News, Sinton, 1969—. Mem. Sinton City Council, 1975—, mayor, 1980-82; foreman San Patricio County Grand Jury, 1979, commr., 1980; mem. Urban Renewal Sinton Commn., 1971-72, Sinton Community Action Agy., 1972-73; exec. com. Sinton Community Concerns, 1964—, chmn., 1968; del. Tex. Democratic Conv., 1978, 80, 82. Mem. Sinton C. of C. (dir. 1967-70), Women in Communication, Am. Assn. Small Cities (dir.-at-large), Tex. Assn. Elected Women (dir.), Tex. Mcpl. League (pres. region II 1982-83), Coastal Bend Council Govts. (treas.), Tex. PTA (life), Sinton Bus. and Profl. Women's Club (Woman of Yr. 1967). Baptist. Home: 802 E Main St Sinton TX 78387 Office: 125 W Sinton St Sinton TX 78387

BROWN, ROSEMARY, Can. govt. ofcl.; b. Jamaica, W.I., June 17, 1930; came to Can., 1950, naturalized, 1969; d. Ralph and Enid Heloise Wedderburn; B.A., McGill U., 1955; M.S.W., U. B.C., 1964; H.H.D., U. Mt. St. Vincent, 1980; m. William Brown, Aug. 12, 1955; children—Cleta, Mary, Jonathan. With Vancouver Neurol. Soc., 1965-68; counselor Simon Fraser U., 1969-72; mem. Legis. Assembly for Vancouver-Burrard, Can., 1972-79, Burnaby-Edmonds, Can., 1979—; vis. lectr. Maritime Sch. Social Work, 1977. UN fellow, 1973. New Democrat. Office: Parliament Bldg Victoria BC V8V 1X4 Canada

BROWN, RUTH CUNNINGHAM, club woman; b. Brooksville, Miss., Jan. 6, 1914; d. George William and Ruth (Hambrick) Cunningham; student Sophie Newcombe Coll., 1933-34, U. Tex., 1934-36; m. William Russell Brown, Apr. 19, 1941; children—Betsy (Mrs. Thomas M. Smith III), Virginia, Russell. Bd. dirs. Houston Community Council, 1962-63; bd. dirs., mem. women's aux. Houston Bar Assn., 1956; horticulture chmn. Garden Club of Houston, 1955-57; bd. visitors Sullins Coll., Bristol, Va., 1966-67, 69-75. Mem. D.A.R. (dir. John-McKnitt Alexander chpt. 1963), Kappa Kappa Gamma (v.p. Houston alumnae assn. 1961). Republican. Episcopalian. Clubs: Houston, Houston Country. Address: 5816 Bayou Glen Rd Houston TX 77057

BROWN, RUTH GEISLER, microelectronic engr.; b. Beaver Falls, Pa., Mar. 17, 1924; d. Carl Charles and Emily (Pletz) Geisler; student math. Johns Hopkins U., 1960-70; m. Stuart Fife Brown, Apr. 13, 1944. Service rep. Bell Tel. Co. of Pa., Pitts., 1942-43; from draftsman to sr. draftsman Martin Marietta Co., Middle River, Md., 1944-49, from jr. engr. to group engr., 1950-63; design draftsman Bendix Corp., Balt., 1949-50; engring. staff asso. Missile Programs and Microelectronics, Johns Hopkins U. Applied Physics Lab., Laurel, Md., 1963-75, sr. staff, supr. hybrid ops., 1975-79, div. staff engr., 1979-81, asst. supr. engring. design group, 1981—. Mem. Internat. Soc. Hybrid Microelectronics. Republican. Home: 7724 Hanover Pkwy Apt 301 Greenbelt MD 20770 Office: Applied Physics Lab/Johns Hopkins U Johns Hopkins Rd Laurel MD 20707

BROWN, RUTH PARKS, musician; b. Beaumont, Tex., Oct. 20, 1924; d. Jesse and Juanita (Haynes) Parks; B.S. in Music Edn., U. So. Calif., 1945; B.Metaphysics, Metaphys. Bible Inst. Progressive Christianity, Los Angeles, 1950, D.Psychology in Metaphysics, 1955, Minister Mus. (hon.), 1955; m. Robert Brown, June 15, 1947; children—Jessica Denise, Maynard William. Concert pianist, 1933—; dir. Parks Sch. Music, Los Angeles, 1941-77; tchr. piano Gray's Conservatory Music, Los Angeles, 1942-47; tchr. elementary schs., Calif., 1945—; tchr. kindergarten Parmelee Ave. Elementary Sch., Los Angeles, 1962-72, tchr. music, 1972-77, music resource specialist, 1977—; mem. testing and eval. com. tchr. exams Los Angeles Unified Sch. Dist. Recipient various service awards, certs. appreciation. Mem. Music Educators Nat. Conf., Calif. Music Educators Assn., Los Angeles City Elementary Schs. Music Assn., U. So. Calif. Alumni Assn., Practitioners Guild Metaphys. Bible Inst. Progressive Christianity, Jack and Jill Am. (chpt. v.p. 1965-66), Zeta Phi Beta. Democrat. Mem. Ch. Religious Sci. Internat. Author syllabus student kindergarten tchrs.; composer children's operettas, songs. Home: 13322 McKinley Ave Los Angeles CA 90059 Office: 1338 E 76th Pl Los Angeles CA 90001

BROWN, SAMMYE SCOTT, music educator; b. Dublin, Ga., Nov. 21, 1939; d. Sidney Augustus and Anne Scott; A.A., Brewton-Parker Jr. Coll., Mt. Vernon, Ga., 1960; B.A., U. So. Miss., Hattiesburg, 1962; M.M.E., U. Houston, 1981; m. William Kenneth Roberts, Oct. 11, 1980. Public affairs specialist Skylab Program, Johnson Space Center, 1973-74; adminstrv. aide to chief U.S. Astronaut Corps, Apollo-Soyuz Test Project, Houston, 1974-75; adminstr., Houston, 1975—; music cons., piano, organ, Houston, 1975—. Mem. Cultural Arts Council Houston. Mem. Nat. Guild Piano Tchrs., Music Tchrs. Nat. Assn., LWV, NOW, Gulf Coast Music Assn., AAUW, Young Women of the Arts of Houston, Houston Symphony League. Address: 18100 Nassau Bay Dr Houston TX 77058

BROWN, SANDRA M., corp. exec.; b. Mineola, N.Y., Oct. 7, 1938; d. Edgar P. and Dorothy M. Senne; B.A., Mt. Holyoke Coll., 1960, Ph.D., 1964; M.Ed., Springfield Coll., 1961. Tchr., East Windsor, Conn., 1960-63; reading supr., Middletown, Conn., 1964-66; editor My Weekly Reader, Middletown, 1966-67; dir. dissemination Ednl. Lab., W.Va., 1967, 68; pres. Sandra Brown Advt., Inc., N.Y.C., 1969—, First Women's Funding Corp., N.Y.C., 1976—. Mem. Women's Forum. Mem. com. on rights and responsibilities of women, sec. HEW, 1977; first woman in U.S. licensed to start small bus. investment co. by SBA. Address: 134 E 38th St New York NY 10016

BROWN, SARA MAE, psychologist, educator; b. Monessen, Pa., Aug. 11, 1927; d. Clark Power and Grace (Allen) B.; B.A., Wellesley Coll., 1949; B.Ed., U. Miami, Coral Gables, Fla., 1952; M.S., U. Pa., 1962, Ed.D., 1964. Asst. buyer John Wanamakers, Phila., 1949-51, 53-57; tchr. Lower Merion Twp., Ardmore, Pa., 1957-62; research asst. Carter Found., U. Pa., Phila., 1962-64; asst. prof. U. Del., Newark, 1964-67; asso. prof. psychology So. Conn. State Coll., New Haven, 1967-70, prof. psychology, 1970—. Mem. Am. Psychol. Assn., Am. Statis. Assn., Am. Ednl. Research Assn., Psi Chi, Phi Delta Kappa, Pi Lambda Theta. Presbyterian. Home: 149 Patton Dr Cheshire CT 06410 Office: So Conn State Coll 501 Crescent St New Haven CT 06515

BROWN, SARAH E. (MRS. RALPH JASON TEMPLE), lawyer; b. Topeka, Kans., Aug. 9, 1936; d. Paul Shannon and Alice (Rafter) B.; A.B., Vassar Coll., 1958; LL.B., Georgetown U., 1963; m. Ralph J. Temple, July 17, 1960; children—Katherine Esme, John Anthony. Admitted to D.C. bar, 1964; staff mem. U.S. Senator Estes Kefauver, Washington, 1958; legis. aide U.S. Senator Vance Hartke, Washington, 1959-60; staff asst. John F. Kennedy Presdl. Campaign, Washington, 1960; asst. to dir. compliance surveys and research Pres.'s Com. on EEO, Washington, 1961-65; cons. Migrant div. Office Econ. Opportunity, Washington, 1965-66; practiced in Washington, 1968-71; staff atty. Pub. Defender Service, Washington, 1971—; adj. prof. criminal law George Washington U. Grad Sch., Washington, 1974-76; faculty Nat. Inst. Trial Advocacy Georgetown U. Law Center, 1980-81; mem. D.C. Bar Com. on D.C. Cts.; treas., dir. N.W. Investment Co., Washington, 1964-66; vol. atty. ACLU, Washington, 1969-71; bd. dirs. Women's Legal Def. Fund, 1976-77; mem. criminal justice com. D.C. Commn. on Status of Women; bd. dirs. Washington Halfway House for Women; mem. Criminal Practice Inst. Com.; exec. com., bd. dirs. Law Students in Ct., 1979-82. Mem. Fed., Women's bar assns., Washington Council Lawyers (dir. 1979-82), Women's Legal Def. Fund. Home: 300 11th St NE Washington DC 20002 also Dillons Run Rd Capon Bridge WV Office: 451 Indiana Ave NW Washington DC 20001

BROWN, SARAH MITCHELL, investment co. exec.; b. Ennis, Tex., Mar. 22, 1941; d. Jack Alexander and Elizabeth Anne (Staton) Mitchell; B.A., U. Tex., 1967; m. June 3, 1967; children—Donna Chappell, Laura Chappell, Sarah Lynn Brown. Dir. computer services Mudge Rose Guthrie & Alexander, N.Y.C., 1975-79; firm adminstr. Kramer Levin Nessen Kamin & Soll, N.Y.C., 1979-81; adminstrv. dir. and v.p. capital markets group Dean Witter Reynolds, N.Y.C., 1981—. Vice pres. Brooklyn Heights Assn., 1972-75; mem. bd. Willoughby House, 1982—; nominating chmn. Jr. League of Bklyn., 1971. Democrat. Club: Heights Casino. Office: Dean Witter Reynolds 130 Liberty St New York NY 10006

BROWN, SHARON GAIL, data processing exec.; b. Chgo., Dec. 25, 1941; d. Otto and Pauline (Lauer) Schumacher; B.G.S., Roosevelt U.; 1 dau., Susan Ann. Info. analyst Internat. Minerals & Chems., Northbrook, Ill., 1966-71, programmer analyst, 1971-74; programmer analyst Procon Internat. Inc. subs. UOP Inc., Des Plaines, Ill., 1974-76, systems analyst, 1976-77, project leader, 1977-78; mgr. adminstrv. services, 1978-82; spl. cons. to pres. IPS Internat., Ltd., 1982—; data processing cons. Mem. Buffalo Grove (Ill.) Youth Commn., 1978-82; mem. adv. com. UOP Polit. Action Com., 1979-82. Mem. Am. Mgmt. Assn.

BROWN, SHERRI RUTH, dental student; b. Evansville, Ind., Mar. 14, 1953; d. Charles Samuel and Helen LaVerne (Maraman) Brown; B.S., Miss U. for Women, 1975; M.T., U. Louisville, 1976; postgrad. U. Louisville, 1979—. Med. technologist, supr. hematology Hopkins County Hosp. Madisonville, Ky., 1976-79; sr. dental student U. Louisville. Sch. Dentistry, 1982—, continuing edn. chmn. lab., Madisonville, 1977-79. Mem. Ky. Assn. Women Dentists, Acad. Gen. Dististry, Am. Soc. Cin. Pathologists, Am. Student Dental Assn., Beta Beta Beta, Lambda Tau, Pi Tau Chi. So. Missionary Baptist. Home: Rural Route 1 Clay KY 42404 Office: Apt 2B S Preston Louisville KY 40202

BROWN, SHIRLEY ANN, fundraising exec.; b. St. Louis, Jan. 9, 1943; d. Laura B. Couzart; M.S., So. Ill. U., 1969. Tchr. St. Louis Pub. Schs., 1965-66; coordinator residential living St. Louis Job Corps, 1966-69; resident dir. So. U., Baton Rouge, 1969-71; coordinator-tutor counselors Rutgers U., New Brunswick, N.J., 1973-74; dean women Jersey City Job Corps, 1971-74; asso. area dir. United Negro Coll. Fund, Atlanta, 1974-75, area dir. Ala. Birmingham, 1975-78, asst. nat. campaign dir., 1978—; adv. bd. Campfire Teen Age Girls; chmn. Ala. caucus Nat. Black Women's Polit. Leadership Caucus, 1977; mem. adv. bd. Ala. Women's Campaign Fund, 1978—; bd. dirs. Birmingham Urban League, 1976—; Birmingham Regional Planning Commn., 1977—, Birmingham Regional Health Systems Agy., 1977—, Jefferson County Mental Health Assn., 1977—. Recipient outstanding merit award Booker T. Washington Bus. Coll., Birmingham, 1978. Mem. Nat. Soc. Fundraising Execs. (dir.), Am. Mgmt. Assn., Delta Sigma Theta, Iota Phi Lambda. Baptist. •

BROWN, STELLA CHANEY, advt. agy. exec.; b. East St. Louis, Ill., Apr. 1, 1924; d. James Oscar and Lela Elizabeth (Hartill) Chaney; student Northwestern U., 1941-42, Jefferson Coll., 1942-45; m. A. Harvey Brown, Nov. 1, 1946 (div. Nov. 1960); children—Wendy Alexandra Brown Kennedy, Deborah Elisabeth Brown Garrity. Advt. mgr. Sonnenfelds, St. Louis, 1943; dir. men's wear advt. Stix, Baer & Fuller, St. Louis, 1944; account exec., copy writer Hillman Shane Breyer Agy., Los Angeles, 1945; copy dir. Harry Serwer Agy., N.Y.C., 1945-46; advt. mgr. Libson Shops, St. Louis, 1946-47; asst. advt. dir. Edison Bros. Stores, Inc., 1947-53; copy dir., account exec. Hirsch-Tamm & Ullman Agy., 1957-58; pres. Stella Chaney Brown Advt., Inc., Clayton, Mo., 1959—; dir. St. Louis Broadcasting Co., Inc.; fashion editor Prom Mag., 1946—. Mem. Am. Fedn. Astrologers. Editor: Wheelspin, 1953-58. Address: 9180 Ladue Rd Saint Louis MO 63124

BROWN, SUZANNE GOLDMAN, art historian, gallery owner; b. N.Y.C., Sept. 8, 1929; d. Maurice Elwell and Agnes (Wilson) Goldman; B.A. cum laude, Radcliffe Coll., 1951; postgrad. Harvard U. Sch. Law, Tufts U., Ariz. State U.; m. Jack Edward Brown, Aug. 27, 1950; children—Charles, Abigail, James, Amanda. Owner, operator Art Wagon Gallery, doing bus. as Suzanne Brown Gallery and Suzanne Brown Collection, Scottsdale, Ariz., 1963—; lectr. art history various univs., museums, pvt. orgns.; docent Phoenix Art Mus. League, 1969-73. Bd. dirs. Ariz. Women's Caucus, Seven Coll. Conf., Ariz. Acad., Ariz. Theatre Co. Mem. Main St. Art Assn. (pres. 1976-77). Home: 6645 N Central St Phoenix AZ 85012 Office: 7156 Main St Scottsdale AZ 85251

BROWN, SUZANNE WILEY, mus. exec.; b. Cheyenne, Wyo., Aug. 28, 1938; d. Robert James and Catharine Helen (Schroeder) Wiley; B.S. with honors, U. Wyo., 1960, M.S., 1964; postgrad. U. Cin. Med. Sch., 1965-66, U. Ill., 1969-72; m. Ralph E. Brown, July 19, 1968; 1 dau., Nina M. Research asst. Harvard Med. Sch., 1962-63; research asst. U. Cin. Med. Sch., 1964-65; sr. lab. asst. U. Chgo., 1966-67; research asso. U. Colo. Med. Sch., 1968; teaching asst. U. Ill., 1971-73; exec. asst. Chgo. Acad. Scis., 1974—. NDEA fellow, 1960-62. Mem. Mus. Educators of Greater Chgo., Am. Assn. Museums, Internat. Council Museums, Phi Beta Kappa, Sigma Xi, Phi Kappa Phi. Office: 2001 N Clark St Chicago IL 60614

BROWN, THELMA ETHELDA, psychologist; b. Glouster, Ohio, Feb. 16, 1908; d. John Wright and Kathryn Ethelda (Shevlin) Grubb; B.S., Ohio U., 1930; M.S., U. Ill., 1931; Ph.D., U. Ky., 1938; m. Ralph Roxborough Brown, July 2, 1931; children—Craig Milton, Kathryn Kay Brown Weber. Chief psychologist Longview State Hosp., Cin., 1942-48, VA Hosp., Ft. Thomas, Ky., 1948-53, VA Hosp., Cin., 1953-66; asso. dir., part owner United Indsl. Services, Cin., 1946-73; cons. U.S. Office Hearings and Appeals, Cin., 1966—; asst. prof. dept. psychiatry U. Cin. Med. Sch., 1953-67; lectr. Evening Coll., WCKY, WLW-TV, 1953-59. Diplomate Am. Bd. Examiners in clin. psychology; lic. psychologist, Ohio. Fellow Am. Psychol. Assn., Ohio Psychol. Assn.; mem. Cin. Psychol. Assn. Episcopalian. Contbr. articles in field to profl. jours. Home and office: 83 Miami Pkwy Ft Thomas KY 41075

BROWN, TOTLEE JEANNE DIXON, free lance producer, camerawoman; b. N.Y.C., Dec. 1, 1946; d. Arthur Stanley and Joyce May (Levy) Dixon; B.A. in Theatre and Speech, U. Toledo, 1968; postgrad. CCNY, 1969-70; cert. in TV prodn. Inst. New Cinema Artists, 1976-77; 1 son, Michael. Free lance talent coordinator/producer For You Black Woman, Soul Alive, also fashion shows, beauty pageants, spls., 1967-78; TV camerawoman Sta. WNYC-TV, 1976-77, ABC-TV, 1978—; free lance camerawoman, 1978—; pres. Silver Cloud Communications Inc., T. D. Enterprises, 1979—; dir. M.E. Inc., 1979—. Vice pres. Martin Luther King Day Sch. Adv. Bd., 1977-80; bd. dirs. Community Action Agy., 1978-80. Recipient Public Service award for For You Black Woman, Media Workshop, 1978. Mem. Nat. Assn. TV Arts and Scis., Delta Sigma Theta. Episcopalian. Contbg. editor, feature writer Black N.Y. Illus. Mag., 1977-78. Home: 55 Hamilton Ave New Rochelle NY 10801 Office: 310 Madison Ave Suite 1707 New York NY 10017

BROWN, TRENDA BETH, veterinarian; b. Dumas, Tex., July 26, 1955; d. Walter J. and Elizabeth May (Daniel) Burgess, Jr.; student West Tex. State U., 1973-76; Vet. Scientist, Tex. A&M U., 1978, D.V.M., 1979; m. Mark André Brown, July 27, 1979. Veterinarian, Markham Vet. Clinic, Canyon, Tex., 1979-80, 81; owner, operator Amarillo (Tex.) Mobile Vet. Clinic, 1981—; vol. Animal Rights Assn.; assoc. Canyon Road Animal Hosp. Mem. Citizens Choice, Republican Nat. Dom., Amarillo-Panhandle Humane Soc.; sponsor slow-pitch softball team. Mem. AVMA, Amarillo Vet. Med. Assn. Mormon.

BROWN, VALERIE ANNE, psychiat. social worker; b. Elizabeth, N.J., Feb. 28, 1951; d. William John and Adelaide Elizabeth (Krasa) B.; B.A. summa cum laude (fellow), C.W. Post Coll., 1972; M.S.W. (Silberman scholar), Hunter Coll., 1975. Social work intern Greenwich House Counseling Center, N.Y.C., 1973-74, Metro Cons. Center, N.Y.C., 1974-75; sr. psychiat. social worker, co-adminstr. Saturday Clinic, Essex County Guidance Center, East Orange, N.J., 1975-80; pvt. practice psychiat. social work, psychotherapy, Cedar Grove, N.J., 1979—; psychiat social worker John E. Runneils Hosp., Berkeley Heights, N.J., 1980—; field instr. Fairleigh Dickinson U., Madison, N.J., 1981—, Sch. Social Work, N.Y. U., N.Y.C., 1980—. Mem. N.J. Assn. Clin. Social Workers, (writer in residence Essex County chpt. 1981), Nat. Assn. Social Workers, N.J. Assn. Women Therapists, Am. Soc. Tng. and Devel. Office: 250 N 19th St Kenilworth NJ 07033

BROWN, VERA FRANCES, realtor asso.; b. Cedar County, Mo., Oct. 12, 1916; d. Thaddeus and Janie Frances (Hembree) Achord; B.S., U. Mo., 1940; postgrad. U. Calif., Berkeley, 1958-59; m. Clyde Ellis Brown, Aug. 3, 1940; children—Jane Anne (dec.), Susan Frances, Stephanie Ellis. Tchr., Arcola (Mo.) High Sch., 1940-42; prin. Keats (Kans.) High Sch., 1942-44; realtor asso. Ron Walker Realty, Danville, Calif., 1968—. Mem. DAR (chpt. regent 1977-79, Calif. chmn. DAR schs. 1980), Calif. Vet. Med. Aux. (life), Calif. Assn. Realtors, Contra Costa County Bd. Realtors, Alameda Contra Costa County Vet. Med. Aux. (pres. 1956-58), County Assn. High Sch. Prins. (pres.), AAUW (br. pres.), Children's Home Soc., Diablo Cotillion. Methodist. Clubs: Castlewood Country; Diablo Women's Garden. Home: 29 Mariposa Ct Danville CA 94526 Office: 523 San Ramon Valley Blvd Danville CA 94526

BROWN, WILMA ALENE, educator; b. Mildred, Kans.; d. Scott Robert and Carrie May (Sloan) B.; B.S., Kans. State U., 1943, Ph.D., 1961; M.S., Ohio State U., 1952. Tchr., Mildred, Kans., 1933-42, Colony, Kans., 1942-44, Iola, Kans., 1944-54; chmn. dept. home econs. Youngstown (Ohio) U., 1954-57; asst. prof. foods and nutrition U. Ariz., Tucson, 1957-58, Central Mich. U., Mt. Pleasant, 1961-63; asso. prof. Indiana (Pa.) State U., 1963-64; prof. nutrition and food sci. Tex. Woman's U., Denton, 1964—; asst. dir., dir. food service Campfire Girls of Kansas City (Mo.), summer 1944; dir. food service Girl Scouts Am., Kansas City, summer 1949. Named Piper Prof. of Tex., 1975. Mem. Am. Home Econs. Assn., Tex. Home Econs. Assn., Nutrition Today Soc., Tex. Assn. Coll. Tchs., AAUW, Delta Kappa Gamma, Phi Kappa Phi, Omicron Nu, Phi Delta Gamma. Methodist. Home: 2003 Bell Ave Denton TX 76201 Office: PO Box 20007 TWU Sta Denton TX 76204

BROWNE, CHRISTINE WEBB, sch. counselor; b. Chgo.; d. Alexander and Lucinda Vera (Cole) Webb; B.S., Chgo. State U., 1941; M.A., DePaul U., 1956, postgrad., 1970; m. William H. Browne III, Sept., 1949 (dec.); children—Kristine Julia (Mrs. Stephen B. Colson), William Henri. Tchr., Chgo. Bd. Edn., 1941-54, master tchr., 1954-68, acting asst. prin., 1968-70, counselor, 1970—, instr. classroom mgmt., 1978—, counselor, 1978—; instr. adult edn. Chgo. City Colls., 1980—, panelist All-City Guidance Conf., 1978, vol. Project Cope, 1975-80, mem. adv. com. Pupil Personnel and Spl. Edn. Services, 1980—, mem. regional supt.'s adv. com. Inst. Guidelines, Ednl. Service Region of Cook County, 1978—. Cub Scout den mother Chgo. Area council Boy Scouts Am., 1965-68; mem. com. local council Girl Scouts U.S.A., 1961-64; active PTA, 1960-70, sec., 1979-83; bd. dirs. Camp Martin Johnson, Chgo. Area YMCA, 1972-76. Mem. Secondary Sch. Counselor Council (program chmn. 1981-82, pres. 1982-83), Council Coll. Attendance, Chgo. Guidance and Personnel Assn., Ill. Guidance and Personnel Assn., Am. Personnel and Guidance Assn., Ill. Assn. Coll. Admissions Counselors, Chgo. Area Alliance of Black Sch. Educators, AAUW, Nat. Assn. Female Execs., Mus. Contemporary Art, Chgo. Art Inst., Chgo. Urban League, NAACP, Alpha Kappa Alpha. Episcopalian. also Regents Park Chicago IL 60615

BROWNE, JANE COTTON, family planning cons.; b. St. Paul, Nov. 19, 1912; d. Donald Reed and Grace (Gillette) Cotton; student Wells Coll., 1930-32; m. Harry C. Browne, May 17, 1941 (div. May, 1954); 1 son, Marshall Gillette. Adminstrv. asst. Cargill, Inc., Mpls., 1944-45; office mgr., dir. spl. gifts Am. City Bur., Portland, Oreg., 1947-48; dir. field cons. Planned Parenthood, N.Y. State (Eastern League), 1956-58; exec. dir. Planned Parenthood of Mpls., 1951-56; exec. dir. Planned Parenthood Assn. of Chgo. Area, 1958-69; sr. fellow Adlai Stevenson Inst. Internat. Affairs, 1969; chmn. exec. dirs. council Planned Parenthood-World Population, 1965-68; mem. steering com. N. Cook County Office Econ. Opportunity, 1966-69; gov. bd. Cook County, Office Econ. Opportunity, 1966-69, founder, mem. Family Planning Coordinating Council Met. Chgo., 1967-71; mem. health com., welfare com., Evanston Anti-Poverty Council, 1967-69; mem. Gov.'s State-Wide Advisory Council Ill. Div. Health Planning and Resource Devel., Com. Health Care Facilities, 1968-71; mem. profl. advisory panel Welfare Council Met. Chgo., 1969-71; advisory council Comprehensive Health Planning, Inc., Met. Chgo., 1969-71; family planning cons., research asso. Center for Population Studies, U. Minn., 1970—. U.S. del. Internat. Planned Parenthood Conf., Singapore, 1963 Bangdung, Indonesia, 1969; cons. Near East South Asia div. AID, 1968; project dir. Ark. Family Planning Council, 1970-71, spl. cons., 1971-73; family planning cons. Office Econ. Opportunity, Washington, 1970-73; cons. Nat. Center Family Planning Services, Region VIII, Dept. Health, Edn. and Welfare, 1972-73; program adviser Naomi Gray Assos., 1970—; internat. traveler, lectr. Bd. dirs. Opportunity Workshop, Mpls., 1972—; budget allocations com. United Way of Mpls., 1974-77; bd. dirs., chmn. pub. affairs com. Met. YWCA, Mpls., 1977—. Mem. Mpls. Bd. Realtors (asso.), Am. Pub. Health Assn., Nat. Conf. Social Welfare. Republican. Episcopalian. Home: 205 S Barry Ave Apt #310 Wayzata MN 55391

BROWNE, KATHLEEN GAIL, communications co. exec.; b. Hoboken, N.J., Jan. 24, 1948; d. Joseph Edward and Margaret M. (Finn) B.; B.A., Mackinac Coll., 1970; postgrad. Wake Forest U., 1971, U. Cin., 1975-76, Rensselaer Poly. Inst., 1980; m. John E. Sweeney. Editor tech. publs. Western Electric Co., Winston-Salem, N.C., 1970-73; tng. course devel. supr. Am. Telephone & Telegraph Long Lines, Cin., 1973-76, salesperson, Detroit, 1976-79, data products sales manuals author, Bedminster, N.J., 1979-81, direct response tracking and analysis mgr., 1981—. Mem. Soc. Tech. Communication, AAAS, Direct Mail Mktg. Assn., Beta Sigma Phi. Home: 4 Hamlet Ct Somerset NJ 08873

BROWNE, LESLIE, dancer, actress; b. N.Y.C., June 28, 1957; d. Kelly and Isabel (Mirrow) B.; student pvt. sch., N.Y.C. Mem. corps de ballet N.Y.C. Ballet, 1974-76; soloist Am. Ballet Theatre, N.Y.C., 1976—; appeared in movies: Turning Point, 1976, Nijinsky, 1980; TV shows: The Fonz, 1977, A Tribute to Irving Berlin. Mem. SAG, Am. Guild Mus. Artists, Acad. Motion Picture Arts and Scis. Office: care ICM Artists Ltd 40 W 57th St New York NY 10019 •

BROWNE, PEMA, painter, lit. agt.; b. Atlantic City, Feb. 18, 1928; d. Peter and Katherine (Kendro) Pema; student Moore Coll. Art, 1944-47, Vall State Coll., 1955, New Sch., 1956; m. Perry J. Browne, Nov. 8, 1961; 1 son, Brian Tarquin. Art/traffic coordinator Sudler & Hennessey, N.Y.C., 1954-55; asst. to exec. art dir. Needham & Grohmann, N.Y.C., 1956-61; art buyer, coordinator Grey Advt., N.Y.C., 1962-65; pres. Pema Browne Ltd., N.Y.C., 1966—; numerous one-person exhibits. Recipient Hallmark Fine Arts award, 1952. Republican. Albanian Orthodox. Address: 185 E 85th St New York NY 10028

BROWNING, CAROLYN ELIZABETH, ednl. adminstr.; b. Denver, July 20, 1948; d. Donovan Bruce and Eleanor (Ells) Browning; B.Bus., U. N.Mex., 1975, M.P.A., 1980. Asst. dir. research devel. Office Research Adminstrn., U. N.Mex., Albuquerque, 1975-80, instr., 1977-80; research coordinator Found. of Calif. State U., Sacramento, 1980—; fiscal cons. NIH, 1976—; lectr. in field. Instr., YMCA, Albuquerque, 1978; v.p. Albuquerque United Artists, 1979; sec. bd. dirs. Camp Fire Inc., Albuquerque, 1980. NIH grantee, 1979-80. Mem. Soc. Research Adminstrs. (chpt. sec.-treas. 1978-79), Nat. Council of Univ. Research Adminstrs., Am. Soc. Pub. Adminstrn., World Future Soc. Home: 3418 Viking Dr Sacramento CA 95827 Office: 6000 J St Bldg TAA Calif State U Sacramento CA 95819

BROWNING, COLLEEN, painter; b. Cregg, County Cork, Ireland, 1929; came to U.S., 1949, naturalized, 1956; student (scholar) Slade Sch. of Art (London), 1944-46; m. Geoffrey Wagner, 1949. Set decorater J. Arthur Rank Corp., Eng., 1947-49; one-woman shows include: Little Gallery, London, 1949, Lehigh U., Bethlehem, Pa., 1966; group shows include: Meml. Art Gallery of U. Rochester (N.Y.), 1950 (award), Internat. Exhbn. of Paintings, Carnegie Inst., Pitts., 1952 (award), Butler Inst. Am. Art, Youngstown, Ohio, 1954, Stanford (Calif.) U., 1956 (award), Contemporary Art—U.S., Los Angeles County Fair, 1956 (award), Columbia (S.C.) Mus. Art and Sci., 1957 (award), Milw. Art Center, 1962, 20th Century Realists, San Diego Fine Arts Festival, 1963, Women Artists of Am., Newark Mus., 1965, Twelve Am. Realists, Cleve. Mus. Art, 1975, Painting Today, Indpls. Mus. Art, 1976, Contemporary Landscape Painting, Philbrook Art Center, Tulsa, 1977, Charles H. MacNider Mus., Mason City, Iowa, 1979; Colleen Browning exbns. include: Kennedy Galleries, N.Y.C., 1969, 72, 76, 79, 82, Towson (Md.) State Coll., 1978; represented various shows; commd. for lithographic posters U.S. Olympics Com. and Kent Bicentennial Portfolio Spirit of Independence, 1975, portrait of His Eminence Terence Cardinal Cooke, Archdiocese of N.Y., 1978. Recipient Today's Art Medal of Merit, Butler Art Inst. Am. Art, 1974. Mem. Nat. Acad. Design (Joseph S. Isidor medal, 1953, Julius Hallgarten prize, 1957, purchase award, Henry Ward Ranger Fund, 1963, Adolph and Clara Obrig prize, 1970. Works represented public collections U.S. including Archdiocese of N.Y., Detroit Inst. Arts, Nat. Acad. Design, N.Y.C., N.Y. State Mus., Albany, Randolph-Macon Woman's Coll. Art Gallery, San Francisco Palace of Legion of Honor, St. Louis Art Mus. Address: Kennedy Galleries 40 W 57th St New York NY 10019

BROWNING, HAZEL GAY, educator; b. Greenville, N.C., May 29, 1950; d. Daniel Robert and Helen Nelson (Shelton) Gay; B.S.N., East Carolina U., 1972, M.S. in Rehab. Counseling, 1976, M.S.N., 1979; m. James Fred Browning, Oct. 29, 1972; 1 dau., Lauran Shelton. Staff nurse Pitt Meml. Hosp., Greenville, N.C., 1972-73; office nurse Dr. David Pearsall, Greenville, N.C., 1973; nursing instr. East Carolina U., Greenville, 1973-77, asst. prof. nursing, 1977-80; asst. prof. nursing Duke U., Durham, N.C., 1980—. Mem. Am. Nurses Assn., Nurses Assn. of Am. Coll. Obstetricians and Gynecologists, So. Perinatal Assn., N.C. Nurses Assn. (sec. maternal-child health div. on practice), N.C. Nurses Assn. of Am. Coll. Obstetricians and Gynecologists (mem. adv. council), Rho Lambda, Sigma Theta Tau. Democrat. Presbyterian. Home: 3202A Myra St Durham NC 27707 Office: Sch Nursing Duke U Med Center Durham NC 27710

BROWNING, LOUISE HALL, assn. exec.; b. Science Hill, Ky., June 7, 1934; d. Charles Zack and Ethel Marie (Cassada) Hall; B.A. summa cum laude in Psychology, W.Va. State Coll., 1977, postgrad. 1977-79; children—Tamara Jean, Lisa Kay, John R. Office mgr. Charleston West 76, (W.Va.), 1971-74; asst. comptroller W.Va. Turnpike Commn., Charleston, 1978-80; adminstrv. dir. W.Va. Nurses Assn., Charleston, 1980—. Bd. dirs. Mental Health Assn., 1976—. Mem. W.Va. LWV, Nat. Assn. Female Execs., W.Va. Soc. Assn. Execs., Alpha Kappa Mu, Beta Kappa Chi. Democrat. Editor, The Weather Vane, 1980—. Home: 36 Broadway Gardens Nitro WV 25143 Office: Suite 511 Union Bldg Charleston WV 25301

BROWNING, MELISSA ANN, mech. engr.; b. Steubenville, Ohio, Aug. 31, 1947; d. Milton M. and Mabel (Steele) Trudix; B.S. in M.E., U. Colo., Boulder, 1977. Purchasing agt. Eastman Kodak, Windsor, Colo., 1971-73; mech. engr. Public Service Co. of Colo., Denver, 1978—; cons. Hvar Service, Inc. Mem. ASME. Episcopalian. Home: 11023 Tennyson Pl Westminster CO 80030 Office: 5900 E 39th Ave Denver CO 80207

BROWNING, NORMA LEE (MRS RUSSELL JOYNER OGG), journalist; b. Spickard, Mo., Nov. 24, 1914; d. Howard R. and Grace (Kennedy) Browning; A.B., B.J., U. Mo., 1937; M.A. in English, Radcliffe Coll., 1938; m. Russell Joyner Ogg, June 12, 1938. Reporter, Los Angeles Herald-Express, 1942-43; with Chgo. Tribune, 1944—, Hollywood columnist, 1966-75. Vis. lectr. creative writing, editorial cons., mem. nat. adv. bd. Interlochen Arts Acad., Northwood Inst. Recipient E.S. Beck award Chgo. Tribune. Mem. Theta Sigma Phi, Kappa Tau Alpha. Author: City Girl in the Country, 1955; Joe Maddy of Interlochen, 1963; (with W. Clement Stone) The Other Side of the Mind, 1965; The Psychic World of Peter Hurkos, 1970; (with Louella Dirksen) The Honorable Mr. Marigold, 1972; (with Ann Miller) Miller's High Life, 1972; Peter Hurkos: I Have Many Lives, 1976; Omarr: Astrology and the Man, 1977; (with George Masters) The Masters Way to Beauty, 1977; (with Russell Ogg) He Saw A Hummingbird, 1978; (with Florence Lowell) Be A Guest At Your Own Party, 1980; Face-Lifts: Everything You Always Wanted to Know, 1981; (with Edith Head) Edith Head's Hollywood, 1982. Contbr. articles to nat. mags. Address: 226 Morongo Rd Palm Springs CA 92262 *

BROWNING, RUTH ANNA WRIGHT, educator; b. Indpls., July 7, 1932; d. Charles Parry and Mary Margaret (Miller) Wright; B.A., Earlham Coll., 1953; M.Ed., Ind. U. Pa., 1971; Ph.D., U. Pitts., 1981; m. Scott David Browning, June 8, 1953; children—Donald Wayne, Douglas William. Dietician, Northwestern U., Evanston, Ill., 1953-54; bookkeeper Wright, Coal & Oil Co., Indpls., 1954-56; tchr. Bishop Carroll High Sch., Ebensburg, Pa., 1966-70; faculty Ind. U. Pa., Indiana, 1970—, asso. prof. home econs. and vocat. edn. 1970—. Mem. Am. Vocat. Assn., Am. Home Econs. Assn., AAUP, Pa. Vocat. Assn., Pa. Home Econs. Assn., Pa. Assn. Tchr. Educators, Phi Delta Kappa. Republican. Author: Analyze the Role of a Teacher, A Pre-Student Teaching Field Experience for Pre-Service Teachers, 1979; (with Alma B. Kazmer) Occupational Home Economics, 1980. Editor: Developing Independent Living Skills for the Physically Handicapped 1974. Home: 2592 Shelley Dr Indiana PA 15701 Office: Indiana University of Pennsylvania Ackerman Hall Indiana PA 15705

BROWNMILLER, SUSAN, author, feminist activist; b. Bklyn., Feb. 15, 1935; student Cornell U., 1952-55, Jefferson Sch. Social Sci. Reporter, NBC-TV, Phila., 1965; network newswriter ABC-TV, N.Y.C., 1965-67; former researcher Newsweek mag.; former staff writer Village Voice; free-lance writer mags., newspapers; author books including: Shirley Chilsholm, 1970; Against Our Will: Men, Women and Rape, 1975; founder Women Against Pornography. Office: care Simon and Schuster 1230 Ave of Americas New York NY 10020 *

BRUBAKER, GWENDOLYN LEE, choral condr., educator; b. Leadville, Colo., Feb. 28, 1944; d. Harold Harry and Frances Helen (Frey) B.; B.M., Hastings Coll., 1966; M.M.E., Drake U., 1967; Ph.D., Northwestern U., 1982. Tchr. vocal music kindergarten through 12th grades Central Dallas Sch., Minburn, Iowa, 1967-69; tchr. vocal music Lane Jr. High Sch., West Allis, Wis., 1969-77; vis. lectr. in music edn. Roosevelt U., 1979-80; vis. lectr. in jr. high sch. music Northwestern U., 1980; instr. choral music edn. U. Wis., LaCrosse; dir. music Trinity Lutheran Ch., LaCrosse; musical dir. community theaters, Milw., LaCrosse. Mem. Am. Choral Dirs. Assn., Music Educators Nat. Conf., Wis. Music Educators Conf., Pi Kappa Lambda. Democrat. Choral compositions: Love Is Come Again, 1972; Sing Praise, 1972; The Lone Wild Bird, 1978; Orientale, 1982. Home: 616 Sand Lake Rd Onalaska WI 54650 Office: Fine Arts Bldg U Wis 16th and Vine LaCrosse WI 54601

BRUBECK, ANNE ELIZABETH DENTON, artist; b. Beardstown, Ill., Mar. 5, 1918; d. Harry B. and Helen Jean (Gibbs) Denton; student Christian Coll., 1935-36; B.Design, Newcomb Coll., Tulane U., 1939; postgrad. Art Inst. Chgo., 1939-40; A.A. (hon.), Wabash Valley Coll., 1981; m. William E. Brubeck, Dec. 14, 1940; children—Jean Brubeck Stayman, William E. Instr. painting Wabash Valley Coll., Mt. Carmel, Ill., 1962-67; painter; one-man shows include N.Y.C., 1961, 63-67, Evansville, Ind., 1963-69; retrospective, Wabash Valley Coll., 1980; juried exhbns. include: Evansville Mus., 1963, 64, 65, Swopes Gallery, Terre Haute, Ind., 1964, 68, Nashville, 1967. Trustee, Mt. Carmel Pub. Library, 1954—, chmn., 1975-6; mem. cultural events com. Wabash Valley Coll., 1976—. Brubeck Art Center named in her and her husband's honor, 1976; named to Mt. Carmel High Sch. Centennial Hall of Fame, 1982. Mem. Ill. Library Assn., Nat. League Am. Penwomen, PEO. Methodist. Club: Reviewers Matinee. Home and office: 729 Cherry St Mount Carmel IL 62863

BRUCE, JOYCE PEARL PETERSON, retail exec.; b. Webster County, Mo., Apr. 25, 1941; d. Nay Dean and Phyllis Marie (Jennings) Felkner; student public schs., Fordland, Mo. and Casper, Wyo.; m. Kenneth L. Bruce, Aug. 17, 1979. Kelley girl Buttreys Dept. Store, Great Falls, Mont., 1962-65; 2d asst. mgr. ladies apparel Montgomery Ward, Great Falls, 1965-67; asst. mgr. Paris, Springfield, Mo., 1969-70; asst. mgr., window trimmer Stuarts, Springfield, 1970-71; mgr. Libson Shops, Springfield, 1971-78; mgr., buyer Gift Gallerys, McLeans Enterprises, Springfield, 1978—; bd. dirs. Battlefield Mall, Springfield, 1974-75, mem. promotion bd., 1975-76. Mem. Am. Fox Trotting Horse Assn., Mo. Fox Trotting Horse Assn. Office: 2610 N Glenstone St Springfield MO 65804

BRUCE, MARCIA THOMAS, civic worker; b. Lansing, Mich., Mar. 3, 1939; d. Joseph Earl and Maxine Louella (Mosher) Thomas; student Long Beach State Coll., 1957-61; B.S., U. Md., College Park, 1978; m. Malcolm Charles Bruce, Sept. 5, 1961; children—Lisa-Marie, Wendy Louise. Chmn., Planned Parenthood Montgomery County (Md.), 1977-79; bd. dirs. Planned Parenthood of Met. Washington, 1976-79; coordinator vols. Magruder High Sch., Rockville, Md., 1980-82; worthy advisor Rainbow Girls, 1957; youth coordinator Mill Creek United Meth. Ch., 1978-79; Girl Scout leader, 1973-74. Recipient Margaret Sanger cert., 1979. Mem. Omicron Nu. Club: Redland Homemakers (founder). Home: 7408 Mill Run Dr Derwood MD 20855

BRUCE, MICHELE DOUGLASS, nurse; b. Lake Placid, N.Y., Apr. 14, 1952; d. Raymond Donald and Veronica (Petruce) Douglass; R.N. with honors, Champlain Valley Physician's Hosp. Sch. Nursing, 1977; student N.Y. State External Program, 1981—; m. William Bernard Bruce, July 24, 1971; children—Shelby Anne, Michael Douglass. Admitting sec./acctg. clk. Gen. Hosp. of Saranac Lake (N.Y.), 1970-72; legal sec. Norman L. Hess, Esq., Lake Placid, 1972-73; waitress Howard Johnson Restaurant, Lake Placid, 1973-77; nurse, 11-7 supr. Placid Meml. Hosp., Lake Placid, 1977-79, acting dir. nursing, 1979-80, asst. dir. nursing, discharge planner/infection control nurse, 1980-81, dir. nursing service, 1981—, mem. task force of bd. dirs., 1981—. Lic. R.N., N.Y. State. Mem. N.Y. State Nurses Assn. Dist. 8., Lake Placid Vol. Ambulance Assn. (adminstrv. v.p. 1979-80). Home: Fawn Ridge Dr Lake Placid NY 12946 Office: Placid Meml Hosp Lake Placid NY 12946

BRUCE-WOLFE, VIRGINIA, neuropsychologist; b. Cortland, N.Y., Aug. 13, 1936; d. Warren A. and Marion S. Bruce; student Syracuse U., 1954-56; B.A., U. Mo., Kansas City, 1967, M.A. in Psychology, 1970; Ph.D. in Exptl. Psychology (dissertation fellow), U. Kans., 1977; children—Bruce Wayne Jackson, Brenda Lee Jackson. Research asst. in psychology U. Kans., 1972-74; postdoctoral trainee in neuropsychology VA Med. Center, Kansas City, Mo., 1976-79; asst. prof. psychiatry U. Kans. Med. Center, 1979—; instr. psychology Avila Coll.; vis. asst. fellow J.B. Pierce Found. and Yale U., New Haven, 1980-81. Nat. Inst. Environ. Health Scis. grantee, 1980-85. Mem. AAUP, Bioelectromagnetics Assn. Contbr. articles and revs. to profl. jours. Office: 4801 Linwood Blvd Kansas City MO 64128

BRUCH, CAROL SOPHIE, lawyer, educator; b. Rockford, Ill., June 11, 1941; d. Ernest and Margarete (Willstätter) B.; A.B., Shimer Coll., 1960; J.D. (Bartley Cavanaugh Crum scholar), U. Calif., Berkeley, 1972; children—Margarete Louise Myers, Kurt Randall Myers. Mem. profl. staff San Francisco council Girl Scouts U.S.A., 1960-62, summers 1963, 64; substitute tchr. elem. sch. Oakland (Calif.) Pub. Schs., 1966-67; tchr. primary grades Dependents' Sch., Bendix Field Engring. Corp., Madagascar, 1967-68; law clk. to Assoc. Justice William O. Douglas, U.S. Sup. Ct. 1972-73; admitted to Calif. bar, 1973, U.S. Sup. Ct. bar, 1980; acting prof. law U. Calif., Davis, 1973-78, prof., 1978—; cons. to Ctr. for Family in Transition, 1981—, Calif. Law Revision Commn., 1979—, NOW Legal Def. and Edn. Fund, 1980-81. Mem. adv. com. child support and child custody Calif. Commn. on Status of Women, 1981—; host parent Am. Field Service, Davis, 1977-78. Max Rheinstein sr. research fellow Alexander von Humboldt Found., W.Ger., 1978-79. Mem. ABA (mem. com. on Family Law Quar., 1980—), Calif. State Bar, Am. Law Inst., Order of Coif. Contbr. articles to legal jours.; editor Calif. Law Rev., 1971. Democrat. Jewish. Office: School of Law Univ of California Davis CA 95616

BRUCHAC, CAROL WORTHEN, mag. editor; b. Ithaca, N.Y., Dec. 2, 1942; d. Albert Woolman and Katherine (Haberly) Worthen; ed. U. Okla., 1961; m. Joseph Bruchac, III, June 13, 1964; children—James, Jesse. Lab. asst. Cornell U., 1961-65; lab. technician Syracuse U. Research Corp., 1965-66; sch. librarian, bookstore mgr. Keta (Ghana) Secondary Sch., 1966-69; mng. editor Greenfield (N.Y.) Rev., lit. mag., 1970—; sales mgr. Greenfield Rev. Press, 1971—; dir. prison project Com. Small Mag. Editors and Pubs., 1973—, editor Prison Project Newsletter, 1974—. Mem. dist. cultural arts com. Greenfield Center Sch. PTA. CCLM Editors fellow, 1980. Address: Box 80 Greenfield Center NY 12833

BRUCK, LILLY, consumer adv., broadcaster, columnist; b. Vienna, Austria, May 13, 1918; came to U.S., 1941, naturalized, 1944; d. Max and Sophie M. Hahn; Ph.D. in Econs., U. Vienna; postgrad. Sorbonne, Paris, Sch. of Econs., London, Sch. of Bus., Columbia U., 1941-42, Sch. of Social Work, N.Y. U., 1964-66; m. Sandor Bruck, Mar. 7, 1943; 1 dau., Sandra Lee. Dir. consumer edn. Dept. Consumer Affairs, City of N.Y., 1969-78; project dir. Am. Coalition of Citizens with Disabilities, 1977-78; consumer adv., broadcaster In Touch Networks, N.Y.C., 1978—; consumer affairs commentator Nat. Public Radio, 1980—. Chmn. Westchester County, Bonds for Israel, 1960-64. Recipient Eleanor Roosevelt award Bonds for Israel, 1963; Woman of Yr. award Anti Defamation League, 1972; Community Service award local council Girl Scouts U.S.A., 1974. Mem. Soc. of Consumer Affairs Profls., Am. Women in Radio and TV, Authors Guild, Am. Workers for Blind. Democrat. Jewish. Author: Access, The Guide to a Better Life for Disabled Americans, 1978; contbr. articles on disability and rehab. to books, ency. Home: 55 Secor Rd Scarsdale NY 10583 Office: In Touch Networks 322 W 48th St New York NY 10036

BRUCK, PHOEBE ANN MASON, landscape architect; b. Highland Park, Ill., Nov. 26, 1928; d. George Allen and Louise Townsend (Barnard) Mason; student Bard Coll., 1946-49; B.S., Ill. Inst. Tech., 1954; M.L.A., Harvard U., 1963; m. F. Frederick Bruck, June 30, 1956. Trainee, Nat. Gallery of Art, Washington, 1947, Mus. Modern Art, N.Y.C., 1948; head design dept. Design Research Inc., Cambridge, Mass., 1955-60; cons. The Architects Collaborative & Sert, Jackson Assocs., Inc., 1960-63; v.p. F. Frederick Bruck, Architect & Assoc., Inc., Cambridge; vis. design critic dept. landscape architecture Harvard U. Grad. Sch. Design, 1971-79. Judge, New Eng. Flower Show, Mass. Hort. Soc., 1971-79, Thoreau Awards, Assn. Landscape Contractors, 1980; mem. Sci. Adv. Group for Edn., Cambridge Pub. Schs., 1981-82. Mem. Mass. Bd. Registration of Landscape Architects, Am. Arbitration Assn., Am. Soc. Landscape Architects, Boston Soc. Landscape Architects (pres. 1973-75, examining bd. 1978-81), Harvard U. Grad. Sch. Design Alumni Assn. (officer 1972-78). Episcopalian. Contbr. to New Landscapes for Living, 1980. Home: 148 Coolidge Hill Cambridge MA 02138 Office: 148 B Coolidge Hill Cambridge MA 02138

BRUCKMAN, IDEL RAPOPORT, psychologist; b. San Antonio, June 13, 1920; d. David and Riva (Feldman) Rapoport; B.A. summa cum laude, U. Tex., 1938, M.A. in Psychology, 1951; Ph.D., U. London, 1964; m. Lawrence Bruckman, July 20, 1941; children—Chaddie Kruger, Kathy McClelland. Instr., San Antonio Coll., 1956-60; mem. faculty St. Mary's U., San Antonio, 1965—, prof. psychology, chmn. dept., 1970—, also dir. master's program clin. psychology; vis. prof. U. London, 1971; adj. prof. U. Tex. Med. Sch., 1971—; organizer, chmn. ad hoc com. Bexar County Jail Inmate Probation Rehab., 1970. Mem. Am. Psychol. Assn., Tex. Psychol. Soc., Brit. Psychol. Soc., S.W. Tex. Archaeol. Soc. (exec. com.). Author papers in field. Home: 115 Danube St San Antonio TX 78213 Office: 1 Camino Santa Maria San Antonio TX 78284

BRUDERMANN, SHARON RUTH, sales exec.; b. Bklyn., Aug. 1, 1943; d. Fred Lee and Ruth Marie (Decker) Waite; student public schs., Old Westbury, N.Y.; m. Donald J. Brudermann, Nov. 14, 1963; children—Donald, Christopher. Pres., Sharon Brudermann Corp., Farmingdale, N.Y., 1975-78, Fred L. Waite Corp., Babylon, N.Y., 1978-80; with communications div. Gen. Electric Co., Woodside, N.Y., 1980-82; sales exec. Fawn Vending Inc., Jericho, N.Y., 1982—; owner, operator Islanders Dance Club, Farmingdale, 1971-74; instr. Dale Dance Studio and Arthur Murray Studios, Hempstead, N.Y., 1961-64. Mem. U.S. Senatorial Bus. Adv. Bd., 1981, Presdl. Task Force, 1982. Lic. pvt. single-engine pilot. Mem. Internat. Platform Assn. Republican. Roman Catholic. Home: 4 Larkin St Farmingdale NY 11735 Office: 366 N Broadway Jericho NY 11753

BRUDNER, HELEN GROSS, educator; b. N.Y.C.; d. Nathan and Mae (Grichtman) Gross; B.S., N.Y. U., 1959, M.A., 1960, Ph.D., 1973; m. Harvey Jerome Brudner, Dec. 18, 1963; children—Mae Ann, Terry Joseph, Jay Scott. Tchr., N.Y.C. Bd. Edn., 1959-60; instr. Pratt Inst., Bklyn., 1959-61; asst. prof. history N.Y. Inst. Tech., N.Y.C., 1961-63, dir. guidance, 1962-63; asso. prof. Fairleigh Dickinson U., Rutherford, N.J., 1963-73, prof. history and polit. sci., 1974—, dir. Honors Coll., 1972—, chmn. social sci. dept., 1980—, pres. univ. senate, 1975-76; v.p. HJB Enterprises, Highland Park, N.J., 1970—, vice chmn. WLC Inc., Highland Park, 1976—; cons. auto edml. systems, 1971—. Bd. dirs. NSF Women in Politics project, 1981, Nat. Endowment for The Humanities and Woodrow Wilson Found. project Women in Am. History, Princeton, N.J., 1980. Recipient Woman of Yr. award Am. Businesswomen's Assn., 1980. Mem. Am. Judicature Soc., Am. Hist. Soc., Acad. Polit. Sci. Contbr. articles in field to profl. publs. Home: 812 Abbott St Highland Park NJ 08904 Office: Fairleigh Dickinson Univ Social Sci Dept Rutherford NJ 07070 also HJB Enterprises Inc 333 Montgomery St Highland Park NJ 08904

BRUEL, IRIS BARBARA, psychologist; b. N.Y.C., June 10, 1933; d. Herman and Anna (Cohen) Goldstein; B.A. in Psychology, CCNY, 1956, M.S. in Sch. Psychology, 1961; Ph.D. in Clin. Psychology, U. Miami (Fla.), 1972; m. Robert Bruel, Apr., 1953 (div. 1957); adopted children—Michael Abraham, Russell Emanuel. Child supr. Linden Hill Sch., Jewish Bd. Guardians, Hawthorne, N.Y., 1957-59; tchr.-therapist The League Sch. for Severely Disturbed Children, Bklyn., 1959-61, Assn. for Mentally Ill Children, Yonkers, N.Y., 1961-63; psychology research asst. U. Miami, Coral Gables, Fla., 1964-67; trainee VA Hosp., Miami, 1967-68; intern diagnostic testing and psychotherapy Henderson Clinic, Ft. Lauderdale, Fla., 1968-69; intern child psychol. services San Fernando Valley Child Guidance Clinic, Van Nuys, Calif., 1970-71; cons. Sorensen Group, N.Y.C., 1972; clin. psychologist Dade County Dept. Youth Services, Miami, 1972-77; co-dir. Center for the Whole Family, Inc., Coral Gables, 1976-79; pvt. practice clin. psychology, South Miami, Fla., 1979—; cons. Jewish Vocat. Service, 1980—; dir. psychol. services Sex, Health, Edn. Center, North Miami, Fla., 1981—; affiliate staff Grant Center Hosp., 1977—; adj. prof. Nova U., Ft. Lauderdale, 1977; field supr. practicum students S. Fla. Sch. Profl. Psychology, Miami, 1978—. Sec., Reform Democratic Club, N.Y.C., 1962-63. Cert. profl. psychologist, Fla. Mem. Am. Psychol. Assn., Dade County Psychol. Assn., Fla. Soc. Clin. Hypnosis, Dade County Mental Health Assn., Amnesty Internat., Cousteau Soc. Jewish. Home: 2869 Shipping Ave Miami FL 33133 Office: 7800 Red Rd South Miami FL 33143

BRUEMMER, MARY ADELE, univ. ofcl.; b. Madison, Ill., Feb. 26, 1920; d. Ignatius George and Adele M. (Bergrath) B.; A.B. in Edn., St. Louis U., 1938-42, M.Ed., 1960. Dir. Cath. Youth Orgns., Springfield, Ill., 1943-48; dir. continuity dept. Sta. WCVS, 1948-51; dir. publicity Lincoln Library, 1951-53; dir. adult edn. dept. Springfield Coll. in Ill., 1953-55; dir. Marguerite Hall, St. Louis U., 1956-59, dir. women's housing, 1959-67, dean of women, 1967-73, asst. v.p. student devel., dean of women, 1973-75, dean student affairs, 1975—. Mem. Nat., Mo. (sec.-treas. 1958-64, pres. 1971-78) assns. women deans, adminstrs. and counselors, AAUW, Assn. Coll. Personnel Adminstrs., Am. Personnel and Guidance Assn., Am. Assn. Higher Edn., Pi Lambda Theta, Alpha Sigma Nu (nat. v.p. 1979-82). Roman Catholic. Address: 20 N Grand Blvd Saint Louis MO 63103

BRUFF, BEVERLY OLIVE, assn. adminstr.; b. San Antonio, Dec. 15, 1926; d. Albert Griffith and Hazel Olive (Smith) Bruff; B.A., H. Sophie Newcomb Coll., 1948; postgrad. Our Lady of Lake Coll., 1956, Okla. Center for Continuing Edn., 1960-70. Asst. dir. New Orleans Theatre Guild, 1948-50; dist. dir. San Antonio Area council Girl Scouts U.S.A., 1958-70, public relations dir., 1970—; mem. Council of Pres., (v.p., 1981-82; mem. Council of Internat. Relations. Zoning commr. Hill Country Village, Tex., 1973-76. Mem. Assn. Girl Scout Profl. Workers (exec. bd. 1963-72, pub. relations chmn. 1964-69, v.p. 1969-72, mem. nat. bd. dirs. 1972—, communications chmn. 1972), Tex. Pub. Relations Assn. (Silver Spur award), Women in Communications (historian 1969-70, v.p. 1970-71, treas. 1971-73), Tex. Press Women (recipient state writing contest awards 1971, 72, 73, 74, mem. exec. bd. dirs. 1970-71, 73-74, dist. treas. 1972-73, dist. v.p. 1973), Nat. Fedn. Press Women, Internat. Assn. Bus. Communicators, Speech Arts of San Antonio (v.p. 1963-64, pres. 1964-66, 70-72, dir. 1964-72, chmn. bd. dirs. 1966-69), Am. Women in Radio and TV (dir. chpt. 1974, sec. 1975, pres.-elect 1978, pres. 1979-80), San Antonio Soc. Fund Raising Execs. Home: 508 Tomahawk Trail San Antonio TX 78232 Office: 1017 N Main Ave Suite 300 San Antonio TX 78212

BRUININKS, VIRGINIA LEE, psychologist; b. Temple, Tex., Oct. 30, 1937; d. Luther Patterson and Virginia Lafayette (Wilkins) Walter; B.S., U. Tex. at Austin, 1959, M.Edn., 1967; postgrad. internship program in Spl. Edn. Adminstrn., 1970; Ed.D., U. Houston, 1973; m. Glen Ellis, 1958 (div.); 23, 1975; children—Glen Edward, David Walter; m. 2d, Robert Reinehr, 1963 (div.); 1 son Charles Allen (Bruininks); m. 3d, Robert Bruininks, 1975. Elem. classroom tchr. Austin (Tex.) Ind. Sch. Dist., 1959-60, Houston Ind. Sch. Dist., 1965; teaching asst. and research asst. dept. ednl. psychology U. Tex., Austin, 1965-66; intern Austin State Hosp., 1967; curriculum specialist Spl. Ednl. Instructional Materials Center, U. Tex., 1967-68; dir. field activities Edn. Personnel Devel., Austin, 1969-70; parent trainer-communications coordinator Edn. Service Center, Austin, 1970-71; grad. asst. U. Houston, 1971-72, teaching fellow, summer 1972, evaluator lab. experiences Tchrs. Inst. Program, 1972-73, grad. asst., advisor in curriculum and instrn. student services center, 1972-73, teaching fellow dept. curriculum and instrn., 1973; prof. ednl. psychology Dept. of Psychoeducational Studies, U. Minn., Mpls., 1973—; chmn. State Adv. Council for Inservice Tng. Regular Classroom Tchrs. 1977-79. cons. spl. ednl. various sch. dists. Named Minn. Spl. Educator of Yr., 1978; recipient service award Internat. Council Exceptional Children, 1978; HEW Office of Human Devel. Services grantee, 1976-80. Mem. Council for Exceptional Children, Nat. Assn. Children with Learning Disabilities (dir. Minn. chpt. 1978-80), Nat. Assn. Retarded Citizens, AAUP, Assn. Supervision and Curriculum Devel. Editorial cons. Jour. Ednl. Psychology, 1979; asso. editor Exceptional Children, 1979—; contbr. articles to profl. jours., papers to profl. confs. Home: 4914 Arden Ave S Edina MN 55424 Office: 13 Pattee Hall 150 Pillsbury Dr SE University of Minnesota Minneapolis MN 55455

BRULÉ, A. LORRAINE, comml. property mgr., business exec.; b. Yakima, Wash., Aug. 16, 1925; d. Arthur E. and Helen (Auvé) Brulé; student Seattle U., 1943-44, Dominican Coll. San Rafael, 1944-45; B.S. in Sociology, Seattle U., 1947; m. Nolan D. Roach, Oct. 24, 1959 (div. Jan. 1978); children—Dusty Dean, Gaylen Leigh, Susan Marie, Dean Patrick. Bookkeeper, Harper Meggee, Inc., Seattle, 1947-48; sec.

bookkeeper Griffin Envelope Co., Seattle, 1948-50; with Yukon Investment Co., Inc., Seattle, 1950-59, 75—, treas., 1977—, mgr. comml. properties, 1975—, asst. sec., 1975—. Mem. Seattle U. Alumni Assn., Bldg. Owners and Mgrs. Assn. Seattle, Bldg. Owners and Mgrs. Assn. Internat. Roman Catholic. Clubs: Edmonds Yacht, Wash. Athletic. Home: 17304 Palatine Ave N Seattle WA 98133 Office: Suite 315 Lyon Bldg Seattle WA 98104

BRUMAGIN, SUSAN JOY, exec. search firm exec.; b. N.Y.C., Sept. 8, 1949; d. Mark and Dorothy (Segal) Casper; exec. secretarial degree, Jones Bus. Coll., 1968. Sec. to pres. Koger Properties, Jacksonville, Fla., 1970-71; adminstrv. asst. to pres. Pinebreeze Farms, Inc., Jacksonville, 1971-75; sales rep. Procter & Gamble, Jacksonville, 1975-76; sales search recruiter Bales Sales Recruiters, Jacksonville, 1976-78; owner Exec. Sales Registry, Tampa, Fla., 1978—. Mem. Sales and Mktg. Execs. Tampa. Office: 4100 W Kennedy Blvd Tampa FL 33609

BRUMBAUGH, ELIZABETH PAUL, social worker; b. Phila., Nov. 22, 1910; d. Joseph Archer and Orpha Jane (Miller) Paul; B.S., U. Pa., 1932; M.S.S.W., Smith Coll., 1939; cert. in family therapy Family Inst. of Phila., 1968; m. John McCall Brumbaugh, May 19, 1934; children—Susan Jane, Eileen Elizabeth, Paul Michael. Caseworker, supr. Phila. Fed. Relief Program, 1934-36; social worker supr. Delaware County (Pa.) Poor Bd., 1936; social worker Phila. Family Soc., 1937-40; clin. social worker Norristown (Pa.) State Hosp., 1940-44; co-founder Phila. Fountain House (now Phila. Horizon House), 1951, chmn. bd. dirs., 1951-56, dir., 1956—; clin. social worker Montgomery County (Pa.) Mental Health/Mental Retardation Center, Norristown, 1962—, dir. retardation service, 1966-73, dir. out patient service, 1976-78, chief social worker, 1973—. Fellow Assn. Clin. Social workers; mem. Nat. Assn. Social Workers, AAUW. Home: 111 Owen Ave Lansdowne PA 19050 Office: 1100 Powell St Norristown PA 19401

BRUMFIELD, DEBORAH JAGERS, med. sociologist; b. McComb, Miss., Sept. 16, 1954; d. Hugh Fitzhugh and Mary Francelia (Moore) Jagers; B.S., U. So. Miss., 1975, M.A., 1981; 1 dau., Autumn Richelle. Med. sociologist, dir. public relations SW Miss. Regional Med. Center, McComb, 1976—; cons., med. recruiter. County demographic cons. senatorial campaign of Thad Cochran; active March of Dimes; vol. Crippled Children's Clinic. Mem. Am. Soc. Hosp. Public Relations Dirs., Nat. Assn. Nurse Recruiters, Women in Communication, Miss. Soc. Hosp. Public Relations, Dirs. Republican. Methodist. Home: 7-A Pine Terr Apt McComb MS 39648 Office: 215 Marion Ave McComb MS 39648

BRUMFIELD, PEGGY DARLINE, oil co. exec.; b. Washington, May 27, 1948; d. Stanley Warren and Bessie C. (Grant) Tapscott; B.A. in French, Ind. State U., Terre Haute, 1970; m. James Irving Brumfield; children—Koren, James Irving, Jonathan, Colette. Human relations rep. Pa. Human Relations Commn., Pitts., 1972-74; with Gulf Oil Corp., Pitts., 1974—, mgr. programs and systems devel., 1977-78, mgr. EEO support systems, 1978—; tchr., lectr., speaker in field. Mem. Am. Soc. Tng. and Devel., Orgn. Resource Counselors. Baptist. Author articles in field. Office: Gulf Oil Corp PO Box 1166 Pittsburgh PA 15230

BRUMMER, BARBARA JOAN, chem. mfg. co. exec.; b. Passaic, N.J., Mar. 5, 1947; d. Charles Francis and Rose Theresa (Mangone) Flenner; B.A., Montclair State U., 1968; M.S., N.Y. U., 1975, Ph.D., 1980; m. Thomas Brummer, Aug. 11, 1968; children—Judith, Laurie. Clin. microbiologist Paterson Gen. Hosp., 1966-69; microbiologist Airwick Industries, 1971-73, mgr. research services, 1973-76, asso. dir. product devel., 1976; v.p. research and devel. Boyle-Midway, Cranford, N.J., 1976—. Mem. Chem. Specialties Mfrs. Assn. (dir.), AAAS, Assn. Research Dirs. Home: 19 Warfield Upper Montclair NJ 07043 Office: South Ave and Hale St Cranford NJ 07016

BRUNDAGE, DOROTHY JUNE, nurse; b. Cleve., June 18, 1930; d. William David and Isabelle Josephine (Porter) Palmer; B.S. Nursing, Western Res. U., 1953; M.Nursing, Emory U., 1968; Ph.D., Walden U., 1980; m. Donald D. Brundage, Nov. 29, 1952; children—David C., Ellen K. Staff nurse Univ. Hosp., Cleve., 1953, Larimer County Hosp., Ft. Collins, Colo., 1953-54, Euclid-Glenville Hosp., Cleve., 1954-55, Lake County Meml. Hosp., Painesville, Ohio, 1955-61; dir. in-service edn. Anniston (Ala.) Meml. Hosp., 1962-65, instr. Hosp. Sch. Nursing, 1965-67; mem. faculty Duke U. Sch. Nursing, Durham, N.C., 1968—, assoc. prof., 1979—, assoc. dean, 1979—, mem. steering com. U. Regional Research Conf., 1976-77. Fellow Am. Acad. Nursing; mem. Am. Assn. Nephrology Nurses and Technicians (adv. bd. 1981—), Am. Nurses Assn., AAUP, Am. Assn. for Higher Edn., AAAS, Sigma Theta Tau. Author: (with Katina Strauch) Guide to Library Resources in Nursing, 1980, Nursing Management Renal Problems, 1976, 2d edit., 1980. Home: Route 6 Box 215 Mebane NC 27302 Office: Sch Nursing Duke U Durham NC 27710

BRUNER, CHARLOTTE HUGHES, educator; b. Urbana, Ill., May 8, 1917; d. Charles Hughes and Nell Converse (Bomar) Johnson; B.A., U. Ill., 1938; M.A., Columbia U., 1939; m. David Kincaid Bruner, July 16, 1939; children—Nell Kincaid Bruner Sedransk, Charles Hughes. Tchr. French, Iowa State U., 1942-44, 55—, prof., 1980—; instr. U. Ill., 1944-45. Mem. African Lit. Assn. (vice chmn. 1978-79), African Studies Assn., Am. Tchrs. French, Am. Council Teaching Fgn. Langs., Coll. Lang. Assn., MLA, Phi Beta Kappa, Phi Kappa Phi, Phi Sigma Iota. Writer, dir. radio series, 1974, 79, 80—; contbr. articles to profl. jours. Home: 4625 Westbend Dr Ames IA 50010 Office: Dept Fgn Langs and Lits Iowa State U Ames IA 50011

BRUNER, DARLENE HILDAGARDE, indsl. co. ofcl.; b. Creston, Nebr., Oct. 8, 1928; d. Otto Frederick and Hildegard Eleanor (Dasenbrock) Feye; B.A. in Bus. Adminstrn., Midland Luth. Coll., 1949; m. James L. Paulin, Oct. 23, 1949 (div., 1963); children—James D., Jamie L., Kathryn D. Paulin Lackey; m. 2d Robert T. Bruner, Dec. 23, 1970. Acctg. clk. Kavich's Furniture, Fremont, Nebr., 1948-50; asst. acct. Gamble-Skogmo, Fremont, 1950-51; acctg. clk., plant acct. Hydro-Conduit Corp., Fremont, 1962-65; acctg. clk., plant acct., mgr. services CF Industries, Inc., Fremont, 1965—. Mem. Am. Soc. Women Accts., Fremont Personnel Mgrs. Assn., Mensa. Democrat. Presbyterian. Home: 2139 William Fremont NE 68025 Office: PO Box 68 Fremont NE 68025

BRUNER, JANICE D., bank trust adminstr.; b. Arlington, Tex., Aug. 24, 1938; d. Oney C. and Irene L. (Tucker) Tucker; student Am. Inst. Banking, Eastfield Jr. Coll. of Dallas County; children—Kay Danielle Bruner Turney, Perry David Bruner, Jr. Clk.-typist First Nat. Bank, Dallas, 1961-64, adminstrv. sec., 1964-73, adminstrv. asst., 1973-75, trust adminstr., 1975—; v.p., trust officer, mgr. trust ops. Tex. Commerce Bank, Irving, 1981—. Baptist. Club: Altrusa of Dallas (2d v.p., 1981-82). Home: 2361 Larry Dr Dallas TX 75228 Office: PO Box 1285 Irving TX 75060

BRUNER, MADELIN EVE (MADGE), radio sta. exec.; b. Cleve., Sept. 27, 1938; d. Raymond Alphonse and Louise Katherine (Eisele) Bruner; student, U. Fla., 1961. Trumpet player Jacksonville Symphony (Fla.), 1962-70; buyer May-Cohens, Jacksonville, 1963-67; buyer Hoyt High Fidelity, Jacksonville, 1967-70; merchandiser Southland Record Distributors, Atlanta, 1971; buyer classical music Franklin Music, Atlanta, 1971-72; music program dir. Sta. WJCT-FM, Jacksonville, 1972—; publicity dir. Theater Jacksonville, 1974—; tchr. trumpet, flute, saxophone, Jacksonville, 1962-68 free lance concert mgr., 1980—. Mem. Am. Fedn. Musicians, Tau Beta Sigma. Episcopalian. Home: 5811 Atlantic Blvd #252 Jacksonville FL 32207 Office: 100 Festival Park Ave Jacksonville Fl 32202

BRUNNER, SULTRA ELAINE, lawyer, county ofcl.; b. Meridian, Miss., July 20, 1950; d. Moses and Hazel Juanita (Davis) B.; B.A. in Psychology, UCLA, 1973; M.A., Calif. State U., Los Angeles, 1976; J.D., Southwestern U., Los Angeles, 1982. Resource cons. Los Angeles County Dept. Mental Health, 1970-74; with Los Angeles County Dept. Health Services, 1974—, program mgr., 1975-77, legis. analyst, 1977—; admitted to Calif. bar, 1982. Office: 313 N Figueroa St Room 534 Los Angeles CA 90012

BRUNO, LAURETTA J., banker; b. N.Y.C.; d. Michael S. and I. M. B.; B.A., Manhattanville Coll., 1968; M.B.A., Columbia U., 1970. With Morgan Guaranty Trust Co. N.Y., N.Y.C., 1970—, London, 1978-81, now v.p. European corporate group, U.K. and Scandinavia unit head, N.Y.C. Active Jr. League N.Y.C. Office: 23 Wall St New York NY 10015

BRUNS, GAIL ANNE PETTIT, geneticist; b. Butler, Pa., Feb. 9, 1935; d. Grant A. and Isabelle Dorothy (Edwards) Pettit; B.S. in Chemistry, U. Rochester (N.Y.), 1956, M.D. with honors, 1960; Ph.D. in Biochemistry (NIH fellow 1965-69), M.I.T., 1970; m. Romaine R. Bruns, Dec. 27, 1958. Intern in medicine Barnes Hosp., St. Louis, 1960-61; research fellow Albert Einstein Coll. Medicine, 1961-64; guest fellow physiol. chemistry U. Louvain (Belgium), 1964-65; research asso. biology M.I.T., 1969-70; research asso., then sr. research asso. div. clin. genetics Children's Hosp. Med. Center, Boston, also prin. research asso. pediatrics Harvard Med. Sch., 1970—. Mem. Am. Chem. Soc., Am. Soc. Human Genetics, Am. Soc. Cell Biology, Am. Soc. Mirobiology, NOW, Nat. Audubon Soc., Nat. Wildlife Fedn., Sigma Xi. Office: Children's Hosp Med Center 300 Longwood Ave Boston MA 02115

BRUNSON, FLORENCE ALANCE, speech and lang. pathologist; b. Wichita, Kans., Dec. 23, 1934; d. Francis Alan and Florence Patricia Irwin; B.A., Randolph-Macon Women's Coll., 1956; M.S., Vanderbilt U., 1957; m. Harold Brunson, Jr., Jan. 4, 1975. Speech pathologist, Nashville, 1957-64, Michael Reese Hosp., Chgo., 1964-71; dir. speech pathology Cerebral Palsy Center, Atlanta, 1971-74; instr. Emory U. Med. Sch., Atlanta, 1971-74; dir. clin. services Easter Seals, Balt., 1974-75; dir. speech pathology Easter Seal Center, Atlanta, 1976-77; speech pathologist Petersburg (Va.) Gen. Hosp., 1977-78, Archway Programs, Atco, N.J., 1978-81, Elwyn (Pa.) Insts., 1981—; lectr., cons.; cons. speech pathology oral-facial clinic crippled children's service Dept. Public Health, Atlanta, 1972-74; instr. DePaul U., Chgo., 1964-68, Loyola U., Balt., 1974-75. HEW trainee, 1969-70; VA grantee, 1959-60; Children's Bur. fellow, 1956-57. Mem. Am. Speech, Lang. and Hearing Assn., Nat. Spastics Soc., Acad. Aphasia, Assn. Children with Learning Disabilities, Ga., Va., Ill., N.J. speech and hearing assns., Vanderbilt U. Alumnae Assn. So. N.J. (sec. 1979-80), Kappa Alpha Theta. Democrat. Methodist. Club: Nashville Cotillion (pres. 1959-60). Contbr. articles to profl. jours. Home: 47-A Aspen Hill Deptford NJ 08096 Office: 120 E Front St Elwyn PA 19063

BRUNTON, RUTH CAROLYN, home economist; b. Far Rockaway, N.Y., Dec. 14, 1922; d. Elias Nathan and Ida Emelia (Krumwiede) Caplan; B.S. (scholar 1940-44), Cornell U., 1944; M.S., U. Colo., 1948; Ph.D., Colo. State U., 1975; m. Robert L. Brunton, June 8, 1946; children—Judy, Nancy, Barbara, Beth, Robert. Mem. staff Womans Home Companion, N.Y.C., 1944; coop. extension agt. home econs. N.Y. State, Wayne County, 1945-46; instr. U. Colo., 1946-47, Minot State Coll. (N.D.), 1950-51, Elgin (Ill.) Community Coll., 1964-72, Larimer County Vocat. Tech. Center (Colo.), 1973-76; home economist U. Ariz. Coop. Extension Service, Maricopa County, 1978—. Bd. dirs. Elgin YWCA, 1966-72, LWV, 1962; leader Girl Scouts, 1960-70; tchr. Sunday Sch. United Ch. of Christ. Ednl. Profl. Devel. Act fellow, 1973-75; grantee HEW. Mem. Am. Home Econs. Assn., Ariz. Home Econs. Assn., Ariz. Assn. Extension Home Economists, Omicron Nu, Pi Lambda Theta, Pi Delta Gamma, Phi Delta Kappa. Home: 3514 N 26th St Phoenix AZ 85016 Office: 4341 E Broadway Phoenix AZ 85040

BRUSKI, NANCY LEE SHLAES, social worker; b. Chgo., Apr. 6, 1951; d. William Howard and Marjorie (Weishaus) Shlaes; B.A., Washington U., St. Louis, 1971; M.A. (study fellow), U. Chgo., 1975; m. Mitchell Jay Bruski, May 6, 1973; 1 dau., Katy Anne. Ednl. therapist Virginia Frank Child Devel. Center, Jewish Family and Community Service, Chgo., 1975-77, caseworker, ednl. therapist, 1977-80; pvt. practice clin. social work, 1980—; social worker Orchard Center for Mental Health Early Years Program, Skokie, Ill., 1980—; cons. nursery schs. Chgo. area. Cert. Acad. Cert. Social Workers. Mem. Nat. Assn. Social Workers, Chgo. Assn. Ednl. of Young Children, Fedn. Employees Assn. (past pres.), North Shore Choral Soc. Democrat. Jewish. Home: 1617 Judson Ave Evanston IL 60201 Office: 8600 Gross Point Rd Skokie IL 60077

BRUZZONE, NORMA ELAINE, acctg. adminstr., profl. chorister; b. Albany, Calif., Jan. 6, 1937; d. Norman Gale and Mary Aida Schaefer; grad. high sch.; children—Michael Alan, Dana Elaine. Sec., Chevron Research Corp., Richmond, Calif., 1955-61; profl. chorister San Francisco Opera Co., 1967-79; performer San Francisco Symphony Orch., 1967-74; adminstrv. mgr. Warren, McVeigh & Griffin, San Francisco, 1973-79; adminstrv. mgr. profl. liability div. Marsh & McLennan, San Francisco, 1979-80; adminstrv. mgr. Orlando J. Antonini, C.P.A., San Francisco, 1980—. Active PTA. Mem. Am. Guild Musical Artists, AFTRA. Office: 1700 Montgomery St Suite 225 San Francisco CA 94111

BRYAN, ALPHA JEAN, retail dept. store co. exec.; b. Stuttgart, Ark., Nov. 21, 1928; d. James Ray and Gladys Trice Reynolds; B.A., Rice U., 1949; postgrad. So. Methodist U., 1961; M.A., E. Tex. State U., 1967; children—Jan Bryan Burr, James Wingfield, Glenn Etsil. Research technician Baylor U. Coll. Medicine, 1949-52; tchr. Dallas Independent Sch. Dist., 1962-65; corporate tng. dir. Joske's, Dallas, 1967-75; v.p., corporate tng. dir. P.A. Bergner & Co., Rockford, Ill., 1975—. Active Jr. Achievement Dallas and Rockford; tchr. Sunday sch. Redwood Park Methodist Ch., Dallas; leader Boy Scouts Am., Dallas. Mem. Nat. Retail Merchants Assn., Am. Assn. Tng. Dirs. Republican. Methodist. Contbr. articles in field to profl. jours. Home: 5142 E State St Rockford IL 61108 Office: 3600 N Main St Rockford IL 61101

BRYAN, BETTY SUE, violinist; b. Madisonville, Ky., Oct. 23, 1923; d. Herman Pratt and Ada Evelyn (Johnson) Nance; student Ernest Williams Sch. Music, N.Y.C., 1941-43, New Orleans Baptist Theol. Sem., 1947-49; m. Wayne Delmar Bryan, Aug. 15, 1948. With Mobile Symphony Orch. and Civic Opera, 1960-62; concert master Chipola Jr. Coll., Marianna, Fla., 1960-65; violinist Lake Charles Symphony Orch., 1970-80, Rapides Symphony Orch., 1970-80; prin. 2d violinist Baton Rouge Philharmonia Orch., 1972—; prin. violin in string quartet in movie The Toy, 1982; pianist, organist Baton Rouge chs., 1971—; owner Su-Del Publs., 1963—; owner, mgr. Betty Bryan Sheet Music Store, Baton Rouge, 1970-82; rec. and TV personality weekly program; composer several pub. works. Mem. Internat. Platform Assn. Republican. Baptist. Author: Monograms (poetry), 1981. Home: 9642 Rustling Oaks Dr Baton Rouge LA 70811

BRYAN, BILLIE MARIE (MRS. JAMES A. MACKEY), biologist; b. Norfolk, Va., Dec. 30, 1932; d. William B. and Marie (Fortescue) Bryan; B.A. in Biology, U. Richmond, 1954; M.Ed., Am. U., 1966; m. James A. Mackey. Bacteriologist, Arlington County Health Dept., Arlington, Va., 1954-58; med. bacteriologist Walter Reed Army Inst. Research, Walter Reed Army Med. Center, Washington, 1959-62; tchr. Fairfax (Va.) High Sch., 1962-66; biologist NIH, Washington, 1966—. Mem. Am. Public Health Assn., Am. Soc. Info. Sci., Am. Med. Writers Assn., DAR. Contbr. articles to profl. jours. Home: 201 Quaint Acres Dr Silver Spring MD 20904 Office: NIH—NIADDK Westwood Bldg Room 604A Bethesda MD 20205

BRYAN, CLARICE ADINA, lawyer; b. St. Thomas, V.I., Apr. 30, 1923; d. C. Arthur and Iza Anita (Lanclos) B.; A.B., Howard U., 1943; LL.B., Columbia U. and Howard U., 1949; 1 dau., Charlene Smith. Admitted to V.I. bar, 1950; tax assessor Govt. of V.I., 1950-60, asst. atty. gen., 1961-65, asst. commr. of labor, 1965-68, dir. consumer affairs, 1968-73; individual practice law, St. Thomas, 1950—; dir. People's Bank, 1971-75; trustee V.I. Retirement System. Vice pres. V.I. Constl. Conv., 1977, del., 1964, 81; mem. UN Status of Women Commn. Mem. ABA, Internat. Women Lawyers Assn., V.I. Bus. and Profl. Women (state pres. 1964-65). Roman Catholic. Home: 245A Bourne Field Saint Thomas VI 00801 Office: Room B2 Professional Bldg Saint Thomas VI 00801

BRYAN, JANET MAJOR, nutritionist, educator, cons.; b. Barbour County, Ala., Nov. 22, 1922; d. Emmette B. and Virginia (Tillman) Bryan; B.S., Ala. Coll., 1944; M.S., Tchrs. Coll., Columbia U., 1964; postgrad. Iowa State U., 1970-71. Tchr. Roanoke (Ala.) city pub. schs., 1944-45; dir. food and nutrition service ARC, San Francisco, 1947-49, Cin., 1949-61; dir. sch. lunch programs, Norwood (Ohio) Pub. Sch., 1961-63; dir. sch. lunch program Manhasset (L.I., N.Y.) Pub. Schs., 1963-65; asst. prof. Morehead (Ky.) State U., 1965-67, No. Mich. U., Marquette, 1967-69, N.Y. State U., Plattsburg, 1971-73; cons. nutritionist, educator, 1974—. Recipient award of merit, 1973, diploma of honor for community service, 1975. Mem. Am. Dietetic Assn., Am. Pub. Health Assn., Am. Home Econs. Assn., AAUP, AAAS, Soc. Nutrition Edn., Kappa Delta Pi. Author: Learning Exercises and Laboratory Experiences in Quantity Food Production Management, 1973; co-author: Family Cupboard: Lowcost Nutritious Meals, 1950-55. Home: Box 191 Clayton AL 36016 Office: 527 Elberon Ave Cincinnati OH 45205

BRYAN, KATHARINE BYRAM, health services exec.; b. Atchison, Kans.; d. John Charles and Jane (Price) Byram; B.A., U. Mo., Ph.D., 1979; m. John Shelby Bryan, Mar. 12, 1982; children—George H. Gurley, John Austin. Asso. dir. psychology Corporate Health Examiners, N.Y.C., 1979-82, asso. dir., v.p. mktg., 1979—; cons. in field. Bd. dirs. Nelson Art Gallery, Kansas City, Mo., 1965-67. Mem. Am. Psychol. Assn., Biofeedback Soc. Am. Episcopalian. Club: Madistone (East Hampton, N.Y.); Union (N.Y.C.). Contbr. articles to profl. jours. Home: 220 E 63d St New York NY 10021 Office: 650 Fifth Ave New York NY 10019

BRYAN, LELA MAY, home economist; b. Seattle, Jan. 7, 1948; d. Mathew John and May (Johnson) B.; B.S., Central Wash. U., 1970; postgrad. U. Wash., 1975. Tchr. home econs. Granite Falls High Sch., 1970-72, Issaquah High Sch., 1972-76; edn. specialist Wash. State Dairy Council, Seattle, 1976-80; asst. dir. Smokenders of N.W., Bellevue, Wash., 1980; v.p. Valley Auto Electric Corp., Seattle; now moderator/trainer Smokenders, Reno. Mem. Home Economists in Bus., Am. Home Econs. Edn. Assn., Wash. Home Econs. Edn. Assn., Food and Nutrition Council. Club: Wash. State Athletic. Home and office: 3295 S Virginia St Apt 194 Reno NV 89502

BRYAN, SHARON ANN, med. writer, editor; b. Kansas City, Mo., Dec. 18, 1941; d. George William and Dorothy Joan (Henn) Goll; B.J., U. Mo., 1963; diploma Stanford Radio and TV Inst., 1961; postgrad. N.Y.U. Sch. Arts and Sci., 1963-64; m. James Wesley Bryan, Dec. 26, 1962; children—Lisa Ann, Holly Renee. Proofreader, copy editor Cadwalader, Wickersham, and Taft, N.Y.C., 1963-64; manuscript editor, writer nonsci. sects. N.Y. State Jour. Medicine, Med. Soc. State of N.Y., N.Y.C., also mng. editor Staffoscope, 1965-66; manuscript editor Transactions, also editor Perceiver, Am. Acad. Ophthalmology and Otolaryngology, Rochester, Minn., 1969-72, hist. writer, 1972—; v.p., sec. James W. Bryan, M.D., Inc., med. corp.; writer publicity articles Ft. Lee (Va.) Community Theatre. Mem. vol. honor roll Soc. of Meml. Sloan-Kettering Cancer Center; active N.Y. Hosp. Women's League, 1965-67, Doctors' Wives Guild, Little Company of Mary Hosp., Torrance, Calif.; docent Los Angeles County Mus. Natural History. Mem. Am. Med. Writers Assn. (editor conv. bull. 1966), AAAS, Internat. Platform Assn., Kappa Tau Alpha, Kappa Alpha Theta (chmn. membership com. N.Y. chpt. 1966). Club: Stanford. Author: Pioneering Specialists: History of the American Academy of Ophthalmology and Otolaryngology. Home: 533 Via del Monte Palos Verdes Estates CA 90274

BRYANT, ANITA JANE, entertainer; b. Barnsdall, Okla., Mar. 25, 1940; d. Warren Gene and Lenora (Cate) B.; student Northwestern U., Chgo., 1959; m. Robert Einar Green, June 25, 1960 (div. Aug. 1980); children—Robert Einar, Gloria Lynn, William Bryant and Barbara Elisabet (twins). Miss Okla. and runner-up in Miss Am. contest, 1959; guest star Bob Hope's Christmas Tours, 1960-67; sang Star Spangled Banner for Democratic and Republican Nat. Convs., 1968; numerous White House performances, 1964-69; numerous Billy Graham Evangelistic Crusades, 1965—; performed at Orange Bowl and Super Bowl games, 1970-71; TV, rec. artist, author, 1971—; spokeswoman for Coca-Cola Co., 1963-67, State of Fla. Citrus Industry, 1968-80, Friedrich Air Conditioning Co., 1969—. Mem. nat. council USO, 1961-66; bd. mem. Women's USO N.Y., 1965—; hon. chmn. Freedoms Found. at Valley Forge, 1969-70; hon. chmn. First Found. for One Nation Under God, 1969—; mem. Am. Orchid Soc., 1970—, Friends of Art Soc., 1970—; com. mem. Project Survival, 1970—; film narrator Drugs Are Like That, 1970; hon. chmn. Mental Health Assn. Fla., 1970—; pres. Save Our Children, Inc. Recipient USO 25th Ann. Silver Medallion award, 1966, VFW Gold medal and citation award, 1966, Leadership award Freedoms Found. at Valley Forge, 1969, Woman of Year award, 1970; VFW award, 1978; nominated for Grammy award for best religious rec. of How Great Thou Art, 1968; named to Okla. Hall of Fame, 1966; named one of Am.'s 25 Most Influential Women in 1977, World Almanac, 1978; One of Most Admired Women, Good Housekeeping, 1978-80; Mem. U. Tampa Alumni Assn. (hon.), Fla. Future Bus. Leader of Am. Author: Mine Eyes Have Seen the Glory, 1970; Amazing Grace, 1971; Bless This House, 1972; Fishers of Men, 1973; Light My Candle, 1974; Bless This Food-The Anita Bryant Family Cookbook, 1975; Running the Good Race, 1976; Raising God's Children, 1977; The Anita Bryant Story, 1977; At Any Cost, 1978. Recs. include Anita Bryant's Greatest Sacred Hits, All Time Favorite Hymns, Old Fashioned Praying, Singing a New Song. Address: care Project Amer-Children PO Box 899 Selma AL 36701 *

BRYANT, BERTHA ESTELLE, ret. nurse; b. Va., Jan. 11, 1927; d. E.F. and Julia Bryant; diploma Sibley Meml. Hosp., Washington, 1947; B.S., Am. U., 1948; M.A., Tchrs. Coll., Columbia U., 1962. Staff nurse, head nurse, NIH, Bethesda, Md., 1954-59; asst. dir. nursing USPHS Alaska Native Hosp., Mount Edgecumbe, Alaska, 1959-61; instr. Sch. Nursing, U. Mich., 1962-64; chief div. clin. nursing Bur. Nursing, D.C. Dept. Public Health, Washington, 1964-65; commd. Nurse Corps,

USPHS, 1965, nurse dir., 1974-81; nurse cons., hosp. facilities services br., div. hosps. and med. facilities Bur. Health Services, HEW, Silver Spring; nurse cons., social analysis br., div. health services research and analysis, Nat. Center Health Services Research, Health Resources Adminstrn., HEW, Rockville, Md.; nurse cons. div. extramural research, Nat. Center Health Services Research, Office Asst. Sec. Health, HEW, Hyattsville, Md., 1977-81, ret., 1981. Mem. Am. Nurses Assn., Nat. League Nursing, Am. Public Health Assn., Assn. Mil. Surgeons U.S., Am. Sociol. Assn., Commd. Officers Assn. USPHS (dir., treas.). Contbr. articles to profl. jours. Home: 8004 Westover Rd Bethesda MD 20814

BRYANT, BETTY JANE, shopping center exec.; b. Camden, Ind., June 19, 1926; d. Claude Raymond and Louise (Eckert) Wickard; B.S., Purdue U., 1947; m. Harry R. Bryant, Aug. 21, 1949; children—Susan, Patricia. Retail mgmt. and advt. L. S. Ayres, Indpls., 1947-49, Burdine's, Miami, Fla., 1950-51, Joske's, San Antonio, 1968, Dillard's, San Antonio, 1968-70; with Sterling Advt. Agy., N.Y.C., 1949; mktg. dir. Mary Ann Fabrics and Designer's Fabrics By Mail, Evanston, Ill., 1971-75; instr. Ray-Vogue Sch., Chgo., 1976; mktg. dir. Woodfield Shopping Center, Schaumburg, Ill., 1977—. Mem. council Fashion Group of Chgo. Bd. dirs. Northwest Area council Girl Scouts Am., 1982—. Mem. N.W. Suburban Assn. (dir.), Commerce and Industry (v.p. 1981-82), Chgo. Area Shopping Center Mktg. Dirs.'s Assn., Women in Mgmt., Mortar Board, Kappa Kappa Gamma. Home: 2008 Bayberry Ln Hoffman Estates IL 60195 Office: Woodfield Merchants Assn 5 Woodfield Mall Schaumburg IL 60195

BRYANT, BETTY LOU, health care facility exec.; b. Parke County, Ind., Sept. 3, 1929; d. Odus A. and Latitia I. (Swaim) Ratcliff; Lic. Practical Nurse, Ivy Tech. Coll., 1972; B.S. Nursing, Ind. State U., 1980, postgrad. (Vis. Nurses Assn. asst.), 1982-83; m. Bobby L. Bryant, Dec. 7, 1947; children—Taunnie Nelson, Greg, Chris. Nurse's aide Ind. State Sanitorium, Rockville, Ind., 1968-70; Lic. Practical Nurse, Vermillion County Hosp., Clinton, Ind., 1972-79; asst. adminstr. Lee Alan Bryant Health Care Facility, Rockville, 1979-80, dir. nursing service, 1980-82; cons. gerontol. program Ind. State U. Sch. Nursing, Terre Haute, 1981-82, continuing edn. cons.-aging, 1981-82, asst. instr. anatomy, physiology, sci. dept. univ., 1979-80. Sec., Women's Soc. Christian Service, 1960-62; brownie leader Boy Scouts Am., 1961-62; leader Meth. Youth Fellowship, 1969-70, ch. camp counselor, 1968-70; precinct com. person Republican party, 1968-72, active Ind. state senator campaign, 1980-81; diabetes screener, 1979. Mem. Ind. Assn. Quality Assurance Profls., Ind. State U. Alumni Assn., Nat. League Nursing. Home: Rural Route 1 Bloomingdale IN 47832 Office: Lee Alan Bryant Health Care Facility Rural Route 1 Box 7 Rockville IN 47872

BRYANT, BETTYE DAWNE, realtor; b. Burlington, Wash., Mar. 7, 1924; d. Joy and Georgia (Watkinson) Busha; student Skagit Valley Coll., 1942-43, Western Wash. State Coll., 19433 45; m. William T. Addison, Aug. 31, 1945; children—Jackie Addison Voegtlin, Teresa Addison Smith, Eric Addison; m. 2d, William R. Bryant, Dec. 14, 1964; 1 dau., Debra Bryant. Realtor, Bryant's Realty, Anacortes, Wash., 1957-62, mgr., 1962-64, owner, mgr., 1964-76; owner, broker Century 21 Bryant's Realty, Anacortes, 1976—. Mem. Anacortes City Council, 1974-77; mayor City of Anacortes, 1977. Mem. Wash. Assn. Realtors, Nat. Assn. Realtors. Clubs: Anacortes Women's, Elks. Office: 2701 Commercial St Anacortes WA 98221

BRYANT, BEVERLEY BROWN, educator; b. N.Y.C., July 15, 1942; d. Elmo Pope and Madeline (Walker) Brown; A.B., Mt. Holyoke Coll., 1963; M.A., St. Mary's U., 1965; Ph.D. (fellow), Ariz. State U., 1971; m. Alan Willard Bryant, Jr., Dec. 28, 1963; children—Hilary Ann, Christopher Bowman. Instr. dept. polit. sci. SUNY Agrl. and Tech. Coll., Morrisville, 1966-67; field researcher U. N.C. Inst. Research in Social Sci., Chapel Hill, 1971; asst. prof. polit. sci. Old Dominion U., Norfolk, Va., 1972-75, asst. dean Sch. Arts and Letters, 1975-76; vis. prof. polit. sci. U. N.H., Durham, 1976-81, project dir. Women in Polit. and Govtl. Careers Program, 1981—, adj. faculty mem. women's studies dept., 1982—; reviewer McGraw-Hill Book Co., 1975. Mem. Com. on Human Services, Community Action, Portsmouth, Va., 1979—; sounding bd. Town of Madbury (N.H.), 1979-81; clk., mem. Conservation Commn. Madbury, 1978-81; mem. Madbury Planning Bd., 1981—. Recipient Phi Theta Kappa award, 1976; Service to Univ. Women award, Old Dominion U., 1976; Nat. U. Continuing Edn. Creative Programming award, 1982. Mem. AAUW (legis. chmn. 1973-74), Am. Soc. Public Adminstrn. (dir. 1973-75), LWV (dir. Durham-Dover 1980-81), Strafford County Community Concert Assn. (dir. 1981—). Club: Pepperrell Cove Yacht (vice commodore 1981-82). Contbr. to: First Person Female American: A Selected and Annotated Bibliography of the Autobiographies of American Women Living after 1950, 1980; contbr. articles to profl. jours. Home: 18 Garrison LN RFD 4 Dover NH 03820

BRYANT, ELIZABETH LEEDS NOE, nurse; b. Abington, Pa., Apr. 29, 1940; d. William Leeds and Dorothy Donaldson (Roney) Noe; diploma Peter Bent Brigham Hosp. Sch. Nursing, 1961; B.S. in Nursing, Boston U., 1965; M.Ed., Francis Marion Coll., 1979; children—Kimberly Haws, Peter Leeds. Staff nurse Peter Bent Brigham Hosp., Boston, 1961-65, Tufts-New Eng. Med. Center, Boston, 1965-66; dir. inservice McLeod Meml. Hosp., Florence, S.C., 1969-73, dir. nursing service, 1974-76; regional nurse coordinator Pee Dee Area Health Edn. Center, Florence, 1976-79; head nurse alcohol dependence treatment program Seattle VA Med. Center, 1979—; clin. asst. prof. Sch. Nursing U. Wash., 1980—. Bd. dirs. S.C. affiliate Am. Heart Assn., 1975-79, mem. nursing edn. com., 1974-78; bd. dirs. Upper Florence County Heart Unit, 1976-79. Mem. Am., Wash., King County nurses assns., Nat. League Nursing, Sigma Theta Tau. Republican. Office: 8 West Seattle VA Med Center 4355 Beacon Ave S Seattle WA 98108

BRYANT, ELSIE NEAL SHAW, sociologist; b. Lauringburg, N.C., Mar. 7, 1924; d. Gaston and Mildred Juanita (McNeill) Shaw; B.A., Talladega Coll., 1946; postgrad Union Theol. Sem., 1947; M.A., Columbia U., 1948; M.A., SUNY, Stony Brook, 1973; m. Rosecoe W. Bryant Apr. 12, 1953; children—Denise R. Instr., Talladega Coll., 1946-47; dir. religious edn. Presbytery of N.Y., 1949-53; girls work dir. Goodwill Settlement House, 1953-55; housing coordinator, N.Y.C., 1955-57; tchr. Great Neck (N.Y.) Sch. Dist., 1959-69; asst. prof. sociology SUNY, Farmingdale, 1969-74; asso. prof. sociology Brevard Community Coll., Cocoa, Fla., 1974—. Agusta Larned scholar, 1948. Mem. AAUW, Jack and Jill of Am., Fla. Assn. Sociologists, Alpha Kappa Alpha. Democrat. Presbyterian. Club: Links Inc. Office: Brevard Community Coll Liberal Arts Div Cocoa FL 32922

BRYANT, JACQUELINE EOLA, educator; b. Norfolk, Va., Oct. 26, 1949; d. James Thomas and Wincie Jackson B.; B.S. in Edn., Old Dominion U., 1971; M.A. in Human Relations, George Washington U., 1982. Tchr. English, Balt. City Pub. Schs., 1971-75; curriculum developer, cons. tutorial project Norfolk Com. for Improvement of Edn., Inc., 1975; curriculum cons., developer Virginia Beach (Va.) City Schs., 1976-78, tchr. English, chairperson dept. 1979—; team tchr. St. Leo's Coll., Virginia Beach, 1977-78; curriculum developer Combined Agys. Tutorial Project, Norfolk, 1978-79; cons. human renewal resources project FiBaChu Corp.; adv. Va. Dept. Edn. Co-founder Southeastern Coalition of Women, 1971. Mem. Virginia Beach Assn. Tchrs. English (pres. 1978), Va. Assn. Tchrs. English, Nat. Council Tchrs. English, Va. Reading Assn. Democrat. Roman Catholic. Mem. adv. bd. Scholastic Publs., Inc. Office: 860 Churchill Dr Virginia Beach VA 23464

BRYANT, KATHRYN HENRIETTE, educator; b. Eau Galle, Wis.; d. William George and Elizabeth (Bohn) B.; student U. Wis., River Falls, 1918, Valparaiso U., 1922; M.A., U. Berlin, 1931. Tchr. jr. coll. in Minn., 1934—; script writer radio program for children with original plays, 1937-42; tchr. adult edn. and spl. edn., Mpls., 1967—. Bd. dirs. Nat. Police Orgn., Nat. Security Found. Served with USAAF, 1942-44. Recipient Presdl. citation, 1947; named Tchr. of Year, 1965; commendation J. Edgar Hoover. Mem. Nat. C. of C., NEA, Minn. Edn. Assn., Women's Soc. Christian Service. Republican. Clubs: Women's; Asso. Tchrs. Address: Elmwood WI 54740

BRYANT, MARJORIE ESTHER, flight instr.; b. Concord, N.H., June 17, 1926; d. Herbert and Gladys (French) Tittemore; m. Jack Douglas Bryant, Dec. 14, 1945; children—Virginia, Dale, Robert. Flight instr. Pennridge Airport, Perkasie, Pa., 1967—, chief flight instr., fixed base operator; accident prevention counselor FAA, 1973—; speaker in field. Named Flight Instr. of Yr. Eastern Pa., 1974; recipient Pa. Gov.'s trophy for outstanding service to aviation, 1981; apptd. flight examiner FAA. Mem. Aircraft Owners and Pilots Assn., Nat. Pilots Assn., Internat. Flying Farmers, Nat. Assn. Flight Instrs., 99's, Aviation Council Pa. (dir. 1974—). Republican. Clubs: Soroptomist, Order Eastern Star; Woman's (Perkasie). Won last leg of Powder Puff Derby Race, Parkersburg, W.Va. to Wilmington, Del., 1976. Home: 801 Schwenkmill Rd Perkasie PA 18944

BRYANT, PATRICIA SAND, govt. ofcl., psychologist; b. Minot, N.D., July 18, 1940; d. Lawrence and Helen Eloise (Natwick) Sand; B.S., U. Wash., 1961, M.S., 1963, Ph.D., 1964; m. James Alexander Bryant, June 20, 1975; children—James Sand, Marta Evelyn. Teaching asst. U. Wash., Seattle, 1961-64, postdoctoral intern in clin. psychology, 1965, asst. prof. Sch. Nursing, 1966-67, asst. prof. dept. rehab. medicine Sch. Medicine, 1968-73, asso. prof., 1973-75; health scientist adminstr. Nat. Inst. Dental Research, NIH, Bethesda, Md., 1976—; adj. asso. prof. dept. med. psychology Uniformed Services U. Health Scis., 1978—. Mem. Am. Congress Rehab. Medicine (mem. ad hoc com. on rehab. children 1973-75), Am. Psychol. Assn. (legis. and profl. liaisons com. div. health psychology 1978—), Internat. Assn. Dental Research, Am. Assn. Dental Research. Club: Sons of Norway. Contbr. articles in field to profl. jours. Office: Nat Inst Dental Research 5333 Westbard Ave Bethesda MD 20205

BRYANT, SHIRLEY GIBBS, publishing co. exec.; v. Bklyn., June 29, 1935; d. James Vernon and Noridca (Germaine Adamson) Bryant; B.A., Bklyn. Coll., 1972; postgrad. Coll. New Rochelle (N.Y.); m. Robert Gibbs, Aug. 12, 1967; children—Paul, Robert, Scott. Med. technologist Kings County Hosp., Bklyn., 1960-68; child therapist Early Care Clinic, Mt. Vernon, N.Y., 1972-79; real estate sales Kamcho Realty, Mt. Vernon, 1972-79; edn!. sales cons.; rep. Harcourt Brace Jovanovich, N.Y.C., 1979—. Chmn. scholarship com. Progressive Women for Civil Rights, 1972; established tutorial program Friends Negro Ensemble Co., 1967. Mem. N.Y.C. Sales Assn., N.Y. State Realty Bd., Nat. Med. Assn. Aux. (v.p., scholarship chmn. 1982). Home: 528 Forest Ave New Rochelle NY 10804 Office: 757 3d Ave New York NY 10017

BRYFONSKI, DEDRIA ANNE, publishing co. exec.; b. Utica, N.Y., Aug. 21, 1947; d. Lewis Francis and Catherine Marie (Stevens) Bryfonski; B.A. in English, Nazareth Coll. of Rochester, N.Y., 1969; M.A. in English, Fordham U., 1970; m. Alexander Burgess Cruden, May 24, 1975. Editorial asst. Dial Press, N.Y.C., 1970-71; editor Walker & Co., N.Y.C., 1971-73; editor Gale Research Co., Detroit, 1974-79, sr. editor, 1979, v.p., asso. editorial dir., 1979—. Bd. dirs. Friends of Detroit Public Library. Mem. Assn. Am. Publishers (libraries com.), Detroit New Girls Network, Am. Mgmt. Assn. Democrat. Roman Catholic. Author: New England Beach Book, 1974; editor: Contemporary Literary Criticism, vols. 7-14; Twentieth-Century Literary Criticism, vols. 1-2. Home: 18237 Saxon Dr Birmingham MI 48009 Office: Gale Research Company Book Tower Detroit MI 48226

BRYSON, NATALIE ELIZABETH, antique dealer; b. Weymouth, Mass., Feb. 20, 1931; d. Harry Follett and Amy Louise (Hill) Duncan; student public schs.; m. William MacLean Bryson, Feb. 20, 1948; children—Elizabeth Alice, Muriel Anne, William MacLean, Rebecca Jane, David Duncan, James Hill. Owner, Antiques and Epicure, Silverdale, Wash., 1972—; instr. gourmet cooking and antiques Olympic Coll., Bremerton, Wash., 1971—, lectr. on China, 1979—; tour guide trip to China, 1982; cons., mem. Mus. History and Industry, Seattle; rep. Wash. Art Commn. Pres. Olympic View Community, 1978. Recipient Golden Acorn award Wash. PTA, 1970, Outstanding Achievement award Lockheed Mgmt. Assn., 1979; flag officer Keechong Soc., Mus. Am. China Trade, Milton, Mass., 1979—. Mem. Oriental Ceramic Soc. (London and Hong Kong), Nat. Assn. Female Execs., Nat. Assn. Dealers Antiques, Victorian Soc. Am., Kipsap County Hist. Soc., Seattle Antique Study Group, Decorative Arts Council, Seattle Art Mus., U.S. C. of C., Central Kitsap C. of C. Home: 15251 Olympic View NW Silverdale WA 98383 Office: 3392 NW Carlton St Silverdale WA 98383

BRZEZICKI, MARY ELEANORE, mfg. co. exec.; b. Pittsfield, Pa., Mar. 13, 1932; d. Joseph E. and Eleanore Victoria (Battko) Bosko; student Kans. State U., Manhattan, 1952-53, Rosary Hill Coll., Buffalo, 1972, U. Pitts., 1978-79; m. Robert Edward Brzezicki, June 2, 1956 (div. Feb. 1974); children—Michael Joseph, Suzanne Marie. Various secretarial positions, 1956-59, 75; engaged in real estate sales, 1972-74; freelance community corr. Buffalo Evening News, 1972-74; exec. sec. to pres. and chief exec. officer, editor corp. newsletter Struthers Wells Corp., Warren, Pa., 1975—; Warren County corr. Erie Times News, 1981—. Exec. bd. West Falls (N.Y.) Sch. Assn., 1969-72, 2d v.p., public relations chmn. East Aurora (N.Y.) Middle Sch. Assn., 1972-73; pres. New Horizons, Warren, 1977, 80-82; bd. dirs. Warren YWCA, 1982—. Mem. Warren Bus. and Profl. Women's Club (pres. 1982—; Woman of Year award 1982-83), Pa. Assn. Notaries, Kappa Delta. Republican. Roman Catholic. Home: 18 Elm St Warren PA 16365 Office: PO Box 8 Warren PA 16365

BUCHANAN, GWENDOLYN ANN JONES, nurse; b. New Straitsville, Ohio, June 17, 1927; d. Thomas Britton and Gwendolyn (McGrady) Jones; R.N., U. Cin., 1948; B.S. in Nursing, U. Okla., 1967, M.S. (Outstanding Achievement scholar), 1978; m. Jim Charles Buchanan, Oct. 2, 1948; children—Linda Sue Buchanan Laakman, Cynthia Dianne Buchanan Patterson, Jim Charles, Thomas Britton. Staff nurse, then head nurse neurosurgery and neurology VA Hosp., Memphis, 1949-59; head nurse neurosurgery and neurology rehab. VA Med. Center, Oklahoma City, 1960-65, clin. nursing supr. ambulatory care, 1968-80, asst. chief nurse surg./ambulatory care, 1981—; nurse coordinator, cons. Midwest City (Okla.) Hosp., 1966-68; clin. asst. prof. U. Okla. Coll. Nursing. Mem. Am. Nurses Assn., Nat. League Nursing, Emergency Dept. Nurses Assn. (chmn. edn. and program com.), Assn. Ambulatory Care Nursing Service Adminstrs., Okla. League Nursing (recognition award for community service 1980, 81), Okla. Nurses Assn. (dir. 1969-71), Okla. Home Health Care Assn. (standards com. 1979-81, chmn. nominations com. 1981), Okla. Nursing Service Adminstrs., U. Okla. Coll. Nursing Alumni Assn. (chmn. nominating com. 1982), Sigma Theta Tau (chpt. pres. 1982). Lutheran. Club: Order Eastern Star. Author articles in field, chpt. in book. Home: 5301 Listen Circle Spencer OK 73084 Office: 921 NE 13th St Oklahoma City OK 73104

BUCHANAN, MARY ELLA, nurse, army officer; b. Hot Springs, Ark., July 19, 1950; d. Robert Glynn and Georgia Catherine (Dobson) B.; B.S. in Nursing, Vanderbilt U., 1972; M.S., U. Tenn., 1974. Staff nurse Met. Health Dept., Nashville, 1972-73; commd. lt. Nurse Corps, U.S. Army, 1973, advanced through grades to capt., 1975; ambulatory care nurse clinician Family Practice Clinic, Ft. Belvoir, Va., 1974-76, Robinson Barracks Army Health Clinic, Stuttgart, Germany, 1976-77, 5th Gen. Hosp., 1977-79, Acad. Health Scis., Ft. Sam Houston, Tex., 1979-80; ambulatory care nurse clinician Walter Reed Army Med. Center, Washington, 1980-81, nurse researcher Nursing Research Service, 1980-82, Nurse Ward 72, 1982—. Mem. Am. Nurses Assn. (cert. family nurse clinician, div. community health), Am. Pub. Health Assn., Council Primary Health Care Nurse Practitioners, Nurse Practitioner Assn. D.C. (pres.), Sigma Theta Tau. Methodist. Clubs: Smithsonian Assos., Franklin Mint Collectors Soc., Internationale Volkssportverband c.V. Home: 208 Bayou Point Dr Hot Springs AR 71901 Office: Ward 72 Dept Nursing Walter Reed Army Med Center Washington DC 20012

BUCHANAN, MARY ESTILL, state ofcl.; b. San Francisco, Nov. 15, 1934; d. Carl A. and Elizabeth D. (Yager) Henlein; B.A., Wellesley Coll., 1956; M.B.A. with distinction, Harvard, 1962; m. Dodds Buchanan, Sept. 11, 1960; children—David, Stephen, Helen, Eugene, Catharine, Bruce. Sec. of state State of Colo., Denver, 1974—. Dir. Nat. State Bank. Mem. Colo. State Bd. Equalization, 1973—; Colo. State Bd. Agr., 1971-73; chmn. women in govt. Colo. Commn. on Status of Women, 1971-74. Mem. Colo. Fedn. Republican Women, Colo. Law Enforcement Assn., Nat. Assn. Secs. of State. Home: Boulder CO Office: 124 State Captiol Bldg Denver CO 80203 *

BUCHANAN, ROSE MAY, med. technologist; b. Bluefield, W.Va., June 26, 1947; d. Ambrouse Wesley and Lacie Thelma (Marchant) B.; B.A. cum laude, Bluefield State Coll., 1981. Lab asst. Clinch Valley Clinic, Richlands, Va., 1966-71; lab. technologist Bluefield Sanitarium Clinic, 1971-79; supr. chemistry lab. Bluefield Community Hosp., 1979—. Mem. Am. Soc. Clin. Pathologists. Baptist. Home: PO Box 294 Bluefield WV 24701 Office: 500 Cherry St Bluefield WV 24701

BUCHANAN-GILLIAM, RUTH ANN, cytotechnologist; b. St. Louis, July 31, 1942; s. William Washington and Geneva Cornelius Buchanan; B.S., W.Va. State Coll., 1966; postgrad. Charleston Sch. Cytotech., 1966-67; m. Jesse E. Gilliam, Jr., Mar. 14, 1976; 1 son, Jesse Eugene, III. Cytotechnologist, Barnes Hosp., St. Louis, 1978—. Minister youth music St. John A.M.E. Zion Ch., 1960-62, Washington Met. A.M.E. Zion Ch., 1976-77. Mem. Am. Soc. Cytology, Am. Soc. Clin. Pathologists, St. Louis Soc. Cytology, A.M.E. Zion Missionary Soc. (life), Delta Sigma Theta, Phi Theta Kappa. Clubs: Legend Singers. Home: 4400 Lindell Blvd Apt 9j St Louis MO 63108

BUCHANAN-JACKSON, ANGELA MARIE, treas. of U.S.; b. Washington, Dec. 20, 1948; d. William Baldwin and Catherine Elizabeth (Crum) Buchanan; B.A. in Math., Rosemont (Pa.) Coll., 1971; M.S. in Math., McGill U., Montreal, 1973; postgrad. U. New South Wales (Australia), 1975, U. Va., Arlington, 1976-77; LL.D. (hon.), Samford U., Birmingham, Ala., 1981; m. William R. Jackson, Mar. 13, 1982. Bookkeeper, Com. to Re-Elect the Pres., Washington 1972; tchr. math. Georgetown Visitation Prep. Sch., Washington, 1973-74; acct. Bamfield & Co., Sydney, Australia, 1974-75, Citizens for Reagan, Washington, 1976, H.M. Buchanan & Co., Bethesda, Md., 1977; controller Citizens for the Republic, Santa Monica, Calif., 1977-79; nat. treas. Reagan for Pres. Com., Los Angeles, 1979-80, Reagan-Bush Com., Arlington, 1980-81; treas. of U.S., Washington, 1981—. Home: Fullerton CA Office: Treasury Dept 15th and Pennsylvania Ave NW Washington DC 20220

BUCHEN, CHARLOTTE, public relations cons.; b. Canton, Ill., Jan. 11, 1927; d. Bert and Edith (Melgreen) Buchen; profl. journalism fellow Stanford U., 1966-67. Editor house organ Cuneo Press, Inc., Chgo., 1949-51; mag. prodn. coordinator Internat. Harvester Co., Chgo., 1951-52; reporter, writer Canton Daily Ledger, 1953-56, The Arizona Republic, Phoenix, 1956-69; dir. urban affairs Nat. Housing Industries, Inc., Phoenix, 1969-72, dir. communications, 1971-73; asst. to pres. Samaritan Health Service, Phoenix, 1973-79; prin. Charlotte Buchen Communications, Phoenix, 1979-80; partner Buchen, Snell & Co., Phoenix, 1980—. Editorial cons. Ariz. Welfare Study, Ariz. State U., 1970; mem. rate rev. com. Comprehensive Health Planning Council Maricopa County, 1972-74; mem. Blue Ribbon Task Force on Tchr. Cert., Ariz. Dept. Edn., 1978; bd. dirs. Phoenix Opportunities Industrialization Center, 1970-71. Mem. Ariz. Hosp. Assn., Phoenix Press Club (past dir.), Women in Communications (named Woman of Achievement, Phoenix chpt. 1982). Clubs: Kiva; Mountain Shadows Country. Home: 5301 N 45th St Phoenix AZ 85018 Office: 77 E Weldon St Suite 240 Phoenix AZ 85012

BUCHENHORNER, MARIANNE, psychotherapist, psychoanalyst; b. Budapest, Hungary, Sept. 15; d. Tibor and Agnes Aozel (Marks) de Nagy; B.A., Vassar Coll.; M.S.W., Columbia U., 1966; cert. in psychotherapy and psychoanalysis Postgrad. Center for Mental Health, 1975, cert. mental health cons., 1976, cert. in supervision, 1977; m. Walter Buchenhorner, Aug. 16, 1965. Research asst., librarian Psychoanalytic Inst., Columbia U., N.Y.C., 1960-61; asst. to dir. of social sci. and humanities textbooks McGraw Hill Co., N.Y.C., 1961-63; case aide Youth House, N.Y.C., 1963-64; social worker Community Service Service Soc. N.Y.C., 1966-69; supr. State U. Hosp., Bklyn., 1969-71; dir. Multiple Service Center, Big Bros. Inc., N.Y.C., 1971-72; dir. counseling services Postgrad. Center for Mental Health, N.Y.C., 1976-81, tchr., 1974—, supr., pvt. practice psychotherapy, N.Y.C. Mem. Nat. Assn. Social Workers, Soc. Clin. Social Work Psychotherapists, Postgrad. Psychoanalytic Soc. Office: 200 E 33rd St New York NY 10016

BUCHER, MARY ALICE, editor; b. Columbus, Ohio, Jan. 9, 1937; d. Paul and Florence Hale (Burington) B.; B.A. cum laude, Ohio State U., Columbus, 1958, M.A., 1973. Sec., then editorial asst. Ohio State U. Press, 1959-68; asst. editor Jour. Higher Edn., Columbus, 1968-72; public info. specialist Transp. Research Center Ohio, Columbus, 1974; editor Apropos, Nat. Center Ednl. Media and Materials for Handicapped, 1975-77; sr. writer-editor Battelle Columbus Labs., 1978—. Adult Sunday sch. tchr. Maize Manor United Meth. Ch., Columbus, 1974-79. Mem. Women in Communications, Soc. Tech. Communicators, Mensa, Buckeye Singles Council (public relations chmn. 1981—, chmn. Nat. Singles Week 1982), Phi Beta Kappa, Sigma Delta Chi. Home: 102 Glenmont Ave Columbus OH 43214 Office: 505 King Ave Columbus OH 43201

BUCHHOLDT, THELMA GARCIA, state legislator, planning cons.; b. Claveria, Cagayan, Philippines; came to U.S., 1951; B.A., Mt. St. Mary's Coll., Los Angeles, 1956; m. Jon Buchholdt; 4 children. Planning cons., Anchorage, Alaska; mem. Alaska Ho. of Reps., 1974—. Active various civic and service orgns. Democrat. Office: Pouch V Juneau AK 99811 *

BUCHHOLZ, ESTER SCHALER, psychologist, educator; b. N.Y.C., d. Harry and Rose (Hoffman) Schaler; A.B. summa cum laude, Hunter Coll., 1961; Ph.D., N.Y.U., 1968; cert. in psychoanalytic psychotherapy Washington Sq. Inst., 1970; m. Bernard Buchholz, Dec. 14, 1964; children—Gary, David, Phillip. Clin. asst., psychology clinic N.Y.U., 1962-63, intern in clin. psychology, psychology clinic, 1963-64; intern, staff psychologist Met. Hosp., N.Y.C., 1964-65, research fellow, 1966-68; staff psychotherapist Washington Sq. Inst., 1969—; pvt. practice psychoanalysis, 1975—; asst. prof. sch. psychology program N.Y.U., 1975-80, asso. prof., 1980—; cons. to public schs. Sec., Lower West Side Children's Com. for Mental Health; trustee Village Temple; mem. high edn. task force Internat. Yr. of Child, 1979-80. Recipient Founders Day award N.Y.U., 1968; NIMH fellow, 1966-68; Dean's Devel. Fund fellow, 1975, 76, 78-79. Mem. Am. Orthopsychiat. Assn., AAAS, Am. Psychol. Assn., Council for Exceptional Children, Eastern Psychol. Assn., Fedn. Am. Scientists, Nat. Accreditation Assn. for Psychoanalysis, N.Y. Acad. Scis., N.Y. State Psychol. Assn., Sch. Psychology Educators Council N.Y. State (pres.-elect), Phi Beta Kappa. Author: Application of Ego and Self Psychology in Groups with Children, Adolescents, and Parents, 1982. Mem. editorial bd. Clin. Neuropsychology; contbr. numerous articles to edn. and psychology jours. Office: 933 Shimkin Hall NY Univ New York NY 10003

BUCHHORN, BARBARA JEAN, telephone co. sales mgr.; b. Kansas City, Mo., Mar. 3, 1952; d. Robert D. and Garnet L. (Ellis) B.; B.S. in Edn., Central Mo. State U., 1970-74; postgrad. Rockhurst Coll., 1979—. Travelling rep. Sigma Kappa Sorority, 1974-75; conv. coordinator Breckenridge Inn, Kansas City, Mo., 1975-77; dist. staff supr. direct mktg. Southwestern Bell, Kansas City, 1977-82, sales compensation mgr., 1982—. Bd. dirs. Big Bros. and Sisters, 1980. Mem. Dimensions Unltd. Presbyterian. Home: 337 W Argonne Kirkwood MO 63122 Office: 112 N 4th St Rm 610 Saint Louis MO 63102

BUCHSBAUM, BETTY CYNTHIA, psychologist; b. N.Y.C., May 27, 1927; d. Joseph and Kate (Havel) Buchsbaum; B.A., Cornell U., 1948; M.A., U. Pa., 1950; Ph.D., Yeshiva U., 1965; m. William Weinstein, Aug. 20, 1967; 1 son, Daniel. Psychol. intern Flower Fifth Ave Hosp., N.Y.C., 1953-54; sch. psychologist N.Y.C. Bur. Child Guidance, Bd. Edn., 1954-57, 58; staff psychologist Kings County Hosp., Bklyn., 1957-58; staff psychologist, asst. prof. Jacobi Hosp., Albert Einstein Coll. Medicine, Bronx, N.Y., 1958-67; chief psychologist Center for Preventive Psychiatry, White Plains, N.Y., 1967-68; asst. prof. Bellevue Hosp. and N.Y.U. Med. Center, 1968-69; clin. asst. prof. psychology dept. psychiatry Westchester div. N.Y. Hosp., Cornell Med. Center, 1976—; asst. clin. prof. Montefiore Hosp. and Med. Center, 1982—; pvt. practice psychotherapy and diagnostic testing, Rye, N.Y., 1965—. Mem. Am., Westchester psychol. assns., Phi Beta Kappa, Phi Kappa Phi, Psi Chi. Home and Office: 515 Greenhaven Rd Rye NY 10580

BUCHWALD, NAOMI REICE, U.S. magistrate; b. Kingston, N.Y., Feb. 14, 1944; d. Albert and Sylvie Reice; B.A. cum laude, Brandeis U., 1965; LL.B. cum laude, Columbia U., 1968; m. Don Buchwald, Jan. 19, 1974; children—David Evan, Jennifer Anne. Admitted to N.Y. bar, 1968; litigation assoc. firm Marshall Bratter Greene Allison & Tucker, N.Y.C., 1968-73; with U.S. Atty.'s Office, So. Dist. N.Y., N.Y.C., 1973-80, chief civil div., 1979-80, dep. chief civil div., 1976-79; U.S. magistrate So. Dist. N.Y., 1980—. Vice pres. Fed. Bar Council. Recipient spl. citation Commr. FDA, 1978. Mem. N.Y.C. Bar Assn., N.Y. State Bar Assn., Fed. Bar Assn., Phi Beta Kappa, Omicron Delta Epsilon. Editor: Columbia Jour. Law and Social Problems, 1967-68. Office: US Courthouse Foley Sq New York NY 10007

BUCK, BARBARA JAMISON, indsl. co. exec.; b. Pitts., Sept. 21, 1951; d. George Gale and Mary Jane (Butler) Jamison; B.S. in Chem. Engring., Carnegie-Mellon U., 1973; m. John Ashley Buck, May 19, 1973; Process design engr. Union Carbide Corp., Tarrytown, N.Y., 1973-75, sales engr., Tarrytown, 1975-77, asst. region sales mgr., 1977-79, asst. to v.p., bus. analyst, N.Y.C., 1979-81, product mgr. custom catalyst, Tarrytown, 1981—, project coordinator divestiture project. Mem. Soc. Women Engrs. (chmn. nat. conv. 1980, mem. adv. com. nat. conv. 1980, 81, 82, exec. com. 1982-83), Water Pollution Control Fedn., Am. Water Works Assn., Delta Delta Delta (corr. sec. chpt.). Office: Union Carbide Corp Old Ridgebury Rd Danbury CT 06817

BUCK, CAROLYN FELTER, engring. co. exec.; b. Evansville, Ind., Sept. 17, 1941; d. John Vincent and May Louise (Robinson) Felter; student U. Tex., 1959-61; B.A., Parsons Coll., 1964. Tchr., Carpentersville (Ill.) public schs., 1964-73; property mgr. John Felter Co., Houston, 1974-76; advt. mgr. Triangle Engring. Co., Houston, 1974-80, v.p. mktg., gen. mgr., 1980—; partner Fantasy Glass, Houston, 1977—. Mem. Nat. Assn. Female Exec., Am. Ventilation Assn., Beta Sigma Phi, Alpha Omicron Pi. Presbyterian. Home: 15026 Mintz Ln Houston TX 77014 Office: PO Drawer 38271 Houston TX 77238

BUCK, NATALIE SMITH, state ofcl.; b. Carlsbad, N.Mex., Jan. 10, 1923; d. Milton R. and Rosa Adele (Binford) Smith; student William and Mary Coll., 1940-41; B.B.S., U. Colo., 1943; postgrad. U. Tex., 1945-46; m. C. B. Buck, Sept. 12, 1948; children—Warren Z., Barbara Anne. Chief clk. N.Mex. Senate, 1951-53; sec. of state State of N.Mex., Santa Fe, 1955-59; formerly supr. personnel N.Mex. Dept. Public Welfare; formerly chief personnel N.Mex. Health and Social Services Dept. Mem. Kappa Alpha Theta. Democrat. Home: 108 W Alicante Rd Santa Fe NM 87501 Office: PO Box 2183 Santa Fe NM 87501

BUCK, PEGGY SULLIVAN, educator; b. North Augusta, S.C., Aug. 3, 1930; d. Charles Edmund and Ethlene Amanda (Peacock) Sullivan; A.B., Coker Coll., 1961; M.A., Appalachian State U., 1976; m. William D. Buck, Oct. 18, 1954; (div.); children—Wilson E., Deborah Ann. Tchr., Smith's Elementary Sch., Lumberton, N.C., 1964, Butner Elementary Sch., Fort Bragg, N.C., 1965—. Hon. fellow Anglo-Am. Acad.; mem. NEA, N.C. Assn. Educators, Internat. Platform Assn., Internat. Biog. Assn. (ann. fellow). Episcopalian. Author: I'm Divorced—are you listening, Lord?, 1976; I'm Depressed-are you listening, Lord?, 1978; It's So Lovely Here Now Lord-But Not Always, 1980. Home: PO Box 5 Lumberton NC 28358 Office: Drawer A Fort Bragg Dependents Schs Fort Bragg NC 28307

BUCKER, BARBARA JO, arts adminstr.; b. St. Louis, July 29, 1949; d. Gordon M. and Marjorie R. (Hillebrand) Nunnelly; B.S., U. Mo., Kansas City, 1971, M.A., 1975; m. Robert H. Adler, Sept. 20, 1981. Exec. dir. Kansas City (Mo.) chpt., Young Audiences, Inc., 1976-81, assoc. dir., N.Y.C., 1981-82; exec. dir. Chamber Music Am., N.Y.C., 1982—. Office: 1372 Broadway New York NY 10018

BUCKETT, BONNIE-JEAN, educator; b. Port Chester, N.Y., Apr. 23, 1948; d. Victor Robert and Dorothy Jean (Burger) Buckett; student Tampa U., 1967; B.S., Springfield Coll., 1970, M.S., 1976; postgrad. (Mamaroneck Women's Club Chairmanship scholar 1981, doctoral teaching fellow 1981-83) Middle Tenn. State U., 1981—. Tchr. phys. edn., coach Byram Hills Sch. System, Armonk, N.Y., 1970-71; tchr. health, phys. edn., coach Rye (N.Y.) City Sch. System, 1971-75; women's athletic dir., coach Springfield Tech. Community Coll., 1975-76, coach women's basketball and softball, 1976-77; asst. prof. phys. edn., women's athletic dir. Castleton State Coll., 1976—, coach women's basketball, 1976-80, women's lacrosse, 1977-78, women's softball, 1979-81, dir. coll. Girls' Basketball Camp, 1977-81; dir. Springfield Coll. Clinic for Mentally Retarded, 1967-70; dir. recreation Town Newtown (Conn.), 1969-71; dir. Summer 8-13 Year-olds Community Regional Opportunities Program, Chicopee, Mass., 1976-77; cons. for adaptive phys. edn. programs Louisa Devel. Center, Murfreesboro, Tenn., 1981—; ofcl. Amateur Softball Assn. Vt. State Colls. grantee, 1981-83. Mem. AAHPER and Dance, Vt. Assn. Phys. Edn. and Sports, Tenn. Assn. Health, Phys. Edn., Recreation and Dance, Middle Tenn. State U. Health, Phys. Edn. and Recreation Club, Am. Softball Assn., U.S. Field Hockey Assn. (local ofcl.), Nat. Girls' and Women's Sports Assn. (state basketball ofcl.), Am. Fedn. Tchrs., Vt. Women's Golf Assn. Club: Neshove Golf Course. Home: RD 1 Box 176 Castleton VT 05735 Office: Dept Phys Edn Castleton State Coll Castleton VT 05735

BUCKLEY, ANNA PATRICIA, state senator; b. Brockton, Mass., Mar. 21, 1924; d. Michael and Ann (Fitzmaurice) Herman; student Williams Sch. Bus., 1943; student spl. courses Stonehill Coll., Bridgewater State Coll.; m. Daniel J. Buckley, 1946; children—Kevin Michael, Daniel J., Paul, Patrice, Nancy J. Adminstrv. asst. to Lt. Gov., of Commonwealth of Mass., 1962-64, to Auditor, Commonwealth of Mass., 1965-72; mem.-at-large Brockton (Mass.) City Council, 1972-73; mem. Mass. Senate, Boston, 1973—, chmn. com. election laws and legis. research council 1973, mem. counties, ways and means, post audit, oversight coms., 1973—. Sec., Mass. State Democratic Com., 1968—; mem. Dem. Nat. Com.; del. Dem. Nat. Conv., 1980. Served with WAC, 1943-45. Recipient Silver medal Mass. VFW; First Ann. award Mass. City Clks.'s Assn. Mem. Plymouth County Dem. League, Am. Legion, AFL-CIO. Roman Catholic. Office: Room 219 State House Boston MA 02133 *

BUCKLEY, MARY HENDERSON, voice tchr.; b. Longuevuil, Que., Can., Dec. 17, 1912; came to U.S., 1934, naturalized, 1949; d. Jacob Harry and Eva Friedman; Licentiate in music, McGill U., 1932; m. Emerson Buckley, May 27, 1948; children—Robert A., Richard E. Appearing with New Opera Co., N.Y.C., 1942, San Carlo Opera, N.Y.C., 1944-46, Met. Opera, N.Y.C., Cleve., Dallas, 1946-48, Wagner Opera, 1950; numerous concerts with Boston Symphony, N.Y. Philharmonic, Mpls. Orch., Toronto Orch., NBC Orch., Montreal Symphony, Balienkov Symphonetta, Little Orch. Soc., Can. Broadcasting Corp., NBC. Faculty U. Miami, Coral Gables, Fla., 1964-68; pvt. voice tchr., North Miami Beach, Fla., 1978—. Mem. Nat. Assn. Tchrs. Singing, Am. Guild Mus. Arts. Home: 19640 20th Ave North Miami Beach FL 33179

BUCKLEY, PRISCILLA LANGFORD, mag. exec.; b. N.Y.C., Oct. 17, 1921; d. William Frank and Aloise (Steiner) Buckley; B.A., Smith Coll., 1943. Copy girl, sports writer UP, N.Y.C., 1944, radio rewrite, 1944-47, corr., Paris, 1953-56; news editor-Sta. WACA, Camden, S.C., 1947-48; reports officer CIA, Washington, 1951-53; with Nat. Rev. mag., N.Y.C., 1956—, mng. editor, 1959—. Clubs: St. Hubert Soc.; Sharon (Conn.) Country (sec. 1973-77, pres. 1978-80). Columnist One Woman's Voice Syndicate, 1976-80. Home: Great Elm Sharon CT 06069 Office: National Review 150 E 35th St New York NY 10016 *

BUCKLEY, THELMA CLAIRE, guidance counselor; b. Primrose, Pa., Apr. 24, 1927; d. John Harvey and Anna Matilda (Hesselmeir) Weiderhold; student Phila. Bible Coll., 1950; B.A., Glassboro State Coll., 1975, M.A., 1979; m. Harold Donald Buckley, Apr. 8, 1950; children—Donna Buckley Movsovich, Darlene Buckley Gilligan, Deane. Clk., typist Bell Telephone Co., Phila., 1945-52; evening supr. food services dept. Mohawk Valley Community Coll., Utica, N.Y., 1966-67; asst. dir. catering Syracuse U., 1967-68; case assignment, service coordinator, field supr. Vis. Homemaker Service of Cumberland County, Vineland, N.J., 1971-76; spl. instr. N.J. Dept. Health, Trenton, 1977-78; sch. social worker Commercial Twp. Sch. Dist., Port Norris, N.J., 1975-79, Cumberland Regional Bd. Edn., Seabrook, N.J., 1979-81, sch. guidance counselor, 1981—. Dep. v.p. region V, Fedn. Democratic Women, 1975-79; committeewoman Cumberland County Dem. Orgn., 1975—; mem. adv. bd. Cumberland County Home Health Care, 1977—, Cumberland County Coll. Equal Opportunity Fund. Mem. NEA, Am. Personnel and Guidance Assn., N.J. Sch. Guidance Assn., Cumberland County Personnel and Guidance Assn. (pres.). Baptist. Home: 2263 Edgewood Dr Vineland NJ 08360 Office: Cumberland Regional High School Seabrook NJ 08302

BUCKNER, DOROTHY ANNE, public relations exec.; b. Catlin, Ill., Mar. 9, 1934; d. John Allen and Dorothy Rowena Elizabeth (McReynolds) McClure; B.S., U. Ill., 1955; M.S., Ill. Inst. Tech., 1961; m. Donald Morton Buckner, Aug. 23, 1956 (div. 1967); 1 son, Derek Scott. Food technologist Pillsbury Co., Louisville, 1955-56; 4-H club agt. U.S. Dept. Agr. Coop. Extension Service, Trenton, N.J., 1956-57; restaurant supr. Marshall Field & Co., Chgo., 1957-58; mktg. publicist, food technologist Armour Grocery Products Co., Chgo., 1958-65; account exec. Theodore R. Sills, Inc., Chgo., 1965-66; editor recipe and package services Gen. Foods Corp., White Plains, N.Y., 1966-67; account exec. Carl Byoir & Assos., Inc., N.Y.C., 1967-70, 1973-80; pvt. practice public relations cons., N.Y.C., 1980—; account exec. Ruder & Finn, N.Y.C., 1970-72. Mem. Inst. Food Technologists, Am. Women in Radio and TV, Am. Home Econs. Assn., Am. Mgmt. Assn., Internat. Wine and Food Soc., Les Dames des Escoffier, Confrerie des Chevaliers du Tastevin (editor). Home and Office: 350 Central Park W New York NY 10025

BUCKNER, GERALDINE LAREE, nurse; b. Dallas, Jan. 11, 1924; d. Avery Manual and Geraldine Kinney (Macon) Millican; A.D. in Nursing, El Centro Jr. Coll., Dallas, 1974; B.S. in Health Care Adminstrn., E. Tex. State U., 1979; m. Leonard Cooke Buckner, Aug. 11, 1942 (dec. Nov. 1967); children—Janet Laree, Rebecca Sue, Joni Kay. Supr. emergency room East Town Osteo. Hosp., Dallas, 1966-79, dir. nursing, 1979—; ARC nurse. Mem. Am., Tex., Emergency Dept. nurses assns. Democrat. Baptist. Club: Eastern Star. Home: 7515 Lovett St Dallas TX 75227

BUCKNER, KAY LAMOREUX, painter; b. Seattle, Dec. 26, 1935; d. Harvey DeWitt and Mary Eunice (Coble) Lamoreux; B.A. in Fine Art, U. Wash., Seattle, 1958; M.F.A. in Painting, Claremont (Calif.) Grad. Sch., 1961; m. Paul Eugene Buckner, Aug. 15, 1959; children—Matthew, Nathan. Profl. artist, 1961—; one-woman exhbns.: Phoenix Gallery, Seattle, 1963, 12th Ave. Gallery, Eugene, Oreg., 1966, Gallery West, Portland, Oreg., 1973, 75, 77, 80, U. Idaho Gallery of Fine Art, Moscow, 1978, Kerns Art Center, Eugene, 1978, Frye Art Museum, Seattle, 1979, Oreg. Mus. Art, 1981, U. Portland, 1981; group exhbns. include: Exhbn. NW Artists, Seattle, 1963, Am. Drawings '66, Mercyhurst (Pa.) Coll., 1966, Mainstreams '74, 76, Internat. Exhbn., Marietta, Ohio, 1974, 76, Greater Fall River (Mass.) Nat., 1976, 80, New Orleans Internat., 1978, 80, Nat. Small Painting Exhbn., Los Angeles, 1980, exhbn., Springfield, Ill., 1981, N.Mex. Internat., 1981; vis. lectr. fine art U. Oreg., Eugene, 1976-79. Recipient 1st prize Wash. Drawing Exhbn., 1957, 58, Puget Sound painter's award, 1959, 1st prize figure exhbn. Woessner Gallery, Seattle, 1962, spl. jury commendation Salem (Oreg.) Civic Center, 1976, 1st prize Greater Fall River Nat. Exhbn., 1976, N.Mex. Internat., 1981; Avery fellow, 1960-61. Address: 2332 Rockwood Ave Eugene OR 97405

BUCKNER, REBECCA RUTH, ednl. adminstr.; b. Evansville, Ind., May 10, 1948; d. George W. and Lorene (Towler) Buckner; B.S., Ky. State U., 1971; M.S.W., U. Ill., 1973; postgrad. Howard U., 1978—. Sch. social worker Danville (Ill.) Dist. 118 Sch. System, 1973; caseworker II, Crittenton Comprehensive Care Center, Chgo., 1973-74; asst. prof. social work Western Ill. U., Macomb, from 1974, mem. affirmative action council, 1975-76, chairperson Black faculty and staff com., 1975-76; field liaison person BSW program U. Ill., 1976; with Falls Church-Fairfax County Mental Retardation Services, 1978-80, HEW, 1979; child devel. fellow Georgetown U., 1979-80; program coordinator Howard U. Inst. Urban Affairs and Research, Washington, 1980—. Mem. Fulton-McDonough County CMH Adv. Com., 1975-76; mem. McDonough County Youth Services Bur. Youth Guidance Council, 1977-78. Mem. Alpha Kappa Alpha. Home: PO Box 56355 Washington DC 20011

BUDD, ISABELLE AMELIA, fin. cons.; b. Granite City, Ill., Feb. 8, 1923; d. Floyd Harry and Amelia Frederica (Bradvogel) Marx; B.S., U. Mo., 1944; postgrad U. Wis., 1946; m. Louis John Budd, Mar. 3, 1945; children—Catherine Lou, David Harry. Research economist Ralston Purina Co., St. Louis, 1945-46; govtl. adminstr., Durham, N.C., 1975-79; fin. and govtl. cons., Durham, 1972—; co-organizer Downtown Durham Devel. Corp., 1980. Troop leader Girl Scouts U.S.A., 1955-61; co-chmn. environ. concerns com. Duke U., Durham, 1974-75; mem. Durham City Council, 1975-79; Durham del. Council Govts., 1976-78; mem. exec. com. regional govt. criminal justice com., 1976-78; chmn. personnel policy com. regional govt., 1977-78. Mem. N.C. Center for Public Rolicy Research, AAUW (life), Greater Durham C. of C., SW Durham Assn. (charter mem., treas. 1973-76), Nat. Trust for Historic Preservation, Historic Preservation Soc. Durham (charter mem.), N.C. Mus. Life and Sci., Friends of Duke U. Library (life). Home: 2753 McDowell St Durham NC 27705

BUDINGER, PEYTON BAILEY, writer; b. Bronxville, N.Y., Aug. 27, 1939; d. Randolph and Noona (Bibb) Evans; B.A. in English, Skidmore Coll., 1961; m. William Budinger, Nov. 10, 1979; 1 child, Bibb; stepchildren—Susan, William. Trainee, Time, Inc., N.Y.C., 1961-62; advt. copywriter Carson/Roberts, Los Angeles, 1962-65; feature writer Glamour Mag., N.Y.C., 1965-68; freelance writer various mags., 1968-72; articles editor Brides Mag. N.Y.C., 1972-77; columnist Coed Mag. N.Y., N.Y.C., 1975—; freelance writer, editor books and mags., 1977—; workshop leader human relationships Bradford Coll., 1980. Recipient Penney-Missouri Journalism award, 1972. Mem. Am. Soc. Journalists and Authors, Women in Communications (lectr. Career Day). Author: (with James Wagenvoord) Men: A Book for Women, 1978, Women: A Book for Men, 1979; (with Virginia Chamberlain and Jan Jones) Teen Guide, 1981. Contbr. numerous articles to various nat. publs. Home: 16 Southridge Rd Kennett Square PA 19348 Office: 10 Mitchell Pl New York NY 10017

BUDNEY, LINDA MCDONALD, computer analyst; b. Stamford, Conn., Nov. 26, 1946; d. Harold Thomas and Dorothy (Nungesser) McDonald; B.A. in Econs., Cath. U., 1969; postgrad. in tech. of mgmt., Am. U., 1972-75; m. Thomas J. Budney, Mar. 4, 1978. Computer specialist HEW, Washington, 1969-73; area mgr. computer measurement and evaluation Data Mgmt. Center, HEW, 1973-77, chief systems programming br., 1977-79; EDP project coordinator Pension Benefit Guaranty Corp., Washington, 1979—. Mem. Reston (Va.) Chorale, 1976-78, treas., 1977; mem. Rockville (Md.) Community Chorus, 1978-79. Mem. Assn. Computing Machinery, Computer Measurement Group, Ops. Research Soc. Am., Pi Gamma Mu. Home: 9908 Newhall Rd Potomac MD 20854 Office: 2020 K St NW Washington DC 20006

BUDOR, OLGA IRENE, public relations and public affairs cons.; b. Hamtramck, Mich., Mar. 19, 1939; d. William Anthony and Maria (Grabowska) B.; B.A. (Ford scholar), U. Mich., 1960, M.A., 1962; m. Thomas Hawley Moreland, May 1, 1976; 1 son, William Lloyd. Public relations asst. Edison Electric Inst., 1962-66; adminstrv. asst. N.Y. U., 1966-68; public relations positions N.Y.C., 1968-78; dir. Citizen Advs. for Justice, Inc., N.Y.C., 1981—. Adv. com. N.Y.C. Comm. Status of Women; mem. Women in Housing and Fin.; former mem. county exec. com. Democratic Party. Mem. Pi Alpha Kappa. Greek Catholic. Club: Women's City. Author book revs., grants proposals, tng. manuals. Home: 167 E 82d St New York NY 10028

BUDREIKA, JANE P., educator; d. Kostas and Stephanie (Zizniauskas) Paskauskas; came to U.S., 1947, naturalized, 1953; B.S., U. Vytautas the Great, Kaunas, Lithuania, 1943; Med. Technologist, Simmons Coll., 1961; M.S., Northeastern U., 1967; postgrad. in nutrition Harvard U., 1974; m. Ronald R. Budreika, May 7, 1942; children—Raymond A., Edward J., Thomas A. Chief pharmacist U.S. Army Hosp., Muehldorf, Germany, 1946-47; pharmacist Children's Hosp., Boston, 1947-48; lectr. pharmacology Red Cross Sch. Nursing, Munich, Germany, 1946-47; lab asst. Peter Bent Brigham Hosp., Boston, 1957-60; intern Mass. Gen. Hosp., Boston, 1960-61; sci. instr. Mt. Ida Jr. Coll., Newton, Mass., 1962—, fgn. student advisor, 1974-75, dir. med. asst. program, 1975—, instr. continuing edn. pharmacology and chemistry 1977—; mem. Coll. Council, 1979—; mem. adv. bd. med. assisting program Middlesex Community Coll., Bedford, Mass., 1979—. Registered med. technologist, cert. med. asst. and clin. lab. scientist Nat. Cert. Agy. Mem. Am. Soc. Clin. Pathologists, Royal Soc. Health (London), AAUP, Northeastern U. Alumni Assn., Simmons Coll. Alumnae Assn., Mt. Ida Jr. Coll. Faculty Assn., Phi Sigma. Home: 5 Grayfield Ave West Roxbury MA 02132

BUECK, JANE MARGARET, clin. social worker; b. Providence, July 6, 1929; d. James Francis and Mary Gertrude (Foley) Harahan; B.A., St. Mary-of-the-Woods Coll., 1951; M.S.W., Catholic U. Am., 1953; m. Robert Kesler Bueck, Feb. 22, 1958; children—Sharon, Carol, Barbara. Social worker Youth Service Bur., Detroit, 1953-56; agy. supr. Catholic Family and Children's Services, Portsmouth, Va., 1970-72; psychiat. social worker Tidewater Psychiat. Inst., Virginia Beach, Va., 1972-75; supr. Family Counseling Center, Clearwater, Fla., 1975-77; dir. social services Horizon Hosp., Clearwater, 1977-79; pvt. practice clin. social work, Clearwater, 1979—. Served with USNR, 1956-58. Mem. Acad. Cert. Social Workers, Nat. Assn. Social Workers, Fla. Soc. Clin. Social Work. Roman Catholic. Office: 1106 Druid Rd S Suite 201 Clearwater FL 33516

BUEHLER, ANN AGATHA, librarian; b. St. Louis, May 19, 1951; d. Paul F. and Viola R. (Schmitt) B.; A.B., Fontbonne Coll., St. Louis, 1972; M.A. in L.S., Rosary Coll., River Forest, Ill., 1975. With St. Louis County Library, 1967—, supr. Tesson Ferry br., 1981—. Mem. Mo. Library Assn., Greater St. Louis Library Club (dir. 1981-82), St. Louis Regional Network. Roman Catholic. Address: 4707 Seibert Ave Saint Louis MO 63123

BUELL, MARCIA BALDWIN, univ. adminstr.; b. Milford, Conn., Apr. 6, 1923; d. Malcolm Augustus and Rose (Baldwin) Buell; diploma N.Y. Inst. Dietetics, 1943; B.A. in Chemistry, U. Bridgeport, 1965, M.S. in Biology, 1980. Therapeutic dietitian Griffin Hosp., Derby, Conn., 1944-45, dir. food services, 1945-52; dir. food service U. Bridgeport (Conn.), 1952-76, facilities coordinator, 1976-81, dir. spl. events and facilities, 1981—, asso. prof. nutrition, part-time 1959-61. Mem. alumni bd. dirs. U. Bridgeport, 1979—; mem. ad hoc com. Inst. Meals on Wheels, 1973-77; pres. bd. dirs. Candlelight Terrace Condominiums, 1981—. Mem. Nat. Assn. Coll. and Univ. Food Services, Nat. Assn. Bioclin. Nutritionists. Office: Univ of Bridgeport 219 Park Ave Bridgeport CT 06601

BUETHE, MILDRED ROSE, internat. mktg. co. exec.; b. Pawnee City, Nebr., Aug. 16, 1929; d. Joe and Rose (Stepan) Herink; student public schs., Pawnee City; m. Ken Buethe, Jan. 12, 1947; children—Connie Rose, Douglas Carl. Jeweler, Elgin Watch Co., Lincoln, Nebr., 1956-61; interior decorator cons. Montgomery Wards, Lincoln, 1961-63, Sears Roebuck & Co., Lincoln, 1963-65; owner, mgr. Millie Buethe Beauty Salon, Lincoln, 1965-70; office mgr. Lincoln Liberty Life Ins. Co. (Nebr.), 1968-71; joint owner v.p., dir. BZD Livestock Products, Inc., BZD Internat., Inc., Lincoln, 1968—; owner, mgr. investments, 1978—; overseas mktg. rep. Zinpro Corp., Chaska, Minn., 1979—. Lutheran. Home: 1740 Superior St Lincoln NE 68521 Office: BZD Livestock Products Inc 708 W Cornhusker Hwy Lincoln NE 68501

BUFFERD, BARBARA LESLIE, social worker; b. Rockville Centre, N.Y., Oct. 16, 1951; d. Lew and Roslyn Blaustein; B.A., George Washington U., 1973; cert. legal asst. Adelphi U., Garden City, N.Y., 1973, M.S.W., 1976; m. Stephen M. Bufferd, Dec. 10, 1977. Med. social worker, supr. social work assts. and community aides Nassau County (N.Y.) Dept. Health, 1976-79; social worker Bronx (N.Y.) Mcpl. Hosp. Center, 1979—; devel. in-service tng. programs presented at Molloy Coll., Nassau Community Coll. cert. social worker, N.Y. Mem. Acad. Cert. Social Workers, Nat. Assn. Social Workers, Social Work Vocat. Bur.

BUFFINGTON, ANN, mfg. co. exec.; b. Chgo., Mar. 7, 1940; d. James F. and Mary Margaret (Dorsey) Wrigley; ed. U. Okla.; m. Fred Courtney Buffington; children—Christina Lee, Courtney. Stockbroker; interior designer; owner specialty store dealing in fine gifts; pres. Buffington and Assos., Norman, Okla., Ann Buffington Ltd., 1978; exec. v.p., chmn. bd. Buffington Med. Assn., Buffco Inc. (both Norman); past chmn. for Okla., AMA Ednl. and Research Found. Mem. Norman C. of C., Bus. and Profl. Women's Assn., Okla. Women's Med. Aux., Abdominal Surgeons Med. Aux., Cleve. County Med. Aux., Direct Mail Mktg. Assn. Republican. Roman Catholic. Club: Whitehall (Oklahoma City). Home: 2512 Walnut Rd Norman OK 73069 Office: 733 Asp St Suite B Norman OK 73069

BUFFINGTON, LINDA BRICE, interior designer; b. Long Beach, Calif., June 21, 1936; d. Harry Bryce and Marguerite Leonora (Tucciarone) Van Bellehem; student El Camino Jr. Coll., 1955-58, U. Calif., Irvine, 1973-78, Calif. State U., Fullerton, 1979-81; children—Lisa Ann, Phillip Lynn. With Public Fin., Torrance, Calif., 1954-55, Beneficial Fin., Torrance and Hollywood, Calif., 1955-61; interior designer Vee Nisley Interiors, Newport Beach, Calif., 1964-65, Leon's Interiors, Newport Beach, 1965-69; partner Marlind Interiors, Tustin, Calif., 1969-70; owner, designer Linda Buffington Interiors, Villa Park, Calif., 1970—; cons. builders, housing developments. Mem. Bldg. Industry Assn., Home Builders Council, Nat. Assn. Home Builders, Sales and Mktg. Council. Republican. Club: POCA. Office: 17767 Santiago Blvd Villa Park CA 92667

BUFLER, CAROLE ORME, distbg. co. exec.; d. James Erskine and Elisabeth Margaret (Bishop) Orme; B.A., Trinity U., 1961; M.A., Incarnate Word Coll., 1980; m. Raymond Bufler; 1 son, Michael. Tchr. English, Macarthur High Sch., San Antonio, 1961-64; mem. faculty continuing edn. div. San Antonio Coll., 1972-77; program devel. coordinator U. Tex., San Antonio, 1978-79; comml. and investment realtor Owens & Assos., San Antonio, 1979-81; mng. partner Southtex Distbrs., San Antonio, 1981—; mem. bus. adminstrn. faculties San Antonio Community Coll. Dist., Tex. Luth. Coll., St. Mary's U. Div. Continuing Edn. Mem. adv. council on women's programs Incarnate Word Coll., San Antonio; mem. Arts Council of San Antonio; program dir. San Antonio Literacy Council, 1976-78; program dir. Covenant Presbyn. Ch., 1974-76. Mem. Women in Communications, Adult Edn. Assn., AAUW (Outstanding San Antonio Woman in Bus. award 1980), San Antonio Mus. Assn., North San Antonio C. of C. Home: 614 Golfcrest San Antonio TX 78239 Office: 10205 Oasis Dr Suite 120 San Antonio TX 78216

BUFORD, CARMEN, ednl. adminstr.; b. Los Angeles, May 31, 1932; d. George and Gladys (Edgenton) Buford; student Oberlin Coll., 1950-51; B.A. in Music with distinction, Calif. State U., Dominguez Hills, 1975, M.A. in Humanities, 1978; doctoral candidate UCLA; children—Laurine, Jocelyn, Michael, Virginia, Carolyn, Stephanie. Clerical worker in public sector and pvt. industry, 1952-73; job devel. specialist Compton Community Coll., 1976-77; tchr.-discussion leader Project INFO, Whittier, Calif., 1976-79; dir. Disabled Students Service, Vets.' Program, Women's Center, asst. to dean Univ. Coll., Calif. State U., Dominguez Hills, Carson, 1977—; condr. workshops, tchr., lectr. in field; recitalist, organist and music tchr. Los Angeles area coordinator Black Caucus, 1978; conf. chmn. Calif. Advs. for Reentry Edn., 1982; program co-chmn. Calif. Non-White Concerns, 1982. Mem. Calif. Personnel and Guidance Assn. (chairperson women's caucus 1980), Am. Personnel and Guidance Assn., Nat. Assn. Student Personnel Adminstrs., Nat. Assn. Women Deans, Adminstrs. and Counselors, Nat. Assn. Negro Musicians, Choral Condrs. Guild, Am. Guild Organists, Music Tchrs. Assn. Calif., Phi Delta Kappa. Democrat. Mem. African Methodist Episcopal Ch. Home: Carson CA 90746 Office: 1000 E Victoria St Carson CA 90747

BUFORD, EVELYN CLAUDENE SHILLING, printing co. exec.; b. Fort Worth, Sept. 21, 1940; d. Claude and Winnie Evelyn (Mote) Hodges; student Hill Jr. Coll., 1975-76; m. Mar., 1982; children by previous marriage—Vincent Shilling, Kathryn Lynn Shilling Vassar. With Imperial Printing Co., Inc., Fort Worth, 1964-70, 77—, gen. sales mgr. comml. div., 1982—, corp. sec., 1977—; with Tarrant County Hosp. Dist., Fort Worth, 1973-77, asst. to asst. adminstr., 1981-82. Mem. Am. Mgmt. Assn., Exec. Women Internat. (dir., publs. chmn.), Nat. Assn. Female Execs., Presidents Club Tex. Republican. Methodist. Home: 100 Kenneth Ln Burleson TX 76028 Office: 1610 8th Ave Fort Worth TX 76104

BUGBEE-JACKSON, JOAN, sculptor; b. Oakland, Calif., Dec. 17, 1941; d. Henry Greenwood and Jeanie Ogden (Abbot) B.; B.A. in Art, San Jose (Calif.) State Coll., 1964, M.A., 1966; student Nat. Acad. Sch. Fine Arts, N.Y.C., 1968-72, Art Students League, N.Y.C., 1968-70; m. John Michael Jackson, June 21, 1973; 1 dau., Brook Bond. Instr. art Foothill (Calif.) Jr. Coll., 1966-67; instr. design De Anza Jr. Coll., Cupertino, Calif., 1967-68; instr. pottery Greenwich House Pottery, N.Y.C., 1969-71, Craft Inst. Am., N.Y.C., 1970-72, Cordova (Alaska) Extension Center, U. Alaska, 1973-79, Prince William Sound Community Coll., 1979—; one-woman exhbns. in Maine, N.Y.C., Alaska and Calif.; group exhbns. include Allied Artists Am., 1970-72, Nat. Acad. Design, 1971, 74; pres. Cordova Arts and Pageants Ltd., 1975-76; commns. include Marie K. Smith Commemorative Medal, 1973, Bob Korn Pool Commemorative Plaque, 1975, Eyak Native Monument, 1978, Alaska Pioneer's Home Ceramic Mural, 1979, Alaska Wildlife Series Bronze Medal, 1980, sculpture murals and portraits Alaska State Capitol, 1981, also portraits. Scholarship student Nat. Acad. Sch. Fine Arts, 1969-72; recipient J.A. Suydam Bronze medal, 1969; Dr. Ralph Weiler prize, 1971; Helen Foster Barnet award, 1971; Daniel Chester French award, 1972; Frishmuth award, 1971; Allied Artists Am. award, 1972; C. Percival Dietsch prize, 1973; citation Alaska Legislature, 1981. Fellow Nat. Sculpture Soc. Address: Box 374 Cordova AK 99574

BUHL, PAMELA ANNE, purchasing exec.; b. Ada, Okla., July 14, 1951; d. Jack Doylen and Ruby Eleanor (Lowery) Moore; exec. sec. cert. Draughn Sch. Bus., 1969; student Tulsa Jr. Coll., 1974-76, U. Okla., 1982—; student Nat. Purchasing Mgmt. Assn. seminars, 1979-82; m. Dudley Buhl, June 6, 1969; children—James Michael, Douglas Mance. Buyers asst. Elta Corp., Wagoner, Okla., 1973-74; buyer, sales mgr. Harris Jewelers, Tulsa, 1975-76; dir. Tulsa Entertainment Corp., 1977-79; buyer, mgr. Internat. Harvester Co., Wagoner, Okla., 1980-81; sr. buyer SPS Techs., Tulsa, 1981—. Mem. exec. founding com. PTA, Porter, Okla., 1972. Mem. Nat. Purchasing Mgmt. Assn., Purchasing Mgmt. Assn. Tulsa (asst. to program dir. 1981-82, chmn. 1981-82, program chmn., dir. 1982-83), Am. Mgmt. Assn. Club: Western Hills Lodge. Home: RR 2 Box 380 Coweta OK 74439 Office: 4239 S 74th East Ave Tulsa OK 74145

BUIST, JEAN MORFORD, hosp. adminstr.; b. Newton, N.J., Oct. 5, 1951; d. Richardson and Jean (Mackerley) B.; B.A., Cornell U., 1973; M.Ed., Coll. William and Mary, Williamsburg, Va., 1974. Adminstrv. positions Korman Corp., Phila., 1975-77; v.p. ops. Community Assn. Mgmt. Co., Inc., Phila., 1977-78; adminstr. divs. pediatrics, obstetrics and gynecology, psychiatry No. div. Albert Einstein Med. Center, Phila., 1978—, vol. hospice death and dying program, 1978—. Mem. Am. Hosp. Assn., Am. Horse Show Assn., Cornell U. Alumni Assn., Gypsy Ln. Owner's Assn. (treas. 1979-80). Home: 4000 Gypsy Ln #201 Philadelphia PA 19144 Office: Albert Einstein Med Center York and Tabor Rds Philadelphia PA 19141

BUJARSKI, ROSALIE BENISH, communications co. exec.; b. Spokane, Wash., July 11, 1933; d. Frank Joseph and Gertrude Cecelia (Simones) Benish; A.B., San Diego State U., 1971, M.A., 1973; m. Marcel J. Bujarski, Mar. 6, 1957; children—Jerry, Ronald, Michael. Residential supr. Tongue Point Job Corps Center, Astoria, Oreg., 1974-75; mem. staff Clatsop County Mental Health Center, Astoria, 1974-76; mental health specialist, services coordinator, county drug coordinator; instr. psychology Clatsop Community Coll., Astoria, 1973-76; mgmt. positions AT&T Long Lines, Piscataway, N.J., 1979—. Mem. Am. Psychol. Assn., Human Factors Soc., Am. Mgmt. Assn. Club: USCG Officers Wives. Contbr. articles to psychol. jours. Home: 77 Atlas Rd Basking Ridge NJ 07920 Office: 340 Mount Kemble Ave Morristown NJ 07960

BULL, FRANCES ELEANOR, oncologist; b. Ann Arbor, Mich., Jan. 10, 1927; d. Hempstead Stratton and Sarah Elizabeth (Carr) Bull; B.S. with honors in Zoology, U. Mich., 1948, M.D. with honors, 1952; M.S., U. Minn., 1960. Intern, Phila. Gen. Hosp., 1952-53; resident Mayo Found., Rochester, Minn., 1954-57; fellow in hematology Simpson Meml. Inst., U. Mich., Ann Arbor, 1957-59, instr. to prof. internal medicine, 1957—, prof. med. oncology, 1962—; clin. researcher in cancer therapy. Diplomate Am. Bd. Internal Medicine and subspecialty bd. med. oncology. Fellow ACP. Contbr. articles in field to profl. jours. Office: U Mich Med Center Ann Arbor MI 48109

BULL, MARI, clin. psychologist; b. Savannah, Ga., Jan. 27, 1931; d. Ernest Coren and Mamie Em (Allen) B.; student Wesleyan Coll., 1949-50; B.A., Swarthmore Coll., 1953; M.A., Middlebury Coll., 1956; postgrad. Harvard U., 1956-57, Purdue U., 1957, Georgetown U., 1963-64, U. Calif., Riverside, 1968—; Ph.D., Calif. Sch. Profl. Psychology, 1975. Spanish tchr. Fairfax Hall, Waynesboro, Va., 1955-56, Highland Park (Mich.) Jr. Coll., 1957-59, New Trier Twp. High Sch., Winnetka, Ill., 1959-62, Claremont (Calif.) Unified Sch. Dist., 1965-71; psychology trainee West Central Mental Health Center, Los Angeles, 1971-72; counselor So. Calif. Counseling Center, Los Angeles, 1972-74, Brentwood VA Hosp., Los Angeles, 1973-74; psychol. asst. Newton Center Clin. Hypnosis, Los Angeles, 1974-76; pvt. practice clin. psychology, Claremont, Calif., 1976—. Bd. dirs. Rec. for the Blind, 1977—, vice chmn., 1980-81, chmn., 1981-83; founder, chmn. governing bd. Recorded Psychol. Jours., 1978-81. Am. Psychol. Found. grantee, 1979, 80, 81. Mem. Am. Psychol. Assn. (grantee 1978), Am. Soc. Clin. Hypnosis, Calif. Psychol. Assn., Soc. Clin. and Exptl. Hypnosis, So. Calif. Soc. Clin. Hypnosis, NOW, AAUW, Am. Assn. Workers for the Blind. Office: 219 N Indian Hill Blvd Suite 102 Claremont CA 91711

BULL, MARY ANN CHRISTINE, med. social worker; b. Ft. Myers, Fla., Nov. 15, 1944; d. John Henry and Helen Veronica (Menovcik) Shupenko; B.S.W., Mich. State U., 1974, M.S.W., 1982. Cons., Mich. Assn. for Regional Med. Programs, Lansing, 1974-75; exec. asst. to med. dir. Ingham Community Mental Health Center, Lansing, 1976; med. social worker Ingham Med. Center, Lansing, 1976—; mem. clin. faculty Lansing Community Coll., 1979—; cons. Lansing Cath. Archdiocese, 1977—. Faculty adv. Vet. Med. Student Wives, 1970-72; com. mem. Mich. Lung Assn. Mem. Nat. Assn. Social Workers, Mich. Heart Assn. (sci.), Greater Lansing Vet. Med. Aux. (v.p. 1970). Author: The Transplantation Society of Michigan: A Historical Documentary, 1974; co-author: Michigan State University Protocols of Cardiac Rehabitation, 1980. Home: 6224 Brookline Ct East Lansing MI 48823 Office: Mid-Mich Med Group 4015 W Greenlawn Lansing MI 48910

BULLARD, ETHEL MUNDAY, musician; b. Cranston, R.I.; d. Alfred James and Martha Jane (Walker) Munday; Mus. B., Am. Conservatory Music, Chgo., then postgrad.; postgrad. Northwestern U.; attended master classes Am. Conservatory of Music and Chgo. Mus. Coll.; m. Henry Messenger Bullard, Apr. 22; 1 son, Thomas Robert. Tchr. piano, Oak Park, Ill.; piano accompanist Oak Park Musical Theatre, 1967—, music dir., 1971-79; author, compiler music appreciation course Hadley Sch. for Blind, Winnetka, Ill., 1967; cons. in field. Afternoon chmn. Beye Elem. Sch. PTA, Oak Park, 1957, evening v.p., 1958. Recipient Steinway award, 1967; cert. for service to blind Sigma Alpha Iota, 1968. Mem. Soc. Am. Musicians, Music Tchrs. Nat. Assn., Ill. State Music Tchrs. Assn. (Chgo. chmn. 1961-65, 71-72, piano chmn. 1968, Service award 1979), Nat. Fedn. Music Clubs, Am. Fedn. Musicians, Nat. Guild Piano Tchrs., Am. Music Scholarship Assn., MacDowell Artists Assn. Oak Park, Sigma Alpha Iota (editorial bd. 1970-73, nat. editor 1973-79, dir. Music Library at U. Mich. 1973—, honor awards). Congregational. Club: Eastern Star. Address: 228 N Lombard St Oak Park IL 60302

BULLARD, HELEN (MRS. JOSEPH MARSHALL KRECHNIAK), sculptor; b. Elgin, Ill., Aug. 15, 1902; d. Charles Wickliffe and Minnie (Cook) Bullard; student U. Chgo., 1921-29; m. Lloyd Ernst Rohrke, June 11, 1924 (div. Feb. 1931); children—Ann Louise (Mrs. Ross DeWitt Netherton), Barbara Jane (Mrs. Valtyr Emil Gudmundson); m. 2d, Joseph Marshall Krechniak, Jan. 30, 1932 (dec. Feb. 1964); 1 dau., Mariana (Mrs. Wilfred Martin). With research dept. L.V. Estes, Inc., Chgo., 1920-22; operator Square D Co., Detroit, 1922-24; simple research Commerce and Adminstrn. Library, U. Chgo., 1924-25; dir. Crossville (Tenn.) Play Center, 1949-50; creator hand-carved dolls, 1949—, wood sculpture, 1959—; exhibited with Nat. Inst. Am. Doll Artists Exhbns., Los Angeles, 1963, Cin., 1964, Washington, 1965, Chgo., 1966, Boston, 1967, New Orleans, 1969, Detroit, 1970, Los Angeles, 1971, Omaha, 1972, Louisville, 1973, Miami, Fla., 1974, Milw., 1975, Watts Bar Dam, Tenn., 1976, Chgo., 1977, N.Y.C., 1979, also craftsmen's fairs, 1954-65, The Club, Birmingham, Ala., 1963, Oak Ridge Art Center, 1965, Children's Mus., Nashville, 1967, McClung Mus., Knoxville, 1969; one man show Tenn. State Mus., 1972. Campaign chmn. Cumberland County unit Am. Cancer Soc., 1947-52. Mem. So. Highland Handicraft Guild (dir. 1957-59), Nat. Inst. Am. Doll Artists (founder, pres. 1963-67, 69-71, chmn. bd. 1977—), United Fedn. Doll Clubs (2d v.p. 1977-79), Am. Craftsmen's Council, Tenn. Folklore Soc., Mensa. Democrat. Unitarian. Author: (with husband) Cumberland County's First Hundred Years, 1956; The American Doll Artist, 1965, Vol. II, 1974; A Bullard Family, 1966; Dorothy Heizer, the Artist and Her Dolls, 1972; Crafts and Craftsmen of the Tennesee Mountains, 1976; (monograph) People in Wood, 1982.

BULLEN, ADELAIDE KENDALL (MRS. KENNETH SUTHERLAND BULLEN), anthropologist; b. Worcester, Mass., Jan. 12, 1908; d. Oliver Sawyer and Grace (Marble) Kendall; A.B. cum laude, Radcliffe Coll., 1943; postgrad. Harvard U., 1943-48, 50; m. Ripley Pierce Bullen, July 25, 1929 (dec. Dec. 1976); children—Dana Ripley II, Pierce Kendall; m. 2d, Kenneth Sutherland Bullen, Mar. 22, 1980. Research anthropologist Health Center, Radcliffe Coll., 1943-44, Fatigue Lab., Harvard U. Grad. Sch. Bus. Adminstrn., 1944-46; civilian cons. in anthropology U.S. War Dept., 1946; anthropologist Peabody Mus., Harvard U., 1946-48, Fla. State Mus., 1949—. Fellow Am. Anthrop. Assn., AAAS, Royal Anthrop. Inst. London, Soc. Applied Anthropology; mem. Am. Assn. Phys. Anthropologists, Am. Psychosomatic Soc., N.Y. Acad. Scis., Authors League Am., Authors Guild, Soc. Research in Child Devel. Clubs: Gainesville Golf and Country. University Women's, Gainesville Woman's. Author: New Answers to the Fatigue Problem, 1956, paperback edit., 1980; also articles in field; contbg. editor Anthropology, Handbook of Latin American Studies, 1969-71. Home: 2720 SW 8th Dr Gainesville FL 32601 Office: Fla State Museum U Fla Gainesville FL 32611

BULLIS, ELEANOR GROSS, social worker, realtor; b. Akron, Ohio, July 19, 1939; d. Frank R. and Herta (Camerer) Gross; B.A., Ohio Wesleyan U., 1962; M.S.W. (NIMH grantee), Case-Western Res. U., 1966; m. Richard Spencer Bullis, Aug. 28, 1969 (div. 1976); 1 dau., Elizabeth Herta. Teenage program dir. San Francisco YWCA, 1962-64; Fulbright grantee Cleve. Internat. Social Work Exchange Program, Germany, 1965; psychiat. social worker Agnews State Hosp., San Jose, Calif., 1966, Langley Porter Neuropsychiat. Inst., U. Calif., San Francisco, 1967-69; exec. dir. Human Investment Project, Menlo Park, Calif., 1976-81; condr. seminars, cons. in field; Realtor, Grubb & Ellis, Menlo Park, 1981—. Lic. Realtor, Calif. Mem. Nat. Assn. Social Workers, Internat. Assn. Social Workers, Internat. Social Work Edn., Cleve. Internat. Exchange Program Social Workers, Profl. Women's Network, Resource Center Women, Sierra Club, Gamma Phi Beta. Episcopalian.

BULLOCH, BENNIE DUVALL, educator; b. Lakeview, Tex., Apr. 8, 1933; d. Horace J. and Lolo Kathryn (Davenport) DuVall; B.S., W. Tex. State U., 1954; m. Don Kenyon Bulloch, June 30, 1957; children—Don Kenyon, Bryan DuVall, Sarah Kathryn. Exec. sec. Shamrock Oil and Gas Corp., Amarillo, Tex., 1954-57; legal sec. firm Vinson, Elkins, Weems & Searls, Houston, 1957-61; part-time legal sec. J.V. Hammett, Lampasas, Tex., 1964-78; vocat. edn. tchr., coordinator Lampasas Ind. Sch. Dist., 1979—. Pres., Lampasas County Republican Women, 1979. Mem. Vocat. Office Edn. Tchrs. Assn. Tex., Tex. Dental Assn. Women's Aux. (pres. 1973-74). Baptist. Club: Pierian (pres. 1976-77, sponsor Juniorette Pierian Club 1977-82). Home: PO Box 323 Lampasas TX 76550 Office: 902 S Broad St Lampasas TX 76550

BULLWINKEL, IRMA NANCY, real estate agt.; b. Lyndhurst, N.J., Oct. 22, 1920; d. Henry Edgar and Anna Weidner (Dubuy) Clay; student Tulsa U., 1951; A.A., Napa Coll.; grad. Realtor Inst. Calif., 1969; D.D. (hon.), Universal Life Ch., 1965; m. John Henry Bullwinkel, Nov. 1, 1941; children—John David, Douglas Kent. Sales analyst Prudential Ins. Co., Newark, 1937-41; teller Chase Nat. Bank, N.Y.C., 1942; real estate agt., Tulsa, 1950-62, Napa, Calif., 1962—. Vol. aide Napa Coll., 1968—; active ARC, 1942; mem. Easter Seal Soc.; patron Pretenders' Playhouse. Mem. Napa C. of C. (mem. law and order com., pub. com.), Napa County Bd. Realtors, Calif. Real Estate Assn., Nat. Inst. Realtors, Nat. Notary Assn. Presbyterian. Club: Napa Women's (pres. Entre Nous sect. 1972-73). Contbr. poems to newspapers. Home: 2636 W Pueblo Ave Napa CA 94558 Office: 1765 3d St Napa CA 94558

BULSON, CAROLYN JEAN, musician, educator; b. Gloversville, N.Y., Apr. 24, 1928; d. Arthur W. and Ruth C. (Peters) Longfritz; B.Ed. cum laude, SUNY, Potsdam, 1949; m. Walter T. Bulson, June 25, 1949; children—Linda Ruth Bulson Kauffman, Nancy Grace Bulson Shanor. Tchr., Tappan (N.Y.) schs., 1949-51; prin. flutist Rockland (N.Y.) Symphony, 1949-55, Suburban (N.Y.) Symphony, 1951-55, Lancaster (Pa.) Symphony, 1955—, Reading (Pa.) Symphony, 1968-70, Regional Symphony of Pa., 1974—, Lancaster Opera Workshop Orch.; flutist Reading Woodwin Quintet, 1965—, Lancaster Woodwin Quintet, 1977—; pvt. tchr. flute; adj. instr. music Millersville (Pa.) State Coll., 1978; tchr. Youth Symphony Music Camp, 1978, 80, 81, 82. Bd. dirs. Penn Laurel council Girl Scouts U.S.A., York, Pa., 1964-77, v.p., 1972-77, recipient Thanks Badge, 1962; v.p. Musical Art Soc., Lancaster, 1977-78, pres., 1978-80. Mem. Music Tchrs. Nat. Assn., Pa. Music Tchrs. Assn., Lancaster Music Tchrs. Assn., Nat. Fedn. Music Clubs, Pa. Fedn. Music Clubs, Nat. Flute Assn., Piccolo Soc., Inc., Am. Fedn. Musicians, Kappa Delta Pi, Alpha Sigma Omicron. Republican. Presbyterian. Club: Order Eastern Star. Author: Children in Wonderland, 1958. Home: 903 Forest Rd Lancaster PA 17601

BULTMANN, PHYLLIS WETHERELL, writer; b. Ottumwa, Iowa, Aug. 21, 1923; d. Harry Gillette and Venice B. (Lewis) Wetherell; B.A., UCLA, 1944, M.A., 1945, Ph.D., 1950; m. William Arnold Bultmann, Dec. 28, 1949; 1 dau., Janice. Instr. Ark. State U., Conway, 1950-58, Ohio Wesleyan U., Delaware, 1958-64, Western Wash. U., Bellingham, 1966-71, 80—; profl. writer columnist SEA Mag., Newport Beach, Calif., 1973—; columnist Everett (Wash.) Herald, 1981—; public relations officer Press Boat, PITCH Regatta, Bellingham, 1976-78; sr. Fulbright lectr., East Pakistan, 1960-61; dir. Maritime Heritage Found., Bellingham, 1980—. Mem. Conf. Brit. Studies. Episcopalian. Clubs: Bellingham Yacht; Squalicum Yacht. Author: Two Burners and An Ice Chest, 1977; (with Bill Bultmann) Border Boating, 1979; Editor: (with W.A. Bultmann) Current Research in British Studies, 1975; (with Leroy Dresbeck) British Studies Intelligencer, 1972-77. Home and office: 447 14th St Bellingham WA 98225

BUMBRY, GRACE MELZIA, mezzo soprano; b. St. Louis, Jan. 4, 1937; d. Benjamin and Melzia (Walker) Bumbry; student Boston U., 1954-55, Music Acad. West, 1956-59; studied with Lotte Lehmann, Northwestern U., also fgn. countries; H.H.D. (hon.). Operatic debut Paris Opera, 1960; concert and operatic appearances in Europe, Japan, Bayreuth, Germany and U.S., also command performance The White House; performed Met. Opera, N.Y.C., Royal Opera House Covent Garden, London, La Scala Milan, Vienna Stateopera, Teatro Colon Buenos Aires; recs. for Deutsche Grammophon, Angel, London and RCA. Recipient John Hay Whitney award, 1959; Grammy award. Mem. Zeta Phi Beta, Sigma Alpha Iota. Office: care Columbia Artists Mgmt Inc 165 W 57th St New York NY 10019 *

BUMGARNER, MARLENE ANNE, author, educator; b. Yorkshire, Eng., Nov. 6, 1947; came to U.S., 1949, naturalized, 1965; d. Rowland and May (Whittaker) Skirrow; A.A., Coll. San Mateo, 1967; B.A., San Diego State Coll., 1970; M.A., San Jose State U., 1982; m. John Owen Bumgarner, June 17, 1967; children—Doña Ana, John Rowland. Tech. editor electronics firms, 1967-70; coordinator Peer Counseling Center, Las Cruces, N.Mex., 1970-72; tchr. elem. sch., 1974-76; owner, mgr. Morgan Hill Trading Post, natural food store, Morgan Hill, Calif., 1976-78; editor Natural Living Newsline, Morgan Hill, 1979-81; mgr. Natural Living Assos., 1979—; dir. Morgan Hill Country Day Sch., 1980—; instr. Gavilan Coll., 1979—. Leader, founder La Leche League of Morgan Hill, 1977—; supt. Sunday Sch., St. John's Episcopal Ch., 1982—. Mem. Soc. Children's Book Writers, Nat. Newspaper Food Writers and Editors Assn., Calif. Press Women. Author: Book of Whole Grains, 1976; Organic Cooking for (not-so-organic) Mothers, 1980; columnist San Jose (Calif.) Mercury, 1977-80; contbr. People's Cookbook, 1977, Real Food Places, 1981; sr. tech. writer Boole and Babbage, Inc.; contbg. editor Mothering mag., 1981—. Office: PO Box 1326 Morgan Hill CA 95037

BUMP, DOROTHEA ROSE, writer; b. Muncie, Ind., Nov. 22, 1918; d. Leo Bernard and Gladys Melinda (Simpson) Conn; B.S., Ball State U., 1978; m. Richard Earl Bump, Aug. 29, 1941; 1 son, Michael Richard. Continuity writer WBT, WSOC-AM, Charlotte, N.C., 1935-40; reporter, columnist Muncie (Ind.) Evening Press, 1945-50, 56-68; dir. public relations Community Fund Delaware County (Ind.), 1952-55; edn. writer Ball State U., Muncie, Ind., 1968, 72-82. Bd. dirs. Muncie Civic Theatre, 1950's, Delaware County Mental Health Assn., 1958-62; chmn. adv. council Richmond State Hosp., 1968-76; mem. adv. commn. Ind. Dept. Mental Health, 1970-76; pres. Widowed Persons Service Delaware County, 1981—. Mem. Nat. Fedn. Press Women, Women in Communications, Womens Press Club Ind. (v.p. 1959-61), East Central Ind. Women in Communications (pres. 1976-78). Mem. Soc. Friends. Home: 2308 N Janney Ave Muncie IN 47304

BUNCE, LOUISE LONGNECKER, speech/lang. co. ofcl.; b. Linden, N.C., Nov. 19, 1930; d. Albert Franklin and Sara Kathryn (Eason) Longnecker; student public schs., Stedman, N.C.; m. Apr. 30, 1949; children—Gwendolyn Louise, Leon Warren, David children— Matthew, Thomas. Telephone Co., Fayetteville, N.C., 1957—, customer services supr., 1978—. Mem. Fayetteville Heritage Sq. Service Com. Mem. Ind. Telephone Pioneer Assn., Carolina Speakers Bur., Nat. Trust. Club: Woodhaven Garden (sec. 1979). Home: 205 Vivian Dr Fayetteville NC 28301 Office: PO Box 1630 Fayetteville NC 28302

BUNCH, ARLINE HAMMOND (MRS. ALFRED B. BUNCH), educator; b. Lowry City, Mo., Jan. 30, 1907; d. Hardin R. and Minnie (Slavens) Hammond; B.S., Springfield State Tchrs. Coll., 1928; m. Alfred B. Bunch, June 28, 1933; children—Bryan H., Robert Dale, Barbara Bunch Fields (dec.). Tchr., St. Clair County (Mo.) Rural Schs., 1926-28, Springfield Draughon's Bus. Coll., 1928-30; mgr. Sarachon Hooley Secretarial Sch., St. Louis, 1930-35; tchr. advanced secretarial dept. Miss Hickey's Sch. for Secs., St. Louis, 1935-40; owner, mgr. Crescent Hall Secretarial Sch., Peoria, Ill., 1940-47; owner, corp. sec., dir. Midstate Coll., Peoria, 1966—; bd. advs. Internat. Speedwriting Co., N.Y.C.; mem. adv. bd. Ill. State Pvt. Bus. and Vocat. Schs., 1968—; accrediting commr. Assn. Ind. Colls. and Schs., 1968-70, recipient disting. service award for 50 yrs. service, 1979. Trustee Barbara Fields Meml. Scholarship Fund, 1968—. Recipient Charlotte Danstrom award, 1982. Mem. Jubilee Bus. and Profl. Women's Assn. (pres. 1965, 82-83), Nat. Assn. Women Bus. Owners (charter mem. Peoria chpt.), Peoria Advt. and Selling Club (dir. 1967—). Home: Byerly Hills East Peoria IL 61611 Office: 244 SW Jefferson St Peoria IL 61602

BUNCH, MERIBETH ANN, voice cons.; b. Aulander, N.C., Apr. 20, 1938; d. Luther Elmo and Edith Wiley (Pickard) B.; B.M., Salem Coll., 1960; S.M.M., Union Theol. Sem., 1962; Ph.D., U. So. Calif., 1974. Instr. voice, instr. anatomy U. So. Calif., 1968-74; instr. anatomy, cons. Huntington Hosp., Pasadena, Calif., 1970-74; assoc. prof. music and life and health sci. U. Del., Newark, 1974-82; prof. anatomy Royal Acad. Dancing, London, 1981—; cons. voice to opera and mus. theatre cos., U.S. and Eng., 1982—; research fellow Royal Coll. Surgs. Eng., London, 1979-80. Recipient award NIH, 1979-81. Mem. AAUP, Nat. Assn. Tchrs. Singing, Internat. Assn. Logopedics and Phoniatrics, Collegium Medicorum Theatre, Internat. Platform Assn. Author: Dynamics of the Singing Voice, 1982; mem. editorial bd. Nat. Assn. Tchrs. Singing Bull., 1975—. Office: 100 Christiana Med Center Newark DE 19702

BUNCH, ZOE VESTAL, corrugated paperboard mfg. co. exec.; b. Whitewright, Tex., May 28, 1931; d. Rolla Calhoun and Lora Adelaide (Robinson) Vestal; student Baylor U., 1948-49, Houston Community Coll., 1974, Houston Bus. Coll., 1949, Lollie Lowe Career Coll., 1974, Harvard U., 1975; children—Morgan Rainey III, Zoann Marie. Sec., Nifty Tablet Mfg. Co., 1948; sec. to gen. mgr. Gen. Motors Acceptance Corp., Houston, 1950-52; change and reinstatement clk. Prudential Life Ins. Co., 1952-55; clk./tchr. aide William P. Hobby Elem. Sch., Houston, 1967-72; exec. sec. to pres. Krafcor Corp., Houston, 1973-74, mgr. Houston office, 1974, dist. sales rep., 1974-80, mgr. adminstrv. services, 1980-82, v.p., dir., 1982—. Mem. Nat. Secs. Assn. (dir.), Houston Personnel Assn., Purchasing Mgmt. Assn. Houston, Nat. Assn. Fleet Adminstrs., Am. Soc. Profl. and Exec. Women, Women's Network, DAR, UDC, Children of Am. Revolution, Dau. Republic of Tex. Republican. Baptist. Clubs: Chi Omega Mother's, Prayer Key Family, Internat. 700, Exec. Bus. Women's Forum. Home: 5857 Valley Forge Houston TX 77057 Office: 2900 Wesleyan Suite 680 Houston TX 77027

BUNDEALLY, AMINA ESMAIL, microbiologist; b. Bombay, India; came to U.S., 1968, naturalized, 1977; d. Esmail Gulamhusein and Sherbanoo (Alimohamed) B.; B.S., St. Xavier's Coll., 1957; M.S., Haffkine Inst., 1962, Ph.D., 1968. Jr., then sr. Diamond Jubilee fellow Haffkine Inst., 1962-68; Mass. health research fellow Biologic Labs., Jamaica Plains, 1968-70; research officer dept. plastic surgery J.J. Hosp., Bombay, 1971-73; research fellow Burns Research Centre, Cin. Gen. Hosp., 1973-74, jr. research asso. pathology dept., 1974-77; asst. prof. microbiology W.Va. Sch. Osteo. Medicine, Lewisburg, 1977-82, assoc. prof., 1982—. Mem. Am. Soc. Microbiology, Assn. Microbiologists India, Bus. and Profl. Women's Club. Democrat. Moslem. Author papers in field. Home: 107 Greenbrier Ave Lewisburg WV 24901 Office: 400 N Lee St Lewisburg WV 24901

BUNDY, ANNALEE MARSHALL, librarian; b. Chgo., Feb. 11, 1938; d. Warren Elmer and Marie Thresa (Madden) Marshall; B.A., U. N.H., 1960; M.L.S., Simmons Coll., 1961; m. John Willard Bundy, Mar. 11, 1961. Assoc. head librarian Coll. Guam, Agana, 1961-62, head librarian, 1962-63; tech. librarian E. I. duPont de Nemours & Co., Maydown Works, Londonderry, No. Ireland, 1963-65; head librarian children's room Schnectady County (N.Y.) Public Library, 1965-66; documents and periodicals librarian Grad. Sch. Public Affairs, SUNY, Albany, 1966-67; asst. dir. Medford (Mass.) Pub. Library, 1967-73; dir. libraries Somerville (Mass.) Public Library, 1973-78; dir. Providence Public Library, 1978—; mem. adv. com. R.I. Sch. Design, 1979—; mem. accreditation vis. team New Eng. Bd. Higher Edn., 1976, challenge grant panelist Nat. Endowment Humanities, 1980. Commr. Mass. Cable TV Commn., 1975-79. Mem. ALA, PLA/Met. Libraries (pres. 1981-82), New Eng. Library Assn. (sec. 1978-79), R.I. Library Assn. (nominating com. 1982), Providence C. of C., Downtown Providence Improvement Assn. (mem. edn. com.). Clubs: Agawam Hunt, Providence Art, Turk's Head. Compiler: Alternatives in Print, 1972. Office: 150 Empire St Providence RI 02903

BUNDY, ORA BRINKLEY, newspaper editor; b. Houston, Dec. 15, 1915; d. Ellis and Essie Sanchez (Robinson) Mitchell; B.A., U. Wis., 1934; m. Robert Fleming Bundy, Dec. 15, 1973; children by previous marriage—Leon Brinkley, Jr. (dec.), Shirley Ayn Barber. Soc. editor Phila. Tribune, 1945-58, women's and soc. editor, 1975-80, social columnist, 1980—; soc. editor N.Y. Amsterdam News, N.Y.C., 1958-61; fashion editor Sepia Mag., Ft. Worth, 1961-64, Elegant & Elegant Teen Mags., Los Angeles, 1965-67; public relations dir. YWCA, Phila., 1967-75; cons. Music Fair Enterprises, Inc., Bala Cynwyd, Pa., 1979-81. Mem. adv. bd. Afro-Am. students Pa. State U.; mem. public relations bd. Women's Way, Phila., 1978—; bd. dirs. North Central YWCA, 1978-80, S.W. Belmont YWCA, 1982—, Tribune Charities, 1980—; mem. Phila. Crime Commn. Mem. NAACP, Nat. Assn. Media Women, Women in Communications, Phila. Urban League, Continental Socs. (founder, pres. 1950-54), Lambda Kappa Mu. Democrat. Episcopalian. Club: Links. Office: Philadelphia Tribune 520-26 S 16th St Philadelphia PA 19146

BUNKER, NORENE RAE, polit. worker; b. Mobridge, S.D., July 11, 1931; d. Tilford M. and Ethel Florence (Moe) Leverson; student Interstate Bus. Coll., 1949-50; m. Ardis Gray Bunker, June 24, 1961. PBX steno, credit mgr. Store Without a Name, Fargo, N.D., 1950-55; bookkeeper Monarch Lumber Co., Great Falls, Mont., 1955-60, Piggly Wiggly Northland Nash Finch, Fargo, 1960-61; bookkeeper, office mgr. Hagstrom Bros. Clothing, St. Paul, 1961-62; mem.-at-large Nat. Fedn. Republican Women, 1978-79, treas., 1980—. Treas., Fargo Republican Com., 1970-77; pres. N.D. Fedn. Rep. Women, 1975-78; chmn. 46th legis. dist. Rep. Com., 1977-78; mem. N.D. Rep. Exec. Com., 1975-78; hon. bd. dirs. Minnkota chpt. ARC, 1969—; chmn. Fargo Nursing Home Bd., 1981—. Mem. PEO, Sons of Norway, Am. Legion Aux. Republican. Lutheran. Club: Order Eastern Star. Home: 721 Southwood Dr Fargo ND 58103 also 4717 E Ahwalukee Dr Phoenix AZ 85044

BUNN, BEVERLY, lawyer; b. Sacramento, Sept. 2; d. Guy Alvis and Violet (Pelzel) B.; student Portland State U., U. Portland; J.D., Pepperdine U., 1969. Stewardess, United Air Lines, N.Y.C., Los Angeles, 1964, stewardess recruiter, 1964; dir. Airline Stewardess Tng. Sch., Viva Modeling Sch., Riverside, Calif., 1965; social worker Calif. State Dept. Social Welfare, Riverside County, Orange County, 1965-70; admitted to Calif. bar, 1971; practiced in Orange County, Calif., 1971-76; overseas project mgr. econ. devel., project mgr. emergency assistance to war victims and refugees Cath. Relief Services, Yemen Arab Republic, 1976-79, econ. devel., Tunis, Tunisia, 1980-81; supervising atty. NANA region Alaska Legal Services Corp., Kotzebue, 1982—; legal counsel Anaheim Young Republicans, 1971; gen. counsel Calif. Young Republicans, 1972-73; lectr. U. Calif., Irvine, 1973; vice chmn. Calif. Citizens Com. Welfare Reform, 1971. Sec., Orange County Young Republicans, 1972-73. Mem. Am. Bar Assn., Internat. Bar Assn. (London), Am. Soc. Internat. Law, Assn. Immigration and Nationality Lawyers, United Air Lines Stewardess Alumni Assn., Calif. Bar Assn., Santa Ana C. of C. (ambassador). Editor: Clipped Wings, 1964-65, The Double Tau, 1967-69. Home: 864 49th St Sacramento CA 95819 Office: PO Box 316 Kotzebue AK 99752

BUNNELL, JANE SUSAN, product graphic designer; b. St. Louis, Mar. 31, 1951; d. Eugene Allison and Ida (Malaspina) Jackson; student U. Mo., St. Louis, 1970; cert. comml. art Am. Acad. Art, 1972; m. Michael Bunnell, Mar. 10, 1979. Indsl. designer Outboard Marine Corp., Waukegan, Ill., 1972-74; graphic designer Allstate Ins. Co., Northbrook, Ill., 1975-76; indsl. designer, product graphic designer Internat. Harvester Corp., Hinsdale, Ill., 1976—. Recipient 1st Pl. award for watercolors Chgo. Area Art Show, 1977. Mem. Soc. Automotive Engs. (subcom. on human factors). Club: Tennis League (Hinsdale). Office: Components Engring and Devel Internat Harvester Co 16W 260 83d St Hinsdale IL 60521

BUNTE, DORIS, state legislator; b. N.Y.C., July 2, 1933; d. Evelyn C. Johnson; student Boston U., Suffolk U., U. Mass., Amherst; children—Yvette, Harold, Allen. Dir. housing Southend Neighborhood Action Program, Boston, 1969-70, dir. personnel, 1970-72; mem. Mass. Ho. of Reps., 1972—; commr. Boston Housing Authority, 1969-75; mem. Nat. Rent Adv. Bd. for Phase II Econ. Stabilization Act; mem. Exec. Com. to Investigate Mass. Commn. Against Discrimination; participant Loeb Fellowship Program, Harvard U. Grad. Sch. Design. Mem. Mass. Democratic Com.; mem. Boston Dem. Com.; mem. electoral coll. Dem. Nat. Conv., 1976. Named Citizen of Yr., Omega Psi Iota Chi Chpt.; Doris Bunte Day named by City of Boston, 1978; notary public, Mass. Mem. Solomon Carter Fuller Mental Health Center, Roxbury Multi-Service Center, Freedom House, Mas. Black Caucus, NAACP, Citizen's Housing and Planning Ass., Mass. Conf. Human Rights, Mass. Caucus Women's Legislators, Black Polit. Task Force. Author reports, HEW, HUD. Office: Com on Human Services/Elderly Affairs State House Room 22 Beacon St Boston MA 02133 *

BUNTIN, LINDA ANNE, entomologist; b. N.Y.C., Aug. 8, 1953; d. Edward J. and Gladys R. (Bedigian) Bormann; B.S. in Agr. with honors and distinction (Outstanding Sr. Woman Coll. Agr.), U. Del., 1975; M.S., Wash. State U., 1977; Ph.D., Iowa State U., 1983; m. G. David Buntin, Mar. 25, 1978. First woman extension entomologist in U.S., mem. faculty Iowa State U., 1977—; coordinator Iowa Pesticide Applicator Cert. Tng. Program. Mem. Entom. Soc. Am., Can. Entomol. Soc., Kans. Entomol. Soc., Sigma Xi, Alpha Zeta, Phi Delta Gamma. Office: Insectary Bldg Iowa State U Ames IA 50011

BUNTING, JOELLE, psychiatrist, psychoanalyst; b. San Francisco, Feb. 6, 1939; d. John Richard and Adella Virginia (Bristol) Bunting; B.A. with distinction, Stanford U., 1960; M.D., U. Calif., 1964; cert. N.Y. Med. Coll., 1976; m. Leo B. Mazer, Mar. 27, 1977; 1 son, Ross Arthur. Intern, Maimonides Med. Center, Bklyn., 1964-65; resident N.Y. Med. Coll.-Met. Hosp. Center, N.Y.C., 1965-68; pvt. practice medicine specializing in psychiatry and psychoanalysis, Tenafly and Harrington Park, N.J., 1968—; clin. instr. Westchester div., N.Y. Med. Coll., Valhalla, 1979—; mem. staffs Englewood (N.J.) Hosp. Mem. Am. Psychiat. Assn. (br. treas.), Am. Med. Women's Assn., Soc. Med. Psychoanalysts (editor The Forum newsletter 1982—), Am. Acad. Psychoanalysis. Club: Altrusa International. Home and office: 92 Higgins Pl Harrington Park NJ 07640

BUNTING, MARGARET ANNE, state legislator; b. Brownsville, Pa., July 5, 1920; d. Charles Edward and Lillian Mae (Long) Rothrock; student George Washington U., 1943-44, Boise State Coll., 1954; m. Clyde E. Bunting, Nov. 16, 1945; children—Margaret Heidi Mae, Sally Anne. Sec., Hdqrs. Army Service Forces, Washington, 1943; adminstrv. sec. Exec. Office of Pres., Under Sec. of War, Washington, 1944-45; jour. clk. Idaho Ho. of Reps., 1967-70; mem. Idaho Ho. of Reps., 1973—; pres. Bunting Tractor Co., Bunting Bldg. Corp. Chmn., Idaho Concert and Artist Series, 1952-53, Idaho Youth Concert, 1955, St. Lukes Hosp. Ball, 1964, Boise Philharmonic Assn., 1957; sec. bd. Boise Art Assn., 1960-63. Sec. Idaho Gov.'s House Heritage Com., 1969-69; precinct com. woman Republican Party, 1967-72; dir. Ada County Rep. Central Com., 1970—; pres. Ada County Rep. Women's Club, 1972; pres. Idaho Fedn. Rep. Women, 1973, parliamentarian, 1976—; pres. Idaho State Hist. Soc. Aux., 1967-68. Mem. Boise Jr. League, St. Luke's Hosp. Aux., Nat. Order Women Legislators (parliamentarian 1977). Episcopalian. Mem. Women of Rotary. Club: Hillcrest Country. Author: Historical Treasures from Idaho Kitchens, 1967. Home: 944 Lewis St Boise ID 83702

BURBIDGE, ELEANOR MARGARET PEACHEY (MRS. GEOFFREY BURBIDGE), astronomer; b. Davenport, Eng.; came to U.S., 1955; d. Stanley John and Marjorie (Stott) Peachey; B.Sc., Ph.D., U. London; Sc.D. (hon.), Smith Coll., 1963, U. Sussex, 1970, U. Bristol, 1972, U. Leicester, 1972, City U., 1974, U. Mich., 1978, U. Mass., 1978, Williams Coll., 1979; m. Geoffrey Burbidge, Apr. 2, 1946; 1 dau., Sarah. Mem. staff U. London Obs., 1948-51; research fellow Yerkes Obs., U. Chgo., 1951-53, Calif. Inst. Tech., Pasadena, 1955-57; Shirley Farr fellow Yerkes Obs., 1957-59, asso. prof., 1959-62; mem. Enrico Fermi Inst. for Nuclear Studies, 1957-62; prof. astronomy dept. physics U. Calif. at San Diego, 1964—; dir. Royal Greenwich Obs., Herstmonceux Castle, Hallsham, Sussex, Eng., 1972-73, dir. Center for Astrophysics and Space Scis., UCSD, 1979—. Recipient (with husband) Warner prize in Astronomy, 1959; hon. fellow Univ. Coll., London, Girton Coll., Lucy Cavendish Coll., Cambridge Fellow Royal Soc., Nat. Acad. Scis., Am. Acad. Arts and Scis., Royal Astron. Soc., Catherine Wolfe Bruce Medal, Astron. Soc. Pacific, 1982; mem. Am. Astron. Soc. (v.p. 1972-74, pres. 1976-78), Internat. Astron. Union (pres. commn. 28, 1970-73), Am. Assn. for the Advancement of Sci. (fellow 1982, pres. 1982), Am. Philos. Soc., Author: (with G. Burbidge) Quasi-Stellar Objects, 1967. Editor Observatory mag., 1948-51; editorial bd. Astronomy and Astrophysics, 1969—. Address: CASS C-011 UCSD U Calif La Jolla CA 92093

BURCH, PAULA TEMPEST, pharmacy adminstr.; b. Coleman, Tex., May 4, 1949; d. Howard Ray and Geneva Pearl (Hinds) Kilgore; student U. Tex., Arlington, 1973-74, Mountain View Jr. Coll., 1975-76; m. Roy Edward Burch, May 31, 1968; 1 son, Mark Edward. Lab. technician Dr. Ralph L. Buller, Hydro, Okla., 1968-70; bookkeeper, clk. Hilley Pharmacy, Cedar Hill, Tex., 1972-76; owner, mgr. Shell Knob Pharmacy (Mo.), 1977—. Mem. Mo. Pharm. Assn., Nat. Assn. Retail Drug Stores. Republican. Home and office: PO Box 38 Shell Knob MO 65747

BURCHAM, MARY MOSSIE, civic worker; b. Lawrence County, Ohio, Sept. 22, 1925; d. Harlow R. and Elizabeth H. (Bevan) Fuller; student Huntington Bus. Coll., 1944; m. Bernard E. Burcham, Nov. 8, 1947; children—Elizabeth A. Burcham Nibert, Linda Sue, Berna Jean Burcham Hilbert. With Alexander H. Kerr & Co., Inc., Huntington, W.Va., 1944-49; mother adviser Point Pleasant Assembly 23, Rainbow Girls, 1970—, mem. Grand Cross of Color; community worker Cancer Soc., Heart Fund, Muscular Dystrophy Assn., ARC, March of Dimes, Multiple Sclrosis Soc., past PTA officer; sponsor Girl Scouts U.S.A.; chaperone high sch. students on tours to Washington; past mem. bd. edn. United Methodist Ch., past Sunday sch. tchr. Club: Order Eastern Star (Point Pleasant chpt. No. 75). Home: 2301 Jefferson Ave Point Pleasant WV 25550

BURCHETTE, ANN MARIE POWLEY, mfg. co. exec.; b. Los Angeles, Dec. 20, 1942; d. Leo Joseph and Ethel Louise (Fitzgerald) Greenhalgh; student Santa Monica (Calif.) Coll., UCLA extension; m. Donald L. Burchette, Jan. 6, 1980. Field support officer C.O.R.D.S. program AID mission to Vietnam, 1968-71; adminstrv. asst. Manzan & Assos., Inc., Malibu, Calif., 1972-75; supr. sales adminstrn. TRW Datacom Internat., Inc., Los Angeles, 1975-77; nat. logistics mgr. Computer Communications, Inc., Torrance, Calif., 1978-80; materiel mgr. data systems services div. Eaton Corp., Los Angeles, 1981—. Mem. Assn. Field Service Mgrs., Nat. Assn. Purchasing Mgrs., Am. Mgmt. Assn. Home: 12712 Dewey St Los Angeles CA 90066 Office: 6374 Arizona Circle Los Angeles CA 90045

BURCHWOOD, KATHARINE TYLER, writer, educator; b. Portland, Oreg.; d. Lewis Morris and Ellen A. (Richmond) Tyler; A.B. in Edn., Art Inst. Chgo., 1916; Ph.B., U. Chgo., 1927, A.M., 1931; m. Louis F. Burchwood, Nov. 24, 1943. Asst. supr. pub. sch. art, Evanston, Ill.; head art dept. State Tchrs. Coll., Valley City, N.D., summer 1932; lectr. grad. sch. Syracuse (N.Y.) U., summer 1933; tchr. English, art practice and history art Chgo. Bd. Edn., 1923-56. Mem. Nat. Soc. New Eng. Women Daus. Am. Colonists, Nat. Soc. Arts and Letters, D.A.R., Seabury Western Found., Ill. Soc. Mayflower Descs., Daus. Founders and Patriots Am., Colonial Dames Am. Episcopalian. Republican. Co-author: (textbook) Art Then and Now, 1949; Origin and Legacy of Mexican Art, 1972. Contbr. articles to mags. Home: 1305 Lincoln St Evanston IL 60201

BURDE, MARY LOIS (PENNY), labor/mgmt. specialist; b. Newark, May 25; d. Thomas J. and Mae V. (Pennie) Duggan; M.Edn., Rutgers U., 1976, postgrad., 1982—; m. Francis R. Burde, July 4; children—Gregory, Christopher, Tracey. Pres., Bergen Community Coll. Supportive Staff Assos., 1969-72; labor lobbyist, cons. N.J. Indsl. Union Council, AFL-CIO, 1978-79; bd. mem. Pvt. Industry Council, Hackensack, N.J., 1979—; v.p. Penclaire Service Corp., Paramus, N.J., 1973—; chmn. pay equity task force N.J. Coalition Labor Union Women, 1979-82; mem. Com. on Pay Equity, Conf. Alt. State and Local Policies, 1981—; mem. panel Women's Affirmative Action Com., N.J. Indsl. Union Council, AFL-CIO, 1979-81; adv. bd. mem. Women's Inst., Bergen Community Coll., 1978—. Mem. Bergen County Commn. Status of Women, 1976—. Mem. NOW, Coalition Labor Union Women, N.J. Coll. and Univ. Coalition for Women's Edn. Office: Seven Chimneys Westwood NJ 07675

BURDEN, JEAN (PRUSSING), poet, editor, author; b. Waukegan, Ill., Sept. 1, 1914; d. Harry Frederick and Miriam (Biddlecom) Prussing; B.A., U. Chgo., 1936; m. David Charles Burden, Aug. 31, 1940 (div. May 1949). Sec., John Hancock Mut. Life Ins. Co., Chgo., 1937-39, Young & Rubicam Advt. Agy., Chgo., 1939-41; editor, copywriter Domestic Industries, Inc., Chgo., 1941-45; office mgr. Obrion Russell & Co., Los Angeles, 1948-56; mem. public relations staff Meals for Missions Found., Los Angeles, 1956-65; editor Stanford Research Inst., South Pasadena, Calif., 1965-66; owner Jean Burden & Assos., Altadena, Calif., 1966-72; contbg. editor Woman's Day Mag., 1973-82; poetry editor Yankee Mag., 1955—; supr. poetry workshop Pasadena City Coll., 1961-62, 66, U. Calif., Irvine, 1975; lectr. poetry numerous univs. and colls., 1960—. Recipient awards including Silver Anvil award, Public Relations Soc. Am., 1969; MacDowell Colony fellow, 1973, 74, 76. Mem. Poetry Soc. Am., Acad. Am. Poets, Authors Guild. Democrat. Author: Naked as the Glass, 1963; Journey Toward Poetry, 1966; The Dog You Care For, 1968; The Cat You Care For, 1968; The Bird You Care For, 1970; The Fish You Care For, 1971; A Celebration of Cats, 1974; The Classic Cats, 1975; The Woman's Day Book of Hints for Cat Owners, 1980; Contbr. numerous articles to mags. and jours. Home and Office: 1129 Beverly Way Altadena CA 91001

BURDICK, CAROLYN JANE, physiologist; b. Westerly, R.I., Jan. 10, 1938; d. Thomas John and Amy (Eaton) B.; B.A., Smith Coll., 1959; Ph.D., Harvard U., 1965. NIH fellow Harvard U., Cambridge, Mass., 1962-64, dept. cell biology Rockefeller U., N.Y.C., 1964-66; lectr. physiology Hunter Coll., N.Y.C., 1966; asso. prof. biology Bklyn. Coll., 1966—; mem. corp. Marine Biol. Lab, Woods Hole, Mass., 1972—. Mem. Am. Soc. Zoologists, Phi Beta Kappa, Sigma Xi. Author: Laboratory Manual for General Physiology, 1978; contbr. numerous articles in field to profl. jours. Office: Dept Biology Brooklyn Coll Brooklyn NY 11210

BURDUS, JULIA ANN, advt. agy. exec.; b. Alnwick, Eng., Sept. 4, 1933; came to U.S., 1981; d. Gladstone and Julia Wilhelminia (Booth) Beaty; B.A. in Psychology with honours, St. Mary's Coll., Durham U., 1956; m. Ian Robertson, June 11, 1981. Market research exec. Ogilvy & Mather, 1961-67; research dir. Compton Advt., 1967-71; dir. research, vice chmn. McCann Erickson U.K., 1971-77, exec. v.p., 1978-79; chmn. McCann & Co. U.K., 1979-81; sr. v.p. Interpublic Group Cos., N.Y.C., 1981—. Mem. Advt. Assn. U.K., European Soc. Mktg. and Opinion Research, Inst. Practitioners in Advt. Office: 1271 Ave of the Americas New York NY 10020

BURFORD, ANN DESALME, credit exec.; b. San Antonio, Oct. 13, 1938; d. Adolph Joseph and Sophia Edna (Arnold) DeSalme; student public schs. Austin, Tex.; m. Wesley M. Burford, Mar. 20, 1955; children—Scott, Wesley, Donna, Christopher, Jennifer. Office and credit mgr. Gen. Tire Service, Austin, 1964-67; acct. Ching Investment Co., Austin, 1967-70; credit mgr. Evelyn Wood Reading Dynamics, Austin, 1972-73; v.p., gen. mgr. Ednl. Credit Corp., Austin, 1973—; dir. Evelyn Wood Reading Dynamics, Inc., Credit Mgmt. of Tex., Inc. Mem. Internat. Consumer Credit Assn., Credit Women Internat., Credit Mgmt. Assn. of Tex. (president's award for credit edn. 1977, Credit Exec. of Yr. 1978), Credit Mgmt. of Austin (pres., 1977), Credit Women of Austin (v.p., 1977-78). Roman Catholic. Home: 11702 Windermere Meadows Austin TX 78759 Office: 1801 Lavaca St Austin TX 78701

BURFORD, MARY ANNE, med. technologist; b. Paris, Ark., Aug. 24, 1939; d. Anthony John and Julia Elizabeth (Hoffmann) Elsken; B.S. in Biology, Benedictine Coll., 1961; grad. in med. tech. St. Mary's Sch. Med. Tech., 1962; m. Joseph Paul Burford, May 11, 1968; children—Sarah Elizabeth, Shawn Anthony, Joseph Paul, Daniel Aaron. Evening supr. St. Vincent's Infirmary, Little Rock, 1962-65; med. technologist Holt-Krock Clinic, Ft. Smith, Ark., 1966-68, Ball Meml. Hosp., Muncie, Ind., 1971-72, Pathologist Assoc., Muncie, 1972-73; chief technologist Ob-Gyn Inc., Muncie, 1975—; instr. microbiology St. Vincent's Infirmary, 1962-65, Sparks Med. Ctr., Ft. Smith, 1966-68. Chmn. liturgical life, St. Mary's Catholic Ch. Mem. Am. Soc. Clin. Pathologists (affiliate mem., registered med. technologist), Am. Assn. Clin. Chemists, Am. Soc. for Microbiology. Club: Altrusa. Home: 1509 W Buckingham Dr Muncie IN 47302 Office: 2501 W Jackson St Muncie IN 47302

BURG, LORETTA MARIE, pianist; b. Scottville, Mich., Oct. 20, 1907; d. William Matthew and Mary Agnes (O'Donnell) Wagar; tchr.'s cert., Rosary Coll., River Forest, Ill., 1925-26; grad. Eastern Mich. Coll., 1929; m. Martin S. Burg, July 2, 1932; children—William Francis, Mary Ellen Henehan. Tchr. piano class, Hazel Park, Mich., 1930-38; pvt. tchr. of piano, Chgo., 1945—; social activities columnist Beverly Rev., Chgo., 1960-80; organist, choir dir. St. Walter Ch., Chgo., 1949-69. Active local Girl Scouts, 1945-69, dist. chmn., 1960-65, sec. Chgo. bd. dirs., 1966-69; bd. dirs. Archdiocesan Council Catholic Women, 1956-68. Recipient various Girl Scout awards. Mem. Gen. Fedn. Women's Clubs (sec. dist. 3). Republican. Clubs: Western Springs Women's (past pres.), Beverly Hills Woman's (past pres.), St. Walter Woman's (past pres.), St. Cajetan Woman's (past pres.). Address: 5806B Wolf Rd Western Springs IL 60558

BURGE, ETHEL CORRIHER, author, fashion cons.; b. Chgo., Feb. 5, 1916; d. Lon Freeze and Alma (Paape) Corriher; student Chgo. Coll. Commerce, 1934-35, Northwestern U., 1936-38; m. Floyd Burge, June 28, 1941; children—Jeffery Lon, Jon Graham. Exec. dir. Women's Whirl, Chgo., 1957-60; dir. Mrs. America Speaking Services, Chgo., 1960-61; author books: 101 Ways to Be More Attractive, 1959, This Business of Dressing for Business, 1974, What is Your SQ?, 1976, Color-Code Your Personality, 1978; author column: The Fashion Strip, 1961-78; lectr. in field; cons. Met. Sch. Bus., Chgo., Dartnell Inst. Mgmt. Home: 1352 W Pampa Ave Mesa AZ 85202

BURGER, ELISABETH OWEN, economist; b. Naples, Italy, Dec. 7, 1923; d. Frieda Segelke Miller; student Friends Sem., N.Y.C., 1937-41; B.A., Vassar Coll., 1944; certificate Seven Coll. Vocat. Workshop, 1964; m. Arthur David Kemp Owen, Sept. 16, 1950 (dec. June 1970); children—Michael David and Hugh Miller; m. 2d, Chester Burger, Sept. 2, 1971. Mem. staff ILO, Geneva, Switzerland, 1947-49; research analyst N.Y. State Gov.'s Commn. on Edn. and Employment of Women, 1964; spl. researcher Rockefeller Found., N.Y.C., 1966-67; asst. to dep. exec. dir. Council on Fgn. Relations, N.Y.C., 1970-71; asso. program officer UN secretariat for World Population Conf., 1974, also Internat. Women's Year, 1975; research, editorial work U.S. Dept. State, 1973. Bd. dirs. Planned Parenthood, N.Y.C., 1974—. Democrat. Clubs: Cosmopolitan. Home: 33 W 67th St New York City NY 10023

BURGER, MARY LOUISE, psychologist, educator; b. Chgo., Nov. 3; d. Robert Stanley and Margaret Agnes (Brennan) Hirsh; B.A., Mundelein Coll.; M.Ed., Loyola U.; Ed.D., No. Ill. U., 1973; m. William Bronson Burger, Mar. 16, 1968. Tchr., Chgo. Bd. Edn., 1954-68; mem. faculty DePaul U., 1960-61, Roosevelt U., 1967-70; cons. psychologist Worthington-Hurst & Assos., Headstart Program, Chgo., 1972-74; prof. dept. early childhood edn. Northeastern Ill. U., 1968—, chmn. dept., 1968-80; ednl. dir., owner Childhood Edn. Nursery and Day Care Center, Evanston, Ill., 1975—; cons. Chgo. Mayor's Office Child Care Services. Chmn. bd. dirs. Univ. Community Day Care Centers; mem. Chgo. com., chmn. subcom. White House Conf. on Children, 1980; mem. Ill. Priorities for Children, 1981. Mem. Assn. Childhood Edn. Internat. (past pres. Ill. and Chgo. brs.; chmn. nominating com. 1980-81; chmn. tchr. edn. com. 1983—), Nat. Assn. Edn. Young Children, Assn. Higher Edn., NW Assn. Nursery Schs., Nat. Safety Council, AAUP, Phi Delta Kappa (chpt. v.p.), Delta Kappa Gamma (past pres. Gamma Alpha chpt.). Club: Zonta Internat (dir. Chgo. chpt.). Editor bull. and pamphlets Assn. Childhood Edn. Internat., 1975-77. Home: 1 Kittery on Auburn Rolling Meadows IL 60008 Office: Northeastern Ill U 5500 N Saint Louis Ave Chicago IL 60625 also Childhood Edn Center 2727 Crawford St Evanston IL 60201

BURGESS, ANNIE PEARL, cytotechnologist; b. Brookhaven, Miss., Oct. 10, 1945; d. Jerome and Bernice (Calcote) Ratliff; student Malcolm X Jr. Coll., 1972-73, Roosevelt U., 1973-75, U. Chgo. Med. Sch., 1975; certificate Mt. Sinai Sch. Cytotechnology, 1975; A.A., Kennedy-King Jr. Coll., 1975; postgrad. U. Miss., 1981—; children—Terree Terrinda, Kimetta Arlinda, Leander Marcellus. Catalog writer Sears Roebuck & Co., Chgo., 1972; service rep. Ill. Bell Telephone Co., Chgo., 1973-74; cytotechnologist Mason-Barron Labs., Chgo., 1975-76, North Miss. Med. Center, Tupelo, 1976—. Mem. Am. Soc. Clin. Pathologists, Am. Soc. Cytology, Am. Soc. Cytotechnology, Miss. Soc. Cytopathology, Miss. Soc. Med. Technology, So. Assn. Cytotechnologists, Ill. Soc. Cytology. Home: RR1 Box 558 Belden MS 38826 Office: North Mississippi Medical Center Pathology Dept 830 S Gloster St Tupelo MS 38801

BURGESS, BEVERLY JANE, church dept. adminstr.; b. Urbana, Ill., June 8, 1932; d. Ward Edward and Mable Olive (Emmons) Slade; student public schs., Urbana; m. Robert Dean Burgess, July 24, 1950; children—Cindy Kay Speicher, Pamela Jane McKamie. Supr. traffic dept. Ill. Bell Telephone Co., Champaign, Ill., 1952-55; service rep. Southwestern Bell Telephone Co., Little Rock, 1960-64; state rep. Goodwill Book Co., Little Rock, 1964-66; distbr. Bibles, Gideon Internat. Aux., Little Rock, 1965-67; sr. acct. home missions and evangelism depts., gen. bd. Ch. of Nazarene, 1969-76, office mgr., 1976—; tchr., trainer Personal Evangelism Clinics, 1972—. Mem. council Nazarene World Mission Soc.; organizer, leader Prayer Group; organizer Bible Study Group. Republican. Nazarene. Clubs: Clinton Country, Kansas City Phys. Fitness. Home: 9036 Holly St Kansas City MO 64114 Office: Gen Bd Ch of Nazarene 6401 The Paseo Kansas City MO 64131

BURGESS, CAROLINE REICHARDT, real estate exec.; b. Salem, Mass., Dec. 14, 1942; d. Joseph Wallace and Helena M. (Sullivan) Johnson; B.S., Salem State Coll., 1964; M.S., Eastern Conn. State Coll., 1971; m. Gary D. Burgess, Nov. 10, 1965 (div.); 1 dau., Tara Lynn. Elem. tchr. Elizabeth (N.J.) Bd. Edn., 1964-65; tchr. sci. Montville (Conn.) Bd. Edn., 1965—; asso. Ask Mr. Tuthill Agy., real estate, East Lyme, Conn., 1979-80; Realtor asso. McBride Realty (doing bus. as Carriage House Realty), East Lyme, 1980—. Fellow Am. Biog. Inst. (life); mem. Nat. Assn. Female Execs. (network dir. Norwich-New London area 1979—), NEA, Conn. Edn. Assn., Montville Edn. Assn., New London Bd. Realtors, Conn. Sci. Tchrs. Assn., Electronic Realtor Assn., Internat. Platform Assn., Am. Mgmt. Assn. Home: 292 Pequot Ave New London CT 06320 Office: Carriage House Realty 218 Flanders Rd East Lyme CT 06333

BURGESS, JANET HELEN, art gallery dir., interior designer; b. Moline, Ill., Jan. 22, 1933; d. John Joseph and Helen Elizabeth (Johnson) Burgess; student Augustana Coll., 1950-51, U. Utah, 1951-52, Marycrest Coll., 1959-60; m. Richard Everett Guth, Aug. 25, 1951; children—John Joseph, Marshall Claude, Linnea Ann Guth Layman; m. 2d Milan Andrew Vodick, Feb. 16, 1980. Artist, self-employed, El Pao, Estado Bolívar, Venezuela, 1952-62; producer, designer Playcrafters Barn Theatre, Moline, 1963-65; designer, gen. mgr. Grilk Interiors, Davenport, Iowa, 1963—; dir. Fine Arts Gallery, Davenport, 1978—. Bd. dirs. Quad Cities Art Council, Rock Island (Ill.) Art Guild; adv. bd. Interior Design Dept., Scott Community Coll., also tchr. adult edn.; bd. dirs. Village of East Davenport (Iowa) Assn., 1963—, pres., 1981; mem. Mayor's Com. for Historic Preservation, Davenport, 1976-77; bd. dirs. Neighborhood Housing Services, Davenport, 1981; bd. dirs., mem. retail com. Operation Clean Davenport. Recipient Gov.'s award for Leadership, Gov. Ray of Iowa, 1982. Mem. Davenport C. of C., ASID, Interior Designers, Gift & Decorative Accessories Assn. (Nat. merit award for promotion 1969), Nat. Trust for Historic Preservation, The Preservation Group, State of Iowa Hist. Soc., Rock Island Arsenal Hist. Soc., Civil War U.S. Christian Commn. Republican. Design work featured in Gift & Decorative Accessories mag., 1969, 80, Decor mag., 1979; contbr. articles to profl. jours. Home: 2801 34th Ave Ct Rock Island IL 61201 Office: 2200 E 11th St Davenport IA 52802

BURGESS, JOY BELLE, mayor; b. Portland, Oreg., Sept. 20, 1928; d. Claude Sanford and Beulah Essia (Evans) McCoy; student Lewis and Clark Coll., Portland, 1946-47; m. John Alford Burgess, Dec. 17, 1948; children—Cathy, Jeffrey, David, Julie, Jeannie, Randy. Various secretarial positions, 1948-51; poet, contbr. Ideals Pub. Co., 1970—; mem. city council City of Milwaukie (Oreg.), 1972-80, mayor, 1981—; chmn. Milwaukie Parks and Beautification Com., 1971-72; chmn. local ofcl. adv. com. Met. Bd., Portland, 1979-80; mem. citizens policy bd. Clackamas County Coop. Library Systems, 1978-80; del. White House Conf. Libraries, 1979. Recipient Milwaukie Kiwanis Bullfrog award, 1972. Mem. LWV, Oreg. Fair Share, Milwaukie Hist. Soc. Home: 12208 SE 22d Ave Milwaukie OR 97222 Office: 10722 SE Main St Milwaukie OR 97222

BURGESS, MEREDITH NANCY STRANG, advt. agy. exec.; b. Rockland, Maine, Apr. 27, 1956; d. Walter P. and Charlene M. (Perkins) Strang; B.S., U. Maine, Orono, 1978; m. James L. Burgess, June 24, 1978. Store activities rep. McDonald's Corp., Boston, 1978-79; account exec. Arnold & Co., Inc., Portland, Maine, 1979-80, field account supr., 1980-81, account supr. for McDonald's advt. in Maine, 1981—. Mem. Camden (Maine) Republican Town Com., 1974-80, Cumberland (Maine) Rep. Town Com., 1980—; del. Rep. Conv. Maine, 1974, 76, 78, 80; 1st alt. to Rep. Nat. Conv., 1976; com. woman from Knox County, Maine Rep. Party. Mem. Greater Portland Advt. Club, Soil Conservation Soc. Am., Alpha Phi. Home: 12 Country Charm Rd Cumberland ME 04021 Office: 949 Brighton Ave Portland ME 04102

BURGESS, PATRICIA ANN, nurse, educator; b. Carson City, Nev., Oct. 20, 1938; d. Joseph Cecil and Victorine Virginia (Sciarini) Morrison; diploma Mary's Help Coll. Nursing, 1959; B.S.N. (Profl. Nurse trainee), U. Nev., 1974, cert. rural nurse practitioner program, 1976, M.S., 1981; m. William V. Burgess, Jan. 24, 1965; children—Heather, Michael. Staff nurse Marin Gen. Hosp., San Rafael, Calif., 1959; staff nurse Washoe Med. Center, Reno, 1959, head nurse emergency room, 1960, staff nurse ICU, 1961-64, head nurse ICU, 1965-66, staff nurse pediatrics, 1978, 82; lectr. U. Nev., 1974-81, instr. pediatrics, 1982—. Mem. Nev. Task Force on Child Abuse and Neglect. Mem. Am. Nurses' Assn., Nev. Nurses' Assn., Nat. Soc. Profs., Orvis Sch. Nursing Hon. Roman Catholic. Home: 1479 Coronet Circle Reno NV 89509 Office: Orvis Sch Nursing U Nev Reno NV 89557

BURGIO, JANE, state ofcl.; b. Nutley, N.J.; student Newark Sch. Fine and Indsl. Arts; m. John Burgio; children—John E., James. Sec. of state, State of N.J., Trenton, 1982—; chmn. N.J. Voter Registration Adv. Council; clk. N.J. Bd. Canvassars. Devel. com. St. Barnabas Hosp.; trustee North Essex Devel. and Action Council, Planned Parenthood Essex County, Arts Council N.W. Essex, Julie Maloney Dance Co., Support of Free Public Schs.; study commn. Hackensack Meadowlands Cultural Center; mem. N.J. State Assembly, 1973-81; past pres. PTA; former Essex County Republican. Committeewoman; former mem. Essex County Bd. Elections; alt. del. Rep. Nat. Conv., 1972. Recipient Ann. recognition award Alumni Assn. Univ. Coll., cert of appreciation N.J. Humane Soc., Hist. award League Hist. Socs. N.J., 1981. Mem. Millburn-Short Hills Bus. and Profl. Women. Home: 586 Mountain Ave North Caldwell NJ 07006

BURGOON, SANDRA LEIGH, cons.; b. Phila., Mar. 2, 1939; d. David Flegeal and Beatrice Louisa (Mills) B.; B.A., U. Wis., 1960; M.A., U. Kans., 1963; m. Jules Jacob Schwartz, Dec. 18, 1971. Economist, E. I. duPont de Nemours & Co., Wilmington, Del., 1964-69; cons. Arthur D. Little, Inc., Cambridge, Mass., 1969-73; sr. cons. Krall Mgmt., Inc., Phila., 1974-76, prin., 1977; sr. cons. Arthur D. Little, Inc., Cambridge, Mass., 1977-82; v.p. Cons. Resources Corp., Lexington, Mass., 1982—; asst. prof. dept. econs. U. Del. Extension, Newark, 1964-69. Woodrow Wilson fellow, 1960-61. Mem. Am. Econ. Assn., Nat. Assn. Bus. Economists, Am. Mktg. Assn., Delta Gamma Alumnae (pres. Boston 1980-82), Phi Kappa Phi. Home: 96 Radcliffe Rd Belmont MA 02178 Office: Six Northbrook Park Lexington MA 02173

BURGOS-SASSCER, RUTH, educator; b. N.Y.C., Sept. 5, 1931; d. Carmelo and Maria Luisa (Berly) Burgos; B.A., Maryville Coll., 1953; M.A., Columbia U., 1956; student Iowa State U., 1962-63, Interam. U., 1968-71, U. Salamanca (Spain), 1974; m. Donald S. Sasscer, June 14, 1958; children—Timothy, James, Julie, David. Prof. edn. Interam. U. P.R., 1970-72, prof. humanities and social sci. Aguadilla Regional Coll., U. P.R., 1972—, dir. dept. humanities and social sci., 1972-76, dir. non-traditional programs, adminstrn. regional coll., 1976—, dean and dir. of coll., 1981—; cons. creation of humanities TV course, Miami-Dade Community Coll., 1976-78; cons. Coll. Entrance Exam. Bd. P.R., 1974-77, 79-80. Sec., Commn. for Women's Affairs, Office of Gov. P.R., 1977-78, v.p., 1978-79, pres., 1979-81. Nat. Endowment for Humanities summer stipend, 1974, research grantee, 1979; fellow Inst. for Ednl. Leadership, 1981-82. Mem. Nat. Assn. Bilingual Edn., Am. Assn. Ednl. Tech., AAUW, LWV of P.R. (women's rights chairperson 1974-77). Presbyterian. Club: Altrusa Internat. Author: (with Francisca Hernández Giles) La Mujer Marginada por La Historia: Antología de Lecturas, 1978; (with Shirley Williams) Exploraciones Chicanas-riqueñas, 1980; editor: La Mujer Marginada Por la Historia: Ensayos, 1978; Death and Dying: Challenge and Change (Spanish edit.), 1981. Home: D-18 Calle 1 Jardines de Boringuen Aguadilla PR 00603 Office: Aguadilla Regional Coll U PR Box 160 Punta Borinquen PR 00604

BURGOYNE, MARIANNE HARDING, educator; b. Hayden, Colo., June 22, 1948; d. Edward Bailey and Lurean (Stevens) Harding; B.A., Brigham Young U., 1970; M.A., U. Utah, 1981, postgrad., 1981—; m. Robert H. Burgoyne, Sept. 17, 1977. Pvt. practice modeling and dancing instr., Salt Lake City, 1969; tchr. Bryant Intermediate Sch., Salt Lake City, 1972-78, E. Sr. High Sch., Salt Lake City, 1978-79; teaching asst. U. Utah, 1979-81, teaching fellow, 1981—. Mem. Société d'Honneur Française, Pi Delta Phi. Democrat. Office: Orson Spencer Hall U Utah Salt Lake City UT 84112

BURGOYNE, PATRICIA HAWKINS, freelance writer; b. Chgo., May 22, 1953; d. William Emery and Lorraine (Udall) Hawkins; B.A. cum laude, U. So. Calif., 1975; m. David Burgoyne, II, June 23, 1973; children—Michael Lundy, Megan Louise. Staff mem. KUSC-FM Radio, Los Angeles, 1971-73; dir. public relations Tucson Mus. Art, 1975-76; contbg. editor Tucson Mag., 1976-78, Scottsdale (Ariz.) Progress Saturday Mag., 1980—; freelance writer, 1975—. Chmn. public relations Maricopa County Med. Soc. Aux., 1979-80; bd. dirs. Planned Parenthood Central and No. Ariz., 1981-82, 82-83; pres. Planned Parenthood Aux., 1981-83; chmn. publicity Kachina County Day Sch. Aux., 1979-80. Mem. Women in Communications, Inc., Maricopa County Med. Soc. Aux., Scottsdale Med. Wives, Kappa Kappa Gamma (pres. elect) Phoenix Alumna chpt. 1982-83). Club: Village Tennis.

BURGOYNE, SHIRLEY JEAN, lawyer; b. Saginaw, Mich., Oct. 25, 1932; d. Marshall Albert and Beatrice Viola (Clements) Cox; A.B., J.D., U. Mich., 1956; m. Bert Burgoyne, Apr. 22, 1955 (div.); children—Deborah Jeanne, David Edward, Douglas Jeffrey. Law clk. Oreg. Supreme Ct., Salem, 1956-57; admitted to Oreg. bar, 1957, Mich. bar, 1959; practiced in Roseburg, Oreg., 1957-58, Lansing, Mich., 1959-63, Ann Arbor, Mich., 1963—; mem. firm Burgoyne & Burgoyne, Roseburg, 1957-58, Thomas C. Walsh, Lansing, 1959-63, Burgoyne & Morris, Ann Arbor, 1968-69, Burgoyne & Pratt, Ann Arbor, 1977—; legal counsel Mich. Abortion Referendum Com., 1969-73. Mem. Mich. Women's Commn., 1971-72; bd. dirs. Mich. Council for Study of Abortion, 1971-73. Mem. Am. (vice chmn. com. law and mental health family law sect.), Mich. (council family law sect.), Oreg. bar assns., Am. Trial Lawyers Assn., Am. Judicature Soc., AAUW, Kappa Beta Pi. Presbyn. Home and Office: 206 Miller St Ann Arbor MI 48104

BURICK, MARY FRANCES, banker; b. Youngstown, Ohio, Dec. 22, 1952; d. Joseph and Carol Marie (Vlasic) B.; B.A., Youngstown State U., 1975; M.A., U. Okla., 1981. Fin. analyst examiner Ohio Div. Bank Supervision, Columbus, 1975; liquidator FDIC, Washington, 1975—, asst. liquidator, Cleve., 1979—, liquidator-in-charge, 1981—. Mem. Nat. Assn. Bus. Economists, Am. Mgmt. Assn., Nat. Assn. Female Execs., Internat. Platform Assn., Young Profls. of Cleve., Am. Soc. Profl. and Exec. Women. Home: 931 Dravis Ave Girard OH 44420 Office: 550 17th St NW Washington DC 20429 also 629 Euclid Ave Cleveland OH 44114

BURK, BARBARA ELLEN, occupational claims cons.; b. Cleve., July 15, 1944; d. Bernard and Florence (Apple) Burk; B.Sc. in Home Econs., Ohio State U., 1966; M.A. in Edn., U. Mich., 1969. Social Service worker Univ. Hosps. of Cleve., 1966-67; vocat. rehab. counselor/coordinator div. vocat. rehab. Mich. Dept. Edn., Ann Arbor, 1968; vocat. counselor Vocat. Guidance and Rehab. Services, Cleve., 1969-73; mgr. vocat. rehab. dept. Hill House, Cleve., 1974; vocat. expert Social Security Adminstrn., Office Hearings & Appeals, U.S. Dept. Health & Human Services, 1974—; occupational claims cons./rehab. damage evaluator in pvt. practice, Mayfield Heights, Ohio, 1974—; mgr. Client Advocacy Unit, City of Cleve., 1979-80, mgr. client services center, 1980-81; creator/founder Job Hunters United, Mayfield Heights, 1981—; lectr. in field. Mem. N.E. Ohio Rehab. Assn. (pres. 1974-75, dir. 1973-74), Ohio Rehab. Assn., Nat. Rehab. Assn., Nat. Rehab. Counselors Assn., Am. Soc. for Training & Devel. Clubs: City of Cleve., Toastmasters, U. Mich. Alumnae of Cleve. Home: 6809 Mayfield Rd Apt 954 Mayfield Heights OH 44124

BURK, BOBBIE JEAN MCBRIDE, coll. dean; b. Dallas, May 13, 1930; d. Robert Edward and Thelma Edith (Grines) McBride; B.Mus., Oklahoma City U., 1952; M.Ed., U. Mo., 1969; m. James Mack Burk, June 12, 1954; 1 son, James Jeffery. Tchr., Okla. public schs., 1952-65; curriculum cons. Oklahoma City public schs., 1965-67; instr. Univ. Lab. Sch., U. Mo., Columbia, 1967-68, univ. instr. edn., 1967-70; dir. secondary edn. Stephens Coll., Columbia, Mo., 1970-79, asst. dean faculty, registrar, 1979—; cons. in field. Dir. choir First Presbyn. Ch., Fulton, Mo., 1975—. Mem. Am. Assn. Collegiate Registrars and Admission Officers, Soc. Coll. and Univ. Planning, Assn. Higher Edn., Nat. Assn. Women Deans, Adminstrs. and Counselors, Coll. Music Soc., Sigma Alpha Iota (nat. exec. bd. 1974—), Mu Kappa Lambda, Pi Kappa Lambda, Pi Lambda Theta, Delta Kappa Gamma, Phi Delta Kappa. Author articles in field. Home: 3111 Crawford St Columbia MO 65201 Office: Stephens Coll Columbia MO 65215

BURK, MARGUERITE CATHERINE, educator; b. Ottawa, Kans., July 12, 1915; d. Ralph G. and Clara A. (Eberhart) Burk; A.B., U. Kans., 1937, M.A., 1938; Ph.D. (fellow), U. Minn., 1948; postgrad. Am. U., 1938-40, U. Wis., 1940, Cambridge (Eng.) U., 1955-56. Statis. clk., economist U.S. Dept. Agr., Washington, 1939-45; head consumption sec. Bur. Agr. Econs., Washington, 1945-60; agrl. economist Econ. Research Service, Washington, 1960-61; prof. agrl. econs. and home econs. U. Minn., 1961-69; leader food consumption research group Dept. Agr., Washington, 1969-75; prof. program internat. studies in human ecology Howard U., Washington, 1975—; cons. FAO program, Rome, 1961, Philippine Food and Nutrition Research Inst., Manila, 1977, 79; cons. U.S. Dept. Agr., 1980—; cons. in field. Recipient Superior Service award U.S. Dept. Agr., 1954; USOE grantee internat. studies in human ecology, 1975-77. Mem. Am. Econ. Assn., Am. Home Econs. Assn., Soc. Internat. Devel.; fellow Am. Council Consumer Interests (pres. 1961-62). Author handbooks. Contbr. articles to profl. jours. Editor: The Nat. Food Situation, 1945-60. Home: 10209 Gainsborough Rd Potomac MD 20854

BURKA, LESIA ROMANIW, pharmacist; b. N.Y.C., Dec. 9, 1953; d. Omelan and Daria (Szpilman) Romaniw; student Rutgers U., Newark, 1971-73; certs. in piano Ukrainian Music Inst. Am., in Ukrainian lang. Ukrainian Acad., 1972; B.S. in Pharmacy, Temple U., Phila., 1976; m. Eugene Burka, Aug. 11, 1973; children—Adrian, Tanya. Pharmacist, nursing homes cons. Mikes Pharmacy, Erdenheim, Pa., 1976-77; mgmt. trainee, supr. processing depts. McNeil Labs., Inc. and McNeil Consumer Products Co., Ft. Washington, Pa., 1977-80; group supr. multi-shift packaging dept. McNeil Consumer Products Co., 1980-81, group supr. projects in processing ops., 1981—, steering com. quality circle program, 1981—. Mem. Am., Pa., Montgomery County pharm. assns.; Del. Valley Women in Pharmacy, Acad. Pharm. Scis. Ukrainian Catholic. Home: 1375 Harris Rd Dresher PA 19025 Office: Camphill Rd Fort Washington PA 19034

BURKE, BARBARA LOU, librarian; b. Ottumwa, Iowa, Jan. 11, 1942; d. John W. and Dorothy M. (Crans) B.; B. Art Edn., Eastern Mich. U., 1963; M.L.S., State U. N.Y. at Geneseo, 1966. Asso. librarian Merck Sharp & Dohme Research Labs., West Point, Pa., 1966-73; asst. engring. scis. librarian and asst. prof. Colo. State U., Ft. Collins, 1974-78, asso. prof., 1978—. Mem. Spl. Libraries Assn. (chmn. engring. div. 1976-77), Colo. Library Assn., Am. Soc. Engring. Edn. (treas. info. systems com. 1978-80). Author: (with Robert N. Meroney) Energy from the Wind, 1975, supplement, 1977, 79, 82; Cumulative Indexes, 1982. (with others) Water and Soil in Arid Regions, 1976, rev. 1977. Home: 1933 W Lake St Fort Collins CO 80521 Office: Engring Research Center Colo State U Fort Collins CO 80523

BURKE, BEVERLY ANN, psychologist; b. Pulaski, Va., Jan. 31, 1943; d. Jack Edward and Mary (Brewer) B.; B.S. cum laude, David Lipscomb Coll., 1965; M.Ed. summa cum laude, Central State U., 1969; Ph.D. cum laude, U. Okla., 1977. Tchr., David Lipscomb Coll. Demonstration Sch., Nashville, 1964-65, Met. Nashville Public Schs., 1965-66; instr. dept. edn. and psychology Central State U., Edmond, Okla., 1969-71; psychologist S.W. Guidance Center, Wheatland, Okla., 1974-78; psychologist/coordinator Canadian County Guidance Center, El Reno, Okla., 1978-80; cons. child and family therapy, clin. supr. staff tng. Seattle Indian Health Bd., 1980—; pvt. practice, Seattle, 1981—. Mem. Am. Psychol. Assn., Okla. Psychol. Assn., Southwestern Psychol. Assn., Wash. State Psychol. Assn., Nat. Indian Edn. Assn., Okla. Indian Edn. Assn. (dir. 1976-80), Oklahoma City Cherokee Community Orgn. Office: Seattle Indian Health Bd PO Box 3364 Seattle WA 98114

BURKE, CAROL ELIZABETH, lawyer; b. Gt. Bend, Kans., June 23, 1946; d. Robert M. and Virginia (Jaworski) Burk; B.A. with highest distinction, SUNY, 1971, J.D., 1974; 1 dau., Gina Faye. Admitted to Tex. bar, 1974, Hawaii bar, 1981, since practiced privately in Houston, Honolulu; faculty Bryant Stratton Bus. Coll., Buffalo, 1972. Dir. research and evaluation Mayor's Summer Youth Program, Buffalo, 1971. Jaeckle-Abrams research grantee, 1973. Mem. Tex. Trial Lawyers Assn., Am., N.Y. State, Tex. bar assns., AAUW. Club: Toastmasters. Contbr. articles to profl. jours. Office: 1221 Victoria Admiral Thomas Bldg Suite 1701 Honolulu HI 96814

BURKE, KAREN KAESS, journalist; b. Boston, Feb. 12, 1948; d. Kenneth Richard and Marquerite Alice (Welch) Kaess; B.A., Briarcliff, 1969; m. Edwin M. Burke, Jr., June 6, 1970; children—Edwin M., James Van Vleck. Asst. editorial credit editor Glamour Mag., N.Y.C., 1969-70; tchr. Canterbury Sch., Charlottesville, Va., 1970-71; asst. dir. mktg. Vogue Mag., N.Y.C., 1971-72, asst. fashion editor, 1972-73; asst. mdse. editor House and Garden Mag., N.Y.C., 1972; tchr., vol. fund raiser Matheny Sch. Cerebral Palsey, 1976—; mktg. and brokerage Previews Inc., Greenwich, Conn., 1978—, Estates Internat. Corp., Greenwich and New Canaan, Conn., 1978—; pres. Balloons Unltd., New Canaan. Bd. dirs. The Rectory, Newark, 1976—. Mem. Nat. Assn. Realtors, New Canaan Bd. Realtors. Jr. League. Democrat. Home: 33 Father Peter's Ln New Canaan CT 06840

BURKE, MARJORIE H., state legislator; b. Burnsville, W.Va., Nov. 14, 1932; student Glenville State Coll.; m. Billy B. Burke; children—Roberta Diane, Carolyn Sue. Farmer, Gilmer County, W.Va.; mem. W.Va. Ho. of Dels., 1978—. Dist. dir. W.Va. Fedn. Democratic Women; bd. dirs. Gilmer County Farm Bur.; mem. 4-H All Star, Gilmer County 4-H Leaders, Gilmer County Dem. Women's Club, Gilmer County Recreational Council; pres. W.Va. Simmenthal Assn.; v.p. W.Va. Livestock Round-up; mem. Future Farmers Am. Alumni. Baptist. Clubs: Order Eastern Star, Glenville Extension Homemakers, W.Va. Cowbelles (charter pres.). Office: West Virginia Ho of Dels Charleston WV 25305 *

BURKE, MARY ELIZABETH MCCASLIN, secretary, civic worker; b. Havre, Mont., June 3, 1920; d. George Edward and Elizabeth Mary (O'Connor) McCaslin; student parochial schs., Omaha; m. John P. Burke, Aug. 17, 1942 (div. 1969); children—Thomas, James, Mary, Robert, Joseph, Elizabeth, John, Martin. Sec., dept. indsl. engring. U. Nebr., Lincoln, 1971—. Pres. Lincoln chpt. Lit. Council of Nebr., 1977-79, sec. state council, 1978-80, 80-82; mem. state planning and evaluation com. Nebr. Dept. Edn., 1979—. Mem. Nat. Affiliation for Literacy Advance, Inter-Club Council of Lincoln. Democrat. Roman Catholic. Editor newsletter Lit. Council of Nebr., 1977-79. Home: 1520 Dakota St Lincoln NE 68502 Office: Dept Indsl Engring U Nebr 175 Nebraska Hall Lincoln NE 68588

BURKE, MARY JOAN THOMPSON, psychiat. social worker; b. Louisville, Apr. 1, 1933; d. Thomas Earl and Imelda C. (Mattingly) Thompson; B.S., Nazareth Coll., 1955; M.S.W., U. Pitts., 1969; m. Joseph Charles Burke, Sept. 1, 1956; children—Anne Maura, Colleen Elizabeth. Psychiat. social worker Homestead Community Mental Health Center, Pitts., 1969-70, Mental Hygiene Instr., Montreal, Que., Can., 1971-73, Champlain Valley Physicians Hosp., Plattsburgh, N.Y., 1973-79; also pvt. practice psychol. counseling. Bd. dirs. Assn. Retarded Children, Center Emotionally Disturbed, 1974-76, Clinton County Community Services, 1974—; co-chmn. Conf. on Psychiatry and Medicine, 1974-82; mem. Lake Champlain Com. Bd. Mem. Nat. Assn. Social Workers, Am. Assn. Marriage and Family Counselors, Am. Acad. Certified Social Workers, LWV, Internat. Coll. Psychomatic Medicine, N.Y. State Assn. Community Service Bds. (1st v.p.). Roman Catholic. Home: 134 Court St Plattsburgh NY 12901 Office: 60A Oak St Plattsburgh NY 12901

BURKE, MARY LOUISE, instrumentation lab. exec.; b. Holyoke, Mass., May 15, 1936; d. Edmund Anthony and Mary Louise (McCabe) B.; B.A., Elms Coll., 1957; cert in med. tech. Mercy Hosp. Sch. Med. Tech., Springfield, Mass., 1957. Hematologist, Mercy Hosp., Springfield, 1957-66, teaching supr., 1961-66; tech. rep. Hycel Inc., NE and Eastern Can., 1966-69, new product mgr. Houston, 1969, edn. mgr., 1969-71, dir. profl. consultation, 1971-73; product coordinator Instrumentation Lab., Inc., Lexington, Mass., 1973-74, mgr. tech. services, biomed. div., 1974—; mem. lab. adv. panel U. Lowell. Am. Soc. Med. Tech. Clay-Adams research grantee, 1963; recipient Disting. Alumnae Medal Elms Coll., 1982. Mem. Am. Soc. Med. Tech., Am. Assn. Clin. Chemistry, Mass. Assn. Med. Tech. (pres. 1966-67), Elms Coll. Alumnae Assn. (pres. 1963-67, Disting. Alumnae medal 1982). Roman Catholic. Home: 378 Park Ave Arlington Heights MA 02174 Office: 113 Hartwell Ave Lexington MA 02173

BURKE, MARY THOMAS, educator; b. Westport, County Mayo, Ireland, Nov. 28, 1930; d. Thomas and Anne (McGuire) B.; B.A., Belmont (N.C.) Abbey Coll., 1958; M.A., John Carroll U., 1962; M.A., Georgetown U., 1965; Ph.D., U. N.C., Chapel Hill, 1968. Tchr. elem. and high sch., N.C., 1954-64; acad. dean Sacred Heart Coll., Belmont, 1967-70; asso. prof., chairperson counselor edn. U. N.C., Charlotte, 1970-76, prof., chairperson, 1976-79, area head support services and spl. programs, 1979-81, chairperson dept. human services, 1981—; cons. Nat. Bus. Forms, Inc., Duke Power Co., service orgns. and instns., schs. and colls. Mem. exec. com. local chpt. Am. Cancer Soc., 1976—; co-chairperson bd. NCCJ, 1978—, nat. dir., 1979—; pres. bd. dirs. Open House Counseling Service, 1965-68; bd. trustees United Way, 1976—; bd. dirs. St. Joseph's Hosp., Asheville, N.C., 1981—; exec. com. To Life. Named N.C. Counselor Educator of Yr., 1976; recipient Humanitarian award Assn. Non-White Concerns, 1977, Anti-Defamation League, 1978; Woman of Yr., Sta. WBT, 1979. Mem. N.C. Personnel and Guidance Assn. (pres. 1981-82), Assn. Counselor Edn. and Supervision, Assn. Religious Values in Edn., N.C. Personnel and Guidance Assn., N.C. Vocat. Guidance Assn., N.C. Sch. Counselors Assn., N.C. Assn. for Non-White Concerns, Phi Delta Kappa. Republican. Roman Catholic. Editorial bd. NCPGA Jour., 1976-79. Home: Main St Belmont NC 28012 Office: Coll HDL U NC Sta Charlotte NC 28223

BURKE, PATRICIA ANNE, assn. exec.; b. Boston, Apr. 30, 1943; d. Frederick Joseph and Dorothy Ruth (Thomas) Whateley; m. Paul W. Burke, Dec. 7, 1963; 1 son, Matthew Andrew. Mktg. research asst. Avco Corp., Wilmington, Mass., 1970-71, mktg. adminstr. water projects, 1971-75; mktg. coordinator Baird Corp., Bedford, Mass., 1975-76; contract adminstr. Kollsman Instruments, Merrimac, N.H., 1977; exec. dir. Nat. Water Supply Improvement Assn., Ipswich, Mass., 1977—, bd. dirs., 1977—, bus. mgr. jour., 1975—, contracting cons. middle east ops., 1980—; pres. Compass Point, Inc., export cons. co. Mem. Met. Area Planning Council. Real estate lic., Mass. Office: Nat Water Supply Improvement Assn 26 Newbury Rd Ipswich MA 01938

BURKE, YVONNE WATSON BRATHWAITE (MRS. WILLIAM A. BURKE), lawyer; b. Los Angeles, Oct. 5, 1932; d. James A. and Lola (Moore) Watson; A.A., U. Calif., 1951, B.A. UCLA, 1953; J.D., U. So. Calif., 1956; m. William A. Burke, June 14, 1972; 1 dau., Autumn Roxanne. Admitted to Calif. bar, 1956; mem. Calif. Assembly, 1966-72, chmn. urban devel. and housing com., 1971, 72; mem. 93d Congress from 37th Dist. Calif., 94th-95th Congresses from 28th Dist. Calif.; chmn. Congl. Black Caucus, 1976; mem. House Appropriations Com. Dep. Corp. Commr.; hearing officer Police Commn., 1964-66; atty., staff McCone Commn. investigation Watts riot, 1965; mem. Los Angeles County Bd. Suprs., 1979-80. Mem. Women's Democratic Forum; vice chmn. 1984 U.S. Olympics Organizing Com.; vice chmn. Dem. Charter Commn. Bd. dirs. or bd. advisers numerous orgns. including U. Calif. at Los Angeles Found., Nat. Athletic Health Inst., United Negro Coll. Fund. Recipient Profl. Achievement award UCLA, 1974; named one of 200 Future Leaders, Time mag., 1974; recipient Achievement awards C.M.E. Chs., Nat. Assn. Black Women Attys., Nat. Assn. Negro Bus. and Profl. Women's Clubs; numerous other awards, citations. Fellow Inst. Politics John F. Kennedy Sch. Govt. Harvard, 1971-72; Chubb fellow Yale U., 1972. Office: 500 W Temple Los Angeles CA 90012 *

BURKES, SARAH BEATRICE, educator; b. Clarksdale, Miss., Feb. 28, 1948; d. Henry and Eldora (Abshaw) Burkes; student Jackson State U., 1966-68; B.S., Tex. Coll., 1970; postgrad. East Tex. State U. With Progressive Community Center, Chgo., 1970-72; tchr. Chgo. Bd. Edn., 1972—; with Blue Cross-Blue Shield, Chgo., 1972-75; communications counselor Malcolm X Coll., Chgo., 1975-77; instr. reading and English, Accounter Community Center, Chgo., 1977-80; agt. Equitable Life Ins., Chgo., 1980—; rep. World Book-Childcraft Encyclopedia, 1981—. Mem. Internat. Reading Assn., Nat. Council Tchrs. English, MLA, Chgo. Reading Assn., Nat. Life Underwriters Assn., United Ednl. Employees Assn., Alpha Kappa Alpha. Home: 1109 S Troy St Chicago IL 60612 Mailing Address: PO Box 12051 Chicago IL 60612

BURKET, GAIL BROOK, author; b. Stronghurst, Ill., Nov. 1, 1905; d. John Cecil and Maud (Simonson) Brook; A.B., U. Ill., 1926; M.A. in English Lit., Northwestern U., 1929; m. Walter Cleveland Burket, June 22, 1929; children—Elaine (Mrs. William L. Harwood), Anne, Margaret (Mrs. James Boyce). Pres. woman's aux. Internat. Coll. Surgeons, 1950-54, now bd. dirs. mus.; nat. vice chmn. Am. Heritage of DAR, 1971-74; pres. Northwestern U. Guild, 1976-78; sec. bd. Northwestern U. Settlement, 1979-81. Recipient Robert Ferguson Meml. award Friends of Lit., 1973. Mem. Nat. League Am. Pen Women (Ill. state pres. 1952-54, nat. v.p. 1958-60), Soc. Midland Authors, Poetry Soc. Am., Women in Communications Inc., AAUW (pres. N. Shore br. 1961-63), Daus. Am. Colonists (state v.p. 1973-76), Colonial Dames Am. (chpt. regent 1974-80), Zonta, Phi Beta Kappa, Delta Zeta. Author: Courage Beloved, 1949; Manners Please, 1949; Blueprint for Peace, 1951; Let's Be Popular, 1951; You Can Write a Poem, 1954; Far Meadows, 1955; This is My Country, 1960; From the Prairies, 1968. Contbr. articles, poems to lit. publs. Address: 1020 Lake Shore Dr Evanston IL 60202

BURKETT, MARGARET LEE, indsl. belting and plastic exec.; b. Lake City, Fla., June 14; d. Joseph Mortimer and Evelyn Louise (VanLandingham) Burkett; ed. Jones Bus. Coll., Orlando, Fla., spl. courses Ga. State U., U. Pa. Bookkeeping asst. Pan Am. Tire Co., Miami, Fla., 1962-63; NCR operator UPI, N.Y.C., 1964-65, Dodwell & Co., N.Y.C., 1966-69; bookkeeper Angelus Furniture Co., Los Angeles, 1969-71; v.p. adminstrv. services, sec., asst. treas. Atlanta Belting Co., 1971—; dir. Tenn. Belting Co.; sec., asst. treas. Fla. Belting Co. Methodist. Home: 164 Amherst Pl NW Atlanta GA 30327 Office: 560 Edgewood Ave NE Atlanta GA 30312

BURKHALTER, PAULA, med. technologist; b. Manchester, N.H., Aug. 6, 1946; d. William Charles and Kathryn Marion (Torcellini) Fenton; B.S. in Med. Tech., Quinnipiac Coll., New Haven, 1969; postgrad. U. Central Fla., 1978, Central Mich. U., 1980; m. Edward Burkhalter, Dec. 27, 1971; 1 dau., Stacey. Staff med. labortorian Meriden (Conn.) Hosp., 1964-68, Meriden Meml. Hosp., 1968, Gaylord Hosp., Wallingford, Conn., 1967-68; med. tech. intern, then staff med. technologist Yale-New Haven Med. Center, 1968-72; hematology teaching supr. Fla. Hosp., Orlando, 1973-78; hematology specialist Orlando Regional Med. Center, 1979-80, div. mgr., 1980—; also inservice instr.; Recipient various service awards. Mem. Am. Soc. Med. Tech. (chmn. hematology sci. assembly Fla. div. 1978—, public relations chmn. 1978-79, sci. assembly coordinator 1980-81, pres. Central Fla. chpt. 1979-80, Omicron Sigma award 1981). Roman Catholic. Home: 1221 Wilkinson St Orlando FL 32803 Office: 1416 S Kuhl Ave Orlando FL 32806

BURKHARDT, DOLORES ANN, librarian, educator; b. Meriden, Conn., July 28, 1932; d. Frederick Christian and Emily (Detels) Burkhardt; B.A., U. Conn., 1955, 6th year diploma, 1972; M.S., So. Conn. State Coll., 1960; postgrad. Central Wash. State Coll., 1962, Columbia, 1964—. Asst. librarian So. Conn. State Coll. Library, summers 1960, 62; sch. library tchr. Farmington High Sch., Unionville, Conn., 1955-66, North Haven High Sch., 1967-68; media specialist East Farms Demonstration Sch., Farmington, Conn., 1967-70; library coordinator Regional Dist. 13, 1970-72; library media coordinator Regional Dist. 10, Burlington-Harwinton, Conn., 1972-78. Instr. So. Conn. State Coll., New Haven, 1967-68, Boston U. Media Inst., 1970-71. Spl. cons. Conn. Dept. Edn., 1965-68; chmn. Conn. Sch. Library Standards Com., 1968-70. Mem. AAUW (sec. 1956-58, edn. chmn.), NEA, Conn. Edn. Assn., New Eng. (past pres.), Conn. (2d v.p. 1965-68) sch. library assns., Am. Assn. Sch. Librarians, New Eng. Media Assn., New Eng. Sch. Devel. Council, Am. Soc. Curriculum Devel., Nat. Council Tchrs. English, Phi Delta Kappa. Lutheran. Home: 812 Savage St Southington CT 06489 Office: 812 Savage St Southington CT 06489

BURKHART, ARDATH, civic worker; b. Vincennes, Ind., Sept. 2, 1905; d. Bert Hall and Fava (Tolbert) Yates; B.S. in Music, DePauw U., 1927; Litt.D., Tri-State Coll., 1974; m. John Burkhart, June 9, 1929 (div. Nov. 1974); children—John (dec.), Gay Burkhart Brown. Tchr., supr. music pub. schs., 1929-35. Mem. nat. devel. com. Girl Scouts U.S.A., 1951-55, mem. Region VII com., 1951-60, vice chmn. region VII, 1953-58, chmn. internat. work Region VII, 1958-60, Friends of Our Cabana Com. (Mexico), mem. bd. dirs. Hoosier Capital council, 1949-63, pres., 1951-54; v.p., mem. exec. com. Women's Affairs Com. of Civic Theatre, 1969-71; founder Women's Council for Ednl. TV Channel 20, 1970, pres., 1970-72, life mem.; mem. Met. Planning Commn., 1963-65; chmn. women's div. United Fund campaign, 1957, bd. dirs., 1957—, mem. exec. com., 1958-80, mem. allocations com., 1958-69, mem. admission com., 1969-73; chmn. women's div. Community Chest, 1950, 51, 56, bd. dirs., 1951-54; founder, pres. United Fund League, 1958-60, 64-65, chmn. selections com., 1961-63, mem. bd., exec. com., 1958—, chmn. individual gifts and founds. campaign, 1977; mem. Bd. Sch. Commns., 1962-63; chmn. Charity Solicitations Commns., 1955-65; bd. govs. Asso. Colls. Ind., 1966—, chmn., 1972-76; bd. dirs. Hoosier Art Salon, 1965, v.p., 1972-78, pres., 1978-81; bd. dirs. 500 Festival, 1967-73, v.p., 1970-73; bd. dirs. Indpls. Day Nursery Assn., 1964-74, St. Mary's Child Center, 1968-71, Civic Theatre, 1970—, Jr. Achievement, 1970—, Marion County Public Library Found., 1972— (also trustee 1972—), Crossroads council Boy Scouts Am., 1975-79, Indpls. Symphony, 1980—; bd. dirs., pres. Met. Indpls. TV Assn., 1968-72, pres., 1972-75, del. Public Broadcasting Service, 1972—, chmn. bd., 1975—; mem. bd., com. on human resources Pub. Broadcasting Service, 1977—; bd. dirs. Central Ind. Council on Aging; trustee Wenona Meml. Hosp., 1965-76; trustee DePauw U., 1955—, life mem., 1978—, nat. alumni co-chmn. fund campaign, 1959-61; trustee Meth. Hosp. Found., 1977—, v.p., 1979—; trustee New Hope Found., 1977—, United Theol. Sem., 1980—; mem. Indpls. Sesquicentennial Commn., 1971, Greater Indpls. Progress Com., 1971-78; mem. arrangements com. NATO Conf. on Cities, 1971; mem. Mayor's Task Force on Aging, 1972, Mayor's Task Force on Women, 1972—; mem. advisory com. Kennedy Center for Performing Arts; mem. pres.'s council Greater Indpls. Ch. Fedn., 1972-81; pres. Porter Bus. Coll., 1972-74; bd. dirs., chmn. congregational care commn. Meth. Ch., trustee, 1972-80; mem. nat. adv. com. Reagan-1980 trustee Ind. Soc. to Prevent Blindness, 1981; trustee Indpls. Mus. Art, 1982—, also Second Century Soc., 1982—; Named Woman of Year, B'nai B'rith, 1958; recipient Adminstrv. Service award Girl Scouts U.S.A., 1963; TSP award Theta Sigma Phi, 1968, Woman of Year award, 1971; Distinguished Citizen award 11th dist. Am. Legion, 1970; Ind. Acad. Achievement award, 1973. Mem. Mid-Am. World Trade Assn., Inc. (charter), Nat. Friends Pub. TV, Alpha Chi Omega (past pres. Indpls. Alumni; chmn. Nat. Founders fellowship com. 1946-56, nat. conv. mgr. 1960, chmn. nat. nominating com. 1964, Nat. Achievement award for community service 1960). Home: 8461 Quail Hollow Rd Indianapolis IN 46260

BURKHART, DAMA MARTIN, educator; b. Woodsfield, Ohio, Mar. 16, 1926; d. Wilbert Earl and Carrie Mildred (Doan) Martin; B.S. cum laude, Taylor U., Upland, Ind., 1950; M.S., Butler U., Indpls., 1965; Ph.D. (grad. fellow), Purdue U., 1968; m. George F. Burkhart, Apr. 11, 1981; children by previous marriage—Paige Elizabeth Cofield, Malvin Scott Cofield. Mem. public relations dept. Taylor U., 1950-51; tchr., curriculum cons. Howard County (Ind.) Council Chs., 1955-65; staff counselor, psychol. services Purdue U., 1965-68, vis. prof. edn., 1969-70, human devel. specialist, dept. child devel. and family life, 1970-74, staff and program devel. specialist Sch. Home Econs. and Coop. Extension Service, 1974—, asst. dir. Coop. Extension Service, also asso. dean Sch. Consumer and Family Scis.; adult edn. supr. Associated Migrant Opportunities Services, 1967; mem. Task Force on Career Devel. for Women, 1975-76; condr. workshops, cons. in field. Recipient Ecumenical citation Howard County, 1965. Council Chs. grantee. Mem. Nat. Council Family Relations, Ind. Council Family Relations (v.p. 1972-74, pres. 1980-81, dir. 1975-77) Am. Home Econs. Assn. Presbyterian. Author articles, bulls. Home: 222 N Main St Woodsfield OH 43793

BURKHART, ELIZABETH FLORES, govt. exec.; b. Waelder, Tex., July 19, 1935; d. Pablo M. and Helen G. Flores; B.A., Midwestern U., Wichita Falls, Tex., 1966; diploma Southwestern Grad. Sch. Banking, 1978; M.B.A., Houston Baptist U., 1979; m. Jon Mac Burkhart, Mar. 27, 1960. Various secretarial positions, 1960-65; elem. sch. tchr. Houston Ind. Sch. Dist., 1966-68; with Tex. Commerce Bank, Houston, 1968-79, asst. v.p., to 1979; controller George Bush for Pres., Houston, 1980; controller Presdl. Transition Found., 1980-81; asso. dept. adminstr. VA, 1981-82; mem. bd. NCUA, 1982—; adv. bd. Women Work for Work Project, Houston, 1977-79; mem. Pres.'s Task Force on Legal Equity for Women, 1982. Served with USMCR, 1954-56. Cert. profl. sec. Mem. Nat. Assn. Bank Women (trustee ednl. found. 1976-78), Am. Inst. Banking. Republican. Methodist. Office: 1776 G St NW Washington DC 20456

BURKHART, JOYCE M., mfg. co. acctg. mgr.; b. Alliance, Ohio, Sept. 15, 1946; d. James A. and Lenora Holliway; student Maple Woods Community Coll., 1971-73; B.A., Park Coll., 1975; m. Jerry Lee Burkhart, June 8, 1974; children—James, Carrie Renee. Acct., Butler Mfg. Co., agrl. div., Kansas City, Mo., 1964-73, acctg. mgr., 1973—. Mem. Internat. Mgmt. Council (pres. Kansas City chpt., newspaper editor Midwest div., instr. nat. convs., 1976—, condr. seminar nat. conv., 1980, mem.-at-large Midwest div. 1980—, pres. Midwest div. 1981—, gen. conf. chmn. of nat. conv. 1982-83, nat. bd. dirs.), Nat. Assn. Accts., Nat. Assn. Female Execs., Phi Theta Kappa. Clubs: Nat. Women's Bowling Council, local chpt. Bowling Assn., 6 bowling leagues. Home: 6616 NW Park Plaza Dr Kansas City MO 64151 Office: 7400 E 13th St Kansas City MO 64126

BURKS, MARY BURNETT, nurse; b. Birmingham, Ala., Sept. 29, 1955; d. William Popwell and Mary Frances (Collins) Burnett; B.S., Samford U., Ida V. Moffett Sch. Nursing, 1977, A.S. in Nursing, 1976; m. Arthur Leroy Burks, Jr., June 7, 1979. Staff nurse Bapt. Med. Center, Princeton-Birmingham, Ala., 1976-77; inservice dir. Chilton County Hosp. and Nursing Home, Clanton, Ala., 1977-79; nursing supr. Estes Health Care Center, Montgomery, Ala., 1979; asst. dir. nursing Meml. Manor Multiple Care Prattville, Ala., 1979; dir. nursing Chilton County Nursing Home, Clanton, 1979-81; staff nurse Shelby Med. Center, Alabaste, 1981-82, charge nurse, 1982—. Mem. Ala. Nurses Assn., Am. Nurses Assn. Baptist. Address: PO Box 1196 Clanton AL 35045

BURLEY, DEBORAH KAY, utility co. exec.; b. Zanesville, Ohio, Aug. 6, 1947; d. Robert Winfield and Virginia Rose (Summers) B.; B.S., Kent State U., 1969. With Columbia Gas System, various locations, 1969—, gas utilization rep., Sandusky, Ohio, 1974-78, area mgr., Port Clinton, Ohio, 1979-80, area mgr., Bucyrus, Ohio, 1980—. Active Jr. Achievement, 1978-79; sec.-treas. Bucyrus Community Improvement Corp., 1980—. Mem. Bucyrus C. of C., Am. Home Econs. Assn., Ohio Home Econs. Assn., Nat. Home Economists in Bus. (Mid-central regional adv. 1979-81), Bucyrus Bus. and Profl. Women's Assn. (sec. 1981-82, 1st v.p. 1982-83), Cleve. Home Economists in Bus. (chmn. 1978-79, adv. 1979-80, bus. home economist of yr. 1981). Clubs: Bucyrus Altrusa; Sandusky Ski (pres. 1978-79, dir. 1979-80).

BURLINGAME, VIRGINIA SIMS, family therapist; b. Chgo., Mar. 30, 1930; d. Paul J. and Pauline Sims; B.A., Blackburn Coll., 1952; M.S. In Social Service, Boston U., 1955; Ph.D. in Psychology, Northwestern U., 1982; m. Leroy J. Burlingame, July 1954 (div. 1982); children—Elizabeth, John. Tchr., Carlinville (Ill.) Jr. High Sch., 1951-52; child welfare worker Rockford (Ill.) Dept. Child Welfare, 1953-54; caseworker Children's Aid of Boston, 1955-56; sch. social worker Rockford Public Schs., 1956-58; psychiat. caseworker Bacon Clinic, Racine, 1960-62; caseworker Children's Service Soc., Racine and Kenosha, 1966-72; dir. Big Sisters of Racine, 1973-75; clin. therapist Family Service Racine, 1976-78; pvt. practice marital and family therapy, Racine, 1982—; counselor Holy Communion Lutheran Ch., 1980—. Wis. co-chmn. John Anderson for Pres., 1981; pres. bd. Taylor Children's Home; bd. dirs. Family Service Racine, Racine Symphony, Racine Urban League, Girl Scouts, U.S.A., Racine, Unitarian Ch. Racine, also PTAs and nursery sch. bds. Mem. Acad. Clin. Social Work, Am. Assn. Marital and Family Therapy, NOW, Phi Delta Kappa. Unitarian. Address: 4637 Bluffside Dr Racine WI 53402

BURLISON, BEVERLY NADINE, med. adminstr., fin. cons.; b. Los Angeles, Dec. 23, 1937; d. Austin Thomas and Dorothy (Gaby) Hodges; B.A. in Econs., UCLA, 1959; M.B.A. in Fin., Rutgers U., 1972. Mgr. research info. systems Stanford U., 1972-76; asso. dir. Inst. Med. Sci., Heart Research Inst., San Francisco, 1976—; pres., mng. editor Acad. Research Info. Systems, Inc., 1976—; exec. dir. Frank Gerbode Med. Research Found., 1979—, ALS and Neuromuscular Research Found., 1980—; fin. officer program rev. com. NIH, 1978—. Mem. Nat. Council Univ. Research Adminstrs., Soc. Univ. Research Adminstrs., Fedn. Am. Scientists. Republican. Roman Catholic. Home: 1176 Millbrae Ave Millbrae CA 94030 Office: 2200 Webster St A310 San Francisco CA 94115

BURMAN, CEARA SUE, bilingual cons.; b. Arcadia, Ohio, Apr. 23, 1941; d. Woodrow W. and Garnet E. (Wagner) Withrow; B.A. in English and Spanish, Heidelberg Coll., Tiffin, Ohio, 1963; M.A. in Spanish, U. Toledo, 1969; m. Lanny Ross Burman, Feb. 15, 1964. Tchr. English and Spanish, Old Fort (Ohio) Public Schs., 1962-63; chmn. fgn. lang. dept., tchr. Spanish, Port Clinton (Ohio) City Schs., 1963-68; teaching asst. U. Toledo, 1968-69; tchr. Spanish, Maumee (Ohio) City Schs., 1969-76; program coordinator English as 2d lang. Penta County Joint Vocat. Sch., Perrysburg, Ohio, 1977-78; bilingual cons., Toledo, 1979—; pres. Internat. Info. Specialists, Inc., 1981-82; instr. Owens Tech. Coll., 1981—; owner/adminstr. Internat. Lang. Services, 1982—; condr. workshops and seminars, pvt. tutor. Area rep. Youth for Understanding, 1969-76; mem. Operating Bd., First Call for Help. Mem. Am. Assn. Tchrs. of Spanish and Portuguese, Am. Council Teaching of Fgn. Langs., Nat. Assn. Female Execs., Exec. Network (pres. 1981, counselor to bd. 1982—), Toledo Area Internat. Trade Assn., Am. Translators Assn. Address: 2346 Cedarwood Dr Maumee OH 43537

BURNETT, BARBARA ANN, artist; b. Kansas City, Kans., May 7, 1927; d. Roy Ira and Wilma Agnes (Carson) Snyder; student public schs., Shawnee Mission and Enterprise, Kans.; m. W.E. Heiser, May 7, 1946 (dec.); 1 son, W. David; m. John E. Burnett, May 14, 1966. One-person shows at colls., galleries; group shows include: Kans. Tri-State (Main Hurdman award 1982), Wichita, 1976-82, Am. Watercolor Soc., N.Y.C., 1980, Midwest Nat. Watercolor Soc. (Hunt award 1981), Rockford, Ill., 1981, Aqueous, Louisville, 1980, Rocky Mountain Nat., Golden, Colo., 1981, Salmagundi Club, N.Y.C., 1982, Catherine Lorillard Wolfe Art Club (award), 1982, Allied Artists Am., N.Y.C., 1982; represented in permanent collections: Barnard Library, La Crosse, Kans., Blue Valley Sch. Dist., Stilwell, Kans., Shawnee Mission North Gallery, also over 1500 paintings in pvt. collections in U.S., Europe, Can.; owner, operator Burnett Art Studio, Mission, Kans., 1972—; staff corr. Sunshine Artists mag., 1978-82. Recipient 90 regional state and nat. awards, 1972-82. Mem. Kans. Watercolor Soc., Okla. Water Color Soc., Greater Kansas City Art Assn., Nat. League Am. Pen Women, Midwest Watercolor So. (asso.), Am. Watercolor Soc. (asso.). Home and Office: 5430 Lamar Ave Mission KS 66202

BURNETT, BARBARA DIANE, med. social worker; b. Charleston, W.Va., Aug. 20, 1928; d. LeRoy Sparks and Hallie Catherine (Walker) Montague; B.S., U. Wis., 1949; M.S., Pa. State U., 1963; M.S.W., Va. Commonwealth U., 1977; m. Clyde Ray Burnett, Sept. 20, 1947 (div. 1972); children—Beverly, Pamela, Marcia, Janet, Craig. Tchr., Exceptional Child Edn., Palm Beach County, Fla., 1964-75; counselor Project Peace, Boca Raton, Fla., 1977-78; end stage renal disease social worker Artificial Kidney Center of Boca Raton, 1978—; med. social worker Community Home Health Services, Boynton Beach, 1978—. Recipient 5 Yr. Vol. award Center for Group Counseling, Boca Raton, 1978. Mem. Nat. Assn. Social Workers, Acad. Cert. Social Workers, Nat. Assn. Patients on Hemodialysis and Transplantation, Palm Beach County Kidney Assn., Crucible, Mortar Bd., Pi Lambda Theta, Omicron Nu. Democrat. Episcopalian. Home: 4730 NE 5th Ave Boca Raton FL 33431 Office: 2800 S Seacrest Blvd Boynton Beach FL 33435

BURNETT, CAROL, actress, comedienne, singer; b. San Antonio, Apr. 26, 1936; d. Jody and Louise (Creighton) Burnett; student U. Calif. at Los Angeles, 1953-55; m. Joseph Hamilton, 1963; children—Carrie Louise, Jody Ann, Erin Kate. Introduced comedy song, I Made a Fool of Myself Over John Foster Dulles, 1957; Broadway debut in Once Upon a Mattress, 1959; regular performer Garry Moore TV show, 1959-62; appeared several CBS-TV spls., 1962-63, Broadway play Fade Out-Fade In, 1964, play Plaza Suite, 1970, film Pete "n" Tillie, 1972, musical play I Do, I Do, 1973, film Front Page, 1974, films A Wedding, 1977, Health, 1979, Annie, 1982, TV movies The Grass Is Always Greener Over the Septic Tank, 1978, 6 Rms Riv Vu, 1974, Twigs, 1975; club engagements Harrah's Club, The Sands, Caesar's Palace; star Carol Burnett Show, CBS-TV, 1967-78. Recipient outstanding comedienne award Am. Guild Variety Artist, 5 times; Emmy award for outstanding variety performance Acad. TV Arts and Scis., 1961, 62, 72, 73, 74; TV Guide award for outstanding female performer, 1961, 62, 63; Peabody award, 1963; Golden Globe award for outstanding commedienne of year Fgn. Press Assn., 7 times; Woman of Year award Acad. TV Arts and Scis.; People's Choice award for favorite all-round female entertainer, 1975, 76, 77; Critics Circle award, 1977. Address: care Robinson and Associates Inc 132 S Rodeo Dr Beverly Hills CA 90212 *

BURNETT, JUDITH JANE, health care exec.; b. Muncie, Ind., Aug. 21, 1947; d. Albert Ward and Janelyn Mae (Collins) Burnett; student public schs. Saleswoman, Collins Mobile Home Sales, Muncie, 1970-73; sales mgr. HiWay, Inc., Anderson, Ind., 1973-75; service dir., then ops. mgr. Indiana Homemakers, Inc., Indpls., 1975-80, exec. v.p., 1980—, also dir.; exec. v.p., dir. Three—I Homemakers, Inc., Illini Homemakers, Inc.; dir. Home Care Med. Products Co.; mem. council Central Ind. Health Systems Agy., 1980—; mem. Homemaker, Handyman, Home Health Aide Task Force, 1980—, sec., 1980-81. Mem. Nat. League Nursing, Health Systems Agy., Nat. Assn. Female Exec., Network Women in Bus., Ind. Assn. Home Health Agencies, Ind. Citizens League Nursing, U.S. Tennis Assn. Republican. Baptist. Home: 768 Lake Nora South Ct Indianapolis IN 46240 Office: 6356 N Guilford St Indianapolis IN 46220

BURNETTE, NANCY EVERITT, retail co. exec.; b. Hackettstown, N.J., Jan. 8, 1932; d. Isaac Dill and Elizabeth Louise (Lamson) Everitt; B.A., Wellesley Coll., 1953; M.A., U. Calif., Berkeley, 1968; m. Robert W. Burnette, June 9, 1979; children—Elizabeth, James, Samuel. Investment officer Wells Fargo Bank, San Francisco, 1968-74, U. Calif., Berkeley, 1974-79; v.p., corporate sec. Lucky Stores, Inc., Dublin, Calif., 1979—; dir. Yosemite Lab. Mem. adv. bd. Mills Coll. Mem. Am. Soc. Corporate Secs., Sentinel Pension Forum, Pensions West, Women's Forum West, Security Analysts San Francisco. Home: 6668 Charing Cross Rd Oakland CA 94618 Office: 6300 Clark Ave Dublin CA 94566

BURNHAM, LEAH LUCILLE, med. technologist; b. Fergus Falls, Minn., July 31, 1947; d. Dresden Gordon and Helen Lucille (Keller) Taylor; B.S., Millikin U., 1969; M.S., U. Vt., 1972; m. Frederick R. Burnham, II, Dec. 8, 1973; 1 son, Russell Adam. Blood bank technologist Luth. Hosp., Cleve., 1969-70; gen. technologist Lake Forest (Ill.) Hosp., 1970; teaching fellow U. Vt., Burlington, 1970-72; edn. coordinator Tucson Med. Center Sch. Med. Tech., 1972-74; sr. technologist in clin. toxicology U. Ariz. Health Sci. Center, Tucson, 1974—; conductor workshops in field. Mem. Am. Soc. Clin. Pathologists. Contbr. articles to profl. jours. Office: Clin Pathology Univ Ariz Health Sci Center Tucson AZ 85724

BURNLEY, DOROTHY ROCKWELL, state legislator; b. High Point, N.C., Feb. 27, 1927; d. Hubert J. and Ella L. Rockwell; student Hollins Coll., 1944-46; m. James H. Burnley III, Oct. 4, 1947; children—James H., Mary H., Ellen B., Judith L. Sec.-treas. Craftwood, Inc., High Point, N.C.; mem. N.C. Ho. of Reps., 1981—. Trustee, High Point Pub. Library; bd. dirs., past pres. High Point Women's Shelter; bd. dirs. High Point Mental Health Assn. Mem. Furniture City Woman's Club, High Point C. of C., U.S. C. of C. Baptist. Office: NC Ho of Reps State Capitol Raleigh NC 27602 *

BURNS, ANNE MARIE, educator; b. Providence, Apr. 13, 1921; d. James B. and Annie (Hagan) B.; Ph.B., Providence Coll., 1964; M.A., U. Conn., 1965. Tchr., Providence Sch. Dept., 1961—, also nursing asst. R.I. Hosp., Providence, 1972—. Sec. del. to Democratic Nat. Conv., 1980; appeared in BBC TV film on Dem. Nat. Conv., 1980. Mem. Providence Tchrs. Union, R.I. Hist. Soc. Roman Catholic. Club: Cath. Women's. Home: 1 Sheila Ln Smithfield RI 02917 Office: 195 Nelson St Providence RI 02908

BURNS, BARBARA M., editor; b. Evanston, Ill., July 4, 1929; d. Martin Hughes and Miriam (Miller) Burns; B.A., Smith Coll., 1951; diploma U. London (Eng.), 1954, Evanston Bus. Coll., 1958. Researcher for dir. Presdl. Appointments Office, White House, Washington, 1959; personal sec. to Senator Jacob Javits, 1959-60; exec. asst. to asst. chmn. Republican Nat. Com., Washington, 1960-62; adminstrv. asst. to Hon. John Clifford Folger, Washington, 1962-63; spl. asst. to chmn. John F. Kennedy Center, spl. asst. to Pres. on Arts, White House, 1963-66; dir. confs. for corp. execs. Sch. Advanced Internat. Studies, Johns Hopkins, Washington, 1966-69; dep. asst. sec. for consumer services HEW, Washington, 1969-73; asst. to sec. interior for internat. activities Dept. Interior, 1973-77; Washington editor Bus. and Society Rev., 1978—. Mem. consumer council Am. Nat. Standards Inst., 1969-73; mem. nominating com. Am. Stock Exchange, 1972. Profl. chmn. vol. service bd. Washington Jr. League, 1965-66, profl. chmn. bd. dirs., 1966-67, mem. project research com. 1967-68, adv. planning com. 1968-69, mem. nominating com. 1969-70. Sustaining mem. Republican Nat. Com.; v.p., co-founder Georgetown Rep. Club, 1964. Mem. Exec. Women in Govt. (founding mem.), Smithsonian Assos., Corcoran Gallery Art, Nat. Cathedral Assn. Clubs: 1925 F Street, Sulgrave. Home: 6 Pomander Walk Washington DC 20007

BURNS, DEBRA SUE CORT, chem. co. exec.; b. Detroit, July 18, 1952; d. Robert F. and Betty (Johns) Cort; B.S., Mich. State U., 1974; m. John Edward Burns III, June 19, 1982. Sales rep. Dow Chem. USA, Detroit, 1974-78; product sales mgr. Dow Chem. Co., Indpls., 1978—. Office: PO Box 68511 Dow Chem Co Indianapolis IN 46268

BURNS, (DIANA) SUSAN CRAWFORD, vocat. edn. coordinator; b. Chgo., Aug. 7, 1935; d. Robert Brace Penn and Florence (Stiller) Crawford; A.B., U. Ga., 1957; children—Alton Franklin III, Robert Crawford. Asst. account exec. Grant Advt., Miami, Fla., 1958-59; account exec. Mason, Dow & Stone Advt., Jacksonville, 1959-60; with WFGA-TV, Jacksonville, Fla., 1960, WSFA-TV, Montgomery, Ala., 1960-62, Citizens & So. Nat. Bank of S.C., Columbia, 1966-67; asst. to dean journalism sch. U. S.C., Columbia, 1967-70; women's editor Brunswick (Ga.) News, 1970-72; feature writer Coastal Illustrated (bi-monthly), Sea Island, Ga., after 1972; advt. public relations work, to 1978; learning coordinator/communications Glynn Acad. High Sch., Brunswick, Ga., 1976—; columnist Jacksonville (Fla.) Times-Union. Bd. dirs. Brunswick Civic Ballet Co., Easter Seal Speech and Hearing Center, Brunswick, 1972-74, Glynn County A.R.C., 1973-74; publicity chmn. United Way, 1979—; bd. dirs. St. Simons Cotillion, 1976-79. Mem. Ladies Aux. Humane Soc. Glynn County, C. of C. Brunswick (mem. womens affairs com. 1971-72, mktg. com. 1980—), Glynn County Am. Cancer Soc. Mortar Bd., Kappa Alpha Theta, Theta Sigma Phi, Gamma Alpha Chi. Episcopalian. Clubs: Cassina Garden (v.p. program and publicity chmn. 1971-72) (St. Simons Island, Ga.); Brunswick Press (pres. 1976-77). Home: 208 Rivera Dr St Simons Island GA 31522 Office: Glenn Acad High Sch PO Box 1678 Brunswick GA 31521

BURNS, ELLEN BREE, judge; b. New Haven, Dec. 13, 1923; d. Vincent Thomas and Mildred Bridget (Bannon) B.; B.A., Albertus Magnus Coll., 1944, LL.D. (hon.), 1974; LL.B., Yale U., 1947; LL.D. (hon.), U. New Haven, 1981; m. Joseph Patrick Burns, Oct. 8, 1955; children—Mary Ellen, Joseph Bree, Kevin James. Admitted to Conn. bar, 1947; dir. legis. legal services State of Conn., 1949-73; judge Conn. Circuit Ct., 1973-74; judge Conn. Ct. of Common Pleas, 1974-76; judge Conn. Superior Ct., 1976-78, U.S. Dist. Ct. for Dist. of Conn., New Haven, 1978—; Guggenheim fellow Yale Law Sch., 1974-75. Trustee Fairfield U., 1978—. Recipient John Carroll of Carrollton award John Barry Council KC, 1973; Judiciary award Conn. Trial Lawyers Assn., 1978; Cross Pro Ecclesia et Pontifice, 1981. Mem. New Haven County Bar Assn., Am. Bar Assn., Am. Bar Found. Roman Catholic. Office: 141 Church St New Haven CT 06510 *

BURNS, ELLEN WHEELER, oil and gas processing equipment mfg. co. exec.; b. Lovell, Okla., Feb. 22, 1934; d. Ralph Wilson and Myrtle Ellen (Lawyer) Wheeler; student No. Va. Community Coll., 1969-70; A.A., N.E. Miss. Jr. Coll., 1972; now student U. Okla.; m. Erit Lamar Burns, Sept. 10, 1953; children—David Randal, Douglas Regan. Exec. sec. Aerospace Corp., Vandenberg AFB, Calif., 1959-61; office mgr. Bill Gaser Sales Co., Tulsa, 1972-76; tech. services analyst C-E Natco, Tulsa, 1976-77; adminstr. Fenix & Scisson, Tulsa, 1977-78, div. tng. coordinator, 1978-80, supr. learning resources, 1980—; dir. Nursing Services, Inc. Instr. water safety ARC, Washington, 1967-73; coordinator Gt. Raft Race, Tulsa, 1975, 76, 79; sales adv. Jr. Achievement, Tulsa, 1976-77. Named to N.E. Miss. Jr. Coll. Hall of Fame, 1972. Mem. Am. Soc. Tng. and Devel., Leadership Tulsa Alumni, Am. Soc. Personnel Adminstrn., Nat. Assn. Female Execs., Internat. Platform Assn. Phi Theta Kappa. Home: 1103 N 31st St Broken Arrow OK 74012 Office: 5330 E 31st St Tulsa OK 74135

BURNS, FRANCES CAREY, home economist; b. Woodhaven, N.Y., Dec. 7, 1939; d. Robert F. and Florence (Bohne) Carey; B.S., Immaculata Coll., 1961; postgrad. Villanova U., 1964, U. Pa., 1962, Columbia U., 1976, Parsons New Sch., 1979; m. Gerald E. Burns, Apr. 4, 1978; 1 son, Thomas Gerald. Home service dir. mags. Macfadden Barteil Co., N.Y.C., 1971-74; cons. to food dir. Weight Watchers Internat., Inc., Manhasset, L.I., 1974-75; advt. home economist Best Foods Co., Englewood, N.J., 1975-76; restaurants mgr. Lord & Taylor Co., N.Y.C., 1976-77; freelance cons., N.Y.C., 1977-82. Treas., Assn. to Improve Abbington Sq. Park, 1979—. Mem. Am. Home Econs. Assn., Home Economists in Bus., Immaculata Alumnae. Roman Catholic. Home and office: 310 W 11th St New York NY 10014

BURNS, FRANCES HILL, social worker; b. Denver, Sept. 13, 1931; d. David B. and Marzllle (Cooper) Hill; B.A., Bishop Coll., 1970; student Tenn. State U., 1948-51; children-Robert, David Kanoa, Kevin Stuart. With Dallas Housing Authority, 1953-55, 62-66, Tacoma Housing Authority, 1955-57, San Antonio Housing Authority, 1957; with Dallas Post Office Annex, 1966; with W.K. Flowers, Jr., M.D., Dallas, 1966-69; social worker Martin L. King, Jr. Center, City of Dallas, 1969-72, social work supr., 1972-79, mgr. spl. services div., 1979—. Social work chmn. P.C. Anderson Acad. PTA, 1979-82, also life mem.; bd. dirs. Tex. Area 5 Health System Agy. 1977—, Ret. Sr. Vol. Program, 1980—; mem. adv. bd. Black Adoption, 1979—; adv. council East Oak Cliff, 1978—; active Youth Motivation Team, YWCA, Women's Center of Dallas. Recipient cert. of appreciation Boy Scouts Am., 1980; Humanitarian award U. Tex. at Arlington chpt. Kappa Alpha Psi, 1981; spl. award Anheuser-Busch, Inc., 1981; Black Women-Achievement Against the Odds award East Oak Cliff subdist. Dallas Ind. Sch. Dist., 1981. Mem. Nat. Assn. Black Social Workers (sec. 1971—), Nat. Caucus Black Aged, Dallas Black C. of C. (Community Service award 1981), Dallas Urban League, Delta Sigma Theta. Democrat. Mem. A.M.E. Ch. Club: Soroptomists Internat. Office: Martin L King Jr Center 2922 Forest Ave Dallas TX 75215

BURNS, GAYLE S., photojournalist; b. Baton Rouge, La., May 2, 1942; d. Jack Vernon and Dorothy (Gayle) Sams; student Colegio Americano, Caracas, Venezuela, 1958-59, La. State U., 1960-63, New Sch. Social Research, 1974-76; 1 son, Denis Bradly. Freelance photographer, 1969—; photojournalist, advt. and sports photographer, contbr. to nat. and internat. mags. and newspapers. Recipient 3 awards N.J. Press Assn. Mem. Nat. Press Photographers Assn., Nat. Women's Polit. Caucus, Nat. Fedn. Dem. Women, Ky. Cols. Prin. photographer: This is the Day (Judy Collins), The Last Season of Weeb Eubank (Paul Zimmerman). Home: 132 Lakewood Dr Denville NJ 07834

BURNS, JO ANN MITCHELL, psychologist; b. Quanah, Tex., Mar. 31, 1944; d. Alger and Eddie Lovice (Moore) Mitchell; student Okla. Southwestern State U., 1962-63; B.S., Okla. State U., 1966; M.Ed. (HEW fellow), U. Okla., 1973, Ph.D., 1979; 1 son, Jason Mitchell. Social worker, Valley County Dept. Public Welfare, Glasgow, Mont., 1967-68; counselor Meth. Mission Home, San Antonio, 1968-71; tchr. St. Anthony's Spl. Edn. Assn., San Antonio, 1971; staff psychol. asso. Bethany (Okla.) Child Guidance Center, Okla. Dept. Public Health, 1974-76; clin. psychologist, child/adolescent unit Rusk (Tex.) State Hosp., Tex. Dept. Mental Health and Mental Retardation, 1976-77; asst. prof. spl. edn. Pan Am. U., Edinburgh, Tex., 1977—; asso. sch. psychologist McAllen (Tex.) Sch. Dist., part time, 1979-81; mem. adv. bd. Dept. Spl. Edn., McAllen Ind. Sch. Dist. Lic. psychologist, Tex.; registered health service provider, Tex.; cert. sch. psychologist, ednl. diagnostician, Tex. Mem. Am. Psychol. Assn., Southwestern Psychol. Assn., Tex. Psychol. Assn., Council Exceptional Children, Assn. Children with Learning Disabilities, Nat. Assn. Sch. Psychologists. Democrat. Home: 1200 Nolana Loop Apt 111 McAllen TX 78501 Office: Dept Sch Services Pan Am U Edinburg TX 78539

BURNS, MARETTA JO, acct.; b. San Antonio, Nov. 7, 1941; d. Joseph Wallis and Mary (Shepard) Burns; B.B.A., Baylor U., 1962. Supervisory cost acctg. asst. Pueblo (Colo.) Army Depot, 1962-65; employment security advisor U.S. Dept. Labor, Denver, 1965-68, Seattle, 1968-70, cost acctg. task force, 1969-70, budget and acctg. officer, Denver, 1970—, regional automated system redesign task force, 1979-80. Mem. Nat. Assn. Female Execs., Phi Gamma Nu, Beta Alpha Psi, Beta Gamma Sigma. Baptist. Home: 3784 S Quince St Denver CO 80237

BURNS, MARGARET ALICE, nurse; b. New Bedford, Mass., Jan. 19, 1924; d. John S. and Margaret L. (Ring) B.; R.N., Union Hosp., Fall River, Mass., 1945; cert. Yale U., New Haven, 1947. Operating room staff nurse Meml. Hosp. Cancer and Allied Diseases, N.Y.C., 1947-48; operating room supr., instr. Middlesex Hosp., Middleton, Conn., 1948-49; charge nurse operating room Pack Med. Group, N.Y.C., 1949-52; operating room supr., instr., asso. dir. to dir. surg. services New Eng. Deaconess Hosp., Boston, 1952—. Served with Nurse Corps, AUS, 1945-46; PTO. Mem. Assn. Operating Room Nurses (pres. Mass. chpt. 1976-77), Am. Nurses Assn., Mass. Nurses Assn., Nat. Assn. Female Execs., Union Hosp. Alumni Assn., Assn. Diploma Nurses, Am. Assn. Ret. Persons. Democrat. Roman Catholic. Club: Dedham (Mass.) Community House. Author: Teaching the Operating Room Technician, 1968-72; Self-Evaluation of Current Knowledge for the Operating Room Technician, 1973-75. Home: 95 Pine St Dedham MA 02026 Office: 185 Pilgrim Rd Boston MA 02215

BURNS, PATRICIA ANN, state ofcl.; b. Balt., Apr. 12, 1946; d. Willie Rutherford and Annie Lee (Green) Mason; B.S., Morgan State U., 1976; M.A.S., Johns Hopkins U., 1979; m. Clarence Henry Burns, May 6, 1962; children—Clarence Henry, Natasha Lynn, Sean Damon. Credit mgr. Pollack-Blum's Furniture Store, Balt., 1969-77; coordinator Balt. Mayor's Office Manpower Resources, 1977-80; project coordinator Balt. Dept. Human Resources, 1980-81; asst. dir. Md. Occupational Info. Coordinating Com., 1981—. Mem. Nat. Assn. Female Execs. (area dir.), Greater Balt. Bd. Realtors, Delta Sigma Pi. Home: 6725 Fox Meadow Rd Baltimore MD 21207 Office: 1123 N Eutaw St Baltimore MD 21201

BURNS, PHYLLIS-ANNE, clin. and neuropsychologist; b. Montague, Mass., Oct. 19, 1948; d. James Joseph and Claire Marie (Coleman) Burns Tutein; A.B., (Watertown Kiwanis Club scholar), Boston U., 1968, A.M., 1974, Ed.D., (grad. fellow), 1981; M.A. (grad. fellow), U. Chgo., 1978. Social worker Mass. dept. Public Welfare, 1968-71; community affairs coordinator, counselor CETA, Cambridge, Mass., 1973-74; dir. adult work experience program, 1974-75; project intern: Adult Ed and Consl. Ctr., City Colleges of Chgo 1976-78; research asst. Ill. Gov.'s Commn. Mental Health and Devel. Disabilities, 1977-78; acad. counselor, mem. faculty psychology and philosophy, psychotherapist Bradford (Mass.) Coll., 1978-79; tchr. social studies and sci. Belmont (Mass.) High Sch., 1979-80; Intern (Clin. Psy.) Dr. Solomon C. Fuller, Boston, 1980-81; clin. and neuropsychologist House of Affirmation, Inc., Whitinsville, Mass., 1982—. Cert. tchr., Mass.; postdoctoral fellow (Clin. and Neuropsychology) Boston City Hosp., 1981-82, VA Med. Center, Jamaica Plain, Mass., 1982-83, Faculty Dept of Neurology, Univ. of Mass. Med. Sch. 1982—. Mem. Am. Psychol. Assn., Mass. Psychol. Assn., Am. Acad. Religion, Internat. Neurol. Soc., Assn. Humanistic Psychology, Pi Lambda Theta. Roman Catholic. Contbr. articles profl. jours and profl. presentations

BURNS, SHIRLEY DARLENE, legal sec.; b. Decatur, Ill., Oct. 30, 1938; d. Robert and Sylvia Faye (Cowger) Belke; grad. Decatur (Ill.) Public Schs., 1956; m. Richard Lee Burns, Nov. 24, 1956 (div. July 1980); children—Cindi Lynn (Mrs. Thomas A. Diprima), Richard Todd, Scotti Lee, Kristin Annette. With C. N. Gorham & Sons, Decatur, 1956-57; with Burger, Geisler, Fombelle & Wheeler, Decatur, 1961-74; legal sec. Geisler, Waks & Geisler, Decatur, Ill., 1974—; rec. and corr. sec. Macon C. of C., 1974-80; sec.-treas. South Macon Twp. Library Bd., 1975-80. Cert. profl. legal sec. Mem. Macon-Moultrie Counties Legal Secs. Assn., Ill. Assn. Legal secs. (pres. elect, Legal Sec. of Yr. 1977), Nat. Assn. Legal Secs. (Area 5 membership dir. 1980-82), Macon C. of C., Winning as Single Adults (sec.), Parents Without Partners (newsletter editor; regional council sec.). Democrat. Methodist. Home: 240 W Prairie Apt A Decatur IL 62523 Office: 241 S Main St PO Box 1147 Decatur IL 62525

BURNS, SUSAN ANNANETTE, public relations adminstr.; b. Phoenix, June 12, 1951; d. Joseph Kent and Flora Annanette (Newell) (dec.) Burns; B.A. in Journalism and Secondary Edn., U. Ariz., 1973. Reporter, photographer, editor Saddleback Valley News, Mission Viejo, Calif., 1974-77; publs. editor Mission Viejo Co., 1977-79, public relations adminstr., 1979—. Mem. Commn. Status of Women, 1978—, mem. bd., 1981; mem. Jr. League Newport Harbor, 1977—, project chmn., 1981. Recipient award of Merit for publs. Public Relations Soc. Am., 1979, 80; award of Excellence for publs. Internat. Assn. Bus. Communicators, 1980. Mem. Women in Communications (dir. 1978), Internat. Assn. Bus. Communicators, Am. Cancer Soc. (adv. bd. 1978—), Sigma Delta Chi. Republican. Roman Catholic. Office: 26137 La Paz Rd Mission Viejo CA 92691

BURNS-BLAGMON, DJUANA PHAE, public health analyst; b. Little Rock, Oct. 4, 1944; d. James Venice and Cleopatra (Diamond) Burns; student Little Rock U., 1964; B.S. in Zoology, Howard U., 1966; postgrad. U.S. Dept. Agr. Grad. Sch., 1970-71, also Am. Soc. Clin. Pathologists, Hawaii, ISH, Paris and Montreal, Que., Can.; m. Lowell E. Blagmon, Aug. 29, 1981; 1 child, Vache Nieri. Histotechnologist, Georgetown U. Med. Sch., Washington, 1966-68; research technologist Washington Hosp. Center Research Found., 1968-69; cardiopulmonary research technologist Hosp. for Sick Children, Washington, 1969; med. technologist, supr. hematology Bur. of Lab., D.C. Dept. Pub. Health, 1969-77; Medicaid program specialist in lab. sci., pub. health analyst D.C. Commn. Pub. Health, Washington, 1978—; leader surveillance/utilization rev. team for nat. certification of D.C. Medicaid Mgmt. Info. System, 1982; cons./adviser to various orgns. and agys. Dancer, D.C. Recreation Dept. Showmobile, 1967; mem. community modeling group for charitable orgns., 1971-73. Recipient longevity sevice award D.C. Govt., 1980; cert. in histology U.S. Communicable Disease Center. Mem. Am. Soc. Clin. Pathologist (asso. mem., cert. in histology), Am. Pub. Health Assn., Am. Inst. Biol. Scis., AAUW, D.C. Neighborhood Health Center Technologists (rec./corr. sec. 1970-74). Methodist. Club: Bridge. Contbr. article to profl. jours. Home: 9801 Justina Ct Lanham MD 20706 Office: 617 H St NW Suite 707 Washington DC 20001

BURNSIDE, MARY ARDIS, psychologist; b. Milw., May 14, 1950; d. Glenn Grover and Edna Mae Chrystine (Mueller) B.; B.A., Rice U., 1972; M.A., U. Houston, 1976, Ph.D., 1980; m. Bruce Edward Anderson, July 17, 1973; children—Aaron Hunter Anderson-Burnside. Asst. prof. clin. psychology dept. psychiatry Baylor Coll. Medicine, Houston, 1980—. Lic. psychologist, Tex. Mem. Am. Psychol. Assn.,

Houston Psychol. Assn., Phi Kappa Phi. Office: Dept Psychiatry Baylor Coll Medicine Tex Med Center Houston TX 77030

BURRESS, WILHELMINA BAKER, educator; b. Allentown, Pa., May 31, 1937; d. William Samuel and Martha Dorothy (Taliaferro) Baker; student Howard U., 1955-57, George Washington U., 1958-59; student corr. course U.S. Army Adj. Gen. Sch., 1969-71; A.A., U. Md., 1976; B.S. in Early Childhood Edn., Bowie State Coll., 1978, M.A. in Reading Edn., 1981; postgrad. Trinity Coll., 1979, 81, Western Ill. U., 1981; m. George Adams Burress (dec.); 1 dau., Karen LaVerne. Psychiat. nurse aide George Washington U. Hosp., 1957-59, occupational therapy asst., 1959-60; dir. Neighborhood Presch., Council Chs. Greater Washington, 1963-65; U.S. securities processor Bur. Engraving and Printing, Washington, 1965, examiner currency notes, 1965-66, clk., 1966-67, substitute utility clk., 1967-68; mil. personnel clk. Aviation Warrant Officer Br., Washington, 1968-70; mil. personnel clk. Armor Br., Office of Personnel Ops., Dept. Army, Washington, 1970-74, mil. personnel status technician Retirement br., Alexandria, Va., 1974-75; substitute tchr. public schs. Prince George's County, Md., 1975-76; staff mem., records specialist Coll. Continuing Edn., Bowie State Coll., 1976-78, presch. tchr. Campus Center for Early Learning, Prince George's Community Coll., 1978; elem. tchr. Anne Arundel County (Md.) Public Schs., 1979—. Elder, Christian Community Presbyterian Ch., Bowie, Md., 1980—; mem. Hope Circle, Bowie-Crofton Choral Soc., 1981. Recipient Profl. Achievement award Bowie State Coll. Edn. Club, 1978; named Outstanding Alumnus Edn. Club, Bowie State Coll., 1979. Mem. NEA, Md. State Tchrs.' Assn., Tchrs. Assn. Anne Arundel County, Anne Arundel County Reading Council (historian 1981-82), Internat. Reading Council, AAUW, Kappa Delta Pi. Club: Omega Wives, Inc. (chmn. hostess com. 1971-72, corr. sec. 1973, Omega Wife of Yr. 1973).

BURRIE, JACQUELINE JOY, multimgmt. co. exec.; b. Namecolin, Pa., Apr. 20, 1940; d. Joseph William and Helen (Haynali) Yaros; A.A., Harrisburg Area Community Coll., 1971; B.S., Pa. State U., 1973; postgrad. Shippensburg State Coll., 1973-74, Millersville State Coll., 1974-76, Bloomsburg State Coll., 1973, N.Y.U., 1976-77; children—Vicki Lynn, Becki Ann. Tchr., Cumberland Valley Sch. Dist., Mechanicsburg, Pa., 1973-75; legis. dir., publ. relations dir. Pa. Manufactured Housing Assn., Pa Recreational Vehicle and Camping Assn., New Cumberland, 1975-78; pres. Exec. Mgmt. Assos., Lemoyne, Pa., 1978—; govtl. affairs rep. Nat. Fedn. Ind. Bus., San Mateo, Calif., 1979. Mem. Pa. Abortion Law Commn., 1972. Recipient Guy and Helen Swope Leadership award, Harrisburg Area Community Coll., 1971. Mem. Am. Soc. Assn. Execs., Pa. Soc. Assn. Execs., (dir., 1979-80), Pa. Pub. Relations Soc., Delta Tau Kappa. Home: 1113 Nanroc Dr Mechanicsburg PA 17055 Office: PO Box 222 Lemoyne PA 17043

BURRIS, PEGGY PHILLIPS, public relations cons., ret. coll. adminstr.; b. Marengo, Ill.; d. Eugene and Maude (Hoit) Neubauer; student Alderson Jr. Coll., 1926-27, Stephens Coll., 1927-28, U. Mo., 1928-30; A.A. (hon.), Christian Coll., Columbia, Mo., 1964; m. J. Webster Phillips, May 4, 1930 (dec.); 1 dau., Peggy Ann Jennings; m. 2d, Baxter Emmet Burris, Dec. 29, 1972. Reporter, feature writer Fairmont (W.Va.) Times, 1924-26, Columbian (Mo.) Missourian, 1928-29, Columbia Daily Tribune, 1942-45; dir. news bur. Stephens Coll., 1945-58; asso. dir. 50th anniversary Sch. Journalism, U. Mo., Columbia, 1958-59; dir. pub. relations Christian Coll., Columbia, 1959-64; coordinator resources and research Am. Alumni Council and Am. Coll. Public Relations Assns., Washington, 1964-66; publicity chmn. Nat. Cherry Blossom Festival, Washington, 1966-67; dir. public info. Cedar Crest Coll., Allentown, Pa., 1967-76; public relations cons., free lance writer, editor. Mem. N. Whitehall Twp. Bicentennial Com.; mem. asso. bd. Lehigh County Assn. for Blind, 1980—; mem. alumnae bd. Stephens Coll., 1975-79, nat. pres., 1976-79, bd. curators, 1976-79, media advisor, 1974—, mem. sesquicentennial planning com., 1979; adv. council Lehigh County Area Agy. on Aging, 1979; chmn. regional council Pa. Council on Aging, 1980-81, sec., 1981-83. Named hon. alumna Christian Coll., Cedar Crest Coll.; recipient Alumnae Achievement award Stephens Coll., 1979, Alumnae Service award, 1981; Service award Pa. Council on Aging, 1981, Council Advancement and Support of Edn., 1981. Mem. Am. Coll. Public Relations Assn. (nat. program dir. 1956-57, 1st place award for ednl. news and features 1961), Nat. Fedn. Press Women (v.p. membership 1959-61, 3 1st place awards 1972, 25 Yr. Service award 1981; regional dir. 1976), Mo. Press Women (pres. 1958-59), Pa. Press Club (pres. 1982), Lehigh Valley Public Relations Club (pres. 1973-74), Women in Communication (nat. v.p. mems.-at-large 1959-61, pres. Washington chpt. 1965-66), Lehigh County Hist. Soc. (dir. 1976—, editor Town Crier 1976—), Nat. Press Club, Press Congress of World. Co-author: Places, 1972. Editor: Entertaining in the White House, 1966. Contbr. chpts. to books, articles to newspapers, mags. Home: De Olde Haus 1365 Main St Orefield PA 18069

BURROUGHS, CECILLE HOLLOWAY, social worker; b. Seattle, July 9, 1928; d. Albert Cecil and Maude (Hall) Holloway; student U. Wash., 1946-49; B.S., Temple U., 1964; M.S., Bryn Mawr Coll., 1967; m. H. Kelley Burroughs, June 20, 1948; children—Michael, Daniel, John, Brian. Staff social worker LanKenau Child Guidance Clinic, Overbrook, Pa., 1967-69; staff social worker Irving Schwartz Inst. for Youth and Children, Phila., 1969-74; coordinator, chief social worker Child Evaluation and Treatment Unit, Barnet Hosp., Paterson, N.J., 1975-76; dir. profl. services Family Counseling Service of Somerset County, Boundbrook, N.J., 1976—. Mem. Nat. Assn. Social Workers, Acad. Cert. Social Workers. Democrat. Unitarian. *

BURROUGHS, ESTHER RUTH, campus minister; b. Calgary, Alta., Can., Feb. 6, 1937; came to U.S., 1955, naturalized, 1963; d. David George and Neva-Dell (Lecuyer) Milligan; student Mars Hill Bapt. Coll., 1955-57; B.S., Okla. Bapt. U., 1959; m. Bob Lloyd Burroughs, Aug. 28, 1958; children—Melody Jean, David Lloyd. Dir. women's programs YMCA, Muskogee, Okla., 1963-64; youth dir. First Bapt. Ch., Abilene, Tex., 1969-71; dir. campus ministry Samford U., Birmingham, Ala., 1971-80; asst. dir. Dept. Spl. Mission Ministries, Home Mission Bd., So. Bapt. Conv., Atlanta, 1980—; cons. in field. Exec. com. Freedom Family Found. of Am., 1979-80; mem. Christian edn. com. Bapt. Coll. Relations Com., 1979-80. Danforth Found. fellow, 1974-75. Mem. NEA, So. Personnel Coll. Assn., Internat. Platform Assn., AAUW, Internat. Miniature Enthusiasts, Sigma Alpha Iota. Baptist. Club: 20th Century Study. Contbr. articles to profl. jours. Office: 1350 Spring St NW Atlanta GA 30367

BURROUGHS, MARGARET TAYLOR GOSS, museum dir.; b. St. Rose, La., Nov. 1, 1917; d. Alexander and Octavia Pierre Taylor; tchr. cert. Normal Coll., 1937; B.Ed., Art Inst. Chgo., 1946, M.A.Ed., 1948; postgrad. Columbia U., 1960-61; D.H.L., Lewis U., 1972; m. Bernard Goss, 1939 (div. 1949); m. 2d, Charles Burroughs, Dec. 23, 1951; children—Gayle Goss Hutchinson, Paul Burroughs. Tchr., Chgo. Public Schs., 1946-69; instr. Art Inst. Chgo., 1968-70; asso. prof. humanities Kennedy-King Coll., Chgo., 1969-79; founder, exec. dir. DuSable Mus. African-Am. History, Inc., Chgo., 1961—; founder South Side Art Center, 1941. Mem. Chgo. Council Fine Arts, 1976-80. Named Sr. Citizen of Year, Chgo. Park Dist., 1981; recipient citation Pres. Carter, 1980. Mem. Am. Forum Internat. Study (dir.), Phi Delta Kappa, Nat. Conf. Artists (founder). Author: Did You Feed My Cow? (rhymes), 1969; Jasper, The Drumin' Boy, 1947; Whip Me Whop Me Pudding & other stories, 1966; (poetry) What Shall I Tell My Children Who Are Black?, 1968, Africa, My Africa, 1970. Office: 740 E 56th Pl Chicago IL 60637

BURROUGHS, PAULINE HUFF, social worker; b. Carlton, Ga., Mar. 20, 1926; d. Arthur W. and Mattie E. (Huff) Huff; Ph.B., Northwestern U., 1952; M.S.W., Loyola U. Chgo., 1955; M.Ed., DePaul U., 1958; postgrad. U. Chgo. and Smith Coll., 1970-71; m. Stanley A. Burroughs, Mar. 9, 1972. Tchr., Bd. Edn., Chgo., 1956-60, 64; clin. social worker VA Hosp., Buffalo, 1960-62; clin. social worker psychiatry VA Hosp., Tomah, Wis., 1963-65; med. clin. social worker VA Hosp., Hines, Ill., 1965-66; clin. social worker psychiatry VA Hosp., Northport, N.Y., 1966-74; field experience supr. SUNY, VA Hosp., Northport, 1968-74; social worker VA Hosp., Battle Creek, Mich., 1974-76; cons., counseling therapist in pvt. practice, Chgo., 1977—; lectr. in field. Recipient award for superior performance in social work VA Hosp., Northport, 1970, others; cert. social worker, Ill., N.Y. Mem. Nat. Assn. Social Workers (registered clin. social worker), Acad. Social Workers, Council on Social Work Edn., Am. Soc. Profl. and Exec. Women, Nat. Assn. Female Execs., AAUW. Office: PO Box 49365 Chicago IL 60649

BURROWS, MARY MCCAULEY, state legislator; b. Palco, Kans.; d. Carl and Lucille Coddington McCauley; student N.W. Christian Coll., 1950-52; m. Charles Burrows; children—Charles Patrick, Thomas Michael, Candice Shawn, Shane Micah. Mem. Oreg. Ho. of Reps., 1973—. Sec. Western Shasta County (Oreg.) Republican Assembly, 1962-65; treas. Oreg. Young Rep. Fedn., 1966-67, co-chmn., 1967-68; mem. precinct com. Lane County Rep. Party; chmn. Lane County Young Reps., 1967, vice chmn. Lane County Rep. Central Com., 1968-70; campaign chmn. Elect Bob Packwood to Senate, Lane County, 1968, Reelect Gov. Tom McCall, 1970; sec. Oreg. Rep. State Central Com., 1971-72; publicity chmn. Western Lane County Rep. Women; deaconess First Christian Ch., Eugene, Oreg. Office: Oreg Ho of Reps State Capitol Salem OR 97310 *

BURROWS, MURIEL LOWE, hosp. adminstr.; b. Scotland, Sept. 26, 1921; came to U.S., 1924, naturalized, 1929; d. John and Jean (Fleming) L.; A.S., Rutgers U., 1970, B.S., 1972; M.B.A., Fairleigh Dickinson U., 1978; m. June 13, 1942 (div.); children—Gail, Muriel Burrows Simpson, Robin Burrows Sacco. Bookkeeper various firms, 1955-61; bookkeeper Saddle Brook (N.J.) Gen. Hosp., 1961-62, office mgr., 1962-68, adminstrv. asst., 1968-76, asso. dir., 1976—; partner Saddle Brook Mgmt. Services, 1976—; sec. treas. Saddle Brook Health Care Found. Mem. Saddle Brook C. of C. (v.p. 1975, sec. 1976, treas. 1977), N.J. Soc. Hosp., Nat. Assn. Accts., Hosp. Fin. Mgrs. Assn. Home: 181 Canterbury Dr Ramsey NJ 07446 Office: 300 Market St Saddle Brook NJ 07662

BURSTON, SUZANNE HELEN, communications co. exec.; b. N.Y.C., July 19, 1946; d. Ivor John Patrick and Madeline Helen Pruess B.; B.A., C. W. Post Coll., 1976. Customer service rep. Braniff Internat., John F. Kennedy Airport, N.Y.C., 1967; spl. services rep. Pan-Am. World Airways, John F. Kennedy Airport, 1969-76, corp. accounts mgr., Lake Success, N.Y., 1976-81; dir. corp. travel Warner Communications, N.Y.C., 1981—. Mem. L.I. Assn. Commerce and Industry, Nat. Passenger Traffic Mgrs. Assn., Corp. Travel Assn. Republican. Episcopalian. Home: 29 Avalon Rd Garden City NY 11530 Office: 75 Rockefeller Plaza New York NY 10019

BURSTYN, ELLEN, actress; d. Detroit, Dec. 7, 1932; d. John Austin and Coriene Marie (Hamel) Gillooly; student pub. schs., Detroit; 1 son, Jefferson Jack. Appeared in: (films) Tropic of Cancer, 1970; Alex in Wonderland, 1970; The Last Picture Show (Acad. Award nomination for Best Supporting Actress; awards N.Y. Film Critics, Nat. Soc. Film Critics), 1971; The King of Marvin Gardens, 1972; The Exorcist (Acad. award nomination Best Actress), 1973; Harry and Tonto, 1974; Alice Doesn't Live Here Anymore (Acad. award Best Actress), 1974; Providence, 1977; A Dream of Passion, 1978; Same Time Next Year, 1978; Resurrection, 1980; Silence of the North, 1980; (Broadway play) Same Time Next Year, 1974-75 (Tony award Best Actress 1974-75); mem. corp. bd. Actors Studio, 1975—, Actor's Equity (pres. 1982). Office: William Morris Agency Inc 1350 Ave of the Americas New York NY 10019 *

BURSTYN, JOAN NETTA, educator; b. Leicester, Eng., Mar. 6, 1929; d. David Edward and Nellie (Wachman) Jacobs; B.A. with honors, U. London, 1950; Cert. of Edn., U. London, 1952, Acad. Diploma in Edn. 1958, Ph.D., 1968; m. Harold L. Burstyn, Aug. 19, 1958; children—Judith, Gail, Daniel. Teaching fellow edn. Harvard U., Cambridge, Mass., 1959-64; lectr. U. Pitts., 1967; lectr. psychology, edn. Carnegie Mellon U., Pitts., 1967-68, instr., 1968, asst. prof., 1969-74, dir. tchr. edn., 1970-74; assoc. prof., chairperson edn. dept. Douglass Coll., Rutgers U., New Brunswick, N.J., 1974-81, prof. edn., 1981—, dir. women's studies program, 1981—. Mem. adv. bd. nurse-midwifery ednl. program U. Medicine and Dentistry N.J., 1978—; bd. dirs. Children's Sch. Sci., Woods Hole, Mass., 1977-80; assoc. dir. N.E. Council Women in Devel., 1981—; mem. joint com. Am. Hist. Assn. and Can. Hist. Assn., 1978-81. Recipient grant-in-aid John F. Kennedy Sch. Govt. and Bunting Inst., 1964-65; Marion Talbot fellow AAUW, 1965-66; Faculty Merit award Rutgers U., 1977, 81; dir. Nat. Endowment for Humanities pilot grant, 1980-82. Fellow AAAS.; mem. Am. Hist. Assn., History Edn. Soc. U.S., History Edn. Soc. Eng., AAAS, Assn. Study Higher Edn., Conf. Brit. Studies, AAUW. Author: Victorian Education and the Ideal of Womanhood, 1980; Song Cycle, 1976; contbr. articles to profl. jours.; mem. editorial bd. Signs, History of Edn. Quar., History of Higher Edn. Ann. Office: Graduate Sch of Edn Rutgers Univ New Brunswick NJ 08903

BURT, DIANE LEE, property mgr.; b. Detroit, Nov. 15, 1942; d. Leo A. and Ethelyn Ruth (Bailey) B.; B.A. in Social Work, Mich. State U., 1964; m. David L. Coggin (div.). Social worker Fla. Welfare Dept., Miami, 1964-66, supr., 1968-72; social worker Ill. Child Welfare, East St. Louis, 1967; supr. Dade County Welfare Dept., Miami, 1972-80; with GDG Property Mgmt., Miami, 1980—; field adv. Fla. Internat. U. Vice pres. Sabal Chase Condominium Assn. I, Inc., Miami, 1978-79, 80-81, pres., 1979-80; bd. dirs. Sabal Chase Homeowners Assn., 1979-80; sec. Kendall Fedn. Homeowners Assns., Miami, 1979-80. Mem. Fla. Assn. Health and Social Services (Outstanding Service plaque Dade County chpt. 1979), Metro-Dade County Mgmt. and Profl. Assn. (dir. 1978, treas. 1979), Nat. Assn. Female Execs., Dade County Mental Health Assn., Community Assns. Inst. (leadership tng. cert. 1979), Am. Soc. Profl. and Exec. Women. Methodist. Home: 11365 SW 157th Terr Miami FL 33157

BURTNER, SUSAN BURNS, govt. ofcl.; b. Chgo., Nov. 30, 1942; d. William Grady and Margaret (MC Donald) Burns; B.A., Purdue U., 1964; M.S.L.S., U. Ill., 1967; M.A., George Washington U., 1979; m. Carrol E. Burtner, June 7, 1980. Catalog librarian HEW, Washington, 1967; librarian U.S. Air Force, Japan, 1968-70, Dept. Commerce, Washington, 1970-73; chief readers services Gen. Acctg. Office Library, Washington, 1973-75, library dir., 1975-80, dir. Office Info. Systems and Services, 1980-81, dep. dir. gen. services and controller div., 1981—. Mem. Spl. Library Assn., ALA. Roman Catholic. Home: 4013 N Tazewell St Arlington VA 22207 Office: General Services & Controller General Accounting Office Washington DC 20548

BURTON, ANN M., historian, univ. adminstr.; b. Detroit, Mar. 4, 1933; d. Ralph J. and Edith M. Burton; B.A. in History, Duke U., 1954; M.A. in History, U. Mich., 1955; D.Phil. in Brit. Imperial History (Beit sr. research scholar), St. Anne's Coll., Oxford (Eng.) U., 1960. Mem. faculty Bklyn. Coll., 1961, 64-81, prof. history, 1979-81, chmn. dept., 1976-80; chmn. faculty senate City U. N.Y., 1978-81; asso. dean Arts and Sci., N.Y.U., 1981—; instr. Hunter Coll., N.Y.C., 1961-63, asst. vis. prof., summer 1970; vis. asst. prof. Columbia U., summer 1968; mem. doctoral faculty in history city U. Grad. Sch., 1975. Mem. vestry Grace Ch., N.Y.C.; trustee City U. N.Y., Grace Ch. Sch. Grantee Am. Philos. Soc., 1963-64, City U. N.Y., 1971; fellow AAUW, 1963-64. Mem. Am. Hist. Assn., Inst. Hist. Research. Club: Princeton. Office: 5 Washington Sq N New York NY 10003

BURTON, ANNA MARJORIE, nurse; b. Pontiac, Mich., May 1, 1931; d. Harold Vale and Sophia (Eaton) Kelly; student Mich. State U., 1949-51; A.A., Fla. Keys Community Coll., 1976; children—Julie A. Burton Stone, William A., Rory R., Kenneth G. Orthodontic technician Birmingham, Mich., 1960-67; claims rep. Social Security Adminstrn., Lexington, Ky., 1967-71, Key West, Fla., 1972-79; student nurse. Recipient Appreciation award Vets. Council, 1974; hon. Conch and Key, City of Key West, 1974. Mem. U.S. Coast Guard Aux. (comdr. 1976, growth and retention officer 1977-79), Fla. Keys Community Coll. Student Nurses Assn. (Nurse of Yr. 1979-80), Student Nurse Assn. Fla., Nat. Student Nurse Assn.,Bus. and Profl. Women, Handicapped Boaters Assn., Boat Owners Assn. of U.S. U.S. Yacht Racing Union, Key West Art and Hist. Soc., Phi Theta Kappa. Episcopalian. Club: Marathon Yacht. Home: 1420 Von Phister St Key West FL 33040

BURTON, CATE, hosp. adminstr.; b. Chgo., Sept. 6, 1952; d. John Louis and Nancy Virginia (Stine) Burton; student Ithaca Coll., 1970-72, Golden Gate U., 1982—. PBX supr. U. Chgo. and Hosps., 1972-74; PBX operator St. Francis Meml. Hosp., San Francisco, 1974-78; mgr. telecommunications Presbyterian Hosp. of Pacific Med. Center, San Francisco, 1978—. Mem. Am. Soc. Hosp. Engring., Hosp. Telecommunications Mgmt. Assn. (founder, dir.). Democrat. Office: 2333 Buchanan P-1311 San Francisco CA 94115

BURTON, CATHERINE ADAMS, clin. psychologist; b. Detroit, Sept. 23, 1951; d. David Rittenhouse and Louise Romaine (Adams) B.; student Northwestern U., 1969-71; B.A. magna cum laude with highest honors in Psychology, Williams Coll., 1973; M.A., Emory U., 1977, Ph.D., 1979. Clin. psychology intern Sch. Medicine, U. Wash., Seattle, 1976-77; postdoctoral fellow Seattle Family Inst., 1978-80; clin. instr. dept. psychiatry U. Wash., Seattle, 1980-81, adj. faculty, 1981—; adj. faculty Antioch U., John Bastyr Coll. Medicine, 1981—, also supr. tng. and cons.; pvt. practice clin. psychology and psychotherapy, Seattle. Mem. Am. Psychol. Assn., Wash. Psychol. Assn., Citizens for Planetary Initiative (sponsored UN), World Future Soc., Futures Network, Phi Beta Kappa, Alpha Lambda Delta. Research in field; contbr. article to profl. jour. Home: 1122 Grand Ave Seattle WA 98122 Office: 2722 Eastlake Ave E Suite 250 Seattle WA 98102

BURTON, CLELAND PATRICIA, hist. abstractor; b. Detroit, July 15, 1918; d. Fred and Fern Louise (McCloy) B.; student Fairfax Hall, Waynesboro, Va., 1937-39, U. Mich., 1939-40; m. Robert Waller Bragg III, Jan. 25, 1941 (dec.); 1 dau., Melissa. Exec. v.p. Fred Burton Abstract Co., 1947-59; owner Burton Farms for Registered Shetlands, various locations, 1960-64; hist. abstractor Am. Frontier Ltd., Bolar, Va., 1965—; hist. cons. Mason County (W.Va.) Bicentennial Commn., 1974-77, Point Pleasant, W.Va., 1977-79. Recipient award Freedoms Found., 1975. Mem. W.Va. Press Women, Detroit Hist. Soc. Office: PO Box 1774 Bolar VA 24414

BURTON, DOROTHY JO, automation co. exec.; b. Mexico, Mo.; d. Joe Wheeler and Gladys Leah (Robison) Hanson; B.S., Washington U., St. Louis, 1961; postgrad. So. Ill. U., 1980-82; m. W. Wesley Burton, Jr.; children—Carole, Barbara, John, Wesley W. Engr., McDonnell Aircraft, St. Louis, 1952-64; sr. engr. McDonnell Douglas Astron., St. Louis, 1964-70; sr. cons. McDonnell Douglas Automation Co., St. Louis, 1970-80, sect. mgr., 1980—; cons. in field. Mem. Am. Assn. Cost Engrs., Project Mgmt. Inst. Republican. Presbyterian. Home: 16 Rue Grand Lake Saint Louis MO 63367 Office: PO Box 516 Saint Louis MO 63166

BURTON, ELSIE CARTER, educator; b. Rupert, Idaho, Aug. 1, 1930; d. Lawrence and Maudie May (Wilferth) Carter; A.A., Graceland Coll., 1950; B.S., U. Colo., 1952, M.S. U. Wash., 1958; Ph.D., Ohio State U., 1970; postgrad Laban Art of Movement Center, Dartford, Eng., Loughborough Coll., 1973, Orff Inst., Salzburg, Austria, 1975; m. Sept. 6, 1959 (div. 1970); 1 son, Timothy George. Tchr. phys. edn., public schs., Lewistown, Mont. and Lakeview, Oreg., 1952-57; asst. prof. health and phys. edn. Sam Houston Coll., 1958-59; asso. prof. U. Ky., Lexington, 1970-74; vis. prof. Western Mich. U., 1974; prof. Fla. State U., Tallahassee, 1974—; cons. phys. edn. and child devel. Mem. AAHPERD (life), So. Assn. Phys. Edn. Coll. Women, Fla. Assn. Health, Phys. Edn., Recreation and Dance, Delta Psi Kappa. Author: Movement Fundamentals, 1971; Developmental Movement Activities for Pre-School Children, 1976; The New Physical Education for Elementary School Children, 1977; Learning Through Movement, 1979; Physical Activities for the Developing Child, 1980; The Dynamic Self, 1982; contbr. articles to profl. jours. Home: 1112 Richview Rd Tallahassee FL 32301 Office: Dept Phys Edn Fla State U Tallahassee FL 32306

BURTON, JUDITH MARGARET, artist, psychologist; b. Croydon, Eng., Aug. 4, 1939; d. William Henry and Dora Constance (Lyons) B.; diploma U. London, 1970; M.Ed., U. Manchester, Eng., 1972; Ed.D., Harvard U., 1981. Lectr., U. London Inst. Edn., 1966-72; asst. prof. Mass. Coll. Art, 1972-76; assoc. prof. art Boston U., 1976-82, chmn. art edn., 1982—; vis. lectr. N.Y. U., 1974, Lesley Coll., 1974-76; teaching fellow Harvard U., 1977; cons. curriculum; dir. Summer Visual Arts Inst. of Boston U. Travel grantee Harvard U., 1976, Boston U., 1979. Mem. Nat. Art Edn. Assn., Internat. Art Edn. Assn., Am. Psychol. Assn. Roman Catholic. Author: Visualising Experience, 1982. Home: 16 Ware St Cambridge MA 02138

BURTON, OPHELIA WEAVER, govt. tax service adminstr.; b. Athens, Ala., Oct. 6, 1937; d. Joe and Natie E. (Cunningham) Weaver; B.S. (Coll. scholar), Bera Coll., 1959; postgrad. Maxwell Midcareer Devel. Program, Syracuse U., 1978-79, M.P.A., 1981; m. James S. Burton, July 16, 1959; 1 dau., Traci Michelle. Program analyst Dept. Def., Arlington, Va., 1962-70; budget analyst, dir. program planning and budget D.C. Govt., 1970-72; program analyst, br. chief IRS, Washington, 1974-80, asst. dir. Taxpayer Service div., Washington, 1980—. Bd. dirs. Reston (Va.) Children's Center, 1972-74, Nat. Council Negro Women, 1980. Named to Outstanding Young Women Am., U.S. Jaycees, 1971; recipient Spl. Act in Service award U.S. Army Office Personnel Ops., 1963, cert. achievement, 1974, also numerous letters of appreciation and commendation. Mem. Am. Soc. Public Adminstrs. (dir. 1976-77), Federally Employed Women (dir. 1979-80). Mem. United Ch. of Christ.

BURTON, SHERIL DALE, microbiologist, educator; b. Malad, Ida., May 10, 1935; B.S., Brigham Young U., 1959, M.S., 1961; Ph.D., Oreg. State U., 1964; married; 3 children. Research asst. bacteriologist Brigham Young U., Provo, 1959-61; microbiologist U. Nebr., 1961-62; research asst. microbiologist Oreg. State U., 1962-64, asst. prof., 1964-65; asst. prof. Inst. Marine Sci., U. Alaska, 1965-67, asso. prof., 1967-78; prof. microbiology Brigham Young U., 1978—. Mem. Am. Soc. Microbiology. Office: Dept Microbiology Brigham Young U Provo UT 84601 *

BURTT, ELIZABETH ALLENE, public health nurse; b. Exeter, N.H., July 31, 1926; d. William Abbot and Elizabeth Pride (Cole) Burtt; diploma in Nursing, Hillsborough County Gen. Hosp., 1947; B.S., Johns Hopkins U., 1961, M.P.H., 1977; M.S. in Public Health Nursing, Boston U., 1965. Staff nurse Mass. Gen. Hosp., Boston, 1948-49; head nurse, supr. emergency dept. Johns Hopkins Hosp., Balt., 1950-55; resident sch. nurse Oldfields Sch., Glencoe, Md., 1955-60; sr. public health nurse Balt. City Health Dept., 1961-63; instr. public health nursing U. R.I., Kingston, 1965-68; asst. prof. public health nursing U. N.H., Durham, 1968-72; public health nurse epidemiologist N.H. Div. Public Health Services, Concord, 1972-73, ednl. cons., 1973-75, chief Bur. Public Health Nursing, 1975—; N.H. State Tb control officer, 1981—; summer camp nurse Vt., 1955-59, N.Y., 1965, Mass., 1966, R.I., 1968; public health nurse cons. Exeter Vis. Nurse Assn., 1967; adv. N.H. Student Nurse Assn., 1979-81. Chmn. Epping (N.H.) Health Com., 1969-70, N.H. Immunization Task Force, 1977-79. Fellow Royal Soc. of Health; mem. Am. Nurses Assn., N.H. Nurses Assn. (dir. 1979-81, chmn. legis. com. 1978-80). Am. Public Health Assn., Nat. League Nursing, N.H. League Nursing (dir. 1977-78, pres. 1981—), Assn. State and Territorial Dirs. Public Health Nursing, Sigma Theta Tau. Contbr. to Nursing Clinics of North America, 1972. Home: Route 1 Exeter NH 03833 Office: Hazen Dr Concord NH 03301

BURY, MARYELLEN JILL, social worker; b. Paterson, N.J., Aug. 18, 1946; d. Frederick P. and Rita Patricia (Smith) B.; B.S. magna cum laude, Seton Hall U., 1969; M.S.W., Rutgers U., 1973. Caseworker, Bur. Childrens Services, 1969-71; outreach caseworker Catholic Family and Community Services, Paterson, 1973-76; sch. social worker, Clifton, N.J., 1976; chief social worker Mount St. Joseph Children's Center, Totowa, N.J., 1976-81; sch. social worker Essex Career Acad., 1981-82; asst. dir. Mt. St. Joseph Children's Center, Totowa, N.J., 1982—; field instr. Ramapo Coll., 1979—, Rutgers U. Sch. Social Work, 1980—. Mem. Child Placement Rev. Bd., Passaic County, 1979-82, chairperson, 1979-80. Mem. Nat. Assn. Social Workers, Acad. Cert. Social Workers. Roman Catholic. Office: 124 Shepherd Ln Totowa NJ

BUSCHINI, MARGARET MARY, former classified advt. ofcl.; b. Chgo., Sept. 28, 1914; d. John Peter and Rose Domenica (DeGasso) Gellono; student Barclay Bus. Coll., 1932-34, Coll. San Mateo, 1950-55; m. Jerry J. Buschini, Nov. 26, 1933; 1 son, John A. Classified advt. sales San Mateo (Calif.) Times, 1943-55, classified advt. mgr., 1955-80. Treas. El Camino House Orgn. Recipient Charles W. Horn Meml. award for Outstanding Classified Advt. Mgr., 1979; 25 1st pl. honor awards for classified promotions. Mem. No. Calif. Classifield Advt. Mgrs. Assn. (past pres.), Western States Classified Advt. Mgrs. Assn. (past pres.), Assn. Newspapers Classified Advt. Mgrs. (internat. want ad chmn.). Club: Soroptimist of Burlinghame-San Mateo (past pres.).

BUSH, BARBARA PIERCE, wife of Vice Pres. U.S.; b. Rye, N.Y. June 8, 1925; d. Marvin and Pauline (Robinson) Pierce; ed. Smith Coll., L.H.D., Mt. Vernon Coll., Wash. D.C., 1981, LL.D., Cardinal Strich Coll., Milwaukee, 1981; m. George Herbert Walker Bush, Jan. 6, 1945; children—George Walker (1946), John Ellis (1953), Neil Mallon (1955), Marvin Pierce (1956), Dorothy Walker (1959). Lived in China, 1974-75, returned to Peking, 1977, 78; lectr. on China to various univs. and orgns. Bd. of dirs. Reading is Fundamental, Nat. Trust for Hist. Preservation, Soc. for Meml. Sloan-Kettering Cancer Center, Children's Oncology Services of Met. Wash. D.C., Parent's Choice, The Wash. Home, Wash. D.C.; trustee The Kingsbury Center, U.S. Cap. Hist. Soc.; sponsor Laubach Literacy, Inc.; mem. Leukemia Soc. Am. (natl. hon. chmn.), Ladies of the Senate (pres.), Internat. Club II, Rep. Women's Fed. Forum (Wash. D.C.), Women's Nat. Rep. Club (N.Y.C.), Magic Circle Rep. Women's Club (Houston), Tex. Fedn. Rep. Women (life member). Republican. Espiscopalian. Address: The Vice President's House Washington DC 20501 *

BUSH, ESTHER LOREAN, mgmt. cons.; b. Pitts., Oct. 26, 1951; d. Willie Clauzell and Ola Mae (Herbert) B.; B.S., Morgan State U., Balt., 1973; M.S. (William Wallace Lanahan scholar), Johns Hopkins U., 1978. Tchr., Balt. Public Schs., 1973-77; asst. dir./career counselor Career Planning and Placement Center, Coppin State Coll., Balt., 1977-80; cons. Donchian Mgmt. Services, N.Y.C., 1982—; cons. Balt. Urban Tchrs. Center, 1978-79, Career Services, Inc., 1979, Coll. Placement, 1979, Services, Inc., 1979. asst. dir. programs for labor edn. advancement program, women's affairs div., econ. resources dept. Nat. Urban League, N.Y.C., 1980-81. Mem. College Placement Services, Inc., Council Concerned Black Execs., Nat. Council Negro Women, Am. Soc. Tng. and Devel., Adult Edn. Assn., Am. Mgmt. Assn., Coalition of 100 Black Women, Internat. Platform Assn., Assn. Career Devel. in Higher Edn. (exec. com.), Nat. Orgn. Devel. Network, N.Y. Orgn. Devel. Network, NAACP, Balt. Urban League, Pi Lambda Theta (rec. sec. chpt. 1978). Democrat. Baptist. Author curriculum and workshop materials. Home: 725 Riverside Dr Apt 11 New York NY 10031 Office: 49 E 53d St New York NY 10022

BUSH, FREDDIE ANN, educator; b. Greensboro, N.C., June 30, 1942; d. Fred and Elizabeth (Hinton) B.; B.S., N.C. A&T State U., 1969; M.S., Hunter Coll., 1975. Editorial asst. McGraw-Hill Book Co., N.Y.C., 1969-76; instr. Spanish American Inst., N.Y.C., 1976—, also student counselor. Cert. tchr., N.Y.C., N.Y. State, N.J. Mem. Nat. Alumni Assn. N.C. A&T State U. (2d v.p. 1979-81, sec. NE Region 1972-79, pres. N.Y.C. chpt. 1978-80, young alumna award 1973, Chancellor's Council award 1974), Hunter Coll. Alumni Assn. N.Y.C. Club: Century Club of N.C. A&T State U. Alumni Assn. Author: The Woman's Personal Wardrobe Plan Book, 1981. Home: 419 W 34th St New York NY 10001 Office: 215 W 43rd St New York NY 10036

BUSH, GEORGIA ANN, inventory mgmt. specialist; b. Stratford, Okla., Dec. 22, 1920; d. Nathan C. and Ethel Helen (Kates) Pettit; B.M., U. Extension Conservatory, Chgo., 1957; student Oklahoma City U., 1950, Oklahoma City Jr. Coll., 1975; m. Enoch O'Dell Bush, Aug. 10, 1939; 1 son, Nathan O'Dell. Pvt. piano tchr., Oklahoma City, 1936—; with Okla. Bd. Pub. Affairs, Oklahoma City, 1968-72; inventory mgmt. specialist Tinker AFB, Oklahoma City, 1972—; ordained to ministry, Assemblies of God, 1957; pastor University Heights Assembly of God, Oklahoma City, 1958-62, Northwest Assembly of God, Oklahoma City, 1968-72. Recipient Sustained Superior Performance with cash award, Tinker, 1980. Mem. Nat. Guild Piano Tchrs., Okla. Dist. Council Assemblies of God. Democrat. Club: Order Eastern Star. Home: 1040 SW 58 St Oklahoma City OK 73109 Office: MM1FAE/Tinker AFB OK

BUSH, GERALDINE TERESA, mktg. exec.; b. Phila., Apr. 14, 1946; d. Charles William and Marie Frances (Barnes) B.; B.A., Temple U., 1968. Chemist, Union Camp Corp. Research and Devel., Princeton, N.J., 1968-71; asst. scientist N.L. Industries Corp., Hightstown, N.J., 1971-73; sales engr. UPA Tech., Syosset, N.Y., 1973-74, dist. mgr., 1974-75, field sales mgr., 1975-77, dir. sales and mktg., 1977—; lectr. in field. Recipient Salesman of Yr. award, 1973, 74, 75; Recognition award Dept. Commerce, 1978. Mem. ASTM, Am. Electroplaters Soc., Am. Soc. Quality Control, Am. Mgmt. Assn. Club: Internat. Bus. Roundtable (Adelphi U.). Contbr. articles to profl. jours. Office: 60 Oak Dr Syosset NY 11791 *

BUSH, GLORIA K. Y MORAGA, psychologist; b. Huntington Park, Calif.; d. P. and S. (Moraga) Kemerer; A.B., U. So. Calif., 1937, M.A., 1941, Ph.D., 1974; m. William R. Eckles, Oct. 27, 1953 (dec. Sept. 1970). Asst. chief statis. unit ARC, San Francisco, 1942-43, asst. chief nat. hdqrs. statis. unit, Washington, 1943-44; personnel mgr. Bullocks, Los Angeles, 1944; psychologist Juvenile Hall Hosp., Los Angeles, 1948-52; vocat. rehab. worker Dept. Pub. Welfare Los Angeles, 1952-55; domestic relations officer Superior Ct. Los Angeles County, 1955-60; psychologist Meyers Clinic, Los Angeles, 1960-61; psychologist, Van Nuys, Calif., 1961—; cons. Calif. Sch. Profl. Psychology, 1973-74; founder, pres. Multiple Ego State Tng. Inst., 1977. Mem. Am. Psychol. Assn., Internat. Transactional Analysis Assn. Tech. dir. film Youthquake (Golden Globe award as best documentary 1975). Home: 348 Peralta Dr Santa Paula CA 93060 Office: 134 Davis St Santa Paula CA 93060 also 22055 Clarendon St Suite 101 Woodland Hills CA 91367

BUSH, MARGERY PECK, clin. social worker; b. Bristol, Conn., Mar. 22, 1934; d. Seymour Roe and Margery (Earl) Peck; B.A. in Psychology, Wells Coll., Aurora, N.Y., 1956; M.S.W., U. Conn., 1975; m. Edward Wallace Bush, Jr., Feb. 28, 1958; children—Kimberly, Barbara, David. Intern, Family Service Soc., Hartford, Conn., 1973-74, Inst. Living, Adult Outpatient Clinic, Hartford, 1974-75; cons., sch. social worker East Hartford Bd. Edn., 1976; family counselor Family Service, Inc., New Britain, Conn., 1976-79, Glastonbury Youth and Family Resource Center, 1980-82; pvt. practice individual, marital, and family counseling, West Hartford, 1979—; instr. program Living in Fuller Effectiveness (LIFE), 1979—. Corporator, Oak Hill Sch. Blind, 1968—; trustee Larrabee Fund Assn., 1970-73, chmn. Hartford com., 1970-72; bd. dirs. Hartford Interval House, 1977-78. Mem. Nat. Assn. Social Workers, Acad. Cert. Social Workers, Conn. Soc. Clin. Social Workers, Audubon Soc. Congregationalist. Clubs: Hartford Ski, Hartford Tennis. Address: 113 Pioneer Dr West Hartford CT 06117

BUSH, MELINDA JOHNSON, publisher; b. Champaign, Ill., June 14, 1940; d. Maurice R. and Margaret B. Johnson; B.S., U. Colo., 1962; postgrad. London Sch. Econs. and Polit. Sci. With J. Walter Thompson, advt., N.Y.C., 1962-64, Paul Bradley Assns., public relations, N.Y.C., 1964-66; with Ziff-Davis Publishing Co., N.Y.C., 1966—, asst. to pres., 1974-76, pub. Hotel and Travel Index, 1976—; chmn. Hotel and Travel Index work studies program Cornell U., U. Mass. Nat. photography coordinator Model Cities Task Force, 1970-72; founder, chmn. Photography Youth Found., 1973-76. Named Woman of Year in Travel, Travel Industry Assn. Am., 1980. Mem. Hotel Sales Mgmt. Assn. (dir.), Am. Hotel and Motel Assn., Advt. Women N.Y. Club: Wings (N.Y.C.). Author articles in field. Office: 1 Park Ave New York NY 10016

BUSH, NANCY WAGONER, educator; b. Malvern, Pa., Aug. 6, 1934; d. George Sidney and Alverda (Kennedy) Wagoner; B.S. (William Morris Phillips scholar), West Chester State Coll., 1953; A.A., N.J. Coll. Commerce, 1954; M.S., Fla. State U., 1963, AD.M.S., 1969, Ph.D. (Higher Edn. Act fellow), 1972. Columnist, feature writer The Archive, Downingtown, Pa., 194649; art and copy expeditor N.W. Ayer Co., Phila., 1953; instr. Warwick Sch., Pottstown, Pa., 1953-55, Biddle Sch., West Chester, Pa., 1955-56; reference asst., br. librarian Miami (Fla.) Pub. Library, 1960-66; chief of circulation Jacksonville (Fla.) Pub. Library, 1966-68; asst. prof. research Fla. State U., 1972; program dir. asso. prof. Appalachian State U., Boone, N.C., 1972-75, asst. to vice chancellor for acad. affairs, 1975-76; chmn. ednl. media dept. Auburn (Ala.) U., 1976-80; dir. curriculum lab. U. South Ala., Mobile, 1980—; chmn. steering com. for library continuing edn. Ala. Pub. Library Service; cons. various schs. and univs. Harvard fellow, 1972-73. Mem. ALA, Southeastern, Fla. library assns., NEA, AAUP, AAUW, N.C. Assn. Educators, Ala. Library Assn., Ala. Instructional Media Service, Spl. Libraries Assn., League Women Voters, Phi Delta Kappa, Beta Phi Mu, Phi Delta Gamma. Editor: The Pilot Light newsletter, 1966-68, Ala. Instructional Media Service, 1978-80. Home: 101 Foreman Rd Mobile AL 36608 Office: ILB Univ South Ala Mobile AL 36688

BUSH, PHYLLIS IVERSON, univ. dean; b. Centerville, S.D., Oct. 15, 1922; d. Elmer F. and Helen Evangeline (Stubkjaer) Iverson; A.B., Municipal U. of Omaha, 1943; M.A., U. Nebr., 1951, Ed.D., 1957; m. Richard F. Bush, June 30, 1948; 1 son, David. Instr., U. Nebr., 1953-57; prof. edn. Calif. State U., Chico, 1957-71, dean Learning Activities Resource Center, asso. v.p. acad. affairs, 1971-82, dean Sch. Communications, 1982—. cons. New Haven Unified Schs., Union City, Calif.; dir. Title III Project Enterprise, Calif. Chairperson, mem. dist. bd. Chico Area Recreation Dist., 1964-68. Served with USCG Womens Res., 1943-45. Named Woman of Year, Bus. and Profl. Women in No. Calif., 1974. Mem. Western Assn. Schs. and Colls. (accreditation service, sr. div.), Delta Kappa Gamma. Republican. Christian Scientist. Home: PO Box 13 Chico CA 95927 Office: Calif State U Chico CA 95929

BUSH, SUZANNE LOEWENSTEIN, newspaper exec.; b. Wilmington, Del., Aug. 23, 1946; d. Fritz and Virginia (McGuire) Loewenstein; B.A., U. Del., 1969, also postgrad.; m. William Guy Bush, July 31, 1976. With News-Journal Co., Wilmington, 1969—, market research dir., 1979—. Bd. dirs. Del. Assn. for Blind. Recipient 1st Place award Del. Press Women Communication Contest, 1978; 3d Place award Nat. Fedn. Press Women Communication Contest, 1978. Mem. Del. Press Women (treas. 1977-79), Internat. Newspaper Promotion Assn., Nat. Fedn. Press Women, Newspaper Research Council. Office: 831 Orange St Box 1111 Wilmington DE 19899

BUSHBAUM, MARIANNE LUCILLE, social worker; b. Portland, Oreg., June 10, 1923; d. Frank Olaf and Alma Bertina (Dahl) Walbom; student U. Minn., 1942-43, 75-76, St. Mary's Jr. Coll., 1976-77; m. Richard Leonard Bushbaum, Aug. 10, 1944; children—Holly, Timmi Li, Kimla, Joan, Jill, Dirk, Laurie. Mgr. Parkview Pain Rehab. Unit, Mpls., 1977-78; chem. dependency counselor Parkview Treatment Center, Mpls., 1977; counselor Parkview Pain Clinic, Mpls., 1978, asst. dir., 1979-80, treatment dir., 1981—. Eden Prairie (Minn.) chpt. pres. Am. Field Service, 1965-66. Mem. Assn. for Humanistic Psychology, Minn. Assn. Rehab. Providers. Republican. Home: 14230 Chestnut Dr Eden Prairie MN 55344 Office: 3705 Park Center Blvd Minneapolis MN 55416

BUSHELL-PAST, PHYLLIS ANNE, edn1. adminstr.; b. N.Y.C., Aug. 22, 1941; d. John D. and Grace R. (McCabe) Bushell; B.S., Coll. St Rose, 1965; M.S., SUNY, Oswego, 1977, C.A.S., 1979; Ed.D. U. Sarasota, 1982; m. Roger D. Past, Nov. 29, 1975; stepchildren—Lis, Julie, Jeff. Tchr. elem. sch., 1964-70; exec. dir. Learning Founds., Syracuse, N.Y., 1970-73; learning disabilities coordinator Cazenovia (N.Y.) Schs., 1973-74, Title I Coordinator, 1975-76; supr. spl. edn. Onondaga-Madison County Bd. Coop. Ednl. Services, 1974-75; sch. prin. Syracuse City Schs., 1976-77, supr. eelm. edn., reading and lang. arts, 1977-80; dir. Edn. Resource Center, Casper, Wyo., 1982—. Bd. Dirs. Onondaga Pastoral Counseling Service, 1977-78. Cenrt., N.Y., Wyo. Mem. Internat. Reading Assn., Onondaga County Assn. Children Learning Disabilities, Assn. Gifted and Talented Edn., Assn. Profl. Managerial and Exec. Women, Delta Kappa Gamma, Phi Delta Kappa. Home: 7952 Easy St Evansville WY 88636 Office: 970 N Glenn Caspet WY 82601

BUSHNELL, CATHARINE, photographer; b. Pullman, Wash., July 2, 1950; d. David and Catharine Howe (Goodfellow) B.; B.S. in Speech, Northwestern U., 1972; m. H. Michael Sisson, Oct. 31, 1975. Prodn. dept. Mike White Advt., Chgo., 1972; stage actress, Chgo., 1972-73; partner, dir. photography Mome, Raths and Outgrabe, Chgo., 1973-75; prodn. stills photographer Raggedy Ann and Andy, animated film, 1975-77; motion picture stills photographer for various feature films, N.Y.C., 1977—; v.p., creative dir. Sisson Assos., N.Y.C., 1981—; pres. Illusion Gallery, Creative Service Co., N.Y.C., 1981—; judge ann. student photog. portfolio rev. High Sch. Art and Design, N.Y.C., 1979, 80, 81, 82. Mem. Internat. Photographers Motion Picture Industry, Internat. Soc. Photography (charter), Actors Equity Assn., Northwestern U. Alumnae Assn., Delta Zeta. Author: Raggedy Ann and Andy in the Tunnel of Lost Toys, 1980; Raggedy Annand Andy and the Pirates of Outgo Inlet, 1981; Linda's Magic Window, 1981. Office: 300 E 40th St New York NY 10016

BUSSE, PATRICIA ANNETTE, med. technologist; b. Odessa, Wash., Feb. 23, 1935; d. James Gough and Olga Helen (Michaelsen) Ellis; B.S., Gonzaga U., Spokane, Wash., 1957; diploma med. tech. Sacred Heart Hosp., Spokane, 1957; m. Robert John Busse, Aug. 3, 1957; children—Cynthia Lou, Tamara Ann, Jennifer Sue. Med. technologist Med. Center Lab., Yakima, Wash., 1957—, supr., chief med. technologist, 1982—; lectr. Sch. Med. Tech., Central Wash. State U. Pres. Yakima Kindergarten Council, 1965, Gilbert Grad. Sch. PTA, Yakima, 1966; trustee Yakima Allied Arts Council, 1962-65, membership chmn., 1963; vol., parent counseling group leader Yakima County Juvenile Hall, 1966-73; sec. bd. dirs. Yakima Symphony Orch., 1976—. Recipient Outstanding Vol. Action cert., 1973. Mem. Am. Soc. Clin. Pathologists, Am. Soc. Clin. Pathology (affiliate), Yakima Jr. League. Democrat. Roman Catholic. Club: Yakima Tennis. Home: 4502 Avalanche St Yakima WA 98908 Office: 1114 W Spruce St Yakima WA 98902

BUSSER, ANN SHARON, nurse; b. Scranton, Pa., Dec. 9, 1940; d. George Edward and Margaret Mahady) May; student Marywood Coll., 1958; grad. Mercy Hosp., Scranton, 1961; m. Robert Eugene Busser, Oct. 7, 1961; children—Mauri, Lauri, Robert David. Nurse, Mercy Hosp., Scranton, 1961; team leader med. surg. unit San Gabriel (Calif.) Community Hosp., 1961-62; pvt. duty Mercy Hosp., 1963; intermitent pvt. duty, Md., 1964-74; charge nurse, admissions coordinator adolescent psychiat. nursing Edgemeade of Md., Croom, Md., 1975, 76; house supr., patient care supr. Charles County Nursing Home, LaPlata, Md., 1976-79; dir. nursing Clinton Convalescent Center (Md.), 1980—. Republican. Roman Catholic. Club: Mt. Carmel Estates Gourmet. Home: Rt 4 Box 4108 LaPlata MD 20646 Office: 9211 Stuart Ln Clinton MD 20735

BUSTIN, BEVERLY MINER, state senator; b. Morrisville, Vt., Feb. 14, 1936; d. Donald Haze and Della Mae (Kenfield) Miner; B.S., Thomas Coll.; divorced; children—Catherine Margaret, David Wayne. Vice-chmn. Kennebec County (Maine) Democratic Com., 1979—; mem. Maine Senate. Home: 6 Colony Rd Augusta ME 04330 Office: Maine State Senate State Capitol Augusta ME 04330

BUTCHER, JEANIE SUE, personal holding co., real estate cos. fin. exec.; b. Clinton, Mo., Aug. 16, 1947; d. Eugene J. and Freda A. (Wright) Tally; B.S. in Acctg., S.W.Mo. State U., 1970; m. Nov. 25, 1972 (div. 1975). Audit sr. Cooper's & Lybrand, C.P.A.'s, Kansas City, Mo., 1970-73, tax specialist, 1975-76; tax acct. Norman E. Fuller, Atty., Mission, Kans., 1974-75; treas. Kemper Investment Co., Troost Ave. Devel. Co. and Riverside Redevel. Corp. (all Kansas City, Mo.), 1976—. Com. person Women's C. of C. of Greater Kansas City (Mo.), 1972, bd. dirs., 1980—; active Jr. Achievement, 1975-76; treas. South Central region Venture Clubs Am., 1974-75; adminstrv. bd. Central United Meth. Ch., Kansas City, Mo., 1982—. Office: Suite 2222 Commerce Tower Kansas City MO 64105

BUTCHER, JOANNA VAN SMITH, advt. exec.; b. Muskogee, Okla., Jan. 28, 1912; d. Hurxthal Van Valzah and Marie (Simmons) Smith; student U. Minn., 1929-31; m. Robert K. Butcher, May 10, 1936; children—Phillip Hurxthal, John Kimberlin. Sec.-treas. Robert K. Butcher & Assos., Inc., Shreveport, La., 1958—; chmn. bd. Marie Oil Corp., Shreveport, 1959—. Bd. dirs. Shreveport Assn. Blind, Shreveport Civic Opera, Shreveport Symphony Soc., Shreveport Jr. League. Democrat. Episcopalian. Home: 921 Unadilla St Shreveport LA 71106 Office: 1615 Slattery Bldg Shreveport LA 71161

BUTCHKO, KATHRYN ANN, social worker; b. McKeesport, Pa., Feb. 18, 1938; d. Michael and Mary Elizabeth (Yurick) B.; B.A., Seton Hill Coll., Greensburg, Pa., 1959; M.S.W., U. Pitts., 1965. Probation officer Juvenile Ct. Allegheny County, Pitts., 1962-64; social worker, then exec. dir. Girls Service Club, Pitts., 1965-70; dir. social service Three Rivers Youth, Pitts., 1970-72; supr. protective services Allegheny County Adults Services, Pitts., 1973-76; asso. dir. community services Allegheny County Adult Services/Area Agy. on Aging, 1976-78, dir., 1980—; speaker in field. Mem. Nat. Assn. Social Workers, Acad. Cert. Social Workers. Roman Catholic. Home: 2386 Collins Rd Pittsburgh PA 15235 Office: 401 Wood St Pittsburgh PA 15222

BUTEL, JANE FRANZ, consumer/mktg. cons. co. exec.; b. Wamego, Kans., June 23, 1938; d. Sidney L. and Dorothy O. (Krig) Franz; B.S., Kans. State U., 1959; postgrad. U. N.Mex., 1965-68; 1 dau., Amy Elizabeth. Home service dir. Public Service Co. N.Mex., 1959-69; mgr. consumer affairs Consol. Edison Co., N.Y.C., 1969-73; mgr. major appliance bus. group Consumers Inst. Gen. Electric Co., Louisville, 1973-76; v.p. consumer affairs Am. Express Co., N.Y.C., 1976-78; pres. Jane Butel Assos., Inc., N.Y.C., 1978—, Jane Butel's Pecos River Spice Co., N.Y.C., Corrales, N.Mex., 1978—; bd. mem. Am. Nat. Standards Inst., 1977—. Bd. mem. Auburn U., 1976-78. Recipient home appliance mfg. and mag. awards, 1965, 69, 72. Mem. Am. Women in Radio and TV, Soc. Consumer Affairs Profls. in Bus., Women in Communications, Am. Council Consumer Interests, Am. Home Econs. Assn. (past pres. N.Mex. chpt.), Home Economists in Bus. (nat. meeting chmn. 1975), Greater Albuquerque C. of C. (chmn. women's com. 1964-65). Republican. Methodist. Author: Jane Butel's Tex-Mex Cookbook, 1980; Chile Madness, 1980; Tacos, Tortillas and Tostados, 1982; Finger Lickin', Rib Stickin', Great Tastin', Hot 'n Spicy Barbeque, 1982; Jane Butel's Freezer Cookbook, 1977; Favorite Mexican Foods, 1968. Home: 500 E 77th St Apt 2324 New York NY 10162 Office: 45-39 37th St Long Island City NY 11101

BUTERA, ANNE FABBRI, art mus. dir.; b. Norristown, Pa.; d. Remo and Anne W. (Butterworth) Fabbri; A.B. cum laude, Radcliffe Coll.; 1971; m. Joseph Henry Butera; children—Virginia, Remo, Joseph. Art lectr. Villanova U., Pa., 1971-73, Drexel U., Phila., 1974-76; art critic, art editor The Drummer, Phila., 1976-79; art critic The Bulletin, Phila., 1978-80; dir. Alfred O. Deshong Mus., Widener U., Chester, Pa., 1980-82, The Noyes Mus., Oceanville, N.J., 1982—. Mem. Am. Assn. Museums, Artists Equity Assn., Coll. Art Assn., Internat. Assn. Art Critics. Home: 1513 Plymouth Blvd Norristown PA 19401 Office: The Noyes Museum PO Box 283 Lily Lake Rd Oceanville NJ 08231

BUTLER, ANNA MABEL LAND (MRS. FLOYD BUTLER), author; b. Phila.; d. John Weaver and Edith Frances (Jones) Land; student Trenton State Tchrs. Coll., 1920-22, 36, Temple U., 1953, U. Md., 1942-45; m. Maurice Alexander Hayes, June 1925 (div.); 1 son, Maurice Alexander (dec. 1943); m. 2d, Floyd Butler, Mar. 10, 1935. Tchr. pub. schs., Atlantic City, 1922-64; newspaper corr. Pitts. Courier, 1936-65; Atlantic City reporter Phila. Tribune, 1965—. Mem. edn. council Human Resources Atlantic County Anti-Poverty Program, 1965—; pres. Seaboard Council Heritage House, 1954—, Atlantic City Study Center, 1959—; rec. sec. Episcopal Women, Diocese of N.J., v.p. Atlantic dist., also chmn. Christian social relations Atlantic dist. Episcopal Diocese N.J., 1975—; pres. Episcopal Churchwomen of St. Augustine's Ch., v.p. Atlantic dist., 1976—; ednl. dir. Morris Day Care Center; mem. planning com. Bal Masque, Atlantic City; mem. Atlantic County Cultural and Heritage Adv. Bd. Mem. N.J. Fedn. Colored

Women's Clubs (South Jersey state chmn. pub. relations dept.), Northside Bus. and Profl. Women's Club (pres. 1961-65, v.p. 1960-61, trustee 1971), N.J. Orgn. Tchrs. (v.p. 1960—), Nat. Assn. Negro Bus. and Profl. Women, Heritage House (pres. Eastern Seaboard council), Phila. Cotillion Soc. (dir. 1956—), Catholic Poetry Soc., Am. Poets Fellowship Soc., Atlantic City Tchrs. Assn. (life, exec. bd. 1962-64), Nat. Links (nat. chmn. creative writing 1972, pres. Atlantic City chpt. 1971—, poet laureate Eastern area 1977-79, 80-82, mem. chpt. establishment com. 1979—), Atlantic City C. of C. (chmn. judges boardwalk div., planning com. ann. children's parade), Nat. Soc. Lit. and Arts, Phi Delta Kappa. Club: Wednesday Lit. (pres. 1977). Author: Album of Love Letters—Unsent, 1952; Touchstone, 1962; High Noon, 1970; poems pub. in various anthologies; editor: Responsibility, 1955-59, asso. editor 1953—; Eastern area editor Nat. Links Jours., 1968—. Initiator 1st Black history news scrapbook contest for jr. high sch. students, also Butler poetry contest, 1970. Home: 410 N Kentucky Ave Atlantic City NJ 08401

BUTLER, CAROL ANN MARINO, psychotherapist; b. N.Y.C., Mar. 14, 1942; d. Anthony Aloysis and Madeline Gladys (Pearlmuter) Marino; B.A., Queens Coll., 1962; M.A., N.Y. U., 1967, Ph.D., 1970; m. Sept. 10, 1961; children—Adam, Aisha. Correctional vocat. rehab. specialist N.Y. State Employment Service, 1963-65; counselor, supr. Springfield Coll. Guidance Center, N.Y.C., 1965-67; pvt. practice psychoanalysis and psychotherapy, N.Y.C., 1967—; adj. asst. prof. N.Y. U., 1970-72. Recipient Founders Day award N.Y. U., 1970; cert. Washington Square Inst. for Psychotherapy and Mental Health, 1970, Nat. Accreditation Assn. Psychoanalysis, 1976. Mem. Am. Psychol. Assn., Nat. Accreditation Assn. for Psychoanalysis, N.Y. Acad. Sci. Office: 60 W 13th St New York NY 10011

BUTLER, CAROL DENTON, social ins. adminstr.; b. York, Nebr., Apr. 8, 1931; d. Robert Ralph and Fern V. (Mann) Denton; B.A. summa cum laude, York Coll., 1952; m. Charles Farrell Butler, Jan. 17, 1959; children—Robert Charles, Julie Ann. Reporter, staff asst. York (Nebr.) Daily News Times, 1952-54; claims rep. Social Security Adminstrn., Lincoln, Nebr., 1955-57, disability examiner, cons., policy specialist, staff assoc., Balt., 1957-69, sect. chief disability operations, 1970, chief med. policy, 1971-74, chief rehab. div., 1974-76, dep. asst. bur. dir. fed./state programs, 1976-78, dep. asst., bur. dir. systems and methods, 1978-79, dir. office pub. concerns, 1979—. Counselor, Howard County Sexual Assault Center, 1976-79, bd. dirs., 1979-82, pres. bd., 1981-82; mem. Md. Gov's. Adv. Bd. on Rape and Sexual Offenses, 1982-84. Recipient Commrs. Citations, Social Security Adminstrn., 1968, 78. Mem. ACLU, Soc. Preservation Md. Antiquities, Image de Balt., Am. Fedn. Govt. Employees, Alpha Chi.

BUTLER, ELAINE RUTH MARJORIE MALLORY (MRS. HAROLD ARTHUR BUTLER), civic worker; b. North Bergen, N.J., July 2; d. Eugene Lester and Adele May (Reeder) Mallory; A.B., Barnard Coll., 1930; postgrad. Montclair Coll., 1932; M.S., N.Y. Sch. Social Work, 1935; postgrad. Seton Hall U., 1939, 53; M.S., Newark State Coll., Union, N.J., 1959; postgrad. San German U., P.R., 1959; postgrad. No. Ariz. U., 1976, Scottsdale Community Coll., 1978; m. Harold Arthur Butler, Feb. 17, 1928; 1 dau., Dellamay Dorothy Butler Seibold. Tchr., Horace Mann Sch., Tchrs. Coll., N.Y.C., 1926; statistician, confidential sec. Boy Scouts Am., N.Y.C., 1927-30; investigator Tenement Housing Authority for N.Y. Assembly, 1927; tchr. elem. and secondary schs., coll., N.J., 1932-37; social worker N.J. Dept. Instns. and Agys., Trenton, 1937-48; adminstrv. sec. N.J. Heart Assn., Newark, 1948-51; tchr. specialist Montclair Pub. Schs., 1953-64; free-lance writer, artist, 1964—(paints under name Le Boutiliere). Worker, Gompers Rehab. Inst., Phoenix, 1966; mem. aux. Goodwill Industries, Phoenix, 1968—, YWCA, 1972—; chmn. Fun for Funds and Bridge Builders, Phoenix, 1966—, Juvenile Detention Homes For Boys and Girls, 1972—, Half-Way House for Ex-Felons, Phoenix vol. Community Orgn. for Drug Abuse Control; v.p. Ariz. Citizens Self Help Now; adv. bd. Save-A-Child-League, Loretta Young Project; sec. New Brunswick (N.J.) Democratic Club, 1939; campaign mgr. South Orange Village Council, 1955; bd. dirs. 7th Step Found., 1974—, sec., 1977—; treas. Ariz. Women in Transition, 1974—; bd. dirs. Northwoods Inst. Music, 1982—. Recipient cert. of honor Bd. Edn., Montclair, N.J., 1964, numerous service awards. Mem. Nat. Assn. Ret. Fed. Employees (sec. Phoenix chpt. 1965-69, 2d v.p. 1981—, sec. treas. Ariz. Fedn. 1969-71, charter mem. Scottsdale 1972—, sec.-treas. 1972-73, nat. editor monthly newsletter 1979-80, contbg. mem., del., 2d v.p. Phoenix chpt.), Seven Coll. Conf., Nat., N.J. Montclair edn. assns., Scottsdale, Valley Artists leagues, Franklin Mint. Soc. (charter), Friends for Terros Aux. (charter), Phoenix Art Mus., Friends Mexican Art, Internat. Platform Assn., Ariz. Poets, Musicians and Artists Assn., Heard Mus., AAUW. Republican. Presbyterian (fellowship chmn. 1965-66, coordinator for Involvement in Action 1966-68). Clubs: Orange Lawn Tennis (South Orange, N.J.), College of Oranges (West Orange, N.J.); Scottsdale College. Home: 4015 E Sierra Vista Dr Scottsdale AZ 85253 also Las Conchas Puerto Penasco Mexico also Kauii Hawaii

BUTLER, ELENORA STEINMEYER, interior designer; b. Chgo., June 9, 1904; d. Paul George and Anna (Boltz) Steinmeyer; student Northwestern U., 1921-22, U. Ill., 1922-23, Rosary Coll., 1924-25, Art Inst. Chgo., 1925-27; m. Max Clear Butler, Feb. 8, 1930. Tchr. Art Inst. Chgo., 1926; design and instr. Pebbles Decorating Co., Oak Park, Ill., 1930-31, owner, mgr. interior designer div., Oak Park, 1931-42; interior designer Watson & Boaler, Chgo., 1944-54, owner, mgr. firm, Chgo., 1954-74; owner, mgr. Elenora Butler, Oak Park, 1974—; lectr. and cons. in field. Mem. Am. Soc. Interior Designers, Nat. Trust for Historic Preservation, Art Inst. Chgo., Frank Lloyd Wright Found. Republican. Presbyterian. Clubs: Garden, 19th Century (Oak Park). Exibition batik Art Inst. Chgo., 1926, paintings St. Louis Art Mus., 1943. Home and Office: 511 N Grove Ave Oak Park IL 60302

BUTLER, ELIZABETH ANN, oil and gas co. exec.; b. Meridian, Miss., Sept. 10, 1932; d. Franklin Walter and Serena (Hopper) McGee; B.S. in Geology, Millsaps Coll., Jackson, Miss., 1955; M.S. in Geology, La. State U., 1957; m. William Bradley Butler, III, Apr. 21, 1951; 1 dau., Barbara. Research geologist La. Geol. Survey, 1957-63; sr. research geologist, then supr. paleontology Sinclair Research Co., Tulsa, 1963-69; with Atlantic Richfield Co., 1969-81, exec. asst. to exec. v.p. natural resources, 1977-80, sr. planning cons. corp. planning, 1980-81; mgr. stratigraphy and paleontology Arco Exploration Co., Dallas, 1981—. Mem. Am. Assn. Petroleum Geologists, Soc. Econ. Palentologists and Mineralogists, Sigma Xi, Eta Sigma Phi. Republican. Baptist. Clubs: Brookhaven Country, Lancers (Dallas); Petroleum (Los Angeles). Author articles in field. Office: ARB 2857 PO Box 2819 Dallas TX 75221

BUTLER, IDELLE FLINN, social worker; b. Urbana, Ill., Feb. 26, 1943; s. Lewis Edward and Florence Idelle (Bridson) Flinn; B.S., Ill. Wesleyan U., 1964; M.S.W., U. Ill., 1966: m. Edward Saxe Butler, Aug. 22, 1964; children—Edward Travis, Kerry Elizabeth. Social worker Park Ridge Sch. for Girls, 1966-73, Arapahoe Community Services, Englewood, Colo., 1976-77; psychiat. social worker Research Med. Center, Kansas City, Mo., 1980—. Chmn. S.E.L.F. Jobs. NIMH grad. fellow, 1964-66. Mem. AAUW, Acad. Cert. Social Workers, Nat. Register Certified Clin. Social Workers, Nat. Assn. Social Workers. Home: 8820 Carriage Dr Lenexa KS 66215

BUTLER, JOSEPHINE DENATALE, dance educator; b. N.Y.C., Mar. 12, 1911; d. Domenico Tommaso and Maria Adelina deNatale; student Traphagen Sch. Fashion, N.Y.C., 1928-32, N.Y. U., 1939-40; m. Albert Shreve Butler, July 19, 1937. Fashion stylist Amos Parrish Fashion Cons., N.Y.C., 1932-36; tchr., historian Albert Butler Sch. Dancing, N.Y.C., 1936—, also dir. Recipient Dance Masters of Am. awards, 1968, 72. Mem. Inst. Social Dance Studies (pres.), Internat. Dance Council, Dance Masters Am., Am. Alliance Health, Phys. Edn. and Recreation and Dance. Author: (with Albert Butler) Encyclopedia of Social Dance, 1971, 75, 80; contbr. articles in field to profl. jours. Home: 60 W 57th St New York NY 10019 Office: 24 W 57th St New York NY 10019

BUTLER, MARGARET KAMPSCHAEFER, computer scientist; b. Evansville, Ind., Mar. 7, 1924; d. Otto Louis and Lou Etta (Rehsteiner) Kampschaefer; A.B., Ind. U., 1944; postgrad. Dept. Agr. Grad. Sch., 1945, U. Chgo., 1949, U. Minn., 1950; m. James W. Butler, Sept. 30, 1951; 1 son, Jay. Statistician, U.S. Bur. Labor Statistics, Washington, 1945-46, U.S. Air Forces in Europe, Erlangen and Wiesbaden, Germany, 1946-48, U.S. Bur. Labor Statistics, St. Paul, 1949-51; mathematician Argonne (Ill.) Nat. Lab., 1948-49, 51-80, sr. computer scientist, 1980—, dir. Nat. Energy Software Center Dept. Energy Computer Program Exchange, 1960—; cons. AMF Corp., 1956-57, OECD, 1964, 81, Poole Bros., 1967. Treas. Timberlake Civic Assn., 1958; rep. mem. nominating com. Hinsdale (Ill.) Caucus, 1961-62; coordinator 6th dist. Equal Rights Amendment, 1974-82; Ill. del. Nat. Women's Conf., 1977; elected Ill. del. Rep. Nat. Conv., 1980. Fellow Am. Nuclear Soc. (chmn. math. and computation div. 1966-67, dir. 1976-79, mem. exec. com. 1977-78, chmn. bylaws and rules com. 1979-82, publs. reviewer); mem. Assn. Computing Machinery (exec. com., sec. Chgo. chpt. 1963-65, publs. chmn. nat. conf. 1968; publs. reviewer), LWV, Assn. Women in Sci. (pres. Chgo. area chpt. 1982—), Women's Polit. Caucus. Editor: Computer Physics Communications, 1969-79; contbr. chpts. to Problems in Reactor Physics, 1968, Advances in Nuclear Science and Technology, 1976; contbr. articles to profl. publs. Home: 17W139 Hillside Ln Hinsdale IL 60521 Office: 9700 S Cass Ave Argonne IL 60439

BUTLER, MATILDA LOU, psychologist, educator; b. Oklahoma City, Feb. 5, 1942; d. Edward Ainsworth and Flossie Jewel (Calderhead) Butler; student U. Okla., 1960-62; B.S. magna cum laude, Boston U., 1964; M.A., Stanford, 1966; Ph.D., Northwestern U., 1970; m. William John Paisley, Oct. 16, 1970; children—Kenneth Earl, Edward Ainsworth, William John. Research asso. psychology dept. Stanford U., 1970, lectr., research asso. Inst. for Communication Research, 1971-77; research asso. U. Calif. at Berkeley Grad. Sch. Pub. Policy, 1971; v.p. Applied Communication research, 1974-77; v.p. Far West Lab. for Ednl. Research and Devel., San Francisco, 1977—, dir., 1982—, dir. women and minorities mgmt./leadership program, 1977-78, leader women's concerns component, 1977-81, health edn. component, 1977-81, dir. Women's Ednl. Equity Communications Network, 1977-80, chmn. tech. and communications dept., 1980-82, dir. research and devel. div., 1982—; pres. Edupro, 1982—; cons. Coll. Bds., Lockheed-Technicon Info. Systems, Palo Alto Unified Sch. Dist., Nat. Cancer Inst., Nat. Center Health Services Research. NIMH trainee. Mem. Am. Psychol. Assn., Am. Assn. Pub. Opinion Research (program chmn. Pacific chpt. 1972, council mem. 1975), Assn. for Edn. in Journalism (co-chmn. com. status women 1975), Internat. Communication Assn. (co-chmn. com. status women in communications 1975-76), Am. Ednl. Research Assn., ALA, Am. Soc. for Info. Sci. (cabinet rep.), Am. Assn. Higher Edn. Author: (with W. Paisley) Women and the Mass Media: Sourcebook for Research and Action, 1980, Knowledge Utilization in Education: Dissemination, Technical Assistance, Networking, 1982. Home: 717 Charleston Ct Palo Alto CA 94303 Office: PO Box 51346 Palo Alto CA 94303

BUTLER, NATALIE STURGES (MRS. BENJAMIN BUTLER), writer; b. Melrose, Mass., July 13, 1908; d. Dwight Case and Clare (Vaughan) Sturges; student Vesper George Art Sch., 1926-28 M.A. (hon.), U. Maine at Farmington, 1972; m. Benjamin Butler, May 23, 1932; children—Diane-Clare (Mrs. Carl Alexander Brinkman), Benjamin Sturges. Librarian, decorator Irving & Casson-A.H. Davenport Co., Boston, 1928-31; pres. Sturdia Corp., Farmington, Maine, 1955—. County chmn. Maine Sesquicentennial Com., 1970; sec. Maine Citizens for Historic Preservation, 1971; sec., curator Red Schoolhouse Com., 1970—; trustee Farmington Pub. Library Assn., 1950—, treas., 1958-74, sec., 1958-77; trustee Franklin County Meml. Hosp., 1963-70; trustee Maine League Hist. Socs. and Museums, 1973-77; mem. Maine State Mus. Commn., 1974-77; co-chmn. Union Baptist Ch. of Farmington Falls Restoration Project, 1976-78. Recipient (with Ben Butler) Outstanding Service award Maine Historic Preservation Commn., 1973. Mem. Maine Soc. Mayflower Descs., Maine Hist. Soc., New Eng. Historic and Geneal. Soc., John Howland Soc., Delta Kappa Gamma (hon.). Republican. Conglist. (deaconess 1963-68). Author: (with Ben Butler) History of Old South Church Farmington, 5 Historical Farmington Pilgrimage Books (certificate of commendation Am. Assn. for State and Local History 1970), Little Red Schoolhouse Museum, 1971; Dwight Sturges, Etcher on an Era, 1974; (with Ben Butler) Zephaniah Builds a Schoolhouse, 1975, The Falls: Where Farmington, Maine, Began in 1776, 1976; Farmington's Musical Heritage, 1975. Contbr. to newspapers and mags. Home: 93 Main St Farmington ME 04938

BUTLER, PAMELA ELLEN, clin. psychologist; b. Tuscaloosa, Ala., Dec. 1, 1946; d. Henry W. and Chlora B. (Brown) B.; B.S., U. Ala., 1967, M.A., 1969, Ph.D., 1971; NIMH postdoctoral fellow U. Calif., Berkeley, 1971. Asst. dir. Behavior Therapy Inst., Sausalito, Calif., 1972-77, dir., 1977-79; pvt. practice clin. psychology, pres. Pamela E. Butler, Ph.D. Inc., Mill Valley, Calif., 1979—; instr. U. Calif. extensions Davis and Santa Cruz; lectr. on assertive communication to profl. and civic groups. Recipient award for outstanding instr. U. Calif., Davis, 1979. Mem. Am. Psychol. Assn., Calif. Psychol. Assn., Assn. for Advancement of Behavior Therapy, Behavior Therapy and Research Soc. (clin. fellow), Profl. Women's Network, Phi Beta Kappa. Author: Self Assertion for Women, 1976; Talking to Yourself, 1981; contbr. chpt. to book in field. Office: 150 Shoreline Highway A-7 Mill Valley CA 94941

BUTLER, REBECCA BATTS, ednl. cons.; b. Norfolk, Va.; d. William and Gussie Batts; diploma Va. State Coll., 1933; B.S., Glassboro (N.J.) State Coll., 1942; M.Ed., Temple U., 1950, Ed.D., 1965; m. Robert Butler (dec.). Tchr. one room sch., Charlotte County, Va., 1930-32, Caroline County, Va., 1933-35; tchr. Norfolk (Va.) Public Schs., 1935-36; tchr. and guidance counselor, Camden, N.J., 1937-65, supr. guidance, 1966-68; dir. State N.J. Adult Learning Center, Camden, 1968-69; dir. adult continuing community edn. program, Camden, 1969-74; adj. prof. Glassboro State Coll., 1971-82; ednl. cons., 1974—; condr. workshops. Trustee, Thomas Edison Coll., N.J., 1973-76; pres. Vis. Nurses and Health Assn. Camden County, 1974-82; bd. dirs. Camden County chpt. ARC, 1970-82, Planned Parenthood, 1970—; nat. trustee Andrus Found., 1980—; civilian mem. adv. com. on women to Sec. Def., 1972-74; del. 1981 White House Conf. on Aging. Recipient numerous awards, including: Vol. Service award United Way, 1978; Achievement award N.J. Elks, 1977; Woman of Year, Zeta Phi Beta, 1977; Humanitarian award N.J. conf. United A.M.E. Chs., 1977. Mem. Am. Assn. Ret. Persons (chairperson nat. com., nat. dir. 1980—), AAUW, Nat. Assn. Adult Continuing Pub. Edn., Nat. Assn. Negro Bus. and Profl. Women's Clubs (Woman of Year 1982), Nat. Hook-up of Black Women (dir.), Phi Delta Kappa (nat. editor-in-chief 1973-77, nat. and regional chairperson second careers com. 1979—). Mem. African Methodist Episcopal Ch. Club: Cherry Hill Maturity. Address: 15 Eddy Ln Cherry Hill NJ 08002

BUTLER, VIRGINIA STEWART, govt. ofcl.; b. Bracey, Va., Oct. 18, 1926; d. James Andrew and Odell Eunice (King) Stewart; student Am. U., 1949-50; m. Bernard W. Butler, June 6, 1954; children—Eric S., Lisa D. With Dept. State, 1943—, publs. supply officer analysis and reference, 1960-71, chief publs. distbn. br., 1971—; dir., chmn. credit com. Dept. State Fed. Credit Union. Recipient Commendable Service award Dept. State, 1963, Human Rights award, 1975, EEO award, 1982; named Bus. Woman of Yr. 1976. Mem. Potomac Bus. and Profl. Women's Club (pres. 1974-76), Nat. Council Negro Women (life), Credit Women Internat., Pan Am. Liaison Orgn., Urban League, NAACP. Democrat. Episcopalian. Home: 4914 8th St NE Washington DC 20017 Office: 2201 C St NW Washington DC 20520

BUTTERWORTH, NONA ANGEL, artist; b. Spartanburg, S.C., Jan. 28, 1929; d. James Oscar and Joyce (Beatty) Angel; student Randolph Macon's Womans Coll., 1947-49, Ringling Sch. Art, 1949-50, Art Students League, N.Y.C., 1950-51; m. James Ebert Butterworth, Jr., Dec. 18, 1954; children—James Ebert III, Alison Angel, Joy Evans. Jr. curator art Pack Meml. Library, Asheville, N.C.. 1951-52; artist. advt. dept. Ivey's Dept. Store, Asheville, 1952-53; comml. artist Ayer & Gillette advt. agy., Charlotte, N.C. 1953-55; one woman show Charlotte Country Club, 1972, Charlotte Country Day Sch., 1977, Copeland House Art Gallery, 1982; exhibited in group shows First Union Bank, Charlotte, 1973, 74, 75, 76, 77, Wachovia Bank, 1975, WSOC-TV, 1975-78; Lincolnton (N.C.) City Hall, 1974, 75, N.C. Nat. Bank, 1971, 72, 76-77, Charlotte Festival in the Park, 1972-77, Spl. Bicentennial Invitational Exhibit Queens Coll., 1976, N.C. Watercolor Show, High Point, 1976, Greenville, 1977, Davidson Coll., 1979; represented in permanent collections, Phila., Charlotte, Asheville, Gastonia; tchr. art, children Mint Museum, Charlotte, 1973-76, Charlotte Country Day Sch., 1975-76, 77; watercolor tchr. Central Piedmont Community Coll., 1981—; pvt. tchr. art; free-lance writer Charlotte Mag., 1981-82. Pres. Friends of Mint Museum, 1972-73; v.p. Artists Guild, 1973-74, 2d v.p. Womens Aux. Mint Mus., 1975-76, chmn. overseas tours, 1975—; chmn. Christ Episcopal Ch. Fair, 1968; bd. dirs. Womens Assn. Charlotte Symphny, also co-chmn. Symphony Designerhouse, 1975; mem. artists' adv. bd. Mint Mus., 1977—; bd. dirs. Arts and Sci. Council, 1978-81. Recipient Merit award Pa. State Hort. Soc., 1966; Purchase award Mint Mus., 1977; 1st prize WSOC-TV Invitational, 1978. Mem. Guild Charlotte Artists (dir., pres. 1976-77), Affiliates Arts and Sci. Council (sec. exec. com. 1977—), N.C. Watercolor Soc. (sec., dir. 1978-79), Jr. League, Charlotte Writer's Club (pres. 1982-84, 1st prize children's story contest 1981). Republican. Epsicopalian. Club: Charlotte Country. Home: 1438 Queens Rd W Charlotte NC 28207

BUTTERWORTH, PAMELA JEAN, ednl. adminstr., communications cons., human resource cons./trainer; b. Mineola, N.Y., Oct. 17, 1947; d. John F. and Anna L. (Paul) B.; B.S. in Edn., U. Kans., 1969; M.A. with honors in Ednl. Tech., San Diego State U., 1976. Tchr. Aurora (Colo.) primary and secondary public schs., 1969-75, media specialist, 1975—; media cons. to firm Holland and Hart, 1979; cert. cons./trainer Performax Systems Internat., Personal Dynamics Inst., Personal Growth Found., Profl. Edn. Inst. Founder Com. for Denver Arts, 1973, chairperson, 1977-80; mem. planning com. Arapahoe Chamber Orch., 1978—; bd. dirs. Bonfils Theater, Aurora, Colo., 1978—, Republican Assocs., 1976—; founder Fox Hunt, 1977, chmn., 1977-80. Nominated Best Actress award Players Club, 1972. Mem. Am. Soc. Tng. and Devel., Assn. Ednl. Communication and Tech., Nat. Assn. for Female Execs., Colo. Ednl. Media Assn. Club: Internat. Athletic. Home: 105 S Eagle Circle Aurora CO 80012

BUTTNER, ELEANOR HOLLINGSWORTH, educator; b. Balt., Apr. 30, 1953; d. Walter Douglas and Sarah Alexander (Russell) B.; B.A., Hollins (Va.) Coll., 1975; M.B.A., U. Pa., 1977. Instr. Radford (Va.) U., 1977-79; treas., dir. Camp Atahi, Inc., Conway, N.H., 1977-80; asst. prof. mgmt. and stats. Merrimack Coll., North Andover, Mass., 1979—. Recipient Elizabeth Kennedy Chance award Hollins Coll., 1975. Mem. NOW (treas. Greater Lawrence chpt. 1980—), AAUW (corp. rep. 1980—), ACLU. Republican. Presbyterian. Clubs: Appalachin Mountain, Appalachin Trail Conf. Contbr. articles to profl. publs. Home: 413 Hawthorn Rd Baltimore MD 21210 Office: Dept Mgmt Merrimack Coll North Andover MA 01845

BUTTON, MARIAN LUCILLE, mayor; b. Topeka, Oct. 15, 1930; d. Richard Maurice and Lucille Alice (Rose) Sears; B.S., Kans. State U., Manhattan, 1951; m. Donald Jack Button, Dec. 28, 1950; children—Amy Lynn, Daniel Jack, John Compton. Mem. Plainville (Kans.) Sch. Bd., 1959-65; sec. Kans. Corrections Ombudsman Bd., 1978-81; commr. City of Newton (Kans.), 1979-82, vice mayor, 1979-80, mayor, 1982—. Republican precinct woman, 1970-78; mem. Kans. Rep. Exec. Com., 1976-78, del., Rep. Nat. Conv., 1976; chmn. Harvey County Rep. Party, 1980-82; mem. ch. and society com. 1st United Methodist Ch., Newton, 1978-82; mem. Kans. State U. Legis. Network, 1978-82. Mem. Kans. League Municipalities, Newton C. of C. (chmn. legis. affairs com. 1982), Kans. State U. Alumni Assn., Pi Beta Phi. Clubs: Ladies Reading Circle (pres. 1982), Roundtable (pres. 1970). Home: 401 E 2d St Newton KS 67114

BUTTORFF, MERCY LYNNE, home economist, educator, businesswoman; b. Malden, Mo., Apr. 12, 1944; d. Fay Hatch and Mercy (Sargent) Johnson; B.S. in Home Econs., U. Utah, 1967; postgrad. Utah State U., 1970-77; m. Roy John Buttorff, Aug. 29, 1967; children—Mercy Anne, Jefferson Lee, Braxton John. Tchr., curriculum writer Granite Sch. Dist., Salt Lake City, 1967—, Valley Jr. High Sch., 1967-70, Valley Jr. High Sch., 1970-71, Kearns High Sch., 1971-75, Young Mothers Programs, 1970-75; freelance home economist educator, Salt Lake City, 1975—; career tchr. Granger High Sch., 1978—; pres. Buttorff & Johnson Enterprises Inc., 1979—; asst. Dian Thomas Enterprises; cons. Utah Bd. Edn.; commd. curriculum writer; cons. Festival of the Arts; tchr. Utah Girls' Village for delinquent teenage girls; tchr. sr. citizens, low-income mothers; author plays and musicals for schs. and religious groups. Active, Internat. Women's Yr. Named Nat. Home Econs. Tchr. of Yr., 1974, Utah Home Econs. Tchr. of Yr., 1974, by Am. Home Econs. Assn. and Family Circle Mag. Mem. Am. Home Econs. Assn., Utah Vocat. Assn., Delta Kappa Gamma. Mormon. Author: Being On Your Own; The First Six Months of Life; The Fascinating World of Home Economics Careers. Home and Office: 6902 S 2510 E Salt Lake City UT 84121

BUTTS, PRISCILLA ANN, nurse; b. McIntyre, Ga., Feb. 5, 1949; d. James and Eva (Wright) B.; B.S.N. cum laude, Dillard U., 1970; M.S.N., U. Pa., 1972; postgrad. N.Y. U., 1980—. Staff nurse dept. ob-gyn, Baldwin County Hosp., Milledgeville, Ga., 1971; clin. supr. Hosp. of Med. Coll. Pa., Phila., 1972-74; clin. supr. maternal-infant and gynecol. nursing Thomas Jefferson U. Hosp., Phila., 1974-78, acting asst. dir. nursing, cardiopulmonary care program, 1979-80, asst. dir. nursing, women and children care program, 1978-79; preceptor Boston U. Baccalaureate Sch. Nursing, 1977-78; mem. faculty Med. Coll., Thomas Jefferson U., 1977-79; mem. faculty perinatal sect. U. Pa. Sch. Nursing, 1981—; lectr. continuing edn. for nurses. Mem. Garden Ct. Plaza Tenants Assn. Rita E. Miller scholar, 1967; Crown Zellerbach Found. scholar, 1968; Am. Nurses Assn. fellow 1981—. Mem. Am. Nurses Assn. (dist. public relations com. 1974-75, dist. program com. 1974-75, chairperson dist. fund raising com. 1975, chairperson state commn.

nursing practice 1974-77, mem. physician-nurse liaison com. of Pa. Med. Soc. 1974-76; legis. intern D.C.). Nurses Assn. of Am. Coll. Obstetricians and Gynecologists, Internat. Childbirth Edn. Assn., Council High Risk Perinatal Nurses (communication cons., newsletter editor 1982-84), Am. Acad. Polit. Sci., ASPO (Lamaze) (mem nat. conv. and program planning com.), Nat. Black Nurses Assn., Nat. League for Nursing, Sigma Theta Tau (chpt. joint project com. 1972-73, chpt. 2d v.p. and editor newsletter 1974-75, editorial bd. Image mag. 1975-80, nat. ednl. devel. com. 1980-82, regional chpt. coordinating com. 1982—, founders award com. 1977, 79, Alpha Kappa Mu, Alpha Kappa Alpha (scholar 1968). Democrat. Baptist. Author: High Risk Perinatology, 1981. Contbr. articles to profl. jours. Home: 4701 Pine St Philadelphia PA 19143

BUTTS, VIRGINIA, public relations specialist; b. Chgo.; B.A., U. Chgo. TV producer, writer, performer Chgo. CBS Outlet, Dave Garroway's NBC Radio Show; midwest public relations dir. Time-Life Publs., 1956-63; public relations dir. Field Enterprises, Chgo. Sun-Times and Daily News, 1963-74, v.p. public relations and public affairs Field Enterprises, Inc., Chgo., 1974—. Mem. Public Relations Soc. Am. Address: Field Enterprises Inc 401 N Wabash Ave Chicago IL 60611 *

BUTZ, LINDA JENKINS, data processing co. exec.; b. Statesville, N.C., Mar. 5, 1939; d. Horace Yount and Sarah Elizabeth Jenkins; student Mitchell Coll., 1958, Statesville Bus. Sch., 1961; m. Charles Henry Butz, July 13, 1968; children—Thomas Lee, Randal Dean, Martin Scott, Pamela Anne, Kelle Brenning. Model, Marians & Spainhour, Statesville, 1958-62; exec. sec. to pres. Carolina Wire & Cable, Charlotte, N.C., 1967-69, purchasing agt., asst. plant mgr., 1970-72; pres. Computer Oriented Services, Charlotte, 1973—. Mem. Data Processing Mgrs. Assn. (sec., treas. 1979-80, pres. 1980-81). Republican. Episcopalian. Club: Waxhaw Women's. Office: 5435 77 Center Dr 50 Charlotte NC 28210

BUXBAUM, ELAINE LUKACH, social worker; b. New Brunswick, N.J., Aug. 20, 1948; d. Peter and Helen Grace (Molnar) Lukach; B.A., Douglass Coll., 1970; M.S.W., Rutgers U., 1977; m. Kenneth Buxbaum, Jan. 29, 1971; children—Alyssa Kathryn, Stephen Lukach. Evaluator spl. programs New Brunswick Public Schs., 1970-71; caseworker, asst. supr. N.J. div. Youth and Family Services, New Brunswick, 1971-77; social worker, parent trainer Project POPE, Bricktown, N.J., 1978—. Mem. Nat. Assn. Social Workers, Acad. Cert. Social Workers. Democrat. Roman Catholic. Home: RD 5 Box 70-R Jackson NJ 08527 Office: 345 Chambersbridge Rd Bricktown NJ 08723

BUXBAUM, LINDA ZELFMAN, computer co. exec.; b. New Haven, Conn., Aug. 26, 1937; s. Albert A. and Esther H. (Rozen) Zelfman; B.A., Smith Coll., 1959; M.A., Fairleigh Dickinson U., 1968; postgrad. Clark U., 1979—; m. Paul Buxbaum, Sept. 7, 1958; children—Laurel, Mark, Rebecca; m. 2d, Welles Hotchkiss, Oct. 23, 1977. Public info. officer Morristown Public Schs., 1967-68; copywriter W.C. McDade Inc., 1968-69; public info. officer Coll. Entrance Examin. Bd., Waltham, Mass., 1971-74; editor Biomedical Insight, Cambridge, Mass., 1974-76; mktg. mgr. Digital Equipment Corp., Hudson, N.H., 1977—, Mem. Morris County Democratic Com., 1960-64, Sudbury (Mass.) Dem. Town Com., 1972-76; dir. Congregation Bethel, 1972-82. Mem. Assn. Bus. and Profl. Advertisers, Advt. Research Found. Jewish. Clubs: Concord Smith, Action for Soviet Jewry. Author: Biomedical and Health Care Marketplace Guide, 1975. Home: 10 Nashoba Rd Sudbury MA 01776 Office: 5 Flagstone Dr Hudson NH 03051

BUXTON, VIRGINIA MARIE, indsl. psychologist; b. Phila., May 18, 1952; d. Robert Stevens and Dorothy Louise (Miller) B.; B.S., Pa. State U., 1974; M.A., U. Md., 1977, Ph.D., 1979. Research cons. Personnel Decisions Research Inst., Mpls., 1978-79; personnel research specialist Standard Oil Co. (Ohio), Cleve., 1979-81, staff tng. asso., 1981—. Lic. psychologist, Ohio. Mem. Am. Psychol. Assn. (indsl. organizational psychology). Home: 11900 Edgewater Dr Lakewood OH 44107 Office: 5 SI Midland Bldg Cleveland OH 44115

BUYER, SUSAN PATTERSON, health care agy. program exec.; b. Paterson, N.J., Nov. 8, 1949; d. Edward Michael and Marilyn Patterson (Stier) B.; student Wellesley Coll., 1967-69; B.A. in Polit. Sci., George Washington U., 1971, M.A. in Health Care Adminstrn., 1975; m. Eugene A. Slater, Feb. 9, 1980; 1 dau., Laura Patterson. Mgmt. intern. NIH, Bethesda, Md., 1971-72; sr. program analyst planning office, Nat. Library Medicine, Bethesda, Md., 1972—. Recipient Sustained High Quality Work Performance award Nat. Library Medicine, 1980. Mem. Am. Pub. Health Assn., NOW, Nat. Assn. Female Execs., Am. Soc. Pub. Adminstrn., Nat. Abortion Rights Action League. Office: 8600 Rockville Pike Bethesda MD 20209

BUYSE, MARYLOU, pediatrician, clin. geneticist; b. N.Y.C., June 27, 1946; d. George J. and Barbara M. (Sauer) B.; A.B., Hunter Coll., 1966; M.D., Med. Coll. Pa., 1970; m. Carl N. Edwards, Jan. 22, 1982. Intern, U. Mich., 1970-71; resident in pediatrics Los Angeles County-U. So. Calif. Med. Center, 1971-73, fellow, 1973-75; instr. Boston U., 1975; asst. prof. pediatrics U. So. Calif., 1973-75, Tufts U., 1976—; coordinator Myelodysplasia Clinic, Tufts-New Eng. Med. Center, Boston, 1976-79, dir. Cystic Fibrosis Clinic and staff pediatrician Center for Genetic Counseling and Birth Defects Evaluation, 1975-82, med. dir. Center for Birth Defects Info. Service, 1978-82, dir. center, 1982—; mem. med. adv. bd. Mass. Cystic Fibrosis Found.; cons. in field. Recipient Physicians Recognition award AMA, 1975. Diplomate Am. Bd. Clin. Genetics. Fellow Am. Acad. Pediatrics, Mass. Med. Soc.; mem. Am. Assn. Mental Deficiency, Am. Med. Woman's Assn., Am. Soc. Human Genetics, AAAS, N.Y. Acad. Scis., Soc. Med. Decision Making, Am. Cleft Palate Assn., Teratology Soc., Common Cause. Asso. editor Birth Defects Compendium, 2d edit., 1979; asso. editor Syndrome Identification Jour., 1977-82, editor, 1982—. ; editor Jour. Clin. Dysmophology, 1982—. Office: 171 Harrison Ave Boston MA 02111

BYARS, FRANCES CAROL, med. technologist; b. Calhoun City, Miss., Dec. 10, 1932; d. John G. and Elvie I. (Barton) Putman; B.S. in Bacteriology, Miss. State Coll. for Women, 1954; cert. Hendrick Meml. Hosp., 1958; m. Larry Byars, Dec. 17, 1955; children—John Randolph, Donna Dianne. Chief med. technologist Houston Hosp., 1954-56, Hendrick Meml. Hosp., Abilene, Tex., 1956-59; head bacteriology dept., tchr. med. tech. Coahoma County Hosp., Calrksdale, Miss., chief med. tech., 1959-61; med. technologist Jackson (Tenn.) County Hosp., 1961-63, Children's Hosp., Birmingham, Ala., 1963-64, part-time, 1964-68; chief med. tech. Shades Mountain Clinic, 1968-75; head lab. Vestavia Pediatric P.A., Birmingham, Ala., 1975—. Mem. Am. Soc. Clin. Pathologists, Am. Soc. Med. Tech. Baptist. Address: 1915 Buttercup Dr Birmingham AL 35216

BYARS, ILA PEARL, orgn. exec., civic worker; b. Travis, Tex., June 25, 1908; d. William Lafayette and Sibyl Allen (Massey) B.; student public schs. With Mid-west States Telephone Co., Blanco, 1924-53; with Bigden Ins. and Real Estate, Tex., 1953-55; pvt. kindergarten tchr., Blanco, 1955-56; waitress various restaurants, 1956-62, 63-65; with Wall Furniture, also Wall Funeral Home, Blanco, 1952-53, 65-66; staff food dept. Blanco Mill Nursing Home, 1966—. County chmn. Am. Heart Assn., 1957-72, meml. and campaign mgr., 1957-72; bd. dirs. Blanco County unit Am. Cancer Soc., 1959-72, unit sec., 1971-74, pres., 1974-76; trustee Blanco Library, 1950-53, librarian, 1952-53; bd. dirs. Blanco County Tb Assn., 1951-53. Recipient Achievement citations Am. Heart Assn., 1970, 71, 73, Am. Cancer Soc., 1971. Mem. Blanco C. of C. (sec. 1967-72, dir. 1967-71), Daus. of Nile, Wesleyan Service Guild (co-founder 1952, pres. 1968—). Methodist (dir. Vacation Bible Sch. 1968—, Sunday Sch. tchr. 1949—, mem. pastoral com. 1972-75, chmn. commn. on elderly 1974—, sec. council on ministries 1977—, nominating com. 1982—). Club: Order Eastern Star (past matron; past sec. chpt.). Home: PO Box 246 Blanco TX 78606

BYARS, MILDRED RHODES, club woman; b. Sulphur, Okla., May 11, 1929; d. Gilbert Alfred and Alleen Elizabeth (Parker) Rhodes; A.A., Stephens Coll., 1948; B.S., U. Ala., 1950, M.S., 1951; m. Walter Ryland Byars, Jr., Dec. 22, 1950; children—Debra, Walter III, Rebecca, John Baxter. Tchr., New Merkle Sch., Jefferson County, Ala., 1951-52, Troy (Ala.) High Sch., 1954-57. Area chmn. United Way, 1970; area chmn. Cancer Drive, 1972; past treas. Republican Women Montgomery County. Mem. DAR (regents council pres. 1978-79; state registrar 1979-82), Colonial Dames CDXVII Century (state conf. chmn. 1979, pres. chpt., 2d vice regent), Daus. Am. Colonists (chpt. treas. 1979-81, conf. treas. 1979, Lady of Ct. 1979), Dames of Magna Charta, Ala. Hist. Research Soc. (v.p. 1979, pres. 1981-82), Ala. Geneal. Soc., Chi Omega (pres. Birmingham, Ala. alumnae 1964-65, pres. house corp. Lambda Kappa chpt. 1977-79). Methodist. Clubs: Civiette Civic; Edgewood Garden (pres. 1980). Home: 1616 S Hull St Montgomery AL 36104

BYASSEE, JEANNE COCKRELL, fabric center exec.; b. Columbus, Ohio, Mar. 24, 1936; d. Stanley M. and Margaret R. Cockrell; student Sunbury (Ohio) public schs.; m. Richard C. Byassee, Nov. 25, 1960; children—Mark, Timothy, Lisa, Keith. Cashier, office mgr. Mfrs. Life Ins. Co., Columbus, 1955-61; fabric cons. Stretch and Sew Fabrics, Columbus, 1974, owner, operator, 1974—; mem. Stretch and Sew Internat. Franchise Council; cons. in fabric knowledge to high sch. home econs. classes. Presents fashion shows for benefits and fund-raising events. Mem. Nat. Assn. Female Execs., Rochester Area C. of C. Home: 5 Thornwood Dr Rochester NY 14625 Office: 1614 Penfield Rd Rochester NY 14625

BYE, ROSEANNE MARIE, restaurant research and product devel. ofcl.; b. Chgo., Nov. 27, 1946; d. Paul David and Gwen Lucielle (Hipp) Forrester; B.S. in Foods and Nutrition, Western Ill. U., 1969; postgrad. in Mktg. and Mgmt., Calif. State U., Irvine, Long Beach, and Los Angeles, 1970-78; m. Richard Wayne Bye, June 14, 1969. Test kitchen home economist Hunt-Wesson Foods, Inc., Fullerton, Calif., 1969-73; product and recipe devel. home economist Lawry's Foods, Inc., Los Angeles, 1973-74; mgr. research and product devel. Carl Karcher Enterprises, Anaheim. Calif., 1974-81; dir. research and devel. Denny's Restaurants, La Mirada, Calif., 1981—; cons. new products, quality control, others; participant mktg. research, seminars; panelist in field. Sec., publicity chmn. Orange County Music Center, Allegro chpt., 1979—; mem. Calif. Conf. on the Family, 1979—. Recipient Effie awards for new products, 1976, 78; Home Economist in Bus. awards of excellence, 1977, 78, 80; named Outstanding Home Economist in Bus. in Calif., 1977, 78. Mem. Am. Home Econs. Assn., Calif. Home Econs. Assn., Home Economists in Bus., Nat. Restaurant Assn., Women in Mgmt., Mktg. Research Assn., NOW, Soc. Advancement Food Service Research. Anaheim C. of C. (publicity chmn., 1977-78). Republican. Clubs: Soroptimist, Wine, Gourmet Dinner, Tennis and Swim. Mem. editorial council Internat. Foodservice; contbr. articles to Cotempo. Home: 5829 Valencia Dr Orange CA 92669 Office: 1200 N Harbor Blvd Anaheim CA 92803

BYER, SHERRY MARCIA PFEFFER, psychologist; b. Yonkers, N.Y., Nov. 6, 1946; d. Jack and Annette Gertrude (Sachs) Pfeffer; A.A., Dean Jr. Coll., 1966; B.A., Hofstra U., 1968; Ph.D., Ill. Inst. Tech., 1980; m. Lawrence Louis Byer, Feb. 24, 1979; 1 son, David Robert Pfeffer. Clin. psychologist, intern Chgo. Read Mental Health Center, 1977-78; psychotherapist, sch. psychologist Maine Twp. High Schs., Park Ridge, Ill., 1978-79; sch. psychologist, Chgo. Public Schs., 1979-80; pvt. practice psychotherapy, Chgo., 1979—; psychologist Obesity and Risk Factor Program, Chgo., 1980—; cons. behavioral medicine. Mem. Am. Psychol. Assn., Ill. Psychol. Assn., Gerontol Soc., Ill. Sch. Psychologist Assn., Chgo. Psychol. Assn. Home and office: 1039 W Altgeld St Chicago IL 60614

BYER EISENBERG, KAREN SUE, nurse; b. Bklyn., Mar. 11, 1954; d. Marvin and Florence (Beck) Byer; diploma nursing L.I. Coll. Hosp. Sch. Nursing, 1973; B.S. in Nursing, L.I. U., 1976, M.Profl. Studies, 1977; m. Howard Eisenberg, May 11, 1974. Nurse recovery room and surg. intensive care unit Downstate Med. Center, Bklyn., 1973-75; utilization rev. analyst Bezallel Health Related Facility, Far Rockaway, N.Y., 1975-76; utilization rev. analyst, R.N. supr. Seagirt Health Related Facility, Far Rockaway, 1976; staff nurse neurosurg. and rehab. nursing Downstate Med. Center, Bklyn., 1978, nurse intensive care unit, 1978-79, asst. nursing dir. pathology, clin. research asso. Research Found., 1979—. Mem. Oncology Nursing Soc., Am. Nurses Assn., N.Y. State Nurses Assn., N.Y. Acad. Scis., L.I. Coll. Hosp. Alumnae Assn. Contbr. articles to profl. jours. Office: 450 Clarkson Ave Box 25 Brooklyn NY 11203

BYERLY, KATHLEEN MAE, navy officer; b. Newport News, Va., Feb. 5, 1944; d. Joseph Paul and Lucille Virginia (Alessandroni) Donahue; B.A., Chestnut Hill Coll., Phila., 1966; postgrad. Pepperdine U., Los Angeles, 1975-77; grad. Naval War Coll., 1978. Commd. ensign U.S. Navy, 1966, advanced through grades to comdr., 1980; exec. officer Navy Recruiting Dist. N.Y., 1978-81, with Office Chief Naval Ops., Washington, 1981—. Decorated Navy Commendation medal, 1977, 81. Mem. NOW, Nat. Women's Polit. Caucus, U.S. Naval Inst., Navy Women Officer Profl. Network. Roman Catholic. Home: 4449 Flintstone Rd Alexandria VA 22306 Office: Chief Naval Ops Navy Dept Washington DC 20350

BYERS, ADDIE BYRD, edn. cons.; b. Savannah, Ga.; d. Samuel and Rena Byrd; B.S., Savannah Coll., 1941; A.B., Atlanta U., 1946; M.A., Columbia U., 1950; postgrad. N.Y. U., 1955, U. Mich., 1956, U. So. Calif., 1964, UCLA, 1964, Stamford U., 1964, Harvard U., 1967; m. Claude Byers, 1956 (dec.). Sr. high sch. tchr., Liberty County, Ga., 1928-36; asst. Carnegie Public Library, Savannah, 1938-43; jr. high sch. prin., Bartow, Ga., 1943-44; tchr. Beach-Cuyler High Sch., Savannah, 1944-58, Tompkins High Sch., Savannah, 1958-71; faculty Savannah State Coll., part-time 1965-72; tchr. Chatham County Adult Edn. Center, 1978; mem. adv. council Savannah Bd. Edn., 1968-72; mem. adv. council ESAA, Savannah, 1970—. Mem. Chatham County Democratic Exec. Com., 1976—, v.p., 1980, mem. Dem. Fedn. Women, 1975—; mem. nominating com. YWCA, 1969-75; mem. Observation Corps LWV, 1960-69, Chatham County Polit. Action Com., 1965—; bd. dirs. Chatham, Effingham, Liberty Regional Library. Recipient Outstanding Librarian Service award, 1966, 69, Edn. Merit certs., 1959, 60, 67, 71, Bd. Edn. cert., 1971, Tchr. of Year certs., 1968, 69, Ga. Dept. Vets. Appreciation certs., 1954, Ga. C. of C. award, 1968, Ga. Tchrs. and Edn. Assn. award, 1968; apptd. lt. col. a.d.c. Gov.'s Staff, 1975; Addie B. Byers Dr. named in her honor, Savannah, 1979. Mem. NAACP (life, 3d v.p. local chpt. bd. dirs. 1965—, Honors 1965-67), Ret. Tchrs. Assn., NEA (life), AAUW, Chatham-Effingham-Liberty Regional Library (dir. 1968—). Mem. A.M.E. Ch. Clubs: 41st St. Community, Daus. of the World, Elks. Home: 923 W 41st St Savannah GA 31401

BYERS, RITA JEWELL, ins. co. exec.; b. Shelbyville, Ky., Oct. 30, 1947; d. Raymond M. and Wilma (Ragland) B.; student Western Ky. U., 1965-67; B.S., U. Louisville, 1980, postgrad. in bus. adminstrn., 1981—. Unit chief Commonwealth Life Ins. Co., Louisville, 1975-78, supr. policy values, 1978-79, supr. policy payments, 1979-81, mgr. adminstrv. services, 1981—. Adviser, Jr. Achievement. Mem. River City Bus. and Profl. Women, Assn. Records Mgrs. and Adminstrs., Bus. Forms Mgmt. Assn., In-house Printing Mgrs. Assn., Internat. Info./Word Processing Assn., Smithsonian Assos. Democrat. Baptist. Home: 224 Saint Joseph St Louisville KY 40203 Office: 4th St and Broadway Commonwealth Life Ins Co Louisville KY 40202

BYKOWSKI, JO ANN, mgmt. cons.; b. Toledo, Ohio, Feb. 18, 1947; d. Eugene Andrew and Virginia Mae (Hall) B.; Order processing specialist Hunt Wesson Foods, Rossford, Ohio, 1966-68; personnel sec. Sun Oil Co., Toledo, 1968-72; personnel mgr. Velva Sheen Mfg. Co., Cin., 1973-74; pres. Jay Christopher & Assos., Inc., Cin., 1974—; partner Boster Collection, Inc., 1980—. Republican. Roman Catholic. Home: PO Box 492 Put-in-Bay OH 43456 Office: PO Box 6583 Cincinnati OH 45206

BYNUM, ESTHER ANDERSON, art curator, gallery exec.; b. Henderson, Tex., Dec. 19, 1922; d. John Benton and Bertie Lee (Williams) Anderson; student So. Meth. U., Dallas, 1952, Tex. State U., Arlington, 1954; B.A., N.Tex. State U., 1965; M.A., U. Md., 1972, advanced grad. specialist in art edn. and secondary edn., 1973; postgrad. Western Md. U., 1975; m. James Louis Bynum, Mar. 7, 1942; children—James Lynn, John Michael, Marvin Anderson, Karen Melinda. Traveling art tchr. Montgomery County Public Schs., Rockville, Md., 1965-75, art coordinator, 1975-79; art curator, co-owner Four Oaks Gallery, Henderson, 1980—; art cons.; works exhibited juried shows: N.Y. Internat. Art Show, 1970, Laguna Beach (Calif.) Art Mus., 1973, Balt. Mus. Art, 1973-74, Jersey City Mus., 1974, Lowe Art Mus., Miami, Fla., 1975, Tex. Watercolor Soc., San Antonio, 1975-81. Vice pres. Concerned Citizens for Arts in Public Schs., 1973-75. Mem. AAUW, Am. Craft Council, Tex. Watercolor Soc., Henderson Art League, Delta Kappa Gamma, Methodist. Home: 711 Hwy 43 Henderson TX 75652 Office: 709 Hwy 43 Henderson TX 75652

BYRAM, BETTY JONES, accountant; b. Homer, La., Aug. 18, 1926; d. James Carl and Irene (Booth) Jones; B.A. in Econs., La. State U., 1947; postgrad. (acad. scholar), U. Ill., 1947-49; M.B.A., Lamar U., Beaumont, Tex., 1978; divorced; children—Beryl E. Byram Blankenship, Janet, Martha. Instr., researcher U. Ill., 1949; economist OPS, Shreveport, 1951-52; mgmt. analyst USAF, Barksdale AFB, La., 1953-54; sec.-treas. Universal Contractors, Inc., Beaumont, Tex., 1957-66; v.p. Byram-Swain Inc., Beaumont, 1966-73; partner Byram & Assos., C.P.A.s, Beaumont, 1979—; instr. acctg. Lamar U., 1977—; v.p. Beaumont Housing Fin. Corp., 1980-82; chmn. adv. council SBA, 1976-80. Commr., Beaumont Housing Authority, 1974—; bd. dirs. Hospice; chmn. Beaumont Housing Appeals Bd., 1971—; mem. adminstrv. bd. Trinity United Methodist Ch., Beaumont, 1982. C.P.A., Tex. Mem. Am. Inst. C.P.A.s, Am. Women's Soc. C.P.A.s, Tex. Soc. C.P.A.s, AAUW (chpt. treas. 1979-81), LWV (chpt. pres. 1961-63), Tex. Fedn. Republican Women (1st v.p. 1973-75), Beaumont Estate Planning Council, Tex. Gulf Coast Hist. Soc., Beaumont C. of C. (past chmn. econ. edn. com.). Home: 4550 Gladys Beaumont TX 77706 Office: PO Box 1645 Beaumont TX 77704

BYRD, CAROLE FAULKNER, personnel exec., word processing specialist; b. Memphis, Mar. 5, 1944; d. Frank D. and Mary N. (Kelly) Faulkner; student U. Tenn.; 1 son, Eric M. Office mgr. Barber & McMurry, Inc., Architects, Knoxville, Tenn., 1973-76; asst. supr., tech. info. services Union Carbide Corp., X-10 Plant, Oak Ridge, Tenn., 1966-72, 77-79; info. officer, personnel officer, supr. adminstrv. services Comparative Animal Research Lab., Oak Ridge, 1979—. Recipient Women of Achievement award U. Tenn., 1980. Mem. Nat. Assn. Female Exec., Am. Bus. Women's Assn., Beta Sigma Phi. Office: PO Box 117 1299 Bethel Valley Rd Oak Ridge TN 37830

BYRD, HARRIETT ELIZABETH, educator, state legislator; b. Cheyenne, Wyo., Apr. 20, 1926; d. Robert Charles and Sudie (Smith) Rhone; B.S. in Edn., W.Va. State Coll., 1949; M.Ed., U. Wyo., 1976; m. James W. Byrd, Aug. 8, 1947; children—Robert C., James W., Linda C. Elem. tchr. Sch. Dist. 1, Cheyenne, 1959—; mem. Wyo. Ho. of Reps., 1980-82; mem. Marshall Scholarships Com. for Pacific Region, 1972-77, Wyo. State Adv. Council Title III ESEA, 1969-76. Vice pres. Democratic Women's Club Laramie County; City of Cheyenne spl. police woman; mem. Cheyenne Patrons of Dance; adv. bd. Cheyenne Civic Center; mem. Golden Eagle Booster Club Laramie County Community Coll. Student Athletes, NAACP. Recipient Excellence in Teaching award Instr. Mag., 1967-68. Mem. Cheyenne Classroom Tchrs. Assn., Wyo. Edn. Assn., NEA, Wyo. Internat. Reading Assn., U. Wyo. Alumni Assn., LWV, Dem. Women Laramie County, Wyo. Internat. Reading Assn., Kappa Delta Pi, Kappa Kappa Iota. Roman Catholic. Club: Cheyenne Altrusa (past pres.).

BYRD, HELEN MAE, ins. co. exec.; b. Durham, N.C., Feb. 9, 1930; d. Charlie Raymond and Olive Mae (Kelly) Byrd; student U. N.C., intermittently, 1955-65; m. Harry Richard Bray, Jr. With CIA, 1950-51; with Home Security Life Ins. Co., Durham, 1951—, sec. to pres., 1967-76, corp. sec., 1976—; dir. Home Security Fire and Casualty Ins. Co. Bd. dirs. Durham County Mental Health Assn., 1979—. Cert. profl. sec. Fellow Life Mgmt. Inst.; mem. Nat. Secs. Assn. (local pres. 1968-69, internat. rules and bylaws com. 1975). Baptist. Home: 3106 Ithaca St Durham NC 27707 Office: 505 W Chapel Hill St Durham NC 27701

BYRD, MARTHA GOODE, med. technologist; b. Denver, Aug. 30, 1943; d. William Law and Martha Catherine (Pate) Goode; B.S. in Biology, Furman U., 1965; diploma med. tech., Grady Meml. Hosp., Atlanta, 1965; m. Daniel English Byrd, Apr. 7, 1973; children—Susan Catherine, William English. Blood bank night supr. Grady Meml. Hosp., 1965-68, 71-73; research technologist, supr. histocompatability lab. Emory U.-VA Hosp., Atlanta, 1968-71; sr. med. technologist, histocompatability lab. supr. Atlanta Regional Red Cross Blood Center, 1973-80; sr. med. technologist Pathology Services, Profl. Asso., Tucker, Ga., 1980—; lectr. in field. Mem. Am. Soc. Med. Tech., Am. Soc. Clin. Pathologists, Am. Assn. Blood Banks, Area Bloodbankers Orgn. (sec. 1972), Am. Assn. Clin. Histocompatibility Testing. Democrat. Baptist. Home: 4055 Lake Erin Ct Tucker GA 30084 Office: 1777 Montreal Circle Tucker GA 30084

BYRD, MICHAELE ABNER, bus. machine co. exec.; b. Bklyn., June 22, 1949; d. Philip Russell and Yvonne Edythe (Dixon) Abner; student U. Pa., 1966-68, Marymount Coll., 1968-69; B.A., U. Pa., 1971; m. David Caulbert Byrd, III, July 24, 1976. Mktg. support rep. IBM Corp., Washington, 1971-74, mktg. support rep. staff instr., Dallas, 1974-78, mktg. support mgr., McLean, Va., 1978-79, adminstrv. systems ops. mgr., Gaithersburg, Md., 1979-81, mktg. support rep. sch. tng. mgr., Dallas, 1981—. Mem., Big Bros. and Sisters Am. Mem. Am. Soc. Profl. and Exec. Women, Nat. Assn. Female Execs., Internat. Word Processing Assn. Democrat. Roman Catholic. Home 118 Meadowcreek Rd Coppell TX 75019 Office: 2300 One Main Pl Dallas TX 75250

BYRD, ROSEMARY IMBRAGUGLIO, retail ladies apparel exec.; b. Laurel, Miss., Aug. 15, 1927; d. Philip S. and Tena I. (Martello) Imbraguglio; student Ellisville (Miss.) Jr. Coll., So. Methodist U.; m. James P. Byrd, Jr., June 1, 1947; children—James Philip, Elizabeth Ann Byrd Marshall, Mark G. Various retail and secretarial positions,

1947-68; co-owner Rosemary's Kitchen, restaurant, Dallas, 1968-69; sales specialist, fashion coordinator Neiman-Marcus, Dallas, 1970-76; mgr. Carriage Shop, Dallas, 1976; owner Rosemary's Inc., ladies wearing apparel, Dallas, 1980—, Rosemary Byrd Shoes, 1982—. Mem. Nat. Fedn. Ind. Bus., Better Bus. Bur., Dallas C. of C. Roman Catholic. Home: 9926 Greenfield St Dallas TX 75238 Office: 17 Highland Park Village Dallas TX 75205

BYRNE, BEVERLEA PATRICIA MARY, judge; b. Vancouver, B.C., Can., Jan. 29, 1932; d. Ultan Patrick and Dorothy Agnes (Greig) B.; B.A., U. B.C., 1952, LL.B., 1956. Articled with firm Davis and Co., Vancouver, B.C., Can., 1956-57, asso., 1957-65; called to B.C. bar, 1957; asso. firm Hean, Wylie and Co., Burnaby, B.C., 1965-67, partner, 1967-75; apptd. judge Provincial Ct. B.C., 1975—; guest lectr. continuing legal edn. U. B.C., 1964-69. Active Can. Bar Assn., 1956-76, mem. exec. jr. bar, B.C. Sect., 1956-60, exec. real property sub-sect., 1970-75, provincial exec. nat. council, 1974-76. Mem. Provincial Judges Assn. B.C., Can. Assn. Provincial Ct. Judges. Clubs: Vancouver Golf, Vancouver Lawn Tennis and Badminton, Lawyer's Inn.

BYRNE, JANE MARGARET BURKE, mayor Chgo.; b. Chgo., May 24, 1934; d. William and Katharine (Nolan) Burke; ed. Barat Coll.; m. William Patrick Byrne, Dec. 31, 1956 (dec. May 1959); 1 dau., Katherine; m. 2d, Jay McMullen, Mar. 17, 1978. With Chgo. Anti-Poverty Agy., 1964-68; commr. Chgo. Dept. Consumers Sales, Weights and Measures, 1968-77; mayor City of Chgo., 1979—; cons. Underwriters Lab. Chmn. resolutions com. Democratic Nat. Com., co-chmn. Cook County Dem. Central Com., 1975-76. Office: Office of Mayor City Hall 121 N LaSalle St Chicago IL 60602 *

BYRNE, KATHERINE MARIE KILLION, polit. worker; b. N.Y.C., Aug. 15, 1926; d. Robert Vincent and Margaret Ellen (Reilly) Killion; student N.Y. U., 1943; m. Eugene Kevin Byrne, Jan. 15, 1949; children—Maureen, Eugene, Katherine, Kevin. Group supr. FBI, N.Y.C., 1943-52; parish sec. St. Sylvester's Rectory, S.I., N.Y., 1964-70; grand jury reporter Dist. Atty.'s Office, Staten Island, 1970—. Sec., North Shore Democratic Club of Richmond County, 1975—. Mem. Police and Fire Line of Duty Widows of N.Y.C. Roman Catholic. Home: 28 Meadow Ave Staten Island NY 10304 Office: 36 Richmond Terr Staten Island NY 10301

BYRNE, PATRICIA MARY, ambassador; b. Cleve., June 1, 1925; A.B., Vassar Coll., 1946; M.A., Sch. Advanced Internat. Studies, Johns Hopkins U., 1947. Joined Fgn. Service, Dept. State, 1949; assigned to Athens, 1949-52, Saigon, 1952-55; internat. relations officer, Washington, 1955-57, officer-in-charge Laos affairs, 1957-58; assigned to Izmir, Turkey, 1958-60, Ankara, Turkey, 1960-62, Vientiane, Laos, 1962-64; fgn. affairs officer, Washington, 1964, officer-in-charge dependent area affairs, 1964-66, UN policy affairs, 1966, supervisory personnel staffing specialist, 1966-67, spl. asst., 1967-68, detailed to Nat. War Coll., 1968-69; polit. officer, Paris, 1969-73; dep. chief mission, Colombo, Sri Lanka, 1973-77; ambassador to Republic of Mali, 1976-79, to Burma, 1979—. Recipient Commendable Service award Dept. State, 1954, Meritorious Service award, 1958. Office: American Embassy 581 Merchant St Rangoon Burma *

BYRNE, PEGGY, state legislator; b. Mpls., Dec. 17, 1949; d. Joseph Emmett and Anna Mary (Scheller) B.; B.A., U. Minn., 1971. Mem. Minn. Ho. of Reps., 1973—. Democratic Farmer-Labor. Office: Room 220 State Office Bldg St Paul MN 55155

BYRNE, SHIRLEY MAXINE, educator; b. East Liverpool, Ohio, June 12, 1931; d. Burdette J. and Gladys (McMahan) Smith; B.S.Ed. in Elementary Edn., Ohio U., 1954; M.S.Ed. in Reading, U. Mass., 1964; D.Ed. in Curriculum and Instruction, U. Ky., 1972; m. Robert L. Byrne, Jr.; children—Robert L., Susan A., Colleen A. Reading supr. South Hadley (Mass.) Schs., 1962-65; reading specialist Title III pub. schs., Somerset, Ky., 1967-70; supr. Clark County (Ky.) Schs., Winchester, 1972-80; assoc. prof. Eastern Ky. U., 1980—; vis. prof. Eastern Ky. U., 1978. Mem. Am. Assn. Sch. Adminstrs., Internat. Reading Assn., Nat. Reading Conf., Am. Assn. Supervision and Curriculum Devel., Assn. Ednl. Suprs. Specialist in reading and curriculum devel., Assn. Tchr. Educators, Kappa Delta Pi, Phi Delta Kappa. Home: 110 Westwood Dr Richmond KY 40475 Office: Combs 112 Coll of Edn Eastern Kentucky U Richmond KY 40475

BYRNES, BARBARA HELEN, exec. search co. exec.; b. N.Y.C., Feb. 10, 1951; d. Richard Francis and Jeanne Frances (Orchard) B.; B.S., Cornell U., 1973. Chef, The Harbor Ho., Nantucket, Mass., 1976; club mgr. The Tokeneke Club, Darien, Conn., 1977; sr. cons. Hospitality Personnel Inc., Valley Forge, Pa., 1977-79; dir. hospitality recruiting T. A. Davis & Assos. Inc., N.Y.C., 1979—. Mem. Hotel Sales Mgrs. Assn., Cornell Soc. Hotelmen, Nat. Assn. Female Execs., NOW. Home: 12 W 72d St New York NY 10023 Office: 575 Madison Ave New York NY 10022

BYRNES, MURIEL MARIE, research chemist; b. Chgo., Aug. 7, 1925; d. Edward David and Stella Ann (Courney) B.; B.S., Mt. Mary Coll., Milw., 1947. Chemist research labs. Quaker Oats Co., Chgo., 1947-52; dir. quality assurance Xttrium Labs., Chgo., 1952-70; sr. research scientist, sect. head Miles Labs., Chgo., 1970—. Recipient Alumnae award Mt. Mary Coll., 1977. Mem. Internat. Food Technologists, Am. Chem. Soc., Am. Oil Chemists Soc., Vitamin Chemists Soc. Democrat. Roman Catholic. Home: 9717 S Keeler St Oak Lawn IL 60453 Office: 7123 W 65th St Chicago IL 60638

BYRNES, SUZANNE THERESE, govt. ofcl.; b. Central Falls, R.I., Nov. 27, 1926; d. Ernest O. and Rose Alma (LaSalle) Gazaille; student extension Providence Coll., 1946-47, Bryant Coll., U. R.I., 1975—; m. John C. Byrnes, Nov. 6, 1948; children—M. Christine, Maureen P., John C. Office sec., bookkeeper Notre Dame Hosp., 1945-47; clk.-typist City Clerk's Office, Central Falls, R.I., 1947-49, mayor's sec., 1960-64; office sec. Central Falls Housing Authority, 1964-68, adminstrv. asst., 1968-75, acting exec. dir., 1975-76, asst. exec. dir., 1976—; dir. Central Senior Center, Inc., 1969—. Sec., Central Falls Diamond Jubilee, 1970; mem. Mayor's Adv. Council, 1978—; treas. Central Falls Community Sch., 1977-79; bd. dirs. Dexter Credit Union, 1977—, sec., 1978—; trustee Central Senior Center, 1976—, sec., treas., 1976—; troop leader Girl Scouts U.S.A., 1946-48. Recipient Outstanding Community Services award HUD, 1976, Outstanding Citizens award Sta. WICE, 1961. Mem. R.I. Assn. of Exec. Dirs. for Housing (sec. 1975—), Internat. Fedn. of Cath. Alumnae (gov. R.I. chpt. 1961-64). Club: R.I. Catholic Women (pres. 1967-68). Home: 4 School St Central Falls RI 02863 Office: 466 Hunt St Central Falls RI 02863

BYRNSIDE, PRISCILLA HICKS, nurse; b. Madison, W.Va., July 26, 1946; d. Arla Randall and Shirley Madge (Pennington) Hicks; R.N., Charleston Gen. Sch. Nursing, 1967; m. Charles Marshall Byrnside, Aug. 22, 1969; children—Amy Louise, Beth Ann. Staff nurse hematology-urology, W.Va. U. Med. Center, 1967-68; staff nurse med.-surg. unit Meml. div. Charleston Area Med. Center, 1968-69; nurse emergency room Boone Meml. Hosp., Madison, W.Va., 1969—, inservice dir., 1980—; pre-hosp. care advisor Boone County Ambulance Authority, 1981—; EMT instr. Boone County Bd. Edn. 1970—; mem. adv. bd. Boone Career Center Allied Health, 1970—; affiliate faculty basic cardiac life support Am. Heart Assn., 1975—. Mem. rescue squad Madison Vol. Fire Dept. 1974—; civic chairperson fund drive Am. Heart Assn., 1981—. Mem. Emergency Dept. Nurses Assn. Baptist. Home: Route 1 Box 642 Danville WV 25053 Office: Boone Meml Hosp 701 Madison Ave Madison WV 25130 also Boone County Ambulance Authority PO Box 586 Madison WV 25130

BYRON, BEVERLY BUTCHER, Congresswoman; b. Balt., July 27, 1932; d. Harry C. and Ruth Butcher; student Hood Coll., 1962-64; m. Goodloe E. Byron, 1952 (dec.); children—Goodloe E. Jr., Barton Kimball, Mary McComas. Mem. 96th-98th Congresses from 6th Md. Dist. State treas. Md. Young Democrats, 1962, 65; bd. assos. Hood Coll.; bd. dirs. Frederick County chpt. ARC: sec. Frederick Heart Assn., 1974-79; chmn. Md. Phys. Fitness Commn.; mem. Frederick County Landmarks Found.; bd. dirs. Am. Hiking Soc.; bd. visitors Air Force Acad. Episcopalian. Office: 1216 Longworth House Office Bldg Washington DC 20515

BYSIEWICZ, SHIRLEY RAISSI, lawyer; b. Enfield, Conn.; d. Kyriakos and Anna (Gavala) Raissi; B.A., J.D., M.S. in L.S., U. Conn.; m. Stanley J. Bysiewicz, July 18, 1959; children—Susan, Walter John, Karen, Gail. Admitted to Conn. bar, 1954; mem. firm Raissi & Raissi, Enfield, 1954—; mem. faculty U. Conn., West Hartford, 1956—, prof. law, 1965—, also law librarian. Mem. Permanent Commn. on Status Women for Conn., 1976-80, pres., 1978-79; mem. Conn. Law Library Adv. Com., 1976—; law revision commr. for Conn., 1980—. Mem. Bar Assn. Conn. (treas. 1975-78), Nat. Assn. Women Lawyers, Am., Hartford County (exec. com.), Conn. (chmn. juvenile justice coms.) bar assns., Am. Bar Assn. Women Lawyers, Am. Assn. Law Schs. (co-presider sect. on status of women, sect. legal research 1974), Am. Assn. Law Librarians (law library jour. com., sec. 1980—), U. Conn. Law Sch. Alumni Assn. (exec. sec. 1958-68), New Eng. Law Librarians (pres. 1970), Women's Equity Action League. Author: (with Max R. White) Forms of Town Government in Connecticut, 1954; Survey of County Law Libraries in Connecticut, 1967; co-author Selected Annotated Bibliography on Education for Professional Responsibility, 1968; (with Price & Bitner) Effective Legal Research, 1979. bus. mgr. Law Library Jour., 1968-72; co-editor Materials on Estate Planning, 1969. Contbr. law articles to profl. jours. Office: 1800 Asylum Ave West Hartford CT 06117

BYSTRYN, SARA WOLSKI, importer; b. Brest Litovsk, Russia; d. Charles and Louba (Prilouk) Wolski; student Sorbonne, Paris, 1930-33; m. Iser Bystryn, Dec. 23, 1930; children—Denise (Mrs. Eric Kandel), Jean-Claude. Came to U.S., 1949, naturalized, 1954. Owner, pres. Ibis Export Import Co., N.Y.C., 1951—. Active mem. French Resistance, 1942-44. Home: 800 West End Ave New York NY 10025 Office: 250 W 57th St New York NY 10019

BYUS, LELA HUTCHISON, guidance counselor; b. Morganton, Ark.; d. William Joshua and Willie Beatrice (Graddy) Hutchison; B.S. in Edn., U. Central Ark. (formerly Ark. State Tchrs. Coll.), 1941; M.S. in Edn., U. Tex., El Paso, 1966; postgrad. U. Md., 1952-53, U. Philippines, 1957-59; m. John Byus, Jr., Apr. 24, 1946; children—John, Kent, Tina, Fred. Tchr. home econs. and sci. Pine Bluff (Ark.) Schs., 1941-42; chem. insp. Ordnance Depot, Little Rock, 1942-44; personnel officer Air Force Specialized Depot, Little Rock, 1944-46; tchr., counselor Am. Sch., Manila, Philippines, 1957-59; tchr., elem. supr., counselor El Paso (Tex.) Pub. Schs., 1960-80; elem. guidance counselor Houston Elem.-Intermediate Sch. 1966—. Leader Am. Sch. Council Boy Scouts Am. and Am. Sch. Council Girl Scouts U.S.A., Manila. Recipient Life Membership award PTA Mem. NEA, Tex. State Tchrs. Assn., El Paso Educators Assn., Tex. Personnel and Guidance Assn., Am. Personnel and Guidance Assn., Trans-Pecos Guidance Assn., El Paso Guidance Assn., AAUW, Assn. Children with Learning Disabilities, Alpha Delta Kappa (Appreciation award 1968). Republican. Presbyterian. Clubs: Gideons Aux., Army Officers Wives. Office: 2851 Grant Ave El Paso TX 79930

CABATIT-SEGAL, BETSY ROZELLS, ednl. adminstr.; b. Penang, Brit. Malaysia, Feb. 27, 1932; came to U.S., 1957, naturalized, 1969; d. Fructoso Ramos and Mathilda (Rozells) Cabatit; B.S. in Nursing, U. Philippines, 1955; M.A. in Edn., U. Chgo., 1960; m. Marvin Segal, Dec. 17, 1976. Instr. U. Philippines, Quezon City, 1955-56; chmn. med./surg. nursing U. Nueva Caceres, (Philippines), 1956-57, Philippine Women's U., Manila, 1961-64; USA exchange vis. staff nurse Cook County Hosp., Chgo., 1957-60, instr., 1960-61, 64-65; instr. U. Ill., Chgo., 1965-68; dir. staff devel. Rush-Presbyterian St. Luke's Hosp., Chgo., 1968-69; instr. Coll. of DuPage, Glen Ellyn, Ill., 1970-74, asst. dean, 1970-78, asso. dean health and public services, 1978—. Mem. bd. dirs. Edn. Network for Older Adults, Chgo., 1980—, DuPage County (Ill.) Heart Assn., 1980—. Public Adminstrn. scholar, 1961. Mem. Am. Nurses' Assn., Ill. Nurses' Assn. (del. to INA conv. Chgo. 1978), Nat. League Nursing, Ill. League Nursing, Am. Soc. Allied Health Professions', Ill. Assn. Allied Health Professions' (treas. 1981-82), Health Edn. Resources Council for No. Ill. (pres. 1980-81), Philippine Nurses Assn. Chgo. (pres. 1967-68, 75-76), Am. Assn. Community and Jr. Colls. Women Adminstrs., Ill. Vocat. Assn. (mem. council of local adminstrs. 1980—). Democrat. Roman Catholic. Office: Main Campus Adminstrn Coll of DuPage 22nd St and Lambert Rd Glen Ellyn IL 60137

CABLE, JOAN MARIE, beauty salon exec.; b. Levittown, N.Y., Apr. 1, 1931; d. Joseph J. and Mae (Kennedy) Blank; student CCNY, 1949-51, Pohs Inst., 1970; children—Pamela, Audrey, Georgianna. Pres., Joan M. Cable's La Femmina Beauty Salons, Inc., Levittown, 1973—, Lemon Tree Haircutting Establishments, 1976—. Chmn. Town Beautification Com., Bethpage, N.Y. Recipient numerous letters and certs. of appreciation. Republican. Roman Catholic. Office: 3301 Hempstead Turnpike Levittown NY 11756

CABOT, TRACY, cable television co. exec.; b. Chester, Pa., Mar. 4, 1941; d. Ben and Ruth (Burston) Blank; B.A., Whittier Coll., 1964. With Universal Studio, 1964-65; editor Get Smart TV Show, 1965-66, Overdrive mag., 1966-67, Confidential mag., 1968-71, Parliament Press, North Hollywood, Calif., 1972-74; staff reporter National Enquirer, Los Angeles, 1975-76; editor Human Insight mag., 1980; story coordinator Real People TV Show, 1979; creative affairs dir., feature film prodn. Entertainment Software, Inc., Hollywood, Calif., 1980-81; creative dir. cable TV programming, vice-pres. Cableshows, Inc., Van Nuys, Calif., 1982—; cons. Com-Aware Inst., Los Angeles, 1979—. Author: Letting Go, 1978; Inside the Cults, 1971; The Parkhursts, 1967. Contbr. articles to various mags. Address: 6937 Sunnyslope Ave Van Nuys CA 91405

CACACE, MAERY MORIARTY, nurse; b. Nashua, N.H., Jan. 30, 1911; d. Denis Francis and Amanda Bernedette (Caron) Moriarty; student Revier Coll., 1933, Columbia U., 1936-38, Elizabeth Seton Coll., 1976-77; m. Orlando E. Cacace, July 20, 1940; children—Denise, Caron, Rosemary, Michelle. Tchr. practical arts Nashua Meml. Hosp., 1932-34; sch. nurse, Nashua, 1934-40; maternal child care Nashua Health Dept. nurse in Tb, Diabetic and V.D. clinics, 1968-72; asst. supr. St. John Riverside Hosp., Yonkers, N.Y., 1956-66, sr. supr., 1974—; healing minister, 1981—. Mem. Am. Nurses Assn. Republican. Roman Catholic. Office: 967 N Broadway Yonkers NY 10701

CACCAMISE, GENEVRA LOUISE BALL (MRS. ALFRED E. CACCAMISE), librarian; b. Mayville, N.Y., July 22, 1934; d. Herbert Oscar and Genevra (Green) Ball; B.A., Stetson U., DeLand, Fla., 1956; M.S. in L.S., Syracuse U., 1967; m. Alfred E. Caccamise, July 7, 1974. Tchr. grammar sch., Sanford, Fla., 1956-57, elem. sch., Longwood, Fla., 1957-58; tchr., librarian Enterprise (Fla.) Sch., 1958-63; librarian, media specialist Boston Ave. Sch., DeLand, 1963—; area dir. for Volusia County, Fla. Edn. Assn., 1963-65. Charter mem. West Volusia Meml. Hosp. aux., DeLand, 1962—; Girl Scout leader, 1955-56. Bd. dirs. Alhambra Villas Home Owners Assn., 1972-75; trustee, pres. DeLand Public Library. Mem. AAUW (2d v.p. chpt. 1965-67, rec. sec. 1961-65, 78-80, pres. 1980-82), Assn. Childhood Edn. (1st v.p. 1965-66, corr. sec. 1963-65), DAR (chpt. registrar 1969—; asst. chief page Continental Congress, Washington 1962-65), Bus. and Profl. Women's Club (corr. sec. DeLand 1968-71, 2d v.p. 1969-70), Stetson U. Alumni Assn. (class chmn. for ann. fund drive 1968), Volusia County Assn. Media in Edn. (treas.), Colonial Dames XVII Century, Magna Charta Dames, Soc. Mayflower Descs., Delta Kappa Gamma (pres. Beta Psi chpt.). Democrat. Episcopalian. An author Volusia County manual Instructing the Library Assistant, 1965. Home: PO Box 241 DeLand FL 32720 Office: 340 N Boston Ave DeLand FL 32720

CACY, LORA BELLE, educator; b. Bristow, Okla., Sept. 9, 1918; d. Ernest Edwin and Willa Mae (Wyatt) Greer; B.S. Okla. State U., 1952, M.S., 1954, Ed.D., 1962; m. King Washington Cacy, Jr., Nov. 2, 1941; children—Judith Juanita Brightwell, Linda Fern Scott. Tchr., elem. schs., Noble County, Okla., 1947-50; instr. vocat. home econs., public schs., Yale, Okla., 1953-56; asst. prof. home econs. edn. Okla. State U., Stillwater, 1963-72, asso. prof., 1972—. Mem. Am. Home Econs. Assn., Okla. Home Econs. Assn., Am. Vocat. Assn., Okla. Vocat. Assn., Nat. Assn. Tchr. Educators, Okla. Assn. Tchr. Educators, Nat. Assn. Vocat. Home Econs. Educators, Payne County Genealogical Assn., Payne County Hist. Soc., Okla. Genealogical Assn., Delta Kappa Gamma, Phi Upsilon Omicron. Democrat. Baptist. Home: 1323 Skyline Dr N Stillwater OK 74074 Office: HEW 125 Okla State U Stillwater OK 74078

CADART-RICARD, ODETTE MARIE-HÉLÈNE, educator; b. Romilly, France, Sept. 8, 1925; came to U. S., 1946, naturalized, 1949; B.A., LL.B., U. Paris, 1945; B.A., Dominican Coll., 1947; M.A., Sacramento State Coll., 1959; Ph.D., U. Oreg., 1970; m. Jacques Louis Ricard, Feb. 7, 1948 (div. 1970); children—Suzanne Madeleine, Michèle Odette. Instr., French, Dominican Coll., San Rafael, Calif., 1947-48, French and history Sacramento City Sch. Dist., 1960-65; asst. prof., asso. prof. French and edn. Oreg. State U., Corvallis, 1965-76, dir. modern lang. edn., 1965-75; prof. French, 1976—, dir. Oreg. Studies Center, U. Poitiers, France, 1971-73. Vol. French Forces of Interior, 1942-44. Decorated knight of French Order of Acad. Palms, 1972. Mem. Am. Assn. Profs. of French, MLA, Internat. Courtly Lit. Soc., Western Soc. for French History, Am. Assn. Tchrs. of French (pres. Oreg. chpt. 1967-68), Oreg. Assn. Fgn. Lang. Tchrs. (pres. 1970-71). Author: The French Verb System: A Programmed Text, Vol. I, 1971; co-author: Les Gammas, Introductory French Text, 1982. Office: Dept Fgn Langs and Lits Oreg State U Corvallis OR 97331

CADDEL, DORIS KAY, textile researcher; b. Hydro, Okla., Mar. 6, 1937; d. William Arthur and Merle (Goodwin) Wildman; B.S., Southwestern State U., Okla., 1965; M.S., Tex. Tech. U., 1966; postgrad. U. R.I., Tex. Tech., Okla. State U.; m. Jerry Louis Caddel, Oct. 6, 1956; 1 son, Christopher Louis. Substitute tchr. public schs., Okla., 1956-63; instr. home econs. dept. clothing and textiles Tex. Tech. U., Lubbock, 1965-74, research asso., textile research center, supr. student affairs in textile engrng. Coll. Engrng., 1974—; designer patterns for individuals with handicaps. Dist. officer United Methodist. Ch. Women, 1975; leader, 4H, 1975-82. Mem. Southwest Textile Assn., Am. Assn. Textile Technologists, Assn. Coll. Profs. Textiles and Clothing, Phi Psi, (sec. grand council). Democrat. Author: Measurements, Guidelines and Solutions, 1977. Home: 1712 Norwich St Route 8 Box 12T2 Lubbock TX 79407 Office: PO Box 4150 Tex-Tech U Lubbock TX 79409

CADIGAN, HELEN ELISE, social worker; b. Topeka, Mar. 8, 1947; d. Grattan Crowe and Virginia Christine (Ross) Huckabee; B.A., Washburn U., 1972; M.S.W., Kans. U., 1977; m. Rufus Jones Cadigan, Aug. 17, 1979; children—Kent Bradley, Matthew Ryan. Social worker Family Service and Guidance Center, Topeka, 1972-76; instr. Ottawa (Kans.) U., 1977-78; exec. dir. Trinity Children's Services, 1978-79; social worker United Sch. Dist. 497, Lawrence, Kans., 1978-79; social worker Harlem Consol. Sch. Dist. 122, Rockford, Ill., 1979—; clin. social worker Glenwood Evaluation and Treatment Center, Rockford, 1980—. Chmn. bd. dirs. Trinity Children's Services, Lawrence, 1977-78; bd. dirs. Big Bros./Big Sisters of Rockford. Mem. Nat. Assn. Social Workers (mem. exec. bd. Jane Adams chpt.), Acad. Cert. Social Workers, St. Anthony's Med. Center Aux., Phi Delta Kappa. Episcopalian. Clubs: Jr. League of Rockford, Rockford Woman's. Home: 6878 Paddock Ln Rockford IL 61111 Office: 2823 Glenwood Ave Rockford IL 61111

CADOVICH, JOANN CATHERINE, educator; b. Highland Park, Mich., Sept. 22, 1956; d. Joseph Mitchell and Ann Barbara (Woitko) C.; B.S. with honors in Edn., Central Mich. U., 1978. Volleyball coach Redford (Mich.) Union Sr. High Sch., 1978; instr. health and phys. edn. Benedictine High Sch., Detroit, 1979-80; bus. edn. instr. Bishop Foley High Sch., Madison Heights, Mich., 1980—; volleyball coach Madonna Coll., Livonia, Mich., 1980—; volleyball ofcl. Named Outstanding Phys. Edn. major Central Mich. U., 1977. Mem. Mich. Assn. Health, Phys. Edn. and Recreation, Mich. Alliance for Health, Phys. Edn. and Recreation, Am. Alliance Health, Phys. Edn., Recreation and Dance, Nat. Cath. Educators Assn., Mich. Bus. Educators Assn., Delta Psi Kappa (nat. dir. Psi Kap of Yr. award 1979). Home: 29191 Hemlock Ct Farmington Hills MI 48018 Office: 32000 Campbell Rd Madison Heights MI

CADY, BARBARA BUIVID, publisher; b. Milw., Feb. 20, 1942; d. Raymond and Janina Marie (Celichowski) Buivid; student Marymount Coll., Tarrytown, 1957-58; B.A., Marquette U., 1962; m. 1962 (div.); children—Stephanie, Monica and Jennifer (twins). Producer, host Dealing program Sta. KPFK, Los Angeles, 1971—; editor in chief Playgirl mag., 1976-78; publisher, editor-in-chief Flowers & mag., Redondo Beach, Calif., 1980—. Mem. Western Publs. Assn., Soc. Am. Bus. Editors. Democrat. Contbr. articles (interviews with John Dean, Norman Lear) to Playboy mag.; regular contbr. Los Angeles Times Book Rev. Sect., 1972—. Office: 12233 W Olympic Blvd Los Angeles CA 90064

CADY, JANET ARLENE, assn. exec.; b. Atlanta, Mich., Aug. 19, 1949; d. Arthur F. and Jean M. (Maanika) C.; student Oakland U., 1967-69; B.A. with high honors, Mich. State U., 1971; postgrad. Taiwan Normal U., 1972-74; M.A., U. Mich., 1975. Pub. relations officer Chinese Acupuncture Sci. Research Found., Taipei, Taiwan, 1972-74; project asst. Chinese econ. studies program U. Mich., 1975-77; program dir. internat. Asian studies program Yale-China Assn., New Haven, 1977-78; program asso. Nat. Com. U.S.-China Relations, N.Y.C., 1978—. Mem. Assn. Asian Studies, Nat. Assn. Fgn. Student Affairs, Yale-China Assn., Phi Beta Kappa, Phi Kappa Phi. Editor: Understanding China newsletter, 1974-75; (with E.A. Winckler) Urban Planning in China: Report of the U.S. Urban Planners Delegation to the People's Republic of China, 1980. Office: 777 UN Plaza 9B New York City NY 10017

CAFFERATA, PATRICIA DILLON, state legislator; b. Albany, N.Y., Nov. 24, 1940; d. Kenneth Price and Barbara Farrell (Vucanovich) Dillon; student Mills Coll., 1958-61; B.A., Lewis and Clark Coll., 1963; m. H. Treat Cafferata, June 17, 1961; children—Elisa, Janet, Reynolds. Mem. Nev. State Assembly, 1980—. Former pres. Drs. Wives of Washoe County; bd. dirs. St. Mary's Hosp. Guild. Named Outstanding Freshman Legislator, Nev. Med. Assn., 1980. Mem. Nev. State Order Women Legislators (charter), Republican State Legislators Assn. Episcopalian. Club: Rep. Women's (Reno). Home: 205 Urban Rd Reno NV 89509

CAFRITZ, PEGGY COOPER, communications exec.; b. Mobile, Ala., Apr. 7, 1947; d. Algernon Johnson and G. Catherine (Mouton) C.; B.A. in Polit. Sci., George Washington U., 1968, J.D., 1971. Founder, Workshops for Careers in Arts (name later changed to Duke Ellington Sch. Arts), Washington, 1968, developer, chmn. bd., 1968—; admitted to D.C. bar, 1972; dir. Arrowstreet, Architects and Planners, Inc., Cambridge, Mass. and Washington, 1972-74, Nat. Bank Washington; spl. asst. to pres. Post-Newsweek Stas., Inc., Washington, 1974-77; programming exec., producer documentary films Sta. WTOP-TV, Washington, 1974—; cons. arts; mem. exec. com. D.C. Commn. Arts and Humanities, 1970-75, chmn., 1979—; trustee Am. Film Inst., 1972-74; fellow Woodrow Wilson Internat. Center for Scholars, 1971-72; bd. govs. Corcoran Gallery Art, Washington, 1972-74; exec. dir. Gt. issues project D.C. Bicentennial Commn., 1974; mem. exec. bd. Nat. Assembly State Arts Agys., 1980—. Mem. conv. staff Democratic Nat. Com., 1972, 76; mem. steering com. Carter/Mondale, Washington, 1976; mem. nat. panel Arts, Edn. and Ams., 1975—; mem. internat. com. UNICEF, 1976—, bd. dirs. U.S. com., 1978—; bd. dirs. Nat. Guild Community Schs. of Arts, 1976—, Pennsylvania Ave. Devel. Corp., Washington. Recipient John D. Rockefeller III award, 1972, Geroge F. Peabody award, U. Ga., 1976; Emmy award, 1977; 27th Ann. Broadcast Media award, 1977; named Washingtonian of Yr., Washingtonian Mag., 1972, Woman of Yr., Mademoiselle Mag., 1973. Mem. Am., D.C. bar assns. Home and Office: 2900 44th St NW Washington DC 20016

CAGNEY, JUDITH ANNE, coll. pres.; b. Evanston, Ill., July 26, 1938; d. Richard DeMarais and Mary Cecelia (Lynch) Cagney; B.A., Barat Coll., 1966; M.A., Fordham U., 1968; L.H.D. (hon.), Maryville Coll., St. Louis, 1980. Tchr., Hardey Prep. Sch., Chgo., 1962-65, Duchesne Acad., Omaha, 1966-67; tchr. philosophy Barat Coll., Lake Forest, Ill., 1968-69, trustee, 1972—, pres., 1975—; dir. personnel Chgo. Province, Soc. Sacred Heart, 1970-74. Trustee, Glen Oak Sch., Cleve., 1970-74. NDEA grantee Catholic U., 1967. Hon. scholar Newton Coll, 1956. Office: Barat Coll Lake Forest IL 60045 *

CAHILL, EDNA W., educator; b. St. Louis, Jan. 6, 1945; d. Samuel and Sarah (Brown) C.; B.A., Washington U., St. Louis, 67; M.A., U. Ill., 1969. Tchr. pub. schs., Clayton, Mo., 1969-74, Columbus, Ohio, 1974-77, Memphis, 1977-80, Atlanta, 1980—. Vol., ARC, Am. Cancer Soc. Mem. NEA, Ga. Edn. Assn., Atlanta Edn. Assn., Nat. Council Tchrs. English, Phi Beta Kappa, Delta Gamma. Club: Atlanta Tennis. Address: Werik Apts 3116 Maple Dr NE Atlanta GA 30305

CAHNERS, SUE SCHWARTZ, clin. social worker; b. New London, Conn., Feb. 16, 1925; d. Joseph R. and Harriet B. Schwartz; B.A., Smith Coll., 1946; M.S.W., Simmons Coll., Boston, 1974; m. Walter J. Cahners, Oct. 15, 1951; children—Amy Sue, Catherine Jane. Exec. asst. Reynolds Metals Co., N.Y.C., 1948-51; home service asst., bd. dirs. Bangor (Maine) chpt. ARC, 1953-57; founding dir. Boston Ballet Soc., 1963-70; bd. dirs. women's aux. Beth Israel Hosp., Boston, 1960-70; researcher Mass. Dept. Drug Rehab., Boston, 1974; dir. social service Shriners Burns Inst., Boston, 1975—; clin. social worker Gen. Med. Assos., Weston, Mass., 1978—; vis. lectr. Simmons Coll. Sch. Social Work, Harvard U. Sch. Public Health. Mem. Acad. Cert. Social Workers, Nat. Assn. Social Workers, Internat. Soc. Burn Injuries, Am. Burn Assn. Jewish. Club: Smith Coll. (pres. 1967-69) (Boston). Author papers in field. Office: 51 Blossom St Boston MA 02114

CAHOON, MARGARET CECELIA, nurse, educator; b. Hallowell, Ont., Can., May 5, 1916; d. Gordon Milton and Mary Maude (Black) C.; grad. Women's Coll. Hosp. Sch. for Nurses, 1943; B.A., Queen's U., 1950; M.Ed., U. Toronto, 1960; Ph.D., U. Mich., 1967; postgrad. U. Edinburgh, 1975-76. Community health nurse, 1946-49; fellow, asso. prof. Sch. Hygiene, U. Toronto, 1950-68, prof. faculty of nursing, 1961—, prof. faculty of medicine, 1970—, Rosenstadt prof. health research, 1980-82, mem. univ. governing council, 1979-82; prin. investigator Sunnybrook-U. Toronto Nursing Project, 1980—. Vice chmn. East York Bd. of Health, 1971-75. WHO fellow 1963-64. Mem. Registered Nurses Assn., Can. Public Health Assn. (mem. governing council 1960-64), Am. Public Health Assn. (mem. governing council 1979—), Ont. Public Health Assn. (pres., bd. dirs.). Presbyterian. Author textbooks, teachers manuals on health sci.; contbr. articles to profl. jours. Mem. editorial bd. Advanced Nursing, Research in Nursing and Health Care; former mem. editorial bd. Research in Nursing and Health Care. Office: 50 St George St Toronto ON M5S 1A1 Canada

CAIN, JOYCE TAYLOR, cosmetics sales exec.; b. Houston, Sept. 20, 1931; d. Clarence George and Rena Mae (Flannery) Taylor; grad. Elliott Bus. Coll., 1945; grad. U. Houston, 1953; m. Ward H. Cain, Nov. 25, 1950; children—Eva, Ward H., June, Kenneth, Daniel, Gayle, Alice. Asst. purchasing agt. Sinclair-Arco, Houston, 1950-51; asst. to plant mgr. deepwater plant Houston Light & Power, 1951-54; sales rep. Avon Cosmetics, Pasadena, Tex., 1961-68, dist. sales mgr., Houston, 1968—. Pres., sec.-treas. PTA. Mem. Nat. Assn. Female Execs., Am. Soc. Profl. and Exec. Women, Christian Bus. Woman's Club. Democrat. Baptist. Clubs: Toastmistress, Soroptomist, Delphian Soc.

CAIN, LINDA CHARLOTTE, communications co. exec., educator; b. Boston, Oct. 5, 1941; d. Charles Cummings Cain and Edna Augusta Cain Clark; B.A. in History and Govt., Boston U., 1963; M.Ed., Northeastern U., 1967. Admissions officer Children's Hosp. Med. Center, Boston, 1964-65; exec. asst. to mgr. Mass. Republican. State Com., 1965-67; tchr. Dover (Mass.) Public Schs., 1967-81; owner, mgr. Cain and Clark, Medfield, Mass., 1971—; pres. Beehive Communications, Inc., Medfield, 1982—; corp. clk., dir. Bay Shores Homeowners Assn., Inc., North Falmouth, Mass., 1978-82. Chairperson com. Sta. WGBH-TV Auction, 1973-76. Mem. NEA, Mass. Tchrs. Assn., Dover Sherborn Edn. Assn. (past pres.). Republican. Author: Blast-Off, 1973; author, developer Keep One Step Ahead info. series. Home: 11 Pleasant St Medfield MA 02052

CAIN, MADALENE FLORES, securities rep.; b. Floresville, Tex., June 15, 1913; d. John N. and Mary Clara (Edds) Flores; div. Sec., Metzger Dairies, San Antonio, 1942-55; office mgr. Exec. Aircraft Co., San Antonio, 1955-61; real estate broker, San Antonio, 1957-61; account exec. Dempsey Tegeler & Co., San Antonio, 1962-70, Rauscher Pierce Refsnes, Inc., San Antonio, 1970—. Mem. Arts Council San Antonio, Tex. Arts Alliance, Greater San Antonio C. of C., Internat. Platform Assn. Roman Catholic. Home: 663 McDougal Ave San Antonio TX 78223 Office: 400 San Antonio Bank & Trust Bldg San Antonio TX 78205

CAIN, VIRGINIA HARTIGAN, jud. orgn. exec., educator; b. Bklyn., May 1, 1922; d. James Gerard and H. Virginia (Williams) Hartigan; A.B., N.Y.U., 1943; M.Ed., U. Del., 1963; postgrad. U. Nev., 1972; m. Edmund Joseph Cain, Dec. 3, 1944; children—Edmund Joseph III, Mary Ellen Cain McMullen, James Michael. Personnel counselor Research and Devel. Labs., Ft. Monmouth, N.J., 1943-47; elem. and secondary tchr. and counselor, Reno, 1968-73; project dir. children in placement project Nat. Council Juvenile and Family Ct. Judges, Reno, 1974-76, curriculum dir., asst. tng. dir., 1976—; adj. asst. prof. U. Nev., Reno; mem. adv. bd. Com. To Aid Abused Women, Nat. Assn. Family Counselors in Juvenile Ct., 1981-82; del.-at-large White House Conf. on Families, 1980. Mem. Nev. Gov.'s Commn. on Status of Women, 1966-70, 72-81; del. Nat. Democratic Convs., 1970, 72, 80; Dem. chmn. Nev. chpt. ERA, 1980-82; mem. Dem. Nat. Com., 1980-82; mem. Platform Accountability Commn., 1982; 1st vice chmn. Nev. Dem. Com., 1980-82; mem. adv. bd. Mental Health Assn. Nev., 1966-72; mem. Nev. Gov.'s Commn. on Girl's Tng. Sch., 1972-76; mem. exec. com. Washoe County Dem. Central Comm., 1966-80; Nev. mem. Compliance Rev. Commn., 1972-76; mem. Nev. Charter Com., 1972-74; No. Nev. coordinator for Senator Edward Kennedy, 1979-80; active campaign worker for Adlai Stevenson, John F. Kennedy, Jimmy Carter; bd. dirs. United Way No. Nev., Planned Parenthood Nev.; mem. Nat. Com. for Support Pub. Schs.; mem. Sr. Citizens Adv. Bd. Washoe County; former chmn. early childhood edn. and legis. com. Del. PTA Bd.; former mem. adv. bd. Washoe Assn. for Mentally Retarded; co-program chmn. 21st Ann. South Pacific Regional Conf., Child Welfare League Am.-Nat. Council Juvenile Ct. Judges, 1976; numerous other civic and polit. activities. Recipient various service and profl. awards. Mem. Internat. Soc. Family Law, Children's Def. Fund, Women's Polit. Caucus, Nat. Assn. Counsel for Children, AAUW, LWV, Reno Bus. and Profl. Women (legis. chmn.). Nev. Art Gallery, Croesus Corp. Investment Club (pres.). Roman Catholic. Club: U. Nev. Faculty Wives. Home: 3710 Clover Way Reno NV 89509 Office: Box 8978 U Nev Reno NV 89507

CAINE, ELIZABETH S., clergywoman; b. Boston, July 7, 1947; d. Jacobus J. and Shirley H. Snel; B.A., U. Conn., 1972; M.A., U. Hartford, 1975; postgrad. Divinity Sch. Yale U., 19—; children—David Scott, Susan Alexandra. Clin. psychologist, 1975-78; part time lectr. in psychology Manchester (Conn.) Community Coll., 1978-80; sch. psychologist East Hampton, Conn., 1978-80; asso. First Congl. Ch., Coventry, Conn., 1981—; co-founder, bd. dirs. Human Growth Services of Coventry, Inc.; developer Adolescent Hot Line; adult educator, condr. workshops. Mem. Am. Psychol. Assn. Mem. United Church of Christ. Home: 110 Slocum Rd Hebron CT 06248

CAIRD, HELEN G., tech. communicator; b. Vienna, Austria, Jan. 10, 1922; d. Ernest and Lucy (Heinsheimer) Geiringer; came to U.S., 1941, naturalized, 1941; B.A. in Modern Langs., Brown U., 1943; student U. Grenoble, 1939, U. London, 1940, Cambridge U., 1941; m. Kenneth A. Caird, Aug. 22, 1964; 1 dau., Rochelle Sharon. Asst. to mgr. Stanford Research Inst., Los Angeles, 1948-56; tech. editor So. Calif. Air Pollution Found., Los Angeles, 1956-58; publs. mgr. Electro-Optical Systems, Inc., Pasadena, Calif., 1958-65; staff asst. tech. documentation Jet Propulsion Lab., Pasadena, 1966-78, documentation supr., 1978—; cons. in field. Fellow Inst. Advancement of Engring., Soc. Tech. Communication (pres. 1973-74); mem. Calif. Inst. Tech. Mgmt. Club. Home: 3573 Yorkshire Rd Pasadena CA 91107 Office: Jet Propulsion Lab 4800 Oak Grove Dr Pasadena CA 91109

CAIRNS, SHIRLEY ANNE, fin. planner; b. Hundred, W.Va., Sept. 26, 1937; d. John Martin and Thelma Irene Stiles; B.S., W.Va. U., 1959, M.A., 1964; children—John Michael, Lyle Dennis, Glynis Ann. Tchr. public schs., Alliance, Ohio, 1958-60, Morgantown, W.Va., 1960-61; receptionist Strand Realty, Coronado, Calif., 1962-63; tchr., head bus. edn. dept. Sutherlin (Oreg.) High Sch., 1964-80; fin. planner IDS, Sutherlin, 1980—. Mem. Democratic Central Com., Oreg. Dem. Platform Com., Oreg. Women's Polit. Caucus, Nat. Women's Polit. Caucus, Oreg. Dem. Women's Fedn.; sec. Calapoola Rural Fire Dist. Mem. Internat. Assn. Fin. Planning, Inst. Cert. Fin. Planners (asso.), Am. Bus. Women's Assn., Sutherlin C. of C. (dir.), Nat. Assn. Female Execs., AAUW, LWV, Umpqua Basin Life Underwriters Assn. (v.p.). Clubs: Women's Civic, Toastmistresses. Home: Box 76 Oakland OR 97462 Office: 1273 W Central Sutherlin OR 97479

CALABIA, DAWN T., legislative asst.; b. Bklyn., May 22, 1941; d. Thomas Michael and Alice Brady (Diver) Tennant; B.A., St. John's U.; M.S.W., Fordham U., 1967; m. Florentine Calabia; children—Florentine Christopher, Theodore Rizal, Alison Maria Clara. Local area analyst N.Y.C. Planning Commn., 1967-68; urban planner Manoussoff Assos., 1969-72; fundraiser, cons. N.Y. State ADA, 1973-74; legis. asst. to Rep. Solarz (N.Y.), Washington. Mem. Nat. Assn. Social Workers, NOW, Lambda Kappa Phi. Office: Room 1536 Longworth House Office Bldg Washington DC 20515 *

CALABRESE, PAULA ANN, ednl. adminstr.; b. Pitts., Mar. 4, 1942; d. Nicholas Anthony and Esther Marie (Morsillo) Calabrese; B.S. in Edn., Duquesne U., 1976, M.Ed., 1969; Ph.D., U. Pitts., 1981. Reading specialist Plum Boro Sch. Dist., Pitts., 1968-69, Churchill Area Sch. Dist., 1969-74; ednl. cons. MacMillan Pub. Co., Riverside, N.J., 1974-77; coordinator of staff/program devel. North Allegheny Sch. Dist., Pitts., 1977—. Cert. elem. tchr., reading specialist, guidance counselor, elem. and secondary sch. prin., reading supr., supr. curriculum and instrn., Pa. Mem. Women in Communications, Inc., Assn. of Supervision and Curriculum Devel., Phi Delta Kappa. Democrat. Roman Catholic. Office: 350 Cumberland Rd Pittsburgh PA 15237

CALABRESE, REBECCA SUSAN, social worker; b. N.Y.C., Jan. 19, 1953; d. Bernard and Ann Hoch (Kubie) R.; A.B. in Sociology, Washington U., St. Louis, 1975, M.S.W. (Comprehensive Care Corp. fellow), George Warren Brown Sch. Social Work, 1977; cert. Rutgers U. Summer Sch. Alcohol Studies, 1979; m. Frank M. Calabrese, June 7, 1981. Chief psychiat. social worker alcohol treatment program Inst. Psychiatry, Northwestern Meml. Hosp., Chgo., 1977-78; exec. adminstr., spl. health cons. Atlantic Chem. Corp., Nutley, N.J., 1978-79; exec. asst. to exec. dir. Post-Grad. Center for Mental Health, N.Y.C., 1980—; asst. to dir. Madeleine Borg Counseling Services, N.Y.C., 1980-81; chief therapist/asst. program coordinator CAREUNIT, Buena Park, Calif., 1981-82; pvt. practice psychotherapy, cons. alcohol, Montclair, N.J., 1979—; exec. dir. N.J. Alcoholism Assn., 1982—; social work instr. Northwestern U. Med. Sch., 1978; condr. alcoholism in-service workshops. Active in numerous polit. campaigns, local, and nat.; active in local N.J. tenants rights movements. Cert. social worker, Ill. Mem. Nat. Assn. Social Workers, Acad. Cert. Social Workers, Assn. Labor-Mgmt. Adminstrs. and Cons. on Alcoholism, Ill. Alcoholism and Drug Dependence Assn., Am. Soc. Profl. and Exec. Women, Am. Public Health Assn., Alumni-Parents Assn. Washington U. (local coordinator).

CALCAGNI, MARIA MINGOLA, cons., educator; b. New Bedford, Mass., Jan. 19, 1954; d. Bartholomew Canto and Lillian Ferriera (Belmarce) Mingola; B.S. in Biology, Simmons Coll., 1976; M.B.A. in Bus. Analysis, San Francisco State U., 1982; m. Dean E. Calcagni, June 26, 1976. Lectr. bus. math. San Francisco State U., 1980—, also research cons. Kuehne, Rock & Mazour Options Mgmt. Co., San Francisco, 1981—. Recipient Grad. Student Disting. Achievement award San Francisco State U., 1982. Mem. Beta Gamma Sigma. Home: 1440B Battery Caulfield Rd Presidio of San Francisco CA 94129 Office: 1600 Holloway Ave San Francisco CA 94132

CALDEMEYER, M. JANET, conservationist; b. Evansville, Ind., Aug. 17, 1952; d. Daniel Freidrich and Marjorie June (Lamble) C.; B.S., St. Mary's Coll., Notre Dame U., 1974; M.A. in Coll. Teaching, Murray State U., 1979; m. Richard O. Meier, Oct. 18, 1980. Recreation specialist TVA, Land Between the Lakes, Golden Pond, Ky., 1974-76, conservationist environ. edn., 1976—; mgr. Big Bear Resort and Marina, Benton, Ky.; dir. Mgmt. Recruiters, Inc., Evansville, Ind. Named hon. Ky. Col. Mem. Nat. Assn. Environ. Edn., Ky. Recreation and Parks Soc., Nat. Recreation and Parks Soc., Nat. Assn. Female Execs., Ky. Assn. Environ. Edn. Republican. Club: West Ky. Performance Boat (bd. dirs.). Home: Route 4 Box 155F Benton KY 42025 Office: TVA Land Between the Lakes Golden Pond KY 42231

CALDEN, GERTRUDE BECKWITH, civic worker; b. Santa Paula, Calif., Apr. 18, 1909; d. Ralph Leslie and Bernice (Hart) Beckwith; grad. Woodbury Coll., 1928; postgrad. U. Calif., Santa Barbara, UCLA; m. Raymond A. MacMillan, Nov. 7, 1928 (div. 1948); 1 son, Thad C.; m. 2d Guy C. Calden, Jr., Dec. 16, 1961 (dec. 1967). Assoc. dir. Students Internat. Travel Assn., N.Y.C., 1949-51; lectr. on self-improvement to schs., colls., women's clubs So. Calif., 1951-54; cons., tchr., counselor Marymount Sch., Santa Barbara, 1953-54; adminstrv. asst. to pres. Resin Industries, Santa Barbara, Calif., 1954-58; adminstrv. asst. to corp. cons. Grant C. Ehrlich, Santa Barbara, 1958-61; treas. Wire Co. Am., Goleta, Calif., 1959-60. Pres. Roosevelt Sch. PTA, 1944-46; sec. Jefferson Sch. PTA, 1941-42; chmn. tchr. recognition div. Santa Barbara County Selective Tchrs. Recruitment Council, 1960-61; mem. adv. com. to bd. govs. Calif. Community Colls., 1970; bd. dirs. community council Santa Barbara City Coll., 1958-66, pres., 1961-62; bd. dirs. U. Calif., Santa Barbara Affiliates, 1975, pres., 1978-80; trustee Found. for Santa Barbara City Coll., 1975—, pres., 1977-79; trustee Found. for U. Calif., Santa Barbara, 1978-80; appropriations com. Santa Barbara Found., 1981—; pres. Santa Barbara Citizens Adult Edn. Adv. Council; women's bd. Santa Barbara Mental Health Assn.; bd. dirs. Work Tng. Program, Inc., 1968—, Central Counties USO, 1969-71, Channel City Women's Forum, 1966—; mem. Citizens Commn. Civil Disorders U. Calif., Isla Vista, 1970-71; mem. Pres.'s Nat. Adv. Council on Adult Edn., 1974-80; mem. Am. Friends of Wilton Park, 1974—; bd. dirs. Rec. for Blind, Santa Barbara Unit, 1974-78, Alexander House, 1976-81; pres. bd. dirs. Friends for Hospice, Santa Barbara, 1981; pres. Montecito Republican Women's Club, 1963-65; bd. dirs. Santa Barbara Rep. Assembly, 1963-66, v.p., 1964; bd. dirs. Santa Barbara County Fedn. Rep. Women's Clubs, 1963—, pres., 1966-69; bd. dirs. So. div. Calif. Fedn. Rep. Women, 1966-69; mem. 13th Congl. Dist. Rep. Com., 1965—; asso. mem. Calif. Rep. Central Com., 1967-68, mem., 1969—; mem. Santa Barbara County central com., 1970-74, sec., 1971-74. Named Women of Yr., Greater Santa Barbara Area, 1974; fellow Wilton Park Internat. Conf., Sussex, Eng., 1972. Mem. Santa Barbara Personnel Assn. (sec. 1957-58), Santa Barbara C. of C. (edn. com. 1955, 57-61), Am. Assn. for UN (dir. Santa Barbara chpt. 1953-57), Family Service Agy., Am. Field Service, Mental Health Assn., Santa Barbara Hist. Soc., Citizens Planning Assn. of Santa Barbara County, St. Francis Hosp. Guild, LWV, Santa Barbara Council Women's Clubs, Calif. Hist. Soc., Univ. Affiliates U. Calif. Santa Barbara. Club: Zonta (pres. Santa Barbara 1956-57, 59-60, chmn. IX dist. Amelia Earhart Scholarship com. 1957-58). Contbr. poems to anthology Gossamer Wings. Address: 819 E Pedregosa St Santa Barbara CA 93103

CALDERON, LINDA CARON, nurse; b. Newark, Nov. 22, 1951; d. Arthur Donovan and Lillian Thomas; B.S.N., Calif. State U., Los Angeles, 1974, M.A., 1982; grad. nurse midwifery program, 1982; m. Rudy J. Calderon, May 3, 1975; children—Mikel Louis, John Matthew. Nurse, Huntington Meml. Hosp., Pasadena, Calif., 1975, nurse clinician, 1980, labor/delivery asst. head nurse, 1981—. Mem. ACLU Found. Reproductive Project, 1981—. Mem. Calif. Perinatal Assn., Am. Coll. Nurse Midwives (asso.), Consortium for Nurse Midwives. Democrat. Roman Catholic. Home: 1145 Leonard St Pasadena CA 91107 Office: 100 Congress St Pasadena CA 91105

CALDERONE, MARY STEICHEN, physician; b. N.Y.C., July 1, 1904; d. Edward J. and Clara (Smith) Steichen; B.A., Vassar Coll., 1925; M.D., U. Rochester, 1939; M.P.H., Columbia U., 1942; D.Med. Sci. (hon.), Women's Med. Coll., 1967; L.H.D. (hon.), Newark State Coll., 1971; Sc.D. (hon.), Adelphi U., 1971, Worcester Found. Exptl. Biology, 1974, Brandeis U., 1975, Haverford Coll., 1978; LL.D. (hon.), Kenyon Coll., 1972; Dr. Pedagogy (hon.), Hofstra U., 1978; children—Linda Martin Hodes, Francesca Stuart, Maria S. Intern Bellevue Hosp., N.Y.C., 1939-40; med. dir. Planned Parenthood Fedn. Am., 1953-64; co-founder, dir., pres. Sex Info. Edn. Council U.S. (SIECUS), N.Y.C., 1964—; lectr. human sexuality, 33d Lower lectr. Acad. Medicine and Cleve. Clinic, 1970; Rufus Jones lectr. Friends Gen. Conf., 1973; Hundley lectr. gynecology, Balt., 1973; Alpha Omega Alpha vis. prof. U. Colo. Med. Sch., Denver, 1980. Recipient 4th Ann. award for disting. service to humanity Women's Aux. Albert Einstein Med. Center, Phila., 1966; Woman of Conscience award Nat. Council Women, 1968; citation Merrill-Palmer inst. Human Devel. and Family Life, Detroit, 1969; Woman of Achievement award Greater N.Y. chpt. women's div. Albert Einstein Coll. Medicine, Yeshiva U., 1969; Haven Emerson award N.Y.C. Pub. Health Assn., 1970; named one of Am.'s 75 Most Important Women, Ladies Home Jour., 1971; one of 50 Most Influential U.S. Women, Newspaper Enterprises Assn., 1975; Elizabeth Blackwell award Hobart and William Smith Coll., 1977; Margaret Sanger award Planned Parenthood Fedn. Am., 1980. Fellow Am. Public Health Assn. (hon. life; Edward W. Browing Achievement award 1980), Soc. Sci. Study Sex; mem. Am. Assn. Marriage and Family Counselors (hon. life) Am. Assn. World Health (dir.), AMA (hon. life), Am. Med. Women's Assn. (hon. life), Alpha Omega Alpha. Quaker. Author: Release From Sexual Tensions, 1960; (with Eric W. Johnson), The Family Book About Sexuality, 1981; editor: Abortion in U.S., 1958; Manual of Family Planning and Contraceptive Practice, rev. edit., 1970; Sexuality and Human Values, 1974; contbr. articles to profl. jours., mags., encys., textbooks. Office: SIECUS 80 Fifth Ave Room 801 New York NY 10011

CALDERONE, PAULA KAY, ins. agy. exec.; b. Odgen, Utah, July 28, 1945; d. Richard E. and Mabel Patricia (Byrne) Pickens; student Culver Stockton Coll., 1963-66; m. Dennis R. Calderone. Rate clk. INA, St. Louis, 1967-68; sec. Charles Crane Agy., St. Louis, 1968-69; with Transamerica Ins. Co., Arlington Heights, Ill., 1969-71; asst. treas. Assurance Agy., Arlington Heights, 1972—. Mem. Bus. and Profl. Women. Mem. Christian Ch. (Disciples of Christ). Home: 614 Bayview St Schaumberg IL 60195 Office: 1114 N Arlington Heights Rd Arlington Heights IL 60004

CALDICOTT, HELEN MARY, pediatrician; b. Melbourne, Australia, 1938; M.B.B.S., U. South Australia, Adelaide, 1962. Intern, Royal Adelaide Hosp., 1962-63; intern Adelaide Children's Hosp., 1972-73, resident, 1973-75, mem. staff, 1975-76; fellow in nutrition Children's Hosp. Med. Center, Boston, 1967-68, fellow in cystic fibrosis, 1975-76, asso. in cystic fibrosis, 1977—. Mem. Am. Thoracic Soc., Royal Australasian Coll. Physicians, Physicians for Social Responsibility (pres. 1981—). Office: Children's Hosp Med Center 300 Longwood Ave Boston MA 02115 *

CALDWELL, BENNATTA WILLIAMS (MRS. ANDREW F. CALDWELL), coll. adminstr.; b. Albany, Ga., Mar. 16, 1942; d. Robert James and Birnelle (Johnson) Williams; B.S. in Bus. Edn., Albany State Coll., 1964; M.Bus. Edn., Ga. State U., 1976; m. Andrew Franklin Caldwell, May 28, 1967; children—Quintard Stephone, Andrew Franklin. Sec. div. arts and scis. Albany (Ga.) State Coll., 1964, 80—, sec. dept. music, 1965-78, adminstrv. supr., bus. instr., Albany State Coll. and Albany Jr. Coll., 1979—. Pres., Hazard Pre-Sch. Center and Lincoln Heights Elementary Sch. Parent Tchr. Orgn., 1979-80. Mem. Profl. Secs. Internat. (pres. Albany chpt. 1979-80), Nat. Bus. Edn. Assn., Music Educators Nat. Conf., Albany State Coll. Keyboarders Orgn. (pres. 1978-80), Iota Phi Lambda. Founder, dir. TV Gospel program The

Sound of Pentecost. Home: 1507 Henri Ave Albany GA 31705 Office: 504 College Dr Albany State Coll Albany GA 31705

CALDWELL, DIANNE DEE, home industry exec.; b. Youngstown, Ohio, Jan. 24, 1946; d. Leo William and June Marie (Gakel) Difford; B.S. in Edn., Kent (Ohio) State U., 1968; m. Thomas R. Caldwell, June 22, 1968; children—Ryan Thomas, Reed Jason. High sch. English tchr., Mogadore, Ohio, 1968-69; librarian Ann Arbor (Mich.) Public Schs., 1969-72; cons. Jafra Cosmetics, Inc.-Gillette, Saline, Mich., 1974-79, cons., mgr., 1977-79, regional dir., 1979-82; v.p. The Creative Circle, Saline, 1982—. Pres. Ann Arbor Police Wives Assn., 1971-75; mem. Republican Nat. Com.; mem. Saline Vocat. Edn. Adv. Com., 1979-80; spl. events chmn. Saline March of Dimes, 1973-75. Named Outstanding Mgr., Jafra Cosmetics, Inc.-Gillette, 1978; recipient Jan Day award, 1978, Saline Edn. Adv. award, 1979, 80. Mem. Nat. Assn. Female Execs., Nat. Ruffed Grouse Soc. Methodist. Office: 213 E Michigan Ave Saline MI 48176

CALDWELL, ELEANOR, artist; b. Kansas City, Mo., May 1, 1927; d. Earl Kendrick and Etta (Clark) C.; B.S. magna cum laude, in Edn., SW Mo. State U., 1948; M.A., Columbia U. Tchrs. Coll., 1953, Ed.D. (Alumni fellow, Dow scholar 1958-59), 1959. Tchr. art high schs. in Mo. and Iowa, 1948-52; instr. art SW Mo. State U., 1953-54; asst. prof. Ft. Hays (Kans.) State U., 1954-57; instr. Columbia U. Tchrs. Coll., lectr. art edn. Queen's Coll., also supr. children's art carnival Mus. Modern Art, N.Y.C., 1957-59; prof., chmn. dept. art NW Mo. State Coll., Maryville, 1959-60; asso. prof. Edinboro (Pa.) State Coll., 1960-62, Pa. State U., 1962-63; asso. prof. No. Ill. U., DeKalb, 1963-64, prof. art, 1967—; asso. prof. Ft. Hays State U., 1964-67; dir. Oakbrook (Ill.) Invitational Crafts Exhbn., 1968—; cons., tchr. Arrowmont Sch. Arts and Crafts, Gatlinburg, Tenn., 1974-77; represented in permanent collections Denver Public Schs., Colo. Women's Coll., Denver, Ft. Hays State Coll., No. Ill. U., Sheldon Meml. Art Mus., Lincoln, Nebr., Arrowmont Sch. Arts and Crafts. Recipient Public Service award Ill. Sesquicentennial Commn., 1968; grantee No. Ill. U., 1968, 70, 74-80. Mem. Soc. N.Am. Goldsmiths, Am. Crafts Council, Artists Equity, AAUP, Delta Kappa Gamma, Pi Lambda Theta, Kappa Delta Pi. Editor: Contemporary Jewelry, 1970. Office: Visual Arts Bldg No Ill U DeKalb IL 60115

CALDWELL, (JANET) TAYLOR, author; b. Preswick, Manchester, Eng., Sept. 7, 1900; d. Arthur F. and Anna (Marks) Caldwell; A.B., U. Buffalo, 1931; Litt.D., D'Youville Coll., Bufallo, 1964; L.H.D., Niagara U., 1971; m. William Fairfax Combs, May 27, 1919 (div. 1931); 1 dau., Mary Margaret (Mrs. Gerald Fried); m. 2d, Marcus Reback, May 12, 1931 (dec. Aug. 1970); 1 dau., Judith Ann (Mrs. Theodore Roosevelt Goodman); m. 3d, William E. Stancell, June 1973; m. 4th, William Robert Prestie, July 6, 1978. Began as stenographer, ct. reporter; ct. reporter Workmen's Compensation Div., N.Y. State Dept. Labor, Buffalo, 1923-24; sec. Bd. Spl. Inquiry, U.S. Immigration and Naturalization Service, Dept. Justice, Buffalo, 1924-31. Served as yeomanette, USNR, 1918-19. Recipient nat. award D.A.R. 1956; McElligott medal Marquette U., 1964. Fellow Internat. Inst. Arts and Letters; mem. Am. Legion, St. Francis Guild, Nazareth Guild, Legion of Mary. Republican. Roman Catholic. Club: Women's Nat. Republican. Author: Dynasty of Death, 1938; others include: Melissa, 1948; Let Love Come Last, 1949; The Balance Wheel, 1951; The Devil's Advocate, 1952; Never Victorious, Never Defeated (Grand Prix, Prix Chatrain, Paris), 1956; Tender Victory, 1956; The Sound of Thunder, 1957; Dear and Glorious Physician, 1959; The Listener, 1960; A Prologue to Love, 1961; Grandmother and The Priests, 1963; A Pillar of Iron, 1965; No One Hears But Him, 1966; Dialogues with the Devil, 1967; Testimony of Two Men, 1968; Great Lion of God, 1970; Captains and Kings, 1972; Glory and the Lightening, 1974; Ceremony of the Innocent, 1976; Bright Flows the River, 1978; Answer as a Man, 1981. Contbr. to nat. mags. *

CALDWELL, LEONA IOLA WILL (MRS. OLIVER CROMWELL CALDWELL), clergyman, writer; b. Sabina, Ohio, Apr. 13, 1903; d. Silas Joseph and Luella Marie (Reed) Will; B.S., Ohio State U., 1925; M.A., Columbia U., 1933; D.H.L., Capitol Coll., 1965; m. Oliver Cromwell Caldwell, June 20, 1938. Ordained to ministry Methodist Ch., 1954; lectr. Swarthmore (Pa.) Chautauqua, 1925-29; tchr. speech Sabina High Sch., 1930-34; minister, Franklin Square (Ohio) Meth. Ch., 1957-58; minister, Leetonia, Ohio, 1959—; spiritual dir. Hospitality House, Tampa, Fla., 1959-61. County v.p. ARC, Lisbon, Ohio, 1940-48; vol. St. Stephens (Wyo.) Indian Sch., Wind River Indian Reservation, 1972-78; bd. dirs. County Health, Lisbon, 1943-47. Mem. Internat. Platform Assn. (hon. life mem.; bd. govs. 1950-65, 68-69, chaplain 1956-76), Am. Assn. Women Ministers, Nat. League Am. Pen Women (pres. br., state chaplain 1968-79, service award 1981), Internat. Poetry Assn., Am. Poetry League, London Poetry Soc., Versewriters Guild Ohio (life), Epsilon Sigma Alpha (hon. life). Methodist. Mem. Order Eastern Star (past matron). Address: 6 Lake Hunter Dr Lakeland FL 33803

CALDWELL, MARY ALICE, nurse; b. Los Angeles, Nov. 21, 1949; d. Jack B. and Patricia A. (Towey) C.; B.S. in Nursing, U. San Francisco, 1971; cardiovascular nurse specialist Ariz. Heart Inst., 1976. Intensive care nurse St. Mary's Hosp., San Francisco, 1971-75; clin. instr. cardiovascular intensive care Stanford (Calif.) U. Hosp., 1976-79; clin. research specialist Oximetrix, Inc., Mountain View, Calif., 1979; nurse tchr. practitioner, critical care spl. projects Kaiser Found. Hosp., Los Angeles, 1980; profl. edn. services edn. mgr. Am. Edwards Labs., Irvine, Calif., 1980—; cons. critical care edn. groups; lectr. Registered nurse. Mem. Am. Assn. Critical Care Nurses (pres. elect local chpt. 1979), Am. Heart Assn. Contbr. articles to profl. jours. Office: Am Edwards Labs PO Box 11150 Santa Ana CA 92711

CALDWELL, PEGGY THURSTON, regulatory analyst; b. Cleveland, Tex., Aug. 21, 1945; d. Homer S. and Dorothy Jane (Bailes) Gilbert; m. Bob L. Caldwell, Apr. 12, 1967; children—Brian Lee, Brandon Lee. Vice pres., dir. Agri-Sul, Inc., Mineola, Tex., 1969-78; v.p., dir. Agri-Sul Canada, Ltd., Calgary, Alta., Can., 1974-78; owner Hickory Hut, Mineola, Tex., 1973-75; regulatory analyst Tex. Eastern Transmission Corp., Houston, 1978—; owner Resource Mgmt. Dynamics, Humble, Tex., 1981—. Mem. Am. Entrepreneurs Assn., Exec. Female, Am. Mgmt. Assn. Republican. Methodist. Home: 7019 Foxfield Lane Humble TX 77338 Office: PO Box 1105 Humble TX 77347

CALDWELL, SARAH, opera producer, condr.; b. Maryville, Mo.; student violin New Eng. Conservatory. Mem. faculty Tanglewood (Mass.) Sch. Music; created dept. of music theater at Boston U. and conducted Am. premiere of Hindemith's Mathis der Maler; founder, artistic dir., condr. Opera Co. of Boston which has produced 45 operas including Schoenberg's Moses and Aaron, 1966, Stravinsky's Rakes Progress, 1967, Mussorgsky's Boris Godunov, Offenbach's Voyage to the Moon, Berlioz' The Trojans, 1972 and Benvenuto Cellini, 1975, Prokofiev's War and Peace, 1974, Sessions' Montezuma, 1976, Tippett's Ice Break, 1979, Zimmermann's Die Soldaten, 1982; also former artistic dir. Am. Nat. Opera Co. presenting Falstaff, Tosca and Berg's Lulu in San Francisco, Chgo., Dallas and N.Y.C.; condr. La Traviata, Beijing, China, 1981. Address: care Opera Co Boston 539 Washington St Boston MA 02111 *

CALDWELL, VERNETTE MIRIAM, broadcast exec.; b. N.Y.C., Apr. 25, 1953; d. Charles Wesley and Gloria Dolores (Todd) C.; B.B.A., Pace U., 1976. Intermediate auditor Citibank, N.Y.C., 1974-75; systems engr. developer Electronic Data Systems, Dallas, 1975-76; asst. bus. mgr. ABC, N.Y.C., 1977-81; supr. computer ops. ABC Video Enterprises, N.Y.C., 1981—. Mem. Nat. Assn. Female Execs., Internat. Radio and TV Soc. Office: 825 7th Ave New York NY 10019

CALHOON, JANET ELAINE, chiropractor; b. Hershey, Pa., June 15, 1948; d. William Harvey and Geraldine Romaine (Heisey) C.; student John Brown U., 1966-68, Palmer Jr. Coll., 1970-71; B.S., Palmer Coll. Chiropractic, 1971, D.C., 1971; m. John F. Seavers, Jan. 20, 1979. Gen. practice chiropractic health care Stillwagon Chiropractic Offices, Monongahela, Pa., 1972-73, Fitterer Chiropractic Center, Hershey, Pa., 1974-78; pvt. practice, Hummelstown, Pa., 1978—. Qualified in applied Kenesiology. Mem. Internat. Chiropractors Assn., Am. Chiropractors Assn., Parker Chiropractic Research Found., Pa. Palmer Coll. Alumni Assn. (past pres.). Club: Internat. Toastmistress (speech contest winner 1976, 80, past pres., v.p. council 5 Canusa region). Home: 258 E Main St Hummelstown PA 17036 Office: 2 W Main St Hummelstown PA 17036

CALHOON, OLIVIA CLEO, assn. exec.; b. Eldon, Mo., Jan. 6, 1910; d. George Earl and Audra Nell (McClure) Hite; R.N., St. Luke's Hosp., 1931; m. Nathan Moore Calhoon, Sept. 24, 1936; children—Audra May, Barbara Jane, Frank Hite. Pvt. duty nurse, Kansas City, Mo., 1931-36; partner Calhoon Furniture, Eldon, 1950-74. Mem. Mo. Nurses Assn., D.A.R. (state chmn. mag. advt. 1974-80). Republican. Mem. Christian Ch. Clubs: Order of Eastern Star, Federated Garden, Federated Women's. Home: 630 E Newton St Eldon MO 65026

CALHOUN, ERNESTINE ABNEY, editor; b. Copiah County, Miss., Jan. 14, 1923; d. Tommie and Ollie H. (Hilliard) Abney; B.S. in Elementary Edn., Jackson State Coll., 1958; M.A., Scarritt Coll., Nashville, 1974; m. Walter L. Calhoun, Apr. 27, 1945; children—Thomas Charles, Paulette. Tchr., Meridian (Miss.) Pub. Schs., 1958-70; editor Kindergartner, Methodist Pub. House, Nashville, 1970-72, editor children's books Abingdon Press, 1973—. Bd. dirs. Black Meth. for Ch. Renewal, 1973-77; chmn. Vocat. Services, 1976-77. Mem. ALA, Nat. Council Tchrs. English, Internat. Reading Assn., Woman's Nat. Book Assn. (dir. 1975-77), Assn. Childhood Edn. Internat. Club: Altrusa Internat. (Nashville). Home: 615 39th Ave N Nashville TN 37209 Office: 201 8th Ave S Nashville TN 37202

CALHOUN, FAYE JOHNSON, fed. agy. adminstr.; b. Washington, Sept. 27, 1941; B.S. in Zoology, Howard U., 1963, M.S. in Endocrinology and Biochemistry, 1965; M.P.A., U. So. Calif., 1977, now postgrad.; children—Robin Renee, Raymond Levy. Research asso. Howard U., 1964-67; pharmacologist FDA, Rockville, Md., 1967-69, supervisory pharmacologist, 1969-71, acting chief clin. lab. br., 1971, equal opportunity officer, 1971-73, spl. asst. to dir. Bur. Drugs, 1973-75, health scientist adminstr., 1976-78, acting chief extramural programs br., 1978-79, chief grants adminstrn. and rev. br. Nat. Inst. Occupational Safety and Health, 1979—; exec. sec. toxicology study sect., div. research grants NIH. Mem. Am. Soc. Public Adminstrs., Group Health Assns. of Rockville Center (adv. council), Gamma Sigma Sigma. Contbr. articles to profl. jours. Home: 2202 Westview Dr Silver Spring MD 20910

CALHOUN, GLORIA LYNN, exptl. psychologist; b. Mpls., Nov. 12, 1951; d. Robert Willard and Wilma Marie (Schmoock) Alrutz; B.A., Coll. Wooster, 1974; postgrad Wright State U., 1979—; m. Kevin Paul Calhoun, Apr. 20, 1974; children—Mark Allan, Brian Patrick. Document research analyst Bunker Ramo Corp., Dayton, Ohio, 1974-75; human factors engr., Dayton, Ohio, 1975-81; research psychologist Systems Research Lab., Dayton, 1981-82; engring. research psychologist Air Force Aerospace Med. Research Lab., Dayton, 1982—. Wright State U. scholar, 1980; NSF grantee, 1973. Recipient Leach Meml. prize in psychology Coll. Wooster, 1974. Mem. Human Factors Soc., Soc. Info. Display, Union Concerned Scientists, Sigma Xi (asso.). Contbr. numerous articles to profl. publs. Home: 2814 Bahns Dr Beavercreek OH 45385 Office: AMRL/HEA Wright-Patterson AFB Dayton OH 45433

CALHOUN, NANCY BOLTON, gerontologist; b. South Orange, N.J., Nov. 12, 1935; d. John Hill and Sarah (Pierpont) Holton; B.A., Mt. Holyoke Coll., 1957; postgrad. Boston U. Sch. Theology, 1960-61; M.S.W., Syracuse U., 1973, cert. in gerontology, 1973; children—James, Elizabeth, Douglas, Kristin Bolton. Dir. religious edn. Parkway Community Ch., Milton, Mass., 1957-59; coordinator resident services and admissions Bernardine Apts., Syracuse, N.Y., 1973-75; coordinator admissions Loretto Geriatrics Center, Syracuse, 1974-76, supr. social services Intermediate Care Facility, 1975-77, dir. social work services, 1978—; instr. Syracuse U. Sch. Social Work, 1974—; pvt. practitioner, 1977—. Mem. Nat. Assn. Social Workers (vice chmn. Central N.Y. 1975—), Acad. Cert. Social Workers, Am. Gerontol. Soc., Nat. Council Social Welfare, Coalition Social Workers in Long Term Care. Home: 876 Genesee St W Skaneateles NY 13152 Office: 700 Brighton Ave E Syracuse NY 13205

CALHOUN, SALLY HANSON, clin. psychologist; b. Wauwatosa, Wis., July 7, 1939; d. Lee Delbert and Olive Elizabeth (Congdon) Hanson; B.A. with distinction in English, U. Mich., 1961, M.A. in English, 1963; M.A. (USPHS fellow), Northwestern U., 1967, Ph.D. in Clin. Psychology, 1970; m. David Redfearn Calhoun, Sept. 5, 1964; children—Douglas David, Julie Katherine. Clin. clk. Hines VA Hosp., 1964; psychologist Ill. State Psychiat. Inst., 1965-69; cons. Nelson Hall Pub. Co., 1972-78, also lectr. Northeastern Ill. U., 1972-77; with Assoc. Psychotherapists of Chgo., 1973-74; pvt. practice clin. psychology, Glenview, Ill., 1978—; asst. prof., core faculty Forest Inst. Profl. Psychology, 1979—; dir. Glenview Youth Services. Recipient awards for fiction Scholastic Mag., 1954, 56, Avery Hopwood writing award U. Mich., 1958. Mem. Am. Psychol. Assn., Ill. Psychol. Assn., Nat. Council Health Service Providers Psychology, Am. Assn. Arts and Lhtters, Mortar Bd., Pi Beta Phi. Office: 1717 Glenview Rd Suite 200 Glenview IL 60025

CALISHER, HORTENSE (MRS. CURTIS HARNACK), author; b. N.Y.C., Dec. 20, 1911; d. Joseph Henry and Hedvig (Lichstern) Calisher; A.B., Barnard Coll., 1932; Litt.D. (hon.), Skidmore Coll., 1980; m. Curtis Harnack, Mar. 23, 1959; children by former marriage—Bennet Hughes, Peter Heffelfinger. Adj. prof. English, Barnard Coll., N.Y.C., 1956-57; vis lectr. State U. Iowa, 1957, 59-60, Stanford U., 1958, Sarah Lawrence Coll., Bronxville, N.Y., 1962, 67; adj. prof. Columbia U., N.Y.C., 1968-70, CCNY, 1969; vis. prof. lit. SUNY, Purchase, 1971-72, Brandeis U., 1963-64, U. Pa., 1965; Regent's prof. U. Calif., 1976; vis. prof. Bennington Coll., 1978, Washington U., St. Louis, 1979; lectr. W. Ger., Yugoslavia, Rumania, Hungary, 1978. Guggenheim fellow, 1952, 55; Dept. of State Am. Specialists's grantee to S.E. Asia, 1958; recipient Acad. of Arts and Letters award, 1967, Nat. Council Arts award, 1967. Mem. AAAL. Author: In the Absence of Angels (short stories), 1951; False Entry (novel), 1961; Tale for the Mirror (novella and short stories), 1962; Textures of Life (novel), 1963; Extreme Magic (novella and short stories), 1964; Journal form Ellipsia (novel), 1965, The Railway Police and The Last Trolley Ride (novellas), 1966; The New Yorkers (novel), 1969; Queenie (novel), 1971; Standard Dreaming (novel), 1972; Herself (autobiog. work), 1972; Eagle Eye (novel), 1973; The Collected Stories of Hortense Calisher, 1975; (novel) On Keeping Women, 1977; (novel) Mysteries of Motion, 1953; editor Best American Short Stories, 1981; contbr. short stories, articles, revs. to New Yorker, Harper's, Harper's Bazaar, Mademoiselle, Reporter, N.Y. Times, Am. Scholar, New Criterion, anthologies, others. Office: c/o Candida Donadio 111 W 57th St New York NY 10019

CALKIN, ABIGAIL BURGESS, ednl. adminstr., educator; b. Boston, June 30, 1941; d. John Burgess and Ruth Witmer (Lichty) C.; B.A., U. Colo., 1963; postgrad. U. Edinburgh (Scotland), 1963-65; M.A. (Elks Found. fellow 1966, Office Edn. Fellowship grantee 1967-68), U. Oreg., 1969; Ph.D., U. Kans., 1979; m. Robert Barry Giese, May 25, 1973; 1 son, Seth McKenzie Koch. Counselor, Wallace Village for Children, Broomfield, Colo., 1959-62; tchr. Children's Hosp. Sch., Eugene, Oreg., 1965-67, program coordinator, 1968-70; research asst. U. Oreg., 1970-72; asst. prof. spl. edn., psychology Oreg. Coll. Edn., 1970, 72-75; sch. psychologist Topeka Public Schs., 1977-78, asst. prin. Capital City Schs., Topeka Public Schs., 1978-82, prin., 1982—; asst. prof. ednl. adminstrn. Kans. State U., 1980—; condr. numerous workshops, 1966—; cons. in field, 1966—. Bd. dirs. U. Oreg. YWCA, 1971, Mt. Hood Community Coll. Nursing Program, 1971-73. Cert. elem. tchr., Oreg., Kans.; cert. sch. psychologist, supt., Kans. Mem. Council Exceptional Children, United Sch. Adminstrs. Kans., Assn. Behavior Analysis. Democrat. Quaker. Author books, including: Pebbles, Mops and Thimigs, 1974; (with others) Toilet Training: Help for the Delayed Learner, 1978; bd. editors Behavior Analyst, 1980-81, Jour. Precision Teaching, 1981—; research on use of operant procedures, behavior modification, and precision teaching to investigate thoughts, feelings, and other inner behavior. Home: 631 Lane Topeka KS 66606 Office: 2700 W 6th St Topeka KS 66606

CALKINS, JOANN RUBY, nursing adminstr.; b. Mich., June 28, 1934; d. William Russell and Imajean (Dunkle) Armentrout; A.S., Delta Coll., 1964; B.S., Central Mich. U., 1972, M.A., 1977; m. James Calkins, Feb. 2, 1952; children—Russell, Jill, Cindy. Staff nurse, L.P.N. clin. instr., asst. dir. Sch. Nursing, Midland (Mich.) Hosp., 1964-71; dir. nursing, dir. substance abuse unit Gladwin (Mich.) Hosp., 1972-76; prin. Calkins Profl. Counseling & Cons., Harrison, Mich., 1976-78, part-time, 1978—; dir. nursing service Central Mich. Community Hosp., Mt. Pleasant, 1978—; condr. workshops Mich. Dept. Public Health; Mich. Hosp. Assn.; exec. dir. Holistic Health Agy., 1977—. Trustee, Mid-Mich. Community Coll. Recipient Murial A. Grimmason Nursing Scholarship award, 1962; Cert. nursing adminstr. Mem. Mich. Soc. Hosp. Nursing Adminstrs. (mem. steering com. 1979-80, dir., 14 county rep. 1980—), Mich. Nurses Assn., Am. Nurses Assn., Am. Hosp. Assn. Nursing Adminstrs. Methodist. Home: 3581 E Mostetler St Harrison MI 48625 Office: 1221 South Dr Mount Pleasant MI 48858

CALKINS, SUSANNAH EBY, economist; b. Bucyrus, Ohio, Jan. 16, 1924; d. Samuel L. and Mae (McClure) Eby; A.B., Goucher Coll., 1945; M.S. in Econs. (Univ. scholar 1946-47), U. Wis., 1947; m. G. Nathan Calkins, Nov. 19, 1949; children—Helen E. (dec.), Margaret S., Sarah A., Abigail C. Fiscal analyst U.S. Bur. Budget, 1945-50; economist U.S. Council of Econ. Advisors, 1950-51, U.S. Office Price Stabilization, 1951-53, U.S. Bur. Budget, 1953-55; cons. U.S. Adv. Commn. on Intergovernmental Relations, Washington, 1972-73, 74-75, cons. on counter-cyclical aid programs, 1977-78, sr. analyst, 1979—; cons. revenue sharing Brookings Instn., Washington, 1973-74. Sponsor, S.S. Goucher Victory, Balt., 1945. Mem. Am. Econs. Assn., Phi Beta Kappa. Presbyterian. Author: (with R. Nathan, and A. Manvel) Monitoring Revenue Sharing, 1975. Home: 6504 Dearborn Dr Falls Church VA 22044 Office: US Adv Com Intergovtl Relations Washington DC 20575

CALKINS, VIRGINIA BRADY, physician; b. Balt., Oct. 8, 1924; d. Leo and Lucy McCormick (Jewett) Brady; student Vassar Coll., 1942-43; B.A., U. Mich., 1945; M.D., Johns Hopkins U., 1949; m. Evan Calkins, Sept. 9, 1946; children—Sarah, Stephen, Lucy, Joan, Benjamin, Hugh, Ellen, Geoffrey, Timothy. Physician Med. Care Clinic, Balt., 1950-51; staff physician McLean Hosp., Belmont, Mass., 1953-61; clin. physician Gowanda Psychiat. Center, Helmuth, N.Y., 1962—. Bd. dirs. 4-H, Erie County, N.Y., 1970-78; del. Republican Nat. Conv., 1976; mem. Hamburg (N.Y.) Central Sch. Bd., 1977-82, pres., 1981-82. Presbyterian (deacon). Club: Vassar (pres. 1980-82). Home: 3799 Windover St Hamburg NY 14075 Office: Gowanda Psychiatric Centre Helmuth NY 14079

CALLAGHAN, VERONICA KASTRIN, psychiat. social worker; b. El Paso, Tex., Sept. 14, 1942; d. William Janke and Socorro (Lozano) Kastrin; B.A., H. Sophie Newcomb Coll., 1964; M.S.W., Tulane U., 1968; m. Richard D. Callaghan, Nov. 3, 1973. Staff psychiat. social worker DePaul Community Mental Health Center, New Orleans, 1967-68; staff psychiat. social worker El Paso (Tex.) Child Guidance Center, 1968-73; Cons. St. Margaret's Center, 1973; pvt. practice individual and group psychotherapy, El Paso, 1973—; dir., Kasco Investments, Southwestern Sheet Metal Works, Inc., Urban Gen. Contractors. Mem. Acad. Cert. Social Workers, Am. Group Psychotherapy Assn., Am. Acad. Psychotherapists, Nat. Assn. Social Workers. Office: 5862 Cromo Dr Suite 100 El Paso TX 79912

CALLAHAM, BETTY ELGIN, state librarian; b. Honea Path, S.C., Oct. 8, 1929; d. John Winfred and Alice (Dodson) Callaham; B.A., Duke U., 1950; M.A., Emory U., 1954, M.Librarianship, 1961. Tchr. public elem. and high schs., N.C., Ga. and S.C., 1950-60; field service librarian S.C. State Library, 1961-65, dir. field services, 1965-74, dep. librarian, 1974-79, state librarian, Columbia, 1979—; S.C. rep. White House Conf. on Library and Info. Services, 1979. Mem. Am. Library Assn., S.C. Library Assn., Southeastern Library Assn. Baptist. Office: South Carolina State Library Box 11469 Columbia SC 29211

CALLAHAN, ELAINE SHAW, retail jeweler; b. Gilmer, Tex., July 14, 1926; d. Ellie Hugh and Emily Ethel (Campbell) Shaw; student public schs.; m. J. Carroll Callahan, Mar. 19, 1949; children—J. Kim, J. Elaine. Founder, 1953, since owner Carolane Co., jewelers, Longview, Tex.; owner Carolane Investment Co., 1953—, Carolane Fin. Co., 1953—. Mem. Longview Lawyers Wives, Longview Women's Forum, Longview Fedn. Women's Clubs, Christian Women's Fellowship. Mem. Christian Ch. (Disciples of Christ). Club: Order Eastern Star. Office: PO Box 1428 Longview TX 75606

CALLAHAN, MAUREEN ANNE HAVIKEN, psychologist; b. N.Y.C., Feb. 12, 1939; d. Joseph Patrick and Catherine B. (Dunne) Haviken; B.A., Catholic U. Am., 1961; M.S., Hofstra U., Hempstead, N.Y., 1970; Ph.D., St. John's U., Jamaica, N.Y., 1978; m. Edward P. Callahan, June 30, 1962; children—Jennifer, Christina. Tchr. high and elem. schs.; also career counselor, sch. psychologist; ind. practice psychotherapy; mem. faculty C.W. Post Coll.; now asst. prof. psychology Webster Coll., St. Louis. NDEA fellow. Mem. Am. Psychol. Assn., Am. Personnel and Guidance Assn., Nassau County Psychol. Assn., Orthopsychiat. Assn., Mo. Historic Soc. Address: 6 Fair Oaks St Saint Louis MO 63124

CALLAHAN, SIDNEY DESHAZO, psychologist, educator, author; b. Washington, Mar. 6, 1933; d. George Sidney and Lethama Sara (Jones) deShazo; B.A. in English magna cum laude (scholar), Bryn Mawr Coll., 1955; M.A. in Psychology, Sarah Lawrence Coll., 1971; Ph.D. in Psychology CUNY, 1980; D.Litt. (hon.) Regis Coll., Weston, Mass., 1966, St. Mary's Coll., Notre Dame, Ind., 1970; m. Daniel Callahan, June 5, 1954; children—Mark, Stephen, John, Thomas (dec.), Peter, Sarah, David. Nationally syndicated columnist, 1969-72; staff psychologist Echo Hills Mental Health Services, Dobbs Ferry, N.Y., 1973-75, pres. bd. trustees, 1976; adj. faculty Mercy Coll., Dobbs Ferry, 1976,

New Rochelle (N.Y.) Coll., 1977; faculty Coll. of New Resources of New Rochelle, 1977; asst. prof. psychology grad. sch. edn. Fairfield (Conn.) U., 1977; asso. prof. psychology Mercy Coll., 1980—; participant ednl. films, tapes, TV and radio programs in field of women's role, family, bioethics, 1965—; lectr., leader workshops colls. and univs. in U.S., 1965—; trustee Mercy Coll., 1970-74; lay rep. commn. on higher edn. Middle States Assn. of Colls. and Secondary Schs., 1972; cons. Nat. Council Chs., United Ch. Women, Inst. Soc., Ethics and Life Scis., 1969—, NSF, Nat. Endowment Humanities; mem. Nat. Conf. Cath. Bishops' Com. for Bicentennial on the Family, 1976. Bishops' Com. for Ecumenical and Interreligious Affairs, 1978—; adv. com. for sci. and soc. NSF, 1979—; adv. bd. Kennedy Inst. Bioethics, 1971—; author: The Illusion of Eve: Modern Women's Search for Identity, 1965 (French, German, Spanish, Italian, Portuguese, Japanese edits. 1965-75); Beyond Birth Control: Christian Experience of Sex, 1968 (paperback under title Exiled to Eden, 1970); The Working Mother, 1971 (paperback 1972); Parenting: Principles and Politics of Parenthood, 1973 (paperback 1974); contbr. essays to books in field. Recipient Rosary Coll. alumnae medal, 1966, disting. alumna award Holton Arms Sch., 1978, award for best column Cath. Press Assn., 1971. Fellow Soc. for Values in Higher Edn.; mem. Am. Psychol. Assn. (asso.). Democrat. Roman Catholic. Home: 50 Summit Dr Hastings-on-Hudson NY 10706 Office: Mercy Coll Dobbs Ferry NY 10522

CALLAHAN, THELMA, pianist, educator; b. Sweetwater, Tenn., Feb. 2, 1908; d. Alvin S. and Ressa E. (Collins) Callahan; student Peabody Conservatory of Music, Balt., Eastman Sch. Music, Sherwood Music Sch., Chgo., N.Y.U.; studied with LaSalle Spier, Austin Conradi, James Friskin, Harold Bauer. Broadcast piano program, Washington radio stas. WRC, WJSV, WOL, WMAL, 1924-36; pvt. piano tchr., Washington, 1924—; D.C. chmn., adjudicator Nat. Piano Playing Auditions, 1948—; adjudicator broadcasting cos.; mem. extension faculty Sherwood Music Sch., 1936. Mem. Washington Piano Tchrs. Forum (past pres.), Nat. Fedn. Music Clubs, D.C. Fedn. Music Clubs (past pres.), Nat. Guild Piano Tchrs. (chmn. Washington chpt.), Washington Music Tchrs. Assn., Am. Coll. Musicians (nat. dir.). Methodist. Address: 3803 Ingomar St NW Washington DC 20015

CALLAS, GWEN HOOBLER, univ. adminstr.; b. Zanesville, Ohio, Dec. 14, 1951; d. Joseph and Jane L. Miles; B.A. cum laude, Kent State U., 1974, M.A., 1975. Sr. counselor Bur. Vocat. Rehab., Akron, Ohio, 1975-76; dir. handicapped student services, conf. planner Kent State U., 1976—, also adj. faculty rehab. counseling dept.; cons. univs., agencies and corps.; adv. council Ohio Rehab. Services Commn. Del. White House Conf. on Handicapped Individuals; mem. Kent Affirmative Action Council, Ohio Gov.'s Com. Employment of Handicapped. Cert. rehab. counselor; named Young Career Woman, Cuyahoga Falls Bus. and Profl. Women, 1980; recipient Dedicated Service award Nat. Assn. Handicapped Student Services, 1980, Kent State U., 1980. Mem. Assn. Handicapped Student Service Programs in Postsecondary Edn., Nat. Rehab. Assn., Ohio Rehab. Assn., Ohio Counseling and Personnel Assn., Nat. Assn. Female Execs., Nat. Rehab. Counseling Assn., Omicron Delta Kappa. Methodist. Home: 1547 Stratford St Kent OH 44240 Office: 102 Administration Bldg Kent State U Kent OH 44242

CALLAWAY, MARY MCDOWELL, lawyer, educator; b. Tallahassee, June 26, 1929; d. Charles G. and Mary M. (Hogan) McDowell; A.A., Pensacola Jr. Coll., 1972; B.A., U. West Fla., 1972; J.D., Fla. State U., 1974; LL.M., Emory U., 1981; children—Sara, Julia, Mark. Admitted to Fla. bar, 1975; asst. states atty. Fla. First Jud. Dist., Pensacola, 1975-76, chief asst. states atty., 1977-78; individual practice law, Pensacola, Fla., 1978—; asst. prof. dept. fin. and acctg. U. West Fla., Pensacola, 1978—; arbitrator Community Juvenile Arbitration Program for Escambia County. Mem. N.W. Fla. Creek Indian Council, 1981—. Mem. Am. Inst. C.P.A.s, Fla. Inst. C.P.A.s, Am. Bar Assn., Fla. Bar Assn., Escambia-Santa Rosa Bar Assn., Estate Planning Council N.W. Fla., Phi Delta Phi. Democrat. Methodist. Clubs: Pilot, Pensacola Fedn. Garden, VWF Women's, Panhandle Tiger Bay. Office: PO Box 3697 Pensacola FL 32506

CALLAWAY, RHEA EVA HALL, journalist, public speaker; b. Thomson, Ga.; d. Nathan and Eva Jennie (Hawes) Hall; pvt. studies in music, 1928-39; student CCNY, 1941-44, Pohs Inst., 1958-59, U. Md.; cert. public relations and journalism New Sch. Social Research, 1960; cert. in Christian ministry N.Y. Theol. Sem., 1979; L.H.D., Miller U., 1976, Southeastern U. of V.I., 1979; m. Robert L. Glenn, Mar. 20, 1971; 1 dau., Sharon Callaway McCall. Owner, Miss R. Hall, N.Y.C., 1937-46; dir. Peerless Advt. Corp., N.Y.C., 1946-51; women's editor N.Y. Age, N.Y.C., 1958-59, ch. editor, 1973—; women's editor N.Y. Citizen Call, N.Y.C., 1960-61; mgr. N.Y. Amsterdam News, N.Y.C., Bklyn., 1963-73; pub. Cameo Mag., 1975—; ordained to Gospel ministry, 1978; pastor Good News Baptist Ch.; pres. Mt. Zion Congress of Christian Edn. Dir. public relations Mt. Morris Park Hosp., N.Y.C., 1959-60; cons. pub. relations Camp Minisink, N.Y.C., 1957-63. Mem. adv. council Medgar Evers Coll., Bklyn.; mem. adv. bd. Harlem Inst. Fashion, N.Y.C.; vice chmn. adv. bd. Harlem Center chpt. ARC; exec. dir. Glendale Women's Guild, N.Y.C., 1971—; bd. dirs. Manhattan Cluster Fed. Credit Union, mgr., 1977—. Recipient various honors, citations. Mem. Nat. Assn. Media Women, Nat. Council Negro Women (pres. Manhattan sect. 1968-70), Nat. Assn. Negro Bus. and Profl. Women (chmn. pub. relations 1957-60), Internat. Platform Assn., Nat. Assn. Media Women (founder 1965, pres. 1965-67), Iota Phi Lambda (chpt. pres., nat. journalist 1975-77). Mng. editor Women's Interfaith Reporter, 1973—. Home: 225-08 135th Ave Laurelton NY 11413

CALLEN, SUSAN MANIS, social worker; b. Fond du Lac, Wis., Oct. 13, 1948; d. Jacob Maurice and Lillian (Rudoy) Manis; student U. Wis., 1966-68; B.A. in Psychology, U. Mich., 1969, M.S.W., 1971; m. Jeffrey Phillip Callen, Dec. 21, 1968; children—Amy, David. Caseworker, adolescent unit Ypsilanti (Mich.) State Hosp., 1969-70; caseworker adoption and foster care Child and Family Service Mich., Ann Arbor, 1970-71; counselor Crisis Walk-In Clinic, Ann Arbor, 1974-76; pvt. practice social work, Louisville, 1978—. Docent Louisville Speed Art Mus., 1979—; bd. dirs. Bur. Jewish Edn., Temple Sisterhood; major, community div. Louisville Fund for Arts, 1980, Community div. leader, 1982; chmn. joint study groups women's com. Jewish Community Fedn., 1982; program chmn. Nat. Council Jewish Women, 1981-83, also dir., fine arts chmn.; bd. dirs. Jewish Hosp. Guild, 1981-83. Mem. Nat. Assn. Social Workers, B'nai B'rith Women, U. Mich. Alumni Assn. (dir. 1979—), Phi Kappa Phi. Home: 5404 Pueblo Rd Louisville KY 40207

CALLENS, CHARLOTTE LOSERO, educator; b. Boston, July 24, 1931; d. John Joseph and Dorothy Frances (Taylor) Losero; B.A., U. Md., 1965, Ph.D., 1977; M.A., George Washington U., 1968; m. Ramon Francis Callens, July 25, 1965; children—Susan Victoria White, Johann Rober White, Laura Charlene. Psychologist, D.C. Public Schs., 1966-68; with Prince Georges Community Coll., Largo, Md., 1968—, prof., 1978—; therapist Glass Mental Health Center. Fellow Md. Psychol. Assn.; mem. Am. Psychol. Assn., Eastern Psychol. Assn., D.C. Psychol. Assn. Clubs: Atlantis Rangers Skin and Scuba. Home: 11001 Belton St Largo MD 20772 Office: 301 Largo Rd Largo MD 20772

CALLIHAN, DOROTHY JEANNE, educator; b. Belton, Tex., Mar. 16, 1930; d. Loyd Whitfield and Jewel Earline (Moss) Glazener; B.S., Mary Hardin-Baylor U., 1951; M.S., Iowa State U., 1955; Ph.D., U. Ala., 1966; m. Milton Louis Callihan, Dec. 29, 1957; 1 dau., Debra Ann. Kindergarten tchr. College Nursery, Belton, 1950-51; tchr. Albin (Wyo.) Consol. Sch., 1951-54; Ford Found. appointee, dir. child devel. Am. Coll. for Girls, also Am. U., Cairo, Egypt, 1955-57; instr. U. Ky., 1957-59, U. Ill., Urbana, 1960-61, Miss. State Coll. for Women, Columbus, 1961-64; grad. asst., instr. dept. edn. U. Ala., 1964-66, asst. prof., 1969-71; asso. prof. edn. U. Houston, 1969-71; asso. prof. edn. Trinity U., San Antonio, 1971-79, prof., 1979—, dir. early childhood, 1971—; coordinator San Antonio Area Found. Kindergarten/Early Childhood Edn. Breakfast Conf., 1976—. Mem. screening com. Am. Field Service Student Exchange, 1978-80. Cert. clin.-counseling psychologist, VA; cert. psychologist, Tex.; lic. psychologist, Tex. Am. Assn. for Childhood Edn. Internat., World Orgn. for Childhood Edn., Tex. Assn. for Childhood Edn. (state editor 1975-78), San Antonio Assn. for Childhood Edn. (pres. 1978-80), Tex. Elem.-Kindergarten-Nursery Educators (pres. 1980-82), NEA, Tex. Assn. for Supervision and Curriculum Devel., Nat. Assn. for Edn. of Young Child, Am. Home Econs. Assn., Delta Kappa Gamma (past v.p.), Kappa Delta Pi. Author: Kindergarten Resource Guide, 1970; (with Stinson Worley) Folktales and Footprints—Stories From The Old World, 1973, Texans All—The People in Texas, 1973; Children's Stories from Texas History, vol. I, 1980, vol. II, 1981. Home: 241 E Sunset Rd San Antonio TX 78209 Office: Trinity U Dept Edn 715 Stadium Dr San Antonio TX 78284

CALLISON, NANCY FOWLER, nurse; b. Milw., July 16, 1931; d. George Fenwick and Irma Esther (Wenzel) Fowler; diploma Evanston (Ill.) Hosp. Sch. of Nursing, 1952; B.S., Northwestern U., 1954; m. B.G. Callison, Sept. 25, 1954 (dec. Feb. 1964); children—Robert, Leslie, Linda. Staff nurse, psychiat. dept. Downey VA Hosp., 1954-55; staff nurse Camp Lejeune Naval Hosp., 1955, 59-61; obstetrical supr. Tri-City Hosp., Oceanside, Cal Calif., 1961-62; public health nurse San Diego County, 1962-66; sch. nurse Rich-Mar Union Sch. Dist., San Marcos, Calif., 1966-68; head nurse San Diego County Community Mental Health, 1968-73; dir. patient care services Southwood Mental Health Center, Chula Vista, Calif., 1973-75; program cons. Comprehensive Care Corp., Newport Beach, Calif., 1975-79; dir. Manpower Health Care, Culver City, Calif., 1979—; dir. nursing services Peninsula Rehab. Center, Lomita, Calif., 1980-81; supr., authorizations coordinator Hawthorne Community Med. Group, 1981—; clinic coordinator, translator Flying Samaritans, 1965—, mem. internat. bd. dirs., 1975-77, 79, pres. South Bay chpt., 1975—. Registered nurse, Calif. Mem. Am. Nurses Assn., Alcoholism Nurses Assn., Nat. Assn. Female Execs., Aircraft Owners and Pilots Assn. Office: 4455 W 117th St Hawthorne CA 90250

CALLOWAY, CONNIE GRASER, constrn. co. exec.; b. Palestine, Tex., Dec. 19, 1934; d. Herman William and Hattie Louise (Carroll) Graser; student Anderson Center Coll., 1976-77; m. James Edward Dunnahoe, Sept. 5, 1953 (div.); children—Durenda, Dan D., Duane C.; m. Howard Wesley Calloway, Nov. 6, 1971; stepchildren—Judy, Brenda, Howard L. Gen. office worker various firms, 1954-62; dist. adminstr. Pool Oil Well Service, div. Enserch Corp., Palestine, 1963-76; ind. bus. cons., real estate sales asso., Palestine, 1977; v.p. C & E Builders, Inc., Palestine, 1978-79, pres., 1980—. Industry rep. Anderson County Job Betterment Com. Mem. Nat. Assn. Female Execs. (network dir.), Tex. Assn. Realtors, Palestine Bd. Realtors. Democrat. Baptist. Clubs: Civic Music Assn., Harvey Women's, 21. Author: How to Think Creatively. Home: 715 Inwood Dr Palestine TX 75801 Office: PO Box 1430 Palestine TX 75801

CALLOWAY, DORIS HOWES, ednl. adminstr.; b. Canton, Ohio, Feb. 14, 1923; d. Earl John and Lillian Ann (Roberts) Howes; B.S., Ohio State U., 1943; Ph.D., U. Chgo., 1947; m. Nathaniel O. Calloway, Feb. 14, 1946; children—David Karl, Candace Mary; m. 2d, Robert Olaf Nesheim, July 4, 1982. Researcher, Armed Forces Food and Container Inst., Chgo., 1951-61; chmn. Stanford U. Research Inst., Menlo Park, Calif., 1961-62; prof., chmn. dept. nutrition U. Calif., Berkeley, 1962—; provost Profl. Schs. and Colls., 1981—; cons. FAO, 1974-75, Nat. Adv. Council on Aging, 1978-82. Recipient Meritorious Civilian Service award Dept. Army, 1959. Mem. Am. Inst. Nutrition (pres. 1982-83), Am. Dietetic Assn. Author: Nutrition and Physical Fitness, 10th edit., 1979; contbr. articles to profl. jours. Office: 200 California Hall U Calif Berkeley CA 94720

CALLOWAY, FRANCES AMANDA, hotel exec.; b. Birmingham, Ala., July 6, 1950; d. John Clyde and Nettye M. (Phillips) C.; student U. Ala., 1969-73, Hotel Sch., U. Houston, 1978. Mem. mgmt. staff Jolly Inns, Inc., Birmingham, 1971-72; gen. mgr. Airways Inn, Jackson, Miss., 1972-80; sec.-treas. Intergulf Motels Inc., Jackson, 1975-80, exec. ops. officer, 1980—; exec. v.p. Motor Hotel Investors Inc., Jackson, 1979-80, exec. ops. officer, 1980—. Chmn., Miss. Tourist Promotion Com., 1978-79; mem. adv. bd. Travel South, 1979-80. Mem. Miss. Hotel/Motel Assn. (dir. 1978-79, v.p. 1979-80, pres. 1981—), Jackson Hotel/Motel Assn. (pres. 1979), Jackson C. of C. Democrat. Presbyterian. Club: The Club (Birmingham). Office: 1 Flowood Pl Jackson MS 39208

CALLY, MARY GENEVIEVE, fashion designer; b. N.Y.C., Dec. 23, 1951; d. James John and Helene Victoria (Walterska) C.; B.F.A., Pratt Inst., 1973; A.A.S. in Merchandising, Fashion Inst. Tech., 1975, A.A.S. in Advt. and Communications, 1978. Merchandiser, Val D'or Industries, N.Y.C., 1973-75; cons. Adidas U.S.A. Athletic Apparel, 1974-77; designer, cons. Lumiere Fashions, São Paulo, Brazil, 1975-76; critic awards com. Pratt Inst., 1974-81; owner, designer Mary Cally Inc., N.Y.C., 1975-78; design dir. Salvation div. Thomson Co., 1978-80; v.p., designer Cassant by Mary Cally, apparel mfrs., N.Y.C., 1981—; mem. mdsg. bd. Mademoiselle mag., 1974; cons. in field; designer, cons. Asher Co., N.Y.C., 1982, Regent Internat., N.Y.C., 1982. Recipient Collins & Aikman Design award, 1975, Fashion Show award Pratt Inst., 1973. Mem. Fashion Group Internat., Am. Women Entrepreneurs, Am. Women Econ. Devel. Corp., N.Y. Fashion Designers Council. Home: 144-23 29th Rd Flushing NY 11354 Office: 1411 Broadway Suite 1233 New York NY 10018

CALVERT, ETTA JOHNSON, nurse; b. Cleve., Mar. 19, 1947; d. Robert Lee and Grace Edna (Raines) Johnson and T. Peter Graham; B.S. in Nursing, Carlow Coll., 1969; M.Ed., U. Pitts., 1972, Ph.D. candidate (scholar), 1973; m. Benjamin Calvert; children—Eric Ingram, Benjamin Lester, Nia Donnell. Dir. student activities Community Coll. Allegheny County, Pitts., 1973-76; with Univ. Hosps. of Cleve. and MacDonald House Hosps., 1969-70; nurse U. Pitts. Community Mental Health/Mental Retardation, 1970-73; staff nurse Med. Personnel Pool, 1975-78, asst. dir. nursing service, 1978; dir. nursing service Abbey Nursing Home, Cleve. Chi Eta Phi nursing scholar, 1964; R.N., Pa., Ohio. Mem. Nat. League Nursing, Nat. Assn. Female Execs., Cleve. Area Citizens League Nursing, Hospice Council No. Ohio, Alpha Kappa Alpha. Home: 4779 Walford Rd Warrensville Heights OH 44128 Office: 8205 Euclid Ave Cleveland OH 44103

CAM, VINH, scientist; b. Vietnam, July 8, 1948; M.S., N.Y.U., 1973, Ph.D. in Cellular Immunology-Toxicology, 1977; M.B.A., Bernard M. Baruch Coll., 1977. Postdoctoral fellow dept. bacteriology and immunology Rockefeller U., N.Y.C., 1977-79, research asso., 1979-80; adj. asst. prof. Bernard M. Baruch Coll., N.Y.C., 1978-80; Congressional Sci. fellow U.S. Senate, Washington, summer 1979; environ. scientist, project leader Office of Drinking Water, EPA, Washington, 1980-81, sr. environ. scientist, sr. program mgr. Region II, Water Div., N.Y.C., 1981—. NIH fellow, 1977-79; Nat. Multiple Sclerosis Soc. grantee, 1979-80. Mem. Am. Soc. Microbiology, N.Y. Acad. Scis., Sigma Xi. Office: EPA Region II 26 Federal Plaza New York NY 10278

CAMARILLO, LINDA LOU, petroleum co. exec.; b. Chgo., Dec. 18, 1944; d. George Emry and Betty Jane (Carper) Jamison; student Calif. State U., Bakersfield, 1981—; m. James Daniel Camarillo, Jan. 10, 1969; children—Daniel James, David Scott. With Tosco Corp., Bakersfield, Calif., 1974—, telecommunications analyst, 1979—. Clk., First Baptist Ch., Bakersfield, 1976, sec. long range planning com. and bldg council, 1973-76; life mem. Republican Nat. Com. Mem. Internat. Info. Word Processing Assn. (v.p. programs Bakersfield chpt. 1978-79, pres. 1979-80, 82-83, achievement award), Telecommunications Assn., Assn. Records Mgrs. and Adminstrs. Clubs: Safari Internat., Kern County Gun. Home: 9910 Palm Ave Bakersfield CA 93308 Office: PO Box 2860 Bakersfield CA 93303

CAMBER, DIANE WOOLFE, art and achtl. historian; b. Miami Beach, Fla., Aug. 16, 1934; d. A. Ernest and Betty (Miller) Woolfe; B.A., Barnard Coll., 1956; M.Ed., Boston State Coll., 1973; m. C. Isaac Camber, Aug. 26, 1956; children—Oren, Rachel, Michael. Lectr., Albright-Knox Mus., Buffalo, 1962-64, DeCordova and Dana Mus., Lincoln, Mass., 1967-68; art specialist Holliston (Mass.) Public Schs., 1970-74; exhibiting artist, Mass., La., and Fla., 1972-79; asso. dir. Miami Design Preservation League, Miami Beach, 1978-80; acting dir. Bass Mus. Art, Miami Beach, 1980—; lectr. history of furniture design, arch. and hist. preservation. Mem. Am. Assn. Mus., Nat. Trust Hist. Preservation, Fla. Trust Hist. Preservation, Archtl. Club Miami, Met. Mus. Miami, Friends of Bass Mus., Am. Crafts Council, Smithsonian Assos. Clubs: Barnard Coll. of South Fla., Miami Beach Pioneers. Asso. editor: Portfolio, 1979; Time Past, Time Present, 1980. Office: Bass Mus Art 2100 Collins Ave Miami Beach FL 33139

CAMERA, FRANCES ANN, banker; b. N.Y.C., Mar. 2, 1949; d. Anthony Joseph and Cecile Elizabeth (Merritt) C.; B.B.A., Pace U., 1977, postgrad. fin. mgmt., 1982—. Sec. to dean Sch. Edn. Pace U., N.Y.C., 1968-72; service asst. leasing div. Chem. Bank, N.Y.C., 1972-75, officer's asst., 1975-78, asst. mgr., 1978-81, asst. sec. mktg. officer, 1981—. Recipient Outstanding Achievement award Republican Adv. Com., 1978. Mem. Concern, Inc., Nat. Assn. Female Execs., Phi Chi Theta. Office: 55 Water St New York NY 10041

CAMERON, ALISON STILWELL, artist; b. Peking, China, Feb. 5, 1921; d. Joseph Warren and Winifred Alison (Smith) Stilwell; studied under P'u Ju and Yu Fei-an, 1936-39; m. William Roderick Cameron, Dec. 27, 1947; children—Catherine, Laurie, Bruce. One woman shows: Peking Inst. Fine Art, 1938, William Rockhill Nelson Gallery, Kansas City, Mo., Currier Gallery, N.H., C.T. Loo Gallery, N.Y.C., Syracuse Mus. Art, Columbus (Ohio) Gallery Fine Art, Bonestell Gallery, N.Y.C.; group shows; represented in permanent collections Syracuse Mus., Currier Gallery, Nelson Gallery; owner Stilwell Studio, Carmel, Calif., 1974—; pvt. practice teaching techniques of Chinese painting, 1956—. Fellow Monterey Inst. Internat. Studies; mem. Carmel Art. Assn., Am. Women Internat. Understanding, Nat. Com. on U.S.-China Relations Inc. (dir. 1977—), Soc. Woman Geographers. Author-illustrator: Chin Ling, The Chinese Cricket, 1947, 2d edit., 1981; Chinese Painting Techniques, 1967. Office: PO Box 50 Carmel CA 93921

CAMERON, CHARLOTTE ELAINE, office mgr.; b. Tucson, July 4, 1940; d. David Lee and Doris Arlene (Griffith) Burrows; student Consumnes River Community Coll., 1975, 76; m. Davi Paul Cameron III, Mar. 4, 1961; children—Judith Lynn, Barbara Anne. With Calif. State Dept. Edn., 1958-63, New Hosp Sch. Dist., 1964-67, Calif. Canners & Growers, 1969-70, Beckman & Co., 1971; stenographer local environ. health services sect. Calif. Dept. Health Services, 1973-76; sec. to dir. residency tng. U. Calif. at Davis Med. Center, 1976-79; office mgr. Psychiat. Assocs. and Cons. of Sacramento Valley, Inc., 1979—. Mem. governing bd. New Hosp Sch. Dist., 1975—, now also pres. Mem. Calif. Sch. Bds. Assn., San Joaquin County Sch. Bd. Assn. Democrat. Home: 29280 N Cameron Rd Galt CA 95632 Office: 711 University Ave Sacramento CA 95825

CAMERON, DONNA WELK, real estate developer; b. Muscatine, Iowa, Nov. 9, 1943; d. Edward Reinholdt and Vera Madge (Bird) Welk; A.A., Muscatine Community Coll., 1963; B.S., B.A. in English, U. No. Iowa, 1965; M.S. in Vocat. Rehab. Counseling, Mankato (Minn.) State U., 1973. Instr. English, drama coach Frost (Minn.) High Sch., 1966-68; instr. English, Spanish, Writing Groves High Sch., Savannah High Sch., Savannah, Ga., 1968-70; reporter Daily Reporter, program developer Minorities Studies Center, Mankato State U., cons. Mankato High Sch., 1970-73; counselor, office supr., program developer Opportunities Industrialization Center of R.I., Providence; real estate buyer, 1975—; fin. cons., ins. and mut. funds sales N. D. Erickson & Assos., Providence, 1977-80, Barclay Douglas, Providence, 1980—, real estate developer; instr. R.I. Coll., 1971-73. Corp. mem. Newport County Community Mental Health Center, Inc., 1981—, Roger Williams Coll., Bristol, R.I., 1981; bd. dirs. Human Rights Commn., Mankato, 1974-75; mem. Family Service, Inc. bd., Providence, 1981—; appointee R.I. Bd. Internat. Women's Year, 1976; asso. mem. Jamestown Republican com.; mem. R.I. Rep. Leaders Council. Mem. R.I. Builders Assn. Office: 20 Union St Jamestown RI 02835

CAMERON, ELEANOR FRANCES, author; b. Winnepeg, Man., Can., Mar. 23, 1912; d. Henry and Florence Lydia (Vaughan) Butler; student UCLA, 1931-33; m. Ian Stuart Cameron, June 24, 1934; 1 son, David Gordon. Clk., Los Angeles Pub. Library, 1930-36, Los Angeles Sch. Book Depository, 1936-42; spl. librarian advt. Foote Cone & Belding, Los Angeles, 1942-43; research asst. Batten, Barton, Durstine & Osborn, Los Angeles, 1956-58; spl. librarian Dan B. Miner Co., Los Angeles, 1958-59; mem. editorial bd. Cricket Mag., LaSalle, Ill., 1973—. Mem. adv. bd. Center for Study of Children's Lit., Simmons Coll., Boston, 1977—; judge children's book category Nat. Book Awards, 1978-79. Recipient Nat. Book award for Ct. of the Stone Children, 1973. Mem. Save-the-Redwoods League, Sierra Club, Audubon Soc., Wilderness Soc., Authors League. Author: The Unheard Music, 1950; The Wonderful Flight to the Mushroom Planet, 1954; A Room Made of Windows, 1971; The Court of the Stone Children, 1973; To the Green Mountains, 1975; The Green and Burning Tree; On the Writing and Enjoyment of Children's Books, 1969; Julia and the Hand of God, 1977; Beyond Silence, 1980; That Julia Redfern, 1982; also others; mem. editorial bd. Children's Lit. in Edn., 1982—. Office: EP Dutton and Co 2 Park Ave New York NY 10016

CAMERON, IDA JANE, state govt. ofcl.; b. St. Paul, June 2, 1937; d. Bernis James and Elizabeth Mae Arcand; B.S., Eastern Mich. U., 1962; m. Don R. Cameron, Aug. 16, 1958; children—Amanda Marie, Benjamin David. Tchr., Mich. schs., 1962-76; exec. Fla. chpts. NOW, 1977-79; adminstrv. asst. State of Fla., 1979-80; exec. staff dir. Fla. Dept. Profl. Regulation, Tallahassee, 1978-81, div. dir. adminstrv. services, 1981—. Chmn. Tallahassee Area ERA fundraising, 1978; mem. founding bd. Tallahassee Center Victims Spouse Abuse, 1979-80. Mem. NOW (chmn. Tallahassee chpt. 1977-79). Home: 1511 Belleau Wood Tallahassee FL 32312

CAMERON, SUZANNE HAYDEN, market analyst/broker; b. Newark, Ohio, Sept. 28, 1949; d. George Allen and Virginia (Scott) Hayden; B.A., (U. Rehab. scholar), Ohio State U., 1972, postgrad., 1976-78; postgrad. U. Chgo., 1973-78; 1 son, Allen. Orthodontic research Ohio State U., Columbus, 1972-76, Plikerd & Assos., Newark, 1973-77; barrier-free market research design, sales Sea Pines Plantation, Hilton Head Island, S.C., 1979-80, market research, developer coordination mktg., sales program Daufuskie Island, 1980; cons. barrier-free design, time-sharing, 1979—. Area chmn. United Appeal, Ohio, 1972; philanthropic chmn. Ohio State U., 1972; chmn. Easter Seals campaign, 1973. Mem. Am. Dental Hygienists Assn., Am. Land Devel. Assn., Alda-Timesharing Council, S.C. Bd. Realtors, Hilton Head Island Bd. Realtors, Ohio State U. Alumni Assn., Kappa Kappa Gamma. Republican. Presbyterian. Club: Twentieth Century. Home: 2027 Sealoft St Hilton Head Island SC 29938 Office: PO Box 4890 Hilton Head Island SC 29938

CAMMAROTA, MARIE ANN, real estate developer; b. N.Y.C., May 2, 1927; d. Nicholas and Isabelle Mary (Sellaro) Roccanova; B.A., St. Joseph's Coll. for Women, 1947; M.A., Columbia U., 1951; Postgrad. St. John's U., 1952, CCNY, 1953, Fordham U., 1953, Sacramento State Coll., 1950-51; m. Frank Cammarota, Sept. 28, 1957; children—Isabelle, Nicholas, Francis. Tchr., N.Y.C. Bd. Edn., 1948-57; tchr. San Juan (Calif.) Unified Sch., 1950-51; real estate developer, Sacramento, Calif., 1982—. Roman Catholic. Home: PO Box 255488 Sacramento CA 95825

CAMPANELLA, YVETTE LYNN, cosmetic products co. exec.; b. Rockland County, N.Y., May 31, 1952; d. John Alfred and Marie Christine (Hill) Johnson; B.A. in Psychology, Vassar Coll., 1974; m. John Deloach Campanella, Sept. 22, 1978; 1 son, Jon Thomas. Sr. mgmt. cons. Met. Life Ins. Co., N.Y.C., 1975-78; indsl. engr. Security Pacific Bank, Los Angeles, 1979; new product introductions and promotion system dir. Max Factor, Hollywood, Calif., 1979—. Mem. Am. Mgmt. Assn., Nat. Assn. Female Execs. Congregationalist. Home: 3212 Oakhurst Ave Cheviot Hills CA 90034 Office: Max Factor 1655 N McCadden Pl Hollywood CA 90028

CAMPBELL, CAROL CANDY, accountant; b. Vermillion, S.D., Mar. 12, 1948; d. Wyatt T. and Ruby G. (Drafhal) C.; grad. Barnes Sch. Commerce, Denver, 1971. Public acct., 1971—; pvt. practice acctg., Denver, 1979—. Mem. Nat. Soc. Enrolled Agts., Colo. Soc. Enrolled Agts. (sec. 1978-79), Nat. Soc. Public Accts., Colo. Soc. Public Accts., Nat. Assn. Female Execs. Episcopalian. Clubs: Women of St. John's, Pilot Internat. (dir. Denver 1980-81), Pilot Bridge Marathon. Home: 2621 S Green Ct Denver CO 80219 Office: 4800 Happy Canyon Rd Suite 150 Denver CO 80237

CAMPBELL, CAROL JEAN, mgmt. info. cons.; b. Lubbock, Tex., May 17, 1955; d. Harold Eugene and Norma Jean (Isom) Campbell; B.S. in Math. Edn., Tex. Tech U., 1976; M.B.A., 1981. Adminstrv. intern NASA/Johnson Space Center, Houston, 1979; systems engr. Phase I, Electronic Data Systems, Columbus, Ohio, 1977; tchr. math. Frenship Ind. Sch. Dist., Wolfforth, Tex., 1976-77; mgmt. info. cons. Arthur Andersen & Co., Ft. Worth, 1981-82. Adviser Jr. Achievement, 1982. Mem. Bus. Grad. Student Soc. (pres. 1979), Tech. Acctg. Soc., Am. Assn. M.B.A. Execs. Methodist. Home: 1204 Dovercliff Ct Apt 1505 Fort Worth TX 76112

CAMPBELL, CAROLINE KRAUSE, retail drug co. exec.; b. Praha, Tex., May 5, 1926; d. Charles Joseph and Mary Victoria (Havrde) Krause; student U. N.Mex.; diploma Alexander Hamilton Inst., N.Y.C., 1969; widow; children—Richard Elton, Don Michael, Scott Gary, Jonathan Miles, Candace Kay. Various secretarial positions, 1945-49; survey researcher Winona Research Co., Mpls., 1953-54; merchandiser, buyer Campbell Drug, Inc., Albuquerque, 1961-77, gen. mgr., 1978—, pres., 1978—, also dir. Active campaign Congressman Manuel Lujan. Mem. Nat. Fedn. Ind. Bus., Nat. Assn. Retail Druggists, N.Mex. Pharm. Assn., Albuquerque Symphony Women's Assn., Albuquerque C. of C. (congressional action com., state legis. com., city govt. com.), Albuquerque Rose Soc., Internat. Platform Assn., Assn. Commerce and Industry of N.Mex. Republican. Clubs: Italian Cultural, Elks. Office: 8252 Menaul Blvd NE Albuquerque NM 87110

CAMPBELL, CARY ELIZABETH, editor-in-chief; b. Dallas, Nov. 10, 1954; d. Jefferson Holland and Shelia Ann (Trapp) Campbell; B.A. in Humanities summa cum laude, Southwestern U., 1974; 1 son, Christopher Randolph. Editor, Southwestern Mag., Southwestern Univ., Georgetown, Tex., 1973-74; community resources specialist Tex. Research Inst. Mental Scis., Houston, 1974-77; editor Viva!, mag. for older adults, Houston, 1976-78, Wichita Falls (Tex.) Mag., 1979-80; editor-in-chief 8 Living Mags., Baker Publs., Dallas, 1980—; instr. art history St. Paul's Acad., 1976, St. Luke's Continuing Edn. program, Houston, 1975-76; instr. SW Writers Conf., Houston, and Fla. Suncoast Writers Conf., St. Petersburg, 1981-82, Fla. Mag. Assn., Tampa, 1982. Vice pres. Harris County Com. Aging, 1977, treas., 1976. Recipient Poetry award Southwestern Mag., 1972; Student Leadership award Southwestern U., 1974; Disting. Service award, Harris County Com. Aging, 1975; 1st Place Feature Writing, Tex. Press Women, 1981, Matrix award Women in Communication, 1982, 1st pl. advt. media award, 1982; 1st pl. print media advt. Nat. Fedn. Press Women. Mem. Tex. Press Women, Am. Soc. Mag. Editors, Internat. Bus. Communicators, Nat. Writers Club. Methodist. Contbr. articles to various mags. Home: 61 S Pennsylvania St Denver CO 80209 Office: 2280 S Xanadu Way Suite 305 Aurora CO 80014

CAMPBELL, D'ANN MAE, historian; b. Denver, Dec. 30, 1949; d. Bernard Edward and Eleanor Louise (Mahoney) C.; B.A., Colo. Coll., 1972; Ph.D., U. N.C., 1978; m. Richard Jensen, July 16, 1976. Historian, Forest Service, U.S. Dept. Agr., Washington, 1972; teaching asst. U. N.C., 1973-75; adj. prof., research asso. Office Social and Demographic History, U. Ill., 1977-79; asst., then asso. dir. family and community history center Newberry Library, Chgo., 1976-79; dean women's affairs, asst. prof. history Ind. U., Bloomington, 1979—. Newberry Library fellow, 1975-76; Pi Gamma Mu fellow, 1972-73; grantee Nat. Endowment Humanities, Rockefeller Found., HEW, Office of Edn., 1976-80. Mem. Orgn. Am. Historians, Nat. Hist. Communal Assns. (pres. 1981), Am., So., Social Science hist. assns., Phi Beta Kappa. Contbr. articles to scholarly jours. Home: 1109 Longwood Dr Bloomington IN 47401 Office: Ind U Bloomington IN 47405

CAMPBELL, ELAINE JOSEPHINE, writer, critic, educator; b. Phila., Aug. 6, 1932; d. William Maxwell and Anna Maria (Roller) Bauer; B.A. with maj. honors (Univ. scholar), U. Pa., 1954; M.A., Simmons Coll., 1973; Ph.D. (Univ. scholar), Brandeis U., 1981; m. John Bruce Campbell, Dec. 21, 1957; children—Jennifer Ann, Rebecca Ellen, Sabrina Frances. Soc. editor Main Line Times, Ardmore, Pa., 1954-55; adminstrv. asst. dean Sch. Nursing, U. Pa., 1955-57; teaching asst. dept. English and Am. lit. Brandeis U., 1974-80; lectr. English, Regis Coll., Weston, Mass., 1980-81, asst. prof. English, 1981—, dir. freshman writing program, 1981—; author introduction: The Orchid House (P. Allfrey), 1982; book reviewer Commonwealth Novel in English, Kunapipi; contbr. articles, revs., reports to profl. jours., U.S., Can., Jamaica, Denmark, Eng.; panelist at profl. meetings, convs. Mem. MLA, African Lit. Assn., Assn. Caribbean Studies, Kappa Delta. Home: 63 Puritan Ln Sudbury MA 01776 also Havers care Gen Delivery Roadtown Tortola British Virgin Islands Office: Box 1033 College Hall Regis Coll 235 Wellesley St Weston MA 02193

CAMPBELL, HELEN ZOTT, writer, lectr.; b. Des Moines, Feb. 7, 1919; d. John Henry and Perna A. (Jones) Zott; student Fairmont Jr. Coll., 1938, Strayer Bus. Coll., 1939-40, George Washington U., 1943-45, Orgn. Mgmt. Inst., U. Del., 1973, Mgmt. Inst., Notre Dame U., 1978; m. Robert A. Campbell, Jr., Sept. 4, 1948; children—Karen Leigh, Debra Arlene. Acctg. clk. George Washington U., Washington, 1940-46; sec., bookkeeper NEA, Washington, 1946-47; sec., acct. W. E. Cumberland, Washington, 1947-52; acct. Am. Apparel Mfrs. Assn., Inc., Arlington, Va., 1967-72, asst. treas., 1972-79, dir. fin. services, 1973-79; free-lance artist, writer and lectr., 1979—. Jr. bd. George Washington U. Hosp., Washington, 1948-50, pres., 1950-52; bd. govs. English Speaking Union, Sydney, Australia, 1963-65. Recipient citation Philippine Govt., 1958, citation Children of Libya, 1963. Mem. Nat., Am., Washington socs. assn. execs., Nat. Assn. Execs. Clubs, Soc. Preservation Va. Antiquities, Assn. Fgn. Service Women, Arlington C. of C. (assn. council 1975-79), Zonta Internat., Kappa Delta. Republican. Presbyterian. Clubs: Capital Speakers, Washington, Nat. Press, Capitol Hill. Home: 5312 Westpath Way Fort Sumner Hills MD 20816

CAMPBELL, HOPE, author; b. Seattle, June 17; d. Howard R. and Genevieve E. (Talbot) McDonald; ed. Punahou Sch., Honolulu, Dominican Convent, Calif., Monticello Sch., Calif., John Marshall, Calif.; m. Charles Wallis (dec.); children—Christopher M., John Talbot. Actress, artist stage, radio and TV, Calif. and N.Y.; author: (plays) Fantasy of a Day in Court, 1980, Zekle's Wife, 1980, Why Not Join the Giraffes?, 1968, Mystery at Fire Island (adapted for CBS Children's Mystery Theater), 1981; books include: The Light of Lilith, 1961, Liza, 1965, Home to Hawaii, 1967, Why Not Join the Giraffes?, 1968, Meanwhile, Back at the Castle, 1970, No More Trains to Tottenville, 1971, There's a Pizza Back in Cleveland (with Mary Anderson), 1972, Peter's Angel: A Story About Monsters, 1976, Mystery at Fire Island, 1978, Legend of Lost Earth, 1977, A Peak Beneath the Moon, 1979; co-creator War is the Enemy radio series. Served with USO. Mem. Authors Guild, Dramatists Guild, AFTRA, Actors Equity Assn.

CAMPBELL, JEAN WINTER, educator; b. Chgo., Feb. 6, 1918; d. Olice and Freeda M. (Mercer) Winter; B.S., Northwestern U., 1938, M.A., 1939; m. Angus Campbell, June 29, 1940 (dec.); children—Bruce, Joan, Carol. Secondary sch. reading specialist, Ill., 1938-42; editor United World Federalist, Washington, 1944; tech. aide joint services com. vision OSRD, 1944-46; engaged in various community orgn. positions, 1947-64; dir. Center Continuing Edn. Women, U. Mich., Ann Arbor, 1964—. Mem. Ann Arbor Citizens Council, 1946—, pres., 1954-55. Recipient Disting. Service award Nat. U. Continuing Edn. Assn., 1981. Mem. Am. Assn. Higher Edn., Nat. Assn. Women Deans, Adminstrs. and Counselors, LWV (chpt. v.p. 1950-52), Mortar Bd., Phi Beta Kappa. Home: 1009 Berkshire Rd Ann Arbor MI 48104 Office: 350 S Thayer St Ann Arbor MI 48109

CAMPBELL, JOANN CAVO, social worker; b. Cetara, Italy, Dec. 2, 1950; came to U.S., 1951, naturalized, 1965; d. Simone and Yolanda (Battista) Cavo; B.A., SUNY, Oneonta, 1972; M.S.W., Ariz. State U., 1977; m. Bradley Richard Campbell, Aug. 10, 1974. Counselor/researcher intern Phoenix Indian Center, 1975-77; social work intern Jane Wayland Center, Phoenix, 1976-77; social worker Family Services of Greater Utica (N.Y.), Inc., 1977—; psychiat. social worker Oneida County Dept. Mental Health 1980-81; case mgr. supr. Community Support System, Rome, N.Y., 1980—. Vol. counselor, drug abuse program Insight House, Utica, 1971-73; vol. phys. therapist aide Utica State Hosp., 1973-74; mem. exec. bd., vice chmn. social work adv. com. Utica Coll.; chmn. sexual abuse task Force, bd. dirs. Mohawk Valley Com. for Prevention of Child Abuse and Neglect, Inc., 1977—. Recipient cert. of appreciation Neighborhood Youth Corps, Oneonta, N.Y., 1971, Utica State Hosp., 1973, 74, Phoenix Indian Center, 1976; cert. social worker, N.Y. State. Mem. Nat. Assn. Social Workers (rec. sec. Mohawk Valley div. N.Y. State chpt. 1980-82). Office: Cath Social Services 212 W Liberty St Rome NY also Family Services of Greater Utica 239 Genesee St Utica NY 13501

CAMPBELL, JUANITA (NITA), educator; b. Ionia, Mich., Sept. 10, 1928; d. Wayne H. and Ernestine M. (Green) Bradley; student Yuba Jr. Coll., Marysville, Calif., 1957-58; m. Kenneth W. Campbell, Sept. 10, 1978; children—Suzanne Foster, Edward A. Odgen, Jr., Dawne Marie Ogden. Owner, pres. Mid-State Coll. and Secretarial Service of Stanislaus, Modesto, Calif., 1974—. Mem. Nat. Fedn. Ind. Bus., Better Bus. Bur. Modesto, Modesto C. of C., Bus. and Profl. Women's Club (v.p. Sonora, Calif. 1973). Republican. Office: Muir Med Park 817 Coffee Rd Modesto CA 95355

CAMPBELL, JUANITA SUE, banker; b. Ogemaw, Ark., Sept. 17, 1927; d. Charles Hughey and Mabel (Lockhridge) C.; student public schs.; m. William Dawson Poindexter, Sept. 14, 1944; children—Judy Ann, Gloria Sue, Debra Lynn. With Stephens Security Bank (Ark.), 1961—, v.p., 1972—, also security officer, inside auditor. Mem. Nat. Assn. Bank Women, Bus. and Profl. Women's Club (chpt. treas. 1972—, membership chmn. 1974). Bank Adminstrn. Inst., Am. Bankers Assn. Baptist. Club: Stephens Country. Home: 501 Chert St Stephens AR 71764 Office: 108 Ruby St Stephens AR 71764

CAMPBELL, JUDITH LOWE, child psychiatrist; b. Indpls., Jan. 21, 1946; d. Albert St. Clair and Adele V. (Lobraico) Lowe; B.S. in Zoology, Butler U., 1967; M.D., Ind. U., 1971; m. Robert Frank Campbell, Nov. 30, 1968; children—Christiaan Robert, Kevin Lowe, Geoffrey Ford. Resident in psychiatry Ind. U. Sch. Medicine, 1971-73, fellow in child psychiatry 1973-75; asst. dir. Riley Child Guidance Clinic, Indpls., 1975-79, dir. child psychiatry consultation, liaison service to pediatrics, 1975-79; dir. child psychiatry services Riley Hosp. for Children, 1979—; child psychiatry cons. Center for Mental Health of Madison County (Ind.), Anderson, 1975-77, Lutheran Child Welfare Assn., Indpls., 1974—, Lutherwood Children's Home, Indpls., 1974—; instr. Ind. U. Sch. Medicine, Indpls., 1974-75, asst. prof. dept psychiatry, 1975—. Vol., Ind. State chpt. Cystic Fibrosis Found., 1977. Recipient Physician's Recognition award in Continuing Edn. AMA, 1974, 77; Helen McQuiston award in sci., 1967. Mem. Am. Psychiat. Assn., Ind. Psychiat. Soc. (councilor 1978-80, sec. 1981—, editor newsletter 1981—), Am. Burn Assn., Am. Acad. Pediatrics (Ind. br.), Am. Med. Women's Assn., Am. Acad. Child Psychiatry, Am. Assn. Psychiat. Services for Children, Smithsonian Assos., Field Mus. Natural History, Indpls. Mus. Art, Indpls. Zool. Soc., U. Psychiat. Assos., Pi Beta Phi, Beta Sigma Phi. Clubs: Carmel Racquet, Eastern Star. Contbr. articles on child psychiatry to profl. jours. Research on emotional aspects of burns in children. Office: Riley Hosp 702 Barnhill Dr Indianapolis IN 46223

CAMPBELL, JUDITH MAY, educator; b. Terre Haute, Ind., May 13, 1938; d. O. H. and D. Juanita Campbell; B.S. in Phys. Edn., Ind. State U., 1960, M.S., 1963; D. in Phys. Edn., Ind. U., 1978. Recreational dir. Terre Haute Park Dept., summers 1958-60; tchr. St. Louis public schs., 1960-61; instr. dept. phys. edn. Ind. State U., Terre Haute, 1961-66, asst. prof., 1968-75, asso. prof., 1975-79, prof., 1979—, also dir. undergrad. preparation; coach volleyball and basketball teams, 1970-74, girl sports dir., 1974-78, founder Ind. Spl. Olympics, 1970; basketball chmn. Wabash Valley Bd. of Women Ofcls., 1963-65, 68-74; nat. adv. bd. Spl. Olympics, Inc.; nat. adv. bd. Joseph P. Kennedy, Jr. Found., 1972-74, also chmn. Bd. dirs. Ind. Spl. Olympics, 1968-74, state co-dir., 1970-74; bd. dirs. Girls Sports Adv. Bd., 1975-77. Recipient Lambert award Ind. State U., 1960, Outstanding Phys. Fitness Leadership award Vigo County Jaycees, 1968, Service award Vigo County Assn. for Retarded Citizens, 1971; Community Service award Vigo County Jaycees, 1974, Eleanor St. John Disting. Alumni award, 1977; Lilly Found. grantee, 1974, Chismar Found. grantee, 1972. Mem. AAUP (v.p. 1980-81, pres. 1981—), AAHPER, Ind. AAHPER (Leadership award 1974), Delta Kappa Gamma (pres. 1980—), Phi Delta Kappa, Delta Psi Kappa. Club: Faculty Women's Contbr. articles on phys. edn. to profl. publs.; developer phys. edn. program in sch. curriculums. Home: RR 22 PO Box 90 Terre Haute IN 47802

CAMPBELL, KARLYN KOHRS, educator; b. Blomkest, Minn., Apr. 16, 1937; d. Meinhard and Dorothy (Siegers) Kohrs; B.A., (Tozer scholar), Macalester Coll., 1958; M.A. (Tozer fellow), U. Minn., 1959, Ph.D., 1968; m. Paul Newell Campbell, Sept. 16, 1967. Asst. prof. SUNY, Brockport, 1959-63, Calif. State U., Los Angeles, 1966-71; asso. prof. SUNY, Binghamton, 1971-73, CUNY, 1973-74; prof. communication studies U. Kans., Lawrence, 1974—; Gladys Borchers lectr., U. Wis., Madison, 1974. Mem. Speech Communication Assn., Central States Speech Communication Assn., Nat. Womens Studies Assn., Phi Beta Kappa, Pi Phi Epsilon. Author: Critiques of Contemporary Rhetoric, 1972; Form and Genre, 1978; The Rhetorical Act, 1982; Interplay of Influence, 1983; editorial bd. Today's Speech, 1972-75, The Speech Teacher, 1973-75, Central States Speech Jour., 1977-79, Communication Monographs, 1978-80, Quarterly Jour. Speech, 1980-85; contbr. articles to profl. jours. Office: Dept Communication Studies U Kans Lawrence KS 66045

CAMPBELL, LINDA MARGARET DILLOWAY, textile co. exec.; b. Howell, Mich., Sept. 22, 1947; d. Robert Joseph and Marian Maxine (Schubel) Dilloway; student Kent (Ohio) State U., 1966, Hammell Actual Bus. Coll., Akron, Ohio, 1966; divorced; 1 dau., Cynthia Diane. With Louis Allis Co., Greenville, S.C., 1967-71; charge accounts payable Indsl. Scrap Inc., Greenville, 1972; sec. to pres. Horizon Apts. Ltd., Greenville, 1972-73; with Crosrol Inc., Greenville, 1973—, sales coordinator, 1980—. Home: 121 Canebrake Dr Greer SC 29651 Office: Box 6488 Tower Dr Greenville SC 29606

CAMPBELL, LUCINDA SOLOMON, educator; b. Palestine, Tex., Jan. 11, 1925; d. Henry Symuel and Kitty (Durham) Solomon; B.S., Tex. So. U, 1955, M.Ed., 1969; m. Morris Campbell, Mar. 5, 1949; children—Marvis Aundria, Linda Dureyea, Sonia Veronica, Marcus Devereaux. Tchr., Houston Ind. Sch. Dist., 1958—, reading specialist, 1979—; cons. Weddings by Campbell, Houston, 1973—. Ann. sponsor, dir. Hartsfield Fine Art Exhibit, Houston, 1968—; mem. 4th Ward Neighborhood Council, Houston, 1977-82; commr. 4th Ward Montrose, Houston, 1978-82; del. Nat. Democratic Conv., N.Y.C., 1980; mem. exec. adv. council Houston Handicap Center, 1980-82; mem. Nat. Citizens' Participation Commn., 1981. Recipient Wakan award Camp Fire Girls, 1966. Mem. Tex. So. U. Alumni Assn. (life), Fedn. Tchrs., Houston Residence Citizens Participation Commn., Tex. Coalition Black Dems. Mem. Ch. of Christ. Club: Century. Home: 1613 Robin St Houston TX 77019

CAMPBELL, LYLA JUNE, psychologist; b. South Gate, Calif., June 20; d. George Malcolm and Glora Hazel (Bruce) Campbell; B.A., Loma Linda U., 1959; M.A., UCLA, 1968, Ph.D., 1971; 1 dau., Shelley Lynn Bates. Instr., counselor UCLA Extension, 1971-72; cons. Insgroup, Inc., Long Beach, Calif., 1971-72; counseling psychologist VA Regional Office, Los Angeles, 1972-74; program developer, mgr., instr. VA Med. Center, Sepulveda, Calif., 1974—; oral commr. Calif. State Psychology Licensing Exam., Bd. Med. Examiners, 1978-81. Cert. sex therapist. Mem. Am. Psychol. Assn., Western Psychol. Assn., Am. Assn. Sex Educators, Counselors and Therapists, Pi Lambda Theta. Office: VA Med Center Sepulveda CA 91343

CAMPBELL, (MARGARET) ANNE, state ofcl.; b. Denver, Nov. 13, 1917; d. Earl Ogilvie and Vera E. (Mallon) Linger; A.B., U. No. Colo., 1938; M.Sc., Wayne State Coll., Nebr., 1959; Ed.D., U. Nebr., 1969; hon. degrees Midland Luth. Coll., 1974, Central Meth. Coll., 1972; m. Leonard E. Campbell, July 4, 1938; children—Margilee Sauer, Beverly Fortin, Marilyn Waak. County supt. Madison County (Nebr.), 1955-63; dir. profl. services, lobbyist Nebr. State Edn. Assn., Lincoln, 1963-65; adminstrv. asst. Lincoln Pub. Schs., 1965-72; dir. pub. affairs U. Nebr., Lincoln, 1972-74; commr. edn. State of Nebr., Lincoln, 1974—; mem. adv. bd. UCLA, 1980. Trustee, State Coll., Doane Coll.; bd. dirs. Lincoln Action Program, 1965-72, Lincoln Community Services, 1972-75. Named Woman of Yr., Midland mag., 1973; Woman of Achievement, Nebr. Bus. and Profl. Women, 1974; recipient Disting. Service award Nebr. Council Sch. Adminstrs., 1979; others. Mem. Lincoln C. of C. (legis. affairs and edn. com. 1966—), AAUW (div. pres. 1952-54, regional v.p. 1962-71, pres. 1971-75), Am. Assn. Sch. Adminstrs., Assn. Supervision and Curriculum Devel., Nebr. State Edn. Assn., Assn. Tchr. Educators, NEA, Bus. and Profl. Women, PEO. Republican. Presbyterian. Club: Order Eastern Star. Contbr. articles to newspapers. Home: 7500 South St Apt 8 Lincoln NE 68506 Office: PO Box 94987 Lincoln NE 68509

CAMPBELL, MARGARET LETITIA, banker; b. Belfast, No. Ireland, July 13, 1947; d. John and Margaret Irene Campbell; M.A., Cambridge (Eng.) U., 1969; M.B.A., Manchester (Eng.) Bus. Sch., 1971; m. John Sinclair Gillespie, Oct. 13, 1973; 1 son, Iain Campbell. Asst. treas. Morgan Guaranty Trust Co., N.Y.C., 1973-75, asst. v.p., 1975-77, v.p., 1977—, London, 1973—, dept. head London office, 1977—. Mem. Cambridge U. Appointments Bd., 1977-81. Presbyterian. Home: 15 College Gardens London SE21 England Office: Morgan Bank 1 Angel Ct London EC2 England

CAMPBELL, MARIE MALLORY, human relations specialist; b. Bronwood, Ga., Jan. 5, 1939; d. Clarence and Lula Mallory; B.S., Bethune-Cookman Coll., 1960; M.S., Nova U., 1982; 1 dau., Monique Patrice. Math. tchr. Carver High Sch., Naples, Fla., 1960-64, Dunbar High Sch., Ft. Myers, Fla., 1964-66, North Ft. Myers High Sch., 1966-70, 73-80, Dunbar Middle Sch., 1970-73; human relations specialist Lee County Sch. Bd., Ft. Myers, 1980—. Mem. Dunbar Community Action Com., Ft. Myers Community Relations Commn.; mem. Ft. Meyers Democratic Com.; mem. Dunbar Day Care Adv. Bd.; mem. Suncoast Middle Sch. Adv. Com.; mem. affirmative action com. Sch. Bd. Lee County. Mem. Fla. Teaching Profession, Nat. Edn. Assn., Nat. Council Tchrs. Math, Tchrs. Assn. Lee County, NAACP, Delta Sigma Theta. Baptist. Club: Traveleer. Home: 3175 Guava St Fort Myers FL 33901 Office: Sch Bd Lee County 2055 Central Ave Fort Myers FL 33901

CAMPBELL, MARILYN RUTH, state legislator; b. Salem, N.H., July 31, 1932; s. Howard E. and Ruth K. Turner; B.S. in Occupational Therapy, U. N.H., 1954; m. Bernard W.M. Campbell, Apr. 3, 1955; children—Bernard H., Kevin, Kenneth. With Easter Seal Agy., 1958-61; substitute tchr. Salem Sch. Dist., 1961-66; farmer, Salem, 1966—; mem. N.H. Ho. of Reps., Gen. Ct., 1971—; dir. Farmers Market (Flame). Chmn. adv. com. N.H. Vocat.-Tech. Coll., Manchester, 1980. Recipient Hon. State Farmer award N.H. Future Farmers Am., Friend of Agr. award New Eng. Assn. County Extension Agts. Mem. AAUW, Salem Bus. and Profl. Women (Woman of Achievement 1978), N.H. Farm Bur., Assn. of Women of N.H. Farm Bur. (pres., life mem. Young Farmers). Republican. Methodist.

CAMPBELL, MARY ANN, journalist; b. Portland, Oreg., Mar. 25, 1920; d. David Beasley and Margueritte (Dosch) C.; B.A., U. Oreg., 1943; M.S., Joseph Pulitzer Grad. Sch. Journalism, Columbia U., 1946. Reporter, Oreg. Jour., 1943-50; free-lance reporter, Portland, 1959; reporter Portland Reporter, 1960-64; editor Ontario (Oreg.) Argus-Observer, 1966-69; editor Polk Sun, Monmouth, Oreg., 1970-72; women's editor, reporter, feature writer Medford (Oreg.) Mail Tribune, 1972—, art, music critic, editor, feature writer, 1974—; tchr. Upward

Bound Oreg. Prison Project, New Gate, 1965. Mem. Oreg. Environ. Council, Sierra Club, Friends of the Earth, 1000 Friends of Oreg., Nat. Wildlife Fedn., Defenders of Wildlife, Nat. Trust. Hist. Preservation, Oreg. Hist. Soc., So. Oreg. Hist. Soc., So. Oreg. Humane Soc., Oreg. Humane Soc., Greenpeace, Amnesty Internat., Oreg. Wilderness Coalition, ACLU, Theta Sigma Phi, Sigma Delta Chi. Democrat. Office: PO Box 1108 Medford OR 97501

CAMPBELL, MARY KATHRYN, educator; b. Phila., Jan. 20, 1939; d. Henry Charles and Mary Kathryn (Horan) C.; A.B. in Chemistry, Rosemont Coll., 1960; Ph.D., Ind. U., 1965. Instr. Johns Hopkins U., 1965-68; asst. prof. chemistry Mt. Holyoke Coll., 1968-74, assoc. prof., 1974-81, prof., 1981—; vis. scholar U. Paris VIII, 1974-75, VII, 1977-79; vis. prof. U. Ariz., 1981-82; mem. panel on grad. fellowships NSF, 1980-81. Hon. Woodrow Wilson fellow, 1960, NSF fellow, 1960-64, NIH fellow, 1964-65; grantee in field. Mem. Am. Chem. Soc., AAAS, AAUP, AAUW, Sigma Xi. Contbr. articles to profl. jours. Office: Carr Laboratory Department of Chemistry Mount Holyoke College South Hadley MA 01075

CAMPBELL, PATRICIA ANNE, handicrafts co. exec.; b. Pitts., Dec. 30; d. John A. and M. Lucille (Park) Campbell; B.S., Duquesne U., 1968; M.Ed., U. Pitts., 1969, Ph.D., 1974. Tchr., Avonworth Schs., 1968, Beaver County Community Coll., 1969, Northgate Schs., Pitts., 1974-75; mgmt. trainee Pitts. Nat. Bank, 1974-75; pres. Patpourri Enterprises, Sewickley, Pa., 1975—. Keiki concert chmn. Honolulu Symphony, 1978-80; mem. bd. Women's Symphony Assn., Honolulu, 1978-80; bd. dirs. women's guild Pitts. Ballet Theater, 1981-82. Recipient U. Pitts. Student Research award, 1974. Mem. Doctoral Assn. U. Pitts., AAUW, Pi Lambda Theta. Republican. Club: Pitts. Athletic Assn. Author: Prosocial Television Programming for Children: Expressions of Anger By Children During the Cognitive Revolution Period of development, 1974. Home: 216 Pine Rd Sewickley PA 15143

CAMPBELL, SALLY, data processing exec.; b. Pomona, Calif., Nov. 16, 1949; d. Richard Sewall and Dorothy Jean (Thomason) C.; B.A. in Applied Physics and Info. Sci., U. Calif., San Diego, 1972. From programmer to sr. sci. programmer Sperry Univac, San Diego and Blue Bell, Pa., 1972-80; sr. analyst, tng. specialist Datagraphix, Inc., San Diego, 1980-81; mgr. systems and programming Pepperdine U., Malibu, Calif., 1981—; cons. in field; past mem. extension faculty U. Calif., San Diego. Mem. Data Processing Mgmt. Assn., IEEE, Nat. Assn. Female Execs., Mensa. Home: 13920 Northwest Passage Apt 104 Marina del Rey CA 90291 Office: 24255 Pacific Coast Hwy Malibu CA 90265

CAMPBELL, SALLY WORTHINGTON, freelance writer, editor, public relations cons.; b. Pitts., Jan. 3, 1947; d. Aubrey Walter and Marie Ruth (Henningsen) Worthington; B.A. in Journalism, Auburn U., 1968; m. John Jette Campbell, Aug. 31, 1968; children—Ashley, Heather, John Jette, Jr. Reporter-intern Montgomery, Ala. Jour., 1968; asst. editor Auburn (Ala.) Extension Service, 1968-69; tchr. lang. arts Nichols Jr. High Sch., Tuskegee, Ala., 1969-70; editor Where Mag., Houston, 1971-79, southwestern editorial supr., 1979; dir. public relations Austin (Tex.) Civic Ballet, 1980—, also bd. dirs.; cons. public relations Retinitis Pigmentosa Found., Houston, 1979. Vice pres. Austin Jr. Forum, 1980-82; mem. Laguna Gloria Mus. Women's Art Guild, 1980—; writer for KTBC-TV 1st place award Region II public service announcement competition, Tex. Broadcasters Assn., 1981. Mem. Women in Communications, Alpha Omicron Pi. Republican. Presbyterian. Home and Office: 7705 Bramblewood Circle Austin TX 78731

CAMPBELL, VERONICA MARIE, auditor, govt. ofcl.; b. Phila., Aug. 30, 1952; d. Charles F. and Virginia M. (Hibbits) C.; B.A., Barat Coll., Lake Forest, Ill., 1973. With Office Insp. Gen., Dept. Agr., 1973-82, auditor-in-charge fgn. ops. staff, Washington, 1979-82; supervisory auditor Office of Insp. Gen., U.S. Dept. Interior, 1982—. Mem. Delta Epsilon Sigma, Kappa Gamma Pi. Roman Catholic. Office: Room 401 800 N Quincy St Arlington VA 22217

CAMPBELL-GOYMER, NANCY RUTH, psychologist, educator; b. Florala, Ala., July 1, 1949; d. T.C. and Nora Ella (Conner) Campbell; B.A. magna cum laude (Nat. Merit scholar), Fla. State U., 1971; M.A. (NDEA fellow) U. Ala., 1972, postgrad., 1974—; m. George Goymer, Mar. 10, 1978. Psychol. asst. II, Okla. Dept. Instns., Social and Rehab. Services, Oklahoma City, 1973-74; clin. psychology intern U. N.C., Chapel Hill Med. Sch., 1976-77; asst. prof. psychology Birmingham So. Coll., 1977—, co-dir. Counseling Center, 1978-81; speaker in field; vis. prof. Western Mental Health Center, summer 1979; mem. Jefferson County (Ala.) Child Abuse and Neglect Task Force, 1979—. Recipient Martin S. Wallach award U. N.C. Med. Sch., 1977. Mem. Am. Psychol. Assn. (asso.), Ala. Psychol. Assn., Phi Beta Kappa, Phi Kappa Phi, Psi Chi, Alpha Lambda Delta. Contbr. articles to profl. jours. Office: Psychology Dept Box A-37 Birmingham-So Coll 800 8th Ave W Birmingham AL 35204

CAMPION, EILEEN, lawyer; b. Great River, N.Y.; d. Patrick and Mary (Gaughan) Campion; J.D., U. Miami, 1961. Admitted to Fla. bar, 1962, U.S. Supreme Ct. bar, 1968; practiced in Miami, Fla., 1962-64, 81—; law editor Lawyers Co-op. Pub. Co., Rochester, N.Y., 1964-65; atty. U.S. Treasury Dept., Miami, 1965-80. Founding pres. Women's Com. of One Hundred, Miami, 1970-73; mem. fed. exec. bd. Miami Consumers Com., 1972-74, chmn., 1974-75; mem. exec. com. Miami br. Fla. Consumers Fedn., 1978-79; mem. Met. Dade County Water and Sewer Bd, 1973-75; city rep. Bd. Legal Services Greater Miami, 1974—; invited participant Women's Tour of China, 1978. Recipient Outstanding Service award Fed. Bar Assn., 1968, 69; award for untiring efforts for community betterment Womens Com. of One Hundred, 1973; highest award for legal writing in internat. competition, 1963; highest award for article AAUW, 1982. Mem. Am., Dade County (Outstanding Service award 1971) bar assns., Fla. Bar, AAUW (fellowship gift 1976), Am. Arbitration Assn. (panel arbitrators), Bus. and Profl. Women's Club. Editor: The Short End, 1976-77. Home: 453 Brickell Ave Miami FL 33131 Office: 51 SW 1st Ave Miami FL 33130

CANADA, HELEN, univ. adminstr.; b. Monett, Mo., May 18, 1934; d. Virgil Hubert and Edith Brooks (Salyer) C.; B.S., St. Louis U., 1961, M.S., 1968, Ph.D., 1977. Engaged in merchandising, 1953-56; mem. profl. staff Girl Scouts U.S., 1961-69; mem. adminstrv. staff St. Louis U., 1969—, registrar, 1977—, mem. adj. faculty dept. history, 1979—. Mem. Am. Assn. Coll. Registrars and Admissions Officers. Democrat. Presbyterian. Office: 221 N Grand St Saint Louis MO 63103

CANADA, MARY WHITFIELD, librarian; b. Richmond, Va., June 13, 1919; d. Waverly Thomas and Ruth Bradshaw (Smith) Canada; B.A., magna cum laude, Emory and Henry Coll., 1940; M.A. in English, Duke, 1942; B.S. in L.S., U. N.C., Chapel Hill, 1956. Asst. circulation dept. Duke U. Library, 1942-45, undergrad. librarian, 1946-55, reference librarian, 1956—, asst. head reference dept., 1967-79, head dept., 1979—. Mem. exec. com. Friends of Duke Univ. Library. Duke U. grantee, Can., 1979, 81. Mem. ALA (life; reference services in large research libraries discussion group), Southeastern (sec. coll. and univ. sect., chmn. nominating com. reference services div., also chmn. div.), N.C. (chmn. nominating com., chmn. newspaper com., chmn. coll. and univ. sect.) library assns., Alumni Assn. Sch. Library Sci. U. N.C. (pres.), AAUP, Va. Hist. Soc. (life), Va. Geneal. Soc., DAR, Trinity Coll. Hist. Soc., Va. Mus., Beta Phi Mu, Tau Kappa Alpha, Alpha Psi Omega, Delta Kappa Gamma. Methodist. Contbr. to profl. publs. Home: 1312 Lancaster St Durham NC 27701

CANALES, GUILLERMINA BRAVO, modern dance co. choreographer and exec.; b. Veracruz, Mex., Nov. 13, 1920; d. Guillermo Bravo Avila and Dolores Canales Mondragon; student Williams Sch., 1927-35; student in Piano, Nat. Conservatory of Music, 1938-45; student Martha Graham Dance Sch., 1963-64; m. Carlos Sanchez Cardenas, Aug. 15, 1945; children—Claudia, Lucio. Founder, developer, dir. Ballet Nacional de Mexico (Danza Contemporanea), 1948—, artistic dir., 1948—, prin. choreographer, 1948—; choreography includes: Homenaje a Cervantes, 1973, Epicentro, 1977, Juego de Pelota, 1968, Vision de muerte, 1980, Los Comicos, 1981. Recipient nat. prize for arts, 1979. Roman Catholic. Condr. research ethnic and related areas. Office: 4-3 deg Calle del 57 Mexico DF 06010 Mexico

CANARINA, MARY, artist; b. N.Y.C., Feb. 2, 1904; d. Karol and Xenia Anna (Sczmaydy) Gruber; student Cooper Union, 1922-24, N.Y. Sch. Indsl. Design, 1924-30, Art Students League, 1958-59; m. John Baptiste Canarina, Feb. 6, 1930; children—John Baptiste, Arnold Romano. Freelance artist Cosmopolitan Photographers, N.Y.C., 1936-42, Yuster Studio, N.Y.C., 1936-42, Superior Studios, N.Y.C., 1943-53, Rikshaw Assos., N.Y.C., 1954-64; artist, muralist; works include mural for sr. citizen bldg., 1972, landscape arch. bldg., 1973. Mem. Mt. Vernon Art Assn. (pres.), New Rochelle Art Assn., Hudson Valley Art Assn. (dir.), Nat. League Am. Pen Women, Am. Artist Profl. League. Club: Salmagundi.

CANATSEY, SANDRA DAVIS, bldg. and devel. co. exec.; b. Trussville, Ala., Dec. 30, 1940; d. Samuel Robert and Beulah Gladys (Shook) Davis; B.S. in Edn., U. Kans., 1962; m. Steven Michael Canatsey, July 5, 1974; children—Kimberley, Kacee, Kevin, Kristine, Kip. Kindergarten tchr., Kansas City, Kans., 1962-64; elem. tchr. Larkspur Elem. Sch., Paradise Valley, Ariz., 1964-65; office mgr. Canatsey & Co., Tucson, 1976-78; sec., dir. Canatsey Bldg. & Devel. Co., Inc., Tucson, 1978—; sec., dir. Canlove Enterprises, Inc. Pres. Pathfinder Republican Women, 1980; mem. Five Star Rep. Women, 1982; exec. bd., treas. Tucson Symphony Women's Assn., 1981—; mem. Tucson Med. Center Aux., 1973—; exec. com., sec. Ariz. Fedn. Rep. Women, 1981—; chmn. vols. Barry Goldwater for Senate, 1980. Life cert. substitute tchr., Ariz. Mem. So. Ariz. Home Builders Aux. (exec. com., v.p.), Alpha Phi Mothers Club. Home: 2520 Camino Principal Tucson AZ 85715 Office: 1625 N Alvernon Way Tucson AZ 85712

CANAVAN, ELLEN MCGEE, state legislator; b. San Antonio, Dec. 26, 1941; d. Edward Francis and Eleanor Mary (Mullen) McGee; B.A., Regis Coll., 1963; M.Ed., Boston Coll., 1975, C.A.E.S., 1978; m. M. Christopher Canavan, Jr., Apr. 18, 1965; children—Elizabeth Ann, Michael Edward. Personnel asst. Avco-Everett Research Lab., Everett, Mass., 1963-65; dir. rehab. Mass. Rehab. Commn., Chestnut Hill, 1977-78; dir. community edn. Norfolk Mental Health Assn., Norwood, Mass., 1978-80; mem. Mass. Ho. of Reps., 1980—. Bd. dirs. YMCA; adv. bd. Glover Meml. Hosp., Mount Pleasant Hosp.; mem. Town Meeting, 1976—, chmn. spl. com. on mental health, 1976-77; mem. Needham (Mass.) Planning Bd., 1975-80. Mem. Nat. Fedn. Republican Women, Today's Women, Mass. Caucus Women Legislators, Mass. Legislators Assn., Boston Women. Republican. Roman Catholic. Club: Brae Burn Country. Office: Room 26 State House Boston MA 02133

CANCILLA, ELISABETH ANN, computer systems analyst; b. Pittsfield, Mass., Oct. 25, 1951; d. Vincent William and Yolanda (Campoli) C.; A.A., Bradford Jr. Coll., 1971; B.A. in Computer Sci., Elmira Coll., 1973; M.B.A. in Systems Analysis, SUNY, Binghamton, 1975. Asso. mgmt. systems analyst Burroughs Corp., Detroit, 1975-76; programmer analyst Handelman Co., Clawson, Mich., 1976-77; programmer analyst Chrysler Corp., Detroit, 1977-79, Transam. Life Ins. and Annuity Co., Los Angeles, 1979—. Mem. Nat. Assn. Female Execs. Home: 15115 Parthenia Apt 265 Sepulveda CA 91343

CANDLER, ANN CLIFFORD, educator; b. Galveston, Tex., Sept. 23, 1947; d. Patrick Michael and Ellen Marie (Salmon) Clifford; B.S.Ed., Lamar U., 1970; M.Ed., U. Houston, 1976, Ed.D. (Am. Bus. Club Monterey chpt. grantee), 1981; 1 dau., Millicent. Spl. edn. tchr. Texas City (Tex.) Ind. Sch. Dist., 1970-72; research asst. Coll. Edn., U. Houston, 1974-76; asso. prof. spl. edn. Tex. Tech. U., 1976—, acting asso. chairperson specializations area and chairperson spl. edn., 1980-81. Recipient award for teaching excellence Amoco, 19 ; Am. Bus. Club Monterey Chpt. grantee, 1981, 82; Tex. Tech. U. Coll. Edn. grantee, 1976-77, 78-79; Dept. Edn. Office Edn. for Handicapped grantee, 1979-81. Mem. Council Exceptional Children, Assn. Children with Learning Disabilities, Assn. Severely Handicapped. Roman Catholic. Contbr. articles to profl. jours. Office: PO Box 4560 Lubbock TX 79409

CANDON, VERA ANNE, psychologist; b. Cleve., Jan. 26, 1910; d. William F. and Frances (Skerl) C.; B.S., Ohio State U., 1932, M.A., 1937, Ph.D., Western Res. U., 1954. Authorized sci. texts units Cleve. Bd. Edn., 1934-38, head sci. dept., sci. tchr., 1933-37, psychologist, 1937-56; lectr. Western Res. U., Cleve., 1949-59, Ohio State U., 1963-64, Cleve. State U., 1966-72; supr. psychol. services Berea (Ohio) Bd. Edn., 1956-60, coordinator spl. services, 1960-64; pvt. practice psychology, 1964—; cons. Lorain County Child Study, 1968—; lectr. child devel., adolescence, drug problems; cons., lectr. mental health problems in schs. John Hay fellow, 1963. Mem. NEA, AAAS, Internat. Council Psychologists, Am. Psychol. Assn., Ohio Psychol. Assn., Cleve. Psychol. Assn., World Mental Health Assn., Nat. Mental Health Assn., Cleve. Mental Health Assn., Ohio Acad. Cons. Psychologists, Cleve. Acad. Cons. Psychologists. Office: Med Center Gt No Mall North Olmsted OH 44070

CANFIELD, CAROL KATHRYN, horse breeder; b. Columbus, Ohio, July 29, 1929; d. Karl McKinley and Esther (Eileen (Enright) Koveleski; A.B., U. Chgo., 1951; postgrad. Purdue U., 1953-54; Ohio State U., Newark, 1962-65; m. Sheldon Arthur Canfield, Jan. 29, 1949; children—Karl Herbert, Peter Andreas, Benjamin Arthur. Statis. clk. Purdue Statis. Labs., Lafayette, Ind., 1951-52, draftsman, 1952-53, research asst., 1953-54; tchr. piano, organ Summers & Sons Piano Sales, Newark, Ohio, 1969-70; horsemaster Canfield Farm, Newark, 1971—. Violinist, Licking County Symphony Orch., 1956-59; active League of Women Voters. Mem. Ohio Horsemen's Council (pres. Licking County chpt. 1973—), Blazing Saddles Horse Club (sec. 1977-78, 80, pres. 1981). Clubs: Broken Arrow Riders, Flint Ridge, Cutters (sec.-treas. 1970), Apache Trails Horse (sec. 1973—). Researcher status of horse trails in Ohio. Home: 2041 Hickman Rd NE Newark OH 43055

CANFIELD, JUDY OHLBAUM, psychologist; b. N.Y.C., May 15, 1947; d. Arthur and Ada Evelyn (Werner) Ohlbaum; B.A., Grinnell Coll., 1963; M.A., New Sch. Social Research, 1967; Ph.D., U.S. Internat. U., 1970; children—Oran David, Kyle Danya. Psychologist Mendocino State Hosp., Talmage, Calif., 1968-69, Douglas Coll., New Westminster, B.C., Can., 1971-72, Family and Childrens Clinic, Burnaby, B.C., 1971-72; tng. cons. VA Hosp., Northampton, Mass., 1972-75; dir. New Eng. Center, Amherst, Mass., 1972-76, Gateways, Lansdale, Pa., 1977-78; asst. prof. psychology Hahnemann Med. Coll., Phila., 1978—; pvt. practice psychology, Phila. and Bala-Cynwyd, Pa., 1977—; dir., pres. Inst. for Holistic Health, Phila., 1978—. Mem. Internat. Acad. Preventive Medicine, Am. Acad. Psychotherapists, Am. Psychol. Assn., Pa. Psychol. Assn., World Future Soc., Nat. Register of Health Service Providers in Psychology, Assn. Humanistic Psychology. Home and Office: 345 Llandrillo Rd Bala Cynwyd PA 19004

CANFIELD, JULIE ANN, land devel. and brokerage co. exec.; b. Colorado Springs, July 28, 1951; d. Thomas Lee and Mary Katherine (Brewer), C.; A.A., Pikes Peak Community Coll., 1974; student Brown Mackie Sch. Bus., 1970, Jones Real Estate Sch., 1981, Wichita State U., 1982—. Credit mgr., Cotten Jones Watson Agy., Colorado Springs, 1971-73; on site coordinator Washburn Woods Corp./Ocho Caballos, 1973-74; bookkeeper L.T. Smith Inc., Colorado Springs, 1974-75; bus. mgr. Cellular Product Services, Inc., Colorado Springs, Colo., 1975-82, adminstrv. mgr. Olive Co., Colorado Springs, 1982; acct. adminstr. Fin. Mgmt. Inc., 1982—. Counselor vol. staff, Chins Up Program; vol. Big Sisters. Mem. Colorado Springs Bd. Realtors, Home Builders Assn. Colorado Springs, North End Comml. Assn., Nat. Assn. Credit Mgmt. Republican. Home: 421 Turquoise Wichita KS 67209 Office: 4510 W Central Wichita KS 67212

CANINO, JANE H., ins. agt.; b. Beacon, N.Y., Jan. 24, 1922; d. Joseph J. and Anna (Region) Hiko; student Poughkeepsie Bus. Inst., 1939-40; m. Gabriel P. Canino, Oct. 4, 1947; children—John R., Gabrielle. Ind. contractor, ins. agt. Nationwide Mut. Ins. Co., Highland, N.Y., 1955—; mut. funds rep. Heritage Securities Inc., 1970—. Master Life Rep., mem. Challenger Club, recipient 25 year service award Nationwide Mut. Ins. Co., 1980. Mem. Hudson Valley Agent's Forum. Roman Catholic. Home: 100 Bellevue Rd Highland NY 12528 Office: 24 Main St Highland NY 12528

CANN, CARLTON HELENE, psychologist; b. Greensboro, N.C., Feb. 16, 1944; d. Jesse Eris and Dorothy May C.; student U. N.C., Greensboro, 1961-63, B.S., Chapel Hill, 1965; Ph.D., U. Colo., 1975. Systems analyst Colo. Dept. Social Services and Dept. Adminstrn., Denver, 1966-69; instr. psychology U. Colo., Colorado Springs, 1976; instr. social scis. El Paso Community Coll., Colorado Springs, 1975-76; asso. prof. psychology N.Mex. Highlands U., Las Vegas, 1977—, also chmn. dept. behavioral scis.; founding mem. Quadra Assos. Recipient grants N.Mex. Highlands U., 1978, 79, 80; Ford Found. fellow, 1980. Mem. Am. Psychol. Assn., Rocky Mountain Psychol. Assn., Assn. Women in Psychology, AAUW (rep.), NOW. Home: 2034 Cassidy Dr Las Vegas NM 87701 Office: Dept Behavioral Scis N Mex Highlands U Las Vegas NM 87701

CANN, DOROTHY KILE, trade sch. adminstr.; b. N.Y.C., Aug. 25, 1949; d. John Reynolds and Helen Lily (Kuzmyak) C.; B.A. with honors, U. Newcastle-Upon-Tyne (Eng.), 1971; m. Lowell Hutchison Kile, Nov. 19, 1974. U.S. Peace Corps vol., instr. Mahidol U., Bangkok, Thailand, 1972-74; financial aid officer Apex Tech. Sch., N.Y.C., 1974-78, sch. dir., 1978—, instr. basic grant tng. project, 1977-79. Mem. Nat. Assn. Trade and Tech. Schs. (sec.), Student Aid Coalition. Office: 635 Ave of the Americas New York NY 10011

CANN, MARJORIE MITCHELL, former educator, personnel cons.; b. Moncton, N.B., Can.; d. Douglas Robert and Maude (Dunham) Mitchell; B.S., Acadia U., N.S., 1940; M.A., Mich. State U., 1953; Ph.D., U. Mich. 1957. Tchr., prin. public elem. schs., N.S., Ont., Can., 1936-48; tchr. secondary schs., N.S., Que., Can. and East Lansing, Mich., 1950-56; instr. math. Acadia U., 1957-61; dir. math. Delta Coll., Bay City, Mich., 1961-63; adminstrv. head Greater Cleve. Math. Program, 1963-64; asso. prof. math.-edn. and research U. Akron (Ohio), 1964-67; prof. edn., chmn. behavioral scis. Pensacola (Fla.) Jr. Coll., 1967-79; personnel cons. to orgns. and instns., Pensacola. Ednl. adviser Pensacola Cerebral Palsy Center, 1967-71, bd. dirs. NW Fla. Center, 1971-74, chmn. profl. adv. com., 1971-76, chmn. program devel. com. Fla. state bd. dirs., 1974—, treas. state bd. dirs., 1977—; pres. Mitchell-Meriwether Corp., 1969—. Mem. Nat. Council Tchrs. Math., Math. Assn. Am., NEA, Canadian Edn. Assn., Nat. Soc. Programmed Instrn., Pensacola C. of C. (com. on edn. 1972-74). Author: (with other) A Synthesis of Teaching Methods, 1964-67, 72; author-editor: An Introduction to Education, 1972; contbr. articles to profl. jours. Home: 4740 Peacock Dr Pensacola FL 32504

CANNADY, ROSEMARIE SARAH, nursing adminstr.; b. Gary, Ind., Oct. 31, 1928; d. Patsy and Rose (Roppola) Marando; student Glendale Coll., 1978; Practical Nurse, Harlem Valley State Hosp., 1948; m. Earl W. Cannady, May 30, 1964; 1 son, Earl W.; children by previous marriage—Linda, Karen, Marie. Pvt. nurse, Bridgeport, Conn., 1954-60; dept. mgr., head cashier W. T. Grant Co., 1961-64; pvt. nurse, Naples, Fla., 1966-67; owner, mgr. Glendale (Calif.) Nurses Registry, 1968—; land developer, Las Vegas, Nev., 1977-80. Mem. Nat. Fedn. Ind. Bus., U.S. C. of C., Calif. Employment Assn., Glendale C. of C. Republican. Roman Catholic. Office: 440 W Colorado St Glendale CA 91204

CANNIE, JOAN KOOB, author, learning systems exec.; b. Phila., Aug. 6, 1927; d. Edward T. and Alma (Yergens) Koob; student public schs. Upper Darby, Pa.; m. Allen F. Cannie, Dec. 17, 1949; children—Eva, Edward. Advt. dir. Walter J. Black, 1949-52; partner Steiner & Koob, 1952-55; pres. Joan M. Koob Assos., N.Y.C., 1955-70; co-founder, partner Investment Mgmt. Trust Boston, 1965-67; co-founder, chmn. Learning Dynamics, Inc., Needham, Mass., 1968—. Mem. Nat. Soc. Performance and Instrn., Instructional Systems Assn. Editor-in-chief Personal Success Report, 1970-73; author: The Woman's Guide to Management Success, 1979; Take Charge, 1980. Office: PO Box 323 Needham MA 02192

CANNING, MARGARET GRAEME, opera singer; b. Knoxville, Tenn., Aug. 19, 1941; d. Graeme Alexander and Mary Margaret (Hoskins) C.; B.Mus. with honors, U. So. Calif., 1963, M.Mus. in Opera, 1970; certificate Mozarteum, Salzburg, Austria, 1963-64, 72. Opera singer performances U.S. and Europe including Bayerischen Staatsoper, Nationaltheater, Munich, W. Ger., Detmold Pforzheim, Bremerhaven, W. Ger., Russe, Stara Zagora, Varna, Sofia, Bourgas, Pleven, Bulgaria, Bruxelles (Belgium) Nat. Opera, Tucson Opera, San Diego Opera; recording artist Deutschen Grammophone Gelleschaft; pvt. voice teacher. Tour. dir. Am. Armed Forces Recreation Center, Chiemsee, Germany, 1976-77. Austrian govt. scholar Mozarteum, 1963; Deutschen Grammophone Gelleschaft scholar, 1963-64; Martha Baird Rockefellow Fund for Music grantee, 1966-67; recipient scholarship award Nat. Soc. Arts and Letters, Los Angeles, 1963, Kathy Popova gold medal, Pleven, Bulgaria, 1970. Concurso International de Canto, Barcelona, Spain, 1970, Najla Jabor silver medal, Rio de Janeiro, Brazil, 1971, World Opera Star, Antwerp, Belgium, 1972, vocal winner Internat. Sommerakademie, Mozarteum Salzburg, 1972, awards of merit U. Ariz., 1956, 57, 58, 59; first place winner Artist of Future, dept. mcpl. art, City of Los Angeles, 1963; winner San Francisco Opera Auditions, 1966; Merola Opera Program, San Francisco, 1969. Mem. Sigma Alpha Iota. Presbyterian. First singer to receive Najla Jabor silver medal; only American to receive World Opera Star, title from Benelux countries; only person from Western world to receive Kathy Popova gold medal. Home: 2000 Camino Miraval Tucson AZ 85718

CANNON, BARBARA EVELYN MARIE, ednl. adminstr.; b. Big Sandy, Tex., Jan. 17, 1936; d. Archie and Jimmie Cannon; B.A., San Francisco State U., 1957, M.A. in Music, 1965; postgrad. in French, Monterey Inst. Fgn. Studies, summer 1966, U. Paris, 1966-67; M.A., Stanford U., 1975, Ed.D. (Ednl. Policy fellow 1975-76), 1977. Tchr. music, French, English, history, social studies Berkeley (Calif.) Public Schs., 1958-74, tchr. chorus, piano and orch., 1973-74, staff devel. asso.,

1972-74; teaching fellow and coordinator Sch. Edn., Stanford (Calif.) U., 1974-75; adminstrv. asst. to nat. dir. Tchr. Corps, U.S. Office Edn., Washington, 1975-76; research asst. Center for Ednl. Research, Stanford U., 1976-77, research asso., 1977-78; asst. dean fine, applied and lang. arts Coll. of Alameda (Calif.), 1978—; cons. to U.S. Office Edn., 1978, State Dept. Edn., Calif., 1978, Far West Ednl. Lab., 1978; project coordinator Calif. State Dept. Edn., 1977-78. Govtl. fellow U Ghana, W. Africa, 1968. Mem. Assn. of Calif. Community Coll. Adminstrs., Nat. Assn. Black Psychologists, Phi Delta Kappa, Pi Lambda Theta. Home: 2101 Shoreline Dr #458 Alameda CA 94501 Office: Coll of Alameda 555 Atlantic Ave Alameda CA 94501

CANNON, ELAINE WINIFRED ANDERSON, author, lectr.; b. Salt Lake City, Apr. 9, 1922; d. Aldon Joseph and Minnie (Egan) Anderson; B.S., U. Utah, 1943; m. Donald James Cannon, Mar. 25, 1943; children—James Quayle, Carla, Christine (Mrs. Heber Jacobsen), Su (Mrs. Bryant McOmber), Holly (Mrs. Richard Metcalf), Anthony Joseph. With Deseret News, Salt Lake City, 1943-69, feature writer, columnist, 1944-47, editor teen dept., 1947-69; asso. editor New Era mag., Salt Lake City, 1970-73; asso. editor Era of Youth mag., 1960-70; moderator It's a Date, Sta. KSL-TV, Salt Lake City, 1952-55, Focus on Youth, Sta. KUTV, 1961-65, 67-69, Public Pulse for Youth, Sta. KSL, 1966-67. Instr. continuing edn. Brigham Young U., Provo, Utah, 1958—, U. Utah, Salt Lake City, 1964, Utah State U., Logan, 1968-70. Del. White House Conf. on Children and Youth, 1950-51; mem. adv. bd. Juvenile Ct., Salt Lake City, 1970-71, Boy's Ranch Utah, Salt Lake City, 1966—; mem. spl. program com. Am. Cancer Soc., Salt Lake City, 1965-66. Bd. dirs. Women Unlimited Conv. Program Bur., Salt Lake City; internat. pres. Young Women Ch. Jesus Christ of Latter-day Saints, also mem. coordinating council; bd. dirs. Deseret Gymnasium, Promised Valley Theatre. Recipient 1st prize writing youth div. Nat. Press Women Assn., 1958, service to youth citation Seventeen mag., 1955; named Woman Year, Ricks Coll., 1965, Weber State Coll., 1971, Idaho State U., 1972. Mem. Authors Club, Am. Press Women Assn., Nat. Council Women of U.S.A. (exec. bd. 1979—, v.p.), Mortar Bd., Internat. Platform Assn., Alpha Lambda Delta, Chi Omega. Republican. Mem. Ch. Jesus Christ Latter-day Saints (All-Ch. Honored Woman 1967). Author: Time of Your Life, 1954; Corner on Youth, 1963; Teens and Their Times, 1964; How Glorious is Youth, 1969; A Time for Living; After the Manner of Happiness; It's A Great Idea; Woman, Her Hope and Her Heritage, 1975; Summer of My Content, 1976; The Mighty Change, 1981; Putting Life in Your Life Story, 1981; The Seasoning, 1981. Weekly radio show You and Your World. Home: 1283 E South Temple Salt Lake City UT 84102 Office: 50 E N Temple Salt Lake City UT 84150

CANTEEN, JEANNE T., communications co. ofcl.; b. N.Y.C., June 4, 1944; d. Eugene Simon and Mary Elizabeth (Trulove) Recker; B.A., Smith Coll., 1965; M.B.A., Harvard U., 1976; m. Richard Russell Gordon, Nov. 26, 1977. With New York Telephone Co., 1965—, asst. mgr. operator services, N.Y.C., 1965-69, traffic supr., 1969-72, traffic supt., 1972-74, planning mgr. envison. analysis div., 1976-79, mktg. mgr., retail, N.Y.C., 1976—. Pres. bd. dirs. Gramercy 29 Coop., 1979-80, 82—; Alumni Assn. of Halsted Sch., 1972-74; mem. Senator Goodman's Task Force in Transp., 1981; active Met. Rep. Club. Mem. Planning and Devel. Forum (vice chmn.), Nat. Retail Mchts. Assn., N.Y. Harvard Bus. Sch. Club, N.Y. Smith Club. Episcopalian. Home: 29 E 22nd St New York NY 10010 Office: 1515 Broadway New York NY 10036

CANTY, MARY LOUISE, pub. co. exec.; b. Somerville, Mass., Mar. 14, 1934; d. Cornelius Francis and Mary Ann (McCarthy) C.; With New Eng. Telephone Co., Boston, 1951-62; office mgr., purchasing agt. Cambridge Plating Co. (Mass.), 1962-65; with Shelby Pub. Corp., Wellesley, Mass., 1965—, now v.p., asst. treas., circulation mgr. John Liner Letter, also dir. Mem. Nat. Assn. Female Execs., Mass. Assn. Ins. Women, Nat. Assn. Ins. Women. Roman Catholic. Club: Irish Am. Office: 555 Washington St Wellesley MA 02181

CAPITMAN, BARBARA BAER (MRS. WILLIAM CAPITMAN), author, editor; b. Chgo., Apr. 9, 1920; d. Herschel I. and Myrtle (Bacharach) Baer; student Wash. Sq. Coll.; B.A. with honors in English, N.Y. U., 1941; postgrad. Columbia, 1941-42, U. Pitts. Sch. Fine Arts, 1972-73; m. William Capitman, July 1, 1948 (dec.); children—Andrew William, John Amson. Feature writer Modern Plastics, N.Y.C., 1945-46; editor Modern Lamps and Accessories, N.Y.C., 1946-52, Design Sense, 1955-57; dir. info., editor mag. Ponder Center for Research in Mktg., Inc., Center for Research in Social Dynamics, Peekskill, N.Y., from 1957, now pres. center, Miami, Fla., N.Y.C.; So. editor Designer mag.; editor Portfolio, Art Deco Dist., 1979, Time Present, Time Past, 1980; lectr. art deco Am., N.Y.C., Washington, Chgo. Mem. Am. Soc. Interior Designers, Miami Design Preservation League (pres.), Art Deco Socs. Am. (founder, pres.), Preservation Action (Fla. dir. 1978—). Author several books in field of interior design, 1949-53; author: (with others) Dynamics of the Negro Market, 1968; American Trademark Designs, 1976. Home: 1211 Pennsylvania Ave Miami Beach FL 33139 Office: 1300 Ocean Dr Miami Beach FL 33139

CAPLAN, SYLVIA DAVIS, audio/visual producer/cons., film maker, broadcaster, writer, sculptor; b. Mexico City, Nov. 21, 1936 (parents Am. citizens); d. Irving and Bertha (German) Davis; student U. Mex., 1952, Houston Mus. Fine Art, 1975-77; m. Arthur Morris Caplan, Oct. 12, 1952; children—Curtis Ray, Marcia Dianne, Mark David. Pres. Caplan/Rawley and Assocs., 1977—; owner, operator The Houston Cons. Group, Houston, Dallas, 1977—, also Intermedia Corp., Executrend Internat.; on-air personality and writer Sta. KRIO, McAllen, Tex., Sta. KURV, Edinburg, Tex., Sta. KPAB, Laredo, Tex.; feature editor, columnist Edinburg Daily Rev.; cons. Women in Bus., Audio-Visual Ind. Producers. Active March of Dimes. Recipient awards March of Dimes, 1963, 65, Am. Heart Assn., 1969, Tex. B'nai B'rith, 1967. Mem. Am. Soc. Tng. and Devel., Am. Film Inst., Motion Picture Council Houston, Assn. Multi-Images, Contemporary Women in Am. Art, Artes Internacionales de las Americas, Houston Art League, Am. Women in Radio and TV, Nat. Assn. Women Bus. Owners, Houston C. of C. Jewish. Clubs: B'nai B'rith Women, Sisterhood Temple Emanuel.

CAPLOW, HARRIET MCNEAL, art historian; b. Highland Park, Ill., July 26, 1928; d. Morley Daniel and Julia (Allison) McNeal; M.A., Columbia U., 1966, Ph.D., 1970; children from previous marriage—James, Julie, Firenze. Mem. faculty Ind. State U., Terre Haute, 1967—, asso. prof., 1972-79, prof. humanities and art history, 1979—. Bd. dirs. Eugene V. Debs Found., Planned Parenthood Wabash Valley, Ind. Civil Liberties Union, Farrington Grove Historic Preservation. Grantee Ind. State U., Kress Found.; recipient Caleb Mills award Disting. Teaching, 1981. Mem. Coll. Art Assn. Am., Renaissance Soc. Am., Soc. Archlt. Historians. Author: Michelozzo, 1977. Home: 825 S 7th St Terre Haute IN 47807 Office: Dept Humanities Ind State U Terre Haute IN 47809

CAPODILUPO, ELIZABETH JEANNE HATTON, public relations ofcl.; b. McRae, Ga., May 3, 1940; d. Lewis Irby and Essee Elizabeth (Parker) Hatton; grad. Dale Carnegie Inst., 1976; m. Raphael S. Capodilupo, Jan. 21, 1967. Sec., A.R. Clark Acct., 1959; receptionist, girl Friday, Channel 13, Sta. WNDT-TV, N.Y.C., 1960-62, Coy Hunt and Co., N.Y.C., 1962-69; clk. Woodlawn Cemetery, Bronx, N.Y., 1969-71, historian, community affairs coordinator, 1971—, editor Woodlawn Cemetery News newsletter, 1979—, also dir. public relations; grad. asst. Dale Carnegie Inst., 1977-78. Chairwoman Ann. Adm. Farragut Honor Ceremony, Bronx, 1976—; chmn. Nelly Bly Honor Ceremony, 1978; bd. dirs. Bronx Mus. Arts, 1981—. Recipient awards, including award citation VFW, 1976, Voice of Democracy Program judge's citation, 1980; cert. of appreciation Dale Carnegie Inst., 1977; Outstanding Citizenship award Bronx N.E. Kiwanis Club, 1981. Mem. Women in Communication, Bronx County Hist. Soc., Network Orgn. Bronx Women, Bronx C. of C. (co-chmn. Indsl. Directory 1981). Methodist. Clubs: N.Y. Press, Women's City, Order Eastern Star. Researcher Woodlawn Cemetery's Hall of Fame. Office: The Woodlawn Cemetery PO Box 12 Bronx NY 10470

CAPOLUNGO, BARBARA ANN, U.S. customs officer; b. Mpls., Jan. 27, 1933; d. George Charles and Signa Amanda (Sherve) Larsen; B.A. magna cum laude, U. Calif., San Diego, 1973; M.S.W., U. Calif., Berkeley, 1977; children—Ronald G. Burghall, Brandt E. Burghall, Dirk F. Burghall. Social worker Ct. Dependency div. Dept. Public Social Services, County of Riverside, Riverside, Calif., 1978; community devel. intern City of Oakland (Calif.), 1976-77, planning cons., 1977, mgmt. and budget analyst, 1977-78; inspection and control officer U.S. Customs Service, San Ysidro, Calif., 1978-80, San Francisco, 1980—. Bd. dirs. San Diego Interfaith Housing Found., 1979-80; mem. allocations com. panel United Way of San Diego County, 1978-80; mem. exec. com. Alameda County Supr., Oakland, 1977-78; legis. com. Alameda County chpt. Nat. Assn. Social Workers, 1977-78. U. B.C. fellow, Vancouver, Can., 1975; Adminstrn. of Aging grantee U. Calif., Berkeley, 1975; Outstanding Service award Oakland Econ. Devel. Council, 1970. Mem. Federally Employed Women, Nat. Assn. Social Workers. Democrat. Mem. United Ch. of Christ. Home: 4 Captain Dr Apt E-208 Emeryville CA 94608 Office: US Customs Service San Francisco Dist 555 Battery St San Francisco CA 94104

CAPORAL, CHRISTY CAYE, data processing cons.; b. Oklahoma City, Aug. 17, 1952; d. Chris and Helen Caporal; B.S., Okla. State U. Implementation analyst Standard Oil Ind., 1973-76; programmer/analyst Mitchell Energy & Devel., 1976-77; analyst/mktg. rep. Automated Systems Corp., 1977-78; data processing cons. Berger, Vernay & Co., 1978-79; owner, Guenther, Bautista & Caporal, Inc., Houston, 1980—. Office: 2000 N Loop W #100 Houston TX 77018

CAPP, IRENE M., mgmt. cons.; b. Yonkers, N.Y., June 26, 1949; d. Harry and Anna (Chanas) Capp; B.A., U. Rochester, 1971; M.A., U. Chgo., 1974, M.B.A., 1976; m. Donald E. Kerr, Jr., Nov. 17, 1979; 1 dau., Mariel Ames. With Booz Allen & Hamilton, Chgo., 1976—, sr. assoc., 1979—. Lectr., U. Chgo. Bus. Sch. Home: 1201 Richmond Ln Wilmette IL 60091 Office: 2900 Three First National Plaza Chicago IL 60602

CAPPADONA, MARIE V., univ. food service ofcl.; b. Boston, Sept. 1, 1943; d. Joseph A. and Marie V. (Harlan) C.; B.S., U. Mass., 1966, M.S., 1970. With univ. food services U. Mass., Amherst, 1966—, beginning as asst. dietitian, successively dietitian, mgr. test kitchen, mgr. mktg. and menu services, asst. dir. adminstrn., 1966-80, dir. food services, 1980—; cons. dietitian Amherst Coll., 1969-78. Mem. Am. Dietetic Assn. (registered), Mass. Dietetic Assn. (chmn. Western Mass. div.), Nat. Assn. Coll. and Univ. Food Services (pres. Region I). Home: Plain Rd South Deerfield MA 01373 Office: Worcester Commons University of Massachusetts Amherst MA 01003

CAPPEL, LEONA RUBINSTEIN (MRS. NORMAN O. CAPPEL), microbiologist; b. Cleve., Jan. 14, 1913; d. Benedict and Dora (Molinoff) Rubinstein; B.S. in Chemistry, Ohio State U., 1936, M.S. in Microbiology (Eli Lilly fellow), 1938, Comley research fellow in pathology, 1938-40; m. Norman O. Cappel, Mar. 17, 1939; children—Andrea Cappel Remington, Neils, Bruce, Kim. Pres., Cappel Labs., Cochranville, Pa., 1940-80; cons. immunologist Cooper Labs., Palo Alto, Calif., 1980—. Mem. Am. Soc. Microbiology, AAUW, Patentee in field. Address: 2300 Golden West Lane Norco CA 91760

CAPPELLETTI, NORMA LEONE, state legislator; b. Waterbury, Conn., June 26; d. Ralph and Teresa (Schiavoni) Leone; R.N., Waterbury Hosp. Sch. Nursing, 1947; A.S., Metteluck Community Coll., 1981; m. A. Joseph Cappeletti, 1950; children—Joseph, Robert, Richard, John. Asst. instr. nursing arts Waterbury Hosp., 1948-49, instr. med.-surg. nursing, 1949-50; mem. Conn. Ho. of Reps., 1981—. Mem. Waterbury Charter Revision Commn., 1975, 77; bd. dirs. Waterbury Girls Club, 1970, Waterbury Day Nursery, 1970; mem. McTernan Sch. Bd., St. Margaret's, 1970; mem. adv. bd. Banking Center, 1981—. Mem. Conn. Women's Caucus, Waterbury Hosp. Aux. (dir. 1950-81). Roman Catholic. Office: Conn Ho of Reps Hartford CT 06115 *

CAPPLEMAN, CAROLYN MANCL, educator; b. Detroit, July 12, 1946; d. Alois Paul and Elida (Nelson) Mancl; B.S. in Edn., Fla. Atlantic U., Boca Raton, Fla., 1969, M.Ed. in Reading, 1971; m. Lawrence Eugene Cappleman, Jr., July 26, 1969; children—Lawrence Eugene, III, Holt McLean. Elem. sch. tchr., Fla., 1969—; program coordinator elem. reading Orange County Public Schs., Orlando, 1978—; speaker, cons. in field. Mem. Internat. Reading Assn., Assn. Supervision and Curriculum Devel., Fla. Assn. Sch. Adminstrs., W. Orange Jr. Service League, Phi Delta Kappa. Republican. Presbyterian. Home: 1302 Kelso Blvd Winter Garden FL 32787 Office: 434 N Tampa Ave Orlando FL 32805

CAPPS, BARBARA LOUISE, respiratory therapist; b. Fresno, Calif., Dec. 11, 1933; d. Eugene Victor and Ruth (Lankford) Thalman; med. asst. diploma Fresno Tech. Coll., 1965; m. Ronald Dean Capps, Aug. 9, 1968; children—Rochelle Ruth Pope, Jeffra Lynn Pope, Karen Kay Pope, Jeannie Louise Briggs, Jay Eugene Pope, Ronald Lee Pope, Lisa Dianne Capps. From nurses aide to shift leader respiratory therapy Fresno Community Hosp., 1965-70; staff technician, then shift leader St. Agnes Hosp., Fresno, 1970-71; coordinator Hosp. Pulmonary Services, Modesto, Calif., 1972-73, regional mgr., 1973—; instr., trainer Am. Heart Assn. Mem. Am. Assn. Respiratory Therapy, Calif. Soc. Respiratory Therapy (chpt. membership chmn. 1972-73). Democrat. Office: 1400 Lone Palm Dr Modesto CA 95353

CAPUTI, LILLIAN F., telecommunications exec.; b. N.Y.C., July 28, 1932; d. Charles Galeano and Mary C. (McNamara) Galeano O'Brien; student public schs.; m. Richard J. Meyer, Feb. 15, 1975; children by previous marriage—Patrick J. and Frederick L. Caputi. Asst. office mgr. Nestle LeMur, N.Y.C., 1959-60; spl. services mgr. N.Y. Yankees, 1960-61; telecommunications mgr. N.Y. Mets, 1961-68; telecommunications analyst Allied Chem. Co., N.Y.C., 1968-70; sr. telecommunications analyst N.Y. Stock Exchange, 1970-71; telecommunications mgr. Young & Rubicam, N.Y.C., 1971-72; sr. tech. rep. MCI Communications Corp., N.Y.C., 1972-75; pres. Bandwidth Services, Inc., N.Y.C., 1975-77; v.p. voice telecommunications Mfrs. Hanover Trust Co., N.Y.C., 1977—. Team sponsor Vets. Little League. Mem. Communications Mgrs. Assn. (dir.), Internat. Communications Assn. Home: 1546 Laguna Ln Lakewood NJ 08701 Office: 55 Water St New York NY 10041

CAPUZZI, MARY PHYLLIS, ins. co. ofcl.; b. Phila., Apr. 3, 1949; d. Rocco Nicholas and Grace Delores (Lee) C.; student evening div. Pierce Jr. Coll., 1967-69. Mail clk., clk. typist, sec., Presbyn. Ministers' Fund, Phila., 1967-77, corp. sec., asst. to pres., 1977—. Sec., Upper Darby Twp. govt. study commn., 1973-74; sec. polit. campaigns, 1975, 78; sec. Monsignor Bonner Crew Assn., 1976-77; Republican committeewoman, 1982—; vice-chmn., sec. Yeadon Rep. Com., 1982—; corr. sec. Upper Darby Twp. Council Rep. Women, 1980; active Pa. Acad. Fine Arts, Women's Aux. Yeadon Fire Co. #1. Mem. Life Office Mgmt. Assn. Roman Catholic. Home: 1019 Serrill Ave Yeadon PA 19050 Office: 1809 Walnut St Philadelphia PA 19103

CARABO-CONE, MADELEINE, violinist, author, educator; b. St. Louis, June 2, 1915; d. Charles and Marie Coffman; student Juilliard Sch. of Music (grad. sch. fellow), 1938; student of Georges Enesco, Carl Friedberg, Mischakoff, Nathan Milstein; m., Apr. 25, 1945; children—John Oliver, Claribel. Concert violinist, recitalist, soloist Chgo. Symphony Orch., 1937; 1st woman mem. 1st violin sect. Cleve. Orch., 1943-45; recitalist Town Hall, N.Y.C., 1939, 47, three concert series, Columbia U., N.Y.C., Wigmore Hall, London, Eng., 1970; creator original music teaching method: Carabo-Cone Method; author: How to Help Children Learn Music, 1953; Concepts for Strings (foreword by George Szell), 1966; The Playground As Music Teacher, 1955; A Sensory-Motor Approach to Music Learning, 1971; contbr. articles in field to publs. U.S. and abroad; lectr. U.S. and Can.; guest faculty Eastman Sch. of Music, 1968; presenter workshops U. Calif., Berkeley, 1967-71; lectr. Temple U., U.N.C., Chapel Hill, U. N.C., Greensboro, La. State U., Baton Rouge, Can. univs., 1973. Founder pilot programs day care centers. Recipient Frederick Stock award, Chgo., Nat. Fedn. Music Clubs award of merit. Mrm. Mu Phi Epsilon, The Bohemians. Club: The Woman Pays. Guest appearances various TV programs including Today Show, 1970.

CARBINE, PATRICIA THERESA, editor, publisher; b. Villanova, Pa., Jan. 31, 1931; d. James T. and Margaret (Dee) Carbine; B.A. in English, Rosemont Coll., 1952. With Look mag., 1953-70, mng. editor, 1966-69, exec. editor, 1969-70; editor McCall's mag., 1970-72; pub., editor-in-chief Ms. mag., N.Y.C., 1972—; dir. N.Y. Life Ins. Co.; trustee Dry Dock Savs. Bank. Founder, bd. dirs. Ms. Found. for Women, Inc., 1972—, Ms. Found. for Communication and Edn., Inc., 1979—; trustee Rosemont Coll., 1972—. Mem. Am. Soc. Mag. Editors, Mag. Pubs. Assn. (dir. 1973—), Advt. Council (dir. 1975). Office: Ms Found for Edn and Communication Inc 119 W 40th St New York NY 10018 *

CARBONE, MARTHA CLAIRE, fgn. service officer; b. Yakima, Wash., Oct. 16, 1927; d. Frank K. and Martha E. (Stacy) C.; B.A., U. Wash., Seattle, 1949; postgrad. Stanford U., 1961-62. Joined U.S. Fgn. Service, 1950; service in Bolivia, Peru, Afghanistan, Hungary, Spain, Haiti; comml. attache, Paraguay, 1976-78; consul, Perth, Australia, 1978-82. Address: Dept State Washington DC 20521

CARD, SANDRA DICKINSON, speech pathologist; b. Biddeford, Maine, Mar. 20, 1950; d. John Clinton and Pauline (Derham) Dickinson; B.A. in English, U. Maine, 1972; M.A. in Linguistics (Univ. fellow), U. Rochester (N.Y.), 1974; M.S. in Communication Disorders, Emerson Coll., Boston, 1977; postgrad. in linguistics N.Y. U.; m. Robert Card, Aug. 16, 1975. Speech and lang. pathologist Boston public schs., 1977-79; speech and lang. cons. Forest Hills Nursing Home, Jamaica Plain, Mass., 1978-79; speech and lang. cons. E. River Montessori Sch., N.Y.C., 1979-81, asst. dir., 1982—; teaching asst. articulatory phonetics U. Rochester, 1972-74; adj. instr. English as 2d lang. program Bklyn. Coll., City U. N.Y., 1980—. Mem. Am. Speech and Hearing Assn., New Eng. Child Lang. Assn., Phi Beta Kappa, Phi Kappa Phi. Home: 350 W 55th St New York NY 10019 Office: 570 Grand St New York NY 10002

CARDE, MARY DEBORAH, clin. psychologist; b. Los Angeles, July 15, 1951; d. Millard and Lorraine Ruth (Paley) Kaufman; A.B., Yale U., 1972; M.A., U. So. Calif., 1975, Ph.D., 1977; m. Richard Scott Carde, June 30, 1973. NIMH tng. grantee, 1973-78; intern Thalians Community Mental Health Center, Cedars-Sinai Med. Center, Los Angeles, 1976-77, postdoctoral fellow, 1977-78, attending staff, 1978—; staff psychologist Ross-Loos Med. Group, Torrance, Calif., 1978-79, So. Calif. Permanente Med. Group, Woodland Hills, Calif., 1979-81; staff research asso. dept. psychiatry UCLA, 1982—; pvt. practice clin. psychology, 1981—; cons. Wright Inst., 1978—. Mem. Am. Psychol. Assn., Nat. Register Health Service Providers in Psychology (mem. council).

CARDIA, ELSIE HELEN, real estate exec.; b. N.Y.C., May 3, 1927; d. Simone and Assunta (Badaracco) Garaventa; grad. Bus. Sch., Genova, Italy, 1947; m. Ubaldo Cardia, June 23, 1951; children—Vivian, Aldo Leonardo. Restaurant owner, mgr. Beatrice Inn, N.Y.C., 1955—; real estate owner, mgr. 317 W 12th St. Realty, N.Y.C., 1953—. Mem. Am. Italy Soc. Democrat. Roman Catholic. Former Columnist Italian Weekly. Home: 48 Carmine St New York NY 10014 Office: 285 W 12th St New York NY 10014

CARDIFF, MAUREEN FRANCES, social worker; b. Phila., Nov. 1, 1945; d. Frank M. and Gladys E. (Bensel) C.; B.S., Spring Hill Coll., Mobile, Ala., 1967; M.S. in Social Work, U. Louisville, 1969. Med. social worker Los Angeles County/U. So. Calif. Med. Center, 1969-74, sr. med. social worker, 1974-79; now staff mem. Dept. Clin. Social Work, UCLA; psychiat. social work supr. San Fernando Valley Child Guidance Center, Northridge, Calif., 1979-80; pvt. practice psychotherapy, Woodland Hills, Calif., 1980—; lectr. in field. Lic. clin. social worker, Calif. Mem. Nat. Assn. Social Workers, Am. Orthopsychiatric Assn. Contbr. articles in field. Office: 10833 Le Conte Ave Los Angeles CA 90024 also 23241 Ventura Blvd Suite 224-D Woodland Hills CA 91364

CARDINALE, KATHLEEN CARMEL, med. center adminstr.; b. Donegal, Ireland, July 13, 1933; came to U.S., 1958, naturalized, 1966; d. Denis and Mary (Cannon) O'Boyle; R.N., Walton Hosp., Liverpool, Eng., 1955; B.A., Jersey City State Coll., 1971, M.A., 1973; m. Anthony Cardinale, Aug. 28, 1965. Staff nurse, acting-in-charge Manhattan Gen. Hosp., N.Y.C., 1958-59; charge nurse, acting-in-charge, Met. Hosp., N.Y.C., 1959-60; charge nurse, relief supr. Manhattan Gen. Hosp., N.Y.C., 1960-64, asst. dir. nursing, 1964-68, staffing coordinator, 1968-70; acting asso. dir. nursing Bernstein Inst., N.Y.C., 1970; clin. supr., clin. specialist Beth Israel Med. Center, N.Y.C., 1971-73; asst. dir. nursing Cabrini Med. Center, N.Y.C., 1974-77, asso. dir. nursing, 1977-78, sr. vice-pres. nursing services, 1978—. Mem. Am. Nurses Assn., Greater N.Y. Hosp. Assn. (mem. profl. affairs policy com.), Am. Hosp. Assn., Am. Soc. Nursing Service Adminstrs. Home: 545 E 14th St New York City NY 10009 Office: 227 E 19th St New York City NY 10003

CARDINALE, MARIAN FRANCES, med. technologist; b. Independence, La., June 21, 1933; d. Isadore Thomas and Rosalie Marretta Cardinale; B.S. in Zoology and Chemistry with honors, Southeastern La. U., 1955; M.B.A., U. New Orleans, 1977. Staff technologist Charity Hosp., New Orleans, 1955-56, chemistry supr., 1956-62; chemistry supr. Mercy Hosp., New Orleans, 1962-68; chief med. technologist Pendleton Meml. Meth. Hosp., New Orleans, 1968-81, lab. mgr., 1981—. Mem. Am. Soc. Med. Tech. (dir. 1980—), La. (pres. 1969-70), New Orleans socs. med. tech., Am. Assn. Blood Banks, Sierra Club. Democrat. Roman Catholic. Home: 2704 Whitney Pl #723 Metairie LA 70002 Office: Pendleton Meml Methodist Hosp 5620 Read Blvd New Orleans LA 70127

CARDMAN, CECILIA NEAL, artist; b. Soveria Mannelli, Italy; d. Samuel and Maria (Mendicino) Cardman; B.F.A., U. Colo., 1934, B.A., 1934; student Instituto dei Belli Arte, Naples, Italy, 1921-23, Denver Art Mus., 1930-31, with Leon Kroll, Nat. Acad., 1945-46, others. Head dept. painting Mesa Coll., Grand Junction, Colo., 1930-40; one-man shows: Naples, Italy, Grist Mill Gallery, Chester, Vt., Bergdorf-Goodman, 1978, Jarvis Gallery, Sandwich, Mass., 1975, Elliott Mus., Stuart, Fla.; group shows include: Nat. Arts Club, 1975-76, Nat. Acad., 1945,

Knickerbocker Artists, 1979, Nelson Gallery, 1937-38, Denver Art Mus., 1924-25, Nat. League Am. Pen Women, 1979, Grand Central Art Gallery, 1977, Am. Artist Profl. League, 1979-80. Recipient awards. Mem. Jackson Heights Art Club, Coll. Women's Club, Salmagundi Club (dir., Lay Jury prize 1979), Nat. League Am. Pen Women (dir.), Artist Fellowship, Inc., Pen and Brush (dir.), Knickerbocker Artists, Catherine Lorillard Wolfe Art Club (pres., dir., Best in Show award 1980), Am. Artists Profl. League (nat. dir.). Roman Catholic. Home: 34-06 81st St Penthouse Jackson Heights New York NY 11372

CARDONI, CHARLA DIANNE SHIVE, mgmt. cons.; b. Cape Mirardeau, Mo., Sept. 2, 1942; d. Cecil Ray and Jewel Nita (Tyler) Shive; B.S. in Nursing, U. Ky., 1964; M.A., U. Del., 1972; M.A., LAB at Krisheim, Phila., 1975; m. Anthony Ralph Cardoni, July 8, 1973; 1 dau., Cari Dianne Shive. Staff developer Wilmington (Del.) Med. Center, 1971-72; cons. research div. Procter & Gamble Co., 1974-76; polit. campaign mgr. for Del. state rep., 1976; adj. prof. master's program Antioch U., Phila., 1977-79; ind. mgmt. cons., Miami, Fla., 1979—; dir. testing Am. Welding Soc., Miami, 1981—; mem. steering com. Nat. Orgn. Devel. seminar, 1976. Mem. Del. Adv. Com. Childhood and Adolescence, 1977-79. Mem. Nat. League Nursing (chmn. ways and means com. Md. chpt. 1968), Am. Nurses Assn. Republican. Unitarian.

CARDUCCI, LINDA OSBURN, mgmt. services co. exec.; b. San Diego, Dec. 18, 1948; d. William Harold and Yvonne (Bennett) Osburn; student Radford Coll., 1967-68; B.S. in Elementary Edn., George Mason U., 1971, postgrad., 1976-80; m. Dominick Carducci, June 23, 1972; 1 dau., Sonya Marie. Tchr., Fairfax (Va.) Pub. Schs., 1971-73; with Bank of Va., 1973-79, asst. br. mgr., Arlington, 1974-75, br. mgr., Rosslyn, 1975-78, v.p., dist. mgr., Falls Church, 1978-79; v.p., gen. mgr. Snack Hostess div. Coffee Butler Service, Inc., Fairfax, Va., 1979-80; pres. Mgmt. & Fin. Support Services, Inc., 1980—; instr. banking, bus. and math. No. Va. Community Coll., 1975—. Mem. Adminstrv. Mgmt. Soc. (v.p. programs Washington chpt. 1979—), Greater Rosslyn Bus. and Profl. Assn., Nat. Assn. Bank Women (asst. program chmn. 1978—), Young Bankers Assn., Fairfax C. of C. (membership com. 1978-79). Democrat. Methodist. Office: 7297 Lee Hwy Falls Church VA 22042

CARDULLO, MARIA ANN, educator; b. Boston, Apr. 11, 1942; d. Anthony Orlando and Rosina Margaret (Matthews) Cardullo; A.B. in Chemistry, Emmanuel Coll., 1963, A.B. in Biology, 1964; M.S., Boston Coll., 1967, Ph.D., 1971. Postdoctoral research asso. in bacteriology and molecular biology Boston Coll., Chestnut Hill, Mass., 1971-77; chmn. dept. sci., tchr. biology and chemistry Christopher Columbus High Sch., Boston, 1977—. Mem. Am. Soc. Microbiology, Nat. Assn. Biology Tchrs., NEA, Sigma Xi. Roman Catholic. Contbr. articles to profl. jours. Office: 20 Tileston St Boston MA 02113

CARDWELL, SUE POOLE, environ. cons.; b. Clearfield, Pa., Oct. 31, 1952; d. Robert Thomas and Mary B. (Edwards) Poole; B.A., Transylvania U., Lexington, Ky., 1973; m. Charles Howard Cardwell, Nov. 26, 1979; children—Jonathan Aaron, Jacqueline Leigh. Chief clk.-typist Ky. Dept. Mines and Minerals, Lexington, 1974; sr. reclamation insp. div. reclamation Ky. Dept. Natural Resources, Madisonville, 1974-77; pres. Reclamation Services Unltd., Inc., Madisonville, 1977—; former mem. bd. dirs. West Ky. Coal Operators Assn.; chmn. West Ky. adv. group to Office Strip Mining, 1979-81; mem. exec. bd. Ann. Sedimentology Symposium, U. Ky., 1979—; mem. Ky. Adv. Com. on Strip Mining, 1979—; subcom. chmn. Mining and Reclamation Council Am., 1977—. Served with WAC, 1973-74. Mem. W.Va. Surface Mine and Relamation Assn. Home: Route 4 Central City KY 42431 Office: 12 Hartland Ave Madisonville KY 42431

CARENS, MARILYN EILEEN, stockbroker; b. Boston, Sept. 30, 1944; d. Edward Barrett and Mary Louise (McManus) Daily; B.A. cum laude, Regis Coll., 1965; M.B.A., Babson Coll., 1977; m. Edward M. Carens, Oct. 30, 1965; children—Kelley M., Mark J., Heidi E. Lectr. on South Korea, 1969-75; with Xerox Corp., Boston, 1978-80; account exec. E. F. Hutton, Chestnut Hill, Mass., 1980—. Mem. Bus. Women's Assn. Boston. Clubs: Longwood Cricket, Sagamore Beach Colony. Home: 15 Leighton Rd Wellesley MA 02181 Office: One Chestnut Hill Plaza Chestnut Hill MA 02167

CAREY, BROOK FARRON, bus. cons.; b. Detroit; d. Farron Lowe and Valerie (Gates) Stevens; postgrad. in bus. U. Detroit, 1971; M.S.O.D., Pepperdine U., 1981; m. William K. Carey, 1972; children—Valerie Brook Noon, Kelly David Noon, Susan Michele Carey, Sharla Ann Becker. Asst. to pres. Grand Steel & Mfg. Co., Clawson, Mich., 1965-70; pres. Executeam Inc., Southfield, Mich., 1970-75; asst. v.p. Advance Mortgage Corp., Southfield, 1972-74; supt. Calif. Inst. for Women, Frontera, Calif., 1975-76; v.p. adminstrn. Century 21, Real Estate Corp., Irvine, Calif., 1976-78; pres. Executeam West, Inc., Santa Ana, Calif., 1978—; exec. v.p. dir. Franchise Am. Corp., Santa Ana, Calif., 1979—; mem. evening faculty dept. bus. Macomb County (Mich.) Community Coll., 1972-73; adj. faculty continuing edn. dept. U. So. Calif., Los Angeles, 1979—; seminar developer, leader Centro de Especialización Profesional, S.C.P., Monterey, Mexico, 1979-80. Recipient certs. of appreciation Toastmasters, 1979, Lions, 1979. Mem. Nat. Assn. Women Bus. Owners, Orgn. Devel. Network, Nat. Speakers Assn., Am. Soc. Tng. and Devel., Nat. Assn. Female Execs. Office: 9778 Katella St Suite 117 Anaheim CA 92804

CAREY, ERNESTINE GILBRETH, author, lectr.; b. N.Y.C., Apr. 5, 1908; d. Frank Bunker and Lillian (Moller) Gilbreth; B.A., Smith Coll., 1929; m. Charles Everett Carey, Sept. 13, 1930; children—Lillian Gilbreth Carey Clark, Charles Everett. Buyer, R.H. Macy & Co., N.Y.C., 1930-44, James McCrerry, N.Y.C., 1947-49; lectr., author book revs., 1951. Bd. dirs. Right to Read, Inc., 1967—, co-chmn., 1967; mem. lay adv. com. Manhasset (N.Y.) Bd. Edn., 1954-56; trustee Manhasset Pub. Library, 1953-59, v.p., 1956-59; trustee Smith Coll., 1967-72. Co-recipient (with Frank B. Gilbreth, Jr.) Prix Scarron French Internat. Humor award for Cheaper By The Dozen, 1951, (with Lillian M. Gilbreth) McElliogott medallion Assn. Marquette U. Women, 1966; Montgomery award Friends of Phoenix Library, 1981. Mem. Authors Guild Am. (life, mem. guild council 1955-60), PEN, Seven Coll. Conf. Council Phoenix. Republican. Congregationalist. Clubs: Smith Coll. (asst. chmn. scholarship com. L.I. club 1950-59; chmn. scholarship com. Phoenix club 1967). Author: Jumping Jupiter, 1952; Rings Around Us, 1956; Giddy Moment, 1958; (with Frank B. Gilbreth, Jr.) Cheaper By The Dozen, 1949; Belles on Their Toes, 1951. Address: 6148 E Lincoln Dr Paradise Valley AZ 85253

CAREY, MARY VIRGINIA, writer; b. New Brighton, Cheshire, Eng., May 19, 1925; d. John Cornelius and Mary Alice (Hughes) Carey; B.S., Coll. of Mt. St. Vincent, 1946. Editorial asso. Coronet Mag., N.Y.C., 1948-55; asst. editor publs. Walt Disney Productions, Burbank, Calif., 1955-69; author: Mystery of the Flaming Footprints, 1971; Mystery of the Singing Serpent, 1972; Mystery of Monster Mountain, 1973; Secret of the Haunted Mirror, 1974; Mystery of the Invisible Dog, 1975; Mystery of Death Trap Mine, 1976; Mystery of the Magic Circle, 1978; Mystery of the Sinister Scarecrow, 1979; Mystery of the Scar-Faced Beggar, 1981; Mystery of the Blazing Cliffs, 1981; Love is Forever, 1975; Step-by-Step Candlemaking, 1972; Step-by-Step Winemaking, 1973; The Owl Who Loved Sunshine, 1977; editor: Grandmothers are Very Special People, 1977; author: (with George Sherman) A Compendium of Bunk, 1976. Mem. Author's Guild, Soc. Children's Book Writers. Roman Catholic. Address: 645 Hampshire Rd Apt 137 Westlake Village CA 91361

CARGILE, MARY CHASTEEN, railroad co. exec., sales exec.; b. New London, Conn., Apr. 24, 1939; d. William H. Chasteen and Viola Mae (Coburn) Chasteen Chadwick; student Duke U., 1959; A.A. in Psychology, Ga. State U., 1962; m. Walter J. Cargile, Nov. 28, 1966; 1 son by previous marriage, William H. Nichols III. Sec. and real estate agt. Economy Homes, Morehead City, N.C., 1961; exec. sec. Lloyd A. Fry Mfg. Co., Atlanta, 1961-64, asst. office mgr., 1964-65; data processor So. Ry. System, Atlanta, 1966-74, car locator, 1974-80; personnel mgr., sales analyst Hal Eason Assos., Atlanta, 1974—; cons. to small bus. firms and minority groups, 1968—; inter-racial family counselor, 1970—. Vol., Atlanta Labor Council, 1973-74. Recipient Danforth Found. award, 1957. Mem. Nat. Assn. Female Execs. Democrat. Contbr. articles on interracial families to local publs. Home: 1902 Maywood Place NW Atlanta GA 30318 Office: 5188 Roswell Rd NE Atlanta GA 30342

CARGILL, PAULA MARIE, social worker; b. Henrietta, N.C., Sept. 18, 1943; d. John Edwin and Mabel Anne (Bridges) C.; B.A. in Sociology, Winthrop Coll., 1965; M.R.E., So. Bapt. Theol. Sem., 1973; M.S.S.W., Raymond A. Kent Sch. Social Work, 1975. Social worker child care Connie Maxwell Children's Home, Greenwood, S.C., 1965, 70-71; secondary tchr. Rutherford County (N.C.) Schs., 1965-67, Camden (S.C.) City Schs., 1967, Greenville County Schs., 1967-70; instr. sociology North Greenville Coll., Tigerville and Greenville, S.C., 1973-74; clin. social worker South Greenville Mental Health Center, Simpsonville, S.C., 1975-77; dir. social services J Health Care Center, Inc., Simpsonville, 1978—; field placement supr., adj. asst. prof. social work U. S.C., Columbia, 1979—; exchange social worker to France, Council Internat. programs, summer 1980; instr. adult edn. Greenville County Schs., 1979-81. Flutist Greenville Civic Band, 1975—; mem. Greater Greenville Community Concert Assn., 1978—, Lucille Wall Music Club, 1965-67, Bus. and Profl. Women's Club Greenwood, 1970-71; chmn. Bapt. Women Mission Action, Greenville Bapt. Assn., 1979-81; mem. program and budget rev. com. United Way Greenville County, 1981; mem. Greenville County Commn. on Alcohol and Drug Abuse, 1981—. Registered social worker, S.C. Mem. Acad. Cert. Social workers, Nat. Assn. Social Workers (dir. S.C. chpt. 1976-77, 79-81), S.C. Social Welfare Forum, S.C. Gerontol. Soc. (dir. 1980—), Social Workers of S.C. Health Care Assn., So. Bapt. Social Service Assn., Gerontol. Soc. Am., Leadership Greenville, C. of C. VII, Alpha Kappa Delta, Pi Delta Phi, Kappa Delta Pi. Home: 1 Kenilworth Dr Greenville SC 29615 Office: J Health Care Center Inc PO Box 757 Simpsonville SC 29681

CARITHERS, JEANINE RUTHERFORD, educator; b. Boone, Iowa, Sept. 26, 1933; d. John Twedt and Catherine Elizabeth (Dornan) Rutherford; B.S. in Zoology, Iowa State U., 1956, M.S. in Physiology, 1965; Ph.D. (USPHS fellow) in Anatomy, U. Mo., 1968; m. Robert William Carithers, Sept. 23, 1953; children—Jeffrey Scott, Brian Reid, Douglas Sean. Tchr. sci., Union, Iowa, 1964-65; asst. prof. vet. anatomy Iowa State U., Ames, 1968-72, asso. prof., 1972-76, prof., 1976—, chairperson vet. anatomy; professeur associe Ministre del'Education Nationale, France, 1976. Mem. Soc. of Neurosci., Am. Assn. Anatomists, AAAS, Am. Assn. Vet. Medicine Colls., Congress of European Comparative Endocrinologists, N.Y. Acad. Scis., World Assn. Vet. Anatomists, Sigma Xi, Gamma Sigma Delta. Contbr. articles in field to profl. jours. Office: 1092 Vet Medicine Dept Anatomy Ames IA 50011

CARL, TOMMIE EWERT, orgn. exec.; b. Marion, Kans., Sept. 23, 1921; d. Andrew A. and Orpha (Ratzlaff) Ewert; B.A., Am. U., 1970, M.A., 1972; m. Leo D. Carl, Jan. 1, 1943; 1 son, David Richard. Acct. comptroller's office Hammer Galleries, N.Y.C., 1946-48; chief acctg. div. central purchasing office Exchange Systems, Tokyo, 1949-52; mem. com. for a women's bank Women's Nat. Bank, Washington, 1974-76; tchr. medieval theory Am. U., Washington, 1971-72; founder, pres. Am. Women Composers, Inc., Washington, 1976—; broadcaster WQXR, N.Y.C., 1978, WNYC, N.Y.C., 1978, WBHM, Birmingham, Ala., 1979; composer: Anagrams, 1972; Contemporary Mass, 1972; Piano ad Lib, 1973; Bells, 1974; Illusions, 1974; Chromosynthesis, 1974; Futurama I, 1974; Futurama II, 1974; Sands, 1975; Anagrams, 1976. Office: American Women Composers Inc 6192 Oxon Hill Rd Suite 406 Washington DC 20021

CARLILE, OLGA GIZE, journalist; b. East Chicago, Ind., Jan. 9; d. Walter Edward and Emma Gize; B.A., Ind. U.; m. Robert Leslie Carlile, Aug. 24; children—Byron Thomas, Bradley Robert. Writer, Inland Steel Co., East Chicago; copy editor Freeport (Ill.) Jour. Standard, also soc. editor, now women's editor. Bd. dirs. Am. Cancer Soc., Vis. Nurse Assn., Wa-tan-Ye Service Club, Community Chest, Community Concert Assn., YWCA; exec. bd. Boy Scouts Am.; v.p. Shakespeare Soc., 1975-76. Recipient Silver Feather awards Ill. Women's Press Assn., 1974, 76, 77, 81; also awards Nat. Fedn. Press Women, UPI, AP; Sci. Writers award ADA. Mem. Bus. and Profl. Women's Club (pres. 1960), Ill. Women's Press Assn. (v.p. 1978, 79, 80, pres. 1981—, Woman of Yr. 1981), AAUW, Women in Communications, PEO (v.p. 1980), LWV, Gamma Alpha Chi. Methodist. Author: Heritage Cookbook, 1976. Home: 1713 Manor Dr Freeport IL 61032 Office: 27 State Ave S Freeport IL 61033

CARLIN, MYRNA LOUISE, psychologist; b. Glace Bay, N.S., Can., Jan. 26, 1944; d. Joseph George and Bessie Renee (Lubetzki) C.; B.A., McGill U., 1963, M.Sc.Appl., 1965. Psychologist, Banstead Hosp. Commn., London, 1967; cons. Protestant Regional Sch. Bd. of Chateauguay Valley, Chateauguay, Que., Can., 1970-73; psychologist Queen Elizabeth Hosp., Montreal, Que., 1965-66, sr. psychologist child psychiatry, dir. Learning Clinic, 1967—; cons. Westmount (Que.) Assn. Psychol. Services, 1973—; occasional lectr. McGill U., Concordia U., pres. B.T.C. Investments, 1980—. Mem. Corp. of Psychologists of Province Que., Can. Psychol. Assn., Am. Psychol. Assn., Provincial Assn. Protestant Tchrs. Contbr. articles to profl. jours. Home: 4116 Beaconsfield Ave Montreal PQ H4A 2H3 Canada Office: 2100 Marlowe Ave Montreal PQ H4A 3L6 Canada

CARLISLE, CAROL WHITT JONES, educator; b. May 11, 1919; B.A., Wesleyan Coll., Ga., 1940; M.A., U. N.C., Chapel Hill, 1941, Ph.D. in English, 1951; m. 1942; 2 children. Instr. English, Pearl River (Miss.) Jr. Coll., 1942-43; acting asst. prof. Wesleyan Coll., Ga., 1943; instr. to assoc. prof. U. S.C., 1946-69, prof. English, 1969—. Coop. Program Humanities fellow U. N.C., Duke U. and Ford Found., 1967-68; cons. editor Explicator, 1977—. Mem. Shakespeare Assn. Am., Renaissance Conf. (pres. 1974-75). Contbr. articles to profl. jours. Office: Dept of English University of South Carolina Columbia SC 29208 *

CARLISLE, LILIAN MATAROSE BAKER (MRS. E. GRAFTON CARLISLE, JR.), author, lectr.; b. Meridian, Miss., Jan. 1, 1912; d. Joseph and Lilian (Flournoy) Baker; student Dickinson Coll., 1929-30, Pierce Coll. Bus. Adminstrn., 1930-31; B.A., U. Vt., 1981; m. E. Grafton Carlisle, Jr., Jan. 9, 1933; children—Mrs. E. S. Schwerdtle, Penelope. Legal sec. A. W. Sanson, Phila., 1931-35; adminstrv. sec. RAF Ferry Command, Montreal, Que., Can., 1942; exec. staff mem. in charge collections, research Shelburne (Vt.) Mus., 1951-61; exec. sec. Burlington Area Community Health Study, 1963, coordinator, 1964; asst. coordinator Vt. Mental Retardation Planning Project, 1965; project dir. 4-county Champlain Valley Medicare Alert, 1966; dir. public relations Champlain Valley Agrl. Fair, 1968-77; lectr. U. Vt. Elder Hostel program, 1976-77, mem. faculty Vacation Coll., 1980—. Pres., Burlington Community Council for Social Welfare, 59-61, 71-73; chmn. bd. Interfaith Sr. Citizens, 1977-79; justice of peace, 1979-81; pres. Chittenden County Extension Adv. Com., 1977-78; lay mem. Gov.'s Conf. on Problems of Aging for White House Conf., 1960; chmn. publs. com. Vt. Bicentennial Commn., 1974-77; mem. Gov.'s Commn. on Mobile Homes, 1973—; mem. Vt. Ho. of Reps., 1968-70. Recipient Community Council Disting. Citizen award, 1978. Mem. Vt. (trustee, chmn. mus. com. 1967), N.Y. (faculty seminar) Chittenden (pres. 1969-72, editor Heritage Series of 10 books about Chittenden County towns 1972-76) hist. socs., Vt. Old Cemetery Assn., Vt. Folklore Soc., League Vt. Writers (dir. 1962; v.p., pres. 1967-69). Am. Pen Women (pres. Green Mountain br. 1980-82), Order Women Legislators (pres. Vt. br. 1972-74), Chi Omega. Conglist. (clk.). Club: Zonta (pres. 1964-65). Co-author: The Story of the Shelburne Museum, 1955; Profile of the Community, 1964; Environmental and Personal Health of the Community, 1964; Vermont Clock and Watchmakers, Silversmiths and Jewelers, 1970; also numerous catalogs on collections at Shelburne Mus.; editorial cons. Burlington Social Survey, 1967; contbr. articles to profl. jours. Home: 117 Lakeview Terr Burlington VT 05401

CARLISLE, MARGO DUER BLACK, mem. U.S. Republican senatorial staff; b. Providence, Aug. 18, 1936; d. Thomas F. and Margaret Duer (MacCormick) Black; B.A., Manhattanville Coll., 1957; postgrad. Boston U., 1959; m. Miles Carlisle, Sept. 21, 1960; children—Mary Duer, Miles Tristram Coffin. Legis. asst., speechwriter to Senator James McClure, U.S. senator from Idaho, 1973-75; exec. dir. Senate Steering Com., Washington, 1976-80; staff dir. Republican Conf. of Senate, Washington, 1980—. Trustee Phila. Soc., 1981-82. Roman Catholic. Contbr. articles to profl. jours. Home: 3221 Garfield St Washington DC 20008 Office: 333 Russell Senate Office Bldg Washington DC 20013

CARLOS, JANICE THERESA, cons. data processing analyst; b. Detroit, May 18, 1940; d. Hushel and Cora P. (Perkins) Bryant; cert. Automation Inst., 1962. Programmer, San Francisco Naval Radiol. Def. Lab., 1961-69; programmer/analyst Blue Cross of No. Calif., Oakland, 1969-79; data base adminstr. Automobile Club of Mich. Dearborn, 1980; cons. analyst computer programming gas facilities data base Mich. Consol. Gas Co., Detroit, 1980—, mem. polit. action com., 1980—; owner Carlos Internat. Trade, exporting, Detroit. Commr., Status of Women Commn., State of Calif., 1977-78; reporter Democratic Nat. Conv., 1976. Mem. Am. Mgmt. Assn., Nat. Assn. Female Execs., Black Women Entrepreneurs, Black Data Processing Assos., Nat. Council of Negro Women (rec. sec. 1977-78). Home: 18901 St Marys St Detroit MI 48235 Office: PO Box 35-349 Detroit MI 48235

CARLOW, PHYLLIS JEAN, retail furniture store exec.; b. Madison, Ind., Jan. 3, 1938; d. Avery and Rubye Leora (Lightfoot) Brooks; student pub. schs., Carrollton, Ky.; m. Arno Walker, Nov. 24, 1955 (dec. 1971); children—Candance Ann, Michael Anthony, Nolan Edward; m. 2nd Charles Edwin Carlow, Aug. 18, 1973. Radio announcer WARU, Peru, Ind., 1956-57, WOCH, N. Vernon, Ind., 1957-58, WAXU, Georgetown/Lexington, Ky., 1958-63; with First Nat. Bank, New Castle, Ind., 1963-68; traffic mgr., women's dir. WCTW, New Castle, 1968-73; partner Carlow Discount Furniture & Carpet, Taylor, Temple, Tex., 1973—. Mem. Country & Western Band, Taylor, Tex., 1975—. Mem. C. of C. Christian Ch. Clubs: Bus. and Profl. Women's (treas. 1977), Taylor Music. Home: 1500 Ellen St PO Box 111 Taylor TX 76574 Office: 114 W Lake Dr Shopping Center Taylor TX 76574

CARLSEN, MARY BAIRD, clin. psychologist; b. Salt Lake City, Aug. 31, 1928; d. Jesse Hays and Susannah Amanda (Bragstad) Baird; student St. Olaf Coll., 1946-47; B.A., Whitworth Coll., 1950; M.A., U. Conn., 1967; Ph.D. (PEO research grantee 1972, U. Wash. Women's Guidance Center research grantee 1972), U. Wash., 1973; m. James C. Carlsen, May 1, 1949; children—Philip, Douglas, Susan, Kristine. Profl. organist, piano tchr., Wash., Oreg., Ill., Conn., 1949-68; staff counselor Presbyn. Counseling Service, Seattle, 1976-79; clin. psychologist, marriage therapist, career devel. specialist in pvt. practice, Seattle, 1978—. Chmn., Sr. Adult Adv. Council, Seattle Parks Dept., 1975-76. Mem. Am. Psychol. Assn., Wash. State Psychol. Assn., Assn. Humanistic Psychology, Am. Assn. Marriage and Family Therapy. Office: 1107 NE 45th St Suite 405 Seattle WA 98105

CARLSON, BARBARA COIN, psychologist; b. Davenport, Iowa, July 27, 1927; d. William and Jule I. (Mulcahy) Coin; A.A., Los Angeles Valley Coll., 1964; B.S., Calif. State U., Los Angeles, 1969, M.A., 1975; Ph.D., U.S. Internat. U., San Diego, 1976; m. Douglas D. Carlson, May 8, 1948; children—Eric, Matt, Kurt. Prof. nursing Cerritos Coll., Norwalk, Calif., 1972—; staff psychologist Spectrum Counseling Services, Arcadia, Calif., 1975—; pvt. practice clin. psychology, Rowland Heights, Calif., 1977—; pres. Profl. Assn. for Continuing Edn. Mem. Am. Psychol. Assn., Calif. Psychol. Assn., NEA, Calif. Tchrs. Assn., Am. Nurses Assn., Calif. Nurses Assn.

CARLSON, CAROLIN FURST, civic worker; b. Williamsport, Pa., Apr. 20, 1934; d. S. Dale and Esther Caroline (McCormick) Furst O'Brien; B.A. cum laude, Smith Coll., 1955; m. Elton Frederic Carlson, Sept. 15, 1956; children—Eric Dale, Margaret Cora, Dwight Leonard. Caseworker, McKean County Child Welfare Services, Smethport, Pa., 1955-57; dir. First Nat. Bank of Port Allegany, Pa. Class fund sec. Abbot Acad., Phillips, Andover, 1951—; Jr. choir dir. Gethsemane Evangelical Lutheran Ch., Port Allegany, 1971—, congregational sec., 1973—, Theos chpt. exec. dir. and grief counselor, 1972-76, chmn. bicentennial celebration com., 1975-76, pres. Lutheran Ch. Women, 1959-61, treas., 1962-65, program chmn. 1976-80, 82—; chmn. noon hour cultural series S.W. Smith Meml. Public Library, 1972-74, 77-78, bd. dirs., 1977—, v.p. spl. events, 1978—, book selection, 1977—, pres. elect, 1982—; active Port Area Community TV, 1981—; den mother Allegheny Highland council Boy Scouts Am., Port Allegany, 1967-70, 76-79, sec., 1976-79; asst. troop leader Keystone Tall Tree council Girl Scouts U.S.A., 1969-74; charter driver Meals on Wheels, 1972—; adv. bd. dirs. McKean County Children and Youth Services, 1980—; v.p. Port Allegany High Sch. Band Boosters, 1982—. Recipient award Luth. Ch. Am., 1975. Mem. Smith Coll. Alumnae Assn., Abbot Acad. Alumnae Assn. Clubs: Coudersport Country, Port Allegany Woman's (treas. 1957-60, 66-67, auditor 1965, 82, sec. 1963-65, 70-71, 2d v.p. 1967-68, 71-72, pres. 1977-79, choir 1961—), McKean County Women's (sec. 1958-60, 66-68, treas. 1970-72, 1st v.p. 1972-76), Order Eastern Star. Contbr. articles to weekly paper Reporter-Argus, 1961—. Home: 45 Church St Port Allegany PA 16743

CARLSON, DALE BICK, author; b. N.Y.C., May 24, 1935; d. Edgar M. and Estelle (Cohen) Bick; B.A., Wellesley Coll., 1957; children—Daniel, Hannah. Author children's books, 1961—, including: Perkins the Brain, 1964; The House of Perkins, 1965; Miss Maloo, 1966; The Brainstormers; 1966; Frankenstein, 1968; Counting is Easy, 1969; Your Country, 1969; Arithmetic 1, 2, 3, 1969; The Electronic Teabowl, 1969; Warlord of the Genji, 1970; The Beggar King of China, 1971; The Mountain of Truth (Spring Festival Honor book), 1972; Good Morning Danny, 1972; Good Morning, Hannah, 1972; The Human Apes, 1973; Girls Are Equal Too, 1973; Baby Needs Shoes, 1974; Triple Boy, 1976; Where's Your Head?, 1977; The Plant People, 1977; The Wild Heart, 1977; The Shining Pool, 1979; Lovingsex for Both Sexes, 1979; Boys Have Feelings Too, 1980; Call Me Amanda, 1981; Manners that Matter, 1982; The Frog People, 1982; Charlie the Hero, 1983. Vice pres. Parents League of N.Y., editor-in-chief Parents League Bull., 1967-72. Mem.

Authors League Am., Authors Guild. Address: 35 E 75th St New York NY 10021

CARLSON, EVELYN ANNE, pilot, nurse; b. Santa Monica, Calif., Oct. 10, 1944; d. James Vernon and Laura Marie (Jennings) C.; B.S.N., UCLA, 1967; M.S.N., Case Western Res. U., 1974; postgrad aerospace tech. Kent (Ohio) State U., 1979—. Nurse, Stanford U. Med. Center, Palo Alto, Calif., 1967-68; nurse educator Peace Corps, Kenya, 1968-70; instr. nursing Ursuline Coll., Pepper Pike, Ohio, 1974-79; asst. prof. nursing Kent State U., 1979—; pvt. comml. instrument and cert. flight instr. Kent State U., 1981—, Kent State U. Airport, 19 —; nurse educator cons. State Ohio, 1974—. NIMH grantee, 1971-73; recipient Amelia Earhart award Nat. Intercollegiate Flying Assn. meet, N.D., 1979. Mem. Airplane Owners and Pilots Assn., Sigma Theta Tau. Clubs: Sierra, Kent State Flying, 99's. Home: 238 E College Ave Kent OH 44240 Office: Sch Nursing/Sch Technology Kent State U Kent OH 44242

CARLSON, HARRIET EUNICE, newspaper pub., writer; b. Evanston, Ill., Nov. 15, 1922; d. Conrad and Eunice L. Carlson; student Northwestern U., Chgo. Comparison shopper, asst. to head of dept. Marshall Field & Co., Chgo., 1941-44; copywriter, head home furnishings advt. Carson Pirie Scott & Co., Chgo., 1944-47; group copy dir. Tatham-Laird Advt. Agy., Chgo., 1947-56; free-lance writer, 1956—; owner, operator Harriet Carlson Newspaper Syndicate, Wilmette, Ill., 1956—; tchr. non-fiction writing, adult edn. New Trier High Sch., Winnetka, Ill., 1973-74. Mem. Nat. League Am. Pen Women (state sec. 1980-82, nat. historian 1982-84), Women in Communications Inc. Republican. Author: New Horizons for the Housewife, 1970. Office: 1943 Lake Ave Wilmette IL 60091

CARLSON, HELEN LOUISE, educator; b. Duluth, Minn., Oct. 20, 1940; d. Erling Emil and Ethel Florence (Lindberg) Nelson; B.S. summa cum laude, U. Minn., Duluth, 1961, M.A., 1975; Ph.D., U. Minn., Mpls., 1981; m. Gordon Jerome Carlson, Aug. 4, 1961; children—David J., Amy L., John D. Elem. tchr., public schs., Brockton, Mass., St. Paul and La Mesa, Calif., 1961-66; tchr. early child care provider, 1970-75; research asst. U. Minn., Duluth, 1975-77, instr., 1977-81, asst. prof. profl. edn., 1981—; cons. St. Mary's Child Care Center, 1981-82, Midwest Regional Trainer Communication Model, 1982; bd. dirs. Duluth Early Childhood Consortium, 1981-82; mem. adv. bd. Duluth Community Schs. Parent and Family Life Programs, 1980-82, U. Minn. at Duluth Child Care Center, 1980-82; mem. edn. adv. bd. Duluth Head Start, 1979-80. Ednl. Devel. Program grantee, 1981-82, 82-83; lic. tchr., Minn. Mem. Nat. Assn. Edn. Young Children, Nat. Council Social Studies, Phi Delta Kappa (research grantee 1978; treas. chpt. 1978-81, v.p. chpt. 1981-82), Alpha Delta Kappa. Contbr. articles to profl. jours. Research in tchr. edn. methodology, 1981-82, social interactions of infants and toddlers and their parents, 1982. Home: 2344 Woodland Duluth MN 55803 Office: 229 Bohannon Hall U Minn Duluth MN 55812

CARLSON, JOAN ELIZABETH, banker; b. Jamestown, N.Y., Apr. 18, 1935; d. Ernest L. and Irene L. (Lloydahl) Danielson; student Jamestown Bus. Coll., 1955; A.A., Jamestown Community Coll., 1982; student Am. Inst. Banking, 1965; m. John L. Carlson, Mar. 28, 1973; children—Lee, Bruce, Lou Ann, Robert, Johnny. With Lincoln First Nat. Bank, Jamestown, N.Y., 1965—, drive-in supr., 1972-74, mgr. Bemus Point (N.Y.) br., 1974-80, mgr. Jamestown-South Side br., 1980—. Mem. Bus. Profl. Women's Assn. Baptist. Home: 32 Pearl St Frewsburg NY 14738 Office: 457 Foote Ave Jamestown NY 14701

CARLSON, JUDITH ELIZABETH, nurse; b. Penn Yan, N.Y., Aug. 26, 1946; d. Frank and Carmaletta (Wyman) Van De Mortel; R.N., Highland Hosp. Sch. Nursing, 1967; m. Dennis R. Carlson, June 3, 1967 (div.); children—Hope Stephanie, Christiaan Dennis. Staff nurse surg. unit Oceanside (Calif.) Community Hosp., 1967; staff nurse med. unit E. J. Noble Hosp., Canton, N.Y., 1968; staff nurse emergency room Corning (N.Y.) Community Hosp., 1968-70, New Hanover Meml. Hosp., Wilmington, N.C., 1972-75; staff nurse coronary care unit Duke U. Med. Center, Durham, N.C., 1975, head nurse urology clinic, supr. catheter audit team, 1976—; mem. faculty Travenol Labs., Inc., Deerfield, Ill., 1981. Co-leader, leader Girl Scouts, 1975-78. Mem. Am. Urology Allied Assn. Democrat. Methodist. Club: Duke Faculty (sec. bd. dirs. 1982). Home: 5604 Genesee Dr Durham NC 27712 Office: Box 3707 Duke U Med Center Durham NC 27710

CARLSON, KAREN ANTHONY DONAHUE, real estate and mortgage broker; b. Miami, Fla., Jan. 2, 1954; d. John Joseph and Marilyn Zint Donahue; m. Richard Carlson, Oct. 10, 1970; children—Theresa, Cariann. Realty agt. Keyes Co. Real Estate, North Miami Beach, 1975, World Realty, Miami, 1976-77, Thor Corp. sales Lakes of Acadia, Miami, Fla., 1978-82; owner, mgr. Karen A. Carlson, Inc., Real Estate and Mortgages, North Miami, Fla., 1978—. Mem. Nat. Soc. Fee Appraisers, Greater Miami Real Estate Exchangors. Clubs: Biscayne Gardens Jr. & Sr. (arts chmn. 1978, conservation chmn. 1979, internat. affairs chmn. 1980-81), Gen. Fedn. Women (1st place State Internat. Affairs award 1981), Am. Water Ski Assn. Home: 16401 NE 2d Ave North Miami FL 33162 Office: 12840 NE 6th Ave North Miami FL 33161

CARLSON, LOUISE NEVILLE, writer; b. Kilgore, Tex., Nov. 16, 1936; d. Louis Otto and Hazel (Warthan) Neville; student Tyler Jr. Coll., 1954-55, Weaver Inst., 1955-56, U. Miami, 1956; B.S. with high distinction, U. Minn., 1971; m. John Clarence Carlson, Aug. 28, 1957; 1 dau., Sharon Louise. Ops. communications specialist Eastern Airlines, Miami, Fla., 1956-58; freelance writer Fla., N.C., 1958-59; asst. to dir. salary adminstrn. 3M Co., Mpls., 1961; freelance writer, aviation specialist, So. Calif., Minn., 1962-69; tchr. journalism and mass communications, Mpls., St. Paul, 1971-77; freelance writer, editor, photographer, contbg. writer Lakewood Publs., Airport Services Mgmt. mag., Communicator quar., Mpls. Star, Community weekly, 1982; co-author: Yearbook, Do's, Dont's, and Maybe's. Mem. Women in Communications, Journalism Edn. Assn., Journalism Advisors of Minn. Episcopalian. Club: Shorewood Yacht. Address: 5425 Woodcrest Dr Edina MN 55424

CARLSON, NANCY L., counseling psychologist; b. Kane, Pa., Dec. 15, 1936; d. Stanley H. and Elizabeth J. (Pratt) Carlson; B.S., Edinboro State Coll., 1959; M.A., Ohio U., 1964; Ph.D., U. Kans., 1970. Asst. dean women Edinboro (Pa.) State Coll., 1959-64; program adviser U. Wis., Madison, 1964-66; counselor U. Kans., Lawrence, 1966-70; counselor, asst. prof. U. Md., College Park, 1970-74; dir. counseling SUNY, New Paltz, 1975-78; dir. counseling and career services U.R.I., Kingston, 1978—; mem. Kent County Mental Health Prevention Com., R.I., Ulster County (N.Y.) Health Planning Bd. Danforth grantee, 1961, 62. Mem. Am. Psychol. Assn., Assn. of Univ. and Coll. Counseling Center Dirs., Am. Personnel and Guidance Assn., R.I. Coll. Personnel Assn. (pres. 1982-83), Am. Coll. Personnel Assn., NE Counseling Center Dirs., Coll. Placement Council, Eastern Coll. Personnel Officers. Contbr. articles in field to profl. jours. Office: 219 Roosevelt Hall Univ RI Kingston RI 02881

CARLSON, PATRICIA LAURENE EISING, naturalist; b. Detroit, Jan. 19, 1938; d. Lawrence John and Blanche Hazel (Addicott) Eising; B.S., Mich. State U., 1959, M.A., 1968; m. Gerald E. Carlson, Oct. 27, 1975. Naturalist, Nature Unit, Detroit Dept. Parks and Recreation, 1959-65; naturalist Huron-Clinton Metropolitan Authority, Stony Creek Park, 1965-68, naturalist supr. Kensington Park, Milford, Mich., 1968—; mem. faculty Wayne State U., 1972-75, Univ. Center for Adult Edn., 1972-75. Mem. Natural Areas Council of Mich., 1972—, sec., 1977; leader 4-H, 1960-66, county conservation leader, 1962-64; mem. State of Mich. Bd. Forestry Registration, 1980—. vol. leader trainer Girl Scouts U.S.A., 1964-75. Recipient Meritorious Service award Assn.-Interpretive Naturalists, 1972. Fellow Assn. Interpretive Naturalists (dir. 1967-81. internat. pres. 1975-77); mem. Soc. Am. Foresters, Am. Nature Study Soc., Mich. Recreation and Park Assn. Presbyn. Home: 30030 Cherry Ln New Hudson MI 48165 Office: 2240 W Buno Rd Milford MI 48042

CARLSON, PHYLLIS W. SWAINE, social work adminstr.; b. Boston, Aug. 8, 1936; d. Hedley St. Clair and Mary Elizabeth (Reynolds) Swaine; R.N., New England Deaconess Hosp. Sch. Nursing, 1957; B.S. in Nursing summa cum laude, Boston U., 1963; M.S.W., Simmons Coll., 1969; m. Robert Carlson, June 6, 1958; children—Kari Lee, Kristin Jan. Sr. instr., staff nurse intensive care, 1957-66; caseworker profl. service Family Service, Dedham, Mass., 1969-75, supr., 1975-80, dir. profl. service, 1980-81; pvt. practice clin. social work, West Roxbury, Mass., 1976-81; asso. instr. Simmons Coll., Smith Coll., Regis Coll. Mem. Nat. Assn. Social Workers, Acad. Certified Social Workers, Sigma Theta Tau. Home: 15 Ravenna Rd West Roxbury MA 02132 Office: 18 Norfolk St Dedham MA 02026

CARLSON, WILDA MAY, real estate saleswoman; b. Rome, N.Y., Dec. 10, 1920; d. Percy Lloyd and Pearl Jessie (Huey) Bucklin; R.N., Buffalo Deaconess Hosp. Sch. Nursing, 1942; Public Health Nurse, SUNY, Buffalo, 1961; m. LeRoy E. Carlson, June 14, 1947; children—Nancy Carlson Stone, Carol Carlson Yannie. Admissions, supr. nurse YWCA Hosp., Jamestown, N.Y., 1942-45; indsl. nurse Proto Tool Co., Jamestown, 1963-65, 70-72, Marlin Rodewell div. TRW Corp., Falconer, N.Y., 1969-70; real estates saleswoman, 1973-74, 77—; dir. Fenton Park Nursing Home, 1965-67; nurse Chautauqua County Resource Center, Jamestown, 1981-82. Pres., Kiantone Mothers Club, Stillwater Ch.; Republican com. woman Kiantone Twp., 1950. Jamestown Vis. Nurse Assn. grantee, 1960-61. Mem. Chautauqua County Grad. Nurses Assn. Club: Women's Bus. and Profl. (Marvin) House. Home: 512 Barr St Jamestown NY 14701

CARLSON-RECKNER, SHARON ANNE, nurse; b. Providence, Feb. 26, 1949; d. Gustav Edward and Barbara Ann (Monroe) Carlson; B.S. in Nursing, B.A. in Psychology, Salve Regina Coll., Newport, R.I., 1976; M.S. in Nursing, Russell Sage Coll., Troy, N.Y., 1981; m. William T. Reckner, Nov. 11, 1978. Staff nurse VA Hosp., Providence, 1974-78; in service coordinator Eden Park Nursing Home, Albany, N.Y., 1978-79; instr. Maria Coll., Albany, 1978-82; substance abuse edn. specialist Rensselaer County Mental Health Dept. Unified Services, Troy, N.Y., 1981—; pvt. practice psychotherapy, 1982—; v.p. Performance Mgmt. Systems Cons. & Tng. Chmn. Poestenkill Youth Commn.; adv. bd. Rensselaer County Dept. Youth. Mem. Am. Nurses Assn., Assn. Advancement Behavior Therapy, N.Y. State Nurses Assn., Capital Area Psychiat. Nurses Assn., Sigma Theta Tau. Roman Catholic. Home: RD 2 Box 355 Averill Park NY 12018 Office: County Office Bldg Troy NY 12180

CARLSON WEST, DONNA JEAN, state legislator; b. Emmett, Idaho, Feb. 19, 1938; d. William B. and Florejce (Lappin) Burchfield; B.S., U. Idaho, 1961; m. David William West, 1979; children—Daniel, Richard, John, Kevin, Douglas. Mem. Ariz. Ho. of Reps., 1975—, chmn. counties and municipalities com., 1977—. State committeewoman Ariz. Republican Party, 1968—; pres. Coordinating Council, Rep. Women, 1971-73; del., mem. rules com. Rep. Nat. Conv., 1976; Ariz. chmn. Am. Legis. Exchange Council, chmn. suggested state legis. com., 1976-78, nat. chmn., 1978—; pres. Nat. Com. Status Women. Office: Capitol Bldg Ho of Reps Wing Phoenix AZ 85007 *

CARLSTON, MARY LYNN, mfg. co. exec.; b. Long Beach, Calif., Aug. 2, 1946; d. Robert B. and Nellie I. (Engle) Reinhart; B.S., Brigham Young U., 1970; m. Greg Carlston, Sept. 7, 1968; children—Camber, Kelsi, Tyler. Salesperson, Bryman Schs., 1975; sales and mktg. dir. Long Beach Coll. Med. and Dental Assn., 1976-78; developer R & R Public Relations Firm, 1978; mfr.'s rep. Automated Pool Covers, 1979-80; pres. Solar Safe Pool Covers, Los Alamitos, Calif., 1981—. Chmn. 1981 Internat. Festival, Long Beach. Mem. Nat. Assn. Female Execs., Long Beach C. of C. (women's council). Republican. Mormon. Club: Belmont Racquet Ball. Home: 4845 E 6th St Long Beach CA 90814 Office: 10631 Bloomfield Suite 14 Los Alamitos CA 90720

CARLTON, FRAN S., state legislator; b. Steinhatchee, Fla., Jan. 19, 1936; d. Danial James and Delma (McCall) Stewart; A.A., U. Fla., 1956; B.S., Stetson U., 1958; m. Ernest E. Carlton, Feb. 12, 1956; children—Lynne, Julie. Mem. faculty Stetson U., Deland, Fla., 1959-65; host nat. syndicated TV show The Fran Carlton Show, 1963—; mem. Fla. Ho. of Reps., 1976—, chmn. tourism sub-com., 1979— , appropriations com. Chmn. Govs. Task Force on Phys. Fitness, 1975. Recipient Disting. Alumni award Stetson U., 1974; Outstanding Legislator award Classroom Tchrs. Assn., 1977, Central Fla. Restaurant Assn., 1979, Orlando Area Tourism Trade Assn., 1979. Mem. Nat. Conf. State Legislature Com., Nat. Order Women Legislators, U. Fla. Nat. Alumni Assn. (pres. 1982). Democrat. Baptist. Author: A Time for Fitness, 1978; writer newspaper column on fitness Orlando Sentinel and Today newspapers, 1972-74; contbr. numerous articles to mags. Office: 5151 Adanson St Orlando FL 32804

CARLYLE, MABLE SEARCY, nurse, educator; b. Polk County, N.C., Aug. 2, 1931; d. Alfred and Vinetta Eliza (Hyder) Searcy; diploma nursing Greenville (S.C.) Gen. Hosp., 1953; B.S. in Nursing magna cum laude, Western Carolina U., 1973; M. Psychiatric Nursing, Emory U., 1976; children—Edward Carlyle, Constance Carlyle, Catherine Carlyle, Christopher Carlyle. Staff nurse Johnson County Meml. Hosp., Franklin, Ind., 1954-57, 60-61; indsl. nurse Bigelow-Sanford Carpet Co., Landrum, S.C., 1957-58; staff nurse VA Hosp., Asheville, N.C., 1962-71, head nurse, 1972-74; asst. prof. psychiat. nursing Western Carolina U., Cullowhee, N.C., 1974—; cons. in field. Named nurse of the Yr., Dist. 1, N.C. Nurses Assn., 1973. Mem. Am., N.C. State (Nurse of Year Dist. 1 1973) nurses assns., Advance Council Psychiat. Nurses, Nat. League for Nursing, AAUW, Bus. and Profl. Women's Orgn., Am. Assn. Sex Educators, Counselors and Therapists, N.C. Beekeepers Assn., Alumni Assn. Western Carolina, Emory U. Alumni Assn., Phi Kappa Phi. Contbr. articles to profl. jour. Home: 807 Holly Ave Black Mountain NC 28711 Office: Sch Nursing Western Carolina U Callowhe NC 28723

CARMEL, CATHERINE AP, mktg. exec.; b. Oakland, Calif., June 6, 1939; d. Joseph Bartholomew and Carmella Helen Canciamilla; student Sophia U., 1957-58, U. Hawaii, 1962-63, San Jose State U., 1965-66, Cabrillo Coll., 1970-71; m. Feb. 3, 1957 (div. 1965); children—Michelle Ann Wheeler, Donna Lynn Wheeler. Tech. copywriter Mikon Export Co., Tokyo, 1958-59; tech. advt. coordinator Associated Advt., Inc., San Jose, Calif., 1965-69; engring. documentation cons. NOVAR/GTE, Cupertino, Calif., 1970-71; dir. tech. communications Reizes, Wechsler & Wheeler, Palo Alto, Calif., 1971-75; v.p. mktg. Mercury Communications Corp., Santa Cruz, Calif., 1975—, chmn. bd., 1977—. Mem. Am. Mgmt. Assn., Assn. Am. Mktg. Execs., Smithsonian Assos., Electronic Def. Assn., Am. Assn. Small Research Cos. Co-author: How to Create a Winning Proposal, 1976; Getting Your Share of the R & D Funds, 1978; Info-sources Directory, 1978; author: Pure and Simple Proposal Preparation, 1978; The War on Fat, 1976; You Can Do It, 1977. Home: PO Box 342 Boulder Creek CA 95006 Office: 734 Chestnut St Santa Cruz CA 95060

CARMEN, ELAINE, psychiatrist; b. N.Y.C., Mar. 26, 1939; d. Louis Ben Kay and Rose (Tekulsky) Katz; B.S. in Chemistry magna cum laude, CCNY, 1959; M.D., N.Y.U., 1964; 1 son, Joshua Hilberman. Intern, then resident in medicine N.C. Meml. Hosp., Chapel Hill, 1964-66; staff physician John Umstead Hosp., Butner, N.C., 1967-69, resident in psychiatry, 1969-72; mem. faculty U. N.C. Med. Sch., Chapel Hill, 1972—, assoc. prof. psychiatry, 1979—, asst. dir. psychiat. residency tng., 1977—, dir. inpatient psychiat. ward, 1979—; mem. task panel spl. populations, subpanel on women President's Commn. Mental Health, 1977-78. Diplomate Am. Bd. Psychiatry and Neurology. Fellow Am. Psychiat. Assn. (chmn. com. on women 1978-80); mem. Am. Med. Women's Assn., Am. Orthopsychiat. Assn., Assn. Acad. psychiatry, Nat. Women's Health Network, Psychiatrists for ERA (a founder), N.C. Neuropsychiat. Assn. (v.p. 1976-77), Order Valkyries. Author: The Rape Victim, 1976; also articles, chpts. in books. Office: Dept Psychiatry U NC Med Sch Chapel Hill NC 27514

CARMICHAEL, BEULAH FRANCES, nurse; b. Stutsman County, N.D., Feb. 9, 1921; d. Summerville and Inda Isabell (Smith) Bunker; R.N., St. Mary's Sch. Nursing, 1947; m. Donald Ray Carmichael, Dec. 20, 1947; children—Susan Lynn, Daniel Ray, Catherine Joan, Rodger Ora, Patricia Ann. Staff nurse Meth. Hosp., Indpls., 1947-49; head nurse Waddell Hosp., Galax, Va., 1959-62; occupational health nurse Am. Olean, Jackson, Tenn., 1967-75; occupational health nurse Eaton Corp., Humbolt, Tenn., 1975-78; dir. nursing Hilltop Convalescent Center, Charleston, Ill., 1979—. Docent, Tarble Arts Center, Charleston, 1979—. Cert. C.P.R. tchr. Mem. W. Tenn. Occupational Health Nurses (chmn. bd. 1974-78), Health Occupations Vocat. Edn. Adv. Com. Republican. Methodist. Clubs: Women's, Zonta (dir.), Hoe and Hope Garden. Home: 1001 Williamsburg St Charleston IL 61920 Office: 910 W Polk St Charleston IL 61920

CARMICHAEL, ELEANOR JOHNSON (MRS. CHARLES WESLEY CARMICHAEL), librarian; b. Mooresville, Ind., Aug. 31, 1916; d. Howard Vinson and Cora Alta (Newman) Johnson; B.A., Earlham Coll., 1938; B.L.S., Columbia, 1941; M.L.S., Ind. U., 1970; m. Charles Wesley Carmichael, July 2, 1948; 1 dau., Ann Bromley (Mrs. George H. Biada, Jr.). Librarian, Coll. Architecture, Cornell U., Ithaca, N.Y., 1942-46; librarian dept. physics Purdue U., Lafayette, Ind., 1946-49; librarian Indpls. Mus. Art, 1956-60; tech. services librarian with rank asso. prof. Roy O. West Library, DePauw U., Greencastle, Ind., 1960—. Mem. project task force Coop. Bibliographic Center for Ind. Libraries, 1972-74. Mem. AAUW, DAR, Am., Ind. library assns., Ohio Valley Group Tech. Service Librarians (sec. 1962-63), Beta Phi Mu, Alpha Phi, Tri Kappa. Author: (with K. Lark-Horowitz) A Chronology of Scientific Development, 1848-1948, 1948. Home: 702 Highwood Ave Greencastle IN 46135

CARMICLE, LINDA HARPER, marriage and family counselor, social worker; b. Westmoreland, Tenn., Oct. 20, 1937; d. Noel Franklin and Mary Frank (Caldwell) Harper; B.S. in Social Work, Tex. Woman's U., Denton, 1975, M.A. in Psychology, 1977; m. Jerrel B. Carmicle, June 2, 1956; children—Roxanna, Jerry Noel. Dir., counselor Galaxy Center, Garland, Tex., 1975-78; family ct. counselor Dallas County Juvenile Dept., 1978—; pvt. practice marriage and family therapy, 1978-81; adj. faculty Tex. Woman's U., 1977, 78. Vice pres. Las Colonitas Home Owners Assn., 1981—. Mem. Nat. Assn. Social Workers, Coalition Juvenile Justice, Mental Health Assn. (task force on child abuse 1980-81), Am. Assn. Marriage and Family Therapists clin. mem.), Alpha Kappa Delta. Methodist. Home: 12830 Midway Rd Suite 1119 Dallas TX 75234 Office: 3d Floor Old Courthouse Dallas TX 75202

CARMINE, SHEILA KAMINOW, public relations practitioner; b. N.Y.C., July 17, 1931; d. Nathan I. and Martha (Greenwald) Kaminow; student Colo. Coll., 1948-49; A.B., Syracuse U., 1952, M.A., 1953, M.A., Columbia U., 1970; postgrad. Fairfield U., 1973-76; children—James, Steven, Michael. Tchr. English, social studies, jr. and sr. public high schs., Stamford, Conn., 1953-54; 1967-72; profl. fund raiser United Jewish Appeal, N.Y.C., 1973; pres. Sheila Carmine Public Relations, public affairs, product mktg., Stamford, 1973—; instr. in public relations U. Conn., Stamford Br. Bd. dirs. YMCA, Stamford, 1980—; chmn. Task Force on Conn. Expenditures, Southwestern Area Commerce and Industry Assn., 1981—. Recipient award for brochures Nat. Press Women, 1977, award for news releases, 1978, cert. for excellence Graphics Gallery, 1981. Mem. Public Relations Soc. Am. (sec. Tri-State Region), Fairfield County Public Relations Assn., Conn. Presswomen (5 awards 1979, pres. 1979-80), Women in Communications, Conn. Bus. and Industry Assn., Norwalk C. of C. (chmn. legis. reception), Southwestern Area Commerce and Industry Assn. (dir. govtl. council 1982—, Voluntary Bus. Service award 1982), LWV; Syracuse U. Alumni Assn., Colo. Coll. Alumni Assn. Democrat. Jewish. Clubs: Roxbury Swim and Tennis, Twelve Powerful Women, Mastersingers Home and Office: 59 Denise Dr Stamford CT 06905

CARMON, MARY ANN, photographer; b. Knoxville, Tenn., Oct. 2, 1939; d. Relley and Geneva (Conner) Ogle; student U. Tenn., 1957-58; m. John Carmon, June 16, 1966; children—Mary-John, Jason, James. Bookkeeper, Citizens Realty Co., Knoxville, 1958-60; with Appalachian Nat. Life Ins. Co., Knoxville, 1960-63, Prudential Life Ins. Co., Knoxville, 1963-64; office mgr. H.Y. Dunaway Co., Charlotte, N.C., 1965-67; acct. Peat, Marwick, Mitchell & Co., Greenville, S.C., 1967-68; bookkeeper Crescent Electronics, Bowling Green, Ky., 1969-73; gen. mgr., partner John Carmon Photography, Bowling Green and Elizabethtown, Ky., 1975—. Served with USCGR, 1962-63. Mem. Bowling Green C. of C., Lisel Ramsey Network of Photographers, Profl. Photographers Am., Beta Sigma Phi (Order of Rose award 1975). Republican. Baptist. Home: 438 Grinstead Way Bowling Green KY 42101 Office: 650 31-W Bypass Bowling Green KY 42101 *

CARNABY, ANN JUDSON, costume co. exec.; b. Providence, May 26, 1942; d. Erland L. and Olive W. Sandberg; B.S., U. R.I., 1963; A.M. in Nursing and Child Psychiatry, N.Y. U., 1969; m. Michael John Carnaby, July 31, 1967; 1 stepson, Neal. Asst. prof. nursing Trenton (N.J.) State Coll., 1970-71; clin. psychiat. nursing dir. Community Mental Health Center, Hunterdon Med. Center, Flemington, N.J., 1971-73; legis. agt. N.J. State Nurses' Assn., Montclair, N.J., 1974; asst. prof. nursing, project dir. U. N.H. dept. nursing, Durham, 1975-77; project dir. Statewide Interdisciplinary Planning Project for Nursing and Nursing Edn., N.H. Nurses Assn., Concord, 1977-79; exec. dir. N.H. Nurses Assn., Concord, 1979-80; mem. State Health Plan Implementation Com., 1979-80; mem. State N.H. Dept. Welfare Med. Care Adv. Com., 1979-80; owner, gen. mgr. Tracy Costumes, Boston, 1981—. Recipient Spaulding Potter Community Services Trust Fund award, 1976, HEW Div. Nursing grantee, 1978, 79. Mem. Am. Nurses Assn., Nat. League for Nursing, United Health Systems Agy., N.H. Nurses Assn. Author: Nursing Manpower: Planning Activities in New Hampshire, 1979; Foundations for Growth: Nursing Resources and Requirements in New Hampshire, 1979; Guidelines for Growth: A Plan for Nursing in New Hampshire, 1980. Office: 63 Melcher St Boston MA

CARNEVALE, FRANCA NELKEN, trade co. exec.; b. Rome, Feb. 10, 1937; came to U.S., 1968, naturalized, 1977; d. Leone Boris and Annita

(Budin) Nelken; D. Pharm. cum laude, Rome U., 1959; m. Dario Carnevale, Feb. 28, 1959; children—Daniela, Flavia, Fulvia, Dario. Pharmacology tchr. Rome U., 1952-62; researcher on drugs, Suez Hosp., Egypt, 1963, Beirut (Lebanon) Italian Hosp., 1964-65; researcher children's allergies Bucharest Children's Hosp., 1966; internat. coordinator European lit. and publs. Pharmacology Inst. of Rome, Des Plaines, Ill., 1970; internat. coordinator S.Am. lit. and publs. Pharmacology Inst. of Bogota (Colombia), Miami, Fla., 1972; exec. v.p. Dafra Internat., Inc., Miami, 1978—; tchr., cons.; dir. Mem. Pharmacist Assn. Rome. Roman Catholic. Clubs: Ionosphere, B.A. Exec., Sons of Italy.

CARNEY, BARBARA JOYCE, exec. search cons.; b. Chgo.; d. Maurice David and Celia (Baylen) Sachnoff; B.A. cum laude, UCLA, 1964; M.Ed., Nat. Coll. Edn., 1968; children—Michael, Michelle. Tchr., North Suburban Chgo. pub. schs., 1965-68; mfrs. rep. Shardon Mktg. Inc., Chgo., 1976-78; Midwestern regional sales mgr. Superscope, Inc., Chatsworth, Calif., 1977-80; nat. spl. markets sales mgr. Ronco, Inc., Elk Grove Village, Ill., 1980-81; exec. search cons. Womack & Assos., Inc., Chgo., 1982—. Bd. dirs. North Shore Mental Health Assn., 1975-76; chpt. v.p., chmn. LWV, 1968-76. Mem. Women in Mgmt., AAUW, Am. Soc. Profl. and Exec. Women, Nat. Assn. Female Execs. Home: 2020 Lincoln Park W Chicago IL 60614 Office: 919 N Michigan Ave Suite 2408 Chicago IL 60611

CARNEY, CLAIRE T., real estate devel. co. exec.; b. New Bedford, Mass., June 18, 1922; d. Philippe Oriance and Roseanne Louise (Belhumeur) Galipeau; B.A., Southeastern Mass. U., 1973; m. Hugh J. Carney, Feb. 19, 1944 (dec. May 1962); children—Doreen, Patrick, Mark, Hugh James. Various positions Air Force, Naval Hosp. and Treasury Dept., 1942-46; cost acct. Morse Twist Drill & Machine Co., New Bedford, 1960-68; founder, comptroller, treas. Claremont Co., Inc., New Bedford, 1969—; partner Lord Philip, Car Barn, Claremont Co. Trust; partner Clarkwood Realty, 1968—, Solemar II, N Dartmouth Cross Rd. Assos. Pres., Southeastern Mass. U. Library Assos., 1977-78, trustee univ., 1980-84, chmn. ann. fund drive Southeastern Mass. U., 1979-80. Mem. Southeastern Mass. U. Alumni Assn. (awards chmn. 1979-80, chmn. scholarship Com.), Mass. Bd. Real Estate Brokers, New Bedford Women Realtors, Nat. Assn. Female Execs., Nat. Assn. Home Builders, N.H. Assn. Home Builders, Dartmouth (Mass.) Hist. Commn. (chmn. 1980-82). Roman Catholic. Club: Cath. Women. Home: 966 Tucker Rd North Dartmouth MA 02747 Office: 628 Pleasant St New Bedford MA 02742

CARNEY, KAY, actress, educator; b. Rice Lake, Wis., Aug. 2, 1933; d. Rexford Hugh and Margot Caroline (Haanstad) C.; B.S., U. Wis., 1955; M.A., Mt. Holyoke Coll., 1958; postgrad. Centre du Théâtre Nationale, 1970, Columbia U. and Case-Western Res. U., 1957-63; Creative Arts fellow U. Colo., 1963. Actress performing in London, Paris, Istanbul, Ankara, Tel Aviv and Nicosia, 1970-72, performing in Off Off-Broadway! An Anthology with Kay Carney, N.Y.C., Chgo., San Francisco, Vancouver, Balt., Phila., Boston and various U.S. colls., 1973—; dir. Mourning Pictures, Broadway and Lenox Arts Center, 1974; tchr. acting, directing and psychophys. work Hunter Coll., Henry St. Playhouse, SUNY, Purchase, U. Calif., Santa Cruz, 1977-80; assoc. prof. dept. theatre Smith Coll., Northampton, Mass., 1980-82, Bklyn. Coll., 1983—; condr. workshops for profls. in U.S. and abroad; organizer, trainer La Mama theatre groups, Paris and Tel Aviv; bd. dirs. Bear Rep. Theatre, 1977-79; performed with Open Theatre, 1965-67; seminarian with Jerzy Grotowski, 1970. Moratorium organizer, performer Angry Artists Against the War, 1966-70; mem. Performing Artists for Nuclear Disarmament, 1981—, St. Clements Arts in Religious Action Com., 1972-75; organizer Bay Area Women in Theatre Orgn., 1978-80. Kosciuszko Found. grantee, 1979; SUNY Research Found. grantee, 1976. Mem. Soc. Stage Dirs. and Choreographers, Actors Equity, AFTRA, New Eng. Theatre Conf., Am. Theatre Assn. (exec. com. women's program, presenter nat. convs.), Women in Theatre. Democrat. Episcopalian. Contbr. articles to profl. jours. Office: Theatre Dept Smith College Northampton MA 01063

CARNINE, MARGARET LEE, editor; b. Madison, Ind., Oct. 4, 1925; d. Raymond McKinley and Eva Lena (Cole) C.; R.N., Bethesda Hosp. Sch. Nursing, 1946. Head nurse men's surg. ward Bethesda Hosp., Cin., 1946-50; supr. indsl. nursing Trailmobile, Inc., Cin., 1950-67; exec. editor Charles B. Slack, Inc., Thorofare, N.J., 1968—. Mem. Am. Assn. Occupational Health Nurses. Editor: Occupational Health Nursing, 1968—, Jour. Nursing Edn., Jour. Pediatric Ophthalmology and Strabismus, Jour. Ophthalmic Nursing and Tech., Nursing Leadership, Ophthalmic Surgery. Home: 522 Crafton Ave Pitman NJ 08071 Office: 6900 Grove Rd Thorofare NJ 08086

CARO, BARBARA JEAN, personnel agy. exec.; b. Blount County, Tenn., May 22, 1949; d. Grayson Jake and Edith Lucille (Ward) Russell; B.B.A. in Mktg. cum laude (Equifax scholar), Ga. State U., 1980; m. Luis P. Caro, Aug. 23, 1968; children—Cristina Michelle, Paul Anthony. Teletype operator Shell Chem. Co., Atlanta, 1971-73; with Sales Cons. Atlanta div. Mgmt. Recruiters Internat. Inc., 1973—, adminstrv. asst., 1973-80, mgr. bus. devel., adminstrv. mgr., 1981—; trainer, condr. seminars in field. Active Smyrna (Ga.) Athletic Assn. Served with USAF, 1967-70. Lic. in real estate, Ga. Mem. Ga. Assn. Personnel Services, Ga. Assn. Realtors, Cobb Bd. Realtors, Rho Epsilon (social coordinator 1977-80). Home: 17 Judy Dr SW Marietta GA 30060 Office: 3300 Buckeye Rd Suite 850 Atlanta GA 30341

CARON, LESLIE (LESLIE CLARE MARGARET CARON), film and stage actress; b. Boulogne, France, July 1, 1931; d. Claude and Margaret (Petit) Caron; student Convent of Assumption, Paris; m. George Hormel, May 1953; m. 2d, Peter Reginald Frederick Hall, Aug. 6, 1956; children—Christopher John, Jennifer Caron; m. 3d, Michael Laughlin, Jan. 1, 1969. With Ballet des Champs Elysees, 1947-50, Ballet de Paris, 1954; appeared in motion pictures, including American in Paris, Lili, Glass Slipper, Daddy Long Legs, Gigi, The Doctor's Dilemma, The Man Who Understood Women, Fanny, The L Shaped Room, Father Goose, The Favour, Promise Her Anything, Is Paris Burning, Head of the Family, The Beginners, Madron, Chandler, Purple Night, That's Entertainment—Part 2, Valentino, The Man Who Loved Women, Golden Girl; TV appearances include Carola, 1973, QB VII, 1974; also appeared in Renoir play Orvet, Paris, 1955; Gigi, London, 1956; Ondine, 1961. Address: care Blake Agy Ltd 409 N Camden Dr 202 Beverly Hills CA 90210 *

CAROTHERS, JANE HOUGHTON, fine arts auction firm adminstr.; b. Corning, N.Y., Nov. 28, 1930; d. Arthur Amory and Jane Olmsted (McMillan) Houghton; grad. Foxcroft Sch., 1948, Katherine Gibbs Sch., 1950; student Wells Coll., 1948-49; children—Susan, Jane, Hope, Peter Hadley Exec. asst. Sotheby Parke Bernet, 1981—. Mem. women's com. N.Y. Public Library, 1958-60; mem. adv. com. Sawtooth Nat. Forest, 1971; chmn. Sun Valley Village Hosp. Emergency Room Aux., 1969-71; vol. pediatric recreation N.Y. Hosp., 1974-75; vol., mem. benefit com. Hosp. Spl. Surgery, 1974-75; mem. adv. bd. Exec. High Sch. Internships Am. Chmn., Vols. for Nixon-Lodge, Blaine County, Idaho, 1960; Republican precinct committeeman Blaine County, 1968-73; del. Idaho State Rep. Conv., 1968, 70; page Rep. Nat. Conv., 1968; chmn. Vols. for Nixon-Agnew, Blaine County, 1968; co-chmn. host com. Lt. Gov.'s Conv., 1971; Idaho chmn. Regional Women's Western States Conf., Phoenix, 1972; mem. N.Y. com. U.S. Ski Team. Trustee Blaine County Sch. Dist. 61; chmn. bd. trustees Corning (N.Y.) Public Library, 1957-60; bd. dirs Ketchum Community Library, 1965, chmn. bd. dirs., 1969, 70; trustee Sun Valley Ski Edn. Found., 1968-73, pres., 1969-73; trustee African-Am. Inst. (nominating com. 1975—, vol. 1975—, co-chmn. benefit com. 1977). Club: Sun Valley (Idaho) Ski (gov. 1969-73). Home: 1010 S Ocean Blvd Pompano Beach FL 33062

CAROZZOLO, SHIRLEY JEAN, constrn. co. exec.; b. Buffalo, Nov. 21, 1935; d. Albert A. and Jean Louise (Hanna) La Chiusa; m. Vito A. Carozzolo, Sept. 17, 1966; children—Michael John Kurban, David Charles Kurban. Various secretarial positions, 1953-55, 68-74; office mgr. Haney Erection Services Inc., Tonawanda, N.Y., 1975-76, corp. sec., 1975—, EEO officer, 1980—. Mem. Niagara Frontier Subcontractors Assn. (membership chmn. 1978), Am. Soc. Profl. and Exec. Women. Republican. Episcopalian. Club: Kenmore Zonta (1st v.p. 1979-81, pres. 1981-82). Home: 426 Ashford Ave Tonawanda NY 14150 Office: 199 Wales Ave PO Box 476 Tonawanda NY 14150

CARPENTER, ARLENE CARROLL, advt. exec.; b. Bridgeport, Conn., Dec. 4, 1943; d. Richard John and Fedela Mary (Grasso) C.; B.A., U.Bridgeport, 1965; postgrad Sacred Heart U., 1975. Adminstr. gypsy moth program U.S. Forest Service, Hamden, Conn., 1969-72; mktg. asso. Flaherty-Giavara Assos. New Haven, Conn., 1972-75; sr. research analyst de Kadt Mktg. & Research, Greenwich, Conn., 1975-78; asst. dir. research BBDO, N.Y.C., 1978-80; asst. research dir. Grey Advt., N.Y.C., 1980-81; partner Carpenter/Pampalone Advt., Southport, Conn., 1981—. Mem. NOW, Women in Communication, Ad Club Fairfield County. Roman Catholic. Home: 106 Harlem Ave Bridgeport CT 06606 Office: PO Box 754 Southport CT 06490

CARPENTER, BETTE MARIE (MRS. HERBERT LARSON CARPENTER), Realtor, bldg. contractor; b. Hemet, Calif., Mar. 8, 1927; d. Scott William and Eugenia LeProhon (de Beaufert) Carl; student Oceanside Jr. Coll., 1943-45, UCLA, 1945-47; A.A., Rutledge Coll., 1982; postgrad. in law; m. Herbert Larson Carpenter, May 6, 1944; 1 dau., Carolyn Lee (Mrs. Kenneth Ray Dabbs). Propr., Bette M. Carpenter, Realtors, Carlsbad and Riverside, Calif., 1954-60; pres. Interstate Equities Corp., Carlsbad, 1960—; v.p., sec. LanInCo Corp. Nev., Las Vegas, 1964-72; v.p. mktg. Parkside Devel. Co., Santa Ana, Calif. Mem. Carlsbad Bd. Realtors (charter mem.), Calif. Real Estate Assn., Nat. Assn. Real Estate Bds., Nat. Inst. Real Estate Brokers, Urban Land Inst., Women Council Realtors, San Diego Assn. Legal Assts., Carlsbad C. of C. Republican. Home: PO Box 254 Carlsbad CA 92008 Office: El Camino Real Carlsbad CA 92008 also San Luis Rey Downs CA

CARPENTER, CECELIA ANN, nurse; b. Adrian, Mich., Aug. 23, 1941; d. Charles Edwin and Helen Jean (Ranger) Earles; R.N., St. Vincent's Hosp., Toledo, 1962; B.S., Defiance (Ohio) Coll., 1976; m. Wayne Sidney Carpenter, Aug. 11, 1962; children—Matthew, Caroline. Staff pediatric nurse William Beaumont Hosp., Royal Oak, Mich., 1962-63; staff nurse Morenci (Mich.) Area Hosp., 1963-70, inservice dir., 1970-76, supr., 1970-77, dir. nurses, 1977—; CPR instr., A.R.C. disaster nurse; mem. Mid-Mich. Health Planning Services Bd., 1977-79; adv. bd. Lenawee County Bd. Public Health. 4-H leader; adv. bd. Adrian Assembly Rainbow Girls. Cert. advanced cardiac life support. Mem. Mich. Soc. Hosp. Nursing Adminstrs., NW Ohio Dir. Nurses Assn., Madison Grange, DAR, Croswell Opera House Assn. Baptist. Clubs: Christian Women's, Eastern Star. Home: 1700 Fairfield Rd Adrian MI 49221 Office: Sims Hwy Morenci MI 49256

CARPENTER, DOROTHY FULTON, state legislator; b. Ismay, Mont., Mar. 13, 1933; d. Daniel A. and Mary Ann (George) Fulton; B.A., Grinnell Coll., 1955; m. Thomas W. Carpenter, June 12, 1955; children—Mary Ione, James Thomas. Tchr. elem. schs., Houston, and Iowa City, 1955-58; mem. Iowa Ho. Reps., 1980—, asst. minority floor leader, 1982—. Pres. Planned Parenthood of Iowa, 1970; bd. dirs. Planned Parenthood Fedn. Am., 1977-80; fin. chmn. Episcopal Diocese of Iowa, 1979-80. Recipient Grinnell Coll. Alumni award, 1980. Mem. NOW, Common Cause. Republican.

CARPENTER, ELIZABETH SUTHERLAND, journalist, author; b. Salaso, Tex., Sept. 1, 1920; d. Thomas Shelton and Mary Elizabeth (Robertson) Sutherland; B.J., U. Tex., 1942; m. Leslie Carpenter, June 17, 1944; children—Scott Sutherland, Christy. Reporter, United Press, Phila., 1944-45; propr. with husband of news bur. representing nat. newspapers, Washington, 1945-61; exec. asst. to Vice Pres. Lyndon B. Johnson, 1961-63; pres. sec., staff dir. to Mrs. Johnson, 1963-69; v.p. Hill & Knowlton, Inc., Washington, 1972-76; cons. L.B.J. Library, Austin, Tex.; co-chmn. ERAmerica, 1973-82. Recipient award Ladies Home Jour., 1977. Mem. Nat. Women's Polit. Caucus (nat. policy council 1971—), Women's Nat. Press (pres. 1954-55), Alpha Phi, Theta Sigma Phi (Nat. Headliners award 1962). Author: Ruffles and Flourishes, 1970. Office: LBJ Library 2313 Red River Austin TX 78705 *

CARPENTER, GEORGANN, radiation therapy technologist; b. New Albany, Ind., Apr. 22, 1947; d. Orlan Cleveland and Gertrude Wiltha (Everbach) C.; student nursing, Ind. Central Coll., 1965-66; A.S. in Radiol. Tech., Ind. U., 1968; postgrad. Purdue U., 1969—. Staff technologist St. Elizabeth Hosp., Lafayette, Ind., 1968-73, chief of radiation therapy technologists, 1973—. Sec. Bd. Christian Edn., 1st Bapt. Ch. Recipient 1st prize essay Ind. Soc. Radiol. Technologists, 1974; registered radiol. technologist. Mem. Ind. Soc. Radiol. Technologists (pres. 1982), Am. Soc. Radiol. Technologists. Home: 3316 Hanover Dr Lafayette IN 47905 Office: 1501 Hartford St Lafayette IN 47904

CARPENTER, GRACE HERRING, fin. exec.; b. Hazelton, W.Va., Aug. 19, 1935; d. Harold Clayton and Mabel Virginia (Niner) Herring; A.Bus., Davis & Elkins Coll., 1957; m. Norman Eugene Carpenter, Apr. 1, 1956. With Davis Meml. Hosp., Elkins, W.Va., 1956-61; account exec. Wyllie & Thornhill, Inc., Charlottesville, Va., 1968-71, Mason & Lee, Charlottesville, 1971-76, Wheat First Securities, Charlottesville, 1976-79; asst. v.p. Thomson McKinnon Securities, Charlottesville, 1979—. Pres., Charlottesville Family Y., 1974-76; mem. adv. com. bus. tech. Piedmont Community Coll., 1978; sec.-treas. Greater Charlottesville Area Devel. Corp., 1980—; v.p. Thomas Jefferson Area United Way, 1980—. Mem. Charlottesville Albermarle C. of C. (v.p. 1980, chmn. 1982), Soc. Advancement Mgmt. (pres. 1977-78). Republican. Clubs: Order Eastern Star, White Shrine. Home: 670 Chapel Hill Rd Charlottesville VA 22901 Office: 401 E Water St Charlottesville VA 22902

CARPENTER, MARION PHYLLIS, govt. ofcl.; b. Seattle, Feb. 17, 1931; d. Kenneth Alden and Lora Catherine (Scott) Sprague; student U. Oreg., 1948-49; children—Linda Marie Jenson, Kenneth Frederick, Nancy Lynn. Receptionist, med. clk. Adult and Family Services, State of Oreg., McMinnville, 1964-68, assistance worker, 1968-73, supr., 1973-77, br. mgr., Florence, Oreg., 1974—. Mem. Florence Activity Center Bd., 1977-78; mem. McMinnville Planning Commn., 1975-77; asso. mother adviser Knowles Rainbow Girls, 1971-77; mem. Lane County Council Govt. Rural Transp. Com., 1981—; vice chmn. Florence Area Coordinating Council, 1982—. Mem. Oreg. Mgmt. Assn., Nat. Assn. Female Execs., Am. Mgmt. Assn., Wilderness Soc., Oreg. Gerontol. Assn., Oreg. Assn. Retarded Citizens. Republican. Presbyterian. Clubs: Soroptomists, Jr. Matrons, Eastern Star, Daus. of Nile. Home: PO Box 1166 Florence OR 97439 Office: 1870 Hwy 126 Florence OR 97439

CARPENTER, PHYLLIS MARIE ROSENAU, physician; b. Hastings, Nebr., Aug. 2, 1926; d. Alvin Benjamin and Sophia Helen (Schmidt) Rosenau; B.S., Hastings Coll., 1948; M.D., U. Nebr., 1951; cert. Gestalt Inst. Cleve., 1970; m. Charles Robert Carpenter, Mar. 24, 1956 (dec. Mar. 1972); children—Charles Robert, Carole Rose, Lucinda Joy. Intern, St. Luke's Hosp., Chgo., 1951-52; resident in pediatrics Children's Meml. Hosp., Chgo., 1952-54; asst. med. dir. clin. supr. EEG lab., Mcpl. Contagious Disease Hosp., Chgo., 1955-60; tchr. parenting; staff Well Baby Clinics, Infant Welfare, 1960-70; practice medicine specializing in Gestalt therapy preventive medicine and biofeedback Chgo. and Clarendon Hills, Ill., 1970—; founding fellow, mem. faculty Gestalt Inst. Chgo., 1970—, faculty chmn., 1981—; mem. faculty Coll. DuPage, 1975-79, No. Ill. U., 1979-80, George Williams Coll. Center Extended Programs, Chgo., 1979—; therapist Martha Washington Alcoholic Rehab. Clinic, Chgo., 1969-75. Organizer Community Presbyn. Ch. Nursery Sch., 65 1966. Recipient cert. appreciation Gestalt Inst. Chgo., 1981. Mem. AAUW, Am. Assn. Biofeedback Clinicians (cert. clinician), Nat. Writers Club. Author articles in field. Home: 35 Norfolk St Clarendon Hills IL 60514 Office: 35 Norfolk St Clarendon Hills IL 60514 also 2057 N Sedgewick Ave Chicago IL 60614

CARPENTER, SUSAN, modeling and finishing sch. exec.; b. Montgomery County, Tenn.; d. William Dallas and Ellie Ruth (Mann) Chester; diploma John Robert Powers Sch.; m. William Carpenter, Feb. 16, 1973. Former dir. John Robert Powers Sch., San Jose, Calif.; owner, dir., tchr. Jo Susan Sch., Nashville, 1959—. Active Vanderbilt Childrens Hosp., YWCA; chmn. United Cerebral Palsy. Named one of ten best dressed women in Nashville, Nashville Banner, 1980; recipient awards Sta. WSM-TV, 1965, 1967. Mem. Modeling Assn. Am., Better Bus. Bur., Assn. Preservation Tenn. Antiquity, Cheekwood Bot. Gardens and Fine Arts Center, Nashville Symphony Guild. Club: Hillwood Country. Office: Continental Apts Suite 8 3415 W End Ave Nashville TN 37203

CARPENTIER, POSEY (MRS. CHARLES NELSON CARPENTIER), real estate exec.; b. Hillsboro, Tex., Apr. 2, 1919; d. Homer H. and Itylene (Moore) Posey; A.A., Hillsboro Jr. Coll., 1939; B.A., UCLA, 1975, M.A., 1979; m. Charles Nelson Carpentier, Nov. 14, 1953; children—Carla, Nelson. Dept. head Air Assos., Dallas, 1940-43, Los Angeles, 1943-45; personnel mgr. N.Am. Aviation Co., Los Angeles, 1947-50; dir. clerical personnel dept. Hughes Aircraft Co., Culver City, Calif., 1951-57; pres. Posey Carpentier Realty, Inc., Malibu, 1968—, Car-Nel Properties Investment Co., 1976—, Carpentier Mgmt. Co., 1978—; mgr. Pointe Dume Shopping Center, Malibu; founding dir., chmn. audit com. 1st Women's Bank of Calif., Los Angeles; mem. faculty Santa Monica (Calif.) Coll., 1975—; lectr. on property mgmt. and real estate. Pres. PTA, Webster Sch., Malibu, 1968-69, Malibu Park Jr. High Sch., 1971-72; historian Santa Monica PTA Council, 1972-73; bd. dirs. Bay Area Drug Abuse Council, 1971-73, Malibu Drug Action Bd., chmn., 1971-73; founder Music Center, Los Angeles. Certified property mgr. Grad. Realtors Inst. Mem. Nat. Assn. Realtors (dir., mem. econs. and research com.), Calif. Assn. Realtors (dir. 1973-79, exec. com. 1979, chmn. property mgmt. div. 1980, regional v.p. 1978, mem. faculty, seminar speaker, editor Property Mgmt. mag. 1976-78), Malibu Bd. Realtors (dir. 1971-75, pres. 1972-73), Women in Bus., Los Angeles County Mus. (sustaining), Los Angeles Women's Polit. Com. Contbr. articles to profl. publs. Democrat. Home: 3868 Rambla Orienta Malibu CA 90265 Office: 21361 Pacific Coast Hwy Malibu CA 90265

CARPER, ANNA MARY, librarian; b. Palmyra, Pa., Aug. 13, 1919; d. Frank S. and Ella M. (Ebersole) C.; A.B. cum laude, Elizabethtown (Pa.) Coll., 1941; M.S., Columbia U., 1951. Tchr., librarian Fredericksburg (Pa.) High Sch., 1941-47; tchr. South Lebanon (Pa.) Schs., 1947-50; head cataloger U. Md., College Park, 1951-60; dir. library Elizabethtown Coll., 1960—. Hist. com., deacon Ch. of the Brethren. Recipient award for service to Elizabethtown Coll., Elizabethtown Coll. Alumni, 1970. Mem. ALA, Pa. Library Assn., Lancaster County Library Assn., Delta Kappa Gamma. Home: 316 E Plum St Apt A Elizabethtown PA 17022 Office: Zug Memorial Library Elizabethtown College Elizabethtown PA 17022

CARPER, GLENDA JOY, bus. exec.; b. San Angelo, Tex., July 21, 1939; d. Sam Bruce and Lethia (McGilvray) Lambert; B.A., West Tex. State U., 1971; m. Donald Clayton Carper, July 29, 1956; children—LaDon, Kelli Lin. Billing clk. Gen. Telephone Co., San Angelo, 1957-59; bookkeeper Margarets, Lubbock, Tex., 1959-62; sec., treas. Bearings and Materials Handling Co., Inc., Amarillo, Tex., 1968—, Bamco of Amarillo, Bamco of Dumas, Bamco of Hereford; pres. Amarillo Credit Women Internat., 1980-81, also mem. pres.'s task force com. Second v.p. Lone Star Regional Council, 1981-82; v.p. Credit Women Internat., 1980-81, treas., 1979-80. Republican. Presbyterian. Home: 3908 Eaton Dr Amarillo TX 79109 Office: 108 Crockett St Amarillo TX 79106

CARPIO, LUZ MENDOZA, real estate sales agt.; b. Juarez, Mex., Aug. 3, 1924; came to U.S., 1930, naturalized, 1946; d. Feliciano and Maria Bonilla (Avalos) Mendoza; student Bowie (Tex.) public schs., real estate courses; m. Pedro Carpio, Aug. 3, 1947; children—Cecilia, Pedro. Gen. office clk. Triangle Elec. Co., El Paso, Tex., 1946-66; sales agt. D & R Realtors, El Paso, 1969—; with Tex. Dept. Human Resources, 1981—. Pres. local PTA; bd. dirs. Pan Am. Pilot Club, 1967-69; various chairmanships Bowie Alumni, 1970-79; pres. Nat. Democratic Women's Club, El Paso, 1971-80; chmn. El Paso Women's Polit. Caucus, 1977-80; bd. dirs. Trinity Coalition, 1977-79; com. mem. Police Dept. Youth Div., 1977; mem. Mexican-Am. Dems., 1976-80, Goals for El Paso, 1977. Mem. El Paso Bd. Realtors, Tex. Assn. Realtors, Progressive Dems. Roman Catholic. Club: Cathedral Sch. Mothers. Address: 3511 Russell St El Paso TX 79930

CARR, ANNA WEAVER, cytogenetic technologist; b. Hickory, N.C., Dec. 8, 1930; d. Robert and Mary Beatrice (Simms) Weaver; B.S. cum laude, Va. Union U., 1957; divorced; children—Inga Maria, Troi Lovette. Lab. technician child devel. study project NIH, 1958-64; with Va. Health Dept., Med-Coll. Va.-Va. Commonwealth U., Richmond, 1964—, cytogenetic lab. specialist, 1976—, supr. cytogenetic lab., 1980—. Bd. dirs. Richmond Community Hosp., 1971—; rec. sect. Va. Crusade for Voters Meetings, 1974-75. Mem. Assn. Cytogenetic Technologists (dir.), Continental Socs. (chpt. fin. sec. 1978-80), NAACP, Delta Sigma Theta. Baptist. Home: 1502 Sharpsburg Ct Richmond VA 23228 Office: Sanger Hall 11th and Marshall Sts Richmond VA 23298

CARR, BERNADETTE PATRICIA (CARROZZA), editor; d. Francis and Elizabeth (O'Donnell) C.; B.A., In English Lt., Mercy Coll., Dobbs Ferry, N.Y., 1966; M.A. in Am. Lit., Fordham U., 1968. Mng. editor Photoplay mag., N.Y.C., 1969-70, editor, 1971-73; editor-in-chief MacFadden Fan Titles mag., N.Y.C., 1973-74; editor Weight Watchers mag., N.Y.C., 1975-80; editor-in-chief Everywoman mag., N.Y.C., 1980-81; asso. pub., editor CPDA News, N.Y.C., 1982—. Mem. Nat. Acad. TV Arts and Scis. (asso.), Sigma Delta Chi, Sigma Phi Sigma. Office: CPDA News 488 Madison Ave New York NY 10022

CARR, ELIZABETH, fine arts appraiser; b. Chgo., Sept. 24, 1922; d. Charles Columbus and Grace (Marlor) Zurick; student public schs., Chgo.; m. Peter J. Caracci, Jan. 29, 1944; children—Joann Caracci Pelka, Linda Caracci Lastowski. Tabulation operator U.S. Govt. IBM Tabulation Dept., Chgo., 1941-42; sec./dir. Caracci & Caracci Ins., Grand Western Currency Exchange; paralegal firm Arvey, Hodes, Costello, Burman, Chgo., 1971-74; appraiser fine arts, cons. in antiques, River Forest, Ill., 1962—; lectr. in field; instr. in antiques Loyola U. Chgo., 1978-80, St. Xavier Coll., 1980-82, Triton Coll., 1980-81. Served with WAVES, USN, 1943-44. Mem. Nat. Auctioneers Assn., Ill. State

Auctioneers Assn., Victorian Soc., Wedgwood Soc. Chgo. (dir. public relations), Internat. Wedgwood Soc., Hadji Baba Soc., Armenian Rug Soc., Chgo. Rug Soc. (sec. 1967-82), Old Lacers Soc., Netsuke Soc., Internat. Snuff Bottle Soc., New Eng. Appraisers Assn., Internat. Soc. Fine Arts Appraisers (founder 1979, pres. 1970-82), Nat. Assn. Female Execs., Nat. Home Based Women, Future Women, Nat. Women Bus. Owners. Roman Catholic. Club: Nineteenth Century Women's. Contbr. articles to profl. jours.; publisher, editor The Evaluator, 1979—. Office: PO Box 280 River Forest IL 60305

CARR, JANE DEELEY, dental hygienist, child care center ofcl.; b. Mt. Vernon, Ohio, Jan. 8, 1943; d. George E. and Marian E. Deeley; student Miami U., 1961-63; A.A., Forsyth Sch. for Dental Hygienists, 1965; B.S., Northeastern U., 1966; M.A. in Clin. Psychology, St. Mary's U., 1976; m. Donald M. Greer, July 17, 1981. Pvt. practice dental hygiene, 1965-68; instr. Forsyth Dental Hygiene Sch., 1968-70; instr. Ohio State U., Columbus, 1970-71; pvt. practice dental hygiene, Wichita Falls, Tex., 1971-72; co-developer dental hygiene program Midwestern State U., Wichita Falls, 1972-74; pvt. practice dental hygiene, San Antonio, 1974-75; asst. prof. U. Tex. Health Sci. Center, San Antonio, 1974—, acting coordinator dental hygiene edn. program, 1977-78; pres. Humanistic Resources Inc., San Antonio, 1979—; mem. dental hygiene adv. com. to Tex. State Bd. Dental Examiners, 1977—; cons. to Tattletooth Program, regional SW, Health and Human Resources. Recipient service award, Tex. State Bd. Dental Examiners, 1982. Mem. Am. Dental Hygienists' Assn. (chair council on ednl. services and research), Tex. Dental Hygienists' Assn., San Antonio Dist. Dental Hygiene Soc., Am. Assn. Dental Schs., San Antonio Women in Bus., Sigma Phi Alpha. Episcopalian. Author, co-producer videotape series. Home: Route 4 Box 4509 Boerne TX 78006 Office: 7703 Floyd Curl Dr San Antonio TX 78284

CARR, MARIJANE, cellist; b. Oak Park, Ill., May 8, 1928; d. Vivian Emil and Lucille (Butcher) C.; student Juilliard Sch. Music; M.M., Roosevelt U., 1975; m. Frity Siegal, Sept. 12, 1953; children—Paul Vivan, Elise Fonchon, Peter Eric. Cellist, Tanglewood Music Festival, 1948, Grant Park Symphony, Chgo., 1953-68, Lyric Opera Orch. Chgo., 1954—, Lyric Arts String Quartet; instr. Wheaton Coll., 1956-72, Elmhurst Coll.; cellist Orch. III., 1958-82; tchr. music history Coll. DuPage, 1976-77. Mem. Soc. Am. Musicians. Unitarian. Clubs: Nordmanss Forbundet, Bjornsen Lodge Sons of Norway. Office: 20 N Wacker Dr Chicago IL 60606 *

CARR, MYRA REUSS, writer, crossword puzzle creator; b. East Chicago, Ind., Jan. 3, 1904; d. Howard Gerald and Constance (Reuss) Stevens; student Bohlinger Bus. Coll., 1921-23; A.B. in Lit. and Social Sci., Antioch Coll., 1927; postgrad. San Francisco State U., 1960-61; m. Raymond W. Carr, June 1, 1929; 1 son, Richard R. Free-lance feature writer, 1933-55, contbr. articles to various publs., including Parents, Saturday Evening Post, Look Cosmopolitan mags., Des Moines Register and Tribune, Phila. Inquirer; copychief Phillips, Reick Fardon Advt. Agy., Kansas City, Mo., 1950-55; free-lance advt., editorial and public relations writer for San Francisco firms, 1956-60; crossword puzzle creator Dell Publs., Gen. Features and Publishers Hall syndicates, 1960—; researcher, U. Chgo., U. Calif.; merchandiser Farmer's Wife Mag. Recipient awards Mo. Women's Press, 1953-54. Mem. Calif. Press Women, Nat. Fedn. Press Women (awards 1953-54), AAUW (Calif. state publicity bd. 1965), Westlake Improvement Assn., San Francisco Philatelic Soc., Feature Writers Am. (hon.), Gamma Alpha Chi. Republican. Presbyterian. Home and Office: 378 Glenwood Ave Daly City CA 94015

CARR, NANCY PHARES, ch. ofcl.; b. Hamilton, Ohio, Dec. 15, 1930; d. Anthony Earl and Marietta (Dilg) Phares; B.S. in Edn., Miami U., Oxford, Ohio, 1952; m. Harry Kendall Carr, Dec. 23, 1950; children—Michael, Cheryl, Patricia, Nancy, Jennifer, Mary, Harry, Christine, Anthony, Carolyn, David. Exec. dir. Manchester (Conn.) Area Conf. Chs., 1972—; exec. sec. commn. ecumenical affairs Roman Cath. Archdiocese Hartford (Conn.), 1976—; chmn. Greater Hartford Interfaith Com. Soviet Jewry; pres. adv. council CHRISCON, Christian Conf. Conn., 1981—; v.p. Conn. bd. mgrs. Ch. Women United. Recipient Humanitarian award B'nai B'rith, 1980, Spiritual Leadership award Manchester C. of C., 1981; named Burton's Woman of Yr. Manchester clubs and orgns., 1969, Jr. Women's Club, Manchester, 1972. Democrat. Roman Catholic. Author, editor in field. Home: 40 Coburn Rd Manchester CT 06040 Office: PO Box 773 Manchester CT 06040

CARR, PAQUITA RUIZ, psychologist; b. Aguada, P.R., Mar. 27, 1914; d. Andres C. and Josefina G. Ruiz; B.S., U. P.R., 1936; postgrad. U. Columbia, 1939-40; Ph.D., Fordham U., 1946; postgrad. U. Chgo., 1946-47; m. Randolph Carr, May 1, 1947 (dec.); children—Jan Randolph, Howard Rene. Prof., U. P.R., 1938-40, chief psychol. center, 1947; head dept. psychology VA, San Juan, P.R., 1948; staff psychologist Maywood Vets. Hosp., Chgo., 1949; dir. Psychol. Center, Washington, 1949-50, Asia Research Center, Washington, 1949-50; pvt. practice clin. psychology, Washington, 1949—; chief clin. psychologist dept. psychiatry Group Health Assn., Inc., Washington, from 1973, now dir. family and child services-psychiatry; cons. in field. Cert. psychologist, D.C., Md. Mem. Am. Psychol. Assn., D.C. Psychol. Assn., Puerto Rican Am. Womens League (past pres.), Latin-Am. Psychol. Assn. Club: Univ. Womens. Contbr. articles to profl. jours. Home: 2405 49th St NW Washington DC 20007 Office: 2121 Pennsylvania Ave NW Washington DC 20037

CARR, VIKKI, entertainer; b. El Paso, Tex.; d. Carlos Cardona; hon. doctorates St. Edwards U., 1974, U. San Diego, 1975; m. Michael Nilsson, Aug. 18, 1979. Recorded 33 albums including One Hell of a Woman, 1975; appeared in nightclubs throughout U.S., Europe, Mexico, Japan; appeared in every major network variety show including Dean Martin Show, Ed Sullivan Show, Carol Burnett Show, Bob Hope show, Tonight Show. Pres., Vikki Carr Scholarship Found.; v.p. Muscular Dystrophy Assn., 1973-78; nat. chmn. Am. Lung Assn., 1975-76. Named Woman of Year, Los Angeles Times, 1970. Office: Care of Personal Mgr Arnold Mills & Assos 8721 Sunset Blvd Los Angeles CA 90069

CARRAGHER, AUDREY ANN, state legislator; b. Jamaica Plain, Mass., Jan. 27, 1924; d. Daniel Joseph and Frances Louise (Wright) McLeod; R.N., Faulkner Hosp., 1945; postgrad. Northeastern U., 1968-76; B.Gen. Studies, U. N.H., 1978, postgrad., 1979; m. John C. Carragher, Nov. 11, 1947; children—John C., Janice, Daniel, Lawrence. Library trustee, mem. Bicentennial Commn., 1974; mem. New Eng. Bd. Library Trustees, 1975; chmn. Chelmsford Hist. Commn., 1975; mem. Growth Policy Commn., 1976; student rep. Lifelong Learning Council U. N.H., 1977; planner Nashua (N.H.) Human Services Council, 1978; mem. county Adv. Council on Aging, 1979; mem. N.H. Ho. of Reps., 1980—, mem. exec. dept. com., adminstrn. com., constl. revision com., subcom. chmn. for state reapportionment and for children and youth legis. Pres. Chelmsford Friends of Library, 1973, Republican Women's Club of Nashua, 1980-82; bd. dirs. N.H. Sch. Vols., 1980-81; mem. State Conf. on Aging-Social Services, 1981; v.p. N.H. Fedn. Rep. Women, 1981—; mem. Nat. Fedn. Rep. Women, Nashua Fedn. Rep. Women; pres. Nashua Friends of Library, 1982; active ARC Blood Bank, 1970-82. Served with Cadet Nurses Corps, 1945. Mem. Nat. Order Women Legislators, N.H. Order Women Legislators. Roman Catholic. Clubs: Vesper Country, Women's Guild of Parish, Dartmouth Coll. Women's, Nashaway Women's. Office: Legislative Office Bldg Concord NH 03301

CARRINGTON, JOY HARRELL, artist; b. Jacksonville, Tex.; d. Benjamin G. and Mollie Elizabeth (Anderson) Harrell; student Kansas City Art Inst., 1924-26, Am. Acad. Art, Chgo., 1927, Nat. Acad. Art, 1928, Chgo. Art Inst., 1946, Art Students League, 1948-51, Phoenix Sch. Design, N.Y.C., 1950-51; m. William Lorrin Carrington, Sept. 20, 1934. Comml. artist Montgomery Ward & Co., Kansas City, Mo., Ft. Worth and Chgo., 1925-28; staff artist Hartman Furniture, Chgo., 1928-29; free-lance artist Bloomingdales, N.Y.C., Frank Bros., San Antonio Public Co., 1931-34; artist Handelan & Staff Shoe Agy., Chgo., 1935-36; one-woman shows include: Jr. League Art Center, Tyler, Tex., 1962, Witte Meml. Mus., San Antonio, 1963, Meinhard Galleries, Houston, 1973, St. Marys U., San Antonio, 1964; group shows include: Witte Meml. Mus., 1958-66, McNamara-O'Connor Hist. and Fine Arts Mus., Victoria, Tex., 1968, U. Tex., San Antonio, 1976-77, Am. Artists Profl. League, N.Y.C., 1969-80, Panhandle Plains Mus., Canyon, Tex., 1960-80, Meinhard Galleries, 1970-75, Coppini Acad. Fine Arts, San Antonio, 1955-80; represented in permanent collections: Long Barrack Mus., Alamo, San Antonio, State Capitol Bldg., Austin, Tex.; illuminated Meml. book First Meth. Ch., Jacksonville, Tex.; illuminated manuscript Daus. of Republic of Tex. Library, Coppini Acad. Fine Arts, San Antonio; bicentennial illumination DAR; lectr., tchr. Vol. therapist Kerrville (Tex.) State Home. Recipient Coppini Acad. award Witte Meml. Mus., San Antonio, 1958, 65; Grumbacher award Am. Artists Profl. League, 1969; San Antonio Watercolor award U. Tex., 1976; cert. of appreciation Vol. Council of Kerrville State Home. Mem. Nat. Soc. Arts and Letters, Am. Artists Profl. League, Coppini Acad. Fine Arts, San Antonio Watercolor Group. Club: Kerrville Art. Home: T-Anchor Ranch Route 16 Box 30 Medina TX 78055

CARRINGTON, JUDITH, interior designer, TV producer; b. N.Y.C., Dec. 3, 1939; d. John Claiborne and Elizabeth (Meusebach) Carrington; student Vassar Coll., 1958-60; B.A., N.Y. U., 1962; postgrad. in environ. design Parsons Sch. Design; children by previous marriage—Claiborne Marshall, Blair Marshall; m. 2d, Bernard Green, Jan. 22, 1976; 1 son, Tyler Green. Publicity aide Farrar, Straus & Giroux, N.Y.C., 1962-65; owner, operator Judith Carrington/Interiors, N.Y.C., 1965—, partner, 1976—; producer design series cable TV, N.Y.C., 1976-79; environ. interviewer Sta. WOR; mktg. and communications cons. Haas Group, N.Y.C., 1978-80; account exec. Siesel Co., Inc. Community rep. Hist. Dists. Council, 1972-74. Mem. Allied Bd. Trade, Nat. Fedn. Local Cable Programmers (founder N.Y. chpt.). Episcopalian. Home and Office: 1136 Fifth Ave New York NY 10028

CARROLL, DIAHANN, actress, singer; b. N.Y.C., July 17, 1935; d. John and Mabel (Faulk) Johnson; student N.Y. U. Began career as model; actress motion pictures including: Carmen Jones, Porgy and Bess, Hurry Sundown, Paris Blues, Claudine; on Broadway in House of Flowers, No Strings, Agnes of God, 1982; appeared in play Same Time, Next Year; TV series Julia; appeared in made for TV movie Sister, Sister, 1982. Nominated for Acad. award as best actress (Claudine) Acad. Motion Picture Arts and Scis., 1974. Address: care Roy Gerber 9200 Sunset Blvd Los Angeles CA 90069 *

CARROLL, EDITH BANE, polit. worker; b. Wadsworth, Ohio, June 15, 1930; d. Walter and Mary (Cahill) Bane; student Wittenberg U., 1948-50, UCLA, 1954; m. Patrick Colin Carroll, Mar. 9, 1952; children—Michael Walter, Lisa Ann. Exec. sec. to Maj. Gen. D. H. Baker, comptroller Wright Patterson AFB, Ohio, 1951-53, Dr. Sorenson, Calif. Inst. Tech., 1953-54; with Heritage High Sch., Littleton, Colo., 1974. Mem. budget review com. Littleton Sch. Dist., 1971; pres. PTO, 1967-68; block worker Republican Party, 1967—; Rep. committeewoman Precinct 502, Littleton, Colo., 1967—; sec. Colo. Rep. State Conv., 1974; mem. Arapahoe County Rep. Exec. Com., 1975-80; pres. Littleton Rep. Women's Club, 1975-77; chmn. Pres. Ford Vols., Arapahoe County, 1976; mem. Colo. Rep. State Exec. Com., 1977; chmn. 22nd Senatorial Dist. Colo. Rep. Party, 1979—; vice chmn. Arapahoe County Rep. Party, 1977-81. Mem. Colo. Fedn. Rep. Women (chmn. public relations 1976—, bd. dirs. 1976—). Address: 6775 S Penrose Ct Littleton CO 80122

CARROLL, FRANCES LAVERNE, educator; b. Scammon, Kans., Dec. 6, 1925; d. Robert Allen and Truda Hilda (Flanagan) Carroll; B.S., Kans. State Tchrs. Coll., 1948; M.A., U. Denver, 1956; postgrad. Western Res. U., 1957; Ph.D., U. Okla., 1970. Bank bookkeeper Baxter Springs Bank (Kans.), 1944; tchr. English and journalism high sch., Caney, Kans., 1947-49; librarian Field Kindley Meml. High Sch., Coffeyville, Kans., 1949-54; librarian Coffeyville Jr. Coll., 1954-62, supr. elem. sch. libraries, 1957-62; asst. prof. library sci. U. Okla., Norman, 1962-67, asso. prof., 1971-75, prof., 1975—, acting dir. sch. library sci., 1974-75; head library studies Nedlands Coll. Advanced Edn. (formerly Western Australian Secondary Tchrs. Coll.), Perth, 1977-81; guest lectr. Drexel Inst. Tech., Phila., 1964, U. London, 1972, Pahlavi U., Shiraz, Iran, 1976; dir. U.S. Office Edn. Inst., 1966, 67, 69. U.S. Office Edn. grantee, 1969. Mem. AAUW, AAUP, Internat. Assn. Sch. Librarians, ALA, Internat. Relations Round Table (chmn. membership 1970-74), Internat. Fedn. Library Assns. (chmn. sect. sch. libraries 1973-77), Southwestern, Okla. library assns., Delta Kappa Gamma, Phi Delta Kappa, Beta Phi Mu. Author: (with Mary Meacham) The Library at Mount Vernon, 1977; (with Pat Beilke) Guidelines for the Planning and Organization of School Library Media Centers, 1979; nat. series editor Reading for Young People, 1979—, Recent Advances in School Librarianship, 1981; contbr. articles to profl. jours. Office: 401 W Brooks St Norman OK 73019

CARROLL, JANE ELIZABETH, packaging co. mgr.; b. New Rochelle, N.Y., Aug. 20, 1946; d. Paul Bertrand and Ann Joyce (Cramer) C.; A.B. in History, Boston Coll., 1968; M.B.A., Iona Coll., 1976; m. Donald R. Trojan, June 4, 1977. Tchr., Boston Public Schs., 1968-69; systems analyst Am. Can Co., Greenwich, Conn., 1970-73; adminstr. nat. accounts, 1976-77, mgr. mktg. services Dixie/Marathon div., 1978—. Bd. dirs. Arbors Assn., 1979—; sec.-treas. Rye Town/King Civic Assn., 1979—. Mem. Nat. Assn. Female Execs., Am. Mgmt. Assn., Women in Mgmt. Home: Flora Pl Stamford CT 06903 Office: American Ln Greenwich CT 06830

CARROLL, JEANNE (MRS. HAROLD M. KASS), public relations exec.; b. Oak Park, Ill., May 20, 1929; d. John P. and Mary (Noonan) Carroll; B.A., U. London, 1950; M.A., Northwestern U., 1951; m. Harold M. Kass, Apr. 1966. Bus. girls editor Charm Mag., N.Y.C., 1951-53; public relations dir. Rosary Coll., River Forest, Ill., 1953-66; chmn. publicity Am. Cancer Soc., bd. dirs. W. and S.W. Suburban Unit, 1967—; med. adminstr., asst. to Dr. Harold Kass, Oak Park, Ill., 1969—. Public relations counselor in Midwest for Brown U., 1962; dir. public relations Mundelein Coll., 1968; producer radio show for teen-agers, Chgo., 1954; lectr. sci. devels. Bell Labs. for AT&T, 1954; participant annual Sun-Times seminars for coll. journalists MacMurray Coll., Jacksonville Ill. Chmn., March of Dimes campaign for Chgo., ednl. TV Channel 11, River Forest, 1963; bd. trustees DePaul U., Chgo., chmn. Soc. Fellows dinner; chmn. Oak Park Hosp. Ben Din Dan, 1971-80; mem. com. library Internat. Relations, 1975-82. Recipient Excellence award for coll. brochures Am. Coll. Pubs. Com., 1957; medal of recognition for work in public relations Bishop Fulton Sheen, 1960; Humanitarian award Performing Arts Center and Citizens Com., Chgo., 1976. Mem. Ill. Assn. Coll. Admissions Counsellors (pres.), Assn. Coll. Public Relations Assn., Family Service Assn. Am. (past dir.), Acad. Hosp., Public Relations, Ill. (pres.), Chgo. (public relations dir.), med. soc. auxs. Address: 712 Courtland Circle Springdale Western Springs IL 60558 Office: 715 Lake St Oak Park IL 60301

CARROLL, LISA, Psychologist; b. Pt. Arthur, Tex., Feb. 6, 1954; d. Charles Bryant and Joyce (Rather) C.; B.S., Lamar U., 1975, M.S. with honors, 1977. Adminstr. neuropsychol. tests, condr. group therapy dept. neuropsychiatry, pvt. practice psychol. group, Beaumont, Tex., 1976—; psychol. evaluator various agys. Mem. Am. Psychol. Assn., Tex. Psychol. Assn., SE Tex. Psychol. Assn., Alpha Lambda Delta. Democrat. Home: 2318 12th St Port Neches TX 77651 Office: 3240 Fannin Beaumont TX 77701

CARROLL, LOIS MAE, nurse; b. Scranton, Pa., Oct. 29, 1929; d. Robert George and Mae Fietta (Richards) Fenstermacher; R.N., L.I. Sch. Nursing, Southampton, 1951; B.S. in Nursing, U. Ala., 1976, M.A., 1978; m. Joseph C. Carroll, Jan. 13, 1950; children—Joseph, Jeffrey, Robert. Staff nurse Crestwood Hosp., Huntsville, Ala., 1966-70; supr. occupational health Dunlop Tire & Rubber Co., Huntsville, 1970-78; student health coordinator No. Va. Community Coll., Manassas, 1978—, also chmn. coll. health and safety com.; CPR and first aid instr. Mem. Am. Assn. Occupational Health Nurses, Am. Coll. Health Assn., Bus. and Profl. Women's Club (dist. dir. 1973), Manassas Olde Town Assn., Alpha Lambda Delta. Republican. Unitarian. Home: 9301 Grant Ave Manassas VA 22110 Office: 6901 Sudley Rd Manassas VA 22110

CARROLL, LYNDA LOU, fine art dealer, fashion designer; b. Kansas City, Mo., Jan. 6, 1941; d. Frank and Marteen (Council) Bean; student Kansas City Community Coll., 1966-67, U. Mo., Kansas City, 1967-68; m. R. Barnes, 1957 (div.); Carroll, Nov. 23, 1968 (div. 1982); children—Sandi Quenelle, Michael Carroll, Audrey Harris, Timothy Carroll, Buddy Carroll, Erin Carroll, Nikki Carroll. Free-lance fashion model, 1964-67; owner, designer Genuine Article Boutique, Kansas City, Mo., 1967-68; purchasing agt., trouble shooter Hagemann & Webb Interiors, Kansas City, 1968-71; office supr. Insured Accounts Co., Kansas City, 1979-80; owner, mgr. Carroll Collection, Kansas City, 1980—; designed gowns/costumes for Miss Mo./USA, Miss Kans./USA, Miss Nebr./USA, 1982; lectr. fine art and antique prints; tchr. in decorating with fine art. Officer, Lee's Summit (Mo.) Jaycee Wives, 1975-76; bd. dirs. Lee's Summit Jaycee Bicentennial Com., 1976; mem. Starlight Women's Com., Kansas City, Mo., Independence (Mo.) Neighborhood Council; mem. spl. events com. Gillis Home for Children, Kansas City, Mo., 1980. Recipient New Bus. of Yr. award Sta. KMBC, Kansas City, 1968, Women in Bus. award Squire Publs., Kansas City, 1981. Mem. Nat. Assn. Female Execs. (network dir.), Soc. Profl. and Exec. Women, Waldo Area Bus. Assn., Art Dealers Assn. Am., Antique Dealers Am. Home: 326 N Cedar Independence MO 64053 Office: 200 W 74th Terr Kansas City MO 64114

CARROLL, MARGUERITE RUTH, educator; b. Medford, Mass., June 25, 1926; d. Harry Anthony and Rose (Melanson) C.; B.S., Boston U., 1947; M.Ed., Boston Coll., 1954; Ed.D., St. John's U., 1974. Tchr., Great Mills (Md.) High Sch., 1947-51; dir. guidance Ware (Mass.) High Sch., 1953-54; sch. counselor North Jr. High Sch., Waltham, Mass., 1954-58, Darien (Conn.) High Sch., 1958-64; dir. guidance Weston (Conn.) Public Schs., 1964-68; asst. prof. Fairfield (Conn.) U. Grad. Sch. Edn., 1969-75, asso. prof., 1975-81, prof., 1981—, dept. chmn. div. counseling and sch. psychology, 1972-75, coordinator Tomorrow's Woman Today program div. counseling and commmunity services, 1975-78. Bd. dirs. Woman Place, Darien, 1974-77. Mem. Am. Sch. Counselor Assn. (treas. 1969-70, nat. cons. task force group procedures 1969-71), Conn. Sch. Counselor Assn. (pres. 1967-68), Am. Psychol. Assn., Am. Personnel and Guidance Assn. (chmn. bd. jour. editors, mem. research awards com. 1971-72, media com. 1979—), Conn. Personnel and Guidance Assn., Fairfield County Personnel and Guidance Assn. (pres. 1962-63), New Eng. Guidance Conf. (exec. com. 1968-70), Assn. Counselor Edn. and Supervision (chmn. licensure research com. 1975-76), Conn. Assn. Counselor Edn. and Supervision (pres. 1978-79), Assn. Specialists in Group Work (sec. 1976-77, senator 1977-79, publs. chmn. 1977-78, pres.-elect 1982), New Eng. Assn. Specialists in Group Work (pres. 1979-81). Asso. editor: The School Counselor, 1971-72, editor, 1972-81; poetry editor Jour. for Humanistic Education and Development, 1982—; editorial bd. Counseling and Human Development, 1982—. Home: 9 Longview Dr Ridgefield CT 06877 Office: Fairfield Univ Fairfield CT 06430

CARROLL, MARY JOSEPHINE, speech pathologist; b. Buffalo, Feb. 22, 1948; d. John Patrick and Katherine Ann C.; B.A., Rosary Hill Coll., 1970; M.A., SUNY, Buffalo, 1975. Service adv. N.Y. Tel. Co., N.Y.C., 1970-73; trainee Buffalo VA Hosp., 1974; div. head speech pathology services Mercy Hosp., Buffalo, 1975—; adj. instr. SUNY, Buffalo, 1979—; instr. Literacy Vols. Western N.Y. Office Edn. grantee, 1974-75. Mem. Speech and Hearing Assn. Western N.Y., Am. Speech, Lang. and Hearing Assn., AAUW, Pi Gamma Mu. Roman Catholic. Home: 241 Lamont Dr Amherst NY 14226 Office: 565 Abbott Rd Buffalo NY 14220

CARROLL, MAURA, state legislator; b. Concord, N.H., Mar. 30, 1956; d. Charles Thomas and Arlene Elizabeth (Byrne) C.; B.A., Coll. Holy Cross, 1979. Field coordinator Carter/Mondale Pres. Com., 1979-80; clk. Orr and Reno, 1981, paralegal, 1981—; mem. N.H. Ho. of Reps., 1976—, chmn. pensions com., 1979-82, asst. minority leader, 1981-82. Bd. dirs. Community Services Council, Opportunity House; sec. N.H. Democratic State Com., 1981-82. Named Young Career Woman, Bus. and Profl. Women's Club. Democrat. Roman Catholic. Office: 95 N Main St Concord NH 03301

CARROLL, NINA JANNETTE (JENNIFER MOORE), TV journalist; b. Bethlehem, Pa., May 27, 1950; d. Robert Albright and Nancy Jannette (Bahnsen) Brunell; B.A., Pa. State U., 1972; m. Michael Carroll, Sept. 28, 1974; 1 son, Michael Adain. Announcer-reporter Sta. WHLQ-FM, Canton, Ohio, 1973-75; reporter, anchorwoman Sta. WJR, Detroit, 1976-78; co-anchorwoman, bus. editor Sta. WDIV-TV, Detroit, 1979—. Hon. chmn. Detroit Cystic Fibrosis Assn., 1982. Recipient Detroit Emmy award, 1979, citation of distinction Martin S. Gainsbrugh Found., 1980, Mich. UPI award investigative reporting, 1980; named Broadcast Woman of Year, Detroit chpt. Am. Women in Radio and TV, 1978. Mem. Women in Communications, Am. Women in Radio and TV, Sigma Delta Chi. Office: 622 W Lafayette St Detroit MI 48034

CARROLL, PAT, actress; b. Shreveport, La., May 5, 1927; d. Maurice Clifton and Kathryn Angela (Meagher) C.; student Immaculate Heart Coll., 1944-47, Catholic U., 1950; Litt.D. (hon.), Barry Coll., Miami, Fla., 1969; children—Sean, Kerry, Tara. Profl. debut in stock prodn. with Gloria Swanson in A Goose for the Gander, 1947; supper club debut at Le Ruban Bleu, N.Y.C., 1950; appeared on numerous television shows, 1950—, including Red Buttons Show, 1951, Caesar's Hour (Emmy award), 1956-57, Danny Thomas Show, 1961-63, Busting Loose, 1977; Broadway debut in Catch a Star (Tony award), 1955; appeared in motion picture With Six You Get Eggroll, 1968; producer, actress Gertrude Stein Gertrude Stein Gertrude Stein for colls. and univs., 1979—, The Last Resort, 1979; pres. Sea-Ker, Inc., Beverly Hills, Calif., 1979—; bd. dirs. Hyde Park Theatre, N.Y.C. Mem. Dist. Atty.'s Citizens Adv. Com., Los Angeles, 1970-75; pres. Center of Films for Children, 1971-73; bd. regents Immaculate Heart Coll., Hollywood, Calif., 1970. Mem. Actors Studio, Actors Fund (life), Actors Equity Assn., Screen

Actors Guild, AFTRA, Acad. Television Arts and Scis. (trustee 1958-59), Am. Youth Hostel (life), Del. and Hudson Canal Hist. Soc., George Heller Meml. Found. Address: care Janice S Morgan 301 W 53d St New York NY 10019 *

CARROLL, ROSILYN MARIE, state edn. specialist; b. St. Paul, Apr. 18, 1950; d. Roland III and Thelma Carroll; B.A. in Sociology, Jamestown Coll., 1971; postgrad. U. Minn., Mpls., 1973-77, 79—. Coordinator, Am. Youth Assn., Wiesbaden, W.Ger., 1971-72; cons. cross cultural curriculum St. Paul Open Sch., 1972-73; investigator compliance, Minn. Dept. Human Rights, St. Paul, 1973-75, coordinator, 1975-76, research analyst, 1976-77; employment rep., dept. personnel U. Minn., Mpls., 1977-78; sales asso. Cushing & Driscoll Real Estate, St. Paul, 1978-79; edn. specialist II, Minn. Dept. Edn., St. Paul, 1979—; condr. numerous workshops on sex equity, affirmative action, desegregation, multicultural edn., human relations, employment and personnel practices; condr. workshops for Greater St. Croix Valley, N.Y. Council Girl Scouts U.S.A.; condr. seminars, camp dir. YWCA; lectr. St. Catherine's Coll., 1979-81, U. Minn., 1979-80. Mem. St. Paul Sch. Bd., 1976—, pres., 1977-78, com. chairwoman, 1977—; chairwoman Citizen Participation Com., St. Paul, 1976-77, Citizen Participation Negotiating Team with St. Paul City Council and Mayor, 1977; mem. Dist. 8 Planning Council, St. Paul City Council, 1977-79; pres. St. Peter Claver Sch. Bd., St. Paul, 1980—; mem. St. Paul-Mpls. Mayors' Task Force on Govt. Fin., 1981—; chairwoman Democratic Farm Labor Precinct Caucus, St. Paul, 1981—. Recipient Spl. Recognition, Congl. Black Caucus Ann. Conf., 1979; Tchrs. Tng. fellow, 1973-76. Mem. Nat. Sch. Bds. Assn. (conf. chairperson Desegregation of 80's Clinic 1980), Minn. Sch. Bds. Assn. (condr. conv. workshops 1980), Am. Assn. Sch. Adminstrs., Nat. Assn. Black Sch. Educators, Assn. County, State and Mcpl. Employees, Minn. Affirmative Action Assn., Nat. Assn. Female Execs., NAACP. Roman Catholic. Home: 924 Hague Ave Saint Paul MN 55104 Office: 550 Cedar St Saint Paul MN 55101

CARROLL, SUSAN ANN, business exec.; b. Seattle, Jan. 5, 1945; d. Weaver and Fern (Ross) Berkman; student Grays Harbor Jr. Coll., 1963-64, U. Puget Sound, 1965, Inst. for Orgn. Mgmt., U. Santa Clara, 1969-70; grad. Pacific Floral Inst., 1978; m. David Carroll; 1 dau., Jennifer. Adminstrv. asst. King County Med. Soc., Seattle, 1968-69, exec. asst., 1969-70, acting dir., 1970-74; assoc. dir. program adminstrn. Wash. State PSRO, 1974-79; owner Country Garden, 1979—. Mem. Greenpeace, Sierra Club. Home: 18625 NE 146th Way Woodinville WA 98072

CARRON, MILDRED LOUISE FRANK, civic worker; b. Detroit, May 6, 1920; d. Maxwell Nathaniel and Annette Kathryn (Harris) Frank; B.A., Wayne State U., 1943; m. Dean Philip Carron, Mar. 26, 1944; children—Neil Allan, Susan Helen, David Frank, Barbara. Substitute tchr., public schs., Detroit, 1943-44; bd. dirs. Washtenaw County Child and Family Service, 1971-77; pres. Mich. Med. Soc. Aux., 1979-80; mem. state extention council, family living edn. Mich. State U.; mem. Mich. br. bd. Women's League, United Synagogue of Am., 1961-69; trustee Ann Arbor Public Schs. Dina Kahn Meml. Fund, 1968—. Named Woman of Yr., Sisterhood of Beth Israel Synagogue, 1967. Mem. Am. Contract Bridge League (life master 1982). Republican. Jewish. Address: Ann Arbor MI 48103

CARROS, CATHERINE FRITTS, educator; b. Batavia, N.Y., Sept. 15, 1955; d. William Russel and Barbara (Beadle) Fritts; B.S., Syracuse U., 1977; M.S., Coll. of St. Rose, Albany, 1981; m. Mark Vincent Carros, Aug. 16, 1980. Tchr. kindergarten, Schenectady Schs., 1977-78; tchr. handicapped, Berne, Knox, Westerlo, N.Y., 1978-81; prevocat. resource tchr. Saratoga (N.Y.) Schs., 1981-82; tchr. handicapped Schuylerville (N.Y.) Central Sch., 1982—. Mem. Council on Exceptional Children, N.Y. Assn. Learning Disabilities, Concerned Parents and Profls. Democrat. Quaker. Home: 5 Frederick Dr Saratoga Springs NY 12866

CARR-RUFFINO, NORMA J., bus. educator; b. Ft. Worth, Dec. 15, 1932; d. Robert Leroy and Lorene (Dickeson) Carr; B.B.A., Tex. Wesleyan U., 1968; M.B.E., N. Tex. State U., 1969, Ph.D., 1973; m. Alfred Ruffino, Jan. 6, 1979; children by previous marriage—Randy, Brian, Carrie. Vice pres. Randy's, Inc., Ft. Worth, 1965-72; vocat. office educator coordinator Ft. Worth Public Schs., 1969-72; asso. prof. bus. San Francisco State U., 1973—; mgmt. cons., 1972—. Mem. Am. Bus. Communication Assn., Internat. Soc. Bus. Educators, Adminstrv. Mgmt. Soc., Internat. Communication Assn., Nat. Bus. Edn. Assn., Western Bus. Edn. Assn., Calif. Bus. Edn. Assn., Delta Pi Epsilon. Author: Theory Reinforcement and Skill Building, 2d edit., 1981; Writing Short Business Reports, 1980; The Promotable Woman, 1982. Editor Calif. Bus. Edn. Assn. Jour., 1975-76. Home: 1414 Alameda de las Pulgas San Mateo CA 94402 Office: Sch Bus San Francisco State U 1600 Holloway St San Francisco CA 94132

CARSEY, MARCIA PETERSON, broadcasting co. exec.; b. South Weymouth, Mass., Nov. 21, 1944; d. John Edwin and Rebecca White (Simonds) Peterson; B.A. in English Lit., U. N.H., 1966; m. John Jay Carsey, Apr. 12, 1969; children—Rebecca P., John P. Prodn. asst. Tonight Show, NBC, N.Y.C., 1966-68; program supr. William Esty Advt., N.Y.C., 1968-69; exec. story editor Tomorrow Entertainment, Los Angeles, 1971-74; program exec. ABC, Los Angeles, 1974-76, v.p. comedy and variety programs, 1976-77, sr. v.p. comedy and variety programs, 1977-79, sr. v.p. prime time series, 1979-80; co-founder Carsey-Werner Co., West Los Angeles, TV series, film devel. and prodn., 1981—. Office: 1130 Westwood Blvd West Los Angeles CA 90024

CARSON, BONNIE L(OU), chemist; b. Kansas City, Kans., Aug. 11, 1940; d. Harold Lee and Lorene Marie (Draper) Bachert; student U. Kansas City, 1958-61; B.A. in Chemistry summa cum laude, U. N.H., 1963; M.S. in Organic Chemistry, Oreg. State U., 1966; m. David M. Carson, June, 1961 (div. 1973); 1 dau., Catherine (Katie) Leslie. Grad. teaching asst. Oreg. State U., 1963-66; organic chem. lab. instr. U. Waterloo, Ont., Can., 1968-69; asst. abstractor in macromolecular chemistry Chem. Abstracts Service, Columbus, Ohio, 1969-71; freelance Russian translator, 1971-73; asst. chemist Midwest Research Inst., Kansas City, Mo., 1973-75, asso. chemist, 1975-80, sr. chemist, 1980—. Mem. Am. Soc. Info. Scientists, Am. Chem. Soc., Am. Inst. Chemists, AAAS, N.Y. Acad. Sci., Soc. Environ. Geochemistry and Health, Soc. Scholarly Pub., Am. Translators Assn. Author and Editor: (with others) Trace Metals in the Environment, 1977-81; contbr. in field. Home: 5501 Holmes St Kansas City MO 64110 Office: 425 Volker Blvd Kansas City MO 64110

CARSON, CAROL FRANCES, psychologist; b. Lakewood, Ohio, Feb. 12, 1950; d. Sylvester and Madelyn Frances (Melson) C.; B.S., Middle Tenn. State U., 1971; M.S., U. Ky., 1973, Ph.D., 1976; m. James Warren Hicks, May 31, 1975. Coordinator spl. edn. Bourbon County Schs., Paris, Ky., 1976-77; sch. psychologist Ky. Dept. Edn., Frankfort, 1977-78; pvt. practice as sch. psychologist, Central and No. Ky., Newport, 1976—; due process coordinator Newport City Schs., 1978-80, sch. psychologist/due process, 1980-81; cons. Bur. Edn. Exceptional Children, Ky. Dept. Edn. asso. advocate Citizens Advocacy Program of No. Ky., 1981—. Bd. dirs. Citizens Advocacy Program, 1982—. Mem. Am. Psychol. Assn., Southeastern Psychol. Assn., Ky. Psychol. Assn. (task force on sch. psychology, 1976-77, asst. editor Ky. Psychologist 1981), Ky. Assn. Psychology in the Schs. (treas. 1978-79), Council Exceptional Children, Nat. Assn. Sch. Psychologists, Bluegrass Area Task Group for Children With Emotional Problems. Methodist. Editorial cons. Jour. Cons. and Clin. Psychology, 1978. Home: 612 Rosemont Ave Park Hills KY 41011

CARSON, CLARICE, soprano; b. Montreal, Que., Can., Dec. 23, 1939; d. Philip and Regina (Singer) Katz; came to U.S., 1977; student Sir George Williams U.; children—Melanie Ornstein, Neil Ornstein. Appeared with Met. Opera Nat. Co., 1966, Met. Opera, 1967, Chgo. Lyric Opera, 1969, Gran Teatro de Liceo, Barcelona, Spain, 1970-71, Scottish Opera, 1970, Vancouver, Edmonton and Toronto operas, 1970—, Houston Grand Opera, 1973, 76, Netherlands Opera, Dehinsop, 1977, San Francisco Opera, 1977. Washington Opera, 1977, also Torno Reggio Bordeaux Opera, Los Angeles Philharmonic, Montreal Symphony, Toronto Symphony, Rotterdam Philharmonic, Israel Philharmonic, Ravinia Festival, Robin Hood Dell, Temple U. Festival, Schwenigen Festival, Caramoor and Stratford Festival; pres. Clarice Carson Enterprises, Inc. Mem. Canadian Actors Equity.

CARSON, HELEN SUE, chem. co. exec.; b. Stamford, Tex., June 24, 1943; d. George Rupert and Lottie Pearl (Hanson) Raley; B.S. in Chemistry and Math., Wayland Bapt. Coll., Plainview, Tex., 1971; postgrad. Eastern N.Mex. U.; m. W. Richard Carson, Sept. 3, 1961; children—William Wayne, Misti Beth. Lab. instr. chemistry Wayland Bapt. Coll., 1969-71; high sch. tchr., Dexter, N.Mex., 1971-72; chemist Champion Chem. Co., Houston, 1973; with Amoco Chem. Corp., Houston, 1974—, research chemist product devel. and tech. service, corrosion inhibitors, 1979-80, sr. research chemist corrosion inhibitors, 1980, product specialist internat. oil production chems., 1981, product specialist internat. oil chems., 1981—. Mem. Nat. Assn. Corrosion Engrs. (tech. coms.), Am. Bus. Women's Assn. (Bay Area Am. Bus. Woman of Yr. award 1980), Assn. Female Execs., Soc. Petroleum Engrs., Beta Sigma Phi (pres. 1975-76, Girl of Yr. award 1976). Republican. Author, patentee in field. Home: 207 Parliament St Houston TX 77034 Office: 5450 NW Central Dr Houston TX 77040

CARSON, KATHRYN SINCLAIR, banker; b. N.Y.C., Jan. 18, 1947; d. John Howard and Helen (Fiesel) Carson; B.S., Appalachian State U., 1969; M.M.C., U. S.C., 1978. Tchr., Charlotte (N.C.) public schs., 1969-72; grad. asst. U. S.C., Columbia, 1972-73; dir. info. Columbia Coll., 1973-76; mgr. external communications S.C. Edn. Assn., Columbia, 1976-77; asst. v.p. public relations First Nat. Bank of S.C., Columbia, 1977—. Mem. Central Midlands Regional Commn. Transp. adv. com., 1981—; mem. Downtown Action Club, Central Bus. Alliance, 1981. Mem. Public Relations Soc. Am., (chpt. v.p. 1982—), Kappa Tau Alpha. Democrat. Roman Catholic. Address: PO Box 111 Columbia SC 29202

CARSON, LILLIAN G., psychotherapist; b. N.Y.C., Mar. 22, 1933; d. Joseph and Helen E. (Tucker) Gershenson; B.A., UCLA, 1968, M.S.W., 1970, D.S.W., 1979; m. Ralph Carson, July 19, 1978; children by previous marriage—Susan Gevirtz, Steven Gevirtz, Carrie Gevirtz. Psychotherapist parent-infant consultation program, dept. child psychiatry Cedars Sinai Hosp., Los Angeles, 1970; dir. counseling Zahm Sch. Individual Edn., Los Angeles, 1970-72; dir. clinic Los Angeles Psychoanalytic Soc., 1972—; pvt. practice psychotherapy, Los Angeles, 1970—; case supr. So. Calif. Counseling Center; instr. Calif. State Mental Health Tng. Center; cons. Santa Monica Child Devel. Centers; mem. exec. com., sec.-treas. Psychiat. Med. Group So. Calif., 1973-74; mem. profl. bd. Los Angeles County Mental Health Assn., 1974; bd. dirs. Friends of UCLA Child Care Services, 1981; mem. adv. council Los Angeles Child Devel. Center, 1981; staff mem. Westwood Psychiat. Hosp.; invited guest 20th birthday celebration meetings Hempstead Clinic, London, 1972, participant seminar by Anna Freud, 1978. Lic. clin. social worker, Calif. Mem. Nat. Assn. Social Workers, Acad. Cert. Social Workers, Calif. Soc. Clin. Social Work (nominating com. 1974-77), Am. Orthopsychiat. Assn., Center Improvement of Child Caring, Nat. Assn. Edn. of Young Children. Research in parenting and preschool children. Office: 11665 W Olympic Blvd Los Angeles CA 90064

CARSON, PAMELA, restauranteur, promoter; b. Springfield, Mass., Apr. 29, 1944; d. Parker Cooke and Earla (Rowley) C.; student Skidmore Coll., 1962-65; B.A., U. Denver, 1966. Mem. market research dept. Procter & Gamble Co., Cin., 1967-68; promoter Nat. Antiques Show, N.Y.C., 1969-70; pres., founder Boston Flea Market, Inc., 1971—; pres. Phila. Flea Market, Inc., 1972-74; pres., founder, Friends & Co. Restaurant, Boston, 1977—; owner Cash Conv. Cons. Co.; promoter Lifestyles Show, Boston, 1982. Office: 199 State St Boston MA 02109

CARSTEN, ARLENE DESMET, orgn. exec.; b. Paterson, N.J., Dec. 5, 1937; d. Albert F. and Ann (Greutert) Desmet; student Alfred U., 1955-56; m. Alfred John Carsten, Feb. 11, 1956; children—Christopher Dale, Jonathan Glenn. Piano tchr., 1964-71; exec. dir. Inst. for Burn Medicine, San Diego, 1972-81, mem. bd., 1981—. chief fin. officer A.J. Carsten Co., San Diego, 1981—; dir. Nat. Burn Fedn., 1975—. Organizer, mem. numerous community groups; chmn. San Diego County Mental Health Adv. Bd., 1972-74, mem., 1971-75; chmn. community relations subcom., mem. exec. com. Emergency Med. Services Com., San Diego, Riverside and Imperial Counties, 1973-75; pub. mem. psychology exam. com. Calif. Bd. Med. Quality Assurance, 1976-80, chmn., 1977; San Diego County Bd. Suprs. rep. Health Services Agy. Governing Body, 1980-81. Mem. Calif. Democratic State Central Com., 1968-74, exec. com., 1971-72, 73-74; mem. San Diego Dem. County Central Com., 1970-76, treas., 1972-74; chmn. edn. for legislation com. women's div. So. Calif. Dem. Com., 1972; dir. Muskie for Pres. Campaign, San Diego, 1972; councilwoman City of DelMar, Calif., 1982—; organizer, dir. numerous local campaigns. Bd. dirs. San Dieguito Family Service Assn., 1969-71, San Dieguito Dem. Club, 1965-71, San Diego Mental Health Assn., 1977-79. Recipient Key Woman award Dem. Party, 1968, 72, Spl. award of recognition San Diego Soc. Clin. Psychologists, 1975, 1st Ann. Community award Belles for Mental Health, San Diego County Mental Health Assn., 1974, Alfred U. Alumni Assn. citation, 1979, Spirit of Community Service award Inst. Burn Medicine, 1982. Mem. Info. Council on Fabric Flammability, Nat. Fire Protection Assn., Am. Burn Assn., Republican Assos. Contbr. articles to profl. jours. Home: 1415 Via Alta Del Mar CA 92014 Office: 7007 Carroll Rd San Diego CA 92121

CARSTENS, PHYLLIS ANN, occupational health nurse; b. Cisco, Ill., June 16, 1936; d. Melvin Elmer and Dorothy Pearl (Evey) Long; diploma St. Joseph's Hosp. Sch. Nursing, Bloomington, Ill., 1958; m. John M. Carstens, Sept. 6, 1958. Staff nurse St. Elizabeth's Hosp., Lafayette, Ind., 1959-60; supr. phys. therapy dept. Ind. Soldiers and Sailers Hosp., West Lafayette, 1960; nursing service St. Joseph's Hosp., 1960-61; occupational health nurse Ill. Agrl. Assn., Bloomington, 1961-71; occupational health nurse Gen. Telephone Co. Ill., Bloomington, 1971—; mem. adv. bd. chem. dependency unit Brokaw Hosp., 1981—; instr. CPR, ARC, 1977—. Bd. dirs. McLean County Heart Assn., 1973-78, pres., 1976-77; instr. 1st aid ARC, 1976—, bd. dirs., 1977-80; trustee Village of Downs (Ill.), 1981—; active Christian Neighbors Orgn. Cert. audiometric, spirometric technician. Mem. Am., Ill. nurses assns., Am., Ill., Central Ill. (v.p., program chmn., nominating com. chmn., dir., pres. 1980-82) assns. occupational health nurses, St. Joseph's Hosp. Alumnae Assn. Home: 307 E Dooley Ave Downs IL 61736 Office: 1312 E Empire St Bloomington IL 61701

CARTE, JEWEL LAMBERT, banker; b. Atenville, W.Va., May 13, 1936; d. Van Don and Elizabeth (Slade) Lambert; student Mountain State Coll., 1953-54; m. Donald Keith Carte, June 3, 1955. Sec., Kanawha Banking & Trust Co. N.A., Charleston, W.Va., 1955-71, trust officer, 1971-79, v.p. trust adminstrn., 1979—; publs. bd. Warner Press, Inc., Anderson, Ind., 1978. Bd. dirs. bd. ch. ext. and home missions, Ch. of God, 1973-76. Mem. Nat. Assn. Bank Women. Clubs: Mem. Order Eastern Star, Quota. Home: 507 Montrose Dr South Charleston WV 25303 Office: 107 Capitol St Charleston WV 25301 *

CARTER, ANNA CURRY (MRS. E. KEMPER CARTER), civic worker; b. Kansas City, Mo.; d. William Adams and Susan Maud (Machette) Curry; B.S., U. Mo., 1918; M.A., Columbia U., 1930; postgrad. Oxford U., (Eng.), 1935; m. E. Kemper Carter, Feb. 22, 1936 (dec. Dec. 1951); 1 son, E. Kemper (dec.). Tchr., research Kansas City Pub. Schs., 1919-21; dir. speech and dramatics Westport Jr. High Sch., Kansas City, 1921-26; dir. speech and drama S.W. High Sch., Kansas City, 1926-36. Bd. govs. Kansas City Mus. History and Sci., 1960-76; parliamentarian women's div. Kansas City Philharmonic Assn., 1954—; mem. exec. bd., mem. at large Community Children's Theatre, 1955—. Trustee Kansas City Art Inst. and Sch. of Design, Conservatory of Music, U. Mo. at Kansas City, Rockhurst Coll., Kansas City, Mo., Kansas City Philharmonic Assn., Kansas City Museum History and Sci.; hon. dir. Ch. St. Mary Aldenmanburg, Winston Churchill Meml., Fulton, Mo. Sponsor Winston Churchill Meml.; donar Lenox Hill-Skawhegan Art Projects, N.Y.C. Recipient numerous citations and awards including Skowhegan Sch. Art, Kansas City Art Inst., Rockhurst Coll., others. Hon. fellow Harry S. Truman Library Inst.; Soc. fellows William Rockhill Nelson Gallery Art. Mem. AAUW (del. nat. convs.), Alliance Francaise (parliamentarian 1974—), English Speaking Union, Pres. and Past Pres. Gen. Assembly, Sci. Pioneers, Am. Inst. Parliamentarians, ANTA, Speech Assn. Am., Alpha Phi. Baptist. Clubs: University, Woman's City, Carriage, Mission Hills Country, River, Kansas City, Rockhill Tennis; Capitol Hill (Washington). Home: Wornall Plaza 310 W 49th St Apt 507 Kansas City MO 64112

CARTER, BETSY L., mag. editor; b. N.Y.C., June 9, 1945; d. Rudy and Gerda Cohn; B.A., U. Mich., 1967; m. Malcolm Carter, Oct. 5, 1968. Editorial asst. McGraw Hill, 1967-68; editor co. mag. Am. Security & Trust Co., 1968-69; editorial asst. Atlantic Monthly, 1969-70; researcher Newsweek, N.Y.C., 1971-73, asst. editor, 1973-75, assoc. editor 1975-80; sr. editor Esquire Mag., N.Y.C., 1980-81, exec. editor, 1982—; freelance contbr. to Atlantic, Washington Post, Family Weekly. Office: 2 Park Ave New York NY 10016

CARTER, CAROLYN HOUCHIN, advt. agy. exec.; b. Louisville, Nov. 2, 1952; d. Paul Clayton and Georgia Houchin C.; B.S.J., Northwestern U., 1974, M.S.J., 1975. Asst. account exec. SSC&B Advt., Inc., N.Y.C., 1975-76, account exec., 1976-77; account exec. Grey Advt., Inc., N.Y.C., 1977-79, account supr., 1979-81, v.p., account supr., 1981-82, v.p. mgmt. supr., 1982—. Mem. March of Dimes Media Adv. Council, 1981-82. Mem. Am. Mktg. Assn., N.Y. Women in Communications, Inc. (pres. 1982-83). Office: Grey Advt Inc 777 3d Ave New York NY 10017

CARTER, CAROLYN MCCRAW, nurse, educator; b. Monessen, Pa., Nov. 25, 1932; d. Harry K. and Ruby E. McCraw; diploma St. Francis Hosp. Sch. Nursing, 1953; B.S. in Nursing, U. Pitts., 1958, M.S. in Nursing, 1966, Ph.D. in Higher Edn. Adminstrn., 1981; m. Alphonse H. Carter, May 2, 1955; 1 dau., Cynthia Susan. Staff nurse St. Francis Hosp., Pitts., 1953-54; staff nurse, head nurse, relief supr. VA Hosp., Leech Farm, Pitts., 1954-62; asst. dir. nurses Western Psychiat. Inst. and Clinic, Pitts., 1960-66; instr. Coll. Nursing, U. Cin., 1969-70, asst. prof., 1970-76, asso. prof., 1976; asst. prof. Sch. Nursing, U. Pitts., 1976-81, asso. prof., 1981—, asst. dean for student affairs and spl. projects Sch. Medicine, 1981—; cons. to U. Cin. Coll. Nursing, 1976-78, VA Hosp., 1973-76, Spl. Action Office of Drug Abuse Prevention, Exec. Office of the White House Assignment, Clark AFB, Philippines, 1973. Bd. dirs. Pa. United Way; mem. Pitts. chpt. Girl Friends. Recipient Black Achievers award Cin. Mental Health Assn., 1976. Mem. Am. Nurses Assn. (Mary Mahoney award 1976), Pa. Nurses Assn. (dir. 1977—, 1st Humanitarian award 1981), Sigma Theta Tau, Chi Eta Phi, Alpha Kappa Alpha. Democrat. Clubs: Churchill Women's, 21, Jack & Jill. Home: 2016 Garrick Dr Pittsburg PA 15235 Office: Univ of Pittsburgh School Medicine M247 Scaife Hall Victoria St Pittsburgh PA 15261

CARTER, CHARLENE ANN, clin. psychologist; b. Marshall, Mich., Apr. 7, 1941; d. Charles and Eva (Hesling) Hampton; B.A. cum laude, Albion (Mich.) Coll., 1962; M.A., Mich. State U., 1964, Ph.D., 1968; m. Ross Edward Carter, Jan. 15, 1966; children—Laura, Paul. Clin. intern VA Hosp., Battle Creek, Mich., 1963-65; assessment officer Peace Corps Nigeria Project, Mich. State U., East Lansing, summer 1965, clin. intern psychol. clinic, 1965-66, counseling center, 1966-68, asst. prof. counseling center, 1968-69; dir. clin. tng. Wis. Sch. for Girls, Oregon, 1969-70; cons. psychologist Bangor (Maine) City Schs., 1971; pvt. practice psychology, Bangor, 1971; staff psychologist Adult Community Service, Child Guidance and Mental Health Clinics Delaware County, Media, Pa., 1971-75; pvt. practice, Media, 1973-75. Active PTA. Cert. Mich.; lic. psychologist, Pa., Wis., Maine; USPHS fellow, 1962, 65, 66. Mem. Nat. Register Health Service Providers in Psychology, Milw. Area Women in Clin. Psychology, Am. Psychol. Assn. Contbr. articles to profl. jours. Home: 8924 Jackson Park Blvd Wauwatosa WI 53226

CARTER, CHRISTINE MAUDETTE, securities trader; b. Chgo., Jan. 6, 1948; d. James Young and Beatrice Frances (Turner) C.; B.A., Scripps Coll., 1968; M.A., U. Chgo., 1969, M.B.A., 1972. Asst. v.p., mcpl. bond trader First Nat. Bank of Chgo., 1969-77; v.p., mcpl. bond sales First Boston Corp., N.Y.C., 1977-81; mcpl. bond sales Lehman Bros. Kuhn Loeb, N.Y.C., 1981—. Office: 55 Water St New York NY 10041

CARTER, DELORIS JUANITA, clin. social worker; b. Freeman, Va., Oct. 23, 1948; d. Clarence and Martha Alease (Wyche) C.; student Bergen Community Coll., Paramus, N.J., 1972-74; B.S.W., Fairleigh Dickinson U., 1977; M.S.W., U. Conn., 1980. Sr. social service aide N.J. State Div. Youth and Family Services, Hackensack, 1969-76; cottage coordinator, social work supr. Greer-Woodycrest Residential Sch., Hope Farm, Millbrook, N.Y., 1977-78; social worker Neighborhood Legal Services, Hartford, Conn., 1979; income maintenance technician Bergen County Welfare Bd., Paramus, N.J., 1978; mental health law social worker Neighborhood Legal Services, Hartford, 1980—; case mgr. N.J. Div. Youth and Family Services, Newark, 1981—. Mem. Nat. Assn. Black Social Workers (Outstanding Service award 1976), Conn. Soc. Clin. Social Workers, Nat. Assn. Social Workers, Nat. Fedn. Student Social Workers (pres. Orgn. Black Social Work Students 1979-80). Baptist. Home: 149 Passaic St Hackensack NJ 07601

CARTER, DONNA LEE, nurse; b. Shelby, Mont., Nov. 8, 1932; d. Gothardt and Sara (McCracken) Bauer; diploma Presentation Sch. Nursing, Miles City, Mont., 1954; m. Glen T. Carter, Jan. 20, 1956; children—Tom, Leonard, Teresa. Nurse, inservice dir. Toole County Hosp., Shelby; public health nurse Toole County Mont., 1960-63; clin. instr. Columbus Sch. Nursing, Gt. Falls, Mont., 1963-69; staff nurse Pondera Hosp., Conrad, Mont.; Lamaze instr.; active blood program ARC, 1960—, chmn. home nursing, Columbus Hosp., Great Falls, Mont., 1969—. R.N., Mont. Mem. Am. Soc. Psychoprophylaxis in Obstetrics, Lutheran. Home: Star Route Shelby MT 59475 Office: Toole County Hosp Shelby MT 59474

CARTER, DOTIAN, harpist; b. Salem, Mass., June 2, 1943; d. Curtis Leavitt and Audrey Lois (Sargent) Bushby; grad. Curtis Inst. Music,

1964; m. William Daniel Carter, Sept. 3, 1965; children—Lisa Dianne, Janice Elizabeth. Prin. harpist Phila. Lyric Opera Co., 1964-69, Pa. Ballet Co., 1965-69; 2d harpist Robin Hood Dell, Phila., 1966-69; prin. harpist Phila. Chamber Orch., 1966; prin. harpist Nat. Symphony Orch., Washington, 1969—; soloist Lincoln Center Chamber Music Soc. Democrat. Episcopalian. Office: Kennedy Center Washington DC 20566

CARTER, EDITH HOUSTON, statistician; b. Charlotte, N.C., Oct. 12, 1936; d. Z. and Ellie (Hartsell) Houston; B.S., Appalachian State U., 1959, M.A., 1960; Ph.D., Va. Poly. Inst. and State U., 1976; m. Fletcher F. Carter, Apr. 2, 1961. Transcript analyst Fla. Dept. Edn., Tallahassee, 1961-65; instr. Radford U., 1969-70; prof. New River Community Coll., Dublin, Va., 1970—, dir. instl. research, 1974-78, asst. dean Coll. Arts and Scis., 1978-79, statistician, 1979. Violist Va. Poly. Inst. and State U. Orch., Radford U. Orch., S.W. Va. Opera Soc. Orch. Mem. Am. Ednl. Research Assn., Assn. Instl. Research (exec. bd. 1976-78), Southeastern Assn. Community Coll. Research (exec. bd. 1976-78, Outstanding Service award, Disting. Service award 1981), Nat. Council Research and Planning, Coll. Music Soc., Am. String Tchrs. Assn., Va. Fedn. Women's Clubs (dir. 1968-70). Methodist. Clubs: Radford Garden, Radford Jr. Woman's (pres. 1967-68). Editor Community Coll. Jour. Research and Planning, 1981—, Newsletter Southeastern Assn. Community Coll. Research, 1972—. Home: Box 5781 RU Radford VA 24142 Office: New River Community College Dublin VA 24084

CARTER, ETHEL ANNETTE, govt. exec.; b. St. Louis; d. Beulah and Betty Caroline (Perkins) Berry; student Forest Park Coll., 1974-76, various govt. sponsored mgmt. courses, 1974—; m. Fred Edward Carter; children—Regina Horton, Phyllis McMurtry, Keith Carter. File clk. U.S. Army Fin. Center, St. Louis, 1950, mil. allotment clk. St. Louis, 1951-52; supply clk. U.S. Army Transp. Materiel Command, St. Louis, 1956-58; acctg. technician U.S. Army Aviation Systems Command, St. Louis, 1959-66, adminstr. officer St. Louis, 1967-68, budget analyst/program analyst, St. Louis, 1969-79; program analysis officer U.S. Army Aviation Research and Devel. Command, St. Louis, 1979—. Chmn. supervisory com. Gateway Fed. Employees Fed. Credit Union, St. Louis, 1968-79, bd. dirs., 1979—. Recipient various job performance recognition awards U.S. Govt., 1974-78.

CARTER, FRANCES MONET, psychiat. nurse; b. Mayfield, Ky., Aug. 6, 1923; d. Orlando Lee and Hattie Lois (Buckingham) C.; R.N., Louisville Gen. Hosp., 1944; B.S., UCLA, 1948; M.A., San Francisco State U., 1957; Ed.D., U. San Francisco, 1978; m. Carl Gwin Baker, 1946; children—Donald L. Matthies, Henry H. Evans. Head nurse psychiat. dept. Louisville Gen. Hosp., 1945; psychiat. nurse Langley Porter Clinic, San Francisco, 1946, 52-57; instr., supr. psychiat. nursing Compton (Calif.) Sanitarium, 1948-49; mem. faculty U. San Francisco, 1957—, prof. psychiat. nursing, 1970—; pres. City and County of San Francisco Mental Health Adv. Bd., 1976. Served with Cadet Nurse Corps, 1943-44. Recipient Disting. Teaching award U. San Francisco, 1972; WHO fellow, 1961-62, 70. Mem. Am. Nurses Assn., Nat. League Nursing, Am. Assn. Social Psychiatry, Council Specialists Psychiat. Nursing, AAUP, Sigma Theta Tau, Alpha Sigma Nu (hon.). Author: The Role of the Nurse in Community Mental Health, 1968; Psychosocial Nursing: Theory and Practice in Hospital and Community Mental Health, 3d edit., 1981. Office: 2130 Fulton St San Francisco CA 94117

CARTER, FRANCES TUNNELL, home economist; b. Springville, Miss., May 21; d. David Atmond and Mary Annie (McCutcheon) Tunnell; B.S., U. So. Miss., 1946; A.A., Wood Jr. Coll., 1942; M.S., U. Tenn., 1947; Ed.D., U. Ill., 1954; postgrad. Ursuline Coll., U. Dayton, Fla. State U., Samford U., U. Ala.-Birmingham, LeVerne Coll., N.Y. Sch. Interior Design; m. John T. Carter, Mar. 16; children—Wayne, Nell. Tchr. elem. sch., Thaxton, Miss., 1942-43, Cumberland, Miss., 1943-44; tchr. home econs. Randolph (Miss.) High Sch., 1944-45, Maben (Miss.) High Sch., 1946-47; instr. home econs., art Wood Jr. Coll., 1947-48; head dept. home econs. E. Central Jr. Coll., 1948-49, Clarke Meml. Coll., 1950-56; mem. faculty Samford U., Birmingham, Ala., 1956—, asso. prof., 1957-63, prof., 1963—; vis. prof. Hong Kong Bapt. Coll., 1965-66; instr. charm classes Rocky Ridge Community Sch., 1976—; reading cons., Talladega City Schs., 1978—; mem. early childhood edn. adv. com. Ala. Dept. Edn., 1973—. Named Birmingham Woman of Yr., Birmingham Bus. and Profl. Women, 1977, Vol. of Yr. Greater Birmingham, Cystic Fibrosis Orgn., 1980. Mem. Assn. Childhood Edn. (adv. 1960-80), (pres. Ala. 1970-73), Ala. Writers Conclave (pres. 1978-79), Birmingham Womens C. of C. (pres. 1976-77), Ala. Edn. Assn., CAP (lt. col. 1971-79, asst. info. officer S.E. 1979—), Ala. Assn. Tchr. Educators (editor 1976-77), Nat. League Am. Pen Women (pres. Birmingham 1976-78), Ala. Pen Women (pres. 1980-82), Ala. Poetry Soc. (pres. 1979-82), Ala. WA KA PA Lit. Club (pres. 1980-82), AAUW (v.p. Birmingham 1976-77), DAR (recording sec. 1976-78), Antiques and Allied Arts (pres. 1982-83), Am. Home Econs. Assn., Kappa Delta Epsilon, (nat. pres. 1980-83), Kappa Delta Pi, Alpha Delta Kappa, Pi Gamma Mu, Phi Delta Kappa, Kappa Omicron Phi. Clubs: Women's Civic (pres. 1982-83), Bus. Profl. Womens. Author: (for children) Sammy in the Country, 1960; 'Tween-age Ambassador, 1970; Sharing Times Seven, 1971; Ching Fu and Jim, 1978; contbr. articles to profl. jours. Home: 2561 Rocky Ridge Rd Birmingham AL 35243 Office: Dept Home Econs Samford U Birmingham AL 35229

CARTER, GERALDINE RIDGE, ins. agt.; b. Tampa, Fla., Apr. 30, 1927; d. Irby S. and Irene A. (Clement) Ridge; student Peabody Coll. for Tchrs., 1945-46, U. Tenn., 1975-77; m. George C. Carter, June 25, 1949; children—George C., Michael J., Katherine Carter Sandlin, Marie Carter McKenzie, Paul C. With U.S. Dept. Agr. Statis. Reporting Service, Nashville, 1961-68; owner Carter-Demarcus Calculating, Inventory Service, Nashville, 1961-69; sr. fin. statement analyst First Am. Nat. Bank, Nashville, 1969-73; with Middle Tenn. Heart Assn., Nashville, 1973-74; agy. office mgr. State Mut. Assurance Co. Am., Nashville, 1974, career agt., 1977—. Founder, Metro. Nashville's Youth Govt. Day, 1958; pres. Madison Dem. Women, 1962-63. Recipient U.S. Dept. Agr. citation for meritorious service, 1968. Mem. Nat. Assn. Life Underwriters, Nashville Songwriters Assn., Am. Bus. Women's Assn. Roman Catholic. Author: Mini Poems, 1971. Home and Office: 815 Hamblen Dr Madison TN 37115

CARTER, HEATHER LILIAN, educator; b. Chelmsford, Eng., Dec. 3, 1932; came to U.S., 1957, naturalized, 1962; d. Edgar and Lilian Susan (Bradley) C.; tchrs. cert., Whitelands Coll., London, 1953; Ph.B., Northwestern U., 1962; postgrad. Cornell U., 1965-66; Ph.D., U. Md., 1969. Tchr., London, 1953-57, Harris Sch., Chgo., 1957-62, U. Chgo. Lab. Sch., 1962-65; research asst. AAAS, 1966-69; mem. faculty U. Tex., Austin, 1969—, asso. prof. curriculum and instrn., 1972—, research scientist Research and Devel. Center Tchr. Edn., 1969-72, 80—; sec. Internat. Com. Sci. Edn., 1970-71; cons. in field. Recipient Palmer award Cornell U., 1965; grantee Nat. Inst. Edn., 1980-81. Fellow AAAS; Mem. Am. Ednl. Research Assn., Assn. Tchr. Edn., Nat. Council Tchrs. Math., Phi Delta Kappa, Delta Kappa Gamma. Author articles in field. Cons. editor Jour. Ednl. Research, 1977-80. Home: 8509 Alverstone Way Austin TX 78759 Office: EDB 406 U Tex Austin TX 78712

CARTER, HELEN MEARYLEANE, ednl. adminstr.; b. Detroit, Apr. 29, 1925; d. Julian and Helen (Ray) Appling; B.S., Wayne State U., 1947, M.Edn., 1952; m. Ulysses Carter, July 25, 1947; children—Debra Denise, Julian Appling, Tyrone M. Tchr., Garfield Jr. High Sch., Detroit Bd. Edn., 1947-59, Cleve. Jr. High Sch., 1959-63, Post Jr. High Sch., 1963-68, counselor, 1968-73, asst. prin. Wilson Jr. High Sch., 1973-74, Post Jr. High Sch., 1974-75, Von Steuben Jr. High Sch., 1976-77, prin. Ann Arbor Trail Jr. High Sch., 1977—. Named Outstanding Counselor, Parents of Post Jr. High Sch., 1968. Episcopalian. Office: 7635 Chatham St Detroit MI 48239

CARTER, JOAN PAULINE, cardiac med. services co. exec.; b. Pitts., July 2, 1943; d. Paul Joseph and Hazel Elizabeth (Hykes) Carter; B.A., Coll. of Wooster, 1966; m. John Aglialoro, Aug. 17, 1979; children—Mark David Henderson, Liesl Ann Henderson. Tchr. fgn. langs. Washington Twp. Schs., Washington, Pa., 1966-68; tchr. Mt. Lebanon public schs., Pitts., 1968-69; with United Med. Corp. (and predecessor firm), Haddonfield, N.J., 1973—, v.p., 1977—. Bd. dirs. Planned Parenthood. Mem. Am. Coll. Sports Medicine, World Affairs Council. Republican. Unitarian. Home: 76 Lane of Acres Haddonfield NJ 08033 Office: 56 Haddon Ave Haddonfield NJ 08033

CARTER, JOYCE ELAINE ARNDT, writer, editor, photographer; b. Bellevue, Ohio, Jan. 9, 1944; d. Bryce Leroy Arndt and Agnes Arline (Rudicel) Arndt Chellis; student Gonzaga U., 1962-63, Phoenix Coll., 1963-66, U. Wash., Seattle, 1966-67; m. Zane Hartson Carter, Jan. 16, 1965 (div. 1971). Editor de Paul Speaks mag., St. Vincent de Paul Parish, Phoenix, 1971-74; editor Ultreya internat. mag. Mt. Claret Cursillo Center, Phoenix, 1971-72; pub. info. photographer Phoenix Coll., 1972—; free lance writer. Mem. Nat. League Am. Pen Women, Poetry Soc. Democrat. Roman Catholic. Club: Phoenix Writers (pres. 1972-73). Contbr. poetry and fiction to nat. profl. and popular publs. Home: 1725 E Catalina Dr Phoenix AZ 85016

CARTER, JUDY SHARON, city ofcl.; b. Miami, Fla., Dec. 22, 1951; d. James and Ola (Johnson) C.; B.S. in Edn., Fisk U. 1973; M.A. in Edn. Adminstrn., U. Mich., 1974. Adminstrv. asst. City of Miami, 1975-77, personnel officer, 1977-78, sr. personnel officer, 1978-79, exec. sec., dir. Civil Service Bd., 1979—, trustee Retirement Systems Bd., 1980—; union rep. United Tchrs. Dade, 1974-75. Mem. young adult choir New Way Fellowship, Miami, 1982. Mem. Internat. Personnel Mgmt. Assn., Fla. Public Personnel Assn., Internat. Found. Employee Benefit Plans, Nat. Assn. Bus. and Profl. Black Women Clubs, Nat. Assn. Female Execs., AAUW Leadership in Miami Alumni Assn., Delta Sigma Theta. Democrat. Baptist. Club: Miami Fisk Alumni. Office: 1145 NW 11th St Miami FL 33136

CARTER, LILA MAE, artist; b. Long Beach, Calif., June 10, 1930; d. Thomas Nathan and Blanche Isabel (Springer) Shore; student Long Beach City Coll., 1948-49, Victor Valley Coll., San Bernardino City Coll., 1969-76; m. Lavale Thomas Carter, Jan. 20, 1951; children—Thomas Richard, Stanley Miles, Kenneth Calvin, Randall Scott. Tchr. art, illustrator books, Wrightwood, Calif., 1968—; illustrator local newspaper; works exhibited San Bernardino County fairs, San Bernardino County Mus., Victorville Mus.; paintings represented in permanent collections: Four Seasons Gallery, Gallerie 200, Chgo., Cosgrift Restaurant Gallery (Colo.), Steamboat Springs, Colo.; presented bi-centennial painting to U.S. Ambassador Ann Armstrong, London, 1976; co-owner Four Seasons Gallery, Wrightwood, Calif. Recipient Gold Seal, Internat. League Am. Pen Women, 1975, 1st place award Calif. Fedn. Fine Arts Festivals, 1962-77, 2d place award, 1962, best of show trophy Art Festival of Oak Creek, 1975. Mem. Nat. League Am. Penwomen (past br. pres., So. Calif. v.p. 1980—, 1st and 2d awards So. Calif. Show Fine Arts 1981), Tri Community Art Assn., San Bernardino County Mus. Fine Arts Assn. Democrat. Methodist. Club: Women's of Wrightwood (past pres. Calif. Fedn.). Author: Color It Wrightwood (Woman of Achievement award 1976-78), 1975; illustrator: The Forrest Creatures Celebrate, 1976; Mountain Loves, 1979. Address: PO Box 312 Wrightwood CA 92397

CARTER, MAE RIEDY, univ. adminstr.; b. Berkeley, Calif., May 20, 1921; d. Carl Joseph and Avis Blanche (Rhodehaver) Riedy; B.S., U. Calif., Berkeley, 1943; m. Robert C. Carter, Aug. 19, 1944; children—Catherine, Christin Ann. Ednl. adv., then program specialist div. continuing edn. U. Del., Newark, 1968-78, spl. asst. to provost, exec. dir. commn. status women Office Women's Affairs, 1978—; adv. bd. Rockefeller Family grant project, 1979—. Regional v.p. Del. PTA, 1960-62; pres. Friends Newark Free Library, 1968-69; mem. fiscal planning com. Newark Spl. Sch. Dist., 1972. Recipient Outstanding Service award Women's Coordinating Council, 1977, 79; Spl. Recognition award, Nat. U. Extension Assn., 1977, award for credit programs, 1971, Creative Programming award, 1971; AAUW grantee, 1968; Fulbright grantee, 1976. Mem. AAUW (past br. pres.), Women's Equity Action League, Nat. Assn. Women Deans, Adminstrs. and Counselors, NOW, Women's Studies Assn. Republican. Author: (with Geis and Butler) Seeing and Evaluating People, 1982, Research on Seeing and Evaluating People; also papers, reports in field. Home: 604 Dallam Rd Newark DE 19711 Office: Office Women's Affairs Univ Del Newark DE 19711

CARTER, MARGARET REITMAN, wholesale co. exec.; b. Newark, Apr. 28, 1914; d. William and Erna Lindeman Harris; B.A., Wellesley Coll., 1935; m. Raymond E. Reitman, 1938; m. 2d, Neil Carter, May 18, 1979; children—Margaret Jacobs, Elizabeth Lowenstein, Kathryn Reitman. Chmn. bd. Reitman Industries, West Caldwell, N.J., 1976—. Vice pres. N.J. Symphony, 1975-80, trustee, 1965-81; pres. Theresa Grotta Center, 1955-58, trustee, 1945—; chmn. women's div. United Jewish Appeal Essex County; Republican candidate Freeholder Essex County, 1960, 61. Decorated dame abbesse Ordre des Chevaliers de Provence. Mem. Met. Opera Guild, Nat. Ballet, N.Y.C. Opera Guild, Met. Mus. Art, Mus. Modern Art, Newark Mus. Assn., Wine and Spirits Wholesalers Assn. Am. Clubs: Mountain Ridge Country, Augusta (Maine) Country. Office: 10 Patton Dr West Caldwell NJ 07006

CARTER, MARY EDDIE, govt. ofcl.; b. Americus, Ga., Mar. 14, 1925; d. Walker G. and Mary Esther (Steward) C.; B.S., LaGrange (Ga.) Coll., 1946; M.S., U. Fla., Gainesville, 1949; Ph.D. (Rockefeller and Alex Cowan & Sons, Ltd. grantee), U. Edinburgh (Scotland), 1956. Microscopist, Callaway Mills, LaGrange, 1947-48; textile chemist So. Research Inst., Birmingham, Ala., 1949-51; chemist West Point Pepperel (Ga.), 1951-53; research asso. Am. Viscose div. FMC Corp., Phila., 1956-71; lab. chief textiles and clothing lab. Dept. Agr., Knoxville, Tenn., 1971-73, dir. So. Regional Research Center, 1973-80, assoc. adminstr. Agrl. Research Service, Washington, 1980—; prof. chemistry U. Tenn., Knoxville, 1971-73; instr. LaGrange Coll., 1946-47. Mem. Am. Chem. Soc. (Herty award Ga. sect. 1979), Am. Assn. Textile Chemists and Colorists, Fiber Soc., Inter-Color Soc., Inst. Food Technologists, Am. Assn. Cereal Chemists, Fed. Exec. League, Fedn. Women, Fed. Exec. Inst., Sigma Xi. Author: Essential Fiber Chemistry, 1971; contbr. articles to tech. jours. Patentee in field. Office: ARS Room 302A Administration Bldg Washington DC 20250

CARTER, NANCY A., editor; b. Flint, Mich., Feb. 18, 1949; d. Lowell Walter and Theresa Ann (Quinn) C.; A.B., W.Va. Wesleyan Coll., 1971; Ph.D. (fellow), Am. U., 1975; postgrad. Union Theol. Sem., N.Y.C., 1979. Literature editor Bd. Global Ministries, United Methodist Ch., N.Y.C., 1976—; dir. Washington Sq. Press. Recipient Zeta Tau Alpha Found. grant, 1970-72. Mem. AAUW, MLA, Religious Public Relations Council, NOW, Zeta Tau Alpha (v.p. Washington alumnae chpt. 1973-74). Methodist. Club: Salisbury Dist. United Methodist Women (v.p. 1975-76). Home: 501 W 123d St New York NY 10027 Office: 475 Riverside Dr Room 1356 New York NY 10115

CARTER, NANCY CAROL, librarian, educator; b. Tacoma, Nov. 12, 1942; d. Walter Martin and Lois Elsie (Wilson) Schwebel; B.S., Tex. A. and I. U., 1963, M.S., 1969; M.L.S., U. Okla., 1967, J.D., 1975. Admitted to Okla. bar, 1975; asst. acquisitions librarian, asst. prof. U. Okla. Libraries, 1967-71; dir. Law Library, prof. law Golden Gate U., San Francisco, 1975—; mem. Calif. Law Library Adv. Com., 1977—. Recipient Distinguished Service award Golden Gate U., 1976. Mem. Am., Okla. bar assns., Am. Assn. Law Libraries, Beta Phi Mu, Phi Alpha Theta. Editor: American Indian Law Rev., 1975. Home: 921 Minnesota St San Francisco CA 94107 Office: 536 Mission St San Francisco CA 94105

CARTER, NANCY JEAN, human resources exec.; b. Sandusky, Ohio; A.B., Duke U., 1954; M.A., La. State U., 1970; m. Richard D. Carter; 1 child. Asst. to personnel mgr. Higbee Co., Cleve., 1954-55; asst. personnel mgr. Univ. Hosp. and Clinics, U. Ala., Birmingham, 1956-57; personnel analyst UCLA, 1964-68; pres. UN Women's Guild, Vienna, Austria, 1974-75; mgr. human resources programs Bus. Internat. Corp., N.Y.C., 1977-79, program adminstr., research and cons. services program in internat. human resources, 1979-81; mgr. internat. personnel Emery Worldwide, Wilton, Conn., 1981-82; v.p. corp. human resources Chase Manhattan Bank, N.Y.C., 1982—; v.p. Internat. Mgmt. Consortium, 1976—. Mem. exec. bd. Internat. Com. for Social Welfare, Vienna, 1971-75. Ford Found. fellow, 1967-68. Mem. Indsl. Relations Research Assn., Am. Soc. Personnel Adminstrs., Am. Soc. Tng. and Devel., Human Resources Planning Soc., Phi Gamma Phi. Office: Chase Manhattan Bank 80 Pine St New York NY 10081

CARTER, ONETA WILSON, county ofcl.; b. Durham, N.C., Nov. 21, 1922; d. Alvis Huel and Mary (Wilson) Wilson; student Mary Washington Coll., 1941; m. Marvin Owen Carter, July 26, 1947; children—Martha Carter Moss, Elizabeth Carter Dupree. Auditing dept. asso. Reynolds Metals, Richmond, Va., 1943-44; bookkeeper Thalhimer's, Inc., Richmond, 1945-47; chief dep. commr. County of Mecklenburg (Va.), 1954-80, commr. of revenue, 1981—. Mem. Commrs. of Revenue Assn. Va., Va. Assn. Assessing Officers, Nat. Assn. Female Execs., Mus. Early So. Decorative Arts. Methodist. Club: Boydton Garden (charter).

CARTER, ROSALYNN SMITH, wife of former Pres. U.S.; b. nr. Plains, Ga., Aug. 18, 1927; d. Wilburn Edgar and Allethea (Murray) Smith; grad. Ga. Southwestern Coll.; H.H.D. (hon.), Tift Coll., 1979; L.H.D. (hon.), Morehouse Coll., 1980; m. James Earl Carter, Jr., July 7, 1946; children—John William, James Earl III, Donnel Jeffrey, Amy Lynn. Past mem. Ga. Gov.'s Commn. to Improve Service for Mentally and Emotionally Handicapped; past hon. chmn. Ga. Spl. Olympics for Retarded Children; past vol. Ga. Regional Hosp.; past hon. chmn. Pres.'s Commn. Mental Health. Recipient Merit award NOW; Vol. of Yr. award Southwestern Assn. Vol. Services; Vol. of Decade award Nat. Mental Health Assn., 1980; presdl. citation Am. Psychol. Assn., 1982. Baptist. Home: 1 Woodland Dr Plains GA 31780 *

CARTER, RUTH B. (MRS. JOSEPH C. CARTER), assn. exec.; b. Charlotte, Vt.; d. Ira E. and Sadie M. (Congdon) Burroughs; Ph.B., U. Vt., 1931; m. Joseph C. Carter, June 28, 1935. Prin., Newton Acad., Shoreham, Vt., 1931-35; substitute tchr. Spaulding High Sch., Barre, Vt., also Woodbury (Vt.) High Sch., 1935-36; tchr. Craftsbury Acad., Craftsbury Common, Vt., 1936-38; sales mgr., buyer Vt. Music Co., Barre, 1939-44; statistician Syracuse U., 1944-46; instr. English, Temple U., Phila., 1946-47; records clk. sec., 1947-56; tchr. English, Central High Sch., Phila., 1957, Springfield Twp. Sr. High Sch., Montgomery County, Pa., 1964-65; sec. Women's Univ. Club, Phila., 1961-64, treas., 1965-67; exec. dir. White-Williams Found., 1966—. Recipient Humanitarian award Chapel of Four Chaplains, 1981. Mem. AAUW (admissions chmn.; treas.; rec. sec. Phila. br.), DAR (treas., historian, com. chmn., budget dir. Germantown chpt.), New Eng. Historic Geneal. Soc., Geneal. Soc. Vt., Soc. Mayflower Descs. Republican. Methodist. Clubs: Temple University Faculty Women's (pres. Center City group), Temple University Women's. Author: (with Joseph C. Carter) Anchors Aweigh Around the World with Ernest Vail Burroughs, 1960. Home: D-4 Glenside House Glenside PA 19038 Office: The Pkwy at 21st St Philadelphia PA 19103

CARTER, SALLY (SOPHIA), art shows cons.; b. Buffalo, Dec. 28, 1914; d. Frank and Caroline Walski; B.A., D'Youville Coll., 1936; postgrad. in Art, So. Ill. U., Edwardsville, 1969-75; m. Thad Robert Carter, Nov. 10, 1945; children—Susan V. Carter Penney, Robert Lloyd. Promoter, cons., curator local art shows, Alton, Ill., 1974—; v.p. bd. dirs. Friends of Art, dept. art and design So. Ill. U., Edwardsville, 1981. Served to capt. USAF, 1942-45. Mem. Greater Miss. River Art Council (chmn. 11th ann. show 1981). Republican. Roman Catholic. Home: 3750 Aberdeen Ave Alton IL 62002

CARTER, SARALEE LESSMAN, immunologist, microbiologist; b. Chgo., Feb. 19, 1951; d. Julius A. and Ida (Oiring) Lessman; B.A., National Coll., 1971; m. John B. Carter, Oct. 7, 1979. Supr. lab. immunology Weiss Meml. Hosp., Chgo., 1973-80; lab. immunology supr. Henrotin Hosp., Chgo., 1980—; mem. nat. workshop faculty Am. Soc. Clin. Pathologists. Mem. Am. Soc. Clin. Pathologists (subspecialty cert. in microbiology and immunology, cert. med. technologist). Researcher Legionnaires Disease and mycoplasma pneumonia World Soc. Pathologists, Jerusalem, Israel, 1980. Office: 111 W Oak St Chicago IL 60610

CARTER, SUSAN MONTGOMERY, actress, bus. woman; b. Gt. Falls, Mont., Apr. 12, 1939; d. A. Raymond and Jean (Anderson) Montgomery; B.A., UCLA, 1961; postgrad. Stanford U. Bus. Sch.; m. George Robert Carter, III, July 15, 1961; children—George Robert, IV, Anne Strong. Profl. model, 1969-75; with Harper's Bazaar, 1976-79; actress on stage, screen and TV, 1969—; featured actress TV commls., 1970—; mktg. and adminstrv. dir. Landor Assos., Los Angeles and Hawaii, 1979—. Trustee Strong Center Dental Clinic, Honolulu, 1963-69; bd. dirs. Hawaii Child and Family Service, 1963-69, Big Bros., Chgo., 1973-75, Northwestern U. Med. Center, Chgo., 1973-75; dir. Hawaii Air/Water Pollution campaign, 1967; bd. govs. Burlington House, N.Y.C., 1969-75; mem. Los Angeles Olympic Com., UCLA Chancellors Assocs. Mem. Los Angeles Jr. League (bd. dirs. Hawaii 1963-70), Prytanean Soc., Friends of Vatican, Nat. Charity League. Clubs: San Francisco Metropolitan; Hawaii Outrigger Canoe; Beach (Santa Monica, Calif.)

CARTER, VIRGINIA MILNER, fin. mgmt. exec.; b. Atlanta, July 1, 1919; d. Willis Justus and Virginia Amanda (Cohen) Milner; B.A., Agnes Scott Coll., 1940; student Smith Coll., 1943, Radcliffe Coll., 1944, So. Meth. U., 1959-60, Wharton Bus. Sch., 1978; children—Alverson, Ida Richards (Mrs. Joseph N. Consola, Jr.), Virginia Seixas (Mrs. J.R. Cissell), Robert Milner. Dist. mgr. Prestige Silver Co., Atlanta, Charlotte, N.C. and Richmond, Va., 1947-58; agt. Ga. Internat. Life Ins. Co. and predecessor co., Atlanta, 1959-61, agy. dir., 1961-69, asst. corp. sec., 1965-69; v.p. Employee Benefit Plans, Rome, Ga., 1969; acct. exec. Planned Equity, Atlanta, 1971; v.p. Profl. Investment Counselors, Atlanta, 1970; div. mgr. Waddell & Reed, Atlanta, 1972-76; sr. v.p. A.L. Williams, Tucker, Ga., 1976—, also dir.; dir. Mario's Ristorantes, Inc., Nelco Enterprises. Bd. dirs. Atlanta YWCA, 1966-69; trustee N. Atlanta Presbyn. Ch., 1978-79. Served to lt. USNR, 1942-45. Mem. AAUW, LWV, Bus. and Profl. Women, Internat. Assn. Fin. Planners, DAR, Nat. Assn. Life Underwriters, Cert. Fin. Planners. Republican. Clubs: Dunwoody Country, Horseshoe Bend Country, West Paces Racquet.

Home: 1786 Trapnall Dr Dunwoody GA 30338 Office: 3785 Northeast Expressway Suite 118 Atlanta GA 30340

CARTIER CHRISTENSEN, GRETE, travel agt.; b. Borup, Denmark, June 28, 1931; came to U.S., 1952, naturalized, 1957; d. Niels Frederik and Alida Emilie (Nielsen) Jensen; student Galileo Adult Sch., San Francisco, 1954-58; cert. travel counselor Inst. Cert. Travel Agts., 1979. Sec., Omaha, 1952-54; sec. Schilling Spice Co., San Francisco, 1954-56; sec., passenger agt. East Asiatic S.S. Co., San Francisco, 1956-58; self-employed, 1959-61; travel agt., spl. promotions and Eastern mgr. Farmer-to-Farmer Tours, Berkeley, Calif., 1961—. Active Merola Opera Fund, San Francisco and Oakland Symphony. Mem. Inst. Cert. Travel Agts. and Study Forum No. Calif. Democrat. Lutheran. Club: Danish Lodge (Thyra No. 5, San Francisco). Author research paper in field. Home: 329 Middle Rd Belmont CA 94002 Office: 2855 Telegraph Ave Berkeley CA 94705

CARTLAND, BARBARA HAMILTON, authoress, playwright; b. 1901; d. Bertram Cartland; student pub. schs.; m. Alexander George McCorquodale, 1927 (div. 1933); 1 dau.; m. 2d, Hugh McCorquodale, 1936 (dec. 1963); 2 sons. Designer, organizer numerous charity pageants, including Britain and her Industries at Brit. Legion Ball, Albert Hall, 1930; carried first aeroplane-towed glider-mail in her glider The Barbara Cartland from Mauston to Reading, 1931; lectr. tours in Can., 1940; hon. jr. comdr. A.T.S. and lady welfare officer and librarian to all services in Bedfordshire, 1941-49; county cadet officer St. John Ambulance Brigade, Bedfordshire, 1943-47; county v.p. Cadets, Bedfordshire, 1948-50; organizer, producer St. John Ambulance Brigade Exhbn., 1945-50, chmn. exhbn. com., 1944-51; county v.p. Nursing Div., Hertfordshire, 1966; chmn. St. John Council, Hertfordshire, 1974—; pres. Herts Brigade, Royal Coll. Midwives, 1957; founder Barbara Cartland-Onslow Romany Gypsy Fund, 1961; dep. pres. Nat. Assn. Health, 1965, pres., 1966; appeared on numerous radio and television programs throughout the world. Dec. dame St. John, 1972. Author: (novels) Lord Ravenscar's Revenge, 1978, A Runaway Star, 1978, A Princess in Distress, 1978, The Judgement of Love, 1978, Lovers in Paradise, 1978, The Race for Love, 1978, Flowers for the God of Love, 1978, The Irresistible Force, 1978, The Duke and the Preacher's Daughter, 1978, The Drums of Love, 1978, numerous others; (historical) Bewitching Women, 1955, The Outrageous Queen (The Story of Queen Christina of Sweden), 1956, The Scandalous Life of King Carol, 1957, The Private Life of King Charles II, 1958, The Private Life of Elizabeth, Empress of Austria, 1959, Josephine, Empress of France, 1961, Diane de Poitiers, 1962, Metternich-the Passionate Diplomat, 1964; (sociology) The Many Facets of Love, 1963, Sex and the Teenager, 1964, The Book of Charm, 1965, Living Together, 1965, The Youth Secret, 1968, The Magic of Honey, 1970, Barbara Cartland's Book of Beauty and Health, 1972, Men are Wonderful, 1973, Barbara Cartland's Book of Useless Information, 1977, Woman, the Enigma, 1965, others; (cooking) Barbara Cartland's Health Food Cookery Book, 1971, Food for Love, 1975, Recipes for Lovers, 1977, Magic of Honey Cookbook, 1976; (verse) Lines on Life and Love, 1972; (plays) Blood Money, 1925, French Dressing (with Bruce Woodhouse), 1943; (radio play) The Caged Bird, 1957; (television in Am.) The Merv Griffin Show 1946-76, To Tell the Truth, 1976, 60-Minute Show, 1977; (philosophy) Toward the Stars, 1971. Address: c/o Bantam Books 666 Fifth Ave New York NY 10019 *

CARTON, MARY FRANCIS REGIS, educator; b. N.Y.C.; d. Myles L.B. and Anna C.; B.A. Hunter Coll., 1944; M.A., Catholic U. Am., 1959, Ph.D., 1963. Joined Sch. Sisters of Notre Dame, 1945; tchr. St. James Sch., Balt., 1945-46; tchr. religion and social studies Inst. of Notre Dame High Schs., Balt., 1947-54; instr. dept. religious studies Coll. Notre Dame of Md., Balt., 1954-57, asst. prof., 1957-62, asso. prof., 1962-64, prof., 1964—, chairperson bd. trustees, 1971-75; mem. bd. ecumenical inst. St. Mary's Sem. and Univ., Roland Park, Balt., 1977—. Mem. Coll. Theology Soc. (v.p. 1972-74, editor newsletter 1968-70), Religious Edn. Assn. U.S. and Can. (dir. 1980), Cath. Theol. Soc. Am., Delta Epsilon Sigma. Democrat. Contbr. in field. Home and office: 4701 N Charles St Baltimore MD 21210

CARTRIGHT, MARGARET SHARON, editor; b. Chgo., May 31, 1953; d. Rayfield and Willie (Dixon) Blackmon; student Dominican Coll., 1970-71, U. Ill., Chgo., 1971-74; m. Ralph E. Cartright, Oct. 30, 1972 (div.); 1 son, Alexander Emanuel. Ednl. dir. Pivot Point Internat., Chgo., 1976-81; editor Aura mag.; cons. Dena Corp.; U.S. rep. World Hairdressing Congress, London, 1981; internat. traveling lectr. Chmn. philanthropy Christian Singles, 1980—. Mem. Nat. Assn. Female Execs. Developed henna cream color chart, 1977; conceived and developed underwrapping technique in permanent waving, 1978; author ednl. program hairsculpture, 1980, lexicon for beauty industry, 1980; editor: Long Hair Graphics, 1980. Address: 316 Albert Terr Wheeling IL 60090

CARTWRIGHT, CAROL ANN, univ. dean; b. Sioux City, Iowa, July 19, 1941; d. Carl Anthony and Kathryn Marie (Weishapple) Becker; B.Ed., U. Wis., Whitewater, 1962; M.Ed. (U.S. Office Edn. grad. fellow 1964-66), U. Pitts., 1965, Ph.D., 1968; m. G. Phillip Cartwright, June 11, 1966; children—Catherine Ellen, Stephen Richard, Susan Denise. Classroom tchr., then remedial tutor and spl. class tchr., Pitts., 1962-65; instr. ednl. psychology U. Hawaii, 1966-67; mem. faculty Pa. State U., 1968—, prof. early and spl. edn., 1979—, asso. dean acad. affairs commonwealth ednl. system, 1981—; research fellow Plymouth Poly.-U. London, 1974-75; pres., bd. dirs. Child Devel. Council Centre County (Pa.), 1978-80; Title XX day care coordinator, 1978-80; cons. in field. Grantee U.S. Office Edn., 1969-80; named Outstanding Young Alumni, U. Wis., Whitewater, 1971. Mem. Am. Ednl. Research Assn., Nat. Assn. Edn. Young Children, Council Exceptional Children, AAUW, Phi Delta Kappa. Author books, articles on childhood edn. Producer, host TV programs in field. Office: 111 Old Main Pa State U University Park PA 16802

CARTWRIGHT, MARY LOU, clin. lab. scientist; b. Payette, Idaho, Apr. 5, 1923; d. Ray J. and Nellie Mae (Sherer) Decker; B.S., U. Houston, 1958; M.A., Central Mich. U., 1976; m. Chadwick Louis Cartwright, Sept. 13, 1947. Med. technologist Methodist Hosp., Houston, 1957-59, VA Hosp., Livermore, Calif., 1960-67, Kaiser Permanente Med. Center, Hayward, Calif., 1967-71, United Med. Lab., San Mateo, Calif., 1972-73; sr. med. technologist Oakland (Calif.) Hosp., 1974—; cons. med. lab. tech. Oakland Public Schs. Chmn., Congressional Dist. 11 steering com. Common Cause, 1974-77; consumer mem. Alameda County (Calif.) Health Systems Agy., 1977-78. Served with USNR, 1945-53. Mem. Calif. Soc. Med. Tech., Calif. Assn. Med. Lab. Tech. (Technologist of Yr. award 1968, 78, Pres.'s award 1977, Service award chpt. 1978, 79), Am. Soc. Med. Tech. (by-laws chmn. 1981-83), Am. Bus. Women's Assn., Nat. Assn. Female Execs. Democrat. Home: 1539 Delemos Ave Hayward CA 94544 Office: 2648 E 14th St Oakland CA 94601

CARTWRIGHT, STEPHANIE (ZAVELL) (DOROTHEA COY), textile designer; b. N.Y.C., Feb. 18, 1914; d. James Joseph and Esther (McGrann) Coy; William K. Vanderbilt scholar, France and Italy, 1931; ed. Paris br. Parsons Sch. Design, N.Y. Sch. Fine and Applied Art, 1932, Columbia U.; Arnold Zevell, Feb. 15, 1946; children—Margot, A. Stephen. Designer window and interior displays Bonwit Teller; designer, stylist Susquehanna Silk Mills; pres. Fabrics by Cartwrights div. Roth Fabrics; v.p. Coutoure Fabrics, Ltd., 1945-54, pres., 1954—, also dir.; v.p., dir. Pavillon Fabrics Corp., Fabric Mart Corp.; lectr. textile design, oversser Parsons Sch. Design, Fashion Group Am. Career Course. Office aux. N.Y. Infirmary; asso. bd. dirs. Assn. Home; vice chmn. adv. council LaGuardia House Nursery; vol. painting class Yorkville Youth Council; past bd. govs. Boys and Girls Service League. Recipient Cover Design award Art et Inudstire, 1932; gold medal Calif. Fair Textile Expn., 1953-55; Mem. Parsons Alumni Assn. (council, pres. 1959), Republican Women in Industry and Professions (past pres. N.Y. chpt), Women's Nat. Fashion Group Am. (legis. com., past chmn. membership com. N.Y.), Nat. Council Women, Internat. Platform Assn., N.Y. Advt. Club. Club: York. Contbr. chpt. to Your Future in Fashion Design, 1966. *

CARVAINIS, MARIA, lit. agt.; b. Brisbane, Australia, Mar. 24, 1946; came to U.S., 1952, naturalized, 1965; d. Nicholas John and Edith Maude (Dent) Carvainis; B.A., CCNY, 1967; m. Ian Ross Jenkins, June 24, 1979. Editorial asst. MacMillan Inc., N.Y.C., 1967-69; interpreter, ITT, N.Y.C., 1969; asst. editor Basic Books, Inc., N.Y.C., 1970-72; freelance cons. to mags., book pubs., 1972-73; editor, spl. asst. to pub. Avon Books, Inc., N.Y.C., 1973-75; freelance author, editor, 1975-76; sr. editor Crown Pubs., Inc., N.Y.C., 1976-77; owner Maria Carvainis Agy., N.Y.C., 1977—. N.Y. State Merit scholar, 1963-67. Mem. Authors Guild, Authors League Am., The Writers Guild of Am. Author: Crepes and Omelettes, 1976; co-author: Moustache, 1979. Address: 235 W End Ave New York City NY 10023

CARVALHO, JULIE ANN, psychologist; b. Washington, Apr. 11, 1940; d. Daniel H. and Elizabeth Cecilia (Gardiner) Schmidt; B.A. magna cum laude, U. Md., 1962, postgrad., 1973; M.A., George Washington U., 1966; postgrad. Va. Poly. Inst., 1979—; m. João M.P. de Carvalho, June 7, 1977; children—Alan R., Dennis M., Melanie D., Celeste A., Joshua E. Psychologist, VA, 1961-62; psychologist research grants NIMH, 1962-63, social sci. research analyst Mental Health Study Center, 1963-67; edn. and tng. analyst Computer Applications, Inc., 1967-68; edn. program specialist Nat. Center Ednl. Research and Devel., U.S. Office of Edn., Washington, 1969-70, program analyst, 1970-73; equal opportunity specialist Office of Sec., HEW, Washington, 1973-77, legis. and program analyst Office for Civil Rights, 1977-78, program analyst evaluation br., 1978—; freelance editor, 1961—. Mem. steering com. Alliance for Child Care, 1975-80; bd. dirs. Child Care Centers, 1970-76, HEW Employees Assn., 1973—. Mem. Am. Psychol. Assn., Soc. Psychol. Study of Social Issues, Am. Soc. Public Adminstrn., Federally Employed Women (nat. editor 1975-79), Fairfax County Assn. for Gifted (pres. 1980), Psi Chi, Phi Alpha Theta. Contbr. articles on ednl. programs to profl. publs. Home: 11668 Mediterranean Ct Reston VA 22090 Office: 330 Independence Ave SW Washington DC 20202

CARVEL, MARY JANE, real estate broker; b. St. Louis, Aug. 23, 1920; d. Conrad Arthur and Otillia Mary (Brefeld) Wellings; student selected courses U. Houston, Houston Conservatory Musoc; m. Vincent Carvel, Apr. 25, 1941 (dec. 1943). Various secretarial positions in oil industry, 1937-39; appraiser Nat. Bank Commerce (now Tex. Commerce Bank), Houston, 1949-55; asst. to pres. Weaver Drilling Co., Houston, 1955-59; co-owner, builder 1st garden apts. in Houston, 1959-60; founder, pro-pr. Mary Jane Carvel, Interiors, Houston, 1960—; owner, founder Mary Jane Carvel Realtors, Houston, 1974—; co-own Bayou on the Bend Apts., Timberline Office Bldg. and owner 17 miscellaneous propoerties. Founder, chmn. bd., bd. dirs. Sanctuary for Unwanted Animals, Houston, 1981—; bd. dirs. Carvel Animal Relief Fund.; charter mem. Republican Presdl. Task Force. Mem. Nat Assn. Realtors, Tex. Bd. Realtors, Houston Bd. Realtors, Houston Apt. Assn. Roman Catholic. Office: 5213 Memorial Dr Houston TX 77077

CARVER, DOROTHY LEE ESKEW (MRS. JOHN JAMES CARVER), bus. coll. dean; b. Brady, Tex., July 10, 1926; d. Clyde Albert and A. Maurine (Meadows) Eskew; student So. Oreg. Coll., 1942-43, Coll. Eastern Utah, 1965-67; B.A., U. Utah, 1968; M.A., Calif. State Coll. at Hayward, 1970; postgrad. Mills Coll., 1971; m. John James Carver, Feb. 26, 1944; children—John James, Sheila (Mrs. Joseph English), Chuck, David. Instr., Rutherford Bus. Coll., Dallas, 1944-45; sec. Adolph Coors Co., Golden, Colo., 1945-47; instr. English, Coll. Eastern Utah, Price, 1968-69; instr. speech Modesto (Calif.) Jr. Coll., 1970-71; instr. personal devel. men and women Heald Bus. Coll., Oakland, Calif., 1972-74, dean students Walnut Creek, Calif., 1974—; dir. curricula Heald Colls. Communications cons. I. Magnin's, U.S. Steel Corp., Crocker Bank, Artec Internat., Analysts Internat., 1980-81. Mem. Gov's. Conf. on Higher Edn. in Utah, 1968; mem. fin. com. Coll. Eastern Utah, 1967-69; active various community drives; judge election Republican party, 1960, 64; bd. dirs. dirs. Opportunity Center, 1965-66, Symphony of Mountain, Foster Children, Battered Women. Mem. AAUW, Profl. Bus. Women, Delta Kappa Gamma (regional sec., founder region). Episcopalian (supt. Sunday Sch. 1967-69). Club: Order Eastern Star. Clubs: Internat. Toastmistress (chmn. council 4, program edn. com.), Soroptimist Internat. (pres.) (Walnut Creek). Home: 20 Coronado Ct Walnut Creek CA 94596 Office: 2085 N Broadway Walnut Creek CA 94596

CARVER, JUANITA (NITA), plastic co. exec.; b. Indpls., Apr. 8, 1929; d. Willard H. and Golda M. Ashe; student Ariz. State U.; children—Daniel Charles, Robin Lewis, Scott Alan. Asst. librarian, sec., dir. CAMSCO, 1962—; pres. Carver Corp., Phoenix, 1971—. Fund raiser cancer and heart fund campaigns; active PTA; den mother Cub Scouts; bd. dirs. Scottsdale Meml. Hosp. Aux., 1964-65, asso. mem., 1980—. Republican. Methodist. Patentee Yarner latch hook rug yarn organizer. Home: 6255 E Avalon St Scottsdale AZ 85251

CARVER, NANCY AILSTOCK, safety and health mgr.; b. Washington, Jan. 25, 1944; d. Vernon Lynnwood and Catherine W. Ailstock; R.N., Alexandria (Va.) Hosp., 1966; Audiometric Technician-Hearing Conservationist, N.Y. U., 1975; B.S. in Bus. Adminstrn., St. Joseph's Coll., Maine, 1978; postgrad. Antioch Sch. Law, 1978; m. Anthony M. Carver; children—Catherine E., Owen L. Nurse, Dr. J.C. Bateman, 1966-67, Dr. Frank A. Carroll, 1967-69, Vis. Nurse Assn., 1969-72; occupational health nurse Hazleton Labs., 1974-75, safety coordinator, 1975-76; corporate mgr. safety and health communications Satellite Corp., Washington, 1976-79; v.p. Innovation Mgmt. Concepts, 1980—; cons. mgmt. and occupational safety and health. occupational safety and health cons. Curriculum adv. bd. occupational safety and health div. No. Va. Community Coll., 1976-78. Certified hazard control mgr.; recipient Achievement award Va. Safety Assn., 1977. Mem. Am. Indsl. Hygiene Assn., Am. Soc. Safety Engrs., Nat. Safety Mgmt. Soc., Va. Safety Assn. (exec. bd., bd. dirs.). Contbg. editor to Nat. Safety Mgmt. Soc. Jour., 1978. Home and office: 1332 Valley Rd Stirling NJ 07980

CARVER-BRODIE, DEBORAH, pub. co. exec.; b. Phila., May 30, 1942; d. Jacob and Rebecca (Epstein) Weiss; student Temple U., 1959-60; m. James Thomas Brodie, Nov. 13, 1975; 1 son, Jason Carver. Asst. to dir. public relations Fedn. Jewish Agys., Phila., 1960-62; asst. pub. Brentwood Pub. Corp., Los Angeles, 1962-71; owner, pub. Creative Age Publs., North Hollywood, Calif., 1971—; v.p. Creative Power Mgmt., Los Angeles, 1976—. Recipient award of merit Illustrators West, 1976. Mem. Am. Trauma Soc., Western Publs. Assn. (Maggie award 1978, Eddie award 1975), Western Dialysis Assn., Kidney Found. So. Calif., Advt. Club Los Angeles, Los Angeles Women in Bus.

CARY, ARLENE D., hotel co. sales exec.; b. Chgo., Dec. 19, 1930; d. Seymour S. and Shirley L. (Land) C.; student U. Wis., 1949-52; B.A., U. Miami, 1953; m. Elliott D. Hagle, Dec. 30, 1972 (div.). Public relations account exec. Robert Howe & Co., 1953-55; sales mgr. Martin B. Iger & Co., 1955-57; sales mgr., gen. mgr. Sorrento Hotel, Miami Beach, Fla., 1957-59; gen. mgr. Mayflower Hotel, Manomet, Mass., 1959-60; various positions Aristocrat Inns of Am., 1960-72; v.p. sales, McCormick Inn, Chgo., 1972—. Active Nat. Women's Polit. Caucus, Internat. Orgn. Women Execs., membership promotion chmn., 1979-80, bd. dirs., 1980-81. Recipient disting. salesman award Sales and Mktg. Execs, Internat., 1977. Mem. Profl. Conv. Mgmt. Assn., Nat. Assn. Exposition Mgrs., Hotel Sales Mgmt. Assn., Meeting Planners Internat., Chgo. Soc. Assn. Execs. Jewish. Home: 1130 S Michigan Ave Apt 3203 Chicago IL 60605 Office: Mc Cormick Inn 23rd and Lake Shore Dr Chicago IL 60616

CARY, CHRISTIE ROBINSON, med. supply co. exec.; b. Miami Beach, Fla., July 21, 1952; d. Joseph and Dorothy Elizabeth (Peterson) Robinson; B.S. in Speech and Hearing Sci., U. Ill., Urbana, 1974; M.A. in Speech and Lang. Pathology, Central Mich. U., 1975; m. Robert Philip Cary, Sept. 8, 1979. Regional sales mgr. Bendix Corp., Chgo., 1977-79; account exec. Frank J. Corbett Co. div. BBDO Internat., Chgo., 1979-80; pres. Caramed, Inc., Chgo., 1981—. Office of Edn. scholar, 1975. Mem. Nat. Assn. Female Execs., Profl. Orgn. Speech and Arts, U. Ill. Alumni Assn., Zeta Phi Eta. Home and office: 738 W Schubert St Chicago IL 60614

CARY, FRANCES WOLFSON, ins. co. exec.; b. Miami, Fla., June 9, 1932; d. Mitchell and Frances Louise (Cohen) Wolfson; B.A., Bennington (Vt.) Coll., 1953; m. Elton M. Cary, July 26, 1968; children—Jeri Louise, Jacquelyn Frances. Sec., treas., dir. Gen. Ins. Co., Miami Beach, Fla., 1974—; owner Frances W. Cary Antiques, 1978—; pres. Marine Reins. Corp., Miami Beach, 1981-82; dir. Wometco Cable TV, Miami 1981. Past mem. nat. adv. bd. Big Bros.-Big Sisters Am.; bd. dirs. Up With People, 1981-82; past pres. women's guild U. Miami. Mem. Daus. Confederacy. Clubs: Ocean Reef, Palm Bay, Princeton. Home: 5500 Collins Ave Miami Beach FL 33140 Office: 1815 Purdy Ave Miami Beach FL 33139

CARY, ROSEANNA, sales and mktg. exec.; b. Los Angeles, June 21, 1939; d. Richard Eugene and Frances Ann (Egan) Cramer; B.A., UCLA, 1974; m. Walter W. Cary, June 21, 1956; children—Walter W., Laura Lee, Cynthia Lynn, Paul Richard. Saleswoman, Sears, Roebuck & Co., Alhambra, Calif., 1970-72, Bushnell Optical Co., Pasadena, Calif., 1972-77; sales rep. Pitney Bowes Co., Los Angeles, 1977-78; dist. sales mgr. Van de Kamp's Bakery, Los Angeles, 1978-79; co-owner Copy Plus, Pasadena, 1979—, W.W.C. Mktg. Group, Pasadena, 1977—; speaker. Mem. Women in Mgmt. (1st v.p. San Gabriel Valley chpt. 1979-80), Bus. and Profl. Women, Pasadena C. of C., Women's Econ. and Career Advancement Network, Nat. Speakers Assn. Republican. Author: The Pearl of Potentiality, 1980. Home: 1114 F Magnolia South Pasadena CA 91030 Office: 121 W California St Pasadena CA 91105

CARY, SYLVIA, psychotherapist, writer; b. Norwalk, Conn.; d. John Hyde and Barbara Allen (Knapp) Preston; B.A., Boston U., 1959, M.A., 1960; student Sarah Lawrence Coll., 1953-55; children by previous marriage—Jessica Eve Hartman, Claudia Leslie Hartman. Staff clin. psychologist Boston State Hosp., 1960-63, Somerville (Mass.) Guidance Center, 1965-68; asst. dir. public relations Hollywood Presbyn. Hosp., Los Angeles, 1973; counselor, alcohol detoxification and rehab. center Vols. of Am., Los Angeles, 1974; staff psychotherapist Beverly Manor Hosp. for Alcoholism and Other Drug Problems, Orange, Calif., 1975-76; dir. Alcoholism Council South Bay, Inglewood, Calif., 1976-77; dir. public info. Nat. Council Alcoholism, Los Angeles County, 1977-79; now psychotherapist Pathways Alcoholism Unit, Valley Presbyn. Hosp., Van Nuys, Calif.; pvt. practice psychotherapy Santa Monica, Calif.; freelance writer, photographer; contbr. articles to Ms., McCall's, Mademoiselle, TV Guide, Radical Therapist, Screen Actors Guild mag., London Daily Mail, London Sun, Everywoman (also editor). Lic. marriage, family and child counselor, Calif., 1970. Mem. Mensa, Assn. Labor Mgmt. Adminstrs. and Cons. on Alcoholism, Women in Communications, Am., Assn. Humanistic Psychology. Scriptwriter documentary Pandora's Bottle.

CARYER, JANE HATHEWAY, interior designer; b. Ottawa, Ill., Apr. 15, 1924; d. Elanathan P. and Vera (O'Connell) Hatheway; B.A., U. Wis., 1946; postgrad. Madison Bus. Coll., 1946-47. Sr. interior designer Hendrickson's, Inc., Madison, Wis., 1946-59; sr. interior designer, mgr., pres., treas. Jane H. Caryer, Inc., Madison, 1959-79; founder Caryer Interiors, Ltd., Madison, 1980—. Mem. Dane County Community Welfare Council, 1966-70; bd. dirs. Madison Westside YMCA, 1975-81; bd. dirs., pres. Madison Opportunity Center, Inc., 1966-73, 79—; bd. dirs. Madison Civic Opera Guild, 1980—, v.p., 1982-83. Mem. Am. Soc. Interior Designers, D.A.R., U. Wis. Alumni Assn., Madison Art Assn., Aircraft Owners and Pilots Assn. Clubs: Altrusa Internat. (chpt. pres. 1966-68), Blackhawk Country (Madison). Home: Winchester Bay 102 Ferchland Pl Monona WI 53714 Office: 301 S Bedford St Madison WI 53703

CASACELI, MARILYN, audiologist; b. Rochester, N.Y., Sept. 1, 1946; d. Frank J. and Rose M. Casaceli; B.A., SUNY, Albany, 1968; M.A., Syracuse U., 1969. Audiologist Nat. Tech. Inst. for the Deaf, Rochester, N.Y., 1969-70; audiologist Cleve. Hearing and Speech Center, 1970-71; audiologist Sunnyview Hosp. and Rehab. Center, Schenectady, 1971-74; speech and hearing cons. N.Y. State Dept. Health, Albany, 1974-79; regional med. care adminstr. N.Y. State Dept. Health, Albany, 1980-81, health program adminstr. physically handicapped children's program, 1981—; mem. steering com. women's issues group, 1980; lectr. audiology SUNY, Albany, 1972-74. Mem. Dept. Health and Human Services-MCH Task Force, 1979; bd. dirs. N.Y. Spl. Olympics, 1982. Mem. Am. Speech-Lang.-Hearing Assn. (com. on govtl. affairs 1977, cert. in audiology), N.Y. State Speech and Hearing Assn. (Disting. Service award 1978). Contbg. author: Cancer Nursing—A Developmental Approach, 1980. Home: 18 Bauer Dr Albany NY 12205 Office: Empire State Plaza Tower Bldg Albany NY 12237

CASALS, ROSEMARY (ROSIE), profl. tennis player; b. San Francisco, Sept. 16, 1948. Profl. tennis player, 1969—; played in U.S. Open doubles, 1967, 71, 74, U.S. Open mixed doubles, 1975, Wimbledon doubles, 1967, 68, 70, 71, 73, Wimbledon mixed doubles, 1971, 73, Italian doubles, 1967, 70, Family Circle Cup singles, 1973, Wightman Cup, 1967, 76, 77, 78, 79, Spalding mixed doubles, 1976, 77, Atlanta doubles, 1976, Fedn. Cup, 1967, 76-80; finalist U.S. Open singles, 1970-71, Wimbledon mixed doubles, 1976, Bridgestone Doubles Championship, 1975; winner 1st Virginia Slims tournament in Houston, 1970; finished 3d in Virginia Slims Championship, 1976, 4th, 1977, 4th, 1978; player Los Angeles Strings, 1975-77, Anaheim Oranges, 1978; winner U.S. Open Doubles, 1982, U.S. Indoor Doubles, 1982; winner Pro-Am Tournament sponsored by Colgate Inaugural Series, Mission Hills, Calif., 1976; former pres. Women in Tennis div. Women in Sports, Inc., Beverly Hills, Calif.; founder Sportswoman Inc.; appeared on numerous television shows, including Love American Style, Get Christy Love, Pro-Fan and Dean Martin Comedy Hour; back up singer on first album by Patti Labelle. Chairwoman sports com. Nat. Leukemia Assn., 1978. Named Player of Week, Commr. World Team Tennis, 1977. Mem. Women's Tennis Assn. (dir.), Women's Internat. Pro Tennis Council. Contbr. articles to World Tennis mag. Address: Sportswoman Inc 1505 Bridgeway Suite 209 Sausalito CA 94965

CASAS, LILLIAN, med. librarian; b. Cayey, P.R., Oct. 31, 1924; d. Guillermo and Maria (Llera) C.; B.A., U. P.R., 1951, M. Health Edn., 1973; M.S. in L.S., Syracuse U., 1958; m. Guillermo Lopez, May 3, 1956. Tchr. P.R. Dept. Edn. 1950; asst. librarian U. P.R. Sch. Medicine, San

Juan, 1951-57, head cataloger, 1959-60, librarian, 1961-65, dir. Med. Scis. Campus Library, 1966-79; library cons., 1979—. Mem. P.R. Library Assn. (pres. 1964), Med. Library Assn.

CASBER, SANDRA K., govt. ofcl.; b. Mpls., July 3, 1946; d. Walter Whitten and Irene Dorothy Casber; B.A., Macalester Coll., 1969; J.D., U. Minn., 1972. Admitted to Minn. bar, 1973; law clk. Minn. Supreme Ct., 1972-73; atty. FTC, 1973-74; legis. asst. to Rep. Richard Nolan (Minn.), 1975-76; legis. asst. to Rep. Martha Keys (Kans.), 1977-78; profl. asst. Ho. Com. on Ways and Means, U.S. Ho. of Reps., Washington. Office: Room 1104 Longworth House Office Bldg Washington DC 20515 *

CASBURN, DEBORAH LYNN, trucking co. exec.; b. Lufkin, Tex., Jan. 28, 1951; d. Gervinus P. and Ella Bourrous; grad. Lufkin Secretarial and Bus. Coll., 1970; m. Archie Ronald Casburn, Mar. 9, 1979; 1 dau., Bridget Leah. Billing agt., Drs. Denman, Rowland & Smith, Assos., Lufkin, 1972-73; owner, Ronnie's Western Store, Lufkin, 1976-77; personnel asst. Louisiana Pacific Corp., Lufkin, 1978; v.p. G.P. Bourrous Trucking Co., Diboll, Tex., 1979—; sec., treas. New Waverly Truck & Trailer Inc., Diboll, 1979—. Mem. Profl. Rodeo Cowboys Assn., Nat. Assn. Female Execs. Methodist. Club: East Tex. Rodeo. Home: Route 1 Box 381 Diboll TX 75941 Office: 508 Burke St Diboll TX 75941

CASCIO, ANGELINA GIOVINO, histotechnologist; b. Birmingham, Ala., June 13, 1930; d. Sam and Josephine (Baldone) Giovino; B.S. in Biology, Birmingham So. Coll., 1951, B.A. in Psychology, 1952. Histotechnologist, U. Ala. Hosps., Birmingham, 1960-63, research asst., 1963-67, chief histotechnologist anatomic pathology, 1967—. Named Histotechnologist of Year, 1981. Fellow Royal Soc. Health; mem. Nat. Soc. Histotech. (charter), Am. Soc. Clin. Pathologists, Am. Soc. Med. Tech., Am. Chem. Soc., Ala. Soc. Histotech. (chmn. licensure com.), Bus. and Profl. Womens Club. Home: 2765 20th Pl W Birmingham AL 35208 Office: UAB 502 LHR 619 S 19th St Birmingham AL 35294

CASE, ANN CLAIBORNE, assn. exec.; b. Balt., Sept. 8, 1945; d. Robert Claiborne and Julia Reckord (Smith) C.; U. Del., 1966; postgrad. West Chester State Coll., 1970-71. Tchr., Mt. Pleasant Sch. Dist., Wilmington, Del., 1966-74; sec. to state auditor, Dover, Del., 1975-76; adminstrv. asst. Del. Ho. of Reps. Republican Caucus, 1977-78; exec. dir. Del. Sch. Bds. Assn., Dover, 1978—. Sec., Hamlet Homes Assn., 1979-81; state coordinator Ford-Dole Com., 1976; scheduling sec. Sullivan for Atty. Gen. Com., 1974; mem. adv. bd. Del. Edn. Policy Sem. Presbyterian. Home: 75 Village Dr Dover DE 19901 Office: PO Box 1277 Dover DE 19901

CASE, ELIZABETH, artist, writer; b. Long Beach, Calif., July 24, 1930; d. Nelson and Sarah Lee (Odend'hal) Case; student French Inst., 1946, Art Students League, 1948-49, Elmira Coll., 1949-51, Syracuse U., 1951, Chaffey Jr. Coll., Ontario, Calif., Scripps Coll., Claremont, Calif., 1954; children—Walter J. Zwicker, Jr., Keith Allen Zwicker, Pat James Cioffi, Susan Karin Cioffi. Asst. animator Walt Disney Prodns., Burbank, Calif., 1956-58; faculty Lighthouse Art and Music Camp, 1961; faculty New Hope (Pa.) Art Sch., 1961; asst. promotion mgr., copywriter Reinhold Pub. Co., N.Y.C., 1962-63; copywriter Columbia U. Press, 1963; advt. coordinator Orbit Imperial Design Corp., 1964; prin. Gadfly Prodns., art, writing, promotions, 1969—; faculty Ft. Lee Adult Sch., 1975-79; sr. copywriter/designer spl. projects coll. textbook advt. Prentice-Hall, Inc., Englewood Cliffs, N.J., 1975-77; U.S. Navy combat artist, 1974—; with promotion and design dept. Rutherford Mus. (now Meadowlands Mus.), 1979—; sales promotion mgr. M. Grumbacher, Inc., N.Y.C., from 1979; one-man shows research library exhbn. facility Walt Disney Prodns., 1957-58, Swain's Gallery, New Hope, Pa., 1963, D'Alessio Gallery, 1963, Gallery 8, N.Y.C., 1969, Ft. Lee Pub. Library, 1975, Ridgefield Pub. Library, 1977, Old Bridge Pub. Library, 1978; exhibited in group shows at Friends Central, Phila., 1960, Hist. Soc. Ann. Exhbn., Philips Mill, Pa., 1962-63, Englewood (N.J.) Armory Show, 1967, 68, Hadassah, Paramus, N.J., 1969, Bergen Community Coll., 1970; traveling exhbn. Bicentennial Am. Freedoms, Wilmington Opera House, Nat. Arts Club, 1975-76, Submarine Exhbn., Boat Show, Bergen County Mall, 1977; represented in permanent collections at Washington Navy Yard Combat Art Collection, Ch. of Christ, Jersey City; executed murals at INSCON, San Dimas, Calif., 1956, Los Angeles County Hosp., 1958, Delaware Canal, New Hope, 1959; mural design Allegheny Airlines, Lumberville, Pa., 1960; mural corner Main and 202, New Hope, 1960, Lumberville Meth. Ch., 1961, swimming pool, Jerico Valley, Pa., 1961, Orbit Imperial Design Corp., N.Y.C., 1965, Fabric Shop, Ft. Lee, 1969, 72, Ch. of Good Shepherd, 1971, Horizon Apts., Ft. Lee, 1972, Palisadium restaurant Winston Towers Complex, Cliffside Park, N.J., 1974, Old Bridge Pub. Library, 1977; exterior frieze Met. Plant Exchange, Ft. Lee, N.J., 1979; group shows, Nat. Soc. of Mural Painters; Green Mountain Boys Vets. Home, 1981; illustrator cover Bucks County Life, Doylestown, Pa., 1961; Vanity Fair Books, 1962, Am. Scandinavian Rev., 1962, books Molecular Kinetic Theory, 1963, Theory of Lanthinides and Chemical Energy, 1963, Harle Publs., 1969-70, Programmed Algebra, Vols. 1 and 2, 1977, Vol. 3, 1980; Use and Misuse of Statistics, 1978; assignment paintings for USN, 1974—; lectr. Women of Brandeis U., 1964. Recipient spring concours award Art Students League, 1949, Outstanding Achievement award Elmira Coll., 1976, Merit award Edgewater (N.J.) Council, 1976, Edgewater Arts Council Festival, (1st and 2d prize), 1981. Mem. Miniature Art Soc. N.J., Navy League, Nat. Soc. Mural Painters (publicity chmn. 1973-75, sec. 1975, chmn. public relations 1980-81). Studio: PO Box 58 Edgewater NJ 07020 *

CASE, JANET WILLSON, fast food exec.; b. Pocatello, Idaho, July 1, 1939; d. Ernest and Leone (Edmonds) Willson; children—Michael, Robert, Cathryn, Kelly. Staff, Va. Wesleyan Coll., Virginia Beach, 1969-71; pub. relations staff, account exec. Redmond Amundson & Rice Advt., Norfolk, Va., 1971-75; mktg. dir. Mil. Circle Shopping Mall, Norfolk, 1975-78; regional dir. mktg. Chart House, Inc., Norfolk, 1978-80, dir. mktg. So. div., Lafayette, La., 1980—. Bd. dirs. Safety City, Norfolk Sister City Assn. Mem. Norfolk C. of C. (dir.), Pub. Relations Soc. Am., Internat. Assn. Bus. Communicators, Sales and Mktg. Execs., Advt. Club Tidewater, La. Restaurant Assn. (dir.), Lafayette C. of C. (exec. bd.). Office: 666 Jefferson Lafayette LA 70506

CASE, JUDITH LINDA, ednl. adminstr.; b. Bklyn., Apr. 24, 1940; d. George and Betsy (Posner) C.; B.A., N.Y.U., 1962; M.A., Bklyn. Coll., 1967; postgrad. New Sch. Social Research, 1969-70. Caseworker, Dept. Social Services, N.Y.C., 1962-63; tchr. N.Y.C. Bd. Edn., 1963-68; dir. tng. Addiction Services Agy., N.Y.C., 1968-71; co-dir. Bklyn. Coll. Drug Abuse Program, 1971-72; asst. prof. health and drug edn. Adelphi U., 1972-74; asst. prof. Grad. Div. Human Resources Biscayne Coll., Miami, Fla., 1974—; cons. U.S. Office of Edn., 1974—; co-founder, cons. Profl. Devel. Specialists, 1980—; tng. cons. Switchboard of Miami, 1980—; owner, coordinator Yale Sch., N. Miami Beach, Fla., 1981—. Mem. Am. Soc. Tng. and Devel., Nat. Assn. Female Execs. Office: 70 NE 167th St North Miami Beach FL 33162

CASELLA, JOANNE MARY, med. technologist; b. Boston, May 8, 1942; d. John Vincent and Mary E. (Kapantis) Macdonald; A.B., Northeastern U., 1965, M.S., 1974; m. J. Dennis Casella, Sept. 18, 1966; 1 dau., Lisa. Med. technologist New Eng. Deaconess Hosp., Boston, 1965-67, asst. chief med. technologist, 1971-74, chief med. technologist, 1974—; instr. Coll. Liberal Arts Northeastern U., Boston, 1967-71, clin. instr. med. lab. sci.; cons. Mass. Dept. Pub. Health Lab. Improvement Program. Mem. Am. Soc. Clin. Pathologists, Clin. Lab. Mgmt. Assn. Home: 207 S Main St Sherborn MA 01770 Office: 185 Pilgrim Rd Boston MA 02215

CASELLAS, ELIZABETH REED (BRANNON), author, researcher; educator, author; b. New Orleans, Jan. 7, 1925; d. Dallie Reed and Elizabeth (Robinson) Brannon; B.M., Chgo. Mus. Coll., 1948; M.A., Columbia U., 1949, Profl. Diploma, 1950; postgrad. U. Paris (Sorbonne), 1953-54; M.S., Columbia U. Sch. Library Service, 1964; m. Joaquin Casellas, Mar. 16, 1954. Instr., Valparaiso U., 1946-47; asst. librarian J. M. Mathes, Inc., N.Y.C., 1955-57; librarian Communications Counselors, Inc., N.Y.C., 1957-59; head librarian Cresap, McCormick & Paget, Inc., mgmt. cons., N.Y.C., 1959-60; head librarian Stewart, Dougall & Assos., mktg. mgmt. cons., N.Y.C., 1960-65; asst. prof. Grad. Sch. Library Studies, bibliographer in bus. U. Hawaii, Honolulu, 1965-66; head bus., sci. and tech. dept. Orlando (Fla.) Pub. Library, 1966-69; asso. prof., dir. library Grad. Sch. Bus. Adminstn., Tulane U., New Orleans, 1969-77; author and researcher, 1977—. Recipient Composition award for Piano Sonata, No. 2, Phi Mu Gamma, 1948. Mem. Spl. Libraries Assn. (pres. La. chpt. 1974-75, founder Fla. chpt. 1968, past lectr. N.Y. chpt. advt. group 1957, rep. McKinsey Found. mgmt. book awards com. 1963), ALA, La. Library Assn., AAUP, AAUW, Beta Gamma Sigma, Kappa Delta Pi, Phi Mu Gamma. Republican. Episcopalian. Author: Guide to Basic Information Sources in Business Administration, 1974; Academic Business Librarians in the United States, 1979; contbr. articles on bus. librarianship and classification to profl. jours. Office: 2442 Dauphine St New Orleans LA 70117

CASEMIER, CAROLYN FURGASON, archtl. designer; b. St. Johns, Mich., June 14, 1938; d. Lionel Lyle and Dortha Ione (Kirkey) Furgason; A.S. in Archtl. Drafting, Ferris State Coll., 1958; m. Jay Richard Casemier, May 7, 1960; children—Cynthia, Camella, Christine, Archlt. draftsperson Vander Meiden & Koteles, Architects, Grand Haven, Mich., 1958-60; archtl. draftsperson Gray/Lundwall, Architecture & Land Planners, Grand Haven, 1977-78; archtl. designer and space planner Swart & Assos., Inc., Architecture, Grand Haven, Mich., 1978-79, partner, 1979—. Mem. bldg. and grounds com., bd. dirs. North Ottawa Community Hosp., 1974—; officer, LWV, 1965-74; leader, Girl Scouts, 1968-71. Mem. Dutch Reformed Christ Community Ch. Clubs: Counterpart, Spring Lake Country. Office: 600 Park Ave Grand Haven MI 49417

CASEY, CHERRELYN ANN, communications exec.; b. Fairfield, Iowa, Sept. 16, 1944; d. Edward M. and Hazel Louise (Supalla) Chuck; B.A. in Math., U. Iowa, 1966; m. Donald Patrick Casey, Aug. 8, 1970; 1 son, Michael. With IBM Corp., 1966—, systems analyst, White Plains, N.Y., 1968-69, tech. writer, Boulder, Colo., 1970-74, project mgr. tech. writing, 1974-76, devel. mgr. info. planning and editing, 1976-78, devel. mgr. internal communications, 1978-80, adv. planner, 1981—; lectr. in field.; speaker Internat. Tech. Communications Conf., 1982; pres. Concreative Contracting, Boulder, 1976—. Mem. communications com. St. John's Cath. Ch., 1980. Mem. Longmont C. of C. (edn. com. 1980), No. Colo. Home Builders Assn. Aux. (pres. 1980), Colo. Home Builders Assn. (legis. task force 1980), Soc. Tech. Communication, Young Execs. Inst., U. Iowa Alumni Assn., Women in Communications (v.p. programming 1980), Delta Delta Delta. Republican. Roman Catholic. Home: 1627 Twin Sisters Dr Longmont CO 80501 Office: PO Box 1900 Boulder CO 80302

CASEY, DONNA MILLER, govt. ofcl.; b. Oroville, Calif., Feb. 15, 1949; d. Richard Kendall and Mary Ann (Russell) Miller; B.A. in English Lit., Stanford U., 1971; m. Lyman Henry Casey, Aug. 1, 1970; children—Lyman Robert, Charles Ranieri. Corp. sec., dir. Bank of San Francisco, 1977—; pres. San Francisco Opera Guild, 1979-80, exec. com., 1974-81; dir. devel. Internat. Hospitality Center, San Francisco, 1981—; dir. San Francisco Reception Center, U.S. Internat. Communication Agy., 1982—. N.W. regional dir. Opera Guilds Internat., 1980-82. Republican. Roman Catholic. Club: Francisca (San Francisco). Editor: What Aria Cooking? The San Francisco Opera Cookbook, 1974. Office: 312 Sutter St Suite 402 San Francisco CA 94104

CASEY, EVA LYN M., lawyer; b. Modesto, Calif., Oct. 31, 1929; d. J. Hugh and Martha (Kuhlman) C.; B.S. in Law, Glendale (Calif.) U., 1974, J.D., 1975. County law librarian, San Luis Obispo, Calif., 1960-69, Santa Barbara, Calif., 1969-77; jury commr., San Luis Obispo, 1961-69; admitted to Calif. bar, 1976; head law librarian Glendale U. Coll. Law, 1977—, asst. prof., 1977—; program dir. Glendale Coll. Legal Arts, 1978—; pvt. practice, 1976—; sec. Calif. Jury Commrs. Assn., 1967-68. Mem. Am. Bar Assn., Am. Assn. Law Librarians, State Bar Calif., Calif. Conf. County Law Librarians (sec. 1976-77), So. Calif. Assn. Law Librarians (dir. 1979), Los Angeles County Bar Assn., Los Angeles Paralegal Assn., Alumni Assn. Glendale Coll. Law (rec. sec. 1977-80). Author articles in field. Office: PO Box 90731 Los Angeles CA 90060

CASEY, JACQUELINE SHEPARD, design dir.; b. Quincy, Mass., Apr. 20, 1927; d. Roy and Helen (Kingston) Shepard; B.F.A., Mass. Coll. Art, 1950. With M.I.T., Cambridge, 1955—, design dir. design services, 1970—; design cons. Nat. Endowment for Arts, Washington, 1972—. Mem. Alliance Graphique Internationale, Am. Inst. Graphic Arts (dir. 1978—), Boston Art Dirs. Designs exhibited: Phila. Coll. Art, 1968, M.I.T., 1972, 79, Chelsea Sch. Art, London, 1978, London Coll. Printing, 1980, 8th Poster Biennale, Warsaw, Poland, 1980, Lahti IV Poster Biennale, Finland, 1981, Cooper Hewitt Mus., N.Y.C., 1981, Colo. State U., 1981; work included in: The Cultural Resources of Boston, 1965; Design Through Discovery, 1970; The Design of Advertising, 1973; A Primer of Visual Literacy, 1973; Images of an Era, 1976; Print Case Books, 1975-76. Home: 90 Harvard Ave Brookline MA 02146 Office: MIT Design Services Rm 5-133 77 Massachusetts Ave Cambridge MA 02139

CASEY, LADEANE OSLER, psychologist; b. Griswold, Iowa, May 27, 1926; d. Alonzo A. and Delia Emma (Sasse) Osler; B.A. cum laude, Grinnell Coll., 1947; M.A., Drake U., 1974; Ph.D. in Ednl. Psychology, Ariz. State U., 1977; m. Donald John Casey, June 21, 1947; children—Kent, Robert, Janice, Diane, Donna, Mark. Instr. physics lab. Grinnell (Iowa) Coll., 1947-48; tutor in chemistry and math. Iowa State U., 1954-58; behavior modification intern Center for Human Devel., Des Moines, 1973-74; instr. behavior modification practicum Ariz. State U., Tempe, 1974-75; instr. stats. dept. psychology Mesa (Ariz.) Community Coll., 1976-78; asso. Human Resource Associates, Tempe, Ariz., 1977-78; psychologist God's Little People, Mesa, 1977-79; clin. counselor Outreach Services, Inc., Mesa, 1977-79; pvt. practice counseling, Scottsdale, Ariz., 1978—; mem. staff Family Counseling and Psychol. Services, Scottsdale, 1979—. Exec. v.p. Lakota council Girl Scouts U.S.A., 1968-71. Recipient Outstanding Youth Leadership award Nat. Cath. Conf., 1971; lic. psychologist, Ariz. Mem. Am. Psychol. Assn., Southwestern Psychol. Assn., Ariz. State Psychol. Assn., Soc. for Research in Child Devel., Nat. Soc. for Autistic Citizens, Am. Assn. of Sex Educators, Counselors and Therapists, Phi Beta Kappa, Iota Sigma Pi. Home: 5939 E Hummingbird Ln Paradise Valley AZ 85253 Office: 10620 N 71st Pl Suite C Scottsdale AZ 85254

CASEY, M. DIANE, ARC exec.; b. Shakopee, Minn., May 30, 1942; d. Robert Joseph and Mary Esther (Graves) C.; B.S. in Biology, Coll. St. Catherine, St. Paul, 1964; M.A. in Health Care Adminstrn., Central Mich. U., Mt. Pleasant, 1982. With hosp. transfusion services, Seattle and St. Paul, 1965-72; edn. coordinator Red Cross Center, St. Paul, 1972-77, dir. tech. services, St. Louis, 1977-82, asst. chief blood services ops., 1982—; clin. instr. U. Minn., 1974-77, St. Louis U., 1979-81. Mem. Am. Assn. Blood Banks, Am. Soc. Med. Tech., Clin. Lab. Mgmt. Assn. Author articles in field. Home: 826 Alexandra St Saint Louis MO 63122 Office: 4050 Lindell Blvd Saint Louis MO 63108

CASEY, MARIE C. (MRS. JOHN J. CASEY), mng. editor; b. New Haven, Jan. 13, 1917; d. James Edward and Mary (Lonergan) Coogan; B.A., Coll. New Rochelle, 1938; m. John J. Casey, Aug. 20, 1946; 1 dau., Eileen Mary. Advt. mgr. Brock-Hall Dairy, Hamden, Conn., 1946-53; mng. editor Am. Jour. Sci., Yale U., 1962—, asso. mng. editor Radiocarbon. Sec., Rec. for the Blind, New Haven chpt., 1962-65; editor bull. ch. Women United of Conn., 1975-82. Mem. AAUW (corr. sec. Conn. div. 1963-69, past pres. local br., chmn. fellowships and scholarships coms. local br., former editor Conn. div. Nutmeg News), Am. Field Service (former chmn.). Roman Catholic. Home: 835 Grassy Hill Rd Orange CT 06477 Office: Yale Univ Kline Geology Lab New Haven CT 06511

CASEY, NANCY ANN, social psychologist; b. Cambridge, Ohio, Nov. 13, 1913; d. Charles Leslie and Clara Rogers C.; student Coll. of Wooster (Ohio), 1930-32; B.A., Am. Internat. Coll., 1965; M.A., Boston U., 1966, Ph.D., 1969. ARC worker S.W. Pacific area, Japan, and Germany, 1943-47; Command Service Club dir. 5th Air Force, Korea, 1952-54; command recreation dir. 8th Air Force, U.S., Can., Greenland, and P.R., 1955-63; social psychologist VA Med. Center, Northampton, Mass., 1969-81, research cons., 1981—; instr. Boston U., 1968-69; asso. prof. Am. Internat. Coll., 1976. Mem. Am. Psychol. Assn., Soc. Psychol. Study Social Issues, Soc. Advancement Social Psychology, Fedn. Am. Scientists, New Eng. Psychol. Assn., NOW. Club: Zonta (Northampton, Mass.). Contbr. articles to profl. jours. Office: VA Med Center Northampton MA 01060

CASEY, PATRICIA LYNNE, mng. editor; b. Beaumont, Tex., June 11, 1955; d. David Patrick and Katherine (Kolb) Casey; B.S. in Agrl. Journalism, Tex. A&M U., 1976. Staff writer Edna (Tex.) Herald Pub. Co., 1977-78, mng. editor, asst. pub., 1979—; asst. editor Am. Rose Mag., Shreveport, La., 1978, Am. Rose Ann., 1978. Mem. adv. bd. Peggy Seale Found. for Deprived Tex. Children, publicity div. chmn. Edna-Ganado Twin Centennial Celebration, 1982. Mem. Tex. Press Assn., Gulf Coast Press Assn., South Tex. Press Assn., Jackson County C. of C. (mem. com. 1980), Ganado Mchts. Assn. (sec. 1980, 81-82). Roman Catholic. Office: Drawer K Ganado TX 77962

CASEY, PATRICIA MARIE, auditor; b. Framingham, Mass., Oct. 6, 1955; d. William Francis and Eileen Theresa (McCarthy) C.; B.S. cum laude in Mgmt., Northeastern U., 1978; M.B.A., Suffolk U., 1982. Head teller Framingham Trust Co. (Mass.), 1975-78; br. asst. Guaranty-First Trust Co., Waltham, Mass., 1978-79; payroll asst. Baybank Newton-Waltham Trust Co., Waltham, 1979; asst. controller The Dow Service Group, Boston, 1979-80; sr. auditor Multibank Fin. Corp., Worcester, Mass., 1980—. Recipient cert. of achievement Inst. Internal Auditors, 1980, 81. Mem. Nat. Assn. Female Execs., Inst. Internal Auditors, AAUW, Nat. Assn. Bank Women. Democrat. Roman Catholic. Home: 3 Wakefield St Worcester MA 01605 Office: Multibank Fin Corp 46 W Boylston St Worcester MA 01606

CASEY, PAULA FLORA, journalist; b. Jacksonville, N.C., Dec. 10, 1953; d. Paul J. and Frances Frost (Flora) C.; B.S., U. Tenn., Knoxville, 1975. People editor Clarksville (Tenn.) Leaf Chronicle, 1975-78; sports slot copy editor Jackson (Tenn.) Sun, 1979-80; editor Donelson News Diary, 1980-81; pres. Culinary Creations, Inc., 1982—; freelance journalist, 1982—; instr. journalism continuing edn. dept. Austin Peay State U., 1977-78. Co-convenor, Clarksville Womens Polit. Caucus, 1978; del. Nat. Womens Conf., Houston, 1977. Recipient award Tenn. Press. Assn., 1976, Tenn. Edn. Assn., 1978, Tenn. Assn. Retarded Citizens, 1977. Mem. Tenn. Womens Press and Authors Club Affiliate of Nat. Fedn. Press Women (state pres. 1977-79; nat. dir.), Soc. Profl. Journalists, Bus. and Profl. Women, NOW, Nat. Resources Def. Council, Americans for Democratic Action, Planned Parenthood, Nat. Abortion Rights Action League, Tennesseans for Keeping Abortion Legal and Safe, Common Cause, Tenn. Women's Network. Methodist. Home: Nashville TN

CASEY, ROSEMARY ALICE, editor; b. Bklyn., Jan. 5, 1922; d. George J. and Lillian J. (O'Haire) Christmann; B.A., St. Joseph's Coll., Bklyn., 1944; postgrad. N.Y. U., 1945; m. Michael T. Casey, Jan. 22, 1944; children—Brigid, Maura. Field sec. Girl Scouts of Greater New York, 1945-49; with Dodd, Mead & Co., Inc., N.Y.C., 1955—, editor children's books, 1970—. Vol. worker Mary Manning Walsh Home, 1974-77, Xavier Soc. for Blind, 1975—. Mem. Assn. Am. Geographers, Kappa Gamma Pi. Republican. Roman Catholic. Author: The Cousinly Cousins, 1961; (with Michael T. Casey and Sigmund A. Lavine) Water Since the World Began, 1965. Home: 226 Clinton St Brooklyn NY 11201 Office: Dodd Mead & Co 79 Madison Ave New York NY 10016

CASEY-MOORE, ROSE ANN, psychologist; b. Des Moines, Sept. 25, 1946; d. Otho Beryl and Mary Edna (McMenamy) Casey; B.S., Drake U., 1972, M.S., 1974; m. Raymond E. Moore, Aug. 14, 1977; stepchildren—James B., Susan, Megan Casey. Counseling psychologist Iowa Methodist Med. Center, Des Moines, 1974-81. Mem. Am. Psychol. Assn., Iowa Psychol. Assn., Iowa Womens Polit. Caucus, NOW, Womens Sports Found., Animal Protection Inst. Am., Des Moines Symphony Guild, Ames Internat. Orch. Festival Assn. Roman Catholic.

CASH-HOLLOWAY, ERNESTINE, mfg. co. exec.; b. Lawley, Ala., Jan. 19, 1951; d. Otis Charles and Ruby Mae (Waters) Cash; B.A. in French, Mich. State U., 1973, M.B.A., 1978; m. Marcel Holloway, Aug. 13, 1977. Edn. technician Mich. Dept. Edn., Lansing, 1974-75; program analyst Mich. Dept. Commerce, 1975-77; adminstrv. asst. Mich. Dept. State, 1977-79; sales rep. Xerox Corp., Lansing, 1979—. Acctg. advisor Jr. Achievement, Lansing, 1979—. Mem. Nat. Assn. Female Execs., Delta Sigma Theta. Home: 323 N Walnut St #104 Lansing MI 48933 Office: 6545 Mercantile Way Lansing MI 48910

CASHIN, BONNIE, designer; b. Oakland, Calif., 1915. Designer, ballet co.; costume designer Roxy Theatre, N.Y.C., 1934-37; sportswear designer Adler & Adler, N.Y.C., 1937-43; fashion designer Twentieth Century Fox Studios, Calif., 1943-49, Adler & Adler, 1949-52; own bus. Bonnie Cashin Designs, Inc., N.Y.C., 1952—. Invited by Indian govt. to assist in revitalization program for handloom industry, 1956. Recipient Nieman Marcus award, N.Y.C. Fashion Critics Winnie, Sports Illus. award, Knitwear Industry award, Phila. Mus. Coll. of Art citation, Woolknit Assn. award, 1961, N.Y. Fashion Critics award, 1961, 68; London Sunday Times Fashion award, 1966; named Woman of Year, Lighthouse for Blind, 1961. Address: 866 UN Plaza New York NY 10017 *

CASHMAN, MARGARET ANNE, psychiatrist; b. San Rafael, Calif., May 26, 1951; d. George Arnold and Mary Adele (Ditmas) Cashman; B.A. with distinction in English, U. Wash., 1973; M.D., Mt. Sinai Sch. Medicine, 1977. Intern, U. Pitts., 1977-78; resident in psychiatry Western Psychiat. Inst. and Clinic, U. Pitts., 1978-82, chief resident in child psychiatry, 1981-82; asst. prof. child psychiatry U. Pitts., 1982—, asso. dir. adolescent and young adult module, Inpatient Unit, 1982—; psychiat. cons. No. Communities Mental Retardation Programs, 1979—; invited participant NIMH workshop on child psychiatry research devel., Yale U., New Haven, 1982. Mem. Am. Psychiat. Assn. (resident rep. bd. trustees 1979-80, mem. Falk fellowship selection/program com. 1981-82, chmn. com. of residents 1981-82), Am. Acad. Child Psychiatry, AMA, Am. Soc. Clin. Hypnosis, AAAS, N.Y. Acad. Sci., Hastings Inst. of Soc., Ethics and the Life Scis. Methodist. Contbr. articles to profl. jours. Office: 3811 O'Hara St Pittsburgh PA 15213

CASPERSEN, BARBARA MORRIS, food co. exec.; b. Phila., Feb. 27, 1945; d. Samuel Wheeler and Eleanor May (Jones) Morris; B.A., Wellesley Coll., 1967; m. Finn M.W. Caspersen, June 17, 1967. Treas., dir. Westby Corp., Wilmington, Del., 1971—, Westby Mgmt. Inc., Andover, N.J., 1967—, Tri-Farms, Inc., Andover, 1967—; pres., dir. Clark Hill Sugary Inc., Canaan, N.H., 1971—; dir. Newton Trust Co. Bd. dirs. v.p. O.W. Caspersen Found., 1967—; trustee Hoosac Sch., 1968-76, Shipley Sch., 1980—, Peck Sch., 1981—; trustee Hilltop Sch., 1974—, pres., 1976-80, prin., 1980-81. Mem. English-Speaking Union U.S. (dir. 1972-73, dir. N.Y. chpt. 1970-75). Presbyterian. Club: Colony (N.Y.C.). Office: Westby Corp PO Drawer W Andover NJ 07821

CASPERSEN, FREDA R., bus. exec.; b. N.Y.C., Oct. 10, 1908; d. Benjamin and Rose (Budson) Resika; L.H.D. (hon.), Pace U., 1976; m. Olaus Westby Caspersen, Mar. 3, 1928; children—John Westby, Finn Michael Westby. Chmn. bd. Westby Corp. and Westby Mgmt., 1972—, TriFarms, Inc., 1972—; dir. Beneficial Corp., Wilmington, Del. Chmn. bd. O.W.C. Found., Venice, Fla., 1966—; bd. dirs. Beneficial Found., 1972—; trustee Venice Hosp., also hon. bd. dirs. Mem. Friends of Venice Library, Sun Coast Symphony, Venice Taxpayers League, Palm Springs Desert Mus., Met. Mus. Art, Gulf Shores Assn. Clubs: Venice Yacht, Univ. of Sarasota, Women's of Upper Montclair, Glen Ridge Women's, Montclair Women's. Office: 333 W Venice Ave Venice FL 33595

CASS, LORETTA KEKEISEN, psychologist; b. Decatur, Ill., Feb. 3, 1912; d. Frank Joseph and Ida E. Kekeisen; B.A. summa cum laude, Colo. Coll., 1934, M.A., 1942; Ph.D., Ohio State U., 1950; m. John J. Seleski, Sept. 27, 1977 (dec. Aug. 1979); children—Barbara, Judith; stepchildren—Robert, John, Maria, Joan. Instr. clin. psychology Colo. Coll., 1944-48, Ohio State U., 1948-50; sr. clin. psychologist, child guidance clinic, chief psychologist, asst. prof. med. psychology Washington U., St. Louis, 1950-75, asso. prof. grad. sch. psychology, 1967-75, asst. prof. emeritus, 1975—, prin. investigator NIMH research project, 1974-77. Chmn. Children's Mental Health Services Council, St. Louis, 1968-70, 79—. NIMH grantee, 1974-78; diplomate Am. Bd. Profl. Psychology. Fellow Am. Psychol. Assn. (sec.-treas. sect. on clin. child psychology div. 12), Mo. Psychol. Assn., Phi Beta Kappa. Democrat. Roman Catholic. Author: Childhood Pathology and Later Adjustment, 1979; contbr. articles to profl. jours. Home: 7616 Lindbergh Dr Richmond Heights MO 63117 Office: 369 N Taylor St Saint Louis MO 63108

CASSAI, MILDRED ANN, acct.; b. Denver, Jan. 15, 1928; d. Pasquale and Josephine (James) Serravo; student Denver Opportunity Sch., 1964, 75—, Community Coll., 1974; m. Elmer Cassai, Oct. 31, 1948; children—Shirley (Mrs. Michael Demery), Gary, Michael, Pamela, Larry. With Denver & Rio Grande Western R.R., Denver, 1945-50; acct. Central Bookkeeping & Tax Service, 1964-73, partner, 1971-73; pvt. practice acctg., Denver, 1975—; legal sec. Justin D. Hannen, Atty., 1975—. Mem. Assn. Enrolled Agts. (chmn. seminar com., dir. Colo. soc., membership chmn.), Nat., Colo. socs. pub. accts., Colo., Denver legal secs. assns., Epsilon Sigma Alpha (chpt. treas.). Republican. Roman Catholic. Club: Ports of Call Travel. Home: 1823 W 39th Ave Denver CO 80211 Office: Symes Bldg Denver CO 80202

CASSEL, CHRISTINE KAREN, physician; b. Mpls., Sept. 14, 1945; d. Charles Moore and Virginia Julia (Anderson) C.; A.B., U. Chgo., 1967; M.D., U. Mass., 1976. Intern, resident in internal medicine Children's Hosp., San Francisco, 1976-78; fellow in bioethics, Inst. Health Policy Studies, U. Calif., San Francisco, 1978-79; fellow geriatrics Portland (Oreg.) VA Hosp., 1979-81; asst. prof. medicine and public health U. Oreg. Health Scis. U., 1981—. Woodrow Wilson fellow, 1967; Henry J. Kaiser Family Found. faculty scholar, 1982-85; diplomate Am. Bd. Internal Medicine. Mem. Am. Genetics Soc. (dir. Western region), Assn. Advancement Med. Edn., Physicians Social Responsibility (v.p. 1981-82), ACP, Soc. Health and Human Values. Author: Ethical Dimensions in the Health Professions, 1981; Pediatric Medicine: Principles and Practice, in press. Office: 3710 Veterans Hosp Rd Portland OR 97201

CASSEL, SYLVIA ANN, market research exec.; b. Potsdam, N.Y., June 28, 1938; d. Fredrick Mott and Lillian (Walker) C.; B.S., SUNY, Potsdam, 1960; postgrad. N.Y. U., 1960-61; M.B.A., Baruch Coll., 1980. Systems engr. IBM, 1961-63; systems and programming mgr. Diners Club, 1963-64; data processing mgr. Katz Agy., 1965-69; mgr. spl. projects Arbitron, N.Y.C., 1970-72; mgr. computer client service Axiom/Simmons Market Research Bur., N.Y.C., 1972-78; v.p. advt. agy. sales/data services Mediamark Research Inc., N.Y.C., 1978; teaching fellow SUNY Coll., 1960-61. Alcoa Found. scholar, 1956-60. Mem. Advt. Data Processing Assn. (pres. 1979-80), Am. Mgmt. Assn., Advt. Women N.Y., Radio and TV Research Council. Republican. Club: D.A.R. Office: 341 Madison Ave New York NY 10017

CASSELL, DANA KAY, communications co. exec.; b. Hornell, N.Y., Dec. 12, 1941; d. Robert William and Mayadell Louise (Reubens) Amacher; children—William, Denise, Jody, Robert. Copywriter Sta. WTOC-TV, Savannah, Ga., 1965-67; ins. agt. Liberty Nat. Life Ins. Co., Savannah, 1967-70; dist. mgr. LaSalle Extension U., Fla., 1972; mgr. Stuart Domestic Service (Fla.), 1974-75; pres. Cassell Communications Inc., Port St. Lucie, Fla., 1977—. Served with USAF, 1960-61. Mem. Internat. Bus. Writers, Nat. Writers Club, Fla., Freelance Writers Assn. (founder 1982, exec. dir. 1982—), Mensa. Republican. Clubs: Parents Without Partners (chpt. pres. 1978, regional council pres. 1979, 80, dist. supr. 1981, asso. zone adminstr. 1982; Outstanding Performance & Leadership award 1981), Indian River Acad. Boosters (pres. 1979-80). Contbr. over 650 articles to various publs. Home and Office: 214 Solaz Ave Port Saint Lucie FL 33452

CASSIDY, CLAUDIA, radio critic-at-large; b. Shawneetown, Ill.; d. George Peter and Olive (Grattan) Cassidy; A.B., U. Ill.; m. William John Crawford, June 15, 1929. Music, dance and drama critic Chgo. Jour. of Commerce, 1925-41, Chgo. Sun, 1941-42; music, drama critic Chgo. Tribune, 1942-65, critic-at-large, 1966-69; weekly program Critic's Choice, WFMT, Chgo.; film critic The Chicagoan mag. (now Chicago mag.), 1973-74; contbg. editor: The Arts, Chicago mag., 1974—; spl. commentator radio Lyric Opera, Chgo. Named to Chgo. Press Club Journalism Hall of Fame, 1980.

CASSIDY, EMMA STEVENS, pub. co. exec.; b. Spottsylvania County, Va., Jan. 3, 1920; d. Charles Campbell and Sarah Catherine (Samuels) Stevens; grad. Strayer Coll., Washington, 1937; m. Carlton Cassidy, Mar. 19, 1947; 1 dau., Carol Ann. With Public Utilities Reports, Inc., Arlington, Va., 1938—, sec., 1962—, treas., 1966—, v.p. circulation, 1980—, asst. sec. utilities publ. com., 1952—. Baptist. Home: 6802 Pamela Ln Clinton MD 20735 Office: 1700 N Moore St Rosslyn Center Bldg Suite 2100 Arlington VA 22209

CASSIDY, MARY BARBARA (MARIBEE) (MRS. GEORGE R. CASSIDY), journalist, C. of C. ofcl.; b. Leadville, Colo., Aug. 22, 1914; d. Nicholas and Barbara (Rogina) Frankovich; diploma in stenotypy and bus. English, La Salle Extension U., 1942; m. Joseph George Bost, Sept. 26, 1933 (dec. Oct. 1939); children—Barbara M., Joseph A.; m. 2d, George R. Cassidy, June 4, 1947 (dec. Sept. 1978). Clk., reporter Lake County Ct., 1941-43; r.r. cashier, steno-clk., reporter for r.r. mag. Green Light, 1943—; columnist Leadville Herald Democrat, 1958-68, feature writer, 1958—; exec. sec. Leadville C. of C., 1978—; owner personal mus. of Leadville artifacts, 1964—, theatre based on Leadville history with old-fashioned ice cream parlor, 1970—; established summer theatre to portray Leadville history; tchr. machine shorthand Colo. Mountain Coll., 1971—. Reporter, Lake County Democratic Central Com., 1968—, sec., 1967-69; publicity chmn. Leadville Boom Days, 1975—, sec., 1976—, parade grand marshall, 1981; sec. Leadville Crystal Carnival Assn., 1975—; organizer events Leadville Centennial, 1978; organist St. Joseph Ch. Recipient recognition Order Eastern Star, 1982. Mem. Smithsonian Instn., Am. Hist. Soc., Leadville C. of C. (corr. sec. 1970-81, exec. sec. 1981—). Clubs: Jane Jefferson (sec.), R.R. Vets. (sec.), Lion (hon.) (Leadville). Author: St. Joseph's Church and Parish, 1973; centennial booklet of Leadville, 1978; writer booklet on Leadville history, 1976—. Home: 129 W 4th St Box 911 Leadville CO 80461

CASTAGNETO-DAMRON, CARINA KAY, educator; b. Longview, Wash., Dec. 26, 1942; d. William James and Beverly Jean (Marshall) Castagneto; B.S.Ed. in Child Devel., Brigham Young U., 1965; postgrad. U. Utah, 1965-76; m. William E. Damron, June 11, 1973. Tchr., Salt Lake City Bd. Edn., 1965-76, Centennial Sch. Dist., Portland, Oreg., 1976—. Active March of Dimes, United Fund, Am. Cancer Soc.; vol. Primary Children's Med. Center, Salt Lake City, 1966-68; active Big Sisters Program, 1967-68; mem. Com. for Defeat of Oreg. Initiative to Limit Property Taxes, 1980. Named Tchr. of Yr., Golden Gleanner Outstanding Woman award Ch. Jesus Christ of Latter-day Saints, 1972. Mem. Salt Lake Tchrs. Assn., Utah Tchrs. Assn., Centennial Edn. Assn., NEA, Oreg. Edn. Assn., Assn. of Early Childhood Educators, Assn. Early Childhood Edn. Republican. Mem. Ch. Jesus Christ of Latter-day Saints. Club: Women's Century. Home: 15640 SE Millmain Dr Portland OR 97233 Office: 1546 SE 169th Pl Portland OR 97233

CASTANO, ELVIRA PALMERIO, art historian, gallery dir.; b. Cin., July 23, 1929; d. John and Josephine Castano; B.A., Emerson Coll., Boston, 1950; postgrad. (Cardinal Spellman scholar), Pius XII Inst., Florence, Italy, 1954-55; m. Carlo Palmerio, June 1, 1958; 1 dau., Marina. Curator, Castano Art Gallery, Boston, 1965-78; dir. Castano Art Gallery, Needham, Mass., 1978—; Vatican translator; interpreter Italian art, specialist in Macchiaioli art; Italian lang. translator. Mem. Boston Mus. Fine Arts, Brockton (Mass.) Art Mus. (adv. bd.), Fogg Art Mus. of Harvard U., San Francisco Mus. Roman Catholic. Address: 245 Hunnewell St Needham MA 02194

CASTELLETT, MARISA DEL RE, art dealer; b. Rieti, Italy; d. Mario and Elena (Colantoni) Del Re; student U. Naples, 1953-55; m. Antonino Castellett, Nov. 25, 1967; 1 son, Leonardo. Pres., Marisa Del Re Gallery, N.Y.C., 1969—; dir. Delta Mktg. & Shipping, Delta Resources. Trustee, St. Luke's Sch., New Canaan, Conn., 1979-80. Pub. lithograph edits. of De Chirico, Guttuso; pub. Andre Masson, 1941-45: Water, Air, Earth, Fire. Office: 41 E 57 St New York NY 10022

CASTELLINI, ADELAIDE GLORIA (ADELE GLORIA CASTLE), hotel exec.; b. Hoboken, N.J., Feb. 6, 1926; d. Armando Louis and Mary Antoinette (Caligiure) C.; student Sch. World Trade, N.Y.C., 1965. Outside saleswoman Schaeffer Travel Service, Livingston, N.J., 1970-71; self-employed singer Mello-Larks, 1958-65; asst. mgr. internat. dept. Englewood Travel Service (N.J.), 1968-70; asst. dir. sales Las Vegas Hilton, 1974-76, dir. agy. and tour sales, 1971-74; dir. sales Golden Nugget Hotel and Casino, Las Vegas, 1976-79, v.p., gen. mgr., 1979—. Mem. Hotel Sales Mgmt. Assn. (v.p.). Democrat. Roman Catholic. Office: 129 E Fremont St Las Vegas NV 89101

CASTILLO, ELIZABETH ZIPF, mech. engr.; b. Grossheubach, Germany, June 22, 1938; came to U.S., 1957, naturalized, 1963; d. Ludwig and Erna (Hoger) Zipf; degree in Mech. Engring., Kreisberufsschule and Technische Hochschule Miltenberg (W.Ger.), 1957; 1 son, Ricky Mario Star. Sr. product designer Ling Electronics, Anaheim, Calif., 1958-61; sr. electro-mech. design engr. Astrodata, Inc., Anaheim, 1961-68; mech. engr. McDonnel Douglas Corp., Long Beach, Calif., 1968-70; mech. design engr. Comarco Engring., Ridgecrest, Calif., 1972-73; mem. tech. staff Hughes Helicopters, Inc., Culver City, Calif., 1973-81, project engr., 1981—. Mem. Am. Helicopter Soc. (dir. 1977-81, chpt. pres. 1982-83, nat. dir. 1978-79). Clubs: Hughes Helicopters Inc. Mgmt. (v.p. 1981-82, pres. 1982-83). Home: 7280 W 85th St Los Angeles CA 90045 Office: Hughes Helicopters Inc Centinela and Teale Sts Culver City CA 90230

CASTILLO, LUCY NARVAEZ, real estate broker; b. Guayaquil, Ecuador, June 25, 1943; came to U.S., 1965, naturalized, 1972; d. Jose N. and Teresa (Sanchez) Narvaez; student St. Peters Coll., 1971, Emory Riddle U., 1977; Ph.D. in Psychology, Kensington U., 1981; m. Boris Castillo, Apr. 20, 1964 (div.); children—Sylvia, Boris M. Sales agt. Globe Travel Bur., Bklyn., 1967; asst. supr. files Franklin Nat. Bank, N.Y.C., 1968; corp. sec. Castillo Med. Assos., P.A., Panama City, Fla., 1972-74; mgr. Bell Med. Group Med. Clinic, Los Angeles, 1974-76; pres. Lunar Enterprises, Inc., import-export co., Daytona Beach, Fla., 1976-78; real estate broker Watson Realty, Inc., Ormond Beach, Fla., 1978—; pres. Lucy Motors Cia. Lta. Recipient award of merit Challenge to Am., 1979. Mem. Daytona Beach Bd. Realtors. Republican. Author: (fiction) For Better or For Worse, 1979; Home: 40 Riverside Dr Ormond Beach FL 32074

CASTILLO, MARY HELEN MARQUEZ, nurse; b. El Paso, May 27, 1936; d. Jose Anselmo and Irene Maria (Federico) Marquez; diploma St. Vincents Coll. Nursing, 1957; B.S.N., U. Tex., 1974; M.S.N.U. Tex., Austin, 1977; postgrad. N.Mex. State U., 1982—; m. William Richard Castillo, Dec. 28, 1957; children—Carole Angel, William Richard II, Cesar Orlando. Nurse, St. Vincents Hosp., Los Angeles, 1957; office nurse, staff nurse critical care, El Paso, 1958-61; nursing supr. Providence Meml. Hosp., El Paso, 1961-64, dir. edn. dept., 1964-65, dir. nursing services, 1965-76; asst. prof. nursing U. Tex. El Paso, 1976—; nursing services cons.; dir., officer, W.Tex. Health Systems Agy., 1975—; mem. Profl. Adv. Council Mental Health-Mental Retardation. League United Latin Am. Citizens scholar, 1980. Mem. U.S.-Mex. Border Health Assn. (sec.), Dirs. of Nursing Services in El Paso (chmn. 1975), Tex. Nurses Assn. (v.p., pres.) Council Hosp. Nursing Tex. Hosp. Assn., Am. Hosp. Assn., Am. Nurses Assn., Tri Delta, Phi Delta Kappa, Sigma Theta Tau. Democrat. Roman Catholic. Clubs: U. Tex. Womens Aux., El Paso Womens. Contbr. articles to profl. jours. Home: 6544 Fiesta Dr El Paso TX 79912 Office: Coll Nursing U Tex El Paso TX 79902

CASTILLO, ORALIA JOSEPHINE, home economist; b. Brownsville, Tex., Oct. 14, 1950; d. Douglas Ernest and Maria del Pilar (Gonzalez) C.; B.S., Tex. Womens U., 1973. Dietitians asst. Mercy Hosp., Brownsville, 1969-70; tchr. Brownsville High Sch., 1973-74; mgr. Elson's Gift Shop, Del Monte Hyatt House, Monterey, Calif., 1974; parent edn. coordinator Jose Vasconelos Pre-Sch., Houston, 1974; tchr. home econs. Houston Ind. Sch. Dist., 1974-79; home economist Microwave Oven Center, Houston, 1979—. Mem. Am. Home Econs. Assn., Houston Home Econs. Assn., Houston Tchrs. Home Econs. Assn. Democrat. Roman Catholic. Home: Apt 5 4227 Bettis St Houston TX 77027 Office: Microwave Oven Center Katy Freeway Houston TX 77024

CASTLE, KATHRYN, educator; b. Oklahoma City, Jan. 20, 1948; d. Robert F. and Lorene A. (Bentley) C.; B.A., U. Okla., 1970; M.A. in Ednl. Psychology, Emory U., 1971; Ed.D., U. Va., 1975; m. Douglas B. Aichele, Jan. 7, 1977; children—Adam Douglas, Clint Philip. Research asst. dept. psychology U. Okla., Norman, 1967-70; substitute tchr. Oklahoma City public schs., 1970; teaching asst. dept. psychology Emory U., Atlanta, Ga., 1970-71; pvt. tutor elem. children, Atlanta, 1971-72; chief learning supr. Learning Foundations, Inc., Atlanta, 1971, dir. test evaluation, 1971-72; diagnostician Dallas (Tex.) Ind. Sch. System, 1972; instr. psychology Macon (Ga.) Jr. Coll. 1972-73; research asst. dept. curriculum and instruction U. Va., Charlottesville, 1973-74, tchr. Child Devel. Center, 1974-75; instr. early childhood edn. Piedmont Community Coll., Charlottesville, Va., 1974-75; asst. prof. dept. curriculum and instruction Coll. Edn., Okla. State U., Stillwater, 1975-79, asso. prof., 1979—; guest speaker profl. groups in edn., 1977—. Named Outstanding Tchr. of the Year, Coll. Edn., Okla. State U., 1977; Young Ednl. Leader, Phi Delta Kappa, 1981. Mem. Nat. Assn. Educators of Young Children, Okla. Assn. Educators of Young Children, Assn. of Early Childhood Tchr. Educators, Okla. Kindergarten Tchrs. Assn., Soc. for Research in Child Devel., Parents and Tchrs. for Young Children, Okla. Assn. for Childhood Edn. Internat. (v.p. 1979-81), Parents and Tchrs. for Young Children, Friends of Day Care, Southwestern Soc. for Research in Human Devel., So. Assn. on Children Under Six, Okla. Assn. on Children Under Six (v.p. 1979-81), Phi Delta Kappa. Contbr. articles on ednl. practice and child devel. to profl. jours. Office: Dept Curriculum Instruction Okla State Univ Stillwater OK

CASTLEMAN, (ELISE) MARIE TUCKER, govt. analyst; b. Duquesne, Pa., May 30, 1925; d. Guy Lester and Fannie Mae (Ridley) Tucker; B.A. magna cum laude, Howard U., 1943; M.S.W. (Family Assn. Pitts. fellow), U. Pitts., 1949; m. John Blair Castleman, Dec. 20, 1959; 1 son, John Clair II. Various social work positions Family and Children Services, Pitts., 1951, Family and Child Services, Washington, 1951-52, D.C. Health and Med. Assistance, 1954-57, Wayne County Gen. Hosp. and Infirmary, Eloise, Mich. and hosp. clinic, Detroit, 1957-59, social service dept. Ohio State U. Hosp., 1960-61, United Cerebral Palsy of Columbus and Franklin County, Ohio, 1961-66; dir. health care services Franklin County Welfare Dept., 1966-67; outpatient and clinic social worker Outpatient Clinic, VA, Columbus, 1967-82; mgmt. analyst Def. Constrn. Supply Center, Dept. Def., Columbus, 1982—. Mem. exec. adv. com. Office Minority Affairs, Ohio State U., 1972-73, mem. adv. bd. Nigerian Edn. Program, 1981—; bd. dirs. YWCA, Columbus, 1974-77; mem. Ohio Gov.'s Manpower Services Council, 1975-78; mem. Columbus Bd. Edn., 1971-79. Recipient Superior Performance award VA, 1968; Public Service award Columbus Bd. Edn., 1971-79, Alpha Kappa Alpha, 1973, Ohio State U. Office Minority Affairs, 1973; award for outstanding vol. service Ohio Sch. Bds. Assn., 1976; award for outstanding service in field public edn. Queen Etta Ct. No. 1, Order Calanthe, Columbus, 1976; award for public service Inner-City Sertoma Club, 1978, cert. of appreciation NAACP, Columbus, 1980; award of appreciation Kent State U., Edn. Devel. Services, 1980; award for disting. community service and community involvement Ohio Ho. of Reps., 1981. Developed guidelines for vol. health agys. in use of client records for interagy. communications, 1962. Home: 384 Noe-Bixby Rd Columbus OH 43213 Office: 3990 E Broad St Columbus OH 43215

CASTRO, EDNA CARLENE, personnel exec.; b. Twin Falls, Idaho, Mar. 25, 1942; d. Leo Walter and Joy Pauline (Rugh) Wright; A.A., Coll. So. Idaho, 1980; m. Robert G. Castro, Jr., June 30, 1971; children—R. Jeffrey, Leslie Joy. Personnel clk. Glendale div. Kellwood Corp., Twin Falls, 1969-71; office mgr. Snake River Area council Boy Scouts Am., Twin Falls, 1972-74; mgr. Nat. Car Rental Co., Twin Falls, 1974-78; personnel mgr. F. W. Woolworth Co., Twin Falls, 1978—; calligrapher, personnel cons.; vocat. instr. Coll. So. Idaho. Adv. bd. Distributive Edn. Club Am., 1980—. Mem. Am. Soc. Personnel Adminstrn., Nat. Assn. Female Execs., Alma Soc., Life Study Fellowship Am. Soc. Profl. and Exec. Women, Am. Entrepreneurs Assn., Internat. Entrepreneurs Assn. Republican. Mem. Ch. of Christ. Home: 207 Caswell Ave Twin Falls ID 83301

CASWELL, PATSY LOU, ednl. adminstr.; b. Priceville, Ky., June 7, 1938; d. Raymond and Orene Jane (Gibson) C.; B.S. in Phys. Edn., Western Ky. U., 1960; M.A. in Phys. Edn., No. Colo. U., 1966; postgrad. U. Louisville, 1975-77. Tchr. phys. edn. and health Pleasure Ridge Park High Sch., Louisville, 1960; tchr. swimming Wilson Jr. High Sch., Rockford, Ill., 1961-67; tchr. phys. edn., coach gymnastics Palo Verde High Sch., Tucson, 1967-68; tchr. phys. edn. Ahrens Trade Sch., 1968-70; chmn. dept. health and phys. edn., coach cross country and track, asst. athletic dir., then athletic dir. Thomas Jefferson High Sch., Louisville, 1970-79; Title IX compliance specialist Jefferson County Public Schs., Louisville, 1979—. Named hon. Ky. col. Mem. Nat. Coalition for Sex Equity in Edn., AAUW, Ky. Alliance Health, Phys. Edn. and Recreation, Women in Adminstrn., Jefferson County Adminstrs. Assn., Daus. of Am., NOW, Delta Kappa Gamma, Phi Delta Kappa. Democrat. Methodist. Home: 3509 Hanover Rd Louisville KY 40207 Office: VanHoose Edn Center 3332 Newburg Rd Louisville KY 40218

CATALANA, ROSEMARY, fin. co. ofcl.; b. Balt., Aug. 21, 1945; d. Paul Joseph and Adele Joan (Hromadka) C.; B.A. in Psychology, Washington Coll., Chestertown, Md., 1967; M.A.S. in Mktg. and Orgn. Behavior, Johns Hopkins U., 1973. Project leader Md. Dept. Transp., Balt., 1971-73; asst. v.p. Citibank N.A., N.Y.C., 1973-78; mgr. orgn. and mgmt. resources Am. Express Co., N.Y.C., 1978-81; v.p. personnel and adminstrn. Manning, Selvage & Lee, N.Y.C., 1981—; trustee Process, Inc. Instr., counselor Planned Parenthood Assn. Md., 1970-73; cons. Am. Cancer Soc. of Md., 1969-72; adj. prof. New Sch. Social Research. Recipient cert. of disting. contbn. Citibank N.A., 1977. Mem. Am. Soc. Personnel Adminstrn., Am. Soc. Tng. and Devel., Orgn. Devel. Network, Human Resources Planning Soc. Contbr. articles to profl. jours. Home: 275 Baltic St New York NY 11201 Office: 99 Park Ave New York NY 10016

CATANIA, SUSAN KMETTY, state legislator; b. Chgo., Dec. 10, 1941; d. John and Helen Kmetty; B.A. in Chemistry, St. Xavier Coll., 1962; postgrad. in chemistry Northwestern U., 1962-63; m. Anthony Edward Catania, Dec. 28, 1963; children—Susan, Rachel, Sara Ellen, Melissa, Amy, Anne-marie, Margaret. Tech. writer, editor, info. dir. chem. research firm, Chgo., 1963-70; pvt. practice free-lance and tech. editor, 1970-73; mem. Ill. Ho. of Reps., 1973—; lectr. U.S. Internat. Communication Agy., Europe, S.Am., Carribbean. Active LWV of Ill.; co-chmn. Women's Commn., Ind. Voters Ill., 1972-73; bd. dirs. Beatrice Caffrey Youth Services. Recipient awards various groups and orgns. Mem. Am. Chem. Soc., Soc. for Tech. Communications, Ill. Women's Polit. Caucus (chmn. 1975-76), League of Black Women, Republican Bus. Women's Club Chgo., Ill. Status of Women (chmn. 1974—), NOW, Nat. Order Women Legislators (regional dir. 1980-81). Office: 2043 Stratton Bldg Springfield IL 62706

CATCHINGS, YVONNE PARKS, artist, educator; b. Atlanta, Aug. 17; d. Andrew Walter and Hattie Marie (Brookins) Parks; A.B. in Art, Spelman Coll., 1955; M.A. in Art Edn., Columbia U., 1958; M.A. in Mus. Practice, U. Mich., 1970, Ph.D. in Edn., 1981; m. James A. A. Catchings, May 30, 1960; children—Andrea Yvonne Catchings Tramble, Wanda Elaine Catchings McLean, James Albert A. Tchr. art Atlanta Bd. Edn., 1955-59; instr. in art spelman Coll., 1956-57; tchr. art

Detroit Bd. Edn., 1959-75, art specialist, 1976—; lectr. Marygrove Coll., 1970-72; one-woman show: Black Artist South, Huntsville (Ala.) Mus., 1978; group shows: Forever Free: Art by African Am. Women, 1862-1980, traveling show, 1981; Fulbright-Hayes grantee for study, Zimbabwe, 1982; trustee Afro Am. Mus., 1970-72. Program chmn. Nat. Aux. to Nat. Dental Assn., 1966, chmn. art and craft, 1976; chmn. reception com. United Negro Coll. Fund, Detroit, 1980. Recipient Spirit of Detroit award Detroit Common Council, 1978, Mayor's award of Merit, City of Detroit, 1978; James D. Parks Art award Nat. Conf. Art, 1979. Mem. Nat. Art Edn. Assn., Nat. Conf. Artists, Your Heritage House Mus., Children's Mus., Mich. Art Therapist Assn., Phi Delta Kappa, Delta Sigma Theta (chmn. Founders Day 1965). Clubs: The Links, The Moles, Smart Set, Carrousels. Author: You Ain't Free Yet Notes From a Black Woman, 1976; author geneal. publs. Home: 1306 Joliet Pl Detroit MI 48207

CATERINO, LINDA CLAIRE, psychologist; b. N.Y.C., June 25, 1949; d. Carl Peter and Marie Veronica (Dughi) Caterino; B.A., Fordham U., 1971; M.A., Ariz. State U., 1975, Ph.D., 1977; m. Raymond William Kulhavy, July 17, 1977. Diagnostic psychologist Good Samaritan Hosp., Phoenix, 1975-76; psychologist Tempe (Ariz.) Elem. Sch. Dist., 1976-77; head psychologist Kyrene Sch. Dist., Tempe, 1977—; pvt. practice psychology, Tempe, 1977—; faculty asso. Ariz. State U., Tempe, 1979-80; adj. clin. asst. prof. ednl. psychology U. Ariz., 1979—. Mem. Am. Psychol. Assn., Nat. Assn. Sch. Psychologists (editorial staff Sch. Psychology Rev., 1979—). Contbr. articles to profl. jours. Home: PO Box 26321 Tempe AZ 85282 Office: 8700 S Kyrene Rd Tempe AZ 85284

CATHCART, LINDA LOUISE, museum dir.; b. Lafayette, Ind., Oct. 20, 1947; d. Robert S. and Dolores J. Cathcart; B.A. in Fine Arts, Calif. State U., Fullerton, 1969; M.A. in Art History, Hunter Coll., City U. N.Y., 1972; Fulbright fellow Courtauld Art Inst., 1973-74. Curatorial asst. Whitney Mus. Am. Art, N.Y.C., 1971-73; instr. Sch. of Visual Arts, N.Y.C., 1971-73, 75; instr. Cambridge (Eng.) U., 1974; coordinator spl. programs Bklyn. Mus., 1974-75; curator Albright-Knox Art Gallery, Buffalo, 1975-79; dir. Contemporary Arts Mus., Houston, 1979—; adj. prof. SUNY, Buffalo, 1975-78. Mem. Am. Assn. Museums, Internat. Council Museums, Am. Assn. Mus. Dirs. Contbr. essays to catalogues in field. Office: 5216 Montrose Blvd Houston TX 77006

CATHER, LETHA MAE, constrn. co. exec.; b. Stratford, Okla., May 2, 1941; d. Hollis Floyd and Lillie Lorene (Austin) Ford; diploma Draughons Sch. Bus., Oklahoma City, 1960; student Okla. State U., Okla. Bapt. U.; divorced. With Hartford Ins. Co., Oklahoma City, 1966-67; with Cowen Constrn., Inc., Tulsa, 1967—, head acctg., sec.-treas., dir., 1970—; sec.-treas., dir. Stevco Inc., Rock Ridge Devel. Co.; asst. sec. United Builders, Inc.; mem. adv. com. constrn. tech. dept. Tulsa Jr. Coll., 1977-81. Mem. Nat. Assn. Women in Constrn. (pres. Tulsa chpt. 1977-81, dist. dir. 1982-83). Democrat. Baptist. Office: 822 E 6th St Tulsa OK 74120

CATHEY, KARIN, ednl. adminstr.; b. Marblehead, Mass., Feb. 9, 1942; d. Hermann Wilhelm and Stella Ruth (Peterson) Stieglitz; student Tufts U., 1959-61, U. Munich (W.Ger.), 1961-63; B.A., U. Wash., 1963, M.A., 1964, postgrad., 1980—; m. Frederick Lee Munro, Oct. 25, 1975. Tchr., Glacier High Sch., Seattle, 1965-67; tchr., chairperson dept. fgn. langs. Amherst (Mass.) High Sch., 1967-74; asst. prin. Newport High Sch., Bellevue, Wash., 1974-78; prin. Sammamish High Sch., Bellevue, 1978—; cons. edn.; condr. inservice workshops, contract negotiations. Dist. chairperson Am. Heart Assn., Kirkland, Wash., 1978-82; bd. dirs. to chairperson Planned Parenthood, Bellevue, 1979-82; bd. dirs. Bellevue Probation Dept., 1980-83, chairperson, 1982-83. Recipient Friendoof Coll. award Bellevue Community Coll., 1982. Mem. Nat. Assn. Secondary Prins., Wash. Assn. Sch. Adminstrs., N.W. Women in Ednl. Adminstrn., Phi Lambda Theta, Delta Kappa Gamma. Republican. Episcopalian. Clubs: Soroptimists, Juanita Bay Athletic. Office: 100 140th Ave SE Bellevue WA 98005

CATLIN, MARIAN WOOLSTON, physician; b. Seattle, Jan. 20, 1931; d. Howard Brown and Katharine Nichols (Dally) Woolston; B.A. cum laude, Vassar Coll., 1951; M.D. (Vassar fellow), Harvard U., 1955; m. Randolph Catlin, July 5, 1959; children—Laura Louise, Jennifer Woolston, Randolph III. Intern and resident pediatric medicine Children's Hosp., Boston, 1956; resident psychiatry Mass. Mental Health Center, Boston, 1957-59; clin. fellow psychiatry Harvard U., 1957-59, Commonwealth fellow child psychiatry, 1975-78, clin. instr. psychiatry, 1975—; clin. instr. psychiatry Tufts U., 1957-59; pvt. practice child and adolescent psychiatry, Wellesley Hills, Mass., 1978—; speaker Rhodes House, Oxford (Eng.) U., 1961. Mem. bd. preparatory div. New Eng. Conservatory Music, 1972-75. Mem. Am. Acad. Child Psychiatry, Am. Psychiat. Assn., New Eng. Council Child Psychiatry (mem. chmn.), Mass. Psychiat. Soc. Episcopalian. Clubs: Vassar (mem. bd. 1963-75) (Boston); Board-Hills Garden (design cons. 1973-75) (Wellesley Hills, Mass.). Home: 314 North St Medfield MA 02052 Office: 316 Washington St Wellesley Hills MA 02181

CATO, BETTE MAXINE, state legislator; b. Odessa, Wash., May 9, 1924; d. William Dallas and Ann (Reimer) Millhorn; B.A. in Edn., Eastern Wash. Coll., 1960; postgrad. Alaska Meth. U., U. Alaska, Lawrence U.; m. John F. Cato, June 14, 1962; 1 son, Peter Duane Weber. Tchr., Kenai (Alaska) High Sch., 1960-63, East High Sch., Anchorage, 1965-69, Valdez (Alaska) High Sch., 1969-79; mem. Alaska Ho. of Reps., 1981—, chmn. transp. com., mem. leadership policy com. Mem. Am. Fedn. Tchrs., Am. Legion (Wash. dep. vice comdr. 1955, comdr. Post 2 Valdez 1972-82), Beta Sigma Phi. Served with USN, 1943-44. Home: PO Box 775 Valdez AK 99686 Office: Pouch V Juneau AK 99811

CATO, MARY LEE GRADY, educator; b. Cannelburg, Ind., July 24, 1924; B.A. in Social Scis., San Diego State U., 1958, M.A. in Curriculum and Instrn., 1969; married; 1 child. Classroom tchr. Bostonia Sch., El Cajon, Calif., 1958-68, Title I resource tchr., 1968—. Treas., People for People, 1970-72. Mem. NEA, Calif. Tchrs. Assn., El Cajon Edn. Assn. (pres. 1970-72), Calif. Assn. Compensatory Edn., AAUW. Contbr. articles to profl. jours. Certified elementary tchr., adminstr., Calif.; reading specialist, multicultural coordinator. Home: 13050 Ha Hana Rd Lakeside CA 92040 Office: 533 S 1st St El Cajon CA 92020

CATOE, BETTE LORRINA, physician; b. Washington, Apr. 7, 1926; d. John Booker and Laura Beola (Adams) C.; B.S. cum laude, Howard U., 1948, M.D., 1951; m. Warren J. Strudwick, Sept. 17, 1949; children—Laura Christina, Warren J., William J. Intern, Freedmen's Hosp., Washington, 1951-52; pediatric resident Howard U. Freedman's Hosp., 1952-55; practice medicine specializing in pediatrics, Washington, 1956—; instr. bacteriology Howard U., 1955-57; mem. staff Providence Hosp., Cafritz Hosp., Columbia Hosp., Howard U. Hosp., Washington Hosp. Center; sch. health officer Dept. Health, Washington, 1960-64; clin. instr. Howard U., 1956—. Mem. D.C. Health Planning Adv. Council, 1967-77, chmn., 1973-77; chmn. D.C. Devel. Disabilities Adv. Council, 1970-74; mem. D.C. Mayor's Commn. on Food and Nutrition, 1971-72, Mayor's Commn. on Maternal and Child Health. 1978—, D.C. Commn. Jud. Tenure and Disabilities, 1977—; bd. dirs. United Way of Nat. Capital Area, 1974-76, chmn. social planning com., 1974-75; bd. govs. St. Alban's Sch., 1978—; bd. dirs. D.C. Health and Welfare Council, 1968-73, pres., 1973-74; del. Democratic Nat. Conv., 1976; bd. dirs. Met. Washington Health and Welfare Council, 1970-72, Parent Council of Washington, 1974-75, Met. Med. Founds., Inc., Silver Spring YMCA, 1977-80. Mem. Am. Acad. Pediatrics, AMA, Nat. Med. Assn., D.C. Chirurg. Soc., D.C. Med. Soc., Am. Med. Women's Assn. (chmn. pediatric com. 1981-83), NAACP, Urban League, Am. Assn. Comprehensive Health Planners (dir. 1975-77), Women's Aux. Medico-Chirurg. Soc., Jack and Jill Am., Century Club of Nat. Assn. Negro Bus., Alpha Kappa Alpha. Baptist. Clubs: Links, Carrousels, Women's Nat. Dem. Home: 1748 Sycamore St NW Washington DC 20012 Office: 5505 5th St Washington DC 20011

CAUFIELD, PATRICIA JANE, artist; b. Gross Pointe, Mich., Oct. 2, 1944; d. Wade Arnold and Elizabeth Betty (Melitshka) C.; B.A., Calif. State U., Dominguez Hills, 1975; M.F.A., Calif. State U., Long Beach, 1981. Group exhbns. include: So. Calif. Expo, Del Mar, Calif., 1975, Tex. Tech. U., 1977, Calif. State U., Dominguez Hills, 1977, 82, Crafts As Art, El Camino Coll. Gallery, 1977, Brand Library, Glendale, Calif., 1978, Calif. Metals Invitational, Long Beach Gallery, 1978, Long Beach Mus. Art, 1981, Riverside (Calif.) Art. Mus., 1981, Wild Blue Contemporary Craft Gallery, 1982; owner Patricia J. Caufield Designs, San Pedro, Calif., 1972—; instr. Joslyn Center of the Arts, Torrance, Calif., 1972-80; instr. City of Manhattan Beach, 1975-79; project graphic coordinator TRW Systems, Redondo Beach, Calif., 1979—. Mem. Enamel Guild West, Soc. N. Am. Goldsmiths, Alpha Delta Phi. Address: 934 Weymouth Ave San Pedro CA 90732

CAUGHLAN, GEORGEANNE ROBERTSON, educator; b. Montesano, Wash., Oct. 25, 1916; d. George Duncan and Anna (McLeod) Robertson; B.S. in Physics, U. Wash., 1937, Ph.D., 1964; m. Charles Norris Caughlan, June 21, 1936 (div. 1975); children—Cheryl Karen, Kevin Michael, Kerry Jan, Deirdre Norrine. Instr. physics Mont. State U., 1957-61, asst. prof., 1961-65, asso. prof., 1965-74, prof., 1974—, acting dean grad. studies, 1977-79, acting v.p. academic affairs, 1978-79. Fellow Am. Phys. Soc.; mem. Am. Astron. Soc., Internat. Astron. Union, Am. Assn. Physics Tchrs., Sigma Xi. Episcopalian. Contbr. in field. Home: 1002 E Kagy Blvd Bozeman MT 59715 Office: Department of Physics Montana State University Bozeman MT 59717

CAULKINS, JANET HILLIER, coll. dean, educator; b. Sutton, Surrey, Eng.; came to U.S., 1962; d. S.J. and W.B. Hillier; B.A. with honours, Reading U., 1962; M.A., U. Mich., 1964; Ph.D. summa cum laude, U. Caen (France), 1969; m. David R. Caulkins, 1963; children—Juliette, Jennifer, James. Mem. faculty U. Wis., Madison, 1968—, asso. prof. French, 1974—, asst. dean Coll. Letters and Sci., 1977—; cons. UNESCO, 1976—. Postdoctoral fellow Am. Council Learned Socs., Paris, 1975-76. Mem. MLA, Internat. Arthurian Soc., Mediaeval Acad. Am., Société Rencesvals. Author books and articles on medieval French lit. Address: Dept French and Italian 658 Van Hise Hall Univ Wis Madison WI 53706

CAUTHEN, DELORIS VAUGHAN, artist; b. Wilmington, N.C.; d. Robert S. and Margaret (Hurst) Vaughan; student U. S.C., 1950-52, Richland Art Sch., 1960-63, 75-76, Robert Brackman, Madison, Conn., 1976-77; student of Frank Allen, Rock Port, Mass., 1955; m. John Kelley Cauthen, Dec. 28, 1925 (dec. 1973); children—John Vaughan, Henry Jennings. One-woman shows of paintings and/or sculpture include: U. S.C., Florence, 1968, U. S.C., Aiken, 1970, Francis Marion Coll., Florence, 1980, S.C. Ednl. TV, Columbia, 1966, 70, Columbia (S.C.) Town Theater, 1960, Union County Library, Monroe, N.C., 1969, S.C. Fed. Savs. & Loan Assn., Columbia, 1979 Columbia Coll., 1981, Spring Mills, Ft. Mill, S.C., 1981; numerous group shows including: Mint Mus. Art, Charlotte, N.C., 1962, 65, 66, Columbia Mus. Art, 1964, 70, 73, 77, Gibbs Art Gallery, Charleston, S.C., 1966, 67, 69, Telfair Acad. Art, Savannah, Ga., 1969, Beaufort (S.C.) Art Assn., 1969, S.C. State Fair, 1959, Columbia Coll.; represented in permanent collections: Mint Mus. Art, S.C. Nat. Bank, Columbia, U. S.C., Columbia, Columbia Mus. of Art, Columbia City Schs., Darlington (S.C.) City Schs., S.C. Gov.'s Mansion, Columbia, others. Mem. S.C. Gov.'s Council of Advs. on Consumer Credit, 1974-78. Recipient S.C. Nat. Bank award, 1969-73, also numerous show awards. Mem. Columbia Artists Guild, Guild S.C. Artists, Internat. Soc. Artists, Trenholm Artist Guild, Dutch Gork Art Assn. Methodist. Address: 2407 Wheat St Columbia SC 29205

CAVALLARO, ANN ELLEN, advt. and pub. exec.; b. Beaumont, Tex., Nov. 17, 1947; d. Carmen George and Mildred Jean Gustin (Galatian) C.; student Lamar Tech. U., 1966-68, U. Tex., 1968-69, Hunter Coll., 1972-74. Mktg. researcher Marsteller, Inc., N.Y.C., 1970; public relations asst. Mt. Sinai Med. Center, N.Y.C., 1971-78; account exec. Larick Mfg. Co., N.Y.C., 1978; mng. editor Mt. Sinai Jour. Medicine, N.Y.C., 1978-81; pres. Cavallaro Communications, N.Y.C., 1981—; editor-in-chief Med. Advt. News, 1982—; staff mem. Writing Workshop, Hunter Coll., 1979-82. Mem. Pharm. Advt. Council, Health Care Bus. Women's Assn., Women in Communications, NOW, DAR, Bus. and Profl. Women's Assn. Democrat. Methodist. Club: LaPetite. Editor: Divorce Aide Inc. Newsletter, 1976-78. Home: 302 E 88th St Apt 7H New York NY 10028

CAVALLO, MILDREDA, counselor; b. Summit, Ill., Dec. 29, 1912; d. Charles and Mary (DiViggianp) Cavallo; R.N., St. Joseph Sch. Nursing, 1938. Nurse, St. Joseph Hosp., Concordia, Kan.; med. tech. supr. St. Joseph Hosp., Belvidere, Ill., 1948-75, head pastoral care dept., 1978—; counseler Persons in Crisis, Pastoral Ministry. Mem. Nursing in Kan., No. Ill. Acad. Pastoral Services, Boone County Ministerial Assn., Am. Soc. Clin. Pathologists, Am. Soc. Med. Technologists, Nat. Assn. Cath. Chaplains. Roman Catholic. Home: 1005 Julien St Belvidere IL 61008 Office: Saint Joseph Hosp Belvidere IL 61008

CAVENDER, DELMA MAE, retail exec.; b. Charleston, W.Va., May 23, 1918; d. Mayford Clarence and Lydia Ellen (Ray) Chapman; student public schs., Charleston; m. Apr. 23, 1935 (dec.); children—Ruth Marie Cavender Fouty, Donald. With Morrisons Dept. Store, Charleston, 1945—, mgr. ladies accessories, 1950—, buyer, 1980—. Clk., Advent Christian Ch., 1972-80; asst. leader 4-H Club, 1950-54. Mem. Am. Bus. Womens Assn. (pres. Almost Heaven chpt. 1978-79, woman of yr. 1979, del. nat. conv. 1979). Democrat. Home: PO Box 416 Big Chimney WV 25302 Office: 231 Capitol St Charleston WV 25301

CAVEY, JUDY MARIE, real estate broker; b. Balt., Sept. 2, 1947; d. DeSales Michael and Marie Inez (Buckley) C.; B.A., Inter Am. U., San Juan, P.R., 1969, postgrad., 1970. Leasing dir. The Glimcher Co., Columbus, Ohio, 1972-74; leasing rep. Feist & Feist, N.Y.C., 1974-75; v.p. Yogi Shops, Inc., N.Y.C., 1976-77; leasing dir. Rosenshein Assos., New Rochelle, N.Y., 1977—; real estate broker Cavey-McFall. Mem. Internat. Council Shopping Centers, Yonkers C. of C. Lutheran. Home: 245 E 40th St New York NY 10016 Office: 77 Quaker Ridge Rd New Rochelle NY 10804

CAVNAR, MARGARET MARY (PEGGY), former state legislator, bus. exec., nurse; b. Buffalo, July 29, 1945; d. James John and Margaret Mary Murtha Nightengale; B.S. in Nursing, D'Youville Coll., 1967; m. Samuel M. Cavnar, 1977; children—Heather Anne, Heide Lynn, Dona Cavnar Hambly, Judy Cavnar Bentrim. Utilization rev. coordinator South Nev. Meml. Hosp., Las Vegas, 1975-77; v.p. Ranvac Publs., Las Vegas, 1976—; partner Cavnar & Assos., Reseda, Calif., 1976—, C & A Mgmt., Las Vegas, 1977—; pres. PS Computer Service, Las Vegas, 1978—. Mem. Clark County Republican Central Com., 1977—, Nev. Rep. Central Com., 1978-80; mem. Nev. Assembly, 1979-81; dir., treas. Nev. Med. Fed. Credit Union; v.p. Community Youth Activities Found., Inc., Civic Assn. Am.; mem. utilization rev. bd. Easter Seals; trustee Nev. Sch. Arts, 1980—. Club: Cosmopolitanly Hers Info. (pres.). Office: PO Box 26073 Las Vegas NV 89102

CAWEIN, KATHRIN (MRS. SEABORY CONE MASTICK), artist; b. New London, Conn., May 9, 1895; d. Henry and Barbara (Franz) Cawein; M.A. (hon.), Oberlin Coll., 1966; D.F.A. (hon.), Pacific U., Forest Grove, Oreg.; student Art Students League; m. Seabury Cone Mastick, Apr. 3, 1964. Music roll editor, music interpreter with various musicians, 1911-32; tchr. County Center Work Shop, 1935-36; owner studio for children, 1950-55; one man shows: County Center, White Plains, N.Y., 1935, Village Art Center, N.Y.C., 1945, Town Hall, N.Y.C., 1950, 8th St. Playhouse, N.Y.C., 1953, Sarasota, Fla., 1973, U. Tampa (Fla.), 1973, Oberlin (Ohio) Coll., 1975, St. John's Ch., Pleasantville, N.Y., 1976, Berea (Ky.) Coll., 1977, Pacific U., Forest Grove, Oreg., 1979, 80, 81; exhibited group shows U.S., Eng., France, Italy, Ecuador, including Century of Progress, 1934, Tex. Centennial, 1937, World's Fair, 1939; represented in permanent collections at Met. Mus., Nat. Mus., Washington, Pa. State U., Tampa U., Oberlin Coll.; illuminated books St. Marks Ch., Van Nuys, Calif.; illuminated manuscripts Pacific U. Recipient Frank Talcott Non-Mem. prize Soc. Am. Etchers, 1936, prize for lithography Village Art Center, 1944, prize for etching Nat. Assn. Women Artists, 1947, price for dry point Pleasantville Woman's Club, 1950, prize for etching, 1952, prize for dry point Westchester Fedn. Women's Clubs, 1951, others. Mem. Nat. Assn. Women Artists, Art Students League (life), Chgo. Soc. Etchers, Soc. Graphic Artists. Home and Studio: 35 Mountain Rd Pleasantville NY 10570

CAWOOD, ELIZABETH JEAN, public relations counselor; b. Santa Maria, Calif., Jan. 6, 1947; d. John Stephen and Gertrude Margaret (Shelton) Dille; B.A., Whitworth, Coll., 1968; m. Neil F. Cawood, Jan. 4, 1975; 1 son, Nathan Patrick. Adminstrv. asst. N.W. Assn. of Rehab. Industries, Seattle, 1973-74; dir. public info. Inland Empire Goodwill Industries, Spokane, Wash., 1967-72; public relations counselor, owner Cawood Communications, Eugene, Oreg., 1974—. Coordinator, Bus. Owners Network, Eugene, 1980-81; bd. dirs. Eugene Inst. Managerial and Profl. Women, 1980-81. Recipient Goodwill Industries of Am. Public Relations Achievement award, 1971. Mem. Eugene Pvt. Industry Council (chair 1979-81) LWV of Central Lane County (treas. 1979), Counselor's Acad. of Public Relations Soc. Am. (pres. 1980-82, accredited), Nat. Rehab. Assn. (pres. Oreg. chpt. 1980-81), Women in Communications (v.p. program Eugene profl. chpt.), Rehab. Internat., Nat. Assn. Rehab. Facilities, Nat. Assn. for Retarded Citizens, Eugene Action Forum Presbyterian. Editor, Intercom, 1973-80; editor: Work-Oriented Rehabilitation Dictionary and Synonyms (Words), 2nd edit. 1979; Directory of Rehabilitation Acronyms, 1977; editor Family Communicator, 1979-80, Oregon Focus, 1980-81. Office: 144 E 14th St Suite 1 Eugene OR 97401

CAWS, MARY ANN, educator, critic; b. Wilmington, N.C., Sept. 10, 1933; d. Harmon Chadbourn and Margaret Devereux (Lippitt) Rorison; B.A., Bryn Mawr Coll., 1954; M.A., Yale U., 1956, Ph.D., U. Kans., 1962; m. Peter Caws, June 2, 1956; children—Matthew, Hilary. Asst. instr. Romance langs. U. Kans., 1957-62, asst. editor univ. press, 1957-58, vis. asst. prof. spring 1963; lectr. Barnard Coll., 1962-63; mem. faculty Sarah Lawrence Coll., 1963-64; mem. faculty Hunter Coll., N.Y.C., 1966—, prof. 69—; exec. officer comparative lit. program CUNY Grad. Center, 1977-79, French program, 1979—; Phi Beta Kappa vis. scholar, 1982-83. Fellow Guggenheim Found., 1972-73, Nat. Endowment Humanities, 1979-80; Fulbright travel fellow, 1972-73. Mem. MLA (exec. council 1973-77, v.p. 1982-83, pres. 1983-84), Am. Assn. Tchr. Frech, Internat. Assn. Philosophy and Lit. (exec. bd. 1982—), Am. Comparative Lit. Assn. (exec. com. 1981—). Author 20 books in field; contbr. articles to profl. jours. Editor Dada/Surrealism, 1972, Le Siecle eclate, 1974. Home: 140 E 81st St New York NY 10028 Office: CUNY Grad Center 33 W 42d St New York NY 10036

CAYLOR, MARIE LOUISE, pub. relations exec.; b. Kansas City, Mo., Jan. 31, 1906; d. Joseph Valentine and Marie Anna (Weth) Straub; journalism certificate St. Teresa Coll., 1926; student U. Ill., 1927, U. Berlin, 1928-29; m. Harry Ernest Caylor, June 10, 1933; children—Mary (Mrs. Walter Altmayer), Sarah Ann Jestadt. Mgr., TELAD, 1931-32; account exec., co-pub. relations counsel Am. Osteo. Assn., 1937-45; probate genealogist W.C. Cox & Co., 1945—; pub. relations Nat. WCTU, 1944-81, Chgo. Symphony Orch., 1946-52, Ill. Congress PTA, 1948-53, Am. Fedn. Tchrs., 1953-65, Tchr. Publs., 1955-65, World Forum, 1971—; owner pub. relations firm Harry E. Caylor Orgn. Mem. legis. com. edn. AFL-CIO, 1960; mem. Mt. Prospect (Ill.) Village Plan Commn.; mem. Mt. Prospect Bd. Trustees, 1974-75; exec. bd. Wheeling Twp. Republican Orgn. Mem. Indsl. Research Assn., Am. Fedn. Tchrs., N.W. Suburban Council Assn., Mt. Prospect C. of C. (dir.), Euclid Lake Assn. (pres., editor), Chgo. Newspaper Guild (past v.p. treas. credit union 1969-72), Internat. Labor Press Assn. (past v.p.), Chgo. Labor Editors Round Table (founder, 1st pres.), Union Tchr. Press Assn. (founder, 1st pres.). Club: Altrusa of No. Cook (pres. 1975-76). Address: 1308 Pima Ln Mount Prospect IL 60056

CAYRUTH, CAROLYN SPRY, govt. ofcl.; b. Columbia, S.C., Oct. 17, 1949; d. Bernard David and Henrietta Sally (Corley) Spry; B.S., Benedict Coll., 1971; m. Thomas Lee Cayruth Jr., Dec. 19, 1970; 1 son, Taukuss LaMonte. Teletypist, Columbia Newspaper Co., 1971-72; substitute tchr. Greenview Elem. Sch., Columbia, 1972; social worker Midlands Center, S.C. Dept. Mental Retardation, Columbia, 1972-73, dir. admissions and discharge, 1973—; counselor So. Women Services, 1978—; instr. Midlands Tech. Coll., 1981—. Mem. gov's. legis com. Mental Health and Mental Retardation, 1979—. Mem. Assn. for Retarded Citizens, Am. Bus. Women Assn. Baptist. Office: Midlands Center South Carolina Dept Mental Retardation 8301 Farrow Rd Columbia SC 29203

CAZAN, SYLVIA MARIE BUDAY (MRS. MATTHEW JOHN CAZAN), realtor; b. Youngstown, Ohio, Nov. 17, 1915; d. John J. and Sylvia (Grama) Buday; student U. Bucharest (Rumania), 1933-35, Youngstown Coll., 1936-38, Georgetown U. Inst. Langs. and Linguistics, 1950; m. Matthew John Cazan, July 14, 1935; 1 son, Matthew John G. Adminstrv. asst. statistics U.S. Dept. Def., 1941-52; spl. employee Dept. Justice, 1956-58; mgr. James L. Dixon & Co. Realtors, Falls Church, Va., 1959-70; mgr. Lewis & Silverman Inc., Chevy Chase, Md., 1970—. Mem. bd. examiners Georgetown U., 1950. Bd. dirs. Magnolia Internat. Debutante Ball. Recipient Commendation and Meritorious award Dept. Justice, 1958. Mem. Gen. Fedn. Women's Clubs (pres. 1955-56), Interscholastic Debating Soc., Washington, No. Va. real estate bds. Mem. Rumanian Orthodox Ch. Home: 6369 Lakeview Dr Lake Barcroft Estates Falls Church VA 22041 Office: 8401 Connecticut Ave Chevy Chase MD 20015

CECIL, SISTER, GEORGE ANN, coll. pres.; b. West Louisville, Ky., Dec. 30, 1927; d. Charles Leo and Georgia Ann (Mattingly) C.; B.A., Brescia Coll., 1964; M.Ed., St. Louis U., 1967; Ed.S., George Peabody Coll. Tchrs., 1974. Joined Ursaline Order Roman Catholic Ch. 1947; tchr. Sts. Joseph and Paul Sch., Owensboro, Ky., 1949-55, Seven Holy Founders Sch., Affton, Mo., 1955-65; dir. spl. edn. Brescia Coll., Owensboro, Ky., 1967-74, pres., 1974—. Officer Ky. Ind. Coll. Fund, Inc. Mem. Council Advancement of Small Colls., Council Ind. Ky. Colls. and Univs., Delta Kappa Gamma. Office: 120 W 7th St Owensboro KY 42301

CEDERQUIST, DENA CAROLINE, former educator; b. Madrid, Iowa, Aug. 29, 1910; d. Clarence John and Clara (Bork) Cederquist; B.S., Iowa State Coll., 1931, M.S., 1935; Ph.D., U. Wis., 1945. Asst. dietitian Monmouth Meml. Hosp., Long Branch, N.J., 1932-33; instr. Kans. State Coll., Manhattan, 1937-41, U. Wis., 1941-42; with Mich. State U., 1944—, asst. prof., asso. prof., 1944-56, prof., head dept. foods and nutrition, 1956-71, prof. food sci. and nutrition, 1971-78, prof. emeritus, 1978—. Mem. Am. Dietetic Assn., Am. Home Econ. Assn., Sigma Xi, Omicron Nu, Phi Kappa Phi, Sigma Delta Epsilon. Home: 545 University Dr East Lansing MI 48823

CEDERQUIST, ELEANOR NICHOLAS (MRS. STANLEY G. CEDERQUIST), civic worker; b. Toledo, Aug. 24, 1918; d. Ralph Forest and Marguerite (Wright) Nicholas; A.B., Ind. U., 1941; m. Stanley G. Cederquist, May 10, 1942; children—Eric Stanley, Robert Alan. Sec. The Nicholas Co., Inc., 1953-75. Indpls. exec. chmn. Met. Opera Nat. Co., 1966, mem. nat. council, 1966-67; mem. nat. bd. Am. Nat. Opera Co., 1967; mem. Friends of Kennedy Center, 1966—. Salvation Army Aux., 1965—, Indpls. Mus. of Art Alliance, 1961—, St. Margaret's Hosp. Guild, 1960—, Boys Club Aux., 1960—; pres. women's com. Clowes Meml. Hall, 1965-66, 66-67, adv. bd., 1978-79; residential chmn. Marion County (Ind.)-Am. Cancer Soc. Crusade, 1970—; bd. dirs. Women's Com. Ind. Symphony Soc., 1972—, Crossroads council Boy Scouts Am., 1975—, Ind. Endowment for Arts, 1977-78; trustee Indpls. Mus. Art, 1975—, Civic theatre Indpls., 1977-79; gen. chmn. operating fund campaign Indpls. Mus. Art. Home: 8502 Bent Tree Ct Indianapolis IN 46260

CEGLES-COMSTOCK, KATHLEEN ANNE, phys. therapist; b. Niagara Falls, N.Y., June 15, 1953; d. Frank William and Esther Patricia (Ciezkewicz) Cegles; student U. Buffalo, 1971-73, Miami-Dade Coll., 1973-74; B.S., Fla. Internat. U., 1976; m. John Daniel Comstock, Sept. 9, 1978. Chief phys. therapist Barlow Hosp., Los Angeles, 1976-78; owner C-C Med. Systems, Erie, Pa., 1978-79; chief phys. therapist Shriners Hosp., Erie, Pa., 1978-80; coordinator phys. therapy Home Health Services, Erie, Pa., 1980-82; pres. Health Cons. Assos., Inc., Erie, 1982—. CPR instr., ARC, 1978—, asst. instr. adapted aquatics, 1981-82. Recipient vol. hrs. achievement cert. ARC, 1981. Mem. Pa. Phys. Therapy Assn. N.W. Dist. (publs. chmn. 1980—), Am. Coll. Sports Medicine, Am. Phys. Therapy Assn., Calif. Thoracic Soc., Fla. Internat. U. Alumni Assn., Nat. Indsl. Recreation Assn., Calif. Gov.'s Council on Wellness and Physical Fitness, Coalition for Health and the Environ., Nat. Wellness Assn., AAUW, Am. Running and Fitness Assn., Respiratory Care Assembly, Zonta II, Am. Assn. Fitness Dirs. in Bus. and Industry. Home: 12 Ferncliff Beach Erie PA 16505 Office: 1946 W 26 St Suite 6 Erie PA 16508

CELLA, PHYLLIS ANN, ins. co. exec.; b. Revere, Mass., Aug. 31, 1920; d. Richard and Matilda (Sarno) C.; B.S., Boston U., 1941. With John Hancock Mut. Life Ins. Co., Boston, 1943—, asst. to sr. v.p., 1968-70, gen. dir. spl. projects and research, 1970-72, 2d v.p., 1972-75, v.p., 1975-79, sr. v.p., 1979-82; v.p. Hanseco Ins. Co. subs. John Hancock Mut. Life Ins. Co., 1971-75, pres., chief exec. officer, 1975—, also dir.; chmn. Hanseco (U.K.) Ins. Co., Ltd., Hanseco Reins Co.; dir. John Hancock Subs., Inc., Boston Personal Res. Ins. Co. (Guernsey). Trustee Bentley Coll., Waltham, Mass.; mem. adv. com. grad. program in mgmt. Simmons Coll., Boston. Fellow Life Office Mgmt. Assn. Inst.; mem. Am. Coll. Life Underwriters. Office: John Hancock Pl Boston MA 02117

CELLUCCI, MARGARET ANN, real estate and arts mgmt. exec.; b. Edgerton, Ohio, Sept. 16, 1934; d. Crinus Peter and Bertha Clair (Siebenaler) Goebel; m. Orlando Kent Cellucci, Oct. 12, 1963; children—Camille, Cynthia, Sabrina. Practical nurse, various hosps., Edgerton, Ohio, 1953-59, Colorado Springs, Colo., 1954-55, Ann Arbor, Mich., 1955-57, San Francisco, 1957-58, Boston, 1958-63; with Orlando K. Cellucci Co., Reno, Nev., 1973—; gen. mgr. Lakemill Group, Reno, 1973-80; asst. to state Senator Cliff McCorkle, 1980—. Charter mem. Nev. Opera Assn., 1966—, pres., 1977-79. Mem. Nev. Assn. Realtors, Sierra Arts Found., Reno Philharm. Orch. Roman Catholic. Asst. editor, pub. Mzuri Drumbeat, 1970-72. Office: 200 Mill St Reno NV 89501

CELMER, RACHEL TWENTE (MRS. ERNEST V. CELMER), home economist; b. Darjeeling, India, May 19, 1923 (parents Am. citizens); d. Theophil Henry and Almeta (Wolf) Twente; B.A. in Home Econs., Heidelberg Coll., Tiffin, Ohio, 1945; M.S. in Home Econs. (grad. fellow), Ohio U., Athens, 1949; design opera costumes and textiles, Berkshire Sch. Music, Tangelwood, Mass., 1951-52; m. Ernest Victor Celmer, June 9, 1954; children—Cisley, Kelly Casimer. Asst. prof. home econs. DePauw U., Greencastle, Ind., 1949-52; Ednl. stylist Simplicity Pattern Co., 1952-54; pub. relations cons. Chgo. Pub. Relations Bd., 1954-56; tchr. home econs. Lakeview High Sch., Chgo., 1964, Schurz High Sch., Chgo., 1965-74; tchr. cons. home econs. Chgo. Bd. Edn., 1974—; v.p. Scholar Systems, Inc., Chgo., 1973—, Astro-Occult Press, Inc., Chgo., 1969-73; cons. Zodiac Book Studios; pub. relations dir. Orgn. Northeast, Uptown, Chgo., 1975-76. Life mem. Chgo. PTA; mem. Am. Home Econs. Assn., Am. Vocat. Assn., Chgo. Home Econs. Club, Textile Clothing and Related Arts Forum, Restaurant Women's Club of Chgo. (pres. 1977-79), Friends of Adler Planetarium. Club: Caxton (Chgo.). Asst. editor: Chores of Life, 1965; asso. editor Book Collecting World, 1961-65. Home: 913 W Cullom Ave Chicago IL 60613 Office: Bur Home Econs Chgo Bd Edn 228 N LaSalle St Chicago IL 60601

CENTENO, PILAR AQUINO, physician, pub. health ofcl.; b. Lapog, Ilocos Sur, Philippines, Dec. 11, 1915; d. Isaac A. and Asuncion G. (Aquino) C.; came to U.S., 1951, naturalized, 1958; A.A., U. of the Philippines, 1934, M.D., 1939; M.P.H., Harvard U., 1948; m. Bohdan Jelinek, July 27, 1965. Intern, Philippine Gen. Hosp., 1938-39; resident in obstetrics New Eng. Hosp. for Women and Children, Boston, 1948; resident St. Joseph's Hosp., South Bend, Ind., 1948-49; resident in pediatrics Manila (Philippines) Children's Hosp., 1949-50, St. Mary's Hosp., San Francisco, 1952-53, Children's Hosp., San Francisco, 1953-54; fellow in pediatrics Children's Hosp., San Francisco, 1954; fellow in hematology City of Hope Med. Center, Duarte, Calif., 1954-55, acting chief of pediatrics, 1955-56; physician Student Health Services Associated Colls., Claremont, Calif., 1957-58; sch. physician (part-time) El Monte (Calif.) Sch. Dist., 1958-70; practice medicine specializing in pediatrics, Azusa, Calif., 1957-60, Monrovia, Calif., 1960-70; dep. dist. health officer El Monte Health Dist., 1970-71, Whittier Health Dist., Los Angeles County, Calif., 1971-73; dist. health officer East Los Angeles Health Dist., 1973—. Served to lt., M.C., U.S. Army, 1944-45. Diplomate Am. Bd. Pediatrics. Fellow Am. Acad. of Pediatrics, Am. Coll. Preventive Medicine; mem. Physicians Assn. Los Angeles County, Los Angeles Heart Assn., Nutrition Today Soc. (charter), Am. Pub. Health Assn.; Phi Kappa Phi. Republican. Roman Catholic. Home: 231 N Primrose Ave Monrovia CA 91016 Office: 245 S Fetterly Ave Los Angeles CA 90022

CENTER, INGRID GWYNNETH CATHERINE, city ins. exec.; b. Farnham, Eng., Jan. 12, 1945; came to U.S., 1962; d. G.A. and V.G. (Jones) Bessette; student Carleton U., Ottawa, Ont., Can., 1960-61, U. Oslo, 1964; B.A., Cornell U., 1966, Assoc. in Risk Mgmt., 1981; m. Alfred M. Center, June 25, 1966. With Gen. Motors Corp., N.Y.C., 1967-68; faculty Meiji U., Tokyo, 1968-69, Gulf Tech. Coll., Bahrain, 1971-73; with Sony Corp. of Am., N.Y.C., 1976-78; budget analyst Barclays Bank of N.Y., N.Y.C., 1978-79, ins. analyst, 1980-82; risk mgr. City of Stamford (Conn.), 1982—. Marguerite Bourgeois scholar, 1957-60; U. Oslo summer scholar, 1964. Mem. Bahrain Archaeol. Soc., Risk and Ins. Mgmt. Soc., Kappa Kappa Gamma. Club: Awali Pony. Author: Batangas: The Holiday Province, 1975. Home: 97 Madison Ave Larchmont NY 10538 Office: 429 Atlantic St Stamford CT 06904

CENTERS, LOUISE VAN CORE, clin. psychologist; b. Huntington Park, Calif.; B.A., U. So. Calif., 1953, Ph.D., 1958; J.D., Detroit Coll. Law, 1979. Admitted to Mich. bar, 1979, Fla. bar, 1980; chief clin. psychology sect. Sinai Hosp. of Detroit, 1970—; adj. asso. prof. psychology U. Windsor (Ont.); mem. Mich. State Bd. Psychology, 1975-80, chair, 1978-79. Diplomate in clin. psychology Am. Bd. Profl. Psychology. Mem. Am. Psychol. Assn., Mich. Psychol. Assn. (past state pres.), Mich. Soc. Lic. Psychologists (past state pres.), Kappa Delta. Contbr. articles profl. jours. Office: Dept of Psychiatry 14800 W McNichols Rd Detroit MI 48235

CENTURIONI, M(ARY) KATHLEEN, audiologist; b. Pitts., July 15, 1941; d. Gilbert Anthony and Catherine Margaret (Sprung) Carney; B.S. in Edn., Duquesne U., 1963; M.S., Wayne State U., 1965, Ph.D., 1971; postgrad. Villanova U., 1977, Pa. State U., 1980-81; m. Dominick X. Centurioni; 1 dau., Kierstin. In-service tchr. DePaul Inst. for Sensory Handicapped, Pitts., 1959-62; tchr. Pitts. pub. schs., 1963-64; grad. asst. Wayne State U., Detroit, 1964-65, pediatric audiologist/supr. presch. program for hearing impaired, 1965-68; supr. presch. programs for deaf, hard of hearing Detroit Bd. Edn., 1968-71; pediatric audiologist/supr. presch. lang. program St. Christopher Hosp. for Children, Phila., 1971-72; dir. speech/hearing services Child Devel. Center, Norristown, Pa., 1972-76, assoc. dir. profl. services, 1976-77, dir. profl. services, 1978—; cons. pub. sch. speech therapists Detroit Bd. Edn., 1968-71. Mem., Local Home/Sch. Assn., Wayne, Pa., 1976—, Montgomery County Day Care Assn., Ardmore, Pa., 1971-73; chmn. profl. devel./entertainment com. Main Line Day Care Assn., Ardmore, 1973-74. Nat. Merit fellow (HEW), 1964-65. Mem. Am. Speech, Lang. and Hearing Assn., Pa. Speech and Hearing Assn., Council for Exceptional Children, Alexander Graham Bell Assn. for Deaf. Catholic. Contbr. articles to profl. jours. Home: 615 Stonybrook Dr Jeffersonville PA 19401 Office: 1605 W Main St Norristown PA 19403

CERCIELLO, CAROL CHRISTINE, wallcovering design exec.; b. Teaneck, N.J., Aug. 8, 1945; d. Charles Everett and Alice (Larsen) Nord; student Glassboro State Tchrs. Coll., 1963-64; m. Vincent Cerciello, Nov. 2, 1968; 1 dau., Christina Karen. Order analyst Westinghouse Electric Corp., Succasunna, N.J., 1965-73; order clk. Nils Anderson Studios, Mt. Arlington, N.J., 1976-78, v.p., 1978—; color cons. to various wallcovering cos., 1980—. Mem. Smithsonian Assos., Nat. Assn. Female Execs. Office: 11 Prospect St Mt Arlington NJ 07856

CEREGHETTI, SALLIE DYKMAN, cosmetics co. exec.; b. White Plains, N.Y., Nov. 11, 1936; d. Harry T. and Sallie (Dodson) Dykman; B.A., Ohio State U., 1958; m. C. Armand Cereghetti, May 7, 1960; children—Michelle Diane, Marc Armand. Account exec. James Seikses Co., N.Y.C., 1959-61; asst. prodn. mgr. Dreher Advt., N.Y.C., 1961-63, traffic mgr., 1963, account exec., 1965-68; with Bio-Pharma, Inc., Kansas City, Mo., 1977—, pub. edn. dir., 1980, nat. dir. pub. edn., 1981—. Mem. AAUW. Republican. Christian Scientist. Home: 7501 W 97th St Overland Park KS 66212 Office: 1102 Grand Ave Kansas City MO 64106

CERNEA, CAROLYN ROSE HOOVER, govt. ofcl.; b. Stark County, Ohio, Nov. 19, 1941; d. Edward Lehr and Sadie (Schandel) Hoover; B.S. in Edn., Ohio State U., 1968; M.A. in English, Case Western Res. U., 1970; m. John Gene Cernea, Apr. 3, 1965 (div. 1974). Investigator, EEO Commn., Cleve., 1970-71; with Dept. Labor, 1971—, asst. regional adminstr. Labor Mgmt. Services Adminstrn., Chgo., 1975-78, dep. dir. Office Vets. Reemployment Rights, Washington, 1978—. Recipient Disting. Achievement award Dept. Labor, 1980. Mem. AAUW, Assn. Fed Investigators, Nat. Capital Fedn. Garden Clubs. Address: 200 Constitution Ave NW Room N5414 Washington DC 20216

CERNEY, CAROL ANN, devel. exec.; b. Cleve., Sept. 25, 1933; d. Charles James and Helen Ann (Koenig) Cerney; B.A. cum laude, Ursuline Coll., 1955; M.A., John Carroll U., 1963; postgrad. Cleve. Marshall Law Sch. of Cleve. State U., 1957-58, Harvard U. Tchr. history Beaumont Sch., Cleveland Heights, Ohio, 1955-65; asst. prin. Brecksville (Ohio) Sr. High Sch., 1967-72; prin. St. Augustine Acad., Lakewood, Ohio, 1972-73; dean, dir. devel. Ursuline Coll., Pepper Pike, Ohio, 1973-79; dir. univ. spl. projects Cleve. Bd. Edn., 1979-80, dir. univ. involvement, 1980—; mem. lay adv. bd. Beaumont Sch. Active, Cleve. Mus. Art; mem. Cleve. Area Citizens' League for Nursing Bd.; bd. dirs. Council for Econ. Opportunity, bd. dirs. Parmadale Children's Village; pres. Marymount Rehab. Services, 1980-82; mem. Bishop's Budget Com., Cath. Diocese of Cleve. Mem. AAUW. Republican. Club: Cleve. Athletic.

CEROVIC-DIXON, MARIJA ANDJELA, clin. social worker, psychotherapist; b. Yugoslavia, Oct. 2, 1932; came to U.S., 1963, naturalized, 1968; d. Ivan and Ivka (Benic) Cerovic; B.A., Wayne State U., Detroit, 1973, M.S.W., 1975; m. Fred W. Dixon, June 9, 1973; 1 son, Peter. Lab. technician, research asst. Doctors Hosp., Cleve., 1963-65, Western Res. U. Med. Sch., 1965-67; head pulmonary function lab. St. Luke's Hosp., Cleve., 1967-68; sr. med. technician, research asst. Wayne State U. Med. Sch., Detroit, 1968-71; psychotherapist, dir. ednl. com. Robinwood Clinic Ltd., Detroit, 1975-77; pvt. practice psychotherapy, Bloomfield Hills, Mich., 1977—. Lic. marriage counselor. Mem. Acad. Cert. Social Workers, Nat. Assn. Social Workers, Nat. Inst. Alcohol Abuse and Alcoholism, Mich. Soc. Clin. Social Workers, N.Y. Acad. Scis., Internat. Council for Advancement of Pvt. Practice in Clin. Social Work and Social Psychotherapy. Home: 130 Waddington St Birmingham MI 48009 Office: 1575 Woodward Ave Bloomfield Hills MI 48013

CERRA, GLORIA JEAN, educator; b. Tampa, Fla., May 25, 1945; d. Emilio Anacio and Marina (Diaz) C.; B.S., Fla. State U., 1967; M.A., U. Iowa, 1969. Tchr. jr. high sch. phys. edn., Miami, Fla., 1966-67; instr. phys. edn., coach U. Iowa, 1969-71, Stephens Coll., Columbia, Mo., 1971-76; asst. athletic dir. U. Mo., Columbia, 1976-79, asso. dir., 1979—; cons. in field. Mem. Nat. Assn. Collegiate Dirs. Athletics, Council Collegiate Women Athletic Adminstrs., Nat. Collegiate Athletic Assn., Assn. Intercollegiate Athletics Women. Democrat. Roman Catholic. Club: Altrusa. Office: Box 677 U Mo Athletic Dept Columbia MO 65202

CERTAINE, EVELYN REBECCA, ret. social work adminstr.; b. Phila.; d. Lawrence and Sadie (Hall) C.; B.S. in Edn., Temple U., 1938, postgrad., 1960-63; M.S.W., U. Pa., 1965, postgrad., 1968. With Pa. Dept. Public Assistance, 1940—, now adminstrv. asst. Vol., Big Sisters, 1932-38, Armstrong Assn. (Urban League), 1932-36, ARC, USO, 1942-67, Hawthorne Neighborhood Council, 1960-63; fund raiser for alumni Sch. Social Work, 1968-79; now pvt. social work practioner; active YWCA, various other community groups; bd. dirs. Dowingtown (Pa.) Indsl. and Agrl. Sch., 1977. Recipient Hon. citation for vol. work Chapel Four Chaplains, 1965; also plaques, awards, certs. USO, ARC, Dept. Army, Air Force. Mem. Nat. Assn. Social Workers, Nat. Acad. Cert. Social Workers, Otto Rank Psychoanalytical Soc., Alpha Kappa Alpha (sec. 1942-43, reporter 1945-46). Republican. Episcopalian. Club: Temple U. Mid-City Alumni.

CERUTTI, EILEEN HELEN, civic worker; b. Chgo., July 17, 1920; d. Arthur Reese (Hoskins) and Mary Francis (Weith) Hoskins; student U. Wis., Eau Claire, 1946, Patricia Stevens Modeling Sch., 1948, Tech. Inst. Eau Claire, 1963, U. Wis., 1979; m. Robert Leo Cerutti, Jan. 18, 1943 (div.); children—Mary Frances, Robert, Eileen Helen, Kevin Joseph, Patricia. Insp., Nat. Presto, Eau Claire, 1966-74; tchr. upholstering 1964—. Served with USNR, 1942-45. Mem. Am. Legion (dist. chmn. 1976-77; mem. state com. law and order 1978—, mem. nat. com. law and order 1978-79), Honor Soc. Women-Legionnaires, United Prospectors, Inc. (life). Roman Catholic. Club: Commanders (Eau Claire). Address: 1511 Bartlett Ave Altoona WI 54720

CESTNIK, SANDRA KAY COPELAND, librarian; b. Oklahoma City, Mar. 26, 1944; d. Donald Eugene and Marjorie Lucile (Groves) Copeland; B.A., Grinnell Coll., 1966; postgrad. Tulane U., 1966-67; M.S., La. State U., 1969; M.A. in Humanities, Calif. State U., Dominguez Hills, 1980; m. Teri Jacob Cestnik, Aug. 21, 1971; 1 son, Benjamin Rile. Asst. reference librarian U. Mont. Library, Missoula, 1969-73, asst. humanities librarian, 1973-78, acting humanities librarian, 1978-81, humanities librarian, 1981—, asst. prof., 1973—. Mem. AAUP, Pacific N.W., Mont. library assns., Phi Kappa Phi, Beta Phi Mu. Home: 119 Beverly St Missoula MT 59801 Office: U Mont Library Humanities Div Missoula MT 59812

CESTONE, CAMILLE ANTOINETTE, mktg. rep.; b. St. Louis, Dec. 6, 1953; d. Patrick Brian and Elaine Elizabeth (Favre) C.; B.S. in Journalism, Bowling Green State U., 1975. Editorial asst. Phi Kappa Tau, Oxford, Ohio, 1975-76, asso. editor, 1976-77, dir. communications, 1977-78, editor The Laurel, 1977-78; communications specialist Am. Inst. Plant Engrs., Cin., 1978-79; mktg. rep. Xerox Corp., Chgo., 1980—; condr. communications workshops; coll. adviser. Trustee, exec. com. Bowling Green State U. Alumni Bd. Mem. Women in Communications, Am. Bus. Women's Assn. (charter mem. Oxford chpt., pub. relations chmn.), Coll. Frat. Editor's Assn., Bowling Green State U. Alumni Assn., Gamma Phi Beta (internat. officer, chmn. internat. pub. relations, chmn. pledge com.). Office: 55 W Monroe St Chicago IL 60603

CETLIN, ISABELLE GENTILE, psychologist; b. Bklyn., Apr. 15, 1933; d. Joseph and Antoinette Gentile; B.A., Bklyn. Coll., 1956; M.A., U. Pa., 1958, Ph.D., 1964; m. Robert Cetlin, May 9, 1958; children—Andrea, Michele. Intern, Devereux Inst. Tng. and Research, Devon, Pa., 1959-60; psychologist Suffolk County (N.Y.) Mental Health Bd., Hauppauge, 1965-68; prin. psychologist N.E. Nassau Psychiat. Hosp., Kings Park, N.Y., 1969-70; cons. prin. psychologist Suffolk Developmental Center, Melville, N.Y., 1971-73; psychologist in pvt. pracice, Ft. Salonga, N.Y., 1969—, Smithtown, N.Y., 1976—; asst. adj. prof. C.W. Post Coll., Greenvale, N.Y., 1976-77. NIH fellow, 1956-60; Dexereux Inst. fellow, 1960—. Mem. Am. Psychol. Assn., N.Y. State Psychol. Assn., Suffolk County Psychol. Assn., Sigma Xi, Psi Chi, LWV, NOW. Office: 285 Middle Country Rd Smithtown NY 11787

CHABY, DIANE BLOCK, public relations agy. exec.; b. N.Y.C., Oct. 2, 1935; d. Irving and Tillie Block; B.A. in English, N.Y. U., 1956, M.A. in English, 1968; postgrad. Yeshiva U. Grad. Center, 1972-73, John Clarke Acad., London, 1973; m. June 3, 1956 (div.); 1 son, Alan Seth. Free-lance columnist Westwood (N.J.) News, 1961-63; tchr., cons., trainer N.Y.C. Bd. Edn., 1966-78; free-lance writer and publicist, 1978; publicist, media specialist Peter Rothholz Assos., N.Y.C., 1979, dir. media relations, 1979-81; account group supr. Van Vechten & Assocs., N.Y.C., 1981-82; founder pres. Chaby Communications, N.Y.C., 1982—; free-lance mag. writer, 1981—; condr. career change workshops; tchr. trainer, lab. mgmt. cons. Right To Read; mem. Right To Read Task Force; cons. ednl. systems. Mem. Women in Communications, Bus. and Profl. Women. Office: 6 Peter Cooper Rd New York NY 10010

CHADWICK, DONNA MADDEN, music therapist, speech pathologist; b. Malden, Mass., May 17, 1947; d. John Richard and Miriam (Kelly) Madden; Mus.B., Anna Maria Coll., 1969; M.S., Emerson Coll., 1975; m. William Chadwick, Nov. 7, 1969. Music therapist Hogan Regional Center, Hathorne, Mass., 1969-74; dir. music therapy and speech pathologist North Shore Spl. Edn. Consortium, Salem, Mass., 1975-78; pvt. practice music therapy and speech pathology, Boston area, 1978—; instr. music therapy Northeastern U., Boston, 1978—, Anna Maria Coll., Paxton, Mass., 1979; dir. music therapy Dean Jr. Coll., Franklin, Mass., 1977-79; asst. prof., dir. music therapy curriculum Emmanuel Coll., Boston, 1979—. HEW fellow, 1974-75. Lic. med. provider, Mass.; cert. music educator Mass. Mem. Am. Assn. Music Therapy (nat. com.; cert. music therapist), Nat. Assn. Music Therapy (New Eng. del., registered music therapist), Am. Speech and Hearing Assn. (cert. clin. competence, also state and local socs.), Mass. Music Therapy Alliance (co-founder 1980, exec. chmn. 1980—), Animal Betterment Citizens Action League, Defenders of Animal Rights, Friends of Animals. Roman Catholic. Author: (with Cynthia Clark) Clinically Adapted Instruments for the Multiply Handicapped), 1979; contbr. articles to profl. jours.; work appears in documentary The Music Child. Home: 9 Sawmill Dr Westford MA 01886 Office: Emmanuel Coll 400 The Fenway Boston MA 02115

CHADWICK, ROSALIND, ednl. adminstr.; b. Woodbury, N.J., Nov. 8, 1947; d. Gus G. and Lillian (Morlachetta); B.S. magna cum laude, Trenton (N.J.) State Coll., 1975, M.Ed. in Bus. and Econs., 1978. Adminstrv. asst. to plant mgr. Essex Chem. Corp., Clifton, N.J., 1966-74; tchr. coll. typewriting, assertiveness tng., speed writing Katherine Gibbs Sch., Phila., Glassboro (N.J.) High Sch., also Gloucester County (N.J.) Sch., 1978—; tchr.-coordinator Eastern High Sch., Gibbsboro, N.J., 1975-80; dean acad. affairs Taylor Bus. Inst., Pomona, N.J., 1980—; exec. chmn. Camden County Coop. Office Edn. Mem. exec. bd. Services to Overcome Drugs Among Teenagers; mem. fin. com. United Way Gloucester County; active Big Sisters. Mem. N.J. Coop. Office Edn. Coordinators Assn. (exec. bd.), Nat. Bus. Edn. Assn., Bus. and Profl. Women Atlantic City, Atlantic City Women's C. of C. Club: Woodbury Jr. Woman's (public relations chmn., v.p., treas.). Home: 76 Harmony Rd Mickleton NJ 08056

CHAFFEE, ESTHER RIDENOUR (MRS. THOMAS K. CHAFFEE), ch. organist; b. Lima, Ohio; d. Joshua Mechling and Jennie (Hitchcock) Ridenour; student Wittenberg U., 1929-30, Ball State U., 1956-57, Bluffton Coll., 1932-33, U. Mich., 1950-51; B.A. in Music Edn. Lawrence U., 1963; m. David R. Meily, May 23, 1934 (dec. 1972); children—Helen Adelia (Mrs. Melvin L. Bayer), Martha Frances (Mrs. Edward C. Senechal), Sara Elizabeth (Mrs. David C. Hayden); m. 2d, Thomas K. Chaffee, Jr., Aug. 1975. Elem. vocal music tchr., Lima, 1932-34, Morgan Sch., Appleton, Wis., 1963-75; substitute tchr., Washington, 1934-36, Pontiac and Birmingham, Mich., 1945-55; high sch. music tchr., Marion, Ind., 1955-58. Asst. organist Nat. City Christian Ch., Washington, 1934-36; organist, choir dir. First Bapt. Ch., Birmingham, 1950-53, All Sts. Episcopal Ch., Appleton, 1958-64, St. Thomas Episcopal Ch., Menasha, Wis., 1964-75; organist, choir master St. Albans Episcopal Ch., Olney, Ill., and St. Mary's Episcopal Ch., Robinson, Ill., 1975-77, St. Anne's Ch., De Pere, Wis., 1977—. Vol. tchr., programmer Children's Hosp., Detroit, 1950-54; dir. Civic Music Series, Marion, 1952; music tchr. Retarded Children's Sch., Marion, 1954-55; asst. music therapist Winnebago State Hosp., Oshkosh, Wis., 1967-71; music coordinator Opportunity Centers, SE Ill. Daycare Center. Mem. Organ Guild, Wis. Acad. Arts, Nat., Wis. music educators guilds, Am. Contract Bridge League (life master). Composer: St. Thomas and St. Anne Mass, other sacred works. Home and office: 2600 Riverside Dr Green Bay WI 54301

CHAFFEE, JEAN ANN, dental hygienist; b. Houston, Oct. 17, 1947; d. Claud and Georgia Lee (Wilson) Cochran; student DelMar Coll., 1965-67; certificate in dental hygiene, U. Tex., 1969; B.A., Dominican Coll., 1975; M.S.H.P., S.W. Tex. U., 1977; 1 son, Clinton Jared. Clin. coordinator Wharton (Tex.) Jr. Coll., 1975-76; dental hygienist J.R. Alexander, D.D.S., Austin, Tex., 1976-77; dental hygienist, coll. adminstr. St. Louis Community Coll., 1977—. Active Women's Commerce Assn., Arts and Edn. Council St. Louis, Mo. Bot. Garden. Mem. Greater St. Louis Dental Hygiene Soc., Mo. Dental Hygiene Assn., Am. Dental Hygiene Assn. Republican. Episcopalian. Address: 7711 Ravensridge St Saint Louis MO 63119

CHAIKIN-GELTMAN, BONNIE PATRICIA, lawyer; b. N.Y.C., Apr. 4, 1953; d. Max and Paula (Blechman) Chaikin; student Cornell U., 1970-73; B.A., Hofstra U., 1974; J.D., St. John's U., 1977; m. Joseph Mark Geltman, Aug. 7, 1976. Law intern Queens Supreme Ct., 1977; admitted to N.Y. bar, 1978, Fla. bar, 1979, U.S. Customs Ct. bar, 1979, U.S. Tax Ct. bar, 1979, U.S. Dist. Ct. bar for Eastern and So. dists. N.Y., 1979, U.S. Ct. Customs and Patent Appeals bar, 1979; law asst. firm Weingold & Berman, N.Y.C., 1977-78; asso. firm Dollinger, Gonski and Grossman, Carle Place, N.Y., 1978-79; mng. atty. firm Marsha Edelman, N.Y.C., 1979-80; individual practice law, Oceanside, N.Y., 1980—; dep. county atty. Nassau County, 1982—; profl. fashion model Other Dimensions, N.Y.C., 1980-82. . Mem. adv. bd. South Shore Planning Council; mem. membership com. L.I. Women's Network. Mem. Fla. Bar Assn., N.Y. County Lawyers Assn., Nassau County Bar Assn. (sec. immigration law com.), Nassau-Suffolk Womens Bar Assn., Am. Immigration Lawyers, Am. Bar Assn. Office: 2681 Sheldon Pl Oceanside NY 11572

CHAISSON, ELSA A., constrn. co. exec.; b. Bridgeport, Conn., Aug. 27, 1924; d. Paul and Sebastiana (D'Alesio) Pantaleon; student Nassau Community Coll., 1963-68; B.S., N.Y. State U., 1975; postgrad. div. continuing edn. N.Y. U., 1978; m. Bernard J. Chaisson, Oct. 17, 1942 (div. 1971); 1 son, Paul B. Adminstrv. asst. Gen. Electric Co., Bridgeport, Conn., 1950-54; adminstrv. technician Am. Bosch div. Arma Corp., Garden City, N.Y., 1958-62; fin. v.p. John Grace & Co., Inc., Hicksville, N.Y., 1964-72, v.p., 1972—. Mem. Democratic Com., Mineola, N.Y., 1968-70. Mem. Nat. Assn. Women in Construction, NOW, AAUW, Internat. Roster Experts UN Programmes Tech. Coop. (designate 1978). Home: 29 10th St Carle Place NY 11514 Office: 34 Washington Pkwy Hicksville NY 11801

CHALLENER, ALICE KATHRYN, musician, educator; b. McKeesport, Pa.; d. Frank Samuel and May (Phillips) Edge; pupil of Dallmyer Russell, Hans Barth, Guy Maier; student Pitts. Mus. Inst., 1932-35; m. James M. Challener, Sept. 12, 1929; 1 dau., Carol Ann Berniece. Pvt. tchr. of piano and organ McKeesport; pres. Pitts. Piano Tchrs. Assn., 1946-48; founder, pres. McKeesport Music Club, 1948-50, 55-56, 78; founder, head adviser McKeesport Youth Music Club, 1972; v.p. for certification S.W. dist. Pa. Music Tchrs. Assn., 1970-76; v.p. Pa. Fedn. Music Clubs, 1972-74, pres., 1974-78, parliamentarian, chmn. pres.' council, 1978—, chmn. president's council, 1980—, chmn. Aikens-Cadman Meml. award for Pa. student, 1980—; bd. dirs. Nat. Fedn. Music Clubs, chmn. Dorothy Dann Bullock award in music therapy, 1979-83, chmn. Northeastern region nat. music week, 1979—. Mem. Music Tchrs. Nat. Assn., Am. Guild Organists, Pa. Music Tchrs. Assn., Friends of Music Library Pitts. (dir.), McKeesport Symphony (dir. women's com.). Baptist. Co-author: Pittsburgh Piano Teachers Auditions. Address: 1404 California Ave McKeesport PA 15131

CHAMBERLAIN, CHARLOTTE APPEL, govt. ofcl.; economist; b. N.Y.C., Apr. 30, 1946; d. Henry and Marie (Lugscheider) Appel; Ph.D. in Econs., Cornell U., 1971; Prof. econs. Northeastern U., Boston, 1971-73; br. chief forecasting and modeling U.S. Dept. Transp., Cambridge, Mass., 1973-79; v.p., mgr. dept. econs. Glendale Fed. Savs. and Loan Assn. (Calif.), 1979-81; dir. Office of Policy and Econ. Research, Fed. Home Loan Bank Bd., Washington, 1981—. Bd. dirs. Real Estate Center, U. Calif., Berkeley. Lehman fellow. Mem. Am. Econ. Assn., Nat. Assn. Bus. Economists, Western Econs. Assn., Phi Beta Kappa, Phi Kappa Phi. Editor Jour. Housing Fin. Office: 1700 G St NW Washington DC 20552

CHAMBERLAIN, IMOGENE KEHN, pilot, flight instr.; b. Butte, Nebr., Dec. 25, 1926; d. Loue Emil and Martha M. (Laible) Kehn; B.F.A., U. Nebr., 1949; postgrad. U. So. Calif., 1952-53; M.Ed., Tex. A&M U., 1973; m. Howard E. Chamberlain, Nov. 29, 1957. Tchr. arts and crafts, Spanish sch. dists., Woodland, Calif., San Lorenzo, Calif., Napa, Calif., Corvallis, Oreg., Edmonds, Wash., 1953-70; flight instr. airplanes, instrument and ground Oreg. State U. Flying Club, Corvallis, 1965-67, Tex. A&M U. Flying Club, College Station, 1973—, dir. driver edn. teaching assts. program, 1972-74. Cert. secondary tchr., Calif., Oreg., Wash., Tex.; fed. aviation certs. pvt., comml. instr. with instrument, single and multi-engine-land, single engine sea ratings. Mem. Ninety-Nines, Inc., Internat. Orgn. of Women Pilots, AAUW, Iota Lambda Sigma. Republican. Pilot, Inter-continental Aircraft Delivery, Inc.; pilot Tex. to Australia, Tex. to Switzerland in a Mooney 201; mem. Lake Buccaneers.

CHAMBERLAIN, JEANETTE GOODWIN, nurse; b. Robinson, S.D., Dec. 23, 1923; d. Aaron and Hazel Mattie (Dulin) Goodwin; B.S. in Nursing, Ind. U., 1956; M.S. (USPHS grantee 1957-58), U. Colo., 1959; Ed.D., George Washington U., 1976; m. Ernest W. Chamberlain, Dec. 22, 1972 (div.). Sch. nurse, Avon, Ind., 1948-51; staff nurse Peoria (Ill.) Regional Blood Center, 1951-53; Supt. Marion County Health Dept., Indpls., 1953-57; mem. faculty U. Wash., Seattle, 1959-68, asso. prof., dir. psychiat. nursing depy., 1963-68; chief psychiat. nursing edn. br., div. manpower and tng. programs NIMH, 1968—. Served with USNR. Recipient Meritorious Achievement award Alcohol Drug Abuse and Mental Health Adminstrs., 1979. Mem. Am. Nurses Assn., Nat. League Nursing, Am. Public Health Assn., Council Continuing Edn., Phi Delta Gamma. Author papers in field. Home: 3510 Chiswick Ct Silver Spring MD 20906 Office: 5600 Fishers Ln Room 8C-16 Rockville MD 20857

CHAMBERS, ANNE COX, newspaper exec., former ambassador; b. Dayton, Ohio, Dec. 1, 1919; d. James M. and Margaretta P. (Blair) Cox; student Finch Coll., 1937, pvt. sch., Paris, 1938; m. Robert W. Chambers, Sept. 12, 1956; children—Margaretta Taylor Rich, Katharine Anne Johnson, James Cox. Former chmn. Atlanta Newspapers, dir. Cox Broadcasting Corp., Cox Enterprises, Inc.; former Am. ambassador to Belgium; now chmn. of bd. Atlanta Newspapers; dir. Fulton Nat. Bank. First pres. Forward Arts Found.; mem. internat. council Mus. Modern Art; mem. internat. sponsoring com. Charles A. Lindbergh Meml. Fund; sponsor Ducks Unlimited; bd. dirs. Instl. Devel. Corp., Atlanta, Atlanta Music Festival Assn.; mem. hon. bd. United Fund of Belgium; trustee Atlanta Hist. Soc., So. Center for Internat. Studies; bd. sponsors Atlanta Symphony; mem. exec. com. Central Atlanta Progress. Mem. Belgian Am. Ednl. Found., English Speaking Union of Belgium, Societe d'Etudes et d'Expansion, Institut Jules Bordet, English Comedy Club Brussels (hon. pres.), Atlanta C. of C. (dir., hon. pres.). Democrat. Episcopalian. Clubs: Marks (London); Societe de L'Ommegang (Brussels); Garden of Am.; Jr. League (Atlanta). Office: Atlanta Newspaper 72 Marietta St NW Atlanta GA 30303 *

CHAMBERS, BETTE, assn. exec.; b. Seattle, July 31, 1930; d. Ralph George and Edda Sommers Johnson; student U. Wash., 1946-52, Humboldt State U., Arcata, Calif., 1956-57, Sacramento State U., 1959-60, Eastern Wash. State U., 1966-67; m. Charles M. Chambers, Sept. 19, 1949; children—Janice E. Chambers-Sharar, Martha J., Patrice L. Pres., Humanist Assn. Minn., 1961-64; bd. dirs. Am. Humanist Assn., Amherst, N.Y., 1968—, pres., 1973-79, pres. emeritus, 1979—, exec. dir., 1978-79, 81—; co-founder Com. for Sci. Investigation of Claims of the Paranormal, 1976, fellow, 1976—; lectr., freelance writer. Recipient Humanist Merit award Am. Humanist Assn., 1979, Humanist Pioneer award, 1981; cert. sr. humanist counselor Am. Humanist Assn. Mem. AAAS, N.Y. Acad. Scis., ACLU, Planetary Soc. Democrat. Unitarian. Editorial bd. The Humanist, 1973—; editor Free Mind, Am. Humanist Assn. newsletter, 1975—; contbr. articles profl. jours. Home: 4116 Candlewood Dr SE Lacey WA 98503 Office: American Humanist Assn 7 Harwood Dr Amherst NY 14226

CHAMBERS, IMOGENE KLUTTS, sch. adminstr.; b. Paden, Okla., Aug. 6, 1928; d. Odes and Lillie (Southard) Klutts; B.A., East Central State U., 1948; M.S., Okla. State U., 1974, Ed.D., 1980; m. Richard Lee Chambers, May 27, 1949. High sch. math. tchr. Marlow (Okla.) Sch. Dist., 1948-49; with Bartlesville (Okla.) Sch. Dist., 1950—, asst. supt. bus. affairs Ind. Sch. Dist. 30, 1977—. Bd. dirs. Mutual Girls Club, 1981—. Mem. Am. Assn. Sch. Adminstrs., Okla. Assn. Sch. Bus. Ofcls., Assn. Sch. Bus. Ofcls. of U.S. and Can., Okla. Assn. Sch. Adminstrs., Okla. State U. Alumni Assn., Phi Delta Kappa. Democrat. Methodist. Club: Bartlesville Garden. Home: 911 Greystone Place Bartlesville OK 74003 Office: Bartlesville Ind Sch Dist 301100 S Jennings St Bartlesville OK 74005

CHAMBERS, JOAN GARDINER, home economist; b. Maxine, Ala., Oct. 30, 1935; d. Robert and Curtice Daisy (Vance) Gardiner; B.S. in Vocat. Home Econs. Edn., U. Montevallo (Ala.), 1968, M.A. in Teaching Home Econs., 1972; m. Carl Warmath Chambers, June 10, 1955; children—Rita Elaine, Dale Gardiner. Tchr. home econs., then home econs. coordinator Minor High Sch., Birmingham, Ala., 1968-76; instr. home econs. Samford U., Birmingham, 1976—, mem. univ. instructional improvement com., 1978—. Bd. dirs., sec. Katherwood Christian Sch., Birmingham; v.p. McDonald's Chapel Sch. PTA, 1967; adult Sunday sch. tchr., sec. ch. council, ch. hostess, asst. organist, mem. adult choir Katherwood Baptist Ch., Birmingham. Mem. Am. Home Econs. Assn. (nat. del. 1979, 80), Ala. Home Econs. Assn. (dir. 1979-80, chmn. coll. and univ. sect., chmn. home econs. edn. 1982-83), So. Assn. Colls. and Schs., Kappa Omicron Phi (Samford U. sponsor), Delta Kappa Gamma (chmn. profl. affairs com.). Home: Route 15 Box 1061 Birmingham AL 35224 Office: 800 Lakeshore Dr Birmingham AL 35209

CHAMBERS, LOIS I., ins. agent and exec.; b. Omaha, Nov. 24, 1935; d. Edward J. and Evelyn B. (Davidson) Morrison; m. Frederick G. Chambers, Apr. 17, 1981; 1 son by previous marriage, Peter Edward Mscichowski. Ins. clk. Gross-Wilson Ins. Agy., 1955-57; ins. sec., bookkeeper Reed-Paulsen Ins. Agy., 1957-58; office mgr., asst. sec., agt. Don Biggs & Assos., Vancouver, Wash., 1958—. Mem. Citizens Com. Task Force, City of Vancouver, 1976, Block Grant Rev. Task Force, 1978—; chmn. adv. com. Clark Coll. Mem. Ins. Women of S.W. Wash., Nat. Assn. Ins. Women. Roman Catholic. Club: Soroptimist (sec. Vancouver). Home: 8770 SW Umatilla St Tualatin OR 97062 Office: 916 Main St PO Box 189 Vancouver WA 98666

CHAMBERS, MARY PEYTON, state legislator; b. Poca, W.Va., Aug. 31, 1931; d. Henry Hanna and Hilda Claudia (Cary) Peyton; A.B., W.Va. Wesleyan Coll., 1952; M.A. in Spl. Edn., George Peabody Coll., 1955; m. Wilbert Franklin Chambers, July 6, 1957; children—Henry Peyton, James Erland, Jane Cary. Elem. tchr., W.Va. public schs., 1952-56; ednl. supr. Baird Childrens Center, Burlington, Vt., 1956-62; dir., counselor Upper Valley Adult Basic Edn., Lebanon, N.H., 1975—; mem. N.H. Ho. of Reps., 1972, dep. minority leader, 1974—; chmn. Democratic Policy Com., 1975—. Office: New Hampshire State House Room 306 Concord NH 03301

CHAMBLISS, MADELON ELAINE AHERNE, bus. exec., columnist; b. Buffalo; d. Charles Patrick and Emilie (Beaumont) Aherne; student U. Buffalo; grad. Bryant and Stratton Coll., Buffalo; m. Willard Eugene Wagner (dec.); 1 dau., Patricia Wagner Rose; m. 2d, Phiroze Nazir, Mar. 16, 1963 (div. 1970); m. 3d, William Campbell Chambliss, 1971 (dec.). Sales Rep., Coldwell, Banker & Co., Beverly Hills, Calif., 1957-59; with Century City Alcoa, 1965, Internat. Tower, Long Beach, Calif., 1966, Coldwell, Banker & Co., Securities Beverly Hills, 1969-71; poet; painter, sculptor, works, exhibited Ambassador Hotel; exec. bd. Ebell of Los Angeles. Pres., co-founder Sisters and Servants of Mary Guild, 1960-62; co-founder Mary Health of the Sick Hosp. Guild, Lady of Africa Guild. Mem. Hancock Park Art Council (co-founder), Am. Composers and Condrs. Assn. (nat. adv. bd. 1957-58, 61), Navy Belles, Internat. Platform Assn., Navy League, Assistance League. Republican. Clubs: Overseas Press, Greater Los Angeles Press, Wilshire Country. Columnist: This Changing World. Home: 510 Sierra Bonita Ave Los Angeles CA 90036

CHAMORRO, MARY LOUISE, social work cons.; b. Los Angeles, Sept. 4, 1940; d. Emanuel Goodman and Lydie Hopkins (Kuykendall) Farley; A.A., Peace Coll., 1960; B.S.W., Va. Commonwealth U., 1963; M.S.W., U. Tenn., 1966; m. Jaime E. Chamorro, June 28, 1969; children—Luis, Laura, Pamela, Jaime. Psychiat. social worker Emory U., Atlanta, 1966; med. social worker NIH Clin. Center, Washington, 1967-68, Med. Coll. Va., Richmond, 1968-69, Mass. Gen. Hosp., Boston, 1969-70; social work cons. Washington County Public Health Nurses, Peace Dale, R.I., 1978—. Mem. Nat. Assn. Social Workers (women's issues com. R.I. chpt.), AAUW. Roman Catholic. Home: 72 Oakwoods Dr Peace Dale RI 02879

CHAMPION, DOROTHY MARIE, sch. adminstr.; b. Smithville, N.J., Nov. 8, 1920; d. Robert Allen and Anna Mary (Lovett) Leeds; student N.J. Coll. Commerce, Atlantic City, 1937-38; B.A. summa cum laude, Glassboro State Tchrs. Coll., 1976, grad. student, 1976—; m. Clair E. Champion, July 31, 1939; children—Ruth Ann Champion Hirons, Elaine Champion Nesselroade, Lois Champion Waggoner, Paul. Mem. staff Mt. Carmel High Sch., Jackson, Ky., 1960-68; founder, prin. Bethel Christian Sch., Port Republic, N.J., 1968—, v.p. bd. trustees, 1968—. Mem. Internat. Assn. Christian Schs., Am. Assn. Christian Schs., Mid Atlantic Assn. Christian Schs., Garden State Assn. Christian Schs. Methodist. Address: PO Box 196 Genoa Ave Port Republic NJ 08241

CHAMPION, JUDY ANN, govt. ofcl.; b. Mayaguez, P.R., Oct. 19, 1945; d. Albert A. and Angela Maria (Gonzalez) C.; B.B.A., U. P.R., 1967; M.S. in Acctg., World U., Rio Piedras, P.R., 1976; div.; 1 dau., Shirley Elizabeth Santiago. Chief acct. U.S. Naval Sta., San Juan, 1968-72; fin. mgr. S.C. Johnson Co., Inc., San Juan, 1973-74; chief acct. North Atlantic Mediterranean Freight Conf., N.Y.C., 1973-74; comptroller Ramada San Juan Hotel, 1974; chief acctg. officer Central Acctg. Office, U.S. Army, Ft. Buchanan, P.R., 1974-77; chief Central Acctg. Office-Fin. and Acctg. Office/DRM-U.S. Army, Ft. Gordon, Ga., 1978-80; systems acct. budget analysis div. U.S. Army Fin. and Acctg. Center, Indpls., 1980-81; budget analyst Hdqrs. Army Corps Engrs., Washington, 1981-82; systems acct. fin. and acctg. div. Resource Mgmt. Office, Hdqrs. V Corps., Frankfurt, W.Ger., 1982—. Recipient Outstanding Performance award U.S. Army, 1976, 77, 80. Mem. Nat. Assn. Female Execs., Am. Soc. Mil. Comptrollers. Office: Hdqrs V Corps ACSRM F&A Div APO New York NY 09079

CHAMPION, MARGE (MARJORIE CELESTE BELCHER), actress, dancer; b. Los Angeles, Sept. 2; d. Ernest and Gladys (Basquette) Belcher; student pub. schs., Los Angeles; m. Art Babbitt (div.); m. 2d, Gower Champion, Oct. 5, 1947 (div. 1973); children—Blake, Gregg; m. 3d, Boris Sagal, Jan. 1, 1977. Stage debut Los Angeles Civic Opera, 1936; movie debut (under name Marjorie Bell), The Castles, 1938; model for cartoon heroines in Snow White, Blue Fairy in Pinocchio, Walt Disney Prodns., 1938; appeared Broadway musicals Dark of the Moon, Beggar's Holiday, 1947; first profl. appearance with Gower Champion as Gower and Bell, Montreal, Que., Can., 1947, N.Y. debut in Hotel Plaza, 1947; night club tours, 1948; weekly show Admiral Broadway Review, Dumont and NBC TV Network, 1949; appeared with Bing Crosby in movie Mr. Music. Paramount Pictures, 1950; with husband staged dances for revues Lend an Ear, 1949, Make A Wish, Broadway, 1951; movies inlcude Show Boat, Lovely to Look Author: Everything I Have is Yours, 1952, Give the Girl a Break, 1952, Three for the Show, 1955, Jupiter's Darling, 1955, The Swimmer, 1968, The Party, 1968, The Cockeyed Cowboy of Calico County, 1970; That's Entertainment, Part 2, 1976; various nightclub, TV appearances, including TV show Toast of the Town, 1953, Three for Tonight, 1955, Shower of Stars, 1956, GE Theatre, 1957, Dinah Shore Show, 1958, Telephone Hour, We Four, 1960; acting debut Hemingway and All Those People, Indpls., 1958; title role Sabrina Fair, 1960; choreographer Queen of the Stardust Ballroom (Emmy award), 1975, Day of the Locust, 1975. Author: (with Marilee Zdenek) Catch the New Wind, 1972, God is a Verb, 1974; dialogue coach and choreographer: The Awakening Land, NBC-TV, 1978, Masada, ABC-TV, 1979, Diary of Ann Frank, NBC-TV, 1980. When the Circus Comes to Town, CBS-TV, 1980. Address: care Mercader & Paperny 10889 Wilshire Blvd Suite 1160 Los Angeles CA 90024 *

CHAN, AMY AI-MEI, physician; b. Muar, Malaysia; d. Shi-shi and Lilliam (Lee) Chan; student U. Adelaide (Australia), 1958-60; M.B., B.S., U. Singapore, 1964; m. Wan H. Chan; children—Evelyn, Jennifer, Donald. Tng. Queen's U., Belfast, No. Ireland, and Royal Belfast Hosp. Sick Children, 1967, Belfast City Hosp., 1968-71, Marthin Luther King-UCLA Med. Center, 1973-74; resident, then attending pediatrician, cons. Los Banos (Calif.) Community Hosp. Diplomate in child health Royal Coll. Physicians and Surgeons (Scotland); diplomate Am. Bd. Pediatrics. Fellow Am. Acad. Pediatrics, Calif. Med. Assn. Methodist. Office: 600 W I Los Banos CA 93635

CHAN, JANE, systems analyst; b. Hong Kong, Nov. 12, 1949; came to U.S., 1949, naturalized, 1953; d. Woodrow and Chon How (Tam) C.; B.S. in Chemistry, Bklyn. Coll., 1970; M.S. in Chemistry, N.Y. U., 1973; postgrad. N.Y.U. Sch. Medicine. Chemist radioactivity lab. Merck, Sharpe & Dohme Research Labs., 1970-73; systems analyst Sperry Univac, 1973-75; sr. market research systems analyst Linde div. Union Carbide Corp., N.Y.C., 1975-81. Mem. Am. Chem. Soc., Nat. Assn. Female Execs., N.Y. Acad. Scis., Jung Found. Home: 222 E 56th St Apt 2J New York NY 10022

CHAN, JULIE MAY LEE TANG, educator; b. Los Angeles, July 23, 1941; d. Chester and Lee Tang; B.A., UCLA, 1963; M.S. in Edn., U. So. Calif., 1965; Ed.D. in Reading, U. Colo., 1970; m. Lyman Gordon Chan, June 20, 1965. Elem. sch. tchr., 1963-70; producer radio series for Am. Forces Network Radio, Getting Your Child Off to a Good Start in Reading, 1973-74; mem. faculty Calif. State U., Long Beach, 1975-81; founder, owner, dir. COMPUKIDS, Inc., computer learning center children and adults, Los Angeles, 1981—. Mem. Computer Using Educators, Internat. Reading Assn., Calif. Reading Assn., Calif. Profs. Reading (pres. 1978-79), Pi Lambda Theta (chpt. pres. 1977-79), Kappa Delta Pi (counselor 1976-82). Author: Getting Your Child Off to a Good Start in Reading, 1974; Why Read Aloud to Children?, 1974; mem. editorial bd. Proc. Calif. Reading Assn., 1977-80; mem. nat. reading adv. bd. Eagle Edit., Harcourt Brace Jovanovich, 1982-85. Home: 6921 Dresden Circle Huntington Beach CA 92647 Office: 1798 Kelton Ave Los Angeles CA 90024

CHAN, LINDA WAI SIM, fin. and investment analyst; b. Hong Kong, Aug. 20, 1945; came to U.S., 1970, naturalized, 1975; d. Lam K.C. and Fung Ming (Chan) Leung; B.S.S. in Econs. cum laude (Cheung Chun Shun scholar), Chinese U. of Hong Kong (United Coll.), 1967; M.A. in Econs., U. Colo., 1971; m. Shu Mui Chan, June 22, 1971. Chief research statistician Far Eastern Econ. Rev., 1967-70; sr. acct. C.R. Cushing & Co., Inc., 1972-76, 78-79; asst. controller Soros Assos., N.Y.C., 1979—; project asst. Econ. Research Center of Hong Kong, 1964-65. Bd. deacons Broadway Presbyn. Ch., 1979-80; bd. elders Queens Chinese Presbyn. Ch., 1981—. Lic. ins. examiner N.Y. Mem. Econ. Soc. Hong Kong, Nat. Assn. Female Execs., Leadership Found. Republican. Editor Seedling, 1964-65.

CHAN, ROSALIE YUK-KUEN, med. technologist, chemist; b. Canton, China, Apr. 26, 1938; came to U.S., 1961, naturalized, 1966; d. Shong-Ching and Ying-Wah (Leung) Lau; B.S. with high honors, Taiwan U., 1960; postgrad. Calif. State U., 1970; m. Tom Chan, Dec. 30, 1962; 1 dau., Jane W. Tchr. Chinese Community Center, Oakland, Calif., 1961-63; research asst. U. Calif., Berkeley, 1967-68; real estate broker Century 21, San Leandro, Calif., 1978-79; med. technologist Kaiser Hosp., Oakland, 1972-78; sr. med. technologist Kaiser Permanente Med. Group, Berkeley, 1978—. Mem. Chinese Community Center Bd., 1965; active YWCA, Oakland. Mem. Apt. Owners Assn. of So. Alameda County, Am. Soc. Clin. Pathologists (affiliate mem., cert. med. technologist), Calif. Assn. for Med. Lab. Tech. Democrat. Club: Bay O Vista Country. Office: 1725 Eastshore Hwy Berkeley CA 94710

CHANCE, ELIZABETH MARGARET WINANS (MRS. R. ROBINSON CHANCE, JR.), businesswoman, civic worker; b. Linden, N.J., Apr. 7, 1926; d. Raymond Wood and Cora (Spillinger) Winans; B.A. in Econs., Tufts U., 1948; m. R. Robinson Chance, Jr., June 11, 1955; children—Elizabeth Margaret, Raymond Robinson III, Lawrence Winans. With prodn. expdn. dept. Weston Electric Co., Elizabeth, N.J., 1948-49; tchr. Vaile Deane Sch., 1949-50, Short Hills (N.J.) Country Day Sch., 1950-57; v.p. dir. Robinson Chance Enterprises, Inc., Ocean City, N.J., 1958—; cons., acting mgr. Michelle Whitney Skin Care Products, Colorado Springs, Colo., 1978-82; partner Chance Investment Adv. Service, 1979—; asst. to pres. Sassie Lassie Designs, 1980—. Founder Ocean City (N.J.) Christmas Tour of Homes, 1962, chmn., 1962-69; co-founder Ocean City Cultural Arts Center, 1963, entertainment chmn., 1963-69; mem. Meth. Women's Soc. Christian Service; active community drives; chmn. Wheeling Country Day Antique Show, 1971, 72, Woodmoor Women's Club Antique Show, 1977, 78, Broadmoor Antique Show, 1980-81; coordinator Colorado Springs Sch. Christmas Mart, 1978, 79; trustee Ocean City Vis. Homemaker-Home Health Aide Service, 1962-69, Wheeling Country Day Sch., 1972-74; bd. dirs. Wheeling Salvation Army Women's Aux., 1972-74, Florence Crittenton Home, Wheeling, 1972-74. Mem. Cape May County Art League, Colorado Springs Fine Arts Center, Friends of Ocean City Hist. Mus., Cape May County Hist. and Geneal. Soc., Sigma Kappa. Republican. Clubs: Woodmoor Country. Home: 5 1st St-Broadmoor Colorado Springs CO 80906 summer St Joseph Settlemetn Proctor WV 26055

CHANCE, JANET MACLAREN, clin. social worker; b. Seattle, Sept. 3, 1913; d. Clyde Athol and Myra (Wait) Maclaren; B.A., U. So. Calif., 1940; M.S.W., Bryn Mawr Coll., 1955-59; m. Lee Chance, Nov. 8, 1941;

1 dau., Jean Chance Oberholtzer. Psychiat. social worker Norristown (Pa.) State Hosp., 1955-57; caseworker Family Service of Montgomery County (Pa.), Ardmore, 1957-62; chief psychiat. social worker child guidance clinic Lankenau Hosp., Phila., 1962-73; pvt. practice psychosocial therapy, Wayne, Pa., 1973-81; ret., 1981. Fellow Pa. Soc. Clin. Social Workers; mem. Acad. Cert. Social Workers, Nat. Assn. Social Workers. Home: 170 Conestoga Rd Wayne PA 19087

CHANDLER, A. FAYE, interior designer; b. Petrolia, Kans., Apr. 26, 1918; d. Louis Edmund and Eula Faye (Hughes) C.; student Frances Shimer Girls Coll., Mt. Carroll, Ill., U. Ariz., U. Hawaii. With Lou Regester's Design Studio, Phoenix and Tucson, 1958-71, 74-77, Mayo's Design Studio, Scottsdale, Ariz., 1971-74; propr. Faye Chandler Interiors, Phoenix, 1977—. Recipient award in residential design competition Ariz. chpt. Am. Soc. Interior Designers, 1981. Mem. Internat. Soc. Interior Designers (pres. Ariz. chpt. 1971-72, nat. dir. 1973-74), Internat. Soc. Interior Designers, Am. Soc. Interior Designers nat. dir. 1977-78; nat. medal 1981). Republican. Methodist. Club: Order Eastern Star. Home: 3310 E Camelback St Phoenix AZ 85018

CHANDLER, ALICE, univ. adminstr.; b. Bklyn., May 29, 1931; d. Samuel and Jenny (Meller) Kogan; A.B., Barnard Coll., 1951; M.A., Columbia U., 1953, Ph.D., 1960; m. Horace Chandler, June 10, 1954; children—Seth, Donald. Instr., CCNY, 1961-65, asst. prof., 1965-69, asso. prof., 1970-72, prof., 1973-80, v.p. instl. advancement, 1974-76, provost, v.p. acad. affairs, 1976-79, acting pres., 1979-80; pres. SUNY, New Paltz, 1980—; instr. Skidmore Coll., 1953-54; lectr. Barnard Coll., 1954-55, Hunter Coll., 1956-57. Lizette Fisher fellow, 1955-56. Bd. dirs. Revson Found., 1979; mem. Higher Edn. Adv. Com., N.Y. State Senate, 1979; trustee Wave Hill Center Environ. Studies, 1977—. Mem. MLA, Phi Beta Kappa. Club: Lotos. Author: The Prose Spectrum: A Rhetoric and Reader, 1968; The Theme of War, 1969; The Rationale of Rhetoric, 1970, The Rationale of the Essay, 1971; A Dream of Order, 1970; From Smollett to James, 1980. Office: Haggerty Adminstrn Bldg State Univ Coll New Paltz NY 12561

CHANDLER, ELISABETH GORDON (MRS. LACI DE GERENDAY), sculptor, harpist; b. St. Louis, June 10, 1913; d. Henry Brace and Sara Ellen (Sallee) Gordon; grad. The Lenox School, 1931; pvt. study sculpture and harp; m. Robert Kirtland Chandler, May 27, 1946 (dec.); m. Laci de Gerenday, May 12, 1979. Exhibited sculptures N.A.D., National Sculpture Soc., Allied Artists Am., Nat. Arts Club, Pen and Brush, Lyme Art Assn., Mattatuck Museum, Catherine Lorillard Wolfe Art Club, Am. Artists Profl. League, Hudson Valley Art Assn., USIA, 1976-78, Lyme Art Center, 1979; represented in permanent collections Aircraft Carrier USS Forrestal, Gov. Dummer Acad., James Forrestal Research Center of Princeton U., Lenox Sch., James L. Collins Parochial Sch., Tex., Storm King Art Center, Columbia U., Forrestal Meml. Medal, Timoshenko Medal for Applied Mechanics, Benjamin Franklin Medal, Albert A. Michelson medal, Jonathan Edwards Medal, Shafto Broadcasting Award Medal, Woodrow Wilson Sch. of Princeton U., Georgia Pacific Bldg., Portland, Oreg., Messiah Coll., Grantham, Pa., Adlai E. Stevenson High Sch., Ill., Queen Anne's County, Md., Pace U., N.Y.C., Soc. Medalists, George Washington 250th Anniversary Medal, U.S. Capitol Hist. Soc., also represented in pvt. collections; performed as concert harpist on stage, radio, TV, 1933-45; mem. Mildred Dilling Harp Ensemble, 1934-46. 1942-45; instr. portrait sculpture Lyme Acad. Fine Arts, 1976—. Dir. Abbott Coin Counter Co., Inc., 1941-55. Chmn. Asso. Taxpayers Old Lyme, 1969-72. Trustee The Lenox Sch., 1953-55. Served with mus. therapy div. Am. Theatre Wing. Recipient 1st prize Bklyn. War Meml. competition, 1945; 1st prize sculpture Catherine Lorillard Wolfe Art Club, 1951, 58, 63; Founders prize Pen and Brush, 1954, 76, 78, Gold medal, 1957, 61, 63, 69, 74, Am. Heritage award, 1968, Solo Show award, 1961, 69, 75, Thomas R. Proctor prize N.A.D., 1956, Dessie Greer prize, 1960, 79; sculpture prize Nat. Arts Club, 1959, 60, 62, Gold medal, 1971; Gold medal Am. Artists Profl. League, 1960, 73, 75, Anna Hyatt Huntington prize, 1970, 76, Harriet Mayer Meml. prize, 1961, sculpture prize, 1969; Gold medal Hudson Valley Art Assn., 1956, 69, 74, Mrs. John Newington award, 1976, 78; Lindsey Morris Meml. prize Allied Artists Am., 1973, Tallix Foundry award, 1978; sculpture prize Acad. Artists, 1974; Sydney Taylor Meml. prize Knickerbocker Artists, 1975; New Netherlands D.A.R. Bicentennial medal, 1976; Tallix Foundry award, 1979, Nat. Sculpture Soc., 1979. N.A. Fellow Nat. Sculpture Soc. (council 1976—), Am. Artists Profl. League (prize 1981), Internat. Inst. Arts and Letters; mem. Nat. Arts Club, Allied Artists of Am., Pen and Brush, Catherine Lorillard Wolfe Art Club, Lyme Art Assn. (pres. 1973-75), Council Am. Artist Socs. (dir. 1970-73), Am. Artists Profl. League (dir. 1970-73), Lyme Acad. Fine Arts (trustee 1976—). Home and Studio: Mill Pond Ln Old Lyme CT 06371

CHANDLER, GWENDOLYN MASON, med. technologist; b. Nashville, July 25, 1941; d. James and Bertha Louise (Hadley) Mason; B.S. in Med. Tech. Tenn. State U., 1963; cert. med. tech. Meharry Med. Coll., 1963; M.S. in Zoology, Tenn. State U., 1972; postgrad. U. Tenn., 1965-66; m. Donald S. Chandler, Dec. 23, 1969; 1 son, Donald S. Med. technologist, lab. instr. Meharry Med. Coll., Nashville, 1963-66, cytopathology lab., 1967-69, ednl. coordinator Sch. Med. Tech., 1969-71, lab. instr. clin. pathology lab., 1969-71; lab. supr. clin. chemistry lab. Hubbard Hosp., 1970-71; instr. Menelik Hosp., Peace Corps, Addis Ababa, Ethiopia, 1966-67; grad. teaching asst. Tenn. State U. dept. biol. scis., 1971-72; part-time med. technologist, Kalamazoo, Mich., 1976-81; med. technologist Reproductive Health Care Center of Kalamazoo, 1977-78, part-time Headstart program, 1978; instr. microbiology of infectious disease lab. physician's asst. program Western Mich. U., Kalamazoo, 1978, instr. methods of inquiry, 1979-80; med. technologist Blood Bank VA Med. Center, Dallas, 1981-82. Cert. lab. supr.-gen., Tenn.; cert. med. lab. technologist. Mem. Registry of Med. Technologists (lic.), Am. Soc. Clin. Pathologists (affiliate mem., cert. med. technologist), Am. Soc. Med. Tech., Tex. Soc. Med. Tech., NAACP, Gamma Chi (1st pres., co-founder). Baptist. Author: Some Bible Friends; Heroes of Faith; The People Called Baptists. Home: 1453 Bar Harbor Dr Dallas TX 75232

CHANDLER, KARLYN DOROTHY, computer ops. profl.; b. Pitts., Mar. 28, 1943; d. Wilbert and Theresa O. (McClenny) Scott; A.S. in Bus. Mgmt., Allegheny Community Coll., 1979; cert. Internat. Data Processing Inst., 1966; student in bus. mgmt. Point Park Coll.; m. James R. Chandler, Feb. 17, 1979; 1 dau., Tina Marie. Name taker for city directory, R. L. Polk Co., Cleve., 1966; keypunch operator Higbee Co., Cleve., 1968-69; keypunch operator Westinghouse Elec. Corp., Forest Hills, Pa., 1970-76, sr. keypunch operator, 1976-80, fin. projects clk., 1980, supr. computer ops. Pitts., 1980—. Mem. Nat. Assn. Female Execs. Office: 777 Penn Center Blvd Pittsburgh PA 15235

CHANDLER, KATHLEEN LEONE, city councilwoman; b. Detroit, Sept. 19, 1932; d. Telford R. and Beatrice L. (Smith) McRae; B.A. cum laude, Mich. State U., 1956, M.S., 1957; postgrad. in public adminstrn. Kent State U., 1980—; m. Charles C. Chandler, July 12, 1958; children—Susan, Beth, Jenny. Tchr. public schs., Macomb County, Mich., 1952-54, Irving, Tex., 1959-60, Marquette, Mich., 1960-62; reading cons., dir. reading clinic Livonia (Mich.) Public Schs., 1957-59; mem. Kent (Ohio) City Council; tchr. summer courses Mich. State U., 1958-61. Bd. dirs. Portage County (Ohio) ARC, 1972—, chairwoman, 1979-81; mem. N.E. Ohio council ARC, 1976-81, sec., 1977-79; bd. dirs. LWV, Kent, 1976-79, fin. chairperson, 1977, voter service chairperson, govt. fin. chairperson, 1978-79; chairperson Kent City Cancer Dr., 1977; pres. Univ. Women of Kent State U., 1979; pres. Davey Jr. High Sch. PTA, Kent, 1979; mem. Portage County Council Health and Social Agys. Recipient cert. appreciation, N.E. Ohio ARC, 1979, Portage County ARC, 1979, 80. Mem. Ohio Mcpl. League, Kappa Delta Pi, Phi Kappa Phi, Delta Zeta. Democrat. Clubs: Kent Area Dem., Federated Woman's of Portage County. Home: 455 Dansel Kent OH 44240

CHANDLER, LINDA CLINE, investment broker; b. Sioux Falls, S.D.; d. Lawrence Alphonse and Wilba Nell (Leatherwood) Dhaemers; B.S., Iowa State U., 1968, M.A., 1972; m. Terence E. Chandler, Oct. 16, 1976. With Sutro & Co., San Jose, Calif., 1974—, asso. v.p., 1977-78, v.p. investments, 1978—. Named winner San Jose Mercury News Bay-Area Investment Contest, 1979, Fin. Planner of Yr., Am. Home Properties, 1980-81, One of 18 Outstanding Women Brokers in Nation, Registered Rep., 1981. UN fellow. Mem. Santa Clara County Profl. Brokers Assn., Santa Clara County Profl. Young Women, AAUW, Phi Kappa Phi, Phi Delta Theta, Alpha Delta Pi. Methodist. Club: Sutro Second Century (pres.'s council 1978-82). Featured in February 1982 issue Money Mag. Office: 2700 Augustine Dr Suite 101 Santa Clara CA 95051 *

CHANDLER, VIRGINIA GOODMAN, occupational therapist; b. Evanston, Ill., Jan. 10, 1930; d. Daniel Guy and Helen (Schneider) Goodman; B.A. in Art and Psychology, So. Methodist U., 1951; postgrad. in occupational therapy Tex. Women's U., 1953; children—Ron Lee, Chuck Lee. Occupational therapist Beverly Hills Sanitarium, Dallas, 1953-55; dir. occupational therapy Baylor U. Med. Center, Dallas, 1956-60, 68—, Fla. Sanitarium and Hosp., Orlando, 1962-65; staff therapist Parkland Meml. Hosp., Dallas, 1965-68; cons. Arthritis Found., 1974—, Easter Seals Found., 1975—; dir. clin. edn. internship program univs. Kans., Ind., Puget Sound, Va., Ark., Colo., N.Y., 1972—. Mem. coordinating bd. Tex. Coll. and Univ. System, 1980. Mem. Am. Occupational Therapy Assn. (del. Fla. 1964, Tex. 1980—), World Fedn. Occupational Therapists (participant 8th Internat. Congress, Hamburg, Germany, 1982), Am. Heart Assn., Chi Omega. Club: Boomerang (dir. 1971—). Author: (manual) Lightcast II Splints, 1976; Adult Visual Perceptual Evaluation, 1981. Home: 11106 Shortmeadow Dallas TX 75218 Office: Baylor Univ Medical Center 3500 Gaston Ave Dallas TX 75246

CHANDOR, KAREN KAYSER, mktg. exec.; b. Los Angeles, Feb. 13, 1950; d. Ernest and Kathleen (Adams) Kayser; B.A., Wellesley Coll., 1970; M.B.A., Babson Coll., 1974, also postgrad. Vice pres. Tech. Steel Corp., Newton, Mass., 1971-73; asst. v.p. Thorndike, Doran, Paine & Lewis, Boston, 1973-76; v.p. Colonial Mgmt. Assos., Boston, 1976-77; v.p. mktg. Gardner and Preston Moss, Inc., Boston, 1977—. Mem. corp. Babson Coll., 1982—. Cert. employee benefit specialist. Mem. Assn. Investment Mgmt. Sales Execs. (dir.), Internat. Found. Employee Benefits. Home: 28 Cartwright Rd Wellesley MA 02181 Office: One Winthrop Sq Boston MA 02110

CHANEY, ROSEMARY SULLIVAN, musician, educator; b. Clever, Mo., Jan. 15, 1925; d. Earl Tom and Rosa Ethel (Maples) Sullivan; B.S., S.W. Mo. State U., 1949; M.Ed., U. Mo., 1959; postgrad., U. Cin., Miami U., Oxford, Ohio, 1963-64; m. Donald Samuel Chaney, Dec. 21, 1957; 1 son, Tom Donald; stepchildren—Donna Chaney Roemer, Robert Edward. Tchr. music Clever Consol. Schs. and dir. music First Bapt. Ch., Clever, 1949-53; tchr. Aurora (Mo.) Elem. Schs. and dir. music First Bapt. Ch., Aurora, 1953-57; bass violinist Springfield (Mo.) Symphony Orch., 1949-56; social dir. S.W. Mo. State U., summers 1955-56 and 1957-58; early childhood music specialist Indian Hills Exempted Village Schs., Cin., 1961-80, ret., 1980, on spl. assignment Fine Arts Project, 1980—; writer curriculum materials for Cin. Symphony Orch. In-Sch. Music Program and dir. tng. docents, 1978—; speaker at numerous confs., workshops, radio programs. Named Tchr. of Yr., Indian Hill Schs., 1969; recipient award of appreciation Cin. Public Schs., 1981. Mem. NEA, Music Educators Nat. Assn., Am. Orff Schulwerk Assn. (bd. govs. Greater Cin. chpt. 1973-77), Mo. State Tchrs. Assn. (pres. 1948-49), Nat. Assn. State Tchrs. Assns.' Pres. (pres. 1949-50), Delta Kappa Gamma, Pi Beta Phi (pres. 1943-44), Sigma Alpha Iota (pres. 1943-44). Clubs: Cin. Woman's (dir. 1982—), Coll. Cin. (pres. 1979-80), PEO (local pres., dir. Greater Cin. chorus). Compositions include: Clever High Sch. Alma Mater for Band and Chorus, 1949; prepared, presented numerous original children's musicals; contbr. articles to profl. jours. Home: 6605 Rollymeade Cincinnati OH 45243

CHANG, ALICE FRANCES, clin. psychologist; b. Ithaca, N.Y., Feb. 17, 1943; d. C.W. and Y.C. Chang; B.A., UCLA, 1968; postgrad. Calif. State U., Los Angeles, 1969-70; Ph.D., U. So. Calif., Los Angeles, 1973. Psychol. asst. Los Angeles Remedial Services, Culver City, Calif., 1968-73; psychometrist Clin. Psychol. Services, Santa Monica, Calif., 1969-70; statis. asst. VA Domiciliary, West Los Angeles, 1971; teaching asst. U. So. Calif., Los Angeles, 1970-72; clin. trainee intern Brentwood Neuropsychiat. Inst., Los Angeles, 1972-73; asst. prof. psychology U. Ariz., Tucson, 1973-75; asst. prof. and staff psychologist U. Kans. Med. Center, Kansas City, 1975-77, asst. clin. prof., 1977-79, clin. asso. prof. dept. surgery Sch. Medicine, 1979—; staff med. psychologist Kansas City VA Med. Center, 1977-79; pvt. practice clin. psychology Shawnee Mission, Kans., 1977—; dir. Northland Pain Clinic, N. Kansas City, Mo., 1981—; cons. to various social service and ednl. orgns., 1968—; guest lectr. various schs., med. and social service orgns., 1969—; mem. sci. adv. bd. Shawnee Mission East High Sch., 1978—; supr. Marana (Ariz.) Community Mental Health Clinic, 1973-75. Mem. Am. Psychol. Assn., Kans. Psychol. Assn., Mo. Psychol. Assn., Western Psychol. Assn., Assn. for Advancement of Psychology, Kans. Assn. for Profl. Psychologists, Greater Kansas City Psychol. Assn., Am. Soc. for Psychical Research, Acad. of Parapsychology and Medicine, Am. Schizophrenia Assn., Am. Orthopsychiat. Assn., AAAS, AAUP, Sigma Xi. Presbyterian. Contbr. numerous articles to profl. jours. Office: 1900 W 75th St Shawnee Mission KS 66208

CHANG, HWA YING, accountant; b. Hupeh, China, May 1, 1930; d. Chung An and Chun Hua (Lin) C.; came to U.S., 1965, naturalized, 1974; B. Comm., Soochow U., Taipei, 1958; M.B.A., N.Y. U., 1971, postgrad., 1974-77. Asst. mgr. Hua Nan Comml. Bank, Taipei, Taiwan, 1954-65; accountant Motor Vehicle Accident Indemnification Corp., N.Y.C., 1966-67; asst. to chief accountant Standard & Poor's Corp., N.Y.C., 1968, Dairylea Coop., Inc., N.Y.C., 1971, U.S. Steel Internat. Co., N.Y.C., 1969-70; sr. accountant Internat. Nickel Co., N.Y.C., 1972-79; asst. controller Am. Union Transport Forwarding, Inc., N.Y.C., 1980—; cons. in field. Mem. Am. Mgmt. Assn., Nat. Assn. Accountants, Am. Accounting Assn. Home: 77 E 12th St New York NY 10003

CHANG, KISOOK, psychiatrist; b. Pyungbuk, Korea, Aug. 22, 1934; came to U.S., 1966, naturalized, 1972; d. In-Uk and Un-Wha (Moon) Paik; M.D., Korea U., 1961; m. Pongkeun Chang, Apr. 29, 1961; 1 dau., Carolyn. Intern, Somerset Hosp., Sommerville, N.J., 1973-74; pediatrician Holt Adoption Program, Seoul, Korea, 1962-63; resident John Umstead Hosp., Butner, N.C., 1974-77; pediatrician Clinica Americana, LaPaz, Bolivia, 1965-66; staff physician Western State Hosp., Staunton, Va., 1968-73; practice medicine specializing in psychiatry, Fayetteville, N.C., 1977—; staff psychiatrist Cumberland Mental Health Center, Fayetteville, 1977—; mem. staffs Cape Fear Valley Hosp., Cumberland Psychiat. Hosp.; cons. Fayetteville Family Center. Mem. U.S. Korean Med. Assn. Methodist. Club: Gates Four Country. Home: 2118 Clinchfield Dr Fayetteville NC 28304 Office: 3425 Melrose Rd Fayetteville NC 28304

CHANG, WEINING CHU, psychologist, educator; b. Nanking, China, May 1, 1945; d. Sze-yi and Chung-ying (Chang) Chu; B.A. in Law, Nat. Taiwan U., 1967; Ph.D. in Psychology, U. Houston, 1973; m. Donald C. Chang, Nov. 24, 1968; 1 child, Sishir. Vis. Asst. prof. U. Houston, 1977-78, vis. lectr., 1974-77, 78-81; cons. Stress and Family Project, Harvard Grad. Sch. Edn., Cambridge, Mass., 1978-79; asso. prof. psychology Tex. So. U., Houston, 1973—; columnist, dir. S.W. Chinese Jour., Houston, 1979—. Mem. U.S. China People's Friendship Assn., Nat. Assn. Chinese Ams., Internat. Assn. Cross-Cultural Psychology, Am. Psychol. Assn. Contbr. articles, short stories, essays to various publs. Office: Dept Psychology Tex So Univ Houston TX 77004

CHANGAR-SHAW, ILENE, county adminstr.; b. St. Louis, Feb. 20, 1937; d. Ely and Leona (Rosenblatt) Saphian; student U. Wis., Madison, 1956; B.A. summa cum laude, St. Louis U., 1977, M.A., Center Urban Programs, 1981, postgrad. in public policy analysis and adminstrn., 1981—; m. William J. Shaw, Sept. 24, 1976; children—Cynthia Gay Changar, Michael David Changar, Daniel Ely Changar, Amy Beth Changar. Office mgr. Metro Housing Resources, St. Louis, 1973; adminstrv. asst. Community Behavioral Agys., St. Louis, 1974; supr. County Older Resident Program, St. Louis County (Mo.) Dept. Human Resources, 1975-78, mgr. field ops. County Older Resident Programs, 1978—; practicum instr. Washington U.; producer Accent on Age, Cable TV; mem. steering com. Operation Weather Survival, Metro St. Louis. Chmn. Univ. City House and Garden Tour, St. Louis, 1968-70; chmn. Congl. Action Fund, St. Louis, 1972; bd. dirs. New Democratic Coaligion, St. Louis, 1972; mem. exec. com. Alliance for Community Togetherness, 1973; presenter Mid-Am. Congress on Aging, St. Louis, 1982. Recipient Achievement award Nat. Assn. Counties, 1978, 81. Mem. Am. Planning Assn., Am. Soc. Public Adminstrn., Alumni Assn. St. Louis U. Author service handbooks, profl. papers. Home: 24 S Rock Hill Rd Saint Louis MO 63119 Office: 555 S Brentwood Saint Louis MO 63105

CHANGHO, AURORA DIEGO, dietitian; b. Manila, Dec. 2, 1941; d. Montano Estrella and Florencia (Domingo) Diego; B.S., U. Santo Tomas, 1961; M.S., Howard U., 1966; m. Casto Ong Changho, Sept. 12, 1970; children—Christine Theresa, Emelyn Michelle, Kathleen Marie, Alexander Tien-Si. Instr., U. Santo Tomas, Manila, 1962-64; clin. dietitian George Washington U. Hosp., Washington, 1964-67; research dietitian U. Mo. Med. Center, Columbia, 1967-70; clin. dietitian Menorah Med. Center, Kansas City, Mo., 1970-72; cons. dietitian Bowens Health Center, Raytown, Mo., 1981-82; instr., program dir. Penn Valley Community Coll., Kansas City, Mo., 1972—. Mem. Am. Dietetic Assn., Kans. Dietetic Assn., Mo. Vocat. Assn., Mo. Assn. Community Jr. Colls., Alpha Delta Kappa. Home: 2920 W 93d St Leawood KS 66206 Office: 3201 Southwest Trafficway Kansas City MO 64111

CHANIN, ANN S., office systems cons.; b. St. Joseph, Mo., Dec. 6, 1946; d. Albert and Edith Chanin; B.A. in Sociology and Journalism, No. Ill. U., 1968; postgrad. Loyola U., 1972-74. Social worker Cook County Dept. Public Aid, 1968-69; tchr. Chgo. Public Schs., 1969-70; mem. mktg. staff Breadbasket Comml. Assn., Chgo., 1970-71, Parker House Sausage Co., Chgo., 1972; sales rep. Ralston Purina, Chgo., 1972-74; sales rep. Xerox Corp., Chgo., 1974-76, cons., Chgo., 1976, sales rep., Washington, 1977-80, cons., Washington, 1980—; on leave as tchr., Jamaica, W.I., 1976-77. Winner Ralston Purina Nat. Sales Contest, 1973; named to Xerox Pres.'s Club, 1975, 78, 79. Mem. Nat. Fedn. Bus. and Profl. Women (local legis. chmn., state UN world affairs chmn.). Office: 1616 Fort Myer Dr Arlington VA 22209

CHANNING, CAROL, actress; b. Seattle, Jan. 31, 1923; d. George and Adelaide (Glaser) C.; student Bennington Coll.; m. 3d, Charles F. Lowe, Sept. 5, 1956; 1 son, Channing George. Appeared Broadway prodns. No for an Answer, 1941, Let's Face It, 1941, Proof Through the Night, 1942, So Proudly We Hail, Lend an Ear, 1948, Show Business, 1959, Show Girl, 1961, George Burns-Carol Channing Musical Revue, 1962, The Millionairess, 1963, Carol Channing with Her Stout-Hearted Men (London Critics award), 1970, Four on a Garden, 1971, Cabaret, 1972, Festival at Ford's, 1972, Carol Channing and Her Gentlemen Who Prefer (Blondes (revue), 1972, star of Gentlemen Prefer Blondes, 1949, 51-53, Wonderful Town, 1953, Pygmalion, 1953, The Vamp, 1955, Hello Dolly, 1964-67, 77—; actress with RKO Studios, Hollywood, Calif., pictures include First Traveling Saleslady; appeared in Thoroughly Modern Millie, 1967, Skidoo, 1968; TV prodns., Svengali and the Blonde, Three Men on a Horse, Crescendo, also guest star appearances; toured with Lorelei (play), 1973-75. Recipient Theatre World award, Critics Circle award for play Lend an Ear; award for Best Night Club Act of 1957; 1964 Tony award and N.Y. Drama Critics award as starring actress in Hello Dolly; Golden Globe award as best supporting actress in Thoroughly Modern Millie, 1967; Tony Spl. award, 1968; Bronze medallion City of N.Y., 1978. Christian Scientist. Office: care William Morris Agy 151 El Camino Blvd Beverly Hills CA 90212 *

CHANT, DALE ANN, nurse; b. Woodbury, N.J., July 18, 1953; d. Howard Roy and Dale Ann (Moore) Verfaillie; A.A.S., Gloucester County Coll., 1978; student Stockton State Coll.; m. Frank Chant III, Apr. 11, 1969; children—Michael Frank, Bryan Scott. Nurse intensive care and coronary unit Our Lady of Lourdes Hosp., Camden, N.J., 1978-80; nurse Western Med. Services, Cherry Hill, N.J., 1980; dir. client services/continuing edn. Staff Builders Health Care Services, Mount Laurel, N.J., 1980-81; nurse emergency room Our Lady of Lourdes Hosp., Camden, 1981—; cons. Staff Builders Health Care Services, 1981; instr. nursing Gloucester County Vocat. Sch., 1982—. Mem. Nursing Edn. Com. Camden County, 1981. Mem. Am. Nurses Assn., N.J. State Nurses Assn. Democrat. Methodist. Editor, contbg. editor Aspect, 1975. Home: 5 Hill Ln Woodbury NJ 08096

CHANTILES, VILMA LIACOURAS (MRS. NICHOLAS G. CHANTILES), home economist, editor, writer; b. Phila., Aug. 11, 1925; d. James Peter and Stella (Lagakos) Liacouras; B.S., Drexel U., 1947; M.A., N.Y. U., 1970; m. Nicholas G. Chantiles, Mar. 2, 1952; children—Dean, James, Maria Nicole. Designer Rosenau Bros., Phila., 1948-50; reporter Women's Wear Daily, Phila., 1950-53; tchr. home econs. Scarsdale (N.Y.) Jr. High Sch., 1968-69; lectr. Herbert Lehman Coll., 1970-71, 76-77; instr. N.Y.U., 1973-74; instr. Deree-Pierce Coll., Athens, summer 1979; food editor Athenian Mag., Athens, Greece, 1975—; free-lance researcher and writer, 1974—; author: The Food of Greece, 1975, 2d edit., 1979, reprinted, 1981; columnist, contbg. editor Needle Arts quar., 1980—; editor Needle Joy: A Guide to Teaching Embroidery to Children, 1981; contbr. to The Good Cook series, The Great Cook series; contbr. articles to various publs. Bd. dirs. Westchester County (N.Y.) Choral Soc., 1977-80, membership sec. 1978-80. Mem. Am. Home Econs. Assn., Home Economists in Bus., Embroiderers Guild Am., Pi Nu Epsilon, Omicron Nu. Democrat. Greek Orthodox. Home and Office: 13 Circle Rd Scarsdale NY 10583

CHAPÉ, LINDA MAURINE, office services mgr.; b. Glendale, Calif., Nov. 17, 1943; d. Allen James and Dorothy Dell (Folbré) C.; M.Ed., Antioch U., 1979; student Cerritos Coll., 1968-69, Long Beach City Coll., 1967, Northeastern U., 1976, Whittier Coll., 1971. Owner/operator Jene-Linn Equestrian Stables, Norwalk, Calif., 1968-71; teen coordinator Gardena (Calif.) Recreation Dept., 1967-68; spl. activities supr. Gorton Group div. Gen. Mills, Gloucester, Mass., 1974-77; dean external affairs Graham Jr. Coll., Boston, 1977-79; dean adminstrn. Bay State Jr. Coll., Boston, 1979; mgr. office services The Gorton Group, Gloucester, 1980—. Served with USAF, 1962-66. Mem. Nat. Assn. Female Execs., Chi Kappa Rho. Club: Soroptimists. Home: 2 Stage Hill Rd Ipswich MA 01930 Office: 327 Main St Gloucester MA 01930

CHAPEY, GERALDINE DONNELLY, ednl. adminstr.; b. Bklyn., Nov. 21, 1920; d. Peter Joseph and Teresa Gertrude (Killen) Donnelly; B.A., St. Joseph's Coll., 1940; M.A., City U. N.Y., 1962; Ed.D., Fordham U., 1975; m. Robert Chapey, Aug., 1940; children—Geraldine, Roberta. Mem. adminstrn. N.Y.C. Bd. Edn., 1950—, dir. Title I speech therapy, 1966—, speech program in day high schs., 1969—, office funded programs Div. Spl. Edn., 1975-78; prof. St. John's U., 1980—; cons. in field. Pres. Regular Democratic Club Rockaways, also chmn. polit. sect. com., civic affairs and spl. events com., now pres.; trustee Douglaston Coll. Named Educator of Yr., N.Y.C. Bd. Edn. Emerald Soc., 1980, Assn. Tchrs. of City N.Y., 1980, Lady of Holy Sepulchre of Jerusalem. Mem. N.Y.C. Adminstrv. Women in Edn. (pres. 1978-80), NCCJ, N.Y. Acad. Public Edn., Council Dirs. and Asst. Dirs., Nat. Council Adminstrv. Women Edn. (exec. bd., disting. service award), Am. Speech and Hearing Assn., Fordham U. Sch. Adminstrs. Assn., Theodore Roosevelt Assn. Author articles in field. Office: St John's Univ 300 Howard Ave Staten Island NY 10301

CHAPEY, ROBERTA, speech pathologist; b. Bklyn., Dec. 9, 1942; d. Robert and Geraldine C.; B.A., Marymount Coll., 1964; M.A., N.Y. U., 1965; Ed.D. (Office Edn. fellow), Columbia U., 1975. Instr., Marymount Manhattan Coll., N.Y.C., 1969-70; asso. prof. speech dept. Bklyn. Coll., 1974-80, prof., 1981—, dep. chmn. div. grad. studies in speech, 1979-80. Recipient grant, 1979. Mem. Am. Speech and Hearing Assn., N.Y. State Speech and Hearing Assn., Acad. of Aphasia. Editor, contbr. Language Intervention Strategies for Adult Aphasia, 1981; contbr. articles to profl. jours. Home: 225 E 66th St New York NY 10021

CHAPIN, DIANA DERBY, city ofcl.; b. St. Joseph, Mich., Nov. 15, 1942; d. David Norman and Gladys Ruth (Henke) Derby; B.A. cum laude (Woodrow Wilson fellow), U. Mich., 1964; M.A., Cornell U., 1966, Ph.D. (Woodrow Wilson dissertation fellow), 1971; m. James Burke Chapin, Mar. 16, 1968; children—James Derby, David Sheffield. Asst. prof. Queens Coll., N.Y.C., 1969-74; dist. adminstrn. 8th Congl. Dist., N.Y.C., 1974-76; asst. commr. N.Y.C. Dept. Parks and Recreation, 1978-81, Queens Borough commr., 1981—. Del. Democratic Nat. Conv., Miami, Fla., 1972; dist. leader 35th Assembly Dem. Dist., N.Y.C., 1972-78; mgr. various campaigns, 1977-78. Recipient ann. employee award N.Y.C. Dept. Parks and Recreation, 1982. Congregationalist. Contbr. articles to profl. publs. Home: 35-46 79th St Jackson Heights NY 11372 Office: 80-30 Park Ln Kew Gardens NY 11415

CHAPIN, JOAN BEGGS, entomologist; b. St. Louis, Feb. 8, 1929; d. Thomas Putnam and Myra Barbara (Huntington) Beggs; B.S., Kans. State U., 1950; M.S., La. State U., 1959, Ph.D., 1971; m. Bobie T. Chapin, Dec. 23, 1949 (div. Mar. 1971); children—Larry T., M. Roger, Martha H. Research asst. entomology La. State U., Baton Rouge, 1957-51, research asso., 1961-73, asst. prof., 1973-77, asso. prof., 1977—. Mem. Capital City Bus. and Profl. Womens Club (chmn. legis. com. 1973-74), La. Entomol. Soc. (pres. 1980-81), Entomol. Soc. Am. (standing com. common names of insects 1981-83), Coleopterists Soc., Sigma Xi. Club: Bonaire Garden (pres. 1966-67). Office: Dept Entomology La State U Baton Rouge LA 70803

CHAPIN, ROBERTA JANE, civic worker; b. Saginaw, Mich., July 12, 1943; d. Burton Lee and Verna Ilene (Brand) Thompson; student Delta Coll., 1977-78; m. Gary Arnold Chapin, June 12, 1965; children—Wade Arnold, Dana Kristin, Jon Arnold (adopted), Amy Kristin (adopted). Sales rep. Nugent Drugs, Midland, Mich., 1963-64; asst. mgr. Lerner Dress Shop, Santa Barbara, Calif., 1964-65; credit mgr. Nugent's, Midland, 1965-66; claims processor Dow Corning Corp., Midland, 1966-69; Avon rep., Midland, 1972-78. Sec. Lee Twp. Planning Commn. for Zoning, 1975-76; leader Brownies, 1977-78, Girl Scouts U.S.A., 1977-78; sec. Sunday Sch. Bd.; sec. bd. Floyd-Pleasantview PTA, 1976-78; mem. sex edn. adv. bd. Bullock Creek Sch. Dist., 1980-81; mem. Transp. Task Force, 1981-82, Title I Adv. Com., 1982. Democrat. Mem. Missionary Ch. Home: 2070 W Isabella St Midland MI 48640 Office: Box 1592 S Saginaw St Midland MI 48640

CHAPIN, VIRGINIA, hand analyst, graphologist; b. Mass., Aug. 29, 1915; d. Gerard and Lilian E. (Sleicher) C.; B.A., Vassar Coll., 1937; postgrad. Inst. Fine Arts N.Y., 1960-62, New Sch. Social Research N.Y., 1972-76; children—Arnold M. Combrinck-Graham III, Lee Combrinck-Graham. Dir. hospitality com. UN Dels., 1963-73; hand analyst, 1970—; graphologist, 1973—; tchr. Graphology New Sch. Social Research, 1976; tchr. hand analysis Bucks County Community Coll., 1974. Thresholds counselor Bucks County Prison, 1975—; Former bd. mem. Nat. Council Community Services to Internat. Visitors, Washington, Council Internat. Visitors Phila.; former chmn. Bucks County Assn. Corrections and Rehab., vice chmn.; student C.G. Jung Found. N.Y., 1973-80; officer Round Table Assos. of C.G. Jung Found. and C.J. Jung Center Phila. Mem. LWV, Arab-Am. Women's Friendship Assn., Fortune Soc., Pa. Prison Soc., ACLU. Address: Box 95 Solebury PA 18963 *

CHAPLIN, GERALDINE, actress; b. Santa Monica, Calif., 1944; d. Charles and Oona (O'Neill) C.; ed. pvt. schs., Royal Ballet Sch., London; 1 son, Shane. Motion pictures include Doctor Zhivago, 1965, Stranger in the House, 1967, I Killed Rasputin, 1968, The Hawaiians, 1970, Innocent Bystanders, 1973, Buffalo Bill and the Indians or Sitting Bull's History Lesson, The Three Musketeers, 1974, The Four Musketeers, 1975, Nashville, 1975, Welcome to L.A., 1977, Cria, 1977, Roseland, 1977, Remember My Name, 1978, A Wedding, 1978, The Mirror Crack'd, 1980. Address: care William Morris Agy 151 El Camino Beverly Hills CA 90212 *

CHAPMAN, BARBARA BIGGS, med. writer; b. Rockford, Ill., May 17, 1929; d. Vernon Earl and Mildred Lucille (Bertch) Biggs; student Rockford Coll., 1946-47, 64-65; m. Chester V. Chapman, Oct. 24, 1948 (dec.); 1 son, David Ralph. Med. writer Rockford Morning Star and Register-Rep., 1971-74; dir. public relations Rockford Meml. Hosp., 1975-76; asso. dir. Office of Public Relations, AMA, Chgo., 1977-80; speaker agrl. health and safety; condr. physicians seminars in media relations. Bd. dirs. Rockford Jail Reachout Chaplaincy Program, 1975-76, Blackhawk Area council Boy Scouts Am., 1975-77, Boys Club Assn. Rockford, 1975-77, Kidney Found. of Ill., 1977-79; program chmn. Mendelssohn Club Fellowship, 1981—. Nat. Endowment for Humanities fellow, 1972-79; recipient 55 awards in writing, 1972-79. Mem. Am. Agrl. Editors Assn., Am. Med. Writers Assn., Ill. Woman's Press Assn. (v.p. 1982-83), Am. Agriwomen, Am. Assn. History of Medicine, Nat. Assn. Sci. Writers, Nat. Fedn. Press Women, Nat. Inst. Farm Safety, Internat. Assn. Bus. Communicators. Episcopalian. Author: That Men Know So Little of Men, a History of the Negro in Rockford, Illinois, 1975; This, the Noblest Charity, the Centenary History of Rockford Memorial Hospital, 1983. Home and Office: 1212 Cosper Av Rockford IL 61107

CHAPMAN, CAROLYN, media exec.; b. Portsmouth, Ohio, Feb. 4, 1933; d. Roger Donald and Flowery Alice (Callaway) Carr; diploma Portsmouth Interstate Bus. Coll., 1954, S. Ohio Manpower Tng. Ctr., 1965; m. Edward J. Chapman, May 13, 1966; children—Cheryl, Roger, Lisa, Mark, Edmond, Sean. Dep. probation officer Scioto County Juvenile Ct., Portsmouth, 1960-63; coder II, Aid for Aged, Ohio Dept. Public Welfare, Columbus, 1964; clk. typist II, Bur. Vital Statistics, Dept. Health, Columbus, 1964, clk.-stenographer II, CD Div., 1966; clk.-stenographer ABC, Los Angeles, 1967, ops. coordinator, 1968-72, asso. dir., on-air dir., 1972—; cons. in video tape and TV prodn.; mem. negotiating com. Teamsters Union, Los Angeles, 1970. Ch. sec. Findlay St. Meth. Ch., Portsmouth, 1959-63, chmn. women's day program, 1962, chmn. commn. on missions, 1959-62, del. ann. conf., Cleve., 1963, sec. ofcl. bd., 1959-62; pres. local chpt. Ohio Republican Council, 1959-62, mem. state bd., 1962, del. from Scioto County to State Rep. Conv., Ohio, 1962; mem. film editing com. Social Health and Hygiene Assn., 1961-62; tribute com. for Tribute to Dorothy Arzner, 1975; Los Angeles Jr. C. of C., 1977. Mem. ABC Employees Assn. (pres. Hollywood branch, 1971-73), Dirs. Guild Am. (ad council 1981-82). Address: PO Box 43025 Los Angeles CA 90043

CHAPMAN, ELEANOR HOWELLS, coll. adminstrv. asst.; b. Durham, N.C., Feb. 19, 1938; d. John Lloyd and Callie Gertrude (Neighbors) Howells; student U. N.C., Chapel Hill, 1960-61; div.; 1 dau., Laura Ann. Bookkeeper, sec.-receptionist Ricca, Nelson and Gantt, C.P.A.s, Durham, N.C., 1958-60; legal sec. Haywood, Denny and Miller, Chapel Hill, 1961-62; sec. to dir. Cytology Lab. dept. pathology Duke U. Med. Center, Durham, 1962-63; sec. Noble Truck Leasing, Richmond, Va., 1963-64, Pitts. Plate Glass Co., Richmond, Va., adminstrv. asst. dept. chemistry, sec. dept. biophysics Med. Coll. Va., Richmond, 1966-67, housestaff sec., 1967, departmental sec. dept. pathology, 1967-68; adminstrv. sec., asst. office mgr. Office of Chief Med. Examiner, State N.C., Chapel Hill, 1968-70; adminstrv. sec. dept. zoology U. N.C., Chapel Hill, 1970-73, adminstrv. asst. dept. chemistry, 1973-74, 1973-74; adminstrv. sec. div. neurology Duke U. Med. Center, Durham, N.C., 1974-77; acting adminstrv. asst. dept. neurology Baylor Coll. Medicine, 1977, adminstrv. asst., 1978-81, sr. adminstrv. asst., 1981—. Mem. exec. com. Houston Gulf Coast chpt. Muscular Dystrophy Assn., 1978—; bd. dirs. Houston Area Parkinson Disease Soc., 1981—; sec. Neurology A Study Sect., NIH, 1979-82; vol. Camp Mission Possible, 1981. Mem. Beta Sigma Phi. Office: 6501 Fannin St Houston TX 77030

CHAPMAN, ERNA MARTA RIEDEL (MRS. RAY F. CHAPMAN), home economist; b. Dresden, Germany, May 20, 1909 (brought to U.S. 1914, naturalized 1923); d. Joseph and Elsa (Mueller) Riedel; B.S., U. Md., 1934, M.S., 1936; postgrad. Ind. U., D.C. Tchrs. Coll., U. Md.; m. Ray F. Chapman, Sept. 5, 1942. Sales, acting asst. buyer The Hecht Co., Washington, 1928-30; card punch operator Census Bur., 1930-31; grad. asst. U. Md. Coll. Home Econs., College Park, 1934-36; corr. editor Social Security Bd., Balt., 1936-38; vocat. home econs. tchr. D.C. public schs., Washington, 1938-56, state supr. home econs. edn., 1960-65; asst. prin. Roosevelt High Sch., Washington, 1956-60; state supr., supervising dir. home econs. edn. D.C. Public Schs., Washington, 1967-75; free lance home economist, farmer, 1975—; chmn. agrl. land preservation adv. bd. Anne Arundel County, Md., 1978-79; trustee Md. Agrl. Land Preservation Found., 1979-80, 80—; acting dean U. Md., College Park, 1965-67; mem. nat. adv. com. J.C. Penney Co., Inc. Family life cons. Teamwork Found.; mem. Gov.'s com. State of Md., Status of Women in Higher Edn., 1965-67; trustee U. Md. Mem. NEA, Am. Vocat. Assn., Am. Home Econs. Assn., AAUW, Nat. Council Adminstrs. of Home Econs., Assn. Home Econs. Adminstrs., Nat. Assn. State Univs. and Land Grant Colls., D.C. Home Econs. Assn., Omicron Nu, Phi Kappa Phi, Phi Delta Gamma. Club: Research (D.C.). Contbr. articles to profl. jours. Home: 1660 Riedel Rd Gambrills MD 21054

CHAPMAN, EUGENIA SHELDON, state legislator; b. Fairhope, Ala., Jan. 10, 1923; d. Chauncey Bailey and Rose (Donner) Sheldon; B.Ed., Chgo. State U., 1944; m. Gerald M. Chapman, Nov. 24, 1948; children—George, John, Katherine, Andrew. Tchr. public schs., Cicero, Ill., 1944-47, Chgo., 1947-51; mem. Ill. Ho. of Reps., 1964—, minority whip, chmn. human resources com., standing com. on appropriations. Mem. Dist. 214 Bd. Edn., Cook County, Ill. Named Best Legislator Independent Voters. Ill., 1966, 68, 70, 74, 76, 78, 80, 82. Mem. LWV (pres. Arlington Heights 1957-59), Bus. and Profl. Women's Club. Democrat. Address: 16 S Princeton Ct Arlington Heights IL 60005

CHAPMAN, FRANCES ELIZABETH CLAUSEN (MRS. WILLIAM JAMES CHAPMAN), civic worker; b. Atchison, Kans., Feb. 27, 1920; d. Erwin W. and Helen (Hackney) Clausen; B.A., Wellesley Coll., 1941; m. W. MacLean Johnson, Aug. 31, 1940 (dec. Nov. 1965); children—Stuart MacLean, Duncan Scott, Douglas Hamilton; m. 2d, William James Chapman, Dec. 5, 1970. Project dir. Women in Community Service, Inc., St. Louis, 1965-66; pres. Nursery Found., St. Louis, 1956-58, dir., 1953-59, 65-68; adv. com. Mo. State Children's Day Care, 1963—; chmn. day care com. Mo. Council Children and Youth, 1961, chmn. foster care sect., 1961-63, mem. steering com., 1967-69; spl. asst. to the pres. Webster Coll., 1966-68. Bd. dirs. New City Sch., 1967-69, Mid-County YMCA, 1967-70, St. Louis Conservatory and Sch. Arts, 1978—; trustee Jr. Coll. Dist., St. Louis-St. Louis County, 1968-80, pres. bd. trustees, 1971-73, 76-77; trustee John Burroughs Sch., 1973-79, Wellesley Coll., 1976-82; bd. dirs. Assn. Governing Bds. Univs. and Colls., 1970-80, v.p., 1977-78, chmn. bd., 1978-79, hon. trustee, 1982—; bd. commrs. Nat. Commn. on Accrediting, 1971-72; bd. overseers Center for Research on Women in Higher Edn. and Professions, Wellesley, Mass., 1977-82; mem. Coordinating Bd. for Higher Edn. State of Mo., 1982—. Mem. Nat. Soc. Arts and Letters, Wellesley Coll. Alumnae Assn. (sec., dir. 1958-61). Club: Wellesley Coll. (pres. 1965-67). Home: 10 Overbrook Dr St Louis MO 63124

CHAPMAN, JEAN RUSS, publishing exec.; b. Pitts., Aug. 11, 1928; d. John Monroe and Constance (Clarke) Russ; B.A., U. Mich., 1950; postgrad. L.I. U., 1969-71; m. Robert David Rust, Mar. 4, 1957 (div.); 1 dau., Constance Clare; m. 2d, Francis Allan Chapman, Mar. 11, 1972; stepchildren—Allan, Kenneth, Jeanne Chapman Berg. Asst. to editor Ladies Home Jour., N.Y.C., 1950-51; asst. editor Child Life Mag., Boston, 1951-55; tchr., Stirling, Scotland, 1955-57; sr. editor, project mgr., then cons. Harcourt Brace Jovanovich, N.Y.C. and San Francisco, 1971-75; adminstr. dept. anesthesiology U. Wash. Med. Center, Seattle, 1976-82; chief book editor Alaska N.W. Pub. Co., Edmonds, Wash., 1982—; instr. Nassau Community Coll., part-time 1970-71. Clk., Congressional Ch., Huntington, N.Y., 1968. Mem. Network Exec. Women, Alpha Phi (chpt. pres. 1967-69). Democrat. Presbyterian. Club: Mercerwood Shore. Sr. editor, project mgr. Bookmark Reading Series, 1973-75. Home: 4307 E Mercer Way Mercer Island WA 98040 Office: 130 2d Ave S Edmonds WA 98020

CHAPMAN, PHYLLIS WAGNER, assn. exec.; b. Jeffersonville, Ind., May 2, 1938; d. Joseph Edward and Jane Elizabeth (Stringe) Wagner; grad. Columbia Sch. Nursing, 1960; student U. S.C., 1960-62; Geriatric Certificate, Grady Hosp., 1962; m. Henry William Chapman, Dec. 23, 1961 (dec. May 1980); children—Joseph Henry, Rebekah Lewe, Sarah Kline. Med. surg. nursing instr. Columbia (S.C.) Hosp., 1960-61; med. surg. instruction coordinator S.C. Bapt. Hosp., Columbia, 1961-63; office asst. Charlotte (N.C.) Sales & Mktg. Execs., Inc., 1975-76, exec. dir., 1976—; nurse ARC Blood Center, Charlotte, 1975—. Mem./historian exec. com. Char-Meck PTA Council, 1970-75; N.C. Amateur Athletic Union jr. olympic diving chmn., 1972—; mem. competitive diving com. Nat. Amateur Athletic Union and U.S. Olympic Com., 1979-80. Fed. grantee in geriatric nursing, 1961; Charlotte Central YMCA Leadership award, 1975. Mem. Sales and Mktg. Execs. Internat. (internat. vice chmn. 1979-81), N.C. Amateur Athletic Union, Telephone Pioneers of Am. (chpt. 35). Republican. Lutheran. Clubs: Gyminis Gymnastics (pres. 1976-78), Order of Rainbow. Home: 4302 Silo Ln Charlotte NC 28211 Office: 1409 E Boulevard PO Box 3186 Charlotte NC 28203

CHAPMAN, SANDRA JOAN, assn. exec.; b. Honolulu, Jan. 21, 1950; d. Richard James and Dorothy Helen (Burke) Buckley; B.S., Colo. State U., 1972; m. Mervin L. Chapman, Aug. 30, 1969. Asst. dir. Make It Yourself with Wool program Am. Sheep Producers Council, Denver, 1973-75, asst. dir. public relations, 1975-79; exec. Colo. Cattle Feeders, Denver, 1979—. Mem. Am. Home Econs. Assn., Colo. Home Econs. Assn., Rocky Mountain Assn. Meeting Planners Internat., Home Economists in Bus. Home: 11341 W Berry Ave Littleton CO 80123 Office: 326 Livestock Exchange Bldg Denver CO 80216

CHAPPELL, ALICE MERCKENS, glass co. exec.; b. Buffalo, Oct. 9, 1942; d. E. August and Betty Ruth (Merckens); B.A., Vassar Coll., 1964; M.A., U. Pa., 1968; M.B.A. with honors, Columbia U., 1973; m. Richard Lee Chappell, Sept. 6, 1968; children—Carol Lee, Phoebe Dreux. Lectr., Albright-Knox Art Gallery, Buffalo, 1964-65; dir. F. Roten Gallery, Inc., Balt., 1968-70; product mgr. Avon Products, Inc., N.Y.C., 1973-77; dir. sales and mktg. Steuben Glass Co., N.Y.C., 1977—. Mem. Beta Gamma Sigma. Club: Vassar (N.Y.C.). Office: 717 Fifth Ave New York NY 10022

CHAPPELL, CLAUDIA BOTTS, realtor; b. Ft. Worth, Oct. 12, 1929; d. Claud A. and Lena M. (Pope) Botts; student Stephens Coll., Columbia, Mo., 1946-48; grad. Realtors Inst., 1973; m. J.W. Chappell, Apr. 12, 1948; children—Glenna Chappell Downing, Neil, Nancy Chappell Stanfa, Chris. Pres., Chaparral Properties, Inc., Oklahoma City, 1973—; chmn. exec. com. Oklahoma City Multiple Listing Service, 1977. Named Okla. Realtor of Yr., 1980; cert. residential specialist. Mem. Nat. (dir., Omega Tau Rho award 1980), Okla. (dir. 1975—, regional v.p. 1979, sec.-treas. 1980) assns. realtors, Women's Council Realtors (v.p. Oklahoma City 1974), Oklahoma City Bd. Realtors (dir. 1975-80, v.p. 1976—, Realtor of Yr. 1978), Realtors Nat. Mktg. Inst. (state chmn. 1976-79 recipient 2 Nat. Membership awards 1978), Nat. Fedn. Bus. League, Better Bus. Bur., Home Builders Assn., Okla., Oklahoma City chambers Commerce, Geol. Soc. Aux. Okla., Home Builders Aux. Methodist. Clubs: Oklahoma City Gun, Stephens Coll. Alumnae (pres. 1976-77) (Oklahoma City). Home: 4616 NW 61st St Oklahoma City OK 73122 Office: 5770 NW Expressway Oklahoma City OK 73132

CHAPPELL, RUTH, personnel exec.; b. Calif., Apr. 20, 1932; d. George and Helen (Finley) Rax; B.A. in Communication, Calif. State U., Sacramento, 1977, B.A. in Psychology, 1977; m. Joseph Chappell, May 10, 1952; children—Valinda, Patricia, Jerome, Kevin. With San Francisco Public Health Dept., 1954-63; lab. technician, technologist Calif. Dept. Food and Agr., 1963-75, affirmative action officer, women's program officer, 1975-76, tng. officer, 1976-77; prof. devel. cons., 1977-79; mgr. adminstrv. services personnel devel. div. Calif. Personnel Bd., 1979-81, asst. mgr. Calif. State Women's Program, 1981-82, mgr. appeals div., 1982—. Vice chmn. legis. com. Calif. State Employees Assn., 1977; legis. chmn. Sacramento Community Commn. on Status of Women, 1976; No. vice chmn. Women's Coalition Calif., 1979; Calif. chmn. Womens' Equity Action League, 1977. Recipient cert. merit (3) Calif. State Govt. Mem. Am. Soc. Tng. and Devel., Labor Relations Assn., Nat. Womens Polit. Caucus, Black Women Organized for Polit. Action, Black Women's Polit. Caucus. Methodist (human rights chmn.). Club: Toastmistresses (regional public relations chmn.). Address: 2551 5th Ave Sacramento CA 95818

CHARAK, BETTY JANE, plastics co. exec.; b. N.Y.C., June 7, 1941; d. Nathan and Sylvia (Jandorf) C.; B.F.A., Boston U., 1962; postgrad. U. Florence, 1962-63. Asst. art editor Columbia Records, N.Y.C., 1963-65; asst. accessories editor Seventeen Mag., N.Y.C., 1965-66; exec. sales dir. Personality Plastics, Inc., N.Y.C., 1966-81, v.p., 1981—. Address: Personality Plastics 225 W 34th St New York City NY 10001

CHARD, DOROTHY ALICIA, counselor; b. Elizabeth, N.J., July 28, 1938; d. Edward Joseph and Dorothy Josephine (Delhagen) Guinee; B.S., Coll. Misericordia, 1960; M.A., Seton Hall Coll., 1966. With East Brunswick (N.J.) Sch. System, 1967—, asst. dir. adult and continuing edn. program, 1978—, chmn. guidance dept., 1971—. Mem. N.J. Sch. Counselor Assn. (v.p. middle sch., exec. com.), N.J. Edn. Assn., East Brunswick Edn. Assn., N.J. Personnel and Guidance Assn. Democrat. Roman Catholic. Home: 500 Adams Ln Apt 16Y North Brunswick NJ 08902 Office: Churchill Jr High Sch Norton Rd East Brunswick NJ 08816

CHARISSE, CYD (TULA ELLICE FINKLEA), actress, dancer; b. Amarillo, Tex., Mar. 8, 1923; d. Ernest E. and Lela (Norwood) Finklea; student Hollywood Profl. Sch.; m. Nico Charisse, Aug. 12, 1939 (div. 1947); 1 son, Nicky; m. 2d, Tony Martin, May 9, 1948; 1 son, Tony. Toured U.S. with Ballet Russe, also in Europe; dancer in motion picture, Something to Shout About, Columbia Pictures, 1942; other films include: Mission to Moscow, 1943, Ziegfeld Follies, Harvey Girls, 1945; Three Wise Fools, Fiesta, The Unfinished Dance, Till the Clouds Roll By, 1946, On an Island With You, 1947, Words and Music, 1948, The Kissing Bandit, East Side West Side, 1949, Tension, Adventures of Don Renegade, Singin' in the Rain, The Wild North, Sombrero, 1952, The Band Wagon, 1953; Silk Stockings, 1957; Black Tights, 1962; Two Weeks in Another Town, 1962; The Silencers, 1966; Mardoc 7, 1968; Warlords of Atlantis, 1978. Elected Star of Tomorrow, 1948. Home: Beverly Glen Los Angeles CA 90024 Office: care Contemporary-Korman Artists Ltd 132 Lasky Dr Beverly Hills CA 90212 *

CHARKEY, CAROLYN LOUISE, newspaper exec.; b. Cheyenne, Wyo., Nov. 23, 1939; d. John Frederick and Frances Louise (Riddell) LoSasso; student Colo. State U., 1957-58; m. Norman Alan Charkey, Feb. 22, 1959 (dec. Sept. 1979); children—Mark Alan, Martin Todd. Freelance writer, public relations cons., 1958—; continuity dir. Sta. KCOL, Ft. Collins, 1964-65; reading tutor Ft. Collins Public Schs., 1965-69; owner, mgr. Carolyn's Interiors, Ft. Collins and Cheyenne, Wyo., 1970-77; sect. editor Wyo. Eagle, Cheyenne, 1972-74; info. officer State of Wyo., Cheyenne, 1974-77; dir. public relations programs Coors Distbg. Co., Tustin, Calif., 1978-82; mgr. public relations The Register, Santa Ana, 1982—; public relations cons. Leukemia Soc., Sr. Citizens Council. Bd. dirs. Leukemia Soc., Sr. Citizens Adv. Council, United Cerebral Palsy Assn.; pres. The Register Charities, Inc., 1982—. Mem. Orange County C. of C. (council dir.), Tustin C. of C. (v.p.), Internat. Assn. Bus. Communicators (accredited), Public Relations Soc. Am., Nat. Fedn. Press Women, So. Calif. Assn. Philanthropies. Republican. Office: 625 N Grand Ave Santa Ana CA 92711

CHARLES, MARGOT GRATZ, nurse; b. Phila., June 23, 1938; d. Earl Jay and Margaret Greil (Gerstley) Gratz; B.S.N., Cornell U., 1961; m. David Jay Charles, Aug. 29, 1965; children—Daniel Jay, Margery Gratz. Staff nurse Hosp. U. Pa., Phila., 1961-62; head nurse cardiopulmonary renal research unit Einstein No. Div., Phila., 1962-64; instr. Hosp. Sch. Nursing Temple U., 1964-65; part time positions, 1965-72; instr. Miami Dade Community Coll., 1972-74; nurse epidemiologist Coral Reef Gen. Hosp., Miami, Fla., 1974-77; instr. Jackson Meml. Hosp. Sch. Nursing, Miami, 1977-78; nurse epidemiologist Am. Hosp., Miami, 1978—. Unit leader LWV, 1971-72, tel. chmn. Dade County, 1972; active Boy Scouts,

Girl Scouts. Mem. Nat. League Nurses, Assn. Practitioners Infection Control (chmn. ways and means Dade County 1977, dir. Dade County chpt. 1982—), Fla. Practitioners Infection Control (treas. 1981—), Beta Sigma Phi, Republican. Jewish. Home: 7701 Palmetto Ct Miami FL 33156 Office: 11750 Bird Rd Miami FL 33175

CHARLES, MARY LOUISE, social worker, columnist; b. Los Angeles, Jan. 24, 1922; d. Louis E. and Mabel I. (Lyon) Kusel; B.A., San Jose State U., 1964; A.A., Los Angeles City Coll., 1941; m. Henry Loewy Charles, June 19, 1946; children—Susan Lynn, Henry Loewy, Robert Louis, Carol Lisa. Social worker Sutter County, Calif., 1954-57, Santa Clara County, Calif., 1957-61, manual coordinator, 1961-73, community planning specialist, 1973-81; columnist Sr. Grapevine, 1981—; founder, pres. Triple A Council of Calif., 1978-80; chmn. social service subcom. of adv. com. Calif. Health and Welfare Agy., 1976—. Bd. dirs. Outreach and Escort, Inc., 1980—; mem. City of Santa Clara Sr. Citizens Adv. Commn., 1975, chmn., 1980—; chmn. bd. Family Planning Alternatives, 1976-79; mem. adv. bd. Ind. Aging Program, 1977—, chmn., 1980—; mem. adv. bd. Friends Outside, 1970—; pres. Council on Aging of Santa Clara County, 1977-79; mem. Santa Clara County Social Service Adv. Commn., 1979—, Paratransit Coordinating Council, 1979—. Served with WAVES, 1942-45. Recipient Daniel E. Koshland Found. award in Social Welfare, 1973. Mem. Nat. Assn. of Social Workers, Mental Health Assn. of Santa Clara County, Am. Public Welfare Assn., Calif. Children's Lobby, Western Gerontol. Soc., Calif. Social Services Union Local 535 of AFL-CIO (state exec. bd.). Editor, pub. Calif. Legislation, 1968-74. Home and Office: 2527 Forbes Ave Santa Clara CA 95050

CHARLESWORTH, MARION HOYEN, educator; b. Lowell, Mass., Jan. 1, 1918; d. Francis Emmanuel and Elizabeth (Donabed) Hoyen; A.A. in Acctg. summa cum laude, Worcester Jr. Coll., 1950; B.A. cum laude, Worcester State Coll., 1976; m. Donald W. Charlesworth, Sept. 7, 1952 (dec. May 1974); 1 son, Donald W. Office mgr. Worcester Shoe Co. (Mass.), 1945-46; asst. fin. sec. YMCA Worcester, 1946-56; substitute tchr. Haverhill (Mass.) Public Sch. System, 1965—, acctg. tchr. adult continuing edn. evening div., 1979—. Vol. clk. Haverhill Public Library Fund Raising, 1966-69; mem. Haverhill Skating Rink Com., 1969-70; vol. Merrimack Wastewater Mgmt. Study, U.S.C.E., Commonwealth of Mass. and Merrimack Valley Planning Commn. in cooperating with EPA, 1973-75; vol. Haverhill Recycling, 1971-75; vol. hostess USO, 1941-52; deaconess First Congregational Ch., Haverhill, 1967-70, 74-75, 81-83, mem. outreach com., 1978-81; bd. dirs. Steven-Bennett Home, Inc., Haverhill, 1977—, Winnekenni Found., Inc., 1977—; mem. Widow's Lifeline, 1974—, vol., 1980—. Mem. NAM, Mature Students Orgn. (chmn. parliamentary procedure 1974), Haverhill Parent Tchr. Assns. (exec. bd. 1964-71, pres. 1968-71, co-chmn. project People and Their Environment 1972), Mass. Congress PTA, Friends of Haverhill Public Library, Merrimack River Wastewater Council, Tau Lambda Omega. Clubs: Haverhill Garden (pres. 1973-75, chmn. public relations 1972—, dir. 1975-81, recipient awards), Women's City of Haverhill (2d v.p. 1971-73); Assyrian-Am. Ind. (treas. 1948-72) (Worcester). Mass. reporter The Assyrian Star, 1963-64. Instrumental while pres. in numerous awards being bestowed on Haverhill Garden Club. Home: 35 Columbia Park Haverhill MA 01830

CHARLTON, BETTY JO, state legislator; b. Reno County, Kans., June 15, 1923; d. Joseph and Elma (Johnson) Canning; B.A., U. Kans., 1970, M.A., 1976; m. Robert Sansom Charlton, Feb. 24, 1946; children—John Robert, Richard Bruce. Asst. instr. U. Kans., Lawrence, 1970-73; legis. adminstrv. services employee State of Kans., Topeka, 1977-78, legis. aide gov's. office, 1979; mem. Kans. Ho. of Reps., 1980—.

CHARLTON, MARGARET ELLEN JONSSON, civic worker; b. Dallas, Aug. 7, 1938; d. John Erik and Margaret Elizabeth (Fonde) Jonsson; student Skidmore Coll., 1956-57, So. Meth. U., 1957-60; m. George Volk Charlton, Jan. 23, 1960; children—Laura, Emily, Erik. Dir. KRLD radio, Dallas, 1970-74; 1st woman dir. First Nat. Bank Dallas, 1976—, also vice-chmn. trust com. First woman trustee Meth. Hosp., 1972—, mem. exec. com., 1977-81, mem. corp. bd., 1981—; bd. dirs., chmn. exec. com. Lamplighter Sch., 1967—; bd. dirs. Winston Sch., 1973—; bd. dirs., exec. com. Episcopal Sch. Dallas, 1976—; bd. dirs. Callier Center for Communications Disorders, 1967—, v.p., 1974—; mem. vis. com. dept. psychology M.I.T., 1978—; past chmn. Crystal Charity Ball; past bd. dirs. Children's Med. Center, Hope Cottage, Children's Bur., Baylor Dental Sch., Dallas Health and Sci. Mus., Dallas YWCA, Dallas Day Nursery Assn. Margaret Jonsson Charlton Hosp. named in her honor, Dallas, 1973. Republican. Club: Dallas Woman's.

CHARLTON, MARJORIE BEVERLY, govt. ofcl.; b. Elgin, Ill., Feb. 27, 1925; d. Donald and Pauline (Hagelow) Beverly; B.S., Miami U., Oxford, Ohio, 1948; student U. Dubuque, 1942-43, Wright State U., 1959-60, 81, Air Force Inst., 1965—; m. Thomas E. Charlton, Dec. 15, 1961; 1 dau., Catherine; children from previous marriage—Lawrence Landaker, Peter Landaker; stepchildren—Russell, Carol, Bruce, Elizabeth. Advt. asst. McGraw Electric Co., Elgin, Ill., 1948-49; research asst. Ohio State U., 1950-52; With USAF, Ohio, 1960—; sr. contract negotiator, 1967—. Bd. dirs. Buckeye Cabinets Inc., 1975—; v.p. Xenia Area Human Relations Council, 1970-73. Recipient spl. achievement and outstanding performance awards, USAF, Mem. Nat. Contract Mgmt. Assn., AAUW, Nat. Assn. Female Execs., DAR, Pi Beta Phi. Democrat. Presbyterian. Home: 425 Winding Trail Xenia OH 45385

CHAROF, EILEEN JOAN, personnel services exec.; b. Bronx, N.Y., July 2, 1947; d. Robert Gerard and Rosalie Fortuna (Nasta) Stickley; B.A. in Psychology, St. John's U., 1969; m. Alan I. Charof, Nov. 15, 1969. Regional adminstr. Am. Sign and Indicator Corp., N.Y.C., 1970-72; dir. adminstrn. Direct Mail Mktg. Assn., N.Y.C., 1972-74; mgr. Allied Temporary Service, N.Y.C., 1974-78; nat. ops. mgr. Temp Force, East Meadow, N.Y., 1978-80; v.p. Cyberway, N.Y.C., 1980—; owner, pres. E.J.C. Assos., 1981—. Active Vol. Services for Children, N.Y.C. Mem. Nat. Assn. Female Execs., Nat. Assn. Personnel Cons., Nat. Assn. Temporary Services, Internat. Word Processing Assn. Home: 81-53 263 St Floral Park NY 11004 Office: 405 Lexington Ave New York NY 10174

CHARREN, GABRIELLE, dental technologist; b. Berlin, Germany, Nov. 15, 1937; came to U.S., 1959, naturalized, 1965; d. Hans Manfred and Margot (Kaufmann) Purucker; Masters degree cum laude in Dental Tech., Berufschule Hannover, W. Ger., 1959; postgrad., U. Madrid, 1970-71; 1 dau., Stefanie. Head ceramist Beverly Dental Ceramics, Beverly Hills, Calif., 1959-64; dept. mgr. Wolfsen Dental Lab., Los Angeles, 1964-66, Park Dental Lab., Inglewood, Calif., 1966-68; art. mgr., rep. artists J. Zuniga, Manolo, Coronado, Mallorca, Spain, 1968-70; disc jockey 3-lang. radio show, Mallorca, 1971-72; owner Oak Grove Dental Lab., Palo Alto, Calif., 1975-79; mgr. Capital City Dental Lab., Sacramento, 1980-81; owner Novadent Ceramics, Sacramento; condr. clinics in ceramic staining and anatomy. Pres., Parent Council, Keys Family Day Sch., Palo Alto, 1976-78; v.p. Parent Council Waldorf Sch., Sacramento, 1981—. Cert. dental technician, 1977. Mem. Nat. Assn. Dental Labs., Nat. Assn. Female Execs. Republican. Club: Arden Hills Swim and Tennis (Sacramento). Contbr. daily column Who's Who Daily Bull., English lang. newspaper, Mallorca, 1971-72; guest contbr. Spanish newspapers: Dairio Mallorca, Balleares, 1971-79. Home: 921 Castec Dr Sacramento CA 95825 Office: Novadent Ceramics 577 Arden Town Ct Sacramento CA 95825

CHARTER, MARILYN ANN, bookkeeping services exec.; b. Defiance, Ohio, June 26, 1937; d. Aaron Ivan and Alice Imogene (Cubberly) Russell; student schs., Perrysburg, Ohio; m. Fred Charter, Jr., June 27, 1959; children—Russell Keith, Richard Fred, Timothy Jay. Bookkeeper, I.R. Miller & Assos., C.P.A.s, Toledo, 1967-71; bookkeeping supr. Moak, Hunsaker & Rouse, C.P.A.s, Oklahoma City, 1973-78; bookkeeper F. Dail Harper, Investments, Oklahoma City, 1978; now owner Marilyn A. Charter Bookkeeping Services, Oklahoma City. Address: 6161 N May Ave Suite 124 Oklahoma City OK 73112

CHARTERS, ANN, educator; b. Bridgeport, Conn., Nov. 10, 1936; d. Nathan and Kate (Schultz) Danberg; A.B., U. Calif., Berkeley, 1957; M.A., Columbia U., 1960, Ph.D., 1965; m. Samuel B. Charters, Mar. 14, 1959; children—Mallay, Nora Lili. Mem. faculty Colby Jr. Coll., New London, (N.H.), 1962-64; lectr. Columbia U., 1964-65; asst. prof. Am. lit. N.Y.C. Community Coll., 1967-70; prof. Am. lit. U. Conn., Storrs, 1974—. Author: Nobody-Life and Times of Bert Williams, 1967; Kerouac, 1973; I Love-Story of Vladimir Mayakovsky and Lili Brik, 1979; The Story and Its Writer, 1983; The Beat Generation, 1983. Address: Dept English U Conn Storrs CT 06268

CHARTOCK, PATRICIA OWENS, gerontol. psychologist; b. Berkeley, Calif., Apr. 9, 1943; d. Donald Fish and Jean (Hoagland) Owens; A.B., Mt. Holyoke Coll., 1965; M.A.T., Northwestern U., 1966; postgrad. U. S.C., 1974; Ph.D., Columbia U., 1980; m. Lewis C. Chartock, Sept. 11, 1966; children—Donald, Andrea. Biology and chemistry tchr. high schs. Chgo., 1965-66, N.J., 1966-68; research technician Worthington Biochems., N.J., 1968-69, John S. Sharpe Research Found., Pa., 1969-71; field rep. malnutrition and parasite project OEO, Columbia, S.C., 1971-74; program evaluation, research cons. Florence Heller Jewish Welfare Bd. Research Center, N.Y.C., 1977-78; asst. dir. research Brookdale Center on Aging, Hunter Coll., N.Y.C., 1977-78, acting dir. research, 1978-79, dir. Inst. of Work and Retirement, 1979—, cons. to Hunter Coll. Sch. of Nursing; adj. asst. prof. Adelphi Sch. of Social Work. Mem. Am. Psychol. Assn., Gerontol. Soc. Am., Sigma Xi, Pi Lambda Theta. Author, co-author papers presented profl. confs.; chmn., organizer symposium in field. Home: RFD 1 Box 440 Croton-on-Hudson NY 10520 Office: 440 E 26th St New York NY 10010

CHARY, ERIKA MAGDA, pianist, educator; b. Vienna, Feb. 8, 1923; came to U.S., 1966, naturalized, 1977; d. Ignaz and Mariska (Gonda) Weiner; Assoc. Royal Coll. Music, Eng.; Licentiate Royal Acad. Music; diploma in edn., U. London; m. Henry Chary, Nov. 3, 1945. Concert pianist, performing in Eng. and U.S.; mem. Fidelio Trio, Eng.; artist/tchr., voice coach, head music dept. Radlett Prep. Sch., 1957-66; founder Opera Group with children, 1960; head music dept. Marymount Sch., 1967-72; artist tchr., Palos Verde Peninsula, Calif., 1968—; founder, dir. Young Artists Peninsula Music Festival, 1977. Mem. Music Tchrs. Assn. Calif., Nat. Guild Piano Tchrs., Am. Coll. Musicians, European Piano Tchrs. Assn. Home and office: 6931 Vallon Dr Palos Verdes Peninsula CA 90274

CHASE, DORIS TOTTEN, artist; b. Seattle, Apr. 29, 1923; d. William Phelps and Helen Mae (Feeney) Totten; student U. Wash., 1941-42; Ph.D. (hon.), U. Colo., 1974; div.; children—Gregary Totten Chase, Randall Totten Chase. Exhibited one-woman shows: Formes Gallery, Tokyo, 1970, Portland (Oreg.) Art Mus., 1976, 80, Mus. Modern Art, N.Y.C., 1978, 80, Hirschhorn Mus., Washington, 1974, 77, Wadsworth Atheneum, Hartford, Conn., 1973, U. Wash., Seattle, 1971, 78, 81, 82, Erica Williams/Ann Johnson Gallery, Seattle, 1980; represented in permanent collections: Mus. Fine Arts, Boston, Hudson River Mus., Yonkers, N.Y., Milw. Art Mus., Seattle Art Mus., Art Inst. Chgo., Mus. Modern Art, Kobe, Japan, Mus. Fine Arts, Houston, Smithsonian Instn., Washington, Pa. Acad. Fine Arts, Vancouver (Can.) Art Gallery, Nat. Collection Fine Arts, Washington, N.C. Mus. Art, Raleigh; monumental kinetic sculpture commns.: Expo 70, Osaka, Japan, Atlanta Sculpture Park, Kerry Park, Seattle, Lakeside Park, Anderson, Ind., Sculpture in the Park, N.Y.C., Open Eye Theatre, N.Y.C., Playground of Tomorrow, Los Angeles, Sculpture for Dance, Seattle, 1968, 69, Seattle Opera, 1972, Mus. Art, Montgomery, Ala.; guest lectures and presentations: Carpenter Center, Harvard U., 1975, SUNY, Purchase, 1978, UCLA, 1974, 80, 82, San Francisco State U., 1979, Winthrop (N.C.) Coll., 1978, CUNY, Bklyn., 1976, 77, 78, N.Y. U., 1977, Fordham U., 1976, U. Cin., 1978, Sarah Lawrence Coll., 1977, U. Mich., 1977, 79, New Sch. Social Research, N.Y.C., 1979, Calif. Inst. Arts, 1976, 80, 82, M.I.T., 1976, Seattle Art Mus., 1972, 77, Lincoln Center Performing Arts Mus., N.Y.C., 1977, Brit. Film Inst., Cornell U., 1982, Steddeljck Mus., Amsterdam, 1982; producer/dir. films and video. Recipient awards, Mannheim, Ger., 1975, U. Mich., 1977, 78, 80, Ithaca, N.Y., 1978, 80, Chgo., 1977, 80, Bellevue, Wash., 1976, 77, 78, 80, Cannes, France, 1976, Deauville, France, Santa Clara, Calif., Northwestern U., Lille, France, N.Y. Film Festival, 1979, Am. Film Festival, N.Y.C., 1980, Filmex, Los Angeles, 1981, numerous others. Mem. Women Artist Filmmakers, Whitney Mus., Mus. Modern Art, N.Y. Film Council, Assn. Ind. Video and Film. Home: 222 W 23d St New York NY 10011

CHASE, ELIZABETH WAGNER (MRS. HAROLD F. CHASE), former librarian; b. Susquehanna, Pa., Aug. 14, 1917; d. Charles Tingley and Marion Elizabeth (Dimock) Wagner; B.S., Phila. Coll. Pharmacy and Sci., 1939; M.S. in Library Sci., Drexel Inst., 1950; m. Elof Fritiof Johnson, Nov. 23, 1939 (dec. Sept. 16, 1962); m. 2d, Harold F. Chase, Sept. 2, 1966. Librarian Phila. Coll. Pharmacy and Sci., 1946-63, 64-81, acting dean women, 1946-62; acquisition librarian Drexel Library Sch., Phila., 1963-64, instr. library sci., 1959-62. Mem. Med. Library Assn., Spl. Libraries Assn., Am. Assn. Colls. Pharmacy, AAUW, Lambda Kappa Sigma. Republican. Episcopalian. Home: 1945 Greenlawn Dr Englewood FL 33533

CHASE, FRANCES WALKER, psychiatric social worker; b. Youngstown, Ohio, May 25, 1916; d. Alexander Edward and Marie (Gaston) Walker; A.B., Conn. Coll., 1938; M.S.W., Columbia U., 1944; asso. Tavistock Inst. Human Relations, London, 1970; m. Richard V. Chase, Jr., July 27, 1940; children—Elizabeth Chase Millett, Richard A., Elliott, Nathaniel C. Social worker Pub. Welfare Dept., Fairfield, Conn., 1940-42; social worker, immigration counselor Christian Com. for Refugees, N.Y.C., 1942-44; psychiat. social worker Family Counseling Service, Hackensack, N.J., 1963-69; sr. psychiat. caseworker London (Eng.) Youth Adv. Centre, 1970-76; prin. psychiat. social worker Canonbury Child Guidance Unit, Inner London Edn. Authority, 1976-81, child guidance cons., 1982—; tchr. courses, pvt. diagnostic cons. for referral to psychiat. resources, speaker, discussion leader in field. Vol. adoption worker, home finder Bus. Children's Services, Hackensack, 1960-63. Mem. Nat. Assn. Social Workers (U.S.), Brit. Assn. Social Workers (chairwoman Nat. Assn. Social Workers European chpt.), Group for Advancement of Psychotherapy in Social Work (U.K.) (chairwoman 1978-81), Alumni Assn. Columbia U. Sch. Social Work (bd.). Home: Flat 1 47 Netherhall Gardens London NW3 5RJ England Office: Canonbury Child Guidance Unit 15 River Pl London N1 England

CHASE, JEAN ANNA, accountant; b. Rumford, Maine, Oct. 30, 1948; d. Paul Willard and Constance Margaret (Fowler) Salonen; student public schs., Quincy, Mass.; James Gordon Chase, Feb. 17, 1968; children—Paul Carroll, Eric Jon. Internal auditor, tax preparer tax dept. Howard Johnson's, Braintree, Mass., 1969-71; bookkeeper subs. co. PGA Nat. Venture Ltd., W. Palm Beach, Fla., 1973-75, acctg. supr. 1976-77, controller, 1977-81, corp. sec., treas., 1981—; dir., corp. sec., treas. PGA Nat. Venture Ltd. dir., sec. treas. corps. Treas. W. Palm Beach Soccer League, 1981—; active Cub Scouts, 1977. Mem. Nat. Assn. Accts. (Palm Beach chpt.). Home: 1188 Fernlea Dr West Palm Beach FL 33409 Office: P O Box 3267 West Palm Beach FL 33402

CHASE, JOYCE ELAINE, accountant, ins. co. exec.; b. Benton Harbor, Mich., Dec. 4, 1931; d. Richard I. and Evelyn Pauline (Hahn) Winney; student Lake Mich. Coll., 1974-75, Mich. State Ins. Sch., 1974, m. Ernest Arthur Chase, July 21, 1951; children—Ernest L., Arthur M., Robert J., William R., James R. Clk. Gillespie's Drug Store, Benton Harbor, 1945, WoolWorth's Store, Benton Harbor, 1946-47; bookkeeper Reeder's Bookkeeping Service, Benton Harbor, 1949; assembler VM Corp., Benton Harbor, 1950; telephone operator Mich. Bell Co., Benton Harbor, 1951; bookkeeper I & M Electric Co., Buchanan, Mich., 1952, Auto Specialties Co., St. Joseph, Mich., 1953; clk. Galien Drug Store, Galien, Mich., 1955; assembler Electro-Voice Corp., Buchanan, Mich., 1958-62; bookkeeper Chase Bookkeeping & Tax Service, Galien, Mich., 1963-67 , sr. tax accountant, 1968—; ins. agt. Chase Ins. Service Center, Galien, Mich., 1974—; emergency med. technician and ambulance driver Galien Vol. Ambulance Service, 1974—. Cub. Scout den mother S.W. Mich. council Cub. Scouts Am., 1963-69; mem. Galien Twp. election bd., 1971-73; mem. Galien Sch. Election Bd., 1971—; pres. Galien Athletic Boosters, 1969; mem. Galien High Sch., PTA, 1966—, adv. com., 1965-68. Mem. Nat. Soc. Pub. Accountants, Mich. Emergency Services Health Council, Am. Legion Aux. Republican. Methodist. Home: US Route 12 East at Garwood Lake Galien MI 49113 Office: 112 N Main St Galien MI 49113

CHASE, LUCLA, ballet dancer; b. Waterbury, Conn., Mar. 24, 1907; d. Irving Hall and Elizabeth Hosmer (Kellogg) Chase; student St. Margaret's Sch., Waterbury, Theatre Guild Sch., N.Y.C.; D.F.A., U. Wis., 1977, Williams Coll., 1977, L.I.U., 1979, Yale U., 1980, Goucher Coll., 1981, others; m. Thomas Ewing, Jr.; children—Thomas III, Alexander Cochran. Ballerina Mordkin Ballet 1937-39; ballerina The Ballet Theatre, N.Y.C., 1940-60, co-dir., 1945—. Recipient 17th ann. Capezio Dance award, 1968 City of N.Y. Mayor's award, 1978, award State of Conn., 1980, Chgo. Mayor's award, 1980, Presdl. Medal of Freedom, 1980. Mem. grand council Royal Acad. Dancing, 1946. Office: Am Ballet Theatre 890 Broadway New York NY 10003 *

CHASE, MARY JANE, jewelry mfg. co. exec.; b. Glouster, Ohio, July 16, 1938; d. Cecil Nelson and Juanita Marie (Anderson) McCafferty; grad. Andrews Sch., 1957; m. Robert Vincent Chase, Oct. 16, 1971; 1 son, Robert Vincent. Sec. to v.p. accessories div. TRW, Cleve., 1957-63; office mgr. Kaufman & Reynolds Constrn. Co., Sacramento, Calif., 1964-67; asst. to med. staff Roseville (Calif.) Community Hosp., 1967-69; asst. to v.p. ops. Intel Corp., Mountain View, Calif., 1969-70; exec. asst. to pres. Catamore Co., Inc., E. Providence, R.I., 1971-74, dir. adminstrn., 1978-81, v.p. adminstrn., 1981—. Bd. dirs. Nat. Fedn. Republican Women, mem. nominating com., 1979; alt. del. Rep. Nat. Conv., 1976, 80; bd. dirs. E. Providence unit Am. Cancer Soc., 1979-81; mem. Meml. Hosp. Aux., 1978—. Episcopalian. Home: 201 Wilson Ave Rumford RI 02916 Office: 1 Catamore Blvd East Providence RI 02914

CHASE, PAMELA LOUISE, banker; b. Mineola, N.Y., May 27, 1954; d. James Raymond and Valborg Louise (Mortenson) Quinn; B.S. in Acctg., SUNY, Albany, 1974; m. Robert Chase, Dec. 22, 1974. Acct., Price Waterhouse & Co., N.Y.C., 1974-75; asst. sec. Mfrs. Hanover Trust Co., N.Y.C., 1975-78; asst. v.p. Marine Midland Bank, N.Y.C., 1978-80, v.p. credit and tng., 1980—. Mem. N.Y. Inst. Credit, Robert Morris Assos., Inc., Bank Credit Assos. Home: 246 Stonegate Nissequogue NY 11780 Office: 140 Broadway New York NY 10015

CHASE, SHIRLEY EVELYN, editor, pub.; b. Montrose, Colo., Feb. 24, 1949; d. Donald Chester and Nellie Louise (Scott) Neal; student Western State Coll., Gunnison, Colo., 1967-68, Colo. Western Coll., Montrose, 1970-71; hypno-technician Colo. Hypnosis Inst., Cedaredge, 1979; m. Thomas Leo Chase, July 10, 1968; 1 dau., April Jenette. Graphic designer, copy editor J.M.E. Bus. Service, Denver, 1974-75; freelance copywriter, graphic artist, 1975-77; founder, pres. Ironstone Pub. Co., Olathe, Colo., 1977—; pres. Ironstone-Chase Enterprises. Adult vol. Girl Scouts U.S.A., 1976—; mem. accountability com. Montrose County Sch. Bd., 1982—. Mem. World Naturopathic Assn. (founding com.). Exec. editor: Drugless Health Care, 1979. Home: 6647 57 50 Rd Olathe CO 81425 Office: PO Box 610 Olathe CO 81425

CHASE, SYLVIA B., journalist; b. St. Paul, Feb. 23, 1938; d. Kelsey David and Sylvia (Bennett) C.; B.A., UCLA, 1961. Aide to assembly fin. and ins. investigative com. and Sen. Thomas Rees, Calif. Legislature; coordinator Kennedy for Pres., 1968; advance person Atty. Gen. Tom Lynch, 1966; action reporter Sta. KNX, Los Angeles, 1969-71; news corr., anchorwoman CBS News, 1971-77, ABC News, N.Y.C., 1977—. Recipient Emmy award for news and documentary report VW Beetle: The Hidden Danger, 1980. Office: ABC News 77 W 66th St New York NY 10023 *

CHATFIELD, HELEN ELIZABETH, photo-journalist, writer; b. El Paso, Tex., Jan. 15, 1925; d. William Henry and Mary Alice (Kelleher) Fryer; B.A., Northwestern U., 1946; m. James David Lloyd Chatfield, July 9, 1948 (dec. June 1969); children—Camelia, David, Jim, John, Linda, Tom. Women's program dir. Sta. KROD, El Paso, 1946-48; stringer Skagit Valley Herald, Mt. Vernon, Wash., 1971-75; newscaster Sta. KBRC, Mt. Vernon, 1972-78, Sta. KWYZ, Everett, Wash., occasionally, 1978-80. Pres. No. deanery Archdiocesan Council Catholic Women, 1976-80, St. Augustine's Altar Soc., 1973-75; sec. bd. mgmt. Armed Forces YMCA, 1978-80; v.p. St. Augustine's Parish Council, 1980-82; 1st women mem. bd. Oak Harbor Council Navy League, 1975-80; pres. Scenic Heights Water Assn., 1977-80. Recipient 1st Place award for news story Nat. Assn. Press Women, 1981. Mem. Nat. Assn. Press Photographers, Wash. Press Assn. (1st pl. award photography 1977), Nat. Assn. Mil. Widows, Tri-Delta. Clubs: Soroptimists Internat. (charter Oak Harbor, Wash. 1981); Ret. Officers Wives (chpt. pres. 1973-75). Home: 764 W Mount Baker Blvd Oak Harbor WA 98277 Office: 1000 College Way Mount Vernon WA 98273

CHAUVIN, CLARICE BLANCHE, educator; b. Webster, Mass., Nov. 13, 1913; d. Jean Baptiste and Emma (Carmel) Chauvin; B.A., B.E., U. Montreal (Que., Can.), 1942, M.A., 1946; Ph.D. in English, Catholic U. Am., 1951. Joined Sisters of St. Ann, Roman Catholic Ch., 1931; tchr., elem. and secondary schs., Montreal, 1933-43; prof. Marie Anne Coll., Montreal, 1943-46; prof., chmn. English dept. Anna Maria Coll., Paxton, Mass., 1951-72, registrar, prof., 1972-75, prof., chmn. div. lang. and lit., 1975—. Mem. Nat. Conf. of Tchrs. of English, Coll. English Assn., MLA, Am. Soc. Aesthetics, Delta Epsilon Sigma. Home and office: Anna Maria Coll Paxton MA 01612

CHAUVIN, DORIS GAUTREAUX, banker; b. Houma, La., June 9, 1932; d. Alex Paul and Maggie Margaret (Pitre) Gautreaux; student public schs.; student Am. Inst. Banking; m. Ollen Anthony Chauvin, Nov. 4, 1951; children—Ollen, Alex A., Barry D., Denise L. Retail saleswoman, 1951-54; hairdresser, Houma, 1954-71; with Raceland Bank (La.), 1972—, asst. cashier, loan officer, 1977—, asst. v.p., 1980-81, v.p., br. mgr. Bayou Blue br., 1981—; notary public, 1975—. Sec.-treas. fair com. St. Louis Roman Cath. Ch., Houma, 1974-80, chmn. fin. com., 1978-80. Democrat. Address: Route 5 Box 275-B Houma LA 70360

CHEAIRS, CLAUDIA DENISE, mfg. co. ofcl.; b. Hamtramck, Mich., Apr. 21, 1951; d. Sidney Minrose and Rosa Eileen (McKinney) Jones; B.S., Mich. State U., East Lansing, 1973; m. John W. Cheairs, Sept. 15, 1979; 1 dau., Gianna Denise. With IBM Corp., Detroit, 1973—, staff asst., 1977-78, adminstrn. ops. mgr., 1978—; cons. in field. Mem. Brazeal Dennard Chorale, 1978—. Democrat. Mem. A.M.E. Ch. Home: 12030 Montrose St Detroit MI 48227 Office: 200 Renaissance Center Suite 1800 Detroit MI 48243

CHEATHAM, KATHIE BALLON, banker; b. Memphis, Sept. 24, 1943; d. David and Polly (Weaver) Ballon; A.B., Randolph-Macon Woman's Coll., 1969; postgrad. N.Y.U. Grad. Sch. Bus. Adminstrn., 1970-72; 1 son, William W. With AT&T, N.Y.C., 1960-70; asst treas., asst. v.p., v.p. Morgan Guaranty Trust Co. N.Y., N.Y.C., 1970-81; v.p., treas. AVCO Community Developers, Inc., San Diego, 1981-82; v.p., gen. mgr. Morgan Guaranty Internat. Bank, Houston, 1982—, also dir. Mem. Internat. Bus. Council, Houston C. of C., 1982-83. Home: 5308 Piping Rock Ln Houston TX 77056 Office: 1100 Milam St Suite 830 Houston TX 77056

CHEATHAM, NORMA ROSETTA, advt. co. exec.; b. Indpls., Oct. 21, 1942; d. William Rozell and Frances (Britt) C.; B.A., Ind. U., 1964. Editor, Che Che Publs., Indpls., 1970-76; advt. cons. Calif. Good Life Publs., Sepulveda, 1977-80; advt. cons., 1980—. Bd. dirs. NAACP, 1973-75. Club: Order of Eastern Star. Home: 719C N Eucalyptus Ave #12 Inglewood CA 90302 Office: 1110 S Inglewood Ave Inglewood CA 90301

CHEATUM, BILLYE ANN, educator; b. Oklahoma City, Jan. 27, 1933; d. Leon Thomas and Agnes Mabel Cheatum, B.S., Okla. Coll. for Women, 1955; M.S., Smith Coll., 1957; Ph.D., Tex. Womans U., 1967. Tchr. phys. edn. U. Okla., Norman, 1957-60; instr. Syracuse U., 1960-61; instr., chmn. phys. edn. women Fla. So. Coll., 1961-63; mem. faculty Midwestern U. Wichita Falls, Tex., 1965-67; mem. faculty Western Mich. U., Kalamazoo, 1967—, prof. phys. edn., 1979—, coordinator spl. phys. edn., 1972—, chmn. dept. womens phys. edn., 1967-72, also adv. gerontology program; mem. nat. sport devel. com. U.S. Assn. for Blind Athletes. Nat. bd. dirs. Womens Equity Action League. Named to Alumnae Hall of Fame Mem. Am. Coll. Sport and Medicine Am. Assn. Gerontology in Higher Edn., AAHPER, Am. Assn. Children with Learning Disabilities, AAUP, Nat. Wheelchair Athletic Assn., Mich. assn. Learning Disabilities. Democrat. Christian Ch. Author: Golf, 1969; Basketball-Five Player, 1972; contb. articles to profl. jours. Home: 2614 Taliesin St Kalamazoo MI 49008 Office: Phys Edn Dept Western Mich U Kalamazoo MI 49008

CHEATUM, LINDA ROSE, health assn. exec.; b. San Antonio, July 3, 1943; d. Raoul Armand and Rosemarie (Cardenas) Berlanga; B.S. in Journalism, Tex. Woman's U., 1964; M.L.S., 1970; m. Dan Earl Cheatum, Apr. 23, 1966; children—Carole Diane, Candy Ann. Asst. editor Tex. Agrl. Experiment Station, Tex. A&M U., College Station, 1964-66; periodicals reference librarian Tex. Woman's U. Denton, 1970-73; acquisitions librarian Sci.-Engring. Library So. Meth. U., Dallas, Tex., 1973-75; librarian Am. Heart Assn. Nat. Center, Dallas, 1975-78, info. analyst div. research programs, 1978-82, chief data mgmt. Office of Research and Med. Programs, 1982—. Active Richardson Assn. for Children with Learning Disabilities. Mem. Spl. Library Assn., Med. Library Assn., Tex. Library Assn. (mem. publs. com.), Dallas County Library Assn. (pres., v.p., editor newsletter), U.S. Figure Skating Assn. (trial judge). Editor Dallas-Tarrant County Health Sci. Consortia: Union List of Periodicals, 1979. Home: 3301 Shield Ln Garland TX 75042 Office: 7320 Greenville Ave Dallas TX 75231

CHEELY, WILMA CANNON, personnel co. exec.; b. Savannah, Tenn., Feb. 7, 1910; s. Thomas Riley and Katie Strickland (Russell) Cannon; student Athens Woman's Coll., 1930, Robin Adair Sch. Oral Hygiene, 1931-32, Ga. State U., 1951; m. Lamar Joseph Cheely, June 28, 1935 (dec.); children—Mary Eugenia and Jane Gray (twins). Dental hygienist Dr. Gerald Mitchell, 1934-36; salesperson Gene Craig Realtors, Atlanta, 1951-52; pres. Temporary Office Personnel Services, Inc., Atlanta, 1953—. Mem. Atlanta C. of C., Nat. Women Bus. Owners Assn., Bus. and Profl. Women, Ind. Office Service Inst., Nat. Assn. Personnel Cons., Nat. Assn. Temporary Services, Ga. Assn. Temporary Services (past pres.). Club: Quota. Home: 147 15th St Hanover House #11 B Atlanta GA 30361 Office: 100 Colony Sq #2100 Atlanta GA 30361

CHEEVER, ELLEN, kitchen designer; b. Ukiah, Calif., Jan. 29, 1949; d. Howard Allen and Katharine Mary (Donohue) Cheever; B.A. in Home Econs., Calif. State U., Sacramento, 1971; m. Joseph W. Aievoli, Aug. 4, 1973. Kitchen designer Kitchen Center, Sacramento, 1971-73; gen. mgr. Kitchens Inc., Sacramento, 1973-77; propr. Kitchens by Ellen, Sacramento, 1978—; instr. Calif. State U., Sacramento; speaker, cons. in field. Mem. Am. Inst. Kitchen Dealers (dir., hon. mention design award 1976, 78, 79, pres. No. Calif. chpt. 1976-78, Kitchen Designer Merit award 1979, 80), Am. Soc. Interior Designers, Sacramento Better Bus. Bur. (dir.), Sigma Kappa. Democrat. Roman Catholic. Club: Soroptomist. Author: Beyond the Basics: Advanced Kitchen Design, 1978; also numerous articles. Address: 1617 18th St Sacramento CA 95814

CHELSTROM, MARILYN ANN, ednl. inst. exec.; b. Mpls., Dec. 5; d. Arthur Rudolph and Signe (Johnson) C.; B.A., U. Minn., 1950; L.H.D., Oklahoma City U., 1981. Staff asst. Mpls. Citizens Com. Public Edn., 1950-57; coordinator, policies and procedures Lithium Corp. Am., Inc., Mpls., N.Y.C., 1957-62; exec. dir. The Robert A. Taft Inst. Govt., N.Y.C., 1962—, exec. v.p., 1977-78, pres., 1978—. Active LWV, Mpls., 1950-60, N.Y.C., 1972—; charter mem. Citizens League Greater Mpls., 1952-60; del. White House Conf. on Edn., 1955; vice chmn. Minn. Women for Humphrey, 1954. Recipient Cert. of Recognition for Service to Mpls. Public Schs., Mpls. Citizens Com., 1957; named Town Topper, Mpls. Star, 1958. Mem. Am. Polit. Assn., Minn. Alumni Assn. (gov. N.Y. 1963—, pres. 1971-73; nat. dir. 1971-75), Lutheran (treas. councilman). Club: Minn. Alumni (Mpls.). Home: 155 E 38th St New York NY 10016 Office: The Robert A Taft Inst Govt 420 Lexington Ave New York NY 10017

CHEN, CHING-CHIH, info. specialist, educator; b. Foochow, China, Sept. 3, 1937; came to U.S., 1959, naturalized, 1974; d. Han-chia and May-ying Liu; B.A. (Rotary scholar), Nat. Taiwan U., China, 1959; A.M. in L.S. (Barbour scholar), U. Mich., 1961; Ph.D., Case-Western Res. U., 1974; m. Sow-Hsin Chen, Aug. 20, 1962; children—Anne, Cathy, John. Asst., Sch. Library Sci., U. Mich., 1960-61, service librarian, 1961-62; sci. reference librarian Windsor (Ont., Can.) Pub. Library, 1962; reference and circulation librarian McMaster U., Hamilton, Ont., 1962-63, head Sci. Library, 1963-64; sr. sci. librarian U. Waterloo (Ont.), 1964-65, head Sci., Engring. and Math. Library, 1965-68; assoc. sci. librarian M.I.T., Cambridge, 1968-71; asst. prof. Sch. Library Sci., Simmons Coll., Boston, 1971-75, asso. prof., 1975-79, prof., 1979—, assoc. dean Grad. Sch. Library and Info. Sci., 1979—; cons. to WHO, 1980-82, Abt Associates, Inc., 1980-81; mem. U.S. del. on biomed. info. to China, summer, 1980; guest lectr. on info. sci. to various professional orgns., 1971—. Recipient Disting. Service award Chinese Am. Library Assn., Disting. Alumnus award Sch. Library Sci., U. Mich., 1980; Jasper Whiting Found. travel grantee, 1976, Emily Hollowell research fund grantee, 1972—. Mem. ALA (councilor 1981—), Am. Soc. for Info. Sci. (edn. com. 1979—, nomination com. 1981-82, dir. 1981—), Med. Library Assn. (chmn. surveys com. 1980-82), Spl. Library Assn., New Eng. Library Assn., Assn. of Am. Library Schs., Mass. Library Assn., AAUP, Assn. of Coll. Libraries, Beta Phi Mu. Author 12 books on library and info. sci., latest being: Health Sciences Information Sources, 1981; Online Bibliographic Searching: A Learning Manual, 1981; (with Peter Hernon) Information Seeking, 1982; (with Stacey Bressler) Microcomputers in Libraries, 1982; contbr. articles on library research and continuing edn. to profl. publs.; contbr. book revs. on library references to profl. jours. Home: 11 Nassau Dr Winchester MA 01890 Office: Graduate Sch Library and Information Sci Simmons College 300 The Fenway Boston MA 02115

CHEN, CONCORDIA CHAO, mathematician; b. Peiping, China; came to U.S. 1955, naturalized 1969; d. Chun-fu and Kwie Hwa (Wong) Chao; B.A. in Bus. Adminstrn., Nat. Taiwan U., 1954; M.S. in Math., Marquette U., 1958; postgrad. Purdue U., 1958-60, M.I.T., 1961-62; m. Chin Chen, July 2, 1960; children—Marie Hui-mei, Albert Chao. Teaching asst. Purdue U., Lafayette, Ind., 1958-60; system analysis engr. electronic data processing div., Mpls.-Honeywell, Newton Highlands, Mass., 1960-63; mgmt. planning asst. Lederle Labs., Am. Cyanamid Co., Pearl River, N.Y., 1964-68, computer applications specialist, 1967, ops. analyst, 1967-68; staff programmer IBM, Sterling Forest, N.Y., 1968-78, adv. programmer, data processing mktg. group, Poughkeepsie, N.Y., 1978-80, mgr. systems programming and systems architecture, Princeton, N.J., 1980—. Mem. Am. Math. Soc., Soc. Indsl. Applied Maths. Home: Mountain Pass Box 34 Route 6 Hopewell Junction NY 12533 Office: IBM PO Box 390 Poughkeepsie NY 12602

CHEN, CONNIE S. P., fin. planner; b. Shanghai, China; came to U.S., 1967; d. Gin-Sun and Yuen Chuen-Lan C.; B.A., Providence Coll. Liberal Arts, Taiwan, 1964; student N.Y. U., 1968-69, Advanced Mgmt. Program Harvard U., 1982-83. Dist. mgr. Investors Diversified Services, N.Y.C., 1968-74; account exec., product specialist Merrill Lynch, N.Y.C., 1975-77; fin. planning cons. Personal Capital Planning Group, N.Y.C., 1977-79; pres. Chen Planning Cons., Inc., N.Y.C., 1979—; asso. prof. Fin. Planning Inst., Adelphi U., N.Y.C. Cert. fin. planner. Mem. Internat. Assn. Fin. Planners (dir.), Fin. Women's Assn., Women's Econ. Round Table. Office: 527 Madison Ave New York NY 10022

CHEN, DIANE TZE-SUN, physician, pharm. co. exec.; b. Chgo., Jan. 30, 1951; d. York Yueh and Irene Fei-Fei (Hu) C.; B.S. in Chemistry, U. So. Calif., 1970; M.D., N.Y.U., 1974. Internal medicine intern L.I. Jewish-Hillside Med. Center, New Hyde Park, N.Y., 1974-75; resident in neurology North Shore-Meml. Sloan-Kettering Cancer Center, N.Y.C., 1975-76; asst. dir. profl. services Hoffmann-LaRoche Inc., Nutley, N.J., 1976—; adj. attending physician dept. neurology Meml. Sloan-Kettering Cancer Center, 1977—. Mem. Am. Med. Women's Assn., Am. Acad. Neurology, Am. Pain Soc. (exec. adminstr.), Eastern Pain Assn. (treas.), Internat. Assn. for Study Pain, Assn. for Psychophysiologic Study Sleep. Office: 340 Kingsland St Nutley NJ 07110

CHEN, IRENE GEE, food stylist; b. N.Y.C., Aug. 17, 1950; d. Jimmy Set and Lin Fung (Ng) G.; B.A., Hunter Coll., 1971; M.S. in Family and Consumer Studies, Lehman Coll., 1974, M.S. in Guidance and Counseling, 1978; m. Oct. 17, 1981. Tchr., Olinville Jr. High Sch., Bronx, N.Y., 1971-75, Lehman Coll., Bronx, 1975-77, Harry Eiseman Jr. High Sch., Bklyn., 1978-80; food stylist, recipe developer Ladies Home Jour., 1977-78; food stylist, recipe developer Woman's Day Mag., 1979—, home economist, 1980—; food coordinator Evander Childs High Sch.; food cons. Corn Products Corp., 1978—; food stylist Nabisco, 1978; cons. food cos. and publs.; comml. model Mauna Loa Macadamia Nuts, Lewis & Neale. Mem. Am. Home Econs. Assn., Home Economists in Bus., Am. Counseling Assn., Omicron Nu.

CHEN, JANEY C., linguist; b. China, Feb. 5, 1922; d. Ching Choi and Sik Yu (Li) Chou; B.Sc., Nat. South-West Associated Univs., Yunnan, China, 1944; M.R.E., Heavenly People Theol. Sem., 1968, Golden Gate Baptist Theol. Sem., 1980; m. Ti Kang Chen, July 25, 1943; children—David, Julia, Helen. Instr. English, 1st Middle Sch., Kuangchouwan, 194S-46; sr. instr. Taipei Lang. Inst., Taiwan, 1957-64; sr. instr. Chinese U., Hong Kong, 1964-71; founder, prin. Hong Kong Lang. Inst., 1971-75; tchr. German Swiss Internat. Sch., 1975-78; instr. Chinese Tiburon (Calif.) Baptist Ch., 1979—; dir. English/Chinese lang. and Bible classes Lang. Mission, 1981—; dir. H.K. World Home Bible League, 1972-77; owner J.C. Publs., 1968-78. Author: A Language Bridge for John, 1967; Cantonese for Foreign Children, 1968; Conversation Drills in Everyday Cantonese, 1969; A Practical English-Chinese Pronouncing Dictionary, 1970. Home: 19 Miwok Way Shelter Hill Apt Mill Valley CA 94941

CHEN, MARJORIE WONG, airline exec.; b. Los Angeles, Oct. 28, 1940; d. Thomas A. and Mayme M. (Moe) Wong; B.A., Goucher Coll., 1962; M.A., U. Calif. at Berkeley, 1965; m. Joseph Tao Chen, July 10, 1966; children—Barbara Joanne, Cynthia Anne. Research economist Fed. Reserve Bank San Francisco, 1964-65; bus. cons., travel industry, 1968-74; marketing analyst The Flying Tiger Line, Inc., Los Angeles, 1974-76, systems analyst, 1976-77, mgr. mgmt. reporting and performance analysis, 1977-78; mgr. passenger pricing and fare devel. Continental Airlines, 1978-80, mgr. internat. pricing, 1980—. Mem. Calif. Republican Assembly, 1976. Danforth Found. asso., 1968-79. Mem. Nat. Mgmt. Assn. (membership chmn.), U. Calif., Marlborough alumni assns. Republican. Conglist. Club: Goucher. Home: 640 N June St Los Angeles CA 90004 Office: 7300 World Way W Los Angeles CA 90009

CHEN, SHIRLEY CHIH-HSUAN, nutritionist; b. Kweichow, China, Sept. 10, 1944; d. Joseph S. and Olivia Ch.; came to U.S., 1966, naturalized, 1977; B.Sc., Taiwan Normal U., 1966; M.S., Mich. State U., 1969; Ph.D., U. Calif., Davis, 1973; Research chemist, dept. envron. health and engring. U. N.C., Chapel Hill, 1970-71; postdoctoral fellow biol. chemistry UCLA, 1973-74; research asso. div. nutritional scis. Cornell U., 1974-76; asst. prof. food and nutrition Iowa State U., Ames, 1976-82, asso. prof., 1982—. Grantee Iowa State U. Agrl. Expt. Sta., Best Food Inc., CPC Internat. Mem. N.Y. Acad. Scis., Am. Oil Chemists Assn. Contbr. articles to profl. jours.; research in areas of fatty acid assimilation and vitamin E functions. Office: Dept Food and Nutrition Iowa State U Ames IA 50011

CHENAULT, JACQUELINE, telephone co. ofcl.; b. Cin., May 25, 1946; d. Leonard Arnold and Thelma Ruth (Gentry) C.; student U. Cin., 1965. With ATT Long Lines, Cin., 1964—, data processing asso., Cin., 1975-77, staff acct., mgr., Bedminster, N.J., 1977-79, mgr. circuit and trunk assignment, Cin., 1979-80, mgr. network assignment, Cin., 1980—. Active Usher Bd., Jr. Achievement, NAACP, March of Dimes, Am. Cancer Soc., Cin. Zoo; asst. sec. Christian Women's Fellowship. Mem. Nat. Assn. Female Execs. Home: 3919 Holman Circle Cincinnati OH 45236 Office: 15 W 6th St Cincinnati OH 45202

CHENG, ANNA, real estate investment service co. exec.; b. Taipei, Taiwan, Oct. 15, 1954; came to U.S., 1973; d. Nunsai and Aisun Cheng; B.A. in Econs., Whitman Coll., 1976; M.B.A., U. Santa Clara, 1981. Fin. analyst Frontier Mgmt. Corp., Menlo Park, Calif., 1977-79; real estate exec. Fox & Carskadon Fin. Corp., San Mateo, Calif., 1980. Mem. Am. Mgmt. Assn., Fin. Mgmt. Assn., Am. Fin. Assn., Real Estate Securities and Syndication Inst., World Affairs Council, Center Democratic Instns., Asian Am. Theatre Co., San Francisco Mus. Modern Art, Smithsonian Instn., Signet Table, Mortar Bd. Contbr. articles to profl. publs. Office: 2755 Campus Dr San Mateo CA 94403

CHENG, JENNIFER (JENNIE) VICTORIA, investment mgr.; b. Hong Kong, Dec. 13, 1949; d. Ya Tsing and Chun Hung C.; student Lewis and Clark Coll., 1967-69; B.A., U. Oreg., 1971; M.B.A., Columbia U., 1972; m. Stefan R. Bothe, Oct. 16, 1976. Asso. firm Donaldson Lufkin & Jenrette, N.Y.C., 1973, jr. analyst, 1974-75, sr. analyst, 1975; asst. dir. investments Mut. Life Ins. Co. N.Y., N.Y.C., 1976-78, dir. equity investment, 1978-79; sr. analyst Morgan Stanley, N.Y.C., 1979-82; investment mgr. Cole Yeager & Wood, N.Y.C., 1982—. Mem. N.Y. Soc. Security Analysts, Fin. Analysts Fedn., N.Y.C. Ballet Guild, Met. Mus. Art. Home: Allyn Rd Goshen CT 06756 Office: 630 Fifth Ave New York NY 10111

CHENG, LUCIE, sociologist, univ. adminstr.; b. Hong Kong, Feb. 11, 1939; came to U.S., 1960, naturalized, 1965; d. She-Wo and Tsung-jang (Shaw) Cheng; M.A., U. Chgo., 1964; Ph.D., U. Hawaii, 1971. Lectr., U. Hawaii, Honolulu, 1966-70; asst. prof. UCLA, 1970-76, acting dir. Asian Am. Studies Center, 1972-76, dir., 1976—, assoc. prof., 1976-82, prof., 1982—, dir. China Exchange Program, 1978—, spl. asst. to vice chancellor, 1980—; cons. in field. Mem. Census Adv. Com. on Asia and Pacific Am. Population for the 1980 census, 1976-80; bd. dirs. Chinese Hist. Soc. of So. Calif., 1978-80; mem. Calif. Council for the Humanities, 1981-85. Social Sci. Research Council grantee, 1972; Assn. for Asian Studies grantee, 1974-75; NIMH grantee, 1979-81; NEH grantee, 1982; East-West Center grantee, 1982. Mem. Am. Sociol. Assn. Author: Chinese Immigrant Women in 19th Century California, 1979; Mental Illness Among the Chinese, 1973; Toward a Political Economy of Chinese America, 1975.

CHENG, SYLVIA LAM, physician; b. China, Aug. 15, 1946; d. Thomas H. and Helen W. (Yung) Lam; M.D., Kaohsiung Med. Coll., Taiwan, 1972; m. Francis Cheng, Oct. 5, 1973; 1 son, Michael. Resident in medicine Mercy Hosp., Chgo., 1972-75; practice medicine specializing in internal medicine, Hoffman Estates, Ill., 1975—. Mem. AMA, Chgo. Med. Assn., ACP (physician utilization com.). Club: Meadow. Office: 1000 Grand Canyon Pkwy Hoffman Estates IL 60194

CHENNAULT, ANNA CHAN (MRS. CLAIRE LEE CHENNAULT), airlines exec., author; b. Peking, China, June 23, 1925; d. Y. W. and Bessie (Joung) Chan; B.A., Ling Nan U., Hong Kong, 1944; Litt.D., Chungang U., Seoul, Korea, 1967; LL.D., Lincoln U., 1970; H.H.D., Manahath Ednl. Center, 1970; m. Claire Lee Chennault, Dec. 21, 1947 (dec. July 1958); children—Claire Anna, Cynthia Louise. Came to U.S., 1948, naturalized, 1950. War corr. Central News Agy. (then located in Kunming, China and Shanghai, China), 1944-48, spl. Washington corr., 1965—; feature writer Hsin Ming Daily News, Shanghai, 1944-49; with Civil Air Transport, Taipei, Taiwan, 1946-57, editor bull., 1946-57, pub. relations officer, 1947-57; chief Chinese sect. Machine Translation Research Georgetown U., 1958-63; broadcaster Voice of Am. USIA, Washington, 1963-66; U.S. corr. Hsin Shen Daily News, Washington, 1958—; v.p. Flying Tiger Line, Inc., Washington, 1968-76; pres. TAC Internat. Inc., 1976—; dir. D.C. Nat. Bank; lectr., writer, fashion designer, U.S. and Asia; aviation cons. adv. com. Fed. Energy Adminstrn. Mem. Pres.'s Adv. Com. on Arts, John F. Kennedy Center for Performing Arts; mem. U.S. Nat. Commn. for UNESCO; spl. rep. of Pres. to Philippine Aviation Week celebrations, 1973; spl. asst. to chmn. Asian-Pacific council Am. C. of C.; vice chmn. Pres.' Export Council, 1981—; mem. women's adv. com. on aviation Dept. Transp., 1982—. Pres. Chinese Refugee Relief, Washington, 1962-74, Gen. Claire Lee Chennault Found., Washington, 1961-74; bd. govs. Am. Acad. Achievement, Dallas; trustee Center for Study of Presidency, Library Presdl. Papers; mem. Washington Republican Com., 1960—, mem. Nat. Rep. Fin. Com.; cons. heritage groups, nationalities div. on Asian affairs Rep. Nat. Com.; co-chmn. Fin. Com. to Re-elect Pres., 1972; chmn. Nat. Rep. Heritage Groups Council, 1979; chmn. U.S. Citizens in Asia to Re-elect Pres., 1972; del. Rep. Nat. Conv., 1972. Recipient Woman of Distinction award Tex. Tech. Coll., Lubbock, 1966; Freedom award Order of Lafayette, Washington, 1966; Freedom award Free China Assn., Taipei, 1966, Golden Plate award Champion Democracy and Freedom Am. Acad. Achievement, 1967. Mem. Overseas Press Club, Nat. League Am. Pen Women, Writers Assn., Free China Writers Assn., 14th Air Force Assn. (chmn. awards), U.S. Air Force Wives Club, Flying Tiger Assn., Internat. Platform Assn., Am. Newspaper Club, U.S. C. of C. (internat. policy com.), Theta Sigma Phi. Clubs: Internat., F St., Capitol Hill (Washington). Author: Chennault and the Flying Tigers: Way of a Fighter, 1949, translated into Chinese, 1955; A Thousand Springs, 1962; The Education of Anna, 1979; numerous books in Chinese including Song of Yesterday, 1961, M.E.E., 1963, My Two Worlds, 1965, The Other Half, 1966, Letters from U.S.A., 1967; author Chinese-English dictionaries. Home: 2510 Virginia Ave NW Washington DC 20037 Office: 1511 K St NW Washington DC 20005

CHENOWETH, ARLENE JOYCE, constrn. co. exec.; b. Cass City, Mich., Apr. 1, 1941; d. Robert Melvin and Geraldine Thelma (Bell) Milner; B.S., Olivet Nazarene Coll., Kankakee, Ill., 1963; postgrad. U. Mich., 1963-65; m. Robert R. Chenoweth, Sept. 1, 1962; children—Timothy, Eric, Gregg. Tchr. bus. edn. Swartz Creek (Mich.) Sr. High Sch., 1963-67, Flushing (Mich.) Sr. High Sch., 1969-74; pres., co-owner, office mgr. Chenoweth Constrn. Co., Inc., Fenton, Mich., 1974—; co-owner Chenoweth & Assos. Architects, Inc., Fenton, 1978—; v.p. A&B Enterprises. Sunday sch. tchr.; lectr. on marriage and communication; mem. steering com. Vineyard Ladies Ministries, 1981-82; co-founder Fenton Christian Women's Breakfast Fellowship, 1981. Mem. Nat. Assn. Female Execs., Am. Mgmt. Assn., Fenton Area Bus. and Profl. Women's Club (charter mem., treas. 1979), Boynestat Assn., Chenhen Flying Assn. Nazarene. Clubs: University (Flint, Mich.); Spring Meadows Country. Home: 12050 White Lake Rd Fenton MI 48430 Office: Chenoweth Constrn Co Inc 101 N Ally Dr Fenton MI 48430

CHENOWETH, JEAN, health info. co. exec.; b. Washington, Ill., Dec. 18, 1946; d. Irving Shoemacher, Jr. and Mary Elizabeth (Nickel) C.; B.A. in Psychology, Northwestern U., 1969; B.S. in Med. Record Adminstrn., U. Ill., 1970. With Hosp. Assn. N.Y., 1977-81, v.p., 1980-81; v.p. Commn. Profl. and Hosp. Activities, Ann Arbor, Mich., 1981—; mem. faculty Joint Commn. Accreditation Hosps., 1974-78; bd. dirs. N.Y. State Study Unified Data System, 1976-78; health adv. bd. N.Y. State Dept. Correctional Services, 1977-80; council health info. policy N.Y. State Statewide Planning and Research Coop. System, 1979-81. Mem. Am. Assn. Health Data Systems (pres. 1978-79), Am. Med. Record Assn. (chmn. cons. com. 1978-80), Chgo. Med. Record Assn. (pres. 1972-73), Med. Record Assn. N.Y. State (dir., treas. 1975-76, 79-80), Am. Hosp. Assn. Mem. Christian Ch. Author articles in field. Office: 1968 Green Rd Ann Arbor MI 48106

CHER, singer, rec.artist; b. El Centro, Calif., May 20, 1946; d. Georgia and Gilbert LaPiere; student drama coach Jeff Corey; m. Sonny Bono, Oct. 27, 1964 (div.); 1 dau. Chastity; m. 2d, Gregg Allman (div.), June 1975;1 son, Elijah Blue. Singer with husband as team Sonny and Cher, 1964-74; star TV show Cher, 1975-76, The Sonny and Cher Show, 1976-77; concert appearances with husband, 1977; numerous recs., TV, concert and benefit appearances with Sonny Bono; TV appearances ABC-TV, 1978; appearance with Sonny Bono in motion picture Good Times, 1966, Chastity, 1969; N.Y., Martin Beck Theater, appearances Come Back to the 5 & Dime, Jimmy Dean, Jimmy Dean, 1982; formed rock band Black Rose; recorded album Black Rose, 1980. Address: care Katz-Gallin-Cleary Enterprises Inc 9255 Sunset Blvd Los Angeles CA 90069 also Press Office Ltd 555 Madison Ave New York NY 10022*

CHERNOCK, MARIA CIULLA, consumer products co. exec.; b. S.I., N.Y., Dec. 19, 1951; d. Joseph John and Josephine Marie (LaBita) Ciulla; B.A. in Psychology and English magna cum laude, L.I.U., 1974; m. Joseph Chernock, Sept. 4, 1976. Asst. credit mgr. Stinnes Steel Corp., 1974-76; with Johnson & Johnson Products, Inc., 1976—, ter. mgr., 1978-79, merchandising mgr. health care div., dist. mgr. N.J., 1979-80, mgr. field sales services, New Brunswick, N.J., 1980—. Mem. Nat. Assn. Female Execs., Am. Mgmt. Assn., Variety Service Club, Resource Bur. Corp./Coll. Relations. Office: 501 George St New Brunswick NJ 08903

CHERNOK, NORMA B., social worker; b. N.Y.C., Aug. 15, 1928; d. Louis and Sadie C.; B.S., L.I. U., 1949; M.Ed., Fla. Atlantic U., 1968; M.S.W., Rutgers U., 1978. Dir. med. assisting program Broward (Fla.) Jr. Coll., 1965-66; asst. prof. Coll. of S.I., 1969—, also adminstr. S.I. Women's Crisis Center, 1978-80; teaching asst. social work Rutgers U., 1978; cons. Hudson Valley Community Coll., N.Y.C. Bd. Edn. Pres. Richmond Sr. Centers, Inc., 1978-80; exec. dir. Project SHARE, 1980-81; chmn. health com. N.Y.C. Human Resources Adminstrn. Adv. Com. Dist. 40, pres., 1980-82. Mem. Nat. Assn. Social Workers (chmn. S.I. council 1980-81), Am. Assn. Med. Assts. (past pres. N.Y. State). Author: Your Future in Medical Assisting rev. ed., 1979; Domestic Violence: A Family Matter of Public Concern, 1980. Home: 212 Clermont Pl Staten Island NY 10314 Office: 130 Stuyvesant Pl Staten Island NY 10301

CHERNUCHIN, ELAYNE LINK (MRS. PAUL CHERNUCHIN), mgmt. cons. co. exec.; b. N.Y.C., Oct. 8, 1928; d. Sydney and Lillian (Kalish) Link; B.A., Bklyn. Coll., 1950, M.A., 1952; Ph.D., U. London, 1957; M.A. in Computers, Columbia U., 1979; m. Paul Chernuchin, Sept. 12, 1952; children—Michael Scott, Cindy Jo. Tchr. math., N.Y.C. Public Sch. System, 1950-52; math. analyst Nat. Security Agy., 1952-54; instr. math. USAF, 1955-57; officer Chernuchin Assos., N.Y.C., 1965—. Mem. Am. Statis. Assn., Assn. Computing Machinery, Operational Research Soc. Research in applications specific statis. problems to high speed electronic equipment, comparative course in geometry for high school. Home: 108-19 67th Rd Forest Hills NY 11375

CHESHIRE, MAXINE (MRS. HERBERT W. CHESHIRE), columnist; b. Harlan, Ky., Apr. 5, 1930; d. M.F. and Sylvia (Cornett) Hall; student Union Coll., Barbourville, Ky., 1951-52, U. Ky., 1949-50; m. Herbert W. Cheshire, Apr. 25, 1954; children—Marc, Hall, Paden, Leigh. Reporter Knoxville (Tenn.) News-Sentinel 1951-54; reporter Washington Post, 1954-65; columnist Los Angeles Times Syndicate, 1965—. Author: (with John Greenya) Maxine Cheshire, Reporter, 1978; contbr. articles to popular mags. Office: Times Mirror Square Los Angeles CA 90053 *

CHESLOCK, ROSALIND PLEET, tech. info. mgr.; b. Balt., Aug. 6, 1946; d. Samuel and Anne (Rubin) Pleet; B.A. magna cum laude in Latin and Greek, Goucher Coll., 1967; M.A. in Latin and Greek, Johns Hopkins U., 1968; M.L.S., U. Md., 1974; m. Arthur S. Cheslock, Sept. 5, 1967. Young adult specialist Enoch Pratt Free Library, Balt., 1968-71, asst. dir. bookmobiles, 1971-73; asst. librarian Martin Marietta Labs., Balt., 1974-75, info. specialist, 1975-76, sci. and tech. librarian, 1976-79, mgr. tech. info. services, 1979—. Mem. Neighborhood Bus. Adv. Com., 1980—; bd. dirs. People Encouraging People, 1981—. Dean's scholar Goucher Coll.; Gilman fellow Johns Hopkins U., 1967-68. Mem. Aluminum Assn. (tech. info. com. 1979—; chmn. subcom. World Aluminum Abstracts 1981—), Interlibrary Users Assn. (dir. 1981—), Dept. Def. Remote On-line System Users Council, Am. Soc. Info. Sci., Spl. Libraries Assn. (various coms.), Associated Info. Mgrs., Md. On-line Users Group, Phi Beta Kappa, Beta Phi Mu. Mgmt. adv. panel Modern Plastics, 1981; joint editor: Guide to Metallurgical Information, 3d edit., 1983, Jour. Holdings in the Washington-Baltimore Area, 1983. Home: 2510 Smith Ave Baltimore MD 21209 Office: 1450 S Rolling Rd Baltimore MD 21227

CHESNEY, PATRICIA JOAN (COOK), pediatrician; b. Kingston, Ont., Can., Sept. 23, 1941; came to U.S., 1956, naturalized, 1962; d. Leslie Gladstone and Alfreda Mary (Crutcher) Cook; B.A., U. Rochester, N.Y., 1962; M.D., McGill U., 1966; m. Russell Wallace Chesney, June 8, 1968; children—Karen McColl, Christopher Paton, Gillian Leslie Russell. Intern, Strong Meml. Hosp., Rochester, 1966-67, resident, 1967-68, Johns Hopkins Hosp., Balt., 1971-72, fellow in microbiology, 1968-71, fellow in pediatric infectious disease, 1972-73; med. research council fellow Montreal Children's Hosp. McGill U. med. school, que., 1973-75; asst. prof. dept. pediatrics U. Wis., Madison, 1975-80, asso. prof., 1980—. Mem. Am. Acad. Pediatrics, Infectious Disease Soc. Am., Am. Soc. Microbiology, Midwest Soc. Pediatric Research. Contbr. in field. Office: Dept Pediatrics Clinical Science Center 600 Highland Ave Madison WI 53792

CHESNICK, JOYCE BAILES (MRS. JOSEPH CHESNICK), retail furniture and interiors exec.; b. Memphis, June 6, 1925; d. George W. and Jean Y. Bailes; student U. Tex., 1943-45, U. Houston, 1954-56; m. Joseph Chesnick, Feb. 28, 1945; children—Joan Chesnick Dinerstein, Joseph, Jr., Robert G. Vice pres. Georgetown Manor, Houston, 1968—, San Antonio, 1971—, Beaumont, Tex., 1974—, Houston, 1977—, Robert Joseph Interiors, Corpus Christi, Tex., 1981—, Houston, 1982—. Mem. Am. Soc. Interior Designers (asso.), Houston Retail Furniture Assn., S.W. Home Furnishings Assn., UDC. Club: Westwood Country (gov. 1977-81). Home: 8 Inwood Oaks Houston TX 77024 Office: 1801 N Loop W Houston TX 77008

CHESNUT, CAROL FITTING, economist; b. Pecos, Tex., June 17, 1937; d. Ralph Ulf and Carol (Lowe) Fitting; B.A. magna cum laude, U. Colo., 1971; m. Dwayne A. Chesnut, Dec. 27, 1955; children—Carol Marie, Michelle, Mark Steven. Research asst. U. Colo., 1972; head quality controller Mathematica, Inc., Denver, 1973-74; cons. Mincome Manitoba (Can.), Winipeg, 1974; cons. economist Energy Cons. Assos. Inc., Denver, 1974-80, exec. v.p., 1979-80, also dir.; exec. v.p. ECA/Intercomp, 1980-81; mng. partner The Chesnut Consortium, Denver, 1981—; dir. Critical Resources, Inc.; on leave with staff Senator Gary Hart, 1978. Rep., Lakehurst Civic Assn., 1968. Precinct capt. Republican Party, 1960, 64; now committeewoman Dem. Precinct. Mem. Am. Mgmt. Assn., Soc. Petroleum Engrs., Assn. Women Geoscientists, Assn. Tng. and Devel., Opera Colo., ACLU, NOW, Phi Beta Kappa, Phi Chi Theta. Unitarian. Club: City of Denver, Friends of Phreatophytes. Office: 419 A Saint Paul Denver CO 80206

CHESNUTT, CAROLYN CRAWFORD, assn. exec.; b. Maryville, Tenn., Sept. 16, 1933; d. John Calvin, Jr. and America Arey (Moore) Crawford; B.A. (Presser Found. Music scholar), Agnes Scott Coll., 1955; M.Ed. (Ednl. Research fellow), U. S.C., 1972; M.S., Ga. Inst. Tech., 1979; children—John Calvin, Thomas Walter, Margaret America, Carolyn Christian. Asst. librarian, Hartsville, S.C., 1965-66; instr. math. and psychology secondary schs., Ga. and S.C., 1966-75; asst. to dean engring. Ga. Inst. Tech., Atlanta, 1975-77; exec. dir. Southeastern Consortium for Minorities in Engring., Atlanta, 1977—, also organist, choirmaster various churches, 1951—. Campaign chair Community Concert Assn., 1968-70, pres., 1972-74; v.p. Hartsville Arts Council, 1968-72; com. to restructure bds. and agencies Presbyterian Ch. U.S., 1968-71; gen. exec. bd. Presbyn. Ch. U.S., 1971-72; pres. PTA, 1973. Alfred P. Sloan Found. grantee, 1977-81; NASA grantee, 1982. Mem. Nat. Assn. Pre-Coll. Dirs. (charter), Soc. Women Engrs., Am. Soc. Engring. Edn., Am. Guild Organists, NEA, S.C. Edn. Assn., Atlanta C. of C. Office: Southeastern Consortium for Minorities in Engineering Georgia Institute of Technology Atlanta GA 30332

CHESSHER, FAYE BATEY, bank exec.; b. Dewville, Tex., July 28, 1921; d. William Whitfield and Harriet Mary (Callison) Batey; B.S., Tex. Luth. Coll., 1962; M.A., S.W. Tex. State U., 1968; m. Daniel Simpson Chessher, Apr. 22, 1943. With Sta. KWED, Seguin, Tex., 1949-80, women's dir., 1950-62, 68-80, public affairs dir., 1976-80; community services dir. Nolti Nat. Bank, Seguin, 1980—; tchr. Joe F. Saegert Jr. High Sch., Seguin, 1962-68. Chmn., Sch. Vocat. Nursing, New Braunfels, Tex., 1968—; sec. Coliseum Bd., 1972-80; vocat. ednl. adv. bd. Seguin High Sch. Methodist. Club: Zonta. Home: 1436 Mockingbird Ln Seguin TX 78155

CHESTER, CHARLOTTE WANETTA, artist; b. Columbus, Ohio, Oct. 27, 1921; d. Charles William and Edna May (Casteel) Harper; student Capitol U., 1953-54, Oklahoma City U., 1958-59, Pa. Acad. Fine Arts, 1968-69, Phila. Coll. Art, 1971, workshops, 1968-69; B.F.A., Ft. Wright Coll., 1977; m. David Murel Chester, Sept. 27, 1939; children—Carol (Mrs. Verne Landt), Janet (Mrs. Ronald Cocklereece), David Murel. With U.S. Govt., 1955-71; propr. Char's Studio and Gallery, Ventnor, N.J., 1968-69; tchr. advanced painting Atlantic Community Coll., N.J., Fed. Art Assn. N.J., 1968-69, chmn. So. sect., 1971; co-owner gallery Art Is the Key, West Orange, N.J., 1972-73; paintings in permanent collections Nat. Air and Space Mus., Smithsonian Instn., Frankfort, Germany, Yearbook Ocean City, Kerr Mus. Recipient honorable mention A.C. Art Center, Atlantic City, 1965, 70, merit award Atlantic City C. of C., 1970, hon. mention Cultural Art Center, Ocean City, 1973. Mem. League South Jersey Artists (pres. 1968), Nat. Polit. Caucus, NOW. Unitarian-Universalist (program chmn. 1973). Address: Route 1 Box 53 Reardan WA 99029 also Route 1 Box 53 Reardon WA 99029

CHESTERFIELD, RHYDONIA RUTH EPPERSON, fin. co. exec.; b. Dallas, Apr. 23; d. Leonard Lee and Sally Evelyn (Stevenson) Griswold; B.S., Southwestern U., 1952; B.S., North Tex. U., 1954, M.Ed., 1956; Ph.D., Bernadean U., 1974; D.Litt. (hon.), Calif. Christian U., 1974; m. Chad Chesterfield, Apr. 21, 1979. Personal appearances, radio, evang. worker Griswold Trio, to 1958; public sch. tchr., Dallas, Los Angeles, 1954-74; pres. Griswold-Epperson Fin. Enterprise, Los Angeles, 1974—. Fellow Internat. Naturopathic Assn.; mem. Los Angeles Inst. Fine Arts, Hon. Assn. for Women in Edn., Kappa Delta Pi, Pi Lambda Theta. Clubs: Internat. Bus. and Profl. Women, Nat. Bus. and Profl. Women. Author: The Little Citizens (film series). Address: Griswold-Epperson Fin Enterprise Box 24648 Village Sta Los Angeles CA 90024

CHESTNUT, DELMA LOU, acct., rancher; b. Graham, Tex., July 8, 1940; d. Arnold B. and Nellie Faye (Mayes) McGlothlin; B.B.A., Midwestern U., 1971; postgrad. in acctg. Tex. Tech. U., 1979—; children—Ronnie Mac, Larry Everett, Delmarie. Dep. dist. clk. Young County, Tex., 1963-68; bookkeeper Karper & Glass, 1968-70; acct., gen. mgr. oil ops., ranching and investments LeSage Industries, Graham, 1970—; farmer, rancher. Mem. March of Dimes Com., 1968-69; adult leader 4-H Clubs in Young County, 1966—. Mem. Nat. Assn. Female Execs., West Tex. Oil and Gas Assn., Tex. Mid-Continent Oil and Gas Assn., Desk and Derrick (pres. 1970). Baptist. Home: Bunger Route Graham TX 76046 Office: Box 928 Jacksboro Hwy Graham TX 76046

CHEVERS, WILDA ANITA YARDE (MRS. KENNETH CHEVERS), probation officer; b. N.Y.C.,; d. Wilsey Ivan and Herbertlee (Perry) Yarde; B.A., Hunter Coll., 1947; M.S.W., Columbia, 1959; Ph.D., N.Y.U., 1981; m. Kenneth Chevers, May 14, 1950; 1 dau., Pamela Anita. Probation officer, 1947-55; supr. probation officer, 1955-65; br. chief Office Probation for Cts. N.Y.C., 1965-72, asst. dir. probation, 1972-77, dep. commr. dept. probation, 1978—; conf. faculty mem. Nat. Council Juvenile and Family Ct. Judges. Sec. Susan E. Wagner Adv. Bd., 1966-70. Sec., bd. dirs. Allen Community Day Care Center, 1971-75; bd. dirs. Allen Sr. Citizens Housing, Allen Christian Sch., Queensboro Soc. for Prevention Cruelty to Children. Mem. Nat. Council on Crime and Delinquency, Nat. Assn. Social Workers, Acad. Cert. Social Workers. Middle Atlantic States Conf. Correction, Alumni Assn. Columbia Sch. Social Work, NAACP, Am. Soc. Pub. Adminstrn. (dir.), Counseliers, Delta Sigma Theta. Club: Hansel and Gretel (pres. 1967-69) (Queens, N.Y.). Home: 105-62 132d St Richmond Hill New York NY 11419 Office: NYC Dept Probation 115 Leonard St New York NY 10013

CHEZEM, ESTHER MAE TIMBERLAKE, nurse; b. Riverside, Calif., Apr. 6, 1926; d. Warren Everett and Gladys Marie (Myers) Timberlake; R.N., Ind. U., 1947; student St. Mary of Woods Coll., 1979, 80; m. Ralph Chezem, Jr., Apr. 26, 1947; children—Mary Jeanne, David Michael, Susan Elizabeth. Office nurse, Richard S. Bloomer, M.D., Rockville, Ind., 1947-77; dir. nursing Vermillion Convalescent Center, Clinton, Ind., 1977—. Mem. Parke County Health Bd., 1966—, chmn., 1970-72, 78-80. Mem. Ind. U. Alumni Assn., Ind. U. Nursing Alumni Assn., VFW Aux. Democrat. Mem. Rockville Christian Ch. Clubs: Order Eastern Star, Ladies of Elks. Home: 402 McCune Ave Box 75 Rockville IN 47872 Office: 1705 S Main St Clinton IN 47842

CHI, LOTTA CHAI JUI, engring. research exec.; b. N.Y.C., Dec. 5, 1930; d. Chen Pien and Han Chih (Tang) Li; B.S., Heidelberg Coll., Tiffin, Ohio, 1953; M.S., Rutgers U., 1955; m. Michael Chi, June 15, 1957; children—Loretta Elizabeth, Maxwell Michael. Virologist, NIH, 1956-63; v.p. Chi Assos., engring. research, Arlington, Va., 1974—. Mem. N.Y. Acad. Scis., Am. Soc. Microbiologists, Nat. Assn. Women Bus. Owners, Sigma Xi. Democrat. Home: 2721 N 24th St Arlington VA 22207 Office: 956 N Monroe St Arlington VA 22201

CHIARELLO, DOROTHY ELIZABETH, nurse; b. Phila., Oct. 14, 1948; d. Raffella and Elizabeth Dorothy (Rambo) C.; diploma Roxborough Meml. Hosp. Sch. Nursing, Phila., 1969; B.S. with honors in Nursing, Fla. Internat. U., 1974, M.S. in Adult Edn., 1978; cert. in health occupations edn.; postgrad in edn. Staff nurse emergency dept. Roxborough Meml. Hosp., Phila., 1969, charge nurse ICU, 1969-71; staff nurse, relief charge nurse med. ICU, Jackson Meml. Hosp., Miami, Fla., 1971-73; staff and relief charge nurse emergency dept. Parkway Gen. Hosp., Miami, 1973-79, ednl. instr., 1979-80, ednl. coordinator/spl. care area, 1980—; home health nurse Am. Home Health, Miami, 1976-80; matron U.S. Marshall's Office, Miami, 1978—; mem. asso. faculty Nursing Unlimited, Miami Dade Community Coll.; mem. Dade County Disaster Team, 1980. Recipient service award Parkway Gen. Hosp., 1979; cert. of achievement Am. Heart Assn., 1979; registered nurse, Fla.; registered emergency med. technician, Fla.; cert. critical care nurse; registered advanced life support provider, advanced cardiac life support provider; emergency med. systems adminstr. certs.; jr. coll. tchrs. cert., Fla.; emergency nurse specialist cert.; CPR instr.-trainer. Mem. Nat. Assn. Female Execs., Am. Assn. Critical Care Nurses, Am. Heart Assn., Adult Edn. Assn. U.S.A., Emergency Dept. Nurses Assn., Emergency Med. Technicians Assn. (Meritorious service and pres. awards EMTA-Paramed. Soc. Fla.), chpt. pres. 1981, state treas. 1981), S. Fla. Inservice Educators, Emergency Med. Technicians and Paramedic Soc. (dir., sec. 1980, edn. chmn. 1980). Home: 262 S Biscayne River Dr Miami FL 33169 Office: 160 NW 170th St North Miami Beach FL 33169

CHIBUCOS, NIKI, coll. adminstr.; b. Chgo., Mar. 30, 1949; d. Harry Nick and Sophia Lue (Toscas) Petrakos; B.A. cum laude, Rosary Coll., 1971; M.S., George Williams Coll., 1975; m. Alexander Nicholas Chibucos, Aug. 25, 1979. Admissions counselor Rosary Coll., River Forest, Ill., 1972-74; grad. asst. George Williams Coll., Downers Grove, Ill., 1974-75, asst. dir. admissions, 1975-76, asso. dir. admissions, 1976-79, acting dir. admissions, 1979. Mem. Coll. Entrance Exam. Bd., Nat. Assn. Women Deans, Adminstrs. and Counselors, Nat., Ill. assns. coll. admissions counselors, Nat., Ill. assns. collegiate registrars and admissions officers, Am. Assn. U. Adminstrs., Women in Mgmt., Pi Gamma Mu, Sigma Delta Pi. Greek Orthodox. Home: 3913 S Saratoga Ave Apt 205G Downers Grove IL 60515 Office: George Williams College 555 31st St Downers Grove IL 60515

CHICAGO, JUDY, artist; b. Chgo., July 20, 1939; d. Arthur M. and May (Levenson) Cohan; B.A., UCLA, 1962, M.A., 1964. An organizer Feminist Studio Workshop, Los Angeles, 1970—; numerous one-artist exhbns., numerous group shows; The Dinner Party exhbn. at San Francisco Mus. Modern Art, 1979, U. Houston at Clear Lake City, 1980, Cyclorama Theater, Boston, 1980, Bklyn. Mus., 1980, Musée de l'Art Contemporain, Montreal, 1982, Sculptural Arts Mus., Atlanta, 1982; represented in permanent collections. Recipient Mademoiselle Woman of Yr. award, 1973. Mem. Phi Beta Kappa. Author: Through the Flower, 1975; The Dinner Party: A Symbol of Our Heritage, 1979; Embroidering Our Heritage: The Dinner Party Needlework, 1980. Address: PO Box 842 Benicia CA 94510

CHICAGO, JUDY RAELENE, assn. adminstr.; b. Safford, Ariz., Nov. 8, 1946; d. Ralph Newton and Fayrene (Goodner) Johnson; student Biola Coll., 1964-65; B.A. in Christian Edn., Southwestern Coll., 1970; m. Jan. 21, 1978 (div. June 1981). Editorial asst. Baptist Publications, Denver, 1970-73; expediter Phelps Dodge Corp., Douglas, Ariz., 1974-78; office mgr. So. Ariz. Internat. Livestock Assn., Inc., Tucson, 1978-80; supt.'s sec. Phelps Dodge Corp., 1981—. Mem. adv. bd. Ariz. Lung Assn.; leader 4-H, Douglas. Recipient Am. Legion Good Citizen award, 1964. Mem. Nat. Assn. Female Execs., Inc., So. Ariz. Internat. Livestock Assn. Sigma Lamba Delta. Repubican. Baptist. Clubs: Trunk & Tusk, Pima County Republican, Centre Ct., Westerners Internat., So. Ariz. Depression Glass. Home: PO Box 65 Playas NM 88009

CHICHINSKAS, PAMELA OLIVE, publishing exec.; b. Montreal, Que., Can., July 27, 1952; d. Michael and Doreen (O'Brien) C.; diploma in arts, Dawson Coll., 1971; B.A. in Lit., McGill U., 1974. Pub. asso. Take One mag., Montreal, 1974-76; asst. editor Canadian Business mag., Montreal, 1976-77; pub. dir. Eden Press Women's Publs., Montreal, 1978—. Recipient Lionel Shapiro award, McGill U., 1973. Office: 245 Victoria Ave Suite 12 Montreal PQ H3Z 2M6 Canada

CHICO, BEVERLY ANN BERGHAUS, historian, educator; b. Boston, May 14, 1931; d. Theodore Francis and Genevieve Valentine (Mahoney) Berghaus; B.A., Boston Coll., 1962; M.L.A., Johns Hopkins U., 1965, C.A.S.L.A., 1973; D.A., U. No. Colo., 1979; m. Raymundo J. Chico, July 25, 1959; children—Christian James, Gregory John, Raymund Matthew, Martha Vida M. Free lance journalist Radio Nacional de Espana UN, 1958-64; instr. social scis. dept. Community Coll. Balt., 1965-69, asst. prof. history, 1969-73, asso. prof., 1973-76; vis. prof. history Met. State Coll., Denver, 1976-79; vis. prof. history U. Colo., Denver, 1976-77; adj. faculty history U. No. Colo., Greeley, 1977—. Observer UN Commn. on Status of Women, Buenos Aires, 1960; ofcl. observer Nat. Conf. Women, Houston, 1977; bd. dirs. YWCA, Denver. Mem. Am. Hist. Soc., AAUP, Oral History Assn., Nat. Women's Studies Assn. Democrat. Roman Catholic. Author numerous articles on women's history. Home: 9600 E Grand Ct Englewood CO 80111 Office: Dept History U No Colo Greeley CO 80639

CHICOREL, MARIETTA, pub. co. exec.; b. Vienna, Austria; came to U.S., 1939, naturalized, 1945; B.A., Wayne State U., 1952; M.A., U. Mich., 1960. Chief editor Ulrich's Internat. Periodicals Directory, R. R. Bowker Co., N.Y.C., 1966-68; project mgr. Info. Scis., Inc., Macmillan Pub. Co., Inc., N.Y.C., 1968-69; pres. Chicorel Library Pub. Corp., N.Y.C., 1969-79; prof. library sci. Queens Coll., 1971-72; pres. Am. Library Pub. Co., Inc., N.Y.C., 1979—. Bd. govs. Booksellers League of N.Y., 1968-79. Mem. ALA, Am. Soc. Info. Scientists. Office: American Library Publishing Co Inc 275 Central Park W New York NY 10024

CHILCUTT, DORTHE MARGARET, educator, artist; b. Fond du Lac, Wis., Jan. 29, 1915; d. John William and Pearl Evelyn (Bennett) Trummer; B.S., U. Wis., 1940, M.S., 1952; postgrad. N.Y. U., 1975-78, Instituto Allende, Mexico, summer 1958, La Romita Sch. Art, Italy, 1978-82, Schohegan Sch. Painting and Sculpture, 1959; m. Booth Chilcutt, Feb. 14, 1942; children—Karen Chilcutt Hulett, Booth, Cindy Jo Chilcutt Underhill, Debra Ann Chilcutt-Flippo. Layout artist DeVry Corp., Chgo., 1941-42; tchr. art St. Louis public schs., 1951-53, Monroe County Schs., Key West, Fla., 1957-62, Okeechobee (Fla.) Jr. High Sch., 1963-82; one woman shows: Little Gallery, Key West, 1960, Martello Gallery, Key West, 1963, Ft. Pierce (Fla.) Art Gallery, 1970; exhibited in group shows: Jacksonville (Fla.) Art Mus., 1959, Tampa Art Mus., 1960, Norton Art Gallery, West Palm Beach, Fla., 1960, Ft. Pierce Art Gallery, 1977-82, St. Louis Art Mus., 1951, Wis. Salon of Art, Madison, 1947, Key West Art and Hist. Soc., 1957—, Key West Art Center, 1959; represented in permanent collections Ft. Pierce Art Gallery, Martello Galleries. Recipient Best of Show awards Fla. Fedn. Art, 1974, Ft. Pierce Art Gallery, 1977, Ybor City Ann. Fiesta Day, 1980, 1st pl. awards Highlands Art League 8th Ann., 1974, Jensen Beach Ann., Elliot Mus., 1974, Ft. Pierce Scholarship Show, 1972, 73, 74, 75, Four-County Art Show, Ft. Pierce, 1972, 73, 74, 75, 82, others. Mem. Okeechobee Art League (pres. 1975-80), Fla. Watercolor Soc. (sec. 1975-82), Nat. Art Edn. Assn., Fla. Art Edn. Assn., Miami Watercolor Soc., Key West Art and Hist. Soc. Democrat. Clubs: Ft. Pierce Art, Okeechobee Art. Contbr. articles to profl. jours. Home: 506 SW 15 St Okeechobee FL 33472

CHILD, JULIA MCWILLIAMS (MRS. PAUL CHILD), author, TV performer; b. Pasadena, Calif., Aug. 15, 1912; d. John and Julia Carolyn (Weston) McWilliams; B.A., Smith Coll., 1934; hon. degree Boston U., 1978; m. Paul Child, Sept. 1, 1945. With advt. dept. W. & J. Sloane, N.Y.C., 1939-40; with OSS, Washington, Ceylon and China, 1941-45; condr. TV program The French Chef, WGBH-TV, Boston, 1962—, Julia Child & Co., 1978, Julia Child & More Co., 1980. Recipient Peabody award, 1964, Emmy award, 1966; decorated Ordre de Merite Agricole, Ordre National de Merite (France). Author: (with Simone Beck and Louisette Bertholle) Mastering the Art of French Cooking, 1961; The French Chef Cookbook, 1968; (with Simone Beck) Mastering the Art of French Cooking, Vol. II, 1970; From Julia Child's Kitchen, 1975; Julia Child & Company, 1978; Julia Child & More Company, 1979; monthly columnist From Julia Child's Kitchen, McCall's Mag., 1975-82; food editor Parade, 1982—. Weekly TV appearances ABC Good Morning Am., 1980—. Office: WGBH 125 Western Ave Boston MA 02134

CHILD, LOUISE AVERY, public relations exec.; b. N.Y.C.; d. William Bradford and Gertrude (Sykes) C.; B.A., Wellesley Coll., 1924. Mem. editorial staff Time, 1924; asst. editor Delineator and Fashions Art, 1925-35; free-lance publicity, newspaper article writing, 1934-35; public relations dir. Youth Consulation Service, N.Y.C., 1936-41; public relations dir. Big Bros., Inc., 1941-57, Berkshire Farm for Boys, 1958-59, United Bd. Christian Higher Edn. in Asia, 1959-67; now cons. Mem. Steering com. Assn. Fund Raising Dirs. N.Y.C., 1946-56, v.p., 1955; public relations com. Episcopal Service for Youth, 1947-56; vice chmn. Wellesley-Yenching Com., 1951-68. Mem. Citizens Union, Shakespeare

Soc., Wellesley Coll. Alumnae Assn., Religious Public Relations Council (v.p. N.Y. chpt. 1965-66). Home: 1 University Pl New York NY 10003

CHILD, MARGARET SMILLIE, govt. ofcl.; b. Yonkers, N.Y., July 14, 1929; d. Harold Baxter and Marie (Maloney) Smillie; B.A., Mount Holyoke Coll., 1951; M.A., Cornell U., 1952; Ph.D., U. Md., 1972; m. James Robert Child, Dec. 30, 1955; children—Peter Truesdale, Elizabeth Baxter, Anne Margaret. Intelligence officer on Indonesia, CIA, Washington, 1952-61; editor, Monthly Indonesian Press Survey, Joint Publs. Research Service, Dept. Commerce, Washington, 1961-64; teaching asst. U. Md., College Park, 1964-68, instr. history, 1971-74; asst. prof. Am. U., Washington, 1973-75; asst. dir. div. research programs Nat. Endowment for the Humanities, Washington, 1974-82; asst. dir., chief research services Smithsonian Instn. Libraries, Washington, 1982—. Office: Smithsonian Instn Libraries Washington DC

CHILDERS, JEAN CAROLE, social worker; b. St. Louis, Feb. 5, 1932; d. Otto C. and Lillian B. (Puls) Scheffels; B.S., Washington U., St. Louis, 1968, M.S.W., 1970; m. Gerald V. Childers, Nov. 5, 1955. From caseworker to staff tng. specialist Mo. Div. Family Services, 1955-73; social worker Parkway Sch. Dist., Chesterfield, Mo., 1973—; part-time asst. prof. St. Louis U. Sch. Social Work, 1972-78. Mem. Nat. Assn. Social Workers, Midwest Sch. Social Workers Assn., Alumni Assn. George Warren Brown Sch. Social Work. Congregationalist. Home: 1905 Pine Run Dr Chesterfield MO 63017 Office: 455 N Woods Mill Rd Chesterfield MO 63017

CHILDERS, NEIDA GENEIEVE, nurse; b. Chgo., Dec. 18, 1940; d. Louis Phillip and Phyllis Grace (Tutt) Bebo; student St. Bernard Coll., 1972-73; A.S., John C. Calhoun Jr. Coll., 1975; m. Bobby Childers, Feb. 28, 1958; children—Susan Ann, Bobby Ray, Betty Lynn. With Ill. Bell Telephone, Chgo., 1956-57, Western Electric, Chgo., 1965-66; patient care asst. Huntsville (Ala.) Hosp., 1974-75; staff nurse Pineview (Ala.) Hosp., 1975-78; dir. nursing Flint Nursing Home, Flint City, Ala., 1978-80; supr. Med. Park Convalescent Center, Decatur, Ala., 1980—. Mem. Am. Nurses Assn., Ala. Nurses Assn., Am. Heart Assn. Democrat. Baptist. Home: Route 5 PO Box 17F Hartselle AL 35640 Office: 1306 14 Ave SE Decatur AL 35601

CHILDRES, MARY ROSE, univ. bus. adminstr.; b. Livingston, Ala., Apr. 13, 1936; d. Simon and Mary Magdalene (Sanders) Childress; A.S. in Secretarial Sci., U. Cin., 1973, B.S. in Adminstrv. Mgmt., 1976; m. Robert W. Greene. Secretarial positions Hamilton County (Ohio) Welfare Dept., 1954-S9, VA Hosp., Cin., 1959-63, Mut. Benefit Life Ins. Co., Cin., 1965-66, Ky. State U., Frankfort, 1966-68; nutrition program asst. W.Va. U., Charleston, 1969-70; with U. Cin., 1970—, bus. adminstr., office of vice provost for continuing edn. and met. services 1978—; fin. chmn. Nat. Univ. Continuing Edn. Conf., Cin., 1982. Chmn. Cornelius Van Jordan Scholarship Fund, U. Cin. Mem. Nat. Secs. Assn. (charter mem., co-founder Frankfort chpt.), AAUW, United Black Assn. of Faculty, Adminstrs. and Staff U. Cin. (treas.), Mid-Level Mgrs. Assn. U. Cin., Adminstrv. Women's Assn. U. Cin., Nat. Assn. Female Execs., Delta Tau Kappa. Mem. Ch. of God. Author: Handbook of Office Procedures, 1973, 75. Home: 838 Crowden Dr Cincinnati OH 45224 Office: 8 McMicken Hall Clifton U Cin Cincinnati OH 45221

CHILDRESS, PHYLLIS ANN, constrn. co. exec.; b. Fort Wayne, Ind., Feb. 28, 1937; d. Paschal J. and Pietrina M. (Ceccanese) Pallone; B.S. in Commerce, Internat. Coll., 1955; postgrad. Pima Community Coll., 1978-80; m. Kelly W. Childress, Aug. 24, 1973; children—Patricia, William, Jeffrey. Sec. to v.p. trust dept. Lincoln Nat. Bank, Ft. Wayne, Ind., 1955-57; sec. to pres. adminstrn. dept. Internat. Coll., Ft. Wayne, 1957-60; dir., sec. Lightning Homes, Inc., Homebuilders and Developers, Ft. Wayne, 1960-63; sec. to v.p., fin. dept., office mgr. fleet maintenance dept. N.Am. Van Lines, Inc., Ft. Wayne, 1963-71; asst. mktg. dir. ITT Electro-Optical Products, Ft. Wayne, 1972-76; asst. v.p. Empire West Builders, Inc., Tucson, 1977-80; staff constrn. mgmt. Akins Co., Tucson, 1981-82, Landeco, Inc., Tucson, 1982—. Recipient Appreciation Cert. Nat. Assn. Women Constrn., 1978; named Sec. of yr. Tawasi chpt. Nat. Secs. Assn., 1967, recipient plaque for outstanding service, 1977. Mem. Bus. and Profl. Women, Nat. Assn. Women Constrn. (chpt. pres.). Democrat. Baptist. Club: Internat. Toastmistresses. Contbr. articles to various publs. Home: 2833 N Laurel Ave Tucson AZ 85712 Office: Landeco Inc 2302 E Speedway Suite 106 Tucson AZ 85719

CHILDS, ALTA VICTORIA, auto club ofcl.; b. Gunnison, Utah, Nov. 26, 1922; d. Lovell Lorenzo and Susan Almira (Swain) C.; student Latter Day Saints Bus. Coll. Bookkeeper, 9th Service Command, 1943-44, Lovinger Disinfectant Co., 1944-52; asst. corp. sec., bookkeeper Automobile Club of Utah, Salt Lake City, 1952—. Del., Republican State Conv., 1978, 79. Mem. Exec. Women Internat., Nat. Assn. Exec. Secs., Mormon Tabernacle Choir. Mormon. Home: 861 Downington Ave Salt Lake City UT 84105 Office: 560 E 5th St S Salt Lake City UT 84102

CHILDS, MARJORIE M., lawyer; b. N.Y.C., July 13, 1918; d. Charles William and Eva May (Tarrant) C.; student Hunter Coll., 1942-46; B.A., U. Calif., Berkeley, 1948; postgrad. Hastings Coll. Law, 1948-49; J.D., U. San Francisco, 1956; LL.D., Iowa Wesleyan Coll., 1973. Econ. research analyst Fgn. Service, U.S. Dept. State, Paris, 1949-50, Frankfurt, Germany, 1950-51; legal asst. Dept. Navy, San Francisco, 1956-60; admitted to Calif., bar, 1957, U.S. Supreme Ct. bar, 1969; practiced in San Francisco, 1962-64, 79—; asst. county counsel Humboldt County (Calif.), Eureka, 1960-62; mem. firm Berry, Childs & Berry, San Francisco, 1962-64; commr., referee, judge Juvenile Ct. San Francisco, 1964-79. Bd. dirs. United Cerebral Palsy Assn. San Francisco, United Cerebral Palsy Assn. Calif.; bd. govs. U. San Francisco, 1978-81. Recipient James Harlan award Iowa Wesleyan Coll., 1969. Fellow Am. Bar Found.; mem. Calif. State Bar (com. juvenile justice 1969-76, chmn. 1970-72, adviser 1972-76), Internat. (council 1975-76, del. 1978, 82), Am. (del. 1975-77, sec. family law sect. 1980-82), Fed. (pres. 1976-77) bar assns., Nat. Assn. Women Lawyers (pres. 1974-75), Queen's Bench (pres. 1967-68), AAUW (pres. br. 1970-72), Bar Assn. San Francisco. Club: Met. Contbr. articles to profl. jours. Home: 64 Turquoise Way San Francisco CA 94131 also PO Box 31430 San Francisco CA 94131 Office: 301 Junipero Serra Blvd Suite 260 San Francisco CA 94127

CHILDS, PEGGY, state legislator; b. Tallulah Falls, Ga., Nov. 17, 1937; d. Samuel Trebble and Bertha Harvey Maxwell; B.A., U. Ga., 1958, M.Ed., 1961; m. Mobley Free Childs, 1957; children—Mobley F., Jr., Christy El Lena. Mem. Democratic Reorgn. Com., 1974; mem. Ga. Ho. of Reps., 1975—, mem. judiciary, state insts. and properties and retirement coms., mem. spl. com. on crime and drugs, asst. majority whip, sec. DeKalb del.; chmn. bd. Tallulah Products, Inc., 1968-70. Chmn., Trinity Child Devel. Center, 1974-75; sponsored Walldena Walk Across Tallulah Gorge, 1970. Mem. Ga. Congress Parents and Tchrs., Ga. C. of C. (goal com. 1975). Methodist (social concerns com.). Office: Ga Ho Reps State Capitol Atlanta GA 30334 *

CHILDS, SHIRLE MOONE, early childhood specialist; b. N.Y.C., Aug. 2, 1936; d. Harold McDaniel and Bessie Mary (Batts) Moone; student Queens Coll., 1953-55; B.S., U. Hartford, 1968, M.S., 1970; Ph.D. (Rockefeller fellow, Kettering Found. fellow), U. Conn., 1978; m. William Henri Childs, Sept. 5, 1971; children—Duane Kelby Milner, David Kent Milner. Claims rep. Travelers Ins. Co., Hartford, Conn., 1960-66; tchr. Hartford Public Schs., 1968-71, acting prin., 1973-76, coordinator early childhood edn., 1978—; adj. prof., lectr. Eastern Conn. State Coll., Willimantic, 1974-76; bd. dirs. lang. readiness program U. Hartford Child Care Center; bd. dirs. Women's League Day Care Center. Mem. Am. Assn. Sch. Adminstrs., Assn. Supervision and Curriculum Devel., Council Exceptional Children, Council Basic Edn., Conn. Assn. Suprs. and Instrs. Spl. Edn., Hartford Women's Network, Delta Sigma Theta (nat. sec.), Pi Lambda Theta, Phi Delta Kappa. Democrat. Methodist. Club: Eastern Star (officer). Research on affective and behavioral correlates of reading in urban primary classrooms. Home: 26 Regency Dr Windsor CT 06095 Office: 249 High St Hartford CT 06103

CHILMAN, CATHERINE EARLES STREET, educator; b. Cleve., Sept. 20, 1914; d. Elwood Vickers and Augusta (Jewitt) Street; A.B., Oberlin Coll., 1935; M.A., U. Chgo., 1938; Ph.D., U. Syracuse, 1958; m. C. William Chilman, Sept. 27, 1936 (dec. 1977); children—Margaret Chilman Carpenter, Jeanne Chilman Klovdahl, Catherine Chilman Brown. Caseworker, United Charities Chgo., 1937-39, Family Services, Roanoke, Va., 1939-40; psychiat. cons., ARC, Syracuse, N.Y., 1943-44; tchr. dept. child devel., family relations, Syracuse U., 1947-49, instr., 1949-57, asst. prof., 1957-61; sr. social worker, N.Y. State Mental Health Research Unit, Syracuse, 1955-57; parent edn. specialist, Children's Bureau, U.S. Dept. HEW, Washington, 1961-64; research adminstr. U.S. Welfare Adminstrn., 1964-69; dean faculty Hood Coll., Frederick, Md., 1969-71; curriculum dir. Internat. Population Planning and Social Work Edn. Project, U. Mich., Ann Arbor, 1971-72; prof. Sch. Social Welfare, U. Wis., Milw., 1972—; pres. Nat. Groves Conf. on the Family, 1975-78; speaker, cons. on research, family life, public policy to univs., fed. govt. and profl. orgns. U.S. Office Edn. grantee, 1960-62; Wis. State grantee, 1973-75; Nat. Inst. Child Devel. grantee, 1976-77; recipient Hon. Alumni award Sch. Social Services Adminstrn., U. Chgo., 1978. Fellow Am. Psychol. Assn.; mem. Nat. Council on Family Relations (exec. com.), Council on Social Work Edn. (adv. bd.), Council Social Work Edn., Internat. Conf. on Social Welfare (exec. com. on U.S. com.). Assoc. editor Journal of Marriage and the Family, 1963-69. Author: Your Child: Six to Twelve; Moving Into Adolescence; Growing Up Poor; (with others) Mental Health Crises and the Nation's Children; Adolescent Sexuality in a Changing American Society. Contbr. chpts. to books, articles to profl. jours. Home: 4424 N Frederick Milwaukee WI 53211

CHILTON, ALICE PLEASANCE HUNTER (MRS. ST. JOHN POINDEXTER CHILTON), state ofcl., vocat. counselor; b. Boyce, La., Apr. 16, 1911; d. Albert Eugene and Maggie (Texada) Hunter; B.A., La. Coll., 1931; M.S., La. State U., 1934, Ph.D., 1982, Guidance Counselor certificate, 1954; m. St. John Poindexter Chilton, Mar. 2, 1935. Tchr. secondary sch., Glenmora, La., 1931-35; with La. Div. Employment Security and USES, Baton Rouge, 1937-74, employment interviewer and supr., 1937-43, personnel officer, 1943-46, ops. analyst, 1946-55, supr. counseling and tech. services, 1955-74. Vice pres., dir. LaPlace Enterprises, Inc., Belle Pointe Enterprises, Inc. Mem. curriculum study com. East Baton Rouge, Parish Sch. Bd., 1968—; rec. sec. Quota Internat., 1961-62, 2d v.p., 1963-64. Bd. dirs. YWCO. Recipient certificate of merit La. Acad. Sci., 1960; certificate-35 years meritorious service La. Div. Employment Security, 1972. Mem. Am. Personnel and Guidance Assn., Nat. Vocat. Guidance Assn., Am. Sch. Counselor Assn., Assn. for Counselor Edn. and Supervision, Nat. Employment Counselors Assn., La. Personnel and Guidance Assn., Internat. Assn. Personnel in Employment Security, Nat. Trust Historic Preservation, La. Geneal. and Hist. Soc. (pres. 1957), La. Landmarks Soc., Found. for Hist. La., Kent Plantation House, Inc. (sec.). Clubs: Campus La. State U. (Faculty Wives). Methodist. Address: Route 2 Box 431 Boyce LA 71409

CHIN, JANET S., computer scientist; b. Hong Kong, July 27, 1949 (parents Am. Citizens); d. Arthur Q. M. and Jenny N. C. (Loo) C.; B.S. in Math. with honors, U. Ill., 1970; M.S. in Computer Sci., U. Ill., Urbana, 1972. Computer scientist research in secured operating systems group Lawrence Livermore (Calif.) Nat. Lab., 1972-75; applications programmer laser research program, 1975-77, systems programmer computer graphics group, 1977-79; project leader spl. projects unit Tymshare, Inc., Cupertino, Calif., 1979, mgr. computer graphics unit, 1979-82, mgr. system products sect., 1982—; internat. rep., vice chmn. tech. com. on computer graphics Am. Nat. Standards Insts. Judge, AAU. Mem. Assn. Computing Machinery, Spl. Interest Group in Graphics, Spl. Interest Group in Operating Systems, Nat. Computer Graphics Assn., World Computer Graphic Assn., Sigma Xi. Office: 20705 Valley Green Dr Cupertino CA 95014

CHIN, JENNIFER YOUNG, public health educator; b. Honolulu, June 22, 1946; d. Michael W.T. and Sylvia (Ching) Young; B.A., San Francisco State Coll., 1969; M.P.H., U. Calif., Berkeley, 1971; m. Benny Chin, Nov. 16, 1975; children— Kenneth Michael, Lauren Marie, Catherine Rose. Edn. asst. Am. Cancer Soc., San Francisco, 1969-70; intern Lutheran Med. Center, Bklyn., 1971; community health educator Md. Dept. Health and Mental Hygiene, Balt., 1971-74; community health educator Northeast Med. Services, San Francisco, 1975; public health educator Child Health and Disability Prevention, San Francisco Public Health Dept., 1975—. USPHS grantee, 1970-71. Mem. Soc. No. Calif. Public Health Edn. (treas. 1976, 77), Am. Public Health Assn. Home: 1057 Holly St Alameda CA 94501 Office: CHDP 101 Grove St Room 402 San Francisco CA 94102

CHIN, SUE S. (SUCHIN), artist, photographer, community affairs activist; b. San Francisco; d. William W. and Soo-Up (Swebe) Chin; grad. Calif. Coll. Art, Mpls. Art Inst., (scholar) Schaeffer Design Center; student Yasuo Kuniyoshi, Louis Hamon, Rico LeBrun. Photojournalist, All Together Now show, 1973, East-West News, Third World Newscasting, 1975-78, KNBC Sunday Show, Los Angeles, 1975, 76, Live on 4, 1981, Bay Area Scene, 1981; graphics printer, exhbns. include Kaiser Center, Zellerbach Plaza, Chinese Culture Center Galleries, Chinese Culture Center Galleries, Capricorn Asunder Art Commn. Gallery (all San Francisco), Los Angeles County Mus. Art, Peace Plaza Japan Center, Calif. Mus. Sci. and Industry, Lucien Labaudt Gallery, Sacramento State Fair, AFL-CIO Labor Studies Center, Washington, Asian Women Artists (1st prize for conceptual painting, 1st prize photography), 1978; represented in permanent collections Los Angeles County Fedn. Labor, Calif. Mus. Sci. and Industry, AFL-CIO Labor Studies Center, Australian Trades Council, Hazeland and Co., also pvt. collections. Del. nat., state convs. Nat. Women's Polit. Caucus, 1977-80, San Francisco chpt. affirmative action chairperson, 1978-81, nat. conv. del., 1978-81, Calif. del., 1976-81 Recipient Honorarium AFL-CIO Labor Studies Center, Washington, 1975-76; Bicentennial award Los Angeles County Mus. Art, 1976, 77, 78. Mem. Asian Women Artists (founding v.p., award 1978-79, 1st award in photography of Orient 1978-79), Calif. Chinese Artists (sec.-treas. 1978-81), Japanese Am. Art Council (chairperson 1978-81, dir.), San Francisco Women Artists, San Francisco Graphics Guild, Pacific/Asian Women Coalition Bay Area, Chinatown Council Performing and Visual Arts, Coyote. Address: PO Box 1415 San Francisco CA 94101

CHINITZ, JODY ANNE KOLB, computer systems analyst; b. Bay City, Mich., July 8, 1953; d. Adam H. and Evelyn I. (Sylvester) Kolb; student Saginaw Valley State Coll., 1972, Bklyn. Coll., 1973-76; B.A. in Russian Lang. and Lit. summa cum laude, Hunter Coll., 1980; m. William A. Chinitz, Feb. 11, 1979. With personnel dept. N.Y. Life Ins. Co., N.Y.C., 1972-77, computer programmer, 1977-80; computer systems cons. Soroban Data Systems, Inc., N.Y.C., 1980-82; sr. analyst Midatlantic Nat. Bank, West Orange, N.J., 1982. Mem. Am. Assn. Advancement of Slavic Studies, Montclair Camera Guild. Home: 31 Norwood Ave Upper Montclair NJ 07043 Office: 95 Old Short Hills Rd West Orange NJ 07052

CHINOY, HELEN KRICH, theatre historian, educator; b. Newark, Sept. 25, 1922; d. Benjamin and Anne (Kalen) Krich; B.A. with honors, N.Y.U., 1943, M.A., 1945; cert. U. Birmingham, Shakespeare Inst., 1947; Ph.D., Columbia U., 1963; m. Ely Chinoy, June 6, 1948 (dec.); children—Michael, Claire. Instr. dept. English, N.Y.U., N.Y.C., 1944-45, Queens Coll., N.Y.C., 1945, Newark (N.J.) Coll. of Rutgers U., 1946-48; instr. English, Smith Coll., Northampton, Mass., part-time, 1953-55, lectr. dept. theatre, 1956-60, faculty, 1965—, prof. theatre history, criticism, 1975—, chmn., 1968-71, vis. lectr. dept. English, U. Leicester (Eng.), 1963-64; lectr. colls. and cultural instns. Fellow AAUW, Nat. Endowment for Humanities, Am. Theatre Assn. (asso. editor jour.); mem. Am. Soc. Theatre Research (chmn. research com.). Author: (with T. Cole) Actors on Acting, 1949, 3d edit., 1980; Directors on Directing, 1953, 2d edit., 1973; Reunion: A Self-Portrait of the Group Theatre, 1977; (with L. W. Jenkins) Women in American Theatre, 1981; also chpts. in books, articles and program for ednl. TV. Home: 230 Crescent St Northampton MA 01060 Office: Center for Performing Arts Smith Coll Northampton MA 01060

CHIPMAN, DEBORAH GONDEK, journalist; b. Phoenix, Apr. 6, 1953; d. Joseph H. and Dorothy E. (Bradac) G.; B.A. cum laude in Journalism, Duquesne U., 1975; m. John A. Chipman, Oct. 6, 1979. Dir., performer The Young Tamburitzans ensemble, Phoenix, 1968-71; reporter Phoenix Gazette, 1970-71; newswriter, broadcaster Sta. WDUQ, Pitts., 1973-74; ensemble performer Duquesne U. Tamburitzans, nat. folk arts ensemble, Pitts., 1971-75, European tours, 1971-72; communications/planning Chipman Design, Chgo., 1979—; writer-editor Fairburn Assos., Inc., Phoenix, 1977-79. Recipient Piano Solo Excellence award Nat. Fedn. Musicians, 1971; Quill and Scroll nat. editorial writing award, 1971. Mem. Women in Communications (treas. Phoenix chpt. 1976-77), Internat. Assn. Bus. Communicators (Phoenix award of merit 1979, dist. award of excellence for design 1981), Am. Planning Assn., Photog. Soc. Am., Sigma Delta Chi (sec. Duquesne chpt. 1974), Chgo. Art Inst., Nat. Trust Historic Preservation, Kappa Tau Alpha, Duquesne U. Tamburitzans Alumni Assn. Editor Horizons, 1976-77. Home: 400 S Home Ave Park Ridge IL 60068 Office: 5725 E River Rd Chicago IL 60631

CHISHOLM, BARBARA ANN, child welfare cons.; b. Boston, May 30, 1924; d. Arthur Gerald and Elinor Decatur (McManus) C.; B.A. in Sociology, Regis Coll., Weston, Mass., 1946; M.S.W., Simmons Coll., 1948. From caseworker to supr. N.H. Children's Aid Soc., 1948-54; dept. supr. Children's Aid Soc. Met. Toronto (Ont., Can.), 1954-60; sr. social worker East York/Leaside Mental Health Clinic, Toronto, 1960-61; exec. dir. Victoria Day Care Services, Toronto, 1961-70; child welfare cons., Toronto, 1971—; lectr. U. Toronto Sch. Social Work, 1971—, McMaster U., 1971-74, also various community colls.; cons. to govt. and pvt. agys., 1978—. Bd. dirs. numerous agys. Recipient 1st Children's Service award Ont. Assn. Early Childhood Edn., 1979. Mem. Acad. Cert. Social Workers, Nat. Assn. Social Workers, Can. Assn. Social Workers, Can. Assn. for Young Children, Internat. Assn. for Prevention Child Abuse and Neglect, Internat. Soc. on Family Law, Internat. Assn. Youth Magistrates, Def. for Children, Can. Centre Films for Children. Co-author: Admittance Restricted, 1979; contbr. articles on children's rights and child abuse to profl. jours. Home: 221 Russell Hill Rd Apt 402 Toronto ON M4V 2T3 Canada Office: 1867 Yonge St Suite 600 Toronto ON M4S 1Y5 Canada

CHISHOLM, JUNE FAYE, clin. psychologist; b. N.Y.C., Apr. 29, 1949; d. Wallace P. and Luretta (Brawley) Chisholm; B.A., Syracuse U., 1971; M.S., U. Mass., Ph.D., 1978. Asst. prof. psychology Fordham U., 1978—; practice clin. psychology, N.Y.C., 1980—; sr. psychologist Harlem Hosp., 1982—; cons. N.Y.C. Bd. Edn. Mem. Am. Psychol. Assn., N.Y. State Psychol. Assn., N.Y. Soc. Clin. Psychologists, Chamber Music Assos. Home: 792 Columbus Ave New York NY 10025 Office: 113 W 60th St New York NY 10025

CHISHOLM, SHIRLEY ANITA ST. HILL, educator, congresswoman; b. Bklyn., Nov. 30, 1924; d. Charles Christopher and Ruby (Seale) St. Hill; B.A. cum laude, Bklyn. Coll.; M.A., Columbia U.; hon. doctorates Talladega Coll., N.C. Coll., Wilmington Coll., Hampton Inst., LaSalle Coll., William Patterson Coll., Capitol U., U. Maine, Coppin State Coll., Pratt Inst., Kenyon Coll., Aquinas Coll., Reed Coll., U. Cin., Smith Coll.; m. Conrad Chisholm, Oct. 8, 1949 (div. Feb. 1977); m. 2d, Arthur Hardwick, Jr., Nov. 26, 1977. Former nursery sch. tchr., and dir. nursery sch.; ednl. cons. Div. Day Care, Bur. Child Welfare; mem. N.Y. State Assembly, 1964-68; mem. 91st-97th Congresses from 12th Dist. N.Y., mem. Rules com., Edn. and Labor com., 1971-77, sec. Democratic Caucus, mem. Congressional Black Caucus. Candidate primary elections Democratic nominee Pres. U.S., 1972; mem. Nat. Commn. UNESCO; prof. Mt. Holyoke Coll., S. Hadley, Mass., 1982—. Named Alumna of Year, Bklyn. Coll. Alumni Bull., 1957; recipient award for outstanding work in field of child welfare Women's Council of Bklyn., 1957; key woman of year award, 1963; woman of achievement award Key Women, Inc., 1965; Humanitarian award of family counselling Youth in Action, 1969; Achievement award women's div. Albert Einstein Coll. Medicine, 1969; Woman of Year, Soc. Afro Am. Postal Workers, 1969; Deborah Gannett award Nat. Media Women, 1969; Golden Doughnut award Salvation Army, 1969; Dr. Martin Luther King award Bottle and Cork Sales Club, 1970; hon. life mem. Women's Com. of 1000, 1969; hon. citizen City of Kansas, 1970. Mem. Nat. Assn. Coll. Women, Bklyn. Coll. Alumni, League Women Voters. Methodist. Author: Unbought & Unbossed, 1970; The Good Fight, 1973. Office: Mt Holyoke Coll South Hadley MA 01075 *

CHISM, SYLVIA CHARLOTTE, nursing adminstr.; b. Boston; d. Francis and Amy Hilda (Ramsey) Skidmore; diploma Margaret Pillsbury Hosp. Sch. Nursing, Concord, N.H., 1943; B.A. in Psychology, San Diego State Coll., 1952; M.S. in Nursing, U. Calif. at Berkeley, 1958, postgrad. in hosp. and nursing adminstrn., 1962—; Ph.D. in Nursing and Health Services Adminstrn., Columbia Pacific U., 1981; m. Henry George Chism, Aug. 31, 1946; children—Henry George, Scott Ellis. Asst. dir. nursing Palomar Meml. Hosp., Escondido, Calif., 1958-60; dir. nursing edn. Children's Hosp., San Diego, 1960-62; adminstr. Pacific Hosp., Oakland, Calif., 1954-55; dir. nursing Ross Gen. Hosp., 1955-57, Balt. City Hosp., 1968-71; asst. adminstr., dir. nursing Washoe Med. Center, Reno, Nev., 1971-73; v.p. nursing Bauer Hosp., St. Mary Med. Center, Long Beach, Calif., 1973-75; asst. adminstr., dir. nursing St. Joseph Med. Center, Burbank, Calif., 1976-77; asst. adminstr., dir. nursing Providence Hosp., Oakland, Calif., 1977-78; faculty mentor advanced degree student Columbia Pacific U. mem. advisory coms. U. Md., U. Nev. Served to lt. U.S. Navy Nurse Corps, 1943-47. Fed. Pub. Health Title II grantee, 1957-58, 62-63. Mem. Am. Nurses Assn., Nat. League for Nursing, AAUW (Alameda br.) Republican. Episcopalian. Leader many workshops and seminars in nursing adminstrn. Office: 1105 Park Ave Apt A Alameda CA 94501

CHISUM, GLORIA TWINE, research psychologist; b. Muskogee, Okla., May 17, 1930; d. Chauncey Depew and Nadine Marian (Davis) Twine; B.S., Howard U., 1951; M.S., U. Pa., 1953, Ph.D., 1960; D.Sc. (hon.), Med. Coll. Pa., 1981, Ursinus Coll., 1981; m. Melvin Jackson Chisum, Sept. 10, 1955. Asst. instr. Howard U., 1953; asst. U. Pa., 1953-55, asst. instr., 1955-60, lectr., 1960-68; research psychologist U.S. Naval Air Devel. Center, Warminster, Pa., 1960—, head environ.

physiology research team, 1980; dir. Fischer & Porter Co.; trustee Phila. Savs. Fund Soc.; cons. Dept. Transp., 1972-73, NASA, 1978. Trustees U. Pa.; bd. dirs. World Affairs Council Phila., 1974—, Phila. Orch., 1979—; bd. govs. Arthritis Found., 1971—, 2d v.p., 1976-79; bd. overseers U. Pa. Social Work, chair, 1979—; bd. dirs. Free Library of Phila., 1978—; bd. overseers Faculty Arts and Scis. U. Pa. Mem. Aerospace Med. Assn. (Raymond F. Longacre award 1979), Am. Psychol. Assn., Optical Soc. Am., Eastern Psychol. Assn., AAAS, SAFE, Sigma Xi, Psi Chi, Alpha Kappa Alpha. Contbr. articles to profl. jours. Patentee in field. Home: 4120 Apalogen Rd Philadelphia PA 19144 Office: Code 6003 Naval Air Development Center Warminster PA 18974

CHITTENDEN, CORA LEA, clin. social worker; b. Denver, July 11, 1942; d. Herbert F. and Grace (Thornton) Lovisone; B.A., Ottawa U., 1965; M.S.W., U. Kans., 1968. Clin social worker Marillac Home and Sch. for Children, Kansas City, Mo., 1968-71; clin. dir. day treatment program Hearnes Youth Center, Mo. Div. Mental Health, Fulton, Mo., 1971-75; clin. social worker Colorado Springs (Colo.) Public Schs., 1975-79; pvt. practice social work, specializing in child, adult, family and marital psychotherapy, Colorado Springs, Colo., 1979—; faculty mem. U. Mo. Grad. Sch. Social Work, 1974-75; field instr. U. Denver Grad. Sch. Social Work, 1975-76. Lic. social worker II, State of Colo. Mem. Colo. Soc. Clin. Social Work (state bd. 1977-81, sec. Colorado Springs chpt-1977-81, pres. 1981), Acad. Cert. Social Workers, Nat. Assn. Social Workers. Office: 2411 N Tejon St Colorado Springs CO 80907

CHITTICK, ELIZABETH LANCASTER, assn. exec., women's rights activist; b. Bangor, Pa., Nov. 11, 1918; d. Benjamin H. and Flora Mae (Mann) Lancaster; student Columbia U., 1944-45, N.Y. Inst. Fin., 1950-51, Hunter Coll., 1952-56, Upper Iowa U., 1976—. Adminstrv. asst. to comdg. officer and chief clk. U.S. Naval Air Stas., Seattle, 1941-42, Banana River, Fla., 1942-45; v.p., treas. W. A. Chittick & Co., Manila, 1945-52; real estate sales, La Jolla, Calif., 1949; broker Bache and Co., N.Y.C., 1950-62, Shearson and Hamill, N.Y.C., 1961-62; cons. investments, N.Y.C., 1965; revenue officer IRS, N.Y.C., 1965-72; pres. Nat. Woman's Party, Washington, 1971—, Woman's Party Corp., Washington, 1978—, Sewall-Belmont Home Restoration Fund, 1976—; bd. dirs. Nat. Council Women U.S.; 1st v.p. Pan Am. liaison com. OAS, Washington; mem. adv. com. U.S. Center for Internat. Women's Yr., Meridian House, Washington, 1973-76; mem. Internat. Women's Yr. Continuing Com., 1978—, del. conf., Mexico City, 1975; active Women's Campaign Fund Washington, 1975—, Coalition for Women in Internat. Devel., 1978—; mem. Women's History Center Task Force, Am. Revolution Bicentennial Adminstrn., 1973-76; lectr., TV commentator, cons. ERA. Chmn., UN dr. for orphans and widows, Manila, 1947. Recipient letter commendation Sec. Navy, 1944. Mem. Gen. Fedn. Women's Clubs, Nat. Fedn. Bus. and Profl. Women's Clubs. Clubs: Am. Newswomen's (Washington); Order Eastern Star (La Jolla, Calif.). Author: Answers to Questions about the Equal Rights Amendment, 1971, 73. Office: Nat Women's Party 144 Constitution Ave NE Washington DC 20002

CHIU, ANNETTE, med. technologist, hematologist; b. Canton, China, Dec. 20, 1933; came to U.S., 1949, naturalized, 1952; d. C. C. and Dorothy (Wong) Chend; B.S. in Med. Tech., U. So. Calif., 1954; m. Seymour S. Chiu, Feb. 2, 1957 (dec.); children—Mark, Tina, Debbie, Stanley. Intern. St. John's Hosp., Santa Monica, Calif., 1954-55; med. technologist St. Elizabeth's Hosp., N.Y.C., 1955-56, St. John's Hosp., Santa Monica, 1956-58; supr. hematology clin. lab. Inter-Community Med. Center, Covina, Calif., 1960—. Cert. med. technologist, Calif. Mem. Am. Soc. Clin. Pathologists (cert. med. technologist), Calif. Assn. Med. Lab. Technologists, Internat. Photography Soc., Associated Photographers Internat. Clubs: Mercedes Benz of Am. (San Gabriel), Glendora Camera (dir.). Home: 774 Rancho Simi Dr Covina CA 91724 Office: Inter-Community Med Center 303 N Third St Covina CA 91723

CHMELIR, SANDRA BURKHALTER, psychologist, educator; b. Macon, Ga., Jan. 30, 1948; d. George Lewis and Helen (Wood) Burkhalter; B.S., U. Ga., 1968; M.A., Emory U., 1973, Ph.D. (NDEA fellow), 1975; m. Frank James Chmelir, June 29, 1974; children—Gregg, Cathy. Clin. intern Chgo. Read Mental Health Center, 1974-75; asst. prof. psychology Ill. Benedictine Coll., Lisle, 1977-80, asso. prof., 1980—; psychol. tester Student Devel. Center, 1979—. Mem. Am. Psychol. Assn. Unitarian. Home: 201 39th St Downers Grove IL 60515 Office: Procopian Hall Ill Benedictine College Lisle IL 60532

CHMIELOWSKI, NORMA JEAN, govt. ofcl.; b. Ewen, Mich., Dec. 19, 1940; d. Alex and Martha (Niemala) Tyyska; student U. Md., 1963; children—Marie, Beth. With U.S. Civil Service, Washington, 1959-66; chief funds mgmt. sect., Elmendorf AFB, Alaska, 1980—; fed. women's program mgr. Alaskan Air Command, 1979-80. First v.p. Alaska Congress of Parents and Tchrs., 1981—. Recipient Sustained Superior Performance award, U.S. Civil Service, 1975, 79, Spl. Achievement award, 1980, Squadron Historian of the Yr. award, 1980, Alaskan Air Command Supply Mgr. of the Yr. award, 1979, Outstanding Fed. Employee of the Yr. award, Elmendorf AFB, 1979; named Toastmaster of the Yr., 1980. Mem. Anchorage C. of C., Nat. Assn. Female Execs. Republican. Clubs: Toastmasters (pres. 1979-80, gov. Yukon-Alaska council 1981-82). Editor, No. Mouthpiece, 1980-81. Home: 2704 Lovejoy Dr Anchorage AK 99504

CHOATE, LILLIE MCCOOL, interior designer; b. Vaiden, Miss., Mar. 6, 1929; d. John William and Allie Earlene (Curtis) McCool; student Chgo. Sch. Interior Design, 1964; m. Walter Lamar Choate, 1950 (dec. 1975); children—Walter Lamar, Carolyn Choate Higdon; m. 2d, William D. Ferrell, 1979 (dec. Mar. 1982). Interior designer, Greenville, Miss., 1964—; dir. Miss. Marine Towboat Corp., Greenville, 1976—; pres. Chocox Barge Inc., Greenville, 1975—, Choate Furniture Co., Greenville, 1975—; sec. Cox Marine Corp., Greenville, 1975—. Mem., officer PTA, Greenville, 1959-73, Band Aux., Greenville, 1963-70; Sunday sch. tchr. First United Meth. Ch., 1958-74, bd. stewards, 1976. Mem. Greenville C. of C. (dir. 1978-79, div. v.p., dir. 1979-80). Clubs: Triad (life; sec. 1963-64), Greenville Golf and Country, Tennis League, Colonial Garden. Home: 248 Rose St Greenville MS 38701 Office: 402 Hwy 1 South Greenville MS 38701

CHODORKOFF, JOAN, clin. psychologist; b. N.Y.C., Feb. 17, 1929; d. Jacob Ludwig and Cora (Berger) Rosmarin; B.A. cum laude, Marietta Coll., 1950; M.A., U. Wis., 1954; Ph.D., Wayne State U., 1960; m. Bernard Chodorkoff, June 11, 1951; children—Cathi, David Jacob. Psychologist, Children's Center Wayne County, 1954-60; chief psychologist Children's Psychiat. Unit, Detroit Gen. Hosp., 1960-62, chief psychologist pediatrics, 1967-69; chief psychologist Downriver Guidance Clinic, Lincoln Park, Mich., 1975—; adj. faculty univs.; pvt. practice psychology. Mem. Oak Park Youth Guidance Bd., 1963-54. NIMH research fellow, 1960-61. Mem. Am. Psychol. Assn., Mich. Assn. Lic. Psychologists, Am. Assn. Orthopsychiatry, Nat. Assn. Jewish Women, Hadassah. Office: 26300 Outer Dr Lincoln Park MI 48146

CHODOROW, JOAN, dance and movement psychotherapist; b. N.Y.C., May 29, 1937; d. Eugene Aaronovitch and Lillian Mikofsky (Kleidman) Chodorow; student in dance therapy Trudi Schoop and Mary Whitehouse, Los Angeles, 1963-65; M.A. in Dance Therapy, Goddard Coll., 1972; postgrad. C.G. Jung Inst., Los Angeles, 1977—; 1 dau., Laurene Kim Smallwood. Founder, owner, operator Community Dance Studio, East Los Angeles, Calif., 1957-64; dance therapist County Gen. Hosp., Los Angeles, 1964-66, Santa Barbara (Calif.) Psychiat. Med. Group, 1968-73; pvt. practice Jungian approach dance and movement psychotherapy, Santa Barbara, 1973—; dance therapist, intern supr. Cottage Hosp., Santa Barbara, 1973—; lectr. continuing edn. program Santa Barbara Community Coll., 1973—; lectr., educator in field; vis. faculty mem. various schs.; cons. in field. Cert. community coll. educator, lic. marriage, family and child therapist, Calif. Mem. Am. Dance Therapy Assn. (registered dance therapist 1971, pres. 1974-76, co-chairperson programming nat. conf. 1980), Am. Psychol. Assn., Internat. Assn. Social Psychiatry, Am. Assn. Social Psychiatry, Am. Assn. Marriage and Family Therapy, Calif. Assn. Marriage, Family and Child Therapists, Calif. Dance Educator's Assn., Laban Inst. Movement Studies. Jewish. Author: Dance Therapy and the Transcendent Function, 1978; Dance/Movement and Body Experience in Jungian Analysis, 1982; editor: Proc. 1st Calif. Regional Conf. Am. Dance Therapy Assn., 1972; co-editor: What Is Dance Therapy, Really?, 1973. Home and Office: 1821 La Coronilla Dr Santa Barbara CA 93109

CHOITZ, DOROTHY G., buyer; b. Ness City, Kans., July 12, 1942; d. John F. and Florence E. (Holm) C.; B.S., Valparaiso U., 1964; M.S., Pa. State U., 1968; J.D., Fordham U., 1980. Head home econs. dept. Lutheran High Sch. South, St. Louis, 1964-66; grad. asst. Pa. State U., 1966-68; fashion cons. Talon Co., N.Y.C., 1968-69, ednl. dir., 1969-74; mgr. instructional schs. J.C. Penney Co. Inc., N.Y.C., 1974-76, pattern buyer, fabric coordinator, 1976-78, yarn and art needlework buyer, 1978-80, cosmetics buyer, 1980—; admitted to N.Y. bar, 1981; guest lectr. St. John's U., Hunter Coll., Queens Coll. Vol. TV Public Braodcast System; mem. Mus. Modern Art. Mem. Am. Home Econs. Assn., Home Economists in Business (chmn. N.Y. group 1975-76, nat. program com., 1976), Women's Fashion Fabric Assn., Omicron Nu. Home: 200 E 82d St PH B New York NY 10028 Office: JC Penney Co Inc 1301 Ave of Americas 6th Floor New York NY 10019

CHONG, DOROTHY BIERMA, trading and cons. co. exec.; b. Detroit, Mar. 27, 1925; d. Charles Allen and Jessica (Griffiths) Bierma; student Los Angeles City Coll., 1942-43, U. Mich., 1946-47; m. Richard Seng-Hoon Chong, Jan. 9, 1980; step-children—David C.S., Stephen C.L., Daniel C.Y. Adminstrv. asst. to plant mgr. Monsanto Co., Trenton, Mich., 1952-65; adminstrv. asst. to pres. Adache Assos., Inc., Engrs., Cleve., 1965-69; credit mgr. Hawaiian Crane & Rigging, Ltd., Honolulu, 1969-70; adminstrv. mgr. East Central region Booz, Allen & Hamilton, Inc., Cleve., 1970-73; v.p. Amer-Asia Trading Co., Inc., Orlando, Fla., 1973—; asso., co-owner Sungold Realty Internat., Inc., Orlando, 1979—. Mem. Chinese-Am. Assn. Central Fla. (sec., dir. 1980-81), World Trade Council for Central Fla., Nat. Assn. Realtors, Fla. Assn. Realtors, Orlando-Winter Park Assn. Realtors. Presbyterian. Club: Citrus. Home: 9652 Woodmont Pl Orlando FL 32811 Office: Amer-Asia Trading Co Inc Suite 112 7201 Lake Ellenor Dr Orlando FL 32809

CHONG, MARY DRUZILLEA, nurse; b. Fairview, Okla., Mar. 8, 1930; d. Charles Dewey and Viola Haddie (Ford) Crawford; A.A. (Bells scholarship), El Camino Jr. Coll., 1950; R.N., Los Angeles County Hosp. Sch. Nursing, 1953; B.S. in Nursing, Calif. State U., 1968; M. Nyuk Choy Chong, Aug. 24, 1952 (div. 1968); children—Anthony, Dorlinda. Staff nurse neurosurgery Los Angeles County Gen. Hosp., Los Angeles, 1957-58; staff nurse Harbor Gen. Hosp., Torrance, Calif., 1958-59, emergency room staff nurse, 1959-61, asst. head nurse, 1963-64, supr. neurosurgery intensive care unit, 1964-67, part-time relief nurse, 1967-69, head nurse chest medicine, 1969-72; tchr. YWCA Job Corps, 1972-74; emergency room staff nurse mobile intensive care nurse Victor Valley Hosp., Victorville, Calif., 1974-79; dir. nursing San Vicente Hosp., Los Angeles, 1980-82. Leader, South Bay council Girl Scouts Am., 1968. Mem. Am. Nurses Assn., Nat. Assn. Female Execs., Calif. State U. Los Angeles Alumni Assn. Home: PO Box 697 Lucerne Valley CA 92356

CHOOKASIAN, LILI, mezzo-soprano, contralto; b. Chgo.; student Philip Manuel, Chgo., Ludwig Donath, N.Y.C., Armen Boyajian, Paterson, N.J.; m. George Gavejian; 3 children. Voice tchr. Northwestern U.; debut La Cieca (Gioconda), Met. Opera, 1962; roles major cos., Argentina, Canada, Hamburg, Germany, Turin, Italy, Mexico City, Barcelona, Spain, Balt., Chgo., Cin., Dallas, Ft. Worth, Houston, Miami, N.Y. City Opera, Met. Opera, Phila. Lyric Opera, Portland, San Francisco Opera, Washington; rec. artist Deutsche Grammophon; appearances with symphony orchs.; coach repertoire. Office: care Thea Dispeker Artists Reps 59 E 54th St New York NY 10002 *

CHOP, ROSE MARIE, nurse; b. Kans., Mar. 4, 1955; d. John and Helen Ann (Sachen) C.; B.S. Nursing, Fort Hays State U., 1978, postgrad. Kans. U. Med. Center, 1979-81, Wichita State U., 1982—. With Providence-St. Margaret Health Center, Kansas City, Kans., 1973—, staff charge nurse med.-surg. unit, 1981—; staff faculty mem. Providence-St. Margaret's Health Center, 1980—; instr. CPR, 1981—; aerobic dance instr., 1981—. Mem. Am. Nurses Assn., Am. Heart Assn., Fort Hays State U. Alumni Assn. (life). Democrat. Roman Catholic. Club: Croation Federal Union. Home: 2221 Orville Ave Kansas City KS 66102 Office: Providence-St Margaret Health Center 8929 Parallel Ave Kansas City KS 66102

CHORBA, MARY CATHERINE, account exec.; b. Phila., Aug. 15, 1955; d. George Joseph and Mildred Mary (Hazinski) C.; B.A. in Sociology, Villanova U., 1977. Sales rep., fin. systems specialist TAB Products, N.J., 1977-78; personnel cons. Shaw & Shaw, Inc., Torrance, Calif., 1978-80; sales, mktg. recruitment cons., Torrance, 1980—; now account exec. Bell System; cons. to bus. Mem. coordinating council City of Redondo Beach; mem. task forces Redondo Beach Sch. Bd. Recipient Pres.'s award Shaw & Shaw, Inc., 1979, Volt Info. Scis., N.Y.C.; cert. personnel cons., Calif. Mem. Nat. Assn. Female Execs., Calif. Assn. Personnel Cons., Women in Mgmt. South Bay, Women in Telecommunications, Nat. Assn. Bus. and Profl. Women, Torrance C. of C., Redondo Beach C. of C. Office: 24035 Ocean Ave Suite 7 Torrance CA 90505

CHORPENNING, NANCY ELLEN, pub. co. exec.; b. Columbus, Ohio, Nov. 29, 1953; d. Harry Row and Margaret Ellen (Hayes) C.; B.A., Denison U., 1975; postgrad. in mgmt. Northwestern U., 1979—. Ednl. rep. Year Book Med. Pubs. subs. Times Mirror, Inc., Chgo., 1975-77, field editor, 1977-79, med. editor, 1979-82; dir., exec. editor G.K. Hall Med. Pubs. subs. ITT Pub., Boston, 1982—. Mem. Nat. Assn. Female Execs., Chgo. Women in Pub., Denison U. Alumni Assn., Alpha Phi Alumnae Assn. Republican. Congregationalist. Home: 67 Saint Germain St Boston MA 02115 Office: 70 Lincoln St Boston MA 02111

CHOU, IRIS LI-YIN, Taiwanese govt. ofcl.; b. Taiwan, Jan. 11, 1951; came to U.S., 1978; d. Chun Chi and Shen Chen (Jen) Chou; B.A., Nat. Cheng-chi U., Taipei, 1974; M.A., Am. U., 1981. Sr. staff Ministry of Fgn. Affairs, Taipei, Taiwan, 1975-79; 3rd sec. Taiwan embassy, Washington, 1978; asst. Coordination Council for N.Am. Affairs, Washington, 1979-82, sec. (consul), N.Y.C., 1982—. Clubs: Capital Speakers, Welcome to Washington, China Tiffin, Asian Am., Asia Soc. Home: 41-40 Union St Apt 10H Flushing NY 11355 Office: 801 2d Ave New York NY 10017

CHOUINARD, JACQUEL-ANNE, state commr.; b. Barre, Vt., Aug. 16, 1939; d. J. Leon and Dolores C.; student Trinity Coll., Burlington, Vt., 1981—. Adminstrv. asst. to personnel commr. State of Vt., Montpelier, 1963-68, mgmt. adv., 1968-73, dir. personnel policies and procedures, 1972-74, commr. personnel State of Vt., 1974—; chairperson N.E. Public Personnel Council, 1977-79; mem. Vt. State Employee Relations Bd., 1975—. Mem. Vt. Coll. Adv. Bd., 1978-80; mem. Vt. Mental Health Adv. Council, 1976-79; mem. exec. bd. Vt. Coalition for Health, 1982—; bd. dirs. Women in Polit. and Govt. Careers, Burlington. Mem. Am. Soc. Personnel Adminstrn., Am. Soc. Public Adminstrn., Internat. Personnel Mgmt. Assn. Club: Bus. and Profl. Women (Career woman of Yr. 1978). Office: 110 State Montpelier VT 05641

CHOW, EILEEN SIU-HA, wholesale co. exec.; b. Kowloon, Hong Kong, Jan. 18, 1951; came to U.S., 1969; d. HinTo and Oi (Kuen) Choi; B.A. cum laude, UCLA, 1972, M.S., 1973; m. Chun P. Chow, Aug. 25, 1973; children—Connie, Sandra. Systems analyst Gen. Motors Research Lab., Warren, Mich., 1973-77; v.p. Cougar of Calif., Inc., S. San Francisco, 1977—, Choice Investment Co. N.V., 1978—. Mem. Soc. Women Engrs., IEEE, Exec. Females. Office: 380 Swift Ave #1 South San Francisco CA 94080

CHOYKE, PHYLLIS MAY FORD, ceiling co. exec., editor; b. Buffalo, Oct. 25, 1921; d. Thomas Cecil and Vera (Buchanan) Ford; B.S. summa cum laude (Bonbright scholar), Northwestern U., 1942; m. Arthur Davis Choyke, Jr., Aug. 18, 1945; children—Christopher Ford, Tyler Van. Reporter, City News Bur., Chgo., 1942-43; reporter met. sect. Chgo. Tribune, 1943-44; feature writer OWI, N.Y.C., 1944-45; sec. Artcrest Products Co. Inc., Chgo., 1951-63, v.p., 1963—; founder, dir. Harper Sq. Press, Chgo., 1967—. Mem. Chgo. Press Vets. Assn., Soc. Midland Authors, Phi Beta Kappa. Club: Arts (Chgo.). Editor: Gallery Series One/Poets, 1967; Gallery Series Two/Poets—Poems of the Inner World, 1968; Gallery Series Three/Poets (Levitations and Observations), 1970; Gallery Series Four/Poets—I Am Talking about Revolution, 1973; Gallery Series Five/Poets-To an Aging Nation (with occult overtones), 1977; (under name Phyllis Ford with J. Kachmar and H. Winter) Apertures to Anywhere (poems), 1979. Home: 29 E Division St Chicago IL 60610 Office: 401 W Ontario St Chicago IL 60610

CHRIST, LILY ESTHER SHIH (MRS. DUANE MARLAND CHRIST), educator; b. Korea, Sept. 19, 1936; came to U.S., 1955, naturalized, 1968; d. Whan-Chang and Shin-Tze (Lin) Shih; B.S., U. Minn., 1960; M.A., Western Res. U., 1962; Ed.D., Columbia U., 1967; m. Duane Marland Christ, Sept. 14, 1963. Tchr. math. Cleve. Public Schs., 1960-62; asst. statis. lab. Columbia U. N.Y.C., 1964-66; asst. prof. math. and edn. Coll. Mt. St. Vincent, N.Y.C., 1966-68; asst. prof. math. John Jay Coll. Criminal Justice, City U. N.Y., N.Y.C., 1969-73, assoc. prof., 1974—. Vol. math. tutor Task Force, Riverside Ch., 1966-69; vol. math. fair judge L.I. Math. Fair, 1966-69, Greater Met. N.Y. Math. Fair, 1970—. Fulbright-Hays sr. scholar, 1972-73. Mem. Nat. Council Tchrs. Math., Math. Assn. Am. (del. assembly Met. N.Y. sect. 1966, 67, 71, 72, sec. 1976—), Am. Statis. Assn. (mem. exec. council N.Y. area chpt. 1978-80), Am. Ednl. Research Assn., N.Y. Acad. Scis., Lambda Alpha Psi, Kappa Delta Pi. Office: 445 W 59th St New York NY 10019

CHRISTENSEN, ANNA MAE PARKER (MRS. EDGAR W. CHRISTENSEN), pianist, composer; b. Alexandria, Va., Apr. 15, 1899; d. Charles William and Evelyn Virginia (Henry) Parker; student public schs., Washington, Md., Ind., Nebr.; student Inst. Mus. Art, N.Y.C., 1924; m. Edgar W. Christensen, May 31, 1928. Pvt. piano tchr., Omaha, 1921—; performer, composer piano solos for elem. grades: Slumber Song, Mazurka, Dream Castles, Birthday Candles, Snow Fairy, Yankee Shuffle, Silver Ship, Swedish Dance, Loneliness, Chinese Tinkle Glass, Persian Chant, Tyrolian Holiday, Holiday Festival. Recipient honor awards competitions young composers. Mem. PEO. Congregationalist. Compositions and plaque buried in 2076 Time Capsule at Gerald Ford Birthsite, Omaha, 1976. Home and Studio: 5635 Emile St Omaha NE 68106

CHRISTENSEN, CAROLE CECILE PIGLER, educator; b. Bklyn., Mar. 14, 1939; d. Samuel and Georgia Mae (Williams) Pigler; B.A. in Sociology, Howard U., 1960; M.S.W., U. Mich., 1963; D.Ed. in Counseling Psychology, McGill U., 1980; m. Torkild Vejby Christensen, Sept. 21, 1963; children—Karin, Michael, Lisa. Instr. social work Danish Sch. Social Work, 1964-66; mental health counselor Danish Women's League Counseling Service, Copenhagen, 1964-68; lectr. social work McGill U., 1970-80, asst. prof., 1980—. Fulbright fellow, 1960-61, Can. Council fellow, 1977-80. Mem. Am. Psychol. Assn., Canadian Assn. Social Workers, Soc. Intercultural Edn. Tng. and Research, Am. Assn. Sex Educators Counselors and Therapists (cert.), Afro-Asian Assn. Can. (co-founder), Phi Beta Kappa, Phi Kappa Phi. Office: McGill University School of Social Work 3506 University St Montreal PQ H3A 2A7 Canada

CHRISTENSEN, RUTH ELLEN, physician; b. Terre Haute, Ind., Feb. 18, 1928; d. Leo Martin and Eva Inez (Patterson) Christensen; B.A. in English and Zoology, U. Nebr., 1950, M.D., 1954. Intern, Touro Infirmary, New Orleans, 1954-55, resident internal medicine, 1955-58, chief resident, 1957-58; staff physician Central Colo. Med. Center, Colorado Springs, 1959-60, Vets Hosp., Wadsworth, Kans., 1961; cons. staff Good Samaritan Hosp., Kearney, Nebr.; practice medicine specializing in internal medicine, Miller, Nebr., 1962—; bd. dirs., v.p. Mid-Nebr. Family Health Services, 1978-80. Co-organizer Citizens Against the Dam, Miller, 1971; mem. Miller Women's Improvement Club, 1963—; chmn. bicentennial flag raising com., Miller; chmn. Miller Area Heritage Com. Mem. Nebr., Buffalo County med. socs., Internat. Platform Assn., Nat. Audubon Soc., Nat. Wildlife Fedn., Nat. Smithsonian Assn., Am. Med. Women (asso.), Buffalo County Hist. Soc. Methodist. Home and Office: Miller NE 68858

CHRISTENSEN, VERDA ANN, accountant; b. Amite, La., Sept. 24, 1945; d. Marvin Virgual and Olga Henrietta (Kauss) C.; student La. State U., 1963-65. Acct., Public Welfare, State of La., 1965-78, Dept. Health and Human Resources, Office of Human Devel., Baton Rouge, 1978—. Mem. Assn. Govt. Accts. Lutheran. Office: 1755 Florida Blvd Baton Rouge LA 70802

CHRISTENSON, EVELYN CAROL, writer, lectr.; b. Muskegon, Mich., Jan. 31, 1922; d. Edward F. and Edna B. Luhman; A.A., Bethel Coll., St. Paul; student Moody Bible Inst., Chgo.; m. Harold Christenson, Feb. 14, 1942; children—Jan Christenson Johnson, Nancy Christenson Thompson, Kurt. Sec. to pres. Bethel Coll. and Sem., 1946-50; founding pres. United Prayer Ministries, St. Paul, 1976, chmn. bd., 1976—; internat. lectr. Australia, N.Z., Eng., Ireland, Scotland, Taiwan, Japan, India; mem. com., lectr. Am. Festival of Evangelism, Kansas City, Mo., 1981; co-prayer chmn., lectr. Internat. Council Bibl. Inerrancy, San Diego, Calif., 1982; consultation com. Internat. Conf. Lutheran Evangelists, Amsterdam, 1983; writer; books include: What Happens When Women Pray (Top Ten list Christian Booksellers), 1975; Lord Change Me (Top Ten list Christian Booksellers), 1977; Gaining Through Losing, 1980; teaching cons. colls. Mem. Prison Fellowship Bd. (Washington). Named Pacesetter of Yr., Bethel Coll., 1976; books rated top two by woman author Booksellers Jour., 1979; named Churchwoman of Yr., Religious Heritage of Am., 1980. Mem. Alumni Assn. Bethel Coll., Bethel Coll. Aux., Sem. Wives Assn. Bethel Sem. Home and Office: 4265 Brigadoon Dr Saint Paul MN 55112

CHRISTENSON, FABIENNE FADELEY, jet engine mfg. co. exec.; b. Washington, June 20, 1951; d. James McNelledge and Catherine Shirley (Sweeney) Fadeley; B.S. cum laude, U. Md., 1976; M.B.A. with honors, Boston U., 1979; m. Gordon A. Christenson, Sept. 16, 1979. With Gen.

Electric Aircraft Engine Group, Evendale, Ohio, 1979—, contract adminstr., foreman, prodn. control specialist, now configuration control specialist; pres. Mfg. Tng. Program, 1980. Home: 3737 Clifton Ave Cincinnati OH 45220 Office: Mail Drop B-108 Neumann Way Evendale OH 45215

CHRISTIAN, DOLLY LEWIS, civic affairs adminstr.; b. N.Y.C.; d. Daniel Webster and Adeline (Walton) Lewis. Dir. civic affairs equal employment affirmative action program Sperry & Hutchinson Co., N.Y.C., 1968—. Chmn. bd. N.Y. Urban League, 1977-78, pres., 1978—; panel of arbitrators Am. Arbitration Assn., N.Y.C., 1973—; adv. com. master's degree program in fund raising mgmt. New Sch. for Social Research, N.Y.C., 1978—. Bd. dirs. Coalition of 100 Black Women, 1981. Recipient scroll of honor Nat. Council Negro Bus. and Profl. Women's Clubs, 1975, community service award, 1974, ombudswoman award, 1975; youth salute to black corp. execs. award Nat. Youth Movement, 1975, corp. recipient Mary McLeod Bethune award Nat. Council Negro Women, 1976; spl. corp. recognition award Met. Council of Brs., NAACP, 1981. Mem. Council Concerned Black Execs. (vice chmn. 1970-77), NAACP, N.Y. Personnel Mgmt. Assn., Edges Group (v.p. 1981), Nat. Urban Affairs Council (dir. 1977—). Home: Jamaica NY 11435 Office: 330 Madison Ave New York NY 10017

CHRISTIAN, MARY BLOUNT, author; b. Houston, Feb. 20, 1933; d. George Dickerson and Anna Belle (Dill) Blount; B.S., U. Houston, 1954; m. George L. Christian, Jr., Sept. 22, 1956; children—Scott, Karen, Devin. Reporter, U. Houston Newsservice, 1952-54; columnist Houston Post Newspaper, 1954-57; feature writer Barthelmer Moore Advt., Houston, 1963-65; author children's books, 1973—; lectr., tchr. Rice U. Inst. Children's Lit. U. Houston, Houston Press Club scholar, 1952; Lilly Kaiser Lewis Found. grantee for pub. TV program, 1976. Mem. Authors Guild, Author's League, Mystery Writers Am. (Spl. Edgar Allan Poe award, 1981), Soc. Children's Book Writers. Democrat. Baptist. Author numerous books including The Lucky Man, 1979; The Devil Take You, Barnabas Beane, 1980; The Doggone Mystery, 1980; The Ventriloquist, 1982; Sebastian Super Sleuth and the Hair of the Dog Mystery, 1982. Home and office: 1108 Danbury Rd Houston TX 77055

CHRISTIAN, MAUREEN MAHER, clin. psychologist; b. Poughkeepsie, N.Y., Mar. 30, 1947; d. Thomas Francis and Linda Maher; B.A. (scholar), Trinity Coll., 1969; M.A., Am. U., 1971, Ph.D., 1979; m. James H. Christian, Aug. 8, 1970. Staff psychologist Youth Center One, D.C. Dept. of Corrections, Lorton, Va., 1971-74, chief psychologist Youth Center Two, 1974-80; clin. psychologist St. Elizabeth's Hosp., Washington, 1980—, mem. gerontology com., 1981—. Cons., bd. dirs. Isaiah House, Washington, 1979-80; bd. dirs. Shadowalk Home Assn., Fairfax Sta., Va., 1981—, v.p., 1982—; mem. exec. bd. Boy Scouts Am., 1982—. Recipient award of excellence D.C. Dept. Corrections, 1979, 80. Mem. Am. Psychol. Assn., Med. Soc. St. Elizabeth's Hosp., Psi. Chi, Phi Kappa Phi. Contbr. articles in field to profl. publs. Office: Saint Elizabeth Hosp John Marr Div 2700 Martin Luther King Ave SE Washington DC 20032

CHRISTIAN, SHIRLEY ANN, journalist; b. Windsor, Mo., Jan. 16, 1938; d. Herbert Walsh and Minnie Lucille (Acker) C.; B.A., Pittsburg (Kans.) State U., 1960; M.A., Ohio State U., 1966; Nieman fellow, Harvard U., 1973-74. UN corr. AP, 1970-73, copy editor fgn. desk, N.Y.C., 1974-77, chief of bur., Santiago, Chile, 1977-79; Latin Am. corr. Miami (Fla.) Herald, 1979—; adj. prof. journalism Columbia U., 1977. Recipient Pulitzer prize for internat. reporting, 1981, George Polk Meml. award for fgn. reporting, 1981. Mem. Overseas Press Club. Congregationalist. Home: 4726 SW 67th Ave Apt F8 Miami FL 33155 Office: Miami Herald 1 Herald Plaza Miami FL 33101

CHRISTIAN, SUSAN HENDRICK, educator; b. Denver, Feb. 24, 1954; d. Warren Frederick and Doris (Hostetter) Hendrick; B.S. in Edn., Baylor U., Waco, Tex., 1976; M.R.E., New Orleans Bapt. Theol. Sem., 1979; m. John Marion Christian, May 16, 1978. Organist, pianist radio program Little Country Ch., Can. and U.S., 1971-73; guest artist Sta. WSLS-TV, Roanoke, Va., 1971-76; asst. Roanoke Valley Christian Schs. day camp, 1973; music and youth leader Meadowbrook Bapt. Ch., Waco, 1974-76; asst. day care dir. First Wesleyan Children's Center, Roanoke, 1977; minister to youth Woodley Bapt. Ch., Montgomery, Ala., 1979—, organist, 1981—; pvt. tchr. piano and organ, 1976—; dir. tchrs. Campo Bros., Inc., music co., New Orleans, 1977-79. Sec., 8th Dist. Young Republicans Va., 1972. Mem. Am. Educators Assn. Bapt., Am. Harpists Soc. (sec. Baylor U. chpt. 1976). Home: 3861 MacLamar Rd Montgomery AL 36111 Office: 3920 Antoinette Rd Montgomery AL 36111

CHRISTIAN, VIRGINIA DAVISON, data systems specialist; b. Washington, Oct. 29, 1929; d. Archie R. and Marie (Burke) Davison; B.S. in Physics, Howard U., 1951; postgrad. U. Conn., 1951-52; m. William M. Christian, Jr., 1952; children—William M. III, David G., Marie F. Scientist, mathematician Gen. Dynamics Corp./Electric Boat div., Groton, Conn., 1956-57, 59-63, nuclear project engr., 1965-78; data systems specialist So. New Eng. Telephone Co., New Haven, 1978—. Mem. Conn. Joint Fedn. Engrs., 1972—; mem. Gov.'s Council for Human Rights and Opportunities, Gov.'s Council for Youth Opportunity, Conn. State Police Adv. Council; mem. United Negro Coll. Fund Com., 1971—; mem. econ. devel. coordinating com. Norwich Community Devel. Corp.; mem. West Side Community Action Com., 1966—; mem. Conn. Bd. Edn., 1967-73; mem. Norwich (Conn.) City Council, 1965-67, sec. Citizens Conf. on Gen. Assembly, 1968-70; mem. adv. council Thames Valley Regional Tech. Coll., 1973-77; mem. Norwich Sch. Bd., 1973-77; trustee Thames Valley Council for Community Action, 1965-71, ARC, Norwich, 1967-69; bd. dirs. State Tech. Colls., 1967-73, 75—, Easter Seal Rehab. Center S.E. Conn., 1970-75; adv. council Mohegan Community Coll.; 2d v.p., chmn. fin. com. Fedn. Black Democrats of New London County. Recipient Dr. Martin Luther King, Jr. Community Service award; recognition award NAACP. Mem. Nat. Council of Women, Nat. Council Negro Women, Norwich Area C. of C., Nat. Soc. Women Engrs. (public relations chmn. 1971-73), NAACP (public relations chmn. br., mem. emeritus Conn. State Conf. NAACP brs.). Soc. Founders Norwich, Black Mgmt. Assn. (steering com. 1980-81), Nat. Mgmt. Assn. (dir. Electric Boat div. 1974-76). Presbyn. Home: 118 McKinley Ave Norwich CT 06360

CHRISTIANSEN, JOYCE L. SOELBERG, newspaper writer; b. Salt Lake City, May 25, 1924; d. Lloyd LeRoy and Irene (Lindberg) Soelberg; student public schs.; m. Ernald Christiansen, Sept. 7, 1947; children—Melodie Joyce, Lynda Lee, Lloyd Randall, Catherine Jill. Sec., COBUSCO Steel, Salt Lake City, 1941-42, Universal Film, Inc., Salt Lake City, 1942-43, Delivery Service Co., Salt Lake City, 1946-47; legal sec. Clearfield Naval Supply (Utah), 1943-45; editor Sunset News, Bountiful, Utah, 1972-75; photographer, journalist Deseret News, Salt Lake City, 1976—, religious editor, 1976-81; writer, photographer Spectrum Press, 1981-82. Active Girl Scouts U.S.A., 1965—, originator Girl Scout Baby Award, Utah, 1980, writer/narrator slide presentation, 1980; safety chmn. Backman Elem. Sch., 1958-60, pres. PTA, 1960-62; 1st v.p. N.W. Jr. High Sch. PTA, 1963-64; mem. adv. bd. Northwest Multi-Purpose Center, 1972—, sec., 1973—; mem. Salt Lake Library Bd., 1980—, mem. ops., bldgs. and grounds coms.; mem. Sunday sch. bd. Riverside state Ch. Jesus Christ of Latter-day Saints, 1954-55, primary officer and tchr., 1962-78. Recipient 3d place award Nat. Fedn. Press Women Communication Contest, 1977; numerous first and second place awards Utah Press Women. Mem. Nat. Fedn. Press Women, Utah Press Women (sec. 1978—). Clubs: Women's Democratic, Jane Jefferson, Lady Lions (2d v.p. 1979-80). Home: 755 N 1400 W Salt Lake City UT 84116 Office: Desert News 30 E First S Salt Lake City UT 84110

CHRISTIE, ALICE PATRICIA, indsl. designer; b. Bklyn., Apr. 21, 1934; d. Joseph Francis and Mary Martha (Coon) Buck; B.S. in Indsl. Design, Phila. Coll. Art, 1978; m. 3d, Richard Dunstan Christie, May 19, 1959; children—Patricia J., Joseph Buck, Mary Ellen. Free lance artist Ogontz Press, Phila., 1953; asst. recreation leader Phila. Dept. Recreation, 1957-59; engring. employment counselor APS Employment Agy., 1967-68; employment counselor and various positions in drafting and design, 1973-77; design cons. CCA Electronics Co., 1977-80, Westinghouse Electric Co., 1978-82; pres. A. Christie Design, Lester, Pa., 1978—; group exhbns. include Print Club Phila., 1955, Art Alliance Phila., 1977. Active local Boy Scouts Am., ARC. Recipient Design in Steel award, 1969, also various service awards. Mem. Indsl. Design Soc. Am., Human Factors Soc., Delaware County C. of C. (women in bus. com.), N.Am. Benefits Assn., D.C. Women's Coalition. Episcopalian. Address 207 Pontiac St Lester PA 19113

CHRISTIN, VIOLET MARGUERITE, cons.; b. Chgo., Oct. 4, 1903; d. Charles A. and Eva M. (Bosse) C.; student Northwestern U., 1936-37, Am. Inst. Banking, 1955-75. With Nat. Bank of Austin, 1922-76, asst. sec., 1953-57, sec., 1957-65, sec., asst. v.p., 1965-76, sec. mktg. com., 1977-79; cons. Mem. Am. Inst. Banking, Ill. Bankers Assn. (50 year club), Assn. Chgo. Bank Women, Nat. Assn. Bank Women, Chgo. Fin. Advertisers (treas. 1964-65, 69-81, dir., treas. 1973-81, Eagle award 1977, First Lady Life Mem. 1981). Clubs: Chgo. Press, Execs., Chgo. Advt. Home: 805 N Grove Ave Oak Park IL 60302

CHRISTISON, DOROTHY F., real estate broker, dance tchr.; b. South Bend, Ind., Jan. 21; d. Elmer Thomas and Julia Rose (Zimmerman) Freed; student U. Ariz., 1943-44; U. Conn., Stamford, 1966; grad. Real Estate Inst., 1971; m. George Lee, July 10, 1938; children—Pamela Lee Christison Stivers, Julie Irene. Founder, tchr. dance studio, Moline, Ill., 1938; dance tchr., Tucson, 1940-44; Green Fields Sch., Tucson, 1940-43, 44; Vero Beach, Fla., 1944-45; Moline, 1946-53; Burlington, Iowa, 1953-59; St. Katherine's Episcopal Sch., Davenport, Iowa, 1958-59; Wilton, Conn., 1962—; dance tchr. YMCA, Moline, Tucson, Burlington, Ridgefield Community Center, 1975-79; asso. Realtor Wilton Country Homes, Wilton, 1966-69; Realtor, partner Wilton Real Estate Agency, 1969-71; owner, operator Christison Assos., Realtors, Wilton, 1971-81; mgr. William Pitt Real Estate, Wilton, 1981—; choreographer Burlington Community Playhouse, 1958-59; Wilton Community Playhouse, 1969, 72, 74. Chmn. voters' service LWV, 1964; nurse's aide ARC, Vero Beach, Fla., 1944-45, Moline, 1942-43; founding mem. Young Horizons of Wilton, pres., treas., 1964, 65, 66, 67; active Jr. Service League, pres., 1952-54. Cert. residential specialist. Mem. Dance Educators of Am., Conn. Assn. (state dir. 1975-76), Women's Council Realtors (fin. chairperson 1973-74), Wilton Bd. Realtors (membership chairperson 1972-76, dir. 1970-76), Nat. Assn. Realtors, Realtors Nat. Mktg. Inst., Internat. Assn. Realtors, Chgo. Assn. Dance Tchrs. (faculty mem. 1969). Congregationalist. Clubs: Wilton Women's (charter mem.), Wilton Garden. Office: 146 Danbury Rd Wilton CT 06897

CHRISTISON, MURIEL BRANHAM, museum exec.; b. Mpls.; d. Garold D. and Helen (Ferguson) Brenham; B.A., U. Minn., 1933, M.A., 1940; diplome, U. Paris, 1936, U. Brussels, 1938; m. 1933; children—Evelyn, Carolyn. Curatorial research Mpls. Inst. Arts, 1936-42, head edn., 1944-47; asso. dir. Va. Mus. Fine Arts, 1948-61; operating dir. Krannert Art Mus. U. Ill., 1962-64, asso. dir., 1962-74, dir., 1975—; lectr. cons. in field. Fellow Belgian-Am. Ednl. Found.; Carnegie scholar. Mem. Am. Assn. Mus. (council), Internat. Council Mus., Assn. Art Mus., Midwest Mus. Conf., Assn. Preservation Va. Antiquities. Club: Cosmopolitan (N.Y.C.). Contbr. articles to profl. jours., mags. Home: 508 S Mattio Apt 20 Champaign IL 61820 Office: 500 E Peabody Dr Champaign IL 61820 *

CHRISTOLON, BLAIR KAY BIRKHOLZ, librarian; b. Oak Park, Ill., Oct. 1, 1947; d. William Howard and Evelyn Weinkauf (Mueller) Birkholz; B.A., U. Denver, 1969; M.L.S., Brigham Young U., Provo, Utah, 1976; m. Warren Kenneth Christolon, Aug. 12, 1972; children—Christopher Warren, Niklas Winston. Librarian, Johns Hopkins U., USIS, Bologna, Italy, 1972-73; tchr. Denver public schs., 1969-74; asst. dir. children's services Weber County Library, Ogden, Utah, 1975-77; dir. govt. library Overseas Pvt. Investment Corp., Washington, 1978; library cons. Dept. Edn., Washington, 1979—; admissions dir. Alphabet Sch., Manassas, Va., 1981—. Mem. parent adv. com. Va. Coop. Extension, 1981—, editor newsletter, 1981—; cons. Parent Infant Handicapped Edn., 1979. Recipient Outstanding Woman award U. Denver, 1969. Mem. ALA, Delta Gamma. Home: 8396 Briarmont Ln Manassas VA 22111

CHRISTOPHER, DOLORES LEE, govt. ofcl.; b. N.Y.C., Feb. 5, 1940; d. Ernest Charles and Ethel Margrita (Cox) C.; A.A.S., Borough Manhattan Community Coll., 1970; B.A., Fordham U., 1978. Various clerical positions, 1956-62; with U.S. Postal Service, 1965—, jr. acct. internat. accts. center, N.Y.C., 1976-77, supr. settle sect., 1977-81, mgr. center, 1981—, EEO counselor, 1977—; shop steward Am. Postal Workers Union, 1974-77. Bd. dirs. Manhattan Community Coll., 1964—, vice chmn., 1974; bd. dirs. Esplanade Gardens Coop., 1967-75, parlimentarian, vice chmn., treas., 1967-75. Recipient various service awards. Mem. Alumni Assn. Fordham U. Democrat. Roman Catholic. Home: 101-125 W 147th St New York NY 10039 Office: GPO Bldg Room 4519 New York NY 10099

CHRISTOPHER, MAURINE BROOKS, writer, editor; b. Three Springs, Tenn.; d. John Davis and Zula Pangle Brooks; B.A., Tusculum Coll., 1941; m. Milbourne Christopher, June 23, 1949. Reporter, entertainment editor Kingsport (Tenn.) Times, 1941-43; reporter, feature writer Balt. Sun, 1943-45; TV radio editor Advt. Age, 1947-51, sr. editor, head broadcast dept., 1951-77, dep. exec. editor, N.Y.C., 1977-79, dep. exec. editor, Videotech columnist, 1979—. Mem. Am. Women in Radio and TV (past pres. N.Y.C. chpt., cert. of merit), Women in Communications, Women's Econ. Council, Assn. Study Afro-Am. Life and History. Author: America's Black Congressmen, 1971; Black Americans in Congress, 1976. Home: 333 Central Park W New York NY 10025 Office: 220 E 42d St New York NY 10017

CHRISTOPLOS, FLORENCE WOLLMAN, educator; b. N.Y.C., Oct. 29, 1928; d. Isidore and Tillie (Green) Wollman; B.A., Hunter Coll., 1951; M.A., U. Md., 1965, Ph.D., 1968; m. George Christoplos, Nov. 11, 1947; children—Laura, Ian Keith. Asst. prof. spl. edn. Johns Hopkins U. Sch. Medicine, Balt., 1969-74; dir. edn. program Kennedy Inst., Balt., 1968-69; cons. on admissions and programming Calverton Sch., Huntingtown, Md., 1967-81; prof., coordinator grad. programs in learning disabilities Coppin State Coll., Balt., 1967-72; prof. Bowie State Grad. Coll., 1972—; cons. staff tng. Edgemeade Sch., Md., 1971-75; vis. prof. George Mason U., Fairfax, Va., 1976-79. Mem. Council for Exceptional Children, Nat. Assn. for Edn. of Young Children, Assn. for Childhood Edn. Internat. Contbr. articles on learning disabilities and ednl. programs to profl. jours.; editor Preventing Physical and Mental Disabilities, 1979, Inter-Disciplinary Approaches to Human Services, 1977. Home: 6410 Sandy St Laurel MD 20707 Office: Edn Div Bowie State College Bowie MD 20715

CHRYSTAL, GAIL KATZ, marketing exec.; b. Chgo., Mar. 17, 1949; d. Bernard and Lucille Jean (Zuckerman) Katz; B.A., U. Ill., 1973; m. James J. Chrystal, Apr. 4, 1971; 1 dau., Sarah Eden. With prodn./editing, Fred Niles Studios, Chgo., 1972-74; disc jockey Sta. WSDM, Chgo., 1969-72; with Glenn-Warren Studios, Chgo., 1974-75; list promotion mgr. Cosmetique Golden 50, Chgo., 1975-77; account group mgr. Stone & Adler, Inc., Chgo., 1977-81; pres. Chrystal Direct Mktg. Group, 1981—; speaker profl. groups; pres. Research to Women; mem. vis. execs. program. Mem. Chgo. Assn. Direct Mktg., Women's Direct Response Group Chgo. (founding officer), Direct Mail Mktg. Assn., Women's Advt. Club of Chgo. Democrat. Jewish. Home: 1667 Ottowa Ct Wheeling IL 60090 Office: 3227 N Frontage Rd Suite 2703 Arlington Heights IL 60004

CHU, BILLIE MAE, engr., mfg. co. exec.; b. Dawsonville, Ga., May 1, 1930; d. William Thomas and Ida Mae (Hill) Redd; B.A., Agnes Scott Coll., 1948; M.A., Emory U., 1949; Ph.D., Calif. Inst. Tech., 1970; M.B.A., U. Detroit, 1977; m. Hugh N. Chu, June 23, 1961; children—Stephen, Edward, Nancy. Design specialist Martin Marietta Corp., Denver, 1956-61; research fellow Calif. Inst. Tech., Pasadena, 1969-72; research engr. Gen. Motors Corp., Warren, Mich., 1972-78; sr. engr. Ford Motor Co. , Dearborn, Mich., 1978—. Anthony scholar, 1963-64; Douglas Aircraft fellow, 1966-67; NIH grantee, 1967-69. Mem. IEEE (editorial bd. Proc. 1978-80), AAAS, Am. Burn Assn., Biophys. Soc., Biomed. Engring. Soc., Sigma Xi, Beta Gamma Sigma, Sigma Pi Sigma. Developed miniature force-displacement transducers to measure in situ mech. properties of living skin, 1972. Home: 22877 Nottingham Dr Birmingham MI 48010

CHUANG, CYNTHIA REN-YI, biochemist, educator; b. Shanghai, Sept. 21, 1941; d. Zenith Chien-Nei and Ching-Chuan (Chen) C.; came to U.S., naturalized, 1976; B.S., Nat. Taiwan U., 1962; Ph.D., Purdue U., 1967. Research chemist Union Carbide Corp., South Charleston, W.Va., 1967-69; vis. asso. prof. Nat. Taiwan Normal U., Taipei, 1969-70; postdoctoral fellow U. Tex. System Cancer Center, Houston, 1971-73, research asso., 1973-74, asst. prof. biochemistry, asst. biochemist, 1975—. Recipient award Nat. Sci. Council Republic of China. Mem. Biophys. Soc., Am. Soc. Cell Biology, Sigma Xi. Baptist. Contbr. articles to profl. jours. Address: 7700 Creekbend No 11 Houston TX 77071 *

CHUN, CONNIE CASPE, state legislator; b. Iloilo City, Philippines, June 2, 1928; came to U.S., 1956, naturalized, 1962; R.N., Manila Sanitarium and Hosp., 1953; B.S. in Nursing, Loma Linda U., 1958; M.P.H. in Comprehensive Planning and Adminstrn., U. Hawaii, 1972, J.D., 1978; m. Hing Hua Chun, Apr. 10, 1970; children—May Lynne, Jerry, June, Hingson, Joy, Daven. Dir. nursing Golden Gate Hosp., San Francisco, 1962-68; asst. dir. nursing St. Francis Hosp., Honolulu, 1968-70; health planner Rehab. Hosp. of the Pacific, Honolulu, 1970-72; admitted to Hawaii bar, 1979; individual practice law, Honolulu, 1979; mem. Hawaii Ho. of Reps., 1980—, chmn. com. on public assistance and human services, mem. coms. on consumer protection and commerce, corrections, health, housing, judiciary, youth and elderly affairs, 1980—. Trustee sr. cardiovascular rehab. program Honolulu Med. Group, 1980-81, Filipino Garden, Inc., East-West Center, 1981—; chmn. Honolulu Police Commn., 1979-80; v.p. Leeward Marathon Clinic, 1980; rev. bd. Mid Pacific Road Runners Club, 1980; mem. Women Democrats of Hawaii. Fulbright scholar, 1956; R.N., Hawaii, Calif. Mem. Am. Bar Assn., Hawaii State Bar Assn., Am. Nurses Assn., Hawaii Nurses Assn., Am. Pub. Health Assn., Hawaii Pub. Health Assn., Filipino C. of C., U. Hawaii Law Sch. Alumni Assn., Bus. and Profl. Women's Club. Club: Filipino Women's. Co-author: Hawaii State Health Facilities Plan, 1975; Master Plan Rehabilitation Hospital of the Pacific, 1976; contbr. articles to legal jours. Office: State Capitol Room 438 Honolulu HI 96813

CHUN, RAMONA IWALANI TANIYE, editor; b. Manhattan, Kans., July 23, 1955; d. Raymond K. and Sachiko (Taniguchi) C.; B.A. in English, Colo. Women's Coll., 1977. Editorial intern Am. Sch. Food Service Assn., Denver, 1977—, asst. editor, 1977-79, mng. editor, 1979-81, editor, 1981—; dir. public relations Adams County Community Theatre, 1979-81. Mgr. public relations Robert Morise for Rep., 1977-78. Mem. Women in Communications. Office: Am Sch Food Service Assn 4101 E Iliff Ave Denver CO 80222

CHURCH, BETTY JUANITA, educator; b. Clinton, Ill., Mar. 29, 1932; d. William Otis and Nora May (Brighton) Johnson; B.S., U. Ill., 1954, M.S., 1959; m. Glenn J. Church, Aug. 12, 1954 (div. July 1981); children—Susan Jo, Zackary William. Extension trainee Ford County (Ill.), Melvin, summer 1952; home adv. DeWitt County (Ill.), Clinton, summer 1953; asst. home adv. Logan County (Ill.), Lincoln, summer 1954; tchr. home econs. Parma (Mo.) Public Schs., 1954-55; camp dir., sec. Camp Fire Girls, Wichita Falls, Tex., summer 1955; field dir., camp dir. San Bernardino (Calif.) council Girl Scouts U.S.A., 1955-57; tchr. vocat. home econs. Unity High Sch., Tolono, Ill., 1957-59; part-time instr. home econs. Bradley U., Peoria, Ill., 1965-73, half-time instr., 1973-81, full time instr., 1981—; dir. Ill. Make it Yourself with Wool Program, 1969-74; supt. modeling Heart of Ill. Fair, 1965—; demonstration cons.; instr. mgmt. classes State Hosp., Bartonville, 1964-66; occasional guest Town and Country TV Show, Channel 31, 1976—; mem. North Central Evaluation Team, 1977; mem. Ill. home econs. planning com. of Home Econs. Vocat. Curriculum Project, 1979—. Active fund drives Lakeview Center, United Fund, Arthritis and Rheumatic Found., Heart Fund, U. Ill. Found., Mothers March, 4-H House; mem. Lakeview Mus. Arts and Sci., Neighborhood House Women's Aux.; active Girl Scouts U.S.A., Boy Scouts; mem. women's adv. bd. Peoria Jour. Star, 1975—. Mem. Am. Home Econs. Assn. (public relations com. 1968-70), Ill. Home Econs. Assn. (pres. 1970-71, newsletter editor), Peoria Area Home Econs. Club (past pres.), Peoria County Home Economists in Homemaking (past pres.), AAUW (coms.), Ill. Nutrition Com. (chmn. by-laws com. 1980), Nat. Home Fashion League, Elec. Women's Round Table, Internat. Fedn. Home Econs., Ill. Vocat. Home Econs. Tchrs. Assn., Four-H House Assn., U. Ill. Home Econs. Alumni Assn. (dist. dir. 1976—, pres. 1980-82), Phi Upsilon Omicron, Kappa Omicron Phi (Alpha Tau adv. and conclave mgr. 1980), Delta Kappa Gamma, Gamma Sigma Delta. Republican. Methodist. Home: 313 Glencrest Dr Peoria IL 61614 Office: Bradley U Room 208 Peoria IL 61625

CHURCH, IRENE ZABOLY, personnel services co. exec.; b. Cleve., Feb. 18, 1947; d. Bela Paul and Irene Elizabeth (Chandas) Zaboly; student public schs.; children—Irene Elizabeth, Elizabeth Anne. Personnel cons., Cleve., 1965; sec., Cleve., 1966-68; personnel cons., Cleve., 1968-70; owner, pres. Oxford Personnel, Euclid, Ohio, 1973—; v.p. Oxford Temps., Inc., Euclid, 1979-81, chmn. bd., 1981—; guest lectr. in field; lectr. on work and family life. Fund raiser Better Bus. Bur., 1973. Mem. Nat. Assn. Personnel Cons. (co-chmn. ethics com. 1977-78), Ohio Assn. Personnel Cons. (trustee 1975—, 1st v.p., chmn. bus. practices and ethics 1976-78), Greater Cleve. Assn. Personnel Cons. (1st v.p., chmn. bus. practices and ethics 1974-76, pres., recipient Vi Pender award 1976-77, adv., chmn. Vi Pender award 1977-78, chmn. award 1980, chmn. arbitration 1980—, chmn. fund raising 1980—), Euclid C. of C. Home: 8 Ridgecrest Dr Chagrin Falls OH 44022 Office: Oxford Personnel 711 Babbitt Rd Euclid OH 44123

CHURCH, MARTHA ELEANOR, coll. pres.; b. Pitts., Nov. 17, 1930; d. Walter Seward and Eleanor (Boyer) C.; B.A., Wellesley Coll., 1952; M.A., U. Pitts., 1954; Ph.D., U. Chgo., 1960; D.Sc. (hon.), Lake Erie

Coll., 1975; D.Litt. (hon.), Houghton Coll., 1980; L.H.D. (hon.), Queen's Coll., N.C., 1981, Ursinus Coll., 1981, St. Joseph Coll., 1982. Lectr. geography Mt. Mercy Coll. (now Carlow Coll.), Pitts., 1953; instr. geology and geography Mt. Holyoke Coll., South Hadley, Mass., 1953-57; lectr. geography Ind. U. Gary Center, 1958; instr., then asst. prof. geography, Wellesley Coll., 1960-65; dean coll., prof. geography Wilson Coll., 1965-71; assoc. exec. sec. Commn. Higher Edn., Middle States Assn. Colls and Secondary Schs., 1971-75; pres. Hood Coll., 1975—; dir. Farmers and Mechanics Nat. Bank; vice-chmn. Am. Council on Edn., 1978-79; cons. for Choice: Books for College Libraries; adv. bd. Project Noncollegiate-Sponsored Instruction, 1974-77, HEW Fund for Improvement of Postsecondary Edn., 1976-79; mem. Sec. Navy's Adv. Bd. on Edn. and Tng., 1976-81. Bd. dirs. Four-Year Servicemen's Opportunity Project, 1973-75; chmn. Md. state adv. com. U.S. Commn. on Civil Rights, 1981-82; bd. dirs. Nat. Center Higher Edn. Mgmt. Systems, 1980-84, Inst. Edn. Leadership, 1982—; trustee Bradford Coll., 1982—, Peddie Sch., 1982—; mem. Higher Edn. Colloquium, 1981—; Edn. Commn. of the States, 1981—. Recipient Christian R. and Mary F. Lindback Found. Disting. Teaching award Wilson Coll., 1971. Mem. Assn. Am. Colls. (steering com. baccalaureate degree project), Md. Ind. Coll. and Univ. Assn. (pres. 1979-81), Am. Assn. Higher Edn. (pres. 1980-81), Am. Assn. Advancement Humanities (dir. 1979-83), Council Internat. Exchange of Scholars, AAUW, Am. Conf. Acad. Deans (sec., editor 1969-71), Am. Home Econs. Assn. (public mem. council profl. devel. 1981-83), Council Protestant Colls. and Univs. (dir. 1969-71), Sigma Delta Epsilon. Clubs: Cosmopolitan, Mount Vernon. Author: The Spatial Organization of Electric Power Territories in Massachusetts, 1960; co-editor: A Basic Geographical Library: A Selected and Annotated Book List for American Colleges, 1966; cons. editor Change Mag., 1980—. Home: President's House Hood Coll Frederick MD 21701

CHURCH, OLIVE DOROTHY, educator; b. Fort Collins, Colo., Jan. 19, 1932; d. Roe B. and Violet (Auld) Vincent; B.S., Central Mo. U., 1959; M.S., Eastern N.Mex. U., 1969; Ph.D., U. N.D. 1973; m. S. L. Gehring, Nov. 10, 1973; children—Sherrill, Kimberly, Lori, Russell, Julia. Office mgr. Internat. Minerals and Chems., Midland, Tex., 1954-55; exec. sec. to pres. Graceland Coll., 1955-57; tchr., Kansas City, 1959-62, St. Mary's Acad., 1962-63, instr. bus. adminstrn. Southwest Coll., Hobbs, N.Mex., 1963-65; dir. intensive adult skills program N.Mex. Jr. Coll., Hobbs, 1969-71; dir. fed. project N.D. U., Grand Forks, 1971-73; coordinator bus. edn., Office Adminstrn. U. Wyo., Laramie, 1973-81; head dept. vocat. edn., 1981—, prof., 1981—. Named Tchr. of Yr., N.Mex., 1971. Mem. Adminstrn. Mgmt. Soc., NOW, Nat. Bus. Edn. Assn., Am. Vocat. Assn., Wyo. Vocat. Assn., Delta Pi Epsilon. Democrat. Author: (novel) A Time of Rebellion, 1968; Secretarial Services, 1978; Office Procedures, 1978; Interpersonal Communications, 1979; Shadow Mountain Lodge, 1979; Getting Involved with Business, 1981; Office Systems, 1981. Home: PO Box 3835 University Station Laramie WY 82071 Office: Dept Vocat Edn U Wyo Laramie WY 82071

CHURCH, ROBERTA, ret. govt. ofcl.; d. Robert R. Jr. and Sara (Johnson) Church; A.B., Northwestern U., 1935, M.A., 1937. Social worker Family and Child Welfare div. Chgo. Welfare Adminstrn., 1940-43, adoption div. Ill. Children's Home and Aid Soc., Chgo., 1943-53; cons. for minority groups U.S. Dept. Labor, 1953-61; cons. Rehab. Services Adminstrn., HEW, Washington, 1961-81, ret., 1981. Mem. Pres.'s Nat. Adv. Council on Adult Edn., 1970-75. Mem. Tenn. Republican Exec. Com., 1952-53. Recipient Certificate of Merit, Alpha Phi Alpha, 1956. Mem. AAUW, Nat. Assn. Social Workers, Delta Sigma Theta. Republican. Episcopalian. Co-author: The Robert R. Churches of Memphis. Home: 99 N Main St Memphis TN 38103

CHURCHILL, DOROTHY HELEN KING (MRS. WALTER AUGUSTUS CHURCHILL, SR.), supermarket chain exec.; b. Evansport, Ohio, Nov. 24, 1906; d. Edward Nicholas and Olide (Spangler) King; student Defiance Coll., 1924-25; m. Walter Augustus Churchill, June 9, 1928; children—Walter Augustus, Carolyn Ann Churchill Colwell. Sec.-treas. Churchill's Super Markets, Inc., Toledo, 1953—, Certified Leasing Co., Inc., Toledo, 1967—. Republican. Mem. Order Eastern Star. Home: 3007 Cheltenham Rd Toledo OH 43606 Office: 5700 Monroe St Toledo OH 43560

CHURCHVILLE, LIDA HOLLAND, librarian; b. Dallas, May 5, 1933; d. Norbert R. and Agnes J. (Buckley) Holland; B.A. in History, Russell Sage Coll., Troy, N.Y., 1965; M.L.S. (SUNY Library fellow 1966-67), SUNY, Albany, 1967; m. Joseph J. Churchville, Oct. 6, 1952 (dec. 1974); children—Lisa, Zoe, Stephen. Legis. libararian Office Legis. Research, N.Y. Senate, Albany, 1967-75; chief law library U.S. Army Library, Washington, 1975-78; coordinator fed. women's program Dept. Defence, The Pentagon, 1976-78; chief library Nat. Archives and Records Services, 1978-81; reference and spl. project librarian Nat. Archives Library, 1981—. Mem. Women's Issues Task Force, Women's Nat. Democratic Club, 1981-82. Recipient Outstanding Performance award The Pentagon, 1977. Mem. Am. Soc. Info. Sci., D.C. Library Assn., Law Librarians Soc. Washington, DC Online Users Group. Home: 905 6th St SW Washington DC 20024 Office: Room 302 Nat Archives Library 8th and Pennsylvania Ave NW Washington DC 20408

CHUSID, JUDITH FRANCINE, psychologist, psychoanalytic psychotherapist; b. N.Y.C., Dec. 3, 1947; d. Harry and Phyllis A. C.; B.A., Queens Coll., 1971; M.A., N.Y.U., 1974, A.B.D., 1981; P.D., St. John's U., 1978; grad. Manhattan Center for Psychoanalytic Studies. Program supr. East N.Y. YM-YWHA, 1970; tchr. Lexington Sch. for Deaf, N.Y.C. Bd. Edn., 1971-76; instr. Adelphi U., Garden City, N.Y., 1976-80; pvt. practice psychoanalytic psychotherapy, Jackson Heights and N.Y.C., 1974—; founder, pres., chmn. bd. Positive Approaches to Sports Success, Inc., Jackson Heights, 1980—; mem. teaching faculty, tng. analyst Rockland Inst. for Psychoanalysis and Psychotherapy, Suffern, N.Y.; condr. workshops, lectr. field sports psychology. Co-founder, Actor's Voice, N.Y.C., 1982. Recipient Otto Klitgord award N.Y., 1967; cert. sch. psychologist, N.Y. State. Mem. Am. Psychol. Assn., Nat. Accreditation Assn. Psychoanalysis (cert.), Council Exceptional Children, AAUP, N.Y. State Assn. Sch. Psychologists, N.Y. State Educators Deaf, N.Y. State Tchrs. Emotionally Disturbed. Contbr. articles to profl. jours. Home: 79-10 34th Ave Jackson Heights NY 11372

CHUTE, MARCHETTE, author; b. Wayzata, Minn., Aug. 16, 1909; d. William Young and Edith Mary (Pickburn) Chute; A.B., U. Minn., 1930; Litt.D., Western Coll. for Women, 1952, Carleton Coll., 1957, Dickinson Coll., 1964. Author: Rhymes About Ourselves, 1932; The Search for God, 1941; Rhymes About the Country, 1941; The Innocent Wayfaring, 1943; Geoffrey Chaucer of England, 1946; Rhymes About the City, 1946; The End of the Search, 1947; Shakespeare of London, 1950; An Introduction to Shakespeare, 1951; Ben Jonson of Westminster, 1953; The Wonderful Winter, 1954; Stories from Shakespeare, 1956; Around and About, 1957; Two Gentle Men: The Lives of George Herbert and Robert Herrick, 1959; Jesus of Israel, 1961; (with Ernestine Perrie) The Worlds of Shakespeare, 1963; The First Liberty: A History of the Right to Vote in America, 1619-1850, 1969; The Green Tree of Democracy, 1971; P.E.N. American Center: A History of the First Fifty Years, 1972; Rhymes About Us, 1974. Mem. exec. com. Nat. Book Com.; judge non-fiction Nat. Book Awards, 1952, 59. Recipient Author Meets the Critics award for best non-fiction of 1950; Chap-Book award Poetry Soc. Am., 1954; N.Y. Shakespeare Club award, 1954; Secondary Edn. Bd. book award, 1954; Oustanding Achievement award U. Minn., 1957. Fellow Royal Soc. Arts, Soc. Am. Historians; mem. Am. P.E.N. (pres. 1955-57), Am. Acad. Arts and Letters, Renaissance Soc. Am., Phi Beta Kappa. Home: 450 E 63d St New York NY 10021

CHUTIS, LAURIEANN LUCY, social worker; b. Detroit, Nov. 30, 1942; d. Paul J. and Helen Marie (Shilakes) C.; A.B., U. Mich., 1964, M.S.W., 1966. Community worker Tuskegee (Ala.) Inst., 1966; social worker Catholic Sch. Bd. Head Start, Chgo., 1966; community worker Cath. Charities, Chgo., 1966-70; asst. to dir. Ravenswood Hosp. Community Mental Health Center, Chgo., 1970-72, coordinator consultation and edn. dept., 1972, dir. consultation and edn. dept., 1972—; instr. Chgo. Bd. Edn., 1974—; guest lectr. various profl. assn. groups, 1975—; cons. NIMH, also various mental health centers, 1977—; pvt. practice individual group and family therapy; 1976—; region V coordinator Consultation-Edn. Conf., 1979-81; coordinator Nat. Consultation-Edn. Network, 1980—. Mem. Salvation Army Community Services Bd., 1978—. Mem. Nat. Assn. Social Work, Acad. Certified Social Work, World Fedn. Mental Health, Registry Clin. Social Workers, Nat. Council Community Mental Health Centers (council on Prevention 1976-79), Assn. Consultation-Edn. Service Providers (pres. 1978-79). Contbr. chpt. to To Your Good Health, 1980. Office: 4550 N Winchester Chicago IL 60640

CHVATAL, PATRICIA JOAN, lawyer; b. Walla Walla, Wash., July 6, 1950; d. Joseph J. and Mary R. (Doherty) C.; B.A. magna cum laude, Carroll Coll., 1972; J.D. cum laude, Gonzaga U., 1976. Admitted to Wash. bar., 1976; asso. firm Bennett and Carroll, Richland, Wash., 1976-78; jr. partner firm Bennett, Carroll and Chvatal, Richland, 1978-79; partner firm Carroll and Chvatal, Richland, 1979-81, Carroll, Chvatal and Heye, Richland, 1981—; lectr. seminars on law, State of Wash. Mem. Richland City Council Planning Commn.; bd. dirs. United Way, 1979-80, N.W. Women's Law Center, Seattle. Mem. Wash. State Bar Assn., Wash. Women Lawyers, Tri-City Women Lawyers (past pres.), AAUW, LWV, Cath. Daus. Am., Wash. Women United, Wash. Women's Polit. Caucus (pres. 1981), Altrusa. Democrat. Roman Catholic. Club: Bus. and Profl. Women's (pres. Richland chpt. 1977-79). Contbr. articles to legal jours. Home: 2120 Duportail Richland WA 99352 Office: PO Box 966 Richland WA 99352

CIANFARANI, CAROL MARGARET, real estate co. exec.; b. Cleve., May 4, 1945; d. Alfred George and Grace Gloria (Guzzo) C.; B.S. in Edn., Bowling Green State U., 1967; M.S. in Edn., Springfield (Mass.) Coll., 1974. Realtor asso. McCullough & Williams Realtors, Long Meadow, Mass., 1972-73; office mgr. Robert J. Davis Real Estate, East Longmeadow, Mass., 1973-75; officer mgr., dir. tng. George and Green Real Estate Co., Inc., Southwick, Mass., 1975-79; dir. personnel and edn. Whyte Co. Realtors, West Springfield, Mass., 1979-81; sales mgr. Boileau & Johnson, Inc., La Jolla, Calif., 1981—; seminar instr. U. Mass., Amherst, 1978-81; instr. Am. Internat. Coll., 1980-81. Mem. park and recreation commn. Town of Southwick, Mass., 1976-77. Mem. Greater Springfield Bd. Realtors (Realtor of Yr. 1980), Greater Westfield Bd. Realtors, San Diego Bd. Realtors, San Dieguito Bd. Realtors (program chmn.), Calif. Assn. Realtors, Mass. Assn. Realtors, Nat. Assn. Realtors, Internat. Platform Assn., Realtors Nat. Mktg. Inst. Home: 190 Del Mar Shores Terrace Apt 83 Solano Beach CA 92075

CIANI, SUZANNE ELIZABETH, composer; b. Ind., June 4, 1946; d. A. Walter and Ruth (Bowman) C.; B.A., Wellesley Coll., 1964-68; M. Mus., U. Calif., Berkeley, 1970; postgrad. Stanford U., 1969-70. Free-lance composer, performer, 1968-74; pres. Electronic Center for New Music, 1974-76: pres. Ciani/Musica Inc., N.Y.C., 1976—. Hertz fellow in music; Nat. Endowment of Arts composers grantee; Creative Artists Public Service grat. Mem. Audio Engring. Soc., ASCAP, Screen Actors Guild, AFTRA. Club: Wellesley. Albun: Seven Waves, 1981; composer music score Incredible Shrinking Woman, 1980. Office: 1650 Broadway New York NY 10019

CIENCIAIA, ANNA MARIA, educator; b. Gdansk, Poland, Nov. 8, 1929; d. Andrew M. and Wanda M. (Waissmann) C.; came to U.S., 1965, naturalized, 1970; B.A., U. Liverpool, 1952; M.A., McGill U., 1955; Ph.D., Ind. U., 1962. Lectr. European history U. Ottawa, 1960-61, U. Toronto (Ont., Can.), 1961-65; asst. prof. history U. Kans., Lawrence, 1965-67, asso. prof., 1967-71, prof. history and Soviet and Eastern European area studies, 1971—; cons. HEW, 1972. Recipient prize Pilsudski Inst. Am., 1968; Ford Found. fellow, 1958-60; Can. Council grantee, 1963; Fulbright-Hays fellow, 1968-69; U. Kans. gen. research grantee, 1965-75; Am. Council Learned Socs. grantee, 1980; Irex fellow, Poland, 1979-80. Mem. AAUP, AAUW, Am. Assn. Advancement Slavic Studies, Am. Hist. Assn., Kosciuszko Found., Pilsudski Inst. Am., Polish-Am. Inst. Arts and Scis., Polish-Am. Hist. Assn., Hist. Preservation. Author: Poland and the Western Powers, 1938-39, 1968; editor: (with A. Headlam-Morley and R. Bryant) A Memoir of the Paris Peace Conference 1919, 1972; American Contributions to the Seventh International Congress of Slavists, 1973; contbr. articles to profl. jours. Home: 3045 Steven Dr Lawrence KS 66044 Office: Dept History U Kans Lawrence KS 60045

CIESINSKI, KATHERINE, mezzo soprano; b. Newark, Del.; B.Mus., M.Mus., Temple U.; postgrad. Curtis Inst. of Music. European operatic and concert debut Internat. Festival, Aux-en-Provence, 1976; U.S. opera debuts include: Countess Geschwitz in Lulu, Santa Fe Opera, Siebel in Faust, Chgo. Opera 25th anniversary opening; other roles include Erika in Vanessa, Spoleto Festival U.S.A., 1978; concert debut with Phila. Orch., 1974, other performances: Acad. of Music, Ann Arbor, Mich., Saratoga Springs, Robin Hood Dell, performance with Phila. Orch. of Beethoven's Ninth Symphony. Second place winner Met. Opera Nat. Auditions, 1974; winner Auditions of the Air, Sta. WGN, Chgo., 1974, Sr. Student Auditions, Phila. Orch., 1974; winner first prize Geneva Internat. Competition, 1976, Concours Internat. de Chant de Paris, 1977.

CIFANI, ELIZABETH BURKE, harpist; b. Pensacola, Fla., July 22, 1944; d. James Edmund and Pearl Elizabeth (Brookfield) Burke; B.Mus., Northwestern U., 1967, M.Mus., 1968. Prin. harpist Lyric Opera Chgo., 1968—; co-founder Orch. Ill., Chgo., 1978, v.p., 1979-81; tchr. harp. Northwestern U., 1981—, No. Ill. U., 1981—. Mem. Am. Fedn. Musicians, Am. Symphony Orch. League.

CIMO, CORINNE J., controller, accountant; b. N.Y.C., July 13, 1930; d. Peter and Rose J. (Giorno) Caracaus; B.S. cum laude, Mercy Coll., 1978; A.A.S. with high honors, Elizabeth Seton Coll., 1977; m. Louis J. Cimo, Jan. 22, 1949; children—Kenneth, Karen, Lisa. Acctg. clk., exec. sec. Atwell Vogel & Sterling, Inc., 1969-73; adminstrv. asst. to pres. Combe Inc., White Plains, N.Y., 1973-77; Controller, acct. Human Relations Media, Inc., Pleasantville, N.Y., 1978—. N.Y.C. drama coach to underpriveleged, 1965-68; sec. to coordinator Little League Baseball, N.Y.C., 1966-67; N.Y.C. coordinator for Drug Abuse Confs., State Assembly, 1965-67. Recipient awards for public service, 1966-68. Mem. Nat. Assn. Female Execs., Nat. Assn. Female Accts. Democrat. Home: 68 Foxwood Dr Pleasantville NY 10570 Office: 175 Tompkins Ave Pleasantville NY 10570

CINTRON, MARLENE, lawyer; b. N.Y.C., Apr. 14, 1951; d. Lorenzo and Isabel (Ramos) C.; B.A., SUNY, Old Westbury, 1972; M.S., Fordham U., 1977; J.D., Georgetown U., 1980. With Model Cities, Bronx, N.Y., 1973-76, El Congreso, Washington, 1976-77; exec. dir. dist. office of Congressman U.S. Ho. Reps., Bronx, N.Y., 1980—. Mem. bd. East Harlem Music Sch. Nat. Hispanic Scholarship Fund scholar; Model Cities Acad. scholar; Aspira-Rockefeller fellow. Democrat. Mem. Pentecostal Ch. Office: 890 Grand Concourse Bronx NY 10451

CIOLLI, ANTOINETTE, librarian; b. N.Y.C., Aug. 20, 1915; d. Pietro and Mary (Palumbo) Ciolli; A.B., Bklyn. Coll., 1937, M.A., 1940; B.S. in L.S., Columbia U., 1943. Tchr. history and civics Bklyn. high schs., 1943-44; circulation librarian Bklyn. Coll. Library, 1944-46; instr. history Sch. Gen. Studies, Bklyn. Coll., 1944-50, asst. prof. library dept., 1965-72, asso. prof., 1973-81, prof. emerita, 1981—; reference librarian Bklyn. Coll. Library, 1947-59, chief sci. librarian, 1959-70, chief spl. collections div., 1970-81, hon. archivist, 1981—. Mem. ALA, Am. Hist. Assn., AAUP, Spl. Libraries Assn. (museum group chpt. sec. 1950-51, 52-54), N.Y. Library Club, Beta Phi Mu. Author: (with Alexander S. Preminger and Lillian Lester) Urban Educator: Harry D. Gideonse, Brooklyn College and the City University of New York, 1970. Contbr. articles to profl. jours. Home: 1129 Bay Ridge Pkwy Brooklyn NY 11228

CIOTOLA, LINDA ANN, mgmt. and fitness cons.; b. Balt., Sept. 17, 1947; d. Lawrence Andrew and Virginia (Wertley) Miller; B.A., Mt. St. Agnes Coll., 1969; M.Ed., Loyola Coll. of Balt., 1975; hon. broadcasting degree, Broadcasting Inst. Md., 1977; m. Joseph A. Ciotola, Jr., July 26, 1969; children—Joseph John, Alyson Marie. Tchr. English, public speaking Cath. High Sch., Balt., 1969-73; cons., editor textbooks, workbooks Local Union 24 Internat. Brotherhood Elec. Workers, Balt., 1973-75; tchr. English, Atholton High Sch., Howard County., Md., 1975-76; dir. activities and spl. events Villa Julie Coll., Stevenson, Md., 1976-79; cons., sec.-treas. Bus. Brokers Bldg. Maintenance & Mgmt., Inc., Ellicott City, Md., 1981—; founder The Fitness Movement, exercise studio, Balt. County, 1982—; instr. fitness Howard County YMCA, 1981-82; lectr. in field; faculty Broadcasting Inst. Md., 1976-77. Bd. dirs. Theatre Loyola Workshop, 1974-74, Theatre Incarnate, 1976—. Loyola Coll. grantee, 1974-75; Villa Julie Coll. grantee, 1977-78, 78-79. Mem. Nat. Wildlife Fedn., LWV, NOW, Nat. Assn. Female Execs., NEA, Nat. Assn. Coll. and Community Arts Adminstrn., Nat. Assn. Am. Coll. Unions, Nat. Assn. Philosophy of Edn., Sigma Phi Sigma. Address: 3986 View Top Rd Ellicott City MD 21043

CIRKER, BLANCHE, publisher; b. N.Y.C., Oct. 3, 1918; d. Frank and Tillie (Jager) Brodsky; B.A., Hunter Coll., 1939; M.S.W., U. Pa., 1941; m. Hayward Cirker, Aug. 11, 1939; children—Steven, Victoria. Family social worker intake office Jewish Child Care Assn., 1948-50; med. social worker Joint Disease Hosp., N.Y.C., 1950; book pub., 1950—; now v.p. Dover Publs., N.Y.C. Mem. Otto Rank Assn. (dir.). Author: Monograms and Alphabetic Devices, 1970; Dictionary of American Portraits, 1967; Golden Age of Poster, 1971; Book of Kells, 1982. Home: 199 Woodside Dr Hewlett Bay Park NY 11557 Office: Dover Publications 180 Varick St New York NY 10014

CIRUTI, JOAN ESTELLE, educator; b. Ponchatouia, La., Aug. 8, 1930; d. Joseph Aloysius and Olga (Jordan) Ciruti; B.A., Southeastern La. Coll., 1950; M.A., U. Okla., 1954; Ph.D., Tulane U., 1959. Instr. modern langs. U. Okla., Norman, 1957-59, asst. prof., 1959-63; research asst. U.S. Office Edn., Washington, 1959-60; asst. prof. Spanish, Mt. Holyoke Coll., South Hadley, Mass., 1963-66, asso. prof., 1966-71, chmn. dept. Spanish, 1965-71, prof., 1971—, now Helen Day Gould Found., dean of studies, 1971-74, chmn., dept. Spanish and Italian, 1975-81. Cons. Ednl. Testing Service, 1968-79. Named Distinguished Alumnus, Southeastern La. Coll., 1973. Mem. Am. Council on Teaching of Fgn. Langs., MLA (nomination, adv. com., 1962-64, nominating com. 1979-80, com. on acad. freedom 1980-83), Latin Am. Studies Assn. (mem. steering com. consortium Latin Am. studies programs 1969-72, com. on women 1973-74, nominating com. 1975), New Eng. MLA, Am. Assn. Tchrs. Spanish and Portuguese, New Eng. Council on Latin Am. Studies, AAUP, AAUW, Phi Sigma Iota, Sigma Delta Pi. Co-author: Modern Spanish, 2d edit., 1966; Continuing Spanish, 1967. Contbg. editor: Handbook of Latin-American Studies, vol. 28, 1966, vol. 30, 1968, vol. 32, 1970. Home: 21 Jewett Ln South Hadley MA 01075

CITRIN, JUDITH, painter, sculptor, counselor; b. Chgo., May 29, 1934; d. Harvey and Estelle (Lieberman) Goldfeder; student Art Inst. Chgo., 1943, 47-48, U. Ill., 1951-53, Am. Acad. Art, 1953-54, Adler Inst., 1975, C.G. Jung Center, 1979—, Esalen Inst., 1981; m. Phillip M. Citrin, Dec. 23, 1967; 1 son by previous marriage, Jeffrey Scott Levin. Asst. producer, researcher WTTW Channel 11, Chgo., 1963-68; free-lance interior designer, jewelry designer, fabricator, clothing designer, 1963—; freelance painter and sculptor, 1968—; cert. Reiki practitioner and transformational counselor, 1978—; group facilitator, tchr. Oasis Center, 1981—; facilitator Healing Circle; artist in residency Cultural Ministry, Marrakech, Morocco, 1979-80; works exhibited Musee des Oudaias, Rabat, Morocco, 1980, Art Inst. Chgo., 1973, 77, 81, Nat. Mus. Am. Art of Smithsonian Instn., 1982, Nat. Acad. Design, N.Y.C., 1982, Chgo. Cultural Center, 1979, Mus. Art of U. Okla., 1978. Ill. Arts Council grantee, 1977; Royal Air Maroc funding grantee, 1980-81. Mem. Assn. Holistic Health, Arts Club Chgo., Spiritual Emergency Network of Esalen Inst., Am. Reiki Assn., Artists Circle Chgo. Contbg. writer to Under the Sign of Pisces, 1972; contbg. artist to Black Maria, 1972; contbg. editor The New Art Examiner, 1978. Home: 423 Greenleaf Ave Wilmette IL 60091 Studio: 927 Noyes St Evanston IL 60201

CITRON, HELEN ROOME, librarian; b. Eden, N.Y., Oct. 21, 1941; d. Floyd Kenneth and Helen Elizabeth (Fuller) Roome; B.A., Fla. State U., 1963; M.A., Emory U., 1966; Ph.D., Ga. State U., 1980; 1 son from previous marriage—David. With Ga. Inst. Tech. Library, Atlanta, 1963—, head adminstrv. services, 1973-79, asso. dir. tech. services, 1979—; bd. dirs. Universal Serials and Book Exchange, Inc., 1972-83. Mem. ALA, Assn. Coll. and Research Libraries, Ga. Library Assn., Southeastern Library Assn., Nat. Micrographics Assn. Home: 2749-2 Briarcliff Rd NE Atlanta GA 30329 Office: Ga Inst Tech Library Atlanta GA 30332

CLABAU, LAUREL JANE, social worker; b. Havana, Cuba, Jan. 10, 1917; d. Clarence E. and Mina O. (Brown) Sample (parents Am. citizens); B.A., So. Meth. U., 1938; M.S.W., Our Lady of Lake U., 1969; cert. U. Tex., Austin, 1974, U. Tex., Arlington, 1972. Geol. sec. E. Allan Graham, Dallas, 1954-57; sec.-asst. Bernard Brister, Public Relations Cons., Dallas, 1957-67; with child welfare protective services Dept. Human Resources, Dallas, 1967-82, supr., 1970-72, instl. licensing rep., 1967-82; ret., 1982; group therapist State Mental Health Clinic, Dallas, 1969-71; lectr. in field. Recipient letter of commendation Office of Gov., Tex., 1976. Mem. Tex. Assn. for Services to Children (organizer meeting to honor social worker of yr. 1975), Acad. Cert. Social Workers, So. Regional Inst. of Nat. Assn. Social Workers, Zeta Phi Eta, Alpha Omicron Pi. Home: 6830 Merrilee Ln Dallas TX 75214 Office: 2727 Inwood Rd Dallas TX 75235

CLAGETT, VIRGINIA MARIE, mfg. co. exec.; b. Meza, Ariz., Aug. 3, 1938; d. Westall Irwin and Elna Jeanne (Smith) Harmon; B.A., U. Ariz., 1959. Engring. aide numerical analysis lab. U. Ariz., Tucson, 1959-61; systems analyst Gen. Electric Co., Phoenix, 1961-70; project leader Honeywell Info. Systems, Inc., Phoenix, 1970-73, project engr., 1973-78, mgr. comml. compiler, 1978-81, mgr. multi-environ. process control 1982—. Mem. Am. Bus. Women's Assn., Nat. Assn. Female Execs., Epsilon Sigma Alpha (pres. Ariz. council 1979-80). Republican. Episcopalian. Home: PO Box 3044 E Cannon Dr Phoenix AZ 85028 Office: PO Box 6000 Phoenix AZ 85005

CLAIR, CAROLYN GREEN, civic worker; b. Boston, Sept. 18, 1909; d. James Maddocks and Marietta Cecelia (Foeley) Green; B.S., Boston U., 1930, postgrad., 1933; m. Miles Nelson Clair, June 16, 1928; children—Cynthia York Clair Norkin, Valerie DeLuce Clair Stelling, Ardith Monroe Houghton. Translator, Am. Concrete Inst., Chgo., 1930-37; dir. Thompson & Lichtner Co. Inc., cons. engrs., 1960-78. Regent Mass. soc. D.A.R., 1933-35, state and nat. page Mass. soc., 1932-36; pres. Mass. soc. Children Am. Revolution, 1936-38, historian, 1937-39; v.p. Mass. chpt. Daus. Colonial Wars, 1969-71; active Salvation Army Aux., 1970—, v.p. thrift shop, Boston, 1970-72; active Asso. Country Women World, 1968—, lectr., 1972—, alt. to UN, 1974-77, rep. to UN, 1977—; mem. bd., service league, lying-in div. Boston Hosp. Women, 1966-76, treas., 1969-71, v.p., 1971-74, pres., 1974-76, trustee bd. overseers Boston Hosp. Women, 1974—; pres. New Eng. Farm Garden Assn., 1968-71; mem. bd. Boston Morning Musicales Tuft U., 1966—; mem. council Boston Symphony Orch., 1969—; pres. Woman's Nat. Farm Assn., 1972-74, chmn. adv. bd., 1974—; mem. corp. Affiliated Hosps. Center, Boston, 1975—; mem. adv. bd. Nat. Arboretum, Washington, 1974-80; exec. bd. Country Women's Council, 1972-74; v.p. Coll. Culb Boston, 1970—, Mass. Hort. Soc., 1970—. Recipient Brit. War Relief award, 1945. Mem. New Eng., Mass. hist. socs., Pam Am. Soc., Internat. Platform Assn., People to People, Boston Mus. Fine Arts, Internat. Womens Ednl. Indsl. Union, Audubon Soc., Nat. Wildlife Fedn., Friends of Libraries of Boston U., Nat. Trust Historic Preservation, Bostonian Soc., Arnold Arboretum. Republican. Episcopalian. Contbr. articles to Women's Farm Garden Assn. mags. Address: 17 Dorset Rd Waban MA 02168 also Cataumet MA 02534

CLAMAGE, SANDY, photographer; b. Chgo., Aug. 8, 1945; d. Robert and Elza Ann (Shapiro) C.; student Northwestern U., 1963-64, Laurence Merrick Studios, Hollywood, Calif., 1970-72, Los Angeles City Coll., 1975-76, Nikon Sch. Photography, 1976; 1 son, Eric Ray. Personal photographer to TV actor, Hollywood, Calif., 1975-76; ofcl. photographer Muscular Dystrophy Assn., Fresno, Calif., 1976-78; sports photographer All Am. Color, Culver City, Calif., spring 1979; sch. photographer Thompson Photography, Glendale, Calif., fall 1979; staff photographer San Fernando Valley Fair Housing Council, Van Nuys, Calif., 1980; free-lance photojournalist, 1979—; owner, mgr., photographer Reflections Photography, Burbank, Calif., 1979—; tchr. photography; cons. darkroom techniques.; exhibited works in Burbank Fine Arts Fedn. Multi-Media Exhibit, 1980; Central Library, Burbank, 1982. Recipient 3d Pl. award North Hollywood Arts and Crafts Show, 1977. Mem. Nat. Press Photographer's Assn. Home: 6617 Orange St #302 Los Angeles CA 90048 Office: 1736 N Buena Vista Burbank CA 91505

CLAMAR, APHRODITE J., psychologist; b. Hartford, Conn., Sept. 26, 1933; d. James John and Georgia (Panas) C.; B.A., CCNY, 1953; M.A., Columbia U., 1955; Ph.D., N.Y. U., 1978; m. Richard Cohen, June 24, 1973. Mgmt. cons., psychologist Milla Alihan Assos., N.Y.C., 1957-62; research psychologist, coordinator Inst. Devel. Studies, N.Y. Med. Coll., 1964; intern psychologist Bellevue Psychiat. Hosp., N.Y.C., 1964-66; asso. prof. Fashion Inst. Tech., 1966-69; supervising psychologist Lifeline Center for Child Devel., N.Y.C., 1966-67; chief psychologist Beth Israel Med. Center, N.Y.C., 1967-70; dir. community-sch. mental health programs Soundview Community Services, Albert Einstein Coll. Medicine, Yeshiva U., 1970-73; dir. treatment program for ct.-related children, dept. child psychiatry Harlem Hosp. Med. Center, 1973-76; mem. faculty dept. psychiatry Columbia U., 1973-76; pvt. practice psychotherapy, N.Y.C., 1976—; cons. public health and mental health agys. Fellow AAAS; mem. Am. Psychol. Assn. (chair com. for women, div. psychotherapy 1980-82), Eastern Psychol. Assn., N.J. Psychol. Assn., Soc. Clin. and Exptl. Hypnosis, Am. Acad. Psychotherapists, NOW, Assn. Women in Psychology. Democrat. Greek Orthodox. Author: (with Budd Hopkins) Missing Time, 1981; contbr. articles to profl. jours. Home: 162 E 80th St New York NY 10021 Office: 30 E 60th St New York NY 10022

CLANCE, PAULINE ROSE, educator; b. Welch, W.Va., Oct. 19, 1942; d. George W. and Gladys (Riley) Rose; B.S. cum laude Lynchburg Coll., 1960; M.S., U. Ky., 1964, Ph.D., 1969; m. Lanier Clance, Dec. 14, 1959. Clin. psychologist G.B. Dinmick Child Guidance Clinic, Lexington, Ky., 1965; psychologist Univ. Hosp. Cleve., 1966-68, Brecksville VA Hosp., 1969-71; clin. psychologist Psychol. Services, Oberlin Coll., 1971-74; asst. prof. Oberlin Coll., 1971-74; asso. prof. psychology Ga. State U., Atlanta, 1974—; pvt. practice clin. psychology, Atlanta, 1974—; cons. in field. Adv. bd. Odyssey Family Service, 1979—; mem. Com. on Minority and Poverty Groups, Coll. Entrance Examination Bd., 1972-75; peer reviewer grants nat. Endowment for Humanities, Washington, 1972—; reviewer curriculum materials Appalachian Center for Ednl. Equity, U. Tenn., 1978—. Oberlin Coll. leadership tng. grantee, 1973; Urban Life Center grantee, 1977; others. Mem. Southwestern Psychol. Assn. (pres. 1982-83), Am. Acad. Psychotherapists, AAUP, Assn. Women in Psychology, Am. Psychol. Assn. Co-author: The Teaching Sourcebook, 1980; contbr. articles to profl. jours. Office: Dept Psychology Ga State U Atlanta GA 30303

CLAPP, CYNTHIA LOUISE, nurse; b. Kankakee, Ill., May 5, 1949; d. LaVern Walter and Beverly Evon (Hills) Schwark; B.S. in Nursing, No. Ill. U., 1971; postgrad. in Bus., Kankakee Community Coll.; m. Larry J. Clapp, Aug. 21, 1971; children—Shawn Larry, Adam Joseph. Staff nurse, Riverside Hosp., Kankakee, Ill., 1971-72, edn. instr., 1972-74, coordinator nursing edn., 1974-76, asst. dir. nursing, 1976—; cons. area hosp. in devel. nursing quality assurance program. Mem. Nat. League Nursing. Lutheran. Club: Cabery Jr. Women's. Contbr. articles to profl. publs. in field. Home: Route 1 Cabery IL 60919 Office: Riverside Medical Center 350 N Wall St Kankakee IL 60901

CLAPP, MARILYNN PATRICIA, govt. ofcl.; b. Wallace, Idaho, Nov. 25, 1942; d. Louis E. and Margaret R. Clapp; B.A., Boise (Idaho) State U., 1979. Account clk. II, Idaho Auditors Office, 1966-68; with staff Payette Nat. Forest, McCall, Idaho, 1968-69; with IRS, 1969—, br. chief taxpayer service, Boise, 1975-78, sect. chief, also public affairs mgr., 1978—. Advisor The Women's Club Ltd. Recipient various govt. awards. Address: IRS Box 041 Boise ID 83724

CLAPPER, JEAN MONROE, artist; b. Phila., Oct. 14, 1926; d. Newton Elvin and Frances Eugenia (Monroe) Zartman; student Fleischer Art Inst., 1940-41, Dobbins Tech. Inst., 1941-43, Froman Sch. Art, 1964-75; m. Russel William Clapper, Feb. 17, 1945; children—Robert William, Douglas Neil. Artist helper Woodington Art Agy., Phila., 1942; auctioneer's clk. Roswell, N. Mex., 1954-63; nurse San Jacinto Hosp. Baytown, Tex., and Chambers Meml. Hosp., Anahuac, Tex., 1970-73; exhibited in one-person shows Nell Gallery, Baytown, 1972, Gates Gallery, Port Arthur, Tex., 1977, Simpatico Gallery, Houston, 1977; group shows Nell Gallery, 1971-78, Simpatico Gallery, 1976, NW Gallery, Houston, 1978; commns. include wildlife paintings Kelsey Seybold Clinics, Houston; represented in permanent collections; lectr. in field. Recipient purchase prize Tex. Rice Festival Art Show, 1973-74, 2d. place prize Baytown Civic Center Show, 1975, 2d. pl. prize SW Watercolor Soc., 1974. Home and Office: Box 1453 Anahuac TX 77514

CLARAMUNT, PATRICIA ANN, educator; b. Detroit, June 16, 1938; d. Joseph Dwino and Leona Rosalie (Machesky) C.; B.A., U. Detroit, 1963; M.Ed., Oakland U., 1976. Tchr., Fremont, Calif., 1963-66, Dearborn, Mich., 1969—; chmn. Dearborn Tchr. Center Policy Bd., 1977-79. Mem. Am. Fedn. Tchrs., NOW, Mich. Fedn. Tchrs., Internat. Reading Assn., Mich. Reading Assn., Wayne County Reading Assn., Dearborn Fedn. Tchrs. (v.p., chair polit. action com.), Nat. Women's Polit. Caucus, ACLU, Gray Panthers, Alpha Delta Kappa. Democrat.

CLARIDGE, LOIS WESSLUND, social worker, nurse; b. Paxton, Ill., Oct. 8, 1921; d. Anton Edgar and Ellen Esther (Pearson) Wesslund; B.S., Northwestern U., 1945; diploma in nursing Evanston (Ill.) Hosp., 1945; m. Samuel Ray Claridge, Oct. 8, 1948; children—Clifford, Lynne, Lois. Clin. instr. in med. and surg. nursing Evanston Hosp. Sch. Nursing and Northwestern U., 1945-46; office nurse Safford Clinic (Ariz.), 1946-50; cattle rancher Bonita Creek Ranch, Safford, 1949-72; sch. nurse Safford Schs., 1953-65; caseworker Ariz. Dept. Public Welfare, 1965-72, eligibility and payments supr., 1972—; office coordinator Ariz. Dept. Econ. Security, 1978—. Bd. dirs. Ariz. Eastern Seal Soc., 1955—; mem. Gov.'s Adv. Com. on Mental Health, 1963-65; vice chmn. Graham Greenlee Comprehensive Health Planning Council, 1974. Mem. Ariz. Nurses Assn., Am. Nurses Assn., Ariz. Cattle Growers Assn., Am. Nat. CowBelles (pres. 1962). Republican. Methodist. Home: 1507 W Relation St PO Box 388 Safford AZ 85546 Office: 106 8th Ave PO Box 1019 Safford AZ 85546

CLARK, ALICE BILLINGS THOMPSON, educator, coll. adminstr.; b. Preston, Idaho, Mar. 2, 1926; d. Melvin Billings and Hazel Kirk (Justesen) Thompson; B.S., U. Utah; M.S., Brigham Young U., 1960, Ph.D., 1965; children—Frederick Selby, Sherrie Ellen, Gordon Thomas, Terrence Andrew, Laurie Anne, Riley Gamet. Tchr., McKinley Sch., Salt Lake City, 1947-48, Arsonal Sch., New Brighton, Minn., 1948-49; instr. Brigham Young U., 1954-55; asst. prof. psychology U. N.D., 1965, then asso. prof., prof., to 1975, dean grad. sch., 1975-77, asst. v.p. academic affairs, 1977-80, v.p. acad. affairs, 1980—. NDEA fellow, 1962-65. Mem. Am. Psychol. Assn., N.D. Psychol. Assn., Midwest Psychol. Assn., AAUP, Nat. Assn. Retarded Children, Sigma Xi, Psi Chi, Phi Kappa Phi, Pi Lambda Theta, Alpha Phi. Republican. Mormon. Home: 622 23d Ave S Grand Forks ND 58201 Office: PO Box 8232 University Station University North Dakota Grand Forks ND 58202

CLARK, ANN HAMMOND, med. instrument co. exec.; b. San Francisco, Jan. 21, 1941; d. Howard and Elizabeth (Fallows) Hammond; A.B. in Biology, Stanford U., 1962; m. Phillip Wayne Clark, June 28, 1981. Laser researcher in ophthalmology N.Y. U. Med. Center, N.Y.C., 1964-66, S.R.I. Internat., Menlo Park, Calif., 1966-70; with Palo Alto Med. Clinic, 1970-74; exec. dir. Health Edn. Center, Palo Alto, Calif., 1974-79; product mgr. Spectra Physics, Inc., Mountain View, Calif., 1979-81; sales mgr. western region Cooper Med., Mountain View, 1981-82; area sales mgr. Xanar, Inc., 1982—; cons. in laser surgery, health edn., 1971-79. Recipient Citation for contributions to Patient and Health Care Edn. Am. Group Practice Assn., 1979. Mem. AAAS. Republican. Contbr. articles in field to profl. publs. Home: 2241 W Settlers Way The Woodlands TX 77380

CLARK, BETTY CAROL PACE, bank exec.; b. Bowling Green, Ky., Apr. 3, 1930; d. J. Fred and Alcie (Kinslow) Pace; B.S., U. Ky., 1952; postgrad. Program Bus. Adminstrn. Harvard-Radcliffe Coll., 1954; m. Robert O. Clark, Oct. 4, 1958; children—Fred Anson, Heather Pace. Sales exec. Hilton Hotels, N.Y.C., 1954-59; v.p. J.F. Pace Constrn. Co., Glasgow, Ky., 1960—; owner Glasgow Holiday Inn, 1966—; pres., chmn. Bank of Marrowbone, Ky., 1979—, also dir. Trustee, sec. bd. U. Ky., 1971—; bd. dirs. Ky. Bldg. Mus., Bowling Green. Mem. U. Ky. Alumni Assn. (dir., recipient Distinguished Service award 1976), Ky. Bankers Assn., Ky. Hotel Motel Assn., Ky. State C. of C. (dir. 1979—), Chi Omega (chpt. visitor 1952-54), Omicron Delta Kappa. Democrat. Presbyterian. Clubs: Glasgow Country, Spindletop, DAR. Home and Office: 111 Leech Ct Glasgow KY 42141

CLARK, BETTY JEAN, state legislator; b. Kansas City, Kans., Apr. 18, 1920; d. Raymond Carlisle and Mary Priscilla (Hunt) Walker; student Ft. Hays State U., 1937-38, U. Utah, 1939-40, U. Pacific, 1942-45, Garrett Evangelical Sem., 1948; m. Homer Orville Clark, Sept. 3, 1950; children—Peggy, Mark, Paul. Dir. student program Wesley Found., Ames, Iowa, 1948-51; dir. Christian edn. First United Meth. Ch., Mason City, Iowa, 1963-75; mem. Iowa Gen. Assembly, Des Moines, 1977—. Mem. Republican Women's Task Force. Mem. Bus. and Profl. Women, Women's Polit. Caucus, LWV, Fedn. Republican Women. Methodist. Clubs: P.E.O., Ch. Women United, United Meth. Women. Author: (with Harriet Ann Daffron) Nearer to Thee, 1956. Office: State Capitol Des Moines IA 50319

CLARK, CAROLYN CHAMBERS, nurse, educator; b. Superior, Wis., Mar. 25, 1941; d. John and Phyllis (Olsen) Stark; B.S. in Nursing, U. Wis., 1964; M.S. in Psychiat. Nursing (NIMH trainee 1964-66), Rutgers U., 1966; Ed.D. (NIMH trainee 1974-75), Columbia U., 1976. Psychiat. mental health nursing clinician N.Y. Med. Coll. Community Mental Health Center, 1966-71; psychiat. mental health nursing cons., individual and family therapist Nursing Service, Inc., Ridgewood, N.J., also Vis. Nurses No. Bergen County, Mahwah, N.J., 1971—; mem. faculty Bergen Community Coll., 1972-74, Pace U., 1976-78; ednl., mgmt., wellness and mental health cons., 1972—; founder, 1979, since dir. Wellness Inst., Sloatsburg, N.Y., also editor, pub. Wellness Newsletter. Author: Nursing Concepts and Processes, 1977, The Nurse as Group Leader, 1977, Mental Health Aspects of Community Health Nursing, 1978, Assertive Skills for Nurses, 1978, Classroom Skills for Nurse Educators, 1978, The Nurse as Continuing Educator, 1979, Enhancing Wellness: A Guide for Self-Care, 1981; co-author: Management in Nursing: A Vital Link in the Health Care System, 1979; contbr. articles to profl. publs. Address: 48 Johnsontown Rd Sloatsburg NY 10974

CLARK, CATHLEEN DIANE, bus. exec.; b. Houston, Aug. 8, 1945; d. Baron Cecil and Baroness Margo Von Hagen; B.S., U. Tex., 1968. Sales rep. Hendreks & Co., Houston, 1968; pres. Land Analysis and Investment Co., Houston, 1969-71; researcher Marney, Orton & Huitt, Houston, 1972-74; gen. mgr. Radio Paging, Inc., Houston, 1974-76; internat. sales rep. ITT, Houston, 1976-77; pres., chief exec. officer Galleria Secretariat, Inc., Corp. Group Internat., Houston. Mem. Nat. Assn. Female Execs. (dir.), Nat. Assn. Security Dealers, Houston Assn. Personnel Cons., Greater Houston Builders Assn., Nat. Assn. Personnel Cons., Houston C. of C., Galleria Bus. and Profl. Womens Assn. Episcopalian. Home: 5107 Del Monte St Apt 1 Houston TX 77056 Office: 3000 S Post Oak St Suite 100 Houston TX 77056

CLARK, CHARLENE KERNE, energy info. specialist, educator; b. Thibodaux, La., Apr. 15, 1947; d. Francis Lloyd and Ethel (Walker) Kerne; B.A., U. Southwestern La., 1969; M.A., U. Ark., 1970; Ph.D., La. State U., 1974; m. William B. Clark, Dec. 22, 1972; children—Mary Frances Lyons, Eleanor Kerne. Instr. in English, U. N.C., Greensboro, 1975-77; instr. bus. communication N.C. A&T State U., Greensboro, 1976-77; vis. asst. prof. English, Tex. A&M U., College Station, 1977-78; energy info. specialist Center Energy and Mineral Resources, Tex. A&M U., 1978—. Mem. Brazos County Humane Soc., Citizens Hist. Preservation, Internat. Assn. Bus. Communicators, Am. Bus. Women's Assn., Phi Kappa Phi. Roman Catholic. Home: 1009 Winter St Bryan TX 77801 Office: Tex A&M U College Station TX 77843

CLARK, DIANE CELESTE, health services adminstr.; b. July 20, 1949; B.S., Dallas Bapt. Coll., 1971; diploma Sch. of Perfusion, Tex. Heart Inst., 1972; postgrad. U. Houston at Clear Lake City, 1977—. Staff perfusionist, instr. Sch. Perfusion, Tex. Heart Inst., Houston, 1971-80, asso. dir. Sch. of Perfusion, 1973—. Recipient Polystan Edn. and Travel award, 1975. Cert. Am. Bd. Cardiovascular Perfusion (dir. 1975-80). Mem. Am. Soc. Extracorporeal Tech. (dir. 1975-76, mem. exec. bd. 1977-79, named Perfusionist of Yr. 1979), Am. Acad. Cardiovascular Perfusion (charter). Author: (with Charles C. Reed) Cardiopulmonary Perfusion, 1975; asso. editor Jour. Extracorporeal Tech., 1975-79. Contbr. articles to profl. jours.

CLARK, DOROTHY JEAN, child devel. specialist; b. Portsmouth, Ohio, Feb. 5, 1926; d. Carl and Marguerite Anna (Ressinger) Warner; B.S. in Edn., Wittenberg Coll., 1950; M.Ed., Bowling Green State U., 1979; m. Edward Clark, Dec. 21, 1946 (dec.); children—Dawn, Roy Hamilton II, Scott Timothy, Eric Edward. Elem. sch. tchr., Springfield, Ohio, 1950-51, Yellow Springs, Ohio, 1970-72; presch. tchr. Community Children's Center, Yellow Springs, 1953-54, 59-60, 68-70, Antioch Sch., Yellow Springs, 1964-67; dir. Head Start, Greene County, Ohio, 1972-81; child devel. dir. Wright Patterson AFB, Ohio, 1981—; instr. Antioch Coll., Sinclair Coll.; child devel. cons. Mem. Nat. Assn. Edn. of Young Children, Mil. Early Childhood Alliance, Nat. Assn. Female Execs., Sigma Alpha Iota. Unitarian. Home: 131 E Davis St Yellow Springs OH 45387 Office: 2750 ABW SSRC Wright Patterson Air Force Base OH 45433

CLARK, DOROTHY RODELLA, auto. dealership exec.; b. Elm Grove, W.Va., Apr. 2, 1926; d. S. Edward and Mary R. (Sheets) Lively, student public schs., Wheeling, W.Va.; m. Ivan G. Clark, Feb. 22, 1969; children—Cassandra, Victoria. Office mgr. Zeiss Motor Co., Sebring, Fla., 1955-68; dep. Highlands County Tag Agy., Sebring, 1969-72; title supr. Ross Backus Pontiac-Buick-Cadillac-GMC, Inc., Sebring, 1972—. Bd. dirs. Girl Scouts U.S.A., Sebring, 1956-76; chmn. Highlands County Sch. adv. commn., 1975-76; pres. Fla. PTA, 1956-57; life mem. VFW Nat. Children's Home. Recipient Heart of Fla. Girl Scout award, 1960; S.E. Youth Community Career Mother of Year, 1976; Youth Activities award VFW Aux., 1958, 60. Mem. Ladies Aux. VFW (pres. 1957-62, 74-77, dep. chief staff 1959-60). Democrat. Methodist. Home: PO Box 588 Sebring FL 33870 Office: Alt 27 S Sebring FL 33870

CLARK, EDYTHE SEYMOUR, club woman; b. N.Y.C., Oct. 12, 1903; d. Howard Gates and Maria Louise (Seymour) C.; student pub. and pvt. schs., N.Y.C. Joined DAR, 1941, treas. and regent N.Y.C. chpt., 1947-52, 64-67, v.p., 1967-70, pres., 1967-70, mem. nat. finance com., 1962-65, state treas., 1959-62; chaplain gen. New Eng. Women, 1972-75, v.p. gen., 1975-78, corr. sec., 1978—; treas. N.Y. State chpt. Daus. Colonial Wars, 1968-80; treas. Washington Hdqrs. Assn.; treas. Women Descs. Ancient and Honorable Arty. N.Y. State, 1974-80; treas. Sorosis, 1971-80, v.p., 1980-82; treas. N.Y. State Soc. Dames of Ct. of Honor. Pres., treas. ch. com. St. Lukes Hosp. Social Service; 25 yr. vol. worker St. Lukes Hosp. Episcopalian. Home: Hotel Surrey 20 E 76th St New York NY 10021

CLARK, ELOISE ELIZABETH, biologist; b. Grundy, Va., Jan. 20, 1931; d. J. Francis Emmett and Ava Clayton (Harris) C.; B.A., U. Va., 1951; Ph.D. in Zoology, U. N.C., 1958; D.Sc., King Coll., 1976; postdoctoral research Washington U., St. Louis, 1957-58, U. Calif., Berkeley, 1958-59. Research asst., then instr. U. N.C., 1952-55; instr. physiology Marine Biol. Lab., Woods Hole, Mass., summers 1958-62; mem. faculty Columbia U., 1958-69, asso. prof. biol. sci., 1966-69; with NSF, Washington, 1969—, head molecular biology, 1971-73, div. dir. biol. and med. scis., 1973-75, dep. asst. dir. biol., behavioral and social scis., 1975-76, asst. dir. biol., behavioral and social scis., 1976—. Mem. alumnae bd. Mary Washington Coll., U. Va., 1967-70; bd. regents Nat. Library of Medicine, 1975—; mem. policy group competitive grants program U.S. Dept. Agr.; mem. White House interdepartmental task force on women and interagy, 1978-80, task force for conf. on families, 1980; mem. com. on health and medicine, 1976-80; vice chmn. com. on food and renewable resources, 1977-80. Named Disting Alumnus, Mary Washington Coll., 1975; Wilson scholar, 1956; E.C. Drew scholar, 1956; USPHS postdoctoral fellow, 1957-59; recipient Disting. Service award NSF, 1978. Mem. Soc. Gen. Physiology (sec. 1965-67, council 1969-71), AAAS (council 1969-71, dir. 1978-82), Biophys. Soc. (council 1975-76), Am. Soc. Cell Biology (council 1972-75), Am. Inst. Biol. Scientists, Phi Beta Kappa, Sigma Xi. Contbr. articles to profl. jours. Home: 2450 Virginia Ave NW Washington DC 20037 Office: Nat Sci Found 1800 G St NW Washington DC 20550

CLARK, ELSIE SNYDER, educator, cons.; b. Portsmouth, Va., July 16, 1926; d. Francis Marion and Annie May (Irving) Snyder; B.A., Carson Newman Coll., 1949; M.Ed., Tex. Wesleyan Coll., 1965; m. Elijah Garland Clark, Aug. 4, 1946; children—Garland Bruce, Kenneth Wayne, Debbie Sue. Tchr. English, sch. librarian Keller (Tex.) Ind. Schs., 1956-57; serials and aquisitions librarian LTV Aerospace Co., Dallas, 1957-67; research librarian Tex. Instruments, Inc., Dallas, 1967-71; microfilm librarian Shop Rite Foods, Inc., Grand Prairie, Tex., 1972-74; librarian James A. Lewis Engring., Dallas, 1974-78; records adminstr. Delhi Internat. Oil Corp., Dallas, 1978-79; substitute tchr., records mgmt. cons., 1979—. Librarian Lamar Elem. Sch. PTA, Grand Prairie, 1959-61, v.p., 1961-62, program chmn., 1962-63; 1st v.p. membership Crow Elem. Sch. PTA, 1980-81; den mother Boy Scouts Am., Grand Prairie, 1958-66, recipient Den Mother's award, 1961. Named Tchr. of Yr., Keller High Sch., 1957, Den Mother's award Boy Scouts Am., 1961, Service award PTA, 1981. Mem. ALA, Spl. Libraries Assn., Nat. Assn. Female Execs., Am. Council on Alcohol Problems, Bible-A-Month Club, PTA (life). Baptist. Home and office: 2714 Roberts Circle Arlington TX 76010

CLARK, ESTHER FRANCES (MRS. JOHN H. CLARK, JR.), legal educator; b. Phila., Aug. 29, 1929; d. John and Lucy (Scapula) Giaccio; B.A., Temple U., 1950; J.D., Rutgers U., 1955; m. John H. Clark, Jr., June 12, 1954; 1 dau., Jacqueline. Admitted to Pa. bar, 1956, practiced in Chester, to 1976; prof. law Del. Law Sch., Widener U., Wilmington, 1976—. Mem. adv. bd. Project Prepare, Widener Coll., 1972—. Recipient Citizenship award Chester NAACP, 1973. Fellow Am. Bar Found.; mem. Am., Pa. (chmn. com. legal edn. and bar admission), Delaware County (pres. 1982) bar assns., Am. Trial Lawyers Assn., Delaware County Legal Assistance Assn. (dir. 1972-77, pres. bd. dirs. 1974-76). Club: Soroptimists. Roman Catholic. Asso. editor Rutgers U. Law Rev., 1954-55. Home: 207 Knoll Rd Wallingford PA 19086 Office: PO Box 7474 Wilmington DE 19803

CLARK, EVE VIVIENNE, educator; b. Surrey, U.K., July 26, 1942; came to U.S., 1967; d. Desmond Charles and Nancy (Aitken) Curme; M.A. with honors, U. Edinburgh, 1965; Ph.D. in Linguistics, 1969; m. Herbert H. Clark, July 21, 1967; 1 son, Damon A. Research asso. Lang. Universals project Stanford U., 1969-71, asst. prof. linguistics, 1971-77, asso. prof., 1977—; fellow Center for Advanced Study in the Behavioral Scis., 1979-80. Mem. Linguistic Soc. Am., Soc. Research in Child Devel., Internat. Assn. Study of Child Lang. Author: (with H.H. Clark) Psychology and Language, 1977; The Ontogenesis of Meaning, 1979; contbr. articles in field. Office: Department of Linguistics Stanford Univ Stanford CA 94305

CLARK, GEORGIA ANN MARIE, law librarian; b. Duluth, Minn., Sept. 19, 1942; d. George Oscar and Josephine (Scanlon) Berglund; B.S., Coll. St. Scholastica, Duluth, 1965; M.A. in L.S., U. Mich., 1965; m. George S. Clark, May 11, 1968. Circulation librarian, then serials librarian U. Mich. Law Library, 1965-73; asst. dir. law library Wayne State U., Detroit, 1973-75, dir., law librarian, 1975—; bd. dirs. Law Library Microform Consortium, 1977—. Mem. Am. Assn. Law Libraries, Mich. Assn. Law Libraries, Ohio Regional Assn. Law Librarians, Irish Setter Club Am., Irish Setter Club Mich. Republican. Roman Catholic. Office: 115 Law 468 W Ferry Mall Detroit MI 48202

CLARK, JANE COLBY, educator; b. Smith County, Kans., July 22, 1928; d. Noel Barclay and Velma Matilda (Helfinstine) Colby; B.S., Kans. State U., 1951; postgrad. Colo. State U., 1955-56, U. Colo., summers 1957-59; m. William Kline Clark, May 27, 1951; children—Courtney, Hilary. Tchr. rural sch., Smith County, 1946-47; sec., home service worker ARC, Boulder, Colo., 1952-55; tchr. public schs., Manhattan, Kans., 1956-59; temporary instr. in English, Kans. State U., 1968-74, instr., 1974—, asst. dir. writing lab. dept. English, 1974—; pvt. tchr. piano, 1944-45. Mem. Kans. Assn. Tchrs. English, Nat. Council Tchrs. English, Mortar Bd. Alumnae (pres. 1965-66), Delta Kappa Gamma. Methodist. Contbr. book revs. to newspaper, Manhattan Mercury. Home: 1801 Ranser Rd Manhattan KS 66502 Office: 102 Denison Hall Kans State U Manhattan KS 66506

CLARK, JANET H., state legislator; b. June 13, 1941; B.S. in Edn. and Music, Westminster Coll. Tchr. public schs.; owner, operator day care center; mem. Minn. Ho. of Reps., 1974—, vice-chairperson criminal justice com., mem. edn., energy, health and welfare coms. Mem. Democratic-Farmer-Labor Party. Office: 291 State Office Bldg Saint Paul MN 55155 *

CLARK, JANET MORRISSEY, polit. scientist, educator; b. Kansas City, Kans., June 5, 1940; d. Edward Francis and Mildred Lois (Mack) Morrissey; A.A., Kansas City Community Coll., 1960; A.B., George Washington U., 1962, M.A. (Wolcott fellow 1963-64), 1964; Ph.D. (NDEA fellow 1967-70), U. Ill., 1973; m. Caleb Morgan Clark, Sept. 28, 1968; children—Emily Claire, Grace Ellen, Evelyn Adair. Social sci. research analyst Dept. Labor, Washington, 1962-64; instr. social sci. Kansas City Community Coll., 1964-67; instr. polit. sci. Parkland Coll., Champaign, Ill., 1970-71; asst. prof. govt. N.Mex. State U., Las Cruces, 1971-75, asso. prof., 1975-81; asso. prof. polit. sci. U. Wyo., Laramie, 1981—. Recipient summer seminar stipend Nat. Endowment for Humanities, 1977. Mem. Am., Western polit. sci. assns., Western Social Sci. Assn., NEA, Phi Beta Kappa, Phi Kappa Phi, Beta Sigma Phi. Democrat. Lutheran. Contbr. articles in field. Home: 519 S 12th St Laramie WY 82070

CLARK, JANICE, educator; b. Chgo., Oct. 7, 1941; d. Okley and Bessie (Scruggs) C.; A.A.S., Meharry Med. Coll., 1963; B.S. (HEW grantee), Lindenwood Coll., 1978, M.S. in Health Care Adminstrn., 1980; children—Richard A. Franklin, Lea C. Franklin. Clin. dental hygienist Labor Health Inst., St. Louis, 1963-64, Med. Assos. Doctors Rogers Tanner & Kimbrough, Chgo., 1964-67; clin. instr. Forest Park Jr. Coll., 1969-76; clin. dental hygiene instr. in periodontics Washington U. Sch. Dental Medicine, 1976-81; asst. prof. dental hygiene Tex. Women's U., 1981—; mem. Gen. Assembly, Greater St. Louis Health Systems Agy., 1975-80; grantee U. Pa. Expanded Functions Dental Auxs. Faculty Inst., 1979; co-sponsor Dental Explorer Post, Boy Scouts Am. Mem. Am. Dental Hygienists' Assn., Sigma Phi Alpha. Mem. A.M.E. Ch. Office: Dental Hygiene Tex Women's U PO Box 22665 Denton TX 76204

CLARK, JANICE DIANNE, banker; b. Alexandria, La., Apr. 27, 1942; d. Gilbert Dupree and Lois Albiana (Peart) C.; student La. Banking Sch. for Supervisory Tng., 1974. With Security 1st Nat. Bank, Alexandria, La., 1959—, asst. ops. officer, 1974-77, asst. cashier, 1977—. Mem. Nat. Fedn. Bus. and Profl. Women, Alexandria Bus. and Profl. Women (1st v.p., membership chmn. 1976, pres. 1981-82), Nat. Assn. Female Execs., Nat. Assn. Bank Women (chmn. Cenla chpt. 1978-79). Democrat. Baptist. Home: Route 2 Box 266 Alexandria LA 71301

CLARK, JOAN M., ambassador; b. Ridgefield Park, N.J., Mar. 27, 1922; attended Katherine Gibbs Sch., N.Y.C. With Fgn. Service, Dept. State, 1945—, clk., then adminstrv. asst., Berlin, beginning in 1945; econ. asst., London, 1951-53; adminstrv. asst., Belgrade, 1953-57; placement officer Dept. State, beginning in 1957, adminstrv. officer, to 1962; adminstrv. officer, Luxembourg, 1962-68; coordinator adminstrv. tng. Dept. State Sch. Profl. Studies, 1962-68; personnel officer, then adminstrv. officer Bur. Inter-Am. Affairs, Dept. State, 1969-71; dep. exec. dir., then exec. dir. Bur. European Affairs, 1971-77; dir. Office Mgmt. Ops., Dept. State, 1977-79; AEP, Republica of Malta, 1979-81; dir. gen. Fgn. Service, Dept. State, 1981—. Address: Fgn Service Dept of State 2201 C St NW Washington DC 20520 *

CLARK, JOCELYN KAY COFFMAN, accountant, civic worker; b. Fairfield, Iowa, June 23, 1940; d. Harold Samuel and Wanneitta Mae (Fitch) Coffman; student pub. schs., Tucson; m. Donald Eugene Clark, Sept. 10, 1960; 1 dau., Renee Ann. With Sears, Roebuck and Co., 1958-62; dental asst., Tucson, 1963-70; staff acct., office mgr. Donald E. Clark, C.P.A., Tucson, 1978—. Past pres. Parent Tchr. Council, Gale Sch.; mem. Dist. 1 Adv. Bd. for Home Econs. Studies; bd. dirs. Pima County 4-H Leaders Assn., 1970-80, clothing dir., 1970-72, gen. home econs. dir., 1972-74, v.p., 1974-77, pres., 1977-80. Recipient Friend of 4-H award, 1975. Mem. C.P.A. Aux. (past pres.). Republican. Episcopalian. Home: 845 S Santa Ana Dr Tucson AZ 85710 Office: 40 N Swan St Suite 109 Tucson AZ 85711

CLARK, KAREN, state legislator; B.S. in Nursing, Coll. of St. Teresa, Winona, Minn., 1967. Staff Migrant Health Project, 1967-68; nurse-practitioner, Hennepin County (Minn.) Hosp. and Health Dept., 1973-80; mem. Minn. Ho. of Reps., St. Paul, 1980, mem. govtl. ops., health and welfare, local and urban affairs, regulated industries coms. Mem. Phillips Neighborhood Improvement Assn., Vista, Parent's Assistance Funds of Greater Mpls. Daycare, Coalition for Affordable Housing, Minn. Com. for Gay/Lesbian Rights, No. Sun Alliance, Democratic-Farmer-Labor Feminist Caucus, Farmer-Labor Assn., Hennepin County Women's Polit. Caucus, Am. Fed. State, County and Mcpl. Employees. Office: 255 State Office Bldg Saint Paul MN 55155

CLARK, LOUISE RHODES, educator; b. DeArmanville, Ala., Nov. 2, 1919; d. Henry Grady and Willie Elsie (Hewett) Rhodes; student U. Ala., 1937-40; B.S. in Home Econs., Jacksonville State U., 1958; M.A. in Home Econs., U. Ala., 1963, Ed.D. in Secondary Edn., 1968; m. Edward Wilson Clark, Jan. 23, 1941; children—Edward Wilson II, Robert Henry, Alan Benjamin. High sch. tchr. home econs., Jacksonville, Ala., 1958-66; prof. home econs., head dept. Jacksonville State U., 1967—; mem. com. for curriculum revision in home econs. Ala. State Dept. Edn., 1961; bd. advs. Seventeen Mag., 1962-64; mem. state com. to study home mgmt. residence in instns. higher learning Ala. State Dept. Edn., 1970-71; sec. Ala. State Nutrition Council, 1971-73; chmn. nutrition com. White House Conf. Aging, 1971; mem. home econs. adv. council Ala. Commn. Higher Edn., 1972-74; mem. com. for revision certification requirements vocat. tchrs. Ala. State Dept. Edn., 1971-73. Adv. bd. Faith Outreach for Christ, 1977-79. Mem. Am. Home Econs. Assn. (chmn. research com. 1974-76), Internat. Fedn. Home Econs. (Ala.-Tenn. rep. 1968-70), Future Homemakers Am. (hon. life), Ala. Vocat. Assn., Ala. Edn. Assn., Jacksonville State U. Alumni Assn. (life mem.), Alpha Eta Epsilon, Kappa Delta Pi, Delta Kappa Gamma, Phi Delta Kappa. Baptist. Club: Altrusa (Anniston, Ala.). Home: Route 1 Box 207 Jacksonville AL 36265 Office: Jacksonville State U Jacksonville AL 36265

CLARK, M. CORINNE, coll. dean; b. Ottawa, Ill., Sept. 28, 1923; d. Roger H. and Marcia (Brown) C.; B.S., Ill. State U., 1947; M.A., Columbia Tchrs. Coll., 1950; Dr. Phys. Edn., Ind. U., 1968. Tchr. phys. edn. secondary sch., East Peoria, Ill., 1947-49, West Aurora High Sch., Aurora, Ill., 1950-51; supr. student tchrs. elem. and secondary sch. Kans. State Tchrs. Coll., Pittsburg, 1951-54; dept. chmn. Maine Twp. High Schs., Des Plaines and Park Ridge, Ill., 1954-66; coordinator phys. edn. for women U. Wis., Whitewater, 1966-69, prof. phys. edn., 1969—, chmn. dept. health phys. edn. and recreation-women, 1969-75, chmn. dept. health, phys. edn. and recreation, 1975-82, asso. dean Coll. Edn., 1982—. Served with WAVES, 1943-46. Mem. Nat., Wis. edn. assns., Am., Midwest (sec.-treas. 1967-72; pres. 1973-74), Ill. (dist. pres.), Wis. (div. v.p. 1969-70), Midwest assns. health, phys. edn. and recreation, Sch. Health Assn., Nat., Midwest (pres. 1981-82) assns. phys. edn. for coll. women, Pi Lambda Theta, Tri-Sigma. Contbr. articles to profl. jours. Home: Route 4 Whitewater WI 53190

CLARK, MARIANNE J. M., trade assn. adminstr.; b. Clifton, N.J., Nov. 19, 1956; d. Michael and Marie (Scserbak) Marcisin; B.A., Bucknell U., 1977; m. Paul S. Clark, July 29, 1978. Permissions mgr. Charles Scribner's Sons, N.Y.C., 1978, subs. rights mgr., 1978-79; adminstr. Nat. Assn. MDS Service Co., Inc., Washington, 1979—. Mem. Am. Mgmt. Assn., Assn. Am. Publs. Home: 1600 S Joyce St C-1213 Arlington VA 22202 Office: 1629 K St NW Suite 520 Washington DC 20006

CLARK, MARIE TRAMONTANA, modeling agency exec.: b. Tampa, Fla., Apr. 21, 1940; d. Joseph S. and Nadean (Weeks) Tramontana; student U. Fla., 1958-59, U. Tampa, 1960-62; B.A., U. South Fla., 1976, B.A. in Bus. Adminstrn., 1980; m. Robert Julian Clark Jr., Jan. 28, 1961; children—Julie Ann, Robert Julian. Tchr. dance City of Tampa Recreation Dept., 1966-70; dir. Wendy Ward Modeling Sch., Montgomery Ward Co., Tampa, 1974-78; dir., owner T-Clark Modeling & Talent Agency, Lutz, Fla., 1978—. Named nat. sophisticate model of yr. Models Assn. Am., 1972. Mem. U. South Fla. Alumnae Assn., Mass Communication, Latin Am. Fiesta Assn. Democrat. Presbyterian. Clubs: Krewe of Venus, Carrollwood Swim and Tennis, Christian Women's Tampa, Tampa Jr. Women's (pres. 1969). Home and Office: 16350 Hanna Rd Lutz FL 33549

CLARK, MARY ALICE, nurse; b. Gouverneur, N.Y., Jan. 7, 1946; d. Reginald Bush and Betty Jane (Best) Smith; R.N., Royal Victoria Hosp., Montreal, 1966; B.S.P.A., St. Joseph's Coll., 1982; div.; children—Heather Elizabeth, Anthea Marie. Nurse Montreal Neurol. Inst., 1966-67; successively staff nurse, head nurse EEG nurse specialist, neurol. research U. Calif., Los Angeles, 1967-77; sr. research nurse in EEG/Epilepsy Lab., Wadsworth VA Hosp., 1978—; mem. profl. adv. bd. Calif. Epilepsy Soc., bd. dirs., 1981—; mem. steering com. State Implementation Task Force; nurse coordinator Internat. Symposium on Status Epilepticus, 1980; cons. Calif. Comprehensive Epilepsy Program, 1981—. Mem. Can. Nurses Assn., Royal Victoria Hosp. Alumnae Assn. Republican. Methodist. Club: Antelope Valley Corvette (sec. 1982—). Home: 38715 2d St E Palmdale CA 93550

CLARK, MARY HIGGINS, novelist. Founding v.p. Aerial Communications, N.Y.C., 1971—; author: Aspire to the Heavens, 1969; Where Are the Children, 1975; A Stranger is Watching, 1978; The Cradle Will Fall, 1980; editor: Best Post Stories, 1962, 63. Address: 2508 Cleveland Ave Washington Township NJ 07675 *

CLARK, MARY TWIBILL, philosopher; b. Phila., Oct. 23; d. Francis S. and Regina Holland (Twibill) C.; B.A., Manhattanville Coll., Purchase, N.Y., 1939; M.A., Fordham U., 1952, Ph.D., 1955; postdoctoral fellow Yale U., 1968-69; L.H.D. (hon.), Villanova (Pa.) U., 1977. Joined Soc. Sacred Heart, Roman Cath. Ch., 1939; tchr., supr. studies secondary schs. in N.Y. and Pa., 1941-5; mem. faculty Manhattanville Coll., 1951—, prof. philosophy, 1961—, chmn. dept., 1962-64, 66-68, 72-79; vis. prof. Villanova U., 1980, Fordham U., 1981; vis. prof. U. San Francisco Grad. Sch., summers 1964—; vis. prof. U. Santa Clara, 1983. Recipient Interracial Justice award, 1967. Mem. Am. Cath. Philos. Assn. (pres. 1976-77), Am. Philos. Assn. (chmn. conf. of chmn. 1974-76), Metaphys. Soc., Internat. and N. Am. Patristic Assn., Soc. Medieval and Renaissance Philosophy (sec.-treas. 1978—), Am. Maritain Assn. (v.p. 1981—), Conf. Philos. Socs. (exec. com. 1976—), Soc. Christian Philosophers (exec. com. 1981—), AAUW. Author: Augustine, Philosopher of Freedom, 1959; Logic, 1963; Discrimination Today, 1966; Augustinian Personalism, 1970; An Aquinas Reader, 1972; The Problem of Freedom, 1973; author introduction, translator: Theological Treatises of Marius Victorinus, 1981. Adv. bd. Dionysius, Logos. Address: Manhattanville Coll Purchase NY 10577

CLARK, MARY WILLIAMS, pediatric orthopaedic surgeon; b. Charlotte, Mich., July 30, 1942; d. Weldon Miles and Esther Alice (Richard) Williams; B.A. (Nat. Merit scholar), Swarthmore Coll., 1963; M.D., Yale U., 1967; m. Jeffrey Wayne Clark, Apr. 11, 1971 (dec.); 1 dau., Kathryn Williams. Intern, U. Pitts. Health Center Hosps., 1967-68, resident in gen. and orthopedic surgery, 1967-72, asst. prof. orthopedics and allied health professions, 1972-77; dir. rehab. unit Children's Hosp., New Orleans, also clin. asso. prof. orthopedics La. State U. and Tulane U., 1977-80; co-dir. Children's Rehab. Center of U. Va., also asso. prof. orthopaedics and pediatrics U. Va., 1980—; examiner Am. Bd. Orthopaedic Surgery; mem. med. adv. bd. Nat. Wheelchair Athletic Assn. Grantee Richard King Mellon Found. and Sarah Scaife Found., 1976, La. Planning Council on Devel. Disabilities, 1978-79. Fellow Am. Acad. Orthopaedic Surgeons; orthopaedic fellow Am. Acad. Pediatrics; mem. Am. Orthopaedic Soc. Sports Medicine, Am. Congress Rehab., Am. Spinal Injury Assn., Assn. Prosthetic and Orthotic Clinics (dir.), Pediatric Orthopedic Study Group, Am. Acad. Cerebral Palsy and Devel. Medicine, Rehab. Engring. Soc. N.Am., Am. Med. Women's Assn. Unitarian. Contbr. articles profl. jours., chpt. in book. Office: Children's Rehabilitation Center 2270 Ivy Rd Charlottesville VA 22901

CLARK, MAXINE, retail exec.; b. Miami, Fla., Mar. 6, 1949; d. Kenneth and Anne (Lerch) Kasselman; B.A. in Journalism, U. Ga., 1971. Exec. trainee Hecht Co., Washington, 1971, hosiery buyer, 1971-72, misses sportswear buyer, 1972-76; mgr. mdse. planning and research May Dept. Stores Co., St. Louis, 1976-78, dir. mdse. devel., 1978-80, v.p. mktg. and sales promotion Venture Stores div., 1980-81, sr. v.p. mktg. and sales promotion, 1981—. Sec., Lafayette Sq. Restoration Com., 1978-79. Mem. Nat. Assn. Female Execs., St. Louis Women's Commerce Assn., St. Louis Forum, Advt. Club St. Louis, Advt. Fedn. St. Louis. Home: 1912 Rutger St Saint Louis MO 63104 Office: 615 Northwest Plaza Saint Ann MO 63074

CLARK, MYRNA BAKER, ednl. adminstr.; b. Sturgis, S.D., July 25, 1937; d. Glenn Phillip and Holly Isabell (Howie) Baker; B.F.A. in Comml. Art and Edn., U. S.D., 1959; M.Ed. (Delta Kappa Gamma Scholar), Mont. State U., 1981; 1 son, Brooks. Art supr. West Sioux Community Schs., Hawarden, Iowa, 1959-61; sec. to dir. library services Rocky Mountain Coll., Billings, Mont., 1967-68; proof reader Vermillion (S.D.) Plain Talk, 1965-66; tchr. art Ross High Sch., Hamilton, Ohio, 1968-70; art cons. Sch. Dist. 2, Billings, 1970-80; art supr. Anchorage Sch. Dist., 1981—; art cons. State of Mont., also Mont. Migrant Workers Program. Bd. dirs. Midland Empire Council for Arts and Humanities; mem. steering com. Artrain, State of Alaska, 1981—. Delta Kappa Gamma scholar, 1979-80. Mem. Nat. Art Edn. Assn. (awards 1979, 80), Mont. Art Edn. Assn., Billings Art Assn., Mont. Inst. of Arts, Delta Kappa Gamma. Republican. Episcopalian. Clubs: Kappa Alpha Theta Alumnae (pres. 1976-78), Gourmet, Thread Benders. Home: 1790 Morningside Ct Anchorage AK 99501 Office: Dept Art Anchorage Sch Dist 5100 E 4th Ave Anchorage AK 99504

CLARK, NANCY DEANNA, oil co. exec.; b. Miami, Fla., Jan. 25, 1938; d. Michael and Ruth Burns; B.S. in Bus. Adminstrn., San Fernando Valley State Coll.; m. Don W. Clark, Oct. 13, 1962. Owner, operator Pacifica Realty Co.; owner Pacifica Oil Co., Tarzana, Calif., 1974—. Active Republican Party. Mem. Independent Producers Assn. Am. (dir.), Calif. Independent Producers Assn. Club: Toastmasters. Office: 18344 Oxnard St Tarzana CA 91356

CLARK, NANCY RANDALL, state senator; b. Portland, Maine, May 6, 1938; d. Willis Shaw and Marthajane (Lund) Randall; B.S., Husson Coll., 1962; M.Ed., U. Maine, Orono, 1968. Tchr. bus. edn. Scarborough High Sch., 1962-67, Freeport (Maine) High Sch., 1968—; mem. Maine Ho. of Reps., 1972-78; mem. Maine Senate, 1978—. Mem. exec. com. Muscular Dystrophy Assn. Maine; mem. exec. com., vice-chmn. Arthritis Found., Maine chpt.; bd. trustees Husson Coll., Freeport Conservation Trust; corporator Maine Savs. Bank. Recipient Vets. Service award Am. Legion Maine, 1978; named Outstanding Legislator, 1977, Woman of Year, Bus. and Profl. Women's Club, 1982. Mem. NEA, Nat. Order Women Legislators, League Women Voters, AAUW, Maine Tchrs. Assn. (past pres. 1974-75), Bus. Edn. Assn. Maine, New Eng. Bus. Educators Assn. Brunswick Bus. and Profl. Women's Club, Freeport Hist. Soc. Democrat. Congregationalist. Club: Order Eastern Star. Office: State House Sta 3 Senate Chamber Augusta ME 04333 also Holbrook St Freeport ME 04032

CLARK, PATRICIA ANNE, stockbroker; b. Trieste, Italy, Apr. 20, 1951; d. Robert Sterling and Pia (D'Auria) C. (parents Am. citizens); student Orange Coast Coll., 1969-72. Guide, hostess Disneyland, Anaheim, Calif., 1969-72; mgr. Architekton, Newport Beach, Calif., 1972-73; adminstrv. asst. KMA & Assos., Los Angeles, 1973-74; mgr. Petrick's Gallery, Newport Beach, Calif., 1974-75; v.p. Letterman Transaction Services, Inc., Irvine, Calif., 1976—. Bd. dirs. So. Calif. Counseling Center, Los Angeles. Cert. lay therapist, Ariz. Mem. Nat. Assn. Securities Dealers. Office: 19742 MacArthur Blvd Irvine CA 92715

CLARK, PETULA, singer; b. Epson, Surrey, nr. London, Nov. 15, 1934; d. Leslie Clark; m. Claude Wolff, 1961; children—Barbara Michele, Catherine Natalie, Patrick Philippe. Formerly child star in Eng., then in Europe; recs. in four langs., best known being Downtown (Grammy award 1964), also Don't Sleep in the Subway, Darlin', I Couldn't Live Without Your Love, My Love, A Sign of the Times, Round Every Corner, I Know A Place (Grammy award 1965); numerous concert, nightclub and TV appearances; appeared in motion pictures Finian's Rainbow, 1968, Goodbye, Mr. Chips, 1969; also appeared in 25 films in Eng.; star, theatre prodn. Sound of Music, London, 1981. Recipient France's Bravos du Music Hall award for outstanding woman in show bus., 1965, 2 Grammy awards, 10 Golden Discs. Address: care Internat Creative Mgmt Inc 22 Grafton St London W1 England *

CLARK, RUTH, personnel cons.; b. N.Y.C., Oct. 16, 1942; d. William B. and Pauline Cheek; student public schs.; div. Pres. Hour Power Temporary Agy., N.Y.C., 1972-74, Clark Unlimited Personnel, Inc., N.Y.C., 1974—, Clark Unlimited Placement, Inc., 1977—; franchised agt. Cup Stars, Inc., talent agy., 1977; seminar leader, 1979—. Bd. dirs. Nat. March of Dimes, 1980—. Recipient Role Model award New Future Found., 1979, Bus. Achievement award Black Action Retail Group, 1979; named Bus. Woman of Yr., Laurelton Club, Nat. Assn. Negro Bus. and Profl. Women's Clubs, 1978. Mem. Nat. Assn. Temporary Services, N.Y. Assn. Temporary Services (dir.), Women's Forum. Office: 527 Madison Ave New York NY 10022

CLARK, SHARON ANN, univ. pub. affairs adminstr.; b. Toledo, Jan. 14, 1939; d. Stanley Joseph and Anna Dorothy (Zulka) Gosik; B.A., U. Miami, 1974; m. John H. Clark, Aug. 23, 1961 (div. 1968); 1 dau., Tania Elizabeth. Staff writer U. Miami (Fla.), 1970-79; dir. News Bur., U. Miami, 1979-82, assoc. dir. pub. affairs, 1982—. Trustee, Dade Heritage Trust, 1979—. Mem. Women in Communication, Public Relations Soc. Am., Beaux Arts. Roman Catholic. Club: Zonta. Home: 4712 SW 67th Ave Miami FL 33155 Office: PO Box 248105 Coral Gables FL 33124

CLARK, SHERYL MARIE, nurse practioner; b. Dallas, Nov. 12, 1944; d. William Stanford and Thelma Marie (Johnson) C.; B.S. in Nursing, U. Colo., 1967. Office nurse, supr. Dr. S.E. Wood, Charleston, S.C., 1970-72; staff nurse VA Hosp., Charleston, S.C., VA Hosp., Long Beach, Calif., 1972-73; family nurse practitioner Family Health Program, Long Beach, Calif., 1973-78; research nurse practitioner U. Calif., Irvine, 1978-79; mgr. health services Martin-Marietta Aluminum Corp., Torrance, Calif., 1979-81; mgr. health services TRW, Redondo Beach, Calif., 1981—. Served with USNR, 1967-70. Mem. Calif. Nurses Assn. (chairperson interregional standing com. nurse practitioners), Am. Nurses Assn., Am. Public Health Assn., Nat. Assn. Exec. Females, Am. Assn. Occupational Health Nurses, Harbor Area Assn. Occupational Health Nurses. Republican. Home: 17701 Avalon Blvd Apt 146 Carson CA 90746 Office: One Space Park S/1459 Redondo Beach CA 90278

CLARK, SUSAN ATKINSON, social worker, educator; b. Paterson, N.J., Jan. 28, 1942; d. Edward Francis and Evelyn (Moore) Atkinson; student Fairleigh Dickinson U., 1959-61; B.A., Hope Coll., 1963; M.S.W., U. Conn., 1965; postgrad. Boston U.; M.B.A., U. New Haven, 1982; m. Albert Miles Clark III, Aug. 24, 1968; children—David Miles, Albert Miles IV, Jonathan Edward. Psychiat. social worker Mendocino (Calif.) State Hosp., 1963; program dir. West Haven (Conn.) Community House, 1963-70; asst. prof. edn. So. Conn. State Coll., New Haven, 1970-72, asst. prof. social work, 1972—, also chmn. admissions div. of social work, dir. field edn. Chairperson allocations com. United Way of New Haven; bd. dirs. YMCA Camp Hazen, Health Systems Agy.; v.p. Eastern Seal Goodwill Rehab. Center Aux. Bd.; sec. bd. dirs. West Haven Community House, 1971-78; mem. Human Service Com., Town of Orange, 1978—; bd. dirs. Met. New Haven YMCA, 1974-77, Orange Community Nursery Sch.; mem. Orange Public Health Nursing Bd., 1971-77; mem. Gov.'s Adv. Council for New Haven Regional Center, 1974—; chmn. Orange Youth Service Com., 1975-81; chairperson Long Range Planning Com., Town of Orange; mem. adv. bd. R.E.S.P.O.N.D., New Haven Cerebral Palsy Assn., 1978-79. Mem. Nat. Assn. Clin. Social Workers, Nat. Assn. Social Work, Acad. Certified Social Workers, Council of Social Work Edn., AAUP, AAUW (v.p. Milford-Orange br. 1974-77). Republican. Mem. United Churches of Christ. Home: 580 Orange Center Rd Orange CT 06477 Office: 501 Crescent Ave New Haven CT 06515

CLARK, WYNONA GARRETT, mfg. co. exec.; b. Lewisburg, Tenn., Nov. 10, 1927; d. Connie Clayton and Ola Luna (Bryant) Garrett; student public schs., Marshall County, Tenn.; m. Wilburn Eugene Clark, Dec. 16, 1950; children—Deborah Kay, Delores Fay. Sec., Jimmy Joe Murray, Murray Farm, Tenn., 1945; sec. Tenn. Walking Horse Mag., 1945-46, sta. WJJM-AM, 1946-57, commentator Listen Ladies, 1948-57; sec. Cathey Furniture Mfg. Co., Lewisburg, 1957—, sec.-treas., 1963—, also dir.; corr. Nashville Banner, 1955-76, Daily Herald Columbia, 1955-65. Chmn. publicity United Givers Fund, 1964-65; tchr. Sunday sch. Ch. of Christ, 1965—. Democrat. Clubs: Pilot (v.p. 1977-78, pres. 1978-79, dir. 1977-80), Lewisburg Music (project chmn. 1978-79), Marshall County Woman's (v.p. 1971-72). Home: Rt 2 Lewisburg TN 37091 Office: Box 12 Lewisburg TN 37091

CLARK-BOURNE, KATHRYN, diplomat; b. Fort Collins, Colo., Oct. 15, 1924; d. Andrew Giles and Orpha Mae (Spielman) Clark; student (scholar) Colo. State U., 1942; B.A., U. Wash., 1947; M.A., U. Minn., 1950. Intelligence research analyst Dept. State, Washington, 1952-56; polit. officer Am. embassy, Teheran, Iran, 1956-58; consul U.S. consulate gen., Rotterdam, Netherlands, 1960-62, Bombay, India, 1962-67; dep. dir. Office Fisheries Affairs, Washington, 1975-77; counselor polit. affairs Am. embassy, Lagos, Nigeria, 1977-80; dep. dir. Office West African Affairs, Washington, 1980-82; dep. chief mission Am. embassy, Conakry, Guinea, 1982—; supr. Coopers & Lybrand, N.Y.C., 1969-74; cons. George B. Buck, Inc., N.Y.C., 1974-75. Mem. State Dept. Commn. and Tenure Bd., 1982. Mem. Am. Fgn. Service Assn., NOW, Kappa Alpha Theta, Sigma Delta Chi, Theta Sigma Phi, Kappa Tau Alpha. Home and Office: American Embassy Conakry Guinea

CLARKE, CAROL SUE, psychologist; b. Washington, Dec. 25, 1946; d. Denzil Cope and Frances Louise (Hall) Bywaters; A.A.S., No. Va. Community Coll., 1972; B.A., Calif. State U., Los Angeles, 1974, M.A., 1976; Ph.D., U. So. Calif., 1978; m. Thomas D. Clarke, Dec. 18, 1971. Various secretarial and adminstrv. positions, Washington, 1964-71; counselor Am. Inst. Family Relations, Los Angeles, 1978-79; psychotherapist and seminar leader Transactional Analysis Inst. San Fernando Valley, 1978—; pres., chief exec. officer Assn. Women in Psychology, Counseling and Edn., Glendale, Calif., 1980—; instr. U. La Verne. Mem. Glendale C. of C., Am. Psychol. Assn., Calif. Psychol. Assn., Nat. Bus. and Profl. Women's Assn., ASTD, Am. Personnel and Guidance Assn. Office: 611A E Glenoaks Blvd Glendale CA 91207

CLARKE, CORDELIA KAY KNIGHT MAZUY, ins. co. exec.; b. Springfield, Mo., Nov. 22, 1938; d. William Horace and Charline (Bentley) Knight; A.B. with honors in English, U. N.C., 1960; M.S. in Stats., N.C. State U., 1962; m. Logan Clarke, Jr., July 22, 1978; children by previous marriage—Katharine Michelle Mazuy, Christopher Knight Mazuy. Statistician, Research Triangle Inst., Durham, N.C., 1960-63; statis. cons. Arthur D. Little, Inc., Cambridge, Mass., 1963-67; mktg. research project mgr. Polaroid Corp., Cambridge, 1967, dir. mktg. research, 1968-69, mgr. mktg. planning and analysis, 1969-70; dir. mktg. and bus. planning Transaction Tech. Inc., Cambridge, 1970-72; pres. Mazuy Assos., Boston, 1972-73; v.p. Nat. Shawmut Bank, Boston, 1973-74; sr. v.p., dir. mktg. Shawmut Corp., 1974-78; sr. v.p., dir. retail banking Shawmut Bank, 1976-78; v.p. corp. devel. Arthur D. Little, Inc., 1978-79; v.p. Conn. Gen. Life Ins. Co., 1979—; dir. McGraw-Hill, Blue Shield Mass., 1976-79; tchr. Amos Tuck Grad. Sch. Bus., 1964-65; mem. faculty Williams Sch. Banking, 1975-78; exec.-in-residence Wheaton Coll., 1978; vis. prof. Simmons Grad. Sch. Mgmt., 1978; mem. corp. adv. bd. Hartford Nat. Bank & Trust Co., 1980—. Trustee Aeroflex Found., 1973—; mem. Mass. Gov.'s Commn. on Status of Women, 1977-79; mem. doctoral adv. com. Boston U. Sch. Mgmt.; mem. bus. adv. bd. Boston Mayor's Office Cultural Affairs, 1977-79; mem. adv. com. Bur. Census; exec. in residence Amos Tuck Grad. Sch., Dartmouth Coll., 1978, now bd. overseers; corporator Babson Coll., 1977-81; bd. dirs. Greater Hartford Arts Council, 1979—, Inst. Criminal and Social Justice. Children's Mus. Hartford, 1980—; corporator Inst. of Living, 1981—, Hartford Hosp., 1981—. Recipient Women '76 award Boston YWCA, 1976; Disting. Alumni award U.N.C., 1982. Mem. Am. Mktg. Assn., Phi Beta Kappa, Phi Kappa Phi, Kappa Alpha Theta. Columnist, Am. Banker, 1976-78. Home: 31 Main St Farmington CT 06032 Office: Conn Gen Life Ins Co Hartford CT 06152

CLARKE, FRANCES MARGUERITE, psychologist; b. Lorain County, Ohio, Nov. 11, 1905; d. Carl Thomson and Miriam E. (Price) C.; A.B., Barnard Coll., 1924; A.M., Columbia U., 1925, Ph.D., 1928; postgrad. Yale U., 1931-33; grad. U. Balt. Law Sch., 1953. Practice psychology, New London, Conn., 1931-36, Towson, Md., 1950-60; faculty U. Md. overseas and Western Md. Coll., Westminster; admitted to Md. bar, 1954. Fellow Am. Psychol. Assn.; mem. Conn., Md. psychol. assns., Internat. Applied Psychotherapists, Soc. Mayflower Descs. in Conn., Md. Bar Assn., Women's Bar Assn. Md. Home: 506 Locksley Rd Towson MD 21204

CLARKE, GRETA FIELDS, dermatologist; b. Detroit; d. George William and Willa (Wright) Fields; B.A., U. Mich., 1962; M.D., Howard U., 1967; m. Robert Mines, May 6, 1979; 1 son, Richard Clement Clarke. Resident in dermatology N.Y. U., 1969-72, clin. instr., 1972-77; practice medicine specializing in dermatology, N.Y.C., 1972-66; dermatologist Arlington Med. Group, Oakland, Calif., 1977-79; practice medicine specializing in dermatology, Berkeley, Calif., 1979—. Diplomate Am. Bd. Dermatology. Mem. Women of Nat. Med. Assn. (pres.), Golden State Med. Assn., Am. Acad. Dermatology, San Francisco Dermatol. Club: Jack and Jill Am. Office: 2500 Milvia St Berkeley CA 94704 *

CLARKE, JEANNE CAROL, sales exec.; b. Rochester, N.Y., May 27, 1945; d. Harold Miller and Katherine Carol (Nowack) Kentner; B.S. in Bus. Mgmt., Rochester Inst. Tech., 1966; m. Joel Edgar Clarke, Feb. 12, 1966; children—Amy Carol, Bryan Joel. With Coppercraft Guild by Castlebleu, 1969—, North Deighton, Mass., dist. mgr., 1973-76, regional mgr., 1976-79, area mgr., 1979-81, field v.p., Waukesha, Wis., 1981—. Mem. Alpha Sigma Alpha. Republican. Presbyterian. Home: 19695 Timberline Dr Waukesha WI 53186

CLARKE, KIT HANSEN, radiologist; b. Louisville, May 24, 1944; d. Hans Peter and Katie (Jones) Hansen; A.B., Randolph-Macon Woman's Coll., 1966; M.D., U. Louisville, 1969; m. Dr. John M. Clarke, Feb. 14, 1976; children—Brett Bonnett, Blair Hansen, Brandon Chamberlain; stepchildren—Gray Campbell, Jeffrey William John M. Intern, Louisville Gen. Hosp., 1969-70; resident in internal medicine and radiology U. Tenn., Knoxville, 1970-73; resident in radiology U.S. Fla., Tampa, 1973-74; staff radiologist, chief spl. procedures Palms of Pasadena, Lake Seminole hosps., St. Petersburg, Fla., 1974—. Active Fla. Competitive Swim Assn. of AAU. Diplomate Am. Bd. Radiology. Fellow Am. Coll. Radiology; mem. Fla. West Coast Radiology Soc., Radiol. Soc. N.Am., AMA, Fla. Med. Assn., Pinellas County Med. Soc., Fla. Radiology Soc. Episcopalian. Home: 7171 9th St S Saint Petersburg FL 33705 Office: 1609 Pasadena Ave S Saint Petersburg FL 33707

CLARKE, MARY ELIZABETH, ret. army officer; b. Rochester, N.Y., Dec. 3, 1924; d. James M. and Lillian E. (Young) Kennedy; student U. Md., 1962; D.Mil.Sci., Norwich U., Northfield, Vt., 1978. Joined U.S. Army as pvt., 1945, advanced through grades to maj. gen., 1978; exec. asst. to Chief of Plans and Policies, Office of Econ. Opportunity, 1966-67; comdr. WAC Tng. Bn., 1967-68; office dep. chief of staff for personnel, 1968-71; WAC staff adviser 6th Army, 1971-72; comdr., comdt. U.S. Women's Army Corps Center and Sch., 1972-74; chief WAC Adv. Office, U.S. Army Mil. Personnel Center, Washington, 1974-75, dir. Women's Army Corps, Washington, 1975-78; comdr. U.S. Army Mil. Police and Chem. Sch. Tng. Center, Ft. McClellan, Ala., 1978-80; dir. human resources devel. Office of Dep. Chief of Staff for Personnel, Washington, 1980-81, ret.,1981; hon. prof. mil. sci. Jacksonville (Ala.) State U., Decorated D.S.M. Mem. Assn. of U.S. Army, WAC Assn., WAC Mus. Found., Bus. and Profl. Women's Club. Address: 80 Fairway Dr Jacksonville AL 36265

CLARKE, MARY WHATLEY, writer; b. Palo Pinto, Tex., June 11, 1899; d. Cephas Vachel and Narcie Isabella (Abernathy) Whatley; student N.Mex. State Normal Sch., 1925; m. James Coltman Dunbar, Oct. 27, 1920 (dec. 1923); 1 dau., Mary Murray Dunbar Harper; m. 2d, Joe A. Clarke, Nov. 15, 1941 (dec. 1971). Owner, pub. Norwood (Man.) Press, 1924-26; advt. dept. Hudson's Bay Co., Winnipeg, Can., 1926-27; advt. mgr. Mineral Wells (Tex.) Daily Index, 1928-33, Breckenridge (Tex.) Am., 1939; pub. Palo Pinto (Tex.) County Star, 1933-44; writer; books include: The Palo Pinto Story, 1957; Life in the Saddle, 1963; David G. Burnet, First President of Texas Republic, 1969; Thomas J. Rusk: Soldier, Statesman, Patriot, 1971; Chief Bowles and the Texas Cherokees, 1971; The Swenson Saga and SMS Ranches, 1976; A Century of Cow Business, 1976; The Slaughter Ranches and Their Makers, 1979; contbr. numerous stories and articles to the Cattleman. Woman's bd. Ft. Worth Children's Hosp., pres., 1955-56. Mem. Lecture Found., Tarrant County Hist. Soc. (past pres., award), W. Tex. Press Assn. Republican. Presbyterian. Club: Ft. Worth Woman's. Home: 3605 Bellaire Dr S Fort Worth TX 76109

CLARKE, URANA, writer, amateur astronomer, music educator; b. Wickliffe-on-the-Lake, Ohio, Sept. 8, 1902; d. Graham Warren and Grace Urana (Olsaver) Clarke; artists and tchrs., diploma Mannes Music Sch., N.Y.C., 1925; Dalcroze cert. Sch. Music, N.Y.C., 1950; passed navigators exam. U.S. Power Squadron, 1943; student Pembroke Coll., Brown U.; B.S., Mont. State U., 1967, M.S., 1970. Mem. faculty Mannes Music Sch., 1922-49, Dalcroze Sch. Music, 1949-54; adv. editor in music The Book of Knowledge, 1949-61; v.p., dir. Saugatuck Circle Housing Devel., 1950-58; host Skies over the Big Sky Country, daily radio astronomy show, 1964-79, weekly radio programs Birds of Big Sky Country, 1972-79, Great Music of Religion, 1974-79; writing monthly astron. forecast; instr. continuing edn. Mont. State U.; guest lectr. celestial navigation, nautical astronomy, Hayden Planetarium, 1945; guest lectr. Roger Williams Planetarium, Providence, 1959-63. Adv. com. Nat. Rivers and Harbors Congresses, 1947-58; co-chmn. Barrington Town Blood Assurance Program, 1960-64; chmn. Park County chpt. ARC, 1965—, co-chmn. blood program, 1965—, 1st aid instr., 1941—, Red Cross first aid instr. trainer, 1969—, instr. cardiopulmonary resuscitation, 1976—; vice chmn. Park County Local Govt. Study Commn., 1974-76; rep. Westport (Conn.) Town Meeting, 1955-57; treas. Park County Wilderness Coalition, 1977—; bd. dirs. Friends Livingston Library, 1978—; chmn. Park County Refugee Com., 1979—. Mem. Am. Acad. Polit. Sci., Music Library Assn., Royal Astron. Soc. Can., Inst. Nav., Maria Mitchell Soc. Nantucket, N.A. Yacht Racing Union, R.I. Meteor Research Orgn. (dir.), Internat. Soc. Mus. Research, Big Sky Astron. Soc. (dir.), Renaissance Soc., Am., Internat. musicological socs., Sierra Club, Trout Unltd., Mont. Wilderness Soc., Am. Guild Organists. Lutheran. Club: Cedar Point Yacht. Author: The Heavens Are Telling (astronomy), 1951; Skies Over the Big Sky Country, 1965. Weekly newspaper columnist Big Skies; contbr. to mags. on music and astronomy. Pub. music elem. two-piano pieces, Five Chorale Preludes for Organ, 1975. Inventor, builder of Clarke adjustable piano stool. Address: Log-a-Rhythm 9th St Island Livingston MT 59047

CLARKSON, CHERYL LEE, hosp. supply co. exec.; b. Chgo., Apr. 14, 1953; d. George M. and Carol A. (Fertig) C.; B.A. with distinction, Ariz. State U., 1975; M. Richard C. Carton. Sales rep. Dietary Products div. Am. Hosp. Supply Corp., Ariz., 1975-78, sales mgr. Southwestern area, Arlington, Tex., 1978-79, Eastern area sales mgr., Edison, N.J., 1979-81, Boston, 1981—, regional sales mgr., Boston, 1982—. Mem. DAR, Alpha Delta Pi. Office: Am Dietary Products 22 Wiggins Ave Bedford MA 02115

CLARKSON, ELISABETH ANN HUDNUT, civic worker; b. Youngstown, Ohio, Apr. 20, 1925; d. Herbert Beecher and Edith (Schaaf) Hudnut; A.B., Wilson Coll., 1947; M.A., State U. N.Y., 1973, also postgrad.; m. William M.E. Clarkson, Sept. 23, 1950; children—Alison H., David B., Andrew E. With J.L. Hudson Co., Detroit, 1947-50; writer The Minute Parade, daily Sta. WGR, Detroit, 1948-50; chmn. Garret Seminars, Buffalo, 1975—; trustee Wilson Coll., Chambersburg, Pa., 1970—, chmn. bd. trustees, 1979-82; vice-chmn. Women for Downtown; bd. dirs. Buffalo Mus. Sci., Trinity Center, Soc. Companion of the Holy Cross; past chmn. jr. group Alright Knox Art Gallery; collector, curator Graphic Controls Corp. collection art, 1976—; dir. Bischoff Clarkson Hudnut Corp., North Creek, N.Y., 1973—. Episcopalian. Clubs: Garret, Buffalo Tennis and Squash. Author: You Can Always Tell a Freshman, 1949; also articles, dramatic presentations, archival materials Adirondack Mus., 1950-77. Home: 156 Bryant St Buffalo NY 14222

CLARKSON, SHIRLEY ANNE, assn. exec.; b. Sterling, Ill., Sept. 14, 1934; d. Charles S. and Juliet (Darland) Long; B.A., U. Chgo., 1957; m. June 14, 1957 (div.); 1 son, James M. Adminstr., com. for comparative study of new nations U. Chgo., 1960-64; dir. info. office S.E. Asia Regional Council, Ann Arbor, Mich., 1969-72; program officer Am. Council on Edn., Washington, 1972-75; asso. dir. Council Internat. Cooperation in Higher Edn., Washington, 1976—; staff Commn. Internat. Relations, Nat. Acad. Scis., Washington. Mem. Assn. Asian Studies, Assn. African Studies. Home: 2007 Kalorama Rd NW Washington DC 20009 Office: 2101 Constitution Ave Washington DC 20418

CLARY, ROSALIE BRANDON STANTON, timber farm exec., civic worker; b. Evanston, Ill., Aug. 3, 1928; d. Frederick Charles Hite-Smith and Rose Cecile (Liebich) Stanton; B.S., Northwestern U., 1950, M.A., 1954; m. Virgil Vincent Clary, Oct. 17, 1959; children—Rosalie Marian, Frederick Stanton, Virgil Vincent, Kathleen Elizabeth. Tchr., Chgo. Public Schs., 1951-55, adjustment tchr., 1956-61; faculty Loyola U., Chgo., 1963; v.p. Stanton Enterprises, Inc., Adams County, Miss., 1971—; author Family History Record, genealogy record book, Kenilworth, Ill., 1977—. Leader, Girl Scouts, Winnetka, Ill., 1969-71, 78-82, Cub Scouts, 1972-77; badge counselor Boy Scouts Am., 1978—; election judge Republican party, 1977—. Mem. Nat. Soc. DAR (Ill. rec. sec. 1979-81, nat. vice chmn. program com. 1980-83, dir. Ill. 4th div. 1981-83, Ill. State chmn. sch. com. 1983—), Am. Forestry Assn., Forest Farmers Assn., North Suburban Geneal. Soc. (v.p. 1979-82), Winnetka Hist. Soc. (governing bd. 1978—, pres. 1982—), Delta Gamma. Roman Catholic. Home: 509 Elder Ln Winnetka IL 60093 Office: PO Box 401 Kenilworth IL 60043

CLASTER, BARBARA LEINER, psychologist, psychoanalyst; b. Cleve., Feb. 11, 1931; d. Philip A. and Della Florence (Berkowitz) L.; A.B., Ohio U., 1953; M.A., Northwestern U., 1954, Ph.D., 1966; m. Jay B. Claster, Apr. 28, 1963; 1 dau., Saundra Margaret. Counselor, Northwestern U., 1953-54, 1958-60; tchr., Warrenville Heights, Ohio, 1954-55; counselor Div. Child Welfare, Cuyahoga County, Cleve., 1955-56; dir. ednl. counseling Cleve. Coll., Western Res. U., Cleve., 1956-58; med. psychology intern Washington U. Sch. Medicine, St. Louis, 1960-61; psychologist Pa. State U., 1961-64; staff asst. Pa. State U., v.p. for student affairs, 1968-71, tutoring coordinator, 1971; with Postgrad. Center for Mental Health, N.Y.C., 1973—, chmn. Forum for Women and Psychoanalysis; pvt. practice as psychotherapist, State Coll., Pa., 1976—, N.Y.C., 1977—. Pres. Centre County Council for Human Services, 1970-72; chmn. Women's Forum State College, 1977-79; mem. Pa. Adv. Com. for Mental Health/Mental Retardation; mem. Temple Emanu-El Religious Sch. Com. Lic. psychologist, Pa. Mem. Pa., Am., Eastern, N.Y. State psychol. assns., N.Y. Soc. Clin. Psychologists, Pi Lambda Theta. Home and Office: 433 Ridge Ave State College PA 16801 also 1065 Park Ave New York City NY 10028

CLAUSEL, NAN DONEY, newspaper exec.; b. Houston, Aug. 24, 1926; d. Louden Charles and Mary Nan (Gaynor) Doney; student Mary Baldwin Coll., 1943-44, Barnard Coll., 1945-47; B.S., U. Houston, 1948; m. Calvin L. Clausel, Jr., Oct. 19, 1951 (div. 1965); children—Caroline Clausel Peter, David Louden. Public relations dir. Houston Soc. for Prevention Cruelty to Animals, 1965-66; promotion copy chief Houston Post, 1966-67; promotion copywriter St. Petersburg (Fla.) Times & Ind., 1967-69; asst. promotion mgr., promotion coordinator San Antonio Light, 1969—, free-lance music reviewer, 1973-80. Active San Antonio Symphony Mastersingers, 1981—. Mem. Women in Communications, San Antonio Advt. Fedn. (dir. 1979-81), Mensa. Republican. Episcopalian. Home: 272 Emporia St San Antonio TX 78209 Office: San Antonio Light 420 Broadway San Antonio TX 78205

CLAUSON, ALBERTA LILLIAN AYER (MRS. BRUCE KENMORE CLAUSON), former librarian; b. Deer River, Minn., May 5, 1913; d. Charles Edward and Inez Mildred (Randall) Ayer; B.E., St. Cloud State Coll., 1935, postgrad., 1936; postgrad. Moorhead State Coll., 1953-55, U. Minn., 1956-57, Columbia, 1958, Mont. State U., 1960, Brigham Young U., 1967; m. Bruce Kenmore Clauson, Dec. 31, 1938 (dec. 1982); children—Bruce Edward, Kathryn C. Ayer, Christopher Charles. Elem. sch. tchr., Ashby (Minn.) Public Schs., 1935-38; prin. jr. high sch., math. and English instr. Gaylord Public Sch., 1938; treas. sch. bd. rural sch., St. Olaf Twp.-Ottertail County, Minn., 1939-46; tchr. English, Alexandria Jr. High Sch., 1945-51; tchr. English, librarian Underwood High Sch., 1952-55, Hoffman High Sch., 1955-56; tchr. English, Elbow Lake Jr. High Sch., 1957-58; librarian, Henning High Sch., 1958-62, Fergus Falls Elem. Sch., 1962-65; librarian Media Center, Fergus Falls (Minn.) Jr. High Sch., 1965-75; owner, mgr. Century Farm. Taped programs for radio program, Minn. State Service for Blind, 1968-76, also taped textbooks. Life mem., vol. librarian Otter Tail County Hist. Mus.; vol. driver Ashby Sr. Citizens, community worker, mem. outreach com., 1974—; v.p. Grant County Commn. on Aging. Mem. NEA, Minn., Fergus Falls (treas. 1963-64), Henning (pres. 1961), and local edn. assns., Am., Minn. (chmn. Western div. 1969-70) assns. sch. librarians, ALA, Nat., Minn., Fergus (v.p.) ret. tchrs. assns., Sr. Citizens Fedn. (v.p. state chpt., state sec. 1983), Delta Kappa Gamma (charter mem. local chpt.). Lutheran (Sunday sch. supt. and tchr. 1949-51). Home: Route 1 Box 168 Ashby MN 56309

CLAUSON, ELSA JUNE, nurse; b. Lorain, Ohio, June 19, 1938; d. John Dominic and Marie (Tenne) Difilippo; B.S. in Nursing, Ohio State U., 1960; m. Jerome K. Clauson, June 17, 1961; children—Mary, Tammy, Cindy. Staff nurse Ohio State U. Hosp., 1960; mem. faculty Mt. Carmel Sch. Nursing, Columbus, Ohio, 1961-62, Akron (Ohio) Gen. Hosp. Sch. Nursing, 1962-64; supr. Ceauga Community Hosp., Chardon, Ohio, 1964-67; mem. faculty, coordinator jr. level Mt. Carmel Sch. Nursing, 1971-74; mem. faculty, coordinator sr. students Marion (Ohio) Tech. Coll., 1974-76; dir. Tri-Rivers Marion Gen. Hosp. Sch. Nursing, 1976-81; asso. dir. nursing Marion Gen. Hosp., 1981—; CPR instr., cons. and adv. in field. Mem. Am. Nurses Assn., Nat. Assn. Nurse Recruiters, Ohio Nurses Assn., Ohio Hosp. Assn., AAUW, Am. Soc. Nursing Adminstrs., Altrusa Internat., Ohio State U. Alumni Assn. (life). Republican. Roman Catholic. Home: 310 Cottswold Dr Delaware OH 43015 Office: Marion Gen Hosp McKinnley Park Dr Marion OH 43302

CLAUSS, CHERRYL A., interior designer; b. Oswego, N.Y., July 13, 1942; d. George D. and Geraldine P. (Heimhilger) Arden; B.S., Syracuse U., 1964; postgrad. N.Y. Sch. Interior Design, 1979—; m. Karl J. Clauss, July 18, 1964; 1 dau., Jennifer A. Owner, The Designer's Touch, Warsaw, Ind. Pres., Washington Sch. Parent Tchrs. Orgn.; sec., mem. exec. bd. Humane Soc. Kosciusko County; art adv., cookie chmn. Warsaw jr. troop 73 Lakeland Council Girl Scouts U.S.A.; Sunday Sch. tchr. United Meth. Ch. Warsaw. Mem. Ind. Soc. Interior Designers, AAUW (sec. Warsaw br.), Kappa Kappa, Kappa.

CLAWSON, KATHERINE LOUISE, health services assn. exec.; b. Boston, Sept. 24, 1949; d. Paul Francis and Martha Johanna (Laudeman) B.; A.B., DePauw U., 1971; M.S.W., Ind. U., 1973. Med. social worker Ind. U. Med. Center, Indpls., 1973-76; social services analyst Blue Cross-Blue Shield of Ind., Indpls., 1976—. Mem. adminstrv. bd. North United Methodist Ch., 1976-80; vol. Alliance Rental Gallery, Indpls. Mus. Art, 1975—. Mem. Acad. Cert. Social Workers, Nat. Assn. Social Workers, Central Ind. Bicycling Assn. (dir. 1980-81), Delta Delta Delta (adv. bd. DePauw chpt. 1971-78). Republican. Home: 2517 Bennett Rd Lafayette IN 47905 Office: Blue Cross-Blue Shield of Ind 120 W Market St Indianapolis IN 46204

CLAY, CELINA MAY, psychologist; b. Nashville, Feb. 26, 1951; d. Ambrose W.J. and Rosie May (Hawkins) C.; B.S., Tenn. State U., 1972, M.S., 1973; Ed.D., U. Tenn., 1978. Sch. psychologist Met. Nashville Public Schs., 1973—; part-time instr. U. Tenn., Nashville, 1978; part-time asst. prof. Tenn. State U., 1979; cons. in field. Lic. psychol. examiner, Tenn. Mem. Am. Psychol. Assn., NEA, Tenn. Edn. Assn., Tenn. Psychol. Assn., Middle Tenn. Edn. Assn., Metro Nashville Edn. Assn., Psi Chi. Mem. Ch. of Christ. Office: PO Box 22642 Nashville TN

CLAYBROOK, JOAN B., govt. ofcl.; b. Balt., June 12, 1937; B.A., Goucher Coll., 1959; J.D., Georgetown U., 1973. Research Analyst Social Security Adminstrn., 1959-65; spl. asst. to adminstr. Nat. Hwy. Traffic Safety Assn., 1966-70; researcher Pub. Interest Research Group, 1970-73; atty. Pub. Citizen, Washington, 1973-77; adminstr. Nat. Hwy. Traffic Safety Adminstrn., Dept. Transp., Washington, 1977-81; now consumer rights advocate. Founding mem. Trial Lawyers for Public Justice, 1982; pres. Public Citizen, 1982—. Am. Polit. Sci. Assn. fellow, 1965-66. Office: care Public Citizen PO Box 19404 Washington DC 20036 *

CLAYMAN, JULIE ANN, thoracic surgeon; b. Cleve., 1942; M.D., Case Western Res. U., 1966. Intern, Univ. Hosps. of Cleve., 1966-67, resident, 1967-71, thoracic surgeon, 1975—; trainee U. Toronto Hosps., 1971-72. Diplomate Am. Bd. Surgery, Am. Bd. Thoracic Surgery. Office: 2065 Adelbert Rd Cleveland OH 44106

CLAYTON, JAN BYRAL, actress; b. Alamogordo, N.M., Aug. 26, 1917; d. Gessie Verner and Vera (Carter) Clayton; student Gulf Pk. Coll., 1937-39; m. Robert W. Lerner, Apr. 14, 1946; children—Robin, Karen, Joseph Clayton. Starred as Julie, orig. prodn. Rodgers & Hammerstein's Carousel, 1944-45; starred as orig. mother long-running —Lassie— TV series, 1956-59; most recent TV appearances incl.: Scruples, Dukes of Hazzard, Insight; starred in Turn to the Right, 1981; other stage credits incl.: Meet the People, They Can't Get You Down, Music in the Air, Rose Marie, Once More with Feeling, Marriage Go Round, Gigi, My Fair Lady, A Majority of One, The Glass Menagerie, Show Boat, Guys and Dolls, King and I.; lectr. in field; cons. Schick Labs., Los Angeles, 1975-82. Bd. dirs. Nat. Council on Alcoholism, 1970-80; mem. Detoxification Rehab. Center of Vols. of Am., 1971-81. Recipient Bronze Key award, 1975, 77. Named Mother of the Yr., Helping Hand Orgn., 1959. Democrat. Episcopalian. Author: Bewitched, Bothered and Bedeviled, 1975. Address: 9018 Elevado Ave Los Angeles CA 90069

CLAYTON, JANE ELLEN, (STERNBERG), nurse, marriage, family and mental health counselor; b. Chisholm, Minn., Jan. 4, 1948; d. Vincent P. and Eleanor Jane (Grigg) Gregorich; R.N., Los Angeles County Gen. Hosp., 1975; B.S., U. Wis., 1972; M.S., UCLA, 1975; m. Ira David Sternberg, Aug. 6, 1977; children— Michael Charles, Aaron Samuel. Instr., U. Nev., Las Vegas, 1976-79; pvt. practice marriage and family counseling, Los Angeles and Las Vegas, 1975-79; exec. dir. Suicide Prevention Center, Las Vegas, 1978—; co-chmn. bd. dirs., exec. dir. Growth Found.; bd. dirs. Rape Crisis Center. Mem. Am. Nurses

Assn., Am. Assn. Suicidology. Pub., contbg. writer Growth Found. monthly jours.; author: Parents Drug Abuse Handbook. Office: 2408 Santa Clara Dr Las Vegas NV 89104

CLAYTON, MARGARET LEE, interior designer; b. Durham, N.C., Mar. 15, 1952; d. Lonnie Lee and Mary (Moser) Clayton; B.F.A., Va. Commonwealth U., 1974. Dir. store planning and showroom display Horizons Inc., Hickory, N.C., 1974-75; freelance showroom display cons., High Point, 1975-76; sr. designer store planning dept. Drexel Heritage Furnishings Inc. (N.C.), 1976-79, store design coordinator, 1979-81, dir. display planning, 1981—. Mem. adv. council Western Carolina U. Mem. Am. Soc. Interior Designers (profl. mem.), Inst. Bus. Designers (profl. mem.), Nat. Trust Historic Preservation. Republican. Methodist. Home: 253 Camelot Dr Camelot Acres Morganton NC 28655 Office: Display Planning Dept Drexel Heritage Furnishings Inc Drexel NC 28619

CLAYTON, PHYLLIS LARUE, sales exec.; b. Coffeyville, Kans., Nov. 27, 1946; d. Clyde E. and J. Lorene Hancock; ed. real estate courses, Coffeyville Jr. Coll.; m. Don Clayton, Jr., Aug. 2, 1964 (div. 1975); children—Tom, Melissa. Realtor, 1976—; owner, dealer franchise Happy Housekeepers of Coffeyville, 1979—. Mem. Nat. Real Estate Assn., Kans. Real Estate Assn., Coffeyville Real Estate Assn., Nat. Assn. Female Execs. Home: 505 Cline Coffeyville KS 67337 Office: 702 W 11th St Coffeyville KS 67337

CLAYTON, STUART DORTHEA, real estate exec.; b. Berkeley, Calif., May 5, 1948; d. William F. and Sally D. Clayton; B.S., U. S.D., 1970; student Chapman Coll. World Campus Afloat, 1969, 72; grad. Realtors Inst., 1976; Tchr. Jefferson County Public Schs., 1970-72; liaison around the world cruises Orient Overseas Line, 1972-73; leasing agt. John Madden Co., Denver, 1974, Highline Med. Bldg., Denver, 1975; comml. leasing specialist Van Schaack & Co., Denver, 1975-80; mgr. Office Leasing div. Fuller & Co., Denver, 1980—; speaker real estate workshops. Mem. Million Dollar Roundtable, 1975-88; named one of Colo.'s leading bus. women Colo. Bus. Mag., 1977. Lic. real estate broker, Colo. Mem. Colo. Assn. Realtors, Nat. Assn. Realtors, Denver C. of C., Profl. Bus. Women's Orgn., Jr. Symphony Guild. Contbr. articles on office bldgs. to profl. jours., newspapers. Office: 1515 Arapahoe St Suite 1600 Denver CO 80202

CLAYTON, VERNA ANN LEWIS (MRS. FRANK RODGERS CLAYTON, JR.), city ofcl.; b. Hamden, Ohio, Feb. 28; d. Matthews L. and Yail K. (Miller) Lewis; Okla. State U., 1954-55; m. Frank Rodgers Clayton, Jr., Feb. 4, 1956; children—Valerie Suzanne, Barry Lewis. Sec. Okla. Gas & Electric Co., Oklahoma City, 1955-56; cashier Denver Amarilla Express, Oklahoma City, 1956-57; sec. to asso. dean arts and scis. U. Okla., 1957-58; sec. Torklson Assos., Indpls., 1968-69; salesperson Avon, Buffalo Grove, Ill., 1969-71; village clk., Buffalo Grove, 1971-79, village collector, 1972-78, office mgr., 1972-78, village pres., 1979—; chmn. transp. com. Northwest Mcpl. Conf., 1980-82, v.p., 1982—; vice chmn. Council of Mayors, 1981. Inter-club council chmn. YWCA, Winston-Salem, N.C., 1961, Y-Teen adviser, 1961; sec., parents exec. council Western Ill. U., 1976-78; precinct chmn. Republican party, 1965. Mem. Internat. Inst. Mcpl. Clks. (cert. mcpl. clk.; mem. election adminstrn. com. 1977-79), Mcpl. Clks. Ill. (registered mcpl. clk.; dir. 1977), Mcpl. Clks. North and NW Suburbs Cook County, Mcpl. Clks. Lake County (legis. chmn. 1973-74, sec. 1975, pres. 1977-79), Strathmore Homeowners Assn. (schs. com. chmn. 1969), Women's Soc. Christian Service (pres. 1963), LWV Delta Zeta. Methodist (mem. edn. commn. 1972). Home: 911 Twisted Oak Ln Buffalo Grove IL 60090 Office: 50 Raupp Blvd Buffalo Grove IL 60090

CLEAR, CAROLYN HILL, sales exec.; b. Memphis, May 21, 1937; d. Owen Landale and Sylvia Mae (Walter) Hill; B.J., U. Mo., 1959; children—Stacey Alan, Sylvia Lee. Asst. to asst. advt. dir. MFA Ins. Cos., Columbia, Mo., 1958, 59-60; traffic directory, copywriter, on-air announcer Sta. WENE, Endicott, N.Y., 1960-61; weekly columnist, advt. salesman Fort Bend Mirror, Stafford, Tex., 1970-71; advt. sales rep., promotion dir., nat. accounts mgr. Suburbia, Houston, 1972-76; dir. rep. advt. sales, mgr. directory sales Southwestern Bell, Houston, 1976-80, staff mgr. directory premise tng., 1981—. Counselor, Youth Emergency Hot Line. Recipient Gold Key award Southwestern Bell, 1977. Republican. Presbyterian. Home: 2 Bitterfield Ct Ballwin MO 63011 Office: Room 520 112 N 4th St St Louis MO 63102

CLEARY, BEVERLY ATLEE (MRS. CLARENCE T. CLEARY), author; b. McMinnville, Oreg.; d. Chester Lloyd and Mable (Atlee) Bunn; B.A., U. Calif., 1938; B.A. in Librarianship, U. Wash., 1939; m. Clarence T. Cleary, Oct. 6, 1940; children—Marianne Elisabeth, Malcolm James. Children's librarian, Yakima, Wash., 1939-40; post librarian Regional Hosp., Oakland, Calif., 1942-45. Mem. Authors Guild of Authors League Am. Author: Henry Huggins, 1950; Ellen Tebbits, 1951; Henry and Beezus, 1952; Otis Spofford, 1953; Henry and Ribsy, 1954; Beezus and Ramona, 1955; Fifteen, 1956; Henry and the Paper Route, 1957; The Luckiest Girl, 1958; Jean and Johnny, 1959; The Real Hole, 1960; Hullabaloo ABC, 1960; Two Dog Biscuits, 1961; Emily's Runaway Imagination, 1961; Henry and the Clubhouse, 1962; Sister of the Bride, 1963; Ribsy, 1964; The Mouse and the Motorcycle, 1965; Mitch and Amy, 1967; Ramona the Pest (Georgia Children's Book award 1970), 1968; Runaway Ralph, 1970; Socks, 1973; Ramona the Brave, 1975; Ramona and her Father (Honor Book for U.S., Internat. Bd. and Books for Young People), 1977; Ramona and her Mother, 1979; Ramona Quimby, Age 8 (Newberry honor book 1982), 1981, Land of Enchantment (N.Mex. Library Assn. Children's book award 1981); Ralph S. Mouse, 1982. Recipient Young Reader's Choice award Pacific N.W. Library Assn., 1957, 60, 68, 71, 80; Dorothy Canfield Fisher Children's Book award Vt. Congress of Parents and Tchrs., 1958, 66; Nene award Hawaii Assn. Sch. Librarians and Hawaii Library Assn., 1968, 69, 71, 72, 79; Sue Hefley award La. Assn. Sch. Librarians, 1973, William Allen White award Kans. Assn. Sch. Librarians and Kans. Tchrs. Assn., 1968, 75; Sequoyah Children's Book award Okla. Library Assn., 1971; Charlie May Simon award Ark. Elem. Sch. Council, 1973; Laura Ingalls Wilder award Children's Services div. ALA, 1975; Golden Archer award U. Wis., 1977; Newbery Honor Book, 1978; Regina medal Cath. Library Assn., 1980; Utah Children's Book award Children's Lit. Assn. Utah, 1980; Tenn. Children's Book award Tenn. Library Assn., 1980; Garden State award N.J. Library Assn., 1980; Tex. Bluebonnet award Tex. Library Assn. Tex. Assn. Sch. Librarians, 1981; Am. Book award, 1981. Address: care William Morrow 105 Madison Ave New York NY 10016

CLEARY, CATHERINE BLANCHARD, banker; b. Madison, Wis., Dec. 19, 1916; d. Michael J. and Bonnie (Blanchard) C.; A.B., U. Chgo., 1937; LL.B., U. Wis., 1943; LL.D., Ripon Coll., 1955, Alverno Coll., 1970, Marquette U., 1972, Smith Coll., 1973, U. Wis., 1974, Lawrence U., 1974, U. Notre Dame, 1977; L.H.D., Lakeland Coll., 1975, Russell Sage Coll., 1975, Beloit Coll., 1976. Apprentice Shady Hill Sch., Cambridge, Mass., 1937-38, tchr., 1938-39; tchr. New Canaan (Conn.) Country Sch., 1939-40; admitted to Wis. bar, 1943, Ill. bar, 1945; legal dept. Kohler Co. (Wis.), 1943-44; asso. Defrees, Fiske, O'Brien & Thomson, Chgo., 1944-47; with First Wis. Trust Co., Milw., 1947-78, asst. trust officer, trust officer, exec. v.p., pres., chmn. bd., chief exec. officer, now dir.; adj. prof. Sch. Bus. Adminstrn. U. Wis.-Milw., 1978-81; dir. AT&T, Dart & Kraft, Inc., Gen. Motors, Kohler Co.; trustee Northwestern Mut. Life Ins. Co. Asst. treas. U.S., 1953; asst. to sec. treasury, 1953-54. Mem. Wis. (ho. of govs. 1951-52, chmn. com. fed. legis. 1952-53), Am. bar assns. Clubs: University; Woman's of Wis.; Milwaukee Country; Cosmopolitan (N.Y.C.). Home: 924 E Juneau Ave Milwaukee WI 53202 Office: 735 N Water St Milwaukee WI 53202

CLEAVE, MARY LOUISE, astronaut; b. Southampton, N.Y., Feb. 5, 1947; d. Howard E. and Barbara A. (Toy) C.; B.S. in Biol. Scis. with honors, Colo. State U., 1969; M.S. in Microbial Ecology, Utah State U., 1975, Ph.D. in Civil and Environ. Engring., 1980. Researcher, Ecology Center, also Utah Water Research Lab., U. Utah State U., 1971-80; astronaut candidate NASA, 1980-81, astronaut, 1981—. Mem. ASCE, Phycological Soc. Am., Water Pollution Control Fedn., Sigma Xi, Alpha Delta, Tri-Beta, Tau Beta Pi. Address: Lyndon B Johnson Space Center Houston TX 77098

CLEAVER, CLAIRE MARIE, public relations and mktg. cons.; b. Reading, Pa., Mar. 4, 1943; d. Edward John and Arlene Elvira (Wenrich) C.; B.A. in English, Pa. State U., 1966. Tchr. English, Daniel Boone Area High Sch., Birdsboro, Pa., 1966-78, chmn. dept., 1971-76; saleswoman Met. Life Ins. Co., 1978-79; dir. field devel. Creative Expressions, div. Caron Internat., Robesonia, Pa., 1979-80, nat. sales dir., v.p. sales communications and tng., 1980-81; founder, 1981, since pres. Concepts by Claire, Inc., Boyertown, Pa.; asst. Dale Carnegie Mgmt. seminars, speaker in field. Pres., Pa. Jr. Miss, Inc., 1978-79, bd. dirs., choreographer for state pageant. 1972-80, sr. v.p. scholarship, 1982. Mem. Am. Mgmt. Assn., Nat. Assn. Female Execs., Nat. Alliance Homebased Businesswomen, AAUW. Author: Step Into Sales, 2d edit., 1982. Address: 174 Popoickon Dr Boyertown PA 19512

CLEGG, SUE WALL ROBERSON (MRS. CHARLES MYRON CLEGG), realtor, civic worker; b. Franklinton, N.C., June 4, 1904;; d. John Sachel and Florence (Tomlinson) Roberson; A.B., U. N.C., 1926; postgrad. Georgetown U. Grad. Sch. Govt., 1954-56; m. Charles Myron Clegg, Sept. 17, 1943 (dec. Jan. 1970); stepchildren—Charles Myron (dec.), Myles Standish, Eleanor Standish (Mrs. John Ennis Holloway). Washington corr. for Reese River Reveille newspaper, Nev., 1956-62; with Metzler, Realtor, Washington. Sec. Georgetown Citizens Assn., del. Fedn. Citizens Assns., Washington; mem. Zoning and Planning Com., chmn. Home Beautification Com.; mem. Nat. Trust for Historic Preservation. Publicity chmn. League Republican Women Washington, 1950's. Mem. Montgomery County, Washington (asso.) bds. realtors, UN Assn. U.S.A., Georgetown U. Alumni Assn., Nat. Wildlife Fedn., Acad. Polit. Sci., Amnesty Internat., Internat. Platform Assn. Home: 2800 Woodley Rd NW Washington DC 20008

CLELAND, JUNE ELIZABETH, govt. ofcl.; b. Santa Rosa, Calif., May 28, 1922; d. Marion Wilson and Ethel Blossom (Woods) Harvey; B.A., U. Calif., Berkeley, 1946; m. Thomas William Cleland, Apr. 24, 1966; 1 son, David. Office mgr. human relations area files project U. Calif., Berkeley, 1954-55; editorial asst. Commn. Race and Housing, Berkeley, 1955-61; with HUD, 1961—, regional fed. women's program coordinator, San Francisco, 1970-75, program analyst, 1975—; co-chmn. interagy. com. women No. Calif. Personnel Council, 1973; co-chmn. interagy. women's com. San Francisco Fed. Exec. Bd., 1974-75. Recipient cert. appreciation San Francisco Fed. Exec. Bd., 1975; Spl. Achievement award HUD, 1979, Outstanding Performance award, 1982. Mem. AAUW, Federally Employed Women, NOW, U. Calif. Alumni Assn., Calif. Scholarship Fedn. (life). Democrat. Presbyterian. Home: 6821 Aitken Dr Oakland CA 94611 Office: PO Box 36003 450 Golden Gate Ave San Francisco CA 94102

CLEMENS, ELIZABETH MALM, educator; b. New Orleans, Oct. 4, 1928; d. William A. R. and Madeline Elizabeth (Dietz) Malm: B.A., Tulane U., 1965; M.Ed., Loyola U., 1970; m. Harold A. Clemens, Oct. 3, 1953; children—Barry Michael, Susan Elizabeth. Tchr., St. Bernard and Orleans Parish (La.) Public Schs., 1958-71; founder, tchr., dir. Barry Acad., Chalmette, La., 1974—; pres. Potential Devel. Assn., Chalmette; ednl. cons., 1972—; chmn. edn. com. The Chamber, New Orleans and River Region, 1978-80, bd. dirs., 1982—; mem. State Task Force on Compensatory Edn., 1980—; adv. bd. New Orleans Regional Vocat.-Tech. Sch., 1982—. Chmn., United Fund, Cancer Drive, 1978-80. EDPA fellowship participant for reading specialists, Loyola U., 1969-70. Mem. New Orleans C. of C. (chmn. St. Bernard council 1976-78), Greater New Orleans Reading Assn., AAUW. Republican. Presbyterian. Club: Chalmette Lions Aux. Home: Route 2 Box 140 Saint Bernard LA 70085 Office: PO Box 45 Chalmette LA 70044

CLEMENS, JACQUELINE BETTE-RAE BOUDER, home economist; b. Woodlyn, Pa., Jan. 15, 1937; d. Raymond S. and Elizabeth Veronica (Dengler) Bouder; B.S. cum laude in Home Econs. Edn., Fla. State U., 1958, M.S. in Early Childhood Edn., 1975; m. Leslie Eugene Clemens, Dec. 30, 1960; children—Laurie Dawn, Scott, Anthony. Tchr. home econs. and sci. schs. in Fla. and Ga., 1958-72; tchr. child guidance, care and mgmt. services, also coordinator Lively Child Care Center, Leon County Public Schs., Tallahassee, 1972—; bd. dirs. Leon County Community Coordinated Child Care, 1978; cons. in field. Mem. choir St. John's Episcopal Ch., Tallahassee, 1977—; vol. Lemoyne Art Found., Tallahassee, 1976-78; instr. first aid local ARC, 1976—; Fla. del. White House Conf. on Families, 1980. Recipient various service awards; scholar Fla. Home Demonstration Council, 1954-58, Pilot Club, 1954, Scholarship Cup, 1956. Mem. NEA, Am. Vocat. Assn., So. Assn. Children Under Six, Fla. State U. Home Econs. Alumni Assn. (pres. 1980—), Fla. Vocat. Assn. (chmn. auditing com. home econs. sect. 1978-79), Fla. Tchrs. Assn., Leon County Tchrs. Assn., Leon County Vocat. Assn. (pres. 1978-79), Fla. Assn. Children Under Six (state adv. bd. 1975-77, 78-79, corr. sec. 1981-82), Leon County Assn. Children Under Six (pres. 1975-76), Fla. Child Devel. Assn. (planning com. 1977—), Omicron Nu, Delta Kappa Gamma, Phi Kappa Phi. Republican. Episcopalian. Club: Killearn Golf and Country. Office: 500 N Appleyard Dr Tallahassee FL 32304

CLEMENTS, BARBARA EVANS, historian; b. Richmond, Va., May 26, 1945; d. Lorenzo Sibert and Champe Carter (Winston) E.; B.A., U. Richmond, 1967; M.A., Duke U., 1969, Ph.D., 1971. Asst. prof. history U. Akron, 1971-78, asso. prof., 1978—. Am. Council Learned Socs./ Social Sci. Council grantee, 1972-73. Mem. Ohio Acad. History (pres. 1981-82), Am. Hist. Assn., Am. Assn. Advancement Slavic Studies, Ohio Acad. History, Coordinating Com. Women in Hist. Profession, Phi Beta Kappa. Author: Bolshevik Feminist: The Life of Aleksandra Kollontai, 1979. Office: Dept History U Akron Akron OH 44325

CLEMENTS, LYNNE ETHEL, psychotherapist, social worker; b. Bklyn., Aug. 8, 1945; d. Gillies M. and Dorothy F. (Zitzmann) Fleming; B.A., Bradley U., 1967; postgrad. Mus. Fine Arts Evening Sch., Boston, 1969-70, Columbia Grad. Sch. Social Work, 1970-71; M.S.W., Fordham U., 1973; m. Louis Clements, Feb. 19, 1972; children—Ryan Louis, Glenn Fleming. Computer programmer Employer's Union Group Ins. Cos., Boston, 1967-69, Harvard Bus. Sch., Cambridge, Mass., 1969-70, Volkswagen of Am., Inc., Englewood Cliffs, N.J., 1970-71; vol. social work aid Community Center Mental Health, Inc., Dumont, N.J., 1970-71; psychiat. social worker Associated Cath. Charities Family and Children's Services, Paramus, N.J., 1973-74; inpatient psychiat. social worker Christian Health Care Center, Wyckoff, N.J., 1974-76; bd. dirs., chmn. bd. Community Play Center, Bergenfield, N.J., 1977-78; owner, originator Wicker Wagon, Bergenfield, 1977—; psychotherapist The Psychotherapy Counseling Center, Bergenfield, N.J., 1982—. NIMH grantee, 1971-73. Home and Office: 67 Reid Ave Bergenfield NJ 07621

CLEMMONS, FRANCES ANNE MANSELL (MRS. SLATON CLEMMONS), govt. ofcl.; b. Camden, Miss., Dec. 21, 1915; d. Otho Franklin and Pearl (Dunlap) Mansell; B.S., Belhaven Coll., 1937, Mus.B., 1937; m. Rowe Sanders Crowder, Dec. 17, 1938 (div. Mar. 1954); children—Rowe Sanders, Frances Elizabeth; m. 2d, Slaton Clemmons, Nov. 21, 1965. Owner, operator Crowder Art Gallery, Jackson, Miss., 1946-50; dept. mgr., buyer Valley Dry Goods Co., Vicksburg, 1954-56; with Social Security Adminstrn., 1956—, asst. dist. mgr., Rome, Ga., 1962—. Charter mem. Citizens Adv. Council on Energy; mem. Rome Little Theatre, Rome Community Concert Assn., Rome Area C. of C., Interagy Council, Floyd County Merit Bd., Salvation Army Aux., Mayor's Com. Employment of Handicapped. Democrat. Presbyterian. Club: Quota Internat. (pres. Rome 1974-76, dist. 8 lt. gov. 1979-80, gov. 1980-82). Home: 412 E 3d Ave Rome GA 30161 Office: Federal Bldg Rome GA 30161

CLEMMONS, PENNY, psychologist, educator; b. Chgo., Aug. 16, 1947; d. Trefin D. and Garnet Hope (Murray) Paganis; B.A., U. Ill., 1970; M.A., Roosevelt U., 1976; Ph.D., Calif. Grad. Inst., 1979; m. Marty Cottler, Dec. 9, 1979. Tchr., Archdiocese of Chgo., 1967-69; outpatient treatment coordinator Grant Hosp., Chgo., 1969-74; marriage/family and child counselor, 1977—; clin. psychologist in pvt. practice, Los Angeles, 1981—; asso. prof. psychology, dean admissions Calif. Grad. Inst., Los Angeles, 1979-82; asst. program dir. Fielding Inst., Santa Barbara, Calif., 1982—; clin. dir. Inst. for Psychotherapy and Counseling, Los Angeles, 1980—. Pres., bd. dirs. San Fernando Valley Counseling Center, 1978-80; v.p. bd. dirs. Ill. Alcoholism and Drug Dependence Assn., 1972-76. Recipient Pub. Service award, State of Ill., 1976; lic. clin. psychologist, Calif. Mem. Calif. Psychol. Assn., Nat. Assn. Advancement Psychoanalysis, Am. Orthopsychiat. Assn., Assos. for Interdisciplinary Studies, Am. Personnel and Guidance Assn. Contbr. articles to profl. jours. Office: 10884 Santa Monica Blvd Suite 403 West Los Angeles CA 90025

CLEMONS, ELIZABETH CAMERON (MRS. NELSON T. NOWELL), author; b. Berkeley, Calif.; d. Alfred George and Edith (Catton) Cameron; A.B San Jose State Coll., 1928; M.A., Stanford U., 1937; m. Wood Clemons, Dec. 22, 1946 (div. Dec. 1958); m. 2d, Arthur G. Robinson, May 27, 1961 (dec. Jan. 1967); m. 3d, Nelson T. Nowell, Feb. 15, 1969 (dec. Sept. 1973). With edn. dept. San Jose State Coll., 1928-39, in service tng. U. Calif. Extension Div., 1939-42; elem. editor The John C. Winston Co., 1942-43, Silver Burdett Co., 1943-44, D.C. Heath, 1944-46; instr. English dept. U. Minn., 1947; writing, editing publs. services Gen. Mills, 1947-50; freelance writer, 1950—; reading cons. Monterey City Sch., 1959-62, asso. editor Calif. edit. Am. Home Mag., 1965-70; mem. seminar faculty Embroiderers Guild, 1980, Monterey Peninsula Coll., 1978—; exhibited needle-work Good Samaritan Hosp., Los Angeles, 1977, 79, 83 Montalvo Center for Arts, Saratoga, Calif., 1980, 82, Status Needle Art Show, Burlingame, Calif., 1982, Altrusa Needlework Exhbn., Santa Maria, Calif., 1982, others. Bd. dirs. Community Hosp. Aux.; bd. dirs. Harrison Meml. Library, 1971-76, Monterey Symphony Assn., 1974-75; vestryman St. Dunstan's Episcopal Ch., 1974-77. Mem. Nat. League Am. Pen Women, Authors Guild, LWV, Nat. Embroidery Tchrs. Assn. (nat. dir. 1978—), Embroiderers Guild Am. (nat. dir. 1978—; pres. chpt. 1977-78; judge needlework exhbns.), Kappa Alpha Theta, Pi Lambda Theta, Delta Phi Upsilon, Kappa Delta Pi, Delta Kappa Gamma. Republican. Clubs: Casa Abrego (historian 1979—), Carmel Valley Golf and Country, Monterey Peninsula Country, Soroptimist. Author: The Pixie Dictionary, 1953; the Catholic Child's First Dictionary, 1954; The Winston Dictionary for Canadian School Children, 1955; Away I Go, 1956; All About Baby, 1956; I Live on A Farm, 1956; A Wish for Billy, 1956; Wings, Wheels, and Motors, 1957; The Big Book of Real Fire Engines, 1958; The Big Book of Real Trains, 1958; The Big Book of Real Trucks, 1958; Rodeo Days, 1960; Shells Are Where You Find Them, 1960; Rocks and The World Around You, 1960; Big and Little, 1961; Tide Pools and Beaches, 1964; Tides, Waves, and Currents, 1967; Here and There Stories; Now and Then Stories; Near and Far Stories; A Source Book for the Teaching of Literature for Children (all 1967); The Seven Seas, 1971; The Friendly Frog, 1971; What I Like, 1971; also feature articles in nat. mags. Address: PO Box 686 Carmel CA 93921

CLENDANIEL, ANNE LUCILLE EVANS, health agy. exec.; b. Harrington, Del., Aug. 30, 1918; d. John Franklin and Bertha (Collison) Evans; student U. Del., 1936-37, spl. courses in writing, leadership and communications; m. Harry Edgar Clendaniel, Jr., Sept. 6, 1941; children—Mary Catherine Clendaniel Culver, John Evans. Exec. sec. Beacom Bus. Coll., 1939; legal sec., tax dept. duPont Co., 1939-45, Maguire, Voorhees & Wells, Orlando, Fla., 1943-45; vol., study group leader Great Books, 1945-61; legal sec. Young, Conaway, Stargatt, 1962-63; dir. communications Episcopal Diocese of Del., 1963-73; exec. dir. Del. chpt. Arthritis Found., Wilmington, 1974—. Mem. Del. Press Women, Profl. Staff Assn. Arthritis Found. Republican. Club: Wilmington Quota (pres. 1977-78), Contbr. poetry and verse, to newspapers, mags., anthologies, 1939-55; founder, writer Communion Diocesan paper, 1967-73; author The Arthritis Report, 1974—.

CLEVELAND, HELEN BARTH, teaching cons., civic worker; b. Alliance, Ohio, Aug. 28, 1904; d. Luther Martin and Ella Mae (Forest) Barth; A.B., Mt. Union Coll., 1927; postgrad. Kent State U., 1929-32, Akron U., 1946-48, N.Y. U., 1950-53; M.A., Syracuse U., 1955, Ph.D., 1958; postgrad. London Acad. Arts, 1970, U. San Juan, 1972, Acad. Arts Honolulu, 1973; m. Harold J. Cleveland, Oct. 26, 1946; children—Carol, Ronald, Marilyn, George, Donald. Tchr., cons. Alliance Public Schs., 1927-74; instr. crafts Syracuse U., 1953-60; instr. art, Sierra Leone, 1963-64; pres., dir. Chautauqua (N.Y.) Art Gallery, 1963-76, pres. emeritus, bd. dirs., 1977—; chmn. bd. missions Christ United Methodist Ch., 1981-82; bd. dirs., cons. adminstr. Mabel Hartzel Mus., Alliance, 1974—; bd. dirs. Lighthouse Gallery, Tequesta, Fla., 1970-72, Canton (Ohio) Culture Center, 1970—; trustee Alliance Art Center, Wildwood Art Gallery; mem. Keating (Mich.) Antique Village. Recipient Bronze plaque Community Alliance Bi-Centennial Com., 1976, Community Service award Am. Legion Aux., 1975; named Outstanding Alumna, Alpha Delta Pi, 1981. Mem. AARP, (chpt. pres. 1981-82), Am. Fedn. Art, Ohio Fedn. Art; life mem. NEA, Ohio Edn. Assn. Republican. Methodist. Clubs: Mt. Union College Women, Alliance Woman, Chautaqua Woman, Univ. Women, Order Eastern Star, K.T. Ladies, Shrine Ladies, DeMolay-Rainbow (Mom of Year 1959). Author: Arts and Crafts, 1955; Art in Poetry, 1959; Creativity in Elementary Schools, 1963. Home: 1192 Parkside Dr Alliance OH 44601

CLEVELAND, PEGGY R., cytotechnologist; b. Cannelton, Ind., Dec. 9, 1929; d. —Pat— Clarence Francis and Alice Marie (Hall) Richey; cert. U. Louisville, 1956; m. Peter Leslie Cleveland, Nov. 25, 1948 (dec. 1973); children—Pamela Cleveland Litch, Paula Cleveland Bertloff, Peter L. Cytotechnologist cancer survey project NIH, Louisville, 1956-59; chief cytotechnologist Parker Cytology Lab., Inc., Louisville, 1959-75; mgr. cytology dept. Nat. Health Labs., Inc., Louisville, 1978—; clin. instr. cytology Sch. Allied Health U. Louisville, 1960—, cytology adv. com., 1980-81, chmn., 1982, ednl. coordinator Nat. Health Labs., Inc. with cytology program U. Louisville; owner, operator Broke N. Bent Farm thoroughbred horse breeding and racing. Mem. Am. Soc. Clin. Pathologist (cert. cytotechnologist), Internat. Acad. Cytology (cert. cytotechnologist), Am. Soc. Cytology (pilot program continuing edn. certification), Horseman's Benevolent and Protective Assn. Democrat. Roman Catholic. Office: Nat Health Labs Inc 634 S Floyd St Louisville KY 40202

CLEVER, ELAINE COX, librarian; b. N.Y.C.; d. Russell Scarlott and Estelle Ruth (Gilliland) Cox; B.A., Pa. State U., 1944; M.S., Drexel U., 1961; Cert. IBM Systems Research Inst., 1962; postgrad. Drexel U., 1976-78; m. Fred E. Clever, Feb. 18, 1944; 1 son, Eric Conrad. Instr. reading Avon Sch., Barrington, N.J., 1954-59; librarian Woodland Sch. Barrington, 1959-63; librarian Hadden (N.J.) High Sch., 1963-64; head circulation dept. Temple U. Library, Phila., 1964-81, librarian innovative projects, 1981—. Office Edn. grantee, 1969-70. Mem. AAUP (membership chmn. 1979—nat. council 1980—, v.p. chpt.), Phila. Women's Network, Nat. Com. Pay Equity (collective bargaining and organizing com.), Nat. Librarians Assn. (cert. standards com.), Theta Sigma Phi, Beta Phi Mu. Mem. Society of Friends. Club: Engrs. (Phila.). Office: Barton Hall Temple U Philadelphia PA 19122

CLEWIS, CHARLOTTE WRIGHT STAUB, educator; b. Pitts., Aug. 20, 1935; d. Schirmer Chalfant and Charlotte Wright (Rodgers) Staub; student Memphis State Coll., 1953-54, U. Wis., 1957-59; B.A., Newark State Coll., 1963; M.A.T., Loyola Marymount U., 1974; m. John Edward Clewis, Aug. 11, 1954; 1 dau., Charlotte Wright. Asst. to dir., housemother Leota Sch. and Camp, Evansville, Wis., 1957-59; math. tchr. Rahway Jr. High Sch. (N.J.), 1963-70, Torrance (Calif.) Unified Sch. Dist., 1970—, coordinator math. dept., 1977—, mem. math. steering com., 1978—, mem. proficiency exam writing com., 1977—. Sec., pres. Larga Vista Property Owners Assn., 1975—; mem. Rolling Hills Estates City Celebration Com., 1975—; treas. adult leaders YMCA, Metuchen, N.J., 1967-69; bd. dirs. Peninsula Symphony Assn., 1978—; commr. Rolling Hills Estates Parks and Activities, 1981—. Named Tchr. of Year, Rahway Jr. High Sch., 1966. Mem. Nat. Council Tchrs. Math., Calif. Math. Council. Club: Phidippides Track (sec. 1980—) (Los Angeles). Marathon runner Home: 1 Gaucho Dr Rolling Hills Estates CA 90274 Office: 23751 Nancy Lee Ln Torrance CA 90505

CLIFFORD, SISTER, ADELE, educator, biologist; b. Chillicothe, Ohio, Aug. 29, 1906; d. Timothy and Ellen (Murphy) Clifford; A.B., Coll. Mt. St. Joseph (Ohio), 1933; M.S., Fordham U., 1946, Ph.D., 1949. Grade sch. tchr., Cleve., 1930-33; grade sch. prin., Royal Oak, Mich., 1933-35; high sch. tchr., Cin., 1935-42; instr. biology Coll. Mt. St. Joseph, 1942-67, pres., 1967-72, pres. emeritus, 1973—, prof. biology, 1972-79, prof. emeritus, 1979—. Research Marine Biol. Lab., Woods Hole, Mass., 1946-48, summers 1961-67, 73-77. Named one of ten women of achievement Cin. Bus. and Profl. Women's Club, 1973. Mem. Am. Inst. Biol. Scis., Bot. Soc. Am., Coll. Biology Tchrs. Conf. (sec. 1966-67), Am. Soc. Zoologists, AAAS, Ohio Acad. Sci., Am. Genetic Assn. Club: Zonta (sec. 1975-76) (Cin.). Home: Mount Saint Joseph OH 45051

CLIFFORD, CATHY ANN, mktg. exec.; b. St. Marys, Ohio, June 6, 1947; d. William Eugene and Kathleen Bertha (McNally) C.; B.S., U. Dayton, 1969. Biomedical sales supr. VWR Sci., Columbus, Ohio, 1970-74; mktg. rep. J.T. Baker Instruments, Cin., 1974-76; sr. mktg. rep. clin. systems div. E.I. DuPont, Dallas, 1976—. Mem. Nat. Assn. Female Execs., U. Dayton Alumni Assn. Home: 9144 Chimney Corner Dallas TX 75243

CLIFT, ULYSSINE GWENDOLYN GIBSON (MRS. JOSEPH WILLIAM CLIFT), social worker; b. Port Arthur, Tex., Aug. 12, 1937; d. Ulysses Grant and Matilda Louise (McShann) Gibson; B.A., Fisk U., 1958; M.A., U. Chgo., 1960; m. Joseph William Clift, Aug. 10, 1963; children—Kory Grant, Nathalie Louise-Gibson. Med. Social worker social service dept. U. Tex. Med. Br., Galveston, 1960-65; caseworker Family Service, Berkeley, Calif., 1965-67; dist. dir. Family and Childrens Service Assn., Dayton, Ohio, 1967-69; caseworker, field work supr. Family Service, Berkeley, Calif., 1969-72; field work supr. U. Calif., Berkeley, 1969-72; pvt. practice, 1972— Chmn. function and service com., Lincoln Center, Oakland; bd. dirs. Lincoln Child Fin. sec. No. Calif. Med., Dental and Pharm. Assn. Aux.; sec.), Sinkler-Miller Med. Assn. Aux.; vol. Samuel Merritt Hosp., Oakland, Am. Heart Assn. Lic. clin. social worker. Mem. Nat. Assn. Social Workers, Acad. Cert. Social Workers, No. Calif. Med., Dental, Pharm. Assn. Aux. (fin. sec.), Sinkler-Miller Med. Assn. Aux. (sec.), Alpha Kappa Delta, Alpha Kappa Alpha. Home: 14030 Broadway Terrace Oakland CA 94611 Office: 3300 Webster St Suite 308 Oakland CA 94609

CLIFTON, ANNE RUTENBER, psychotherapist; b. New Haven, Dec. 11, 1938; d. Ralph Dudley and Cleminette (Downing) Rutenber; B.A., Smith Coll., 1960, M.S.W., 1962; m. Roger Lambert Clifton, Sept. 9, 1961; 1 dau., Dawn Anne. Psychiat. case worker adult psychiatry unit Tufts-New Eng. Med. Center, Boston, 1962-68, supr. students, 1967-68; pvt. practice psychotherapy, Cambridge, Mass., 1966—; supr. med. students, staff social workers out-patient psychiatry Tufts New Eng. Med. Center, 1973—, also mem. adv. bd. Women's Resource Center. Lic. social worker, Mass. asst. clin. prof. psychiatry Tufts U. Med. Sch., 1974—, research dept. psychiatry, 1966-68, 73, 77—. Mem. Acad. Cert. Social Workers, Nat. Assn. Social Workers, Phi Beta Kappa, Sigma Xi. Clubs: Cambridge Tennis, Mt. Auburn Tennis. Contbr. articles to profl. jours. Home: 126 Homer St Newton Center MA 02159 Office: 51 Brattle St Cambridge MA 02138

CLIMO, BETH LUCRETIA, lawyer; b. Cleve., Oct. 24, 1951; d. James O. and Thea K. C.; B.A., Wittenberg U., 1973; J.D., Wake Forest U., 1976. Admitted to Ohio bar, 1976, D.C. bar, 1978; govt. relations counsel Am. Bankers Assn., Washington, 1977-79; counsel U.S. Senate Com. on Banking, Housing, and Urban Affairs, Washington, 1979-82, sr. counsel, 1982—. Mem. Am. Bar Assn., Fed. Bar Assn. Club: Women in Housing and Fin. Contbr. articles to publs. in field. Office: 5300 Dirksen Senate Office Bldg Washington DC 20510

CLINE, ANITA ALBERTS, talk show personality, corp. exec., actress, fashion and beauty cons.; b. Hollywood, Calif., Feb. 18, 1944; d. Maxwell Sergis and Ruth Laura (Cathey) Alberts; B.A. (acad. scholar), Mills Coll., 1964; m. Wayne Nelson Cline, Feb. 18, 1978. Asso. fashion editor Mademoiselle Mag., N.Y.C., 1964-67; actress, 1968—; movies include House Calls, 1978, Prime Time, 1976, The Steagle, 1971, The Sterile Cuckoo, 1969; TV appearances include lead roles in Hawaii Five-O, two episodes of Cannon, Banyon, Dr. Kildare; other roles include Of Men and Women - ABC Anthology; two episodes of Man and the City, three episodes Bracken's World, also Room 222, That Girl, Why Marry?, Sta. KTLA Comedy Spl.; account exec. Jay Bernstein Public Relations, Los Angeles, 1971-74; news broadcaster Sta. KPFK, Los Angeles, 1975; appeared in numerous commercials; dir. Fashion Office, spokesperson Carnation Co., Los Angeles, 1977-79; featured as leading career woman in Stern Mag., Cosmopolitan Mag.; appearances also include over 250 radio and TV talk shows throughout U.S. Mem. Screen Actors Guild, AFTRA, Mills Coll. Alumnae Assn., UCLA Alumni Assn. Democrat.

CLINE, ANN, artist, designer; b. Greensboro, N.C., Apr. 7, 1934; d. Grady Alton and Mae Josephine (Karsten) Merriman; scholar Cooper Union, N.Y.C., 1954, Fashion Inst. Tech., 1957, Arts Students League, 1961-62, Fine Arts Acad., 1962-63, Joachim Simon Atelier, Tel Aviv, 1962; A.B., N.E. La. U., Monroe, 1971; m. S.C. Johananoff, Mar. 9, 1959 (div. 1973); 1 dau., Pamela; m. 2d, Francis X. Cline, Feb. 14, 1973. Asst. designer Adele Simpson Couture, 1959; pres. Johananoff Designs, 1967-70, Ann Cline Art Objects, Monroe, La., 1975—; pres. 165 North Properties; artist; works exhibited in group shows Haifa Mus., 1961, Am. Watercolor Soc., 1962; one person shows include: Barzansky Gallery, 1962, La. Polytech. U. Art Gallery, 1967, Mittel's Art Gallery, 1969, N.E. La. U., 1973, 71, Am. Consulate, Tel Aviv, 1962, Contemporary Gallery, Dallas, 1970, 22d Ann. Delta Exhbn., Ark. Arts Center, 1979, Mayor's Show, Monroe, 1979, Wesley Found. Award Show, 1979, 80, 81, others. Bd. dirs. La. Council Performing Arts, 1974; rep. Gov.'s Conf. Arts; bd. adjustments Monroe Zoning Commn.; trustee Masur Mus., 1974-75; bd. dirs. Little Theater of Monroe, 1975-76; bd. dirs. Women of the Ch., Episcopal Ch., 1977-78, mem. Daus. of the King, 1979-82, chmn. meml. com. Recipient Young Designer competition award Fontana of Rome, 1957, 1st prize Fashion Inst. Tech., 1959, Young Designer's award Women's Wear Daily, 1960, 1st prize, Arts Students League, 1961, 2d prize, 1963, 2d prize Fine Arts Acad., 1962, 1st prize, Woodstock Gallery, 1962, 1st prize, La. Folk Art Festival, 1966, 68, 72, prize awards Temple Emmanuel Ann., Dallas, 1969, 71, 74. Clubs: Bayou Desiard Country, Lotus, Illustrator: Jessie Strikes Louisiana Gold, 1969. Home and Office: 503 Speed Ave Monroe LA 71201

CLINE, JUDY ELIZABETH, writer, artist; b. Franklin, Ky., Dec. 24, 1944; d. Drew Saunders and Reba Mae (Webb) Gibson; student David Lipscomb Coll., 1963-64, Western Ky. U., 1965-66; m. Oliver Lawson Cline, Jan. 7, 1967; 1 dau., Cheryl-renee. Adminstrv. asst. to purchasing mgr. Kendall Co., Chgo. div., 1964-65, adminstrv. asst. to mgr., Franklin, 1966-67; expeditor, asst. mgr. Malone and Hyde Distbn. Center, Franklin, 1976-81; writer, artist Whimsies Unltd., Franklin, 1975—; exhibited in group shows including Parthenon, Nashville, 1975-76, Berry Hill, Frankfort, Ky., 1978, Capitol Bldg., Carson City, Nev., 1979; cons. Right to Read Ednl Program., Franklin, 1971-81. Speaker, Ky. Democratic Conv., Frankfort, 1980; del. Dem. Nat. Conv., N.Y.C., 1980; alt. del. White House Conf. on Families; leader 4-H Club. Mem. Nat. Soc. Pub. Poets, So. Ky. Guild Artists and Craftsmen, Barren River Area Arts Commn. Mem. Ch. of Christ. Clubs: Ky. Extension Homemakers. Asst. editor Voices, 1965-66. Home and Office: 111 Archwood Pl Madison TN 37115

CLINT, ANE DOROTHY, fin. exec.; b. Denver, Jan. 6, 1914; d. William Charles and Lillian Christina (Jacobsen) Ohrstedt; B.B.A. (coll. scholar) cum laude, Colo. Coll., 1933; m. David K. Clint, Jr., Dec. 15, 1950; stepchildren—David, Daniel. Acctg. clk. Am. Med. & Dental Assn., Denver, 1935-40; clk. local bd. 5, U.S. Selective Service, Denver, 1940-46; acctg. clk. Farmers Mktg. Assn., Denver. 1947—, asst. treas., 1965-69, treas., 1969—. Sec., Colo. R.R. Hist. Found., 1971—. Mem. Colo. Hist. Soc., Nat. Soc. Accts. for Coops., Historic Denver, Nat. R.R. Hist. Soc., Phi Beta Kappa. Republican. Clubs: Rocky Mt. R.R. (treas. 1959-70), Colo. Ghost Town (treas. 1977—), Rocky Mountain Jim Beam and Splty., Internat. Jim Beam Bottle and Spltys., Antique Bottle Collectors (treas. 1969-72), Mt. Vernon Country. Home: 815 Adams St Denver CO 80206 Office: 4545 Madison St Denver CO 80216

CLINTON, ANITA LOVELACE, community nutritionist; b. Charlotte Court House, Va., Aug. 6, 1935; d. Theodore R. and Sara (Thomas) Lovelace; B.S., U. Conn., 1957, M.S., 1974; m. Rodney D. Clinton, Dec. 6, 1958; children—Rodney D., Derek Lovelace. Head therapeutic dietitian Bridgeport (Conn.) Hosp., 1958-66; teaching dietitian, nutrition cons. Waterbury (Conn.) Hosp. and Mattatuck Community Coll. Schs. of Nursing, 1969-74; asso. prof. nutritional scis. U. Conn., Storrs, 1974-75, asso. extension agt., nutritionist, Bridgeport, 1975—; nutrition resource person Urban League Workshop, Rochester, N.Y., 1978. Bds. dirs. Bridgeport Symphony, 1962-64, Hall Neighborhood House, 1979—, Fedn. Neighborhood Councils, 1979—; vice chmn. allocations for social devel. United Way, 1980. Recipient service citation Major Appliance Consumer Action Panel, Chgo., 1978, service award United Way Eastern Fairfield County, 1979. Mem. Am. Dietetic Assn., Conn. Dietetic Assn. Republican. Baptist. Club: Links (Waterbury). Home: Pastors Walk Route 2 Newtown CT 06470 Office: 171 Golden Hill St Bridgeport CT 06604

CLINTON, LINDA PENELOPE HAMILTON, editor; b. Bklyn., Dec. 23, 1949; d. Alfred M. and Leona M. (Stokes) H.; A.A., Queensborough Community Coll., 1969; B.A., CCNY, 1971; m. Marcus Bethea Clinton, Mar. 3, 1973; 1 son, Marcus Hamilton. Paralegal-adminstrv. asst. Simpson Thacher & Bartlett, N.Y.C., 1971-74; asst. editor McCall's Mag., N.Y.C., 1974-78; sr. editor Working Mother Mag., N.Y.C., 1978—. Mem. Am. Soc. Mag. Editors, Delta Sigma Theta. Office: 230 Park Ave New York NY 10169

CLIPSHAM, JACQUELINE ANN, artist; b. Welwyn Garden City, Hertfordshire, Eng. (parents Am. citizens), July 27, 1936; d. George Frederick and Helene Lucille (Lees) C.; B.A., Carleton Coll., 1958; postgrad. Universita per Stranieri, Perugia, Italy, 1959; M.A., Western Res. U., 1962. Mem. Clay Art Center, Port Chester, N.Y., 1963-66; dir. ceramics program and art workshop CORE Community Center, Sumter, S.C., 1965; mem. faculty Bklyn. Mus. Art Sch., 1968-79, Essex County Coll., Newark, 1979-80; mem. Atlantic Gallery, N.Y.C., 1974—; mem. crafts task force Nat. Endowment for Arts, 1980; Culpeper Found. project coordinator, dept. community edn. Met. Mus. Art, N.Y.C., 1981—; mem. grants panel for crafts N.J. State Council Arts, 1982; works exhibited: Cleve. Mus., Bklyn. Mus., Mus. Contemporary Crafts, N.Y.C., Butler Inst. Art, Youngstown, Ohio, Hunterdon Art Center, Clinton, N.J., Greenwich House Pottery, N.Y.C., Pratt Inst., Bklyn., Atlantic Gallery, N.Y.C., 1980, Webster Coll., St. Louis, 1981; work loaned to Dept. Acad. Affairs, Met. Mus. Art, 1978. Recipient awards for ceramics and sculpture Butler Inst. Am. Art, 1963, 64, 65, nat. merit award for ceramics Mus. Contemporary Crafts, 1966. Mem. Coll. Art Assn., Am. Crafts Council, Women's Caucus for Art, Artists Equity N.Y., NOW, Alumni Assn. Cleve. Inst. Art, ACLU. Featured in Women Artists' Book, Women's Caucus for Art Exhbn., 1982, Artists' Books, From the Traditional to the Avant Garde, 1982. Home: 232 Warren St Brooklyn NY 11201 Studio: PO Box 387 Califon NJ 07830

CLOHERTY, PATRICIA MARY, investment banker; b. San Francisco, July 2, 1942; d. John Joseph and Doris (Dawson) Cloherty; B.A. (Calif. State scholar), San Francisco Coll. Women, 1963; M.I.A., M.A. (Ford Found. fellow), Columbia U., 1968; m. Daniel Tessler, May 24, 1977. Peace Corps vol., Brazil, 1963-65; asst. to pres. Inst. Internat. Edn., N.Y.C., 1969; analyst, then v.p. Alan Patricof Assos., Inc., pvt. investments, N.Y.C., 1970-77; dep. adminstr. SBA, Washington, 1977-78; pres. Tessler & Cloherty, Inc., investment bankers, N.Y.C., 1980—; dir., exec. com. Technoservice, Inc.; dir. Local Initiative Support Corp., Econ. Capital Corp. Bd. dirs. N.Y.C. Partnership, Internat. House, Green Hope, Services for Women, Women's Action Alliance. Recipient Outstanding Public Service award Nat. Council Women U.S., 1976. Roman Catholic. Home: 1 University Pl New York NY 10003 Office: 420 Madison Ave New York NY 10017

CLOHESY, STEPHANIE JUNE, assn. exec.; b. Morgantown, W.Va., Sept. 23, 1948; d. Edward John and Josephine J. (Pytlak) Jagucki; B.A., Loyola U., 1970; m. William W. Clohesy, June 19, 1971. Adminstr., Rome Center of Loyola U., Chgo., 1970-72; adminstrv. dir. Center for Policy Research, N.Y.C., 1972-77; exec. dir. NOW Legal Def. and Edn. Fund, N.Y.C., 1977—. Mem. Community Adv. Bd., Bklyn. Mem. Soc. Research Adminstrs., Nat. Assn. Public Service Orgn. Execs. Office: 36 W 44th St New York NY 10036

CLOPINE, MARJORIE SHOWERS, librarian; b. N.Y.C., June 25, 1914; d. Ralph Walter and Angelina (Jackson) Showers; B.A., Pa. State U., 1935; M.S., Drexel U., 1936; M.S., Columbia U., 1949. Gen. asst. Library, Drexel U., Phila., 1937-42; asst. librarian Gen. Chem. Div., Allied Chem. Corp., Morristown, N.J., 1943-46; bibliographer U.S. Office Tech. Services, Washington, 1946; med. librarian VA Hosp., Washington, 1946-49; asst. librarian U.S. Naval Obs., Washington, 1949-52, librarian, 1952-63; asso. librarian Bethany (W.Va.) Coll., 1967-69; asso. librarian Marine Research Lab. Fla. Dept. Natural Resources, St. Petersburg, 1971-73; cons. in astronomy Dewey Decimal Classification Editorial Office, Library of Congress, Washington, 1956. Chmn., Community Improvement program, Fla. Dist. 14, Gen. Fedn. Women's Clubs, 1980-82; library cons. Garden Center, Oglebay Park, Wheeling, W.Va., 1965-69. Alice B. Kroeger Meml. scholar, 1935-36. Mem. AAUW, Nat. Assn. Ret. Fed. Employees, Spl. Libraries Assn. (consultation officer Fla. chpt.), Beta Phi Mu. Unitarian. Clubs: Friends of the Arts and Scis., Internat. House, Woman's of Sarasota. Contbr. articles to profl. jours.

CLOSE, ELIZABETH SCHEU, architect; b. Vienna, Austria, June 4, 1912 (came to U.S. 1932, naturalized 1938); d. Gustav and Helene (Riesz) C.; student Technische Hochschule, Vienna, 1931-32; B.Arch., Mass. Inst. Tech., 1934, M.Arch., 1935; m. Winston A. Close, Apr. 11, 1938; children—Anne Miriam (Mrs. Milton Ulmer), Roy Michel, Robert Arthur. Draftsman Oscar Stonorov, Architect, Phila., 1935-36; designer Magney & Tusler, Mpls., 1936-38; partner, architect Close & Scheu (name changed to Close Assos., Inc., 1969), Mpls., 1938—; instr. Mpls. Sch. Art, 1936-37; instr. design U. Minn. Sch. Arch., 1938-39. Mem. Gov.'s Commn. on Minn.'s Future. Bd. dirs. Civic Orch. Mpls., 1951-68; bd. dirs. Minn. Opera Co.; pres. New Friends Chamber Music, 1973-74. Recipient Honor award Pub. Housing Adminstrn., 1964; hon. mention F.D. Roosevelt Meml. competition, 1960; honor award Minn. Soc. Architects, 1975. Fellow AIA (dir. Mpls. chpt., 1964-69); mem. Minn. Soc. Architects (v.p., pres. elect). Prin. works include Garden City Devel., Brooklyn Center, Minn., 1957; Duff House, Wayzata, Minn., 1959; variety structures Met. Med. Center Complex, 1960—, Golden Age Homes, 1960, both Mpls.; Peavey Tech. Center, Chaska, Minn., 1970; Gray Freshwater Biological Institute, 1973; Windslope Housing Project, Eden Prairie, Minn., 1978; Family Practice Clinic, Vadnais Heights, Minn., 1979. Home: 1588 Fulham St St Paul MN 55108 Office: Close Assos Inc 3101 E Franklin Ave Minneapolis MN 55406

CLOSTER, CATHERINE CAUTHORNE, psychologist; b. Richmond, Va., Dec. 16, 1949; d. Thomas Gordon and Jean Parrish (Luck) Cauthorne; B.A. (Algenon Sydney Sullivan award 1972), U. N.C., Chapel Hill, 1972, Ph.D., 1979; m. David Stanley Closter, Aug. 29, 1981. Psychologist, Family Resource Center, Albuquerque, 1977-78, Bernalillo Mental Health Center/Programs for Children, Albuquerque, 1978-79, Indian Childrens Program, Indian Health Service, Albuquerque, 1979-81; clinic instr. psychology U. R.I., Kingston, 1981—; pvt. practice psychology, Narragansett, R.I., 1981—; bd. dirs. Parentcraft; cons. in field. Mem. Am. Psychol. Assn., N.Mex. Psychol. Assn., R.I. Psychol. Assn., Order Old Well. Democrat. Episcopalian. Author articles in field. Home: 391 Forest Ave Middletown RI 02840 Office: 302 Chafee U RI Kingston RI 02881

CLOUD, CYNTHIA EUGENIA, banker; b. Martinsburg, W.Va., Jan. 6, 1943; d. Calvin Siler and Almira Eugenia (Coffinbargar) Knott; student Strayer Bus. Coll., Washington; m. Bernard Lee Cloud, Mar. 4, 1961; children—Tisha Annette, Marsha Ellen, Melissa Gaye. With FHA, Washington, 1960-64; with Shepherd Coll., 1964-66; with C & P Tel. Co., Martinsburg, W.Va., 1966-67; with Smith-Nadenbousch Instrument Co., Martinsburg, 1967-68; bookkeeper C & S Bank, Winchester, Va., 1970-72; adminstrv. asst. Shenandoah Valley Nat. Bank, Winchester, 1972-75; with Bank of Frederick County, Stephens City, Va., 1975—, now v.p., cashier; admissions dir. Shawnee Springs Nursing Home. Pres., Apple Pie Ridge Elem. Sch. PTO, 1979-80; chmn. bus. persons adv. council bus. dept. James Wood High Sch., 1979-80. Mem. Bank Adminstrn. Inst. (voting rep.), Nat. Assn. Bank Women (ednl. chmn. 1979-80), Am. Inst. Banking. Democrat. United Methodist (Sunday sch. tchr., mem. pastor-parrish com.). Clubs: Jaycettes, James Wood Band Boosters. Home: 1703 Valley Ave Winchester VA 22601 Office: 380 Millwood Ave Winchester VA 22601 *

CLOUD, DELORES ONA, educator; b. Ponemah, Minn., Aug. 6, 1941; diploma in bus. tng. Haskell Inst., Lawrence, Kans., 1962; student U. Minn., Bemidji (Minn.) State U. Sec., Hotel and Restaurant Workers Union Local #458, Mpls., 1968-72; tchr., coordinator ojibwe lang. program Am. Indian studies U. Minn., 1969-74; tchr., coordinator ojibwe tchrs. tng. and linguistic workshop Bemidji State U., 1974; cons. S. St. Paul Schs., 1973-74, Interstate Research Assos., Indian Day Care Project, Washington, 1973, Bur. Indian Affairs, 1972, Nat. Indian Edn. Assn., 1971; chmn. adv. council St. Paul Arts and Sci. Mus., 1973-74; panel speaker Nat. Indian Edn. Conf., Seattle, 1975; mem. Red Lake Edn. Task Force; tng. for Title IV staff Minn. Dept. Edn., also tng. for curriculum devel., coordinator Indian adult basic edn. program. Bd. dirs. Ams. for Indian Opportunity, 1970-73; mem. Red Lake Band of Chippewa Indians, Red Lake (Minn.) Indian Reservation. Mem. Nat. Indian Edn. Assn., Am. Indian Student Assn. (pres. U. Mnn. chpt. 1970-71, dir. 1973-74). Democrat. Address: PO Box 20 Red Lake MN 56671

CLOUGH, ELAINE BUCHHOLZ, librarian; b. Green Bay, Wis., July 2, 1921; d. Helmuth Henry and Lenora Elizabeth (Augustine) Buchholz; B.A., U. Wis., 1943; B.L.S., Simmons Coll., Boston, 1944; m. Robert Francis Clough, June 5, 1943; children—Betty Elaine, Jeanette Marie. Research librarian Turck, Hill & Co., N.Y.C., 1944-48; br. librarian Conejo Library, Thousand Oaks, Calif., 1967-70; bus. research librarian Ventura County Library Services Agy., Ventura, Calif., 1970—; bus. librarian Calif. Lutheran Coll., Thousand Oaks, 1978—. Trustee, Pequannock Twp. Public Library, Pompton Plains, N.J., 1961-65, pres., 1963-65; Pequannock Twp. neighborhood chmn. Morris Area council Girl Scouts U.S.A., 1962-65; SCORE/ACE Counseling Program, SBA, 1974—; v.p. LWV, Pompton Plains, 1959-62. Mem. Spl. Libraries Assn., Calif. Library Assn., Am. Library Assn., AAUW, Wis. Alumni Assn., Simmons Coll. Library Sch. Alumni Assn. Home: 1324 Buckingham Dr Thousand Oaks CA 91360 Office: PO Box 771 651 E Main St Ventura CA 93002

CLOVER, LOIS SMITH, public relations cons.; b. Starkville, Miss., Mar. 6, 1926; d. Floyd Rowan and Myrtle (Davis) Smith; B.A., La. Coll., 1947; m. Charles Chandler Clover, Jan. 24, 1948; children—Chandler Clare, Jane Arthur. News and feature writer Mobile Press and Register, summers 1945-46; editor Pineville (La.) News, 1948-49; feature writer Alexandria (La.) Town Talk, 1949-53; dir. public relations Belhaven Coll., Jackson, Miss., 1958-67, 72-76; editor Jackson mag., 1978; freelance cons., Jackson, 1978—. Pres., Jackson Symphony League, 1971, Miss. Opera Guild, 1973; chmn. Miss. Arts Festival, 1976. Recipient Beautiful Activist award, 1970, Outstanding Alumna award La. Coll., 1975. Mem. Nat. Press Women, Miss. Press Women (Woman of Achievement award 1978), Jackson Jr. League. Republican. Baptist. Address: 326 Glenway St Jackson MS 39216

CLOVIS, BARBARA FLIPSE, histopathologic technologist; b. Flushing, N.Y., Nov. 8, 1948; d. Robert Charles and Margaret Emily (Oehler) Flipse; H.T., N. Shore Hosp. Sch. Histologic Technique, 1968; student Eckerd Coll., 1970-71; m. Arnold J. Dazinis, June 3, 1978 (dec. 1980); 1 dau., Theresa Lee Dazinis; m. 2d, Ralph Clovis, Jan. 2, 1982; stepchildren—Ralph David, Suzanne Virginia. With Lane Bryant, Miami, Fla., 1966-67; histotechnologist N. Shore Hosp., Miami, 1967-70; mgr. thoroughbred breeding Kromor Farm, Reddick, Fla., 1971-73; histotechnologist, dir. Mid-Fla. Labs., Inc., Ocala, 1973-76; dir. Histopathology Lab., Marion Community Hosp., Ocala, 1976-80; mgr. comml. thoroughbred breeding facility Just-A-Farm, Dunnellon, Fla., 1980—; cons. dept. histopathology, Munroe Regional Med. Center, 1973-81. Youth coordinator, Holy Faith Episcopal Ch., 1981—. Mem. Am. Soc. Clin. Pathologists, Nat. Soc. Histotechnology, Fla. Soc. Histotechnologists, Fla. Thoroughbred Breeders Assn. Republican. Episcopalian. Club: Elks (hon. mem.). Address: Route 1 Box 384 Dunellon FL 32630

CLOW, TONI WIRKLER, nurse, educator; b. Monona, Iowa, Jan. 7, 1944; d. Merle Joseph and Helen Dorothea (Hazlett); B.S. in Nursing, U. Iowa, 1966, M.A., 1975; m. Donald Alan Clow, Sept. 11, 1965; children—Tanya Anne, Nathan Donald. Public health nurse Vis. Nurses Assn., Iowa City, 1966-68; asst.-in-instrn. U. Iowa Coll. Nursing, 1968-70, teaching asst., 1974-75; instr., nursing co-dir. pediatric nurse practitioner program, 1976-78, asst. prof., nursing co-dir., 1978-81, asso. prof., nursing co-dir., 1981—; instr. Mt. Mercy Coll., Cedar Rapids, Iowa, 1971-74, instr. pediatrics, community health nursing, 1975-76; chairperson task force Iowa Bd. Nursing, 1978—; cons. Iowa State Health Dept., 1978; mem. primary care tech. task force Iowa Health Systems Agy., Inc., 1977. Mem. Assn. of Faculties of Pediatric Nurse Assos./Practitioners Programs (officer-at-large 1981—), Nat. Assn. Pediatric Nurse Assos./Practitioners (disting. fellow award 1981), Iowa Assn. Nurse Practitioners (legis. com., co-chmn. 1980—), Am. Public Health Assn., Nat. League for Nursing and Iowa Citizens' League for Nursing, Inc., Am. Nurses Assn., Iowa Nurses Assn. (joint practice com. Iowa Med. Soc. 1978—), Sigma Theta Tau. Contbr. articles in field to profl. jours. Home: 4511 Twin Pine Dr NE Cedar Rapids IA 52402 Office: Coll Nursing U Iowa Iowa City IA 52242

CLUNIES, SANDRA MACLEAN, alcoholism counselor; b. Boston, Jan. 23, 1936; d. Daniel Fraser and Phyllis Cass (Wardrobe) MacLean; B.S., Simmons Coll., Boston, 1957; m. David A. Clunies, Oct. 12, 1957; children—Jonathan, Katherine. Caseworker, Balt. Dept. Public Welfare, 1957-58; research psychologist USAF, Bedford, Mass., 1958-60; vol., 1960-71; mem. staff Seneca House, Poolesville, Md., 1971—, counselor, 1975-78, dir., chief exec. officer, 1978—; chmn. Montgomery County Alcoholism Adv. Council, 1981-83; mem. Md. Alcoholism Counselors Cert. Bd., 1978—; chmn. com. ad hoc task force drinking and driving Montgomery County Govt., 1981; mem. Md. Task Force Women and Addictions, 1975—; com. chmn. Md. Congress Councils on Alcoholism, 1981. First exec. dir. Gaithersburg (Md.) HELP, 1967-69. Recipient Outstanding Citizen award community service Montgomery County Press Assn., 1968. Mem. Washington Area Council Alcoholism and Drug Abuse, Gen. Fedn. Women's Clubs. Office: 13025 Riley's Lock Rd Poolesville MD 20837

CLUTTER, MARY ELIZABETH, botanist, govt. ofcl.; b. Charleroi, Pa.; B.S., Allegheny Coll., 1953; M.S., U. Pitts., 1957, Ph.D. in Botany, 1960; married. Research assoc. Yale U., 1961-73, lectr. biology, 1965-78, sr. research assoc., 1973-78; program dir. NSF, Washington, 1976-81, sect. head, 1981—. Mem. AAAS, Am. Soc. Cell Biology, Am. Soc. Plant Physiologists, Scandinavian Soc. Plant Physiology, Soc. Devel. Biology. Office: National Science Foundation 1800 G St NW Washington DC 20550 *

CLYBURN, LINDA L., nurse; b. Williamson, W.Va., Nov. 5, 1945; d. Opal Ferne (Chapman) C.; diploma St. Mary's Hosp. Sch. Nursing, Huntington, W.Va., 1966; postgrad. W.Va. U., 1969, Marshall U., 1971, St. Joseph's Coll., North Windham, Maine, 1978, U. Central Fla., 1982—; m. Steven Edward Randall, Oct. 12, 1974. Charge nurse ICU and CCU, St. Mary's Hosp., Huntington, 1966-68; supr. ICU and CCU, Drs. Meml. Hosp., Huntington, 1968-73; team leader CCU, Community Hosp., Springfield, Ohio, 1973-74; charge nurse Urbana (Ohio) Care Center, 1974, dir. nursing services, 1974-78; dir. nursing services The Palms Health Care Center, Sebring, Fla., 1978-79; asst. head nurse, emergency and employee health services Ringling Bros., Barnum & Bailey Circus World, Orlando, Fla., 1979-80; asst. charge nurse emergency dept. Halifax Hosp. Med. Center, Daytona Beach, Fla., 1980-82; supr. operating room and post anesthesia Daytona Beach (Fla.) Gen. Hosp., 1982—; mem. med. staff Daytona Beach Internat. Speedway, 1981—. Bd. dirs. Ohio Hi-Point Joint Vocat. Sch. Allied Health Fields. Mem. Nat. League Nursing, Am., Fla. nurses assns., Emergency Dept. Nurses Assn., Am. Heart Assn. (basic life support instr. 1981, advanced cardiac life support 1982), Am. Assn. Critical Care Nurses, Defenders of Wildlife, Nat. Audubon Soc., Nat. Wildlife Found., Fund for Animals, Cousteau Soc. Republican. Methodist. Home: 5500 Ocean Shore Blvd Condo #17 Ormond Beach FL 32074

CLYBURN, ROSE MARY REED, chem. mktg. rep.; b. New London, Conn., July 31, 1954; d. Raymond Morgan and Bernice Joan (Zaugg) R.; B.S. in Zoology, U. R.I., 1976; M.B.A. in Fin., Northwe. U., 19 ; m. Collins G. Clyburn, Aug. 14, 1982. Market research assoc. PPG Industries Chems. Group, Pitts., 1976-77, field sales rep., Houston, 1977-78, sales rep. Chems. div., Chgo., 1978-80, sales devel. rep. Splty. Products Unit, Chgo., 1980—. Advisor Pitts. Jr. Achievement, 1976-77. Mem. Chgo. Fed. Socs. Coatings Tech., Chgo. Paint and Coatings Assn. Home: Rd #1 Sheldon Rd St Albans VT 05478 Office: 80 Main St W Orange NJ 07052

COATS, MARCY ISNER, histologist; b. Kansas City, Mo., Jan. 19, 1953; d. Rennix Joseph and Margaret Mary (McCloskey) Isner; student Brevard Hosp. Sch. Histology, 1970-71; m. John Vincent Coats, Aug. 10, 1974. Histologist, Brevard Hosp., Melbourne, Fla., 1970-74, Fla. Hosp., Orlando, 1974-75, Pathology Assos., Tampa, Fla., 1975-77, Tampa Gen. Hosp., 1977-78, Women's Hosp., Tampa, 1978—. Mem. Am. Soc. Clin. Pathologists, Fla. Histology Soc. Home: 1708 Orange Hill Dr Brandon FL 33511 Office: 3030 W Buffalo Ave Tampa FL 33607

COBB, CAROLYN ANN, telephone co. exec.; b. St. Louis, Feb. 21, 1950; d. Vincent Atlee and Margaret Elizabeth (Ottinger) Knopp; B.A., Harris Tchrs. Coll., 1973; M.A., Webster Coll., 1975; m. Richard Joseph Cobb, Aug. 7, 1976; 1 son, Richard Joseph. Tchr., St. Louis Public Schs. 1973-74; programmer Gen. Am. Life, 1974-75, Mercantile Trust Co., N.A. 1975-78; programmer/analyst Mo. Pacific R.R. 1979-81; data base adminstr, asst. staff mgr. Southwestern Bell, St. Louis 1981—. Home: 6520 Galewood Ct St Louis MO 63129 Office: 915 Olive St Suite 700 Saint Louis MO 63101

COBB, JENNIFER EVANS JONES, educator; b. Cin., Sept. 16, 1945; d. Harley Arthur and Jeanne Miriam (Evans) Jones; B.A., Ottawa U., 1970; M.S., Kans. State U., 1972, Ph.D., 1978; m. Ronald Lee Cobb, Sept. 9, 1966; 1 son, David Albert. Tchr., Louisburg (Kans.) High Sch., 1970-71; grad. teaching asst. Kans. State U., Manhattan, 1974-75; chmn., asst. prof. home econs. Washburn U., Topeka, 1975—. Cons., United Way of Topeka on Day Care for Children, 1979-80; chmn. Task Force on Aging, Topeka N. Outreach, 1972-74; founder, dir. VIP Luncheon, 1972-74. Mem. Nat. Council Family Relations, Am. Home Econs. Assn., Nat. Council Adminstrs. Home Econs., AAUP, Kans. Home Econs. Assn., Topeka Home Econs. Assn., Phi Delta Kappa. Mem. Disciples of Christ. Office: Home Econs Dept Washburn U Topeka KS 66621

COBB, LLEWELLA JEAN BESS, nursing adminstr.; b. Bradford, Pa., May 23, 1934; d. Charles Benjamin and Eva Marie (Koch) Bess; R.N., Arnot-Ogden Meml. Hosp. Sch. Nursing, Elmira, N.Y., 1955; student Tex. Woman's U., 1972-73, St. Thomas U., 1973, Ottawa U., 1980. Med.-surg. nurse VA, Bath, N.Y., 1955-56; operating room nurse Olean (N.Y.) Gen. Hosp., 1956-57; operating room nurse St. Francis Hosp., Olean, N.Y., 1957-59; operating room nurse Roswell Park Meml. Inst., Buffalo, 1960-61; occupational health nurse Niagara Machine and Tool Works, Buffalo, 1963-65; occupational health nurse T. Smith & Sons, New Orleans, 1966; hemodialysis and operating room nurse VA, New Orleans, 1967-69; head nurse hemodialysis and ICU Unit, Ochsner Found. Hosp., New Orleans, 1969-72; hemodialysis nurse VA, Houston, 1972; dept. head hemodialysis Diagnostic Clinic of Houston, 1973-77; operating room nurse VA, Houston, 1977-78; dir. Kidney Disease Center, North Miss. Med. Center, Tupelo, 1978-80; adminstr. renal disease services Meth. Hosp. of Ind. Inc., Indpls., 1980—; dir. Immunetics, Houston, 1982—. Mem. Am. Assn. Nephrology Nurses and Technicians, Nat. Renal Adminstrs. Assn., Nat. Kidney Found., Nat. Assn. Patients on Hemodialysis and Transplantation. Republican. Home: 10919 Fondren Rd #1701 Houston TX 77096

COBBETT, DOROTHY COLBERT, assn. exec.; b. Bartow, Fla., June 4, 1947; adopted dau. Ethel Stewart Colbert; B.S., Fla. So. Coll., 1969; M.A. in Teaching, Rollins Coll., Winter Park, Fla., 1975; Ed.S., Tenn. State U., 1979; m. Edward Cobbett, June 1, 1973; 1 dau., Ethel Marie. Tchr., Polk County (Fla.) Schs., 1969-77; master distbr. Holiday Magic Cosmetics, Polk County, 1972-77, instr., 1973-77; dir. field services Metro Nashville Edn. Assn., 1977—; prof. in residence Project Upward Bound, U. South Fla., Tampa, 1971; instr. Nashville State Tech. Inst., 1980—; with Registered Lobbyists for Educators in Tenn., 1977—. Active Girl Scouts U.S.A., Project PENCIL Found. Mem. NEA, Nat. Assn. Female Execs., Assn. Tchr. Educators, Nat. Staff Orgn., Nat. Local Profl. Staff Assn., Tenn. Edn. Assn., Middle Tenn. Edn. Assn., Met. Nashville Edn. Assn., Nashville Urban League, LWV, Phi Delta Kappa. Democrat. Methodist. Home: 100 In A Vale Dr Brentwood TN 37027 Office: 2730 Larmon Dr Nashville TN 37204

COBBIN MURPHY, EARLEAN, lawyer; b. Chgo., July 15, 1943; d. Eddie and Lucinda (Watts) Slaughter; A.A. with honors, Thornton Jr. Coll., 1969; B.S.Ed. cum laude (Legal Opportunities scholar, 1970), Chgo. State U., 1970; J.D., DePaul U., 1976; children—Kenneth, Alonzo, Charlean Renee, Twanda Lekecia. Sec., Samuel Miller & Co., Chgo., 1963-66, Sears Roebuck & Co., Chgo., 1966-68; tchr. Chgo. Vocat. High Sch., Chgo. Bd. Edn., 1971-75; admitted to Ill. bar, 1976; individual practice, Harvey, Ill., 1976—; part time instr. Chgo. State U.; part time atty. Ill. Sec. of State. Mem. ABA, Nat. Bar Assn., Ill. Bar Assn., Cook County Bar Assn., Chgo. Bar Assn., South Suburban Bar Assn., Women's Bar Assn. Unitarian. Office: 15402 S Center Suite 3 Harvey IL 60429

COBEY, ARLENE ANNE, cosmetics sales co. exec.; b. Fairfax, Va., May 16, 1955; d. John Anthony and Ida Mary (Wanke) Cobey; student Continential B.B. Inst., 1973; lic. Stamford U., 1974. Group mgr. Seligman & Latz, Inc., Syracuse, N.Y., 1974-77; asst. regional mgr. Syntex, Upstate N.Y., Maine, Mass., 1977-81; pres. Michel-Arlen Sales & Assos., Syracuse, 1981—; edn1. advisor Matrix Essentials, Inc., Solon, Ohio, 1981-82. Ednl. advisor United Way Agy., Syracuse, 1982—. Recipient Advisor of Yr. award Syntex Beauty Care, Inc., 1978. Mem. Am. Soc. Bus. Profl. Women, Am. Barber Beauty Supply Inst., Artistic Skating of Am., Bus. and Profl. Women, Am. Soc. Profl. and Exec. Women. Democrat. Roman Catholic. Home: 311 Molloy Rd East Syracuse NY 13211 Office: 311 1/2 Molloy Rd East Syracuse NY 13211

COBURN, DENISE CAPPS, educator; b. Lucama, N.C., Nov. 6, 1920; d. George C. and Amy Alta Capps; A.B., U. Akron, 1943; M.S. S.A., Case Western Res. U., 1951; cert. clin. practice in transactional analysis Internat. Transactional Analysis Assn., 1973; m. L. Paul Coburn, Aug. 9, 1941; children—Christopher, Leslie, Ann, Cal. Psychiat. social worker Child Guidance Center, Cleve., 1952-56; med. social worker Sparrow Hosp., Lansing, Mich., 1962-69, asst. dir. med. social services, 1968-69; asst. prof. social work Mich. State U., 1969—; cons. transactional analysis and social problems of children and families. HEW grantee, 1974-75. Mem. Acad. Cert. Social Workers, Nat. Assn. Social Workers, Internat. Transactional Analysis Assn. (exam. bd. 1976-77), Council Social Work Edn., AAUP (exec. bd. 1974-76), Am. Orthopsychiat. Assn. Author: The Heart of Intimacy, 1982; Social Treatment: A Transactional Analysis Model, 1983. Office: Michigan State University East Lansing MI 48823

COBURN, MARJORIE FOSTER, psychotherapist; b. Salt Lake City, Feb. 28, 1939; d. Harlan Arnold and Alma (Ballinger) Polk; B.A. in Sociology, UCLA, 1960; asso. Montessori internat. diploma Washington Montessori Inst., 1968; M.A. in Psychology, U. No. Colo., 1979; doctoral candidate in counseling psychology U. Denver; m. Robert Byron Coburn, July 2, 1977; children—Robert Scott, Polly Klea Foster, Matthew Ryan Foster, Kelly Anne. Probation officer Alameda County (Calif.), 1960-62, Contra Costa County (Calif.), 1966, Fairfax County (Va.), 1967; dir. club for recovering mental patients Orange County (Fla.) Mental Health Assn., 1963-65; tchr. Va. Montessori Sch., Fairfax, 1968-70; spl. edn. tchr. Leary Sch., Falls Church, Va., 1970-72, sch. adminstr., 1973-76; sch. adminstr. Aseltine Sch., San Diego, 1976-77, Coburn Montessori Sch., Colorado Springs, Colo., 1977-79; supervised pvt. practice psychotherapy, Colorado Springs, 1979-82; psychology intern U. Calif., San Diego, 1982—; cons., condr. workshops in spl. edn.; bd. dirs. Calif. Assn. Pvt. Spl. Edn. Schs., 1976-77; mem. Leary Edn. Adv. Bd., 1977-80. Mem. Am. Orthopsychiat. Assn., Phobia Soc., Council Exceptional Children, El Paso Psychol. Assn., AAUW, NOW, Mensa Internat. Democrat. Episcopalian. Author: (with R. C. Orem) Montessori: Prescription for Children with Learning Disabilities, 1978. Home: 2180 Calle Frescota La Jolla CA 92037 Office: 16766 Bernardo Center Dr Rancho Bernardo CA 92128

COCA, IMOGENE, actress, comedienne; b. Phila., Nov. 18; d. Joe and Sadie (Brady) Coca; m. Bob Burton, 1935; m. 2d, King Donovan, Oct. 1960. Made first appearance as tap dancer in N.Y.C. vaudeville at age of 11; debut as comedienne, New Faces of 1934; appeared in Straw Hat Revue, 1939; played in summer shows, Pa., 1938-42; first appearance on TV in Broadway Revue, 1949; on Your Show of Shows (Emmy 1952), NBC-TV, 1950-54; TV series Grindl, 1963-64; TV shows Imogene Coca Show, 1954-55, Sid Caesar Invites You; appeared in stage plays The Four Poster, 1973, Prisoner of Second Avenue, 1973, also Once Upon a Mattress, Plaza Suite, I Can't Hear You When the Water is Running, Twentieth Century; toured with Sid Caesar, Las Vegas and N.Y.C., 1978-79; films include Under the Yum Yum Tree, 1963, Ten from Your Show of Shows, 1973, Rabbit Test. Address: care Blake Agy Ltd 409 N Camden Dr Suite 202 Beverly Hills CA 90210 *

COCCARI, BARBARA MOONEY, ednl. cons.; b. Greenburg, Pa., Sept. 28, 1946; d. Richard L. and Matilda M. (Barton) Mooney; student U. Ams., Mexico City, 1970; B.S., Calif. State Coll., 1966; M.A., N.Y. U., 1972; postgrad. U. Pitts., 1980—; m. David P. Coccari, May 26, 1973. Caseworker, N.Y.C. Dept. Social Service, 1966-70; community social worker N.Y.C. Human Resources Adminstrn., 1970-72; tchr., operator Adult Edn. Program, Intermediate Unit I, Waynesburg, Pa., 1975—; with Comoco Cons., Pine Bank, Pa., 1973—; counselor, social and community services Cath. Diocese of Pitts., 1980—; dir. Operation Outreach, Bowlby Public Library, Waynesburg, 1976-78. Treas., bd. dirs. Parents Anonymous of Greene County, 1979-80; sec. Health and Welfare Council, Greene County, 1980-81, pres., 1981-82; notary public, Pa. Recipient Golden Key award, Greene County. Democrat. Roman Catholic. Home: RD 1 Pine Bank PA 15354 Office: 243 E High St Waynesburg PA 15370

COCHÉ, JUDITH ABBE, psychologist; b. Phila., Sept. 2, 1942; d. Louis and Miriam (Nerenberg) Milner; B.A., Colby Coll., 1964; M.A., Temple U., 1966; Ph.D., Bryn Mawr Coll., 1975; m. Erich Coché Oct. 16, 1966; children—Juliette Laura, Raymond Erich. Clin. research asst. Jefferson Med. Coll., 1965-66; diagnostician Law Court, Aachen, W. Ger., 1967-68; staff psychologist N.E. Community Mental Health Center, Phila., 1969-74; family clinician Inst. Pa. Hosp., 1974-76; instr. psychology Drexel U., 1976-77; lectr. Med. Coll. Pa., 1977-78; asst. clin. prof. Hahnemann Med. Coll., Phila., 1979—; psychologist in pvt. practice, Phila., 1974—; clin. cons. Hilltop Prep. Sch., 1977—. Bd. dirs. Whitemarsh Art Center, 1977-78; program cons. WHYY-TV, 1978; mem. profl. adv. bd. Parents Without Partners, 1977—. Grantee, Del. Childrens Bur., Bryn Mawr Coll., 1974-75, Pa. Hosp., 1975-77. Mem. Phila. Soc. Clin. Psychologist (pres. 1980-81), Family Inst. Phila., Am. Assn. Marriage and Family Therapists, Am. Group Psychotherapy Assn., Am. Psychol. Assn., Pa. Psychol. Assn. (chmn. legis. com. 1982), Soc. Research in Psychotherapy. Contbr. articles to profl. jours., chpts. to books. Address: 2037 Delancey Pl Philadelphia PA 19103

COCHRAN, DEBORAH RAND, state legislator; b. N.Y.C., Nov. 18, 1939; d. James Henry, III and Mary Banks (Page) Rand; student Wellesley Coll., 1957-58; B.A., N.Y. U., 1962; postgrad. Smith Coll., 1963-64; children—Thomas Charles, Christine Rand, Stephen Rand, Diana Banks. Advisor Child Abuse Task Force, Jr. League of Boston, Inc., 1974-78; child abuse investigative coordinator, office Dist. Atty., 1977-78; mem. Mass. Ho. of Reps., 1979-82, v.p. freshman legis. class, 1979-80, house ethics com., 1981-82, mem. Mass. Commn. on the Elderly, legis. com. on election laws, legis. com. on human services and elderly affairs; ex-officio mem. gov.'s Commn. on Status of Women; chmn. Norfolk County Mental Health Legis. Caucus; treas. Mass. Caucus Women Legislators, 1979-80; co-chmn. Republican Study Group, 1979. Bds. dirs. Mass. Soc. for Prevention of Cruelty to Children, 1977-82, Dedham (Mass.) Family Service, 1976-82; founding dir. Human Services Council of Dedham; mem. Town Meeting, Dedham, 1977-78, Citizens Adv. Com., Dedham, 1976-78; vice chmn. Dedham Olde Time Community Fair, 1977; mem. King Philip Elder Services Adv. Com., 1980-82, South Norfolk Council for Children, 1976-81; chmn. Dedham Rep. Town Com.; mem. Mass. Rep. State Com. Episcopalian. Home: 902 High St Dedham MA 02026

COCHRAN, JANICE LOUISE, mktg. exec.; b. Cin., June 3, 1946; d. Raymond L. and Edna (Roy) Cochran; B.S., Jacksonville U., 1970. With Ford Motor Co., Cin., 1970-74; with IBM Corp., various locations, 1974—, sales rep., Cin., 1974-76, product planning mgr., Lexington, Ky., 1977-79, mktg. account mgr., Atlanta, 1979—. Active, Big Bros./Big Sisters of Am., 1980-81. Served with USN, 1964-67. Mem. Nat. Orgn. Female Execs. Republican. Roman Catholic. Club: Women's Commerce. Home: 1105 Berkshire Rd Atlanta GA 30306 Office: 2690 Cumberland Pkwy Atlanta GA 30339

COCHRAN, JULIENNE VRADENBURGH, librarian; b. San Anselmo, Calif., June 19, 1907; d. Preston Hickok and Juliet Burroughs (Cochran) Vradenburgh; A.B., Mills Coll. 1930; M.A., Stanford U., 1946; M.L.S., Case Western Res. U., 1960; postgrad. U. Ill., 1972—; m. Dennis G. McQuade, June 19, 1932; m. 2d, Stefan A. Wade, Jan. 4, 1971. Librarian, Pasadena (Calif.) Star-News and Post, 1932-42; safety engr. U.S. Naval Air Sta., Moffatt Field, 1944-46; librarian Stanford (Calif.) U., 1948-50, Tacoma Public Library, 1950-52; instr. Coll. Puget Sound (Wash.), summer 1952; librarian Miss Hall's Sch. for Girls, Pittsfield, Mass., 1953-54; documents librarian Whitman Coll., 1954-55; asst. librarian S.D. Tchrs. Coll., Aberdeen, 1956-57; law librarian U. Idaho, Moscow, 1957-58; ref. librarian Case Western Res. U., Cleve., 1958-60; law librarian Akron (Ohio) Law Library, 1960-62, Cook County Law Library, Chgo., 1966-68; Ill. Research Librarian, Champaign, Ill., 1972—; library cons. Ill. Continuing Edn., 1972—. Recipient Cert. of Achievement, No. Ill. U., 1971, 72; Social Sci. Research Council grantee, 1946, 52, 58-60, 68-72, 74—; cert. tchr., Ill. Mem. Women in Communication, DAR, Theta Sigma Phi, Sigma Delta Chi, Kappa Delta Pi, Sigma Iota Epsilon, Delta Gamma Sigma, Phi Beta Lambda, Alpha Phi Omega, Phi Delta Kappa. Republican. Clubs: Order Eastern Star, Women's, Wici. Author: Guaranteed Annual Wage, 1946; State Sources to School Libraries, 1965; Internat. Ednl. Orgn., 1952; Guide to Thomas Beer 1977; Paul Monroe Writings, 1966; Books on Financial History of U.S., 1970; Guide for Business Research, 1975; Civil Disturbances and Civil Disorders, 1976; Tunis Wortmen and Freedom of the Press, 1981; Continuing Education Law, 1982. Home: 1107 W Green St Urbana IL 61801 Office: PO Box 2979 Sta A Champaign IL 61820

COCHRAN, LEONA JEAN, cons. engr.; b. Gary, Ind., Nov. 2, 1936; d. Willie and Minnie Lee (Greer) Stroud; B.A., Mundelein Coll., 1981; M.S., Nat. Coll. Edn., 1982; m. Christopher C. Cochran Jr., Sept. 8, 1957; children—Karen Alise, Ronald Kevin. Exec. sec. Dr. Brian Berry, U. Chgo., 1974; adminstrv. asst. Dr. John Sheaffer of Bauer, Sheaffer & Lear, Chgo., 1977; dir. adminstrn., treas., dir. Sheaffer & Roland, Inc., Chgo., 1982—; dir. Energy Harvest, Inc. Mem. Chgo. Bd. Edn., 1982—. Mem. Am. Mgmt. Assn. Unitarian. Home: 8916 S Harper Chicago IL 60619 Office: Sheaffer & Roland Inc 130 N Franklin St Chicago IL 60606

COCHRAN, STEFANI DEIRDRE, social worker; b. Manila, Philippines, Oct. 22, 1940; d. Robert Edgar and Susan Elizabeth (Jurika) Cecil; B.A., Stanford U., 1961; M.S.W., Cath. U. Am., 1975; m. Garrett Cochran, Dec. 22, 1962; children—Suzita, Heather; m. 2d, Daniel Couch, Nov. 6, 1975. Econ. analyst CIA, Langley, Va., 1961-66; social worker Fairfax County (Va.) Schs., 1975-79; exec. dir. Marriage and Family Clinic, Silver Spring, Md., 1979-80; clin. dir. Family Counseling and Evaluation Center, Oakton, Va., 1980—; lectr. in field. Founder, No. Va. Stepfamily Assn., 1980. Carnegie Found. fellow, 1960. Mem. Nat. Assn. Social Workers, Acad. Cert. Social Workers, Am. Orthopsychiat. Assn., Stepfamily Assn. Am., Soc. Clin. Social Work. Unitarian (pres. ch.). Clubs: RunHers, Potomac, Old Dominion Dancers, Reston Flute Quintet, Reston Chorale. Home: 2005 Cutwater Ct Reston VA 22091 Office: 2519 Hunter Mill Rd Suite 19 Oakton VA 22124

COCHRANE, BETSY LANE, state legislator; b. Asheboro, N.C.; d. William Jennings and Brodus Inez (Campbell) Lane; B.A., Meredith Coll., 1958; m. Joe Kenneth Cochrane, June 14, 1958; children—Lisa Lane, Craig Campbell. Tchr., Winston-Salem (N.C.) Sch. Dist., 1958-61, 66-67, Highland Presbyn. Ch. Sch., Winston-Salem, 1969-76; mem. N.C. Ho. of Reps., 1980—; dir. Jeffries Engring. & Equipment Co., 1981—. Mem. Nat. Conf. State Legislators, Meredith Coll. Alumni Assn., Kappa Nu Sigma. Republican. Baptist. Office: 1015 Legislative Bldg Raleigh NC 27611

COCHRANE, ELIZABETH BRANTLY, oil co. exec.; b. Birmingham, Ala., Jan. 22, 1945; d. William Minge and Mary Kate (Jemison) C.; B.S., U. Ala., 1967. Dept. mgr. Sears Roebuck, Bel Air Mall, Mobile, Ala., 1967-69, fashion coordinator, 1969-70; sec. treas. McGuire Engring. Co., Tuscaloosa, Ala., 1970-80; pres. Douglas Exploration Co., Inc., Tuscaloosa, 1981—, also dir.; sec. treas. Talbot & Co., Inc., 1980—, also dir. Pres. bd. dirs. Spouse Abuse Network Tuscaloosa, 1981—; bd. dirs. Tuscaloosa County Preservation Soc., 1977-80; chmn. public relations Tuscaloosa Jr. League, 1972-78; pres. bd. dirs. Tuscaloosa County

Humane Soc., 1979—. Episcopalian. Home: PO Box 1275 Tuscaloosa AL 35403 Office: 611 Hwy 82 West Northport AL 35476

COCHRANE, PEGGY, architect, writer; b. Alhambra, Calif., July 9, 1926; d. E. Elliott and Gladys (Moran) C.; B.A., Scripps Coll., 1945; postgrad., U. So. Calif., 1951-52, Columbia U., 1954; m. Hugh Bowman, Nov. 24, 1954 (div.). Job capt. Kahn and Jacobs, N.Y.C., 1954-55; project architect Litchfield, Whiting, Panero & Severud, Teheran, Iran, 1956; archtl. designer Daniel, Mann, Johnson and Mendenhall, Los Angeles, 1956-59; individual practice architecture, Sherman Oaks, Calif., 1966—. Recipient Architecture prize Scripps Coll., 1945. Mem. Assn. Women in Architecture (life), Union Internationale des Femmes Architects. Republican. Episcopalian. Club: Dionysians (S. Pasadena). Author mus. Yucatan, 1979, play I Gave at the Office, 1980; mem. editorial bd. Los Angeles Architect, 1978—; contbr. to Contemporary Architects. Home and office: 3888 Sherview Dr Sherman Oaks CA 91403

COCKER, BARBARA JOAN, marine artist, interior designer; b. Uxbridge, Mass.; d. Frank Blessing and Mary (Anderson) Cassidy; A.A., Becker Jr. Coll., 1943; student Mt. St. Mary Coll., 1944-45, Clark U., summer 1945, N.Y. Sch. Interior Design, 1965-67; m. John T. Cocker, June 26, 1948; children—David John, Neil Joseph. Owner, operator Barbara J. Cocker, Interior Design, Rumson, N.J., 1966—; owner Barbara J. Cocker Paintings of the Sea Gallery, Nantucket, Mass., 1975—; tchr. adult edn. courses in interior design, 1965-68; artist, pvt. instr. marine art; pres. Maximus Praetorius Corp., Nantucket, Mass., 1979—; exhibited one-man shows marine paintings Little Gallery, Barbizon, N.Y., 1971, Old Mill Assn., 1971, Pacem en Terris Gallery, N.Y.C., 1972, Central Jersey Bank & Trust Co., Rumson, 1971, 72, 74, 77, 79, Little Gallery, Nantucket Art Assn., 1975, 77, 79, 81, Caravan House Galleries, N.Y.C., 1975, 79, Guild of Creative Art, Shrewsbury, N.J., 1976, 81, IBM Corp., N.J., 1977, South St. Seaport Mus., N.Y., 1977, 80, Provident Nat. Bank, Phila., 1978, Gallery 100, Princeton, 1978, Bell Telephone Research Labs., 1982; exhibited group shows including Burr Artists N.Y., Guild Creative Art N.J., Composers, Authors and Artists Am. NAD, Salmagundi Club N.Y.C., Monmouth Coll. Festival of Arts, Caravan House Galleries, Pen and Brush Club, N.Y.C., N.Y.C., Lever House Galleries, N.Y.C., Nat. Arts Club, N.Y.C. Mem. Burr Artists, Cutharine Lorillard Wolfe Arts Club, Am. Artists Profl. League N.Y. Guild Creative Arts, Nantucket Art Assn., Composers, Authors and Artists of Am., Allied Artists Am., Monmouth Arts Found. (N.J.), So. Vt. Artists Inc., Dayrells Art Center (Barbados). Address: 3 Rumson Rd Rumson NJ 07760 also Paintings Of Sea Galery Old South Wharf Nantucket MA 02554

COCKRAM, DARNELL HUGHES, nursing edn. adminstr.; b. Stuart, Va., Aug. 30, 1940; d. James Roy and Vada Gay (Pendleton) Hughes; R.N., U. Va., B.S., 1971; M.S. in Nursing, Emory U., 1977; m. Douglas L. Cockram, Aug. 30, 1958; 1 dau., Linda Dawn. Staff nurse Martinsville (Va.) Gen. Hosp., 1965-66, head nurse, 1966-68, nursing supr., 1971-72, coordinator inservice edn., 1972-77; dir. Sch. Nursing, Meml. Hosp., Danville, Va., 1978—. Chmn., Va. State Public Health Scholarship Com., 1981—. Mem. Am. Nurses Assn., Nat. League Nursing, Am. Heart Assn. (sci. council for cardiovascular nursing), Am. Assn. Critical Care Nurses, Sigma Theta Tau. Baptist. Club: Pilot (sec. 1981). Home: Route 8 Box 84 Martinsville VA 24112 Office: 142 S Main St Danville VA 24541

COCKRELL, PEARL HAND, poet; b. Gadsden, Ala., Jan. 2, 1921; d. Arthur H. and May (Jones) Hand; student Massey Bus. Coll., Cleve. State Community Coll.; m. Harold R. Cockrell, May 11, 1946; children—Pamela Cockrell White, Jan Cockrell Mitchell, Donis E. Schweizer. Author: Sing On, America (poems), 1976, Of Men and Seasons, 1978; contbr. poems to mags. including Sci. of Mind, Home Life, Modern Maturity, Music Ministry, Grit, The Volunteer Gardener, Tennessee Voices Anthology, The American, Ch. Musician, Progressive Farmer, Nat. Daffodil Jour., Missionary Messenger, Camellia Jour., Poet's Monthly, Encore; also anthologies: Pegasus, The Sampler, Nat. Fedn. State Poetry Socs.; weekly columnist So. Democrat, 1973-80. Prize Poems, Clover Collection Verses, Tenn. Voices, Sandcutters, Rose Garden, Garden Prayers, Alalitcom, others. Recipient Tenn. Fedn. Garden Clubs, Inc. Poet Laureate award, 1973, 74, 75, 76, 77; 1st place poetry award Authors and Artists Club Chattanooga, 1972; Am. Legion award, 1974; 1st place awards Nat. Fedn. State Poetry Socs., 1974, 79, also Walter R. Lovel Meml. award, 1974; Tenn. Poet Laureati's 1st place Mid South Poetry Festival, 1976, 1st place lyric poetry award, 1977, Miss. Poet Laureate prize, 1978; Nat. Contest 1st place award Ky. State Poetry Soc., 1976; Freedoms Found. award, 1977; Nat. Contest 1st place award Utah State Poetry Soc., 1977; Young and Collier award Deep South Writers and Artists Assn., 1978; 1st place Mid-South Poetry Festival Competitions, 1976, 77, 78(2), 81(2); numerous other awards. Mem. Nat. League Am. Pen Women (historian Chickasaw br., letters contest 1st place numerous articles award, 1975, 77, 1st place narrative poetry award, 1977), Tenn. Woman's Press and Authors Club, Poetry Soc. Tenn., Ala. Writers Conclave (literary competitions 2 first place awards 1975, humorous poetry 1st place award 1977, lyric award 1977, 2 1st place awards 1978), Tenn. Writers Guild (1st v.p.), Ala. State Poetry Soc., Cleve. Creative Arts Guild (children's fiction 1st place award 1973, poetry 1st place award 1974, gen. articles 1st place award 1974, Catriona Dow award 1974, poetry award 1979). Baptist. Home and Office: PO Box 16175 Chattanooga TN 37416

CODER, RACHEL REED, social worker; b. Lexington, Ky., Oct. 17, 1940; B.A., Rollins Coll., 1962; M.S.W., Fordham U., 1965; married; 1 son. Social worker field placement Spence Chapin Adoption Agy., N.Y.C., 1962-64, obstet. unit St. Luke's Women's Hosp., N.Y.C., 1965-66; sr. social worker surg., orthopaedic and ENT units Lenox Hill Hosp., N.Y.C., 1966-70; dir social services Silver Hill Found., New Canaan, Conn., 1971-77, Bethesda Meml. Hosp., Boynton Beach, Fla., 1980—; mem. faculty Grad. Sch. Social Work, U. Conn., 1975-76, Grad. Sch. Social Work, Barry U., 1981-82. Vol. group therapist USAFB, Glyfada, Athens, Greece, 1978-79; bd. dirs. Hospice of Boca Raton, Fla., 1980. Cert. social worker, N.Y.; lic. clin. social worker, Fla. Mem. Am. Hosp. Soc. for Dirs. Social Services, Nat. Assn. Social Work, Acad. Cert. Social Workers, Register Clin. Social Workers. Address: 6217 Celadon Circle Eastpointe Country Club Palm Beach Gardens FL 33410

CODERE, HELEN FRANCES, anthropologist, educator; b. Winnipeg, Man., Can., Sept. 10, 1917; came to U.S. 1919, naturalized 1924; d. Charles Francis and Mabelle (Prosser) Codere; B.A. summa cum laude, U. Minn., 1939; Ph.D., Columbia U., 1950. Instr., Vassar Coll., 1946-50, asst. prof., 1951-53, asso. prof., 1955-57, prof., 1958-63; vis. lectr. anthropology U. B.C., 1954-55; vis. lectr. Northwestern U., winter 1963; mem. faculty Bennington (Vt.) Coll., 1963-64; prof. anthropology Brandeis U., Waltham, Mass., 1964—, dean Grad. Sch. Arts and Scis., 1975—; anthrop. fieldwork Kwakiutl Indians of B.C., 1951-55, Rwanda, Africa, 1959-60. Faculty fellow Vassar Coll., 1956; Social Sci. Research Council fellow, 1956, 62-63; Guggenheim fellow, 1959-60. Fellow Am. Anthrop. Assn. (exec. council. 1966—), AAAS, African Studies Assn., N.Y. Acad. Scis.; mem. Am. Ethnol. Soc. (pres. 1971-72), Phi Beta Kappa. Author: Fighting with Property: a study of Kwakiutl Potlatching and Warfare, 1792-1930, 1950. Contbr. articles to profl. jours. Office: Dept Anthropology Brandeis U Waltham MA 02154

CODY, JANE MERRIAM, classicist; b. Chgo., Oct. 20, 1941; d. John Henry and Charlotte (Orr) Merriam; A.B., Randolph-Macon Women's Coll., 1963; M.A., Bryn Mawr Coll., 1964, Ph.D., 1968; children—Erin Elizabeth, Thomas Edan. Instr., Pomona Coll., 1967-68; asst. prof. classics U. So. Calif., from 1968, asso. prof., chmn. dept. classics, 1971-74, 80—; pres. Summa Galleries, Inc. Am. Council Learned Socs. fellow, 1975-76. Mem. Am. Philol. Assn., Archaeol. Inst. Am., Royal Numis. Soc., Am. Numis. Soc. Contbr. articles on Roman coins, history and lit. to profl. jours. Office: Taper Hall 224 U So Calif Los Angeles CA 90089 *

CODY, PATRICIA ELIZABETH, librarian; b. San Francisco, Feb. 3, 1922; d. William Francis and Lucille Hawley (Gignoux) C.; A.A., U. Calif., Berkeley, 1942, B.A. (with highest honors), 1943; M.A. (fellow in anthropology), U. Oreg., Eugene, 1945; M.L.S., U. Calif., Berkeley, 1956, gen. secondary teaching credential, 1946. Tchr. high sch., Calif., 1946-48; field worker among Paiute Indians, Nev., also teaching asst. anthropology U. Calif., Berkeley, 1948-52; clk. U. Calif. Library, 1952-54; cataloger U. Portland Library, Oreg., 1954-56; asst. librarian, cataloger, public services librarian Modesto (Calif.) Jr. Coll., 1956—; lectr. Charter mem. Calif. Democratic Council, sec. Stanislaus County, 1957-58; mem. Stanislaus County campaign com. Gov. Pat Brown, 1958; sec. Unitarian Fellowship of Stanislaus County. Fellow in U.S. History, Stanford U., 1948. Mem. AAUP, NEA, Calif. Tchrs. Assn., AAUP (pres. Modesto Jr. Coll. chpt. 1969-70, state bd. dirs. 1970-74), Modesto Jr. Coll. Faculty Assn. (sec. 1963-64, NEA del. 1979-80), Phi Beta Kappa, Sigma Xi, Pi Lambda Theta, Beta Phi Mu. Organizer shows of aboriginal art Modesto Jr. Coll., 1974-75. Home: 538 College Ave Modesto CA 95350 Office: Library Modesto Jr Coll Modesto CA 95350

COE, ILSE G., lawyer, former banker; b. Koenigsberg, Germany, May 28, 1911; came to U.S., 1938, naturalized, 1946; Referendar, U. Koenigsberg, 1935, J.S.D., 1936; LL.B., Bklyn. Law Sch., 1946. Dir. econ. research Internat. Gen. Electric Co., Berlin, 1936-38; asst. to sales promotion and advt. mgrs. Ralph C. Coxhead Corp., N.Y.C., 1940-44; law clk. Mendes & Mount, N.Y.C., 1944-46; admitted to N.Y. bar, 1946; atty. Hill, Rivkins & Middleton, N.Y.C., 1946-50, McNutt, Longcope & Proctor, N.Y.C., 1950-52, Chadbourne, Hunt, Jaeckel & Brown, N.Y.C., 1952-54; asst. v.p., asst. trust officer Schroder Trust Co. and J. Henry Schroder Banking Corp., N.Y.C., 1954-76; dir., sec., editor Fgn. Tax Law Assn., Inc., L.I., N.Y., 1945-55; tchr. Drakes Bus. Sch., N.Y.C., 1946-49; lectr. on estate planning to ch., women's and bar assn. groups, 1947—; tutor literacy vols., 1977—; lectr. wills and photography Pace U.; exec. bd. Active Retirement Center, Pace U., 1977-79, pres., 1982—. County com. woman Republican Party, 1948-50; former deacon, now ruling elder, chmn. investment com. 1st Presbyterian Ch., Bklyn. Recipient Human Relations award NCCJ, 1979. Mem. Bklyn. Women's Bar Assn. (past treas., dir. 1960—), Protestant Lawyers Assn. N.Y. Inc. (sec. 1960-75, 1st v.p. 1976-77, pres. 1978—), Internat. Fedn. Women Lawyers, Bklyn. Heights Assn., L.I. Hist. Soc. (investment com.), N.Y. Color Slide Club (by-laws chmn., dir. 1973-74). Home: 187 Hicks St Brooklyn Heights NY 11201

COE, WILLA D., ednl. adminstr.; b. Martinsville, Tex., July 27, 1928; d. William D. and Elma N. (Ellison) Brown; B.A., Stephen F. Austin State U., 1948, M.A., 1950; postgrad. Lamar U., 1965-66, Tex. A&M U., 1967-69; m. Henry Allen Coe, Jr., Nov. 25, 1955; children—Laura Lea, Mary Virginia, Henry Allen III. Coach, Kountze, Tex., 1953-67; biology instr., 1967-69; elem. prin., Kountz, 1969-71; distributive edn. coordinator, Kountze, 1971-78; high sch. prin. Kountze High Sch., 1978—. Del., Democratic State Conv., 1980. Lamar U. fellow, 1967. Mem. NEA, Tex. Assn. Distributive Edn. Tchrs., Tex. Assn. Classroom Tchrs. (state bd. mem. 1965-67), Tex. Educators Assn., Tex. Assn. Secondary Prins., Tex. State Tchrs. Assn. (state com. 1969-71, pres. dist. V 1969-70), Kountze C. of C. (pres. 1980), Tex. High Sch. Rodeo Assn. (state sec. 1979-81, dir. region V 1976-82), Kountze Bus. and Profl. Women's Club (pres. 1975), Delta Kappa Gamma. Democrat. Methodist. Clubs: Woman's (pres. 1965-66) (Kountze, Tex.). Home: PO Box 519 Kountze TX 77625 Office: PO Box 460 Kountze TX 77625

COE-HAUSKINS, CAROLE VIVIAN, lawyer, city ofcl.; b. Los Angeles, Aug. 16, 1937; d. Philip and Bonnie Belle (Currey) Brown; B.A., U. Puget Sound, 1968; J.D., (William Wallace Wilshire scholar) U. Wash., 1971; m. William E. Hauskins, Sept. 28, 1980; children by previous marriage—Curtis David, Craig David. Office mgr. social services sect., VA Hosp., American Lake, Wash., 1957-59; sec. to warden U.S. Fed. Penitentiary, McNeil Island, Wash., 1959-61; sec. to supt. Milw. R.R., Tacoma, Wash., 1961-68; admitted to Wash. bar, 1971; dep. dir. city affairs Office of the Ombudsman, Seattle-King County, Seattle, 1971-72, acting dir., 1972-74; atty., dir. adminstrv. services Lighting Dept., City of Seattle, 1974—, adj. faculty labor history and law U.S. Fire Acad., Emmetsburg, Md. Mem. Wash. Bar Assn., Seattle-King County Bar Assn., Seattle Mgmt. Assn. (v.p., bd. trustees), Am. Arbitration Assn., Am. Public Power Assn., Women's Profl. and Managerial Network, Phi Alpha Delta. Club: Wash. Athletic. Contbr. articles to profl. jours. Home: 2502 28th St W Seattle WA 98199 Office: 1015 3d Ave Seattle WA 98104

COELHO, JUDITH CAROL PRICE, med. technologist; b. Shelbyville, Ill., Aug. 20, 1942; d. Maurice Ray and Naomi Aileen (Milner) Price; B.S. in Med. Tech., Millikin U., 1970; cert. in med. tech. St. Mary's Sch. Med. Tech., 1969; m. Patrick S. Coelho, Jan. 16, 1971; children—Kawiki, Uilani. Lab. technician State of Ill. Dept. Agr., div. feeds, fertilizer and standards, 1961-63; lab. asst. Shelby County Meml. Hosp., Shelbyville, Ill., 1963-67, St. Mary's Hosp., Decatur, Ill., 1967-68, staff med. technologist, 1969-70; lab. supr. Molokai (Hawaii) Gen. Hosp., 1970-81; staff technologist Blood Bank of Hawaii, Honolulu, 1981—; instr. in field. Mem. infection control com. Molokai Gen. Hosp., sec., 1975-81, vice chairperson, mem. safety com., 1980-81; mem. safety com. Blood Bank of Hawaii, 1982; v.p. Kaunakakai Sch. PTA, 1979, pres., 1980-81; Cub Scouts leader, 1981-82; tchr. Bible Sch., 1981-82. Mem. Am. Soc. Med. Tech., Hawaii Soc. Med. Tech. (scholarship chairperson 1977-78). Mem. Chs. of Christ. Clubs: Malia Alanon, Molokai Saddle (sec. 1981). Office: 2043 Dillingham Blvd Honolulu HI 96819

COERR, ELEANOR BEATRICE, author; b. Canada, May 29, 1922; came to U.S., naturalized, 1958; d. William Thomas and Mabel (Selig) Page; B.S., Am. U., M.A. in Library and Info. Sci. U. Md., 1971; postgrad. Monterey (Calif.) Peninsula Coll.; m. Wymberley D. Coerr, June 10, 1965; children—Robert, Bill. Editor, illustrator youth page Montgomery (Ala.) Advertiser-Jour., 1953-57; editor children's column Manila Times, 1958-60; contbg. editor Civil Air Transp. mag., also contract writer USIS, 1960-63; contract writer spl. English div. Voice of Am., 1963-65; children's librarian David Meml. Library, Bethesda, Md., 1971-72; contract author G.P. Putnam's Sons, N.Y.C., 1972-79; high sch. librarian Santa Calatina Sch. Girls, Monterey, Calif., 1978-79; lectr. Chapman Coll., Ft. Orde, Calif., also Monterey Peninsula Coll., 1979—; author: Circus Day in Japan, 1954; The Mystery of the Golden Cat, 1968; Twenty-Five Dragons, 1971; Biography of a Giant Panda, 1975; Jane Goodall, 1976; Biography of a Kangaroo, 1976; The Mixed-Up Mystery Smell, 1976; Waza Wins at Windy Gulch, 1977; Sadako and the Thousand Paper Cranes (Best Children's Book of Year in W. Australia 1981), 1977; Gigi, a Baby Whale, 1980; The Big Balloon Race, 1981; also articles. Recipient Outstanding Sci. Writing award, 1976; award for Best Children's Book of 1981, West Australia. Mem. Soc. Women Geographers, Children's Book Guild, Children's Lit. Assn., Internat. Inst. Children's Lit. and Reading Research, Beta Phi Mu. Address: 1360 Josselyn Canyon Rd Apt 34 Monterey CA 93940

COFFEE, CHARLENE DAUGHERTY, accountant; b. Athens, Tenn., Feb. 3, 1943; d. Charles McGee and Alma (Millsaps) Daugherty; B.S., U. Tenn., Knoxville, 1964; m. Joe Donald Coffee, Apr. 9, 1966. Buyer trainee, Castner-Knott Co., Nashville, 1964-66; asst. buyer, buyer Harvey's, Nashville, 1966-67; mdse. control clk., supr. Sears Roebuck, Nashville, 1967-73, acctg. mgmt. trainee, 1973-74, mem. point of sale implementation team So. ter., 1974-77, controller acctg. and processing center, Atlanta, 1977-80, staff asst., field report consolidation, Chgo., 1980-81, staff asst. acctg. policy and procedure, 1981—. Mem. DAR, AAUW, Delta Zeta. Lutheran. Home: 5930 Bradley Ct Hanover Park IL 60103 Office: Sears Tower BSC 22-12 Chicago IL 60684

COFFEE, CHARLOTTE EVELYN LONG, social worker; b. Evansville, Ind., Sept. 13, 1926; d. Thomas Jackman and Helen Dorinda (Buckner) Long; student Ind. U., Bloomington, 1943-45; B.S., U. Louisville, 1971, M.Ed., 1974; m. J. C. Coffee, Oct. 27, 1947 (div.); children—Paul Thomas, Karen Lynn. Sec., Registrar's Office, Md. State Coll., 1947-48; gen. asst. in transcripts Registrar's Office, Tenn. State U., 1951-56, sec. Div. Health and Phys. Edn., 1958-67, Sch. Engring., 1967-69; sch. social worker Div. Pupil Personnel Jefferson County (Ky.) Public Schs., 1971—. Bd. dirs. ARC, Louisville, 1973-80, mem. youth com., 1976—, mem. staff Leadership Camp, 1977—; vice chmn. bd. trustees Plymouth Congregational Ch., Louisville, 1980—. Recipient cert. appreciation ARC, 1973-80; Gen. Electric Co. Bridging The Gap Program fellow, 1979. Mem. Jefferson County Tchrs. Assn., Nat. Assn. Social Workers, Ky. Assn. Sch. Social Workers (Social Worker of Yr. 1981), Midwest Sch. Social Work Council, Ky. Edn. Assn., NEA. Democrat. Home: 5710 Hamburg Pike Jeffersonville IN 47130 Office; 3332 Newburg Rd Louisville KY 40218

COFFEE, VIRGINIA CLAIRE, civic worker, former mayor; b. Alliance, Nebr., Dec. 8, 1920; d. James Maddigan and Adelaide Mary (Forde) Kennedy; B.S., Chadron State Coll., 1942; m. Bill Brown Coffee, June 21, 1942; children—Claire, Sara, Virginia Anne, Sue. High sch. prin., Whitman, Nebr., 1942; sec., bookkeeper Coffee & Son, Inc., Harrison, Nebr., 1965—, officer, 1967—; mayor City of Harrison, 1978-80. Leader, Girl Scouts U.S.A., 1953-63; mem. Harrison Elem. Sch. bd., 1958-64; mem. liaison com. Chadron State Coll., 1975—; public relations chmn. Nebr. Cowbelles, 1968; sec. N.W. Stock Growers, 1971-73; corp. officer Ft. Robinson Centennial, 1973—; officer Gov.'s Fort Robinson Centennial Commn., 1973-75; hon. gov. Nebr. Centennial, 1967; chmn. Sioux County Bicentennial, 1973-77; trustee Nebr. State Hist. Soc. Found., 1975—, Village of Harrison, 1973-80. Mem. Nebr. State Hist. Soc. (dir. 1979—, 2d v.p. 1982—), Sioux County Hist. Soc. (past pres.), Wyo. Hist. Soc. Cardinal Key Honor Frat. Roman Catholic. Clubs: Sioux County Cowbelles, Nebr. Cowbells, Community. Contbr. articles to area newspapers; chmn. compilation com. book Sioux County Memoirs of Its Pioneers, 1967. Address: PO Box 336 Harrison NE 69346

COFFEY, KATHRYN (KAY) R(OBINSON), civic worker; B.S. in Govt., West Tex. State U., 1937; m. Clarence W. Coffey; children—Clarence William, Kathryn Ann. Active Lakeview Presbyterian Ch., New Orleans, 1944—, deacon, 1968-71, bd. dirs. kindergarten and nursery sch., 1965-68; mem. com. on home and family nurture Presbytery South La., 1967-69; mem. exec. com., chmn. dept. relation to public schs. Greater New Orleans Fedn. Chs., 1970-76; mem. Presbyn. campus life com. Presbytery New Orleans, 1978-82; mem. various coms. Orleans Parish (La.) Sch. Bd., 1953-77; active PTA, including bd. dirs. New Orleans council, 1956-75, pres., 1965-67, v.p., chmn. legis. services and pres. Dist. One La., 1967-72, mem. legis. com. Nat. Congress, 1969-72; mem. New Orleans Public Library Bd., 1956-62; v.p., chmn. membership com. Civic Council New Orleans, 1952-75; organizer, exec. sec. New Orleans Citizens for Support of Public Schs., 1968-76; bd. dirs., mem. coms. La. Assn. Mental Health, 1968-71; mem. La. Commn. Law Enforcement and Adminstrn. Criminal Justice, 1968-70; pres. La. Orgns. for State Legis., 1972-76; com. mem., bd. dirs. regional adv. group La. Regional Med. Program, Inc., 1970-76; numerous activities for gifted edn. and spl. edn., including: founder, v.p., legis. chmn. Greater New Orleans Spl. Edn. PTA, 1971-77; mem. exec. com. La. Adv. Council for Learning Disabilities, 1972-76; co-chmn. Speak Out for Spl. Children, New Orleans, 1972-77; mem. Task Force for Implementation of Act 368 of 1972, La., 1972-76; spl. hearing officer Fed. Dist. Ct., New Orleans, 1973-77; chmn. La. Adv. Com. for Gifted and Talented, 1973-76; pres., organizer Assn. Gifted and Talented Students, Inc., 1973—, editor newsletter, 1973-81, contbg. editor, 1981—; com. mem., chmn. nomination com. La. Gov.'s 4-C Policy Bd., 1974-77; project reader Office Gifted and Talented, Office Edn., 1975-76; mem. La. Coalition on Handicapped, 1975—; mem. U. New Orleans Task Force on Gifted and Talented, 1976—; regional rep. La. Gov.'s White House Conf. on Handicapped, 1977; bd. dirs. Nat. Assn. Gifted Children, 1977—; mem. La. Gov.'s Adv. Com. on Edn. of Handicapped, 1978-81; mem. adv. bd. Gifted Advocacy Info. Network, 1979—; mem. adv. bd. Inst. Gifted and Talented Edn., N.J. Dept. Edn., 1979-81; rev. editor Jour. Edn. of Gifted, Assn. for Gifted, 1980-82; vice-chmn. bd. dirs. La. Sch. for Math., Sci. and the Arts, Natchitoches, 1981—; mem. adv. bd. Gifted Children's Newsletter, 1981—; mem. Gov.'s Adv. Com. Ednl. Block Grants. Recipient Life Membership in La. PTA, Edward Hynes PTA, 1954; cert. of merit Mayor New Orleans, 1969; Life Membership of Nat. Congress Parents and Tchrs., New Orleans Council PTAs, 1970; award for outstanding service Gov.'s Commn. on Law Enforcement and Adminstrn. Criminal Justice Juvenile Delinquency Com., 1970; Outstanding Scouter award Greater New Orleans Fedn. Chs., 1972, Outstanding Citizen award Council Exceptional Children, 1974; award for outstanding service Dir. Office Gifted and Talented, Office Edn., 1976; award of appreciation Assn. Gifted and Talented Students, 1980; award for outstanding service Inst. Gifted and Talented Edn., N.J. Dept. Edn., 1980; named Hon. Senator, Lt. Gov. and Pres. of La. Senate, 1975; award for outstanding service Inst. Arts and Humanities, Inc., Kansas City, Mo., 1982; Conv. Parent of Yr., Nat. Assn. Gifted Children, 1982. Home: 1627 Frankfort St New Orleans LA 70122

COFFEY, LESLIE KNELLER, advt. agy. exec.; b. Washington, Feb. 14, 1947; d. Chester and Edna W. Kneller; B.S., Boston U., 1968; m. Charles F. Coffey, Jr., Dec. 19, 1976. Broadcast prodn. asst. Geyer-Oswald Advt., N.Y.C., 1968-69; copywriter/broadcast producer Weightman, Inc., Phila., 1969-73, v.p., asso. creative dir., 1973-79; v.p., Weightman Advt., Phila., creative dir. 1979—; dir. Manhattan Satin, Inc.; lectr. in field. Recipient Clio award, Hollywood-Internat. Broadcasting award, Phila. TV-Radio Advt. Club awards. Clubs: Spring Lake (N.J.) Golf and Country; Cat Cay (Bahamas); Poinciana (Palm Beach, Fla.). Contbr. article to profl. jour. Office: 1818 Market St 33d Floor Philadelphia PA 19103

COFFILL, MARJORIE LOUISE (MRS. WILLIAM CHARLES COFFILL), civic worker; b. Sonora, Calif., June 11, 1917; d. Eric J. and Pearl (Needham) Segerstrom; A.B. with distinction in Social Sci., Stanford, 1938, M.A. in Edn., 1941; m. William Charles Coffill, Jan. 25, 1948; children—William James, Eric John. Asst. mgr. Sonora Abstract & Title Co. (Calif.), 1938-39; mem. staff Dean of Women, Stanford, 1939-41; social dir. women's campus Pomona Coll., 1941-43, instr. psychology, 1941-43; asst. to field dir. ARC, Le Moore AFB, Calif., 1944-46; partner Riverbank Water Co., Riverbank Hughson, Calif., 1950-68; mem. Tuolumne County Mental Health Adv. Bd., 1963-69; mem. Central adv. council Supplementary Edn. Center, 1966-68; mem. Pres.'s adv. bd. Columbia Jr. Coll., chmn., 1972, 80, bd. dirs. found., 1973—; mem. Tuolumne County Bicentennial Com.; bd. dirs. Lung Assn. Valley Lode Counties, Tuolumne County Salvation Army,

1974—; clk. bd. trustees Sonora Union High Sch., chmn. bd. trustees, 1969-71; pres. Tuolumne County Republican Women; asso. mem. Calif. Rep. Central Com., 1950; active PTA, ARC. Recipient Pi Lambda Theta award, 1940. Mem. AAUW (charter mem. Tuolumne County br., pres. Sonora br. 1965-68), Tuolumne County, Calif. hist. socs., Book Club Calif., Friends of Huntington Library, Friends Bancroft Library, Assos. Stanford Libraries (adv. com.), Oakland Mus. Episcopalian (sr. warden 1970-71, mem. vestry). Home: 376 E Summit Ave Sonora CA 95370

COFFIN, LINDA LEE, govt. ofcl.; b. Hutchinson, Kans.; d. Ralph B. and Virginia (Richards) L.; B.A., U. Calif., 1964; M.A., U. Okla., 1965. Mgmt. intern U.S. AEC, Richland, Wash., 1965-67, adminstrv. asst., 1967-68, contract adminstrn. asst., 1968-69, contract specialist, 1969-72; contract negotiator, acting chief Office Bus. Devel., SBA, Boston, 1972-74; sr. contract adminstr./negotiator Electric Power Research Inst., Palo Alto, Calif., 1974-76; contracting officer U.S. Geol. Survey, Menlo Park, Calif., 1976-78, nat. minority bus. officer and small bus. adviser, Reston, Va., 1978-79; dir. Office Small and Disadvantaged Bus., Dept. Treasury, Washington, 1979—; cons. Richland Flying Service, 1971-72. Bd. dirs. Campfire Girls, Richland Civic Light Opera. Mem. Am. Polit. Sci. Assn., Am. Acad. Arts and Scis., Nat. Contract Mgmt. Assn. (dir.), Calif. Alumni Assn., Wash. Pilots Assn. (dir.), Pi Sigma Alpha, Phi Alpha Theta, Zeta Tau Alpha. Home: PO Box 124 Sterling VA 22170 Office: Dept Treasury 15th and Pennsylvania Ave NW Suite 1320 Washington DC 20220

COFFMAN, JEAN ELIZABETH, investment rep.; b. North English, Iowa, June 9, 1920; d. Richard G. and Rose C. (Grauer) Owen; student U. No. Iowa, 1938, Kirkwood Community Coll., 1978; m. William J. Coffman, June 29, 1940; children—Helen J. Coffman Murray, Kathy A. Coffman Stevens. Rural sch. tchr., 1938-41; with Bill Coffman Ins., 1947-77, Evans Photography, 1955-59; registered rep. Investors Diversified Services of Mpls., 1979—, dir., 1979. Mem. North English (Iowa) City Council, 1976-79; Republican precinct committeewoman; lay del. ann. conf. United Methodist Ch., 1978, 9; mem. Federated Women's Club: twp. assessor, 1955-71; formerly active Girl Scouts U.S.A.; mem. ch. bd. Meth. Ch. Mem. Nat. Assn. Security Dealers, SEC, Iowa Security Dealers, Iowa Ins. Commn. Clubs: Eastern Star, Am. Federated Women, VFW Aux., DAV Aux. Home and Office: 108 E Oak St North English IA 52316

COGAN, DOLORIS COULTER, pharm. co. exec.; b. Potter, Nebr., July 28, 1924; d. George A. and Margaret (Jensen) Coulter; B.A., Nebr. Wesleyan U., 1945; M.S., Columbia U., 1946; m. Thomas James Cogan, Oct. 6, 1950; children—Thomas J., Richard B., Douglas G. Editor, Inst. Ethnic Affairs, Washington, 1946-49; research dir. Nat. Indian Inst., Dept. Interior, Washington, 1949-50, adminstrv. asst. Pacific Affairs, Office of Territories, 1950-55; free-lance writer, 1955-65; asst. public relations mgr. Pepperidge Farm, Inc., Norwalk, Conn., 1965-67, mgr. public relations, 1967-72; dir. public relations Miles Labs. Inc., Elkhart, Ind., 1972—. Mem., U.S. del. to 2d Inter-Am. Indian Congress, Cuzco, Peru, 1949; sec. Norwalk (Conn.) Charter Rev. Commn., 1959, sec. Fact-Finding Com. on Sch. Bldg. Requirements, 1962; mem. econ. devel. commn. Elkhart, Ind., 1981. Mem. Public Relations Soc. Am., Am. Women in Radio and Television (pres. Hoosier chpt. 1977), Pharm. Mfrs. Assn., Elkhart C. of C. Democrat. Unitarian Universalist. Club: Altrusa. Home: 1616 North Bay Dr Elkhart IN 46514 Office: 1127 Myrtle St Elkhart IN 46515

COGGIN, CHARLOTTE JOAN, physician, educator; b. Takoma Park, Md., Aug. 6, 1928; d. Charles Benjamin and Nanette (McDonald) Coggin; B.A., Columbia Union Coll., 1948; M.D., Loma Linda U., 1952. Intern, Los Angeles County Gen. Hosp., 1952-53, resident in medicine, 1953-55; fellow in cardiology Children's Hosp. Los Angeles, White Meml. Hosp., Los Angeles, 1955-56, Hammersmith Hosp., London, 1956-57; resident in pediatrics, pediatric cardiology Hosp. for Sick Children, Toronto, Ont., Can., 1965-67; cardiologist, co-dir. heart surgery team Loma Linda (Calif.) U., 1963—, asst. prof. medicine 1961-73, asso. prof. medicine, 1973—, asst. dean internat. programs, 1973-75, asso. dean internat. programs, 1975—; pvt. practice medicine specializing in pediatric and adult cardiology, Los Angeles, 1957-67, Loma Linda, 1967—; mem. staff Loma Linda U. Med. Center; cardiologist, heart surgery mission to Pakistan and Asia, 1963, Greece, 1967—, Saigon, Vietnam, 1974-75, Saudi Arabia, 1976—; trustee Tel-Med, Inc., 1972-80, pres., 1977-78. Mem. U.S. Pres's. Adv. Panel on Heart Disease, 1972—; gov.'s appointee Calif. Bd. Med. Quality Rev., dist. 12, 1976-79. Recipient awards for service in open heart surgery City of Karachi (Pakistan), 1963, Evangelismos Hosp., Athens, Greece, 1967-69; Golden Eagle Cine award Venice Film Festival for motion picture Arterial Septal Defect, 1964, 1st prize, 1964; named Outstanding Women of Yr. in Sci., Calif., Mus. Sci. and Industry, 1969; Gold medal of health Ministry of Health, Republic of Vietnam, 1974; Outstanding Woman award Gen. Conf. Seventh-day Adventists, 1975, Charles E. Weniger award for excellence, 1976; CASS grantee, 1974—. Diplomate Am. Bd. Pediatrics. Mem. San Bernardino County Med. Soc. (vice chmn. communications com. 1974-75, chmn. communications com. 1975-76, editor 1975—), Loma Linda U. Sch. Medicine Alumni Assn. (pres. 1978), AMA (mem. physicians adv. com. 1969—), Am. Acad. Pediatrics, Am., Calif. heart assns., Am. Med. Women's Assn., AAUP, Calif. Med. Assn. (com. on mem. services 1980—, chmn. com. on med. schs. 1980—), Am. Coll. Cardiology, Internat. Platform Assn., Democrat. Home: 11495 Benton St Loma Linda CA 92354 Office: Loma Linda U Med Center Loma Linda CA 92354

COGGIN, ELINOR LOUISE, banker; b. Melrose, Mass., Oct. 10, 1930; d. Fred N. and Elizabeth (Rattray) C.; grad. Grad. Sch. Savs. Banking, Brown U., 1971. With Mut. Bank for Savs., Boston, 1950—, v.p., 1976, sr. v.p., 1977—, trustee, 1979—. Bd. dirs. Boston Center for Adult Edn., 1979—. Mem. Am. Inst. Banking Boston (bd. govs.), Savs. Bank Assn. Mass., Nat. Assn. Bank Women. Club: Zonta. Office: 45 Franklin St Boston MA 02110

COGGS, MARCIA P., state legislator; b. Kansas City, Kans., Apr. 5, 1928; d. Harold C. and Elizabeth D. (Patton) Young; student Sumner Jr. Coll., Kansas City, 1945-46, Milw. State Tchrs. Coll., 1955-56; B.S., U. Wis., Milw.; 1 dau., Elizabeth. Mem. Wis. Assembly, 1977—, chmn. com. aging, women and minorities. Bd. dirs. Women's Community Correctional Center, Child Labor, Labor Standards and Adult Edn. Center Councils; chmn., treas., sec. Northside Democratic Unit, Milw., 1952—; v.p., treas. Black Women's Polit. Orgn., 1971-74; mem. Manpower Area Planning Council, 1974-76, State Ins. Consumer Advocate Council, 1975—; state chmn. Wis. Black Polit. Caucus, 1975—; del. Dem. Nat. Conv., 1978; mem. Nat. Caucus Black State Legislators, Nat. Order Women Legislators; exec. bd. Harambee Revitalization Project, 1973—, Milw. United Sch. Integration Com., 1965—; bd. dirs. YWCA, 1972—; mem. Milw. Caucus on Black Aged, NAACP. Baptist. Office: Wisconsin Gen Assembly Madison WI 53702

COGLEY, SCARLET CARDWELL, social worker; b. Welch, W.Va., Aug. 28, 1950; d. Billy and Bessie (Spears) Cardwell; B.A. in Psychology and English, Marshall U., 1972; M.S. in Social Work, U. Tenn., 1974; m. Floyd Cogley, June 25, 1977. Therapist, Lansdowne Comprehensive Mental Health Center, Ashland, Ky., 1972-73; social planner U. Tenn. Sch. Architecture, Managua, Nicaragua, 1974; research assoc. health planning and implementation project Boston Coll. Sch. Social Work, Chestnut Hill, Mass., 1974-75; health service specialist United Mine Workers of Am. Health and Retirement Funds, Middlesboro, Ky., 1975-77; adminstr. asst. Letchworth Village Devel. Center, Thiells, N.Y., 1977-78; social work cons. N.Y. State Dept. Health, White Plains, 1978-79, health program adminstr., 1979-80; dir. med. social work Presbyn. Hosp., Charlotte, N.C., 1980—. Bd. dirs. Child Day Care Center for Nyacks, Inc., Nyack, N.Y., 1979-80. Cert. social work, N.Y. Mem. Nat. Assn. Social Workers, Acad. Cert. Social Workers, Nat. Soc. for Hosp. Social Work Dirs. of Am. Hosp. Assn., N.C. Soc. for Hosp. Social Work (v.p., dir. 1982-83). Democrat. Episcopalian. Office: 200 Hawthorne Ln Charlotte NC 28204

COHEN, ANN RHONDA, psychologist; b. N.Y.C., May 8, 1952; d. Sidney and Judith C.; B.S. with honors in Human Devel. and Family Studies, Cornell U., 1973; M.A., Hofstra U., 1975, Ph.D. (doctoral fellow, 1974-75), 1976; m. Howard Marc Rombom, Aug. 19, 1979. Research psychologist NIMH, Bethesda, Md., summer 1973; grad. asst. in statistics, Hofstra U., Hempstead, N.Y., 1974-76; sch. psychologist Valley Stream (N.Y.) Dist. #30, 1976-77; postdoctoral fellow Inst. for Rational-Emotive Therapy, N.Y.C., 1977-79, staff psychologist, approved supr., 1979—; asso. dir. Center for Human Behavior, Bayside, N.Y., 1979—. Mem. Am. Psychol. Assn., N.Y. State Psychol. Assn., Nassau County Psychol. Assn., Assn. for Advancement of Psychology. Jewish.

COHEN, ANNE SILBERSTEIN, psychotherapist, clin. social worker; b. Balt., Aug. 12, 1928; d. Louis M. and Marie Rita (Adlin) Silberstein; B.A., Goucher Coll., 1949; M.A., Montclair State Coll., 1974; M.S.W., Rutgers U., 1975; cert. N.J. Acad. Group Psychotherapy, 1976-78; postgrad. N.Y. Center for Psychoanalytic Tng., 1978—; m. Robert J. Cohen, Sept. 7, 1952; children—Laura Marjorie, Michael Louis. Social worker children's div. Dept. Public Welfare, Balt., 1950-53, Children's Protective Services, Pa. Soc. to Protect Children from Cruelty, Phila., 1953-56; mem. staff Social Work Family Life Improvement Project, Rutgers U. Grad. Sch., New Brunswick, N.J., 1964-68; social worker Catholic Family and Community Services, Paterson, N.J., 1974-75; psychotherapist, clin. social worker Essex County Guidance Center, East Orange, N.J., 1975—; pvt. practice psychotherapy, marriage and family counseling, Livingston, N.J., 1980—. Mem. planning com. Mental Health Assn. N.J., 1980; bd. dirs. Community Psychiat. Inst. Inst., East Orange, N.J. Lic. marriage counselor, N.J. Mem. Acad. Cert. Social Workers, N.J. Acad. Group Psychotherapy, N.J. Soc. Clin. Social Work (dir., membership chairperson), Nat. Assn. Social Workers, Am. Assn. Marriage and Family Therapists, N.J. Assn. Women Therapists, LWV, Nat. Council Jewish Women. Jewish. Office: Roosevelt Plaza Suite 305 2 W Northfield Rd Livingston NJ 07039

COHEN, BETTE PETERS, counselor; b. Chgo., Jan. 20, 1947; d. John Ahrvin and Anna Katherine (Felde) Peters; B.A., Lakeland Coll., Sheboygan, Wis., 1969; postgrad. U. Wis., Madison, 1975-78; M.A., Calif. State U., Bakersfield, 1982; m. David Chestney Cohen, Jan. 3, 1980. Tchr., New Glarus, Wis., 1969-70; team leader Lakeshore Manor, Madison, Wis., 1970-78; group home coordinator Bakersfield (Calif.) Assn. Retarded Citizens, 1978-79; client program coordinator Kern Regional Center, Bakersfield, 1979—. Mem. Calif. Profl. Guidance Assn. Democrat. Home: 2001 Westminster Dr Bakersfield CA 93309 Office: 501 40th St Bakersfield CA 93309

COHEN, DEBORAH HARRIET, employment co. exec.; b. N.Y.C., Nov. 8, 1948; d. Max J. and Anne (Deaner) Epstein; B.A., Queens Coll., 1969, M.L.S., SUNY, Stony Brook, 1972. Tchr. elem. schs., N.Y. and Md., 1969-73; asst. dir. grad. edn. SUNY, Buffalo, 1974-78; dir. health care div. Manpower Temporary Services, Buffalo, 1978-80, area mgr. Richmond and Petersburg, Va., 1980—. Mem. adult services com. Jewish Community Center, Buffalo, mem. budget com., Richmond. Mem. Adminstrv. Mgmt. Soc., Richmond C. of C., Va. Mus. Home: 1507 Regency Woods Rd Apt 204 Richmond VA 23233 Office: Pocoshock Sq Office Park 7637 Hull St Rd Suite 200 Richmond VA 23235

COHEN, EDITH MILLER, nutritionist; b. Bklyn., Apr. 8, 1923; d. Samuel and Hannah Miller; B.A., Hunter Coll., 1950; M.S. in Pub. Health, Tchrs. Coll., Columbia U., 1955; m. Marvin Cohen, Jan. 21, 1968. Dietitian Columbia Presbyterian Med. Center, N.Y.C., 1955-56; pub. health nutritionist, Bureau of Nutrition N.Y.C. Dept. of Health, N.Y.C., 1957-75; nutrition services cons. N.Y. State Dept. of Health, N.Y., 1975-82. Mem. Am. Dietetic Assn., Am. Pub. Health Assn. Home: 75 Henry St Apt 4E Brooklyn NY 11201

COHEN, ELAINE RUTHFIELD, editor, social work cons.; b. Boston, May 30, 1937; d. Edward and Esther Mildred Ruthfield; student Barnard Coll., 1955-56; B.S., Simmons Coll., 1960, M.S., 1966; m. Joseph Meyer Cohen, June 9, 1956; children—Lawrence, Bruce, Steven. Psychiat. social worker Jewish Family and Children's Service, Boston, 1968-70, Travelers Aid Soc., Boston, 1970-76; social work cons. to nursing homes in Boston area, 1975—; editor and writer articles Focus publ., Boston, 1972-77; lit. editor Brooklines lit. mag., 1979—; tchr. creative writing Brookline (Mass.) High Sch., 1979—. Mem. Nat. Assn. Social Workers, Acad. Cert. Social Workers, Playwright's Platform. Jewish. Author: (plays) Poor Ida, 1979; Room to Grow, 1980. Home: 156 Lancaster Terr Brookline MA 02146

COHEN, ELIZABETH ANNE, lawyer; b. Ft. Benning, Ga., July 21, 1946; d. William Andrew, Jr., and Mildred Hilda (Phillips) Jackson; B.A. cum laude, Anderson (Ind.) Coll., 1967; postgrad. U. Hamburg, W. Ger., 1969-70; J.D., Seton Hall U., 1976; 1 son, Matthew Ezra. Claims rep. Social Security Adminstrn., Chgo. and Perth Amboy, N.J., 1967-68, 70-73, field rep., Elizabeth, N.J., 1973-76; clk. Hong Kong and Shanghai Bank, Hamburg, W. Ger., 1970; clk. Middlesex County (N.J.) Ct., 1976-77; admitted to N.J. bar, 1976; asso. firm Sachar, Bernstein, Rothberg, Sikora & Mongello, Esqs., Plainfield, N.J., 1977-78; individual practice law, Westfield, N.J., 1979—. Recipient outstanding performance award HEW, 1975. Mem. Am. Bar Assn., N.J. State Bar Assn., Women's Equity Action League. Home: 213 Montgomery St Highland Park NJ 08904 Office: PO Box 1221 Highland Park NJ 08904

COHEN, HARRIET NEWMAN, lawyer; b. Providence, Dec. 8, 1932; d. Morris and Marion Newman; B.A. in Latin and Greek, Barnard Coll., 1952; M.S. in Latin and Greek (Tuition scholar), Bryn Mawr Coll., 1953; J.D. cum laude, Bklyn. Law Sch., 1974; 4 daus. Admitted to N.Y. bar; asso. Squadron, Gartenberg, Ellenoff & Plesent, N.Y.C., 1974-76, Phillips, Nizer, Benjamin, Krim & Ballon, N.Y.C., 1976-80, Golenbock & Barell, N.Y.C., 1980—; tchr. domestic relations law Continuing Edn. div. CUNY, 1980—, adv. bd., 1982—; lectr. Assn. Bar City N.Y., 1982, N.Y. Women's Bar Assn., 1981, 82, N.Y. State Trial Lawyers Assn., 1981, 82. Mem. N.Y. Women's Bar Assn. (dir.), Assn. Bar City N.Y., N.Y. State Bar Assn., Bklyn. Law Rev. Alumni Assn. (trustee). Office: 645 Fifth Ave 10th Floor New York NY 10022

COHEN, HELEN ANN, psychologist; b. Duluth, Minn.; d. Barney and Belle (Karon) C.; Ph.D., U. Chgo., 1964; m. Gerald Rose, Sept. 7, 1968; children—Barney, Sarah. Prof., Roosevelt U., Chgo., 1960-67, Ill. Inst. Tech., Chgo., 1968-71; dir. psychol. services Cook County Hosp., Chgo., 1971-77; pvt. practice psychology, Chgo., 1975—; cons. nursing edn. Cook County Hosp.; dir. Psychol. Registration Bd. State of Ill. Mem. Am. Psychol. Assn., Ill. Psychol. Assn., World Health, Psi Sigma Tau. Jewish. Author: Nurses Quest for Professional Identity, 1981; contbr. numerous articles to profl. jours. Office: 664 N Michigan #715 Chicago IL 60611

COHEN, IDA BOGIN (MRS. SAVIN COHEN), warehousing exec.; b. Bklyn.; d. Joseph and Yetta (Harris) Bogin; student St. Johns U.; B.S., N.Y.U.; m. Barnet Gaster, June 26, 1941 (div. May 1955); m. 2d, Savin Cohen, Aug. 30, 1964. Sec.-treas. J. Gerber & Co., Inc., N.Y.C., 1942-54, v.p., dir., 1954-73; pres., dir. Austracan U.S.A., Inc., N.Y.C., 1960-73; v.p. Parts Warehouse, Inc., Woodside, N.Y., 1970-72, sec.-treas., 1972—; also engaged in pvt. investments. Contbr. articles to S. African Outspan, newspapers. Home: 12 Shorewood Dr Sands Point NY 11050 Office: 58-25 Brooklyn-Queens Expressway Woodside NY 11377

COHEN, JANE ELIZABETH WATKINS, health educator; b. Corsicana, Tex., Dec. 16, 1942; d. Charlie and Elna (Mitchell) Watkins; B.S. in Home Econs. (Collins scholar), N. Tex. State U., 1965; M.Ed., Tex. A&M U., 1975; doctoral candidate Tex. Tech U., 1979—; m. Robert Strib Cohen, Dec. 2, 1967. Asst. county home demonstration agt. Tex. Agrl. Extension Service, Ellis County, 1965-66, county home demonstration agt., Jack County, 1966-67; caseworker Tex. Dept. Public Welfare, Eastland County, 1968-69; expanded food and nutrition program specialist Tex. Agrl. Extension Service, College Station, 1969-78, extension agt.-home energy specialist, Lubbock, 1978-79; instr. food and nutrition Tex. Tech. U., 1982—; health educator Lubbock Health Dept., 1982—; legis. chmn. Tex. State Nutrition Council; mem. youth com. Farm Bur. Registered dietitian. Mem. Tex. Agrl. Extension Service Specialists Assn. (membership chmn.), Brazos Valley Home Econs. Assn. (scholarship chmn.), Am. Home Econs. Assn., Tex. Home Econs. Assn., Lubbock Dietetic Assn. (sec. 1982—), Am. Dietetic Assn., Tex. Dietetic Assn., DAR (chpt. program chmn. 1978-79), Epsilon Sigma Phi, Phi Upsilon Omicron, Beta Sigma Phi. Democrat. Baptist. Author articles in field. Home: 5609 70th St Lubbock TX 79424 Office: 1202 Jarvis Lubbock TX 79408

COHEN, JOAN O'BRIEN, social work adminstr.; b. Neptune City, N.J., Oct. 28, 1934; d. William G. and Emily (Pyott) O'Brien; B.A., Rutgers U., 1972, M.S.W., 1977; m. Jerome J. Cohen, Oct. 23, 1961 (dec. 1978); children—Stephen, Mark. Coordinator, Vol. Tutor Program, Camden, N.J., 1964-68; intake counselor Opportunities Industrialization Center, Camden, 1966-68; counselor adult edn. pilot project Camden Learning Center, 1968-72; dir. Gatehouse, Inc., Phila., 1972-77; personnel dir. Impact Services Corp., Phila., 1977—; cons. Heritage House, Cherry Hill, N.J. Bd. dirs. Gatehouse Inc., Phila.; mem. adv. bd. Rutgers U. Sch. Social Work, Camden, 1979-81; rep. Haddonfield Democratic Com., 1979—; v.p. Lila Kaplan City of Hope, 1966-68. Recipient Community Service award Phila. Jaycees, 1978. Mem. Nat. Assn. Social Workers, Acad. Cert. Social Workers. Democrat. Presbyterian (del. gen. assembly 1970). Home: 400 Haddon Ave 111 Haddonfield NJ 08033 Office: 134 E Indiana Philadelphia PA 19134

COHEN, JOYCE E., state legislator; b. McIntosh, S.D., Mar. 27, 1937; grad. Coll. Med. Tech. Minn., 1955; student UCLA, 1957-58, Santa Ana Coll., 1961-62; m. Stanley N. Cohen, 1959; children—Julia Jo, Aaron J. Med. research technician, dept. surgery U. Minn., 1955-58; department technician U. Calif., 1958-59, dep. bacteriologist, 1959-61; med. research scientist Allergan Pharms., Santa Ana, Calif., 1961-70; partner Co-Fo. Investments, Lake Oswego, Oreg., 1978—; mem. Oreg. Ho. of Reps., 1979—, chmn. housing and urban devel. com., chmn. judiciary subcom. 3. Chmn. environ. service citizens adv. com. Columbia Regional Assn. of Govts., 1977-78; vice chmn. Oreg. Energy Policy Rev. Commn., 1977-78. Mem. Assn. Family Conciliation Cts., LWV, Oreg. Women's Polit. Caucus. Office: Oreg House of Reps State Capitol Salem OR 97310 *

COHEN, JUDITH LOVE, elec. engr.; b. Bklyn., Aug. 16, 1933; d. Morris Bernard and Sarah (Roisman) C.; student Bklyn. Coll., 1950-52; B.S. in Elec. Engring., U. So. Calif., 1957, M.S. in Elec. Engring., 1962; m. Bernard Siegel, Aug. 2, 1952 (div. 1965); children—Neil Gilbert, Howard Karl, Constance Rachel; m. 2d, Thomas W. Black, 1966 (div. 1980); 1 son, Thomas Jacob; m. 3d, David A. Katz, 1981. Jr. engr. N.Am. Aviation, Downey, Calif., 1952-56, research engr., 1956-57, guidance engr., 1957-59; mem. tech. staff guidance, nav. and controls depts. Space Tech. Labs., Redondo Beach, Calif., 1959-62, project engr. Minuteman missile platform controls, 1962-68, group leader guidance software engring., 1969-71, real time software design and mgmt., 1971-77; dir. computer systems Western Union Spacecom, Redondo Beach, 1977-80; project mgr. digital communications software TRW Systems Group, Redondo Beach, 1980-81, systems engr. space telescope sci. ops. ground system, 1981—; cons. Burroughs Electrodate Div., 1959. Lectr. Explorer Scouts, 1961-62; lectr. on women in engring., 1957—. Recipient Woman's badge Tau Beta Pi, 1957. Registered profl. engr., Calif. Mem. IEEE, Soc. Women Engrs. (profl. guidance and edn. 1962-63), pres. Los Angeles chpt. 1963-64), Eta, Kappa Nu. Jewish (v.p. temple sisterhood 1962). Contbr. articles to profl. publs.; columnist Engr. Mag.; research on ballistic missile and space systems. Address: 1 Space Park Redondo Beach CA 90278

COHEN, LAUREN BEVERLY, lawyer; b. Passaic, N.J., Aug. 11, 1946; d. Morris and Sharon C.; B.A., Rutgers U., 1969; J.D., Seton Hall U., 1973; postgrad. N.Y. U., 1978—. Jud. clk. to judge Superior Ct., Appellate Div. State of N.J., Newark, 1973-74; admitted to N.J. bar, 1973; asso. atty. Newark Housing & Redevel. Authority, 1974-76; asso. firm Ravin & Kesselhaut, West Orange, N.J., 1976-77; house counsel, sec. Agfa-Gevaert, Inc., Teterboro, N.J., 1977—. Mem. N.J. Bar Assn., Bergen County Bar Assn., Women Lawyers in Bergen County, Assn. Corp. Counsel N.J. Club: Mensa. Home: 79 Clifton Ave Clifton NJ 07011 Office: Agfa-Gevaert Inc 275 North St Teterboro NJ 07608

COHEN, MARION GERRICK, artist; b. Cedarhurst, N.Y., Nov. 11, 1923; d. Edward and Gertrude(Harris) Gerrick; degree in illustration Pratt Inst., 1945; pvt. student Victor White, Raphael Soyer, Anthony Toney, Jack Levine, Seong Moy, Jack Rabinowitz, Betty Holliday; m. Norman Louis Cohen, Apr. 18, 1948; children—Gary Alan, Andrew J., Jacqueline. Exhibited in one man shows including: Gallery Soho 7 Ltd., Gt. Neck, N.Y., 1976, 78; exhibited in group shows including: F.A.R. Gallery, N.Y.C., 1974; represented in corp. and pvt. collections including: Anne Frank Meml. Mus., Amsterdam; staff artist Screen Stars mag., 1945-48; with Bourgois Perfumes, 1943; exec. v.p. Soho 7 Gallery Ltd., Gt. Neck, N.Y., 1976-78, v.p., 1979-81; executed mural Internat. Flower Show, N.Y. Coliseum, 1961; Recipient Certificate of Service, Jewish Welfare Bd., 1942; Wings award Civil Aeronautics Administration, 1942; 1st prize Hempstead Town Hall, 1973; Greenwich Savs. Bank award Malverne Art League, 1974, 75; Lever House award, 1975, 77; 3d prize Chung Cheng Cultural Center, 1979. Mem. Nat. League Am. Pen Women (1st prize, 1974, 2d prize, 1975, 3d prize, 1975, Spl. award, 1976, 1st prize Winter Festival 1976, award of merit N.Y. State Pre-biennial 1980, 81), Five Towns Music and Art Found., Long Beach Art Found. Club: Salmagundi. Home: 1166 Harbor Rd Hewlett Harbor NY 11557

COHEN, MICHELLE ERLICH, exptl. psychologist; b. Phila., Oct. 25, 1950; d. Marvin and Ann (Liss) Erlich; B.A., Beaver Coll., Glenside, Pa., 1972; M.Ed., Temple U., 1974, Ph.D. in Ednl. Psychology (Univ. scholar 1974-75), 1981. Instr., Beaver Coll., 1972-73; teaching asst., then research asso. Temple U., 1976-79; research asso., teaching asst. psychology Bryn Mawr Coll., 1979—; instr. Rosemont (Pa.) Coll., 1979; cons. in field. Mem. Am. Psychol. Assn., Jean Piaget Soc., Eastern Psychol. Assn. Author papers in field. Office: Dept Psychology Bryn Mawr Coll Bryn Mawr PA 19010

COHEN, PENNIE MYERS, psychologist; b. Phila., Aug. 16, 1939; d. William Lee and Roberta B. (Appel) Myers; B.A. magna cum laude, Wichita State U., 1973, M.A., 1975; children—Susan Lee, Robert Lewis. Counselor, Wichita (Kans.) State U., 1975-78, coordinator consulting, 1978—. Chairperson Wichita Sedgewick County Women's Task Force on Alcohol Abuse, 1979; mem. Wichita Sedgewick County Task Force on Drug Abuse, 1976-79; bd. dirs. Residential Homes for Boys, Mid-Kans. Jewish Welfare Fedn., Family Consultation Service. Mem. Am. Psychol. Assn., Am. Assn. Marriage and Family Counselors, Kans. Psychol. Assn., Kans. Alcoholism Counselors Assn. Office: Box 91 Wichita State Univ Wichita KS 67208

COHEN, PHYLLIS LINDA, alcoholic beverage co. ofcl.; b. Passaic, N.J., June 20, 1946; d. Louis Nathan and Florence (Schnitzer) C.; B.S., Monmouth Coll., 1972. Store mgr. Eatontown (N.J.) Wines & Liquors, 1972-76; food service rep. Inglenook Wines, Met. N.J., 1976-77, field rep., Met. N.Y. and N.J., 1977, dist. mgr., N.J. and Del., 1977-78; state mgr. Schenley World T & I Co., N.J., 1978-81; Eastern regional mgr. Asbach Uralt & Co., 1981—. Recipient innovative sales award, 1979. Mem. N.J. State Mgrs. (of Alcoholic Beverage Industries) Club. First woman dist. mgr. Inglenook Wines; first woman state mgr. Schenley. Home: 16 Seymour St Apt 14 Montclair NJ 07042 Office: 22 Law Dr Fairfield NJ 07006

COHEN, RITA S., real estate broker; b. Montreal, Ont., Can., Jan. 11, 1934; came to U.S., 1959, naturalized, 1964; d. Meyer and Annie (Black) Friedman; ed. Grad. Realtors Inst.; m. Arthur Cohen, May 29, 1956; children—Mara Susan, Dana Sherril, Marcia Gayle. Vice pres., relocation dir. Robert Martin's Condo Mart Inc., Hartsdale, N.Y., 76-82; pres. Rita Cohen Realty Services Ltd., White Plains, N.Y., 1982—; tchr. condo and coop. course for real estate brokers Pace U. and White Plains High Sch. Bd. dirs. March of Dimes, Westchester County 1981. Mem. Nat. Assn. Realtors, Westchester County Bd. Realtors, Women's Council Realtors, Hadassah (v.p. edn. 1978). Jewish. Home: 12 Ritchey Pl White Plains NY 10605 Office: 601 Eagle Bay Dr Ossining-on-the-Hudson NY

COHEN, ROBERTA, audiologist; b. N.Y.C., Jan. 3, 1951; d. Abraham and Ruth (Finkelstein) Schiffman; B.A. summa cum laude, Queens Coll., 1972; M.A. (Fellow 1972-73), Hofstra U., 1973; m. Harvey Alan Cohen, June 4, 1972. Clin. audiologist Hofstra U., Hempstead, N.Y., 1973-76, clin. audiology supr., 1976-77, instr. Hofstra U., 1974-76; C.W. Post Coll. of L.I. U., 1975; audiol. cons. Zenetron Inc., Chgo., 1979—. Mem. Am. Speech-Lang.-Hearing Assn. (cert. clin. competence), N.Y. State Speech-Lang.-Hearing Assn., L.I. Speech-Lang.-Hearing Assn., Phi Beta Kappa, Sigma Alpha Eta.

COHEN, SALLY ANN, ednl. counselor, univ. adminstr.; b. Zanesville, Ohio, Mar. 20, 1942; d. Walter W. and Helen Jean (Bateman) Seifert; B.S. in Edn., Miami U., Oxford, Ohio, 1964; M.A. in Counseling and Guidance, Loyola Marymount U., 1976; m. Donald B. Cohen, Sept. 16, 1967. Tchr. English and journalism secondary schs., Ohio, 1964-71; acctg. supr. med. group clinic, Los Angeles, 1971-73; adminstrv. asst. Loyola Marymount U., 1973-76; counselor, departmental supr. UCLA, 1976—. Active in preserving ecology and landmarks in Huntington Beach (Calif.) area; bd. govs. Condominium Project, Huntington Beach; career counselor to young adults. Recipient cert. for superior managerial capabilities USAF, 1979; cert. secondary tchr. and sch. counselor, Calif., Ohio. Mem. Nat. Assn. Female Execs., Calif. Personnel and Guidance Assn., Am. Personnel and Guidance Assn., UCLA Staff Assn. (chairperson career advancement, devel. com.), Alpha Chi Omega. Libertarian. Unitarian. Editor community newsletter, 1975-77. Home: 17166 Bluewater Ln Huntington Beach CA 92649 Office: 251 Dodd Hall UCLA Los Angeles CA 90024

COHEN, SHIRLEY S., social worker; b. Columbus, Ohio, Dec. 5, 1926; d. Meyer and Libbie (Silverman) Schottenstein; B.S., Ohio State U., 1974; M.S.W., Barry Coll., 1976; m. Albert Cohen, Feb. 22, 1948; children—Jeri Beth, Jeffrey, Jay. Caseworker, Franklin County Welfare Dept., Columbus, Ohio, 1949-53; counsellor Methodone Clinic, Miami, Fla., 1975-76; therapist Childrens Psychiat. Clinic, Miami, 1976-77; pvt. practice psychotherapy, North Miami Beach, Fla., 1977—. Chmn. bd. women's div. Greater Miami Jewish Fedn., 1973. Mem. Nat. Assn. Social Workers, Nat. Council Family Relations, Fla. Clin. Social Workers, Am. Jewish Congress. Democrat. Office: 16800 NW 2d Ave #501 North Miami Beach FL 33169

COHN, ANN ROCHELLE, psychologist; b. N.Y.C., Apr. 16, 1941; d. Harry and Eleanor Rochelle; B.S., Temple U., 1962; Ph.D. in Psychology, Ill. Inst. Tech., 1975; m. Ronald I. Cohn, Dec. 20, 1970; 1 son, Henry Ian. Editorial asst. Babcock & Wilcox, N.Y.C., 1962-64; creative dir., account supr. Comdine Corp., N.Y.C., 1964-68; v.p. Rowland Co., N.Y.C., 1968-70; psychology intern Ill. Masonic Med. Center, Chgo., 1974-75; psychologist Rehab. Inst., Chgo., 1975-77; pvt. practice clin. and cons. psychology, Chgo., 1977—; tchr. Ill. Inst. Tech., 1977-78; cons. Ill. Masonic Med. Center, 1978-79. Bd. dirs. Mental Health Assn. Greater Chgo., 1978-80. Mem. Am. Psychol. Assn., Ill. Psychol. Assn., Soc. Clin. and Exptl. Hypnosis, Nat. Register Health Service Providers in Psychology. Home: 20 E Cedar St Chicago IL 60611 Office: 1030 N State St Chicago IL 60610

COHN, CECELIA ILENE, accountant; b. Kansas City, Mo., Jan. 25, 1939; d. Phillip and Jeanette (Skoler) Gilberg; student Tex. State Coll. for Women, 1957, Tusculum Coll., 1958; B.A. in Econs., Met. State Coll., Denver, 1975; m. Gershon George Cohn, Aug. 31, 1958; children—Howard Allan, Barbara Richelle. Mgr., Greeneville Pool, 1957, swimming instr., 1961-69; tax cons., mgr. exec. tax service, adminstrv. asst., coordinator real estate sch. Met. Denver area H & R Block, 1969-80; owner, operator Block Bookkeeping, Denver, 1978—. Pres. Northglenn Jaycee-ettes, 1965, 67, Northglenn Toastmistress Club, 1968, br. 65 Nat. Assn. Postal Suprs. Aux., 1970, 75, Colo.-Wyo. Bi-state pres., 1976-78; ednl. v.p., pres. Orators TM Club, 1978, dist. 26 Met. 2 area gov., 1979-80, gov. dist., 1981-82, adminstrv. lt. gov., 1980-81. Recipient Girl of Yr. award Northglenn Jaycee-ettes, 1963, 64; Outstanding Area Gov. award Dist. 26, 1979-80; named Able Toastmaster, 1981, Disting. Toastmaster, 1982. Mem. Colo. Public Accts. Soc., Omega Rho Alpha. Democrat. Jewish. Home: 771 S Holly St Denver CO 80222

COHN, FRIEDA SELMA, librarian, acad. specialist; b. Princeton, Wis., Jan. 15, 1915; d. Hyman and Clara Louise (Feldman) Swed; B.S.Ed., U. Wis., 1935, M.A. in Math., 1936; m. Herbert E. Cohn, Mar. 17, 1946. Librarian, U. Wis., Madison, 1936-43, Forest Products Lab., Madison, 1943-48; librarian, acad. specialist, tutor U. Wis., Madison, 1948—. Bd. dirs. Temple Beth El. Recipient Spl. Achievement award Temple Beth El, 1972. Mem. Madison Area Library Council, Spl. Univ. Libraries Group, Assn. Computing Machinery. Clubs: Winged Foot (Tom Jones award 1978), Blue Line, Basketball Boosters, Hadassah. Home: 937 S Midvale Blvd Madison WI 53711 Office: 1210 W Dayton St Madison WI 53706

COHN, MILDRED, biophysicist, educator; b. N.Y.C., July 12, 1913; d. Isidore M. and Bertha (Klein) Cohn; B.A., Hunter Coll., 1931; M.A., Columbia U., 1932, Ph.D., 1938; Sc.D. (hon.), Women's Med. Coll., 1966, Radcliffe Coll., 1978, Washington U., St. Louis, 1981; m. Henry Primakoff, May 31, 1938; children—Nina, Paul, Laura. Research asst. biochemistry George Washington U. Sch. Medicine, 1937-38; research asso. Cornell U., 1938-46; research asso. Washington U., 1946-50, 51-58, asso. prof. biol. chemistry, 1958-60; asso. prof. biophysics and phys. biochemistry U. Pa. Med. Sch., 1960-61, prof., 1961-78, Benjamin Rush prof. physiol. chemistry, 1978-82; sr. mem. Inst. Cancer Research, Phila., 1982—; Chancellor's disting. prof. biophysics U. Calif., Berkeley, spring 1981; research asso. Harvard U., 1950-51; established investigator Am. Heart Assn., 1953-59, career investigator, 1964-78. Recipient Garvan medal; Cresson medal Franklin Inst., 1976; award Internat. Assn. Women Biochemists, 1979. Mem. Am. Philos. Soc., Nat. Acad. Scis., Am. Chem. Soc., Harvey Soc., Am. Soc. Biol. Chemists, Am. Biophys. Soc., Am. Acad. Arts and Scis., Phi Beta Kappa, Sigma Xi. Editorial bd. jour. Biol. Chemistry, 1958-63, 67-72. Address: Inst Cancer Research 7701 Burholme Ave Fox Chase Philadelphia PA 19111

COHN-ISAACSON, SHIRLEY, psychologist; b. Bklyn., Feb. 13, 1931; d. Max and Rose Cohn; B.A., Bklyn. Coll., 1953; M.A., Calif. State U., Northridge, 1972; Ed.D., Brigham Young U., 1976; children—Cory Michael Isaacson, Dean Robert Isaacson. Sch. psychologist Los Angeles Unified Schs., 1972—; pvt. practice marriage, family and child counseling, ednl. psychology, Los Angeles, 1973—; condr. workshops. Mem. Am., Calif. psychol. assns., Los Angeles Assn. Sch. Psychologists, PTA, Center for Improving Child Caring. Jewish. Co-author filmstrip, Affective-Effectiveness, Springboard to Learning. Home and Office: 350 S Fuller Ave Los Angeles CA 90036

COHRAC, PATRICIA ANN, med. devices mfg. co. exec.; b. Orange, Calif., Aug. 4, 1940; d. Ray Timothy and Shirley (Caufield) Ellis; A.A., St. Joseph Tchrs. Coll., 1960; B.A., Immaculate Heart Coll., 1970; m. George Thomas Cohrac, Oct. 5, 1975. Research and development technician, hosp. pathologist Central Lab. of Orange County, Garden Grove, Calif., 1968-69; research technician U. Calif., Irvine, 1969-70; med. technologist St. Joseph Hosp., Orange, 1971-76; prodn. services mgr. Accugenics, Inc., Garden Grove, Calif., 1976—. Mem. Am. Soc. Clin. Pathologists (asso.), Am. Kennel Club. Home: 11321 Salinaz Dr Garden Grove CA 92643 Office: Accugenics Inc 7272 Chapman Ave Garden Grove CA 92642

COIN, JANE, radiologist; b. Ardmore, Okla., Sept. 7, 1922; d. James Walter and Grace (Allen) C.; M.D., U. Okla., 1947, M.D., 1951. Rotating intern Letterman Army Hosp., San Francisco, 1951-52; resident in radiology U. Okla. Hosps., 1956-58; radiologist St. Anthony Hosp., Oklahoma City, 1958-62; asst. prof. U. Okla. Med. Sch., 1962; dir. radiology Providence Hosp., Anchorage, 1962-65, Columbus Hosp., Gt. Falls, Mont., 1965-67, Alaska Hosp., Anchorage, 1967-70; fellow cardiovascular radiology U. Oreg. Med. Center, 1970-71; dir. radiology Eisenhower Med. Center, Palm Desert, Calif., 1974-76; fellow neuroradiology UCLA Harbour Hosp., 1978-79; radiologist Kodiak (Alaska) Island Hosp., 1979—. Served with USAAF, 1942-45, USAF, 1951-53. Decorated Air medal with 2 oak leaf clusters; grantee Am. Heart Assn., 1956; diplomate Am. Bd. Radiology, Am. Bd. Nuclear Medicine. Mem. AMA, Am. Med. Women's Assn., Alaska Med. Assn., Am. Coll. Radiology, Am. Coll. Nuclear Physicians, Radiol. Soc. N.Am., Am. Soc. Neuroradiology. Republican. Club: Tower (Anchorage). Home: 18 Alderwood St Kodiak AK 99615 Office: Kodiak Island Hosp Box 1187 Kodiak AK 99615

COKER, CORINNE, nurse, nursing home adminstr.; b. DeQueen, Ark., July 17, 1932; d. Roy L. and Clarice M. (Brizendine) Johnson; diploma St. Joseph's Sch. Nursing, 1953; cert. in nursing home adminstrn. Grayson County Coll., 1974; m. Noble E. Coker, Dec. 3, 1977; children by previous marriage—Steven Qualls, Stacy Gaston, Shelta Qualls, Sherri Qualls. Operating room, emergency room nurse Leflore County Hosp., Poteau, Okla., 1953-54; pvt. duty nurse, Okla. and Calif., 1954-63; night supr. Van Buren (Ark.) Hosp., 1963-65, Broken Bow (Okla.) Nursing Home, 1967-68; dir. of nurses, asst. adminstr. Morgan Nursing Home, Broken Bow, 1968-70; pres., owner Yes-Ter-Year, Inc., Saint Jo, Tex., 1970—, Muenster Manor, Inc., Saint Jo, 1977—. R.N., Tex., Ark., Okla., Calif.; lic. nursing home adminstr., Tex. Republican. Baptist. Clubs: 20th Century (pres. 1973-74), St. Jo Band Booster (pres. 1972-73), St. Jo Riding. Home: 2 Capps Corner Rd Saint Jo TX 76265 Office: 405 W Boggess St Saint Jo TX 76265

COKER, JEAN CARR, lawyer; b. Fort Riley, Kans., Jan. 11, 1945; d. Jefferson D. and Helen Auld Carr; B.A. cum laude, Wake Forest U., 1966; J.D., Duke U., 1970; LL.M. in Taxation, U. Fla., 1979; children—Hannah Carr, Elizabeth Auld. Admitted to Fla. bar, 1970, U.S. Supreme Ct., also Tax Ct. bars, 1975; asso. firm Mahoney, Hadlow, Chambers & Adams, Jacksonville, Fla., 1970-75; partner firm Coker & Coker, Jacksonville, 1975-80; asso. firm Smathers & Thompson, Jacksonville, 1980—; dir. Jacksonville Area Legal Aid Assn., 1975-77; faculty mem. Jacksonville U. Dawn Program, 1975—; guest lectr. Fla. Jr. Coll., Center for Continuing Edn. Women, 1975—. Commr. Jacksonville Mayor's Commn. on Status of Women, 1975-80, chmn. legal rights com., 1975-76; dir. Travelers Aid Soc. Jacksonville, 1975—. Mem. Am. Bar Assn., Jacksonville Bar Assn., Fla. Assn. Women Lawyers, Fla. Bar (mem. exec. council real property, probate and trust law sect. 1974-77, chmn. law sch. workshop com. 1974-77, mem. probate and guardianship rules com. 1974—), Phi Beta Kappa. Home: 1118 Holly Ln Jacksonville FL 32207 Office: 3103 Independence Sq Jacksonville FL 32202

COKER, SYBIL JANE THOMAS, journalist, educator; b. Elizabeth, La., Aug. 16; d. Andrew Jackson and Lillie Mae (Miller) Thomas; A.A., Los Angeles City Coll., 1952; B.A., Calif. State U., Los Angeles, 1955; B.A., Pepperdine U., 1957; M.S., Mount St. Mary's Coll., 1980; m. Charles M. Dolo Coker, July 1978. With Amos 'n Andy TV series, 1952; elem. tchr. Barton Hill Sch., 1957-58, 96th St. Sch., 1958-63, Hooper Ave. Sch., 1963-65, Vermont Ave. Sch., 1965-68, Hooper Sch., 1968-70, Angeles Mesa Sch., 1970—; entertainment and soc. editor Los Angeles Gazette, 1972-73; soc. editor Herald-Dispatch, Los Angeles, 1966-67, 75—, women's page editor, movie critic, 1970—; writer Los Angeles Entertainment Digest, 1970-71, Los Angeles Defender, 1974, A.C.C. Ch. and Community News, 1969-70, Celebrity Newspaper, 1970-71, CRS mag., 1978—; free-lance writer; fashion show commentator-coordinator, wedding cons. Founder 2d Baptist Drama Guild, 1957-67. Commended in resolutions U.S. Congress, Calif. Senate. Mem. NEA, Calif. Tchrs. Assn., United Tchrs. Los Angeles, Women in Communications, PTA (hon. life), Nat. Assn. Grad. Women, Nat. Fedn. Press Women, Nat. Assn. Media Women (pres. Beverly Hills/Hollywood chpt., Nat. Pres.'s award 1977), NAACP (life), Nat. Council Negro Women (life), Black Women's Forum, Am. Personnel and Guidance Assn., Christian Women on the Move, United Tchrs. Los Angeles, Greater Los Angeles Press Club, Delta Sigma Theta (Communications award Los Angeles Alumnae chpt. 1977, charter mem. Century City Alumnae chpt., journalist 1981—), Sigma Delta Chi. Democrat. Club: Emanon.

COLABELLA, BETTY MARIE, engring. co. exec.; b. Mt. Carmel, Pa., May 27, 1925; d. Philip Christ and Edith Lavinia Wagner; student public schs. Mount Carmel, Pa.; m. Alfred V. Colabella, Jr., Aug. 28, 1945; children—Alfred V. III, Robert Clark, Edith Ann, Scott Michael. Sec.-treas. A.V. Colabella Engrs., Bordentown, N.J., 1955—, also dir. Mem. Bordentown Bd. Edn., 1965-75, pres., 1968-69, 73-74. Mem. Profl. Engrs. Soc. Mercer County Aux. (pres.), PTA Bordentown (pres.), Republican. Home: 19 Prince St Bordentown NJ 08505 Office: 138 Farnsworth Ave Bordentown NJ 08505

COLACHICO, JEANNE MARIE, lawyer, govt. ofcl.; b. Medford, Mass., Mar. 1, 1951; d. Charles Anthony and Margaret Leona (Harvey) C.; B.A. magna cum laude, Regis Coll., Weston, Mass., 1973; M.Urban Affairs, Boston U., 1977; J.D., Suffolk U., Boston, 1981. Asst. to dir. consumer protection Office Atty. Gen. Mass., 1973-74; EEO specialist Def. Contract Adminstn., Boston region, 1974-81, EEO mgr. 1981—; admitted to Mass. bar, 1981, Fed. Dist. Ct. bar, 1982, Ct. Appeals, 1982. Recipient numerous certs., service awards. Mem. ABA, Mass. Bar Assn., Middlesex Bar Assn., Mass. Assn. Women Lawyers, Nat. Assn. Female Execs., Boston Fed. Execs. Bd. (chmn. coms.), Federally Employed Women, Pan Am. Soc., Greater Boston Civil Rights Coalition, Phi Delta Phi. Author articles in field. Home: 109 Mitchell Ave Medford MA 02155 Office: 495 Summer St Boston MA 02210

COLANGELO, GEMMA FIORILLO, clin. social work psychotherapist; b. Bklyn., Sept. 14, 1924; d. Aniello and Gemma (Giordano) Fiorillo; B.S., Hunter Coll., 1947; M.S.S. (fellow, grantee), Smith Coll., 1950, cert. in Family Therapy, 1979; m. Salvatore F. Colangelo, Dec. 23, 1950; children—Joan, Lynn (dec.), Susan, Lisa. Social investigator N.Y.C. Dept. Welfare, 1947-48; caseworker psychiat. clinic Ellis Hosp., Schenectady, 1950-51; caseworker Jewish Family Service, N.Y.C., 1960-63, Queens (N.Y.) Child Guidance Center, 1963-64, Jamaica Center for Psychotherapy, 1964-66, Hillside Hosp., Queens, affiliate Queens Gen. Hosp., 1966-67; psychotherapist Jewish Community Services of L.I., Queens, 1967-79; pvt. practice family, marital counseling and psychotherapy, N.Y.C., 1973—; cons. Les Clochettes, Bayside, N.Y.; instr. social work Sch. for Social Work, Hunter Coll. and N.Y. U., 1969-76. Diplomate N.Y. State Soc. Clin. Social Work Psychotherapists (membership chmn., 1977-82. Mem. Nat. Assn. Social Workers, Acad. Certified Social Workers. Club: Smith Coll. Alumni. Home: 175-20 Wexford Terrace Jamaica Estates NY 11432 Office: 2 E 85th St New York NY 10028

COLASURDO, ELLEN MARIE, ins. broker exec.; b. Bklyn., Mar. 24, 1944; d. George Thomas and Mary Ellen (Bolger) Brady; B.A. in History, Coll. of New Rochelle, 1965; m. Anthony Colasurdo, Sept. 14, 1968; 1 son, Anthony. Ins. underwriter Chubb & Son, Inc., N.Y.C., 1967-69; ins. marketer Schiff-Terhune, Inc., N.Y.C., 1969-72; mgr. instl. dept. Corroon & Black, N.Y.C., 1972-78; v.p. Alexander & Alexander, Ins. Broker, Greenwich, Conn., 1979—. Recipient Bravo award, Greenwich YWCA, 1980. Asso. in Risk Mgmt., Conn. Ins. Cons. Mem. C.P.C.U. (Conn. chpt.). Republican. Roman Catholic. Home: 93 Buckingham Dr Stamford CT 06902 Office: 1 Pickwick Plaza Greenwich CT 06902

COLBERT, CLAUDETTE (LILY CHAUCHOIN), actress; b. Paris; d. Georges and Jeanne (Loew) Chauchoin; brought to U.S., 1910; grad. Washington Irving High Sch., 1923; m. Norman Foster, Mar. 13, 1928; m. 2d, Joel Pressman, 1935. Debut as Sibyl Blake in Wild Westcotts, Frazee Theatre, 1924; later appeared in plays including The Marionette Man, Leah Kleschna, High Stakes, The Kiss in a Taxi, The Ghost Train, Pearl of Great Price, Tin Pan Alley, See Naples and Die, Eugene O'Neill's Dynamo, A Talent for Murder; 1st appearance in London, in the Barker, 1928; appeared in motion pictures, 1929—, including The Lady Lies, Manslaughter, The Smiling Lieutenant, Sign of the Cross, Cleopatra, Private Worlds, Maid of Salem, It Happened One Night, The Gilded Lily, I Met Him in Paris, Bluebeard's Eighth Wife, Zaza Midnight, Drums Along the Mohawk, Skylark, Remember the Day, Palm Beach Story, No Time for Love, So Proudly We Hail, Parrish, Since You Went Away, Three Came Home, Bride for Sale, Arise My Love, Sleep My Love; starred in Broadway plays Marriage-Go-Round, 1958-60, The Irregular Verb To Love, 1963, The Kingfisher, 1978; tour A Community of Two, 1973-74, Chgo. performances Marriage-Go-Round, 1976; appeared in TV spls. Best of Broadway, including Royal Family, The Guardsman, Blythe Spirit, Private Worlds, 1954-56. Recipient Oscar award for best actress Nat. Acad. Motion Picture Arts and Scis., 1934. *

COLBERT, LINDA ELAINE, nurse; b. Merced, Calif., Aug. 15, 1947; d. William Ralph and Elaine R. (Murray) Phelps; B.S., Calif. State U., Fresno, 1969, postgrad. 1981—; m. Gary Colbert, Aug. 24, 1968; children—Tamara, Rebecca, Valerie. Staff nurse Valley Med. Center, Fresno, Calif., 1969-72; night supr. Coalinga (Calif.) Dist. Hosp., 1973-75, dir. nurses, 1978—; coordinator med. assisting and emergency med. tech. program W. Hills Coll., 1975-78. Bd. trustees Coalinga Dist. Hosp., 1975-76.

COLBORNE, PATRICIA BECKER, publishing ofcl.; b. Evansville, Ind., Jan. 10, 1929; d. Julius A. and Georgiana (Fischer) Becker; B.M.E., DePauw U., 1950; postgrad. Washington U., St. Louis; m. James B. Colborne, Dec. 28, 1950 (div. 1973); 1 dau., Gwendolyn Colborne Arthur. Producer/talent Sta. WEHT-TV, Evansville, Ind., 1958-60, Sta. WCET-TV, Cin., 1967; co-owner, pub. Auto and Flat Glass Jour., Cin., 1967-73; circulation dir. Signs of the Times Pub. Co., Cin., 1973—; guitar instr., 1966-70. Exec. com. Cin. Postal Customers Council; docent Cin. Art Mus., 1964-67; bd. dirs. Jr. League Cin., 1963-64. Mem. Ohio Valley Direct Mktg. Club (pres. 1977-78). Presbyterian. Home: 6993 Wooster Pike Cincinnati OH 45227 Office: 407 Gilbert Ave Cincinnati OH 45202

COLBURN, BARBARA LAMBERT, dietitian; b. Lowell, Mass., Aug. 15, 1950; d. Donald G. and Miriam I. (Asquith) Lambert; B.S. in Foods and Nutrition Teaching, Framingham State Coll., 1972; postgrad. Notre Dame Coll., Manchester, N.H.; m. Robert J. Colburn, Nov. 21, 1975; 1 dau., Jennifer. Diet clk. Lawrence (Mass.) Gen. Hosp., 1969-72, diet therapist, 1972; dietetic trainee in community nutrition New Eng. Dairy and Food Council, Boston, 1972-74, nutrition edn. cons., Bedford, N.H., 1974-80. Mem. Lowell (Mass.) Consumers Council, 1971-72; trustee Litchfield (N.H.) Library. Named Young Dietitian of Yr. in N.H., N.H. Dietetic Assn. and Am. Dietetic Assn., 1979; registered dietitian, N.H. Mem. Am. Dietetic Assn., N.H. Dietetic Assn. (past pres.), LWV. Episcopalian. Home: 63 Nesenkeag Dr Litchfield NH 03051

COLBURN, KATHLEEN GRAHAM, univ. adminstr.; b. Decatur, Tex., Aug. 10, 1945; d. Richard Walker and Ayleen (Barrett) Graham; B.S., N. Tex. State U., 1968; postgrad. U. Tex. at Arlington, 1974-76; children—Jimaleen, Richard. Dir., Denton County (Tex.) Mental Health Clinic, 1970-72; asst. to dean edn. N. Tex. State U., Denton, 1972-74; dir. continuing edn. U. Tex. at Arlington, 1974-79; cons. insts. energy devel. and Tex. Paralegal insts., 1975—; program developer Office Continuing Edn., Div. Public Service, Lamar U., 1979-81; ednl. cons. Casey, Inc., 1981—. Mem. Ft. Worth Regional Council on Alcoholism, 1972-74; pres. Denton County Council on Alcoholism, 1972-74; adv. council Denton (Tex.) City Day Nursery, 1971-74; adv. bd. Arlington Conv. and Visitors Bur., 1974—. Danforth awardee, 1963. Mem. Arlington (ambassador 1974-79), Arlington Women's (v.p. 1975-76), chambers commerce, Am. Bus. Women's Assn., Am., Tex. med. records assns., Tex. Tchrs. Assn., Tex. Assn. Community Service and Continuing Edn., Med. Group Mgmt. Assn., Beta Sigma Phi. Republican. Methodist. Club: Altrusa. Home and office: 4413 Windsor Dr Garland TX 75042

COLBURN, NORMA ELAINE WHEELER, city ofcl.; b. St. Johnsbury, Vt., June 26, 1933; d. Clayton Wallace and Ida Minerva (Lang) Wheeler; student Burdett Coll., 1951, Rutgers U., 1968, 75; m. James Austin Colburn, Jan. 19, 1952; children—Candice Margaret, James Austin. Exec. sec. Oswald L. Sanborn C.P.A.'s, Ridgewood, N.J., 1952; exec. sec. archtl. div. Am. Brakeshoe Co., Mahwah, N.J., 1952; postal clk. U.S. P.O., Lyndon Center, Vt., 1956-60; partner Colburn's Store, Lyndon Center, Vt., 1956-60; corr., feature writer Burlington (Vt.) Free Press, 1959-60; dep. borough clk., ct. clk., Allendale, N.J., 1968-70, sec. planning bd., dep. water collector, 1969-70, borough clk., 1970—, borough adminstr., 1972—. Active Girl Scouts U.S.A., 1965-66. Recipient Time Mag. Current Events award, 1950, 51. Mem. Municipal Clks. Assn. N.J., Bergen County Municipal Clks., Internat. Inst. Municipal Clks. Assn. Mem. Order Eastern Star. Home: 310 Brookside Av Allendale NJ 07401 Office: Office City Clk City Hall Allendale NJ 07401

COLBY, ANNE, psychologist; b. Galveston, Tex., Feb. 10, 1946; d. Malcolm Young and Emily Jane (Armacost) Colby; B.A., McGill U., 1968; Ph.D., Columbia U., 1972. Research asso., lectr. Harvard U., Cambridge, Mass., 1972-80; dir. Henry A. Murray Research Center of Radcliffe Coll., Cambridge, 1980—; dir. research Clin. Devel. Inst. Lic. psychologist, Mass. Mem. Nat. Council of Centers for Research on Women (dir.). Author: The Measurement of Moral Judgment, 1983. Office: H A Murray Research Center Radcliffe Coll 10 Garden St Cambridge MA 02138

COLBY-HALL, ALICE MARY, educator; b. Portland, Maine, Feb. 25, 1932; d. Frederick Eugene and Angie Fraser (Drown) Colby; B.A., Colby Coll., 1953; M.A., Middlebury Coll., 1954; Ph.D., Columbia, 1962; m. Robert A. Hall, Jr., May 8, 1976; stepchildren—Philip, Diana Hall Goodall, Carol Hall Erickson. Tchr. French, Latin Orono (Maine) High Sch., 1954-55; tchr. French Gould Acad., Bethel, Maine, 1955-57; lectr. French Columbia, 1959-60; instr. romance lit. Cornell U., Ithaca, N.Y., 1962-63, asst. prof., 1963-66, asso. prof., 1966-75, prof. romance studies, 1975—. Fulbright grantee, 1953-54. Mem. Modern Lang. Assn., Medieval Acad. Am., Internat. Arthurian Soc., Societe Rencesvals, Phi Beta Kappa. Republican. Conglist. Author: The Portrait in Twelfth Century French Literature: An Example of the Stylistic Originality of Chretien de Troyes, 1965. Mem. editorial bd. Speculum, 1976-79, Olifant, 1974—. Home: 308 Cayuga Heights Rd Ithaca NY 14850 Office: Dept Romance Studies Cornell U Ithaca NY 14853

COLD, BARBARA ANN, fin. planner; b. Cleve., Jan. 14, 1933; d. C. Christian and Elvyra (Von Kanel) Nelson; student U. Ohio, 1950 51, Joliet Jr. Coll., 1963, 65, U. Ill., 1966; m. Wallace Partridge Cold, Dec. 16, 1950 (div.); children—Deborah, Christian, Jennifer, Laura, Craig, Mark. Land salesperson Am. Central Corp., Lansing, Mich., 1970-71, mktg. mgr., 1972, 74; mktg. mgr. Russwood Corp., Peoria, Ill., 1973, Charleston, S.C., 1975; owner, mgr. Equity Planning, Joliet, Ill., 1975-81, Peoria, Ill., 1981—; counselor, condr. seminars on fin. planning. Mem. Nat. Assn. Fin. Planners, Nat. Assn. Truth in Life Ins., Assn. Bd. Dirs. La., LWV, Theosophical Soc. Am. Democrat. Unitarian. Home: 805 Moss Ave Peoria IL 61606

COLE, ADELAIDE MEADOR, educator; b. Hinton, W.Va., June 6, 1923; d. Vollmer A. and Josephine F. (Ratliff) Meador; A.B., Marshall U., 1946; M.A., Duke U., 1947; Ed.D. Tchrs. Coll. Columbia U., 1950; m. James Lewis Cole, Nov. 29, 1965; children—John Aden Hunter, W. Alexandra Hunter, Mary Adelaide Hunter, Tanya Sean. Prof. phys. edn. Cedarville Coll., 1951-52; assoc. prof. Pan Am. Coll., 1953-60; asso. prof. Calif. Western U., 1960-61; asso. prof. N.Mex. Highlands U., 1961-65; prof. Ball State U., Muncie, Ind., 1967—, dir. grad. studies Sch. Phys. Edn. Recipient ARC Outstanding Service award, 1958. Mem. AAH-PERD (sec. 1981-82, chmn. research Midwest dist. 1982-83), Ind. Assn. Health Phys. Edn. and Recreation, Kappa Delta Pi (pres. 1945-46), Phi Epsilon Kappa, Pi Lambda Theta, Phi Delta Kappa, Sigma Sigma Sigma. Democrat. Episcopalian. Clubs: Elks Aux., Rotary, Eagles Aux. Contbr. in field. Home: 968 Mary Lee Ave New Castle IN 47362 Office: Ball State U Muncie IN 47306

COLE, A(NNA) RUTH, vol. church worker, former educator; b. Eaton, Ohio; d. George Washington and Esther (Akel) Cole; B.S., Miami U., Oxford, Ohio, 1939; M.A., Ohio State U., 1953; summer student U. Colo., 1937, Vassar Coll., 1963. Tchr., Morris Sch., Hamilton, Ohio, 1921-23, 24-25, Edison Elem. Sch., Columbus, Ohio, 1925-26, Robert Louis Stevenson Sch., Columbus, 1926-71; mem. arithmetic textbook selection com. Grandview Heights Public Schs., 1967-68. Mem. commn. on edn., youth counselor, mem. adminstrv. bd. Trinity United Methodist Ch., chmn. global concerns, 1974-78; sec. Wesleyan Service Guild, 1971-74, chmn. program resources, 1973-77, mission coordinator Christian global concerns, 1974-77, work area on missions, 1974-76; sec. program resources Columbus N. Dist. United Meth. Ch., 1973-77. Mem. Grandview Heights Tchrs. Assn. (dir. 1947-50, pres. 1954-56) (social chmn. 1969-70), Assn. for Childhood Internat. (v.p. 1956-58, pres. 1958-60), NEA (life), Ohio Edn. Assn., Central Ohio Tchrs. Assn., Wesleyan Service Guild (pres. 1943-45, 62-64, 64-65, dist. sec. 1957-61; v.p. 1968-69), Grandview Heights PTA, Ohio Conservation and Outdoor Edn. Assn., Ohio State U. Alumni Assn. (life), Nat., Ohio, Franklin County ret. tchrs. assns., Am. Assn. Ret. Persons, Nat. Fedn. Republican Women, Am. Contract Bridge League, Upper Arlington Sr. Activities (desk vol. 1981-83), United Meth. Women (coordinator prayer chains 1978-79, v.p., dist. and conf. officer 1979-81), Franklin County Hist. Soc., Center Sci. and Industry, Kappa Phi (life), Phi Delta Gamma (life, pres. 1955-57), Delta Kappa Gamma (chpt. membership chmn. 1962-64, recruitment com. 1964-66, initiation chmn. 1974—, rec. sec. 1978-80, membership com. 1980—). Life mem. Silhoutte Nat. Health Studios. Republican. Home: 1314 W 7th Ave Columbus OH 43212

COLE, CAROLYN JO, brokerage co. exec.; b. Carmel, Calif., Apr. 22, 1943; d. Joseph Michael, Jr., and Dorothea Wagner (James) C.; A.B., Vassar Coll., 1965. Mgr. tech. services Aims Group, N.Y.C., 1965-67; editor Standard & Poor's Corp., N.Y.C., 1968-74; corp. v.p. Paine Webber Jackson & Curtis, also 1st v.p. Paine Webber Mitchell Hutchins, N.Y.C., 1975—; guest lectr. Harvard U. Bus. Sch. Mem. N.Y.C. Commn. on Status of Women. Named to YWCA Acad. Women Achievers. Mem. N.Y. Soc. Security Analysts, Fin. Analysts Fedn., Soc. Fgn. Analysts, Fin. Women's Assn., Women's Econ. Roundtable, Econ. Club N.Y., NOW, DAR. Democrat. Episcopalian. Club: Vassar (N.Y.C.). Contbr. to Ency. Americana. Home: 197 Amity St Brooklyn NY 11201 Office: Paine Webber Mitchell Hutchins Inc 140 Broadway New York NY 10005

COLE, CLARANN MAE FRONCZAK, educator; b. Turlock, Calif., Mar. 17, 1947; d. Thaddeus Francis and Lola Mae (Curtis) Fronczak; A.A., Merced Jr. Coll., 1967; B.A., Fresno State Coll., 1970, Standard Tchr. Credential, 1971; 1 dau., Suzanne Lydia. Sec./aide Merced Coll., 1966-67; tchrs. aide Fresno (Calif.) State Coll., 1967-68; tchr. Atwater (Calif.) Sch. Dist., 1971—; elem. migrant summer sch. tchr., 1979-80. Recipient Calif. 4-H Club Leadership award, 1979. Mem. Atwater Elem. Tchrs. Assn. (sec. 1976), Calif. Indian Edn. Assn., AAUW, Calif. Tchrs. Assn. Republican. Roman Catholic. Home: 2328 Redwood St Atwater CA 95301 Office: PO Box 775 Mitchell K-6 Atwater CA 95301

COLE, DONNA ALBERTSON, temporary manpower services co. exec.; b. Waverly, N.Y., Jan. 20, 1934; d. Donald Charles and Cecile Mae (Clarke) Albertson; B.S., Elmira Coll., 1956; m. Donald Dennis Cole, Jan. 27, 1956; children—Elizabeth Marie, Marjorie Cecilia, Lucinda Grace, Raymond Charles. Chemist, Thatcher Glass Mfg. Co. Inc., Elmira, N.Y., 1956-57; chemist Corning Glass Works (N.Y.), 1957-59; mgr. Manpower Temporary Services, Elmira, N.Y., 1976-81, area mgr., 1981—; teaching asso. organic chemistry lab. Elmira Coll., 1974; tchr. Corning Community Coll., 1981. Bd. dirs. Southerntier Economic Growth, 1981; mem. Adv. Council Elmira Coll.; Chemung County chpt. ARC. Mem. Adminstrv. Mgmt. Soc., Chemung County C. of C. (v.p.), Am. Soc. Profl. and Exec. Women. Republican. Methodist. Clubs: Ithaca Yacht, Twin Tier Racquet. Home: 651 Euclid Ave Elmira NY 14901 Office: Mark Twain Bldg Elmira NY 14901

COLE, ELMA PHILLIPSON (MRS. JOHN STRICKLER COLE), social welfare exec.; b. Piqua, Ohio, Aug. 9, 1909; d. Brice Leroy and Mabel (Gale) Phillipson; A.B., Berea Coll., 1930; M.A., U. Chgo., 1938; m. John Strickler Cole, Oct. 3., 1959. Various positions in social work, 1930-42; dir. social service dept. Children's Hosp. D.C., 1942-49; cons. public cooperation Midcentury White House Conf. Children and Youth, 1949-51; exec. sec. Nat. Midcentury Com. Children and Youth, 1951-53; cons. recruitment Am. Assn. Med. Social Workers, 1953; asso. dir. Nat. Legal Aid and Defender Assn., 1953-56; exec. sec. Marshall Field Awards, Inc., 1956-57; dir. asso. orgns. Nat. Assembly Social Policy and Devel., 1957-73; asso. exec. dir. Nat. Assembly Nat. Vol. Health and Social Welfare Orgns., 1974; dir. edn. parenthood project Salvation Army, 1974-76, asst. sec. women's and children's social service dept., 1976-78, dir. research project devel. bur., social services dept., 1978—, also mem. Manhattan adv. bd., 1975—, hist. commn., 1978—; cons. nat. orgns. Golden Anniversary White House Conf. Children and Youth, 1959-60; mem. adv. council public service Nat. Assn. Life Underwriters and Inst. Life Ins.; mem. judges com. Louis I. Dublin Public Service awards, 1961-74; mem. com. public relations and fund raising Am. Found. for Blind Commn. on Accreditation, 1964-67; mem. adv. bd. sexuality edn. project Center for Population Options, 1977—; mem. task force vol. accreditation Council Nat. Orgns. for Adult Edn., 1974-78; v.p. Blue Ridge Inst. of So. Community Service Execs., 1977-79, exec. com., 1979-81; bd. dirs. Values and Human Sexuality Inst., 1980—; mem. nat. adv. panel Planned Parenthood Fedn. Family Life Edn. Project, 1981—. Mem. Public Relations Soc. Am. (accredited), Nat. Assn. Social Workers (accredited), Nat. Conf. Social Welfare (com. public relations 1961-66, 69—; chmn. adminstrn. sect. 1966-67), Jr. League Washington, Pi Gamma Mu, Phi Kappa Phi. Club: Women's of N.Y. Contbr. articles to profl. jours., encys. Home: 19 Washington Sq N New York NY 10011 Office: 120 W 14th St New York NY 10011

COLE, ELSIE MAY, psychologist; b. East St. Louis, Ill., Sept. 24, 1919; d. Charles Arthur and Nettie Jane (Young) Holt; student Long Beach City Coll., 1955-57; B.A. with distinction, Calif. State Coll., Long Beach, 1959; M.A. in Psychology (grad. scholar), U. Ariz., 1961; m. Fabian Monroe Cole, Apr. 10, 1937; children—Virginia May Cole Mahan, Carol Cole Cormack (dec.). Adminstrv. asst. U.S. Navy Ordnance Test Sta., China Lake, Calif., 1945-50; with VA, Poplar Bluff, Mo., 1950-51, Bonham, Tex., 1951-52, Long Beach, 1952-54; cost analyst U.S. Naval Sta., Long Beach, 1954-57; child welfare worker Pinal County, Florence, Ariz., 1960-61; research engr. N.Am. Aviation, Inc., Downey, Calif., 1962-67; research psychologist Joint Task Force-2, Sandia Base, N.Mex., 1967-69; research psychologist U.S. Air Force Human Resources Lab., Brooks AFB, Tex., 1969-76, coordinator fed. women's program, 1972-76; cons. in human factors research and documentation, aerospace tech. and life scis., 1976—. Cert. psychologist, Tex. Mem. Am. Psychol. Assn., Human Factors Assn., Mensa Internat. Soc., Am. Mensa. Contbr. articles to profl. publs. Home and office: Route 2 Box 195A Doniphan MO 63935

COLE, EVELYN MARIE, day care center owner, adminstr.; b. Alvon, W.Va., Sept. 14, 1928; d. Melvin Arthur and Lillie Mae (Fifer) Cole; student pub. schs.; m. Delford Lee Cole, Jan. 31, 1950; children—Karen Lee, Phillip Quinton, Jonathon Avery. Owner, adminstr. Evelyn's Home Away from Home Day Care, Roanoke, Va., 1975—; owner, adminstr. Foster Home and Shelter Home for State Va., Roanoke, 1969-72. Mem. Ch. of Christ. Home: 2122 Berkley Ave SW PO Box 4656 Roanoke VA 24015 Office: 1731 Grandin Rd SW Roanoke VA 24015

COLE, HELEN, state legislator; b. July 13, 1922. Mem. Okla. Ho. of Reps., 1979—. Republican. Office: Okla Ho Reps State Capitol Oklahoma City OK 73105 *

COLE, JEANINE MAE MONDEVILLE, religious assn. exec.; b. Belleville, Ont., Can., Mar. 19, 1938; came to U.S., 1958, naturalized, 1970; d. Harry J. and Marion E. (McNeil) Mondeville; m. Philip Edward Cole, Nov. 4, 1966; children—Mike, Patti, Marion. Sec., Phoenix Real Estate Bd., 1965-67; sr. sec. Wackenhut Corp., Oklahoma City, 1980-81; sr. exec. sec. So. Satellite Systems, Tulsa, 1981-82; exec. dir. United Trinity Ministries, Inc., Bixby, Okla., 1978—; lectr., condr. seminars and cons. in ministries mgmt. Mem. Am. Soc. Profl. and Exec. Women. Office: 6730 E Mcdowell Rd Suite 116 Scottsdale AZ 8257

COLE, JOAN HAYS, social worker, social clin. psychologist; b. Pitts., Sept. 4, 1929; d. Frank L. Wertheimer and Edith H. Einstein; B.A., Western Res. U., 1951; M.S.S.A. in Social Work, Case Western Res. U., 1962; Ph.D., Wright Inst., 1975; children—Geoffrey F. Cole, Douglas R. Cole, Peter Hays Cole. Social group worker Alta House Settlement House, Cleve., 1958-59; housing dir. Cleve. Urban League, 1961-62; dir. Citizens for Safe Housing, Cleve., 1963; housing dir. United Planning Orgn., Washington, 1963-68; asst. prof. community orgn. U. Md., Balt., 1968-72; asso. prof. Lone Mountain Coll., San Francisco, 1975-78; psychotherapist, Berkeley, Calif., 1977—; cons. various public and vol. social welfare, health and housing agys., 1969-80; mem. adj. faculty Union Grad. Sch. and Antioch West Coll., 1978-80; lectr. U. Calif. Sch. Social Welfare, Berkeley, 1980—; mem. faculty Berkeley Psychotherapy Inst., 1981—. NIMH grantee, 1971-72, Sr. Social Work Career Devel. grantee, 1973-75. Mem. Nat. Assn. Social Workers, Soc. Clin. Social Work, Am. Orthopsychiat. Assn., Soc. Study of Social Issues, ACLU, NOW, Nat. Welfare Rights Orgn., Acad. Cert. Social Workers. Home: 1377 Campus Dr Berkeley CA 94708 Office: 1905 Berkeley Way Berkeley CA 94704

COLE, JOYCE COUCH, educator; b. Mobile, Ala., Apr. 26, 1954; d. Robert Chesley and Barbara Allen (Joyce) Couch; B.S., Auburn U., 1976, M.A., U. Ala.-Birmingham, 1980; postgrad. Memphis State U., 1982—; m. Stanley George Cole, Aug. 22, 1981. Research asst. Center for Devel. and Learning Disorders, Birmingham, 1976; work adjustment specialist Delgado Vocat. Rehab. Center, New Orleans, 1976-77; vocat. evaluator for deaf and blind E.H. Gentry Spl. Tech. Facility, Talladega, Ala., 1977-80; instr., coordinator vocat. evaluation Memphis State U., 1980—; pvt. practice vocat. evaluation specialist and cons. Memphis, 1980—. Bd. dirs., sec. Interpreting Services for the Deaf, Memphis. Cert. vocat. evaluation specialist. Mem. Nat. Rehab. Vocat. Evaluation and Work Adjustment Assn., Nat. Rehab. Counseling Assn., Nat. Council Rehab. Educators, World Future Soc. Episcopalian. Home: 485 Patterson St Memphis TN 38111 Office: Dept Spl Edn and Rehab Memphis State U Memphis TN 38152

COLE, JUDITH ANN, writer, govt. ofcl.; b. Parsons, Kans.; d. John Cotterman and Marguerite Maria (Jones) C.; B.A. in Sociology, St. Mary's Coll., Notre Dame, Ind., 1961; M.A. in Polit. Sci., U. Mo., Kansas City, 1972; grad. program for mgmt. devel. Harvard Grad. Sch. Bus. Adminstrn., 1977; law student George Mason U., 1980—. Elementary sch. tchr., 1961-64; legis. asst. U.S. Ho. Reps., 1965-67; chief adminstrv. officer Presdl. Campaign Nat. Hdqrs., Washington, 1967-69; staff asst. to Pres. U.S., 1972; staff asst. to dir. ACDA, 1973; dep. asst. adminstr. for legis. affairs NASA, 1974-79; mgr. regulatory affairs Philip Morris, Inc., Washington, 1979-80; writer for White House, 1981—. Recipient Exceptional Service award NASA, 1979. Mem. Exec. Women in Govt. (a founder), Fed. Exec. Inst. Alumni Assn. (class rep.). Roman Catholic. Office: White House 1600 Pennsylvania Ave Washington DC 20500

COLE, MARTHA ELIZABETH, med. technologist; b. Corpus Christi, Tex., Apr. 27, 1941; d. Robert Lenear and Helen Degge (Sumners) McCall; B.S., S.W. Tex. State U., 1963; M.T., Valley Bapt. Hosp. Sch. Med. Technology, 1964; m. Fred L. Cole, Jr., Oct. 27, 1973; children—Allison, Elizabeth Ann. With S.W. Blood Bank, Harlingen, Tex., 1964; chief technician Valley Diagnostic Clinic, Harlingen, 1964-69; chief technologist PAR Lab., Corpus Christi, Tex., 1969-71; treas. Cole's The Cash Register Co., Harlingen. Bd. dirs. St. Alban's Day Sch., 1979—; mem. vestry St. Alban's Ch., 1980—. Mem. Am. Soc. Clin. Pathologists, Jaycettes. Democrat. Episcopalian. Home: 2609 Lotus St Harlingen TX 78550 Office: 317 5 77 Sunshine Strip Harlingen TX 78550

COLE, MERCEDES THERESE, med. technologist; b. Schenectady, Dec. 14, 1946; d. Ramon V. and Charlotte F. (Lachner) Azua; B.S. in Med. Tech., Gwynedd-Mercy Coll., 1969; M.S., Thomas Jefferson U., 1977; m. Richard L. Cole, Jr., Aug. 10, 1968; 1 dau., Maria Mercedes. With Clinica Samper, Bogota, Colombia, 1967; microbiologist Rolling Hill Hosp. and Diagnostic Center, Elkins Park, Pa., 1969-73, edn. coordinator for med. lab. technician program, 1973-75, program dir., 1976—; site surveyor/team mem. Nat. Accrediting Agy. for Clin. Lab. Scientists, 1978—. Mem. med. lab. technicians adv. com. Gwynedd-Mercy Coll., 1978—; chmn. Games June Fete, Abington Meml. Hosp., 1977-81; mem. emergency med. service adv. com. Abington Twp., 1977-78; chmn. ARC Bloodmobile, Rolling Hill, 1972-75, 77—. Mem. Am. Soc. Med. Technologists (student bowl coordinator regional playoffs 1978, 79), Pa. Soc. Med. Technologists (bd. dirs. 1982-84, chmn. ann. conv. 1981), Thomas Jefferson U. Grad. Alumni (dir. 1982-84, mem. nominating com. 1978-80). Home: 65 Shady Ln Philadelphia PA 19111 Office: 60 E Township Line Rd Elkins Park PA 19117

COLE, NORMA JEAN, educator; b. Slick, Okla., Mar. 18, 1941; d. Norman and Lela Florence (Steward) C.: B.S., Langston U., 1963; M.S., Central State U., 1970; M.S., U. Okla., 1975. Tchr., Chickasha (Okla.) Public Schs., 1963-65; tchr. Oklahoma City Public Schs., 1965-77, curriculum cons., 1977-81; instr. dept. curriculum and instrn. Okla. State U., Stillwater, 1981—. Active March of Dimes. Recipient J. Andrew Holley Meml. Scholarship award, 1982. Mem. Reading Council, Assn. Supervision and Curriculum Devel., Okla. Edn. Assn., Delta Kappa Gamma, Sigma Gamma Rho. Democrat. Baptist. Office: 306A Gundersen St Stillwater OK 74078

COLE, PATRICIA JEANNEANE, nurse; b. Caldwell, Kans., Dec. 20, 1929; d. Roscoe Aubry and Dorothy (Walker) Cornwall; grad. St. Mary's Sch. Nursing, Enid, Okla., 1950; children—Doran, Janet, Lisa, Jay. Staff nurse Santa Rosa Hosp., San Antonio, 1951-52; surg. nurse St. Mary's Hosp., Enid, 1952-53; staff nurse Caldwell Gen. Hosp., 1956-66; staff nurse Sumner County Dist. No. 1 Hosp., Caldwell, 1966-79, dir. nursing, 1979—; mem. adv. bd. mobile continuing edn. program for nurses Wichita State U. Mem. Kans. Assn. Hosp. Edn. Coordinators, Kans. Soc. Nursing Services Adminstrs. Methodist. Home: 603 N Young St Caldwell KS 67022 Office: 601 S Osage St Caldwell KS 67022

COLE, PATRICIA RUTH, speech pathologist; b. Stamford, Tex., Dec. 27, 1940; d. Ben B. and Patsey D. Cole; B.S., U. Tex., 1963, M.A. (Vocat. Rehab. Commn. grantee), 1966, Ph.D., 1976. Speech pathologist Abilene (Tex.) Ind. Sch. Dist., 1963-64; supr. speech pathology U. Tex. Speech and Hearing Clinic, Austin, 1966-71; co-dir. Austin Speech, Lang. and Hearing Center, 1971—; cons. Austin Ear, Nose and Throat Clinic, various schs., health agencies, and state programs. Recipient Disting. Service award Tex. Occupational Therapy Assn., 1978; Presdl. citation Tex. Assn. Deaf., 1979. Fellow Am. Speech, Lang. and Hearing Assn. (legis. council, state licensure com. 1975-78, resolutions com. 1976-77, congl. action contact 1976-80, sci. and profl. meetings bd. 1979-80, assn. adv. com. 1978-80, com. state-nat. relations 1980, ad hoc com. communication standards 1979, asso. editor 1979-80, v.p. planning), Tex. Speech and Hearing Assn. (pres. 1976-78, cert. of appreciation 1977, honors 1979), Phi Kappa Phi. Methodist. Home: 3519 Westchester St Austin TX 78759 Office: 1209 W 34th St Austin TX 78705

COLE, SALLY R., ednl. testing exec., counselor; b. Oklahoma City, Oct. 28, 1946; d. C. Ralph and Ruth I. (Longfellow) White; B.S. in Edn., U. Okla., 1968, M.S. in Edn., 1971, Ph.D. in Edn., 1977. Spl. edn. tchr. Classen High Sch., Oklahoma City, 1968-70, Harmony Elem. Sch., Oklahoma City, 1970-72; tchr. coordinator Douglass High Sch., Oklahoma City, 1972-75, asst. prin., 1975-77; asst. prin. John Marshall High Sch., Oklahoma City, 1977-78; prin. Classen High Sch., 1978-82; pvt. counselor, testing adminstr., Oklahoma City, 1982—. Named Mar. Employee of Month, Oklahoma City Pub. Schs., 1981, also recipient Outstanding Adminstr. award, 1981; Sally R. Cole Day named in her honor by Okla. gov., 1982. Mem. Council Exceptional Children, Oklahoma City Assn. Secondary Sch. Prins., Nat. Assn. Secondary Sch. Prins., Oklahoma City C. of C., Phi Delta Kappa. Contbr. articles to profl. publs. Home: 5517 N Billen St Oklahoma City OK 73112 Office: 4101 N Classen St Oklahoma City OK 73118

COLE, STEPHANIE BARRY, ins. co. exec.; b. Bangor, Maine, Apr. 4, 1943; d. Stephen A. and Marvia P. Barry; B.A. in Math. magna cum laude, U. Maine, 1965. EDP tng. coordinator Eastman Kodak, Rochester, N.Y., 1965-67; data processing cons. Arthur D. Little, Cambridge, Mass., 1967-73; with New Eng. Life Ins. Co., Boston, 1974—, asst. v.p., 1978-79, 2d v.p. corp. planning and research, 1979—. Mem. Commonwealth of Mass. Gov.'s Mgmt. Task Force, 1975. Mem. Planning Execs. Inst., Assn. Internal Mgmt. Cons. Office: 501 Boylston St Boston MA 02117

COLE, VIRGINIA ADELAIDE, educator; b. Hinton, W.Va., June 6, 1923; d. Vollmer Aden and Josephine Florence (Ratliff) Meador; A.B., Marshall Coll., 1946; M.A., Duke U., 1947; Ed.D., Columbia U., 1950; m. James Lewis Cole, Nov. 29, 1964; children—John, Alexandra, Mary Adelaide, Tanya Sean. Instr. phys. edn. Columbia U., 1950; prof. Cedarville (Ohio) Coll., 1951-52; asso. prof. Pan Am. Coll., Edinburg, Tex., 1953-60, Calif. Western U., San Diego, 1960-61, N.Mex. Highlands U., Las Vegas, 1961-65; prof. phys. edn. Ball State U., Muncie, Ind., 1967—, dir. grad. studies Sch. Phys. Edn., 1971-82, also adminstrv. asst. to chmn. sch., 1977-82. Recipient ARC Outstanding Service award, 1958. Mem. Am., Ind. assns. for health, phys. edn. and recreation, Nat. Assn. for Phys. Edn. for Coll. Women, LWV, DAR, Sigma Sigma Sigma, Phi Delta Kappa, Pi Lambda Theta. Democrat. Episcopalian. Clubs: Elks, Eagles, Rotarian women's auxs. Home: 968 Mary Lee Ave New Castle IN 47362 Office: Ball State U Muncie IN 47306

COLEBURN, PAMELA LYNNE, ins. co. exec.; b. Washington, Oct. 24, 1948; d. Robert Custis and Cornelia Lynne (Becker) C.; B.S. in Bus. Edn., Longwood Coll., Farmville, Va., 1975. Sec., receptionist, then inventory control clk. Kloman Hosp. Industries, Fairfax, Va., 1971-74; instr. bus. Bristol (Tenn.) Coll., 1975-76; acct. Gibson & Turner Co., Inc., ind. ins., Bristol, 1976—. Mem. Ins. Women's Club, Bristol Jaycettes (treas.), Phi Mu. Presbyterian. Office: 1252 W State St Bristol TN 37620

COLECHIO, PENELOPE ROSE, restaurant exec.; b. Harrisburg, Pa., Dec. 22, 1944; d. Samuel Dominic and Myrtle Kinney (McDonough) C.; student Rochester Bus. Inst., 1963-65. Ins. adminstr., payroll Carolando

Corp., Orlando, Fla., 1972-73; mgr. Ireland's Restaurants, Nashville, 1973-74; bartender Dutch Pantry Restaurants, Orlando, 1974-75; field supr. Holiday House Restaurants, Inc., DeLand, Fla., 1975-81; owner, operator Longwood Village Inn (Fla.), 1982—. Recipient certs. Nat. Restaurant Assn., Mem. Nat. Restaurant Assn., Fla. Restaurant Assn. Democrat. Roman Catholic. Home: 820 Jamestown Dr Winter Park FL 32792 Office: Longwood Village Inn Longwood FL 32750

COLEMAN, ARLENE HAMLETT, reading specialist; b. Newark, Apr. 17, 1946; d. Edwin and Helen Hamlett; B.A. in Elem. Edn., William Paterson Coll., 1967; M.S. in Reading, Queens Coll., City U. N.Y., 1977; m. Gregory D. Coleman, Jr.; children—Candice Arlene, Naniette Helene, Aaron Gregory. Elem. sch. tchr., East Orange, N.J., 1967-70; Fulbright-Hays exchange tchr., Halifax, N.S., Can., 1970-71; lang. arts tchr., East Orange, 1971-72; sch. service rep./cons. Westinghouse Learning Corp., N.Y.C., 1972-73; pvt. reading cons., writer, Westbury, N.Y., 1977—; instr. Adelphi U., 1980; adj. prof. SUNY Coll., Old Westbury, 1980—. Vice pres. Westbury chpt. LWV, 1979-80, membership/conf. dir., 1978-79, program dir., 1980-81; mem. membership com. Soc. Gifted and Talented Children, 1979-80; mem. Greater Westbury Coalition, Greater Westbury Arts Council, Sherwood Civic Assn.; bd. dirs. Day Care Council Nassau County, 1981—; mem. arts council Westbury Public Library, 1982—; mem. gifted and talented com. Westbury Schs., 1978-79. Mem. AAUW (dir., chairperson creative writing group), Nat. Assn. Negro Bus. and Profl. Women's Clubs (dir. Westbury 1979—, chpt. Pres.'s award 1980), Internat. Reading Assn., Soc. Children's Book Writers, Soc. Gifted and Talented Children (v.p. 1982—), Nassau Reading Council, Nat. Writers Club, N.Y. State Reading Assn., Kappa Delta Pi. Methodist. Author: (poetry) U.S. in Clover '76, 1976; The Clover Collection of Verse, 1975. Home and Office: 813 Eastfield Rd Westbury NY 11590

COLEMAN, CLAIRE KOHN, public relations exec.; b. New Castle, Pa., Nov. 19, 1924; d. Louis and Florence (Frank) K.; B.A., Pa. State U., 1945; m. Frederick H. Coleman, Mar. 10, 1957; children—Franklin, Elliot. Market editor Fairchild Publs., N.Y.C., 1945-48; asst. home editor N.Y. Times, 1949-50; public relations dir. United Wallpaper, Chgo., 1950-53; public relations dir. Asso. Am. Artists, N.Y.C., 1953-54; dir. Wallpaper Info. Bur., N.Y.C., 1954; dept. head Roy Bernard, Inc., N.Y.C., 1955-58; public relations dir. The Siesel Co., N.Y.C., 1972—, sr. v.p., 1981—. Mem. central steering com., Sch. Dist. Critical Assessments, New Rochelle, N.Y., 1969-71; bd. dirs., v.p. Beechmont Assn., 1960-74; mem. Mayor's Adv. Council on Aging, 1966; mem. Mayor's Adv. Com. on Bd. Edn. Appointments, 1969; v.p. Council of PTAs, 1969-70; chmn. women's div. United Jewish Appeal, New Rochelle, 1971. Fellow Nat. Home Fashions League (founder 1947, nat. treas. 1977-78, pres. 1980-81); mem. Public Relations Soc. Am., Women in Communications, Women Execs. in Public Relations. Office: 845 3d Ave New York NY 10022

COLEMAN, DEBORAH LEWIS, telephone co. exec.; b. Birmingham, Ala., June 21, 1949; d. James and Gearline (Banks) Lewis; B.A., Va. State U., 1974; m. Winson R. Coleman, Jr., Sept. 3, 1977; 1 son, Kevin Lewis. Communications rep. C & P Telephone, Richmond, Va., 1977-78, account exec., industry cons. in banking, 1978-81, staff mgr. advanced mktg. tng., 1981—. Named Salesperson of the Yr. Sales and Mktg. Execs., 1979. Mem. Va. Savs. and Loan League, Savs. Inst. Mktg. Soc. Am., Nat. Assn. Female Execs., NAACP, Nat. Soc. Profl. Instrs. Home: 6391 Wishing Bridge Columbia MD 21045 Office: 1825 I St NW Washington DC 20006

COLEMAN, DONNA ANN, state legislator; b. Sao Paulo, Brazil, Mar. 11, 1949; d. John M. and Donna (Hendricks) C.; B.S., U. Utah, 1974; postgrad. U. Mo., Washington U. (both St. Louis). With Stanford Research Inst. (Calif.), 1975-76; corp. sec.-treas., fin. officer Engineered Fire Protection, Inc., St. Louis, 1977—, bd. dirs., trustee employee profit sharing trust. Mem. Mo. Ho. of Reps., 1981—; dir. speakers bur. Mo. Citizens Council; del. Mo. Republican Conv., 1980. Mem. Ch. Jesus Christ of Latter-day Saints. Home: 570 Meadow Bridge Saint Louis MO 63011 Office: Room 105-C State Capitol Bldg Jefferson City MO 65101

COLEMAN, EDITH WETHERILL, med. assn. exec.; b. Edgewater Park, N.J., Feb. 14, 1918; d. Edwin Howard and Edith Roberts (Scott) Frazier; student public schs., Burlington, N.J.; m. Samuel Roger Wetherill, Jr., Oct. 11, 1941 (dec. May 1959); children—Samuel Roger III, Stephen Frazier; m. 2d, Loren Otis Coleman, Jr., Sept. 15, 1967. Sec. to adminstr. Collingswood, (N.J.) Public Schs., 1959-63; asst. to exec. sec. Camden County Med. Soc., Collingswood, N.J., 1963-70, exec. sec., 1970-72, mng. editor Bull., 1970—, exec. dir., 1972—; notary public, 1967—. Mem. Am. Med. Soc. Execs., Haddonfield Hist. Soc., DAR (regent Collingswood chpt. 1977-81, historian 1981—). Republican. Presbyterian. Office: Camden County Med Soc 900 Haddon Ave Suite 202 Collingswood NJ 08108

COLEMAN, JENNIFER WALKER, meeting planner, group travel and internat. trade cons. co. exec.; b. San Francisco, Feb. 9, 1949; d. Leon and Rebecca (Hudson) Walker; B.A. in Social Sci., Calif. State U., San Jose, 1973; m. Curley Coleman, Sept. 4, 1976. Fiscal technician NASA Ames Research, Moffit Field, Calif., 1972-73; account technician Oakland (Calif.) Head Start, 1973-74; free-lance cons., 1974-76; sr. accountant San Francisco Housing Authority, 1976-78, internal auditor, 1977-78; group travel coordinator Atlas Travel Service, San Francisco, 1977—; controller D.D.&A., Cons., San Francisco, 1978-79, also dir.; owner, operator Bus. Interaction Exchange, Oakland, 1979—; affirmative action counselor NASA; bd. dirs. Oakland Small Bus. Export Task Force. Exec. sec. East Bay chpt. Black C. of C.-Oakland, 1980—; mem. conv. activity com. Oakland-Conv. and Tourist Bur., 1980—. Recipient Sales award Norwegian Caribbean Cruise Line, 1978. Mem. Am. Entrepreneurs Assn., Black Am. Polit. Assn. Calif., Black C. of C., Black Women Organized for Polit. Action, Inst. Reading Devel., NAACP, Oakland C. of C. (internat. trade com. 1980—), Oakland Together, Meeting Planners Internat. Democrat. Baptist. Choreographer for plays Calif. State U., San Jose, 1971-72. Home: 4136 Carrington St Oakland CA 94601 Office: 1247 5th Ave Suite 4 Oakland CA 94606

COLEMAN, KAYE MARTIN, univ. adminstr.; b. Ogden, Utah, Sept. 25, 1931; d. Frank Leonard and Donna Margaret (Ramsden) Martin; B.S., U. Utah, 1969, M.S.W., 1971, Ph.D., 1976; m. Clair Flygare Coleman, Aug. 26, 1949; children—Rich Flygare, John Patrick, Jolie Ann Coleman Howard. Counseling dir. Women's Resource Center, U. Utah, 1971-81, asso. dir. OEO, 1981—, also clin. asso. prof. Grad. Sch. Social Work, adj. asst. prof. Coll. Health; mgmt. trainer, cons. in field. Bd. dirs. Phoenix Inst., Salt Lake City, 1971—, Children's Center, Salt Lake City, 1975-77; past pres. Salt Lake City Jr. League. Recipient Outstanding Tchr. award U. Utah Mortar Bd. chpt., 1977; grantee VA, U.S. Office of Edn., others. Mem. Am. Psychol. Assn., Nat. Assn. Women Deans, Adminstrs. and Counselors, Nat. Assn. Social Workers, Am. Soc. Tng. and Devel. Home: 1321 South 1500 East St Salt Lake City UT 84105 Office: 207 Park Bldg U Utah Salt Lake City UT 84112

COLEMAN, LINDA ANN, editor; b. St. Louis, July 7, 1947; d. Sylvester and Virginia (Kumke) Coleman; student Bert Rodgers Sch. Real Estate, 1978. Asso. dir. No. Ednl. Seminars, Sr. Citizen Mag., St. Petersburg, Fla., 1970—; asso. editor Guidebook to Mobile Home Living in Fla., St. Petersburg, 1979—, Sunshine State Sr. Citizen Mag., St. Petersburg, 1969—; lectr. in field of mobile home living. Mem. Yoga Soc. Fla., Assn. Sr. Citizen Mags., World Hunger Found., EST. Democrat. Home: 1640 Manor Way S Saint Petersburg FL 33712 Office: 2820 First Ave N Saint Petersburg FL 33713

COLEMAN, LUCILE LEWIS, poet; b. N.Y.C., Apr. 4; d. Myron H. and Della (Konski) Lewis; m. Denzil R. Coleman; 1 son, Joseph (dec.). Out-of-print and antiquarian bookseller, propr. A to Z Book Service, North Miami, Fla., since 1961; author: Strange Altar, 1947; This Laughing Dust (India Journalist's award 1962), 1951; The Lyric Return, 1977; December 25th: Christmas Verses and Safety Signposts, 1978; Once Upon a Rhyme (for children), 1957; From Where I Sit (play) (Lajos Egri award), 1951; contbr. over 1000 poems to mags., newspapers and lit. jours. in U.S., Australia, Belgium and Eng. Founder N.Y. State and S.I. Poetry Day, 1949. Mem. Antiquarian Booksellers Assn., Internat. League Antiquarian Booksellers, Fla. State Poetry Soc. Editor Singing Warriors, Anthology of War Poetry, 1952, also various anthologies for S.I. Poetry Soc., newspaper columns. Address: PO Box 610813 North Miami FL 33161

COLEMAN, MARILYN RUTH (ADAMS), poultry sci. cons.; b. Lancaster, S.C., Mar. 27, 1946; d. Coyte and Jill J.D. (Lyon) Adams; B.S. in Biology, U. S.C., 1968; Ph.D. in Physiology, Auburn U., 1976; postgrad. U. Va., summer, 1971, 72, Va. Poly. Inst., 1972; m. George Edward Coleman III, Jan. 27, 1968; children—Jill Ann Marie, George Edward IV. Teaching asst. U. S.C., 1967-68; research technician Va. Poly. Inst. and State U., Blacksburg, 1968, teaching asst. biology, 1970-72; tchr. biology and basketball coach Brunswick County (Va.) Pub. Schs., 1968-69; research asst. poultry sci. Auburn (Ala.) U., 1973-76; asst. prof. poultry sci. Ohio State U., Columbus, 1977—, adj. asso. prof., 1982—; propr. MAC Assos., Columbus, Ohio, 1974—; cons. to poultry industry, 1974—. Pianist, New Cut Presbyn. Ch., Lancaster, 1960-64; tchr.'s aide Mountview Baptist Ch., Upper Arlington, Ohio, 1964. Nat. winner 4-H, 1964; NSF grantee, 1967, 71-72. Mem. Poultry Sci. Assn., Am. Physiol. Assn., World's Poultry Sci. Assn., Assn. of Southeastern Biologists, Auburn U. Alumni Assn., U. S.C. Alumni Assn., Sigma Xi, Phi Sigma. Republican. Contbr. numerous articles poultry sci. to profl. publs. Home and office: 2532 Zollinger Rd Columbus OH 43221

COLEMAN, MARTHA ANNE, maternal child nurse cons.; b. Madison, Wis., Oct. 27, 1932; d. Willis Prague and Anne (Wyles) Coleman; B.S.N., U. Wis., 1956; M.S.N. with Eliot honors, Washington U., St. Louis, 1965; postgrad. U. Pitts., 1965-66, Pa. State U., 1978; m. John Penrose Ambler, Dec. 26, 1965 (div. Dec. 1981). Staff nurse U. Wis. Hosp., Madison, 1955-56, St. Louis Children's Hosp., 1959-61, instr., 1965-66; instr. Children's Hosp., Pitts., 1965-66; dir. nursing edn. Hollidaysburg State Hosp., 1966-71; asst. prof. Mt. Aloysius Jr. Coll., Cresson, Pa., 1971-76; instr. Pa. State U., 1976-78; course coordinator Mercy Hosp., Altoona, Pa., 1978-79; nurse cons. Home Nursing Agy., Altoona, 1979-81; psychiat. nurse cons. VA Med. Center, Altoona, 1978-81; asst. prof. Henderson State U., Arkadelphia, Ark., 1981—; pediatric cons. Mercy Hosp., Johnstown, Pa., 1971, Lee Hosp., Johnstown, 1974. Former chmn. Blair County NOW, Woman of Yr. for Blair County, 1974. Mem. Am. Nurses Assn., Ark. Nurses Assn., Nat. League Nursing, Ark. League Nursing, Forum Death Edn. and Counseling, Blair County Mental Health Assn., Ouachita Children's Center Aux. Episcopalian. Club: Blair County Rock and Mineral (past v.p.). Home: 117 Robinhood Rd Hot Springs AR 71913 Office: Henderson State U Arkadelphia AR 71923

COLEMAN, MARY CATHERINE, educator; b. Buffalo, N.Y., May 16, 1929; d. Leo Walter and Anne Grace (Klemach) C.; B.S., Mich. State U., 1951, Ph.D., 1966; M.S., U. Iowa, 1953. Therapeutic dietitian U. Mich. Med. Center, Ann Arbor, 1952-54; head therapeutic dietitian Mount Sinai Hosp., Cleve., 1954-55; instr. food and nutrition Mich. State U., East Lansing, 1955-66, asst. prof. food and nutrition, 1966-68; asso. prof. experimental foods Pa. State U., University Park, 1968-74, prof., 1974—; cons. Recipe Testing div. Gen. Foods. Gen. Foods Corp. fellow, 1963-65. Mem. Am. Dietetic Assn., Inst. Food Technologists, Coll. Tchrs. Food and Nutrition. Contbr. in field. Office: The Pennsylvania State University 214 Human Development Bldg University Park PA 16802

COLEMAN, MARY LEE, dietitian; b. Richmond, Ky., Mar. 4, 1922; d. Leonard and Lillie (Hocker) Yates; grad. Ky. State U., 1972; postgrad. N.Y.U.; m. George H. Coleman, Dec. 20, 1946; 1 dau., Micheline Jackson. With N.Y.C. Health and Hosp. Corp., 1952—, dir. food service, 1977—, asst. dir. psychiat. food service, 1980—; tchr. student nurses Central Sch., N.Y.C., 1968-75. Mem. Am. Dietetic Assn., Am. Soc. Hosp. Food Service Adminstrs., Pan Hellenic Council N.Y., NAACP (chpt. rep.), Nat. Council Negro Women, Am. Home Econs. Assn., Soc. Nurtrition Edn., N.Y.C. Managerial Employees Assn., Exec. Female, Alpha Kappa Alpha. Democrat. Roman Catholic. Home: 645 E 14th St New York NY 10009

COLEMAN, MARY STALLINGS, state supreme ct. chief justice; b. Forney, Tex.; d. Leslie C. and Agnes B. (Huther) Stallings; B.A., U. Md., 1935; J.D., George Washington U., 1939; hon. degrees: L.H.D. Nazareth Coll., 1973; LL.D., Eastern Mich. U., 1974, Western Mich. U., 1974, U. Md., 1978, Alma Coll., 1973, Olivet Coll., 1973, Adrian Coll., 1976, Detroit Coll. Law, 1975, Saginaw Valley State Coll., 1979; m. Creighton R. Coleman, June 24, 1939; children—Leslie (Mrs. Donald J. Hagan), Carol. Admitted to D.C. bar, 1940, Mich. bar, 1950; practiced in Washington, 1940-46; partner firm Wunsch & Coleman, Battle Creek, Mich., 1950-61; probate and juvenile ct. judge Calhoun County, Mich., 1961-73; justice Mich. Supreme Ct., 1973—, chief justice, 1979-80, 81—; guest lectr. various univs., police schs., Mich. public and pvt. schs. Trustee Albion (Mich.) Coll., 1971—; mem. Nat. Commn. for Observance Internat. Women's Year, 1975-76; mem. diocesan canons com. St. Thomas Episcopal Ch. Recipient Disting. Career award George Washington U., 1973, Disting. Alumna award, 1980; Disting. Alumni award U. Md., 1973, Disting. Mem. award Phi Kappa Phi, 1973; award Calhoun County Bd. Edn., Frat. Order Police, NAACP Young Adults; Newspaper George award; Outstanding Mich. Alumna award, Internat. Wyman award Alpha Omicron Pi; Disting. Woman award Mich. Bus. and Profl. Women's Club, 1973; Religious Heritage of Am. award, 1974; DAR medal, 1978; named Woman of Yr., Mich. Assn. of Professions, 1976, One of Top 10 Michiganians of Yr., Detroit News, 1980; Disting. Citizen award Mich. State U., 1977; Disting. Service award Mich. Juvenile Detention Assn., 1980; award of merit Am. Judges Assn., 1980; Disting. Vol. Leadership in Birth Defects award March of Dimes, 1981; Mich. Pine and Dunes Law Day award Girl Scouts Am., 1981; Disting. Woman award Northwood Inst., 1981; named hon. mem. Jr. League, Big Sisters, Big Brothers, Altrusa Internat. Fellow Am. Bar Found.; mem. Am., Mich., D.C. bar assns., Am. Judicature Soc., Nat. Probate Judges Assn. (life), Nat., Mich. women lawyers assns., Bus. and Profl. Women's Club, AAUW (Mich. Disting. Service award 1979), Am. Legion Aux., PEO, Beta Sigma Phi (hon.), Alpha Delta Kappa (hon.). Club: Battle Creek Country. Contbr. articles to profl. publs. Office: Supreme Ct Law Bldg Lansing MI 48901

COLEMAN, PAMELA, investment advisor; b. Wichita, Kans., July 17, 1938; d. Clarence William and Emry Regester (Inghram) Coleman; student U. Okla., 1956-57, U. Mo., 1962-65, Wichita State U., 1972-73; children— Cristy Jeanne Coleman, Cathryn Coleman. Teller, Union Nat. Bank, Wichita, 1959, 1st Nat. Bank, Charleston, S.C., 1959-61, 1st Nat. Bank of New London (Conn.), 1961-62; acct., bookkeeper Greenbaum & Assos., Sydney, Australia, 1966-68; pres., chief exec. officer Sweet Peach Prodns. Pty., Ltd., Sydney, 1968-72; fin. mgr. Clarence Coleman Investments, Wichita, 1972-75, registered investment adv., office mgr., 1976—. Formerly active Project Bus. of Jr. Achievement; bd. dirs. Goodwill Industries of Wichita, 1978-80, sec., 1978-79, treas., 1979-80. Mem. Midwest Geneal. Soc., DAR, Soc. Mayflower Descs., Daus. Am. Colonists, Nat. Soc. Colonial Dames of Am. Clubs: Wichita, Wichita Country. Office: 1005 Union Center Wichita KS 67202

COLEMAN, PATRICIA JOANNE, educator; b. Mpls., June 25, 1941; d. Arthur Patrick and Catherine Ann (Janoweic) C.; B.A., Coll. St. Catherine, 1965; M.A., U. Minn., 1973; M.F.A., Va. Commonwealth U., 1983. Tchr. art secondary parochial schs., St. Paul, 1965-68; free lance graphic artist St. Paul Catechetical Guild, 1968-71; tchr. art, arts area leader Edina (Minn.) Public Schs., 1969-78; free lance graphic designer/photographer Mpls., 1978-80; elem. art specialist Edina Public Schs., 1979-80; tchr. design Va. Commonwealth U., 1981-83. Mem. Edina Educators Assn. (sec. 1977-78), Nat. Art Edn. Assn., Art Educators Minn., NEA, Minn. Edn. Assn., Va. Edn. Assn., NOW, Graphic Artist Guild, Edina Edn. Assn., Am. Computer Machinery-Spl. Interest Group Graphics, NOW, Mpls. Inst. Art, Sierra Club. Democrat. Roman Catholic. Home: 2519 Floyd Ave Richmond VA 23220

COLEMAN, SYLVIA ETHEL, biologist; b. Gainesville, Fla., Mar. 23, 1933; d. John Melton and Jessie Lee (Coleman) C.; B.S., U. Fla., 1955, M.S., 1956, Ph.D., 1972; m. Henry Carl Aldrich, Jan. 1, 1978. Med. bacteriologist, St. Petersburg, Fla., 1959-60; research microbiologist VA Center, Bay Pines, Fla., 1960-67; electron microscopy lab. supr. U. Fla., 1972; research biologist VA Med. Center, Gainesville, 1972—; adj. asst. prof. microbiology and cell sci. U. Fla., 1976—. Pres. adv. bd. Gainesville chpt. Nat. Multiple Sclerosis Soc., 1979—. NDEA fellow, 1969-70; NIH grantee, 1977. Mem. Am. Soc. Cell Biology, Am. Soc. Microbiology, Am. Assn. Pathologists, Electron Microscopy Soc. Am., N.Y. Acad. Sci., Fla. Acad. Sci., Am. Soc. Microbiologists, Histochem. Soc., S.E. Electron Microscopy Soc., Am. Soc. for Microbiology, Sigma Xi. Democrat. United Ch. Christ. Contbr. articles to sci. jours. Home: 122 NW 28th Terr Gainesville FL 32607

COLEMAN, TAMARA ELISE, sausage co. exec.; b. Balt., Feb. 26, 1941; d. Arthur and Rosearle Moore (Reid) Gaither; student Lackawanna Jr. Coll., 1959, Community Coll. Balt., 1970, Essex Community Coll., 1978; m. Donald J. Coleman, Dec. 18, 1976; children by previous marriage—Derrick L. Clapp, Darryl T. Clapp. Receptionist, switchboard operator H. G. Parks, Inc., Balt., 1964-67, sales clk., 1965-67, sec. to sales staff, 1967-70, exec. sec. to pres., 1970-77, exec. sec. to chmn. bd., 1977-79, asst. to chmn. bd., 1979-80, exec. adminstrv. asst., part owner, 1980—. Mem. Exec. Women Internat., Nat. Assn. Female Execs., Profl. Secs. Internat. Democrat. Office: 501 W Hamburg St Baltimore MD 21230

COLES, ANNA LOUISE BAILEY, nurse adminstr., coll. dean; b. Kansas City, Kans., Jan. 16, 1925; d. Gordon Alonzo and Lillie Mai (Buchanan) Bailey; diploma Freedmen's Hosp. Sch. Nursing, 1948; B.S. in Nursing, Avila Coll., Kansas City, Mo., 1958; M.S. in Nursing, Catholic U. Am., 1960, Ph.D. in Higher Edn., 1967; children—Margot, Michelle, Gina. Instr., VA Hosp., Topeka, 1950-52; supr. VA Hosp., Kansas City, Mo., 1952-58; asst. dir. in-service edn. Freedmen's Hosp., Washington, 1960-61, adminstrv. asst. to dir. nursing, 1961-66, asso. dir. nursing services, 1966-67, dir. nursing, 1967-69; dean Coll. Nursing, Howard U., Washington, 1968—; cons. Gen. Research Support Program, NIH, 1972-76, VA health care com. NRC-Nat. Acad. Scis., 1975-76, VA Gen. Office continuing edn. com., 1976—; pres. Nurses Exam. Bd., 1961-68; mem. Inst. Medicine, Nat. Acad. Scis., 1974—. Mem. D.C. Health Planning Adv. Com., 1968-71, Tri State Regional Planning Com. for Nursing Edn., 1969, Health Adv. Council, Nat. Urban Coalition, 1971-73; bd. dirs. Iona Whipper Home for Unwed Mothers, 1970-72, Nursing Edn. Opportunities, 1970-72; trustee Community Group Health Found., 1976-77, cons., 1977—; bd. regents State U. System Fla., 1977; mem. adv. bd. Am. Assn. Med. Colls., 1970-72. Recipient Sustained Superior Performance award HEW, 1962, Meritorious Public Service award Govt. D.C., 1968, Avila Coll. medal of honor, 1969. Mem. Nat. League Nursing (chmn. legis. adv. com. 1975-77, dir. 1977—, exec. com. council baccalaureate programs), Am. Nurses Assn., Freedmen's Hosp. Nursing Alumni Assn., Am. Congress Rehab. Medicine, Am. Assn. Colls. Nursing (sec. 1975-76), Sigma Theta Tau, Alpha Kappa Alpha. Contbr. articles to profl. jours. Home: 627 G St SW Washington DC 20024 Office: Howard U Coll Nursing 2400 6th St NW Washington DC 20059

COLES, BARBARA ANN, broadcasting exec.; b. Nashville, Jan. 15, 1942; d. Charles Richard and Catherine Estelle (Rukert) Butz; B.A., Washington Coll., 1964; m. John Marshall Coles, May 1, 1965; children—Diana Darnell, Ian Kennedy. Asst. to public relations dir. Head Ski Co., Timonium, Md., 1964-65; tchr. Pennsauken (N.J.) Schs., 1965-66; reporter Suburban Newspaper Group, Cherry Hill, N.J., 1967-71; free-lance writer, 1971-75; news and public affairs dir., talk show host Sta. WOTW, Nashua, N.H., 1975-80; exec. producer N.H. Radio News Network, 1980-81; TV journalist Sta. WENH-TV, Durham, N.H., 1981—; dir. Rukert Terminals Corp., Balt. Sec., Moorestown United Fund, 1968-71; mem. Moorestown Zoning Bd., 1973-75; mem. Burlington County Meml. Hosp. Aux.; bd. dirs. Nashua YWCA, Moorestown Youth Coordinating Orgn., Moorestown Vis. Nurse Assn. Mem. AAUW. Quaker. Home: 18 Corduroy Rd Amherst NH 03031 Office: Sta WENH-TV Box 2 Durham NH 03824

COLFAX, JANE A., physician; b. Paterson, N.J., June 21, 1923; d. Richard S. and Elsye (Schoonmaker) C.; student U. Vt., 1941-42; R.N., Flower-Fifth Ave. Sch. Nursing, 1945; student Columbia U., 1946-47; B.A., Hunter Coll., 1950; M.D., Woman's Med. Coll. Pa., 1955; m. Michael DeNike, 1962. Intern, Kings County Hosp., Bklyn., 1955-56; resident Woman's Hosp. div. St. Luke's Hosp., N.Y.C., 1956-60, mem. staff, 1960-66, asst. attending obstetrician and gynecologist Woman's Hosp. div., 1962; attending obstetrics and gynecology St. Joseph Hosp., Paterson, 1960—; attending gynecologist Preakness Hosp., Wayne, N.J., 1966—; practice medicine specializing in obstetrics and gynecology, Wayne, 1960—. Diplomate Am. Bd. Obstetrics and Gynecology, Nat. Bd. Med. Examiners. Fellow Am. Coll. Obstetricians and Gynecologists; mem. Internat., Am. med. women's assns., N.J., Passaic County med. socs., Woman's Med. Coll. Alumni Assn., N.J. Obstet. and Gynecol. Soc., Zeta Phi. Club: Soroptimists. Home: 2411 Hamburg Turnpike Wayne NJ 14893 Office: No 4 2411 Hamburg Turnpike Wayne NJ 07470

COLFLESH, MARIE ADELE, audiologist; b. Phila., Apr. 19, 1950; A.S., Brandywine Coll., 1970; B.S., East Tenn. State U., 1973, M.A. in Audiology, 1975. Grad. asst. in audiology East Tenn. State U., Johnson City, 1974-75; audiology trainee VA Center, Mountain Home, Tenn., 1975; audiologist Audiological Cons., Inc., Jenkintown, Pa., 1975, Speech & Hearing Center, Hosp. of U. Pa., Phila., 1975-77, ENT Associated, Penndel, Pa., 1977-80, Phila. Coll. Osteo. Medicine, Phila., 1981-82, Dahlberg Electronics, 1982—. Recipient Alumni award Brandywine Coll., 1970; Dean's award E. Tenn. State U., 1974; cert. tchr., Tenn. Mem. Am. Speech and Hearing Assn. (cert. clin. competence in audiology), Pa. Speech and Hearing Assn., Phi Kappa Phi, Kappa Delta Pi, Zeta Mu Epsilon (past chpt. pres.). Democrat. Roman Catholic. Home: 3603-2 Fenn Dr Philadelphia PA 19154

COLGAN, MARY CRESWELL, graphic artist; b. Augusta, Ga., Dec. 12, 1918; d. George Washington and Bennie George (Johnson) Summers;

student Louisville Inst. Tech., 1937-40; m. Arthur Rudolf Colgan, July 6, 1953; 1 dau., Dorothy Anne (dec.). Adminstrv. asst., sec. to pres. S.D. Sch. Mines and Tech., Coll. of Engrng. and Sci., 1949-54; exec. sec., office mgr. Dr. Joseph S. Knight, D.C., Hawthorne, Calif., 1970-73; partner ARCI Enterprises, Palos Verdes, Calif., 1969-73; editor, artist MARCI originals for ARCI Assos., Rapid City, S.D., 1973—; sec.-treas. A.R. Colgan, Inc., Edgemont, 1964—; dir., curator Colgan's Old Gen. Store Mus., Edgemont, 1968-78. Dist. chmn. Los Angeles County dist. 8, Am. Cancer Soc., 1965-66. Mem. Geneal. Soc. Pa. Republican. Episcopalian. Home and Office: Spring Canyon Trail at Sheridan Lake Rd Box 2724 Rapid City SD 57709

COLIN, JOAN DEUEL, banker; b. Summit, N.J., Apr. 3, 1936; d. Franklin S. and Marion Grace (Elton-Miller) Deuel; B.A. in Fine Arts and Architecture, Smith Coll., 1958; cert. Oxford (Eng.) U., 1957; cert. N.Y. Sch. Design, 1960; m. David T. Colin, Aug. 17, 1969; children—Elizabeth, David Elton Deuel. Interior designer Lord & Taylor, 1958-69; co-founder, asst. dir. Am. U. Rome, 1969-79, dean students, 1975-79; co-founder, pres. Joan Colin & Assos., corp. relocation, Rome, 1977-79; mgr. adminstrv. services Nat. Consumer Coop. Bank, Washington, 1979-82; pres. Joan Colin & Assos., corp. and diplomatic relocation, 1982—; founder, dir. Fin. Services Unlimited, 1980—. Trustee Overseas Sch. Rome, 1976-79. Episcopalian. Club: Smith Coll. (Washington). Home and Office: 7705 Westfield Dr Bethesda MD 20817

COLISH, MARCIA LILLIAN, educator; b. Bklyn., July 27, 1937; d. Samuel and Daisy (Kartch) Colish; B.A. magna cum laude, Smith Coll., 1958; M.A., Yale U., 1959, Ph.D., 1965. Instr. history Skidmore Coll., Saratoga Springs, N.Y., 1962-63; instr. Oberlin (Ohio) Coll., 1963-65, asst. prof., 1965-69, assoc. prof., 1969-75, prof. history, 1975—, chmn. history dept., 1973-74, 78-81; lectr. history Case Western Res. U., Cleve., 1966-67; editorial cons. W.W. Norton & Co., 1973, John Wiley & Sons, Inc., 1981; cons. history dept. Grinnell Coll., 1974 Knox Coll., 1981, St. John's U., 1981, Whitman Coll., 1982; mem. exec. bd. Ohio Program in Humanities, 1976-81, exec. bd., 1978-81, vice chmn., 1979-81. Mem. exec. bd. ACLU, 1970-74, chmn., 1972-74, rec. sec., 1976-77, vice chmn., 1979-80; exec. bd. Oberlin YWCA, 1966-70. Recipient Hazel Edgerly Prize, Smith Coll., 1958; Samuel S. Fels fellow Yale U., 1961-62; younger scholar fellow Nat. Endowment for Humanities, 1968-69, sr. fellow, 1981-82; vis. scholar Am. Acad. Rome, 1968-69; fellow Inst. for Research in Humanities, U. Wis., 1974-75; Nat. Humanities Ctr. fellow, 1981-82. Mem. Am. Hist. Assn., Medieval Acad. Am., Medieval Assn. Midwest (council 1978-81), Midwest Medieval Conf. (pres. 1978-79), Renaissance Soc. Am., Central Renaissance Conf., Societe Internat. pour l'Etude de Philosophie medievale, Phi Beta Kappa. Author: The Mirror of Language: A Study in the Medieval Theory of Knowledge, 2nd rev. edit.; The Stoic Tradition from Antiquity to the Early Middle Ages, 1983. Home: 143 E College St Apt 310 Oberlin OH 44074 Office: Dept of History Oberlin College Oberlin OH 44074

COLL, HELEN FRYE (MRS. ROBERT FRANCIS COLL), banker; b. nr. Lovettsville, Va., Dec. 2, 1921; d. Raymond C. and Minnie (Peters) Frye; grad. Wash. Sch. Secs., 1940, Sch. Financial Pub. Relations Northwestern U., 1963; grad. Stonier Grad. Sch. Banking Rutgers U., 1966; m. Lee Stanley Sherline, Sept. 1, 1942 (div. Feb. 1955); m. 2d, Robert Francis Coll, May 25, 1957. With Nat. Savs. & Trust Co. (now NS & T Bank, N.A.), Washington, 1940—, sec. to pres., 1948-51, asst. sec., 1951-55, sec., 1955—, v.p., 1963—, v.p., sec. bd., 1966-72, sr. v.p., sec. bd., 1972—. Mem. Met. Bd. Trade, Nat. Assn. Bank Women, D.C. Bankers Assn., Bank Marketing Assn. Club: City Tavern (Washington). Home: 1310 29th St Washington DC 20007 also Fantasy Farm Round Hill VA 22141 Office: NS & T Bank NA 15th St And New York Ave Washington DC 20005

COLLART, MARIE ETHEL, assn. exec.; b. Clarksburg, W.Va., Nov. 23, 1945; d. Richard C. and Ethel Collart; B.S., Ohio State U., 1967, M.S., 1970, Ph.D., 1979. Staff nurse Case Western Res. U. Hosp. Cleve., 1967-70; instr. Sch. Nursing Ohio State U., Columbus, 1971-72, dir. computer assisted instrn. program devel., 1972-73; dir. Ohio Thoracic Soc., 1973-81, dir. prof. edn. Ohio Lung Assn., 1973-81, exec. dir. Am. Lung Assn. Central Ohio, 1981—; adj. asst. prof. Ohio State U. Allied Medicine div. Med. Coll., 1981—; mem. advanced faculty Creative Edn. Found. SUNY, Buffalo, 1975—; chmn. health medicine and safety category Columbus Internat. Film Festival, 1980-82. Mem. City Upper Arlington Cultural Arts Com., 1971—. Recipient Allied Health Profl. Educator award Am. Lung Assn., 1976, Chris Bronze plaque Columbus Internat. Film Festival, 1977. Mem. Am. Thoracic Soc., Assn. Ednl. Communication Technicians, Health Scis. Communications Assn., Nat. Soc. Fund Raising Execs., Phi Delta Kappa, Sigma Theta Tau. Republican. Photography: Nursing Care of Adults and Orthopedic Conditions (Leona Mourad), 1979. Home: 4063 Fairfax Dr Columbus OH 43220 Office: 1770 Arlingate Columbus OH 43228

COLLETTE, MARTHA ANN, psychologist; b. Boston, Mar. 22, 1945; d. Richard Louis and Margaret Campbell (Wall) C.; B.A. in Psychology, Clark U., Worcester, Mass., 1967; M.A., U. Hawaii, 1974, Ph.D., 1976; postdoctoral studies neuropsychology Tufts U.; m. Christopher Harris, Mar. 2, 1968; 1 son, Peter. Asso. prof. psychology Emerson Coll., Boston, 1976—; staff neuropsychologist Youville Hosp., Cambridge, Mass., 1981—; clin. asso. Mass. Gen. Hosp., Boston, 1980—; instr. Harvard U. Med. Sch. NIMH grantee, 1979-80. Mem. Am. Psychol. Assn., Am. Assn. Behavior Therapy, Soc. Research in Child Devel., Internat. Neuropsychol. Soc., Mass. Psychol. Assn. Roman Catholic. Author: Clinical Neuropsychological Reporting Package (software), 1982; also articles. Home: 51 Parker Terr Newton Center MA 02159 Office: Emerson College 148 Beacon St Boston MA 02116

COLLIER, ALEXIS CHRISTINA, psychologist, educator; b. Norton, Va., July 10, 1951; d. S. Alexander and L. Belle (Robinett) Collier; B.S., Va. Poly. Inst. and State U., 1973; postgrad. Princeton U., 1973-74; Ph.D., U. Wash., 1976. Teaching and research asst. Princeton U., 1973-74, U. Wash., Seattle, 1974-76; asst. prof. psychology Ohio State U., Columbus, 1976-82, asso. prof., 1982—; cons. to profl. jours. and firms, 1976—. NIMH grantee, 1980, mem. grant rev. com., 1981-83. Mem. Am. Psychol. Assn., Eastern Psychol. Assn., Midwestern Psychol. Assn., Psychonomic Soc., Internat. Soc. Developmental Psychobiology, NOW, Colony, Mortar Board, Alpha Lambda Delta, Phi Kappa Phi, Delta Zeta. Democrat. Baptist. Club: Order Eastern Star. Contbr. articles to jours. in psychology. Home: 5015 Hibbs Dr Columbus OH 43220 Office: 1945 N High St Columbus OH 43210

COLLIER, ELLEN CLODFELTER, fgn. policy specialist; b. Lawrence, Kans., Oct. 19, 1927; d. Harve Malone and Martha June (Lambert) Clodfelter; B.A. cum laude with highest distinction, Ohio State U., 1949; M.A., Am. U., 1951; grad. Nat. War Coll., 1978; m. Edwin Collier, May 25, 1951; children—Stephen Harve, Martha Lambert Collier Riva, Sarah Reiner, John Reiner, Catherine Clodfelter. U.S. fgn. policy analyst, fgn. affairs div. Congressional Research Service, Library of Congress, Washington, 1949-55; mem. staff subcom. on disarmament U.S. Senate Fgn. Relations Com., 1955-59; U.S. fgn. policy analyst Congressional Research Service, 1960-69, specialist, 1969—, head spl. project sect., 1972-75, head fgn. issues and nat. security policy sect., 1975-76, head global issues sect., 1976-77. Mem. Internat. Studies Assn., Am. Soc. Internat. Law, Soc. Internat. Devel., Exec. Women in Govt., Phi Beta Kappa, Pi Sigma Alpha. Club: Potomac Pedalers. Author report. Editor: Congress and Foreign Policy, 1979, 80, 81. Home: 9905 Holmhurst Rd Bethesda MD 20817 Office: Congressional Research Service Library of Congress Washington DC 20540

COLLIER, GAYLAN JANE, educator; b. Fluvanna, Tex.; d. Ben V. and Narcis N. (Smith) Collier; B.A., Abilene Christian U., 1946; M.A., U. Iowa, 1949; Ph.D., U. Denver, 1957. Instr., U. N.C., Greensboro, 1946-47; asst. prof., acting chmn. dept. speech and drama Greensboro Coll., 1949-50; asst. prof., dir. theatre Abilene Christian Coll., 1950-57, asso. prof., dir. theatre, 1957-60; asso. prof., chmn. acting studies Idaho State U., 1960-63; asso. prof. drama Sam Houston State U., 1963-65, prof., 1965-67; prof., chmn. acting/directing studies Tex. Christian U., Ft. Worth, 1967—; dir. summer theatre programs Parkway Playhouse, Greensboro, 1951; guest lectr. Idaho State U., summers 1958, 59; staff dir. Scott Actors Repertory Co., Ft. Worth, summers 1968, 69; guest dir. U. Denver Theatre Festival, 1962; dir. Ft. Worth Repertory Co., 1972; dir. The Imaginary Invalid, rep. U.S. at Am. Festival in Britain, 1970. Named Best Actress, Abilene Christian Coll., 1944, 45, 46. Faculty grantee seminar Stratford (Ont.) Festival, summer 1979. Mem. Am. Theatre Assn., Children's Theatre Assn., S.W. Theatre Conf., Tex. Ednl. Theatre Assn., AAUP, Alpha Psi Omega, Zeta Phi Eta. Democrat. Mem. Ch. of Christ. Author: Assignments on Acting, 1966; also articles on theatre. Home: 2616 S University Dr Fort Worth TX 76109 Office: Tex Christian Univ Fort Worth TX 76129

COLLIER, HELEN VANDIVORT, counseling psychologist; b. Nagpur, India; d. William Boardley and Stephena Ruth (Hecker) C.; A.B., Ohio Wesleyan U.; M.Ed., Ed.D., U. Toledo; grad. San Diego Gestalt Tng. Center; children—Keith Vandivort, Daniel Vandivort, Heidi Vandivort Childress; m. Gary J. Scrimgeour. Tchr. elem. schs., Itasca, Ill., 1950-53; ednl. cons. Toledo Bd. Edn., 1960-67; elem. counselor Toledo Public Schs., 1968; counseling psychologist, asst. prof. U. Toledo, 1968-74; asst. dir. adult counseling project Sch. Continuing Studies, Ind. U., Bloomington, 1975-76; dir. Human Devel. Assos., Bloomington, Ind., 1974-79, HVC Assos., Bloomington. cons. tng. and orgnl. devel., 1980—; pvt. practice psychotherapy. Lic. psychologist, Ohio. Mem. Am. Psychol. Assn., Assn. for Women in Psychology, Am. Personnel and Guidance Assn., Nat. Vocat. Guidance Assn., Assn. for Counselor Edn. and Supervision, Am. Soc. Tng. and Devel., Women's Equity Action League, Nat. Women's Polit. Caucus. Co-editor: Meeting the Educational and Occupational Planning Needs of Adults, 1975; author: Freeing Ourselves: Removing Internal Barriers to Equality, 1979; Counseling Women: A Guide for Therapists, 1982; also articles. Office: 706 N Walnut St PO Box 464 Bloomington IN 47402

COLLIER, VICKI JEAN, mgmt. cons.; b. Wichita Falls, Tex., Feb. 6, 1952; d. Perry Dale and Peggy Jo (Graham) Stogner; B.S. in Bus., Cameron U., 1974; M.A. in Mgmt., U. Okla., 1978. Office mgr. Shelco Corp., Wichita Falls, Tex., 1974-75; sr. mgmt. tng. specialist FAA-U. Okla. Mgmt. Tng. Sch., Lawton, Okla., 1975-77; orgn. devel. mgr. ITT Hartford Ins. Group, Hartford, Conn., 1977-79; v.p., cons., mgr. Chase Manhattan Bank, N.Y.C., 1979—. Mem. Orgn. Devel. Network, Am. Soc. Tng. and Devel., Beta Gamma Sigma, Phi Kappa Phi. Democrat. Methodist. Home: 230 W 55th St New York NY 10019 Office: 80 Pine St New York NY 10081

COLLINS, ANN ELIZABETH AVERITT (MRS. GALEN FRANKLIN COLLINS), civic leader; b. Peru, Ind., July 28, 1934; d. Robert Chancellor and Cleo (Hite) Averitt; B.A., Fla. Internat. U.; m. Galen Franklin Collins, Sept. 30, 1956; children—Galen Robert, Amelia Lynn, Scott Franklin, Daniel Chancellor. Co-soc. editor Elkhart (Ind.) Truth, 1955-56; mem. Elkhart Civic Theatre, 1957-60; mem. Chenango County Community Players, N.Y., 1960-63; co-founder Dogwood Playhouse, Bristol, Va.-Tenn., 1964, bd. dirs., 1964-69; co-founder Collero Puppets, Bristol, 1967; writer, Miami, Fla., 1972—; free lance writer, 1972—; dir. Christian edn. United Ch. Christ, Miami, 1978—. Musical compositions include Why Am I Old, 1969; Little Boy, My Dear Son, 1969; Color, 1969; Willows, 1969; Soldier Boy, 1969; Is That Your Voice I Hear?, 1969. Home: 10800 SW 69th Ave Miami FL 33156

COLLINS, ANNIE LAURA, educator; b. Cocoa, Fla., Nov. 11, 1929; d. Osborne Herman and Rosa Lee (Campbell) Jones; B.S., Bethune-Cookman Coll., 1951; m. Samuel Deampus Collins, Feb. 26, 1955; children—Greta Ann, Raymond Bruce. Tchr., Brevard County (Fla.) Public Sch. System, 1951-55; clk. typist Army-Air Force Exchange Service, Elmendorf AFB, Alaska, 1955-58; tchr. Vallejo (Calif.) Unified Sch. Dist., 1958-63, 78—, Medical Lake (Wash.) Sch. Dist., 1974-75, Albuquerque Public Schs., 1975-78; tchr. Dept. Def., Clark AFB, Philippines, 1970; mem. Vallejo Unified Sch. Dist. Adv. Council. Baptist. Mem. Nat. Council Negro Women, PTA. Democrat. Home: 1045 Sheridan St Vallejo CA 94590

COLLINS, BARBARA-ROSE, city councilwoman; b. Detroit, Apr. 13, 1939; d. Lamar and Versa Richardson; student Wayne State U., 1957; widow; children—Cynthia, Christopher. Bus. mgr. physics dept. Wayne State U., Detroit, 1964-73, office asst. OEO and Neighborhood Relations, 1973-74; mem. region I dist. Detroit Sch. Bd., 1970-73; mem. Mich. Ho. of Reps., 1974-81; mem. Detroit City Council, 1981—. Mem. Inner-City Parents Council and Black Parents for Quality Edn.; chmn. Constl. Revision and Women's Rights Com.; mem. Detroit Human Rights Commn.; mem. City Wide Citizen's Action Council; mem. adv. bd. Housing Centers; trustee Internat. Afro-Am. Mus.; bd. govs. Jefferies Day Care and Cultural Center; mem. state coordination com. Internat. Women's Yr., also del. conv., 1978. Mem. Nat. Order Women Legislators, LWV, Ams. for Democratic Action, ACLU, Shrine of Black Madonna. Democrat. Office: Detroit City-County Bldg Detroit MI

COLLINS, CARDISS, congresswoman; b. St. Louis; d. Finley and Rosia Mae (Robertson) Robertson; certificate bus. Northwestern U., 1966, diploma in profl. accounting, 1967; m. George Collins (dec.); 1 son, B. Kevin. Stenographer, then sec. employment service Ill. Dept. Labor, 1950-58; sec., then revenue auditor Ill. Dept. Revenue, 1958-72; mem. 93-98th congresses from 7th Ill. Dist., chmn. Congl. Black Caucus. Vice pres. Lawndale Youth Commn., Chgo. Committeewoman 24th Ward Regular Democratic Orgn., Chgo.; adv. bd. Ill. Dem. Central Com. Office: 2438 Cannon House Office Bldg Washington DC 20515 *

COLLINS, CAROLYN JANE, molecular biologist; b. White Plains, N.Y., Sept. 18, 1942; d. John Gordon and Barbara Jane (Harris) C.; B.A., Skidmore Coll., 1964; Ph.D., Duke U., 1970. Postdoctoral fellow German Center Cancer Research, Heidelberg, W.Ger., 1970-72, U. Mich., Ann Arbor, 1973-76; asst. prof. microbiology U. Va., Charlottesville, 1976—. F.G. Novy fellow, 1974-75; USPHS fellow, 1975-76; NSF grantee, 1978-81. Mem. Am. Soc. Microbiology, N.Y. Acad. Sci., AAAS, Phi Beta Kappa. Contbr. articles to profl. jours. Office: Dept Microbiology U Va Med Center Charlottesville VA 22908

COLLINS, CARRIE BEATRICE HOLLOWAY, educator, composer; b. Meridian, Miss., Nov. 14, 1930; d. Clem and Maude Lee (Booker) Holloway; B.S., Tenn. A. and I. State Coll., 1950, M.S., 1957; M.A., U. Denver, 1977; m. Clinton Clarence Collins, Sr., Dec. 29, 1957; children—Rosalyn Benitra, Clinton Clarence, Beatrice Renee. Music tchr. Meridian (Miss.) Sch. System, 1950-57; music specialist Jones County (Miss.) Schs., 1959-61; music tchr. Littleton (Colo.) Public Schs., 1965—; prof. music black studies dept. U. No. Colo., Greeley, 1974-75; dir. Littleton Elem. Music Festival, 1970; mem. Colo. Commn. Tchr. Edn. and Cert., 1975. Committeewoman precinct Democratic party. Recipient Cert. of Merit, Miss. Tchrs. Assn., 1961, Service to Mankind award Arapahoe Sertoma Club, 1973, Community Leaders and Noteworthy Ams. award Hist. Preservations Am., 1976, Notable Ams. award, 1977, Cert. of Recognition award Colo. Music Educators, 1976, Cert. of Appreciation, State Colo. Centennial-Bicentennial Commn., 1976, Honor award Colo. Music Educators, 1982; U. Denver Sch. Librarianship fellow, 1976. Mem. Nat. Assn. Negro Musicians, Inc. (Midwestern regional dir. 1979, Disting. Achievement award 1978), ASCAP, Music Educators Nat. Conf., Rocky Mountain Musicians Assn., Colo. Educators Assn., Colo. Music Educators Conf., Littleton Educators Assn., Alpha Delta Kappa. Baptist. Composer: Look to Jesus, 1973; Love for Mankind, 1973; Mother-Dear, 1973; This is My Home, 1973; Love Me Always, 1974; Two Hundred Year Ago, 1975; Black Folks Music, 1975. Home: 5820 E Florida Ave Denver CO 80224

COLLINS, COLLENE, mktg. exec.; b. Leavenworth, Kans., Oct. 11, 1948; d. James Thomas and Vera (Gibson) Collins; student Briar Cliff Coll., 1966-67; B.F.A., U. Kans., 1970; postgrad. Dallas Coll., 1971; M.B.A. (Harriman scholar), Columbia U. Grad. Sch. Bus., 1978. With product mgmt. dept. Seven Seas Salad Dressings, Anderson Clayton Foods, Dallas, 1970-72; asso. mgr. market research Frito Lay Inc., Dallas, 1972-73; investment mgr. Henry S. Miller Co., Dallas, 1973-75; mem. corporate mktg. dept. AT&T, Basking Ridge, N.J., 1976-78; corp. dir. market devel. Harte-Hanks Communications, 1979; dir. mktg. Citicorp Ind. Corr. Banks, 1980—; vice chmn. future banking adv. bd. Citicorp, 1980—. Mem. cultural affairs task force Goals for Dallas, 1970-75; bd. dirs. Dallas Civic Ballet, 1973-76; patron Mus. Am. Folk Art, N.Y.C. Mem. Am. Bankers Assn., Bank Mktg. Assn., Am. Mktg. Assn., Nat. Assn. Real Estate Brokers, Mgmt. Sci. Inst., Am. Assembly, Nat. Congress Am. Indians, Am. Horse Shows Assn., U.S. Equestrian Team, Victorian Soc. Am. Clubs: Dallas Cotillion, Dallas Slipper, Dallas 500 Inc., Dallas Womens, Garden, Jockey, Willow Bend Polo and Hunt; Burnt Mills Polo (Far Hills, N.J.). Home: 33 Fifth Ave New York NY 10003 also Cedar Grove San Antonio TX 78247 Office: 4th Floor One Citicorp Center New York NY 10043

COLLINS, CORLISS JEAN, social worker, family counselor; b. El Reno, Okla., Apr. 7, 1938; d. Corliss B. and Katherine (Evans) Allen; student Okla. Bapt. U., 1956-58; B.S. summa cum laude Southwestern State Coll., 1966; M.S.W., Okla. U., 1968; m. William E. Collins, June 20, 1970; children—Bryan Dwayne Barnes, Bryson Allen Barnes, Corliss Adora Collins. Welfare aide Cheyenne-Arapaho Indian Agy., Concho, Okla., 1964; family counselor Sunbeam Home and Family Service, Oklahoma City, 1968-72; pvt. practice family and child counseling, Oklahoma City, 1972—; founder, dir. Show Biz Kids, God's Kids, talent groups. Mem. child devel. study group U. Okla. Health Scis. Center, 1969-72; mem. Oklahomans for Gifted and Talented, 1977—; pres. Lincoln Sch. PTA, El Reno, 1968-69; vol. Cerebral Palsy Drive, Mothers' March on Birth Defects, March of Dimes, 1979, Multiple Sclerosis, 1981. Lic. social worker, Okla. Mem. Nat. Assn. Social Workers (registered clin. social worker), Okla. Health and Welfare Assn. (life), Okla. Edn. Assn., Acad. Cert. Social Workers, Okla. Assn. Children with Learning Difficulties, Okla. Geneal. Soc., Okla. Hist. Soc., Canadian County Geneal. Soc., DAR, Alpha Phi Sigma. Baptist (Sunday sch. tchr.).

COLLINS, DIANA JOSEPHINE, psychologist; b. Potsdam, N.Y., Apr. 27, 1944; d. Philip Joseph and Janet Dorothy (Lynke) C.; grad. with high honors, SUNY; Psy.D., Mass. Sch. Profl. Psychology, 1981. Psychologist, N.H. Hosp., Concord, 1974-79; asst. dir. forensic unit, 1979-80; founder, dir. Victim/Witness Service County of Hillsborough, Manchester, N.H., 1980—; adj. asso. prof. U. N.H., 1974; adj. asso. prof. Antioch Coll. of New Eng. N.H. Crime Commn. grantee, 1979-80. Mem. AAUW, N.H. Psychol. Assn., Am. Assn. Female Execs., Roman Catholic. Home: RFD 2 Contoocook NH 03229 Office: 300 Chestnut St Manchester NH 03101

COLLINS, DOROTHY LANHAM, interior designer; b. Chgo., Sept. 26, 1926; d. Cecil Ray and Elizabeth (Billow) Lanham; children—Judith Collins Hunerberg, Tom, John, Patricia Collins Gruggen, Susan. Founder, pres. Dorothy Collins Interiors, Inc., Edina, Minn., 1950—; owner Dorothy Collins Retail Design Studio, Edina, 1968—. Mem. Nat. Home Fashion League (v.p., pres. elect), Fashion Group. Republican. Club: Calhoun Beach. Home: 6432 Red Fox Ct Edina MN 55436 Office: Dorothy Collins Interiors Inc 7010 France Ave S Edina MN 55435

COLLINS, DOROTHY (MRS. AKIBA EMANUEL), advt. and public relations agy. exec.; b. Salt Lake City; d. Joseph L. and Dorothy (Frey) Collins; A.B., U. Denver; m. Akiba Emanuel; 1 dau., Lynn Collins. Woman's page editor Rocky Mountain News, Denver; fashion editor NBC, N.Y.C.; pub. relations dir. Shwayder Bros., Denver; account exec. Ellington & Co., N.Y.C.; v.p. Infoplan, N.Y.C.; v.p., mgr. consumer group Burson-Marsteller, N.Y.C.; sr. v.p., chief exec. officer Public Relations div. Sam Lusky Assos., Inc., Denver, 1981—. Former nat. dir. women's activities Nat. Jewish Hosp., Denver; active Girl Scouts U.S.A.; trustee Marymount Coll., 1979-80. Mem. Nat. Home Fashions League (pres. N.Y. chpt. 1977-79), Women's Forum, Am. Women in Radio and TV, Exec. Women in Pub. Relations. Club: Denver Women's Press. Home: 2950 Albion St Denver CO 80207 Office: First of Denver Plaza Bldg Denver CO 80202

COLLINS, EARLEAN, state senator; b. Miss.; B.A., U. Ill., Chgo. Child welfare exec. Chgo. Dept. Children and Family Services; now mem. Ill. Senate. Mem. parent adv. com. Sch. Dist. 19; mem. Commn. on Youth Welfare; bd. dirs. Lawndale Mental Health Clinic, Operation Brotherhood. Mem. League Black Women, Chgo. Assn. Edn. of Young Child, Black Child Devel. Assn., NAACP. Office: Ill Senate State Capitol Springfield IL 62706 *

COLLINS, EILEEN LOUISE, economist; b. Chillicothe, Ohio, Dec. 15, 1942; d. Theodore Milton and Louise Alma (Suess) C.; B.A. (regional scholar), Bryn Mawr Coll., 1964; M.A., U. Wis., Madison, 1967, Ph.D., 1975. Lectr. dept. econs. U. Waterloo (Ont., Can.), 1971-73; asst. prof. dept. econs. Barnard Coll., N.Y.C., 1975-76; asst. prof. dept. econs. Fordham U., N.Y.C., 1976-78; economist NSF, Washington, 1978—. Recipient NSF Outstanding Performance award, 1979, 81; NIMH fellow, 1969-71; Nat. Inst. Public Affairs fellow, 1966-67. Mem. Am. Econ. Assn., Nat. Tax Assn., Washington Women Economists. Office: NSF 1800 G St NW Room 1229 Washington DC 20550

COLLINS, ÉLISE GUIGNON, research asso.; b. St. Louis, Aug. 11, 1895; d. Emile Simon and Julia Rose (Miltenbérger) Guignon; B.A. in European Cultural History, U. Mo., Kansas City, 1963, postgrad., 1968—; m. Tom Collins, Aug. 30, 1924; children—Joan Collins Nugent, Philip K. Editor, Woman's Page, Kansas City (Mo.) Jour.-Post, 1921-22; writer, salesperson advt. copy Ferry Hanley Co., Kansas City, Mo., 1922-24; teaching asst. art dept. U. Mo., Kansas City, 1964-72, research asso., archtl. papers Spl. Collections Library, 1979-80. Mem. Coll. Art Assn. Am., Soc. Archtl. Historians, Women in Communications. Democrat. Roman Catholic.

COLLINS, ELIZABETH, occupational therapist; b. New Orleans, Aug. 4, 1921; d. Clark Wilkins and Madeleine (Fuller) C.; A.F.A., Colby Jr. Coll., 1941; occupational therapy cert. Boston Sch. Occupational Therapy, 1944; B.A., U. Iowa, 1953. Dir. occupational therapy Salem (Mass.) Hosp., 1945-46, Robert B. Brigham Hosp., Boston, 1946-49; dir. occupational therapy U. Iowa Hosp., 1949-62, asst. prof. occupational therapy, chmn. occupational therapy curriculum, 1954-71; asst. prof., chmn. occupational therapy U. Wis., Eau Claire, 1971-72; coordinator rehab. services Rock Island (Ill.) Franciscan Hosp., 1972-73; asst. prof., fieldwork coordinator Wayne State U., 1974-76, asst. prof., chmn. occupational therapy, 1976-77; asso. prof. U. Kans., Lawrence, 1978—. Mem. Am. Occupational Therapy Assn. (editorial bd. Am. Jour. Occupational Therapy 1946-51, Roster of Fellows 1979—), Registry Occupational Therapists, Kans. Occupational Therapy Assn., World Fedn. Occupational Therapists, AAUP, Univ. Women's Assn., Bus. and Profl. Women's Assn. Unitarian. Home: G-3 Regency Pl Lawrence KS 66044 Office: 318 Blake Hall U Kans Lawrence KS 66045

COLLINS, ELLA GARRETT, ins. agy. exec.; b. Cedartown, Ga., Sept. 25, 1933; d. Albert Columbus and Katie (Smith) Garrett; grad. Polk Bus. Coll., 1958; m. Jack Brealand Collins, Nov. 26, 1958 (dec.); 1 son, David Douglas. Ins. sec. Edwards Ins. Agy., Rockmart, Ga., 1954-58; corp. sec., accounts rep. Ins. Underwriters, Inc., Atlanta, 1958-61; office mgr. Ryals Ins. Agy., Inc., Atlanta, 1961-63; adminstrv. asst. Ins. Agts., Inc., Atlanta, 1963-65; corp. sec., office mgr. Chancey Agy., Inc., Atlanta, 1965-74; account exec. Hamilton-Dorsey-Alston Ins., Atlanta, 1974-75; corp. sec., account exec. Graham-Naylor Agy., Inc., Marietta, Ga., 1975—; asst. sec., dir. Charter Oak Devel. Co. Mem. Nat. Assn. Ins. Women (cert. profl.), Atlanta Assn. Ins. Women (Ins. Woman of Yr. award 1977), Ind. Ins. Agts. Am., Ga. Assn. Ind. Ins. Agts. Cobb County Ind. Ins. Agts., Nat. Assn. Parliamentarians, Ga. Assn. Parliamentarians. Club: Pilot (Marietta). Office: Graham-Naylor Agy Inc 1885 Leland Dr PO Box 6818 Marietta GA 30065

COLLINS, EVA MAE LOMERSON, ins. co. exec.; b. Lake Orion, Mich., July 10, 1930; d. J.M. Lomerson and Thelma Marie (Kimmery) Winter; student U. Mich., Wayne State U.; m. John Armstrong Collins, Feb. 24, 1968. Div. mgr. Sears, Roebuck & Co., 1951-69; with Bimgham & Bingham, Inc.-Ins., Birmingham, Mich., 1970—, underwriting mgr. Intercede Group, v.p., 1979—. Mem. Ins. Women Met. Detroit (adv. chmn. 1976-77, rec. sec. 1977-78, corr. sec. 1978-79, treas. 1979-80, 2d v.p. 1980-81, 1st v.p. 1981-82, pres. 1982-83), Nat. Trust Historic Preservation, Women's Econ. Club Detroit, Nat. Assn. Female Execs., Hist. Soc. Mich., Detroit Soc. Geneal. Research, DAR (chpt. regent 1967-69, chpt. pres. 1964-65, chpt. librarian 1977-79, chmn. chpt. good citizens com. 1979—, state chmn. pages 1967-69, state chmn. jr. membership 1969-70, state chmn. good citizens 1982—), Nat. Wildlife Fedn., U. Mich. Alumni Assn. (life), Nat. Audubon Soc., Nat. Hist. Soc., Mich. Hist. Soc., Daus. Colonial Wars, Am. Bus. Women's Assn. (Chpt. Woman of Yr. award 1965, pres. chpt. 1964-65), Am. Soc. Profl. and Exec. Women. Club: Detroit Econ. Home: PO Box 734 Rochester MI 48063 Office: 30700 Telegraph Rd S-4535 Birmingham MI 48010

COLLINS, GAIL PETTY, educator; b. Bronx, N.Y., June 11, 1947; d. Edward Joseph and Virginia (Lattmann) Petty; B.A., Mt. St. Mary Coll., 1969; M.S., Herbert H. Lehman Coll., 1973; postgrad. Cornell U., 1978. Tchr., Newburgh (N.Y.) City Sch. Dist., 1969-71; tchr. Clarkstown Central Sch. Dist., West Nyack, N.Y., 1971—. Commr. Rockland County Park Commn., Clarkstown, 1978-82, vice-chairperson, 1981; mem. Town of Clarkstown Bicentennial Commn., 1976; vol. Meals on Wheels; bd. dirs. Clarkstown United Way. Mem. Rockland County Tchrs. Assn. (dir. 1977—, v.p. 1978-79, pres. 1979-82), N.Y. State United Tchrs. (alt. del., del. 1977—), Am. Fedn. Tchrs. (alt. del., del. 1977—), Rockland County Bldg. and Central Trades Council (del. 1976—), Rockland County Hist. Soc., Coalition of Labor Union Women. Democrat. Home: 449 Sierra Vista Ln Valley Cottage NY 10989 Office: Lakewood Elem Sch 77 Lakeland Ave Congers NY 10920

COLLINS, GLENDA BARDWELL, educator, civic worker; b. Grenada, Miss., Sept. 21, 1941; d. Robert Lee and Irene (James) Bardwell; B.F.A., Miss. State Coll. for Women, 1963; M.Ed., U. New Orleans, 1975; m. M. B. Collins, June 30, 1963 (div.); 1 dau., Cathleen Kelly. Tchr. art Memphis City Sch. System, 1964-68, Met. Nashville-Davidson County Schs., 1969-72, St. Bernard Parish Schs., 1973-76, St. Tammany Parish, Salmen High Sch., Slidell, La., 1976—; co-chmn. Bicentennial Festival of Arts for Children, New Orleans, 1976; exhibitor Internat. Trade Mart, New Orleans, 1976; tchr., cons. State-wide Inservice Program. Co-founder, pres. Council for Victims of Family Violence in St. Tammany Parish, 1979-80; organizer, pres. Parish President's Commn. on Needs of Women, 1981-82; active ERA, United, ERAmerica, Speakers Bur. Slidell, Talent Bank of Women; active polit. campaigns; photographer La. Women's Conf., Baton Rouge; works include La. Internat. Women's Yr. banner cover photograph. Mem. NEA, La. Assn. Educators, St. Tammany Parish Assn. Educators (v.p.), Nat. Assn. Art Educators, La. Art Educators Assn., St. Tammany Parish Assn. Art Educators (pres.), Slidell Art League. Methodist. Club: Bus. and Profl. Women's (Woman of Yr. 1978-79). Home: PO Box 916 Slidell LA 70459 Office: Salmen High School PO Box 787 Slidell LA 70459

COLLINS, JUDITH NAN, economist; b. Melrose, Mass., Jan. 9, 1954; d. Ivor Winter and Shirley Nan (Rhea) C.; B.S. in Agrl. Econs., U. Wis., 1976, M.S. in Agrl. Econs. (Vilas fellow), 1978. Economist, Econ. Research Service, U.S. Dept. Agr., Washington, 1979-82; research assoc. United Way Am., Alexandria, Va., 1982—. Mem. Am. Agrl. Econs. Assn., Northeastern Agrl. Econs. Council. Contbr. articles to profl. publs. Home: 1138 Valley Dr Alexandria VA 22302 Office: United Way Plaza Alexandria VA 22314

COLLINS, JUDY MARJORIE, singer; b. Seattle, May 1, 1939; d. Charles T. and Marjorie (Byrd) Collins; pvt. study piano, 1944-56; m. Peter A. Taylor, Apr. 1958 (div.); 1 son, Clark Taylor. Made debut as profl. folk singer, Boulder, Colo., 1959, since has appeared in numerous clubs in U.S. and Can.; performer in concerts including Newport Folk Festival, Orch. Hall, Chgo., Carnegie Hall, N.Y.C., also appeared radio and TV; tours in Europe; producer, co-dir. documentary film Antonia: A Portrait of the Woman (nominated for Acad. Award, recipient Silver medal Atlanta Film Festival, Blue Ribbon award Am. Film Festival, Christopher award); acting debut as Solveig in Peer Gynt, N.Y. Shakespeare Festival, 1969. Rec. artist Elektra albums A Maid of Constant Sorrow, Golden Apples of the Sun, Judy Collins 3, The Judy Collins Concert, Judy Collins 5, In My Life, Wildflowers, Who Knows Where The Time Goes, Recollections, Whales and Nightingales, Living, Colors of the Day, True Stories and Other Dreams, Judith, Bread and Roses, So Early in the Spring/The First Fifteen Years, 1977, Hard Times for Lovers, 1979, Running for My Life, 1980, Times of Our Lives, 1982. Recipient 6 gold LPs, hit singles. Author: Judy Collins Songbook. Office: care Rocky Mountain Prodns 1775 Broadway New York NY 10019

COLLINS, KAREN LYNN WISLER, psychologist; b. Oklahoma City, Mar. 25, 1949; d. Charles C. and Frances Joan (Higgins) Wisler; B.A. with honors, Stephen F. Austin State U., Nacogdoches, Tex., 1973; M.A., Tex. Christian U., 1978, Ph.D., 1979; m. David C. Eiland. Asst. prof. Dickinson (N.D.) State Coll., 1979-80; research asst. prof. psychiatry U. Tex. Med. Br., Galveston, 1980-81, asst. prof. dept. ob-gyn and sr. research asso. Office Ednl. Devel., 1981—. Mem. Am. Psychol. Assn., Southwestern Psychol. Assn., Am. Ednl. Research Assn., So. Soc. Philosophy and Psychology, Psi Chi, Alpha Kappa Delta, Alpha Chi, Delta Zeta. Methodist. Contbr. articles to profl. jours. Office: Dept Ob-Gyn U Tex Med Br Room 313 MW E-87 Galveston TX 77550

COLLINS, KATHRYN PATRICIA, property mgmt. co. ofcl.; b. Charleston, S.C., Nov. 27, 1953; d. Frederick Burtrumn and Jeanne Marie (Hicks) C.; B.A. in Edn., U. S.C., 1974. Adminstrv. asst. psychiatry dept. U. S.C., Charleston, 1977-79; asst. dir. office property adminstrn. Seabrook Island Co., Charleston, 1979-82, dir. property adminstrn., 1981. Vol. planning for fund raising March of Dimes, Charleston, 1979-80; mem. People Against Rape, 1978-79. Lic. real estate sales, S.C. Mem. Community Assns. Inst. Author: To Understand the Nature of Man, 1978. Home: Route 1 Box 68A Yonges Island SC 29494

COLLINS, LEILA B., county ofcl.; b. High Spring, Fla., July 9, 1933; d. Harvey Arnold and Pansy Henreitta (Bugg) C.; student public schs., High Springs. Dir. purchasing Pinellas County (Fla.), 1961-81; purchasing dir. Met. Dade County, 1981—; mem. Gen. Services Adminstrn., 1974-75. Recipient Disting. Service award Kiwanis of Tyrone, St. Petersburg, Fla., 1977. Mem. Nat. Assn. Purchasing Mgrs. (pres. Fla. West Coast chpt. 1965-66, 67-68, Purchasing Agt. of Yr. 1968), Nat. Inst. Govtl. Purchasing, Fla. Assn. Govtl. Purchasing Officers (pres. 1977-78). Home: 1129 Mariposa Ave Coral Gables FL 33146 Office: 315 Court St County Courthouse Clearwater FL 33516

COLLINS, LINDA GREENE, hotel service adminstr.; b. Danville, Va., Aug. 5, 1944; d. Charlie T. and Novella (Kendrick) Greene; student Ferrum Jr. Coll., 1963-64; grad. Holiday Inn U., 1975; m. Paul David Collins, July 31, 1965. Various clerical positions Danville Foods (Va.), 1965-71; with Allen-White, Inc., Shelby, N.C., 1972-80, asst. gen. mgr.; 1974, gen. mgr., 1974—, innkeeper, 1980; gen. mgr. Holiday Inn, Wilkesboro, N.C., 1980—. Young adult tchr. Wesley Chapel United Meth. Ch., 1969, high choir leader, 1970. Cert. hotel adminstr. Mem. Nat. Innkeepers Assn., Internat. Orgn. Hotel and Motel Mgrs., N.C. Motel Assn. (Merit award 1978, W. Capers White award 1980; dir. 1975—, pres. 1980), N.C. Innkeeper Assn. (dir. 1974—), N.C. Restaurant Assn., Nat. Notary Assn. Methodist. Address: 1001 Oak Towers North Wilkesboro NC 28697

COLLINS, MARION SMITH, writer; b. Carrollton, Ga., Jan. 25, 1936; d. John Tuggle and Katherine Lee (King) Smith; A.B.J., U. Ga., 1957; m. Robert Lee Collins, Jr., Dec. 23, 1956; children—Katherine Collins Dooley, Robert Lee III. Owner, operator This Old House, Calhoun, Ga., 1975-77; pub. relations dir. Calhoun City Sch. System, 1978; free-lance decorator, 1975-79; writer of fiction; books include: The 'dolce far niente' Girl, 1982; The Beachcomber, 1983. Pres. Gordon County chpt. Am. Cancer Soc., 1962, Gordon County Woman's Club, 1964, Calhoun-Gordon County LWV, 1965, Calhoun Elem. PTA, 1967, Line St. PTA, 1970, Cherokee Dames Investment Club, 1974, Friends of Gordon Hosp., 1980; dist. sec. Ga. Fedn. Women's Clubs, 1965. Recipient 1st place for novel Southeastern Writers Assn. Conf., 1982. Mem. Southeastern writers Assn., Romance Writers Am. (S.E. advisor), Ga. Romance Writers (organizational pres.).

COLLINS, MARTHA LAYNE, lt. gov. Ky.; b. Shelby County, Ky., Dec. 7, 1936; d. Everett Larkin and Mary Lorena (Taylor) Hall; student Lindenwood Coll.; B.S., U. Ky., 1959; m. Bill Collins, July 3, 1959; children—Stephen Louis, Marla Ann. Tchr., Fairdale High Sch., Louisville, Seneca High Sch., Louisville, Woodford County Jr. High Sch., Versailles, Ky.; now lt. gov. of Ky., Frankfort. Exec. dir. Friendship Force, 1977—. Mem. Nat. Conf. Appellate Ct. Clks., Bus. and Profl. Womens Club, Ky. Commn. on Women, U. Ky. Alumni Assn., Psi Omega. Baptist. Club: Order of Eastern Star. Office: Lieutenant Governor's Office State Capitol Frankfort KY 40601 *

COLLINS, MARVA DELOISE NETTLES, educator; b. Monroeville, Ala., Aug. 31, 1936; d. Alex L. and Bessie Maye (Knight) Nettles; B.A., Clark Coll., Atlanta, 1957; postgrad. Chgo. Tchrs. Coll. and Columbia Coll., 1965-67; hon. degrees, Howard U., Wilberforce U., 1980, Amherst Coll., 1981. m. Clarence Collins, Sept. 2, 1961; children—Eric Tremayne, Patrick, Cynthia. Tchr., Monroeville, 1957-59, Chgo. Public Schs., 1960-75; founder Westside Prep. Sch., Chgo., 1975—; featured on Phil Donahue Show, Good Morning America, 60 Minutes, mags., newspapers throughout U.S.; subject of film The Marva Collins Story, 1981; condr. workshops U.S. and Europe; dir. local Right to Read Program. Recipient Watson Washburne award, 1979, West Garfield Image award, 1980, United Negro Coll. Fund award, 1980, Sears Week of the Child award, 1980, Sojourner Truth award, 1980, West Garfield Park award, 1980, Educator of Yr. award, 1981. Mem. Internat. Platform Assn., Alpha Kappa Alpha. Baptist. Contbr. articles to newspapers and mags. Office: 3819 W Adams St Chicago IL 60624

COLLINS, MARY ALICE, psychiat. social worker; b. Everett, Wash., Apr. 20, 1937; d. Harry Edward and Mary (Yates) Caton; B.A., Sociology, Seattle Pacific Coll., 1959; M.S.W., U. Mich., 1966; Ph.D., Mich. State U., 1974; m. Gerald C. Brocker, Mar. 24, 1980. Dir. teenage, adult and counseling depts. YWCA, Flint, Mich., 1959-64, 66-68; social worker Cath. Social Services, Flint, 1969-71, Ingham Med. Mental Health Center, Lansing, Mich., 1971-73; clin. social worker Genesee Psychiat. Center, Flint, 1974—; instr. social work Lansing Community Coll. and Mich. State U., 1974; vis. prof. Hurley Med. Center, Flint, 1980—; cons. Ingham County Dept. Social Services, 1971-73. Advisor human relations Youth League, Flint Council Chs., 1964-65; sec. Genesee County Young Democrats, 1960-61. Mem. Nat. Assn. Social Workers, Acad. Cert. Social Workers, Registry Clin. Social Workers, Registry Health Care Workers, Phi Kappa Phi, Alpha Kappa Sigma. Contbr. articles to profl. jours. Home: 5945 Round Lake Rd Laingsburg MI 48848 Office: PO Box 7179 Flint MI 48507

COLLINS, MARY BETH, assn. exec.; b. Detroit, Jan. 3, 1925; d. James Edward and Mildred Ina (Barding) Hughes; B.A., Manhattanville Coll. Sacred Heart, 1947; M.A., Ariz. State U., 1970; m. Taber Loree Collins, Aug. 7, 1947; children—Louise Collins Alton, James, Suzanne Collins Giroux, Mary Beth Collins Brenner, Mildred Collins Hittner, Marguerite Collins Zeller, Miriam Collins Huston, Frank, Jesse, Kathleen Collins Cheo, Martha Willing. Community services coordinator Alcohol and Drug Abuse div. Ariz. Health Dept., Phoenix, 1967-68, acting dir., 1968-70; coordinator City of Phoenix Drug Control, 1970-73; exec. dir. Drug Action Coalition, Montgomery County, Md., 1973-74; exec. dir. Community Orgn. for Drug Abuse Control, 1974-76; adminstr. Office Substance Abuse Services, Mich. Dept. Pub. Health, Lansing, 1977-78; chmn. N.Y. State Commn. Prevention and Edn. of Alcohol and Substance Abuse, Albany, 1978-79; exec. dir. Internat. Assn. Prevention Programs, 1974—. Pres. Ariz. Family, Inc., 1970-71; bd. dirs. Community Orgn. for Drug Abuse Control, 1969-73; mem. adv. bd. Good Samaritan Hosp., Mental Health Services; mem. bd. Nat. Coordinating Council on Drug Edn., 1974-76. Mem. Internat. Council on Alcoholism and Addictions, Drugs, Alcohol and Women's Health Coalition (regional chmn.), Ariz. Alumnae of Sacred Heart (founding pres. 1963-64), Pi Lambda Theta. Home: PO Box 1825 Cave Creek AZ 85331 Office: PO Box 812 Carefree AZ 85377

COLLINS, MARY ELIZABETH STEINHEIMER, pediatrician; b. Nanking, China, Jan. 9, 1921; d. Herman Carl and Ella Frances (Jones) Steinheimer; A.B., Syracuse U., 1942; M.D., Syracuse Med. Coll., 1944; m. William A. Collins, Jr., Apr. 19, 1968; 1 dau., Emma Lou. Intern, Johns Hopkins Hosp., Balt., 1944-45; resident in pediatrics Bellevue Hosp., N.Y.C., 1945-46, Syracuse Meml. Hosp., 1946-47; pediatrician Soochow (China) Hosp., 1948-50; commd. capt. U.S. Army, 1951, advanced through grades to col., 1968; pediatrician Walter Reed Army Inst. Research, 1962-63, 2d Gen. Hosp., Europe, 1963-68, William Beaumont Gen. Hosp., El Paso, Tex., 1968-71; ret., 1971; pvt. practice medicine specializing in pediatrics, Tucson, 1971—; pediatric cons. USAF Europe, 1965-68. Decorated Legion Merit. Mem. Am. Med. Women's Assn. (sec. 1981), Acad. Pediatrics, Ariz. Pediatric Soc., Pima County Pediatric Soc., Los Angeles Pediatric Soc., Am. Med. Womens Assn. Address: 234 S Country Club Tucson AZ 85716

COLLINS, NANCY WHISNANT, med. found. adminstr.; b. Charlotte, N.C., Dec. 20, 1933; d. Ward William and Marjorie Adele (Blackburn) Whisnant; student Queens Coll., Charlotte, 1951-53; A.B. in Journalism, U. N.C., 1955, M.S. in Personnel Adminstrn., 1967; postgrad. (fellow) Cornell U., 1955-56; m. James Q. Collins, Jr., Apr. 25, 1959; (div. 1974) children—James Quincy III, Charles Lowell, William Robey; m. 2d, Richard F. Chapman, May 29, 1982. Personnel asst. R.H. Macy & Co., Inc., N.Y.C., 1955; jr. exec. placement dir. Scofield Placement Agy., San Francisco, 1956-57; free-lance journalist, London, Paris, and Frankfort, W.Ger., 1957-59; program dir. Girl Scouts U.S., Hampton, Va., 1959-61; tour dir., Tokyo, Hong Kong, Singapore, 1965-66; asst. dir. Sloan exec. program Stanford U., 1968-78; asst. dir. Hoover Instn., 1979-81; asst. to pres. Palo Alto (Calif.) Med. Found., 1981—. Mem. council Trinity Episcopal Ch., Menlo Park Calif., 1975—, fund-raising Cornell U., 1975—; exec. council Stanford area Boy Scouts Am., 1980—; mem. San Mateo County Charter Rev. Com.; mem. personnel bd. City of Menlo Park, 1979—, women's program bd. Coro Found. Richardson Found. grantee, 1967. Mem. AAUW, Am. Mgmt. Assn., Peninsula Profl. Women's Network (adv. council), Overseas Press Club, Kappa Delta. Episcopalian. Contbr. articles, short stories and poems to mags. and newspapers. Home: 1850 Oak Ave Menlo Park CA 94025 Office: Office of the Pres Palo Alto Med Found 400 Channing Ave Palo Alto CA 94301

COLLINS, NATALIE ANNE, chemist, health products co. exec.; b. Vancouver, B.C., Can., Mar. 15, 1928; came to U.S., 1951, naturalized, 1958; d. Walter P. and Eugenie (Ferley) Koohtow; B.S., McGill U., Montreal, Que., Can., 1949. Neurophysiol. research asst. Allan Meml. Inst., Montreal, 1949-51; physiol. research asst. Harvard U. Sch. Public Health, Boston, 1951-53; in new product devel. Gillette Co., Boston, 1954-69, sr. project chemist, 1967-69, internat. clearance officer, 1969—; U.S. rep. to exec. bd. Internat. Fedn. Congress Cosmetic Chemists, Tokyo, 1969. Mem. Soc. Cosmetic Chemists (dir. 1968-69, chmn. New Eng. chpt. 1967), Internat. Fedn. Soc. Cosmetic Chemists, Kappa Alpha Theta (Beta Psi chpt.). Research, publs. in field; devel. consumer products, including foam shave cream. Office: Gillette Co Prudential Tower Bldg Boston MA 02199

COLLINS, NELIA ANNE, missionary nurse; b. Crawfordsville, Ind., Aug. 31, 1941; d. G. Neil and Helen Alice (Grantham) C.; diploma Meth. Hosp. Sch. Nursing, 1962; student Ind. Bapt. Coll., evenings 1966-70. Staff nurse Meth. Hosp., Indpls., 1962-63, 64-66, Espanola (N.Mex.) Hosp., 1963-64, Community Hosp., Indpls., 1966-75; Christian counselor mission to cancer patients Colonial Hills Bapt. Ch., Indpls.,1974—. Home: 671 Village Pl N Dr Indianapolis IN 46280 Office: 8151 Union Chapel Rd Indianapolis IN 46240

COLLINS, REBA NEIGHBORS, museum dir.; b. Shawnee, Okla., Aug. 26, 1925; d. Robert Luther and Susie Ione (Peek) Neighbors; B.A. in English, Central State U., Edmond, Okla., 1958; M.S. in Journalism, Okla. State U., 1959, Ed.D. in Journalism for Higher Edn., 1968; m. Delmar Leroy Collins, Aug. 26, 1941; children—Rebecca Collins Jones, Wanda Jean Collins Johnson, Dennis Mikel. Mem. faculty Central State U., Edmond, 1958-75, prof., 1970-75, dir. public relations, 1969-75; dir. Will Rogers Meml., Claremore, Okla., 1975—. Bd. dirs. Edmond Guidance Center; an organizer first July 4th Ann. Celebration, Edmond; mem. Gov.'s Mini-Cabinet for Tourism and Recreation. Recipient Okie award Gov. Bartlett, 1967; Service award VFW, 1968; Disting. Alumni award Central State U., 1979; named Outstanding Communicator, Okla. Women in Journalism, 1976. Mem. Okla. Museum Assn. (dir.), Daus. Am. Colonists, Daus. of Confederacy, D.A.R., Rogers County Hist. Assn., Delta Kappa Gamma (sec.). Democrat. Club: Pilot (pres.) (Claremore). Author: Janes-Peek History; Will Rogers Centennial; co-author: In the Shadows of Old North; contbr. articles to various newspapers and mags.

COLLINS, ROSEMARY A., librarian; b. Muncie, Ind.; d. Cary Jackson and Ruby Mae (Johnson) C.; B.S., Ind. U., 1954; M.Ed. (fellow), Am. U., 1966; postgrad. U. Md., 1968-74, D.C. Tchrs. Coll., 1967-76, Trinity Coll., 1978—, George Washington U., 1980-81. Tchr. public schs., Eau Claire, Mich., 1953-54, Bedford, Ind., 1954-55, Jeffersonville, Ind., 1955-57; librarian, media specialist Washington Public Schs., 1958—. Mem. D.C. Human Relations Commn., 1963-64; fund-raiser Heart Assn., 1969-70. U.S. Office of Edn. grantee, 1974-75. Mem. ALA, AAUW, Phi Kappa Phi, Alpha Xi Delta, Phi Delta Gamma. Clubs: Zonta; Christian Women's (exec. bd.); Order of Eastern Star. Home: 3535 Chevy Chase Lake Dr Chevy Chase MD 20815

COLLINS, RUTH HARVEY, social worker; b. Rochester, Minn., June 4, 1917; d. Clair Lloyd and Iva Bell (Whiton) Harvey; B.A., Lawrence U., Appleton, Wis., 1945; M.A., Mich. State U., East Lansing, 1966, M.S.W. (NIMH scholar), 1967; m. T. T. Collins, Jr., June 12, 1939 (div.); children—Theresa Ruth, Theron Tilford, Jane Elizabeth. Social worker Head Start, Lansing, Mich., 1967; group worker Methodist Community House, Grand Rapids, Mich., 1968-69; regional sec. women's div. United Meth. Ch., Atlanta, 1968-71; supr. day care licensing Ga. Dept. Human Resources, 1971-78, state tng. officer, 1978—; adv. com. dept. econs. Morehouse Coll., Atlanta; cons. curriculum Ga. Vocat./Tech. Sch. Chmn. United Fund campaign, Jacksonville Beach, Fla., 1952; mem. SE regional com. internat. programs YMCA. AAUW grantee, 1974. Mem. Nat. Assn. Social Workers, Ga. Assn. Young Children, So. Assn. Children Under Six, Nat. Assn. Edn. Young Children, AAUW, Acad. Cert. Social Workers. Democrat. Presbyterian. Club: Altrusa. Author: Resources for Children in Georgia, also papers, articles in field. Home: 1433 Willivee Dr Decatur GA 30033 Office: 618 Ponce de Leon Ave NE Atlanta GA 30308

COLLINS, SHERRY DELLE, C. of C. exec.; b. Mason City, Iowa; d. Lionel Francis and Dorothy Delle C.; grad. Hamilton Bus. Coll., 1961; student No. Iowa Community Coll., 1967, U. Okla., Norman, 1977, U. Colo., 1971—. Adminstrv. sec. Mason City (Iowa) C. of C., 1965; sec. devel. div. Iowa Devel. Co., Des Moines, 1968-71; exec. v.p. Glencoe (Minn.) C. of C., 1971-75; pres. Broomfield Area C. of C., 1975—. Chmn. bd. Greeters Inc.; active Minn. Republican Com., 1972-75. Mem. Colo. C. of C. Execs. (dir.), Am. C. of C. Execs., Mountain States Assn., Met. C. of C. Execs., C. of C. U.S. Methodist. Club: Order Eastern Star. Home: 1147 Sequerra Broomfield CO 80020 Office: PO Box 301 Hwy 287 and Midway Blvd Broomfield CO 80020

COLLINS, ZELMA MITCHELL, ednl. adminstr.; b. Newark, June 16, 1930; d. James Hugo and Pattie Evelyn (Booker) Mitchell; B.S., Newark State Tchrs. Coll., 1951; M.A., Seton Hall U., 1973, postgrad., 1973-78; m. Charles M. Collins, Sr., Nov. 10, 1951; 1 son, Charles M. Tchr., Oliver St. Sch., Newark, 1951; tchr. South 17th St. Sch., Newark, 1952, helping tchr., 1969, organizer Title I Program, 1970, vice prin., 1972-74, prin., 1974—. Recipient award Essex County Civic Club, 1977, South 17th St. PTA, 1977, Newark Bd. Edn., 1978; Disting. Alumnus award Seton Hall U., 1980. Mem. Nat. Assn. Elem. Sch. Prins., Newark Prins. Assn., Kean Coll. Alumni Assn., Seton Hall Alumni Assn., Seton Hall Prep. Alumni Mothers Assn., N.J. Assn. Elem. Sch. Prins., Essex County Council Sch. Adminstrs., City Adminstrs. and Suprs. Assn., Nat. Assn. Negro Bus. and Profl. Women, Phi Kappa Phi, Kappa Delta Pi (chpt. pres. 1980-81), Phi Delta Kappa. Baptist. Clubs: Women's

League N.J., Four Seasons. Home: 64 Girard Pl Newark NJ 07108 Office: South 17th St School 619 South 17th St Newark NJ 07103

COLLINSWORTH, FRANCES MARIANNE, cytotechnologist; b. Lay, Colo., July 17, 1921; d. Charles Howard and Mary Campbell (Brodie) Webb; B.S., Colo. State U., Ft. Collins, 1943; grad. Parkland Hosp. Sch. Cytotechnology, Dallas, 1969; m. J.D. Collinsworth, Aug. 4, 1945; 1 son, Ross Brian. Tchr. home econs. Sidney (Nebr.) High Sch., 1943-44; stewardness United Airlines, 1944-45; tchr. sci. Taipei Am. Assn. Sch., Tien Mou, Taiwan, 1959-61; chief cytotechnologist, sr. instr. Parkland Meml. Hosp., Dallas, 1969-70; supr. dept. cytology Damon Lab., Phoenix, 1982—. Vol., ARC, 1959-65. Mem. Am. Soc. Cytology, Am. Soc. Clin. Pathologists, Am. Soc. Cytotechnology, Ariz. Cytology Assn., Colo. State U. Alumni Assn., Nat. Ret. Tchrs. Assn. Democrat. Episcopalian. Club: Delta Delta Delta. Home: 310 E Sharon Ave Phoenix AZ 85022 Office: 210 N 24th St Phoenix AZ 85006

COLL-PARDO, ISABEL HARRISON, ednl. adminstr.; b. Greenwood, S.C., May 22; d. Lloyd Bratton and Mary Lucile (Stoney) Harrison; A.A., Chevy Chase Jr. Coll., 1943; B.A., George Washington U., 1945; postgrad. Am. U., 1970-71; m. Max Luis Coll-Pardo, Mar. 17, 1945; children—Anne Coll-Pardo Yuhasz, Mary Luisa Coll-Pardo Heymann. Soloist, Washington Nat. Ballet Co., 1939-47; sec., translator French Govt., Washington, 1945-47; ballet tchr., Ga., 1945, Washington, 1952-55; conf. coordinator, office mgr. Am. Assn. Jr. Colls., Washington, 1960-67; staff asst. Nat. Assn. Coll. and Univ. Bus. Officers, Washington, 1967-69; program asso., seminar leader Am. Council on Edn., 1969-80; now conf. cons. Sch. Continuing Studies U. Miami (Fla.). cons. role of coll. and univ. pres.'s wife. Mem. S.C. Hist. Soc., Kappa Kappa Gamma, Phi Theta Kappa. Presbyterian. Editor: (with C.F. Fisher) Guide to Leadership Development Opportunities for College and University Administrators, 1979-80; compiler Selected Bibliography for the College and University President's Spouse, 1976, 79. Home: 20422 SW 85th Ave Miami FL 33189

COLOGNE, EVELYN ALBERTA, sch. sec.; b. Toronto, Ohio, Apr. 21, 1921; d. Redmond and Olive Gertrude (Dunlap) Lewis; student W.Va. No. Community Coll., 1976; B.A., West Liberty State Coll., 1979; children—Barbara Cologne Eddy, Maxine June Guz. Sec., H.J. Mark Co., Steubenville, Ohio, 1943-45, Jefferson County Soldiers' Relief Commn., Steubenville, 1945-46; dispatcher D & B Truck Terminal, Weirton, W.Va., 1950-55; food server Hancock County Bd. Edn., New Cumberland, W.Va., 1965-68; sr. sec. Weirton Heights (W.Va.) Elem. Sch., 1968—. Active, Hancock County Easter Seal Soc., Weirton Heights PTA. Mem. W.Va. Sch. Service Personnel Assn., W.Va. No. Community Coll. Alumni Assn., West Liberty State Coll. Alumni Assn. Democrat. Clubs: Am. Legion Aux., Eagles Aux., Women of the Moose. Home: 207 Murphy Ave Weirton WV 26062 Office: Weirton Heights Elem Sch 160 S 12th St Weirton WV 26062

COLOMBO, MARY JO, mgmt. cons.; b. Denver, Mar. 26, 1947; d. Arnold Melford and Coral (Bailiff) Sathre; A.D., Community Coll. Denver, 1973; B.S., Met. State Coll., 1978; m. Daniel Leonardo Colombo, July 4, 1966 (div. 1970); children—Michael Kevin, Jeffery Scott. Staff nurse emergency room Beth Israel Hosp., Denver, 1973-79; adult nurse practitioner W.K. Podleski, M.D., Inc., Denver, 1979-80; pres. Rocky Mt. Stone Co., Denver, 1981—; v.p. Murphree-Palmer Adv. Group, Ltd., Denver, 1982—; dir., officer Mannering Oil Co., Novel Ideas, Inc., Murphree Palmer Adv. Group. Mem. Assn. Women Govt. Contractors, Women's Bus. Owners Assn., Nat. Assn. Female Execs., Colo. Nurses Assn. Democrat. Lutheran. Office: 601 Broadway Suite 112 Denver CO 80203

COLON, JOYCE EDNA, mfg. co. exec.; b. Va., Oct. 22, 1942; d. Herbert and Viola Wooden; B.S., Va. State U., 1965; M.B.A., Pace U., 1975. Dir. residence life Va. State U., Petersburg, 1971-72, dir. fin. aid, 1972-73; with Equitable Life Assurance Soc., 1965-71, 73—, new bus. mgr., Milford, Conn., 1978-79, asst. v.p., N.Y.C., 1979-80; exec. asst. Constrn. Group, Westinghouse Electric Corp., Pitts., 1980—; instr. mktg., mgmt. Collegiate Inst., N.Y.C., 1974-76. Founding mem., pres., bd. dirs. Minority Interchange, 1975—; bd. dirs. Conn. Housing Investment Fund, 1979—. Recipient Disting. Service award Urban League, 1975, Va. State U., 1973, Nat. Alliance Bus., 1971. Mem. Am. Mgmt. Assn.

COLQUITT, BETSY FEAGAN, educator; b. Fort Worth, Mar. 4, 1926; d. Belton Dial and Eddie Howard (Young) Feagan; B.A., Tex. Christian U., 1947; M.A., Vanderbilt U., 1948; postgrad. U. Kans., U. Wis.; m. Landon Augustus Colquitt, May 29, 1954; children—Clare Elizabeth, Catherine Amanda. Instr. English, Ala. State Coll. for Women (name changed to U. Ala. at Montevallo), 1948-49, U. Kans., Lawrence, 1949-52; teaching asst. U. Wis., Madison, 1952-53; mem. faculty Tex. Christian U., Fort Worth, 1953—, prof. English, 1978—; prof. summer teaching U. Americas, Puebla, Mex.; Tex. Commn. on Arts 1981-82; ; Frost Found. grantee, 1981-82. Mem. AAUP, South Central MLA, Tex. Assn. Creative Writing Tchrs. (past pres.), Coll. Conf. Tchrs. of English, Mortar Bd., Phi Beta Kappa (officer Tex. Christian U. chpt.). Democrat. Editor: Descant, 1963—; editor: Jerome Moore's Tex. Christian U.: A Hundred Years History, 1973; A Part of Space: Ten Texas Writers; 1969; author book of poems: Honor Card, 1981; contbr. essays, poems, fiction to various mags. Home: 2601 McPherson St Fort Worth TX 76109 Office: Tex Christian U Station Fort Worth TX 76129

COLSON, ELIZABETH FLORENCE, anthropologist; b. Hewitt, Minn., June 15, 1917; d. Louis Henry and Metta Louise (Damon) C.; B.A., U. Minn., 1938, M.A., 1940; M.A., Radcliffe Coll., 1941, Ph.D., 1945. Research officer Rhodes-Livingstone Inst., Zambia, 1946-47, 56-57, 62-63, dir., 1948-51; sr. lectr. Manchester (Eng.) U., 1951-53; asso. prof. Goucher Coll., Towson, Md., 1954-55; asso. prof., research asso. African studies program Boston U., 1955-59; prof. Brandeis U., Waltham, Mass., 1959-63, U. Calif., Berkeley, 1964—. Fellow Am. Anthrop. Assn., Royal Anthrop. Inst. (hon.), AAAS; mem. Nat. Acad. Scis., Am. Acad. Arts and Scis., Assn. Social Anthropologists, Am. Ethnol. Soc., Internat. African Inst., Am. Assn. African Studies, Soc. Sci. Study of Religion, Assn. Study of Law and Society, PEO, AAUW. Author: The Makah, 1953; Marriage and the Family Among the Plateau Tonga, 1958; Social Organization of the Gwembe Tonga, 1960; The Plateau Tonga, 1962; The Social Consequences of Resettlement, 1971; Tradition and Contract: The Problem of Order, 1974; (with Thayer Scudder) Secondary Education and the Formation of an Elite. Office: Dept Anthropology U Calif Berkeley CA 94720

COLSTON, MARION JANE, counselor; b. Darby, Pa., Jan. 27, 1950; d. Joseph Stanley and Ruth Louise (Robinson) Bradley; B.S., Cheyney State Coll., 1976; M.Ed., Antioch U., 1982; m. Jackie Colston, Jan. 7, 1978; 1 son, Jackie. Dir. creative arts dept. So. Home for Children, Phila., 1975-78; career edn. tchr. Delaware County Intermediate Unit #25, Media, Pa., 1979-81; counselor/instr. Upward Bound, Widener U., Chester, Pa., 1981—; instr. career edn. class for unemployed adults, 1981. Cert. spl. edn. tchr., Pa. Mem. Mid-Eastern Assn. Ednl. Opportunity Program Personnel, Nat. Assn. Female Execs. Democrat. Office: Loveland Hall Widener Univ 14th and Chestnut St Chester PA 19013

COLT, JULIE GUION GEORGE HEWITT (MRS. S. BARCLAY COLT), civic worker; b. Princeton, N.J.; d. Charles Albert and Mary Leslie (Guion) George; student Vassar Coll., 1921-23; m. Edward Cooper Hewitt, June 11, 1927 (dec. Aug. 1966); children—Mary Leslie Guion (Mrs. David Waddell Bird), Edward Cooper, Jr.; m. 2d, Sackett Barclay Colt, Sept. 15, 1973. Social reporter, social editor Elizabeth (N.J.) Daily Jour., 1920-35, N.Y. Herald Tribune, 1925-37, Charm mag., Newark, 1928-33, Sportsman Mag., Summit, N.J., 1933-36, Newark Sunday Call, 1930-40, Newark Evening News, 1940-45; saleslady Morrell Studio Portraits, Plainfield, N.J., 1932-38. Vice pres. Elizabeth Dramatic Club, 1942-43; pres. Jr. League, Elizabeth, 1941-43; pres., exec. com. N.J. Jr. Leagues, 1943-45; trustee Vail Deane Sch., Elizabeth, N.J., 1967—, chmn. centennial com., 1967-69, pres. alumna assn., 1939-41; asso. vestry Trinity Ch., Elizabeth, 1968—; chmn. 1st ann. grandparents fund-raising com. Suffield (Conn.) Acad.; 4th Ward Republican committeewoman, Elizabeth, 1980—. Named Alumna of Yr., Vail Deane Sch., 1981. Clubs: Jr. League of Elizabeth and Plainfield, Elizabeth Town and Country, Vassar (Essex County chpt.), Baltusrol Golf, Bay Head Yacht, Elizabethtown Cotillion. Home: 50 Georgian Ct Elizabeth NJ 07208 also 634 East Ave Bay Head NJ 08742

COLTON, MARIE WATTERS, state legislator; b. Charlotte, N.C., Oct. 20, 1922; d. John Piper and Sarah (Thomas) Watters; student St. Mary's Jr. Coll.; B.A., U. N.C., Chapel Hill; postgrad. Mars Hill Coll., U. N.C., Asheville; A.S. in Humane Letters (hon.), St. Mary's Coll., 1979; m. Henry Elliott Colton, Sept. 4, 1943; children—Marie Jaqueline Pelzer, Sarah Prince Villeminot, Walter Stokes, Elizabeth Overton. Vice-pres. Democratic Women of N.C., 1976, 77; dist. dir. 11th Congressional Dist. Dem. Women, 1974-76; mem. N.C. Ho. Reps., 1979—, chmn. cultural resources com., vice-chmn. health com., vice-chmn. small bus. com., appropriations base budget com. on natural and econ. resources, appropriations expansion budget com., natural and econ. resources com. Bd. dirs. Thomas Rehab. Hosp., Historic Preservation Soc. N.C. Inc., Vagabond Sch. Drama, United Way Buncombe County, N.C. Agy. for Public Telecommunications; bd. visitors U. N.C., Chapel Hill. Mem. Bus. and Profl. Women, LWV, AAUW, Sir Walter Cabinet, Children's Welfare League. Episcopalian. Office: NC Ho Reps State Capitol Raleigh NC 27602 *

COLWELL, RITA ROSSI, educator, univ. adminstr.; b. Beverly, Mass., Nov. 23, 1934; d. Louis and Louse G. (Di Ralma) R.; B.S., Purdue U., 1956, M.S., 1958; Ph.D., U. Wash., 1961; m. Jack H. Colwell, May 31, 1956; children—Alison E.L., Stacie Anne. Research asst. U. Wash., 1957-58, predoctoral asso., 1959-60, asst. research prof., 1961-64; guest scientist div. applied biology NRC Can., Ottawa, 1961-63; vis. asst. prof. biology Georgetown U., 1963-64, asst. prof. biology, 1964-66, asso. prof., 1966-72; prof. microbiology U. Md., 1972—, dir. Sea Grant Program, 1977—, acting dir. Center Environ. and Estuarine Studies, 1980-81; mem. ad hoc commn. on Klebsiella-Enterobater-Hafnia-Serratia div. WHO, 1975—; mem. numerous coms. NSF, 1970—; bd. dirs. Upper Bay Survey, Md. Dept. Natural Resources, 1974-75. Fellow Washington Acad. Sci. (bd. mgrs. 1976-79), AAAS, Am. Acad. Microbiology (bd. govs. 1979), Can. Coll. Microbiologists; mem. Am. Soc. Microbiology (v.p. 1971-72, pres. Wash. Br. 1972-73), Am. Type Culture Collection (trustee 1970-83, sec.-treas. 1971-78, vice chmn. 1978-80, chmn. 1980-81), Marine Tech. Soc. (exec. com. 1978—), Soc. Indsl. Microbiology (bd. govs. 1976-79), Am. Inst. Biol. Sci. (bd. gov. 1976-82), U.S. Fedn. Culture Collections (governing bd. 1978—), Soc. Gen. Microbiology, Soc. Applied Bacteriology, Systematics Assn., Classification Soc., Soc. Invertebrate Pathology, Am. Soc. Limnology and Oceanography, Am. Oceanic Soc., Estuarine and Brackish Water Scis. Assn., Atlantic Estuarine Research Soc., Am. Littoral Assn., World Fedn. Culture Collections, Sigma Xi, Sigma Delta Epsilon, Phi Beta Kappa. Asso. editor Can. Jour. Microbiology, 1972-75, asst. editor, 1975-79; editorial bd. Microbiology Ecology, 1972—, Applied and Environ. Microbiology. 1969-81, Oil & Petrochem. Pollution, 1980—, Jour. Washington Acad. Sci., 1981—, Johns Hopkins Univ. Oceanographic Series, 1981—, Revue de la Fondation Oceanographique Ricard, 1981—, J. Diarrheal Dis 1982—; contbr. chpts. to books and numerous articles to profl. jours. Office: Dept Microbiology U Md College Park Md 20742 *

COLWELL, ROBBIE ELENA, lawyer; b. Hiawassee, Ga., Feb. 12, 1956; d. Robert England and Doris Winifred (Collins) Colwell; student Young Harris Coll., 1973-75; B.S.Ed. cum laude, U. Ga., 1977, M.Ed., 1978; J.D., Mercer U., 1982. Tchr. elem. schs., Blairsville, Ga., 1979-80; admitted to Ga. bar, 1982; pvt. practice law, Blairsville, Ga., 1982—. Del. Democratic Nat. Conv., 1980; vice chmn. Heart Fund Drive, 1980; chmn. Townlift Project, Blairsville, 1982. Mem. Ga. Bar Assn., Am. Bar Assn., Ga. Fedn. Dem. Women, Blairsville C. of C., Ga. Assn. Edn. Democrat. Methodist. Address: PO Box 126 Gainesville Hwy Blairsville GA 30512

COMAS-DÍAZ, LILLIAN, psychologist; b. Chgo., July 18, 1950; d. Filiberto and Maria (Díaz) Comas; B.A., U. P.R., 1970, M.A., 1973; NIMH predoctoral psychology fellow, Yale U., 1979; Ph.D., U. Mass., 1979. Tchr. Yabucoa (P.R.) Public Sch., 1971-72; instr. psychology U. P.R., 1973; project dir. Clinica Hispana de Evaluación y Orientación, New Britain, Conn., 1976; psychologist Mental Health Clinic of New Britain Gen. Hosp., 1976-78; asst. prof. psychology Yale U., also asst. dir. Hill Mental Health Clinic, New Haven, 1979—. Recipient Humanitarian award Omega Psi Phi, 1981. Mem. Am. Psychol. Assn., Am. Orthopsychiat. Assn., Nat. Hispanic Psychol. Assn. Research and publs. on transcultural psychology, mental health services to ethnic minorities. Home: 431 Orange St New Haven CT 06511 Office: 464 Congress Ave New Haven CT 06519

COMBI, CLAIRE ABRUZZO, mktg. cons.; b. N.Y.C., Oct. 16, 1932; d. Serafino Frank and Mae (Romano) Abruzzo; diploma Grace Downs Modeling Sch., 1954, N.Y. Sch. Advt., 1958; m. John Vincent Combi, Dec. 26, 1959; 1 dau., Christine. Production mgr. Promenade Mag., N.Y.C., 1954-59; columnist Houston Post, 1960-64; freelance mktg. rep. Houston, 1965—; former rep. Allied Chem., Hoescht, Owens-Corning; now rep. Celanese Fibers Mktg. Co., others; cons. Kinkaid Sch., Houston Community Coll. Founder Musical Theatre Guild of Houston, Inc., 1976—, chmn. bd., 1981—; founding mem. Alley Theatre Guild; active Houston Grand Opera (recipient Gold Medal), Houston Symphony. Mem. Fashion Group (past officer). Roman Catholic. Home and Office: 1110 Marshall St Houston TX 77006

COMBIER, ELIZABETH IRENE, communications exec.; b. N.Y.C., July 11, 1949; d. Philibert Hodges and Julia Elizabeth C.; B.A. in Psychology, Northwestern U., 1971; cert. in internat. politics Johns Hopkins U., 1976; postgrad. in interactive telecommunications N.Y. U. Bus. mgr. sales and service Memorex Corp., 1971-72; ind. mgmt. cons. DeMaris Investment Co., 1972-74; producer Cue Mag. Show, TV, N.Y.C., 1975-76; pres. Combier Communications, N.Y.C., 1976—; pres. Combier Solar Communications; seminar leader on solar communications UN Conf., Vienna, 1979. Campaign vol. Eugene McCarthy, Wis., 1967; mem. N.Y. Inds. for Govt. Recipient hon. mention Washington Sq. Outdoor Art Exhibit, 1975, 76. Mem. Internat. Radio and TV Soc., Internat. Solar Energy Soc., Assn. Ind. Film and Videomakers, Am. Film Inst., Solar Lobby, Internat. TV Assn., Nat. Acad. TV Arts and Scis., English Speaking Union, French Inst., N.Y. Jr. C. of C. Clubs: St. Bartholomew's Community, Edwardian, Excelsior. Research on solar communications, media applied to Third World rural villages. Address: 315 E 65th St Apt 4C New York NY 10021

COMBS, BETTY JANE, educator; b. Nassau County, N.Y., Dec. 18, 1932; d. Raymond George and Elsie Jane Elliott; B.A., Pace U., 1972; M.A., Manhattanville Coll., 1976; M.S., Pace U., 1980; m. LeRoy Charles Combs, Mar. 22, 1952; children—Donald Charles, David Charles, James Robert, Jeffrey Raymond. Dir., Meml. Nursery Sch., White Plains, N.Y., 1959-68; substitute tchr., Westchester County, N.Y., 1968-72; head tchr. Lab Sch., asst. prof. early childhood edn. Pace U., Pleasantville, N.Y., 1972—. Vice pres. PTA, 1970-71; vice chmn. North Castle Republican Town Com., 1976—. Mem. Nat. Assn. Edn. Young Children, Assn. Supervision and Curriculum Devel., Nat. Assn. Early Childhood Educators, Phi Delta Kappa. Methodist. Home: 23 Washington Pl North White Plains NY 10603 Office: Sch Edn Pace U Pleasantville NY 10570

COMBS, BRENDA CHRYSTEL, educator; b. Fargo, N.D., Jan. 14, 1953; d. Virgil Booker T. and Eva Charles (Hooks) Combs; B.A. in Psychology, U. Redlands, 1975. Tchr., Monrovia (Calif.) High Sch., 1975—; minority relations rep. Calif. Tchrs. Assn., 1981-82; sch. rep. Monrovia Tchrs. Assn., 1980-81. Mem. Calif. Tchrs. Assn., Nat. Assn. Female Execs., Pi Lambda Theta. Home: 340 W Scenic Dr Monrovia CA 91016 Office: 845 W Colorado Blvd Monrovia CA 91016

COMBS, JANET CONSTANCE, social worker; b. Birmingham, Ala., Nov. 25, 1949; d. Eugene Columbus and Lillian Odessa (Bunn) Combs; B.A. in Sociology/Anthropology, Morgan State Coll., Balt., 1971; M.S.W. in Casework, U. Utah, 1973; cert. John Marshall Law Sch., 1979. Social Rehab. Services trainee, 1972; clin. social worker Levinson Center for Mentally Handicapped Children, Chgo., 1974-75, VA West Side Med. Center, Chgo., 1975—; preceptor social work students U. Ill., Chgo., 1976-79. Mem. Nat. Assn. Social Workers, Ill. Continuity of Care Orgn. Baptist. Home: 505 N Lake Shore Dr Apt 807 Chicago IL 60611 Office: 820 S Damen Ave Chicago IL 60612

COMBS, JULIA CAROLYN, oboist; b. Topeka, July 11, 1950; d. Joe Denton and Fay Magel (Meshew) C.; Mus.B., Memphis State U., 1972, Mus.M., 1974; now postgrad. in oboe N.Tex. State U. Sch. Music; m. William Barney Stacy. Aug. 2, 1981. Oboist, solo English horn Memphis Opera Theater, 1971-74; 2d oboist Memphis Symphony, 1972-74; solo English horn Norfolk (Va.) Symphony, 1974-75; prin. oboe Norfolk Opera, 1974-75; asst. prof. oboe U. Wyo., Laramie, 1978—; oboist New World Wind Quintet, 1978—; oboe and oboe d'amore soloist, 1976—. Served with U.S. Army, 1975-78. U. Wyo. grantee, 1981. Mem. Internat. Double Reed Soc., Nat. Assn. Coll. Wind and Percussion Instrs., Women in the Arts (founding mem.), Music Educators Nat. Conf., DAR, Puppetters Am., Union Internat. de la Marionnette, Sigma Alpha Iota, Pi Kappa Lambda, Phi Kappa Phi, Alpha Lambda Delta. Home: 1123 S 7th St Laramie WY 82070 Office: PO Box 3037 Univ Sta Music Dept U Wyo Laramie WY 82070

COMBS, MARY JIM, educator; b. Carrollton, Ga., Dec. 13, 1933; d. Lewis Lee and Floy Burson Combs; B.S. in Home Econs., Ga. State Coll. for Women, 1955; M.Ed., U. Ga., 1963, Ed.S., 1967, Ed.D., 1974; m. Curtis E. Tate, Jr., Aug. 28, 1977; stepchildren—C. Emory, Milton O. Tchr., Cedartown (Ga.) High Sch., 1955-58, Carrollton (Ga.) High Sch., 1958-66; research asst. in vocat. edn. U. Ga., Athens, 1966-68, asst. prof., tchr. educator in home econs., 1968—. Mem. Ga. Assn. Future Homemakers Am. (hon.), Phoenix Soc., NEA, AAUP, Am. Home Econs. Assn., Ga. Home Econs. Assn., Am. Vocat. Assn., Ga. Vocat. Assn., Nat. Assn. Tchr. Educators in Home Econs., Home Econs. Edn. Assn., Ga. Assn. Educators, Phi Upsilon Omicron, Phi Kappa Phi, Kappa Delta Pi, Delta Kappa Gamma. Contbr. articles to profl. publs. Home: 130 Wells Dr Athens GA 30606 Office: 604 Aderhold Hall U Ga Athens GA 30602

COMBS, MAXINE CLARA, educator, artist, real estate salesperson; b. Belington, W.Va., May 13, 1922; d. Ernest Lee and Ocie Norma (Talbott) Turner; B.S. in Elem. Edn., Alderson Broaddus Coll., 1941; postgrad. U. Akron, 1967; m. Elwood Combs, July 26, 1941; children—Sheridan Lee, Sheron Maureen. Elem. tchr. Milroy Sch., Akron, Ohio, 1953-79; salesperson Wm. Kay Realty Co., Akron, 1957—. Recipient award Martha Holden Jennings Found., 1966; Valley Forge Freedom Found. award, 1978. Mem. NEA (life), Ohio Edn. Assn. (life), Internat. Reading Assn. (life), Am. Bus. Women's Assn. (pres. 1979-80, Summit chpt. Woman of Yr. 1980), AAUW, Am. Golf Assn., Women's Internat. Bowling Congress, Kappa Kappa Iota (local pres. 1972, state pres. 1973, 74, nat. officer 1976), Akron Symphony Women's Guild. Presbyterian. Clubs: Coll. (Akron); Univ. Home: 652 Lakemont Ave Akron OH 44314

COMDEN, BETTY, writer, lyricist, performer; b. Bklyn., May 3, 1919; d. Leo and Rebecca (Sadvoransky) Comden; student Bklyn. Ethical Culture Sch., Erasmus Hall High Sch.; B.S., N.Y. U.; m. Steven Kyle, Jan. 4, 1942; children—Susanna, Alan. Performer, writer nightclub act Revuers. Writer book and lyrics (with Adolph Green) Broadway shows On the Town, 1944-45, Billion Dollar Baby, Two on the Aisle, Bells are Ringing, Fade-Out—Fade-In, Subways are for Sleeping, On the 20th Century (2 Tony awards), 1978, A Doll's Life, 1982; lyrics Wonderful Town, Peter Pan, Say, Darling, Do Re Mi, Hallelujah, Baby!; book for Applause; screen plays for Good News, Barkleys of Broadway, Band Wagon, Singing in the Rain, Auntie Mame; screenplay and lyrics for Bells are Ringing, On The Town, It's Always Fair Weather, What a Way to Go; A Party (performed with A. Green in show of their works), 1959, 77; also appeared in On the Town, 1972; lyricist, dir. (with Adolph Green) Lorelei, 1973. Recipient Donaldson award and Tony award for Wonderful Town, as co-lyricist best score, 1953; Tony award for Hallelujah, Baby, as co-writer best score, 1968; Tony award for Applause, 1970. Mem. Dramatists Guild (council). Office: care The Dramatists Guild 234 W 44th St New York NY 10036

COMET-EPSTEIN, SHARON, coll. adminstr.; b. Cleve., Oct. 25, 1950; d. Sol S. and Fay (Shochet) Comet; B.S. cum laude, Ohio State U., 1972; M.S., Case Western Res. U., 1974, postgrad., 1974—; m. Robert E. Epstein, Sept. 1, 1974; children—Adam Scott, Rachel. Instr., Columbus Jr. Theatre Arts, summer 1971; instr., designer allied health scis. Ohio State U., Columbus, 1971-72; ednl. project dir. Sch. Dentistry Case Western Res. U., Cleve., 1972-76, dir. ednl. resources and public affairs, 1976—, sr. instr., 1980—; mgmt. cons., 1982—. Recipient 2d place award Health Scis. Communications Assn., 1974. Mem. Women in Communications, Health Scis. Communications Assn., Am. Assn. Dental Schs., Profl. and Instructional Devel. Assn. Northeast Ohio, Pi Lambda Theta. Jewish. Clubs: Hasassah, ORT. Editor, Focus, 1975—, Off The Cusp, 1976—. Office: 2123 Abington Rd Cleveland OH 44106

COMFORT, IRIS TRACY, author; b. Racine, Wis.; d. Arnold Thomas and Iva (Dorothea) Tracy; student U. Minn., U. Wis.; m. James D. Comfort, Apr. 19, 1941; 1 son, Alain James. Reporter, St. Paul Dispatch, 1939-40; mem. public relations staff Allis-Chalmers Co., Milw., 1941-45; editor-in-chief Chgo. edit Where mag., 1945-46; owner, operator public relations agy., Milw. and Chgo., 1947-49; freelance writer, 1950—; author: Let's Grow Things, 1967; Let's Read About Rocks, 1968; Joey Tigertail, 1974; Echoes of Evil, 1978; Shadow Masque, 1981; owner wildlife sanctuary, Lake Helen, Fla., 1970—. Mem. Mystery Writers Am., Nat. League Am. Pen Women, Nat. Speleological Soc., Spiritual Frontiers. Address: 2902 Oxford St Orlando FL 32803

COMINI, ALESSANDRA, educator, author; b. Winona, Minn., Nov. 24, 1934; d. Raiberto and Megan (Laird) Comini; B.A., Barnard Coll., 1956; M.A., U. Calif., Berkeley, 1972; Ph.D., Columbia U., 1979. Teaching asst. U. Calif., Berkeley, 1964, vis. instr., 1967; vis. asst. prof. Yale U., New Haven, 1973; preceptor Columbia U., N.Y.C., 1965-66,

1967-68, instr., 1968-69, asst. prof., 1969-74; vis. asst. prof. So. Meth. U., Dallas, 1970, 72, assoc. prof., 1974-75, prof. art history, 1975—; lectr. to various orgns., 1972—. Alfred Hodder fellow Princeton U., 1972-73. Mem. ASCAP, Coll. Art Assn. Am. (Charles Rufus Morey Book award 1976), Women's Caucus for Art, Assn. Central European Art Studies. Democrat. Author: Schiele in Prison, 1973; Egon Schiele's Portraits (Nat. Book award nominee 1975), 1974; Gustav Klimt, 1975; Egon Schiele, 1976; The Fantastic Art of Vienna, 1978; The Changing Image of Beethoven: A Study in Myth-Making, 1982. Home: 2900 McFarlin Dallas TX 75205 Office: Art History Dept Southern Meth Univ Dallas TX 75275

COMISKEY, DONNA JEAN ARNDT, social worker, human devel. ofcl.; b. Hazleton, Pa., Aug. 26, 1949; d. Paul William Stein and Lucille Jane (Albano) Arndt; B.A. in Sociology, St. Francis Coll., Loretto, Pa., 1971; M.S.W., Marywood Coll., Scranton, Pa., 1975; postgrad. Temple U., Phila., 1978, Menninger Found., Topeka, 1979; m. Walter Phillip Comiskey, Aug. 4, 1973; children—Jeffrey Scott, Lisa Sue. Phys. medicine and rehab. vol. Perry Point VA Hosp., Md., 1965-68; caseworker trainee, child welfare (Md.), 1970; caseworker trainee Cresson State Sch. Hosp. (Pa.), 1970-71; community and residential caseworker Dept. Public Welfare, White Haven (Pa.) Center, 1971-73; social worker, criminal justice trainee Dallas (Pa.) State Correctional Inst., 1973-74; psychiat. social worker trainee VA Hosp., East End, Wilkes Barre, Pa., 1974-75; mental retardation, devel. disability specialist Hazleton-Nanticoke Mental Health/Mental Retardation Center, Nanticoke, Pa., 1975-78, dir., 1978—; field instr. social work program Coll. Misericordia, Dallas, Pa.; pres. Comiskey Enterprises, Larksville, Pa. Active Cath. War Vets. Aux., 1969—, Luzerne County Vocat. Rehab. Task Force, 1979—. Recipient Juliette Low World Friendship award, internat. Girl Scout ambassador and participant Experiment in Internat. Living, Australia, 1967; grantee, Bur. of Correction, Pa. Dept. Justice, 1973-74, VA Rehab., 1974-75. Mem. Acad. Cert. Social Workers, Nat. Assn. Social Workers, Assn. for Retarded Citizens, Am. Assn. on Mental Deficiency, Alpha Delta Mu, Alpha Psi Omega. Roman Catholic. Coordinator, presentor, facilitator workshops in field; radio, TV, film panelist, conf. panelist. Home: 445 Carver St Larksville PA 18651 Office: W Washington St Nanticoke PA 18634

COMPTON, MARY BEATRICE BROWN (MRS. RALPH THEODORE COMPTON), public relations exec., writer; b. Washington, May 25, 1923; d. Robert James and Abie Eliza (Stone) Brown; grad. Thayer Acad., Chandler Sch., Leland Powers Sch. Radio, TV and Theatre, Boston, 1942; m. Ralph Theodore Compton, Mar. 18, 1961; stepchildren—Ralph Theodore, Patricia (Mrs. William R. Schnitzler). Radio program dir. Converse Co., Malden, Mass., 1942-45; head radio continuity dept. Sta. WAAB, Yankee Network, Worcester, Mass., 1945-46; asst. dir. radio Leland Powers Sch. Radio, TV and Theatre, Boston, 1946-49, dir., 1949-51; program asst. Sta. KNBH, Hollywood, Calif., 1951-52; v.p. Acorn Film Co., Boston, 1953-54; dir. women's communications, editor Program Notes, radio interviewer NAM, 1954-61; cons. on women's communications to N.Y. advt. agys., 1961—. Celebrities pub. relations Nat. Citizens for Nixon, 1968. Mem. Montgomery County Art Assn., Smithsonian Assos., Sch., Soc. Old Plymouth Colony Descs., Magna Carta Dames. Club: Congressional Country (Bethesda, Md.). Home: Watergate at Landmark Apt 807 203 Yoakum Pkwy Alexandria VA 22304

COMPTON, MARY FRANCES, educator; b. Paris, Tenn., July 3, 1931; d. William Thomas and Lena Mai (Smith) C.; B.S., George Peabody Coll., Nashville, 1953; M.A., 1960; Ed.D., U. Fla., 1967. Tchr., prin. Fla. schs., 1953-64; research asso. U. Fla., 1964-67; mem. faculty U. Ga., Athens, 1967—, asso. prof. middle sch. edn., 1972-82, asso. prof. curriculum and supr., 1982—; cons. in field. Mem. Nat. Middle Sch. Assn. (pres. 1981-82), Assn. Supervision and Curriculum Devel., Am. Ednl. Research Assn., Ga. Middle Sch. Prins. Assn. (hon. life), Phi Delta Kappa. Democrat. Episcopalian. Author articles in field. Home: 119 Canterbury Dr Athens GA 30606 Office: 124 Aderhold Hall U GA Athens GA 30602

COMPTON, MARY GAIL, immunologist; b. Balt., Oct. 14, 1946; d. Nicholas Ernest and Marjorie Mary (Simon) Sylvester; B.S. magna cum laude, U. Md., 1981; m. Robert Compton; children—Robert, Karen. Mem. lab. staff Greater Balt. Med. Center, 1970—, tech. supr. immunology/coagulation, 1976-80, supr. immunology/coagulation, 1980—, also chmn. pathology intradeptl. edn. com., chmn. records retention com. Mem. Am. Soc. Clin. Chemists, Am. Soc. Clin. Pathologists (affiliate). Democrat. Roman Catholic. Home: 3101 Brandon Hunt Ln Baldwin MD 21013 Office: 6701 N Charles St Towson MD 21204

COMRAS, REMA, library dir.; b. N.Y.C., Oct. 26, 1936; d. Manuel and Zita (Kessel) C.; B.A., U. Fla., 1958; M.L.S., Syracuse (N.Y.) U., 1960; m. Jose Simonet, June 22, 1981. Librarian, Queensborough (N.Y.) Pub. Library, 1960-61, Spl. Services, U.S. Army, W.Ger. and France, 1962-64; asst. head librarian City of Hialeah (Fla.), 1964-73, library dir., 1973—. Mem. ALA, Fla. Library Assn., Beta Phi Mu. Office: 190 W 49th St Hialeah FL 33012

COMSTOCK, PATRICIA HAMILTON, sch. food service adminstr.; b. Gary, Ind., Sept. 26, 1926; d. Robert Crow and Roma Jane (Earnest) Hamilton; student Milw.-Downer Coll., 1946-48; B.S., Purdue U., 1951; m. Jess Adamson Comstock, Sept. 1, 1955; children—Thomas Edward, Janeann, Robert Andrew. With Swift & Co., St. Louis, 1952-54, Chgo. and Atlanta, 1954-55; asso. home demonstration agt. La. Agrl. Extension Service, New Orleans, 1955-56; with New Orleans Public Schs., 1958-73, supr., 1973-74, asst. dir. food services dept., 1974—. Mem. New Orleans Dietetic Assn., La. Dietetic Assn., Am. Dietetic Assn. (registered dietitian), New Orleans Sch. Food Service Assn., La. Sch. Food Service Assn., Am. Sch. Food Service Assn. (cert. specialist), New Orleans Home Econs. Club, Internat. Food Service Exec. Assn. (cert.). Democrat. Episcopalian. Author tng. manual. Home: 4910 Music St New Orleans LA 70122 Office: 4300 Almonaster St New Orleans LA 70126

COMTOIS, MARY ELIZABETH, educator; b. Pitts., Mar. 14, 1927; d. Walter R. and Helen M. (Jones) Hart; B.A., Wellesley Coll., 1948; postgrad. Royal Acad. Dramatic Art, London, 1948-50; M.A., San Francisco State U., 1961; Ph.D., U. Colo., 1970; m. Richard J. Comtois, Nov. 21, 1961; children—Katherine Ann, Elizabeth Josephine. Casting dir. Young & Rubicam, Inc., N.Y.C., 1950-53; co-founder, mgr. Group 20 Players Inc. of Mass., 1953-55; play and story editor Kermit Bloomgarden Prodns., N.Y.C., 1955-60; instr., lectr. San Francisco State U., 1961-64, 70; chmn. theater arts dept. Mason Gross Sch. Arts Rutgers U., 1970—. Mem. Dramatists Guild, Am. Theatre Assn. Author: Contemporary American Theater Critics, 1977; The Accident (play), 1979. Home: 110 N 5th Ave Highland Park NJ 08904 Office: Theater Arts Department Mason Gross School of the Arts Rutgers University New Brunswick NJ 08904

CONAGHAN, DOROTHY DELL, state legislator; b. Oklahoma City, Sept. 24, 1930; d. John Joseph and Wilhelmina Elizabeth (Boyer) Miller; student U. Okla., 1949-51; m. Brian Francis Conaghan, June 10, 1951 (dec. Apr. 1973); children—Joseph Lee, Charles Alan, Roger Lloyd. Mem. Okla. Ho. of Reps., 1973—minority caucus sec., 1977-82, asst. minority leader, 1983-84. Bd. dirs. Alpha II, Community Liaison Council Juvenile Services, Ponca City, Okla.; pres. Washington Sch. PTA, Tonkawa, 1965; vice chmn. Kay County Republican Com., 1960-64, 6th Dist. Congl. Rep. Com., 1967; del. Rep. Nat. Conv., 1968. Recipient Women Helping Women award Ponca City Soroptimist Club, 1975, hon. mem., 1978. Mem. Nat. Order Women Legislators, Am. Legis. Exchange Council (state dir.), Tonkawa C. of C., Am. Legion Aux., P.E.O., Beta Sigma Phi (hon.). Mem. Christian Ch. (Disciples of Christ). Clubs: Delphi Study, Order Eastern Star (past matron). Office: Room 541 State Capitol Bldg Oklahoma City OK 73105

CONANT, DORIS KAPLAN, sculptor, civic worker, real estate developer; b. Phila., Apr. 28, 1925; d. Benjamin A. and Rae (Shander) Kaplan; B.A., U. Pa., 1945; postgrad. U. Havana, 1945, Art Inst. Chgo., 1962; m. Howard R. Conant, Dec. 14, 1947; children—Alison, Howard, Meredith Ann. One man shows Glenview Public Library, Northbrook Library,; exhibited in group shows Art Inst. Chgo. Sales and Rental Gallery, Design Unlimited, New Horizons in Sculpture, Old Orchard Art Fair, Lake Forest Coll. Exhbn. Sec. to consul Argentine Consulate, Phila., 1945-47; sec., dir. Interstate Steel Co., Des Plaines, Ill., 1948—; organizer proposed 1st Women's Bank Chgo.; dir. Upper Ave. Nat. Bank, Chgo., 1976-81; pres. Urban Innovations Ltd., Loftworks Two. First pres. ERA Ill.; mem. Chgo. Network. Recipient Glenview Brotherhood award, 1965; named one of outstanding women P.U.S.H., 1975. Club: Carlton. Home: Glenview IL also 180 E Pearson St Chicago IL 60611

CONANT, GLORIA A., state legislator; b. Syracuse, N.Y., Jan. 14, 1926; student Burlington Bus. Coll.; widow; 4 sons, 2 daus. Dir., Milk Promotion Services, Inc., Champlain Valley Milk Producers Coop, Fed. Land Bank and Prodn. Credit Assn.; mem. Vt. Ho. of Reps., 1979-80, 81—; chmn. Gov.'s Agrl. Adv. Bd. Mem. Vt. Council, U. Vt.; bd. govs. Med. Center Hosp. Vt.; mem. Vt. Travel Adv. Council; chmn. Richmond Zoning Bd. Adjustment, 1974-78; mem. Richmond Planning Commn., 1962-72. Mem. Chittenden County Bus. and Profl. Women. Roman Catholic. Office: Vt Ho Reps State House Montpelier VT 05602 *

CONANT, MARY PLACIDA, hosp. adminstr.; b. Modesto, Calif., Apr. 5, 1910; d. Daniel Frederick and Magdaleine Anne (Kaal) C.; grad. St. Mary's Coll. Nursing, San Francisco, 1931; B.S., San Francisco Coll. Women, 1936. Joined Sisters of Mercy, Roman Catholic Ch., 1931; nursing supr., instr. St Mary's Coll. Nursing, San Francisco, 1936-42, dir. nursing, 1942-52, receptionist, 1982—; adminstr. Notre Dame Hosp., San Francisco, 1952, St. Joseph's Hosp., Phoenix, 1953-65, Mercy Hosp. and Med. Center, San Diego, 1965-74, exec. dir., 1974-77; adminstr. Mercy Hosp., Bakersfield, Calif., 1976-82; bd dirs. Notre Dame Hosp., San Francisco, 1952-53; pres. bd. dirs. St. Joseph's Hosp., Phoenix, 1953-65, Mercy Hosp., San Diego, 1965-77, Mercy Hosp., Bakersfield, 1976-82. Recipient Disting. Pub. Service award Maricopa County (Ariz.) Med. Soc., 1962; Disting. Leadership and Service award NCCJ, 1972; Disting. Service award Comprehensive Health Planning Assn. San Diego and Imperial County, 1976; Cert. of Recognition Calif. State Legislature, 1977; Recognition award City of San Diego, 1977; registered nurse, Calif., Ariz. Fellow Am. Coll. Hosp. Adminstrs. Home: 2215 Truxtun Ave Bakersfield CA 93301

CONAWAY, JANE ELLEN, educator; b. Fostoria, Ohio, July 9, 1941; d. Robert and Virginia Conaway; B.A. in Elem. Edn., Mary Manse Coll., Toledo, 1966; M.Ed. in Elem. Edn., U. Ariz., Tucson, 1969; postgrad. in Reading, U. Toledo, 1975—. Tchr. Sandusky (Ohio) public schs., 1966-67, Bellevue (Ohio) City Schs., 1969-70; coordinator 1st grade small group instrn. program St. Marys Grade Sch., Sandusky, 1970-71; tchr. Title 1 remedial reading Eastwood Local schs., Pemberville, Ohio, 1971—, also dist. dir. Right to Read program. Mem. NEA, Ohio, Eastwood edn. assns., Ohio, Martha Weber Local reading assns., Ohio Assn. Gifted Children, Toledo Area Assn. for Gifted, Delta Kappa Gamma. Cert. as reading supr., reading tchr., Ohio; specialist in diagnostic and remedial reading. Home: 2615 Eastwood Dr Sandusky OH 44870 Office: 4800 Sugar Ridge Rd Pemberville OH 43450

CONAWAY, ROSEANNE, med. technologist; b. Charleroi, Pa., Apr. 22, 1952; d. Ardil Michael and Joan (Bruno) Zanardelli; B.A., Calif. State Coll., 1972; med. tech. Western Pa. Hosp., 1974; m. Jason Conaway, Dec. 18, 1971; children—Jeremy Michael, Jennifer Marie. Med. technologist Brownsville (Pa.) Hosp., 1974-80, quality control technologist, 1980—. Sec., California Police Wives Aux., 1975-76. Cert. med. technologist. Mem. Pa. Soc. Med. Technologists, Am. Soc. Clin. Pathologists. Home: 757 Hickory St California PA 15419 Office: 125 Simpson Rd Brownsville PA 15417

CONCEPCION, ELSA SIGAYA, med. technologist; b. E.B. Magalona, Negros Occidental, Philippines, June 12, 1938; came to U.S., 1969, naturalized, 1972; m. Sofronio Lagaran Concepcion and Madalena (Sigaya) Concepcion; B.S. in Agr., U. Philippines, 1961; Cytotechnologist, Brooke Gen. Hosp., 1971. Researcher, Hamunganya Experiment Sta., Liganes, ILoilo, Philippines, 1962; tchr. Bur. Edn., Div. Negros Occidental, 1962-69; plant pathologist Hydro Farms, Inc., Winters, Calif., 1970; cytotechnologists 6th Army Area Lab., Ft. Baker, Calif., 1972-75; med. technologist reference lab. Letterman Army Med. Center Presidio of San Francisco, 1975—. Served with U.S. Army, 1970-74. Mem. Am. Soc. Clin. Pathologists, Farm Bur. of Calif., Am. Soc. Cytotechnologists. Roman Catholic. Home: 7555 Geary Blvd 202 San Francisco CA 94121 Office: Dept Pathology Reference Lab Letterman Army Med Center Presidio of San Francisco CA 94129

CONDELL, YVONNE CORKER, biologist; b. Quitman, Ga., Aug. 29, 1931; d. Draughty Rawlin and Gwendolyn Cecil (Harvey) Corker; B.S., Fla. A&M U., 1952; M.A., U. Conn., 1958, Ph.D., 1965; m. James F. Condell, July 15, 1952. Tchr. biology, public schs., Ft. Lauderdale, Fla., 1955-57; tchr. sci., public schs., Underwood, Minn., 1958-60; instr. in biology Minn. Community Coll., Fergus Falls, 1960-65; instr. biology and multidisciplinary studies Moorhead State U., 1965-68, asst. prof., 1968-80, asso. prof., 1980—; mem. panel judges Bush Leadership Program, Bush Found., St. Paul; mem. program rev. com. Office Nuclear Waste Isolation, Dept. Energy; vis. scientist Minn. Acad. Sci. Bd. dirs. Plains Art Museum, Moorhead, 1968-82, United Way, Moorhead, 1972-78, Red River Valley Mental Health Assn., Fargo, N.D.-Moorhead, 1980—. Named Outstanding Vol., AAUW and Germaine Monteil, 1975; recipient Women Helping Women award Moorhead Internat., 1982; Bush Leadership fellow, 1974; AAUW Yvonne C. Condell Am. fellow established, 1982. Mem. AAAS, Minn. Acad. Sci., NEA, Fargo-Moorhead Women's Sci. Assn., AAUW. Methodist. Contbr. articles to profl. jours.; editor: Nuclear Energy: What's the Score?, 1977. Office: Moorhead State U Moorhead MN 56560

CONDIT, MARTHA OLSON (MRS. MILTON ARMSTRONG CONDIT), ednl. cons.; b. East Orange, N.J., Sept. 8, 1913; d. Olof and Ida Christina (Johnson) Olson; certificate Pratt Inst., 1934; B.A., Rutgers U., 1953, M.L.S., 1958; supervisor's certificate Montclair State Coll., 1971; m. Milton Armstrong Condit, June 17, 1944. Children's librarian, pub. libraries, Nutley, N.J., 1936-43, Passaic, N.J., 1943-45, East Orange, 1945-56; sch. librarian Montclair (N.J.) Pub. Schs., 1956-65, coordinator media services, 1965-72, cons. media services, 1973. Mem. coadj. staff Sch. Edn., Rutgers U., 1961-62, Grad. Sch. Library Service, 1962-64; cons. Scholastic Book Services, 1963—, Elementary Sch. Library Collection, Mayor's Com., Montclair, N.J. Cable TV, 1973; v.p. Cable Car Playhouse, West Orange, N.J. Mem. ALA, Am. Assn. Sch. Librarians, Essex County Sch. Librarians (pres. 1961). Presbyterian (elder). Club: Operetta (life) (Montclair, N.J.). Author: Something to Make, Something to Think About, 1975; Easy to Make, Good to Eat, 1976; Koala, 1981. Contbr. articles to profl. jours. Home and Office: 17 Lincoln Ave Florham Park NJ 07932

CONDON, KATHLEEN A., pension cons.; b. Worcester, Mass., Aug. 29, 1948; d. William and Dorothy H.; A.B., Mt. Holyoke Coll., 1970; M.B.A., N.Y. U., 1973. With Bankers Trust Co., N.Y.C., 1970—, mgr. investment process cons. group, 1977-79; v.p. and mgr. employee benefit cons. sect., 1979—. Bd. dirs. Inst. Quantitative Research in Fin. Mem. N.Y. Soc. Security Analysts, Inst. Chartered Fin. Analysts. Author articles in field. Office: 280 Park Ave New York NY 10017

CONDON, MARIE POWERS, state legislator; b. North Bennington, Vt., June 21, 1927; d. Michael Francis and Marion (Church) Powers; A.B. in English, U. Vt., 1949; m. Robert Condon, June 21, 1949; children—Robert P., Kate C. Owner, operator New Englander Motor Inn, Bennington, Vt., 1955-78; mem. Vt. Ho. of Reps., Montpelier, 1981—. Pres., Bennington Day Care Center, 1968-70; mem. Vt. Bd. Edn., 1974-80; mem. Bennington Democratic Com. Mem. Vt. Women's Polit. Caucus. Quaker. Clubs: Bennington Garden, Bus. and Profl. Women's. Home: 10 Main St North Bennington VT 05257

CONDON, MAYBETTE ZUPKO, speech pathologist; b. Yonkers, N.Y., Oct. 16, 1948; d. George Arthur and Mae Theresa Zupko; B.S., U. Bridgeport (Conn.), 1970; M.S., So. Conn. State Coll., 1972. Tchr., Valley Regional Assn. Retarded Children and Adults, Derby, Conn., 1971-74; sr. speech pathologist Derby Bd. Edn., 1973-78; speech pathologist Stamford (Conn.) Bd. Edn., 1980—. Co-chmn. socials Monroe (Conn.) Republican Town Com., 1979; mem. Monroe Pres.'s Council. Mem. U. Bridgeport Alumni Assn. (dir. 1978—, edn. council 1979-80, v.p. student affairs 1980), Am. Speech and Hearing Assn. (cert. clin. competency), Conn. Speech and Hearing Assn., Conn. Council of Speech, Lang. and Hearing Coordinators, Council Exceptional Children, AAUW, NEA, Derby Edn. Assn. Roman Catholic. Club: Jr. Women's (pres. 1979-80). Home: 144 Richards Dr Monroe CT 06468

CONE, MARTHA CAROLINE, TV prodn. co. exec.; b. Columbus, Ohio, Apr. 11, 1933; d. Francis Edward and Freda Katherine (Ehlers) Clymer; student Ohio State U., 1951-52; children—Denise Danielle Buyaky, David Douglas DeVoe. Asst. to program mgr. Sta. WLW-C-TV, Columbus, Ohio, 1952-53, Sta. WBNS-TV, Columbus, 1953-55; dir. women's programming Sta. WPTA-TV, Ft. Wayne, Ind., 1963-65; asst. to dir. press/publicity Sta. KNBC-TV, Los Angeles, 1965-69; comml. mgr. Lawrence Welk Show, Don Fedderson Prodns., Los Angeles, 1971-77; mgr. syndication ops. West Coast, Goodson-Todman Prodns., Los Angeles, 1977—. Res. police officer City of Burbank (Calif.), 1979; vol. Burbank Community Hosp. Republican. Club: Foothill Civitan (Burbank, Calif.). Office: 6430 Sunset Blvd Los Angeles CA 90028

CONE, MOLLY ZELDA, author; b. Tacoma, Oct. 3, 1918; d. Arthur A. and Frances Dorothy (Sussman) Lamken; student U. Wash., 1936-38; m. Gerald J. Cone, Sept. 9, 1939; children—Susan, Gary, Ellen. Advt. copy writer, co-dir. Cone Mail Advt., Seattle, 1944-46; author 37 books, 1960—, including Mishmash series, 1962, 63, 65, 68, 76, 81, 82; A Promise Is a Promise, 1964; Annie Annie, 1969; Number Four, 1972; Dance Around the Fire, 1974; Call Me Moose, 1978; The Amazing Memory of Harvey Bean, 1980. Recipient numerous awards, 1966—, including Matrix Table honor award Women in Communications, Inc., 1968, 1st place juvenile book award for Simon, Nat. Fedn. Press Women, 1970, Shirley Kravitz Children's Book award Assn. Jewish Libraries, 1973. Mem. Authors Guild, Soc. Children's Book Writers, Seattle Free Lances. Address: PO Box 1005 Suquamish WA 98392

CONE, VIRGIE HORNE HYMAN (MRS. EDWARD E. CONE), former educator, civic worker; b. Brooksville, Fla.; d. George G. and Virgie (Horne) Hyman; B.S., Fla. State Coll. Women, 1945; M.Ed., U. Fla., 1956; m. Edward Elbert Cone, Dec. 20, 1930 (dec. Feb. 1962); children—Molly Gentile, Edward Elbert. Tchr., Meml. Jr. High Sch., Hillsborough County, 1929-31; tchr. Duval County Robert E. Lee Sr. High Sch., Jacksonville, Fla., 1943-55, dean, 1955-70; prin. Lee High Sch. (1st woman secondary sch. prin. in county), 1971-74; owner Cone's Antiques. Chmn., ARC night vols. St. Vincent's Hosp., 1969-71; mem. task force Mayor's Community Planning Council, 1969; pres. Hamilton County unit Am. Cancer Soc., 1974-76; v.p. Hamilton County Meml. Hosp. Aux., 1975-76; mem. adv. council Health and Rehabilitative Services, Dist. 3, Fla.; dir. Area Agy. on Aging, 1977-82, bd. dirs., 1982—; del. White House Conf. on Aging, 1981; mem. adv. council Social Security; pres. North Fla. Mental Health Bd., 1978-80; mem. Hamilton County Planning Council, Gov.'s Commn. on Status Women; exec. bd. North Central Fla. Health Planning Council, 1979—. Mem. Fla. Council Tchrs. Math. (curriculum chmn. 1952, sec. 1949), AAUW (Jacksonville v.p. 1953), Duval Tchrs. Assn. (chmn. profl. rights and responsibilities com. 1965-66), Jacksonville Panhellenic Assn. (pres. 1959-60, mem. scholarship com. 1963-68), Duval Personnel and Guidance Assn. (organizing chmn. 1966-69), Nat., Fla. assns. secondary prins., Hamilton Ret. Tchrs. (pres.), Fla. Assn. Area Agy. Dirs. (pres.), Delta Kappa Gamma (chpt. pres. 1959-61), Sigma Kappa (nat. scholarship chmn. 1963-77). Clubs: Pilot of Jacksonville, Suwannee Valley Country (dir. 1978-80). Home: NW 3d St Jasper FL 32052

CONFINO, SHIRLEY ROSE LEWIS, interior designer; b. Albuquerque, Oct. 20, 1940; d. Benjamin Milton and Lena (Abrin) Lewis; B.A. magna cum laude, Queens Coll., 1977; diploma N.Y. Sch. Interior Design, 1973; div.; children—Steven Howard, Lizabeth Dara. With Aluminium Ltd., 1959-62; ind. artist, Queens, 1963-64; owner Ideas Unltd., Queens, 1970-79, Shirley Confino Interiors, Norfolk, Va., 1980—; tchr. Norfolk Vocat. High Sch. Bd. dirs. Tidewater Jewish Community Center, 1981—, Cultural Experiences, 1981—; co-founder L.I. chpt. Dysautonomia Found., 1972. Mem. Am. Soc. Interior Designers, Bus. and Profl. Women, Women in Constrn., Women's Forum, Norfolk C. of C. Office: 2210B Hampton Blvd Norfolk VA 23517

CONFORTI, CAMILLE, advt. exec.; b. Chgo., Jan. 21, 1944; d. John and Connie C.; B.Mus., North Central Coll., Naperville, Ill., 1966; cert. advt. specialist U. Houston; 1 son, Laddie Fromelius. Exec. sec. Bell Labs., Naperville, 1966-67; co-owner mason contracting co., 1969-79; account exec. CK & Assos., mktg. and advt., Naperville, 1979—; pvt. piano instr., 1966-74. First v.p. North Central Coll. Community Concert Assn., 1979-80; mem. President's Club, North Central Coll. Mem. North Central Coll. Alumni Assn. (dir.), Sigma Alpha Iota (chpt. pres. 1965-66, pres. alumnae chpt. 1977-80; Sword of Honor 1977). Home: 25W431 Johnson Dr Naperville IL 60540 Office: 216 S Washington St Naperville IL 60540

CONGER, ROWENA GAIL, savs. and loan assn. exec.; b. Parkersburg, W.Va., Apr. 10, 1929; d. Wesley and Tura Ann (Price) Reed; student public schs.; m. Lester LeJeune Conger, Feb. 15, 1948; children—Brenda Diane Conger Brown, Michael LeJeune. With First Fed. Savs. & Loan Assn., Parkersburg, 1956—, controller, 1961, treas., 1963-80, mgr. customer service dept., 1963—, v.p., 1981—. Bd. dirs. Parkersburg YWCA, 1950-54; sec. Sparettes Bowling League, 1958-60; treas. Bethel Pl. Homeowners Assn., 1978-81. Mem. Nat. Soc. Controllers and Fin. Officers of Savs. Instns., W.Va. Fin. Mgrs. Assn. (sec.-treas. 1963-67, v.p. 1980-81), Nat. Assn. Female Execs., Women's Internat. Bowling Congress. Democrat. Baptist. Clubs: Eagles Aux., Altrusa. Home: 62

Bethel Pl Washington WV 26181 Office: First Fed Savs and Loan Assn 8th and Avery Sts Parkersburg WV 26101

CONGRESS, ELAINE PILLER, psychiat. social worker; b. Hartford, Conn., Feb. 14, 1942; d. Arthur John and Marion Frances (Luree) Piller; B.A. magna cum laude (Elisha Benjamin Andrews scholar), Brown U., 1963; M.A. in Teaching, Yale U., 1964; M.S. in Social Work (VA fellow), Columbia U., 1969; M.A. in Psychology, New Sch. Social Research, 1974. Secondary sch. tchr., 1964-65; caseworker Conn. Welfare Dept., 1965-67; psychiat. social worker Luth. Med. Center Family Health Clinic, N.Y.C., 1969-72, clinic coordinator Mental Health Clinic, Bklyn., 1972—; field supr. social work Adelphi U., N.Y. U., Sch. Social Work Hunter Coll., 1978—; part-time therapist Washington Sq. Inst. Mental Health, 1975-78. Bd. dirs., sec. Greenwich and Perry St. Housing Corp. Mem. Nat. Assn. Social Workers (women's issues com. N.Y.C. chpt.), Acad. Cert. Social Workers, Phi Beta Kappa. Co-author: The Clinic, 1980. Office: 514 49th St Brooklyn NY 11220

CONIGLIO, FAITH BOULT, social worker; b. Sault Ste. Marie, Mich., Apr. 19, 1926; d. James Ben and Grace Anne (Corrigan) Boult; A.B., U. Mich., 1948; M.S.W., U. Denver, 1952; m. Gioacchino Charles Coniglio, Sept. 1, 1951; children—Gina Mari, Giuli Anna. Social worker Sedgwick County Welfare Bd., Wichita, Kans., 1949-50; psychiat. social worker Topeka (Kans.) State Hosp., 1952-56; social worker Youth Center at Topeka, 1973-78, social work supr., 1978—. Kans. Bd. Social Welfare grad. scholar, 1950-51; NIMH grantee, 1951-52. Mem. Nat. Assn. Social Workers (charter). Office: 1440 NW 25th St Topeka KS 66608

CONKLIN, CARA LOUISE MCMILLAN, educator; b. Riverdale, Md., Oct. 19, 1924; d. Norman Ellis and Josephine Owens (Purdy) McMillan; diploma Milw. Bible Inst., 1948; B.S., Milw. State Tchrs. Coll., 1950; M.A., U. Minn., 1967; m. John Davis Conklin, June 13, 1959 (dec.). Tchr. of deaf Mpls. Public Schs., 1950-59; tchr. orthopedically handicapped, blind and deaf Gillette State Hosp., St. Paul, 1959-62; supervising tchr. Minn. Sch. for Deaf, Faribault, 1962-79; itinerant tchr. hearing impaired Minn. River Valley Spl. Edn. Coop., New Prague, 1979—. Faribault Family YMCA Big Sister, 1976—; vol. tchr. Bible classes for deaf children, 1951-77. Cert. tchr. elem. deaf students Council Edn. of Deaf. Mem. Minn. Edn. Assn. (pres. spl. tchrs. sect. 1965-66), Alexander Graham Bell Assn. for Deaf, Am. Instrn. of Deaf, Council Exceptional Children (state dir. 1962-66), AAUW, Minn. Fedn. Bus. and Profl. Women's Clubs (state 1st v.p. 1979-80, pres. 1980-81). Club: Faribault Woman's (pres. 1976-77). Faculty editor Companion, 1975-79. Home: 1155 S Willow St Faribault MN 55021 Office: 405 1st Ave NW New Prague MN 56071

CONKLIN, CAROL MARIE, automotive exec.; b. Jamaica, N.Y., Dec. 7, 1931; s. Raymond Jerome and Caroline Veronica C.; student U. Detroit, 1949-51, LL.B., 1955. Admitted to Mich. bar, 1955; sr. title officer Lawyers Title Ins. Corp., 1972; dep. atty. in charge real estate for legal staff Gen. Motors Corp., 1974-77, sec., N.Y.C., 1978—; sec. Gen. Motors Acceptance Corp., 1977. Honoree nat. bd. YWCA First Tribute to Women in Internat. Industry, 1978. Mem. ABA, Am. Soc. Corp. Secs., Inc., Mich. Bar Assn., Kappa Beta Pi. Office: 767 Fifth Ave New York NY 10153

CONKLIN, LYNN SUMMERS, EDP co. exec.; b. Balt., Feb. 4, 1936; d. Harry Ricks and Doris Louise (Sturm) Summers; A.A., Valencia Community Coll., 1981; B. G.S., Rollins Coll., 1982; children—Vicky Lee, David Travis. Office mgr. Norrell Temporary Service, Winter Park, Fla., 1976-77, clerical div. mgr., 1977-79; office systems supr. Martin Marietta Data Systems, Orlando, 1979-80, office automation system adminstr., 1980—; lectr. in field. Mem. Internat. Info. Word Processing Assn., Nat. Assn. Exec. Females, Gamma Phi Beta. Home: 5888 Peregrine Ave Orlando FL 32805 Office: 5401 Kirkman Rd Orlando FL 32805

CONLAN, SISTER MARY SAMUEL, educator; b. San Francisco, Mar. 10, 1927; d. Samuel Leo and Gertrude Margaret (O'Brien) Conlan; B.A., Dominican Coll., 1948; M.A., Cath. U. Am., 1957; Ph.D., Stanford, 1963. Tchr., 1952-57; mem. faculty Dominican Coll., San Rafael, Cal., 1957—, acad. dean, 1967-68, pres., 1968-80, prof. English, 1980—. *

CONLEY, CAROLYN PATTON, accountant; b. Detroit, Mar. 5, 1944; d. Carl D and Roberta Jean (Kennedy) Patton; B.B.A., Wichita State U., 1966, M.S., 1967; m. Norman Eddy Conley, Nov. 19, 1967; 1 son, Sean Peter. Mem. audit staff Fox & Co., C.P.A.s, Wichita, 1967-69; controller Central Computing Inc., Wichita, 1969-70, Campus Activity Center, 1970-72, Inst. Logopedics, 1972-74; mgr. mgmt. services George U. Landis C.P.A., Wichita, 1974-76; tax analyst Dynatax div. Tymeshare, Wichita, 1976-78; pvt. practice acctg., Wichita, 1978—. Mem. Commn. Status of Women, 1975-81, pres., 1976; bd. dirs. Historic Wichita, 1981—, sec.-treas., 1982-83; bd. dirs. YWCA, 1978—, treas., 1978—; campaign treas., local polit. campaigns; treas. Wichita Free U., 1981-83. Mem. Nat. Assn. Women Bus. Owners (pres. 1982-83), Adminstrv. Mgmt. Soc. (membership chmn. 1981-82, v.p. fin. 1982-83), Nat. Assn. Accts., Am. Inst. C.P.A.s, Kans. Soc. C.P.A.s. Clubs: Sports Car Am. (treas. dir.; Midwest div. Class A Rallye champion, 1974, 75, 76). Address: 2916 W 21st St Wichita KS 67203

CONLEY, FRANCES KRAUSKOPF, neurosurgeon, educator; b. Palo Alto, Calif., Aug. 12, 1940; d. Konrad Bates and Kathryn (McCune) Krauskopf; B.A., Stanford U., 1962, M.D., 1966; m. Philip Conley, July 5, 1963. Intern, Stanford U. Hosp., 1966-67, resident, 1967-75; chief sect. neurosurgery Palo Alto Veterans Hosp., 1975—; asst. prof. neurosurgery, Stanford U., 1975-81, asso. prof., 1981—; mem. Dist. VII Med. Quality Rev. Com. State of Calif., 1976—; mem. adv. panel neurol. devices FDA, 1978—, chmn., 1980-81. Fellow ACS; mem. Calif. Assn. Neurol. Surgeons, Am. Assn. Neurol. Surgeons, Congress Neurol. Surgeons, Am. Spinal Injury Assn., Santa Clara County Med. Assn. Office: Division Neurosurgery Stanford University School Medicine Stanford CA 94305

CONLEY, MARJORIE TAYLOR, constrn. co. exec.; b. Chgo., Nov. 14, 1920; d. Myron DeLoss and Margaret Elizabeth (Heppner) Taylor; grad. Walton Coll. Commerce, Chgo., 1939; m. Robert John Kostka, July 4, 1942 (div. 1963); children—Beverly Kostka Elk (dec.), Kent Allen, Kurt Stanton; m. 2d, George L. Conley, Jr., Mar. 13, 1964. Exec. sec. Jackson & Curtis and Boettcher & Co., Chgo., 1940-42; office mgr., asst. sec.-treas. Redwood Empire Savs. & Loan Assn., Petaluma, Calif., 1952-59; asst. indsl. advt. mgr. Fluor Corp., Santa Rosa, Calif., 1959-60; exec. v.p., mng. officer Bear Flag Builders Control Co., Santa Rosa, 1960-64; co-owner Conley Constrn. Co., Santa Rosa, 1964-75; sec.-treas. Conley Homes, Inc., Santa Rosa, 1975—, Timberidge Enterprises, Inc., 1975—, Highland House, Inc., 1975—. Mem. Women in Constrn. (charter pres.), Las Rosas Bus. and Profl. Women's Club (past pres.), Santa Rosa C. of C., Congress for Community Progress, Building Industry Assn. (bd. dirs.), Credit Women (past pres.), Psi Sigma Alpha. Republican. Clubs: Soroptimist Internat. (past pres. Santa Rosa; regional gov., founder, dir. Soroptimist Founds., Inc.). Order Eastern Star (past gov. founder region). Home: 5174 Blank Rd Sebastopol CA 95472 Office: 3187 Coffee Ln Santa Rosa CA 95401

CONLEY, MARTHA BERNICE MCCLENNY, home economist; b. Zuni, Va., Sept. 25, 1944; d. Theodore Bernard and Portia Bernice (Wilson) McClenny; B.S., Hampton Inst., 1970; M.S., Va. Poly. Inst. and State U., 1972, Ph.D., 1979; Ed.S., George Washington U., 1974; 1 dau., Angela Yvette. Family specialist Coop. Extension Service, Petersburg, Va., 1972-73; asst. prof. home econs. Norfolk (Va.) State U., 1974-80; research asst. Va. Poly. Inst. and State U., Blacksburg, 1976-78; project dir. Norfolk Adolescent Pregnancy Prevention and Services Project, 1980; mem. state task force Va. Conf. on the Family. Pres., Ivor (Va.) PTA, 1972-73; active polit. campaigns, Human Relations Council, 1970-72, Boosters Club, 1979. Served with USAF, 1963-64. Recipient Betty Crocker award, 1970, Va. Home Econs. grad. student award, 1977, Outstanding Ednl. Achievement award Little Gilfield Bapt. Ch., 1979; Office of Edn. fellow, 1973. Mem. Va. Council Family Relations, Nat. Council Family Relations, Southeastern Council Family Relations, Va. Home Econs. Assn., Am. Home Econs. Assn., Tidewater Assembly Family Life, Tidewater Council Human Sexuality, Tidewater Childcare Assn. Baptist. Club: Eastern Star. Author: Kidstuff, 1976; Motivation for Parenthood, Need Perception and Romantic Love: A Comparison Between Pregnant and Nonpregnant Teenagers, 1979, others. Mem. editorial bd. Family Relations jour. Home: 1030 Bryce Ln Virginia Beach VA 23464 Office: 2401 Corprew Ave Norfolk VA 23504

CONLEY, MYRA ANN, bus. exec.; b. Ft. Wayne, Ind., Jan. 23, 1939; d. Elvin Edwin and Etheldra Marie (Schultz) Rehklau; B.S., Purdue U., 1973; student Christian Coll., Columbia, Mo., 1957-58, St. Francis Coll., 1969, Ind. U. Purdue U., Ft. Wayne, 1969-72; children by previous marriage—Scott David Gilliom, Steven Lee Gilliom. Corp. sec. Reliable Stores, Inc., Reliable Oil, Inc., and Rehklau Realty, Inc., Ft. Wayne, 1963-78; pvt. practice speech pathology, Ft. Wayne, 1975—; pres. More Prodns., Inc., Ft. Wayne, 1981—. Vol., Allen County Cancer Soc., 1974-77. Mem. Ft. Wayne Bd. Realtors, Nat. Assn. Realtors, Ind. Assn. Realtors, Ind. Speech and Hearing Assn., NE Ind. Speech Pathologists, Council Exceptional Children, Am. Bus. Woman's Assn. Clubs: Ft. Wayne Woman's, Order Eastern Star.

CONLIN, PATRICIA PETERS, bank exec.; b. Santa Monica, Calif., Sept. 17, 1943; d. John Dennis and Dorothy Amanda (Tydeman) Peters; B.A. in econs. Magna Cum Laude, Cornell U., 1965; M.A. in econs., Stanford U., 1966; m. John W. Conlin, Sept. 20, 1980. With Morgan Guaranty Trust Co. of N.Y., N.Y.C., 1966—, asst. treas., 1968-70, asst. v.p., 1970-73, v.p., 1973—. Dir. Public Devel. Corp. City of N.Y. Mem. Phi Beta Kappa. Club: Mid-America (Chgo). Office: 23 Wall St New York NY 10015

CONLIN, ROXANNE BARTON, lawyer; b. Huron, S.D., June 30, 1944; d. Marion William and Alyce Muraine (Madden) Barton; B.A. (Readers Digest scholar), Drake U., 1964, J.D. (Fischer Found. scholar), 1966, M.P.A., 1979; m. James Clyde Conlin, Mar. 21, 1964; children—Jacalyn Rae, James Barton. Admitted to Iowa bar, 1966; asso. firm Davis, Huebner, Johnson & Burt, Des Moines, 1966-67; dep. indsl. commr. State of Iowa, Des Moines, 1967-68, asst. atty. gen., 1969-76; U.S. atty. for So. Dist. Iowa, Des Moines, 1977-81. Mem. Iowa Commn. on Status of Women, 1972-77. State chmn. Iowa Women's Polit. Caucus, Des Moines, 1973-76, del. nat. steering com. 1973-77; mem. adminstrv. com. Nat. Women's Polit. Caucus, 1975-77; nat. committeewoman Iowa Young Democrats, pres. Polk County Young Dems., 1965-66; del. Iowa Presdl. Conv., 1972. Named to Iowa Women's Hall of Fame, 1981. Mem. Am. (mem. individual rights and responsibilities com. 1971-79), Iowa (mem. career day panel 1971-76, mem. bar rev. com. 1972-73) bar assns., Women's Equity Action League, NOW (dir. 1969), Phi Beta Kappa, Alpha Lambda Delta, Chi Omega (Social Service awards), Pi Alpha Delta. Office: Suite One Stephens Bldg Des Moines IA 50309

CONN, (TISHIE) LOUISE, mfg. co. exec.; b. Beaumont, Tex., Jan. 18, 1931; d. John Calvin and Lillie Mae (Wood) Smith; B.B.A., Tex. State Coll. for Women, 1952; postgrad. U. Houston, 1968-69, Nat. Inst. Credit, 1973-76; m. Robert C. Conn, June 16, 1948; children—Constance E. Conn Garnett, Robert C., Debra E., Preston D. With Gen. Electric, Houston, 1955-60; with Living Windows Corp., Houston, 1962—, personnel mgr./office mgr., 1966, dir./corp. sec. and credit mgr., 1968, dir./corp. sec. and adminstrv. asst. to pres., 1978, dir., 1st v.p., chief fin. officer, 1981—. Pres., Houston Credit Women Group, 1967-68; pres. PTA, Matzke Elem. Sch., 1968-69; team capt. surrogate speaker Jack Heard for Mayor, Houston, 1981; mem. Houston Livestock Show Com., 1979-81; sec. Future Farmers of Am., Cypress Creek, 1979. Recipient Presdl. award Houston Assn. Credit Mgmt., 1968. Mem. Nat. Credit Women's Assn. (exec. com. vice chmn.), Houston Assn. Credit Mgmt. (dir. 1977-80), Houston C. of C., Bus. and Profl. Women. Republican. Baptist. Clubs: Future Farmers Am., Order Eastern Star, Boosters, Petticoat Pilots Houston. Home: 1923 Mayweather Ln Richmond TX 77496 Office: 13211 Old Westheimer St Houston TX 77082

CONNALLY, ALMA VIRGINIA SHAFFER, freight co. ofcl.; b. Torrance, Calif., May 28, 1935; d. Eugene Robert and Marion Evelyn (Famous) Shaffer; B.S., Utah State U., 1956; m. Joseph M. Connally, Jr., June 17, 1961 (div. Aug. 1971); 1 son, David McClain. Sec. to pathologist, also med. asst.-sec. to plastic surgeon, 1956-58; sec. to pres. Tex. Woman's U., 1958-61, Gen. Telephone Co. of Wis., 1964-67; office mgr. archtl. firm, 1961-62; secretarial position ETMF Freight System, Dallas, 1970-79, staff asst., mktg. and sales, 1979-81, staff asst. for ops., 1981—; chmn. bd. East Tex. Motor Freight Employees Fed. Credit Union, 1979—. Mem. com. on mgmt. for girls adventure trails program YWCA; chmn. pack com. Circle 10, Boy Scouts Am.; judge Jr. Achievement, Dallas. Cert. profl. sec. Mem. Profl. Secs. Internat. (Sec. of Yr., Big D chpt. 1973), Traffic Clubs Internat., Unitarian-Universalist Women's Fedn., Unitarian-Universalist Assn., Nat. Wildlife Fedn., Women's Alliance of Dallas. Club: Women's Transp. (Dallas). Office: ETMF Freight System 2355 Stemmons Freeway PO Box 10125 Dallas TX 75207

CONNALLY, CATHERINE EVERETT, fin. cons.; b. Middletown, Conn., July 28, 1956; d. Aaron and Mary (Rogolino) Everett; B.S., U. Colo., Boulder, 1977; m. Kenneth Edward Connally, Aug. 14, 1982. Internal auditor to sr. auditor Atlantic Richfield Co., Denver, 1978-81; on-site audit supr. Brit. Petroleum Alaska Exploration, San Francisco, 1981-82; pres. Connally Cons., Little Rock, 1982—. Cert. internal auditor. Mem. Inst. Internal Auditors, Little Rock C. of C., Republican. Home: 11 Old Forge Ct Little Rock AR 72207 Office: 2024 Arkansas Valley Dr Suite 807 Little Rock AR 72212

CONNELL, SUZANNE (SPARKS) MCLAURIN, ret. librarian; b. Bennettsville, S.C., Sept. 12, 1917; d. John Bethea and Aleine (McLeod) McLaurin; A.B., Woman's Coll. of U. N.C., 1938; A.B. in L.S., U. N.C., 1940; 1 son, John Alexander (dec.). Library asst. Mt. Pleasant br. D.C. Pub. Library, Washington, 1940-41; post librarian Camp Sutton, N.C., 1943-44; post librarian McGuire Gen. Hosp., Richmond, Va., 1945-46, chief librarian McGuire VA Hosp., 1946-52, 59-62; chief librarian VA Hosp., Lake City, Fla., 1952-56; cataloger, chief books acquisitions, chief books circulation, asst. chief documents acquisitions Air U. Library, Maxwell AFB, Ala., 1956-59; head extension, head circulation Greensboro (N.C.) Pub. Library, 1962-63; reference librarian, asst. and acting base librarian Marine Corps Base, Camp Lejeune, N.C., 1963-66; part time cataloger Wilmington (N.C.) Pub. Library, 1967-75; now hist. researcher, author, vol. worker. Mem. ALA (pres. assn. hosp. and instn. libraries 1955-56), N.C., Southeastern library assns., Phi Beta Kappa. Contbr. articles to Brit. and Am. periodicals. Home: 502 Brunswick St Southport NC 28461

CONNELLY, CLAIRE ANNCHILD, writer, editor; b. Bklyn., Sept. 16, 1935; d. Harry Joel and Edith Ann (Egelhofer) Spatz; B.A., Eastern Conn. State Coll., 1976; cert. in graphic arts N.Y. U., 1965; cert. in computer programming Manchester Community Coll., 1981; 1 son, Christopher. With Hartford (Conn.) Times, 1974-78; staff, freelance writer Sales Mgmt. mag. McGraw-Hill Book Co., 1964-68; legis. analyst, tech. writer Travelers Ins. Co., Hartford, 1979—; freelance editor. Candidate for Conn. State Legislature, 1982; mem. Windham Regional Planning Agy., 1980—, Coventry Planning and Zoning Commn., 1978-82. Mem. Soc. Tech. Communication, Nat. Assn. Ins. Women, NOW, Humane Soc. U.S. Club: Travelers Women's. Contbr. numerous articles to newspapers and mags. Home: 232 Plains Rd Coventry CT 06238

CONNELLY, DORRIS DAWN, real estate exec.; b. Abilene, Tex., Jan. 6, 1934; d. Thomas Armour and Roberta Mae Patterson; B.Mus., Hardin Simmons U., Abilene, 1955; M.R.E., Southwestern Baptist Theol. Sem., Ft. Worth, 1958; M.Mus., New Orleans Bapt. Theol. Sem., 1965; m. James M. Connelly, Nov. 6, 1979; children—Renee Annette, Amara Dawn. Head music dept. Mexican Bapt. Bible Inst., San Antonio, 1966-68; music editor Crescendo Music Publns., Dallas, 1968-70; pres. Postlude and Psaltry Music Pub. Co., Dallas, 1970-78; real estate broker ERA Hughes D'Angelo Inc., Dallas, 1978—. Mem. Nat. Assn. Realtors, Tex. Assn. Realtors, Greater Dallas Bd. Realtors, Am. Guild Piano Tchrs., Broadcast Music Inc., John Birch Soc. Republican. Baptist. Club: D.A.C. Country. Composer choral works, arranger works for womens voices. Home: 800 Via Altos Mesquite TX 75150 Office: 130 Casa Linda Plaza Dallas TX 75218

CONNELLY, ELIZABETH ANN, state legislator; b. Bklyn., June 19, 1928; d. John and Alice (Mallon) Keresey; grad. high sch.; m. Robert V. Connelly, Sept. 6, 1952; children—Alice, Robert, Margaret, Therese. Sales rep. Pan Am. World Airways, N.Y.C., 1946-54; mem. N.Y. State Assembly, 1974—, chairperson com. mental health, mental retardation/developmental disabilities, alcoholism and substance abuse, chairperson sub. drunk driving. Trustee, S.I. Hosp.; del. Democratic Nat. Conv., 1980; bd. govs. S.I. Inst. Arts and Sci. Mem. Nat. Order Women Legislators, S.I. Mental Health Soc., S.I. Amputee Club (hon. dir.), S.I. Bot. Garden Assn., S.I. Arts Council, Bus. and Profl. Women, N.Y. Women's Group for Soviet Jewry. Recipient numerous civic awards. Club: Pilot's. Home: 94 Benedict Ave Staten Island NY 10314 Office: Legislature Bldg Room 826 Albany NY 12248

CONNELLY, LINDA LEE, coll. info. specialist; b. Tacoma, Nov. 21, 1937; d. Norman J. and Dorothea Esther (Voorhies) Arrington; B.A., Western Wash. U., 1960, postgrad., 1980—; m. Ralph Stanton Connelly, Dec. 26, 1959; children—Colleen Tracy, Jeffrey Wayne. Tchr., Port Orchard and Tacoma Schs., 1960-63; feature writer Tacoma Rev., 1973-74; coordinator Mother's March, Tacoma-Pierce County March of Dimes, 1974-75; info. asst. Ft. Steilacoom Community Coll., 1975-78, public info. officer, 1978—; community coll. adv. Dist. VIII Conf., Council for Advancement and Support Edn., 1979-80. Exec. bd. March of Dimes, Tacoma, 1975-77. Mem. Nat. Council for Community Relations (dist. trustee 1980-81, nat. sec. 1981-82, v.p./pres.-elect 1982-83), Wash. Assn. Community Coll. Public Info. Officers, Wash. State Info. Council, Tacoma C. of C. (edn. com.). Clubs: Jr. Woman's of Tacoma (Clubwoman of Yr. 1973), Peninsula Fedn. Women's Clubs (dist. chmn. 1971-73), Veleda Federated Woman's (v.p. 1974), Tacoma Outboard Assn. Office: 9401 Farwest Dr SW Tacoma WA 98498

CONNELLY, LYNETTE MAXINE, jewelry co. exec.; b. Madison, Ill., Oct. 21, 1937; d. Theodore Alfred and Nettie Bell (Graham) Werner; student City U. N.Y.; divorced; children—Gregory, Monica, Kurt, Cheryl. With Foley's, Houston, 1972-75, buyer robe and loungewear, 1973-75; with Ciani Div., Monet Jewelers, N.Y.C., 1975—, exec. v.p., dir. ops., 1976-80, v.p., dir. merchandising Monet Jewelers, 1981—.

CONNER, CAROL MAE, nurse; b. Jamestown, N.Y., Sept. 21, 1933; d. Percy M. and Levina M. (Heminger) Barlow; Lic. Practical Nurse, Erie Sch. Dist. Practical Nursing, 1969; R.N., Hamot Hosp. Sch. Nursing, 1976; m. Clarence L. Conner, Dec. 5, 1953; 1 dau., Terry Ann. Telephone operator Bell Telephone, Erie, Pa., 1952-56; Practical nurse Hamot Med. Center, Erie, 1969-76, staff nurse, 1976-78, asst. head nurse telemetry unit, 1979—. Mem. Am. Assn. Critical Care Nurses. Democrat. Presbyterian. Home: 406 California Dr Erie PA 16505

CONNER, LOLA PHYLLIS (MRS. MERLIN L. CONNER), dept. store exec.; b. Grand Rapids, Mich., Feb. 5, 1930; d. Wesley Louis and Effie Mabel (Stephens) Crips; grad. Felt & Tarrant Comptometer Sch., 1950; m. Merlin L. Conner, Aug. 13, 1948; children—Kristi Louise, Robert Lee, Mary Lyn. Payroll clk. Keeler Brass, Grand Rapids, 1947-55; with Rogers Dept. Store, Wyoming, Mich., 1957—, dept. mgr., buyer, mdse. mgr., auditor, 1960—; fashion coordinator. Campfire, Bluebird leader, dist. chmn., 1955-65; mag. chmn. Wyoming High Sch. PTA, 1958-59, mother v.p., 1960-61; conducts style shows for charitable orgns., 1968—; bd. dirs. fashion mdse. and retail mgmt. Davenport Coll.; bd. dirs. Kent Skill Center Retail Marketing. Home: 2000 Melvin St Wyoming MI 49509 Office: 959 28th St SW Wyoming MI 49509

CONNERLY, DIANNA JEAN, office mgr.; b. Urbana, Ill., June 7, 1947; d. Ellsworth Wayne and Imogene (Sundermeyer) Connerly; student Ill. Comml. Coll., 1967. Bookkeeper, Jerry Earl Pontiac, 1968-72; officer mgr. Jack Nicklaus Pontiac, 1972-76; office mgr. Simon Motors Inc., Palm Springs, Calif., 1977—. Office: 78611 Highway 111 LaQuinta CA 92253

CONNERTH, WENDIE FAY, nurse; b. Chgo., Feb. 5, 1951; d. Willard Frederich and Alice Marie (Esnorff) Helsdon; A.A., Coll. of DuPage, 1973; Student North Central Coll., 1973-74; B.S., No. Ill. U., 1975, M.S., 1979, postgrad., 1980—; m. Robert William Connerth, Aug. 23, 1975; children—Mary Anna (dec.), Robert William (dec.), Clifton Morgan (dec.), Christian Daniel. Staff nurse Loyola Hosp., Maywood, Ill., 1973-77; staff nurse ICU, Westlake Hosp., Melrose Park, Ill., 1978-79; research technician U. Ill., Chgo. Ill. Sch. Nursing, 1979-80; clin. coordinator gynecology Mt. Sinai Hosp., Chgo., 1979-80; staff nurse Ill. Hosp. Assn. Med. Registry, 1979-81, Kimberly Nurses, 1982—, Suburban Hosp. and Sanitarium of Cook County, 1982—. Commentator, Be Healthy, It's Good For You, Sta. WGCI, 1980. Ill. State Scholarship Commn. grantee, 1969-73. Mem. Am. Nurses Assn., Ill. Nurses Assn. Republican. Christ Ch. Home: 771 S Chatham Elmhurst IL 60126

CONNERY, CAROL JEAN, ednl. adminstr.; b. Amarillo, Tex., Oct. 22, 1948; d. William Wayne and Joyce Jean (Forney) Connery; A.A., Christian Coll., 1969; B.J., U. Tex., Austin, 1971. Asst. dir. admissions Columbia (Mo.) Coll., 1971-80; exec. dir. nat. office Teenworld Scholarship Program, Overland Park, Kan., 1980—; cons. in field. Mem. C. of C. of Greater Kansas City, Johnson County Bd. Realtors, Kans. Bd. Realtors, Mid-Am. Soc. Assn. Execs., Zeta Tau Alpha. Methodist. Club: Columbia Coll. Alumni Assn. Office: 4550 W 109 St Suite 300 Overland Park KS 66211

CONN-LEVIN, NANCY BARBARA, health cons., sex educator; b. Newark, Mar. 16, 1952; d. Ralph Irving and Gertrude (Zacks) Conn; B.A., Sarah Lawrence Coll., 1974; postgrad. Princeton U., 1974-75; M.A., Goddard Coll., 1980; m. Eric M. Levin, Dec. 17, 1972; 1 dau., Amanda Conn-Levin. Cons. women's health, Manahawkin, N.J., 1976-80; cons. Ocean County Coll., CEA of Ocean County, Ocean County

NOW, Women's Counseling and Community Services, Childbirth Edn. Assn. Ocean County, La Leche League of Tuckerton, 1977-80, S.H.A.R.E. Center, Inc., 1982; dir. Health Info. Assos., Inc., Plantation, Fla., 1982—. Co-coordinator East Windsor (N.J.) NOW, 1974-75. Mem. Nat. Women's Health Network, Am. Public Health Assn., AAUW, Internat. Childbirth Edn. Assn., Cesaran Support Edn. Concern, Am. Personnel and Guidance Assn., Sex Info. and Edn. Council U.S., Am. Assn. Sex Educators, Counselors and Therapists. Compiler women's health info. and resources; cons. health info. Home: 9680 NW 11th St Plantation FL 33322 Office: PO Box 16323 Plantation FL 33318

CONNOLLY, ARLENE FRANCES, nurse; b. Groton, Mass., Nov. 25, 1930; d. Gerard Joseph and Mabel Frances (Connell) C.; B.S., Boston U., 1953, M.S., 1961, Ed.D., 1971. Mem. faculty Boston U. Sch. Nursing, 1961-78, chmn. gen. course unit grad. program, 1978-80, acting asst. dean grad. affairs, 1980-81, prof. nursing, prin. investigator Maine Outreach Project, 1980—; cons. Simmons Coll., Northeastern U., U. Lowell, Curry Coll. Mem. Am. Nurses Assn., Nat. League Nursing, Am. Assn. Higher Edn., AAUP, Sigma Theta Tau. Democrat. Roman Catholic. Author: Promotion of Physical Comfort and Safety, 1970; contbr. articles to profl. jours. Home: 60 Commerford Rd Concord MA 01742 Office: 635 Commonwealth Ave Boston MA 02215

CONNOLLY, LINDA LEE, ins. agt.; b. Wichita, Kans., Dec. 31, 1946; d. Keith Leroy and Zada Mae (Carlson) England; student Wichita State U., 1965-67; grad. Wichita Bus. Coll., 1965, South Jersey Profl. Sch. Ins., 1979; student Comml. Lines Sch., U. Nev., 1981; m. Jan. 6, 1968; children—Robert, Michael. Asst. office supt. 3M Corp., Englewood, N.J., 1970-71; v.p. Heritage Ins. Agy., Vineland, N.J., 1974—. Mem. Ind. Agts. Assn., Profl. Agts. Assn. Methodist. Club: Vineland Jr. Soccer League. Home: 1609 Wills Pl Vineland NJ 08360 Office: 606 Landis Ave Vineland NJ 08360

CONNOLLY, PATRICIA MARY, acctg. firm exec.; b. Bronx, N.Y., Feb. 17, 1932; d. Eugene Joseph and Mary Catherine (Travers) C.; B.S., St. Joseph's U., Phila., 1963; M.S.W., Fordham U., 1965. With Catholic Social Services, Phila., 1954-63, 65-66; supr. homemaking services Bronx (N.Y.) Cath. Charities, 1966-68; dir. South Bronx Project, 1968-72; cons. Fedn. Protestant Welfare Agys., 1972-81; asst. partner-in-charge govt.-edn.-med. services, adminstrv. mgr. Touche, Ross & Co., C.P.A.s, N.Y.C., 1981—; field instr. N.Y.U.; adj. lectr. Lehman Coll.; cons. in field. Bd. mgrs. Citizens Advice Bur.; Sec. Bowery Planning Task Force, 1973-76, V.p., 1977-79; mem. community adv. bd. Montefiore Hosp., N.Y.C.; mem. Neighborhood Com. Asphalt Green, Carl Schurz Park Assn. Mem. Acad. Cert. Social Workers, Nat. Assn. Social Workers, Fordham U. Alumni Assn., Nat. Assn. Female Execs., Am. Soc. Tng. and Devel., Greater N.Y. Com. Women and Alcoholism, Regional Coalition on Services to Women with Drug and Alcohol Problems. Author manuals, chpts. in books. Home: 75 East End Ave New York NY 10028 Office: 1 World Trade Center 93d Floor New York NY 10048

CONNOR, JUDITH TURNER, govt. ofcl.; b. Toronto, Ont., Can., Mar. 6, 1939; (parents Am. citizens); d. Harold M. and Esther Diana Turner; B.A., Wellesley Coll., 1961; M.B.A., Columbia U., 1965; m. James Edward Connor, June 30, 1972. With Pacific Telephone Co., San Francisco, 1965-68, Trans World Airlines, N.Y.C., 1968-69, Excalibur Assos., N.Y.C., 1969-71; policy adviser OEO, Washington, 1971; dir. bus. policy analysis Dept. Commerce, 1972; spec. asst. and acting chmn., urban transp. Adm., 1973-75; asst. sec. for environment, safety and consumer affairs Dept. Transp., 1975-77; dir. internatl. and reg. affairs, Pan Amer. World Airways, 1977-81; asst. sec. for policy and internatl. affairs, Dept. Transp. 1981—. Mem. Fed. Exec. Women Assn. Republican. Clubs: Capitol Hill, Gt. Cove Golf and Country. Office: Dept Transp 400 7th St SW Washington DC 20590 *

CONNOR, MARLENE, city fin. investigator; b. N.Y.C., Nov. 11, 1937; d. Marcellus and Vivian (Marsh) C.; B.B.A., Bernard M. Baruch Coll., City U. N.Y., 1979. Sr. auditor-investigator Office Spl. Prosecutor for Medicaid Fraud Control, N.Y. State Dept. Law, N.Y.C., 1978-80; sr. acct. Beth Israel Med. Center, N.Y.C., 1980-81; confidential investigator Office Insp. Gen., N.Y.C. Dept. Mental Health, 1981—. Mem. N.Y. State Soc. for C.P.A. Candidates. Office: 125 Worth St New York NY 10013

CONNOR, MARY ANNE, civic worker; b. Watertown, Wis., Aug. 18, 1930; d. Arthur Robert and Esther Florence (Mittag) Jaeger; student schs. Watertown; m. William Thomas Connor, Sept. 6, 1952; 1 dau., Mary Kay. Billing clk. Watertown Daily Times, 1955-72; machine operator, Owen Glove Lining, Watertown, 1973-75; office mgr. Feisst Liquor Co., Watertown, 1975-76; cook, Elks Club, Watertown, 1974—. Sec., Watertown Municipal Band, 1950—; pres. local chpt. Am. Legion Aux., 1959-61, 77-79, county pres., 1960-62, dist. pres., 1965-67, dist. bowling chmn., 1966—, WALA state bowling dir., tournament mgr., 1979—; corr. sec. Watertown Meml. Hosp. Aux., 1980-81, membership chmn., 1978-79, chmn. fund raiser, 1981; active Watertown Hist. Soc., St. Mark's Ladies Aid; bd. dirs., blood bank chmn. ARC, 1977—; exec. sec. Watertown chpt. ARC, 1981—, also mem. speakers bur.; chmn. Jefferson County Govt. Day, 1972—; vol. VA Hosp., Madison, Wis. Recipient plaques Am. Legion, 1977, 78. Mem. Watertown Women's Bowling Assn. Lutheran. Clubs: Saturday, Watertown VFW, Elks Ladies, Watertown Musicians Assn. Local 469 (rec. sec. 1977—), Wethonkitha, Oconomowoc Band. Home: 307 9th St Watertown WI 53094 Office: 314 Main St Watertown WI 53094

CONNORS, DORSEY (MRS. JOHN E. FORBES), TV and radio commentator, newspaper columnist; b. Chgo.; d. William J. and Sara (MacLean) Connors; B.A. cum laude, U. Ill.; m. John E. Forbes; 1 dau., Stephanie. Appeared on Personality Profiles, Sta. WGN-TV, Chgo., 1948, Dorsey Connors Show, Sta. WMAQ-TV, Chgo., 1949-58, 61-63, Armchair Travels, Sta. WMAQ-TV, 1952-55, Home Show, NBC, 1954-57, Haute Couture Fashion Openings, NBC, Paris, France, 1954, 58, Dorsey Connors program, Sta. WGN, 1958-61, Tempo Nine, WGN-TV, 1961, Society in Chgo., Sta. WMAQ-TV, 1964; floor reporter Sta. WGN-TV, Republican Nat. Conv., Chgo., Democratic Nat. Conv., Los Angeles, 1960; writer column Hi! I'm Dorsey Connors, Chgo. Sun Times, 1965—. Founder Ill. Epilepsy League; mem. women's bd. USO; mem. woman's bd. Children's Home and Aid Soc. Mem. AFTRA, Screen Actor's Guild, Nat. Acad. TV Arts and Scis., Soc. Midland Authors, Chgo. Hist. Soc., Chi Omega. Author: Gadgets Galore, 1953; Save Time, Save Money, Save Yourself, 1972. Office: Chgo Sun Times 401 N Wabash Chicago IL 60611

CONOLEY, JOANN SHIPMAN, ednl. adminstr.; b. Bartlesville, Okla., July 19, 1931; d. Joe and Frances Loomis (Wall) Shipman; B.S. in English and Edn., Midwestern State U., Wichita Falls, Tex., 1968, M.S. in English and Edn., 1971; m. Travis A. Conoley, Oct. 29, 1976; children by previous marriage—James F. Lane, Joe Scott Lane, Kimberly Diane Lane. Tchr. 3d grade Queen of Peace Sch., Wichita Falls, 1968-69; lang. arts team leader, jr. high sch. Wichita Falls Public Schs., 1969-74; fed. programs dir., reading coordinator Rockdale (Tex.) Public Schs., 1974-78, adminstrv. asst. to supt., 1978-79, asst. supt. adminstrn. and instrn., 1979—; reading cons. ALCOA, 1977—. Bd. dirs. Rockdale Public Library, 1975-79, pres., 1976-77. Cert. elem. tchr., reading tchr., reading/lang. arts coordinator, reading cons., adminstr., Tex. Mem. NEA, Tex. State Tchrs. Assn., Nat. Council Tchrs. English, Internat. Reading Assn., Assn. Compensatory Edn. Tex. (exec. bd. 1977—), Assn. Supervision and Curriculum Devel., Alpha Chi, Delta Kappa Gamma, Kappa Delta Pi. Home: 405 Bounds St Rockdale TX 76567 Office: Box 632 Rockdale TX 76567

CONOLY, DARLENE CROWELL, travel exec.; b. Glendale, Calif., Feb. 5, 1933; d. Dee Howell and Rose Mae (Whitley) Crowell; B.A., U. Tex., 1952; postgrad. U. Houston, Trinity U., U. Oreg., Bee County Coll.; children—Dona, Clay, Patrick. Owner, Darlene Conoly-Travel, Beeville, Tex.; co-owner Dixie Dude Ranch, Bandera, Tex. Vice pres. Beeville Ind. Sch. Dist., 1970-80; chmn. St. Philips Episcopal Sch., 1964-81; pres. Beeville Little Theater, 1981; mem. fine arts bd. Bee County Coll., 1976-81; bd. mem. Art Mus. South Tex., 1975-80, Japanese Art Mus., 1977, Boy's Club Beeville, 1978-80, Bee Community Action Agy., 1978-80, Community Concerts, 1965-81, Upjohn Health Service, 1981. Mem. Navy League Am., Bee County C. of C. (bd. mem. 1981-83). Episcopalian. Clubs: Rosetta (pres. 1969-70); Pan Am. Roundtable (dir. 1971). Home: 9 Country Club Pl Beeville TX 78102 Office: 110 N St Marys St Beeville TX 78102

CONOVER, NELLIE COBURN, retail furniture co. exec.; b. Lebanon, Ohio, Dec. 21, 1921; d. Frank C. and Isabel (Murphy) Coburn; student public schs.; m. Lawrence E. Conover, Jan. 11, 1941; children—Lawrence R., Carol, David C., Constance, Christina. Co-founder, 1949, since exec. sec.-treas. Larry Conover Furniture & Appliance, Inc., and predecessor, Milford, Ohio, also trustee co. pension fund. Mem. Milford C. of C., Cin. Hist. Soc., Milford Hist. Soc., DAR. Democrat. Roman Catholic. Address: 438 Main St Milford OH 45150

CONRAD, CAROLYN HOPE, educator; b. Denver, Oct. 22, 1932; d. Hans Frans and Laura (Breeden) Schuelke; B.A. in English, U. Tex., Arlington, 1966, M.A., 1974; m. Kenneth Earl Conrad, June 20, 1952 (div. May 1961); children—Anna Belle, Alexander Benjamin, Loralyn Faith. Tchr. English, Calhoun County Ind. Sch. Dist., Port Lavaca, Tex., 1966-67, Arlington (Tex.) Ind. Sch. Dist., 1970—; dir. programs and edn. Parents Without Partners, Internat., 1976-78. Mem. Democratic Nat. Com., 1978. Mem. NEA, Tex. Tchrs. Assn., Classroom Tchrs. Assn., South Central Renaissance Conf., AAUW, Delta Zeta. Baptist. Club: Arlington Bicycle. Home: 2119 Reever St Arlington TX 76010 Office: 2101 Browning St Arlington TX 76010

CONRAD, MARIAN RIDEOUT, elem. sch. tchr.; b. Salt Lake City, July 15, 1925; d. Lawrence Joseph and Lidy Henreitta (Sorensen) Rideout; B.S. in Edn., U. Utah, 1947; postgrad. U. Mo., U. Nev.; m. Charles Arthur Conrad, Aug. 27, 1946; children—Rae Lyn Conrad Burke, Lawrence Charles, Byron Rideout. Tchr. home econs., McClure, Ill., 1947-48; elem. sch. tchr. Washoe County Sch. Dist., Sparks, Nev., 1956-81; pres. Nev. Edn. Assn., 1981—. Vice chmn. Washoe County Democratic Central Com., 1976-78. Mem. NEA (dir. 1968-70, 75-81; Disting. Service award 1981), Nev. Edn. Assn., Washoe County Tchrs. Assn. (pres. 1964-66; Outstanding Leadership award 1965), Alpha Delta Kappa. Mormon. Office: 151 E Park St Carson City NV 89701

CONRAD, NANCY RIEDEL, painter, educator; b. Houston, Jan. 29, 1940; d. Alfred E. and Mildred S. (Schlafke) Riedel; B.A., Randolph Macon Woman's Coll., 1961; m. Friedrich Walter Conrad, Aug. 5, 1961; children—Jennifer Anne, Paul Barth. One woman shows: Marjorie Townley Gallery, Austin Tex., 1962, Houston Art and Frame, 1967, Montrose Gallery, Houston, 1968, 69, Erdon Gallery, Houston, 1971, 72, Canary Hill Galleries, Houston, 1973, Ars Longa Galleries, Houston, 1975; group shows include: Tex. Painters and Sculptors, Dallas Mus., 1971, Abilene (Tex.) Mus., 1975, Port Arthur (Tex.) Galleries, 1976, Blaffer Galleries, Houston, 1975-76, Internat. Women's Yr., 1977, Adelle M. Taylor Fine Arts, 1979, Women and Their Work touring exhbn., 1980-81; represented in permanent collections El Paso (Tex.) Mus., Harris County (Tex.) Library System, Randolph Macon Mus., Dresser Industries, Continental Oil Co. Recipient 1st prize Assistance League, 1973; competition awards S.W. Watercolor Soc., 1972, 73. Mem. Art League Houston (v.p. 1975), Mus. Fine Arts, Contemporary Arts Mus., Artists Equity Assn., Nat. Art Edn. Assn. Home: 819 Wade Hampton Houston TX 77024

CONRAD, REBECCA LOU, veterinarian; b. Hutchinson, Kans., June 7, 1957; d. Harold D. and Lillian Lucille (Davis) C.; B.S., Kans. State U., 1979, D.V.M., 1981. Resident radiologist Vet. Med. Center, Kans. State U., 1981-82, clin. instr., 1981—. Mem. Am. Animal Hosp. Assn., AVMA, Kans. Vet. Med. Assn., Phi Zeta. Office: Vet Med Center Radiology Kans State U Manhattan KS 66506

CONRARD, PATRICIA ANN, public info. specialist; b. Seattle, Dec. 9, 1947; d. Peter A. and Ann (Rohr) Hollinger; B.A., Seattle U., 1970; m. Donald J. Conrard, June 24, 1972. News reporter The Highline Times, Burien, Wash., 1970-72; public relations dir. Am. Heart Assn. of Wash., 1972-76; public info. specialist Bellevue (Wash.) Public Schs., 1976—. Recipient Pacific N.W. Bus. Communicators Assn. award of Excellence, 1978, award of Merit, 1976; First Place awards, Wash. Press Woman, 1974, 76. Mem. Wash. Press Women, Nat. Press Women, Women in Communications, Internat. Assn. Bus. Communicators, Nat. Sch. Public Relations Assn., Public Relations Soc. Am. Home: 12021 NE 67th St Kirkland WA 98033 Office: 310 102d Ave NE Bellevue WA 98004

CONSOLA, MARY FRANCES, actuary; b. Chgo., Aug. 29, 1946; d. Anthony Patsy and Mary Frances (Reilly) C.; B.A., Mundelein Coll., 1968. Actuarial student Globe Life Ins. Co., Chgo., 1968-73; John McLaughlin Cons. Actuary, Chgo., 1973-74; asst. v.p. support PolySystems, Inc., Chgo., 1974-80; asst. actuary Nat.-Ben Franklin Life Ins. Corp., Chgo., 1980-82; sr. actuarial programming analyst Am. Bankers Ins. Group, Miami, Fla., 1982—. Mem. Chgo. Council Fgn. Relations, Chgo. Hist. Soc., Chgo. Public TV, Chgo. Art Inst., Chgo. Arch. Found., Chgo. Actuarial Club. Roman Catholic. Office: 600 Brickell Ave Miami FL 33131

CONSTANT, RUTH LAVERN, nurse, educator; b. Port Arthur, Tex., Jan. 14, 1932; d. Carl Leon and Mary (O'Grady) Ellerbee; B.S. in Nursing, U. Tex., 1966, M.S. in Nursing, 1972; Ed.D., Tex. A and M U., 1982; m. George A. Constant, Apr. 16, 1971; children—Melinda, Jame Dewit, Rebecca. Exec. dir. Schlesingers Home Health Service, Beaumont, Tex., 1964-65; exec. v.p. Beaumont Home Health, Inc., 1969-79, pres., 1979—; exec. v.p. Port Authur Home Health, 1969—, also Sta. KAVU-TV; v.p., adminstrv. cons. Wichita Home Health, Wichita Falls, Tex., 1969; bus. mgr. Constant Clinic, Victoria, Tex., 1973—; dir. asso. degree nursing program Victoria (Tex.) Coll., 1975-78. Fellow Am. Coll. Nursing Home Adminstrs.; mem. Nat. (dir. 1970-77), Tex. (pres. 1970) assns. home health agencies, Am. Nurses Assn., Nat. League Nursing, Nat. Nursing Forum Adminstrs., Tex. Nursing Home Assn., Am. Acad. Med. Adminstrs., Nat. Public Relations Assn. Democrat. Methodist. Club: Pilot. Home: 2206 E Loma Vista Victoria TX 77901 Office: 2710 Hospital Dr Victoria TX 77901

CONTREARAS, DARLENE ROWELL, rancher; b. Seneca, Mo., June 16, 1926; d. Myrlen and Ada (Ruggles) Rowell; grad. high sch.; m. John L. Contreras, Feb. 15, 1957 (dec. 1978); children—Patricia, Pamela. Service rep. Pacific Telephone Co., 1955-66; bookkeeper Mobil Oil plant, Fairfield, Calif., 1967-75, distbr., 1978-81; rancher, owner, 1978—. Mem. Calif. Farm Bur. Fedn., Internat. Platform Assn. Address: 507 Buck Ave Vacaville CA 95688

CONWAY, IRENE RUNKLE, nursing home adminstr., acct.; b. York County, Pa., July 26, 1921; d. Paul Sylvester and Gertie Irene (Geisler) Runkle; m. Samuel A. Conway, Feb. 6, 1944; 1 son, Samuel A. Acct., Foreman Realty Corp., Chgo., 1948-51, S.A. Conway, D.C., Hanover, Pa., 1953-61; adminstr. Golden Age Nursing Home, Hanover, 1961—, bd. dirs., sec.-treas., 1961—; adv. com. practical nursing program Hanover Sch. Dist., 1970—; traveler South Africa and Rhodesia with group from Nat. Coll. of Chiropractic, Chgo., for public relations work Chiropractic Union of South Africa, 1972; traveler to Mex. with Am. Coll. Nursing Home Adminstrs., 1973. Active ARC, York County Hist. Soc., Conservation Soc. York County. Mem. Health Care Facilities Assn. of Pa., Am. Chiropractic Alumni Aux., Pa. Assn. of Drugless Physicians Aux. (pres., 1969-70), Nat. Coll. Chiropractic Alumni Aux. (charter), Hanover C. of C. (editing com. Hanover Penna. 1973), Lambda Chi. Democrat. Clubs: Order Eastern Star (Hanover chpt.), Soroptimist Internat. (1st. v.p. 1974-76, dir. 1971—). Home: 230 Primrose Ln Hanover PA 17331 Office: 267 Frederick St Hanover PA 17331

CONWAY, JILL KATHRYN KER, coll. pres.; b. Hillston, New South Wales, Australia, Oct. 9, 1934; d. William Innis and Evelyn Mary (Adames) Ker; B.A., U. Sydney (Australia), 1958; Ph.D., Harvard U., 1969; hon. degrees: U. N.B., 1974, Mt. Holyoke Coll., 1975, Amherst Coll., 1976, York U., Toronto, 1977, U. N.H., 1977, Westfield State Coll., 1979, Mt. St. Vincent U., Halifax, N.S., 1980, Wesleyan U., 1980, U. Mass., Amherst, 1981, Williams Coll., 1982; m. John James Conway, Dec. 22, 1962. Asst. prof. history U. Toronto (Ont., Can.), 1964-71, assoc. prof., 1971-75, v.p., 1973-75; pres. Smith Coll., Northampton, Mass., 1975—; dir. Center for Communication, Inc., 1980—; dir. IBM World Trade Ams./Far East Corp., Merrill Lynch & Co., Arthur D. Little, Inc. Trustee Hampshire Coll., Clarke Sch. for Deaf, William H. Donner Found., 1976-82 Acad. Music, Northampton, Coll. Retirement Equities Fund; bd. overseers Harvard U., 1976-82; bd. dirs. Council Fin. Aid to Edn., Inc., 1981—; 2d v.p. New Eng. Colls. Fund, Inc., 1981—; mem. nat. com. Nat. Resource Center for Girls Clubs Am., Inc., 1981—; mem. Ind. Sector, Washington, 1981—. Mem. Am. Antiquarian Soc., Am., Can. hist. assns., Assn. Ind. Colls. and Univs. in Mass. (vice chmn. 1982—). Research, numerous publs. on Am. social and intellectual history, history of family life and sex roles, history of edn. Office: Office of the President Smith Coll Northampton MA 01063

CONWAY, JOAN ELIZABETH BONNER, med. social worker; b. Balt., Aug. 29, 1920; d. James Michael and Elizabeth (Lukes) Bonner; B.A., Rosemont Coll., 1941; M.S. in Social Work (A.R.C. scholar 1943), Cath. U. Am., 1943; advanced cert. social work adminstrn. U. Pa., 1967, postgrad., 1967—; m. Thomas Agnew Conway, Jan. 6, 1968 (dec. July 1968). Med. social worker, then asst. casework supervisor ARC, 1943-48; psychiat. social worker VA, 1948-50; med. social worker U. Pa. Hosp., Phila., 1950-53, Misericordia Hosp., Phila., 1953-55; Albert Einstein Med. Center, Phila., 1957-58; dir. social service dept. Magee Meml. Hosp. for Convalescents Rehab. Center, Phila., 1958-71; dir. social service dept. Hosp. of U. Pa., 1971—. Tchr. history Collegio Americana. Caracas, Venezuela, 1956, Merici Acad., 1956-57. Mem. Council for Internat. Visitors Phila., 1957—; mem. St. Vincent's Aux., 1948—; mem. sch.-agy. relations com. U. Pa. Sch. Social Work, 1962-65; mem. rehab. com. S.E. Pa. chpt. Am. Heart Assn., 1972-74, bd. dirs. Main Line Council Alcoholism, 1961-67; mem. social work adv. com. Phila.-Montgomery County chpt. Am. Cancer Soc. Mem. Nat. Assn. Social Workers (charter mem., chmn. med. social work Phila. 1962-64, chmn. nat. com. local council relationship com. 1963-64, chmn. nominating com. 1964-66, 1st vice chmn. exec. com. 1971-73, chmn.-elect Phila. area chpt. 1973-74, chmn. 1974-76; Pa. dir. 1975—, chmn. state nominating com. 1979—, regional rep. nat. nominating com. 1979—), Am. Public Health Assn., Pa. Public Health Assn., Nat. Rehab. Assn., Pan Am. Assn., Alumni Assn. Cath. U. Am. (bd. govs. 1975—), Council on Social Work Edn. (ho. of dels. 1974—), Acad. Certified Social Workers, Rosemont Coll. Alumnae Assn. (rec. sec. 1964-66, pres. Phila. 1969-70, 2d v.p. gen. assn. 1971-74), Am. Hosp. Assn., Nat. Conf. on Social Welfare, Am. Soc. Hosp. Social Work Dirs. (charter mem., area rep. Phila. and Eastern Pa. region 1968-70, chmn. Phila. area chpt. 1971-73). Home: 603 Ballytore Rd Wynnewood PA 19096 Office: 34th and Spruce Sts Philadelphia PA 19104

CONWAY, KATHRYN LOUISE, univ. media adminstr.; b. Henry County, Va., Jan. 30, 1950; d. Richard Earl and Josephine Hope (Leftwich) C.; B.F.A., U. N.C., Chapel Hill, 1975, postgrad. in communication, 1980—, cert. univ. mgmt. devel. program, 1981; Advt. writer Sta. WTOB, Winston Salem, N.C., 1969; research asst. U. N.C., Chapel Hill, 1971, 73, photographer Photo Lab., 1974-75, asso. dir. Media and Instructional Support Center, 1976—, dir. telecommunications devel., 1982—; chairperson bd. Sta. WXYC-FM; mem. steering com., interim bd. dirs. N.C. Public Radio Assn.; lead actress Desperadoes, Pocket Theatre, off-off-Broadway, 1978, The Fate of my Joy teleplay Sta. WUNC-TV, Chapel Hill, 1978; mem. Chapel Hill Adv. Com. on Cable TV, 1979. Mem. Am. Mgmt. Assn. (cert. Fundamentals Data Communication), Am. Assn. Higher Edn., N.C. Ind. Film and Video Assn., Assn. Ednl. Communications and Techs. Democrat. Home: Route 7 Box 2 Chapel Hill NC 27514 Office: 07 Smith Bldg 128A Chapel Hill NC 27514

CONWAY, MARIE CORSO, mgmt. cons.; b. Bklyn., Dec. 10, 1949; d. Anthony and Sophie (Coraci) Corso; B.B.A., Bernard Baruch Coll., 1971; M.B.A., Adelphi U., Garden City, N.Y., 1976; m. John Conway, Aug. 16, 1980. Research asso. William E. Hill & Co., mgmt. cons., 1972-75; procedures analyst Doubleday & Co., 1975-76; cons. Robert Bell & Co., mgmt. cons., Balt., 1976-78, Irving Trust Co., N.Y.C., 1978-81; pres. Laiser Corp., N.Y.C., 1981—. Mem. Am. Soc. Profl. Cons. Republican. Roman Catholic. Home: 178 E Mineola Ave Valley Stream NY 11580 Office: 1 Wall St New York NY 10015

CONWAY, MARY E, nurse, educator, univ. adminstr.; b. Albany, N.Y., Nov. 4, 1923; B.S., Columbia U., 1947; M.N.A., U. Minn., 1958; Ph.D., Boston U., 1972. Prof., dean Sch. Nursing, Med. Coll. Ga., Augusta, 1980—; cons. Guyana Project, WHO, 1969, N.Y. State Dept. Civil Services, 1968-69; Gov.'s Adv. Council on Vocat. Rehab., N.Y. State, 1966-68; chmn. Nurse Adv. Council to selective Service System, 1966-68; cons. VA Hosp., West Roxbury, Mass., 1973-75; mem. peer rev. panel health resources adminstrn., Dept. Health and Human Services. Fellow Am. Acad. Nursing; mem. Am. Assn. Colls. Nursing, Am. Nurses Assn., Am. Sociol. Assn., Sigma Theta Tau. Author: (with Margaret Hardy) Role Theory: Perspectives for Health Professionals, 1978; (with O. Andruskiw) Administrative Theory and Practice: Issues in Higher Education in Nursing, 1983; mem. editorial bd. Jour. Research in Nursing and Health; contbr. articles to profl. jours. Office: Sch Nursing Med Coll Ga Augusta GA 30912

CONWAY, MAUREEN ANN, mgmt. cons.; b. Hoboken, N.J., July 25, 1945; d. Michael A. and Margaret (Spiegel) C.; B.A. William Paterson Coll., 1966; M.A., Montclair State Coll., 1971; M.B.A., Temple U., 1980. Tchr. math. high sch., Palisade Park, N.J., 1966-68; mem. tech. staff Bell Tel. Labs., Whippany, N.J., 1968-75; dir. info. systems IUIMC, Phila., 1975—. Bd. dirs. Penns Landing Sq. Condominium, 1977—. Mem. Am. Mgmt. Assn., Beta Gamma Sigma. Office: 1500 Walnut St Philadelphia PA 19102

CONWELL, ESTHER MARLY, physicist; b. N.Y.C., May 23, 1922; d. Charles and Ida (Korn) C.; B.A., Bklyn. Coll., 1942; M.S., U.

Rochester, N.Y., 1945; Ph.D., U. Chgo., 1948; m. Abraham A. Rothberg, Sept. 30, 1945; 1 son, Lewis J. Instr., Bklyn. Coll., 1946-51; mem. tech. staff Bell Telephone Labs., 1951-52; physicist GTE Labs., Bayside, N.Y., 1952-61; mgr. dept. physics, 1961-72; Abby Rockefeller Mauze prof. M.I.T., 1972; prin. scientist Xerox Corp., Webster, N.Y., 1972-80, research fellow, 1981—; vis. prof. U. Paris, 1962-63; mem. adv. commn. engring. NSF, 1978—. Fellow IEEE, Am. Phys. Soc. Author: High Field Transport in Semiconductors, 1967; mem. editorial bd. Jour. Applied Physics, IEEE, Nat. Acad. Engring.; contbr. numerous articles in field; patentee in field. Office: 800 Phillips Rd Webster NY 14580

COOK, ALICE E., social worker; b. Chgo., Mar. 2, 1951; d. Carl R. and Alice Jane (Forester) C.; B.A., U. Ill., Chgo., 1974; M.S.W., Loyola U., Chgo., 1977. Social worker, dir. after sch. program Erie House, Chgo., 1977-80, child care coordinator, 1980—; condr. workshops; dir. Bickerdyke Redevel. Corp., Humbolt Constrn. Co. Mem. Acad. Cert. Social Workers, Nat. Assn. Social Workers, Nat. Assn. Edn. Young Children, Chgo. Assn. Edn. Young Children (after sch. task force). Office: 1347 W Erie St Chicago IL 60622

COOK, CAROL ANN, univ. contracting officer; b. Bridgeport, Conn., Aug. 28, 1932; d. Anthony and Evelyn Mary (Oviatt) C.; B.S., Ga. State U., 1975, postgrad. in govtl. adminstrn. Asst. to dir. Yerkes Regional Primate Research Center, Atlanta, 1969-79; asst. dir. grants and contracts N.Mex. State U., Las Cruces, 1979; contracting officer Ga. Inst. Tech., Atlanta, 1979—; asst. to v.p. and gen. mgr. Ga. Tech. Research Inst. Mem. Feminist Alliance, 1978-79. Served with WAC, U.S. Army, 1959-63. Mem. Nat. Contract Mgmt. Assn., Soc. Research Adminstrs., Nat. Council Univ. Research Adminstrs. Roman Catholic. Club: Northwood Country. Home: 1614 Stonecliff Dr Decatur GA 30033 Office: Ga Inst Tech Office of Contract Adminstrn Atlanta GA 30332

COOK, DORIS MARIE, acctg. educator; b. Fayetteville, Ark., June 11, 1924; d. Ira and Mettie Jewell (Dorman) Cook; B.S. in Bus. Adminstrn., U. Ark., 1946, M.S., 1949; Ph.D., U. Tex., 1968; Staff acct. Haskins & Sells Tulsa, 1946-47; instr. acctg. U. Ark., Fayetteville, 1947-52, asst. prof., 1952-62, assoc. prof., 1962-69, prof., 1969—. C.P.A., Okla., Ark. Mem. Fayetteville Bus. and Profl. Womens Club (pres. 1973-74, 75-76, Woman of Yr. award 1977), Ark. Fedn. Bus. and Profl. Women's Clubs (chmn. found. com., 1975-77, treas. 1979-80), Ark. Soc. C.P.A.s (v.p., 1975-76, sec. student loan found. 1981—), Am. Acctg. Assn., (chmn. Ark. membership com. 1981-82, nat. chmn. membership com. 1982-83), N.W. Ark. Chpt. C.P.A.s, (pres. 1980-81), Am. Inst. C.P.A.s, Am. Womans Soc. C.P.A.s, Mortar Board, Beta Gamma Sigma, Beta Alpha Psi (mem. nat. council 1973-80, editor newsletter 1973-77, nat. pres. 1977-78, dir. regional meetings 1978-79), Phi Gamma Nu, Alpha Lambda Delta, Delta Kappa Gamma (chpt. pres. 1978-80), Phi Kappa Phi. Editor newsletter Ozarks Econ. Assn., 1982-85. Contbr. profl. jours. Home: 1115 Leverett St Fayetteville AR 72701 Office: Dept Acctg Univ Ark Fayetteville AR 72701

COOK, EVELYN BURNEY, former hosp. pharmacist; b. Langdale, Ala., May 7, 1920; d. Sylvanus Leonidus and Emma Eulalia (Meadows) Burney; B.S. in Home Econs., Auburn U., 1942, B.S. in Pharmacy, 1957, M.S., 1961; Ph.D. in Phys. Pharmacy (fellow, 1964-65), U. Fla., 1965; m. Glenn Draper, Sept. 1, 1942; children—Carolyn, Daniel G.; m. 2d, Edward A. Cook, June 16, 1968. Owner, mgr. retail pharmacy, Lanett, Ala., 1953-59; instr., asst. prof. coll. pharmacy, Auburn (Ala.) U., 1959-62; lab. instr., fellow, coll. of pharmacy U. Fla., Gainesville, 1962-65; asst. prof. coll. of pharmacy, U. S.C., Columbia, 1965-69; pharmacist Emory U. Hosp., Atlanta, 1970-79, Lanier Meml. Hosp., Langdale, Ala., 1979-80. Rec. sec. Dem. Women of DeKalb, 1974. Mem. Am. Pharm. Assn., Am. Public Health Assn., Ga. Pharm. Assn., Am. Assn. Hosp. Pharmacists, Ga. Assn. Hosp. Pharmacists, Drug Info. Assn., Sigma Xi, Kappa Epsilon, Phi Kappa Phi, Rho Chi. Methodist. Clubs: Breckenridge Garden (pres. 1975), Altrusa. Home: 93 Hamilton Dr West Point GA 31833

COOK, FRANCES D., ambassador; b. Charlestown, W.Va., Sept. 7, 1945; student Université d'Aix-Marseille, 1965-66; B.A., U. Va., 1967; M.P.A., Harvard U., 1978. With USIA (now ICA), Paris, 1967-69; spl. asst. to Ambassador Sargent Shriver, Jr., Paris, 1969-71; mem. U.S. del. to Vietnam treaty meetings, Paris; cultural affairs officer, Sydney, Australia, 1971-73, Dakar, 1973-75; fgn. service personnel officer, Washington, 1975-77; dir. Office of Public Affairs, Bur. African Affairs, U.S. Dept. State, 1978-80; apptd. fgn. service officer, 1980; U.S. ambassador to Burundi, 1980—. Mem. Am. Fgn. Service Assn. Club: Harvard. Office: US Embassy Chaussee Prince Louis Rwagasore BP 1720 Bujumbura Burundi

COOK, HELGA GISELA, chem. corp. exec. asst.; b. Koenigsberg, E. Prussia, Ger., June 12, 1941; came to U.S., 1964, naturalized, 1974; d. Albert and Maria (Wunderlich) Woelk; bi-lingual bus. grad. in English and French, Vorbeck Lang. Inst., W.Ger., 1959; 1 son, Raymond J. Sec. EDP div. U.S. Army, Pirmasens, 1959-62, Internat. Leather Exhbn., Pirmasens, 1962-63; with comml. div. Honeywell, Pitts., 1966-70; with Mobay Chem. Corp., Pitts., 1970—, pricing clk., mktg., 1970-71, bilingual exec. sec., polyurethane div., 1971-74, exec. asst. to pres. and chief exec. officer, 1974-81, to chmn. and pres., 1981—. Chpt. sec. Beaver-Lawrence-Butler County chpt. Muscular Dystrophy Assn., 1973-74; asso. Merrick Art Gallery, New Brighton. Mem. Am. Soc. Profl. and Exec. Women, Nat. Assn. Female Execs. Office: Penn Lincoln Pkwy W Pittsburgh PA 15205

COOK, JACQUELINE NELL, home economist; b. Mpls., Apr. 28, 1921; d. Findley Earl and Nelle Maude (Kingston) C.; B.S. in Textiles and Clothing, Iowa State U., 1942; M.S. in Family Living/Nutrition, Drexel U., 1965; children—Kingston Owens, Gregory Owens, Linell Owens. Tchr., chmn. home econs. Gt. Valley High Sch., Malvern, Pa., 1962-71; adminstr. diabetes clinic Soufriere, St. Lucia, W.I., 1974-76; asst. mgr. Money Savers Dept. Store, Levittown, Pa., 1976-77; home economist Coop. Extension Service, Pa. State U. and U.S. Dept. Agr., 1977—; woman's editor and commentator Sta. WDNH. Trustee Serendipity Day Care Center. Mem. AAUW, Pa. Extension Home Econs. Assn. (Radio Communications award 1979, 81), Pa. Wool and Sheep Growers Assn., Northeast Artisan's Guild, Woodland Weavers and Spinners Guild. Christian Scientist. Home: PO Box 662 Honesdale PA 18431 Office: Wayne County Extension Service Courthouse Honesdale PA 18431

COOK, JEANNINE SALVO (MRS. DONALD CARTER COOK), librarian; b. N.Y.C., Apr. 11, 1929; d. Ernest August and Edith Agatha (Lombardo) Salvo; A.B., Hunter Coll., 1951; M.L.S., Columbia, 1958, advanced library degree, 1973; m. Donald Carter Cook, June 9, 1962; 1 son, Carter Steven. Chemist, Charles Pfizer & Co., Inc., Bklyn., 1951-56; lit. chemist, 1956-58; central med. librarian Am. Cyanamid Co., N.Y.C., 1958-60; sr. profl. adminstr. Columbia U. Engring. and Phys. Scis. Library, N.Y.C., 1960-62; asso. librarian SUNY, Stony Brook, 1962-63; dir. Emma S. Clark Meml. Library, Setauket, N.Y., 1967—. Co-chmn. ednl. com. Assn. Community/Univ. Coop., 1973-76; exec. bd., personnel com. Community Youth Services, 1977—; bd. dirs. Three Village Community and Youth Services; mem. bd. council ministries Setauket United Methodist Ch. Mem. Adminstrs. Assn. Suffolk Coop. Library System (exec. bd.), Adminstrs. Assn. Brookhaven and Riverhead Public Libraries (pres.), ALA, Spl. Libraries Assn., Med. Library Assn., Am. Chem. Soc., LWV, Suffolk County Library Assn. (chmn. public libraries sect. 1978—), Public Library Dirs. Assn. Suffolk County (exec. bd. 1976—), Suffolk Coop. Library System Dirs. Assn. (co-chmn. budget com. 1975), Assn. for Coalition of Exceptional (bd. dirs.), Three Village Hist. Soc. (library com.). Methodist (trustee 1971-73). Home: 40 Seabrook Ln Stony Brook NY 11790 Office: 120 Main St Setauket NY 11733

COOK, LOIS JEAN, cosmetologist; b. Alamosa, Colo., Sept. 19, 1948; d. Harold L. and Betty J. (Jack) Workman; grad. Americana Beauty Coll., 1967; children—Marty Wayne, Tammy Lynn, Brent David. Hairdresser, House of Duke, Alamosa, 1971-76, propr., cosmetologist, 1976—; cons. various style-shows. Mem. Nat. Fedn. Ind. Businesses, Nat. Hairdresser and Cosmetologists Assn. Home: 7378 Harmony St Alamosa CO 81101 Office: 421 Hunt St Alamosa CO 81101

COOK, LYNN MAUREEN, public relations exec; b. Bremerton, Wash., Feb. 19, 1942; d. Hance and Frances Lucille (Teachout) Jacobson; student Olympic Coll.; B.F.A., U. Hawaii, 1972; m. David L. Cook, 1963 (div.); 1 dau., Elizabeth Louise. Asst. women's editor Bremerton Sun, Wash., 1966-68; display/advt. dir. Kramer's Men's Stores, Honolulu, 1971-74; public relations cons. Pacific Adminstrv. Devel. Corp., Honolulu, 1975-77; public relations asst. dir. Aloha United Way, Honolulu, 1977-79; public relations account supr. Fawcett McDermott Cavanagh, Inc., Honolulu, 1979—. Spl. projects dir. Visitor Industry Edn. Council, 1979—, Bus. Communications Council, 1979-81; mem. Honolulu Neighborhood Bd. Council, 1977-79. Recipient Mayor's award, Artists of Hawaii, City of Honolulu, 1976, 77, 78. Mem. Public Relations Soc. Am., Women in Communications, Honolulu Advt. Fedn., Internat. Assn. Bus. Communicators, Honolulu Printmakers (pres. 1979-80), Honolulu Press Club, Theta Sigma Phi. Home: 1868 Puowaina Dr Honolulu HI 96813 Office: 1441 Kapiolani Blvd Suite 1500 Honolulu HI 96814

COOK, MARLENE FRANCES, editor; b. Chgo., June 5, 1934; d. Menno and Margaret (Ooms) Boersma; student Thornton Community Coll., Calumet Coll., No. Ill. U., also journalism seminars; m. Henry Cook, Apr. 4, 1953; children—Kenneth Jay, Kevin John, Keith Jerrold-Kraig Jerrard. Columnist, feature writer Star Publs., Chicago Heights, Ill., 1970—, entertainment editor, 1972—; speaker, condr. workshops in field. Founding mem. bd. dirs. Quad City Blood Council, 1973-77; pres. Berger-Vandenberg Sch. PTA, 1969-72, Community Reformed Women's Guild, 1972-74; bd. dirs. S. Cook County council Girl Scouts U.S.A., 1980-82; active local Boys Baseball, Boy Scouts Am. Recipient various certs. of appreciation. Mem. Nat. Fedn. Press Women, Ill. Women's Press Assn. (7 1st pl. awards), Nat. Writers Club, Women's Network. Mem. Community Reformed Ch. Clubs: Illiana Traditional Jazz, Pointe East Recreational. Home: 14428 Ellis St Dolton IL 60419 Office: 1526 Otto Blvd Chicago Heights IL 60411

COOK, PATRICIA STILLWELL, banker; b. N.Y.C., June 5, 1947; d. Irving Lawrence and Elizabeth Anderton (Brown) C.; B.S., Wheelock Coll., Boston, 1969; M.Ed., Boston U., 1970, Ph.D. (NDEA teaching fellow), 1976; m. William C. Bush, Nov. 29, 1975. Sr. project dir. Abt Assos., Cambridge, Mass., 1970-75; asso. Booz-Allen & Hamilton, Inc., N.Y.C., 1976; sr. v.p. Louis Harris & Assos., Inc., N.Y.C., 1977-79; v.p. Chem. Bank, N.Y.C., 1979—. Mem. Am. Mktg. Assn., Am. Psychol. Assn., Bank Mktg. Assn. Club: River (N.Y.C.).

COOK, PHYLLIS WILSON, psychologist; b. Beckley, W.Va., June 12, 1941; d. Philip Hart and Barbara Ann (Hoke) Wilson; B.A., Morris Harvey Coll., 1972; M.S., Radford U., 1973, postgrad., 1974; postgrad. W.Va. U., 1978—; 1 son, Philip. Registrar vital statistics Raleigh County, Beckley, W.Va., 1970-72; homebound tchr. Raleigh County Public Schs., 1972-73, sch. psychologist, 1974-75; asst. prof. psychology Bluefield (W.Va.) State Coll., 1977-79; psychologist Fayette County Schs., Fayetteville, W.Va., 1979-80, N.C. Dept. Corrections, Rocky Mount, 1980-81; self-employed sch. psychologist, 1981—; adj. faculty W.Va. Coll. Grad. Studies, 1979-80, Bluefield State Coll., 1979-80. Mem. Raleigh County Republican Exec. Com., 1963-72, Beckley Republican Exec. Com., 1963-72. Mem. Nat. Assn. Sch. Psychologists, W.Va. Assn. Sch. Psychologists, Am. Psychol. Assn. (asso.). Republican. Episcopalian. Home: 7 Heritage Hills Rocky Mount NC 27801

COOK, ROSA LEE, nurse; b. Covington, Ky., Oct. 17, 1937; d. Lewis Edison and Margaret Lee (Robinson) Cook; B.R.E., Piedmont Bible Coll., 1958; R.N., Ky. Bapt. Hosp. Sch. Nursing, 1961; B.S.N., U. Pa., 1972; M.S., Ohio State U., 1976. Operating room staff nurse Ky. Bapt. Hosp., Louisville, 1961-62; missionary Central Am. Mission, 1962-64; nurse Georgetown (Ky.) Coll., 1964; staff nurse St. Elizabeth Hosp., Covington, Ky., 1964-66; commd. 1st lt. Nurse Corps, U.S. Air Force, 1966, advanced through grades to maj., 1977—, staff nurse March AFB, Calif., 1966-68, supr. operating room England AFB, La., 1968-70, supr. Central Nursing Service, Ramey AFB, P.R., 1972-73, asst. supr. operating room Wright-Patterson AFB, Ohio, 1973-75, nursing supr. Brooks AFB, Tex., 1977-81, chief nurse, dir. nursing services Loring AFB, Me., 1981—; lectr. in field; cons. in field. Recipient Am. Jour. Nursing and Tex. Nurses Assn. Excellence in Writing award, 1977; Chief Nurse Badge, USAF, 1979; Brigadier Gen. E.A. Hoefly award for excellence in clin. nursing research, 1980; Nat. Teaching Inst. scholar, 1980. Fellow Am. Acad. Nursing; mem. Am. Nurses Assn., Maine State Nurses Assn., Am. Assn. Critical Care Nurses, Nat. League Nursing, Council of Nurse Researchers, Aerospace Med. Assn. (flight nurse sect.), Assn. Mil. Surgeons of U.S., Nat. Critical Care Inst., Air Force Assn., Sigma Theta Tau. Baptist. Contbr. articles to profl. jours. Home: 20 Westwind Dr Caribou ME 04736 Office: USAF Hosp SGHN Loring AFB ME 04751

COOK, RUTH E., state legislator; b. Berlin, Nov. 11, 1929; d. Samuel and Ilse (Meyer) Mohr; student N.Y. U.; m. John Oliver Cook, Oct. 31, 1954 (dec.); children—Roger Mohr, Judith Ellen. Exec. dir. State Council for Social Legis.; mem. N.C. Ho. of Reps., 1975-76, 77-78, 79-80, 81—, mem., chmn. appropriations base budget com. on human resources, vice-chmn. appropriations base budget com., vice-chmn. appropriations expansion budget com., vice-chmn. human resources com., vice-chmn. mental health com. Bd. dirs. N.C. Housing Finance Agy., Women's Center Raleigh; chmn. N.C. Council for Hearing Impaired. Mem. N.C. Consumers Council (1st v.p.), Raleigh Wake LWV (past pres.). Office: NC Ho Reps State Capitol Raleigh NC 27602 *

COOK, SHARON OLLERENSHAW, social worker; b. Rochester, N.Y., June 10, 1948; d. Harold James and Gladys Jean (Cook) Ollerenshaw; B.A., Lycoming Coll., 1970; M.S.S.W. (scholar), U. Tex., Arlington, 1976; m. Paul Stuart Cook, Feb. 26, 1977; 1 dau., Katherine. Med. case aide U. Rochester Med. Center, 1970-74; supr. Family Service of Tarrent County, Ft. Worth, 1976; dir. supportive services Parenting Guidance Center, Ft. Worth, 1976-77; dir. social work services Good Shepherd Hosp., Longview, Tex., 1978-79; counselor East Tex. Pastoral Counseling Center, 1978-79, Longview Family Counseling Center, 1979-81; cons. dialysis unit Good Shepherd Hosp., 1978-80; psychol. cons., bd. dirs. Parents Anonymous, 1980—. Assn. Am. Businesswomen grantee, 1974-75; cert. Acad. Cert. Social Workers; cert. social worker, Tex. Mem. Nat. Assn. Social Workers, Methodist. Contbr. article to Group Psychotherapy, Psychodrama and Sociometry. Home: PO Box 3528 Longview TX 75606

COOK, SUSAN PAULA, retail exec.; b. Rochester, N.H., Feb. 16, 1947; d. Israel Jack and Molly (Landes) C.; A.B. cum laude (scholar), N.Y. U., 1968; scholar U. Madrid, 1967. Dept. mgr. Bloomingdale's, 1968, personnel mgr., 1969-70, corp. tng. dir., 1971-72; asst. personnel dir. I Magnin Co., San Francisco, 1971; personnel mgr. Macy's Calif., Palo Alto, 1973-74, staff tng. mgr., 1974-75, adminstr. tng., 1975-77, v.p. personnel devel., 1977-80, v.p. exec. personnel and devel., 1980—. Mem. United Way mgmt. assistance program United Jewish Appeal. Recipient Priscilla Lieber Kaufman Swimming medal. Mem. Am. Soc. Tng. and Devel., Internat. Assn. Bus. Communicators, Nat. Soc. Performance Improvement, Nat. Retail Mchts. Assn., Am. Soc. Personnel Adminstrs., No. Calif. Indsl. Relations Council, Profl. Women's Alliance. Democrat. Jewish. Editor: Israel's Numismatic Mag., 1970; editor, developer Faces, Bloomingdale's internal mag., 1971-72; contbg. writer NE Training News, 1982. Home: 21100 Gary Dr Apt 309 Hayward CA 94546 Office: PO Box 7888 San Francisco CA 94120

COOK, WANDA JOHNSON, sch. counselor; b. Houston, Nov. 21, 1919; d. Levi Hazlett and Hope Moutray (Mashaw) Johnson; B.A., Denver U., 1940; M.A., N.Mex. Highlands U., 1949; summer postgrad. Tex. Tech. U., 1962, N.Mex. State U., 1968-69, Eastern N.Mex. U., 1956, 59, 68, 73, Western N.Mex. U., 1969, U. Tex., El Paso, 1965; m. George Gayle Cook, Dec. 31, 1953; 1 dau., Karen Hope Dennis. Elem. sch. tchr. Carlsbad (N.Mex.) Mcpl. Sch., 1940; mgr. Sprouse-Reitz Store, 1941-42; asst. statistician Blue Cross-Blue Shield, Dallas, 1949; counselor N.Mex. Employment Security Commn., Carlsbad, 1952-53; math. tchr., counselor Carlsbad Mcpl. Schs., 1953—, head counselor Carlsbad Sr. High Sch., 1964—; psychology instr. N.Mex. State U., Carlsbad, 1967—; test examiner Ednl. Testing Service, 1967—. Bd. dirs. Hacienda de Esperanza Boys Home, 1970-78, pres., 1970-72, 77-78; bd. dirs. United Fund, 1967-70, citation, 1967. Recipient Eastern N.Mex. cert. of award Youth Problems Seminar, 1968; NDEA Counseling and Guidance Inst. fellow, 1962. Mem. AAUW, NEA, NEA-N.Mex. (constn. com. 1969-72), Am. Personnel and Guidance Assn., Am. Sch. Counselors Assn., N.Mex. Personnel and Guidance Assn., N.Mex. Sch. Counselors Assn. (pres. 1980-81), N.Mex. Classroom Tchrs. Assn. (sec. 1961-62), Southeastern N.Mex. Edn. Assn. (sec.-treas. 1970-77), Carlsbad Edn. Assn. (pres. 1968-69), Carlsbad Classroom Tchrs. Assn. (pres. 1959-60), Kappa Delta Pi, Psi Chi, Tau Kappa Alpha, Delta Kappa Gamma (pres. 1968-70), Delta Zeta (pres. 1939-40). Democrat. Methodist. Clubs: Order Eastern Star (Grand Cross Color 1961); Altrusa (pres. Carlsbad 1978-79, dist. conf. chmn. 1980). Home: 1207 N Country Club Circle Carlsbad NM 88220 Office: Carlsbad Sr High Sch 3000 W Church St Carlsbad NM 88220

COOKE, ANNA LOUISE, librarian; b. Jackson, Tenn., Feb. 14, 1923; d. Thurston and Effie (Cage) Lee; A.B., Lane Coll., Jackson, 1944; M.L.S., Atlanta U., 1955; m. James A. Cooke, Apr. 11, 1956; 1 dau., Elsie Louise. Prin., Douglas Jr. High Sch., Haywood County, Tenn., 1944-46; tchr., then librarian Jackson City Sch. System, 1947-63; catalog librarian, 1963-67, alumni affairs exec. sec., 1966-69, library dir., 1967—; columnist Tri-State Defender, Memphis, 1951-63. Bd. dirs., sec. Jackson Arts Council, 1972-74; v.p., bd. dirs. Reelfoot Girl Scout Council, 1980—; v.p. Jackson Fedn. Democratic Women, 1972. Recipient various service plaques; hon. fellow Philos. Soc. Eng., 1969. Mem. ALA, Southeastern Library Assn., Tenn. Library Assn., W. Tenn. Library Assn., Assn. Coll. and Research Libraries, So. Assn. Colls. and Schs. (eval. teams), Delta Sigma Theta (chpt. pres. 1951-52). Mem. Methodist Episcopal Ch. Club: Links (pres. Jackson 1979—). Author, editor in field. Home: 120 Hale St Jackson TN 38301 Office: Lane Coll 545 Lane Ave Jackson TN 38301

COOKE, CYNTHIA GAIL, univ. ofcl.; b. N.Y.C., June 19, 1943; d. Edmund F. and Laura M. (Swetman) Cooke; B.A. cum laude in Psychology, U. Ariz., 1969; M.A. magna cum laude, Ariz. State U., 1978, postgrad., 1978—; 1 dau., Elizabeth. Program developer Pima Community Coll., Tucson, 1970-75; conf. coordinator Ariz. State U., Tempe, 1977-78; program officer U. So. Calif., Los Angeles, 1978-79, asst. dir. community and profl. programs, 1979—, now dir. Inst. for Personal and Profl. Achievement; dir. program devel. Sold-Out Inc., 1979—; pres. Cooke & Assos., Oxnard, Calif., 1979—; instr. psychology Pima Community Coll., Tucson, part-time, 1970-74; cons. to industry; condr. workshops, 1978—. Chmn. Commn. Status of Women Adult Edn. Assn., 1980; sec. Valley of Sun Adult Edn. Roundtable, 1978; chmn. So. Ariz. Women's Polit. Caucus, 1972-73; coordinator Ventura County Businesswomen's Network. Mem. Nat. Univ. Extension Assn., Adult Edn. Assn., Am. Soc. Tng. and Devel. (program chmn.), Psi Chi. Home: 345 W Deodar St Oxnard CA 93030 Office: Univ Park Los Angeles CA 90007

COOKE, EDNA MARIE, fire protection co. exec., restaurant owner; b. Hogansburg, N.Y., Dec. 27, 1935; d. Thomas and Agnes E. (Jock) Lazare; student Pasadena Coll., 1965, Citrus Coll., 1966-67; m. Charles Ronald Cooke, July 2, 1955 (div.); children—Leanna Jane, Ramona Gale, Craig Ronel. Various positions, 1953-65; sec.-treas., part owner Vanguard Automatic Sprinkler Co., Santa Fe Springs, Calif., 1967-74; owner LaZar House of Beauty, Glendora, Calif., 1974—, Jacques Restaurant, Glendora, 1974—; pres., owner Eagle Fire Protection, Glendora, 1974—. Ways and means chairperson San Gabriel Valley Symphony Assn., 1966. Mem. Glendora C. of C., Calif. Restaurant Assn. Democrat. Roman Catholic. Club: Glendora Country. Office: 2264 E Alosta Glendora CA 91740

COOKE, EVELYN KATHLEEN CHATMAN, educator; b. Jackson, Tenn.; d. Charles Elijah and Josie (Bond) Chatman; B.A. cum laude, Lane Coll., 1955; M.Ed., Xavier U.; m. James T. Cooke, Apr. 21, 1954 (div. Aug. 1970); 1 dau., Madelyn LaRene. Tchr. pub. schs., Chattanooga, 1957-67, Cin., 1967—; cons. career edn. Pub. Schs., Cin. Pres., Harriet Tubman's Black Women's Democratic Club; mem. upper grade sch study council. Mem. Fellowship United Meth. Musicians, NAACP, Council for Co-op Action, Am., Ohio, Cin. fedns. tchrs., Nat. Council Negro Women, Top Ladies of Distinction (nat. corr. sec., chmn. info. com.), Sigma Gamma Rho, Gamma Theta, Sigma Rho Sigma. Methodist (dir. music ch.). Club: Top Ladies of Distinction, Inc. Home: 6748 Elwynne Dr Cincinnati OH 45236

COOKE, HELEN HEMLIN, editor, writer; b. N.Y.C.; d. Valentine and Katherine (Fischer) Hemlin; student U. N.Mex., 1925-26, Columbia, 1927-29; m. Charles Cooke, Jan. 29, 1931 (div. Sept. 1955); 1 son, Harris Craig. Mem. staff writers Lowell Thomas, 1929-33; reporter New Yorker Mag., N.Y.C., 1933-35; publicity dir. Douglas Leigh, Inc., N.Y.C., 1938-45; publicity dir. Monroe Dreher Advt. Agy., N.Y.C., 1941-45; free-lance editor, writer, Washington, 1948—; asst. to exec. v.p. Aerospace Med. Assn., Washington, 1960-61. Clubs: Am. Newspaper Womens, Nat. Press (Washington). Author: (with Evelyn D. Boyer) Distinguished Women of Washington, D.C., 1964. Contbr. articles to various newspapers, mags. including Washington Star Sunday mag., Balt. Sun, Aerospace Medicine, Cue mag., others. Patentee in field toys. Home: 2244 N Nottingham St Arlington VA 22205

COOKE, MICHELE LOUISE, editor; b. Gary, Ind., Dec. 4, 1950; d. John and Elizabeth Sara (Kaczorowski) Opalak; student Ind. State U., 1968-69; grad. in religious philosophy Ind. U., 1969-73; 1 son, Erik Peter. Asst. editor Nat. Enquirer, Lantana, Fla., 1975-77, cartoon and short articles editor, 1977—. Office: 600 SE Coast Ave Lantana FL 33464

COOKE, PHYLISS SWANSON, psychologist; b. Cleve., Sept. 6, 1933; d. Reuben and Margaret (Oldach) Swanson; B.A., Baldwin Wallace Coll., 1969; M.A., Cleve. State U., 1971; Ph.D., Kent State U., 1975; m.

Thomas Lee Cooke, Apr. 19, 1952 (div. 1975); 1 son, Thomas Lee II. Instr. Patricia Stevens Modeling Agy., Cleve., 1964-66; free-lance profl. model, 1962-68; sch. psychologist pub. schs., Cleve., 1970-77; instr. Grad. Edn., Kent (Ohio) State U., 1973-75; cons. to Assn. of Humanistic Edn.; pvt. practice clin. psychology, 1971-78; pvt. mgmt. cons., 1974-78; dir. profl. services Univ. Assos., San Diego, 1978—, mem. cons. staff, 1975—, now also dean tng. program, dean masters human resource devel. program. Mem. Am. Psychol. Assn., Calif. Psychol. Assn., Acad. Mgmt. AAUP, Mensa. Home: 17666 Cumana Terr Rancho Bernardo CA 92121 Office: Univ Associates 8517 Production Ave San Diego CA 92121

COOLBAUGH, LOUISE CLAUD, life ins. co. exec.; b. Danville, Va., Aug. 9, 1935; d. Jesse and Lorraine (Walker) Claud; ed. bus. sch.; m. Donald J. Coolbaugh, Aug. 4, 1962; children—Donald J., Eric. Ins. mgr. Lane & Fentriss, Danville, 1955-57; bookkeeper First & Mchts. Bank, Pensacola, Fla., 1957-59; sec. Mass. Mut. Life Ins. Co., Richmond, Va., 1959-62, office mgr., N.Y.C., 1962—. Republican. Club: Pine Ridge Women's. Home: 2628 Woods Ave East Meadow NY 11554 Office: 201 E 50th St 10th Floor New York NY 10022

COOLBRITH, ALISON GALLAGHER, ins. co. exec.; b. N.C., July 16, 1945; d. Francis Michael and Gladys (Rolfe) Gallagher; A.A., Hartford Coll. for Women, 1965; B.A., U. Wis., 1967. Ins. underwriter Aetna Life and Casualty, Hartford, Conn., 1967-71, compensation adminstr. and mgr., 1972-76, mgr. compliance Aetna Variable Annuity Life Ins. Co., 1976-78, asst. dir. pension and profitsharing sales Aetna Life and Casualty, 1978-80, dir. corp. social responsibility, 1980-81, v.p. corp. public involvement, 1982—. Bd. dirs. Urban League. Mem. Alumnae Assn. Hartford Coll. Women (pres. 1977-80). Home: 22 Charter Oak Pl Hartford CT 06106 Office: 151 Farmington Ave Hartford CT 06156

COOLEY, ADELAIDE NATION, painter, potter, writer; b. Idaho Falls, Idaho, Apr. 18, 1914; d. Carl DeLos and Ivo Ethel (Miller) Nation; student Stephens Coll., Columbia, Mo., 1931-33; B.S., U. Wis., Madison, 1935; m. William Cooley, Jr., Aug. 24, 1937; children—Marcia Jean Cooley Blevins, Susan Adelaide Cooley Fargo, William Carl. Freelance artist and potter, Peoria, Ill., 1965—; judge art exhibits and awards; cons. Carson Pirie Scott & Co. Art Exhibits; tchr. YWCA, art chmn. Jubilee Coll. Restoration Com., 1975—; mem. selection com. sculpture for Peoria Civic Center, 1979; exhbn. chmn. Joseph Petarde sculpture exhibit Peoria Art Guild, 1976; chmn. Peoria Collects: Prints and Drawings, Lakeview Mus., 1964; art cons. Peoria Hist. Soc., 1980—; reviewer area art exhibits New Art Examiner, Chgo., 1981—; appraiser art collections for estates and ins., 1980—. Named Outstanding Woman in Art, Peoria YWCA, 1973, recipient Leadership in Arts award, 1978; Ill. Arts Council grantee, 1977. Mem. Ill. Art League, Peoria Art Guild, Fine Arts Soc. Peoria, Peoria Hist. Soc., NOW, Jr. League Peoria, Peoria Med. Soc. Aux., Meth. Hosp. Service League, Kappa Alpha Theta. Republican. Methodist. Club: Peoria Woman's. Author: The Monument Maker, 1978. Home: 808 Chalon Dr Peoria IL 61614

COOMBES, TERRI LEE, polit. cons.; b. Robinson, Ill., Oct. 15, 1954; d. Raymond Lee and Betty Keith (Moore) Coombes; BS, So. Ill. U., 1977; m. David Charles Hawkinson, June 14, 1979. Campaign scheduler Com. to Elect R. Troy Atty. Gen., Chgo., 1978; corp. treas., adminstrv. asst. D.G. Group, Inc., Chgo., 1979; campaign scheduler, asst. mgr. Com. to Elect John Curry State Rep., Galesburg, Ill., 1980; dep. county clk. Knox County, Galesburg, 1981—; campaign cons. Del., Nat. Dem. Conv., 1980, Ill. Dem. Conv., 1980, 82; treas. Knox County Dem. Orgn., 1982—. Mem. League Women Voters. Home: 2762 Springer Rd Apt 8 Galesburg IL 61401 Office: Knox County Courthouse Galesburg IL 61401

COOMBS, HOPE CHANDLER BENTON (MRS. CHARLES EDWARD COOMBS, JR.), civic leader; b. Seattle, Mar. 30, 1910; d. Paul Amasa and Ruth (Chandler) Benton; B.S. in Textiles, U. Wash., 1932; m. Charles Edward Coombs, Jr., Apr. 14, 1934; children—Charles Paul, Marcia Joan (Mrs. John Tadlock Howe). Vol. St. Luke's Hosp. Aux., San Francisco, 1955-66; mem. Mother's Milk Bank, Inc., 1948—, aux. bd., 1956, 69; mem., club photographer Century Club of Calif., 1962—; mem. bd. dirs., docent council M.H. de Young Museum, San Francisco, 1966—; mem. San Francisco Garden Club, 1948—, historian, 1966-68, photographer, 1965-68, bd. dirs., 1954-56; mem. DAR, Calif., 1954—, bd. dirs., 1958-76, regent, 1964-65. Mem. U. Wash. Alumni Assn., Calif. Geneal. Soc., Photog. Soc. Am., Soc. Asian Art, M.H. de Young Mus. Soc., Nat. Soc. Magna Charta Dames, Soc. Mayflower Descs., Nat. Soc. Daus. of Founders and Patriots Am., Sovereign Colonial Soc. Ams. Royal Descent, Nat. Soc. Colonial Dames Am., Order of Washington, Alpha Chi Omega. Club: Photochrome (San Francisco).

COOMBS, SUSAN M. GLISSON, soft drink co. exec.; b. Atlanta, Sept. 3, 1928; d. S. T. and Sue (Harrison) Maughon; student U. Ga., Atlanta, 1951, 53, 54, Greenleaf Bus. Sch., Atlanta; m. L. G. Dalon, Apr. 21, 1952; children—Lynn Dalon Sutton, David J.; m. Robert France Coombs, Oct. 11, 1972 (dec.). Mgr., Kelly Girls, Atlanta, 1957-58; asst. to dir. market devel. Phillips Petroleum Co., Tampa, Fla., Atlanta, exec. sec., adminstrv. asst. Coca-Cola Co., U.S.A., Atlanta, 1958-78, dir. guest relations, 1978—. Mem. Atlanta Hist. Soc., Atlanta Arts Festival Assn., Atlanta Childrens Theatre, Atlanta Art Alliance. Republican. Methodist. Office: 310 North Ave NW Atlanta GA 30313

COOMER, GLADYS, corp. exec.; b. Juan, Ky., June 18, 1937; d. John and Arkie (Hall) Vires; student Computer Programming Inst., 1967; 1 dau., Katrina Lynne. Recreation supr. City of Middletown, Ohio, 1957-60; clk. Park N Save Inc., Germantown, Ohio, 1967, sec., 1967-74, sec.-treas., 1974—. Active ARC. Mem. Internat. Assn. Fin. Planners. Democrat. Home: 345 E Market St Germantown OH 45327 Office: 1375 W Market St Germantown OH 45327

COONEY, JOAN GANZ, television exec.; b. Phoenix, Nov. 30, 1929; d. Sylvan C. and Pauline (Reardan) Ganz; B.A., U. Ariz., 1951, hon. degree, 1975; hon. degrees: Boston Coll., 1970, Hofstra U., Oberlin Coll., Ohio Wesleyan U., 1971, Princeton, 1973, Russell Sage Coll., 1974, Harvard, 1975, Allegheny Coll., 1976, Georgetown U., 1978; m. Peter G. Peterson, Apr. 26, 1980. Reporter, Ariz. Republic, Phoenix, 1953-54; publicist NBC, N.Y.C., 1954-55; TV publicist U.S. Steel Hour, N.Y.C., 1955-62; producer pub. affairs documentaries Channel 13, WNET, N.Y.C., 1962-67; TV cons. Carnegie Corp. of N.Y., N.Y.C., 1967-68; exec. dir. Children's TV Workshop, producers Sesame St. and Electric Co., others, N.Y.C., 1968-70, pres., trustee, 1970—; dir. Xerox Corp., May Dept. Stores Co., Johnson & Johnson, Met. Life Ins. Co.; trustee Channel 13 (Ednl. Broadcasting Corp.); mem. Pres.'s Commn. on Marijuana and Drug Abuse, 1971-73, Pres.'s Commn. for Nat. Agenda for Eighties, 1980—; mem. Nat. News Council, 1973-81; Recipient numerous awards for Electric Company, Sesame Street, other TV programs including Gold Key award Nat. Sch. Pub. Relations Assn.; Distinguished Service medal Columbia Tchrs. Coll., Soc. for Family of Man; Gold medal Nat. Inst. Social Scis., Frederick Douglass award N.Y. Urban League, Quest medal, Friends of Edn. award NEA, Disting. Service award Nat. Assn. Ednl. Broadcasters, named Woman of Yr. in Edn., Ladies Home Jour., 1975; Woman of Decade award Ladies Home Jour., 1979. Mem. Nat. Acad. TV Arts and Scis., Council Fgn. Relations (adv. com. trade negotiations 1978-80), Internat. Radio and TV Soc., Am. Women in Radio and TV, NOW, Nat. Inst. Social Scis. Office: 1 Lincoln Plaza New York NY 10023

COONEY, PATRICIA JANE, lawyer; b. Englewood, N.J., Jan. 20, 1953; d. Thomas Bernard and Doris (Ettore) C.; B.A. summa cum laude, Fordham U., 1973; J.D. cum laude, Seton Hall U., 1976. Admitted to N.J. bar, 1976; law clk. to chief judge U.S. Dist. Ct. for N.J., 1976-77; asso. firm Shanley & Fisher, Newark, 1977-81; partner firm Giblin, Combs and Cooney, Morristown, N.J., 1981—; adj. faculty Seton Hall U. Sch. Law, 1978-79. Life mem. Ft. Lee (N.J.) Vol. Ambulance Corps, 1972—; mem. Ft. Lee Bd. Ethics, 1980—. Recipient Outstanding Grad. award Seton Hall U. Sch. Law, 1976. Mem. Am. Bar Assn., N.J. State Bar Assn., Trial Attys. N.J., Fed. Bar Assn. Democrat. Roman Catholic. Office: 550 Broad St Newark NJ 07102

COONS, DOROTHY HEETER, gerontologist; b. Lewisburg, Ohio, Dec. 28, 1914; d. Charles Allen and Meta (Van Ausdal) Heeter; B.S. in Edn., Wittenberg U., Springfield, Ohio, 1936; postgrad. U. Mich., 1940; m. George Douglas Coons, May 8, 1943. Program dir., then dir. tng. in milieu therapy Inst. Gerontology, U. Mich., Ann Arbor, 1962-74, asst. prof. edn., then dir. continuing edn. 1973-81, program dir. Inst. Gerontology, 1981—, asso. prof., 1979—; cons., workshop condr. in field. Grantee Nat. Endowment Arts, 1978, 79-80, Rehab. Services Adminstrn., 1978-79, Am. Assn. Retired Persons, 1982. Mem. Internat. Psychogeriatric Assn., Geront. Soc. Am., Am. Geriatrics Soc. Democrat. Lutheran. Author papers in field. Co-editor: Special Senses in Aging, 1979. Home: 2031 Winsted Ct Ann Arbor MI 48103 Office: 520 E Liberty St Ann Arbor MI 48109

COONS, RUNELL S., TV exec.; b. Amarillo, Tex., July 11, 1944; d. Larry Burgie and LaRue (McCanne) Stitt; A.A., Amarillo Coll., 1963; B.S. cum laude, U. Houston, 1965; postgrad. West Tex. State U., 1966—; m. David Russell Coons, Aug. 23, 1968; children—Courtnay, Kevin. Copy writer McCormick Advt., Amarillo, 1965-67; continuity dir. KFDA-TV, Amarillo, 1967-73, KAMR-TV, 1973-75; traffic dir. KAMR-TV, Amarillo, 1975—; free lance advt. cons., 1975—; part-time instr. West Tex. State U., Canyon, 1977-80. Bd. dirs. Domestic Violence Council, Amarillo, sec. speakers bur., 1981-82; active Amarillo Little Theatre. Recipient Public Affairs award Up Internat., Amarillo Ad Club and Tex. Med. Assn., 1973; Addy award Amarillo Advt. Club, 1974; Mayes Advt. award for Superior Service, 1981. Mem. Nat. Fedn. Press Women, Tex. Press Women (state publ. chmn. 1979-80), Amarillo Advt. Club (chmn. speakers bur. 1980-81), Amarillo C. of C. Baptist. Club: Altrusa (v.p., sec.) (Amarillo, Tex.). Home: 3505 Barclay St Amarillo TX 79109 Office: PO Box 751 Amarillo TX 79189

COOPER, AGNES PEARSON (MRS. DAVID ACRON COOPER), educator; b. Bonner Springs, Kans., Oct. 18, 1910; d. James P. and May B. (Luther) Pearson; B.S., Pittsburg (Kans.) State U., 1932; M.S., U. Denver, 1938; postgrad. Harvard, 1939, 40; m. David Acron Cooper, Oct. 15, 1941 (dec. 1974); 1 son, David Acron. Tchr. high schs., Kan., Mo., 1929-37; tchr. Wyandotte High Sch., Kansas City, Kans., 1937-39; instr. secretarial sci. Alfred U., 1939-41; instr. U. Tenn., 1941-42; dir. edn. and placement Knoxville (Tenn.) Bus. Coll., 1942-48; dean student services, also treas. Cooper Inst., Inc., Knoxville 1948—. Mem. Knox County adv. com. Tenn. Dept. Human Services, Knoxville, 1955—, chmn., 1959, 76-77; mem. East Tenn. Community Improvement Central Com., 1952—, vice chmn., 1954, pres. 1968; dir. spelling match TVA Agrl. and Indsl. Fair, 1972—; mem. nat. bd. Women's Med. Coll., Phila.; mem. emergency energy policy com. Knoxville-Knox County Community Action Com., 1975-76. Mem. East Tenn. Edn. Assn. (chmn. bus. sect. 1958, sec. 1957), Nat. Office Mgrs. Assn., AAUW, Am. Bus. Women's Assn., Better Bus. Bur., Internat. Platform Assn. (dir. 1977). Baptist. Club: Quota Internat. (1st v.p. 1963-64, 2d v.p. 1961-63, gov. 23d dist. 1956-57, gov. 8th dist. 1949-51, trustee ednl. revolving fund Knoxville 1962-63, internat. pres. 1965-66). Home: Box 225 Route 2 Kodak TN 37764

COOPER, ALVA CRITCHLEY, career counselor; b. N.Y.C.; d. Alfred Edward and Jeanne Marie (Malplate) Critchley; B.A., Hunter Coll., N.Y.C., 1931; M.A., N.Y.U., 1941; Ph.D., Columbia U., 1954; m. James Cooper, June 21, 1936. Instr., then prof. counseling and student devel. Hunter Coll., 1956-76, dir. career counseling and placement, 1956-76; cons. profl. devel. Coll. Placement Council, Bethlehem, Pa., 1976-80, pres., 1973-74; cons. careers and career services, Bayville, N.Y., 1980—; pres. Met. N.Y. Coll. Placement Assn., 1961-63, Eastern Coll. Personnel Assn., 1966, Personnel Club N.Y., 1960-61; pres. Coll. Placement Services, 1978-81, bd. dirs., 1976—. Mem. Am. Psychol. Assn., Am. Personnel and Guidance Assn., Am. Coll. Personnel Assn., Nat. Vocat. Guidance Assn., N.Y. Personnel Mgmt. Assn. Co-author: A Model Career Counseling and Placement Program, 3d rev. edit., 1980. Address: 1 Adams Ave Bayville NY 11709

COOPER, BEATRICE GITTEL ZIPPERMAN, cable TV exec.; b. N.Y.C., June 11, 1922; d. Casiel Von and Rachele Countess (Vortzvogel) Zipperman; ed. pvt. tutors; m. Herman A. Cooper, Feb. 17, 1945; children—Michele, Brian. Treas., dir. Cooper Cable Service Corp., Long Island City, N.Y., 1970—; officer, dir. T.L.C. Women's Services. Pres., Young Women's League Cerebral Palsy, 1975-76. Recipient meritorious service award N.Y. Cerebral Palsy Soc. Republican. Jewish.

COOPER, BERNICE RUTH STEINBERG, film editor; b. N.Y.C.; d. Joseph and Nettie Steinberg; student Juilliard Sch. Music; m. Sidney Cooper, July 1, 1956; 1 dau., Diane. With Famous Studio div. Paramount Pictures, 1945-48, Tempo Prodns., 1948-52, Acad. Pictures, 1952-55; owner Ani-Live Film Service Inc., N.Y.C., 1955—; dir. Multicolor Film Lab. Recipient editing awards including: Clio award, Am. Film Festival award, Internat. Film Festival award. Mem. Film Editors Union, Nat. Acad. TV Arts and Scis. Club: Woodcrest Country. Contbr. articles to mags., weekly newspapers; concert piano recitalist. Home: 40 Fairway Ct Roslyn Harbor NY 11576 Office: 45 W 45th St New York NY 10036

COOPER, CAROLYN, market research exec.; b. Portal, Ga., Aug. 17, 1939; d. Collie Mann and Olga Vivian (Brannen) Usher; student Los Medanos Coll., 1974-76; m. Alfred Cortley Cooper, Oct. 2, 1976; children—Phyllis Carolyn Russell, Vivian Colleen Russell. Exec. sec. Colonial Oil Industries, Inc., Savannah, Ga., 1966-67; supr. Calif. Employment Devel. Dept., 1973-77; interviewer Gallup Poll, Grass Valley, Calif., 1978; owner, supr. Cooper Research, Savannah, 1978; poet, photographer's model. Soprano, Savannah Symphony Chorale, St. John's Ch. Choir, Savannah, Mikve Israel Synagogue. Mem. Mktg. Research Assn. Am., Poetry Soc. Ga., Telfair Acad. Arts, Historic Savannah Found., Better Bus. Bur., Ga. Hist. Soc., Nat. Trust Hist. Preservation. Episcopalian. Home and Office: 108 W Manta Cove Savannah GA 31410

COOPER, CATHERINE CAMERON, hotel corp. ofcl.; b. Tulsa, Apr. 27, 1950; d. William Ennis, Jr., and Catherine Calhoun (McLeod) Cameron; B.S. in Mgmt., U. S.C., 1971; m. David S. Cooper, Aug. 20, 1977; 1 son, William Saunders. Flight attendant Delta Airlines, Atlanta, 1971-73; sales mgr. Hyatt Regency Atlanta, 1973-76, sales mgr. Hyatt Worldwide Sales, Atlanta, 1976-78, dir. sales and mktg. Hyatt Hotels Worldwide Sales, Atlanta, 1978—. Active U. S.C. Alumni Council, 1979-80. Recipient All Hyatt award, 1982. Mem. Hotel Sales Mgmt. Assn. Internat., Ga. Hotel Sales Mgmt. Assn., Ga. Soc. Assn. Execs., Ga. Passenger Traffic Assn., Atlanta Women's C. of C. U. S.C. Alumni Assn. Republican. Presbyterian. Home: 2476 Oldfield Rd NW Atlanta GA 30327 Office: 233 Peachtree St NE Suite 1511 Atlanta GA 30303

COOPER, DIANE ELIZABETH, home economist; b. Chgo., Feb. 2, 1942; d. Donald Howard and Margaret (Kingsley) C.; B.S. in Home Econs., U. Ariz., 1969. Home economist, research test kitchen supr. Sunbeam Appliance Co., Oak Brook, Ill., 1970-77; product devel. research home economist Ore-Ida Foods, Inc., Ontario, Oreg., 1977—. Mem. Am. Home Econs. Assn., Home Economists in Bus., Oreg. Home Econs. Assn. (dist. dir.), Treasure Valley Home Economists. Office: 175 NE 6th Ave Ontario OR 97914

COOPER, DORIS JEAN, market research prodn. co. exec.; b. N.Y.C., Dec. 17, 1934; d. James N. and Georgina N. (Cassidy) Breslin; student Sch. of Commerce, N.Y. U., 1953-55, Hunter Coll., 1956-57; m. S. James Cooper, June 17, 1956; 1 son, David Austin. Asst. coding supr. Crossley S-D Surveys, N.Y.C., 1955-57; asst. field supr. Trendex, Inc., N.Y.C., 1957-59; coding dir. J. Walter Thompson Co., N.Y.C., 1960-63, Audits & Surveys, N.Y.C., 1964-65; pvt. practice cons., N.Y.C., 1965-73; pres. Cooper Services, Hastings-on-Hudson, N.Y., 1973—; cons. market research prodn. problems. Mem. Am. Mktg. Assn. (N.Y. chpt.), Nat. Bus. Women Owners Assn., Hastings C. of C. Republican. Episcopalian. Office: Cooper Services 419 Warburton Ave Hastings-on-Hudson NY 10706

COOPER, JOSEPHINE SMITH, govt. adminstr.; b. Raleigh, N.C., Aug. 2, 1945; d. Joseph W. and Marie (Peele) S.; B.A. in bus. and econs., Meredith Coll., Raleigh, 1967; M.S. in mgmt. Duke U., 1977. Program analyst Office of Air & Quality Planning and Standards EPA, Research Triangle Park, N.C., 1968-78, environ. profl. specialist Office of Research and Devel., Washington, 1978-80; mem. profl. staff majority leader Howard H. Baker, Jr., U.S. Senate Com. on Environ. and Public Works, Washington, 1980—; treas. RTP Fed. Credit Union, 1969-72, pres., 1975. Congressional fellow, 1979-80. Mem. Federally Employed Women (treas., pres. 1972-77). Mem. Disciples of Christ. Club: Cts. Royal Racquetball. Office: 4204 Dirksen Senate Office Bldg United States Senate Washington DC 20510

COOPER, LENNIE ALICE, chem. co. exec.; b. Chattanooga, Oct. 13, 1948; d. Marvin S. Cooper and Imogene Lenora (Westfield) Rowe; B.S. in Math., Lane Coll., Jackson, Tenn., 1970; M.S. in Computer Sci., Purdue U., 1972. Asso. Programmer IBM Corp., Boca Raton, Fla., 1972-76; sr. systems engr. E.G.&G. Co., San Ramon, Calif., 1976-77; service mgr. Commodore Bus. Machines Co., Palo Alto, Calif., 1977-78; project mgr. So. Pacific Communication Co., Burlingame, Calif., 1978-79; systems analyst, then sr. systems analyst E.I. duPont de Nemours & Co., Inc., Chattanooga, 1980-81, staff asst., 1981—; instr. engring. and computer sci. Diablo Valley Coll., Pleasant Hill, Calif., 1978; cons. Cooper Computer Cons., Oakland, Calif., 1977-79. Active local Cub Scouts, reading programs; trustee St. Phillips Luth. Ch., Chattanooga, 1980-81. Mem. Nat. Assn. Female Execs., Nat. Council Negro Women, Nat. Bus. League, Purdue U. Alumni Assn. Home: 3131 Mt Creek Rd Apt 4A3 Chattanooga TN 37415 Office: 4501 Access Rd Chattanooga TN 37415

COOPER, LOIS BLOUNT, educator; b. Jackson, Miss., Feb. 18, 1939; d. Clarence Malcolm and Viola (Murray) Blount; B.S., Miss. U. Women, 1961; m. Carl Baxter Cooper, Aug. 13, 1961; children—Douglas (dec.), Michael, Tamara. Various bookkeeping and secretarial positions, 1961-66; tchr. bus. Decatur (Miss.) High Sch., 1967-69, Newton County Acad., Decatur, 1971-72, 76-81; staff writer Newton Record, 1965—; co-owner So. Fashions, Newton, 1979-82, Decatur, 1982—. Chmn. Newton County March of Dimes, 1976-82, mem. dist. bd., 1976-82; charter mem., past pres. Decatur Jaycettes; mem. Newton County Jury Commn., 1976—; mem. adminstrv. bd. Council on Ministries; children's coordinator Decatur United Meth. Ch.; active Girl Scouts U.S.A. Recipient various certs. of appreciation. Mem. Nat. Fedn. Press Women, Miss. Press Women (3 awards), Newton County C. of C. (sec.-treas., dir. 1978—), Miss. Pvt. Sch. Assn., Miss. Bus. Tchrs. Assn., Decatur Devel. Assn., East Central Jr. Coll. Alumni Assn. (sec.-treas. 1972—). Methodist. Club: Garden. Home: PO Box 223 Decatur MS 39327 Office: So Fashions 422 Broad St Decatur MS 39327

COOPER, MARY ADRIENNE, publishing co. exec.; b. Bklyn., Jan. 27, 1927; d. James H. and Helen (Hofeditz) C.; B.S., SUNY, Albany, 1948; postgrad. in bus. N.Y. U., 1949-50, Columbia U., 1976. With McGraw Hill, Inc., N.Y.C., 1953—, asst. v.p. fin. ops., 1973-75, v.p. adminstrv. services, 1976—. Bd. dirs. McMahan Services for Children, N.Y.C., 1976—. Mem. Fin. Execs. Inst., Nat. Investor Relations Inst. Office: 1221 Ave of the Americas New York NY 10020

COOPER, NANCY JOAN, delivery co. exec.; b. Bronx, N.Y., June 26, 1953; d. Gerald and Dolores I. (Hakoun) Hass; B.A. in Philosophy, Hunter Coll., N.Y.C.; M.B.A. in Corp. Fin., Adelphi U., 1981; m. George E. Cooper, Aug. 25, 1971. Record keeper Millimeter mag., N.Y.C., 1973-75; clerical supr. Aquarius Transfer Ltd., N.Y.C., 1974-75; with Can Carriers, Inc., N.Y.C., 1971-80, controller, 1975-80, exec. v.p., 1981—, also dir.; chief acct. Liberty Engraving Co., N.Y.C., 1980—. Mem. Assn. Messenger Services, Nat. Assn. Female Execs.

COOPER, PATRICE O'HEGARTY COBB, business exec.; b. Collooney, Sligo, Ireland, July 5, 1909; d. Timothy and Honorah E. (Scanlon) O'Hegarty; came to U.S., 1922, naturalized, 1943; student Bay State Inst. Commerce, 1926, St. Mary's Coll., 1927-29, Rutgers U. Sch. Bus. Adminstrn., 1944-45, Berkeley Secretarial Sch., 1951; m. Francis Cutter Cobb, Oct. 30, 1943 (dec. Jan. 1965); 1 dau., Patricia Cobb Oliver; m. 2d, J. Gilbert Cooper, Feb. 20, 1971. Fashion and beauty exec. Best and Co., N.Y.C., 1935-43; personnel mgmt. Heil Co., N.J., 1945-49; staff Lord and Taylor, 1950; fashion coordinator and commentator, Fla., 1957-69; fashion writer, soc. writer Pompano Beach (Fla.) Town News, Sun Sentinel, Pompano and Palm Beach Post Times, 1960-68; travel cons. Erin Gardner Travel, Boca Raton Fla., 1961—; pres., owner Irish Imports Galore, Ltd., Boca Raton, 1967—; co-owner Personnally Yours, public relations, 1962-64. Chmn., Community Concerts Assn., Short Hills, N.J., 1952-55; com. head Project Hope, Palm Beach and Broward Counties, 1961-62; mem. adv. bd. Ft. Lauderdale Forum, 1963-70; chmn. art exhibit Boca Raton Art Guild, 1967; life mem., past pres. North Broward Symphony Soc.; life mem. Ft. Lauderdale Symphony Soc., Debbie Rand Service League; charter, life mem. Fla. Atlantic Music Guild, Civic Ballet Ft. Lauderdale, Round Table Palm Beach; chmn. Le Premier Bal a Boca Raton, 1970, El Segundo Baile de Boca Raton, 1971; chmn. Symphony Ball, 1973, mem. com., 1974; chmn. Heart and Harness at Pompano Park, Heart Fund, 1972, mem. com., 1973; reservations chmn. Tiara Ball, Royal Dames, 1972; mem. Royal Dames Cancer Research; mem. landscaping com. Gold Circle of Nova U.; founder-donor Caldwell Playhouse, Boca Raton, 1975; social chmn. Friends of Playhouse; founder Stars for Caldwell. Recipient Internat. award for individual achievement on behalf of Ireland, 1981. Mem. Soc. of Ireland in Fla. (founder, past pres., hon. chmn.), Nat. Soc. Arts and Letters (life; ways and means chmn. Boca Raton chpt. 1981). Clubs: La Coquille (Palm Beach); Boca Raton; Royal Palm Yacht. Home: 1200 S Ocean Blvd Boca Raton FL 33432 Office: 403 Golf View Dr Boca Raton FL 33432

COOPER, PATRICIA DAWKINS, assn. exec.; b. Houston, Feb. 5, 1944; d. Austin Eli and Sarah Lorraine (Rountree) Dawkins; B.A., Columbia Coll., 1965; children from previous marriage—Catherine Sloane, Sarah Riley, Patricia Daily. Appointments sec. to Congressman Tom Gettys, Washington, 1965; tchr. Lugoff (S.C.) Elem. Sch., 1967-68, Camden (S.C.) Elem. Sch., 1969-70; ombudsman State of S.C., 1970-73;

asst. dir. Carolina Cup and Colonial Cup Internat., Camden, 1973—; adminstr. Camden Feed Co., 1973—; office mgr. Camden Tng. Center, thoroughbreds, 1973—asst. sec. Mulberry Resources, Inc., 1980-82; sec.-treas. Equistar Products Co., 1980—. Mem. Kershaw County Fine Arts Center; sustaining mem. Camden Jr. Welfare League; bd. dirs. Kershaw County unit Am. Cancer Soc., 1980—. Mem. Nat. Steeplechase and Hunt Assn., Nat. Hay Assn. Democrat. Methodist. Clubs: Camden Country, Sprindale Hall. Home: 401 Greene St Camden SC 29020 Office: Knights Hill Rd Camden SC 29020

COOPER, PAULETTE MARCIA, author; b. Antwerp, Belgium, July 26, 1944, came to U.S., 1948, naturalized, 1950; d. Ted S. and Stella R. (Toepfer) C.; B.A. with honors, Brandeis U., 1964; M.A., City U. N.Y., 1968. Free-lance writer, 1968—. Recipient Edgar Allan Poe spl. award Mystery Writers Am., 1975. Mem. Am. Soc. Journalists and Authors, N.Y. Press Club, Investigative Reporters and Editors, Nat. Acad. TV Arts & Scis., Travel Journalists Guild, Sigma Delta Chi. Author 6 books including: The Scandal of Scientology; The Medical Detectives; Growing Up Puerto Rican, also 350 articles. Address: 300 E 40th St New York NY 10016

COOPER, REBECCA, art, real estate dealer; b. Phila., July 11, 1947; d. Frank and Bernice (Lewis) C.; B.A., N.Y. U., 1969, M.A., 1971; m. Michael J. Waldman, June 27, 1982. Owner, operator Gallery Rebecca Cooper, Washington and N.Y.C., 1974-90; pres. Rebecca Cooper, Inc., N.Y.C., 1980—; conceptual art investment; conceptual artist; N.Y. Mayor's Adv. Com. on Interior Furnishings and Design Industry, 1981-82. Program com. Women's Campaign Fund. Mem. N.Y. Assn. Woman Bus. Owners-Artsroundtable, Friends Whitney Mus. Am. Art, Am. Ballet Theatre. Home: 929 Park Ave New York NY 10028 Office: PO Box 364 207 E 85th St New York NY 10028

COOPER, THEODOSHIA SARAH MAE, rehab. social worker; b. Eudora, Ark., Mar. 26, 1925; d. James Weldon and Leola (Simon) Johnson; B.S. in Edn., Ark. Bapt. Coll., 1951; M.Ed., U. Ark., Fayetteville, 1980; m. J.V. Cooper, Apr. 12, 1944 (dec. Sept. 1980); children—Mary Louise, Patricia Ann. High sch. tchr., Ark., 1946-47; prin., tchr. Gravel Hill Elem. Sch., Benton, Ark., 1947-48; spl. edn. tchr. Children's Convalescent Center, Jacksonville, Ark., 1948-56; tchr., social worker Ark. Sch. Deaf, Little Rock, 1957-58; psychiat. social worker Ark. State Hosp., Little Rock, 1958-66, Easter Seal Agy., Little Rock, 1966-69; rehab. social worker, then supr. Ark. Rehab. Services, 1969-74, adminstr. facilities program, 1979—; Bd. dirs. Ark. Youth Planning Council; mem. Ark. Mental Health Adv. Bd.; bd. dirs. Little Rock YMCA; bd. dirs., sec. Little Rock Legal Aid Soc.; mem. Little Rock Community Concert Assn. Recipient award Ark. conf. Social Welfare, 1976, also numerous certs. and service awards; grantee Ark. Alcoholic Found., Yale U., Nat. Found. Infantile Paralysis, Eastern Mich. Coll., George Washington U. Mem. Nat. Rehab. Assn. (v.p. Ark. chpt. 1978), Ark. Assn. Mental Health (dir.), Ark. Rehab. Assn. (v.p. 1978), Am. Personnel and Guidance Assn., Am. Rehab. Counselor Assn., Nat. Rehab. Counseling Assn., Nat. Assn. Social Workers, Ark. Juvenile Correctional Assn. (past pres.), Ark. Council Social Welfare (past pres.), Am. Assn. Workers Blind, Am. Council Blind, Nat. Rehab. Adminstrn. Assn., Ark. Assn. Human Services, AAUW, Am. Public Welfare Assn., LWV. Baptist. Home: 1915 Battery St Little Rock AR 72202 Office: 1320-H Brookwood Dr Little Rock AR 72203

COPELAND, CAROLYN ABIGAIL, univ. dean; b. White Plains, N.Y., May 5, 1931; d. Robert Erford and Mary Terwilliger; B.A. (CEW scholar), U. Mich., 1973, M.A. (Rackham Grad. Student scholar), 1979; m. William E. Copeland, Aug. 16, 1964; children—Rob Cameron, Diana Elizabeth Bosworth. With dean's office Coll. Lit., Sci. and the Arts, U. Mich., Ann Arbor, 1967—, asst. dean, 1980—. Mem. Mortar Bd., Phi Beta Kappa. Author: Tankas from the Koelz Collection, 1980; Walter Norman Koelz, A Biography, in progress. Research in Buddhist art history. Home: 520 Darwin Rd Pinckney MI 48169 Office: University of Michigan Ann Arbor MI 48109

COPELAND, KATHLEEN GAYLE, fitness cons.; b. Altadena, Calif., Oct. 12, 1949; d. Gilbert M. and Dolores (Charron) Rascon; student U. Calif., Davis, 1968-69; B.A., Calif. State U., Long Beach; m. Michael Calhoun, June 12, 1982. Guest relations Disneyland, Anaheim, Calif., 1967-72; loan officer First Hawaiian Bank, Honolulu, 1972-76; v.p. Fitness Cons. Parcourse Ltd., San Francisco, 1976—. Advisor, Jr. Achievement, 1974-76. Mem. Am. Assn. Fitness Dirs. in Bus. and Industry. Office: 3701 Buchanan St San Francisco CA 94123 *

COPELAND, LOIS JACQUELINE (MRS. RICHARD A. SPERLING), physician; b. Malden, Mass., Sept. 16, 1943; d. Arnold Alan and Ann (Goldfarb) C.; B.A. magna cum laude with distinction, Cornell U., 1964, M.D., 1968; m. Richard A. Sperling, June 7, 1970; children—Mark, Larissa, Lauren Anne. Intern N.Y. Hosp., N.Y.C., 1968-69, resident, 1969-70; resident Bellevue Hosp., N.Y. U. Med. Center, 1970-72; teaching asst. internal medicine N.Y. U. Med. Center, 1971-72; asst. attending physician Pascack Valley Hosp., Westwood, N.J., 1974—. Mem. AMA, Med. Soc. N.J., Bergen County Med. Soc., Phi Beta Kappa, Phi Kappa Phi, Alpha Lambda Delta. Home: 25 Sparrowbush Rd Upper Saddle River NJ 07458 Office: 47 Central Ave Hillsdale NJ 07642

COPELIN, KAY SUE, mgmt. cons.; b. Cin., Apr. 5, 1933; d. Carl W. and Linda F. (Jamison) Kaucher; student Miami (Ohio) U., U. Cin., 1958, Coll. Mt. St. Joseph, 1981; m. Howard L. Copelin, June 30, 1951; children—Howard L., David, Gary, Ray. Br. mgr. Hunter Savs. Assn., Cin., 1963-73; mortgage loan underwriter Liberty Mortgage Ins. Corp./Verex Corp., Cin., 1973-77; regional dir. Foremost Guaranty Corp., 1978-80; pres. KSC Assos., 1980—; v.p. Percept Assos., 1981—. Chmn. bd. dirs. Northeastern YMCA, 1981-82; bd. dirs. Meml. Community Center, 1982—, Cin. Women Investors, 1980—; trustee Kenwood Baptist Ch., 1980-82. Mem. Nat. Assn. Profl. Saleswomen, Cin. Bus. and Profl. Womens Club. Home: 5850 Bayberry Dr Cincinnati OH 45242 Office: 1527 Madison Rd Cincinnati OH 45206

COPLEY, HELEN KINNEY, newspaper publisher; b. Cedar Rapids, Iowa, Nov. 28, 1922; d. Fred Everett and Margaret (Casey) Kinney; student Hunter Coll., N.Y.C., 1945; m. James S. Copley, Aug. 16, 1965 (dec.); 1 son, David Casey. Asso. Copley Newspapers, 1953—; chmn. corp., dir., mem. exec. com. Copley Press, Inc., 1973—, chief exec. officer, exec. compensation com., chmn. ops. com., 1974—, sr. mgmt. bd., 1974—; chmn. bd. Copley News Service, San Diego, 1973; chmn. bd., dir., mem. exec. com. Union-Tribune Pub. Co., 1973; editor editorial page San Diego Union, 1973; pub. San Diego Union and Evening Tribune, 1973; chmn. bd., dir., mem. exec. com. Communications Hawaii, Inc., 1973. Mem. Friends of Internat. Center, La Jolla, La Jolla Mus. Comtemporary Arts, La Jolla Town Council Inc.; life patroness Makua Aux., Childrens Home Soc.; charter mem. San Diego Womens Council, Navy League U.S.; life mem. San Diego Hall of Sci.; mem. San Diego Opera Guild, San Diego Soc. Natural History; mem. womens com. San Diego Symphony Assn., Scripps Meml. Hosp. Aux., Social Service League of La Jolla; life mem. Star of India Aux., Zool. Soc. San Diego; mem. YWCA. Chmn. bd., trustee James S. Copley Found., 1973; hon. chmn., bd. dirs. Washington Crossing Found.; mem. adv. council Freedom of Info. Center, U. Mo.; bd. dirs. Fine Arts Soc. San Diego, Putnam Found., Wells Fargo Bank; trustee, bd. dirs. Freedoms Found. at Valley Forge; trustee, trustee devel. com. Scripps Clinic and Research Found.; trustee U. San Diego. Mem. Inter Am. (dir.), Calif. press assns., Newspaper Advt. Bur. (dir.), Am. Soc. Newspaper Editors, Am., Internat. press insts., Calif. Newspaper Pubs. Assn., Greater Los Angeles, Nat., San Diego, San Francisco press clubs, Nat. Newspaper Assn., Pres.'s Assn., Western Newspaper Found., Calif. C. of C. (dir.), Sigma Delta Chi. Republican. Roman Catholic. Clubs: Aurora (Ill.) Country; Cuyamaca, San Diego Yacht, Stadium, University, U. San Diego Presidents (San Diego); De Anza Country (Borrego Springs, Calif.); La Costa Country (Carlsbad, Calif.); La Jolla Beach and Tennis, La Jolla Country; Menlo Coll. Mothers (Menlo Park, Calif.). Office: Copley News Service PO Box 190 San Diego, CA 92112 *

COPP, LAUREL ARCHER, univ. dean; b. Sioux Falls, S.D., Nov. 12, 1931; B.S. in Nursing Edn., Dakota Wesleyan U., 1956; M. Nursing Edn., U. Pitts., 1960, Ph.D., 1967; cert. program health systems mgmt., Harvard U., 1974; m. John Dixon Copp. Asso. prof., acting head nursing dept. Pa. State U., 1966-72; vis. prof. abnormal psychiatry Thiel Coll., Greenville, Pa., 1969-75, also chief nursing research div. VA Sch. Nursing, Washington, 1972-75; dean Sch. Nursing, prof. U. N.C., Chapel Hill, 1975—; lectr.; mem. policy bd. Health Services Research Center; former chmn. Va./Carolinas' Doctoral Consortium; interdisciplinary tng. for humanistic health care Health Manpower; RFP writers for nat. cancer program planning Nat. Cancer Inst.; adv. com. clin. center NIH. Chmn. alumni council program health systems mgmt. Harvard U., 1981-82. Named Alumnus of Yr., Dakota Wesleyan U., 1981. Fellow Am. Acad. nursing; mem. Am. Assn. Colls. of Nursing, Am. Nurses Assn., Nat. League Nursing, Sigma Theta Tau, Delta Kappa Gamma, Pi Lambda Theta. Editor: (with others) Recent Advances in Nursing (series); overseas mem. editorial bd. Jour. Advanced Nursing, London; contbr. articles to profl. jours. Office: 107 Carrington Hall Chapel Hill NC 27514

COPPERSMITH, MARIAN UNGAR (MRS. W. LOUIS COPPERSMITH), mag. pub. exec.; b. Wilkes-Barre, Pa., June 11, 1933; d. Max H. and Tillie (Landau) Ungar; B.A., Pa. State U., 1953; m. Sy Barash, Jan. 31, 1954 (dec. Feb. 1975); children—Carol Lynn, Nan Ruth; m. 2d, W. Louis Coopersmith, Apr. 29, 1978. Tech. writer Kling Studios, Chgo., 1951; editorial dir. Daily Collegian, State College, Pa., 1953; grad. asst. dept. speech Pa. State U., State Coll., 1953-55; writer, salesman Friedman & Barash, State College, 1956-59; pub. State College Town-Gown, 1959—, pres., 1975—; cons. mktg. and public relations to various fin. instns.; instr. mktg. Pa. State U., University Park, 1973—. Chmn., Art Alliance Fund Campaign, 1971; mem. public relations com. Central Pa. Heart Assn., 1973; chmn. Cancer Crusade, State College, 1973-74; mem. Pa. Commn. for Women, 1980—; bd. govs. Pa. Free Enterprise Week, 1981—; vice chmn. bd. govs. Centre County Community Found., 1981—; pres. Nittany Council of Republican Women, 1960-61; bd. dirs. United Fund, 1965-70, asst. chmn., 1969; trustee Pa. State U., 1976—; bd. dirs. Pennsylvanians for Effective Govt., 1978; bd. dirs. United Way Pa., 1977—, treas., 1978; bd. dirs. Capital Blue Cross, 1978—, Women's Campaign Fund, 1982—. Recipient Kiwanis award, 1976. Mem. Nat. (public relations com. 1972-73), Pa. (public relations counsel 1967-75) cable TV assns., Women in Communications, C. of C. (dir. 1973-79, pres. 1974-75), Pa. C. of C. (dir. 1974—), Phi Sigma Sigma. Mem. B'nai B'rith (pres. 1956). Contbr. articles to profl. jours. Home: 620 Toftrees Ave Apt 359 State College PA 16801 also 900 Parkview Dr Johnstown PA 15905 Office: 403 S Allen St State College PA 16801

CORAZA, MARY CATHERINE, psychologist; b. Newton, N.J.; d. Alfred J. and Alice R. (Reynolds) C.; Ed.D., Lehigh U., 1977. Staff psychologist Pa. Hosp., Phila., 1980—; asst. prof. psychology depts. pediatrics and mental health sci. Hahnemann Med. Coll., Phila., 1974—. Mem. Am. Psychol. Assn., Pa. Psychol. Assn., Phila. Soc. Clin. Psychologists, Psi Chi. Home: 409 S Croskey St Philadelphia PA 19103 Office: Pa Hosp 8th and Locust Sts Philadelphia PA 19106

CORBETT, GWEN ANN, telephone answering service co. exec.; b. Chgo., Aug. 24, 1938; d. Wesley Francis and Marie Ruth (Johnson) Evans; m. George Raymond Corbett, June 25, 1960; children—June Ellen, Lori Louise, Kim Elizabeth, Kristi Lee, Matthew William. Pres., Answer-All Secretarial Service Inc., Westminster, Colo., 1964—, Print-All Services, 1976—. Vocat. adv. com. Adams County Sch. Dist. 50. Mem. Adams County C. of C., Asso. Telephone Answering Assn. (internat. dir. 1977—, sec.-treas. 1979-80, v.p. 1980-81, pres.-elect 1981-82, pres. 1982—), Telephone Answering Services Mountain States (dir. 1973—, pres. 1975-76, exec. sec. 1978), Bus. and Profl. Womens Club, Am. Soc. Profl. and Exec. Women. Democrat. Mem. Reorganized Ch. Jesus Christ Latter-day Saints. Home: 10914 Pearl Ct Northglenn CO 80233 Office: 7145 Lowell Blvd Westminster CO 80030

CORBETT, RUTH ALLEEN, artist, writer; b. Northville, Mich., Jan. 24, 1912; d. Howard James and Rhoda Alice (Fuller) Corbett; student Cranbrook Acad., 1932, Meinzinger Found. Art Sch., 1935-36, Famous Writer's Sch., 1967-69; m. Roy Brent, Feb. 23, 1958; children—Jana Loi Janczarek, Paton. Illustrator Simons-Michelson Advt. Co., Detroit, 1935-37, Bass-Luckoff, Inc., Detroit, 1937-39, Detroit Times, 1939-40, Canfield Assos., Detroit, 1947-53, Dow Chem Co., Midland, Mich., 1950-53, Creative Services, Detroit, 1953-56, Parke-Davis Pharm. Co., Detroit, 1954-56, H.J. Heinz Co., 1950, Mich. Bell Telephone Co., 1954-56, Detroit Edison Co., 1950-53, various automobile mfg. cos., 1947-53; advt. illustrator Universal Pictures Co., Universal City, Calif., 1956-74; tchr. art as pvt. tutor, also adult classes Pontiac (Mich.) High Sch., 1933-34; one woman show Freeman Gallery, Montrose, Calif., 1964; group shows Art Instrn., Mpls., 1935-65; exhibitor, lectr. on movie advt. art, 1979; columnist, cartoonist Sun City (Calif.) Times; executed mural Pontiac C. of C., 1934. Recipient Grand prize, numerous 1st prizes Art Instrn., Mpls., 1935-64, 1st, 2d, 3d prizes San Fernando Valley Club, 1961-63; Nonfiction Book award for Dying for a Cigarette?, Nat. Writers Club, 1976, Book award for Some Doctors Make Me Sick, 1980. Mem. Soc. Illustrators, Nat. Writers Club, Sun City Creative Writer's Group, Arts and Crafts Guild, Pontiac Sketch Club (pres. 1932-33), San Fernando Valley Art Club, Canyon Lake Art Assn. (award for water color). Republican. Mem. Methodist-Episcopalian Ch. Author and illustrator: Daddy Danced the Charleston, 1970; Art as a Living, 1982; contbr. numerous articles on motion picture advt. to various mags. Home: 25681 Sun City Blvd Sun City CA 92381

CORBIN, ANDREA HEINZLE, real estate corp. adminstr.; b. Kansas City, Mo., Aug. 23, 1945; d. Ferd Bernard and Adeline P. (Castello) Heinzle; B. in Photojournalism, U. Mo., 1967; student St. Mary Coll., Xavier, Kans., 1964-65; m. Arthur V. Corbin, Jr., Apr. 28, 1973. Asst. documents librarian Linda Hall Library, Kansas City, 1968-69; asso. editor Am. Family Physician Mag., 1969-71; public relations dir. Studio Sales & Service, Kansas City, 1971-72; successively creative writer, art dir., prodn. coordinator, mgr. customer service br. offices and Telecommunications div. United Farm Real Estate, Kansas City, 1972—. Mem. Kansas City Bd. Realtors, Nat. Assn. Female Execs., Am. Soc. Female Execs., Greater Kansas City C. of C., Women's C. of C. Office: 612 W 47th St Kansas City MO 64112

CORBIN, CATHERINE WHEELER, clin. psychologist; b. Toledo, Feb. 23, 1951; d. Everett William and Margaret Mary (Johannsen) Wheeler; B.A. (Phi Gamma Mu scholar), U. N.H., 1972; M.S. (NIMH grantee), Syracuse U., 1974, Ph.D., 1976; postgrad. psychoanalysis Westchester Center Psychoanalysis and Psychotherapy, 1981—; m. John Noyes Corbin, July 18, 1981. Staff psychologist VA Hosp., Montrose, N.Y., 1976—, coordinator neuropsychology clinic, 1977—; pvt. practice psychotherapy, 1977—; tchr. Pace U., 1978-81; adj. lectr. in psychiatry N.Y. Med. Coll., 1977—. Recipient Quality Increase award VA, 1981; cert. psychologist, N.Y. Mem. Am. Psychol. Assn., N.Y. State Psychol. Assn., Eastern Psychol. Assn., Westchester County Psychol. Assn., N.Y. Neuropsychology Group, Phi Beta Kappa, Phi Kappa Phi. Democrat. Presbyterian. Home: 139 Washington Ave Pleasantville NY 10570 Office: Psychology Service VA Medical Center Montrose NY 10548

CORBIN, KAREN SUE, office systems mfg. co. exec.; b. N.Y.C., Dec. 12, 1945; d. Arnold L. and Claire Cynthia (Rothenberg) C.; B.S., N.Y.U., 1967, M.A., 1971. With Xerox Corp., 1973—, mgr. office systems cons. program, Dallas, 1977-79, br. mgr., Chgo., 1979-81, mgr. dealer sales planning, Dallas, 1981-82, mgr. mktg. ops., 1982—. Mem. Internat. Word Processing Assn. Home: 17659 Sun Meadow Dr Dallas TX 75252 Office: 1341 W Mockingbird Ln Dallas TX 75247

CORBIN, KRESTINE MARGARET, author, fashion designer, columnist; b. Reno, Nev., Apr. 24, 1937; d. Lawrence Albert and Judie Ellen (Johnston) Dickinson; B.S., U. Calif., Davis, 1958; m. Lee D. Corbin, May 16, 1959; children—Michelle Marie, Sheri Karin. Asst. prof. Bauder Coll., Sacramento, 1974—; columnist Sacramento Bee, 1976-81; owner Creative Sewing Co., Sacramento, 1976—; cons. in field. Mem. Crocker Art Gallery Assn., 1960-78; mem. Republican Party election com., Sacramento, 1964, 68. Mem. Home Economists in Bus., Am. Home Econs. Assn., Internat. Fashion Group, Women's Fashion Fabrics Assn., Omicron Nu. Author: Suede Fabric Sewing Guide, 1973; Creative Sewing Book, 1978; (audio-visual) Fashions in the Making, 1974; producer: Cream of the Cream Collections, (nat. show in 40 cities), 1978—; Style is What You Make It!, (nat. buyers show). Address: 1448 Tradewinds Ave Sacramento CA 95822

CORBITT, ROBERTA DAY, educator; b. Blue Mound, Kans., Oct. 20, 1902; d. Everett Webster and Anna Lucile (Bundy) Day; student Asbury Coll., 1921-23, Emory U., 1924-26; A.B., U. Chgo., 1941, M.A., 1941; Ph.D., U. Ky., 1955; m. Duvon Clough Corbitt, June 3, 1924; 1 son, Duvon Clough. Prof., Candler Coll., Havana, Cuba, 1937-43, 45-46; instr. history Columbia (S.C.) Coll., 1943-45; prof. Spanish, Asbury Coll., Wilmore, Ky., 1946—, chmn. div. langs., 1955-65, 66-68; dir. Wildwood Chapel Mission in Ky. Mountains, 1959—. Named to Order of Ky. Cols., 1965; named Outstanding Lady Tchr., Asbury Coll., 1972; bldg. on Asbury Coll. campus named in her honor. Mem. Am. Assn. of Tchrs. of Spanish and Portuguese, Latin Am. Studies Assn., Midwest Council for Latin Am. Studies, NEA, Ky. Edn. Assn., Carribean Studies Assn., Asbury Alumni Assn. (recipient A award 1972), Phi Sigma Iota. Republican. Methodist. Club: Asbury Anns. Contbr. articles to profl. jours. Home: 205 E Morrison St Wilmore KY 40390 Office: Asbury College Wilmore KY 40390

CORCORAN, AGNES RUTH, businesswoman; b. Ada, Minn., Oct. 16, 1938; d. August Paul and Anna Fredricka (Sittko) Blau; student Augsburg Coll., 1956-58, Moorhead State Coll., 1962-63; m. Richard Michael Corcoran, Aug. 31, 1963; children—Beri Lynn, Michael Eugene. Advt. sec. Archer & Daniels, Mpls., 1959-60; service rep. Northwestern Bell Telephone Co., Mpls., 1960-62; exec. sec. No. Fed. Savs. and Loan Assn., St. Paul, 1964-65; exec. sec. Walter Butler Engr. and Architect, St. Paul, 1965-66; legal sec. McMenomy Hertogs & Fluegel, Attys., Rosemount, Minn., 1966-68; sec.-treas. Corcoran Hardware and Implement Co., Inc., Rosemount, 1973—. Adv., Dakota County Vocat. Sch., Rosemount; mem. exec. bd. ARC; mem. Ind. 196 Rosemount Elem. Adv. Bd. Mem. Highland Profl. and Bus. Women's Club, Female Execs. Nat. Assn., Am. Soc. Profl. and Exec. Women, Female Execs. Am. Republican. Roman Catholic. Home: Box 301 3355 Upper 143d St W Rosemount MN 55066 Office: 2975 145th St W Rosemount MN 55068

CORCORAN, ALICE FOLEY, bus. cons.; b. Roslindale, Mass., Jan. 1, 1941; d. Francis Gerard and Alice Elizabeth (Hayes) Foley; grad. Boston Sch. Bus. Edn., 1960; children—Candace Marie, Dennis Scott. Exec. sec., adminstrv. asst. various firms, 1960-68; asst. to pres. Am. Apparel Mfrs. Assn., Arlington, Va., 1968-77, asst. treas. Polit. Action Com., Fairfax, Va., 1973-78, dir. Apparel Polit. Edn. Com., 1976-78; pres. Polit. Action, Inc., Fairfax, 1976—, ACS Assos., Fairfax, 1977—; treas. Allied Realty Corp., Chevy Chase, Md., Orgn. Mgmt., Inc., Washington. Mem. Nat. Assn. Female Execs. Roman Catholic. Office: 13234 Pleasantview Ln Fairfax VA 22033

CORCORAN, EILEEN LYNCH, educator; b. Newark, Mar. 12, 1917; A.B. in English, Montclair (N.J.) State Coll., 1938, Litt.D. (hon.), 1976; M.S. in Elementary Edn., State Univ. Coll., Brockport, N.Y., 1953; spl. edn. cert. U. Rochester, 1958; Ed.D., SUNY, Buffalo, 1970. High sch. tchr., 1957-65; coordinator spl. edn. Bd. Coop. Ednl. Services, 2d Supervisory Dist., Monroe County, N.Y., 1965-67; asst. prof., then asso. prof. D'Youville Coll., Buffalo, 1967-72, dir. spl. edn., 1969-72; dir. edn. Children's Psychiat. Centre, N.Y. State Dept. Mental Hygiene, 1970-71; mem. faculty SUNY, Brockport, 1972-81, prof. curriculum and instrn., 1977-81, prof. emeritus, 1981—; bd. visitors Monroe Developmental Center, Rochester; cons. in field. Fellow Am. Assn. Mental Deficiency; mem. Council Exceptional Children (pres. N.Y. State 1971, pres., 1979-82, gov. 1979-82, Disting. Service award 1977), AAUW, AAUP, Assn. Children Learning Disabilities, Soc. Research Child Devel., Delta Kappa Gamma. Author curriculum materials, articles. Address: 17442 105th Ave Sun City AZ 85373

CORCORAN, MARY BARBARA, educator; b. Pasadena, Calif., May 22, 1924; d. George Ernest and Ina Pearl (Thomas) Morrison; B.A., Wellesley Coll., 1946; M.A., Radcliffe Coll., 1949; postgrad. U. Munchen, 1949-50; Ph.D., Bryn Mawr Coll., 1958; m. James Leonard Corcoran, Dec. 22, 1956; children—Ann Morrison, Elizabeth Phippen. Translator, U.S. War Dept., Nurenberg, Germany, 1946-47; instr. German, Wellesley Coll., Mass., 1947-48; faculty Vassar Coll., Poughkeepsie, N.Y., 1953—, prof., chmn. German dept., 1977—. Mem. Am. Assn. Tchrs. German, AAUP, MLA. Republican. Mem. United Ch. of Christ. Office: Vassar College German Dept Poughkeepsie NY 12601

CORCORAN, MARY (ELIZABETH), educator; b. Providence, Aug. 15, 1921; d. Charles and Katherine (Weeden) C.; B.A., Hunter Coll., N.Y.C., 1947; M.A., Stanford U., 1948, Ph.D., U. Minn., 1957. Instr. psychology U. Vt., 1948-50; asso. Ednl. Testing Service, 1950-53; mem. faculty U. Minn., 1953—, prof. higher edn. and ednl. psychology, 1967—, dir. grad. studies higher edn., 1976-81; vis. prof. Ont. Inst. Studies in Edn., 1968-69, Ind. U., 1975-76; research dir. Internat. Study Univ. Admissions, 1961-63; cons. in field. Mpls. Woman's Club fellow, 1954-55. Mem. Assn. Instl. Research (Disting. Mem. award 1981), Assn. Study Higher Edn. (Meritorious Service award 1980), Am. Ednl. Research Assn., Am. Psychol. Assn., Comparative Edn. Soc. Europe. Author, editor in field. Home: 716 3d Ave SE Minneapolis MN 55414 Office: 221 Burton Hall U Minn 178 Pillsbury Dr SE Minneapolis MN 55455

CORD, VIRGINIA KIRK THARPE, radio sta. exec.; b. Shreveport, La., Oct. 21, 1905; d. Edgar Allen and Rachel Virginia (Kirk) Tharpe; ed. UCLA, U. Nev.; m. Brett Lobban Cord, Jan. 3, 1931; children—Nancy Cord Phelps, Sally Cord Hummel, Susan Cord Pereira. Owner radio Sta. KCRL-AM, Reno, Nev. Recipient numerous citations for outstanding radio programming. Mem. Jr. League of Reno. Christian Scientist. Club: Reno Executives. Home: 1700 Coronet Circle Reno NV 89509

CORDER, BILLIE FARMER, clin. psychologist, artist; b. Dundee, Miss., Sept. 12, 1934; d. Lee Kennith and Jimmy Louise (Hawkins) Farmer; B.S., Memphis State U., 1957; M.A., Vanderbilt U., 1959; Ed.D., U. Ky., 1966; student Memphis Acad. Art, 1959, Sch. Design, N.C. State U., 1971-75; m. Robert Floyd Corder, July 11, 1961. Intern, U. Tenn. Sch. Medicine, Memphis, 1959; staff psychologist Eastern State Hosp., Lexington, Ky., 1960-65, Child Guidance Clinic, Lexington, 1965-67; asst. prof. psychology Inter-Am. U., P.R., 1967-68; dir. psychology adolescent day care Area Community Mental Health Center, Washington, 1968-70; dir. psychol. services Alcoholic Rehab. Center, Butner, N.C., 1970-71; co-dir. psychol. services in child psychiatry Dix Hosp., Raleigh, N.C., 1971—; mem. adv. bd. Raleigh Developmental Evaluation Clinic, 1976—; adj. faculty psychology dept. N.C. State U., Raleigh, 1975—, U. N.C. Sch. Medicine, 1975—. Mem. Wake County Youth Adv. Bd., 1979-80; mem. adv. com. Raleigh Arts Commn.; bd. dirs. Haven House for Children, Nazareth House for Children. Recipient best research award N.C. Dept. Mental Health, 1965, cert. of appreciation Washington Tchrs. Assn., 1969; numerous awards for art, including Purchase award N.C. Mus. Art, 1976, awards N.C. Watercolor Soc., 1978, 79; numerous research grants. Mem. Am. Psychol. Assn., Southeastern Psychol. Assn., N.C. Psychol. Assn., Am. Assn. Psychiat. Services for Children (program chmn. i976-77), Raleigh Artists Guild, Raleigh Fine Arts Soc., N.C. Art Soc., Women's Equity Action League. N.C. Women's Polit. Caucus, Durham Artists Guild, N.C. Watercolor Soc. (v.p.), AAUW. Democrat. Baptist. Club: Raleigh Racquet. Contbr. articles to profl. jours.; dir. editorial bd. N.C. Jour. Mental Health, 1974—; adj. editorial rev. bd. Hosp. and Community Psychiatry, Quar. Jour. Studies on Alcohol. Office: Child Psychiatry Clinic Dix Hospital Raleigh NC 27611

CORDES, LOVERNE CHRISTIAN, interior designer; b. Cleve., Feb. 13, 1927; d. Frank Andrew and Loverne (Brown) Christian; B.S., Purdue U., 1949; m. William Peter Cordes, Nov. 14, 1959; children—Christian Peter, Carey Pomeroy. Interior designer, buyer, Fred Epple Co., Cleve., 1949-67; owner Loverne Christian Cordes, Chagrin Falls, Ohio, 1967—, also mgr., buyer; faculty John Carroll U., Cleve., 1976-77; cons. Cleve. Mus. Art, Western Res. Hist. Soc. Bd. dirs. Dunham Tavern Mus., 1961-62; pres. Dunham Dames, 1971-72; mem. Soc. of Collectors, Western Res. Hist. Soc., Am. Furniture Collectors, Cleve. Mus. Art, Chagrin Falls Hist. Soc., Nat. Trust for Historic Preservation. Fellow Am. Soc. Interior Designers (nat. bd. dirs. 1969-75, nat. v.p. E. Central Region 1972-75, recipient first presdl. citation 1973, 74, 75, soc. rep. to first Russian design seminar 1975 and Internat. Fedn. Interior Design, Sweden 1975); mem. AIA (profl. affiliate), Nat. Home Fashions League (pres. Ohio chpt. 1962-63), Am. Inst. Interior Designers (pres. Ohio chpt. 1969-72). Republican. Mem. United Church of Christ. Clubs: Chagrin Valley Country, Bowling Green (Milford, N.J.), Cleve. Garden Center, Audubon Soc., Arcadian Garden (pres. 1980-81), Dogwood Valley Garden, Kappa Kappa Gamma (pres. Cleve. alumni assn. 1966-68). Home and Office: 60 S Franklin St Chagrin Falls OH 44022

CORDIER, MARY ELLEN HURLBUT, educator; b. Davenport, Iowa, Dec. 24, 1930; d. Irving William and Evelyn Hazel (Bolte) Hurlbut; B.A., U. No. Iowa, 1955; M.A., Mich. State U., 1958; Ed.S., Western Mich. U., 1972; m. Sherwood S. Cordier, June 21, 1959; children—Ann Marie, Gail Renee. Tchr., elem. and jr. high schs., Iowa, 1950-56; tchr., school camp, Battle Creek, Mich., 1956-58; tchr. Univ. Campus Sch., Western Mich. U., Kalamazoo, 1958-60, asso. prof. edn., 1967—; tchr. edn. multicultural edn., environ. edn. Mem. Nat. Sci. Tchrs. Assn., Council Elem. Sci. Internat. Contbr. articles to profl. jours. Home: 1115 Cherry St Kalamazoo MI 49008 Office: Dept Edn and Profl Devel Western Mich U Kalamazoo MI 49008

CORDOVA, RITA ELAINE, banker; b. Old Hickory, Tenn., Dec. 16, 1949; d. James Frey and Beth (Merrill) Shelton; student public schs., East Nashville, Tenn.; m. Ross Cordova, June 25, 1968; children—Lori Beth, Lila Jane. Drawing clerk South Central Bell Telephone Co., Nashville, 1967-69, service rep., 1969-70; bookkeeper 1st Nat. Bank, Walsenburg, Colo., 1970, head bookkeeper, 1971-74, jr. officer, asst. cashier, 1974-80, cashier, personnel officer, 1981—. Roman Catholic. Office: 501 Main St Walsenburg CO 81089

CORDOVA JENSEN, CYNTHIA MOUREEN, publicist; b. Seattle, June 15, 1948; d. Michael and Colleen (Tacher) Cordova; student U. Wash., 1966-70; B.A. in Art and Edn., Western Wash. State Coll., 1972; m. Paul R. Jensen, Aug. 3, 1980. Tchr., Shoreline Sch. Dist., Seattle, 1972-77; printer, production asst. Pelican Press, Seattle, 1977; graphic artist Liberty Press, Seattle, 1977-78; sign and poster designer Nordstrom's Dept. Store, Seattle, 1978; asst. public relations Dorothy Matin Advt. Agy., Seattle, 1979; self employed publicist, 1979—; owner Media Tours West, Seattle, 1980—. Mem. No. Calif. Book Publicists, So. Calif. Book Publicists, Seattle Women Advt., Seattle Edn. Assn., Nat. Assn. Female Execs. (dir.), Pubs. Publicity Assn. Contbr. articles to ednl. mags. Home: 11032 14th St NE Seattle WA 98125 Office: PO Box 7 Northgate Station WA 98125

CORE, JANE ANN BOGGS, psychiat. social worker; b. Franklin, W.Va., Aug. 31, 1944; d. Richard Hopkins and Dorothy Virginia (Trumbo) Boggs; B.A. in Sociology, W.Va. U., 1966; M.Social Sci. Adminstrn. (HEW grantee 1969), Case Western Res. U., 1969; m. Harry Michael Core; 1 dau., Jennifer Trumbo Hess. Caseworker children's and adoptive services W.Va. Dept. Welfare, Martinsburg, 1966-67; social worker Lake County Mental Health Center, Mentor, Ohio, 1969-71; dir. social services Family Planning Assn., Lake and Geuaga County (Ohio), 1973; psychiat. social worker Simon & Bertschinger, M.D.'s, Inc., Willoughby, Ohio, 1974—; instr. Lake Erie Coll. Women; condr. seminars, cons. in field. Mem. Acad. Cert. Social Workers, Nat. Assn. Social Workers. Mem. Christian Ch. (Disciples of Christ). Home: 6707 Stratford Rd Painesville OH 44077 Office: 35104 Euclid Ave Willoughby OH 44094

CORE, MARY CAROLYN W. PARSONS, radiologic technologist; b. Valpariso, Fla., Dec. 8, 1949; d. Levi and Mary Etta (Elliott) Willey; student Peninsula Gen. Hosp. Sch. Radiologic Tech., Salisbury, Md., 1969, U. Del. Extension, 1969-73, Del. Tech. Community Coll., 1973-79; m. Joel Kent Core, Aug. 3, 1979; 1 dau., Candace W. Parsons. Technologist, Peninsula Gen. Hosp., Salisbury, 1967-72, tech. dir. edn. Sch. Radiologic Tech., 1973-75; technologist Johns Hopkins Hosp., 1972-73, Nanticoke Meml. Hosp., Seaford, Del., 1975-79; adminstrv. chief technologist, imaging depts. Shady Grove Adventist Hosp., Rockville, Md., 1979-81; adminstrv. technologist dept. radiol. scis. Anne Arundel Gen. Hosp., Annapolis, Md., 1981—; condr. profl. seminars. Mem. Am. Soc. Radiologic Technologists, Md. Soc. Radiologic Technologists (pres. 1980-81, sr. bd. mem. 1982-83, various awards including 1st Pl. Essay award 1974, 76), Soc. Nuclear Medicine Technologists, Am. Hosp. Radiology Adminstrs., Nat. Assn. Female Execs., Eastern Shore Dist. Radiologic Technologists (pres. 1976-78). Republican. Methodist. Home: 8231 Coatsbridge Ct Severn MD 21144 Office: Franklin and Cathedral Sts Annapolis MD 21401

CORELL, BELLE OLIVER, educator, club and civic worker; b. Suffolk, Va., July 30, 1902; d. Samuel Columbus and Eureka (Ashburn) Oliver; student Mary Washington Coll., Fredericksburg, Va., 1920-22; A.B., George Washington U., 1944; m. James Wesley Simmons, Apr. 27, 1926 (div. Apr. 1929); children—Belle Oliver (Mrs. Wm. E. Traver II), John Oliver; m. 2d, Harold Clifford Hart, Oct. 15, 1934 (dec.); m. 3d, Archibald Gerald Corell, Nov. 2, 1974 (dec. 1980). Tchr., Martha Washington Coll., Abingdon, Va., 1922-23, Harpers Ferry (W.Va.) High Sch., 1923-24, Hopewell (Va.) High Sch., 1924-26, 28-29; asst. prin., Tenacre, Mass., 1938-39; asst. state service officer Dept. Public Welfare, Richmond, Va., 1929-31; adminstrv. asst. Dept. Justice, Washington, 1931-33; sec. NRA, Fed. Emergency Relief Adminstrn., U.S. Govt., 1933-34; nat. def. WPB, Washington, 1940-44; exec. sec. woman's aux. Episcopal Diocese Mass., Boston, 1945-48; asso. John M. Hancock, Lehman Bros., N.Y.C., 1948-54. Pres. Boston chpt. U.D.C., 1945-47, 58-59, rec. sec. gen., 1955-57; pres., Wellesley Council Ch. Women, 1958-60; mem. bd. Northfield League, 1955-64; bd. dirs. Mass. N.E. Grenfell Assn.; sec. Belleair Beach Property Owners Assn., 1965—; dir. Bellaire Beach Park Bd., 1978-79. Mem. DAR (regent Amos Mills chpt. Wellesley 1961-63), Mary Washington Coll. Alumnae Assn. (pres. 1941-44), AAUW, Belleair Beach Garden Club (pres. 1967-69), Federated Hills Garden Club (rec. sec. 1956, pres. 1961-62, sustaining mem.), Power Squadron of CAP. Episcopalian (dir. ch. altar guild). Clubs: Bath (St. Petersburg Beach, Fla.); No. Lake George Yacht; Clearwater Country. Author: Foot Prints—A History of the United Daughters of the Confederacy. Address: 117 5th St Belleair Beach FL 33535

COREY, ANITA, designer; b. Albuquerque, Mar. 2, 1935; d. Clark M. and Anita (Osuna) Carr; student Scripps Coll., 1957-59, Washington U., 1960; B.A., U. N. Mex., M.A., 1975; children—Clark, Ana, Maria Virginia. Archtl. draftsman, 1958-68; project architect, Mexico City, 1969; project designer JFN Assos., 1966-70; partner Nicholson, Wilson, Corey & Wilhelm, 1970-73; pres. CHS Planning & Design Corp., N.Y.C., 1973—. Recipient Best Architecture award N.Mex., 1960; Indsl. design award; Gold Medal award. Office: 225 W 57th St New York NY 10019 *

COREY, JOSEPHINE, broadcasting exec.; b. Charleston, W.Va., Dec. 15; d. George N. and Behia (Jorge) C.; student Morris Harvey Coll., Charleston, Ohio U., Athens, U. Dayton (O.), Wright State U., Dayton. With sta. WCHS radio and TV, Charleston, 1960-63; hostess TV program Romper Room, sta. WTVN-TV, Columbus, Ohio, 1964-65; weathercaster, co-hostess-co-producer 22 Kidoo news, children's shows, producer, deliverer commls. sta. WKEF-TV, Dayton, 1965-73, program dir. commls., 1974-81; weathercaster, co-anchor news sta. WBBH-TV, Ft. Myers, 1974-76; ops. mgr. sta. WCHS-TV, 1981—. adv. bd. Jr. League Charleston; bd. dirs. Literacy Vols. Kanawha County. Mem. TV Programmers Conf. (past dir.). Mem. Eastern Orthodox Ch.

CORICH, MARIE ESTHER, mayor; b. Trinidad, Colo., Sept. 27, 1932; d. John and Soletta Rose (Frazzini) Toti; student public schs., Trinidad; m. A. Frederick Corich, Mar. 3, 1950; children—Frederick, Caroline, Michael, Glori, William, Melanie. Pres. Title I programs Trinidad Public Schs., 1976-77; bookkeeper Mike's Electric Co., Trinidad, 1975—; acting mayor Town of Starkville (Colo.), 1977-79, mayor, 1980—. Democrat. Roman Catholic. Home: Route 1 Box 418 Trinidad CO 81082 Office: 828 W Kansas St Trinidad CO 81082

CORLETT, EMMA JEAN, social worker; b. Knox City, Tex., Aug. 4, 1926; d. LeRoy and Luella (Burns) Massey; B.A. in Secondary Edn. cum laude, N.W. Nazarene Coll., 1965; M.S.W. with honors, U. Utah, 1972; m. John Paul Corlett, Jan. 1, 1946 (dec. 1969); children—Jeanne Marie, Thomas Lee, Jan Louise. Feature writer Statesman Newspaper, Boise, Idaho, 1960-63; caseworker Idaho Dept. Pub. Assistance, Boise, 1965-68; mental health counselor Community Inst. Human Resources, Boise, 1969-70; dir. patient and family counseling Mercy Med. Center, Nampa, Idaho, 1972-75; edn. counselor U.S. Army, Seoul, S. Korea, 1975-76; med. social worker Kern Med. Center, Bakersfield, Calif., 1976-78, dir. med. social services, 1978-79; dir. med. social services Santa Barbara (Calif.) Cottage Hosp., 1979—. Named Mrs. Idaho, 1959; licensed clin. social worker, Calif. Mem. Nat. Assn. Social Workers, Acad. Certified Social Workers, Internat. Register Clin. Social Workers, AAUW, Soc. Hosp. Social Worker Dirs., Am. Hosp. Assn., U.S. Postal Clks. Aux. (nat. v.p. 1959-63). Phi Delta Lambda. Office: Santa Barbara Cottage Hosp Pueblo at Bath St Santa Barbara CA 93105

CORLEW, ELIZABETH MAINES, ednl. adminstr.; b. Greensboro, N.C., May 20, 1928; d. Thomas Richard and Catherine (Dooley) Maines; B.A. in Liberal Arts, U. Tenn., 1949; m. Sept. 16, 1948 (div.); children—Elizabeth Jean (dec.), Deborah Ann, Susan Maines. Sec., Schs. Guidance Office Knox County, 1959-62; sec. Coop. Engring. Program, U. Tenn., Knoxville, 1962-67, coordinator, 1967-78, dir., 1978—. Mem. Am. Soc. Engring. Edn. Republican. Episcopalian. Club: PEO. Office: Estabrook Hall University Tennessee Knoxville TN 37996

CORLISS, GLADYS LOUISE, Realtor; b. Greeley County, Kans., July 8, 1934; d. Ted and Bertha Marie (Dyberg) Reeves; acctg. and data processing certs. Tech. Vocat. Inst., Albuquerque, 1969; student U. N.Mex., 1972—; m. James Henry Faulconer, 1950 (div. 1956); children—Doris Louise, Katherine Marie; m. 2d, Jack Oliver Corliss, 1956 (div. 1972); children—Charlie Ross, Joe Clifford (dec.), Wesley Leland. Sales asso., asso. broker with various brokerages, Albuquerque, 1972-77; owner, broker Lady Luck Real Estate and Ins., 1977—; vol. state Republican Hdqrs.; com. chmn. Bus. Profile Sheet, Albuquerque, 1979. Lic. broker, life and casualty agt., realtor, Okla., N.Mex. Mem. Albuquerque Symphony Women, Nat. Assn. Realtors, N.Mex. Assn. Realtors, Albuquerque Bd. Realtors, Beta Sigma Phi (past sec.). Republican. Clubs: Toastmasters (sec.), Duke City Bridge. Office: PO Box 3564 Albuquerque NM 87190

CORN, ANNE LESLEY, educator; b. Bklyn., June 29, 1950; d. Jay and Claire (Skolnick) C.; B.S., Syracuse U., 1972; M.A., San Francisco State U. 1973; Ed.D., Tchrs. Coll., Columbia U., 1980. Tchr. Multihandicapped-visually impaired Oak Park (Ill.) Public Schs., 1973-74; tchr. visually handicapped Intermediate Sch. 27, N.Y.C. Public Schs., 1974-76; instr., practicum supr. Tchrs. Coll., Columbia U., 1976-79; asst. prof. spl. edn. and rehab. U. Tex., Austin, 1979—. Frederic Burk Found. fellow, 1972-73; U.S. office Edn. grantee, 1976. Mem. Council for Exceptional children (bd. dirs. div. Visually Handicapped), Assn. for Gifted (chairperson com. for gifted/handicapped), Assn. for Edn. Visually Handicapped. Author: Monocular Mac, 1977; (with Iris Martinez) When You Have A Visually Handicapped Child in Your Classroom: Suggestions for Teachers, 1977, also Dutch and German translations. author profl. papers; editorial adv. bd. Jour. Visual Impairment and Blindness, 1981—. Office: EDB 306 U Tex Austin TX 78712

CORNELIUS, ALICE CATHERINE, consu.; b. Washington, Pa., June 10, 1929; d. Charles Arthur and Daphne Catherine (Connolly) Schuck; B.A., Vassar Coll., 1951; J.D., Yale U., 1954; English Speaking Union fellow, Oxford (Eng.) U., 1953; m. Benjamin F. Cornelius, Aug. 27, 1955; children—Charles Asher, Brian James, Bruce John, Dana Elisabeth. Admitted to Conn. bar, 1954, Mich. bar, 1956; atty. HEW, 1954-55; economist, city planner, community organizer Detroit City Plan Commn., 1956-61; partner firm Cornelius & Cornelius, Detroit, 1956-61; community organizer Model Cities program Detroit Housing Commn., 1962, Gt. Cities program Ford Found., also Detroit Bd. Edn., 1963; dir. Duluth (Minn.) Fair Employment and Housing Practices Com., 1964-68; cons. paralegal edn. Nat. Coll. Edn., Evanton, Ill., 1979—; dir. Legal Asst. Program, Mallinckkrodt Coll., Wilmette, Ill., 1974-79; bd. dirs. Northshore Paralegal Assn., 1979—. Trustee Wilmette Hist. Museum; mem. comml. aears com. Village of Wilmette; mem. family adv. bd. Loyola Acad., 1980-82. Mem. Nat. Assn. Paralegal Educators (dir.), Ill. Paralegal Assn. (dir.), Women in Mgmt. (dir.), Yale Law Sch. Alumni Assn. Chgo. (dir.), Conn. Bar Assn., Mich. Bar Assn. Roman Catholic. Address: 1030 Ashland Ave Wilmette IL 60091

CORNELIUS, LORETTA, govt. ofcl.; b. Hopkinsville, Ky., Apr. 1, 1936; d. Arlett Clifton and Lura Belle (Wade) C.; B.A., Bowie Coll., 1970; M.A., George Washington U., 1981; m. Francesco A. Calabrese, June 17, 1980; children—Charles, Cavin, Caroline. Vice pres. adminstrn. PRC Data Services Co., McLean, Va., 1967-81; dep. dir. Office Personnel Mgmt., Washington, 1981—. Chief adv. orgn. Hospice Fauquier County (Va.), 1980—. Republican. Roman Catholic. Office: 1900 E St NW Washington DC 20415

CORNETTE, MARY ELIZABETH, art gallery exec.; b. Logan County, Ky., Sept. 9, 1909; d. John Henry and Hallie Irene (Brister) Lawson; student Logan Coll., 1928; B.S., Bowling Green U., 1932; M.A., Western Ky. U., 1942; m. James Percival Cornette, Feb. 26, 1930; children—Marvin Brister, James Lawson, William Richard. Faculty, Bowling Green (Ky.) Bus. U., 1932-44; dir. Canyon Art Gallery, Canyon, Tex., 1965—, now pres., dir. Recipient West Tex. C. of C. Culture Award for Outstanding Achievement, 1972. Baptist. Home: 3312 Linda Ln Canyon TX 79015 Office: 2710 4th Ave Canyon TX 79015

CORNING, MARY ELIZABETH, scientist, govt. ofcl.; b. Norwich, Conn., Oct. 19, 1925; d. Horace Francis and Mary Teresa (Sullivan) C.; B.A., Conn. Coll. for Women, 1947; M.A., Mt. Holyoke Coll., 1949, D.Sc. (hon.), 1982. Chemist, Nat. Bur. Standards, Dept. Commerce, 1949-58; spl. asst. to sci. adv. Dept. State, 1958-60; program dir. Internat. Activities Planning Group, NSF, 1960-61, spl. asst. to head Office Internat. Science Activities, 1961-62, asso. program dir., 1962-64; chief publs. and translations div. Nat. Library Medicine, HEW, 1964-66, spl. asst. to dep. dir., 1966-67, apl. asst. to dir., 1967-72, asst. dir. internat. programs, 1972—; mem. chemistry panel U.S. Civil Service Bd. Examiners, 1953—, tech. editor, writer, 1955-60; mem. Internat. Commn. Optics, 1961—; U.S. nat. liaison officer OECD, 1962; dir., mem. exec. com. Gorgas Meml. Inst. Tropical and Preventive Medicine, Inc., 1972—, sec., 1974—; cons. biomed. communications to orgns., fgn. govts. Recipient Dir.'s award Nat. Library Medicine, 1974, 77; Silver medal HEW, 1971; Regent's award Nat. Library Medicine, 1980; Fed. Exec. fellow Brookings Inst., 1977. Fellow Optical Soc. Am., AAAS (chmn. sect. T); mem. Med. Library Assn., Am. Chem. Soc., Nat. Acad. Sci. (internat. commn. optics, internat. council sci. unions abstracting bd., internat. fedn. documentations), Phi Beta Kappa. Roman Catholic. Author book on internat. biomed. research and communication. Contbr. chpts., articles to books and jours. on colors and chem. constn., organic absorption spectra, spectrophotometry; orgn. of sci.; sci. communications and internat. sci. cooperation. Home: 8200 Wisconsin Ave Bethesda MD 20814 Office: Nat Library Medicine 8600 Rockville Pike Bethesda MD 20209

CORONA, LAVERNE MARY, controller; b. Chgo., Sept. 22, 1925; d. Dominick and Antionetta (Sangermano) Cribari; B.S.C., DePaul U., 1949; m. Joseph Corona, Oct. 22, 1949; children—Sandra Lee, Lynn Suzann, Vincent Joseph. Cost acct. Warwick Corp., 1949-52; substitute tchr. Chgo. Public Schs., 1956; acct. N.W. Community Hosp., 1960, Indsl. Research Products, Elk Grove, Ill., 1960-70; acct. Packaging Systems, Inc., Itasca, Ill., 1970-74, controller, 1974-78, sec., 1978-79, v.p., 1978-79; controller Packaging Systems, Inc. div. Nat. Can Corp., Itasca, Ill., 1979—, also dir. Mem., officer N.W. Council, 4-H, 1973-76; mem., sec. Cook County Exec. Council, 1972-74. Mem. Am. Soc. Women Accts. Home: PO Box 64 Medinah IL 60157 Office: Bedford Park IL 60638

CORONADO, ROSA, restaurant and food mfg. co. exec.; b. St. Paul, July 27, 1938; d. Arthur Morquecho and Elvira (Gamez) C.; B.A. in Public Relations, U. Mexico, 1960. With La Casa Coronado Restaurant, Mama Coronado Food Products, Mpls., 1960—, sec., 1973—, owner, 1974—; cons. food; mem. adv. bd. Dakota County Vocat. Trade Sch. Food Dept.; vol. tchr. fgn. foods Mpls. Sch. System; condr. seminar on Mexican foods Gen. Mills. Co., 1977. Mem. adv. bd. City Center Redevel., City of Mpls.; bd. dirs. Met. Econ. Devel. Assn., Mpsl; mem. Minn. Small Bus. Task Force; mem. ch. council, pres. soc. Our Lady of Guadalupe' Ch., St. Paul; chmn. food com. Ch. Parish Council, 1979-82. Recipient Letter of Merit, Amoco Co., 1976. Mem. Internat. Geneva Assn. (ann. trophies for food displays 1970-77, plaque spl. recognition 1979), Geneva Exec. Chef Assn. (dir.), Midwest Chefs Soc. (rec. sec. bd. dirs.), Minn., Nat. restaurant assns., Minn. Hispanic C. of C., Nat. Assn. Cooking Sch. Instrs. Democrat. Author: Cook in Mexico. Home: 2733 France Ave S Minneapolis MN 55416

CORPUZ, TITA DURAN, health care assn. exec.; b. Manila, Philippines, Mar. 16, 1938; came to U.S., 1964, naturalized, 1973; d. Constante F. and Florentina (Buenavista) Duran; B.S. in Nursing, U. Philippines, 1959; M.S. in Nursing, U. Ill., 1974; m. Oscar D. Corpuz, May 24, 1961; 1 son, Oscar D. Chief public health nurse Philippine Rural Reconstrn. Movement, Manila, 1959-60; asst. chief public health nurse Filipro Inc., Manila, 1960-64; staff nurse Albert Einstein Med. Center, Phila., 1964-65; staff nurse Michael Reese Hosp., Chgo., 1965-66; instr. edn. dept. Victory Meml. Hosp., Waukegan, Ill., 1966-69, adv. to hosp. adminstr., 1969-70; asso. chmn., instr. dept. nursing Evanston (Ill.) Hosp., 1969-75; dir. nursing and patient and community services Am. Hosp. Assn., Chgo., 1975-78, V.P. 1978—; nursing adv. U.S. Employers Del. to Internat. Labor Orgn., Geneva, Switzerland, 1976-77; nursing cons. various hosps., 1975—. Fellow Inst. Medicine of Chgo.; mem. Am. Nurses Assn., Sigma Theta Tau. Home: 250 Glenview Rd Glenview IL 60025 Office: 840 N Lake Shore Dr Chicago IL 60611

CORREA, EILEEN ISRAEL, clin. psychologist; b. New Orleans, Sept. 26, 1950; d. Norman Charles and Jeannette (Simison) Israel; B.S., U. Southwestern La., 1972; M.S. (USPHS grantee 1973-75), U. Ga., 1975, Ph.D., 1977; m. John Henry Correa, Jan. 28, 1978. Psychologist, Biloxi (Miss.) Gulfport VA Med. Center, 1977-79; acting chief psychology service New Orleans VA med. Center, 1980-81, clin. psychologist, 1979—, dir. psychology tng. program, 1981—. Mem. Am. Psychol. Assn., Assn. Advancement Behavior Therapy, La. Psychol. Assn., Southeastern Psychol. Assn. Democrat. Methodist. Office: 1601 Perdido St New Orleans LA 70146

CORREA, ELSA ISABEL, psychiatrist; b. Guayaquil, Ecuador, Jan. 8, 1941; came to U.S., 1973; d. Telmo O. and Victoria L. (Franco) Abril; B.S., San Marcos U., Lima, Peru, 1964; M.D., 1971; m. Pelayo Correa, 1962; children—Patricia, Luz, Elsa, Fernando, Christopher. Intern, St. Mary of Nazareth Hosp., Chgo., 1974-75; resident Spring Group Hosp., Balt., 1975-77, Johns Hopkins Hosp., Balt., 1977-79; clin. and research fellow in psychiatry Johns Hopkins U. Sch. Medicine, Balt., 1977-81, asst. prof. psychiatry, 1981—; practice medicine specializing in psychiatry, Balt., 1977—; psychiatrist, mem. staff Johns Hopkins Hosp., Balt. City Hosp., 1977—; dir. acute psychiat unit Balt. City Hosp., 1982—, asst. chief psychiatry, 1981—. Diplomate Am. Bd. Psychiatry and Neurology. Mem. Am. Psychiat. Assn., Md. Psychiat. Soc. Roman Catholic. Office: Dept Psy Balt City Hosps 4940 Eastern Ave Baltimore MD 21224

CORREA, MAIDA E., educator; b. Havana, Cuba, Nov. 4, 1949; came to U.S., 1961, naturalized, 1968; d. Juan I. and Silvina (Millan) Perez; A.A., Miami Dade Community Coll., 1971; B.S. in Bus. Edn., Barry Coll., 1972; B.S., Fla. Internat. U., 1973, M.S., 1976; postgrad. Fla.

Atlantic U., 1978, Nova U., 1978, Fla. A&M U., 1981; m. Lazaro C. Correa, May 6, 1966; 1 dau., Raquel Marta. With Marvin Stein, C.P.A., Miami, Fla., 1968-69; bilingual exec. sec. Miss Jane of Miami, Inc., 1969-70; tchr. asst. Miami Beach (Fla.) Sr. High Sch., 1970-72; with Western-Girl, Inc., Miami, 1972; sec. intensive lang. dept. Fla. Internat. U., 1972-73, intensive lang. instr., 1972-73; vocat. bus. edn. tchr. Nautilus Jr. High Sch., Miami Beach, 1974-76, tchr., chmn. bus. and vocat. edn. dept., 1976—. Mem. Dade County Equipment Evaluation Standards Com., 1976—; mem. Nat. Republican Congressional Com., 1979—. Named Tchr. of Yr., Miami Beach Sr. High Sch., 1979, 80, Dade County Vocat. Assn. Bus. Edn. Tchr. of Yr., 1980, Bus. Edn. Star Tchr. of Yr., 1978; recipient Dade Vocat. Assn. Appreciation award, 1978, 80; Vocat. Office Edn. Tchr. award, 1977; Mainstreaming Tchr. of Yr. award Council for Exceptional Children, 1977; Future Bus. Leaders Am. award of appreciation, 1977; Dade County Bus. Edn. Assn. cert. of appreciation, 1980; others. Mem. Miami Beach Sr. Faculty Council (sec. 1977—), Miami Beach Sr. Articulation Com., Fla. Vocat. Assn., Fla. Bus. Edn. Assn., Nat. Bus. Edn. Assn., So. Bus. Edn. Assn., Fla. Internat. Alumni Assn., Dade County Schs. Curriculum Writers, AAUW, Dade County Bus. Edn. Assn., Dade Vocat. Assn. (sec. 1977-78, v.p. 1979-80), Coop. Bus. Edn., Future Bus. Leaders Am. (Project of Yr. dedicated to her 1980-81), Phi Delta Kappa. Roman Catholic. Club: Coop. Bus. Edn., Home: 3987 SW 2d St Miami FL 33134 Office: 2231 Prairie Ave Miami Beach FL 33139

CORRIERE, ROSEMARY, interior designer; b. Milw., Sept. 17, 1947; d. Sebastian H. and Josephine A. Corriere; B.S., U. Wis., Madison, 1970. Designer, salesperson The Slater Co., Chgo., 1972-78; pres. Laird & Corriere Design Assos., Chgo., 1978-81, Corriere Design Assos., 1981—. Mem. Inst. Bus. Designers (v.p. Chgo. regional chpt.), Nat. Assn. Women Bus. Owners (co-chmn. corp. relations com. 1980—). Office: 22 W Erie St Chicago IL 60610

CORRIGAN, DENISE MAY, retail exec.; b. Abington, Pa., Mar. 31, 1947; d. John J. and Mildred B. Corrigan; B.Mus.Edn., Temple U., 1971. Asst. sales mgr. J.W. Pepper & Son, Inc., Valley Forge, Pa., 1970—, choral specialist, editor ann. choral catalogue, 1975—. Choir dir. Ch. of Christ, 1977—. Club: Mendelssohn of Phila. Home: 117 Meadowview Ln Mont Clare PA 19453 Office: J W Pepper & Son Inc Box 850 Valley Forge PA 19482

CORRIGAN, JANE MCGARA, veterinarian; b. Detroit, Dec. 2, 1946; d. Homer Joseph and Esther Lockwood (Skelding) McGara; A.B., Ind. U., 1968; D.V.M., Ohio State U., 1972; m. Lewis Corrigan, Apr. 8, 1972. Assoc. veterinarian Village Vet. Clinic, 1972-73; assoc. veterinarian Pacific Beach Vet. Clinic, San Diego, 1973-77; owner, mgr., 1977—. Mem. AVMA, Am. Animal Hosp. Assn., Calif. Vet. Med. Assn., San Diego County Vet. Med. Assn. (past membership chmn. and chmn. animal seminar, pres. 1981-82; past rep., sec., treas. Beach Mesa chpt.). Home: 2107 Calle Guaymas San Diego CA 92037 Office: 1362 Garnet Ave San Diego CA 92109

CORSBERG, DOROTHY JEAN, educator; b. Greeley, Colo., July 25, 1924; d. John Hermon and Inez Christine (Salberg) Corsberg; B.A., Colo. State Coll., 1946, M.A., 1952; postgrad. U. No. Colo., 60-81. Tchr., Oakesdale Consol. High Sch., Oakesdale, Wash., 1946-49; mem. faculty Northeastern Jr. Coll., Sterling, Colo., 1949—, dean women, 1949-62, chmn. humanities div., 1962—; critical reader/reviewer for ednl. materials; N.E. Colo. field cons. Colo. Humanities Program, 1982; mem. Colo. State Dept. Adv. Bd. Social Studies, 1966-68; chmn. Anna C. Petteys Scholarship Com., 1971—; mem. rural libraries and humanities com. Colo. Planning and Resource Bd., 1982—. Bd. dirs. Community Concert Assn., 1971-81. Named Outstanding Female Educator, U. No. Colo., 1968, Community Coll. Faculty Mem. of Yr., State Bd. Community Colls. and Occupational Edn. in Colo., 1981-82. Mem. NEA, Colo. Assn. Higher Edn. (program chmn., dir. 1965-67), P.E.O. Democrat. Home: 1113 Beattie Dr Sterling CO 80751 Office: Northeastern Jr Coll Sterling CO 80751

CORSER, SUSAN L., investment co. exec.; b. Detroit, Nov. 25, 1927; d. Oliver T. and V. Lyvonne (Van Matre) Dyer; grad. Patricia Stevens Models Finishing Sch., 1949; diploma N.Y. U., 1958; student Roberts Sch. of Beauty Culture, 1960-61, Phoenix Coll., 1962-67, Ariz. State U., 1978; children by previous marriage—Sharon, Lester J., Kimme. Photographer's model Galbraith Studio, Ft. Wayne, Ind., 1949-52; fashion model Patterson/Fletcher, dept. Store, Ft. Wayne, 1949-52; model for various fashion shows, Chgo., 1948-49; appeared on various fashion shows on TV, 1949-60; pres., dir. Charm and Models Finishing Sch., Lockport, N.Y., 1957-61; appeared on Nat. Biscuit Co. program Sta. WBEN, Buffalo, 1959-60; photographer's model for various studios and advt. agys. in Buffalo, 1954-60, Chgo., 1949-52; sales mgr. Ray Warriner Realty Co., Phoenix, 1963-67; pres. Biwi Investments Co., Phoenix, 1967—; also mortgage broker; guest speaker to various women's clubs and civic orgns., 1949—; beauty cons., 1949-60; free-lance fashion coordinator, 1949-60. Chmn. Our Year of History Celebration, Upstate N.Y. Centennial, 1950-60. Mem. Big Sisters Ariz., Nat. Assn. Realtors, Buffalo Models Guild. Office: 4750 N Central Ave Phoenix AZ 85012

CORSINI, NAOMI, nurse; b. Joliet, Ill., Nov. 17; d. Elmer and Barbara (Hutchison) Larson; R.N., Silver Cross Hosp., Joliet, 1946; B.A. in Psychology, N. Central Coll., Naperville, Ill., 1964; m. Frank S. Corsini, Mar. 29, 1952 (dec.); children—Pamela Sue, David Frank. Surg. nurse Silver Cross Hosp., 1946-48; polio nurse John Seeley Hosp., Galveston, Tex., 1948; pvt. surg. nurse Collins Belles Clinic, Peoria, Ill., 1948-50; instr. Silver Cross Hosp. Sch. Nursing, 1950-53, dir. nursing edn. Silver Cross Hosp., 1957-70, initiator, dir. vol. program, 1959—, dir. fire, safety and disaster programs, 1970-83; mem. health occupations com. Joliet Central High Sch., 1972-78; nursing edn. adv. com. Joliet Jr. Coll., 1977—; pres. Joliet Community Services Council, 1975-77; chmn. nursing com. Pub. Health Council Joliet, 1970-78; vice chmn. bd. Drug Coordination Info. Council Joliet, 1978; mem. healthcare services adv. bd. Upjohn Co., 1978-83. Mem. Ill. Hosp. Assn. (dir. region 2-C, recipient leadership award 1980), Am. Nurses Assn., Ill. Nurses Assn. (past dist. pres., past chmn. coms.), Ill. Soc. Dirs. Vol. Services (chmn. 1979-81). Author tng. curriculum in field. Address: 1007 Highland Ave Joliet IL 60435

CORT, DIANA, social worker; b. N.Y.C., Oct. 27, 1934; d. Arthur and Augusta Deutsch; B.S., N.Y.U., 1955; M.S.W., Columbia U., 1957; m. Leonard Van Arsdale, Sept. 17, 1978; children by previous marriage—Hayley, Daniel. Clinician, Payne Whitney Clinic, N.Y. Hosp., N.Y.C., 1957-59, psychiat. clinic Jewish Bd. Guardians, N.Y.C., 1959-61; founder, pres. Big Six Towers Nursery Sch., N.Y.C., 1962-67; dir. intake and social service L.I. Consultation Center, Forest Hills, N.Y., 1966—; supr., faculty mem. L.I. Inst. Mental Health, 1973—; cons. in social work Bergen Center for Child Devel., 1981—; dir. Seniors Option Service, Allendale, N.J., 1980—. Mem. Nat. Assn. Social Workers, N.Y. Soc. Clin. Social Workers. Address: 97 29 64th Rd Forest Hills NY 11374

CORTÁZAR, MERCEDES, editor; b. Havana, Cuba, May 15, 1940; came to U.S., 1961, naturalized, 1970; d. Filiberto and Flora Jiménez de Ayala Cortázar. Editorial dir. La Nueva Sangre mag., 1968-69; free-lance writer, 1969-76; editor-in-chief Fascinación mag., Miami, Fla., 1978-80; founding editor-in-chief Mar Abierto, internat. yachting mag., 1980—. Cintas fellow, 1971. Mem. Nat. Assn. Female Execs., Miami Design Perservation League. Author books of poems; El largo canto, 1959, Deux Poèmes de Mercedes Cortázar, 1965; contbr. poetry, short stories and articles to various publs. including: Protesta, Mundo Nuevo, Revista Exilio, La nueva sangre, Fascinación. Office: Mar Abierto Mag 1975 NW S River Dr Miami FL 33125

CORTNER, KAY LAMARR, computer hardware specialist, army officer; b. Kansas City, Mo., July 28, 1944; d. Robert Lee and Pearle Emogene (Willis) C.; B.A., Kans. State Coll., 1966; M.A., U. Tex., 1969; postgrad. U. Mo., 1976-78. Commd. 2d lt. U.S. Army, 1966, advanced through grades to maj., 1977; personal affairs officer, Ft. Jackson, S.C., 1967; comdr., Ft. Knox, Ky., 1968; computer specialist U.S. Forces, Korea, 1972, III Corps, Ft. Hood, Tex., 1973; personnel officer U.S. Retrograde Force, S.E. Asia, 1973; automatic data processing officer 1st Inf. Div., Ft. Riley, Kans., 1978; personnel and adminstrn. officer Saudi Arabian Nat. Guard Modernization Program, Riyadh, 1979—. Decorated Meritorious Service Medal, 3 Army Commendation Medals; recipient award for leadership DAR, 1971. Mem. Assn. U.S. Army, Promotion Research Com. Democrat. Home: 444 E Cedar St Olathe KS 66061 Office: Hdqrs US Army Armament Materiel Readiness Command Rock Island IL 61299

CORTRIGHT, JOAN EISENBREY, market research ofcl.; b. Phila., July 5, 1953; d. Nathan Dillingham and Eleanor (Beitler) C.; B.A. in Econs., Colo. Coll., 1977; M.B.A. (mktg. fellow), Keller Grad. Sch. Mgmt., Chgo., 1979. Owner, operator concession stand, Bryn Mawr, Pa., 1974-75; sr. research analyst Tech. Cons., Chgo., 1977-79; mktg. research analyst R.H. Donnelley Co., Chgo., 1979-81; mgr. market research Datacomp Corp., Phila., 1981—. Mem. Am. Mktg. Assn., Nat. Assn. Female Execs., Pi Gamma Mu.

CORWIN, JOYCE ELIZABETH STEDMAN, constrn. co. exec.; b. Chgo.; d. Cresswell Edward and Elizabeth Josephine (Kimbell) Stedman; student Fla. State U., U. Miami; m. William Corwin, May 1, 1965; children—Robert Edmund Newman, Jillanne Elizabeth Newman. Investment rep. A.M. Kidder & Co., N.Y.C., 1954-56; pres. Am. Properties, Inc., Miami, Fla., 1966-72; v.p. Stedman Constrn. Co., Miami, 1971—; owner, proprietor Joy-Win Horses. Gray lady ARC, 1969-70; guidance worker Youth Hall, 1969-70; sponsor Para Med. Group of Coral Park High Sch., 1969-70, hostess, Republican presdl. campaign, 1968; aide Rep. Nat. Conv., 1972. Mem. Dade County Med. Aux. (chmn. directory com. 1970), Fla. Psychiat. Soc. Aux., Vizcayans, Fla. Morgan Horse Assn., Fla. Thoroughbred Breeders Assn. Clubs: Coral Gables Junior Women's (chmn. casework com. 1959-63), Riviera Country, Golden Hills Golf and Turf, Coral Gables Country, Royal Palm Tennis. Home: 3929 Granada Blvd Coral Gables FL 33134 Farm: Windrift Ocala FLA 32686

CORWIN, RITA P., psychiat. social worker; b. N.Y.C., d. Michael H. and Clara D. (Gluck) Schwartz; B.S., Ind. No. U., 1974; M.S.W., Adelphi U., 1976; postgrad. Donsbach U., 1983—; m. Irving J. Corwin, Sept. 19, 1948; children—Lynn, Jan. Community and parent coordinator N. Shore Child Guidance Assn., Manhasset, N.Y., 1976-81; dir. Herricks Community Life Center, Williston Park, N.Y., 1973-75, Option Center for Psychotherapy, Williston Park, 1976—; pvt. practice psychiat. social work, Williston Park, 1976—; adj. prof. Stony Brook U., 1977—, Brookport U., N.Y.C., 1977—. Mem. Nat. Assn. Social Workers, Acad. Clin. Social Workers. Contbr. articles in field to profl. publs. Office: 79 Hillside Ave Williston Park NY 11596

CORYELL, MARY EDNA, distbg. co. exec.; b. Harrison, N.J., Jan. 25, 1908; d. Wilbur J. and Mary H. (Tilden) Shupe; student public schs., Livingston, N.J., West Orange, N.J.; m. Albert E. Coryell, Oct. 27, 1928. Stenographer, N.J. State Regional Planning Commn., 1926-30; legal stenographer Fitzsimmons, McGovern & Farrell, Newark, 1930-36; legal sec. Herman & Amsterdam, Orange, N.J., 1936-50; with Sub Tool Machine Supply Corp., Fairfield, N.J., 1961—, office mgr., co-owner, 1968—. Baptist. Club: Order Eastern Star (past matron N.J.). Home: 1-A DeBaun Ave West Caldwell NJ 07006 Office: 1275 Bloomfield Ave Fairfield NJ 07006

CORYLELL, JANE FRANCES, phys. therapist; b. South Bend, June 19, 1936; d. Andrew James and Helen Louise (Kinyon) C.; A.B., Oberlin Coll., 1958; cert. in phys. therapy, U. Iowa, 1959; M.S., Boston U., 1971, Ph.D., 1977. Staff phys. therapist Children's Seashore house, Atlantic City, 1960-63; staff phys. therapist Children's Specialized Hosp., Westfield, N.J., 1963-65; sr./phys. therapist Children's Seashore House, Atlantic City, 1965-69; asst. prof. to asso. prof. phys. therapy Boston U., 1974—. Mem. Am. Phys. Therapy Assn., Soc. Research in Child Devel., Soc. Behavioral Kinesiology. Editor: Body Senses and Perceptual Deficit, 1973; asso. editor Phys. and Occupational Therapy in Pediatrics, 1980—; contbr. articles to profl. jours. Home: 14 Parmenter Terr West Newton MA 02165 Office: Sargent College of Allied Health Professions 1 University Rd Boston MA 02215

COSCARELLO, BARBARA ANNE, econ. devel. cons.; b. Phila., July 22, 1941; d. Joseph A. and Carmela Mildred (Bossone) C.; B.A. with honors, Temple U., Phila., 1971; M.S., Drexel U., Phila., 1977. Mgr., Phila. Redevel. Authority, 1971-78; dir. Office Econ. Devel., City of York (Pa.), 1978-82; econ. devel. cons., 1982—; partner Devel. Cons.; bd. dirs. Pvt. Industry Council York County, York Rehab. and Industrialization Tng. Center; bd. dirs., sec. York County Visitors and Tourist Bur.; instr. York Coll. Bd. dirs. Open, Inc., 1967-69, Older Ams. Center of Haddington, 1972-74. Mem. Nat. Council Urban Econ. Devel., Pa. Council Urban Econ. Devel. (Edward Deluca award 1981), Women's Network York. Author articles in field. Office: 13 Market Way E York PA 17401

COSGROVE, CHRISTINE, coll. dean; b. Langley Field, Va., Feb. 14, 1944; d. Thomas Francis and Muriel Edmonde (Dinneen) C.; A.B. magna cum laude, Mt. Holyoke Coll., 1965; M.A. with distinction, Georgetown U., 1969, Ph.D. in Physics, 1970. Jr. physicist reactor br., nuclear physics div. Naval Research Lab., 1967; asst. prof., then asso. prof. math. Fitchburg (Mass.) State Coll., 1971-76, dean undergrad. studies, 1976—. Georgetown U. fellow, 1965-68; NSF trainee, 1968-69. Mem. AAUP, Assn. Women in Math., Math. Assn. Am., Phi Delta Kappa. Home: 83 Lancaster Ave Lunenburg MA 01462 Office: 160 Pearl St Fitchburg State Coll Fitchburg MA 01420

COSHO, KELLIE GREEN, artist; b. Seattle, Sept. 24, 1927; d. Lester Charles and Cornelia (Patzold) Green; B.A., U. Idaho, 1949; m. Louis Harrison Cosho, Aug. 28, 1948; children—Marilyn Teria, Ann L'Argent, James Harrison. Artist, gallery owner, Boise, Idaho, 1968—; group exhbns. include: Sun Valley Invitational, 1965-70, Idaho Biennial, Flathead Internat. Arts Festival, No. Idaho Coll., 1968, Women Artists of Idaho, Boise State U., 1969, Boise State Gallery, 1981, U. Idaho, 1981; mem. Idaho Commn. on the Arts, 1976—, chmn. 1978-80; adv. bd. U. Idaho Coll. Art and Architecture, 1981—; bd. Idaho Artistry, 1972-73. Chmn. citizens adv. com. Boise Redevel. Agy., 1978-80; mem. bd. visual arts panel Western States Arts Found., 1978-80. Mem. Nat. Assembly State Art Agys., Am. Fedn. Art, Idaho Watercolor Soc., Am. Council for the Arts, Idaho Art Assn. (dir. 1976-78), Boise Gallery of Art Assn. (trustee, 1972-78), Gamma Phi Beta. Club: Boise Jr. League (adv. bd., 1978-80). Home: 531 Warm Springs Boise ID 83702

COSIMANO, GLADYS NEATROUR, customs broker; b. Cambria County, Pa., Nov. 16, 1926; d. Frank Joseph and Sadie Mae (Hellman) Neatrour; grad. pub. schs.; m. Kenneth Joseph Cosimano, Nov. 11, 1945; children—Kenneth James, Michael Vincent, Toni Marie, Terri Ann. With FBI, Washington, 1944-46, 47-49; with Samuel Shapiro (D.C.) Inc., 1951-57; import mgr. Milton S. Kronheim & Co., Washington, 1957-58; customs broker, fgn. freight forwarder, Washington, 1959—; pres. G. Cosimano Inc., Washington, 1971—. Mem. Nat. Customs Brokers and Forwarders Assn. Am. Inc., Fairfax County C. of C. Office: Cargo Bldg 3 Door 76 Dulles Airport Washington DC 20041

COST, KAREN MAE, clin. immunologist; b. Port Clinton, Ohio, June 2, 1943; d. Earl Charles and Lillian Beatrice (Harrod) Dreier; B.S., Ohio State U., 1964, M.S., 1968, Ph.D., 1973; m. Chester L. Davidson, Jr., Jan. 1, 1977. Postdoctoral fellow in microbiology U. Louisville Med. Sch., 1973-74, clin. instr. medicine and pediatrics, 1974-77; chief immunology lab. Norton/Kosair Children's Hosps., Louisville, 1977—. Chmn. counseling com. Metro United Way Louisville, 1979-80, bd. dirs., v.p., 1980—. Research grantee Ky. Tobacco and Health Inst., 1976-78, Sta. WHAS-TV Crusade for Children, 1977, 81; diplomate Am. Bd. Med. Lab. Immunology. Mem. Arthritis Found., Am. Soc. Microbiology, Am. Rheumatism Assn., S.Central Assn. Clin. Microbiology, N.Y. Acad. Scis., Bus. and Profl. Women's Club. Club: Nat. Skeet Shooting Assn. Home: 8201 Salford Way Louisville KY 40222 Office: PO Box 35070 Louisville KY 40232

COSTA, MARY, soprano; b. Knoxville, Tenn.; student Los Angeles Conservatory of Music. Film voice of Sleeping Beauty by Walt Disney; appeared TV commls., 1955-57; debut Los Angeles Opera, 1958, in La Boheme, San Francisco Opera, 1959, as Violetta in La Traviata at Met. Opera, N.Y.C., 1964; appeared Glyndebourne Opera House, Royal Opera House Covent Garden, Teatro Nacional de San Carlos, Grand Theatre de Geneve, Vancouver, Lisbon, Kiev, Leningrad, Tbilisi, Boston, Cin., Hartford, Newark, Phila., San Antonio, Seattle; toured U.S. with Bernstein's Candide; appeared English prodn. Candide; revival Bernstein's Candide at John F. Kennedy Center for Performing Arts, 1971; tour Soviet Union, 1970; Bolshoi debut in La Traviatta, 1970; starring role motion picture The Great Waltz, 1972; appeared internat. recitals, orchs.; v.p. Hawaiian Fragrances, Honolulu, 1972. Vice pres. Calif. Inst. Arts. Named Woman of yr., Los Angeles, 1959; recipient DAR Honor medal, 1974; Mary Costa Scholarship established at U. Tenn., 1979. Address: care Shaw Concerts 1995 Broadway New York NY 10023 *

COSTANTINO, LORINE PROTZMAN, woodworking co. exec.; b. Chattanooga, Feb. 8, 1921; d. John Edgar and Rosa Jane (Ellis) McClelland; student U. Balt., U. Ill.; m. Conrad Protzman, 1937 (dec. 1958); children—Rosa Lorine, Charles Conrad, James Paul, Sharon Lee; m. 2d, Anthony A. Costantino, Feb. 27, 1960. With Conrad Protzman, Inc., Balt., 1954—, pres., chief exec., 1958—; developer apprenticeship programs for woodworking industry. Mem. Archtl. Woodworking Inst. (dir.), Bldg. Congress and Exchange Balt., Am. Sub-Contractors Assn., Nat. Assn. Women Bus. Owners, Iota Lambda Sigma (hon. mem. Nu chpt.). Republican. Roman Catholic. Club: Hillendale Country. Office: Conrad Protzman Inc 2325 Banger St Baltimore MD 21230

COSTELLO, JOAN, psychologist; b. Lawrence, Mass., Jan. 16, 1937; d. William Agustine and Helen Mary (Dolfe) C.; B.S., Boston Coll., 1959; M.S., Ill. Inst. Tech., 1963, Ph.D., 1967; 1 dau., Cathleen. Clin. psychologist Cath. Charities Chgo., 1960-70; research scientist Ill. Inst. Juvenile Research, 1964-70; asst. prof. psychology dept., Child Study Center, Yale U., 1970-77; dean, Erikson Inst., Chgo., 1977-79; asso. prof. Sch. Social Service Adminstrn., U. Chgo., 1979—; cons. U.S. Dept. Health and Human Services. Mem. Am. Psychol. Assn., Soc. Research Child Devel., Am. Orthopsychiat. Assn. Office: 969 E 60th St Chicago IL 60637

COSTELLO, MARILYN CLEODOMIRA, musician, educator; b. Cleve., July 17, 1926; d. George D. and Diana (Bevilacqua) C.; artists diploma Curtis Inst. Music, 1949; m. L.D. Dannenbaum, July 12, 1958; 1 son, Daniel George. Prin. harpist Phila. Orch., 1946—; instr. harp Curtis Inst. Music, Phila., 1961—, Temple U., Phila., 1961—. Recipient Italian Phonographic Critics award, 1967. Mem. Am. Harp Soc.

COSTOMIRIS, LOIS JEAN KAISER, writer; b. Noblesville, Ind., June 6, 1921; d. Everett E. and Ethel (Kepner) Kaiser; student pub. schs., Noblesville; m. Mar. 1, 1941; children—Wanda, Becky, Tonja, Dennis (adopted), John (adopted), William (adopted). Telephone operator, 1939-41; free-lance writer, 1970—; weekly columnist Tri-Town Topics, 1970—; contbr. articles to various publs. including: Good Old Days, Farm Wife, Indpls. Star, Fate. Recipient 1st place award for feature article Ind. State Home Econs. Orgn., 1974; writing awards Ind. State Press Club, 1977. Mem. Nat. Writers Club, Woman's Press Club of Ind. Republican. Quaker. Clubs: Home Econs., Book, Writers. Author: (with others) Cicero, Indiana, History Book, 1976. Home: Rural Route 1 Cicero IN 46034

COTANCH, PATRICIA HOLLERAN, nurse; b. Pitts., Aug. 26, 1945; d. Jerome Joseph and Delia Francis (Connelly) Holleran; B.S.N., U. Pitts., 1969, M.Ed., 1972, Ph.D., 1979; m. Stephen R. Cotanch, May 20, 1976; 1 dau., Kaitlyn Holleran. Staff nurse Braddock (Pa.) Hosp., 1966-68; instr. U. Pitts., 1974-76; asst. prof. nursing Duke U., Durham, N.C., 1976-79, asso. prof., 1979—; clin. nursing research cons., 1979—. Am. Nurses Found. scholar, 1980; Nat. Cancer Inst. grantee, 1981-84. Mem. Oncology Nurses Soc., N.C. Clin. Hypnosis, Soc. Behavioral Medicine. Home: 729 Blenheim Dr Raleigh NC 27612 Office: Sch Nursing Duke U Durham NC 27710

COTE, EVA, Can. govt. ofcl.; b. Rimouski, Que., Can., Jan. 1, 1934; d. Leonidas and Maria-Anna (Belanger) Lachance; comml. studies diploma Soeurs du Saint-Rosaire et Soeurs de la Charite, 1951; m. Robert Cote, Aug. 20, 1955; children—Elaine, Bruno, Ann. Law sec. Casgrain, Tessier et Casgrain, 1951-55; sec. Provincial Police, 1955-58; sec. legal dept. Phone Co., 1958-66; sec. Life Ins. La Sauvegarde, Rimouslu, Quebec, 1968-76; adm. sec., Loto, Quebec, 1976-80; M.P. for Rimouski-Temiscouata, 1980—, chmn. agr. com., 1981—. Mem. Commerce Chambre. Liberal. Roman Catholic. Office: House of Commons Ottawa ON Canada K1A 0A6

COTE-BEAUPRE, CAMILLE YVETTE, artist, educator; b. Worcester, Mass., May 21, 1926; d. Harvey and Blanche (Trahan) Cote; B.A. cum laude, Am. Internat. Coll., 1949; cert. in fine arts, Walker Studio Group, 1952; M.S., U. Bridgeport, 1967. Dir. arts and crafts South End Community Center, Springfield, Mass., 1955-58; art tchr. YWCA, Springfield, 1958-61; dir. workshops Hall Neighborhood House, Bridgeport, Conn., 1961-64, Jewish Community Center, Bridgeport, 1964-69; tchr., chmn. art dept. Notre Dame High Sch., Fairfield, Conn., 1970—; one man shows: Bridgeport Cath. Center, 1978, Creative Mind Gallery, Stratford, Conn., 1978, Burroughs Library, Bridgeport, 1979, Trumbull (Conn.) Library, 1981, St. Vincent's Hosp., Bridgeport, 1981, St. Joseph Manor, Trumbull, 1981; group shows include: Stamford (Conn.) Mus., 1977, Slade Mus., Norwich, Conn., 1975, Mus. Sci. and Industry, Bridgeport, 1974, Sacred Heart U., Bridgeport, 1979, Fairfield (Conn.) U., 1979, others; represented in permanent collections: Eastern Conn. State Coll., Trumbull Library Assn., St. Vincent's Hosp., St. Joseph's Manor. Mem. Conn. Classic Artists, Bridgeport Art League, Branfort Art League, Diocesan Bridgeport Edn. Assn., Newtown Soc. for Creative Arts, Nat. Arts Club. Home: 12 Melon Patch Ln Monroe CT

06468 Office: Notre Dame High School 220 Jefferson St Fairfield CT 06430

COTTER, ANNE MARIE KELLEY, home economist; b. Scranton, Pa., Jan. 24, 1935; d. Joseph Patrick and Genevieve (Murphy) Kelley Carey; B.S., U. Calif., Berkeley, 1956; M.S., U. Wis., Milw., 1977; children—David John, Paul Joseph, Linda Jean (dec.), Brian James. Tchr., chmn. dept. home econs. Marian High Sch., Mishawaka, Ind., 1966-71; home service adv. Wis. Gas Co., Milw., 1971-73; asso. prof., extension home economist U. Wis.-Extension, Racine County, 1973-82, S.E. dist. coordinator expanded food and nutrition edn. program, Milw., 1982—, mem. faculty senate, 1978-80, mem. univ. com., 1979-82. Mem. Nat. Assn. Extension Home Economists (Florence Hall award 1979), Wis. Assn. Extension Home Economists (scholarship 1974, fellowship 1976). Home: 1150 S Bobolink Dr Brookfield WI 53005 Office: 204 North Hall 929 N 6th St Milwaukee WI 53203

COTTER, MAUREEN HELEN, exec. search co. exec.; b. Lawrence, Mass., Jan. 25, 1943; d. John Joseph and Helen Theresa (Kavanagh) C.; B.A. in Theatre Arts, Pasadena Playhouse, 1963; B.A., Calif. State Coll., 1970. Chaplain's asst. Pacific State Hosp., Pomona, Calif., 1967-68; correctional counselor Calif. State Penintentiary for Women, Frontera, 1969-70; mgr. Forum, Los Angeles, 1971-72; exec. recruiter V.I.P., Los Angeles, 1972-74; owner, pres. Actuarial Search Assos., Los Angeles, 1974—. Mem. NOW, Nat. Assn. Female Execs., Am. Entrepreneurs Assn., Women in Bus. Los Angeles. Home: 902 S Curson Los Angeles CA 90036 Office: 910 S Curson Los Angeles CA 90036

COTTINGHAM, MARION DIANE, nurse; b. Milw., Dec. 22, 1943; d. Archie Rude and Francis Ilene (Thompson) Manson; R.N., St. Luke's Hosp., Racine, Wis., 1975; student Parkside U., Kenosha, Wis., 1972-75, also specialized nursing courses; div.; children—David, Diana. R.N., So. Wis. Center, Union Grove, 1975; patient care coordinator Brookside Geriatrics Center, Kenosha, 1977; inservice coordinator charge tng. and edn. Westview Nursing Home, Racine, 1978; dir. staff devel. Lincoln Luth. Home, Racine, 1979; dir. nursing Shady Lawn West, Kenosha, 1981—; real estate saleswoman, also owner, operator floral design shop Rose Palace. Mem. Gateway Bd. Fire Tng. State of Wis. grantee, 1972-75; lic. nursing home adminstr., Wis. Mem. Wis. Soc. Health, Manpower, Edn. and Tng., Long Term Care Dirs. Greater Milw., Kenosha Dirs. Long Term Care, Nat. Assn. Female Execs. Lutheran. Address: 15941 Durand Ave Lot 30C Union Grove WI 53182

COTTLE, ELEANOR CRAY (MRS. EDGAR WILLIS COTTLE), lumber co. exec.; b. Quincy, Mass., Oct. 13, 1891; d. John D. and Mary Ann (Sullivan) Moriarty; student Boston U.; m. Edgar Willis Cottle, Jan. 17, 1929. Credit mgr. Quincy Lumber Co., 1924-28, pres., treas., 1944—; former pres., treas. Rhines Lumber Co., Weymouth, Mass. Trustee, Edgar W. Cottle Found., Boston, Eleanor Cray Cottle Charitable Trust. Home: Woodchuck Hill Rd Harvard MA 01451 Office: 176 Newbury St Boston MA 02116

COTTMAN, IRYS JUANITA, food mfg. co. exec.; b. Bethesda, Md., June 10, 1950; d. George Greensbury and Alice Yvette (Williams) C.; B.S., Drexel U., 1972; M.B.A. (Quaker Oats Co. fellow), U. Chgo., 1974. Mktg. asst. L'Eggs Products Inc., Winston Salem, N.C., 1974-75, asst. product mgr., 1976-78; asso. product mgr. new products Pet Inc., St. Louis, 1978-79, product mgr. Pet Evaporated Milk, 1979-80; mgr. new products devel. Keebler Co., Elmhurst, Ill., 1980—. Mem. Am. Mgmt. Assn., Am. Mktg. Assn., Assn. M.B.A. Execs., Assn. Female Execs., Internat. Platform Assn., Alpha Kappa Alpha. Democrat. Baptist. Home: 231 N Kenilworth St Apt 1 Oak Park IL 60302 Office: 677 Larch St Elmhurst IL 60126

COTTON, CATHRYN BERNICE, nurse; b. Chattanooga, Aug. 30, 1935; d. Hubert McKinnley and Thelma Lousie (Cothran) Young; A.A., Kankakee Community Coll., 1970; B.S., Governors State Coll., 1974; m. Jonathan Arthur Cotton, June 24, 1965; children—Carlo LaVante, Jackie LaRue. Surg. tenchician Cook County Hosp., Chgo., 1960-69; dir. nurses Threshold Drug Abuse Center, Kankakee, Ill., 1971-72; shift coordinator Shapiro Devel. Center, Kankakee, Ill., 1972-77; dir. nurses Golden Age Convalescent Hosp., Pasadena, Calif., 1978; supervising staff nurse I with duties of asst. head nurse Los Angeles County-U. So. Calif. Med. Center, Los Angeles, 1977—; profl. cons. YWCA, Kankakee, 1971-74. Mem. AFL-CIO (Los Angeles County Union Shop Steward of Yr. Local 660 1981). Republican. Home: Pasadena CA 91103 Office: Los Angeles CA 90031

COTTON, CHARLA JANETTE, home economist, educator; b. DeFuniak Springs, Fla., Mar. 8, 1944; d. Adolphus Edgar and Callie Etta (Hood) Wambles; student Tenn. Poly. Inst., 1962-64; B.S. in Home Econs., Fla. State U., 1966, M.S. in Home Econs. Edn., 1969; postgrad. U. Ala., 1973; m. Ernest L. (Buddy) Cotton, Aug. 30, 1969; children—Bryon Ernest, Stephanie Suzanne. Asst. home econs. agt. Fla. Co-op. Extension Program, Okaloosa County, 1966-68; tchr. Walton Jr. High Sch., DeFuniak Springs, 1969-71; instr. home econs. Samford U., Birmingham, Ala., 1971-73; instr. Jefferson State Jr. Coll., Birmingham, 1972-74; extension 4-H agt. Fla. Co-op. Extension Service, Okaloosa County, 1975-82; instr. Okaloosa-Walton Jr. Coll., 1982—; cons. Okaloosa County Schs., 1977-80, Okaloosa County Council on Aging, 1978-80; guest appearance radio talk shows, 1975-79. Recipient Martha White award, 1977, Appreciation award Okaloosa County Shrine Fair, 1977. Mem. Am. Home Econs. Assn., Fla. Home Econs. Assn., Nat. Assn. Extension Home Economists, W. Fla. Home Econs. Assn., Omicron Nu, Nat. Assn. 4-H Agts., Fla. Assn. 4-H Agts., Gamma Sigma Delta. Democrat. Methodist. Clubs: Okaloosa-Walton Legal Aux. (pres.), Ft. Walton Beach Woman's, Elkettes (Fort Walton Beach). Author 4-H leaders guides, clothing and textiles pamphlets. Home: 719 Kris Ave Fort Walton Beach FL 32548

COTTON, ELEANOR LOVE, educator; b. El Paso, Tex., Jan. 30, 1923; d. William Dement and Eleanor Love (Martin) Greet; B.A., Tex. Western Coll. (name changed to U. Tex., El Paso), 1950, M.A., 1952; Ph.D., U. N.Mex., Albuquerque, 1973; m. Donald Reed Cotton, Feb. 26, 1944; 1 dau., Cabell Gillette. Instr. English, U. Tex., El Paso, 1960-71, instr. linguistics, 1971-73, asst. prof., 1973-79, asso. prof., 1979—, coordinator freshman English for fgn. students, 1973-81, asso. mem. grad. council, 1973—, mem. faculty senate; evaluator El Paso Pub. Schs. for So. Assn. Colls. and Univs., 1973; cons. in field. Mem. El Paso Central Council Social Agys., 1945; chmn. jr. bd. St. Luke's Hosp., Mpls., 1947; aide Mpls. Gen. Hosp., 1948; occupational therapy aide William Beaumont Army Hosp., El Paso, 1950-52; vol. worker Providence Meml. Hosp., El Paso, 1953; coordinator free immunization program for elem. sch. children, Van Horn, Tex., 1955; troop leader Girl Scouts U.S.A., Van Horn, 1956-58; pres. PTA, Van Horn, 1955-57; coordinator lang. instrn. program for adults, English for Spanish-speakers, Spanish for English-speakers, Van Horn, 1955; bd. dirs. Head Start, 1974-76, El Paso Assn. Day Care Center, 1975-76. Named Outstanding Faculty Woman of Yr., U. Tex., El Paso, 1970-71. Mem. MLA, S.W. Area Lang. and Linguistics Orgn., Tex. Joint English Com., S.W. Council Fgn. Lang. Tchrs., Mexican-Am. Edn. Assn. (sec. 1969), Nat., Tex. (pres. 1975), assns. Teaching English to Speakers of Other Langs., Linguistic Assn. S.W., Chi Omega. Democrat. Episcopalian. Club: Jr. League. Contbr. articles to profl. publs. Home: 613 Mississippi St El Paso TX 79902 Office: Linguistics Dept U Tex El Paso TX 79968

COTTON, MARY ELIZABETH, state legislator, nurse; b. Springfield, Ohio, Nov. 7, 1945; d. Justin LeRoy and Alwilda Catherine (Paden) Fagan; grad. Mercy Central Sch. Nursing, 1964; m. John Newell Cotton, Oct. 17, 1969. Nurse Mercy Hosp., Springfield, Ohio, 1964-68, Dr. Milton Berliner, N.Y.C., 1968, Drs. C. Jenkins and D. Scott, Springfield, 1969; campaign coordinator Muskie for Pres., 1972; mem. N.H. Ho. of Reps., 1973—, ranking mem. com. on state instns., mem. Dem. house policy com., 1979—, house edn. com., 1973-76. Del., N.H. Democratic Conv., 1972, 74, 76, 78, 80, 82; Portsmouth Dem. City Com.; ward 3 clk. Portsmouth, N.H., 1975-76, 1980—; selectman Ward 3, Portsmouth, 1977-79; nat. committeewoman for Young Dems. N.H., 1973-74; del. Nat. Fgn. Policy Conf. for Outstanding Young Polit. Leaders Am., Washington, 1975, 78. Recipient award Boy Scouts Am., 1973. Mem. N.H. Orgn. Women Legislators, NOW, Nat. League Nursing. Club: Seacoast Figure Skating. Home: Office: State House 2-18 Ho of Reps Concord NH 03301

COTTONE, VERA MARIAN, ednl. adminstr.; b. S.I., N.Y., June 19, 1937; d. Anthony Joseph and Vera Marian D'Alecy; B.A., Notre Dame Coll. of S.I., 1970; M.A., Richmond Coll., 1972; profl. diploma St. Johns U., 1977; Ed.P., Fairleigh Dickinson U., 1981; m. Richard Cottone, Oct. 18, 1958; children—Richard, Marc. Tchr. social studies, N.Y.C. public schs., 1970-72, tchr. spl. edn., 1972-77, tchr. trainer spl. edn., 1977-79, supr. spl. edn. Region V1, S.I., 1979—. Title IV-B grantee. Mem. N.Y.C. Council Adminstrv. Women in Edn., Assn. Supervision and Curriculum Devel. Office: 777 Seaview Ave Bldg C South Beach Psychiat Center Staten Island NY 10305

COTTRELL, MARY-PATRICIA TROSS, banker; b. Seattle, Apr. 24, 1934; d. Alfred Carl and Alice-Grace (O'Neal) Tross; B.A. in Bus. Adminstrn., U. Wash., 1955; m. Richard Smith Cottrell, May 17, 1969. Systems service rep. IBM, Seattle, also Endicott, N.Y., 1955-58, customer edn. instr., Endicott, 1958-60, 62-65, edn. planning rep., San Jose, Calif. and Endicott, N.Y., 1960-62; cons. data processing, Stamford, Conn., 1965-66; asst. treas. Union Trust Co., Stamford, 1967-68, asst. v.p., 1969-76, v.p., 1976-78, v.p., head corp. services, 1978—. Bd. dirs. Family and Children's Aid of Greater Norwalk (Conn.). Mem. Electronic Funds Transfer Assn. (vice chmn., dir.), Fairfield County Bankers Assn. (dir.), West Norwalk Assn. (dir.). Republican. Roman Catholic. Club: Grad. Office: Union Trust Co 300 Main St Stamford CT 06904

COUCH, SUZAN KULP, communications co. exec.; b. Pottstown, Pa., May 5, 1938; d. Harry Monroe and Bessie (Weaver) Kulp; B.A., Wilson Coll., Chambersburg, Pa., 1960; m. Andrew G. Couch, Oct. 13, 1962. Dir. sales devel. CBS-TV Stas., 1969-72; v.p. broadcast advt. R.H. Macy Co., 1972-75; v.p. advt. and sales promotion Am. Express, 1975-80; v.p. mktg. Warner Amex Cable Communications, N.Y.C., 1980—; dir. Corp. Theatre Fund. Recipient Clio award, 1973, Internat. Bus. Tribute to Women award YWCA, 1978, Corp. Image of Year award Vogue mag., 1979. Mem. Women in Cable, Am. Women in Radio and TV, Cable TV Mktg. and Advt. Assn., Nat. Cable TV Assn. Home: 1 Forest Ct Larchmont NY 10538 Office: 641 Lexington Ave New York NY 10022

COUGHLAN, PHILIPPA MATHIEU, clin. psychologist; b. Boston, Oct. 13, 1937; d. Philippe D. and Anne (Reynolds) Mathieu; A.B., Boston U., 1956, M.A., 1957; Ph.D., U. Wis., Madison, 1965; m. Neil Patrick Coughlan, June 25, 1967; 1 son, John Patrick. NIMH postdoctoral research fellow Wis. Psychiat. Inst., 1964-65; asst. prof. U. Wis., Madison, 1965-68; asst. clin. prof. dept. psychiatry Yale U. Sch. Medicine, 1968-70, asso. prof., 1970—; dir. Office of Student Mental Health, adj. prof. dept. psychology Wesleyan U., Middletown, Conn., 1971—; cons. State of Conn. div. mental hygiene, Conn. Valley Hosp., 1975-78. Vice pres., bd. trustees Ind. Day Sch., Inc., Middlefield, Conn. Diplomate Am. Bd. Profl. Psychology in Clin. Psychology; lic. clin. psychologist, Conn. Fellow World Assn. for Social Psychiatry; mem. Am. Assn. Sex Educators and Counselors, AAUW (Wesleyan U. rep. 1972-76), Am. Psychol. Assn. (CHAMPUS peer review project, peer reviewer), Assn. for Women in Sci., Conn. Psychol. Assn. (chairperson profl. standards review com.), Middlesex County chpt. of Planned Parenthood League of Conn., Inc., New Eng. Assn. Schs. And Colls., Inc., Soc. for Psychotherapy Research (charter mem.). Bd. dirs. Gilead House, Inc., 1971-78; mem. NIMH advisory com., Mental Health Services and Women, U. S. Figure Skating Assn. (judge). Democrat. Roman Catholic. Contbr. numerous articles in field to profl. jours. Home: 47 Red Clover Circle Middletown CT 06457 Office: Office of Student Mental Health Wesleyan U Middletown CT 06457

COUGHLIN, MAGDALEN, nun, coll. pres.; b. Wenatchee, Wash., Apr. 16, 1930; d. William J. and Cecilia (Diffley) C.; B.A. in History, Social Sci. Coll. of St. Catherine, St. Paul, 1952; postgrad. (Fulbright scholar), U. Nijmegen, The Netherlands, 1952-53; M.A. in Medieval History. Mt. St. Mary's Coll., Los Angeles, 1962; Ph.D. in Am. History (Haynes fellow). U. So. Calif., 1970. Tchr. history Alemany High Sch., San Fernando, Calif., 1960-61; tchr. history St. Mary's Acad., Los Angeles, 1961-63; asst. prof. history Mt. St. Mary's Coll., 1963-69, dean acad. devel., 1970-74, pres., 1976—; provincial councilor, regional superior Sisters of St. Joseph of Carondelet, Los Angeles, 1974-76. Mem. Am. Hist. Soc., Calif. Hist. Soc., Phi Alpha Theta, Pi Gamma Mu, Delta Epsilon Sigma, Kappa Gamma Pi, Lambda lota Tau. Roman Catholic. Contbr. reviews and articles to profl. jours. Home and office: 12001 Chalon Rd Los Angeles CA 90049 *

COUGHLIN, MARYROSE, nurse; b. Springfield, Mass., Oct. 21, 1956; d. Robert William and Margaret Mildred C.; B.S.N. cum laude, Boston Coll., 1978. R.N., U. Va. Med. Center, Charlottesville, 1978-79; asst. head nurse Baystate Med. Center, Springfield, 1979-80, clin. supr. surg. nursing service, 1980—. Del., Democratic State Conv., 1982; asso. mem. Dem. City Com. Mem. Am. Nurses Assn., Mass. Nurses Assn. (bd. dirs., chmn. legis. com.), LWV, Sigma Theta Tau. Roman Catholic. Mem. editorial bd. Nursing Perspectives, 1981. Home: 20 Ashbrook St Springfield MA 01118 Office: Baystate Med Center Chestnut St Springfield MA 01107

COULTER, ELIZABETH, psychiat. social worker-adminstr.; b. Champaign, Ill., Apr. 18, 1942; d. Lyle H. and Elizabeth (Russell) Bean; B.A., U. Iowa, 1975, M.S.W., 1976; m. Charles R. Coulter, Dec. 16, 1961; 1 dau., Anne Elizabeth. Various secretarial positions, 1961-63; office mgr. Trinity Episcopal Ch., Iowa City, 1963-65; sch. social worker Miss. Bend Area Edn. Agy., Muscatine, Iowa, 1976-80; exec. dir. Gt. River Mental Health Center, Muscatine, 1980—; mem. Eastern Iowa Juvenile Justice Commn., 1978-80, Muscatine Child Abuse Com., 1977—; bd. dirs. Gt. River Mental Health Center, 1975-76, 78-80, pres., 1979-80; chmn. child abuse task force com. Muscatine Community Health Assn., 1977; pres. bd. dirs. Trinity House Group Home, 1971-72. Mem. Christian social concerns com. Episcopal Diocese Iowa, 1969-71; bd. dirs., mem. vestry Trinity Episcopal Ch., Muscatine, 1969-72; bd. dirs. Muscatine Community Sch. Dist., 1969-70; mem. Citizens Adv. Com. Improvement Muscatine, 1968-69; mem. Muscatine Adv. Com. on Substance Abuse, 1981—. Mem. Nat. Assn. Social Workers, Acad. Cert. Social Workers, Register Clin. Social Workers, Muscatine Community Health Assn., LWV (dir. 1965-68). Home: 607 Sunrise Circle Muscatine IA 52761 Office: 415 E 4th St Muscatine IA 52761

COULTER, ELIZABETH JACKSON, biostatistician; b. Balt., Nov. 2, 1919; d. Waddie Pennington and Bessie (Gills) Jackson; A.B., Swarthmore (Pa.) Coll., 1941; A.M., Radcliffe Coll., 1946, Ph.D., 1948; m. Norman Arthur Coulter, Jr., June 23, 1951; 1 son, Robert Jackson. Asst. dir. health study Bur. Labor Stats., San Juan, P.R., 1946; research asst. Milbank Meml. Fund, N.Y.C., 1948-51; economist Office Def. Prodn., 1951-52; research analyst Children's Bur., HEW, 1952-53; statistician, then chief statistician Ohio Dept. Health, 1954-65; lectr. econs., then clin. asst. prof. preventive medicine Ohio State U., 1954-65; asst. clin. prof. biostats. U. Pitts. Sch. Public Health, 1958-62; asso. prof. biostats. U. N.C., Chapel Hill, 1965-72, prof., 1972—, asso. dean undergrad. public health studies, 1979—, asso. prof. econs., 1965-78; adj. asso. prof. hosp. adminstrn. Duke U., 1972-79. Mem. Am. Public Health Assn. (governing council 1970-72), Am. Econ. Assn., Am. Statis. Assn., Am. Acad. Polit. and Social Sci., AAAS, Biometric Soc., Sigma Xi, Delta Omega. Methodist. Author articles in field. Home: 1825 N Lake Shore Dr Chapel Hill NC 27514 Office: Sch Public Health U NC Chapel Hill NC 27514

COULTON, MARTHA JEAN GLASSCOE (MRS. MARTIN J. COULTON), librarian; b. Dayton, Ohio, Dec. 11, 1927; d. Lafayette Pierre and Gertrude Blanche (Miller) Glasscoe; student Dayton Art Inst., 1946-47; m. Martin J. Coulton, Sept. 6, 1947; children—Perry Jean, Martin John. Dir. Milton (Ohio) Union Pub. Library, 1968—. Active West Milton (Ohio) Cable TV Com. Recipient Outstanding Woman award Jaycees, 1979. Mem. ALA, Ohio Library Assn., Miami Valley Library Orgn. (sec. 1981, v.p. 1982), Internat. Platform Assn., DAR. Home: 1910 N Mowry Rd Pleasant Hill OH 45359 Office: 560 S Main St West Milton OH 45383

COUMANTAROS, STELLA THEO, lay religious orgn. adminstr.; b. N.Y.C., Apr. 4, 1923; d. Constantine and Angeliki (Mangican) Pilarinos; B.A., Douglas Coll., 1940; M.A., New Sch. for Social Research, 1958; m. Theodore Coumantaros, June 20, 1937 (dec.); children—George, Olga Maria. Dir. social health and welfare center, Greek Orthodox Archidiocese of N.Am. and S.Am., N.Y.C., 1971, nat. exec. dir. Greek Orthodox Ladies Philoptochos Soc., Inc., N.Y.C., 1972—. Mem. Philoptochos Soc., Daus. of Penelope, Order of Ahepa. Greek Orthodox. Office: 8 E 79 St New York NY 10021

COUNCE-NICKLAS, SHEILA JEAN, biologist; b. Hayes Center, Nebr., Mar. 18, 1927; d. Hardy Melva and Florence Ruth (Enyeart) Counce; B.A., U. Colo., 1948, M.A., 1950; Ph.D. (Fulbright fellow 1950-52, AAUW fellow 1952-53), Edinburgh (Scotland) U., 1953, Macauley fellow, 1954-55; NSF postdoctoral fellow, U. Zurich, 1955-56; m. (Robert) Bruce Nicklas, Sept. 17, 1960. Mem. staff Jackson Lab., Bar Harbor, Maine, 1954; research asso. Yale U., 1956-65; mem. faculty Duke U., 1965—, prof. anatomy, 1978—; mem. panel NIH, 1978-80. Grantee NSF, 1956-81. Fellow AAAS; mem. Genetics Soc., Soc. Devel. Biology, Am. Soc. Naturalists, Am. Soc. Zoologists, Am. Soc. Cell Biology, AAUP, N.C. Acad. Sci., S.E. Assn. Biologists, Sigma Xi. Democrat. Author numerous articles in field. Co-editor: Developmental Systems, Isects, 2 vols., 1972-73. Office: Dept Anatomy Duke U Med Center Durham NC 27710

COUNIHAN, DARLYN JOYCE, educator; b. Cumberland, Md., May 1, 1948; d. Joseph Paul and Clara Kathryn (Miller) C.; A.B., Hood Coll., 1970, M.A., 1982; postgrad. U. Md., 1971-73; m. Mark W. Chambré, Jan. 20, 1979. Tchr. math. Cabin John Jr. High Sch., Montgomery County, Md., 1970-75, coach girls volleyball team, 1975; math. resource tchr. Takoma Park (Md.) Jr. High Sch., 1975-77; math. resource tchr. Ridgeview Jr. High Sch., Gaithersburg, Md., 1977-81; tchr. Kennedy High Sch., Silver Spring MD 20902 mem. Area 3 adv. council Montgomery County Public Schs., 1972-73; coach boys basketball team Montgomery County Recreation Assn., 1971. Recipient various acad., athletic awards in high sch., coll.; NSF grantee, 1971-72. Mem. Am. Fedn. Tchrs., Nat. Assn. Female Execs., Nat. Council Tchrs. Math. Clubs: Capts. Cove Golf and Yacht, Lake Holiday Country. Home: 18913 Goldmine Ct Brookeville MD 20729 Office: Kennedy High Sch 1901 Randolf Rd Silver Spring MD 20902

COUNTEE, SANDRA FLOWERS, social services adminstr.; b. Oklahoma City, Feb. 15, 1943; d. LeRoy and Minnie Ola Flowers; B.S., Kans. U., 1965; M.S., Columbia U., 1975; M.P.A., N.Y.U., 1979. Staff occupational therapist D.C. Gen. Hosp. Community Mental Health, 1965-68; supr. occupational therapy Columbia U.-Harlem Hosp. Center, N.Y.C., 1968-76, chief occupational therapy, 1976-78; asst. prof., dir. field work edn. Temple U., Phila., 1978-81; dist. mgr. N.Y. Commn. Blind and Visually Handicapped, N.Y. State Dept. Social Services, N.Y.C., 1981-82; dist. mgr. Office of Vocat. Rehab., N.Y. State Dept. Edn., White Plains, 1982—; clin. instr. rehab. medicine Columbia U., 1977-78; cons. Trinity Ch. and St. Margaret's House Devel., N.Y.C., 1979. Adv. bd. Community Home Health Services of Phila., 1980-81. Cert. social worker, N.Y.; lic. occupational therapist, N.Y. Mem. Am. Public Health Assn., Am. Occupational Therapy Assn. Home: 30 New Holland Village Bldg 3 Nanuet NY 10954

COUPE, JOAN, bookkeeper, travel agt.; b. Maple Creek, Sask., Can., July 25, 1938; came to U.S., 1959, naturalized, 1973; d. Sidney and Jean (Wilnechenko) Hanchar; grad. Allen Bus. Coll., Saskatoon, Sask., 1956; m. Joseph R. Coupe, Jan. 27, 1961; children—Janelle, Jeff, Kevin. Office mgr. Champion Feeders, Inc., Hereford, Tex., 1968-72; pvt. practice bookkeeping, Hereford, 1972—; owner, gen. mgr. Hereford Travel Center, 1976—. Bd. dirs. Deaf Smith County United Way, 1978-80, treas., 1979. Mem. Tex. Cattle Feeders Assn., Hereford CowBelles (sec. 1973), Deaf Smith C. of C. (dir. 1979—, treas. 1980, chmn. public affairs com. ladies' div. 1978), Am. Soc. Travel Agts. Home: 300 Westhaven Dr Hereford TX 79045 Office: 144 W Second St Hereford TX 79045

COURSHON, CAROL BIEL, civic worker; b. Cleve., Sept. 5, 1923; d. Maurice and Rita (Glueck) Biel; student Wesleyan Coll., Macon, Ga., 1941-42; m. Arthur Howard Courshon, Feb. 20, 1943; children—Barbara Mills, Deanne. With Washington Savs. & Loan Assn., Miami Beach, Fla., 1979-80, chmn. adv. bd., 1979-80, dir., 1980-82. Chmn. hotel-motel div. Mothers March Dimes, 1948-53; co-chmn. bus. div. Greater Miami Heart Fund campaign, 1977-78; bd. dirs. Children's Service Bur. of Dade County, 1960-70, Nat. Family Service Assn. Am., 1977—, United Family and Childrens Service Dade County, 1970—; vol. tchrs. aide handicapped Dade County (Fla.) public schs., 1960-81; del. Democratic Nat. Conv., 1968; adv. bd. Jefferson Nat. Bank, Miami Beach, 1981—. Mem. Nat. Savs. and Loan League (exec. women's group), Nat. Council Jewish Women (v.p. Bay div. 1953-55), Hadassah. Office: 301 41st St Miami Beach FL 33140

COURT, MARGARET, profl. tennis player; b. Albury, New South Wales, Australia, July 16, 1942; d. Lawrence William and Maud (Beaufort) Smith; ed. St. Augustine's Convent, Wodonga, Victoria, Australia; m. Barry M. Court, Oct. 28, 1967; children—Daniel Lawrence, Marika Margaret, Teresea Ann. Australian tennis champion, 1960-66, 69, 70, 71, 73; French tennis champion, 1962, 64, 69, 70, 73; winner Wimbledon (Eng.) tennis championship, 1963-65, 70; U.S. champion, 1962, 65, 68, 69, 70, 73; winner Va. Slims championships, 1973; cons. tennis fashion David H. Smith, Inc. Lynn, Mass., 1973—; cons. phys. fitness for women Deversified Products Corp., Opelika, Ala., 1975—. Author: (with Don Lawrence) The Margaret Smith Story, 1965; Court on Court: A Life in Tennis 1975. Author several monographs various phases instl. tennis. Office: care L W Krieger 295 Madison Ave New York NY 10017

COURTEAU, JOANNA, educator; b. Lwow, Poland, Apr. 15, 1939; d. Ryszard and Lidia Wojtowicz; B.A. cum laude, U.Minn., 1960, M.A., 1962; Ph.D. (NDEA fellow), U. Wis., 1970. Instr., Sullins Coll., Bristol, Va., 1963-65; asst. prof. U. Ark., Fayetteville, 1967-71; asst. and asso. prof. Iowa State U., Ames, 1971-78, prof. Spanish and Portuguese, 1980—; vis. prof. U. Warsaw, 1979. Vice pres. publicity ACTORS 1978; leader Democratic Precinct Com., 1976-80, coordinator fundraising, 1980-81; founding mem. Amnesty Internat., Ames. Ford Found. fellow, Brazil, 1967; Nat. Communication grantee, 1979; recipient FISH award Ames City, 1980. Mem. Sierra Club, NOW, Women's Internat. League of Peace and Freedom, Midwest MLA, Midwest Latin Am. Studies Assn., Assn. Tchrs. Spanish and Portuguese, Latin Am. Studies Assn. Roman Catholic. Contbr. articles to profl. jours. Home: PO Box 1158 ISU Sta Ames IA 50010 Office: Dept Modern Langs and Lit Iowa State U Ames IA 50011

COURTENAY, IRENE DORIS, nursing cons.; b. Regina, Sask., Can., July 1, 1920; d. Thomas Greer and May Elizabeth (York) C.; R.N., Princess Alice Meml. Hosp., Eastbourne, Eng., 1942; B.S. in Nursing, U. Western Ont., 1956; M.P.H., U. Mich., 1957. Occupation health nurse Chrysler of Can., 1948-50, 52-55; cons. occupational health nursing N.C. Bd. Health, 1958-61; occupational health nursing specialist Nat. League for Nursing, 1961-64; cons. occupational health nursing Dept. Nat. Health and Welfare, Ottawa, Ont., Can., 1966-69; asst. prof., dir. grad. program occupational health nursing U. N.C., Chapel Hill, 1971-75; asso. prof. occupational health N.Y. U., 1975-78; pvt. practice cons. occupational health nursing, 1978—. Mem. Am. Nurses Assn., Nat. League Nursing, Am. Assn. Occupational Health Nurses, Am. Bd. Occupational Health Nurses (dir.), Am. Indsl. Hygiene Assn. (asso.), Permanent Commn. and Internat. Assn. Occupational Health, AAUP, Am. Public Health Assn. Mem. Anglican Ch. Author several publs. Home: 5110 Wyandotte St E #X14 Windsor ON N8S 1L2 Canada

COURTNEY, LOUISE, educator; b. Somerst, Pa., June 19, 1934; d. James Orval and Dorothy (Burleigh) C.; B.S., U. Pa., 1956; M.A. in Occupational Therapy Adminstrn., Western Mich. U., 1968, M.A. in Spl. Edn., 1970; div.; children—Barbara, Judith. Founder, dir. occupational therapy program United Cerebral Palsy, Jamestown, N.Y., 1957, Monroe, La., 1963; occupational therapist Del. Bd. Health, 1958-59; dir. occupational therapy and vocat. edn. depts. Emily Bissell Hosp., Wilmington, Del., 1961-62; supr. spl. classes, adminstr. New Rosedale Sch. Learning Disabled Students, Coatesville, Pa., 1971-74; learning disabilities cons., diagnostician Phila. Sch. Dist., 1975-77, adminstr. Title VI project DELP, 1977-78, coordinator spl./vocat. programs, 1978-79, instructional advisor, 1979—; owner/mgr. apt. bldg. Mem. Gov.'s Adv. Council Exceptional Children, 1974; mem. Pa. In-Service Com. Physically Handicapped, 1974, Pa. Dept. Health Task Force Establishing Occupational Therapy Standards, 1979, Phila. Past, Present and Future Housing Task Force, 1981; chmn. Liquor Licensing Com., Zoning Bd. Mem. Am. Occupational Therapy Assn., Friends of Independence Nat. Park, Queen Village Homeowners Assn., Homeowners Assn. Phila. (dir.), Society Hill Civic Assn., English Speaking Union. Author curriculum materials. Home: 514 G South Randolph St Philadelphia PA 19147 Office: Dist 2 Adminstrn Office Phila Sch Dist 16th and Moore Sts Philadelphia PA 19145

COURTNEY, NORMA ISABELLE, systems analyst; b. New Albany, Ind., Oct. 17, 1927; d. William and Mary Isabelle (Emery) Hagmann; B.S. in Computer Sci., Wright State U., Dayton, Ohio, 1975; m. Robert Lee Courtney, Dec. 2, 1950; children—Deborah Lynn Courtney Smyth, Ellen Ann Courtney Irvin, Jennifer Lee Courtney Lightcap, Lisa Marie. With C.E., U.S. Army, Louisville, 1945-46, Ky. Actuarial Bur., Louisville, 1947-52; with NCR Corp., Dayton, 1976—, sr. prin. systems analyst, 1981—. Home: 4893 Archmore Dr Kettering OH 45440 Office: 2d Floor Bldg 31 Main and K Sts Dayton OH 45479

COURTOIS, CHRISTINE ANN, counseling psychologist; b. Providence, Aug. 29, 1949; d. Normand Albert and Dorice Irene (Dufort) Courtois; B.A. in History and Secondary Edn. (R.I. State scholar, Herbert Pell award), R.I. Coll., 1971; M.A. in Counseling (grad. asst., fellow), U. Md., 1973, Ph.D., 1979; m. Banks R. Chamberlain, Aug. 7, 1976. Asst. dir. orientation office U. Md., 1975-77, counseling psychology intern, 1977-78, counselor, 1978-81; with Counseling and Testing Center, Cleve. State U., 1978-80; counseling psychologist U. Md., 1980-81, GAO, Washington, 1981-82, Women's Med. Center, 1981—; pvt. practice counseling psychology, 1981—. Past mem. parish council St. Mathew's Roman Cath. Ch., Central Falls, R.I.; trustee Cleve. Rape Crisis Center, 1979-80; co-founder, dir. Univ. Women's Crisis Hotline, U. Md., 1972-76. Mem. Am. Psychol. Assn., Am. Personnel and Guidance Assn., Am. Coll. Personnel Assn., Assn. Women Psychology, Va. Personnel and Guidance Assn. Democrat. Author articles in field. Office: 8321 Snowden Oaks Pl Laurel MD 20708

COURY, ELAINE MARIE, linguist, educator; b. Cumberland, Md., Sept. 2, 1947; d. Joseph George and Rose Theresa (Beshara) C.; B.A., St. Joseph Coll., West Hartford, Conn., 1969, Ph.D. (Condon fellow 1974-75, Arthur J. Schmitt fellow 1975-76), Loyola U. Chgo., 1976. Tchr. Latin, Litchfield (Conn.) High Sch. and tchr. French, Bantam (Conn.) Elem. Sch., 1969-71; teaching asst. Loyola U. Rome Center Liberal Arts, 1972-73; teaching asst. Loyola U. Chgo., 1971-72, lectr. in classical mythology, summer 1976; asst. prof. classics Creighton U., 1976-77, Loyola U. Rome Center, 1977-79; asst. prof. Cardinal Newman Coll., 1979-82, assoc. prof., 1982—. leader tours to Greece, Italy. Mem. Am. Philol. Assn., Archaeol. Inst. Am., Am. Classical League, Classical Assn. Middle West and South, Ill. Classical Conf., St. Louis Classical Club, MLA, Alpha Sigma Nu. Author: Terence: Bembine Phormio: A Palaeographic Examination, 1982; editor: Phormio: A Comedy by Terence, 1982; research on comparative mythology. Home and Office: 7701 Florissant Rd Saint Louis MO 63121

COUSINS, BERNICE BRIGANDO, map co. exec.; b. Flushing, N.Y., Nov. 2, 1937; d. August and Olympia (Tortora) Brigando; B.F.A. in Interior Design, Pratt Inst., 1955, postgrad. 1959; postgrad. City U. N.Y., 1966; children—David Bruce, Jason Bruce. Asst. to dir., tchr., Mus. Modern Art, Dept. Edn., N.Y.C., 1963-72; tchr. N.Y.C. Bd. Edn., 1966-73; with Am. Map Corp., N.Y.C., 1975—, dir cartographic services; co-dir. CW Assos., Flushing, N.Y.; lectr. in field. Curriculum Adv. Com., Public Sch. 85Q, 1976-77. Mem. Nat. Assn. Female Execs., Assn. for Research and Enlightment, Am. Fedn. Astrologers. Contbr. articles to profl. jours.; researcher, compiler, editor: Nutritive Value of Common Foods, 1978; researcher, editor: Art Work: Schick-Colorprint Anatomy Charts, 1976—. Home: 4505 Astoria Blvd Astoria NY 11105 Office: PO Box 310 Flushing NY 11352

COUSINS, ELIZABETH ANNE, investment broker; b. Paso Robles, Calif., Feb. 12, 1922; d. James Ignatius and Cecile Catherine (Crouse) C.; A.A., San Luis Obispo Jr. Coll., 1942; R.N., Knapp Coll. Nursing, Santa Barbara, Calif., 1945; B.S. in Nursing, U. San Francisco, 1950. Surg. nurse Santa Barbara Cottage Hosp., 1945-46; owner, agt. Fire & Casualty, 1950-80; life and health ins. sales rep., 1980-81; investment broker 1st Affiliated Securities, Inc., Paso Robles, 1981—; founder, dir., asst. Heritage Oaks Bank, Paso Robles, 1981—; pub. speaker. Mem. Paso Robles Citizens Scholarship Found.; mem. San Luis Obispo Grand Jury, 1967-68; bd. dirs. Paso Robles Meml. Hosp., 1973-77; dir. Infant Hearing Screening Clinic, Paso Robles Meml. Hosp., 1961. Mem. Knapp Coll. Nursing Alumnae Assn., Nat. Assn. Security Dealers, Ind. Ins. Agts. Am., Paso Robles C. of C. (Personality of Week 1969), Paso Robles Women's Golf Assn. (pres. 1967-68, 80-81). Republican. Roman Catholic. Clubs: Quota of Paso Robles (pres. 1958-59, Dist. lt. gov., 1965-66, 2d v.p. 1981-82), Paso Robles Golf and Country (dir. 1958-62). Home: PO Box 65 1351 Chestnut St Paso Robles CA 93446 Office: PO Box 65 1227 Pine St Paso Robles CA 93446

COUSINS, JANE CAMPBELL, real estate exec.; b. Camden, S.C., June 29, 1924; d. Herbert Allison and Mabel (Henning) Campbell; student Katherine Gibbs Sch., N.Y.C., 1945; m. James Lee Cousins, Dec. 19, 1949; children—Charles Henning, James Lee, Julie Elizabeth, Mary Allison. Field rep. ARC, 1943-44; stewardess Pan Am. Airways, 1947-49; engaged in real estate, 1964—; founder, 1967, pres., chief exec. officer Cousins Assos., Miami, Fla., 1967-81; pres., chief exec. officer Merrill Lynch Realty/Cousins, Miami, 1981—; dir. Miami br. Fed. Res. Bank Atlanta, 1976-81; dir. Fed. Res. Bank Atlanta. Bd. dirs. Jr. Achievement Miami; trustee Fairchild Tropical Gardens, Bascom Palmer Eye Inst., Fla. Meml. Coll., S. Miami Hosp.; mem. citizens bd. U. Miami; past pres. Beaux Arts of Lowe Gallery, U. Miami. Mem. Nat. Assn. Real Estate Bds., Jr. League Miami, Greater Miami-Dade County C. of C. (exec. bd.). Republican. Episcopalian. Office: 5830 SW 73d St Miami FL 33143

COVAL, NAOMI MILLER, orthodontist; b. Bayonne, N.J.; d. Jacob Paul and Bertha (Blumstein) Miller; student U. Chgo., 1931-35; B.A., N.Y.U., 1939; D.D.S., Columbia U., 1943. Children—Ilya Sandra, Payson Rodney, Mark Lawrence. Private practice dentistry, specializing in orthodontics, N.Y.C., 1943-44, Bklyn., 1944-59, Lawrence, N.Y., 1959—; postgrad. lectr. Pam-Am. Med. Assn., 1960; lectr. to profl. groups throughout world, 1947—; attending staff Peninsula Gen. Hosp., Queens, N.Y.; attending dentist N.Y. Infirmary, N.Y.C., 1946-50, Peninsula Hosp. Center, 1967—; instr. N.Y.U., N.Y.C., 1948-49; vis. lectr. orthodontics, various S.Am., European, Asian and Australian univs., 1969—. Chairlady L.I. Com. for Fluoridation Water; del. Oral Hygiene Com., 1948-51; lectr. to Women's Clubs on Worldwide anthrop. and archaeol. tours. Active PTA, 1948—, pres. Lawrence High Sch. PTA, 1966-67; leader Girl Scouts U.S.A., 1950-58; group leader Jane Addams' Hull House, Chgo., 1933-35; charter patron, sponsor Island Concert Hall; pres. Five Towns Aux. Penninsula Gen. Hosp., 1964-66; v.p. B'nai B'rith, Nat. Council Jewish Women; v.p. Pulse of Women, 1971. Bd. dirs. Am. Cancer Soc., Lawrence (chmn. art show); chpt. pres. Am. Jewish Congress, 1968-72, del. nat. conv., 1970. Fellow Soc. for Oral Physiology and Occlusion, Royal Soc. Health; mem. Fedn. Dentaire Internat. (lectr. Rome 1957, Tel Aviv 1966, Australia 1973), Acad. Dental Medicine, Internat. Acad. Orthodontics (v.p. 62-66, sec.), Fedn. Am. Orthodontists (charter), AAAS, Am. Acad. Oral Medicine, Internat. Platform Assn. (charter), UN Assn. U.S.A., Fellowship Reconciliation, Nat. Geog. Soc., Am. Mus. Natural History, ADA, 10th Dist., Rockaway dental socs., Nassau-Suffolk Acad. Dentistry, Am., Brit. socs. for study orthodontics, Pan-Am. Med. Assn., Nat. Assn. Women Dentists, William Jarvie Soc. for Dental Research, N.Y. Assn. Women Dentists (editor Dentistae 1948, v.p. 1962-66), Am. Assn. Dental Editors (only woman dentist elected to assn.), N.Y. State Assn. for Professions (charter), Am. Soc. for Preventive Dentistry, Columbia U. Dental Alumni Assn. (publicity chmn.), Assn. Women in Sci., Nat. Women's Polit. Caucus (charter; mem. bd.), Pulse of Women (v.p.), NOW, Am. Assn. for Study Psychoanalysis, Am. Red Mogen David Soc., Met. Opera Guild, Jacques Cousteau Soc. (charter), Lawrence Assn., Rapa-Nui Soc. for Easter Islanders, Wildlife Soc. Kenya, Am. Field Service, Internat. Soc. Artists. Clubs: Wayfarers, Atrium, Intrepids. Editor: Internat. Jour. Orthodontics, 1962-66, Internat. Acad. Orthodontics, 1961; contbr. numerous articles to dental and sci. jours. First women dentist invited to lecture in Bucharest, 1971; 1st woman elected by organized dentistry to be on TV, 1964. Developed technique for repositioning the mandible; research on thyroidectomies in rat; designed and exhibited original gold jewelry executed from dental materials; sculptress, photographer. Address: 30 Westover Pl Lawrence NY 11559

COVEN, LINDA S., banker; b. Detroit, Dec. 3, 1950; d. Sorrel Maurice and Barbara (Rose) C.; student Mich. State U., 1969-70, U. Calif., Santa Barbara, 1970-72. Mgr. info. services I. Magnin, San Francisco, 1974-79; mgr. output control Crocker Nat. Bank, San Francisco, 1979, mgr. distbn., 1979-80, mgr. br. service ops., 1980-81, project mgr. ops. div., 1981—. Mem. Am. Soc. Profl. and Exec. Women, Nat. Assn. Female Execs. Home: 2645 Sacramento St Suite 6 San Francisco CA 94115 Office: 155 5th St San Francisco CA 94103

COVINGTON, MAE RUFFIN, public relations ofcl., entrepreneur; b. Meridian, Miss., May 11, 1940; d. Ernest Howard and Ethel Earline Ruffin; A.A. (coll. scholar), Compton Jr. Coll., 1972; student in sociology UCLA, 1972-75; m. Morris Covington, May 23, 1957 (div. 1972); children—Rickey, Phyllis, Janet, Schanille, Morris, Angela, Kenyatta, Marquetta, Jonathan. Mgr. Covington's Decorating, Los Angeles, 1963-72; owner, prin. Mae Covington & Co., Charm Workshop, Compton, Calif., 1972-77; owner, founder, Black Tie Expressions, Profl. Bus. Club, Altadena, Calif., 1980—, pub., editor in chief newsletter, 1981—; dir. Watts Writer's Workshop, 1975, dir., coordinator Showcases to Prisons, 1973-76; fashion coordinator Sheen Way Culture Center, Los Angeles, 1975. Vol. state PTA, Calif.; vol. dir. Repertoire Theater, talent promoter, 1973—; vol. entertainment cons., 1980-81. Named outstanding fashion coordinator, Los Angeles Profl. Guild, 1975. Mem. Tarry Town (N.Y.) Group, Interval Internat., Nat. Assn. Female Execs., Profl. Writers Club, Am. Film Inst., Golden Banclub, So. Calif. Publicist Club. Clubs: Palm Desert Country, Showcase Social (pres. 1980, award 1980), Gamma Phi Delta. Writer, contbr. to Black Tie Expressions Newsletter. Home: 2770 N Olive Ave Altadena CA 91001 Office: PO Box 6048 Altadena CA 91001

COVINGTON, NORMA JONES, clin. social worker; b. Mebane, N.C.; d. Leonard J. and Nannie (Pinnix) Jones; B.A., Bennett Coll., Greensboro, N.C., 1973; M.S.W., W.Va. U., 1975; m. James Michael Covington, May 28, 1977. (div.). Case mgr. Alderson (W.Va.) Fed. Reformatory, 1973, Loysville (Pa.) Youth Devel. Center, 1974; protective services investigator Alamance County Dept. Social Services, Burlington, N.C., 1975-76; clin. social worker Alamance County, 1976-81; psychiat. social worker Charter Hills Hosp., Greensboro, N.C., 1981—; instr. Alamance Tech. Coll., Haw River, N.C.; vol. Burlington Suicide and Crisis Services; mem. Alamance County Human Relations Council. Named An Outstanding Young Woman Am., 1979. Mem. Acad. Cert. Social Workers, Nat. Assn. Social Workers, Interat. Transactional Analysis Assn., N.C. Group Behavior Soc., N.C. Assn. Mental Health Social Workers, Delta Sigma Theta. Baptist. Home: 507 College St Graham NC 27253 Office: Charter Hills Hosp Greensboro NC

COVINGTON, VICTORIA LOUISE, educator; b. Bennettsville, S.C., Feb. 11, 1946; d. Harry Poindexter and Sarah Christine (Benfield) C.; B.Mus., St. Andrews Presbyn. Coll., 1968; M.Mus., U. Ill., Urbana, 1971, Ed.D., 1981. Instr. piano St. Andrews Presbyn. Coll., Laurinburg, N.C., 1970, 75-76; lectr. group piano U. Ill., Urbana, 1974-75; asst. prof. piano Baldwin-Wallace Coll. Conservatory Music, Berea, Ohio, 1976—; performances include solo recitals, guest recitals, chamber music recitals, telecast S.C. ETV Network, 1969—. Recipient Handicapped Profl. Woman of Year award S.C. dist. Pilot Clubs Internat., Sears Roebuck & Co., 1980. Mem. Music Educators Nat. Conf., Pi Kappa Lambda. Methodist. Home: 55 Barrett Rd 307 Berea OH 44017 Office: Baldwin-Wallace Conservatory Music Berea OH 44017

COWAN, CHARITY ALLENE, educator, adminstr.; b. Lancaster, Ky., Oct. 1, 1924; d. John Theo and Julia Mae (Stevens) Cowan; B.S., Eastern Ky. U., 1946; M.A., U. Ky., 1952, Rank I, 1960. Grade Sch. tchr. Locust Street Sch., Erlanger, Ky., 1946-58; gen. supr. Erlanger-Elsmere Bd. Edn., 1958-76, asso. supt., 1976-81, gen. supr., 1981—. Mem. Assn. Childhood Edn. (state sec. 1956-58, chpt. pres. 1968-70), NEA (life mem., br. pres. 1967-68), Eastern State U. Alumni Assn. (life), U. Ky. Alumni Assn. (life), Ky. Edn. Assn., Assn. for Childhood Edn. (life), Ky. Assn. for Ednl. Suprs., Assn. for Supervision and Curriculum, AAUW (v.p. 1964-66; program chmn. 1964-66), Ky. PTA (life), Ind. Order Foresters, Order Ky. Cols., Ky. Assn. Sch. Adminstrs., Ky. Assn. Supervision and Curriculum Devel., Council for Exceptional Children, Kappa Delta Pi, Delta Kappa Gamma (pres. Zeta chpt. 1974-76) Phi Delta Kappa (1st v.p. 1981-82). Baptist (sec. chmn. kindergarten 1964-78). Home: 440 B Graves Ave Erlanger KY 41018 Office: 500 Graves Ave Erlanger KY 41018

COWAN, MARGUERITE ROSS (MRS. HUBERT RANDOLPH COWAN), educator; b. Talisheek, La., Dec. 30, 1919; d. P.A. and Sara (Owen) Ross; B.S. in Edn., U. Ark., 1946, M.Ed., 1978, postgrad., 1978—; m., Nov. 11, 1945; children—Sara Margaret Cowan Rodgers, Morris Randolph. Tchr., Fayetteville (Ark.) High Sch., 1963-67, head bus. edn. dept., 1968—, tchr. adult edn., sponsor Future Bus. Leaders of Am. Mem. Ark. State Council on Econ. Edn., 1978—. Recipient award Internat. Paper Co. Found., 1976-77. Mem. NEA, Ark. Ednl. Assn., Fayetteville Ednl. Assn., Nat. Bus. Edn. Assn., Am. Vocat. Ednl. Assn., Am. Vocat. Bus. Ednl. Assn., Ark. Bus. Edn. Assn., Nat. Am. Vocat. Ednl. Spl. Needs Persons, AAUW. Methodist. Clubs: Altrusa, Delta Gamma. Contbr. article to publ. in field. Office: Fayetteville High School 1001 Stone St Fayetteville AR 72701

COWAN, SALLY JANE, audio visual co. exec.; b. Denver, May 7, 1942; d. Robert Reed and Vivian Louise (Cone) Cook; student Dana Coll., 1960-61, U. Nebr., 1972-76; children—Kevin Michael, Christine Elizabeth. Office mgr. Nebr. State Dept. Health, Lincoln, 1963-67; mng. dir., corp. sec., dir. Cartel, Inc., Lincoln, 1976-81; owner, pres. Tavco, Inc., Lincoln, 1981—. Mem. Nat. Assn. Female Execs., Adminstrv. Mgmt. Soc. (publicity com.), Lincoln Ind. Bus. Assn., Nat. Audio Visual Assn. Democrat. Rec. 2 albums. Home: 1830 Sunny Hill Rd Lincoln NE 68502 Office: 830 R St PO Box 2731 Lincoln NE 68508

COWAN, TRUDI, newspaper editor; b. N.Y.C., May 29, 1925; d. William and Ida Berger; student Art Students League, 1943-45, Columbia U., 1945-46; m. George Cowan, June 10, 1950; children—Stephen Scott, Jill Ellen. With N.Y. Times, 1943-50; editor Bellmore (N.Y.) Life, 1964—; lectr. on community newspaper to schs. and cls. Officer, PTA, 1960-70; mem. North Bellmore Library Bd., 1962-65; founder, pres. Bellmore Hist. Soc. 1964-66, 81-82; mem. Girl Scouts U.S.A. com. Recipient hon. life membership PTA; award N.Y. State Bar Assn., 1972, L.I. Press Club, 1981; named Bellmore Citizen of Yr., 1975; hon. asst. chief North Bellmore Fire Dept. Mem. N.Y. State Press Assn. (awards for service to edn., awards for writing), Sigma Delta Chi. Office: 2717 Grand Ave Bellmore NY 11710

COWDEN, JULIANAN, steel co. exec., craftsman; b. Midland, Tex.; d. Robert Edwin and Jett (Baker) Cowden; student Hockaday Jr. Coll., 1940-41; B.A., U. Tex., 1944. Rancher, oil investments JAL Co., Alvarado, Tex., 1950—, chmn. bd., 1970—; treas. J & M Steel Co., Inc., Ft. Worth, 1971—; v.p. Western Tool and Mfg. Co., Inc. Instr. jewelry and silversmith Ft. Worth Art Center, 1963-66; exhibited jewelry and sculpture in one-man shows at Simpson Gallery, Amarillo, 1969, Sq. House Mus., Panhandle, 1971; exhibited in group shows at Ft. Worth Art Center, Carlin Gallery, Mus. Internat. Folk Art, Santa Fe, Wichita Falls (Tex.) Art Mus., Tex. Tech U. Mus., Lubbock, Artist's Jamboree, San Antonio. Trustee, pres. Tex. Sch. Bd. Assn.; mem. Tex State Bd. Edn.; mem. Fed. Relations Network; pres. Alvarado Ind. Sch. Dist. Bd., 1966—; del., mem. rules com., Democratic Nat. Conv., 1968, del., mem. credentials com., 1972; sec. Tex. Dem. Com. 1972-78; pres. Tex. Fedn. Dem. Women; Dem. precinct chmn., Alvarado, 1970-76; mem. Nat. Fedn. Republican Women; sustaining mem. Rep. Party, 1979—; mem. Task Force Com. on Sch./Coll. Articulation; trustee Hockaday Sch., 1971-73. Mem. Nat. Sch. Bd. Assn., Nat. Petroleum Council, Tex. Designer Craftsmen, U. Tex. Ex-Students Assn. (life), Tex. Artists Craftsmen Guild (pres. 1970-72), S. W. Cattleraisers Assn., Ranch Heritage Assn., Zeta Tau Alpha. Episcopalian. Clubs: Amarillo, Fort Worth. Home: JAL Ranch Alvarado TX 76009

COWDEN, MARGARET GISONDI, state ofcl.; b. Gloversville, N.Y., Mar. 21, 1929; d. Harvey and Dorothy (Desmond) Gisondi; B.S., Columbia U., 1957; 1 dau., Nina Lucia. Adminstrv. asst. to dean of grad. faculties Columbia U., N.Y.C., 1951-53; tchr. public schs., N.Y.C., 1956-63; sect. supr. Basic Systems, Inc., N.Y.C., 1963-64; writer Holt, Rinehart and Winston, 1964-65; free lance writer, 1966-71; partner Hasty Pudding Catering Service, Macomb, Ill., 1972-74; exec. dir. Ill. Commn. on Status of Women, Springfield, 1974-80; exec. Ill. Dept. Children and Family Services, Springfield, 1980-82, Ill. Dept. Commerce and Community Affairs, Springfield, 1982—. Mem. coordinating com. Internat. Women's Yr., 1976-77, Ill. del. nat. conf., 1977; mem. adv. bd. Ill. Women's History Week, 1980; mem. Adv. Council on Edn. of Handicapped Children, 1980-81; mem. Gov.'s Adv. Com. on Statewide Displaced Homemakers Program, 1979—; mem. Ill. Council on Nutrition, 1981—; mem. health edn. adv. com. Ill. Bd. Edn., 1981—, mem. early childhood services com., 1980—. Mem. Nat. Women's Polit. Caucus, AAUW, LWV, Ill. Women's Polit. Caucus (past dir.), Springfield Women's Polit. Caucus. Republican. Unitarian. Office: Ill Dept Commerce and Community Affairs 222 S College St Springfield IL 62706

COWEN, JANET CATHERINE CRAIG, genealogist; b. Madison, Ind., June 16, 1919; d. Robert J. and Mary Elizabeth (Young) Craig; student Hanover Coll., 1937-39, A.B., 1941; postgrad. U. Wis.; m. Carl Claudius Cowen, Sr., June 29, 1944; 1 son, Carl Claudius. Bus. tchr. Saluda High Sch., Hanover, Ind., 1941-43, Bourbon (Ind.) High Sch., 1943-44; typist M.I.T. Underwater Sound Lab., Boston, 1944-45; typist and salesperson, Madison, Wis., 1947-50; sec., Indpls., 1951-52; bus. tchr. Mooresville (Ind.) High Sch., 1952-63, Decatur High Sch., Indpls., 1965-75; profl. genealogist, Indpls., 1975—. Recipient 4-H awards, also from local ch. and DAR. Mem. DAR (Ind. state chmn. geneal. records 1970-79, founder Greenwood chpt. 1979, state chmn. Yorktown Bicentennial, 1980-81), Ind. Hist. Soc., Palentine Soc., Sigma Delta Pi. Republican. Presbyterian. Indexed cemetery data Morgan County (Ind.); others. Home: 349 E Dixie St Indianapolis IN 46227

COWEN, SONIA SUE, univ. adminstr.; b. Wichita Falls, Tex., Sept. 30, 1952; d. Jackson Thompson and Shirley Isabel (Skerritt) C.; B.A. magna cum laude, East Wash. U., 1973; M.F.A. in Creative Writing, U. Mont., 1975; postgrad. U. Utah, 1981-82. Adminstrv. sec., ednl. program devel. and sch. services Eastern Wash. U., Cheney, 1970-73, grants adminstr., 1978-81, 82—, mem. adj. faculty, 1979, exec. sec. N.W. Inst. for Advanced Study, 1978-81, 82—; teaching asst. U. Mont., Missoula, 1974-75; instr. head journalism program Coll. of Siskiyous, Weed, Calif., 1975-76; spl. asst. in adminstrn. Ednl. Service Dist. 101, Spokane, Wash., 1976-78; teaching fellow U. Utah, Salt Lake City, 1981-82; freelance writer; cons. grants and contracts to hosps. and state govts. Del. to Mont. State Land Use, 1974, Bend in the River Council, 1974-75; publicity chmn. Wash. State 4th Ann. Very Spl. Arts Festival for Handicapped Children and Adults, 1978, Nat. Theatre of Deaf Spokane

Tour, 1978. Recipient Gov.'s Commendation, State of Wash., 1979; scholar Bread Loaf Writers Conf., 1973. Mem. Nat. Council Univ. Research Adminstrs., Nat. Assn. Coll. and Univ. Bus. Officers, Nat. Assn. Univ. Women Deans, Adminstrs. and Counselors, Am. Assn. State Colls. and Univs., LWV. Club: Panhandle North Star Yacht (Coeur D'Alene, Idaho). Author: (with B. Mitchell and L. Triplett) Something About China, 1971; contbr. poems to various publs. Home: PO Box 172 Cheney WA 99004 Office: Eastern Washington U Cheney WA 99004

COWEN-MILLER, SANDRA LYNN, advt. and public relations agy. exec.; b. Mpls., July 26, 1944; d. Edward Thomas and Marie Elizabeth (Swank) Brandy; student public schs.; m. Robert S. Cowen, Oct. 11, 1965; 1 son, Jonathan David; m. 2d, Steven P. Miller, Apr. 28, 1978. Traffic mgr. Sta. KOOL, Phoenix, 1962; systems analyst Sta. KHJ, Los Angeles, 1965; media dir. Owens & Assos. Advt., Phoenix, 1966-69; part owner record distributorship ENDISCO, 1968-71; public relations dir. Owens & Assos. Advt., Phoenix, 1970-73; pres., owner Sandy Cowen Agy., Inc., Phoenix, 1973—; mem. Phoenix Media Adv. Bd.; speaker, lectr. in field. Vice pres. Samaritan Health Services Bd., Phoenix, 1980—; bd. dirs. Youth Evaluation Treatment Centers 1981-82. Recipient Public Relations award Nat. Hotel/Motel Assn., 1979. Mem. Am. Advt. Fedn., Retail Mktg. Group (chmn.), Nat. Acad. TV Arts and Scis., Phoenix Advt. Club, Phoenix Press Club, Ariz. C. of C., Phoenix C. of C., Phoenix Better Bus. Bur. Home: 1809 N 13th Ave Phoenix AZ 85007 Office: 15 E Garfield St Phoenix AZ 85004

COWGILL, MARY LU, psychologist; b. Newton, Kans., Nov. 20, 1932; d. George David and Marian Chase (Axtell) Hanna; A.B., Stanford U., 1954; M.A., Tufts U., 1972; m. F. Brooks Cowgill, Dec. 22, 1954; children—David, Ann. Head tchr. Red Barn Nursery Sch., Weston, Mass., 1968-69; elem. tchr. Stoneham (Mass.) Pub. Schs., 1969-71; psychologist Fernald Lang. grant study Mass. Dept. Health and Welfare, Belmont, 1972-75; sch. psychologist learning disorders unit Mass. Gen. Hosp., Boston, 1976—. Mem. Mass. Assn. for Children with Learning Disabilities (founder), Am. Psychol. Assn., Mass. Psychol. Assn., Stanford U. Alumni Assn. Congregationalist. Contbr. articles to profl. jours. Home: 75 Lawson Rd Winchester MA 01890

COWLES, MILLY, coll. dean; b. Ramer, Ala., May 29, 1932; d. Russell Fail and Sara (Mills) Cowles; B.S., Troy State U., 1952; M.A., U. Ala., 1958, Ph.D. (grad. fellow), 1962. Tchr. public schs., Montgomery, Ala., 1952-59; asst. then asso. prof. Grad. Sch. Edn., Rutgers U., 1962-66; asso. prof. U. Ga., 1966-67; prof., dir. early childhood devel. and edn. Sch. Edn., U. S.C., Columbia, 1967-73; prof. U. Ala., Birmingham, 1973—, asso. dean Sch. Edn., 1973-80, dean, 1980—. Dir. Williamsburg County Schs. Career Opportunity Program, 1970-73; cons. So. Edn. Found., Atlanta, Ga. Inst. Higher Edn. U. Ga., also numerous sch systems throughout Northeast and South. Pres. bd. dirs. 2d Reformed Ch. Nursery Sch., New Brunswick, N.J., 1963-66; bd. dirs. S.C. Assn. on Children Under Six, 1969-73. Recipient Outstanding Public Educator award Capstone Coll. Edn. Soc., U. Ala., 1977; Alumna of Yr. award Troy State U., 1981. Mem. Am. Ednl. Research Assn., Soc. for Research Child Devel., AAAS, AAUP, Nat. Council Tchrs. English, Internat. Reading Assn., Assn. for Supervision and Curriculum Devel. (mem. council on early childhood edn. 1969—, dir. 1978-82), Nat. Assn. for Edn. Young Children, Assn. for Childhood Devel. Internat., N.Y. Acad. Scis., Kappa Delta Pi (chpt. treas. 1964-66), Delta Kappa Gamma. Author: Taming the Young Savage, 1981; Developmental Discipline, 1982; editor, contbg. author: Perspectives in the Education of Disadvantaged Children, 1967. Research and publs. on psycholinguistic behaviors of rural children.

COWLEY, E. GERALDYN, accountant; b. Phila., June 9, 1907; d. Leo and Anna (Van Dexter) Lustig; ed. N.J. Coll. Commerce, LaSalle Inst., bus. courses; m. Harry J. Josephsen, Sept. 27, 1923; children—Bernice Martina, Harry Leo. Paymaster, Howard Johnson's, Atlantic City, 1946-49; owner employment office, 1949-52; acct., 1953-59; owner, operator E.G. Cowley Acctg. Office, Pleasantville, N.J., 1960—; cons. bus. and taxes. Mem. Nat. Assn. Tax Consultors, Nat. Small Bus. Assn., Am. Notary Assn., Nat. Soc. Public Accts. (asso.), Greater Mainland C. of C., Better Bus. Bur. South Jersey. Republican. Methodist. Home and Office: 702 W Adams Ave Pleasantville NJ 08232

COX, ANGELA LOUVENIA, ednl. adminstr.; b. Balt., Feb. 23, 1953; d. George Marion and Harriett McDonald (Pennington) C.; student (Md. minority scholar 1972, Md. state scholar 1973) U. Md.—Baltimore County, 1972-75; B.S. in Early Childhood Edn., Towson State U., 1977. Coordinator City-Wide Peer Counseling Program, Balt. Office Guidance and Placement 1978-79; asst. to acad. dean Md. Inst. Coll. Art, 1979—; pvt. tutor in reading, 1978-70; interviewer Project Growing Opportunity; cons. student facilitator program Balt. City Schs., 1979-81. Vol., YMCA, Balt., 1979-80. Cert. tchr., Md. Mem. Am. Assn. Higher Edn., Nat. Acad. Advising Assn. Roman Catholic. Office: 1300 Mount Royal Ave Baltimore MD 21217

COX, BARBARA BOLL, ednl. adminstr.; b. N.Y.C., Oct. 9, 1943; d. George L. and Madeline F. (Foody) Boll; B.A., Coll. Mt. St. Vincent, N.Y.C., 1965; M.S., Fordham U., 1967; postgrad. Yeshiva U. Tchr., then counselor Yonkers (N.Y.) Sch. Dist., 1965-73, adminstr., 1973—, dir. adminstrv. services, 1979—; chmn. Yonkers City Wide Comprehensive Youth Plan, 1978—; adv. bd. Westchester County Dept. Community Mental Health. Mem. Assn. Women Adminstrs. Westchester, Am. Soc. Profl. and Exec. Women, Nat. Assn. Female Execs., Assn. Supervision and Curriculum Devel., N.Y. State Assn. Pupil Personnel Adminstrs. (exec. bd.). Home: 76 DeHaven Dr Yonkers NY 10703 Office: 145 Palmer Rd Yonkers NY 10701

COX, BEVERLEY LENORE, zoologist; b. Huntington, Pa., Jan. 11, 1929; d. Elwood Beck and Orlee Arcola (Davis) C.; B.S., Pa. State U., 1951, M.S., 1953; Ph.D., U. Okla., 1960; NIH fellow, research asso. U. Oreg., 1961. Instr., U. Okla., 1959-60; mem. faculty Central State U., Edmond, Okla., 1961—, asso. prof. zoology, 1965-70, prof. biology, 1970—; vis. asso. prof. U. Okla., 1967, 68, 69, 74. NDEA fellow, 1959-60; NIH fellow, 1960-61, 63; NSF fellow, 1963, 64, 65. Mem. Am. So. Zoologists, AAUP, AAAS, Sigma Xi. Contbr. articles to profl. jours. Home: Rt 1 Box 184 Oklahoma City OK 73111 Office: Dept Biology Central State U Edmond OK 73034

COX, EILEEN FRANCES HINSHAW, bus. exec.; b. Washington, Oct. 24, 1935; d. Max O. and Marguerite Mary (Wootton) Hinshaw; B.A. with honors, U. Md., 1967; M.A., Rutgers U., 1971; M.A., Columbia U., 1973; m. Robert Gene Cox, July 10, 1953; children—Ann Rebecca, Allan Robert. Staff asst. to dir. U.S./Mex. Border Devel. Commn., Exec. Office of Pres., Washington, 1967-68; asst. to Am. ambassador Conf. on Mex. Border Devel., San Diego, 1968; office mgr. Am. Acad. Cons., N.Y.C., 1971; devel. assoc. Found. Center, Inc., N.Y.C. and Cleve., 1975-78, cons., 1979; pres. Sloane & Hinshaw, Inc., N.Y.C., 1979-80, All Souls Music Soc., 1981—; mng. dir. Hinshaw Cox Ltd.; mem. U.S. del. U.S.-Mex. Trade Conf., Washington, 1967; Mem. N.Y.C. area council Unitarian Universalist Assn., 1979-80, mem. service com., 1979—. Mem. Center for Study of Presidency, Fgn. Policy Assn., Met. Opera Guild, Center Inter-Am. Relations, Women's Econ. Round Table, Legal Aid Soc. N.Y., Pi Sigma Alpha, Phi Kappa Phi. Democrat. Office: Hinshaw Cox Ltd 225 Central Park W Suite 1207 New York NY 10024

COX, ELIZABETH FOWLER, computer programmer; b. Norton, Kans., Nov. 16, 1944; d. Roy Newton and Von Lee (Hendrickson) Fowler; student Kans. U., 1962-63; m. Steven Lloyd Cox, Aug. 9, 1964; children—Stephanie, Nicolette, Camille, Christopher. Bd. dirs. Norton County Arts Council, Norton, 1979-81, pres., 1979-81, sec.-treas. S & L Cox Farms, Inc., Long Island, Kans., 1975-80; v.p. C & C. Swine Equipment, Inc., Long Island, 1979—. Music chmn. Long Island United Meth. Ch., 1973-75; active Community Choir, Norton. Mem. DAR (membership chmn. Phebe Dustin chpt., dist. sec., state flag chmn.), Norton County Geneal. Soc. Republican. Methodist. Club: Wednesday Study. Home: 914 Westridge Ave Norton KS 67654 Office: Rural Route 1 Long Island KS 67647

COX, ENID ELAINE, home economist; b. Eugene, Oreg., Feb. 28, 1935; d. James Artie and Bessie Agnes (Foster) Tanner; student Central Oreg. Coll., 1956; B.S., Oreg. State U., 1958, M.S., 1964; m. Manuel Ernest Cox, Jan. 7, 1950; children—Kathryn A., Carol A. Tchr. vocat. homemaking, chmn. dept. Scappoose (Oreg.) High Sch., 1958-67; instr. home econs. Marylhurst (Oreg.) Coll., 1967-68; coop. ext. agt. Wash. State U., Pullman, 1968; ext. agt. 4-H youth Clark County, Wash., 1968-75, home economist, 1975-81; home economist Walla Walla County and 4-H Youth, 1982—. Mem. Nat. Elec. Women's Round Table (dir., chmn. Oreg. chpt. 1978-79), Nat. Extension Home Economists Assn., Am. Econs. Assn., Blue Mountain Home Econs. Assn. (pres. 1982-83). Lutheran. Clubs: Daughters of Pioneers of Wash., Scappoose Woman's (past pres.), Wash. State Friendship Force. Address: 314 W Main St Walla Walla WA 99362

COX, GLORIA LU, health center adminstr.; b. Sac City, Iowa, Mar. 18, 1952; d. Calvin Carl and Helen Lucille C.; Ph.D., Purdue U., 1979. Asst. dir. research and evaluation Mental Health Center, Fort Wayne, Ind., 1979-80, dir. research and evaluation, 1980—. Mem. Am. Psychol. Assn. Home: 706 Three Rivers E Fort Wayne IN 46802 Office: 909 E State Blvd Fort Wayne IN 46805

COX, HATTIE MAE, mgmt. exec.; b. Utica, Miss., Feb. 26, 1931; d. Walice Field and Nora Mae (Ford) Collins; student Jackson Comml. Coll., 1948-50; m. James Elijah Cox, Feb. 27, 1950 (div. 1960); children—Martha Patricia, James Michael, Cynthia Delaine. Sec., Miss. State Tax Commn., Jackson, 1950-56; sec. Multi-Copy Letter Shop, Jackson, part-time, 1957; sec.-bookkeeper Cook & Co., Jackson, 1957-64; office mgr. Jackson Mack Sales, Inc., 1964-67, v.p., 1967-72, sec.-treas., 1972—. Christian Ch. Clubs: VFW Ladies Aux. (dept. pres. 1964-65), Am. Legion Ladies Aux. Home: 545 Greenmont Dr Jackson MS 39212 Office: 412 Hwy 49 S Jackson MS 39208

COX, JULIE ANN, blood bank adminstr; b. Bartlesville, Okla., Oct. 15, 1950; d. Roger and Barbara Mary (Simmons) Weigl; B.S., Okla. State U., 1972; Med. Technologist cert., St. Francis Hosp., Wichita, 1972; Specialist in Blood Banking cert., Wesley Med. Center, Wichita, 1976; M.B.A., Corpus Christi State U., 1981. Staff technologist Blood Bank, Wesley Med. Center, Wichita, Kans., 1974-76, edn. coordinator, 1976-78; tech. dir. Nueces County Med. Soc. Community Blood Bank, Corpus Christi, Tex., 1978-79, exec. dir., 1979—. Long range planning com. United Way; med. lab. technologist adv. com. DelMar Coll. Cert. med. technologist and specialist in blood banking, Am. Soc. Clin. Pathologists. Mem. Am. Assn. Blood Banks, S.Central Assn. Blood Banks. Methodist. Club: Zonta. Home: 3401 Crest Lake Corpus Christi TX 78415 Office: 5025 Deepwood Circle Corpus Christi TX 78415

COX, LEONA KRIESEL, ednl. writer; b. Hudson, Wis., Apr. 5, 1915; d. Frederick Gustave and Nettie Emma (Jones) Kriesel; B.S., U. Minn., 1938; postgrad. U. Cin., 1961, Miami U., 1962-63; m. John Joseph Cox, Sept. 1, 1944; 1 dau., Kathleen. Sec., Dayton-Hudson, Mpls., 1938-39; tchr. bus. high sch., Houston, Minn., 1939-41, Red Wing, Minn., 1941-42; instr. bus. Allegheny Coll., Meadville, Pa., 1942-43; tchr., Greenhills-Forest Park, Ohio, 1961-75; writer ednl. books and filmstrip scripts, Cin., 1975—; books include: Outlining, Note Taking and Report Writing Skills, Book I, 1979, Book II, 1982; High Interest Grammar, 1979; Rhymes and Numbers with Mother Goose, 1980; Fairy Tales and Numbers, 1980; Tall Tales and Numbers, 1980; Holiday Dot to Dot with Trolls, Numbers and Letters, 1980; Learning to Write Sentences, 1982; Learning to Write Paragraphs, 1982; Learning to Write Reports, 1982; Sound filmstrip: Why People Differ-A Study of Cultures; About the World at Hanukkah and Christmas, 1982. Served with ARC, 1943-45. Mem. Women in Communication, Nat. Writers Club, Nat. Ret. Tchrs. Assn., Ohio Ret. Tchrs. Assn., Am. Overseas Assn., Delta Kappa Gamma. Repubican. Presbyterian. Clubs: Wyoming (Ohio) Women's, Nat. Rep. Home and Office: 8816 Falmouth Dr Cincinnati OH 45231

COX, LINDA CEDRONE, state legislator; b. Washington, Apr. 18, 1946; d. Aldo Joseph and Lucretia (Capursi) Cedrone; B.A., U. S.C. Mem. consumer affairs task force Broward County (Fla.) Democratic Exec. Com., 1975-76; mem. Broward County Young Democrats; mem. Fla. Ho. of Reps., 1976—; tchr. Broward County Sch. Bd. Bd. dirs. Spectrum Program, 1977—, Here's Help, 1977—, Broward County Affirmative Action Com.; mem. Concerned Democrats North Broward. Episcopalian. Office: Fla Ho Reps State Capitol Tallahassee FL 32304 *

COX, MARGARET JANE, speech pathologist; b. Bklyn., Jan. 28, 1947; d. Jere Coleman Cox and Jane Dunseath (O'Neill) C.; student Chatham Coll., 1965-67; B.A. cum laude and with distinction, Mt. Holyoke Coll., 1969; M.A., Northwestern U., 1971. Speech pathologist Berkshire Rehab. Center, Pittsfield, Mass., 1972-78, clin. supr., 1978; speech pathologist Hosp. U. Pa., Phila., 1979—; instr. dept. otorhinolaryngology Med. Sch. U. Pa., 1979—; cons. Ashmere Manor Nursing Home, Hinsdale, Mass., 1975-78, Bennington (Vt.) Convalescent Center, 1975-77. Rehab. Services Adminstrn. trainee, 1969-71. Mem. Am. Speech Lang. and Hearing Assn. (cert. clin. competence 1973), Pa. Speech and Hearing Assn., Aphasia Study Group Phila. Republican. Club: Mendelssohn. Home: 7300 Cresheim Rd B-6 Philadelphia PA 19119 Office: 3400 Spruce St Philadelphia PA 19104

COX, MARGARET STORKE (MRS. EXUM MORRIS COX), civic worker; b. Santa Barbara, Calif., Apr. 15, 1908; d. Thomas More and Elsie (Smith) Storke; A.B., Scripps Coll., 1931; m. Exum Morris Cox, Sept. 6, 1934; children—Cynthia (Mrs. Huntting), Susan More (Mrs. James T. Fousekis), Thomas Storke. Dir. Santa Barbara News Press Pub. Co. 1957-64. Mem. women's bd. San Francisco Mus. Art, pres., 1962-64; bd. dirs. San Francisco Players Guild, 1960-64; San Francisco Planning and Urban Renewal, 1964-66, Stern Grove Festival Assn. Com. 1965—, Music Acad. of West, Santa Barbara, 1962-64; trustee Scripps Coll., 1971-76; trustee World Affairs Council No. Calif., 1974—, v.p., 1978-80. Clubs: Social, Town and Country. Home: 2361 Broadway San Francisco CA 94115

COX, MARGIE HADDOCK, univ. adminstr.; b. Vicksburg, Miss., Apr. 5, 1952; d. William Hershel and Mary Jane (Gill) Haddock; A.A., Hinds Jr. Coll., Raymond, Miss., 1972; B.S., U. So. Miss., 1974, M.S.W., 1976; m. James K. Cox, Jr., Mar. 27, 1976. Supr. residential program Ellisville (Miss.) State Sch. for Mentally Retarded, 1976-79, regional coordinator univ. affiliated program, 1980-81; coordinator adult services U. So. Miss., Hattiesburg, 1981—. Mem. Nat. Assn. Social Workers, Miss. Conf. on Social Welfare, Acad. Cert. Social Workers, Am. Assn. Mental Deficiency, Miss. Assn. Women in Higher Edn. United Methodist (tchr. Sunday sch.). Home: Route 9 Box 347E Hattiesburg MS 39401 Office: So Sta Box 5112 Hattiesburg MS 39401

COX, MARY BLANCHE, clin. psychologist; b. Orange, N.J., May 10, 1945; d. William Roe and Mary Sophia Cox; A.B. Barnard Coll., 1968; Ph.D., Adelphi U., 1972. Staff psychologist VA, N.Y.C., 1972-76; pvt. practice clin. psychology, cons., N.Y.C., 1974—. Mem. Am. Psychol. Assn., N.Y. Inst. Gestalt Therapy, Am. Soc. Psychical Research. Office: 350 Central Park W Suite 1F New York NY 10025

COX, MARY E., physicist, educator; b. Detroit, Mich., Nov. 11, 1937; A.B., Albion Coll., 1959; M.A., U. Mich., 1961; m. Kendall B. Cox, July 1, 1961; 1 son. Instr. in physics U. Mich., Flint, 1966-71, acting dir. instl. research, 1971-73, asst. prof. physics, 1971-76, asso. prof. physics 1976—, chmn. dept. physics, 1976-77, asso. dean Coll. Arts and Scis., 1980-81, acting dean, 1981—; tutor in physics Sommerville Coll., U. Oxford, England, 1977-78; cons. biomed. applications of coherent optics, 1970—. NSF grantee, 1977-78. Mem. Am. Assn. of Physics Tchrs., Optical Soc. Am., Soc. of Photo-Optical Instrumentation Engrs. Contbr. articles on holography and optics to sci. jours.; contbr. book revs. in laser expts. Office: Office of the Dean Univ Michigan Flint MI 48503

COX, MERIDITH BRITTAN, risk mgmt. cons., publisher; b. Bklyn., Oct. 25, 1941; d. Virgil McLeod and Elizabeth Joan (Maxey) C.; B.A., Golden Gate U., 1974, M.P.A., 1975. Exec. dir., Info. Center, San Francisco Hosp. Conf., 1967-69; research adminstr. ASME, N.Y.C., 1970-72; patient rep. Vis. Nurse Assn., San Francisco, 1972-73; cons. med. malpractice, 1973-76; risk mgmt. cons., prin. Meridith B. Cox Assos., El Cerrito, Calif., 1977—; editor, pub. The Nurse, The Patient and The Law, 1977—, Public Sector Health Care Risk Mgmt., 1980—, The Risk Mgmt. Report: Med. Records, 1982—, The Cox Report: Risk Mgmt. for Female Execs., 1982—; professorial lectr. Golden Gate U. Commr., El Cerrito Appeals Bd., 1979-80; mem. El Cerrito Parks and Recreation Commn., 1980-81, El Cerrito Safety Commn., 1981—. Served with U.S. Navy, 1960-63. Mem. Calif. League Nursing (chmn. state legis. and public affairs com.), Am. Soc. Hosp. Risk Mgmt., Am. Soc. Hosp. Edn. and Tng., Am. Soc. Public Adminstrn., Am. Soc. Law and Medicine, Assn. Western Hosps., Nat. Assn. Female Execs., Nat. League Nursing, Patient Care Assessment Council, Media Alliance, Golden Gate U. Alumni Council. Episcopalian. Office: PO Box 935 El Cerrito CA 94530

COX, NANCY JANE, microbiologist; b. Emmetsburg, Iowa, July 21, 1948; d. Emmett Stanley and Verna Lucille (Olson) Cox; B.S. with honors, Iowa State U., 1970; Ph.D., Cambridge, (Eng.) U., 1975; m. Milton Evan Lindsay, Apr. 11, 1981. Postdoctoral fellow Muscular Dystrophy Assn., Balt. and Atlanta, 1975-77; staff fellow Centers for Disease Control, Atlanta, 1978-80, research chemist, 1980—. Recipient Marshall Scholarship for study abroad, 1970; postdoctoral fellow Muscular Dystrophy Assn. Am., 1970. Mem. AAAS, Am. Soc. Microbiology, Sigma Xi. Methodist. Contbr. articles to various publs. Office: Viral Diseases Div 7-111 Centers for Disease Control 1600 Clifton Rd Atlanta GA 30333

COX, RACHEL DUNAWAY, clin. psychologist; b. Murray, Ky., Jan. 20, 1904; d. Enoch T. and Khadra Dunaway (Fergeson) C.; B.A., U. Tex., 1925; M.A., Columbia U., 1930; Ph.D., U. Pa., 1943; m. Reavis Cox, Feb. 18, 1928; children—David Jackson, Rosemary Cox Masters. Reporter, editorial work N.Y. Herald Tribune, N.Y.C., 1926-30; tchr., dir. edn. West Side YWCA, N.Y.C., 1930-35; hosp. case worker ARC, Walter Reed Hosp., Washington, 1944; lectr. psychology and edn. Bryn Mawr (Pa.) Coll., 1944-45, asst. prof., 1945-49, asso. prof., 1949-55, prof., 1955-71, dir. Child Study Inst., 1944-70, vis. prof., 1976; clin. psychologist Manchester (Eng.) Royal Infirmary, Gaskell House Unit, 1972; pvt. practice clin. psychology and research, Wallingford, Pa., 1972—. Mem. adv. com. Center for Early Childhood Services, Phila., 1977-81, trustee, 1981—; bd. dirs. Sleighton Sch., 1955-79, Devel. Center for Autistic Children, Phila., 1960-81. Recipient Disting. Service award Pa. Psychol. Assn., 1975; B'nai B'rith award for Service to Youth, 1960; Lindbach award, 1970. Mem. Am. Psychol. Assn., Eastern Psychol. Assn., Pa. Psychol. Assn., Soc. Personality Assessment (past sec.), Nat. Assn. Social Workers, Am. Personnel and Guidance Assn., Phi Beta Kappa, Theta Sigma Phi, Sigma Xi. Republican. Presbyterian. Club: Media Book. Author: Youth Into Maturity, 1970; Counselors and Their Work, 1945; contbr. numerous articles to profl., lay jours., mags.

COX, THELMA BANKS, ednl. adminstr.; b. Cambridge, Md., July 21, 1928; d. Charles Monroe and Ida Mae (Slacum) Banks; B.S., Morgan State U., 1948, M.S., 1972; Ph.D., Union Grad. Sch., Cin., 1980; m. Leonard Cox, June 25, 1949. Social caseworker Phila. Dept. Public Assistance, 1948-49; sci. tchr., Annapolis, Md., 1949-50; English tchr., Balt., 1950-65, reading tchr., 1965-66, dept. head, 1966-67, coordinator community schs., 1967-68, spl. projects coordinator, 1968-72, project mgr., 1972-73, regional supt., 1973-79, asst. supt. intergovtl. relations, 1980—; mem. Md. Council Higher Edn., 1970-76, State Bd. Higher Edn., 1976—. Named Woman of Year, Greyhound Bus Co., 1972. Mem. Am. Assn. Sch. Adminstrs., Nat. Assn. Black Sch. Educators, Assn. Tchr. Educators, Delta Sigma Theta. Democrat. Editor: The Heritage of the Baltimore Chapter of Delta Sigma Theta, 1979. Home: 3344 Dolfield Ave Baltimore MD 21215 Office: 3 E 25 St Baltimore MD 21218

COYE, DOROTHY HELEN, hosp. adminstr.; b. Sturgis, Mich.; d. Charles Willard and Harriet Marie (Ruud) C.; diploma Henry Ford Hosp. Sch. Nursing, 1938; B.S. in Nursing, Wayne State U., 1963, M.S. in Nursing, 1964. Head nurse Henry Ford Hosp., Detroit, 1949-55, supr., 1955-63, asst. dir. nursing edn., 1963-68; asso. dir. nursing edn. William Beaumont Hosp., Royal Oak, Mich., 1968-69, dir. nursing edn., 1969—. Mem. Am., Mich. (chmn. com. on continuing edn. 1973-76, dir. 1978—), Oakland (Mich.) Dist. (chmn. program com. 1966-67) nurses assns., Mich. League Nursing, Henry Ford Sch. Nursing, Wayne State U. alumni assns., Sigma Theta Tau. Contbr. articles to profl. jours. Mem. editorial bd. Jour. Continuing Edn. in Nursing, 1976—. Home: 10505 Talbot St Huntington Woods MI 48070 Office: 3601 W 13 Mile Rd Royal Oak MI 48072

COYE, JANET LOPER, mental health adminstr.; b. Lihue, Kauai, Hawaii, Jan. 20, 1926; d. W. Harold and Violet Jane (Grinols) Loper; B.A., Bennington Coll., 1947; M.A., U. Rochester, 1951; div.; children—Joel Chapin, Peter Loper, Carol Loomis. Asst. to dir. Sch. Social Work, U. Wis., 1965-69, asst. dir., 1969-72; research analyst Wis. Coordinating Council for Higher Edn., Madison, 1968; staff analyst, adminstrv. cons. Wis. Gov.'s Health Planning and Policy Task Force, Madison, 1971-72; cons. Am. Public Health Assn. related project on formation Nat. Com. on Prison Health Reform, Detroit, 1973; project dir., cons. Office Health and Med. Affairs, Mich. Dept. Mgmt. and Budget, Lansing, 1973-74, health planning cons., 1974-75; health planning cons. Wis. Div. Health Policy and Planning, Madison, 1974; mental health cons. Mich. Dept. Mental Health, Lansing, 1974-75, interim dir. Office Recipient Rights, 1975-76, dir., 1976—; mem. commn. on mentally disabled Am. Bar Assn., 1980—, mem. criminal justice mental health standards project, 1981—. Contbr. articles to profl. jours. Office: Lewis Cass Bldg Lansing MI 48926

COYLE, BERTHA M., nurse; b. Galion, Ohio, Dec. 25, 1912; d. Edward E. and Blanche E. (Keiffer) Eichhorn; diploma, Fairview Gen. Hosp., Sch. Nursing, 1933; m. Charles W. Coyle, Oct. 5, 1946; children—Christine E. Coyle Snyder, Deborah A. Coyle Barron. Staff nurse Fairview Hosp., Cleve., 1933-35, Cleve. City Hosp., 1935-38; pvt. duty nurse Galion, Ohio, 1938-42; staff nurse Galion Hosp., 1947-66, coronary care head nurse, 1966-78; active nurse ARC, Galion, 1954-78; cons. in field. Chmn. Galion chpt., ARC, 1962, instr. prepared parenthood, 1954-78, mem. disaster program, blood bank, nursing service, 1954-78; counselor Girl Scouts of Am., Galion, 1956-65. Served to capt. with U.S. Army, Nurses Corps, 1943-46. Decorated 3 overseas service bars, victory medal. Recipient commendation for Nursing Services, ARC, 1962; woman of yr. award, Business and Profl. Women's Club, 1962. Mem. ARC, Ohio, Nurses Assn., Am. Nurses Assn., Am. Heart Assn. Presbyterian (elder). Clubs: Am. Legion, Eastern Star. Address: 202 S Columbus St Galion OH 44833

COYLE, JOAN DEGOT WASHBURN, editor; b. N.Y.C., Aug. 29; d. Arthur Lawrence and Sona Jeanne (DeGot) Washburn; B.A., Manhattanville Coll., 1948; m. Eugene F. Coyle, June 8, 1957; children—Nancy Wickes Washburn, Laura Philbin Cooke. Publicity dir. Duell, Sloan & Pearce, N.Y.C., 1948-50, G.P. Putnam's Sons, Coward-McCann, Inc., John Day Co., pubs., 1951-54; picture researcher Time mag., N.Y.C., 1956-62, Can. edit., 1962-63; pres. DeGot, Washburn, Inc., Fashion Idea Co., 1970-73; asst. editor Darien Rev., 1968-69; picture editor Money mag., Time, Inc., N.Y.C., 1974-81; free-lance picture editor ABC-TV, NBC-TV. Vice chmn. United Fund, Darien, Conn., 1971-72; editor Council of Sch. Parents Newspaper, Darien, 1970-71. Republican. Roman Catholic.

COYNE, SARAH THERESA, educator; b. Pitts., Feb. 23, 1941; d. Matthias F. and Sarah A. Coyne; B.A. in English, Wheeling (W.Va.) Coll., 1962; M.A., Duquesne U., Pitts., 1967; postgrad. U. Pitts., W.Va.U., Univ. Coll., Dublin, Ireland. Elementary sch. tchr. S.S. Simon and Jude Sch., Pitts., 1962-66; instr. English, Edinboro (Pa.) State Coll., 1966-68; assoc. prof. English, chmn. dept. W.Liberty (W.Va.) State Coll., 1968—. Founder, supr. W.Liberty Coop., 1980-82; vol. Spl. Olympics, Wheeling Long Distance Race. Mem. AAUP, Sigma Tau Delta. Home: 302 Lakeview Dr West Liberty WV 26074 Office: L36 W Liberty State Coll Library West Liberty WV 26074

COZZOLINO, DOROTHY MARIE, law librarian; b. Flushing, N.Y., Jan. 9, 1938; d. William George and Anna Amelia (Brignole) Aramini; student U. Conn., 1955-58; B.S. in Geography, Trenton State Coll., 1973; M.S., Drexel U., 1975; m. Joseph M. Cozzolino, Nov. 30, 1957; children—Suzan, Alison, Matthew. Asst. librarian U.S. Ct. Appeals 3d Circuit, Phila., 1975-79, chief librarian, 1979—. Trustee, Morrisville (Pa.) Vis. Nurse Assn., 1972-75; fin. chairperson, treas. Morrisville Jr. Women's Club, 1970-74. Mem. Am. Assn. Law Libraries, Greater Phila. Law Library Assn. (treas. 1979-81, dir. 1978). Office: US Ct Appeals Library 22409 US Courthouse Philadelphia PA 19067

CRABB, BARBARA BRANDRIFF, U.S. dist. judge; b. Green Bay, Wis., Mar. 17, 1939; d. Charles Edward and Mary (Forrest) Brandriff; A.B., U. Wis., 1960, J.D., 1962; m. Theodore E. Crabb, Jr., Aug. 29, 1959; children—Julia Forrest, Philip Elliott. Admitted to Wis. bar, 1963; asso. firm Roberts, Broadman, Suhr & Curry, Madison, 1962-64; research asst. U. Wis. Law Sch., 1968-70, Am. Bar Assn., Madison, 1970-71; U.S. magistrate, Madison, 1971-79; dist. judge U.S. Dist. Ct. Western Dist. Wis., Madison, 1979—, chief judge, 1980—; mem. Gov.'s Task Force Prison Reform, 1971-73. Membership chmn., v.p. Milw. LWV, 1966-68; mem. Milw. Jr. League, 1967-68. Mem. Am. Bar Assn., Nat. Council Fed. Magistrates, Nat. Assn. Women Judges, Dane County Bar Assn., U. Wis. Law Alumni Assn. Office: PO Box 1724 Madison WI 53701

CRADDOCK, PATRICIA BLAND, educator; b. New Orleans, Oct. 28, 1938; d. French Hood, Jr. and Winifred Jane (Bland) C.; B.A., Ind. U., 1959; M.A., Stanford U., 1960; M.A., Yale U., 1963, Ph.D., 1964. Instr. English, Ala. Coll., Montevallo, 1960-61; instr., then asst. prof. Conn. Coll., New London, 1963-66; asst. prof., then asso. prof. Goucher Coll., Balt., 1966-72; mem. faculty Boston U., 1972—, prof. English, 1981—, dir. grad. studies in dept., 1975-80, chmn. dept., 1980—; vis. prof. M.I.T., fall 1981. Mem. choir, cantor St. Mary Assumption Roman Cath. Ch., Brookline, Mass.; v.p. Sylacauga (Ala.) Cemetery, 1973. Fellow Guggenheim Found., 1971-73, Nat. Endowment Humanities, 1978-79; grantee Ford Found.-Goucher Coll., 1969, Am. Council Learned Socs., 1977. Mem. AAUP, MLA, Am. Soc. 18th Century Studies, Coll. English Assn., Northeastern Soc. 18th Century Studies, Northeastern Coll. English Assn. Democrat. Author: The English Essays of Edward Gibbon, 1973; Young Edward Gibbon: Gentleman of Letters, 1982; also articles. Home: 8 Littell Rd Brookline MA 02146 Office: 236 Bay State Rd Boston MA 02215

CRAFT, BETTY VANCE, med. technologist; b. Second Creek, W.Va., Apr. 20, 1938; d. Paul Gray and Etta Blanche (Bostic) Vance; B.S., Concord Coll., Athens, W.Va., 1959; M.A. in Health Care Adminstrn., U. Central Mich., 1975; m. Donald David Craft, June 6, 1959; 1 son, Kevin Don. Med. technologist Beckley (W.Va.) Meml. Hosp., 1959-61; secondary sch. tchr., Lewisburg, W.Va., 1961-62, Wytheville, Va., 1968-70; chief med. technologist Greenbrier Valley Hosp., Ronceverte, W.Va., 1962-67; substitute tchr., Princeton, W.Va., 1968; asso. prof. med. tech., program head Wytheville Community Coll., 1970—. Mem. Am. Soc. Med. Tech., Am. Soc. Clin. Pathologists (affiliate), AAUW (v.p. programs 1977-79, v.p. membership 1980-82, legis. rep. 1979-80), Va. Assn. Allied Health Profls. (dir., chmn. edn. com., nomination com., sec. 1981-83), Va. Soc. Med. Tech., Wytheville Community Coll. Faculty Govt. Assn. Presbyterian. Club: Wytheville Community Coll. Faculty Wives. Author papers in field. Home: 825 N 3d St Wytheville VA 24382 Office: 1000 E Main St Wytheville VA 24382

CRAFT, CAROL LEIGH, univ. ofcl.; b. Dallas, Jan. 20, 1954; d. Herbert Gray and Dorothy Evelyn (Dickson) C.; B.A. in Radio-TV, Baylor U., 1975; postgrad. in architecture Tex. Tech. U., 1982—. Reporter, Tyler (Tex.) Courier-Times-Telegraph, 1975-77, women's editor, 1977; reporter Waco (Tex.) Tribune-Herald, 1977-82; writer Tex. Football mag., 1980-82; head resident Wall Hall, Tex. Tech. U., Lubbock, 1982—. Mem. Zeta Phi Eta, Sigma Delta Chi. Baptist. Home and office: Wall Hall Tex Tech U Lubbock TX 79406

CRAFT, DOROTHY ANN, librarian; b. Kinsley, Kans., Sept. 23, 1936; d. Joseph Olaf and Rubie Helen (Hatfield) C.; B.S., Kans. State U., 1958; M.L.S., Emporia (Kans.) State U., 1968. Tchr. public schs., Anaheim, Calif., 1958-60, Casper, Wyo., 1960-61, Wichita, Kans., 1961-63, Syracuse, Kans., 1963-66; fed. documents librarian Linda Hall Library, Kansas City, Mo., 1968-71, asst. acquisitions librarian, 1971-73, acquisitions librarian, 1973-82, research librarian, 1982—. Mem. Spl. Libraries Assn. (past chpt. sec. and pres., mem. nominating com. 1979, chmn. 1980, chpt. exec. bd. 1981-82, co-editor chpt. newsletter 1980-81), Area Wide Orgn. Librarians (exec. bd. 1978-80).

CRAFT, ELIZABETH ANN, educator; b. Lexington, Ky., Jan. 14, 1943; d. Richard P. and Beatrice (Coles) Harris; B.F.A. (Alumni Sesquicentennial scholar 1963-64, Univ. Upperclass scholar 1964-65), Ohio U., 1965; M.A., Ariz. State U., 1979; m. John Edward Craft, Dec. 18, 1965; children—Lauren Kelly, Jennifer Lavonia. Teaching asst. in speech Ohio U., 1964-65, in English, 1964-65; tchr. English, Steubenville (Ohio) High Sch., 1965, 68; debate coach, 1966-68; teaching asst. in communication Ariz. State U., 1978-79, faculty asso. in communication, 1980-82, instructional TV coordinator, 1982—; speaker for civic orgns. Sec., Ariz. State Button Soc., 1980-82. Mem. Kappa Delta Pi. Mem. Christian Ch. (Disciples of Christ). Co-editor Ariz. State U. Faculty Wives Club newsletter, 1975-76. Home: 218 E Carter Dr Tempe AZ 85282 Office: Univ Media Systems Ariz State U Tempe AZ 85281

CRAFT, PEARL SARAH DIECK SERBUS, former editor; b. Riverdale, Ill.; d. Emil Edwin and Pearl (Kaiser) Dieck; m. Gerald Serbus, Jan. 26, 1946 (dec. Aug. 1969); children—Allan Lester, Bruce Alan, Curt Lyle; m. 2d, James E. Craft, Jan. 16, 1974. Mem. home econs. staff, writer Chgo. Herald Examiner, 1934-39; operator test kitchen Household Sci. Inst., Mdse. Mart, Chgo., 1940-45; free-lance writer grocery chains, Chgo., 1945-49; Riv.-Dolton corr. Calumet Index, Chgo., 1953-58, editorial asst., 1958-60, asst. editor, 1960-68, editor, 1968-72; with Suburban Index, Chgo., 1959-72, editor, 1960-72; mng. editor Index Publs., 1972-74; free lance writer, 1974—. Public relations vol. New Hope Sch., 1959-67; bd. dirs. United Fund of Riverdale, Roseland Mental Health Assn., Thornton chpt. Am. Field Service. Recipient Disting. Service Meml. scroll PTA, 1959, Sch. Bell award Ill. Edn. Assn., 1965, Outstanding Citizen award Chgo. South C. of C., 1972. Named Outstanding Civic Leader Am. Mem. Ill. Woman's Press Assn. (past pres. Woman of Distinction 1968, recipient 46 state awards, 3 nat. awards), Nat. Fedn. Press Women (pres. parlay past presidents 1981), Riverdale (v.p. 1966-68), Chgo. South (v.p., dir.) chambers commerce. Home: Rt 4 Box 223 Walkerton IN 46574

CRAFT, SHIRLEY FRANCES BROWN, data processing services co. exec.; b. Honey Grove, Tex., Oct. 2, 1950; d. Everette Layton and Elizabeth Ann (Burnsed) Brown; student N. Tex. State U., 1970, Eastfield Jr. Coll., 1971, Richland Coll., 1978, 1981-82; div. Comml. bldg. mgr. for pres. Plano (Tex.) Title Co., 1973-75; property mgr., Garland, Tex., 1971-73; asst. dir. ops. Murray Fin. Corp., Dallas, 1973-75; gen. mgr. adminstrn. Ins. Adminstrn. div. E.D.S. Fed. Corp. subs. Electronic Data Systems, Dallas, 1977—. Mem. Am. Business-women's Assn., Nat. Assn. Health Care Adminstrs., Nat. Hosp. Assn., So. Assn. Medicaid Adminstrs. Republican. Office: 7171 Forest Ln Dallas TX 75230

CRAFTON-MASTERSON, ADRIENNE, real estate exec.; b. Providence, Mar. 6, 1926; d. John Harold and Adrienne (Fitzgerald) Crafton; student No. Va. Community Coll., 1971-74; m. Francis T. Masterson, May 31, 1947 (div. Jan. 1977); children—Mary Victoria Masterson Powers, Kathleen Joan, John Andrew, Barbara Lynn. Mem. staff Senator T.F. Green of R.I., Washington, 1944-47, 54-60; mem. staff U.S. Senate Com. on Campaign Expenditures, 1944-45; clk. Ho. Govt. Ops. Com., 1948-49, Ho. Campaign Expenditures Com., 1950; asst. appointment sec. Office of Pres., 1951-53; with Hubbard Realty, Alexandria, Va., 1962-67; owner, mgr. Adrienne Investment Real Estate, Alexandria, 1968—. Mem. No. Va. Bd. Realtors (chmn. comml. and indsl. com. 1981-82), Nat. Assn. Realtors, Va. Assn. Realtors, Internat. Investment and Bus. Exchange. Exchange, Alexandria C. of C., Friends of Kennedy Center (founding), Nat. Hist. Soc., Nat. Trust Hist. Preservation. Home: 8200 Rolling Rd Springfield VA 22153 Office: 421 King St PO Box 1271 Alexandria VA 22313

CRAHAN, ELIZABETH SCHMIDT, med. assn. adminstr.; b. Cleve., Oct. 6, 1913; d. Edward and Margaret (Adams) Schmidt; student Wellesley Coll., 1931-32; B.Arch., U. So. Calif., 1937, M.L.S., 1960; m. Kenneth Acker, 1938 (div. 1968); children—Margaret Miller Johanningmeier, John Acker, Steven Acker, Charles Acker; m. 2d, Marcus E. Crahan, Dec. 16, 1968. Reference librarian Los Angeles County Med. Assn., 1960-61, head reference librarian, 1961-67, asst. librarian, 1967-78, dir. library services, 1978—. Founder, Med. Library Scholarship Found., 1967; pres. Friends of the UCLA Library, 1977-79. Mem. Spl. Libraries Assn., Med. Library Assn., Med. Library Group, So. Calif. and Ariz. Office: 634 S Westlake Ave Los Angeles CA 90057

CRAIG, BLANCHE MAE, educator; b. Glendive, Mont., May 20, 1936; d. Chris and Josephine E. (Richert) Christensen; B.A., Dickenson State Tchrs. Coll., 1957; M.A., Mount Marty Coll., 1969; M.A., U. S.D., 1972; m. Raymond M. Craig, May 24, 1958; children—Leasa Anne, Jodene Bess, Chauna Rae. Tchr. rural schs., N.D., 1954-56, Irene (S.D.) Public Schs., 1957-58, Turner, and Yankton County, S.D., 1958-67; tchr. Yankton Public Schs., 1969—, intermediate sci. instr. Stewart Elementary Sch., 1969—; cons. U. S.D. NSF projects, 1972-76. Mem. AAUW, NEA, S.D. Edn. Assn., Yankton Edn. Assn., V.F.W. Aux. (safety chmn., pres. dist. 1, nat. award), Delta Kappa Gamma, Phi Delta Kappa. Democrat. Methodist. Home: 2009 Cedar St Yankton SD 57078

CRAIG, BRENDA HARDIN, nurse; b. Lancaster, S.C., Nov. 9, 1944; d. Robert Calvin and Sarah Frances (Collins) Hardin; B.S. in Nursing, Duke U., 1968; M.A. in Teaching, The Citadel, Charleston, S.C., 1971; M.S. in Nursing, Med. U. S.C., 1982; m. Thomas Lee Craig, III, June 11, 1967; children—Lee Hardin, Kathryn Elizabeth. Public health nurse S.C. Dept. Health, Columbia, 1968-69; mem. faculty Med. U. S.C., Charleston, 1969—, instr. nursing, 1979—. Tchr. ch. sch. Mt. Pleasant (S.C.) Presbyn. Ch., 1973-79, treas. Women of Ch., 1978-80, v.p., 1982. Mem. AAUW (treas. Charleston chpt. 1977-79), Am. Nurses Assn., S.C. Nurses Assn. (fin. com.), Trident Nurses Assn., Assn. Children with Learning Disabilities. Clubs: Cooper Estates Garden (pres. 1978), Cooper Estates Civic. Home: 631 Pelzer Dr Mount Pleasant SC 29464 Office: 171 Ashley Ave Charleston SC 29425

CRAIG, GENEVA ELLEN (GENE CRAIG), airline exec.; b. Aberdeen, Wash., July 11, 1918; d. Traverse and Thelma (Howell) Radcliffe; student Grays Harbor Jr. Coll., 1938-39, Grays Harbor Bus. Coll., 1939-40; m. William Craig, July 7, 1944. Librarian, Aberdeen Public Library, 1937-41; jr. aircraft mechanic Spokane Army Air Depot (Wash.), 1942-44; recruiter Guy F. Atkinson Constrn. Co., Anchorage, 1945; sec. Alaska Dept. Engrs., Anchorage, 1945-46; chief procurement Army and Air Force Exchange Service, Anchorage, 1946-54; with Reeve Aleutian Airways, Inc., Anchorage, 1955—, v.p. passenger service, dir., 1976—. Mem. NOW, Aux. U.S. Army, Gray Panthers, Salvation Army Aux. Clubs: Soroptimist; Pioneers of Alaska. Home: Box 82 SRA Anchorage AK 99507 Office: 4700 W International Airport Rd Anchorage AK 99502

CRAIG, GRACE J., developmental psychologist; b. Newton, Mass., July 9, 1937; d. Charles Edgar and Lucille (Burnham) Johnson; B.A., U. Mass., 1959, M.S., 1962, Ph.D., 1967; m. Ralph P. Craig, June 20, 1959; 1 dau., Talli Lynn. Sch. psychologist Dalton (Mass.) Public Schs., 1962-64; lectr. Smith Coll., Northampton, Mass., 1966-70; asst. prof. human devel. U. Mass., Amherst, 1970-74, assoc. dean Sch. Edn., 1975-79, prof., chmn. human devel. and edn., 1979—. Mem. Nat. Assn. for Edn. Young Children, Am. Psychol. Assn., Soc. for Research Child Devel. Author: Human Development, 1975, 2d edit., 1980, 3d edit., 1983; Child Development, 1979; Human Development: A Social Work Perspective, 1982. Office: U Mass 365 Hills South Amherst MA 01003

CRAIG, KAREN, univ. adminstr.; b. Pitts., Apr. 17, 1936; d. Charles Homer and Bertha Mercedes (Barr) Craig; B.S. in Edn., Carlow Coll., 1964; M.Ed., Pa. State U., 1970; Ed.D., U. N.D., 1973; Cert., Saffron Walden, Eng., 1972; B.S. in Psychology St. Joseph Coll., Rensselaer, Ind., 1982. Entered Sisters of St. Joseph, Roman Cath. Ch., 1954; elem. sch. tchr., Pitts., Greensburg, Altoona-Johnstown Diocese, 1958-70; reading coordinator Ind. Unit 8, Pa., 1973-74; grad. sch. adminstr. St. Patrick's Sch., Gallitzer, Pa., 1974-75; arts/drama instr. Pitts. Diocesan Schs., 1975-76; asst. prof. edn. St. Joseph Coll., Rensselaer, Ind., 1977-82, dean of students, 1979-81, chmn. dept. edn., asst. prof. edn., 1981—; ednl. cons. local schs. Active Girl Scouts U.S.A. U. N.D. grantee, 1971-73; State of Pa. grantee, 1976-77. Mem. Internat. Reading Assn., Nat. Assn. Am. Deans, Adminstrs. and Counselors, Am. Assn. Group Psychotherapy and Psychodrama. Contbr. articles to profl. jours. Home: 610 N College St Rensselaer IN 47978 Office: PO Box 935 Saint Joseph Coll Rensselaer IN 47978

CRAIG, MARIAN ELEANOR, social worker; b. N.Y.C., Feb. 24, 1948; d. Robert Stirling and Mary Elizabeth (Hobbie) C.; B.A., Wells Coll., 1970; M.S.W., Boston U. Sch. Social Work, 1975. Social work asst. Odd Fellows' and Rebekah's Home for Aged, Lockport, N.Y., 1971-72; admissions coordinator Niagara Falls (N.Y.) Meml. Nursing Home, 1972-73; program dir. Don Orione Adult Day Health Center, East Boston, Mass., 1975-80; orgnl. cons. Project Homespun, Boston, 1981; dir. Greater Lynn (Mass.) Sr. Services Adult Day Health Centers, 1982—. Bd. dirs. Project Homespun; selective service counselor Draft Counseling Center, Buffalo, 1971-73. Mem. Acad. Cert. Social Workers, Nat. Assn. Social Workers, Mass. Audubon Soc., New Eng. Historic Geneal. Soc. Home: 4 Washington Ave Cambridge MA 02140 Office: Briarcliff Lodge 112 Kernwood Dr Lynn MA 01904

CRAIG, MARJORIE REED (MRS. JOHN THOMAS CROWLEY), phys. therapist, author; b. Bangor, Maine, Mar. 9, 1912; d. Warren Everet and Harriet (Humphrey) C.; B.S. in Phys. Edn., Arnold Coll., 1932; postgrad. in phys. therapy Columbia, 1932-33; m. John Thomas Crowley, Sept. 9, 1935. Inst., Neurol. Inst., Columbia-Presbyn. Med. Center, 1935-42; supr. exercise Richard Hudnut Salon, N.Y.C., 1942-52, Elizabeth Arden Salon, N.Y.C., 1952—. Author: Miss Craig's 21-Day Shape-Up Program; Miss Craig's Face-Saving Exercises; Miss Craig's Growing Up Exercise, 1973; Miss Craig's 10 Minute a Day Spot Reducing Program, 1979. Office: care Random House 201 E 50th St New York NY 10022

CRAIG, NANCY, paralegal, univ. adminstr.; b. St. Louis, Feb. 28, 1928; d. Charles Wallace and Ruth Jorndt (Craig) Begeman; B.A., DePauw U., 1949; postgrad. U. Wis., 1949-50; M.H.A., Washington U., St. Louis, 1963. Asst. buyer Stix Baer & Fuller, St. Louis, 1951-54; pub. relations dir. St. Louis council Girl Scouts Am., 1954-60; asst. dir. Barnes Hosp., St. Louis, 1963-71; adminstrv. asst. records Mallinckrodt Inst. Radiology, St. Louis, 1971-78; para-legal asst., 1978—; sec.-treas. grad. program in health care adminstrn. Washington U., St. Louis, 1976-78. Bd. dirs. St. Louis YWCA, 1970-74, Family Planning Council, St. Louis, 1978-80, Kirkwood (Mo.) Old Folks Home, 1979—; vol. worker Barnes Hosp.; active St. Louis Art Mus., St. Louis Symphony Soc. Mem. Am. Coll. Hosp. Adminstrs., Mo. Nursing Home Adminstrs., Am., Mo. hosp. assns., Women in Communications, Assn. Univ. Programs in Health Adminstrn., Mo. League Nursing, AAUW, Mo. Correction Assn., Assn. Programs Female Offenders, Mo. Bot. Assn., Mo. Hist. Soc., DePauw U. (pres. 1959-63, dir. 1967-69), Washington U. (bd. govs. 1975-81) alumni assns., Mortar Bd., Nat. Cathedral Assn., Smithsonian Assos. Episcopalian. Home: 44 Hill Dr Kirkwood MO 63122

CRAIG, REBECCA ALICE, nurse; b. Sacramento, June 24, 1948; d. John Francis and Cora Murl (Quick) C.; A.S. in Nursing, Loma Linda (Calif.) U., 1970; B.A. in Humanities, Calif. State U., Sonoma, 1972; M.P.A., Golden Gate U., 1982. Head nurse, supr. recovery room Eisenhower Med. Center, Palm Desert, Calif., 1973; staff nurse Community Hosp., Santa Rosa, Calif., 1973-77, head nurse emergency dept., 1977-80; staff nurse Petaluma Valley Hosp., 1980-81; Coro Found. intern, 1981; staff nurse U. Calif.-San Francisco Med. Center, 1981—; mem. staff public affairs program Coro Found. Mem. Disaster Planning Task Force, 1979, Sonoma County Emergency Services Utilization Bd., 1980; mem. exec. com. Sonoma County Public Employees Union. Mem. Nat. Women's Polit. Caucus (state steering com.), NOW, Am. Soc. Public Adminstrn., Acad. Polit. Sci., Phi Alpha Theta. Democrat. Address: 1272 34th Ave San Francisco CA 94122

CRAIG, SHARON ALANE, labor union ofcl.; b. Noblesville, Ind., Sept. 28, 1947; d. Ralph E. and Virginia K. Craig; student Ind. U., 1970-77; with Ind. Bell Telephone Co., Kokomo, 1968-77; with Communications Workers of Am., AFL-CIO, Indpls., 1977-80, Chgo., 1981—, staff rep., 1977—; mem. labor studies adv. com. Ind. U.; mem. Ind. AFL-CIO community services adv. com. NAACP, Indpls.; mem. union busters com. Ill. State AFL-CIO, 1981. Bd. dirs. City of Hope, 1977-80, Howard County Mental Health, 1973-76; mem. planning com. United Way of Howard County, 1976-77; sec. Citizens Action Coalition, 1980—; mem. Juvenile Justice Task Force; precinct committeeman Democratic Party, Kokomo, 1978; mem. CWA C.O.P.E. Quorum, 1977-82. Recipient gold award United Way, 1978. Mem. Coalition of Labor Union Women, NOW. Episcopalian. Club: Ind. U. Alumni and Women's. Home: 1031 Maple Ln Elk Grove Village IL 60007 Office: 790 Busse Rd Elk Grove Village IL 60007

CRAIN, E(LLA) MARIE, electrologist, cosmetologist; b. nr. Tekoa, Wash., July 12, 1919; d. Phillip Gerald and Anna Margaret (Harms) Harnisch; student Wash. State Coll., 1938, Butler Beauty Sch., 1939-40, Western Hair Coll., 1940-41; m. Warren Eugene Crain, Apr. 6, 1947; children—Constance Ann, Susan Marie Crain Hansen. Elec. accessories insp., Galena, Wash., 1941-45; electrologist Kree Inst., N.Y.C., 1945; with Alexander's Beauty Salon, Spokane, Wash., 1945-50; clk.-typist welfare dept., 1950-52; electrologist, cosmetologist, owner M. Crain Beauty Salon, Spokane, 1957—; guest lectr. electrolysis Community Coll. First alt. Republican County Conv. Mem. Nat. Hairdressers and Cosmetologists Assn., Wash. State Cosmetologists Assn. (pres. 1979-81, Community Leadership award 1973, 80), Wash. State Electrologists (pres. 1976-78), Am. Inst. Parliamentarians (past pres. Spokane chpt.), Spokane Area C. of C. Club: Hillyard Comml. (past exec. sec.-treas.). Home and office: N 6317 Market St Spokane WA 99207

CRAIN, EMMA JO, educator; b. Newburg, Mo., May 14, 1936; d. Alfred Chistopher and Margaret Elizabeth (Shank) Crain; B.S. in Edn., S.E. Mo. State U., 1968; M.Spl.Edn., La. State U., 1970; postgrad. U. New Orleans, 1972; Ed.D., U. Ala., 1979; children—David, Walter. Tchr. mentally retarded Spl. Sch. Dist., St. Louis County, Mo., 1968-70, East Baton Rouge (La.) Sch. Dist., 1970-71; spl. edn. cons. East Baton Rouge, 1971-72; ednl. cons. La. State U., Baton Rouge, 1972-73, instr., 1973-77, asst. prof., 1978-81; dir. spl. edn. Springfield (Mo.) public schs., 1981—. Bd. dirs. Easter Seals of SW Mo. Mem. Internat. Council for Exceptional Children, Am. Assn. Mental Deficiency. Presbyterian. Author: (with Horn, Callander & Henderson) Ethical - Legal Aspects of Special Education: A Book of Readings, 1977; contbr. articles to profl. jours. Home: 2149 E Sunshine St Springfield MO 65804 Office: 940 N Jefferson St Springfield MO 65802

CRAMER, CYNTHIA JEANETTE, charitable orgn. exec.; b. N.Y.C., May 7, 1943; d. Morgan J. and Miriam Jeanette (Fuchs) C.; student Katherine Gibbs Secretarial Sch., 1961-62. Exec. comml. producer Lennen & Newell, Inc., N.Y.C., 1962-68; asst. to dir. public info. Lehigh U., Bethlehem, Pa., 1969-70; adminstrv. asst. to pres. Morgan J. Cramer Assos., Inc., N.Y.C., 1970-72; public relations dir. Greater Bethlehem Area United Fund, 1972-73; v.p. Cramer Assos., Inc., Allentown, Pa., 1973-77; asst. to convention coordinator Girl Scouts U.S.A., 1977-78; realtor asso. Ernie Palmer Realty, Fountain Hills, Ariz., 1979-80; broker Fountain Hills Real Estate Center, 1980-81; exec. dir. Chandler (Ariz.) United Way, 1981—. Bd. dirs. Sayre Child Center, 1973-76, Lehigh Valley of Performing Arts, 1973-76; stewardship com. Shephard of Hills Luth. Ch., 1980-81. Mem. Fountain Hills Real Estate Assn., Fountain

Hills Civic Assn., Dalmatian Club of Greater Phoenix (dir. 1980—). Republican. Lutheran. Home: Chandler AZ 85224 Office: PO Box 567 Chandler AZ 85224

CRAMER, MARGARET SULLIVAN, mfg. co. exec.; b. Jackson County, Iowa, Nov. 3, 1933; d. Joseph M. and Margaret (Downey) Sullivan; B.S. in Bus. Adminstrn., N.Y. Inst. Tech., 1979, M.S., 1982; m. Robert E. Cramer, Feb. 14, 1953; children—Robert E., Laura Downey. With Chgo. Motor Club, Eastern Air Lines, Chgo., 1952-54, Robert F. Silverstein Agy., Midwest Steel Corp., Charleston, W.Va., 1956-60; with ILC Data Device Corp. subs. ILC Industries, Inc., Hicksville, N.Y., 1965-74, Bohemia, N.Y., 1974—, v.p. indsl. relations, 1978—. Treas., Cultural Arts Soc. Farmingdale, 1970-71, publicity chmn., 1971-72; mem. adv. council vocat. edn. adv. programs SUNY, Farmingdale, 1982—. Mem. L.I. Electronic Wage and Salary Council (pres. 1977-78, exec. com. 1978-79), Personnel Dirs. Council L.I. Assn., Electronic Industries Assn. (human resources council). Club: Nissequoque Golf. Office: 105 Wilbur Pl Bohemia NY 11716

CRANDALL, KATHLEEN MARGARET, univ. ofcl.; b. Lowell, Mass., Aug. 4, 1943; d. Kenneth John and Anne Francis (Doonan) Crandall; B.S. in Biology, Tufts U., 1964; Ph.D. in Physiology, Columbia U., 1972; m. Joseph Tomasulo, Oct. 8, 1966 (div.); children—Michael, Stephen, Elizabeth Anne. Lectr. physiology Coll. Medicine, U. Calif., Irvine, 1974-77, lectr., vice-chmn. physiology, 1976-77, asst. research psychobiologist, 1977-79; asso. dir. admissions Calif. Inst. Tech., Pasadena, 1979—, lectr. biology, 1980—. Mem. AAAS. Democrat. Club: Sierra. Office: Office of Admissions 109-40 Dabney Hall Calif Inst Tech Pasadena CA 91104

CRANDALL-STOTLER, BARBARA JEAN, educator, writer; b. Jamestown, N.Y., Mar. 4, 1942; d. Arthur John and Margaret Alice (Pangborn) Crandall; B.A., Keuka Coll., 1964; M.S., U. Cin., 1966, Ph.D., 1968; m. Raymond E. Stotler, July 28, 1969. Postdoctoral fellow U. Tex., Austin, 1968-69; asst. prof. botany So. Ill. U., Carbondale, 1969-76, assoc. prof., 1976-82, prof., 1982—. Recipient Alumnae Profl. Achievement award Keuka Coll., 1975-76; Am. Philos. Soc. grantee, 1981. Mem. Am. Bryological and Lichenological Soc. (sec.-treas.), Bot. Soc. Am., Brit. Bryological Soc., Bryological Soc. Japan, Dutch Bryological Soc., Internat. Assn. Bryologists, Nordic Bryological Soc. Author: Bios—Process and Diversity, 1976; Bios-Process and Diversity, 1978; contbr. articles to profl. jours. Office: Botany Dept Southern Il Univ Carbondale IL 62901

CRANE, BARBARA BACHMANN, photographer, educator; b. Chgo., Mar. 19, 1928; d. Burton Stanley and Della (Kreeger) Bachmann; student Mills Coll., 1945-48; B.A. in Art History, N.Y. U., 1950; M.S. in Photography, Inst. Design, Ill. Inst. Tech., 1966; children—Elizabeth, Jennifer, Bruce. Chmn. photography dept. New Trier High Sch., Winnetka, Ill., 1964-67; prof. photography Sch. Art Inst. Chgo., 1967—; vis. prof. Phila. Coll. Art, 1977, Sch. Mus. Fine Arts, Boston, 1979; panelist Ill. Arts Council, 1981. Photography fellow Nat. Endowment for Arts, 1975; Guggenheim Meml. fellow in photography, 1979-80. Mem. Soc. Photog. Edn., Friends of Photography (trustee 1974—), Chgo. Network. Author retrospective monograph: Barbara Crane: 1948-80, 1980; traveling exhbn. Barbara Crane, 1948-80. Home: 3164 N Hudson St Chicago IL 60657

CRANE, DENA T., media artist; b. Bklyn., Dec. 14, 1949; d. Benjamin Jules and Ruth Dianne Hochberg; B.A. in Humanities, U. Chgo., 1972. Ind. media artist, Windham, N.Y., 1969—; creator, exec. dir. Greene County Council on the Arts, Windham, 1976-79; instr. media Sch. Visual Arts, N.Y.C., 1979—; cons. Am. the Beautiful Fund, 1976-80. Recipient Nat. Thespian award, 1966; Creative Artists Public Service grantee, 1978-79, Nat. Endowment Arts grantee, 1980-81. Mem. N.Y. State Council Arts (production grantee, mem. rev. panel in media). Address: PO Box 115-B Windham NY 12496

CRANE, ELIZABETH ANN, educator; b. N.Y.C., Jan. 7, 1943; d. Clifford Murray, Jr. and Ruth Charlotte (Rieder) C.; B.A. in Biol. Scis., San Jose (Calif.) State U., 1966, M.A. in Early Childhood Edn., 1978. Tchr. 3d grade Moreland Sch. Dist., San Jose, 1967—; presider Asilomar Math. Conf., 1977, 78; mem. Moreland Dist. Adv. Com. Early Childhood Edn., 1975. Mem. NEA, Nat. Council Tchrs. Math., Calif. Tchr. Assn., Moreland Sch. Dist. Assn., Home and Sch. Club, Calif. Math. Council (life), Santa Clara Valley Math. Assn. (rep. to exec. bd. 1979—), Computer Using Educators, Santa Clara Reading Assn., San Jose State U. Alumni Assn. (life). Office: 4710 Campbell Ave San Jose CA 95130

CRANE, HENRIETTA PAGE, Republican nat. committeewoman; b. Skowhegan, Maine, Jan. 1, 1913; d. Blin Williams and Edith (Nay) Page; B.A., Wellesley Coll., 1935; children—Kennedy, III, Trudi, Tobey. Tchr. Latin, Cape Elizabeth (Maine) High Sch., 1935-37; Republican nat. committeewoman for Maine, 1972-80. Mem. exec. com. Gov.'s Adv. Com. on Edn., 1958-63; vice chmn. Knox County Rep. Party, 1966-69; del. Rep. Nat. Convs., 1968, 76, mem. Platform Com., 1976, Rules Com., 1980; mem. exec. com. Maine Rep. Com., 1969—; bd. dirs. Tri-County Community Health Services; trustee Knox County Gen. Hosp., Rockland, Maine; hon. trustee Penobscot Bay Med. Center, Rockland. Honored by Knox Fedn. Rep. Women, 1977. Home and office: 30 Shaw Ave Rockland ME 04841

CRANE, JULIANNE GRANDIN, journalist; b. Charleston, W.Va., Mar. 29, 1943; d. James Franklin and Mary Frances (East) Grandin; B.J. (scholar), U. Tex., Austin, 1970, M.A., 1972. Communicator, journalist; freelance writer, broadcast reporter, producer, 1972—, media outlets include San Diego, Aspen, Colo., Washington, and Seattle, 1973—; asst. promotion dir. Regional Shopping Center, San Diego, 1972-73; public info. dir. San Diego County Mental Health, 1973-77; instr. journalism and communication U. Nebr., Omaha, 1979-80; program dir., instr. journalism and mass media Highline Coll., Midway, Wash., 1980—; media and mktg. cons.; mktg. cons. King County East Conn. and Visitors Bur., Seattle, 1981. Media cons. Center on Aging, San Diego, 1974; publicity dir. UN Week, San Diego, 1975; media relations v.p. NOW, San Diego, 1973-77; organizing com. Nat. Women's Polit. Caucus, San Diego, 1977; bd. dirs. Inst. Managerial and Profl. Women, Seattle, 1981-82. Recipient awards Nat. Press. Women, 1976, Calif. Press Women, 1976, San Diego Press Club, 1974, 75, 76; exemplary status award Wash. State Commn. Coll. Humanities Project, 1982. Mem. Internat. TV Assn., Women in Communications, Inc., LWV, Nat. Women's Polit. Caucus, Women's Inst. Freedom of the Press, Seattle Women's Network, Sigma Delta Chi. First woman reporter awarded credentials San Diego Padres Press Box, 1973. Home: PO Box 98263 Seattle WA 98188 Office: Highline College 18 1 Midway WA 98032

CRANE, KATHARINE ELIZABETH, editor, writer; b. Kenton, Ohio; d. George Edward and Kate (Rhodes) Crane; A.B., Smith Coll., 1916; Ph.D., U. Chgo., 1930. Tchr., St. Katherine's Sch., Davenport, Ia., 1916-17, Shippen Sch., Lancaster, Pa., 1920-22, Women's Coll., U. N.C., 1925-26; asst. editor Ency. Social Scis., 1929-30; asst. editor Dictionary Am. Biography, 1930-36, Social Studies and Social Edn., 1936-39; state supr., state guide, Va. Hist. Survey. Library Services, 1940-43; officer Dept. State, 1943-50; historian Mil. Air Transport Service, 1950-60; free-lance writer, 1960—. Author: Status of Countries in Relation to the War, 1944; Blair House, 1946; Mr. Carr of State, 1960. Contbr. articles to profl. jours. Home: 500 North Main St Kenton OH 43326

CRANE, PHYLLIS, artist; b. San Diego, Apr. 14, 1903; d. William Anderson and Mabel (Ray) C.; B.S., U. So. Calif., 1935, M.A., 1945; postgrad. Noyes (N.Y.) Sch. Rhythm and Creative Arts Studios, Portland, Conn., 1955. Tchr. schs. Pasadena, Calif., 1927-56, Peekskill, N.Y., 1958-60, Brewster, N.Y., 1960-62; one-woman shows: Contemporary Artists Gallery, Kingston, Jamaica, 1971, Dawson's Grist Mill Gallery, Chester Depot, Vt., 1974, 76, Port Chester (N.Y.) Library Gallery, 1975, Wood Pavalion Gallery, White Plains, N.Y., 1978; group shows include: Nat. Arts Club, 1965-79, Hansen Galleries, 1979, Pen and Brush Galleries, 1978-82, Sotheby Park Bernet Galleries, 1980, 81, Custom House Mus., World Trade Center, 1981, Lever House, 1980, 82, Salmagundi Club (all N.Y.C.); represented in permanent collections U.S., Europe; chmn. art shows No. Westchester, 1969-72, 77; co-chmn. art shows Hendrick Hudson Library, Montrose, N.Y., 1977; chmn. art show Lever House, N.Y.C., 1982. Bd. dirs. YWCA. Anglo-Am. Acad. hon. fellow, 1980. Mem. Pen and Brush (Emily Nichols Hatch award 1979, dir. 1980-85), Nat. League Am. Pen Women, Composers, Authors and Artists Am. (corr. sec. 1978-80), Burr Artists, Gotham Artists, DAR, Pi Beta Phi, Delta Kappa Gamma. Author: Fundamental Exercises Most Beneficial for Relaxation, 1943; contbr. articles in field to profl. jours. Home and studio: Boscobel Point Croton-On-Hudson NY 10520

CRANE, VALERIE, research cons. communications; b. N.Y.C., Apr. 24, 1945; d. Kent and Marguerite (Gillison) Crane; B.A., Bennington Coll., 1966; M.Ed., U. Vt., 1968; Ph.D., Fordham U., 1972; m. Donald Stern, July 4, 1972; children—Hilary Crane-Stern, Erika Crane-Stern. Tchr., Dorset (Vt.) Elem. Sch., 1966-69; research asst. N.Y.C. Bd. Edn. and Fordham U., 1972-73; research cons. in desegregation and childrens TV, San Francisco, 1974-75; research asso. Heuristics, Inc., Wellesley, Mass., 1975-78; dir., media div. Public Affairs Research Inst., Wellesley, 1978-80; pres. Research Communications Inc., Chestnut Hill, Mass., 1980—. Vice pres. Baker Sch. Extended Day Kindergarten, 1978-79. Mem. Nat. Assn. Ednl. Broadcasters (planning com. for research council 1978-81), Am. Ednl. Research Assn., Am. Psychol. Assn., Assn. Ednl. Communication and Tech., Kappa Delta Pi. Address: 384 Newton St Chestnut Hill MA 02167

CRANE, VIRGINIA MARIE, nurse; b. Honolulu, Aug. 31, 1933; d. John C. and Virginia (Roderiges) Cortez; A.A., San Jose City Coll., 1972; student in health arts Coll. of St. Francis, Joliet, Ill.; m. Albert E. Crane, Dec. 30, 1972; children—Colleen, Arthur, Susan, Edith, Margaret, Katherine. Housekeeper, San Jose (Calif.) Hosp., 1959, nursing asst., 1960, surg. technician, 1960-72, staff nurse, 1972-74, asst. head nurse, 1974-77, staff nurse and cons. surg. center, 1977-79; staff nurse operating room Santa Clara Valley Med. Center, San Jose, 1979-80, asst. head nurse, 1980—. Mem. Assn. Operating Room Nurses, Am. (cert.), Calif. nurses assns., Registered Nurses Profl. Assn. Calif. Baptist. Home: 3601 Millicent Ct San Jose CA 95148 Office: Santa Clara Valley Med Center 751 S Bascom Ave San Jose CA 95128

CRANSHAW, REBECCA JEAN, educator; b. Brunswick, Ga., Sept. 20, 1943; d. Aaron Joseph and Emojene (Drawdy) C.; B.A. in Edn., Trevecca Nazarene Coll., Nashville, 1965; M.S. in Spl. Edn. (Tenn. Dept. Edn. fellow 1971, 72-73, United Comml. Travelers scholar 1977), George Peabody Coll. Tchrs., 1977. Classroom tchr., Tenn. and Ind., 1966-70; spl. edn. tchr., 1970-79; ednl. specialist Wilson County-Lebanon schs., Lebanon, Tenn., 1979—; pres. Insight Publns., Inc., 1978—; dir. Cheryl Lynn Tng. Center, Sembach, Ger., 1973; instr. Trevecca Nazarene Coll., 1981, 82, cons. in field, condr. workshops. Mem. NEA (life), Nat. Assn. Female Execs., Tenn. United Teaching Profession, Tenn. Edn. Assn., Lebanon Edn. Assn., Delta Kappa Gamma. Mem. Ch. of Nazarene. Author manuals and books on diagnostic and prescriptive math.; illustrator teaching manuals. Home: 709 Braidwood Dr Donelson TN 37214 Office: Spl Edn Dept N Cumberland Edn Center Lebanon TN 37087

CRAPIVINSKY-JUTKOWITZ, BETTY, pub. exec.; b. Santiago, Chile, May 20, 1936; came to U.S., 1967, naturalized, 1975; d. Benjamin and Clara (Meirovich-Henin) Crapivinsky-Huberman; student U. Chile, 1958-60; m. Joel M. Jutowitz, July 22, 1966; children—Edward Andre, Monica Regina, Alexander Steven. Pub., Benjamin Crapivinsky Publs. Ltd., Santiago, Chile, 1960-73; dir. publs. Inst. for Study of Human Issues, Phila., 1974—. Mem. research publs. rev. panel Nat. Endowment for Humanities, Washington, 1980-81. Nat. Endowment for Humanities grantee, 1979-82. Mem. Phila. Publs. Group (founding mem. 1982). Democrat. Jewish. Home: 1420 Locust St Philadelphia PA 19102 Office: 3401 Market St Suite 252 Philadelphia PA 19104

CRASSWELLER, RUTH ODEGARD, savs. assn. exec.; b. Princeton, Minn., June 8, 1922; d. Odin James and Mabel Elizabeth Odegard; B.S., U. Minn., 1944; m. Donald B. Crassweller, Aug. 5, 1944; children—James Richard, Thomas Mark. Producer/hostess TV talk show The Scene Today, WDSM-TV, Duluth, Minn., 1971-73; fashion coordinator/public relations dir. Glass Blook Stores, Duluth, 1973-75; interviewer Only for Girls, KBJR-TV, Duluth, 1975-76; community club awards dir. WDSM Radio, Duluth, 1976-79; area service mgr. Savs. Plus Mid-Am., Inc., Duluth, 1979—; account exec. Internat. Diamond Corp., 1981-82. Mem. Duluth Bd. Edn., 1965-69, pres., 1965-69; active PTA, ARC; mem. Duluth Airport Authority; dir. Salvation Army Adv. Bd.; mem. State Adv. Council for Vocat. Edn., v.p., 1968-69; co-chmn. Northeastern Minn. Traffic Safety Conf.; mem. Nat. Adv. Council on Extension and Continuing Edn., pres., 1973-74; mem. Nat. Adv. Council on Apprenticeship Programs for Police Officers, sec., 1978—; mem. U.S. Magistrate Merit Selection Panel, 1980, N.G. Adv. Com., 1980—; bd. dirs. Miller Divan Med. Center Found.; active various community drives. Mem. Am. Women in Radio and Television, AAUW (scholarship/fellowship chmn.), Arrowhead Home Econs. Assn., Duluth Women's Inst. (naturalization chmn.), Minn. Sch. Bd. Assn. (dist. dir.), Lawyers Advs. and Wives (v.p. Minn.), Delta Kappa Gamma (hon.). Clubs: PEO (pres.), Newcomer's (pres.), Lawyer's Wives (pres. 1978-79), Soroptimists (hon.). Home and Office: 3810 Gladstone St Duluth MN 55804

CRATER, FLORA MARINA TRIMMER, editor, women's rights orgn. exec.; b. San Jose, Costa Rica, Apr. 19, 1914; d. Horace Curtis and Albertina Frances (Benard) Trimmer; grad. George Mason U., 1980; m. Walter James Crater, Apr. 29, 1935; children—Walter James, Horace William, Vivian Crater Gray. Editor, The Woman Activist, Falls Church, Va., 1971-80; pres. The Woman Activist Fund, Inc., 1978—, The Woman Activist Inc., 1971-80. Candidate for lt. gov. State of Va., 1972, Democratic candidate for U.S. Senator, 1978. Mem. NOW (convened 1st chpt. in Va.), Va. Women's Polit. Caucus, Women's Equity Action League, Nat. Woman's Party. Democrat. Unitarian. Co-author: The Almanac of Virginia Politics; also articles. Home: 2310 Barbour Rd Falls Church VA 22043

CRAWFORD, ALICE LOCICERO, psychologist; b. Paterson, N.J., Aug. 7, 1945; d. Thomas and Rose (Farah) Locicero; B.A., Coll. St. Elizabeth, 1966; Ph.D., Cath. U. Am., 1974; m. James Logan Crawford, Feb. 4, 1979; 1 dau., Emily Dawn. Tchr. public sch., Fair Lawn, N.J., 1966-69; intern in psychology Fairfax-Falls Church (Va.) Mental Health Center, 1972-73; postdoctoral intern in psychology Children's Hosp. and Judge Baker Guidance Center, Boston, 1973-74; coordinator mental health services for children Marth M. Eliot Health Center, Boston, 1974-75; supervising staff psychologist Judge Baker Guidance Center, Boston, 1975-76; psychologist in pvt. practice, 1976—; sr. staff psychologist Children's Hosp., Boston, and instr. psychology Harvard Med. Sch., Boston, 1976-80; cons. Day Care Service, U. Mass., Boston, 1974-75, Carroll Hall Sch., Lesley Coll., Cambridge, Mass., 1976-81, Roxbury Children's Service, Boston, 1978-80; instr. Northeastern U., Boston, 1974-76; lectr. Mass. Sch. Profl. Psychology, Newton, 1977-78, Simmons Coll., Boston, 1977-78. NDEA fellow, 1969-72; NIMH fellow, 1973-74. Mem. Am. Psychol. Assn., U.S. Orienteering Fedn., New Eng. Orienteering Club, Mass. Audubon Soc., Boston Mus. Sci. Research papers presented at profl. meetings. Address: 439 Huron Ave Cambridge MA 02138

CRAWFORD, ANNA LEE, dean; b. Washington, Feb. 26, 1942; d. Lamar Sparks and Aline (McDaniel) C.; B.A., Austin Coll., 1964; M.Ed., The Citadel, 1977; Ph.D., U. Ala., 1982. Dir. student activities and placement Trident Tech. Coll., Charleston, S.C., 1974-77; coordinator placement/career devel. activities Loyola U., New Orleans, 1977-79; acting dir. counseling and career devel. center Loyola U., New Orleans, 1980; cons. continuing edn. U. Ala., Tuscaloosa, 1981-82; dean student affairs St. Mary's Dominican Coll., New Orleans, 1982—; cons. Mayor's Office, City New Orleans, 1978-79, Internat. Yr. of the Child, 1979, others; spl. scholar, Project Growth, Inst. Higher Edn. Research and Services, U. Ala., 1978-82. Trustee Resolution for Excellence, Trident Tech. Coll., 1977. Mem. Ala. Assn. Women Deans, Adminstrs. and Counselors, Am. Assn. Higher Edn., AAUW, Am. Coll. Personnel Assn., Am. Personnel and Guidance Assn., Am. Vocat. Guidance Assn., Capstone Women's Network, Am. Council Edn., Nat. Assn. Women Deans, Adminstrs. and Counselors, Nat. Assn. Student Personnel Adminstrs. Office: PO Box 904 7214 Saint Charles Ave New Orleans LA 70118

CRAWFORD, CHRISTINA, author; b. Los Angeles, June 11, 1939; adopted dau. of Joan Crawford; B.A. in Communication magna cum laude, UCLA, 1974; M.A. in Communication Mgmt., U. So. Calif., 1975; m. C. David Koontz, Feb. 14, 1976. Actress, 1958-72; tchr., 1973-75; with corp. communications dept. Getty Oil Co., 1975-77; freelance author, 1978—; pres. Hermitage Co., Inc., 1978—; lectr., speaker in field; author: (non-fiction) Mommie Dearest, 1978; (fiction) Black Widow, 1982; also mag. articles. Rep., Annenberg Sch., 1975-77; trustee Christina Crawford Found., 1974—; pres. ICAN Assos., 1979—. Recipient various commendations and certs. of recognition. Mem. Writers Guild Am., Screen Actors Guild. Republican. Clubs: Braemar Country, Knights of Vine.

CRAWFORD, DANA HUDKINS, real estate co. exec.; b. Salina, Kans., July 22, 1931; d. Dale Carlin and Josephine Dana Hudkins; A.B. in English, U. Kans., Lawrence, 1953; postgrad. Radcliffe Coll., 1954; m. John William Roy Crawford, Oct. 12, 1955; children—John, Thomas, Peter, Duke. Public relations cons. William Kostka & Assos., Denver, 1954-55; public relations cons., 1955-57; vol. mgmt. Denver Art Mus., Jr. League of Denver, 1958-64; pres. Larimer Square, Inc., mng. gen. partner Larimer Square Assos., Denver 1964—; gen. partner Oxford Hotel, Ltd. Mem. Platte River Devel. Com.; v.p. Downtown Denver, Inc. Recipient Disting. Alumnae award Radcliffe Coll., 1969. Mem. Nat. Trust for Hist. Preservation (trustee emeriti), Colo. State Hist. Found. (pres.), Urban Land Inst. (mem. comml. and retail devel. council). Club: Jr. League. Office: 1463 Larimer St Denver CO 80202

CRAWFORD, FRANCES FREEMAN, musician, educator; b. Birmingham, Ala., Apr. 17, 1933; d. James Lewis and Flavia W. (DeVan) Freeman; B.Music Edn., U. Montevallo (Ala.), 1957; M.Mus., Fla. State U., 1963; m. Kenneth Herbert Crawford; children—James Freeman, Carolyn Redding, Kenneth DeVan. Tchr., Murphy High Sch., Mobile, 1954-61; mem. faculty Berea (Ky.) Coll., 1962-67; mem. faculty U. Ill. Sch. Music, Champaign-Urbana, 1967—, prof. voice, 1979—; recitalist, soloist with oratorio and orch., 1965—; maj. roles include Cio Cio San in Madame Butterfly, Donna Anna in Don Giovanni, Ariadne in Ariadne auf Naxos; judge, adjudicator, cons. in field, also tchr. master classes. Deacon, Univ. Pl. Christian Ch. (Disciples of Christ). Mem. Nat. Assn. Tchrs. Singing, Pi Kappa Lambda, Mu Phi Epislon. Democrat. Home: 12 Golfview Ct Savoy IL 61894 Office: 200B Smith Music Hall Sch Music U Ill Urbana IL 61820

CRAWFORD, JANICE ANN, bus. exec.; b. Russell County, Ky., Sept. 9, 1943; d. Floyd and Ano Pearl Conatser; student U. Louisville, 1962. With Morrison Food Services, Mobile, Ala., 1961-75, catering mgr./home office and tng. mgmt., 1974-75; v.p. Sunshine Food Services, Mobile, 1975-79; tng. dir. A & G Cafeterias, New Orleans, 1979-80, cons. quality and cost control; owner, operator Gourmet Caterers, Mobile, 1980—, Wimberly Hory Catering Inc., Mobile, 1980—. Mem. travel and conv. com. Mobile Area C. of C. Mem. Nat. Assn. Exec. Women, Mobile Restaurant Assn. (dir.), Ala. Restaurant Assn. (dir.), Methodist. Club: Order Eastern Star. Author: Gourmet Caterers Party-Fare Cook Book, 1981. Home: PO Box 6574 Mobile AL 36660 Office: 5456 Old Shell Rd Mobile AL 36608

CRAWFORD, JOAN LARAWAY ROSS, newspaper publisher; b. Catskill, N.Y., Dec. 25, 1919; d. Webster Mace and Frances Elizabeth (Weed) Laraway; diplomas in bus. and music, U. N.Mex., 1941; m. William Albert Ross, Apr. 2, 1943 (dec. Mar. 12, 1949); children—Jeanette Margaret Ross Blaschke Attaway, William Albert Ross, Jr.; m. 2d, Richard Wallace Crawford, Mar. 5, 1955. Clerical and secretarial positions Sta. KAFB, 1949-50, Crawford Ins. Agy., 56-58; bus. mgr. Health City Sun Newspaper, Albuquerque, 1960-72; publisher Health City Sun Legal Newspaper, 1972—; publicity chmn. Albuquerque Legal Secs. Assn., 1979. Mem. Alpha Chi Omega. Democrat. Methodist. Clubs: Daus. of Nile, Women's Golf Assn. Home: 3418 Harwood Ct NE Albuquerque NM 87110 Office: 900 Park Ave SW Albuquerque NM 87102

CRAWFORD, JOSEPHINE LACKEY, nurse; b. Ripley, Tenn., Apr. 28, 1921; d. George Henry and Maggie Lue (Richardson) Lackey; R.N., St. Mary's Infirmary, St. Louis, 1944; B.S. in Nursing, St. Louis U., 1972; M.S. in Counselor Edn., So. Ill. U., Edwardsville, 1976; m. Brice Crawford, Sept. 10, 1950 (div.). Nurse, Homer G. Phillips Hosp., St. Louis, 1945-56; nurse Malcolm Bliss Mental Health Center, St. Louis, 1956—, dir. nursing edn., 1971—; cons., speaker in field. Chmn., Valada Barnes-Nina Williams Scholarship Fund, 1978-82; bd. dirs. Hubert Wheeler Sch. for Retarded; mem. screening com. Rudolph McNair Scholarships, 1982; mem. radiothon com. Annie Malone Children's Home, 1981-82. USPHS trainee, 1966; recipient Service award ARC, 1977; Community Service award Harmony Grand chpt. Order Eastern Star, 1978; cert. of appreciation Congressman William Clay, 1st Dist. Mo., 1978; Community Service award Cotillian de Leon, Union Meml. Meth. Ch., 1979. Mem. Am., Mo., 3d Dist. nurses assns., N. Am. Assn. Alcohol and Drug Programs, NAACP, Sigma Gamma Rho (George Washington Carver award 1978), Sigma Theta Tau. Democrat. Baptist. Clubs: Les Femmes, Daus. Isis (imperial dep. 1977-80, hon. past imperial comandress deg., Service award 1967, 75, 77, 78), Eureka Assembly, Order of Cyrenes Heroines of Jericho. Author articles. Address: 4562A Cote Brilliante St Saint Louis MO 63113

CRAWFORD, JUNE JUSTICE, coll. adminstr.; b. North Tonawanda, N.Y., Nov. 13, 1941; d. James Clinton and Jennette June (Smith) Justice; A.A. in Liberal Arts, SUNY, Buffalo, 1971; B.A. in English, SUNY, 1973, Ed.M. in Elem. and Remedial Edn., 1977; m. Duane Crawford, May 28, 1960; children—Martin, Jennifer. Tech. asst. Niagara County Community Coll., Sanborn, N.Y., 1973-75; instr. Medaille Coll.,

Buffalo, 1976-77; instr. Niagara U., Niagara Falls, N.Y., 1977-80, dir. Learning Center, 1980—; cons. various bus. and colls. Voter service chmn. LWV, Kenmore, N.Y., 1971-72; Republican committeewoman Town of Tonawanda, 1975-80; mem. adv. bd. Ken-Ton Schs. Continuing Edn., 1976—. Recipient Thomas Galley award U.S. Assn. Evening Students, 1972; James Cummings Found. grantee 1978; U.S. Dept. Edn. Title III grantee, 1980. Mem. N.Y. Coll. Learning Skills Assn. (pres. 1979-80; mem. exec. bd. 1980-81), Coll. Reading Assn., Internat. Reading Assn., N.Y. State Reading Assn., Niagara Frontier Reading Council. Republican. Methodist. Clubs: Shawnee Country; Ken-Ton Republican Couples; Niagara U. Faculty. Home: 119 Northwood Dr Buffalo NY 14223 Office: Alumni Hall Niagara U Niagara Falls NY 14109

CRAWFORD, KATHERYN ALICE, psychologist; b. Monroe, La., Dec. 17, 1940; d. Thomas Jimmy and Ruby Irene (Salley) Reagan; secretarial cert. NE La. Vocat. Sch., 1960; B.A., N.E. La. U., 1970, M.S., 1974; Ph.D. in Psychology, U. Ala., Tuscaloosa, 1980; m. Kenneth Dale Crawford, Nov. 29, 1957; children—Karen Lynette, Stephen Arlen, Bryan Scott. Billing clk. REA, Winnsboro, La., 1960-63; temp. operator Cities Service Oil Co., Winnsboro, 1965; clk.-typist III, La. Dept. Public Welfare, Winnsboro, 1965-67; tchr. Winnsboro Upper Elem. Sch., 1970-72; psychol. asst. Columbia (La.) State Sch., 1973-75, now psychologist, program dir., dir. inservice tng. Mem. Am. Psychol. Assn., La. Psychol. Assn., Am. Assn. Mental Deficiency, Alpha Lambda Delta, Phi Kappa Phi, Beta Sigma Phi. Democrat. Baptist. Contbr. articles to profl. jours. Home: Star Route S Box 25 Winnsboro LA 71295 Office: PO Box B Columbia LA 71418

CRAWFORD, KAY POPENHAGEN, psychotherapist; b. Webster Iowa, Feb. 22, 1950; d. Carl William and Ethel (Dickson) Popenhagen; B.S.W., U. No. Iowa, 1972; M.S.W., U. Iowa, 1973; m. Michael Dennis Crawford, Mar. 8, 1975. Psychiat. social worker Blackhawk County Mental Health Center, 1971-72; psychiat. social worker, clin. cons. Des Moines Child Guidance Center, 1973-77; group home dir. Lutheran Social Services Iowa, Des Moines, 1977, dir. southwest br., 1978-81; pvt. practice psychotherapy, Des Moines, 1981—; vis. prof. sociology Simpson Coll., Indianola, Iowa. Bd. dirs. Des Moines Rape Center. Mem. Nat. Assn. Social Workers, Group Home Personnel Assn., Acad. Cert. Social Workers. Democrat. Lutheran. Home: 2115 46th St Des Moines IA 50310 Office: 2130 Grand Ave Des Moines IA 50312

CRAWFORD, MARIA LUISA, geologist, educator; b. Beverly, Mass., July 18, 1939; d. William Theodore Buse and Barbara (Kidder) Aldana; B.A., Bryn Mawr Coll., 1960; postgrad. U. Oslo, 1960-61; Ph.D., U. Calif., Berkeley, 1965; m. William A. Crawford, Aug. 29, 1963. Asst. prof. Bryn Mawr (Pa.) Coll., 1965-73, asso. prof., 1973-79, prof., 1979—, chmn. dept. geology, 1976—; chmn. women geoscientists com. Am. Geol. Inst., 1976-77; mem. U.S. Nat. Com. for Geochemistry, 1980-82. NASA grantee, 1973-76, NSF grantee, 1967—. Fellow Geol. Soc. Am., Mineral Soc. Am.; mem. Mineral. Assn. Can., Am. Geophys. Union, Norwegian, Phila. geol. socs., Microbeam Analysis Soc., Assn. Women in Sci. Office: Dept Geology Bryn Mawr Coll Bryn Mawr PA 19010

CRAWFORD, NORMA VIVIAN, nurse; b. Cleveland, Tex., Dec. 29, 1936; d. Ira Wesley and Lizzie Augusta (Godejohn) C.; student Lee Jr. Coll., 1971-72; R.N., Cumberland County Coll., 1977; m. Arthur B. Crawford, Sept. 20, 1956; children—Pamela, Desiree. Charge nurse Patrick Henry Hosp., Newport News, Va., 1972-73; staff nurse Salem (N.J.) County Nursing Home, 1975-77, Nicholson Nursing Home, Penns Grove, N.J., 1977; staff nurse ICU, Metroplex Hosp., Killeen, Tex., 1977-79; dir. nurses Wind Crest Nursing Center, Copperas Cove, Tex., 1979—. Baptist. Club: Order Eastern Star. Home: 604 Yucca Dr Copperas Cove TX 76522 Office: 607 W Ave B Copperas Cove TX 76522

CRAWFORD, SANDRA KAY, lawyer; b. Henderson, Tex., Sept. 23, 1934; d. Obie Lee and Zilpha Elizabeth (Ash) Stalcup; B.A., Wellesley Coll., 1957; LL.B., U. Tex., 1960; m. Dec. 21, 1968. Admitted to U.S. Supreme Ct. bar, 1965, Ill. bar, 1974; editor, research asst. to Herbert Hoover, 1961-62; trial atty. SEC, 1962-66; asst. v.p./legal Hamilton Mgmt. Corp., 1966-68; v.p., gen. counsel, sec. Transam. Fund Mgmt. Co., Los Angeles, 1968; cons. to law dept. Met. Life Ins. Co., N.Y.C., 1969-71; counsel Touche Ross & Co., Chgo., 1972-75; v.p., asso. gen. counsel Continental Ill. Nat. Bank and Trust Co. of Chgo., 1975—. Mem. Midwest Regional Marshall Scholarship Com. Mem. Am. Bar Assn., Ill. Bar Assn., Tex. Bar Assn., Colo. Bar Assn. Clubs: Saddle and Cycle, Carlton. Office: Continental Ill Nat Bank and Trust Co of Chgo 231 S LaSalle St Chicago IL 60693

CRAWFORD, SUSAN YOUNG, educator, med. library adminstr.; b. Vancouver, B.C., Can.; d. James Y. and S.C. Young; B.A., U. B.C., 1948; M.A., U. Toronto, 1952; M.A., U. Chgo., 1957, Ph.D., 1970; m. James Weldon, July 5, 1956; 1 son, Robert James. Dir. div. library and archival services AMA, 1960-81; asso. prof. Sch. Library Service, Columbia U., N.Y.C., 1971-75; prof. biomed. communication, dir. Washington U. Sch. Medicine Library, St. Louis, 1981—; . Bd. regents U.S. Nat. Library of Medicine. USPHS grantee, 1969-81, cert. of recognition. Fellow AAAS; mem. ALA, Spl. Libraries Assn., Am. Soc. for Info. Sci., Med. Library Assn. (Eliot prize), Soc. for Social Studies of Medicine, Sigma Xi, Pi Lambda Theta. Contbr. numerous articles in field to profl. jours.; editor Perspectives (Jour. Am. Soc. Info. Sci.), 1980-82; editor-in-chief Bull. Med. Library Assn. Home: 2418 Lincoln St Evanston IL 60201 Office: 4580 Scott Ave St Louis MO 63110

CRAWFORD, TWILA JEAN, mgmt., edn. and communications cons.; b. Sylvan Grove, Kans.; d. Walter W. and Irma J. (Ziegenbalg) Von Fange; B.A., Kans. State U., 1967, M.S., 1971; children—Rachel Shelle, Curtis Stanley. News dir. Sta. KMAN, Manhattan, Kans., 1964-69; corr. Topeka (Kans.) Daily Captila, 1964-69; instr. journalism Kans. State U., Manhattan, 1969-71, communications specialist Coop. Extension Service, 1971-77; mgmt., edn. and communications cons., Washington, 1977—. Bd. dirs. Lutheran Hosp. Assn., Manhattan, 1973-77, treas., 1974-77. Mem. Women in Communications, Agrl. Communicators in Edn., Nat. and Capitol Hill Women's Polit. Caucus. Washington Women's Network, Washington Ind. Writers, Sigma Delta Chi. Clubs: Nat. Press, Georgetown Women's. Home: 4515 Willard Ave Chevy Chase MD 20815

CRAWFORD-ORTIZ, RUTH AUSTIN, artist; b. Slaton, Tex.; d. Charles Freeman and Bertha Elizabeth (Henry) Austin; student Tex. Tech. U., 1945-48, N.Y. Sch. Interior Design, 1960-63, Eastern N.M. U., 1965-67; m. William Conner Crawford, June 13, 1948; children—Michael Conner, William Charles, Camille Louise, Christopher Austin; m. 2d, Leo P. Ortiz. Owner, The Gallery, 1969-74; group exhbns. include: Southwester Arts and Crafts Show, 1970-74, Best Western Show, San Antonio, 1973, Best of the SW, 1973-74, also numerous pvt. shows. Charter mem. Arts Council, Clovis, N.Mex.; mem. Mayors Com. Devel. Fine Arts, 1969-73; mem. Council for Devel. of Fine Arts, 1970-73. Mem. Bus. and Profl. Womens Club, N.Mex. Art League, Art League Clovis (past pres.), Artists Equity. Methodist. Home: 1021 San Lorenzo Dr Santa Fe NM 87501

CRAWLEY, PHYLLIS GAIL, mag. pub. co. exec.; b. Omaha, Feb. 3, 1941; d. Fred Joseph and Mary Catherine Knipping; B.S., U. Nebr., 1964; div. Dir. advt. and publicity Pegasus Books, also dir. Western Pub. Co., 1967-70; publicity dir. Esquire mag., 1970-75; v.p. corp. communications Esquire, Inc., 1977-79; communications dir. CBS Consumer Pub. div. CBS Inc., 1979—. Mem. Nat. Investor Relations Inst., Profl. Women's Found., Women's Econ. Round Table. Office: CBS Publns 1515 Broadway New York NY 10036 *

CRAWLEY-CROWE, BARBARA KAY, hosp. adminstr.; b. Washington, Sept. 21, 1951; d. Bradley and Katie L. (Randall) Crawley; student St. Francis Coll., 1969-70, D. C. Tchrs. Coll., 1971-76; B.S., Trinity Coll., 1978; postgrad. Howard U. Grad. Sch. Bus. and Public Adminstrn., 1979-81. Med. technician Howard U. Hosp., Washington, 1975-77; counselor Trinity Coll., Washington, 1977-78; mental health specialist D.C. Dept. Health and Human Services, Washington, 1979-80; nuclear medicine research technologist NIH, Dept. Health and Human Services, Washington, 1980-81; asst. to dir. nuclear medicine Albany (N.Y.) Med. Center Hosp., 1981—. Lay minister/choir directress Nativity Cath. Ch., Washington, 1976-81; gospel Choir directress/layminister St. John's-St. Ann's Cath. Ch., 1981—; active D.C. Assn. Retarded Citizens. Named Parishioner of Year, Nativity Cath. Ch., 1980. Mem. Am. Chem. Soc. (pres. Trinity Coll. chpt. 1977-78), Nat. Assn. Female Execs., Assn. M.B.A. Execs., Delta Sigma Theta Sorority. Roman Catholic. Home: 4M Independence Square Apts East Greenbush NY 12061 Office: Albany Med Center Hosp New Scotland Ave Albany NY 12208

CRAYNE, NANCY ANN, computer cons. b. Toledo, Aug. 27, 1942; d. Richard Vernor and Arlene Edna (Thull) Crayne; B.S., Bowling Green (Ohio) State U., 1964. Analytical chemist Stauffer Chem. Co., Adrian, Mich., 1964-76; ind. computer programming cons., Westland, Mich., 1976-78; systems analyst Ford Motor Co., Dearborn, Mich., 1978-81; project mgr. Powderhorn Assos., Hamtramck, Mich., 1981-82; computer cons. Mich. Cons. in Data Processing, Birmingham, Mich., 1982—. Mem. Nat. Assn. Female Execs., Mich. Profl. Women's Network (pres. 1981—).

CREAGER, VIRGINIA MARY, town ofcl.; b. Grand Rapids, Mich., Nov. 8, 1926; d. Charles Grover and Helen Sarah (Stephens) Batson; student Davenport Bus. Coll., 1946-48; m. Donald Ross Creager, Aug. 17, 1949; children—Charles, Frederick, Daniel, Kenneth, Richard, Michael, Frances Helen. Mem. office staff Ford dealership, 1948-50; treas. Chester Twp., Conklin, Mich., 1976—. Mem. council Roman Catholic Ch., Conklin, 1972-73, 81-82; chmn. local bicentennial, 1975-76; active Boy Scouts Am., girls softball, 4-H Clubs, FFA. Mem. Mich. Twp. Assn., Am. Legion Aux., Ottawa County Treas. Assn. (sec-treas. 1981-82), Community Brotherwood Assn. Republican. Address: 4635 Harding St Conklin MI 49403

CREASON, NANCY STENCE, nurse; b. Elkader, Iowa, Aug. 7, 1938; d. Francis H. and Murrel (Cords) S.; B.S.N., U. Iowa, 1960; M.S.N., Wayne State U., 1964; Ph.D., U. Mich., 1977; children—James, Michael. Staff nurse, neurology-neurosurgery VA Hosp., Iowa City, 1960-61; rehab. field nurse Liberty Mut. Ins. Co., Chgo., 1961-63; instr., med. surg. nursing Coll. Nursing U. Ill., Chgo., 1965-66; instr., Sch. Nursing U. Mich., Ann Arbor, 1966-67, 69, asst. prof., 1973-74, asst. prof., chmn. fundamentals area instrn., 1975-77; asso. prof., asso. dean, dir. baccalaureate program Coll. Nursing U. Utah, Salt Lake City, 1977-78; asso. prof. nursing U.Ill., Urbana, 1978—; mgmt. cons., 1978-81. Pres., Tiffin LWV, 1970-72; mem. Washtenaw County Commn. Status of Women, 1973-75; treas. troop Boy Scouts Am., 1979—. Merit scholar U Iowa, 1955-57; U. Mich. fellow, 1974-75; Danforth asso., 1980—; USPHS grantee, 1981; recipient Golden Apple award U. Ill., 1966. Mem. Am. Nurses Assn., Ill. Nurses Assn., Dist. 15 Nurses Assn. (dir.), State Nurses Active in Politics in Ill., Nurses Coalition for Action in Politics, NOW, Midwest Soc. Nurse Researchers, Sigma Theta Tau. Episcopalian. Contbr. articles to profl. jours. Home: 1820 Sadler Dr Champaign IL 61820 Office: 1115 1/2 W Oregon St Urbana IL 61801

CREEL, JANE ESTELLA, soap mfg. co. exec.; b. Reno, Apr. 20, 1923; d. Cecil and Laura B. (Stevens) C.; B.S., U. Nev., 1945; postgrad. N.Y. U. Service mgr. Macy's Dept. Store, San Francisco, 1947-51; mgr. home econs. Monsanto Chem. Co., St. Louis, 1951-57; dir. home econs. dept. Lever Bros. Co., Inc., N.Y.C., 1957-70, mgr. consumer affairs, 1970—; dir. Gerber Life Ins. Co.; mem. Women's Council, N.Y. State Dept. Commerce, 1962-70; mem. adv. com. Coll. Human Ecology, Cornell U., 1962-72; mem. Nat. Com. on U.S.-China Relations, 1975—. Bd. dirs. Am. Philharmonia, Inc., 1980—. Mem. Am. Home Econs. Assn., Home Economists in Bus., Soap and Detergent Assn., Nat. Council Women, Grocery Mfrs. Am., Am. Advt. Fedn., Advt. Women N.Y.C. (dir. 1978—), Soc. Consumer Affairs Profls., Women Execs. in Public Relations (pres. 1972), Kappa Alpha Theta. Office: Lever Bros Co Inc 390 Park Ave New York NY 10022

CREELMAN, MARJORIE BROER, psychologist; b. Toledo, Dec. 5, 1908; d. William F. and Ethel (Griffin) Broer; student Pine Manor Jr. Coll., 1926-27, U. Wis., 1927-28; A.B., Vassar Coll., 1931; M.A. (Vassar Coll. fellow), Columbia U., 1932; Ph.D., Western Res. U., 1954; m. George Douglas Creelman, June 29, 1932 (div. Dec. 1958); children—Carleton Douglas, Stewart Elliott, Katherine George. Asst. psychologist N.Y. Psychiat. Inst., N.Y.C., 1932-33, Sunny Acres Sanitorium, Cleve., 1947-48; clin. asst. dept. psychology Western Res. U., Cleve., 1947-49, supr. field work, dir. practicum tng. program, dept. psychology, 1949-54; asst. to dir. parent edn. program Children's Aid Soc., Cleve., 1951-53; cons. Edward A. Berk & Assos., Cleve., 1952-53; partner, sr. asso. Creelman Assos., Cleve., 1954-58; pvt. practice psychology, Cleve., 1954-64, 69-79, Washington, 1964-69; research psychologist behavioral studies St. Elizabeth's Hosp., Washington, 1963-65, dir. psychophysiology, clin. and behavioral studies, 1965-67; asst. clin. prof. psychiatry George Washington U., Washington, 1965-69; dir. psychol. services Alexandria Community Mental Health Center, 1967-69; mem. policy and planning com. Midwest Tng. Center in Human Relations, 1954-60; prof. psychology Cleve State U., 1969-76, prof. emeritus, 1976—; mem. profl. staff Gestalt Inst. Cleve., 1969-81, hon. fellow, 1981—; mem. citizens adv. bd. Western Res. Psychiat. Habilitation Center, 1979-81. Fellow Internat. Council Psychologists (sec. 1964-65), Am. Soc. Group Psychotherapy and Psychodrama, Ohio Psychol. Assn.; mem. Internat. Soc. Gen. Semantics (v.p. Cleve. 1950-61), Am. Acad. Psychotherapists (life mem., publications com. directory editor 1963-67), Cleve. Acad. Cons. Psychologists (pres. 1957-58), Sigma Delta Epsilon, Psi Chi, Alpha Chi Omega. Club: Vassar (Cleve.). Author: The Experimental Investigation of Meaning, 1965; editor: Ohio Psychologist, 1956-59; contbr. articles to profl. jours.

CREIGH, DOROTHY WEYER, educator, writer; b. Hastings, Nebr., Dec. 4, 1921; d. Frank E. and Mabelle (Carey) Weyer; A.B., Hastings Coll., 1942; M.S., Columbia U., 1945; m. Thomas Creigh, Jr., July 17, 1948; children—Mary Elizabeth, Thomas, John Weyer, James Carey. Soc. editor Hastings Daily Tribune, 1941-42; tchr. Central City (Nebr.) High Sch., 1942-43; editor weekly newspaper Naval Ammunition Depot, Hastings, 1943-44; news and radio AP, Richmond, Va., 1945-46; with UNRRA, Hankow and Shanghai, China, 1946-48; tchr. Hastings Coll., 1952, 61-68; garden editor Hastings Daily Tribune, 1960; editor Stringing Along music quar., 1967, Adams County Hist. monthly, 1968—. Mem. Nebr. Bd. Edn., 1974—; mem. Nebr. Coordinating Commn. for Post-Secondary Edn., 1978—; dir. Nebr. Arts Council, 1967-80; mem. council Am. Assn. State and Local History, 1978—; bd. dirs. Hastings Civic Symphony, 1950-60, Nebr. Hist. Soc. Found., 1971—. Recipient Mari Sandoz award Nebr. Library Assn., 1981. Mem. Adams County Hist. Soc. (dir.), PEO. Presbyterian. Editor Hastings Coll. Alumni Quar., 1949-51; author: (with C. Brock) Journalism for Nebraska High Schools, 1943; (with F.E. Weyer) Hastings College, 75 Years, 1958; Bellevue College, 1962; Tales from the Prairie, Vol. I, 1970, Vol. II, 1973, Vol. III, 1976, Vol. IV, 1979; Adams County: The People, 1971; Adams County: A Story of the Great Plains (Merit award Am. Assn. for State Local History), 1972; The First Hundred Years (Presbyn. history), 1973; Where in the World Have We Been?, 1973; A Primer for Local Historical Societies, 1976; Nebraska Bicentennial History, 1977; A Handbook for the Great Plains Movies, 1979; Nebraska, Where Dreams Grow, 1980; author, dir. 6 part TV documentary on Gt. Plains, 1978; author cassettes for Exec. Inst., 1973; contbr. articles to mags. and newspapers, chpts. to Rolling Rivers, ann. ency. on Ind. state history. Address: 1950 N Elm St Hastings NE 68901

CREMER, ALMA GRACE FORD, nurse, educator; b. Winnipeg, Man., Can., Sept. 12, 1914; d. Thomas Walter and Mabel Ethel (Duncan) Ford; R.N., State U. Iowa Hosps., 1936; B.Sc. and cert. with honors in Public Health Nursing, U. Calif., Los Angeles, 1949; M.A., Ohio State U., 1962, Ph.D., 1970; m. Gordon D. Cremer, May 21, 1950; children—Gordon D. II, Peter B.R. Staff and head nurse Barnes Hosp., St. Louis, 1936-40, Kapiolani Hosp., Hawaii, 1942; pub. health nurse Santa Barbara County Health Dept., 1949; instr. Ohio State U., 1962-73; dir. allied health and nursing edn. W.Va. No. Community Coll., 1973-74; asso. prof. community health nursing Ohio U., Athens, 1976-80. Sr. bd. dirs. Florence Crittenton Services, Wheeling, W.Va., also pres. bd., 1974-75. Served to 1st lt. Nurse Corps, USAAF, 1943-46, 49. Recipient Ohio State U. Deptl. grant for research in obesity, 1967. Fellow Am. Sch. Health Assn., Am. Public Health Assn., Royal Soc. Health; mem. Am. Nurses Assn., AAHPER, Nat. League Nursing, Alpha Tau Delta. Republican. Episcopalian. Home: 3 Ball Dr Athens OH 45701

CRENSHAW, MARGARET PRICE, lawyer; b. Eugene, Oreg., Apr. 16, 1945; d. Warren Charles and Lillian Irene (Shidell) Price; B.A., Stanford U., 1967, M.A., 1968; J.D., Georgetown U., 1975; m. Albert Burford Crenshaw, Aug. 11, 1973; children—David Ollinger, Caroline Abbey. Admitted to D.C. bar, 1975, D.C. Ct. Appeals bar, 1976, U.S. Ct. Claims bar, 1976; reporter Eugene Register-Guard, 1965, 66; press asst. Californians for Humphrey San Francisco, 1968; newswoman AP, New Haven, Conn., 1969; press asst. Rep. Jeffery Cohelan, Washington, 1969; research writer Congl. Quar., Washington, 1969-70; asst. editor Washington Post, 1970-72; law clerk firm Harrison, Lucey, Sagle & Solter, Washington, 1974-75; legis. counsel Senator Philip A. Hart, Washington, 1975-77; legis. counsel Senator Paul S. Sarbanes, Washington, 1977; asso. firm Brownstein, Zeidman & Schomer, Washington, 1977-79; counsel Senate Subcom. on Govt. Efficiency and the D.C., 1979-81, minority chief counsel, 1981—; adj. prof. journalism U. Md., College Park, 1975. Ford Found. fellow, 1967-68. Mem. Am. Bar Assn., D.C. Bar Assn. Democrat. Congregationalist. Office: 6206 Dirksen Senate Office Bldg Washington DC 20510

CRESPIN, REGINE, soprano; b. Marseilles, Frace; d. Henri and Margherite (DiMeirone) C.; student Lycée Francais, Conservatoire de Paris. Appeared in numerous operas including Lohengrin, Mullhouse, France, 1950, Paris, 1951, N.Y.C., 1964, Tosca, Il Trovatore, Otello, Die Walkuere, Oberon, Fidelio, Der Rosenkavalier, Marseilles, Le Nozze di Figaro, Paris, 1956, Dialogues of the Carmelites, 1957, Parsifal, 1958, Ballo in Maschera, 1958, Fedra, Milan, Italy, 1959, Die Walkuere, Vienna, 1959, Der Rosenkavalier, Berlin, 1960, as the Marshallin, London, 1961, Les Troyens, Paris, 1961, Penelope, Buenos Aires, 1961, Otello, Ballo in Maschera, Die Walkuere, Der Rosenkavalier, Vienna, also Rosenkavalier, N.Y.C., 1962, Flying Dutchman, N.Y.C., 1962, Ballo in Maschera, N.Y.C., 1962, La Vestale, N.Y.C., 1962, Herodiade, N.Y.C., 1963, Fidelio, Ballo in Maschera, Tannhauser, Fidelio, Chgo., 1963, Carnegie Hall, 1973, Met. Opera, 1973, Carmen, Met. Opera, 1975, Cavalleria Rusticana, San Francisco Opera, 1976, Dialogues of the Carmelites, Met. Opera, 1977, 78; soloist N.Y. Philharm., 1964-65; appeared in recital Hunter Coll., 1965. Office: Herbert H Breslin 119 W 57th St New York NY 10019 *

CREWS, RUTHELLEN, educator; b. McCaysville, Ga., July 3, 1927; d. Robert Harvey and Della P. (Mason) Crews; B.A., Maryville Coll., 1949; M.S., U. Tenn., Knoxville, 1959; Ed.D. (Delta Kappa Gamma Scholar), Tchrs. Coll., Columbia U., 1966. Tchr. English and speech Cradock High Sch., Portsmouth, Va., 1949-50; elementary tchr. Rose Sch., Morristown, Tenn., 1951-54; tchr. English and Speech Morristown High Sch., 1954-58; elementary sch. librarian Knox County Schs. Materials Center, Knoxville, Tenn., 1958-60; supr. of instrn. Knox County Schs., Knoxville, 1960-65; prof. edn. U. Fla., Gainesville, 1966—; cons. curriculum devel. in pub. schs.; lectr. in field. Mem. Nat. Council Tchrs. of English, Assn. for Supervision and Curriculum Devel., Internat. Reading Assn., Delta Kappa Gamma. Author: (with others) The World of Language, textbook series, 1970, rev. edit., 1973; (with others) Pathfinder, textbook series, 1978. Contbr. articles in field of edn. to profl. jours. Home: 1719-4B NW 23d Ave Gainesville FL 32605 Office: Coll of Edn U Fla Gainesville FL 32611

CRIDER, FRANCES CAROLYN, inst. exec., educator; b. Dawson, Tex., Apr. 27, 1933; d. Robert Lee and Carrie (Lee) C.; B.S. in Edn., McMurry Coll., 1954; M.Ed. in Reading and Psychology, Eastern N.Mex. U., 1968, postgrad., 1969; Ed.S. in Elem. Edn. and Reading, U. Colo., 1973; Ed.D. in Reading and Multi Disciplinary Clinic Adminstrn., U. No. Colo., 1975; children—Catherine Dean, Elizabeth Gail. Instr. phys. edn. McMurry Coll., Abilene, Tex., 1954-55, Greiner Jr. High Sch., Dallas, 1955-56; tchr. Walker Elem. Sch., Roswell, N.Mex., 1965-67; grad. asst. Eastern N.Mex. U., Portales, 1967-68, teaching asst., 1968-69, coordinator reading edn., asso. prof. edn., 1975-79; asst. prof. edn. Adams State Coll., Denver, 1969-70; instr. in reading, dir. Reading Services Clinic, Colo. State U., Ft. Collins, 1970-75; asst. prof. U. N.Mex., Albuquerque, 1979-80; pres. Dean Inst., Albuquerque, 1980—; dir. instrn. Sunset Mesa Schs., Albuquerque, 1982—; cons. Colo. Right-to-Read, Erie Community Unit, Title III, Colo. Migrant Edn., Portales Mcpl. Schs.; adj. faculty U. Portland, 1981-82; dir. Project ACT, Portland, 1980-82; panel mem. KENM-TV, 1976. Active sch. parents adv. bds., CAP, United Fund. Recipient merit award Eastern N.Mex. U., 1977. Mem. N.Mex. Internat., Portales, Western Coll. reading assns., Council Exceptional Children, Am. Council Univ. Faculty, AAUW, AAUP, Delta Kappa Gamma. Democrat. Methodist. Author: Foundations of Reading Syllabus, 1973-74; Study Skills Manual, 1973-74; Reading Clinic Manual, 1973-74. Home: 12236-A Menaul NE Albuquerque NM 87112 Office: Sunset Mesa Schs 3020 Morris St NE Albuquerque NM 87111

CRIDER, RUBY N., graphic arts shop exec.; b. Hugo, Okla., June 29, 1938; d. Charlie E. and Dorothy Ellen (Chappell) Wadley; student Comml. Bus. Sch., Odessa, Tex., 1964-66, Odessa (Tex.) Jr. Coll., 1966-68; m. Gary C. Crider, May 15, 1971; 1 son, Michael Wayne. Operator, Southwestern Bell Telephone Co., 1958-62; credit clk. Nationwide Advt. Co., Arlington, Tex., 1971-73; printing sales sec., advt. cons. Citizen Jour., Arlington, Tex., 1973-75; owner, mgr. Web Graphics, Inc., Ft. Worth, 1976—; adv. com. Tarrant County Jr. Coll., 1979-81, bd. dirs., 1981—. Mem. Full Gospel Ch. Office: 461 S Jennings St Fort Worth TX 76104

CRIGLER, PATRICIA WOODALL, clin. psychologist, naval officer; b. Nashville, Jan. 27, 1939; d. Horace and Willie (Holleman) Woodall; B.A., Miss. State U. for Women, 1961; M.S., Ga. State U., 1968; Ph.D., Northwestern U., 1973. Commd. lt. (j.g.) U.S. Navy, 1973, advanced through grades to lt. comdr., 1979; dir. psychology Naval Hosp., San

Diego, 1973-75; sr. psychologist Pacific area, 1975-77; clin. dir. alcohol rehab. service Naval Regional Med. Center, Long Beach, Calif., 1978-81; with Naval Regional Med. Center, San Diego, 1981—; author, cons., lectr. Recipient Presdl. citation for work in field of alcoholism, 1979. Mem. Am. Psychol. Assn., Calif. Psychol. Assn., Humanistic Psychol. Assn., Mil. Psychologists Assn. Episcopalian.

CRISALLI, ANN MARIE, consumer products mfg. co. exec.; b. Glendale, Calif., Oct. 31, 1956; d. Emanuel and Elsie Lucille C.; B.S. in Biomed. Engring., U. So. Calif., 1978. Supr. packing/process area Procter and Gamble Mfg. Co., Long Beach, Calif., 1978-79, plant safety mgr., 1979—. Mem. Republican Nat. Com. Mem. Am. Soc. Profl. and Exec. Women, Nat. Assn. Female Execs., Nat. Safety Mgmt. Soc., U.S. Senatorial Club, Am. Security Council, Second Amendment Found., Conservative Caucus. Office: 1601 W 7th St Long Beach CA 90813

CRISHAL, MARGARET ANN, coll. dean; b. Youngstown, Ohio, Oct. 9, 1931; d. Flora Elizabeth Crishal; B.S., Youngstown State U., 1953; M.Ed., Kent (Ohio) State U., 1956; Ed.D. (AAUW scholar 1979), Andrews U., Berrien Springs, Mich., 1981. Tchr., Girard (Ohio) Sch. Dist., 1953-56; program dir. YWCA, Cin., 1956-62, exec. dir., St. Joseph, Mich., 1965-73; asst. prof. phys. edn. DePauw U., Greencastle, Ind., 1962-65; dean Lake Michigan Coll., Benton Harbor, Mich., 1973—. Trustee, Benton Twp., 1974—. Recipient Disting. Community Service award Bahai's of St. Joseph-Benton Harbor, 1978; named Woman of Year, Twin Cities Bus. and Profl. Women's Club, 1981. Mem. Mich. Personnel and Guidance Assn., Mich. Assn. Women Deans, Adminstrs. and Counselors, Berrien, Cass, Van Buren Counties Counselors Assn., Phi Delta Kappa. Home: 220 Higman Park Benton Harbor MI 49022 Office: 2755 E Napier Ave Benton Harbor MI 49022

CRISP, LORENA ANN, newspaper editor; b. Marion, N.C., Mar. 16, 1947; d. Furman and Dorothy Evelyn (Wells) Fincher; student U.N.C.; m. Neal Kyle Crisp, July 20, 1979; 1 dau., Tina Lisa Vess. Asst. to mayor City of Brewton (Ala.), 1972-73; newspaper reporter, photographer Marion McDowell (N.C.) News, 1973-75, asst. mng. editor, 1975-77, mng. editor, 1977—. Alt. mem. Marion Bd. Adjustment; mem. capital fund bd. Marion Gen. Hosp.; mem. policy making bd. McDowell County Sheriff's Dept., 1974-76. Mem. N.C. Press Assn., Sigma Delta Chi. Democrat. Baptist. Club: Order Eastern Star. Home: 20 New St Marion NC 28752 Office: PO Box 610 Marion NC 28762

CRISP, MARY DENT, cons.; b. Allentown, Pa., Nov. 5, 1923; d. Harry Cortland and Elizabeth Patch Dent; B.A., Oberlin Coll.; M.Polit. Sci., Ariz. State U., 1975; children—William D., Barbara, Anne. Worker, Republican party, 1961-77; co-chmn. Rep. Nat. Com., 1977-80; chmn. John Anderson for Pres., Nat. Unity; owner M. D. Crisp Enterprise, Washington. Mem. ACLU (mem. adv. bd.), Population Action Council (chmn.), Nat. Abortion Rights Action League (bd. mem.), Women's Campaign Fund, Nat. Woman's Polit. Caucus, Women's Nat. Bank, Nat. Security Council. Republican. Unitarian. Home and Office: 2555 Pennsylvania Ave NW Washington DC 20037

CRISPIN, MILDRED SWIFT (MRS. FREDERICK EATON CRISPIN), civic worker; b. Branson, Mo.; d. Albert Duane and Anna (Harlan) Swift; student Galloway Woman's Coll., 1922-24; m. Herbert William Kochs, Dec. 1, 1928 (div. Mar. 1955); children—Susan Kochs Judevine (dec.), Herbert William, Judith Ann (Mrs. Nelson Shaw); m. 2d, George Walter King Snyder, Oct. 6, 1962 (dec. 1969); m. 3d, Frederick Eaton Crispin, May 20, 1972. Bd. dirs. Travelers Aid Soc., Chgo., 1936-68, nat. dir., 1948-71; bd. dirs. U.S.O., Chgo., 1944-65, nat. dir., 1951-57; bd. dirs. John Howard Assn., 1958-67, Community Fund Chgo., 1950-56, Welfare Council Met. Chgo., 1950-56; chmn. woman's div. Crusade of Mercy, Chgo., 1964. Mem. U.S. Women's Curling Assn. (co-founder 1947, pres. 1950, founder Indian Hill Women's Curling Club, Winnetka, Ill., 1945, chmn. 1945-46), DAR, Daus. Am. Colonists. Republican. Methodist. Clubs: Woman's Athletic, Saddle and Cycle, Town and Country Arts (pres. 1957-58) (Chgo.); Everglades (Palm Beach, Fla.); Venice (Fla.) Yacht; Coral Ridge Yacht (Ft. Lauderdale, Fla.). Home: Box 68 Osprey FL 33559

CRIST, JUDITH KLEIN, film, drama critic; b. N.Y.C., May 22, 1922; d. Solomon and Helen (Schoenberg) Klein; A.B., Hunter Coll., 1941; teaching fellow State Coll. Wash., 1942-43; M.Sc. in Journalism, Columbia U., 1945; m. William B. Crist, July 3, 1947; 1 son, Steven Gordon. Civilian instr. 3091st AAFBU, 1943-44; reporter N.Y. Herald Tribune, 1945-60, editor arts, 1960-63, assoc. theater critic, 1965-63, film critic, 1963-66; film, theater critic NBC-TV Today Show, 1963-73; film critic World Jour. Tribune, 1966-67; critic at large Ladies Home Jour., 1966-67; contbg. editor, film critic TV Guide, 1966—, N.Y. mag., 1968-75, The Washingtonian, 1970-72, Palm Springs Life, 1971-75; contbg. editor, film critic Saturday Rev., 1975-77, 80—, N.Y. Post, 1977-78, MD/Mrs., 1977—, 50 Plus, 1978—, L'Officiel/USA, 1979-80; instr. journalism Hunter Coll., 1947, Sarah Lawrence Coll., 1958-59; asso. journalism Columbia Grad. Sch. Journalism, 1959-62, lectr. journalism, 1962-64, adj. prof., 1964—. Trustee Anne O'Hara McCormick Scholarship Fund. Recipient Page One award N.Y. Newspaper Guild, 1955; George Polk award, 1961, N.Y. Newspaper Women Club awards, 1955, 59, 63, 65, 67, Edn. Writers Assn. award, 1952, Columbia Grad. Sch. Journalism Alumni award, 1961, named to 50th Anniversary Honors List, 1963; Centennial Pres.'s medal Hunter Coll., 1970; named to Hunter Alumni Hall of Fame, 1973. Mem. Columbia Journalism Alumni (pres. 1967-70), N.Y. Film Critics, Nat. Soc. Film Critic, Sigma Tau Delta. Author: The Private Eye, The Cowboy and the Very Naked Girl, 1968; Judith Crist's TV Guide to the Movies, 1974; contbr. articles to mags. Office: 180 Riverside Dr New York NY 10024

CRISWELL, ELEANOR CAMP, psychologist; b. Norfolk, Va., May 12, 1938; d. Norman Harold Camp and Eleanor (Talman) David; B.A., U. Ky., 1961, M.A., 1961; Ed.D., U. Fla., 1969. Asst. prof. edn. Calif. State Coll., Hayward, 1969; prof. psychology Calif. State Coll., Sonoma, 1969—; faculty adviser Humanistic Psychology Inst., San Francisco, 1970-77; mng. editor Somatics jour.; cons. Venturi, Inc., Autogenic Systems, Inc. Founder Humanistic Psychology Inst., 1970. Mem. Am. Psychol. Assn., Biofeedback Soc. Calif. (dir.), Aerospace Med. Assn., Assn. for Transpersonal Psychology. Patentee optokinetic perceptual learning device. Office: Psychology Dept Calif State Coll at Sonoma Rohnert Park CA 94928

CRITES, LINDA JO, real estate co. exec.; b. Sacramento, Aug. 18, 1947; d. John Arthur and Virginia Rae (Brake) McCurry; grad. Realtors Inst., 1978, cert. residential specialist, 1980; m. Michael Crites; 1 dau., Angela Jean. Customers service rep. Security Pacific Nat. Bank, Rancho Corodova, Calif., 1972-74, office bookkeeper escrow; receptionist Vogel & Co. Realtors, Sacramento, 1974-75, salesman, 1975-77; salesman Bohannon Realtors, Inc., Sacramento, 1977-78, mgr. Roseville office, 1978-79; now owner, mgr. Vintage Investment Properties, Carmichael, Calif.; area rep., mgr. Resort Mktg. Internat. Sacramento Bd. Realtors, El Dorado Bd. Realtors. Democrat. Episcopalian. Home: 3130 Mayer Way Carmichael CA 95608

CRITZER, ROSE MARIE, telephone co. mktg. exec.; b. Quakertown, Pa., Nov. 21, 1946; d. Samuel W. and Rose Marie (Garcia) Critzer; B.S. in Elem. Edn., Gwynedd Mercy Coll., 1968. Tchr. St. Jude Elem. Sch., Chalfont, Pa., 1968-69; service rep. Bell Telephone, Norristown, Pa., 1970-75, service adviser, Ft. Washington, Pa., 1975-77, staff asso., Phila., 1977-78, asst. mgr., 1978-80; asso. staff mgr. mktg. Bell of Pa., Reading, 1980—. Mem Women in Mgmt., Telephone Future Pioneers, Nat. Assn. Female Execs. Republican. Roman Catholic. Home: 23 Winding Rd Pottstown PA 19464 Office: 147 N 5 St Reading PA 19601

CRIVELLI, GIOCONDA MARIA CATHERINE (MRS. ERIC R. RIPPEL), jewelry designer, artist; b. Florence, Italy, Sept. 15, 1939; d. Lorenzo and Catherine Anderson (Lester) Crivelli; student Istituto Santa Reparata, Istituto della Santissima Annunziata al Poggio Imperiale Florence; m. Eric Richards Rippel, Nov. 6, 1974; 1 dau., Schoenly Shearer Alexandra. Mem. pub. relations staff S. Ferragamo, Florence, 1959-63; pub. relations fashion coordinator Irene Galitzine couture, Rome, 1963-67, Titti Brugnoli, 1967-69; owner, mgr. Gioconda, N.Y.C., 1969-83; editor Harpers Bazaar, Italy, 1969-71; jewelry show Aaron Faber Gallery, N.Y.C., 1978; coordinator Pompei Show, Am. Mus. Natural History, N.Y.C., 1979; jewelry show Am. Mus. Natural History, 1979-80; collages exhibited Rizzoli Gallery, N.Y.C., 1980; collage show Il Borro Gallery, Florence, 1981—, Art Students League, 1982. Mem. president's council Vis. Nurses N.Y.; mem. organizing com. Scuola d'Italia, N.Y.C., 1977; mem. coms. N.Y. Infirmary-Beekman Downtown Hosp., N.Y.C. Club: Circolo Nautico E Della Vela, Porto Ercole, Italy.

CROAFF, MARVA JOAN, mktg. exec.; b. Phoenix, May 19, 1950; d. Vernon B. and Velma L. (Love) Croaff; B.S. in Zoology, Ariz. State U., 1972; postgrad. San Francisco State U., 1973-75, Syracuse U., 1978, U. Wis.-Milw., 1976. Mgr. data control Health Application Systems, Burlingame, Calif., 1972-74, mgr. planning and evaluation, 1974-75; mgr. product devel. Blue Cross/Blue Shield, Milw., 1976-78, mgr. individual plans, No. Calif., Oakland, 1978-79; ins. mktg. mgr. Durango Systems, Inc., San Jose, Calif., 1979-81; dir. mktg. Insurnet, Inc., Emeryville, Calif., 1981—. Chmn. corp. innovation task team Blue Cross/Blue Shield, Milw., 1977-78; participant in seminars on preventive health; solicitor, Milw. County Easter Seal Soc., 1977-78. Mem. Blue Cross/Blue Shield Assn. (nat. product adv. panel 1976-77, adv. panel worksite hypertension 1977-79), Sales and Mktg. Execs. Internat. Alumna, Sales and Mktg. Execs. Assn. San Francisco, Internat. Orgn. Women Execs. (dir. 1978-79), Am. Mktg. Assn., Am. Mgmt. Assn. Club: Commonwealth. Office: 1900 Powell St Emeryville CA 94608

CROCE, ARLENE LOUISE, writer; b. Providence, May 5, 1934; d. Michael Daniel and Louise Natalie (Pensa) C.; student U. N.C., 1951-53; B.A., Barnard Coll., 1955. Founder, editor Ballet Review, 1965-78; dance critic The New Yorker, N.Y.C., 1973—; dance panelist Nat. Endowment for Arts, 1977-80. Recipient Janeway Prize, Barnard Coll., 1955, Am. Acad. and Inst. Arts and Letters award, 1979, Arts and Culture award Mayor N.Y.C., 1979; Hodder fellow Princeton U., 1971; Guggenheim fellow, 1972. Author: The Fred Astaire & Ginger Rogers Book, 1972; Afterimages, 1977; Going to the Dance, 1982. Office: 25 W 43d St New York NY 10036

CROCKER, VIRGINIA LEAMAN, coll. adminstr., state legislator; b. Clinton, S.C., Sept. 9, 1951; d. Claude Arthur and Myra Leaman (Adair) C.; B.A., Columbia Coll., 1973; postgrad. U. S.C. Dir. spl. projects Presbyn. Coll.; mem. S.C. Ho. of Reps., 1978—. Bd. dirs. area 6 S.C. Lung Assn., 1978, Clinton Family YMCA; alt. del. Democratic Nat. Conv. Named Young Careerist, Clinton Bus. and Profl. Women, 1977. Mem. Women Adminstrs. in Higher Edn., Clinton Bus. and Profl. Women's Club, Am. Legion Aux., Columbia Coll. Alumnae Assn., Alpha Psi Omega. Episcopalian. Office: 404A Blatt Bldg Columbia SC 29211 *

CROCKETT, ETHEL PUTNAM STACY, librarian; b. Mt. Vernon, N.Y., Jan. 19, 1915; d. Henry P. and Marian (Putnam) Stacy; B.A., Vassar Coll., 1936; M.A., San Jose State Coll., 1962; postgrad. U. Calif. at Berkeley, 1964-65, San Francisco State Coll., 1966; m. Clement Wirt Crockett, Aug. 17, 1936 (div. 1969); children—Patricia, Richard; m. 2d, Jack H. Aldridge, June 22, 1973. Children's librarian Corning (N.Y.) Meml. Library, 1958; gen. reference librarian San Jose (Calif.) City Coll., 1962-68; dir. library services City Coll. San Francisco, 1968-72; librarian State of Calif., Sacramento, 1972-80; dir. Inst. Tng. and Evaluation, San Francisco, 1971; vice chmn. Western Interstate Commn. on Higher Edn. Library Council, 1974-76; chmn. Calif. Intersegmental Task Force on Library Automation, 1974-76; chmn. Calif. Bd. Library Examiners, 1974-76; mem. adv. council edn. stats. Nat. Center Edn. Stats. 1975-79; adviser bd. Friends of Calif. Libraries; Adv. Com. on Libraries to Librarian of Congress, 1976-77. Mem. Sir Francis Drake Commn., Calif., 1974-80; mem. vis. com. Stanford U. Libraries, 1975-82; mem. adv. bd. BALLOTS; adv. com. Ohio Coll. Library Center; adv. council Pacific SW Regional Med. Library Service, 1978-80; bd. dirs. Book Club Calif., 1981—, Seadrift Property Owners Assn., 1980—, Marin Income Property Owners Assn., 1980—; mem. adv. council Center for the Book, Library of Congress, 1980—. Mem. ALA, Calif. Library Assn. (chmn. library devel. standards com. 1970-71), Spl. Libraries Assn. (dir. 1970-72), Calif. Inst. Libraries (pres. 1973-74), Calif. Assn. Sch. Librarians (chmn. community coll. sect. 1966-67), Pvt. Libraries Assn. (Eng.), Chief Officers of State Library Agys. (chmn. 1974-77), Apt. House Consol. Assns., Calif. Media and Library Educators Assn. Home: PO Box 457 Stinson Beach CA 94970 Office: Library and Courts Bldg Sacramento CA 95809

CROCKETT, JEAN A., educator; b. Tucson, Apr. 20, 1919; B.A., M.A., Ph.D. in Econs., U. Chgo.; M.A. in Math., U. Colo.; married; 3 children. With fin. dept. Wharton Sch., U. Pa., 1954—, prof., 1966—, chmn. dept., 1977—; mem. Office Bus. Econs., Dept. Commerce, U. Ill.; mem. Cowles Commn.; dir. Fed. Res. Bank of Phila., Pennwalt Corp. Mem. Am. Fin. Assn. (dir.). Author: (with others) Financial Effects of the Capital Tax Reforms, 1978; (with others) Mutual Funds and Other Institutional Investors: A New Perspective, 1970; Consumer Expenditures and Incomes in Greece, 1967; editor: (with others) Economic Activity and Finance, 1982; contbr. articles to profl. jours., chpts. in books. Office: Wharton School University of Pennsylvania Philadelphia PA 19104 *

CROCKETT, MARY SWANSON, educator; b. Louisville, June 11, 1922; d. Arthur Gray and Marie (Rhoads) Bulter; B.A., Westminster Coll., 1943; M. Nursing, Yale U., 1946; D. Nursing Sci. (USPHS fellow), U. Calif., San Francisco, 1977; m. Guy E. Swanson, Mar. 20, 1948; children—Emily Swanson Berndt, Elisabeth H., Mary Alice, Sarah C.; m. 2d, David Crockett, Aug. 14, 1977. Research asst. Mental Health Research Inst., U. Mich., 1952-63; instr. psychiat. nursing U. Mich., 1966-69, prin. investigator psychotherapy project, 1966-69; psychiat. public health nurse, instr. mental health nursing Alameda County Health Care Services Agy., 1969-74; clin. asst. prof. nursing U. Calif., San Francisco, 1971-74; pvt. practice as nurse psychotherapist, Oakland, Calif., 1975-78; prin. investigator, asst. prof. nursing U. Tex., Austin, 1978—; cons. psychiat. nursing VA, 1967-77, 79-80, Calif. Dept. Mental Hygiene, Napa. Bd. dirs. New Directions Low Cost Counselling Service, 1975-78, pres., 1977-78; mem. Tex. Legis. Council Mental Health Task Force, 1981—. Recipient Teaching Excellence award U. Tex., 1980, Summer Research award, 1980. Mem. Am. Nurses Assn., Am. Orthopsychiat. Assn., Sigma Theta Tau. Presbyterian. Clubs: Onion Creek, Internat. Task Force. Contbr. articles profl. jours. Home: 10613 Pinehurst Dr Austin TX 78747 Office: 1700 Red River St Austin TX 78701

CROCKETT, VERLYS MOSER, mfg. co. exec.; b. Rock Rapids, Iowa, Dec. 15, 1928; d. Dick and Violet (Holland) Moser; B.A. in Edn., Denver U., 1952; m. Olen C. Crockett, Nov. 5, 1952; children—Deborah, David, Holly, Jamie, Emily. Tchr., Iowa, S.D. and Colo., 1948-52, Ark., 1952-53; mem. summer faculty Denver U., 1952; owner Master's Gallery, Denver, 1973-74; pres. Colo. Moulding Co., Englewood, 1974—. Mem. Profl. Pictures Framers Assn. (chpt. bd. dirs. 1973-83, sec.-treas. 1973-75), Framer's Guild (trustee 1981-83), Englewood C. of C. Republican. Lutheran. Home: 870 Reed Ct Lakewood CO 80215 Office: 2606 S Raritan Circle Englewood CO 80110

CROCKETT-GALLO, BARBARA, dancer; b. Berkeley, Calif., Sept. 19, 1920; d. Earl Warner and Elsie Bliss (Kennedy) Wood; student public schs.; m. Deane Crockett, Dec. 7, 1941; children—Leslie Deane Crockett, Allyson Deane Crockett Schwennesen; m. 2d, Albert Gallo, Nov. 23, 1978. Dancer, San Francisco Ballet, 1938-43; artistic dir., instr. Crockett Dance Studio, Sacramento, 1945—; founder, 1965, since prin. dancer, artistic dir. Sacramento Ballet; bd. dirs. Sacramento Regional Arts Council, 1974-77; mem. dance panel Calif. Arts Council, 1981-82. Recipient Community Service award Sacramento Regional Arts Council. Mem. Nat. Assn. Regional Ballet (pres. 1972-74, dir. 1974-82), Pacific Regional Ballet Assn. (co-founder 1966, pres. 1975). Office: 4050 Manzanita Ave Carmichael CA 95608

CROFFORD, HELEN LOIS, coll. adminstr.; b. Mesa, Ariz., Sept. 1, 1932; d. Elmer Earl and Lillian Irene (Williams) C.; grad. Lamson Bus. Coll., Phoenix, 1952. Acct., Bob Fisher Enterprises, Inc., Holbrook, Ariz., 1964-78; office mgr. for physician, Holbrook, 1978-79; office mgr. Trans Western Services, Inc., Holbrook, 1979; acct., Northland Pioneer Coll., Holbrook, 1980—. Squadron comdr. CAP, 1965-67, mission coordinator, 1970-79, group comdr., 1972-77, mem. regional staff, 1977-79; mem. Navajo Fair Commn., 1966-75; mem. Navajo County Natural Resource Conservation Dist., 1970—, sec.-treas., 1971—, chairperson, 1981-82. Mem. Ariz. Assn. Conservation Dists. (exec. bd. 1977-78, sec., 1979-80, v.p. 1981-82), Nat. Assn. Conservation Dists. (edn. and youth com. 1981), D.A.R. Democrat. Home: Box 36 Woodruff AZ 85942 Office: 1200 E Hermosa Dr Holbrook AZ 86025

CROFT, BARBARA YODER, physicist; b. Port Chester, N.Y., Aug. 11, 1940; d. Paul Henry and Harriet French (Postle) Yoder; B.A., Swarthmore Coll., 1962; M.A., Johns Hopkins U., 1964, Ph.D., 1967; m. Joseph Edward Croft, Dec. 15, 1977. Sr. scientist Johnston Labs., Inc., Balt., 1967-69; instr. radiology U. Va., Charlottesville, 1969-72, asst. prof., 1972—; cons. radiopharm. adv. com. FDA. Mem. Am. Chem. Soc., Am. Assn. Physicists in Medicine, Soc. Nuclear Medicine (trustee), Am. Coll. Nuclear Physicians, Pattern Research Soc., Sigma Xi. Episcopalian. Author: Basics of Radiopharmacy, 1978. Home: Rt 2 Box 565 Scottsville VA 24590 Office: Dept Radiology Box 170 Univ Va Charlottesville VA 22908

CROFT, CAROLINE JANE, govt. ofcl.; b. Durham, N.C., Oct. 27, 1947; d. Isadore Coleman and Mary Elizabeth (McDonald) Croft; B.A., U. N.C., 1971 postgrad. U. Mich., 1979, Harvard U., 1979, Oberlin Coll., 1980, 81. Mem. staff subcom. on adminstrv. practice and procedure, Hon. Edward M. Kennedy, Washington 1971-77; cons. Youthwork, Inc., Washington, 1978; dir. Runaway Youth Programs, Dept. Health & Human Services, Washington, 1979—; editorial cons. Jour. Early Adolescence, 1981-82; field instr. U. Mich., Ann Arbor., 1979-80. Active Women's Campaign Fund, 1979-82; vol. Spl. Olympics, 1979-82; advisor Youth Policy Inst., 1979-82. Mem. Childrens Def. Fund, N.C. State Soc., People for the Am. Way, Pi Beta Phi. Home: 4540 MacArthur Blvd Washington DC 20007 Office: 400 6th St SW Washington DC 20201

CROFTS, INEZ ALTMAN, composer, contralto; b. Portsmouth, Ohio; d. John Louis and Hazel Opal (Walters) Altman; B.Mus., Chgo. Conservatory, 1958, Mus.M., 1960; m. Philip Hague Crofts; 1 son, Philip Hague. Tchr. piano, Portsmouth; organist, choir dir. Temple Bapt. Ch., Portsmouth; TV program Twilight Time, Sta. WNHC, New Haven, 1951-53; dir. Woman's Dept. Club Chorus, Terre Haute, Ind., 1953-55; toured with N.Y.C. Opera Co. in role of Bertha in Barber of Seville, 1957; contralto soloist North Shore Bapt. Ch., 1959-81; composer opera Mission in Burma, premiered Judson Coll., Elgin, Ill., 1970; faculty mem. music dept. Judson Coll., 1968-74, Chgo. Conservatory Coll., 1967-74; dir. choral activities Sigma Alpha Iota (Sword of Honor 1959, Rose award 1971); composer music centennial pageant, Riverside, Ill., 1975. Active Heart Assn. solicitations. Mem. Internat. Soc. Contemporary Music (dir. Chgo. chpt. 1961—), Lake View Mus. Soc. (pres. 1977-78, dir.), Chgo. Artists Assn. (pres. 1960-62), Musicians Club of Women (pres. 1982—, program chmn). Home: 277 Gatesby Rd Riverside IL 60546

CROMIE, THETIS RACHAEL, clergywoman; b. Orlando, Fla., Oct. 12, 1947; d. Edgar Davidson and Aldene (Bott) C.; grad. with distinction Marion Coll., 1967; honors A.B. in Theology, grad. with distinction, Valparaiso U., 1969; M.A. with distinction, U. Chgo., 1972, D.Min., 1981. Ordained minister Lutheran Ch. in Am., 1976; hosp. chaplain Augustana Lutheran Hosp., Chgo., 1976—; co-instr. fieldwork course McCormick Presbyn. Sem., Chgo.; mem., chmn. Luth. Ch. Am. Ill. Synod Subcom. on Women and Men; mem. Luth. Women's Caucus, 1980—; mem. religious com. ERA. Mem. Inst. Soc., Ethics and Life Scis., Soc. Health and Human Values, NOW. Contbr. articles to Cresset, A Rev. of Lit., the Arts, and Public Affairs, Christian Century. Home: 411 W Dickens St Chicago IL 60615 Office: Augustana Hosp Chaplaincy Dept 411 W Dickens St Chicago IL 60614

CRONENBERGER, JO HELEN, immunologist; b. LaGrange, Tex., Mar. 17, 1939; d. Glasys Frances Legler; B.S., B.A., U. Tex., Austin, 1962; Ph.D., U. Houston, 1972. Med. technologist Methodist Hosp, Houston, 1961-64; research asst. Baylor Med. Sch., Houston, 1964-68; postdoctorate fellow Max Planck Inst., West Berlin, 1972-75; asst. prof., dir. med. tech. U. Tex. San Antonio Health Sci. Center, 1975-80; asso. prof., dir. med. technology U. N.C. Med. Sch., Chapel Hill, 1980—. Robert Welch fellow, 1970-72; Deutscheforschungs Gemeinschaft research fellow, 1975; Mem. Am. Soc. Med. Tech. Am. Soc. Microbiology, Am. Soc. Clin. Pathology, Am. Assn. Clin. Chemistry, Am. Soc. Cell biology, Reticuloendothelial Soc. Home: 100 Boulder Ln Chapel Hill NC 27514 Office: Dept MAHP Med Sch U NC Chapel Hill NC 27514

CRONIE, BARBARA, public relations and publishing cons.; b. Youngstown, Ohio; d. Joseph B. and Dorothy M. (Saluga) Cronie; student Kent State U., 1956-58; B.S., Youngstown State U., 1960; postgrad. John Carroll U., 1967. Tchr., English and journalism Jackson Milton High Sch., Youngstown, Ohio, 1960-62, Boardman (Ohio) High Sch., 1963; news reporter Fairchild Pub. Co., Cleve., Women's Wear Daily, Cleve., 1964; instr. English, Dyke Coll., Cleve., 1964-68; asst. editor Where Mag., N.Y.C., 1968; copywriter Random House, N.Y.C., 1969-70; instr. English and communications, seminar dir. Katharine Gibbs Sch., N.Y.C., 1971-72; editor Modern Hi-Fi & Stereo, N.Y.C., 1973-75; mng. editor Gallery Mag., 1975-82; owner, pres. Barbara Cronie Public Relations and Publishing Services, 1982—, exec. dir. Your Bus. Image, N.Y.C., 1982—. Mem. Am. Soc. Mag. Editors, Bus. and Profl. Women's Club N.Y. Club: Publicity.

CRONIN, KATHLEEN ANNE, exec. search co. exec.; b. Oak Park, Ill., Sept. 17, 1933; d. Brendan C. and Rose J. (Mangini) Powell; B.A., DePaul U., 1977; m. Richard J. Cronin, May 29, 1954; children—Anne, Patrick, Richard J., Edward, John, Michael, Eileen. Sec. to credit mgr. Hills Bros. Coffee, Inc., Chgo., 1951-53; estimator Alpha Portland

Cement Co., Chgo., 1953-54; v.p. adminstrn. and research Hodge-Cronin & Assos., Inc., Rosemont, Ill., 1977—, sec. corp., 1977—. Mem. Des Plaines Safety Council, 1965-66, Des Plaines Human Relations Com., 1971-72; asso. researcher Ill. Center Psychol. Research, 1973-78; conciliator Office Conciliation and Arbitration, Archdiocese Chgo., 1970-74. Cert. CPR instr. Club: St. Mary Women's (v.p. 1968). Author: Psychic Ability of the Aborigines, 1977. Office: 9575 W Higgins Rd Rosemont IL 60018

CRONIN, MARTHA PATRICIA, coll. adminstr.; b. St. Louis, Feb. 22, 1927; d. William Dennis and Bridget Delia (Rogers) C.; student Washington U., St. Louis, 1944-45; B.A., Harris Tchrs. Coll., 1948; M.A., Stanford U., 1958. Tchr., St. Louis Public Schs., 1948-66; asst. publs. editor St. Louis U., 1966-68; dir. public info. Lindenwood Colls., St. Louis, 1968-73; dir. public relations Mo. Bot. Garden, 1974-76; writer, editor, public relations cons., St. Louis, 1976-80; dir. publs. Humanities Programs for Older Adults, St. Louis Area Agy. on Aging, Mo. Com. on Humanities, 1978-80; dir. public relations Fontbonne Coll., St. Louis, 1980—. Bd. dirs. St. Louis Network Gray Panthers, 1979—, also media cons. Served as officer USMCR, 1950-56. Fulbright awardee, London, 1959-60. Mem. Women in Communications, Mo. Press Women, St. Louis Press Club. Roman Catholic. Home: 3516 Russell Blvd Saint Louis MO 63104

CROOKS, BARBARA JEANNE, broadcasting rep.; b. Dallas, Aug. 30, 1936; d. Frank Orlando and Joni (Jungman) Starz; B.A., So. Meth. U., 1957, postgrad., UCLA, 1957-58; m. Stanley S. Crooks, May 31, 1964; children—Beverly Jeanne, David Grant. Traffic and continuity dir. Sta. KLIF, 1957-58, Sta. KBOX, 1958-59, account exec., 1959-65; account exec. Sta. KIXL AM-FM, 1965-71; account exec., sales mgr., Sta. KOAX, Dallas, 1971-74; mgr. Selcom, Dallas, 1974-78, v.p., mgr., 1979-81, v.p., Western regional mgr., 1981—. Mem. Am. Women in Radio and TV, Assn. Broadcaster Execs. in Tex., Tex. Assn. Broadcasters, Southwestern Broadcast Rep. Assn. (treas. 1982), Kappa Alpha Theta. Republican. Roman Catholic. Club: Park Cities Women's Republican. Home: 4661 Mockingbird Ln Dallas TX 75209 Office: 3626 N Hall St Suite 822 Dallas TX 75219

CROOKSHANKS, BARBARA MALONE (MRS. ROBERT V. CROOKSHANKS), editor; b. South Charleston, W.Va., Nov. 16, 1928; d. Joseph William and Lucy (Caldwell) Malone; student Mary Washington Coll., U. Va., 1946-48; B.S. in Journalism, W.Va. U., 1950; postgrad. U. Pa., 1953-54; m. Robert Vincent Crookshanks, Dec. 29, 1951; children—Lee Pelham, Virginia Anne. Asst. editor W.Va. Farm News, Morgantown, 1950-51; asst. soc. editor Charleston (W.Va.) Gazette, 1951; asst. to makeup editor Ladies' Home Jour., Phila., 1952-55; reporter Free-Lance Star, Fredericksburg, Va., 1956-61; editor Fredericksburg Times, 1974—; cons. editor Personal Selling Power bi-monthly, 1981—. Publicity chmn. Fredericksburg Bicentennial Commn., 1975-77. Mem. Nat. Fedn. Press Women, Va. Press Women, Children Am. Revolution (sr. pres. Surgeon Lawrence Brooke Soc. 1969—), DAR, Colonial Dames 17th Century, Mary Washington Coll. Alumni Assn., Alpha Delta Pi, Kappa Tau Alpha. Home: 1300 Washington Ave Fredericksburg VA 22401 Office: 604 William St Fredericksburg VA 22401

CROOKSHANKS, BETTY DORSEY, state legislator; b. Rainelle, W.Va., Oct. 27, 1944; d. Talmage Lee and Gilda Marie (Sovine) Dorsey; B.A., W.Va. Inst. Tech., 1968; M.A., W.Va. U., 1973; m. Donald Eugene Crookshanks, Sept. 1, 1972. Sec., NIH, 1965-66; tchr., coach Fayette County Bd. Edn., Meadow Bridge, W.Va., 1968-78; life underwriter Farm Family Life Ins. Co., 1979-82; tchr. Greenbrier (W.Va.) West High Sch., 1981—; mem. W.Va. Ho. of Dels., 1977—. Mem. adv. bd. W.Va. Woman's Commn., 1977—, Greenbrier Valley Domestic Violence Com.; treas. Rupert Community Library, 1977—; bd. dirs. Seneca Mental Health/Mental Retardation Council, 1978-82, treas., 1979-80, pres., 1980-82; bd. dirs. W.Va. Health Systems Agy., 1980-82; bd. dirs. W.Va. div. Am. Cancer Soc., 1981—; pres. Greenbrier County Cancer Soc., 1981-82. Recipient meritorious award W.Va. div. Isaac Walton League of Am., 1978; Disting. Service award W.Va. Osteo. Sch. Medicine, 1982; named Outstanding Young Woman of W.Va., 1980. Mem. Order of Women Legislators, Farm Bur., Rainelle Bus. and Profl. Women's Club (treas. 1982—), Delta Kappa Gamma (sec. 1980-82, 1st v.p. 1982—). Democrat. Baptist. Clubs: Quota (bd. dirs. 1981-82), Rupert Woman's (pres. 1979-80), Order of Eastern Star, Rebekah.

CROSBY, CHRISTINE CURRIER, office equipment mktg. co. exec.; b. Utica, Aug. 3, 1945; d. Wayne Arthur and Bernadette (Townley) Currier; student King Coll., 1976-80; children—Michele, Tiffany. With Delta Bus. Systems, Inc., Orlando, Fla., 1976—, exec. v.p., 1980—. Mem. Sales and Mktg. Execs. Assn., C. of C. Republican. Home: 101 Red Cedar Dr Longwood FL 32750 Office: 4601 Parkway Commerce Blvd Orlando FL 32804

CROSBY, GERRY WORTH, assn. exec.; b. Savannah, Ga., Mar. 17, 1929; d. John and Ida Worth; B.A., Armstrong Coll., 1950; student U. Miami, U. Ga.; children—Glenn R., Pamela J. Credit and collections mgr. Variety Children's Hosp., Miami, Fla., 1951-52; substitute tchr. Dade County (Fla.) Sch. Bd., 1964-69; reporter, asso. editor S. Dade County News Leader, 1964-70; exec. dir. South Dade C. of C., Miami, from 1970—, now exec. v.p.; freelance writer, contbr. to UPI, Miamian, Fla. Bankers, 1965—. Mem. Public Safety Dept. Adv. Council. Recipient Outstanding Citizens award Fla. Jr. C. of C., 1968; 1st and 2d place awards AP Fla., Armed Service pub. relations award, POW award, mental health award, others. Mem. Women in Communications, Mental Health Guidance Center, Am. C. of C. Execs., Zool. Soc. Dade County. Lutheran. Home: 8450 201st St SW Miami FL 33189

CROSBY, RAMONA CONCHITA THOMPSON, chem. co. exec.; b. Bklyn., May 18; d. Samuel Duncan and Adina Priscilla (Eustace) Thompson; B.S., Bklyn. Coll., 1955; M.S. (teaching fellow), Howard U., 1957; postgrad. teaching fellow Poly. Inst. Bklyn., 1966-69; postgrad. Purdue U., 1957-59; m. Gordon Crosby, July 27, 1963. Research asst. Purdue U. Research Found., 1958-59, N.Y.U. Med. Center, 1960-66; lit. scientist, then sr. lit. scientist Warner Lambert Research Inst., Warner Lambert Co., Morris Plains, N.J., 1969-73; supr. info. services Stauffer Chem. Co., Dobbs Ferry, N.Y., 1973—; instr. N.Y. Community Coll. Mem. council Grad. Sch. Library and Info. Sci., Pratt Inst. Mem. Am. Chem. Soc., Am. Soc. Info. Sci. (sec.-treas. spl. interest group on automated lang. processing), Am. Mgmt. Assn., Asso. Info. Mgrs. (co-chmn. career devel. com.), Sigma Delta Epsilon, Beta Kappa Chi, Zeta Phi Beta (past chpt. pres.). Democrat. Author articles. Office: Stauffer Chem Co Livingstone Ave Dobbs Ferry NY 10522

CROSS, BARBARA LOUISE ANNE, truck equipment co. ofcl.; b. Canton, Ohio, Jan. 8, 1954; d. Glenn Griffin and Mary Lucille (Bamberger) Cross; B.S. in Elem. and Early Childhood Edn., B.A. in English, U. Tampa, 1975; M.S. in Ednl. Adminstrn., U. Akron, 1978. Prin., St. Paul's Sch., Canton, 1978-82; exec. sec. to pres. Cross Truck Equipment Co. and Crosco, Inc., Canton, 1982—. Mem. Republican Nat. Com., 1978—. Mem. Stark County Wilderness Soc., Kappa Delta Pi, Phi Delta Kappa, Omicron Delta Kappa, Alpha Chi Omega. Roman Catholic. Clubs: Jr. League Canton, College (Canton). Home: 3925 Southway Ave SW Massillon OH 44646 Office: 1801 Perry Dr SW PO Box B Sta C Canton OH 44708

CROSS, DOROTHY ABIGAIL, librarian; b. Bangor, Mich., Sept. 9, 1924; d. John Laird and Alice Estelle (Wilcox) C.; B.A., Wayne State U., 1956; M.A. in Library Sci., U. Mich., 1957. Jr. librarian Detroit Public Library, 1957-59; adminstrv. librarian U.S. Army, Braconne, France, 1959-61, Poitiers, France, 1961-63; area library supr., 1963, asst. command librarian, Kaiserslautern, Germany, 1963-67, acquisitions librarian, Aschaffenburg, Germany, 1967, Munich, Germany, 1967-69, sr. staff library specialist, Munich, 1969-72, command librarian, Stuttgart, Germany, 1972-75, dep. staff librarian, Heidelberg, Germany, 1975-77; chief librarian 18th Airborne Corps and Ft. Bragg (N.C.), 1977-79; chief ADP sect. The Army Library, Pentagon, Washington, 1979-80, chief readers services br., 1980—. Mem. ALA, Spl. Libraries Assn., U. Mich. Alumni assn., Delta Omicron. Methodist. Home: 6008 Old Landing Way Burke VA 22015 Office: The Army Library Room 1A518 Pentagon Washington DC 20310

CROSS, DOROTHY FREEMAN, clergywoman; b. Little Rock, Sept. 16, 1923; d. Robert Alfonso and Mattie Hopson Freeman; B.A., Va. Union U., 1954; M.S. in Edn., Chgo. State U., 1968; cert. tchr. tng. Northwestern U., 1972; M.Div., McCormick Theol. Sem., 1976; m. William Edward Cross, Dec. 29, 1943; children—William, Robert, James. Tchr. Chgo. Public Schs., 1954-74, instructional team leader, adminstrv. asst., 1974; ordained to ministry United Presbyn. Ch., 1976; pastor 1st Presbyn. Ch., Benton Harbor, Mich., 1976-80; asso. exec. Synod of Lincoln Trails, Indpls., 1980—; mem. adv. council discipleship and worship United Presbyn. Ch. in U.S.A. Recipient Mother of Yr. award Chgo. Boys Clubs, 1955-56. Mem. Presbyn. Health, Edn. and Welfare Assn. (dir. 1981-84), Internat. Assn. Women Clergy, Racial/Ethnic Clergywomen's Assn., Alpha Kappa Alpha. Home: 7473 Country Brook Dr Indianapolis IN 46260 Office: Synod of Lincoln Trails United Presbyn Ch 1100 W 42d St Indianapolis IN 46208

CROSS, GERTRUDE ANN, educator, gerontology cons.; b. Flint, Mich., Oct. 12, 1925; d. Warren Edwin Carl and Leona Marie (Gallinat) Carl Dahljelm; B.S., Central Mich. U., 1976, M.S., 1980; m. Henry George Cross, Feb. 15, 1942; children—Kathleen, John, Cindi, Sandra, Margaret. Recreation profl. Flint Recreation Dept., 1943-77; instr. Central Mich. U., Mt. Pleasant, 1976—; cons. on aging Charles Stewart Mott Found., Flint, 1978—; sec. Flint Retirement Homes, Inc., 1967-75; bd. dirs. Center for Ind. Living, 1978—, Sr. Adults, Inc., 1963—, Sr. Adventurers, Inc., 1970—; mem. Genesee County Commn. on Aging. Recipient Golden Deeds award Flint Exchange Club, 1967; Mich. Recreation and Park Assn. fellow, 1971. Mem. Nat. Council on Aging, Nat. Caucus for Black Aged, Am. Assn. Ret. Persons, Gerontol. Soc. Am., Western Gerontol. Soc., Mich. Soc. Gerontology. Presbyterian. Club: Birch Pointe Country. Author: Program Ideas for Senior Citizens, 1970; editor Sr. Citizen News, 1963-82. Home: 4395 E Coldwater Rd Flint MI 48506 Office: Mott Found Bldg Flint MI 48502

CROSS, JUDITH ANN, state records ofcl.; b. Beech Grove, Ind., Dec. 30, 1951; d. A.R. and Betty Ann Cross; A.B. (Ind. State scholar), Ind. U., 1973, M.L.S., 1976. Librarian, Ind. State Library, Indpls., 1974-79; crime analyst U. Tex. Police Dept., Arlington, 1979, Security Gov., Indpls., 1979-82; records analyst Commn. on Pub. Records, State of Ind., Indpls., 1982—. Office: 4750 N Meridian St Indianapolis IN 46208

CROSS, JULIA BAUMGARDNER, govt. ofcl.; b. Bristol, Tenn., Aug. 28, 1923; d. John Dixon and Bessie Gertrude (Kegley) Baumgardner; student Va. Intermont Coll., 1941-43; B.S., U. Tenn., 1946; m. Ralph Edgar Cross, Sept. 3, 1949 (dec.); children—William Mitchell (dec.), Charles Duane, Julianne (dec.). Sec. to pres. Va. Intermont Coll., Bristol, 1946-49; sec. to editor Methodist Pub. House, Nashville, 1966-68, editorial asst., 1968-69; dep. clk. U.S. Dist. Ct., Nashville, 1969-73, courtroom dep. clk., 1973-78, chief dep. clk., 1978, clk., 1978—. Active Tenn. Performing Arts Center, Tenn. State Mus., Nashville Symphony Assn.; chmn. ch. chpt. Episcopal Ch. Mem. Mental Health Assn. Nashville, Am. Judicature Soc., Fed. Ct. Clks. Assn., Assn. of Records Mgrs. and Adminstrs., Middle Tenn. Fed. Exec. Assn., Phi Mu (life). Club: Zonta Internat. Home: 112 Royal Oaks Condominium 4505 Harding Rd Nashville TN 37205 Office: 800 US Courthouse 801 Broadway Nashville TN 37203

CROSS, JUNE VICTORIA, reporter; b. N.Y.C., Jan. 5, 1954; d. James and Norma Cross; B.A. Harvard U., 1975. Reporter various newspapers, Mass., 1973-76; asst. dir., prodn. mgr. Sta. WGBH-TV, Boston, 1977-78; reporter MacNeil/Lehrer Report, WETA-TV Shirlington, Va., 1978—. Sch. Urban and Pub. Affairs fellow Carnegie-Mellon U., 1981. Mem. Am. Film Inst., Nat. Assn. Black Journalists, Coalition of One Hundred Black Women, Assn. Black Harvard Alumni (dir. 1980-81). Club: Radcliffe. Writer, producer Simple is Harlem, 1975. Home: 1614 G St SE Washington DC 20003 Office: 3620 27th St S Shirlington VA 22206

CROSS, KAREN SUE MOSLEY, realtor; b. Detroit, Feb. 10, 1942; d. Jeffie Terrance and Frances Eleanore (Mack) Mosley; student (Roseville Federated Tchrs. Scholar) Central Mich. U., 1960-61; student Southwestern Bapt. Theol. Sem., 1962-65, DeKalb Community Coll., 1977; m. Dale Wesley Cross, June 17, 1961; children—John, Crystal, Jeffrey. Recreation dir., Roseville, Mich., 1960, 61; tchr. Shadywood Elem. Sch., Warren Woods, Mich., 1961; currency sorter Fed. Res. Bank, Dallas, 1965-67; mem. credit and sales audit staff Montgomery Ward and Co., Detroit, 1968-69, account rep., Lombard, Ill., 1975-76; decorating cons. House of Decorating Accessories, Detroit, 1971-74; account mgr. BWS Credit Services, Oak Brook, Ill., 1977-78; realtor asso. Century 21 Raymond Morris, Tucker, Ga., 1978-80; realtor Classic Properties, Decatur, Ga., 1980—; resident mgr. Royal Vines Apts., Clarkston, Ga., 1980—; owner Cross & Assos., 1980—. Sec., Youth Adv. Council State of Mich., 1961; pres. PTA, Idlewood Sch., Tucker, 1979-81. Mem. Nat. Assn. Realtors, State Assn. Realtors, DeKalb and Gwinnett Bd. Realtors, Nat. Assn. Female Execs. Club: Twilight Tillers Garden (Tucker). Baptist (nat. adv. bd. women on evangelism 1980—). Editor: Dogwood Legend, New Neighbors League Club, Atlanta, 1978-79, Idlechatter, monthly neighborhood newsletter, 1978—. Home: 1080-4 Noblevines Dr Clarkston GA 30021 Office: 10864 Montreal Rd Clarkston GA 30021

CROSS, KATHRYN PATRICIA, educator; b. Normal, Ill., Mar. 17, 1926; d. Clarence LeRoy and Katherine Delia Cross; B.S. in Math., Ill. State U., 1948, LL.D. (hon.), 1970; A.M., U. Ill., 1951, Ph.D., 1958; Sc.D. (hon.), Loyola U., Chgo., 1980, Northeastern U., 1975; L.H.D. (hon.), Hood Coll., 1979, Grand Valley State Coll., 1975, Marymount Manhattan Coll., 1982; D. Pedagogy (hon.), Our Lady of the Lake U., 1977. Tchr. math. Harvard (Ill.) Community High Sch., 1948-49; research asst. dept. psychology U. Ill., Urbana, 1949-53, asst. dean of women, 1953-59; dean of women Cornell U., Ithaca, N.Y., 1959-60, dean of students, 1960-63; program dir. comprehensive coll. tests Ednl. Testing Service, Princeton, N.J., 1963-65, program dir. research program for higher edn., 1965-66, sr. program dir. coll. and univ. programs, 1966-69, sr. research psychologist, 1969-76, disting. research scientist, 1976-82; research educator (part-time) Center for Research and Devel., U. Calif., Berkeley, 1966-77; vis. prof. U. Nebr., 1975-76; lectr. higher edn. U. Calif., Berkeley, 1977-80; sr. lectr. Harvard Grad. Sch. Edn., Cambridge, 1980—; mem. nat. adv. bd. Inst. for Acad. Improvement, Memphis State U., Tenn., 1978-81; mem. nat. res. bd. Carnegie Found. Advancement Teaching, 1981-85. Bd. dirs. Nat. Center for Higher Edn. Mgmt. Systems, 1980—. Recipient Medallion of Honor, Mother's Assn., U. Ill., 1973, Delbert Clark award West Ga. Coll., 1979; Disting. Alumni award Ill. State U., 1980. Mem. Nat. Acad. of Edn. (vice chmn. 1981—), Assn. for the Study of Higher Edn. (dir. 1979-81), Am. Assn. of Higher Edn. (dir. 1973-75, pres. 1974-75). Author: Beyond the Open Door (Citation award 1981), 1971; The Junior College Student (Pi Lambda Theta Best Books award 1968), 1968; Planning Non-Traditional Programs (with J. R. Valley and Associates), 1974; Accent on Learning: Improving Instruction and Reshaping the Curriculum (Am. Council Edn. Nat. Book award 1976), 1976; Adults as Learners, 1981; contbr. numerous articles on higher edn. to profl. publs.; contbr. chpts. to books on edn.; editorial bd. Jour. Higher Edn., 1974—, Community/Junior College Research Quar., 1976—. Office: Harvard Grad Sch of Education 337 Gutman Library Cambridge MA 02138

CROSS, LAURA ELIZABETH, lawyer; b. Lathrop, Mo.; d. Pross T. and Nina (Peel) C.; A.B., Lindenwood Coll., 1923; B.Litt., Columbia Sch. Journalism, 1925; J.D., George Washington U., 1939. Bibliog. research Library of Congress, Washington, 1931-42; admitted to D.C. bar, 1940; atty. Office Chief of Engrs., U.S. Army, 1942-73; practiced in Washington, 1973—. Mem. Am., Fed. bar assns., Am. Judicature Soc., Women in Communications, Kappa Beta Pi, Theta Sigma Phi. Home and Office: 2500 Wisconsin Ave NW Washington DC 20007

CROSS, MIRIAM HELEN, sales rep.; b. Port Orchard, Wash., July 17, 1943; d. Arthur Emerson and Helen Lucille (Furseth) Cross; B.S., Wash. State U., 1964; M.S., Oreg. State U., 1972; postgrad. Olympic Coll., 1962, Portland Community Coll., 1969-70, U. Nebr., 1974, Kans. State U., 1975-77, Central State U., 1978, U. Okla., 1979. Home econs. tchr. Wahkiakum High Sch., Cathlamet, Wash., 1964-66, Portland public schs., 1966-68; dept. mgr. fashion accessories/sml. leathers Meier & Frank, Portland, 1968-70; instr. home econs. S.W. Tex. State U., San Marcos, 1971-73; instr./fashion mktg. coordinator Kan. State U., Manhattan, 1973-77; asst. prof. home econs. U. Okla., Norman, 1977-80; coll. sales rep. Scott, Foresman, Inc., Norman, 1980—; cons. in field; lectr. in field; contest judge, various locations, 1965, 69, 71-72; faculty Kans. State U. free Univ. for Man, 1974. Mem. NOW, Am. Home Econs. Assn., Assn. Coll. Profs. Textiles and Clothing, Fashion Group Inc., Internat. Arabian Horse Assn., Am. Horse Shows Assn. Lutheran. Club: Okla. Arabian Horse. Author: A Retailing Internship Laboratory Manual, 1975, 3rd edit. 1980; contbr. articles to profl. jours. Home: 17 F St Norman OK 73071

CROSSLAND, HARRIET KENT, portrait painter; b. Cleve., Sept. 8, 1902; d. Carl and Harriet Emily (Bacon) Dueringer; pupil of Margaret McDonald Phillips; m. Paul Marion Crossland, Sept. 20, 1959. Portrait painter, 1952—; freelance editor med. papers, 1953-70; represented in permanent collection John F. Kennedy Library, Boston. Fund raiser Am. Cancer Soc.; mem. fund raising com. Vol. Action Bur.; mem. Santa Rosa Symphony League; mem. visual arts com. Luther Burbank Center for the Arts, Santa Rosa, 1982—. Recipient award of merit Am. Cancer Soc., 1979. Mem. Nat. League Am. Pen Women, Artists Round Table, Sonoma County Med. Assn. Aux., Am. Med. Women's Assn. (friend), Am. Cancer Soc., DAR. Clubs: Ret. Officers Wives, Sonoma County Press, Sat. Afternoon. Editor, illustrator: X-Rays and Radium in Treatment of Diseases of the Skin, 1967. Address: 2247 Sunrise Dr Santa Rosa CA 95405

CROSSLEY, LINDA SUSAN, univ. adminstr.; b. New Brunswick, N.J., July 21, 1950; d. Richard Lawrence and Mary Vee (Adams) Crossley; B.A., Ohio State U., 1972. Adminstrv. asst. news and info. services Ohio State U., Newark, 1972-77, also Central Ohio Tech. Coll.; dir. info. services Olivet (Mich.) Coll., 1977-80; asst. dir. news bur. Ball State U., Muncie, Ind., 1980—. Recipient Gorton R. Riethmiller Outstanding Adminstr. award Olivet Coll., 1980. Mem. Ball State U. Art Gallery Alliance (co-editor newsletter), Council Advancement and Support of Edn. (co-editor dist. 5 newsletter), Office: Public Info Services Ball State U Muncie IN 17306

CROSSLIN, LOUISE, real estate broker; b. Sallisaw, Okla., May 29, 1927; d. Alvon A. and Maye M. (Burton) Diffee; student Oklahoma City U., 1949, 50; m. Paul L. Crosslin, July 18, 1943; children—Alvon Paul, Norman Randy. With CRE, Tahlequah, Okla., 1952—, owner, broker, 1955—. Mem. Rural Water Dist., Tahlequah, 1972-75. Mem. C. of C. (sec. 1952-82), Home Builders Assn., Okla. Real Estate Commn., Am. Legion Aux., VFW Aux., Beta Sigma Phi. Democrat. Baptist. Club: Sportsmen Acres Devel. Co. (pres. 1970-82). Home: PO Box 164 Tahlequah OK 74464 Office: 400 S Muskogee Tahlequah OK 74464

CROSWELL, ANNE PEARSON, lyricist, playwright, author, poet; b. Tuscaloosa, Ala., Dec. 12; d. John Hale and Eudora Maxwell (Yerby) Pearson; B.A., Randolph-Macon Woman's Coll., 1951. Theater lyrics for Tovarich, Broadway musical winning Tony award for Vivien Leigh; book and lyrics for Ernest in Love, 1960, I'm Solomon, 1968, Chips 'n Ale, 1974; TV lyrics for Who's Earnest, 1957, Washington Sq., 1957-58, Sesame St., 1980-82; concerts at Carnegie and Philharmonic Halls; numerous record albums, songs rec. by the Muppets, Julie Andrews, Johnny Mathis, Andre Previn, The Vienna Boys' Choir, others; songs in revues, N.Y., London; photo-caption humor book Some of My Best Friends are Runners, 1979; copy/jingles for J. Walter Thompson Co. and Leo Burnett. One of founders, Village Ind. Democrats, 1956, county committeewoman, N.Y. Recipient ASCAP Popular awards. Mem. ASCAP, Authors Guild, Dramatists Guild.

CROUCH, EVELYN, nurse, educator; b. Ponce, P.R., May 18, 1945; d. Everett Irvin and Juanita Victoria (Ruiz) C.; diploma St. Luke's Epis. Sch. Nursing, 1966; B.S.N. cum laude, Cath. U. P.R., 1972; M.S.N., U. Tex., Austin, 1978, postgrad., 1981—; m. Julio M. Rivera, Aug. 8, 1970; children—Evelyn Aixa, Julio Irvin, Alex Raul. Staff clin. nurse St. Luke's Episcopal Hosp., Ponce, P.R., 1966-67; clin. nurse Columbia Presbyn. Med. Center, N.Y.C., 1967-69; pvt. duty nurse, Ponce, 1969-72; nursing instr. Cath. U. P.R., Ponce, 1972-80; clin. nurse USPHS Hosp., Houston, 1980-81; asst. instr. U. Tex., Austin, 1981—; cons. labor and delivery Castaner (P.R.) Hosp., Damas Hosp., Ponce, P.R., 1978-80; dir. cultural and social activities Delicias, Ponce, P.R., 1980; chmn. recruitment Coll. Profl. Nurses, Ponce, 1979-80; coordinator Assoc. Degree Nursing Program, Regional Coll., Ponce, 1980—. Mem. Assn. Nurses Grad. Sch. (research rep.), Coll. Profl. Nurses P.R. Democrat. Episcopalian. Office: 1700 Red River Austin TX 78701

CROUCH, LOIS (ELIZABETH), civic worker; d. Richard C. and Willie A. (Howard) Kimbrough; B.A. in Polit. Sci., UCLA, M.A. in Polit. Sci.; m. Winston W. Crouch; 1 dau. Active Calif. Fedn. Woman's Clubs, 1967—, chmn. state leadership devel., 1972-74, dist. del., 1976, 77, pres. Marina Dist. 18, 1976-78, parliamentarian Pacific Palisades (Calif.) Women's Club, 1974-76, pres. Parliamentary Law Study Club, 1978-79; pres. Los Angeles LWV, 1950, Calif. LWV, 1951-53; mem. Coordinating Council Pacific Palisades, 1968-78, sec., 1969; mem. Civic League Pacific Palisades; chmn. Los Angeles Citizens Urban Renewal Adv. Com., 1963-66; bd. dirs. Palisades Homeowner's Assn., 1970-78, sec.-treas., 1970, treas., 1979-82; mem. adv. bd. YWCA of UCLA, 1963, sec., 1964; scout leader Girl Scouts U.S., 1946-48; deacon Pacific Palisades Presbyn. Ch., 1967-69, elder, 1982—, mem. ch. and soc. com., 1967-68, co-editor monthly bull., 1967-68; mem. western region planning bd., corp. planning council United Way of Los Angeles; adv. bd. Santa Monica Westside Sr. Multiservice Center; participant/del. to many polit. sci., urban renewal, pub. personnel, citizen participation confs. Recipient award Gen. Fedn. Women's Clubs, 1974; named One of 6 Outstanding Clubwomen in Bay Area-West Los Angeles, 1975. Clubs: Faculty

Womens UCLA (sect. chmn.), Eastern Star (chmn. grand chpt. coms. 1972-73, 74). Home: 1035 Anoka Pl Pacific Palisades CA 90272

CROUSHORE, SUSAN RITA, microbiologist; b. Phila., Mar. 24, 1954; d. Charles Matthew and Catherine Mary (Finchen) Ott; B.S. in Med. Tech., Pa. State U., 1976; M.S. in Clin. Microbiology (grantee), Thomas Jefferson U., 1982; postgrad. LaSalle Coll., 1979—; m. Edward Croushore, Oct. 18, 1975; 1 dau., Amy. Microbiologist, Pa. Hosp., Phila., 1976-79, microbiology supr., 1979-82; lab. mgr. Met. Hosp., Phila., 1982—. Mem. Am. Soc. Clin. Pathologists, Am. Soc. for Microbiologists, Clin. Lab. Mgrs. Assn., Clin. Master's Alumni Group of Thomas Jefferson U., Phi Kappa Phi. Republican. Roman Catholic. Home: 2916 Cambridge St Philadelphia PA 19130 Office: Met Hosp 201 N 8th St Philadelphia PA 19106

CROUT, ELEANOR MUECKE (MRS. G. STANLEY CROUT), civic worker; b. N.Y.C., Jan. 13, 1938; d. Berthold Muecke, Jr. and Eleanor B. Thalmann; B.A., Mt. Holyoke Coll., 1959; M.A., Columbia, 1960; m. G. Stanley Crout, May 14, 1960; children—Alexandra Lynn, Stephen Andrew, Charles Merrill. Tchr., Walnut Hill Sch., Natick, Mass., 1960; DeWitt Clinton High Sch., Bronx, N.Y.C., 1961-62. Mem. Jr. Welfare Assn., Santa Fe, 1962-68, program chmn., 1963-64, treas., 1964-65, pres., 1965-66, pub. relations chmn., 1967-68; chmn. Community Christmas Store, Santa Fe, 1965; co-chmn. ticket sales Heart Fund Benefit, 1969; active March of Dimes drive, 1964, Heart Fund, 1965, Am. Cancer Soc. Drive, 1969; mem. St. Vincent Hosp. Aux., 1967-68, chmn. com., benefit, 1965, 69; mem. Santa Fe Council Internat. Relations, 1968—; chmn. Girl Scout Expn., 1972. Bd. dirs. Jr. Welfare Assn., 1964-68, Girl's Club, 1965-66, 79—; bd. dirs., chmn. personnel services Sangre de Cristo council Girl Scouts U.S.A., 1972-75; bd. dirs. St. Michael's High Sch., Santa Fe, 1975-77; coordinator City Elementary Sch. Competitive Swimming Program, 1973-79. Mem. Mt. Holyoke Alumnae Assn., Sch. Am. Research, Friends of St. John's Coll., Delta Kappa Pi, Phi Lambda Theta. Club: Santa Fe Garden (co-chmn. house and garden tours 1972, sec. 1974-75, dir. 1972-76, publicity chmn. 1974-76). Episcopalian. Address: Old Arroya Chamisa Rd Box 32 Santa Fe NM 87501

CROWDER, LENA BELLE, educator; b. Winston-Salem, N.C., Apr. 4, 1931; B.S. in Elem. Edn., Winston-Salem (N.C.) State U., 1952; M.S. in Edn., N.C. A. and T. U., Greensboro, 1959; postgrad. Appalachian State U., Boone, N.C., 1972—; married; 1 child. Spl. edn. tchr. Winston-Salem/Forsyth County Sch. System, 1962-72, resource tchr., 1972-73, spl. edn. task force, 1974-75, placement adminstr., spl. edn. tchr., 1975—; co-organizer, designer lang. arts curriculum guide for tchrs. educable mentally retarded classes; spl. edn. rep. Early Childhood Inst.; mem. evaluation team assn. appraisal spl. edn. instructional material devel. center N.C. Dept. Pub. Instrn.; mem. planning com. Spl. Olympics; mem. arts in basic curriculum steering team Kimberley Park Sch., 1979-80. Named Tchr. of Year Walkertown Elementary Sch. faculty, 1970-71, Kimberley Park Intermediate Sch. faculty, 1979; recipient Christian Service award Mt. Zion Bapt. Ch.; certs. of recognition for excellence in teaching Winston-Salem/Forsyth County Bd. Edn., 1979, Sta. WSJS, 1980; named outstanding tchr. Winston-Salem/Forsyth County System Newspaper, 1981; cert. N.C.; specialist in mental retardation. Mem. Winston-Salem Arts Council, Council for Exceptional Children (Excellence in Teaching award 1982), Assn. Retarded Citizens, NEA, Assn. Classroom Tchrs., N.C. Assn. Educators, Winston-Salem State Alumni Assn. Home: 1140 Rich Ave Winston-Salem NC 27101 Office: Kimberley Park Elementary Sch Winston-Salem NC 27105

CROWELL, PEARL TROUTZ, summer resort exec.; b. Clay County, Mo., Nov. 7, 1908; d. James Walter and Carrie Lottie Rose (Vanderhoef) Troutz; student William Jewell Coll., 1926-27, Kansas City Art Inst., 1927-29, Purdue U. seminars, 1941-60; m. Wilbur Gale Crowell, Feb. 10, 1934 (dec. 1977); children—Gayle Ann Crowell Boyer, James Elliott. Owner-operator Crestwood Flowers, Kansas City, Mo., 1934-42; farmer, 1942-82; owner-operator Big Chief Lodge, Monticello, Ind., 1957—; real estate salesperson, Burnettsville and Monticello. Democratic precinct committeeman, 1948-72; bd. dirs. White County Hosp. Aux., 1954—. Mem. Monticello C. of C. (dir. 1970-82). Mem. Ch. of Christ. Clubs: Adams Home Econs. (past pres.), Bus. and Profl., Monticello Women of Moose, Twin Lakes Senior Citizen, Carroll County Democratic Women's. Address: Big Chief Lodge 207 Indiana Beach Rd Monticello IN 47960 also Rural Route 1 Burnettsville IN 47926

CROWLEY, ELLEN, lawyer; b. Cheyenne, Wyo., July 26, 1916; d. Frank J. and Miriam (Keliher) C.; B.A., U. Wyo., 1938; B.S. in Library Sci., U. Denver, 1942; LL.B., Fordham U., 1948; m. Toshiro Suyematsu, Apr. 30, 1954. Asst. state librarian Wyo., Cheyenne, 1939-42; law librarian Mc Lanahan, Merritt & Ingraham, N.Y.C., 1942-49; Wyo. state librarian, ex-officio state historian, 1949-51; law librarian U. Nebr. Coll. Law, 1951-53; admitted to Wyo. bar, 1953; pvt. practice law, Cheyenne, 1953—; asst. atty. gen., dep. atty. gen. State of Wyo., 1955-59; law clk. U.S. Dist. Ct. Judge, Dist. Wyo., 1960-69. Dir., Security First Savs. & Loan Assn., Cheyenne. Mem. Wyo. Ho. of Reps., 1973-74, 77-82, mem. ho. standing coms. on corps., elections and polit. subdivs., labor, health and welfare, judiciary com., chmn. judiciary com. 1979-82; regional v.p. Wyo. Assn. for Retarded Citizens, 1980—. Mem. Wyo. State Bar, Laramie County Bar Assn. (v.p. 1973-74, pres. 1974-75), Am. Bar Assn., Nat. Assn. Women Lawyers, Kappa Kappa Gamma. Republican. Roman Catholic. Home: 1050 Road 214 Carpenter WY 82054 Office: PO Box 287 Cheyenne WY 82001

CROWLEY, ELLEN MARION, psychologist; b. Glen Ridge, N.J., Dec. 8, 1946; d. John Francis and Marion Theresa C.; B.S., U. Pitts., 1967; M.A., Fairleigh Dickinson U., 1974; Ed.S., Seton Hall U., 1982. Sch. psychologist, Cumberland County, N.J., 1974-79, dir. spl. services, 1979-80; psychologist, chmn. Bridgewater (N.J.)-Raritan High Sch., 1980-81; pediatric psychologist Urban Hosp., Newark, 1981—, Child Devel. Ctr. of United Hosps., Newark, 1981—; marriage and family counselor; adviser Neofite. Mem. Am. Psychol. Assn., N.J. Psychol. Assn., N.J. Acad. Psychology. Home: 166 Broughton Ave Bloomfield NJ 07003 Office: 15 S 9th St Newark NJ 07107

CROWLEY, PATRICIA CARON, civic worker, travel agy. exec.; b. Chgo.; d. O.J. and Marietta (Higman) Caron; A.B., Trinity Coll. 1936; student Sorbonne, Paris, France 1935, Litt.D. St. Mary's Coll. 1961; m. Patrick F. Crowley, Oct. 16, 1937; children—Patricia, Mary Anne, Patrick, Catherine, Theresa. Pres., Space Inc. travel agy. Chgo.; dir. CaronnInternat. Pres. Internat. Confedn. of Christina Family Movements, 1949-78; pres. Chgo. Internat. Visitors Center 1972-75; mem. women's bd. Cath. Interracial Council 1961-65; co-organizer Wilmette Human Relations Com. 1963; bd. dirs. Found. for Internat. Cooperation1960—, Nat. Conf. Religion and Race 1963, World Lay Congress, Rome 1957, 67; mem. Spl. Commn. of Pope Paul VI to Study Population Problems; sec., chmn. Little Bros. of the Poor, Chgo. Trustee, Citizens Info. Service, Chgo. Mem. nat. bd. dirs. Women for McCarthy 1968. Recipient Magnificat medal Mundelein Coll. 1962; co-recipient Laetare medal Notre Dame U. 1966. Mem. The Family Inst. Chgo., UN Assn. Chgo., Chgo. Friends of the Pub. Library (pres. 1977-79). Contbr. articles to profl. jours. Home: 175 E Delaware St Chicago IL 60611 Office: Space Inc Travel 875 N Michigan Ave Chicago IL 60611

CROWLEY, REIDUN MARIE, electric utility mgr.; b. Bergen, Norway, July 29, 1945; came to U.S., 1957, naturalized, 1962; d. Reidar and Konny Fammestad; B.A. in Home Econs., U. Wash., 1968, edn. cert., 1968; m. David N. Crowley, Dec. 6, 1969; 1 dau., Britt Lindsey. Home economist Puget Sound Power & Light Co., Bellevue, Wash., 1969-76, energy info. supr., 1976-77, mgr. energy info., 1977-78, mgr. edn. and consumer relations, 1980, corp. planning adminstr., 1980-81, mgr. conservation services, 1981—. Recipient Seattle Salute award Seattle Conv. and Visitors Bur., 1976, Alma award Assn. Home Appliance Mfgrs., 1976. Mem. Elec. Women's Round Table (chpt. achievement award 1975, nat. pres. 1975-78), Home Economists in Bus. (internat. relations chmn. 1974-75), Am. Home Econs. Assn., Internat. Microwave Power Inst., Soc. Consumer Affairs Profls. N.W. Electric Power Assn., Seattle C. of C., Bellevue C. of C., Washington State Home Econs. Assn. Address: 13456 64th Terr Kirkland WA 98033

CROWLY, MARY, home furnishing co. exec.; b. Slater, Mo., Apr. 1, 1915; d. L.. and Mrs. Weaver; student U. Ark., 1931-32, So. Meth. U., 1940-41; L.H.D., Grand Canyon Coll., 1976; m. Joseph Carter, May 4, 1932; children—Donald J., Ruth Carter Shanahan; m. 2d, David M. Crowley, Apr. 17, 1948. Accountant, Republic Ins. Co., 1941-46, Purse Furniture Co., 1946-50; unit mgr. Stanley Home Products, 1950-54; sales mgr. World Gift Co., 1954-55; v.p. in charge sales, 1955-57; with Home Interiors and Gifts, Dallas, 1957—, now pres., sales mgr.; bd. dirs. Direct Selling Assn.; lectr. Am. Mgmt. Assn. Seminars, So. Meth. U. Bd. dirs. Inst. for Blind, Billy Graham Evangelistic Assn., Am. Cancer Soc., Dallas Services for Visually Impaired Children; trustee Dallas Bapt. Coll. mem. adv. bd. Community Chest. Recipient Oscar of Salesmanship Am. Salesmaster Orgn., 1966; named Mature Woman of Year, Altrusa Club, 1969; Woman of Year Baylor Univ., 1973. Mem. Dallas C. of C., Am. Mgmt. Assn. Republican. Baptist. Author: Moments with Mary; Be Somebody; Think Mink, 1976. Contbr. articles to profl. jours. Office: 4550 Spring Valley Rd Dallas TX 75240

CROWNINGSHIELD, SHARON KAY, savs. and loan assn. exec.; b. Cedar Rapids, Iowa, Dec. 1, 1948; d. Marvin John Henry and Maxine Harriet (Barlow) Rathje; student in acctg. Mesa Jr. Coll., 1974-75; m. Gary Crowningshield, Sept. 9, 1967; children—Scott, Vicki. With Home Fed. Savs. & Loan Assn., San Diego, 1968—, mgr., 1974-80, v.p., asst. controller, 1980—, mem. polit. action coms. for fed. and state, 1980—. Mem. Fin. Mgrs. Soc. for Savs. and Loan Assn. (sec.). Office: 701 Broadway Suite 900 San Diego CA 91101

CROWTHER, SUZANNE DELEFOSSE, info. scientist, translator; b. Paris, Feb. 21, 1934; came to U.S., 1955, naturalized, 1957; d. Marcel and Jeanne (Thevenot) Delefosse; Baccalaureate in Philosophy and Langs., U. Paris, 1953; postgrad. London U., 1953-54, Berlitz Sch., Italy, 1957-58, Poitiers France U., 1965, U. Md. at Pirmasens, Germany, 1967; m. Lloyd Ridgeway Crowther, Jan. 11, 1980; children by previous marriage—Anne Elizabeth Osborne, Marc James Osborne. Accounts supr. French Social Security, Paris, 1955; tchr. French Berlitz Sch. Langs., Verona, Italy, 1957-58; librarian Spl. Services Libraries, U.S. Army, Poitiers, France, 1964-65; spl. tech. library asst. Goddard Space Flight Center, Greenbelt, Md., 1969, John I. Thompson & Co., Washington, 1969-70; librarian Flight Safety Found., Arlington, Va., 1970-71; rail info. specialist Nat. Acad. Scis., Washington, 1971—, translator hwy. engring., 1977—, urban transit specialist, 1981—. Mem. AAAS, N.Y. Acad. Scis., Am. Translators Assn., Internat. Platform Assn., U.S. Coast Guard Aux. Office: 2101 Constitution Ave NW Washington DC 20418

CROXFORD, LYNNE LOUISE, social services adminstr.; b. Schenectady, N.Y., Nov. 9, 1947; d. Frederick William and Elizabeth Elger (Irish) C.; B.A., Kalamazoo Coll., 1969; M.P.A., Wayne State U., 1975; m. Daniel Roderick Talhelm; 1 son, Alan Frederick. Caseworker dept. social service County of Calhoun, Battle Creek, Mich., 1969-70; caseworker, supr. County of Oakland, Pontiac, Mich., 1970-76; program specialist Mich. Dept. Social Services, Lansing, 1976-78; exec. coordinator for programming Mich. State Planning Council for Devel. Disabilities, 1978-79; staff coordinator Gov. Com. on Unification of Public Mental Health System, Lansing, 1979-80; dir. dept. social service County of Ingham, Lansing, 1980—; adv. Mich. Assn. Non-Profit Residential Facilities, 1976-78. Trustee, Unitarian Universalist Ch. of Greater Lansing, 1979—, v.p., 1980—. Mem. Am. Soc. Public Adminstrn. (trustee chpt.), Assn. Mental Health Adminstrs., Michigan County Social Services Assn., Detroit Inst. Arts. Contbr. in field. Home: 531 Gainsborough St East Lansing MI 48823 Office: 930 W Holmes Rd Lansing MI 48910

CROY, HAZEL CATHERINE, nurse; b. Chgo., Sept. 30, 1925; d. Eugene Clyde and Dorothy Ella (Meyer) Cory; R.N., Wesley Meml. Hosp., Chgo., 1946; B.A., Judson Coll., Elgin, Ill., 1971; M.S. in Nursing, No. Ill. U., DeKalb, 1974; m. Vernon Dale Croy, Oct. 19, 1946; children—Carol, Paul, Kathy. Staff nurse hosps. in Ohio, Colo. and Ill., 1946-55; office nurse, 1959-72; public health nurse adv. adult day care centers Mass. Dept. Public Welfare, Boston, 1974—; bd. dirs. Hospice of Mass. WHO fellow, 1981. Mem. Am. Nurses Assn., Mass. Nurses Assn., Am. Public Health Assn. Methodist. Editor: Resource, nat. newsletter for adult day care. Home: 21 Rice Rd Maynard MA 01754

CROYLE, BARBARA ANN, oil co. exec.; b. Knoxville, Tenn., Oct. 22, 1949; d. Charles Evans and Myrtle Elizabeth (Kellam) C.; B.A. cum laude in Sociology, Coll. William and Mary, 1971; cert. corp. tax and securities law Inst. Paralegal Tng., 1971; J.D., U. Colo., 1975; cert. program mgmt. devel. Colo. Women's Coll., 1980; postgrad. U. Denver, 1982—. Admitted to Colo. bar, 1976; paralegal firm Holland & Hart, Denver, 1972-73; law clk. Colo. Ct. Appeals, Denver, summer 1976; asso. firm Shaw Spangler & Roth, Denver, 1976-77; title analyst Petro-Lewis Corp., Denver, after 1977, now supr. acquisitions/lands; tchr. oil and gas law Colo. Paralegal Inst., 1978, 79; arbitrator Am. Arbitration Assn.; vol. arbitrator Better Bus. Bur. Bd. dirs., vol. mediator Denver Center Dispute Resolution; bd. dirs. Women and Bus. Enterprises, Inc.; vol. Legal Info. Center, YWCA-Colo. Women's Bar. Recipient Community Services award Petro-Lewis Corp., 1981. Mem. Am. Bar Assn., Colo. Bar Assn., Denver Bar Assn., Colo. Women's Bar Assn., Exec. and Profl. Women's Council, Denver Assn. Petroleum Landmen, Nat. Assn. Female Execs. Home: 1835 S Linden Way Denver CO 80224 Office: 717 17th St Denver CO 80202

CRULL, ANNA WELCH, chem. cons. co. exec.; b. Centerville, Miss., Oct. 30, 1934; d. George Ashbel and Marian Jones Welch; B.S., U. Miss., 1955; M.S., U. Mo., 1959; m. Carroll Marshall Crull, Dec. 18, 1954; children—Frank, Wayne. Mem. research and devel. staff Redstone Arsenal and instr. U. Ala., Huntsville, 1959-69; pres. Chem. Tech. Cons., Houston, 1970—; offshore evaluator, Norway. Mem. Am. Chem. Soc., Soc. Petroleum Engrs., Sigma Xi. Methodist. Editor Energy Mag. (organizer Internat. Energy Conf.); contbg. editor and co-mgr. Enhanced Energy Recovery, Applied Genetics News.

CRUM, KAY MCDONALD, mktg. cons.; b. Greeneville, Tenn., Sept. 16, 1935; d. John Kidwell and Ina Frances (Reeser) McDonald; student Hiwassee Coll., 1954, Steed Bus. Coll., 1955, E. Tenn. State U., 1970-71, U. Tenn., 1977; m. Daniel R. Crum, Aug. 18, 1956; children—Debra Kay, Darren Russell, David Michael. With Formex div. Huyck Corp., Greeneville, 1961-81, mktg. communications mgr., 1977-79, mktg. communications mgr. forming and drying div., 1978-81; pres., owner CEI Mktg. Cons., Greeneville, Tenn., 1981—; lectr. in field. Publicity chmn. United Way bd. dirs., 1963-77; bd. dirs. Greene County Mental Health Assn., 1974-77; charter mem. Formex Employees Credit Union, 1964; founder Greeneville City Employees Credit Union, 1966. Recipient awards Nat. Small Bus. Adminstrn., 1977, Lions, 1977; Fosdick award Jour. TAPPI, 1981, others. Mem. Internat. Mktg. Communications Group, Paper Industry Mgmt. Assn., TAPPI, Assn. Indsl. Advertisers, Tri-Cities Metro Advt. Fedn., Nat. Assn. Female Execs., Am. Advt. Fedn. Republican. Clubs: Greene County Republican Women, Ladies of Elk. Contbr. articles to profl. jours.

CRUMBAKER, MARY KATHRYN (MRS. WILLIAM GOODMAN WILLIAMSON), bus. coll. exec.; b. Gt. Falls, Mont.; d. Calvin and Kathryn Elizabeth (Harbaugh) Crumbaker; student U. Mont., 1939, Southwestern U. at Memphis, 1942-43, Whitman Coll., 1939-41; B.S., U. Oreg., 1946; postgrad. Hochschule for Music, Vienna, Austria, 1947-48; M.Ed., Oreg. State U., 1966; Ph.D., Nat. Christian U. Dallas, 1974; m. William Goodman Williamson, Dec. 17, 1941 (dec. Oct. 1970); children—James Calvin, Albert Jerome, Kathryn Erilda. Sec., exec. sec. Granada (Miss.) Elem. Sch., also U.S. C.E., 1941-44; substitute sec. U. Oreg., 1944-46; head comml. studies Internat. Trade Coll., Chgo., 1948-51; tchr. Mich. Dept. Rehab., Am. Legion Tb Hosp., Battle Creek, 1952-53; tchr. U.S. Army, Kokura, Japan, 1954-56; tchr. Clark Bus. Coll., Topeka, 1956-58; charm sch. dir., dir. tng. Eugene (Oreg.) Bus. Coll. 1959-70, mgr., corp. sec.-treas., 1970—, pres., 1974—; prof. U. System Found., Ltd., Beliz City, Beliz, Nat. U., Houston; lectr., Am. econ. system and music Austro-Am. Soc., Vienna, 1946-48. Mem. exec. bd. S.W. Oreg. Mus. Sci. and Industry, 1972-75; den mother Oreg. Trail council Boy Scouts Am., 1959-69; chmn. West Univ. Neighborhood, 1981; mem. Neighborhood Leaders Council, 1981; treas. Eugene WCTU, 1980-82; precinct committeeman Republican party, 1960—; pres. Central Lane Rep. Women, 1970. Named Troop Mother of Yr. Boy Scouts Am., 1971. Mem. Nat. Fedn. Bus. and Profl. Women's Clubs, Am. Bus. Women, Am. Inst. Profl. Cons., Rubicon Soc., Eugene Bus. and Profl. Women's Club (pres. 1966, 79), DAR, Daus. of Nile, Am. Forestry Assn., Nat. Rifle Assn., PEO, Beta Gamma Sigma, Mu Phi Epsilon. Clubs: Order Eastern Star (musician), White Shrine of Jerusalem (musician), Order of Amaranth (musician; condr. 1982-83), Clubs: Eugene City (life mem.), Zonta, Dial (pres. Eugene 1973-74). Author: Typing with Less Than 2 Hands, 1962. Home: 1031 Mill St Eugene OR 97401 Office: 383 E 11th St Eugene OR 97401

CRUMBO, MINISA, artist; b. Tulsa, Sept. 2, 1942: d. Woodrow and Lillian (Hogue) C.; student Tex. Western U., El Paso, 1961-62, U. Colo., Boulder, 1970-71, Taos (N.Mex.) Acad. Fine Arts, 1972-74, Sch. Visual Arts, N.Y.C., 1974-75, Wasatch (Utah) Acad.; children—Woody Carter, Chris Carter. One-woman shows: Gilcrease Inst. Am. History and Art, Tulsa, 1976, Tulsey Town Gallery, Tulsa, 1975, USSR, 1978-79, Roy Clark Ranch Party-TV Spl., 1976, Pottawatomie Agrl. and Cultural Center, Shawnee, Okla., 1977, Okla. Gov.'s Spl. Showing, 1976, Adobe Gallery, Las Vegas, 1977; traveling exhbn. Indian Art Show, U. Oreg., 1977; other exhbns.; Pushkin Mus., Moscow, Montreux (Switzerland) Jazz Festival, 1979, Harwelden, Tulsa, 1979, Oklahoma City U., 1981, Independence (Kans.) Community Coll., 1981; represented in permanent collections at Heard Mus., Phoenix, Gilcrease Inst. Am. History and Art, Philbrook Art Center, Tulsa, U. Tulsa Art Center, Pushkin Mus., Moscow, Wasatch Acad., Oklahoma City U., Baker U., Baldwin, Kans., Independence (Kans.) Community Coll., also pvt. collections in U.S. and Europe; guest artist instr. Taos Pueblo Day Sch. Center. Recipient Graphics award for pencil drawing Creek Woman, 29th Am. Indian Exhbn. at Philbrook Art Center; Disting. Alumni award Wasatch Acad., 1980; Disting. Service award Baker U., 1982. Mem. Native Am. Ch. Home: 515 N 2d St Independence KS 67301 Office: 3225 S Norwood St Tulsa OK 74135

CRUM DE GROOT, SUSAN LOUISE, ins. agt.; b. Queens, N.Y., Mar. 16, 1953; d. James Robert and Louise Madeline (Yaeger) Crum; B.S. in Psychology and Religion (Pompton Lake Rotary scholar, 1971; Nat. Ladies Aux. scholar 1971), Evangel Coll., 1975; M.A. in Psychology, Montclair State Coll., 1978; postgrad. Rutgers U., 1979—; m. Bruce Anthony De Groot, Aug. 11, 1973; 1 son, Ross Hamilton. Vol. counselor, instr. Good Samaritan Boys Ranch, Springfield, N.J., 1975; income maintenance worker Passaic County (N.J.) Welfare Bd., 1975-76; grad. asst. psychology dept. Montclair (N.J.) State Coll., 1976-77, acting dir. second careers program, 1977; adj. Kean Coll., Union, N.J., 1978; devel. counselor Counseling Services, Nutley, N.J., 1977-78; coordinator career decision program Bergen Community Coll., Paramus, N.J., 1978-80; spl. agt. Prudential, Wayne, N.J., 1980—; owner Oxford Ins. Agy., 1982—. Pres., Opponents of Hunger, 1970-71; patient companion Essex County Mental Hosp., 1971-72; vol. child aide St. Mary's Hosp., Passaic, N.J., 1976-77. Mem. Am. Psychol. Assn. (asso.), N.J. Coll. and Univ. Coalition Women's Edn., Assn. Adult Edn. N.J., Psi Chi. Mem. Assembly of God Ch. Home: 53 Grist Mill Rd Wanaque NJ 07465 Office: 573 Valley Rd Wayne NJ

CRUMP, MARJORIE VIRGINIA DODSON, univ. adminstr.; b. Smithville, Tex., Sept. 12, 1924; d. P.J. and Marjorie (Dietz) Dodson; B.A., Baylor U., 1946. M.A., 1962; m. Stephen Henry Crump, Jr., Oct. 24, 1947. Adminstrv. asst. to librarian Baylor U., Waco, Tex., 1946-60, research asst. devel. dept., 1960-61, asst. dean women, 1961-64, asst. dean students, 1964-72, asso. dean students, 1972-80, dean student life programs, 1980-81, asst. v.p. student affairs, 1981-82, emeritus dean student life, 1982—, chmn. univ. council, 1972-74. Mem. Women's council Waco Symphony Assn.; exec. bd. Wesley Found. at Baylor U.; bd. dirs. Bluebonnet council Girl Scouts U.S.A., 1975-77; bd. dirs. Heart of Tex. br. Arthritis Found., 1977—, pres., 1979-81. Named Outstanding Alumna, Baylor U., 1966, recipient H.H. Reynolds award for disting. service, 1982. Mem. Nat. (nominating com. 1971-72, 77-81, com. concerns for students 1972-74, univ. sect. adv. council 1975-77), Tex. (membership chmn. 1963-64, sec. 1964-66, 2d v.p. 1967-69, program chmn., pres. 1969-71) assns. women deans and counselors, AAUW (bull. editor Waco br. 1962-64, 1st v.p. Waco 1966-67, pres. 1967-68), Waco C. of C. (vice chmn. youth council 1972-73, mem. image com. 1976-78), Friends Waco Public Library, Historic Waco Found., Waco Art Center, Angel Flight, Mortar Bd., Phi Gamma Nu, Alpha Lambda Delta, Kappa Alpha Theta. Baptist. Home: Route 10 Box 368 Waco TX 76708

CRUNICK, HELEN LOUISE BARTLEY, educator; b. Parkersburg, W.Va., May 24, 1929; d. Adam Harvey and Beatrice Elizabeth (Watts) Bartley; B.A., U. Pitts., 1969, M.Ed., Reading Specialist, 1970; m. Michael Leonard Grunick, Aug. 28, 1949; children—Michael Leonard, Lisa Chancellor, Eric Stephen. Reading specialist Houston (Pa.) Sch. Dist., 1970-74, dir. Right to Read program, 1974-76, career program developer, 1976-81, dir. Quest program, drug and alcohol prevention, 1981, reading supr. Chartiers, 1981—; mem. reading council Intermediate Unit I Pa.; workshop leader, cons. in field. Chmn., Washington (Pa.) Mayor's Beautification and Revitalization Com., 1980-82; initiator City of Washington (Pa.) Flag Com., 1980-81; moderator First Baptist Ch. Washington, 1982, also trustee. Mem. Internat. Reading Assn., Keystone Reading Assn., Three Rivers Reading Council, Quest, Inc. (charter), AAUW, Bus. and Profl. Women, Washington (Pa.) Opera Assn., Monday Music Club Delta Kappa Gamma, Beta Zeta. Home: 603 N Main St Washington PA 15301

CRUPI, FRANCESCA A., business ofcl.; b. Mileto, Italy, Mar. 26, 1952; came to U.S., 1956, naturalized, 1958; d. Nicholas R. and Maria A. (Ruffa) C.; grad. in liberal arts Ottawa (Kans.) U., 1971. N.E. dist. mgr. Mary Quant Cosmetics, N.Y.C., 1972-73; post prodn. coordinator Winkler Video Assos., Inc., N.Y.C., 1974-76; dir. ops. Nat. Video Center, N.Y.C., 1976-80; ops. mgr. Devlin Prodns., Inc., N.Y.C.,

1980—; ops. mgr. Magno Video. Mem. Nat. Assn. Female Execs., Nat. Acad. TV Arts and Scis. Democrat. Roman Catholic. Home: 279 E 44th St New York NY 10017 Office: 212 W 48th St New York NY 10036

CRUSE, IRMA BELLE RUSSELL, writer, ret. telephone co. exec.; b. Hackneyville, Ala., May 3, 1911; d. Charles Henry and Nellie Dunn (Ledbetter) Russell; student Birmingham-So. Coll., 1927-28; corr. student U. Chgo., U. Wis., U. Minn., intermittently 1958-68; A.B., U. Ala., 1976; M.A. in English, Samford U.; m. Jesse Clyde Cruse, Dec. 22, 1931; children—Allan Baird, Howard Russell. With So. Bell and successor South Central Bell, Birmingham, Ala., 1928-44, 54-76, pub. relations supr., 1965-68, rate supr., 1968-76; free lance writer, 1956—. Bd. dirs. Festival of Arts, Birmingham, 1970-73, Birmingham Council Christian Edn.; v.p. Birmingham Council Clubs, 1973-74; pres. Jefferson County Radio and TV Council, 1971-72; mem. Gov.'s Commn. Employment of Handicapped. Recipient numerous awards including Freedoms Found. award, 1967-69; Beautiful Activist, 1972; nominated Women of Yr., Birmingham, 1971, 72, 74-76, 82, Woman of Achievement Met. Bus. and Profl. Women's Club, 1970-71. Mem. Birmingham Bus. Communicators, Ala. Writers' Conclave (pres. 1973-74), Birmingham Bus. and Profl. Women (pres. 1970-71), Women in Communications (pres. 1970-71), Birmingham Bus. Communicators (pres. 1968-69), Telephone Pioneers Am. (editor newsletter 1970-74), Ala. State Poetry Soc. (program chmn. 1972-74, editor newsletter 1976-78), Women's C. of C. (2d v.p. 1978—), Ala. Bapt. Hist. Commn., Freedoms Found. of Valley Forge (Birmingham Area chpt.), Birmingham Geneal. Soc., Salvation Army Women's Aux., Women's C. of C., Nat. Soc. Am. Pen Women, Sigma Tau Delta, Phi Kappa Phi, Sigma Tau Delta. Club: Quota of Birmingham (pres. 1976-77). Contbr. articles to various publs. Home: 136 Memory Ct Birmingham AL 35213

CRUZ, MIRIAM COSCA, psychiatrist; b. Philippines, Jan. 18, 1946; d. Raymundo Mota and Sofia Veloso (Martin) Cosca; B.S., U. Philippines, 1965, M.D., 1970; m. Paulino S. Cruz, July 19, 1970; children—Jonathan, Christian, Maria Elena. Straight pediatric intern, 1970-71; sch. physician, pediatrician well baby clinics Balt. Health Dept., 1971-73; resident in psychiatry SUNY, Stony Brook, 1973-76; attending psychiatrist Central Islip (N.Y.) Psychiat. Center, 1976—, treas. med. staff, 1982-83; cons. psychiatrist Crest Hall, 1979—, Oak Hollow Nursing Home, 1979—; practice medicine specializing in psychiatry, Lake Ronkonkoma, N.Y., 1979—. Mem. Am. Psychiat. Assn. Home: 35 Homestead Circle Hauppauge NY 11788 Office: 276 Smithtown Blvd Lake Ronkonkoma NY 11779

CSERESZNYE, GEORGINA MARIE, ednl. adminstr.; b. Detroit, June 27, 1944; d. George Armand and Dorothy Elizabeth (McKee) Daubresse; B.A., Eastern Mich. U., 1966, M.A., 1969; Ed.D., Wayne State U., Detroit, 1980; children—Lisa Marie, Renee Lynn. Mem. staff Wayne-Westland (Mich.) Community Schs., 1966—, co-prin. P.D. Graham Elementary Sch., 1978-80, exec. asst. to supt. schs., 1980—. Bd. dirs. Wayne-Westland Found.; v.p. Wayne-Westland Arts Assn., 1981-82. Mem. Nat. Assn. Sch. Prins., Mich. Assn. Sch. Adminstrs., Mich. Elementary and Middle Sch. Prins. Assn., Mich. Council Women Ednl. Adminstrn., Wayne C. of C., Alpha Delta Kappa, Phi Delta Kappa. Roman Catholic. Contbr. articles to profl. jours. Home: 37593 Hillcrest Dr Wayne MI 48184 Office: 36745 Marquette St Westland MI 48185

CUDDY, MARIAN PAGE, editor; b. Covington, Ky., Aug. 23, 1943; d. Clyde R. and Marian G. (von Beushausen) Tipton; B.A., Ohio State U., 1962. Dir. subs. rights G.P. Putnam's Sons, N.Y.C., 1972-75; editor-in-chief, exec. v.p. Berkley Pub. Co., N.Y.C., 1975-78; asst. pub. Simon & Schuster, N.Y.C., 1978-79; sr. editor Avon Books, N.Y.C., 1979—. Mem. Women's Media Group. Home: 34 Perry St New York NY 10014 Office: 959 8th Ave New York NY 10019

CUDJOE, VERA MARIE, artistic dir.; b. Trinidad, W.I., May 19, 1928; d. Venice Adolphus and Carmen Anastasia (Joseph) C.; R.N., Mile End Hosp., 1955; student Ryerson Poly. Inst., 1961-62, U. Toronto, 1964. Registered nurse, Can., 1963-68; dist. mgr. sales Can. Security Mgmt., 1968-71; founder, artistic dir. Black Theatre Can., Toronto, Ont., 1972—. Mem. parish council St. Basils Roman Catholic Ch., 1976. Recipient Canadian Silver Jubilee award for cultural work, 1977, Can. Council Arts award, 1978. Mem. Theatre Ont. (Toronto), Assn. Canadian TV and Radio Artists, Canadian Actors Equity Assn., Ont. Black History Soc., NBCC, AMORC. Contbr. poems to The New Voices, Landscape, 1977, One Out of Many. Home: 201 Sherbourne St Apt 905 Toronto ON M5A 3X2 Canada Office: Black Theatre Can 109 Vaughan Rd Suite 1 Toronto ON M6C 2L9 Canada

CUELLAR, LOURDES MATIANA, pharmacist; b. San Antonio, Oct. 10, 1950; d. Celso and Matiana (Medina) Cuellar; student St. Mary's U., 1968-70; B.S., U. Houston, 1973, M.S., 1979. Pharmacy intern/extern VA Hosp., Houston, 1971-73; relief pharmacist Foley's Pharmacy, Pasadena, Tex., 1973-74; staff pharmacist Inst. for Rehab. and Research, Houston, 1974-79, dir. pharmacy services, 1979-82, asst. adminstr. clin. services, 1982—; adj. instr. U. Houston, Coll. Pharmacy, 1979—. Active Big Sister in Assn. for Advancement of Mexican Ams., 1980—. Mem. Am. Soc. Hosp. Pharmacists, Tex. Soc. Hosp. Pharmacists, Houston-Galveston Area Soc. Hosp. Pharmacists, Kappa Epsilon, Alpha Sigma Tau. Roman Catholic. Contbr. articles to profl. jours. Home: 6666 Chetwood St Apt 231 Houston TX 77081 Office: 1333 Moursund Ave Houston TX 77030

CULBERT, ALICE AINBINDER, sculptor; b. Chgo.; d. Max and Anna (Rozet) Ainbinder; student U. Chgo., 1929-31, Art Inst. Chgo., 1931-33; m. Robert Richheimer, Sept. 15, 1933 (div. 1968); children—Robert H., Laurie Ann Richheimer Bender (dec.), Kathie Ruth Richheimer Cohen; m. 2d, Richard E. Culbert, Feb. 1, 1970 (dec.). Artist-in-residence Valparaiso U., 1961; tchr. sculpture North Shore Art League, 1971-74, Urban Gateways, Chgo., 1974-78; one-woman exhbns. include: Chgo. Public Library, 1960, Valparaiso (Ind.) U., 1961, Judson Community Coll., Elgin, Ill., 1971, One Ill. Center, 1978; 2-person show Art Inst. Chgo., 1978; group shows include: Art Inst. Chgo., 1965, State Bldg., Springfield, Ill., 1968, U. Ill. Med. Center, 1969, 1st Chgo. Invitational Sculpture Exhbt., 1974, Sears Tower, Chgo., 1978, Harmon Gallery, Naples, Fla., 1978; prin. works include 24 foot sculpture B'nai Torah Temple, Highland Park, Ill., sculpture in Peace Center, Hiroshima, Japan, 14 foot sculpture Community Center, New Orleans, 10 foot sculpture in lobby Elgin (Ill.) Community Coll., 12 foot sculpture Woodstock (Ill.) Cultural Center, Rosary Coll., River Forest, Ill., Kankakee (Ill.) Community Coll. Recipient prize New Horizons in Ill., 1973; 1st prize Women in Art, N. Shore Art League, 1977, Longboat Key Art Center, 1978. Mem. Artists Equity San Diego, Chgo. Arts Council, Arts Club Chgo. Address: 1596 Vista Claridad La Jolla CA 92037 *

CULBERTSON, BARBARA JEAN, bus. services exec.; b. Kirksville, Mo., July 3, 1943; d. Warren and Ruth Genevieve (Mervin) Dawson; B.A., U. Mo., 1964; 1 son, Michael David. Owner, mgr. Mission Bus. Services, Shawnee Mission, Kans., 1978—, also office sales mgr., v.p., sec. Deay Industries, Inc., 1981—; data rev. technician Social Security Adminstrn., 1974-78; conf. leader Woman and Bus. Regional Conf., 1980. Election clk. and judge, 1964, 66; active Mothers March of Dimes, 1980-81; v.p. Am. Legion Aux., 1968; mem. Republican Presdl. Task Force, 1982; sec., regional del. Pres.'s White House Conf. on Small Bus., 1980. Mem. Johnson-Wyandotte Life Underwriters Assn. (exec. sec.), Nat. Assn. Women Bus. Owners (treas. Mid-Am. chpt.), Kansas City C. of C., Mission C. of C., Bus. and Profl. Women's Assn. (sec. 1972), Legal Secs. Assn. Presbyterian. Home: 10404 W 70th St Shawnee KS 66203 Office: 5000 Johnson Dr Suite 102 Shawnee Mission KS 66205

CULBERTSON, KATHERYN CAMPBELL, state librarian; b. Tom's Creek, Va., Aug. 14, 1920; d. Robert Fugate and Mary E.V. Campbell (Leonard) C.; B.S., E. Tenn. State U., 1940; B.S. in Library Sci., George Peabody Library Sch., 1942; J.D., YMCA Night Law Sch., 1968. Librarian, Bur. Ships Tech. Library, U.S. Navy Dept., Washington, 1945-49, 51-53; librarian Lincoln Elem. Sch., Kingsport, Tenn., 1949-50, 50-51; librarian Regional Library, Tenn. State Library and Archives, Johnson City, 1953-61; dir. extension services library Met. Govt. Nashville and Davidson County, 1961-71; Tenn. state librarian and archivist, 1972—; admitted to Tenn. bar, 1969; since practiced in Nashville. Mem. library com. Pres.'s Com. Employment of Handicapped, 1966—; mem. library com. Nat. Bus. and Profl. Women's Found., 1968-70; pres. Tenn. Fedn. Bus. and Profl. Women's Clubs, Inc., 1974-75. Mem. ABA, Tenn. Bar Assn., ALA, Southeastern Library Assn., Tenn. Library Assn., DAR. Republican. Club: Bus. and Profl. Women's (pres. Nashville 1970-71). Contbr. to Ency. of Edn. Office: 403 7th Ave N Nashville TN 37219

CULBREATH, ELIZABETH JOSEPHINE, chem. cleaning co. exec.; b. Portland, Tenn., Jan. 7, 1927; d. John Garnett and Ola (Hardin) White; student Vol. Community Coll., 1980-82; m. Bob R. Culbreath, Oct. 21, 1944; children—Georgia, Robert, Elizabeth Ann. Sec., A&P Tea Co., 1944-50; exec. sec. Indpls. Morris Plan, 1950-56; bookkeeper Whittington Fabricating Co., 1956-59; bookkeeper Imperial Fabricating Co., Portland, Tenn., 1964, sec.-treas., 1964-78; sec.-treas. Imperial Chem. Cleaning, Inc., Portland, 1978—; partner, bookkeeper Culbreath Dairy Farms, Cottontown, Tenn., 1979—; acct. Fleet Design & Engring., Inc., Portland, 1980—; owner, operator E. J. C. Real Estate, Portland, 1981—. Mem. civic adv. bd. Highland Hosp. Mem. Nat. Assn. Exec. Secs., Sumner County Bd. Realtors. Baptist. Clubs: Blue Grass Country, Silver Springs Country, Order Eastern Star. Home: Rural Route 2 Cottontown TN 37048 Office: PO Box 429 Portland TN 37148

CULBREATH, MYRNA LOU, author; b. Dodge City, Kans., June 1, 1938; d. Noel Galen and Anna Leota (Lickteig) Culbreath; B.A. cum laude, Colo. U., 1960, postgrad., 1961. Founder, mgr. Culbreath Schs., Colorado Springs, Colo., 1962, Los Angeles, 1980; books include: Culbreath School Phonics 44 Games and Methods; (with Sondra Marshak) The Price of the Phoenix, 1977; The Fate of the Phoenix, 1979; The Prometheus Design, 1982; (with S. Marshak and W. Shatner) Shatner: Where No Man..., 1980; editor: The Fire Bringer, 1971-73, Star Trek, The New Voyages, I, 1976, II, 1977. Founding mem., co author 1st platform Libertarian Party, 1972. Mem. Nat. Assn. Female Execs. Home: 1101 LaBoice Dr Glendale CA 91205

CULBRETH, MARTHA ELIZABETH, lawyer; b. Winston Salem, N.C., June 23, 1942; d. Marvin Trawick and Mildred Louise (Warren) C.; B.A., Berea Coll., 1964; LL.B., Vanderbilt U., 1967. Admitted to D.C. bar, 1968, Tenn. bar, 1974; atty. FTC, Washington, 1967-68; trial atty. TVA, Knoxville, Tenn., 1968-75, 76-81; counsel U.S. Senate Select Com. to Study Govtl. Activities with respect to Intelligence, Washington, 1975-76; dep. senate legal counsel U.S. Senate, Washington, 1981—. Trustee, Berea (Ky.) Coll., 1978-84, Pine Mountain (Ky.) Settlement Sch., 1980-84. Mem. AAUW, Fed. Bar Assn. (chpt. pres. 1972-73), Berea Coll. Alumni Assn. (pres. 1975-76). Methodist. Office: 1413 Dirksen Senate Office Bldg Washington DC 20510

CULL, LURA ELIZABETH, hosp. adminstr.; b. Sherman, Tex., Apr. 22, 1907; d. Emerson Ethridge and Grace Dawn (Hilger) Mathis; A.S., Southeastern State U., 1927; m. Robert O. Cull, May 9, 1929; children—Carol Elizabeth, Robert Emerson. Tchr. elem. sch., Frederick, Okla., 1927-33; dir. vols., public relations and social services Tillman County Meml. Hosp., Frederick, Okla., 1960-81; ret., 1981. Active ARC, Cancer Soc., Boy Scouts Am., Girl Scouts, U.S.A., United Way, Tillman County Youth Services; elder Presbyn. Ch., 1960, 80. Recipient Service award Frederick Lions Club, 1948. Mem. Okla. Soc. Dirs. Vols. (past pres.), Am. Soc. Dirs. Vol. Services, Okla. Public Relations Soc. (past pres.), PEO. Democrat. Club: Order Eastern Star. Home: 520 N 16th St Frederick OK 73542

CULLEN, JONNA LYNNE, govt. ofcl.; b. Memphis, Oct. 10, 1941; d. John Nolan, Jr. and Louise Bunnell (Shipp) C.; student U. Miss. Asst. Republican counsel rules com. U.S. Ho. of Reps., 1967-81; asso. dir. legis. affairs Office Mgmt. and Budget, 1981—. Mem. entertainment com. Nat. Rep. Club, 1968-81. Baptist. Home: 1300 Army Navy Dr Apt 209 Arlington VA 22202 Office: 243 Old Executive Office Bldg Washington DC 20503

CULLEN, KARON NUNNALLY, public relations co. exec.; b. Richmond, Va., Jan. 27, 1947; d. Moses Washington and Alice Maude (Emory) Nunnally; B.A., Mary Baldwin Coll., 1968; postgrad Radcliffe Coll. Pub. Sch., 1968. Dir. publicity Americana Hotels, Inc., N.Y.C., 1970-71; dir. public relations Princess Hotels Internat., N.Y.C., 1971-74; chmn. Cullen and Taylor, Ltd., N.Y.C., 1974-82; pres. Cullen and Casey, Ltd., N.Y.C., 1982—. Bd. dirs. Irvington House for Med. Research, N.Y.C. Mem. Public Relations Soc. Am., Soc. Am. Travel Writers (sec. N.Y.C. chpt.), Pride and Alarm (public relations corp. leaders N.Y.C.). Club: Doubles (N.Y.C.). Office: Cullen and Casey Ltd 232 Madison Ave New York NY 10016

CULLEN, SUSAN ELIZABETH, immunologist; b. N.Y.C., Jan. 12, 1944; d. Myles B. and Margaret (Krell) C.; B.S., Coll. Mt. St. Vincent, 1965 Ph.D., Albert Einstein Med. Coll., 1971; m. Benjamin D. Schwartz, June 19, 1974; children—Michael J., Daniel R. Research asso. Basel (Switzerland) Inst. Immunology, 1971-72, Albert Einstein Med. Coll., Bronx, 1972-74; vis. fellow Nat. Cancer Inst., Bethesda, Md., 1974-76; asst. prof. microbiology and immunology Washington U. Med. Sch., St. Louis, 1976-80; asso. prof., 1980—; mem. allergy and immunology study sect. NIH, 1980—. Leukemia Soc. Am. fellow, 1973-75; NIH fellow 1975-76, research career devel. awardee, 1977-82. Mem. AAAS, Am. Assn. Immunologists. Asso. editor Jour. Immunology, 1977—; editorial bd. Molecular Immunology, 1981—; contbr. articles to profl. jours. Office: Med Sch Washington U St Louis MO 63110

CULLINGFORD, HATICE SADAN, chem. engr.; b. Konya, Turkey, June 10, 1945; came to U.S., 1966, naturalized, 1971; d. Ahmet and Emine (Kadayifcioglu) Harmanci; student Middle E. Tech. U., 1962-66; B.S. with high honors, N.C. State U., 1969, Ph.D., 1974; m. Tod S. Johnson, Oct. 5, 1981. Statis. clk. Research Triangle Inst., 1966; reactor engr. U.S. AEC, Washington, 1973-75; spl. asst. ERDA, Washington, 1975; mech. engr. Dept. Energy, Washington, 1975-78; staff mem. Los Alamos Nat. Lab., 1978-82; engring. cons., Houston, 1982—; lectr. in field. Mem. U. N.Mex., Los Alamos curriculum review com., 1980. Recipient Woman's Badge, Tau Beta Pi, 1968, ERDA Spl. Achievement award, 1976; Cities Service fellow, 1969-72. Mem. Am. Nuclear Soc. (chmn. elect Trinity sect. 1981-82), Am. Inst. Chem. Engrs. (organizer, 1st chmn. No. N.Mex. club 1980-81), Am. Chem. Soc. (adviser), Am. Vacuum Soc., Internat. Assn. Hydrogen Energy, Phi Kappa Phi, Pi Mu Epsilon. Club: No. N.Mex. Chem. Engrs. Editor, author tech. reports; contbr. articles to profl. jours.; inventor in field.

CULLINS, DORIS CRAWFORD, ednl. adminstr.; b. Fate, Tex., Aug. 14, 1922; d. J. Reagan and Leila (Welch) Crawford; B.S. in Elem. Edn., East Tex. State U., 1943, M.E. in Elem. Edn., 1956; m. Walter Cullins, Jan. 31, 1953; 1 son, John W. Tchr. elem. schs., Ennis, Tex., 1943-46, Royse City, Tex., 1946-53, Rockwall, Tex., 1953-55, 60-73, Garland, Tex., 1958-60; instructional team leader Rockwall Elem. Sch., 1970-73; prin. Rockwall Elem. Sch., 1973—. Mem. Tex. Elem. Prins. and Suprs. Assn., Nat. Assn. Elem. Sch. Prins., Assn. Tex. Educators, Tex. Congress Parents and Tchrs. (hon. life), Friends of Library, Delta Kappa Gamma. Baptist. Club: Order Eastern Star. Home: 318 Highland Dr Rockwall TX 75087 Office: Route 3 Box 1215 Rockwall TX 75087

CULLITON, BARBARA JANE, journalist; b. Buffalo, May 2, 1943; d. Richard Joseph and Marion (Holmes) Culliton; A.B., Vassar Coll., 1965; m. Wallace K. Waterfall, Nov. 22, 1974. Reporter, Sci. News, Washington, 1965-70, Med. World News, 1970-71; reporter Science, 1972-79, news editor, 1979—. Recipient George Polk journalism award, 1982. Mem. Nat. Assn. Sci. Writers (pres. 1981—), Council for Advancement Sci. Writing (dir. 1976—). Office: Science 1515 Massachusetts Ave NW Washington DC 20005

CULLOM, DELORES MAE, histologist; b. Denton, Tex., Apr. 9, 1935; d. Noval P. and Gracie Mae (Oliver) Roach; student Tex. Christian U., 1959-62; m. Thomas Edward Cullom, Feb. 18, 1972; children—Juanita Hamilton, Aletha Ballenger. Histologist, Harris Hosp., Ft. Worth, 1956-66, Tex. Med. Labs., Ft. Worth, 1966-71, Ft. Worth Med. Lab., 1971-75; chief histologist Tex. Coll. Osteo., Ft. Worth, 1975—. Mem. N. Tex. Soc. Histologists, Am. Soc. Clin. Pathologists, Nat. Soc. Histologists, N. Tex. Soc. Histotechnologists. Home: 3050 Bird St Fort Worth TX 76111 Office: Camp Bowie at Montgomery Fort Worth TX 76111

CULLUM, JOAN M., psychotherapist; b. N.Y.C.; d. Rocco Michael and Teresa Delores (Drennan) Famileth; B.A., Coll. New Rochelle (N.Y.), 1957; M.A., Boston Coll., 1960; Ph.D., St. Andrews Internat. U., London, 1968; m. William H. Cullum, Sept. 7, 1963; children—Bill, Candace. Pvt. practice psychotherapy, Calif., 1974—; dir. clin. services San Fernando Valley Ednl. Center, Canoga Park, Calif., 1978—; mem. faculty Suffolk U., Boston, 1962-63, U. So. Calif., 1964-66, Calif. State U., Northridge, 1969-71, Moorpark (Calif.) Coll., 1972-77. Lic. psychotherapist, Calif. Mem. Am. Assn. Marriage and Family Therapists, Calif. Asssn. Marriage and Family Therapists, Am. Assn. Sex Educators and Therapists, So. Calif. Assn. Marriage and Family Therapists, Calabasas Hist. Soc., Psi Chi. Clubs: Calabas Park Country, Calabasas Park Swim and Tennis. Home: 23109 Park Contessa Calabasas Park CA 91302 Office: 4869 Topanga Canyon Blvd Suite 8 Woodland Hills CA 91364

CULOTTA, WINIFRED IMOGENE (JEANNE) RICHARDSON (MRS. JAMES J. CULOTTA), civic-philanthropic worker; b. Midway, Ala. Mar. 11, 1922; d. James Fred and Sybil Irene (Tucker) Richardson; grad. Draughons Bus. Coll., 1939-40; m. James Joseph Culotta, Apr. 18, 1942; children—James Joseph II, Sybil Richelle. Exec. sec., Hartford Life and Accident Ins. Co., Montgomery, Ala., 1940-41; exec. sec., personnel dept. Michoud USAF, New Orleans, 1943; pres. Home Builders Assn. Greater New Orleans Aux., 1954, 55, bd. dirs., 1953—; pres. Nat. Assn. Home Builders Women's Aux., 1966, bd. dirs., 1955, 62-82; bd. dirs. Lit. Study Group, 1975, Crippled Children's Hosp. Guild, 1974-75, The Pontalbans, 1976-78, Workers of Magnolia Sch. for Retarded, 1977-78; organizing pres., bd. dirs. East Jefferson Gen. Hosp. Aux., 1972-81; 2d and 3d v.p. bd. dirs. Womens Aux. Goodwill Industries, 1972—, pres., 1980-81; bd. dirs. Crippled Children's Hosp. Guild, 1969—; Lit. Study Group, 1972-81, St. Mary's Dominican Coll. Assos., 1975-79, Archbishop's Community Appeal, 1975—, Women's Aux. Eye and Ear Inst. La., 1975-79, corr. sec., 1979-80; bd. dirs. Sara Mayo Hosp. Guild, 1976-78, St. Charles Gen. Hosp. Aux., 1977, 80, East Jefferson Gen. Hosp. Found., 1977—, Inst. Human Understanding, 1979—, Sophie Gumbel Guild, 1979—, Les Quarante Ecoliers, 1979-82. Recipient ABC Radio award community service, 1966; Jefferson Parish Outstanding Woman award 1971, Great Lady award, 1977; named to Town & Country's Nationwide Honor Roll Vol. Women, 1979, Vol. Activist, 1980, one of Ten Outstanding Persons in Greater New Orleans, 1981. Democrat. Roman Catholic. Club: Metairie Woman's (dir. 1952-58, 67-72, 74-81, pres. 1968-69).

CULPEPPER, DOROTHY JUNE, aviation exec.; b. San Angelo, Tex., Aug. 30, 1933; d. James Ross and Mary Lena (Hooper) C.; student public schs., Jacksonville, Fla.; children—J. Michael Miller, Matthew T. Miller, Richard E. Miller. Sec. to junket masters Dunes Hotel, Las Vegas, Nev., 1971-72; asst. to Howard Hughes staff Summa Corp., Miami, Freeport, Bahamas, 1972-76; adminstrn. mgr. aviation div. Resorts Internat., North Miami, Fla., 1976—. Recipient Spl. award FAA, 1980. Mem. Nat. Assn. Female Execs. Democrat. Baptist. Home: 5830 SW 94th Ct Miami FL 33173 Office: 915 NE 125th St North Miami FL 33161

CULTON, KAREN JOYCE, research center adminstr.; b. Stillwater, Okla., Sept. 5, 1949; d. James Albert and Ethyl Joann (Boyce) Austell; cert. secretarial sci. Okla. State U., 1970, student, 1979—; m. Robert Mark Culton, May 28, 1972; 1 dau., Dana Gabrielle. Sec., C.E. Donart High Sch., Stillwater, Okla., 1966; with Okla. State U., Stillwater, 1968—, adminstrv. sec. Fluid Power Research Center, 1977-78, adminstrv. supr., 1978-80, adminstrv. asst., 1980—; alt. coordinator FES Inc., cons. in fluid power engring., 1979—. A.E. Scroggs scholar, 1967-68. Mem. Bus. and Profl. Women's Club (charter), Nat. Assn. Female Execs., Alpha Lambda Delta. Republican. Presbyterian. Home: 2420 N Park St Stillwater OK 74074 Office: 112 Fluid Power Research Center Okla State U Stillwater OK 74078

CULVER, DOROTHY CLARK, assn. exec.; b. San Antonio, Oct. 1, 1928; d. Thomas Lawrence and Rose Mary Clark; A.B., Barnard Coll., 1950; certificate Harvard-Radcliffe Sch. Bus. Adminstrn., 1956; M.A., Columbia U., 1964; m. Ralph J. Culver, Jan. 28, 1954 (dec.); 1 dau., Rosemary Clark. Personnel mgr. Bank of N.Y., 1956-59; v.p. Assn. of Pvt. Schs. and Colls., 1959-63; edn. cons. Assn. Jr. Leagues, 1965-66, 71-72; placement dir. Katherine Gibbs Sch., N.Y.C., 1966-71; dir. human resources Girl Scouts U.S.A., N.Y.C., 1972-78; nat. dir. personnel Jr. Achievement, Inc., 1978—. Mem. Am. Mgmt. Assn., China Inst., Asia House. Republican. Club: West Side Tennis. Home: 134 Rowayton Ave Rowayton CT 06853

CUMMIN, SYLVIA ESTHER, educator; b. N.Y.C., Mar. 15; d. Harry and Sarah (Josephson) Smolok; B.S., N.Y. U., 1946, M.A., 1947; m. Alfred S. Cummin, Mar. 24, 1946; 1 dau., Cynthia Katherine. Mktg. adminstr. Ayerst Labs. div. Am. Home Process, N.Y.C., 1946-55; tchr. Queensbury (N.Y.) High Sch., 1955-57, Corfu (N.Y.) Central Sch., 1957-59, Brookline (Mass.) High Sch., 1959-63; tchr. bus. Westfield (N.J.) Secondary Sch., 1963—. Active, Westfield PTA, 1963—, YWCA, 1966—; sponsor, committeewoman Nat. Debutante Assembly, N.Y.C., 1972—, Internat. Debutante Ball, N.Y.C., 1973—, Debutante Cotillion, Washington, 1973—, Ball of the Silver Rose, Vienna, Austria, 1973—; Cert. tchr., Mass., N.Y., N.J. Mem. NEA, N.J. Edn. Assn., Mass. Tchrs. Assn., N.Y. Educators Assn., Eastern Bus. Tchrs. Assn., Nat. Bus. Edn. Assn., N.Y. U. Alumni Assn., N.Y. U. Faculty Wives Assn., Am. Platform Assn. Clubs: Westfield Coll. Women's, Glens Falls Country, Garden. Contbr. articles to profl. jours. Home: 2 Naworth Pass Westfield NJ 07090 Office: Edison Jr High Sch Rahway Ave Westfield NJ 07090

CUMMINGS, CONSTANCE PENNY, pub. relations exec.; b. Morristown, N.J., Feb. 12, 1948; d. Renwick Speer and Juliana Diane (Novotny) C.; B.A., U. Md., 1970. With Kaiser Aluminum, Washington, 1970-71, Manning, Selvage & Lee, pub. relations, Washington, 1971-77; dir. pub. relations Sheraton Washington Hotel, 1977-82, area dir. public relations Sheraton Corp., Washington, 1982—. Recipient Sheraton Corp. Pres. award, 1978, Pub. Relations award, 1981. Mem. Am. News Women's Club (pres. 1982-83), Am. Women in Radio and TV (pres. 1976), Advt. Club Washington, Public Relations Soc. Am. (dir. 1977). Contbr. articles in field. Office: Sheraton Washington Hotel 2660 Woodley Rd NW Washington DC 20008

CUMMINGS, FAY THOMAS, tax practitioner, enrolled agt.; b. Midland, Tex., Apr. 3, 1929; d. William Emmett and Vernon M. (Lee) Thomas; ed. U. Ark., 1945-46, U. Ga., 1951; B.A. in Acctg., U. Okla., 1954; m. Neale Stinner (dec. 1951); children—Jerry Neale, Fay Marie, Charley Ray, Teryl Lee. Controller, Garrett Corp., Oklahoma City, 1952-63, Condor Pacific, Canoga Park, Calif., 1963-69; individual practice acctg. and tax service, Redondo Beach, Calif., 1974—; lectr. in field. Mem. various scholarship bds. Mem. Assn. Bus. and Tax Cons. (pres. 1977-79), Inland Soc. Accts. (v.p. 1978). Republican. Mem. Ch. of Religious Sci. Office: 909 N Aviation Suite 3 Manhattan Beach CA 90266

CUMMINGS, JEANETTE GLENN, social worker, ins. rep.; b. Cyrene, Ga., Aug. 11, 1949; d. Asbery and Euzera (Humphrey) Glenn; B.S., Tuskegee Inst., 1972; M.S.W. (Univ. fellow), Atlanta U., 1973; m. Jesse Cummings, Dec. 30, 1978. Dir. resident services Wesley Homes Inc., Atlanta, 1973-78; sr. citizen planner/coordinator Central Savannah River Area Planning Commn., Augusta, Ga., 1979, dir. Area Agy. on Aging, 1979—; ins. agt. A. L. Williams, Augusta, 1981—; cons. on group work with elderly, organizing social service programs. Vice pres. Mental Health/Mental Retardation Assn., Augusta; chairperson Mental Health/Mental Retardation Adv. Council; mem. exec. bd. Leadership Augusta; sec. Sr. Enrichment Assn., Augusta. Elected Employee of Yr., Central Savannal River Area Planning Commn., 1980; named Social Worker of Yr. Augusta unit Nat. Assn. Social Workers, 1982; Citizen of Yr. Sr. Enrichment Assn., 1982. Mem. Nat. Assn. Social Workers (chairperson Augusta unit), Acad. Cert. Social Workers, Ga. Gerontology Soc., Southeastern Assn. Area Agy. on Aging Dirs. (dir.), Nat. Assn. Found. Execs., Delta Sigma Theta. Democrat. Mem. Unity Ch. Club: Tuskegee Alumni (sec. Augusta chpt.). Home: 2715 Vernon Dr. W Augusta GA 30906 Office: 2123 Wrightsboro Rd Augusta GA 30904

CUMMINGS, LOIS MARJORIE, elem. prin., acad. coordinator; b. Beaver Falls, Pa., Apr. 18, 1931; d. Alfred and Freda (Behringer) Tyson; cert. Bob Jones U., 1952; B.S. in Elem. Edn., Geneva Coll., 1955; M.A. in Edn., U. Ga., 1972; m. Buhl Cummings, June 25, 1955; children—Timothy, Susan, Steven. Sec., Bob Jones U., Greenville, S.C., 1950-52; sec., treas. Cummings Evang. Assn., Athens, Ga., 1956—; tchr. English Korean Bible Coll., Seoul, 1956-57; sec.-treas., acad. coordinator Athens Christian Sch., 1970—. Mem. Ga. Assn. Christian Schs. Home and Office: 1270 Hwy 29 N Athens GA 30601

CUMMINGS, SUSAN NULL, educator: b. Oak Park, Ill., Sept. 6, 1920; d. Howard Ellsworth and Marie (Kapps) Null; B.S., U. Chgo., 1944; M.A., Ariz. State U., 1963, Ph.D., 1967; m. Edward Albert Cummings, Oct. 4, 1947; 1 stepson, John Bruce. Field dir., Girl Scouts USA, Oak Park, Ill., 1944-45, Kalamazoo, 1945-47, exec., Maricopa County, Ariz., 1948-50, camp dir. Santa Monica, Calif., 1950-60; instr. psychology Phoenix Coll. Evening div., 1963-68; instr. ednl. founds. Ariz. State U., Phoenix, 1964-67, asso. prof. secondary edn., 1969—; cons. human relations. Title XI grantee, 1968. Mem. Ariz. Edn. Assn. (Tchr. of Yr. 1970), World Council Curriculum and Instrn., World Futurist Soc., Assn. Supervision and Curriculum Devel., Am. Psychol. Assn., Assn. Humanistic Psychology, Mineral. Soc. Ariz. (dir. 1951-57). Editor newsletter World Council Curriculum and Instruction, 1981—, Communication in Education, 1970. Home: 1743 E Beth Dr Phoenix AZ 85040 Office: Coll Edn Ariz State U Tempe AZ 85287

CUMMINGS, THERESA FAITH, social service corp. exec.; b. Springfield, Ill., Feb. 27; d. Nelson Mark and Mary Jeanette (Irvine) C.; B.S., Winston-Salem State Tchrs. Coll., 1956; M.S., So. Ill. U., 1967. Classroom tchr. St. Louis Public Sch. System, 1957-67; dir. Neighborhood Service Centers, Springfield, 1967-69; exec. dir. Springfield/Sangamon County Community Action, Inc., Springfield, 1969—. Chmn. Union Baptist Day Care Center; chmn. state adv. com. U.S. Commn. on Civil Rights; mem. exec. com. Central Ill. Health System Agy.; commr. region 14 Ill. Law Enforcement Commn.; mem. Ill. Internat. Year of the Child Com.; mem. Ill. adv. com. to White House Conf. on Families; past pres. Consumer Credit Counseling Service. Recipient award Ministerial Alliance, 1973; medallion March of Dimes, 1979. Mem. Nat. Community Action Agy. Exec. Dirs. Assn. (past treas.), Ill. Assn. Community Action Agys. (past treas.), Am. Soc. Public Adminstrs. (past mem. local exec. bd.), Ill. Assn. Manpower Mgmt., Ill. Affirmative Action Officers Assn., Ill. Child Care Assn., Nat. Women's Polit. Caucus, AAUW, NAACP (life mem., award), LWV, Iota Phi Lambda (past regional dir., past pres. chpt.), Alpha Gamma Pi. Mem. African Methodist Episcopal Ch. Club: Altrusa. Office: Springfield/Sangamon County Community Action Inc 1101 S 15th St Springfield IL 62703

CUMMINGS, YVONNE EUTRELDA, physician; b. Columbus, Ohio, Oct. 2, 1947; d. Joseph William and Sarah Julia (Armstrong) C.; B.S., Ohio State U., 1969; M.D., Howard U., 1973; m. Robert R. Colbert, June 6, 1981; children—Rhonda, Nancy, Robin, and Rodrick Colbert, Rhonda. Intern, Freedmen's Hosp., Washington, 1973-74; med. resident Howard U. Hosp., Washington, 1974-75, chief med. resident, 1975, fellow in nephrology, 1976-78; asst. prof. medicine renal div. U. South Fla. Coll. Medicine. Mem. med. adv. bd. Suncoast chpt. Lupus Found. Am., Inc. Diplomate Am. Bd. Internal Medicine. Fellow ACP; mem. AMA, Am. Soc. Nephrology, Fla. Soc. Nephrology (sec.-treas.), Ohio State U. Alumni Assn. Episcopalian. Home: 3306 W Leona St Tampa FL 33609 Office: 12901 N 30th St Tampa FL 33612

CUMMINS, EVELYN FREEMAN, social agy. exec.; b. Beatrice, Nebr., Mar. 24, 1904; d. John Allen and Irene (Townsend) Freeman; student Nebr. Wesleyan, 1920-23; B.A., U. Nebr., 1928; postgrad. U. Chgo., 1934-36, 41; M.S., Columbia, 1946; m. Paul Otto Cummins, Oct. 8, 1927 (dec. Sept. 1943); 1 dau., Beverly Anne (Mrs. Cummins Spangler). Tchr. rural Gage County, Nebr., 1921-22, Wilber, Nebr., 1923-25, Lincoln, Nebr., 1925-27; sch. social worker Lincoln, 1930-36; supr. Fla. Dept. Pub. Welfare, Orlando, 1936-42, dist. dir., 1942-45; dir. Nebr. Gov.'s Com. to Study Services to Blind, Lincoln, 1946-47; field rep. Fla. Dept. Pub. Welfare, Jacksonville, 1948-51, appeals officer, 1950-51; exec. dir. Community Council Oklahoma City Area, 1952-61; exec. dir. spl. projects Chgo. Community Fund, 1962-63; exec. dir. Family Service Assn. La Porte County (Ind.), 1964—; lectr. social problems Purdue North Central; field supr. Valparaiso U., Loyola U., Jane Addams Sch. Social Work, Chgo. Del. Area II Adv. Council on Aging, 1976-80; mem. housing com. Mayor of Michigan City (Ind.), 1973; pres. Community Service Council Michigan City, 1966-68; chmn. residential campaign United Way Michigan City, 1966-68. Diplomate Conf. Advancement Pvt. Practice in Social Work. Mem. Nat. Assn. Social workers, Acad. Certified Social Workers, Council Social Work Edn., Family Service Assns. Ind., Ind. Conf. on Social Concerns, Internat. Platform Assn., LaPorte County Council on Aging (pres. 1978). Democrat. Methodist. Home: 1317 Washington St Michigan City IN 46360 Office: Suite 228 Warren Bldg Michigan City IN 46360

CUMMINS, PATRICIA ANN WILLETT, educator; b. Worcester, Mass., Oct. 16, 1948; d. Warren Joseph and Mary Margaret (Shannon) Willett; B.A. cum laude, Smith Coll., 1970; M.A., U. Rochester, 1971, Ph.D. (Dissertation grantee), U. N.C., Chapel Hill, 1974; m. Christopher James Cummins, Oct. 4, 1975; children—John, Mary. Asst. prof. French, Lafayette Coll., 1973-74; asst. prof., asso. prof. W.Va. U., Morgantown, 1974—, acting asst. dean Grad. Sch., 1981-83. Recipient Holmes prize U. N.C., 1974; grantee Lafayette Coll., 1973-74, W.Va. U. Faculty, 1975-77, Govt. Que., 1979; Nat. Endowment Humanities fellow, 1976-77; named Fgn. Lang. Dept. Outstanding Tchr., 1979, 81. Mem. Southeastern Medieval Assn. (v.p. 1981-82, exec. council 1978-81), MLA (del. assembly 1979-81), Am. Assn. Tchrs. French, Internat. Courtly Lit. Soc. (bibliographer 1974-82, N.Am. chief bibliographer 1979). Am. Council Teaching Fgn. Langs., Medieval Acad., Am. Assn. Tchrs. French, Internat. Fedn. Modern Langs. and Lit., Societe Internationale du Theatre Medievale, W.Va. Fgn. Lang. Tchrs. Assn., W.Va. Assn. Humanities. Democrat. Roman Catholic. Editor: Critical Edition of LeRegime tresutile, 1976, Commerical French, 1982; editor: Procs. Council So. Grad. Schs., 1982; (with others) Literary and Historical Perspectives of the Middle Ages, 1982. Home: 10 Yorkshire Pl Rt 9 Morgantown WV 26505 Office: Dept Fgn Langs W Va U Morgantown WV 26506

CUNEGIN, FLORETTA BROWN, nurse; b. Orlando, Fla., Sept. 9, 1927; d. Lee Andrew and Fannie K. (Hicks) C.; R.N., St. Philip Hosp. Sch. Nursing, Richmond, Va., 1951; B.S.N., Wayne State U., 1957, M.S.N., 1958; postgrad. U. Mich. m. Paul Joseph Cunegin, Jan. 31, 1958. Asso. dir. in-service edn. Plymouth (Mich.) State Home and Tng. Sch., 1959-61; mem. faculty Flint (Mich.) Community Jr. Coll., 1961-66; mem. nursing faculty Oakland Community Coll., Union Lake, Mich., 1966—, head dept., 1978—; mem. Mich. Bd. Nursing, 1979—. Served to capt. Nurse Corps, USAF, 1951-61. Recipient Tchr. of Yr. award in minority nursing, 1972, Students of Mich. Concerned Tchr. award, 1973; USPHS grantee, 1957-48. Mem. Am. Nurses Assn., Nat. League Nursing, Nat. Black Nurses Assn., Am. Psychiat. Assn., Mich. Occupational Edn. Assn., Mich. Nurses Assn., Mich. Heart Assn., Mich. Epilepsy Found., Mich. Edn. Assn., Mich. Black Nurses Assn., Oakland Dist. Nurses Assn., Oakland County Council Black Nurses (founder, pres. 1971; Mary E. Mahoney award 1978). Roman Catholic. Author articles in field. Office: 7350 Cooley Lake Rd Union Lake MI 48085

CUNNINGHAM, SISTER, CATHARINE JULIE, coll. chancellor; b. San Francisco, Oct. 22, 1910; d. John Francis and Mary Cecilia (McCarthy) Cunningham; B.A., U. Calif., Berkeley, 1932; M.A., Catholic U. Am., 1954; L.H.D. (hon.), U. San Francisco, 1978. Mem. Sisters of Notre Dame de Namur, 1932—; prin. high sch., 1942-56; pres. Coll. of Notre Dame, Belmont, Calif., 1956-80, chancellor, 1981—, also trustee. Bd. dirs. Far West Lab. for Ednl. Research and Devel. Mem. NEA (past dir.), Nat. Catholic Ednl. Assn. Address: 1500 Ralston Ave Belmont CA 94002 *

CUNNINGHAM, CATHY DIANE, equipment rental co. exec.; b. Buffalo, May 4, 1954; d. Harry Oden and Lillian Louise (Tillis) Roberts; student Central Ariz. Coll., 1971-72; m. Jerry Dewayne Cunningham, Mar. 10, 1978. Acct., office mgr. Speedy Devil Enterprises, Phoenix, 1972-77; bookkeeper LeVine & Eckstein, Boston, 1977-78; acct., corp. sec.-treas. R.J.&M. Vacuum Service Co., Bakersfield, Calif., 1978-79; acct. Rebels Equipment Rental Co., Parker, Ariz., 1979—. Youth dir. Community Bapt. Ch., Earp, Calif., 1979—. Mem. Exec. Female Assn. Democrat. Home: PO Box 165 Earp CA 92242 Office: 1405 Joshua St Parker AZ 85344

CUNNINGHAM, CAY, psychotherapist; b. Port Arthur, Tex., Sept. 8, 1939; d. Arthur Troy and Rachel Blanche (McGill) C.; B.A., U. Calif., Berkeley, 1967; M.A., U. Houston, 1973. Counselor, Day Care Assn., Houston, 1967-68; research asst. dept. psychiatry Baylor Coll., Houston, Tex., 1969-70; asso. planner, coordinator early childhood projects Harris County Dept. Edn., Houston, 1970-71; dir. early childhood div. Houston Child Guidance Center, 1971—. Mem. Am. Psychol. Assn., Tex. Psychol. Assn. Home: 411 Euclid St Houston TX 77009 Office: 3214 Austin St Houston TX 77004

CUNNINGHAM, DIANA PINSON, clin. psychologist; b. Dallas, Dec. 3, 1936; d. Roscoe Henderson and Margaret (Churchwell) Pinson; B.S., Tex. Woman's U., 1958, M.S., 1970; Ph.D., N.Tex. State U., 1981; m. Morris Cunningham, June 20, 1958; children—Cheryl Diane, M. Craig. Mem. faculty Coll. Nursing, Tex. Woman's U., Denton, 1958-68; clin. specialist, dir. staff devel. Children's Med. Center, Dallas, 1968-72; clin. specialist Psychiat. Mental Health Nursing, 1972-76; staff psychologist Dallas Child Guidance Clinic, also pvt. practice stress mgmt.; condr. seminars on stress mgmt. for corps. Lic. psychologist, R.N., Tex. Mem. Dallas Psychol. Assn., Tex. Psychol. Assn., Southwestern Psychol. Assn., Am. Psychol. Assn., Sigma Theta Tau. Home: 934 Whitestone Ln Dallas TX 75232 Office: 8215 Westchester St Suite 228 Dallas TX 75225

CUNNINGHAM, ISABELLA CLARA MANTOVANI, mktg. specialist, educator; b. Milan, Italy, Apr. 1, 1942; d. Fortunato and Anna (Sinigaglia) Mantovani; came to U.S., 1967; J.D., Universidade Catolica de Sao Paulo (Brazil), 1964; M.B.A. in Mktg., Mich. State U., 1968, Ph.D. in Mktg., 1972; m. William H. Cunningham, Dec. 31, 1970; 1 son, John William. Admitted to Brazilian bar, 1965; teaching asst. in mktg. Mich. State U., 1968-69; asst. prof. mktg. Escola de Administracao de Empresas de Sao Paulo da Fundacao Getulio Vargas, 1969-71; asst. prof. mktg. St. Edward's U., Austin, Tex., 1971-72, acting dean Center Bus. Adminstrn., 1972-73; vis. asst. prof. mktg. U. Tex., Austin, 1973-74, asst. prof. advt., 1974-76, asso. prof. advt., 1976-81; prof., 1981—, chmn. dept., 1978—; bd. dirs. Univ. Co-op.; cons. to bus. Univ. Research Inst. grantee, summer 1977, fall 1977. Mem. Am., So. mktg. assns., Am. Acad. Advt. Women in Communications, Austin Advt. Club (pres. 1978-79), Phi Kappa Phi. Author: (with W. H. Cunningham and W. J.E. Crissy) Selling: The Personal Force in Marketing, 1977, Effective Selling, 1977; (with G. Kozmetsky) Investment Management a Book of Readings, 1978; (with W.H. Cunningham) Marketing: A Management Approach, 1980; (with W.J.E. Crissy) Metodos Efectivos de Venta, 1980; contbr. articles to profl. publs. Home: 6509 Mesa Dr Austin TX 78731 Office: Dept Advt U Tex Austin TX 78712

CUNNINGHAM, MADONNA MARIE, nun, coll. pres.; b. Trenton, N.J., Aug. 31, 1933; A.B., Villanova U., 1961; M.A., Fordham U., 1964, Ph.D., 1968. Joined Sisters of St. Francis, Roman Catholic Ch., 1953; intern in psychology St. Elizabeth's Hosp., Washington, 1965-66; elem. tchr., Spokane, Wash. and Elsmere, Del., 1956-60; dir. counseling, asst. prof. psychology Our Lady of Angels Coll. (now Neumann Coll.), Aston, Pa., 1967-71, pres., asso. prof., 1971—; lectr. dept. edn. St. Joseph's Coll., Phila., 1968-70; staff psychologist Phila. Archdiocesan Counseling Service for Religions, 1969-76. Trustee, St. Joseph Hosp., Towson, Md., 1976-81, Archmere Acad., Claymont, Del.; exec. com., chmn. instl. survey com. Pa. Commn. Ind. Colls. and Univs.; bd. dirs. Franciscan Health System, Sisters of St. Francis of Phila. Mem. Am. Psychol. Assn., Pa. Psychol. Assn., Psychologists Interested in Religious Issues, Sigma Xi. Office: Neumann College Aston PA 19014

CUNNINGHAM, MARY, public relations cons.; b. Los Angeles, Feb. 9, 1932; d. Paul LaFrance and Ina (Decoto) Johnson; A.A., Sacramento Coll., 1951; children—David, Diane, Denise. Loan supr., teller, bookkeeper various banks, Calif., Wash., 1951-61; singer, actress, publicist, dir. concert, light opera, civic theatre, 1948-71; free-lance writer, 1975-79; owner PR Northwest, Renton, Wash., 1980—; seminar leader community colls., Wash., Small Bus. Adminstrn. Founder, Shasta Civic Theatre, 1959; actress, publicist. Stockton Civic Theatre, 1966-68; dir., publicist Santa Rosa Players, 1970-71; fund-raising chmn. Children's Home Soc., 1964-69. Mem. Women Entrepreneurs Network (founder), Women's Bus. Exchange, Women in Communications, Pacific N.W. Writers, Tukwila-Sea Tac C. of C. (media rep.). Contbr. articles to profl. jours.; author: The Nuts and Bolts of Promoting Your Business, 60 min. cassette tape, 1981. Address: 15450 SE Fairwood Blvd Renton WA 98055

CUNNINGHAM, NANCY CAROL, legal sec.; b. Idaho Falls, Idaho, Dec. 17, 1944; d. Gordon L. and Opal Dene (Miller) Nadauld; student Utah State U., 1963-65, Georgetown U., 1965-66, Highline Community Coll., 1977-79; m. Brent L. Cunningham, Feb. 17, 1967; children—Kristin, Rebecca. Sec. to Idaho br. office dir. AEC, 1963-64; sec. to dir. Soviet and racial divs. FBI, Washington, 1965-66; sec. firm Peterson, Moss & Olson, Idaho Falls, 1966-67, Irwin, Friel & Myklebust, Pullman, 1967-70; adminstrv. asst., office mgr., firm Wimer, Harpold & Phillipson, Seattle, 1975-81; legal sec. Joyce J. Cresswell, Atty. at Law, Oregon City, Oreg., 1982—. Sec., Kent Juvenile Ct. Conf. Com., 1976-78; v.p. PTA, 1976-77; young women's pres. Ch. of Jesus Christ of Latter-day Saints, 1973-74, 82, sem. tchr., 1974-80, young women's pres. Gresham (Oreg.) south stake, 1982—. Mem. Nat. Assn. Legal Adminstrs., Seattle Assn. Legal Adminstrs., Idaho Falls Legal Secs. Assn., Profl. Bus. Women. Home: 1560 SW 24th Dr Gresham OR 97030 Office: 1511 Orbanco Bldg Portland OR 97204

CUNNINGHAM, PATRICIA MARIE REEDY, nurse; b. Scranton, Pa., Nov. 9, 1940; d. John Walter and Mary Zita (Dempsey) Reedy; R.N., Highland Hosp. Sch. Nursing, 1963; B.S., Chapman Coll., 1980, postgrad. 1980—; m. Harold W. Cunningham, Oct. 30, 1971; children—Marie, David, Wayne, Deborah. Indsl. nurse Walt Disney World, Lake Buena Vista, Fla., 1973-74; staff charge nurse Mercy Hosp., Orlando, Fla., 1972-73, asst. head nurse emergency room, 1974-76; nursing services supr. Kaiser Found. Hosp., Hayward, Calif., 1976-78, asst. nursing adminstr., 1978—, co-coordinator method improvement program, instr. behavior modeling, supr. basic life support system program, 1977—. Lic. nurse, Fla., N.Y., Calif. Mem. Patient Care Assessment Council, Calif. Soc. Nursing Service Adminstrs. Democrat. Roman Catholic. Clubs: St. Leonards Sch. Parent, Shaklee Salesman, Kaiperm. Home: 35355 Blackburn Dr Newark CA 94560 Office: 27400 Hesperian Blvd Hayward CA 94645

CUNNINGHAM, ROSE ANN, communication cons.; b. Jamaica, W.I.; came to U.S., 1965, naturalized, 1972; d. Alfred and Angela (Vidal) Chambers; B.S., Pace U., 1973; m. Wilford Alexander Cunningham, (div.); children—Dwight, Michael. Zone systems engring. mgr. NCR Corp., N.Y.C., 1977-80; communication cons. AT&T Long Lines, Somerset, N.J., 1981—; chairperson bd. PMSSI, Inc., N.Y.C., 1981—, also mgmt. cons. Mem. Am. Mgmt. Assn., Assn. Computing Machinery, Nat. Assn. Female Execs., Assn. M.B.A. Execs., Women in Data Processing. Office: 115 Belmont Dr NJ 07888

CUPIDO, RAFFAELLA ELIZABETH, social worker; b. Rochester, N.Y., Apr. 12, 1929; d. Salvatore and Elizabeth (Squilla) Cupido; B.A. in Sociology, U. Rochester, 1951; M.Social Service, U. Buffalo, 1954, Group worker Lewis St. Center, Rochester, 1951-53; with Baden St. Settlement House, Rochester, 1952-53; Council Social Agys., 1953, Neighborhood House, 1953-54 (both Buffalo); asst. dir. Neighborhood House, Auburn, N.Y., 1954-55; 1st group worker House of Providence, 1955-58, supr. group work Huntington Family Center, 1958-61 (both Syracuse, N.Y.); staff cons. recreation and group work R.I. Council Community Services, Inc., Providence, 1961-65; coordinator pub. and profl. edn. mental retardation Child Health and Devel. Center, faculty Brown U., Providence, 1965-66; exec. dir. Federal Hill House Assn., Providence, 1966-70, Smith Hill Center, Providence, 1970—, organizer new br., 1975; Field instr. Syracuse U. Sch. Social Work, 1958-61, Boston Coll., 1963-64, 71—, U. Conn., 1967; mem. R.I. Bd. Registration Social Workers, 1970—, sec., 1971—. Mem. R.I. Gov.'s Com. on Youth Employment, 1962, Gov.'s Task Force on Youth Employment, 1963; mem. Attys. Gen.'s Youth Adv. Bd., 1967-70, R.I. Youth Opportunity Council, 1968-70 (award 1964); treas. United Fund Execs., 1967-69, vice chmn., 1969-71; mem. Bd. Registration Social Workers, 1970-75, sec. bd., 1971—, mem. capital funds com. United Way Southeastern New Eng., 1971-76; founder, v.p. Citizens for Preservation Waterman Lake, 1970-72, pres., 1972-73; mem. Glocester Democratic Town Com., 1971-73; bd. dirs. Tri Town Econ. Com., 1973-76, Mayor Providence Anti-Litter Campaign, 1981—; mem. Glocester Conservation Commn., 1974-78, vice chmn., 1975-76. Mem. Nat. Assn. Social Workers (chmn. membership Syracuse chpt. 1958-61, editor newsletter R.I. chpt. 1967-70, sec. 1969-73, pres. 1973-75), Acad. Certified Social Workers, Assn. Community Service Execs., Multi-Service Center Exec. Dirs. Assn. Home: Waterman Lake Shore Dr Harmony RI 02829 Office: 110 Ruggles St Providence RI 02908

CUPP, JULIA ANTONIA ESSENIYI, guidance counselor, educator; b. Youngstown, Ohio, Sept. 12, 1952; d. Alex Joseph and Julia Josephine (Soriano) E.; A.B., Youngstown State U., 1974, M.S. in Guidance and Counseling, 1977; m. N. Scott Cupp, Aug. 8, 1980. Tchr., Spanish and drama Ontario (Ohio) Middle Sch., 1974-76; grad. asst. Youngstown State U., 1976-77; guidance counselor, student council advisor Reed Middle Sch., Hubbard, Ohio, 1977-79; component coordinator career devel. program Mahoning County Schs., Canfield, Ohio, 1979-80; guidance counselor Poland (Ohio) Local Sch. Dist., 1980—; cons. World of Work program Warren City Schs., 1977. Mem. AAUW, Am. Vocat. Assn., Career Edn. Assn., Eastern Ohio Counselors Assn., Nat. Assn. Gifted Children and Adults, Northeastern Ohio Personnel and Guidance Assn., Northeastern Ohio Tchrs. Assn., Ohio Assn. Gifted Children, Ohio Assn. Women Deans, Adminstrs. and Counselors, Ohio Personnel and Guidance Assn., Ohio Sch. Counselors Assn., Youngstown Panhellenic Assn., Alpha Sigma Tau. Presbyterian. Home: 7120 Glendale Ave Youngstown OH 44512 Office: 2731 Center Rd Poland OH 44514

CUPP, MARY KATHERINE HYER, psychiat. social worker; b. Clay, W.Va., Jan. 17, 1932; d. Oral Otis and Icie Hyer (Barsotti-McCracken) Hyer; B.A., W.Va. State Coll., 1967; M.S.W., W.Va. U., 1970; div. Service rep. Chesapeake & Potomac Tel. Co. of W.Va., Charleston, 1948-67; statistician W.Va. Dept. Welfare, Charleston, 1967-68; psychiat. social worker Calif. Dept. Mental Hygiene, Southgate, 1970-73; adoptions worker Los Angeles County Adoptions, 1973; psychiat. social worker Calif. Dept. Health, Camarillo State Hosp., 1973—. Pres., Camarillo Save Our Streetlights Orgn., 1980—. Licensed clin. social worker, Calif. Mem. Nat. Assn. Social Workers, Acad. Cert. Social Workers. Methodist. Home: 1091 Dara St Camarillo CA 93010 Office: Box A Unit 77 Camarillo CA 93010

CURIE, EVE, author, lectr.; b. Paris, Dec. 6, 1904; d. Pierre (Nobel prize winner for work in radium 1903) and Marie (Skiodowska) (Nobel prize winner in radio-active substances, 1903, in chemistry 1911) Curie; B.S., Ph.B., Sevigne Coll.; D.H.L. (hon.), Mills Coll., 1939, Russell Sage Coll., 1941; Litt.D. (hon.), U. Rochester, 1941; m. Henry Richardson Labouisse, Nov. 19, 1954. Took up study of music and gave first concert as pianist, Paris, 1925; later concerts in France and Belgium; mus. critic for Candide (weekly jour.) for several years; also wrote articles on motion pictures and the theater; made first visit to U.S. with mother, 1921; on 2d visit lectured in 10 U.S. cities (speaks English, French and Polish), 1939; witnessed fall of France, 1940, went to London to work for cause of Free France; came to U.S., 1941, lectured on war in France and Eng.; because of pro-ally activities deprived of French citizenship by Vichy Govt., 1941. Served in Europe with Fighting French as officer in Women's div. of army; one of pubs. Paris Presse (daily), resigned to return to ind. writing, 1949. Spl. adviser Sec. Gen., NATO, 1952-54. Decorated Chevalier Legion of Honor (France), 1939; Polonia Restituta (Poland), 1939; Croix de Guerre (France), 1944. Author: Madame Curie (selection of Lit. Guild, Jr. Guild, Book-of-the-Month Club, Scientific Book of the month; Nat. book award for non-fiction), 1937; Journey Among Warriors (Lit. Guild Selection), 1943. Home: 1 Sutton Pl S New York NY 10022

CURLEE, DOROTHY SUMNER, social worker; b. Coleman, Tex., July 31, 1921; d. Thaddeus Pickett and Lena (Pierson) Sumner; B.A., Howard Payne Coll., 1942; postgrad. Tulane U., 1944; M.S. in Social Work, Columbia U., 1963; m. A. Wesley Curlee; 1 dau., Lenae. Supr. child welfare Tex. Dept. Human Resources, 1944-54, 59-60; dir. adoptions Hope Cottage Children's Bur., Dallas, 1961-69; cons. Adoption Resource Exchange N.Am., Child Welfare League Am., 1969-70; asso. dir. Children's Home Soc. N.C., Greensboro, 1970-72; med. psychiat. social worker Tex. Dept. Mental Health and Mental Retardation, Denton, 1972-78; program mgr. crippled children's div. Tex. Dept. Health, Abilene, 1978—; field instr. social work U. Tex., 1950-52, 69. Mem. Acad. Cert. Social Workers, Nat. Assn. Social Workers, Tex. Assn. Mental Health (dir. 1957-59), Daus. Republic Tex. Home: PO Box 3643 Abilene TX 79604 Office: Old Courthouse Abilene TX 79604

CURLER, (MARY) BERNICE (MRS. ALBERT ELMER CURLER), writer; b. Los Angeles, Dec. 4, 1915; d. Charles Ether and Josephine Babetta (Meier) Davis; student Woodbury Coll., 1934-35; m. Albert Elmer Curler, Apr. 10, 1938; children—Daniel Jay, Dawna Dee. Freelance writer of short stories and articles for various nat. mags. including McCalls, Parents Mag., Modern Maturity, Success Unlimited, Progressive Women, Christian Sci. Moniter, Small World, Ladys Circle, Chevron USA, Writer's Digest, National Enquirer, 1957—; author: (play) Mazle's Red Garter, 1962; Story of a Medal, 1976; contbg. author: Creative Congregations, 1972. Instr. article writing Cosumnes River Evening Coll., Sacramento, 1971—; asst. dir. Sierra Writing Camp; condr. writing seminars. Recipient Achievement award Sacramento Regional Arts Council. Mem. Calif. Writers Club (pres. 1960-61, dir. 1960—, Jack London award 1981), Am. Soc. Journalists and Authors. Home and Office: 8156 Waikiki Dr Fair Oaks CA 95628

CURLEY, LOIS LONG, editor, pub. cons.; b. Portland, Oreg., May 6, 1921; d. Ward Willis and Evangeline Burlette Long; B.A., Coll. of Pacific, 1943; M.A., Pasadena Coll., 1968; postgrad. Fuller Theol. Sem.; m. Richard DeLos Curley, Oct. 12, 1943; children—David Wayland, Michelle Curley Eastburn. Tchr., Stockton High Sch., 1943, Modesto Jr. Coll., 1947; dir. religious edn. St. Charles Ave. Presbyn. Ch., New Orleans, 1944-45; asst. program dir. Mt. Hermon (Calif.) Assn., 1946-47; writer ch. sch. curriculum Gospel Light Publs., Glendale, Calif., 1950-54, editor early childhood dept., 1954-60, coordinating editor editorial dept., 1961-70, exec. editor, 1971-79; owner Lois Curley Enterprises, pub. project devel., Santa Cruz, Calif., 1979—; chmn. coordinating bd. Extension Edn., Los Angeles County, Fuller Theol. Sem., 1977—. Nat. bd. dirs. HANMI, Los Angeles, 1979—; bd. dirs. Pioneer Girls, Inc., Wheaton, Ill., 1979—; bd. dirs., publs. editor Conservative Congl. Christian Conf. U.S. and Can.; chmn. Fuller Theol. Sem. Aux., 1966-72. Mem. Evang. Press Assn., Nat. Assn. Women Execs. Co-editor: Women and the Ministries of Christ, 1979; mng. editor Family Life Today, 1977-79. Office: Lois Curley Enterprises 1700 Escalona Dr Suite K Santa Cruz CA 95060

CURNUTT, ESTHER CLARK, cons. public relations, advt.; b. Texon, Tex., June 16, 1935; d. J. Linton and Ann Martin Clark; B.J., U. Tex., Austin, 1957; M.A., Sul Ross State U., 1959; postgrad Ind. U., 1963, U. Miss., 1966; m. Harry O. Curnutt, Feb. 11, 1966; 1 son, Clark Denton. Society editor, Pecos (Tex.) Enterprise, 1957-58; with San Antonio Independent Sch. Dist., 1959-66, NE Independent Sch. Dist., San Antonio, 1966-67; faculty, public relations staff San Antonio Coll., 1967-71; cons. public relations, mktg., advt., San Antonio, 1976—. Pres., Women Interested in Govt., 1972-73; mem. Mayors Commn. on Status of Women, 1973-74; chmn. Upton County Bicentennial, 1976; 1st v.p. LWV, 1977-79. Mem. Women in Communications, Bexar County Women's Polit. Caucus, San Antonio C. of C., Women's Polit. Action Com., Women in Bus. (founder, pres.), San Antonio Conservation Soc. Methodist. Clubs: Suburban Bankers, Headliners. Wives (past pres.). Address: 126 Five Oaks St San Antonio TX 78209

CURRAN, ANITA STILES, physician, county ofcl.; b. Northampton, Mass., July 11, 1929; d. Charles Linfield and Rita Agnes (Equi) Stiles; B.A., U. Conn., 1951; M.D., N.Y. Med. Coll., 1955; M.P.H., Columbia U., 1974; m. John P. Curran, Aug. 10, 1953; children—Maureen, Kathryn, Michael, John Patrick. Intern, Mountainside Hosp.; Montclair, N.J., 1955-56; resident in preventive medicine and public health N.Y.C. Dept. Health, 1975; physician, pediatric ambulatory care unit Met. Hosp., N.Y.C., 1963-66; child health conf. physician N.J. Dept. Health, 1966-73, also physician child evaluation center Hackensack, Hosp. (N.J.), 1970-73; asst. dir. Bur. Handicapped Children N.Y.C. Dept. Health, 1974-75, dir. Bur. Lead Poisoning Control, 1975-78, asso. dept. commr. environ. health services, 1972-76; dep. commr. dist. health services, 1977-78; health commr. Westchester County (N.Y.), White Plains, 1978—; clin. asst. prof. pediatrics N.Y. Med. Coll., 1974—, clin. asst. prof. community and preventive medicine, 1976—; adj. prof. Columbia U. Sch. Public Health, 1976—; mem. Mayor's Adv. Bd. Lead Poisoning Control; cons. Center Disease Control; cons. adv. bd. EPA, HUD; nat. health and safety cons. Girl Scouts U.S.A. Diplomate Am. Bd. Preventive Medicine. Fellow Am. Coll. Preventive Medicine, N.Y. Acad. Medicine, N.Y. Acad. Sci.; mem. Am. Public Health Assn., AAAS, N.Y. County Health Services Rev. Orgn. Contbr. articles to profl. jours. Home: 1321 Prospect St Westfield NJ 07090 Office: 150 Grand St White Plains NY 10601

CURRAN, CAROL ANNE, comml. real estate co. ofcl.; b. San Francisco, Nov. 2, 1943; d. Andrew Joseph and Verna Maude (Woodman) Geiser; A.A. in Bus., City Coll. San Francisco; A.A. in Bus. Adminstrn., Foothill Coll.; B.S. in Bus. Adminstrn., San Jose State U., M.B.A., 1978; teaching credential Calif. Community Coll. System, 1980. Employee recruiter, employment rep., asst. mgr. Pacific Telephone Co., San Francisco, 1962-65; with Stanford U., 1965-68; with mktg. dept. Varian Assocs., Palo Alto, Calif., 1968-71; with Michael C. Fields, Menlo Park, Calif., 1971-72; adminstrv. asst. editor co. newsletter Time/Data Corp., Palo Alto, Calif., 1972-74; ind. cons. Olson Labs., Anaheim, Calif., 1977-78; office bldg. specialist Coldwell Banker, San Jose, Calif., 1978—. Mem. Peninsula Profl. Women's Network, Assn. South Bay Brokers (dir. 1981—), World Affairs Council No. Calif. Office: 226 W Brokaw Rd Suite 150 San Jose CA 95110

CURRAN, EILEEN MARY, educator; b. Ann Arbor, Mich., May 11, 1927; d. Edward and Laura Barbara (Meyer) Curran; B.A., Cornell U., 1948, Ph.D., 1958; B.A., Cambridge (Eng.) U., 1950, M.A., 1953. Instr. English, U. N.H., 1951-54, Ohio U., Athens, 1956-58; instr. English, Colby Coll., Waterville, Maine, 1958-60, asst. prof., 1960-66, asso. prof., 1966-73, prof., 1973—, dir. Miller Library, 1973-76. Asso. editor, The Wellesley Index to Victorian Periodicals, I, 1966, Vol. II, 1972, Vol. III, 1978. Contbr. articles to profl. jours. Home: 29 Averill Terr Waterville ME 04901 Office: Dept English Colby Coll Waterville ME 04901

CURRAN, HELEN, educator; b. Chgo., Aug. 6, 1916; d. Samuel Audley and Edna (Sandiford) Curran; student Lewis Inst. Tech., 1935-37; B.S., Ill. Inst. Tech., 1946; M.E. in Guidance and Counseling, U. Ill., 1952; postgrad. Internat. Inst. Edn., 1957, U. Maine, 1962, U. London, 1963, No. Ill. U., 1964; Advanced certificate in ednl. adminstrn., U. Ill., 1966; m. William Zorn, 1937 (div.); 1 dau., April; m. 2d, J.W. Fenner, Aug. 21, 1949 (div.); m. 3d, J.W. Fenner, May 10, 1972. Tchr. public schs., Maywood, Ill., 1946-47, tchr., Fox Lake, Ill., 1947-49, guidance dir., dean girls, 1949-57; dean girls, Peoria Heights, Ill., 1957-59, dir. guidance, 1959-63, administrv. asst., dir. curriculum, McHenry (Ill.) Pub. Schs., 1963-66, asst. supt., 1966-71; asst. supt. instrn. Tech. Info. Center, Charleston, S.C., 1972—; instr. The Citadel, Charleston, summer 1973; asst. prof. psychology Baptist Coll., Charleston, 1974—. Mem. adv. council Advocacy for Retarded Citizens; bd. dirs. Orphans of Storm. Mem. Ill. Assn. Sch. Adminstrs., N.E.A., Ill. Edn. Assn., Am. Assn. Sch. Personal Adminstrs., Nat. Assn. Su ervision and Curriculum, Internat. Transactional Analysis Assn., Am. Legion Aux., Delta Kappa Gamma. Office: 64 Society St Charleston SC 29401

CURRAN, HILDA PATRICIA, social worker; b. Patterson, N.J., Jan. 15, 1938; d. James Patrick and Hilda Lucille (Walsh) C.; A.B., Hiram Coll., 1959; M.S.W., Ohio State U., 1963; m. Robert S. Kennon, Nov. 1980. Tchr., Cin. Bd. Edn., 1960; caseworker Franklin County Welfare Dept., Columbus, Ohio, 1960-61; mem. relocation staff Springfield (Mass.) Redevel. Authority, 1963-64; neighborhood organizer Community Council Greater Springfield, 1964-65; mem. program devel. staff United Community Centers, Bklyn., 1965-67; facilities devel. specialist in vocat. rehab. Mich. Dept. Edn., Lansing, 1967-70; program devel. specialist Bur. Community Services, Mich. Dept. Labor, Lansing, 1970-78, dir. Office Women and Work, 1978—. Mem. Ingham County Housing Commn., 1977-79, Ingham County Social Services Bd., 1979-82; bd. dirs., officer Big Bros.-Big Sisters Greater Lansing, 1968-82; charter mem. bd., officer Big Bros.-Big Sisters Am., 1977—, Big Sisters Internat., 1973-77, pres. 1976-77. Recipient Diana award in govt. YWCA, 1977; ann. award for outstanding achievement Hiram Coll., 1980. Mem. Nat. Assn. Social Workers (mem. del. assembly 1977, 81, pres. Lansing-Jackson chpt. 1978-80, named Lansing-Jackson Social Worker of Yr. 1977), AAUW (women as agent of change award 1981), Phi Kappa Phi (life). Clubs: Zonta, Torch (pres. 1979-80) (Lansing). Home: 1505 Osborn St Lansing MI 48915 Office: 309 N Washington St Lansing MI 48909

CURRIE, BARBARA FLYNN, state legislator; b. LaCrosse, Wis., May 3, 1940; d. Frank T. and Elsie R. (Gobel) Flynn; A.B. cum laude, U. Chgo., 1968, A.M., 1973; m. David P. Currie, Dec. 29, 1959; children—Stephen Francis, Margaret Rose. Asst. study dir. Nat. Opinion Research Center, Chgo., 1973-77; part time instr. polit. sci. DePaul U., Chgo., 1973-74; mem. Ill. Ho. of Reps., 1979—, chmn. House Democratic Study Group; mem. Ill. Council Nutrition, Commn. Status of Women. Mem. adv. bd. Harriet Harris YWCA; v.p. Chgo. LWV, 1965-69; mem. ACLU, Hyde Park-Kenwood Community Conf., South Shore Commn., South Shore Hist. Soc., Ind. Voters of Ill.-Ind. Precinct Orgn., Hyde Park Coop. Soc., Ams. for Dem. Action. Named best legislator Ind. Voters of Ill., 1980, 82, Ethel Parker award, 1982, best legislator Ill. Credit Union League; recipient Ill. Environ. Council award, Ill. Community Action Agys. award, Ill. Women's Polit. Caucus Lottie Holman O'Neill award. Mem. Ill. Conf. Women Legislators, Nat. Order Women Legislators. Contbr. article to publ. Office: 2107 Stratton Office Bldg Springfield IL 62706

CURRIER, CAROL BEVERLY, clin. psychologist; b. Cleve., June 8, 1926; d. Harold Thomas and Elsie Margaret (Boma) Currier; B.A., Allegheny Coll., 1948; M.A., Northwestern U., 1949; Ph.D., U. Fla., 1963. Asst. dir. nursing, counselor The Johns Hopkins U. Hosp. Sch. Nursing, Balt., 1953-60; clin. asst. in psychol. services health center, teaching asst., research asst. interim instr. U. Fla., Gainesville, 1960-63; asst. prof. clin. psychology depts. psychology and psychiatry U. Ky. Med. Center, Lexington, 1963-68; clin. psychologist mental health div. U. Ga. Health Service, asso. prof. psychology, Athens, 1968—. Mem. Am. Psychol. Assn., Nat. Assn. Women Deans, Adminstrs., Counselors, Southeastern Psychol., Ga. Assn. of Women Deans, Adminstrs., Counselors, Phi Beta Kappa. Co-author: The Clergyman and The Psychologist: When to Refer, 1978. Home: 150 Ravenwood Run Athens GA 30605 Office: Univ Health Service U Ga Athens GA 30602

CURRY, ANITA SAUVEUR, biologist; b. Washington, Feb. 23, 1930; d. Clarence Victor and Minnie (Bryant) Sauveur; B.S., George Washington U., 1952; divorced; 1 dau., Shannon M. Tech. writer Nat. Acad. Scis.-NRC, 1951-52; research asso. Hazleton Labs., Vienna, Va., 1952-55, 64-65, regulatory affairs cons., tech. writer, 1965-72; librarian Office Adj. Gen., Dept. Army, 1956-57; research asso. toxicology dept. Cosmetic Toiletry and Fragrance Assn., Washington, 1972—. Mem. Nat. Assn. Female Execs. Author article, petitions to FDA for listing of food and color additives. Editor: Food and Color Additives Directory, 1965-72, author index, 1969; asso. editor jours. in field. Home: 102 W Greenway Blvd Falls Church VA 22046 Office: 1110 Vermont Ave Washington DC 20005

CURRY, ELIZABETH REICHENBACH, educator; b. Evanston, Ill., Jan. 31, 1934; d. William George and Alice Mary (Martel) Reichenbach; B.A., Northwestern U., 1956; Ph.D., U. Wis., Madison, 1963; m. Stephen Jefferis Curry, June 10, 1958; 1 son, Geoffrey. Instr. U. Wis., Milw., 1963-65; asst. prof. Alfred (N.Y.) U., 1965-69; asst. prof. Slippery Rock (Pa.) State Coll., after 1969, asso. prof., to 1976, prof., 1976—. Knapp fellow, 1961-62; recipient Presdl. Research award, 1975-76. Mem. NOW, Assn. Pa. State Coll. and Univ. Faculties, Pa. Coll. English Assn., Phi Beta Kappa. Contbr. in field. Office: 308 Eisenberg Bldg Slippery Rock State College Slippery Rock PA 16057

CURRY, EVALINE JULIANA, life ins. co. exec.; b. Hopeville, Iowa, Mar. 4, 1926; d. Niels and Lena M. (Nelson) Karstensen; m. Raymond V. Curry, Apr. 12, 1948 (dec.). With Mut. of Omaha Ins. Co., 1957—; with United Omaha Life Ins. Co., 1957—, asst. sec., 1979—, 2d v.p., 1980—. Office: Mutual of Omaha Plaza Omaha NE 68175

CURRY, JANE LOUISE, author; b. East Liverpool, Ohio, Sept. 24, 1932; d. William Jack, Jr. and Helen Margaret (Willis) C.; B.S., Indiana (Pa.) U., 1954; A.M. (Fulbright grantee 1961-62), Stanford U., 1962, Ph.D., 1969; Leverhulme fellow, U. London, 1965-66. Tchr. art, East Liverpool, 1955, Los Angeles, 1956-59; teaching asst. English, Stanford U., 1959-61, 64-65, acting instr., 1967-68; freelance writer, 1968—; author: Down From the Lonely Mountain, 1965; Beneath the Hill, 1967; The Sleepers, 1968; The Change-Child, 1969; The Daybreakers (Outstanding Book award So. Calif. Council Lit. Children and Young People 1970), 1970; The Housenapper, 1970; Over the Sea's Edge, 1971 Buch des Monats award Deutsche Akademie Kinder und Jugendliteratur, 1976); The Ice Ghosts Mystery, 1972; The Lost Farm, 1974; Parsley Sage, Rosemary and Time, 1975; The Watchers, 1975; The Magical Cupboard, 1976; Poor Tom's Ghost (Ohioana Book award 1977), 1977; The Birdstones, 1977; The Bassumtyte Treasure, 1978; Ghost Lane, 1979; The Wolves of Aam, 1981. Recipient award disting. contbn. to field So. Calif. Council Lit. Children and Young People, 1979. Mem. Authors Guild, Children's Lit. Assn., So. Calif. Council Lit. Children and Young People, Internat. Arthurian Soc., Soc. Children's Book Writers, Philol. Assn. Pacific Coast, MLA. Office: Atheneum Publishers 597 Fifth Ave New York NY 10017

CURRY, LINDA WILSON, video introductions service exec.; b. Long Branch, N.J., Mar. 17, 1945; d. Sidney and Josephine Barbara (Dremel) Meadow; B.S., Bucknell U., 1966; m. James Prescott Curry, Aug. 22, 1980. Mathematician, Vitro Labs., Silver Spring, Md., 1966-67, Booz Allen, Bethesda, Md., 1968, TRW Systems Group, McLean, Va., 1969-70; ops. research analyst Dept. Transp., Washington, 1970-72; mgr. Planning Research Corp., McLean, 1972-74; exec. v.p. Automated Sci. Group, Inc., Silver Spring, 1974-77; pres. Excel Corp., Reston, Va., 1978; mgr. info. systems Commonwealth Research Corp., Reston, 1978; pres., chmn. bd. Wilson Hill Assocs., Inc., Washington, 1978-81; pres. S. Bay Introductions, Inc., Manhattan Beach, Calif., 1981—; cons. in field; dir. Back Bay Restaurant. Mem. Manhattan Beach C. of C., Nat. Assn. Women Bus. Owners, Am. Mgmt. Assn., Ops. Research Soc. Am., Am. Mktg. Assn., Am. Entrepreneurs Assn., Women's Referral Service, Women in Bus., Phi Beta Kappa. Club: Soroptomists. Home: 2027 Via Nova Lomita CA 90717 Office: 3770 Highland Ave Suite 206 Manhattan Beach CA 90266

CURRY, MARGARET ANN, nurse educator; b. Terrell, Tex., Dec. 15, 1926; d. Curtis Herbert and Jetty Bell (Moreland) Gourley; A.A., Victor Valley Coll., 1970; B.S.N., Calif. State U., 1972; M.Nursing, UCLA, 1974; Ph.D., Kans. State U., 1983; m. Earl Dean Curry, Dec. 25, 1970. Office nurse, Houston, 1947-49; psychiat. technician Wash. State Hosp., 1958-59; physician asst., Spokane, Wash., 1959-65; camp nurse Wash. Summer Camp, Medical Lake, 1962-64; office nurse, Sacramento, 1965-69; psychiat. nurse Neuro-Psychiat. Inst., Los Angeles, 1973; asst. prof. nursing Kans. State Coll., 1974-75; asst. prof. Radford Coll., 1975-76, 78-79; asst. prof. U. Tex., 1976-77, 77-78; asso. prof. St. Mary of the Plains Coll., 1979; asst. prof. Pittsburg (Kans.) State U., 1980; asst. prof. nursing Wichita State U., 1980—; ARC nurse, Va., Tex., and Kans., 1974—. Mem. NEA, AAUP, Am. Nurses Assn., Nat. League Nursing, Internat. Transactional Analysis Assn., Am. Assn. Mental Deficiency, Kans. State Nurses Assn., UCLA Nurses Alumni, Tex. Nurses Assn., AAUW, Sigma Theta Tau, Phi Delta Kappa, Nat. Council Family Relations. Democrat. Contbr. in field. Office: Department Nursing PO Box 41 Wichita State U Wichita KS 67208

CURRY, NANCY ELLEN, educator; b. Brockway, Pa., Jan. 26, 1931; d. George R. and Mary F. (Covert) C.; B.A., Grove City Coll., 1952; M.Ed., U. Pitts., 1956, Ph.D., 1972. Tchr. public schs., East Brady and Oakmont, Pa., 1952-55; presch. demonstration tchr. Arsenal Family and Children's Center, U. Pitts., 1955-79, asso. dir., 1971-79; instr. Sch. of Health Related Professions, U. Pitts., 1956-61, asst. prof., 1961-72, asso. prof., 1972-75, prof., 1975—, acting chmn. dept. child devel./child care, 1972-73, chmn. dept., 1973—; asso. Pitts. Psychoanalytic Inst., 1974—; Fulbright exchange tchr. North Oxford Nursery Sch., Oxford, Eng., 1957-58; asso. dir. early childhood project Edn. Professions Devel. Act, U.S. Office Edn., 1970-74; cons. in field. Lic. psychologist, Pa. Mem. AAUP, Assn. for Care of Children in Hosps., Nat. Assn. for Edn. of Young Children, Am. Psychol. Assn., Am. Psychoanalytic Assn. Producer child devel. films, also articles in field. Office: 213 Pennsylvania Hall U Pitts Pittsburgh PA 15261

CURTIS, ANNA BLAIR, banker; b. Crawford, W.Va., Jan. 28, 1918; d. Thomas Jackson and Emma (Davisson) Blair; student Coll. William and Mary, 1936; A.B., W.Va. U., 1941; m. Harry Edward Curtis, June 21, 1941; children—Harry Edward, Emma Blair Curtis Bramble. With Weston (W.Va.) Nat. Bank, 1976—, also dir. Mem. St. Albans Parks and Recreation Commn., 1969-72; mem. women's com. Charleston (W.Va.) Symphony Orch. Mem. DAR, Chi Omega. Democrat. Episcopalian.

CURTIS, CHARLOTTE MURRAY, editor, columnist; b. Chgo.; d. George Morris and Lucile (Atcherson) Curtis; B.A. in Am. History, Vassar Coll., 1950; H.H.D., St. Michael's Coll., 1974; LL.D. (hon.), Denison U., 1976; L.H.D. (hon.), Bates Coll., 1977, Union Coll., 1979. Reporter, soc. editor Columbus (Ohio) Citizen, 1950-61; reporter N.Y. Times, 1961—, family/style editor, 1965-73, asso. editor, 1974—, editor Op-Ed page, 1974-82, columnist, 1982—; free-lance writer, 1950—; tchr. narrative and short story writing, Columbus YWCA, 1952-54; radio commentator, Sta. WMNI, Columbus, 1959-60, Sta. WQXR, N.Y.C., 1970-71. Founder, pres. Young Assos. Columbus Symphony Orch.; chmn. edn. Columbus Jr. League, 1958-60; mem. N.Y. Jr. League 1964—; mem. Manhattan adv. bd. N.Y. Urban League; mem. Princeton Adv. Council for Sociology, U. Chgo. adv. Council Nat. Humanities Inst. Recipient various awards for reporting, writing N.Y. Newspaper Women's Club, Ohio Newspaper Women's Assn.; Ohio Gov.'s award for journalism, 1973, awards N.Y. and Los Angeles Women in Communications, Newspaper Journalism award U. So. Calif.; Journalism award Am. Newspaper Women's Club, 1969. Author: First Lady, 1963; The Rich and Other Atrocities, 1976; Ohio Humanitarian award ACLU, 1979. Contbr. to The Soviet Union: The Fifty Years, 1967; Mafia: U.S.A., 1972; Assignment; America, 1974. Home: 40 E 10th St New York NY 10003 Office: 229 W 43d St New York NY 10036

CURTIS, DOROTHY (DOLLY) POWERS, textile artist; b. N.Y.C., Apr. 25, 1942; d. David C. and Miriam Roger (Harvey) Powers; B.S. in Edn. (Alumni Meml. scholar), Pa. State U., 1963; M.A., N.Y.U., 1966; student Brookfield Craft Center, 1971-78; m. John Edwin Curtis, June 15, 1963; children—Kara Aimee, Jason Andrew. Tchr. public secondary schs., Milesburg, Pa., and Rye, N.Y., 1963-68; owner, operator Contemporary Fibers/Textile Studio, Easton, Conn., 1972—; exhibited in one-woman shows: Silvermine Guild, Conn., 1978, Design Research, Conn., 1979, Pindar Gallery, N.Y.C., 1979, Waveny Carriage Barn, Conn., 1980; group shows include: Elements, Conn. and N.Y., 1975-79, Julie's, N.Y.C., 1977, U. Bridgeport (Conn.), 1977, Conn. Coll., 1975, Silvermine Guild, 1975-70, Marymount Coll., N.Y., 1975, 76, Wesleyan U., Conn., 1974, 79; represented in permanent collections: Marymount Coll., Meredith Assos., Conn.; represented by Pindar Gallery, N.Y.C. Recipient Various exhbn. awards, 1973-77; Conn. State grantee, 1976. Mem. Am. Crafts Council, Soc. Conn. Craftsmen, Handweavers Guild Conn., Handweavers Guild Westchester County, Handweavers Guild N.Y., Handweavers Guild Boston, Surface Design Assn., Silvermine Artists Guild. Subject of articles in profl. publs. Home and Studio: 35 Flat Rock Rd Easton CT 06612

CURTIS, FRANCES JO, real estate broker-developer; b. Winnepeg, Man., Can., Oct. 17, 1923; d. William and Anna (Strelecki) Curnell; brought to U.S., 1925, naturalized, 1951; student U. Detroit, 1952-54, Oakland U., 1974-76; grad. Specs Howard Sch. Broadcast Arts, 1979; children—Carol (Mrs. Bill Lowery), Dennis Curtis, Bradley. Founder, prin. Troy Realty (Mich.), 1954—; founder, pub. Tri-City Messenger, Troy, 1956-61; owner Meadowbrook Realty & Mortgage, 1976—, Sta. WTIQ (radio), 1982—, host radio program. Sec. of Incorporation, City of Troy, 1955; founding mem. Indsl. Com. Troy, 1957-62, Library Com., 1959-65, Sewer Com., 1958-62, Civic Center Com., 1960-65 (all Troy); mem. Crittenton Hosp. Com., Rochester, Mich., 1958-62. Mem. Coast Guard Aux., 1980. Lic. broadcaster, ham operator. Mem. Troy C. of C. (founder 1959), Air Force Assn. (Mich. aerospace chmn.), Internat. Platform Assn. Former editor Mich. Bus. and Profl. Women's Mag. Home: 1039 N Woodward PO Box 475 Birmingham MI 48012 Office: 2820 W Maple Troy MI 48084

CURTIS, JEANNETTE, ins. co. rep.; b. Washington, Feb. 6, 1948; d. Samuel Leroy and Elmira (McAbee) Curtis; B.S., U. D.C., 1972, M.S., 1973. Clin. speech pathologist Hackensack (N.J.) Hosp., 1972-79; sales rep. John Hancock Life Ins. Agy., Cresskill, N.J., 1979—; speech cons. Holley Ctr., Leonard Johnson Nursery, 1972-79, vol., 1975—; lectr., condr. workshops Prisoner's Accelerated Creative Exposures, 1980; intern asst. to curator Community Gallery, Bklyn. Mus., 1980. Bd. dirs. Afro Ednl. Center, Teaneck, N.J., 1979; exec. dir. Afro Am. Ednl. Center, 1980; ednl. and art coordinator Bergen County Ad Hoc Com. Black Women's Orgns., 1981-83; adviser Benevolent Leadership Assn. of Cultural Knowledge, Dwight Morrow High Sch., 1981-82; mem. child evaluation team spl. services dept. Englewood (N.J.) Bd. Edn., 1981-82. Mem. Am. Speech and Hearing Assn., N.J. Speech and Hearing Assn., Bergen Passaic Assn. Life Underwriters, Internat. Soc. Artists, Greater Paterson Art Council, Cultural Vistiors to Africa, Nat. Conf. Artists. Democrat. African Methodist Episcopalian. Poetry readings, 1977—; exhibited in group art shows at various galleries. Home: 77 Mattlage Pl Apt 5 Englewood NJ 07631 Office: 50 Spring St Cresskill NJ 07626

CURTIS, LINDA KAY, accountant; b. Washington, Aug. 16, 1954; d. Robert Albert and Beverly Joyce (Rounds) Sargent; B.S. with honors, George Mason U., 1975; m. Timothy Rolin Curtis, Jan. 3, 1976. Staff acct. Soza & Co., Ltd., Falls Church, Va., 1974-75, sr. acct., 1976-78; sr. auditor James C. Jones, Alexandria, Va., 1979; mgr. M.D. Oppenheim & Co., C.P.A.s, Washington, 1979—. C.P.A., Va. Mem. Am. Inst. C.P.A.s, Va. Soc. C.P.A.s, Am. Soc. Women Accts., No. Va. C.P.A.s. Methodist. Home: 7423 Shreve Rd Falls Church VA 22043 Office: 1629 K St Suite 600 Washington DC 20006

CURTIS, RUBY BAHNER, tax shelter specialist; b. Nanticoke, Pa., Dec. 30, 1948; d. Howard John and Viola Jane (Rosencrans) Chapin; B.S., Pa. State U., 1970; M.A., U. Md., 1977; m. Arthur V. Curtis, Jr., May 23, 1981. Tchr., Gov. Mifflin Jr. High Sch., Shillington, Pa., 1970-73; data analyst, computer programmer ITT Electro-Physics Lab., Columbia, Md., 1973-75; grad. asst. U. Md., College Park, 1975-77; systems devel. mgr. Future Shapes, Inc., Pikesville, Md., 1977-79; account exec. H.C. Copeland & Asso. Columbia, Md., 1979—, dist. mgr., 1981—; lectr. in field. Coach, Jr. Tennis Team, Columbia, Md., 1976-77; active Nat. Jr. Tennis League, 1976-77. Mem. Nat. Assn. Female Execs., U.S. Tennis Assn., Old English Sheepdog of Am. Home: 6259 Bright Plume Columbia MD 21044 Office: 10227 Wincopin Circle Suite 818 Columbia MD 21044

CURTIS, SHIRLEY ANN, educator; b. Nauvoo, Ala., Sept. 25, 1943; d. Edward Herbert and Grace (Rhoden) C.; B.A. in English and Speech, U. S.Fla., Tampa, 1964, M.A. in English, 1969; Ph.D. in Higher Edn., Fla. State U., 1979; m. Frederick Cameron Sumner, Dec. 16, 1972 (div.); 1 son, Matthew Frederick Curtis. Jr. and sr. high sch. tchr., Fla. and Calif., 1965-67; resident counselor, instr. English U. S.Fla., 1967-70; prof. communications and humanities Polk Community Coll., Winter Haven, Fla., 1970— , pres. faculty senate, 1982—. Vice pres., program chmn. Unitarian-Universalist Fellowship, Lakeland, Fla., 1980—, pres., 1982—; del. Fla. Democratic Conv., 1978; co-founder Cinema Six, 1972-74. Mem. Internat. Transactional Analysis Assn., Nat. Assn. Bus. and Profl. Women, Fla. Women's Network, Nat. Assn. Female Execs., NOW, Fla. Assn. Community Colls., Sierra Club. Democrat. Office: Dept Communication and Fine Arts Polk Community Coll 999 Ave H NE Winter Haven FL 33880

CURTISS, FLORENCE MARIE, ret. nurse; b. Flushing, Ohio, June 7, 1922; d. John William and Sara Bell (Anderson) Evans; R.N., Ohio Valley Gen. Hosp. Sch. Nursing, 1943; B.S. in Nursing, Ohio State U., 1948; m. John Stuart Curtiss, Dec. 4, 1949; children—Sandra Lynn, Philip Evan, Alan Stuart. Supr., VA Hosp., Battle Creek, Mich., 1949-51, instr., 1958-82; trustee VA Employees Credit Union, 1977—. Chmn. bd. dirs. McKay Library, Augusta, Mich., 1967—; chmn. Bicentennial Com., 1976; treas. Augusta Mus. Served with Nurse Corps, USN, 1944-46. Mem. Mich. Library Assn., Federally Employed Women, Inc., Nurses Orgn. VA. Republican. Methodist. Home: 412 N Augusta Dr Augusta MI 49012

CURTISS, GAYL MARUEEN, mktg. exec.; b. Seattle, Apr. 21, 1951; s. Robert Roy and Patricia Lee C.; B.A., Central Wash. U., Ellensburg, 1975, postgrad., 1975-76. Account mgr. Brittania Sportswear Inc., Seattle, 1976; advt. mgr. B and J Industries, Inc., Marysville, Wash., 1976-81; mktg. dir. Cardinal Recreation, Everett, Wash., 1982—. Pres. Marysville Fine Arts Assn., 1981; 1st v.p. Marysville Strawberry Festival, 1980, Marysville YMCA, 1980. Recipient United Way Community award, 1979; Marysville Friendship Award, 1980. Mem. Direct Mail Mktg. Assn., Central Wash. U. Alumni Assn., (dir.), Snohomish County Public Relations Roundtable. Democrat. Lutheran. Editor: Country Living News, 1981-82. Home: 822 129th Pl NW Marysville WA 98270 Office: PO Box 9002 Everett WA 98206

CURTISS, VIENNA IONE, author, designer, illustrator; b. Eau Claire, Wis., 1909; d. Frederick and Esther Pearl (Scott) Curtiss; grad. in interior architecture Parsons Sch. Design, N.Y.C., 1930; Ed.D. in Fine Arts, Columbia U., 1960. Profl. designer, Hollywood, Calif., 1930-37; prof. design in art Ariz. State U., 1937-40, U. Md., 1940-75; author-designer-illustrator Life's Great Show and, Zip, Zing, Ping, Pop (companion vols.), 1966; I Should Be Glad to Help You, Madame, 1977; Pageant of Art: A Visual History of Western Culture (internat. award graphic arts competition Printing Industries Am.), 1977; Cappy-Rollicking Rancher Atop Arizona's Mighty Rim (1st prize non-fiction. Nat. League Am. Pen Women), 1980. Address: 1727 Massachusetts Ave NW Washington DC 20036

CURTRIGHT, GLADYS STEELE, real estate broker; b. Evansville, Wis., May 13, 1904; d. Robert L. and Mamie L. (Haley) Steele; student Rockford (Ill.) Coll., Beloit (Wis.) Coll.; m. Walter L. Curtright, Dec. 22, 1923; children—Lois Rae Curtright Henderson, Jay B. Cosmetologist, Cin., 1922-28; agt. Prudential Ins. Co., Beloit, 1930-33; various acctg. positions, 1942-50; owner refail gift shop and real estate office, Beloit, 1950-64; broker, salesman J.R. Schuster Agy., Beloit, 1964-72, Exec. Services, Sanibel, Fla., 1974-78; v.p., broker Bluebill Properties, Inc., Sanibel Island, 1978—; past pres. Beloit Bd. Realtors. Mem. Nat. Assn. Relators, Fla. Assn. Realtors, Ft. Myers Bd. Realtors, Naples Area Bd. Realtors. Methodist. Home: 896 Angel Wing Dr Sanibel Island FL 33597 Office: 2422 Periwinkle Way Sanibel Island FL 33957

CURVIN, KENYA JOYCE, oil co. and geol. service co. exec.; b. Oklahoma City, June 15, 1938; d. T. Clinton and A. Jean (Coulter) Wallace; student Belhaven Coll., Jackson, Miss., 1957, Oklahoma City U., 1958, Okla. U., 1976-78; m. James Daniel Curvin, June 9, 1977; 1 child, Cimarron Trace Anthony Curvin; children by previous marriage—Derek Jerome Sanderson, Gina Rachelle Sanderson. New accounts rep. Fidelity Bank N.A., Oklahoma City, 1964-68; geol. asst. G.B.K. Co., Oklahoma City, 1968-72; psychiat. unit mgr. Queens Hosp., Honolulu, 1972-74; exec. officer Standard of Wewoka, Inc., Oklahoma City, 1974—, also dir.; naturalist Okla. Tourism and Recreation Dept., 1977-78; owner, operator Wildcat Geol. Services, Oklahoma City, 1979—, teaching dir. Wildcat Geol. Mapping Seminars; v.p. Scissortail Oil Corp., 1982—; asst. v.p. G.B.K. Co., 1982; drafting coordinator GADSCO, Inc.; ecology and conservation lectr. Mem. Nat. Assn. Female Execs. (network dir.), Okla. Petroleum Drafting Assn. Democrat. Author: Manna-Mana (poetry), 1977; composer: Red Land (musical play), 1980; Milky Way Galaxy, 1981; ballads; photographer. Office: 1343 First National Center W Oklahoma City OK 73102

CUSACK, MARY JOSEPHINE, lawyer; b. Canton, Ohio, Mar. 3, 1935; d. Edward Thomas and Mary (O'Meara) Cusack; A.B, Marquette U., 1957; J.D., Ohio State U., 1959. Admitted to Ohio bar, 1959, U.S. Supreme Ct. bar, 1962; mem. firm Cotruvo and Cusack, Columbus, Ohio; atty. for Indsl. Commn. Ohio, Columbus, 1960-61, Office Tax Commr., Columbus, 1961-65. Pres., E.T. Cusack, Inc., Canton, 1963-64, dir., 1960-64; spl. counsel to Atty. Gen. William J. Brown. Mem. Ohio Commn. on Status of Women. Mem. Am. Bar Assn., Ohio Bar Assn. (past chmn. workmen's compensation com., mem. council dels.), Columbus Bar Assn. (profl. ethics com., adv. com. fees, workmen's compensation, Women Lawyers Club Columbus (past pres.), Ohio Acad. Trial Lawyers (workmen's compensation com.), Franklin County Trial Lawyers (sec.), Nat. Assn. Women Lawyers (rec. sec.), Ohio Assn. Attys. Gen. (past pres.), Am. Arbitration Assn. (nat. panel arbitrators), Thomas More Soc., Kappa Beta Pi (past internat. pres., del. Profl. Frat. Assn.), Theta Phi Alpha. Clubs: Columbus Toastmistress (past pres.), Columbus Met. Home: 229 W Southington Ave Worthington OH 43085 Office: 50 W Broad St Columbus OH 43215

CUSHMAN, HELEN BAKER, cons., historian; b. Perth Amboy, N.J.; d. Ivan Franklin and Lucile (Atkinson) Baker; B.A., Barnard Coll.; postgrad. N.Y. U.; m. Robert Arnold Cushman, June 2, 1945; children—Lucinda, Robert. Route analyst Air Transport Command, Washington, 1942-44; personnel asst. Gen. Cable Corp., N.Y.C., 1944-45; sr. staff asst. to chmn. Trans World Airline, Inc., N.Y.C., 1946-50; mng. assoc. H. M. Baker Assocs., Westfield, N.J., 1958—; cons. to various corps., 1958—. Pres. Barnard Coll. Club North Central, N.J., 1962-64; pres. PTA, 1964-65. Recipient Literary award Am. Records Mgmt. Assn. 1972. Mem. N.J. Hist. Soc., Soc. Am. Archivists. Club: PEO. Office: 266 E Dudley Ave Westfield NJ 07090

CUSNIR, MARION, physician; b. Nova Sulota, Switzerland, Mar. 19, 1915; came to U.S., 1946, naturalized, 1952; d. Aron and Sima (Gonikman) Cusnir; student U. Berlin, 1930-33, U. Freiburg (Germany), 1934-36; M.D. cum laude, U. Frankfurt (Germany), 1936; m. Herbert Wyatt, Apr. 15, 1939; 1 son, Robert. Intern, Hosp. for Skin Diseases, London, 1943-44: asst. med. officer London Hosp., 1942; med. officer Hollymoor Emergency Hosp., Birmingham, Eng., 1942-44; practice medicine, London, 1944-46; resident in medicine Meriden (Conn.) Hosp., 1947-48; practice medicine specializing in internal medicine and allergy, Meriden, 1948—; mem. staff Vets. War. Meml. Hosp., Meriden. Mem. Pan-Am. Med. Assn., New Haven County Med. Assn., Conn. Med. Soc. Club: Order of Eastern Star. Home: 912 Kingfisher Ln Westbrook CT 06498 Office: 21 Colony St Meriden CT 06450 also 135 Whitney Ave New Haven CT 06510

CUTHBERTSON, MRS., GEORGE RAYMOND, club woman; b. Liberty, Mo., Apr. 2, 1911; d. Edgar and Mary Jane (Anderson) Archer; student William Jewell Coll., 1929-31; m. George Raymond Cuthbertson, Sept. 3, 1931. Dist. capt. Mothers' March of Dimes, 1959-60; mem. Bergen County Panhellenic Council 1957-60; mem. woman's com. William Jewell Coll. Mem. Mo. Hist. Soc., Clay County Hist. Soc., DAR, Huguenot Soc. S.C., Clay County Mus. Assn., Alpha Delta Pi. Baptist. Clubs: Liberty Hills Country, Fortnightly, P.E.O. Home: 1921 Clay Dr Liberty MO 64068

CUTLER, MORENE PARTEN, civic worker; b. Waxahachie, Tex., July 27, 1911; d. Bedford Taylor and Lofie Mae (Stockton) Parten; student Trinity U., 1929, U. Okla., l1931, U. Tex., Austin, 1933; m. Robert Ward Cutler, Apr. 27, 1954. Asst. to dir. N.Y. Sch. of Interior Decoration, N.Y.C., 1938; chief cons. Hilton Hotels Corp., Chgo., 1946-48; interior designer, 1948-54; founder aux. N.Y. chpt. AIA, 1958, 1st pres. Chmn., Salado Bicentennial Commn., 1974—; dir. Central Tex. Bicentennial com., 1974—; vice chmn. Internat. Debutante Ball, N.Y.C., 1975-78; mem. Beautify Tex. Council, 1976—; chmn. Beautify Salado Com., 1979-80; founder Tex. Bluebonnet com., 1961. Recipient Tex. Good Will awards, 1960—, citation AIA, 1966; named hon. mem. Ellis County Hist. Mus. and Art Gallery, Waxahachie, 1967. Trustee Central Tex. Area Mus., Salado, 1968-75. Mem. Chautauqua Preservation Soc. (dir. Waxahachie 1975), Newport Preservation Soc., Nat. Trust Hist. Preservation, Bell County Hist. Soc., Salado C. of C. (dir. aux. bd. 1974-75), Tex. Soc. of Washington. Episcopalian. Clubs: Met. (N.Y.C.), Tex. Ex-Students Assn. Author: Stagecoach Inn—Iron Skillet and Velvet Potholder, 1981. Home: PO Box 26 Salado TX 76571

CUTLER, RHODA DAWN, human resources specialist; b. Phila., Dec. 11, 1944; d. Allen Robert and Mary (Satinoff) C.; B.S., Emerson Coll., 1966. Tng. supr. Hilton Reservation Service, subs. Hilton Hotels, Inc. and Hilton Internat., N.Y.C., 1966-69; asst. tng. dir. Loews Hotels, N.Y.C., 1969-70; promotion mgr. Lawrence Schiff Silk Mills, Inc., N.Y.C., 1970-73; with Chem. Bank, N.Y.C., 1973—, mgr. mgmt. devel., 1977-79; human resources officer human resources systems devel., 1980—; cons. Vol. Urban Cons. Group, 1978—; alumni recruiting rep. Emerson Coll., 1978—. Mem. Am. Soc. Tng. and Devel. (vice-chmn. bd. dirs. N.Y. met. chpt. 1977-80). Jewish. Home: 301 E 47th St New York NY 10017 Office: 52 Broadway New York NY 10004

CUTLER, RUTH ELLEN LEMON, aircraft co. ofcl.; b. York, Nebr., Feb. 26, 1928; d. Harry Oliver and Ruby Elizabeth (Hartgrave) Lemon; student Latter-day Saints Bus. Coll., 1946; m. Harold Max Cutler, Nov. 17, 1944 (div. 1971); children—Sheryl, Harold Max, Pamela. Sec., photostat operator IRS, Salt Lake City, 1951-54; sec. Purdue U. Sch. Civil Engring., West Lafayette, Ind. and engring. firms, 1954-60; exec. sec. Rico Argentine Mining Co., Salt Lake City and Rico, Colo., 1960-63; exec., legal sec. Manpower, Inc., Salt Lake City, 1959-71; owner, operator Mountain View Motel and Country Club Motel, Salt Lake City, 1963-64; exec. sec., adminstrv. asst. to clin. psychologist in pvt. practice, Salt Lake City, 1964-70; legal sec., head office staff Watkins & Faber, attys., Salt Lake City, 1971-73; adminstrv. sec. F-15 Radar div. Hughes Aircraft Co., Culver City, Calif., 1973—; dir., v.p., sec. Cutler Enterprises, Inc., Salt Lake City, 1963-71. State del. Utah Republican party, 1967-69; active various community drives. Mem. League Utah Writers.

CUTLER, SEENA NORMA, psychiat. social worker; b. N.Y.C., Apr. 18, 1928; d. Nat and Rose S. Schwartz; B.A., N.Y. U., Washington Sq. Coll., 1951; M.S.W., Columbia U., 1955; m. B. Robert Cutler, Nov. 24, 1954; children—Andrew Neale, Matthew Steven. Social worker Bklyn. VA Hosp., 1955-59, Roosevelt Hosp., N.Y.C., 1974-77; sr. social worker, supr. Community Health Program, Queens-Nassau, Inc., New Hyde Park, N.Y., 1977—; cons. VA Div. of Handicapped, Kansas City, Kans., 1976; guest lectr. Nassau County Dept. Sr. Citizens Affairs, 1980-81, Am. Cancer Soc., 1981; group therapist, various groups, 1979-81. Bd. dirs. and com. mem. Temple Emanuel of Gt. Neck, N.Y., 1965-76, v.p. Sisterhood, 1969-71; com. mem. Gt. Neck Public Schs., 1964-79. Recipient award, Bklyn. VA Hosp., 1959; cert. social worker. Mem. Nat. Assn. Social Workers. Democrat. Home: 48 Berkshire Rd Great Neck NY 10023 Office: 410 Lakeville Rd New Hyde Park NY 10042

CUTLER, VIRGINIA FARRER, educator; b. Park City, Utah, Dec. 17, 1905; d. Robert and Mary (Jensen) Farrer; B.A., U. Utah, 1926; M.A., Stanford U., 1937; Ph.D., Cornell U., 1946; postgrad Vassar Coll., 1938, 39, Wharton Sch. U. Pa., 1953; m. Ralph Garr Cutler, July 10, 1929 (dec. 1931); children—Robert, Ralph Garr. Tchr. home econs. schs. Manti, Jordan, 1926-29, Taylorsville, Utah, 1932-35, Durham, Calif., 1936-38; home demonstration agt. U. Calif., 1938-44; head dept. home econs. U. Utah, 1946-54; teaching advisor S.E. Asia, Thailand and Indonesia, 1954-61; dean Coll. Family Living Brigham Young U., Provo, Utah, 1961-66, Disting. prof., 1969-72, emeritus prof., Fulbright 1972—; prof. U. Ghana, 1966-69; chmn. Major Appliance Consumer Action Panel, Chgo., 1970-75; mem. Pres. Nixon Consumer Adv. Council, 1972-74. Recipient Outstanding Womanhood award Brigham Young U., 1974. Mem. AAUW (Utah pres. 1972-74, named Utah Woman of Yr. 1966), Am. Home Econs. Assn., Sigma Xi, Pi Lambda Theta, Phi Kappa Phi, Omicron Nu. Republican. Mormon. Author pamphlets in field. Home: 1173 Princeton Ave Salt Lake City UT 84105

CUTNAW (CUGNEAU), MARY-FRANCES, educator, writer; b. Dickinson, N.D., June 15, 1931; d. Delbert A. and Edith (Calhoun Pritchard) Cutnaw; B.S., U. Wis.-Madison, 1953, M.S., 1957, Ph.D. candidate, 1959-60, 67-68. Tchr., Displaced Persons Vocat. Sch., Stevens Point, Wis., 1951-52, Pulaski High Sch., Milw., 1953-55; teaching asst. dept. speech U. Wis.-Madison, 1956-57, spl. asst. Sch. Edn., summer 1957; instr. speech and English, U. Wis.-Stout, Menomonie, 1957-58, dean of women, 1958-59, asst. prof. speech, 1959-64, asso. prof., 1964-74, prof. emeritus, 1974—; hon. scholar, teaching asst. dept. speech U. Wis.-Madison, 1959-60, hon. scholar dept. speech, 1967-68. Organizer, past adviser Young Democratic Orgn., U. Wis.-Stout. Mem. Internat. Platform Assn., U. Wis. Alumni Assn., Assn. U. Wis. Faculties, Wis. Acad. Scis., Arts and Letters, Wis. Women's Network, Am. Personnel and Guidance Assn., Linus Pauling Inst., Am. Quarter Horse Assn., Nat. Soc. Prevention Cruelty to Animals, Nat. Anti-Vivisection Soc., Nat. Ret. Tchrs. Assn., Smithsonian Asso., Center for Study Democratic Instns., ACLU, Common Cause, NOW, Walker Art Center, Phi Beta, Sigma Tau Delta, Pi Lambda Theta, Gamma Phi Beta. Roman Catholic. Club: Lake City Yacht, Blaisdell Pl (dir.), Calhoun Beach. Contbr. articles to profl. jours. Research in speech proficiency and teaching success, curricular speech for spl. occupational groups, speech as guidance tool. Founder, Edith and Kent P. Cutnaw Scholarship, U. Wis.-Stevens Point. Home: Red Cedar Farm Box 282 Menomonie WI 54751 Winter: Key West FL 33040

CUZA, PATRICIA ANN, feminist; b. Massillon, Ohio, Dec. 18, 1936; d. Charles V. and Anna (Gergel) Cuza; A.B., Oberlin (Ohio) Coll., 1958; student Katharine Gibbs Sch., N.Y.C., 1960; M.A., Mich. State U., East Lansing, 1969; M.P.A., Western Mich. U.; children—Cybele, Sabrina Silea. Exec. dir. Mich. Women's Com., Lansing, 1972-77; adminstr. Crime Victims Compensation Bd., Lansing, 1977—; mem. women's adv. council Learning and Career Center for Women, Lansing Community Coll., 1974-77; mem. task force on status of female offender Nat. Council Crime and Delinquency, 1974-76; mem. reference bd. Cultural Pluralism project Mich. Dept. Edn., 1974-76; founding mem. Mich. Women's Polit. Caucus, 1972; cons. in field. Fiscal officer Mich. coordinating com. Nat. Internat. Women's Year Commn., 1976-77; del. Nat. Women's Conf., 1977; pres. Lansing Ballet Assn., 1980-81; vice chmn. E. Lansing Cable Communications Commn. Mem. NOW (Positive Action award 1975), Ingham Women's Polit. Caucus (charter), Mich. Fed. Bus. and Profl. Women, Profl. Women's Caucus, YWCA (award of recognition 1975), Women in Cable. Home: 730 Chittenden Dr East Lansing MI 48823 Office: Crime Victims Compensation Bd Plaza Hotel Suite 809 Lansing MI 48933

CYPESS, SANDRA MESSINGER, educator; b. Bklyn., Jan. 5, 1943; d. Morris and Florence Messinger; B.A. magna cum laude, Bklyn. Coll., 1963; M.A., Cornell U., 1965; Ph.D., U. Ill., 1968; m. Raymond Cypess, Aug. 15, 1964; children—Aaron, Joshua. Vis. asst. prof. Duke U., 1967-70; asst. prof. Romance studies Point Park Coll., 1970-74; vis. asst. prof. Carnegie Mellon U., 1975-76; asso. prof. SUNY, Binghamton, 1976—; vis. prof. Haifa U., 1982. Mem. MLA, Am. Assn. Tchrs. Spanish and Portuguese, Latin Am. Studies Assn., North East Modern Lang. Assn. (mem. exec. council 1977-79), Phi Beta Kappa, Sigma Delta Pi, Pi Delta Phi. Jewish. Editor: Studies in Romance Languages & Lits.: Essays Critical & Contextual, 1979; mem. editorial bd. Latin American Theatre Review; contbr. articles in field. Office: Department of Romance Languages and Literatures SUNY Binghamton NY 13901

CZAYA, MARY THERESA, ednl. adminstr.; b. Carteret, N.J., June 2, 1917; d. Francis and Theresa (Mezglewski) Dylag; B.S., N.J. State Tchrs. Coll., 1947; M.Ed., Rutgers U., 1957; postgrad. U. Mexico, 1958; m. Francis Czaya, June 22, 1946; 1 son, Paul. Tchr., Nathan Hale Sch., Carteret, N.J., 1940-46, Columbus Sch., Carteret, 1946-61, prin., 1961-70; prin. Washington & Cleveland Schs., Carteret, 1970-79, Minue Sch., Carteret, 1979—. Trustee Carteret Public Library, 1972-78; mem. Middlesex County Mental Health Bd., 1961-66, Carteret Juvenile Delinquency Bd., 1974-75; trustee Middlesex County Coll., 1972—, bd. sec., 1978-81, bd. v.p., 1981—. Recipient cert. of merit VFW Aux., 1978. Mem. N.J. Congress Parents and Tchrs. (life), Nat. Elem. Prins. Assn., N.J. Elem. Prins. Assn., Kappa Delta Phi. Home: 75 Edgar St Carteret NJ 07008 Office: Post Blvd Carteret NJ 07008

CZECH, ELIZABETH SHIMER, broadcasting educator; b. Bethlehem, Pa., Oct. 18, 1919; d. William Robert and Grace Felicia (Penner) Shimer; B.A. magna cum laude, Georgian Court Coll., 1941; M.A., Lehigh U., 1954; Ph.D., Ohio State U., 1972; m. Valentine Anthony Czech, Sept. 1, 1962 (dec. 1974). Broadcaster, WGPA, Bethlehem, 1945-54; tchr. Liberty High Sch., Bethlehem, 1954-59; head radio-TV dept. Centenary Coll. for Women, 1959-66; instr. Ohio State U., 1966-68; head radio-TV-film dept. Shaw U., Raleigh, N.C., 1968-72; assoc. prof. communications U. Kans., Lawrence, 1972-75; assoc. prof. radio TV U. N.C., Chapel Hill, 1975—, asst. dean Coll. Arts and Scis.; cons. establishing ednl. radio stas.; cons. broadcast mgmt. of non-comml. radio stas., minorities in broadcast media. Mem. Broadcast Edn. Assn., Nat. Assn. Ednl. Broadcasters, Women in Communications, Speech Communication Assn., Internat. Communication Assn., Assn. Edn. in Journalism, Kappa Gamma Pi. Roman Catholic. Club: Altrusa. Home: 105 Yorktown Dr Chapel Hill NC 27514 Office: Dept Radio TV Univ NC Swain Hall 044A Chapel Hill NC 27514

CZERWINSKI, BARBARA SHELDEN, nurse, health care mgmt. cons.; b. Albany Calif., Nov. 27, 1940; d. Roger Francis and Lucinda Elizabeth (McCulla) Shelden; R.N., S. Merritt Hosp., Oakland, Calif., 1961; B.S. in Nursing, St. Louis U., 1974, M.S., 1977; m. Edmund W. Czerwiski, June 24, 1961; children—Melinda Jane, Mary Ann. Staff nurse Children's Hosp. East Bay, Oakland, 1961-62; office nurse, Berkeley, Calif., 1962-63; from staff nurse to head nurse Community Hosp. Indpls., 1965-72; ICU staff nurse St. Louis U. Hosps., 1972-73; cardiovascular clin. specialist dept. surgery St. Louis U. Med. Center, 1974-78; asst. dir. nursing-surgery U. Tex. Med. Br., Galveston, 1978-80, dir. inpatient nursing-surgery, 1980; clinic adminstr. Advanced Health Systems, Inc., Houston, 1980-81; health care mgmt. cons. B. Czerwinski and Assos., Houston, 1981—; dir. Nursing Diagnostic Center Hosp., Hosp. Corp. Am., Houston, 1982—; clin. instr. U. Tex. Med. Br. Sch. Nursing, 1978-80. Mem. Am. Assn. Critical Care Nurses (treas. St. Louis chpt. 1974-75), Am. Heart Assn., Am. Nurses Assn., Nat. Assn. Female Execs., Nat. League Nursing, Sigma Theta Tau. Presbyterian. Author book, articles in field. Address: 1907 Port Royal Houston TX 77058

DABBS, MIRIAM ADAIR, artist, journalist; b. Rialto, Calif., May 6, 1908; d. Watts McIntosh and Betty (Pearson) Adair; B.A., Miss. State

Coll. for Women, 1930; m. Chester Norwood Dabbs, Dec. 24, 1933; 1 son, Willis Norwood. English instr., Jones County Jr. Coll., Ellisville, Miss., 1933-34, also Am. history Northwest Jr. Coll., Senatobia, Miss., 1935-36; soc. editor Clarksdale (Miss.) Daily Register, 1942-47; feature writer, corr. Clarion-Ledger, Jackson, Miss., 1964-75, Jackson Daily News, 1968-75, Memphis Press-Scimitar, 1969-74; one-woman shows: Galeries Raymond Duncan, Paris, France, 1970, 71, 74, 77, 78, 79, 80, Originals Only Gallery, Memphis, 1971, Ligoa Duncan Gallery, N.Y.C., 1971, 76, Christ Only Mus., Eureka, Springs, Ark., Robinson-Carpenter Library, Cleveland, Miss., 1971, others; group shows include: Municipal Mus. Modern Art, Paris, 1974, Luxemburg Palace Mus., Paris, 1977, Festival Internat. d'Art de St. Germaine-de-Pres, 1974, 78, Internat. Festival, Barcelona, Spain, 1980. Missionary Soc., Bapt. Ch., 1952-53; mem. Clarksdale Beautification Commn., 1952-54, 56-63, sec., 1955, 68. Recipient Beautification Merit award, Miss. C. of C. community program at Clarksdale, 1961; recipient Art award Prix de Paris competition, 1970, 74, 77, 78; Gold medal Accademia Italia, 1979; Palmes de Oro al Merito Belgo-Hispanico, 1974; Internat. prize St. Germaine de Pres Exhbn., 1974. Mem. Nat. League Am. Pen Women (award; editor Pen Drifts, 1957), Ulster-Scot Hist. Soc. (Belfast, Ireland), DAR, Accademia Italia delle Arti e del Lavora. Clubs: Clarksdale Woman's (past pres.), Town and Country Garden (Clarksdale). Author: Idyls of the Delta; Coahoma, 1948; The Passing Storm; Sepaled Horns; Sonnets From India, 1962. Contbr. articles on founding families of Miss. to tech. lit. Research in genealogy. Home: 321 Maple St Clarksdale MS 38614

DABICH, LYUBICA, hematologist; b. Detroit, May 15, 1929; d. Milan and Mildred Dabich; B.S. in Chemistry, U. Mich., Ann Arbor, 1950; M.D., C.M., McGill U., Montreal, Que., Can., 1960. Intern, then resident in hematology U. Mich. Hosp., 1960-64, fellow, 1964-66; mem. faculty U. Mich. Med. Sch., 1966—, assoc. prof. hematology, 1973—; cons. in field. Elsa U. Pardee fellow, 1964-65; diplomate Am. Bd. Internal Medicine (hematology). Fellow A.C.P.; mem. Am. Fedn. Clin. Research, Am. Soc. Clin. Oncology, Am. Soc. Hematology. Author papers in field. Home: 2919 Park Ridge St Ann Arbor MI 48103 Office: Univ Hosp 1006 Catherine St Ann Arbor MI 48109

DABNEY, JUNE BOSLEY, educator, singer; b. St. Louis, Apr. 13, 1935; d. Preston Tyler and Alma Jean (Thompson) Bosley; B.M.E., Lincoln U., 1956; postgrad. Harris-Stowe State Coll., summers 1964-68, St. Louis U., summer, 1964, Webster Coll., 1980—; children—Diane Charisse Hawkins, Dellarese Carmen Hawkins, Marion P. Hawkins, Raphael Franklin Dabney. Tchr. vocal music and voice S.W. High Sch., 1976-77; tchr. vocal music, founder Honors Concert Choir, Visual and Performing Arts High Sch., St. Louis, 1977-80; tchr. vocal music, dir. student activities, Honors Music High Sch., 1980-82; music dir. Peacock Alley Cultural Art Center Workshops, St. Louis, 1982—; performing concert artist. Democratic committeewoman 1st Ward, St. Louis, 1974-76. Met. Opera audition winner, 1966; Ted Mack Original Amateur Hour winner, 1966-67; Recipient service award Chick Finney Assocs., 1970, Meritorious award in music St. Louis Silhouettes, 1967, Black Women of Unity award, 1974, Key to City and Gateway, Mayor A.J. Cervantes, 1975; Sumner High Sch. Alumni soloist 30th Anniversary, 1980; recipient Katz Radio Service award, 1966, service award Honors Music High Sch., 1982. Mem. Nat. Assn. Female Execs., Clarence Wilson Music Guild, Delta Sigma Theta. Club: St. Louis Div. Devel. Treatment Center Parents. Home: 5024 Durant Ave Saint Louis MO 63115

DABOLL, EVELYN LOUISE KENYON, tax and fin., real estate cons.; b. Old Mystic, Conn., Feb. 22, 1927; d. Anson Surber and L. Maude (Tinker) Kenyon; student Jackson (Miss.) Sch. Law, 1954; m. H. Merle Witt, Oct. 29, 1945 (div. Apr. 1956); m. 2d, Frederick A. Daboll, Feb. 9, 1962. Instr. traffic dept. So. New Eng. Telephone Co., New Britain, Conn. and Mystic, Conn., 1943-45; residential designer Frank Kincannon, AIA, Tupelo, Miss., 1949-51; chief dep. Chancery clk. Chancery Clk's Office, Tupelo, 1951-54; jr. partner Sadler Oil Co., Jackson, Miss., 1954-61; owner, operator Witt Enterprises, bookkeeping and secretarial services, 1961-62; adminstr. asst. Copp, Brenneman & Tighe, attys., New London, Conn., 1961-62; owner, operator Daboll Enterprises, Noank, Conn., 1963—. Moderator, Town of Groton Rep. Town Meeting, 1969-70, rep., 1968-70; mem. Bd. Selectmen Groton, 1980-81. Mem. New London Bd. Realtors, VFW Aux. Democrat. Baptist. Address: 206 Seneca Dr Noank CT 06340

DACE, TISH, ednl. adminstr.; b. Washington, Sept. 13, 1941; d. Edward Durnford and Claude Marshall (Russell) Skinner; B.A. magna cum laude, Sweet Briar Coll., 1963; M.A., Kans. State U., 1967, Ph.D., 1971; children—Hal, Ted. Instr. speech and drama Kans. State U., Manhattan, 1967-71; asst. prof. speech and drama John Jay Coll. Criminal Justice, City U. N.Y., N.Y.C., 1971-74, assoc. prof., dep. chmn., 1974-77, acting chmn., 1978, chmn., 1979-80; dean Coll. Arts and Scis., prof. English, Southeastern Mass. U., North Dartmouth, 1980—; theatre critic for The Villager, 1982—, The Advocate, 1982—, The Soho News, 1977-82, Other Stages, 1978-82; judge design awards Joseph Maharam Found., 1979—. Mem. Am. Theatre Critics Assn., Am. Soc. Theatre Research, Brit. Theatre Inst., New Drama Forum, Outer Critics Circle (exec. com.), Drama Desk, Theatre Library Assn., MLA, Women's Caucus for Modern Langs., Phi Beta Kappa (chpt. pres. 1969-70). Author: LeRoi Jones (Imamu Amiri Baraka): A Check List of Works by and About Him, 1971; (with Wallace Dace) The Theatre Student: Modern Theatre and Drama, 1973; contbr. articles to numerous publs. including mags. Office: College of Arts and Scis Southeastern Mass Univ North Dartmouth MA 02747

DACEY, EILEEN M., lawyer; b. N.Y.C., Dec. 15, 1948; d. Gabriel A. and Mary (Breen) D.; B.A. in Sociology, SUNY-Stony Brook, 1970; J.D., St. John's U., 1975. Assoc. Mendes & Mount, N.Y.C., 1976-80, jr. ptnr., 1980—. Mem. Vol. Lawyers for the Arts. Mem. ABA, Assn. Bar City N.Y., Council N.Y. Law Assocs. Republican. Episcopalian. Home: 208 E 35th St New York NY 10016 Office: 3 Park Ave New York NY 10016

DACEY, KATHLEEN RYAN, judge; b. Boston; A.B. with honors, Emmanuel Coll., 1941; M.S. in L.S. (Mass. Library Assn. scholar), Simmons Coll., 1942; LL.B., Northeastern U., 1945, J.D., 1945; postgrad. Boston U. Law Sch., 1945-46. Admitted to Mass. bar, 1945, U.S. Supreme Ct. bar, 1957; law clk. to justices Mass. Supreme Jud. Ct., 1945-47; practiced in Boston, 1947-75; asst. atty. gen., chief civil bur. Mass. Dep. Atty. Gen., Boston, 1975-77; U.S. Adminstrv. law judge, 1977—; auditor, master Commonwealth of Mass., 1972-75, Suffolk and Norfolk Counties (Mass.), 1972-75; asst. dist. atty. Suffolk County, 1971-72; mem. panel def. counsel for indigent persons U.S. Dist. Ct., Dist. Mass.; lectr., speaker in field. Bd. dirs. Mission United Neighborhood Improvement Team, Boston; mem. Boston Sch. Com., 1945-46, chmn., 1946-47. Recipient Oratorical Contest prize Am. Legion; Silver Shingle award Boston U. Sch. Law, 1980; named Alumnae Woman of Year Northeastern U. Law Sch. Alumni Assn., 1976. Mem. Internat. Bar Assn., Am. Bar Assn. (ho. of dels. 1981—), Mass. Bar Assn., Boston Bar Assn., Norfolk Bar Assn., Middlesex Bar Assn., Am. Trial Lawyers Assn., Mass. Trial Lawyers Assn., Nat. Assn. Women Lawyers (pres.), Mass. Assn. Women Lawyers, Internat. Fedn. Women Lawyers, Boston U. Law Sch. Alumni Assn. (corr. sec. 1974-76), Boston U. Nat. Alumni Council. Contbr. articles to legal jours. Office: Health and Human Services Bur Hearings and Appeals 55 Summer St Boston MA 02110

DACOSTA, JACQUELINE, advt. exec.; b. N.Y.C., Jan. 21, 1927; d. Joachim and Tirsa (Olmeda) DaCosta; B.A. in Bus. Adminstrn., Hunter Coll., 1952. Asst. export mgr. Morse Internat., N.Y.C., 1946-52; supr. media research Biow, Beirn, Toigo, Inc., N.Y.C., 1952-55; media research analyst Ted Bates & Co., N.Y.C., 1955-63, asst. v.p. media research, 1963-65, coordinator internat. media, 1965—, v.p., dir. media info. and analysis, 1965—, sr. v.p., 1977—, media dir., 1978—; cons. media, research, mktg., govt. and pvt. orgns.; internat. lectr. Mem. adv. bd. Nat. Urban Coalition; bd. govs. Nat. Conf. Puerto Rican Women, 1975-77, Puerto Rican Family Inst., 1977—; Hamilton Madison Settlement House, 1977—, pres., 1981; bd. dirs. Bus. Council for UN Decade for Women, pres., 1979; bd. dirs. Broadcast Pioneers Found. Mem. Am. Advt. Fedn. (dir., named Advt. Woman of Yr. 1974), Advt. Research Found. (dir.), Advt. Women N.Y. (pres. 1973-74). Internat. Radio TV Soc., Internat. Radio TV Found., Hispanics in Communications (founder, pres. 1980-81). Contbr. articles to trade jours. Home: 340 E 64th St New York NY 10021 Office: Ted Bates & Co 1515 Broadway New York NY 10036 *

DAEN, PHYLLIS HELENE, clin. psychologist; b. N.Y.C., Feb. 22, 1931; d. Herbert M. and Esther Deutsch; B.S., Queens Coll., 1950; Ph.D. (AAUW fellow 1955), Adelphi U., Garden City, N.Y., 1960; m. Jerome Daen, Dec. 25, 1952; children—Jonathan, Matthew, Meris. Researcher, N.Y. State Psychiat. Inst., 1950-54; chief psychologist Children's Home, Easton, Pa., also Northampton County Child Guidance Clinic, 1958-66; chief psychologist South County Mental Health Clinic, Springfield, Va., 1968-72; dir. tng. Woodburn Mental Health Clinic, Annandale, Va., 1972-78, bd. govs., 1982—; mem. faculty Georgetown U., 1973—, George Washington U., 1973—; clin. affiliate Am. U., 1973—; ind. practice psychology, 1978—; lectr. George Mason U.; cons. in field. Bd. dirs. N. Va. Colls. Daycare Centers, 1972-81; adv. bd. N. Va. Colls. Human Resources, 1974-79. Mem. Am. Psychol. Assn., AAAS, D.C. Psychol. Assn. (Disting. Contbn. award 1980), Md. Psychol. Assn., Washington Soc. Study Hypnosis (pres. 1982). Jewish. Club: Kenwood Country. Author papers in field. Home: 4700 Langdrum Ln Chevy Chase MD 20815 Office: 4300 Chain Bridge Rd Fairfax VA 22030

DAFFIN, CAROL FARWELL, mfg. co. exec.; b. Harrison, N.Y., Oct. 21, 1953; d. Edward B. and Frances R. (Brown) Farwell; student Chesapeake Coll., 1981, U. Md., 1976-77; m. Ronald Wayne Daffin, July 9, 1977; children—Jenny Alice, Kate Frances. Salesman, Easton (Md.) Pub. Co., 1973-74; sales mgr. Chesapeake Products, Inc., Easton, 1974-75; v.p. Helm Distbrs., Inc., Easton, 1975-78, now dir.; pres. Daffin Disposables, Inc., Secretary, Md., 1977—, also dir.; dir. Daffin Corp., Secretary. Recipient Md. tng. grant, 1980. Mem. NOW, Nat. Safety Council, Nat. Assn. Women in Bus., Safety Equipment Mfrs. Assn., Nat. Safety Equipment Dealers Assn., Am. Nuclear Soc., Am. Apparel Mfrs. Assn., Nat. Assn. Bus. and Profl. Women (Young Career Woman award 1982), Internat. Non-Woven Dealers Assn., Talbot County C. of C., Dorchester County C. of C. Republican. Home: 707 S Morris St Oxford MD 21654 Office: 1 Daffin Square Secretary MD 21664

DAGEL, LOU TOMLINSON, family counselor; b. Emporia, Kans., May 7, 1930; d. Lloyd H. and Josephine K. Tomlinson; B.A., B.S., Trinity U., San Antonio, 1965, M.S., 1968; m. A. Gene Dagel, June 28, 1951; children—Gena E., Tomlinson J., Karl M. Instr. psychology, dir. counseling and testing Tex. Lutheran Coll., 1969-81; practice family counseling, Seguin, Tex., 1968-82; bilingual psychol. tester Good Samaritan Center, San Antonio, also mem. bd. dirs.; 1st pres. Guadalupe County Mental Health-Mental Retardation Bd.. Vice pres. Guadalupe County United Fund; bd. dirs. Neighborhood Center Assn., San Antonio. Recipient various service awards. Mem. Am. Psychol. Assn., AAUP, Tex. Psychol. Assn., 99s, Psi Chi, Kappa Kappa Gamma. Republican. Episcopalian. Clubs: Seguin Zonta (area dir. 1980-81), Seguin Study (pres. 1981-82), Daus. of the King. Address: 1327 Keller Ln Seguin TX 78155

DAGGETT, MARSHA LEA, home economist, educator; b. Ft. Stockton, Tex., Feb. 10, 1917; d. Marsh and Artie (McLeod) Lea; B.S., Tex. Women's U., 1938; M.Ed., Sam Houston State U., 1957; Ph.D., Tex. Woman's U., 1972; m. Walter M. Daggett, June 19, 1938 (div. 1964); 1 son, Merrell. Tchr. sci. Calvert (Tex.) High Sch., 1954-57; tchr. vocat. home econs. Bremond (Tex.) High Sch., 1960-61; instr. home econs. Sam Houston State U., Huntsville, 1962-63, Stephen F. Austin State U., Nacagdoches, Tex., 1963-64; instr. to asst. prof. home econs. Lamar U., Beaumont, Tex., 1964-71; asst. to asso. prof. home econs. S.W. Tex. State U., San Marcos, 1972-77. Recipient teaching excellence award S.W. Tex. State U., 1975. Mem. Am., Tex. (exec. council 1966-72, 77—) home econs. assns., Jefferson, Tex. hist. assns., Internat. Nutrition Congress, Internat. Fedn. Home Econs., Internat., Am. dietetic assns., AAUP, AAUW, Inst. Food Technologists, Soc. Nutrition Edn., Nutrition Today, Tex. Nutrition Council (exec. council 1965-72), Internat. Gem Finders Soc., Ft. Stockton Hist. Soc. (dir. 1978-84, pres. 1980-82), Tex. Sheep and Goat Raisers Assn., Pecos County Livestock Show Assn., Pecos County Hist. Com., Tex. Womans U. Alumnae Assn., Nat. Wildlife Fedn. (world asso. mem.), Kappa Lambda Kappa (Tchr. of Yr. 1974, Appreciation award 1977), Delta Kappa Gamma, Kappa Omicron Phi, Phi Epsilon Omicron. Presbyn. Club: Pioneer (Ft. Stockton), Fort Stockton Lit. Editor Pecos County History, 1978-83. Home: Box 1545 Fort Stockton TX 79735

DAGLE, JULIE CLAUDELL, accountant; b. Springfield, Mass., Mar. 13, 1938; d. E. Joseph and Josephine M. (Field) Claudell; A.S. with high honors in Acctg., Manchester Community Coll., 1973; m. Robert John Zukas, Apr. 16, 1955; children—Julie, Robert, Susan, Laurence, Virginia; m. 2d, Thomas Jeffrey Dagle, June 24, 1977; children—Jennifer Lynn, Lindsey Jeanne. Office mgr. H & R Block, 1968-73; taxpayer service rep. IRS, Hartford, Conn., 1973-75, taxpayer service specialist, 1975-76, problem resolution officer Hartford dist. N. Atlantic region, 1976-77; owner Julie C. Dagle acct., Portland, Conn., 1971-77; co-owner Dagle and Dagle Assos., Portland, 1981—; tchr. adult edn. tax courses. Mem. Nat. Assn. Female Execs. Republican. Roman Catholic. Home and Office: Upper Cox Rd Portland CT 06480

D'AGNESE, HELEN JEAN (MRS. JOHN J. D'AGNESE), artist; b. N.Y.C., July 6, 1922; d. Leonardo and Rose (Redavid) De Santis; student CUNY, 1940-42, Oakland Art Inst., 1954-56; m. John J. D'Agnese, Oct. 29, 1942; children—John, Linda, Diane, Michele, Helen, Gina, Paul. One-man shows: Maude Sullivan Gallery, El Paso, 1964, John Wanamaker Gallery, Phila., 1966, U. N.Mex., 1967, Karo Manducci Gallery, San Francisco, 1968, Tuskegee Inst. Carver Mus., 1968, Lord & Taylor Gallery, N.Y.C., 1969, Harmon Gallery, Naples, Fla., 1970, Fountainbleau, Miami, 1970, Reflections Gallery, Atlanta, 1972, Williams Gallery, Atlanta, 1973, Americana Gallery, Mineola, Tex., 1977, E. M. Howard Gallery, Amelia Island, Fla., 1978, Haitian Primitives Gallery, 1981, others; group shows: Musseo des Artes, Juarez, Mexico, 1968, Benedictine Art Show, N.Y.C., 1967, Southeast Contemporary Art Show, Atlanta, 1968, Atlanta U., 1969, Red Piano Gallery, Hilton Head, S.C., Terrace Gallery, Atlanta, Ann. Bible Heritage Art Exhibit, Marietta, Ga., 1976, Nat. Judaic Theme Exhbn., Atlanta, 1976; represented in permanent collections: Pres. Jimmy Carter, Juarez (Mexico) Art Mus., Vatican Mus., Rome. Judge art show Mt. Loretto Acad., El Paso, 1967; art demonstration and lectr. Margaret Harris Sch., Atlanta, 1970; artist-in-residence Montessori Sch., Atlanta, 1978-79. Recipient Gold medal Accademia Italia delle Arti, Italy, 1979; 1st place sculpture award Tybee Island Art Festival, 1982. Mem. Atlanta Lawn Tennis Assn. Club: Tennis (Atlanta). Address: 1683 Knob Hill Ct NE Atlanta GA 30329

DAGUE, LINDA JO CLARK, research asst.; b. Muncie, Ind., Apr. 12, 1947; d. Gene Phillip and Dorothy Catherine (Griffin) Clark; A.B., Ind. U., 1968, law student, 1980—; m. Jerry Halsey Dague, June 15, 1968 (div. May 1979); children—Mary Louise, Robert Clark. Reporter, Tri City Jour., Delaware County, Ind., 1968; teaching asst. Ind. U. Sch. Journalism, 1968-69; editor RCA, Bloomington, Ind., 1969-70, Tri City Jour., 1970-71; asst. editor Pi Lambda Theta, Bloomington, 1974-75, nat. editor, 1975-80; research asst. Ind. U., 1981—. Vice pres. Friends of Library, Martinsville, 1975-76; bd. dirs. Tulip Trace council Girl Scouts U.S., 1981—. Mem. Women in Communications (pres. chpt. 1978-79), Soc. Profl. Journalists, Ednl. Press Assn. Am. (regional rep. 1979-80), Am. Soc. Assn. Execs. (communicators sect.), Ind. U. Sch. Journalism Alumni Assn. (dir., treas., class agt. 1975-77, pres. 1982-83), Pi Lambda Theta, Zeta Tau Alpha. Republican. Editor Ednl. Horizons, 1975-80; asso. Ind. U. Law Jour., 1981-82. Home: 610 N Hawthorne Dr Muncie IN 47304

DAHL, ARLENE, actress, author, fashion designer; b. Mpls., Aug. 11, 1928; d. Rudolph and Idelle (Swan) Dahl; student (1st, 2d, 3d scholastic prizes for fashion designs) U. Minn., Mpls. Inst. Art, Mpls. Coll. Music, Mpls. Bus. Coll.; m. Rounsevelle W. Schaum, 1969; 1 son, Rounsevelle Andreas; children by previous marriage—Lorenzo Lamas, Carole Christine Holmes. Broadway appearances include Mr. Strauss Goes to Boston, 1946, Cyrano de Bergerac, 1953, Applause, 1972; 28 motion pictures include My Wild Irish Rose, 1947, Three Little Words, 1950, Sangaree, 1953, Woman's World, 1954, Journey to the Center of the Earth, 1959, Kisses for My President, 1963, The Land Raiders, 1969; TV series Arlene Dahl's Beauty Spot, ABC-TV, 1965-66, Arlene Dahl's Starscope, 1979-80 H.B.O. and Arlene Dahl's Lovescope, ABC, 1982; guest appearances Jig Saw John, Burke's Law, Chrysler Theater, Love Boat, Fantasy Island, One Life To Live, also nat. talk and quiz shows; syndicated beauty columnist Chgo. Tribune—N.Y. News Syndicate, 1950-71; designer sleepwear A. N. Saab & Co., 1951-57; v.p. Kenyon & Eckhardt Advt. Agy., Inc., 1967-72, pres. woman's world div., 1967-72; nat. beauty dir. Sears, Roebuck & Co., 1970-75; pres. Arlene Dahl Enterprises, 1965-75, Dahlia Parfums, Inc., 1975—, Dahlia Prodns., Inc., 1978—, Dahlmark Prodns. Internat., 1981—; designer Vogue Pattern, 1980—; Hon. life mem. Father Flanagan's Boys Town, Hollywood Mus.; bd. dirs. Pearl Buck Found; ambassadress City of Hope. Decorated comdr. Order de Bontemps de Bordeaux; named Woman of Yr. in Communications, N.Y. Advt. Club, 1969; Mother of Yr., 1980; Todays Woman, 1981; winner 8 Laurel box office awards for motion pictures. Mem. Acad. Motion Picture Arts and Scis., Authors League. Author: Always Ask a Man, 1965; 12 Beautyscopes, 1968, rev. edit., 1978, Secrets of Hair Care, 1970; Secrets of Skin Care, 1970; Beyond Beauty, 1980. Address: PO Box 911 Beverly Hills CA

DAHL, DONNA M., cleaning and waterproofing co. exec., state legislator; b. Salt Lake City, Sept. 20, 1930; d. Ellis Reed and Lavera Bailey (Evans) Maxfield; student John Powers Finishing Sch., 1960, Hall Inst., 1979; m. Rulon W. Dahl, Nov. 26, 1948; children—Paula Sue Dahl Knight, Carolyn Jo, Mark Rulon, Scot Guy. Office and sales mgr. Utah's Great Game Preserves, Salt Lake City, 1977-78; with Pressure Systems, Inc., Salt Lake City, 1978—, sec., treas., dir., 1979—; dir. Utah Pump Co. Bd. dirs. Freedom Found. at Valley Forge, 1982; bd. dirs. SSS, Denver, 1981; mem. Utah Ho. of Reps., 1980—. Republican. Mormon. Office: Pressure Systems Inc 51 E Oakland Ave Salt Lake City UT 84115

DAHL, ELEANOR CARMAN, weaver; b. Quogue, N.Y., Mar. 31, 1931; d. Russell Vail and Marguerite (Campbell) Carman; student Dowling Coll.; m. Per Fridtjof Dahl, Oct. 15, 1966; stepchildren—Erik Johan, Thomas Fridtjof. Crafts coordinator Bellport (N.Y.)-Brookhaven Hist. Soc., 1975-78; instr. The Weaving Place Ltd., Huntington, N.Y., 1980-81; exec. sec. Brookhaven N.Y. Nat. Lab., 1981—; weaver, Brookhaven, 1980—. Chmn. Brookhaven Nat. Lab. Art Com. Home: 20 Highview Blvd Brookhaven NY 11719

DAHL, FLORENCE ISABEL, nurse; b. Bottineau, N.D., Aug. 2, 1930; d. John Jackson and Margaret Minnie (Randahl) Hiatt; diploma Trinity Hosp., Minot, N.D., 1953; student Minot State Coll., 1950-51, Alaska Meth. U., 1966-67, U. Alaska, 1967-68, Coll. of the Desert, 1978-81; m. Howard Clinton Dahl, Mar. 3, 1954; children—Marcus, Marsha, Matthew, Michael. Pct. duty nurse, St. Josephs and St. Lukes Hosp., Fargo, N.D., 1955-56; surgery and emergency nurse Providence Hosp., Anchorage, Alaska, 1956-68; surgery nurse Alaska Native Med. Center, Anchorage, 1974-75; nurse Einsenhower Hosp., Palm Desert, Calif., 1980-81. Vice pres. PTA, Anchorage, 1962-63; chmn. Precinct Election Bd., 1961-77; bd. dirs. Alaska Campfire, 1965-66; den mother Boy Scouts Am., 1962-67; tchr. Sunday Sch., 1958-67; chmn. pvt. kindergarten, 1960-67. Republican. Club: Shadow Mountain Palette. Home: 1414 Otter St Anchorage AK 99504

DAHL, NANCY SUE (FIFE), nursing adminstr.; b. Charleston, W.Va., Oct. 4, 1947; d. Ernest Dara and Dorothy Ann (Lipscomb) Fife; R.N., Grace Hosp., 1970; grad. Mercy Coll., 1970; m. Earl D. Dahl, Aug. 30, 1972; children—Dale Shannon, Rachael Elizabeth. Staff nurse Grace Hosp., Detroit, 1970; intensive care nurse Peralta Hosp., Oakland, Calif., 1970-72; head nurse Mineo Detoxification Center, Cass Lake, Minn., 1972-75; home care coordinator, home health aide instr. Inter County Nursing Agy., Bagley, Minn., 1975-77; nurse evaluator Minn. Dept. Health, Bemidji, 1977-79; dir. nursing services, interim adminstr. Beltrami Nursing Home, Bemidji, 1979-80; dir. nursing service Ah Gwah Ching (Minn.) State Nursing Home, 1980—; nursing instr. vocat. nursing programs; mem. policy task force for long term care com. Found. for Health Care Evaluation. Chmn. North Central Planned Parenthood Bd., 1974-76. Mem. Minn. Gerontol. Soc., Bus. and Profl. Women. Republican. Presbyterian. Home: Route 3 Box 924 Bemidji MN 56601 Office: Ah Gwah Ching Nursing Home Ah Gwah Ching MN 56430

DAHLBERG, SOPHIA FLORANCE, writer; b. Tulsa, Sept. 4, 1928; d. Hayes Louis and Lorraine Mary (Ivers) Little Bear; student Okla. Coll. Liberal Arts, 1973; m. Willis N. Overton, Dec. 30, 1944; children—Mickie Chouteau, Hayes Neil, Roger Dean, Michael Anthony, Nakomis Ann; m. 2d, Gilbert Harry Dahlberg, Oct. 29, 1960. With Smoot-Holman, Inglewood, Calif., 1950-51, Am. Aviation, Compton, Calif., 1959-60; restaurant mgr. Catalina Island, Calif., 1964-66; mgr. Authentic Am. Indian Singers and Dancers, 1961-64; dancer, 1944-81; bail bondsman Stuyvesant Ins., Davenport, Iowa, 1977-80; lectr. in field. Mem. Stephens County Hist. Soc., Duncan, Okla., 1972-82. Mem. Am. Legion Aux., Okla. Hist. Soc. Democrat. Roman Catholic. Clubs: Klash-Kah-she Indian Woman's, Cher-O-Kan Gateway Soc., others. Contbr. biographies to hist. soc. publs., articles to profl. jours.

DAHLIN, ELIZABETH CARLSON, univ. adminstr.; b. Worcester, Mass., July 26, 1931; d. Alden Gustaf and Elizabeth Christine (Peterson) Carlson; B.A., Wellesley Coll., 1953; postgrad. Harvard U., 1953, 64; M.A., George Washington U., 1971; m. Douglas Gordon Dahlin, June 27, 1953; children—Christine Elizabeth, Cynthia Jean, Constance May. Substitute tchr. Fairfax County, Va., 1958-77; asst. folklife specialist, concessions mgr. Smithsonian Instn., Washington, 1976-77; asst. to exec. dir. Nat. Sch. Vol. Program, Alexandria, Va., 1978-80; asst. to v.p. devel. George Mason U., Fairfax, Va., 1980—. Treas., bd. dirs. Nation's Capital Council Girl Scouts U.S., 1972-78, award, 1978; chief election judge Fairfax County Electoral Bd., 1967-75; mem. Fairfax County

Democratic Com., chmn. Belle Haven precinct Mount Vernon dist.; deacon United Ch. of Christ; mem. alumni council Wellesley Coll., 1970, 81. Brown U. grad. fellow, 1953. Mem. Va. Women's Polit. Caucus, Council Advancement and Support Edn., Profl. Women's Network, Textile Mus., Smithsonian Assos., Nat. Aviation Club, AAUW, George Washington U. Alumni Council (edn. council), Phi Delta Kappa. Democrat. Clubs: Wellesley (bd. dirs. 1969—, treas. 1978-82, pres. 1980-82), Harvard (Washington); Fort Myer Officer's. Home: 6041 Edgewood Terr Alexandria VA 22307 Office: Finley 102 George Mason U 4400 University Dr Fairfax VA 22030

DAHLIN, ELSIE U., metal fabrication co. exec.; b. Portadown, N. Ireland, Mar. 1, 1936; came to U.S., 1946, naturalized, 1964; d. William Walker and Marguerite Lily (Chambers) Whiteside; student public schs.; m. Eugene Leroy Dahlin, Aug. 24, 1955; children—Leah Marguerite, Kevin Harold. Exec. sec. Pasadena (Calif.) Jaycees, 1951-56; office mgr. Merritts Hardware Co., Pasadena, 1960-65; sec.-treas. Best Fluorescent Maintenance Corp., El Monte, Calif., 1965-75; chmn. bd., pres. Ladd Fabrication Inc., El Monte, 1975—; dir. Linder Caster & Truck Co., El Monte, 1978-79. Mem. Los Angeles C. of C. Republican. Office: 4323 N Rowland Ave El Monte CA 91731

DAHLIN, ROSALIE JULE ROWE, artist, designer; b. Hopkins, Minn., June 2, 1911; d. Joseph F. and Anna Mary (Novak) Rowe; student Mpls. Sch. Art and Design; m. T. Leroy Dahlin, Dec. 12, 1938; children—Carol Lee, Lee Edward. Beauty cons. Walgreen Co., Mpls., 1937-74; freelance artist, designer Bloomington, Minn., 1938—; exhibited in one-person shows: Control Data Co., Mpls., 1974, 75, 76, 79, 80, 81, 82, Cinema Gallery, Edina, Minn., 1976; group shows include: Sky Gallery, St. Paul, Normandale Coll., Bloomington, Bloomington Art Center, Southdale Fine 81, 82, Cinema Uptown Art Show, Sky Gallery, St. Paul, Minn. Mus. Art, St. Paul, Twin City Fed. Savs. and Loan, St. Paul and Mpls., Anoka-Ramsey Community Coll., 1979; represented in permanent collections. Mem. Mpls. Soc. Fine Arts, Minn. Art Assn., Minn. Rural Art Assn., Fine Art Soc. Dakota County, Minnetonka, Bloomington art socs., Hopkins Hist. Soc., Internat. Soc. Artists., North Star Watercolor Soc., Nat. League Am. Pen Women.

DAIGNEAULT, WENDY, harness racing driver, owner, trainer; b. N.Y.C., July 21, 1951; d. Bertram David and Annette Knapp; student Nassau (N.Y.) Community Coll., 1969-71; m. Rejean Daigneault, Sept. 29, 1974; 1 dau., Christina. Groomer standardbred racehorses Del Isko Stable, 1970-72; pres. Storybook Stables of L.I., Inc., owner, trainer and driving harness horses, 1972—. Mem. U.S. Trotting Assn., Standardbred Owners Assn. N.Y. (dir.), Standardbred Owners Assn. N.J. Office: Barn AA Roosevelt Raceway Westbury NY 11590

DAIL, HILDA LEE, psychologist; b. Ga., Aug. 23, 1920; d. Ransom Harvey and Mattie (Gray) Lee; B.A., Piedmont Coll., 1941; postgrad. Duke U., 1943, Columbia U., 1957-68, U. Utah, 1968; Ph.D., Union Grad. Sch., 1979; m. F. Roderick Dail, Dec. 27, 1941; children—Janice Sylvia, Roderick Lee. Tchr. public schs., Ga., Tenn., N.C., 1939-53; assoc. sec. fgn. dept. Bd. Missions, United Methodist Ch., 1954-60, missionary to India and on faculty Leonard Thebl Coll., 1960-64, editor lit., 1964-70; exec. dir. Internat. Found. Ewha U., Seoul, Korea; dir devel. Ch. Women United; dir. Resource Center on Women; devel. cons., N.Y.C. and Briarcliffe Acre, S.C., 1975—; mem. faculty Marymount Manhattan Coll., N.Y. U., Johns Hopkins U., U. S.C., Coastal Carolina Coll.; bd. dirs. Enablement, Inc., Boston; radio, TV appearances. Bd. dirs. Green Chimney Sch., Assn. Cooperating Agys. of Asian Women's Univs. Recipient Creative Communications award Public Relations Council, 1971, citation Women's Bur., U.S. Govt., 1974. Mem. Am. Soc. Tng. and Devel. (dir. N.Y. chpt. 1977-79, chairwoman spl. interest group career devel. 1980—, mem. task force for internat. div.), Am. Assn. for Artists-Therapists (cert. experiential psychotherapist), Internat. Transactional Analysis Assn., Met. N.Y. Assn. Applied Psychology, Bus. and Profl. Women (pres. Gotham chpt. 1979, N.Y. State Profl. Woman of Yr. 1978). Democrat. Methodist. Club: Zonta Internat. (dir.). Author books, the most recent being: Lotus and Pool, Creativity and Career Development, 1983; editor books; clients include cos., assns., religious groups, govt. and colls. and univs. Office: 140 E 56 St Suite 10F New York NY 10022 also 154 Pinetree Ln Briarcliffe Acre SC 29527

DALE, JIMME KATHRYN, journalist; b. Morrilton, Ark., Aug. 13, 1943; d. E.E. and Gwendolyn Louise (Williams) Kirtley; m. Johnnie F. Dale, July 27, 1959; children—Tommy Lynn, Cathi Jayne, Jeffery Lane. Owner, operator wedding cake bus., Alamogordo, N.Mex., 1962—; women's editor Alamogordo Daily News, 1975—; owner Hypnosis Center. Organizer, past pres. Sunshine Aux.; chmn. women's div. United Way, 1978. Named Woman of Distinction, Otero County, 1980; registered hypnotist. Mem. Am. Bus. Women's Assn. (named local Woman of Yr. 1978). Democrat. Baptist. Clubs: Jr. Woman's (outstanding mem. 1975). Home: Route 1 Box 194 Alamogordo NM 88310 Office: PO Box 870 Alamogordo NM 88310

DALE, NANCY LEE, religious edn. adminstr.; b. Franklin, N.J., Mar. 4, 1936; d. Thomas Francis and Helen Louise (Greene) Sullivan; student U. Wis., Milw., 1954-56; m. George D. Dale, Mar. 1, 1958; children—Susan Ann, Carol Lynn, Wesley Thomas. Polit. columnist, feature writer Dominguez News, Dominguez Hills, Calif., 1963-65; early childhood ednl. aide Palos Verdes Peninsula (Calif.) Schs. Dist., 1974-78, chair spl. edn. adv. com., 1982—; adminstrv. asst. religious edn. program St. John Fisher Catholic Ch., Rancho Palos Verdes, Calif., 1978—. Active Calif. PTA; sec. Palos Verdes Library Dist., 1975-76, v.p., 1976-77, pres., 1977-78, trustee, 1975—; mem. Palos Verdes Peninsula Community Center Assn.; Palos Verdes North Homeowners Assn.; Peninsula Friends of Library; scout leader Angeles council Girl Scouts Am., 1969-74; producer, actor Palos Verdes Players. Mem. Nat. Assn. Female Execs., ALA, Calif. Library Assn. Roman Catholic. Home: 3741 Palos Verdes Dr N Rolling Hills Estates CA 90274 Office: 5400 Crest Rd Rancho Palos Verdes CA 90274

D'ALENE, ALIXANDRIA FRANCES, corp. exec.; b. Buffalo, Oct. 21, 1951; d. Francis and Fern (Hill) D'A.; B.A., Canisius Coll., Buffalo, 1973, M.S., 1975, M.B.A., 1980. Tchr., Buffalo public schs., 1973-76; personnel cons. Sanford Rose Assos., Williamsville, N.Y., 1976-78; mgr. benefits adminstrn. Service Systems Corp., Clarence, N.Y., 1978-80; mgr. employee relations Del Monte Corp., Walnut Creek, Calif., 1980—. Mem. Assn. Personnel Adminstrs., Indsl. Personnel Soc., Phi Alpha Theta. Episcopalian. Home: 340 N Civic Dr Walnut Creek CA 94596 Office: 205 N Wiget Ln Walnut Creek CA 94598

D'ALESSIO, KITTY, cosmetic and clothing co. exec.; b. Sea Girt, N.J., 1929; B.A., Upsala Coll., 1951. Formerly with B. Altman and Co., N.Y.C.; mem. wardrobe staff NBC, N.Y.C.; sr. v.p., dir. Craig, and Hummel, until 1980; pres. Chanel, Inc., N.Y.C., 1980—. Office: Chanel Inc 9 W 57th St New York NY 10019 *

DALIA, VERA, clin. psychologist; b. Brno, Czechoslovakia, Nov. 19, 1935; d. Aharon and Helen (Grun) Wollner; student Hebrew U. Jerusalem, 1956-58; B.A., U. Toronto, 1961; M.A., U. Evansville, 1971; Ph.D., U. Mich., 1974; m. Zol F. Muskovitch, Dec. 23, 1958 (dec. 1969); children—David, Debby. Clin. community psychologist Sudbury (Ont., Can.) Algoma Sanatorium, 1974-76; clin. coordinator Bangor (Maine) Mental Health Inst., 1976-78; dir. behavioral sci. family practice residency St. Joseph Hosp., Flint, Mich., 1978-79; clin. and cons. psychologist, Flint, Birmingham and Southfield, Mich., 1979—; clin. faculty U. Maine, 1978. Horace H. Rackham grantee, 1973-74. Mem. Am. Psychol. Assn., Mich. Psychol. Assn., Mich. Soc. Cons. Psychology, Soc. Tchrs. Family Medicine. Office: 1621 E Court St Flint MI 48503

DALLY, ALICE GERTRUDE GHERKE, author, educator; b. Defiance, Ohio, Feb. 18, 1910; d. William Ernest and Emma Amelia Ort Gherke; student Wausau Coll., 1927-29, U. Wis., 1930-38, Bryan Stenotype Coll., 1965-66, San Bernardino Valley Coll., 1960-79, Chaffey Coll., 1965-66, U. Calif., Riverside, 1966; Ph.D., Golden State U., 1981; m. John Wesley Dally, Sept. 17, 1938 (dec.). Ct. reporter; asst. credit mgr., interviewer U. Wis.; acct. State of Wis.; sr. interviewer, investigator fed. govt.; mgr. kennel; legal sec.; clk. of ct.; med. sec.; legal sec. to dist. atty.; exec. sec.; adminstr.; univ. tchr., coll. tchr.; tchr. adult edn.; substitute tchr. Mem. Nat. Ret. Tchrs. Assn., Polish Am. Hist. Assn., Calif. Tchrs. Assn. (life), Calif. Ret. Tchrs. Assn., NEA (life), U. Wis. Alumni Assn. (life). Club: San Bernardino Coin. Author: Suzanne's Family; Suzanne's Merry Chase; also poetry.

DALMUS, ELINORE JOSEPHINE, ins. broker; b. Astoria, N.Y., Mar. 15, 1922; d. Joseph Franz and Catherine (Yongen) D.; B.B.A., Coll. of Ins., 1974, masters degree, 1976. With Continental Ins. Co., 1939-66; ins. broker John C. Paige, N.Y.C., 1966-70, Johnson & Higgins, N.Y.C., 1970—; tchr. Coll. of Ins., 1976—. Vol. Salvation Army. Served with U.S. Army, 1942-44. C.P.C.U. Mem. Ins. Inst. Am., Assn. C.P.C.U.s, Bus. and Profl. Women (past pres. Wall Street Club), Am. Inst. Mgmt., NOW. Republican. Club: Ins. Women's. Home: 42-19 218 St Bayside NY 11361 Office: Johnson & Higgins 95 Wall St New York NY 10005

DA LOMBA, DOLORES WINIFRED, ins., brokerage exec.; b. Norfolk, Va., Dec. 24, 1932; d. Joseph and Lucy Lavinia (Price) Da Lomba; Ed.M., Harvard U., 1973, C.A.S., 1975, Ed.D., 1977; m. Edward Mendelson, (div.); children—Mark, Don, Aaron. Dir. public service careers Cambridge (Mass.) Econ. Opportunity Com., 1971-73; asso. dir. Citywide Coordinating Council, Boston, 1977-78; dir. office of energy conservation Commonwealth of Mass., Boston, 1978-79; exec. dir. Nat. Community Action Exec. Dirs. Assn., Washington, 1979-82. Mem. editorial adv. bd. Jour. of Community Action, Washington, 1981—. Edn. Profl. Devel. fellow, 1973, Nat. Fellowship Fund fellow, 1973-74; Ford Travel grantee, 1974. Mem. Am. Soc. Assn. Execs., Nat. Assn. Female Execs. Contbr. articles to profl. publs. Office: 100 Crown St New Haven CT 06510

DALRYMPLE, JEAN, theatre producer-dir.; b. Morristown, N.J., Sept. 2, 1910; d. George Hull and Elizabeth Van Kirk (Collins) D.; educated privately; m. Ward Morehouse, Mar. 31, 1932 (dec.); m. 2d, P. D. Ginder, Nov. 1951 (dec.). 1951 (dec.). Producer, dir. numerous plays, musicals and operas, 1939—; mgr., publicist various stage personalities, singers, 1933— ; dir. Am. Theatre, Brussels World's Fair, 1958; tour of Latin Am. with Teahouse of August Moon in Spanish for Dept. State, 1956; dir. N.Y.C. Ctr. Drama and Musicals, 1943-69; a founder N.Y.C. Opera, 1944, N.Y.C. Drama Ctr. 1943, N.Y.C. Ballet, 1948; chmn. bd. dirs. Light Opera Manhattan, Friends Theatre Collection, Mus. City of N.Y.; Decorated Order Crown Belgium; recipient citation N.Y.C. Mem. Am. Theatre Wing (dir.), ANTA (dir.). Presbyterian. Club: Silver Spring Country (Ridgefield, Conn.). Author: September Child, 1963; Careers and Opportunities in the Theatre, 1968; Dalrymple's Pinafore Farm Cookbook, 1970; From The Last Row, 1976; The Complete Handbook for Community Theatres, 1979; co-author: The Folklore and Facts of Natural Nutrition, 1974. Home and Office: 150 W 55th St New York NY 10019 Home: Pinefore Farm Brushy Hill Rd Danbury CT 06810

DALRYMPLE, PATRICIA KENNEDY, real estate asso., civic worker; b. Amsterdam, N.Y., Feb. 1, 1926; d. John Joseph and Marie (Kennedy) K.; student Ithaca Coll., 1944-46; m. William Edward Dalrymple, Dec. 27, 1946; children—Sharon, William, Marie, Mark, Peter, Michael, Tara. Waitress, 1968-78; real estate asso. Bardino Realty, Saratoga Springs, N.Y., 1971-76, Fireside Realty, Saratoga Springs, 1976-77, ERA-McNeary Realty, Saratoga Springs, 1978—. Active Jerry Lewis Muscular Dystrophy; founder, pres. Hartwick Literary Club, 1947-48; pres. Saratoga County Childrens Com., 1975-77; mem. N.Y. State Legis. Women's Forum Edn., chmn., 1968-69; dist. legis. chmn. PTA Council, 1958-60; pres. Div. St. Sch. PTA, 1968, Sch. 2, 1960; v.p. Cooperstown Nat. Council Cath. Women, 1950; city chmn. Saratoga Springs Heart Fund, 1969; candidate Saratoga Springs Bd. Edn., 1966; coach girls' basketball Harwick High Sch., 1949; mem. com. preservation of Congress Park Casino, Saratoga Springs Hist. Soc.; bd. dirs. United Fund, 1969, Kenwood, Albany, N.Y., 1956-57, LWV of Saratoga Springs, 1966-70. Mem. Nat. Assn. Realtors, Saratoga County Bd. Realtors, N.Y. State Realtors Assn., Saratoga Bus. and Profl. Women (pres. 1976-78), Am. Assn. Ret. Persons. Republican. Roman Catholic. Office: 12 Circular St Saratoga Springs NY 12866

DALTON, JULIE ANN, sports editor, writer; b. Omaha, Mar. 18, 1947; d. James Leo and Alice Cecilia (Carville) Dalton; B.A. in English Lit., U. Iowa, 1968; M.A. in English Edn., SUNY, Albany, 1973. Tchr., English Bellport (L.I.) Middle Sch., N.Y., 1968-70, Westlake High Sch., Thornwood, N.Y., 1971-72; sports reporter The Evening Times, Pawtucket, R.I., 1976-78, sports editor, 1978-82; copy editor Providence Jour., part-time 1982—. Mem. Soc. Profl. Journalists, Newspaper Guild, (Pawtucket Newspaper Guild (v.p.). Democrat. Home: 24 1/2 Fletcher St Central Falls RI 02863

DALTON, SHARON LEE, hosp. adminstr.; b. Bakersfield, Calif., Dec. 15, 1936; d. Vern and Lillian Ruth (Zimmerman) Wilson; B.A., Calif. State U., Fresno, 1969; divorced; children—Jeffry Scott, Laura Dawn, Craig Adam, Eric Vern. Social worker Kern County Welfare Dept., Bakersfield, 1969-70; asst. exec. dir. Kern County Cancer Soc., 1970; dir. med. social services Menominee County-Lloyd Hosp., Menominee, Mich., 1970-73, St. Francis Hosp., Escanaba, Mich., 1973—; instr. Mich. State U., No. Mich. U., Marquette; bd. dirs. Bay de Noc Hospice, 1978-80, Half-Way House, Escanaba, 1977-80, Delta County Easter Seals, 1973-80; mem. Mich. Bd. Examiners Social Work, 1975—, vice chmn., 1979—. Mem. Nat. Assn. Social Workers (chpt. exec. com. 1976, Upper Peninsula Social Worker of Yr. 1973). Democrat. Lutheran. Home: 1600 S 30th St #69 Escanaba MI 49829 Office: 1018 13th St S Escanaba MI 49829

DALY, BARBARA KRUEGER, interior designer; b. Wauwatosa, Wis., June 8, 1945; d. Harry Albert and Beverly Edna (Reediger) Krueger; student U. Miami (Fla.), 1963-64; grad. Parsons Sch. Design., 1967; m. John Neal Daly, Apr. 2, 1966; children—John Gorman, Cristina Reed. Head interior decoration May Co. Dept. Stores, N.Y.C., 1968-70; free-lance interior designer, 1970—. Mem. Am. Inst. Interior Design, Am. Soc. Interior Designers, Silvermine Guild Artists, Art Soc. Old Greenwich, Greenwich Art Soc. Club: The Stanwich. Home: 390 Stanwich Rd Greenwich CT 06830

DALY, FREDERICA YOUNG, psychologist; b. Washington; d. Samuel P. and Geneva A. (Sharper) Young; B.S., Howard U., 1947, M.S., 1948; Ph.D., Cornell U., 1956; m. Michael E. Daly, Mar. 15, 1972. Instr., Howard U., Washington, 1950-53, dir. social services George Jr. Republic, Freeville, N.Y., 1955-73; assoc. prof. SUNY, Empire State Coll., N.Y.C., 1973-81; coordinator Juvenile Forensic Program dept. psychiatry U. N.Mex., Albuquerque, 1979-81; coordinator alcohol program VA Med. Center, Albuquerque, 1981—. Bd. dirs. YWCA, 1979-80; active Street Ministry, 1980-82. Mem. Am. Psychol. Assn., Internat. Council of Psychologists, Am. Orthopsychiat. Assn., Nat. Women's Polit. Caucus, 1981-82, N.Mex. Women of the 80's. Democrat. Home: 526 Hermosa NE Albuquerque NM 87108

DALY, VALERIE A., educator; b. N.Y.C., June 23, 1942; d. Elbert and Mildred A. (Hall) Moses; B.A., U. Akron (Ohio), 1966; M.S., CCNY, 1977; 1 dau., Michelle. Exec. dir. Police Athletic League project Head Start, Bklyn., 1966-71; exec. dir. E. Bronx (N.Y.) NAACP Day Care Center, 1971—; cons. in field; field instr. Fairleigh Dickinson U. Mem. Council Suprs. and Adminstrs., Nat. Assn. Edn. Young Children, Coalition 100 Black Women, NAACP (br. v.p. 1973), Bronx Council Arts, Phi Delta Kappa. Office: 1113 Colgate Ave Bronx NY 10472

DAMANDA, CARLOTTA, ednl. adminstr.; b. Rochester, N.Y., Aug. 18, 1927; d. Christopher and Marie (West) Damanda; B.A., Sarah Lawrence Coll., 1948; M.A., Columbia U., 1950, Ph.D., 1965; postgrad. U. San Francisco, 1952-53. Faculty, Harley Sch., Rochester, 1945-46, Womens Inst., Yonkers, N.Y., 1945-48, King St. Sch., Greenwich, Conn., 1948-50, Blythedale Rehab. Hosp., Valhalla, N.Y., 1950-52, Sarah Lawrence Coll., Bronxville, N.Y., 1953-59; exec. dir. LWV, San Francisco, 1952-53; adj. prof. Columbia U., 1955-65; asst. dir. Inst. for Religious and Social Studies, N.Y.C., 1959-65, asso. dir., 1965—; coordinator Conf. on Sci., Philosophy and Religion, 1960—; asso. dir. dept. intergroup activities Jewish Theol. Sem. Am., N.Y.C., 1968—, community affairs dir., 1970—, officer of adminstrn.; sec., mem. exec. com., bd. dirs. Morningside Renewal Council, 1970—; mem. exec. com., bd. dirs. Morningside Area Alliance, 1970—, chairperson community services com., 1974—, v.p., 1976-80, pres., 1980—; bd. dirs. Manhattanville Community Centers, 1971—, mem. exec. com., 1972—, v.p., 1974—, chairperson personnel com., 1975—; cons. Manhattan Community Planning Bd. 9, 1970—, mem., 1976—, mem. maj. instns. com. 1979—, public relations com., 1980—, ethics com., 1981—, transp. com., 1980—. Mem. Am. Sociol. Assn., Acad. Polit. and Social Scis., Brit. Assn. Sociologists. Clubs: Faculty, Princeton (N.Y.C.). Lit. editor numerous annals and yearbooks. Home: 251 Lexington Ave New York NY 10016 Office: 3080 Broadway New York NY 10027

DAMASHEK, ZELDA GUTTMAN, mental health planner; b. N.Y.C., July 14, 1924; d. Max Mendel and Sally Helen (Wolf) Guttman; B.A. with honors in Sociology, Cornell U., 1944; M.S.W., N.Y. Sch. Social Work, 1947; m. George Damashek, June 19, 1949; children—Sandra, Robert, Ronald. Caseworker, Jewish Child Care Assn., N.Y.C., 1946-48; field staff mem. Health Council Greater N.Y., N.Y.C., 1948-50; nat. adviser young adults and bus. and profl. women's groups Nat. Council Jewish Women, N.Y.C., 1950-51; exec. dir. Planned Parenthood Eastern Westchester, Port Chester, N.Y., 1962-63; mem. editorial staff Nat. Assn. Social Workers, N.Y.C., 1965; coordinator Project Enable, Port Chester, 1966-67; field rep. Westchester Community Mental Health Bd., White Plains, N.Y., 1967-78; coordinator Westchester Community Support System, Westchester Dept. Community Mental Health, White Plains, 1978-79, program dir. Westchester Community Support System, 1980—; cons. to mental health agys. Bd. dirs. Heathcote PTA, 1960-62; mem. adv. council Scarsdale Adult Sch., 1961-62. Cert. social worker, N.Y. State. Mem. Nat. Assn. Social Workers (dir. Westchester chpt. 1968-70), Acad. Cert. Social Workers, Nat. Council Jewish Women (dir. Cooper Stuyvesant br.). Jewish. Home: 25 Wynmor Rd Scarsdale NY 10583 Office: Dept Community Mental Health Room 234 COB 1 148 Martine Ave White Plains NY 10601

DAMASKA, SHIRLEY HORNBERGER, dental corp. exec.; b. Williamsport, Pa., Jan. 14, 1940; d. Oren L. and Gertrude E. (Bastian) Hornberger; student parochial schs., Williamsport; children—Steven Michael, David Patrick. Sec. to sales mgr. Bell Telephone Pa., Williamsport, 1957-59; sec. to treas. Chestnut Fleet Car Leasing Co., Phila., 1961-62; sec. to personnel mgr. R.L. Polk & Co., Cin., 1963-64; disc jockey, news announcer radio sta. WKKY-FM, Ky., 1966-67; sec. to pres. Harmeyer & Brand Dental Supply Co., Cin., 1968-69; adminstr., asst. treas. Cin. Dental Services, Inc., 1969—, partner, 1975—. Recipient Good Citizen's Cert., DAR, 1957. Mem. Nat. Assn. Female Execs. Democrat. Roman Catholic. Home: 7491 Quail Hollow Dr Cincinnati OH 45243 Office: 121 E McMillan St Cincinnati OH 45219

D'AMATO, BARBARA STEKETEE, writer, lyricist; b. Grand Rapids, Mich., Apr. 10, 1938; d. Harold Arthur and Yvonne Virginia (Watson) Steketee; student Cornell U., 1956-58; B.A., Northwestern U., 1972, M.A., 1973; m. Anthony D'Amato, Sept. 4, 1958; children—Brian Richard D'Amato, Paul Steketee D'Amato. Freelance author, lyricist, 1973—; musical comedies include The Magic Man, Chgo., 1974, London, 1977; The Magic of Young Houdini, Niles, Ill., 1975-77, London, 1976, RSVP Broadway, Chgo., 1980-81; author detective novels The Hands of Healing Murder, 1980; The Eyes on Utopia Murders, 1981; contbr. article to profl. jour. Office: 716 Greenwood Glencoe IL 60022

D'AMBROSIO, LILLIAN MARIE, judge; b. Boston, Dec. 27, 1920; d. Michele Angelo and Rose Raffaele (Sammarla) D'A.; B.B.A., Boston U., 1946; J.D., 1950, LL.M., 1952. Admitted to Mass. bar, 1950; practiced in Boston, 1950-66; commr. Mass. Indsl. Accident Bd., 1966-73; mem. firm Parker, Coulter, Daley & White, 1973—; spl. justice Dist. Ct., Chelsea, Mass., 1973—; adminstrv. sec. to Gov., 1957-58, adminstrv. sec., legal counsel, 1958-59; tax counsel Mass. Dept. Corps. and Taxation, Boston, 1959-66. Mem. women's council Don Orione Home, East Boston, 1973—; dir., clk. Social Service Credit Union, Boston, 1953—; sec. Young Democrats, 1952-54; bd. dirs. Christopher Columbus Community Center. Recipient Golden Lady award Amita, 1969-70; Circolo Lettario Italiano Soc. award, 1973. Mem. Mass., Boston bar assns., Justinian Law Soc. (sec. 1950-78, pres. 1978—), Am. Justinian Soc., Nat., Mass. assns. women lawyers, Sons Italy in Am. (state chmn. charity drive for birth defects 1969-70), Profl. and Bus. Woman's Lodge (venerable 1972-74), Boston U. Law Sch. Alumni Assn. Roman Catholic. Club: Women Grads. Boston U. (dir. 1973-76). Home: 37 Union St Charlestown MA 02129 Office: Chelsea Dist Ct Chelsea MA 02150

DAME, PHYLLIS JEAN, writer, editor; b. Somerville, N.J., Feb. 10, 1935; d. James Joseph and Evelyn L. (Shrope) Corrigan; student Valley Jr. Coll., 1955, Cerro Coso Community Coll., 1981; m. Pieter A. Dame, Dec. 10, 1964; children—David Scott, Brian Robert, Kathleen Lydia, Pieter James. Sec., Lyons VA Hosp., N.J., 1953-55, VA Hosp., Jackson, Miss., 1961-62, Sepulveda, Calif., 1955-58, 62-69; with NASA Redstone Arsenal, Huntsville, Ala., 1959-61; writer, editor. Naval Weapons Center, China Lake, Calif., 1969—. Mem. Inyokern C. of C. (sec. 1972-73), Soc. Tech. Communications (sec. 1982), Nat. Assn. Female Execs. Pub., editor Inyokern Chatterbox, weekly newspaper, 1969-71. Home: 5225 Inyokern Rd PO Box 6 Inyokern CA 93527 Office: Code 3464 Naval Weapons Center China Lake CA 93555

D'AMICO, VIRGINIA ANN, fund raiser; b. Youngstown, Ohio, Apr. 26, 1948; d. Samuel and Ann T. (DeCola) D'Amico; student Notre Dame Coll., Cleve., 1966; B.A., Youngstown U., 1970; postgrad. U. Hawaii, 1971; M.Ed., Boston U., 1975; m. Larry D. Myer, Jan. 8, 1977 (div.). Health and phys. edn. instr. St. Mary's High Sch., Sandusky, Ohio, 1970-73; teaching asst. Boston U., 1973-74; instr. psychology Newbury Jr. Coll., Boston, 1974; Kellogg fellow, planning asso. United Way, Louisville, and United Way of Wichita, Kans., 1975, asst. campaign dir., Wichita, 1976-78, campaign dir., 1979-82; asst. campaign dir. United Way of Tex. Gulf Coast, Houston, 1982—. Bd. dirs. Maize (Kans.) Community Bldg., 1980-81; ARC vol., 1967-70, water safety instr.,

1967-70, emergency social service com., 1977-82. Mem. Am. Mgmt. Assn., Kappa Delta Pi, Sigma Sigma Sigma. Republican. Roman Catholic. Office: 1010 Waugh Dr Houston TX 77019

DAMMANN, KATHLEEN ELLEN, bus. mgr.; b. Chgo., June 18, 1954; d. Robert D. and Joanne G. D.; B.Mus.Edn., Northwestern U., 1975. Freelance musician, 1969—; med. sec. to physician, Chgo., 1975-78; bus. mgr. pharmacy dept. Rush-Presbyn.-St. Luke's Med. Center, Chgo., 1978—. Active Skokie Fine Arts Commn., 1977-80, chmn. goals com., 1978-80, vice chmn. commn., 1979-80; vol. Passavant Meml. Hosp., Chgo. Recipient service award pins Passavant Meml. Hosp. Mem. Women in Mgmt. (Chgo. Loop chpt.). Lutheran. Home: 7836 Kildare Ave Skokie IL 60076 Office: Pharmacy Dept 1753 W Congress Pkwy Chicago IL 60612

DAMSBO, ANN MARIE, psychologist, clinic adminstr.; b. Cortland, N.Y., July 7, 1931; d. Jorgen Einer and Agatha Irene (Schenck) D.; B.S., San Diego State Coll., 1952; M.A., U.S. Internat. U., 1974, Ph.D., 1975; 6 foster children. Commd. 2d lt. U.S. Army, 1952, advanced through grades to capt., 1957; staff therapist Letterman Army Hosp., San Francisco, 1953-54, 56-58, 61-62, Ft. Devers, Mass., 1955-56, Walter Reed Army Hosp., Washington, 1958-59, Tripler Army Hosp., Hosp., Hawaii, 1959-61, Ft. Benning, Ga., 1962-64; chief therapist U.S. Army Hosp., Ft. McPherson, Ga., 1964-67, ret., 1967; med. missionary So. Presbyterian Ch., Taiwan, 1968-70; psychology intern, burn center Univ. Hosp., San Diego, 1975; pre-doctoral intern Naval Regional Med. Center, San Diego, 1975-76, postdoctoral intern, 1975-76, chief, founder pain clinic, 1976—; cons. on forensic hypnosis, fed. investigation agys.; lectr. in field, U.S., Can., Eng., France, Australia. Fellow Am. Soc. Clin. Hypnosis (faculty); mem. San Diego Soc. Clin. Hypnosis (pres. 1980), Am. Psychol. Assn., Am. Phys. Therapy Assn., Calif. Soc. Clin. Hypnosis (bd. govs.), Internat. Platform Assn., Internat. Soc. Clin. and Exptl. Hypnosis. Republican. Methodist. Club: Job's Daus. Contbr. articles to profl. pubs.; also cht. in book. Home: 1062 W 5th Ave Escondido CA 92025 Office: Chief Pain Clinic Naval Regional Med Center San Diego CA 92134

DAMSGAARD, KATHERINE STARK, personal and office support co. exec.; b. Milw., Nov. 13, 1952; d. William Fredrick and Judith (Zentner) Stark; B.A. cum laude, Bryn Mawr (Pa.) Coll., 1974; M.B.A., Wharton Sch., U. Pa., 1978; m. Kell Marsh Damsgaard, June 17, 1972; 1 son, Peter Kjeld. Comml. credit analyst Girard Bank, Phila., 1974-76, mem. comml. credit rev. staff, 1976; operational planner, then mgr. customer service Gen. Electric Co., Phila., 1979-81; co-pres. The Support System, Inc., Phila., 1981—. Home: Route 2 Horseshoe Trail Chester Springs PA 19425 Office: 1701 Arch St Suite 406 Philadelphia PA 19103

DAMSKER, BECA, microbiologist; b. Jassy, Romania, Jan. 15, 1923; came to U.S., 1969, naturalized, 1974; d. Jacques and Rose Grünspan; M.A., Bucharest U., 1950; M.S., U. Montreal (Que., Can.), 1969; m. Mircea Damsker, May 11, 1944. Intern, resident and fellow, Bucharest, 1950-59; specialist physician, clin. lab. Hosp. Extrapulmonary Tb, Bucharest, 1959-63; research physician Hadassah Hebrew U., dir. clin. lab., Jerusalem, 1966-67; clin. lab. supr., asst. dir. Mt. Sinai Hosp., N.Y.C., 1969-80, asso. dir. microbiology, 1980—; instr., then asst. prof. Mt. Sinai Med. Sch., 1970—. Recipient Physicians Recognition award AMA, 1971, 81. Mem. Am. Soc. Microbiology, N.Y. Soc. Film, Met. Mus. Contbr. articles to profl. jours. Office: 1 Gustave Levy Pl New York NY 10029 *

DANA, JEANNE MARIE, fin. analyst; b. Los Angeles, Mar. 31, 1941; d. Martin and Anita (Alcala) Lassos; student UCLA; 1 dau., Pilar Janine. Research asst. Delafield & Delafield Co., N.Y.C., 1965-67; fin. analyst Graham Loving & Co., N.Y.C., 1968; sr. transp. cons., exec. v.p. Connaught Research Corp., N.Y.C., 1969-75; pres. The Dana Group, Inc., N.Y.C., 1975—. Mem. N.Y. Soc. Security Analysts, Conf. Bd., Am. Mgmt. Assn., Fin. Analysts Fedn., Transp. Assn. Am. Club: Met (N.Y.C.). Office: 10 E 53d St New York NY 10022

DANART, KAREN MILLY, govt. ofcl.; b. N.Y.C., Nov. 12, 1942; d. Jacob J. and Dors L. Steinberg; B.A., Hunter Coll., N.Y.C., 1965; J.D., N.Y. Law Sch., 1968; m. Arthur Danart, Aug. 24, 1968; 1 son, Joshua P. Admitted to D.C. bar; staff atty. Am. law div. Library of Congress, 1968-69; with EEOC, 1970—, spl. asst. Office Commn., 1976-77, dep. dir. Office Policy Implementation, 1977—. Mem. D.C. Bar Assn.

DANBURG, DEBRA, state legislator; b. Houston, Sept. 25, 1951; d. Stanley and Barbara Jean (Hamilton) D.; B.A., U. Houston, 1974, J.D., 1979. Asst. dir., lobbyist Texans for ERA, 1974-75; atty. pvt. practice, Houston, 1979—; mem. Tex. Ho. of Reps., 1981—. Mem. Harris County Democratic Exec. Com., 1976-80. Named Outstanding feminist NOW, 1975. Mem. Tex. Bar Assn. Home: 1201 McDuffie St Houston TX 77019 Office: Texas House of Representatives State Capitol Austin TX 78769 *

DANDOY, MAXIMA ANTONIO, educator; b. Santa Maria, Philippines; d. Manuel A. and Isidra (Mendoza) D.; A.B., Nat. Tchrs. Coll., Manila, 1947; M.A., Arellano U., 1949; Ed.D., Stanford U., 1952. Elem. tchr. Philippines, 1927-37; lab. tchr. Philippine Normal Coll., Manila, 1938-49; instr. Arellano U., Manila, 1947-49; curriculum writer/gen. officer supr. Dept. Edn., Manila, 1944-45; lab. sch. prin. U. of East, Manila, 1953-54, assoc. prof. edn., 1952-55; vis. prof. UCLA, summer, 1956; prof. edn. Calif. State U., Fresno, 1956—. John M. Switzer scholar, Stanford U., 1950, Newhouse Found. scholar, 1951; Philippine scholar, Calif. Fedn. Bus. and Profl. Women's Clubs, 1952; named Disting. Profl. Woman of Yr., Fresno Bus. and Profl. Women's Club, 1958; Bicentennial award Kappa Delta Pi, 1976; Dr. Jose Rizal Outstanding Filipino award Filipino-Am. Assn. of Fresno, 1981. Mem. Internat. Platform Assn., Orgn. Filipino-Am. Educators of Fresno (pres. 1977-82), State Filipino-Am. Coordinating Council (resource person 1968), Nat. Council Social Studies, AAUW (liaison officer for Calif. State U., Fresno), Calif. Fedn. Bus. and Profl. Women's Clubs (treas. 1960-61), state chmn. Calif. state scholarships 1961-62), Pi Lambda Theta, Kappa Delta Pi, Phi Delta Kappa. Clubs: Filipino-Am. Women's. Home: 1419 W Bullard Ave Fresno CA 93711 Office: Calif State Univ Fresno CA 93740

DANDOY, SUZANNE EGGLESTON, physician, educator; b. Los Angeles, Jan. 2, 1935; d. Leonard Lester and Catherine (Wheelwright) Eggleston; B.A., UCLA, 1956, M.D., 1960, M.P.H., 1963; m. Jeremiah Richard Dandoy, June 14, 1958; children—Kevin, Bret, Jolyn. Intern, Harbor Gen. Hosp., Los Angeles, 1960-61; resident Los Angeles Health Dept., 1961-62, 63-64; epidemiologist San Diego Dept. Public Health, 1967-68; chief Bur. Preventive Health Services, Ariz. Dept. Health, Phoenix, 1970-73, asst. commr., 1973-74; asst. dir. Ariz. Dept. Health Services, Phoenix, 1974-75, dir., 1975-80 asso. prof. community medicine U. Ariz., 1970—; prof. health services adminstrn. Coll. Bus. Adminstrn., Ariz. State U., Tempe, 1981—, adviser Mortar Bd., 1981—; mem. immunization practices adv. com. HEW, 1977-80, mem. adv. com. on policy and programs Center for Disease Control, 1978; mem. council on trustees Am. Hosp. Assn. Trustee, Tempe St. Luke's Hosp., 1981—. Recipient Clarence Salsbury medal Maricopa County Med. Soc., 1980; diplomate Am. Bd. Preventive Medicine. Fellow Am. Public Health Assn., Am. Coll. Preventive Medicine; mem. Ariz. Med. Assn., Ariz. Public Health Assn. Democrat. Mormon. Contbr. articles to med. jours. Office: Center for Health Services Adminstrn Ariz State U Tempe AZ 85287

DANEK, MARITA MCKENNA, ednl. adminstr.; b. Garden City, N.Y., June 7, 1942; d. James A. and Mary Rita (Noble) McKenna; B.A., Catholic U., 1964; M.Ed., U. Md., 1970, Ph.D., 1979; m. Joseph Gerard Danek, June 18, 1966; children—Joseph, Jennifer, Geoffrey. Vocat. rehab. counselor State of Md., Bladensburg, 1966-70; counselor Model Secondary Sch. for Deaf, Washington, 1970-73; asst. prof. rehab. counseling Dept. Counseling, Gallaudet Coll., Washington, 1979—, dir. rehab. counseling (deafness) program, 1981—. Rehab. Services Adminstrn. fellow, 1976-78, D.C. Services for Independent Living grantee, 1982; Women's Ednl. Equity Act grantee, 1982. Mem. Am. Psychol. Assn., Nat. Rehab. Assn., Am. Personnel and Guidance Assn., Am. Deafness and Rehab. Assn., Am. Ednl. Research Assn., Capitol Area Rehab. Educators, Evaluation Network. Contbr. articles to profl. publs. Office: Gallaudet Coll 113 Fowler Hall Washington DC 20002

DANER, REBA ENGLER, lawyer; b. Key West, Fla., June 21, 1911; d. Abram and Anna (Schechtman) Engler; student U. Fla., 1927; A.B., U. Miami, 1930, J.D., 1936; m. Leonard Epstein, 1930 (dec. 1943); m. 2d, Jack L. Daner, Feb. 1, 1948; children—Ann Daner Anderson, Leonette E. Admitted to Fla. bar, 1936, since practiced in Miami. Chmn. bd. trustees Miami Beach Public Library, 1958-72, 80-82; mem. Met. Dade County Library Bd., 1962-72, chmn. bd., 1966; bd. dirs. Brandeis U. Women's Assn.; trustee Bass Mus. Art, Miami Beach; founder Mt. Sinai Hosp., Miami Beach, 1981. Mem. Fla. Bar, Am., Dade County (chmn. resolutions com. 1965-67, mem. library com. 1959-70) bar assns., ALA, Southeast Library Assn. (chmn. 1970-72), Am., Fla. (pres. 1959-60) library trustees assns., Nat. Assembly Library Trustees (Fla. rep. 1958), Hadassah (pres. Greater Miami chpt. 1936), Fla. Women's Golf Assn. (sec. 1948), Soc. Founders U. Miami. Jewish (pres. Sisterhood temple 1944-48). Clubs: Westview Country, Miami Woman's (dir. 1978—), Fla. Women's Golf Assn. (sec. 1948); Lawyers (dir. 1969-71); Century. Home: 303 E San Marino Dr Miami Beach FL 33139 Office: Alfred I DuPont Bldg Miami FL 33131

DANFORTH, FRANCES MUELLER (MRS. WILLIAM PAUL DANFORTH), civic worker; b. Austin, Tex., Mar. 23, 1914; d. Rudolph George and Laura Emma (Von Boeckmann) Mueller; B.J., U. Tex., 1935, B.A., 1936; M.S., Columbia U., 1938; m. William Paul Danforth, Aug. 16, 1942; children—William Paul, Douglas Mueller, Donald Lee. Grader dept. journalism U. Tex., Austin, 1934; asst. dir. Interscholastic League Press Bur., U. Tex., 1936-37; asst. editor Alcade, monthly alumni mag., 1936-37, 38-42; editor Star Points, nat. papers Delta Delta Delta Chgo., 1968-70. Pres., Austin Symphony League, 1967-68; state v.p. Tex. Women's Assn. Symphony Orchs., 1970; pres. Austin Vol. Bur., 1966-68; bd. dirs., sec. USO, 1971-72; bd. dirs. Symphony Orch. Soc.; bd. dirs., sec. Cen-Tex. chpt. ARC, pres. Altenheim, 1961-62. Mem. Women in Communications, Mortar Board (Austin alumna pres. 1978—) Delta Delta Delta, Lutheran (pres. ch. women 1972-74). Clubs: Settlement, Lawyers Wives (mem. bd., sec. 1973-74), Woman's (sec. 1972-74, v.p. 1977-79) (all Austin). Home: 1400 West Ave Austin TX 78701

D'ANGELO, ANTONIA BILLETT, social worker, editor; b. Phila., Nov. 17, 1928; d. Marc and Alma (Scott) Billett; B.A., U. Pa., 1947, M.S.W., 1950; m. George A. D'Angelo, Sept. 3, 1949; children—Marc Scott, Christopher Scott, David Steven, Victoria Scott. Social worker Children's Aid Soc. Montgomery County, 1947-51, Sleighton Farm Sch. for Girls, Phila., 1954-55, Haverford (Pa.) State Hosp., 1962-67; founder alcoholism treatment program, cons. on alcoholism and addictions Inst. of Pa. Hosp., Phila., 1973-81; mng. editor Focus on Women, Jour. Addictions and Health, Phila., 1980—; pres. Delaware Valley area Nat. Council on Alcoholism, 1978-82, chmn. bd., 1982—, nat. v.p., N.Y.C., 1978-80; chmn. sect. on women Internat. Council on Alcohol and Addiction; mem. UN Non-Govtl. Orgns. Com. on Women and Health, and del. Mid-Decade Conf. on Women, Copenhagen, 1980; mem. women's bd. Jefferson Hosp. Mem. Nat. Assn. Social Workers, Acad. Cert. Social Workers, Alcohol and Drug Problems Assn., Am. Public Health Assn., Nat. Assn. Social Psychiatry, English-Speaking Union, AAUW. Clubs: Cosmopolitan, Merion Cricket, Phila. Skating, Phila. Art Alliance. Office: 1315 Walnut St Suite 905 Philadelphia PA 19107

DANGREMOND, LUCILLE MARTIN (MRS. HARLEY L. DANGREMOND), civic worker; b. St. Louis; d. George H. and Julia (Blattner) M.; B.A., Washington U., St. Louis, 1922; M.A., Tchrs. Coll., Columbia, 1940; m. Harley L. Dangremond, June 28, 1924 (dec. June 4, 1979); children—Jack M., Dorothy J. (dec.). Tchr., Bogota (N.J.) High Sch., 1940-43; substitute tchr. Teaneck (N.J.) High Sch., 1943-60; tchr. Englewood (N.J.) High Sch., 1940-55; profl. mag. writer, 1946-48. Mem. adv. com. Sch. Edn., Rutgers U., 1957-59; former mem. adv. panel pub. health services HEW; liaison officer Am. Mothers Com.; mem. Bergen County (N.J.) Easter Seal Com., 1971—. Recipient citation Nat. Police Officers Assn. Mem. N.J. State Fedn. Women's Clubs (pres. 1960-62, Cecilia Gaines Holland award 1976), Gen. Fedn. Women's Clubs (chmn. religion 1962-64, dir. 1960-70, chmn. vets. div. 1968-70, v.p. past state pres. club 1980-82; State Jewel 1966; recipient award for leadership, 1964-66, for longest outstanding record leadership N.J. 1966), Am. Mothers Com., Inc. (regional dir. 1958-60), Middle Atlantic Conf. Gen. Fedn. Women's Clubs (pres. 1964-66, chmn. home life dept. 1964-66) PEO (chpt. pres. 1967-69). Clubs: Past Presidents' (pres. 1949-51), Washington University Alumni, Teachers College Alumni. Home: 753 Larch Ave Teaneck NJ 07666

DANIEL, CYNTHIA DORSEY, telephone co. exec.; b. Mexia, Tex., Sept. 24, 1950; d. Thurman Edward and Dorothy Marie (Jones) Dorsey; B.A., N. Tex. State U., Denton, 1972; postgrad. So. Meth. U., Dallas, 1975—. Mktg. rep. Southwestern Bell Telephone Co., Waco, Tex., 1972-73, project clk., Dallas, 1973-75, service cons., 1975-76, account exec. securities industry, 1976-78, market mgr. securities industries, St. Louis, 1978—. Mem. Dallas Black C. of C. (dir. 1978—), Am. Mgmt. Assn., Nat. Assn. Female Execs., Alpha Kappa Alpha, Dallas Pan Hellenic Council (sec. 1978—). Democrat. Baptist. Office: Southwestern Bell Telephone Co 112 N 4th St Room 1410 Saint Louis MO 63102

DANIEL, ELEANOR SAUER, economist; b. Bklyn., Feb. 8, 1917; d. Charles P. and Elsie (Dommer) Sauer; B.A. magna cum laude, Mt. Holyoke Coll., 1936; M.A., Columbia U., 1937; m. William C. Bagley, Jr., June 11, 1937 (div. 1951); m. 2d, John Carl Daniel, Dec. 31, 1952; children—Victoria Ann, Charles Timothy. Research economist U.S. Steel Corp., 1938; lectr. econs. Bklyn. Coll., 1939-40; supr. research div. Mut. Life Ins. Co. N.Y., 1940-44, research asso., 1945-55, dir. econ. research, 1955-72, asst. v.p., sr. econ. adviser, 1972-74; economist Fed. Home Loan Bank N.Y., 1974-75; v.p., dir. Daniel Realty Cos.; dir. Atlantic Electric, Atlantic City; bd. mgrs. U.S. Savs. Bank of Newark. Mem. joint subcom. on monetary and fiscal policy Life Ins. Assn. Am.-Am. Life Conv., 1962-74, mem. life ins. investment research com., 1957-60, 64-67; mem. econ. growth com. bus. research adv. council U.S. Bur. Labor Stats., 1966—; mem. various tech. coms. Nat. Bur. Econ. Research; research review panel HEW; mem. coms. Project Econs.; mem. Pres.'s Task Force on Fed. Credit Programs, 1968-69; mem. econ. adv. bd. U.S. Sec. of Commerce, 1970-72; past vice chmn. bd. trustees Mt. Holyoke Coll.; trustee N.J. Blue Shield; past treas. Family Service Assn. Middlesex County. Mem. Downtown Economists (treas. 1962-64, chmn. 1964-66), Am. Fin. Assn. (dir. 1957-59), Am. Statis. Assn. (fin. com. 1968-74), Am. Econ. Assn., Acad. Polit. Sci., Nat. Assn. Bus. Economists, Forecasters Club N.Y. (sec.-treas. 1970-72, pres. 1975-76), Nat. Planning Assn., Women's Bond Club (v.p. 1970-72, pres. 1972-74), Atlantic Council, Phi Beta Kappa. Author: (with J.J. O'Leary and S. Foster) Our National Debt and Our Savings, 1949; contbr. articles to profl. jours. Home: 34 N Drive East Brunswick NJ 08816

DANIEL, JAMIE, business cons.; b. Grand Junction, Tenn., Nov. 16, 1921; d. Doctor Newton and Helen Beatrice (Nabers) Daniel; student U. Miss., 1954-56; m. Paul J. Phyfer, Aug. 1940 (dec. 1954); children—Paul J., Daniel W., Kathryn Anne, David Laird; m. 2d, Donald Lindenberg, June 1956 (div. 1974); children—Jon Ward, James Frank. Pub. info. officer Mark VII Corp., Geneva, Ill., 1973-75; v.p. BASIC, Geneva, also Washington, Va., 1975—; pres. Miscella Inc., Geneva, 1976—; vice chmn. Twin Silos Hydrofarms, Inc., St. Charles, Ill., 1981—; pres. Dansko, Inc., Washington, Va., 1980—. Vice pres. LWV Ill., 1967-71; sec. Landmarks Preservation Service, Chgo., 1975-77; dir. Landmarks Preservation Council of Ill., 1975-81; chmn. daily procedures No. Ill. Conf. United Meth. Ch., 1972-77. Mem. Chgo. Assn. Commerce and Industry, Mid Am. Arab C. of C., Internat., No. Ill. solar energy socs. Club: Plaza (Chgo.). Home: 41W906 Hughes Rd Elburn IL Office: Box 145 Geneva IL 60134

DANIEL, LINDA MARIE, microbiologist; b. Abilene, Tex., Aug. 19, 1944; d. James Marcus and Mary Marie (Hill) Daniel; B.S., U. Tex., 1969. Microbiologist, instr., Good Samaritan Hosp., Phoenix, 1967-70; supr., ednl. coordinator Desert Samaritan Hosp., Mesa, Ariz., 1970-73; surveyor/cons. Ariz. Dept. Health, Phoenix, 1973-76; owner, cons. Lab. Cons., Ltd., Tempe, Ariz., 1976-77; owner, pres., supr. Mobile Microbiology Services, Inc., Tempe, 1977—; tchr. Maricopa County Jr. Colls., 1972-73; cons. in field; lectr. in field. Mem. Nat. Registry of Microbiologists, Am. Soc. Microbiology, Am. Soc. Med. Technologists, Am. Public Health Assn. Home: 507 W Manhatton Dr Tempe AZ 85282 Office: 915 S 52 St Suite 2 Tempe AZ 85281

DANIEL, SUSAN MARIE, program analyst; b. Frederick, Md., May 18, 1949; d. Mansfield White and Mary Waters (White) Daniel; B.A. (Montgomery County Edn. Assn. scholar), Towson State U., 1971; M.P.A., George Washington U., 1980; m. Lawnie Henderson Taylor, Mar. 31, 1979; 1 dau., Liza Marie. Info. specialist Battelle Columbus Labs., Washington, 1972-74; program officer Am. Revolution Bicentennial Adminstrn., Washington, 1974-76; tech. cons. Internat. Bus. Services, Inc., Washington, 1977-80; program analyst U.S. Dept. Health and Human Services, Washington, 1980-81. Mem. Am. Soc. Public Adminstrn., Nat. Assn. Female Execs., Women's Equity Action League, Federally Employed Women, Phi Alpha Theta. Episcopalian. Home: 305 N St Washington DC 20024

DANIEL-DREYFUS, SUSAN B. RUSSE (MRS. MARC ANDRE DANIEL-DREYFUS), civic worker; b. St. Louis, May 30, 1940; d. Frederick William and Suzanne (Mackay) Russe; student Smith Coll., 1958-60, Corcoran Sch. Fine Arts, 1960-61, Washington U., St. Louis, 1961-62; m. Don B. Faerber, Nov. 27, 1962 (div. Nov. 1968); 1 dau., Suzanne Mackay; m. 2d, Marc Andre Daniel-Dreyfus, Aug. 9, 1969. Mem. St. Louis-St. Louis County White House Conf. on Edn., 1966-68; mem. Mo. 1st Gov.'s Conf. on Edn., 1966, 2d Conf., 1968; bd. dirs. St. Louis Smith Coll.; hon. bd. dirs. New Music Circle; mem. woman's bd. dirs. Washington U., New Music Circle, 1963-67; mem. woman's bd. Mo. Hist. Soc.; bd. dirs. Non-Partisan Ct. Plan for Mo., Young Audiences Inc., 1967-69; bd. dirs. Childrens Art Bazaar, 1968-70; founder St. Louis Opera Theater; chmn. Art. Mus. Bond Issue election St. Louis, 1966; jr. bd. dirs. St. Louis Symphony, 1966-68, Opportunities Indsl. Center, Boston; legis. chmn. bd. dirs. Boston LWV, 1969-72, 74-76; mem. council, bd. dirs. Jr. League Boston, 1970-72, Family Counseling-Region West, Boston, 1979—; pres. Family Counseling Bd., Brookline, Mass.; bd. govs. Tunbridge Sch.; trustee Chestnut Hill Sch., Boston, Brookline Friendly Soc.; mem. steering com. ann. fund Boston Children's Hosp. Med. Center; v.p. Nat. Friends Bd., Joslin Diabetes Found.; mem. corp. bd. Joslin Diabetes Center; v.p. bd. dirs. Boston Center Internat. Visitors, 1979-81; Boston bd. dirs. Mass. Soc. Prevention of Cruelty to Children. Mem. Colonial Dames, Soc. Art Historians. Clubs: Women's City (dir.) (Boston); Vincent (dir.). Home: 120 Middlesex Rd Chestnut Hill MA 02167

DANIELS, BETTIE MARIE, assn. exec.; b. Ponca City, Okla., Apr. 14, 1933; d. William Homer and Edith Marie (Gambill) Sharpton; student LaSalle U., 1966-68; m. Jess Harold Daniels, Oct. 3, 1951; children—Susan Marie Daniels Jorensen, Ronald Bradley, Karen Kay. Mgr. fire ins. dept. Farmers Ins. Group, Colorado Springs, 1951; bookkeeper Torrino Constrn. Co., Torrance, Calif., 1964-66; sec., bookkeeper Livingston Engrng. Co., Cody, Wyo., 1966, 68-69; bookkeeper Colo. Cartage Co., Denver, 1967; bookkeeper, acct. Nielson Enterprises, Inc., Cody, 1969-75; field exec. Wyo. council Girl Scouts U.S.A., Cody, 1975—; pvt. practice bookkeeping, 1977—. Mem. parish paster relations com. Cody United Meth. Ch., 1979—, chmn. youth activities, 1969-71. Republican. Clubs: Soroptimist, Newcomers, Eastern Star, Daus. of Nile. Author histories. Home: PO Box 1275 Cody WY 82414 Office: PO Box 293 Casper WY 82602

DANIELS, DEMETRIA, spl. events co. exec.; b. Bklyn., Nov. 12, 1941; d. James and Nora D.; B.S., Columbia U., 1967. Columnist, Fairchild Publs., N.Y.C., 1967; reviewer Arts Mag., N.Y.C., 1968-69; public relations mgr. Fritzsche Dodge & Olcott, Inc., N.Y.C., 1970-71; publicist to the arts, 1972; pres. Demetria Daniels, Inc., spl. events, N.Y.C., 1979. Dir.-in-charge N.Y. Big Apple Awards Banquet, 1978, 79; bd. dirs. N.Y. Jr. C. of C., 1978, 79, Columbia U. Gen. Studies, 1980, 81. Mem. N.Y. Assn. Women Bus. Owners, Gotham Bus. and Profl. Women's Club, N.Y. Women in Communications, N.Y. Mcpl. Art Soc., N.Y. Archtl. League, Nat. Assn. TV Arts & Scis., Met. Mus. Art. Clubs: Womens City Club N.Y., Princeton of N.Y. Address: 140 Riverside Dr New York NY 10024

DANIELS, DOROTHY, writer; b. Waterbury, Conn., July 1, 1915; d. Judson Richard and Mary (Guilfoile) Smith; student Central Conn. State Coll., 1932-36; m., Oct. 7, 1937. Tng. tchr., New Britain, Conn., 1937-39; actress, 1939-40. Author 132 books under name Dorothy Daniels, 1962—, most recent including: House of Silence, 1980, Nicola, 1980, Monte Carlo, 1981, Sisters of Valcour, 1981; seven books under name Suzanne Somers, 1961-73, including: The Caduceus Tree, 1961, Image of Truth, 1963, Romany Curse, 1971, House on Thunder Hill, 1973; other books under names Cynthia Cavanaugh, Angela Gray, Daniella Dorsett. Active Citizens Adv. Com. Ventura Sch., Calif. Youth Authority, Republican Women's Club. Mem. Nat. League Am. Pen Women (nat. hon.), Authors Guild, Ventura County Writers' Club.

DANIELS, ELAINE MAKRIS, public relations cons.; b. S. Bend, Ind., Nov. 17, 1938; d. Peter C. and Dorothy Makris; B.A. in Comparative Lit., Ind. U., 1960; m. Michael Paul Daniels, Sept. 1, 1964; children—Anthony, Maria, Alexander. Senatorial campaign coordinator, 1976; mem. staff select com. population U.S. Ho. of Reps., 1977-78; congl. and public affairs officer select commn. immigration and refugee policy Joint Congl. and Presdl. Commn., 1979-81; public relations cons., 1981—. Mem. Nat. Assn. Female Execs. Mem. Greek Orthodox Ch. Author chpts. in reports. Address: 5615 Bent Branch Rd Bethesda MD 20816

DANIELS, ELISABETH ANN MICHAEL, mayor; b. Kansas City, Mo., Oct. 12, 1944; d. Archie Washigton and Elizabeth Virginia (Moreland) Michael; student Central Mo. State U., Warrensburg, 1963-66; m. Joseph Ames Daniels, Sept 1, 1963; children—Jeffrey Michael, Christopher Ames. Adminstrv. sec., dean women Central Mo. State U., 1966-68; minister youth and music First Baptist Ch.,

Carrollton, Mo., 1970-73; propr. Ann's Catering Service, Carrollton, 1973—; mayor Town of Carrollton, 1977—; v.p., bd. govs. Area II Health Systems Agy., 1979—; exec. com., v.p., chmn. personnel com. Mo. Valley Regional Planning Commn., 1977—; chmn. Sub Area Health Council, 1980—, Regional Manpower Adv. Council, 1981—; mem. Mo. Older Adults Transp. Bd., 1981—. Pres. community adv. bd. Sta. KMOS-TV, 1980—. Mem. Mo. Mcpl. League, PEO, Federated Woman's Club, Beta Sigma Phi. Home: 1112 Hilltop Dr Carrollton MO 64633 Office: 201 W Benton St Carrollton MO 64633

DANIELS, ELIZABETH ADAMS, educator; b. Westport, Conn., May 8, 1920; d. Thomas Davies and Minnie Mae (Sherwood) Adams; B.A., Vassar Coll., 1941; M.A., U. Mich., 1942; Ph.D., N.Y.U., 1954; m. John L. Daniels, Mar. 21, 1942; children—John, Eleanor, Sherwood, Ann. Mem. faculty Vassar Coll., 1948—, prof. English, 1965—, Helen D. Lockwood prof., 1972—, chmn. dept., 1974-76, 81—, dean freshmen, 1955-58, dean studies, 1965-73, acting dean faculty, 1976-78, dir. self-study, 1978-80; mem. Middle States Evaluation Teams. Vassar Coll. fellow, 1942; recipient summer stipend Nat. Endowment Humanities, 1981; named Grad. Student of Year, N.Y.U., 1954. Mem. MLA, AAUP, Northeastern Victorian Assn., Brit. Studies Assn., Research Soc. Victorian Periodicals (exec. bd.). Democrat. Club: Poughkeepsie Tennis. Author: Jessie White Mario, Risorgimento Revolutionary (translated into Italian), 1972; also articles. Office: Vassar Coll Poughkeepsie NY 12601

DANIELS, JANICE EMILY, electric co. ofcl.; b. Pitts., Oct. 2, 1943; d. Lawrence C. and Ugirtha Johnson; B.S. magna cum laude in Adminstrv. Mgmt. (Presdl. Merit scholar), Point Park Coll., Pitts., 1976; m. LeRoy J. Daniels, Jr., Dec. 12, 1964; children—Terri Y., Carol Ann. Sec. to v.p. Pitts. Brewing Co., 1963-66; adminstrv. sec. Rust Engring. Co., Pitts., 1970-71; exec. asst. Allegheny Opportunities Industrialization Centers, McKeesport, Pa., 1976-78, bd. dirs., 1981—; personnel and labor relations supr. large rotating apparatus and plant services divs. Westinghouse Electric Corp., East Pittsburgh, Pa., 1978—; public speaker. Jr. Achievement advisor, 1980; mem. Wilkinsburg image com. of Wilkinsburg Sch. Dist.; chmn. edn. com. Wilkinsburg chpt. NAACP, 1977-78. Recipient Black Achiever award Talk Mag., 1977. Mem. Pitts. Personnel Assn., Westinghouse Foremen's Assn. Democrat. Episcopalian. Home: 525 Holmes St Pittsburgh PA 15221 Office: 1G Annex 700 Braddock Ave East Pittsburgh PA 15112

DANIELS, JESSICA MARIE, journalist; b. Portsmouth, Va., Sept. 6, 1951; d. Joe Allen and Mary Therese (Clos) D.; B.A. in Journalism and Anthropology, Ind. U., 1973. Research asst. Ind. Center on Law and Poverty, Indpls., 1973; asst. news editor The Record newspaper, Louisville, 1974-78; employee communications supr. Humana Inc., Louisville, 1978—; free-lance writer, editor. Trustee Cherokee Triangle Assn., 1978-80; v.p. Louisville Hist. League, 1978, bd. dirs., 1979. Editor: Sensory Stimulation Kit: A Teacher's Guidebook, 1978. Office: Humana Inc PO Box 1438 Louisville KY 40201

DANIELS, LESLIE BETH, city ofcl.; b. Kansas City, Mo., July 14, 1951; d. Charles Lee and Helen Atanasoff D.; B.A., U. Ariz., 1972; M.A., U. Phoenix, 1981. Copywriter public relations, Tucson, 1972-74, graphic artist/electronic typesetter, 1974-75, polit. campaign mgr., 1972-77; adminstrv. asst. City Mgrs. Office, City of Tucson, 1978—. Editor, State Republican Com. newspaper, 1975-76; chmn. Pima County Young Rep. League, 1973-74; dist. 9 chmn. Pima County Rep. Central Com., 1974. Mem. Ariz. Assn. Indsl. Developers, Kappa Tau Alpha, Delta Sigma Pi. Republican. Methodist. Club: Pima County Trunk 'n Tusk (publicity chmn. 1974-77). Home: 7369 E 20th St Tucson AZ 85710 Office: PO Box 27210 Tucson AZ 85726

DANIELS, MADELINE MARIE, clin. anthropologist; b. Newark, Oct. 14, 1948; d. William and Dorothy Barlow; B.A. cum laude, CCNY, 1971; Ph.D., Union Grad. Sch., Yellow Springs, Ohio, 1975; m. Peter W. Daniels, Oct. 18, 1976; children—Jonathan, Jedediah. Lectr., Westchester Community Coll., also Bronx Community Coll., 1973-74; mem. adj. faculty SUNY, Purchase, 1974-76; data processing coordinator GTE Internat., 1976-78; lectr. div. continuing edn. U. N.H., 1979—; exec. dir. Crossroads Center Human Inregration, Kingston, N.H., 1979—; psychotherapist, lectr., cons. in field. Cert. ind. biofeedback practitioner. Mem. Am. Psychol. Assn., Biofeedback Soc. Am., Soc. Psychol. Athropology, Soc. Sci. Study Sex N.H. Psychol. Assn., NOW, Author: Realistic Leadership, 1982. Office: Crossroads Center East Kingston NH 03827

DANIELS, MARIONETTE SANDERS (MRS. EDWARD DANIELS), social worker; b. Union, S.C., Aug. 25, 1927; d. William and Essie (Moorehead) Sanders; B.S., W.Va. State Coll., 1948; M.S.W., Columbia U., 1965; m. Edward Daniels, Aug. 25, 1949. Social worker D.C. Govt., 1955-62; social work supr. and psychiat. program coordinator Harlem Hosp. Med. Center, N.Y.C., 1965-70; clin. coordinator White Plains (N.Y.) Hosp., 1971-72; asst. dir. social work dept. Mt. Sinai Med. Center, N.Y.C., 1972-75; instr. and coordinator community program planning, dept. community medicine Mt. Sinai Sch. Medicine, City U. N.Y., 1975—; tchr. New Sch. Social Research, N.Y.C., 1971-73; instr. Nat. Assn. Social Workers, Mental Health Tng. Inst., Chgo., 1972-74; cons., group therapist Hillcrest Center for Children, Bedford Hills, N.Y., 1968-74. Founding mem., steering com. mem. E. Harlem Coordinating Com. on Child Abuse, 1974—; bd. dirs. E. Harlem Health Council, 1974-76; mem. N.Y. Citywide Adv. Council on Sch. Health, 1975—; steering com. mem. E. Harlem Coordinating Com. on Awareness of Human Services, 1975—; chairperson membership com. Health Systems Agency N.Y.C., 1978—; mem. health adv. com. Taft-Madison Headstart Program, 1978; mem. Mt. Bethel Baptist Ch., Washington. Recipient Exceptional Service award D.C. Govt., 1959; certified social worker, N.Y. Mem. Nat. Assn. Social Workers, Internat. Council Social Welfare, Nat. Conf. Social Welfare, Am. Pub. Welfare Assn. Club: The Fashionettes, Inc. (hon. mem. D.C.). Contbr. articles in field to profl. jours.; presentations and workshops for profl. meetings and insts. Home: 7524 Piney Branch Rd Silver Spring MD 20910

DANIELS, MAXINE LOREAT, counselor; b. Columbus, Tex., Oct. 27, 1926; d. Earl Preston and Elizabeth (Wright) Harris; B.A. Music, Prairie View U., 1946; postgrad. U. Iowa, 1947-48, Rutgers U., 1956-58, Newark State Tchrs. Coll., 1957, 67-70; M.S.Ed. magna cum laude, Monmouth Coll., 1974; m. Thomas Edward Daniels, Aug. 8, 1948; children—Michael E., Karen E. Daniels Alston, Kevin E., Daryl E., Larrick E., Danita E., Raun E. Instr. in music Lane Coll., 1948-49, Tillotson Coll., 1949-50; tchr. Neptune Twp. (N.J.) Sch. System, 1956-68, guidance counselor, 1967-70; chmn. dept. guidance Asbury Park (N.J.) Middle Sch., 1970—; tchr. piano, guitar; cons. Head Start. Dist. bd. dirs. Ocean Twp. (N.J.) Democratic Club, 1972—; mem. lay council, deaconess African Methodist Episcopal Zion Ch. Recipient cert. of appreciation Whitesville PTA, 1965, 67, N.J. Jaycettes, 1964, Nat. Assn. Negro Bus. and Profl. Women's Clubs, 1977, N.J. Orgn. Tchrs., 1974; letter of appreciation Neptune Supt. Schs., 1969, Brookdale Community Coll., 1969, 70, Bur. Children's Services, Red Bank, N.J., 1969; certified in pupil personnel services, adminstrn., supervision, music, elem. teaching, N.J.; cert. tchr., Tex. Mem. NAACP (Civil Rights Person of Yr. 1979), Nat. Council Negro Women, NEA, N.J. Edn. Assn., N.J., Am. personnel and guidance assns., Monmouth County Guidance Assn., Nat. Assn. Negro Bus. and Profl. Women's Clubs (Chpt. Civil Rights Person of Yr. 1982), Bus. and Profl. Women's Council, U. Iowa (life), Monmouth Coll. alumni assns., Asbury Park Suprs. Assn., N.J. Prins. and Suprs. Assn., Nat. Assn. Secondary Sch. Prins., N.J. State Fedn. Colored Women's Clubs, Alpha Kappa Alpha. Author: Directory of Monmouth County Minorities in Non-Traditional Areas, 1979; research in field. Home: 52 Fredric Dr Oakhurst NJ 07755 Office: 1200 Bangs Ave Asbury Park NJ 07712

DANIELS, NANCY PATRICIA, health care exec., potter; b. Milw., Oct. 1, 1934; d. Harry Donald and Janet Ione (Nemacheck) Altman; B.S. with honors, Mich. Tech. U., 1956; postgrad. Ft. Wright Coll., Spokane, Wash., 1965-66, U. Mont., 1967-68; children—Peter, Jeffrey, Erik. Med. technologist County Indian Hosp., Albuquerque, 1956-57, Peninusula Hosp., Burlingame, Calif., 1957-58, Clinic of Leo Bell, San Mateo, Calif., 1958-60, St. Mary's Hosp., Madison, Wis., 1962-65, now at Boulder (Mont.) River Sch. and Hosp.; tchr. pottery Spokane YWCA, 1965-66; tchr., owner Pot Shop, Missoula, Mont., 1970-78; partner Basin (Mont.) Sun Works Pottery. Mem. Basin Community Action League. Nat. Endowment Arts grantee, Danish island Bornholm, 1976. Mem. Am. Soc. Clin. Pathology. Home: Box 37 Basin MT 59631 Office: Box 87 Bounder MT 59632

DANIELS, SUZANNE MADELEINE, med. technologist; b. Worcester, Mass., July 23, 1941; d. George Edward and Ruth Bernadette (St. Martin) Brodeur; student Central New Eng. Coll. Tech., 1959-62; M.T., Worcester City Hosp. Sch. Med. Tech., 1962; m. Charles Daniels; children—Edward, Jennifer. Flight exam technician Pratt & Whitney, E. Hartford, Conn., 1962-63; sect. head chemistry/radioisotopes Mt. Sinai Hosp., Hartford, Conn., 1963-65; gen. technician Meml. Hosp., Worcester, 1965-69; blood bank supr. Milford-Whitinsville Regional Hosp., Milford, Mass., 1969-70; asst. clin. supr., sect. head chemistry Worcester Hahnemann Hosp., 1970-75; lab. supr. Weeks Meml. Hosp., Lancaster, N.H., 1975—; clin. teaching staff Vt. Coll. Sch. Med. Lab. Technicians, 1975—. Mem. Am. Soc. Clin. Pathologists, Clin. Lab. Mgmt. Assn. Roman Catholic. Clubs: Twin Mt. Snowmobile, Bethlehem Country. Home: PO Box H Twin Mountain NH 03595 Office: Middle St Lancaster NH 03584

DANIELS, TINA FANTO, fund-raising mgmt. cons.; b. Vienna, Austria, June 16, 1929; came to U.S., 1952, naturalized, 1956; d. Richard and Anna (Weissbacher) Fanto; candidate Ph.D., U. Vienna, 1950; m. Arthur Daniels, Oct. 13, 1952 (dec.); 1 dau., Ricki. Exec. asst. Amicale Co., Inc., 1953-57; asso. dir. Leukemia Soc. Am., 1960-66; with Brakeley, John Price Jones Inc., Stamford, Conn. and N.Y.C., 1966—, exec. v.p., corp. sec., 1978—; lectr. in field of computers. Sec., Westchester County Bridge Assn., 1975—. Mem. Nat. Assn. Hosp. Devel. Home: 1514 N James St Mamaroneck NY 10543 Office: 1600 Summer St Stamford CT 06905

DANIELSON, JEANETTE MARILYN, oil co. ofcl.; b. Windsor Twp., Wis., Oct. 24, 1940; d. Albert Edward and Linda Josephine (Davidson) Moe; student Madison Area Tech. Coll., 1970-80, E.R.T.I. Bus. Sch., 1960; children—Russell Alan, Jeffrey Peter, Eric Lee. Exec. sec. Kerr-McGee Oil Co., Madison, Wis., 1965-70, Atlantic-Richfield Oil Co., Madison, 1970-75; adminstrv. sec. Skelly Oil Co., Madison, 1975-76; adminstrv. asst. Getty Oil Co., Madison, 1976—; mgr., stylist Beeline Fashions, Madison, 1963—. Hostess, Greater Madison Conv. Bur., 1980—. Named March of Dimes Coordinator of Yr., 1976; recipient God-Home-Country award, 1960; State of Wis. Key award, 1960. Mem. Am. Bus. Women's Assn. (nat. bd. dirs. 1978-79, pres. Wis. chpt. 1981-82, Woman of Yr. award 1976, 80), Nat. Assn. Female Execs., Direct Selling Assn., Four Lakes Secs. Assn. (pres. 1980—). Lutheran. Club: Toastmistress. Home: 918 Moorland Rd Madison WI 53713 Office: Suite 211 2934 Fish Hatchery Rd Madison WI 53713

DANIELSON, PHYLLIS IRENE, ednl. adminstr.; b. Marion, Ind.; d. Alta V. (Norris); B.A., Ball State U., 1953; Ed.S., Mich. State U., 1966; Ed.D., Ind. U., 1968; 1 son, Matthew T. Tchr. pub. schs. in Mich., 1953-60; adult dir. YWCA, Lansing, Mich., 1960-62; dept. chmn. pub. schs., Lansing, 1962-66; asst. prof. Ball State U., Muncie, Ind., 1966-67, U. N.C., Greensboro, 1968-70; assoc. prof. Ind. U.-Purdue U., Indpls., 1970-76; pres. Kendall Sch. Design, 1970—; adv. bd. Mich. Nat. Bank, Grand Rapids. Bd. dirs. St. Mary's Hosp., John Ball Zoo; lay reader Episcopal Ch. Mem. NOW Nat. Art Edn. Assn., Am. Council Edn., Nat. Council Art Adminstrs., Furniture Designers Assn., Grand Rapids C. of C. (v.p., bd. dirs. found.), Furniture Mfg. Assn. (dir.). Clubs: Pen, Charlevioux, Economic (v.p.). Office: 1110 College Ave NE Grand Rapids MI 49503

DANIS, FRAN STILLERMAN, social worker; b. Bklyn., July 22, 1953; d. Melvin and Suzanne Mary (Danis) Stillerman; B.A. (N.Y. State Regents scholar), SUNY, Stony Brook, 1974, M.S.W., 1976. Social work intern Westbury (N.Y.) Sch. Dist., 1974-75, Pilgrim Psychiat. Center, Brentwood, N.Y., 1975-76; caseworker II, Dallas County Mental Health and Mental Retardation Center, Dallas, 1976-77; vol. coordinator Denton County Big Bros. and Sisters, Denton, Tex., 1979-80; exec. dir. Denton County Friends of the Family, Inc., 1980—; supr. social work students Tex. Woman's U., 1979—, North Tex. State U., 1980—; coordinator public edn. Tex. Council on Family Violence. Bd. dirs. Denton County Big Bros. and Sisters, 1980—; mem. health and welfare com. City of Denton Directions and Decisions for the 80s. Mem. Nat. Assn. Social Workers (Social Worker of Yr.), Acad. Cert. Social Workers, Bus. and Profl. Women's Club. Democrat. Jewish. Home: 433 Fulton St Denton TX 76201 Office: PO Box 623 Denton TX 76201

DANISKAS, BARBARA (LEE), elec. engr.; b. Oakmont, Pa., Jan. 15; d. Louis Fred and Mary Lillian (Norris) Sokol; A.S., Community Coll. Allegheny County, 1976; B.S.E.E., U. Pitts., 1982. Research technician research and devel. dept. ARCO/Polymers, Monaca, Pa., 1976-80; engr. Orbital Engring., Carnegie, Pa., 1980—; engr. on loan for spl. project Parsons, Brinckerhoff-Gibbs & Hill, Pitts., 1981—. Vice pres. coll. women's council Boyce Campus Community Coll. of Allegheny County, 1975, also mem. returning student's council, 1975. Mem. IEEE. Mem. Christian Ch. Home: 827 Highview St Pittsburgh PA 15206 Office: 101 W Mall Plaza Pittsburgh PA 15106

DANNER, BLYTHE KATHARINE (MRS. BRUCE W. PALTROW), actress; b. Phila.; d. Harry Earl and Katharine Danner; B.A. in Drama, Bard Coll., 1965; m. Bruce W. Paltrow, Dec. 14, 1969; children—Gwyneth Kate, Jake. Appeared as Laura in Glass Menagerie, 1965; repertory at Theatre Co. Boston, The Knack and 7 new Am. Plays, 1965-66; N.Y.C. debut 81st St. Theater, The Infantry, 1966; repertory in R.I., Trinity Sq. Playhouse, appearing as Helena in Midsummer Night's Dream, Irena in Three Sisters, 1967; off-Broadway shows include Collision Course, 1968, Up Eden, 1968; Someone's Commin Hungry, 1969; Lincoln Center Repertory Co. included Summertree, 1968, Cyrano de Bergerac, 1968, Elise in the Miser, 1969 The Philadelphia Story, 1980; appeared on Broadway as Jill Tanner in Butterflies Are Free (Tony award); also plays Major Barbara, 1971, Twelfth Night, 1972, The Seagull, 1974, Ring Around The Moon, 1975, Betrayal, 1980; TV spls. include To Confuse the Angel (with Lee J. Cobb), George M. (with Joel Grey), 1970, Doctor Cook's Garden (with Bing Crosby), To Be Young, Gifted and Black, 1971, F. Scott Fitzgerald and 'The Last of the Belles', 1974, The Seagull, 1975, Eccentricities of a Nightingale, 1976, The Scarecrow, Adam's Rib (series 1973), You Can't Take It With You, 1979, Too Far to Go (John Updike adaptation), 1979; movies include 1776, 1972, To Kill a Clown, 1972; Lovin' Molly, 1974, Hearts of the West, 1975, Futureworld, 1976, The Great Santeni, 1980. Recipient Theatre World award, 1969. Home and Office: 333 W 71st St New York NY 10023 also care Agy for Performing Arts Inc 888 7th Ave New York NY 10106 *

DANSER, ELLEN SPENCER, publishing co. exec.; b. Mancelona, Mich., Mar. 15, 1922; d. Edward C. and Emma (Maffitt) Shafer; student Bliss Bus. Coll., 1939-43; m. Harold W. Danser, Jr., June 22, 1969. Treas. SSS Corp., North Adams, Mass., 1950-63; v.p., treas. Paper Service Co., Holyoke, Mass., 1963-69; nat. sales mgr. F. Weber Co., Phila., 1969-71; cons. sales promotion Wall St. Transcript, N.Y.C., 1970-72; owner, pres., treas. Elan Pub. Co., Inc. and Elan Products, Meredith, N.H., 1972—. Treas., First Congl. Ch. of Meredith, 1978—; pres. Community Garden Club, 1975. Republican. Home: Oak Island Meredith NH 03253 Office: PO Box 683 Meredith NH 03253

D'ANTONIO, LINDA MARY, retail store ofcl.; b. Bklyn., July 8, 1954; d. Frank M. and Rita C. (Allegra) D'A.; student St. John's U., 1972-74, Fashion Inst. Tech., 1975-76. Asst. buyer, asso. buyer Martin's Dept. Store, Bklyn., 1976-78; sr. asst. buyer Lord & Taylor, N.Y.C., 1978-80, buyer, 1980—. Home: 80 Spencer Ave Lynbrook NY 11563 Office: 424 Fifth Ave New York NY 10018

DANY, MARIE-LOUISE, hotel exec.; b. Strasbourg, France, Jan. 23, 1929; d. Robert Adolph and Fanny (Walter) Roser; grad. College Technique Hotelier, Strasbourg, 1947; m. Guy Dany, Feb. 5, 1958. Mgmt. trainee Societe des Hotels and Casino de Deauville (France), 1946-52, Hoteles Unidos Madrid, 1952-59; exec. Terrass' Hotel, Paris, 1959-62; auditor Fairmont Hotel Co., San Francisco, 1974—. Office: Fairmont Hotel and Tower 950 Mason St San Francisco CA 94106

DANZIG, KATHRYN ALICIA, social worker; b. Somerville, N.J., Oct. 1, 1943; d. Samuel and Anne (Boriek) D.; student Wilmington Coll., 1961-64; B.A., Central State Coll., 1966; postgrad. Okla. State U., 1966-67; M.S.W., U. Okla., 1973; m. William Gates Fink, Apr. 2, 1964 (div. 1974). Social worker div. social services Okla. Dept. Human Services, Oklahoma City, 1967-72, social services supr., 1973-74, acting county adminstr., 1974-76, staff asst. for program devel., 1976-77; cons. div. youth and family services N.J. Dept. Human Services, Trenton, 1977, supervising systems analyst and adminstrv. analyst, 1977-79; asst. dir. Region III Adoption Resource Center, Phila., 1979-80; with Office of Refugee Resettlement, U.S. Dept. Health and Human Services, Washington, 1980-81; project dir. Center for Social Policy and Community Devel., Sch. Social Adminstrn. Temple U., Phila., 1981—. Bd. dirs. Mid-City br. YWCA of Phila. Mem. Zool. Soc. Phila., Friends of Rittenhouse Sq., Nat. Assn. Social Workers, Am. Public Welfare Assn. Office: Sch Social Adminstrn Temple U Philadelphia PA

DANZIG, MARILYN ESTHER, real estate co. exec.; b. Cleve., June 30, 1933; d. Albert Louis and Violet Irene Taylor; student public schs.; 1 son, Glenn Frank Grahl. Sales mgr. Bay Islands Condominiums, St. Petersburg, Fla., 1973-76, Envoy Point and Yacht and Tennis Club of St. Petersburg Beach, 1976-81; sales, mktg. mgr. Silver Sands Beach and Racquet Club, St. Petersburg, 1981—. Pres., Big Sisters of Pinellas County, 1975. Named Salesman of Yr. Sales and Mktg. Execs., 1975. Mem. Gulf Beach Bd. Realtors. Republican. Mem. St. Petersburg Beach C. of C. Home: 7100 Sunset Way #1106 Redington Saint Petersburg Beach FL 33706 Office: Silver Sands Beach and Racquet Club 600 66th Ave Saint Petersburg Beach FL 33706

DANZIGER, GERTRUDE, metal fabricating mfg. co. exec.; b. Chgo., Oct. 24, 1919; d. Isidor and Clara (Fuchs) Seelig; student Northwestern U., 1937-40, U. Wis., 1945; m. Sigmund H. Danziger (dec.). Sec., Homak Mfg. Co., Chgo. 1955-78, pres., 1979—, also dir. Patentee mech. and design process. Office: 4433 S Springfield St Chicago IL 60032

DARAKANANDA, CHONGRAKSA, bus. exec.; b. Nakhon Srithammaraj, Thailand, Dec. 21, 1933; came to U.S., 1977, permanent resident, 1979; d. Hen Jen Lim and Francim Wen; 10th grade cert. Sukit Coll. Sch., 1954; 12th grade cert. Triam-Udom Prep. Sch., 1956; m. Damri Darakananda, Aug. 10, 1957; children—Chutindhon, Aksornprasit, Pinipjporn, Bovornrat, Vacharaphong. Bus. woman, mgr., exec. various trading and mfg. cos., Thailand, 1956-77; dir., treas. Saha-Union Internat. (U.S.A.) Inc., San Francisco, 1977-78, pres., Daly City, Calif., 1978—, exec. dir. fin. and personnel Saha-Union Corp. Ltd., Bangkok, Thailand, 1972—, guest lectr. middle mgmt., supr. tng. of group, chmn. com. for grievances of group. Mem. Personnel Mgmt. Assn. Thailand (life), Thai Mgmt. Assn. (corp.), Am. Mgmt. Assn. Thailand Chpt. (corp.). Buddhist. Club: Royal Bangkok Sports. Home: 455 37th Ave San Francisco CA 94121 Office: 419 Allan St Daly City CA 94014

DARANY, MAUDALEA JANE, nurse, educator; b. Marshall, Mich., May 22, 1945; d. William Oscar and Susie Mae (Hamlin) Fausz; A.D.N. summa cum laude, Lansing Community Coll., 1969; B.S., Mich. State U., 1971; m. Theodore S. Darany, July 2, 1966. Instr. maternal child nursing Lansing Community Coll., 1972-74; supr. maternal child nursing Rolling Hill Hosp., Elkins Park, Pa., 1975; maternal child patient care coordinator Helene Fuld Med. Center, Trenton, 1976; staff nurse St. Mary Hosp., Langhorne, Pa., 1977; staff nurse St. Bernardine (Calif.) Hosp., 1978-80, head nurse, 1980-81; asst. prof. nursing Calif. State Coll., San Bernardino, 1981—; instr. Lamaze Childbirth Edn. Classes, 1971—. Mem. Nurses Assn. Am. Coll. Ob-Gyn (chpt. coordinator 1982—), Internat. Childbirth Edn. Assn., Calif. Perinatal Assn., Internat. Platform Assn. Author: (with others) Childbirth Preparation Handbook, 3d edit., 1979; newspaper columnist To Your Health. Home: PO Box 230 San Bernardino CA 92402

D'ARBANVILLE, PATTI, actress; b. N.Y.C., May 25, 1951; d. George Maurice and Jean Lynn (Giacomini) D'A.; student acting Herbert Berghof, N.Y.C.; m. Roger Mirmont, 1975. Winner beautiful baby contest Bloomingdale's, N.Y.C.; Ivory soap baby in TV commls.; profl. model Wilhemina modelling agy., N.Y.C., other agys., Brit., France, W.Ger.; appeared in films: La Maison, La Saignee, L'Amour, Rancho Deluxe, The Crazy American Girl, Big Wednesday, Bilitis, The Main Event, Hog Wild (as Angie). Office: care Belson and Klass Assos 211 S Beverly Dr Beverly Hills CA 90212

DARBY, JUNE SCOTT, public relations cons.; b. Topeka, 1917; d. Harry F. and Alberta F. (Sellers) Darby; B.J., Kans. State U., 1940; m. Jay Ellison, Dec. 30, 1944 (div.); children—Jeremy Jodi, David Scott, John Michael. Broadcaster-writer WMBH Radio, Joplin, Mo., 1940-43; writer KSD Radio, St. Louis, 1943-47; broadcaster, writer KXLW Radio, St. Louis, 1947-50; writer KWK Radio, St. Louis, 1954-57; public relations officer Merc. Trust Co., St. Louis, 1957-75; public relations officer Merc. Bancorp., Inc., St. Louis, 1975-78; owner Ellison Communications, St. Louis and San Francisco, 1978—. Mem. consumer adv. council Better Bus. Bur. Greater St. Louis, 1967-72; adv. council Downtown Activities Unltd. for Downtown St. Louis Inc., 1965-70. Named Advt. Woman of Year St. Louis, 1974-75, Advt. Woman of Year Midwest, 1975-76 (both Am. Advt. Fedn). Mem. Nat. Assn. Bank Women (regional v.p. 1974-75), Mo. Bankers Assn. (chmn. bank mktg. and public relations com. 1975-76), Advt. Women St. Louis Inc., Public Relations Soc. Am., Bank Mktg. Assn., Mo. Press Women, St. Louis Press Club, Women in Communications, Inc., Women's Polit. Caucus. Religious Scientist. Home and Office: 437A Vermont Ave San Francisco CA 94107

DARDEN, MARY DUNLAP, computer software devel. co. exec.; b. Richmond, Va., Aug. 10, 1952; d. Oscar Bruton and Ann Wingfield

(Johnson) D.; B.S. in Math. and Edn., Va. Poly. Inst. and State U., 1974; M.B.A. candidate U. Richmond, 1979—. Mktg. rep. IBM, Richmond, 1974-78; territorial saleswoman Swan, Inc., Richmond, 1978, dir. ops., 1978—; pres. Cygnet, Inc., computer software devel., Richmond, 1980—. Named to 100 Percent Club, IBM, 1976, 77. Mem. St. Mary's Hosp. Aux., Richmond Assn. Women Bus. Owners. Presbyterian. Home: 2435 Crowncrest Pl Richmond VA 23229 Office: Cygnet Inc PO Box 29768 Richmond VA 23229

DARDEN, MELLYE DENSMAN, real estate broker; b. Kilgore, Tex., Mar. 5, 1935; d. James Randolph and Evelyn (Christain) Densman; student Bish Mathis Inst., 1954, Kilgore Coll., 1978-79; m. Doyle L. Darden, Oct. 1, 1954; children—Douglas, Gina Lee, Leigh Ann, Dee Laine. With Tex. Welfare Dept., 1953-56, Braniff Airways, 1957-60, Tex. Instruments, 1962-65, Zack William Real Estate, 1967-74; broker, mgr. R.B. Williams Real Estate, Longview, Tex., 1974—. Mem. Nat. Bd. Realtors, Tex. Assn. Realtors, Longview Bd. Realtors, Longview C. of C., Realtors Nat. Mktg. Inst. Baptist. Home: 705 Honeysuckle St PO Box 459 White Oak TX 75693 Office: PO Box 3266 Longview TX 75606

DARITY, EVANGELINE ROYALL, educator, dean; b. Wilson, N.C., June 16, 1927; B.Sc. in Religious Edn., Barber-Scotia Coll., Concord, N.C., 1949; M.Ed., Smith Coll., 1969; Ed.D., U. Mass., Amherst, 1978; m. William A. Darity; children—William, Janki Evangelia. Various YWCA positions 1949-53; tchr., Egypt, N.C. and Mass., 1953-67; asst. to class deans Smith Coll., Northampton, Mass., 1968-75; v.p. student affairs Barber-Scotia Coll., 1978-79; exec. dir. YWCA, Holyoke, Mass., 1979-81; assoc. dean studies, assoc. dean third world affairs, asst. prof. psychology and edn. Mt. Holyoke Coll., South Headley, Mass., 1981—; corp. mem. Community Savs. Bank, Holyoke. Mem. Amherst Town Meeting, 1971-80. Mem. AAUW (br. pres. 1971-74), Am. Personnel and Guidance Assn., Nat. Assn. Women Deans, Counselors and Adminstrs., LWV, Alpha Kappa. Phi Delta Kappa. Home: 105 Heatherstone Rd Amherst MA 01002 Office: Mount Holyoke College South Hadley MA 01075

DARKEN, MARJORIE ALICE, editor; b. Bklyn.; d. William Henry and Gertrude (Stamper) D.; B.S. cum laude, St. Lawrence U., Canton, N.Y., 1936; M.A., U. Mich., 1937. Research technician U. Mich. Hosp., 1937-39; research asst. Inst. Living, Hartford, Conn., 1939-41, chief labs., 1941-43; research microbiologist Am. Cyanamid Co., Princeton, N.J., 1943-55, sr. tech. writer, N.Y.C., 1955-56, sr. research scientist, Pearl River, N.Y., 1956-63, pharmacology editor, then med. editor, 1963-74, cons. editor, 1974—; research investigator Stetson U., Deland, Fla., 1977—. Fellow AAAS; mem. AAUW, Phi Beta Kappa, Sigma Xi. Editorial bd. Applied Microbiology, 1961-74; editorial reviewer Reinhold Pub. Co., 1966-74; contbr. articles to profl. jours. Address: Four Seasons Apt 103D 600 N Boundary Ave Deland FL 32720

DARKIS, MILDRED LEE MORRIS (MRS. FREDERICK RANDOLPH DARKIS), civic worker; b. nr. Salisbury, Md.; d. Elisha Purnell and Martha Florence (Bailey) Morris; A.B., U. Md., 1924; m. Frederick Randolph Darkis, Oct. 6, 1928; children—Frederick Randolph, Thomas Morris, Barbara Lee (Mrs. James Frederick Blake). Tchr. English and Am. history high sch., Pittsville, Md., 1924-25, Salisbury, 1925-28. Pres. Durram Parent-Tchr. Council, 1945-47, Hope Valley Garden Club, 1962-64; bd. dirs. Durham YWCA, 1946-48, v.p., 1948; bd. dirs. Durham Child Guidance Clinic, 1945-47, Girl Scout Council, 1944-48; chmn. woman's div. Community Chest, Durham, 1946-47. Mem. D.A.R. (N.C. chmn. nat. honor roll 1961-64, chpt. regent 1968-70), Phi Kappa Phi, Alpha Omicron Pi. Republican. Methodist (tchr. adult Bible class, v.p. Durham dist. Woman's Div. Christian Service 1957-59, steward 1960, bd. stewards 1972—). Club: Hope Valley Country. Address: 3010 Surrey Rd Durham NC 27707

DARLICH, JOANN JOENSEN, nurse; b. Batavia, N.Y., June 8, 1931; d. Anker Peter and Gertrude Will Joensen; R.N. diploma Sister of Charity Sch. Nursing, Buffalo, 1952; postgrad. (USPHS grantee) U. Buffalo Grad. Sch. Nursing for Pub. Health, 1957-64; m. 2d, Herschel Darlich, June 8, 1961; children—David, Lisa, Peter, Gigi, Jay. Instr. in sch. nursing U. Buffalo, 1959-60; tchr. public health nursing Niagara County (N.Y.) Public Health Nursing Service, 1960-62; night supr. nursing Wheelchair Home, Kenmore, N.Y., 1977—; pvt. duty nurse, 1966-78; indsl. nurse TRW, 1979-80. Bd. dirs. B. Franklin Jr. High Sch. PTA, Kenmore, 1973-79, pres., 1976-79; vol. ARC, 1952-80, 82; leader Buffalo and Erie County council Girl Scouts U.S.A., 1969-75, Greater Niagara Frontier council Boy Scouts Am., 1960-77, Buffalo and Erie County Camp Fire Girls, 1961-69; active fund raising campaign Jr. Olympic Synchronized Swimming Team, Tonawanda, N.Y.; mem. synchronized swim team Huff and Puff. Cert. ofcl. synchronized swimming AAU; accredited in testing and counseling Occupational Hearing Conservation Council. Research publs. on medicine, home, parents. Home: 2195 Parker Blvd Tonawanda NY 14150

DARLING, CAROL ANDERSON, home economist, educator; b. Virginia, Minn., Apr. 13, 1946; d. Harry Arthur and Eileen Signe (Lampela) Anderson. Tchr., dept. chmn. Col. E. Brooke Lee Jr. High Sch., Silver Spring, Md., 1968-71; instr. U. Minn., Duluth, 1973-76, Utah State U., Logan, 1972-73; legis. aide Mich. Ho. of Reps., Lansing, 1977-78; asst. prof. home and family life Fla. State U., Tallahassee, 1979—; cons. Children's Lit. Project, Tallahassee, 1980-81, staff analysis Duluth Public Sch. System, 1981. Bus. and Profl. Women's Orgn. fellow, 1975; Omicron Nu fellow, 1977-78; Mich. State U. fellow, 1979; Phi Upsilon Omicron Founders' fellow, 1978-79. Mem. Am. Home Econs. Assn., Fla. Home Econs. Assn., Nat. Council Family Relations, Southeastern Council Family Relations, Fla. Council Family Relations, Nat. Assn. Edn. Young Children, Am. Assn. Sex Educators, Counselors and Therapists, Sex Info. and Edn. Council U.S., Fla. Network Family and Parent Edn., Fla. Center Children and Youth. Contbr. articles to profl. jours. Home: 2436 Lanrell Dr Tallahassee FL 32303 Office: Dept Home and Family Life Coll Home Econs Fla State U Tallahassee FL 32306

DARLING, JOAN KUGELL, film dir.; b. Boston, Apr. 14, 1935; d. Simon Harris and Helen (Kerner) Kugell; student Carnegie Mellon U., 1953-54, U. Tex., 1955-56; m. Willard H. Suanoe, Mar. 12, 1966. Actress, roles include: Viola in Twelfth Night, Stratford, Conn., 1966, The Premise, N.Y.C., 1960-64, London; dir. TV series, including Mary Hartman, Mary Hartman, 1976, Mary Tyler Moore Show (Emmy award), 1976, Phyllis, Doc, Rhoda, MASH (Emmy nomination), 1977; film dir.: 1st Love, 1977. Mem. Screen Actors Guild, AFTRA, Women in Film, Actors Equity, Dirs. Guild Am. Address: 13319 Mulholland Beverly Hills CA 90210 *

DARLING, MARTHA ANN, banker; b. Portland, Oreg., May 20, 1944; d. Richard Williams and LuAnn (Williams) D.; B.A., Reed Coll., 1966; M.A. (NDEA fellow), Boston U., 1967; M.P.A. Woodrow Wilson Sch. Pub. and Internat. Affairs, Princeton U., 1970. Cons. OECD, Paris, and European N.Am. Com., Brussels, Belgium, 1970-74; research social scientist Battelle Seattle Research Center, 1974-76; exec. dir. Gov.'s Select Panel, Wash. State Dept. Social and Health Services, Olympia, 1976-77; White House fellow exec. asst. to W. Michael Blumenthal, Sec. of Treasury, Washington, 1977-78; cons. to commr. U.S. Customs Service, Washington, 1978-79; legis. asst. fin. and budget to U.S. Sen. Bill Bradley, Washington, 1979-82; v.p. corp. strategy div. Seattle 1st Nat. Bank, 1982—; speaker NATO Symposium, Lisbon, Portugal, 1980; vis. faculty Salzburg (Austria) Seminar in Am. Studies, 1980. Bd. trustees, exec. com. Reed Coll., 1978—; adv. council Woodrow Wilson Sch. Public and Internat. Affairs, Princeton U., 1979—; nat. adv. com. Hubert H. Humphrey North-South Fellowship Program, 1979—; Bd. trustees Seattle Youth Symphony Orch., 1976—; vis. com. U. Wash. Sch. Social Work, 1982—. Mem. Reed Coll. Alumni Assn., White House Fellows Alumni Assn., Salzburg Seminar Alumni Assn., Council European Studies. Democrat. Unitarian. Author: The Role of Women in the Economy, 1975; (with others) A World of Children: Day Care and Preschool Institutions, 1979. Office: Corporate Strategy Div Seafirst Bldg 1001 4th Ave Seattle WA 98124

DARLINGTON, BETH MARY, educator; b. Berlin, Wis., Mar. 17, 1941; d. Ernest and Mildred Darlington; B.A., U. Wis., 1963; M.A., Cornell U., 1965, Ph.D., 1970; With Vassar Coll., 1967—, prof. English, dir. women's studies, 1980—. Woodrow Wilson fellow, 1963-64, Dissertation fellow, 1966-67; NEH fellow, 1979, grantee, 1981-82; Am. Council Learned Socs. fellow, 1982-83. Mem. Modern Lang. Assn., AAUP, C. G. Jung Found., Phi Beta Kappa. Office: Vassar Coll Box 323 Poughkeepsie NY 12601

DARLINGTON, SUSAN BARNET, social worker; b. Chgo., Feb. 8, 1942; d. Donald Danks and Vivian Ann (Kimpler) Barnet; B.A., Barry Coll., Miami, Fla., 1965; M.S.W., Loyola U., Chgo., 1969; m. Larry G. Darlington, Mar. 20, 1971; children—Scott William, Laurel Nell. Caseworker, Cook County Dept. Public Aid, Chgo., 1965-67; adoption social worker Catholic Charities, Chgo., 1968; med. social worker Northwestern Meml. Hosp., Chgo., 1969-71; adoption social worker Bensenville (Ill.) Home Soc., 1980-82; respite worker Community Support Services, La Grange, Ill., 1982; neo-natal social worker Loyola U. Med. Center, Maywood, Ill., 1982—; mem. Suburban Health Systems Agy., Oak Park, Ill. Children's Bur. fellow, 1967-69. Mem. Acad. Cert. Social Workers, Nat. Assn. Social Workers, AAUW. Roman Catholic. Home: 1430 Sunset Terr Western Springs IL 60558

DARNALL, ROBERTA MORROW, univ. ofcl.; b. Kemmerer, Wyo., May 18, 1949; d. C. Dale and Eugenia Stayner (Christmas) Morrow; B.S., U. Wyo., Laramie, 1972; m. Leslie A. Darnall, Sept. 3, 1977. Tariff sec., ins. adminstr. Wyo. Trucking Assn., Casper, 1973-75; asst. clerical supr. Wyo. Legislature, Cheyenne, 1972-77; congl. campaign press aide, 1974; pub. relations dir. in Casper, Wyo. Republican Central Com., 1976-77; asst. dir. alumni relations U. Wyo., 1977-81, dir. of alumni, 1981—; exec. com. Higher Edn. Assn. Rockies. Mem. Council Advancement and Support Edn., Higher Edn. Assn. Rockies, Am. Soc. Assn. Execs., Laramie C. of C., PEO, Sigma Delta Chi. Republican. Episcopalian. Home: 1172 Frontera Dr Laramie WY 82070 Office: Box 3137 Univ Station Laramie WY 82071

DARNEILLE, SARAH ANN, oil and gas co. exec.; b. Houston, May 26, 1950; d. George Joseph and Roberta Shepherd (Higgins) Darneille; B.A., U. Colo., 1972; M.B.A., U. Houston, 1980. Various mktg. positions, to 1976; adminstr. Westates-Italo Co., and Westates Petroleum Co. Liquidating Trust, 1976—, also sec.-treas.; dir. Westate Offshore Energy Ltd. Episcopalian. Home: 4237 S Judson St West University Houston TX 77005 Office: One Houston Center Suite 1504 Houston TX 77010

DARNELL, CHARLOTTE DEANE, psychologist; b. Lamar, Mo., Jan. 15, 1934; d. P.L. and Mary Ambrosia (Burt) Potter; B.A., William Jewell Coll., 1955; M.A., U. Mo., 1958; Ph.D., U. Colo., 1968; m. Donald K. Darnell, Nov. 23, 1951; children—Kelleen, Diana, Kimberly, Daniel. Tchr. elem. sch., Lansing, Mich., 1955-59; social worker, East Lansing, Mich., 1960-62; psychologist, Manhattan, Kans., 1962-65; dir. spl. edn., Manhattan, 1962-65; vis. prof. U. Iowa, 1969-70; coordinator early childhood edn., Boulder (Colo.) Valley Schs., 1971-75; researcher and program evaluator Jefferson County Schs., Lakewood, Colo., 1975—; cons. Colo. Dept. Edn., Colo. Legislature; vis. scholar Harvard U., 1974. Mem. Am. Ednl. Research Assn., Am. Psychology Assn., Nat. Assn. Young Children, Colo. Assn. Edn. Young Children, Assn. Colo. Ednl. Evaluators, Evaluation Network, Phi Delta Kappa. Democrat. Baptist. Contbr. articles to profl. jours. Home: 4497 Grinnell Ave Boulder CO 80303 Office: 1211 Quail St Lakewood CO 80215

DARROW, KATHARINE PRAGER, lawyer; b. Chgo., Dec. 26, 1943; d. Frank D. and Herta Prager; A.B., U. Chgo., 1965; J.D., Columbia U., 1969; m. Peter H. Darrow, June 29, 1968; children—Alexander, Jessica, James. Admitted to N.Y. State bar, 1970; assoc. N.Y. Times Co., N.Y.C., 1968, staff atty. 1970-71, 73-76, asst. gen. atty. 1976-80, gen. atty. 1980-81, gen. counsel, 1981—; assoc. firm Gottesman, Evans & Van Merkeanstein, 1971-73. Trustee U. Chgo. 1982—. Mem. ANPA (Press/Bar Relations Com.), ABA/ANPA (Joint Task Force), Bar Assn. City N.Y. Office: 229 W 43d St New York NY 10036

DART, CAROL ANNE, cons. co. exec., lobbyist; b. Bloomfield, Mo., July 21, 1950; d. Frank M. and Rita (Decelis) Hodge; B.A., Sangamon State U., 1982; m. William Edward Dart, June 28, 194. Asst. to program dir. EICS-TV, NBC, Springfield, Ill., 1973-75; adminstrv. asst. Air Time, Inc., Chgo., 1975-76; v.p. Dart & Assocs., Springfield, 1976-78; pres. C. Dart, Cons., 1979—; legis. and govt. affairs cons. Bd. dirs. Juvenile Diabetes Found., publicity chmn., 1980-81. Mem. Am. Soc. Assn. Execs., Chgo. Soc. Assn. Execs., Women in Mgmt. (founder, 1st pres.), Ill. Soc. Assn. Execs. (exec. dir). Roman Catholic. Office: PO Box 1964 Springfield IL 62705

DATAN, NANCY, psychologist, educator; b. Chgo., Feb. 17, 1941; d. John R. and Jeraldine I. (Kepner) Gordon; B.S. (Ill. State Regional Latin scholar) magna cum laude, Shimer Coll., 1959; M.A., U. Chgo., 1961, Ph.D. (fellow), 1971. Research asst. com. on human devel., U. Chgo., 1960-61, research asso., 1971-72; research asst. dept. psychology The Hebrew U. of Jerusalem, 1963-66; vis. lectr. Shimer Coll., Mt. Carroll, Ill., 1966-67; lectr. Am. Coll. of Jerusalem, 1967-70; research asso. Israel Inst. of Applied Social Research, 1967-70; lectr. dept. psychology De Paul U., Chgo., 1971; asst. prof. div. behavioral scis. Ben-Gurion U. of the Negev, Israel, 1972-73; asst. prof. dept. psychology W.Va. U., Morgantown, 1973-74, assoc. prof., 1976-80, prof., 1980—, acting dir. Gerontology Center, 1980-81; vis. assoc. Ctr. for Studies in Higher Edn., U. Calif., Berkeley, 1980. Fellow Am. Orthopsychiat. Assn., Gerontol. Soc. (mem. task force on humanities 1977—); mem. Am. Psychol. Assn. (mem. program com. 1977), Internat. Soc. for Study of Behavioral Devel., Internat. Assn. of Gerontology, Am. Anthrop. Assn., AAAS, Israel Sociol. Assn., Israel Assn. of U. Women, Am. Profs. for Peace in the Middle East, AAUP (v.p. W.Va. chpt. 1980-82), Sigma Xi. Contbr. numerous articles to jours. in psychology; contbr. chpts. to books in psychology; editorial bd. Jour. of Mind and Behavior, 1978—, Internat. Jour. of Aging and Human Devel., 1982—. Home: 361 Webster Ave Morgantown WV 26505 Office: Dept Psychology WVa U Morgantown WV 26506

DATTA, BHAKTI, pathologist; b. Calcutta, India, Jan. 28, 1937; came to U.S., 1965, naturalized, 1979; d. Nagendra Gopal and Hemlata (Samaddar) Biswas; student Lady Brabourne Coll., 1954-56; M.B.B.S., Calcutta U., 1961; m. Ranajit Kumar Datta, Dec. 12, 1964; 1 dau., Rakhi. Asst. surgeon B.R. Singh Hosp., Calcutta, 1962-64; intern N.Y. Infirmary, N.Y.C., 1965-66; resident, fellow in pathology Beth Israel Med. Center, N.Y.C., 1966-71; asst., asso. pathologist St. Barnabas Hosp., Bronx, N.Y., 1971-79, asst. dir. pathology, 1979—; asst. clin. prof. pathology Albert Einstein Coll. Medicine, 1980—. Trustee, East Coast Durga Puja Assn., 1978—. Diplomate Am. Bd. Pathology. Mem. Am. Soc. Clin. Pathologists, Am. Assn. Blood Banks, N.Y. Path. Soc. Collaborating editor The Clinician (India), 1971—. Home: 101 Iden Ave Pelham Manor NY 10803 Office: St Barnabas Hospital Bronx NY 10457

DATTA, GOURI, psychiatrist; b. Varanasi, India, May 15, 1949; d. Birendra Nath and Gita (Sen) Das-Gupta; B.Sc.I., Chandradhari Mithila Coll., 1965; M.B.B.S., Darbhanga Med. Coll., 1971; m. Sanjay Datta, Mar. 15, 1973; 1 dau., Nandini. Intern, Beverly (Mass.) Hosp., 1974-75; resident St. Elizabeth's Hosp., Brighton, Mass., 1976-79; practice medicine specializing in psychiatry, Georgetown and Newton, Mass., 1979—; mem. staffs St. Elizabeths Hosp., Baldpate Hosp.; clin. instr. psychiatry Tufts Med. Sch., Boston. Diplomate Am. Bd. Psychiatry and Neurology. Mem. AMA, Am. Psychiat. Assn., Mass. Med. Soc., Mass. Psychiat. Soc. Hindu. Author book of poems (in Bengali). Office: Baldpate Hosp Georgetown MA 01833

DATZ, RUTH ELIZABETH, educator, musician; b. Greensburg, Pa., June 10, 1936; d. Robert Albert and Ruth Elizabeth (Bates) Datz; B.A., Indiana (Pa.) U., 1958; M.A., N.Y. U., 1961; postgrad Pa. State U., 1962-63, U. Colo., 1971, SUNY, Potsdam, 1978. Tchr. music public schs., Middletown Twp., N.J., 1958-61, Tyrone, Pa., 1961-65, Ann Arbor, Mich., 1965—; counselor, recreation dir., dir. jr. girls div. Interlochen (Mich.) Nat. Music Camp, 1956-69; head womens counselor New Eng. Music Camp, Maine, 1970, 72; flutist, pit orchestras, N.Y.C., 1959-61; conductor spl. chorus. Mem. Republican. Com., Tyrone, 1962-65. Mem. Music Educators Nat. Conf., Mich. Music Educators Assn., Mich. Sch. Vocal Assn., Am. Choral Dirs. Assn., Nat. Assn. Humanities Edn., Delta Zeta. Mem. United Ch. of Christ. Clubs: Ann Arbor Dog Tng., Eastern Star, Job's Daughters. Home: 1564 Barrington Pl Ann Arbor MI 48103 Office: 2727 Fuller Rd Ann Arbor MI 48105

DAUBENAS, JEAN DOROTHY TENBRINCK, librarian; b. N.Y.C., Apr. 4, 1940; d. Eduard J.A. and Margaret Dorothy (Schaffner) Tenbrinck; A.B., Barnard Coll., 1962; grad. Am. Acad. Dramatic Arts, 1963; M.A., N.Y. U., 1965; M.L.S., U. Ariz., 1972; postgrad U. Utah, 1975—; m. Joseph Anthony Daubenas, May 29, 1965. Tchr., Beth Jacob Tchrs. Sem. Am., Bronx, 1965-66; caseworker, Dept. Social Services, N.Y.C., 1966-67; actress Boothbay (Maine) Playhouse, others, 1967-70; reference librarian Ariz. State U., Tempe, 1972-75; asst. librarian, asst. prof. library sci. Avila Coll., Kansas City, Mo., 1979—. N.Y. State Regents scholar, 1958-62; U. Ariz. scholar, 1971-72. Mem. ALA, Actors Equity Assn., Beta Phi Mu, Phi Kappa Phi. Roman Catholic. Home: 11525 Baltimore Ave Kansas City MO 64114 Office: 11901 Wornall Rd Kansas City MO 64145

DAUBENDIEK, BERTHA ANTONIE, assn. exec.; b. Poplar, Mont., Jan. 31, 1916; d. Carl Henry and Bertha (Krejci) D.; B.A., Grinnell (Iowa) Coll., 1936. Court reporter Detroit, Mt. Clemens, Saginaw, Mich., 1937-71; founder, exec. sec. Mich. Nature Assn., Mt. Clemens, 1951-71, part time, 1971—, full time. Recipient 1 of Top Ten Vols., Mich. Week State award, 1974; named Michiganian of Year, Detroit News, 1979. Methodist. Pioneer in establishing 75 new nature preserves in Mich., 1960-82. Address: 7981 Beard Rd Avoca MI 48006

DAUBENMIRE, MARTHA LAVERN, civic worker; b. Lebanon, Ohio, Dec. 5, 1940; d. Leonard Mounts and Bernice LaVern (Pursley) McKinney; student Miami (Ohio) U., 1968-72, Akron U., 1974; m. David Stanford Daubenmire, Feb. 20, 1957; children—David Wayne, Joseph Daniel, Julia Ann. Sch. tchr. Clinton-Massie Schs., Cadette cert., 1970-72; substitute tchr, Rittman (Ohio) Sch. System, 1973-79; co-owner wholesale distbn. co. Sec.-treas. Rittman (Ohio) United Way, 1977—; treas. Muskingum Valley Presbyterial. Mem. Rittman C. of C. (exec. sec. 1977-79), C. of C. Execs. Ohio, Gen. Fedn. Women's Clubs. Republican. Presbyterian. Club: Olla Podrida Federated Women's (program chmn., chmn. ways and means com., past sec.). Home: 124 Woodland Ave Rittman OH 44270

DAUGHERTY, ALMA JOAN, elec. equipment mfg. co. ofcl., accountant; b. Louisville, Sept. 17, 1931; d. Stanley G. and Alma S. (Mosier) D.; B.S.C., U. Louisville, 1967, M.B.A., 1970; cert. Bellarmine Coll., 1972. Page, substitute librarian Louisville Free Public Library, part-time 1946-49; legal sec. Bullitt, Dawson & Tarrant, Louisville, 1951-53; sec. acctg. Gen. Electric Co., Appliance Park, Louisville, 1953-56, acctg. clk., 1956-67, specialist acctg., 1967-72, supr. gen. accounts, 1972-81, specialist budgets and estimates, 1981—. Clk., City of Forest Hills, Ky., 1975-78, city trustee, 1978-80, mayor (chmn. bd. trustees), 1980—; vol. worker Republican party, 1954—, precinct clk. for gen. elections, 1956—. Mem. Am. Bus. Women's Assn. (nat. pres. 1977-78), Nat. Assn. Accts. (dir. publicity 1980-81, dir. personnel devel. 1981-82), Phi Kappa Phi, Zeta Tau Alpha. Clubs: Filson, U. Louisville Alumnae (exec. com. 1980-81, Merit award 1970, Disting. Alumnus award 1979), Jeffersontown Alumnae (pres. 1979-82), Order Eastern Star. Home: 2112 Canterbrook Dr Jeffersontown KY 40299 Office: Gen Electric Co Appliance Park 4-218 Louisville KY 40225

DAUGHERTY, JUDITH KATHERINE, patient services adminstr., educator; b. Philipsburg, Pa., May 16, 1940; d. David T. and Mary K. Minto; diploma Persbyterian Hosp. Sch. Nursing, 1961; B.S. cum laude in Nursing Duquesne U., 1971; M.P.A., U. Pitts., 1973, Ph.D., 1982; children—Dawn Karen, William David. Staff, head nurse Magee Woman's Hosp., Pitts., 1961-63; staff nurse U.S. Steel Corp., Pitts., 1965-67; supr., v.p. nursing service and edn. Monsour Med. Center, Jeannette, Pa., 1967-73; adminstrv. asst. for patient services Mercy Hosp. of Johnstown, Pa., 1975-80, asso. adminstr., 1980—; mem. grad. faculty nursing edn./adminstrn. U. Pitts., 1982—. Mid-Career for Women Carnegie fellow, 1974. Lic. nursing home adminstr. Mem. Nat. League for Nursing, Am. Hosp. Assn., Am. Soc. Nursing Service Adminstrs., Hosp. Council of Western Pa., Forum for Hosp. Nurse Adminstrs., Am. Heart Assn. (past chmn. bd. dirs. Pa. affiliate), Profl. Nurses at Mercy, Sigma Theta Tau. Club: Am. Legion Aux. Home: RD 1 Box 14AA Ligonier PA 15658 Office: 1020 Franklin St Johnstown PA 15905

DAUGHTREY, MARTHA CRAIG, judge; b. Covington, Ky., July 21, 1942; d. Jacob Wykoff and Martha (Craig) Piatt; B.A. cum laude, Vanderbilt U., 1964, J.D., 1968; m. Larry G. Daughtrey, 1963; 1 dau., Sarah Carran. Admitted to Tenn. bar, 1968; practiced in Nashville, 1968; asst. U.S. atty., Nashville, 1968-69; asst. dist. atty., Nashville, 1969-72; asst. prof. law Vanderbilt U., 1972-75, lectr. law, 1976—; judge Tenn. Ct. Criminal Appeals, Nashville, 1975—; mem. faculty Appellate Judges Seminar, N.Y.U., 1977—. Chmn. chancellor's commn. on status of women Vanderbilt U., 1975; v.p. Council on Alcohol and Drug Abuse, 1972; chmn. Nashville Women's Polit. Caucus, 1975; bd. dirs. Planned Parenthood Assn. Nashville, 1978-80; mem. adv. bd. Cable, 1978-80; bd. visitors Sch. Law, Memphis State U., 1978—. Mem. Am. Bar Assn. (exec. com. appellate judges conf. 1979—, sec., 1978-80), Nat. Assn. Women Judges (dir. 1979—), Tenn. Jud. Conf. (exec. com. 1977-80), Inst. Jud. Adminstrn., Tenn. Bar Assn., Nashville Bar Assn., Order of Coif, Phi Beta Kappa. Mem. bd. of editors Judges Jour., 1979-81, sec., 1981-82; contbr. articles to law jours. Office: Tenn Ct Criminal Appeals Supreme Ct Bldg Nashville TN 37219

DAVENPORT, BARBARA LYNN, home economist; b. Navasota, Tex., Apr. 1, 1947; d. Jearl and Dorothy Louise (Pool) Gresak; B.S. in Home Econs., Southwest Tex. State U., 1969; m. Duane Thomas Davenport, Sept. 26, 1970; 1 dau., Ashley Elizabeth. Home economist La-Co, Inc., Houston, 1969-70, N.C. Extension Service, Charlotte,

1971-72, Gold Kist Research Center, Atlanta, 1970-71, 1973—. Chmn., Ga.'s. Teenage Nutrition Program, 1976-77; mem. adv. com. Ga. Nutrition Edn. Program, 1978-80. Recipient Acad. Excellence award S.W. Tex. State U., 1968. Mem. Am. Home Econs. Assn., Ga. Home Econs. Assn., Ga. Home Economists in Bus. (chmn. 1979-80), Ga. Nutrition Council, Ga. Teenage Nutrition Program, Elec. Womens Round Table. Baptist. Home: 1110 Feagin Dr NE Atlanta GA 30319 Office: 2230 Industrial Blvd Lithonia GA 30058

DAVENPORT, DEBORAH ANNE, retail co. exec.; b. Port Jefferson, N.Y., July 2, 1948; d. Francis M., Jr., and Nell Sperry (Brown) D.; A.B., Ind. U., 1970; M.B.A., Cleve. State U., 1981. Mktg. services mgr. Premier Indsl. Corp., Cleve., 1974-75, prodn. mgr., 1975-76, distbn. sales ops. mgr., 1976-78; dir. planning services Mr. Wiggs Dept. Stores, Inc. (SDC Inc.), Beachwood, Ohio, 1978-79, asst. v.p. planning and info. services, 1979-82, v.p., 1982—; guest lectr. Cleve. State U. Mem. N.Am. Soc. Corp. Planning (officer Cleve.), Assn. M.B.A. Execs., Beta Gamma Sigma. Club: City (Cleve.). Software designer. Office: 23700 Commerce Park Rd Beachwood OH 44122

DAVENPORT, JOANNA, educator; b. Salem, Mass., Jan. 17, 1933; d. Carleton and Virginia (Price) D.; B.S., Skidmore Coll., 1954; M.S., Smith Coll., 1958; Ph.D., Ohio State U., 1966. Instr., Mt. Holyoke Coll., South Hadley, Mass., 1954-56; tchr. public schs., Colo. and Maine, 1956-59; instr. U. Vt., Burlington, 1959-62, Colo. State U., Ft. Collins, 1962-63, Ohio State U., Columbus, 1963-65; asst. prof., chmn. dept. U. Vt., Burlington, 1965-67; asso. prof. U. Ill., Urbana, 1967-76; asso. prof., women's athletic dir. Auburn (Ala.) U., 1976—; vis. prof., cons. phys. edn. and athletics U.S. Mil. Acad., West Point, N.Y., 1968-79; coordinator U.S. delegation to Internat. Olympic Acad., 1981; mem. Edn. Council of U.S. Olympic Com., 1977—. Sec. Class of 1954 Skidmore Coll. Recipient 2d prize internat. writing contest Internat. Olympic Com., 1981. Mem. Nat. Assn. Girls and Women in Sport (pres. 1976-77), N.Am. Soc. Sport History, Nat. Assn. Sport and Phys. Edn. (pres. history acad. 1982-83), Nat. Assn. Phys. Edn. in Higher Edn. (necrologist), So. Assn. Phys. Edn. of Coll. Women, AAHPERD. Contbr. chpts. in books, articles in encys. Home: 308 Shelton Rd Auburn AL 36830 Office: Memorial Coliseum Auburn University Auburn University AL 36849

DAVEY, GLORIA DELORIS, polit. campaign exec.; b. Batesville, Ark., Feb. 14, 1950; d. Ermal H. and Lura A. (Martin) Bowman; student State Coll. Ark., 1969-70; A.A., Ark. Polytechnic Coll., 1972; B.A., U. Tex., 1979; m. Thomas Paul Davey, Apr. 20, 1974. Bookkeeper, sales and catering mgr. Ramada Inn, North Little Rock, Ark., 1972-74; teller Worthen Bank & Trust, Little Rock, 1974-75; credit clk. Tex. Industries, Arlington, 1975-77; teller Mansfield (Tex.) State Bank, 1977-81; orgnl. dir. Congl. campaign, 1981—; instr. voice, Mansfield. Mem. Mansfield Planning and Zoning Commn.; pres. Mansfield Library Bd. Mansfield C. of C. (dir.), Mansfield Ladies Chamber (officer). Methodist. Club: Walnut Creek Country. Editor Insider Transaction, 1979-81. Home: 1011 Westminister Ln Mansfield TX 76063 Office: 1011 Westminster Mansfield TX 76063

DAVID, JULY BREINER, advt. writer and producer; b. Milw., May 26, 1938; d. James Mirko and Fannie (Apple) Breiner; student Washington U., St. Louis, 1956-58; m. Sept. 4, 1960 (div.); children—Rod Alan, Donna Lyn. Dir./producer amateur theatricals Empire Producing Co., Kansas City, Mo., 1959; supr. pub. relations, tours, promotions, program guides Sta. KETC-TV, St. Louis, 1959-62, also producer/host interview show; pub. relations writer, St. Louis, 1966-69; copywriter George Johnson Advt., Inc., St. Louis, 1968, Ridgeway Advt., St. Louis, 1969; copywriter/producer Gardner/Wells, Rich, Greene, Inc., St. Louis, 1970-74; sr. writer McCann-Erickson, Inc., Atlanta, 1974-77; freelance writer/producer/promotions cons., doing bus. as A Functional Literate, Atlanta, 1977—; judge CLIO Awards, 1982, Addy Awards, 1980, 81; panelist, lectr. Ga. State U., 1979, 80. Vol., Atlanta Soc. for Blind, 1975, 76, Ga. Press Assn. Gridiron, 1978, 79, 80, Jewish Vocat. Services, 1982, others. Named ADWEEK Writer of Yr., 1982; recipient Addy awards, 1974, 75, 77, 80, 81, Phoenix award, 1974, 75, 76, 78, 81, 82, Andy awards, 1976, 78, 80, 81, CLIO, 1981, numerous other industry awards. Mem. Atlanta Soc. Communication Artists (dir. 1974-75), Women Bus. Owners. Cartoonist; radio and stage performer; comedy writer; product designer. Author: Moonlighter's Guide to Success, 1978. Address: 2324 Bry-Mar Dr Atlanta GA 30345

DAVID, LENORA MILDRED, educator; b. Scio, Ohio, Mar. 3, 1923; d. John James and Inez Margaret (Pfouts) Scott; B.S., Ohio State U., 1944; postgrad. Brigham Young U., 1962, Mo. So. Coll., 1968-70, Sch. of Ozarks, 1970, Ohio U., 1976; m. Clayton Cunningham David, Feb. 11, 1945; children—Lynn Allen, James Scott. News reporter Sta. WGRV, Greenville, Tenn., 1948; home economist C.W. Justis Co., Greeneville, 1956-58; tchr. Public Schs. Greeneville, 1958-61, Wasatch Jr. High Sch., Salt Lake City, 1961-63; chmn. spl. edn. Neosho (Mo.) Jr. High Sch., 1966-74; mgr. YOUCAN Co., St. Clairsville, Ohio, 1975—; coordinator wider opportunities for women W.Va. No. Community Coll., 1978-80. Leader, Girl Scouts, 1950-53; bd. dirs. Newton County OEO, 1967-72; officer PTA, Tenn., Utah, Mo. Mem. Assn. Children with Learning Disabilities, Ohio State U. Alumni Assn., Ohio State Edlums, AAUW (chpt. treas., v.p. 1969-73), Delta Kappa Gamma. Republican. Presbyterian. Clubs: Belmont Hills Country, Res. Officers Wives, Women's of Wheeling. Address: 215 Dennis Ln Saint Clairsville OH 43950

DAVID, MARSHA LYNN GUNDY, sch. guidance counselor; b. Bronx, N.Y., Mar. 10, 1949; d. Nathan and Trussie Louise (Anderson) Gundy; B.A. in Edn., Howard U., 1971; M.A., Tchr.s Coll., Columbia U., 1974, M.Ed. in Pupil Personnel Services, 1974; m. Abel David, Aug. 25, 1973. Tchr. first grade, public schs., Teaneck, N.J., 1971-74, guidance counselor Emergency Sch. Aid Act Group, jr. high sch., 1974-76, sch. guidance counselor Thomas Jefferson Jr. High Sch., 1976—; tchr. Summer Head Start Program, Teaneck, 1975-77; mem. adjustment com. Youth Guidance Council, 1976—. Sec. bd. dirs. Teaneck Group Care Home, 1978—. Recipient award Fair Housing Council Bergen County (N.J.), 1981. Mem. N.J. Edn. Assn., NEA, Bergen County Edn. Assn., Nat. Assn. Female Execs., Teaneck Tchrs. Assn. Presbyterian. Home: 82 Lexington Ave Dumont NJ 07628 Office: 655 Teaneck Rd Teaneck NJ 07666

DAVID, VIRGINIA LEA, mktg. exec.; b. Mitchell, Ind., Mar. 13, 1931; d. Noble and Jeanette Rose (Gordon) Smith; student Ind. U., 1949-51; B.A., Butler U., 1954; m. Lewis M. Grabhorn, Jr., Nov. 23, 1951; children—Karen Lea, Lewis M. Fashion coordinator, model William Block Co., Indpls., 1960-65; cons., tng. dir. Revlon Inc., N.Y.C., 1960-65; West Coast account exec. Swank Inc., N.Y.C., 1970-72; founder, owner, pres. Calif. Girls Co., Los Angeles, 1973—; founder, owner Virginia David & Assos., Los Angeles, 1974—; owner Models Registry, Promotional People. Named Mrs. Ind. as rep. to Mrs. Am. Contest, 1954; presented Key to City of Indpls., 1954. Mem. Santa Monica C. of C., Nat. Fedn. Ind. Bus., Western States Delicatessen (bd. dirs. 1977-79), Food Industries Circle, The Illuminators, Frozen Food Council So. Calif., Los Angeles Mktg. and Merchandising Assn. Republican. Club: Los Angeles Bus. Women's. Office: 1855 Lincoln Blvd Santa Monica CA 90404

DAVID-NELSON, MARGIT ANTONIA, pathologist; b. Szeged, Hungary, Apr. 9, 1931; d. Lajos Antal and Szaniszla Korodi (Biro) David; came to U.S., 1966, naturalized, 1970; M.D., Med. U. Szeged, 1955; m. Neal Stanley Nelson, July 7, 1966; children—Arlane, Tamar. Research asst. pathology Med. U. Szeged, 1953-57, resident in internal medicine, 1957-60, asst. prof. internal medicine, 1960-66; vis. scientist Royal Free Hosp., London, 1964; research fellow pharmacology U. Milan (Italy), 1964-65; postgrad. fellow physiology U. Cin. Med. Sch., 1967-69; resident in pathology Alexandria (Va.) Hosp., 1970-74, asst. pathologist, 1974—, invited scholar 2d Internat. Congress Endorinology, 1964; invited scholar 2d Internat. Congress Steroid Congress, 1966. Bd. dirs. Alexandria unit Am. Cancer Soc., 1977—. Diplomate Am. Bd. Clin. and Antomic Pathology. Fellow Am. Soc. Clin. Pathologists, Coll. Am. Pathologists; mem. AMA, Tissue Culture Assn., Med. Soc. Va., Alexandria Med. Soc. Roman Catholic. Home: 8102 Ashtonbirch Dr Springfield VA 22152 Office: Alexandria Hosp Alexandria VA 22304

DAVIDSON, GENEVA UPCHURCH, assn. dir.; b. San Antonio, Dec. 7, 1931; d. Littleton Hershal and Delia (Adams) Upchurch; student S.W. Tex. State U., 1949-51; m. James Madison Davidson, III, Aug. 28, 1949; children—Robert John, William Allan, James Brian. Program dir. Ret. Sr. Vol. Program, Kennewick, Wash., 1973-79; exec. dir. Voluntary Action Center, Kennewick, 1979—; cons. State Office Voluntary Action, Wash.; mem. region 2 adv. com. Wash. Dept. Social and Health Services. Bd. dirs. Kennewick Sch. Dist. 17, 1971-73; pres. bd. dirs. Benton-Franklin United Way, 1973; trustee Columbia Basin Community Coll., 1979. Recipient Golden Acorn award PTA, 1973. Mem. Nat. Center Citizen Involvement (vol.), Western Gerontol. Soc. Baptist. PEO. Home: 1101 S Irby Kennewick WA 99336 Office: Voluntary Action Center 205 N Dennis Kennewick WA 99336

DAVIDSON, GRACE EVELYN, nursing service cons.; b. Wabash, Ind., Aug. 2, 1920; d. William Alexander and Jennie Lavinia (Baker) D.; diploma Columbia Presbyn. Sch. Nursing, 1942; B.S., U. Minn., 1948; M.A., Tchrs. Coll. Columbia U., 1954, postgrad. 1963-64. Instr., Sch. Nursing, Columbia U., N.Y.C., 1948-51; asso. prof. Skidmore Coll., Saratoga Springs, N.Y., 1954-66; asst. adminstr., dir. nursing Univ. Hosp. N.Y. U. Med. Center, 1966-79, asso. prof. part time, 1977-79, prof. 1979—; cons. nursing service adminstrn., N.Y.C., 1980—. Served with Army Nurse Corps, 1943-46, 51-53. Recipient Alumni Fedn. medal Columbia U., 1981. Mem. Nursing Edn. Alumnae Assn. Tchrs. Coll. Columbia U. (achievement award 1977), NOW, Nat. Assn. Female Execs., Inc., Am. Nurses Assn., Nat. League Nursing, Columbia U.-Presbyn. Hosp. Sch. Nursing Alumnae Assn. (pres. 1970-76, Disting. Alumnae award 1981), Am. Hosp. Assn., Soc. Nursing Services Adminstrs., Am. Hosp. Assn. Republican. Presbyterian. Contbr. articles to profl. jours. Home: 1608 Pea Pond Rd Bellmore NY 11710

DAVIDSON, JESSICA URSULA, music educator; b. Rome, N.Y., Jan. 10, 1914; d. Jay Sidney and Lucy Adelaide (Clarke) Brown; student Potsdam State Coll., 1931-34; B.Mus. in Music Edn., U. Del., 1972, M.Ed. in Music Edn., West Chester State Coll., 1973; Ph.D. in Secondary Edn., U. Md., 1978; m. Alexander Clyde Davidson, June 8, 1936; children—Shirley Anne, Nancy Jeannette. Tchr. music Adams Center High Sch., 1934-36, 42-43; dir. music Ave. Methodist Ch., Del. 1946-75; dir. Student Nurses Choir, Del., 1965-75; tchr. piano, organ Kimball Music Co., 1967-69; tchr. music Milford Spl. Dist., Del., 1969-70; tchr. music New Castle County (Del.) Sch. Dist., 1970-77, 78-79; tchr. music edn. U. Md., 1977-78; dir. music edn. and area music program for Council on Aging Inter-Disciplinary Center for Research in Gerontology, U. Ky., 1979—. Class rep. U. Del., 1977—. Mem. Music Educators Nat. Conf., Ky. State Music Edn. Assn., Nat. Ret. Tchrs. Assn., Am. Assn. Ret. Persons, Delta Kappa Gamma (chmn. music com. Newcastle, Del 1975-77, mem. program com. Lexington 1980). Republican. Methodist. Clubs: Order Eastern Star (matron 1942), Univ. Composer: Christmas Cantata: The Birth of Christ According to Saint Luke, 1970, The Night the Christ Child Came to Earth, 1965, The Greatest of These Is Love, 1973 Mothers of the World, 1965, Christmas in Kentucky, 1980. Home: 1043 Cross Keys Rd Lexington KY 40504 Office: Ligon House University of Kentucky Lexington KY 40506

DAVIDSON, JO ANN, state legislator, assn. ofcl.; b. Ft. Wayne, Ind., Sept. 28, 1927; d. Ralph and Bernice (Kraus) Benington; student Nat. Inst. Comml. and Trade Orgn. Execs., 1945-50; children—Julie Lynn, Jenifer Lee. Asst. sec. Findlay (Ohio) C. of C., 1945-53; research asst. Ohio C. of C., Columbus, 1974-75, fin. specialist, 1977-78, dir. legis. services, 1978-79, dir. legis. affairs, 1980-81, dir. spl. programs, 1981—; mem. Ohio Ho. of Reps. from 27th Dist., 1981—. Mem. lifelong learning adv. com. Ohio Bd. Regents, 1979-80; mem. Ohio Turnpike Commn., 1978-80, Franklin County Mental Health and Mental Retardation Bd., 1979-81, Reynoldsburg City Council, 1968-77; chmn. Franklin County Republican Central Com., 1979-80, chmn. for Franklin County, 1973-80; trustee Ohio Mcpl. League; mem. Columbus Sewer and Water Rate Bd., 1975-78; exec. dir. Pres. Ford Com. in Ohio, 1976; del. Rep. Nat Conv., 1976, mem. platform com. from Ohio, 1976. Mem. Nat. Women's Polit. Caucus, Ohio Assn. Trade Orgn. Execs. Lutheran. Home: 6870 E Livingston Ave Apt B Reynoldsburg OH 43068 Office: 17 S High St Columbus OH 43215

DAVIDSON, JOYCE, TV personality; b. Saskatoon, Sask., Can., Apr. 14, 1931; came to U.S., 1962; d. Eric Arthur and Myrtle Irene (Johnson) Brock; m. Douglas P. Davidson, 1948 (div. 1959); children—Shelley Irene, Constance Barbara; m. 2d David Susskind, Apr. 22, 1966; 1 dau., Samantha Maria. Co-host Tabloid, CBC, 1956-61; appeared on Close-Up, CBC, 1958-61, Today Show, 1959-60, Jack Benny Show, 1959-60, PM East, 1962-63, Joyce Davidson Show, Can., 1974—, Authors, CBC, 1978-80, The World of Mother Teresa spl., 1981; pres. Joyce Davidson Prodns., 1980—. Mem. AFTRA, Assn. Can. TV and Radio Artists. Office: care Assn Can TV and Radio Artists 105 Carlton St Toronto ON M5B 1M2 Canada

DAVIDSON, JOYCE LOUISE, fuel co. exec.; b. Detroit, Apr. 1, 1950; d. Stuart E. and Louise Davidson; B.S. in Psychology, Eastern Mich. U., 1972. Geol. technician, then land-file technician Am. Natural Resources Co., Detroit, 1973-77; project controls adminstr. subs. ANG Coal Gasification Co., Detroit, 1977-82, systems engr., 1982—; speaker in field. Mem. Grosse Pointe (Mich.) Community Choir, 1979-81. Mem. Am. Assn. Cost Engrs. Roman Catholic. Club: Gasco Tennis (v.p. 1977). Author project mgmt. plans. Office: 600 Renaissance Tower 600 Floor 10 Detroit MI 48226

DAVIDSON, LEAH, psychiatrist; b. Chelm, Poland, June 1, 1926; d. Israel and Frajda (Englender) Zygielbaum; came to U.S., 1963, naturalized, 1969; B.S., U. Witwatersrand, Johannesburg, S. Africa, 1946, M.D., 1951; m. Esmond Davidson, June 25, 1947 (div. 1972); children—Fay Joyce Davidson Leighton, Martin Leslie, Allan Roy. Intern, Empangeni Hosp., Zululand, S. Africa, 1951-53, Simonstown Hosp., Cape Town; resident in psychiatry Bronx VA Hosp., N.Y.C., 1965-68, Psychiat. Inst. N.Y., 1967-68; physician Nursery Sch., Muizenberg Cape, S. Africa, 1954-57, med. students clinic U. Cape Town, 1954-57; practice medicine specializing in psychiatry and psychoanalysis, N.Y.C., 1969—; liaison cons. spinal cord injury service, cons. dept. psychiatry Bronx VA Hosp., 1969-82; supervising and tng. analyst Psychoanalytic Inst. Nassau County Med. Center, 1977; supr. psychotherapy and faculty William Alanson White Inst. Fellow Am. Acad. Psychoanalysis; mem. Am. Psychiat. Assn., AMA. Contbr. articles to profl. jours. Home: 602 W 231st St New York NY 10463 Office: 125 E 87th St 9D New York NY 10028

DAVIDSON, RITA CHARMATZ, judge; b. Bklyn., Sept. 1, 1928; d. Michael and Eiga (Rokeach) Charmatz; B.A. with honors, Goucher Coll., 1948, LL.D. (hon.), 1979; LL.B., Yale U., 1951; m. David Sternheimer Davidson, Aug. 27, 1951; children—Minna Kohn, Leo Charmatz. Admitted to D.C. bar, 1952, Md. bar, 1963; individual practice law, Washington and Montgomery County, Md., 1951-67; vice chairperson, chairperson Montgomery County Bd. Appeals, 1960-64; commr. Md. Nat. Park and Planning Commn., 1967; zoning hearing examiner Montgomery County, 1967-70; sec. Md. Dept. Human Resources, 1970-72; asso. judge Ct. Spl. Appeals Md., 1972-79, Ct. Appeals Md., Annapolis, 1979—; chairperson Gov.'s Commn. on Jobs for Vets., and Gov.'s Interagy. Com. on Childhood Devel., 1970-72. Recipient Woman of Yr. award Balt. Bus. and Profl. Women, 1971; Disting. Citizen's award State of Md., 1973; Leadership award Silver Spring C. of C., 1973; others. Mem. Am. Bar Assn., Md. Bar Assn., Montgomery County Bar Assn., D.C. Bar Assn., Women's Bar Assn., Nat. Assn. Women Lawyers, Am. Judicature Soc., Md. Jud. Conf., Com. on Juvenile and Family Law. Address: Jud Center 50 Court House Sq Rockville MD 20850 *

DAVIDSON, ROSALIE CAROL, author; b. Paoli, Ind., July 25, 1921; d. Roger Carl and Annabel (McIntosh) D.; student U. Louisville, 1939-41; B.A., U. Denver, 1948, M.A., 1950; postgrad. U. Calif. at San Diego, 1950-60. Mem. staff quality lab. Seagrams Distillery, Louisville, 1941-43; tchr. Denver Pub. Schs., 1948-50; tchr., sci. curriculum adv. San Diego Unified Schs., 1950—; owner Used Books By Mail, San Diego; author: Dinosaurs, The Terrible Lizards, 1969; When the Dinosaurs Disappeared, 1973; Animals of the Tidepools, 1982; also articles. Served with USNR, 1943-46. Mem. Nat. Sci. Tchrs. Assn., Soc. Children's Book Writers, San Diego, Calif. tchrs. assns., NEA, Calif. Assn. Tchrs. of Gifted, Com. of 100, Mus. Natural History, Space Mus., Zool. Soc., Sea World. Presbyterian. Home: 6315 Connie Dr San Diego CA 92115 Office: John Forward Sch 6460 Boulder Lake Ave San Diego CA 92119

DAVIDSON, SHARON MARIE, educator; b. Bronx, N.Y., May 6, 1955; d. Robert Eugene and Lillie Jane Rowe Davidson; B.S. in Early Childhood Edn., D.C. Tchrs. Coll., 1977; M.A., Trinity Coll., Washington, 1978. Dir. Parent-Child Center, D.C. Public Schs., 1978-80; tng. coordinator parenting and employability skills for teenage parents D.C. Dept. Labor, also Assn. for Renewal in Edn., 1979; cons. St. Ann's Infant and Maternity Home, Hyattsville, Md., 1980; tng. coordinator, early childhood devel. specialist Parent Focus, Assos. Renewal in Edn., 1980; coordinating instr. Trinity Coll., 1980-81; dir. The Children's Center, early childhood devel. specialist Arlington (Va.) Hosp., 1981-82; mem. D.C. Task Force Adolescent Sexuality and Parenting, 1978—; mem. D.C. Mayor's Task Force Internat. Yr. of Child, 1978—; bd. dirs. Blacks in Urban Am. Recipient certs. and plaques of recognition. Mem. Assn. Childhood Edn. Internat., Coalition Children and Youth, Day Care and Child Devel. Council Am., Nat. Assn. Edn. Young Children, Nat. Black Child Devel. Inst., Council Exceptional Children, Com. Internat. Profl. Women, Nat. Center Clin. Infant Programs, AAUW Kappa Delta Pi, Phi Delta Kappa. Democrat. Roman Catholic.

DAVIES, MIRIAM HELEN, Christian Science nurse; b. Colwyn Bay, Wales, July 17, 1922; came to U.S., 1972, naturalized, 1980; d. David Francis and Miriam Alice (Higginbottom) D.; S.R.N., Royal Infirmary Manchester, 1943; C.S. Nurse, Chestnut Hill, Mass., 1968; diploma in Mgmt. Katharine Gibbs Sch., Boston, 1977; first class diploma Good Housekeeping Sch. Cookery, 1950. Regular commn. Queen Alexandria Imperial Mil. Nursing Service, 1945-49, served India, 1945-47, in charge operating theatres, Aldershot, Eng., 1947-49; served with Brit. Red Cross Soc., 1949-54; owner hotel, 1954-66; C.S. nurse, U.K., 1968-72, with hdqrs., Boston, 1972-77; with Tenacre Found., Princeton, N.J., 1977-79, dep. dir. nursing, Riverdale, N.Y., 1979—. Recipient Gold Thanks badge Boy Scouts Gt. Britain, 1949. Life mem. Brit. Red Cross Soc. Republican. Club: V.A.D. (London). Co-author tng. program for C.S. nurses, 1972. Home and office: 805 Belle Park Dr Champaign IL 61820

DAVIES-RODGERS, ELLEN (MRS. HILLMAN P. RODGERS), club woman, planter, author; b. Brunswick, Tenn., Nov. 13, 1903; d. Gillie M. and Frances Ina (Stewart) Davies; B.S., George Peabody Coll., 1924; M.A., Columbia U., 1927; m. Hillman P. Rodgers, Dec. 21, 1932; foster-children—Sarah B. Gandy, adv. council CD; Mary Gandy Hardee. Critic tchr. campus sch., Memphis State U., 1924-26, also prof. early childhood edn.; prof. elem. edn., Evansville (Ind.) Coll., summer 1926; prin. Arlington High Sch., 1928-29, Lausanne Sch. Girls, 1953; state elem. supr. West Tenn. 1938-40; mem. Shelby County Bd. Edn., 1961-65; dir. Tenn. Sch. Bds. Assn., 1963-65; 1st Shelby County (Tenn.) historian, 1965—; founder-owner Plantation Press, Memphis, 1964. Organized Pleasant Hill Cemetery Assn., 1937, pres. 1937—; founder Davies Meml. Library for Children (name now Davieshire Library), 1937, chmn. bd. 1973—; clk. St. Philip Episcopal Mission, 1977; 1st pres. Davies Manor Assn., 1976; del. Dem. Nat. Conv., 1956; del. Tenn. Constl. Conv., 1953, 59; hon. del. Tenn. State Constl. Conv., 1977; state exec. vice chmn. Woman's adv. council, CD; organized Zachariah Davies chpt. DAR (organizing regent 1945-46, chpt. regent, 1946-48; state regent, 1956-59, hon. regent 1959, nat. vice chmn. Am. history month 1964-67). Named Woman of Yr., Memphis Kiwanis Club, 1965; one of 10 women cited by Memphis Comml. Appeal, 1969; hon. Shelby County Squire, 1976; hon. Memphis City Councilman, 1979. Mem. Tenn. Assn. Childhood Edn. (past pres.), Memphis and Shelby County Council Garden Clubs (past pres.), Memphis State U. Alumni Assn. (past pres.), Alumni Assn. Memphis St. U. (life; Disting. Alumnus award 1977), Daus. Am. Colonists, Children Am. Revolution (state and nat. promoter), Memphis Geneal Soc., Ladies Hermitage Assn., Tenn. Hist. Soc. (v.p. West Tenn. 1967), Tenn. Poetry Soc., So. Dames Am. (nat. parliamentarian 1965-67), Am. Assn. State and Local History, Nat. Congress PTA (life), Nat. Council State Garden Clubs (life), Tenn. Fedn. Garden Clubs (life mem.; past pres.), YWCA, Internat. Platform Assn., Huguenot Soc. (life), AAUW, Nat. Hist. Soc. (founding mem.), Nat. Trust for Historic Preservation, Am. Heritage Soc. (charter), Phi Mu (life mem.; pres. Memphis Kappa Lambda House Corp. 1960, treas. 1961, woman of yr. award 1966), Beta Sigma Phi (internat. hon. mem.). Episcopalian. Clubs: Brunswick Road Garden (organizing pres. 1965—); Quota (hon. mem.; past pres.) (Memphis); Nineteenth Century; Tenn. Woman's Press and Authors; Stonebridge Country (hon.). Author (under name Ellen Davies-Rodgers): The Romance of the Episcopal Church in West Tennessee, 1964; The Holy Innocents, 1966; The Casket Case, 1970; Education, Then, Now and Yon, 1971; The Great Book, Calvary Protestant Episcopal Church 1832-1972, 1973. Contbr. numerous articles and items to mags. Home: Davies Plantation (Brunswick) Memphis TN 38134

DAVIS, ALICE ELIZA MORSE (MRS. GEORGE ARTHUR DAVIS), club woman; b. Milo, Maine; d. John Willis and Mabel (Martin) Morse; student U. Maine, 1919-21; grad. Gilman Comml. Sch., Bangor, Maine, 1936; m. Maynard Havey, Dec. 22, 1921 (dec. Dec. 1930); 1 dau., Gloria (Mrs. Lee Baker); m. 2d, George Arthur Davis, Aug. 18, 1947 (dec. Jan. 10, 1969). Tchr. public schs. Maine, 1922-25; sec. Agrl. Mktg. Service, USDA, Washington, 1936-46; mem. community adv. com. Maine Hwy. Safety Com., 1962-64; mem. adv. council Maine Civil War Centennial Commn., 1961-65; mem. nat. adv. bd. Am. Security Council, Washington, 1971—; charter mem. Security and Intelligence Fund, Washington, 1977—; Maine chmn. nat. def. com. D.A.R., 1958-65, resolutions com., 1958-75, regent chpt., 1962-64, 72-76, area rep. speakers staff com., 1968-74; nat. vice chmn. Northeastern div. Americanism and D.A.R. Manual for Citizenship Com., 1965-68; Maine pres. Daus. Colonial Wars, 1965-68, nat. vice chmn. program com. 1st div. states, 1968-71, mem. Nat. Officers Club, 1966—; nat. chmn. Am. def. and legislation, Nat. Soc. New Eng. Women, 1966-69, nat. vice chmn. resolutions com., 1966-69, v.p. Augusta Colony, Maine, 1966-72; pres. 1972-75, registrar, 1979—; nat. mem. Smithsonian Assn., 1977-83; mem. Nat. Travel Club, Soc. Mayflower Descs., Nat. Rifle Assn.; charter mem. Mason (N.H.) Hist. Soc., 1969—; mem. Pine Tree Soc. for Crippled Children and Adults, 1975—; mem. Ret. Officers Assn., 1977—. Mem. Order Eastern Star. Home: Twin Coves Southport ME Mailing address: PO Box 117 Boothbay ME 04537

DAVIS, ALICE ELLIOTT, banker; b. Sidon, Miss., Nov. 1, 1902; d. Archibald Stuart and Ruby (Elliott) D.; B.A., William Carey Coll., Hattiesburg, Miss., 1922. Asst. cashier Peoples Bank, Mendenhall, Miss., 1926-60, v.p., dir., 1960—. Pres. trustees Mendenhall Public Library, 1975-79. Recipient Outstanding Citizen's award Mendenhall C. of C., 1977, Disting. Service award Miss. Lung Assn., 1978. Republican. Baptist. Address: Peoples Bank Maude Ave Mendenhall MS 39114

DAVIS, ALICE VIRGINIA GUNN, educator; b. Daingerfield, Tex., July 24, 1918; d. Walter Harrison and Lena Belle (Porter) Gunn; student pub. schs., Daingerfield; m. Joseph Marion Davis, Dec. 25, 1938; children—Joe Lane, Jerrol Porter. Pvt. instr. piano, Omaha, Tex., 1962—; organist Meth. Ch., 1965—, dir. children's music, tchr. Sunday sch., Bible study leader. Mem. Nat. Guild Piano Tchrs. (sr. collegiate diploma, hall of fame), Nat. Music Tchrs. Assn. (officer), N.E. Tex. Music Tchrs. Assn. Home and Office: Route 1 Box 57 Omaha TX 75571

DAVIS, ALMA BRITTON, govt. ofcl.; b. Pitts., Dec. 11, 1924; d. Horace Roland and Della Britton; B.A., U. Pitts., 1974, M.P.A., 1974; m. James Davis, June 16, 1940 (dec.); children—Clarence, Jamie. Mem. staff Community Action Pitts., Inc., 1969-73, asst. dir. community affairs, 1970-73; project dir. Mark V Assos., Inc., N.Y.C., 1973-75, 76; expert EEO specialist EEO Commn., Washington, 1975; adminstrv. liaison officer Washington Urban League, 1977; edn. specialist Office Fed. Procurement Policy, Office Mgmt. and Budget, 1977—. Bd. dirs. Lincoln Park Community Center, 1953-59, Child Welfare League Am., 1966-72, Nat. Council Illegitimacy, 1967-70; bd. dirs. Family and Children's Service Assn. Allegheny County, 1960-72, sec., 1970; co-chmn. neighborhood services com. Community Fund Allegheny County, 1971; trustee Community Services Pa., 1970-79; chmn. nat. advs. Nat. Student Bus. League, 1974—. Recipient various service awards. Mem. Am. Soc. Public Adminstrn., Nat. Council Negro Women (life), Phi Delta Gamma. Episcopalian. Club: Foxtrappe (Washington). Home: 1515 Jefferson Davis Hwy Arlington VA 22202 Office: OFPP/OMB 726 Jackson Pl NW Washington DC 20503

DAVIS, ANN MARIE HOUSTON, nurse; b. Knoxville, Tenn., Nov. 21, 1946; d. Robert Lockhart and Ruth Wilda (Fincannon) Houston; B.S. in Nursing, U. Tenn., 1968; children—Shane Houston, Britt Woodroff, Carrie Nicole. Staff nurse, emergency room Bapt. Hosp., Memphis, 1968-69: charge nurse U. Tenn. Hosp., Knoxville, 1969-70, relief charge nurse, 1970-71, adminstrv. supr. nursing service, 1971-74, clin. supr. pre- and post-operative care, 1974-75; asst. dir. nursing service Eastern State Psychiat. Hosp., Knoxville, 1970-71; dir. sudden infant death syndrome counseling and info. project Met. Nashville-Davidson County Health Dept., Nashville, 1976-77; dir. nursing River Park Hosp., McMinnville, Tenn., 1977-81; office mgr./nurse, McMinnville, 1981—; nursing cons. ARC, 1969-70, dept. psychol. services and spl. edn. Little Tennesee Valley Ednl. Coop., Alcoa, Tenn., 1974-75, Motlow State Community Coll., Tullahoma, Tenn., 1977—, THA, 1978—. Vol. instr., supr. jr. hosp. aides ARC, Knoxville, 1969—, nurse-in-residence, leadership instr. for area high schs., 1969—; bd. dirs. Knoxville Rape Crisis Center, 1973-75, treas., 1973-74, counselor, 1973-75; pres. Warren County Diabetes Assn.; mem. edn. com. Greater Tenn. Diabetes Assn.; den leader Cub Scouts. Recipient Vol. Service award ARC, 1969. Mem. Am., Tenn. socs. nursing service dirs., Tenn. Hosp. Assn., ARC, Am. Nurses Assn. Home: 204 Boyd Ave McMinnville TN 37110 Office: River Park Hosp Sparta Rd McMinnville TN 37110

DAVIS, ANNA GRAY, banker, farm mgr.; b. Josephine, Tex., Dec. 17, 1897; d. Robert Lee and Lillian (Wright) Gray; student Burleson Coll., 1915-16; m. Richard Clinton Davis, Aug. 29, 1917; children—Jack Gray, Dorothy (Mrs. Robert J. Cannon). Pioneer in orgn. Womens Home Demonstration Clubs in Hunt County, 1935; mgr. farm properties, 1964—; instrumental in securing rural water lines for community Indsl. Found. Devel., 1965-66; dir. Citizens State Bank, Royse City, Tex. Active, ARC, Am. Cancer Soc.; bd. dirs. Area Concert Assn. Mem. DAR (regent Thomas Wynne chpt. 1961-64, organizing registrar Rockwall chpt.), Royse City C. of C., UDC, So. Meml. Dallas, Tex. Fedn. Womens Clubs Dallas (Heritage div. chmn. Trinity dist. 1975—). Republican. Baptist. Clubs: Book Lovers (pres. 1971-73); Martha Bible (treas.). Home: Route 1 Box 88 Royse City TX 75089

DAVIS, BARBARA AVENT, govt. ofcl.; b. Durham, N.C., Sept. 22, 1935; d. Dallas Gaston and Elsie Amelia (Baugh) Avent; B.S. magna cum laude in Bus. Adminstrn., U. Tenn., Chattangooga, 1979, M.B.A., 1981; m. Jack Davis, May 30, 1954; 1 son, David Jack. Various secretarial positions, 1953-65; with TVA, Chattanooga, 1973—, mgmt. asst., 1979-82, supr. records and sales, 1982—. Pres. Brainerd United Meth. Women, Chattanooga, 1972-74, trustee ch., 1980-83. Mem. Nat. Mgmt. Assn., Federally Employed Women, Alpha Soc. Home: 4604 Rocky River Rd Chattanooga TN 37416 Office: 355 Lupton Blvd Chattanooga TN 37401

DAVIS, BARBARA JANE, med. technologist; b. New Britain, Conn., Sept. 30, 1937; d. Anthony Joseph and Mary Ann (Nargi) Fallo; cert. med. tech. New Britain Gen. Hosp. Sch. Med. Tech., 1958; A.S., Galveston Coll., 1978; B.S. in Marine Sci., Tex. A&M U., 1981; m. George D. Davis, Sept. 12, 1959; children—Peter Anthony, George Dewey, Sandra Louise. Med. technologist Rancho Los Amigos Hosp., Downey, Calif., 1959-63, Lawrence and Meml. Hosps., New London, Conn., 1963-65, Bapt. Hosp., Pensacola, Fla., 1965-66, Hollywood (Fla.) Meml. Hosp., 1966, Bay Harbor Hosp., Harbor City, Calif., 1971-73, Miami Dade Gen. Hosp. (Coral Reef Gen. Hosp.), Miami, Fla., 1975-77, U. Tex. Med. br. Galveston, 1977, County of Galveston 4c's Clinic, 1981-82. Lic. med. technologist, Calif., Fla. Recipient of appreciation Elks Lodge 126, 1982. Mem. Am. Soc. Clin. Pathologists (cert. med. technologist), Delta Zeta. Home: 6421 Princeton Woods Dr N Mobile AL 36618 also 419 Anderson Dr Destin FL 32541

DAVIS, BARBARA LYDON, banker; b. Detroit, Aug. 4, 1932; d. Robert Carlton and Olive Norman (Speers) Lydon; B.A., Wilson Coll., 1954; M.B.A., N.Y.U., 1982; m. Ralph Glenn Davis, Aug. 14, 1954 (div. 1977); children—Brenda Lynn, Stephen Glenn, Karen Ann. Prof., Sasebo (Japan) Tech. Coll., 1971-73; asso. Donaldson, Lufkin & Jenrette, Inc., 1976-82; asst. v.p./leveraged buyout specialist Nat. Bank Can., N.Y.C., 1982—; asst. sec. Sinclair & Rush, Inc., 1979-62, Ill. Coil Spring Co., 1980-82. Bd. dirs. N.Y.U Bus. Forum, Ikebana Internat. Mem. AAUW. Republican. Clubs: Met. Rep., Eastside Rep. Home: 80 Park Ave New York NY 10016 Office: 535 Madison Ave New York NY 10022

DAVIS, BARBARA M(AE), librarian; b. Cranston, R.I., Dec. 23, 1926; d. Harrie S. and Marguerite M. (Cameron) D.; Sc.B. in Chemistry, Brown U., 1948; M.S. in L.S., Simmons Coll., 1956. Asst. research librarian research and devel. dept. Cabot Corp., Cambridge, Mass., 1948-57, research librarian, 1957-61, research librarian Billerica (Mass.) Research Center, 1961-68, head tech. info. services, 1968-81, mgr. tech. info. center, 1981—. Dir. Cabot Boston Credit Union, 1956-59, 61-64, 72-78, clk., 1961-64, 72-77, v.p., 1977-78; chmn. research com. Greater Boston Young Republican Club, 1959-61. Mem. Am. Chem. Soc. (sec. div. chem. lit. 1961-65), Spl. Libraries Assn. (chmn. Boston chpt. 1965-66, chmn. chemistry div. 1971-72), Simmons Coll. Library Sch. Alumni (v.p. 1965-66). Home: 37 Drummer Boy Way Lexington MA 02173 Office: Cabot Corp Concord Rd Billerica MA 01821

DAVIS, BERTHA GERMIZE, artist; b. Vilno, Lithuania; came to U.S., 1940, naturalized, 1941; d. Abraham and Dvora Germaize; student Stewart Van Orden, Pan Am. Coll., 1960-61, Fred Samualson and James Pinco, Art Inst. of San Migual Allende, Mex., 1965, Harold Phenix, 1972-73, Ed Whitney, 1973-74, Bud Shackelford, 1976, Zoltan Szabo, 1977, Morris Shubin, 1977; children—Sylvia Davis Caplan, Doryn. Owner, operator art gallery, Houston, 1969-72; asst. mgr. Art Internat., Houston, 1972-75; asst. mgr. Kirt Niven Gallery, Dallas, 1977-78; one woman shows: Pan Am. Coll., 1960, Jewish Community Center, Houston, McAllen State Bank, 1974, La Culdadela, Monterey, Mex., Houston Public Library, U. Tex. Health Sci. Center, Dallas, 1979, Gallery of Discovery, Dallas, 1981, Channel 13 TV Gallery, Dallas, 1981, Sol Del Rio Gallery, San Antonio, 1982, others; group shows include: Watercolor Soc. Houston, S.W. Watercolor Soc., Am. Painters in Paris, Cooperstown Art Exhibit, Issac Delgado Mus. Art, New Orleans, Corpus Christi Art Found., Salmagundi Club Art Show, N.Y.C., 1979, Gallery Two, Old Town, Dallas, Laguna Gloria Mus., 1979, Catharine Lorillard Wolfe Art Club, N.Y.C., 1980, Houshangs Gallery, Dallas, 1980, Nimbus Gallery, Dallas; showings in Marsha London Gallery, N.Y.C., Nat. Design Center, N.Y.C., Fonteinbleau Gallery of N.Y., Deportive Israelita de Mexico, Laguna Gloria Mus; represented in permanent collection Shell Oil Co., Houston. Mem. Tex. Fine Art Assn., S.W. Watercolor Assn., Richardson Civic Art Assn., Artist Sculptors Contemporary Assn., Art League Houston, Houston Art Assn. Prin. illustrator: Open Dallas, 1976; works reproduced in various publs. Home: 715 Gaylewood Dr Richardson TX 75080

DAVIS, BETTE RUTH ELIZABETH, actress; b. Lowell, Mass., Apr. 5, 1908; d. Harlow Morrell and Ruth (Favor) D.; ed. Cushing Acad., Ashburnham, Mass.; m. Harmon Oscar Nelson, Jr., Aug. 18, 1932 (div.); m. 2d, Arthur Farnsworth, Dec. 1940 (dec. Aug. 25, 1943); m. 3d, William Grant Sherry, Nov. 30, 1945; 1 dau., Barbara Davis; m. 4th, Gary Merrill, Aug. 1950 (div.); adopted children—Margot, Michael. Began as motion picture actress, 1931; leading pictures include Of Human Bondage, Bordertown, Dangerous (Acad. award Best Actress 1935), The Petrified Forest, Jezebel (Acad. award Best Actress 1938), Dark Victory, Juarez, The Old Maid, The Private Lives of Elizabeth and Essex, The Great Lie, The Bride Came C.O.D., All About Eve, 1950, Payment on Demand, 1951, Phone Call from a Stranger, 1952, The Star, 1953, The Virgin Queen, 1955, Storm Center, The Catered Affair, 1956, John Paul Jones, 1959, The Scapegoat, 1959, What Ever Happened to Baby Jane, Dead Ringer, Painted Canvas, 1963, Where Love Has Gone, Hush, Hush, Sweet Charlotte, 1964, The Nanny, 1965, The Anniversary, 1967, Connecting Rooms, 1969, Bunny O'Hare, 1970, Madam Sin, 1971, The Game, 1972, Burnt Offerings, 1977, Death on the Nile, 1979, Watcher in the Woods, 1979; TV movies Sister Aimee, 1977, The Dark Secret of Harvest Home, 1978, Strangers (Emmy award), 1979, White Momma, 1980, Skyward, 1980, Family Reunion, 1981, A Piano for Mrs. Cimino, 1982; Little Gloria Happy At Last, 1982; (play) The Night of the Iguana. Recipient Am. Film Inst. Life Achievement award, 1977. Author: The Lonely Life, 1962; co-author: Mother Goddam, 1974. Office: care Gottlieb Schiff Ticktin Sternklar and Harris 555 Fifth Ave New York NY 10017

DAVIS, BETTY BARTLETT, librarian; b. Wedowee, Ala., July 1, 1927; d. James Donald and Addie Lou (Roop) Bartlett; B.A., Ga. Coll., 1946; M.A., Emory U., 1952. Tchr., librarian, pub. schs., Ga., 1946-49; librarian, lab. sch., Ga. State Coll. for Women, 1949-53, instr. library sci., summers 1952, 53; dir. Uncle Remus Regional Library, Madison, Ga., 1953-54; various library positions Fla. State U., 1954-58; head humanities social scis. div. Library Clemson U., 1958-61; cataloger U. Wis., Madison, 1961-64, Va. Poly. Inst., Blacksburg, 1964-68; cataloger Frostburg (Md.) State Coll., 1968-71, head cataloger, 1971-77; tech. services librarian Salem Coll., Winston Salem, N.C., 1977-78; head Online Computer Library Ctr., Kans. State U., Manhattan, 1978-80; dir. library tech. services Ind. State U., Terre Haute, 1980—. Recipient McCants award Ga. Library Assn., 1949. Mem. ALA, Library and Info. Tech. Assn., Assn. Coll. and Research Libraries, Resources and Tech. Services Div. ALA, Library Adminstrn. and Mgmt. Assn., Ohio Valley Group Tech. Services Librarians, Ind. Library Assn., AAUW. Episcopalian. Home: 406 S Brown St Terre Haute IN 47803 Office: Cunningham Meml Library Ind State U Terre Haute IN 47809

DAVIS, BETTY JEAN BOURBONIA, real estate co. exec.; b. Ft. Bayard, N.Mex., Mar. 12, 1931; d. John Alexander and Ora M. (Caudill) Bourbonia; B.S. in Elem. Edn., U. N.Mex., 1954; children— Janice Ann Cox Plagge, Elizabeth Ora Cox. Gen. partner BJD Realty Co., Albuquerque, 1977—. Bd. dirs. Albuquerque Opera Guild, 1977-79, 81-83, membership co-chmn., 1977-79; mem. Friends of Art, 1978—, Friends of Little Theatre, 1973—. Recipient Matrix award for journalism Jr. League. Mem. Maxwell Mus. Assn., Albuquerque Mus. Assn., N.M. Hist. Soc., Albuquerque Symphony Women Assn., Jr. League Albuquerque, Alumni Assn. U. N.Mex. (dir. 1973-76), Alpha Chi Omega. Republican. Methodist. Clubs: Alpha Chi Omega Mother's, Tanoan Country, Internat., Century (U. N.Mex.), Order Eastern Star, Order Rainbow for Girls (past grand worthy adv. N.Mex., past mother adv. Friendship Assembly 50), Alpha Chi Omega (chpt. adv. 1958 building corp. 1962-77). Home: 7816 Vista Del Arroyo NE Albuquerque NM 87109

DAVIS, BEVERLY WANDA, nurse; b. Greenville, Pa., July 17, 1924; d. Glenn Insly and Agnes Mae (Reagle) Blair; grad. Cleve. City Sch. Nursing, 1945; m. Roy Aaron Davis, Apr. 11, 1949 (dec. Jan. 1967); 1 dau., Jane Ann. Asst. supr. in-service tng. Cleve. State Hosp., 1948-50, supr. in-service tng., personnel dir., 1950-52; pvt. duty nurse, Miami Beach, Fla., 1952-60; supr. group nursing Mt. Sinai Hosp., Miami Beach, Fla., 1960-76; supr. Total Care Home Health Agy., Miami, 1976; head nurse, coordinator surg. services, adminstrv. supr. Lake Community Hosp., Leesburg, Fla., 1976-82; staff nurse Marion Community Hosp., Ocala, Fla., 1982—. R.N., Fla. Mem. Fla. Nurses Assn., Assn. Intravenous Therapists. Democrat. Club: Rosicrucians. Home: 950 145th St SW Ocala FL 32671

DAVIS, BILLIE JOHNSTON, sch. counselor; b. Charleston, W.Va., Sept. 24, 1933; d. William Andrew, Jr. and Garnet Macil (Johnston) D.; B.S., Morris Harvey Coll., Charleston, W.Va., 1954; M.A., W.Va. U., 1957. Tchr. math. Kanawha County schs., Charleston, 1954-59, counselor, 1959—; mem. public edn. study commn. W.Va. Legislature, 1980; mem. W.Va. Commn. on Juvenile Law, 1982. Mem. W.Va. Personnel and Guidance Assn. (pres. 1964-66, legis. chmn., 1974—; spl. award legis. services 1981), W.Va. Edn. Assn. (past legis. chmn.), Kanawha County Personnel and Guidance Assn. (pres., legis. chmn. 1974—), Alpha Delta Kappa (past chpt. pres.), Phi Delta Kappa. Democrat. Baptist. Home: 915 Breezemont Dr Charleston WV 25302 Office: Dunbar Jr High Sch 1300 Myers Ave Dunbar WV 25064

DAVIS, BONITA CAROLE, social worker, state grants officer; b. Spartanburg, S.C., July 12, 1941; d. Calvin, Jr. and Johnnie Maude (Jones) D.; B.A., Bennett Coll., Greensboro, N.C., 1966; M.S.W., Adelphi U., Garden City, N.Y., 1972. Successively caseworker, supr., adoption coordinator, adoption div. N.Y.C. Dept. Social Services, 1966-70, 72-73; dir. edn. and career hdqrs. N.Y. Community Tng. Inst., 1973-79; part-time lectr. Adelphi U. Sch. Social Work, 1974-80; mgr. gov.'s discretionary grant program N.Y. State Dept. Labor, Albany, 1980—; cons. career and organizational devel., 1973—. Incorporating officer East-West Interlock Inc., 1978; bd. dirs., fund raiser Women's Liberation Center, N.Y.C., 1977-79. United Negro Coll. Fund scholar, 1959-60. Mem. Nat. Assn. Black Social Workers, Am. Personnel and Guidance Assn., Assn. Non-White Concerns, Nat. Women's Referral Network, NAACP, Urban League, Public Employees Fedn. Club: Order Eastern Star. Home: 10 Park Hill Albany NY 12204 Office: Bldg 12 State Campus Albany NY 12240

DAVIS, CAROL LYN, ceramics cons.; b. West Palm Beach, Fla., Oct. 22, 1953; d. Robert Lee and Barbara Jean (Collett) D.; B.F.A., Tex. Christian U., Ft. Worth, 1975, M.A. in Am. Studies, 1977. Research and devel. product line designer Am. Handicrafts/Merribee Needlearts, Ft. Worth, 1977-81; ceramics/china sales cons. Dillard's, Ft. Worth, 1981—, dept. mgr., 1981-82; free lance ceramic and string art designer, 1982—. Mem. mgmt. adv. panel Chem. Week, 1981. Mem. Am. Craft Council, Nat. Trust Historic Preservation, Cousteau Soc. Democrat. Episcopalian. Contbr. pamphlets in field. Office: 131 E Exchange St Fort Worth TX 76106

DAVIS, CAROLE ANN, speech and hearing therapist; b. Bklyn., Oct. 6, 1946; d. Benjamin and Elsie (Steinberg) Honigman; student Emerson Coll., 1965-66; L.I. U., 1966-68; M.S., Bklyn. Coll., 1972; postgrad. City U. N.Y., 1971-72, Adelphi U., 1978-79; m. Mark George Davis, Sept. 1, 1968; children—Rachel, Buffy. Speech tchr. Bur. for Speech Improvement, Bklyn., 1968-71; cons. to devel. clinic L.I. U., 1971; supr. speech and hearing pediatric unit Suffolk Devel. Center, 1972-75, coordinator Outpatient Clinic, mem. admissions com., 1972-75; cons. Assn. for Down's Syndrome Children, West Islip, N.Y., 1975-76; cons. Port Jefferson Nursing Home and Health Related Facility, 1976; tchr. speech and hearing impaired BOCES, James E. Allen Learning Center, Melville, N.Y., 1977-81; elem. sch. Counselor, 1981-82; tchr. speech and hearing impaired, Dix Hills, N.Y., 1982—. Vice pres. Dix Hills Hadassah Fundraiser, 1976, Brandeis U. Nat. Women's Com. Fundraiser, 1978. City U. N.Y. Clin. fellow, 1971. Mem. L.I. Speech and Hearing Assn., N.Y. State Speech, Hearing, Lang. Assn., L.I. Speech, Lang., Hearing Assn., Am. Speech and Hearing Assn. Jewish. Home: 21 Ground Pine Ct Dix Hills NY 11746 Office: Half Hollow Hills Sch Dist 5 Dix Hills NY 11746

DAVIS, CAROLYN BELL, systems analyst; b. Martinsville, Va., Sept. 20, 1950; d. Daniel W. and Marie (Vaughn) Bell; A.A.S., Danville Community Coll., 1970; m. James Michael Davis, Nov. 6, 1970; 1 son, Michael Andrew. Programmer analyst, prodn. support Tultex Corp., Martinsville, 1978-79; with Bassett (Va.) Furniture Industries, 1970-78, 79—, sr. programmer analyst, designing on-line computer systems, 1979—. Mem. Nat. Assn. Female Execs., Nat. Soc. Published Poets, Beta Sigma Phi. Author: A Concise Treasury of Virginia, Nevada and R.I. Poets and Their Poems, 1976. Home: 609 Forest St Martinsville VA 24112 Office: Bassett Furniture Industries Main Office Bassett VA 24055

DAVIS, CAROLYN BRANDT, mgmt. cons. co. exec.; b. Atlanta, Apr. 4, 1936; d. Marion Henry and Margaret (Blitchington) Brandt; student Brenau Coll., 1955; B.A., Emory U., 1957; M.B.A., Fla. State U., 1976; m. Frank M. Davis, Aug. 21, 1957 (div. July 1975); children—Margaret Norine, Kathryn Amelia, Frank Massey. Tchr. English, Chapelle High Sch., Metairie, La., 1964-67; systems analyst Data Design Labs., Norfolk, Va., 1976-78; sr. systems analyst Advanced Tech., Inc., Arlington, Va., 1978-79; ops. analyst Sci. Applications Inc., McLean, Va., 1979; pres. ANA-LOG, Inc., McLean, 1979—, also chmn. bd.; instr. logistics George Mason U., 1981-82. Bd. dirs. Fla. Heritage Found., 1971-73, publicity chmn., 1972; antique show chmn. Tallahassee Jr. Mus., 1973, dance camp dir. 1975; program chmn. Fla. Sesquicentennial, 1973; v.p. Tallahassee Civic Ballet, 1975, choreographer, 1973-76; editor Springtime Tallahassee, 1974; docent LeMoyne Art Gallery, 1972-75. Cert. profl. logistician. Mem. Soc. Logistics Engrs. (edn. chmn. 1979, treas. 1980, v.p. 1981), Nat. Assn. Women Bus. Owners, Nat. Small Bus. Assn., Fairfax C. of C., Federally Employed Women, Nat. Assn. Female Execs., Ga. Soc., Delta Delta Delta. Co-author, dir. (with Cheryl Richardson) Southern Educational TV series, 1969-70. Home: 2301 Jefferson Davis Hwy #732 Arlington VA 22202 Office: 7655 Old Springhouse Rd McLean VA 22102

DAVIS, CATHERINE CORNICK, dental hygienist; b. Omaha, Jan. 16, 1956; d. John Henry Dickinson and Constance Patricia (McGinness) D.; B.S. with distinction, U. Nebr., 1978; M.S., in Pathology, Washington U., St. Louis, 1978-80; postgrad. U. Iowa, 1981—; m. Steven C. Scheffel, Aug. 25, 1979. Pathology extern St. John's Mercy Med. Center, St. Louis, 1979; instr. dental hygiene Forest Park Community Coll., St. Louis, 1980; asst. prof. denistry U. Iowa, 1981—. Am. Dental Hygienists Assn. Grad. fellow; 1978-79; grantee Clin. Cancer Edn., 1979-80, Am. Dental Health Assn. Found, 1981-82. Mem. Internat. Assn. Dental Research, Am. Dental Hygienists Assn., Iowa Dental Hygienists Assn., Mortar Bd., Sigma Phi Alpha, Gamma Gamma, Alpha Lambda Delta, Phi Eta Sigma. Club: P.E.O. Editorial adv. bd. Dental Hygiene, 1981—. Research on radiosensitivity of parotid gland. Office: DSB S248 Iowa City IA 52242

DAVIS, CELESTIA BRANNEN, reading cons.; b. Swenson, Tex., June 20, 1915; d. Calvin Ernest and Iva (Galloway) Brannen; B. Religious Edn., Southwestern Baptist Sem., 1946; M. Ed., Eastern N. Mex. U., 1965, edn. specialist, 1968; Ed.D., Tex. Woman's U., 1976; m. Paul Wendelin Davis, Oct. 6, 1935; one dau., Wendelin Ann (Mrs. William Arden Taylor). Prin. Stonewall County Sch., Aspermont, Tex., 1932-34; head tchr. Sacaton (Ariz.) Pub. Sch., 1953-59; elem. tchr. Carlsbad, N. Mex., 1962-63; remedial reading tchr. Marton, Tex., 1963-67; reading cons. Tex. Edn. Agency, Austin, 1968—, edn. grantee, 1976-77. Mem. Assn. State English and Reading Suprs. (pres. 1975-76), Internat. Reading Assn. (state orgn. chmn. 1968-76, Founders award Tex. council 1976), DAR, Tex. State Council Reading and Supervision, Tex. Council Lang. Arts Suprs., Nat. Council Tchrs. English (cons. to CEE commn. on supervision and curriculum devel. 1982—), Delta Kappa Gamma. Democrat. Baptist. Contbr. articles to profl. publs. Home: 9610 Covey Ridge Ln Austin TX 78758 Office: 201 E 11th St Austin TX 78701

DAVIS, CYNTHIA ANN, acct.; b. Independence, Mo., June 11, 1952; d. Billie Buel Harper and Martha Rae (Brewer) Thrutchley; B.A., Graceland Coll., 1973, cum laude. Acctg. office supr. Southwestern Bell Telephone Co., Wichita, Kans., 1973-75; staff acct. McGladrey Hendricksen & Co., Des Moines, 1975-78; profl. staff acct. Deloitte Haskins & Sells, Davenport, Iowa, 1979; pvt. practice public acctg., Davenport, 1979-81; mgr. Carpentier, Mitchell, Goddard & Co., Moline, Ill., 1981—; instr. Scott Community Coll., 1980—; lectr. in field. Recipient cert. of hon. recognition, U.S. SBA, 1978. Mem. Am. Inst. C.P.A.s, Iowa Soc. C.P.A.s, Ill. Soc. C.P.A.s. Soc. Mem. Reorganized Ch. Jesus Christ of Latter-Day Saints. Office: 1600 30th Ave Moline IL 61265

DAVIS, DERALYN RILES, acct.; b. Corsicana, Tex., Dec. 23, 1935; d. Roy and Juanita Jeanetta (Williams) Riles; B.S., Huston-Tillotson

Coll., 1953; B.B.A., U. Tex., Arlington, 1978; m. Jefferson Davis, Jr., Aug. 25, 1956; children—Jefflyn Dorsai, Jock Kevin. Tchr. public schs., Tex., 1954-60, 61-75; office mgr. Jones Realty, Washington, 1960; asst. to controller Transport Ins., Ft. Worth, 1978-79; acct. DRD Bookkeeping & Tax Service, Ft. Worth, 1981—. Vice chmn. Tex. Democratic Com., 1978—; chmn. Tex. Coalition of Black Dems., 1979—. Mem. Am. Soc. Women Accts., Tex. Assns. Realtors, Nat. Assn. Realtors. Home: 4528 Moorview St Fort Worth TX 76119 Office: PO Box 15126 Fort Worth TX 76119

DAVIS, DIANNE CHRISTINE, former dept. store exec.; b. Berkeley, Calif., Sept. 6, 1945; d. Vincent John and Islea Ann (Negus) Vabri; B.S. in Bus. Adminstrn., U. Calif., Berkeley, 1963-67; m. James Critser Davis, Dec. 17, 1966; children—Scott Edward, Stephanie Lynn. Asst. area adminstr. Bank of Am., San Francisco, 1967; asst. buyer, dept. mgr. Emporium Dept. Store, San Francisco, 1967-68; sales analyst Varian Aerograph, Walnut Creek, Calif., 1969-70; chmn. fashion merchandising dept. Northwood Inst., Midland, Mich., 1976-79; area sales mgr. J.L. Hudson Dept. Store, Lansing, Mich., 1979-82; cons. in field. Treas. Midland Montessori Sch., 1976-77, pres. 1977-78. Mem. AAUW. Home: 6000 Bradford Way Hudson OH 44236

DAVIS, DOROTHY LOUISE, jewelry store and art gallery exec.; b. Falls County, Tex., Sept. 22, 1928; d. John Lee and Ina (Martin) Schneider; student Midland Coll.; m. James Lee Davis, Aug. 4, 1946; children—Sandra Lea, David Lynn, Michael Keith, Lori Kay. Sec., C. Roy Chambers, lawyer, Mart, Tex., 1946-47; sec. J.L. Davis Cons. Firm, Midland, Tex., 1966-70; owner, operator Shop of the Blue Gem and Art Gallery, Ruidoso, N.Mex., 1977—, Blue Gem of Lafonda, Santa Fe, 1981—, Shop of the Blue Gem and Art Gallery, Midland, 1981—. Precinct 26 coordinator Midland County (Tex.) Ronald Reagan for Pres., 1976; pres. Women's Aux. Midland County Hosp. Dist., 1980-81; v.p. bd. dirs., co-founder Permian Basin High Sch., Midland, 1981—. Mem. Exec. Female, Nat. Assn. Female Execs., Entrepreneurship Inst. Ohio, Tex. Assn. Hosp. Auxs. (records com. 1981-82). Presbyterian. Clubs: Santa Rita of Petroleum Basin Oil Museum, Petroleum Engrs. Wives. Home: 2804 Maxwell Midland TX 79701 Office: PO Box 8488 Midland TX 79703

DAVIS, ELAINE CARSLEY, educator; b. Balt., Apr. 15, 1921; d. Stanley Leon and Corinne Odeal (Baker) Carsley; B.S., Coppin State Coll., 1942, Morgan State Coll., 1943; LL.B., U. Md., 1950; M.Ed., Johns Hopkins U., 1955, Ph.D., 1958; m. Robert Clarke Davis, May 2, 1945 (dec.); children—Robert Clarke, Lisa Corinne. Tchr., supr., asst. prin., dir., sr. ednl. officer to supr. Balt. City Public Schs., 1942-74; assoc. prof., assoc. dir. div. edn. Johns Hopkins U., Balt., 1974-77, assoc. prof., dir. div. edn., 1977—; trustee Morgan State Coll., 1965-67, Md. State Colls., 1967-73, Goucher Coll., 1972-75; dir. Rouse Co. Bd. dirs. LWV of Balt. City, 1962-64; mem. Jail Bd., 1972-73. Fellow AAUW; mem. Nat. Conf. Profs. Ednl. Adminstrn. (planning com.), Nat. Assn. Secondary Sch. Prins., NEA, Nat. Orgn. on Legal Problems in Edn., Phi Beta Kappa. Episcopalian. Guest editor Ednl. Horizons, 1975; co-author: Practical Math., 1979. Office: 34th & Charles Sts Baltimore MD 21218

DAVIS, ELAINE RITA, data processor; b. Washington, Oct. 27, 1946; d. Sidney Lawrence Davidson and Lillian Leibovitch; B.S. in Math., U. Md., 1968; m. Edward A. Davis, Oct. 26, 1969. Systems engr. IBM, Arlington, Va., 1968-70; mgr. computer planning Irving Trust Co., N.Y.C., 1970-78; sr. mgmt. cons. Touche Ross & Co., C.P.A.s, Newark, 1978-81; mgr. tech. services Dell Pub. Co., Pine Brook, N.J., 1981—. Mem. Exec. Women N.J. (a founder), Nat. Council Jewish Women (dir.). Office: Dell Pub Co Change Bridge Rd Montville NJ 07058

DAVIS, ELAINE ROLLINS, health facility adminstr.; b. Rome, Ga., Feb. 3, 1948; d. James R. and Doris M. Rollins; student, DeKalb Community Coll., 1972-74; children—Kelline, Robert, Tamara. With, Hirschfield & Assos., Atlanta, 1975-79; adminstr. Am. Home Health Care of Ga., Inc., Dacatur, 1979—, also dir. Mem. Am. Fedn. Home Health Agencies, Ga. Assn. Home Health Agencies. Republican. Home: Route 3 Loganville GA 30249 Office: American Home Health Care of Georgia Inc 3250 Memorial Dr PO Box 36300 Decatur GA 30032

DAVIS, ELISE MILLER (MRS. LEO M. DAVIS), author; b. Corsicana, Tex., Oct. 12, 1915; d. Moses Myre and Rachelle (Daniels) Miller; student U. Tex., 1930-31; m. Jay Albert Davis, June 27, 1937 (dec. June 1973); 1 dau., Rayna Miller (Mrs. Michael Edwin Loeb); m. 2d, Leo M. Davis, Aug. 23, 1974. Freelance writer, 1945—; merchandiser and dir. Jay Davis, Inc., Amarillo, Tex., 1956-73; instr. mag. writing U. Tex., Dallas, 1978; lectr. creative writing Baylor U., Waco, Tex., 1980, 81. Mem. Am. Soc. Journalists and Authors. Author: The Answer Is God, 1955; articles to periodicals including Reader's Digest, Woman's Day, Nation's Business, others. Home: 3906 Old Mill Rd Waco TX 76710

DAVIS, ELIZABETH BERRY, sales and advt. exec.; b. Columbia, S.C., Nov. 26, 1929; d. Boyd Franklin and Ethel (Crumpton) Berry; student schs. Columbia, S.C.; m. Jimmy L. Davis, Aug. 14, 1948; children—Wade L., Debra Davis Strother, Gayle Davis Shumpert. Med. sec. S.C. State Hosp., Columbia, 1951-52; stenographer E.I. du Pont, Aiken, S.C., 1952-53; exec. asst. Bradley, Graham & Hamby Advt. Agy., Columbia, 1958-76; sales assn. Century 21 Grover Richey Realty, Columbia, 1976-79; sales office mgr., advt. dir. Risdon Enterprises, Inc., Columbia, 1979—. Tchr. adult ladies Sunday sch. class Springhill Wesleyan Meth. Ch., 1980—, women's missionary zone chmn. lower S.C., 1970—, women's missionary pres. local ch., 1971—. Republican. Home: Route 1 Box 494 Columbia SC 29203 Office: PO Box 4599 Columbia SC 29240

DAVIS, ELIZABETH EMILY LOUISE THORPE, psychologist; b. Grosse Pointe Farms, Mich., Aug. 11, 1948; d. Jack and Mary Alvinia (McCarron) Thorpe; B.S., U. Ala., 1972; M.A., Columbia U., 1975, M.Phil., 1976, Ph.D., 1979; m. Ronald Wilson Davis, May 16, 1969. Lectr. Am. Lit. and English composition Nei Ming Inst., Lamtin, Hong Kong, 1969-71; research fellow Columbia U., 1973-77; research assoc., N.Y.U., 1979-81, adj. asst. prof., 1981; prof. exptl. psychology Oberlin (Ohio) Coll., 1981—. Recipient, Nat. Research Services award NIH, 1979; grantee Sigma Xi, 1979, Oberlin Coll., 1981. Mem. AAAS, Am. Psychol. Assn., Assn. Research Vision and Ophthalmology, Soc. Neuroscis., Optical Soc. Am., N.Y. Acad. Scis., Eastern Psychol. Assn., Sigma Xi, Pi Mu Epsilon. Author papers in field. Office: Severance Labs Psychology Dept Oberlin Coll Oberlin OH 44074

DAVIS, ELIZABETH MARDRE (MRS. HARTWELL DAVIS), civic worker, former educator; b. Lumpkin, Ga.; d. Wilson Little and Sarah (Bivins) Mardre; student Coll., Berkeley, 1927; B.S., Auburn U., 1929; m. Hartwell Davis, Feb. 24, 1933; children—Hartwell, Letitia D. Hamill. Tchr., English Clift High Sch., Opelika, Ala., 1929-33, Lanier High Sch., Montgomery, Ala., 1934-36, 39, Robert E. Lee High Sch., Montgomery, 1962-68, Jefferson Davis High Sch., Montgomery, 1968-69; adminstrv. clk. Bur. Census, Ala. 2d Congl. Dist. Office, 1960. Mem. Ala. Citizens Adv. Ednl. Council, Ala. Com. for Better Schs., Inc.; pres. Montgomery Know-Your-Schs. Com., 1951-52; trustee Carnegie Library Assn.; mem. Montgomery County Rep. exec. com., 1956-66, 71-73, 79—; vice chmn. Ala. Rep. Exec. Com., 1961-62, mem., 1956-66. Mem. United Ch. Women (pres. Montgomery 1951-53, pres. Ala. 1955-57, mem. adminstrv. and exec. coms. gen. dept. 1957-58), Rep. Women of Montgomery (pres. 1971-73), LWV (exec. bd. Montgomery 1952-54), DAR, Daus. Am. Colonists, Colonial Dames 17th Century, Magna Charta Dames, Auburn U. Alumni Assn. (v.p. 1946-48), Kappa Delta, Phi Kappa Phi, Kappa Delta Pi. Methodist. (exec. com., sec. promotion Ala.-W. Fla. Woman's soc. 1952-58, mem. exec. com. 1960-64; mem. Ala.-West Fla. Conf. Bd. Missions 1952-56, trustee 1st United Meth. Ch. of Montgomery). Clubs: 20th Century Lit. (pres. 1944-45, 72-73), Hypatia Lit. (pres. 1944-45), Panjandrum Lit. (pres. 1948-49, 74-75). Home: 2216 Allendale Pl Montgomery AL 36111

DAVIS, ELOINE GREENE, interior decorator; b. Bartow County, Ga., Feb. 22, 1924; d. Eulus Llyallen and Vista (Thompson) Greene; student public schs., Cassville, Ga.; m. Jefferson Lee Davis, Apr. 1, 1942; children—Jefferson Lee, Sarah Grace. With Johnson-Davis Ins. Co., Cartersville, Ga., 1958-68, also sec.-treas.; owner, designer Eloine Interiors, Cartersville, 1961—. Chmn. exec. com. Bartow County Heart Unit, 1965-66; bd. dirs. Ga. Heart Assn., 1964-70, mem. public edn. com., 1966-67; bd. dirs. Etowah Valley Hist. Soc., 1977—, pres., 1980-82; bd. dirs. Bartow County unit Am. Heart Assn., 1982—; bd. dirs., curator Roselawn Mus., 1981—. Recipient Gold and Silver medallions, Ga. Heart Assn., 1967-71. Episcopalian. Address: Route 1 Old Alabama Rd Cartersville GA 30120

DAVIS, ETHEL CAIN, ret. computer systems analyst; b. Savannah, Ga., May 6, 1917; d. Adamus and Viola (Handy) Jackson; certificate Hofstra U., 1976; children—Rosalyn Maria, Floyd Anthony. Data processor, key punch operator to supervisory computer systems analyst U.S. Army, Office Dependency Benefits, USAF, 1942-61; chief data processing br. FAA, Jamaica, N.Y., 1962-79, ret., 1979. Vice pres. Hempstead Civic Assn., 1954-56; sec. Hempstead Interracial and Intercultural Council, 1958-59; bd. dirs. Cath. Interracial Council, 1964-70; L.I. regional dir. NAACP, 1973-74. Roman Catholic. Home: 176 Mason St Hempstead NY 11550

DAVIS, EVELYN MARGUERITE B., educator; b. Springfield, Mo., Oct. 5, 1914; d. Philip Edward and Della Jane (Morris) Bailey; student public schs., Springfield; m. James Harvey Davis, Sept. 22, 1946. Tchr., Bible, organist, pianist, vocal soloist and dir. youth choir Bible Bapt. Ch., Maplewood, Mo., 1956-69; pvt. instr. piano and organ, Affton, Mo., 1960-71, St. Charles, Mo., 1971—; Bible instr. 3d Bapt. Ch., St. Louis, 1948-54; pianist, soloist, Bible tchr. Temple Bapt. Ch., Kirkwood, Mo., 1969-71; dir. youth orch., music arranger, organist, pianist, vocal soloist, tchr. Bible, Bible Bapt. Ch., St. Charles, Mo., 1971-78, Faith Missionary Bapt. Ch., 1978—; asst. organist-pianist, vocal soloist, tchr. Bible, Bible Ch., Arnold, Mo., 1969—, also harpist and composer; faculty St. Charles Bible Bapt. Christian Sch., 1976-77; interior decorator and floral arranger. Fellow Am. Biog. Inst. Research Assn. (life); mem. Am. Guild Organists, Nat. Guild Piano Tchrs., Internat. Platform Assn. Executed mural in oils Bible Bapt. Ch., Maplewood (now in Arnold, Mo. Bible Ch.); composer cantata, psalms, other sacred works. Home: RFD 2 Box 178-B Rogersville MO 65742

DAVIS, FRANCES JEAN, fin. exec.; b. Little Rock, Mar. 2, 1950; d. Bob Hammett and Arline Turley Uselton; student Ark. State U., 1968-69; 1 dau., Angela Renee. Adminstrv. asst. Union Nat. Bank of Little Rock, 1969-76; pension plan adminstr. 1st Variable Life Ins. Co., Little Rock, 1976-79; trust mktg. officer 1st Nat. Bank, Little Rock, 1979-81, trust adminstrn. officer employee benefit sect., 1981—. Mem. Am. Inst. Banking, Nat. Assn. Bank Women. Democrat. Baptist. Club: YWCA. Home: 2 Stillman St Little Rock AR 72209 Office: Captiol at Broadway Little Rock AR 72201

DAVIS, FRANCES M., lawyer, corp. exec.; b. 1925; grad. U. Calif., Los Angeles, 1946; J.D., U. Calif., Berkeley, 1953. Partner firm LeProhn & LeProhn, 1960-67; asst. dean Earl Warren Legal Center, Calif. Coll. Trial Judges, 1968-72; asso. firm Pillsbury, Madison & Sutro, 1972-75; v.p., gen. counsel Potlatch Corp., San Francisco, 1975—; dir. Macy's Calif. Bd. overseers U. Calif., San Francisco. Mem. San Francisco C. of C. (dir.). Office: Potlatch Corp 1 Maritime Plaza PO Box 3591 San Francisco CA 94119

DAVIS, FREDERICA MILLER, investment co. exec.; b. Pitts., Jan. 23, 1955; d. William John and Muriel (McKaig) Miller; B.A. in Italian Studies, Trinity Coll., Hartford, Conn., 1976; cert. fin. planner, Coll. Fin. Planning, 1979; m. James Hornor Davis, IV, Aug. 11, 1979. Field service rep. Pioneer Group, Boston, 1977-79; fin. planner, account exec. Bache, Inc., Charleston, W.Va., 1979—; mem. faculty U. Charleston Coll. 2000, 1981—; columnist You and Your Money, Charleston Daily Mail, 1980—. Bd. dirs. Charleston YWCA, 1981—. Mem. Internat. Assn. Fin. Planners, Nat. Assn. Female Execs., Charleston Women's Forum (founder, past pres.). Clubs: Kanawha Sport Horse Assn. (treas.), Kanawha Obedience Tng. Club. Office: 1270 1 Valley Sq Charleston WV 25301

DAVIS, GLORIA ROCKHILL, coll. personnel exec.; b. Malden, Mass., Apr. 18, 1931; d. Herbert Wellington and Lillian May (Barbrick) Rockhill; B.S., Simmons Coll., 1953; M.A., Harvard U., 1955; M.S. in Counseling, Calif. State U., Hayward, 1973; m. John Wood, Aug. 29, 1953; children—Valerie Wood Davis Vaatete, Laura Rockhill. Dir. admissions and placement Graham Jr. Coll., Boston, 1955-57; counselor North Sacramento (Calif.) Sch. Dist., 1977-78; substitute tchr., reader, research asst. Acalanes High Sch. Dist., Lafayette, Calif., 1978-79; placement coordinator S.W. Coll., Los Angeles, 1979—. Vol. Congl. aide, 1978-79. Ford Found. scholar Harvard Grad. Sch. Edn., 1953-54, Carnegie Corp. fellow Yale Grad. Sch. Edn. Mem. NOW (editor newsletter), Nat. Women's Polit. Caucus, Am. Personnel and Guidance Assn., Am. Coll. Personnel Assn., Calif. Personnel and Guidance Assn., Calif. Career Guidance Assn. Office: 1600 W Imperial Hwy Los Angeles CA 90047

DAVIS, GRACE ELIZABETH, sch. adminstr.; b. Washington County, Ga., Aug. 10, 1935; d. Hayes and Nina Latimore; B.S., Ft. Valley State Coll., 1962; M.Ed., U. Ga., 1969, Ed.S., 1982; m. Julian I. Davis, July 29, 1954 (dec.); children—Kenneth Gregory, Darlene Mechelle. Tchr. English, Washington County Bd. Edn., 1962-80, secondary supr., 1980-81, asst. supt. instrn., 1981—; bd. dirs. Headstart. Named Washington County Tchr. of Yr., 1972. Mem. NEA, Ga. Assn. Educators, Nat. Council Tchrs. English, Ga. Assn. Instructional Supervision, Nat. Assn. Negro Bus. & Profl. Women's Club, Inc., NAACP, Ga. Coalition Black Women, Delta Sigma Theta. Home: 310 Oak St Sandersville GA 31082 Office: 210 N Harris St Sandersville GA 31082

DAVIS, HARRIET PARMENTER, brokerage account exec.; b. Ipswich, Mass., Mar. 27, 1942; d. Charles William and Marjorie Alice (Parmenter) D.; A.B., Wheaton Coll., Norton, Mass., 1963; student Sweet Briar Coll. Jr. Yr. in France, 1961-62; M.A., Boston U., 1967; M.B.A., Simmons Coll., 1975. Instr. French, Chamberlayne Jr. Coll., Boston, 1967-71; research asso. Boston Globe, 1973-74; account exec., tax shelter specialist Merrill Lynch, Pierce, Fenner & Smith, Boston, 1976—. Steering com. Wheaton Coll. Ann. Fund; trustee Cambridge (Mass.) YWCA. Mem. Boston Stockbrokers Club. Republican. Episcopalian. Home: 19 Chauncy St Cambridge MA 02138 Office: Merrill Lynch 125 High St Boston MA 02110

DAVIS, HELEN GORDON, state legislator; b. N.Y.C., Dec. 25, 1924; d. Harry Gordon and Doree Gordon; B.A., Bklyn. Coll.; postgrad. U. South Fla., 1967-70; m. Gene Davis; children—Stephanie, Karen, Gordon. Tchr., High Sch. of Commerce, N.Y.C., Hillsborough High Sch., Tampa, Fla.; grad. asst. U. S. Fla., 1968; mem. Fla. Ho. of Reps., 1974—, vice chmn. edn. com., mem. judiciary com. Jud. chmn. Local Govt. Study Commn. Hillsborough County (Fla.), 1964; mem. Tampa Commn. on Juvenile Delinquency, 1966-69, Mayor's Citizens Adv. Com., 1966-69, Quality Edn. Commn., 1966-68, Gov.'s Citizen Com. for Ct. Reform, 1972, Hillsborough County Planning Commn., 1973-74; mem. Gov.'s Commn. on Judicial Reform, 1976; mem. employment com. Commn. Community Relations, 1966-69; by-laws chmn. Arts Council Tampa, 1971-74; 1st v.p. Tampa Symphony Guild, 1974; bd. dirs. U. South Fla. Found., 1968-74, Stop Rape, 1973-74; founder Women's Survival Center, Tampa, 1978. Recipient U. S. Fla. Young Democrats Humanitarian award, 1974; Diana award NOW, 1975; Woman of Achievement in Arts award Tampa, 1975; Tampa Human Relations award, 1976; Hannah G. Solomon Citizen of Yr. award, 1980; St. Petersburg Times/Fla. Civil Liberties award, 1980. Mem. LWV (pres. Hillsborough County 1966-69, lobbyist, Fla. adminstrn. of justice chmn. 1969-74), PTA (past pres.), Temple Guild Sisterhood (past pres.), Am. Arbitration Assn. Home: 45 Adalia Ave Tampa FL 33606 Office: 732 Freedom Federal Tampa FL 33602

DAVIS, HELEN NANCY MATSON (MRS. CHAUNCEY D. DAVIS), real estate broker, civic worker; b. Zanesville, Ohio, Nov. 18, 1905; d. Austin F. and Georgianna (Hale) Matson; grad. high sch.; m. Chauncey D. Davis, May 1, 1924; children—James Harvey, Robert Lee. Real estate broker, South Bend, Wash., 1964—. Exec. sec. Pacific County Tb League, 1936-62; chmn. Park Bd., South Bend, 1955—; ofcl. Pacific County Bicentennial Pageant; trustee Pacific County Hist. Soc. Named Woman of Yr. Pacific County C. of C., 1949, 61. Mem. Propelaeum Study Club, Grange, Chinook Indian Tribe (hon.), Wash. Fedn. Music Clubs, Delta Kappa Gamma. Republican. Methodist. Rebekah. Club: Garden (South Bend). Composer: Washington, My Home (ofcl. state song Wash.), 1959; Eliza and the Lumberjack (mus. play). Home: 606 W 2d St South Bend WA 98586 Office: 705 Robert Bush Dr South Bend WA 98586

DAVIS, IMOGEN ERIKA, conservationist, writer, linguist; b. Troppau, Czechoslovakia, June 21, 1928; came to U.S., 1952, naturalized, 1955; d. Fridges and Olga (Tutmann) Lotz (parents Austrian citizens); Dekanats-Pruefung in Italian, U. Vienna, 1947; student French civilization Sorbonne, Paris, 1948-50, Hispanic-Am. civilization Sacred Heart U., Bridgeport, Conn., 1976-77. Active numerous wildlife conservation groups, U.S. and internat., including Animal Welfare Inst., Defenders of Wildlife, Friends of Animals, Nat. Mustang Assn., Pet and Animal Welfare Soc. Conn., Animal Protection Inst., Save the Whales, also various orgns. to promote world peace and understanding; chmn. Argentine scholarship com. U. Bridgeport, 1973-74; active Bridgeport Area Assn. for UN. Recipient certs. of appreciation Animal Protection Inst., 1975, UN Assn. U.S., 1964. Author poems.

DAVIS, INGER PEDERSEN, educator; b. Holstebro, Denmark, Oct. 16, 1927; came to U.S., 1961, naturalized, 1970; d. Niels Aage and Ansine Wilhelmine (Larsen) Pedersen; B.S., Statens Kursus, Copenhagen, 1948; M.S.W., Copenhagen Sch. Social Work, 1952; M.A. (UN fellow), U. Chgo., 1962, Ph.D., 1972; m. Kenneth Culp Davis, 1962. Dir. reference library Dept. Social Affairs, Copenhagen, 1954-59; lectr. Copenhagen Sch. Social Work, 1959-61; research asst., textbook writer, 1962-64; parent counselor, caseworker Chgo. Child Care Soc., 1965-67; lectr., then asst. prof. Sch. Social Service Adminstrn., U. Chgo., 1971-76; mem. faculty Sch. Social Work, San Diego State U., 1977—, prof. social work, 1981—; mem. regional steering com. Child Welfare Tng. Center, UCLA, 1979—. Fulbright fellow, 1956, 61-62; Fed. Child Welfare Teaching grantee, 1977—. Mem. Internat. Assn. Schs. Social Work, Council Social Work Edn., Nat. Assn. Social Workers. Author articles, monographs in field. Office: San Diego State U San Diego CA 92182

DAVIS, JACQUELINE MARIE VINCENT (MRS. LOUIS REID DAVIS), educator; b. Birmingham, Ala.; d. Jud Fred and Marie (Yates) Vincent; A.B. cum laude, Birmingham-So. Coll., 1943; M.A., Columbia U., 1950; M.S., U. Ala., 1958, Ed.D., 1961; postgrad. U. Va., George Washington U.; m. Louis Reid Davis, July 17, 1943. Tchr., Fork Union (Va.) Mil. Acad., 1943-46, Ft. Belvoir, Va., 1946-48; tchr., adminstrv. asst., supr. Quantico (Va.) Post Schs., 1950-52; instr., prof. dept. child devel. and family life U. Ala. Sch. Home Econs., 1952-57, asso. prof., 1957-67, prof. child devel., dir. Child Devel. Center, 1967—, mem. grad. council, adminstr. head start tng. program; dir. Ala. Presch. Inst., 1964—; mem. NASA scholarship selection bd. U. Ala., 1966; mem. Gov.'s Adv. Com. on Day Care, 1963-66; mem. State Adv. Com. on Children and Youth, 1960—; coordinator Head Start supplementary tng. programs State of Ala. Adviser, mem. selection com. Tombigbee council Girl Scouts U.S.A., 1961-66; cons. Tuscaloosa Community Action Program, 1965-66. Mem. Nat. Assn. Edn. of Young Children (planning bd. 1963-64), U.S. Nat. Com. Early Childhood Edn., World Orgn. Early Childhood Edn., Southeastern Council Family Relations, So. (pres. 1961, mem. exec. bd. 1961—, chmn. 19th ann. conf.), Ala. (pres. 1963-64) assns. children under six, Ala. Home Econs. Assn. (chmn. profl. sect. family life and child devel. 1963—, v.p., mem. governing bd. 1969-70), Comparative Edn. Soc., NEA, Am. Home Econs. Assn., Phi Beta Kappa, Kappa Delta Pi, Kappa Delta Epsilon. Methodist. Contbr. articles to profl. jours. Home: 47 Guilds Wood Tuscaloosa AL 35401 Office: PO Box 1211 University AL 35486

DAVIS, JAN, educator; b. Corpus Christi, Tex., June 29, 1943; d. Reuben T. and Ruby (Englert) Pattillo; A.A., Del Mar Coll., 1963; B.A., U. Houston, 1965; teaching cert. S.W. Tex. State U., 1971; m. William A. Davis, Dec. 26, 1964; children—William A., Wade. Tchr., Edna (Tex.) Jr. High Sch., 1966-67, counselor, 1967-68; tchr. Pleasanton (Tex.) High Sch., 1972—; mem. Pleasanton Public Schs. Supt.'s Com., 1975-77, 78-79; chmn. social studies dept. Pleasanton Public Schs., 1976—. Leader 4-H, 1978-80. Mem. Tex. Classroom Tchrs. Assn. (Tchr. of Year 1979), Pleasanton Classroom Tchrs. Assn. Roman Catholic. Clubs: Pleasanton Jr. Woman's (1st v.p. 1976, pres. 1977), A&M Women's of Atascosa County (Tex.) (pres. 1978-80). Home: Route 1 100 Parsons Rd Pleasanton TX 78064 Office: 831 Stadium Dr Pleasanton TX 78064

DAVIS, JOAN, employment/human resources co. exec.; b. Ft. Worth, Nov. 1, 1952; d. David Howard and Betty Joan (Beck) D.; student U. Tex., Arlington, 1970, Tarrant County Jr. Coll., Ft. Worth, 1971. With Businessmen's Personnel Service, Dallas, 1975-76, mgr. businessmen's personnel, 1976; a founder Diversified Human Resources Group, Inc., Dallas, 1976, Western regional mgr., Los Angeles, 1981—, v.p. sales and prodn., 1982—. Recipient various co. awards. Mem. Nat. Assn. Personnel Cons., Am. Soc. Profl. and Exec. Women, Santa Monica C. of C. Office: 304 Grand Venice CA 90291

DAVIS, JOAN CHRISTIE, writer, cons.; b. Astoria, N.Y.; d. Joseph Francis and Alice Alvina (Plante) Christie; B.A. (Regents scholar), Manhattanville Coll., 1947; 1 son, Michael Evan. Dir. community programming Fgn. Policy Assn., N.Y.C., 1966-77; dir. devel. and alumni affairs Columbia U. Sch. Social Work, 1977-82; free-lance writer, cons., 1982—; program dir. U.S. Com. for Refugees, Cath. Relief Services, U.S. Com. Resettlement of Displaced Profls., 1954-63. Mem. AAUW, Women in Communications. Democrat. Roman Catholic. Contbr. articles to America, Cath. Lawyer. Home: 3200 Park Ave Bridgeport CT 06604

DAVIS, JOYCE CORALIE, mfg. co. exec.; b. N.Y.C., Jan. 7, 1925; d. Samuel Stanley and Florence Leonore (Hay) D.; B.A. in Bus. Adminstrn., St. John's U., Jamaica, N.Y., 1946; postgrad. Katherine Gibbs Sch.; m. Paul L. Roberts, Oct. 5, 1966 (div. 1979); children—Paula Lenore, Bruce Linwood, Valerie Elizabeth. Sec., St. Philip's Episcopal Ch., N.Y.C., 1946-57; with Union Carbide Corp., 1958—, mgr. office and clerical staff, chems. and plastics div., N.Y.C., 1973-76, mgr. profl. recruiting, EEO, agrl. products div., 1976, mgr. compensation, 1976—. Mem. Corp. Women's Network, Assn. Female Execs., Nat. Assn. Negro Women, Gamma Phi Delta (past chpt. pres.). Democrat. Episcopalian. Home: Old Hawleyville Rd Bethel CT 06801 Office: Old Ridgebury Rd Danbury CT 06810

DAVIS, KAREN RUTH, ready to wear designer, sculptor, painter; b. Santiago, Chile, May 21, 1950 (patents Am. citizens); d. Arthur Horace, Jr. and Marion Esther Davis; student Art Students League, 1968, 71, 72, Chelsea Art Sch., London, 1969; student welding Hicio Isolani, 1972; lic. in welding Roberts Tech. and Trade Sch., 1973-74; m. Eric Heller, 1970; 1 dau., Tasha. Designer, producer for boutiques, San Francisco, 1967; painter, Ibiza, Spain and Tangiers, Morocco, 1970; designer, producer Ace, London, 1971; designer Karen Davis Designs, N.Y.C., 1972; apprentice with Lito Cavalcante, welder, 1974-75; created lines for Kensington Blue, also Henri Bendel, Bloomingdales, N.Y.C., 1976; owner, pres. Havona Design Studios, N.Y.C., 1975—. Mem. Mchts. Assn., Citizens Community Police Assn. (pres.), Soho Bus. Assn. (chmn. 1982). Address: 110 Thompson St New York NY 10012

DAVIS, LILLIAN JUANITA, hosp. adminstr.; b. N.Y.C., Jan. 20, 1943; d. Charles and Elva (Sinclair) D.; B.A. in Sociology, CCNY, 1974; M.P.A. (Martin Luther King fellow), N.Y. U., 1976; children—Crystal Cook, Talmadge Cook. Adminstrv. resident N.Y.C. Health and Hosp. Corp., Morrisania Neighborhood Family Care Center, 1975-76, asst. dir., 1976-80; planner Richard A. Harrow Mgmt. Cons. & Assos., 1980-81; dep. dir. Dr. Martin Luther King, Jr., Health Center, Bronx, N.Y., 1981—; chmn. I'm O.K. Health Fair, 1978-79; cons. religious com. on health Riverside Ch.; mem. dep. mayor's task force for South Bronx immunization campaign. Bd. dirs. Bronx Residents to Attain Sponsorship for Housing, 1978—; sec. IPS No. 1 Sch. Bd., 1970-72. Recipient spl. recognition award Rafael Hernandez Bilingual Sch., 1978, cert. of merit N.Y.C. Nat. Work Study Recruitment Program, 1980. Mem. Am. Coll. Hosp. Adminstrs., Am. Hosp. Assn., Am. Public Health Assn., Nat. Assn. Female Execs., Nat. Assn. Health Service Execs. (treas. NE Region chpt.), Nat. Assn. Neighborhood Health Centers, Hosp. Execs., Nat. Black Health Planning Assn., Inc. Home: 105 03 223d St Queens Village NY 11429 Office: 3674 3d Ave Bronx NY 10456

DAVIS, LINDA JANE, gerontologist, occupational therapist; b. Oakland, Calif., Oct. 26, 1939; d. Stanley Spencer and Martha Madeline (Kerwin) D.; B.A., Mills Coll., 1960; M.P.H., U. Mich., 1970, Ph.D., 1974. Research scientist, dir. program in health gerontology Sch. Public Health, U. Mich., 1974-76; research project dir. Phila. Geriatric Center, 1976-79; asst. prof. health related professions and occupational therapy U. So. Calif., 1979—; cons. Pa. Dept. Public Welfare. Served to capt. USNR. Gerontol. Soc. Research fellow, 1976; cert. registered occupational therapist, 1961. Mem. Gerontol. Soc., Western Gerontol. Soc., Am. Occupational Therapy Assn., Am. Public Health Assn. Author: Rape and Older Women: A Guide to Prevention and Protection, 1979; Blood Pressure Control: A Beginning in Detroit, 1975. Office: 12933 Erickson Ave Bldg 30 Downey CA 90242

DAVIS, LOTTIE MAE, educator; b. Lake Providence, La., Nov. 17, 1920; d. Albert Lee and Susie (Harris) Dellar; A.B., Harris-Stowe Coll., 1965; M.A., U. Mo., St. Louis, 1972; m. Calvin Davis, Aug. 9, 1943; children—Vickie, Aurelia, Toni, Denise, Loretta. Tchr. 3d grade, public schs., St. Louis, 1965-72, tchr. 6th grade, 1972-73, tchr. 7th grade, 1973-75; resource tchr. Hempstead Sch., St. Louis, 1975—. Mem. Internat. Reading Assn., Mo. State Tchrs. Assn., Council Exceptional Children, U. Mo. St. Louis Alumnae, Delta Sigma Theta. Democrat. Baptist. Co-author: Profiles in Silhouette, 1981. Address: 10118 Monorch Dr Saint Louis MO 63136

DAVIS, LOUISE MATTOCKS, banker; b. Onslow County, N.C., July 27, 1936; d. William Percy and Rinda Freeman (Howard) Mattocks; Ph.D. in Banking, Bank Regional Tng. Center, 1977; m. Alton C. Davis, July 27, 1955; 1 son, Michael Alton (dec.). Bookkeeper, First Citizens Bank, Camp Lejeune, N.C., 1954-55; with First Citizens Bank & Trust Co., Swansboro, N.C., 1955—, ops. mgr., internal control officer, 1975—. Treas. Onslow County chpt. Cystic Fibrosis; chmn. Swansboro Mullet Festival; past treas. Swansboro Booster Club. Recipient award Onslow County, 1977. Mem. Am. Bus. Women's Assn. (pres. Swansboro chpt., Woman of Yr. award 1974, 78, Boss of Yr. award 1976), Nat. Assn. Bank Women (treas.), N.C. Bankers Assn. Democrat. Baptist. Club: Moose (Swansboro). Home: PO Box 1201 Swansboro NC 28584

DAVIS, LUCY ELIZABETH TOLBERT, educator, psychologist; b. Greenville, S.C., May 10, 1925; d. Joseph Augustus and Margaret (Shirley) Tolbert; B.A., Erskine Coll., 1946; M.A., Columbia, 1948, Ph.D., 1955; m. Ron Willson Davis, Aug. 28, 1948; children—Ronald Redd, Margaret Willson, Elisabeth Southard. Guidance-testing counselor New Trier High Sch., Winnetka, Ill., 1948-50, psychologist, coordinator spl. services Bucks County Schs., 1955-64; research assoc. Ednl. Research Council of Greater Cleve., 1964-67; research assoc., editor N.C. Commn. on Public Sch. System of N.C., 1967-68; ednl. coordinator Therapeutic edn. program Duke U. Med. Ctr. and Durham (N.C.) County Schs., 1968-70, asst. prof. edn., 1970-71, assoc. prof., 1972—, chmn. edn. program, 1982—; clin. assoc. psychiatry, Duke Med. Ctr., 1972; cons. N.C. Bd. Edn.; editor state commn. reports. Mem. coms. for Episcopal Ch.; active fund-raising drives Heart Fund, Am. Cancer Soc. Lic. psychologist, N.C. Mem. Am. Psychol. Assn., Nat. Assn. for Sch. Psychology, Nat. Council for Register of Health Providers, Inter-Univ. Council for Sch. Psychology (chmn.), Am. Sch. Counselor Assn. (chmn. nat. program), Pi Lambda Theta, Kappa Delta Pi, Delta Kappa Gamma. Contbr. numerous articles to profl. jours. Home: 705 Gimghoul Rd Chapel Hill NC 27514 Office: W Duke Bldg Duke U Durham NC 27707

DAVIS, LYNN C. BACKER, speech and lang. pathologist; b. Sussex, N.J., Oct. 7, 1952; d. Albert D. and Grace (Weil) Backer; student Butler U., 1970-72; B.S., SUNY, Geneseo, 1974; M.S., Coll. of St. Rose, Albany, N.Y., 1977; m. Gary R. Davis, June 16, 1973; 1 son, Justin Louis. Speech and lang. pathologist spl. edn. div. Bd. Coop. Ednl. Services of Albany, Schenectady and Schoharie Counties, Albany, 1977—. Lic. profl. speech pathologist, N.Y. State; permanent cert. in speech and hearing handicapped, N.Y. State. Mem. Am. Speech, Lang. and Hearing Assn. (cert. clin. competence), Capitol Area Speech and Hearing Assn. Office: Bd Coop Ednl Services Spl Edn Div at Maywood Sch 1979 Central Ave Albany NY 12205

DAVIS, MARGARET MANN, med. technologist; b. Hutchinson, Kan., July 16, 1936; d. George G. and Kathryn L. (Duvall) Mann; A.A., Colo. Woman's Coll., 1956; B.S., U. Denver, 1958; M.A., Central Mich. U., 1979; m. Jerry Brooks Davis, June 23, 1957; children—Lisa Kay, Kent Fonti, Kevin Duvall. Med. technologist Presbyn. Med. Center, Denver, 1961-73, micro supr., 1963-69, lab. computer coordinator, 1969-73; micro supr. Rose Med. Center, Denver, 1974-75, lab. computer coordinator, 1975-76; product specialist Spear Med. Systems, 1976-77, originator outpatient lab. services, Rose Med. Center, 1978-80; sales rep. Vitek Systems, Inc., Lakewood, Colo., 1980—. Leader, Girl Scouts U.S.A., 1968-70; deacon Presbyn. Ch., 1968-71. Mem. Am. Soc. Clin. Pathologists, Am. Soc. Med. Tech., Am. Mgmt. Assn., Am. Micro. Soc. Delta Gamma. Presbyterian. Clubs: Rebbkah, Colo. Woman's Coll. Alumni (rec. sec. 1966-67, pres. 1967-68). Contbr. articles to profl. jours. Home: 3056 Nelson Ct Lakewood CO 80215

DAVIS, MARGY-RUTH, human rights assn. exec.; b. N.Y.C., Mar. 20, 1949; d. Henry J. and Alice F. Greenbaum; A.B., Barnard Coll., 1970; postgrad. City U. N.Y., 1970-72; m. Perry I. Davis, Sept. 11, 1973; children—Rena Ariela, Chaim Jacob, Josepha Abigail. Founding asst. dir. Greater N.Y. Conf. on Soviet Jewry, N.Y.C., 1971-74, asso. dir., 1974-76, exec. dir., 1976—; founder, coordinator Solidarity Sunday for Soviet Jewry, 1971-79; founding dir. Inst. for Jewish Experience, 1980—. Co-chairperson Salute to Israel Parade, N.Y.C., 1970-71, hon. grand marshal, 1972-80; chairperson N.Am. Jewish Youth Council, 1970-71; mem. exec. bd. N.Y. chpt. Am. Jewish Com.; bd. dirs. Union Orthodox Jewish Congregations Am., 1978—; Mem. Assn. Jewish Community Relations Workers, Am. Jewish Public Relations Soc. Columnist: Jewish Week, 1977-80.

DAVIS, MARIAN BELLE, former museum curator, educator; b. St. Louis County, Mo., Sept. 24, 1911; d. John William and Frances Edith (Walters) D.; A.B., Washington U., St. Louis, 1932, M.A., 1935, postgrad., 1935-36; M.A., Radcliffe Coll., 1939, Ph.D., 1948. Mus. instr. Worcester (Mass.) Art Mus., 1941-44; instr. U. Tex., Austin, 1944-45, asst. prof. art, 1946-50, asso. prof., 1950-60, prof., 1960-78, prof. emeritus, 1978—, chief curator Univ. Art. Mus., 1963-78. Alice Longfellow fellow, 1940-41; U. Tex. at Austin grantee, 1951. Mem. Renaissance Soc., Coll. Art Assn. (editorial advisory bd. Coll. Art Jour., 1953-60, dir., 1951-55), Soc. Archtl. Historians, Archeol. Inst. Am., Nat. Trust, Phi Beta Kappa. Unitarian. Contbr. numerous articles, book and exhbn. revs. to art and hist. jours., to catalogues. Home: 2701 Wooldridge Dr Austin TX 78703 *

DAVIS, MARION PEASE (MRS. PAUL DAVIS), social work adminstr.; b. Derby, Conn., Oct. 9, 1918; d. John Wood and Myrtle Stowe (Humphrey) Pease; B.A. in Psychology, U. Bridgeport (Conn.), 1964; M.S.W., U. Conn., 1969; m. Paul Davis, Oct. 15, 1938; children—Linda Davis Payne, Robert, Richard. Caseworker, Conn. Welfare Dept., Bridgeport, 1964-65, social worker protective service dept., 1965-67, supr. protective service unit, 1969-73, sr. psychiat. social worker, 1973-75, supervisory psychiat. social worker, 1975-78; dir. psychiat. social workers Greater Bridgeport Community Mental Health Center, 1973-82, chmn. housing com., 1974-78, mem. accreditation com., 1974-78, chmn., 1978-81, psychiat. social work chief, 1978-82; pvt. practice, 1982—. Mem. Nat. Assn. Social Workers (exec. com. 1974-75, editorial com. 1975-77), Am. Assn. Marriage Family Counsellors (asso.), Huxley Inst. Biosocial Research (v.p., dir. 1978-81), Conn. Assn. Human Services, Mental Health Services Coordinating Com. (rec. sec., exec. com. 1975—, corr. sec. 1978—), Nat. Assn. Social Work Register Clin. Social Workers.

DAVIS, MARJORIE ALICE, city ofcl.; b. Newton, Mass., July 1, 1917; d. Herbert Francis and Harriet Cole (Dodge) Parmenter; A.B., Wellesley Coll., 1939; spl. grad. student Radcliffe Coll., 1941; cert. Harvard U., 1940; spl. courses in social work Boston U., 1961-62; m. Charles William Davis, Aug. 31, 1940 (dec.); children—Harriet Parmenter, Charles Edwin II. Exec. dir. Mid-Essex Area council Girl Scouts U.S.A., South Hamilton, Mass., 1952-59, Greater Lynn council, 1959-63, Merrimack River council, Andover, Mass., 1963-80; mem. Wenham Bd. Selectmen, 1972—, chmn., 1977—. Mem. Met. Area Planning Council, 1975—, Mass. Com. Criminal Justice, 1974; exec. dir. Essex County Greenbelt Assn., 1980; mem. Salem (Mass.) prime sponsor adv. council CETA, 1980—; bd. dirs. North Shore Family Planning Council, 1981, treas., 1982—; mem. ct./Community Relations Com. for Essex County, 1975; pres. Hamilton-Wenham Community Service, 1970-80; sec. United Fund of Central North Shore, 1969—; pres. Hamilton-Wenham Vis. Nurses Assn., 1963-73; v.p. Mass. chpt. Children Am. Revolution, 1944; mem. Republican Town Com. Mem. Mass. Selectmen's Assn., Women Elected Mcpl. Ofcls., Mass. Mcpl. Assn. Episcopalian. Clubs: Harvard (Boston); Singing Beach (Manchester, Mass.). Home: 143 Grapevine Rd Wenham MA 01984

DAVIS, MARJORIE FRY, patron of arts; b. Natchez, Miss.; d. Louis and Regina G. Fry; student Newcomb Coll., 1936-40; m. Walter Davis, June 15, 1939; children—Patricia, Walter III, Rodney. Exhibits pvt. collection art to benefit small communities. Trustee, Met. Arts Council of New Orleans, New Orleans Mus. of Art, La. Arts and Sci. Center, Washington Opera, La. Arts Council, La. State Mus.; bd. dirs. Women's Com., New Orleans Symphony, New Orleans Women's Opera Guild, Davis Family Fund; bd. dirs. New Orleans Speech and Hearing Clinic, also v.p.; bd. dirs. Council of Arts for Children, New Orleans Ballet; mem. adv. bd. Sculpture Garden, New Orleans City Hall; mem. Pres.'s Com. for Preservation of White House; nat. patron Am. Fedn. Art; mem. Met. Opera Council. Mem. Smithsonian Soc., Golden Circle of Kennedy Center. Clubs: Plimsoll, International House. Home: 1819 Octavia St New Orleans LA 70115 Office: PO Box 6099 New Orleans LA 70174

DAVIS, MARJORIE MAY, developmental anatomist; b. Elkhart, Kans., Mar. 13, 1935; d. Harry and Lena (Lunsford) Smith; B.S. in Biology, Panhandle State U., 1959; M.A. in Zoology, Kans. U., 1962; Ph.D. in Developmental Anatomy and Reproductive Physiology, Kans. State U., 1970; m. Gerald Wade Davis; 1 son, Roger. Instr. dept. of biology Mankato (Minn.) State U., 1962-69; part time instr. Kans. State U., 1964-69, vis. asst. prof., 1971-75; asst. prof. biology Mo. Western Coll., St. Joseph, 1969-71; asst. prof. anatomy Okla. Coll. Osteo. Medicine and Surgery, Tulsa, 1975—; part time faculty Tulsa Jr. Coll.; vol. tchr. planned parenthood. Pres. local PTA, 1966; pres. Modern Oklahomans for Retention of Abortion Rights; curriculum com. YWCA and Planned Parenthood program for teenagers, edn. com. local Planned Parenthood. Mem. AAAS, Soc. for Study of Reproduction, Am. Soc. Zoologists, Kans. Acad. Scis., Okla. Acad. Scis., N.Y. Acad. Scis., Sigma Xi. Methodist. Author: Human Anatomy Lab. Manual, intro. to Gen. Biology Lab. Manual. Home: 3816 E 105th St Tulsa OK 74136 Office: 1111 W 17th St Tulsa OK 74101

DAVIS, MARTHA JANE, civic worker; b. Fairmont, W.Va., Dec. 3, 1923; d. John Ward and Louise Lloyd Brown; B.M., Peabody Conservatory Music, 1941; A.A., Ellen Cushing Jr. Coll., 1942; m. Denver J. Davis, June 9, 1943; children—Connie Jean, John. Exec. bd. Women's Missionary Union, S.C., 1960-66, Md., 1967-69; chaplain Gaffney (S.C.) chpt. DAR, 1958-66, sec. Col. William Preston chpt., Roanoke, Va., 1974-77; regent, 1977-80; asst. to chaplain Friendship Manor, Roanoke, 1980—; active S.C. Mental Health Assn., S.W. Va. chpt. Multiple Sclerosis. Baptist. Club: Garden. Contbr. articles to religious and other publs. Home: 3225 Londonderry Ln SW Roanoke VA 24018

DAVIS, MARY ALYCE, constrn. co. exec., city ofcl.; b. Austin, Tex., Mar. 4, 1927; d. William Cornelius and Jimmie Elaine (Copeland) Hudson; student UCLA, 1945-46, Citrus Jr. Coll., 1951-52; m. William Earl Davis, Dec. 17, 1949; children—Linda Alyce, Billie Sue, Judith Ann, Teresa Marie. With Coast Guard Hdqrs., Washington, 1946-48; drapery hardware mfg. co., Glendora, Calif., 1957-62; with Giannini Controls Co., Monrovia, Calif., 1962-64, Koger Properties, Jacksonville, Fla., 1964-70; rec. sec. City of Jacksonville Beach (Fla.), 1972—, mem. planning-zoning bd., 1972—, mem. civil service bd., 1972—; with WED-CO, Inc., electric utility constrn. co., Jacksonville, 1974—, sec.-treas., 1974—. Fin. officer Valiant Air Command Bd., 1980—. Recipient various flower show design awards; cert. nationally accredited flower show judge Nat. Council State Garden Clubs. Mem. Fla. Fedn. Garden Clubs (life), Am. Bus. and Profl. Women's Assn. Democrat. Presbyterian. Clubs: Jacksonville Beach Woman's; Ribault Garden (pres. 1977-79). Home: 4228 Coquina Dr Jacksonville Beach FL 32250 Office: WED-CO Inc 3031 Herring Rd Jacksonville FL 32216

DAVIS, MARY FRANCES, oil and gas prodn. co. exec.; b. Wilson, Tex., Aug. 28, 1920; d. John Pascal and Esther Lou (Pennington) Turner; student Tex. Technol. U., 1950; m. Richard A. Bird, June 5, 1937 (div.); children—Mary Frances II, Joan Gail, Carolyn Jay, Richard A. Cashier, Walgreen's, Lubbock, Tex., 1946-49; owner, operator real estate co., Lubbock, 1948-50; owner, operator oil field supply and sporting goods store, Lovington, N.Mex., 1950-61; cashier, office worker May Co., Denver, 1962; bookkeeper Gordon M. Cone, ind. oil operator, Lovington, 1965—; mgr. Southwestern Oil Co., Inc., 1967—; mgr., sec.-treas. Southwestern, Inc., Lovington, 1970—. Mem. Lovington Public Library Bd.; active various Heart Fund, Cancer, March of Dimes drives. Mem. Nat. Fedn. Bus. and Profl. Women (Lovington Woman of Yr. 1977-78, Dist. III Woman of Yr. 1977-78). Republican. Methodist. Clubs: Prairie-Lea Grandmother, Susana Guild (Lovington); Altrusa (Humanities award 1979). Home: 1316 W Polk Ave Lovington NM 88260 Office: 208 E Washington PO Box 1116 Lovington NM 88260

DAVIS, MARY SMITH, hotel exec.; b. San Diego, June 10, 1928; d. John Wesley and Susye Belle (Crume) Smith; student public schs. Real estate saleswoman, 1950-56; race car driver, test driver Chrysler Corp., 1957-64; stunt car driver MGM Studios, 1958-60; founder, v.p. Portofino, Redondo Beach, Calif., 1961-63, pres., gen. mgr., 1963—; dir. Bay Cities Nat. Bank. Chmn. Harbor Rev. Bd., 1979-81; adv. bd. Salvation Army, 1979—; bd. dirs. Redondo Beach Round Table, South Bay Cancer Found.; mem. Redondo Beach Beautification Com., 1979—. Served with USMCR, 1944-45. Mem. Redondo Beach C. of C. Republican. Baptist. Clubs: Jockey, Touch, Pips, Portofino Yacht. Address: 260 Portofino Way Redondo Beach CA 90277

DAVIS, MARYLEE, univ. adminstr.; b. Kingsport, Tenn., Sept. 17; d. Harold Jefferson and Lydia Lee (Bloomer) D.; B.S. magna cum laude, U. Tenn., 1965, M.S., 1970; Ph.D. in Adminstrn. and Higher Edn., Mich. State U., 1974. Tchr., Kingsport, Tenn., 1965-69; asst. head resident U. Tenn., 1969-70; grad. asst. Mich. State U., 1970-71, mem. adminstrv. staff, 1971—, assoc. prof. coll. and univ. adminstrn., 1979—, asst. v.p. adminstrn. and public affairs, 1978—; chmn. task force to explore feasibility of external degree program for Mich., Mich. Dept. Edn., 1975-77. Pres. Mich. Capitol Area Girl Scouts Council, 1982—; charter mem. agy. relations com. Mich. Statewide Extension Council United Way, 1982—, vice chmn. Capital Area, 1982-83; adv. bd. East Lansing Salvation Army, 1982—; co-chmn. Diana awards com. East Lansing YWCA, 1982. Recipient Service award Mich. State U. Coop. Extension Service, 1977, cert. merit Diana Dinner, Lansing, 1977, award excellence Mich. State U. Faculty Women's Assn., 1980. Mem. Am. Assn. Higher Edn., Nat. Assn. Women Deans, Counselors and Adminstrs., Am. Assn. Higher Edn., Phi Delta Kappa. Club: East Lansing Zonta (past pres.). Home: 6223 Cobblers Dr East Lansing MI 48823 Office: 484 Adminstrn Bldg Mich State U East Lansing MI 48824

DAVIS, MATILDA SUTTON, assn. exec.; b. Washington, Sept. 1, 1945; d. Alphonso Lafayette and Alice Beatrice (Covington) Sutton; B.A., Antioch Coll., 1977; 1 son, Eric Davis; foster children—Billy Carpenter, Mary Carpenter, Melissa Carpenter. Coordinator program services Liberation for Ex-Offenders Through Employment Opportunities, Washington, 1978-79; client rep. Dist. Line Fin. Center, Washington, 1972—; dir. adminstrv. services Am. Nurses' Assn., Washington, 1980—; prin. Mattie Davis, cons., Washington. Active Washington chpt. People United To Save Humanity. Mem. Nat. Assn. Female Execs., Am. Soc. Profl. and Exec. Women. Club: Met. Women's Dem. (Washington). Home: 1406 Emerson St NW Washington DC 20011 Office: 1101 14th St NW Suite 200 Washington DC 20005

DAVIS, MATTIE BELLE EDWARDS, ret. county judge; b. Ellabell, Ga., Feb. 28, 1910; d. Frank Pierce and Eddie (Morgan) Edwards; student law in law office; m. Troy Carson Davis, June 6, 1937 (dec. Aug. 1948); stepchildren—Jane (Mrs. Robert Gordon Potter), Betsy (Mrs. James W. Clark, Jr.). Legal sec., 1927-36; admitted to Fla. bar, 1936, U.S. Supreme Ct. bar, 1950; practice with husband in Miami, 1936-48; pvt. practice, Miami, 1948-59; judge Met. Ct. Dade County Fla., 1959-72, County Ct. Dade County, 1973-80. Mem. exec. com. Women's Conf. Nat. Safety Council 1960-80, chmn., 1968-70; bd. dirs. Nat. Safety Council, 1965, v.p. women, 1973-80; mem. Fla. Gov.'s Hwy. Safety Com., 1970-81; mem. Nat. Hwy. Safety Adv. Com., 1967-71; mem. registrants adv. bd. SSS World War II; pres. Dade County Tb Assn., 1960-62; exec. com. Fla. Tb and Respiratory Disease Assn., 1960-66; pres. Haven Sch. Mentally Retarded, 1958-60, sec., 1960-69; trustee Andrew Coll., Cuthbert, Ga., 1960-81. Mem. Nat. (treas. 1961-62, corr. sec. 1962-63, v.p. 1963-64, pres. 1965-66), Fla. (pres. 1957-58) assns. women lawyers, Am. (ho. of dels. 1967-75, 77—), Dade County bar assns., Fla. Bar, Internat. Fedn. Women Lawyers, Nat. Assn. Women Judges (a founder), Miami Bus. and Profl. Women's Club (pres. 1952-54), Nat. Fedn. Bus. and Profl. Women's Clubs (dir. dist. Fla. 1956-57), Kappa Beta Pi. Democrat. Methodist (supt. Sunday sch. 1948-54, chmn. ofcl. bd. 1957-60, trustee 1952-67, adminstrv. bd. 1968—). Club: Zonta Internat. Home: 402 Como Ave Coral Gables FL 33146 *

DAVIS, MICHELE STAR, educator; b. Auburn, Ind., Dec. 31, 1946; d. Robert Emmett and April Dawn (Bowser) Davis; B.A. summa cum laude, St. Francis Coll., 1970; M.A., Purdue U., 1972, Ph.D., 1979; m. Richard D. Watman, Sept. 13, 1981. Teaching asst. Purdue U., West Lafayette, Ind., 1970-72, grad. instr., 1973-77; lectr. Ohio State U., Columbus, 1979-80, instr., 1980—, faculty adv. La Hermandad Latina (club for Hispanic students), founder, dir. Teatro Unidad, dir. Ohio State U. summer Spanish Lang. Camp, 1982; leader seminars, workshops Office Hispanic Student Programs, 1979-82. Leader cultural presentations to elem., jr. high and high sch. students through Internat. Council of Mid Ohio. Recipient Hermandad Latina and MECHA award, Ohio State U., 1981. Mem. Am. Assn. Tchrs. of Spanish and Portuguese, Ohio Theatre Affiliation, Ohio Community Theatre Assn., Am. Council of Tchrs. of Fgn. Lang., MLA. Author: A Dramatist and His Characters, 1982; Un Don Juan del Siglo XX: El Conquistador Conquistado, 1981; Del Realismo a la Vanguardia en Tres Dramaturgos Hispanoamericanos, 1981; Dreams and Reflections: The Cycle of Human Existence. Two Plays by Dantes and Giovaninetti; contbr. articles to profl. jours. Home: 29 W Tulane Rd Apt C Columbus OH 43202 Office: 1841 Millikin Rd Columbus OH 43210

DAVIS, MIRIAM DELORES, state social services adminstr.; b. Salisbury, N.C., Oct. 28, 1936; d. Sanford Reid and Rachael Miller (Turner) D.; A.B., Lenoir-Rhyne Coll., 1959; M.S.W., U. N.C., 1969. Dir. Christian edn. St. Andrew's Luth. Ch., Hickory, N.C., 1959-61; child welfare worker Stanly County Dept. Social Services, Albemarle, N.C., 1961-65; child welfare supr. Catawba County Dept. Social Services, Newton, N.C., 1965-66; day care cons. N.C. State Div. Social Services, Raleigh, 1966-70, field services rep., 1970—. Mem. Child Welfare League Am. (planning com. 1971-73, 80—), Am. Public Welfare Assn. (task force on children 1975-76), Acad. Cert. Social Workers, Nat. Assn. Social Workers, N.C. Social Service Assn., N.C. State Employees

Assn. Democrat. Lutheran. Club: Pilot Internat. Home: 1205 Southwood Dr Newton NC 28658

DAVIS, MIRIAM MCGLAMRY, accountant; b. Elmore County, Ala., Nov. 4, 1934; d. Samuel Cobb and Rosa B. (Ernest) McGlamry; student U. Ala., Montgomery, 1966, Auburn U., 1980-81; children—S. Matthew, J. Mark, Morgan S. Acct., sec./treas. Hargrove Supply Co., Montgomery, Ala., 1956-80, now dir.; acct. Gilpin Brokerage Co., Montgomery, 1980-81; acct./office mgr. Copeland, Franco, Screws & Gill, P.A., Montgomery, 1981—. Mem. Am. Soc. Women Accts. (treas./bd. dirs.), Ala. Assn. Credit Execs., Montgomery Assn. Credit Execs. (bd. dirs.). Home: 113 Sterling Dr Montgomery AL 36109 Office: 444 S Perry St Montgomery AL 36101

DAVIS, OLIVE MCFATE, trade show exec.; b. Oakland, Calif., Nov. 16, 1922; d. Thomas Albert and Leana Jewel (Combs) McFate; student Inst. Orgnl. Mgmt., 1980-81; m. Warren L. Davis, Jan. 18, 1942 (dec. 1976); children—Jean, Patricia, Larry, Allan, Bonnie. Partner with husband in farming, Calif., 1943-69; newspaper corr. Stockton (Calif.) Record, 1968-73; urban 4-H coordinator, San Joaquin County, Stockton, 1973; writer-researcher S.T. & E. R.R., Stockton, 1974-76; coordinator Central Valley Agrl. Expo, Stockton, 1976-77; trade show exec. Stockton C. of C., 1976—. Chmn. Stockton Cultural Heritage Bd., 1981-82; regional dir. Am. Field Service, 1970-73; pres. 4-H Leaders Council, 1956; bd. dirs. Linden Devel. Commn., 1975, Linden Peters C. of C., 1974-77. Named Citizen of Year, Linden Lions, 1973. Mem. Nat. League Am. Pen Women, Nat. Assn. Agrl. Mktg., San Joaquin County Hist. Soc. (pres. 1981-82), Calif. Hist. Soc. Club: Linden Garden. Author: Slow Tired & Easy Railroad, 1976. Office: 1105 N El Dorado St Stockton CA 95202

DAVIS, OLIVIA ANNE CARR (MRS. TOM LUCIAN DAVIS), author; b. Leeds, Eng., Dec. 4, 1922; d. Henry Marvell and Olive Frances Kate (Rumble) Carr; student pvt. sch., pvt. tutors; m. Tom Lucian Davis, Oct. 13, 1943; children—Sebastian, Miranda, Penelope. Came to U.S., 1951, naturalized, 1956. Sec., Mil. Intelligence, War Office, London and Oxford, Eng., 1941-44. Recipient Emily Clark Balch award Va. Quar. Rev., 1969. Mem. Authors Guild, Smithsonian Resident Assos., Nat. Trust Historic Preservation, Audubon Soc. Author: The Last of the Greeks, 1968; The Steps of the Sun, 1972; The Scent of Apples, 1973; contbr. short stories to lit. quars. and anthologies in U.S. and abroad. Home: 6828 Floyd Ave Springfield VA 22150 Office: care Curtis Brown Ltd 575 Madison Ave New York NY 10022

DAVIS, PAT HADLEY, accountant, town commr.; b. Wilkes County, N.C., Aug. 16, 1926; d. Jack Alvis M. and Lucy (Vannoy) Hadley; A.A., Wilkes Community Coll., 1969; B. Bus. Tech., Appalachian State U., 1976; m. Brad F. Davis, Feb. 2, 1949 (dec.); children—Brad F., Patsy R. Asst. sec-treas. Foster-Sturdivant Co., 1964-69, Sturdivant Devel. Co., 1969-76; acct. Beacon Ins. Co., Wilkesboro, N.C., 1976-80; mgr. N.C. Profl. Credit Service, North Wilkesboro, 1980—; mem. North Wilkesboro Bd. Commrs., 1975-81, mayor pro-tem, 1977-79. Former mem. Democratic Exec. Com., vice chmn., 1973-79. Democrat. Methodist. Home: 1002 K St North Wilkesboro NC 28659 Office: 918 B St North Wilkesboro NC 28659

DAVIS, PHYLLIS BURKE, cosmetic co. exec.; b. Albany, N.Y., Dec. 24, 1931; d. J. Frank and Mary Catherine (Barnett) Burke; B.A., U. Vt., 1953; LL.D. (hon.), Babson Coll., 1974; m. Edmund R. Davis, Nov. 22, 1968. Account exec. Norman, Craig & Kummel Advt. Agy., N.Y.C., 1965-68; product counselor product mktg. Avon Products, Inc., N.Y.C., 1968-69, group product counselor product mktg., 1969-71, mgr. sales promotion, 1971, dir. sales promotion, 1971-72, v.p. sales promotion/advt., 1972-74, v.p. product mgmt., 1974-77, group v.p. product mgmt., 1977-81, group v.p. product quality and communications, 1981—; dir. Nabisco Brands, Inc., N.Y.C. Trustee U. Vt., 1982—. Recipient Cosmetic Woman Achiever of Yr. award Cosmetic Career Women, 1978, Econ. Equity award Women's Equity Action League, 1979; named to YWCA Acad. of Achievement, 1980. Office: 9 W 57th St New York NY 10019

DAVIS, POLLY ANN, historian; b. Pittsboro, Miss., Nov. 11, 1931; d. Robert Sidney and Olive Marie (Flanagan) Davis; B.A., Blue Mountain Coll., 1953; M.A., U. Miss., 1954; Ph.D. (So. Fellowships Fund dissertation fellow), U. Ky., 1963. Instr. social studies Bethel Coll., Hopkinsville, Ky., 1954-57; instr. history Western Ky. U., Bowling Green, 1961-62; chmn. dept. history and polit. sci. East Tex. Baptist Coll., Marshall, 1963—, asso. prof. history, 1963-68, prof., 1968—, div. chmn., 1964-79. Haggin scholar, 1957-59. Mem. Am. Hist. Assn., Soc. History Edn., Phi Alpha Theta (sponsor Pi Mu chpt. 1970—). Democrat. Baptist. Club: Coll. Women's. Author: Alben W. Barkley: Senate Majority Leader and Vice President, 1979; contbr. to profl. jours. Home: 4301 John Reagan St Marshall TX 75670 Office: N Grove St East Tex Baptist Coll Marshall TX 75670

DAVIS, RUTH ANN, interior designer; b. Centralia, Ill., Aug. 14, 1940; d. Emerson Howard and Olga (Hugo) D.; B.A. in Interior Design, U. Nebr., Omaha, 1970; M.A., Iowa State U., 1972; pupil of M. Alain Leisuitre, Paris. Pres. Ruth Ann Davis Interior Design Inc., Omaha, 1973—; vis. instr. contract interiors and hist. interiors U. Nebr., 1974—; guest lectr. U. Nebr., Iowa State U., U. Iowa; speaker on art deco; bd. dirs. Landmarks, Inc., Met. Arts Council Omaha; hon. bd. dirs., guest lectr. Miami Beach (Fla.) Design Preservation League; mem. Save the Astro Theater City Commn., Save WOW Bldg. Com. Mem. Am. Soc. Interior Designers (pres. Nebr./Iowa chpt. 1980-81, regional v.p. 1982-83), Nat. Trust Historic Preservation. Address: 3817 Dewey Ave Suite 1 Omaha NE 68105

DAVIS, RUTH MARGARET (MRS. BENJAMIN FRANKLIN LOHR), govt. ofcl.; b. Sharpsville, Pa., Oct. 19, 1928; d. W. George and Mary Anna (Ackermann) D.; B.A., Am. U., 1950; M.A., U. Md., 1952, Ph.D., 1955; m. Benjamin F. Lohr, Apr. 29, 1961. Statistician, FAO, UN, Washington, 1946-49, mathematician Nat. Bur. Standards, 1950-51, head ops. research div. David Taylor Model Basin, 1955-61, staff asst. office dir. def. research and engring. Dept. Def., 1961-67; asso. dir. research and devel. Nat. Library Medicine, 1967-68, dir. Lister Hill Nat. Center for Biomed. Communications, 1968-70; dir. Inst. Computer Scis. and Tech., Nat. Bur. Standards, 1970-77; dep. undersec. research and engring. Dept. Def., 1977-79; asst. sec. resource applications Dept. of Energy, 1979-81; pres. The Pymatuning Group, 1981—; dir. Comml. Credit Corp., United Telecomm Inc., Varian Assos.; trustee Con Edison, Aerospace Corp.; lectr. U. Md., 1955-57, Am. U., 1957-58; vis. prof. computer sci. U. Pitts., 1969-72; adj. prof., 1981—; cons. Office Naval Research, Washington, 1957-58. Mem. Md. Gov.'s Sci. Adv. Council, 1972-77; mem. Council of Library Resources; mem. nat. adv. council Electric Power Research Inst., 1972-79; bd. overseers Harvard U.; bd. dirs. Dartmouth Coll., Thayer Sch. Engring, 1980—, Sch. of Engring and Applied Sci. of U. Pa., 1981—. Fellow Soc. Info. Display; mem. AAAS, Am. Math. Soc., Math. Assn. Am., Washington Philos. Soc., Ops. Research Soc. Am., Nat. Acad. Engring., Nat. Acad. Pub. Adminstrn., Phi Kappa Phi, Sigma Pi Sigma. Contbr. articles to profl. jours. Home: 12720 Eldrid Pl Silver Spring MD 20904

DAVIS, SANDRA KAY, educator; b. El Paso, Tex., Nov. 10, 1949; d. Marvin Julius and Valerie Rosa (Taylor) Ward; B.S. in Edn., U. Tex., El Paso, 1971; M.S. in Guidance and Counseling, N.C. Central U., 1982; m. Edward Lamon Davis, Dec. 31, 1969; 1 dau., Tanya Lynn. Tchr. English, Carroll County Bd. Edn., Sykesville, Mo., 1971-73; engring. aide Carolina Power & Light Co., Raleigh, N.C., 1973-74; tchr. math. Raleigh (N.C.) Public Schs., 1974-76; remedial tchr. math. Cin. Public Schs., 1977-79; tchr. math. Chapel Hill (N.C.)-Carrboro City Schs., 1979-80, Lakeshore High Sch., Fulton County (Ga.) Sch. System, 1981-82. Sec., Black Feminist Orgn. Raleigh, 1976; vol. mental health, 1977. Recipient Most Helpful Tchr. award South Carroll High Sch., 1972. Mem. NEA, Am. Assn. Sex Educators, Counselors and Therapists, Math. Tchrs. Assn., Md. Tchrs. Assn., Ohio Educators Assn., Ga. Assn. Educators, Chapel Hill Assn. Educators. Home: 1430 Austin Rd SW Atlanta GA 30331

DAVIS, SARA JANE, utility co. exec.; b. Jackson, Mich., Feb. 24, 1948; d. Leonard William and Margery Barbara (Smith) Lashley; A.A. in Bus. Mgmt. and Data Processing, Lansing Community Coll., 1978; student Spring Arbor Coll., part-time 1978—; m. Don E. Davis, Jan. 4, 1974. Computer programmer Consumers Power Co., Jackson, 1968-79, computer analyst, 1979-82, supr. software services, 1982—, mem. info. systems tng. com., 1981—. Mem. Assn. for Systems Mgmt. Club: Nat. Fedn. Bus. and Profl. Women. Office: Consumers Power Co 1945 Parnall Rd Jackson MI 49201

DAVIS, SUE ANN, educator; b. Huntington, W.Va., Aug. 4, 1954; d. Darrell Duane and Sally Lou (Chapman) D.; B.A., Marshall U., 1975, M.A., 1978. Dental asst., Huntington, W.Va., 1973-74; asst. Marshall U., Huntington, 1976-78; Whitewater boatman Adventure Bound, Craig, Colo., 1979-80; tchr. Barboursville (W.Va.) Jr. High Sch., 1981-82; legis. del. So. Regional Edn. Bd., 1981-82; mem. W.Va. Standards Edn. Com., 1982-83. Mem. W.Va. Ho. of Dels., 1981-83; mem. adv. bd. Time Out Run Away Youths; mem. adv. bd. Branches Domestic Violence Shelter. Mem. NEA, W.Va. Edn. Assn. (chmn. profl. standards com.), Cabell County Edn. Assn. (v.p.). Democrat.

DAVIS, SUSAN ANN, business exec.; b. Wausau, Wis., Nov. 18, 1946; d. Edward L. and Vivian (Chellberg) D.; B.A. in Polit. Sci. (Outstanding Sr. Woman 1968), U. Wis., 1968, postgrad. in Communications, 1969. Asst. to press sec. Office Gov. Wis., 1968-69; spl. asst. to asst. sec. transp., Washington, 1969-70, to asst. sec. OEO, 1970-71, to asst. sec. Cost of Living Council, 1971, 73; advance person for Pres. Nixon, 1972; chmn. hospitality 1973 Inaugural; partner Washington Cons. Group, 1973-74; pres. Susan Davis & Assos., Washington, 1974—, Successful Woman, Inc., Washington, 1979—; pres. Nat. Self-Help Resource Center, Washington, 1974—; women's career advisor Georgetown U.; cons. in field; juror All Am. Cities, All Vol. Cities. Mem. Republican Women's Fed. Forum, Rep. Women's Task Force. Mem. Greater Washington Bd. Trade, Nat. Women's Polit. Caucus, Women in Communications, Common Cause, Nat. Com. Reponsive Philanthropy, Bus. and Profl. Women's Orgn., Nat. Assn. Women Bus. Owners (dir. Capitol Area chpt.). Republican. Roman Catholic. Author: Uplift-What People Themselves Can Do, 1974; Community Resource Centers: The Notebook, 1976; also handbooks, articles in field. Home: 3216 Military Rd NW Washington DC 20015 Office: 1722 Connecticut Ave NW Washington DC 20009

DAVIS, SUSAN ELIZABETH, banker; b. St. Louis, Nov. 9, 1941; d. Tyler Burton and Adelaide (Boyd) Davis; B.A. cum laude, Brown U., 1963; postgrad. Harvard U.; m. Lawrence Edward Hammer, Dec. 20, 1975; children—Blake Davis-Hammer, Julia Steele Davis-Hammer. Publisher, The Spokeswoman, Chgo., 1970-73; v.p. South Shore Bank, Chgo., 1973-81; v.p., div. adminstr. Harris Bank & Trust, Chgo., 1982—; founder, dir. Chgo. Fin. Exchange. Mem. exec. com. March of Dimes. Mem. Nat. Assn. Bank Women, Chgo. Network Inc. (co-founder, exec. com.), Com. of 200 (founder). Contbr. articles to profl. jours. Office: 111 E Monroe St Chicago IL 60690

DAVIS, SUSAN LYNN RABINOWITZ, psychiat. social worker, family therapist, trainer; b. Bklyn., Feb. 27, 1944; d. Murray and Jeanette (Baumgarten) Rabinowitz; B.A., Conn. Coll. for Women, 1964; M.S.S. (NIMH grantee), Bryn Mawr Coll., 1968; m. Donald Irvin Davis, Aug. 16, 1964; children—Kenneth Bernard, Joshua Ian. Caseworker, Phila. State Reception Center, Phila. Gen. Hosp., 1965-66; field work Eastern Pa. Psychiat. Inst., Phila., 1966-67, Child Devel. Center, Bryn Mawr Coll., 1967-68; social worker Mental Devel. Center, Case Western Res. U., 1968-69; clin. instr. Northwestern U. Med. Sch., 1969-70; co-leader parent-student discussion group U. Chgo. Lab. Schs., 1972; trainee in family therapy Family Therapy Inst. Washington, 1975-76; pvt. practice family therapy, Alexandria, Va., 1972-78; co-founder, asso. dir. Family Therapy Inst. Alexandria 1978—; developer, co-dir. Habit Mgmt. Workshops, Alexandria, 1981—; cons. local schs.; workshop presenter and panelist, local, nat., internat. mental health meetings. Co-chmn. Com. To Assess Future of Burgundy Farm Sch., Alexandria, 1977-78; active in campaigning for polit. candidates. Lic. social worker, Md., Va. Mem. Nat. Assn. Social Workers, Acad. Cert. Social Workers, Am. Orthopsychiat. Assn., LWV, NOW, Center for Study Democratic Instns., Common Cause. Contbr. articles to profl. jours. Home: 7805 Elba Rd Alexandria VA 22306 Office: 220 S Washington St Alexandria VA 22314

DAVIS, SUSAN MARIE, graphic arts cons.; b. Lynwood, Calif., Nov. 10, 1951; d. Richard P. and Mary L. Davis; student Cypress (Calif.) City Coll., 1969-71; m. Lawrence A. Sherwin, Feb. 26, 1980. From office mgr. to v.p., sales mgr. Quality Graphics, Santa Ana, Calif. 1974-81; pres. Susan Davis Graphic Services, Inc., Santa Ana, 1981—; seminar leader, 1979—. Mem. Printing Industries Assn. (treas., dir. So. Calif. chpt. 1978—). Address: 10821 Skyline Dr Santa Ana CA 92705

DAVIS, SUSAN SCOTT (MRS. GAYLORD DAVIS), civic worker; b. Kearney, Nebr.; d. Thomas Jefferson and Mary Estelle (Grant) Scott; A.B., U. Nebr., 1918, Nebr. State Tchrs. Coll., 1919; M.A., Columbia U., 1935; m. Gaylord Davis, July 4, 1925; 1 dau., Susanne (Mrs. Daniel Oliver Newberry). Dir. tng. sch., dept. kindergarten Nebr. State Tchrs. Coll., 1914-16; mem. casts plays in N.Y. theatres, 1921-23. Mem. Council Juvenile Planning Group, Asheville and Buncombe County, N.C., 1956-59; sec. exec. com. Buncombe County Com. 1960 White House Conf. Children and Youth; dir. Children's Welfare League, Asheville, N.C., 1949, 52, 60, pres., 1955-57; dir. Family and Children's Service Agy., 1948-55; dir. Asheville Day Nursery, 1960-62, v.p., 1963-64, pres., 1964-66, dir., 1967-73; mem. permanent conf. Buncombe County Planning Council, 1964-67, exec. com., 1965-67, mem. day care council Family and Children's Services div., 1969-71. Dir. United Social Services, 1955-60, Candelight Concerts, Inc., (exec. com. 1959-62). Mem. nat. council Women's Republican Club, 1963-74, membership com., 1969-74; bd. dirs. Asheville Community Concerts Assn., 1972—. Mem. English-Speaking Union, The Duetters (founder), Pi Beta Phi. Republican. Christian Scientist. Clubs: Biltmore Forest Country; Univ. (N.Y.C.). Home: T-4 Crowfields Dr Asheville NC 28803

DAVIS, SYLVIA A., govt. ofcl.; b. Crystal Springs, Miss., Nov. 14, 1944; d. Morris C. and Mary Joe (Solomon) D.; B.S., Tougaloo Coll., 1965; M.S.W., U. Ill., 1970; postgrad. (fellow) U. Calif., Berkeley, 1973, 76. Ill. Legis. Internship fellow, 1964-68; accounts receivable clk. Tougaloo Coll., 1964-68; with contractual services dept State of Ill., 1970; legis. staff asst. Ill. Senate, 1971-77, asst. staff dir. to pres., 1977-81; legis asst. to Senator Dixon of Ill., U.S. Senate, Washington, 1981—. Mem. Springfield (Ill.) City Water. Light and Power Adv. Bd.; mem. Nat. Assn. Black Social Workers, NAACP, Springfield Urban League, U. Ill. Alumni Assn., Lupus Erythematosis Soc. Ill., Tougaloo Alumni Assn. Office: Room 456 Russell Senate Office Bldg Washington DC 20510 *

DAVIS, TERRY SERFASS, psychologist; b. Los Angeles, Nov. 6, 1942; d. George Donald and Mriam Allen (Baisden) Serfass; B.A. with distinction, U. Redlands, 1966; Ph.D. in Clin. Psychology (USPHS fellow 1966-68), U. So. Calif., 1973; children—Sheryl Ann Barak, Janet Lee Barak. Field placement supr. psychology dept. UCLA, 1973-76, dir. family rehab. coordinator project, extension dept., 1976-81; out-patient counselor alcoholism, recovery service San Pedro (Calif.) Peninsula Hosp., 1979-80; lectr. health and safety Calif. State U., Los Angeles, 1975-78; pvt. practice psychology, Torrance, Calif., 1978—; dir clin. services addictive disease unit Charter Pacific Hosp., Torrance; coordinator alcohol/drug tng. programs, extension dept. UCLA; faculty Antioch U.-West, 1981-82; cons. in field. Bd. dirs. CLARE Found., 1977-80, pres., 1979-80; bd. dirs. Felicity House, 1974-80, pres., 1977-78, 79-80; bd. dirs. Valley Women's Center, 1978-79. Mem. Calif. Assn. Alcoholic Recovery Homes (pres. Los Angeles chpt. 1979-80), Am. Psychol. Assn., Western Psychol. Assn., Calif. Psychol. Assn., Assn. Women in Psychology, Alcohol and Drug Problems Assn., Calif. Women's Commn. Alcoholism, Sierra Club. Office: 21150 Hawthorne Blvd Suite 102-3 Torrance CA 90503

DAVIS, VICKI KATHRYN TIGERT, educator; b. Omaha, Tex., May 24, 1943; d. Dee Whitcker and Mae Dorothy (Ball) Tigert; B.S., E. Tex. State U., 1964, M.S., 1966; Ph.D., Tex. Woman's U., 1973; m. Jerry Spencer Davis, Aug. 8, 1964; 1 son, Jerry Spencer. Vocat. homemaking tchr. Lubbock (Tex.) Pub. Schs., 1964-66; asst. instr., assoc. prof. child devel., family living East Tex. State U., Commerce, 1966—. Mem. Am. Home Econs. Assn., Nat. Assn. for Edn. of Young Children, So. Assn. for Children Under Six, Nat. Council for Family Relations, Tex. Assn. Coll. Tchrs., Internat. Fedn. for Home Econs., Assn. of Couples for Marriage Enrichment, Delta Kappa Gamma, Phi Delta Kappa. Baptist. Club: Order of Eastern Star. Home: Route 1 PO Box 114 Campbell TX 75422 Office: Home Econs Dept East Tex State U Commerce TX 75428

DAVIS, VIRGINIA, health care adminstr.; b. N.Y.C., Aug. 6, 1953; d. George T. and Haydee (Quiñones) D.; A.A.S., DeHostos Community Coll., 1973; B.S., C. W. Post Coll., 1979; M.A., Columbia U., 1980; m. Ramon Lavandero, May 27, 1978. Nurse, N.Y.C., 1973-77; dialysis coordinator, researcher Baumritter Kidney Center, Albert Einstein Coll. Medicine, 1977-80; dir. ambulatory services Mt. Sinai Med. Center, Milw., 1980-82; care center adminstr. Health Maintenance Orgn. Del./Blue Cross-Blue Shield, Wilmington, 1982—. Mem. Am. Hosp. Assn., Am. Coll. Hosp. Adminstrs. (nominee), Del. Pub. Health Assn., Wilmington Women in Bus. Author papers in field. Office: 24 A Trolley Sq Wilmington DE 19806

DAVIS, WELDON ALEXANDRIA BEASLEY, ednl. cons.; b. Lake Providence, La., Aug. 13, 1931; d. Weldon A. and Williametta R. (Jordan) Beasley; B.S., Calumet Coll., 1960, Columbia Coll., 1962; M.S., Ind. U., 1965; Ph.D. (Rockefeller Found. fellow), Atlanta U., 1980; m. Robert E. Davis, Jr., June 20, 1952 (div.); children—Robert E. III, Weldon A., Patricia A. Davis Rouse. Edn. resource cons. Gary (Ind.) Public Schs., 1960-78, asst. prin., 1976-78; edn. cons. instructional resources Ga. Dept. Edn., Atlanta, 1980—; cons. local sch. systems, colls.; mem. Ga. Library Media Dept. Active polit. campaign Mayor of Gary, also environ. cleanup problems of Gary; proposal writer HUD funds for city beautification; active polit. campaign Mayor of Atlanta. Recipient Civic award Gary Lions Club, 1973; Sears Found. acad. fellow Purdue U., 1976-77; cert. in guidance and counseling, teaching, media-librarianship, and ednl. adminstrn. and leadership, Ga. Mem. Assn. Supervision and Curriculum Devel., Nat. Sci. Tchrs. Assn., Am. Childhood Edn., ALA, Nat. Council Tchrs. of Math., Ga. Assn. Instructional Tech., Assn. Ednl. Communications and Tech., NAACP, LWV, Urban League, Delta Sigma Theta, Delta Kappa Gamma. Home: 2716 Fern Valley Dr East Point GA 30344 Office: Instructional Media Services Twin Towers East 205 Butler St SE Atlanta GA 30334

DAVIS, WENDY MOIRA, constrn. co. exec.; b. London, Dec. 9, 1929; came to U.S., 1969, naturalized, 1978; d. Bruce John and Rosemary Whyl (Abrahams) Baron; student pvt. schs., Sussex, Eng.; m. William John Davis, Oct. 20, 1951; children—Faith Ilda, William Baron and Waverley Rowena (twins), Kyle Micheal. Code enforcement officer City of Treasure Isle (Fla.), 1976-79; spl. codes insp. Pinellas County (Fla.) Bldg. Dept., 1977-79; plan review analyst City of Dunedin (Fla.), 1979-80, acting bldg. official, 1979—; pres. Wendy Homes, Citrus County, Inverness, Fla., 1981—. Chmn. adv. bd. Largo (Fla.) High Sch., 1972-77; mem. adv. bd. Boy Scouts Am., Rainbow Girls. Served with RAF, 1948-51. Mem. Nat. Inst. Bldg. Scis. (com. mem. Washington), Elec. Council Fla. (state dir., chmn. edn.), So. Bldg. Code Congress (v.p. West Coast chpt.), Citrus County Builders Assn. (chmn. legis. com.). Democrat. Clubs: University, Order Eastern Star. Contbr. articles to profl. jours. Home: Route 2 Box 204 Crystal River FL 32629 Office: 1610 W Main St Inverness FL 32650

DAVIS, WILLIE FAYE, auditor; b. Rockwall, Tex., Aug. 10; s. Willie and Noble B. (Johnson) Wells; student Bishop Coll., 1960-62, So. Meth. U., 1973-74, Richland Jr. Coll., 1975; children—Steven, Reginald. Waitress, Zodiac Restaurant, Neiman Marcus, Dallas, 1959-62, lead operator data entry, 1963-69, mgr. data entry, 1970-77, asst. sales audit mgr., 1978-82, sales audit mgr., 1982—. Mem. Female Execs. Am., Bus. and Profl. Club. Baptist. Home: 5623 312B Belmont St Dallas TX 75206

DAVIS, WILMA JEAN, nursing home adminstr.; b. Goodland, Mo., Apr. 24, 1931; d. Sherman L. and Bessie Keith; cert. housing mgmt., Community Sch. Practical Nursing, Columbia U., 1977, cert. activity dir., 1977, med. records cert., 1978; m. Billy Davis, Mar. 15, 1968; children—Jackie, David, Joey, Kelly. Colonial Nursing Home, Bismarck, Mo., 1958—, Lone Pine Congregate Center, Ironton, Mo., 1977—, Belleview (Mo.) Nursing Home, 1956—. Mem. Am. Health Care Assn., Mo. Assn. Lic. Practical Nurses, Mo. Health Care Assn., Activity Dirs. Assn. Mo. Methodist. Club: Order Eastern Star. Address: Box 24 Star Route Belleview MO 63623

DAVIS-GAVIN, JANE FRANCES, lawyer; b. Boston, Oct. 29, 1945; d. Frank Lyons and Louise (Spiers) Davis; B.A. (Trustees scholar, Edith Lynn Bush Tufts scholar), Tufts U., 1967; J.D., Suffolk U., Boston, 1977; m. Kenneth John Gavin, June 17, 1976. Pub. info. specialist exec. office of Pres., OEO, Washington, 1967-68; nat. project officer, prison inmate and ex-offender tng. Dept. Labor, Washington, 1969-71, employment and manpower specialist, Boston, 1974-76, equal employment officer, 1976-77; spl. asst. to dir. Div. Employment Security, Boston, 1971-74; admitted to Mass. bar, 1977, D.C. bar, 1978, Fed. bar, Boston, 1979; counsel Nat. Treasury Employees Union, rep. employees of Dept. Energy, IRS, Treasury and U.S. Customs, San Francisco, 1977-78; founder, dir. Wider Opportunities for Women, Boston; instr., lectr. domestic relations and legal research Inst. for Legal Asst. and Paralegal Tng. Inc., 1981—; cons., lectr. fair labor standards, civil rights, privacy and freedom of info. acts. Chairperson, Mass. Task Force Employment and Manpower Tng., 1971-73; mem. Mass. Gov.'s Commn. on Status of Women, 1972-76, Gov.'s Drug Abuse Prevention Planning Council, 1972-74, Boston Area Planning Commn., 1972-74; mem. adv. bd. Mass. Social Services Adminstrn.; cons. Hyannis Legal Services. Recipient Am. Legion Ann. Essay award, 1963, Exceptional Performance award Dept. Labor, 1969, Mass. State Brotherhood award NCCJ; named Citizen of Yr., Bedford Civic Club, 1963. Bedford Womens Community Club scholar, 1963-67. Mem. Am. Bar Assn., Mass. Bar Assn., Tufts U., Suffolk U. Law Sch. alumni assns., Leonard Carmichael Soc. Home: 328 Concord Rd Bedford MA 01730 also 379 South St Hyannis MA 02601 Office: 379 South St Hyannis MA 02601

DAVISON, BETSY JANE, charitable orgn. adminstr.; b. Cleve., Dec. 22, 1921; d. Alexander Stuart and Helen Eva (Chapman) D.; student Albion (Mich.) Coll., 1941-43; B.A., U. Chgo., 1943; M.A., Tchrs. Coll., Columbia U., 1952. Civilian recreation dir. U.S. Army and Air Force Overseas, 1945-55; command recreation dir. Hdqrs. U.S. Air Forces in Europe, Ger., 1956-58; coordinator student activities Kean (N.J.) Coll., 1959-66; cons. edn. and tng. Assn. Jr. Leagues, N.Y.C., 1966-70; dir. tng. Mental Health Materials Center, N.Y.C., 1971-76; tng. cons. APC Skills Co., N.Y.C., 1977-78; dir. tng. and confs. Child Welfare League Am., N.Y.C., 1979—. Mem. Am. Soc. Tng. and Devel., Am. Edn. Assn., Kappa Delta Pi, Pi Lambda Theta, Delta Sigma Rho, Alpha Lambda Delta. Author tng. manuals. Home: 333 E 43d St New York NY 10017 Office: 67 Irving Pl New York NY 10003

DAVISON, DOROTHY, urban planner; b. Boston, June 22, 1925; d. Israel and Tillie (Bloom) Goldstein; student Chaffey Coll., 1947, Ind. U., 1948-50, Harvard U., 1952-55, Contra Costa Coll., 1956-59, U. Calif., Berkeley, 1960; B.A. in Urban Studies-Community Devel., San Francisco State U., 1968; postgrad. in basic indsl. devel. Tex. A&M U., 1982; postgrad. Econ. Devel. Inst., U. Okla., 1982; m. Sol Davison, Feb. 3, 1945; children—Scott J., Mark G. With CSC, Mass., Calif., Tex. and Fla., 1942-46; apptd. to Mayor's Citizen Adv. Com., Richmond Urban Renewal Agy., Assn. Bay Area Govts. and Richmond (Calif.) Model Cities, 1956-72; chief planner Harris County Community Devel. Agy., Houston, 1975-82, asst. dir., 1982—. Cons. Tex. A&M U. Agrl. Extension Resource Council; Gulf Coast regional econ. devel. com. Houston/Galveston Area Council; nat. del. White House Conf. on Aging, 1981; Tex. del. Gov.'s Conf. Aging, 1981; chmn. housing for elderly Houston/Harris County Area Agy. Aging, 1981. Cert. housing mgr.; specialist in sr. citizen housing; recipient cert. merit City of Richmond, 1969, Women in Govt. cert. U. Houston, 1978, ct. resolution Harris County Commrs., 1981; lic. real estate broker, Tex. Mem. Am. Planning Assn., Nat. Assn. Housing and Redevel. Ofcls., Tex. Indsl. Devel. Council. Home: 11919 Pebble Rock Dr Houston TX 77077 Office: 3100 Timmons Ln Suite 202 Houston TX 77027

DAVISON, JAQUIE MAY, author; b. Lexington, Ky., May 5, 1938; d. James Abraham and Etta May (Hall) Kirk; student public schs., Lexington; m. Ronald Ray Davison, Jan. 19, 1963; children—John, Mary, Thomas, Regina, Ralph. Founder, pres. Happiness of Womanhood, Kingman, Ariz., 1970—; author: I Am A Housewife, 1972; Cancer Winner, 1977; lectr. on cancer cure to various orgns. Mem. Nat. Press Women's Club. Republican. Mormon. Home: 5182 Danica Way Las Vegas NV 89122 Office: 1335 Hancock Rd Riviera AZ 86442

DAVITO, CHARLENE L., nursing adminstr.; b. Westfield, Ill., Sept. 3, 1947; d. Charles W. and Lola M. Goldsmith; grad. St. Joseph Hosp. Sch. Nursing, 1977; m. Frank L. Davito, July 8, 1967; 1 son, Frank L. Staff nurse Riverside Hosp., Kankakee, Ill., 1977, Morris (Ill.) Hosp., 1977-78; staff nurse Will County Health Dept., Joliet, Ill., 1978-79; dir. nursing Bradley (Ill.) Nursing Centre, 1979; dir. nursing Americana Nursing Center, Joliet, 1980; dir. nursing Briarcliff Manor, Bourbonnais, Ill., 1980-81. Mem. Am. Nurses Assn., Assn. Rehab. Nurses, Ill. Nurses Assn., Psi Chi. Roman Catholic. Home: Box 117 Coal City IL 60416 Office: 300 N Madison St Joliet IL

DAVY, AUDREY, ednl. adminstr.; b. Evanston, Ill., Aug. 6, 1926; d. Royal E. and Rose Ann (Keefe) D.; B.B.A., U. Miami, 1948, M.B.A., 1978. Asst. to the dean, sch. bus. adminstrn. U. Miami, Fla., 1950-75, asst. dean, 1975—, also dir. overseas programs. Active NOW, Sierra Club. Mem. Am. Mgmt. Assn., Assn. Grad. Bus. Dirs. (pres.), Beta Gamma Sigma. Democrat. Office: PO Box 248505 Coral Gables FL 33124

DAVY, DOROTHY JEAN, state ofcl.; b. Portland, Oreg., Feb. 15, 1932; d. Conwell Landis and Constance D.; grad. Good Samaritan Hosp. Sch. Nursing, Portland, 1957; diploma in nursing Lewis and Clark Coll., 1960; postgrad. in bus. adminstrn. Portland State U. City U., 1983—. Dir. nursing service Good Samaritan Hosp. and Med. Center, 1965-73, dir. hosp. edn., 1973-75; dir. provider relations Portland Metro Health HMO, 1976-77; acting adminstr. and dir. nursing Camelot Care Center, Forest Grove, Oreg., 1977-78; exec. dir. Oreg. Bd. Nursing, Portland, 1978—. Mem. Nat. League Nursing, Am. Nurses Assn., State Mgmt. Assn., Am. Mgmt. Assn., Portland C. of C., Sigma Theta Tau. Republican. Methodist. Clubs: Order Eastern Star, City of Portland. Office: 1400 SW 5th Ave Portland OR 97201

DAVY, JANE ANN, real estate broker; b. Falls City, Nebr., Jan. 14, 1935; d. Glen Leslie and Wilma Anna (Bertram) Wachtel; A.A., City Coll. San Francisco, 1974; grad. Realtors Inst., 1978; m. Bruce S. Davy, July 25, 1964; children—James, Leslie Ann, Nanette, Peter. Mutual funds specialist trust dept. Wells Fargo Bank, San Francisco, 1972-76; consumer researcher Corey, Canapary & Galanis, San Francisco, 1976-80; owner, realtor Davy Real Estate, San Francisco, 1980—; mem. Multiple Listing Service, San Francisco. Election officer San Francisco Elections, 1966—. Named Sales Person of Month, Green & Kaufmann Realty, 1977, 78, 79; real estate broker, Calif. Mem. Women's Council Realtors (v.p. San Francisco chpt. 1981), Realtors Nat. Mktg. Inst., San Francisco Real Estate Bd., Republican. Presbyterian. Author, pub. News from Jane Davy. Home and office: 184 Molimo Dr San Francisco CA 94127

DAVY, KAREN LEE, bancorp. exec.; b. Columbus, Ohio, Dec. 2, 1952; d. Richard Lee and Janet Ruth (Seidel) D.; A.A., Manatee Jr. Coll., 1973; B.A., U. West Fla., 1975. Comml. loan note teller Nat. Bank of Sarasota (Fla.), 1973; fin. intern Office Comptroller of Currency, Atlanta, 1974-75, asst. nat. bank examiner, 1976-80, mem. EEO affirmative action com., region 6, 1977-80; consumer compliance asso. First City Bancorp. of Tex., Inc., Houston, 1980-81, consumer compliance rep., 1981—. Named Greek Woman of Yr. Panhellenic Assn., U. West Fla., Pensacola, Fla., 1974-75. Mem. Greater Houston Bankers Compliance Assn., Nat. Assn. Female Execs. Democrat. Mem. Ch. of Christ. Home: Apt 194 9201 Clarewood Dr Houston TX 77036 Office: First City Bancorp of Tex Inc 1001 Fannin St Houston TX 77002

DAWDY, FAYE MARIE CATANIA, photography studio mgr.; b. San Mateo, Calif., Sept. 15, 1954; d. Frank Benjamin and Melba Rita (Arata) Catania; A.A., Coll. San Mateo, 1979; student San Francisco State U., 1979—; m. John Thomas Dawdy, May 5, 1974. With Procter & Gamble Distbg. Co., San Mateo, 1973-78; partner Dawdy Photography, Millbrae, Calif., 1978—; dir., sec.-treas. Millbrae Stamp Co., 1980—; guest speaker, lectr. Mills High Sch., Millbrae, Millbrae Women's Club, Portola Camera Club. Area chmn. Millbrae Am. Heart Assn. Ann. Fund Dr., 1977-82; mem. fund raising com. San Mateo County chpt. Am. Heart Assn., 1980—; co-chmn. Miss Millbrae Pageant, 1981, Queen Isabella Columbus Day Festival Pageant, 1981; judge arts and crafts exhbns.; mem. Millbrae Art Assn., 1979-80. Recipient awards No. Calif. Council Camera Clubs, 1979, 81. Mem. Millbrae C. of C. (sec. women's div. 1979), Wedding Photographers Internat., Portola Camera Club (nature chmn. 1978—), Friends of Millbrae Library, Italian Catholic Fedn., Nat. Assn. Female Execs., Photog. Soc. Am., Calif. Women in Profl. Photography, Profl. Photographers Calif., Fedn. Ind. Bus. Democrat. Roman Catholic. Clubs: Soroptomist of Millbrae-San Bruno (sec. 1981-82), St. Dunstan Women's (Millbrae). Office: 1653 El Camino Real Millbrae CA 94030

DAWIDOWICZ, LUCY S., historian, author; b. N.Y.C., June 16, 1915; d. Max and Dora (Ofnaem) Schildkret; B.A., Hunter Coll., N.Y.C., 1936; postgrad. research fellow Yivo Inst. Jewish Research, Vilna, Poland, 1938-39; M.A., Columbia U., 1961; L.H.D. (hon.), Kenyon Coll., 1978, Hebrew Union Coll.-Jewish Inst. Religion, 1978, Monmouth Coll., 1982; m. Szymon M. Dawidowicz, Jan. 3, 1948. Asst. to research dir. Yivo Inst. Jewish Research, N.Y.C., 1940-46; edn. officer displaced persons camps Am. Jewish Joint Distbn. Com., Ger., 1946-47; research analyst, then research dir. Am. Jewish Com., N.Y.C., 1948-69; mem. faculty Yeshiva U., N.Y.C., 1969-78, prof. social history, 1974-78, Paul and Leah Lewis prof. holocaust studies, 1970-75, Eli and Diana Zborowski prof. interdisciplinary holocaust studies, 1976-78; vis. prof. Jewish civilization Stanford U., 1981; vis. prof. SUNY, Albany, 1982; bd. dirs. Leo Baeck Inst., N.Y.C.; mem. Pres.' Commn. on the Holocaust, 1978-79; mem. adv. council Center for Modern Jewish Studies, Brandeis U.; bd. dirs. library corp. Jewish Theol. Sem. Am. Recipient award Nat. Found. Jewish Culture, 1965, John Slawson Fund Research, Tng. and Edn., 1972, 79, Lucius N. Littauer Found., 1972, 80, Gustav Wurzweiler Found., 1974, 78; Outstanding Achievement award Hunter Coll., 1978; Guggenheim fellow, 1976. Mem. Am. Hist. Assn., Am. Jewish Hist. Soc., Conf. Jewish Social Studies, Assn. Jewish Studies. Author: (with L. J. Goldstein) Politics in a Pluralist Democracy, 1963; The Golden Tradition: Jewish Life and Thought in Eastern Europe, 1967; The War Against the Jews, 1933-1945 (Anisfield-Wolf prize 1976), 1975 (transl. into French, German, Japanese, Hebrew); A Holocaust Reader, 1976; The Jewish Presence: Essays on Identity and History, 1977; The Holocaust and the Historians, 1981; On Equal Terms: Jews in America, 1881-1981, 1982; editor: (with Joshua A. Fishman, others) For Max Weinreich: Studies in Jewish Languages, Literatures and Society, 1964. Home: 200 W 86th St Apt 20L New York NY 10024

DAWKINS, IMOGENE, acct., income tax cons. and preparer; b. Edgefield County, S.C., May 8, 1938; d. Jack and Rebecca (Simmons) D.; B.S., S.C. State Coll., 1960; diploma Inst. Children's Lit., 1980. Adminstrv. asst. Greenwood (S.C.) Sch. Dist. 50, 1960-70; manpower devel. specialist Manpower Adminstrn., Dept. Labor, Washington, 1970-74; manpower devel. specialist Office Adminstrn., Office Gov. S.C., Columbia, 1974-76; magistrate, Edgefield County-Edgefield City, S.C., 1980; owner, operator Dawkins Income Tax and Acctg. Services, Edgefield, 1978—. Candidate for Edgefield County Council. Mem. Am. Legion Aux., Alpha Kappa Alpha. Baptist. Home and Office: PO Box 304 219 Peachtree St Edgefield SC 29824

DAWKINS, MARVA PHYLLIS, psychologist; b. Jacksonville, Fla., Apr. 12, 1948; d. Ralph and Altamese (Padgett) D.; student U. Freiburg (W.Ger.), 1969-70; B.S., Stetson U., 1971; M.S., Fla. State U., 1972, Ph.D., 1975. Research asst. Fla. State U., Tallahassee, 1970-72; clin. intern, psychology dept. Presbyn.-St. Luke's Med. Center and mental health dept. Mile Square Health Center, Chgo., 1973-74; staff psychologist, dir. aftercare treatment program, mental health dept. Mile Square Health Center, Chgo., 1974-75, staff psychologist, coordinator devel. disabilities program, 1976-79; asst. prof. psychology U. North Fla., Jacksonville, 1975-76, Rush U.-Presbyn. St. Luke's Med. Center, Chgo., 1976—; pvt. practice clin. psychology, Oak Park, Ill., 1977—; exec. dir. Inst. for Community Mental Health, 1979—. Registered psychologist, Ill. Mem. Am. Psychol. Assn., Assn. Black Psychologists. Office: 109-1 Harrison St Oak Park IL 60304

DAWLEY, PATRICIA KELLY, bank exec.; b. Seattle, July 27, 1937; d. Gail W. and Edith Kelly; B.A., U. Wash., 1959; M.B.A., N.Y. U., 1979. Exec. v.p., sec. Anchor Savs. Bank, N.Y.C., 1978—. Mem. Nat. Assn. Bank Women, AAUW, Delta Gamma. Office: New York NY

DAWSON, DIANA LEE, advt. co. exec.; b. Miles City, Mont., Sept. 22, 1949; d. John Daniel and Dora Deane (Hudson) D.; B.A. cum laude, Doane Coll., 1971. Client relations Nat. Merchandising Corp., 1972-73, advt. dir., 1973-77, mktg. communications dir., 1977-78; corporate relations dir. Namco Industries, Natick, Mass., 1978—, v.p. corporate relations, 1980—, also dir. Active Mass. Citizen's Legis. Seminars. Mem. Greater Boston Ad Club, S. Middlesex C. of C., Sales and Mktg. Execs. Internat., Am. Mgmt. Assn., Nat. Assn. Telephone Directory Cover Advt. Cos. (dir.), Small Bus. Assn. New Eng., Women West (Boston). Club: Tanheath Hunt. Home: 12 Cross St Hopkinton MA 01748 Office: 7 Strathmore Rd Natick MA 01750

DAWSON, DIANN, social worker; b. Wilson, N.C., Nov. 23, 1950; d. Frank Lee and Elnora (Cotton) D.; B.A. in Sociology and Psychology, Bennett Coll., Greensboro, N.C., 1972; M.S.W., U. N.C., 1973. With S.C. Dept. Social Services, 1974-80, program dir. II, 1977-79, project adminstr. div. assistance payments, Columbia, 1979-80; mem. Central Midlands Dist. Health Adv. Bd., 1979-80, Lexington County Manpower Planning Council, 1979-80; family assistance program specialist Office of Family Assistance, HEW/SSA, Atlanta, 1980—. Delta Sigma Theta scholar, 1968-72; HUD fellow, 1972-73. Mem. Nat. Assn. Black Social Workers (pres. Columbia 1978-79), Acad. Cert. Social Workers, Nat. Assn. Social Workers, Pi Gamma Mu. Baptist. Home: 3737 Peachtree Rd NE Atlanta GA 30319 Office: SSA Office of Family Assistance 101 Marietta Towers Atlanta GA 30323

DAWSON, JEAN ELAINE PACKARD, copywriter; b. Hanover, N.H., Sept. 28, 1938; d. George Clarence and Marjorie E. (Truman) Packard; B.S., U. N.H., 1969; m. Frank Dawson, June 16, 1958; children—Stephen Bryan, Carlton Douglas. Counselor, program coordinator USAF Edn. Center, Athens, Greece, 1970-74; registrar U. Md., Athens, Greece, 1970-74; recreation center program dir. Randolph AFB, Tex., 1974; freelance writer, 1974-76; chief copywriter Tex.-N.Mex. div. Dillard's, San Antonio, 1976—; dir. mktg.-public relations San Antonio Symphony, 1982. Mem. steering com. San Antonio Network Power Coalition, 1981-82, bd. dirs. 1982. Recipient NoRMA award Nat. Retail Mchts. Assn., 1980; Award of Excellence, Haggar Corp., 1977. Mem. Women in Communications (v.p. projects, Proliner awards 1981, dir. 1980-83), San Antonio Advt. Fedn. (Addy Merit awards 1978, 80, 81, 82). Home: 7618 Meadow Green San Antonio TX 78251 Office: 9315 Broadway San Antonio TX 78217

DAWSON, MARY ANN WEYFORTH, fed. commr.; b. St. Louis, Aug. 31, 1944; d. Francis Griffin and Jeanne Gething Weyforth; A.B. in Govt., Washington U., St. Louis, 1966; m. Rhett B. Dawson, Jan. 15, 1976. Legis. asst. Rep. James Symington, Mo., 1969-72; legis. asst., press sec. Rep. Richard Ichord, Mo., 1973; press sec. Senator Packwood, 1973-75, legis. dir., 1975-76, adminstrv. asst., chief of staff, 1976-81; commr. FCC, Washington, 1981—. Mem. Am. Council Young Polit. Leaders, Women's Campaign Fund, Washington U. Alumni Assn. Republican. Roman Catholic. Office: FCC 1919 M St NW Washington DC 20554

DAWSON, PATRICIA ANNE, fin. exec.; b. Tampa, Fla., Sept. 6, 1938; d. Seymour Charles and Casilda (Ladrero) Mickler; B.S. in Edn., Fla. State U., 1959; m. William Penn Dawson, Jr., June 24, 1960; children—William Penn III, Seymour Charles Mickler. Tchr. Citrus Park Sch., Tampa, 1960-68; dir., sec., asst. treas. Mickler Corp., Clearwater, Fla., 1960—. Mem. Tampa Jr. League, 1960-73; mem. admissions com. MacDonald Tng. Center, 1960-62; pres. Elks Pre-Sch., 1966-68, North Ward Sch., 1976-78; pres. Clearwater Jr. League, 1971-72, v.p., 1970-71, bd. dirs., 1963-72; charity ball chmn. Morton F. Plant Hosp., 1977. Republican. Roman Catholic. Clubs: Tampa Yacht and Country, Ye Mystic Krew of Gasperilla, Carlouel Yacht, Casado, Tower, Merrymakers.

DAWSON, SUSAN HUBBELL, social worker; b. Bedford, Ohio, July 29, 1920; d. Charles Edward and Lois Nettie (Wheeler) Hubbell; B.A., Hiram (Ohio) Coll., 1942; M.A. in Social Work, U. Chgo., 1944; m. Joseph Green Dawson, Apr. 2, 1944; children—Joseph Green, III, Stephanie W. Dawson Abell. Home visitor St. Mark's Pl. Settlement House, N.Y.C., 1941; caseworker home service Charleston (S.C.) chpt. ARC, 1944-45; welfare caseworker children's div. St. Tammany Parish (La.) Dept. Public Welfare, 1954-55; psychiat. social worker La. Dept. Hosps., Bogalusa, 1955-58; mem. faculty Sch. Social Welfare, La. State U., Baton Rouge, 1962—, prof. social work, 1975—. Mem. Council Social Work Edn., Am. Group Psychotherapy Assn., Nat. Assn. Social Workers, La. Conf. Social Work Edn., La. Assn. Group Psychotherapy, AAUW (pres. Baton Rouge br. 1969-71, sec. La. div. 1978-79), Internat. Assn. Pupil Personnel Workers, Delta Kappa Gamma (chpt. pres. 1974-76). Democrat. Episcopalian. Author articles in field. Asso. editor Jour. Internat. Assn. Pupil Personnel Workers. Home: 245 Albert Hart Dr Baton Rouge LA 70808 Office: Sch Social Work La State U Baton Rouge LA 70803

DAY, CARMEL MARTI, educator, med. technologist; b. Long Beach, Calif.; d. Julius A. and Leona Monasch LeiBert; B.S., Calif. Poly. U., 1972, M.S., 1974; M.A., Central Mich. U., 1976; M.A.M., A.B.D. in Exec. Mgmt., Claremont Grad. Sch., 1979, Ph.D. in Exec. Mgmt., 1980; children—Alexander Jered, Michele Louise. Program dir. med. tech. City of Hope Med. Center, Duarte, Calif., 1975-79; coordinator lab. services Community Health Projects, West Covina, Calif., 1974-78; mgmt. cons. Health Mgmt. Analysts, West Covina, 1977—; asst. adminstr. technologist/program dir. Brotman Hosp., Culver City, Calif., 1979-80; asso. prof. health care mgmt. U. LaVerne (Calif.), 1980—; mem. adv. bd. Community Health Projects, 1977-80; asst. prof. microbiology and public health Calif. State U., Los Angeles, 1978. Mem. editorial com. West Covina Republican Club, 1978—; show chmn. membership, trophies Ridge Riders, Inc., 1965-75. HEW grantee, 1976-77. Recipient Disting. Alumna award Sch. Sci., Calif. Poly. U., 1980; Profl. Achievement award Am. Soc. Med. Tech., 1981. Mem. Am. Soc. Med. Tech., Am. Soc. Allied Health Professions, Am. Med. Writers, Calif. Assn. Med. Lab. Tech., Women in Mgmt., Beta Beta Beta, Am. Horse Show Assn. (judge 1974-79), Arabian Horse Assn. So. Calif. Asso. editor Am. Jour. Med. Tech. Mgmt., 1979—; mgmt. question and answer adv. panel Med. Lab. Observer, 1978—. Office: 1950 3d St LaVerne CA 91750

DAY, FRAN, mfg. assn. exec.; b. Gulfport, Miss., Nov. 29, 1945; d. James Melbourne and Lucy Eleanor (Elmore) Oakes; B.A., UCLA, 1971; M.A., Univ. Without Walls, 1975; m. Ralph P. Day, Aug. 28, 1975; children—Jeremie Maria, Jason Barry. Tchr., Pinecrest Schs., Northridge, Calif., 1965-71; news dir. Sta. WATO, Oak Ridge, 1971-74; creative dir. Media Graphics, Pitts., 1974-75; talk show host Sta. WDEF-TV, Chattanooga, 1975-76; mng. dir. Cleveland (Tenn.) Associated Industries, 1976—; cons. local govt. and CETA program; instr. Cleveland State Community Coll., 1976-78. Mem. Tenn. Hypertension Adv. Com., 1979-80; chmn. Gov's Com. on Employment of Handicapped, 1977-81; mem. Ga./Tenn. Regional Health Commn., 1979-81. Recipient awards Kiwanis, 1975, Lions Club, 1976. Mem. Am. Soc. of Assn. Execs. (Mgmt. and Achievement award 1980), Tenn. Soc. of Assn. Execs., U.S. C. of C. (inst. program, 1979). Unitarian. Clubs: Civitan Internat., Cleveland Country. Author: Cleveland/Bradley Industrial Sewer Use Ordinance, 1977; CAI Model Health Care Plan, 1980; Guide to Local Government, 1980. Home: 565 Parker NE Cleveland TN 37311 Office: 160 Ocoee St NE Cleveland TN 37311

DAY, GRACE ANNE, violinist; b. Tondo, Belgian Congo, Jan. 4, 1933; (parents Am. citizens); d. George Wesley and Ellen Irene (Peckham) Westcott; B.M., Eastman Sch. Music, 1957; m. Bernard Hoffer, June 1957; children—Kara Hoffer Day, Gilbert Hoffer; m. 2d, Robert Day, Feb. 8, 1972; adopted children—Ronald Day, Robin Day. Violinist, Rochester (N.Y.) Philharmo. Orch., 1953-58, orch. Radio City Music Hall, N.Y.C., 1964-65, N.J. Symphony, Newark, 1965-66, Toledo Symphony, 1966-67, Indpls. Symphony Orch., 1967—, Suzuki and Friends Chamber Orch., Indpls., 1980—; mem. faculty Am. U., 1961; pvt. tchr. violin. Mem. Matinee Musical. Home: 903 W 54th St Indianapolis IN 46208

DAY, KATHERINE MINDLIN, psychologist; b. Scarsdale, N.Y., May 10, 1943; d. Eugene S. and Sarah (Baum) Mindlin; B.A. cum laude, Barnard Coll., 1964; M.A., Columbia U., 1965; Ph.D. (USPHS fellow), U. Wash., 1975; m. Theodore B. Day, Aug. 25, 1967; children—Eleanore Amara, Theodore Eugene, Jennifer Jane. Intern, Astor Home for Children, Rhinebeck, N.Y., 1972-73; psychologist Childrens Orthopedic Hosp., Seattle, 1974-79; pvt. practice psychology, Mercer Island, Wash., 1976—; asst. prof. U. Wash., 1972—; cons. Seattle Public Schs., Wash. Dept. Social and Health Services. Mem. Gov.'s Conf. on Abuse and Neglect, 1978. VA trainee, 1971-72. Mem. Am. Psychol. Assn., Wash. Psychol. Assn., Assn. Profl. Women, Assn. Mormon Counselors and Psychotherapists. Contbr. articles to profl. jours. Office: 2737 77th St SE Mercer Island WA 98040

DAY, MARGARET MCVAY, petroleum co. exec.; b. Royal Oak, Mich., Jan. 25, 1921; d. John Edward and Bessie Dorothy (Kinsey) McVay; B.A., U. Mich., 1943; postgrad. Wayne State U., 1956-57. Sec., translator Gen. Motors Corp., 1943-45; office mgr. Mobile Oil Corp., Chgo., 1947-50, sec. to ops. mgr., Detroit, 1952-62, adminstrv. asst., N.Y.C., 1962-73, corp. asst. sec., 1973-76, mgr. sec.'s dept., 1975-76, corp. sec. Mobil Corp. and Mobil Oil Corp. Mem. Am. Soc. Corp. Secs. (sec.), Stockholder Relations Soc. N.Y. (pres.). Office: 150 E 42d St New York NY 10017 *

DAY, MARKETA FERN, placement cons.; b. Canyon City, Colo., Nov. 14, 1928; d. Edward and Ethel Clista (Smith) Blanton; B.S., State Tchrs. Coll. Mo., 1949; children—Claudia Suski, Dudley Day. With Stanley Home Products, Westfield, Mass., 1953-73; with Washington Exec. Group, 1977-81, v.p. Registry, 1980-81; pres. Marketa Day & Assos., Springfield, Va., 1981—; cons. in field. Mem. VIP Exec. Assn. for Career Women, Washington Trade Assn., EST, Sylva Mind Control. Methodist. Clubs: Order Eastern Star, Sailing of Mt. Vernon. Home: The Fountains 1405 301 N Beauregard St Alexandria VA 22312 Office: 5509 Backlick Rd Springfield VA 22151

DAY, MARYLOUISE MULDOON (MRS. RICHARD DAYTON DAY), appraiser; b. St. Louis; d. Joseph A. and Dorothy (Lang) Muldoon; A.B., Washington U., St. Louis, 1940; postgrad. Air U., 1958, George Washington U., 1963-64; grad. Real Estate Inst. Md., 1972; m. Richard Dayton Day, Aug. 15, 1959. Intelligence specialist U.S. Air Force, Washington, 1947-60; program officer, spl. asst. to dir. project devel. VISTA, OEO, 1965-67; v.p. Culpeper Corp., Wilmington, Del., 1955—; with Joint Intelligence Bur., London, Eng., 1953; appraiser, cons. on antiques, fine arts, 1969—; pres. Agts. For Sales Ltd., 1974—, Marylouise M. Day, Inc., 1978—. Recipient citation U.S. Air Force, 1960. Fellow Inc. Soc. Valuers and Auctioneers (London); mem. Am. Soc. Appraisers (sr., 1st v.p. 1977-78, pres. 1978-79, chmn. fine arts forum 1976-78, gov. Region 3 1980-82) internat. sec. 1982-83), Appraisers Assn. Am., Irish Georgian Soc., Winterthur Guild, Delta Gamma. Club: Kenwood Golf and Country (Washington). Home: 4928 Sentinel Dr Bethesda MD 20816

DAY, MRS., R. ERVEN (STELLA H. DAY), civic worker; b. Fillmore, Utah; d. G. Riley and Hannah (Hanson) Huntsman; tchrs. certificate U. Utah, 1909, student Brigham Young U., Utah State U., Northwestern U.; m. Richard Erven Day, Aug. 4, 1909; children—Erven Vance, Glade Riley, Belva, Daila (Mrs. Wendell Pixton Paxton). Tchr. jr. high sch., Utah. Chmn. A.R.C., Millard County, Utah, 1918-28; pres. East Millard Cancer Assn., 1935-46; sec. Fillmore (Utah) Latter-day Saints Hosp., 1950—; chmn. Civic Improvement. Named Club Woman of Yr. Utah, 1960; Dist. Mother Yr., 1961; awards Utah State U., 1967, 69, 70-71, 72, 73, 74-75, Utah Nurserymen's Assn., 1968, 1st place for environ. improvement in state and Rocky Mountain region, 1973; Woman of Year award Am. Legion Aux., 1975; Spl. Service award Utah Fedn. Women's Clubs, 1976; monument dedicated in her honor City of Fillmore, 1979. Mem. Utah Asso. Garden Clubs (pres. 1957-58, dir. 1945—), Nat. Council State Garden Clubs (dir. 1957-75, 1st nat. accredited flower show judge in Utah), East Millard Fine Arts Guild (pres. 1954-55), Nat. Assn. Daus. of Pioneers (v.p. 1948-72, historian 1958—), Gen. Fedn. Women's Clubs, Am. Rose Soc. (accredited judge, cons. rosiarian), Am. Iris Soc. (judge), Civic Improvement Soc. (v.p.), Utah Hist. Soc. (chmn. bicentennial com. 1975-76), Utah Beautification Soc. Mem. Ch. of Jesus Christ of Latter-day Saints. Compiler: Milestones of Millard History of Millard County. Composer: Builders of Early Millard. Author: Everything Is Relative, 1970. Contbr. articles to profl. jours.; also weekly column for newspaper. Home: 95 E Center St Fillmore UT 84631

DAY, ROSALEE, probation officer; b. Norwood, Ga., Nov. 2, 1943; d. John Kendrick and Louise (Woods) Porter; B.S.W. cum laude, Temple U., 1976, M.S.W. (fellow), 1977; m. Emanuel W. Day, Sept. 23, 1961; 1 dau., Kimberly Ann. Clk.-typist Phila. County Bd. Assistance, 1960-67; adminstrv. asst., counselor, therapist Diagnostic and Rehab. Center, Phila., 1967-76; U.S. Probation officer U.S. Dist. Ct. Eastern Dist. Pa., Phila., 1977—. Bd. dirs. Phila. Youth Leadership Inst., Inc.; adv. bd. Berean Inst. Mem. Nat. Assn. Social Workers, Nat. Assn. Black Social Workers, Nat. Assn. Blacks in Criminal Justice, Vols. in Criminal Justice, Am. Probation and Parole Assn., Am. Corrections Assn., Temple U. Alumni Assn. (dir.), NAACP, Urban League. Baptist. Club: Social. Home: 6654 Cornelius St Philadelphia PA 19138 Office: US Ct House 601 Market St Philadelphia PA 19106

DAYTON, PATRICIA JANE, printer, former pub.; b. Ft. Dodge, Iowa, May 27, 1925; d. Clarence Augustus and Sylvia Ethyl (Bass) Danielson; student Lehigh (Iowa) public schs.; m. Myrle Dayton, Apr. 13, 1944; children—Tony, Delner. Telephone operator, PBX operator, sec., 1943-57; owner, operator Modern Scribe, Mendota, Ill., 1976—; former pub. Dollar Stretcher; columnist The Dollar Stretcher. Christian Scientist. Club: Navy Mothers. Author: The Best of the Dollar Stretcher and More. Office: Modern Scribe 1907 Lincoln Ave Mendota IL 61342

DAYWITT, JEANNE, nursing adminstr.; b. Frankfort, Ind., Jan. 31, 1922; d. Daniel Martin and Mabel (Harmon) D.; student Franklin Coll., 1940-41; grad. nurse Ind. U., Indpls., 1944; B.S. in Nursing Edn., Cath. U. Am., 1949, M.S. in Nursing, 1959. Staff nurse Robert Long Hosp., Ind. U. Med. Center, Indpls., 1944-45, Wakeman Gen. Hosp., Camp Atterbury, Ind., 1945-46; head nurse Riley Hosp., Ind. U. Med. Center, Indpls., 1946-47; staff nurse Children's Hosp., Washington, 1948; staff nurse St. Elizabeths Hosp., Washington, 1952-53, head nurse, 1953-54, acting asst. supr., 1954-55, asst. supr., 1955-59, acting asst. dir. nursing, 1959, asst. dir. nursing, 1959-73, chief nurse Richardson div., 1973; ind. nurse practitioner Rural Delivery Nursing Service, Mechanicsville, Md., 1974—; asst. dir. nursing St. Mary's Hosp., Leonardtown, Md., 1975—. Served as 2d lt. Nurse Corps, U.S. Army, 1945-46. Registered nurse, D.C., Md., Ind. Am. Nurses Assn., Sigma Theta Tau. Methodist. Home: 426 Beach Dr Mechanicsville MD 20659 Office: St Mary's Hosp Leonardtown MD 20650

DEACON, RUTH ELINOR, ednl. adminstr.; b. Bellaire, Ohio, June 4, 1923; d. Floyd Thomas and Madge (Brawley) D.; B.S., Ohio State U., 1943; M.S., Cornell U., 1948, Ph.D., 1954. Tchr., West Carrollton (Ohio) High Sch., 1944-45; home extension agt., Cadiz, Ohio, 1945-47; household mgmt. specialist, instr. Cornell U., Ithaca, N.Y., 1948-52, asst. prof., asso. prof., 1954-58; asso. prof., prof. Ohio Agrl. Research and Devel. Center, Wooster, 1958-74; asso. prof., prof., chmn. mgmt. housing and equipment div. Ohio State U., Columbus, 1962-74; head family environ. dept., Coll. Home Econs., Iowa State U., Ames, 1974-76, prof., 1974—, dean, Coll. Home Econs., 1975—; cons. internat. programs: FAO, 1967, 75, USAID, Brazil, 1973, Netherlands, 1975, Egypt, 1975, 80. Bd. dirs. Ames-Gilbert United Way, 1980—, pres., 1982—. Recipient disting. alumni award Coll. Agrl. and Home Econs., 1977. Mem. Am. Home Econs. Assn., AAAS, Nat. Council on Family Relations, Phi Upsilon Omicron, Omicron Nu, Phi Kappa Phi. Republican. Presbyterian. Co-author: Home Management Context and Concepts, 1975, Family Resource Management, 1981; contbr. articles in field to jours. Office: 123 MacKay Hall Iowa State Univ Ames IA 50011

DEAKINS, DEBORAH SUE, fin. exec.; b. Athens, Tenn., Jan. 1, 1952; d. Daniel Boone and Delois Ann (Rule) D.; B.S. in Acctg. cum laude, U. Tenn., 1974; Staff auditor Peat, Marwick, Mitchell & Co., C.P.A.s, Tampa, Fla., 1974-75; internal auditor Fla. Fed. Savs. & Loan Assn., St. Petersburg, 1975-78; auditor Tenn. Div. State Audit, 1978-80; auditor No. Telecom, Inc., Nashville, 1980-81, sr. auditor, 1982—. C.P.A., Tenn. Mem. Am. Inst. C.P.A.s, Tenn. Soc. C.P.A.s. Methodist. Home: 116 Village Green Dr Nashville TN 37217 Office: 219 Cumberland Bend Nashville TN 37208

DEAL, NANCY ELIZABETH CAMPBELL, constrn. co. exec.; b. Warren, Ohio, Jan. 16, 1929; d. Charles Edmund Campbell and Myrtle Irene (Bowers) Campbell Trout; student public schs., Swissvale, Pa.; m. Charles Joseph Deal, Jan. 1, 1973; children by previous marriage—Gary Robert Martin, Linda Irene Martin Nesky, Kathryn Lee Martin Lemon. Acctg. clk. Benefit Assn., Pitts., 1947-50; adminstrv. asst. Kelly Girl Service, Pitts., 1960-72; mgr. employee benefits Eichleay Corp., Pitts., 1973-75; mgr. market research Dick Corp., Pitts., 1975—. Fin. chmn. Congressional candidate, 1970; mem. steering com. Presdl. candidate; bd. dirs., treas. Big Bros. and Big Sisters, 1980—. Mem. Exec. Women Internat. (life mem., corp. pres. 1971-72), Am. Contract Bridge League, Pa. Assn. Parliamentarians. Presbyterian. Home: 5134 Cherryvale Dr Pittsburgh PA 15236 Office: Dick Corp PO Box 10896 Pittsburgh PA 15236

DEAL, PATRICIA LOU EISENBISE, ednl. adminstr.; b. Reading, Pa., Mar. 25, 1932; d. Jasper Paul and Mae (Rozycki) Eisenbise; B.S., Albright Coll., 1954; M.A., Pacific Lutheran U., 1978; m. Robert Lee Deal, May 31, 1955; children—Robert Lee Jr., David Alan, James Edward. Tchr. aide instr.-coordinator Clover Park Vocat.-Tech. Inst., Tacoma, Wash., 1970-78, asst. to program supr. of secondary vocat. edn., 1979, career edn. asst., fed. and spl. projects asst., 1979-81, asst. dir. Elective High Sch., 1981-82; dir. Singletree Estates, Yelm, Wash. Recipient Community Service award United Way, 1980. Mem. Wash. Vocat. Assn. (pres. Clover Park local unit 1981-82, legis. chmn. 1980-81), Wash. Assn. Career Edn. (mem. exec. bd. 1980-81), Am. Vocat. Assn., C. of C., South Sound Women's Network, Nat. Council Local Adminstrs., Wash. Assn. Vocat. Adminstrs. Home: 8401 Woodlawn Ave SW Tacoma WA 98499 Office: 4500 Steilacoom Blvd SW Tacoma WA 98499

DEAL, THEOLA VIRGINIA, nurse; b. Alleene, Ark., Dec. 2, 1929; d. Floyd Dennis and Coelia Pearl (Anderson) Cleghorn; R.N., William Buchanan Sch. Nursing, 1970; m. James Ray Deal, Nov. 25, 1950; children—Joseph Michael, Dennis Ray, Jo Ann, Floyd Eugene (dec.). Staff nurse McCurtain County Meml. Hosp., Idabel, Okla., 1970-72, 11-7 supr., 1972-74; 3-11 supr. DeQueen Gen. Hosp., DeQueen, Ark., 1974—. Mem. Am. Nurses Assn., Okla. Nurses Assn. Dist. 6. Democrat. Ch. of Christ. Office: Hwy 70 W DeQueen AR 71832

DEALMEIDA, MARCELLA J., banker; d. Floyd Francis and Ruth Elma (Cox) Craig; grad. Sch. Consumer Banking, U. Va., 1973; children—Steven Craig and Victor James (twins). Fashion model, 1941-42; tchr. of voice, piano and organ, 1943-53; with First Nat. Bank & Trust Co., Joplin, Mo., 1953-81, v.p., 1976-81; sr. v.p. Centerre Bank of Springfield (Mo.), 1981—; condr. TV program on banking and fin., 1974-75, workshops for Am. Bankers Assn., 1974-75; speaker in field. Bd. dirs. S.W. Mo. Health Systems Agy., 1975-79; mem. Gov. Mo. Adv. Council, 1971-74; exec. com. Jasper County Devel. Assn., 1969-72; vice chmn. Mo. Health Planning Council, 1976; mem. adv. council U. Mo. Health Services Research Center, U. Mo. Spl. Emphasis Health Care Tech. Center. Named to Hall of Honor, Joplin Ann. Celebration Commn., 1973. Mem. Nat. Assn. Bank Women (past chmn. Ozark group), Mo. (past chmn., dir. women's div.), Am. (adv. bd. installment loan div. 1973-79) bankers assns., Am. Inst. Banking (dir. div., bd. govs.), Joplin C. of C. (chmn. red carpet com. 1970-79). Baptist. Clubs: Briarbrook Golf and Country, Mid-Am. Press (dir. 1975—). Home: 3826 El Aztec Springfield MO 65807 Office: 300 S Jefferson St PO Box 1745SSS Springfield MO 65806

DE AMICIS, MARILYN A(NN), clin. psychologist; b. Leominster, Mass., Mar. 30, 1946; d. Mario and Mary (McInerney) De A.; B.A. magna cum laude, Clark U., 1972; Ph.D. (USPHS fellow 1972-76), U. Rochester, 1977. Postdoctoral fellow U. Rochester Student Health Service, 1976-77, dept. psychiatry Sex Therapy Center, SUNY, Stony Brook, 1978-80; adj. faculty St. Joseph's Coll., 1978-80; dir. clin. services Sexual Diagnostic and Treatment Center, Deaconess Hosp., Milw., 1980—. Scottish Rite fellow, 1976; Nat. Research Service grantee, 1978-80. Mem. Am. Psychol. Assn., Phi Beta Kappa. Contbr. articles to profl. jours. Office: Good Samaritan Med Center Deaconess Hosp 620 N 19th St Milwaukee WI 53233

DEAN, ANABEL LOUISE, author; b. Deming, N.Mex., May 24, 1915; d. Orlee Eugene and Mabel May (Wheeler) Stephenson; B.A., Calif. State U., Arcata, 1958; postgrad. U. Calif., Berkeley, Calif. State U., Chico; m. Edward M. Dean, Sept. 3, 1949; children—David Hummel, Stephen Mason, Denise Dean Mills. Tchr., Enterprise Elem. Sch., Redding, Calif., 1960-80; author 42 children's books, 1968—, including Animals That Fly, 1975; How Animals Communicate, 1977; Fire! How Do They Fight It?, 1978; Up! Up! and Away! The Story of Ballooning, 1980; Windsports, 1982. Recipient award for outstanding sci. book Nat. Assn. Sci. Tchrs., 1976, 80. Mem. NEA, Calif. Tchrs. Assn., Ret. Tchrs. Assn. Republican. Address: 2993 Sacramento Dr Redding CA 96001

DEAN, LOUISE DANFORTH, educator; b. St. Louis, May 1, 1933; d. Carlton Miles and Christine Alice (Danforth) D.; B.A., Calif. State U., Northridge, 1971, M.A. with honors, 1974; Ed.D., Nova U., 1980; children—Deborah Louise, Lee E., Linda Gail, Laura Dean. Dir., Congl. Presch., Chatsworth, Calif., 1971-74; dir. campus child devel. center Los Angeles Valley Coll., Moorpark, Calif., 1974-75, instr. child devel., 1975—; prof. Los Angeles Valley Coll., chmn. dept. family and cons. studies, 1979—; asso. prof. Calif. State U., Northridge, 1977-78; pres., past public policy chair Valley chpt. So. Calif. Edn. Young Children; bd. dirs. Child Care Consortium of San Fernando Valley, 1975—; presenter Nat. Adv. Council on Women Hearings, 1979. Mem. Assn. Supervision and Curriculum Devel., Nat. Assn. Edn. of Young Children (nat. presenter 1977), So. Calif. Assn. Edn. of Young Children (editor newsletter), Child Care Consortium San Fernando Valley, NOW, Phi Kappa Phi, Kappa Kappa Gamma. Presbyterian. Home: 17808 Lemarsh St Northridge CA 91325 Office: 5800 Fulton Ave Van Nuys CA 91401

DEAN, LYDIA MARGARET CARTER (MRS. HALSEY ALBERT DEAN), food and nutrition cons., educator, author; b. Bedford, Va., July 11, 1919; d. Christopher C. and Hettie (Gross) Carter; grad. Averett Coll.; B.S., Madison Coll., 1941; M.S., Va. Poly. Inst. and State U., 1951; postgrad. U. Va., Mich. State U.; m. Halsey Albert Dean, Dec. 24, 1941; children—Halsey Albert, John Carter, Lydia Margerae. Dietetic intern, therapeutic dietitian St. Vincent de Paul Hosp., Norfolk, 1942, physicist, U.S. Naval Operating Base, Norfolk, Va., 1943-45; clin. dietitian, instr. Roanoke Meml. Hosps., 1946-51; asso. prof. nutrition Va. Poly. Inst. and State U., 1951-53; community nutritionist and supr. sch. lunch program Roanoke (Va.) Public Schs., 1953-60; dir. dept. dietetics and nutrition Southwestern Med. Center, Roanoke, 1960-67; food and nutrition cons. Nat. hdqrs. ARC, Washington, 1967-79, vol. food and nutrition cons., 1973-82; nutrition cons. U.S. Dept. Agr., Dept. Army, Washington, ARC, 1973—; dir. coordinated undergrad. degree program U. Hawaii, 1974; cons. Am. Dietetic Assn., 1969—, dir. communications, 1975—; mem. task force White House Conf. Food and Nutrition, 1969—; chmn. fed. com. Interagy. Com. on Nutrition Edn., 1970-71; tech. rep. to AID and Dept. State; chmn. Crusade for Nutrition Edn., Washington, 1970—; food cons. internat. tng. Dept. Agr., 1973; cons., participant U.S. Senatorial Nat. Nutrition Policy Conf., 1974. Fellow Am. Public Health Assn.; mem. Am. Dietetic Assn. (dir. communications ann. meeting program and publs. 1975—), Bus. and Profl. Women's Clubs (cons. 1970—, pres.-elect 1980-81, pres. 1981-82), Am. Home Econs. Assn. (rep. and treas. Joint Congressional Com.), AAUW, Food Service Execs. Assn., Inst. Food Technologists, Soc. for Nutrition Edn., Soc. for Nutrition Today (charter), Internat. Platform Assn. Author: (with Virginia McMasters) Community Emergency Feeding, 1972; (with Stanton and Hatfield) Help! My Child Won't Eat Right, 1973; The Gourmet Nutrition Cookbook, 1978; Stress Survival Foodbook, 1980; The Stress Foodbook, 1982; Your Personal Health Book, 1982. Contbr. articles to profl. jours. Home: 7816 Birnam Wood Dr McLean VA 22101

DEAN, MARGARET GENEVIEVE, lawyer; b. Bklyn., Dec. 30, 1943; d. Richard Gerard and Pearl Dorothy (Olson) D.; B.A., Hunter Coll., 1967; J.D., U. Conn., 1980; m. Norman Dean, Apr. 3, 1966; children—Peter, Richard, Dean. Research asst. dept. pediatric psychiatry Bklyn. Jewish Med. Center, 1965-66; research asst. dept. internal medicine Yale U. Med. Sch., 1974; admitted to Conn. bar, 1980; asso. firm Donald Pogue, Hartford, Conn., 1978-81; individual practice employment rights and labor law, New Haven, 1982—; mem. women's adv. panel Sta.-WTNH-TV, New Haven, 1975-78; commentator Sta. WELI, 1976—. Mem. employment task force NOW, Tucson, 1970-71, founder New Haven chpt., 1973, cons. coordinator employment task force, 1973-77, mem. nat. ins. task force, 1976-77; co-founder Ariz. Women's Polit. Caucus, 1972; mem. public edn. com. Conn. div. Am. Cancer Soc., 1973-74; mem. citizens' adv. bd. Conn. State Police and Sex Crimes Adv. Bd., 1974-75; mem. Orange (Conn.) Democratic Town Com.; bd. dirs., chmn. legis. and by-laws com. Griffin Hosp. Aux., Derby, Conn. Mem. New Haven Bar Assn., Conn. Bar Assn., Unitarian. Home: 888 Indian Hill Rd Orange CT 06477 Office: 152 Temple St New Haven CT 06510

DEAN, MARGO, ballet dir.; b. Ft. Worth, Dec. 9, 1930; d. Arthur Augustus and Margaret (Holliday) Webster; B.F.A., Ward-Belmont Coll., 1947; student Tex. Christian U., 1948; m. Beale Dean, Sept. 3, 1948; children—Webster Beale, Giselle Liseanne. Ballet appearances, Louisville, 1948, Dallas, 1947; prin. dancer, choreographer Ft. Worth Opera Ballet, 1955-60; dir. Ft. Worth Ballet Assn., 1961; artistic dir. Ballet Concerto, Ft. Worth, 1969—. Bd. dirs. Ft. Worth Symphony Orch. Mem. Southwestern Regional Ballet Assn., Nat. Assn. Regional Ballet. Republican. Presbyterian. Clubs: Fort Worth, Fort Worth Boat, Ridglea Country. Home: 3709 Cresthaven Fort Worth TX 76107 Office: 3803 Camp Bowie Fort Worth TX 76107

DEAN, MARJORIE SWANSON, cons.; b. San Diego, Mar. 10, 1931; d. Frans Albin and Edith Marie (Larson) Swanson; B.A. with honors in Social Scis., San Diego State U., 1969, teaching cert., 1971; m. Winfield Albert Dean, Sept. 8, 1951; children—Eric Winfield, Janis Lorraine. Music tchr., 1971-79; ind. contractor for cons. and coordination services for bus., travel, recreational and rehab. programming, Spring Valley, Calif., 1978—; bd. mgrs. Mt. Miguel Covenant Village, Spring Valley, 1977-81. Mem. exec. bd. of bd. evangelism Evang. Covenant Chs. Am., 1974—, mem. exec. bd. of bd. evangelism and ch. growth Pacific S.W. conf., 1974—. Recipient Achievement award Covenant Women, 1977. Address: 3594 Hartzel Dr Spring Valley CA 92077

DEAN, MARY ELIZABETH, ins. exec.; b. Harford County, Md., June 29, 1934; d. Miles Edgar and Elizabeth Zora (Poteet) Robinson; ed. public schs., bus. and ins. seminars; m. Norman J. Dean, Jan. 23, 1954; children—Edgar, Linda. File clk. Harford Mut. Ins. Co., Bel Air, Md., 1952-53, underwriter, 1953-56; agt. O'Brien-Little, Inc., Bel Air, 1957-73; ins. agt., broker, 1973-74; owner Little & Slapak Inc., 1974—; owner, pres. Dean Ins. Agy., Inc., Bel Air, 1974—; v.p. Dean & Donovan Ins. Agy., Inc. Co-chairperson Mandel for Gov., Harford County, 1974. Mem. Harford-Cecil Ind. Ins. Agts. Assn. (past pres.), Harford-Cecil Ins. Women's Assn. (founder), Profl. Women's Assn. Bel Air (founder), Nat. Assn. Ins. Agts., Ind. Ins. Agts. Md., Profl. Ins. Agts. Assn. (regional capt.). Methodist. Club: Md. Golf and Country. Office: 707 N Hickory Ave Bel Air MD 21014

DEAN, PAMELA LOUISE, real estate broker, bakery owner; b. Greenville, Ohio, Jan. 7, 1943; d. Robert Franklin and Edith Elizabeth (Wood) Cook; B.A. in Sociology, U. Wash., 1972, postgrad., 1974; 1 son, Bret Ronald Wright. Parole counselor, Pasco, Wash., 1972; owner Thunderhead Turquoise & Silver Co., Seattle, 1973-75; realtor, asst. mgr., broker, Sherwood & Roberts Inc., Seattle, 1975-80; owner So-Low Sweet Shops, diet bakeries, Seattle, 1980—; speaker in field. Active United Good Neighbor Fund, 1980. Mem. Bus. and Profl. Women's Assn., Bus. Women's Network, Nat. Assn. Female Execs. Home: 2459 S 216th St Des Moines WA 98188 Office: 630 SW 153d St Seattle WA 98166

DEAN, PEGGY POWELL, fin. devel. cons.; b. Birmingham, Ala., Aug. 2, 1951; d. Jason Martin and Peggy (Powell) D.; B.A., U. Ala., 1973; postgrad. Columbia U., 1974, N.Y. U., 1975. Asst. to pres. for devel. Finch Coll., 1974-75; account exec. John O'Donnell Co., N.Y.C., 1975-76, sr. account exec., 1976-77, account supr., 1977-79; pres. Peggy Powell Dean & Co., N.Y.C., 1979—; cons. First Women's Bank, N.Y. Urban Devel. Corp., UN Assn., Inwood House, Girls Clubs Am., Jupiter Symphony, Trailblazer Camps, others. Tech. asst. N.Y. State Council on Arts; bd. dirs. Council Career Planning, 1978-81, Big Sisters, 1981—; mem. exec. council N.Y.C. Opera Guild, 1977—; founding mem., mem. exec. com. Camerata, N.Y.C., 1978-79. Recipient Nat. Alumni Student award U. Ala., 1973. Mem. U. Ala. Alumni Assn. (pres. Greater N.Y. chpt. 1977-78), Nat. Assn. Fund Raising Execs., AAUW (forum com. 1974). Office: 30 Lincoln Plaza New York NY 10023

DEANS, CATHERINE MARIE, mfg. co. mktg. exec.; b. N.Y.C., Dec. 6, 1946; d. Robert Francis and Catherine Patricia (Lynch) Deans; B.A., St. Joseph's Coll., 1968; M.B.A., Babson Coll., 1976; m. Peter Norman Richard, Aug. 14, 1975. VISTA vol., health advocate, Blytheville, Ark., 1968-69; technician Blood Grouping Lab., Boston, 1970-72; chemist Collaborative Research, Inc., Waltham, Mass., 1972-75; cons. Corporate Tech. Planning, Waltham, 1976-78; mktg. analyst Helix Tech. div. Helix Process Systems, Westboro, Mass., 1978-79; applications engr. Helix Tech./CTI Cyrogenics, Waltham, Mass., 1979-80, regional sales/mktg. exec., 1980-82, maj. account mgr., 1982—; dir. Hardric Labs., Inc., Waltham, 1976—. Pres., Palfrey St. Sch., Watertown, Mass., 1979—, trustee, 1978—. Mem. Am. Mktg. Assn., Indsl. Mktg. Group (treas. 1980—), Nat. Assn. Female Execs., Am. Vacuum Soc., Soc. Vacuum Coaters. Contbr. articles to profl. jours. Home: 1 Dexter Ave Waltham MA 02154 Office: 266 2d Ave Waltham MA 02254

DE ARMAS, MAYDA ANA, counselor; b. Havana, Cuba, Feb. 6, 1944; d. Osvaldo and Ana (Leon) de A.; came to U.S., 1961, naturalized, 1971; B.A., Mundelein Coll., 1966; M.A., Mount St. Mary's Coll., 1970; M.Ed., U. So. Calif., 1977. Community worker Venice Community Center, 1967; social worker Los Angeles County Dept. Public Social Services, 1970-72; tchr. Thomas Jefferson Community Adult Sch., 1968-80; pupil services and attendance counselor Los Angeles Unified Sch. Dist., 1972—. Served in USAR, 1977—. Mem. United Tchrs. Los Angeles, Cuban-Am. Tchrs. Assn. Home: 16032 Londelius St Sepulveda CA 91343 Office: 8111 Calhoun Ave Panorama City CA 91402

DEATHERAGE, CLETA, lawyer, state legislator; b. Oklahoma City, Sept. 16, 1950; d. Jack H. and Modean (Lane) D.; B.A. with high honors, U. Okla., 1973, J.D., 1975. Legal asst., then legal counsel Okla. Human Rights Commn., 1973-76; admitted to Okla. bar, 1976; asso. firm Draper, Deatherage and Patten, Norman, Okla., 1976-82; asso. firm English, Patten and Deatherage, 1982—; mem. Okla. Ho. of Reps., 1976—, chmn. appropriations and budget com., 1980—, mem. joint com. on fiscal ops. Chmn. Norman Reapportionment Commn., 1975-76; precinct ofcl. Okla. Dem. Party, 1972—, nat. del., 1972, dist. officer, 1976—, state exec. com.; state adv. council U.S. Commn. on Civil Rights; mem. strategy council Dem. Nat. Com., also mem. commn. on Presdl. nominations; vice chmn. Center for Nat. Policy, Washington. Recipient Redbook Red Ribbon award, 1979; Patron of Higher Edn. award, 1979; Disting. Service award Am. Legion, 1979, 82; Byliner award Oklahoma City Women in Communications, 1980; named to Top Ten Legislators, 1977, 78, 79, 80, 81, 82; fellow Harvard U. Inst. Politics, 1981. Mem. Nat. Conf. State Legislatures (chmn. fiscal oversight com., chmn. assembly on the legislature 1982-83, mem. exec. com. 1982-83), AAUW, Nat. Fedn. Bus. and Profl. Women's Clubs Am. (polit. action com.), Nat. Order of Women Legislators, Nat. Women's Polit. Caucus, Okla. Bar Assn., Cleveland County Bar Assn. Mem. Christian Church (Disciples of Christ). Clubs: PEO, Assistance League of Norman, Chi Omega Alumnae. Office: 210 E Main St 200 Norman OK 73069

DEATHERAGE, MARTHA MARTIN, educator; b. Parsons, Kans.; d. Maxwell Metier and Helen Louise (Ott) Martin; Mus.B. cum laude, Stephens Coll., 1951; Mus.M., U. Tex., 1952; advanced study Dame Maggie Teyte, Madame Lotte Lehmann; m. Bruce H. Deatherage, July 1953; children—Alison Ann, Laura Ellen. Soprano soloist, St. Louis Symphony, St. Louis Philharmonic, Rockefeller Meml. Chapel, U. Chgo.; soloist, oratorio and symphonic concerts, Midwest, 1954-61; concertised, Midwest, 1956-61; radio and TV appearances Los Angeles, 1959-61; instr. voice U. Tex., Austin, then assoc. prof., 1967-80, prof., 1980—, coordinator vocal div., 1980—. Recipient Nat. Young Artist award Nat. Fedn. Music Clubs, 1957. Mem. Nat. Assn. Tchrs. Singing (regional lt. gov. South Tex. 1973-80), Sigma Alpha Iota, Pi Kappa Lambda. Episcopalian. Dept Music U Tex Austin TX 78746

DEATON, FAE ADAMS, psychiat. social worker; b. Phila., Feb. 19, 1932; d. Charles Sizemore and Dorothea Lucia (Adams) Deaton; Mus.B., Salem Coll., Winston-Salem, N.C., 1953; M.S.Ed., Old Dominion U., 1975; M.S.W., Norfolk State U., 1980; postgrad. Ohio U., 1961-62, Oxford (Eng.) U., 1963-64, U. Alaska, 1967-69, Alaska Meth. U., 1969, Wright State U., 1971-73; children—Dorothea Fae Stein Krause-Falloure, Caroline Louise Stein, Erich Charles Stein. Music tchr. Mifflin Twp., Columbus, Ohio, 1953-54; high sch. supr. USN Dependents' Sch., Argentia, Nfld., 1956-57; tchr. USAF Dependents Schs., Eng., 1960-63, 63-64; mag. editor, Scott AFB, Ill., 1966-67; substitute tchr. USAF Dependents Sch., Alaska, 1967-70; arts and music critic, writer Anchorage Evening Times, 1968-70; mem. staff Anchorage Hist. and Fine Arts Mus., 1968-70; publicity chmn. Alaska Council on Arts, 1969-70; counselor Dayton (Ohio) Youth Services Bur., 1973; writer Dayton Daily News, 1973; engrng. aide biophysics lab. Wright-Patterson AFB, Ohio, 1973; researcher Am. Inst. Research, 1974-75; writer, editor Old Dominion U., 1974, grad. asst. to chmn. dept. spl. edn., 1974-75, adminstrv. asst. econs. dept., 1975-76; counselor, patient advocate Norfolk (Va.) Free Clinic, 1975-76; tchr., counselor Blessed Sacrament Sch., Norfolk, 1976-77; mental health worker young adolescent unit Portsmouth (Va.) Psychiat. Center, 1977-79, children's unit, 1979-80; individual and family therapist Pain Treatment Clinic and Program for Young Adults, 1982—; active Tidewater Rape Info. Service; sponsor Parents United, sexual abuse self-help group, 1979—; admissions-release com. Norfolk Lakehouse Girls Detention Home, 1978-79; legis. com. Tidewater Profl. Assn. on Child Abuse, 1978—; chmn. project spl. needs of children Children's Art Center, Norfolk, 1979—; author/adminstr. Sexual Abuse Helpline of Tidewater, 1979-81; mem. Sexual Abuse Treatment Team of Virginia Beach. Troop leader Girl Scouts U.S.A., 1964-69; dir. chapel choir RAF Croughton (Eng.) AFB, 1960-64, dir. jr. choir, 1963-64; mem. Elmendorf (Alaska) Sch. Bd., 1967-68; organist St. Timothy Luth. Ch., Norfolk, 1970-71; bd. dirs. Norfolk Little Theatre, 1977-78. Mem. Nat. Assn. Am. Pen Women, Am., Va., Hampton Roads personnel and guidance assns., Nat., Va. assns. specialists in group work, Va. Council on Social Welfare (dir. Tidewater chpt. 1978-81), Pub. Offenders Counselors Assn., Nat. Assn. Social Workers, Am. Orthopsychiat. Assn., Nat. Public Offender Counselors Assn., Crisis Intervention Coalition, Nat. Coalition on Sexual Abuse, Mid-Atlantic Coalition Sexual Abuse of Children (sec. 1981-82), Tidewater Alliance Sexual Abuse (pres.-elect 1982, pres. 1983), Am., Va. sch. counselors assns., Am., Va. mental health counselors assns., Tidewater Mental Health Assn. (public affairs com.), Va. Elem. Sch. Counselors Assn. (legis. com. 1975-76), Chrysler Mus. Assn., Va. Opera Assn. Guild, Staff Assn. Old Dominion U. (v.p. 1975-76), Alaska Press. Author articles in field; also textbook. Home: 1176 Pickett Rd Norfolk VA 23502 Office: Portsmouth Psychiat Center Sexual Trauma Treatment Center 301 Fort Lane Portsmouth VA 23704

DEAVER, AGNES JEAN, business exec.; b. Mercersburg, Pa., Aug. 2, 1931; d. Russell Ellsworth and Christina Jane (Reeder) D.; student Chambersburg (Pa.) Bus. Coll., 1951, King's Coll., Briarcliff Manor, N.Y., 1958, U. Calif., Santa Barbara, 1969. Various secretarial positions, 1951-70; adminstv. asst. to resident v.p. Sentry Ins. Co., Santa Barbara, Calif., 1964-70; exec. asst. Chi Alpha Mgmt., Inc., Santa Barbara and Ventura, Calif., 1970—; sec.-treas. W.D. Mgmt., Inc., W.W. Mgmt., Inc., Am. Family Services, Inc., United Family Assos., Inc. Mem. Nat. Secretarial Assn. (charter mem. Santa Barbara chpt.). Republican. Home: 3950 Via Real Apt 14 Carpinteria CA 93013 Office: 1486 E Valley Rd Suite F Montecito CA 93108

DEAZLEY, JOAN AUDREY, med. instn. exec.; b. Williamsville, N.Y., Sept. 12, 1920; d. Bernard George and Barbara Caroline (Schultz) D.; student N. Park Bus. Sch., 1939. Sec. to dir. flight research Curtiss-Wright Corp., Buffalo, 1939-44, sec. to asso. dir. Cornell Research Lab., 1944-46; sec. to dept. mgr. Westinghouse Electric Corp., Buffalo, 1947-54; campcraft specialist Camp Seven Hills, Holland N.Y., summer 1954, asst. dir. camp, summer 1955; sec. to purchasing agt. Howard Hughes Med. Inst., Miami Beach, Fla., 1956-62, asst. to adminstr. purchasing and med. library, Miami, Fla., 1962-73, purchasing agt., 1973-79, mgr. Sci. Conf. Center, Coconut Grove, Fla., 1979—. Girl Scout leader, 1940-54; mem. Buffalo and Erie County Girl Scout Leaders Assn., 1945-54, v.p., 1950-52, pres., 1952-54, U.S. rep. to Internat. Conf., 1953. Mem. Soc. Research Adminstrs., Hollywood (Fla.) Power Squadron Aux. (pres. 1964-65). Republican. Roman Catholic. Office: PO Box 330837 Coconut Grove FL 33133

DEBAKEY, LOIS, communications specialist, educator; b. Lake Charles, La.; d. Shaker M. and Raheeja (Zorba) DeB.; B.A. in Math., Tulane U., 1949, M.A. in Lit. and Linguistics, 1959, Ph.D., 1963. Asst. prof. English, Tulane U., New Orleans; asst. prof. sci. communications Tulane Med. Sch., 1963-65, asso. prof., 1965-67, prof., 1967-68, lectr. sci. communications, 1968—, adj. prof., 1981—; prof. sci. communications Baylor Coll. Medicine, Houston, Tex., 1981—; dir. Plain Talk, Inc.; mem. usage panel Am. Heritage Dictionary; cons. communications to various schs. and med. libraries. Recipient Bausch and Lomb Sci. award. Mem. Soc. for Tech. Communication (dir. Houston chpt.), Nat. Council Tchrs. of English (com. on sci. writing), Am. Med. Writers Assn. (Disting. Service award), Internat. Soc. Gen. Semantics, Nat. Assn. Sci. Writers, Soc. Health and Human Values, Soc. Tech. Communications, Council Biology Editors (dir.; com. on grad. tng. in sci. writing), Assn. Tchrs. of Tech. Writing, So. Assn. Colls. and Schs. (exec. council commn.), NIH Alumni Assn., Phi Beta Kappa. Episcopalian. Author: The Scientific Journal: Editorial Policies and Practices; contbr. numerous articles on biomed. communication, sci. writing, editing and publ. to profl. jours.; editorial bd. Excerpta Medica's Core Jours. in Cardiology, Jour. of Cardiology, Health Communications, Forum on Medicine, Grants Mag., Cardiovascular Research Center Bull. Office: Baylor College of Medicine 1200 Moursund Ave Houston TX 77030

DEBAKEY, SELMA, sci. communication specialist, educator; b. Lake Charles, La.; d. S.M. and Raheega (Zorba) DeB.; B.A., Newcomb Coll.; postgrad. Tulane U. Dir. dept. med. communication Alton Ochsner Med. Found., New Orleans, 1942-68; prof. sci. communication Baylor Coll. Medicine, Houston, 1968—; mem. faculty various intensive courses in sci. communication for med. schs., med. socs. Mem. Soc. Tech. Communication, Soc. Health and Human Values. Contbr. numerous articles on sci. writing to profl. jours.; author: (with Segaloff and Meyer) Current Concepts in Breast Cancer, 1967; editor Cardiovascular Research Center Bull., 1970—. Office: 1200 Moursund Ave Houston TX 77030

DEBOER, REBECCA LEANN, state legislator; b. Concord, N.C., July 1, 1947; d. Robert DeWitt Starnes and Leah Ruth (Smith) Moore; student So. Oreg. State Coll., 1967-69; m. Robert Giles DeBoer, July 1, 1966; children—Tamarah Ann, Lezlie Lynn, Robert Walter Collins. Co-owner, Valley Chevrolet dealership, Medford, Oreg., 1980-82; mem. Oreg. Ho. of Reps., 1980—. Pres., Hoover Sch. Parent Club, 1977-78; vol. Dist. 549C Medford Schs., 1975-77, site chmn., adv. bd., 1977-78; mem. Park Devel. Commn. City of Medford, 1975, vice chmn., 1977-78, chmn., 1978-80; vice chmn. Bear Creek Greenway Commn., 1977-78, chmn., 1978-80; chmn. Kennedy Sch. PTA, 1978-79; chmn. John F. Kennedy Elem. Citizens Adv. Com., Citizens Budget Com. Medford, 1979-80; 2d v.p. Jackson County unit Oreg. Republican Women; bd. dirs. Jackson County Red Cross; active Rogue Valley Inst.; provisional mem. Jr. Service League. Lutheran. Office: 820 Cedar Mall Medford OR 97501

DEBOLD, VICKI SUE, ins. broker; b. Macomb, Ill., Sept. 14, 1947; d. Robert Melvin and Laura Mae (Magnuson) Pollock; student public schs.; m. Neil C. Goforth, July 18, 1969 (dec. Mar. 1971); m. 2d, David Loran DeBold, Nov. 18, 1978. Various retail sales and secretarial positions, 1964-70; broker-owner Goforth Ins. Agy., Bushnell, Ill., 1971—, profl. singer with group Life, 1972-74. Named Young Career Woman of Yr., Bus. and Profl. Women Macomb (Ill.), 1972. Hon. mem. Ill. Assn. Nat. Campers and Hikers Assn. (Wild Life Refuge award 1975); mem. Nat. Fedn. Small Businesses, Nat. Assn. Female Execs., Ind. Ins. Agts. Ill., Profl. Ins. Agts. Ill., Bushnell Ind. Ins. Agts. Assn., Macomb Ind. Ins. Agts. Assn. Republican. Presbyterian. Home: 1227 W Adams St Macomb IL 61455 Office: 162 E Hail St Bushnell IL 61422

DEBORD, VIOLA FERNE, nursing adminstr.; b. Dwight, Ill., Oct. 17, 1914; d. Arthur E. and Kathryn (Schroeder) Houck; B.S. in Nursing Adminstrn. (Katherine Densford scholar), U. Minn., 1963; student DePaul U., Chgo., 1964-65; children—Kathleen, Ruth, Sally, Betty. Dir. nursing Brackenridge Hosp., Austin, Tex., 1954-60; nursing supr. Evanston (Ill.) Hosp., 1961-62; asso. dir. nursing Michael Reese Hosp. and Med. Center, Chgo., 1964-66; nursing cons. Tex. State Health Dept., Austin, 1966-68; asst. adminstr. nursing Brackenridge Hosp., Austin, Tex., 1968—. Mem. Am. Soc. Nursing Service Adminstrs., Tex. Soc. Nursing Services Adminstrs., Sigma Theta Tau. Office: 1500 East Ave Austin TX 78701

DEBS, BARBARA KNOWLES, coll. pres.; b. Eastham, Mass., Dec. 24, 1931; d. Stanley F. and Arline (Eugley) Knowles; B.A., Vassar Coll., 1953; Fulbright fellow, Scuola Normale, Pisa, Italy, 1953, U. Rome, 1954; postgrad. Radcliffe Coll., 1956-58; Ph.D., Harvard U., 1967; LL.D. (hon.), N.Y. Law Sch., 1979; m. Richard A. Debs, July 19, 1958; children—Elizabeth, Nicholas. Instr. art dept. Vassar Coll., 1955-56; free lance translator editor Ency. of World Art, McGraw-Hill Pub., N.Y.C., 1959-62; asst. prof. art history dept. Manhattanville Coll., Purchase, N.Y., 1968-73, asso. prof., 1973-77, acting pres., 1975, pres., 1976—, prof. art history, 1977—; dir. AMF, Inc. Bd. dirs., hon. mem. Westchester Chamber Music Soc.; trustee N.Y. Law Sch., 1979—; mem. Westchester County Bd. Ethics; mem. implementation bd. Westchester Med. Center; mem. N.Y. Council on Humanities; adv. com. on higher edn. to Dems., N.Y. Senate, 1979-80. AAUW Nat. fellow and Ann Radcliffe fellow, 1958-59; Radcliffe grant-in-aid, 1966-67; Am. Council Learned Socs. grantee, 1973. Mem. Hundred of Westchester (dir.), Phi Beta Kappa. Contbr. articles on Renaissance and contemporary art to profl. publs. Home and office: Manhattanville Coll Purchase NY 10577

DEBUS, ELEANOR VIOLA, business mgmt. co. exec.; b. Buffalo, May 19, 1920; d. Arthur Adam and Viola Charlotte (Pohl) D.; student Chown Bus. Sch., 1939. Sec., Buffalo Wire Works, 1939-45; home talent producer Empire Producing Co., Kansas City, Mo., sec. Owens Corning Fiberglass, Buffalo; with public relations and publicity Niagara Falls (Ont., Can.) Theatre, 19—; public relations dir. Woman's Internat. Bowling Congress, Columbus, Ohio, 1957-59; publicist, sec. Ice Capades, Hollywood, Calif., 1961-63; sec. to controller Rexall Drug Co., Los Angeles, 1963-67; bus. mgmt. acct. Samuel Berke & Co., Beverly Hills, Calif., 1967-75; Gadbois Mgmt. Co., Beverly Hills, 1975-76; sec., treas. Sasha Corp., Los Angeles, 1976—; bus. mgmt. dir. Dean Martin, Los Angeles, 1976—; pres. Tempo Co., Los Angeles, 1976—. Mem. Nat. Assn. Female Execs., Nat. Notary Assn., Nat. Film Soc., Am. Film Inst. Republican. Club: Order Eastern Star. Contbr. articles to various mags. Office: Tempo Co 9911 W Pico Blvd Suite 560 Los Angeles CA 90035

DE CAMP, CATHERINE CROOK, author; b. N.Y.C., Nov. 6, 1907; d. Samuel and Mary Eliza (Beekman) Crook; A.B. magna cum laude, Barnard Coll., 1933; postgrad. Columbia U., Temple U.; m. Lyon Sprague de Camp, Aug. 12, 1939; children—Lyman Sprague, Gerard Beekman. Tchr. English and history, Conn., Ohio and N.Y., 1934-39; instr. Temple U., 1949-50; editor, bus. mgr. L. Sprague de Camp, 1950—; comptroller Conan Properties, Inc., 1980—; freelance writer, 1950—; vis. lectr. various colls.; author: The Money Tree, 1972; Teach Your Child to Manage Money, 1974; Creatures of the Cosmos, 1977; (with L. Sprague de Camp) Ancient Ruins and Archaeology (retitled Citadels of Mystery), 1964; Spirits, Stars and Spells, 1966; The Story of Science in America, 1967; The Day of the Dinosaurs, 1968; Darwin and His Great Discovery, 1972; 3,000 Years of Fantasy and Science Fiction, 1972; Tales Beyond Times, 1973; Science Fiction Handbook, rev. edit., 1975; Footprints on Sand, 1981; (with de Camp and L. Carter) Conan the Barbarian, 1982. Recipient (with L. Sprague de Camp) 8th Drexel citation for disting. contbr. to lit. young people, 1978. Mem. Authors Guild, Fellows in Am. Studies, Barnard Coll. Alumnae Assn., Hist. Soc. Pa., Acad. Natural Scis. Phila., Cum Laude Soc., Phi Beta Kappa. Episcopalian. Club: Barnard (Phila.). Address: 278 Hothorpe Ln Villanova PA 19085

DECARIE, THERESE GOUIN, educator; b. Montreal, Que., Can., Sept. 30, 1923; d. Leon Mercier and Yvette Ollivier Gouin; B.A., U. Montreal, 1945, L.Ph., 1947, Ph.D., 1960; m. Vianney Decarie, Dec. 24, 1948; children—Pascale, Dominique, Jean-Claude, Emmanuel. Instr. psychology U. Montreal, 1949-51, asso. prof., 1951-65, prof., 1965—. Mem. Societe Canadienne, de Psychologie, Corp. des Psychologues de la Province de Que., Soc. Research in Child Devel., Societe de Psychanalyse. Author: Le developpement psychologique de l'enfant, 1953; De l'adolescence a la maturitie, 1955; L'intelligence et l'affectivite chez le jeune enfant, 1961; contbr. in field. Office: Department of Psychology Universite de Montreal Montreal PQ H3C 3J7 Canada

DECARLO, MARY ANN, mfg. exec.; b. Lakewood, N.J., Dec. 18, 1946; d. Alexander Joseph, Sr., and Gloria Pauline (Gould) DeC.; student bus. adminstrn., Brookdale Community Coll., 1976-79; m. Randolph Henry Adrian, Feb. 2, 1980. Quality control tester Hecon Corp., Tinton Falls, N.J., 1973-74; quality assurance insp. Interdata, Oceanport, N.J., 1974; tester MolecuWire Corp., Wall Twp., N.J., 1974-75; quality control supr. Autodynamics, Inc., Neptune, N.J., 1975—. Mem. Am. Soc. Profl. and Exec. Women, Am. Soc. Quality Control (asso.), Nat. Assn. Female Execs., Inc., Home: 110 Belshaw Ave Eatontown NJ 07724 Office: 1115 Green Grove Rd Neptune NJ 07753

DECICCO, ANNE LOMMEL, assn. exec.; b. N.Y.C., Sept. 27, 1950; d. Richard Arthur and Nancy (Robertson) Lommel; children—Geoffrey Lommel, Melanie Paige. Dir. vol. services Perth Amboy (N.J.) Gen. Hosp., 1975; dir. aux. services and health promotion N.J. Hosp. Assn., Princeton, 1979-81, v.p. human resources and mgmt. practices, 1981—; mem. adv. com. health fairs Sta. WNBC-TV, N.Y.C., Office of Consumer Health Edn., U. Medicine and Dentistry N.J., mem. dietetic internship residency program adv. com. Bd. dirs. Am. Trauma Assn. Mem. Am. Soc. Dirs. Vol. Services, Am. Soc. Health Manpower Edn. and Tng., Am. Public Health Assn. Home: 120 Jackson Ave Dunellen NJ 08812 Office: Center Health Affairs 760 Alexander Rd Princeton NJ 08540

DECKER, ANNE FOLGER, ednl. assn. adminstr.; b. Orange, N.J., Oct. 14, 1925; d. Riley Carlisle and Althea Margaret (Penland) Folger; A.B. cum laude, Salem Coll., 1947; M.A. (scholar), N.Y. U., 1962, Ph.D. (Health Info. Found. grantee), 1967; m. William Butterfield Decker, Oct. 9, 1964. Wage and salary analyst Lockheed Aircraft Corp., Marietta, Ga., 1951-55; adminstrv. asst. So. Regional Edn. Bd., Atlanta, 1955-57; adminstrv. asst. to exec. v.p. N.Y. U., N.Y.C., 1957-59; nat. coordinator Learning Resources Inst., N.Y.C., 1959-63; asst. dir. Nat. Instructional TV Library, N.Y.C., 1963-64; security analyst Francis I. duPont, N.Y.C., 1968-70; adj. asst. prof. Hunter Coll., City U. N.Y., 1971, asst. dean acad. advising, 1971-79; asst. dir. research Council Fin. Aid to Edn. Inc., N.Y.C., 1979-81, asst. v.p., 1981—; cons. Fordham U., 1974, Kirkland Coll., 1975. Co-chairwoman LaGuardia Corner Gardens, 1976-78; bd. dirs. Washington Sq. Corp., 1976-79, pres., 1978-79. Recipient Founders Day award N.Y. U., 1967. Mem. Am. Sociol. Assn., Am. Assn. Higher Edn., Nat. Assn. Women Deans, Adminstrs. and Counselors, Eastern Assn. Coll. Deans and Advs. of Students. Author: (with Ruth Jody, Felicia Brings) A Handbook on Open Admissions, 1976; also articles in profl. jours. Office: 680 Fifth Ave New York NY 10019

DECKER, BETH FRANCIS, nursing adminstr.; b. Croswell, Mich., Sept. 14, 1923; d. Frank William and Delta Ferne (Francis) Gray; diploma St. Joseph Hosp. Sch. Nursing, 1946; m. K. Ward Decker, Sept. 3, 1949; 1 son, Rex A. Staff nurse Good Samaritan Hosp., Cin., 1946, St. Joseph's Hosp., Mt. Clements, Mich., 1946-47; office nurse, Deckerville, Mich., 1947-50; staff nurse Deckerville Hosp., 1950-70; office nurse, Bad Axe, Mich., 1971-73; inservice dir. Huron Meml. Hosp., Bad Axe, 1973-77, dir. nursing service, 1977—; instr. emergency med. technicians, 1973—. Bd. dirs. East Central Mich. Emergency Med. Services, 1976—; pres., 1976—; bd. dirs. Health Systems Agy., 1977—, v.p., 1977-78. Served with Cadet Nurses Corps, 1943-46. Mem. Am., Mich., Sanilac Dist. (pres. 1972-73), ARC nurses assns., Natural Childbirth Assn., Mich. Ambulance Assn., Mich. Hosp. Pub. Relations Assn., Emergency Dept. Nurses Assn., Am. Legion Aux. (pres., sec. local unit 1955-65). Republican. Methodist. Home: 2672 Black River St Deckerville MI 48427 Office: 110 S Van Dyke Bad Axe MI 48413

DECKER, DEBRA ELNORA, librarian; b. Williamsport, Pa., Oct. 25, 1946; d. Herman Thomas and Harriett Lucina (Mullen) Palmer; B.S., Lock Haven State Coll., 1968; M.Ed., West Chester State Coll., 1971; M.S. in Library Sci., Clarion State Coll., 1981; m. Sept. 7, 1969; 1 dau., Moana Kai. Tchr., Owen J. Roberts Sch. Dist., Pottstown, Pa., 1968-73; instr., Becker Research Learning Center, Clarion (Pa.) State Coll., 1976-80, librarian instr., Instructional Materials Center, 1980—. Neighborhood chmn. Brookville Council Girls Scouts U.S., 1976—; bd. dirs. Brookville Area United Fund, 1980—; officer Zion United Methodist Ch., 1977—. Mem. NEA, Pa. Edn. Assn., Assn. Pa. State Coll. and Univ. Faculties, Phi Delta Kappa. Democrat. Home: RD 4 Box 250 Brookville PA 15825 Office: Carlson Library Clarion State Coll Clarion PA 16214

DECKER, JEAN CAMPBELL, fin. exec.; b. Chgo., Mar. 10, 1915; d. Dm and Bertha (Campbell) Decker; B.A. in Bus. Adminstrn., U. Chgo., 1937. With Calco Mfg. Co., Addison, Ill., 1950—, asst. treas., 1967, treas., 1969—, plan adminstr., dir. pension plan, 1976—; treas. Gustafson Enterprises, Inc., Addison, Ill., 1971—, dir., 1971-78, 82—; treas. Environ, Inc., Haines City, Fla., 1971-72. Mem. U. Chgo. Alumni Assn., Phi Delta Upsilon. Republican. Home: 885 Smith St Glen Ellyn IL 60137

DE CLEENE, BETTY JEANE, wholesale fish co. exec.; b. Green Bay, Wis., Dec. 18, 1933; d. Mike Solomon and Ethel Josephine (Isaacson) Buckarma; diploma Vocat. Edn. Bus. Sch., Green Bay, 1953; m. Louis John De Cleene, May 12, 1953; children—Jacob, Jon, Jamie, Jeffrey. With Wis. Telephone Co., 1953-54, Reynolds Tobacco Co., 1955-56; head elec. engrng. estimator Va. Electric Power Co., Norfolk, 1960-61; sec. Buck's Fish Transfer Co., Green Bay, 1973-75, v.p., sec., dir., 1976—. Pres., Elmore Sch. PTA, Green Bay, 1975-76; mem. Green Bay-Brown County Planning Commn., 1976—; active local Cub Scouts, Little League. Mem. Nat. Fedn. Ind. Bus., Green Bay Area C. of C., Northeastern Wis. Fishermen's Assn., Green Bay Area Fishermen's Assn., Wis. Com. Individual Land Rights, Ladies Aux. Fleet Res. Assn. (pres., regional hosp. chmn. 1979—), United Patriotic Soc. Green Bay (sec. 1976—). Home: 727 Neville Ave Green Bay WI 54303 Office: 203 Alexander St Green Bay WI 54303

DECROW, KAREN, lawyer, author, lectr.; b. Chgo., Dec. 18, 1937; d. Samuel Meyer and Juliette (Abt) Lipschultz; B.S., Northwestern U., 1959; J.D., Syracuse U., 1972; m. Alexander Allen Kolben, 1960 (div. 1965); m. 2d, Roger Edward DeCrow, 1965 (div. 1972). Resort editor Golf Digest mag., Evanston, Ill., 1959-60; editor Am. Soc. Planning Ofcls., Chgo., 1960-61; writer Center for Study Liberal Edn. for Adults, Chgo., 1961-64; editor Holt, Rinehart, Winston, Inc., N.Y.C., 1965; editor L.W. Singer, Syracuse, N.Y., 1965-66; writer Eastern Regional Inst. for Edn., Syracuse, 1967-69; nat. bd. mem. NOW 1968-77, nat. pres., 1974-77, also nat. politics task force chairperson; admitted to N.Y. State bar; legal practice specializing in constl. law, lit. and entertainment law, also gender discrimination law; cons. on affirmative action; lectr. colls. and univs., U.S., Can., Mex., Greece, USSR, Finland, Radio Free Europe. Trustee Elizabeth Cady Stanton Found.; a nat. coordinator Women's Strike for Equality, 1970; legis. specialist N.Y. Women's Bar Assn.; nat. bd. dirs. Gay Rights Nat. Lobby; mem. ad hoc com. Women for Human Rights; bd. advisers Working Women's Inst.; endorser Coalition Against Racism. Candidate for mayor Syracuse, 1969; bd. dirs. Schs. for Candidates; mem. chancellor's affirmative action com. Syracuse U.; mem. Dist. Atty.'s Adv. Council. Mem. Am. Arbitration Assn., ACLU. Author: (with Roger DeCrow) University Adult Education: A Selected Bibliography, 1967; The Young Woman's Guide to Liberation, 1971; Sexist Justice, 1974 (with Robert Seidenberg) Women Who Marry Houses: Panic and Protest in Agoraphobia, 1983. Editor: The Pregnant Teenager (Howard Osofsky), 1968; Corporate Wives, Coporate Casualities (Robert Seidenberg), 1973. Contbr. articles to newspapers including N.Y. Times, Los Angeles Times, Chgo. Sun-Times, Miami Herald, Boston Globe, Internat. Herald Tribune, also to mags. including Mademoiselle, Vogue, The Civil Rights Quar. Address: 116 Benedict Ave Syracuse NY 13210

DECTER, MIDGE, writer, editor; b. St. Paul, July 25, 1927; d. Harry and Rose (Calmenson) Rosenthal; student U. Minn., 1945-46, Jewish Theol. Sem. Am., 1946-48; m. Norman Podhoretz, Oct. 21, 1956; children—Rachel, Naomi, Ruth, John. Asst. editor Midstream mag., 1956-58; mng. editor Commentary, 1961-62; editor Hudson Inst., 1965-66, CBS Legacy Books, 1966-68; exec. editor Harper's mag., 1969-71; book review editor Saturday Rev./World mag., 1972-74; sr. editor Basic Books, Inc., 1974—; exec. dir. Com. for Free World, 1980—. Author: The Liberated Woman and Other Americans, 1971; The New Chastity, 1972; Liberal Parents, Radical Children, 1975. Contbr. articles to popular publs. Home: 120 E 81st St New York NY 10028

DE CUEVAS, ELIZABETH, sculptor; b. St. Germain en Laye, France, Jan. 22, 1929 (Am. citizen); d. George and Margaret (Strong) De C.; student Vassar Coll., 1946-48; A.B., Sarah Lawrence Coll., 1952; student John Hovannes, Art Students League, N.Y.C., 1963-68; 1 dau., Deborah Carmichael. Exhibited in one-woman shows: Lee Ault Gallery, N.Y.C., 1977, 78, Tower Gallery, Southampton, N.Y., 1980; group show Art Students League of N.Y., 1982; represented in pvt. collections. Club: Vassar of N.Y.

DEDERICH, SUSAN RUSSELL, harpist; b. Rockville Center, N.Y., Oct. 4, 1951; d. Robert Marwood and Martha Annette (Geffs) D.; B. Performing Arts, Cleve. Inst. Music, 1973; student of Alice Chalifoux. Prin. harpist Oklahoma City Symphony. 1973-74, New Orleans Symphony, 1974-77, Dallas Symphony, 1977—. Office: care Dallas Symphony Orch Music Hall PO Box 26207 Dallas TX 75226 *

DEDERICK, JUDITH GARRETTSON, psychologist; b. St. Louis, Apr. 4, 1943; d. John Alexander and Elizabeth K. (Painter) Garrettson; B.A., Vassar Coll., 1965; M.A., Columbus U., 1966, Ph.D. (NIMH and Heft-Patterson fellow), 1969; m. Warren Emery Dederick, Aug. 3, 1975; 1 dau., Elizabeth Jane. Instr., Hunter Coll., CUNY, 1968-69, asst. prof., 1969-72, assoc. prof., 1972-81, prof., 1982—; pvt. practice psychology, Bklyn., 1977-81, Westfield, N.J., 1981—; psychologist Union County Ct., N.J.; Internat. Inst. for Humanistic Edn., 1978. Mem. Am. Psychol. Assn. Contbr. articles to profl. jours. Home and office: 211 N Chestnut St Westfield NJ 07090

DEDOWICZ, CHRISTINE DOROTHY, nurse; b. Chgo., Mar. 30, 1949; d. Edward Thaddeus and Dorothy Stephanie (Kujawa) Dedowicz; A.A., Morton Coll., 1969; B.S.N., Lewis U., 1982. Staff nurse MacNeal Meml. Hosp., Berwyn, Ill., 1969-74, asst. head nurse, 1974-75, head nurse post partum, 1975-78, head nurse med./surg., 1978—. Mem. Nurses Assn. of Am. Coll. Obstetricians and Gynecologists, Ill. Assn. for Maternal and Child Health. Home: 3721 S Wenonah Ave Berwyn IL 60402 Office: 3249 S Oak Park Ave Berwyn IL 60402

DEE, JOAN MCHUGH, educator; b. Newton, Mass., Dec. 10, 1934; d. Joseph Patrick and Esther Mary (Walsh) McHugh; B.S. in Edn., Framingham (Mass.) State Coll., 1956; M.Ed., Boston U., 1959, Ed.D. (fellow), 1973; m. Norman Edward Dee, Aug. 17, 1957. Elem. tchr. pub. schs., Natick, Mass., 1956-61, Concord, Mass., 1961-70; instr. Lowell (Mass.) State Coll., 1970-71; acting dir. Adaptation Center Boston U., 1971-72, asst. to Dean, 1972-73, asst. dean, asst. prof. Sch. Edn., 1973-80, asso. dean, asst. prof., 1980—. Recipient Outstanding Service award Concord Pub. Schs., 1967; Ida M. Johnston Alumni award Boston U. Sch. Edn.; Alumni Achievement award Framingham State Coll. Mem. Am. Assn. Sch. Adminstrs., Univ. Council for Ednl. Adminstrn., Mass. Assn. Colls. Tchr. Edn. (dir.), Phi Delta Kappa, Pi Lambda Theta. Home: 582 Old Bedford Rd Concord MA 01742 Office: 605 Commonwealth Ave Boston MA 02215

DEEMER, JANET ANN, mktg. exec.; b. Pitts., June 29, 1953; d. Harry Richard and Marion Elizabeth (James) D.; student Kent State U., 1971-73; A.S., Duluth Bus. U., 1975; student in bus. adminstrn. Nat. U. Adminstrv. asst. to v.p. sales and promotions Ringling Bros., Barnum & Bailey Circus World, Orlando, Fla., 1977-78; media and spl. events dir. DuQuoin (Ill.) State Fairgrounds, 1979; dir. ops., spl. assignment ETS Promotional Mktg., San Diego, 1981; bus. mgr. Thorntree Group, Inc., Solana Beach, Calif., 1981—. Mem. Am. Mktg. Assn., Nat. Assn. Female Execs., Nat. Mgmt. Assn. Office: 740 Loma Santa Fe Suite 101 Solana Beach CA 92075

DEEN, EDITH ALDERMAN, author; b. Weatherford, Tex., Feb. 28, 1905; d. James Harris and Sara (Scheuber) Alderman; student Tex. U., 1922-23, Tex. Christian U., 1923-24, Columbia, 1926; B.A., Tex. Woman's U., 1953, M.A., Litt.D., 1959; Litt.D., Tex. Christian U., 1972; m. Edgar Deen, Dec. 30, 1945 (dec.). Woman's editor Daily columnist Fort Worth Evening Press, 1924-54. Mem. Fort Worth City Council, 1965-67; mem. bd. regents Tex. Woman's Univ., 1951-63. Mem. Tex. Inst. Letters, Women in Communications. Author: All of the Women of the Bible, 1955; Great Women of the Christian Faith, 1959; Family Living in the Bible, 1963; The Bible's Legacy for Womanhood, 1970; All the Bible's Men of Hope, 1974; Wisdom from Women in the Bible, 1978. Home and Office: 2420 Refugio St Fort Worth TX 76106

DEEN, FRANCES MAY MAHONEY, former educator; b. St. Charles, Mich.; d. Stephen Phillip and Mary Fleming (Wright) Mahoney; Mus. B., Stetson U., 1925; M.A., Columbia U., 1940; m. George Deen, Dec. 26, 1940 (dec. 1959). Head music edn. dept. Stetson U., 1928-31; dir. choral music Edison Sr. High Sch., Miami, Fla., 1931-58, dean of girls, 1962-63, guidance counselor, 1963-71; acting supr. music Dade County, Fla., 1958-59; head fine arts dept. Miami-Dade Jr. Coll., 1960-62. Sec. recording for blind unit, Miami chpt. Zonta Internat., 1963-64; music chmn. Dade County Fedn. Women's Clubs, 1962-64; chmn. scholarship com. Miami Woman's Club, 1949-52, chmn. edn. dept., 1973-75. Mem. Fla. Coll. Music Educators Assn. (sec.-treas. 1962-64), Fla. Music Educators Assn. (pres. 1955-57), Music Educators Nat. Conf. (life), Fla. Vocal Assn. (pres. 1951-53), Miami Music Club (pres. 1970-73), Nat. League Am. Pen Women, Fla. Fedn. Music Clubs (rec. sec. 1973-75, pres. 1977-79), Zonta Internat. (pres. Miami 1972-73), Nat. Fedn. Music Clubs (extension chmn. 1979-83), Sigma Kappa, Phi Beta, Delta Kappa Gamma (chpt. pres. 1970-72). Club: Coral Gables Country. Home: 1011 Cotorro Ave Coral Gables FL 33146

DEERING, CHERYL ANN, advt. exec.; b. Quantico, Va., Oct. 1, 1950; d. Claude Elliott and Carolyn Ida (Costa) D.; student U. No. Colo., 1968-72. Prodn. mgr. Sidaris Co., Los Angeles, 1972-74; owner, mgr. The Precious Point, Los Angeles, 1974-76; advt. coordinator Hartfield Zodys Inc., Los Angeles, 1976-77; dir. advt. The Federated Group, City of Commerce, Calif., 1977-80; account mgr. W. B. Doner & Co., Advt., Detroit, 1980-81; pres. Deering & Holmes, Inc., advt., N.Y.C., 1981—. Mem. Advt. Club Los Angeles. Home: 1365 York Ave New York NY 10028 Office: 120 E 56th St New York NY 10022

DEESE, ELLIN KRAUSS, univ. ofcl.; b. N.Y.C., Nov. 8, 1930; d. Lawrence and Clara (Freyer) Krauss; A.B., George Washington U., 1949; M.A.T., Johns Hopkins U., 1960; m. James Earle Deese, Dec. 24, 1948; children—Elizabeth Ellin, James Lawrence. Tchr., Homewood Sch., Balt., 1949-51; tchr., asst. prin. upper sch., dir. coll. guidance Park Sch., Brooklandville, Md., 1960-72; asst. dean Coll. Arts and Scis., U. Va., Charlottesville, 1972—, lectr. liberal arts seminar, 1972-79, lectr. dept. religious studies, 1979-82, asso. prof., 1982—. Bd. dirs., sec. Balt. City-County Democratic Club, 1953-56; mem. woman's club Johns Hopkins U., 1948-72; mem. vestry, 1977-80, lay reader St. Paul's Meml. Episcopal Ch., Charlottesville, 1977—; trustee Tandem Sch., Charlottesville, 1981—; bd. dirs. Koinonia of Charlottesville, 1977-82. Recipient Algernon Sydney Sullivan award U. Va., 1980. Mem. Nat. Assn. Women Deans, Adminstrs. and Counselors, Nat. Inst. Campus Ministries. Clubs: Colonnade (gov. 1976-78), Greencroft (gov. 1980—). Author: (with J. Deese) How to Study, 3d edit., 1979. Home: 1829 Westview Rd Charlottesville VA 22903 Office: 106 Garrett Hall U Va Charlottesville VA 22903

DE FAZIO, LYNETTE STEVENS, dancer, choreographer, educator; b. Berkeley, Calif., Sept. 29; d. Honore and Mabel J. (Estavan) Stevens; student U. Calif., Berkeley, 1950-55, San Francisco State Coll., 1950-51; children—Joey Panganiban, Joanna Pang. Contract child dancer Monogram Movie Studio, Hollywood, Calif., 1938-40; dancer, instr. San Francisco Ballet, 1953-64; performer San Francisco Opera Ring, 1960-67; performer, choreographer Oakland Civic Light Opera, 1963-70; owner, dir. Ballet Arts Studio, Oakland, 1960—; instr. Peralta Community Coll. Dist., Laney Campus, Grove St. Campus, 1971—; teaching specialist Oakland Unified Sch. Dist.-Childrens Center, 1968—; fgn. exchange dance dir. Academie de Danses, Paris, France, 1966; cons., instr. U. Calif. at Los Angeles Edn. Extension, Fresno State Coll., Calif. Childrens Centers Dirs. and Suprs. Assn., Fed. Projects Office Pittsburg Unified Sch. Dist., Tulare City Sch. Dist., 1971-73; researcher HEW Ednl. Testing Service, Berkeley, 1974; choreographer San Francisco Children's Opera; ballet mistress Dimensions Dance Theater, Oakland, 1977—; cons. Gianchetta Sch. of Dance, San Francisco and Concord, Calif., Robicheau Boston Ballet, TV series Patchwork Family, CBS, N.Y.C. Recipient credential of eminence in dance edn., life credential Calif. Community Colls., standard services credential, childrens centers credential all from Calif. Dept. Edn.; Notable Ams. award, 1976-77. Mem. Profl. Dance Tchrs. Assn. Am. Author: Basic Music Outlines for Dance Classes, 1960, rev., 1968; Teaching Techniques and Choreography for Advanced Dancers, 1965; Basic Music Outlines for Dance Classes, 1965; A Teacher's Guide for Ballet Techniques, 1970; Principle Procedures in Basic Curriculum, 1974; Objectives and Standards of Performance for Physical Development, 1975. Asso. music composer, lyricist The Ballet of Mother Goose, 1968. Asso. music arranger Le Ballet du Cirque, 1964; Techniques of a Ballet School, 1970, rev. edit., 1974. Choreographer Ravel's "Valses Nobles Et Sentimentales", 1976, Pachelbel's Cannon in D for Strings and Continuo, 1979. Home and Office: 4923 Harbord Dr Oakland CA 94618

DEFILIPPES, MARY KATHERINE WOLPERT, pharmacologist; b. Sioux City, Iowa, Dec. 13, 1939; d. Paul Louis and Katherine Mary (Block) Wolpert; student Duchesne Coll., 1958-60; B.S., Creighton U., 1963, M.S., U. Mich., 1966, Ph.D., 1969; m. Frank M. DeFilippes, June 29, 1973. Postdoctoral fellow Yale U., 1969-70, research assoc., 1970-71; staff fellow Nat. Cancer Inst. NIH, Bethesda, Md., 1971-75, sr. staff fellow, 1975-76, pharmacologist, 1976-81, dep. br. chief drug evaluation br., devel. therapeutics program, div. cancer treatment, 1981—. Recipient NIH award, 1982. Mem. Am. Assn. Cancer Research. Roman Catholic. Asso. editor Cancer Treatment Reports, 1978-82. Home: 4507 Sleaford Rd Bethesda MD 20814 Office: 8300 Colesville Rd Silver Spring MD 20910

DE FILIPPO, RITA MARCELLA, budget analyst; b. N.Y.C.; d. Sal and Margaret (Jaeger) DeF.; student Los Angeles City Coll., 1957, City Coll. San Francisco, 1975, U. San Francisco, 1976; cert. acctg., LaSalle U., 1968. Asst. advt. dir. Gump's, Inc., San Francisco, 1959; research statistician Honig-Cooper & Harrington, advt. agy., San Francisco, 1960-61; salesperson Landau Realty, San Francisco, 1962-63; mgmt. analyst Oakland Army Base (Calif.), 1978-80; budget analyst Dept. Army, San Francisco, 1980—. Recipient Outstanding Performance award Fed. Govt., 1979. Mem. Am. Bus. Women's Assn. (treas. 1978-79), Am. Soc. Mil. Comptrollers, Assn. Women in Sci., Assn. U.S. Army, Nat. Fedn. Fed. Employees (trustee 1972), World Affairs Council. Club: Sierra. Home: 2820 Scott St San Francisco CA 94123 Office: Presidio of San Francisco CA 94129

DEFONZO, DOLORES JENNY, microbiologist; b. New Haven, Aug. 29, 1952; d. Ralph James and Virginia (DeRosa) DeF.; B.S. in Biology, So. Conn. State Coll., 1974, M.S. in Biology, 1977; M.B.A., U. New Haven, 1982. Research microbiologist Olin Chem. Corp., New Haven, 1974-79, indsl. relations mgr. Chems. Research and Devel. Group, 1979—; pvt. tutor sci. and math. Mem. Am. Soc. Microbiology, Am. Soc. Agronomy, Conn. Assn. Dairy and Food Sanitarians, Soc. Indsl. Microbiology, Am. Mgmt. Assn., Sigma Xi. Roman Catholic. Home: 185 Lee St West Haven CT 06516 Office: 275 S Winchester Ave New Haven CT 06511

DE FOOR, MARJORIE KEEN, food co. exec.; b. West Palm Beach, Fla., Oct. 31, 1929; d. Stephen Wesley and Ada Mae Keen; student Stetson U., 1947; A.A., Stephens Coll., Mo., 1948; B.S., U. Ala., 1949; children—James Allison, Stephen Charles, Sheila Keen Monaco. With Keen Fruit Corp., Frostproof, Fla., 1956—, v.p., 1980—, also dir. Republican. Episcopalian. Club: Tower (Tampa, Fla.).

DEFOREST, JUNE (MORGANSTERN), violinist; b. Pitts., June 30, 1939; d. William E. and Isabel (Nameth) DeF.; student Carnegie-Mellon U., 1957-60; Mus.B., Manhattan Sch. Music, 1963, Mus.M., 1974; m. Daniel R. Morganstern, June 19, 1966. Concertmaster, Joffrey Ballet, 1966, Can. Opera, 1968; asst. concertmaster Am. Ballet Theatre and Harkness Ballet, 1967-70; violinist Royal Ballet, Stuttgart Ballet, Musica Sacre, 1967-71; violinist Am. Ballet Theatre, N.Y.C. and Chgo. Lyric Opera, 1971—; mem. Am. Chamber Trio, 1974—. Mem. Coll. Music Soc., Chamber Music Am., Am. Chamber Concerts, Inc. Democrat. Baptist. Home: 890 West End Ave New York NY 10025 also 2300 Lincoln Park W Chicago IL 60614

DEFREES, (MARY) MADELINE, educator; b. Ontario, Oreg., Nov. 18, 1919; d. Clarence C. (dec.) and Mary T. (McCoy) DeF.; B.A., Marylhurst Coll., 1948; M.A., U. Oreg., 1951; Litt.D., Gonzaga U., 1959. Tchr. elem. schs., Oreg., 1938-42, high schs., Oreg., 1942-48; Instr., Holy Names Coll., Spokane, 1950-55, asst. prof., 1955-63, assoc. prof., 1963-67; vis. assoc. prof. U. Mont., Missoula, 1967-69, assoc. prof., 1969-72, prof., 1972-79; prof. English, U. Mass., Amherst, 1979—, dir. M.F.A. program in creative writing, 1980—. Recipient T. Neil Taylor award for journalism research U. Oreg., 1949; Guggenheim fellow for poetry, 1981; Nat. Endowment for Arts grantee, 1982. Mem. Poetry Soc. Am., PEN, Democrat. Roman Catholic. Author: Springs of Silence, 1953; Later Thoughts from the Springs of Silence, 1962; From the Darkroom, 1964; When Sky Lets Go, 1978; Imaginary Ancestors, 1978; Magpie on the Gallows, 1982. Office: Grad English Bartlett Hall Univ Mass Amherst MA 01003

DEGEN, MAUREEN R., mgmt. cons.; b. N.Y.C., 1940; grad. Lenox Hill Sch. Nursing, N.Y.C., 1961; student Ind. U., 1968-70; B.A. magna cum laude, U. Philippines, 1972; M.B.A., U. Utah, 1974; doctoral candidate Golden Gate U., 1980—. Adminstrv. acct. City of Fairfield (Calif.), 1975-76; pres. Maureen R. Degen Mgmt. Cons., Vacaville, Calif., 1976—; mem. faculty Golden Gate U. Grad. Sch. Bus. and Pacific Christian Coll. Sch. Mgmt.; exec. dir. Center Career and Bus. Planning and Devel. Chmn. coordination of agys. com. Vacaville Unified Sch. Dist., 1978—; mem. regional adv. council Region IX, SBA, 1978—; mem. small bus. adv. bd. Calif. Senate Select Com. Small Bus. Enterprises, 1980—; founder, chmn. Ind. Citizens' Adv. Com., 1977—; mem. fin. com., chmn. United Way Crusade, Napa-Solano council Girl Scouts U.S.A., 1976-77; mem. publicity com. Napa-Solano Big Bros.-Big Sisters, 1976-77. Mem. Assn. M.B.A. Execs., AAUW (v.p. Vacaville br.), Inst. Cert. Bus. Counselors, Nat. Assn. Realtors, Internat. Entrepreneurs Assn., Enterprising Woman (co-founder Solano County), Calif. Assn. Realtors, No. Solano Bd. Realtors. Office: 421 Boyd St Suite A Vacaville CA 95688

DEGENHART, PEARL C., artist, educator; b. Phillipsburg, Mont., Feb. 25; d. L.C. and Ellen (O'Neill) Degenhart; A.B., U. Mont., 1923; A.M., Columbia, 1928. Instr. art Arcata (Calif.) Union High Sci., 1928—; one-man shows Stafford Inn, Scotia, Calif., 1954, Humboldt State Coll., 1951, 75, Humboldt Fed. Bldg., 1975, Ramada Inn, 1975, Corta Maderia Art Gallery, 1975; exhibited group shows San Francisco Art Assn., 1932, 37, 40, Contemporary Arts Gallery, N.Y.C., 1939, Denver, 1938, Humboldt State Coll., 1935, 45, 54, Spokane Wash., 1948, Oakland Art Gallery, 1948, Humboldt Fed. Gallery, 1966, Eureka Courthouse, 1968, Trinidad (Calif) Art Show, 1974-75. Mem. Bus. and Profl. Women's Club, Nat. League Am. Pen Women, Alpha Xi Delta, Delta Phi Delta. Contbr. to art, juvenile mags. Address: Box 142 Trinidad CA 95570

DE GHEEST, ANNE, sales exec.; exec.; b. Brussels, Belgium, Feb. 5, 1955; came to U.S., 1977; Jacques and Monique (De Vestel) De G.; Comml. Engr. summa cum laude, Free U. Brussels, 1977; M.B.A., Harvard Bus. Sch., 1979. Course asst. Free U. Brussels, 1974-1977; asst. to v.p. Euro-Currency Treasury, Morgan Guaranty, Brussels, summer, 1978; mfg. planning mgr. Raychem Corp., Menlo Park, Calif., 1979-81, U.S. Sales market mgr. for computer and communication, 1981—. Recipient Felix Le Blanc prize, 1978. Belgian Am. Ednl. Found. fellow, 1977-78. Mem. Harvard Bud. Sch. Assn. No. Calif. Home: 3362 La Mesa St Apt 10 San Carlos CA 94070 Office: 300 Constitution Dr Menlo Park CA 94025

DEGNAN, JUNE OPPEN, publisher; b. N.Y.C., June 7, 1918; d. George August and Seville (Shainwald) Oppen; student U. Calif., Berkeley, Sorbonne U., Paris, U. San Francisco Law Sch.; 1 dau., Aubrey Lindgren. Pub., San Francisco Rev., N.Y.C., San Francisco, 1959—; pub., editor Oceans Mag., publ. Oceanic Soc., 1973-75; cons. Internat. Learning Inst., San Francisco, 1969; pres. Internat. Child Art Center, San Francisco, 1971-72; v.p. Infonet Systems, Inc., San Francisco, 1974-76; sec.-treas. WRD Assos., 1976—. Mem. finance com. Calif. Democratic Central Com., 1956—; nat. finance co-chmn. Sen. Eugene McCarthy's presdl. campaign, 1967-68; nat. vice chmn. Sen. George McGovern presdl. campaign, 1972; mem. Dem. Nat. Com., 1976—; mem. Calif. Dem. Adv. Council, 1977; mem. Mem. San Francisco City and County Adv. Com. for Adult Detention Facilities, 1974-77; trustee Kennedy Center Peforming Arts, Washington, 1981—; bd. dirs. Norman Thomas Endowment Fund, New Sch. Social Research, 1968, E.W. Found., San Francisco, 1968. Mem. Ams. for Dem. Action (nat. dir. 1962-74), Cons. Assn. Lit. Mags., Oceanic Soc. San Francisco. Clubs: Commonwealth, Metropolitan (San Francisco). Address: 1000 Mason St San Francisco CA 94108

DEGORTER, LISA MEYERS, personnel agy. mgr.; b. N.Y.C., Feb. 13, 1955; d. Gilbert and Anita (Hittner) M.; B.A. in Elem. Edn. and Art History, Hofstra U., 1978; m. Richard Daniel DeGorter, Oct. 18, 1981. Office mgr. Starr Personnel, Los Angeles, 1978-79; br. mgr. Tempo Services, Huntington/East Meadow, N.Y., 1979-80; ops. mgr. Temporary Mgmt. Resources, East Meadow, 1980—. Recipient award of Gratitude, Temp Force N.Y., 1980. Mem. Nat. Assn. Personnel Cons. Home: 200 Earl Pl East Meadow NY 11554 Office: 1976 Hempstead Turnpike East Meadow NY 11554

DEGRAFF, JANE ROBERTS, civic worker; b. N.Y.C., Dec. 31, 1939; d. John and Agnes (Murton) Roberts; student Barnard Coll., 1957, Mount Vernon Coll., 1977—; m. Elliott Dodd DeGraff, 1959 (div.); children—Pamela Joyce, Jill Katherine. Active Hospitality and Info. Service, Washington, 1964—, sec. bd., 1971-73; bd. dirs. Jr. League Washington, 1970-71; tour lectr. Corcoran Gallery Art, Washington, 1965-70; vice chmn. UN Concert, Washington, 1971, 50th Jubilee Nat. English Speaking Union, 1971; spl. asst. to chmn. United Givers Fund, Washington, 1971-72; chmn. ball Opera Soc. Washington, 1972; bd. dirs. Nat. Ballet Soc., 1972-74, Washington Performing Arts Soc., 1972-75; mem. D.C. Mayor's Com. on Internat. Visitors, 1972-77; trustee Hosp. for Sick Children, Washington, 1973—; editor Washington Antiques Show Catalogue, 1972-75; mem. D.C. Republican Fin. Com., 1972-75; trustee Meridian House Internat. Center, Washington, 1964—, sec., 1974-75, vice chmn. bd., 1976—; mem. bd. advisers D.C. Lung Assn., 1975—; active fund-raising drive for Washington Cathedral, 1976; bd. dirs. Washington Home for Incurables, Nat. Eye Found., 1976—, Children's Hosp. Nat. Research Found., 1978—, D.C. chpt. ARC, Travelers Aid Soc.; chmn. Washington Antiques Show, 1976-78, Washington Cathedral Flower Mart; dir. fin. devel. YWCA of Nat. Capital Area, 1979. Address: 5316 Blackistone Rd Washington DC 20016

DE GRAFFENRIED, VELDA MAE CAMP (MRS. THOMAS P. DEGRAFFENRIED), clin. lab. exec.; b. Kirwin, Kans.; d. George Robert and Laura (Woodward) Camp; student No. Ill. U., 1959-60; m. Thomas P. deGraffenried, May 23, 1942; children—Donna Rae (Mrs. Kenneth George Pigott), Albert Lawrence II, Nicholas Thomas. Office mgr. deGraffenried & Fisher Clin. Labs., DeKalb, Ill., 1957-64, exec. sec., 1964—; dir. public affairs deGraffenried Med. Cons. Service, Inc. Vice pres. Haish Sch. PTA, DeKalb, 1958-59; den mother cub scouts Chief Shabbona council Boy Scouts Am., 1957-60; supr. Teen Age Club, Louisville, 1949-50; county crusade chmn. Am. Cancer Soc., 1965, mem. exec. bd. DeKalb County, 1964—, dir. public affairs, 1970—, chmn. bd., 1978-80, chmn. Radiothon, 1972-82, 83, sec. DeKalb County Soc., 1969—. Recipient commendations Am. Cancer Soc., 1965, 74, Boy Scouts Am., 1955. Mem. DeKalb County Med. Soc. Aux. (sec. 1959-60, 76—, pres. 1973-74), DeKalb Hosp. Aux. Methodist. Home: 1208 Sunnymeade Trail DeKalb IL 60115

DE GUIO, LYDIA MARIA, corp. ofcl.; b. Phila., Nov. 11, 1930; d. Louis and Louise Madelaine De G.; student Temple U., 1957, U. Pa., 1982. With acctg. dept. Govt. div. Philco/Ford, Phila., 1952-57; with sales/reservations dept. Am. Airlines; exec. sec. Sta. WFIL-AM-FM-TV, Phila., 1964-69; adminstrv. asst. Gen. Electric Co., 1957-64; dist. adminstr. Control Data Corp., Phila., 1969—. Active local, state and nat. polit. campaigns. Mem. U. Pa. Real Estate Soc., U. Pa. Alumni Assn., Am. Italy Soc., Old Acad. Players Theatre Group, Chi Alpha Phi (pres.). Clubs: U. Pa. Luncheon (pres.), Germantown Cricket. Home: 540 W Clapier St Philadelphia PA 19144 Office: Control Data Corp 1900 Market St Philadelphia PA 19103

DEGUIRE, KATHRYN SILBER, psychologist; b. Mankato, Minn., Nov. 16, 1932; d. Ernest Albert and Anna (John) Silber; Mus.B., Eastman Sch. Music U. Rochester, 1954; postgrad. Akademie fur Musik ünd Darstellende Kunst, Vienna, 1954-55, Upsala Coll., 1966-69; M.A., Fordham U., 1971, Ph.D., 1974; m. John Diaz, Aug. 22, 1981; 1 dau., Lise Kathryn. Pianist, organist, instr. piano, 1955-66; clin. asst. psychologist Meml. Sloan Kettering Cancer Center, N.Y.C., 1974—; pvt. practice, N.Y.C. and Fairfield, N.J., 1976—; lectr. Upsala Coll., East Orange, N.J., 1971-72, 78-81. Fulbright scholar, Vienna, 1954-55; USPHS grantee, 1969-71. Mem. Am. Psychol. Assn., N.J. Psychol. Assn., Soc. Psychologists in Pvt. Practice. Rec. artist: Orion. Home: 26 Sand Rd Fairfield NJ 07006 Office: 120 E 34th St Suite 2L New York NY 10016

DE HAAN-PULS, JOYCE ELAINE, sales rep.; b. Grand Rapids, Mich., Dec. 22, 1941; d. Harry Herman and Dorothy Elaine (Kikstra) DeHaan; student Calvin Coll., 1960-61; B.S. with honors, Grand Valley State Colls., 1978; postgrad. U. Sarajevo, Yugoslavia, 1978, Grad. Inst., Siedman Grad. Coll., 1979—; children—Bruce Todd, Daniel Lane, Cristy-Ann Sara Elizabeth Puls. Owner, operator Joyce Elaine's Beauty Parlor, Grandville, Mich., 1960-64; asst. assessor City of Hudsonville, Mich., 1978; dir. displaced homemaker program Women's Resource Center, Grand Rapids, 1979-81; visual products rep. 3M Corp., Grand Rapids, 1982—; mem. Ottawa County (Mich.) CETA Adv. Bd. Bd. dirs. Downtown Day Care Center, Grand Rapids, 1972. Recipient cert. of appreciation Bishop of Saigon, Vietnam, 1969; Phillip Morris scholar, 1975. Mem. Nat. Assn. Fgn. Students, Grand Rapids Council on World Affairs, Am. Soc. Public Adminstrn. Republican. Home: 1515 Ridgewood Dr Jenison MI 49428 Office: 252 State St Grand Rapids MI 49503

DE HART, PANZY HAWK, social worker; b. Cleveland County, N.C., May 18, 1934; d. Henry and Sallie Maude (Hawk) Kilgore; B.A., Howard U., 1956, M.S.W., 1958; postgrad. N.Y.U.; m. Henry Ross DeHart, June 18, 1966; children—Henry, Linda. Sr. clin. social worker VA, Buffalo, 1961-63, VA, Bronx, N.Y., 1963-65; supr. Inwood House, N.Y.C., 1966-68, 70-72; dist. social work cons. N.Y.C. Dept. Health, 1968-70; social worker Spina Bifida Project, Inst. Rehab. Medicine, N.Y. U. Med. Center, N.Y.C., 1976-81, social worker children's div., 1981—.

Recipient Service award Howard U. Alumni Club N.Y.C., 1972. Mem. NAACP, Nat. Assn. Social Workers, Assn. Black Social Workers, Lambda Kappa Mu (Nat. Achievement award 1974). Episcopalian. Clubs: Cambria Heights Lioness (sec. 1979-80); Jack and Jill Am., Inc.; Howard U. Alumni (pres. 1970-74) (N.Y.C.). Home: 110-06 214th St Queens Village NY 11429 Office: 400 E 34th St New York NY 10016

DE HAVILLAND, OLIVIA MARY, actress; b. Tokyo, July 1, 1916; d. Walter Augustus and Lilian Augusta (Ruse) de H. (parents Brit. subjects); ed. in schools and convent in Calif.; awarded scholarship Mills College; m. Marcus Goodrich, Aug. 26, 1946 (div.); 1 son, Benjamin Briggs Goodrich; m. 2d, Pierre Galante, April 2, 1955; 1 dau., Gisele. Naturalized Am. Citizen, 1941. Pres. Jury Cannes Film Festival, 1965. Made stage debut as Hermia in Midsummer Night's Dream (Max Reinhardt prodn.), Hollywood Bowl, 1934; 1st motion picture in same role, 1935; starred in pictures, including: Captain Blood, Anthony Adverse, Robin Hood, Gone With The Wind (nominated for Acad. award 1939), Strawberry Blonde, Hold Back the Dawn (nominated for Acad. award 1941), Princess O'Rourke, To Each His Own (Acad. award for best actress performance, 1946), Dark Mirror, Snake Pit (nominated for Acad. award, 1948, N.Y. Critics award 1948), The Heiress (Acad. award for best actress performance, 1949, N.Y. Critics award), My Cousin Rachel, 1952, Not As A Stranger, 1954, Ambassador's Daughter, 1955 (Belgian Critics Prix Fermina), Proud Rebel, 1957, Light in the Piazza, 1961, Lady in a Cage, 1963 (Brit. films and filming award), Hush, Hush Sweet Charlotte, 1964. The Adventurers, 1969, Pope Joan, 1971, Airport '77, 1976, The Swarm, 1978; appeared in play A Gift of Time, 1962; summer stock; What Every Woman Knows (Westport, Conn., Easthampton, L.I.), 1946; Candida, 1951; 245 performances Transcontinental Tour, 1951-52; 100 performances Juliet, 1951; TV performances Noon Wine, 1966, The Screaming Woman, 1972; TV appearances include Roots, The Next Generations, 1979; lecture tours U.S., 1971-78; toured Army and Navy hosps. in U.S., Alaska, Aleutians, South Pacific, 1943-44, Europe, 1957-61; participant narration of France's Bicentennial gift to U.S., Son et Lumiere; 1976; Bicentennial Service Am. Cathedral in Paris, 1976. Trustee Am. Coll. in Paris, 1970, 71, Am. Library in Paris, 1974-78. Recipient Women's Nat. Press Club award, presented by Pres. Truman, 1950 for outstanding accomplishment in theater; Am. Legion Humanitarian award, 1967. Mem. Screen Actors Guild, Acad. of Motion Picture Arts and Scis. Democrat. Episcopalian (lay reader, mem. altar guild). Author: Every Frenchman Has One, 1962. Address: BP 156 75764 Paris Cedex 16 France *

DEIBLER, BARBARA ELLEN, librarian; b. Pottsville, Pa., Aug. 11, 1943; d. Samuel Elwood and Miriam Elizabeth (Houser) D.; B.A., Pa. State U., 1965; M.S., Drexel U., 1966. Cataloger, State Library Pa., Harrisburg, 1966-82, head cataloger, 1972-82, rare book librarian, 1980—, asst. coordinator collection mgmt., 1982—. Librarian, Hist. Soc. Schuylkill County, 1971-77. Mem. Am. Acad. Polit. and Social Scis., Acad. Polit. Sci., Schuylkill County Allied Artists (dir. 1976-77), Pa. Library Assn., Hist. Soc. Pa. Baptist. Clubs: Pilot of Pottsville (rec. sec. 1974-75, dir. 1975-77), Pilot of Harrisburg (pres. 1979-81, treas. 1978-79, dir. 1981—). Author: Pennsylvania German Barn Signs: For Protection or Just for Nice, 1978; Simplified Cataloging for Libraries, 1978; The State Library of Pennsylvania: The Philadelphia Years, 1982. Home: 2285 W Norwegian St Pottsville PA 17901 Office: Box 1601 Harrisburg PA 17105

DEIBLER, JANE WELLER, mfg. co. exec.; b. Glenroy, Pa., Apr. 23, 1937; d. Jesse M. and Beulah M. (Finney) Reeves; student public schs., also various specialized courses; m. Richard R. Deibler, Sept. 28, 1963; 1 son by previous marriage, Terry Weller; stepchildren—Donna, Craig, Blake. With Armstrong World Industries, Inc., Lancaster, Pa., 1955—, mgr. consumer affairs, customer response center, 1981—. Mem. Am. Bus. Women's Assn. (chpt. pres. 1972-73, 77-78, dist. nat. v.p. 1980-81; Woman of Yr. award Conestoga chpt. 1973, Boss of Yr. award Wheatland chpt. 1978), Adminstrv. Mgmt. Soc., Soc. Consumer Affairs Profls. (chpt. sec., newsletter editor 1980, v.p. membership 1981-82), Nat. Assn. Female Execs., Friends of Fulton Opera House, Armstrong Lab. Assn. Methodist. Club: Armstrong Circle A (pres. 1964). Author manuals. Office: Armstrong World Industries Inc Lancaster Sq Lancaster PA 17604

DEICH, RUTH FRIDA, psychologist; b. Ger.; d. Hugo Z. and Elsie S. Goitein; B.A. in Psychology, N.Y.U., 1950; M.A., Columbia U., 1951; Ph.D. in Exptl. Psychology, New Sch. Social Research, 1962; m. Herbert Deich; 3 children. Staff psychologist Lanterman State Hosp., Pomona, 1964-76; research coordinator Ednl. Devel. Ctr., Claremont, 1972-74, coordinator diagnostic services and career counseling, 1973-75; asst. prof. child psychiatry Loma Linda (Calif.) U., 1977-80; dir. clin. services and tng. Mid-Valley Mental Health Ctrs. and Sch., Duarte-Covina, Calif., 1978-79; pres., dir. Inst. Research Human Growth, Claremont, Calif., 1972—; ind. practice clin. psychology, 1979—; cons. in field, 1971—. Grantee NIMH, HEW, State of Calif. Mem. Am. Psychol. Assn., Western Psychol. Assn., Am. Women in Sci. (chpt. pres. 1981-82), Soc. Research Child Devel., Biofeedback Soc. Author papers in field. Office: 414 Yale Ave Claremont CA 91711

DEIMEL, LOVENA CRUMP, govt. adminstr.; b. Shreveport, La.; d. William Ralph and Mary (Arnold) Crump; student Lake Charles (La.) Bus. Coll., 1939; m. Ludwig Mathias Deimel, June 17, 1943 (dec.). Sec. C.E., U.S. Army, Lake Charles, 1942-51, chief clk., Ft. Worth, 1951-61, adminstrv. services supr., 1961-70, adminstrv. asst., 1971, adminstrv. officer, 1971—, bd. dirs. Employees Credit Union. Sec. Mayor's Com. on Status of Women, Ft. Worth, 1975-78. Recipient Hon. Recognition Achievement award, EEO, 1973. Mem. Tex. Assn. Realtors, Adminstrv. Mgmt. Soc., Fed. Bus. Assn. (named Career Woman of Yr. 1968), Tex. Bus. Edn. Assn. Democrat. Baptist. Clubs: Zonta Internat., Petroleum of Ft. Worth, Press of Ft. Worth, Corps of Engrs. Wives. Home: 3553 W 6th St Fort Worth TX 76107 Office: PO Box 17300 Fort Worth TX 76102 also 819 Taylor St Fort Worth TX 76102

DEINHARDT, CAROL L(UCY), psychologist; b. N.Y.C., Nov. 8, 1946; d. John and Florence (Hoag) D.; student Rutgers U., 1964-66; B.A., Stanford U., 1969; postgrad. Chapman Coll., 1967; M.A., Harvard U., 1972; Ph.D., Calif. Western U., 1982. Research asst. biophysics Johns Hopkins U., 1967; resident tutor Harvard U., 1971-73; psychologist Salem (Mass.) Hosp., 1972-73; dir., psychologist Child Devel. Center, S.E. La. Hosp., Mandeville, 1973-75; asst. prof. City Coll., Loyola U., New Orleans, 1975-80; dir. Women's Center for Greater New Orleans, 1975-80; cons. human devel. programs, health care agencies, ednl. systems, New Orleans, 1976-80; cons. Dept. Edn., Women's Ednl. Equity Act Program, Nat. Endowment for Humanities, La. Human Resources Services Adminstrn. Exec. bd. dirs. La. Cystic Fibrosis Research Found., 1977-80, Opportunity Line, WYES-TV, 1977-80; dir. Inst. Study of Contemporary World Cultures, 1969; VISTA vol., case worker, community organizer, Balt., 1966-67. Nat. Social Sci. Research Council/NIMH fellow, 1972; NSF grad. fellow, 1969-71; Ford Found. research grantee, 1968; recipient bicentennial achievement award YWCA, 1976. Mem. Am. Personnel and Guidance Assn., Am. Psychol. Assn., Am. Mental Health Counselors Assn. Club: Harvard (N.Y.C.). Author: Personality Assessment and Psychological Interpretation, 1982; contbr. articles profl. jours. Home and Office: PO Box 1662 Ojai CA 93023

DEISTER, MICHAELYNNE A., hosp. exec.; b. Dodge City, Kans., Apr. 5, 1946; d. Clarence and Virginia Matheny; B.A. in Bus. Adminstrn., Park Coll., Parkville, Mo., 1982; 1 son, Christopher. Mgr., N. Kansas City (Mo.) Meml. Hosp., 1964-74; v.p. mktg., adminstrv. asst. Quay Corp., comml. real estate devel., Kansas City, Mo., 1974; Kansas City (Mo.) br. sales mgr. Bio-med. Systems, Inc., St. Louis, 1976-77; dir. services devel. Bethany Med. Center, Kansas City, Kans., 1977—. Mem. Am. Mktg. Assn., Acad. Health Care Marketers, Am. Cardiology Technologists Assn. Democrat. Roman Catholic. Home: 8013 NW Stoddard St Kansas City MO 64152 Office: 51 N 12th St Kansas City KS 66102

DEITRICK, HELEN FOSTER, sales engr.; b. N.Y.C., Sept. 18, 1950; d. Ira Hall and Barbara (Matthews) D.; B.A. in Classical Lang., Furman U., 1971; postgrad. in classics U. Conn., 1971-72; postgrad. in mgmt. sci. Greenville Tech. Coll., 1973-74. Adminstrv. asst. Greater Greenville (S.C.) C. of C., 1973-74; ops. mgr., purchasing agent So. Electric Services Co., Greenville, 1974-78; sales engr. Gen. Electric Co., Columbia, S.C., 1978-79, Greenville, 1979-81, lead sales engr., 1981—; instr. mgmt. Greenville Tech. Coll., 1974-78. Active mem. Greenville Zoo Com., 1975, Greenville Young Republicans, 1974-76, Vital Parts choral group, 1975-76; dir. handbell choirs Christ Ch. Mem. Am. Soc. Profl. and Exec. Women, Eta Sigma Phi. Republican. Episcopalian. Home: 17 Poinsett Ave Greenville SC 29601 Office: PO Box 5797 Greenville SC 29606

DEJARNETTE, SHIRLEY SHEA, corp. fin. ofcl.; b. Bradford, Pa., Feb. 21, 1943; d. James Harold and Jean Lorrain (Dennis) Shea; A.A., Stephens Coll., 1963; B.S. in Bus. Adminstrn., U. Mo., 1966; postgrad. Harvard U. Advanced Mgmt. Program; m. Jaquelin Harrison DeJarnette, Mar. 21, 1978; 1 dau., Shea Ann. Trust officer Boatmen's Nat. Bank, St. Louis, 1966-74; mgr. investor relations and pension funds Kraft, Inc., Glenview, Ill., 1974-77; dir. investment research Cummins Engine Co., Columbus, Ind., 1977-78; asst. treas. and dir. pension fund investments Mead Corp., Dayton Ohio, 1978—; dir. DeJarnette Investment Advisors, Inc. Bd. trustees U. Dayton, chmn., investment subcom., fin. com.; bd. dirs. Stephens Coll., mem. alumni fund; Bd. advs. Sentinel Pension Inst.; active Oakwood Republican Council. Chartered fin. analyst. Mem. Inst. Chartered Fin. Analysts, Fin. Analysts Fedn., Investment Analysts Soc. Chgo., Cin. Soc. Fin. Analysts, So. Ohio Pension Group (founder), Phi Chi Theta. Episcopalian. Clubs: Dayton Racquet, Country Club of Va., Wintergreen Country. Office: Courthouse Plaza NE Dayton OH 45463

DE JESUS, JOSEFINA ESTARIS, nursing adminstr.; b. Philippines, Dec. 30, 1945; came to U.S., 1972, naturalized, 1978; d. Policarpio Foronda and Salud Jaramillo (Panlasigui) Estaris; B.S. in Nursing, U. East, Philippines, 1967; candidate M.A. in Mgmt., U. Redlands, 1983; m. Marc V. De Jesus, Jr., Dec. 30, 1972; children—Marc Jonathan, Mary Jo Angelica. Staff nurse, clin. instr. nursing U. East Med. Center, Philippines, 1967-71; staff nurse, charge nurse Cedars of Lebanon Hosp., Los Angeles, 1971-75; nursing coordinator Cedars-Sinai Med. Center, Los Angeles, 1975-79, asst. dir. nursing services, 1979—. Mem. Am. Nurses Assn., Calif. Nurses Assn., Nat. Assn. Orthopedic Nurses (by-laws com.), Am. Nurses Found. Century Club, United Methodist. Home: 1950 Bershire Dr Fullerton CA 92633 Office: Cedars-Sinai Med Center 8700 Beverly Blvd Los Angeles CA 90048

DE JESUS-MCCARTHY, FE TERESA, physician; b. Samar, Philippines, Dec. 31, 1942; came to U.S., naturalized, 1978; d. Felicisimo V. and Baslia E. de J.; M.D., U. Philippines, 1966; m. Thomas J. McCarthy, Mar. 3, 1973; children—Amour Fe, Vida Linda. Practice medicine specializing in ob-gyn, Schenectady; mem. staff Bellevue Maternity Hosp. Mem. AMA, Am. Med. Women's Assn., Am. Fertility Soc., Am. Coll. Ob-Gyn, Am. Assn. Gynecol. Laparoscopists, N.Y. State Med. Soc., Med. Soc. of Schenectady County. Home: 1261 Hempstead Rd Schenectady NY 12309 Office: PO Box 1030 2210 Troy Rd Schenectady NY 12301 *

DEJMEK, LUDMILA MARIE, architect; b. Prague, Czechoslovakia, Jan. 19, 1941; d. Sava and Edita (Sedlackova) Sedlacek; grad. Czech Tech. U., 1962; postgrad. Charles IV U. of Prague, 1963; grad. Acad. of Fine Arts, 1967; postgrad. L'Universite de Paris, La Sorbonne, L'Institute d'Urbanisme, 1964, L'Institute Catholique a Paris, 1967-68; M.Arch., Nova Scotia Tech. Coll., 1971; m. Karel Dejmek, Sept. 20, 1968; children—Mark, Andrea. Constrn. supr. Steel Corp. of Kladno, Czechoslovakia, 1962-63; designer Krushen & Dailey, Waterloo, Ont., also Donald Skinner, Architect, 1967-72; architect Centrel Mortgage & Housing Corp., Hamilton, Ont., 1972-74, program mgr., 1974-76; prin. firm Ludmila Dejmek, architects and engrs., Cambridge, Ont., Can., 1976—. NRC Can. grantee, 1970-71; recipient 2000 Kcs award, City Hall, Czechoslovakia, 1967, 3000 Kcs award CSSR Embassy, New Delhi, India, 1966. Mem. Ont. Assn. Architects, Profl. Engrs. Ont., Canadian Fedn. Univ. Women. Club: Chicopee Ski. Address: 126 Park Ave Cambridge ON N1S 2S6 Canada

DE JOIA, RUTH ANN, county ofcl.; b. Meadville, Pa., Aug. 16, 1927; continuing edn. student Pa. State U., 1976—; m. Joseph F.A. De Joia, June 28, 1947; children—John F., Joanne Marie De Joia Winans. Sec. various lawyers Meadville, Pa., 1945-56; clk.-typist Crawford County Assessment Office, 1956-59, sec. to chief adult and juvenile probation officer, 1959-65; sec. Holiday Inn of Meadville, 1965-66, asst. innkeeper, 1966-68; exec. sec. Crawford County Tourist Assn., 1970-71; with Domestic Relations Sect., Ct. Common Pleas of Crawford County, Meadville, 1971—, adminstrv. asst., 1976, asst. dir., 1977, dir., 1978—. Past officer PTA; mem. Crawford County Mental Health Assn., 1970—, Crawford County Community Council, 1978—, Child Adv. Council Pa., 1979-80; mem. Women's resource group Crawford County Drug and Alcohol Commn., 1980. Mem. Domestic Relations Assn. Pa. (dir. 1978-81, sec. 1980-81), Nat. Reciprocal and Family Support Enforcement Assn., Eastern Regional Reciprocal and Family Support Enforcement Assn., Eastern Regional Council on Welfare Fraud. Mem. United Ch. of Christ. Home: PO Box 248 Meadville PA 16335 Office: PO Box 385 Meadville PA 16335

DE KOONING, ELAINE, artist; b. N.Y.C., Mar. 12, 1920; d. Charles Frank and Mary Ellen (O'Brien) Fried; hon. degree Western Coll. Women, Oxford, Ohio, 1964; m. William de Kooning, Dec. 9, 1943. One-woman shows include Stable Gallery, N.Y.C., 1954, 56, Tibor de Nagy Gallery, N.Y.C. 1957, Graham Gallery, N.Y.C. 1960, 61, 63, 65. U. N.Mex., 1957, Mus. N.Mex., Santa Fe, 1959, Gump's, San Francisco, 1959, Washington Gallery Modern Art (presdl. portraits), 1964, Lyman Allen Mus., New London, Conn., (retrospective), 1959, Montclair (N.J.) Art Mus., 1973, Benson Gallery, Bridgehampton, N.Y., 1973, Ill. Wesleyan U., Bloomington, 1975, Coll. St. Catherine, St. Paul, 1975, Tampa Bay Arts Center, 1975, Image Gallery, U. Ga., 1977, Lauren Rogers Mus. Art, Miss., 1979, Grimaldis Gallery, Balt., 1980, Spectrum Fine Arts Ltd., N.Y.C., 1981, Ruth Schaffner Gallery, Santa Barbara, Calif., 1981, Himmelfarb Gallery, Water Mill, N.Y., 1981, Phoenix II Gallery, Washington, 1982, Greenberg Gallery, St. Louis, 1982, Port Washington (N.Y.) Library, 1982, Gruenebaum Gallery, N.Y.C., 1982; in represented in permanent collections Mus. Modern Art. Loeb Center, N.Y.C., Kennedy Library, Cambridge, Mass., Truman Library, Independence, Mo., Elmira (N.Y.) Coll., Ark. Arts Center, Little Rock, Jewish Community Center, Bayonne, N.J., Montclair (N.J.) Art Mus., CIBA-Geigy Corp., Ardsley, N.Y., Neuberger Mus., Purchase, N.Y., Washington Gallery Modern Art, also pvt. collections; tchr. U. N.Mex., 1959, Pa. State U., 1960, Contemporary Art Assn., Houston, 1952, U. Calif. at Davis, 1963-64, Yale U., 1967, Carnegie-Mellon U., 1969-70, U. Pa., 1970-72, Wagner Coll., 1970, U. Pa., 1971—, N.Y. Studio Sch., Paris, France, 1974—, Parsons Sch. Fine Art, 1974-76; Lamar Dodd chair U. Ga., Athens, from 1976, now Hilton and Sally Avery Chair Bard Coll. Office: care Gruenebaum Gallery 38 E 57th St New York NY 10022

DELACATO, JANICE ELAINE, learning cons.; b. Bklyn., June 6, 1926; d. Frode Siegfried and Vilma (Riis) Fernstrom; A.B., Bryn Mawr Coll., 1948; m. Carl Henry Delacato, June 20, 1951; children—Elizabeth Delacato Putnam, Carl Henry, David Fernstrom. Tchr., Rydal Hall, Ogontz Sch., Pa., 1948-49, The Spence Sch., N.Y.C., 1949-50, Chestnut Hill Acad., Phila., 1950-52; co-dir. The Chestnut Hill Reading Clinic, Phila., 1951-65, Delacato & Delacato, Cons. in Learning, Phila., 1972—; mgr. Morton (Pa.) Book Store, 1972—; co-dir. The Delacato & Delacato Conf. on Autism and Learning Disabilities, 1979—. Chmn. fund-raising com. Springside Sch., 1969-71; treas. Main St. Fair Antiques Booth, Chestnut Hill Hosp., 1965-77. Recipient Main St. Fair award Chestnut Hill Hosp., 1972. Mem. AAUW. Republican. Unitarian. Club: Phila. Cricket. Editor newsletter Temple U. Med. Center Women's Aux., Phila., 1953-65; class editor Bryn Mawr Coll. Alumnae Bull., 1966-79. Home: The Glen Thomas Rd at Northwestern Ave Philadelphia PA 19118 Office: Delacato and Delacato Suite 107 Plymouth Plaza Plymouth Meeting PA 19462

DELANEY, CATHY EILEEN, state ofcl.; b. Binghamton, N.Y., Apr. 5, 1947; d. Martin Frank and Beverly Carolyn (Hamlin) Piza; B.A., Harpur Coll., Binghamton, 1968; M.S.W., Syracuse (N.Y.) U., 1976; m. Frank L. Delaney, June 28, 1969. Public assistance caseworker Seneca County Dept. Social Services, Seneca Falls, N.Y., 1968; psychiat. social worker Willard (N.Y.) Psychiat. Center, 1968-73, Broome Devel. Center, Binghamton, 1973-74, 76; congl. legis. aide, 1975; asst. dir. bur. program and fiscal audits N.Y. State Office Mental Retardation and Devel. Disabilities, Albany, 1976-80, statewide coordinator intermediate care facilities for developmentally disabled, 1980, cert. coordinator Western County service group, 1980—, also mem. office human relations com.; adj. instr. SUNY Sch. Social Welfare, Albany, 1982—. Grantee HEW, 1975-76. Mem. Upstate Assn. Psychiat. Social Workers in State Schs. and Hosps. (sec. 1970), Am. Soc. Public Adminstrn., Am. Assn. Mental Deficiency, Nat. Assn. Social Workers. Office: 44 Holland Ave Albany NY 12229

DELANEY, ELEANOR CECILIA COUGHLIN, educator; b. Elizabeth, N.J.; d. John C. and Eleanor C. (Fadde) Coughlin; B.S., Sch. Edn. Rutgers U., 1930, M.A., 1939; Ph.D., Columbia U., 1954; 1 son, John. Tchr. public schs., Elizabeth, N.J., 1927; prin. Woodrow Wilson Sch., Elizabeth, 1941-55; prof. Grad. Sch. Edn., Rutgers U., New Brunswick, N.J., 1955—, chmn. dept. ednl. adminstrn. and supervision, 1974—; vis. prof. William and Mary Coll., U. N.Mex., Columbia U.; ednl. cons. sch. systems, N.J., N.Y., Va., 1950—. Mem. Elizabeth Charter Commn., 1960-61; chmn. Mayor's Adv. Commn. on Urban Devel., 1962-64, Elizabeth Human Relations Commn., 1968—; mem. Elizabeth Bd. Edn., 1972-79, pres., 1973-76; mem. exec. bd. Union County chpt. ARC; mem. exec. bd. Vis. Nurse and Health Assn., 1977—; pres., 1981—. Mem. AAUW, Nat., N.J. edn. assns., Dept. Elem. Sch. Prins., AAUP, AAAS, Am. Ednl. Research Assn., Kappa Delta Pi, Pi Lambda Theta, Phi Delta Kappa. Author: Spanish Gold, Lands of Middle America, Our Friends in South America, Science-Life Series, Book 4. Contbr. articles to profl. mags. Home: 220 W Jersey St Elizabeth NJ 07202 Office: 10 Seminary Pl New Brunswick NJ 08901

DE LANGE, VICTORIA PUIG, editor; b. Guayaquil, Ecuador, Dec. 3, 1919; d. Carlos Puig Vilazar and Rosa Marie (Parada) Puig; student U. Catolica, Chile, 1955; children—Luis C. Aguirre, Barbara Pereira, Christian Lange. Attache, Embassies of Washington and Chile, 1946-60; consul gen. of Ecuador, Fla., 1962-64; adviser State Fla., 1964-65; Latin Am. syndicated columnist, 1972—; also free lance writer. Founder People to People Com., 1963; mem. Council for Internat. Visitors, 1964-77; mem. Customers Adv. Bd., Burdines, 1975; mem. bd. Summer Star Theatre, 1974. Recipient Keys of Dade County, Fla., and Miami, Medal of Merit, Govt. Ecuador, 1967, Most Outstanding Ecuador born journalist in internat. field medal, 1982; named Hon. Citizen, State Fla., 1966, Woman of Year, Ecuador, 1975. Mem. Internat. Soc. Arts (dir. 1977). Roman Catholic. Clubs: Turnberry, Jockey (Miami). Office: 6401 NW 36th St Virginia Gardens FL 33166

DELANY, GLORIA CATHERINE, personnel exec.; b. St. Augustine, Fla., Dec. 12, 1930; d. Thomas Aldophus and Theodora Lillian (Canova) D.; A.A., S.W. Miss. Jr. Coll., 1952; R.N., Mobile Gen. Hosp. Sch. Nursing, 1960; B.S.N., Marillac Coll., 1971. Staff nurse Mobile (Ala.) Gen. Hosp., 1960; med./surg. instr. Providence Sch. Nursing, 1961-68; mem. Order Daus. Charity, St. Vincent de Paul, 1968-75; staff nurse Springhill Meml. Hosp., Mobile, 1975-76, dir. staff devel., 1976-77, dir. personnel, 1977—; dir. hosp. edn. St. Margaret's Hosp., Montgomery, Ala., 1970, trustee, 1970. Served with USN, 1952-56. Recipient Grant, Spring Hill Coll., 1977. Mem. Am. Mgmt. Assn., Am. Soc. Personnel Adminstrs., Ala. Soc. Personnel Adminstrn. Roman Catholic. Office: 3719 Dauphin St Mobile AL 36608

DE LAPP, MARY HAMILTON, graphoanalyst; b. Detroit Lakes, Minn., Sept. 27, 1909; d. Hubbard Albion and Ethel Holmes (Blanding) Hamilton; B.Ed., St. Cloud State Coll., 1938; M.A., U. Minn., 1941; m. Warren W. DeLapp, June 28, 1942; children—Ann DeLapp Hook, John. Tchr. elem. sch., Staples, Minn., 1929-30; counselor U. Minn. Gen. Coll., 1939-40, Coffman Meml. Union, 1941; mem. press World Council Chs. Meeting, Uppsala, Sweden, 1968; graphoanalyst cons. Juvenile Ct., Boulder, Colo., 1970-79; instr. graphoanalysts adult edn., Boulder, 1970-76; instr. graphoanalysis, U. Colo., 1977-79; cons. graphoanalysis Mgmt. Recruiters, Boulder; instr. Internat. Graphoanalysis Soc. Congress, 1981—; sales rep. Today's Christian Woman; lectr. on Queen Elizabeth II, 1981; lectr. in field. Recipient Pres.'s Merit award Internat. Graphoanalysis Soc., 1977, named Graphoanalyst of Yr., 1978. Mem. Colo. Author League (Top Hand awards 1963, 65, 69, 71, 73), Denver Women's Press Club, Boulder Writers Club, LWV, Salesmen with a Purpose. Democrat. Congregationalist. Contbr. articles to religious publs., other mags. Home and Office: 401 18th St Boulder CO 80302

DE LA ROSA, CATHERINE LOUISE, wholesale giftware co. exec.; b. Phoenix, Oct. 31, 1955; d. Jack Kerwin and Noyla Gayle (Jamison) Augspurger; B.A., Calif. State U., Long Beach, 1979; m. Daniel De La Rosa, Jan. 31, 1976; 1 dau., Cara Marie. Owner, operator De La Rosa's Indian Jewelry, Anaheim, Calif., 1975-77; sales and banquet mgr. Stovall Motor Hotels, Anaheim, 1976—; pres. Delcourval, Inc., Anaheim, 1980—; owner, operator Kingdom Gifts, Anaheim, 1981—. Leader Girl Scouts U.S.A.; active Anaheim Visitor and Conv. Bur. Mem. Nat. Assn. Female Execs., AAUW. Republican. Roman Catholic. Home: 5 Cornwallis St Irvine CA 92714 Office: 1110 W Katella St Anaheim CA 92802

DE LARROCHA, ALICIA DE LA CALLE, concert pianist; b. Barcelona, Spain, May 23, 1923; d. Eduardo and Teresa (De La Calle) de L; grad. (prize extraordinary, Gold medal), Acad. Marshall, Barcelona; m. Juan Torra, June 21, 1950; children—Juan, Alicia. Debut, Barcelona, 1927; solo recitalist, concert pianist major orchs. in Europe, U.S., Can., Central and S. Am., S. Africa, N.Z., Australia, Japan; dir. Acad. Marshall, 1959—; rec. artist Hispavox, CBS, Decca-London, records. Recipient Harriet Cohen Internat. Music award, 1968; Paderewski Meml. medal, 1961; Grand prix du Disque Acad. Charles Cros, 1960, 74; Edison award, 1968; Grammy award, 1974, 75; 1st Gold medal Merito a la Vocacion, 1972; decorated Order Civil Merit, Order Isabel la Catolica (Spain). Mem. Musica en Compostela (dir.), Hispanic Soc. Am. (corr.), Internat. Piano Archives (hon. pres.) Address: 119 W 57th St New York NY 10019 *

DELATTE, ANN PERKINS, educator; b. Statesboro, Ga., Apr. 8, 1934; d. William Donovan and Lalia Dean (Callaway) Perkins; A.A. summa cum laude, Armstrong Coll., 1954; B.A. magna cum laude (William F. Cooper Meml. scholar), Oglethorpe U., 1956; M.A. in English, New Orleans U., 1971; Ph.D. in Ednl. Leadership, Ga. State U., 1978; m. Martin Joseph Delatte, Sept. 2, 1961 (dec.); children—Martin David and Michael William (twins). Tchr. English Atlanta Pub. Schs., 1956-59, Gould Sch., Savannah, Ga., 1959-60; research asst. Am. Inst. Research, Pitts., 1962-64; program writer, staff tng. coordinator Orleans Parish Sch. Bd., New Orleans, 1969-71; dir. ednl. services Ga. Dept. Offender Rehab., Atlanta, 1971-78, dept. liaison with Ga. Legis. Study Com. on Correctional Edn., 1975-76; assoc. prof., acad. dir. Coll. Urban Life, Ga. State U., Atlanta, 1978-81, adj. assoc. prof. urban studies Coll. Pub. and Urban Affairs, 1981—, also project dir. Inst. Indsl. Relations, Coll. Bus. Adminstrn., 1981—; cons. to bus. and govt., 1970—. Mem. Ga. Right to Read Adv. Council, 1973, Ga. State Manpower Planning Council, 1974; mem. planning subcom. Ga. Employment and Tng. Council, 1974-75; nat. trainer Nat. Inst. Corrections and Law Enforcement Assistance Act, 1976-77; mem. So. Regional Adv. Com. on Improved Services to Women, U.S. Dept. Labor, 1979-80; mem. award selection com. for outstanding summer youth CETA, 1979-82; mem. Task Force on Tng., Office of Manpower Assistance, 1980. Recipient Outstanding Service award New Orleans Pub. Schs., 1970; cert. of appreciation U.S. Dept. Labor, 1979, 81; Lisle fellow Internat. Orgn. Study Human Relationships, U. Mich., 1956-57; co-grantee Nat. Inst. Corrections, 1977. Mem. AAUP, AAUW, Am. Mgmt. Assn., Am. Soc. Tng. and Devel., Internat. Correctional Edn. Assn. (officer Region VIII 1973-75), Ga. Assn. Correctional Educators (founder 1973), Omicron Delta Kappa. Contbr. articles to various publs. Home: 2423 Nancy Ln NE Atlanta GA 30345 Office: University Plaza Atlanta GA 30303

DELAUBENFELS, LINDA ELAINE, writer, editor; b. Bklyn., May 23, 1938; d. Harry Greg and Magdalena Susan (Pater) Price; student Katharine Gibbs Sch., 1956; B.S., magna cum laude, Syracuse U., 1978; children—Susan Price Radcliffe, Lynne Patricia Radcliffe. Communications specialist Blood Systems, Inc., Scottsdale, Ariz., 1978-79; editor, public relations rep. Samaritan Health Service, Phoenix, 1979—; Mem. exec., steering com. Greater Alvarado Los Olivos Neighborhood Assn., Phoenix, 1981—. Recipient award including Assn. Western Hosps. Mem. Internat. Assn. Bus. Communicators (dir. Phoenix 1982—, award), Women in Communications (dir. Phoenix 1981-82, award), Am. Soc. Hosp. Public Relations, Ariz. Press Women (award), Nat. Fedn. Press Women (award), Nat. Audubon Soc., Maricopa County Audubon Soc. Editor: Response Mag., 1979—. Home: 140 E Coronado Rd Apt 29 Phoenix AZ 85004 Office: Samaritan Health Service PO Box 25489 Phoenix AZ 85002

DELAUNE, KATHRYN MAE, educator; b. New Orleans, Apr. 2, 1920; d. Arsene Edward and Emma Rosalie (Gatlin) D.; B.A., La. Coll., 1956; M.A., Tex. Woman's U., 1970. Br. dir. YMCA, Jackson, Miss., 1965-66; center supr. Dallas Dept. Recreation, 1967-68; asso. research economist, indsl. econs. research div. Tex. A&M U., 1970-80; head div. spl. programs tng. Tex. Engring. Extension Service, 1980—. Mem. Bus. and Profl. Women San Antonio. Republican. Baptist. Club: Zonta (San Antonio). Home: 9627 S Bend St San Antonio TX 78250 Office: PO Box 40 San Antonio TX 78291

DELAURO, DEBORAH GREENFIELD, high sch. tchr.; b. Phila., Aug. 25, 1951; d. Albert Monroe, Jr. and Barbara (Littman) Greenfield; B.A., Syracuse (N.Y.) U., 1973; M.Ed., Temple U., Phila., 1980; m. James P. Delauro, July 27, 1974. High sch. tchr., N.Y. and Pa., 1973-75; tchr. social studies, coordinator Keith Valley Middle Sch., Horsham, Pa., 1975-81; tchr. social studies Hatboro Horsham High Sch., 1981—; curriculum writer, ednl. cons., 1980—. Mem. Nat. Council Social Studies, Middle States Council Social Studies, Pa. Council Social Studies (Curriculum award 1979), Eastern Montgomery Council Social Studies, Merion Civic Assn. Author: The Earth, 1980; The Community, 1980. Home: 520 Greystone Rd Merion PA 19066 Office: PO Box 15 Bala Cynwyd PA 19004

DE LA VEGA, DIANNE WINIFRED DEMARINIS (MRS. JORGE DE LA VEGA), govt. ofcl.; b. Cleve.; d. Gerald M. and Dorothy (Philp) DeMarinis; student Case Western Res. U., 1948-50, M.A., 1969; B.A., U. Am., 1952; Ph.D. in Psychology, Internat. Coll., Los Angeles, 1977; M.A., Goddard Coll., 1978; m. Jorge Alejandro de la Vega, July 19, 1952; children—Constance, Francisco Javier, Alexandra. Faculty, Western Res. U., Cleve., 1961-62; instr. Instituto Mexicano-Norteamericano de Relaciones Culturales, Mexico, 1967; supr. fgn. press Mexican Olympic Organizing Com., Mexico, 1968; asst. to producer Producciones Ojo, Canal 8 TV, Mexico, 1969; exec. asst. Internat. Exec. Service Corps, Mexico City, 1969-70; asst. to dir. U.S. Internat. U. Mexico, Mexico City, 1970-75; family planning evaluator for Latin Am., AID, 1976; with dept. spl. edn. region IX Nat. Center on Child Abuse and Neglect, Children's Bur., Office Child Devel., HEW, Calif. State U., 1977—. Chmn. Puppet's Jr. League, Mexico City, 1967, chmn. ways and means, 1968; sec. Tlaxcala-Okla. Partner's of Alliance for Progress, 1967—; bd. dirs. Hot Line of Mexico City. Lic. marriage and family counselor. Mem. Inst. Bioenergetic Analysis, Flying Samaritans, Pro Salud Maternal, Transactional Analysis Assn., Club: Jr. League (Los Angeles). Home: 130 Alta Ave D Santa Monica CA 90402

DELCO, WILHELMINA RUTH, state legislator; b. Chgo., July 16, 1929; d. William P. and Juanita M. (Heath) Fitzgerald; B.A., Fisk U., 1950; m. Exalton A. Delco, Jr., Aug. 23, 1952; children—Debbie, Exalton A. III, Loretta, Cheryl L. Service rep. Ill. Bell Telephone, Chgo., 1950-52; clk. Tchrs. State Assn. Tex., Austin, 1958; mem. Tex. Ho. of Reps., 1975—. Del., Democratic Nat. Conv., 1976; mem. So. Regional Edn. Bd., 1978—; mem. Carnegie Found. Advancement Teaching Governance Panel; vice-chmn. adv. panel Advanced Leadership Program Services; trustee Austin Ind. Sch. Dist., Austin Community Coll.; bd. dirs. U. Tex. YWCA; pres. Travis County PTA Council; mem. City of Austin Human Relations Commn.; mem. Well-Child Conf. Bd.; mem. adv. com. Tex. Employment Commn.; mem. nat. bd. dirs. Girl Scouts U.S.A.; mem. adv. council Tex. Music Educators Assn.; bd. dirs. United Way; bd. dirs. Lone Star council Girl Scouts U.S.A.; del. Tex. Assn. Sch. Bds. Recipient Pres.'s award Assn. Compensatory Educators Tex., 1980. Mem. Nat. Conf. State Legislators, Nat. Black Caucus State Legislators (v.p.), Alpha Kappa Alpha. Democrat. Roman Catholic. Club: Links, Inc. Office: State Capitol Austin TX 78769

DEL DUCA, MARILYN F., bus. exec.; b. Camden, N.J., Jan. 13, 1945; d. William G. and Rosa (Dafler) Del D. Contracts adminstr. Drexel Dynamics Co., Horsham, Pa., 1961-67; lease mgr. Colonial Rental Co., Wyncote, Pa., 1967-69; mem. office mgmt. staff BOSS, Blue Bell, Pa., 1970-71; owner, pres. Alcyone Enterprises, Inc., word processing/secretarial services, Cherry Hill, N.J., 1971—; bldg. mgr. Tarragon Office Bldg., Cherry Hill, 1972—; owner, mgr. Haddonfield Properties (N.J.), 1974—. State bd. dirs. NOW, 1977—; task force coordinator ERA, NOW-N.J., 1978-82, also field organizer, consciousness raising coordinator. Named Feminist of Yr. Elizabeth Haddon NOW, 1977, Spirit of Feminism award, 1982. Lutheran. Home: 107 Walnut St Haddonfield NJ 08033 Office: 811 Church Rd Suite 105 Cherry Hill NJ 08002

DE LEONARDIS, MICHELE KATHLEEN, psychologist; b. Chgo., Nov. 8, 1950; d. Jerome A. and Kathleen Marie (Basile) De L.; B.A., Governors State U., 1972, M.A., 1973; A.A., Triton Coll., 1971; Ph.D., Internat. U. Mo., 1979; m. Frank H. Petty, Feb. 14, 1982. Advisor, coordinator career devel. programs Office of Spl. Edn. of South Cook County, Homewood, Ill., 1972-73; pvt. practice counseling, Hinsdale, Ill., 1974-79, Marietta, Ga., 1980—; managerial cons., 1977—. Mem. Assn. for Humanistic Psychology, Am. Assn. Marriage Counselors, Nat. Psychiat. Assn., Nat. Council on Family Relations, Nat. Council on Child Abuse, Soc. Adlerian Psychology. Contbr. articles to profl. jours. Home: Box 724372 Atlanta GA 30339 Office: 1840 Lantern Ridge Marietta GA 30062

DEL FIACCO, JANICE MARIE, fin. exec.; b. St. Paul, Mar. 25, 1942; d. Gust Francis and Katharine (Speciale) Del F.; B.A. cum laude, Mundelein Coll., Chgo., 1965; M.A., U. Calif., Irvine, 1976. French tchr. secondary schs., Los Angeles Archdiocese, 1966-69; internat. flight attendant Trans World Airlines, N.Y.C., Los Angeles, 1969-72; ednl. specialist severely emotionally disturbed and autistic children Children's Mental Health Unit, Huntington Beach, Calif., 1973-75, Fountain Valley (Calif.) Sch. Dist., 1975-79; registered rep. fin. planning Investors Diversified Services, Inc., Newport Beach, Calif., 1980-81; account exec. Equitec Fin. Group., Inc., Irvine, 1981—; v.p., bd. dirs. Regional Center Orange County, Orange, Calif., 1978-80. Mem. bd. community adv. com. West Orange County Consortium Spl. Edn., 1978-80; Mem. U. Calif. Irvine Alumni Assn.(dir.), Newport Harbor Area C. of C., Irvine C. of C. Democrat. Roman Catholic. Club: Far West Ski Assn. Home: 1033 Bayside Cove E Newport Beach CA 92660 Office: 19782 MacArthur Blvd Suite 240 Irvine CA 92715

DEL GALDO, BICE SANTORA, mfg. co. exec.; b. Gioi, Italy, Nov. 4, 1943; came to U.S., 1958, naturalized, 1966; d. Giovanni and Anna (Ferra) Del Galdo; B.S. in Bus. Adminstrn., Montclair State Coll., 1980; postgrad. Seton Hall U.; children—Jeannette, Lori Ann. With Kelp Industries, Inc., Nutley, N.J., 1974-75; employee relations asst. Tri-Chem, Inc., Harrison, N.J., 1976-77, employee relations adminstr., 1977-81; indsl. relations mgr. Moldcast Lighting, Pine Brook, N.J., 1981—. Mem. Am. Soc. Training and Devel., Am. Soc. Personnel Adminstrn., Morris County C. of C., Met. N.Y. Assn. Applied Psychology. Home: 85 Plenge Dr Belleville NJ 07109 Office: I 80 at Maple Ave Pine Brook NJ 07058

DELIBES, CLAUDE BLANCHE, communications co. exec.; b. Paris, Sept. 20, 1932; d. Andre Jean and Simone (Barou) Seligmann; came to U.S., 1940; naturalized, 1954; B.A., Sorbonne U., Paris, 1953; m. Maurice Delibes, Dec. 31, 1961; 1 son by previous marriage, Roger Schwartz; 1 dau., Jacqueline Delibes. Editor Fairchild Publications, N.Y.C., 1961-65; pub. relations dir. West Point Pepperell Corp., N.Y.C., 1968-72; sr. account supr. The Siesel Co., N.Y.C., 1972-75; pres. Delibes Communications, Ltd., N.Y.C., 1975—. Mem. Women Execs. in Pub. Relations, Cosmetic Career Women, French-Am. C. of C. Home: 1601 3d Ave New York NY 10028 Office: 38 E 57th St New York NY 10022

DELLA-GIUSTINA, MARSHA ANN, TV news producer, educator; b. Springfield, Mass., Jan. 27, 1947; d. Joseph Augustus and Jennie Delores (Subotin) Della-G.; B.A. in English, Russell Sage Coll., Troy, N.Y., 1968; M.S. in Broadcast Journalism, Boston U., 1974, postgrad., 1982; m. John R. Wetmiller, Aug. 26, 1972. Jr. high sch. tchr., Agawam and Westfield, Mass., 1968-72; radio public affairs host-producer sta. WBZ-FM, Boston, 1973-74; TV news producer-writer sta. WCVB-TV, Boston, 1976—; journalism program dir., asso. prof. broadcast journalism Emerson Coll., Boston, 1976—; owner, producer Giustina Prodns., Arlington, Mass., 1979—; co-chmn. Freedom of Info. Act Symposium, 1982; cons. in field. Commr., Agawam Youth Commn., 1970-72; mem. Agawam Town Meeting, 1970-72; co-chmn. reunion com. Russell Sage Coll. Alumni Class 1968, 1978—; mem. media com. Mass. ERA Referendum Com., 1974-76; lobbyist NOW, 1973-76. Recipient Emmy award, 1977, 81. Mem. Am. Women Radio and TV, Nat. Acad. TV Arts and Scis., Boston Women's Media Network, Assn. Edn. in Journalism, Internat. Radio and TV Soc., Russell Sage Coll. Alumni Assn., Citizens for Participation in Polit. Action, Sigma Delta Chi. Democrat. Home: 113 Gray St Arlington MA 02174 Office: Emerson Coll 100 Beacon St Boston MA 02116

DELLI, (HELGA) BERTRUN, musicologist, art historian, editor; b. Dresden, Germany, July 17, 1928; came to U.S., 1967; d. Johannes and Elfriede (Tamme) D.; B.A. in Music, State Acad. Music, Dresden, 1949; Ph.D. in Musicology and Art History, Free U., West Berlin, 1957; M.S. in Library and Info. Sci., Pratt Inst., 1978; lang. diplomas, 1967, 68. Various editorial positions music and art, Germany, U.S.; tchr. music, art history, piano, langs., high schs., Germany, 1965-67, U.S., 1968-69, adult schs., N.Y.C., 1970-72; asst. prof. humanities Concordia Coll., Seward, Nebr., 1972-73; asst. editor Art Index, H.W. Wilson Co., N.Y.C., 1973-76, editor Biography Index, 1977-81, editor Art Index, 1981—. Scholar, Studienstiftung des deutschen Volkes, 1955-57; Clawson Mills research fellow, Met. Mus. Art, N.Y.C., 1969-70. Mem. Am. Musicol. Soc., ALA, Am. Art Librarians Soc. Author: Early Music, Dances from 1600, 1960; The Arts in America, a Bibliography, sect. Am. music annotated, 1980; contbr. articles to publs. in field, Germany. Office: 950 University Ave Bronx NY 10452

DELLING, IRIS BEE, mfg. co. contract adminstr.; b. Kansas City, Mo., Mar. 3, 1925; d. Ross B. and Margaret E. (Briley) Smithson; B.Fgn. Service, U. So. Calif., 1948, M.Liberal Arts, 1976; 1 son, Anthony Ross Delling. With Fgn. Service, Dept. State, Washington, 1949-52; sec. Pacific div. Bendix Corp., Burbank, Calif., 1955-64; sec. Librascope div. Singer Co., Glendale, Calif., 1964-73, job control coordinator, 1973-77, contract adminstr., 1977—. Served with USMC, 1945-46. Mem. Phi Beta Kappa, Phi Kappa Phi, Pi Sigma Alpha, Alpha Xi Delta. Clubs: Marine Corps League, NOW, Sierra, Women Marines Assn.

DELLINGER, ANNE MAXWELL, lawyer, educator; b. Omaha, Nebr., July 19, 1940; d. William H. and Margaret M. (Jackson) Maxwell; student Randolph-Macon Woman's Coll., 1958-60; B.A. with honors, U. N.C., 1962; M.A. in English, Tulane U., 1964; J.D., Duke U., 1974; m. Walter E. Dellinger, June 12, 1965; children—Hampton Yeats, Andrew King. Tech. writer and editor Equitable Life Assurance Soc., N.Y.C., 1964-65; instr. English, U. Miss., Oxford, 1966-68; admitted to N.C. bar, 1974; assoc. prof. law and govt. U. N.C., Chapel Hill, 1974—; chief counsel N.C. Commn. to Revise Public Sch. Laws, 1975-77; counsel to House Edn. Com. N.C. Gen. Assembly, 1979-80; spl. asst. to dir. FBI, Washington, 1980-81. Nat. Merit scholar, 1958-62. Mem. N.C. Bar, Nat. Council Sch. Attys., ACLU (mem. state bd. 1970-73), Order of the Coif, Phi Beta Kappa. Democrat. Author: North Carolina School Law: The Principal's Role, 1981; A Legal Guide for North Carolina School Board Members, 1978; contbr. articles on govt. and law to profl. jours. Home: 513 E Franklin Chapel Hill NC 27514 Office: 225 Knapp Bldg Institute of Government Univ North Carolina Chapel Hill NC 27514

DELLINGER, JOYCE ANITA JACKSON, dep. sheriff; b. Commerce, Tex., Feb. 8, 1935; d. James Monroe and Ada Ann (Graham) Newell; student Abiline Christian Coll., 1978-79; cert. dental asst. Baylor Dental Coll., 1958; m. Robert Lee Dellinger, May 23, 1979; children—Kathy Ann Jackson, Jack E. Jackson, James Edward Jackson, Laura Jo Jackson. Dental asst. bus. mgmt. Drs. Swords and Miranda, Dallas, 1954-67; pres., owner Breakaway Enterprises, Dallas, 1967-69; v.p. Emergency Info. Systems, Dallas, 1970-77; part-time dep. U.S. marshall, Dallas, 1978; dep. sheriff Dallas County Sheriffs Dept., 1977—. Mem. Republican Nat. Com., 1980-82. Mem. Am. Dental Asst. Assn., Profl. and Businesswomen's Assn., Dallas County Sheriffs Assn., Beta Sigma Phi. Republican. Office: Dallas County Sheriffs Dept 600 Commerce Dallas TX 75202

DELONG, NANCY GLYN, journalist, public relations and communications cons.; b. Columbus, Ohio, Oct. 2, 1946; d. Glen A. and Reba Z. (Pope) DeL.; B.A. in Journalism and English, Ohio State U., 1969. Exec. dir. Tri-County Dental Health Council, Detroit, 1971-76, reporter The Detroit News, 1970-71, The Columbus (Ohio) Dispatch, 1965-68; editorial photographer, contbg. editor Amusement Bus., 1968-73; producer The Oz of Prevention, Detroit, 1971-74; partner Real to Reel 1973-77; pres. project promotion Glyn Prodn. Ltd., 1977-79; pres. N. Glynn & Assocs., Inc., Southfield, Mich., 1979-82; bus. cons., 1976—; interior designer, 1976—; assoc. Walt Peabody Advt. Service Inc., Ft. Lauderdale, Fla. Profl. boxing judge, State of Mich. Contbr. articles to various mags.; contbg. editor Downbeat, 1966-68, Billboard, 1968-73; producer ednl. films on health and rehab.; producer, dir. Super Party '82. Address: 4779 Musket Way Columbus OH 43228

DELOUGHERY, GRACE, nursing home adminstr.; b. Allison, Iowa, Jan. 17, 1933; d. Ed F. and Alma K. (Kampman) Meinen; B.S., U. Minn., 1955, M.P.H., 1960; Ph.D., Claremont Grad. Sch., 1966; m. Henry O. Deloughery, Nov. 30, 1962; children—Paul Edward, Michael, Kathleen. Staff nurse Mpls. Dept. Pub. Health, 1955-59; research fellow U. Minn. Sch. Pub. Health, 1960-63; sch. nurse Val Verde Sch. Dist., Perris, Calif., part-time 1963-66; community coordinator, nurse in Title I pilot project in San Jacinto, Riverside (Calif.) County Schs., 1966, cons. Title I, 1966-67; asso. prof. U. N.C. Coll. Nursing, 1967-68; asst. prof. U. Calif. Sch. Nursing, Los Angeles, 1968-72; dean Center Nursing Edn., Spokane, 1972-74; prof., head dept. nursing Winona (Minn.) State U., 1975-77; adminstr. Deloughery Home Sr. Adults, 1977—; participant seminars, condr. workshops, cons. in field. Recipient award for research Calif. Edn. Research and Guidance Assn., 1967. Fellow Am. Pub. Health Assn., Am. Assn. Social Psychiatry (treas. 1974-78); mem. Am. Nurses Assn., Nat. League Nursing, Am. Sch. Health Assn., Internat. Mental Health Fedn., Wash. Pub. Health Assn., Acad. Polit. and Social Sci., Acad. Polit. Sci., Pi Lambda Theta. Lutheran. Club: Winona Country. Contbr. to profl. jours. Home: Pleasant Valley Terr Winona MN 55987 Office: Deloughery Home Sr Adults Lewiston MN 55952

DEL PERCIO, GLORIA, banker; b. Corona, N.Y., Oct. 22, 1926; d. Antonio and Filomena Del Percio; student N.Y. U., 1955, Nassau Community Coll., 1964-65, mgmt. studies program Hofstra/Cornell, 1976-77, N.Y. Inst. Tech., 1977, Wabash (Ind.) Coll., 1978-80. Clk., Altmans, N.Y.C., 1944-46; printers helper Bulova Watch Co., 1946-47; data processing operator IBM, 1947-51; sr. tabulator, computer operator Sperry Rand Corp., N.Y.C., 1951-60; data processing operator airborne instruments IBM, 1960-62, Republic Aviation Corp., 1962-64; supr. Avis Rent a Car, N.Y.C., 1964-67; ops. officer Citicorp, N.Y.C., 1967-77; mgr. data processing Citibank, Melville, N.Y., 1977—. Mem. Nat. Assn. Bankwomen, NOW, Amateur Golfer Met. Golf Assn. (tournament chmn.). Office: 100 Baylis Rd Melville NY 11746

DEL ROSARIO, MARIA LUISA TAN GATUE (MRS. DAVID R. DEL ROSARIO), physician; b. Manila, Aug. 25, 1926; d. Pablo de Jesus Tan Gatue and Josefa Navarro Gan; A.A., U. Philippines, 1947; M.D., U. Santo Tomas (Philippines), 1952; m. David R. del Rosario, Oct. 11, 1959; children—David, Jocelissa, Bernard, Andrew. Came to U.S., 1963, naturalized, 1969. Intern, Norwegian Lutheran Hosp., Deaconess Home and Hosp., 1954-55; resident Balt. City Hosps., 1955-58, Lawrence and Meml. Hosps., 1958-59; practice medicine specializing in obstetrics and gynecology, La Plata, Md., also Waldorf, Md.; chmn. dept. obstetrics and gynecology Physicians Meml. Hosp., La Plata. Mem. Charles County Med. Soc., A.M.A., Am. Med. Women's Assn., Philippine-Am. Med. Assn. of Met. D.C., Am. Cancer Soc. Home: PO Box 938 La Plata MD 20646 Office: 101 Saint Mary's Ave La Plata MD 20646 also Charles Profl Center Waldorf MD 20601

DEL VALLE, HELEN CYNTHIA, artist, designer; b. Chgo., Sept. 22, 1933; d. Andrew Jack and Mary Texanna (Cohen) Del Valle; B.F.A., Pa. Acad. Fine Arts, 1952; B.J., Northwestern U., 1960; diploma in profl. modeling Patricia Stevens Sch., Chgo., 1963. Tchr., Bay Hill Sch., Bushnell, Fla., 1952-54; creative artist House of Baldwin Galleries, Chgo., 1954-59; freelance artist, designer, Chgo., 1960—; paintings pub. newspaper Brighton Park Life, Chgo., 1973, Artists/USA, 1974; exhibited in group shows Navy Pier, Chgo., 1982, 909 N. Michigan Ave., Chgo., 1982; one-woman shows Balzekas Mus., Chgo., Chgo. Pub. Library, 1971-74, Combined Ins. Co., 1970-73, 75, also Spain, Italy, London, Israel, Austria; part-time hand, foot model for fashion mags., 1960—. Recipient 1st place award in portraiture N.Y. Profl. Art Show, N.Y.C., 1968; 1971, 3d award for watercolor. Ill. State Art Show, 1981; honorable mention award in still life Mcpl. Art League of Chgo., 1973; Silver plaque Am. Soc. Artists, 1974, other awards. Mem. Nat. League Am. Pen Women (Dingle Meml. award Chgo. chpt. 1971, 1st award for landscape 1973, 2d award in traditional painting 1971, 1st place painting award ann. exhibit 1979, 3d place award for watercolor ann. show 1980, 3d place award for watercolor state exhibit 1981; mem. art. com. Chgo. chpt 1982-84), Mcpl. Art League Chgo., Am. Soc. Artists (v.p., membership chmn.), Internat. Poetry Soc. (Eng.), Poets and Patrons, Citizens Republic, Tax Limitation Com., Internat. Platform Assn., Renaissance Soc. of U. Chgo. Club: The Cordon. Contbr. poems to New Voices in Am. Poetry (prize for Autumn, 1973). Office: PO Box 958 Chicago IL 60690

DELVALLE, JUNE ACKERMAN, occupational therapist; b. N.Y.C., June 3, 1926; d. Maurice and Bertha (Fox) Ackerman; B.S. in Occupational Therapy, N.Y. U., 1947; certificate cerebral palsy, Children's Rehab. Inst., Balt., 1948; m. Hugh Maduro Delvalle, Dec. 25, 1949; children—Kenneth (dec.), Bruce, Margot. Staff therapist Mt. Sinai Hosp., 1947-49; dir. occupational therapy Westchester (N.Y.) Cerebral Palsy Assn., 1949; pvt. case work, Panama and C.Z., 1950; occupational therapist Neustadter Convalescent Center, Yonkers, N.Y., 1952-54; dir.

occupational therapy Blythedale Children's Hosp., Valhalla, N.Y., 1961-64, Miller Center Nursing Care, White Plains, N.Y., 1964-66; chief occupational therapist in psychiatry United Hosp., Port Chester, N.Y., 1966-82, ret., 1982; cons., speaker in field. Past chmn. edn. com. Westchester Occupational Therapy Dist. Licensed occupational therapist, N.Y. State. Mem. Am., N.Y. State, Met. N.Y. Dist., Westchester Dist. occupational therapy assns., World Fedn. Occupational Therapists, Mental Health Assn. Westchester, Center Preventive Psychiatry, YWCA, Smithsonian Instn., Rye Art Center. Author in field. Home: 29 Blackthorn Ln White Plains NY 10606

DELVENTHAL, PRISCILLA JANE, histologist; b. Chgo., July 29, 1938; d. Ralph Daniel and Geneva Mae (Walden) Esterly; student No. Ill. U., So. Ill. U.; diploma histology, St. Anthony's Hosp., Rockford, Ill., 1961; m. LeRoy Earl Delventhal, Sept. 3, 1966; children—Kathryn Lee, Lane Aaron, Daniel Albert. Tchr., Rockford, Ill., 1960-61; asst. supr. surg. pathology-histology lab. U. Colo. Med. Sch., Denver, 1961-64; head histology Lutheran Hosp., Wheatridge, Colo., 1964-65; asst. head histology Colo. State U., Ft. Collins, 1966-68; head histology lab. Pathology Lab. Assos., Lander Who., 1977—; histologist portamedic services Hooper Homes, 1978—. Active local Boy Scout Am.; dir. jr. choir Trinity Lutheran Ch., Riverton, Wy. 1978-81, St. Johns Lutheran Ch., Ft. Collins, Colo. 1967-67. Mem. Am. Soc. Clin. Pathologists (asso.), Colo. Soc. Histotechnology (charter). Home: 829 Sheryl Sue Riverton WY 82501 Office: 906 Main St Lander WY 82520

DELWORTH, URSULA MARIE, psychologist; b. San Diego, Oct. 22, 1934; d. Lee James and Gertrude (Roberts) D.; B.A., Calif. State U., Long Beach, 1956; M.A., Calif. State U., Los Angeles 1962; Ph.D., U. Oreg., 1969. Staffpsychologist, asst. prof., assoc. prof. Colo. State U., 1969-73; program dir. Western Insterstate Commn. Higher Edn., Boulder, Colo., 1973-76; prof., dir. Counseling Service, U. Iowa, Iowa City, 1976—. Fellow Am. Psychol. Assn.; mem. Iowa Psychol. Assn., Am. Coll. Personnel Assn. Author: Crisis Center/Hot Line, 1974; student Services: A Handbook for the Profession, 1980; contbr. articles to profl. jours. Home: 65 Arbury Dr Iowa City IA 52240 Office: Counseling Center Univ Iowa Iowa City IA 52242

DEMAIO, BARBARA PATRICIA, social worker; b. Bronx, N.Y., Oct. 29, 1940; d. Alphonse Joseph and Elizabeth Elsie (Vogel) DeM.; A.A.S. in Human Services, Rockland Community Coll., 1971; B.S.W. summa cum laude, Fairleigh Dickinson U., 1973; M.S.W., Yeshiva U., 1975, cert. advanced gerontol. practice, 1981; m. Joseph G. DeMaio, Aug. 20, 1960 (div. 1967); remarried, 1977; children—Antonio J., Damon L. Drug counselor, counselor for mentally retarded, foster care caseworker various agys., 1970-74; psychiat. social worker Mental Health Clinic, Pomona, N.Y., 1974-75; dir. social work Dept. Health and Hosps., Rockland County (N.Y.) Health Center, Pomona, 1975—; social work cons.; instr. Yeshiva U., 1981. Cert. social worker. Mem. Acad. Cert. Social Workers, Nat Assn. Social Workers, Westchester-Rockland Health Care Social Work Assn., NAACP, NOW, Phi Sigma Omicron, Phi Omega Epsilon. Office: Rockland County Health Center Bldg A Pomona NY 10970

DEMAR, GERALDINE RELIHAN, realty co. exec.; b. Schenectady, June 19, 1927; d. Matthew Peter and Mary Theresa (Sullivan) Relihan; student Ithaca (N.Y.) Coll., Union Coll., Schenectady; B.S. in Psychology and Human Devel., SUNY, Albany; grad. Realtors Inst., Ithaca Coll., 1970; grad. degree in alcoholism and drug abuse counseling and rehab. Russell Sage Coll., 1980; m. Neil Joseph Demar, Aug. 5, 1950; 1 dau., Maureen Ann. Real estate sales asso., Schenectady, 1964-69; dir. Leased Housing Program, Mcpl. Housing Authority, Schenectady, 1969-71; pres. Geraldine M. Demar Realty Co., Schenectady, 1971—; cons. N.Y. State Panel on Housing for Elderly, N.Y. State Panel for Housing for Low Income Families. Vol., Planned Parenthood, Schenectady, 1971-72; mem. Mohawk Pathways council Girl Scouts U.S.A., Schenectady, 1963-69. Cert. counselor-therapist in alcoholism and drug abuse rehab., N.Y. State. Mem. Schenectady Bd. Realtors, N.Y. State Assn. Real Estate Bds., N.Y. State Soc. Real Estate Appraisers, Nat. Assn. Realtors, Nat. Inst. Real Estate Brokers, Women's Council Realtors (Capitol dist.), Realtors Nat. Mktg. Inst., Upstate N.Y. Transactional Analysis Seminar, Friends of Schenectady County Public Library, Friends of Schenectady Mus., Women's League Schenectady Symphony Orch., Schenectady County LWV, Am. Mus. Natural History, Nat. Soc. Lit. and Arts, Nat. Trust Historic Preservation, Schenectady County Council for Arts, Niskayuna Home and Sch. Assn., Rosendale Estates Assn., Schenectady, Capitol Dist. chambers commerce, AAUW, Beta Sigma Phi. Unitarian. Clubs: Schenectady Women's, Soroptimist. Home and office: 2174 Lynnwood Dr Rosendale Estates Schenectady NY 12309

DEMARCO, MARIA ELENA, business exec.; b. N.Y.C., Sept. 6, 1945; d. Joseph Anthony and Antoinette (Schiraldi) DeM.; B.S., cum laude (Regents scholar 1965-68), U. Calif., San Francisco, 1968, M.S., 1974; postgrad. in bus. adminstrn. St. Mary's Coll., Moraga, Calif., 1980-82; m. Frank Wilson Jr., Dec. 31, 1976. Bus. mgr. Pomegranate, Corte Madera, Calif., 1970-74; clin. nurse specialist in psychiatry Prisoners Health Project, San Francisco, 1974-76; exec. dir. Calif. Nurses Assn., Region XI, Oakland, Calif., 1976-79; tng. mgr. computer ops., staff mgr. acctg. dept. Pacific Telephone Co., San Francisco, 1979—. Mem. criminal justice com. Alameda County Mental Health Adv. Bd., 1977-80. Mem. Nat. Assn. Female Execs., Am. Nurses Assn., Calif. Nurses Assn., Bay Area Profl. Women's Network, Sigma Theta Tau. Democrat. Home: 52 La Vuelta Orinda CA 94563 Office: Pacific Telephone Co PO Box 3269 San Francisco CA 94119

DEMAREST, ELIZABETH JANE, govtl. agy. adminstr.; b. N.Y.C., Aug. 27, 1946; d. Winfield James and Helen Anna (Gray) Demarest; B.A. (N.Y. State Regents scholar), Fordham U., 1968; M.A., Columbia U., 1970; m. Leo Vernon Mayer, Apr. 29, 1978. Legis. specialist, budget analyst, edn. specialist HEW, 1973-76, sr. policy analyst, 1976-79; research mgr. U.S. Dept. Edn., Washington, 1979-80, dir. office of planning and program coordination, office of ednl. research and improvement, 1980—. Mem. Belle Haven Citizens Assn., 1979—. Mem. Am. Soc. Public Adminstrn., Am. Edn. Fin. Assn., Am. Edn. Research Assn., Phi Beta Kappa. Home: 6117 Vernon Terr Alexandria VA 22307 Office: US Dept Edn 400 Maryland Ave SW Washington DC 20202

DEMAREST, ROSEMARY REGINA, librarian; b. N.Y.C., Jan. 20, 1915; d. William Gustavus and Rosemary Ann (MacElhinny) Demarest; B.A., Sarah Lawrence Coll., 1936. Asst. librarian The Hanover Bank, N.Y.C., 1940-44, librarian, 1945-53; research asst. OSS, London, Eng., 1944-45; chief librarian Price Waterhouse & Co., N.Y.C., 1953-80. Mem. Spl. Libraries Assn. (pres. N.Y. chpt. 1955-56, chmn. bus. and finance div. 1961-62, dir. 1968-71), Royal Soc. Lit. (London), N.Y. Jr. League. Author: Accounting Information Sources, 1970. Home: 430 E 86th St New York NY 10028

DEMARR, MARY JEAN, educator; b. Champaign, Ill., Sept. 20, 1932; d. William Fleming and Laura Alice (Shauman) Bailey; B.A., Lawrence Coll., 1954; M.A., U. Ill., 1957, Ph.D., 1963; postgrad. Universitaet Tuebingen, 1954-55, Moscow State U., 1961-62. Asst. prof. English, Willamette U., 1964-65; asst. prof. English, Ind. State U., 1965-70, asso. prof., 1970-75, prof., 1975—. Recipient Fulbright assistantship, 1954-55. Mem. Modern Lang. Assn., Modern Humanities Research Assn., AAUP, Nat. Council Tchrs. of English, ACLU, Phi Beta Kappa, Phi Kappa Phi. Presbyterian. Am. editor: Annual Bibliography of English Language and Literature, 1974—. Home: 2841 Mariposa Dr Terre Haute IN 47803 Office: Dept English Ind State U Terre Haute IN 47809

DEMARS, DONNA JEANNE, dietitian; b. Oklahoma City, May 27, 1947; d. Donald E. and Doris A. (Roushkolb) Malum; B.S., Stout State U., 1969; postgrad. St. Cloud State U., 1981—; m. David M. DeMars, Mar. 23, 1968; children—Michael David, Kristen Aimee. Dietetic intern Milwaukee County Instns., 1969-70; sr. dietitian U. Minn. Hosp., Mpls., 1971-73; nursing home cons., central Minn., 1973-74; dietetic traineeship coordinator, clin. relief dietitian St. Cloud (Minn.) Hosp., 1974-80, adminstrv. dietitian, 1980—; asst. dir. Minn. dietetic internship consortium U. Minn. Mem. Am. Dietetic Assn., Minn. Dietetic Assn., Central Minn. Dietetic Assn. Home: RR 5 St Cloud MN 56301 Office: St Cloud Hospital 1406 6th Ave N St Cloud MN 56301

DEMAS, JEAN V., real estate co. exec.; b. Oak Park, Ill., Dec. 30, 1940; d. Charles William and Helen Alice (Kyriakopulos) Demas; B.A., Northwestern U., 1962; student DePaul U. Coll. Law, 1979—; m. Harry T. Dallianis, Dec. 8, 1962 (div. July 1979); children—Irene Lorraine, Thomas Harry. Tchr., Von Steuben High Sch., Chgo., 1962-65; sec.-treas. Ideal Real Estate and Ins. Brokerage, Inc., Chgo., 1965-72, v.p., exec. dir., 1972-79, dir. corp. relocation, 1975-79; dir. Ideal Realty Co. Mem. Lincolnwood (Ill.) Community Council, 1972—; treas. Lincolnwood Homeowners Assn., 1974-75. Precinct capt. Lincolnwood Citizens Action Party, 1977; mem. Lincolnwood PTA, Lincolnwood Bicentennial Com., Lincolnwood Friends of Library; dir. Sts. Peter and Paul Greek Orthodox Ch. Sch. Bd., 1977-79; 15th Ill. dist. coordinator ERA, 1977-78; mem. Lincolnwood Library Steering Com., 1978—; den leader Cub Scout troop Boy Scouts Am., 1978-79. Mem. Nat. Assn. Realtors, Realtors Nat. Mktg. Inst., Ill. Assn. Realtors, Chgo. Real Estate Bd. (chmn. sales council 1980—), North Side Real Estate Bd., NW Real Estate Bd., Nat. Assn. Rev. Appraisers (sr. cert. rev. appraiser), Nat. Assn. Ind. Fee Appraisers, N. Suburban Chicagoland Real Estate Bd. (pres. 1976-77, dir. 1978-80), RELO-Inter City Relocation Services (chairperson Chgo. area 1975-76), LWV, Zeta Tau Alpha. Home: 6842 N Kostner Lincolnwood IL 60646 Office: 3459 W Foster Ave Chicago IL 60625

DEMERITTE, SUSIE HEATH, psychotherapist; b. Dayton, Ohio, Jan. 24, 1925; d. George W. and Mamie Gertrude (Pratt) Heath; student Spelman Coll., 1943-45; B.S., Ohio State U., 1947; M.S., Western Res. U., 1952; m. Samuel Garfield Demeritte, May 24, 1957; children—Samuel Garfield, Mamie Angela. Caseworker, Family and Children's Service, Pitts., 1952-53; psychiat. social worker Lakin (W.Va.) State Hosp., 1953-56, Ancora State Hosp., 1956-57, 59-60; sch. social worker, child study team mem. Kingsway Regional High Sch. Dist., Swedesboro, N.J., 1974—; psychotherapist Salem (N.J.) County Guidance Center, 1976-78. Certified sch. social worker, N.J. Mem. Nat. Assn. Social Workers, Nat. Council Social Workers, N.J. Edn. Assn. Republican. Episcopalian. Home: 827 Garwood Erial NJ 08081

DEMES, LEANNE CECILE, nurse; b. Chgo., Dec. 19, 1941; d. Charles Joseph and Lenore Marie (Green) D.; R.N., Columbus Hosp., Chgo., 1964; B.S. in Nursing, DePaul U., Chgo., 1970, M.S. in Nursing Adminstrn., 1971. Staff nurse, then head nurse Burn Center, Cook County Hosp., Chgo., 1964-66; head nurse, then supr. Columbus Hosp., 1967-71, asso. dir. nursing, 1971-74; dir. nursing N.E. Ga. Med. Center, Gainesville, 1974-76; dir. nursing service St. Mary's Hosp., Huntington, W.Va., 1976—; adj. asst. prof. Marshall U., Huntington; cons., preceptor in field. Mem. Am. Nurses Assn., Nat. League Nursing, Am. Mgmt. Assn., Am. Soc. Nursing Service Adminstrs., Nat. Forum Adminstr. Nursing Service, Nursing Alumni Assn. DePaul U., W.Va. Soc. Hosp. Nursing Service Adminstrs., W.Va. League Nursing, W.Va. Health Systems Agy., W.Va. Nurses Assn. Roman Catholic. Author articles in field. Home: Route 3 Box 383 South Point OH 45680 Office: 2900 1st Ave Huntington WV 25701

DEMETRIADES, DESPINA GUS, human resources devel. cons.; b. Gastonia, N.C.; d. Gus George and Athena (Leventis) D.; B.A. in Psychology, Columbia U., 1966; M.A. in Counselor Edn., Appalachian State U., Boone, N.C., 1967. Instr., Lynchburg (Va.) Coll., 1967-69; dir. inservice edn. Gastonia Meml. Hosp., 1970-77; edn. coordinator Catawba/Wateree Health Edn. Consortium, Lancaster, S.C., 1977-78; pres., devel. analyst Profl. Devel. Systems, Gastonia, 1978—; motivation/performance analyst Despina G. Demetriades Work Performance Systems, Gastonia, 1982—; seminar leader, speaker in field. Mem. Am. Soc. Tng. and Devel., Gaston County Bd. Realtors, N.C. Women's Forum. Mem. Greek Orthodox Ch. Club: Gastonia Altrusa (pres. 1980-82; chmn. vocat. aid Internat. Founders Fund 1981-83, chmn. internat. relations com. 1983-85). Home: 1300 S York St Gastonia NC 28052 Office: PO Box 1414 Gastonia NC 28052

DEMETRIOUS, MARY, ednl. cons.; b. Florence, S.C., Feb. 27, 1950; d. Chris Nicholas and Katina Demetra (Pappas) D.; B.A., Randolph-Macon Woman's Coll., 1972; postgrad. Georgetown U., 1982. Intern, Sen. Ernest Hollings, Washington, 1971; state field coordinator McGovern for Pres., S.C., 1972; field coordinator Jenrette for Congress, Florence, S.C., 1974; regional dir. S.C. Human Affairs Commn., Florence, 1975-76; project coordinator S.C. Reorgn. Commn., Columbia, 1976-78; adminstr. Francis Marion Coll., Florence, S.C., 1979-80; cons. State Bd. Tech. and Comprehensive Edn., 1980—. Mem. exec. com. S.C. Council Human Rights, 1975; alt. del. Democratic Nat. Conv., 1972, del., 1980, 82; mem. steering com. New Dem. Coalition, 1973-74; vice chmn. Dem. Party of S.C., 1976-78; mem. Nat. Dem. Com., 1976-78, mem. alumni council; mem. exec. com. Dem. Women's Council, 1976-78; chmn. Darlington County Dem. Com., 1979—; mem. S.C. adv. com. ERA, 1977—; sec.-treas. 6th Dist. Dem. Caucus; bd. dirs., treas. Transfiguration Greek Orthodox Ch. Mem. Am. Soc. Public Adminstrn., Assn. State Dem. Chairmen, Darlington C. of C., Darlington County Hist. Soc. (dir., exec. com.), Alston Wilkes Soc. Home: PO Box 22 Darlington SC 29532 Office: PO Box 11465 Columbia SC 29211

DEMHARTER, CHERYL ANN MARIE, educator; b. New Orleans, May 20, 1955; d. Anton Irwin and Liliane Irene (Auger) D.; B.A. magna cum laude, U. New Orleans, 1975; M.A., Tulane U., 1978, Ph.D., 1981. Grad. teaching asst. Tulane U., New Orleans, 1977-80, vis. instr. French, 1980-81; asst. prof. French, U. Tex., Austin, 1981—, faculty adv. Le Cercle Français, 1981-82. Recipient Summer Stipends, U. Research Inst., 1982, Nat. Endowment for Humanities, 1982. Mem. Modern Lang. Assn., Am. Assn. Tchrs. French, Internat. Soc. Phonetic Scis., Am. Council Teaching Fgn. Langs., South Central Modern Lang. Assn., South Atlantic Modern Lang. Assn., Council Devel. French in La., Media-Louisiane, Phi Kappa Phi. Office: Dept French and Italian U Tex Austin TX 78712

DE MILLE, AGNES, choreographer; d. William Churchill and Anna (George) de Mille; A.B. cum laude, U. Calif.; Litt.D. (hon.), Mills Coll., 1952, Russell Sage Coll., 1953, Smith Coll., 1954, Western Coll., 1955, Hood Coll., 1957, Northwestern U., 1960, Goucher Coll., 1961, Clark U., 1962, U. Calif. at Los Angeles, 1964, Franklin and Marshall, 1965, Western Mich. U., 1967, Nosson Coll., 1971; L.H.D., Dartmouth Coll., 1974, Duke U., 1975; m. Walter F. Prude, June 14, 1943; 1 son, Jonathan. Dance recitalist, U.S., Eng., France, Denmark, 1928-42; choreographer and dancer The Black Crook, 1929; choreographer; (film) Romeo and Juliet, 1936; (musicals) Nymph Errant, 1933, Hooray for What, 1937, Oklahoma, 1943, One Touch of Venus, 1943, Bloomer Girl, 1944, Carousel, 1945, Brigadoon, 1947, Gentlemen Prefer Blondes, 1949, Paint Your Wagon, 1951, The Girl in Pink Tights, 1954, Goldilocks, 1958, Juno, 1959, Kwamina, 1961; (ballets) OBeah Black Ritual, 1940, Three Virgins and a Devil, 1942, Drums Sound in Hackensack, 1941, Rodeo, 1942, Tally-Ho, 1944, Fall River Legend, 1948, The Harvest According, 1952; Oklahoma (film), 1955; The Bitter Wierd, 1962; The Wind in the Mountains, 1965; The Four Mary's, 1965; The Golden Age, 1967; A Rose for Miss Emily, 1970; choreographer, dir. Allegro, 1947; dir. Rape of Lucrecia, 1949, Out of this World, 1950, Come Summer, 1969; choreographer (musical) 110 In the Shade, 1963,) Texas Fourth, 1976. Head Agnes de Mille Dance Theatre, presented by S. Hurok, 6 mos. tour, 126 cities, 1953-54, Agnes de Mille Heritage Dance Theater, 1973, 74, Conversations About the Dance, 1974, 75. Omnibus lectrs. and ballets, 1956-57; choreographer for Ballet Russe de Monte Carlo, 1942, Royal Winnipeg Ballet, 1972. Recipient N.Y. Critics prize, 1942-46, Donaldson award, 1943-47, Madamoiselle merit award, 1944, Antoinette Perry award, 1947, 62, Lord and Taylor award, 1947, Dancing Masters award of merit, 1950; Dance Mag. award, 1957; Capezio award, 1966; Handel award Mayor N.Y.C., 1976; named Woman of Year by Am. Newspaper Womans Guild, 1946; named to Theatre Hall of Fame, 1973; Agnes de Mille Theatre N.C. Sch. Arts, Winston-Salem named in her honor, 1975. Mem. Soc. Stage Dirs. and Choreographers (pres. 1965-66). Author: Dance to the Piper, 1952; And Promenade Home, 1958; To A Young Dancer, 1962; The Book of the Dance, 1963; Lizzie Borden Dance of Death, 1968; Dance In America, 1970; Russian Journals, 1970; Speak to Me, Dance with Me, 1974. Contbr. to Good Housekeeping, Esquire, Horizon, Vogue, Atlantic Monthly, McCalls mags. *

DEMING, BARBARA, obstetrician-gynecologist; b. New Orleans, Mar. 28, 1942; d. Harry Hayes and Lucille Marie (Jolly) D.; B.S., U. New Orleans, 1963; M.D., La. State U., 1967; m. David Bryan Lemoine, Aug. 4, 1979 (div.) Rotating intern Charity Hosp., New Orleans, 1967-68, resident in ob-gyn, 1968-71; practice medicine specializing in ob-gyn, Metairie, La., 1972—; pres. Deming Woman's Clinic, Inc., 1972—; chief of ob-gyn East Jefferson Hosp., Metairie, 1977-78; mem. Perinatal Practice Com. Greater New Orleans Area, 1977; mem. maternity task force com. Archdiocese of New Orleans, 1977, mem. adv. bd. Archdiocese Group Home Program, 1973—, charter and founding mem. Youth Guild, 1977; mem. profl. adv. bd. New Orleans area March of Dimes, 1979. Diplomate Am. Bd. Ob-Gyn. Mem. La., New Orleans obstet. and gynecol. socs., Jefferson Soc. Obstetricians and Gynecologists, Am. Fertility Soc., La., Jefferson Parish med. socs., Cancer Assn. Greater New Orleans (dir. 1981-82). Democrat. Roman Catholic. Office: 4740 I-10 Service Rd Suite 310 Metairie LA 70001

DEMIRJIAN, ARLENE, social worker; b. Bridgeport, Conn., Mar. 1, 1941; d. John and Sara (Andrikian) D.; B.A., Clark U., 1962; M.S.W. (scholar), Boston U., 1965; cert. in psychoanalytic psychotherapy Inst. for Study of Psychotherapy, 1975. Social worker Bellevue Psychiat. Hosp., N.Y.C., 1965-69, founder pilot program for heroin addicts, 1969; pvt. practice psychotherapy, N.Y.C., 1974—; cons. N.Y. State Div. Substance Abuse Services, 1974—, U.S. Dept. State, 1982. Cert. social worker, N.Y. Mem. Nat. Assn. Social Workers, Armenian Gen. Benevolent Union. Contbr. articles on heroin abuse and on Soviet psychiatry to publs. Home: 308 E 79th St New York NY 10021 Office: 425 E 86th St New York NY 10028

DE MORELOS, PATRICIA ELENA HARMS, interior designer; b. Mexico City, Aug. 16, 1916; d. Hugo von Pein Harms and Elisa Harms de Morelos; M. Philosophy, Cours Dupanloup, Paris, 1937; service diplomatique Ecole Libre des Sciences Politiques, Paris, 1939; student Newspaper Inst. Am., N.Y.C., 1942; m. Henry Thomas Kent Paxson, Mar. 2, 1940; children—Charles Edward, Richard Enrique Morelos. Pres., owner Patricia de Morelos Modeling Sch., Mexico City, from 1949; pres., owner Patricia de Morelos Designs, Los Angeles, 1978—, Style Enterprises, Los Angeles, 1980—. Recipient Best Actress of Yr. award Mexico City, 1967. Mem. Actors Guild. Republican. Episcopalian. Contbr. short stories to popular mags.

DEMOS, KATHLEEN TALBOT, social worker; b. Alameda, Calif., July 28, 1946; d. Russell Roberts and Emma Martha (Bossman) Talbot; student Butler U., 1964-66; B.A., U. Ill., 1968; M.A., U. Chgo., 1970; m. Steven S. Demos, May 1, 1976. Psychiat. social worker Family Service and Mental Health Center, Chicago Heights, Ill., 1970-71, U. Chgo. Hosps. and Clinics, 1971-74, Pritzker Children's Hosp. and Center, Chgo., 1974, Salvation Army Family Service, Chgo., 1975-76, U. Mich. Neuropsychiatric Inst., Adolescent Service, Ann Arbor, Mich., 1976—; field work instr. Kennedy-King Jr. Coll., Chgo., 1971-72, U. Chgo. Sch. Social Service Adminstrn., 1973-74. Certified social worker, Mich. Mem. Acad. Certified Social Workers, Nat. Assn. Social Workers, Registry of Clin. Social Workers. Home and Office: 3739 Highgate Rd Muskegon MI 49441

DEMOTT, DEBORAH ANN, lawyer; b. Collingswood, N.J., July 21, 1948; d. Lyle J. and Frances (Cummings) DeM.; B.A., Swarthmore Coll., 1970; J.D. (AAUW fellow), N.Y.U., 1973. Admitted to N.Y. State bar, 1974; law clk. U.S. Dist. Ct., 1973; assoc. firm Simpson, Thacher & Bartlett, N.Y.C., 1974-75; asst. prof. law Duke U., 1975-78, assoc. prof., 1978-81, prof., 1981—; vis. asst. prof. U. Tex., 1977-78. Mem. fin. com. Law Sch. Admissions Council. Named Best Research Prof., Duke U., 1981; Mem. Am. Bar Assn., Am. Law Inst. Editor: Corporations at the Crossroads: Governance and Reform, 1980. Home: 2320 Prince St Durham NC 27707 Office: Law School Duke University Durham NC 27706

DEMPSEY, BARBARA JEAN, media cons.; b. Winchester, Mass., June 10, 1953; d. John Thomas and Irene Barbara (Geremonte) D.; B.A. (Lantern award 1975), Adelphi U., 1975. Mktg. researcher Grey Advt., N.Y.C., 1975-76; music dir. Sta. WHDH, Boston, 1976-77; newscaster Sta. WORC, Worcester, Mass., 1977; talk show host, newscaster, sportscaster, producer Sta. WKOX/WVBF-FM, Framingham, Mass., 1977-79; M-F public info. officer Essex County Dist. Atty.'s Office, Salem, Mass., 1979-80; anchorwoman, producer news Sta. WGGB-TV, Springfield, Mass., 1979-80; media coordinator Coalition for Auto Ins. Reform, Boston, 1980-81; mem. public info. com. Am. Cancer Soc. Bd. dirs. Quanapowitt Players, Reading, Mass. Mem. Bus. and Profl. Women's Club, Iota Beta Sigma. Roman Catholic. Home: 1 Winter St Salem MA 01970

DEMPSEY, PATRICIA LOUISE, social worker; b. Waterbury, Conn., Sept. 20, 1947; d. James Louis and Phyllis Virginia (Reid) D.; B.A., Fordham U., 1973; M.S. (Mott fellow), Columbia U., 1975. Dir. Youth Services System, East Side Settlement House, Bronx, N.Y., 1975-76; dep. dir. food stamp alert Community Council Greater N.Y., 1976-77; dir. youth services United Neighborhood Houses of N.Y., 1977-78; program dir. Harlem br. YMCA Greater N.Y., 1978-80, dir. spl. projects, 1980—; mem. faculty Adelphi U. Sch. Social Work, 1978—; cons. Cornell U.; cons. Nat. Council Negro Women. Mem. Bronx Council for Advocacy of Children and Youth, 1975—, mem. edn., child abuse and juvenile justice task forces, 1978—; bd. dirs. Juvenile Justice Coalition of N.Y. Cert. social worker. Mem. Nat. Assn. Social Workers, Nat. Assn. Black Social Workers, Riverdale Mental Health Assn., Assn. Profl. Dirs. YMCA Greater N.Y., Columbia U. Alumni Assn. Office: 180 W 135th St New York NY 10030

DEMSKI, LYDIA, business exec.; b. Romania; came to U.S., 1951, naturalized, 1958; student U. Ill., Southwestern Mich. Coll., Andrews

U., Lake Mich. Coll.; children—Michael, Robert. Profl. translater-interpreter, 1960-62; prodn. supr. Ball Rubber Corp., St. Joseph, Mich., 1962-65; br. mgr. Manpower, Inc., Benton Harbor, Mich., 1965-67; pres., owner Scope Services, Inc., employment agy., St. Joseph, 1967—; gen. mgr., partner Lake Mich. Realty, St. Joseph, 1974; co-owner, v.p., sec.-treas. Zantigo Restaurants, St. Joseph, 1978; chmn. for Mich., SBA, 1977. First aid instr. Berrien County chpt. ARC. Mem. Adminstrv. Mgmt. Soc. (pres. Mich. chpt., Chief award Micianaa chpt., Merit award Willow Grove (Pa.) chpt.), Mich. Employment Assn. (regional v.p.), Twin Cities Area C. of C., Nat. Employment Assn., Nat. Assn. Temporary Help, Nat. Personnel Assn., Mich. Assn. Pvt. Detectives and Security Agencies, Southwestern Mich. Econ. Club, Personnel Roundtable, Nat. Assn. Autistic Children, Berrien County Assn. Retarded Children. Clubs: Berrien Hills Country, Point-O-Woods Country (Benton Harbor, Mich.). Address: 420 Main St St Joseph MI 49085

DE MUESY, NANETTE, advt. exec.; b. Canton, Ohio, Nov. 13, 1926; d. Adam Lawrence and Laviora (Gray) DeM.; B.S. in Edn. and Journalism, Northwestern U., 1948. Reporter, art and music editor Canton Repository, 1948-51; tchr. journalism and English, Canton Public Schs., 1951-54; account exec. Frease & Shorr, Advt., Canton, 1954-62; owner, mgr. DeMuesy Advt., Canton, 1962—; resource tchr. Stark County br. Kent State U. Trustee Cultural Center for the Arts; women's adv. bd. Malone Coll. of Canton. Recipient Most Outstanding New Advt. awards Canton Advt. Club, 1975, 79. Mem. Woman's Advt. Club Cleve., Women in Communications, Nat. Fedn. Press Women, Ohio Press Women, Delta Zeta. Republican. Mem. Christian Ch. Office: PO Box 8318 Canton OH 44711

DEMUTH, MARCELLA DAMIECKI, educator; b. Bridgehampton, N.Y., May 15, 1935; d. Marcel J. and Helen (Buckin) Damiecki; B.A. cum laude, Syracuse (N.Y.) U., 1956; B.S. magna cum laude, Hofstra U., Hempstead, N.Y., 1975; m. Henry Wilson Demuth, Nov. 3, 1962; 1 son, Brian Charles. Tchr., N.Y. State public schs., 1956—; supr. fgn. lang. dept. J.F. Kennedy High Sch., Plainview, N.Y., 1977—, also NDEA demonstration tchr., 1960; past pres. Fgn. Lang. Chmns. Assn. L.I.; past mem. N.Y. State Commn. Integration Arts in Gen. Edn. Recipient Ferdinand Di bartolo award, 1978; NDEA grantee, 1959. Mem. Am. Assn. Tchrs. French (past pres. L.I. chpt.), Am. Council Fgn. Lang. Tchrs., N.Y. State Assn. Fgn. Lang. Tchrs. (past pres.), Pi Lambda Theta, Phi Delta Kappa, Pi Delta Phi. Home: 137 Northfield Rd Hauppauge NY 11788 Office: JF Kennedy High Sch Kennedy Dr Plainview NY 11803

DEMUTH, NINA LEWIS, chem. air sterilization co. exec.; b. Benton, Ill., July 14, 1921; d. William Henry and Agnes Clara (Landreth) Lewis; student Nassau Coll., 1976—; m. Herbert Willard Demuth, Feb. 16, 1947; 1 dau., Nina Dale. With Barbour Co., Inc., St. Louis, 1939-47, v.p., 1943-47; pres. Demuth Co., Garden City, N.Y., 1948—, Demuth Service Corp., Garden City, 1955—, Demuth Devel. Corp., Garden City, 1958. Mem. Parenteral Drug Assn. (dir. 1977-79), Parenteral Drug Assn. Found. for Pharm. Scis. (incorporator 1979, pres. 1979—, dir. 1979-82). Methodist. Contbr. articles in field to profl. publs. Office: PO Box 242 Garden City NY 11530

DEMYAN, BARBARA A., cancer center ofcl.; b. Elmira, N.Y., Nov. 22, 1948; d. Thomas Paul and Philomena Rita (Terpolilli) Rhode; student Russell Sage Coll., 1979-80, Elmira Coll., 1966-67; children—Karen Anne, Nicole Lee. With VA, Albany, N.Y., 1969-77; adminstrv. dir. Albany Regional Cancer Center, 1977—; mem. N.Y. Cancer Programs, Nat. Surg. Adjuvant Breast and Bowel Project, Cancer Control.; assoc. Community Cancer Centers. Democrat. Roman Catholic. Office: Doctors Sponzo and Cunningham 317 S Manning Blvd Suite 330 Albany NY 12208

DENAFIO, TERESA LOUISE, state legislator; b. Dover Foxcroft, Maine, July 6, 1957; d. Ralph Albert and Phyllis (Salley) DeN.; B.A. in Polit. Sci., U. N.H., 1981; student Franklin Pierce Law Center, 1982—. Mem. N.H. Ho. of Reps., 1978—; tchr. Dover, N.H., 1981—. Mem. Dover Sch. Com., 1976—, chmn., 1980. Democrat. Address: 7 Hemlock Forest Dover NH 03820

DEN BOER, JENNIEVA, nurse; b. LeMars, Iowa, May 31, 1949; d. Gerrit and Antonia (Fluit) Rozeboom; R.N., Sioux Valley Hosp. Sch. Nursing, 1970; m. Willis Arlin Den Boer, Jan. 12, 1973; 1 son, Andrew. Staff nurse Sioux Center (Iowa) Community Hosp., 1970-75, Hegg Meml. Hosp., Rock Valley, Iowa, 1975-77, dir. nursing, 1977-81, now dir. edn. Mem. Emergency Med. Soc. (del.), Nat. League Nursing, Assn. of Operating Room Nurses. Republican. Mem. Netherland Reformed Ch. Home: R R 1 Rock Valley IA 51247 Office: Hegg Meml Hosp 1200 21st Ave Rock Valley IA 51247

DENEUVE, CATHERINE (CATHERINE DORLEAC), actress; b. Paris, Oct. 22, 1943; d. Maurice Dorleac and Renee Deneuve; ed. Lycée La Fontaine, Paris; m. David Bailey, 1965 (div. 1970); children—Christian Vadim, Chiara Mastroianni. Motion picture appearances include: Les Petits Chats, 1956; Les Collegiennes, 1956; Les portes claquent, 1960; Les Parisiennes, 1961; Et Satan conduit le bal, 1962; Vacances portugaises, 1963; Le Vice et la Vertu, 1963; Les Parapluies de Cherbourg (Golden Palm of Cannes Festival), 1964; La Chasse à l'homme, 1964; Les Plus belles escroqueries du monde, 1964; Un Monsieur de compagnie, 1964; Repulsion, 1965; Coeur à la gorge, 1965; Le Chant de Ronde, 1965; La Vie de Chateau, 1965; Les créatures, 1966; Les Demoiselles de Rochefort, 1966; Benjamin, 1967; Manon 70, 1967; Belle de Jour (Golden Lion of Venice Festival), 1967; Meyerling, 1967; La Chamade, 1968; The April Fools, 1968; La Sirène du Mississippi, 1968; Tristana, 1969; It Only Happens to Others, 1971; Dirty Money; Hustle, 1975; Lovers Like Us, 1975; Act of Aggression, 1976; March or Die, 1977; La Grande Bourgeoise, 1977; The Last Metro, 1980; A Second Chance, 1981. Office: care Artmedia 10 Ave George V 75008 Paris France *

DENHAM, MARY GRAY, bus. exec.; b. Albion, Pa., Sept. 6, 1929; d. Delmer E. and Ruth Audeen (Gray) Beatty; m. Gene E. Denham, Dec. 12, 1969 (dec.); children—Mary Ruth, Susan, 1 step dau., Wendy Koivisto. Catalog writer Gen. Electric, Erie, Pa., 1953-61; with Sperry-Rand Corp., Phoenix, 1961-69; with Motorola, Inc., Scottsdale, Ariz., 1969-79, supr. drafting and data control, 1975-79; configuration/document control supr. ADDA Corp., Campbell, Calif., 1979—. Mem. Am. Bus. Women (past pres.), Nat. Assn. Female Execs., La Societe de Femme (past v.p.), Clowns of Am. (past pres. Clown Alley 7). Home: 2853 Weyers Ct San Jose CA 95148 Office: 1671 Dell Ave Campbell CA 95008

DENKHOFF, ELIZABETH, tractor mfg. co. exec.; b. Madelia, Minn., Oct. 12, 1914; d. Theodore Francis and Anna Maria (Meis) Denkhoff; student St. Louis Conservatory Music, 1929-30, Browns Bus. Coll., Davenport, Iowa, 1934-35. Instr. secretarial sci. Browns Bus. Coll., 1935-37; office staff supr. Motor Club Iowa, Davenport, 1937-44; exec. sec. to pres. Deere & Co., Moline, Ill., 1944-64, exec. sec. to chmn., chief exec. officer, 1964-71, corp. sec., 1971—. Bd. dirs. Miss Valley council Girl Scouts U.S.A., 1974-81. Cert. profl. rating. Mem. Am. Soc. Corp. Secs., Nat. Secs. Assn. Democrat. Roman Catholic. Home: 3510 37th Ave Apt 1 Moline IL 61265 Office: John Deere Rd Moline IL 61265 *

DENLINGER, JANET LOGAN, biomed. scientist; b. St. Petersburg, Fla., May 16, 1945; d. Robert Ross and Mary Elizabeth (Ryder) D.; B.S. in Biology, U. Fla., 1966; M.S. in Endocrine Physiology, Purdue U., 1967; m. Endre Alexander Balazs, July 19, 1977. Sr. research asst. dept. pharmacology Ottawa (Ont., Can.) U., 1968-71; high sch. tchr. biology and physiology Pasco County Sch. System, Zephyrhills, Fla., 1971-73; sr. research asst. Boston Biomed. Research Inst., 1973-75; staff asso. dept. ophthalmology Coll. Physicians and Surgeons, Columbia U., N.Y.C., 1975—; research cons. Biomatrix, Inc., Riverdale, N.Y. Mem. Assn. for Research in Vision and Ophthalmology, N.Y. Acad. Scis., Internat. Soc. for Eye Research, Phi Sigma. Researcher in ophthalmology and arthritis; contbr. chpts. to books, articles to profl. jours. Office: 630 W 168th St New York NY 10032

DENLINGER, MARGARET ANN, credit co. exec.; b. Balt., Dec. 4, 1940; d. William H. and Anna Mary Denlinger; B.S. in Bus. Adminstrn., magna cum laude, Strayer Coll., Washington, 1975. Adminstrv. asst. to dir. alumni relations Catholic U. Am., 1959-67; with Central Charge Service, Washington, 1967—, asst. mgr. data control div., 1977-78, mgr. consumer service dept., asst. credit officer, 1978—; tchr. classes in field. Mem. Credit Women Internat. Democrat. Romal Catholic. Clubs: Shirley Racquet; Washington Soroptimist (2d v.p. 1980-81). Home: 7509 Vernon Sr Dr Alexandria VA 22306 Office: 1120 Vermont Ave NW Washington DC 20005

DENNIS, BARBARA WALDRON, psychiat. social worker; b. Bklyn., Nov. 9, 1945; d. Joseph Grove and Ruth Delilah (Sanford) Waldron; B.A., U. S.C., 1968, M.S.W., 1972; 1 son, Justin Grove. Social worker Traveler's Aid div. Asso. Social Agys., Columbia, S.C., 1969-70; counselor Family Services, Columbia, 1972-74; clin. social worker II, William S. Hall Psychiat. Inst., Columbia, 1974-77; clin. social worker III, S.C. State Hosp., Columbia, 1977—, unit chief social worker; adj. asst. prof. U. S.C. Coll. Social Work. Mem. Nat. Assn. Social Workers (dir. 1977-79, chmn. S.C. chpt. women's issues com. 1980), Assn. Children with Learning Disabilities (dir. Columbia chpt.), Columbia Women's Network, Epsilon Sigma Alpha (chpt. pres. 1980—). Democrat. Episcopalian. Home: 2109 Morninglo Ln Columbia SC 29206 Office: SC State Hosp PO Box 119 Columbia SC 29202

DENNIS, GAIL, govt. agy. ofcl.; b. Phila., Nov. 26, 1943; d. Albert Eugene and Ruth Kathryn (Gruber) D.; B.A., George Washington U., 1966; also numerous profl. schs.; With U.S. Govt., 1966-72, 74—; mgmt. analyst Office Records and Info. Mgmt., Nat. Archives and Records Service, GSA, Washington, 1974—; sr. mgmt. analyst Fed. City Coll., 1972-74. Recipient Superior Achievement award U.S. Govt. Printing Office, 1970, Fed. Paperwork Mgmt. award, 1973. Mem. Am. Fed. Govt. Employees Union (treas., steward), NOW, Nat. Assn. Female Execs., Nat. Assn. Miniature Enthusiasts, Fairfax Assn. Miniature Enthusiasts. Democrat. Episcopalian. Office: GSA Nat Archives and Records Service NRSO Washington DC 20408

DENNIS, GOLDA NAN, oil co. exec.; b. Baird, Tex., Nov. 18, 1938; d. John Leroy and Juanita H. (Holloway) Thornton; grad. Twin City Bus. Coll., 1963; m. James D. Dennis, Sept. 14, 1979; children by previous marriage—Ida Anita, Tena Mari, Benjamin Franklin, Michaelle Lenae. Controller, Authentic Furniture Products, Dallas, 1972-75; data processing mgr., asst. controller, treas. Hart Graphics, Inc., Austin, Tex., 1977-79; credit mgr. Western Mktg., Inc., Abilene, Tex., 1979-80; tax acct. Lajet, Inc., Abilene, 1980—. Mem. U.S. Congressional Adv. Bd., 1982-83. Mem. Nat. Accts. Assn. (dir. recruits 1982-83), Female Execs. Assn. Democrat. Baptist. Home: 2625 S 22d St Abilene TX 79605 Office: Lajet Inc 3130 Antilley Rd Abilene TX 79606

DENNIS, JUANITA, microbiologist; b. New Orleans, June 2, 1929; d. Lawrence Alphonse and Brunetta (Williams) Dennis; B.A., Dillard U., 1951; Cert. in Med. Tech., U. Calif., San Francisco, 1954; Med. technologist Kaiser Found. Hosp., Oakland, Calif., 1954-55; microbiologist virology Viral and Rickettsial Diseases Lab., State Dept. Health Services, Berkeley, Calif., 1955—, supr., 1981—. Mem. Am. Soc. Microbiology, No. Calif. Am. Soc. Microbiologists, No. Calif. Assn. Public Health Microbiologists, Profl. Photographers of Am., Calif. Inventors Council. Contbr. articles to profl. jours. Patentee in field. Home: 1225 Derby St Berkeley CA 94702 Office: 2151 Berkeley Way Berkeley CA 94704

DENNIS, LINDA HIERS, wholesale needlework co. exec.; b. Columbia, S.C., May 30, 1947; d. Clarence Alba and Willie Jean (Bruce) Hiers; student U. S.C., 1965-66, Middlesex Community Coll., 1970-72; m. Richard Ray Dennis, Sept. 9, 1966; 1 dau., Caroline Christine. Pres., Finish Line, Inc., design, mfg., wholesale, Spartanburg, S.C., 1976—; design cons. Mem. Spartanburg County Legal Aux., Nat. Needlework Assn. Methodist. Author: Finishing Techniques for Counted Cross Stitch, 1977; Finishing Variations with Charted Design, 1978; Special Days, 1979; Christmas Treasures, 1980; contbr. articles and designs to mags.; also kit designs; creator Ribband, ribbon to cross stitch. Home: 519 E Main St Spartanburg SC 29302 Office: 2601 E Main St Spartanburg SC 29302

DENNIS, LOUISE AMANDA-COOK, food service co. exec.; b. Tallahassee, July 23, 1943; d. Appie and Addie (Patrick) Cook; B.S. in Instn. Mgmt., Fla. A&M U., 1967; M.S. in Nutrition, Howard U., 1972; postgrad. Howard U., 1973; m. Solomon Dennis, Dec. 31, 1961; children—Deborah, Darrick. Therapeutic dietitian Jacobi Hosp., N.Y.C., 1967-68; food service mgr. Howard U., 1968-74; food service dir. Saga Food Corp., Washington Crossing, Pa., 1974-80, also affirmative action rep.; spl. asst. to pres. Food Mgmt. Concepts, Atlanta, 1980—. Mem. Am. Dietetic Assn., Omicron Nu. Mem. African Methodist Episcopal Ch. Home: 1312 Noble Woods Dr Atlanta GA 30319 Office: 57 Forsyth St Suite 802 Atlanta GA 30303

DENNIS, LUCILLE, artist; b. Terre Haute, Ind., Feb. 10, 1910; d. Max and Anna (Shatsky) Shower; student U. Chgo.,1927-31; Ph.B., Chgo. Acad. Fine Arts, 1932; m. Albert Dennis, Feb. 17, 1946; 1 dau., Martha Dennis Christiansen. Designer, Edson Novelty Co., Chgo., 1933-40; one-man shows Ind. State U., 1966, Rose-Hulman Inst., Terre Haute, 1971; group shows Hoosier Salon, Indpls., 1958-75, Sheldon Swope Gallery, Terre Haute, 1945-75, Evansville Mus., 1959, 63, 64, 65, Ind. Artist, Indpls., 1973-82, Ind. Realists Artists Exhbn., 1980, 81, 2d ann. Nat. League Am. Pen Women, 1980, 81, Ind. State Art Exhibit, 1980; work represented in Artists U/S/A, 1976, 78; represented in permanent collections Ind. U., Bloomington, Psi Iota Pi Sorority, also pvt. collections. Dir. teenage activities YWCA, 1966-67. Recipient numerous art awards. Mem. Hoosier Salon Patrons Assn., Ind. Artists Club, Inc., Ind. Realists Artists, Nat. Literary Soc., U. Chgo. Alumni Assn. (life), Smithsonian Inst. (asso.), Vigo County Mental Health Assn., Fedn. Jewish Women. Jewish. Address: 710 S 8th St Terre Haute IN 47807

DENNIS, ROSEMARY JULIA, assn. exec., producer; b. Bklyn., Jan. 1; d. Fred and Mary (Spezzano) Battaglia; B.A. in Psychology, Columbia U.; children—Paula Butterfield, Peggy Butterfield. Office mgr., advt. dir., program coordinator Philos. Research Soc., Los Angeles, 1965-79; dir. New Age Symposium, Los Angeles, 1979—; lectr., cons. Mem. Nat. Assn. Female Execs., Book Publicists So. Calif., Mensa. Republican. Club: Press (Los Angeles). Author: Path of the Lonely Ones, 1979; TV producer Conspiracy of Fools.

DENNIS, SANDY, actress; b. Hastings, Nebr., Apr. 27, 1937; d. Jack Dennis; student Nebr., Wesleyan U., U. Nebr.; studied acting Herber Berghof Studio, N.Y.C.; m. Gerry Mulligan, June 1965. Stage debut in Bus Stop, Palm Beach, Fla.; N.Y. debut, 1957; appeared on Broadway in Burning Bright, 1960, Face of Hero, 1960, The Complaisant Lover, 1961, A Thousand Clowns, 1962, Any Wednesday, 1964; film debut in Splendor in the Grass, 1961, later appeared in Who's Afraid of Virginia Woolf?, 1965, Up the Down Staircase, 1967, The Fox, 1967, Sweet November, Daphne in Cottage D, The Millstone, Same Time Next Year; appeared in films A Hatful of Rain, Thank You All Very Much, That Cold Day in the Park, The Out-of-Towners, The Four Seasons, 1981; (plays) And Miss Reardon Drinks A Little, toured, 1971, 72, Let Me Hear You Smile, 1973, Streetcar Named Desire, 1974, Born Yesterday, 1974, Absurd Person Singular, 1975, Cat on a Hot Tin Roof, 1975, Nasty Habits, 1977. Recipient Tony awards for A Thousand Clowns, 1963, Any Wednesday, 1964, Oscar award as best supporting actress for Who's Afraid of Virginia Woolf?; N.Y. Critics Poll award, Moscow Film Festival best-actress award for Up the Down Staircase, 1967. Address: care Diamond Artists Ltd 9200 Sunset Blvd Suite 909 Los Angeles CA 90069 *

DENNISON, MARY ELLEN, nurse; b. Dunn Center, N.D., Feb. 20, 1922; d. Michael Joseph and Alice Bridget (Meehan) McGrath; B.S., U. Calif., San Francisco, 1974, M.S., 1975; m. Lyle Dennison, Sept. 18, 1946 (dec.); children—Mary Elizabeth, Michael Vincent, Kathleen Ann, Georgeanne. Pediatric office nurse-mgr., Oakland, Calif., 1953-65; occupational health nurse Am. Can Co., Oakland, 1965-67; instr. nursing Laney Coll., Oakland, 1967-70; public health nurse Humboldt-Del Norte County Health Dept., Eureka, Calif., 1976—; bd. dirs. No. Calif. Health Systems Agy., 1979—. Commr., Humboldt County Commn. on Status of Women, 1981—; bd. dirs. Behavior Devel. Center, Eureka, 1981. Mem. Am. Nurses Assn., Nat. Fedn. Bus. and Profl. Women (chpt. pres. 1980-81), U. Calif. San Francisco Alumni Assn., Sigma Theta Tau. Democrat. Roman Catholic. Home: 1538 Hayes St Eureka CA 95501 Office: 529 I St Eureka CA 95501

DENNISON, WILENE, advt. exec.; b. Chgo., May 24, 1947; d. Norman and Audrey (Tarsch) Yohanna; M.A., Northeastern Ill. U.; m. Marc Bernard Dennison, Apr. 21, 1974; children—Samantha Joy, Erica Hayden, Bradley Randall. Tchr., Weeling, Ill., 1969-72; sr. account exec. Chicagoland Broadcasters, 1973-78; dir. advt., sales, mktg. A.Y. Corp., 1979—; partner Dennison Studios. Mem. NOW, Realtors Nat. Mktg. Inst. Address: 1055 Devonshire Ct Highland Park IL 60035

DENNY, BARBARA ELIZABETH, psychiat. social worker; b. St. Louis, Mar. 19, 1927; d. William Earl and Verna Bianca (Busch) Horsefield; student Vanderbilt U., 1944-46; B.A., U. N.C., 1972, M.S.W., 1975; m. Floyd Wolfe Denny, Jr., Apr. 27, 1946; children—Rebecca, Mark, Timothy. Clin. asso. div. psychiat. social work, dept. psychiatry Duke U. Med. Center, Durham, N.C., 1975—; cons. in field. Mem. Nat. Assn. Social Workers, Acad. Cert. Social Workers, Soc. for Clin. Social Work. Office: Durham Community Guidance Clinic Trent and Elba Sts Durham NC 27705

DENNY, BONNIE ELIZABETH, banker; b. Shelby County, Ind., May 16, 1935; d. James Albert and Valeria Ethel (Gregory) Kelley; student public schs.; m. Billy Denny, Sept. 25, 1953. With State Bank of Waldron (Ind.), 1953—, asst. cashier, 1974-78, asst. v.p., 1978—. Democrat. Baptist. Home: Box 92 Waldron IN 46182 Office: Box 7 Waldron IN 46182

DENNY, ELEANOR, theatrical lighting co. exec.; b. Bklyn., Oct. 8, 1928; d. Sol and Frieda (Dunetz) Schwartz; student public schs.; m. Seymour B. Denbaum, Mar. 16, 1947 (div.); 1 son, Steven M. Various office and bookkeeping positions with lighting designers, theatres and theatrical cons, 1944—; asst. to comptroller, asst. to gen. mgr. Nederlander Prodns., N.Y.C., 1969-70; sec. to v.p. Swett & Crawford and Buffalo Ins. Co., N.Y.C., 1971-72; with Tharon Musser theatrical lighting designer, N.Y.C., 1956—; comptroller Staging Techniques, N.Y.C., 1972-80, Belden Communications, Inc./Lee Lighting Am., Ltd., N.Y.C., 1982—. Mem. Nat. Assn. Female Execs., Nat. Assn. Exec. Secs. Home: 176 E 77th St New York NY 10021 also 10 Bryant St East Hampton NY 11937 Office: 342 E 40th St New York NY 10018 Also 21 Cornelia St New York NY 10014

DENNY, JUDITH ANN, lawyer, fed. govt. ofcl.; b. Lamar, Mo., Sept. 18, 1946; d. Lee Livingston and Genevieve Adelpha (Falke) D.; B.A., La. Tech. U., 1968; J.D., George Washington U., 1972; m. Thomas M. Lenard, May 29, 1976; 1 dau., Julia Lee. Admitted to D.C. bar, 1973; asst. spl. prosecutor Watergate Spl. Prosecution Office, Washington, 1973-75; pros. atty. U.S. Dept. Justice, 1975-78; dir. div. compliance U.S. Office Edn., HEW, 1978-80; acting asst. insp. gen. for investigations U.S. Dept. Edn., 1980; dep. dir. policy and compliance, office of revenue sharing U.S. Dept. Treasury, Washington, 1980—. Mem. D.C. Bar Assn., Women's Legal Def. Fund. Home: 3214 Porter St NW Washington DC 20008 Office: 2401 E St NW 14th Floor Washington DC 20226

DENNY, SUANNE EMILY, med. technologist; b. Rochester, N.Y., Feb. 27, 1947; d. Crawford Alfred and Doris Catherine (Coventry) D.; A.A.S., Rochester Int. Tech., 1967, B.S., 1969; cert. med. tech. St. Mary's Sch. Med. Tech., 1969; postgrad. U. Rochester Med. Sch., 1972, 74, 76, 80. Staff technologist St. Mary's Hosp., Rochester, 1969-70; technologist Soldiers and Sailors Meml. Hosp., Penn Yan, N.Y., 1970-78, sr. technologist, 1978-80, supr. hematology and blood bank dept., asst. lab. supr., 1980—; instr. Finger Lakes Shared Edn. and Tng. Program; cons. technologist Rushville Community Clinic; instr. Keuka Coll. Active Career Day programs Penn Yan Acad., 1976-80; mem. youth com. Penn Yan Area Council of Chs., 1974; deacon 1st Presbyn. Ch., Penn Yan, 1977-80. Mem. Am. Soc. Med. Tech., Empire State Assn. Med. Tech. (Genesee Valley chpt.), Am. Soc. Clin. Pathologists (registered med. technologist), World Wildlife Fund (charter mem.), Animal Protection Inst. Am., Defenders of Wildlife, Greenpeace, Seal and Whale Rescue Funds, African Wildlife Leadership Fund, Center for Environ. Edn., Nat. Cert. Agy. for Med. Lab. Personnel, Yates County Photog. Soc., Alpha Sigma Alpha. Democrat. Home: 1631 Dresden Rd Penn Yan NY 14527 Office: 418 N Main St Penn Yan NY 14527

DENSEN-GERBER, JUDIANNE (MRS. MICHAEL M. BADEN), psychiatrist, lawyer; b. N.Y.C., Nov. 13, 1934; d. Gustave A. and Beatrice (Densen) Gerber; A.B. cum laude, Bryn Mawr Coll., 1956; J.D., Columbia Law Sch., 1959; M.D., N.Y. U., 1963; m. Michael M. Baden, June 14, 1958; children—Trissa Austin, Judson Michael, Lindsey Robert, Sarah Densen Baden. Admitted to N.Y. bar, 1961; rotating intern French Hosp., N.Y.C., 1963-64; resident in psychiatry Met. Hosp., N.Y.C., 1964-65; mem. core staff Addiction Services Agy., N.Y.C., 1966-67; founder, exec. dir., pres. bd. dirs. Odyssey House, Inc., psychiat. hosps. for rehab. of narcotics addicts throughout U.S., N.Y.C., 1967-74, also clin. dir., 1967-69, pres. bd., 1967-74; founder, pres., bd. dirs. Odyssey Inst., Inc., 1974—; founder, pres. Inst. on Women's Wrongs, 1973—; adj. asso. prof. law N.Y. Law Sch., 1973—; vis. asso. prof. law U. Utah Law Sch., 1974-75; guest lectr. narcotics addiction N.Y. U. Sch. Medicine and Sch. Law; del. White House Conf. on Youth, 1971; mem. nat. adv. commn. Criminal Justice Standards and Goals, 1971-74; cons. mem. Pres.'s Commn. on White House Fellows, 1972-76; pub. health services Nat. Center for Health, Research and Devel., HEW, 1972—, mem. drug experience adv. com., 1973-76; mem. president's council Sch. Social Work, N.Y. U., 1977—; mem. N.Y. State Crime Control Planning Bd., 1975—, N.Y. State Gov.'s Task Force on Crime Control, 1977—; bd. advisors Hosp. Audiences, Inc., 1971—, Inst. for Child Mental Health, 1972—, 1st Women's Bank of N.Y., 1974—; dir.

Daitch Shopwell Inc., bd. dirs. Simpson Street Devel. Assn., 1969, Extraordinary Event, Inc., 1973—, Nat. Coalition for Children's Justice, 1975-76, Richmond County Soc. for Prevention Cruelty to Children, 1977—, Mary E. Walker Found., 1978; v.p. Therapeutic Communities Am., 1975-76. Recipient Woman of Achievement award N.Y. br. Am. Assn. U. Women, 1970; Myrtle Wreath award Hadassah, 1970; Women of Greatness award B'nai B'rith, 1971, also Woman of Achievement award, 1971; named hon. N.Y. State Fire Chief, 1974, Dame of Malta, Knights of Malta, 1976; OTTY award Our Town newspaper, 1977; nobless Order of White Cross (Australia), 1977. Fellow Am. Acad. Forensic Scis. (chmn. psychiatry sect. 1974—), Am. Acad. Legal Medicine; mem. AMA, N.Y. State (sub-coms. drug abuse, delivery of health care 1968—) New York County med. socs., Soc. Med. Jurisprudence, Am. Bar Assn., Am. Psychiat. Assn., Am., N.Y. Women's N.Y. County bar assns., Hon. Order Ky. Cols., Women's Forum, Am. Acad. Psychiatry and Law, N.Y. Assn. Vol. Agys. on Narcotics Addiction and Substance Abuse (dir. 1969—, legal cons. 1969-71), Nat. Coalition Children's Justice. Unitarian. Club: Women's City (N.Y.C.). Author: (with daughter) Drugs, Sex, Parents and You, 1972; We Mainline Dreams: The Odyssey House Story, 1973; Walk in My Shoes: An Odyssey Into Womanlife, 1976; Child Abuse and Neglect as Related to Parental Drug Abuse and Other Antisocial Behavior, 1978; columnist Manchester Union Leader, 1971—, N.Y. Law Jour., 1971-72; bd. advisors Contemporary Drug Problems, 1971—; contbr. numerous articles to profl. jours. Office: 208-210 East 18th St New York NY 10003

DENSMORE, ANN, speech pathologist/audiologist; b. Los Angeles, Nov. 24, 1941; d. Ray B. and Margaret M. (Walsh) D.; B.S. cum laude, UCLA, 1963; M.A. in Communicative Disorders, Calif. State U., 1975; student Cape Cod Conservatory of Arts, 1977-79, Harvard U./Radcliffe Coll. graphics-architecture program, 1980—; children—Kristin Ann, Jennifer Ann. Tchr., Santa Monica (Calif.) Unified Sch. Dist., 1973-74; speech pathologist Kennedy Child Study Center, 1975-76; audiologist VA Hosp. Sepulveda, Calif., 1976-77, New Eng. Rehab. Hosp., Woburn, Mass., 1978; audiology cons. Wellesley (Mass.) Public Schs., 1979; speech pathologist Framingham (Mass.) Public Schs., 1979; speech pathologist and audiologist The Learning Center for Deaf Children, Framingham, 1978-80; free-lance photographer, 1979—; exhibited photographs Copley Soc. of Boston, 1979-80. Dir., Ann. Fund Babson Coll., 1981-82. Lic. speech pathologist and audiologist Calif. Mem. Am. Speech and Hearing Assn. (cert. speech pathologist-audiologist), Artists Assn. of Nantucket, Copley Soc. of Boston. Episcopalian. Home: 9 Roanoke Wellesley MA 02181 Office: Babson Coll Babson Park MA 02157

DENSMORE, DANA, computer corp. exec.; b. Washington, Mar. 27, 1945; d. Russell Wykoff and Donna Claire Allen; B.A., St. John's Coll., 1965. Founder, Ja Shin Do Acad., Washington, 1974—, Ja Shin Do Acad., Boston, 1977-78, Ja Shin Do Center, Boston, 1978, Artemis Outings, Boston, 1978—; founder, dir. Artemis Inst., Washington, Boston, 1979—; Sr. product planner Nixdorf Computer Corp., 1980—; founder A Woman of Power, assertiveness tng. for women, 1980—; dir. instrn. Ja Shin Do Fedn.; co-convenor Feminist Computer Tech. Project, 1979. Editor, pub. No More Fun and Games, 1968-73; editor, pub. Black Belt Woman, mag., 1975-76. Home: 22 Ashcroft Rd Medford MA 02155

DENSON, WAVA LUCENE, newspaper pub., comml. printer; b. Seiling, Okla., June 2, 1920; d. William Frederick and Edith Woodward (Clark) Spies; student Seiling public schs.; m. W.W. Denson, Feb. 12, 1939; 1 son, Jerry Lynn. With Gage (Okla.) Record, 1939—, co-owner, pub., 1946-74, owner, pub., 1974-82; co-owner, pub. Ellis County Capital, 1953-74, owner, pub., 1974-82; reporter Ellis County election news Daily Oklahoman, 1975-82. Recipient cert. of appreciation for community service Young Jaycees, 1975, cert. Okla. State Election Bds., 1978. Mem. Okla. Press Assn., Gage Women's Research Club (pres. 1947-48), Am. Legion Aux. Democrat. Mem. Ch. of Christ. Home: 115 N Madison St Arnett OK 73832 Office: 323 E Renfrow St Arnett OK 73832

DENT, ANDREA ELLEN, tng. and communications exec.; b. Detroit, Dec. 31, 1946; d. Alfred and Muriel Lois (Russell) Bell; student econs. Fordham U., 1981—; divorced; children—Kimberly Ellen, William Ellis. Rental rep. Hertz Corp., Detroit, 1972-76, sta. mgr., 1977, zone tng. adminstr., 1977-78, mgr. customer service programs, 1978-79, dir. tng. and communications, 1980-82; dir. tng. Dollar Systems Inc., Los Angeles, 1982—. Mem. Am. Soc. Tng. and Devel. Office: 6141 W Century Blvd Los Angeles CA 90045

DENTON, BETTY F., state legislator; b. Waco, Tex., Aug. 19, 1946; d. Houston and Dorothy Leonard Kirbo; B.A., M.A. in Law, Baylor U., 1977; postgrad. U. Tex., Austin; m. Lane Denton, 1964; 1 dau., Deeann. Tchr. Connolly Ind. Sch. Dist., 1964-65; TV news reporter Sta. KWTX-TV, 1956-66; tchr. Waco Ind. Sch. Dist., 1970-74; atty., 1977—; mem. Tex. Ho. of Reps., 1977—, mem. agr. and criminal jurisprudence coms., 1977—. Mem. Am. Bus. Women's Assn., Democratic Women, Women's Polit. Caucus, LWV, Women in Communications. Home: 501 Franklin St 621 Waco TX 74701 Office: Texas House of Representatives State Capitol Austin TX 78701 *

DENTON, CAROL FORSBERG, ednl. analyst; b. Boston, Mar. 5, 1937; d. Algot O. and Isabel M. Forsberg; B.S. in Geology, U. Okla., 1959; M.A.T. in Counseling, Rollins Coll., Winter Park, Fla., 1970, postgrad., 1971; m. Earle L. Denton, Oct. 11, 1975; children—Susan, Kathleen. Counselor, U. Okla., Norman, 1958-59; tchr. Lee County, 1960-61; counselor U. Fla., Gainesville, 1961-62; tchr. Seminole County Bd. Instrn., Sanford, Fla., 1965-69; personnel mgmt. specialist U.S. Navy, Orlando, Fla., 1969-73; ednl. analyst U.S. Naval Tng. Equipment Center, Orlando, 1973—; tchr. CAP, 1965-69, mission pilot, observer, 1965-75. Mem. human relations commn. City of Orlando, 1972—. Mem. Nat. Human Factors Soc., (pres., dir. Central Fla. chpt.), Sigma Xi. Presbyterian. Club: Winter Park Altrusa (pres.). Author tech. articles and reports. Home: 4222 B Lake Underhill Dr Orlando FL 32803 Office: Naval Tng Equipment Center Code N-252 Orlando FL 32813

DENTON, EMMA MANEY, banker; b. Hiawassee, Ga., Nov. 25, 1905; d. Milton M. and Missouri (Eller) Maney; student pvt. schs., Hiawassee; m. James Young Denton, May 20, 1920 (dec. Jan. 1982); children—J.C., Evelyn Isabel Denton Groves, Ruth Elois Denton Anderson, J. William, Emma Jean Denton Anderson. Asso. cashier Bank of Hiawassee, 1936-70, cashier, 1970—, dir., 1950—. Chmn. county drive Am. Cancer Soc., 1944-60; flower show judge. Recipient Service award Am. Cancer Soc., 1977; Emma Denton Day, Bank of Hiawassee, 1979; awards flower shows. Mem. DAR, Friendship Community Club, Hiawassee Garden Club (charter mem., pres. 1960—), State Garden Club Ga. (hon. life), Nat. Council Garden Clubs (life). Baptist. Address: Bank of Hiawassee Main St Hiawassee GA 30546

DENTON, GISELE ANN, advt. exec.; b. Italy, Oct. 21, 1937; d. Erasmus R. and Amelia Claire (Finamore) Pezzetta; B.S.B.A., U. Denver, 1961; m. Karl Denton, Aug. 26, 1961; children—Lewis Karl II, Lance Kip. Media liason Sat. Evening Post, Phila., 1955-58; mdse. asst. McMurtry Paints div. Valspar Corp., Denver, 1961-66; media research analyst Henderson, Bucknum Inc., Denver, 1966-68, media dir., 1968-73, v.p., media dir., 1973-75; v.p., media dir. Barickman Advt. Inc. div. Doyle, Dane & Bernbach, Denver, 1974-81, v.p., media dir. parent co., 1982—. Del., Arapahoe County Republican Conv., 1974, 76, Douglas County Rep. Conv., 1982. Mem. Colo. Broadcasters Assn., Denver Advt. Fedn., Altrusa Club Denver, AAUW, Sons of Italy, Il Circolo Italiano, Phi Gamma Nu. Roman Catholic. Home: Route 2 Box 3D Sedalia CO 80135 Office: DDB Advt PO Box 9569 Denver CO 80209

DENVER, EILEEN ANN, mag. editor; b. N.Y.C., Nov. 16, 1942; d. Daniel Joseph and Katherine Agnes (Boland) D.; B.A., Coll. New Rochelle, 1964; M.A., Ind. U., 1967. Asst. prof. English, St. Peter's Coll., Jersey City, 1967-70; asst. copy editor Am. Home Mag., N.Y.C., 1970-75; asst. editor Consumer Reports Mag., Mt. Vernon, N.Y., 1975-78, asst. mng. editor, 1978-79, mng. editor, 1979—. Mem. NOW. Office: Consumer Reports Magazine 256 Washington St Mount Vernon NY 10550

DEOME, BETSY WILLIAMS, public relations cons.; b. Oklahoma City, July 25, 1945; d. Floyd Arthur and Berniece Inez (Blasingame) W.; B.A., U. Okla., 1967; M.J., La. State U., 1976; m. David Paul DeOme, Aug. 30, 1969; 1 son, Sean Michael Williams. Cons., tng. supr. Revlon Cosmetics, Chgo., 1967-70; public relations asst. City of New Orleans, 1970-71; promotions supr., mgr. Foley's, Houston, 1971-74; public relations cons., Baton Rouge, 1974-79; public relations dir. Root & Assos., Baton Rouge, 1979-80; pres. Public Relations Orgn., Baton Rouge, 1980—; public relations instr. La. State U., Baton Rouge, 1981—. WRKF Public Radio Underwriter; press sec. Jack Breaux for Baton Rouge Mayor, 1976; public relations chmn. Mayor's Sts. and Drainage Com., 1979; mem. La. Com. for Bus. and Arts, 1976-78; bd. dirs. Baton Rouge Youth, Inc.; public relations adv. Baton Rouge Battered Women's and Children's Shelter. Recipient Gold Key Public Relations award Am. Hotel and Motel Assn., 1980, 81, Gold award Retail Mchts. Assn., 1971, Lantern award So. Public Relations Fedn., 1981, 82. Mem. Women in Communications (pres. Baton Rouge profl. chpt.), Internat. Assn. Bus. Communicators, Public Relations Assn. La., Women in Politics, LWV, Gamma Phi Beta. Republican. Roman Catholic. Clubs: Press of Baton Rouge, Camelot, Exxon Wives. Home: 1869 Applewood Rd Baton Rouge LA 70808 Office: PO Box 80463 Baton Rouge LA 70898

DEPAOLIS, MARY V., health care adminstr.; b. Sewickley, Pa., May 12, 1944; d. Leo F. and Joanna (Loria) DePaolis; R.N. diploma Mercy Hosp., 1965; B.S. in Biology and Edn., U. Pitts., 1974, M.Ed., 1978, postgrad. 1980-82. Staff nurse anesthetist Children's Hosp., Pitts., 1968-72; nurse anesthetist various hosps., Pitts., 1972-74; anesthesia instr., nurse anesthetist Eye and Ear Hosp., Pitts., 1974-75; dir. U. Health Center of Pitts. Sch. of Anesthesia, 1975—; clin. asst. prof. U. Pitts. Sch. of Medicine, 1975—; vis. lectr. anesthesia and health care various nursing orgns., 1975—. Mem. adv. com. Allegheny County Bldg. Better Boards Project, 1982—. Recipient HEW Public Health Service award, 1974. Mem. Am. Soc. Tng. and Devel., Am. Assn. Nurse Anesthetists (edn. cons. 1981—), Pa. Assn. of Nurse Anesthetists (trustee 1975-77, mem. govt. relations com. 1981—), Assn. for Supervision and Curriculum Devel., Soc. of Neurosurg. Anesthesia. Contbr. articles on anesthesiology to profl. jours. Home: 2936 Strachan Ave Pittsburgh PA 15216 Office: University Health Center of Pittsburgh School of Anesthesia 3459 5th Ave Pittsburgh PA 15213

DEPAUW, LINDA GRANT, historian, educator; b. N.Y.C., Jan 19, 1940; d. Phillip and Ruth Grant; B.A., Swarthmore Coll., 1961; Ph.D., Johns Hopkins U., 1964. Asst. prof. history George Mason Coll., U. Va., Fairfax, 1964-65; spl. asst. to archivist U.S., Nat. Archives, Washington, 1965-66; asst. prof. history George Washington U., Washington, 1966-69, asso. prof., 1969-75, prof. Am. history, 1975—; editor-in-chief, project dir. Documentary History of the First Fed. Congress. Woodrow Wilson fellow, 1961. Mem. Am. Hist. Assn. (Beveridge award 1964) Am. Mil. Inst., Assn. Documentary Editing, Authors Guild, Coordinating Com. on Women in the Hist. Profession, Inter-Univ. Seminar on Armed Forces and Soc., Nat. Women's Studies Assn., Orgn. Am. Historians, So. Hist. Assn., U.S. Naval Inst. Author: The Eleventh Pillar: New York State and the Federal Constitution, 1966; Founding Mothers: Women of America in the Revolutionary Era, 1975; Remember the Ladies, 1976; Seafaring Women, 1982. Home: 1101 S Arlington Ridge Rd Arlington VA 22202 Office: Dept History George Washington U Washington DC 20052

DEPAUW, MARY ELIZABETH, psychologist; b. Chgo., Dec. 2, 1948; d. Charles Anton and Beata Marie (Gough) Janovsky; B.S., Loyola U., Chgo., 1970; M.Ed., U. Mo., Columbia, 1977, Ph.D., 1980; m. A. Philip DePauw, III, Sept. 6, 1969; 1 son, A. Philip. Fin. aid asst. U. Chgo. Grad. Sch. Bus., 1972-75; student personnel intern Center for Student Life, U. Mo., Columbia, 1977-78, counselor intern Counseling Services, 1978-80; dir. counseling and career devel. St. Mary's Coll., Notre Dame, Ind., 1980—, adj. asst. prof. psychology, 1981—. Mem. Women's Assn. of S. Bend (Ind.) Symphony, 1981—; mem. aux. St. Joseph County Med. Soc., 1980—; bd. dirs. St. Joseph County Mental Health Assn., 1982—; dir. tng. Abuse Assault and Rape Crisis Center, Columbia, 1978-79. Mem. Am. Psychol. Assn., Ind. Psychol. Assn., Am. Personnel and Guidance Assn., Am. Coll. Personnel Assn., AAUW, Phi Delta Kappa, Phi Mu., U. Mo. Alumni Assn. Roman Catholic. Author: (with Robert Callis, Sharon K. Pope) Ethical Standards Casebook, 3rd edit., 1982. Home: 52817 Brookdale Dr South Bend IN 46637 Office: 165 LeMans Hall Saint Marys Coll Notre Dame IN 46556

DEPETRIS, CARLA NICOLE CAPIRONE, fine arts cons.; b. Torino, Italy; came to U.S., 1956, naturalized, 1961; d. Giovanni Giuseppe and Albina Luigia (Ferraris) Capirone di Montanaro; ed. Italian and Calif. schs.; cert. in arts mgmt. U. Calif.; m. Wilmer Anthony DePetris, Dec. 4, 19S5; 1 son, Walther Gian Carlo. Cons. fine arts, interior design and hist. preservation, Sonoma, Calif., 1969—; owner, dir. Internat. Gallery Contemporary Arts; tchr. art and art appreciation Sonoma Cath. Elem. Sch.; horse breeder. Bd. dirs. Cath. Social Service, 1967-69, treas., 1968; active Pacific Mus. Soc., San Francisco, 1968-69; pres. Sonoma League Hist. Preservation, 1979; sec.-treas. Sonoma Land Trust, 1977-78; founder St. Francis the Ch. Mouse; diocese interior decorator and appraiser; archtl. rev. commr. City of Sonoma; adv. com. Sonoma Parks and Recreation, Sonoma County Art Council; bd. dirs. Pres.'s Assos., Sonoma State U. Recipient award Sonoma Parks and Recreation, 1975; Calif. State Office Preservation grantee, 1978. Mem. Associated Photographers Internat., Am. Mgmt. Assn. Republican. Research on archtl. style and social devel. from 1840-1940 in So. Sonoma County.

DEPHILLIPS, HELEN CATHERINE, personnel agy. exec.; b. Bklyn., Jan. 5, 1929; d. Sabot and Angelina (Ippolito) DeP.; grad. Browne's Bus. Sch., 1948; student Pace U., 1973-75, N.Y. Inst. Fin., 1975-76. Exec. asst. Office of Chief of Staff to N.Y. Gov., 1950-57; office mgr. physician's office, Bklyn., 1958-66; exec. asst. to pres. A. E. Ames & Co., Inc., N.Y.C., 1967-72; asst. compliance officer Abraham & Co., Inc., N.Y.C., 1973-74; office mgr., compliance officer Heine, Fishbein & Co., Inc., N.Y.C., 1975-77; personnel cons., N.Y.C., 1977-80; owner AnSa Personnel Agy., N.Y.C., 1980—, also dir. Cert. registered rep. N.Y. Stock Exchange, Am. Stock Exchange, Nat. Assn. Securities Dealers. Mem. Assn. Personnel Cons. of N.Y., Assn. Registration Mgrs., Suprs. and Adminstrs. Assn. Bus. and Profl. Women's Assn. N.Y. Republican. Roman Catholic. Office: 61 Broadway Suite 2425 New York NY 10006

DE PLANQUE, E. GAIL, physicist; b. Orange, N.J., Jan. 15, 1945; d. Martin William and Edna (Gilroy) de P.; A.B. in Math. cum laude, Immaculata Coll., 1967; M.S. in Physics, Newark Coll. Engring. (now N.J. Inst. Tech.), 1973; doctoral candidate N.Y. U., 1973—. Dep. dir. Environ. Measurements Lab., U.S. Dept. Energy, N.Y.C., 1967—; tutor, substitute tchr. Waynesboro (Pa.) Area Sch. System, 1969; cons. in field. Dep. foreman Essex County (N.J.) 15th Grand Jury, 1978. Catholic U. Am. grantee, 1967; Fordham U. grantee, 1967; AEC grantee, 1967. Fellow Am. Nuclear Soc. (dir. 1977-80, nat. exec. com. 1978-80, chmn. nat. bylaws and rules com. 1982—); mem. Health Physics Soc., Am. Phys. Soc., AAAS, Assn. Women in Sci. (v.p. N.Y. Met. chpt. 1980-82), N.Y. Acad. Sci., AAUW. Contbr. articles to profl. jours. Home: 13 Bowdoin St Maplewood NJ 07040 Office: 376 Hudson St New York NY 10014

DEPREE, JUSTINE ADELAIDE, civic worker; b. Charleston, W.Va., Mar. 18, 1908; d. Charles Harrop and Lillian Alexander (Womeldorf) Combs; cert. W.Va. Dept. Edn., 1943, Corning (N.Y.) Community Coll., 1979; m. Chauncey Marcellous DePree, Nov. 15, 1938; children—Amelia DePree Harrington, Chauncey Marcellous, William Frederick IV, Tchr., foreman Nat. Youth Adminstrn., South Charleston, W.Va., 1938, 43; legis. attache W.Va. Senate, Charleston, 1952; dist. distbr. Beauty Counselors, Inc., Grosse Pointe, Mich., 1958-67; lic. real estate salesman Tom Starke Realty, Binghamton, N.Y., 1964-67; sr. aide Steuben County Equal Opportunity Program, 1975. Bd. dirs. So. Tier Legal Assn., 1976-78; circle chmn. 1st Presbyterian Ch., Corning, 1954-58; den mother Cub Scouts Am., Corning, 1956-60; committeewoman 3d Erwin Dist., Painted Post, N.Y., 1979—; past exec. v.p. Village Sq. Apts. Assn.; pres. So. Tier Golden Age Club; mem. Nat. Council Sr. Citizens; sec. N.Y. State Council Sr. Citizens, 1979—. Democrat. Presbyterian. Club: Order Eastern Star. Address: Village Sq Apt 109 Painted Post NY 14870

DERBY, ANNE RAFTERMAN, biomed. engr.; b. N.Y.C., Feb. 1, 1949; d. Nathan Joseph and Phyllis Fannie (Kerner) Rafterman; A.B., Barnard Coll., 1969; M.S., Columbia U. Sch. Engring. and Applied Scis., 1971; m. Jeffrey Haskell Derby, Sept. 13, 1970; 1 dau., Nina Rafterman. Clin. engr. dept. surgery Bronx (N.Y.) VA Hosp., 1971-75; chief bio-med. engring. Bronx VA Med. Center, 1975-81; dep. dir. facilities engring. service Nat. Insts. Environ. Health Scis., NIH, Research Triangle Park, N.C., 1981—; asst. in surgery Mt. Sinai Sch. Medicine, CUNY, 1973—; cons. hosp. planning, biomed. engring. Adv. council Girl Scouts U.S.A. NSF fellow, 1964-65; VA research fellow, 1973-76. Mem. N.Y. Acad. Scis., IEEE, Assn. Advancement Med. Instrumentation. Democrat. Jewish. Contbr. articles to profl. jours., 1972—. Office: Nat Insts Environ Health Scis mail drop 102-01 PO Box 12233 Research Triangle Park NC 22709

DE REGGI, MARILYN BOYD, musician; b. Pahokee, Fla., Mar. 8, 1941; d. Frederick Tilghman and Jeanette Marion (Dresser) Boyd; student Elena Nikolaidi, Tallahassee, 1959-62; B. Music Edn., Fla. State U., 1962; M.A., U. Fla., 1964; student Conservatoire National de Musique de Paris, 1960-61, Sorbonne, U. Paris, 1960-61, l'Alliance Française, Paris, 1960-61, U. San Francisco, 1964, U. Va., 1968-69. m. Aime S. De Reggi, Dec. 25, 1964; children—John Martin, Thomas Anthony, Lisa Renee. Instr. humanities St. John's River Jr. Coll., 1964-66; studio voice tchr. in cooperation with U. Va., Charlottesville, 1968-74; asst. prof. voice Shenandoah Conservatory Music, Winchester, Va., 1974-78; soprano, exec. dir. Contemporary Music Forum, Corcoran Gallery of Art, Washington, 1979—; solo recital Festival Am. Music, Nat. Gallery Art, Washington, 1973; recitalist Bicentennial Parade of States, Kennedy Center, Washington, 1976. Mem. adv. bd. Master Plan of Boyds (Md.), 1975-78, Nat. Capital Park and Planning Commn; mem. Corby Mansion Devel. Adv. Com.; bd. dirs. Strathmore Hall Arts Center, Concerts in the Country. Mem. Nat. Assn. Tchrs. Singing, Coll. Music Soc., Am. Harp Soc., Chamber Music Am., Cultural Alliance of Greater Washington, Montgomery County Arts Council, Montgomery County C. of C. Lutheran. Home: 21000 Clarksburg Rd Boyds MD 20841

DERELIAN, DORIS VIRGINIA, nutritionist, assn. exec.; b. Palo Alto, Calif., Aug. 8, 1945; d. Sarkis and Susan D.; B.S. in Nutrition and Dietetics, Calif. State U., Fresno, 1969; M.S. in Nutrition Edn., U. Calif., Davis, 1973; m. James J. Sullivan, Sept. 4, 1976; 1 dau., Stacy Ann Sullivan. Intern, VA Hosp., Los Angeles, 1969-70; sr. food service mgr. St. Agnes Hosp., Fresno, 1965-68; chief dietitian Unibetic Camps, San Bernardino, Calif., summers 1969-77; program dir. Dairy Council of Calif., Los Angeles, 1970-78; exec. dir. Calif. Dietetic Assn., Del Rey, Calif., 1978—; cons. med. edn.; bd. dirs. Los Angeles Metaholic Found., Calif. Council Against Health Fraud; lectr. 7th Internat. Congress Dietetics, Sydney, Australia, 1977. Named Young Dietitian of Yr., Am. Dietetic Assn., 1974. Mem. Am. Dietetic Assn., Am. Home Econs. Assn., Nat. Assn. Female Execs., Los Angeles Metabolic Found., UCLA Sch. Edn. Student Assn., Embroiderers Guild. Contbr. articles on patient-tchr. relationships to profl. jours. Office: 7740 Manchester #102 Playa Del Rey CA 90291

DE REMER, KATHLEEN ROSE, internist; b. Princeton, N.J., Dec. 18, 1947; d. Kenneth Ross and Virginia Rachael (Ramacorti) De R.; A.B., Jackson Coll., Tufts U., 1969; M.M.S., Rutgers U. Med. Sch., 1973, M.D., 1975; m. David O. Howard, Oct. 25, 1978. Intern, Los Angeles County-U. So. Calif. Med. Center, 1975-76, resident, 1976-78; practice medicine specializing in internal medicine, San Gabriel, Calif., 1980—; mem. staff Community Hosp. San Gabriel, St. Luke Hosp., Meth. Hosp. So. Calif., Alhambra Psychiat. Hosp.; chmn. San Gabriel Valley Ann. Cancer Project. Mem. Am. Med. Women's Assn., Los Angeles Med. Women's Assn., Am. Soc. Internal Medicine. Office: 225 E Las Tunas Dr San Gabriel CA 91776

DERIVERA, DOROTHY PEARL BEHM, librarian; b. Libertyville, Ill., Mar. 1, 1922; d. Michael L. and Erma Cora (Dryer) Behm; B.A., Mundelein Coll., 1946; M.Ed., Northeastern Ill. U., 1970; postgrad. U. Americas, Mexico City, 1955, U. Ariz., 1957, Tex. Western U., 1961, Northeastern N.Mex. U., 1962; m. James Enriquez de Rivera, Apr. 22, 1946; children—Sue Anne DeRivera Foss, Charles, Michael, James, John. Owner gift shop, Libertyville, 1944-48; story lady, sta. mgr. KNOG, Nogales, Ariz., 1953-55; producer, master of ceremonies Internat. Variety Show, KOPO-TV, Tucson, 1954-55; radio and TV columnist Nogales Herald, 1954-55; tchr. elem. sch., Nogales, 1956-59, El Paso, Tex., 1959-62, Walker AFB, Roswell, N.Mex., 1962-63, Deerfield, Ill., 1963-68; elem. sch. librarian, audiovisual coordinator Deerfield Pub. Schs., 1968-74, Cadwell Elem. Sch., Deerfield, 1968-76, Maplewood Elem. Sch., Deerfield, 1976—. Mem. NEA (life), Ill. Edn. Assn., Nat. Council Tchrs. English, Internat. Reading Assn., ALA, Chgo.-Suburban Audiovisual Roundtable, Chgo. Council Fgn. Relations, Ill. Librarians Assn., Ill. Assn. Sch. Librarians, Ill. Audiovisual Assn. for Ednl. Communications, Deerfield Hist. Soc. (dir. 1969-72), Deerfield Tchrs. Assn. (charter mem., pres. 1967-68, dir. 1963-67, social chmn. 1972-73), United Ostomy Assn. (exec. bd. Highland Park chpt. 1978—, newsletter editor 1978—, v.p. 1980-81, pres. 1981-82), Mundelein Coll. Alumnae Assn. (mem. governing bd. 1971-74, rep. to Internat. Fedn. Cath. Alumnae 1973-74), Alpha Tau Omega Parents Assn. at U. Iowa (pres. 1970-71), Cath. Daus. Am., Alpha Delta Kappa. Roman Catholic. Home: 509 Willow Ave Deerfield IL 60015 Office: 1321 Wilmot Rd Deerfield IL 60015

DERLIN, JANE CAROL, psychologist; b. Sheboygan, Wis., June 19, 1926; d. Edgar Carl and Jennie Rosalie (Knocke) Derlein; B.S., U. Wis., LaCrosse, 1948; M.A., U. Mich., 1961. Tchr. phys. edn., Oconto Falls, Wis., 1950-53, Sheboygan, 1953-61; sch. psychologist, Sheboygan, 1961-68, Plymouth, Wis., 1969-75, Racine, Wis., 1975—; pvt. practice clin. psychology, 1961—; cons. psychologist New Concepts Found. Northeastern Wis., 1968—; dir. Psychol. Services, Racine, 1973—. Exptl. Design Inst. fellow, 1966; U. Wis. fellow, 1968. Mem. Council for Exceptional Children (pres. Lake-to-Lake chpt. 1970-71), Am. Psychol. Assn., Wis. Psychol. Assn., Gateway Assn. Sch. Psychologists, Wis. Sch. Psychologists Assn. Clubs: Altrusa Internat., Sheboygan (v.p. 1972), Wis. Hunter and Jumper Assn. Home and Office: 4832 Alcyn Dr Racine WI 53402

DERMAN, GLENDA BARTEL, market research exec.; b. San Francisco, Apr. 1, 1936; d. Irving P. and Elain (Barker) Bartel; B.A., U. Calif., Berkeley, 1957, M.A., 1958; m. Irwin H. Derman, Mar. 20, 1969; 1 son, Daniel Bartel. Coordinator vol. service Calif. Hosp. Assn., 1964-68; asso. dir. Calif. Heart Assn., 1968, 69; instr. mgmt. San Mateo (Calif.) Jr. Coll. Dist., 1970-78; project mgr. market research high tech. Gnostic Conceps sub. McGraw-Hill, Menlo Park, Calif., 1978—. Adv. bd. Medic Alert Found. Internat. Recipient commendation Calif. Heart Assn. Mem. No. Calif. Electronic Study Group, Robotics Internat. SME. Author: Connector Industry Forecast, 3 Vols., 1981. Office: 2710 Sand Hill Rd Menlo Park CA 94025

DEROSE, CHRISTINE MARIE, guitarist; b. Racine, Wis., Dec. 9, 1953; d. Anthony and Mary (Pownall) DeRose; student North Tex. State U., 1972-77. Freelance studio musician Dallas comml. rec. market, 1979—; guitarist various jazz groups, Dallas, 1979—; tchr. jazz guitar Cedar Valley Coll., 1979—. Recipient Lion's Arion award, 1972. Mem. Dallas Fedn. Musicians, Ft. Worth Profl. Musicians Assn. Democrat. Composer: Quintessence, 1979, True Leaf, 1980, Umduli, 1981, Just Another Samba, 1981; recs. incl. Sazerac Jazz, 1979; Quintessence, 1979; True Leaf, 1980; The Legend-Lou Fischer Rehearsal Band, 1981. Home: 6342 Llano St Dallas TX 75214

DE ROSE, JOAN ANNE, mgmt. cons. co. exec.; b. N.Y.C., Feb. 25, 1929; d. Edward Michael and Anne Gertrude (Armstrong) Gilbert; B.S., Fordham U., 1950; M.S., L.I. U., 1972; student Am. Theatre Wing and Stella Adler Drama Sch., 1967-69; m. Louis James De Rose, Sept. 22, 1950; children—Richard, Jeffrey. Asst. to buyer sportswear De Pinna Dept. Store, N.Y.C., 1947-49; model Harry Conover Agy., N.Y.C., 1949-58; appeared on commls., TV shows, 1950-52; v.p. De Rose Assos. Inc., Carlsbad, Calif., 1962—. Cert. tchr., N.Y., Calif. Mem. AAUW. Roman Catholic. Club: La Costa Country. Home: 7214 Plaza de la Costa Rancho La Costa CA 92008

DERRICK, SARA MARIAN, educator, psychologist; b. Cuthbert, Ga.; d. Joseph and Pearl (Woods) Lee; A.B., Howard U., 1956; M.Ed., Bowling Green State U., 1959; Ph.D., Ohio State U., 1975; m. William A. Derrick, Jan. 3, 1943; children—William A., Norman W. Tchr., Sandusky (Ohio) pub. schs., 1958-67, dir. remedial reading, 1967-68, psychologist, 1969-72; intern psychologist Betty Jane Rehab. Center, Tiffin, Ohio, 1968-69; research asso. Ohio State U., Dept. Pediatrics, Columbus, 1972-73; asst. prof. child/family studies Bowling Green (Ohio) State U., 1975—; pvt. practice developmental psychology, Bowling Green; founder preschool edn. Erie County, Ohio, 1963; dir. Ebenezer Preschool Nursery, 1963-72. Bd. dirs. Ohio Council on Family Relations; mem. Erie County Mental Health and Retardation Bd. Mem. Ohio Psychol. Assn., Nat. Assn. Sch. Psychologists, Soc. for Research in Child Devel., Nat. Council on Family Relations, Alpha Kappa Alpha. Club: Altrusa Internat. (bd.). Alpha Kappa Alpha. Contbr. articles to profl. jours. Home: 1323 Johnson St Sandusky OH 44870 Office: Dept Child/Family Studies Bowling Green State Univ Bowling Green OH 43403

DERRICO, GEORGIA SANTANGELO, bank exec.; b. N.Y.C., Oct. 6, 1944; d. George M. and Rose Mary (Rao) Santangelo; B.A., St. Mary's Coll. (Notre Dame, Ind.), 1966; degree in Internat. Affairs, Johns Hopkins, Bologna, Italy, 1969; M.Internat. Affairs, Columbia U., 1970; m. R. Roderick Porter, Feb. 6, 1982. With Chemical Bank, N.Y.C., 1971—, various positions including lending officer to dist. head corp. div. to chief adminstrv. and credit officer Multinat. Div., sr. v.p., 1982—, dir. corp. affairs, 1982—; bd. dirs. Oneida, Ltd., National Dance Inst. Attended Harvard Exec. Seminar, 1977. Mem. Assn. M.B.A. Execs. Contbr. article to publs. in field. Home: 15 River Rd Unit 220 Cos Cob CT 06807 Office: 277 Park Ave New York NY 10172

DERRY, PORTIA KAY, artist, state ofcl.; b. Louisville, Jan. 18, 1948; d. Stephen Arthur and Laura Ellen (Miller) D.; A.A. in Architecture, U. Fla., 1969; student Western Ky. U., 1969-70; B.S. with honors in Sociology (Dean's Scholar), U. Louisville, 1979. Engring. draftsman City of Gainesville (Fla.), 1968; archtl. draftsman, then dir. interior decoration Knox A. Griffin, AIA, Atlanta, 1969; art tchr., counselor Hearth-Shire Art Center and Ednl. Community, San Francisco, 1970-72; staff asst. Unité Unlimited, San Francisco, 1972; computer program editor Data Applications, Inc., Silver Spring, Md., 1973; with Bur. of Social Ins., Ky. Dept. Human Resources, Louisville, 1973—, fraud hearing officer for Jefferson County, 1979-81, state outreach coordinator program support br. Bur. for Social Ins., Frankfort, 1981—; legal asst., part-time 1973-79; one man shows including: Hearth-Shire Art Center, 1971, 72, Entropy Gallery, San Francisco, 1971; exhibited in group shows including: Hearth-Shire Art Center, 1970, 71, 72, Highlands Festival Art Shows, Louisville, 1979, Allen R. Hite Gallery, Louisville, 1979, Floyd County (Ind.) Mus., 1980, Ky. State Fair, 1980, others in Louisville. Active worker fund drives of various local groups and charitable orgns.; participant fine arts auction Channel 15, Ky. Ednl. TV, 1981, 82. Recipient Silver Knight award Miami Herald, 1966; Service award Art Club, Miami Beach, Fla., 1968; service award North Bay Village Lions Club, 1968; cert. of appreciation Bayshore and Sunny Isles Lions Club, 1969; Critics Club award Art Center Assn., 1980; honored at Gov.'s Salute to Ky. Artists and Craftsmen, 1981. Mem. Ky. Human Services Assn., Ky. Watercolor Soc., Art Center Assn., Lexington Art League, U. Louisville Art League (founding mem.), Nat. Forensic League, English-Speaking Union, Christian Youth Fellowship, Louisville Craftsmen's Guild, Alpha kappa Delta, Chi Omega. Art editor Embryo Lit Mag., 1966-68. Studio: Carriage House 1023 Cherokee Rd Louisville KY 40204 also Box 14 Game Farm Rd Frankfort KY 40601

DERSH, RHODA E., mgmt. cons.; b. Phila., Sept. 10, 1934; d. Maurice S. and Kay (Weiner) Eisman; B.A., U. Pa., 1955; M.A., Fletcher Sch. Law and Diplomacy, Tufts U., 1956; M.B.A., Manhattan Coll., 1980; m. Jerome Dersh, Dec. 23, 1956; children—Debra Lori, Jeffrey Jonathan. Interpreter, Consul of Chile, Phila., 1954-57; teaching and staff positions Albright Coll., Reading, Pa., Mt. Holyoke Coll., Amherst Coll., 1957-64; cons., systems designer non-profit, ednl., bus. and profl. orgns., Reading, 1965—; exec. dir. Public Sch. Budget Study Project, Reading, 1975-79, cons. dir., 1979—; pres., chief exec. officer Profl. Practice Mgmt. Assos., Reading, 1977—; founder, dir. Pace Inst., Reading; chmn. Public Service Cons. Project, 1980—; writer, lectr. exec. com. Inst. Community Affairs, 1975—; chairperson Community Plan Task Force for City of Reading, 1973-75; chmn. budget allocations panel United Way, 1974-76; del. White House Conf. on Children, 1970; co-founder, pres. World Affairs Council of Reading and Berks, 1963-65; chmn. Berks County Children and Youth Com., 1958-72; active AAUW, LWV. Recipient project grant AAUW Ednl. Found., 1975-76, Outstanding Women's award Jr. League of Reading, 1974. Mem. Am. Mgmt. Assn., Am. Acad. Ind. Consultants (dir., accredited ind. cons.), Nat. Com. Citizens in Edn., Nat. Assn. Female Execs., LWV, AAUW, Berks County C. of C. (edn. com.), Am. Acad. Polit. and Social Scis., Author: The School Budget Is Your Business, 1976; Business Management for Professional Offices, 1977; The School Budget: It's Your Money, 1979; Part Time Professionals and Managers, 1979; contbr. articles to periodicals. Office: Profl Practice Mgmt Assos Suite 305 606 Court St Reading PA 19601

DE RUVO, CLAIRE CHARLOTTE KINGSBURY, univ. adminstr.; b. Jersey City, Feb. 18, 1930; d. Owen John, Sr. and May Gertrude (Theurer) Kingsbury; student Fresno (Calif.) City Coll., 1970-72, SUNY, Binghamton, 1979-80; children—Deborah Ann, Frederick Philip, Jr. Adminstrv. asst. Valley Regional Tng. Center, Fresno; personnel interviewer Fresno Community Hosp.; adminstrv. asst. to exec. dir. univ. aux. services SUNY, Binghamton, 1974-81, asst. to exec. dir. for adminstrv. ops., 1981—; notary public. Mem. Nat. Assn. Coll. and Univ. Food Services, Internat. Platform Assn., Am. Mgmt. Assns., Am. Soc. Public Adminstrn. (Central Valley chpt.), Nat. Assn. Coll. Aux. Services, Broome County C. of C., Nat. Restaurant Assn., N.Y. State Restaurant Assn., SUNY Aux. Service Assn. Republican. Baptist. Home: Ketchum Rd Box 67C RD 2 Conklin NY 13748 Office: Auxiliary Campus Enterprises State U NY at Binghamton Vestal Pkwy E Binghamton NY 13901

DESAI, BALWANT G., nursing home adminstr.; b. Gujarat, India, Nov. 15, 1942; d. Bahalshingh B. and Narendra B. Gill; B.S. in Nursing, B.J. Med. Coll., Gujurat, 1970; M.S. in Psychology, Jersey City State Coll., 1975; m. Girish Desai, Apr. 1, 1973; children—Dimple, Tina. Nurse, India, 1964-65; public health nurse, Ahmedabad, Gujarat, India, 1965-68; nurse N.J. Columbus Hosp., 1971-73; pvt. duty nurse, Livingston, N.J., 1973-79; mgr. Royal Hosts Inn, Lexington, Va., 1979-80; adminstr. Home for Adults, Lexington, Va., 1980—. WHO scholar, 1964. Mem. Am. Critical Care Nurses, Hotel-Motel Assn., Home for Adults Assn. Hindu. Home and Office: 409 S Main St Lexington VA 24450

DESALME, WILLA HITCHCOCK, guidance counselor, educator, coach; b. Cisco, Tex., May 30, 1931; d. Thomas Henry and Orphia (Culberson) Hitchcock; B.S. in Edn., Mc Murray Coll., 1953; M.Ed., Tex. Woman's U., 1965; postgrad. Azusa-Pacific Coll.; children—Charles William, Randy Joe. Tchr., Atascosa (Tex.) Pub. Schs., 1953-55; Beeville (Tex.) Pub. Schs., 1955-56; Randolph AFB (Tex.) Pub. Schs., 1957-62, Fallbrook (Calif.) Pub. Schs., 1962—. Mem. Calif., Fallbrook tchrs. assns., NEA, Am. Fedn. Tchrs. Democrat. Baptist. Home: 3237 Carolyn Circle Oceanside CA 92054 Office: Fallbrook High Sch Fallbrook CA 92028

DE SALVO, LORRAINE CONSTANCE, univ. ofcl.; b. N.Y.C., June 15, 1950; d. William Joseph and Elizabeth Agnes De S.; B.S., U. Md., 1972, para-legal cert., 1978. Personnel officer, classification analyst U. Md., College Park, 1974-75, asst. employment mgr., 1975-76, asst. benefits officer, 1976-77, asst. employment mgr., 1977-78, adminstr. personnel and facilities dept. physics and astronomy, 1978—. Mem. Shih Tzu Fanciers Greater Balt. (v.p., program chmn.), Alumni Assn. U. Md., Alpha Xi Delta Alumnae. Clubs: Nat. Capital Area Shih-Tzu, Am. Shih Tsu. Editor: Palace Scrolls newsletter, 1981. Office: Dept Physics and Astronomy U Md College Park MD 20742

DESCHAINE, BARBARA RALPH, real estate broker; b. Syracuse, N.Y., Feb. 16, 1930; d. George John and Dora Belle (Manchester) Ralph; B.A., St. Lawrence U., 1952; postgrad. Pa. State U., 1969-72; grad. Pa. Realtors Inst., 1973; student Realtors Nat. Mktg. Inst., 1974-75; children—Olav Bernt Kollevoll, Kristan George Kollevoll, Eric John Kollevoll; m. 2d, Bernard Richard Deschaine, May 23, 1981. Salesman, Brose Realty, Easton, Pa., 1967-72, asso. broker/mgr., 1973, broker, owner, 1974—; mem. Pa. Real Estate Polit. Edn. Com. Bd. dirs. Easton Area C. of C., 1973-79, v.p. organizational improvement, 1975-76, v.p. econ. devel., 1976-77, pres., 1977-78; mem. Greater Easton Corp. Strategy Group, 1977-78. Mem. Eastern Northampton County Bd. Realtors (dir. 1973—, sec. 1977, v.p. 1980-81, Realtor of Yr. 1978), Bethlehem Bd. Realtors, Pa. Assn. Realtors, Nat. Assn. Realtors, Realtors Nat. Mktg. Inst., Homes for Living Network (state chmn. 1980), Nat. Assn. Female Execs., Sales and Mktg. Execs. (dir. Easton area chpt. 1976—, Disting. Sales award 1982), Phi Beta Kappa. Republican. Presbyterian. Home: 330 Paxinosa Rd W Easton PA 18042 Office: 1311 Northampton St Easton PA 18042

DESCHAMBAULT, DANIELLE EILEEN, owner, mgr. retail store; b. Montreal, Que., Can., Mar. 19, 1947; came to U.S., 1949, naturalized, 1964; d. John Raymond and Yolande (LaFleur) Deschambault; B.A., LeMoyne Coll., 1969; M.S., Syracuse U., 1974. Tchr. French, Jamesville Dewitt (N.Y.) Central Schs., 1969-73; French teaching asst. Syracuse (N.Y.) U., 1973-74; owner, mgr. Handworks Yarn Shop, Dewitt, N.Y., 1975—. Mem. Women's Forum, Syracuse, 1981-82; account exec. United Way Central N.Y., 1981-82. Mem. Nat. Needlework Assn., N.Y. State Assn. Fgn. Lang. Tchrs., LWV. Home: 126 Jamesville Ave Syracuse NY 13210 Office: 4314 E Genesee St Dewitt NY 13214

DESFOSSES, HELEN ROBERTA, univ. adminstr.; b. Dover, N.H., Apr. 24, 1945; d. Robert Louis and Agnes Mary (Mater) D.; B.A., Mount Holyoke Coll., 1965; M.A., Harvard U., 1967; Ph.D., Boston U., 1971; 1 son, Adam Robsohn Cohn. Chmn., Soviet and East European Studies, Boston U., 1970-72; chmn. dept. govt. Emmanuel Coll., Boston, 1972-74; research fellow Harvard U. Russian Research Center, 1974-76; asso. dean Coll. Arts, Scis. and Letters, U. Mich., Dearborn, 1976-78; dean undergrad. studies and asst. v.p. acad. affairs SUNY, Albany, 1978-82, asso. v.p. research and ednl. devel., 1982—; cons. Internat. Communications Agy., Fgn. Service Inst.; mem. exec. com. and bd. dir. Center for Women in Govt., 1979—. Bd. dirs. Detroit Urban League, 1977-78; chmn. Commn. on Peace and Justice, Diocese of Albany, 1981—. NDEA fellow, 1967-70, Coretta Scott King fellow AAUW, 1969-70, Population Council fellow, 1974-75, Nat. Acad. Scis. exchange scholar, 1975, Ford Found. fellow, 1975-76, Andrew W. Mellon Found. fellow, 1980. Mem. Am. Polit. Sci. Assn., African Studies Assn., Am. Assn. Advancement Slavic Studies, ACLU (state bd. Mich. 1977-78), NAACP (legal redress com. Albany 1979—). Democrat. Roman Catholic. Author: Soviet Policy Toward Black Africa, 1972; Socialism in the Third World, 1975; Soviet Population Policy, 1981. Office: SUNY ADM 216 1400 Washington Ave Albany NY 12222

DESHERBININ, BETTY VARVARA, cons. co. exec.; b. Vancouver, B.C., Can., July 30, 1917; d. Andrew Granville and Elizabeth (Tamblyn) deS. With Roger Williams Tech. & Econ. Services, Inc., Princeton, N.J., 1962—, corp. sec.-treas., 1980—, also dir.; dir. Roger Williams Tech. & Econ. Services Inc. U.K., Inc., 1967—. Mem. PEN Internat., Nat. Assn. Accts. Author: Wind on the Pampas, 1941; Bindweed, 1942; By Bread Alone, 1945; The Challenged Lane, 1946; The River Plate Republics, 1947; The Monkey Puzzle, 1956. Home: 86 Olden Ln Princeton NJ 08540 Office: 34 Washington Rd Box 426 Princeton NJ 08540

DESMOND, PATRICIA LEE, mfg. co. exec.; b. Levelland, Tex.; d. Cecil C. and Ira E. (Read) Lee; student journalism Odessa Coll., 1965; 1 dau., Anne Michele. Asst. continuity and traffic dir. Sta. KOSA-TV, 1964-66; bus. page editor, reporter Odessa (Tex.) Am., 1966-68; v.p., gen. mgr. Harshe-Rotman & Druck, Inc., Houston, 1968-79; v.p. corp. affairs Libbey-Owens-Ford Co., Toledo, 1979—; speaker on communications, investor relations, govtl. relations, fund-raising, women in adminstrn. to civic and bus. groups. Mem. Public Relations Soc. Am. (accredited, nat. exec. com. investor relations sect. 1977-79), Nat. Investor Relations Inst. (founding pres. Houston chpt.), Toledo-Lucas County Visitors and Conv. Center Bur., Inc. (dir.), Great Lakes Govt. Affairs Com., Toledo C. of C., Toledo Area Govtl. Research Assn. (dir.). Home: 3637 Indian Rd Toledo OH 43606 Office: 811 Madison Ave Toledo OH 43695

DESOMOGYI, AILEEN ADA, ret. librarian; b. London, Nov. 26, 1911; d. Harry Alfred and Ada Amelia (Ponten) Taylor; immigrated to Can., 1966; B.A., Royal Holloway Coll., U. London, 1936, M.A., 1938; M.L.S., U. Western Ont., 1971; m. Leslie Kuti, Nov. 22, 1958; m. 2d, Joseph DeSomogyi, July 8, 1966. Librarian in spl. and public libraries, Eng., 1943-66; sr. instr. Nat. Coal Bd., 1957; charge regional collection S.W. Ont., Lawson Library, U. Western Ont., 1966-71; cataloger Coop. Book Centre Can., 1971; mem. staff E. York (Ont.) Public Library, 1971-74; librarian Ont. Ministry Govt. Services Mgmt. and Info. Services Library, 1975-78, Sperry-Univac Computer Systems, Toronto (Ont.) Central Library, 1980-81. Mem. ALA, Library and Info. Tech. Assn., Canadian Wildlife Fedn., Ont. Humane Soc., Internat. Fund Animal Welfare, Royal Holloway Coll. Assn. Roman Catholic. Contbr. articles to profl. jours. Home: 9 Bonnie Brae Blvd Toronto ON M4J 4N3 Canada

DE SOMOV, MADELEINE MARGARET, exec. search co. exec; b. Balt., Apr. 30, 1924; d. William Leo Miller and Pearl Ellen Shoop; B.S. in Lang. Arts, Los Angeles State Coll., 1955, M.S. in Speech and Drama, 1957; m. Sergei de Somov, June 21, 1970; children—De Ette Jeannine, Sergei III, Nicholas Peter. Speech instr. Los Angeles Community Coll., 1956-57; English tchr. San Gabriel (Calif.) High Sch., 1957-58; classified sales rep. Los Angeles Times-Mirror Co., 1958-64; account exec. Curray & Staff, Inc., advt. agy., Los Angeles, 1964-65; advt. sales rep. Los Angeles Herald Examiner, 1965-67; dir. sales and advt. Sta.-KADS, McLendon Pacific Corp., Dallas, 1967; account exec. Sta.-KWIZ, Davis Broadcasting Corp., Santa Ana, Calif., 1968-69; sales mgr. Windsor Publs., Encino, Calif., 1969-72; exec. v.p. Internat. Recruiting Systems, Inc., Van Nuys, Calif., 1972-77; chairperson bd. dirs. Worldwide Systems, Inc., Van Nuys, Calif., 1977—; mgmt. cons. Served with Women's Army Aux. Corps, 1943-44, WAC, 1951-53. Recipient various civic awards, 1954-57, Bus. and Profl. Woman's Club award, 1957. Cert. secondary tchr., Calif. Mem. Nat. Assn. Female Execs., Am. Soc. Profl. and Exec. Women, IEEE. Office: 15205 Burbank Blvd Suite B Van Nuys CA 91411

DESOR, JEANNETTE ANN, exptl. psychologist; b. Balt., July 11, 1942; d. Raymond Charles and Evelyn Clara (Geiger) D.; A.B. magna cum laude, Cornell U., 1964, Ph.D., 1969; univ. fellow, Yale U., 1964-65; NIH fellow, U. Pa., 1970-73. Staff scientist Monell Chem. Senses Center, U. Pa., 1973-75, asst. prof. Med. Sch., 1973-75; research assoc. VA Hosp., Phila., 1973-75; sect. head sensory evaluation personal products div., then mgr. sensory evaluation Warner-Lambert Co., 1975-78; mgr. behavioral scis. corp. research Gen. Foods Corp., Tarrytown, N.Y., 1978-81, prin. scientist, 1982—; dir. Mace-Fremont, Inc., 1980—. Ford Found. fellow, 1963-64; NIH grantee, 1973-75. Mem. Am. Psychol. Assn., Assn. Chemosensory Scis., AAAS, Eastern Psychol. Assn. Author papers in field, chpts. in books. Office: Gen Foods Corp 555 S Broadway Tarrytown NY 10591

DESORMEAUX, BRENDA HEBERT, real estate co. exec.; b. Maurice, La., Sept. 30, 1943; d. Wilbert P. and Laurabelle (Bonin) Hebert; asso. degree in secretarial studies U. Southwestern La., 1963; grad. Bob Brooks Real Estate Sch., 1981; m. Harris J. Desormeaux, Dec. 27, 1964; children—John Keith, Kent Jason, Kristie, Kelli Ann, Kalen Faye, Kip Matthew. Sec., Continental Oil Co., Lafayette, La., 1963-71; sales rep. CDT Realty Co., Lafayette, 1971-76, 77-78, mgr. residential div., 1977—; sales mgr., co-owner Lamaison Realty Co., Lafayette, 1976-77; owner, pres. 5-K Agy., Inc., real estate; notary public. Roll-on fund raiser U. Southwest La.; sec., speaker Acadiana Right to Life Com., Lafayette; den mother Cub Scouts; 6th grade catechism tchr., lay reader local Roman Catholic Ch. Lic. real estate broker. Mem. Nat. Assn. Realtors, Realtors Nat. Mktg. Inst., Acadian Homebuilders Assn., Am. Businesswomen's Assn. (chpt. corr. sec. 1973), Lafayette Bd. Realtors (Million Dollar Sales Club), La. Realtors Assn. (membership chmn. 1982-83). Democrat. Clubs: Ragin Rouge; U. Southwest La. Ragin Cajun, Maurice Spinning Wheels, Home Demonstration. Home: Route 1 Box 372 Maurice LA 70555 Office: 4702 Johnston St Lafayette LA 70503

DESPRES, GINA HELEN, lawyer, legis. asst.; b. Sydney, Australia, Sept. 28, 1941; came to U.S., 1964, naturalized, 1972; d. George Alfred and Winifred Florence (Bush) Eviston; B.A. with honors (Commonwealth scholar 1960-64), U. Sydney, 1964; postgrad. (NDEA fellow 1966-68), U. Calif., Berkeley, 1965-70; J.D., UCLA, 1974; m. John Despres, Sept. 23, 1964; children—Sarah, Naomi. Admitted to Calif. bar, 1974, D.C. bar, 1976; atty. firm Irell & Manella, Los Angeles, 1974-75; ind. practice, Washington, 1976-77; with Dept. Energy, 1977-79, dir. internat. energy and energy security policy, 1978-79; sr. legis. asst. tax and def. U.S. Senator Bradley of N.J., 1979. Bd. editors UCLA Law Rev. 1973-74. Mem. D.C. Bar Assn. Author articles in field. Office: 2107 Dirksen Senate Office Bldg Washington DC 20515

DESSASO, DEBORAH ANN, adminstrv. specialist; b. Washington, Feb. 6, 1952; d. Coleman and Virginia Beatrice (Taylor) D.; student public schs., Washington, Clk.-stenographer FTC, Washington, 1969-70; sec. NEA, Washington, 1970-72; sec. Nat. Ret. Tchrs. Assn./Am. Assn. Ret. Persons, Washington, 1972-79, asso. adminstrv. specialist, 1979-80, adminstrv. specialist, 1980—; founding mem., sec. Andrus Fed. Credit Union, 1980. Mem. Nat. Assn. Female Execs. Mem. Worldwide Ch. of God. Home: 3060 Stanton Rd SE Washington DC 20020 Office: 1909 K St NW Washington DC 20049

DETAMORE, RUTH A., personnel mgmt. specialist; b. Marion, Ind., Nov. 20, 1946; d. Ruth May Virginia (Sherman) Henderson; A.A., Ball State U., 1979, B.S. (Cecil Lagle Meml. scholar), 1982. Clk.-stenographer, FDA, HEW, Washington, 1964; sec. Lincoln Nat. Life Ins. Co., Ft. Wayne, Ind., 1964-65; clk.-stenographer ward adminstrn. VA Med. Center, Marion, 1965-69, asst. chief ward adminstrn., 1969-73, ward mgr., 1973-74, chief ambulatory care and processing, 1974-77, personnel mgmt. specialist, 1977—; mem. adv. bd. Marion Occupational Devel. Center, 1982; chmn. supervisory com. Fed. Employees Credit Union, 1981-82. Recipient profl. awards. Mem. Women in Communication, Am. Bus. Women's Assn., Female Execs. Assn., Soc. Advancement of Mgmt., VA Employees Assn., YWCA. Home: 112 E North H St Gas City IN 46933

DETCH, ETHEL ROSALIE STEWART, motel exec.; b. Parkersburg, W.Va., Oct. 8, 1916; d. John Lawrence and Ethel M. (Flesher) Stewart; B.A., W.Va. U., 1936; M.A. in Econs., U. Va., 1937; m. John Lewis Detch, June 8, 1938 (div. 1972); children—John Lewis, Jr., Charlotte Dietz, Paul Stewart, Ethel Rosalie. Instr. econs. W.Va. U., Morgantown, 1937-39; legal sec., Lewisburg, W.Va., 1940-60; mgr. Ft. Savannah Inn, Lewisburg, 1965-79; pres., mgr. Old Red Mill, Inc., Lewisburg, 1965—; dir. Fort Savannah Mus., Lewisburg, 1965—; sponsor Colgate Darden Grad. Bus. Sch., U. Va. Mem. Greenbrier County Bd. Edn., 1951-63, pres., 1961-63. Mem. Nat. Restaurant Assn., Nat. Trust for Hist. Preservation, W.Va. Sch. Bds. Assn. (pres. 1956-60), Phi Beta Kappa, Gamma Phi Beta. Democrat. Episcopalian. Office: 204 N Jefferson St Lewisburg WV 24901

DETE, MARY KATHERINE, health services adminstr.; b. Newark, Ohio, Nov. 17, 1943; d. Joseph Bernard and A. Louise (McWilliams) D.; B.S. in Nursing, Marillac Coll., 1968; m. Lewis R. Winkler, Nov. 1, 1974. Dir., Universal Home Health Agy., Hawaiian Gardens, Calif., 1974; epidemiologist Paramount Gen. Hosp., Paramount, Calif., 1975-77; pub. health nursing supr. Restorative Home Care, Los Alamitos, Calif., 1977; dir. home health care services San Pedro Peninsula Hosp., Calif., 1977—; home health care cons., Meml. Hosp. of Long Beach (Calif.), 1978—; adminstrv. cons. Hosp. Home Care Depts., Inc., 1978—. Co-chmn., Chgo. Cath. Peace Fellowship, 1970-71; mem. Med. Com. for Human Rights, 1971-74; bd. dirs. So. Calif. Hospice Assn., Inc. Mem. Am. Pub. Health Assn., Calif. Assn. for Health Services at Home. Roman Catholic. Home: 6245 Seabreeze Dr Long Beach CA 90803 Office: 1300 W 7th St San Pedro CA 90732

DETRICK, SUSAN POLLY, psychologist; b. San Francisco, Oct. 15, 1948; d. Jack H. and Claire (Morse) Polly; B.A., Stanford U., 1970, M.A., 1972; Ph.D., U. Calif., Santa Barbara, 1975; m. Douglas Detrick, Jan. 21, 1977; 1 son, Bradley W. Sr. psychologist Colo. State U., 1975-76; postdoctoral student Stanford (Calif.) U., 1976-77; cons. health psychologist Stanford Research Inst., 1977-78; pvt. practice clin. psychology, San Francisco. Mem. Am. Psychol. Assn., Soc. Personality Assessment. Republican. Episcopalian. Office: 350 Parnassus St Suite 507 San Francisco CA 94117

DETWILER, CHARLOTTE JANE, acct.; b. Cleve., Oct. 27, 1920; d. Homer and Agnes Ellen Breyley; student Bob Jones U., 1947, Western Res. U., 1953; m. Erving Detwiler, Nov. 26, 1958; children—Joel, John, David. Exec. sec. to pres. Fed. Reserve Bank, Cleve., exec. sec. to pres. Alloys & Chems., Cleve., 1952-55; personnel dir. Carlon Products, Aurora, Ohio, 1956-66; bus. mgr., treas. Cooper Chevrolet, Aurora, 1966-73; bus. mgr. Haydocy Pontiac, Akron, 1973-77; controller, treas. Aubrey McDonald Creations (and predecessor co.), Akron, 1977—, also dir. Served with USAAF, 1942-45. Mem. Credit Women's Internat. (v.P. 1980-81), Nat. Assn. Accts., Akron Credit Women's Internat. Baptist. Home: 2011 W Market St Apts Akron OH 44313 Office: 565 Wolf Ledges Pkwy Akron OH 44311

DEUCHLER, SUZANNE LOUISE, state legislator; b. Chgo., July 21, 1929; B.A. in Spanish and Speech, U. Ill., 1951; m. Walter E. Deuchler, Jr., children—Mark, Maryll. Mem. Kane County Bd. from Dist. 5, 1976-80, Ill. Ho. of Reps. from Dist. 39, 1980—; mem. Ill. Agt. Orange Commn., 1982—. Mem. regional com. Dept. Children and Family Services, 1979-81; bd. dirs., v.p. Kane-Kendall County Mental Health Bd., 1967-75; chmn. edn. legis. adv. com. Sch. Dist. 129, 1979-80; mem. Ill. com. White House Conf. Children, 1979-80. Named Woman of Yr., Beta Sigma Phi, 1978, Aurora (Ill.) YWCA, 1979. Mem. AAUW (dir. Ill. 1973-75), LWV (pres. Aurora 1973-75). Republican. Address: 1345 Garfield Ave Aurora IL 60506

DEUTSCH, BARBARA SUSAN, univ. adminstr.; b. Newark, Nov. 27, 1940; d. Abe and Sophia Elizabeth (Nehemkis) D.; B.A., U. Mich., 1961; M.Ed., Boston U., 1962. Head resident SUNY, Geneseo, 1962-63; asst. dean students SUNY, Cortland, 1963-65; asst. dean students U. Calif., Santa Barbara, 1965-72, adviser for sororities and fraternities, 1972—; adviser Western Regional Interfrat. and Panhellenic Conf., 1979-83; cons. leadership tng. and group devel. Mem. Santa Barbara County Affirmative Action Commn., 1978-80. Mem. Assn. Frat. Advisors (exec. com. 1980, Western regional rep.; v.p. projects 1981), Nat. Assn. Student Personnel Adminstrs., Order Omega, Delta Phi Epsilon, Pi Lambda Theta. Democrat. Club: U. Mich. of Santa Barbara (pres., treas., sec.). Office: Activities Planning Center U Calif Santa Barbara CA 93106

DEUTSCH, ELINOR, interior designer; b. N.Y.C., Apr. 15, 1934; d. George and Dorothy (Ruderman) Kaplan; B.A., Manhattanville Coll., 1977, M.A., 1981; m. Jerome Deutsch, Apr. 29, 1955; children—Paul, Ginny, Amy. Dental hygienist Dr. Bob Gottsegen, N.Y.C., 1955-57; dental office mgr. Dr. Saul Ewen, Forest Hills, N.Y., 1965-67; interior designer Montgomery-Winecoff, N.Y.C., 1967-69; self-employed interior decorator, 1969-77; sales dir., interior designer Arenson Internat., N.Y.C., 1977—. Sec., New Democratic Coalition White Plains, 1970-72; death and dying therapist, Miller Nursing Home, White Plains, N.Y., 1975-77; dist. leader White Plains Dem. Com., 1970-79. Mem. Internat. Soc. Interior Designers, Women Bus. Owners N.Y., Women in Sales Orgn. (corr. sec. 1982), Nat. Home Fashions League Inc. Jewish. Home: 122 E 82d St New York NY 10028 also 177 Hillair Circle White Plains NY 10605 Office: 122 E 82d St New York NY 10028

DEUTSCH, ELLEN SOLOMON, mgmt. analyst; b. Orange, N.J., Aug. 26, 1943; d. Abram Shrier and Mildred Elizabeth (Berger) Solomon; B.A. in Psychology, U. N.C., Chapel Hill, 1965; m. Marshall Albert Deutsch, Aug. 9, 1970. Contract writer Conn. Gen. Life Ins. Co., Bloomfield, 1965-66; mgmt. trainee, asst. buyer G. Fox & Co., Hartford, Conn., 1966-68; account exec. WLAE-FM, Hartford, 1968; sr. analyst Travelers Ins. Co., Hartford, 1968-70; job analyst Conn. Blue Cross, New Haven, 1970-71; sr. ops. auditor Govt. Employees Ins. Co., Washington, 1972-75; employee devel. specialist Employment Standards Adminstrn., U.S. Dept. of Labor, Washington, 1975-81, mgmt. analyst, 1981—; conf. speaker; workshop leader; cons. Recipient Spl. Achievement award U.S. Dept. of Labor, 1977, 78. Mem. Am. Soc. Tng. and Devel., Nat. Assn. Female Execs., Am. Contract Bridge League, Alpha Gamma Delta. Democrat. Jewish. Club: U. N.C. Alumni (Washington). Home: 19 Cullinan Ct Gaithersburg MD 20878 Office: 200 Constitution Ave NW Washington DC 20210

DEUTSCH, HELGA, educator; b. Katowice, Poland, May 20, 1938; came to U.S., 1939, naturalized, 1957; d. Fred and Stella Deutsch; B.A., Hunter Coll., 1959; M.S., U. Ill., 1960, Ph.D., 1969. Instr. dept. phys. edn. U. Ill., Urbana-Champaign, 1962-69, asst. prof., 1969—, asst. dept. head, 1977—; cons. to Ill. State Bd. Edn., 1981. Mem. Midwest Assn. Phys. Edn. for Coll. Women (treas. 1981—), Nat. Assn. Phys. Edn. in Higher Edn. Am. Edn. Research Assn., AAHPER, AAUP. Author: (with Franks) Evaluating Performance in Physican Education, 1973; contbg. author: Laboratory Experiences for the Bioscience Course, 1974; contbg. articles on phys. edn. to profl. jours. Office: Univ Illinois 129 Freer Gymnasium 906 S Goodwin Urbana Il 61801

DEUTSCH, JACKIE MERRILL, mktg. communications cons.; b. N.J., June 21, 1948; d. Kenneth and Bea Demner; B.A., Upsala Coll., 1970; m. Leonard B. Deutsch, Dec. 26, 1972. Copywriter, Lennen & Newell, Advt., N.Y.C., 1970-72; copy dir. Raymond Richards, Springfield, N.J., 1972-74; cotbg. editor Apt. Life mag., Des Moines, Iowa, 1974-76; freelance writer, N.Y.C., 1976-79; writer, producer Burson-Marsteller, N.Y.C., 1979-80; propr. Jackie Deutsch, Writer & Producer, N.Y.C., 1980—; founder Network Resources Group, N.Y.C., 1982—. Recipient Golden Reel of Excellence award ITVA, 1982; Silver Screen award U.S. Indsl. Film, 1982. Mem. Assn. Multi-Image, Am. Film Inst., Mcpl. Art Soc., Nat. Assn. Female Execs., NOW. Address: 345 E 80th St Apt 27J New York NY 10021

DEUTSCH, NINA, concert pianist; b. San Antonio, Mar. 15; d. Irvin and Freda D.; B.S., Juilliard Sch. Music; M.M.A., Yale U., 1973. Concert pianist, 1958—; recording artist Vox Prodns.; only woman to record complete solo piano music of Charles Ives, 1976; recs. include: piano arrangement of Variations on America (Ives); freelance writer on music for N.Y. Times, UPI and mags., 1974—; music cons. Joe Franklin Show, WOR-TV, 1975—; exec. v.p. Internat. Symphony. Bd. dirs. Metzner Found. for Overseas Relief; Ft. Lee coordinator Channel 13, 1974. NEA grantee, 1977; Tanglewood fellow, 1966; recipient award for Am. music Nat. Fedn. Music Clubs, 1975; Oberlin Coll. scholar. Mem. Music Critics Assn., Publicity Club N.Y. Author: How to be a Successful Private Piano Teacher. Home: 410 Hazlitt Ave Leonia NJ 07605

DEUTSCH, SYLVIA, mcpl. ofcl.; b. Bklyn., July 9, 1924; d. Nathan and Dora Schatz; A.B. cum laude, Bklyn. Coll., 1947; m. Leon Deutsch, Dec. 21, 1946; children—Jack, Nathaniel Mark, Jeremy Joseph. Exec. dir. Proportional Representation Edn. Project, 1969-70; dir. N.Y. Met. Council, 1972-78; edn. cons. Am. Jewish Congress, 1972-78, nat. dir. fields ops. and membership, 1978-81; mem. N.Y.C. Planning Commn., 1972—, also chmn. N.Y.C. Bd. Standards and Appeals, N.Y.C., 1981—. Mem. Mayor's Commn. Taxi Regulatory Issues, 1981-82; v.p., chmn. legis. com. United Parents Assns., 1967-72, chmn. orgn. dept., and chmn. high schs., 1962-67; mem. Citizens Commn. City U., 1969-71; co-founder, exec. v.p. Com. for Pub. Higher Edn., 1966-74; mem. Mayor's Commn. Status of Women, 1976-79. Named Alumna of Yr., Bklyn. Coll., 1974; recipient Community Service award NCCJ, 1976. Jewish. Office: 80 Lafayette St New York NY 10013

DEUTZ, NATALIE RUBINSTEIN, modeling schs. exec.; b. Plymouth, Mass., Sept. 26; d. Louis and Lillian Rubinstein; student Simmons Coll., 1937, Modern Sch. Applied Art, 1938-40; m. Nov. 29, 1947 (dec.). Fashion buyer Wm. Filene's Sons Co., Boston, 1940-47; asst. to corp. pres. Columbia Textiles, Inc., N.Y.C., 1956-68; dir. John Robert Powers Sch., N.Y.C., 1968-72; v.p., nat. dir. fashion merchandising, dir. advt. workshop Barbizon Internat., Inc., N.Y.C., 1972—; Mem. Fashion Group, Nat. Acad. TV Arts and Scis., Advt. Women N.Y., Screen Actors Guild, AFTRA. Office: 3 East 54th St New York NY 10022

DEVANNY, MILDRED ELIZABETH SMITH, genealogist, club woman; b. Carrollton, Ill., Nov. 11, 1901; d. Robert Eugene and Mary Elizabeth (Scorggins) Smith; student Lincoln Bus. Coll., 1920; m. John Stormont Devanny, Aug. 5, 1924; 1 dau., Jacquelen Jeanne Devanny Vance. Owner, tchr. Devanny Dancing Sch., Lincoln, Ill., 1942-47; dir. ARC Camp Revues, 1944-45; condr. geneal. seminars throughout Ill., DAR and various geneal. socs., 1970—; library asst., genealogy Lincoln and Springfield libraries, 1970—; state chmn. Ill. Geneal. Seminars, 1970—. Recipient award for short story Fedn. Women's Clubs, 1960. Mem. Ill. Geneal. Soc. (dir. 1970-73), Decatur Geneal. Soc., Logan County Geneal. Soc., DAR (Ill. officer 1964-66, 68-70, regent 1978-79), Colonial Daus. 17th Century (Ill. pres. 1976-79), Huguenot Soc. (charter), Magna Charta Barons, Am. Assn. Ret. Persons. Episcopalian. Club: Lincoln Woman's (pres. 1960). Author: Sarah Margaret Lurton, Her Ancestors and Descendants, 1959; The Genealogy of Lora Mae Hannum, 1975; Revolutionary Soldiers Buried in Illinois, 1975; Revolutionary Soldiers Buried in Logan County Illinois, 1975; Campbell and Allied Families, 1976; Annotated List of Genealogical and Local History Sources in Lincoln County Pub. Library, 1977; Robert Monroe Smith, The Cumberland Presbyterian Minister, 1977.

DEVECCHIO, LOIS CLARICE LINDLEY, civic worker; b. Mulberry, Kans., Aug. 5, 1914; d. David Jahue and Philomena (Gathmann) Lindley; B.A., Fresno State U., 1935; student Art Inst., Florence, Italy, 1947, Sophia U., Tokyo, 1957; m. Roy G. DeVecchio, Dec. 25, 1934; children—Roy Lindley, Warren Jahue. Fashion cons. Vogue of Calif., 1936-40; freelance interior designer, Washington, 1960-72; property mgr. Shapiro Properties and Dreyfus Co., Washington and Bethesda, Md., 1970-74. Chmn., D.C. Adv. Neighborhood Commn., 1980—; mem. Mayor's Budget Oversight Com.; pres. Potomac Republican Club, 1979—; vice chmn. D.C. Rep. Central Com., 1980—; vice chmn., precinct chmn. 3d Ward, Washington; dir. League Rep. Women, 1977-79; Rep. candidate D.C. City Council, 1982; founding mem., pres. Ikebana Internat., Tokyo, 1956-59, pres. Washington chpt., 1962-64; co-founder Overseas Sch. Rome, 1947, bd. dirs., 1948-49; co-founder Armed Forces Hostess Assn., Washington, 1949, active, 1949-53. Recipient Cert. of Appreciation, Army-Navy Coordinating Group of UN Conf., 1945; Commendation, Dept. of State, 1945; Ambassador's award Am. and Brit. Embassy, 1949; Cert. of Appreciation Dept. of Army, Pentagon, 1965; Hon. Service award Sigma Chi, 1966. Mem. Ohara Flower Arrangers (v.p. 1968-69), Ikebana Internat., Armed Forces Hostess Assn. of the Pentagon, Japan Am. Soc. D.C., Dept of Medicine and Surgery Aux. (pres. 1973-75). Roman Catholic. Clubs: VA Wives (pres. 1975-76), Ft. McNair and Ft. Myer Officers, Marine Meml. of San Francisco. Home: 4841 Rodman St NW Washington DC 20016

DEVEREAUX, CHARITA LEE, home economist; b. Cleve., Sept. 28, 1947; d. John F. and Elizabeth A. (Shatto) Page; B.S. in Applied Sci., Miami U., Oxford, Ohio, 1968; m. Terence H. Devereaux, May 1, 1976; 1 dau., Mary Charita. Dietitian, State of N.J., 1968-69; home economist Ohio Edison Co., 1969-77; freelance home economist, substitute tchr., Cleve., 1979—. Mem. Home Economists in Homemaking, Am. Econs. Assn. Home: 1514 Mayview Ave Cleveland OH 44109

DEVEREUX, DOROTHY LOUISE (MRS. JOHN WILLIAM DEVEREUX), civic worker, former state legislator; b. Spokane, Wash., Nov. 8, 1911; d. John P. and Olive (Davis) Nelson; R.N., Calif. Luth. Sch. Nursing, Los Angeles, 1931; postgrad. Chgo. Lying-in Hosp., 1932; m. John William Devereux, Sept. 1, 1934 (dec. Oct. 1968); children—John William, Marvin, Diane, Frederick. Part-time asst. to mgr. Lansing and Wilmar hotels, Chgo., 1931-34; clinic nurse Public Health Inst., Chgo, 1932; dir. info. Hall of Sci., World's Fair, Chgo., 1933; asst. personnel dir., indsl. nurse Wieboldt Dept. Store, Chgo., 1934; active League Rep. Women, 1956; mem. Ho. of Reps., Ter. of Hawaii, 1958-59; mem. Hawaii Ho. of Reps., 1959-72. Ann. Hiscock lectr. U. of Hawaii, 1969. Pres., Manoa Sch. PTA, 1942-43, Punahou Sch. PTA, 1956-57, Hawaii Congress PTA, 1950-51; bd. mgrs. Nat. Congress PTA 1950-51, mem. platform com., 1951; mem. sch. health com. Hawaii Dept. Public Instrn., 1949-51, lay adv. com. ednl. policies, 1950-52; mem. sub-com. exceptional children of Gov.'s Conf. Edn., 1955; Hawaii sch. study adv. com., 1957; pres. Oahu Health Council, 1951-54, exec. com., 1945-55, 56-62, bd. dirs., 1963-67; adv. Oahu Youth Council, 1951-56; chmn. Hawaii adv. com. to Div. Vocat. Rehab., 1957-63; mem. Gov.'s Com. Employment Handicapped, 1954-77, exec. com., co-chmn. legis. and archtl. barriers com., 1964-72; women's com. Pres.'s Com. on Employment Handicapped, 1962—, mem. subcom. on archtl. barriers, 1965-68; adv. com. Job Survey Project, 1962-65; pres. Oahu Soc. Crippled Children and Adults, 1958-60, dir., exec. com., 1960-63, organizer Hawaii chpt.; adv. bd. Hawaii Salvation Army, 1951-70, hon. life mem. adv. bd., 1970—, sec. bd., 1958-59, vice chmn. bd., 1976-78, mem. children's facilities council, 1964—; former bd. dirs. WAIF of Internat. Social Service Hawaii; former rep. from Hawaii women's nat bd. Med. Coll. Pa.; nat. adv. council vocat. rehab. HEW, 1960-62; citizens adv. com. Oahu Transp. Study, 1963-67; adv. council Hawaii Comprehensive Health Plan, 1967-76; policy bd. Hawaii Rehab. Plan, 1967-69; mem. Fed. Council on Aging, 1974-79, mem. spl. aging population com., 1978-79; mem. Gov.'s Task Force on Implementation Nat. Health/Planning and Resources Devel. Act of 1974, 1975-76; bd. dirs. Mental Health Assn. Hawaii, 1972-75, Health and Community Services Council, 1973-79; mem. Hawaii State Health Coordinating Council, 76-82, chmn. plan and application rev. com., 1977-79, mem. proposed use of Fed. funds com., 1980—; mem. aux. Rehab. Hosp. Pacific, 1977—; bd. dirs. Renewed Energy for Active Living, 1977—, outreach worker, 1980—. Named Hawaii's Mother of Yr., 1955; recipient Disting. Vol. Service award Oahu Health Council, 1959; Disting. Service award Hawaii Rehab. Assn., 1967; Ann. Kokua (Help) award, Abilities Unltd., 1968; Masao Kimura Meml. State Service award Hawaii Easter Seal Soc., 1975. Mem. Calif. Hosp. Nurses Alumnae Assn., Woman's Aux. Honolulu County Med. Soc. (past parliamentarian, chmn. by laws com., mem., exec. bd.), Woman's Aux. Hawaii Med. Assn. (pres. 1957-58, parliamentarian), Hawaii Public Health Assn. (hon. life), Honolulu C. of C. (subcom. on public health issues of public health com. 1980—), Free Kindergarten and Children's Aid Assn. Hawaii, Hawaii Assn. Humanistic Psychology, Hawaii Theosophical Soc., Child and Family Service Assn. Hawaii, Kapiolani Children's Med. Center Aux. (chmn. by-laws com. 1953-57), Assn. Research and Enlightenment Found. Republican. Conglist. Home: 2721 Huapala St Honolulu HI 96822

DEVERICK, BARBARA HOLSCLAW, utility ofcl.; b. Lenoir, N.C., July 20, 1924; d. Oscar H. and Mayna (Tuttle) Holsclaw; A.A. in Acctg., Nat. Sch. Commerce, 1942; student U. N.C., 1961-62, U. Mich., 1966; m. Percy Fontz Deverick, Oct. 13, 1944. With Blue Ridge Electric Membership Corp., Lenoir, 1946—, acct., 1956-59, office mgr., 1949-60, adminstrv. asst., 1960-64, mgr. organizational planning and personnel services, 1964—; interviewer Vets. Office, W.Va. U., Morgantown, 1945-46; participant central com. meeting Internat. Co-op Alliance, Copenhagen, 1978; mgmt. cons. to Jamaica Public Service Co., Kingston, 1979-80. Chmn. United Fund, Lenoir-Caldwell County, N.C., 1964-65; pres. Rural Electric Women's Task Force, 1971-73; mem. Caldwell County Bd. Edn., 1968-76, chmn., 1972-76; bd. dirs. ARC, 1965—, pres., 1968-72; bd. dirs. 4-H Devel. Assn., 1966-72, pres., 1968-70; bd. dirs. Western Piedmont Symphony, 1975-79, N.C. Agrl. Found., 1973-76; bd. dirs. Keep N.C. Beautiful, Inc., 1973—, pres., 1981-83; bd. dirs. N.C. Sch. Bd. Assn., 1973-76; trustee Caldwell Community Coll., 1964-73, sec., 1964-73; mem. central com. Internat. Coop. Alliance, 1976-80; mem. exec. com. Coop. League U.S.A., 1978-80, v.p., 1982—. Recipient Advanced Mgmt. Achievement award Nat. Rural Electric Co-op Assn., 1960, L.A. Dysart Citizenship award Lenoir-Caldwell County C. of C., 1964, State of N.C. 4-H Alumni award, 1970; named N.C. Career Woman of Yr., 1981. Mem. Am. Mgmt. Assn., Nat. Assn. Accts., Adminstrv. Mgmt. Soc., Lenoir Bus. and Profl. Womens Club. Republican. Mem. Advent Christian Ch. Contbr. numerous articles on personnel mgmt. to various profl. mags., also articles to religious publs. Home: 128 Echo Dr PO Box 522 Lenoir NC 28645 Office: 1216 Blowing Rock Blvd NE Lenoir NC 28645

DEVILLIERS, JILL GIBSON, educator; b. Eng., June 20, 1948; d. William Wilkinson and Anna (Gray) Dent; B.Sc., U. Reading (Eng.), 1969; Ph.D., Harvard U., 1974; m. Peter A. DeVilliers, June 19, 1970; children—Nicholas, Charlotte. Asst. prof. Harvard U., Cambridge, Mass., 1974-79; asso. prof. Smith Coll., Northampton, Mass., 1979—. Spencer Found. grantee, 1980-82. Mem. Soc. Research Child Devel. Author: Language Acquisition, 1978; contbr. articles in field to profl. jours. Office: Clark Sci Center Smith Coll Northampton MA 01063

DE VINE-KIRK, VALARIA ANN, mag. ofcl.; b. Chgo., June 14, 1951; d. Ralph and Vivian (Rollison) DeV.; student So. Ill. U., 1969, Lewis U., 1976-77; children—Stacy, Stephen, Scott. Asst. gen. mgr. Hilton-Stauffers, Chgo., 1970-73; v.p. Universal Temperature Control, Inc., Glendale Heights, Ill., 1974-77; sales rep. Matthew-Bender & Co., legal pubs., Chgo., 1977-79, D & S Pubs., Clearwater, Fla., 1979—; pres. The Number 1 Successful Woman, 1979—; mktg. and sales dir. Rep-Insider mag., Ft. Lauderdale, Fla., 1980—; lectr. and cons. small bus. Mem. Nat. Assn. Female Execs. Home: 1664 NW 58 Ave Lauderhill FL 33313

DEVOE, VIOLET ANN, systems analyst; b. Chgo., Sept. 27, 1940; d. Lambert Fred and Jean Mary (O'Hagan) Craemer; B.A. in Math., Mt. St. Mary's Coll., 1962; postgrad. in bus. adminstrn. San Diego State U.; m. Daniel Franklin Devoe, Dec. 29, 1962; children—Debra Jean, Alan Daniel, Lambert Theodore. Research asst. RAND Corp., Santa Monica, Calif., 1962-63; sci. programmer Litton Industries, Canoga Park, Calif., 1964; programmer analyst Lockheed-Calif. Co., Burbank, Calif., 1965-66, 69-72; sr. systems analyst County of San Diego (Calif.), 1972-80; sr. systems analyst Acctg. Corp. Am., San Diego, 1980—. Mem. Data Processing Mgmt. Assn., Assn. Systems Mgmt., Coronado Schs. Found., Am. Mensa Ltd. Republican. Roman Catholic. Club: Soroptimists (Coronado, Calif.). Home: 610 First St Coronado CA 92118 Office: 1929 1st St San Diego CA 92101

DEVORE, KIMBERLY K., hospice adminstr.; b. Louisville, June 19, 1947; d. Wendell O. and Shirley F. DeV.; student (Florence Allen Scholar), Xavier U., 1972-76; A.A., Coll. Mt. St. Joseph, 1979. Patient registration supr. St. Francis Hosp., Cin., 1974-76; cons., bus. mgr. Family Health Care Found., Cin., 1976-77; dir. bus. ops. Hospice of Cincinnati, Inc., 1977—; pres. Micro Med., 1979—; v.p. Sycamore Profl. Assn., 1979—; partner, sec. The Enchanted House, nat. hospice orgn. Mem. service and rehab. com. Hamilton County unit Am. Cancer Soc., 1977-78; bd. dirs. Hospice of the Miami Valley, Inc. Mem. Nat. (chmn. long-term planning com.), Ohio (co-founder, pres., state chmn.) hospice orgns., Nat. League for Nursing, Ohio Hosp. Assn., Greater Cin. Soc. of Fund Raisers, Nat., Ohio, fedns. bus. and profl. women's clubs, Cin. Bus. and Profl. Women's Club (pres. 1973-75). Club: Cin. Woman's.

DE VRIES, JANET MARGARET, clergywoman; b. Chgo., Feb. 24, 1950; d. Calvin Thomas and Janet May (Clark) DeV.; B.A., Hope Coll., Holland, Mich., 1972; M.Div., Union Theol. Sem., N.Y.C., 1978; m. William J. Cowfer, Sept. 6, 1980; stepchildren—David E., Jonathan C., Stephanie L. Ordained to ministry United Presbyterian Ch., U.S.A., 1977; coordinator tng. Support Agy., United Presbyn. Ch., N.Y.C., 1980—, program specialist vols. in mission, Program Agy., N.Y.C., 1973-78, coordinator communication and ch. support Synod S. Calif., Los Angeles, 1973-80; instr. Claremont (Calif.) Sch. Theology, 1979. Gannett Newspaper scholar, 1967. Mem. UN Assn., Religious Public Relations Council. Author: Learning the Pacific Way: A Guide for All Ages, 1982; also articles. Home: 9917 Brookside Circle Bloomington MN 55431 Office: Room 930 475 Riverside Dr New York NY 10115

DE VRIES, MARGARET GARRITSEN, economist; b. Detroit, Feb. 11, 1922; d. John Edward and Margaret Florence (Ruggles) Garritsen; B.A. in Econs. with honors (AAUW scholar 1939-42, Univ. scholar 1942), U. Mich., 1943; Ph.D. in Econs. (Inst. fellow), Mass. Inst. Tech., 1946; m. Barend A. de Vries, 1952; children—Christine, Barton. With Internat. Monetary Fund, Washington, 1946—, asst. chief multiple currency practices div., 1953-57, chief Far Eastern div., 1957-59, econ. cons., 1963-73, historian, 1973—; profl. lectr. econs. George Washington U., 1946-49, 1958-63. Recipient Disting. Alumni award U. Mich., 1980. Ford Found. grantee, 1959-62. Mem. Am. Econ. Assn., Internat. Studies Assn., Washington Women Economists Assn., Phi Beta Kappa, Phi Kappa Phi (Nat. Fellowship award 1943). Author: (with Irving S. Friedman) Postwar Foreign Economic Policy of the United States, 1947;

(with J. Keith Horsefield) The International Monetary Fund, 1945-1965, Twenty Years of International Monetary Cooperation, 3 vols., 1969; The International Monetary Fund, 1966-1971, The System under Stress, 2 vols., 1977; contbr. articles to profl. jours. Office: Internat Monetary Fund 700 19th St NW Washington DC 20431

DEVRIES, NANCY GREGORY, graphic arts co. exec.; b. Newark, Jan. 11, 1936; d. Walter LeRoe and Mabel (Broderick) Gregory; student (scholar), Carnegie Mellon U., 1953-54; B.A. with honors, in Econs., Ramapo Coll. of N.J., 1977; m. Roy Frank DeVries, Aug. 13, 1954; children—Karen DeVries Hedman, David Alan, Robert Frank. Co-founder, partner DATCO Design & Typography, Oakland, N.J., 1968—; v.p., founder DeVries Transfer Paper & Printing Co., Inc., Paterson, N.J., 1975-79; cons. Americraft, Inc., Oakland, N.J., 1971-73; dir. DeVries Bros., Inc., 1979—; lectr. in field; seminar leader Woman-to-Woman: The Bus. Experience, 1979—. Trustee, Saddle River Day Sch., 1975-79, chmn. devel. fund, 1978-79; mem. Oakland Mayors Adv. Com., 1972-74; cons., workshop leader YWCA, 1975—. Recipient Tribute to Women and Industry award, 1975, bronze awards Charpex, 1979; others. Mem. Tribute to Women and Industry Mgmt. Forum (1st pres. 1977-79, chmn. bd. 1979—), Typographers Assn. N.Y., C. of C. Contbr. articles to profl. jours.; editor, Forum Focus, 1977-81. Home: 30 Crosby Ln Oakland NJ 07436 Office: 6 Elm St Oakland NJ 07436

DEW, CAROL ANN, info. systems exec.; b. Springfield, Ill., Nov. 30, 1942; d. Jerome Dewitt Colby and Viviam Maxine (Johnson) Irwin; m. Gene Autry Dew, Mar. 18, 1978; 1 son, Paul William Sandefur. With Ill. Dept. Rev., Springfield, 1962-66; comml. artist Spl. Services, Bamberg, Germany, 1966-68; disbursement clk. Pillsbury Co., Springfield, 1968-69; data processing analyst, programmer Ill. Dept. Registration, Springfield, 1969-74; self employed mgmt. cons., Springfield, 1974-76; sales rep. Xerox Corp., Springfield, 1976-77; adminstrv. asst. Ill. Dept. Conservation, Springfield, 1977-80; data processing analyst Ill. Dept. Public Aid, Springfield, 1980-81; info. systems exec. Ill. Depts. Commerce and Community Affairs and Adminstrv. Services, Springfield, 1981-82; dep. dir. dept. acctg. revenue Dept. Sec. State, Springfield, 1982—. Mem. Springfield Human Relations Commn.; mem. Springfield Citizens Adv. Com. to Mayor; mem. New Horizons Housing Task Force; mem. Springfield Water, Light and Power Utility Adv. Bd.; mem. Springfield Tourism and Conv. Commn.; mem. Springfield Housing Devel. Corp. Mem. Nat. Assn. Female Execs., Nat. Assn. Bus. and Profl. Women. Republican. Baptist. Bi-weekly columnist Dew Line Black Voice Newspaper, 1978-80. Home: 1330 E Washington St Springfield IL 62703

DEWALL, KAREN MARIE, advt. agy. exec.; b. Phoenix, May 31, 1943; d. Merle C. and Agnes Marie (Larson) Feller; A.A., Phoenix Coll., 1968; m. Charles E. DeWall, Sept. 3, 1963; 1 dau., Leslie Karen. Mem. display advt. dept. Newspaper Agy. Corp., Salt Lake City, 1963-64; sec., media buyer Wade Advt. Co., Sacramento, 1964-66; sec., media dir. Garland Agy., Phoenix, 1967-71; media dir., account coordinator, owner DeWall & Assos., Phoenix, 1971—. Bd. dirs. Ariz. Council for the Blind Social Services and Rehab., Inc., Phoenix, Jr. League of Phoenix, Florence Crittendon Services, Phoenix Arts Coming Together, Inc. Republican. Club: Phoenix Country. Home: 32 W Marlette St Phoenix AZ 85013 Office: 737 W McDowell St Phoenix AZ 85007

DEWAR, MILDRED (JO) ELLER (MRS. DONALD NORMAN DEWAR), librarian; b. Wilkesboro, N.C., Nov. 9, 1925; d. Charles Franklin and Golda (Velt) Eller; student Brevard Coll., 1942-44; diploma Jr. Coll, 1944; A.B., Berea Coll., 1946; B.L.S., U. N.C., 1948; postgrad. Barry Coll., U. Fla., U. Miami; m. Donald Norman Dewar, Mar. 6, 1954; 1 dau., Heather. Tchr., librarian Mountain View High Sch., Hays, N.C., 1946-47; chief librarian Tenn. Wesleyan Coll., Athens, 1948-50; dept. head U. Tex. Library, Austin, 1951; librarian U.S. Army Spl. Services, Ft. Jackson, S.C., 1951-52; chief post library system, Ft. Stewart, Ga., 1952-54; librarian Olsen Jr. High Sch., Dania, Fla., 1955-56, Lauderdale Manors Sch., Ft. Lauderdale, Fla., 1956-63; head reader's services Miami-Dade Jr. Coll. Library, Miami, Fla., 1963-70, library dir. South Campus, 1970—; vis. instr. U. Ga., summer 1967; co-exec. dir. Nat. Library Week in Fla., 1965-66; mem. Fla. learning resources standing com. Council on Instructional Affairs. Mem. AAUW (past br. v.p.), ALA, Fla. Library Assn., Am., Fla. (past pres.) assns. sch. librarians, SE Fla. Ednl. Consortium (library task force), Delta Kappa Gamma. Contbr. articles to profl. jours.; mem. editorial bd. Community and Jr. Coll. Libraries. Home: 3520 Crystal View Ct Coconut Grove FL 33133 Office: 11011 SW 104th St Miami FL 33156

DEWEY, PAULINE T., newspaper pub., editor; b. Lyons, Kans., Aug. 2, 1913; d. Ivan L. and Betty Maude (Dalton) Stone; student Kans. State Coll., 1931-32, U. So. Calif., 1943; m. J. Sterling Thomas, Feb. 15, 1938 (dec.); children—Betty Claire (dec.), Anthony Thomas (dec.); m. 2d, Franklin Noah Dewey, Jr., Nov. 24, 1952 (dec. June 1968). Editor, Airview News, Douglas Aircraft, Santa Monica, Calif., 1942-45; pub. relations mgr. Calif. Intelligence Bur., Los Angeles, 1945-48; owner Thomas & Assos., realtors, Los Angeles, also Palm Springs, Calif., 1948-52; editor, pub. Nev. Times, Las Vegas, 1960—. Former chmn. local Heart Fund drive; mem. Gov.'s Com. Mobile Homes and Travel Trailers, 1973-75, Citizens' Group Project 701 for City's Master Plan, 1973-75; former trustee Clark County Library, Las Vegas; past chmn. bd. R.S.V.P. Recipient Boise Cascade Woman of Year award Los Angeles br. Boise Cascade Co., 1971, Gov.'s citation, 1971, certificates of appreciation from various local orgns. Mem. So. Nev. Park Operators Assn. (hon.), North Las Vegas C. of C. (former dir.), Better Bus. Bur., Army Athletic Assn., Am. Assn. Ret. Persons, LWV. Clubs: Soroptimist, Wings Jet, Am. Penwomen's (v.p. internat.), Internat. Toastmistress. Office: 1537 Las Vegas Blvd N Las Vegas NV 89101 Address: POB 4142 North Las Vegas NV 89030

DEWEY, REBECCA ARNELL (MRS. CHARLES SHERMAN DEWEY), cons. psychologist; b. Auburn, Wash., Oct. 11, 1902; d. John Robert and Emma (Hanson) Arnell; B.A. magna cum laude, U. Wash., 1926, M.A., 1936; Ph.D. Stanford U., 1946; m. Charles Sherman Dewey, Dec. 26, 1942. Tchr. pub. schs., Auburn, Aberdeen, Seattle, Wash., 1921-38; instr. Stanford U., 1941-44, U. Nev., summer 1941; asst. prof. U. Ill. at Chgo., 1946-49; cons. psychologist Charles S. Dewey and Assos., 1946—. Fellow AAAS; mem. AIM, Am., Midwestern, Ill. (sec. 1964-69) psychol. assns., MLA, Indsl. Relations Research Assn., Chgo. Psychol. Club (pres. 1964-65), Women's Share in Pub. Service (v.p. 1967-69), Chgo. Guidance and Personnel Assn., Am. Personnel and Guidance Assn., Interam. Soc. Psychology, Internat. Assn. Applied Psychology, Pi Lambda Theta. Club: Stanford. Contbr. articles to profl. jours. Home: 3130 N Lake Shore Dr Chicago IL 60657 Office: 135 S LaSalle St Chicago IL 60603

DEWHURST, COLLEEN, actress; b. Montreal, Que., Can.; student Downer Coll., Milw., then at Am. Acad. Dramatic Art; pupil of Harold Clurman and Joseph Anthony; m. James Vickery, 1947 (marriage dissolved); m. 2d, George C. Scott (div.); 2 sons. First profl. appearance in The Royal Family, 1946; Broadway appearances include Desire Under the Elms, 1952, Tamberlain the Great, 1956, Camille, 1956, The Eagle Has Two Heads, 1957, The Country Wife, 1957, All the Way Home, 1960, Great Day in the Morning, 1962, Ballad of the Sad Cafe, 1963; also Taming of the Shrew, appearances Macbeth, Hello and Goodbye, Good Woman of Setzuan, Children of Darkness, Moon for the Misbegotten, The Big Coca-Cola Swamp in the Sky, Mourning Becomes Electra; appearances with N.Y. Shakespeare Festival; motion picture appearance in The Nun's Story, 1959, McQ, 1974, Annie Hall, 1977 Ice Castles, 1979, When a Stranger Calls, 1977, Final Assignment, 1980, Tribute, 1980; numerous TV appearances, 1957—. Dir. Broadway play, Ned and Jack, 1981. Recipient Obie award, 1957, 63; Lola D'Annunzion award, 1961, Tony award, 1961, 74, Sylvania award, 1960, Theatre World award, Sarah Siddons award for A Moon for the Misbegotten, 1974. Address: care STE Representation Ltd 888 7th Ave New York NY 10019 *

DEWITT, SANDRA LOU, fin. exec.; b. Bremerton, Wash., Feb. 2, 1944; d. Miles Eugene and Billie Elizabeth (McLean) Hurley; student public schs., Garden Grove, Calif.; m. William Albert DeWitt, Dec. 30, 1961; children—Rebecca Sue, William Albert. Sec., claims examiner RIMCO, Dallas, 1972-73; casualty claims supr. Am. PetroFina Co. of Tex., Dallas, 1973-77; dir. ins. and risk mgmt. Ramada Inns, Inc., Phoenix, 1977—. Bd. dirs., sec. Ramada Inn Employee Credit Union, 1980—. Mem. Risk and Ins. Mgmt. Soc. (chpt. v.p. 1981-82, pres. 1982—), Am. Bus. Women's Assn., Am. Soc. Profl. and Exec. Women, Nat. Assn. Female Execs., Ariz. Assn. Ins. Adjusters. Republican. Methodist. Club: Order Eastern Star. Home: 5034 E Columbine Dr Scottsdale AZ 85254 Office: 3838 E Van Buren St Phoenix AZ 85001

DEWOLFE, RUTHANNE KATHARINE SOBOTA, lawyer, psychologist; b. Milw., Aug. 14, 1933; d. Erich Max and Mary Elizabeth (Stork) Sobota; student Oberlin Coll., 1951-52; B.A., Heidelberg Coll., 1954; M.S., Northwestern U., 1958, Ph.D., 1960; J.D. summa cum laude, DePaul U., 1976; m. Alan Steyart DeWolfe, Aug. 24, 1952; children—Kyle Arend, Hillary Stuart, Elena Maria. Staff psychologist Hines (Ill.) VA Hosp., 1960-62; pvt. practice psychology, Evanston, Ill., 1962—; admitted to Ill. bar, 1976; staff atty. Legal Assistance Found., 1976-77; regional counsel U.S. Commn. on Civil Rights, Chgo., 1977-80; supervising atty. Legal Assistance Found., 1980—; adj. prof. U. Ill., Chgo., 1980—. Cert. psychologist, Pa.; registered psychologist, Ill. Mem. Am. Psychol. Assn., Am. Bar Assn., Ill. Bar Assn., Chgo. Bar Assn., Women's Bar Assn., Am. Judicature Soc., Am. Trial Lawyers Assn., AAAS, John Howard Assn. (dir. 1980—), Lex Legio, Sigma Xi. Contbr. articles to profl. jours. Home: 811 Colfax St Evanston IL 60201

DEWS-WOOD, DEBORAH, transp. co. mgr.; b. Roanoke, Va., Dec. 22, 1949; d. Hunter Ernest Dews and Louise Annette (Casey) Dews Ramsay; student Miami Dade Jr. Coll., 1968-69; B.A., Fla. State U., 1972; m. Richard A. Wood. Passenger service rep. Amtrak, Miami, 1972-74, specialist station services, Washington, 1974-75, supr. timetables, 1975-76, chief sta. facilities and ops., 1976-80, mgr. sta. ops., 1980—. Pres. bd. dirs. Georgetown Village Community Assn., 1979-81, treas., 1982—. Mem. Fla. State U. Alumni Assn. Republican. Home: 2901 Wetherburn Ct Woodbridge VA 22191 Office: 400 N Capitol St Washington DC 20001

DEXTER, HELEN LOUISE, dermatologist; b. Cin., July 28, 1908; d. William Jordan and Katherine (Weston) Taylor; A.B., Bryn Mawr Coll., 1930; M.D., Columbia U., 1937; postgrad. U. Cin. Coll. Medicine, 1948-50; m. Morrie W. Dexter, Jan. 27, 1937; children—Katharine, Helen, Elizabeth Taylor Dexter Potsubay, William Taylor. Intern, Jersey City Med. Center, 1938-39; internist Cin. Babies Milk Fund, Maternal Health Clinic, 1938-45; clinician U. Cin. Med. Sch., 1938-48, lectr. dept. dermatology, 1948-53; practice medicine specializing in dermatology, Clearwater, Fla., 1954—; dermatology cons. VA, 1955—; investigation of carcinogenic effects of shale oil U.S. Bur. Mines, Rifle, Colo., 1950. Mem. Clearwater Power Squadron Aux.; bd. dirs. Girls Clubs Pinellas County; commr. Town of Belleair, 1980. Recipient Ina Clay trophy Intercollegiate Ski Champion, 1928-30. Mem. AMA, Soc. Investigation Dermatology, Am. Acad. Dermatology, S.E. Dermatol. Assn. (v.p. 1963-64), Fla. Dermatol. Soc. (pres. 1959), Fla. Soc. Dermatology (pres.), Noah Worcester Dermatol. Soc., Am. Archaeol. Soc., Pan-Am. Dermatol. Soc., Soc. Tropical Dermatology. Presbyterian. Club: Clearwater Yacht Carlovel Yacht. Contbr. articles to profl. jours. Address: 409 Bayview Dr Belleair FL 33516

DEYA, LOURDES LENDIAN (MRS. JOSE MIGUEL DEYA), educator; b. Havana, Cuba, Oct. 23, 1925; came to U.S., 1961, naturalized; d. Armando R. Lendian and Alicia L. Colon; student Randolph Macon Woman's Coll., 1943-46, U. Havana, 1959-61; B.A., La. State U., 1962, M.S. in L.S., 1963, postgrad. 1966-67; Second Lang. Specialist degree in French, U. Paul Valery, Montpellier, France, 1977. m. Jose Miguel Deya, Feb. 3, 1950; children—Michael (dec.), George, Alice. Tchr., Dept. Edn., Havana, 1949-61; asst. cataloger La. State Library, Baton Rouge, 1964-66; prof. cataloging and classification La. State U., Baton Rouge, 1967—, instr. library sci. Coll. Edn., 1971—; faculty adviser La. State U. Library Sch. Grad. Assn., 1969—; cons. on sch. libraries to Govt. Peru, 1972; symposium speaker Inst. Latin-Am. Studies of U. Tex. at Austin—OAS, 1974; speaker So. Conf. Lang. Teaching, 1975; cons. on centralized cataloging, Mex., Spain, 1976. U.S. Office Edn. fellow, 1966-67, summer 69. Mem. Baton Rouge Library Club, ALA, AAUP, AAUW, La. Tchrs. Assn., MLA, NEA, La. Edn. Assn., L'Asamble Francaise, Southwestern, La. library assns., Sacred Heart Alumnae Assn. (pres. 1968-70), KC Ladies Aux., Phi Lambda Pi, Phi Sigma Iota, Sigma Delta Pi, Alpha Beta Alpha. Contbr. articles to profl. jours. Home: 5785 Glenwood Dr Baton Rouge LA 70806 Office: Middleton Library Room 230D Baton Rouge LA 70803

DEYMIER, EILEEN ALEXANDRA, editor; b. N.Y.C., Feb. 11, 1944; d. Anthony Robert and Marie Dolores (Baltar) D.; cert. The Lab. Inst. Merchandising, 1965. Asst. buyer Asso. Merchandising Corp., N.Y.C., 1965-66; dept. mgr. jr. sportswear and dresses The Bon Marche, Seattle, 1966-67; fashion dir. Jacobson's, Ann Arbor, Mich., 1967-69; free lance field editor representing Better Homes & Gardens, Women's Day, House Beautiful, Good Ideas for Decorating, Homeowner's How To mags., Washington, Balt., Annapolis, Richmond, 1970—. Vice-pres., bd. dirs. Pavilion in Common, Inc.; dir. Sustaining Fund, Columbia Pro Cantare Chorus. Mem. Nat. Assn. Female Execs., Nat. Home Fashions League, Am. Soc. Profl. and Exec. Women. Episcopalian. Office: 5135 MacArthur Blvd NW Washington DC 20016

DEYOUNG, LILLIAN JEANETTE, nurse educator; R.N., Thomas Dee Hosp., Utah, 1947; B.S. in Nursing Edn., U. Utah, 1950, M.S. in Ednl. Adminstrn., 1955, Ph.D. in Ednl. Adminstrn., 1975. Assoc. dir. nursing edn. Latter Day Saints Hosp., Salt Lake City, 1954-55; dir. Sch. Nursing St. Luke's Hosp., Denver, 1955-72; assoc. prof., curriculum coordinator Intercollegiate Center for Nursing Edn., Spokane, 1972-73; asst. dir. nursing service U. Utah Med. Center, Salt Lake City, 1973-75; prof. nursing U. Akron, Ohio, 1975—, also dean; mem. council deans Ohio Bd. Regents; mem. State of Ohio Bd. Nursing Edn. and Nurse Registration, 1979—, v.p. 1980-82, pres., 1982-83. Trustee Akron Gen. Med. Center, 1978—. Mem. Ohio League Nursing, Midwest Alliance in Nursing, Am. Nurses Assn., Ohio Nurses Assn., Nat. League Nursing (exec. com. council baccalaureate and higher degree program 1981-83, task force on structure 1982-83), ARC, Am. Assn. Higher Edn., Sigma Theta Tau. Author: Foundations of Nursing as Conceived, Learned, and Practiced in Professional Nursing, 1966, 72, 76; Dynamics of Nursing, 1981. Home: 711 Lafayette Dr Akron OH 44303 Office: 209 Carroll St Akron OH 44325

DEZWARTE, MARY CAROLYN, social services adminstr.; b. Elberton, Ga., Apr. 8, 1922; d. James Phillip and Myrtle (Purcell) Carithers; student W. Ga. Jr. Coll., 1939-41, U. Ga., 1941; postgrad. U. Del., 1970-71, 72-74, Ga. State U., 1974, Fed. City Coll., 1974-75, U. N.C., 1968; m. Virgil LaVerne DeZwarte, Sept. 23, 1945; children—Cheryl Lynn, Muriel Lee. Owner, operator nursery sch., Peru, Nebr., 1955-59; asst. comptroller Nebr. State Coll., Peru, 1959-62; asst. dir. public relations Wesley Coll., Dover, Del., 1962-65; sec./payroll clk. Scotton Contracting Co., Dover, Del., 1965-67; dir. Rehab. Homebound Elderly, Dover, Del., 1967—. Vol., VA Hosps., 1947—; pres. Am. Legion Aux., 1952-53, V.F.W. Aux., 1959; mem. Del. Task Force on Aging, 1968; co-chmn. Kent County White House Conf. on Aging, 1970; pres. Del. Aging Projects Assn., 1974-75; mem. Kent County Task Force on Aging, 1973; mem. Kent County Adv. Bd. on Aging, 1972; mem. Del. Nursing Home Quality Care Com., 1979-81; rep. Nat. Council Activity Coordinators, 1977; county committeewoman Republican party, 1965-72. Recipient Winthrop Rockefeller's Nat. Rural award, 1980. Mem. Nat. Council Aging, Nat. Remotivation Assn., Am. Assn. Ret. Persons, Nat. Therapeutic Recreation Assn., Del. Gerontol. Soc., Del. Aging Projects Assn. Office: 42 Kings Hwy E Dover DE 19901

DEZZUTTI, IDA MARIE, speech and lang. pathologist; b. Uniontown, Pa., Oct. 13, 1948; d. Dante and Regina Marie (Cupelli) Leoni; B.S., Carlow Coll., 1970; M.Ed., Calif. State Coll., 1973; m. Ronald John Dezzutti, Sept. 25, 1976; 1 son, Jonathan Ronald. Tchr., Headstart, Uniontown, Pa., summer 1970; speech and lang. pathologist Allegheny Intermediate Unit III, Pitts., 1970-79; speech and lang. pathologist Miners Clinic, New Kensington, Pa., 1976-80, Vis. Nurses Assn., Export, Pa., 1979—. Recipient cert. of clin. competence Am. Speech and Hearing Assn. Mem. NEA, Pa. state Edn. Assn., Allegheny Intermediate Unit Spl. Service Educators, Delta Kappa Gamma. Roman Catholic. Office: Martin Ave New Kensington PA 15068

D'HARNONCOURT, ANNE, museum curator; b. Washington, Sept. 7, 1943; d. René and Sarah (Carr) d'Harnoncourt; B.A., Radcliffe Coll., 1965; M.A. with distinction, Courtauld Inst. Art, U. London, 1967; m. Joseph J. Rishel, June 19, 1971. Curatorial asst. Phila. Mus. Art, 1967-69; asst. curator 20th Century Art, Art Inst. Chgo., 1969-71; curator 20th Century painting Phila. Mus. Art, 1971—. Mem. Phi Beta Kappa. Author (with Walter Hopps): Reflection on a New Work by Marcel Duchamp, 1969. Editor (with Kynaston McShine): Marcel Duchamp, 1973. Office: Philadelphia Museum of Art PO Box 7646 Philadelphia PA 19101 *

DHOLAKIA, RUBY ROY, educator; b. Calcutta, India, Feb. 16, 1948; came to U.S. 1963; d. Somendra Nath and Saila Rani Roy; B.S. in Bus. Adminstrn., U. Calif., Berkeley, 1967, M.B.A., 1969; Ph.D., Northwestern U., 1976; m. Nikhilesh Dholakia, Aug. 30, 1974; 1 son, Ritik. Mktg. analyst Wells Fargo Bank, San Francisco 1969; asst. prof. Indian Inst. Mgmt., Calcutta 1970-73, 76-78; vis. faculty Indian Inst. Mgmt., Ahmedabad, 1977-79; assoc. prof. Kans. State U., 1979-81; assoc. prof. U. R.I., 1981—; cons. in field of consumer research. Am. Mgmt. Assn. fellow, 1975; AAAA fellow 1982. Mem. Am. Mktg. Assn., Assn. Consumer Research. Contbr. articles in field to profl. jours. Office: PO Box 279 Kingston RI 02881 also Ballentine Hall University of Rhode Island Kingston RI 02881

DIAL, CAROLINE DICK (MRS. GEORGE LOUIS DIAL), civic worker; b. Sumter, S.C., July 15, 1900; d. George William and Caroline (Hutchison) Dick; B.A., Winthrop Coll., 1921; postgrad. U. Wis., summer 1928-29, U. S.C., summer 1939-40; LL.D. (hon.), U. S.C., 1969; m. J. Rion McKissick, May 18, 1927 (dec. Sept. 1944); m. 2d, Irvine Furman Belser, June 21, 1947 (dec. Aug. 1969); m. 3d, George Louis Dial, Oct. 3, 1976. Tchr., High Point (N.C.) Grammar Sch., 1921-23, Greenville (S.C.) High Sch., 1923-24, Sumter High Sch., 1924-26. Dir. Alice Mfg. Co., 1945—. Mem. Columbia Jr. League, 1929-40, sustaining mem., 1940—, founder Jr. League Book Club; pres. Dept. S.C., Am. Legion Aux., 1946-47, founder Palmetto Girls' State, 1947, pres. Unit Post 6, 1950-51, nat. v.p. So. div., 1953-54, only life mem. of Girls' State Com.; v.p. Garden Club S.C., 1956-59, chmn. Gardening Symposium, 1960-65. Vice chmn. Democratic Com. S.C., 1960-64. Charter mem. bd. assos. Converse Coll., 1962—; rep. Diocese Upper S.C., Nat. Cathedral Assn., 1962-65; mem. U. S.C. Found., Found. Chair Club, chmn., 1973-74; pres. U. S.C. Caroliniana Soc., 1954-60; chmn. bd. women visitors U. S.C., 1960—; mem. S.C. Am. Mother's Com. Recipient Algernon Sidney Sullivan award, 1951; Hon. S.C. State Mother award, 1968; past col., staff of Gov. Strom Thurmond. Disting. Alumnus award U. S.C., 1972. Mem. English Speaking Union, Mus. of Art, Richland County, Sumter County hist. socs., LWV; hon. mem. S.C. Press Assn. (pres. womens div. 1968-69), U. S.C. Aux., Mortar Board, Tau Kappa Alpha. Episcopalian (pres. Daus. of Holy Cross 1957-59). Clubs: Fortnightly Book (pres. 1944-45), New Century Book, Evening Music. Home: 15 Heathwood Circle Columbia SC 29205

DIAL, ELEANORE MAXWELL, educator; b. Norwich, Conn., Feb. 21, 1929; d. Joseph Walter and Irene (Beetham) Maxwell; B.A., U. Bridgeport (Conn.), 1951; M.A. in Spanish, Mexico City Coll., 1955; Ph.D., U. Mo., 1968; m. John E. Dial, Aug. 27, 1959. Mem. faculty U. Wisc.-Milw., 1968-75, Ind. State U., Terre Haute, 1975-78, Bowling Green (Ohio) State U., 1978-79; asst. prof. dept. fgn. langs. and lits. Iowa State U., Ames, 1979—; reader Latin Am. Theatre Rev., 1973—; cons. pub. co.; participant workshops; del. 1st World Congress Women Journalists and Writers, Mex., 1975, also mem. edn. commn. NDEA grantee, 1967; Center Latin Am. grantee, 1972; Nat. Endowment Humanities summer seminar UCLA, 1982. Mem. Am. Assn. Tchrs. Spanish and Portuguese, Midwest MLA, MLA, N. Central Council Latin Americanists, Midwest Assn. Latin Am. Studies, Caribbean Studies Assn., Phi Sigma Iota, Sigma Delta Pi. Contbr. articles and revs. to scholarly jours. Home: 3219 Ross Rd Ames IA 50010 Office: Iowa State U Ames IA 50010

DIAL, ETHEL FERGUSON, nurse; b. Rixeyville, Va., July 23, 1933; d. Hugh Maxwell and Philippine Mozelle (Anderson) Ferguson; diploma Lincoln Sch. Nurses, Bronx, N.Y., 1958; student Howard U., 1962-64; cert. U. Pitts., 1979; m. William Haywood Dial, Dec. 30, 1954; children—Karen I. Dial Thorne, Glynn Arwin, Ansia Nadia, Kevin Enoch. Staff nurse NIMH, 1958-63; staff nurse Area C Community Mental Health Center, Washington, 1963-65, head nurse, 1965-68; coordinator mental health unit Detention Facility for Juveniles, Washington, 1969—. Asst. sec. Eugene Clark Elementary Sch. PTA, Washington, 1976-78; bd. dirs. D.C. Govt. Fed. Credit Union; active Police Boys and Girls Club, Wade Sch., Washington. Mem. Am. Correctional Assn., D.C. Nurses Assn., Nat. Council Negro Women, NAACP, PUSH, Nat. Urban League. Baptist. Office: 1000 Mount Olivet Rd NE Washington DC 20002

DIAL, MAUREEN, home econs. extension agt. and adminstr.; b. Robeson County, N.C., Feb. 11, 1944; d. Danford and Reece (Graham) Dial; B.S. in Home Econs. Edn., Pembroke State U., 1965; occupational and vocat. cert. U. N.C., Greensboro, 1969; M.S. in Home Econs. Edn., N.C. Central U., 1975. Tchr. home econs., supr. student tchrs., dir. individualized instrn. program Pembroke (N.C.) Sr. High Sch., 1965-72, 74-77; dir. house mgmt., supr. student tchrs., instr. N.C. Central U., Durham, N.C., 1972-73; Robeson asso. home econs. extension agt. N.C. U. Agr. Extension Service, Lumberton, 1977-81; home econs. program leader Coop. Extension Assn., Cornell U., 1981—; dir. Snowflake Shoppe; cons. Robeson County Energy Com., 1977-81. Sec., Robeson County Rural Devel. Panel, Inter-Agy. Com. for Sch. and Community Devel. Robeson County. Recipient award Lumbee Regional Devel. Assn., 1979, Little Miss Pageant, 1979; Am. Indian scholar, 1972-73. Mem. Am. Home Econs. Assn., N.C. Home Econs. Assn., N.Y. Home

Econs. Assn., Nat. Assn. Extension Home Economists, N.C. Assn. Extension Home Economists, N.Y. Assn. Extension Home Economists. Democrat. Baptist. Home: 15 Adams St Salamanca NY 14779 Office: Coop Extension Center Parkside Dr Ellicottville NY 14731

DIALECTIC, GLORIA, feminist therapist; b. Allentown, Pa.; d. Ammon Clinton and Violet Agnes (Nagle) Roth; A.B., Muhlenberg Coll., 1963; M.A. (NDEA fellow), Lehigh U., 1969, Ph.D., 1973; children—Mark Edward Dussinger, Fay Estelle Dussinger. Instr., Muhlenberg Coll., 1970-71; adj. prof. Northampton County Area Community Coll., 1975; intern in psychotherapy Tulsa Psychiat. Center, 1978-79; counselor, casework supr. HELPline, Community Service Council, Tulsa, Reproductive Services, Tulsa; group therapist Arthritis Found., Tulsa; pvt. practice therapy; vol. therapist and counselor various groups, 1974, 77; speaker in field. Mem. Assn. Women in Psychology, Assn. Poetry Therapy, Women Without Walls, Assn. for Advancement Ethical Hypnosis, Am. Mental Health Counselors Assn., Am. Personnel and Guidance Assn., Nat. Abortion Rights Action League. Home: 2508 E 8th St Tulsa OK 74104

DIAMOND, ADELINA, public affairs exec., writer; b. Chgo., Oct. 9, 1927; d. Herbert C. and Jennie (Friedman) Lust; A.B., U. Chgo., 1947; M.P.A., N.Y. U., 1972; m. Edwin Diamond, Dec. 5, 1949; children—Ellen, Franna, Louise. Sportswear buyer Mandel Bros., Chgo., 1947-49, advt. copywriter, 1949-50; fashion reporter Womens Wear Daily, Chgo., 1950-52; editor Hyde Park Herald, Chgo., 1953-56; v.p. Edwin and Adelina Diamond Assos., communications and public affairs, N.Y.C., 1969—; asso. Center for Housing Partnerships, N.Y.C., 1970-72; Eastern public affairs rep. U. Chgo., 1972-78; dir. public relations Carnegie Council on Children, 1978-80; founding mem. Women U.S.A., Friends of NOW, N.Y.C.; founder, chairperson Friends of ERA. Home: 20 Waterside Plaza New York NY 10010

DIAMOND, CORA ANN, educator; b. N.Y.C., Oct. 30, 1937; d. Abraham and Sylvia (Goldhaar) D.; B.A., Swarthmore Coll., 1957; B.Phil., Oxford U., 1961. Asst. lectr. Univ. Coll. Swansea, 1961-62, U. Sussex, 1962-63; lectr. moral philosophy U. Aberdeen (Scotland), 1963-71; asso. prof. philosophy U. Va., 1971-82, prof. philosophy, 1982—. Am. Council Learned Socs. fellow, 1976-1977; Woodrow Wilson fellow, 1957-58. Mem. Am. Philos. Assn., Aristotelian Soc. Editor: Wittgenstein's Lectures on the Foundations of Mathematics, 1976; editor (With Jenny Teichman) Intention and Intentionality, Essays in Honour of G.E.M. Anscombe, 1979. Home: 655 Kearsarge Circle Charlottesville VA 22901 Office: Dept Philosophy U Va Charlottesville VA 22901

DIAMOND, DIANA LOUISE, editor; b. Floral Park, N.Y., Feb. 4, 1937; d. Louis Bartholomew and Helen Stephanie (Strzelecki) Chmielewski; student Middlebury (Vt.) Coll., 1954-56; B.A. in English, U. Mich., 1958; m. Horace Williams Diamond, Jr., June 29, 1958 (div. Dec. 1975); children—Bruce, Scott, Kent, Mark. Editorial asst. dept. higher edn. NEA, 1958-59; art tchr. pvt. students, 1964-68; reporter Pioneer Press, Highland Park, Ill., 1969-70; with Lerner Newspapers, Highland Park, 1970-78, mng. editor, 1972-78, suburban coordinator, 1974-78; editorial writer, mem. editorial bd. San José Mercury News, 1979-81, editor Sunday Opinion sect., 1979-81; editor-in-chief Calif. Lawyer, publ. Calif. Bar Assn., San Francisco, 1981—; part-time corr. New York Times, 1975-78; exhibited in one-woman shows in Sunnyvale and Palo Alto, Calif., 1964-68. Moderator, co-producer LWV television program Left, Right and Center, 1968, bd. dirs., com. chmn. Central Santa Clara Valley chpt., 1965-68; exec. sec. Midpeninsula Citizens for Fair Housing, 1966-68; pres. Sunnyvale Newcomers Club, 1962, W.Valley Parent Pre-Sch., 1963-64; v.p. Sunnyvale Fine Arts Assn., Hollenbeck Homeowners Assn., 1965; chmn. art San Francisco Peninsula for 1967 KQED-TV auction; organizer Citizens for Mut. Understanding, So. San Francisco Peninsula; bd. dirs. Calif. Republican League, 1962-64, del. San Francisco Conv., 1964; precinct committeeman, 1964-66; active Sunnyvale Bond Com., 1966, Sunnyvale Citizens Adv. Com., 1967, Deerfield Human Relations Commn., 1969; pres. Deerfield Area Human Relations Com., 1969-70; bd. dirs. Chgo. Philharm. Soc., 1977—. Recipient 3d place Ill. Editor of Yr. Contest, 1974, 1st place for best feature story Ill. Press Assn., 1974, 3d place for best editorials, 1974; Nat. Blue Ribbon Newspaper award, 1976, 77, 2d place best column Nat. Newspaper Assn., 1977; cert. excellence best feature story Suburban Newspapers Am., 1977. Nat. Endowment for the Humanities profl. fellow Stanford U., 1978-79. Mem. Chgo. Council Fgn. Relations, Sigma Delta Chi. Home: 4146 Thain Way Palo Alto CA 94306 Office: 555 Franklin St San Francisco CA 94102

DIAMOND, HINDI ALTMAN, mag. editor; b. N.Y.C., Sept. 11; d. Saul and Esther (Kijewski) Altman; student C.Z. (Panama) Jr. Coll., 1947-49, U. Miami (Fla.), 1966-69; children—Linda, Stephen, Mark. Reporter, photographer Panama Am., daily English newspaper, 1951-58; Panama corr. for McGraw-Hill Co. and Vision mag., 1951-61; founder, editor Industria Turistica mag. Diamond Pub. Co., South Miami, Fla., 1957—; pres., pub. Jewel Books; pub., editor Panama/This Month, 1958-65; free-lance writer for Miami Herald, Miami News, also other newspapers, 1966-68. Bd. dirs. Am. Jewish Com., 1966-68, 69-71, editor Newsletter, 1969-71. Mem. Am. Soc. Mag. Photographers (chmn. Fla. chpt. 1960—), Women in Communication (pres. Miami chap., 1982-83), Coral Gables C. of C. (public relations dir., sec., bd. dir., 1980-82). Author: Your Name in the News, 1974; Invitation to a Riot, 1982. Home: 2955 Whitehead St PO Box 1701 Coconut Grove FL 33133 Office: Industria Turistica Box 52 South Miami FL 33143

DIAMOND, LOUISA TORREZ, educator; b. N.Y.C., July 13, 1930; d. Max T. and Emma (Meshoulam) Tassler; student Universidad de las Americas, Pueblo, Mexico, 1954-55, 63-64; A.A., Los Angeles Pierce Coll., 1970-72; B.A. summa cum laude, Calif. State U., 1976; postgrad. U. So. Calif., 1976-79; m. Donald A. Diamond, Aug. 1, 1965; 1 dau., Maxine R. Diamond; children by previous marriage—Fortuna Israel, Emily Israel. Tchr., Lang. Acad., Universidad Autonoma Mexico, Mexico City, 1959-63; owner, mgr. Creaciones Fortuna S.A., Mexico City, 1963-65; tchr. English as second language, Spanish Community Adult Sch. Area 8 In-Service, Los Angeles Unified Sch. Dist., 1971-78; tchr. Grant High Sch., 1982—, Reseda Community Adult Sch., 1982—; instr. Calif. State U., Northridge, 1976-78. Recipient Outstanding Ednl. Leadership award Los Angeles Unified Sch. Dist., 1980, First Pl. award for abstract oil painting Northridge Cultural Arts and Hist. Assn., 1970. Mem. United Tchrs. Los Angeles. Clubs: Latin Am. (Los Angeles); City of Hope. Home: 18284 Karen Dr Tarzana CA 91356 Office: 13000 Oxnard St Van Nuys CA 91401

DIAMOND, ROBIN GAY, pub. co. adminstr.; b. Cleve., Sept. 21, 1944; d. Albert E. Winston and Miriam J. Mandell; student Calif. State U., Northridge, 1962-63, 81-82, Santa Monica City Coll., 1966-67, Pierce Community Coll., 1974-75; m. Stephen E. Diamond, Dec. 27, 1981; children by previous marriage—Lisa Michelle Erickson, Stephanie Diane Erickson. Exec. sec. with Dean Witter, Reynolds, Encino, Calif., 1976-77; adminstrv. asst. Paine Webber, Encino, 1977-79; supr. personnel and adminstrn. NILS Pub. Co., Chatsworth, Calif., 1979-81, mgr. adminstrn., 1981—. Mem. Nat. Assn. Female Execs., NOW, Nat. Notary Assn., ABC Employees Assn. (bd. dirs., 1980). Office: 20675 Bahama St Chatsworth CA 91311

DIAMOND, RUTH LOIS, civic worker; b. Albany, N.Y., Oct. 4, 1930; d. William H. and Bess (Sadosky) Abramson; student Met. Jr. Coll., Kansas City, Mo., 1948-49; B.J., U. Mo., 1952, postgrad., 1978—; m. Myron S. Diamond, June 27, 1954; 1 son, Michael Wayne. Advt. copywriter Kansas City Star, 1952, Mid-Continent Jeweler, Kansas City, 1952-54; sec.-treas. Myron S. Diamond, Co., Inc., Kansas City, Mo., 1960—; pres. Young Matron's Group, Hadassah, Kansas City, 1958-59, v.p. fund-raising Kansas City chpt., 1977; pres. Beth Horon chpt. B'nai B'rith Women, 1970-72, cons. Dist. 2, 1975-77, pres. Greater Kansas City (Mo.) Council, 1977-78, mem. regional bd., 1978—; editor Gateway regional newsletter The Gatepost, 1978—; pres. sisterhood Ohev Sholom synagogue, Prairie Village, Kans., 1974-76, religious sch. tchr., 1970—, synagogue bd. dirs., 1976—; tchr. United Religious Sch., 1976-79, Community Religious Sch., 1979—; editor organizational newspapers. Mem. Anti-Defamation League of B'nai B'rith; mem. coordinating council of Sisterhoods (Temple and Synagogue) and Ohev Sholom Centennial Com.; mem. steering com. Mo. Humanities Com., 1978; free lance writer; communications cons.; dir. local prodns. Recipient Honor award State of Israel Bonds, 1977, Dist. awards for community service and newspaper editing B'nai B'rith Women. Mem. Women in Communications, U. Mo. Alumni Assn., Phi Sigma Sigma, Alpha Epsilon Rho. Home: 8217 Briar St Prairie Village KS 66208

DIAMOND, SUSAN Z., mgmt. cons.; b. Okla., Aug. 20, 1949; d. Louis Edward and Henrietta (Wood) D.; A.B. (Nat. Merit scholar, GRTS scholar), U. Chgo., 1970; M.B.A., DePaul U., 1979; m. Allan T. Devitt, July 27, 1974. Dir. study guide prodn. Am. Sch. Co., Chgo., 1972-75; publs. supr. Allied Van Lines, Broadview, Ill., 1975-78, sr. account services rep., 1978-79; pres. Diamond Assocs. Ltd., Melrose Park, Ill., 1978—; condr. seminars Am. Mgmt. Assn. Mem. Nat. Assn. Women Bus. Owners, Nat. Assn. Accts., Internat. Assn. Bus. Communicators, Adminstrv. Mgmt. Soc., Assn. Records Mgrs. and Adminstrs., Bus. Forms Mgmt. Assn., Delta Mu Delta. Author: How to Talk More Effectively, 1972; Preparing Administrative Manuals, 1981; How to Manage Administrative Operations, 1981; How to be an Effective Secretary in the Modern Office, 1982; 1982; editor Mobility Trends, 1975-78. Office: 2851 N Pearl St Melrose Park IL 60160

DIARD, CAY BERMINGHAM, bldg. contractor; b. Chgo., Dec. 27, 1930; d. Alfred Joseph and Marie Barbara (Skord) Taddei; Charles Bermingham, Dec. 31, 1948 (dec.); children—Charles, Clifford, Clyde, Chris, Cary, Cheri; m. 2d, Ted A. Diard, July 19, 1980. Asso. acct. William Perkins Co., Chicago Heights, Ill., 1961-64; pvt. practice acctg. Ability Acctg., Hazelcrest, Ill., 1964-71; v.p., dir. Tilco Internat., Inc., Melbourne, Fla. and Tilco, Inc., Palm Bay, Fla., 1972-79, pres., dir., 1979—; realtor-asso. Nat. Realty, Palm Bay, 1982—; co-instr. contractors prep. course Brevard Community Coll., 1979, 80. Mem. Am. Bus. Womens Assn. (charter v.p. 1978), Home Builders Assn. Brevard, Profl. Women's Orgn., Nat. Assn. Home Builders. Democrat. Roman Catholic. Home: 2121 SW Brantley St Palm Bay FL 32905 Office: 136 NW Babcock St Palm Bay FL 32905

DIAZ, MYRIAM, film distbr.; b. Honduras, Jan. 19, 1940; naturalized, 1967; d. Max and Ana (Laffite) Rivas; C.P.A., Coll. Manuel La Bonilla Honduras, 19 ; m. Nelson Diaz, Nov. 5, 1960; children—Nelson, Ronald, David. Chief acct. Embassy Pictures Overseas Corp., Los Angeles, 1961-75; Latin Am. supr. Rizzoli Film Distbrs., 1975-77, mng. dir., 1977—, now also head world wide sales. Home: 84-20 55th Ave Elmhurst NY 11373 Office: 712 Fifth Ave New York NY 10019

DIBELIUS, NANCY ELIZABETH, mfg. co. exec.; b. Rhinebeck, N.Y., Jan. 3, 1951; d. George James and Marie Lucinda (Cookingham) Masterson; student Goethe Inst., Munich, W. Ger., 1969; B.A. in English and Sociology, SUNY, Albany, 1972; cert. women in mgmt. program Union Coll., 1976, M.S. in Indsl. Adminstrn., 1978; m. David Richard Dibelius, Mar. 31, 1973. Specialist in advanced systems studies Gen. Electric Co., Schenectady, 1972-74, specialist in project planning, 1974-76, resource adminstr., 1976-80, program adminstr., combustion bldg. expansion, 1980-81, program adminstr. process evaluation facility, 1981—. Mem. NOW, Nat. Assn. Female Execs., YWCA, Nat. Wildlife Fedn., United Meth. Women, Project Mgmt. Inst., Gen. Electric Women's Forum (co-founder), No. N.Y. Paddlers, Eastern Ski Assn. Club: Schenectady Wintersports (dir.). Home: MacElroy Rd Ballston Lake NY 12019 Office: K-1/Combustion PO Box 8 Schenectady NY 12301

DI BIETZ, ERICA MARGRETHE, mental health advocate, adminstr.; b. N.Y.C., Nov. 2, 1935; d. August and Elizabeth (Hutka) DiBietz; B.A., Columbia U., 1955; M.S.W. (John F. Kennedy fellow), U. Md., 1976; children—Regina Antunes, Lisette Antunes, Alexander Antunes. Asst. to sec. for trust and estate law Trust div. N.Y. State Bankers Assn., N.Y.C., 1956-59; tchr. child life, counselor Johns Hopkins Hosp., Balt., 1973-74, mem. women's bd., 1966—; med. social worker John F. Kennedy Inst. Habilitation of Children, Balt., 1974-75; adminstrv. officer Md. Dept. Health and Mental Hygiene, Springfield Hosp. Center, Sykesville, Md., 1977—, co-founder, co-leader, editor newsletter Family support group in state hosp., 1979—, chmn. staff devel. com., 1978-79; mem. patient adv. coms. Md. Atty. Gen.'s Office, 1979—; mem. continuing edn. com. U. Md., 1978-80. Mem. women's com. Balt. Symphony Orch., 1965-69; founder Dulaney Symphony Soc., 1968; del. public edn. nominating conv. Baltimore County Bd. Edn., 1977-78. HEW grantee, 1974; lic. cert. social worker, Md. Mem. Nat. Assn. Social Workers, Am. Assn. Mental Deficiency, Nat. Alliance for Mentally Ill. (edn. and curriculum com.), Md. Conf. Social Concern, Epilepsy Assn. of Md. (adv. bd.). Episcopalian. Author works in field. Home: 2309 Foxley Rd Timonium MD 21093 Office: Springfield Hosp Center Sykesville MD 21784

DI CASIMIRRO, DONNA MARIE, audiologist, mental retardation specialist; b. Shenandoah Heights, Pa., Dec. 24, 1954; d. Wassil Frank and Geraldine Ann (Joseph) DiC.; B.S., Marywood Coll., 1976; M.A., U. Fla., 1977. Clin. audiologist ENT Surg. Group, Kingston, Pa., part time 1978; hearing cons. Wyoming Valley Crippled Children's Center, Wilkes Barre, Pa., 1978; clin. and rehab. audiologist Hamburg (Pa.) Center, 1978-81, mental retardation unit mgr., 1981—; former hearing cons. Easter Seals of Schuylkill County, Frackville, Pa. Mem. Am. Speech, Lang. and Hearing Assn., Pa. Speech and Hearing Assn., Northeastern Speech and Hearing Assn. Pa., Nat. Fedn. Bus. and Profl. Women's Clubs (Young Careerist chairperson 1980—), Alexander Graham Bell Assn. Deaf, Centurions Deafness Research Found., Amer-Ind Code Internat. League Delta Epsilon Sigma, Kappa Gamma Pi. Roman Catholic. Home: 508 New Boston Mahanoy City PA 17948 Office: Dogwood Hall Hamburg Center Hamburg PA 19526

DICENZO, ELLA VIRGINIA, bank exec.; b. Pittsfield, Mass., Oct. 22, 1931; d. Salvatore Lawrence and Aquilina (Tangredi) DiC.; student Berkshire Bus. Coll., 1951, Am. Coll., 1975—, Berkshire Community Coll., 1979—. Cashier, office mgr. Berkshire Life Ins. Agy., Pittsfield, 1953-73; real estate broker Richard Tucker Assos., Pittsfield, 1973-74; mgr. life ins. dept. City Savs. Bank, Pittsfield 1974, asst. treas., 1974-76, asst. v.p., 1976—, mgr. life ins. dept., 1974—. Public relations chmn., bd. dirs. Pittsfield Girls' Club; sec., bd. dirs. Citizens Scholarship Found.; mem. allocations com., bd. dirs. United Way of Central Berkshire; public relations dir. five election campaigns State Senator Andrea Nuciforo, 1964-72; v.p. bd. dirs. Berkshire chpt. March of Dimes, 1970-77; co-chmn. YES, 1978-79; co-editor parish newspaper Mt. Carmel Roman Cath. Ch., Pittsfield. Mem. Mass. Ins. Women (pres. Berkshire chpt. 1971-73), Savs. Bank Life Ins. of Mass. Mgrs. Group (vice-chmn. 1979-80, chmn. 1981-82), Savs. Bank Forum of Berkshire County, Western Mass. Savs. Bank Life Ins. Group (past chmn.), Savs. Bank Women of Mass. Democrat. Home: 221 Robbins Ave Pittsfield MA 01201 Office: City Savs Bank 116 North St Pittsfield MA 01201

DICK, FLORENE FAYE, writer/photographer: b. Los Angeles, Jan. 18, 1922; d. Joseph and Wilhelmina Faye (Vivial) Harwich; student Los Angeles City Coll., 1939-41; m. George Oliver Perkins, Mar. 15, 1941 (dec. Apr. 1945); m. 2d, Ernest Lee Dick, Feb. 4, 1946; children—Virginia Faye Perkins Paschke, Barbara Lee Dick Enfield, Frank Joseph. Research librarian Wallace & Tiernan, Monrovia, Calif., 1955-57; editor/proofreader Stanford Research Inst., Menlo Park, Calif., 1959-61; tech. editor ElectroData Corp., Pasadena, Calif., 1961, Aerojet Electro-Systems Co., Azusa, Calif., 1961, 65-67, 78; lit. search editor Jet Propulsion Lab., Pasadena, 1962; sec. to Dr. Linus Pauling, Calif. Inst. Tech., Pasadena, 1963-64; med. sec. Childrens Hosp., Los Angeles, 1964; people editor, then editor Azusa Herald, 1967-73; news writer Citrus Coll., Azusa, 1973-74; freelance writer/photographer, 1972—; publs./news editor Pomona Coll., Claremont, Calif., 1974-76, 79-80; co-owner E.L. Dick Machine Shop, Upland, Calif., 1974—; staff writer/photographer West End Guide (now Night and Day Guide), Upland, Calif., 1980—; vol. proofreader Aid to Visually Handicapped, Pasadena, 1961-64. Bd. dirs. Calif. Clinic Sch., Puente, 1968-70; charter mem. aux. Foothill Presbyn. Hosp., Glendora, Calif., 1968; mem. prodn. com. Miss Azusa Pageant, also chaperone to Miss Calif. Pageant, Santa Cruz, Calif., 1967-72. Recipient various certs. merit. Mem. Press Club So. Calif. (charter), Nat. Fedn. Press Women, Calif. Press Women (1st pl. editor award 1973). Home: PO Box 1407 Upland CA 91786 Office: Night and Day Guide 1153 W 9th St Upland CA 91786

DICK, NANCY E., lt. gov. Colo.; b. Detroit, July 22, 1930; B.A. in Resort Mgmt., Mich. State U.; widowed; children—Margot, Timber, Justin. Worked in resort mgmt., conv. dir., interior design, bookkeeping; mem. Colo. Gen. Assembly, 1974-79, vice chmn. transp. and energy com.; lt. gov. of Colo., 1979—; past fin. chmn. Fedn. Rocky Mountain States; mem. adv. panel U.S. oil Shale Environ. Com.; mem. Colo. rural health com. Colo. Med. Soc. Democrat. Office: Office of Lt Gov State Capitol Bldg Room 144 Denver CO 80203 *

DICKEL, HÉLÈNE RAMSEYER, astronomer; b. Cambridge, Mass., Mar. 19, 1938; d. Frank Wells and Linda Chapin (Marcus) Ramseyer; A.B. magna cum laude, Mt. Holyoke Coll., 1959; M.A. in Astronomy (univ. scholar 1959-60), 1961, Ph.D. (Rackham fellow 1963-64), 1964; m. John Rush Dickel, June 17, 1961; children—Cynthia, Rebecca. Research assoc. astronomy U. Ill., Champaign-Urbana, 1965-70, 71-77, research assoc. prof., 1977—; vis. research fellow div. radiophysics Commonwealth Sci. and Indsl. Research Orgn., Australia, 1970-71; vis. astronomer Sterrewacht te Leiden, Netherlands, 1977-79; Harlow-Shapley vis. lectr., 1981-83. Mem. Internat. Sci. Radio Union, Internat. Astron. Union, Am. Astron. Soc., Astron. Soc. Pacific, Sierra Club, Phi Beta Kappa, Sigma Xi. Author numerous papers in field. Office: 341 U Ill Astronomy Bldg 1011 W Springfield Ave Urbana IL 61801

DICKENS, DORIS LEE (MRS. AUSTIN LECOUNT FICKLING), psychiatrist; b. Roxboro, N.C., Oct. 12; d. Lee Edward and Delma Ernestine (Hester) Dickens; B.S. magna cum laude, Va. Union U., 1960; M.D., Howard U., 1966; m. Austin LeCount Fickling, Oct. 15, 1975. Intern, St. Elizabeth's Hosp., Washington, 1966-67, resident, 1967-70; staff psychiatrist, dir. Mental Health Program for Deaf, St. Elizabeth's Hosp., Washington, after 1970, now chief program; cons. NIMH. Bd. dirs. Nat. Health Care Found. for Deaf. Recipient Dorothea Lynde Dix award, 1980; diplomate Nat. Bd. Med. Examiners. Mem. Am. Psychiat. Assn., Washington Psychiat. Soc., Profl. Rehab. Workers for Adult Deaf, Washington Soc. Adolescent Psychiatry, Alpha Kappa Mu, Beta Kappa Chi. Author: How and When Psychiatry Can Help You, 1972; You and Your Doctor; contbg. author: Hearing and Hearing Impairment, 1979; editor-in-chief Mental Health in Deafness; Home: 12308 Surrey Circle Tantallon MD 20022 Office: 2700 Martin L King Ave Washington DC 20032

DICKER, PHYLLIS DEBORAH, social worker; b. Bklyn., May 1, 1951; d. Sidney and Rosalind (Flatte) Dicker; B.S., Bklyn. Coll., 1976; M.S.W., N.Y.U., 1981. Lab. technician N.Y. Dept. Health, 1973-76; psychiat. social work South Beach Psychiat. Center, 1982—. Cert. social workers. Mem. NOW, Nat. Assn. Social Workers, Nat. Women's Health Network, Women Against Pornography. Home: 1312 E 83d St Brooklyn NY 11236 Office: 777 Seaview Ave Staten Island NY

DICKER, SUSANNE FORBES, real estate broker; b. San Antonio, Jan. 21, 1942; d. Ruby Laverne Doanne Schunk; B.A., SUNY, Geneseo, 1964; m. Albert P. Dicker, Dec. 1, 1967; children—Forbes, Kyle. With Neiman-Marcus, Dallas, 1965-69; pres. Shoppers' League Am., Inc., Dallas, 1977-79; realtor asso. Coldwell Banker Residential Brokerage Co., Dallas, 1979-81; asso. Nobel and Dunn, Realtors, 1981-82, Jan Nobel, Realtors, Dallas, 1982—. Mem. Dallas Mus. Fine Arts, Goals for Dallas; mem. nat. women's bd. Northwood Inst. Recipient co. awards. Mem. Exec. Women of Dallas, North Dallas C. of C., Greater Dallas Bd. Realtors. Methodist. Home: 9410 Moss Farm Ln Dallas TX 75243 Office: 6021 Berkshire Ln Dallas TX 75225

DICKERSON, BETTY JEAN, nurse; b. Cotton Plant, Ark., Dec. 16, 1936; d. Laurence Von and LaVerne Roddy; A.A. in Nursing, Ind. U., 1971; B.S. Nursing, Purdue U., 1976; M.S. in Restorative Nursing Govs. State U., 1980; m. Robert E. Dickerson, Jan. 8, 1954; children—Carolyn, Edward, Monteena. Staff nurse Our Lady of Mercy Hosp., Dyer, Ind., 1971; staff nurse pediatrics St. Mary Med. Center, Gary, Ind., 1971-75, asst. dir. nursing service, 1975—, instr. heart-lung assessment, 1977-79; instr. med. secs. Marion Bus. Coll., 1973-74; clin. nurse instr. Ind. U. N.W., 1980-81. Bd. dirs. Ind. U. N.W., 1981—, Hospice N.W. Ind., 1981—. Recipient Outstanding Nurse of Yr. award Ind. U., 1971. Mem. Ind. State, Am. nurses assns., Nat. League Nursing, Ind. U., Purdue U., Govs. State U. alumni assns., Ind. U. Nurses Soc. (alumni), Young Women's Christian Council. Author hosp. pediatrics teaching manual, 1974. Home: Gary IN 46404

DICKERSON, KITTY GARDNER, educator; b. Willis, Va., Mar. 30, 1940; d. Lonnie K. and Virginia K. Gardner; B.S., Va. Poly. Inst. and State U., 1962, M.S., 1963; Ph.D., St. Louis U., 1972, m. Harman C. Dickerson, Mar. 18, 1962; children—Derek Len, Donya Lyn. Adminstrv. asst. to v.p. Stix, Baer & Fuller, St. Louis, 1963-64; extension home economist U. Mo. extension div. St. Louis County, 1964-69; research fellow St. Louis U., 1970-72; asst. prof. Va. Poly. Inst. and State U., 1976-81; asso. prof. chmn. dept. clothing and textiles U. Mo.-Columbia, 1981—; adv. bd. St. Louis Better Bus. Bur.; edn. adv. bd. Man-Made Fiber Producers Assn.; speaker in field. NDEA fellow, 1970-72; St. Louis U. fellow, 1969-70; Danforth Home Econs. fellow, 1961; grantee Va. Poly. Inst. and State U., 1977-81. Mem. Am. Home Econs. Assn., Assn. Coll. Profs. Textiles and Clothing, Mo. Home Econs. Assn., Phi Kappa Phi, Epsilon Sigma Phi, Phi Delta Kappa. Baptist. Author articles in field. Home: Route 2 Box 56 Columbia MO 65201 Office: 137 Stanley Hall U Mo Columbia Mo 65211

DICKERSON, NANCY HANSCHMAN, news corr., author, lectr.; b. Milw.; d. Frederick R. and Florence (Conners) Hanschman; student Clarke Coll., Dubuque, Iowa; grad. U. Wis., 1948; postgrad. Harvard U.; H.H.D., Am. Internat. Coll., Springfield, Mass.; m. Claude Wyatt Dickerson, Feb. 24, 1962; children—Elizabeth, Ann, Jane, Michael, John. Sch. tchr., Milw.; staff asst. Senate Fgn. Relations Com.,

Washington; prod. CBS News, 1956-60. 1st woman news corr., 1960-63; news corr. NBC, 1963-70; news analyst Inside Washington, syndicated nationally for TV stas., 1971—; producer spl. syndicated TV programs, pres. Dickerson Co., 1971—; polit. commentator Newsweek Broadcasting Service; reporter Pres. Kennedy's funeral, Republican and Democratic convs., Civil Rights March on Washington, Kennedy, Johnson and Nixon inaugurations; represented Pub. Broadcasting Corp. on all-network Conversation with Pres. Nixon, 1970; lectr. Recipient Collegian award LaSalle Coll., Phila.; Spirit of Achievement award Albert Einstein Coll., Yeshiva U.; Sigma Delta Chi award Boston U.; Pioneer award New Eng. Women's Press Assn. Asso. fellow Pierson Coll., Yale U., 1972—. Mem. Radio-TV News Analysts. Clubs: Washington Press (past v.p.), Federal City, Pisces. Author: Among Those Present, 1976. *

DICKEY, JULIA EDWARDS, librarian, mgmt. and organizational cons.; b. Sioux Falls, S.D., Mar. 6, 1940; d. John Keith and Henrietta Barbara (Zerell) Edwards; student DePauw U., 1958-59; A.B., Ind. U., 1962, M.L.S., 1967, postgrad., 1967; m. Joseph E. Dickey, June 18, 1959; children—Joseph E., John Edwards. Asst. acquisitions librarian Ind. U. Regional Campus Libraries, 1965-67; head tech. services Bartholomew County Library, Columbus, Ind., 1967-74; reference coordinator Southeastern Ind. Area Library Services Authority, 1974-78, dir., 1978-80; pres. Pea Patch Airlines div. Jedco Enterprises, 1981—; pres. Ind. Sport Aviation, 1982—; pres. Human Services, Inc., 1976-78, sec. 1975, v.p., 1977; legis. strategy chmn. Ind. Library Coop. Devel., 1975. Mem. Columbus exec. bd. Mayor's Task Force on Status of Women, 1973—; del. Ind. Sch. Nominating Assembly, 1973-75, 75-77; mem. adv. council Ind./Nat. Network Study, 1977-79; bd. dirs. Columbus Women's Center; precinct coordinator Vols. For Bayh, 1974; treas. Hayes for State Rep. Com., 1978, 82; sheriff Columbus 1st precinct, 1975, clk., 1976-77, insp., 1978, judge, 1980, 82. Mem. ALA, Ind. Library Assn. (dist. chmn. 1972-73, pres. library edn. div. 1980-81; legis. chmn. jointly with Ind. Library Trustees Assn. 1978—), Library Assts. and Technicians Round Table (chmn. 1968-69), Tech. Services Round Table (chmn. 1971-72, sec. library planning com. 1969-72), AAUW (pres. 1973-75), Bartholomew County Library Staff Assn. (pres. 1975-76), Internat. Exptl. Aircraft Assn. (founding pres. Columbus chpt. 1981), Psi Iota Xi. Club: Zonta. Home and Office: 511 Terrace Lake Rd Columbus IN 47201

DICKEY, MARGARET STEVENSON LYNCH, lawyer; b. Cleve., June 21, 1929; d. John Joseph and Margaret Louise (Stevenson) Lynch; A.B. cum laude, Smith Coll., 1950; J.D., N.Y. Law Sch., 1963; m. Raymond R. Dickey (dec. 1981). Fgn. affairs officer USIA, Dept. State, 1950-55; free lance writer and editor, 1956-62; admitted to N.Y. State bar, 1963, D.C. bar, 1971; mem. U.S. del. to 19th-22d UN Gen. Assemblies, 1965-68; adviser legal and pub. affairs U.S. mission to UN, 1965-68; fgn. affairs asst. to Senator Claiborne Pell of R.I., 1968-72; sr. adviser U.S. del. to Law of Sea Conf., 1973-76; individual practice law, Washington, 1972—; partner firm Dickey Roadman & Dickey, Washington; v.p., dir. World Food Corp., 1980—; mem. adv. com. on law of sea Nat. Security Council, 1974—; cons. Dept. State, 1972-76, Presdl. Commn. on World Hunger, 1979-80. Mem. Am. Bar Assn., Am. Soc. Internat. Law, Fgn. Service Assn. (pub. mem.). U.S. Com. for Oceans, Smith Coll. Alumnae Council. Clubs: Mid-Ocean (Bermuda); Smith Coll., 1925 F St, Women's Nat. Dem. (Washington); Cosmopolitan (N.Y.C.). Contbr. articles on UN and law of sea to legal jours. Address: 3046 R St NW Washington DC 20007 also Smith's Parish Bermuda

DICKIE, HELEN AIRD, physician, educator; b. N. Freedom, Wis., Feb. 19, 1913; d. Robert Bruce and Anna (Adams) Dickie; B.A., U. Wis., 1935, M.D., 1937. Intern, Los Angeles County Hosp., 1939-40, resident, 1940-42; resident Wis. Gen. Hosp., Madison; faculty U. Wis., Madison, 1942—, prof. medicine, head pulmonary diseases, 1955—; cons. VA, 1952—. Mem. ACP, AMA, Central Soc. Clin. Research, Am. Thoracic Soc., Sigma Delta Epsilon, Alpha Omega Alpha. Contbr. articles to profl. jours. Home: 501 Clifden Dr Madison WI 53711 Office: 600 Highland Ave Madison WI 53792

DICKINSON, ALICE BRAUNLICH, educator; b. N.Y.C., Apr. 11, 1921; d. Hans and Dorothy (Harding) B.; B.A., U. Mich., 1941, Ph.D., 1952; M.A., Columbia U., 1947; m. David J. Dickinson, Dec. 10, 1944; children—Sara, Dan. Asst. project engr. Sperry Gyroscope Co., Garden City, N.Y., 1942-44;; mem. staff. Radiation Lab., M.I.T., Cambridge, 1944-45; lectr. Pa. State U., 1950-56; vis. prof. U. Baroda, India, 1962, 68, 77, U. Aligarh, India, 1961-62; mem. faculty Smith Coll., 1959—, prof. math., 1970—, chmn. math. dept., 1970-73, dean of coll., 1973-77; cons. Hampshire Coll., 1965-68. Recipient Hampshire Coll. Founders award, 1970. Mem. Ely Ringing Guild, N.Am. Guild Change Ringers, AAUW. Author: Differential Equations: A Study in Time and Motion, 1972. Home: Graves Rd Ashfield MA 01330 *

DICKINSON, ANGIE (ANGELINE BROWN), actress; b. Kulm, N.D., Sept. 30; ed. Immaculate Heart Coll., Glendale Coll.; m. Burt Bacharach; 1 dau., Lea Nikki. Motion pictures include Rio Bravo, 1959, Bramble Bush, 1960, The Sins of Rachel Cade, 1961, Jessica, 1962, Captain Newman, M.D., 1963, The Art of Love, 1965, The Chase, 1966, Cast a Giant Shadow, 1966, Point Blank, 1968, Sam Whiskey, 1968, Some Kind of Nut, 1969, The Killers, 1964, The Last Challenge, 1967, Young Billy Young, 1969, Pretty Maids All in a Row, 1971; Big Bad Mama, 1974, Dressed to Kill, 1980, others; star TV series Policewoman, 1974-78. Address: care The Blake Agy Ltd 409 N Camden Dr Beverly Hills CA 90212 *

DICKINSON, CATHERINE SCHATZ, microbiologist; b. Cin., Jan. 6, 1927; d. Ralph Marvin and Mabel (Dare) Schatz; student U. Cin., 1944-46, postgrad. 1952; A.B., Miami U., Oxford, Ohio, 1948; m. Willard C. Dickinson, Jr., June 23, 1956; children—Kellie Dare, Bradley Clark. Supr., Bacteriology Lab., Children's Hosp., Cin., 1948-53; supr., sect. head Microbiology Lab., Ochsner Found. Hosp., New Orleans, 1953—; lectr. in field. Mem. New Orleans Area Soc. for Microbiology (pres. 1979), Am. Soc. Microbiology, Am. Soc. Clin. Pathologists, New Orleans Soc. Microbiology, Nat. Registry for Microbiologists, Delta Zeta. Episcopalian. Club: Order Eastern Star. Home: 10001 Hyde Pl River Ridge LA 70123 Office: 1516 Jefferson Hwy New Orleans LA 70121

DICKINSON, ELEANOR CREEKMORE, artist, educator; b. Knoxville, Tenn., Feb. 7, 1931; d. Robert Elmond and Evelyn Louise (VanGilder) Creekmore; A.B., U. Tenn., 1952; postgrad. San Francisco Art Inst., 1961-63; M.F.A., Calif. Coll. Arts and Crafts, 1982; m. Wade Oakes Dickinson, June 12, 1952; children—Mark Wade, Katherine Van Gilder, Peter Somers. Escrow officer Security Nat. Bank, Santa Monica, Calif., 1953; faculty Calif. Coll. Arts and Crafts, Oakland, 1971—, assoc. prof. art, 1974—, dir. galleries, 1976—; one woman shows at Tenn. State Mus., 1981, Women's Interart Center, N.Y., 1980, The Oakland Mus., 1979, Galeria de Arte y Libros, Monterrey, Mexico, 1978, The Triton Mus., Santa Clara, 1977, Falkirk Cultural Center, San Rafael, 1976; The Fine Arts Mus. of San Francisco, 1975, William Sawyer Gallery, San Francisco, 1975, Wash. State Mus., 1975, Cheney Cowles Mus. Spokane, 1975, Smithsonian Inst., 1975—, Mus. Fine Arts, Tibbits Found., Colo. Springs, 1980, Valparaiso U., 1980, Corcoran Gallery of Art, 1970, 74, Calif. Coll. Art and Crafts, 1974, Dulin Gallery, Knoxville, 1970, De Young Mus., 1968, San Francisco Mus. Modern Art, 1965, others; represented in collections at The Nat. Collection of Fine Arts, The Corcoran Gallery of Art, Butler Inst. Am. Art, Stanford Art Mus., San Francisco Mus. Modern Art, Santa Barbara Mus., Library of Congress, Mich. State U., Oakland Mus., McClung Mus., Dulin Gallery, City of San Francisco, San Francisco Art Inst., Calif. Coll. Arts and Crafts, Smithsonian Inst., U. San Francisco, Triton Mus., Dallas Mus. Fine Art, Home Savs. & Loan Assn.; represented by: Gallery Rebecca Cooper, N.Y., William Sawyer Gallery, San Francisco. Dir., v.p. Coalition of Women's Art Orgns., 1979-81. Recipient Zellerbach Family Fund fellow, 1975; NEH fellow for Nev. Exhibition, 1978, grantee for Tenn. Exhibition, 1981, grantee for Film/Video Festival, 1982. Mem. Coll. Art Assn., AAUP, San Francisco Art Inst. (sec., dir. 1964-67), Women's Caucus for Art (nat. officer), Artists Equity Assn. (nat. v.p. 1980-84), Calif. Confedn. Arts, Center for Visual Arts, Graphic Arts Soc., Sierra Club, ACLU, Friends of Zoo, Amnesty Internat., Am. Folklore Soc., others. Democrat. Episcopalian. Author: Revival, 1974; That Old Time Religion, 1975; The Complete Fruit Cookbook, 1972. Home: 2125 Broderick San Francisco CA 94115

DICKINSON, JANE W. (MRS. E.F. SHERWOOD DICKINSON), corp. exec., club woman; b. Kalamazoo, Sept. 27, 1919; d. Charles Herman and Rachel (Whaler) Wagner; student Hollins Coll., 1938-39; B.A., Duke, 1941; M.Ed., Goucher Coll., 1965; m. E.F. Sherwood Dickinson, Oct. 23, 1943; children—Diane Jane Gray, Carolyn Dickinson Vane. Exec. sec. Petroleum Industry Com., Balt., 1941-43; exec. sec. Sherwood Feed Mills Inc., Balt., 1943-79. Mem. exec. com. Children's Aid Md., 1960-61; mem. bd. women's aux. Balt. Symphony Orch., 1958-60; dist. chmn. Balt. Cancer Drive, 1958; dist. chmn. Balt. Mental Health Drive, 1957; co-chmn. Balt. United Appeal, 1968. Mem. Alpha Delta Phi. Republican. Episcopalian. Clubs: Three Arts (sec. 1958-60, bd. govs. 1960-64, 67—, pres. 1970-72) (Balt.); Women's (bd. govs. 1960-64) (Roland Park); Cliff Dwellers Garden. Home: 1003 Bellemore Rd Baltimore MD 21210

DICKINSON, JUNE MCWADE, found. exec.; b. Rochester, N.Y., June 26, 1924; d. Howard L. and Esther G. (Benz) McWade; privately educated; M.F.A., Internat. U.; L.H.D. (hon.), Calif. Christian U., D.D., 1980; m. Edward Dickinson, May 3, 1946 (dec. 1975). Founder, 1949, since pres. Schumann Meml. Found.; registered music therapist; dir. Casterbridge Village Fine Arts, Conesus, N.Y., 1963——; owner Ink Pen Beacon, weekly newspaper, Conesus, 1962—, Livingston Enterprises, Lakeville, N.Y.; grantsman, pres. Casterbridge Village Devel. Corp.; mem. adj. faculty Calif. Christian U., Internat. U., also Univ. Insts. depts. City Temple Programs. Mem. panel for women's ednl. equity program HEW; bd. dirs. Western Region Bishopric of Ecumenical Religion and Gen. Edn.; mem. steering com. Com. for Whole Ministry of Episcopal Ch., Diocese of Rochester, chairperson Episcopal Women's History Project. Recipient Community Leader of Am. award, 1969; decorated knight's cross Order Merit (Fed. Republic Ger.); named Rochester Citizen of Day (2), Livingston County Citizen of Week. Fellow Internat. Biog. Assn.; mem. Women in Founds./Corporate Philanthropy, Nat. Assn. Music Therapy, ASCAP, Coll. Music Soc., League of Women Composers, Advs. for the Arts, Livingston County C. of C., Western N.Y. Assn. Music Therapy (public relations dir.), Internat. Platform Assn., Rochester Women's Network. Clubs: Conesus Lake Sportsmen, Conesus Lake Water Ski (founder, adviser, sr. mem.); Rochester. Composer: Love's Wine, Sunset Through the Rain, Old Valentines, Glass Balls on a Christmas Tree, High School Memories, My Hand in God's, Happy Pilgrims, My Irish Coleen, In a Bavarian Garden. Address: 2904 E Lake Rd Livonia NY 14487

DICKSON, FLORA SPECTOR, govt. ofcl.; b. Buenos Aires, Argentina, Aug. 10, 1931; d. Goodman Max and Rose C. (Herzlich) Spector; came to U.S., 1950, naturalized, 1960; student Columbia U., 1950; A.A., Miami Dade Community Coll., 1963; B.A., U. Miami, 1965; M.A., 1968, postgrad., 1968-69; children—Glenn, Errol, Robert. Teaching fellow U. Miami, 1967-68; instr. Spanish, Miami Dade Community Coll., 1968-69; social worker, public assistance eligibility specialist Fla. Dept. Health and Rehab. Services, Coral Gables, 1969-80, dist. XI staff adv. council rep., 1977-78, sec., 1979, adminstrv. asst. for client relations, 1980-82, residential placement coordinator for dist. program Office Devel. Services, Miami, 1982—. Sec., Temple Zamora, Coral Gables, Fla., 1974; pres. Friends Unlimited, Temple Beth Am. South Miami, Fla., 1975; facilitator Solo Center Dade County Mental Health Assn., 1977—; vol. Cedars of Lebanon Health Care Center; active various community drives. NDEA/HEW fellow, U. Miami, 1965. Mem. Friends Hispanic Am. Lit., AAUW, Sigma Delta Pi, Iota Tau Alpha. Democrat. Jewish.

DICKSON, GEAN HARVILL, office mgr.; b. Humphrey, Ark., Nov. 9, 1940; d. Clarence Lee and Lillian Pearl (Vanlandingham) Harvill; A.A., Rollins Coll., 1979, postgrad., 1979—; 1 dau., Cynthia. Supr. med. records Orange Meml. Hosp., Orlando, Fla., 1968-70; exec. sec. Gilmer-Uricchio Orthopaedic Assn., Orlando, 1970-72; office mgr. Mumby and Shea, M.D., Orlando, Fla., 1972—. Adv. bd. Webster Sch. Orlando, 1977-82. Mem. Med. Office Mgrs. Assn. (founder, 1st pres.), Med. Group Mgmt. Assn., Am. Soc. Profl. and Exec. Women. Republican. Methodist. Home: 224 E Copeland Dr Orlando FL 32806 Office: 1809 Bellevue Ave Orlando FL 32806

DIDHAM, EDIEANN BIESBROCK, coll. adminstr., educator, cons.; b. Olympia, Wash.; d. Herbert Eugene and Dorothy (Duncan) Freeman; B.S., Utah State U., 1962; M.Ed., U. Ga., 1965, Ed.D., 1968; m. James R. Didham, Sept. 3, 1977; children—Aaron, Laural, Robert. Teaching asso. U. Ga. Coll. Edn., 1966-68; asst. prof. U. Minn. Coll. Edn., 1968-71; asso. prof., dir. tchr. edn. div., then chmn. Community Services Coll., Brenau Coll., Gainesville, Ga., 1971-77; asso. prof. edn., asso. v.p. continuing edn., regional and summer programs Bowling Green (Ohio) State U., 1977—; cons. in field. Mem. local missions bd. and adult edn. adv. council Findlay (Ohio) Presbyn. Ch.; adv. com. Ohio Bd. Regents. Mem. Nat. Univ. Continuing Edn. Assn., Nat. Assn. Edn. Young Children, Am. Ednl. Research Assn., Nat. Council Tchrs. English, AAUW, Ohio Council Higher Edn. (pres. 1981-83) Ohio Assn. Women Deans, Adminstrs. and Counselors, World Future Soc., Sports Car Club Am., Internat. Porsche Racing Assn., Kappa Delta (Outstanding Alumnae award 1968), Kappa Delta Pi, Phi Delta Kappa, Phi Kappa Phi. Presbyterian. Author monographs in field. Home: 430 1st St Findlay OH 45840 Office: 300 McFall Center Bowling Green State Univ Bowling Green OH 43403

DIDION, JOAN, author; b. Sacramento, Dec. 5, 1934; d. Frank Reese and Eduene (Jerrett) Didion; B.A., U. Calif., Berkeley, 1956; m. John Gregory Dunne, Jan. 1964; 1 dau., Quintana. Asso. feature editor Vogue mag., 1956-63; former columnist Saturday Evening Post; former contbg. editor National Review; now freelance writer; novels: Run River, 1963, Play It As It Lays, 1971, A Book of Common Prayer, 1977; author books of essays Slouching Towards Bethlehem, 1969, The White Album, 1979; co-author screenplays for films The Panic in Needle Park, 1971, A Star Is Born, 1976. Recipient 1st prize Vogue's Prix de Paris, 1956; Breadloaf Writers Conf. fellow, 1963; Morton Dauwen Zabel, AAAL, 1978. Address: care Wallace & Sheil 118 E 61st St New York NY 10021 *

DIE, ANN MARIE HAYES, psychologist, educator; b. Baytown, Tex., Aug. 15, 1944; d. Robert L. and Dorothy Ann (Cooke) Hayes; B.S. with highest honors, Lamar U., 1962; M.Ed., U. Houston, 1969; Ph.D., Tex. A&M U., 1977; m. Jerome Glynn Die, June 5, 1971; 1 dau., Meredith Anne. Tchr., Deepwater Elem. Sch., Deer Park, Tex., 1966-69, team leader, tchr., 1969-71; tchr. Lansdowne Elem. Sch., Lexington, Ky., 1971-73; asst. prof. dept. psychology Lamar U., 1977-82, asso. prof., dir. Psychol. Clinic, 1978—, dir. grad. programs in psychology, 1981—; adminstr. adolescent residential unit Mental Health Mental Retardation of S.E. Tex., 1979-80; pvt. practice clin. psychology, Beaumont, Tex., 1979—; mem. community adv. com. Beaumont State Center Human Devel., 1981—, Mental Health/Mental Retardation S.E. Tex., 1980—; cons. in field. Group leader Juvenile Justice Workshop, Beaumont. Cert. tchr., psychologist, Tex. Recipient Regents Merit award, 1979; Coll. Health and Behavioral Sci. Merit award, 1982. Mem. Am. Psychol. Assn., Southwestern Psychol. Assn., Tex. Psychol. Assn., S.E. Tex. Psychol. Assn. (treas. 1978-79, 79-80), Tex. Council Family Relations, Nat. Council Family Relations, Mental Health Assn. Jefferson County, Nat. Register Health Service Providers in Psychology, Beaumont Art Mus. Republican. Methodist. Club: Port Arthur Yacht. Contbr. articles to profl. jours. Home: 855 Belvedere Dr Beaumont TX 77706 Office: PO Box 10036 Lamar U Beaumont TX 77710

DIEB, MAUREEN FADHA NAYFA, nurse; b. Sweetwater, Tex., Apr. 20, 1942; d. Eddie Elias and Ruby (Mallouf) Nayfa; diploma Shannon W. Tex. Meml. Sch. Nursing, 1963; student San Angelo Jr. Coll., 1960-61, Tex. Women's U., 1970, N. Tex. State U., 1976-78; m. James George Dieb, Mar. 12, 1967; children—Michael Dugan Daily, Leah. Pvt. duty nurse Flow Hosp., Denton, Tex., 1963; operating room and emergency room staff nurse Flow Hosp., Denton, 1964-65; head nurse nursery, 1965; dir. nurses Denton Osteopathic Hosp., 1969; sch. nurse Lewisville (Tex.) Ind. Sch. Dist., 1967-74; staff nurse Westgate Hosp., Denton Tex., 1974-81, operating room head nurse, 1977-79, inservice coordinator operating room, orthopedic specialist, staff nurse operating room, 1979—. Active various community drives. Recipient Teaching award ARC, 1968; nursing grantee, 1975. Mem. Nat. Assn. Orthopedic Nurses, Am. Assn. Operating Room Nurses, Beta Sigma Phi. Democrat. Episcopalian. Club: Order Eastern Star. Home: 606 Mimosa St Denton TX 76201 Office: 4405 N I 35 Denton TX 76201

DIEBENOW, ANITA RUTH, nurse; b. San Antonio, Jan. 30, 1946; d. Roland Paul and Ruth (Kunkel) Wiederaenders; diploma Luth. Hosp. Sch. Nursing, St. Louis, 1967; B.S.N., U. Tex., 1975; M.S., Tex. Woman's U., 1977; m. Peter Diebenow, July 1, 1967; children—Steven, Nathan. Staff nurse Moline (Ill.) Luth. Hosp., 1967-68, St. Louis Children's Hosp., 1968-69; asst. head nurse Ft. Worth Children's Hosp., 1970; office nurse W. B. Scroggie, M.D., Ft. Worth, 1971-75; supr. N. Central Tex. Home Health Agy., Ft. Worth, 1975; instr. U. Tex. at Arlington Sch. Nursing, 1976-80; asst. prof. nursing U. Miami, 1981-82; clin. coordinator maternal-child services Broward Gen. Med. Center, Ft. Lauderdale, Fla., 1982—; parent cons. Parenting Guidance Center, Ft. Worth, 1979-81. Mem. Life Issues Task Force, Circle T council Girl Scouts U.S.A., 1979-80. Mem. Am. Nurses' Assn., Nat. League Nursing, Internat. Childbirth Edn. Assn., LeLeche League Internat., Nurses' Assn. of Am. Coll. Ob-Gyn., Sigma Theta Tau. Lutheran. Office: 1600 S Andrews Ave Fort Lauderdale FL 33316

DIEDE, PAULINE NEHER, writer; b. Mercer County, N.D., Oct. 10, 1911; d. Ludwig and Christina (Steinert) Neher; Comml. degree, Dickinson Normal Sch., 1930; m. Jake Diede, Nov. 24, 1932; children—Darlayne Buchli, Audrey Williamson, Rodney. News reporter, linotypist, feature writer Hebron (N.D.) Herald, 1959-69, writer, 1970—; columnist The Echoes, Dickinson (N.D.) Press, 1970-75; author bicentennial pantomime Remember When, 1976. Editor bull. United Ch., Women, United Ch. of Christ, 1976-79, mem. state women's com., 1976-79, pres. Women's Guild St. John United Ch. of Christ, Hebron, 1956-57, 60-62; election precinct insp., 1970-76. Mem. Nat. Fedn. Press Women, N.D. Press Women (awards 1976, 72, 71, 75, 68). Clubs: Hebron Homemakers, N.D. Hist. Soc. Contbr. sect. to book on pioneer prairie. Address: care Hebron Herald Hebron ND 58638

DIEDERICHS, JANET WOOD, public relations co. exec.; b. Libertyville, Ill.; d. J. Howard and Ruth Wood; B.A., Wellesley Coll., 1950; m. John Diederichs, 1953. Sales agt. Pan Am. Airways, Chgo., 1951-52; public relations regional mgr. Braniff Airways, Chgo., 1953-69; pres. Janet Diederichs & Assos., Inc., Chgo., 1970—. Bd. dirs., exec. com. Chgo. Conv. and Tourism Bur.; exec. com. 1983 World Trade Conf.; com. mem. Nat. Trust for Historic Preservation, 1975-79, (Brit.) Marshall Scholars, 1975-79, Art Inst. Chgo.; bd. dirs. Inst. for Wound Healing, Internat. House, U. Chgo., Com. of 200; mem. Vatican Art Council Chgo.; pres. Jr. League Chgo., 1968-69; mem. Chgo. Network. Mem. Econ. Club Chgo., Public Relations Soc. Am., Soc. Am. Travel Writers, Nat. Acad. TV Arts and Scis., Chgo. Press Club, Publicity Club Chgo., Chgo. Assn. Commerce and Industry. Clubs: Woman's Athletic, Casino, Mid-Am. Office: 333 N Michigan Ave Chicago IL 60601

DIEHL, MARY JANE ELLSWORTH, educator; b. Denville, N.J.; d. Robert George and Angennetta (Keeffe) Ellsworth; B.A., Montclair State Coll., 1940, M.A., 1960; Ed.D., Rutgers U., 1967; m. Edwin D. Diehl, Jan. 14, 1940 (dec. Aug. 1962); children—Digby, Michael. Dir. edn. Middlesex County Health League, New Brunswick, N.J., 1946-49; vice prin., tchr. Montville Twp. Sch., Montville, N.J., 1953-59; team tchr. Mountain Lakes (N.J.) High Sch., 1960-61; profl. asst. adv. services Ednl. Testing Service, Princeton, N.J., 1962-67; prof. Monmouth Coll., West Long Branch, N.J., 1967—, regional coordinator Project Head Start Tng. Program, 1968-69; asst. dir. Project Head Start Tng. Program, Rutgers U., summer 1967. Mem. Assn. for Supervision and Curriculum Devel. (nat. bd. mem. 1967—), AAUW (fellowship chmn. Princeton br. 1968—), N.J. Assn. Supervision and Curriculum Devel. (sec. exec. com. 1962—), World Council on Curriculum and Instrn. Home: Poor Farm Rd Harbourton NJ 08534 Office: Monmouth Coll West Long Branch NJ 07764

DIEMER, EMMA LOU, musician; b. Kansas City, Mo., Nov. 24, 1927; d. George Willis and Myrtle (Casebolt) Diemer; student Eastman Sch. Music, 1945-46, Ph.D., 1959; student Central Mo. State Coll., 1946-47; B.Mus., Yale U., 1949, M.Mus., 1950; postgrad. Berkshire Music Center, 1954-55, Royal Conservatory, Brussels, 1952-53. Tchr. music NE Mo. State Coll., summers 1951-52, William Jewell Coll., Liberty, Mo., 1955-57, Kansas City Conservatory Music, 1955-57, Park Coll., Parkville, Mo., 1955-57; Ford Found. composer in residence Arlington (Va.) Secondary Schs., 1959-61; composer-cons. Balt. Public Schs., 1964; Arlington Public Schs., 1964-65; asst. prof. theory and composition U. Md., College Park, 1965-70; organist Ch. of Reformation, Washington, 1962-71; prof. theory and composition U. Calif., Santa Barbara, 1971—; lectr. contemporary music, composition; organ, piano recitalist. Recipient Woods Chandler prize Yale U., 1950, Cert. of Merit, Music Sch., 1977; Delta Omicron composition prize, 1956; prize St. Mark's Ch., Phila.; Edward Benjamin award, 1959; Nat. Presbyn. Ch. award, 1959; Kindler Found. commn., 1963; Nat. City Christian Ch. commn., 1963; Nat. Fedn. Music Clubs award 1969, Fulbright scholar, 1952-53; U. Calif. creative arts grantee, 1973; Nat. Endowment Arts composer fellow, 1980-81. Mem. ASCAP (ann. award 1962—), Am. Soc. Univ. Composers, Am. Guild Organists, Mu Phi Epsilon (chpt. v.p. 1963-64). Pub. numerous compositions including Three Anniversary Chorus for Mixed Voice, 1970; Seven Etudes for Piano, 1971; Madrigals Three, 1972; Sonata For Flute and Piano, 1973; The Prophecy for Women's Chorus, 1974; Three Pieces for Carillon, 1976; Celebration for Organ, 1976; Music for Woodwind Quartet, 1976; Four Poems, 1977; Concerto for Harpsichord, 1978; Concerto for Flute, 1979; Toccata for Piano, 1980; Songs of Reminiscence, 1981; Symphony No. 2, 1981; Suite for Orchestra, 1981; Solo trio for Xylophone, Vibraphone, and Marimba, 1982.

DIENER, MARY ELEANOR MCMATH, business devel., mktg. research and mktg. services exec., metric transition specialist; b.

Washington, July 20, 1929; d. Mercer Bailey and Margaret Therese (Chase) McMath; student Internat. Coll. Tokyo, 1947-48; B.A., Manhattanville Coll., 1951; M.S. in Human Service Adminstrn., U. Antioch U., 1978; m. William Harrison Diener, Sept. 3, 1951; children—Eric, Paul, Lawrence, Valerie. Mem. econ. analysis staff, reporter co. mag. The World, Gen. Motors of Brazil, Sao Paulo, 1951-52; asst. to Am. dir. Cultural Union of Brazil-U.S., Sao Paulo, 1953-54; dir.-mgr. shopping service research, Sao Paulo, 1956-62; feature writer, columnist Brazil Herald, C. of C. and Brazilian Bus., Sao Paulo, 1961-65; pres. Assitencia Social de Vila Alpina, Sao Paulo, 1956-62; editor, display advt. mgr. The Citizen, weekly newspaper, Sarasota, Fla., 1966-67; account rep. Center for Mktg. and Research, Sarasota, 1969-71; pres. Diener & Assos., Inc., bus. devel., mktg. research and mktg. services firm, Research Triangle Park, N.C., 1972—. mem. adv. council to U.S. Senate Com. on Small Bus.; mem. N.C. Gov.'s Advocacy Council on Small Bus.; chmn. N.C. del. White House Conf. on Small Bus.; woman advocate for small bus. SBA, 1981. Recipient Outstanding Am. award Brazilian govt., 1964, Addy award, 1972; cert. of appreciation White House Conf. on Small Bus. Fellow Internat. Poetry Soc., Internat. Acad. Poets; mem. U.S. Metric Assn. (regional dir.), Nat. Assn. Women Bus. Owners (pres. N.C. chpt., dir. nat. orgn., cert. of appreciation), Am. Mktg. Assn., Nat. League Am. Pen Women (local pres. 1972-74), Am. Advt. Fedn., Women in Communications, Am. Assn. Public Opinion Research, Am. Mgmt. Assn., U.S. C. of C. Republican. Roman Catholic. Co-author: Economics Survey of Brazil 1952-53; author: (poetry) When The Sun Goes Down, 1969; Let's Make It Work, 1979; Have You Come a Long Way, Baby?; contbr. poems to anthologies, numerous articles and position papers to bus. and fin. publs. Address: PO Box 12052 50 Park Dr Research Triangle Park NC 27709

DIERS, DONNA KAYE, nurse, univ. dean; b. Sheridan, Wyo., May 11, 1938; d. Don C. and Ilene H. Diers; B.S. in Nursing, U. Denver, 1960; M.S.N., Yale U., 1964. Psychiat. staff nurse Yale Psychiat. Inst., New Haven, 1960-62; mem. faculty Yale U. Sch. Nursing, 1964—, dean, 1972—, prof. 1978—; mem. adv. com. advanced tng. grants, div. nursing Dept. Health and Human Services, 1978—; mem. peer rev. com. Nat. Center Health Stats., 1982; bd. dirs. Health Systems Agy. S. Central Conn., Community Health Care Plan, Yale Health Plan. Fellow Am. Acad. Nursing; mem. Am. Nurses Assn., Am. Assn. Colls. Nursing, Sigma Theta Tau (chpt. charter mem.). Author; Research in Nursing Practice, 1979; also articles, monographs, chpts. in books. Mem. editorial adv. bds. Nursing Outlook, Cancer Nursing, Image. Office: 855 Howard Ave PO Box 3333 New Haven CT 05610

DIETERLE, DIANE SHUTLEY, genealogist; b. Atlanta, Mar. 16, 1939; d. Charles Crosby and Mary Weaver (Williams) Shutley; B.A. in History, Jacksonville (Ala.) State U., 1973; m. John H. Dieterle, June 6, 1960; children—John, Lorraine, Claire, Ben, Charlotte. Pres., Library Prodns., Atlanta, 1978—; founder, 1975, since dir. Geneal. Center Library, Atlanta; tchr. genealogy in U.S. and W. Ger. Mem. Ga. Geneal. Soc., Utah Geneal. Soc., DAR. Republican. Mormon. Author: (text-books) Genealogy Workbook, 1968, Genealogy For Fun, 1976, Easy Genealogy, 1977; editor Genealogy Today, Computerized Surnames mag.; also family histories. Office: 2815 Clearview Pl Atlanta GA 30340

DIETERMAN, BARBARA HAWKINS, acct., food co. exec.; b. Lynchburg, Va., May 16, 1954; d. Clifton Franklin and Virginia Barbara (Johnson) Hawkins; A.A., Central Va. Community Coll., 1974; B.A., Lynchburg Coll., 1977; m. John Raymond Dieterman II, May 24, 1980. Acct., Coleman-Adams Constrn., Forest, Va., 1977-80; asst. mgr. fin. reporting Rich-Sea Pak Corp., St. Simon's Island, Ga., 1980—; chmn. supervisory com., bd. dirs. Rich-Sea Pak Fed. Credit Union. Mem. Inst. Mgmt. Accts., Beta Sigma Phi. Presbyterian. Club: Jaycettes. Home: 243 Alabama St Saint Simon's Island GA 31522 Office: PO Box 667 Saint Simon's Island GA 31522

DIETL, JANE ANN, bus. exec.; b. Manley, Nebr., Mar. 31, 1941; d. John E. and Meredith (Heneger) D.; B.S. in Edn. and Bus., Peru State U., U. Nebr., 1962; M.A. in Adminstrn., Chapman Coll., Orange, Calif., 1967; Ph.D., U.S. Internat. U., San Diego, 1981. Tchr., Santa Ana, Calif., 1960-67, asst. prin., 1967-69; dir. U.S. Dependents Sch., Soesterberg, Holland, 1969-70; v.p. Extraction Systems Corp., Santa Ana, 1970-72; dir. resources instrn. San Joaquin, Calif., Unified Sch. Dist., 1971-72; asst. prin./prin. Fullerton (Calif.) Sch. Dist., 1972-77; pres. Jane A. Dietl Asso. Enterprises, Inc., 1977—; dean Sch. Bus. S.W.U., Phoenix, 1982—; 1981—; cons. in field. Cert. in personnel supervision and evaluation. Mem. Am. Soc. Tng. and Devel., Am. Mgmt. Assn., Nat. Council Internat. Visitors, AAUW, World Furture Soc., NOW, Phi Delta Kappa. Republican. Contbr. articles to profl. jours. Office: 1112 Ironwood Ctr Suite 146 Bellevue NE 68005

DIETRICH, MARLENE (MARIA MAGDALENA VON LOSCH), actress; b. Berlin, Dec. 27, 1901; d. Edward and Josephine (Felsing) von Losch; ed. Augusta Victoria Sch., Berlin; m. Rudolf Sieber, May 13, 1924; 1 dau., Maria. Began as violinist; debut as actress in Broadway, Berlin; 4 years with Max Reinhardt; later in film The Blue Angel (German); came to U.S., 1930, and since starred in motion pictures, including: Martin Roumagnec (French), 1946, Golden Earrings, 1947, Foreign Affair, 1948, Stage Fright, 1950, No Highway in the Sky, 1951, Rancho Notorious, 1952, numerous others the latest including the Monte Carlo Story, 1957, Around the World in 80 Days, 1956, Witness for the Prosecution, 1958, Judgement at Nuremberg, 1961, Just a Gigolo, 1978; also appears in night clubs and theatres. Recipient Spl. Tony award, 1967-68. Author: Marlene Dietrich's ABC, 1962; My Life Story, 1979. Toured Army Service Camps, Europe, 1945; concert tour U.S., 1973. Address: care Regency Artists Ltd 9200 Sunset Blvd Suite 823 Los Angeles CA 90069 *

DIETRICH, MARTHA JANE (SHULTZ), profl. genealogist; b. Brazil, Ind., Aug. 19, 1916; d. Charles Russell and Florence Delilah (McIntire) Shultz; student Ind. State U.; m. E(arl) Donald Dietrich, June 17, 1939; children—Florence Ann Dietrich Harris, Jean Carol Dietrich Litterst, Charles Donald. Clk., CSC, Washington, 1937-43; personnel officer Armed Forces Med. Library, Washington, 1948-54; personnel staffing specialist, Washington, 1954-70, ret., 1970; profl. free lance genealogist, College Park, Md., 1970—. Cert. Am. lineage specialist; authorized Bd. Cert. of Genealogists, Washington. Mem. Ky. Hist. Soc. (life), Md. Hist. Soc., Md. Geneal. Soc., Ind. Hist. Soc., Conn. Geneal. Soc., Va. Geneal. Soc., Wabash Valley (Ind.) Geneal. Soc., Clay County (Ind.) Geneal. Soc., Adams County (Ohio) Geneal. Soc., Berks County (Pa.) Geneal. Soc., Somerset County (Pa.) Geneal. Soc., Geneal. Soc. Pa., Filson Club Louisville, Prince George's County (Md.) Geneal. Soc., DAR, Nat. Officers Club, DAR, (state registrar 1973-76, state vice regent 1976-79), Md. DAR (state regent 1979—), Md. State DAR Officers Club, Colonial Dames XVII Century Nat. Officers Club, Daus. Am. Colonists (state chmn. 1977-79), Daus. Colonial Wars, UDC, Daus. of 1812, Sons and Daus. of Pilgrims, Magna Charta Dames, Order Crown of Charlemagne, Soc. Ind. Pioneers, Order Ky. Cols., Clan MacIntyre (genealogist 1978—), Daus. Barons of Runnymede, Colonial Dames XVII Century (state pres. D.C. state soc. 1975-77, acting registrar gen. 1974-75, registrar gen. 1975-79, service awards 1977, 78), Kappa Kappa, Kappa Kappa Kappa (Ind.). Episcopalian. Home and Office: 4616 Guilford Rd College Park MD 20740

DIETRICH, SHELLE GAIL, clin. psychologist; b. Houston, Nov. 24, 1949; d. Edwin Jerry and Adele Marie (Odom) Dietrich; B.A., Baylor U., 1971, D.Psychology, 1975. Staff, VA Hosp., Region XII Edn. Service Center, Waco-McLennan County Mental-Health-Mental-Retardation Center, Waco, Tex., 1972-74; clin. intern Tex. Research Inst. Mental Scis., Houston, 1974-75; clin. psychologist in pvt. practice, U. Houston, Houston Community Coll., 1975-77; staff psychologist Bur. Prisons, Fed. Correctional Inst., Oxford, Wis., 1977-79, chief psychology services, 1979-80; dir. psychol. services Female Psychiat. Hosp., Fed. Correctional Inst., Lexington, Ky., 1980—, U. Ky; pvt. practice psychology. Bd. dirs. Huaco council Camp Fire Girls, Waco, 1972-73. Recipient Outstanding Performance award Fed. Correctional Inst., Oxford, 1978; nat. spl. commendation Bur. Prisons, 1978; Am. Assn. Sex Educators and Counselors grantee, 1976; lic. clin. psychologist, Ky., Wis., Tex. Mem. Am. Psychol. Assn. Contbr. articles to profl. jours. Home: 3600 Spurr Rd Apt 12 Lexington KY 40511 Office: Fed Correctional Inst Lexington KY 40511

DIETSCH, CORA MARIE (CORKY), consumer products co. exec.; b. Cin., May 18, 1949; d. John George and Melba Leola (Houck) Ehrnschwender; B.S. in Bus. Adminstrn., Findlay Coll., 1975; 1 dau., Tina Marie. Collection mgr. Sears, Roebuck and Co., Findlay, Ohio, 1967-68; employee services asst. Cooper Tire & Rubber Co., Findlay, 1968-78; personnel mgr. Libby, McNeill & Libby, Inc., Leipsic, Ohio, 1978-80; mgr. personnel services The Nestle Co., Burlington, Wis., 1980-81; mgr. labor relations Armour-Dial Co., Montgomery, Ill., 1981, mgr. indsl. relations, 1981—. Adviser, Jr. Achievement, 1968-73; past mem. Lima Area Safety Council; 1st aid instr./trainer. Mem. Nat. Alliance Bus., Am. Soc. Personnel Adminstrs., Personnel Indsl. Relations Assn., Fox Valley Indsl. Assn. Republican. Methodist. Home: 54 Sonora Dr Montgomery IL 60538 Office: Armour-Dial Co 2000 Aucutt Rd Montgomery IL 60538

DIETZ, ARLENE LELIA, economist; b. Eugene, Ore., Feb. 12, 1944; d. Harold Edward and Leona Mae (Johnson) Rice; B.A., Willamette U., 1965; M.A., Colo. U., 1966; postgrad. U. Wis., 1966-68; DePaul U., 1971, Ill. Inst. Tech., 1972, Northwestern U., 1973; m. Charles Harry Dietz, Aug. 29, 1966; children—Jason Edward, Charles Christopher. Econs. instr. U. Wis., Kenosha, 1967-68; chief economist U.S. Army C.E., Chgo., 1968-77, economist, mgr. Nat. Waterways Study, Ft. Belvoir, Va., 1977—; lectr. in field. Mem. Am. Water Resources Assn. (chpt. pres. 1982-83), Transp. Research Forum (nat. bd. 1972-73), Nat. Acad. Sci. (com. mem. transp. research bd. 1980—), Am. Econs. Assn., Internat. Assn. Navigation Congresses, Alpha Lambda Delta, Pi Gamma Mu. Republican. Lutheran. Club: Toastmistress. Contbr. articles to profl. jours. Home: 3225 Woodland Ln Alexandria VA 22309 Office: Casey Bldg Fort Belvoir VA 22060

DIETZ-BORMAN, MARY ROSSWELL, book co. exec.; b. Knoxville, Tenn.; d. Rosswell Bryan and Alice Beatrice (Fitzgerald) D.; B.A., UCLA, 1952; m. R.C. Borman, Dec. 13, 1980. Mgr. textbook personnel UCLA Student Store, 1952-54; inventory control mgr. Tech. Book Co., Los Angeles, 1954-69; acquisitions mgr., sales service mgr. Stacey div. Brodart Inc., San Francisco, 1970-72; dir. mktg. library service div. College Book Co., Los Angeles, 1972-76; owner Dietz Book Co., 1976—. Active Sunset Young Republican Clubs, 1961-62; chmn. Los Angeles County Delegation; recording sec., 1963; v.p., 1964; mem. bd. dirs., 1965-74. Mem. Nat. Women's Book Assn., Spl. Libraries Assn., Med. Library Group., Calif. Library Assn., Assn. of Western Hosps., Catholic Alumni Clubs Internat. (Los Angeles, San Francisco chpts.). Roman Catholic. Clubs: Valley Artist Guild. One woman art show Ont. Pub. Library, 1965; represented in Hollywood Bowl's Festival of Music and Art, 1966, 67. Home: 13360 Maxella Ave Apt 10 Marina del Rey CA 90291 Office: 14528 Hamlin St Van Nuys CA 91411

DIFATE, HELEN KESSLER, architect; b. Mt. Vernon, N.Y., Jan. 23, 1942; d. Lawrence Victor and Helen de Forestal (McKernan) Kessler; B.A., Coll. of New Rochelle, 1963; B.Arch., Cooper Union, 1968; m. Victor George DiFate, Jr., June 5, 1966; children—Eric Victor, Kristen Helen. Designer, Bro. Cajetan J.B. Baumann O.F.M. Architect, FAIA, N.Y.C., 1962-70; project dir. Philip J. Wilker Architect & Assos., Bronxville, N.Y., 1970-71; designer Robert A. Green & Philip G. McIntosh AIA, Architects, N. Tarrytown, N.Y., 1971-72; architect Fleagle and Kaeyer, Architects, Yonkers, N.Y., 1972-74, Anselevicius/Rupe/Assos., St. Louis, 1974-75; architect Helen Kessler DiFate AIA Architect, St. Louis, 1971—; part time faculty engr. div., archtl. option, St. Louis Community Coll. Meramec, 1975-76, also mem. drafting and design tech. adv. com.; mem. jr. div. bd. Women's Assn. of St. Louis Symphony Soc., Friends of St. Louis Art Mus., Friends of St. Louis Sci. Mus., Mo. Bot. Garden. Registered architect, N.Y., Mo., Ill.; certified Nat. Council Archtl. Registration Bds. Mem. AIA (corporate mem.; dir. Westchester, N.Y., chpt., 1974), Mo. Council Architects, Alliance of Women in Architecture, Clayton (Mo.) C. of C. Roman Catholic. Club: Town & Tennis. Archtl. project published in books: Buildings Reborn: New Uses, Old Places (Barbaralee Diamonstein), 1978, The Building Art in St. Louis: Two Centuries (George McCue), 1981. Office: 131 N Bemiston Ave Saint Louis MO 63105

DI GIACOMO-GEFFERS, ELIZABETH ANN, nursing adminstr.; b. Mt. Vernon, N.Y., Nov. 8, 1939; d. Vincent and Angelina (Coviello) DiGiacomo; B.A. in Health Edn. and Nursing, Jersey City State Coll., 1961; M.P.H. in Public Health Adminstrn., Johns Hopkins U., 1967; m. Rodney A. Geffers, Aug. 31, 1973 (dec. 1981). Tchr. health edn. North Bergen (N.J.) High Sch., 1961-62; supr. Long Beach (Calif.) Meml. Med. Center, 1962-63; occupational health nurse Walt Disney Prodns., 1964-65; coordinator sch. health services Huntington (Calif.) Marina High Sch., 1963-65; instr. Sch. Dentistry, U. Md., 1967; asso. dir. public health nursing John F. Kennedy Inst., Md., 1967-68; research asst. Johns Hopkins, Balt., 1968; adminstr., supr., head nurse North Hudson (N.J.), Hosp., 1968-70; asso. dir. nursing Cedars-Sinai Med. Center, Los Angeles, 1970-81; cons. emergency nursing and nursing adminstrn. Monterey Park (Calif.) Hosp., East Los Angeles Doctors Hosp., 1980—. Mem. med. adv. commn. Los Angeles Olympic Organizing Com., 1981, Los Angeles Olympics, 1981—; mem. com. on health and welfare, select com. on health Calif. Senate, 1981—. Cert. in advanced nursing adminstrn. Fellow Am. Sch. Health Assn., Am. Public Health Assn.; mem. Royal Soc. Health, AAUW, Am. Nurses Assn. Contbr. numerous articles to profl. jours.; editorial cons. R.N. Publs., 1976—; reviewer C.V. Mosby Co., 1979-81. Home: 1301 S Atlantic Blvd Monterey Park CA 91754 Office: Cedars Sinai Med Center Los Angeles CA

DIGIOVANNI, JOAN FIMBEL, psychologist, educator; b. Jersey City, June 18, 1935; d. Albert Charles and Selma (Kugler) Fimbel; B.A., Fla. So. Coll., 1954; M.A. in Psychology, Columbia U., 1955; Ph.D. in Psychology, Baylor U., 1961; m. Philip DiGiovanni, June 23, 1956; children—Juliet Paula, Portia Jonquil. Counselor women's residence halls Dean of Women's Office, U. Ill., Champaign, 1955-57; teaching asst. psychology dept. Baylor U., Waco, Tex., 1958-61; asst. prof. Norfolk (Va.) Coll. of William and Mary (name changed to Old Dominion U. 1962), 1961-63; asst. prof. Springfield (Mass.) Coll., 1963-65; dir. counseling services, asst. prof. Western New Eng. Coll., Springfield, 1965-66, asst. prof., dir. counseling services, 1966-69, assoc. prof., 1969-73, prof., 1973—; pvt. practice psychology. Cert. sch. psychologist, Mass.; lic. psychologist, Mass. Mem. Am. Psychol. Assn., Eastern Psychol. Assn., Mass. Psychol. Assn., New Eng. Psychol. Assn., Western Mass. Psychology Interest Soc., Greater Springfield Psychol. Assn., Psi Chi, Alpha Chi, Alpha Kappa Delta. Democrat. Unitarian. Contbr. articles to profl. jours. Home: 910 Plumtree Rd Springfield MA 01119 Office: 1215 Wilbraham Rd Springfield MA 01119

DIGMAN, KATARINA CERNOZUBOV, psychologist; b. Belgrade, Yugoslavia, Sept. 5, 1941; came to U.S., 1967, naturalized, 1974; d. Konstantin N. and Leonila (Yourschenko) Cernozubov; A.B. in Psychology, U. Belgrade, 1964; M.A. in Psychology, U. Hawaii, 1968, Ph.D., 1970; m. John M. Digman, Jan. 23, 1971; 1 dau., Maria-Anna. Teaching asst. dept. psychology U. Belgrade, 1963-64; field asst. Inst. Internat. Studies, U. Calif., Berkeley, 1965, research asst. dept. anthropology, 1965; intern Neuropsychiat. Clinic, U. Belgrade, 1963-66; chief dept. psychology Neuropsychiat. Clinic, U. Novi Sad Med. Sch., Vojvodina, Yugoslavia, 1966-67; grad. asst. dept. psychology U. Hawaii, Honolulu, 1967-70, lectr., 1969, asst. researcher, 1974-78, mem. grad. faculty, 1977-79, asst. prof. women's studies program, 1975-77; cons. psychologist Hawaii State Hosp., 1967-70, clin. psychologist, 1970-71; mem. grad. faculty Outreach program Antioch Coll., Honolulu, 1975-79, Outreach program U. No. Colo., Honolulu, 1975—; founder, dir. Women's Counseling Clinic and Resource Center, Honolulu, 1977—; publisher Everywoman, 1978—; participant archeol. excavation expdn. pre-Colombian sites, 1976-81. Recipient Best Student award Philos. U. Belgrade, 1964. Mem. Am. Psychol. Assn., Hawaii Psychol. Assn., Western Psychol. Assn., Internat. Assn. Applied Psychology, Soc. for Life History Research, Nat. Register of Health Providers, Assn. of Family Conciliation, Yugoslav Clin. Psychol. Assn., Nat. Wildlife Fedn., Friends of Animals, Am. Mus. Natural History, Hawaii Horse Show Assn., Am. Horse Show Assn., Maya Study Club. Contbr. numerous articles on psychopathology, social psychology and exptl. psychology to profl. jours. Office: 1314 S King St Suite 708 Honolulu HI 96814

DIJAK, DENISE GENEVIEVE, psychotherapist; b. Bklyn., July 14, 1951; d. Martin J. and Dolores E. (Ogaard) D.; B.A., Upsala Coll., 1972; M.S.W., Rutgers U., 1975; postgrad. Inst. Psychoanalytic Tng. and Research, 1975-78; m. Matthew P. Mahon, III, May 22, 1981. Psychiat. social worker Straight and Narrow, Paterson, N.J., 1975-77; alcoholism coordinator City of Passaic (N.J.), 1977—; cons. Psychotherapy Counseling Center, Bergenfield, N.J., 1978-80; human resources cons. Mahon's Express, 1981—; sec. Passaic County Title XX Coalition, 1979-80; chmn. Title XX Health/Mental Health Task Force, 1979; mem. mental health task force Health Systems Agy., 1978-80; mem. alcoholism adv. bd. No. Community Hosp., Oradell, N.J., 1979-80. NIMH fellow, 1974. Mem. Acad. Cert. Social Workers, Nat. Assn. Social Workers, N.J. Alcoholism Counselors Assn., Assn. Labor-Mgmt. Adminsrts. and Cons. Alcoholism, Passaic Interagy. Council, Am. Soc. Tng. and Devel. Home: 70 Cutler St Clifton NJ 07011 Office: 114 Prospect St Passaic NJ 07055

DILKS, ELEANOR, zoologist; b. Richmond, Ind., Jan. 29, 1921; d. Williams Wright and B. Grace (Test) D.; B.S., Earlham Coll., Richmond, Ind., 1942; M.S., U. Wis., Madison, 1944, Ph.D., 1948. Instr. biology Earlham Coll., 1942-43, Drury Coll., Springfield, Mo., 1945-47; instr., then asst. prof. U. Buffalo, 1947-52; mem. faculty Ill. State U., Normal, 1952—, prof. zoology, 1961—. NSF Faculty fellow, 1958. Mem. Am. Soc. Zoologists, Am. Microscopial Soc., Marine Biology Assn. U.K. (life), Sigma Xi, Phi Sigma. Club: Altrusa. Author papers in field. Office: Biology Dept Ill State U Normal IL 61761

DILKS, ELIZABETH THOMAS S., poet, clubwoman; b. North Merion, Bryn Mawr, Pa., July 21, 1917; d. Benjamin and Elizabeth Jones (Thomas) Shank; student Louis Shenk Voice Studios, Phila., 1939-42, Pison Acad. of Appreciation of Arts, Phila., 1941-43, Taylor Coll., Phila., 1943-45; m. John Henry Dilks. Restorer antique furniture and old farmhouses, Paoli, Pa., 1947-52, Malvern, Pa., 1952-62, Md., 1962—. Recipient Soc. Am. Citizens award; poem hung at Christian C. Sanderson Mus. Fellow Internat. Acad. Poets, Anglo Am. Acad. (hon.); mem. Acad. Am. Poets, Poets and Writers, Poets and Writers, Inc., Fedn. Women's Clubs, Christian C. Sanderson Mus. (life). Clubs: Whitford Country (Exton, Pa.); Miles River Yacht (St. Michaels, Md.). Author, illustrator: Poetry-His and Hers, 1976; A Drop in the Bucket; contbr. poetry to mags. and newspapers, anthologies.

DILL, ANNE HOLDEN, educator; b. Poplarville, Miss., Mar. 7, 1920; d. James Houston and Florence Elizabeth (Henley) Holden; B.S., U. Ala., 1954, M.A., 1955, Ed.S., 1970; m. Elmer Dill, Jan. 25, 1941; children—Winston Elmer, Jane Anne, Caroll Elizabeth Dill Norman. High sch. tchr. in Ga., 1958-65; instr. Western world lit. U. Ga. Center, Dublin, 1965-66; instr. English, Gadsden (Ala.) Jr. Coll., 1966—. Mem. Nat. Council Tchrs. English, NEA, AAUW, S.Central MLA, Southeastern Conf. English in Two-Year Colls., Conf. Coll. Composition and Communication, Ala. Coll. English Tchrs. Assn., Ala. Council Tchrs. English, Ala. Jr. Coll. Assn., Ala. Edn. Assn., LWV, DAR (vice regent). Democrat. Baptist. Home: 850 Walnut St Gadsden AL 35901 Office: Gadsden Junior Coll George Wallace Dr Gadsden AL 35903

DILL, JANE ROGERS, counselor; b. Tucson, Nov. 27, 1933; d. Charles Fletcher and Josephine (Jenks) Rogers; B.A., U. Redlands, 1955; M.A., Ariz. State U., 1961, Ph.D., 1977; children—John Montgomery, Beatrice Jo. Instr. psychology Fullerton (Calif.) Community Coll., 1975—; tchr., health educator El Modena High Sch., Orange, Calif., 1969—; counseling asso. Town & Country Psychol. Services, Santa Ana, 1979—. Mem. Mayor's Adv. Council, Palm Springs, 1961; mem. Calif. Task Force on Families, 1979-80; Los Angeles Episcopal Diocese del. Nat. Conv. on Families, 1979; mem. vestry St. Paul's Episcopal Ch. Recipient Degree of excellence coach Nat. Forensic League, 1972. Mem. Assn. Supervision and Curriculum Devel., Calif. Council Family Relations (pres. 1978, 79), Am. Psychol. Assn., NEA, Phi Delta Kappa, Beta Sigma Phi. Author: (with V. Strain) Career Exploration in Education, 1972. Office: 864 Town & Country Office Park Orange CA 92668

DILL, LINDA JEAN, ct. reporter; b. Tampa, Fla., June 7, 1947; d. Rutherford Hayes and Blanche Lorena (McRae) Jones; student Charron-Williams Bus. Coll., Tampa, 1974; m. Robert V. Dill, June 5, 1981; 1 son by previous marriage, Charles Allen Keene. Keypunch and key tape operator various cos. Tampa Bay area, 1966-72; dep. ofcl. ct. reporter 6th Jud. Circuit, Pasco County, Fla., 1974—. Mem. Naval Enlisted Res. Assn., Order Rosicrucians, East Pasco County Legal Secs. Assn. (dir. public relations 1981-82). Home: 1676 Seminole Dr Odessa FL 33556 Office: PO Box 1516 705 E Live Oak St Dade City FL 33525

DILLAMAN, AUDREY BOROK, sch. prin.; b. N.Y.C., Feb. 16, 1941; d. Arthur and Ruth (Jaffe) Borok; B.Ed. in Elem. Edn., U. Miami, 1963; M.Ed., U. Md., 1968; postgrad. Fla. Internat. U., 1979; 1 son, Jed Ethan. Elem. tchr. Dade County Schs., Miami, Fla., 1963-74; prin. Beth David Solomon Schechter Day Sch., Miami, 1974—; instr. U. Miami, 1968-69. U. Miami honor scholar, 1959-63; Fla. Tchrs. grantee, 1959-63. Mem. Nat. Assn. Elem. Sch. Prins., Nat. Assn. Edn. of Young Children, Jewish Council of Early Childhood Educators, Miami Mortar Bd. Alumnae, U. Miami Alumnae, Jewish Family and Childrens Service, Dade County Assn. Retarded Citizens, Central Agy. Jewish Edn., South Fla. Assn. Children Under Six, Zool. Soc. Fla., Mental Health Soc. Dade County, Children in Distress, Phi Sigma Sigma. Democrat. Jewish. Club: B'nai B'rith Women. Office: 7500 SW 120 St Miami FL 33156

DILLARD, MARILYNN ELIZABETH, court reporter; b. Detroit, Nov. 8, 1934; d. Earl Travis and Idella (Coates) Adams; B.B.A., U. Detroit, 1981; m. Paul Anthony Dillard, Dec. 6, 1958; children—Paul Anthony, Angela Denise. Freelance sec. and ct. reporter, 1968-70; ofcl. ct. reporter Wayne County Circuit Ct., Detroit, 1970-81; owner, operator Free Lance Ct. Reporting Agy., Southfield, Mich., 1981—;

guest instr. ct. reporting schs. Mem. Nat. Shorthand Reporters Assn., Mich. Shorthand Reporters Assn., Trade Union Leadership Council, NAACP, Detroit C. of C., Phi Gamma Nu. Baptist. Club: Detroit Renaissance Lions Aux. (pres. 1979-81). Home: 19434 Sorrento St Detroit MI 48235 Office: 23077 Greenfield Rd Southfield MI 48075

DILLARD, NORMA JEAN, practical nurse; b. Spartanburg, S.C., Mar. 22, 1938; d. John Marshall and Lena (Boyter) Burnett; R.T., Spartanburg Gen. Hosp., 1959; L.P.N., R.D. Anderson Vocational Sch. Practical Nursing, 1972; m. Howard E. Dillard, May 24, 1966 (dec. 1971); children—Cheryl Jean, Homer Howard. X-ray dept. Spartanburg Gen. Hosp., 1957-62; with x-ray clinic, Spartanburg, 1962-64, Startex Bleachery, S.C., 1964-66; emergency room licensed practical nurse Spartanburg Gen. Hosp., 1972-74, Mountview Nursing Home, Spartanburg, 1975-76, Lakeview Nursing Home, Spartanburg, 1976, Camp Haven Nursing Home, Inman, S.C., 1976-82, Mountainview Family Practice Assocs., Greer, S.C., 1982—. Mem. Greer Community Concert Choir, 1978-79; mem. choir, dir. children's dept. Abner Creek Bapt. Ch.; sec. unit 1235, W.O.W., 1980. Mem. Am. Registry Radiologic Technologists (registered), Nat. Fedn. L.P.N.'s, State Bd. Nursing of S.C. Home: Route 1 Box 38 Duncan SC 29334 Office: Meml Dr Extension Greer SC 29651

DILLE, JEANETTE HELENE, state ofcl.; b. Kenton, Ohio, May 16, 1928; d. Clayton Miller and Helen Claire (Rabberman) Ewing; B.A., Bowling Green State U., 1950; M.S.W., U. Mich., 1960; children—Patrick, Carol Dille Richards, Ronald, Lawrence. Child welfare supr. Wood County Ohio Dept. of Pub. Welfare, Bowling Green, 1954-61, child welfare cons. Northwest area, 1961-62; instr. staff devel. Conn. State Welfare Dept., Hartford, 1962-67, chief div. of staff devel., 1967-69; exec. dir. Conn. Child Welfare Assn., Inc., 1969-75; dep. commr. Conn. Dept. Children and Youth Services, 1975-79; dir. human services planning Conn. Office Policy and Mgmt., 1979—; project dir. Child Advocacy Center, 1971-73. Child Welfare cons. to Judiciary Com., Conn. State Legislature, 1972-75; adj. prof. child advocacy Union Grad. Sch., Yellow Springs, Ohio, 1973-75; lectr. Conn. State and Mcpl. Police Tng. Acad., Meriden, 1971-78; mem. Dean's Advisory Com. U. Conn. Sch. of Social Work; lectr., cons. St. Joseph's Coll. Social work program; chmn. Gov.'s Task Force to Study the Adoption Laws in Conn., 1971-72. Mem. Nat. Assn. Social Workers, Am. Pub. Welfare Assn., Internat. Juvenile Officers Assn., Am. Pub. Health Assn., Acad. of Cert. Social Workers. Office: 80 Washington St Hartford CT 06115

DILLER, IRENE COREY, cancer researcher; b. North Woodstock, N.H., May 19, 1900; d. Herbert M. and Florette (Clark) Corey; A.B., George Washington U., 1925; A.M., U. Pa., 1931, Ph.D., 1933; m. William F. Diller, June 18, 1938. Research asst. dept. zoology, sec. to dir. dept. U. Pa., 1925-33, research asso., 1933-42; research biologist Lankenau Hosp. Research Inst., Phila., 1942-56; sr. mem. Inst. for Cancer Research, Phila., 1956-65, sr. mem. emeritus, 1965—. Mem. corp. Marine Biol. Lab. Fellow Kelo U., Japan, 1933-34. Fellow AAAS, N.Y. Acad. Scis.; mem. AAAS, Am. Soc. Zoologists, Am. Assn. Cancer Research, Soc. Study Growth, Sigma Xi, Kappa Delta, Sigma Delta Epsilon. Baptist. Home: 2417 Fairhill Ave Glenside PA Office: Institute for Cancer Research 7701 Burholme Ave Philadelphia PA 19111

DILLER, MARY ANN, educator; b. Kansas City, Mo., Sept. 13, 1924; d. Edward and Willa Vaughn (Gates) Diller; A.B., MacMurray Coll., 1945; A.M., U. Ill., 1948; Ph.D., Mich. State U., 1973. Tchr. history Roxana High Sch., 1945-46; asst. in rhetoric and history U. Ill., 1946-48; tchr. history and English, Belleville (Ill.) Twp. High Sch. and Jr. Coll., 1948-49; tchr. social scis. Danville (Ill.) Jr. Coll., 1949-66, head social sci. dept., 1958-66, dean adult edn., 1966-75; regional program dir. for continuing edn. and pub. service U. Ill., 1975—. Vice pres. Vermilion County Citizens for Community Action, 1964-66; mem. bd. Children's Home of Vermilion County, 1969-75; mem. faculty adv. com. Ill. Bd. Higher Edn., 1968-70; mem. exec. com. East Central Ill. Agy. Aging, 1971-75. Mem. Nat., Ill., Danville (pres. 1959-60, 63-64) edn. assns., Ill. Adult Edn. Assn. (mem. exec. bd. 1965-78, pres. 1973-74), Ill. Adult and Continuing Educators Assn., Nat. Assn. Pub. Continuing and Adult Edn. Assn. (mem. publs. com. 1975-77, higher edn. com. 1975-76), Adult Edn. Assn. U.S.A., Nat. Univ. Continuing Edn. Assn., AAUW (Danville pres. 1969-70, Ill. bd. mem. 1967-73), Sigma Phi Gamma (pres. 1961-62), Phi Alpha Theta, Delta Kappa Gamma, Kappa Delta Pi, Phi Delta Kappa, Phi Kappa Phi. Presbyn. Co-author: The Guidance Function and Counseling Roles in an Adult Education Program, 1978. Home: 1426 Mayfair Rd Champaign IL 61820

DILLER, PHYLLIS, actress, author; b. Lima, Ohio, July 17, 1917; d. Perry Marcus and Frances Ada (Romshe) Driver; student Sherwood Music Conservatory, Chgo. 1935-37, Bluffton (Ohio) Coll., 1938-39; D.H.L., Nat. Christian U., 1973; m. Sherwood Anderson Diller, Nov. 4, 1939 (div. Sept. 1965); children—Peter III, Sally, Suzanne, Stephanie, Perry; m. Warde Donovan, Oct. 7, 1965 (div. July 1975). Theatrical prodns. include Dark at the Top of the Stairs, 1961, Wonderful Town, 1962, Happy Birthday, 1963; played lead in Hello Dolly, 1970, Everybody Loves Opal, 1972, What Are We Going to Do with Jenny, 1977; numerous appearances TV and radio, concerts, supper clubs and hotels, 1955—; producer, author Phyllis Diller Shows, 1963, 64; rec. artist for Verve Records, Columbia Records; pres. BAM Prodns., Ltd., 1965—, PhilDil Prodns., Ltd., 1966—; motion pictures include Boy Did I Get a Wrong Number!, 1966, The Fat Spy, 1966, Eight on the Lam, 1967, Did You Hear the One About the Traveling Saleslady, 1967, The Private Navy of Sgt. O'Farrell, 1967, The Adding Machine, 1969; star TV series: The Pruitts of Southampton, 1966-67, The Beautiful Phyllis Diller Show, NBC-TV series, 1968-69. Recipient Star of Yr. award Nat. Assn. Theatre Owners, other awards. Hon. life mem. San Francisco Press and Union League Club. Author: Phyllis Diller Tells All About Fang, 1963; Phyllis Diller's Housekeeping Hints, 1966; Phyllis Diller's Marriage Manual; The Complete Mother; The Joys of Aging and How to Avoid Them, 1981. Accompanied Bob Hope entertainment group to South Vietnam, Christmas, 1966; piano soloist with 70 maj. symphonies in U.S. and Can. Office: PhilDil Prodns Ltd One Dag Hammarskjold Plaza New York NY 10017

DILLINGHAM, MARJORIE CARTER, educator; b. Bicknell, Ind., Aug. 20, 1915; Ph.D. in Spanish (Delta Kappa Gamma scholar and fellow), Fla. State U., 1970; m. William Pyrle Dillingham, (dec. 1981); children—William Pyrle (dec.), Robert Carter, Sharon Dillingham Martin. High sch. tchr., Fla.; former instr. St. George's Sch., Havana; former mem. faculty Panama Canal Zone Coll., Fla. State U., U. Ga., Duke U.; dir. traveling Spanish conversation classes. U.S. rep. (with husband) Hemispheric Conf. on Taxation, Rosario, Argentina. Mem. Am. Assn. Tchrs. Spanish and Portuguese (past pres. Fla. chpt.), Fla. Edn. Assn. (past pres. fgn. lang. div.), La Sociedad Honoraria Hispanica (past nat. pres.), Fgn. Lang. Tchrs. Leon County, Fla. (pres.), Delta Kappa Gamma (state legis. chmn.), Phi Kappa Phi, Sigma Delta Pi, Beta Pi Theta, Kappa Delta Pi, Alpha Omicron Pi, Delta Kappa Gamma. Home: 2109 Trescott Dr Tallahassee FL 32312

DILLON, MARY EARHART, educator; b. Kansas City, Mo.; d. Martin L. and Nellie (Edwards) Earhart; Ph.D., Northwestern U., 1940. Instr. Northwestern U., 1941-45, asst. prof. 1946-48; asst. prof. Queens Coll., Flushing, N.Y., 1949-50, asso. prof., 1951-60, prof., 1960-80, prof. emirita, 1980—, chmn. dept., 1949-53; pub. relations cons., 1954—; nat. cons. Women's Archives, Radcliffe Coll., 1955—. Research cons. Hist. Research Found., 1960; dir. City U. N.Y. Pension Conf., 1975. Mem. Am. Polit. Sci. Assn., Council Edn. Research (dir.), Queens Coll. Assn. (v.p., chmn. pub. relations com.), Delta Delta Delta. Author: Frances Willard: From Prayers to Politics, 1944; Biography of Wendell Wilkie, 1952; also articles. Editor paperback series Politics in Government. Home: 45 East End Ave New York City NY 10028 Office: Queens Coll Flushing NY 11367 *

DILLON, MAUREEN, social worker; b. Bklyn., Feb. 4, 1946; d. Edward J. and Elaine (Allen) D.; B.A., SUNY, Stony Brook, 1971, M.S.W., 1975; postgrad. in gerontology, Adelphi U., 1976, postmaster's cert. in advanced clin. practice, 1982; cert. Fordham U. Sch. Social Work, at SUNY, Stony Brook, 1979. Social worker Indsl. Home for Blind, Bay Shore, N.Y., 1973-75; social worker Southside Hosp., Bay Shore, 1975-79, clin. social worker, 1979—; field instr. Sch. Social Welfare, SUNY, Stony Brook; mem. Suffolk Inter-Agy. Coordinating Council, Islip Town Health Council. Cert. social work practice, N.Y. Mem. Acad. Cert. Social Workers, Nat. Assn. Social Workers (div. sec. 1979—), Soc. Hosp. Social Work Dirs. (chpt. sec. 1977-80), Am. Public Health Assn., Orthopsychiat. Assn., Soc. Clin. Social Work Psychotherapists. Home: 30 Lanier Ln Bay Shore NY 11706 Office: Southside Hosp Montauk Hwy Bay Shore NY 11706

DILLON, SALLY IRENE, forensic scientist; b. Joliet, Ill., Mar. 21, 1947; d. Thomas Eugene and Irene Louise (Castelli) D.; B.S., Coll.-St. Francis, Joliet, 1968. Crime lab. analyst I, Ill. Dept. Law Enforcement, Maywood, 1969-71, crime lab. analyst II, 1971-72, supervising criminalist, 1972-77, asst. lab. supr., 1977-78, lab. supr., 1978—. Recipient achievement award Ill. Dept. Law Enforcement, 1977. Mem. Internat. Assn. Identification, Forensic Sci. Soc. Gt. Britain, Am. Soc. Crime Lab. Dirs. (sec. 1982-83), Am. Mgmt. Assn., Midwestern Assn. Forensic Scientists (sec.-treas. 1978-81, pres. 1982); fellow Am. Acad. Forensic Scis. Roman Catholic. Tech. abstracts editor Jour. Police Sci. and Adminstrn., 1978—. Office: 1401 S Maybrook Dr Maywood IL 60153

DILSAVER, DONNA BOLTON, utility exec.; b. Oatville, Kans., July 19, 1932; d. Raymond H. and Juanita J. (Craig) Bolton; B.A. in Sociology, Friends U., Wichita, Kans., 1954; workshops Kans. U., Kans. State U.; m. R.L. Ryan, 1952 (dec.); 1 son, Ron; m. 2d, Dick Dilsaver, June 17, 1961. Sports writer Wichita Eagle, 1948-52; office mgr. John Coultis Interiors, Wichita, 1953-55; public relations adv. Wichita Area Girl Scout Council, 1955-66; mem. public relations staff Kans. Gas and Electric Co., Wichita, 1967—, communications specialist, 1975—; condr. journalism workshops. Mem. Wichita Conv. Tourism Adv. Bd., 1977-81; public relations cons. Wichita United Way, 1956-70; bus. cons. Wichita Jr. Achievement, 1976-79; mem. selections com. Girl Scouts, 1970; mem. Wichita Bicentennial Com., 1976. Recipient various service awards. Mem. Nuclear Energy Women, Women in Energy (founder, regional chmn.), Nat. Fedn. Press Women (awards), Kans. Press Women (awards), Am. Women in Radio and TV, Energy Advocacy Conf. Mem. Christian Ch. (Disciples of Christ). Office: 120 E 1st St Wichita KS 67202

DIMAIO, VIRGINIA SUE, gallery owner; b. Houston, July 6, 1921; d. Jesse Lee and Gabriella Sue (Norris) Chambers; A.B., U. Redlands, 1943; student U. So. Calif., 1943-45, Scripps Coll., 1943, Pomona Coll., 1945; m. James V. DiMaio, 1955 (div. 1968); children—Victoria, James V. Owner, Capistrano Trading Post, San Juan Capistrano, Calif., 1946—; owner, dir. Galeria Capistrano, 1979—; owner LaPinata Mexican Restaurant, 1979—; cons., appraiser Southwestern and Am. Indian Handcrafts. Mem. Indian Arts and Crafts Assn., Southwest Assn. Indian Affairs, Heard Mus., San Juan Capistrano C. of C. Republican. Roman Catholic. Office: 31741 Camino Capistrano San Juan Capistrano CA 92675

DIMICK, SUSAN CAROL, advt. and mktg. agy. exec.; b. Sioux Falls, S.D., June 21, 1947; d. Gerald Douglas and Virginia Lorraine (Stanton) Schwartzle; student Tulsa Jr. Coll., 1970; m. Donald D. Dimick, May 27, 1977 (dec. 1981); 1 child by previous marriage, Carmen Noel Dresch. Continuity writer Sta. KSOO Radio & TV, Sioux Falls, 1965, continuity dir., 1966; copywriter Advt. Inc., Tulsa, 1967-70; copywriter, producer Miller & Bros Advt. and Public Relations, 1970-72; copywriter, broadcast Prodn. dir. Adsociates, Inc., 1972-76; with Hood, Hope & Assos., Tulsa, 1976—, dir. audio visual communications, 1979—, v.p., 1982—; guest lectr. Oral Roberts U., U. Tulsa. Active United Way, Tulsa, 1974-76; active PTA, Tulsa; bd. dirs. Tulsa Zoo Devel./Zoo Friends, 1977-80. Mem. Am. Women in Radio and TV (nat. dir. 1979—, del. to People's Republic of China 1982). Home: 2111 N Vancouver St Tulsa OK 74127 Office: 6440 S Lewis St Tulsa OK 74136

DIMINO, MARY JANE, real estate broker, investment exec.; b. Norristown, Pa., June 21, 1942; d. Elwood Smith and Mary Ellen (Delaney) Horning; grad. Am. Inst. Banking, 1964, Va. Realtors Inst. at U. Va., 1975; student No. Va. Community Coll., 1976—; m. John M. Dimino, Aug. 8, 1964(div. 1982); children—John, Andrew, Mary Teresa, Gregory. Various secretarial positions, 1960-69; sales asso. House & Home Real Estate Corp., Manassas, Va., 1973-74; asso. broker Panorama Real Estate, Manassas, 1974-75, Long & Foster Real Estate, 1975-76; asso. broker Century 21 Capital Realty, Manassas, 1976—, mgr. Fairfax (Va.) Office, 1977, part-owner, sec.-treas., Manassas, 1981—; owner Income Growth Assos. Named to Million Dollar Sales Club, Century 21, 1977, 79, 80, 81; lic. real estate broker. Mem. No. Va. Bd. Realtors, Prince William Bd. Realtors (Million Dollar Sales Club 1977, 80), Nat. Assn. Realtors, Va. Assn. Realtors, Realtors Nat. Mktg. Inst. (cert. residential specialist), Century 21 Investment Soc., Nat. Assn. Female Execs., Real Estate Exchange Group. Office: 8803 Sudley Rd Manassas VA 22110

DIMMICK, CAROLYN REABER, justice Wash. Supreme Ct.; b. Seattle, Oct. 24, 1929; d. Maurice Clifford and Margaret (Taylor) Reaber; B.A., U. Wash., 1951; J.D., 1953; LL.D., Gonzaga U., 1982; m. Cyrus A. Dimmick, Sept. 10, 1955; children—Taylor, Dana. Admitted to Wash. bar, 1953; asst. atty. gen. State of Wash., 1953-54; dep. pros. atty. King County, Wash., 1955-62; individual practice law, Seattle, 1959-60, 62-65; judge dist. ct., 1965-75, judge superior ct., 1976-81; justice Wash. Supreme Ct., Olympia, 1981—. Named Alumni of Yr. John B. Allen Sch., 1978; recipient award World Plan Execs. Council, 1981; recipient Matrix Table award, 1981. Mem. Am. Bar Assn., Am. Judicature Soc., Am. Judges Assn., Nat. Assn. Women Judges, World Assn. of Judges, Wash. State Bar Assn. Clubs: Wash. Athletic, Wing Point Golf. Office: Temple Justice Olympia WA 98504

DIMMITT, BEVERLY JEAN, radio sta. exec.; b. Worthington, Minn., Apr. 15, 1931; d. Merle and Ethelyn Fern (Bixby) Hanson; student public schs., Graettinger, Iowa; m. Robert Lewis Dimmitt, Feb. 14, 1978; children by previous marriage—Victoria Lynn Des Combaz, Dane Lee Des Combaz. Chromologist, Duree Photography, Ottumwa, Iowa, 1965-69; with Sta. KBIZ-AM, Ottumwa, 1969—, women's editor 1969—. Bd. dirs. Wopello County chpt. ARC. Mem. Am. Legion Aux. Democrat. Methodist. Clubs: Ladies Elks; Ottumwa Women's. Author: (cookbook) Coffee Break with Bev. Home: 304 E McLean St Ottumwa IA 52501 Office: Radio Station KBIZ-AM 211 E 2d St Ottumwa IA 52501

DIMONACO, JANIS SUSAN, social service adminstr., social worker, cons.; b. Springfield, Mass., Apr. 20, 1951; d. Vincent and Conchetta Rachel (Lombard) DiM.; A.A., Holyoke Community Coll., 1972; B.A., Westfield State Coll., 1974; M.Ed., C.A.S., Springfield Coll., 1976; Ph.D., Calif. Western U., 1979; m. Henry J. Sobinski, May 2, 1981; 1 stepdau., Andrea Sobinski. Sr. vocat. counselor C&ROP, Inc., Chicopee, Mass., 1975-76, dir. employment and tng., program, 1976-78; founder, exec. dir. Hampden County Women's Center, Inc., Springfield, Mass., 1978—; co-founder, pres. Valley Mental Health Assos., Inc., Springfield, 1978—; prin. Dr. Janis S. DiMonaco & Assos., Springfield, 1980—; founder, pres. Health Mgmt. Center, Inc., 1981; mem. adj. faculty Springfield Tech. Community Coll., Bay State Med. Center, Western New Eng. Coll.; bd. dirs. Community Care Mental Health Center; cons. in field; lectr. violence against women, wellness health promotion programs; mem. Mass. Employment and Tng. Council, 1978—; chairperson Mass. Community Action Programs Dirs. Assn. on Manpower/Youth, 1978. Named Outstanding Young Woman of Yr., U.S. Jaycees, 1977; lic. ind. clin. social worker; cert. vocat./ednl. counselor; cert. secondary sch. guidance counselor, Mass. Mem. Am. Personnel and Guidance Assn., Am. Assn. Sex Educators, Counselors and Therapists, Am. Vocat. Guidance Assn., Am. Assn. Student Personnel, Am. Assn. Marriage and Family Therapists (clin.). Home: 14 Browngate Ln Simsbury CT 06070 Office: 88 Appleton St Springfield MA 01108

DI MUCCIO, MARY-JO, librarian; b. Hanford, Calif., June 16, 1930; d. Vincent and Theresa (Yovino) Di Muccio; B.A., Immaculate Heart Coll., 1953, M.A., 1960; Ph.D., U.S. Internat. U., 1970. Tchr. parochial schs., Los Angeles, 1949-54, San Francisco, 1954-58; tchr. Govt. of Can., Victoria, B.C., 1958-60; asst. librarian Immaculate Heart Library, Los Angeles, 1960-62, head librarian, 1962-72; adminstrv. librarian City of Sunnyvale (Calif.), 1972—. Pres. exec. bd. Sunnyvale Community Services; allocation bd. United Way. Mem. ALA, Catholic Library Assn. (past pres. exec. bd.), Calif. Spl. Libraries Assn., Sunnyvale Bus. and Profl. Womens Assn., Peninsula Dist. Bus. and Profl. Women (1st v.p.), Italian Cath. Fedn. (pres.), Calif. Women in Govt. Club: Soroptomist (past pres.). Home: 720 C Blair Ct Sunnyvale CA 94087

DINALE, MARGHERITA SILVI, educator; b. Pisa, Italy, Oct. 20, 1928; came to U.S., 1957, naturalized, 1961; d. Luigi and Adelia (Savelli) Silvi; Dottore in Lettere, Universita Firenze, Florence, Italy, 1949; m. Franco Dinale, June 18, 1955; children—Martina, Silvia. Instr., Smith Coll., 1955-58; asso. prof. Italian, 1968—, chmn. dept. Italian, 1976—, dir. Sch. In Italy, 1957, 68, 75, 82-83; research scholar Radcliffe Coll., 1958-59; lectr. Wellesley Coll., 1959, Boston U., 1960; lectr. Middlebury Summer Sch. Langs., 1956, 58, 61. Mem. Dante Soc. Am., Am. Assn. Tchrs. Italian, Dante Alighieri Soc. (Rome). Author: Tutti i luoghi che ho visto, 1977; contbr. poetry to Paragone-Letterature, articles to Il Mondo. Home: 20 Round Hill Rd Northampton MA 01060 Office: Wright Hall Smith Coll Northampton MA 01063

DINEZZA, JANICE HELEN, TV media research exec.; b. Buffalo, Mar. 21, 1953; d. Gregory Joseph and Helen Genevieve (Hermon) DiNezza; student Erie Community Coll., 1971-72; B.A., SUNY, 1983. Office mgr. R. H. Stark Co., Buffalo, 1974-76; media dept. mgr. Healy Schutte & Comstock, Ltd., Buffalo, 1976-80; v.p., dir. media Tavco Mktg. and Media, Buffalo, 1980; media research dir. Cable Time Network, Inc., Buffalo, 1980-82; pres. DiNezza Media Services, Buffalo, 1982—. Public service advt. coordinator Erie County Citizens Com. Sexual Assault, 1979—; writer, producer, numerous tv commls. and radio announcements on program services and needs of Vol. Supportive Advocate Program, 1979—; mem. Committees' Speakers Bur., 1980—; solicitor trainer, retail div. United Way Campaign Buffalo and Erie County, 1981-82. Mem. Women in Communications (pres. 1981-83), Buffalo Bus. and Profl. Women's Club, Women in Touch, C. of C. (vice chmn. com.), Center for Women in Mgmt., Women in Cable. Democrat. Roman Catholic. Home: 22 Tomcyn Ln Williamsville NY 14221 Office: 22 Tomcyn Ln Williamsville NY 14221

DI NICOLA, ANN IRVING, educator; b. Detroit, Apr. 28, 1930; d. Wilfred Radcliff and Georgie Mae (Horne) Irving; B.A. in Social Studies, Mac Murray Coll., 1947-51; M.Elementary Edn., Syracuse U., 1956; m. Alex DiNicola, July 23, 1955. Tchr., Muskegon Heights, Mich., 1951-52, Roseville, Mich., 1952-53; tchr., Utica, N.Y., 1953—, coordinator adult basic edn., 1966-67. Pres. Kemble PTA, 1968-71, now bd. dirs., chmn. membership com.; day chmn. bloodmobiles ARC, Utica, 1973—; pres. women of Westminister Presbyn. Ch., Utica, 1976-81, also lay liturgist; chmn. blood replacement Faxton Hosp., Utica, 1976-81, also v.p. exec. council, chmn. membership com.; exec. bd. hosp. council, 1976-82; primary tchr. Westminster Sunday Sch.; scholarship chmn. Faxton Hosp. Council, 1980-82; mem. blood com. ARC. Mem. AAUW (dir. 1979-83), Utica Tchrs. Assn., N.Y. State United Tchrs., N.Y. State Reading Assn., Bus. and Profl. Women (pres. Utica, N.Y. 1972-74), Am. Fedn. Tchrs., Early Am. Soc., PTA (hon., life). Democrat. Clubs: Order Eastern Star (grand historian 1965), Daus. of Nile (trustee 1964-67). Home: New Paris Hill Rd New Hartford NY 13413

DINKEL, JUNE MCCARTY, nurse; b. Hillsdale, Ind., Apr. 2, 1923; d. Bartholomew H. and Della (Self) McCarty; grad. St. Anthony Hosp. Sch. Nursing, Terre Haute, Ind., 1944; m. Ralph R. Dinkel, May 30, 1944; children—Ralph Michael, Margaret Susan. Pvt. duty nursing Terre Haute, 1944-60; office nurse, Terre Haute, 1960-62; staff nurse Student Health Center, Ind. State U., Terre Haute, 1962-68, dir. nurses, 1968—. Mem. Am. Coll. Health Assn., Mid-Am. Coll. Health Assn. Roman Catholic. Home: 1932 S 30th St Terre Haute IN 47803 Office: 567 N 5th St Terre Haute IN 47809

DINKINS, CAROL EGGERT, govt. ofcl.; b. Corpus Christi, Tex., Nov. 9, 1945; d. Edgar H. and Evelyn (Scheel) Eggert; B.S., U. Tex., Austin, 1968, postgrad. Law Sch., 1968-69; J.D., U. Houston, 1971; m. O. Theodore Dinkins, Jr., July 2, 1966; children—Anne, Amy. Admitted to Tex. bar, 1971; adj. asst. prof. law U. Houston Coll. Law, also prin. assoc. Tex. Law Inst. Coastal and Marine Resources, 1971-73; assoc. then ptnr. Vinson & Elkins, Houston, 1973-81; asst. atty. gen. land and natural resources div. Dept. Justice, Washington, 1981—; chmn. Gov. Tex. Task Force Coastal Mgmt., 1979, Gov. Tex. Flood Control Action Group, 1980-81; dir. Nat. Consumer Coop. Bank, 1981. Chmn. President's Task Force Legal Equity for Women, 1981—; Commr. Native Hawaiians Study Commn., 1981—. Mem. Am. Bar Assn., State Bar Tex., Houston Bar Assn., Houston Law Rev. Assn. (dir. 1978—), Tex. Water Conservation Assn. Republican. Lutheran, Author articles in field. Office: Room 2143 Dept Justice 10th and Constitution Ave NW Washington DC 20530

DINKINS, JANE POLING, mgmt. cons.; b. Van Wert, Ohio, Oct. 11, 1928; d. Doyt Carl and Kathryn (Sawyer) Poling; B.B.A., So. Methodist U., 1974. Instr. stewardess Am. Airlines, 1946-50; exec. sec., adminstrv. asst. Southland Royalty Co., 1956-63; exec. sec. Charles E. Seay, Inc. and C.W. Goyer, Jr., Dallas, 1963-68; systems analyst, programmer Southland Life Ins. Co., Dallas, 1968-69, 1st Nat. Bank, Dallas, 1969-72, Occidental Life Ins. Co., Los Angeles, 1972-73; systems analyst, programmer Pacific Mut. Life Ins. Co., Newport Beach, Calif., 1973-74, mgr. mut. fund subs., 1975; systems analyst, programmer, info. services div. TRW, Orange, Calif., 1975-79; EDP auditor Union Bank, Los Angeles, 1979; sr. EDP auditor Security Pacific Nat. Bank, Glendale, Calif., 1979-80, asst. v.p., 1981; systems analyst cons. Fed. Res. Bank, Dallas, 1982—. Mem. Sigma Kappa. Republican. Methodist. Club: Bachelors. Home: 4820 Westgrove Dr #606 Dallas TX 75248 Office: 400 S Akard St Station K Dallas TX 75222

DINO, LORI WRONA, controller; b. Buffalo, Jan. 8, 1953; d. Leonard M. and Bertha Wrona; B.S., SUNY, Buffalo, 1973, M.B.A., 1977. Bus.

mgr. Seneca Sound, Inc., 1973-76; fin. analyst Arrowhead Puritas Waters div. Coca-Cola of Los Angeles, 1978-80; sr. fin. analyst Crocker Nat. Bank, 1980-81; asst. controller Western div. Citcorp USA, Los Angeles, 1981—. Mem. Assn. MBA Execs. Democrat. Roman Catholic. Office: 444 S Flower St Los Angeles CA 90071

DIORIO, CLAUDIA GIOVINA, hotel exec.; b. N.Y.C., Sept. 18, 1945; d. Claudio Guido and Stella Josephine (Maccharulo) D.; student U. Wash., 1967; 1 dau., Caprice. Nat. gen. mgr. Nu-Dimensions Inc., Seattle, 1968-75; mgr. Office Furniture Mart, Seattle, 1975-79; pres. Hoy Inc., Seattle, 1979; now dir. conv. services Park and Seattle Hilton Hotels; cons. women in bus.; lectr. in field, condr. seminars. Pres. bd. dirs. Women's Assn. of Self-Help; bd. dirs. Central Area Alcohol Community Center; active NOW. Recipient store mgr. of year award Cascade Comml. Co., 1977; scholarship to Pasadena Playhouse, 1963-64. Mem. Nat. Assn. Female Execs., Profl. Bus. Women's Assn. Democrat. Roman Catholic. Home: 3266 80th SE #1 Mercer Island WA 98040 Office: 219 Broadway E Seattle WA 98102

DI OTTAVIO, ROSE SCHOLASTICA, cons.; b. West Chester, Pa., July 11, 1950; d. Carlo Arthur and Lena Rose (Mammarella) DiO.; B.S., U. Pitts., 1971, M.S., 1972. Research asst., Regional Comprehensive Health Planning Council, Inc., Phila., 1973-75, planning asso., 1975-77; planning asso. Health Systems Agy. S.E. Pa., Inc., Phila., 1977, dep. dir., 1977-81; with Plante & Moran, Southfield, Mich., 1981—. Senatorial scholar, 1969-71. Mem. U. Pitts. Alumni Assn., Cousteau Soc., Assn. Research and Enlightenment, Amnesty Internat., Nat. Assn. Female Execs., Am. Assn. Hosp. Planners, Am. Planning Assn., Am. Assn. for Hosp. Planning, Found. for Health Care Mgmt., Am. Soc. Profl. and Exec. Women, Career Guild. Home: Greenbrooke Parkhomes 25172 Maplebrook Southfield MI 48034 Office: Plante & Moran 26211 Central Park Blvd Southfield MI 48037

DIPIERO, DIANE PLEVOCK, nutritionist; b. Boston, Oct. 2, 1941; d. Charles and Monica (Alexandravich) Plevock; B.S., Framingham (Mass.) State Coll., 1962; M.S., Simmons Coll., Boston, 1969; divorced; 1 son, David. Field nutritionist Mass. Dept. Edn., Boston, 1962-64; nutrition cons., sch. program coordinator New Eng. Dairy and Food Council, Boston, 1964-67, sr. staff and nutrition edn. cons., program coordinator, Springfield, Mass., 1970—; tchr. Weymouth (Mass.) Schs., 1967-70; mem. faculty Springfield Coll., 1970—, asso. prof. nutrition, 1970—; pres. Food and Nutrition Consignments, 1979—; mem. faculty, cons. Baystate Med. Center, Springfield; producer TV shows, radio and consumer edn. programs. Mem. Home Econs. Assn., Soc. Nutrition Edn., Home Economists in Bus., New Eng. Public Health Assn., Mass. Home Econs. Assn. (exec. bd. 1972—, pres. 1978-79). Roman Catholic. Clubs: Valley Press (asso. dir. 1976-79, chmn. scholarship ball 1977-79), Pioneer Valley Racquet. Home: 43 Plantation Dr Agawam MA 01001 Office: 1499 Memorial Ave W Springfield MA 01089

DIPIETRO, VINCENZINA GIALLO, educator; b. Endicott, N.Y.; d. Sebastiano and Maria (Bongiorno) Giallo; cert. Am. Inst. Banking, 1950; student U. No. Va., 1973, Rocky Mountain Coll., 1976; m. Robert J. DiPietro, Sept. 5, 1953; children—Angela Maria, Mark Andrew. Exec. asst. trust dept. Harvard Trust Co., Cambridge, Mass., 1954-56; bookkeeper animal husbandry dept. Cornell U., Ithaca, N.Y., 1956-60; co-dir. Italian lang. program Italian Cultural Soc. of Washington, 1975—; instr. English as second lang. Fairfax County (Va.) Public Schs., 1975—; translator, interpreter. Mem. Italian Cultural Soc. Washington (v.p., dir.), Am. Assn. Tchrs. of Italian, Tchrs. English to Speakers of Other Langs. Roman Catholic. Contbg. author: Italian Cooking Heritage, 1979. Home and Office: 1706 Woodman Dr McLean VA 22101

DI PONIO, CONCETTA CELIA, automobile co. exec.; b. Detroit, June 2, 1921; d. Antonio and Mary (Franciosi) Di P.; Asso. in Commerce magna cum laude, Henry Ford Community Coll., 1969; B.B.A. magna cum laude, U. Detroit, 1973, M.A. in Econs. of Bus., 1974, M.B.A., 1975. Bakery, peddler, bookkeeper Wabash Bakery, Detroit, 1937-40; clerical positions F.W. Woolworth, Detroit, 1940-41; office mgr., instr. Design and Engring. Inst., Detroit, 1950-52; owner, mgr., civil engr. Tri-D Constrn. Co., Detroit, 1955-68; with Ford Motor Co., Dearborn, Mich., 1942—, div. prodn. surplus liaison, 1952-55, statis. analytical coordinator, 1955-66, parts program coordinator, 1966-74, mgmt. info. systems programmer/analyst, 1974-81, divisional systems security coordinator, 1981—; Italian translator letters and blue prints, 1960—; bus. instr. Detroit Coll. Bus., Madison Heights and Dearborn, Mich., 1975—; mgmt. instr. Henry Ford Community Coll., Dearborn, 1979—. Leader, Met. council Girl Scouts U.S.A., 1960-69. Recipient Lawrence Canjar Woman of Yr. award U. Detroit, 1974-75, Centennial award, 1976; Nat. Town Crier award Ford Motor Co., 1973, Nat. Citizen of Yr. award, 1973, Div. Community Service award, 1973; Top Ten Working Women award Greater Detroit C. of C., 1969, numerous other awards. Mem. Am. Bus. Womens Assn., Nat. Assn. Female Execs., Am. Soc. Profl. and Exec. Women, Am. Mgmt. Assn., U. Detroit Nat. Alumni Assn. (pres. bd. dirs.), Evening Bus. and Adminstrn. Alumni Council (founder, dir.), Alpha Kappa Psi (Service award 1972), Alpha Sigma Lambda, Beta Gamma Sigma, Alpha Sigma Nu (pres.), Phi Gamma Nu (pres. Zeta chpt., pres. Met. Detroit alumnae). Club: Ford Motor Girls (pres.). Home: 22204 W Seven Mile Rd Detroit MI 48219 Office: Ford Motor Co Ther American Rd Room 1540 FMCC Bldg Dearborn MI 48121

DIRKS, HAZEL MARIE, nurse; b. Ellis County, Kans., Nov. 21, 1925; d. Frederick William and Florence Elma (Carter) Mickelson; diploma Halstead Hosp. Sch. Nursing, 1948; m. Fred Dirks Jr., Dec. 5, 1948; children—Jerald Frederick, Duane Daryl. Staff nurse, charge nurse Halstead (Kans.) Hosp., 1966-69, coronary care charge nurse, 1969-72, night house supr., 1972—; staff nurse, relief house supr. Axtell Christian Hosp., Newton, Kans., 1957-66. Methodist. Home: 333 Weaver Ave S Hesston KS 67062 Office: 328 Poplar St Halstead KS 67056

DISALVATORE, ROANNE, banker; b. Frankfurt, W. Ger., May 29, 1950; d. William James and Virginia Frances D.; A.A., U. Md., Munich, 1970; A.B., Wellesley Coll., 1972; M.B.A., U. Mich., 1974. Intern, Citibank, N.A., N.Y.C., 1973; exec. trainee, acct. officer Irving Trust Co., N.Y.C., 1974-78; asst. v.p. internat. corporate banking Southeast Bank N.A., 1979—. Mem. Nat. Assn. Female Execs., Nat. Assn. Bank Women, U. Mich. Alumni Assn., Miami Wellesley Club. Office: 100 S Biscayne Blvd Miami FL 33131

DI SANTO, GRACE JOHANNE DEMARCO (MRS. FRANK MICHAEL DI SANTO), poet; b. Derby, Conn., July 12, 1924; d. Richard and Fannie (DeMarco) De Marco; student N.Y.U. Sch. Journalism, 1941-43; A.B. in English, Belmont Abbey Coll., 1974; m. Frank Michael DiSanto, Aug. 30, 1946; children—Frank Richard, Bernadette Mary, Roxanne Judith. Newswriter, Australian Asso. Press, N.Y.C., 1942-43; staff reporter Ansonia Sentinel, Derby, 1943-45; feature writer, drama critic Bridgeport Herald, New Haven, 1945-46; editor monthly bull. Pa. State Coll. Optometry, Phila., 1947-48; free-lance writer, 1949-54; founder, pres. bd. Investors Ltd., Morganton, N.C., 1966-67. Pres., Burke County chpt. N.C. Symphony Soc., 1968-70; mem. exec. bd. Community Concerts Assn., 1962-71; trustee N.C. Symphony Soc., 1965-68, 69-70, North State Acad., Hickory, N.C., 1974—. Recipient Oscar Arnold Young Meml. award, 1982. Republican. Roman Catholic. Clubs: Grandfather Golf and Country (Linville, N.C.); Mimosa Hills Golf. Author: (poetry) The Eye is Single. Address: 218 Riverside Dr Morganton NC 28655 also Grandfather Golf And Country Club Linville NC 28646

DISMUKES, KAREN ELROD, women's apparel stores exec.; b. Rutherford County, Murfreesboro, Tenn., Jan. 4, 1943; d. Elrod Cecil and Elrod Betty (Garmany) Henson; student Fla. So. Coll., 1965-68, Middle Tenn. State U., 1968-69, U. Tenn., 1978; m. James R. Dismukes, July 14, 1969; children—Tara Elizabeth, Karen A., James Russell. Owner, The Village Sq., Murfreesboro, Tenn., 1965—; poetry editor Murfreesboro Daily News Jour., 1969-70; lectr. on ladies' apparel. Bd. dirs. Charity Circle, Murfreesboro, 1968; trustee, youth chmn. Monteegle Sunday Sch. Assembly, 1981-82; others. Recipient MAZE award Murfreesboro Archtl. and Zoning Commn., 1978. Mem. Alpha Delta Kappa (founder). Club: Stone River Country. Methodist. Contbr. poetry to newspapers. Home: 434 E Main St Murfreesboro TN 37130 Office: 1150 E Maw Murfreesboro TN 37130

DISPEKER, THEA, artists' rep.; b. Munich, Germany; d. Moritz and Emma Schlesinger; Ph.D. in Musicology, U. Munich; m. Lawrence Greig. Dir. music edn. Central Inst. Edn., Berlin, children's div. N.Y. World's Fair; founder, mgr. Little Orch. Soc., N.Y.C.; personal rep. for singers, instrumentalists and condrs., N.Y.C. Recipient Bundesverdienstkreuz Govt W. Ger.; Handel medallion City of N.Y. Mem. Concert Artists Guild, Am. Symphony Orch. League, Internat. Soc. Performing Arts Adminstrs. Inc., Assn. Coll., Univ. and Community Arts Adminstrs. Inc. Home: 175 E 79th St New York NY 10021 Office: 59 E 54th St New York NY 10022 *

DISSTON RAYNOLDS, ELEANOR HURRY, mgmt. cons. exec.; b. N.Y.C., Aug. 20, 1937; d. Renwick Washington and Anna Bailey (Stoddard) Hurry; A.A., Bennett Coll., 1957; m. John F. Raynolds III, Jan. 9, 1982; children—Jay C., Jennifer S. Kuhn. Coordinator coll. relations Squibb Corp., N.Y.C., 1967-68; asst. to owner Meadow Stable, 1973-77; v.p. MSI Internat. Cons., Ltd. (Hay Group), N.Y.C., 1977-81; v.p., mgr. PA Exec. Search Inc., Stamford, Conn., 1981-82; v.p. Boyden Assocs., Inc., 1982—. Adv. bd. Outward Bound. Mem. Internat. Assn. Personnel Women (adv. bd. 1979—), Brit. Am. C. of C. (chmn. activities com., dir.), Group for Strategic Orgnl. Effectiveness. Episcopalian. Clubs: Cold Spring Harbor Beach, Mayflower Soc. Home: 200 June Rd Stamford CT 06905 Office: 260 Madison Ave New York NY 10016

DISTLER, JOAN MARIE, fin. exec.; b. Nassau County, N.Y., Oct. 27, 1951; d. John William and Mary Josephine (Stalzer) Distler; B.A. cum laude in Math., St. John's U., 1973; M.B.A., Columbia U., 1974. With Met. Life Ins. Co., N.Y.C., 1975-76; fin. analyst Texaco, Inc., White Plains, N.Y., 1976-78; bus. analyst Exxon Co. U.S.A., Bayway Refinery, Linden, N.J., 1978-79; mgr. planning and analysis Berkey Mktg. Div., Berkey Photo, Inc., Woodside, N.Y., 1980-81; mgr. budgets and analysis The Penn Central Corp., Greenwich, Conn., 1981—. Adviser, Jr. Achievement, Elizabeth, N.J., 1978-79, recipient participation award, 1979; mem. alumni counseling bd. Columbia U., 1977-79. Mem. Am. Mgmt. Assn., Am. Soc. Profl. and Exec. Women, Nat. Assn. Female Execs. Polit. columnist, The Torch, 1969-70; arts and entertainment critic The Focus, 1980-81. Home: 16 66 Bell Blvd Bayside NY 11360 Office: 500 W Putnam Ave Greenwich CT 06830

DITTO, TANYA BRADY, telephone co. adminstr.; b. Thibodaux, La., Aug. 21, 1934; d. John Ansel and Irene Marie (Landry) Brady; B.S. in English, Speech Edn., La. State U., 1956; m. William Harold Ditto, May 26, 1956; children—Steven, Diana, Susan. Librarian, Del Rio (Tex.) High Sch., 1957-58, Ins. Library, Atlanta, 1958-59; tchr. South Lafourche High Sch., Galliano, La., 1960-63, 67-69; dir. personnel, public, community relations Lafourche Telephone Co., Larose, 1969—; sec.-treas. Latelco. Leader, service unit chmn., area coordinator, mem. pres.'s cabinet S.E. La. council Girl Scouts U.S.A., 1969-79; den mother Plantation dist. Boy Scouts Am., Larose, 1970-72; pres. Larose Elem. Sch. PTA, 1972-73; bd. dirs. Assn. La. Arts and Artists. Recipient Thanks Badge, Girl Scouts U.S.A., 1974. Mem. Ind. Telephone Pioneer Assn., Orgn. Protection and Advancement of Small Telephone Cos., La. Telephone Assn. Republican. Roman Catholic. Author: The Longest Street, A Story of Lafourche Parish and Grand Isle. Home: 122 W 9th St Larose LA 70373 Office: 112 W 10th St Larose LA 70373

DITZION, GRACE, artist; b. Montreal, Que., Can.; B.A., Hunter Coll., 1933: M.A., N.Y. U., 1936; children—Lynn Shaw, Bruce. Tchr., N.Y.C. Bd. Edn., 1937-74; exhibited in one woman shows at Mus. of the Air (Cable TV), 1977, Nat. Arts Club, 1977, Westchester Community Coll., 1977, Horace Mann-Barnard, 1977, Salmagundi Club (award for sculpture), 1977, 1st Fed. Savs. Bank, 1979; group shows include Nat. Acad., Allied Artists of Am., Springfield Mus., Ponce Mus., P.R., Pittsfield Mus., Hudson Valley Art Assn., Chung-Cheng Cultural Center, St. John's U., Lincoln Center Cork Gallery, others; represented in permanent collections at Milford (Conn.) Fine Arts Council, Auburn (N.Y.) Community Coll., City U. Grad. Center; mem. awards jury Washington Sq. Outdoor Art Exhibit, 1977-79, NCCJ, 1977; vice-chmn. awards jury Salmagundi Art Club, 1978, 79, 80; cons. Womanart Gallery, 1976-78; TV appearances, 1977, 78. Recipient numerous art awards including 1st prizes, Gold medal, Purchase prize, Award of Excellence, Council Am. Artists Socs. award, Award of Merit. Mem. Am. Artists Profl. League, Artists Fellowship, Inc., Nat. Arts Club, Internat. Beaux Arts Club of Performing Arts, Internat. Soc. Artists, Women's Press Club of N.Y.C. Important works include portrait of author on dust jacket of book, Club, 1974. Home and studio: 3635 Johnson Ave New York NY 10463

DIXON, CAROLE, mdse. mart dir.; b. Gainsville, Tex., Mar. 21, 1943; d. George C. and Ann C. (Wistrand) Dixon; ed. Keuka Coll. Women, Penn Yan, N.Y., N.Y. U. Real Estate Inst.; children—Kristin, Shaun. Real estate exec. No. Westchester Land Co., Pound Ridge, N.Y., 1970-76; exec. dir. N.Y. Mdse. Mart, N.Y.C., 1979—; adv. bd. N.Y. Tabletop Assn.; mem. Real Estate Bd. N.Y. Bd. dirs. 23d St. Assn. Mem. Nat. Home Fashions League, Bridal Industry Assn. (chmn. Tabletop adv. com.). Home: 25 W 81st St New York NY 10024 Office: 41 Madison Ave New York NY 10010

DIXON, JO ANN, educator; b. Elkhart, Ind., Feb. 24, 1934; d. Lyle West and Josephine Anna (Smith) Kershner; B.S., Ball State U., 1956; M.S., Butler U., 1964, postgrad., 1976-77; m. Herbert P. Dixon, July 21, 1956; children—Randy, Dwight. Tchr., pub. schs. Indpls., 1956-57, 60-65, Omaha Pub. Schs., 1958-59; tchr. 6th grade Spring Mill Sch., Indpls., 1967—; vis. lectr. Butler U., 1975-76, 78; cons. Agy. for Instructional TV. Bd. deacons 2d Presbyn. Ch., Indpls., 1979—. Mem. Ind. Sch. Womens Club, Washington Twp. Edn. Assn. (sec. 1973-74), Ind. Tchrs. Assn., NEA, Delta Kappa Gamma, Beta Alpha Latreian. Presbyterian. Home: 1415 Brewster Rd Indianapolis IN 46260 Office: 8250 Spring Mill Rd Indianapolis IN 46260

DIXON, JO-ANN CONTE, human resources devel. co. exec.; b. Orange, N.J., Aug. 5, 1942; d. Rocco Louis and Antoinette (DeRosa) Conte; student Paterson State Coll., 1960-63; A.A., Thomas A. Edison Coll., 1976, B.A., 1978; m. Michael Eugene Dixon, July 26, 1964; children—Christopher Michael, Peter Eugene. Tchr., St. Raphael's Sch., Livingston, N.J., 1963-68; owner Orgn. Unltd., Glen Ridge, N.J., 1972-78; adminstr. corp. tng. dept. Rapidata, Inc., Fairfield, N.J., 1978-79, mgr. corp. tng. dept., 1980-81; pres., prin. cons. Q, Inc., Essex Fells, N.J., 1981—. Chmn. bd. Passaic River Coalition, Basking Ridge, N.J., 1976-80, regional coordinator, 1971-76; chmn. mayor's com. on environment, Glen Ridge, 1974-75; mem. N.J. Gov.'s Task Force for Passaic River, 1976-78; mem., pres. Home & Sch. Bd., Glen Ridge, 1978-79. Nat. Trust Hist. Preservation scholar, 1977; citation Borough of Glen Ridge, 1975; Kiwanis award for excellence in citizen involvement, 1974. Mem. Am. Soc. Tng. and Devel. (v.p. profl. devel. 1980—, award for profl. excellence 1980, award for spl. projects 1981), Human Resources Planning Soc., Nat. Soc. for Performance and Instrn., Tarrytown Group, LWV, Glen Ridge Hist. Soc. (founder). Republican. Roman Catholic. Home: 29 High St Glen Ridge NJ 07028 Office: 20 New Dutch Ln Fairfield NJ 07006

DIXON, MIRIAM CAROL, developer, property mgmt. co. exec.; b. Spindale, N.C., May 3, 1942; d. Wilburn William and Ruby Viola (Eplee) D.; student Charlotte Coll., 1961-65. Account supr. Fed. Home Loan Bank, Greensboro, N.C., 1967-69; account mgr. Dan C. Turner Constrn. Co., Charlotte, N.C., 1969-72; internal auditor Cameron Fin. Corp., Charlotte, 1972-74; with Dan. C. Austin & Assos., Raleigh, N.C., 1974—, now sec.-treas., chief fin. officer. Real estate broker, N.C.; notary public Wake County (N.C.). Mem. Nat. Assn. Women in Constrn. (past pres.), Nat. Assn. Female Execs. Democrat. Episcopalian. Home: 5201 Shasta Ct Raleigh NC 27609 Office: 5029 Falls of Neuse Rd Raleigh NC 27609

DIXON, PAM, motion picture co. exec.; b. Santa Monica, Calif.; B.S., U. So. Calif. Casting dir. Mary Tyler Moore Show, 1970; dir. West Coast talent CBS-TV, 1970-75, sr. v.p. talent, 1975-79; prodn. v.p. Paramount Pictures, Los Angeles, 1979—. Vol., Robert Kennedy Presidential Campaign. Recipient TV Acad. citation for producing Young Film Makers Show. Mem. Women in Radio and TV, Women in Film. *

DIXON-STREETER, BETTY JEAN, psychiat. social worker; b. Claremont, N.H., Apr. 20, 1950; d. Howard Leslie and Marion (Marquis) Dixon; B.A. cum laude, U. N.H., 1972; M.S.W., Smith Coll., 1974; m. Jonathan Snow Streeter, Apr. 29, 1972; children—Jessica Marion, Hilary Frances. Psychiat. social work intern Adult Outpatient Psychiat. Hosp., U. Colo. Med. Center, Denver, 1973-74; co-trainer for Vt. surrogate parent program div. spl. edn. Vt. Dept. Edn., Springfield, 1979—; psychiat. social worker Vt. Children's Aid Soc., Springfield, 1974-80; mem. steering com. Upper Valley Social Workers-White River Child Protective Team, Springfield Council Social Agys., 1975—. Mem. adv. panel for children's rights com. young lawyer div. Vt. Bar Assn., 1979—; coordinator Lebanon office West Central N.H. Mental Health Services, 1980—. Mem. Acad. Cert. Social Workers, Nat. Assn. Social Workers. Club: N.H. Smith Coll. Home: 200 Hanover St Lebanon NH 03766 Office: 37 Main St Springfield VT 05156

DMYTRIW, OLYA VERONICA, retail exec.; b. Jersey City, Oct. 29, 1922; d. Peter and Eugenia (Dombrowski) D.; B.A., Pratt Inst., 1941. Buyer, Macy's, 1941-58, Darling Shops, 1958-59; merchandiser RTW, 1972-75; fashion dir. Asso. Dry Goods, N.Y.C., 1975-77, dir. sales promotion dir. and communications, 1977-80, v.p., 1980—. Mem. Fashion Group. Roman Catholic. Editor: (with Anne Mitz) Ukrainian Arts 1952. Home: 883 Montgomery St Jersey City NJ 07306 Office: 417 Fifth Ave New York NY 10016

DMYTRYSHAK, CAROLE ANN, banker; b. Altoona, Pa., Mar. 16, 1942; d. Michael and Dorothy Bernia (Garman) D.; B.S. in Math., Drexel U., Phila., 1965; M.S. in Computer Sci., Pratt Inst., 1974. With Bankers Trust Co., N.Y.C., 1967—, now v.p. charge market research and relationship planning; cons. in field. Mem. Bank Mktg. Assn., N.Y. Map Soc., NOW. Home: 118 E 19th St New York NY 10003 Office: Bankers Trust Co 280 Park Ave New York NY 10017

DOAK, JANICE ASKEW, banker; b. Houston, Jan. 18, 1925; d. Andrew Miller and Cleo Elizabeth Askew; B.B.A., U. Tex., Austin, 1944; m. Ira Kennedy Doak, Dec. 9, 1944; children—Barbara Sue, Carolyn M. With Bank of Houston, 1949—, cashier, 1960-62, v.p., cashier, 1962-74, v.p., 1974—. Vol. worker St. Luke's Episcopal Hosp., 1973—; docent Harris County Heritage Soc. Mem. Nat. Assn. Bank Women, Am. Inst. Banking (past dir. Houston chpt.), Credit Women Internat. (dist. treas.), Houston Credit Women (pres. 1977-78), Am. Bus. Women's Assn. (pres. Houston charter chpt. 1980-81), Fedn. Houston Profl. Women (v.p. 1982-83), Alpha Chi Omega (pres. ho. corp. Gamma Upsilon chpt.). Episcopalian. Club: Altrusa (pres. 1967-68)(Houston). Office: Bank of Houston 5115 Main St Houston TX 77002

DOBBS, BETTY JO TEETER, historian; b. Camden, Ark., Oct. 19, 1930; d. Ransom Alexander and Mary Gladys (Greer) Teeter; B.A. with honors, Hendrix Coll., Conway, Ark., 1951; M.A., U. Ark., 1953; Ph.D. (Danforth fellow 1970-72, NSF fellow 1970-72), U. N.C., 1974; m. Dan Byron Dobbs, May 31, 1953 (div. 1979); children—Katherine Roan, George Byron II, Gladys Rebecca, Jean Frances. Mem. faculty Northwestern U., 1975—, assoc. prof. history, 1976—. Fellow NATO, 1974-75, Nat. Humanities Center, 1978-79. Mem. History Sci. Soc., Soc. Study Alchemy and Chemistry, Brit. Soc. History Sci. Democrat. Episcopalian. Author: The Foundations of Newton's Alchemy, 1975. Adv. editor Isis, 1981-83. Office: Dept History Harris Hall Northwestern U Evanston IL 60201

DOBECK, CAROLE FORD, public relations ofcl.; b. Worcester, Mass., June 3, 1938; d. Roderick Hill and Alice (Swenson) Ford; student in Theatre and Drama, Cushing Acad., 1955; m. Charles Loyde Dobeck, Dec. 19, 1957; 1 dau., Rodine Leslie. Asst. to dir., personnel, Hartford Ins. Co., 1961; legal sec., paralegal Neal M. Welch & Rowley Bialla, attys., N.Y.C., 1962-79; asst. to exec. dir., public relations ofcl. Lavanburg Found., N.Y.C., 1979—, public relations ofcl. Daniel & Florence Guggenheim Found., N.Y.C., 1982—. Chmn. lay visitors council First Congl. Ch., River Edge, N.J., active women's fellowship; active Republican Club, River Edge. Mem. Nat. Assn. Female Execs. Club: Order Eastern Star N.J. (Amore chpt.). Home: 369 Kinderkamack Rd River Edge NJ 07661 Office: 950 3d Ave 30th floor New York NY 10022

DOBELIS, INGE NACHMAN, book editor; b. Würzburg, Germany, Nov. 16, 1933; came to U.S., 1938, naturalized, 1951; d. Rudolf Hugo and Resi (Hamburger) Nachman; B.A. in English, U. Ga., 1956; m. Miervaldis C. Dobelis, May 4, 1969; 1 son, Arthur N. Editorial positions Buttenheim Publs. and Crowell-Collier, 1956-64; copy editor Gen. Book div. Readers Digest, N.Y.C., 1965-72, assc. editor, 1973-79, sr. editor, 1979—. Exec. bd., officer Murray Hill Democratic Club, 1968-74; exec. bd. Community Bd. No. 6, N.Y.C., 1973-78, sec., 1976, chmn. health and hosps. com., 1974-78; pres. local PTA; adv. com. Brotherhood Synagogue, 1980—; mem. N.Y. Dem. County Com., 1967-74. Mem. Phi Beta Kappa. Assoc. editor: Reader's Digest Family Encyclopedia of American History, 1975; Reader's Digest Family Health Guide and Medical Encyclopedia, 1976; Reader's Digest Illustrated Guide to Gardening, 1978; editor: Readers Digest Family Legal Guide, 1981. Home: 201 E 17th St New York NY 10003 Office: 750 3d Ave New York NY 10016

DOBERSTEIN, AUDREY K., coll. pres.; b. June 12, 1932; B.S. in Edn., East Stroudsburg State Coll., 1953; M.Ed., U. Del., 1957; Ed.D., U. Pa., 1982; m. Stephen C. Doberstein; children—Carole, Stephen, Anne, Curt. Exec. dir. Title I ESEA, Del. Dept. Public Instrn., 1965-69; pres. Ednl. Research & Services, Inc., 1969-79; mem. faculty Cheyney State Coll., 1969-79; pres. Wilmington Coll., New Castle, Del., 1979—. Mem. NEA, AAUW, Phi Delta Kappa. Office: Wilmington College 320 DuPont Hwy New Castle DE 19720

DOBIE, SHIRLEY IMOGENE, psychologist; b. Grosse Pointe Park, Mich., Jan. 30, 1930; d. Joseph L. and Gwendolyn Kemp; B.A., Wayne State U., 1954, M.A., 1956, Ph.D., 1959; m. Victor Bloom, June 30, 1973; children—Dorcas, Gordon, Elizabeth. Intern, Lafayette Clinic, Detroit, 1957; adj. asst. prof. Wayne State U., 1960-63, adj. asso. prof., 1964—; staff psychologist Lafayette Clinic, 1959-64, chief psychologist adult out-patient dept., 1964-66, acting head dept. psychology, 1968-69, dir. clin. psychology tng. program, 1967-76, dir. psychiat. edn., 1976-78, cons. in individual and group psychotherapy, 1978—; cons. psychologist U. Mich., 1969-71; psychol. cons. Harper Hosp., 1970-78; pvt. practice supervision of psychologists, social workers and psychiatrists in individual and group psychotherapy, 1978—. Recipient Sigma Xi research award, 1959; cert. cons. psychologist, Mich.; diplomate Am. Bd. Profl. Psychology. Mem. Am. Group Psychotherapy Assn. (cert. 1976), Am. Psychol. Assn., Mich. Group Psychotherapy Assn., Mich. Psychol. Assn., Wolverine State Group Psychotherapy Soc. (pres.). Contbr. articles to profl. jours. Home and Office: 1007 Three Mile Dr Grosse Pointe Park MI 48230

DOBLER, NORMA (MRS. CLIFFORD DOBLER), state legislator, civic worker; b. Haines, Oreg., May 2, 1917; d. Lester and Bessie (Bircket) Woodhouse; student U. Cin., 1935-37; B.S. in Bus., U. Idaho, 1939; m. Clifford Dobler, June 14, 1941; children—Sharon Louise Dobler Vega, Carol Marie Dobler Harris, Terry Lee. Sec. to registrar U. Idaho, 1939-41; sec. to judge, Caldwell, Idaho, 1945; sec. Am. Express Co., Seattle, 1943; lab. technician U. Idaho Coll. Forestry, Moscow, 1963-69; mem. Idaho Ho. of Reps., 1973-77, Idaho Senate, 1977—; mem. edn. com. Nat. Conf. State Legislators; mem. Idaho Pvt. Industry Council; mem. Idaho Developmental Disabilities Adv. Council, 1977-81; chairperson Gov.'s Task Force Independence, alternative nursing homes; mem. Commn. on Nursing and Nursing Edn. Mem. LWV, 1951—, bd. dirs. Moscow, 1953-68, pres. Idaho, 1968-71; county adv. bd. trustee Moscow Sch. Dist., 1963-69, vice chmn., 1966-69; bd. dirs. Idaho Sch. Trustees Assn., 1969; leader 4-H Club, 1951-64; pres. Moscow PTA, 1958-59, life mem. Recipient Service award Idaho Home Economists, 1979; named Citizen of Yr. Nat. Assn. Social Workers, Idaho chpt., 1980. Mem. AAUW (hon.), Delta Kappa Gamma (hon.). Methodist (pres. Woman's Soc. Christian Service 1972, supt. ch. sch. 1953-65, mem. ofcl. bd. 1953-67, 72). Home: 1401 Alpowa St Moscow ID 83843

DOBLER, SANDRA MAY, civic worker; b. Albion, Mich., Jan. 30, 1942; d. Edwin Fredrick and Irene Elsie (Mentink) Johnson; student schs. Prescott, Ariz.; m. Whinery Joseph Dobler, June 25, 1960; children—Daniel, Mayannette, Malynda, Kimberly. Tupperware dealer, George, Wash., 1978, mgr., 1979, unit sales mgr., 1979—. Pres. Grant-Adams 4-H Leaders Council, 1976-77, leader George Go-Getters 4-H Club, 1971-80, instr. positive mental attitudes, dating, nutrition; leader Quincey 4-H Club, 1981—; coordinator Grant Adams State Fair, 1976-80; chmn. George Cystic Fibrosis, 1978; zone pres. Luth. Women's Missionary League, 1971-74, pres. Area II Leaders Council, 1974-76; mem. Good Shephard Aux.; Sunday Sch. tchr., Christ the Savior Luth. Ch., 1971-81, supt., 1982—, Easter breakfast chmn., 1971-81; active Toastmistress Club. Recipient 4-H leadership awards Washington State Bankers, 1975, 78, Washington Grange, 1979. Home: 1551 Hwy 28 Quincy WA 98848

DOBLOUG, ASTRID ELISABETH (LISA), spa adminstr.; b. Hamar, Norway, Apr. 26, 1939; came to U.S., 1963; d. Ingvar A. and Alfhild (Kobberstad) D.; A.A., Nordfjoreid Jr. Coll., 1958; student U. Oslo, summer 1961; B.A., Hamar Coll., 1962; postgrad. U. Calif., Riverside, 1963-64. Tchr. phys. edn., English, Norwegian, Nesbyen High Sch., 1962-63; tchr. phys. edn. Desert Sun Sch., Idylwild, Calif., 1963-64; asst. dir. Golden Door Health Spa, Escondido, Calif., 1964-66; program dir., asst. dir. The Green House Health Spa, Arlington, Tex., 1966-70; spa dir. Palm-Aire Spa, Pompano Beach, Fla., 1970-80; owner The Saga Club, Health & Fitness Center, Washington, 1980—; exec. spa dir. Ft. Lauderdale Inter-Continental Hotel & Spa, Bonaventure, Fla., 1981—; fitness cons. Patino Family, Portugal and France; fitness cons. Evian Waters of France; fencing tchr. Broward Community Coll., Ft. Lauderdale. Contbr. articles to Vogue mag., Harper's Bazaar mag., Fla. newspapers. Producer cassette exercise program: Listen to Lisa, 1975. Home: 16541 Blatt Blvd #106 Fort Lauderdale FL 33326 also 3110 N St NW Washington DC 20007 Office: 250 Racquet Club Rd Fort Lauderdale FL 33326 also 1000 Potomac St NW Washington DC 20007

DOBRIANSKY, PAULA JON, polit./mil. analyst; b. Alexandria, Va., Sept. 14, 1955; d. Lev Eugene and Julia D.; B.S.F.S. summa cum laude, Georgetown U., 1977; M.A., Harvard U., 1980, postgrad., 1980—. Adminstrv. aide Dept. Army, Washington, 1973-76; staff asst. Am. Embassy, Rome, 1976; research asst. U.S. Congress Joint Econ. Com., 1977-78; NATO analyst U.S. Dept. State, Washington, 1979; staff mem. Soviet/East European affairs Nat. Security Council, White House, 1980—. Recipient W. Coleman Nevils award, 1977; Fulbright-Hays scholar, 1978; Rotary Found. fellow, 1979-80; Ford Found. fellow, 1980-81; fellow Center Internat. Affairs, Harvard U., 1980-81; Mem. Internat. Inst. Strategic Studies, Royal United Services Inst., Internat. Studies Assn., Am. Polit. Sci. Assn., Council European Studies, Phi Beta Kappa, Phi Alpha Theta, Pi Sigma Alpha. Club: Harvard (Washington). Recipient 1st prize essay contest Internat. Cultural Soc. Korea, 1980. Home: 4520 Kling Dr Alexandria VA 22312 Office: Old Executive Office Bldg Washington DC 20506

DOBSON, BONNIE JEANNE, human resources mgmt. cons. co. exec.; b. Boise, Idaho, Apr. 2, 1951; d. Benjamin Freeman and Maryjane Phyllis (Quinn) D.; B.S. in Psychology, U. Idaho, 1973. Staff asst. Office of Gov., Human Resource Devel. Council, Boise, 1973-75; manpower analyst U.S. Dept. Labor, Seattle, 1975-76; mgmt. cons. Osoro & Assos., Seattle, 1976-80, exec. regional asso., Washington, 1980—, corp. dir. Mem. Am. Soc. Bus. and Profl. Women, Delta Delta Delta. Democrat. Roman Catholic. Author: New Business Look at Employment and Training Programs, 1979. Home: 1718 Corcoran St NW Apt 32 Washington DC 20009 Office: 2025 Eye St NW Suite 1111 Washington DC 20006

DOBSON, JEAN MARILYN, reading specialist; b. San Jose, Calif., Jan. 5, 1930; d. George Leslie and Jean Gordon (Hayes) D.; student U. Calif., Santa Barbara, 1948-50; B.A. in Edn., San Jose State U., 1953; M.Ed., U. Ariz., 1964. Elem. tchr. Franklin-McKinley Sch. Dist., San Jose, 1953-55, U.S. Govt. Dependent Schs. Overseas, Sendai, Japan, 1955-56, Nara, Japan, 1956-57, Bussac, France, 1957-58, Nurenberg, Germany, 1958-59; elem. tchr. Saratoga (Calif.) Elem. Sch. Dist., 1959-63, 1964-66, reading specialist, 1966—; grad. asst. reading devel. clinic U. Ariz., 1963-64. Mem. Saratoga Citizens Com.; chmn. Santa Clara County Young Authors Fair, 1978-81. Named Tchr. of Yr., Saratoga Elem. Sch. Dist., 1966; recipient award for outstanding contbns. to reading, Santa Clara County Reading Council, 1978, award for outstanding contbns. to Reading Council activities, 1982. Mem. Saratoga Tchrs. Assn. (pres. 1966-67), Calif. Tchrs. Assn., NEA, Santa Clara County Reading Assn. (pres. 1971-72), Calif. Reading Assn. (dir. 1972-75, Area IV award for exemplary contbns. 1982-83), Internat. Reading Assn., Saratoga-Los Gatos Contemporary Artists Assn., San Francisco Symphony Valley League, Saratoga Hist. Found., Pi Lambda Theta (nat. v.p. 1971-75), Delta Kappa Gamma, Alpha Delta Kappa. Republican. Christian Scientist. Club: Eastern Star. Editor, Santa Clara County Reading Assn. Newsletter, 1977-79. Office: 14675 Aloha Ave Saratoga CA 95070

DOBSON, JULIA MARGARET (MRS. GERALD S. HAWKINS), linguist; b. Lincoln, Nebr., Aug. 1, 1937; d. Donald Duane and Carolyn Margaret (Van Anda) D.; student Am. U., Cairo, 1955-56, U. Nebr., 1956-57; B.A. with distinction in Anthropology, U. N.Mex., 1959; M.A. with distinction in Linguistics (Ford Found. scholar), Am. U., Washington, 1963; postgrad. (NDEA fellow) Harvard U., 1965; m. Gerald S. Hawkins, June 9, 1979. Instr., Georgetown U., Washington, 1960; English supr. Turkish Air Force Lang. Sch., Izmir, 1960-65; commd. fgn. service officer Dept. State, 1968; English teaching cons. USIA, Washington, 1968-74, fgn. media analyst, 1974-78, fgn. media analyst U.S. Internat. Communication Agy., 1978—; internat. lectr. linguistics and lang. teaching methodology. Mem. Tchrs. English to Speakers Others Langs., Middle East Inst., State Dept. Women's Action Orgn., Phi Kappa Phi, Kappa Alpha Theta. Club: Internat. (Washington). Author: Effective Techniques for English Conversation Groups, 1974; (with Frank Sedwick) Conversation in English: Points of Departure, 1975; (with Gerald S. Hawkins) Conversation in English: Professional Careers, 1978; contbr. articles to profl. jours. Home: 2400 Virginia Ave NW Consul 907 Washington DC 20037 Office: PGM/RC Room 704 USICA 1750 Pennsylvania Ave NW Washington DC 20547

DOBYNS, ZIPPORAH POTTENGER, psychologist, clergywoman; b. Chgo., Aug. 26, 1921; d. William Albert and Martha Cobb (Livingston) Pottenger; B.A. in Anthropology, U. Chgo., 1944; M.A. in Psychology, U. Ariz., 1966, Ph.D., 1969; m. Henry F. Dobyns, Oct. 30, 1948; children—Rique Livingston, William Comstock, Maritha Susan, Mark McClelland. Clin. psychologist VA Hosp., Tucson, 1966-67, Child Guidance Center, Tucson, 1967-68, Los Angeles Psychol. Services Center, 1969-70; minister, counselor Los Angeles Community Ch. Religious Sci., 1970—; tchr., lectr. numerous colls. throughout U.S., 1970—; research asso. Calif. Parapsychology Found., 1969—. Bd. dirs. Internat. Soc. Astrological Research, 1970-73, 77—; mem. adv. bd. Nat. Conf. Geocosmic Research, 1973-81. Mem. Am. Psychol. Assn., Assn. for Humanistic Psychology, Assn. for Transpersonal Psychology, Western Psychol. Assn., Fedn. Am. Scientists, AAAS, Phi Beta Kappa. Author: Evolution through the Zodiac, 1964; The Zodiac as a Key to History, 1968; Node Book, 1972; (with Nancy Roof) The Astrologer's Casebook, 1974; Finding the Person in the Horoscope, 1974; Progressions, Directions and Rectification, 1975; Asteroid Ephemeris, 1977; Exploring Astrology, in press; editor: Astrologer's Annual Reference Book, 1972-81. Home and Office: 838 5th Ave Los Angeles CA 90005

DODD, DARLENE MAE, nurse, air force officer; b. Dowagiac, Mich., Oct. 11, 1935; d. Charles B. and Lila H. Dodd; diploma in nursing Borgess Hosp. Sch. Nursing, Kalamazoo, 1957; grad. U.S. Air Force Flight Nurse Course, 1959, U.S. Air Force Squadron Officers Sch., 1963, Air Command and Staff Coll., 1973. Commd. 2d lt. U.S. Air Force, 1959, advanced through grades to lt. col., 1975; staff nurse, Randolph AFB, Tex., 1959-60, Ladd AFB, Alaska, 1960-62, Selfridge AFB, Mich., 1962-63; Cam Rahn Bay Air Base, Vietnam, 1966-67, Seymour Johnson AFB, N.C., 1967-69, Air Force Acad., 1971-72; flight nurse 22d Aeromed. Evacuation, Tex., 1963-66; chief nurse Danang AFB, Vietnam, 1967; flight nurse Yokotu AFB, Japan, 1969-71; clin. coordinator ob/gyn and flight nurse, Elmendorf AFB, Alaska, 1973-76; clin. nurse coordinator obstetrics-gynecology and pediatric services USAF Med. Center, Keesler AFB, Miss., 1976-79, ret., 1979. Decorated Bronze Star, Meritorious Service medal, Air Force Commendation medal (3). Mem. Am. Nurses Assn., Aerospace Med. Assn. Clubs: Am. Legion, Women of Moose. Home: 712 W 1st St Phoenix OR 97535

DODD, VIRGINIA MARILYN, veterinarian; b. Battle Creek, Mich., Oct. 14, 1950; d. George Vernon and Marilyn (Johnson) D.; B.S., Mich. State U., 1973, D.V.M., 1974. Dir., staff veterinarian Butler Animal Hosp., Charlotte, N.C., 1975—. Active YWCA, 1976-77; area coordinator Explorer's vet. post Boy Scouts Am., 1978; mem. adv. com. Central Carolina Tech. Coll. Mem. Am. Vet. Med. Assn., N.C., Greater Charlotte (pres.) Mecklenberg County (v.p.) vet. med. assns., Am. Animal Hosp. Assn. (affiliate), Am. Heartworm Soc., Vet. Cancer Soc., Am. Vet. Dental Soc., Sierra Club. Republican. Roman Catholic. Home: PO Box 1055 Cornelius NC 28031

DODEN, CORINNE GERNAEY, trucking co. exec.; b. Springfield, Ill., July 30, 1927; d. Gabriel Maurice and Hulda Katerina (Lienhardt) Gernaey; B.M.E. (scholar), Bradley U., Peoria, Ill., 1949; m. Arnold Doden, July 7, 1958 (dec.); children—Arnold G., John D. Pres., Doden Trucking Co., Inc., Woden, Iowa, 1975—; piano instr.; composer music for Christian women's banquets, Woden Centennial. Served to 1st lt., USAF, 1952-55. Mem. Iowa Truckers Assn., Beta Sigma Phi. Roman Catholic. Home and Office: Box 46 Rural Route 1 Woden IA 50484

DODENHOFF, JUDITH TINGLEY, psychologist; b. Norwich, Conn., Nov. 18, 1938; d. John Kinney Tingley and Regina (Fenton) Tingley Burleson; B.S. in Nursing, U. Mich., 1956-60; M.S., U. Wash., Seattle, 1962; Ph.D., Ariz. State U., 1978; children—James, Steven, David, Sara. Instr., Catonsville (Md.) State Hosp., 1965; asst. prof. U. Mich., 1967-69; clin. specialist St. Joseph's Hosp. Mental Health Center, Phoenix, 1970-73; pvt. practice psychology and mgmt. cons., Phoenix, 1978—. Mem. Am. Psychol. Assn., Am. Personnel and Guidance Assn., Ariz. Soc. Clin. Hypnosis. Author articles in field. Home: 1209 E Escondido Dr Phoenix AZ 85014 Office: 1118 E Missouri St Suite A-2 Phoenix AZ 85014

DODERER, MINNETTE FRERICHS, state legislator; b. Holland, Iowa, May 16, 1923; d. John A. and Sophie S. Frerichs; B.A., U. Iowa, 1948; m. Fred H. Doderer, Aug. 5, 1944; children—Dennis, Kay Lynn. Mem. Iowa Ho. of Reps. 1964-69, 80—, minority whip, 1967-68; mem. Iowa Senate, 1969-79, pres. pro tem, 1975-76; vis. prof. Stephens Coll., Iowa State Coll. (both 1979); vice-chairwoman Iowa Interstate Cooperation Commn., 1965-66; Vice-chairwoman Democratic Party Johnson County, 1957-60; mem. Dem. Nat. Com., 1968-69, Dem. Nat. Policy Council Elected Ofcls., 1973-76; chairwoman Iowa del. Internat. Women's Del. Bd. fellows Iowa Sch. Religion. Recipient Disting. Service award Iowa Edn. Assn., 1969. Mem. LWV, Delta Kappa Gamma (hon.). Democrat. Methodist.

DODGE, JESSYMAE, civic worker; b. Berkeley, Calif., Oct. 3, 1902; d. Will Pratt and Carolyn Lavina (Butterfield) Bush; B.A., U. Calif., Berkeley, 1924; student extension and summer sch. courses, 1940-55; m. Warren T. Dodge, Feb. 18, 1928; 1 dau., Norine Dodge Kimmy. Elem. tchr., Berkeley, 1930-35, Palo Alto, Calif., 1941-47, Ravenswood, Pa., 1947-59; ret., 1959. Worthy matron Eastern Star; asst. co-leader Campfire Girls; guardian Jobs Daus.; former pres. Delta Epsilon Upsilon. Mem. Beta Sigma Phi (Girl of Yr. award 1978), Alpha Mu. Republican. Home: 1437 Piedmont Rd San Jose CA 95132

DODSON, CLAUDIA LANE, athletic adminstr.; b. Washington, Aug. 31, 1941; d. Claude James and Edna Vera (Lane) D.; B.S. in Phys. Edn., Westhampton Coll., Richmond, Va., 1963; M.S., U. Tenn., 1966. Tchr., coach, Chesterfield County, Va., 1963-64, 65-71; grad. asst. U. Tenn., 1964-65; girls athletic programs supr. Va. High Sch. League, U. Va., Charlottesville, 1971—; mem. nat., internat. coms. on girls' and women's basketball, 1973—; speaker, clinician in field. Recipient various certs. of recognition. Mem. NEA, AAHPER, Nat. Interscholastic Athletic Adminstrs. Assn., Amateur Basketball Assn. U.S., Va. Edn. Assn., Va. Assn. Health, Phys. Edn. and Recreation (recognition award 1977), Va. Sports Hall of Fame, Westhampton Coll. Alumnae Assn., Delta Kappa Gamma. Presbyterian. Club: Colonnade (U. Va.). Home: 2540 Cedar Ridge Ln Charlottesville VA 22901 Office: VHSL Box 3697 Univ Station Charlottesville VA 22903

DOELP, FLORINDA DONATO, interior designer; b. Phila., Feb. 19, 1936; d. Joseph A. and Rae B. (Mungiole) Donato; B.A.A. summa cum laude, U. Pa., 1959; postgrad. U. Florence and Eurocentro (Italy); m. David W. Doelp, Jan. 25, 1969. Sr. Staff designer Kling Partnership, Phila., 1963-1969; project mgr. Semanko-Bobrowicz, Phila., 1969-1973; pres. Interspace Inc., Phila., 1973-1978; pres. InterData, Phila., 1978-1979; dir. Kling Interior Design, also partner Kling Partnership, Phila., 1979—; guest lectr. Drexel U., Moore Coll., Phila., Phila. Coll. Art. Mem. Interior Design Council (past mem. exec. bd.), AIA (affiliate), Inst. for Bus. Designers, Forum Exec. Women, Society Hill Civic Assn. Republican. Presbyterian. Club: Charlotte Cushman. Home: 100 Pine St Philadelphia PA 19106 Office: 2301 Chestnut St Philadelphia PA 19103

DOEPKEN, KATHERINE JEFFERSON, editor; b. Wheeling, W.Va., Aug. 17, 1920; d. George Jacob and Katherine V. (Ebbert) Jefferson; student Va. Poly. Inst., 1943-45, Wheeling Coll.; widow; children—James J. McLain, David L. Doepken. Family editor Wheeling (W.Va.) News-Register, 1960—. Mem. Upper Ohio Valley Travel Council. Bd. dirs. Jr. League Wheeling, Inc.; mem. theatre coms. Oglebay Inst. Cultural Art. Recipient Nat. Writing awards Stanley Products, Gorham Silver, 1970's. Mem. Presswomen, W. Va. Press Assn., LWV, Internat. Platform Assn. Sigma Delta Chi. Republican. Episcopalian. Club: King's Daus. Home: 1 Vista Ave Wheeling WV 26003 Office: 1500 Main St Wheeling WV 26003

DOHERTY, ANNA MARIE, mag. editor; b. Baldwin, N.Y., Oct. 28, 1929; d. Dennis James and Helen Elizabeth (Koch) Doherty; A.A., Immaculata Coll., 1949; cert. Traphagen Sch. Interior Design, 1950. Asso. food editor This Week mag., N.Y.C., 1952-66, N.Y. Herald Tribune, 1952-66; acting food editor N.Y. World Jour. Tribune, 1966-67; food editor, columnist Suffolk Sun, L.I., N.Y., 1967-69; with Family Circle mag., N.Y.C., 1970—, sr. editor, dir. editorial services, 1971-79, women's service editor, 1979—; food industry cons., 1965—; free lance food writer, 1966—. Mem. Internat. Fund for Monuments (Venice Com.), Met. Mus. Art, Nat. Trust for Hist. Preservation, Met. Opera Guild, Smithsonian Instn. Club: Newswomen's (dir. N.Y.C. 1970-72). Editor, author: Family Circle's 429 Great Gifts To Make, 1977. Contbr. articles to profl. jours. Home: PO Box 185 Laurel NY 11948 Office: 488 Madison Ave New York NY 10022

DOHERTY, DIANA SALTER, investment co. exec.; b. South Gate, Calif., Feb. 5, 1946; d. Morris and Anna (Gvosdiff) Salter; A.A., Cerritos Coll., 1965; postgrad. U. Calif., Long Beach, 1965-67; m. John Doherty, Apr. 23, 1977; 1 dau., Heather Anne. Fin. v.p. Award Meat Packing Co., South Gate, Calif., 1966-68; registered rep., research analyst Blyth Eastman Dillon, Long Beach, Calif., 1968-74, N.Y.C., 1974; registered investment adviser, v.p. Doherty & Salter, Inc., N.Y.C., 1974-76; pres. Salter Investment Co., N.Y.C., 1976—. Mem. N.Y. Soc. Security Analysts (sr.). Home and Office: 1326 Madison Ave New York NY 10028

DOHERTY, JOSEPHINE VARLEY, computer co. ofcl.; b. N.Y.C., Mar. 1, 1940; d. Michael and Elizabeth (O'Donnell) Varley; B.A. (N.Y. State Regents scholar 1958-62), Marymount Manhattan Coll., 1962; M.A., St. John's U., 1970; m. William G. Doherty, Aug. 15, 1970; children—Katherine Varley, Andrew Attwood. English tchr. St. Catherine Acad., Bronx, 1962-67; English dept. adminstr. Christ the King High Sch., boys' div., Queens, N.Y., 1967-72; KEN-MAC div. mgr. Aspen Systems Corp., N.Y.C., 1977-80; dir. classification and tng. Am. Legal Systems, N.Y.C., 1980—. Lic. English tchr., N.Y. Mem. Nat. Assn. Female Execs. Office: 1133 Ave of Americas New York NY 10036

DOHMAN, GLORIA ANN, librarian; b. Vermillion, S.D., June 19, 1949; d. Marlyn Doyle and Dorothy Marie (Peterson) Edman; student Ball State U., 1973; B.A., Sioux Falls Coll., 1971; m. Terry L. Dohman, Aug. 16, 1970; children—Robb Quincy, Kristin LeeAnn. Librarian/audio visual coordinator U.S. Dependent Schs., Hahn AFB, W.Ger., 1973-74; librarian coordinator/dir. Wahpeton (N.D.) Public Schs. and Leach Public Library, Wahpeton, 1974-76; periodicals/media librarian N.D. State Sch. Sci., Wahpeton, 1976—; del. White House Conf. Libraries and Info. Services, 1979; del. N.D. Gov.'s Conf. on Libraries and Info. Services, 1978. Trustee, Leach Public Library, 1977—, chmn. bd., 1978-80. Mem. N.D. Library Assn. (sec. acad. sect. 1981-83), LWV (chpt. dir. 1977-79), Mountain Plains Library Assn., AAUW. Lutheran. Home: 1631 N 5th St Wahpeton ND 58075 Office: ND State Sch Sci Wahpeton ND 58075

DOHRING, GRACE HELEN, chiropractor, med. supply co. exec.; b. Detroit, May 6, 1921; d. Fred Henry and Martha Helen (Thiel) Johnson; acupuncture cert. Hong Kong Med. Coll.; D.Chiropractic, Detroit Coll. Chiropractic, 1942; D.Naturopathy, Am. Coll. Naturopathy, 1944; Dr., Am. Sch. Neuropathy, 1944; postgrad. Nat. Coll. Chiropractic, 1949, Am. Coll. Chiropractic Internists, 1973-75, Palmer Chiropractic Coll., 1977, Ryodoraku Automatic Nervous System Soc. Japan, 1973; m. Albert A. Dohring, June 30, 1951; children—Charles, Deborah, Joan. Gen. practice chiropractic medicine, Detroit, 1942-60, Dearborn, Mich., 1960—; pres. Doctor's Supply Internat., Dearborn, 1972—, pres. research protocol project; mem. faculty Nat. Chiropractic Coll., 1975, Quebec (Can.) Osteo. Coll., 1975; tchr. seminars, Boston, Chgo., Kalamazoo, Toronto, Ont., Can., 1975; ordained minister, 1979; cons. in field; dir. Doctors' Supply Research Soc.; acupuncture lectr., seminar tchr., 1973—. Cert. in basic sci., Minn., Mich.; cert. drugless practitioner, Can. Fellow Am. Coll. Neuropathy; mem. Kyoto Pain Control Inst., Fla. Homeopathic Soc., Internat. Acupuncture Soc., Soc. Chinese Acupuncture and Cautery, Acupuncture and Research Soc., Soc. Chinese Medicine, Am. Center Chinese Medicine (life), Acupuncture Ryodoraku Assn. (charter), Am. (charter), Mich. chiropractic assns., Nat. Small Bus. Assn., Nat. Assn. Female Execs., Acupuncture Center for Chinese Medicine (life), German Acad. Auricular Medicine, Nat. Fedn. Health (life). Club: Eastern Star (pastmatron). Author: Acupuncture-Electric, 1972; Ear Acupuncture Wall Chart, 1974. Patentee acupuncture devices. Office: 24028 Union St Dearborn MI 48124

DOHRMAN, MARGIE MAE, clin. social worker; b. Palisades, Wash., Oct. 23, 1927; d. Charles Joseph and Josie Mae (Gillum) D.; B.A., Seattle Pacific U., 1965; M.S.W., U. Denver, 1968. Engaged in banking, 1946-57; asst. budget analyst Stromberg-Carlson Co., Rochester, N.Y., 1957-59; office mgr. Salvation Army, Rochester, 1959-60; dist. field teller IRS, Anchorage, 1961-64; case worker Denver Dept. Welfare, 1966; social worker VA Neuropsychiat. Hosp., Ft. Lyon, Colo., 1967; sr. clinician, dept. dir. med. social work services, EEO counselor USPHS-Indian Health Service, Alaska Native Med. Center, Anchorage, 1968—; field instr./liason B.S.W. program U. Alaska, 1975—; sec. bd. Anchorage Mental Health Assn., 1970-71; alt. social worker Anchorage Child Abuse Bd., Child Protection Task Force; cons. in field. Recipient Spl. Act award Treasury Dept., 1965. Mem. Acad. Cert. Social Workers, Nat. Assn. Social Workers, Registry Clin. Social Workers, Alaska Soc. Clin. Social Workers, Soc. Hosp. Social Work Dirs., Am. Public Health Assn., Assn. Retarded Citizens Anchorage, Alaska Mental Health Assn., Seattle Pacific U. Alumni Assn., Chugach Gem and Mineral Soc., Alaskan Prospectors Soc., Anchorage Hist. and Fine Arts Mus., Cook Inlet Hist. Soc. Author papers, reports in field. Home: PO Box 6377 Anchorage AK 99502 Office: PO Box 7-741 Anchorage AK 99510

DOIRON, DIANE BOETTIGER, ins. agt.; b. Montclair, N.J., Dec. 22, 1942; d. Russell W. and Elaine N. (Hibbard) Boettiger; B.A. in Sociology, U. of Pacific, 1965; 1 son, Stephen A.; 1 adopted son, R. Neil Royster. With Macy's, San Francisco, 1965-66, S.T.C. Corp., San Francisco, 1966-68; office mgr. Lavia Porsch-Audi, Santa Barbara, Calif., 1971-74; ins. agt. Penn Mut. Life Ins. Co., Santa Barbara, 1975—. Recipient Nat. Quality award. Mem. Life Underwriters Assn. (dir. 1981, 82, edn. chmn.), Life Underwriters Assn. (dir.; editor bull.; chmn. tng. council 1980-82). Editor PULSE assn. bull., 1981-82. Office: 3820 State St Santa Barbara CA 93105

DOLAN, KAREN ELLIOTT, mktg. co. exec.; b. Columbus, Ohio, Jan. 12, 1943; d. William Elliott and Ethelyne Marie (Winland) Stoyle; student Ohio U., 1960-63; m. Joseph A. Dolan, Jan. 14, 1967; children—Kelly Annette, Joseph Andrew. Office mgr. Westside Newspapers, Inc., Cleve., 1963-67; with Dial Am. Mktg., Inc., Cleve., 1973—, asst. br. mgr., 1976-78, br. mgr., 1978—. Leader Girl Scouts U.S.A., 1975-79. Named Mgr. of Yr., Dial Am. Mktg. Inc., 1980. Mem. Cleve. Advt. Club, Sales and Mktg. Club, Nat. Assn. Female Execs. Republican. Roman Catholic. Clubs: Sailing, Edgewater Yacht. Home: 1251 Edwards Ave Lakewood OH 44107 Office: 20800 Center Ridge #415 Rocky River OH 44116

DOLAN, LINDA SUTLIFF, energy mgr., city ofcl.; b. Danville Pa., Sept. 10, 1951; d. William Bruce and June (Mausteller) Sutliff; m. Roderick Norman Dolan. B.A., Clarion State Coll., 1974; M.S. in Forest Mgmt., Oreg. State U., 1977. Exec. asst. Clarion County (Pa.) Conservation Dist., 1972-74; forest researcher-Oreg. State U., Corvallis, 1976-77; dist. mgr. Spokane County Conservation Dist., Spokane, Wash., 1978; chief cons. Dolan & Assos., Seattle, 1978-79; biomass program mgr. Seattle City Light. 1979—; cons., lectr. in field. Asso. supr. King County (Wash.) Conservation Dist., 1979—; program adviser METROCenter YMCA, 1981—; mem. Democratic Women's Caucus, 1982. Weyerhaeuser Found. fellow, 1974-75, 75-76. Mem. Soc. Am. Foresters, Biomass Energy Research Assn., Poplar Council Can., Biomass Invisible Coll.-Brazil, Bio-Energy Council. Methodist. Contbr. articles to profl. jours. Office: Seattle City Light 1015 3d Ave Seattle WA 98104

DOLAN, PATRICIA, business exec.; b. Devon, Pa., Mar. 17, 1935; d. Roger Joseph and Anna Mary (De Cecco) Napoletano; B.J., Temple U., 1957; postgrad. Pa. State U., 1966; children—G. Donald, Cheryl A. Mgr. communications/community relations Gen. Electric Co., Valley Forge, Pa., 1960-81; dir. communications Soc. Holy Child Jesus, 1981-82; co-owner/dir. Meetings Plus, cons., Wayne, Pa., 1982—; cons. in field. Chmn. St. Agnes Med. Center, Phila., 1982-83, trustee, 1976—; trustee Burn Found. Greater Del. Valley, 1976—; mem. Nat. Teen Adv. Com., 1978-81; adv. com. OIC's of Am., 1974-80. Recipient Profl. Recognition Program award, Gen. Electric, 1970; Public Service award, OIC, 1976. Mem. Phila. Public Relations Assn., Nat. Assn. Female Execs., Sons of Italy. Republican. Roman Catholic. Contbr. articles to profl. jours. Home: 239 S Gulph Rd King of Prussia PA 19426 Office: 1200 W Valley Rd Wayne PA 19087

DOLE, ELIZABETH HANFORD, govt. ofcl.; former commr. FTC; b. Salisbury, N.C., July 29, 1936; d. John Van and Mary Ella (Cathey) Hanford; B.A. with honors in Polit. Sci., Duke U., 1958; postgrad. Oxford (Eng.) U., summer 1959; M.A. in Edn., Harvard U., 1960, J.D., 1965; m. Robert Joseph Dole (U.S. Senator from Kans.), Dec. 6, 1975. Admitted to D.C. bar, 1966; staff asst. to asst. sec. for edn. HEW, Washington, 1966-67; practiced in Washington, 1967-68; asso. dir. legis. affairs, then exec. dir. Pres.'s Com. for Consumer Interests, Washington, 1968-71; dep. dir. Office Consumer Affairs, The White House, Washington, 1971-73; commr. FTC, Washington, 1973-79; chmn. Voters for Reagan-Bush, 1980; dir. Human Services Group, Office of Exec. Br. Mgmt., Office of Pres.-Elect, 1980; asst. to pres. for public liaison, 1981—. Trustee, Duke U., 1974—, also mem. bd. advisors Bus. Sch.; trustee Washington Opera; bd. dirs. Am. Council on Young Polit. Leaders; mem. overseers com. to visit J.F. Kennedy Sch. Govt., Harvard U.; mem. council Harvard U. Law Sch. Assos. Recipient Arthur S. Flemming award U.S. Govt., 1972; named one of Am.'s 200 Young Leaders, Time mag., 1974. Office: White House 1600 Pennsylvania Ave Washington DC 20500

DOLE, GRACE FULLER, librarian; b. Cambridge, Mass.; d. John Soper and Margaret Fernald D.; B.A., Bryn Mawr Coll., 1944; M.L.S., Columbia U., 1954; m. Paul E. Kohler, Jr., Jan. 22, 1944 (div. May 1946); 1 dau., Margaret Kohler Nicholson. Tchr. French, librarian Low-Heywood Sch., Stamford, Conn., 1948-50; sch. librarian Greenwich (Conn.) Library, 1950-53; with reference dept. N.Y. Public Library, N.Y.C., 1954-56; asst. librarian then librarian Benton & Bowles, N.Y.C., 1956-62; reference librarian Ferguson Library, Stamford, Conn., 1962-64; librarian U. Conn.-Stamford Br. and Center, 1964-75, asst. librarian, 1975-80, library specialist, 1981—; instr. library research methods, spring 1975. Mem. Spl. Libraries Assn. (head com. new library devel. 1962-63), ALA, Library Group Southwestern Conn. (rec. sec. 1972-73, chmn. publicity 1971-75, chmn. Newsletter 1975—), Catharine Lorillard Wolfe Art Club (dir. 1975-78), Am. Artists Profl. League (hon.), Hudson Valley Art Assn. (rec. sec. 1973-76, historian 1976—), Margaret F. Dole Contemporary Art Club (v.p. 1973-75, pres. 1976—), DAR, Colonial Dames XVII Century, Huguenot Soc. Conn., Panhellenic Assn. (chmn. Fairfield br. 1973-74, v.p. Fairfield br. 1977-78), Fairfield County-City Panhellenic Assn. (ways and means chmn. 1973-74, treas. 1975-76), English Speaking Union, Jr. League N.Y.C., Nat. Arts Club. Home: 503 W Lyon Farm Dr Greenwich CT 06830

DOLE, PATRICIA L., social worker; b. Pullman, Wash., Feb. 12, 1930; d. Arthur William and Zelma Florence (Hatley) D.; B.A., Whitworth Coll., 1952; M.S.W., U. Denver, 1959. Social case worker Dept. Pub. Welfare, Ellensburg, Wash., 1955-57; case work aide VA Hosp., Fort Lyon, Colo., 1958; psychiat. social worker Tulsa Psychiat. Clinic, 1959-65; pvt. practice, Tulsa, 1965-66; psychiat. social worker Community Mental Health, Dept. Mental Health Okla., Tulsa, 1966-69; psychiat. social worker Eastern State Hosp., Tulsa, 1969-73, Okla. Dept. Mental Health Community Mental Health Clinic, Ardmore, Okla., 1973-79; regional social worker Carter County Health Dept., Maternal and Child Health div. S.C. Health Dept., Ardmore, 1979—; mem. adv. com. Sch. Nursing, Murray State Coll., 1979—, Area Aging Agy., So. Okla. Devel. Assn., 1974—. Commr., Indian Nations Presbytery, 1980. Served to 1st lt. WAC, 1953-55. NIMH grantee, 1958. Mem. Okla. Health and Welfare Assn. (dir.; treas. 1974-81), Nat. Assn. Social Workers (registered), Acad. Cert. Social Workers. Presbyterian (chmn. Christian edn. council, ruling elder). Home: 1219 Hall Pl Ardmore OK 73401 Office: 101 1st St SW Ardmore OK 73401

DOLJACK, BARBARA LYNN, pub. co. exec.; b. Cleve., Mar. 14, 1942; d. Rudolph Frank and Mary Jean Doljack; student Ohio Dominican Coll., 1960-62, Tobe-Coburn Sch. Fashion Careers, N.Y.C., 1963. With Bloomingdale's, N.Y.C., 1963-66, asst. fashion dir., 1964-66; sr. merchandising coordinator Seventeen Mag., N.Y.C., 1966-69, merchandising editor, 1969-71, merchandising dir., 1971-76; dir. promotion services Seventeen mag., 1976-82, mktg. dir., 1982—; dir. promotion services Panorama mag., 1979-81. Mem. exec. alumnae com. The Tobe-Coburn Sch., 1976-79, also mem. industry adv. com.; mem. various coms. The Floating Hosp., 1978—; pres. exec. com. Friends of Henry St. Settlement, 1976-78, adv. com., 1979—. Recipient Mehitabel award, 1979; The T award Tobe-Coburn Sch., 1968. Mem. N.Y. Jr. League, Mktg. Communications Execs. Internat. (chpt. bd. dirs. 1977-79), Advt. Women of N.Y., Nat. Home Fashions League, The Fashion Group (v.p. bd. govs. 1981-83). Home: 310 E 70 St New York NY 10021 Office: 850 3d Ave New York NY 10022

DOLLAR, SANDRA MARIE, bus. communications specialist; b. Phila., Feb. 10, 1949; d. Francis William and Marion Beatrice (Gross) D.; B.A., Bryn Mawr Coll., 1971. Editor, publicity coordinator AMP Spl. Industries, Valley Forge, Pa., 1973-75; public info. coordinator Peirce Jr. Coll., Phila., 1975-76; Vistas editor Roswell (N.Mex.) Daily Record, 1977-78; publs. coordinator Penn Mut. Life Ins. Co., Phila., 1979-80; mgr. editorial services INA Corp., Phila., 1980—. Recipient Mary Swindler award, Mary Windsor award Bryn Mawr Coll., 1969, Media award N.Mex. div. Am. Cancer Soc., 1977, Guy Rader award N.Mex. Med. Soc., 1977, Communicators award United Way Am. and SE Pa., 1980, 81, 82, Bell Ringer award Bus./Profl. Advt. Assn., 1981. Bryn Mawr Coll. alumnae regional scholar, 1967-71. Mem. Internat. Assn. Bus. Communicators, Women in Communications, Nat. Writers Club, ASCAP. Office: 1600 Arch St Philadelphia PA 19101

DOLSON, VIVIAN ANTOINETTE, sales exec.; b. Chgo., July 17, 1925; d. Werner Henry and Lillian Rose (Ghilardi) Steger; student DePaul U., 1943-46; m. Sept. 10, 1948 (div.); children—Bill, David. Asst. registrar DePaul U., 1952-55, exec. sec., 1955-58; asst. personnel dir. Stat. Tabulating Co., Chgo., 1958-61; owner, operator Dolson Market Research, Chgo., 1961-75; dist. sales mgr. for Ill. and Wis., Burroughs/Lear Siegler Co., Chgo., 1975-78, asst. nat. sales mgr., Kalamazoo, 1978-81; nat. sales mgr. Marvel Metal Products, Chgo., 1981—; career cons. Triton Jr. Coll. Mem. Am. Market Research Assn., Nat. Office Products Assn. Am. Mgmt. Assn. Home: Apt 318 17W 724 Butterfield Rd Oakbrook Terrace IL 60181 Office: 3843 W 43d St Chicago IL 60632

DOMAN, JANET JOY, assn. exec. b. Phila., Dec. 16, 1948; d. Glenn J. and Hazel Katie (Massingham) Doman; student U. Hull (U.K.), 1969-70; B.A., U. Pa., 1971; certificate in human devel. Insts. Achievement Human Potential, 1973, teaching certificate, 1975. Clinician, Insts. for Achievement of Human Potential Phila., 1971-74; dir. English, Early Devel. Assn., Tokyo, 1974-75; dir. Evan Thomas Inst. Early Devel., Phila., 1975-77, Inst. Achievement of Intellectual Excellence, 1977-80; vice dir. Insts. Achievement Human Potential, 1980-82, dir., 1982—; 1980-82, dir., 1982—; internat. lectr. on treatment of brain injured children and superiority. Recipient Gold medal Centro de Reabilitacion Nosa Senhora da Gloria, Rio de Janeiro, Brazil, 1974; Brit. star Brit. Inst. Achievement Human Potential, 1976; Sakura Korosho medal Japanese Inst. Achievement Human Potential, 1977; statuette with pedestal Internat. Forum for Human Potential, 1980. Office: 8801 Stenton Ave Philadelphia PA 19118

DOMAN, KATHARINE BIGELOW (MRS. NICHOLAS R. DOMAN), civic worker; b. N.Y.C.; d. Mason Huntington and Elisabeth (Macdonald) Bigelow; student Barnard Coll.; m. Carter Chapin Higgins, 1937 (div. 1949); children—Richard Carter, Elisabeth (Mrs. Henry Null IV), Mark Huntington (dec.); m. 2d, Nicholas R. Doman, Aug. 25, 1951; children—Daniel Bigelow, Alexander Macdonald. Co-dir. Boston Sutdio and Art Gallery, 1947; art and drama critic St. Augustine (Fla.) News, 1948-49; editorial writer Baker & Funaro, 1949; with Conde Nast, 1949-50. Mem. cts. com. N.Y. Jr. League, 1951-58; active fund-raising coms. Sheltering Arms Children's Service Aux., 1951—; bd. dirs. N.Y. council Nat. Council Crime and Delinquency, 1963-69; mem. Legal Aid Soc. Women's Aux., 1963—; co-chmn. Gov.'s Conf. Women's Role in Crime Prevention, 1968; mem. men's and women's com. Am. Mus. Natural History, 1971—, vol. tchr., 1979—. Bd. dirs. N.Y. Edn. Inst. for Learning and Research. 1964-70. Clubs: Cosmopolitan, Shelter Island Yacht, Gardiners Bay Country. Home: 1185 Park Ave New York NY 10028

DOMANSKI, TERESA PELAGIA, psychiat. social worker; b. Phila.; d. Vincent Paul and Pelagia Teresa D.; B.S., U. Pa., 1926, M.A. in Sociology, 1929; M.S.S., Smith Coll., 1949, program advanced study, 1959-60. Claims adjustor, caseworker, tng. supr. Dept. Public Assistance, 1930-43; fed. rep. U.S. CSC, 1943; psychiat. caseworker mil. hosps. ARC, Washington, 1943-45, asst. chief nat. personnel adminstrn., 1945-48, casework supr., 1949-57; field instr. Bryn Mawr (Pa.) Coll. Sch. Social Work, 1950-57, asso. prof. social work, 1958-59; lectr. Sch. Nursing, Jefferson Med. Coll. Hosp., Phila., 1961, social work cons. dept. obstetrics, 1961-63, instr. psychiatry, 1962-65, asso. prof. dept. psychiatry and human behavior, 1965—, asso. dir. social service, 1960-62, chief psychiat. social worker, 1962-68; exec. dir. Florence Crittenton Services of Phila., Inc., 1969-81; pvt. practice social work therapy, Phila.; nat. adv. council execs. Child Welfare League Am., 1976-81, F.C. Nat. Com., 1975-81. Pres., Tenants Assn. Sch. House Lane Apts., Phila., 1974—. Recipient Jefferson award Am. Inst. Public Service, 1979. Mem. Nat. Assn. Social Workers, Acad. Cert. Social Workers. Office: 6325 Burbridge St Philadelphia PA 19144

DOMB, AVIVA, educator; b. Dniepropetrovsk, Russia, June 4, 1915; came to U.S., 1958, naturalized, 1964; d. Asher and Hanna (Gotlieb) Hanina; grad. Inst. Music, Haifa, Israel, 1935, Royal Acad. Music, London, 1939; Licentiate, Royal Acad. Music, London as violin performer, 1939, as violin tchr., 1939; m. Solomon Domb, Aug. 20, 1940; children—Uriel, Daniel. Tchr., Inst. of Music, Haifa, 1940-57; concertized in Europe and Israel, 1938-50; regular violin performer Jerusalem radio, 1940-41; dir. E. Tremont Y, Bronx River Y, and Riverdale Y Music Schs., 1960-68; dir. Center Music Sch. of Yonkers (N.Y.) and Mid-Westchester Y Music Sch., Scarsdale, N.Y., 1970—; organizer, dir. 1st Music and Arts Camp, Henry Kaufmann Camp Grounds, Pearl River, N.Y., 1967-72, others. Mem. Nat. Guild Community Schs. of Arts, Nat. Jewish Music Council (exec. bd.). Contbr. articles to profl. jours. Home: 123 Plymouth Dr Scarsdale NY 10583 Office: 999 Wilmot Rd Scarsdale NY 10583

DOMBRO, MARCIA WINTERS, nurse, ednl. adminstr.; b. Clinton, Minn., Dec. 14, 1940; d. Benton Jay and Thelma Elizabeth (Roth) Winters; B.S.N., U. Wash., 1963; M.S. in Adult Edn., Fla. Internat. U., 1976; m. Roy S. Dombro, Sept. 10, 1967; children—Rayna Lisette, Meryl Elana. Public health nurse Seattle-King County Health Dept., 1964-66, N.Y.C. Dept. Health Bur. Nursing, 1966-67; head nurse home care unit Bellevue Hosp., N.Y.C., 1967-68; asst. clin. instr. in obstetrics City Hosp. at Elmhurst, N.Y.C., 1968; clin. instr. obstetrics Miami-Dade Community Coll., 1973-74; instr. U. Miami Sch. Nursing, 1976-80; dir. dept. nursing edn. Baptist Hosp. Miami (Fla.), 1980—; tchr. sex edn. for schs., civic groups, parent edn. groups. Active ERA, NOW, Miami. Mem. Nurses Assn.-Am. Coll. Ob-Gyn., Am. Nurses' Assn., Nat. League for Nursing, Am. Soc. Psychoprophylaxis in Obstetrics (cert. childbirth instr. 1970, coordinator South Fla. 1976-81), Am. Soc. Health Edn. and Tng. Jewish. Author: Post Partum for the Childbirth Educator-A Programmed Text, 1976; contb. articles to profl. jours.; co-producer audiovisual kit: Born Sexy, 1976. Home: 9841 SW 123d St Miami FL 33176 Office: 8900 N Kendall Dr Miami FL 33176

DOMEC, ETHEL MCDONALD, nurse; b. Blackfoot, Tex., Mar. 10, 1920; d. John Walton and Roberta (Epps) McDonald; student Our Lady of Lake Coll., 1937-38; R.N., St. Mary's Sch. of Nursing, 1941; student Lamar U., 1962-63; m. Samuel Domec, Oct. 11, 1941; children—Colleen Clare, Michael Douglas, Robert Neil. Office and pvt. duty nurse, 1941-52; head nurse obstetrics St. Mary's Hosp., Port Arthur, Tex., 1952-60, head nurse medical, 1960-63; pvt. duty nurse, 1963-64; night supr. Park Place Hosp., Port Arthur, Tex., 1964-67, supr. psychiatry, 1967-76, supr. central supply, 1977-78, quality assurance/risk mgmt. coordinator, 1978—. Recipient award So. Writers' Conf., 1962. Mem. Am., Tex. nurses assns., Tex. Poetry Soc., Franklin Mint Collector's Soc., Nat. Poetry Soc., Wedgwood Collectors Soc., Belleek Collectors Soc. (charter). Democrat. Roman Catholic. Contbr. to Our Area Poets column, Anthology of Texas Poets, Anthology of World Peace and Brotherhood. Home: 3898 Dryden Rd Port Arthur TX 77640

DOMI, TANYA LESLIE, army officer; b. Indpls., July 24, 1954; d. John Thomas Domi and Louise Joan Edwards; B.A., Central Mich. U., 1981, M.A. candidate in polit. sci., 1981-82. Grad. asst. Central Mich. U., 1981-82; commd. 2d lt. U.S. Army, 1982; brigade Hdqrs. comdr., 1982—. Mem. exec. bd. Isabella County Democratic Com., 1979-82, 2d vice-chmn. 1981; mem. Mich. Women's Dem. Caucus, 1981—; bd. dirs. Glenn Civic Center, 1978-79. Mem. Res. Officers Assn., ACLU, Sigma Delta Chi, Mu Sigma, Chi Gamma Iota. Contbr. Soldier's mag., Trailblazer; mem. staff Central Michigan Life. Home: PO Box 2006 Mount Pleasant MI 48858

DOMINGO, GLORIA, real estate broker; b. Zamboanga City, Philippines, Apr. 27, 1930; came to U.S., 1968, naturalized, 1976; d. Leovigildo and Paula (Foronda) D.; B.S. cum laude in Edn., U. Manila, 1951; postgrad. in Bus. Adminstrn., U. of East, 1959-62, Nat. Tchrs. Coll. Grad. Sch., 1965-67, U. Calif., Berkeley, 1970-71, Coll. San Mateo, 1974-76; m. Loriga G. Domingo, Aug. 13, 1949; children—Edgardo, Lynn, Marilyne, Ferdinand. Tchr. sci., demonstrator Div. of City Schs., Manila, 1955-68; jr. acct. Calif. Automobile Assn., San Francisco, 1969-72; real estate salesperson Towne & Country Investments, San Francisco, 1972-74, sales mgr., 1974-76; real estate broker, owner, operator Premier Realty Investments, San Francisco, 1976—; sec. bd. dirs. Realty Elite of Am., 1978—; v.p. Multiple Listing Service of San Francisco Credit Union. Mem. Nat. Assn. Realtors, Calif. Assn. Realtors, grad. Realtors Inst., Women Council of Realtors, Calif. Assn. Real Estate Tchrs., Nat. Assn. Female Execs., San Francisco Bd. Realtors, North San Mateo Bd. Realtors, San Mateo-Burlingame Bd. Realtors. Club: Arthur Murray Hobby. Office: Premier Realty Investments 5580 Mission St San Francisco CA 94112

DOMMEL, DARLENE HURST, writer; b. Charles City, Iowa, July 11, 1940; d. Roy and Elsie (Hopkes) Hurst; B.S. with high distinction, U. Minn., 1963, M.S., 1965; postgrad. So. Meth. U., 1976-77; m. James H. Dommel, Oct. 15, 1961; children—Diann, Christine, David. Pub. health nurse Combined Nursing Service, Mpls., 1963-64; contbr. articles on pottery to various collectors and antiques mags., 1967—; organizer, exhibitor of art pottery display touring fin. instns. in upper midwest, 1976—; lectr. and cons. health care, antiques, journalism; health care specialist Health Services Research Center, St. Louis Park Med. Center, 1978-79; instr. Augsburg Coll., 1979-81. Mem. Minn. Adv. Task Force on Epilepsy, 1981—, State Council for Handicapped, 1982—, Dept. Pub. Welfare Adv. Council on Mental Retardation and Phys. Disabilities, 1982—. Mem. Mpls. Inst. Arts. USPHS trainee, 1964-65; Sigma Theta Tau scholar, 1962-63; Martha Ripley scholar, 1961-62: U. Minn. Sch. Nursing Found. scholar, 1962. Mem. AAUW, Am. Nurses Assn., U. Minn. Alumni Assn., Nat. Writers Club, Nat. League Nursing, Christian Writers Guild, Gethsemane Luth. Ch. Women, Minn. Women in Higher Edn., Minn. Women's Polit. Caucus, Sigma Theta Tau, Delta Delta Delta. Lutheran. Home: 510 Westwood Dr N Golden Valley MN 55422

DOMOL, ARLEEN FRANCIS, photo album co. exec.; b. Bklyn., d. Kenneth F. and Mildred Dorothy (Garcia) Nothnagel; student Oakland Community Coll., Mich., 1973-77. With K-Mart Corp., Troy, Mich., 1967-79, asst. buyer cameras and optical equipment, 1974-79; nat. account exec. Chinon Corp., Springfield, N.J., 1979-81; West Coast regional mgr. Holson Co., Wilton, Conn., 1981—. Mem. Nat. Assn. Female Execs. Republican. Home: 33692 Halyard St Laguna Niguel CA 92677

DOMPE, MARILYN ANN, advt. and public relations exec.; b. Newman, Calif., May 17, 1954; d. Peter J. and Nadine C. D.; B.S. with highest honors, Calif. Poly. State U., 1976; postgrad. Golden Gate U., 1978-79. Newspaper columnist Westside Index, Newman, Calif., 1976-78; staff home economist Steedman, Cooper & Busse Advt., 1976-78, sr. home economist, 1978, food publicity dept. head, 1978—; account exec. Busse & Cummins, San Francisco, 1978—. Mem. Home Economists in Bus. (membership chmn. 1977-78, chmn.-elect 1981-82), Am. Home Econs. Assn., Produce Mktg. Women in Advt., Phi Upsilon Omicron. Club: San Francisco Giants Baseball Boosters. Author: The Treasury of Almond Recipes, 1978; The Sweet Potato Lovers Guide to Good Eating, 1979. Office: 690 5th St San Francisco CA 94107

DONADIO, CAROL ANN, advt. and mktg. exec.; b. N.Y.C., June 19, 1951; d. Anthony Robert and Josephine Martha (LaPella) D.; A.A.S., Fashion Inst. Tech., 1968; B.A., N.Y. U., 1970. Spl. events dir. Gimbels, N.Y.C., 1969-76; dir. women's affairs Planned Consumer Mktg., N.Y.C., 1976-77; dir. mktg. services Modern Bride mag., N.Y.C., 1977-80; asso. pub. Talk mag., N.Y.C., 1980; pres. Carol Donadio Assos. Co., advt. and mktg. to careerwomen, N.Y.C., 1980—; instr. Fashion Inst. Tech., 1975-76; guest lectr. Brandeis U., 1973. Bd. dirs. Theatre Dance Collection; mem. public relations staff Internat. Yr. of the Woman, N.Y.C. chpt. 1974. Mem. Nat. Assn. Female Execs.

DONAHEY, GERTRUDE WALTON, state ofcl.; b. Goshen, Ohio, Aug. 4, 1908; d. George Sebastian and Mary Ann (Thomas) Walton; grad. bus. coll.; D.Pub. Service (hon.), Rio Grande U.; m. John W. Donahey, Apr. 12, 1930 (dec.); 1 son, John William. Pvt. sec., until 1930; now treas. State of Ohio. Sec., mem. exec. com., bd. dirs. Ohio Mental Health Assn. Chmn. operations support Ohio Democratic Com., 1963—, mem.-at-large platform com., 1964, 68; field aide in Central and South Ohio for U.S. Senator Young, 1963-69, then staff asst.; del. Dem. Nat. Conv., 1964, del.-at-large, mem. platform and resolutions com., 1968; trustee Better Bus. Bur. Central Ohio. Mem. Municipal Finance Officers Assn. (v.p.), Nat. Assn. Auditors, Comptrollers and Treasurers (treas. 1975—), Delta Kappa Gamma. Episcopalian. Address: State Office Tower 30 E Broad St Columbus OH 43215

DONAHOE, CAROLYN PAULA, dietitian; b. Mankato, Minn., Nov. 14, 1943; d. Harold Lester and Mildred B. Pischner; B.S. in Secondary Edn., Mankato State U., 1964; postgrad. Iowa State U., 1969-70. Tchr. high sch. biology, 1965-66; asst. to dietitian Immanual Hosp., Mankato, 1966-68; cons. dietitian Lake Crystal Nursing Home and Mankato Nursing Home, 1967-69; asst. to dir. fin. Minn. Hosp. Assn., 1970-71; dietetic intern Hennepin County Med. Center, Mpls., 1971-73; dir. nutrition Va. Bapt. Hosp., Lynchburg, 1973-75; dir. nutrition services Hosp. Dietary Services, Inc., Farmington Hills, Mich., 1975-76; dir. Nutrition Plus, Pasadena, Calif., 1976—; dir. clin. nutrition Meml. Hosp., Long Beach, Calif., 1977-80; pres. Carolyn P. Donahoe, R.D., Inc., Pasadena, Calif., 1981—; cons., lectr., seminar leader in field. Mem. Am. Dietetic Assn., Cons. Nutritionists, Practice Group Registered Dietitians Pvt. Practice, Am. Inst. Clin. Nutrition, Am. Heart Assn., Am. Diabetes Assn., Calif. Dietetic Assn. (legis. chmn. 1979). Republican. Lutheran. Author: Realities in Private Practice, 3d edit., 1982; Clinical Nutrition Management, 1983. Office: 10 Congress St Suite 320 Pasadena CA 91105

DONAHOE, RITA LOUISE, Realtor; b. Boston, Jan. 16, 1930; d. Franklin Augustine and Barbara Rita (Coyne) Bannister; student Boston

Coll., 1948-51; m. Robert Francis Donahoe, June 15, 1957; children—Steven Francis, Christopher John. Asst. clk. Suffolk Superior Criminal Ct., Boston, 1948-57; v.p., treas. D&G Constrn. Co., Inc., Merrimack, N.H., 1964-68; broker Fisher Assos., real estate, Nashua, N.H., 1968-71; propr. R. Donahoe Assos., Bedford, N.H., 1971—. Mem. Nashua (v.p. 1975, pres. 1976, Realtor of Year 1977), Manchester bds. Realtors, So. N.H., (v.p. 1975—, award 1973), Greater Manchester multiple listing services, Women's Council Realtors (chpt. pres. 1974), Nat., N.H. (dir. exec. com. 1976—) assns. Realtors, Realtors Nat. Mktg. Inst., Manchester C. of C. Club: Manchester Country. Home: Davis Rd Merrimack NH 03054 Office: RFD 5 Daniel Webster Hwy Bedford NH 03102

DONAHUE, EFFIE MAE, real estate exec.; b. Scott County, Ind., Oct. 24, 1917; d. Clarence Dexter and Eva (Gobin) Polk; student real estate sales and brokerage Ind. U., 1974-75; profl. designation Grad. Realtors Inst., Ind. U., 1978; also student short courses Purdue U., DuPont Lab.; m. Robert Harold Donahue, Apr. 16, 1938; children—Gloria Jean Donahue Bayes, Betty Jo Donahue Lewis, James Harold. Lab. technician Morgan Packing Co., Austin, Ind., 1943-53; E.I. DuPont, Charlestown, Ind., 1953-58; saleswoman Scottsburg United Home Furnishings (Ind.), 1958-59, clk., treas., 1959-60, mgr., 1960-64; caseworker Scott County (Ind.) Welfare, 1964-67, acting dir., 1967-69; broker Watteau Real Estate, New Albany, Ind., 1974-77; broker, mgr. SIR Real Estate, Jeffersonville, Ind., 1977-79; broker, owner Family Real Estate, Scottsburg, Ind., 1979—. Pres., Scottsburg Elem. Sch. PTA, 1948-51, Parent Tchr. Student Assn., Scottsburg High Sch., 1951-52. Recipient Bronze award in real estate and named to Half Million Dollar Club, So. Ind. Bd. Realtors-Womens Council Realtors, 1975, 76, 77; Appreciation award United Meth. Ch., 1980, cert. of recognition Bus. and Profl. Women, 1980. Mem. Women's Council Realtors (pres. 1978-79, Appreciation award 1979), Nat. Assn. Realtors, Nat. Notary Assn., Phi Beta Psi (pres. chpt.). Clubs: Home Econs. (pres. 1948-53), Order Eastern Star (Scottsburg); Ida Rebecca Lodge (Austin). Home: Route 4 Box 314 Scottsburg IN 47170 Office: 1165 N Hwy 31 Scottsburg IN 47170

DONAHUE, ELLEN MARIE, fine arts broker; b. N.Y.C., Jan. 20, 1954; d. George Francis and Joan Marie (Balme) D.; B.A. cum laude in History, Boston Coll., 1976. Curatorial researcher Soc. for Preservation of New Eng. Antiquities, Boston, 1975-76; asst. mng. dir. George F. Donahue Assos., Manhasset, N.Y., 1977-78; asst. curator antiquities, mus. project Sotheby Parke Bernet Tng. Scheme, London, 1978-79; asst. v.p., supr. bi-monthly catalogs, dir. catalog dept. Trosby Auction Galleries, Atlanta, 1979-80; producer, mng. dir. E.M. Donahue Ltd., London, 1979-80, N.Y.C., 1981—. Fellow, Isabel O'Neill Found. for Art of Painted Finish, 1982; folk art curator in residence Washington's Crossing's Historic Park. Mem. Nat. Trust for Hist. Preservation, Winterthur Guild, Met. Mus., Whitney Mus., Mus. of City of N.Y., Am. Craft Mus., Guggenheim Mus., Mus of Am. Folk Art., Cooper-Hewitt Mus., Clubs: N.Y. Jr. League, Women Bus. Owners of N.Y., Manhasset Bay Yacht. Office: 28 E 10th St New York NY 10003 also 30 Sheffield Terr London W8 England

DONAHUE, MARY KATHERINE, librarian; b. Dallas, Jan. 14, 1942; d. Joseph W. and Ellen (Onan) D.; B.A., Our Lady of the Lake U., 1963; M.L.S., U. Calif., Berkeley, 1965; m. John Patrick Hooker, July 29, 1976. Librarian, Dallas Public Library, 1963-64; 1st asst. Lubbock (Tex.) City-County Libraries, 1965-66, asst. dir., 1966-68, acting dir., 1968-69; librarian U. Tex., Arlington, 1969; corp. librarian Univ. Computing Co., Dallas, 1969-72; sr. librarian Corpus Christi (Tex.) Public Libraries, 1973-75, adminstrv. coordinator, 1975-76; coordinator Hidalgo County (Tex.) Library System, McAllen, 1976-80; asst. prof. Tex. A&M U., College Station, 1981—; grant writer HEW, Trull Found., others. Mem. Hidalgo County Hist. Commn., 1978-81, Brazos County Hist. Commn., 1982—, Rio Grande Valley Council for Arts, 1977-81. Recipient Disting. Service award Tex. Hist. Commn. Mem. ALA, Tex. Library Assn., Southwest MLA, Alpha Chi. Episcopalian. Office: Tex A&M U Library College Station TX 77843

DONALDSON, ELAINE WENING, tool supply co. exec.; b. Toledo, Apr. 29, 1923; d. Arthur G. and Dorothy E. (Goodes) Wening; student, U. Toledo; m. Raymond LeRoy Donaldson, Nov. 28, 1942; children—Randall P., Michael R., Shelley Donaldson Lafler. Co-founder, co-owner Donkirk Tool Supply, Inc., Covina, Calif., 1962—, sec.-treas., 1962—, exec. v.p., 1980—; dir. Prudential Savs. & Loan Assn., 1977—. Mem. Covina City Council, 1974-78, mayor, 1976-78; mem. Covina-Valley Unified Sch. Bd., 1963-74, pres., 1966-67, 71-72; bd. dirs. Edgewood Family Counseling Service, 1968-77, Inter-Community Hosp. Found., 1972-79; Los Angeles County rep. Calif. Sch. Bds. Assn. Del. Assembly, 1968-74, mem. sch. instrl. com., 1972-73, sch. personnel com., 1973-74, state dept. edn.'s task forces inter-agy. council on drug abuse, 1972, state dept. edn. curriculum commn., 1973; del. White House Conf. on Small Bus., 1980; mem.-at-large nat. adv. council SBA, 1976-80; del. White House Econ. Summit Conf., 1974; vice chmn. Calif. Product Liability Task Force, 1979—. Named Covina Citizen of Year, Covina C. of C., 1978, Altrusa Club Woman of Year, 1975; recipient Outstanding Community Service Discus award Covina-Valley Bd. Realtors, 1976, Continuing Service award Covina-Valley PTA Council, 1973. Mem. Nat. Indsl. Distbrs. Assn., Nat. Assn. Wholesale Distbrs., U.S. C. of C. (Small Bus. Council 1977—). Republican. Presbyterian. Club: Soroptimist Internat. (hon. life). Home: 785 S Rancho El Fuerte Covina CA 91724 Office: Donkirk Tool Supply Inc 144 W Badillo St Covina CA 91723

DONALDSON, JUDY JOHNSTON, mgmt. cons.; b. Victoria, Tex., July 14, 1943; d. Carl Cameron and Vivian Estelle (Adcock) Johnston; A.B., Wellesley Coll., 1965; M.B.A., Vanderbilt U., 1981; m. Robert Herschel Donaldson, June 27, 1964; children—Jennifer Gwynne, John Andrew. Programmer, Harvard U. Computing Center, Cambridge, Mass., 1966-68; analyst-programmer Vanderbilt U. Computer Center and Med. Center, Nashville, 1971-73, 75-78; sr. systems analyst York (Pa.) div. Borg-Warner Corp., 1978-79; mgmt. cons. Deloitte Haskins & Sells, N.Y.C., 1981—; cons. community devel. Inst. Cultural Affairs, 1976. Bd. dirs. LWV of Nashville-Davidson County, Tenn., 1970-73, Hillsboro-West End Neighborhood Assn., Nashville, 1975-77. Travel grantee Nat. Council Edn. in Politics, 1964. Mem. Assn. Computing Machinery, AAUW. Methodist. Home: 334 Fairway Rd Ridgewood NJ 07450 Office: Deloitte Haskins & Sells One World Trade Center New York NY 10048

DONALDSON, MARCIA JACKSON, educator; b. Athens, Tenn., May 24, 1934; d. Luther Claiborn and Alva (George) Jackson; B.S., Knoxville Coll., 1958; M.S. in Elem. Edn., U. Tenn., 1964; Ed.D. in Curriculum and Instrn. (Scholar), 1973; m. Herbert L. Donaldson, Apr. 28, 1955; children—Herbert L., Cora Annice. Tchr. public schs., Tullahoma and Knoxville, Tenn., 1958-69, asst. prin., 1963-69, head start tchr. tng. dir., 1965-69; teaching asst. U. Tenn., Knoxville, 1970-73, mem. adj. faculty, 1974—; instr. sci. edn. Maryville (Tenn.) Coll., 1974-75; instr., asst. prof. edn. Knoxville (Tenn.) Coll., 1969-73, asso. prof., 1974-75, prof. edn., 1975—, dir. tchr. edn., chmn. dept., 1975-79, dir. div. gen. studies-basic studies, 1980—; chmn. evaluation com. Tenn. State Bd. Edn.; participant profl. confs.; cons. in field. Bd. dirs. nat. NCCJ; mem. adv. bd. Tchr. Center Policy Bd., Helen Ross McNabb Mental Health Center; trustee Knoxville Coll. Mem. AAUP, NEA, Assn. Supervision and Curriculum Devel., Nat. Assn. Young Children, Alpha Kappa Alpha (past pres. Knoxville, nat. officer). Clubs: Jack and Jill (past pres. Knoxville chpt.), Links. Office: 901 College St Knoxville TN 37921

DONATH, THERESE (PHYLLIS THERESE FREEMAN), artist, writer; b. Hammond, Ind., Dec. 14, 1928; d. Arthur Max and Lillian Louise (Donath) Helfer; student Monticello Coll., 1946-47; B.F.A., St. Joseph's Coll., 1975; additional study Oxbow Summer Sch. Painting, Immaculate Heart Coll., Hollywood, Calif., Monticello Coll., Alton, Ill., Penland, N.C., Haystack, Maine; children—Mark, Alex, Kim. Interviewer, producer Viewpoint, Sta. WLNR-FM, Lansing, Ill., 1963-64; reporter, columnist N.W. Ind. Sentinel, 1965; freelance writer Monterey Peninsula Herald and Community Spirit, 1981-82; asst. dir. Michael Karolyi Meml. Found., Vence, France, 1979; one-woman shows include: Ill. Inst. Tech., Chgo., 1971; Pacific Grove Art Center, Calif., 1983; group shows include: Palos Verdes (Calif.) Mus., 1974, Los Angeles Inst. Contemporary Art, 1978, Mus. Contemporary Art, Chgo., 1975, Calif. State U., Fullerton, 1973, No. Ill. U., DeKalb, 1971; represented in permanent collections including Kennedy Gallery, N.Y.C., also pvt. collections; co-dir. Univ. for Man, Monterey, Calif., 1982—; instr., lectr. Penland, N.C., 1970, Haystack Mountain Sch., Deer Isle, Maine, 1974, Sheffield Poly., Eng., 1978. Bd. dirs., sec. Mental Health Soc. Greater Chgo., 1963-64; exec. dir. Lansing (Ill.) Mental Health Soc., 1963-64. Recipient awards No. Ind. Art Mus., 1966, 70, 71, 73; grantee Ragdale Found., Lake Forest, Ill., 1982. Represented in The Mirror Book, 1978; contbr. articles to profl. jours., newspapers; illustrator: Run Computer Run, 1983. Office: UFM Monterey Peninsula Coll Monterey CA 93940

DONATHAN, ANN G., consumer products co. exec.; b. San Francisco, Feb. 18, 1937; d. Ralph Vincent and Bridgie M. (Mullen) D.; student U. San Francisco, 1955-61, Munson's Sch. Bus., 1957-58, D'Youville Coll., 1965, DeAnza Jr. Coll., 1967-68. Clk. typist to buyer F.W. Woolworth Co., San Francisco, 1955-58; asst. law librarian, sec. City Atty.'s Office, San Francisco, 1958-59; sec., girl friday P.J. Rhodes and Co., San Francisco, 1959-61; sec. to Western sales mgr. Firestone Tire and Rubber Co., San Francisco, 1961-64; sec. to pres. Beal's McCarthy & Rodgers, Inc., Buffalo, 1964-67, Pacific Abrasive/Carborundum Co., Santa Clara, Calif., 1967-69; adminstrv. sec. to pres., chmn. bd. Kanda Corp., San Jose, Calif., 1969-73; sec. to v.p. Western div. Am./Dixie Sales, Am. Can Co., Hayward, Calif., 1973-76, sales analyst, 1976-78, sales devel. analyst, 1978; mgr. sales planning Calif. Canners and Growers, San Francisco, 1978-79, mgr. sales planning and control, 1979-80, mgr. sales and mktg. services, 1980—. Mem. Am. Mgmt. Assn., Montalvo Assn. Arts. Democrat. Roman Catholic. Club: Commonwealth (San Francisco). Home: 100 Kinross Dr Apt 17 Walnut Creek CA 94598 Office: 3100 Ferry Bldg San Francisco CA 94106

DONATTO, MARY ANN, city ofcl.; b. Galveston, Tex., Feb. 14, 1949; d. Paul and Cecelia (Morehead) Baszile; B.A., Wiley Coll., Marshall, Tex., 1971; m. James John Donatto, Sept. 24, 1970; children—Laquinta Dawn, James John. Program dir. L.L. Melton YMCA, Beaumont, Tex., 1974-75; adminstrv. asst. to city controller City of Houston, 1975-77, utility coordinator Dept. Public Service, 1977-79, chief energy conservation officer Dept. Public Works, 1979—. Mem. Assn. Energy Engrs., ASHRAE, Assn. Blacks in Energy, Am. Soc. Public Adminstrn. Democrat. Roman Catholic. Home: 3722 Rio Vista Houston TX 77021 Office: 2220 Brazos St Houston TX 77002

DONCHESS, BARBARA BRIGGS, publisher, author; b. New Bedford, Mass., Sept. 26, 1922; d. Carleton Church and Alice Theresa (Dale) Briggs; grad. Kinyon Bus. Coll., New Bedford, 1942; m. Kalman Donchess, Apr. 19, 1947; children—Ann, Carleton, Christine. Mgr., Brayton Portrait Studio, New Bedford, 1942-47; freelance writer, 1964—; owner Perky Publs., Canton, Mass., 1972—; author: How To Cope With His Horoscope, 1977; In Other Women' Houses, 1977; Travel-Write Guide, 1977; lectr. on the occult. Address: 5 South St Canton MA 02021

DONDY, VIRGINIA M., lawyer; b. Ft. Lauderdale, Fla., Feb. 14, 1943; d. David L. and Murray (Lindsley) D.; A.B., Goucher Coll. 1965; J.D., Georgetown U., 1971. Bar admittee: N.Y. 1976, U.S. Appeals Ct. (D.C. cir.) 1971, U.S. Supreme Ct. 1974. Instr. Wells Coll., 1965-68; law clk. Spottswood W. Robinson, Chief judge U.S. Ct. Appeals (D.C. cir.), 1971-72; assoc. Steptoe & Johnson 1972-75; staff counsel ITT 1976-77, dep. asst. sec. Dept. Air Force, 1978; dep. spl. asst. to sec. Dept. Def., 1979, assoc. gen. counsel, 1980-81; ptnr. Reed, Smith, Shaw & McClay, Washington, 1982—. Recipient Disting. Civil Service award Dept. Air Force 1980, Disting. Civil Service award Dept. Def. 1981. Office: 1150 Connecticut Ave NW Suite 900 Washington DC 20036

DONELLAN, JUDY ZIMMER, musician, educator; b. New Orleans, June 17, 1939; d. Robert Frederic and Agnes (Roussel) Zimmer; B.S. summa cum laude, Livingston U., 1979; m. William John Donellan, June 15, 1957; children—William John, Sandy, Nancy, Jill, Mike, Scott. Pvt. tchr. voice, piano, theory, guitar, Butler, Ala., 1967—; organist, choir dir. St. Isidore Ch., Baton Rouge, 1957-65; glee club dir. Patrician Acad., Butler, 1973-78; ednl. adv. Art Publ. Soc., of St. Louis, Choctaw County, Ala., 1970—; dir., arranger High Noon performing group, Butler, 1970—. Pres. Choctaw County Arts Council. Recipient cert. merit Ala. Council on Arts and Humanities, 1980; Ralph Lyons award for acad. excellence, 1980. Mem. Nat. Music Tchrs. Assn., Ala. Music Tchrs. Assn., Nat. Guild Piano Tchrs., Delta Kappa Gamma. Home: 902 E Pushmataha St Butler AL 36904 Office: PO Box 616 Butler AL 36904

DONELSON, ANGIE FIELDS CANTRELL MERRITT, real estate exec.; b. Hermitage, Tenn., Dec. 2, 1914; d. Dempsey Weaver and Nora (Johnson) Cantrell; student public and pvt. schs., Hermitage, Nashville; m. Gilbert Stroud Merritt, Dec. 15, 1934 (dec.); 1 son, Gilbert Stroud; m. 2d, John Donelson, Jr., VII, Apr. 23, 1966 (dec.); step-children—John, Agnes Donelson Williams (dec.), William Stockley. Pres., So. Woodenware Co., Nashville, 1955-61, So. Properties, Inc., Hermitage, 1961—. Chmn. comml. flower exhibits Tenn. State Fair, 1951; committeewoman and v.p. Davidson County Agrl. Soil and Conservation Community Com., 1959-60; bd. mem. Nashville Symphony Assn., 1961-64, regional council mem., 1977-79; chmn. bd. Nashville Presbyn. Neighborhood Settlement House; founding bd. mem. Davidson County Cancer Soc.; bd. mem. Nashville Vis. Nurse Service; dist. chmn., speakers bur. Am. Red Cross. Mem. Vanderbilt U. Aid, Peabody Coll. Aid, Tenn. Hist. Soc., Descs. of Ft. Nashboro Pioneers, English Speaking Union. Presbyterian. Clubs: Ladies Hermitage Assn. (dir. 1949—), DAR, (chpt. regent 1941), Lebanon Rd. Garden Club (pres. 1947), Horticulture Soc. Davidson County (v.p. 1949). Clubs: Ravenwood Country, Centennial, Belle Meade. Contbr. to books and mags. on history of Tenn. Home: Stone Hall Stones River Rd Hermitage TN 37076 Office: Lebanon Rd Hermitage TN 37076

DONENFELD, SHARON ETTA, ednl. and sch. psychologist; b. Bklyn., Sept. 7, 1948; d. Harry and Elsie (Capp) Kamer; student Syracuse U., 1968; B.A. (N.Y. State Regents scholar), Hunter Coll., 1969; M.A., New Sch. for Social Research, 1971; postgrad. Yeshiva U., 1971-72, Fordham U., 1974; m. Kenneth Jay Donenfeld, June 23, 1968; 1 dau., Elissa. Research asso., field team supr. health services mobility study City Univ. Research Found., N.Y.C., 1969-71; psychology intern Coney Island Hosp., Bklyn., 1971-72, psychologist dept. clin. psychology, 1974, staff psychologist dept. child psychiatry, 1978; research asso. regional med. program Asso. Med. Schs. Greater N.Y., N.Y.C., 1971-72; sch. psychologist, chmn. child study team Bridgewater-Raritan (N.J.) Schs., 1972-75; sch. psychologist spl. edn. programs, mem. com. on handicapped Hempstead (N.Y.) Sch. Dist., 1975-77; sch. psychologist Massapequa (N.Y.) Public Schs., 1977; pvt. cons. ednl. psychology, Great Neck, N.Y., 1978—; psychologist Kings Park (N.Y.) Schs., 1980—; condr. in-service ednl. programs Hempstead Parochial Schs., 1975-77. Bd. dirs. Saddle Rock Civic Assn., 1975—; mem. Womens Am. Orgn. for Rehab. and Tng. 1976—. Cert. sch. psychologist, N.Y., N.J., Calif. Mem. Am. Psychol. Assn., N.Y. State Psychol. Assn., Nassau County Psychol. Assn., N.J. Assn. Sch. Psychologists, Somerset County Assn. Psychologists. Home and Office: 90 Emerson Dr Great Neck NY 11023

DON FRANCESCO, PATRICIA ANN, real estate broker; b. Hot Springs, S.D., Mar. 15, 1951; d. Harry Homer and Anna Marie (Wood) Evans; student Charon State Coll., 1969-72; m. Thomas Antony Don Francesco, June 20, 1970; 1 dau., Makayla Michelle. Owner, broker Biddle Creek Realty, Casper, Wyo. Mem. realtors assns. Republican. Roman Catholic. Home: 641 W 50th St Casper WY 82601 Office: 933 W 14 St Suite 3 Casper WY 82601

DONIGAN, CLARA VIRGINIA, social worker; b. Denver, Oct. 6, 1920; d. Anton Theodore and Leah Ann (Dibble) Pape; A.A., A.F.A., Colo. Woman's Coll., 1940; B.S., U. Ill., 1942; M.S.W., U. Wash., 1957; m. Thomas Pattison Donigan, May 19, 1955; children—Thomas P. II (dec.), Mark Lockwood. Hosp. social worker ARC, 1945-51; social worker Asso. Luth. Welfare, 1955-56; acting supr. child therapy Santa Maria (Calif.) Mental Health Clinic, 1963-66; instr. Brevard Community Coll., Cocoa, Fla., 1967-70; dir. social work Wuesthoff Meml. Hosp., Rockledge, Fla., 1970-76; sub-dist. adminstr. Dept. Health and Rehab. Services, Rockledge, 1976—. Mem. Nat. Assn. Social Workers, Council Southeastern Social Service Execs. Blue Ridge Assembly, Health Systems Agy. East Central Fla. (charter), Soc. Hosp. Social Service Execs. (pres. Brevard council, co-founder, program chmn. Fla. chpt.), Council Social Service Execs. Brevard County (charter pres.). Episcopalian. Home: 215 Antigua Dr Cocoa Beach FL 32931 Office: 705 Avacado St Cocoa FL 32922

DONLEVY, COLLEEN THERESA, beverage co. exec.; b. Paterson, N.J., Apr. 29, 1954; d. John William and Anne Marie (Field) D.; student Marymount Coll., 1974; B.A. in Psychology, Manhattanville Coll., 1975; M.B.A., U. Miami, 1978. Mdse. mgr. J.C. Penney, Miami, Fla., 1978-80; exec. v.p., v.p., sales/mktg. dir. King Cola Fla. and Carolinas Corp., Miami Beach, 1980—; dist. sales rep. Kellogg Co., 1981—. Mem. Crime Patrol. Mem. Miami Assn. Food Trade, Gold Coast Exec. Women Network, Miami Beach Jr. C. of C. Republican. Roman Catholic. Home and office: 4101 Pine Tree Dr 1514 Miami Beach FL 33140

DONLEY, BARBARA ELLEN, nurse anesthetist; b. Burlington, Wis., Sept. 1, 1932; d. Arthur W. and Lillian C. (Luhn) Juranek; R.N., St. Francis Sch. Nursing, 1953; cert. registered nurse anesthetist St. Francis Sch. Anesthesia, 1954; B.A., Redlands U., 1976; M.Sci. Health Care Mgmt., Calif. State U., Los Angeles, 1980; m. Clifford A. Donley, June 15, 1963; children—Timothy A., Jennifer A. Staff nurse anesthetist Misericordia Hosp., Milw., 1954-62, Kaiser Permanente, Los Angeles, 1962-65, Bellflower, Calif., 1965-70, chief nurse anesthetist, 1970-80, dept. adminstr., 1980—; clin. supr., didactic lectr. Kaiser Permanente Sch. Anesthesia, 1972-75; instr. CPR, 1975-77. Tchr. religious edn. jr. high level St. Cyprian Catholic Ch., Long Beach, Calif., 1977—. Mem. Am. Assn. Nurse Anesthetists, Calif. Assn. Nurse Anesthetists, Greater Los Angeles Heart Assn., Nat. Assn. Female Execs. Republican. Roman Catholic.

DONNAN, BRENDA COOMBS, city ofcl.; b. Goldsboro, N.C., Dec. 16, 1947; d. Rhem Horace and Mary Kathleen (Davis) Coombs; student Meredith Coll. 1965-67; B.S. in Bus. Adminstrn. U. Central Fla. 1977, M.A. in Econs., 1979; children—Lisa Reed, Christopher Scott. Grad. asst. U. Central Fla. 1978-79; sr. planner manpower div. County of Seminole, Fla. 1979, sr. budget and mgmt. analyst 1979-81; dir. fin. City of Altamone Springs, Fla. 1981—. Recipient Orlando C. of C. Gold Telephone award 1976. Mem. Orlando-Winter Park Bd. Realtors, Nat. Assn. Realtors, Fla. Assn. Realtors, Municipal Fin. Officers Assn., Beta Gamma Sigma, Omicron Delta Kappa. Republican. Presbyterian. Home: 186 Monterey Isle South Longwood FL 32750 Office: 225 Newburyport Ave Altamonte Springs FL 32701

DONNELLY, ANNE MARIE, catering cons.; b. Chgo., Nov. 28, 1938; d. William L. and Anne E. (Gribbon) Earth; student De Paul U., 1956-59; m. Maurice L. Donnelly, Jan. 11, 1964 (dec. 1973); children—Patricia Anne, Michael Jude. With South Shore View Hotel, Chgo., 1953-66, asst. catering mgr., 1960-66; owner Annette's Catering, Chgo., 1966-73; sr. cons. D'Masti Custom Caterers, Blue Island, Ill., 1976—. Den mother cub scouts Chgo. Area council Boy Scouts Am., 1975-78; mgr. Mt. Greenwood Girls Softball Team, 1976-78, coach, 1979—; officer Band Boosters, 1975-79; active Chgo. Policemen's Annuity Fund, Mt. Assisi Parents Assn., St. Christina Home Sch. Guild, choir, Altar and Rosary Soc.; vol. St. Christina Sch., 1973-78. Mem. Nat. Bus. and Profl. Women. (Beverly br.), Nat. Assn. Female Execs., Nat. Restaurant Assn., No. Ill. Food Execs. Assn., Ret. Policemen's Assn., Nat. Hist. Soc. Club: Mt. Carmel's Mothers. Office: 11915 S Western Ave Blue Island IL 60406

DONNELLY, BARBARA SCHETTLER, med. technologist; b. Sweetwater, Tenn., Dec. 2, 1933; d. Clarence G. and Irene Elizabeth (Brown) Schettler; A.A., Tenn. Wesleyan Coll., 1952; B.S., U. Tenn., 1954; cert. med. tech., Erlanger Hosp. Sch. Med. Tech., 1954; postgrad. So. Meth. U., 1980-81; children—Linda Ann, Richard Michael. Med. technologist Erlanger Hosp., Chattanooga, 1953-57, St. Luke's Episcopal Hosp., Tex. Med. Center, Houston, 1957-58, 1962; engring. research and devel. SCI Systems Inc., Huntsville, Ala., 1974-76; cons. hematology systems Abbott Labs., Dallas, 1976-77, hematology specialist, Dallas, Irving, Tex., 1977-81, tech. specialist microbiology systems, Irving, 1981-82, tech. service coordinator microbiology, bio-chemistry, and hematology systems, 1982—. Recipient 5-Yr. Service award, Abbott Labs. Mem. Am. Soc. Clin. Pathologists (cert. med. technologist), Am. Soc. Microbiology. Contbr. articles on cytology to profl. jours. Home: 204 Greenbriar Ln Bedford TX 76021 Office: 1921 Hurd St Irving TX 75061

DONNELLY, MARY MAGDALEN, sch. psychologist; b. Phila., Dec. 15, 1944; d. Edward John and Mary Anna (Scherer) D.; B.A. in Biology, Chestnut Hill Coll., 1973; M.A. in Psychology, Catholic U. Am., 1979, postgrad. (Bd. Trustees scholar), 1979—; spl. trainee in Neuropsychology, VA Med. Center, Washington, 1982—. Tchr., Archdioceses of Phila., Newark, Allentown and Washington, 1964-75; dir. counseling, Drexel Hill, Pa., 1975-79; cons. sch. psychologist, Fairfax County, Va., 1982—. Mem. Multidisciplinary Child Abuse Com., 1979. Mem. Am. Psychol. Assn., Am. Personnel and Guidance Assn., Md. Psychol. Assn., D.C. Psychol. Assn., Nat. Assn. Sch. Psychologists, Md. Sch. Psychologists, Am. Orthopsychiat. Assn., Assn. Counselor Educators and Suprs. Roman Catholic. Home: 5821 Bradley Blvd Bethesda MD 20814

DONNELLY, PHYLLIS BESWICK, reading cons.; b. Elk Point, Alta., Can., Nov. 19, 1939; naturalized, 1966; d. Colin Alfred John and Ruby Ellen (Gudwer) Beswick; student U. Alta., 1957-58, Northwestern U., 1961-62, Ind. U., 1962-63, M.S. in Edn., 1967 B.S. in Edn., Bethel Coll., Mishawaka, Ind., 1964; m. John Vincent Donnelly, Nov. 28, 1975; children—Deirdre, Sean, Patrick. Elem. tchr. Strathearn Elem. Sch., Edmonton, Alta., Can., 1958-61, Harris Sch., Chgo., 1961-62, Culver (Ind.) Community Schs., 1964-66; reading cons., curriculum writer Cleveland Hts.-University Hts. Bd. of Edn., Cleveland Heights, Ohio, 1967—, program dir. Right-to-Read, 1974—. Pres. Judson Park Evening Aux. Vols. Mem. Internat. Reading Assn., Mary C. Austin Reading

Council, Am. Fedn. Tchrs., Ohio Fedn. Tchrs., Cleveland Hts.-University Hts. Fedn. Tchrs., AAUW (elected to Ohio Roster of Women 1977). Democrat. Author: Reading Evaluation, 1974, Primary Reading Writing and Listening Skills, 1977; co-author: Developmental Reading Guides, vols. 1, 2, 1975, vol. 3, 1976. Home: 10494 Lake Shore Blvd Cleveland OH 44108 Office: 2155 Miramar Blvd Cleveland Heights OH 44118

DONNELLY, ROSE ANN, educator; b. Bklyn., Feb. 21, 1925; d. James John and Madeline Lillian (La Tuga) Garone; B.A., Barnard Coll., 1948; M.A., Columbia U., 1949, Ed.D., 1957; m. Albert Joseph Donnelly, July 16, 1955. Tchr., Bklyn. Public Schs., 1950-56, tchr. in charge, 1956-57, asst. prin., 1958-67, prin., 1967—. Served with WAC, 1945-46. Mem. Assn. Supervision and Curriculum Devel., N.Y.C. Elem. Sch. Prins. Assn. (dist. del.), Nat. Council Adminstrv. Women in Edn., Council Suprs. and Adminstrs. (dist. 21 treas.). Club: Barnard Coll. (L.I.). Contbr. articles to profl. jours. Home: 149 Beach 141 St Belle Harbor NY 11694 Office: 345 Van Sicklen St Brooklyn NY 11223

DONNEM, SARAH LUND, civic worker; b. St. Louis, Apr. 10, 1936; d. Joel Y. and Erle Hall (Harsh) Lund; B.A., Vassar Coll., 1958; m. Roland W. Donnem, Feb. 18, 1961; children—Elizabeth Prince, Sarah Madison. Tech. aide Bell Labs., Whippany, N.J., 1959-60; chmn. placement vol. opportunities N.Y. Jr. League, 1972-73, asst. treas. 1974-75, chmn. urban problems relating to mental health, 1967-69, mem. project research com., 1967-71, chmn., 1973-74 bd. mgrs., 1973-74; chmn. community research D.C. Jr. League, 1970-71, mem. bd. mgrs., 1970-71; bd. dirs. East Side Settlement House, Bronx, N.Y., 1972—, v.p., 1975-76; bd. dirs. Stanley M. Isaacs Neighborhood Center, N.Y.C., 1973-76, v.p., 1975-76; bd. dirs. Presbyterian Home for Aged Women, N.Y.C., 1974-76, v.p., 1976; mem. exec. bd. N.Y. Aux. of Blue Ridge Sch., 1971-75, sec., 1965-67, pres., 1973-75; budget and benevolence com. Brick Presbyn. Ch., N.Y.C., 1973-76, mem. social service com., 1973-74, chmn. fgn. students com., 1963-64; women's com. Cleve. Orch., 1979—; bd. dirs. Search and Care, N.Y.C., 1973-76, Project LEARN, Cleve., 1978-82; trustee Council Older Persons Fedn. Community Planning, Cleve., 1978—, Commn. on Social Concerns, 1981—; trustee Cleve. Ballet '80, exec. com., 1981—, fin. com. 1982; trustee Golden Age Centers Greater Cleve., 1978, 1st v.p., 1980, pres., 1981—, exec. bd. Women's Council, 1978—. Named Vol. of Yr., N.Y. Jr. League, 1975. Mem. Nat. Inst. Social Scis. (mem. memberships com. 1972—), Nat. Soc. of Colonial Dames, Western Res. Hist. Soc. (mem. women's adv. council 1977—; corr. sec. 1978; chmn. Antique Show 1979, 80). Republican. Presbyterian. Clubs: Chevy Chase (Washington); Intown, Kirtland, Cleve. Vassar (sec. 1980—) (Cleve.). Address: 2945 Fontenay Rd Shaker Heights OH 44120

DONNER, ALICE WILKINSON, social worker; b. Phila., July 5, 1922; d. William MacIlhenny and Mary (Yost) Wilkinson; B.S. in Edn., U. Pa., 1944; M.A., Villanova (Pa.) U., 1975; M.S.W., Temple U., Phila., 1977; m. William T. Donner, Apr. 12, 1946; children—William W., Marda Elisa, Mary Alice, Margot Ramona. Elementary sch. tchr., 1944-50; renal social worker Abington (Pa.) Meml. Hosp., 1977—. Bd. dirs. Jenkintown Day Nursery, 1966-75, treas., 1969-71, v.p., 1972-74; bd. dirs. Montgonery County Homemaker Home Health Aide, 1965-74, v.p., 1970-72. Mem. Nat. Assn. Social Workers, Acad. Cert. Social Workers, Council Nephrology Social Workers. Home: 314 Wellington Terr Jenkintown PA 19046 Office: Abington Meml Hosp Abington PA 19001

DONOGHUE, CAROL, oil co. ofcl.; b. Phila., Mar. 9, 1950; d. Joseph Francis and Mary Dorothy (Hirst) D.; B.A., Villanova U., 1972; M.B.A., Widener U., 1977; m. Joseph Coleman Hare, Aug. 26, 1972. Law clk. U.S. Atty.'s Office, Phila., 1973-74; mgmt. trainee Mobil Oil Co., Valley Forge, Pa., 1974-78, sr. analyst, N.Y.C., 1978-79, supr. budget dept., Valley Forge, 1979-81, supr. systems and fin. analysis, 1981—. Bd. govs. Villanova U., 1973. Roman Catholic. Home: 102 Burnside Rd Villanova PA 19085 Office: PO Box 839 Valley Forge PA 19482

DONOGHUE, ELIZABETH MARION MACMAHON (MRS. FLORENCE JOSEPH DONOGHUE), mus. curator; b. Castleisland, Kerry, Ireland, Nov. 9, 1896 (parents Am. citizens); d. James and Johanna Mary (Brosnan) MacMahon; B.A., Calvin Coolidge Coll., 1955, M.A., 1956; m. Florence Joseph Donoghue, Apr. 17, 1963 (dec. July 1970). Acct., Boston Wool Trade, 1914-33; tchr. Everett (Mass.) High Sch., 1934-63; trustee Wenham (Mass.) Hist. Assn. and Mus., Inc., 1956—, curator dolls, 1960—. Driver, Red Cross Motor Corps, Boston, 1939-41, Civilian Def. Motor Corps, Everett, 1941-43. Mem. Antique Toy Collectors Am., Doll Club Gt. Britain, Doll Collectors Am., Emerald Isle, L.I., Ginny doll clubs, League Cath. Women, Mus. Fine Arts Boston, Nat. Ret. Tchrs. Assn., United Fedn. Doll Clubs, Am. Irish Hist. Soc. (life), Christ Child Soc. (life), Soc. Preservation N.E. Antiquities (life), Yesteryears Doll Mus. (life), Eire Soc. Boston (life, editor Bull. 1954-64), Worcester Art Mus., Boston U. Alumni Assn. Contbr. articles to profl. jours. Home: 86 Bradford St Everett MA 02149 Office: 132 Main St Wenham MA 01984

DONOHUE, IDA ISABEL, grain rep.; b. Great Falls, Mont., Apr. 11, 1928; d. Matt William and Esther F. (Mattson) Oja; student U. Mont., 1945-47, No. Mont. Coll., 1947-48, Coll. Great Falls, part-time, 1975-79; children—Michael, Marcy Donohue Horning, Mark, Kathleen, Edward. Jour. clk. Mont. Ho. of Reps., Helena, 1955, Mont. Senate, 1959; adminstrv. asst. to pres. Coll. of Great Falls, 1968-80; Outreach counselor, 1980-81; grain rep. Oswego CD&D (Mont.), 1981—; instr. parent effectiveness tng., 1973—; lectr. in poetry, communications skills, personal growth. Pres., Mont. Consumer Affairs Council, 1973-74; dist. supr. Parents Without Partners, 1971-73. Named Phi Sigma Alpha Woman of Yr., 1972. Mem. Common Cause (Eastern dist. coordinator 1972-79), Mont. Inst. Arts (dir. 1978-81), Phi Sigma Alpha. Democrat. Mem. Baha'i Faith. Club: Ind. Order Foresters. Editor: (anthology) Seed in the Soil, 1967; poetry pub. various mags., anthologies including The Arts in Montana, 1978. Home: 315 4th Ave S Wolf Point MT 59201 Office: Oswego CD&D Oswego MT 59201

DONOVAN, KATHLEEN FRANCES, educator; b. Everett, Mass., Feb. 21, 1938; d. Andrew and Mary Ann (Winters) Philbin) B.A. cum laude, Regis Coll., 1959; M.Ed., Boston Coll., 1962; m. Richard Crowley Donovan, Aug. 1, 1964. Tchr. Immaculate Conception Elementary Sch., Everett, Mass., 1959-62, Hale Sch., Everett, 1962-64, Carter Sch., Chelsea, Mass., 1964-68; head tchr. Devens Sch., Everett, 1968-72, prin., 1972-80; supt. Everett Public Schs., 1980—; mem. implementation bd. Bd. Regents Mass. Public Schs. Coordinator United Fund. Mem. Mass. Assn. Sch. Supts., Am. Assn. Sch. Adminstrs., New Eng. Assn. Sch. Supts., Harvard Round Table, NEA, Regis Alumnae, Guild of Infant Savior. Democrat. Home: 79 Harvard St Chelsea MA 02150 Office: 121 Vine St Everett MA 02149

DOODY, MARGARET ANNE, educator; b. St. John, N.B., Can., Sept. 21, 1939; d. Hubert and Anne Ruth (Cornwall) D.; came to U.S., 1976; B.A., Dalhousie U., Can., 1960; B.A. with 1st class hons., Lady Margaret Hall, Oxford (Eng.) U., 1962, M.A., D.Phil. (Can. Council fellow 1964-65, Imperial Oil fellow 1965-68), 1968. Instr. in English, U. Victoria (B.C., Can.), 1962-64, asst. prof. English, 1968-69; lectr. Univ. Coll. Swansea (Wales), 1969-76; asso. prof. English, U. Calif., Berkeley, 1976-80; prof. English dept. Princeton (N.J.) U., 1980—. Guggenheim postdoctoral fellow, 1979. Anglican (Episcopalian). Author: A Natural Passion: A Study of the Novels of Samuel Richardson, 1974; Aristotle Detective, 1978; (novel) The Alchemists, 1980. Office: English Dept Princeton U Princeton NJ 08544

DOOLEY, JO ANN CATHERINE, pub. co. exec.; b. Cin., Nov. 24, 1930; d. Joseph Frank and Margaret Mary (Flynn) Dooley; ed. U. Cin., 1966. Clk., Castellini Co., Cin., 1949-52; IBM operator Kroger Co., Cin., 1952; asst. acct. Gardner Publs., Inc., Cin., 1953-67, treas., sec., 1967—, also sec. employees profit sharing trust, trustee retirement trust. Mem. Am. Soc. Women Accts. (advt. mgr. Woman CPA 1979, pres. 1982-83), Am. Mgmt. Assn., Cin. Women's Forum, Nat. Assn. Female Execs. Roman Catholic. Office: 600 Main St Cincinnati OH 45202

DOOLEY, MARY AGNES, coll. pres.; b. Sommerville, Mass., Mar. 5, 1923; d. Richard and Mary A. (O'Neill) D.; B.A., Elms Coll., 1944; M.A., Assumption Coll., 1960, L.H.D. (hon.), 1982; Doctorat d'Université, U. Paris, 1968; LL.D. (hon.) Am. Internat. Coll., 1981. Joined Congregation of the Sisters of St. Joseph, 1944; tchr. St. Joseph's High Sch., North Adams, Mass., 1944-65; chmn. lang. dept. Elms Coll., Chicopee, Mass., 1968-70, pres., 1979—; pres. Leadership Conf. Women Religious U.S., Washington, 1978-80; pres. Congregation Sisters of St. Joseph, Springfield, Mass., 1971-79; corporator Community Savs. Bank, Holyoke, Mass. Recipient Disting. Alumna award Elms Coll., 1979; decorated chevalier dans l'Ordre des Palmes Academiques (France), 1981. Mem. Assn. Cath. Colls. and Univs. (dir. 1980-85), Leadership Conf. Women Religious, Delta Epsilon Sigma. Roman Catholic. Contbr. articles in field to profl. jours.

DORAN, DORIS JEANNE, librarian; b. Chambersburg, Pa., July 19, 1932; d. John Franklin and Kathleen Elmira (Cooke) Fraker; B.S., Wilson Coll., 1954; M.L.S., U. Md., 1970, postgrad., 1976-77; m. Francis Joseph Foran, Feb. 5, 1955; children—Brenda Lou, Polly Ann. Asst. buyer Joseph Horne Co., Pitts., 1955-56; dir. research library Sears Roebuck & Co., Chgo., 1956-58; project officer contracts John I. Thompson Co., Washington, 1967-69, staff asst. to v.p. info. sci. div., 1969-70; program officer grants div. Nat. Library of Medicine, Bethesda, Md., 1970-79, program analyst Office of Dir., 1980—; project dir. Nat. Med. Audiovisual Center, 1979; co-owner, treas. Gilran Electric Products, Silver Spring, Md., 1969—. Mem. Med. Library Assn., Health Scis. Communications Assn. Home: 14121 Huckleberry Ln Silver Spring MD 20906 Office: 8600 Rockville Pike Bethesda MD 20209

DORAN, EDWINA BEAN, educator; b. Sparta, Tenn., Sept. 16, 1928; d. Robert and Susie (Allen) Bean; B.S., Tenn. Tech. U., Cookeville, 1949; M.A., George Peabody Coll., Nashville, 1960, Ed.S., 1962, Ph.D. in English, 1969; m. William A. Doran, July 10, 1953. Ford teaching fellow George Peabody Coll., 1961-62; high sch. tchr., Tenn., 1949-60; mem. faculty Eureka (Ill.) Coll., 1962—, prof. English, 1969—, coordinator English edn., 1969—. Mem. Nat. Council Tchrs. English, MLA, NEA (life), Ill. Assn. Tchrs. English, Tenn. Folklore Soc., AAUW (past br. pres.), Ill. Poetry Soc. (pres. 1976-82), Eureka Coll. Dames (past pres.). Club: Peoria (Ill.) Poetry (past pres.). Author articles in field, also poems. Co-editor: Leaves Alive for Touching, 1978. Home: Box 47 Route 3 Eureka IL 61530 Office: Eureka Coll Eureka IL 61530

DORE-DUFFY, PAULA, immunologist, educator; b. Hyannis, Mass., Feb. 23, 1948; d. Paul and Doris J. (Hochu) Dore; B.S., Simmons Coll., 1972; Ph.D., La. State U. Sch. Medicine, 1976; m. Michael Charles Duffy, Dec. 27, 1972. Research asst. dept. microbiology and molecular genetics Harvard Med. Sch., Boston, 1970-71; research asso. La. State U. Med. Sch., New Orleans, 1972-76, lab. instr., 1974; fellow U. Conn. Sch. Medicine, Farmington, 1976-77, asst. prof. medicine div. rheumatic diseases, 1978—, asst. prof. neurology, 1979-82, assoc. prof. neurology, 1982—, chief div. neuroimmunology, 1982—; dir. Multiple Sclerosis Center, 1982—. Fellow Nat. Multiple Sclerosis Soc. (bd. dirs. Conn. Valley br. 1980—, Spl. award 1981); mem. Am. Assn. Immunologists, Am. Soc. Microbiology, Am. Fedn. Clin. Research, Union of Concerned Scientists, AAAS, N.Y. Acad. Scis. Contbr. clin. studies on neuroimmunology to sci. jours. Home: 30 Oxford St Hartford CT 06105 Office: Dept Neurology Univ Conn Health Center Farmington Ave 06032

DOREMUS, BERTHA LARSON, social worker, educator; b. Firth, Idaho, Nov. 12, 1913; d. Claus Albert and Hanna Wilhelmina (Carlson) Larson; B.S., U. Idaho, 1938; M.A., U. Chgo., 1943; m. Edward B. Doremus, Dec. 28, 1956. Tchr., Middleton (Idaho) High Sch., 1938-40, Emmett (Idaho) High Sch., 1940-42; med.-psychiat. social worker Letterman Hosp., San Francisco, 1944-46, Harborview Hosp., Seattle, 1947-48, Firland Sanitorium, Seattle, 1948-53; chief social worker U. Wash. Sch. Health Scis., Seattle, 1953-59, Univ. Hosp., U. Wash., 1959-65, clin. asst. prof. rehab. medicine 1962—; lectr. U. Wash. Sch. Social Work, 1966, 67, 77, cons., 1980-81, practicum instr., 1982; dir. social work services N.W. Hosp., Seattle, 1968-80. Bd. dirs. Helpline, Bainbridge Island, Wash., 1976—. Mem. Acad. Cert. Social Workers, Nat. Assn. Social Workers, Soc. Social Work Dirs., Am. Hosp. Assn., Kappa Delta Pi, Delta Delta Delta. Episcopalian. Address: 8910 NE Spargur Rd Bainbridge Island WA 98110

DOREMUS, CHERIE BELLE DEPIETRO, public relations agy. exec.; b. Columbus, Ohio, Oct. 20, 1943; d. Charles James and Margaret Irene (Littlewood) DePietro; student Citrus Coll., 1961-63; m. Rick Doremus; children—Sean, Shannon. Copywriter for homebuilding co., 1969-71; founding mem. The Groundlings, improvisational comedy group, Los Angeles, 1973-74; with Martin Advt., Tustin, Calif., 1971-74; freelance publicist, writer, 1974-78; founder, pres. Kerr & Assos., public relations, Huntington Beach, Calif., 1978—; tchr. improvisational comedy to children; founder Kerr Comedy Co. Mem. Calif. Press Women's Assn. Office: 5142 Warner Ave Suite 201 Huntington Beach CA 92649

DORFMAN, KAREN KING, sales rep.; b. Indpls., Mar. 3, 1950; d. John P. and Margie W. King; B.A., U. Tex., 1972; M.A., Ind. U., 1976. Sales rep. Liberty Mut. Ins. Co., Indpls., 1976-77; sales rep. Commerce Clearinghouse, Inc., Indpls., 1977; sales rep. John H. Harland Co., 1978—; guest lectr. Ind. U.-Purdue U., Indpls. Mem. Nat. Women's Polit. Caucus, Ind. State Symphony Soc., Network of Women in Bus., Marion County Hist. Soc. Republican. Episcopalian. Home: 5678 N Meridian Indianapolis IN 46208

DORIAN, NANCY CURRIER, linguist, educator; b. New Brunswick, N.J., Nov. 5, 1936; d. Donald Clayton and Edith (McEwen) Dorian; B.A. summa cum laude, Conn. Coll. for Women, 1958; postgrad. Yale U., 1959-60; M.A., U. Mich., 1961, Ph.D. (Rackham fellow), 1965. Lectr., Bryn Mawr (Pa.) Coll., 1965-66, asst. prof., 1966-72, asso. prof., 1972-78, prof. linguistics in German and anthropology, 1978—, William R. Kenan, Jr. prof., 1980—; vis. lectr. U. Pa., 1966, 70, U. Kiel, 1967-68. Fulbright scholar to Germany, 1958-59; NSF research grantee, 1978-79. Mem. Linguistic Soc. Am., Internat. Linguistic Assn., N.E. Folklore Soc., Celtic Studies Assn., Scottish Oral History Group, An Comunn Gaidhealach, Phi Beta Kappa. Democrat. Unitarian. Author: East Sutherland Gaelic, 1978; Language Death, 1981; contbr. articles to profl. jours. Office: Bryn Mawr Coll Bryn Mawr PA 19010

DORICH, BERNADINE, coll. ofcl.; b. Czechoslovakia, Apr. 5, 1945; came to U.S., 1949, naturalized, 1954; A.B., West Liberty (Va.) State Coll., 1967; M.A., Kent (Ohio) State U., 1968, postgrad., 1969-71. Secondary sch. tchr. Wells Jr. High Sch., Wellsburg, W.Va., 1966-67; instr. English, Va. Poly. Inst. and State U., Blacksburg, 1968-69, Hancock County br. West Liberty State Coll. Weirton, W.Va., 1971-72; instr., then asst. prof., dir. public relations W.Va. No. Community Coll., Wheeling/Weirton, 1972-75; dir. public relations Schenectady County Community Coll., 1975-79, Gettysburg (Pa.) Coll., 1979—; speaker, cons. in field. Mem. Council Advancement and Support Edn., Coll. and Univ. Public Relations Assn., Women in Communications, Nat. Assn. Female Execs., Ednl. Writers Assn., AAUW (chpt. dir. 1978-79, 80-82). Republican. Mem. Byzantine Catholic Ch. Author: Extending the Campus in Effective Community Relations, 1981. Editor: Democracy's Colleges, 1976; also articles. Office: Gettysburg Coll Gettysburg PA 17325

DORIO, EVELYN, author; b. Duryea, Pa.; d. John and Rose Marie (Canonico) D.; B.A., U. So. Calif.; m. Harold J. Nicolais. Freelance writer, 1952—; author essays in Involvement, 1977, children's story in Courage, 1979; contbr. story to Suspense Stories, 1963; author: (juvenile) Pigalee Pink, 1980; also other articles, essays, short stories, poetry. Vol., Interfaith Servicemen's Center, San Clemente, Calif., 1968—. Recipient 1st pl. award contest Orange County Writers Group, 1974; 2d pl. award (2) contest Press Women Orange County, 1975. Mem. AAUW, Press Women Orange County (awards 1975), Los Escribientes Club. Democrat. Presbyterian. Address: 32741 Mediterranean Dr Laguna Niguel CA 92677

DORLAND, BYRL BROWN, civic worker; b. Greenwich, Utah, Apr. 25, 1915; d. David Alma and Ethel Myrle (Peterson) Brown; teaching certificate, Brigham Young U., Provo, Utah, 1937; B.S., Utah State Coll., Logan, 1940; m. Jack Albert Dorland, June 11, 1944; children—Lynn Elise Dorland Trost, Lee Allison. Sch. tchr. in Utah, 1937-39, 40-42; restored Washington Irving's graveplot in Sleepy Hollow Cemetery, North Tarrytown, N.Y. (named Nat. Historic Landmark 1972); nat. dir. Washington Irving Graveplot Restoration Program, 1968—; designer Nat. Historic Landmark plaque for Irving's grave. Mem. Nat. Council State Garden Clubs, 1959—; pres. Potpourri Garden Club, Westchester, 1968—; founder, pres. Internat. Washington Irving Soc., 1981—. Recipient Mary Duff Walters trophy Nat. Council State Garden Clubs, 1974; Nat. trophy Nat. Historic Landmark Com., 1974; citation Keep Am. Beautiful, 1974, Nat. Trust Hist. Preservation, 1977. Mem. Nat. Trust Hist. Preservation (Pres.'s award 1977), Herb Soc. Am., Gen. Soc. Mayflower Descs., DAR, Nat. Wildlife Fedn., Nat. Hist. Soc. Address: 10 Castle Heights Ave Tarrytown NY 10591

DORMAN, HATTIE LAWRENCE, govt. agy. ofcl.; b. Cleve., July 22, 1932; d. J. Lyman and Claire A. (Lenoir) Lawrence; student Fenn Coll. (Cleve. State U.), part time 1950-58, D.C. Tchrs. Coll., 1960-64, Dept. Agr. Grad. Sch., 1968-69; m. James L. Dorman, May 16, 1959; children—Lydia, Lynda, James Lawrence. Clk., tax specialist, mgmt. analyst, supr., staff advisor IRS, Washington, 1954-79; spl. asst. to dep. asst. sec. adminstrn. Dept. Treasury, Washington, 1978-79; dep. dir. Interagency Com. on Women's Bus. Enterprise, SBA; Task Force on EEO, Dept. Treasury 1978-79; mem. Pres.'s Task Force on Women Bus. Owners, 1979—; speaker in field. Sec. Linton Hall Guild, 1978-80; chmn. trainer, cons., leader Girl Scout Service Unit, 1971-80; ofcl. observer Nat. Women's Conf., Houston, 1977; bd. dirs. YWCA, 1957-62; mem. planning com. Black Women's Summit, 1981; mem. Vestry St. Paul's Episcopal Ch., 1981—. Recipient spl. achievement award Commr. IRS, 1978, thanks badge Girl Scout Nation's Capital, 1977, recognition cert. for work in Christian edn. St. Paul's Episcopal Ch., 1976, Mary McLeod Bethune Centennial award Nat. Council Negro Women, 1975, other awards and certs. of appreciation. Mem. Am. Soc. Public Adminstrs., Federally Employed Women. Club: Delta Sigma Theta. Journalist Neighbor's Inc., 1969-71. Contbr. article to profl. jour. Office: 1441 L St NW Washington DC 20416

DORN, LINDA MARIE, cartographer; b. Phila., Oct. 18, 1948; d. Clifford Franklin and Anna Dorn; student public schs. Sec., Scatton Bros. Awning Co., North Wales, Pa., 1966-67; cartographer Photics Research Corp., Montgomeryville, Pa., 1967-69; cartographer, sr. drafter compiler Vernon Graphics, Inc., Norristown, Pa., 1969—. Mem. Nat. Assn. Female Execs., Women's Sports Found., U.S. Racquetball Assn., Am. Motorcyclist Assn. Baptist. Club: East Penn Motor. Home: 2437 Unionville Pike Hatfield PA 19440 Office: 30 S Montgomery Ave Norristown PA 19403

DORNER, SHARON A. HADDON, educator; b. Morristown, N.J., Nov. 3, 1943; d. William P. and Eleanor (Dygert) Haddon; B.A. in Bus. Edn., Montclair State Coll., 1965, M.A. in Bus. Edn., 1970, M.A. in Guidance and Counseling, 1978; Ed.D. in Vocat.-Tech. Edn., Adminstrn. and Supervision, Rutgers U., 1982; children—Wendy, Meridith. Tchr., Morris Knolls High Sch., 1965-70; tchr. Katherine Gibbs Sec. Sch., Montclair, N.J., 1973-74; tchr. Leonia (N.J.) High Sch., 1974-75; tchr. bus. Woodcliff Sch., Woodcliff Lake, N.J., 1976—, adminstrv. intern to supt., 1980—; tchr. adult sch. Sussex Vocat. Sch., County Coll. Morris, Randolph, N.J. Judge, Election Bd., Montclair, 1972—. Mem. Assn. Supervision and Curriculum Devel., Am. Vocat. Assn., Am. Vocat. Research Assn., N.J. Vocat. Assn., NEA, N.J. Edn. Assn., Bergen County Edn. Assn., Woodcliff Lake Edn. Assn. (sec. 1976—), N.J. Bus. Edn. Assn., Nat. Bus. Edn. Assn., Eastern Bus. Tchrs. Assn., Consumers League (dir. 1979—), Delta Pi Epsilon (pres. Beta Phi chpt. 1979-80, v.p. 1978-79, sec. 1976-78, newsletter editor 1974-76, nat. com. 1980—, nat. council rep. 1981—, chmn. nat. com. 1982—), Sigma Kappa (nat. alumnae province officer 1977-81, nat. alumnae dist. dir. 1981—), Phi Delta Kappa (pres. 1980-82 treas. 1975-79, 82—, council del. 1977-80), Omicron Tau Theta. Clubs: Daus. of Nile, N.J. Eastern Star. Mem. adv. bd. Today's Sec., 1981-82. Home: 28 College Ave Upper Montclair NJ 07043 Office: 134 Woodcliff Ave Woodcliff Lake NJ 07675

DORO, MARION ELIZABETH, polit. scientist, educator; b. Miami, Fla., Oct. 9, 1928; d. George and Alma (Carram) D.; B.A., Fla. State U., 1951, M.A., 1952; Ph.D. (Bennett fellow), U. Pa., 1959. Instr. polit. sci. Wheaton Coll., Norton, Mass., 1958-60; Ford Found. Area Studies fellow U. London, Kenya, Africa, 1960-62; asst. prof. Conn. Coll., New London, 1962-65, asso. prof., 1965-70, prof., 1970—, dir. grad. studies, 1975-79, chmn. dept. govt., 1981—; Fulbright fellow Makerere U., Kampala, Uganda, 1963-64; vis. research fellow, Am. Philos. Soc. grantee East Africa Inst. Social Sci. Research, 1971-72; sr. research fellow Radcliffe Inst., Cambridge, Mass., 1968-69; sr. asso. St. Antony's Coll., Oxford U., 1977-78. AAUW Am. fellow, 1977-78. Mem. Am., New Eng. (chmn. status women com. 1972-75, exec. council 1973-75), N.E. (exec. council 1974-76, 82—) polit. sci. assns., African Studies Assn. (dir. program nat. meetings 1976), AAUP, AAUW, Soc. Fellows Bunting Inst. of Radcliffe Coll. (exec. bd., co-chairperson), Phi Beta Kappa, Phi Kappa Phi, Pi Sigma Alpha. Editor: (with N. Stultz) Governing in Black Africa, 1970; mem. editorial bd. African Studies Rev.; contbr. articles and book revs. to profl. jours. Office: Conn Coll New London CT 06320

DORONIN, MARY CAMILLE, occupational health cons.; b. Jersey City, Mar. 4, 1938; d. Basil J. Meola and Rose G. (Rienzo) Meola Salge; grad. Holy Name Hosp. Sch. Nursing, Teaneck, N.J., 1958; postgrad. in human sexuality N.Y. Med. Coll., 1975-77; B.A. in Psychology, Fairleigh Dickinson U., 1978, postgrad., 1978—; m. William Doronin, June 12, 1971. Gen. duty nurse Fairmount Hosp., Jersey City, 1958-61; sch. nurse Jersey City Bd. Edn., 1961-62; occupational health nurse Port Authority of N.Y. and N.J., N.Y.C., 1961-80, also coordinator seminar for occupational health nurses, employee centered health edn. programs, 1978-80; occupational health cons. eastern U.S., Fireman's Fund Ins.,

Parsippany, N.J., 1980—; vol. Mass Cancer Screening Inner City, 1965. Vol., Big Sister program, N.Y.C., 1967. Mem. Am. Assn. Occupational Health Nurses, N.Y. State Assn. Occupational Health Nurses, Greater N.Y. Assn. Occupational Health Nurses (dir. 1965-71, v.p. 1971-73, chmn. editorial com., editor paper 1963-65), Am. Nurses Assn., N.J. State Nurses Assn., Am. Assn. Sex Educator, Counselors and Therapists, Eastern Assn. Sex Therapists (clin.). Roman Catholic. Office: Fireman's Fund Ins PO Box 221 Parsippany NJ 07054

DOROS, MARIA HECZEY, psychobiologist; b. Budapest, Hungary, Oct. 25, 1937; came to U.S., 1963, naturalized, 1970; d. Gabriel G. and Ethel M. (Tima) Doros; B.A. summa cum laude, Hunter Coll., 1973, M.A., 1975; Ph.D., City U. N.Y.; m. Ivan M. Heczey, Apr. 6, 1963 (div. 1978). Textile designer Leo Art Studio, N.Y.C., 1963-75; pvt. practice biofeedback therapy, N.Y.C., 1975-77; instr. Calif. Sch. Profl. Psychology, Los Angeles, 1977-79, Los Angeles City Coll., 1977-79; program coordinator N. Wis. Center for the Developmentally Disabled, Chippewa Falls, 1979-80; vis. prof. Carthage Coll., Kenosha, Wis., 1980-81; asst. prof. psychology Marietta (Ohio) Coll., 1981—. Mem. N.Y. Acad. Scis., Am. Psychol. Assn., Soc. Behavioral Medicine. Republican. Author: Behavioral Approach to Etiology and Treatment of Primary Dysmenorrhea and Menstral Distress, 1979; contbr. chpts. to books. Office: Marietta Coll Marietta OH 45750

DORR, LORNA BITGOOD, librarian; b. New London, Conn., May 2, 1941; d. Royal Earl and Frances Allen (Minson) Bitgood; B.A., Alfred U., 1963; postgrad. U. Conn., Washington U., St. Louis, 1973-74, Mars Hill Coll., 1980-82, U. S.C., 1982—; m. Darwin Dorr, Apr. 25, 1964; children—Benjamin Paul, Christopher Joseph. Elem. music tchr., Newburgh (N.Y.) Public Schs., 1963-65; library asst. R. M. Strozier Library, Fla. State U., 1965-67, acting head circulation div., 1968-69; book orderer dept. ind. study U. Minn., 1967-68; swimming instr. Asheville (N.C.) YWCA, 1978; circulation supr. Meml. Library, Mars Hill Coll., 1979-82; chief reference asst. Ramsey Library U. N.C., Asheville, 1982—. Mem. Brevard (N.C.) Chamber Orch., 1979, 81; mem. Asheville Symphony, 1981—. Bd. dirs., com. chmn. Community Center for the Arts, Asheville. Mem. Am. String Tchrs. Assn., ALA, N.C. Library Assn., Conn. Soc. Genealogists, R.I. Geneal. Soc. Episcopalian. Home: 54 Briarwood Rd Asheville NC 28804 Office: Ramsey Library U NC Asheville NC 28804

DORRIS, PEGGY RAE, biologist; b. Holly Bluff, Miss., Feb. 27, 1933; d. Hugh B. and Alta Eugenia (Stampley) D.; B.S., Miss. Coll., 1956; M.S., U. Miss., 1960, Ph.D., 1967. Tchr. high schs., Miss. and Ark., 1955-61; mem. faculty Henderson State U., Arkadelphia, Ark., 1966—, prof. biology, 1973—, chmn. dept., 1972. Mem. Arkadelphia Water and Sewer Commn.; bd. dirs. Ark. Simmental Assn. U.S. Army C.E. grantee, 1978. Mem. AAAS, Entomol. Soc., Ark. Acad. Scis., Audubon Soc., Delta Kappa Gamma. Baptist. Home: 125 Evonshire St Arkadelphia AR 71923 Office: H-642 Henderson State U Arkadelphia AR 71923

DORSCH, ROBERTA FUNK, assn. exec.; b. Balt., July 9, 1943; d. Edward Joseph and Roberta E. (Harris) Funk; student U. Md., 1961-63; cert. Johns Hopkins Hosp. Sch. Cytotechnology, 1967; m. Dennis Edward Dorsch, Apr. 26, 1969; 1 dau., Brenda Jean. Staff cytotechnologist Johns Hopkins Hosp., Balt., 1962-69, Meml. Hosp. Easton (Md.), 1969-71; sr. cytotechnologist Johns Hopkins Hosp., 1971-75, VA Hosp., Balt., 1975-78, Sacred Heart Hosp., Cumberland, Md., 1978-80; field dir. Shawnee Girl Scout Council, Martinsburg, W.Va., 1981—; tchr. swimming Cash Valley Sch., La Vale, Md., 1980-82; tchr. water ballet Cumberland Dept. Parks and Recreation, 1980-82. Bd. dirs. Allegany County unit Am. Cancer Soc., 1979-81, 82—; exec. com. PTA, Cash Valley Elem. Sch., 1980-82; active youth activities Ellerslie United Meth. Ch., 1979—. Mem. Am. Soc. Cytology, Md. Assn. Cytotechnologists (pres. 1974-76), Am. Soc. Clin. Pathologists, Am. Soc. Cytotechnologists. Clubs: Frostburg Badminton (v.p. 1981-82). Republican. Roman Catholic. Contbr. articles to profl. jours. Address: PO Box 358 Ellerslie MD 21529

DORSET, PHYLLIS FLANDERS, tech. and hist. writer; b. Tacoma, Sept. 10, 1924; d. William Winchell and Rhea Louise (MacDougall) Flanders; B.A. in Eng. Lit., U. Wash., 1948, M.A. in Eng. Lit., 1949; postgrad. U. N.Mex., 1950-51; m. Donald E. Dorset, Apr. 20, 1963. Tech. writer Sandia Corp., Albuquerque, 1952-54; tech. writer Stanford Research Inst., Menlo Park, Calif., 1966-63, (name changed to SRI Internat. 1977), supr. tech. media services, 1978—; cons. tech. writer Tech. Ops., Inc., Burlington, Mass., Cambridge, Mass., 1963-66, Arthur D. Little Co., Cambridge, Mass., 1964-66, Physics Internat. Co., San Leandro, Calif., 1970-74; cons. audio/visual presentations Menlo Park Arts Commn., 1976-79. Mem. Authors Guild. Author: Historic Ships Afloat, 1967; The New Eldorado, 1970; contbr. articles to various mags. Home: 460 Sherwood Way Menlo Park CA 94025 Office: 333 Ravenswood St Menlo Park CA 94025

DORSEY, DEBORAH WORTHINGTON, artist, educator; b. Alexandria, Va., Nov. 29, 1938; d. Ridgely Corbin and Leona (Fehler) D.; B.A. magna cum laude, Radcliffe Coll., 1960; M.A., M.Phil. in Art History, Columbia U., 1977; m. William A. Trebilcock, Sept. 9, 1961; children—Evelyn Dorsey, Paul Ridgely. Asst. editor Arts mag., 1967; art critic Art News, 1970-71; art researcher, asst. editor Time-Life Films, 1970-73; writer, researcher Filmstrip House, 1974; tchr. art and art history C.W. Post Center, L.I. U., 1974-78; pvt tchr. painting, N.Y.C., 1976—; exhibited in shows at Caravan House Galleries, N.Y.C., 1968, Artists Assn. Nantucket, 1974. Active Girls Club of New York. Recipient art awards No. Va. Profl. Artists, 1963, Nat. Arts Club, 1964, 80, Nat. Acad. Sch. Fine Arts, 1964-65, Artist Assn. Nantucket, 1968; Fulbright scholar, 1960. Mem. Am. Watercolor Soc. (asso.), Women in the Arts, Artists Assn. Nantucket (exhbn. com.). Club: Nat. Arts (exhbn. com.) (N.Y.C.). Home and Studio: 156 E 74th St New York NY 10021

DORSEY, DOLORES FLORENCE, corp. exec.; b. Buffalo, May 26, 1928; d. William G. and Florence R. Dorsey; B.S., Coll. St. Elizabeth, 1950. With Aerojet Gen. Corp., 1953—, asst. to treas., La Jolla, Calif., 1972-74, asst. treas., 1974-79, treas., 1979—. Mem. Cash Mgmt. Assn. San Diego (pres.). Republican. Roman Catholic. Club: Lomas Santa Fe Country. Home: 8218 Caminito Sonoma La Jolla CA 92037 Office: Aeroject-Gen Corp 10300 N Torrey Pines Rd La Jolla CA 92037

DORSEY, MIRIAM JOHNSON, state govt. ofcl.; b. Raleigh, N.C., Apr. 6, 1944; d. William Frederic and Mabel Estelle (Johnson) D.; B.A. in Polit. Sci., U. N.C., Chapel Hill, 1966, grad. Govt. Execs. Inst., Sch. Bus., 1978. Com. clk. N.C. Ho. of Reps., 1967; mem. staff U.S. Ho. of Reps., Washington, 1967-77; dir. N.C. Council Status of Women, also adv. to gov. N.C. on women's issues, 1977—; adv. bd. Nat. Women's Polit. Caucus, ERA; bd. dirs., Pres. Raleigh Women's Center; convener Women's Forum N.C., 1977. Mem. Exec. Dirs. Assn. (dir.), Nat. Assn. Commns. for Women. Democrat. Presbyterian. Author papers, reports in field. Home: 407 Oakwood Ave Raleigh NC 27601 Office: 526 N Wilmington St Raleigh NC 27604

DORSEY, RHODA MARY, coll. pres.; b. Dorchester, Mass., Sept. 9, 1927; d. Thomas Francis and Hedwig (Hoge) D.; B.A., Smith Coll., 1949, LL.D., 1979; B.A., Newnham Coll., Cambridge, 1951, M.A., 1954; Ph.D., U. Minn., 1956; LL.D., Nazareth Coll. of Rochester, 1970; D.H.L. (hon.), Mt. St. Mary's Coll., 1976, Mt. Vernon Coll., 1979. Teaching asst. U. Minn., 1951-53; faculty Goucher Coll., Towson, Md., 1954—, asst. prof., 1957-62, asso. prof., 1962-65, prof., 1965—, asst. dean, 1962-65, dean and v.p., 1968-74, acting pres., 1973-74, pres., 1974—; vis. lectr. Monash U. and Australian Nat. U., 1966-67; adv. com. to Hewlett and Mellon Founds.' Liberal Arts Coll. Self-Renewal Program; mem. Middle Atlantic Dist. Com. of Selection for Rhodes Scholarship; dir. U.S. Fidelity and Guaranty Co., Chesapeake & Potomac Telephone Co., Noxell Corp., First Nat. Bank Md. Mem. gov.'s ad hoc Bus. Adv. Council; active House of the Good Shepherd, Balt.; bd. dirs. Am. Friends of Cambridge U., 1978—, Am. Council on Edn., 1981—; mem. So. Regional Edn. Bd., 1980—; mem. adv. council of pres. Assn. Governing Bds., 1981—; mem. Md. Higher Edn. Supplemental Loan Authority, 1982—. Boston Globe fellow, 1949-50; Fulbright fellow, 1949-51; Fulbright-Hayes grantee, 1966-67. Mem. AAUP, AAUW (fellow, 1954-55), Middle State Assn. Colls. and Schs. (commn. on higher edn., 1st v.p. 1983), Md. Ind. Coll. and Univ. Assn. (v.p.), Phi Beta Kappa. Clubs: Smith of Balt., Hamilton St. (Balt.), Cosmopolitan of N.Y. Office: Goucher Coll Towson MD 21204

DORT-BRYN, STEPHANIE, health agency adminstr.; b. Lincoln, Nebr., June 3, 1943; Douglas M. and Eileen M. (Donley) D.; B.S. in Dental Hygiene, U. Nebr., 1966; M.P.H. in Health Services Adminstrn., U. Tex., 1972; m. John R. Bryn, May 1, 1981; 1 son, Brandon Jory Douglas. Clin. dental hygienist, Mpls., 1967-69; founder dental hygiene program Normandale State Coll., Bloomington, Minn., 1969-70; lectr. Sch. Dentistry, U. Calif., 1972-73; asst. supr. Sch. Dental Medicine, Harvard U., 1973-74, lectr., 1973-74; asst. prof. and clin. coordinator Sch. Dentistry, Northwestern U., 1974-75; asst. prof. Dental Public Health, Boston U., 1975-77, dir. masters degree program, 1975-77; dir. dental community devel. Indian Health Service, USPHS, HEW, Albuquerque, 1977-80; public health cons. div. health services delivery USPHS, HEW, Atlanta, 1980—; guest lectr. Boston U. Mem. Am. Public Health Assn., Am. Assn. Public Health Dentists, Am. Dental Hygienists Assn. Home: 1101 Collier Rd NW Atlanta GA 30318 Office: 101 Marietta Towers Room 1202 Atlanta GA 30323

DOSER, JANICE MARIE, nurse; b. Yankton, S.D., Nov. 27, 1941; d. Harold Henry and Loretta Agnes (Engle) Sonnenfield; B.S. in Nursing, Coll. St. Teresa, Winona, Minn., 1963; postgrad. U. Wis., LaCrosse, summers 1974, 75; m. Robert Francis Doser, Aug. 23, 1969; children—Andrew, Laura, James, Thomas, Sara. Staff nurse St. Mary's Hosp., Rochester, Minn., 1963-64, head nurse, 1964-66, instr. psychiat. nursing, 1966-69; asst. instr. nursing U. Utah, 1969-72; asst. instr. psychiat. nursing Viterbo Coll., LaCrosse, 1973-76; public health nurse State of Wyo., 1976-77; part-time staff nurse Sweetwater Meml. Hosp., Rock Springs, Wyo., 1978-79, 81—; instr. extended degree program registered nurses U. Wyo., 1979—. Brownie leader Girl Scouts U.S. Mem. Am. Nurses Assn., Wyo. Nurses Assn., Dist. 6 Nurses Assn. (treas.), Home and Sch. Soc. Democrat. Roman Catholic. Club: Rock Springs Swim (sec.). Home: 1108 Hilltop Dr Rock Springs WY 82901 Office: Box 184 Western Wyo Coll Rock Springs WY 82901

DOSS, FAYE WILLIAMS, physician; b. Logan, Ala., July 10, 1932; d. Verlon Aurice and Nonnie Claytor (Hudson) Williams; B.A., Judson Coll., 1954; M.D., Women's Med. Coll. Pa., 1958; m. Chriss H. Doss, July 5, 1957; children—William, Reuben, Nonna Dorothea, Faye Dorothea. Intern Chestnut Hill Hosp., Phila., 1958-59, resident internal medicine, 1959-60; resident psychiatry Norristown (Pa.) State Hosp., 1960-63; pvt. practice psychiatry, Birmingham, Ala.; active staff Bapt. Med. Center, Birmingham, 1968—, chief dept. psychiatry, 1973—; cons. Jefferson County (Ala.) Mental Health Clinic, 1964-69, Ala. State Hosp. Aftercare Services, Birmingham, 1964-70, Vocat. Rehab. Services, 1964-70, Jefferson County Mental Assn. Social Club, 1966-70; cons. Occupational Rehab. Center, Birmingham, 1968-70, mem. profl. adv. bd., 1968-71; asst. prof. psychiatry Med. Coll. Ala., Birmingham, 1964-68. Mem. profl. adv. bd. Fellowship House, Birmingham, 1967-69; mem. Ala. Commn. on Alcoholism, 1968-70. Diplomate Am. Bd. Psychiatry. Mem. AMA, Am. Psychiat. Assn., Med. Assn. State Ala., Pa. Psychiat. Soc., Jefferson County Med. Soc. Baptist. Home: 433 Golf Dr Birmingham AL 35226 Office: 801 Princeton Ave Birmingham AL 35211

DOSS, JEANIE, educator; b. Houston, Miss., May 2, 1949; d. Theo and Bonnie (Lucas) D.; B.S., Miss. U. for Women, 1973, M.Ed., 1977. Spl. edn. tchr., West Point, Miss., 1973-76; kindergarten asst. Miss. U. for Women, Columbus, 1976-77; homebound tchr. Columbus City Schs., 1977—; intern Rehab. Center, Columbus, 1976-77. Named Handicapped Woman of Yr., Pilot Club, 1978. Mem. Assn. for Supervision and Curriculum Devel. Democrat. Baptist. Home: 310 8th St S Apt 3 Columbus MS 39701 Office: Columbus City Schs 720 4th Ave N Columbus MS 39701

DOSS, JUDITH HARRIS, food service dir.; b. Memphis, Dec. 7, 1934; d. Wiley Chasteen and Irene Randle (Hodges) Harris; student Memphis State U., 1952-53, seminars U. Tenn., Nashville, 1971-76, Tenn. State U., 1978-81, Vanderbilt U., 1982, Gourmet's Oxford (Eng.) Center for Mgmt. Studies, 1982; m. Leslie Doss, Jr., 1953 (div. 1972); children—Leslie Walter III, Randle Elizabeth. Sec., receptionist James W. Stewart, investor, Dixie Oil Co., 1971-75; food service dir. The Webb Sch., Bell Buckle, Tenn., 1976—, spl. events coordinator 3d Nat. Conf. Nutrition, 1980, Nat. Food Policy Conf., Washington, 1982. Pres. Hillwood Presbyn. Ch. Women, Nashville, 1968-70; mem. Nashville Symphony Guild. Mem. Colonial Dames Am. (chpt. dir. 1981-83), Ladies Hermitage Assn. (life), Cheekwood Fine Arts Center, Assn. Tenn. Antiquities, Nat. Assn. Female Execs., DAR, Alpha Gamma Delta. Club: Shelbyville Women's. Contbr. to The Webb Cookbook, 1977, 79. Home and office: The Webb School Webb Rd Bell Buckle TN 37020

DOSS, NANCY OTWELL, educator, gallery owner, artist; b. Atlanta, July 28, 1938; d. John Davis and Ruth Elizabeth (Sorrow) Otwell; student Stetson U., 1956-57, Mercer U., 1957-59, Med. Coll. Ga., 1962; B.A., Piedmont Coll., 1978; children—Robyn Leigh, John Clinton. Bookkeeper, GMAC, Augusta, Ga., 1959-60; histologist Med. Coll. Ga., Augusta, 1960-63; personnel dir. Belk-Cornelia, Ga., 1979-80; owner The Studio, Toccoa, Ga., 1981—; self-employed art instr. commr. Stephens County Bd. Commrs., 1973-75, chmn., 1974-75; chmn. Stephens County Indsl. Devel. Authority, 1974-75; mem. Stephens County Bd. Health, 1973-75. Named 9th Dist. Ga. Homemaker of the Yr., 1969; recipient Public Servant award, Stephens County, 1974, others. Mem. Am. Soc. Clin. Pathologists, Ga. Artist Directory. Baptist. Club: Toccoa Country. Contbr. articles to profl. jours. Office: 149 E Doyle St Toccoa GA 30577

DOSSETT, BETTY JO, govt. ofcl.; b. Laurel, Miss., Sept. 14, 1931; d. James Daniel and Mary Allen (Ishee) Mooney; B.S., U. So. Miss., 1953, M.Ed., 1972; m. James Roland Dossett, Apr. 5, 1952; children—Linda Gail, Mark Richard. Social ins. rep. Social Security Adminstrn., Hattiesburg, Miss., 1960-66, Holiday, Fla., 1976-78, Dallas, 1978—; bus. cons. to Paul Stephen Lee, concert organist. Tchr., coordinator high sch. Sunday sch. Main St. Baptist Ch., Hattiesburg, 1962-66, 69-71; bd. dirs. aux. So. Bapt. Women's Missionary Union, Whitehaven Bapt. Ch., Memphis, 1967-68. Recipient Fed. Employee Recognition award Tampa Bay Fed. Exec. Assn., 1977, 15-Yrs. Service award Social Security Adminstrn., 1979. Mem. U. So. Miss. Alumni Assn. Home: 409 North St Hattiesburg MS 39401 Office: 1201A W Camp Wisdom Rd Dallas TX 75232

DOSTER, ROSE ELEANOR WILHELM (MRS. JESSE A. DOSTER), artist; b. Balt., May 11, 1938; d. Lewis Milford and Leeanora A. (Naylore) Wilhelm; cert. illustration and design Art Instrn. Sch. Mpls., 1956; cert. design and painting Md. Inst. Coll. Art, 1960, postgrad., 1960-62; m. Jesse Alfred Doster, Feb. 22, 1958; children—Jeffrey Allen, Roxane Elana. One-woman shows: Hampstead Library Gallery, 1969, 70, Aurora Fed. Gallery, Balt., 1969, Goodman Gallery, Ellicott City, Md., 1971, Central Savs. Gallery, Towson, Md., 1971, Parkville (Md.) Library Gallery, 1972, Equitable Trust Bank Reisterstown Gallery, Balt., 1973, Hancock Art Guild Gallery, 1981, Md. Center Public Broadcasting, Owings Mills, 1982, others; exhibited in group shows: St. John's Coll., Johns Hopkins, Goodman Gallery, Slayton House, Columbia, Md., Paynter Gallery, Rehoboth, Del., Hilltop House, Harpers Ferry, W.Va., 1974, Towson Art Festival, 1977, 78, 79, 80, 82, U.S. Ho. of Reps., Washington, 1981, 82, Unicorn Gallery, Balt., 1979; co-chmn. open exhbn. com. Balt. Arts Festival, 1978; tchr. drawing, painting and ceramics, 1968—; organizer art exhbns. and shows, 1969—. Active Boy Scouts Am.; troop leader, troop service dir., community dir. Girl Scouts U.S.A.; pres. Carroll County Arts Council, 1974-75, 2d v.p., 1980—; leader Greenmount 4-H Club, 1975-76, 77-78, 79; trustee Balt. Mus. Art, 1976—. Recipient numerous awards, including George Peabody award Md. Inst. Coll. Art, 1960. Mem. Nat. League Am. Pen Women (br. art chmn. 1970-72, 1st v.p., membership chmn. 1972-74, pres. Carroll br. 1974-76, br. historian 1976-82), Rehoboth Art League, Balt. Watercolor Soc. (asso.), Md. Craft Council, Md. Inst. Art Alumni Assn., Hanover Art Guild. Home: Box 403-A 3913 Shiloh Ave Hampstead MD 21074

DOTSON, BETTY LOU, govt. ofcl.; b. Chgo., June 29, 1930; d. Heber Theodore and Christine Evelyn D.; B.A., Ohio Wesleyan U.; J.D., Lincoln U. Claims adjuster Met. Ins. Agy., Chgo., 1955; claims authorizer Social Security Adminstrn., Chgo., 1955; relocation rep. Dept. Urban Renewal, Chgo., 1958-63; caseworker Cook County Dept. Public Welfare, Chgo., 1963-64, resource cons., 1964-66; clk. legal services trust dept. First Nat. Bank Chgo., 1966-67; community coordinator Community Legal Counsel, Chgo., 1967-68; adminstrv. asst. Nixon-Agnew Campaign Com., N.Y.C., 1968, Office Pres.-Elect Nixon, N.Y.C., 1968-69; dir. civil rights staff Food and Nutrition Service, U.S. Dept. Agr., Washington, 1970-75; asst. dir. equal opportunity Action, Washington, 1975-78; asst. to dir. Office Equal Opportunity, U.S. Dept. Agr., Washington, 1978-79, chief adjudications and complaints, 1980-81; sr. staff asso. Joint Center Polit. Studies, Washington, 1979-80; instr. bus. law U. D.C., 1981—; dir. Office Civil Rights, spl. asst. to Sec. Civil Rights, Dept. Health and Human Services, Washington. Past mem. nat. bd. Urban Concerns, Inc.; past mem. bd. dirs. Nat. Council Urban Affairs, YWCA Met. Chgo.; bd. dirs. YWCA Nat. Capitol Area, Washington. Mem. Alpha Kappa Alpha. Republican. Methodist. Home: 8 Evarts St NE Washington DC 20002 Office: 300 Independence Ave SW Room 5400 Washington DC 20201

DOTSON, JANE MCENDRE, educator; b. Covington, Ky., Sept. 29, 1926; d. Roy Bryan and Ruby Jane McEndre; B.A. in Psychology, U. Cin., 1960, M.A. in Exptl. Psychology, 1961; Ph.D. in Clin. and Social Psychology, U. Ky., 1968; m. Avery O. Dotson, July 23, 1946. Instr. dept. psychology No. Ky. U., Highland Heights, 1971-73, assoc. prof., dir. human services program, 1973-77, assoc. prof., dir. human services program dept. Allied Health, 1978-79, prof. dept. public adminstrn., dir. human services program, 1980—; cons. Holly Hill Children's Home, Cold Spring, Ky. Mem. Am. Psychol. Assn., Nat. Orgn. Human Service Educators, Cin. Psychol. Assn., Gerontology Soc., Ky. Psychol. Assn., No. Ky. Mental Health Assn., Assn. Gerontology in Higher Edn., Nat. Council on Aging, Am. Assn. Ret. Persons, PEO Sisterhood. Democrat. Home: 40 Pleasant St Apt 302 Fort Thomas KY 41075 Office: Human Services No Ky U Highland Heights KY 41076

DOTTS, MARYANN JULIETTE, educator, librarian; b. Pitts., Nov. 11, 1933; d. Charles A. and Mary J. (Dryer) Dreese; B.A., Nat. Coll. Christian Workers, 1956; M.A., Scaritt Coll., 1974; M.L.S. in Sch. L.S., George Peabody Coll. Tchrs., 1975; 1 dau., Ruthann. Dir. Christian edn. 1st Methodist Ch., Erie, Pa., 1956-58, Arlington Heights, Ill., 1958-61; tchr., supr. children's sect. of edn. staff Riverside Ch., N.Y.C., 1965-67; with tech. services dept. Edn. Library, George Peabody Coll. Tchrs., Nashville, 1974; librarian, cataloguer Upper Room Library and Mus., United Meth. Bd. Discipleship, Nashville, 1975; dir. children's ministries, adult ministries, dir. presch. Belle Meade United Meth. Ch., Nashville, Tenn., 1976-79; dir. Christian edn. Andrew Price U., Nashville, 1980—; free lance writer curriculum units for United Meth. Ch., 1963—. Mem. Ch. and Synagogue Library Assn. (pres. 1978-79), Christian Educators Fellowship, Tenn. Conf. Christian Educators Fellowship, Tenn. Assn. Young Children, Nashville Assn. Young Children, Dirs. United Methodist Preschs. Author: I Am Happy, 1971; Clues to Creativity: Providing Learning Experiences for Children, 3 vols., 1974; The Church Resource Library, 1975; When Jesus Was Born, 1979. Home: 2514 Blair Blvd Nashville TN 37212 Office: 2846 Lebonan Rd Nashville TN 37214

DOTY, DELLA CORRINE, fin. exec.; b. Marshalltown, Iowa, Apr. 12, 1945; d. Edwin Francis and Della Edna (Keller) Mack; B.S.B.A. in Acctg., Drake U., 1967; m. Philip Edward Doty, Dec. 23, 1967; children—Sarah Corrine, Anne Elizabeth. Audit staff Alexander Grant & Co., C.P.A.s, Denver, 1967-71; controller Valley View Hosp. and Med. Center, Denver, 1971-75; rate rev. specialist Colo. Hosp. Assn., Denver, 1975-79; pvt. fin. cons., Littleton, Colo., 1979—; lectr. in field. Dir., asst. treas. YWCA of Metro Denver, 1972-74; dir. Colo. Heart Assn., 1974-82; active Jr. League of Denver, 1979—; active various charitable orgns.; v.p. fin. and housing Alpha Phi Internat., 1974-78, trustee, 1980—; dir., treas. Alpha Phi Found., 1978—. Recipient William G. Follmer Merit award Hosp. Fin. Mgmt. Assn., 1976; C.P.A., Colo. Mem. Am. Inst. C.P.A.s, Colo. Soc. C.P.A.s, Hosp. Fin. Mgmt. Assn., Alpha Phi (Ursa Major award 1980). Republican. Baptist. Contbr. articles to profl. jours. Address: 5981 S Coventry Ln W Littleton CO 80123

DOTY, KATHLYN ELAINE, univ. adminstr.; b. Oak Park, Ill., Jan. 12, 1948; d. Paul Stephen and Helen May (Henderson) Mackey; M.B.A., U. Chgo., 1979; m. Richard Lee Doty, Nov. 27, 1973. Programmer trainee Time-Life, Inc., Chgo., 1967-68; jr. systems analyst Aldens Inc., Chgo., 1968-69, sr. systems analyst, 1969-71, project mgr., 1971-76; self-employed data processing cons., Chgo., 1976-78; dir. systems devel. Loyola U. Chgo., 1978—, bd. dirs., chmn. membership and edn. com. Loyola U. Employees' Fed. Credit Union, 1979—. Mem. Coll. and Univ. Systems Exchange, Nat. Assn. Female Execs., Assn. for Systems Mgmt., Assn. Women in Computing (v.p. Chgo. chpt. 1981-82), Assn. Computer Users. Home: PO Box 919 Oak Park IL 60303 Office: 2160 S 1st Ave Maywood IL 60153

DOUGHERTY, IRIS GWENDOLYN, recreational vehicle co. exec.; b. Fairfield, Nebr., Aug. 11, 1917; d. George Allen and Lena Esther (Houston) Croft; student Kansas City (Mo.) Jr. Coll., 1936; grad. in acctg. Kansas City (Mo.) Bus. Coll., 1942; student Hoff Bus. Coll., 1949-50; m. Walter L. Dougherty, July 12, 1957; children—Roberta Lee Raney, Sandra Kay Jones. With Montgomery Ward & Co., 1935-39, Cowie Electric Co., Kansas City, Mo., 1949; owner, mgr. Croft Trailer & R V Center, and predecessor, Kansas City, 1972—. Mem. Am. Rental Assn. (Spl. award 1966, 75), Family Motor Coach Assn. (comml. council), Kansas City Women's C. of C. (past dir.), Am. Bus. Women's Assn. Mem. Christian Ch. (Disciples of Christ). Club: Zonta (chpt. pres.

1956-57). Home: 4424 Larson St Kansas City MO 64133 Office: 4601 Truman Rd Kansas City MO 64127

DOUGHERTY, JUNE EILEEN, librarian; b. Union City, N.J., Mar. 27, 1929; d. Robert John and Jane Veronica (Smith) Beyrer; B.A. in Edn., Peterson State Coll., 1967; postgrad. Rutgers U. Sch. Library Sci., 1959-69; m. Donald E. Dougherty, Dec. 2, 1946; 1 son, Glen Allan. With A. B. Dumont, Paterson, N.J., 1950-54; sch. librarian St. Paul's Elementary Sch., Prospect Park, N.J., 1957—; dir. North Haledon (N.J.) Free Pub. Library, 1957—; sec.-treas. Dougherty & Dougherty, Inc., North Haledon, 1968—. Den mother Boy Scouts Am., 1954-57; mem. Gov. N.J.'s Tercentenary Com., 1962-64. Mem. Am., N.J., N. Haledon library assns., Cath. Library Assn., N.J. Libraries Roundtable, Bergen-Passaic Library Club, Friends N. Haledon Library. Roman Catholic. Club: St. Paul's Social. Home: 155 Westervelt Ave North Haledon NJ 07508 Office: 129 Overlook Ave North Haledon NJ 07508

DOUGHERTY, MARGARET MARY, advt. exec.; b. Bronxville, N.Y., Oct. 15, 1950; d. Bernard John and Marie Antoinette (Hart) Dougherty; student Manhattan Community Coll., 1973-75, Cornell U., 1969-71; m. Robert A. Marcus, May 14, 1978. Adminstrv. asst., sec., nat. personnel and indsl. relations dept., hdqrs. Gt. A & P Tea Co., N.Y.C., 1968-71; adminstrv. asst., account mgr. Dean L. Burdick Assos. Inc., N.Y.C., 1973-75; account mgr. Lavey/Wolff/Swift Inc., N.Y.C., 1975—, media dir., 1976—; v.p., 1982—. Past chmn. Murray Hill Block Assn. Mem. Advt. Women N.Y. (rec. sec. bd. dirs. 1980-81), Pharm. Advt. Club N.Y., Healthcare Businesswomen's Assn. (sec. 1979-80, pres. 1980-82). Home: 343 E 30th St 19C New York NY 10016 Office: 488 Madison Ave New York NY 10022

DOUGHERTY, M(ARY) FRANCES, choreographer, educator; b. Denver, Jan. 12, 1911; d. James and Cora E. (Kelly) D.; B.S., U. No. Colo., 1935; M.A., U. No. Colo., 1940; Ph.D., N.Y. U., 1959. Tchr. Greeley (Colo.) schs., 1935-40; tchr. Denver Public Schs., 1940-46; asso. prof. health, phys. edn. and dance U. No. Colo., 1946-59, prof., head dept. dance U. Oreg., Eugene, 1959-75, prof. emerita, 1975—; dir. recreation War Relocation Authority, Cody, Wyo., 1941; instr. N.Y. U. Grad. Camp, 1958; vis. prof. U. No. Colo., 1962; vis. lectr. U. Calif., Sacramento, 1963. Dedicant M. Frances Dougherty Dance Theatre U. Oreg., 1976; recipient U. No. Colo. Alumni award, 1970. Mem. Nat. Dance Assn. (hon.), Oreg. Assn. Health Phys. Edn. Recreation and Dance, Western Soc. Phys. Edn. Coll. Women, Phi Beta, Kappa Delta Pi. Republican. Choreographer numerous works including: The Donovans, 1948, Sonata, 1949, Street Scene, 1951, Carnival, 1954, Moon Worship, 1957, Spirituals, 1958, Westward Ha!, 1962, Sea Chanteys, 1966, Magnificat, 1967, Archie and Mehitabel, 1969; contbr. articles in field. Home: 907 Woodhill Dr Eugene OR 97405 Office: Dept Dance Univ Oregon Eugene OR 97403

DOUGHERTY, ROBERTA MOORE, childbirth educator; b. Abington, Pa., Feb. 4, 1939; d. Robert and Elizabeth Donaldson (Niblock) Moore; B.S., Drexel U., 1961; postgrad. Calif. State Coll., Fullerton, 1965, Fullerton Jr. Coll., 1966-68, Broome Community Coll., 1978-80, SUNY, Binghamton, 1980—; m. James W. Dougherty, Sept. 30, 1961; children—James, Tracy Lynn. Ind. practice as childbirth educator, 1968—; asst. tchr. Endwell (N.Y.) Nursery Sch., 1969-71; lectr. parent/child communication Broome Community Coll., Binghamton, 1971-73, various community groups including YWCA, Parents Anonymous, Council of Ministries, Headstart Program, 1972-75; developer, tchr. childbirth program, personnel trainer Our Lady of Lourdes Hosp., 1978-80; family life educator, tchr. fitness program for new mothers Binghamton Gen. Hosp., 1978—. Chmn., Roberson Center Art Enrichment for Binghamton Elem. Schs., 1973-74; weekly art aide, grade mother Homer Brink Elem. Sch., 1973-75; chmn. scholarship fund dr. Binghamton Community Music Center, 1974; vol. Tri-Cities Opera, 1973-75, March of Dimes, 1975-78; hostess Art Center Gallery, 1972-75; bd. dirs. Jr. League Binghamton, 1977-78, chmn. various coms., 1975-80. Mem. Internat. Childbirth Edn. Assn. (bd. dirs., chmn. tchrs. div. So. Tier N.Y. 1968-75 Acknowledgement of Service cert. as nat. historian 1978), Am. Soc. for Psychoprophylaxis in Obstetrics, Council Childbirth Edn. Specialists. Home: 601 Valleyview Dr Endwell NY 13760

DOUGHERTY, SARAH ELIZABETH, nurse; b. Mullica Hill, N.J., Nov. 25, 1922; d. John and Ellen D.; R.N., Cooper Hosp., Camden, N.J., 1944; B.S. in Nursing, Seton Hall U., 1956; M.A. in Nursing, Trenton (N.J.) State Coll., 1966. Surg. nurse Cooper Hosp., 1944-45; sch. nurse N.J. Dept. Health, Trenton, 1945-48, Mantua Twp. (N.J.)-Harris Twp.-S. Harrison Twp., 1948-56; nurse Harrison Twp. Little League, 1954-60; public health and sch. nurse Harrison Twp., 1956-60; sch. nurse Clearview Regional High Sch., Mullica Hill, 1960-69; supr. migrant edn., sch. health services N.J. Dept. Edn., Trenton, 1969-77, cons. I, 1977—; adj. instr. Glassboro (N.J.) State Coll., 1970-77; cons. migrant health N.J. Dept. Edn., 1977-80, sch. nurse cons., 1980—. Mem. Am. Nurses Assn., NEA, N.J. Nurses Assn. (pres. 1967-69), N.J. Sch. Nurses Assn. (program chmn. 1963-65, dir. 1969), Gloucester County Sch. Nurses Assn. Club: Mullica Hill Woman's (pres. 1979-80). Contbr. articles to profl. jours.

DOUGHERTY, URSEL THIELBEULE, communications exec.; b. Rotenburg, W. Ger., July 30, 1942; naturalized U.S. citizen, 1965; d. Hugo and Margarete (Marquardt) Thielbeule; B.A. summa cum laude in Polit. Sci., Cleve. State U., 1971; M.A. in Polit. Sci., U. Wis., 1972; M.B.A. in Fin., Case Western Res., 1982; m. Erich A. Eichhorn, Jan. 3, 1979. Journalist maj. daily, women's mag., Germany, 1962-66; asso. editor Farm Chems., 1967; publs. mgr. Trabon Lubrication Systems, 1967-68; research analyst Legis. Council, State of Wis., 1972; public relations adminstr. to mgr. public info. Eaton Corp., Cleve., 1972—; cons. small bus. Trustee, Lake Erie council Girl Scouts U.S.A., 1975-82, Sr. Citizen Resources, 1978-81; ambassador Jr. Achievement, 1979; steering com. YWCA Career Women of Achievement, 1981; adv. bd. Women's Career Networking, 1980—. Mem. Women in Communications, Sales and Mktg. Execs. Cleve., Public Relations Soc. Am., Detroit Press Club, Cleve. Inst. Art, Am. Exec. Women. Home: 1510 Crest Rd Cleveland Heights OH 44121 Office: 100 Erieview Plaza Cleveland OH 44114

DOUGLAS, JANET ELLYN, psychologist; b. Waterloo, Iowa, Dec. 17, 1933; d. George Willis and Aurel Ellyn (Beatty) Berger; B.A., Iowa State Tchrs. Coll., 1957; M.A., State Coll. Iowa, 1962; student Marycrest Coll., 1969, U. Iowa, 1970, Oxford U., 1958; Fla. A&M U., 1973-74; m. Lawrence Douglas, Dec. 21 1963 (dec., 1978); children—Robert James, Bret George. Tchr., Marion and Muscatine, Iowa, 1957-61; guidance counselor, Muscatine and Jacksonville, Fla., 1962-79; pvt. practice psychology, 1971—; instr. psychology Fla. Jr. Coll., Jacksonville, 1975—, Fla. Jr. Coll., Kent Campus, Jacksonville, 1975— ; counselor Andrew Jackson Sr. High Sch., Jacksonville. Named Outstanding Young Educator, Louisa County, Iowa, 1971. Mem. Riverside-Avondale Preservation Soc., 1974-79; mem. Jacksonville Symphony Assn., 1976—; mem. Jacksonville Community Chorus, 1978—. Mem. Am. Psychol. Assn., Am. Personnel and Guidance Assn., Fla. Personnel and Guidance Assn., Duval Personnel and Guidance Assn., Duval Tchrs. United, Phi Delta Kappa, Alpha Delta Kappa. Episcopalian. Clubs: Ladies Golf Assn., Antique Auto Club. Author: The Beck Work-Color Association Test as a Predictor of Juvenile Delinquency, 1962; The Tutorial System - A Look at Reading Problems at Stilwell Junior High School, 1974. Home: 7598 Old Kings Rd S Jacksonville FL 32217 Office: B 252 Kent Campus Fla Jr Coll Jacksonville FL 32205

DOUGLAS, JOY ANNE MARGARET, social services cons.; b. Spokane, Wash., May 20, 1935; d. Walter Franklin and Ella Mildred (Janes) Jones; B.A. cum laude, San Jose State U., 1958; M.S.W., U. Calif., Berkeley, 1972, cert. in gerontology, 1980, postgrad., 1981—; postgrad. U. Calif., Santa Cruz, 1978-80; m. Mark Newell Douglas, July 19, 1954; children—Sheryll Diane Douglas Graff, Carl Herbert, Eric Stuart, Ward Austin. Tchr. elem. schs., San Jose, Calif., 1958-59, Kempsville, Va., 1954-55, Wettengale Junction, Guam, 1959-61; caseworker Aid to Dependent Children, Honolulu, 1964, Childrens Protective Service Prince Georges County (Md.), 1965-68, Childrens Protective Service, Santa Cruz, Calif., 1969-71; dir. med. social services Community Hosp. Santa Cruz, 1972-74; instr. psychology, adult edn. Santa Cruz City Schs., 1971-76; cons. Social Services to Skilled Nursing Facilities, Santa Cruz, 1973-76; chief ombudsman Santa Cruz-San Benito Counties, 1976-81; cons. Calif. sub-state Ombudsman Programs, 1981—; mem. Santa Cruz County Nursing Home Commn., 1980-83; dir. Santa Cruz County Ombudsman-Adv. Program, 1976—; mem. needs assessment task force Mid-Coast Health Systems Agy., 1979-80. Officer, Navy Wives Club, Guam, Hawaii, 1959-65; bd. dirs. Santa Cruz Community Council, 1973-77; mem. adv. bd. Tri-County R.S.V.P., 1975-81, pres., 1975-79; vol. ARC; formerly active PTA, Boy Scouts Am., 4-H. Cert. life adult educator, Calif. Mem. Nat. Assn. Social Workers, Calif. Specialists on Aging, Western Gerontology Soc. (task force on long-term care), Nat. Coalition for Nursing Home Reform, Calif. Long Term Care Ombudsman Assn. (pres. 1979-81, hon. life). Contbr. articles on long-term care for functionally disabled adults to profl. publs. Home and Office: 2905 Pine Flat Rd Santa Cruz CA 95060

DOUGLAS, JUNE ERLINE, sch. adminstr.; b. Bklyn., July 25, 1931; B.A. in Early Childhood Edn., Bklyn. Coll., 1951, M.S. in Early Childhood Edn., 1969; postgrad. in child devel. Bank St. Coll., N.Y.C.; m. Archie Gordon; 1 dau., Kimberly June. Tchr. early childhood Pub. Sch. 243, Bklyn., 1952-67, supr. Kindergarten pilot program Community Sch. Dist. 16, Bklyn., 1967, coordinator dist. Title I, 1967-68; dir. project follow through program Pub. Sch. 243, Bklyn., 1968—; project dir. Follow Through Resource Center, 1977—; proposal writing cons. Bd. dirs. Carver Child Care Center, 1967-70. Mem. Friends of Children's Muse, 1972—, Hansel and Gretel Inc., 1974—, Nat. Assn. Univ. Women, Met. Assn. Childhood Edn., United Fed. Tchrs. Dir. project Follow Through Program Pub. Sch. 243, Bklyn.; sponsor Bank St. Coll. Co-author: Language and Reading, 1979; Social Studies . . . Guides for Teaching, 1978; Parents and Children Share Experiences in Learning, 1980. Office: 1580 Dean St Brooklyn NY 11213

DOUGLAS, KATHARINE, interior designer; b. Columbus, Nebr.; d. Harold and Irma Kramer; B.A., Sarah Lawrence Coll., 1951; cert. N.Y. Sch. Interior Design, 1953; divorced; children—Pamela Mateer. Steele Frederic. Contract designer R.H. Macy & Co., N.Y.C., 1954-57; head dept. interior design Copeland, Novak & Israel, N.Y.C., 1957-63; interior designer Katzman/Kloke Assos., N.Y.C., 1973-76; v.p. Norwood Oliver Design Assos., N.Y.C., 1976—. Vice pres. Bklyn. Heights Community Nursery Sch., 1966-70; bd. dirs. Bklyn. Ind. Democrats. Mem. Inst. Store Planners (exec. com.). Home: 19 Grace Ct Brooklyn NY 11201 Office: 136 E 57th St New York NY 10022

DOUGLAS, SHIRLEY ANN, state ofcl.; b. Columbus, Ohio, Sept. 10, 1936; d. Lloyd and Florence (Cox) Williams; student Ohio U., 1972-73; children—Benita, Florence, David, Lloyd, Deanna, Donald. With State Library Ohio, Columbus, 1968—, adminstrv. aide EEO, 1972-75, adminstrv. asst. supportive services, 1975—. Mem. word processing adv. council Fort Hayes Career Center, 1977-82. Mem. Ohio Library Assn. (sec. personnel functions, edn. and staff devel. 1974), Internat. Word Processing Assn. Presbyterian. Home: 3244 Indian Head Ct Columbus OH 43224 Office: 65 S Front St Columbus OH 43215

DOUGLASS, DONNA NIKSCH, bus. exec.; b. Joplin, Mo., Aug. 4, 1945; d. Donald Edward and Ruth Angelus (Nagel) D.; B.S., Ind. U., 1969, M.S., 1971; postgrad. Emory U., 1972-73, Ga. State U., 1974-75; m. Merrill E. Douglass, June 5, 1971; 1 dau., Jennifer Ruth. Teaching asst. N. Ga. Coll., 1974, 75; asso. dir. Time Mgmt. Center, Grandville, Mich., 1971—, v.p., 1980—; tchr., cons. on time mgmt. Mem. Nat. Speakers Assn. Author: Manage Your Time, Manage Your Work, Manage Yourself, 1980; Choice & Compromise: A Woman's Guide to Balancing Family and Career, 1983; editor-in-chief Time Talk, monthly newsletter, 1978—; columnist on time mgmt. Office: Time Mgmt Center PO Box 5 Grandville MI 49418

DOUGLASS, ELEANOR ELIZABETH, social worker; b. Summit, N.J., May 21, 1921; d. Thomas William and Elizabeth (Hill) Rooney; B.S. in Psychology, Geneva Coll., 1971; M.S.W., U. Pitts., 1974; M.Public Adminstrn., U. So. Calif., 1977, M.Health Services Adminstrn., 1978; m. James Douglass, June 1, 1946 (div. 1976); 1 dau., Gail. Clk., Met. Life Ins. Co., N.Y.C., 1939-46; office mgr. Shoppers World Stores, Beaver Falls, Pa., 1961-65; bookkeeper Beaver County Sch. Bd., Beaver, Pa., 1965-67; acting personnel dir. Rochester (Pa.) Gen. Hosp., 1967-69; supervising psychiat. social worker Calif. Dept. Health, San Bernardino, 1974-77; program mgmt. cons. Calif. Dept. Social Services, San Bernardino, 1977—; pvt. practice social work, Redlands, Calif., 1977—. Lic. clin. social worker, Calif. Mem. Nat. Assn. Social Workers (rec. sec., dist. 16 exec. com.), Am. Pub. Welfare Assn., AAUW.

DOUGLASS, EVA ROSE, bookkeeper; b. Reynolds, Ind., Apr. 16, 1936; d. Samuel and Helen (Burnett) Firth; A.A., Bellevue (Wash.) Community Coll., 1973; m. Robert E. Douglass, July 8, 1955; children—Robert E., June E., Michele E. Acct., owner Douglass Bookkeeping & Tax Service, Bellevue, 1974—; acct. Tom Locks & Assos., Mercer Island, Wash., 1974, Carmar Steel, Inc., Bellevue, 1973-74. Mem. adv. bd., acctg. dept. Bellevue Community Coll. Mem. Wash. Assn. Accts. (chpt. sec.-treas. 1977-78, co-chmn. editorial and publs. com. 1979-80, chpt. v.p. 1981-82), Am. Soc. Women Accts., Nat. Soc. Public Accts. Office: 16608 NE 19th Pl Bellevue WA 98008

DOUGLASS, KAY WHITLOW, KAY WHITLOW, sch. adminstr.; b. Macomb, Ill., June 11, 1938; d. Claude and Evelyn Carol (Stone) Whitlow; B.S., U. Ill., 1960; M.A., U. Minn., 1976; specialist cert., 1977; m. C. William Douglass, Sept. 1, 1957; children—Kathleen Douglass Winter, Julia. Tchr. Pub. Sch. Dists., 68 and 69, Skokie, Ill., 1961-66; dir. Bethany Nursery Sch., Highland Park, Ill., 1968-69; tchr. Am. Internat. Sch., The Hague, 1970-71; dir. Excelsior (Minn.) United Methodist Nursery Sch., 1972-76; adminstrv. intern, tchr. Pub. Sch. Dist. 276, Excelsior, 1976-77; prin. Kimball (Minn.) Elem. Sch., 1977—. Mem. Minn. Alliance for Arts in Edn. (dir. 1979—), Minn. Elem. Sch. Prins. (pres. Central div. 1981-82), Nat. Assn. Elem. Sch. Prins. Democrat. Methodist. Home: 14233 Prince Pl Minnetonka MN 55343 Office: Kimball Elementary School Kimball MN 55353

DOUGLASS, MARGARET ELLEN, phys. therapist; b. Schenectady, N.Y., Feb. 9, 1945; d. Milton John and Mary Ann (McMeel) D.; B.S. in Phys. Therapy, Russell Sage Coll.-Albany Med. Coll., 1967. Staff phys. therapist St. Peter's Hosp., Albany, N.Y., 1967-68, 69-70, asst. chief phys. therapist, 1970-78, phys. therapy supr., 1978—; staff phys. therapist St. Vincent's Hosp., N.Y.C., 1968-69; cons. Kenwood Infirmary; instr. Russell Sage Coll.; prototype research cons. Codman & Shurtleff, Inc. Cons. Task Force on Design of Erastus Corning Fitness Trail, City of Albany, 1981. Mem. Albany YWCA, Capital Dist. Phys. Therapy Mgrs. Forum. Office: 315 S Manning Blvd Albany NY 12208

DOUTHIT, AUDREY HOLZER, social worker; b. Cin., May 2, 1925; d. William Frederick and Emma Elizabeth Holzer; B.A., U. Cin., 1946; M.A., U. Chgo., 1948; m. Harold Henry Douthit, July 14, 1948; 1 dau., Susan Emily Douthit Hollinberger. Social worker Presbyn. Hosp., Chgo., 1948-50; dir. social service dept. Drake Meml. Hosp., Cin., 1952-56; intake supr. Marion County Assn. Retarded Citizens, Indpls., 1966-78, New Hope Found. of Ind., Indpls., 1978—; grad. student supr. Ind. U. Pres., So. Club of Indpls., 1976; mem. North Group Indpls. Symphony, Indpls. Mus. of Art, Second Presbyn. Ch. Mem. Nat. Assn. Social Workers, Clin. Register Social Workers, Assn. Cert. Social Workers, Republican. Club: Kappa Alpha Theta. Home: 8120 N Brent Ave Indianapolis IN 42640 Office: 8450 N Payne Rd Indianapolis IN 46268

DOUTY, MARY LOIS, pharm. co. exec.; b. Lynchburg, Va., Nov. 22, 1946; d. Stafford Windlack and Lucy Marion (Campbell) D.; A.A., Louisburg Coll., 1967; B.S., Radford Coll., 1969; m. Peter John Smith, Apr. 23, 1977. Tchr. art, head art dept. Carroll County High Sch., Hillsville, Va., 1969-71; artist Pre-Ink, Inc., Denver, 1971-72; print prodn. mgr. Neuwirth-Koller, Denver, 1972-79; co-owner, corp. sec.-treas. Frankfort Drug Co., Inc. (Ky.), 1979—. Home: 205 Woodridge Dr Frankfort KY 40601 Office: 238 W Main St Frankfort KY 40601

DOUVAN, ELIZABETH, psychologist; b. South Bend, Ind., Nov. 3, 1926; d. John S. and Janet (Powers) Malcolm; A.B., Vassar Coll., 1946; M.S., U. Mich., 1948, Ph.D., 1951; m. Eugene V. Douvan, Dec. 27, 1947; children—Thomas Alexander, Catherine des Ormiers. Mem. faculty U. Mich., 1951—, prof. psychology, 1968—, Catherine Neaggie Kellogg prof., 1970—. Mem. Ann Arbor Bd. Health, 1973-76; pres. Democratic Women's Club Ann Arbor, 1970-71. Mem. Am. Psychol. Assn., Am. Sociol. Assn., Nat. Women's Studies Assn., AAUP, AAUW (bd. internat. fellowships 1982—). Author: The Adolescent Experience, 1966; Feminine Personality and Conflict, 1970; American Families, 1980; The Inner American, 1981; Mental Health in America, 1981. Editorial bd. Signs, Psychology of Women Quar. Office: Dept Psychology U Mich 580 Union Dr Ann Arbor MI 48109

DOUZEFF, LINDA THERESA, clin. psychologist; b. Jackson, Mich., May 22, 1948; d. Louie G. and Dorothy Elizabeth (Soneff) D.; B.A. in Psychology, UCLA, 1976; M.A. in Psychology, Calif. Sch. Profl. Psychology, Los Angeles, 1978, Ph.D. in Psychology, 1980. Pediatric research asst. Los Angeles County U. So. Calif. Med. Center, 1972; research asst. UCLA Neuropsychiat. Inst., 1975, psychology intern sect. on legal psychiatry, 1977-78; psychologist Met. State Hosp., Norwalk, Calif., 1981-82; psychologist, cons. Charter Baywood Hosp. (formerly Long Beach Neuropsychiat. Inst.), Long Beach, Calif., 1979-82; pvt. practice psychotherapy, psychodiagnostic assessment and cons., Long Beach. Mem. Nat. Forensic League, Am. Psychol. Assn., Calif. State Psychol. Assn., Orange County Psychol. Assn. Office: 4647 Long Beach Blvd Suite D6 Long Beach CA 90806

DOVE, PATRICIA HOLLY, small business and biotech. cons.; b. Mineola, N.Y., Dec. 27, 1949; d. Ronald Garrett and Ruth (Clarke) D.; student Forbes Trail Tech. Inst., 1967; B.S. in Chemistry cum laude, City U. N.Y., 1974; M.B.A., Babson Coll., 1981; m. George M. Patton, Feb. 7, 1970 (div. 1979). Research chemist, product mgr. Collaborative Research, Inc., Waltham, Mass., 1974-78; asst. to dir. corp. devel. Thiokol Corp., Newtown, Pa., 1979; asst. to comptroller Vac Hyd Processing Co., Woburn, Mass., 1979; nat. accounts sales rep. Millipore Corp., Bedford, Mass., 1980-81; cons. small bus. and biotech., Acton, Mass., 1981, Oakland, Calif., 1982—. Mem. Bus. and Profl. Women Boston (Nike award 1980), Am. Soc. Profl. and Exec. Women, Nat. Assn. Female Execs. Address: PO Box 11264 Oakland CA 94611

DOVRING, KARIN ELSA INGEBORG, writer, lectr.; b. Stenstorp, Sweden, Dec. 5, 1919; came to U.S., 1953, naturalized, 1968; d. Bertil Oscar Oberg and Hedvig Eleonora (Broberg-Engstrom); grad. Coll. Commerce, Gothenburg, Sweden, 1936; M.A., Lund (Sweden) U., 1943, Ph.D., 1951; Phil. Licentiate, Gothenburg U., 1947; m. Folke Dovring, May 30, 1943. Journalist several Swedish daily newspapers and weekly mags., 1940-60; tchr. Swedish colls.; research assoc. Yale U., New Haven, 1953-60; fgn. corr. Swedish newspapers, Italy, Switzerland, France and Germany, 1956-60; vis. prof. Internat. U., Rome, 1958-60, Gottingen (W.Ger.) U., 1962; lectr. numerous univs. including Yale U., U. Wis., McGill U., U. Iowa; research assoc. U. Ill., Urbana, 1968-69; free-lance writer, journalist, 1960—; radio and TV interviews; books include Songs of Zion, 1951, Land Reform as a Propaganda Theme, 3d edit. 1965, Road of Propaganda, 1959, Optional Society, 1972; Frontiers of Communication, 1975, (short stories) No Parking This Side of Heaven, 1982; contbr. numerous articles to mags.; writer Ill. Alliance to Prevent Nuclear War. Recipient Swedish Nat. award for short stories Bonniers Pub. House Stockholm, 1951. Mem. NOW, Société Jean Jacques Rousseau (hon. life), Internat. Platform Assn., Acad. Poets, Inst. Freedom of Press (life asso.). Democrat. Address: 613 W Vermont Ave Urbana IL 61801

DOW, HELEN JEANNETTE, art historian; b. Ottawa, Ont., Can., June 13, 1926; d. Gordon Russell and Beatrice (Bott) Dow; B.A., U. Toronto, 1949; M.A., Bryn Mawr Coll., 1951, Ph.D. (Fanny Bullock Workman fellow), 1955. Lectr. Bryn Mawr (Pa.) Coll., 1957-58; asst. prof. Reed Coll., Portland, Oreg., 1958-60; acting chmn. art dept. Sweet Briar (Va.) Coll., 1960-61; curator Owens Mus., Mt. Allison U., Sackville, N.B., Can., 1961-64; assoc. prof. SUNY, New Paltz, 1964-65; vis. prof. U. Iowa, Iowa City, 1965-66; assoc. prof. U. Alta., Edmonton, 1966-71; assoc. prof. U. Guelph (Ont., Can.), 1971-72, prof., 1972—, chmn. fine art, 1973-74; cons. Can. Council. Founding mem. McDonald Stewart Art Ctr., Guelph; librarian Royal Mil. Coll., Kingston, Ont., Can., 1955-56. Served as sgt. Gov. Gen.'s Foot Guards Cadets, Ottawa, 1943-44. Brit. Council scholar, 1956-57. Fellow World Acad. (affiliate of Club of Rome); mem. Univs. Art Assn. of Can., Internat. Center of Medieval Art (N.Y.C.), William Goodenough Fellowship (London), Brit. Council Scholars Assn., Guelph Art History Soc. Conservative. Anglican. Author: The Art of Alex Colville, 1972; contbr. numerous articles to profl. jours.; asst. editor Peregrinatio, 1968-71. Home: 406-89 Raymond St Guelph ON N1H 3S5 Canada Office: Dept Fine Art U Guelph Guelph ON N1G 2W1 Canada

DOW, MARGUERITE RUTH, educator; b. Ottawa, Ont., Can., June 13, 1926; d. Gordon Russell and Beatrice (Bott) Dow; B.A., U. Toronto, 1949, B.Ed., 1971, M.A., 1970. Lab. asst. Nat. Research Council, Ottawa, Ont., Can., librarian, 1947-48; librarian Def. Research Bd., Ottawa, 1949-50; tchr. English and drama Ont. high schs., 1950-65, head Laurentian High Sch., Ottawa, 1959-65; assoc. prof. Faculty Edn., U. Western Ont., London, 1965-72, prof., 1972—; mem. consultative and research coms. Ont. Ministry of Edn., 1958-64; mem. creative and theatre arts coms. Ont. Inst. for Studies in Edn., 1965-69; founder Can. Heritage Writing Competition, 1974; bd. govs. Theatre Found. of Ottawa, 1961. Served with Gov. Gen.'s Foot Guards, Ottawa, 1943-44. Am. Biog. Inst. grantee, 1974. Fellow Internat. Inst. Community Service, World Acad. (N.Z.); mem. Can. Coll. Tchrs., United Empire Loyalists' Assn. of Can. (pres. London br. 1977-79, life mem. 1977, dominion councillor 1976-82), Monarchist League of Can. (chmn London br. 1979-82), Univ. Women's Club (chmn. scholarship com. Ottawa 1961-62), Ont. Secondary Sch. Tchrs. Fedn. (v.p. Brockville 1953-55, Ottawa 1960-62), Eng. Speaking Union, Heraldry Soc., Can. Assn. Univ. Tchrs. Author: The Magic Mask, 1966; co-author: Courses of Study in the Theatre Arts, 1969; contbr. articles in field to profl. jours.;

editor: Light from Other Windows, 1964; We Are Canada/Nous Sommes Canadiens, 1981. Home: 1231 Richmond St Apt 909 London ON N6A 3L9 Canada Office: Althouse Coll 1137 Western Rd U Western Ont London ON N6G 1G7 Canada

DOWBEN, CARLA (LURIE), lawyer, b. Chgo., Jan. 22, 1932; d. Harold Hiram and Gertrude (Geitner) Lurie; A.B., U. Chgo., 1950; J.D., Temple U., 1955; postgrad. cert. Brandeis U., 1968; m. Robert M. Dowben, June 20, 1950; children—Peter Arnold, Jonathan Stuart, Susan Laurie. Admitted to Ill. bar, 1957, U.S. Dist. Ct. bar, 1957, Mass. bar, 1963, Tex. bar, 1974, U.S. Supreme Ct. bar, 1974; asso. firm Conrad & Verges, Chgo., 1957-63; exec. officer M.I.T., Cambridge, 1963-64; legal planner Mass. Health Planning Project, Boston, 1964-69; asso. prof. Life Scis. Inst., Brown U., Providence, 1970-72; vis. asso. sociology U. Bergen (Norway), 1972; asst. prof. health law U. Tex. Health Sci. Center, Dallas, 1973-78, asso. prof., 1978—; cons. in field. Bd. dirs. Ft. Worth Assn. Retarded Citizens, 1980—, Advocacy, Inc., 1981—. Mem. Am., Dallas, Tex. bar assns., Nat. Health Lawyers Assn., Am. Soc. Law and Medicine, Hastings Inst. Ethics, Tex. Family Planning Assn. Quaker. Contbr. articles on civil rights of handicapped, institutionalized patients, child abuse, provision of health services, med. ethics to profl. jours. Active in drafting health, mental health legislation, agy. regulations several states, local govts. Home: 7150 Eudora Dr Dallas TX 75230 Office: Suite 300 5353 Maple Ave Dallas TX 75235

DOWD, ANN MARIE, med. technologist; b. Detroit, Oct. 17, 1924; d. Frank Raymond and Frances Mae (Ayling) Sullivan; B.S., Wayne State U., 1947; m. Thomas Stephen Dowd, Apr. 23, 1949; children—Cynthia Dowd Restuccia, Kevin Thomas Dowd. Med. technologist Woman's Hosp. (now Hutzel Hosp.), Detroit, 1946-52, St. James Clin. Lab., Detroit, 1960-62; supr. histo-pathology lab. Hutzel Hosp., Detroit, 1962-72, Mt. Carmel Mercy Hosp., 1972—. Mem. Am. Soc. Clin. Pathologists, Am. Soc. Med. Technology, Mich. Soc. Med. Technology, Nat. Soc. Histotechnology, Mich. Soc. Histotechnologists, Wayne State U. Alumni Assn., Smithsonian Assos., Detroit Inst. Arts Founders Soc. Home: 29231 Oak Point Dr Farmington Hill MI 48018 Office: 6071 W Outer Dr Detroit MI 48235

DOWDEN, ANNE OPHELIA TODD, artist-author; b. Denver, Sept. 17, 1907; d. James Campbell and Edith Belinda (Brownfield) Todd; B.A., Carnegie Inst. Tech., 1930; postgrad. Art Students League, N.Y.C., Beaux Arts Inst. Design, N.Y.C.; m. Raymond Baxter Dowden, Apr. 1, 1934. Instr., Pratt Inst., 1930-1933; freelance textile designer, 1935-52; head art dept. Manhattanville Coll., 1932-53; bot. illustrator, author, 1952—; latest books include Wild Green Things in The City: A Book of Weeds, 1972; The Blossom on the Bough: A Book of Trees, 1975; State Flowers, 1978; This Noble Harvest: A Chronicle of Herbs, 1979; illustrator: Shakespeare's Flowers, 1969; Wildflowers and The Stories Behind Their Names, 1977; The Golden Circle: A Book of Months, 1977; The Lore and Legends of Flowers, 1982; group exhbns. include Met. Mus. Art., 1940, 48, Newark Mus., 1948, Cooper Union Mus., 1956; one-woman exhbns. Bklyn. Bot. Garden, 1957, 77, Hunt Bot. Library, 1964, 66, 68, 72, 77, Henry Ford Mus., Dearborn, Mich., 1973, Callaway Gardens, Pine Mountain, Ga., 1971, 75. Recipient Notable Book award ALA, 1963, 75, Showcase Book award Children's Book Council, 1972, 75, Children's Book award Am. Inst. Graphic Arts, 1973; fellow Tiffany Found., 1929, 39, 31; named to Order of Rose, Delta Gamma, 1967. Mem. Hort. Soc. N.Y., N.Y. Bot. Garden, Bklyn. Bot. Garden. Address: 205 W 15th St New York NY 10011

DOWDEN, ANNIE MAE, nurse; b. Caney, La., Dec. 17, 1933; d. James Thomas and Fairy Gladys (Lambert) Jones; A.S., La. State U., 1972-75; m. Willard G. Dowden; children—Jimmy B., Gene E. With Sabine Parish Tax Assessors Office, Many, La., 1964-70; staff nurse Hanna Clinic & Hosp., Coushatta, La., 1976-81; dir. nurses Riverside Guest Care Center, Natchitoches, La., 1981—. Mem. La. Registry Nurses. Baptist. Clubs: Order Eastern Star, Bus. and Profl. Women's (pres. 1971-72). Home: Kisatchie Route PO Box 218 Kisatchie LA 71468 Office: 650 Keyser Ave Natchitoches LA 71457

DOWER, CATHERINE ANNE, music educator; b. South Hadley, Mass., May 19, 1924; d. Lawrence F. and Marie B. (Barber) D.; A.B., Hamline U., 1945; M.A., Smith Coll., 1948; Ph.D., Cath. U., 1968. Tchr. music, organist St. Rose Sch., Meriden, Conn., 1949-53; elem. sch. music supr. Holyoke (Mass.) Public Schs., 1953-55; instr. U. Mass., 1955-56; asst. prof., chmn. dept. music Westfield (Mass.) State Coll., 1956-67, assoc. prof., 1970-71, prof., 1972—; lectr. in field; dir. Open Window Book and Gift Shop; corporator Community Savs. Bank. Bd. dirs. Hispanic Inst., Inc., Holyoke; incorporator Springfield (Mass.) Symphony Orch.; pres. Holyoke Council on Human Understanding, 1982—; mem. Women's Symphony League. Mem. Am. Musicol. Soc., Coll. Music Soc., Ch. Music Assn. Am., Acad. Arts and Scis. P.R., Inter-Am. Acad. of P.R., Irish Am. Cultural Inst. (chmn. Holyoke chpt.), Music Assn. of Ireland. Democrat. Roman Catholic. Clubs: Quota, Haiti Mission (sec.). Contbr. articles to profl. publs.; editorial bd. Dateline Puerto Rico, U.S.A. Home: 60 Madison Ave Holyoke MA 01040 Office: Bates 118 Westfield MA 01086

DOWER, ELEANORE OLIVIA, coll. dean; b. Bethlehem, Pa., May 29, 1922; d. James Daniel and Elizabeth Olivia (Dunstan) D.; diploma in nursing Reading (Pa.) Hosp., 1951; B.S. in Nursing Edn., U. Pa., 1956, M.S., 1959. Staff nurse hosps. in Pa., 1951-54; instr., dept. chmn., asst. to dean Sch. Nursing, U. Pa., 1956-67; asso. dean nursing Widener Coll., Chester, Pa., 1967-74, 78-79, asso. prof., 1979—, dean, 1974-78. Mem. Am. Nurses Assn., Nat. League Nursing AAUW, AAUP, Pa. League Nursing (sec., dir. 1973-77; award of merit 1977), Sigma Theta Tau, Pi Lambda Theta. Presbyterian. Home: 29 Fairfield Rd Havertown PA 19083 Office: Widener Coll 14th and Chestnut Sts Chester PA 19013

DOWHOUER, MARIAN MARIE, sch. counselor; b. Friedensburg, Pa., Nov. 15, 1921; d. Charles Elmer and Carrie Irene (Dietrich) Emerich; B.S., West Chester State Coll., 1943; M.S., Temple U., 1955, postgrad. Pa. State U., Temple U., 1964-71, Boston U. (fellow), 1968; m. Walter L. Dowhouer, Dec. 19, 1953 (dec. 1965). Tchr., supr. music Charleston Sch. Dist., Wellsboro, Pa., 1943-47; tech. supr. Calvert Processing Co., Balt., 1947-48; coll. admissions asst. Temple U., Phila., 1948-55; secondary sch. counselor Spring-Ford Sch. Dist., Royersford, Pa., 1955—. Mem. Pa. Personnel Guidance Assn., Pa. Sch. Counselors Assn., Montgomery County Personnel and Guidance Assn. (mem. exec. bd.), NEA, Pa. State Edn. Assn., Springford Edn. Assn., AAUW, Montgomery County Hist. Soc., Goschenhoppen Hist. Soc. Home: 863 Cross Rd Lederach PA 19450 Office: Spring-Ford Area Sch Dist Washington St Royersford PA 19468

DOWLING, BONNIE LAVONNE, retail exec.; b. Sleepy Eye, Minn., July 29, 1925; d. John Raymond and Amelia (Gunderson) Johnson; m. C.W. Dowling, Dec. 22, 1946; children—Patricia, Kathleen, Michelle. Owner, Bonnie's Ladies Apparel, St. Peter, Minn., 1971—. Mem. City council, St. Peter, 1974—, chmn. retail council; mem. St. Peter Planning Commn., 1982—; mem. Community Edn. Council, 1974—. Mem. St. Peter Area C. of C. (dir. 1974-80), Nat. C. of C. Lutheran. Club: Shoreland Country. Home: 816 Lower Johnson Saint Peter MN 56082

DOWLING, DOROTHY RITA, communications co. exec.; b. Bklyn., Oct. 4, 1944; d. Leonard Thomas and Dorothy Mary Dowling; B.A., Montclair State Coll., 1966; postgrad. AT&T exec. M.S. program Pace U., 1967-69. Researcher, Ogilvy & Mather, N.Y.C., 1969-73; dir. research Einstein Assos., N.Y.C., 1973-75; bus. analyst Xerox, Rochester, N.Y., 1975-76; industry analyst EFTS, AT&T, Morristown, N.J., 1975-76, market mgr., 1976, market mgr. systems mktg. Morris Plains, N.J., 1977-79, market mgr. product and services delivery, 1979-81, dist. mgr. bus. mktg. ops., 1980-82, mgr. services delivery, 1982—. Mem. Nat. Assn. Female Execs. Home: 215 W 92d St New York NY 10025 Office: 225 Littleton Rd Morris Plains NJ 07950

DOWLING, JACQUES MACCUISTON, sculptor, painter, writer; b. Texarkana, Tex., Oct. 19, 1906; d. Charles Edward and Viola John (Estes) MacCuiston; Tchrs. Certificate, Coll. Marshall, 1923; studied art Loyola U., Frolich's Sch. Fine Art, Los Angeles, NAD, Art Students League, N.Y.C.; Ph.D., Colo. State Christian Coll. One man shows include: Fedn. Dallas Artists, 1950, 52, Rush Gallery, 1958, Sartor's Gallery, 1958, Sheraton-Dallas Hotel, 1960, Dallas Meml. Auditorium, 1960; exhibited in group shows at Dallas Mus. Fine Arts, Mus. of N.Mex., Fedn. Dallas Artists, Sartor's Gallery, Ney Art Mus., Oak Cliff Soc. of Fine Arts, Sartor's Gallery, Shuttles Gallery, Sheraton-Park Internat. Platform Assn., 1966-68, Phillips Mills Art Assn., 1967-74, Yardley Ann. Exhbn., 1968-73, Tinicum Art Festival, 1968, Woodmere Art Gallery (life mem.), 1972-74, others; selected sculpture 1st S.W. ann. show Mus. N.Mex., 1958; represented in permanent collections several corps., many pvt. homes. Recipient 1st Sculpture Fedn. Dallas Artists, 1950-54, pinned (all awards jewels), 1961; Hon. Cert. award Dallas Fed. Bus. Assn., 1964; two 1st awards N.J. Fedn. Womens Clubs, 1972, two 1st award, 1974, 1st and 2d award 1975, Gold medal Accademia Italia, 1979, many others, including 3 awards for journalism, 1962-63. Fellow Internat. Inst. Arts and Letters (life); mem. Cousteau Soc. (founding), U.S. Chess Fedn., Am. Contract Bridge League, Am. Assn. Ret. Persons, Internat. Acad. Lit., Arts and Sci. (hon. life mem., Tommaso Campanello with gold medal award 1972), C. of C. South Hunterdon (charter). Republican. Episcopalian. Mem. Order Eastern Star (past grand officer; past matron). Address: 335 NW Midway Blvd Port Charlotte FL 33952

DOWLING, JEANNINE MARIE, mfg. co. exec.; b. N.Y.C., Nov. 19, 1952; d. William Donald and Jeanne Dolores (Millet) Dowling; student Mich. State U., 1970-71, Harpur Coll., 1971-72; B.A., cum laude, SUNY, 1974; m. Michael E. Twomey, Sept. 20, 1980. Dir. public info. N.Y. State Div. Human Rights, N.Y.C., 1975-78; mgr. public interest Philip Morris, Inc., N.Y.C., 1978—. Dep. press sec. N.Y. State Carter Presdl. Campaign, 1974-75; mem. N.Y.C. Commn. on Status of Women, 1979—. Recipient Industry award Nat. Conf. Puerto Rican Women, 1981. Mem. Women in Communications (chmn. Matrix com. 1983), Public Relations Soc. Am., Women in Govt. Relations, N.Y. Public Affairs Profls., Nat. Women's Polit. Caucus, Lifelong Learning Council, Women's Econ. Round Table, Internat. Assn. Bus. Communicators, Women's Equity Action League. Office: Philip Morris 100 Park Ave New York NY 10017

DOWLING, NADINE VALERY, univ. ofcl.; b. Weymouth, Mass., Feb. 14, 1947; d. Clayton Ellsworth and Alise R. Dowling; A.S., Northeastern U., 1976, B.S., 1978, postgrad., 1978—. Asst. to dir. Patricia Stevens Career and Finishing Sch., Boston, 1971-72; asst. dir. personnel Northeastern U., Boston, 1972—; cons. Whale Communications, Stanford, Conn.; modeling instr. Barbizon Sch. Modeling, Boston, 1979, Workshop for Actors and Models, Boston, 1980. developer orgn. for pre-retirement program planners in New Eng. area. Mem. pub. relations dept. Boston Com. for Employment of Handicapped; Mem. young achiever bd. Glamour Mag. Recipient award for promoting dignity of others Nat. Alliance Businessmen, 1975. Mem. Coll./Univ. Personnel Assn., Internat. Assn. Personnel Women (newsletter editor), Soc. for Pre-retirement Planners, Sigma Epsilon Rho. Home: 790 Boylston St Boston MA 02199 Office: 101 Hayden Hall Northeastern U 360 Huntington Ave Boston MA 02115

DOWLING, RUBY HEATH, pianist; b. Robinson, Ill., Mar. 26, 1898; d. Lawrence Seymour and Clara Ella (Frye) Heath; B.Mus., Am. Conservatory of Music, Chgo., 1925; studied with Carl Friedberg, Madame Samaroff, Silvio Scionti, Chgo., 1923-35, Rudolph Ganz, Maurice Dumeznil, Paris, 1928; postgrad. Ind. U., 1973-76. Instr. piano and music theory Kansas City Conservatory, 1938-42; studied with Herbert Kuebler, Lincoln Trail Coll., Robinson, Ill., 1971—; recs. include: Piano Music of the Romantic Era, 1976, Piano Music By Bach, Mozart, and Chopin, 1978; dir. L.S. Heath & Sons, Inc., 1946—. Mem. Mu Phi Epsilon. Address: 412 Heath Ln Robinson IL 62454

DOWLING, SYLVIA (MRS. JOHN BENJAMIN DOWLING), broadcasting and advt. exec.; b. Albany, N.Y.; d. Charles and Harriet (Felt) Klarsfeld; student pub. schs.; m. John Benjamin Dowling; children—Susan Dowling Coes, John Benjamin. Broadcaster, Stas. WOKO, WABY, Albany, WGY, Schenectady; advt. copywriter Young & Rubicam, N.Y.C.; TV supr. Sullivan, Stauffer, Colwell & Bayles, N.Y.C.; v.p. Benton & Bowles, N.Y.C.; asso. creative dir. Am. Home Products Corp., N.Y.C.; newspaper columnist Conn. Sunday Herald, Fairfield County; contbg. editor Fairfield County Mag., Westport; v.p. Radio Stamford (Conn.), Inc.; now sta. mgr., dir. pub. and community affairs Stas. WYRS-FM, WSTC, Stamford; adminstrv. aide 21 Club, N.Y.C. Named Outstanding Businesswoman of Year, N.Y. Abbe Inst., 1962. Club: Stamford Yacht. Home: Southfield Point Stamford CT 06902 Office: 117 Prospect St Stamford CT 06901

DOWNES, WINNIE ALLEN SCOTT, human resources exec.; b. Cambridge, Mass., June 18, 1935; d. Leonard Bliss and Kathleen Bulkley (Smyth) Allen; grad. N.Y. U., Harvard U. Inst. Arts Adminstrn., 1969, New Sch. Social Research, 1970, Am. Assn. Accts. 1971; children—John A. Scott, Peter D. Scott, James L. Scott. Pres. Huntington (N.Y.) Arts Council, 1965-66, exec. dir., 1966-72; exec. dir. Westport-Weston Arts Council, Conn., 1972-74, Arts Council Greater New Haven, 1974-76; chmn. Met. Area Council Arts, N.Y.C., 1969; co-founder Levitt Pavilion Performing Arts, Westport, Conn., 1974; founder, co-chmn. Nat. Assembly Community Arts Agys., Associated Councils of the Arts, 1970-75; dir. public affairs Am. Mgmt. Assns., 1976-78; dir. external affairs Inst. Fine Arts, N.Y. U., N.Y.C., 1978-79; prin. Hay Career Consultants div. Hay Assos., 1980—. Adviser Nat. Com. Cultural Resources, 1975; trustee First Congl. Ch., Old Greenwich, Conn. Mem. Inst. Internat. Devel. (dir.) Contbr. articles to profl. jours. Address: 341 Valley Rd Cos Cob CT 06807

DOWNING, CHRISTINE ROSENBLATT, psychotherapist; b. Leipzig, Germany, Mar. 21, 1931; came to U.S., 1935, naturalized, 1952; d. Edgar Fritz and Herta (Fischer) Rosenblatt; B.A., Swarthmore Coll., 1952; Ph.D. (Kent fellow), Drew U., Madison, N.J., 1966; M.A., U.S. Internat. U., San Diego, 1982; m. George V. Downing, June 9, 1951; children—Peter, Eric, Scott, Christopher, Sandra. From instr. to assoc. prof. religion Rutgers U., 1963-75; mem. faculty San Diego State U., 1975—, prof. religious studies, 1977—, chmn. dept., 1975—; mem. core faculty Calif. Sch. Profl. Psychology, San Diego, 1975—; chmn. bd. mgrs. Pendle Hill Grad. Study Center, 1971-74; ind. practice psychotherapy, 1980—. SVHE cross-disciplinary fellow, 1967-68; summer faculty fellow San Diego State U., 1976; Nat. Endowment for Humanities fellow, 1982-83. Mem. Am. Acad. Religion (pres. 1973-74), Soc. Values Higher Edn. (dir. 1966-81), Soc. Sci. Study Religion. Quaker. Author: Face to Face to Face, 1975; The Goddess: Mythological Images of the Feminine, 1981; editor: Quaker Religious Thought, 1969-74. Home: 625 Serpentine Dr Del Mar CA 92014 Office: Religious Studies San Diego State U San Diego CA 92182

DOWNING, ELIZABETH ANN, army officer; b. Ames, Iowa, Dec. 30, 1955; d. James Ray and Maria Tulia (Quiros) D.; B.S., Nebr. Wesleyan U., 1975; postgrad. U. Okla. at Canal Zone, 1978-80. Commd. 2d lt. U.S. Army, 1977, advanced through grades to capt., 1981; chief All Source Intelligence Center, 1st Inf. Div., Ft. Riley, Kans., 1980-81, 2d brigade asst. sr. intelligence officer, phys. security crime prevention officer, 1981—; mem. working women's panel Glamour mag., 1982. Mem. Junction City-Ft. Riley Ambassadors Program, 1981. Mem. Assn. U.S. Army, Soc. Big Red One, Nat. Assn. Female Execs., Mil. Network, Net. Assn. Female Execs., Planetary Soc. Roman Catholic. Club: Ft. Riley Officers. Home: 6003 Vine St Lincoln NE 68505 Office: HHC 2d Brigade 1st ID Fort Riley KS 66442

DOWNING, MARY ELLEN, extension agent, home economist; b. Morgantown, W.Va., Nov. 24, 1936; d. Ellis D. and Ellen Summers; B.S. in Home Econs., W.Va. U., 1958; M.S. in Home Econs., Syracuse U., 1969; children—Marie, Philip. Utility home economist, Ohio, 1958-62; coop. extension agt., 4-H program leader Onondaga County Coop. Extension Program, Syracuse, N.Y., 1964—; guest tchr. Syracuse U. Chmn., Onondaga County Health Edn. Assn., Nutrition Edn. Tng. Program; mem. adolescents needs and services com. Od County Legislature; mem. rehab. for ind. living planning com. Syracuse U.; deacon Presbyterian Ch. Nat. Assn. Extension Agts 4-H scholar, 1967-69. Mem. Am. Home Econs. Assn., Nat. Assn. Extension Agts. 4-H (N.E. regional contact nat. profl. improvement com., Disting. Service award 1980), N.Y. Assn. Extension Agts. 4-H (pres.), Epsilon Sigma Phi. Republican. Club: Eastern Star. Author: Food in the Morning, 1977. Office: 1050 W Genesee St Syracuse NY 13204

DOWNS, BARBARA JANE, govt. exec.; b. Morrisonville, Ill., Apr. 1, 1938; d. Claude S. and Leona P. (Dowdy) Huddleston; student Brown's Bus. Coll., Springfield, Ill., 1957; m. Dale D. Downs, May 8, 1959; children—D. Dean, Douglas D. Sec., State Atty's Office, Sangamon County, Springfield, Ill., 1957-60; with State Treasurer's Office, Springfield, 1963—, sec. to asst. state treas., 1963-66, sec. to chief fin. officer banking div., 1966-77, adminstrv. asst. banking div., 1977—. Pres. Stonington PTA, 1968; mem. Stonington Community Unit Bd. Edn., 1969-79, sec., 1971-79; mem. Old Stonington Bapt. Ch., chmn. bd. Christian edn., 1965-80, co-leader Bapt. Youth Fellowship, 1978—, sr. high sch. Sunday Sch. tchr., trustee ch., adult Sunday Sch. supt.; mem. Lake Springfield Bapt. Camp Bd., 1976—, pres. bd., 1979, 80, sec., 1980—; lit. chmn. Am. Bapt. Women Area III, 1980—. Home: Rural Route 1 Stonington IL 62567 Office: 203 State House Springfield IL 62706

DOWNS, BRANDI ELIZABETH, artist; b. McComb, Miss., Aug. 11, 1932; d. Jack Denson and Martha Ethel (Bornman) Hammack; B.F.A., Miss. State Coll. Women, 1955; m. William K. Douglas, Dec. 23, 1956; children—Martha Anne, William K., Christine Rachel. Artist, WLBT-TV, Jackson, Miss., 1955, Gorden Marks Advt., Jackson, 1955-57, Dallas Times Herald, 1957-58, Whaley Studio, Dallas, 1958; art dir. Jiffy Printing, Dallas, 1958-59; tchr. art Dallas Public Schs., 1959-62; one-man shows Municipal Art Gallery, Jackson, 1955, French Quarter Gallery, New Orleans, 1967—71, Sheraton Gallery, San Juan, P.R., 1968, La Concia Gallery, San Juan, 1972, Our Lady of Holy Cross, 1971, San Geronimo Gallery, San Juan, 1973, French Quarter Design, New Orleans, 1974-75, Symmetry Gallery, New Orleans, 1976-77; exhibited in group shows Norfolk (Va.) Mus., 1953, Nat. Kappa Pi Exhbn., 1954. Recipient 1st prize Colonial Dames Art award, Columbus Miss., 1954; 1st prize Allison Wells, 1955; silver medal Tommaso Campanella Soc., Rome, 1970, Gold medal, 1972. Mem. Am. Artist Profl. League, Soc. N.Am. Artists. Home: Route 1 Box 29 Mount Croghan SC 29727 Office: 832 Orleans Ave New Orleans LA 70116

DOWNS-JACOBS, EILEEN MARGARET, educator; b. Chgo., Aug. 22, 1942; d. John Preston and Eileen Mary (Sheehan) Downs; B.S. in Speech and Hearing Therapy, B.S. in Speech and Drama K-12, Nazareth Coll. Ky., 1964; M.S. in Spl. Edn. K-12, Portland (Oreg.) State U., 1974, postgrad., 1977-78; m. Owen Jacobs, Sept. 19, 1975; children—Shannon (dec.), Kevin. Speech tchr. and therapist schs. in Mich., Colo., Col., Idaho and Oreg., 1964-74; itinerant specialist, mem. ednl. support personnel team Portland Public Schs., 1974-76; Title I specialist Baker (Oreg.) Public Schs., 1976-79, dir. fed./vocat. and testing programs, 1978—; workshop leader, cons. in field. Chmn. bd. dirs. Crossroads Creative and Performing Arts Center, 1976-80; pres. Cystic Fibrosis Assn. Portland, Boise and Denver, 1968-76; com. chmn. Baker Disaster Relief fund raising, 1980. Mem. Am. Soc. Profl. and Exec. Women, Nat. Assn. Female Execs., Oreg. Assn. Vocat. Adminstrs., N.W. Women in Ednl. Adminstrn., AAUW, Blue Mountain Quarter Horse Assn., Oreg. Cowbelle Assn., Baker County Cowbelle Assn. Democrat. Roman Catholic. Club: Lady Elks. Author handbook. Home: PO Box 1004 Evanston WY 82930 Office: 2090 4th St Baker OR 97814

DOYLE, CONSTANCE TALCOTT JOHNSTON, physician; b. Mansfield, Ohio, July 8, 1945; d. Frederick Lyman IV and Nancy Jean Bushnell (Johnston) Talcott; B.S., Ohio U., 1967; M.D., Ohio State U., 1971; m. Alan Jerome Demsky, June 13, 1976; children— Ian Frederick Demsky, Zachary Adam Demsky. Intern, Riverside Hosp., Columbus, Ohio, 1971-72; resident in internal medicine Hurley Hosp. and U. Mich., Flint, 1972-74, emergency physician Oakwood Hosp., Dearborn, Mich., 1974-76, Jackson County (Mich.) Emergency Services, Jackson, 1975—; disaster cons., co-chmn. emergency med. services disaster com. Region II EMS, 1978-79; course dir. advanced cardiac life support and chmn. advanced life support com. W.A. Foote Meml. Hosp., Jackson, 1979—, others; clin. instr. emergency services, dept. surgery U. Mich., 1981—; instr. Jackson County Emergency Med. Technician refresher courses, Jackson Community Coll. Bd. dirs. Jackson County Heart Assn., 1979—. Mem. Am. Med. Women's Assn., Am. Coll. Emergency Physicians (Mich. disaster com., dir. Mich. 1979—, chmn. Mich. disaster com. 1979—; nat. ad hoc disaster com. 1982—; cons. Fed. Emergency Mgmt. Agy. disaster mgmt. course 1982—), ACP, Mich. Assn. Emergency Med. Technicians (dir. 1979-80), Mich. State, Jackson County med. socs., Sierra Club. Jewish. Contbg. author: Clinical Approach to Poisoning and Toxicology, 1983. Home: 1665 Lansdowne Rd Ann Arbor MI 48105 Office: WA Foote Hospital East Emergency Dept Jackson MI 49201

DOYLE, FRANCES CECILE, artist; b. Denver, Aug. 21, 1917; d. Abraham Swartzchild and Maryfrances King (Blackburn) Switzer; student La. State U., 1946-49, Northwestern State Coll., Natchitoches, La., 1947, U. Guanajuanto, 1969; m. Alvin R. Doyle, Jr., June 28, 1935; 1 son, Maurice. Costume designer, Baton Rouge, 1949—; owner, mgr. Frandol's Pottery Studio, Baton Rouge, 1950-55; sec. Alvin Doyle & Assocs., Baton Rouge, 1965—; tchr. pottery Catholic Youth Orgn.; also portrait painter. Mem. Nat. League of Am. Pen Women, La. Art and Artist Guild Gallery, Inc., Internat. Soc. Artists. Presbyterian. Home: 4924 Parkhollow St Baton Rouge LA 70816 Office: 4924 Parkhollow St PO Box 66256 Baton Rouge LA 70896

DOYLE, HELEN ELIZABETH, polit. cons., Democratic nat. committeewoman; b. Worcester, Mass., Nov. 9, 1936; d. Walter Henry and Helen Mary (Berry) McCloskey; B.A., Trinity Coll., Washington, 1958; postgrad. U. Mass., 1959; m. Robert Thomas Doyle, Jr., Aug. 29, 1959; children—David, Robert E., Deirdre, Sarah, Kate, Padraic, Eamon, Liam. Elementary sch. tchr., Northampton, Mass., 1958-59, Washington, 1959-60; polit. cons., Ashfield, Mass., 1970—; Democratic nat. committeewoman for Mass., 1976—. Sec., Ashfield Bldg. Code Bd.

Appeals, 1975—; chmn. Franklin County Dem. Assn., 1972-75, Dem. Town Com., 1972—; mem. Mass. Dem. Com., 1976—. Roman Catholic. Home: Steady Ln Ashfield MA 01330

DOYLE, KATHERINE LEE LEE, educator; b. Sacramento, Sept. 22, 1932; d. Maurice Omar and Lorena Augusta (Merrill) D.; B.A. magna cum laude, Dominican Coll. San Rafael, 1954; M.A., Stanford U., 1961; Ph.D., Tulane U., 1971; m. F. Vincent Brecka, Jr., May 13, 1972. Research asso. Stanford (Calif.) Med. Sch., 1958-62; asso. research specialist U. Calif. Med. Sch., San Francisco, 1962-67; instr. Tulane Med. Sch., New Orleans, 1967-70, asst. prof., 1970-72; adj. scientist Delta Regional Primate Center, Covington, La., 1967—; prof. U. Ark. Coll. Medicine, Little Rock, 1977—, acting chmn. ob-gyn, 1978. Mem. exec. bd. Ark. Family Planning Council, 1977—, bd. dirs., 1977—, pres., 1979—; pres. Spring Valley Property Owners Assn., 1978-79. cons. James Bowman Inc., 1977-78, Battelle Inst., 1977—, HEW, 1979—. Recipient Squibb award for outstanding research, 1963; Population Council grantee, 1963, 73, NIH grantee, 1969-72. Mem. Am. Fertility Soc. (Rubin award 1962), Am. Assn. Planned Parenthood Profls., Am. Public Health Assn., Nat. Family Planning and Reproductive Health Forum, Am. Primatologic Soc., Soc. Study Reproduction. Roman Catholic. Contbr. articles to profl. jours. Home: 211 Gorgeous View Trail Little Rock AR 72210 Office: Dept Obstetrics and Gynecology U Ark Coll Medicine Little Rock AR 72203

DOYLE, VERLA DOHERTY (MRS. JACOBS H. DOYLE), club woman; b. Franklin, Pa., Aug. 12, 1912; d. Wilbur Felix and Walza (Magee) Doherty; A.B., St. Francis Xavier Coll. Women, 1936; m. Jacobs H. Doyle, Nov. 10, 1951. Case worker Pa. Dept. Pub. Assistance, Franklin, 1937-41; with U.S.O., Nat. Catholic Community Service, 1941-47, successively asst. club dir., club dir., rep. Tenn. maneuvers, 1943-44, traveling dir. S.E. region U.S., 1944-46; exec. sec. Cath. Youth Orgn., Nashville, 1949-51; bd. dirs. Nashville Diocesan Council Cath. Women, 1951—, sec., 1955-57, pres., 1959-61; nat. youth chmn. Nat. Council Cath. Women, 1958-62; del. Pres.'s White House Conf. Children and Youth, Washington, 1960; bd. dirs. Cath. Youth Orgn., Nashville, 1951-55, Nat. Multiple Sclerosis Soc., Nashville chpt., 1963-64. Alternate del. Democratic Conv. from Tenn., 1952, 56. Mem. Cath. Daus. Am., Cheekwood Cultural Center, St. Xavier Coll. Alumnae, Tenn., Nashville bar auxs. Clubs: Richland Country, Newman (dir. 1963-64), Colonna (treas. 1956, pres. 1958-60) (Nashville). Address: 6117 Robin Hill Rd Nashville TN 37205

DRAFFIN, NANCY GIANOUKOS, social worker; b. Charleston, S.C., Sept. 11, 1950; d. Anthony James and Katherine (Carabatsos) Gianoukos; B.A., Furman U., 1972; M.S.W., U. S.C., 1974; m. David Scott Draffin, Sept. 20, 1975; children—David Scott, Katherine Connell. Clin. social worker Med. U. S.C., Charleston, 1974-76; staff devel. and tng. specialist S.C. Dept. Social Services, Columbia, 1976-77; dir. outpatient social services Med. U. S.C., Charleston, 1977-78, asst. program adminstrn., 1978—, instr. Coll. Medicine, 1977—. Mem. Charleston County Multidisciplinary Com. on Child Abuse and Neglect, 1974—; bd. dirs. Comprehensive Emergency Services of Charleston County. Mem. Nat. Assn. Social Workers, Acad. Cert. Social Workers. Greek Orthodox. Home: 249 Belfast Rd Charleston SC 29407 Office: 171 Ashley Ave Charleston SC 29425

DRAGE, HELEN LILLIAN, acct.; b. Calgary, Alta., Can., Dec. 26, 1925; d. Eugene Ernest and Clara Elizabeth (Patch) Palmer; student LaSalle Extension U., 1971; m. Cecil Drage May 25, 1944; children—Donna, Gary, David, Julie Ann. Bookkeeper, Drage Trucking Hwy. Constrn., 1947-49, 50-51, 56-60, Drage Trucking Gypsum Quarry, 1952-55, Drage Trucking. Log Haul, 1962-74; acct. Jade Logging Ltd., 1975—. Bd. dirs. Golden Hosp. (B.C., Can.); pres. Donald Home & Sch. Assn. Clubs: Golden Light Horse, Golden Figure Skating (dir. 1972-74). Home: Reeves Rd Donald Station BC V0A 1C0 Canada

DRAGUL, CAROL, securities trader; b. Bklyn., Apr. 7, 1932; d. Max Harry and Blanche (Halperin) Witzer; student U. Cin., 1950-51, Hebrew Union Coll., 1969-74; m. Charles C. Dragul, June 8, 1952; children—Marc Bruce, Barbara Lynn. Mem. exec. tng. program Shillito's, Cin., 1952-54; community resource worker Accent on Youth, Cin., 1962-63; coordinator Sheltered Tng. Program, Preparation and Employment Program for Spl. Youth, Cin., 1965-66; tng. dir. Ring Realtors, Cin., 1969-76; asst. dir. Devel. Corp. for Israel, Cin., 1976-77; exec. dir. State of Israel Bonds for Cin. and Ky., Cin., 1977-80; rep. AMPAL Securities, Inc., 1981—. Vice chmn. Nat. Jewish Community Relations Adv. Com., 1977—; founding mem. Met. Area Religious Coalition of Cin., 1968. Club: B'nai B'rith Women. Home: 5817 Bayberry Ave Cincinnati OH 45242

DRAKE, BETTYE BENNETT, nurse; b. Isle of Wight County, Va., Sept. 25, 1930; d. Herbert M. and Miriam Amelia (Batten) Thacker; R.N., DePaul Hosp. Sch. Nursing, 1951; cert. Louise Obici Sch. Nursing, 1952; student Emory U., 1957-58, Coll. of William and Mary, 1963-70; B.S.N., Hampton Inst., 1972, postgrad. 1979—; m. Thomas E. Drake, Jan. 11, 1953; children—Cynthia K., Cheryl E. (dec.), Donna J., Betty J., Thomas E. Office nurse Dr. Hugh Warren, Smithfield, Va., 1952-53; staff nurse Louise Obici Hosp., Suffolk, Va., 1953, Gibson Hosp., Enterprise, Ala., 1953-54, St. Frances Hosp., Columbus, Ga., 1954-55, Maryview Hosp., Portsmouth, Va., 1955-57, Emory U., Atlanta, 1957-58, Maryview Hosp., 1958-60; asst. to oral surgeon, Norfolk, 1960-61; acting dir. nursing service Williamsburg (Va.) Community Hosp., 1961-62; gen. duty nurse then head nurse Eastern State Hosp., Williamsburg, 1963-64, head nurse, 1966-68, nurse supr., 1968-69, nurse instr., 1969-78, asst. dir. nursing, 1978-80, nurse coordinator/nurse mgr., 1980-81, 81—; pvt. duty nurse Williamsburg, 1964-65; staff nurse William and Mary Infirmary, Williamsburg, 1965-66. CPR instr., Am. Heart Assn., 1978—; bd. dirs. Williamsburg Community Living Group, 1979—; choir mem., asst. pianist Walnut Hills Bapt. Ch., 1966—; mem. Peninsula Assn. Continuing Edn. com., 1980-81. Named Outstanding Nurse, Eastern State Hosp., 1975; VA Med. Center, Hampton, Va. scholar, 19-. Mem. Am. Nurses Assn., Va. Nurses Assn., Dist. X Nurses Assn. (dir. 1961-63). Baptist. Home: 115 Quaker Meeting House Rd Williamsburg VA 23185 Office: Drawer A Eastern State Hosp Williamsburg VA 23187

DRAKE, ELLEN ANN, psychologist; b. New Brunswick, N.J., Mar. 31, 1945; d. Stanley George and Ann F. Ripish; B.A., Drew U., 1967; M.S., U. R.I., 1969; Psy.D., Rutgers U., 1976. Sch. psychologist Madison Twp. (N.J.) Public Schs., 1969-71; dir. spl. services Sayreville (N.J.) Public Schs., 1971-74; educator-clinician Rutgers Community Mental Health Center, Piscataway, N.J., 1974-80; pvt. practice psychology, Kendall Park, N.J., 1976—; field supr. Grad. Sch. Applied and Profl. Psychology, Rutgers U., 1977—. Mem. Am. Psychol. Assn., N.J. Assn. Advancement Psychology, N.J. Psychol. Assn. Co-author book; also numerous articles on children of divorce. Office: 3186 Route 27 Kendall Park NJ 08824

DRAKE, JANET ELAINE, sales exec.; b. Chatham, Ont., Can., Nov. 5, 1948; came to U.S., 1968, naturalized, 1982; d. Cyril Edgar and Esther (Harlick) Strigley; A.Arts and Sci. with honors, No. Collegiate Coll., 1967; A.B., Chamberlain Sch. Retailing, 1968; m. Millard Llewellyn Drake, July 27, 1968. Area rep. Internat. Playtex, Stamford, Conn., 1971-74; nat. field sales coordinator Burlington Hosiery, N.Y.C., 1974-77; dir. sales devel. Natural Wonder Div., Revlon, N.Y.C., 1977-80; dir. sales devel. Lord Jeff Div., Gen. Mills, N.Y.C., 1980-81; mgr. sales tng. and merchandising Danskin Div., Internat. Playtex, Stamford, 1981—. Mem. Am. Mgmt. Assn., Fashion Group of N.Y. Clubs: Metropolitan of N.Y., Union League, Canadian. Home: 41 Flying Cloud Rd Stamford CT 06902 Office: 1114 Ave of Americas New York NY 10036

DRAKE, JOSEPHINE ELEANOR, publisher, writer; b. Yellow Frame, N.J., July 20, 1931; d. John Hall and Bertha Ellen (Messler) Stickle; certificates Rutgers U., 1967-73, English Lang. Inst. of Am., 1971; m. Paul Edmund Drake, 1952; children—Paul Edmund, Judith Ann, Patricia Ann, Robert Edmund. Dietary aide Newton Meml. Hosp., Newton, N.J., 1950-53; founder Jo's Book Service, Andover, N.J., 1973, pres., 1973—; author various books of poetry including: My Lament, 1974, Interference, 1974, Life Happenings, 1977, Evolution, 1977, Silence is Golden, 1978, Alone, 1978, Winter's Horrors, 1978. Home Econs. Extension Advisory Council scholar, 1973. Mem. ASCAP, Internat. Platform Assn., N.J. Turfgrass Assn., Garden State Hort. Soc., Nat. Writers Club, Nat. Wildlife Fedn. Methodist. Address: PO Box 115 Whitehall Rd Andover NJ 07821

DRAKE, JUDITH SUTTON, civic worker; b. Rochester, N.Y., Jan. 13, 1943; d. Charles William and Alice Earl (Taylor) Sutton; B.A., U. Rochester, 1964, M.A.T., 1965; A.C.E., Hartford Sem., 1976-77; m. Daniel Williams Drake, Aug. 7, 1965; children—Constance, David, Sarah. Elem. tchr., 1965-67; bd. dirs. LWV of Greenwich (Conn.), 1971-72; mem. environment com. Jr. League Stamford-Norwalk, 1973-77, mem. nominating com., 1975-77, bd. advisor, 1977-78, chmn. vol. career devel., 1977-78, facilitator, 1979-80, vol. career devel. tchr., 1980-81; ch. sch. coordinator St. Mark's Episcopal Ch., 1976-80, mem. edn. com., 1976—; communications coordinator Fellowship of Christians in Univs. and Schs., 1981—; mem. New Canaan Nature Center, 1973—, fall fair co-chmn., 1977; clothesline sale co-chmn. New Canaan Country Sch., 1979-80, chmn., 1980-81; alumni admissions com. U. Rochester. Republican. Clubs: New Canaan Field, New Canaan Winter. Author: (with others) The River Book, 1977, Follow That Man, 1971. Home: 157 Silvermine Rd New Canaan CT 06840 Office: 139 E Putnam Ave Greenwich CT 06830

DRAKE, LINDA CONTE, public relations exec.; b. Cleve., Dec. 6, 1948; d. Harry D. and Fern D. (Boehm) Conte; B.S. in Edn., Kent State U., 1970; M.A. in Communication, U. Mass., Amherst, 1971; m. Thomas A. Drake, Mar. 17, 1972; 1 son, Thomas Albert. Grad. teaching asst. U. Mass., 1970; word processing cons. adminstrv. services div. FDI Fin. Corp., Wilmington, Del., 1973-74; mktg. rep. office products div. IBM, Wilmington, 1974-77; relocation dir. Patterson Schwartz, Wilmington, 1977-81, v.p., dir. corp. relocation center, 1981-82; asst. v.p. public relations Chem. Bank (Del.), Wilmington, 1982—. Bd. dirs. Women's Center U. Del., Newark, 1981-82; pacesetter chmn. United Way, Wilmington, 1981. Mem. Nat. Assn. Realtors, Wilmington Women in Bus. (founder 1960, pres. 1981-82), Nat. Assn. Female Execs. Lutheran. Contbr. articles in field to profl. publs. Office: Chem Bank (Del) One Rodney Sq Wilmington DE 19807

DRAKE, LYNN ANNETTE, physician; b. Albuquerque, Aug. 4, 1945; d. Olen Lester and Lucille Susan (Henry) Drake; B.A., Adams State Coll., 1966, M.A., 1967; M.D., U. Tenn., 1971. Instr. math. Adams State Coll., Alamosa, Colo., 1966-67; intern City of Memphis Hosp., 1971-72, resident in dermatology, 1972-75, chief resident, 1974-75; mem. faculty dept. medicine, div. dermatology U. Tenn. Center Health Scis., also Med. Practice Group, Inc.; asst. prof. dermatology Emory U., Atlanta; chief dermatology VA Med. Center, Atlanta; chmn. chemosurgery tag group VA; instr. advanced cardiac life support Am. Heart Assn.; mem. emergency room com. St. Joseph Hosp. Vol., Am. Cancer Soc., 1973-75. Diplomate Am. Bd. Dermatology Fellow Am. Acad. Dermatology; mem. Soc. for Investigative Dermatology, Am. Acad. Dermatology (com. on health planning), AMA, Tenn., Women's, Memphis, Shelby County med. assns., ACP, Ga. Dermatology Soc., Atlanta Dermatology Soc. (program chmn.), Am. Assn. Med. Colls., Council Acad. Scis., Women's Dermatology Soc. (housestaff liaison com., nominating com.), Dermatology Found. Home: 2270C Dunwoody Crossing Atlanta GA 30338 Office: Emory U Clinic 1365 Clifton Rd NE Atlanta GA 30322

DRAKE, MARLENE ANN, nurse; b. Hamilton, Ohio, June 19, 1940; d. Herbert Allison and Lucille Elizabeth (Reimer) D.; B.S. in Nursing, Ohio State U., 1962; M.Ed., U. Cin., 1967, M.S. in Nursing, 1976. Asst. instr. Jewish Hosp., Cin., 1962-64, chmn. prins. of nursing, 1964-67, clin. coordinator, 1967-68, asst. dir., 1968-77, clin. specialist gerontology-rehab., nursing dept., 1977-79, adminstrv. dir. patient care, 1979-80, asst. v.p. patient care, 1980-82; asso. adminstr. Med. Center at Bowling Green (Ky.), 1982—; lectr. geriatric care and stress mgmt.; cons. nursing homes. Tng. vol. Jewish Family Service; mem. adminstrv. bd. Forest Chapel United Meth. Ch., 1978-82. Mem. Nat. League Nursing, Ohio League Nursing (nominating com. Cin., dir. 1978-81, accreditation visitor, council of diploma programs 1971), Ky. League Nursing, Am. Nurses Assn., Ohio Nurses Assn., Southwestern Ohio Nurses Assn. (sec. educators, adminstrs., counselors and tchrs. sect., mem. bylaws com. 1970-74, chmn. 1974, del. state conv. 1973, mem. program and continuing edn. com. 1977-79), Ky. Nurses Assn., Greater Cin. Educator Conf. Group (rotating sec. 1968-77), Greater Cin. Staff Devel. Educators, Ohio State U. Alumni Assn., U. Cin. Alumni Assn., Sigma Theta Tau (chmn. research com. 1978-79, historian and exec. com. 1979-82. Club: Order of Eastern Star. Office: PO Box 56 Bowling Green KY 42101

DRAPER, BESSIE THORNTON, govt. agy. exec.; b. Washington, June 15, 1922; d. James Wesley and Gretchen (Ten Eyck) Thornton; A.S.C., St. Louis U., 1953; postgrad. Lincoln U. Law Sch., 1949-50; B.A., Howard U., 1970; m. George W. Draper II, Sept. 9, 1940; children—George W. III, Thornton C., Wesley R. Minority program officer Mo. State Employment Service, St. Louis, 1963-65; parent participation planning officer Nat. Project Head Start, OEO, Washington, 1966-71; dep. asso. exec., dir. communications U.S. Consumer Product Safety Commn., Bethesda, Md., 1973—. Bd. dirs., mem. exec. com. Christian Children's Fund, Richmond, Va. Recipient Superior Performance award U.S. Consumer Product Safety Commn., 1975. Mem. Soc. Consumer Affairs Profls., Nat. Consumer Symposium. Democrat. Episcopalian. Home: 13312 Bea Kay Dr Silver Spring MD 20904 Office: 5401 Westbard Ave Bethesda MD 20207

DRAPER, CATHERINE POINDEXTER, educator; b. Charlotte, N.C., Feb. 10, 1946; d. Robert Lee and Eddis Birdell (Tallent) Poindexter; A.B., High Point Coll., 1967; grad. student East Carolina U., 1968-70; m. H. Dennis Draper, Jr., July 15, 1967; children—Howard Lee, Robert Lee. Tchr., Spring Lake (N.C.) Elem. Sch., 1967-68; tchr. Coats (N.C.) Union Sch., 1968-70; tchr., chmn. English dept. East Montgomery High Sch., Biscoe, N.C., 1970-73; tchr., chmn. English dept. Roanoke Rapids (N.C.) High Sch., 1973—; instr. Montgomery Tech. Inst., 1971-73; instr. Halifax Community Coll., 1975—; instr. Weight Watchers, Inc., 1974-76; mem. instrnl. program com. Roanoke Rapids Grades Schs. Mem. N.C. Tchrs. English, Nat. Edn. Assn., N.C. Assn. Educators. Democrat. United Methodist. Home: 142 Hunting Ridge Rd Roanoke Rapids NC 27870 Office: 800 Hamilton St Roanoke Rapids NC 27870

DRAVIS, BETTY LOUISE, pub.; b. Hamilton, Ohio, Dec. 20, 1928; d. John D. and Felda Mae (Crawford) Barger; student San Diego State U., Foothill Coll. Los Altos, Cabrillo Coll.; children—Debra Rivera, Denyce, Mary Lee, Bob, Mindy Gonzalez, Allison. Soc. editor Imperial Beach News, San Diego, 1960-62; editor Gilroy (Calif.) News Herals, 1972, Labor News Gazette, 1973-78; talk show hostess Gilroy Cable TV, 1972-73; pub., owner Constrn. Labor News, San Jose, Calif., 1978—. Mem. United Way Communications Com. Recipient Santa Clary County Mercury-News Woman of Achievement award; Stanford Heart Disease Prevention award; Gilroy Jaycees award, others. Mem. Internat. Labor Press Assn., San Jose Newspaper Guild, Sigma Delta Chi. Democrat. Author: Zany the Zebra, We're Neat Guitars, 1960. Home: 4644 Calle de Farrar San Jose CA 951118 Office: 2102 Almaden Rd Suite 303 San Jose CA 95125

DRAZNIN, ANNE LOUISE, lawyer; b. Mpls., Mar. 25, 1945; d. Julius Nathan and Yaffa (Bernstein) D.; B.A., Earlham Coll., Richmond, Ind., 1966; J.D., U. Ill., 1971. Admitted to Ill. bar, 1971, D.C. bar, 1972; legal intern HUD, 1971-72; trial atty. FTC, Chgo., 1972-76; pvt. practice, Chgo., 1976-77, 82—; dir. div. legal services Am. Bar Assn., 1977-81; regional dir. Am. Arbitration Assn., Chgo., 1981-82; asso. prof. legal studies Sangamon State U., Springfield, Ill., 1982—; founder, chmn. bd. advs. Loop Legal Clinic, 1976-77; lectr. dispute resolution and arbitration. Recipient Maurice Wiegle award Chgo. Bar Found., 1977. Mem. Am. Arbitration Assn. (adv. council Chgo. region 1981—, mem. labor and comml. panels), Am. Bar Assn., Am. Judicature Aoc., Indsl. Relations Research Assn., Soc. for Profls. in Dispute Resolution, Constrn. Specifications Inst., Ill. Bar Assn. (past vice chmn. membership and bar activities standing com. 1979-81), Chgo. Bar Assn. (vice chmn. young lawyers sect. 1976-77, sec. arbitration com. 1981-82), Execs. Club Chgo., Mensa. Jewish. Author articles in field. Office: 221 N LaSalle St Suite 1776 Chicago IL 60601

DRECHSEL, BETTY FRANCES, nurse; b. Kankakee, Ill., Sept. 19, 1934; d. William Sylvester, Sr., and Dorothy Ann (Herron) Stearns; R.N., Brokaw Hosp., 1955; B.S.N., Ill. Wesleyan U., 1956; spl. course Northwestern U., 1972; m. Marvin E. Drechsel, Dec. 22, 1956; children—Marcia Elaine, Melissa Elline. Instr. newborn nursery technique Brokaw Hosp., Bloomington, Ill., 1956; office nurse to Dr. B.E. Albright, Kankakee, 1957-67; head indsl. nurse Gen. Foods Corp., Kankakee, 1969—; dir., sec. Gen. Foods Credit Union, 1980—. Pres. St. Paul's Luth. Parent-Tchr. League, 1978-80, mem. concerned parents-library com., chmn. fine arts com., 1978-81; v.p. Gen. Foods Recreation Assn., 1979-81, pres., 1981—; community adv. com. on alcoholism City of Kankakee. Mem. Ill. Occupational Nurses Assn., Am. Assn. Occupational Health Nurses. Lutheran. Home: RR 1 Box 280 Kankakee IL 60901 Office: 1551 E Willow St Kankakee IL 60901

DREHLE, CARMA LADINE, corp. exec., civic worker; b. Great Bend, Kans., Mar. 5, 1945; d. Edward Robert and Hildaguard Elizabeth (Boger) D.; student Ft. Hays (Kans.) State U., 1963-64. Receptionist, Gibson, Titus & Stafford, Inc., Great Bend, 1965-68, office mgr., 1968-72, sec.-treas., dir., 1972—, personal sec. to pres., 1973—. Vice pres. Soroptimist Internat. of Great Bend, 1975-77, pres., 1977-79; mem. office edn. adv. com. Barton County Community Jr. Coll., 1976-81; dist. adv. council Distributive Edn., 1980; mem. Blue Cross-Blue Shield State Subscriber Council, 1976—; mem. Trinity Lutheran Ch., 1945—, Sunday sch. supt., 1978-81; pres. Walter League, 1954, del. internat. convs., 1961, 63. Mem. Gamma Delta. Republican. Club: Barton County Luck 4's 4-H.

DREISER, VERA, psychologist, correctional cons.; b. N.Y.C.; d. Edward M. and Mai V. (Skelly) Dreiser; Ed.D., N.Y. U., 1944; m. Alfred E. Scott, July 8, 1939 (dec.); 1 dau., Sheri. Instr., Queens Coll., 1937-44, extension div. adult edn. program, 1940-43; adviser com. on recreation YWCA, 1940-42; vis. lectr. endocrinology, psychology, edn., music and dance, 1940-47; coll. editor Dance News, 1944-54; psychosociol. research Manhattan State Hosp., 1944-45; sr. psychologist Bklyn. Center for Psychotherapy, 1945-47; cons. psychologist, N.Y.C., 1947-61; psychol. expert for TV on The Ella Mason Show, later Food for Thought, guest numerous TV and radio shows, N.Y.C., 1949-61; correctional counselor, staff psychologist Calif. Instn. for Women, 1962-66, adminstr. psychiat. treatment unit, 1966-72; cons. psychotherapy William Beaumont Army Med. Center, El Paso, 1980-81; pvt. practice psychology. Sandy Springs Med. Center, Atlanta, 1982—, also cons. Bd. Offender Rehab.; lectr. Los Angeles Assistance League, Nat. League Am. Pen Women, Pomona Ebell Club, Am. Legion, Los Angeles ily Service Aux., Calif. State Poly. Coll., Mt. San Antonio Coll., Rotary Club of West Covina, Ontario City Library Series, others, 1970-72; appeared on four TV programs for NBC News on prison reform, radio discussion shows KGBS, 1974-75; columnist Let Dr. Dreiser Help You, Screenplay mag.; lectr. Emory U., Atlanta, 1978-79; guest radio talk shows. Mem. Assn. for Advancement Psychotherapy, Nat. Assn. Mental Hygiene, N.Y. U. Alumni Assn., Nat. League Am. Pen Women, Calif. Probation, Parole and Correctional Assn., Greater Los Angeles Press Club, ASCAP, Pi Lambda Theta. Author: My Uncle Theodore, 1976. Contbr. to King Features Syndicate, 1946-74.

DRENNAN, MARIE CATHERINE, newspaper exec; b. Ft. Wayne, Ind., Feb. 5, 1934; d. Matthew Christopher and Marie Katherine (Sommers) D.; student Ft. Wayne Art Sch., 1942-43. Announcer, Radio Ft. Wayne, WANE, 1950-56; traffic mgr. 1952-56, copywriter, 1951-56; hostess Transworld Airlines, Kansas City, Mo., Detroit, 1956-58; co-owner, v.p. Tops 'n' Talent, Detroit, 1959-67; writer, editor, coordinator spl. promotions Ross Roy, Inc., Detroit, 1969-73; writer, editor, coordinator promotion, spl. projects, mktg. services and sales devel. Detroit Free Press, 1975—. Recipient awards for Night Flight radio program as benefit to State tourist industry Mich. Ho. of Reps., 1971, Gov. William G. Milliken, 1972. Mem. Founders Soc. of Detroit Inst. Arts, Nat. Hist. Soc., Nat. Humane Soc., Nat. Writers Club, Nat. Assn. Female Execs., Detroit Press Club. Roman Catholic. Home: 8900 E Jefferson St Apt 304 Detroit MI 48214 Office: 321 W Lafayette St Detroit MI 48231

DRENOWATZ, MARGARET CLARE, librarian; b. Paterson, N.J., Sept. 18, 1927; d. Gustav Adolf and Margarete Lina (Loebbicke) Drenowatz; A.B., Douglass Coll., New Brunswick, N.J., 1954; M.L.S., Rutgers U., 1956. Head tobacco lit. service N.C. State U., Raleigh, 1956-62; editor wheat abstracts service Nebr. Coll. Agr., 1962-65; tech. info. specialist FDA, 1965-69; cataloger Bucks County Community Coll., Newtown, Pa., 1969-70, Princeton U. Library, 1970-73; chief librarian USV Pharm. Corp., Tuckahoe, N.Y., 1974-75; librarian Boehringer Ingelheim Ltd., Ridgefield, Conn., 1975-80, sci. bibliographer, 1980—. Mem. Med. Library Assn., Spl. Libraries Assn. Office: PO Box 368 Ridgefield CT 06877

DRESCHER, JUDITH MCCRERY, rehab. exec.; b. Worcester, Mass., Oct. 14, 1938; d. Harold Taylor and Norma (Fair) McCrery; B.A., U. Louisville, 1965; postgrad. U. San Francisco, 1973; m. Stephen E. Drescher, Nov. 25, 1959; children—S. Edward, Andrew A., Joshua M. Exec. dir. Columbia Gorge Rehab. Center, Hood River, Oreg., 1969—; participant confs. Mem. adv. bd. Rehab. Workshop Adminstrn. Tng. Center, Seattle U. HEW Rehab. Services Adminstrn. grantee, 1971-73. Mem. N.W. Assn. Rehab. Industries (pres. bd.), Oreg. Assn. Rehab. Facilities (officer), Oreg. Assn. Retarded Citizens (treas.), Assn. Retarded Citizens of Wasco County, AAUW. Presbyterian (elder). Club: Dalles Art. Home: 1709 Cherry Heights Dalles OR 97058 Office: 2940 Thomsen Rd Hood River OR 97031

DRESSELHAUS, MILDRED SPIEWAK, elec. engr.; b. Bklyn., Nov. 11, 1930; d. Meyer and Ethel (Teichtheil) Spiewak; A.B., Hunter Coll., 1951; Fulbright fellow Cambridge (Eng.) U., 1951-52; A.M., Radcliffe Coll., 1953; Ph.D. in Physics, U. Chgo., 1958; D.Eng. (hon.), Worcester Poly. Inst., 1976; D.Sc. (hon.), Smith Coll., 1980; m. Gene F. Dresselhaus, May 25, 1958; children—Marianne, Carl Eric, Paul David, Eliot Michael. NSF postdoctoral fellow Cornell U., 1958-60; mem. staff Lincoln Lab., M.I.T., 1960-67, Abby Rockefeller Mauze vis. prof. M.I.T., 1967-68, prof. elec. engring., 1968—, asso. head dept. elec. engring., 1972-74, Abby Rockefeller Mauze chair, 1973—; dir. Center Materials Sci. and Engring., 1977—, also vis. scientist Francis Bitter Nat. Magnet Lab.; vis. prof. Campinas U., Brazil, summer 1971, Israel Inst. Tech., Technion, summer 1972, also Tokyo, 1973, Caracas, Venezuela, 1977; mem. exec. com. Assembly Math. and Phys. Scis., Nat. Acad. Scis., 1975-78; chmn. evaluation panels Nat. Bur. Standards, 1978—; Graffin lectr. Am. Carbon Soc., 1982; mem. sci. adv. com. Allied Corp., 1980—. Recipient Hunter Coll. Hall of Fame award, 1972, Radcliffe Coll. Alumni medal, 1973. Fellow Am. Phys. Soc. (chmn. nominating com. 1975-76, Buckley prize com. 1976-77, chmn. 1977-78, new materials prize com. 1980, v.p. 1982), IEEE; mem. Soc. Women Engrs. (achievement award 1977), Nat. Acad. Engring., Am. Acad. Arts and Scis., Asso. Harvard Alumni (dir. 1974-76, nat. research adv. bd. 1978—), Brazilian Acad. Sci. (corr.). Contbr. articles to profl. jours. Home: 147 Jason St Arlington MA 02174 Office: Mass Inst Tech Cambridge MA 02139

DRESSER, DOLORES ANN, sch. prin.; b. Fairview, W.Va., Sept. 12, 1933; d. James Lester and Mae Kathleen (Miller) Haught; B.A., Fairmont State Coll., 1955; M.A., U. San Francisco, 1978; postgrad. San Jose State U., Long Beach State U., U. Calif.; m. Roderick Arthur Dresser, Sept. 1, 1956; children—Kathleen Allison, Roderick Arthur. Tchr. schs. in Md., Calif., Fla., Conn. and Va., 1955-70; counselor, Carmel, Calif., 1970-80; prin.-counselor Carmel Middle Sch. 1981—. Mem. AAUW, NEA, Nat. Counselors Assn., Assn. Sch. Adminstrs., Calif. Tchrs. Assn., Calif. Personnel and Guidance Assn., Assn. Carmel Tchrs., Carmel Community Hosp. Aux. Episcopalian. Club: Beach and Tennis (Pebble Beach, Calif.). Address: 840 Dry Creek Rd Monterey CA 93940

DRESSER, ROBERTA LEAZENBY, microbiologist; b. Fayette, Mo., Sept. 30, 1940; d. James Daniel and Mary Ann (Bates) Leazenby; B.A., U. Mo., 1961, B.Med.Sci., 1963, M.S. in Med. Microbiology, 1968; m. Steven T. Dresser, Dec. 17, 1959 (dec. Aug. 1973); children—Sara, Steven M., Todd, Thomas; m. 2d, Louis A. Kaufman, Dec. 30, 1977. Various clin. lab. positions with U.S. Army, USPHS and VA hosps., 1963-74; commnd. officer USPHS, 1974—; microbiologist div. in vitro diagnostic device standards Bur. Med. Devices, FDA, 1974-80, supervisory program analyst Office Asso. Dir. Standards, 1980-82, spl. asst. for regulatory analysis, 1982—. Mem. vestry All Saints Episcopal Ch., San Francisco, 1973-74. Mem. Am. Soc. Microbiology, Am. Soc. Clin. Pathologists, Federally Employed Women, Commd. Officers Assn., Nat. Assn. Female Execs., Children Am. Revolution (officer 1980-81). Democrat. Home: 2128 Edgewater Pkwy Silver Spring MD 20903 Office: 8757 Georgia Ave Silver Spring MD 20910

DREW, ELIZABETH, journalist; b. Cin., Nov. 16, 1935; d. William J. and Estelle Jacobs Brenner; B.A., Wellesley Coll., 1957; D.H.L. (hon.), Hood Coll., 1976, D.H.L., Yale U., 1976, Trinity Coll., 1978, Reed Coll., 1979, William, Coll., 1981; LL.D. (hon.), Georgetown U., 1981; m. J. Patterson Drew, Apr. 11, 1964 (dec. Sept. 1970); m. 2d David Webster, Sept. 26, 1981. Writer, Congressional Quar., 1959-64; Washington editor Atlantic Monthly, 1967-73; host TV interview program Thirty Minutes With, 1971-73; commentator Agronsky & Co., Post Newsweek TV and radio stas., nationally syndicated, 1973—; writer New Yorker Mag., Washington, 1973—. Recipient award Soc. Mag. Writers, 1971; Achievement award Wellesley Alumnae, 1973; DuPont award, 1973; Mo. medal, 1979. Club: Federal City. Author: Washington Journal, 1975; American Journal, 1977; Senator, 1979; Portrait of an Election, 1981. Office: 1300 19th St NW Washington DC 20036

DREW, KATHERINE FISCHER, historian, educator; b. Houston, Sept. 24, 1923; d. Herbert H. and Martha Fischer; B.A., Rice Inst., 1944, M.A., 1945; Ph.D., Cornell U., 1950; m. Ronald F. Drew, July 21, 1951; Asst. prof. history Rice U., Houston, 1950-57, assoc. prof., 1957-64, prof., 1964—, chmn. dept. history, 1970-80. Guggenheim fellow, 1959, NEH sr. fellow, 1974-75. Fellow Mediaeval Acad. Am.; mem. Am. Hist. Assn., Am. Soc. Legal History, Internat. Assn. Study Representative Instns., Phi Beta Kappa. Author: The Burgundian Code, 1949; A Study of Lombard Laws, 1956; Barbarian Invasions, 1970; The Lombard Laws, 1974. Editor Rice Studies, 1966-81. Office: Dept History Rice U Houston TX 77251

DREW, LORRAINE MAPLES, utilities co. community relations mgr.; b. Washington, Dec. 30, 1937; d. Frederick Benman and Ella Lucretia (Johnson) Maples; B.S., Howard U., 1960; M.S. in Edn., Pepperdine U., 1976; m. Eric Ridgeley Drew, Aug. 13, 1960; children—Erin Renee, Lynne Michele, Patrice Lorraine, Eric Michael, Graciella Cecelia. Computer operator, programmer David Taylor Model Basin, Carderock, Md., 1959-64; tchr. Taft Jr. High Sch., Washington, 1964-66; tchr. St. Benedict the Moor Sch., Washington, 1966-69, acting vice prin., 1968-69; tchr. Colma Jr. High Sch., Daly City, Calif., 1969-70, chmn. reading lang. dept., 1971-73; coordinator opportunity program San Jose (Calif.) Affirmative Action, 1973-74; public info. coordinator, reading and multicultural edn. cons. Oak Grove Sch. Dist., San Jose, 1976-79; instr. San Jose State U., 1974-75; customer service coordinator Potomac Elec. Power Co., Washington, 1979-82, community relations and ednl. services mgr., 1982—. Mem. bd. dirs. Jr. Achievement, Washington, 1970-72; vice chmn. bd. dirs. Our Lady of Guadalupe Clinic, Daly City, 1970-72. Recipient Community award of Excellence, Oak Grove Sch. Dist., 1979; Black Parents Community award Oak Grove Parents Assn., 1978. Mem. Washington C. of C. (dir. 1982), Ibero-Am. C. of C., Nat. Assn. Female Execs., Women's Exec. Link, Coalition of Black Bd. Mems. and Black Adminstrs., Alpha Kappa Alpha. Home: 5220 Griffith Rd Laytonsville MD 208799 Office: 1900 Penn Ave NW Washington DC 20068

DREW, PATRICIA, social work educator; b. Los Angeles, June 5, 1928; d. John A. and Ruby (Laity) D.; B.A., UCLA, 1950; M.S.W., U. So. Calif., 1956; D.S.W., Washington U., St. Louis, 1972. Clin. social worker City of Hope Med. Center, Duarte, Calif., 1956-59, asst. dir. social services, 1960-64; instr. George Warren Brown Sch. of Social Work, Washington U., 1966-67, asst. prof., 1967-68; asst. dean Sch. Social Work, Smith Coll., 1968-69; dir. continuing edn. Sch. Social Work, Calif. State U., Fresno, 1969-72; asso. prof. Sch. Social Work and Community Planning, U. Md., Balt., 1972—, dir. research, 1972-75, 78-79; social work research cons. to Mass. Gen. Hosp.-Harvard Sch. Public Health, 1966-67, YMCA of Greater Balt., 1973-74, hosp. social service dept. Washington U., 1967-68, Washington U. Hosp., 1966. Cert. social worker, Md. Mem. Acad. Cert. Social Workers, Nat. Assn. Social Workers, Council on Social Work Edn. Contbr. articles to profl. publs.

DREWS, LINDA JANE, Realtor; b. Lakewood, Ohio, June 7, 1948; d. Herman A. and Eva D.; B.S., Bowling Green U., 1971; postgrad U. Akron, 1972-74, John Carroll U., 1977. Restaurant mgr. Holiday Inn, Richfield, Ohio, 1971-77; regional broker services Century 21 Real Estate, Richfield, 1977—, also regional relocation dir., now regional adminstrv. dir. Mem. Nat. Assn. Realtors, Ohio Assn. Realtors, Cleve. Area Bd. Realtors, Greater Cleve. Growth Assn., Akron Regional Devel. Bd., Cleve. Conv. Bur., Akron Conv. Bur., Heights Area C. of C., Am. Soc. Personnel Adminstrs., Employee Relocation Council, Sales and Mktg. Execs. Assn., Kappa Delta. Republican. Lutheran. Office: 4767 Brecksville Rd Richfield OH 44286

DREYFUS, GRACE HAWES (MRS. LOUIS G. DREYFUS, JR.), civic worker; b. Victory, N.Y., Dec. 26, 1892; d. John Bently and Pearl (Van Hoosen) Hawes; student pub. schs. N.Y., Prager Sch., Dresden, Germany, N.Y. U., 1916; m. Louis G. Dreyfus, Jr., June 14, 1917. Founder, Grace Dreyfus Clinic and Orphanage, Teheran, Iran, 1942; hon. life dir. affiliates U. Calif. at Santa Barbara. Bd. dirs. Welfare Blind, Inc., Washington. Decorated Elmi first class (Iran). Mem. Nat. Inst. Arts and Letters (past pres. Santa Barbara br.), Internat. Platform Assn., The Saint Cecilia Soc. of Santa Barbara, Red Lion and Sun (life mem. Iran), Channel City Women's Forum (charter mem., hon. life dir.). Republican. Clubs: Little Town, Valley, Coral Casino (Santa Barbara); Union Interalliee (Paris, France). Home: 370 Hot Springs Rd Santa Barbara CA 93108

DREYFUSS, CARIL EISENSTEIN, writer; b. New Haven; d. Irving and Gertrude (Lax) Eisenstein; B.A., Smith Coll.; postgrad. Am. U.; m. Barney Dreyfuss, II (div. 1967); children—Caryn, Barney, Evan, Andrew; m. James Marshall McHugh, Jr. Researcher, Washington Gallery Modern Art, 1962-66; asst. to curator prints and drawings Nat. Collection Fine Arts, Washington, 1967-69; dir. Studio Gallery, Washington, 1970-75; dir., owner Caril Dreyfuss Gallery, Washington, 1975-76; co-owner Parsons-Dreyfuss Gallery, N.Y.C., 1976-80; dir. Frank Marino Gallery, 1981; art cons., lectr., 1980—; free-lance writer, 1981—. Bd. dirs. Friends of the Corcoran, 1972-75. Mem. Mus. Modern Art. Club: Smith Coll. of N.Y. Author article, essay. Home: 241 Central Park West Apt 9C New York NY 10024

DRIES, ANN NORBERTA, home economist, consumer advisor; b. N.Y.C., Dec. 11, 1925; d. George Andrew and Rose Miriam (Cunningham) D.; A.B. (Borden scholar), Hunter Coll., 1948, M.A., 1950. Tchr. home econs., jr. high sch., Mt. Vernon, N.Y., 1948-49; instr. home econs. Hunter Coll., N.Y.C., 1949-53; writer, star singing kitchen TV show, WOR-TV, N.Y.C., 1952-53; pub. relations home economist Aluminum Co. of Am., N.Y.C., 1953-67; dir. home econs., Doyle, Dane, Bernbach Advt. Agy., N.Y.C., 1967-70; dir. home econs., consumer services Nestle Co., Inc., White Plains, N.Y., 1970—. Named ten-yr. outstanding grad. Hunter Coll., 1958. Mem. Am., N.Y. State home econs. assns., Nat., N.Y.C. home economists in bus., Am. Women in Radio and TV, Nat. Home Fashion League, Advt. Women of N.Y., Electrical Women's Round Table, Soc. Consumer Affairs Profls., Am. Council on Consumer Interests, Conf. of Consumer Orgns., Phi Upsilon Omicron, Omicron Nu. Home: 39-11 210th St New York NY 11361 Office: 100 Bloomingdale Rd White Plains NY 10605

DRIGGS, MARGARET, journalist, public relations exec.; b. Kansas City, Kans., June 30, 1909; d. William Foster and Lillie (Landers) Brazier; A.B., U. Kans., 1930; postgrad. Hofstra Coll., 1960, Pratt Inst. Sch. Library Sci., 1964-65; m. Jack Weems Quarrier, Nov. 26, 1933 (div. July 1945); children—John Chilton II, Philip Harrington, Camille Elizabeth; m. 2d, Howard R. Driggs, Sept. 26, 1948. Corr., Kansas City (Mo.-Kans.) Star, 1930-33; adminstrv. asst. to sec. and dir. public relations Hofstra Coll., 1956-61; asst. to nat. pres. Am. Pioneer Trails Assn., N.Y.C., 1948-63; dir. public relations, yearbook adv., Cathedral Sch. of St. Mary, Garden City, N.Y., 1969-73, librarian, 1972-74; chmn. Morven Guides for lectures and tours of Gov.'s Mansion, Princeton, N.H., 1975—; installed Duchess of Richelieu Collection, St. Mary's Library, 1973; exhibitor Driggs Collection of Americana; speaker on Indians. Active in acquisition of funds for scholarships in univs., Med. Center Princeton, 1975—. Recipient medal Am. Yearbook Co., 1970, Columbia Scholastic Press Assn., 1970. Mem. N.Y.U. Faculty Club (hon.), Nat. Council Coll. Publs. Advs., Friends of Princeton U. Library, Hist. Soc. Princeton, Pi Delta Epsilon (Gold Key 1958). Episcopalian. Clubs: Present Day, Women's Coll. Princeton (chmn. 65th Ann. luncheon and benefit 1981), U. Kans. Gold Medal (citation and pin 1980). Photographer-editor: Vive Rochambeau, Vive Washington: the Bicentennial Celebration in Princeton, 1981 (French-Am. Alliance medal 1981). Home: 135 Princeton Arms S Cranbury NJ 08512

DRIMMER BOWMAN, ARLEEN, fashion designer, corp. exec.; b. Bklyn., July 14, 1945; d. Nathan and Minnie (Goldhor) Drimmer; student N.Y.C. Community Coll., 1962-63. Prodn. coordinator M.P.O., music and film TV commls., N.Y.C., 1966-67; prodn. mgr. Richard Druz and Victor Lukens Assos., music and film TV commls., N.Y.C., 1967-68; producer Flickers Inc., TV commls., N.Y.C., 1969-72; owner, buyer Family Boutique, Amsterdam, Netherlands, 1972-74; owner, designer, public relations dir. Bowman Trading Co., Inc., N.Y.C., 1974—; cons. China Trade; speaker in field. Recipient Clio award, 1970; Effie award, 1970. Guest editor Fashion mag., 1978. Patentee compact for cosmetics, 1975. Office: 1441 Broadway New York NY 10018

DRISCOLL, CONSTANCE FITZGERALD, educator; b. Lawrence, Mass., Mar. 29, 1926; d. John James and Mary Anne (Leecock) Fitzgerald; A.B., Radcliffe Coll., 1946; postgrad. Harvard U., U. Hartford (Conn.), U. Bridgeport (Conn.), Worcester (Mass.) State Coll.; m. Francis George Driscoll, Aug. 21, 1948; children—Frances Mary, Martha Anne, Sara Helene, Maribeth Lee. Secondary sch. tchr., North Andover, Mass., 1946-48; book reviewer N.Y.C. and Boston pubs., 1955-64; asst. conf. edn. dir. U. Hartford, 1964-68; lectr. Pace U., N.Y.C., 1973-74; asst. ednl. adv. Nat. Girl Scouts, 1972-74; pres., owner, dir. Open Corridor Schs. Cons., Inc., Bronxville, N.Y., 1972—. Mem. Nat. Assn. Exec. Women. Author curriculum materials. Home: 338 Main St Oxford MA 01540 Office: Box 433 Bronxville NY 10708

DRISCOLL, GENEVIEVE (JEANNE) BOSSON, mgmt. and orgn. devel. cons.; b. Pitts., Mar. 26, 1937; d. George August and Emma Haling Bleichner; B.S. cum laude, Fla. State U., 1959; postgrad. SUNY, Albany, 1968-71; postgrad. program for specialists in orgn. devel. Nat. Tng. Labs., 1970. m. John Edwin Bosson, June 17, 1959; 1 son, Matthew Edwin; m. 2d Frederick Driscoll, Oct. 7, 1972; stepchildren—Jennifer Locke, Cynthia Hall, Molly Davis, Julie Ann. Planning asst. Center for Planning and Innovation, Dept. Edn. State of N.Y., 1967-71, planning cons. So. Tier Regional Office for Ednl. Planning, Elmira, N.Y., 1971-72; tng. dir. Neusteters, Inc., Denver, 1973-74; orgn. devel. specialist CONNECT, Inc., N.Y.C., 1975-77; cons. Robert H. Schaffer & Assos., Stamford, Conn., 1977-80; partner Driscoll Cons. Group, Williamstown, Mass., 1980—; cons. in field. Mem. Orgn. Devel. Network, Am. Soc. Tng. and Devel., Greater Boston Orgn. Devel. Network, No. Berkshire Women's Network. Office: 24 Lee Terr Williamstown MA 01267

DRISCOLL, IRENE BERKOWITZ, newspaper editor; b. N.Y.C., Mar. 14, 1947; d. Frank Leon and Bessie (Tacktill) Berkowitz; B.A. with honors in English, U. Conn., 1968. With Hartford (Conn.) Courant, 1968—, asst. state editor, 1979-80, asst. mng. editor, 1980—. Address: Hartford Courant 285 Broad St Hartford CT 06115

DRISKELL, DOROTHY L., artist; b. Paris, Ill., Mar. 3, 1908; d. William Mayo and Josephine (Reese) Driskell; Fine Arts degree Herron Art Inst., 1928; student Art Inst. Chgo., 1928-29, Chgo. Acad. Fine Arts, 1930, Ind. U., 1925-28; pvt. study with M.J. Cartier, Calif., 1922; m. E. Ames Holmes, Nov. 28, 1953. With Chgo. Park Dist., 1940-75, park supr., art instr.; tchr. art St. Scholastica Sch., Chgo., 1941, St. Gregory High Sch., Chgo.. 1942; color cons. 3-T Enamel Co., Chgo., 1931; designer toys, novelties Fireside Industries, Adrian, Mich.; designer silk screen for Batiks, N.Y.C., 1929; one woman show: Paris (Ill.) Mus., 1975; exhibited group shows Freer Gallery of Smithsonian Instn., Washington, 1954, 57; Hoosier Salon, Indpls., 1952; 737 Gallery, Chgo., Herron Art Inst., Indpls., 1952, Mandel Bros., Chgo., Palette & Chisel, Chgo., Old Town Art Fair, Chgo., Rush St. Chgo. Art Fair, Wurlitzer Gallery, Chgo., Chgo. Art Festival, Highland Park Woman's Club, Deer Path Art Gallery, Lake Forest, Ill., Ill. State Mus., Springfield, Chgo. Union League Art Show, 1972, Aurelia Gallery, Evanston, Ill., many others. Recipient Blue Ribbon, Nat. League Am. Pen Women, 1954, Dingle award, 1957, 59, 73; Bronze medal Palette and Chisel, Chgo., 1964, others. Mem. Nat. League Am. Pen Women. Illustrator: 80 in the Shade (Janet Bangs), 1966. Address: 1000 Judson Ave Highland Park IL 60035

DRIVING HAWK SNEVE, VIRGINIA ROSE, radio/TV writer and producer, author; b. Rosebud, S.D., Feb. 21, 1933; d. James H. and Rose E. (Ross) Driving Hawk; B.S., S.D. State Coll., 1954; M.Ed., S.D. State U., 1969; Litt.D. (hon.), Dakota Wesleyan U., 1979; m. Vance M. Sneve, July 2, 1955; children—Shirley K., Paul M., Alan E. Tchr., White (S.D.) schs., 1954-55, Pierre (S.D.) schs., 1955-56; guidance counselor Flandreau (S.D.) Indian Sch., 1966-70; cons., writer, producer S.D. Public TV and Radio, Brookings, 1975-79; author: Jimmy Yellow Hawk, 1972; High Elk's Treasure, 1972; When Thunders Spoke, 1974; Betrayed, 1974; The Dakota's Heritage, 1973; They Led A Nation, 1975; That They May Have Life: The Episcopal Church In South Dakota 1859-1976, 1977; contbr. stories to mags.; cons. in field. Sec., Episcopal Diocese of S.D. Council of Advice, 1974-77; historiographer Episcopal Diocese S.D., 1977—; bd. dirs. Native Am. Consortium, Corp. Public Broadcasting, 1976-80; Big Sioux Arts Council, Mem. Nat. League Am. Pen Women, S.D. Press Women (named Woman of Achievement 1974), Nat. Fedn. Press Women (named Woman of Achievement 1975). Republican. Episcopalian. Clubs: Flandreau Indian Sch. Faculty Wives, Shrine Hosp. Aux., Club: Order Eastern Star. Home and office: 111 S Prairie St Flandreau SD 57028

DROB, LINDA CECELIA, speech pathologist; b. Carbondale, Pa., Feb. 22, 1953; d. Joseph Augustine and Helen Dorothy (Ursich) D.; B.A., Marywood Coll., 1975; M.S., Bloomsburg State Coll., 1978. Speech clinician, St. Josephs Children's and Maternity Hosp., Scranton, Pa., 1976-77, Western Wayne Sch. Dist. summer headstart program, 1976-77, Vis. Nurse Assn. and Home Health Maintenance Orgn., Scranton, Pa., 1978-79, Elk Lake Sch. Dist., Dimock, Pa., 1979—. Mem. Center Stage Community Theater Group, Honesdale, Pa., mem. choir St. Mary's Roman Cath. Ch., Waymart, Pa., 1975—. Mem. Am. Speech and Hearing Assn., Pa. Speech and Hearing Assn., Myofunctional Therapy Assn. Am., Pa. State Edn. Assn., Elk Lake Edn. Assn. Home: RD 1 Box 171 Waymart PA 18472 Office: Dimock PA 18816

DROBNER, VIRGINIA BRODKIN, psychiatrist; b. Newark, Apr. 19, 1937; d. Louis A. and Ruth (Miller) Brodkin; B.A., Syracuse U., 1958; M.D., Med. Coll. Pa., 1962; m. Joseph W. Katz, Feb. 6, 1982; children by previous marriage—William Drobner, Ann Drobner, Richard Drobner. Intern, Beth Israel Hosp., Newark, 1962-63; resident VA Hosp., Lyons, N.J., 1964-67; practice medicine specializing in psychiatry, Princeton, N.J., 1982—; mem. staff Clara Maass Hosp.; cons. psychiatry Princeton Family Services, Assn. Advancement of Mentally Handicapped. Mem. Am. Med. Women's Assn., AMA, Med. Soc. N.J., Mercer County Med. Soc. Home and Office: 3 Deer Run Princeton NJ 08540

DROESCH, VIGEE HALL (MRS. THOMAS PATRICK DROESCH), writer; b. Los Angeles, Feb. 1, 1950; d. Jerome Lincoln and Elizabeth Lee (Hall) Seelen; A.A., Stephens Coll., 1969; B.J., U. Mo., 1971; M.Ed., Xavier U., 1975; postgrad. Fordham U.; m. Thomas Patrick Droesch, July 8, 1978; 1 dau., Audrey Elizabeth. Asst. dept. mgr. H & S Pogue Co., Cin., 1975-76; asst. buyer Lord & Taylor N.Y.C., 1976-80; humorous writer Gibson Greeting Cards Co., Cin., 1972; reporter U. Wyo. Communications Service, Laramie, 1972, Northridger Newspaper, Los Angeles, 1970; tchr. Jack and Jill Nursery Sch., 1972; reporter, Ky. women's editor Cin. Enquirer, 1973-74; lang. arts tchr. Sunland Lutheran Sch., Freeport, Bahamas, 1974-75; free lance journalist Cin. newpapers, writer introductory column for evening provisionals Jr. League Newssheet, 1975, 76; publicity chmn. Cin. 4th Ann. Stitchery Fair for benefit Planned Parenthood, 1976; pub. relations writer community relations dept. WCET-TV Pub. Broadcasting, 1975, 76. Supr., Freeport Aquanets Swim Group, 1974-75; radio and TV publicity chmn. Ann. Antiques Festival, Cin. Children's Convalescent Hosp., 1976; admissions alumni adviser Stephens Coll., Cin., 1975-76, Northeastern regional rep., 1976—; hostess 10th Ann. Cin. Antiques Festival, 1975-76. Mem. Nat. Women in Communications, Ohio Newspaper Women's Assn., Nat. Bus. and Profl. Women's Club, Jr. League N.Y.C. (English teaching com.), D.A.R. (N.Y.C. chpt.; conservation com., evening group rec. sec., Am. Indian chairperson), Freeport Players Guild in Bahamas (nominated Best Actress in Cameo Role and Best Newcomer 1974-75). Author, photographer Sunland Luth. Sch. Yearbook, 1974-75, playsbills for Freeport Players Guild, 1974-75. Home: 35 Park Ave New York NY 10016

DROGUETT, GLORIA IRENE, television prodn. co. exec.; b. New Orleans, Feb. 13, 1934; d. Wade Alfred and Naomi Bernice (Nelson) Gremillion; student Burroughs Bus. Sch., 1953; m. Rudy Droguett, Dec. 12, 1953; children—Lawrence Allen, Darrell Alan. Sales mgr. Western Steel Craft, Ingelwood, Calif., 1953-63; sec.-treas. Calif. Toiletries Reps., Los Angeles, 1964-74; sales mgr., sec.-treas., chief fin. officer Syntar Prodns., Los Angeles, 1975-79; v.p., chief fin. officer Fenestra Prodns., Inc., 1979—; bus. cons. Dalar Pub. Corp., 1978—. Mem. Research Inst. Am., Soc. Preservation of Variety and Performing Arts, Ebell of Los Angeles, Nat. Assistance League Am., Girls Club Aux. of Los Angeles Assistance League. Republican. Christian Scientist. Club: Job's Daus. (past honored queen). Home: 2329 Kenilworth Ave Los Angeles CA 90039

DROLL, MARIAN CLARKE, speech writer, issues specialist; b. Muncie, Ind., Jan. 11, 1931; d. Harold Bertrand and Marguerite (Guffigan) Clarke; student DePauw U., 1949-52; B.A., George Washington U., 1954; children—Cynthia E., Stephanie A., Jennifer M., Kristin M. Feature writer Detroit News, 1971; asst. editor Knight-Ridder News Service, 1971; mgr. media and public relations McLeod Advt., 1972-77; exec. speech writer, issues specialist, Washington liaison Mich. Consol. Gas Co., Detroit, 1977—. Bd. dirs. Preservation Wayne; regional chmn. Muscular Dystrophy Soc., 1963; public relations dir. Scholarship Fund for Children, 1982. Mem. Econ. Club Detroit, Public Relations Soc. Am., Jr. League Detroit, Alpha Lambda Delta, Phi Beta Phi. Home: 305 University Pl Grosse Pointe MI 48230 Office: 500 Griswold St Detroit MI 48226

DROPP, JOY MACNEARY, savs. and loan mgr.; b. Milw., May 11, 1950; d. Ludwig L. and Selma (Monhardt) Johnson; student Milton Coll., 1968-71. Sec. property tax dept. Great Midwest Savs. and Loan Assn., Milw., 1971-72, loan sec. tng., 1972, loan sec., Brookfield, Wis., 1972-77, br. mgr., Hartland, Wis., 1978—; officer Hartland Shopping Mall; lectr. Mem. Hartbrook Mchts. Assn. (treas. 1979—), Women in Associated Real Estate Mgmt. (treas. 1979-80, sec. 1980-82, dir.

1982—), Hartland C. of C. (dir. 1982-83). Office: 600 Hartbrook Dr Hartland WI 53029

DROSTEN, MARY LOU, architect; b. St. Louis, July 5, 1910; d. Charles W. and Eleanor Jean (Hall) Martin; B.Arch., Washington U., 1933, postgrad. in sociology, 1935-36, 34-35; postgrad. in edn. U. Tenn., Chattanooga, 1959-60; m. Fred W. Drosten, Apr. 10, 1937; children—Mary Diane Kovel, Eleanor Kushner, Caroline Rivard, Frederika Harmon. 1st supr. Nat. Youth Adminstrn., St. Louis County, 1936-41; social worker St. Louis County Relief, 1934-36; prin. Drosten Designs, Chattanooga, 1953-64, Huntsville, Ala., 1964-69, University City, Mo., 1969—. Mem. AIA (chmn. speakers bur.), Women's Archtl. League (chmn. speakers bur., pres. 1973-74 St. Louis), Assn. Women in Architecture (nat. pres. 1940-41), League Women Voters. Democrat. Unitarian. Address: 945 Old Bonhomme Rd University City MO 63132

DROUGHT, ROSE ALICE, educator; b. Milw.; student U. Ill., 1924-25, Layton Sch. Art, 1931; B.A., U. Wis., 1924, M.A., 1926, Ph.D. (Carnegie fellow), 1931; postgrad. U. Ariz., No. Ariz. U., Ariz. State U. Exec. 137 camp dir. Girl Scouts U.S.A., 1934-48; free lance writer, 1948-54; tchr. spl. edn. Phoenix Elem. Schs., 1954-69; dir. Community Council Project on Aging, 1969-74; dir. Area Agy. on Aging, Region I, Ariz., 1974-78, exec. dir., 1977-82, dir. emeritus, 1982—; cons. Internat. Center Social Gerontology, 1978; del. White House Conf. on Aging, 1971-81; mem. adv. com. curriculum and internships No. Ariz. U., 1978; mem. multidisciplinary com. on gerontology Ariz. State U., 1978-81; adj. prof. Sch. Social Work, 1981—; camp planning cons. YMCA, YWCA, ch. camps, pvt. camps, 1935—; dir. internat. camp Adelboden, Switzerland, 1939-1940, Outdoor Edn. Inst., Marquette, U., Milw., summer 1963; guest lectr. Ariz. State U., 1966-81, Glendale Community Coll., 1970-80, adj. prof. Sch. Social Work, 1981—; guest lectr. U. Sydney (Australia), 1970. Mem. adv. bd. Salvation Army; mem. Phoenix Housing Commn., Phoenix Nutrition Council; chmn. Phoenix Pub. Housing Adv. Bd., 1973-78; cons. Phoenix Chinese Sr. Citizens Assn., 1980—. Recipient Ann. awards Ariz. State Fair, 1953—; Disting. Service award United Cerebral Palsy Ariz., 1962-63, citation, 1965, cert. of appreciation ARC, 1965; Floyd Adams award, 1972; citation Nat. Ret. Tchrs. Assn., 1973; citation of merit Gov. Ariz., 1974, 76. Mem. Ariz. Acad. Pub. Affairs, Am. Camping Assn. (dir. 1945-48, pres. Wis. sect. 1946-48, pres. Coronado sect. 1960-62, v.p. region VIII, 1961-62 lifetime campcraft instr.), NEA (del. to World Assemblies of Teaching Profession, Vancouver, B.C., Can. 1967, Dublin 1968, Sydney 1970, Kingston, Jamaica 1971, London 1972, Nairobi, Kenya 1973, Singapore 1974, Washington 1976), Ariz. Edn. Asn. (editorial bd. 1968-74), Assn. Outdoor Edn., Council Exceptional Children, Assn. Educators Homebound and Hospitalized Children, Nat. Assn. Area Agys. on Aging (dir. 1974-80, v.p. 1979-80), Ariz. Assn. Area Agys. on Aging (pres. 1974-77), Nat. Wildlife Fedn., Nat. Sch. Pub. Relations Assn. (pres. Ariz. chpt. 1968-69), Gerontol. Soc., Western Gerontol. Soc., Nat. Council on Aging, Internat. Platform Assn., Delta Kappa Gamma. Democrat. Author: A Camping Manual, 1943; Services and Facilities for Meeting the Needs of Older Americans, 1973; The Community College-A Resource for Older Americans-Older Americans-A Resource for the Community, 1974; What the Older Person Will be like—A Look to the Future, 1976. Editor: Conservation in Camping, 1952; Phoenix Elementary Classroom Tchrs. Assn. Press, 1965-68; The Elderly Arizonan, 1976, updated 1978; acting editor Camping Mag., 1945-46. Home: 106 W Pierson Phoenix AZ 85013

DROWN, JANE DAVIS, electronic co. exec.; b. Pitts., Oct. 8, 1922; d. Harvey Baker and Ruth (Kesel) Powers; student Conn. Coll., 1938-40; m. Clifford F. Drown; 1 dau. by previous marriage, Susan. Staff mem. Electronic Industries Assn., 1959-70, dir. planning and requirements, govt. products div., 1970-73; dep. Washington rep. GTE Internat. Inc., 1973-77; asst. v.p. govt. relations, products group GTE Service Corp., Washington, 1977-81, chief European Tech. Info. Bur., Brussels, 1981—; mem. industry sectoral advisory com. 22 Dept. Commerce. Mem. Electronic Industries Assn. (chmn. internat. bus. council 1979-80), Washington Export Council. Office: GTE Labs Inc Ave de Tervuren 412 Brussels B-1150 Belgium

DROWNS-ALLEN, KAREN SUE, psychologist, educator; b. Columbus, Ga., Mar. 12, 1943; d. William Arthur and Elizabeth Marie (Juengling) Drowns; B.S., U. Idaho, 1965, M.A., 1967; Ph.D., U. Md., 1973; m. Reuben Michael Allen, Apr. 19, 1974; 1 dau., Brandywyd Michele. Clin. psychology intern Walter Reed Army Hosp., Washington, 1973-74; asst. prof. Tex. Tech. U. Med. Sch., El Paso, 1977-78; asst. prof. family medicine La. State U. Med. Sch., Shreveport, 1978-80, asst. prof. psychiatry, 1980-81; asst. prof. Southwestern Med. Sch., Dallas, 1981—; asso. chief staff for edn. VA Hosp., Dallas, 1981—; pvt. cons., Marshall, Tex., 1979-80. Served to capt. AUS, 1973-76. Mem. Tex. Psychol. Assn., Am. Psychol. Assn., Kappa Alpha Theta. Baptist. Contbr. articles to profl. jours. Home: 2308 Landshire Arlington TX 76104 Office: Dept Psychiatry La State U Med Sch Shreveport LA 71130

DRUCKER, CECILY ANNE, lawyer; b. Bennington, Vt., Aug. 31, 1944; d. Peter F. and Doris S. Drucker; A.B., U. Rochester (N.Y.), 1966; J.D., U. Calif., San Francisco, 1974. Investment banker Adela Investment Co., S.A., Lima, Peru, 1966-68; admitted to Calif. bar, 1974; asso. firm Miller, Starr & Regalia, Oakland, Calif., 1974-79; partner firm Skjerven, Morrill, MacPherson & Drucker, San Francisco, 1979—; lectr. Calif. Continuing Edn. of Bar. Mem. Am. Bar Assn., Calif. Bar Assn. Office: 601 Montgomery St Suite 1900 San Francisco CA 94111

DRUM, SARA RUTH, nursing adminstr.; b. Evanston, Ill., Aug. 6, 1929; d. Raymond Borland and Ruth Armstrong (Pettit) D.; R.N., Ch. Home and Hosp. Sch. Nursing, 1955; postgrad. in gerontology and nursing adminstrn. U. Ariz., Weber State Coll., UCLA, U. So. Calif., U. Calif., Northridge; Dir. nursing, Colonial Convalescent Hosp., Santa Ana, 1967-68; surp. Rio Hondo Meml Hosp., Downey, Calif., 1968-69; dir. nursing Intercommunity Convalescent Hosp., Norwalk, Calif., 1969-76, Southland Geriatric Center, Norwalk, 1976—. Mem. asso. degree nursing adv. com. Cerritos Coll.; adv. bd. baccalaureate degree nurse program Biola Coll.; mem. occupational adv. com. nursing Whittier Union High Sch. Dist. Democrat. Home: 702 S Webster Ave #203 Anaheim CA 92804 Office: 11701 Studebaker Rd Norwalk CA 90650

DRUMMER, DOROTHY J., lawyer; b. Racine, Wis., Apr. 13, 1949; d. Paul Alan and Ruth Ellen (Fanning) Drummer; A.B., Smith Coll., 1970; J.D., Rutgers U., 1975; m. W. Merriman Morton, Oct. 26, 1982. Admitted to bar; v.p., counsel to chmn. Am. Stock Exchange, N.Y.C., 1976-82; exec. dir. Pres.'s Task Force on Pvt. Sector Iniatives, Washington, 1981-82; v.p. Am. Bus. Conf., Washington, 1980—. Mem. Assn. Bar. City N.Y., ABA. Club: Smith Coll. Home: 1005 Broadmoor Dr El Paso TX 79912 Office: 1025 Connectivut Ave Washington DC 20036

DRUMMOND, ELEANOR ELOISE, nurse, educator; b. Los Angeles, Mar. 1, 1925; d. John Albert and Clara (Jacobson) D.; B.S., U. Calif., San Francisco, 1947; Cert. Pub. Health Nursing, UCLA, 1950, M.S., 1954; Ed.D., Columbia U. Tchrs. Coll., 1960; m. Paul Henry Meyer, Dec. 26, 1969. Staff nurse U. Calif. Hosp., San Francisco, 1947-49, Hollywood (Calif.) Presbyn. Hosp., 1950-51; public health nurse Los Angeles City Health Dept., 1951-53; instr. Los Angeles County Gen. Hosp., 1954-56; research fellow U. So. Calif. Sch. Medicine, 1956; asst. Prof. UCLA Sch. Nursing, 1959-64; prof. nursing Boston U. Sch. Nursing, 1964—. Fellow Am. Acad. Nursing; mem. Am. Nurses Assn., Nat. League for Nursing, AAUP, Alpha Tau Delta, Kappa Delta Pi, Pi Lambda Theta. Club: Boston University Women Grads. Home: 88 Little Nahant Rd Nahant MA 01908 Office: 635 Commonwealth Ave Boston MA 02215

DRUMMOND, FAY CAROLINE, nurse; b. Providence, June 16, 1927; d. Raymond James and Elmo Jean Harrison; R.N., Roger Williams Hosp., Providence, 1948; postgrad. U. Bridgeport (Conn.); divorced; children—Pamela, Cheryl, Byron, Laurie. Dir. admission, dir. nursing Courtland Gardens, Stamford, Conn., 1968-78; rev. coordinator PSRO, Fairfield, Conn., 1978-79, dir. long term care, 1979-81; dir. in-service edn. Overlook Manor, Norwalk, Conn., 1981—; prin. firm Health Mgmt. Programs, Inc. Mem. Nat. Assn. Female Execs., Am. Nurses Assn. Home: 7 Whiffletree Way Riverside CT 06878 Office: 2616 Main St Bridgeport CT 06606

DRWAL, DOROTHY K., educator; b. Edison, N.J.; d. John L. and Margaret (Kovacs) Kalman; B.A., Douglass Coll., 1952; m. Matthew J. Drwal, Aug. 16, 1953 (dec.); children—Nancy, Susan, John Matthew. Exec. dir. Edison (N.J.) C. of C., 1965-67; tchr. Edison (N.J.) Sch. System, 1967—. Councilwoman, Edison Twp., 1975-79, 80—; state crusade chmn. Am. Cancer Soc., 1980, pres. N.J. div., 1980-81; pres. Edison Town Council, 1978-79; past pres. local PTAs; past v.p. Middlesex County Council Parents and Tchrs.; pres. Edison Sheltered Workshop, 1980—. Recipient Community Service award, VFW Post 3117, 1963, AAUW, 1964; Service award, Edison Young Dems., 1968; Silver Bowl Am., Cancer Soc., 1972. Mem. NEA, N.J. Edn. Assn., Middlesex County Edn. Assn., Edison Twp. Edn. Assn. Roman Catholic. Clubs: Edison Friends of Library (pres. 1962-66). Home: 14 Overbrook Ave Edison NJ 08817 Office: Clara Barton School 1015 Amboy Ave Edison NJ 08817

DRYER, DOROTHEA MERRILL (MRS. EDWIN JASON DRYER), lawyer; b. Salt Lake City; d. George Edmund and Lillian (Chapman) Merrill; A.B., Stanford, 1936; LL.B., Yale, 1940; m. Edwin Jason Dryer, Feb. 28, 1942; children—Diana Claire Dryer Wright, Faith Ellen. Admitted to Utah bar, 1941, U.S. Supreme Ct. bar, U.S. Ct. Mil. Appeals; clk. to Chief Justice Wolfe, Utah Supreme Ct., 1941; atty. Bur. Immigration, Dept. Justice, Washington, 1941-42; practiced in Salt Lake City, 1943-47, Washington, 1948—; dep. county atty., Salt Lake City, 1947-48. Fellow Am. Assn. Criminology; mem. Am., Fed., Utah bar assns., Jr. League of Washington, Nat. Assn. Women Lawyers, Nat. Assn. for Gifted Children, Assn. for Gifted, Am. Judicature Soc., Internat. Platform Assn., Oral History Assn., Kappa Kappa Gamma. Unitarian. Clubs: Potomac Bus. and Profl. Women's; Nat. Lawyers. Home: 5126 Palisade Ln NW Washington DC 20016 Office: Farm Running Brook Farm Route 1 Bentonville VA 22610

DUANE, CAMILLE (MRS. FRANK DUANE ROSENGREN), bookseller, research cons.; b. San Antonio, Sept. 28, 1926; d. Emmett Thomas and Camille Georgette (Lodovic) Sweeney; B.A., Incarnate Word Coll., 1948; M.S., Our Lady of the Lake Coll., 1951; m. Frank Duane Rosengren, Jan. 13, 1951; 1 dau., Emily (Mrs. Stephen Ferry). Script reader for various N.Y. prodn. firms, 1954-58; reference librarian, cataloger Met. Mus. of Art, N.Y.C., 1959-61; circulation and reference librarian San Antonio Coll., 1964-67; registrar, librarian Inst. of Texan Cultures, San Antonio, 1967-70; freelance research cons. on history and fine arts, San Antonio, 1970—; v.p./mgr. Rosengren's Books, Inc., San Antonio, 1970—. Mem. Citizens for a Better Environment, San Antonio, 1971-74; mem. San Antonio Symphony Soc., 1964-72. Mem. women's com. Bexar County Democratic Women, 1963-74; bd. dirs. San Antonio Conservation Soc., 1964-68, v.p. pub. relations, 1966-68. Mem. ALA, AAUP, ACLU, Am. Booksellers Assn., Ind. Booksellers Assn. (v.p.), Central Tex. Booksellers Assn. (dir.). Home: 801 Garraty Rd San Antonio TX 78209 Office: 312 Bonham St San Antonio TX 78205

DUANE, DIANE ELIZABETH, author; b. N.Y.C., May 18, 1952; d. Edward David and Elizabeth Kathryn (Burke) D.; R.N., Pilgrim State Hosp., Brentwood, N.Y., 1974. Psychiat. nurse Payne Whitney Clinic, Cornell/N.Y. Hosp. Med. Center, N.Y.C., 1974-76; asst. to writer, 1976-78; freelance novel and TV writer, 1978—; mgr. Lioncelle Enterprises, graphics co., 1980—; author: The Door Into Fire, 1979; The Door Into Shadow, 1981; So You Want to Be a Wizard?, 1982; also scripts for TV animated shows; contbg. author Flashing Swords, 1981. Address: 18520 Prairie St Apt 20 Northridge CA 91324

DUANE, MARYELLYN, psychologist; b. N.Y.C., Feb. 7, 1948; d. Daniel J. and Katherine (Cleary) D.; B.A., Newton Coll., 1969; M.A., Villanova U., 1971; Ph.D. (Univ. scholar), Temple U., 1979; postgrad. Am. Inst. Psychotherapy and Psychoanalysis, 1976-82. Instr., N.Y. U. Sch. Continuing Edn. at Mercy Coll., 1977-79; asst. prof. Counseling Center, Bklyn. Coll., 1978-79; chief psychologist Howard Beach (N.Y.) Child Guidance Center, 1977-80; research cons. Internat. Paper Co., N.Y.C., 1981; pvt. practice individual and group psychoanalytic psychotherapy, N.Y.C., 1981—; asst. prof. Grad. Sch., C.W. Post Center, L.I. U., 1979—. Lic. psychologist, N.Y. State. Fellow Am. Inst. Psychotherapy and Psychoanalysis (vol. psychotherapist Community Guidance Service); mem. Am. Psychol. Assn., Eastern Psychol. Assn., Am. Personnel and Guidance Assn. Club: N.Y. Rd. Runners. Research on determinants of retirement satisfaction among profls. Office: 500 West End Ave Ground Floor B New York NY 10024

DUBBRIN, LOLA HENNESY, real estate co. exec.; b. Bogalusa, La., July 7, 1925; d. Esmond Edward and Ethel Loraine (Simmons) Hennesy; student Huffstetler Bus. Coll., 1943, Santa Rosa Jr. Coll., 1964-67; m. Albert Miles Dubbrin, Mar. 2, 1946; 1 dau., Sonya Dubbrin DeLugg. With Foreman & Foreman, Mobile, Ala., 1943-46; with L.E. Castner Agys. Boyes Hot Springs, Calif., 1947—, v.p., treas., 1968—. Bd. dirs. Boyes Springs Village Assn., 1970—. Recipient Insuror's Press award, 1974; C.P.C.U. Mem. Nat. Assn. Real Estate Bds., Calif., Sonoma County real estate bds., Ins. Womens Assn. (pres. 1968), Sonoma Valley Ins. Agents Assn. (v.p. 1973). Clubs: Sonoma County Ins. Women (Boyes Hot Springs). Home: PO Box 335 1224 Alberca Rd Boyes Hot Springs CA 95416 Office: 18298 Sonoma Hwy Boyes Hot Springs CA 95416

DUBE, WALTRAUT FEIGE, health edn. specialist, govt. ofcl.; b. Berlin, Jan. 22, 1927; came to U.S., 1948, naturalized, 1951; d. Paul H. and Leopoldine J. Feige; B.A., U. Mo., Columbia, 1963; M.A. (Woodrow Wilson fellow), Ind. U., 1965, Ph.D., 1981; m. Roland Lionel Dube, Aug. 21, 1948; 1 son, Douglas Clifton. Teaching asso. Ind. U., 1964-65; instr. DePauw U., Greencastle, Ind., 1965-66; adminstrv. supr. Army and Air Force Exchange Service, Alaska, 1966-68; asso. dir. div. student studies Assn. Am. Med. Colls., Washington, 1968-78; asso. chief spl. edn. programs acad. affairs dept. medicine and surgery VA, Washington, 1978—; cons. Mem. AAUW, Assn. History of Medicine, Am. Geriatrics Assn., Phi Beta Kappa. Episcopalian. Contbr. articles to profl. jours., chpts. to books. Home: 4905 Asbury Ln Bethesda MD 20814 Office: Academic Affairs 141B VA Central Office 810 Vermont St NW Washington DC 20420

DUBIN, ELLEN ZAWEL, retail co. exec.; b. N.Y.C., Oct. 20, 1938; d. Joseph and Leona (Snitkoff) Richman; B.A., City U. N.Y., 1970; postgrad. Yeshiva U., 1972, A. K. Rice Inst. Group Dynamics, 1974; m. Howard S. Dubin, Sept. 17, 1978; children by previous marriage—Alyssa Zawel, Leigh Zawel, Reva Zawel, Joshua Zawel. Community advocate, 1961-73; consumer ombudsperson Washington supermarket div. Greenbelt Consumer Services, Silver Spring, Md., 1974-76; founding pres. Nat. Consumers Congress, Washington, 1973-76; pres. Zawel Assos., Inc., Harrington Park, N.J., 1976-78; v.p. external affairs The Stop and Shop Cos., Inc., Boston, 1978—; bd. dirs. Nat. Consumer Resource Center, 1976-80. Mem. Food Mktg. Inst., Public Relations Soc. Am., Am. Nat. Metric Council, Soc. Consumer Affairs Profls., Pi Sigma Alpha. Office: PO Box 369 Boston MA 02101

DUBNOW, BEATRICE, educator. Tchr., Chgo. Pub. Schs., 1954-64, reading clinician Bur. Child Study, 1964-67; asso. prof. Roosevelt U., Chgo., 1967-76, prof., 1976—. Bd. dirs. Citizens' Schs. Com., Chgo., 1974—; pres. Women's Scholarship Assn. Roosevelt U., 1975-78, bd. dirs., 1978—. Roosevelt U. Coll. Edn. fellow, 1981; recipient Kate Maremont Dedicated Tchr. award, 1968. Mem. Internat., Chgo. Area reading assns., Children's Lit. Assn., Nat. Council Tchrs. English, Assn. Childhood Edn. Internat., Nat. Soc. Study Edn., Internat. Council Edn. for Teaching, Nat. Council Children with Learning Disabilities, Ill. Reading Council, Am. Ednl. Research Assn. Contbr. articles to profl. jours.; co-developed The Self-Report-Reading Scale. Office: Coll Edn Roosevelt U 430 S Michigan Ave Chicago IL 60605

DUBOIS, JANET GAIL, card co. sales mgr.; b. Cheyenne, Wyo., Oct. 12, 1949; d. Warren and Ann (Strumbel) Carnes; B.B.A., U. Iowa, 1972. Merchandising asst. Hallmark Cards, Kansas City, Mo., 1972, sales rep., 1972-73, account mgr., 1974-75, account exec., Chgo., 1975-79, retail sales devel. mgr., 1979-81, market mgr., 1981—. Mem. Am. Mgmt. Assn. Home: 3200 N Lake Shore Dr Apt 1508 Chicago IL 60657 Office: 2311 W 22d St Oakbrook IL 60521

DUBOSE, PATSY GERALDINE HANDEY, mil. med. sch. exec. sec.; b. San Antonio, July 9, 1927; d. Jack and Vera Loraine (Staggs) Handey; student Roanoke Coll., Salem, Va., 1946-47, St. Mary's U., San Antonio, 1949; B.A., U. Md., College Park, 1975; m. B.A. DuBose, Aug. 4, 1950 (dec.); children—Paul A., David A., Jack E. With Air Force Research and Devel., 1968-70, Office Sec. of Def., 1971-76; exec. sec. dept. mil. medicine and history Uniformed Services U. of Health Scis., Bethesda, Md., 1976—. Chmn. bd. dirs. United Methodist Ch., 1973-74. Recipient outstanding awards, 1976, 79. Mem. Washington Soc. History of Medicine. Democrat. Co-editor Med. Ops. in Combat, 1978, 79, 80; co-author, editor Welcome Aboard, 1979, 80. Home: 2309 N Gate Terr Silver Spring MD 20906 Office: Medical History 4301 Jones Bridge Rd Bethesda MD 20814

DUBOULAY, CHRISTINE, ballet tchr.; b. London, June 15, 1923; came to U.S., 1952; d. Guy George and Raby DuBoulay; student public schs., London; m. Richard Ellis, Mar. 22, 1947. Co-dir., tchr. Ellis-DuBoulay Sch. Ballet, Chgo., 1954—. Office: Ellis-DuBoulay School Ballet 17 N State St Chicago IL 60602

DUBOW, ELAINE NADLER, non-profit orgn. exec.; b. Montreal, Que., Can.; came to U.S., 1977, naturalized, 1981; d. Gerald Isadore and Anne Chazan (Elias) Nadler; B.A., McGill U., 1962; postgrad. Concordia U., 1969-70; Diploma in Electronic Media Broadcasting, Canadian Nat. Inst. Broadcasting, 1979; children—Wendy Debra, Douglas Brad, Jonathan David. Exec for Soviet Jewry, Can. Jewish Congress, Montreal, Que., 1974-75; owner, operator Galerie Innit, Eskimo Art Gallery, Montreal, Que., 1975-77; infor. counsellor Israel Council Soviet Jewry, Dept. Info., Tel Aviv, Israel, 1977-79; co-ordinator, speaker Nat. United Jewish Appeal, N.Y.C., 1979-81; co-founder, coordinator Jerusalem Women's Seminar, N.Y.C. 1979—; dir. devel. World Jewish Congress, N.Y.C., 1979—; panelist Second World Conf. Soviet Jewry, Brussels, 1976; host radio program Inside the Jewish World, 1982—; cons. United Jewish Appeal, 40th Anniversary Conv., 1978, Zionist Orgn. Am., Internat. Leadership Conf., 1979, Can. Govt. Commn. Soviet Jews, 1977-78; rep. Council Women for Christians and Jews, 1976-77; nat. exec. United Israel Appeal Can., 1979-80. Recipient Israel Bonds award Israel Bonds of Can., 1977; Nat. Film Festival awards for The Last Journey, 1982. Mem. Nat. Assn. Female Execs. Author: They Came to Stay, 1977; History of Project Renewal, 1979. Office: One Park Ave New York 10016

DUBROFF, DIANA D., lawyer, TV producer; b. N.Y.C., Mar. 4, 1909; d. Meyer and Gussie (Ginsburg) Leibow; B.S., Hunter Coll., 1928; J.D., Bklyn., Law Sch., 1931; m. Alexander DuBroff (dec.); children—Elinor, William. Tchr. young children, 1928-61; sole practice law, N.Y.C., 1961—; founder, dean Practising Justice Inst.; producer cable TV series Practical Justice by a Creative Lawyer. Columnist Let's Look at the Law. Designer concept of divorce and homemaker ins.

DUBUC, MARY ELLEN, educator; b. N.Y.C. July 20, 1950; d. Patrick Joseph and Catherine (McKenna) Reynolds; B.A. cum laude (scholar), Marymount Manhattan Coll., 1972; M.A., Columbia U., 1973; m. Leo Dennis Dubuc, Jr., Sept. 9, 1978; 1 son, Brian Robert. Spl. edn. tchr. Cardinal Cushing Sch., Hanover, Mass., 1973-76, Ferncliff Manor Sch., Yonkers, N.Y., 1976-77; program coordinator Bronx Devel. Services, 1977-78; dir. edn. R.I. Assn. Retarded, Woonsocket, 1978—. Fed. trainee, 1971, 72. Mem. Assn. Severely Handicapped, R.I. Assn. Retarded Citizens. Office: 80 Fabien St Woonsocket RI 02895

DUCKWORTH, JANE, psychologist; b. Providence, Mar. 14, 1932; d. James Allison and Gladys Cook; B.A., U. Buffalo, 1951; M.A., U. Mo., 1968; Ph.D., 1970; m. Edwin Duckworth, July 8, 1971 (dec.); children—Dennis Johnson, Christopher Johnson, Wendy Johnson. Staff counselor U. Mo., 1968-69; instr. Stephens Coll., 1969-70; asst. prof. psychology Ball State U., Muncie, Ind., 1970-75, assoc. prof., 1975-79, prof., 1979—; cons., sex therapist Davis Clinic, Indpls. Lilly Faculty fellow, 1977-78. Mem. Am. Psychol. Assn., Am. Personnel and Guidance Assn. Democrat. Episcopalian. Home: 2004 Euclid Ave Muncie IN 47304 Office: Dept Counseling Psychology Ball State U Muncie IN 47306

DUDACK, GAIL MARIE, securities analyst; b. Johnson City, N.Y., Aug. 17, 1948; d. John and Maria (Kostun) D.; B.A. (Wall St. Jour. Student Achievement award), Skidmore Coll., 1970; postgrad. N.Y. U., 1971-72, N.Y. Inst. Fin., 1971-72. With Pershing div. Donaldson, Lufkin & Jenrette, Inc., N.Y.C., and predecessor firm, 1970—, v.p., head tech. analysis, 1977—; panelist Wall St. Week, PBS, 1975—; mem. bus. research adv. council Dept. Labor, 1977—; pres. DLJ, Inc., Fed. Credit Union, 1977-79; arbitrator Nat. Assn. Securities Dealers, 1976—. Co-chmn. bus. dept. adv. council Skidmore Coll., 1978—, fin. adv. to bd. trustees, 1982—. Mem. Fin. Analysts Fedn., N.Y. Soc. Security Analysts, Market Technicians Assn. (treas. 1979-80, sec. 1981-82), Fin. Women's Assn., Am. Econs. Assn. Contbr. articles to profl. jours. Office: 120 Broadway New York NY 10005

DUDARYK, SHARON DIANN, educator; b. Detroit, Aug. 29, 1945; d. Marion and Nettie (Shishka) Slimak; M.Ed. in Counseling, Wayne State U., 1971; m. Peter Dudaryk, Sept. 1, 1965 (div., 1975); children—Jeffrey Michael Dudaryk, Linda Helen Dudaryk, Patricia Marie Kelly. Vol. remedial tchr. Royal Oak Twp., 1966; elem. tchr., Detroit, 1967—, kindergarten tchr. Van Zile Elem. Sch., 1978—, adult edn. tchr. Osborn High Sch., 1977. Active family workshops, PTA, Founders Soc. Detroit Inst. of Art, 4-H activities, LWV, 1978-79. Served as career counselor USNR, 1979—. Mem. Detroit Fedn. Tchrs. Met. Detroit Reading Council, Warren Assn. Gifted and Talented, Wayne State U. Alumni Assn., Navy League. Eastern Orthodox. Club: Federated Russian Orthodox. Condr. research in field of nutrition. Home: 2725 Saratoga Troy MI 48084 Office: 2915 E Outer Dr Detroit MI 48234

DUDDY, JOAN FRANCES, choreographer, business ofcl.; b. Waltham, Mass., June 26, 1937; d. Walter Francis and Gladys Rita (Wallace) D.; student Boston Conservatory Music, 1956-58, Am. Ballet Center, 1959-65, Clark Center Performing Arts, 1967—; m. Isaac Schambelan, Sept. 1975. Asst. dept. physiology Harvard U. Sch. Public Health, 1956-57; dancer Alicia Langford Boston Ballet Co., 1957-59, Boston Opera Co., 1958, Myra Kinch Dancers, 1959, Robert Joffrey Theatre Ballet, 1959-62; ballet tchr. Alicia Langford Sch., Boston, 1957-59, N.Y.C., 1972—, Woodstock, N.Y., 1981—; sec. to dir. Monrovia Port Mgmt. Co., 1963-66; office mgr. Simat, Helliesen & Eichner, Inc., transp. cons. N.Y.C., 1966-72; adminstrv. asst. to dir. Council on Environ. N.Y.C., 1972-75; office mgr. Bedford Health Assocs., Inc., Katonah, N.Y., 1975—; editor cons. reports and various articles, 1977—; choreographer Green Room Theatre Prodns, N.Y.U., 1973; resident choreographer Children's History Theatre, Woodstock, 1981—, dir. summer dance program, 1982—; coordinator Our Daily Planet weekly radio program Sta. WNYC, 1973-75. Mem. wildlife com. Sierra Club, N.Y.C., 1972-74; vol. legis. profiles N.Y. Public Interest Research Group, 1974. Recipient letter of commendation for service to City N.Y. through Council on Environ., Mayor John V. Lindsay, 1973. Mem. Friends of Woodstock Library, Woodstock Guild of Craftsmen. Home: 306 W 18th St New York NY 10011 Office: 223 Katonah Ave Katonah NY 10536

DUDECK, PATRICIA MARIE, state ofcl.; b. Utica, N.Y., Aug. 19, 1953; d. Vincent Michael and Elizabeth Mary (Suhocki) D.; A.A.S. with honors, Herkimer County Community Coll., 1973. Sec., Mohawk Data Scis. Corp., Herkimer, N.Y., 1973-74; adminstrv. asst. Senator Edwyn E. Mason, 1975-76; sec. phys. edn. staff Herkimer County Community Coll., Herkimer, 1974-77; sec., office mgr. N.Y. State Conservation Council, Ilion, N.Y., 1977—. Advanced first aid and emergency care instr. ARC; sec. Frankfort Center Fire Dept. Aux., 1971-74, treas., 1974-78; active Frankfort Center Fire Dept. Rescue Squad, Herkimer County Fire Dept. Aux. Mem. Herkimer County Conservation Alliance (pres., cert. of appreciation 1977), Phi Theta Kappa. Clubs: East Herkimer Fish and Game, Mohawk Fish and Game, West Winfield Rod and Gun. Home: RD 2 Frankfort NY 13340 Office: 8 E Main St Ilion NY 13357

DUDEK, STEPHANIE ZUPERKO, psychologist; b. Lithuania, Dec. 18; came to U.S., 1944, naturalized, 1953; d. Walter J. and Stella (Suplevicius) Zuperko; B.A., McGill U., 1943; M.A., Columbia U., 1948; Ph.D., N.Y. U., 1960; 1 son, Gregory. Research psychologist N.Y. Psychiat. Inst., 1947-48, Skin and Cancer Clinic, N.Y.C., 1948-50; staff psychologist Columbia Med. Center, 1950-58; dir. dept. clin. psychology Allan Meml. Inst., Montreal, 1960-65, research scientist, 1965-69; asso. prof. dept. psychiatry McGill U., 1964-74, asso. scholar, 1974—; asso. prof. U. Montreal, 1969-75, prof. psychology, 1975—; pvt. practice psychotherapy; cons. Mental Hygiene Inst., others. Que. Mental Health grantee, 1964-67; Med. Research Council grantee, 1967-70; Can. Council sr. fellow, 1966; research grantee, 1969-70, 72, 76, 78-79; Local Initiatives-Research Funds, 1971-72; Alma Mater, 1976. Fellow Soc. Projective Techniques, Can. Psychol. Assn. (dir. 1974-76); mem. Am. Psychol. Assn. (pres. Div. 10 1982-83), Corp. Psychologists P.Q. (dir. 1974-77), Internat. Assn. Applied Psychology, Am. Bd. Examiners Profl. Psychology, Internat. Council Psychologists. Roman Catholic. Contbr. to publs. in field. Home: 3476 Vendome Ave Montreal PQ H4A 3M7 Canada Office: 90 Vincent D'Indy Montreal PQ Canada

DUDLEY, ABBIE ANNE, savs. and loan assn. exec.; b. Eucheeanna, Fla., May 24, 1936; d. Duncan Van and Bonnie Victoria (Day) McLean; diploma Massey-Draughon Bus. Coll., 1954, Am. Inst. Banking, 1956; m. Douglas Lavon Dudley, July 3, 1955; children—Deborah Lynn, Dolores Luanne. Loan clk. Fla. Nat. Bank, Pensacola, 1954; sec. to pres. Valparaiso (Fla.) State Bank, 1955-57; payroll clk. Page Aircraft Maintenance, Inc., Ft. Sill, Okla., 1957-58; bookkeeper First Bank of Marianna (Fla.), 1958-59, City of Marianna, 1962-65; field unit sec. Dozier Sch. Boys, Marianna, 1965-66; bookkeeper Malone Grocery Co., Marianna, 1966-72; asst. sec., loan servicing supr. First Fed. Savs. & Loan Assn., Marianna, 1973—. Mem. Nat. Assn. Female Execs., Ins. Women Jackson County (Fla.). Democrat. Presbyterian. Club: Marianna Pilot (1st v.p. 1982-83). Home: 500 Dogwood St PO Box 796 Marianna FL 32446 Office: 203 N Green St PO Box 340 Marianna FL 32446

DUDLEY, BARBARA HUDSON, church ofcl., author; b. St. James, Minn., Feb. 2, 1921; d. Lloyd Edwin and Lois (Hardin) Hudson; B.A., U. Iowa, 1942; M.A., U. So. Calif., 1951; children—Jean Lois Powers Cross, Cathy Colleen Powers. Youth dir. Hollywood Presbyn. Ch., 1945-47; prin. Isabelle Buckley Schs., Van Nuys, Calif., 1948-50; asso. prof. drama, dir. church drama Calif. Luth. Coll., Thousand Oaks, Calif., 1961-77; dir. drama Calvary Community Ch., 1977—; pres. Barbara Hudson Ministries, Inc., 1982—writer, producer, dir. pageants, for convs., synods of Lutheran Ch., 1967-75; works include: Going with God, 1953; Henrietta Mears Story, 1957; Where Is God?, 1973; Bridge of Nothing Less, 1975; God's Power in Your Life, 1975; also numerous radio scripts. Served as lt. USMCR, 1943-45. Recipient Outstanding Actress award U. So. Calif., 1947, 48; winner Story contest Guideposts mag., 1977. Mem. Conejo Players, Am. Ednl. Theater Assn., Nat. Collegiate Players, NEA, AFTRA, Screen Actors Guild, Pi Kappa Delta, Zeta Phi Eta, Gamma Phi Beta. Home: 1851 Village Ct Thousand Oaks CA 91360

DUDLEY, BETTYE WRIGHT WILLIAMS, research specialist; b. Danvilla, Va., Feb. 1, 1929; d. William Henry and Susie Emma (Wright) Williams; A.B. in Chemistry, Randolph-Macon Woman's Coll., 1951; M.A., Mt. Holyoke Coll., 1956; m. William Earl Dudley, Aug. 25, 1956 (dec. Aug. 1981); children—Suevan, William Earl, David. Chemist Dan River Mills, Inc., Danville, 1951-53; tchr. Chatham Hall Sch., Chatham, Va., 1953-54; teaching fellow Mt. Holyoke Coll., South Hadley, Mass., 1954-56; research chemist P. Lorillard, Greensboro, N.C., 1956-63; research technologist Sch. Pharmacy, U. S.C., Columbia, 1967-69, Office of Research, 1969-73, research specialist Belle W. Baruch Inst. for Marine Biology and Coastal Research, Columbia, 1973—; producer films, organizer workshops, symposia in field. Mem. adminstrv. bd. Washington St. Meth. Ch., 1969-77, 80—, council on ministries, 1971-76, 80—, pres. ch. sch. class, 1979-80; co-chmn. Lexington County Beautification Com., 1969-72; v.p. St. Andrew's Woman's Club, 1965-66; sec. Seven Oaks Community Action Council, 1970-71; mem. Woman's Symphony Assn., S.C. Mental Health Assn., Riverbanks Zool. Soc., Lexington County Hist Soc., SPCA. Recipient Employee of Yr. award U. S.C., 1981. Mem. Am. Chem. Soc., Southeastern Estuarine Research Soc., Nat. Oceanographic Found., U. S.C. Alumni Assn., Sigma Xi (chpt. sec. 1977-78, pres. 1980-81), Omicron Delta Kappa, Alpha Delta Pi. Republican. Editor: Malnutrition and Intestinal Parasites: A Guide for Control and Eradication, 1973; contbr. articles to profl. jours. Home: 749 Woodland Hills W Columbia SC 29210 Office: Belle W Baruch Inst for Marine Biology and Coastal Research U SC Columbia SC 29208

DUDLEY, MARGARET JOYCE, sch. prin.; b. McKinney, Tex., Apr. 11; d. Alexander Henry and Lillian Irene (Bruner) Pigg; B.A., Bethany (Okla.) Nazarene Coll., 1950; M.Ed., Okla. U., Norman, 1951; postgrad. Mexico City Coll., 1954, U. Tex., El Paso, 1967, 68, El Paso Community Coll., 1976, 80, Bilingual Inst., El Paso, 1977-78; m. Newel Clyde Dudley, Aug. 29, 1964. Tchr. public schs., Okla., 1947, Tex., 1951—; tchr. El Paso schs., 1956—; asst. prin. Alta Vista Sch., 1974—. Mem. NEA, PTA, Tex. Tchrs. Assn., El Paso Edn. Assn., El Paso Public Schs. Adminstrs. and Cons. Assn., Delta Kappa Gamma. Mem. Ch. of Nazarene. Home: 9417 Album St El Paso TX 79925 Office: 1000 N Grama St El Paso TX 79903

DUDLEY, MARY CATHERINE, mktg. exec.; b. Wausau, Wis., Jan. 27, 1953; d. Richard David and Eileen (Deneen) Dudley; B.A., Tex. Christian U., 1975; m. William David Stotesbery, June 21, 1975. Reporter, Austin (Tex.) Am.-Statesman, 1975-78; polit. columnist Tex. Woman Mag., Austin, 1978-80; media cons., mktg. mgr. Austin Conv. Bur., Austin C. of C., 1980-82; sr. promotion specialist Bausch & Lomb, Austin, 1982—; cons. in field. Bd. dirs. Center for Battered Women, Austin, 1981—; vol. coordinator Austin Symphony Sq., 1980-81, mem., 1980—; mem. Austin Commn. on Status of Women, 1978-79. Recipient Med. Reporting award Tex. Med. Assn., 1977. Mem. Women in Communications (chpt. bd. dirs. 1979-80), Tex. Soc. Assn. Execs., Austin Sister City Assn. Roman Catholic. Home: 1606 W 42d St Austin TX 78756

DUDLEY, VIVIAN INEZ, educator; b. Grimesland, N.C., June 4, 1944; d. Milton Thomas and Ella (Ree) Gatlin; B.S. in Edn., Elizabeth City (N.C.) State U., 1966; grad. N.J. Mil. Acad., Sea Girt, 1979; m. James K. Dudley, Jan. 15, 1973; children—Shelton, Martha, Jacques. Staff, Sch. Edn., N.Y.U., 1968-71; tchr. Paterson (N.J.) Bd. Edn., 1971—; tchr. 7th grade Sch. 21, 1977—; chmn. bd. dirs. St. Joseph Sch., Newark, 1978—. Mem. N.J. Army N.G., 1976—. Home: 440 Washington St Apt 12-B Newark NJ 07102 Office: Sch 21 Madison Ave Paterson NJ 07514

DUER, SHIRLEY POWELL, state legislator; b. Meigs County, Tenn., Dec. 20, 1935; d. John Scott and Dean Sherrill Stanton; student Huntingdon Coll., 1952-55; B.S., Tenn. Tech. U., 1977; m. Carl T. Duer, Sept. 10, 1955; children—Michelle, Elizabeth, Carl Thomas. Tchr., Walker County, Ga., 1955-57; research chemist U. Tenn. Med. Units, Memphis, 1960-65; field rep. Gov's. Office, Cookeville, Tenn., 1979; mem. Tenn. Ho. of Reps., 1980—; mem. State Adv. Council Vocat. Edn., 1981—. Mem. Tenn. Commn. for Humanities; sec. Tenn. Conservation Commn., 1970-76; mem. Cumberland County Beautiful Assn. Mem. Nat. Republican Legislators Assn., Am. Legislative Exchange Council, Orgn. Women Legislators, C. of C., Am. Legion Aux., Phi Kappa Phi, Phi Alpha Theta. Republican. Congregationalist. Home: Route 9 Box 53 Holiday Dr Crossville TN 38555 Office: Room 107 War Memorial Bldg Nashville TN 37219

DUERK, ALENE B., ret. naval officer; b. Defiance, Ohio, Mar. 29, 1920; d. Albert H. and Emma K. (Dietsch) D.; R.N., Toledo Hosp. Sch. Nursing, 1941; B.S., Western Res. U., 1948; D.Public Service, Bowling Green State U., 1973; D.H.L., Marymount Coll. Va., 1974; D.Sc., Iowa Wesleyan Coll., 1975, Med. Coll. Ohio, 1976. Staff nurse Toledo Hosp., 1941-42; 1st aid nurse Kobacker Dept. Store, Toledo, 1942-43; nurse Detwiler Meml. Hosp., Wauseon, Ohio, 1948; clin. instr., supr. med. nursing Highland Park (Mich.) Gen. Hosp., 1948-51; commd. ensign Nurse Corps, U.S. Navy, 1943, advanced through grades to rear adm., 1972; asst. chief nurse U.S. Naval Hosp., Yokosuka, Japan, 1962-63; sr. nurse Naval Sta. Dispensary, Long Beach, Calif., 1963-65; chief nursing br. Naval Hosp. Corps Sch., San Diego, 1965-66; spl. asst. for nursing affairs Office Dep. Asst. Sec. Def., 1966-67; chief nursing service Naval Hosp., Great Lakes, Ill., 1968-70; dir. Navy Nurse Corps, 1970-75; ret., 1975. Recipient mil. award Ohio Gov., 1973; Outstanding Alumni award Case Western Res. U. Sch. Nursing, 1974. Home: 12 Robinwood Dr Longwood FL 32750

DUERR-LEVINE, DIANE, mktg. exec.; b. Tulsa, Mar. 8, 1938; d. Arthur and Reta (Reeves) Duerr; B.A. in Math., U. Mich., 1960; M.B.A., Columbia U., 1963; m. Matthew A. Levine, June 9, 1963. Systems engr. Xerox Corp., N.Y.C., 1963-64; products mgr. Lever Bros. Corp., N.Y.C., 1964-68; sr. br. mgr. Am. Home Products Corp., N.Y.C., 1968-71; supr. Honig-Cooper Herrington, San Francisco, 1971-72; v.p. advt. and sales promotion Continental Airlines, Los Angeles, 1973-76; dir. mktg. and communications San Francisco Bay Area Transit Dist., 1976-78; pres., founder Inst. Health Mgmt., San Francisco, 1978—; prof. San Francisco State U., 1982—. cons. hosp. groups. Bd. dirs. Resource Center for Women, Palo Alto, Calif.; mem. bus. adv. bd. San Francisco State U.; cons. Solar Energy Research Inst., No. Calif. Coalition for ERA. Mem. Columbia U. Grad. Sch. Bus. Alumni Assn., Kappa Kappa Gamma. Recipient numerous mktg. and advt. awards. Democrat. Mem. Soc. of Friends. Author: Vital Living after Fifty, 1982. Office: 101 Lansdale Ave San Francisco CA 94127

DUFF, MARY KATHLEEN, savs. and loan co. exec.; b. Watseka, Ill., May 26, 1945; d. John Wesley and Mary Margaret (Blake) Duff; student Coll. of Wooster, 1963-65, U. Miami (Fla.), 1965-67; B.S., U. Ill., 1968; M.P.A., U. Denver, 1976. Research asst. Tex. Research Inst. Mental Scis., Houston, 1968-69; research asso. Denver Research Inst.-Indsl. Econs., 1970-75; sr. policy analyst City of Denver, Office of Policy Analysis, 1975-77; spl. project dir. Colo. Civil Rights Commn., Denver, 1977-78; govt. loans coordinator Midland Fed. Savs. & Loan Assn., Denver, 1978-80; asso. Richardson-Burgwyn Assos., Inc., 1981—. Bd. dirs., zoning chmn. West Univ. Community Assn., 1976—. Mem. Nat. Assn. Housing and Redevel. Ofcls., Am. Soc. Public Adminstrn. Ofcls., LWV (housing chmn.), Pi Alpha Alpha, Sigma Iota Epsilon. Office: Midland Federal Savings & Loan Assn 444 17th St Denver CO 80202

DUFF, RUTH ELEANOR, coll. dean; b. Alexander County, Ill., Dec. 19, 1934; d. Richard Ernest and Ruth Ethel (Dickerson) D.; B.S. in Edn., S.E. Mo. State Coll., 1961; M.S. in Edn., So. Ill. U., 1968, Ph.D. (Coll. Edn. dissertation fellow 1972), 1973. Primary and elem. sch. tchr., Ill., 1954-65; dir. demonstration presch. program Alexander County Sch. Dist. I, 1965-68; instr., Head Start regional tng. officer So. Ill. U., 1968-70, instr., dir. Head Start supplementary tng., 1970-72; asso. prof. early childhood edn. U. S.C., Columbia, 1973-74, coordinator early childhood edn., 1974-79, asst. dean acad. affairs, 1979-80, asst. dean students and programs Coll. Edn., 1980—; sec. Midlands Human Resources Devel. Commn., 1980—; mem. Gov. S.C. Interagy. Coordinating Council Early Childhood Devel. and Edn., 1981—, Gov. S.C. Adv. Com. Early Childhood Devel. and Edn., 1980—. Fellow, tchr. tng. for disadvantaged, summer 1970. Mem. Assn. Childhood Edn. Internat., U.S. Nat. Com. Early Childhood Edn., Organization Mondiale pour l'Education Prescolaire, Nat. Assn. Edn. Young Children, So. Assn. Children Under Six, S.C. Assn. Children Under Six, Soc. Research Child Devel., Phi Delta Kappa. Co-author: The Parent-Teacher Bond: Relating, Responding, Rewarding, 1978; Early Childhood Education, 1980; others. Contbr. articles to profl. jours., chpts. to books. Office: Coll Edn U SC Columbia SC 29208

DUFFEE, BEVERLY ANN, educator; b. Sharon, Pa., Apr. 18, 1946; d. Kenneth Ira and Edith Belle (Farringer) Duffee; B.A., Roberts Wesleyan Coll., 1968; M.A., Calif. State U., 1973. Personnel adminstr./programmer Newport Electronics, Santa Ana, Calif., 1973-77; personnel counselor Dennis & Dennis Personnel Services, Santa Ana, 1978; sales sec. Gould Inc., Auto. Battery Div., Irvine, Calif., 1979-81; chmn. dept. English, tchr., chorus dir. Leffingwell Christian Jr./Sr. High Sch., Norwalk, Calif., 1981—. Mem. Women's Missionary Fellowship Internat., Alpha Kappa Sigma. Republican. Methodist. Home: 2841 E Lincoln Ave Apt 249 Anaheim CA 92806 Office: 11032 Leffingwell Rd Norwalk CA 90650

DUFFY, BARBARA ANNE, nurse adminstr.; b. Cin., Dec. 16, 1940; d. Louis Conrad and Ruth Mildred (Hunt) Gutwein; A.S. in Nursing, Mt. San Antonio Coll., 1974; B.S., U. Redlands, 1982; postgrad. in adminstrn. Calif. State U., Dominquez Hills, 1982—; m. Thomas Duffy, Aug. 14, 1960; children—Douglass Michael, Kevin Thomas, Gregory Alan. Staff nurse San Dimas (Calif.) Community Hosp., 1974, Pomona Valley (Calif.) Community Hosp., 1975-76, also charge nurse CCU; head nurse cardiac surgery ICU, Cedars-Sinai Med. Center, Los Angeles, 1976-79; clin. specialist critical care Brotman Med. Center, Culver City, Calif., 1979-81, clin. supr. burn unit, CCU, dialysis, 1980-81; asst. dir. nursing St. Francis Med. Center, Lynwood, Calif., 1981—; guest lectr., cons. R.N., Calif. Mem. Calif. Soc. for Nursing Services Adminstrs., Am. Assn. Critical Care Nurses, Nat. Critical Care Inst. Edn. Office: 3630 E Imperial Hwy Lynwood CA 90262 *

DUFFY, BETTY MINOR, owner art gallery; b. Ft. Smith, Ark., Dec. 13, 1920; d. Robert West and Wrnetta M. (Tanner) Minor; B.A., Okla. State U., 1942; postgrad. U. Conn.; art student, Paris, 1947-49; m. Douglas Monteith Duffy, July 3, 1945; children—Wrenetta Ward, Elizabeth Woodford. Tchr. public schs.; owner, operator Bethesda Art Gallery (Md.), 1975—. Home: 5702 Mohican Rd Washington DC 20816 Office: Bethesda Art Gallery 7950 Norfolk Ave Bethesda MD 20014

DUFFY, DOLORES JEAN, civic worker; b. Weirton, W.Va., Nov. 3, 1933; d. Domenic and Lena (Buracchio) DiGregario; student public schs. Weirton; m. Paul T. Duffy, Jan. 28, 1956; children—Paul, Daniel, Terence. With Weirton Steel Co., 1951-56; receptionist Weirton Med. Center, 1956-57; pres. St. Paul's PTA, 1969-70, Madonna PTA, 1976-77, Weirton Hosp. Aux., 1970, 71, St. Paul's Christian Mothers, 1966, Forget Me Not Twig, 1967, 68; bd. dirs. Madonna Summer Players, 1975—; preceptor Omega, Xi Beta Iota, 1968-69; adv. Gamma Iota, 1977—. Home: 3920 Hanlin Way Weirton WV 26062

DUFFY, ESTHER RODGERS (MRS. ROGER FRANCIS DUFFY), librarian; b. Pitts., Aug. 14, 1911; d. Arthur Gregory and Charlotte Catherine (Nagle) Rodgers; B. Music and B.S. in Music Edn., Seton Hill Coll., 1932; postgrad. U. Pitts., 1933, Carnegie Inst., 1935, Simmons Coll., 1941-42; m. Roger Francis Duffy, Nov. 14, 1945; children—Katherine, Mary Anne, Roger. Instr. music Coll. Misericordia, Dallas, Pa., 1932-37; music librarian Cornell U., Ithaca, N.Y., 1937-41; asst. music librarian Columbia U., N.Y.C., 1942-43; research librarian OSS, State Dept., 1943-44, Balkans outpost rep. Office War Info., 1944-46, Balkans regional rep. USIS, 1946; asst. to pres. Juilliard Sch. Music, N.Y.C., 1947-49; asst. to mng. dir. U.S. Internat. Book Assn., N.Y.C., 1945-47; librarian fine arts Greenwich (Conn.) Library, 1961-81. Mem. adv. com. Greenwich Sr. Center; trustee Greenwich Center for Chamber Music. Mem. Greenwich Arts Council. Mem. Music Library Assn., AAUW, Kappa Gamma Pi. Home: 2 Peters Rd Riverside CT 06878

DUGAL, ELIZABETH ANN, lawyer; b. Opelousas, La., Aug. 28, 1954; d. George Louis and Elizabeth Ann (Thoms) D.; student U. Southwestern La., 1971-74; B.A., La. State U., 1977, J.D., 1977. Admitted to La. bar, 1977; legal research asst., expropriation div. La. Dept. Hwys., Baton Rouge, 1976-77; individual practice law, Lafayette, La., 1977—; hostess monthly TV program Sta. KLFY; tchr. courses, workshops. Mem. Acadiana Women's Polit. Caucus; mem. Lafayette Regional Planning Commn., Lafayette Parish Planning Commn., 1981—; vice chmn. Talent Bank of Lafayette, 1982-83. Mem. Am. Bar Assn., La. Bar Assn., La. Trial Lawyers Assn., Lafayette Parish Bar Assn., AAUW (legis. chmn. 1979-80), UDC, Alpha Lambda Delta, Phi Gamma Mu, Phi Kappa Phi, Phi Alpha Delta. Republican. Roman Catholic. Club: Zonta. Author publs. in field. Office: 1207 Lafayette St Lafayette LA 70501

DUGALLY, MAXINE MILDRED, dept. store exec.; b. Monette, Ark., Aug. 29; d. Ewell C. and Mattie L. (Fitzgerald) Newman; grad. Los Angeles Mdse. Inst., 1950; children—Debra, David. Asst. buyer I. Magnin, Los Angeles, 1950-52; salesperson Marston's, San Diego, 1952-53; asst. buyer Buffum's, Long Beach, Calif., 1953-54; buyer, mdse. mgr. Hinshaw's, Whittier and Arcadia, Calif., 1962—. Mem. Fashion Group. Home: 14442 E 7th St Whittier CA 90602 Office: 8480 Quadway St Whittier CA 90607

DUGAN, KIMIKO HATTA (MRS. WAYNE ALEXANDER DUGAN), anatomist, educator; b. Kyoto City, Japan, Oct. 21, 1924; d. Shinzo and Sano (Hatta) Hatta; student U. Md., 1957-58; B.A., Okla. Coll. Women, 1961; M.S., U. Okla., 1965, Ph.D., 1970; m. Wayne Alexander Dugan, Aug. 18, 1947 (dec. Aug. 1971). Grad. fellow dept. anatomy Sch. Medicine, U. Okla., Oklahoma City, 1964-69, instr. dept. anat. sci. Coll. Medicine, 1969-71, asst. prof., 1971-78, asso. prof., 1978—. Recipient Undergrad. Chemistry Achievement award Okla. Coll. Women, 1960; elected to U. Sci. and Arts Okla. (formerly Okla. Coll. Women) Alumni Hall of Fame, 1977. Mem. Am. Assn. Anatomists, AAAS, AAUW, AAUP, Am. Chem. Soc., Am. Soc. Zoologists, Electron Microscopy Soc. Am., N.Y. Acad. Sci., Sigma Xi. Episcopalian. Home: 1139 NW 63d St Oklahoma City OK 73116 Office: Dept Anat Scis Coll Medicine U Okla Health Scis Center PO Box 26901 Oklahoma City OK 73190

DUGAN, RUTH L., county ofcl., Democratic nat. committee woman; b. Eskilstuna, Sweden, Aug. 13, 1947; came to U.S., 1950, naturalized, 1967; d. Meyer and Estera (Michelwitz) Uncyk; A.A., Dean Coll.; B.A., Boston U.; m. Gordon Puglisi, Mar. 18, 1967; children—Eric, Trisha, Kristen; m. 2d, James P. Dugan; 1 son, James. Adminstrv. asst. to N.J. State Senator; campaign mgr. Jimmy Carter for Pres. campaign, N.J.; mem. Democratic Nat. Com., 1976—, dist. chmn., 1973-76; dir. Bergen County (N.J.) Office Energy Conservation. Mem. NOW, Assn. Profl. Women, Nat. Women's Polit. Caucus. Home: 35 Fox Hedge Rd Saddle River NJ 07458

DUGGAN, CAROL PETKUS, adminstrv. asst., civic worker; b. Jersey City, Jan. 22, 1943; d. Nicodemus and Helen (Haduca) Petkus; B.S., Fordham U., 1964; m. Charles Duggan, Nov. 13, 1965; children—Cassandra Joan, Christopher John. Adminstrv. asst. Am. Assn. Advt. Agys., N.Y.C., 1964-67; office mgr. O Neill Row & Co., N.Y.C., 1967-70; adminstrv. asst. Silcoa Products Inc., Bridgeport, Conn., 1978—. Fair chmn. Holland Hill Sch. PTA, 1974-75, hospitality chmn., 1975-76, del. bd. edn., 1966-77, 3d v.p., 1977-78, editor calendar, 1975-77, chmn. by-laws com., 1974, 76, 78; rec. sec. Fairfield PTA Council, 1978—, treas., 1980-81, assembly del., 1981-82, editor newsletter, 1981-82; del. Osborn Hill Sch. PTA, 1978—, 3d v.p., 1979-80, v.p., 1980-81; PTA council rep. and chmn. by-laws com. Fairfield Woods Jr. High PTA, 1979-80, mem. budget com., 1981-82; Fairfield rep. to Conn. PTA Council Assembly, 1979-80; bd. mgrs. Conn. State PTA, 1981-82, v.p. assembly, 1981-82, mem. legis. com., 1981-82; mem. com. on adminstrv. reorganization Fairfield Bd. Edn., 1980-82, mem. calendar com., 1981-82, parents' handbook com., 1981-82; publicity dir. Fifth Wheel, 1975-76; vol. guide Ogden House, Fairfield Hist. Soc., 1977-78; summer fun program dir. St. Pius X, 1971-74; hospitality chmn. Barnum Festival Salute to Fairfield, 1977, 78; Fedn. Day chmn. Jr. Woman's Club, Fairfield, 1975-76; treas. Lake Hills Garden Club, 1975-76, v.p., 1976-77; town-wide Halloween party chmn. Citizens Nat. Bank, 1975, 76; vol. Heart Fund chmn. June Social, Fairfield Woman's Club, 1980-81, chmn. spring fundraising publicity, program chmn., 1980-82. Mem. Aububon Soc., AAUW. Republican. Roman Catholic. Home: 20 Trillium Rd Fairfield CT 06430

DUGGAN, GLORIA LORENE, social services adminstr.; b. Alpine, Utah, July 22, 1927; d. George Alfred and Alice Cleora (Adams) Brown; B.S. with honors, San Diego State U., 1957, postgrad., 1964-74; m. George F. Duggan Jr., Aug. 25, 1972; 1 son, Gregory P. Maynard. Sch. nurse, tchr. Sweetwater Union High Sch., National City, Calif., 1966-68; resident head nurse Mary C. Wheeler Sch., Providence, 1968-70; sub regional trainer Calif. State Drug program Calif. Dept. Edn., 1970-71; hearing conservation program San Francisco Schs., San Francisco Dept. Pub. Health, maternal and child welfare, 1974; clin. lab. instr. community health R.I. Coll., Providence, 1975-76; exec. dir. Pawtucket (R.I.) Neighborhood Health Centers Inc., 1976—; lectr. in field. Publicity dir. LaJolla aux. San Diego Symphony Orch., 1966-68, chmn. symphony summer music festivals, 1967—; past chmn. health adv. com. Dept. Social and Rehab. Services, State of R.I. Mem. Nat. Assn. Community Health Centers (past treas. region 1, program planning com. 1978-82), R.I. Health Center Assn. (publicity dir. 1978), Mass. League Neighborhood Health Centers, New Eng. Community Health Center Assistance Program, AAUW (publicity dir. chpt. 1966), Am. Pub. Health Assn., New Eng. Pub. Health Assn., Blackstone Valley C. of C., Phi Kappa Phi. Mem. Ch. Jesus Christ Latter-day Saints. Home: 7 Gilbert St Warwick RI 02886 Office: 401 Mineral Springs Ave Pawtucket RI 02860

DUGGAN, MAUREEN, govt. health adminstr.; b. Salamanca, N.Y., Feb. 17, 1945; d. William B. and Rita L. (Haley) D.; B.A. (U.S. Office Edn. trainee), SUNY, Albany, 1966, M.A., 1967; postgrad. Temple U., 1967, Union Coll., 1972, U. Md., 1977. With Office Health Systems Mgmt., N.Y. State Dept. Health, 1968—, asso. med. care adminstr. Syracuse Area Office, 1978, hosp. program dir., 1978-79, prin. med. care adminstr., standards unit chief, Albany, 1979—; vis. lectr. Syracuse U., 1978. Weekly vol. Big Bros./Big Sisters Am., Albany, 1978—; mem. affirmative action adv. com. Dept. Health, Center for Women in Govt., Albany, 1979. Mem. Am. Public Health Assn., Nat. Assn. Female Execs., N.Y. State Women Mgrs. Network. Home: 283 Woodlawn Ave Albany NY 12208 Office: Office Health Systems Mgmt Tower Bldg Empire Plaza Albany NY 12237

DUGGAN, WILMA SLEDGE, home economist, dietitian; b. Coushatta, La., Dec. 12, 1921; d. William Dothan and Ada (Dixon) Sledge; B.S. in Home Econs., La. Poly. U., 1942; m. Martin J. Duggan, July 5, 1958 (div. 1979); children—Nancy, Martin J. Dietetics intern, Harper Hosp., Detroit, 1943; indsl. feeding mgr. Safeway Stores, 1947-49, mgr. Hallmark Testing Service, 1953-56; Western regional home economist, Crosley, 1949-52; West Coast public relations Am. Can Co., N.Y. and San Francisco, 1952-53; pvt. practice cons. firm, San Francisco, 1956-70; consumer services rep. Pacific Gas and Electric Co., San Jose, Calif., 1970—; cons. in field. Pres. Los Altos Parent Presch.; bd. dirs. Santa Clara County chpt. Am. Heart Assn. Served to capt. M.C., U.S. Army, 1943-47. Named Tchr. with Great Merit, Pacific Service Employees Assn., 1975. Mem. Am. Dietetic Assn., San Jose Peninsula Dietetic Assn., Am. Home Econs. Assn., Home Economists in Bus. (nat. group and San Francisco group, pres.), Santa Clara-San Mateo Interagy. Nutrition Council, Santa Clara County Heart Assn. Nutrition Com. (outstanding dietitian of year 1977), Consumer Credit Counselors Santa Clara County (dir.). Republican. Columnist Culinary Q & A, San Jose Mercury News. Home: 1891 Newcastle Los Altos CA 94022 Office: 111 Almaden Blvd San Jose CA 95198

DUGGIN, THELMA, govt. ofcl.; b. Mobile, Ala., Dec. 23, 1949; d. Basil and Elizabeth Alberta (Collins) Duggin; B.A., Edgewood Coll., 1971; D.H.L. (hon.), Morris Brown Coll., 1982. Tchr., Holy Family Sch., Mobile, 1971-73; sr. mdse. mgr. J.C. Penney Co., Columbus, Ga., 1973-77; field coordinator Wright McNeill & Assocs., Washington, 1977-81; dep. spl. asst. to pres., Washington, 1981—, dir. 50 States Project, 1981—. Bd. Govs. Health System Agy., 1976-78; sec. Ga. Republican Party, 1977-79; sec. Muscogee County Rep. Party, 1977-78; bd. dirs. Operation Big Vote, 1979-80. Recipient Disting. Service award Nat. Alumni Council; Parren Mitchell Achievement award; named Woman of Yr., Zeta Phi Beta; recipient Appreciation award Nat. Council Black Mayors; Mary McLeod Bethune Legacy award Nat. Council Negro Women. Mem. Nat. Assn. Colored Women's Clubs, Zeta Phi Beta. Roman Catholic. Home: 501 Slaters Ln Alexandria VA 22314 Office: White House 1600 Pennsylvania Ave Washington DC 20500

DUGGLEBY, TAMARA JEAN, fin. cons.; b. Davenport, Iowa, Oct. 7, 1944; d. Reginald Garrett and Marian Lois (Brown) D.; B.A. in Journalism, U. Iowa, 1967; M.A. in Urban Affairs, Loyola U., Chgo., 1976. Asso. public info. dir. Leadership Council Met. Open Communities, Chgo., 1972-73; multifamily housing rep. HUD, Chgo., 1974-77; rehab. project mgr. Chgo. Area Renewal Effort Service Corp., 1977-79; fin. cons. in community devel. Gressel and Slater, Chgo., 1979-80; fin. cons. to developing countries, 1980—. Recipient Marilyn Singleton award HUD, 1976. Mem. Am. Planning Assn., Women in Communications. Presbyterian. Home and Office: 1737 Q St NW Washington DC 20009

DUHAMEL, LORRAINE RITA, hosp. histotechnologist; b. Boston, Oct. 28, 1942; d. Russell Sumner and Doris Mary (Connaughton) Corkum; student Quincy (Mass.) City Hosp. Sch., 1961; Asso. Sci., Massasoit Community Coll., 1981; m. Ronald Joseph Duhamel, Oct. 6, 1962; children—Ann Marie, William Russell, Melinda Beth, David Sumner. Research asst. Harvard Med. Sch., Boston, 1961-62; chief technician Cancer Screening Lab., Brockton, Mass., 1962-63; histology technician South Shore Hosp., South Weymouth, Mass., part-time 1961-70, full time 1970-73, histology supr., 1973—. Asst. leader Rockland Cub Scouts pack Boy Scouts Am., 1973-76, leader, 1976-78; mem. troop com. Rockland Camp Fire Girls, 1975-78; troop leader Rockland Girl Scouts U.S.A., 1975-77, pres., 1979-81, spl. services chmn., 1981—; asst. coach Rockland Youth Soccer, 1980—. Harleco Ednl. scholar, 1981. Mem. Nat. Soc. for Histotech. (charter), Mass. Soc. for Histotech. (charter, editor Newsletter 1976-77, membership chmn. 1976-80, sec. 1978-80, pres. 1980—), Am. Soc. Clin. Pathologists (affiliate). Home: 36 Beal St Rockland MA 02370 Office: S Shore Hosp 55 Fogg Rd South Weymouth MA 02190

DUHIG, VIVIAN IRENE, educator; b. Henrietta, Okla., Oct. 12, 1922; d. Jesse Lawrence and Bessie Devon (Martin) Chesshir; student So. Tex. Jr. Coll., 1954; B.A. (scholar), Rice U., 1961; postgrad McNeese State U., 1976-77; m. William Gordon Duhig, Jan. 18, 1952; children—Michael Lee and Margaret Louise (adopted twins). High sch. English and math. tchr., Houston, 1961-70; asst. dir. community relations St. Patrick Hosp., Lake Charles, La., 1974-77; adminstrv. asst. architect, Sulphur, La., 1977-79; owner Public Relations Secretarial Service, Lake Charles, 1979-82; tchr. English, Houston Ind. Sch. Dist., 1982—; free lance secretarial service, Houston, 1982—; field ops. supr. for 12-parish dist., 1980 census, Lake Charles; Parish exec. com., 1977-79; active polit. campaigns; pres. 7th Dist. Republican Women Club, 1977-79, del. nat. convs., 1977, 79; charter mem., organizing com. La. Preservation Alliance, chmn. public relations com.; pres. Calcasieu Hist. Preservation Soc., 1977-79; chmn. home show, 1975, 76; mem. La. Assn. for Retarded Citizens, 1970-79; vol. St. Patrick Hosp. Aux.; active La. Women Opposed to ERA. Mem. Am. Bus. Women's Assn., C. of C. (legis. affairs and red carpet coms.), Rice Alumni Assn. Mem. Church of Christ. Club: Toastmasters Internat. Contbr. research, hist., news articles to publs. Home: 7990 Locke Ln #1 Houston TX 77063

DUHME, CAROL MCCARTHY, civic worker; b. St. Louis, Apr. 13, 1917; d. Eugene Ross and Louise (Roblee) McCarthy; A.B., Vassar Coll., 1939; m. Sheldon Ware, June 12, 1941 (dec. 1944); 1 son, David; m. 2d, H. Richard Duhme, Jr., Apr. 9, 1947; children—Benton (dec.), Ann, Warren. Tchr. elem. sch., 1939-41, 42-44; moderator St. Louis Assn. Congregational Chs., 1952; dir. Christian edn. First Congregational Ch., St. Louis, 1960-62, trustee, 1964-66, mem. ch. council, 1974-75, bd. deaconesses, 1978-81, bd. deacons, 1982—; former bd. dirs. Community Music Schs., St. Louis, Community Sch., Ch. Women United, John Burroughs Sch., St. Louis Bicentennial Women's Com., St. Louis Jr. League; pres. St. Louis Vassar Club; pres. bd. dirs. YWCA, St. Louis, 1973-76; bd. dirs. North Side Team Ministry, 1968—, Chautauqua (N.Y.) Instn., 1971—, Mo. Bapt. Hosp., 1973—, Eden Theol. Sem., 1979—; sec. bd. dirs. UN Assn., St. Louis, 1976—; pres. bd. dirs. Family and Children's Service Greater St. Louis, 1977-79; mem. chancellor's long-range planning com. Washington U., 1980-81; chmn. Benton Roblee Duhme Scholarship Fund; trustee Joseph H. and Florence A. Roblee Found., St. Louis. Mem. corp. assembly Blue Cross Hosp. Service of Mo., 1978—. Recipient Mary Alice Messerley award for volunteerism Health and Welfare Council St. Louis, 1971; Vol. of Yr. award, YWCA, 1976; Woman of Achievement award St. Louis Globe Democrat, 1980. Home: 8 Edgewood Rd Saint Louis MO 63124

DUHON, HELEN BLOEDORN, editor; b. Franklin, Nebr., Nov. 19, 1915; d. Charles F.W. and Zoe (Schrock) Bloedorn; B.A., U. Colo., 1938; m. S.C. Duhon, June 1940 (div.); children—Joan Duhon Dana, H. Annette Duhon Fenner, S. Jr. Writer alumni office U. Colo., Boulder, The Colo. Alumnus, 1962—, asst. editor, 1974—, editor For Parents, 1974-76. Mem. Colo. Press Women (chmn. writing contest and scholarship 1975-77), Women in Communications, Boulder Press Club, Delta Delta Delta. Home: 675 Cascade Ave Boulder CO 80302 Office: K Alumni Center U Colo Boulder CO 80309

DUIGNAN-WOODS, EILEEN, mech. engr.; b. Chgo., July 6, 1939; d. Arthur Ambrose and Elizabeth Florence (Kelly) Duignan; B.S.M.E., Ill. Inst. Tech., 1970; m. Lee Donald Woods, Sept. 29, 1970. Draftsperson, City of Chgo., 1959-61, Greeley & Hansen, Chgo., 1961-63; asst. contract engr. Borg-Warner Internat., Chgo., 1963-65; mech. designer Childs & Smith, Chgo., 1965-66; mech. design engr. A. Epstein & Sons, Chgo., 1966-69; mech. design engr. Globe Engring., Chgo., 1969-70; project team leader, chief mech. engr., supervisory engr. GSA, Chgo., 1970-79; project mgr. Schal Assos., Chgo., 1979—. Registered profl. engr., Ill. Mem. ASME, Chgo. Women in Architecture, Assn. Women in Sci., ASHRAE (pres. chpt. 1980-81; vice-chmn. regional edn. com., mem. tech. com. fire and smoke control), Nat. Soc. Profl. Engrs., Ill. Soc. Profl. Engrs. Roman Catholic. Contbr. articles to profl. jours. Home: 3150 N Sheridan Rd Chicago IL 60657 Office: 33 W Monroe St Chicago IL 60603

DUKE, JUNE EILEEN LABER CONWAY, advt. agy. exec.; b. Cumberland, Md., June 4, 1936; d. Goerge Lewis and Lola Kathleen Laber; R.N., U. Md., 1956; postgrad. Johns Hopkins U., 1976-79; children—Deborah, Stephen, Diane, Kathy, David; stepchildren—Larry, Randy and Stacey Duke. Head nurse U. Md. Hosp., 1956-57, hosp. coordinator, 1957-58; fashion model, 1952-80; fashion dir. Mano Swartz, Balt., 1977—; pub. relations dir. Wolff Co., Balt., 1975—. Pub. relations chmn. Am. Field Service; mem. adv. bd. Md. Gen. Hosp. Sch. of Nursing; exec. bd., trustee Md. Gen. Hosp., 1979—; pres. Md. Gen. Hosp. Aux., 1972-74, 76-78; pres. Long Quarter Improvement Assn., 1977-79; chmn. Balt. Opera Build Ball, 1977; coordinator Md. Ballet Ann. Gala, 1979; v.p. Metro-Center unit Am. Cancer Soc., 1978. Republican. Home: 1508 Long Quarter Ct Lutherville MD 21093

DUKE, KARLENE KNUTSSON, edn. cons., coordinator; b. Tampa, Fla., May 31, 1933; d. Karl and Ethel Louise (Lindsey) Knutsson; A.A., U. Fla., 1953; B.S., Fla. So. Coll., 1965; M.Ed., Rollins Coll., 1979; m. Oscar C. Duke, June 27, 1953; children—George, Allan, Brian, Kevin. Dir. kindergarten McCoy AFB, Fla., 1964-65; tchr. elem. sch., Orlando, Fla., 1965-66; ednl. adv. McCoy AFB, Fla., 1966-68; tchr. Homebound/Hospitalized, San Bernardino, Calif., 1972-73; tchr. Homebound/Hospitalized, Sanford, Fla., 1973-79, cons., coordinator, 1979—. Scholarship chmn. Pankhurst, 1982-83. Fla. Ho. of Reps. Teaching scholar, 1951. Mem. Council Exceptional Children (chpt. pres. 1975; pres.-elect internat. div. 1982), Fla. Home/Hosp. Tchrs. Assn. (pres. 1980), Kappa Delta Pi, Phi Delta Kappa, Delta, Delta Delta. Democrat. Methodist. Home: 745 Tuscawilla Trail Winter Springs FL 32708 Office: 1211 Mellonvilla Ave Sanford FL 32771

DUKE, VERONICA MURRAY, social worker; b. Cape May, N.J., Sept. 28, 1931; d. Thomas Patrick and Cora Beatrice (Davies) Murray; student U. Tampa, 1949-51; B.S., U. Fla., 1953; M.S.W., U. Mo., 1959; m. Alvah G. Heideman, Jr., 1955 (div. 1976); children—Alvah G. III, Sara Elizabeth; m. 2d, George Duke, Jr., 1979. Caseworker, Hillsborough County, Tampa, Fla., 1954-56; caseworker State of Mo., Fulton, 1956-59; chief social worker Mo. State Sch., 1959-60; psychiat. social worker State of Alaska, Anchorage, 1970-72; chief social worker Alaska Psychiat. Inst., Anchorage, 1972—; field instr. U. Wash.-Yeshiva U. Republican Committeewoman, Columbia, Mo., 1969; pres. Camp Fire Girls Council, 1969-70. Served to ensign USNR, 1953-54: Korea. Mem. Nat. Assn. Social Workers, Soc. Dirs. Hosp. Social Work, Acad. Cert. Social Workers, U.S. Ski Assn., Mo. Alumni Assn., Clin. Social Work Registry. Republican. Episcopalian. Clubs: Soroptimists, Women's of Am. Home: 1710 Eastridge Dr Anchorage AK 90501 Office: 2900 Providence Rd Anchorage AK 99504

DUKES, HARRIETTE WALKER, artist; b. Richmond, Va., Sept. 20, 1921; d. John Henley and Ida Virginia Walker; B.A., Longwood Coll., Farmville, Va., 1942; M.A., Columbia U., 1953; m. Reese Edwin Dukes, Apr. 4, 1953; 1 son, Thomas Edwin. Advt. dept. Thalhimers, Richmond, 1944-48; art tchr., Laurel (Del.) schs., 1948-52, Springfield (Ohio) Art Center, 1964-68, Oglebay Inst., Wheeling, W.Va., 1971—; works exhibited Steubenville (Ohio) Art Show (purchase award), 1974, Bethany Coll. show (fine arts award), 1976, Springfield Art Center, 1977, Mansion Gallery of Oglebay Inst., 1976; design com. needlepoint covers for dining room chairs Gov.'s Mansion, Charleston, W.Va., 1973; lectr. on Oriental painting and watercolor. Sec. Leaf Twig, 1977; executed mural of Wheeling hist. bldgs. for Ogden Newspapers, Inc., 1979; 12 commd. paintings for Reynolds Meml. Hosp., Glen Dale, W.Va., 1981; com. Oglebay Art Inst. Mem. Nat. League Am. Pen Women, DAR. Presbyterian. Clubs: Newcomers (pres. 1970-71), West Liberty Coll. Wives, Seedling Garden (pres. 1974-75). Home: 32 Park Rd Wheeling WV 26003

DULDULAO, FLORENCE MARGARET, hosp. personnel exec.; b. Nogales, Ariz., Dec. 27, 1923; d. Joseph Duffy and Casimira Erang (Portacio) Price; student Skyline Community Coll., 1975-77, La Verne Coll., 1977; B.S. magna cum laude in Bus. Adminstrn., U. San Francisco, 1978; m. Antonio C. Duldulao, June 16, 1942; children—Antonia Maria, Michael David. Riveter, China Aircraft subs. Douglas Aircraft Co., 1945; clk.-sec. Nat. ARC, 1946-61, 63-64; with Mt. Zion Hosp. and Med. Center, San Francisco, 1964—, asst. dir. personnel, 1972-74, acting dir. personnel, 1974-75, personnel dir., 1977—; mem. adv. group on careers and occupations in bus. and industry, disabled student services San Francisco State U.; mem. panel of oral examiners Met. Transp. Commn., 1977; mem. personnel com. San Francisco Filipino-Am. Council. Bd. dirs. ARC, 1980-81. Mem. Am. Soc. Personnel Adminstrn., Am. Soc. Personnel Adminstrs., Calif. Hosp. Personnel Mgmt. Assn. (state bd. 1978-79, pres.-elect 1979-80, pres. state bd. 1980-81, pres. Bay Area chpt. 1979-80), U. San Francisco Alumni Assn. Democrat. Roman Catholic. Club: Toastmasters Home: 999 Higate Dr Daly City CA 94015 Office: Mt Zion Hosp and Med Center 1600 Divisadero St San Francisco CA 94115

DULING, WENDY MCMILLAN, govt. ofcl.; b. N.Y.C., June 16, 1951; d. Bruce Thomas and Jean Converse (Duncan) McMillian; student Ithaca Coll., 1969-70, Wroxton (Eng.) Coll., 1971-72; B.S. in Psychology, St. Lawrence U., 1973; postgrad. George Washington U., 1974-75; m. Thomas Dean Duling, Aug. 31, 1974; children—Shannon McMillian, Jordan Winthrop. Research asst. Revenue Sharing, Washington, 1973-74; mgmt. analyst Office Comptroller of Currency, Washington, 1974-75, program analyst, 1978-80, dep. dir. mgmt. services, 1980—; mgmt. analyst Fed. Home Loan Bank Bd., Washington, 1975-78; sec. EEO Adv. Com. to Comptroller. Recipient Alpha award Fed. Home Loan Bank Bd., 1976, quality and spl. achievement awards Office Comptroller of Currency, Nat. Scholastic award for play Child's Play, 1968. Mem. Psi Chi. Republican. Home: 804 Westview Terr Alexandria VA 22301 Office: 490 L'Enfant Plaza East SW Washington DC 20219

DULZER, M. KENAN, coll. pres.; b. Cleve., Jan. 20, 1925; d. Edward Fred and Sophie (Grill) D.; B.S.E., St. John Coll., 1954; M.A. in Theology, U. Notre Dame, 1959; Ph.D., Kent State U., 1979. Joined Order of St. Ursula, 1944; tchr. Cleve. Parochial Schs., 1946-54; asst. novice dir. Ursuline Order, Cleve., 1954-59, novice dir., 1959-69; instr. speech, drama, English, theology Ursuline Coll., Pepper Pike, Ohio, 1956-59, prof., 1976, pres., 1969—. Recipient Internat. Women's Yr. award, 1975; Amadeus Rappe award Ursuline Alumnae Assn., 1981. Mem. Associated Colls. Cleve. (vice chmn. 1971, chmn. 1973, 1979-82), Ohio Found. Ind. Colls. (chmn. 1980-82), Cleve. Commn. Higher Edn., Orange Area Clergy Assn. (chmn. colls. and univs. div. United Way 1980), Ohio Coll. Assn., Am. Council Edn., Assn. Am. Colls., Nat. Assn. Ind. Colls. & Univs. Office: 2550 Lander Rd Pepper Pike OH 44124

DUMAIS, MONIQUE, theologian; b. Rimouski, Que., Can., Aug. 9, 1939; d. Francois and Doria (Tanguay) D.; Baccalauréat en philosophie U. Laval (Que.), 1968; baccalauréat en théologie, U. Que., Rimouski, 1970; Th.M., Harvard U., 1973; M.Phil., Union Theol. Sem., 1975, Ph.D. in Theology, 1977; Joined Ursulines, Roman Catholic Ch., 1961; prof. theology and ethics U. Que., Rimouski, 1970—, dir., Master in Ethics program, 1978-82; cons. to women's groups. Recipient cert. Le Salon de la Femme, Montreal, Que., 1980; Que. Govt. travel grantee, summer 1981; Social Scis. and Humanities Research Council Can. grantee, 1982-83. Mem. Association canadienne-francaise pour l'avancement des sciences, Société canadienne de theologie, Société canadienne pour l'etude de la religion, Association des théologiens pour l'Etude de la Morale, Am. Acad. Religion, Institut Canadien de recherche pour l'avancement de la Femme, Institut Simone de Beauvoir. Author: L'Eglise de Rimouski dans un contexte de dèveloppement règional (1963-1972), 1978; (with Elisabeth J. Lacelle) La femme et la religion au Canada francais, Un fait socio-culturel, 1979; Devenirs de femmes, 1981; research on women and religion. Office: 300 Ave des Ursulines Rimouski PQ G5L 3A1 Canada

DU MAS, DOROTHY JONES, banker; b. Richmond, Va., Mar. 1, 1922; d. Russell Edward and Etta May (Thompson) Jones; student U. Denver, U. Mont., N.Mex. State U.; m. Frank Maurice du Mas, Nov. 20, 1941; children—Donald Edward, Michael Earl, Mark Maurice, Douglas Frank, Dorothy Mae. Engaged in banking, 1952—; personnel dir. central info. file Ga. RR Bank, Augusta, 1966-69; officer, plan mgr. bank credit card dept. First Nat. Bank & Trust Co., Augusta, 1969-82; with Peachtree Bank and Trust Co., Atlanta, 1982—. Named Outstanding Lady Banker of Yr., Am. Inst. of Banking, 1971. Mem. Am. Inst. Banking (mem. faculty; speaking award 1970), Nat. Assn. Bank Women, Credit Women Internat. Baptist. Contbr. articles to profl. jours. Office: 5008 Buford Hwy Atlanta GA 30341

DUMAS, ELNORA JEANETTE, psychotherapist; b. Elmira, N.Y., Oct. 24, 1938; d. Henry and Ira Mae (Lewis) D.; B.S., Howard U., 1960, M.S.W., 1962; postgrad. New Sch. Social Research, 1979-80. Supr., Bronx (N.Y.) State Hosp., 1968-71; asst. dir., then dir. Project Teen Aid, Bklyn., 1967-68; supr. N.Y.C. Soc. Meth. Ch., Headstart Program/Foster Home Care Div., Bur. Child Welfare, 1964-67; cons. Pre-Kindergarten Headstart, N.Y.C., 1969-71, Maternal and Infant Care Family Planning Project, N.Y.C., 1963-64; caseworker Community Service Soc./Warwick State Tng. Sch., 1962-63; pvt. practice psychotherapy, Bklyn., 1971—; cons. Reed & DiSalvo Assos., N.Y.C., 1971; sec. Psychiat. Outpatient Clinics Am., 1971; asst. sec. Bklyn. Psychiat. Centers, 1974—; pres. Bushwick Mental Health Clinic, 1974—. Den mother Boy Scouts Am., Bklyn., 1975; vol. Internat. Center Fgn. Students and Businessmen, Bklyn., 1977, Vol. Literacy Program, 1980—; transp. hostess Nat. Dem. Conv., 1976. Cert. social worker, N.Y. State. Mem. Nat. Assn. Social Workers, Acad. Cert. Social Workers, Nat. Assn. Black Social Workers, Coalition of 100 Black Women, NAACP, Lambda Kappa Mu (Gamma chpt.). Democrat. Roman Catholic. Club: KC Aux. Home: 361 Clinton Ave Brooklyn NY 11238

DUNA, LOIS RUTH, music tchr., writer; b. Grand Forks, N.D., Mar. 12, 1947; d. Milton Theodore and Clara Olivia (Motland) Bratrud; student Concordia Coll., 1964-66; B.A., U. Minn., 1968; m. William Anthony Duna, Mar. 15, 1972; children—Cory, Geza Scott, Timothy, Christopher. Mem. Singing Sextette, Schiek's restaurant, Mpls., 1968; ednl. asst. Hartford Ins. Group, San Francisco, Oakland, Calif., 1968-69, bond underwriter, 1969-70, editor house organ, 1969-70; office mgr., bond agt. Brindemour-Wooldridge, San Francisco, 1970-71; pres., tchr. Duna Studios, Mpls., 1972—; author, contbg. composer music series and play-along tapes: (with Bill Duna) Let's Play—Right Away, Book 1, 1981, Book 2, 1982. Fund-raising chairperson Lake Harriet Open Sch., Mpls., 1980-82, facilitator whole brain learning project, 1981-82, music option tchr., 1980-82; teaching asst. Childbirth Edn. Assn., Mpls. Mem. Music Educators Nat. Conf., Nat. Assn. Jazz Educators, Minn. Music Educators Assn., Upper Midwest Group Keyboard Assn. Democrat. Lutheran. Office: PO Box 24051 Minneapolis MN 55424

DUNAWAY, FAYE, actress; b. Bascom, Fla., Jan. 14, 1941; student U. Fla., Boston U.; m. Peter Wolf, 1974 (div. 1979). An original mem. Lincoln Center Repertory Co.; appeared in Hogan's Goat, off-Broadway, Curse of an Aching Heart, Broadway, 1982; played Bonnie in motion picture Bonnie and Clyde, 1967; appeared in motion pictures The Happening, 1966, Hurry Sundown, 1966, Extraordinary Seaman, 1967, The Thomas Crown Affair, 1968, Sundown, The Extraordinary Seaman, A Place for Lovers, 1968 The Arrangement, 1969, Puzzle of a Downfall Child, 1970, Little Big Man, 1970, Doc, 1971, Oklahoma Crude, 1972, Three Musketeers, 1973, Four Musketeers, 1973, Towering Inferno, 1974, Chinatown, 1974, Three Days of the Condor, 1975, Network (Acad. award for best actress), 1976, The Voyage of the Dammed, 1976 Eyes of Laura Mars, 1978, The Champ, 1978, First Deadly Sin, 1980, Mommie Dearest, 1981; appeared on TV in After the Fall, Duchess of Windsor, Disappearance of Sister Aimee, Evita and the Country Girl. Recipient Most Promising Newcomer Award Brit. Film Acad., 1968. Address: care William Morris Agy Inc 151 El Camino Dr Beverly Hills CA 90212

DUNBAR, ISOBEL MOIRA, glaciologist; b. Edinburg, Scotland, Feb. 3, 1918; immigrated to Can. 1947, naturalized, 1957; d. William and Elizabeth Mary (Robertson) D.; B.A., Oxford U., 1939, M.S., 1948.

With div. earth sci. Can. Def. Research Bd., Ottawa, Ont., 1947-78, dir. earth scis. div., 1975-77, sr. scientist, 1977-78; mem. Canadian Environ. Adv. Council, 1972-78. Recipient Centennial award Can. Meteorol. Service, 1971; Massey medal Royal Canadian Geog. Soc., 1972. Decorated Order of Can., 1976. Fellow Royal Soc. Can., Arctic Inst. N.Am. (gov. 1966-69), Royal Can. Geog. Soc. (dir. 1974—); mem. Internat. Glaciological Soc. Contbr. articles to profl. jours.

DUNBAR, JACQUELINE MARUS, health psychologist, nurse; b. Detroit, Jan. 7, 1942; d. Donald and Margaret Jean (Henderson) Brashley; R.N., Presbyn. U. Hosp. Sch. Nursing, Pitts., 1962; B.S. in Nursing magna cum laude, Fla. State U., 1968; M.S., U. Calif., San Francisco, 1969; Ph.D., Stanford U., 1977. Staff nurse in adult acute treatment in-patient service Western Psychiat. Inst., Pitts., 1962-63; head nurse acute treatment for adolescents South Fla. State Hosp., Hollywood, 1963-66; staff nurse med.-surg., pediatric, emergency room and intensive care areas Tallahassee Meml. Hosp., 1966-67; lectr. continuing edn. in nursing U. Calif., San Francisco, summers 1968-72; lectr. dept. nursing grad. and undergrad. programs San Jose State U., 1970-72, part-time, 1973-75; asst. prof. dept. family practice U. Iowa Coll. Medicine, Iowa City, 1977-79; dep. dir. Lipid Research Clinics Recruitment and Adherence Cons., Lab. for Study of Behavioral Medicine dept. psychiatry and behavioral scis. Stanford (Calif) U., 1979—; research asst. Lab. for Study Behavioral Medicine, Sch. Medicine, Stanford U., 1974-75, coordinator, 1975-77; mem. working group Nat. Heart, Lung and Blood Inst., 1979—, working group on critical patient behavior in dietary mgmt. hypertension, 1979—; mem. policy bd. Primary Prevention in Hypertension Trial, 1982—; mem. Nat. High Blood Pressure Conf. Planning Com., 1980. Mem. Am. Heart Assn., Am. Psychol. Assn., Assn. for Advancement of Behavior Therapy, Soc. Behavior Medicine (membership com. 1979, publ. com. 1979, com. on profl. liaison and public edn. 1979, bd. mem.-at-large 1981—, editor Behavioral Medicine Updates 1982—, area editor Behavioral Medicine Abstracts 1980—), Phi Kappa Phi, Sigma Theta Tau (v.p. Alpha Eta chpt. 1970-71). Contbr. numerous articles to profl. jours. Home: 6019 Amador Pl Newark CA 94560 Office: Behavioral Medicine Lab Dept Psychiatry Stanford U Sch Medicine Stanford CA 94305

DUNBAR, NANCY LEE, govt. ofcl.; b. Geneva, Ill., Aug. 29, 1931; d. Douglas D. and Grace K. (Grant) Hammond; student UCLA, 1975; children—Robert Alan Burns, David Wayne Burns. Adminstrv. dir. Swiftbird Tng. Center, Gettysburg, S.D., 1969-71; secretarial positions U.S. Navy, Port Hueneme, Calif., 1970-74, adminstrv. asst., 1974-75, fed. women's program mgr. Naval Ship Weapon Systems Engring. Sta., 1975-80, EEO specialist, 1975-80, mgr. handicapped or upward mobility program, 1979-80, personnel specialist, 1980—; adv. to various community groups, 1960—. Vice pres. YWCA, 1978-80; sec. Braille Transcribers, 1966—; pres. Rio Plaza PTA, 1962-64; mem. adv. com. Rio Plaza Sch. Bd., Calif., 1962-64. Mem. Federally Employed Women (pres. Ventura County 1977-79, sec. 1974-77). Home: 1286 Cachuma Ave Ventura CA 93004 Office: Code 006C Naval Ship Weapon Systems Engring Station Port Hueneme CA 93043

DUNCAN, BEVERLY, sociologist educator; b. Pa., Apr. 17, 1929; Ph.D., U. Chgo., 1957; m. Otis Dudley Duncan. Research asst. Population Research and Tng. Center, U. Chgo., 1951-57, research asso., 1957-62; research asso. Population Studies Center, U. Mich., Ann Arbor, 1962-73, prof. sociology, 1972-73; prof. sociology U. Ariz., Tucson, 1973—. Co-author: The Negro Population of Chicago, 1957; Metropolis and Region, 1960; Housing a Metropolis—Chicago, 1960; Statistical Geography: Problems in Analyzing Areal Data, 1961; Metropolis and Region in Transition, 1970; Socioeconomic Background and Achievement, 1972; Social Change in an Metropolitan Community, 1973; Sex Typing and Social Roles: A Research Report, 1978. Office: Dept Sociology Univ Ariz Tucson AZ 85721

DUNCAN, CYNTHIA BERYL, univ. library adminstr.; b. Madison, Pa., Apr. 26, 1932; d. Andrew and Harriet (Morris) D.; B.S., California (Pa.) State Coll., 1953; M.Litt., U. Pitts., 1958; M.S., Fla. State U., 1965; Ph.D. (fellow), Ind. U., 1973. Tchr., Gateway Union Sch., Monroeville, Pa., 1953-64; instr. Fla. State U., 1965, spl. librarian, 1966, acting librarian, 1967; asso. prof. library sci. Mansfield (Pa.) State Coll., 1966-67; asso. prof. library sci. Winthrop Coll., Rock Hill, S.C., 1967-70; adj. prof. library sci. Ind. State U., 1972; prof. library sci., dir. Sandel Library Northeast La. U., 1973-76; dean library services Old Dominion U., Norfolk, Va., 1976—; adj. lectr. library sci. Catholic U. Am., 1979-80. Mem. ALA, La., S.C., Va. library assns., Assn. Am. Library Schs., Med. Library Assn. Office: University Library Old Dominion University Norfolk VA 23508

DUNCAN, FRANCES MURPHY, educator; b. Utica, N.Y., June 23, 1920; d. Edward Simon and Elizabeth Myers (Stack) Murphy; B.A., Barnard Coll., Columbia U., 1942; M.Ed., Auburn U., 1963, Ed.D., 1969; m. Lee C. Duncan, June 23, 1947 (div. June 1969); children—Lee C., Edward M., Paul H., Elizabeth B., Nancy R., Richard L. Head sci. dept. Arnold Jr. High Sch., Columbus, Ga., 1960-63; tchr. physiology, Spanish, Jordan High Sch., Columbus, 1963-64; tchr. spl. edn. mentally retarded Muscogee County Sch. System, Columbus, 1964-65; instr. spl. edn. Auburn (Ala.) U., 1966-69; asso. dir. Douglas Sch. for Learning Disabilities, Columbus, 1969-70; prof. edn. and spl. edn. Columbus Coll., 1970—. Sec. exec. bd. Muscular Dystrophy Assn., 1968-70; 73-74; mem. Gov.'s Commn. on Disabled Georgians; trustee Listening Eyes Sch. for Deaf; chmn. adv. bd. Columbus Health Dept. Tng. Centers; chmn. Consumer Adv. Bd. Vocat. Rehab.; mem. adv. bd. dept. spl. edn. Muscogee County Sch. System; mem. team for evaluation and placement of exceptional children Columbus Public Schs. Fellow Am. Assn. Mental Deficiency; mem. AAUP, AAUW (pres. 1973-75, div. rec. sec. 1975—), Council Exceptional Children (legis. chmn. 1973-74), Kappa Delta Pi, Psi Chi, Delta Kappa Gamma, Phi Delta Kappa. Roman Catholic. Home: 1811 Alta Vista Dr Columbus GA 31907

DUNCAN, JOAN HEATHER, drug co. exec., govt. ofcl.; b. Wakan, Sask., Can., Oct. 30, 1941; d. John W. and Edna V. (Blakley) Tratch; m. D. John Duncan, Oct. 10, 1964; children—William, Heather, Richard, Michael. Ptnr., Duncan Drugs; dir. Maple Creek Holdings Ltd.; mem. Sask. Legislature 1978—, now cabinet minister. Progressive Conservative. Office: 43 Legislative Bldg Regina SK S4S 0B3 Canada

DUNCAN, JOANNE KIRK, lawyer, banker; b. Huntington, W.Va., Jan. 3, 1950; d. Charles Edwin and Peggy (Ward) Kirk; B.A., Centre Coll. Ky., 1971; J.D., U. Ky., 1974; m. Robert Michael Duncan, June 3, 1972; 1 son, Robert Michael. With Inez Deposit Bank (Ky.), 1974—, v.p., cashier, 1977-81, exec. v.p., 1981—, also dir.; admitted to Ky. bar, 1974. Treas., Martin County Devel. Assn., Martin County Heart Fund, Inez Vol. Fire Dept., ARC Martin County. Recipient U.S. Law Weekly award, 1974; U. Ky. fellow, 1976. Mem. Am. Bar Assn., Ky. Bar Assn., Martin County Bar Assn., Centre Coll. Alumni Assn. (sec.), Isaac Shelby Soc., U. Ky. Alumni Assn. (dir. Big Sandy chpt.), Delta Theta Phi. Republican. Methodist. Home: PO Box 331 Inez KY 41224 Office: PO Box 365 Inez KY 41224

DUNCAN, KIT, social worker; b. Anderson, Ind., Jan. 1, 1956; s. Leo and Theda (Robinson) Craig; A.A., Freed-Hardeman Coll., 1975; B.A., Lubbock Christian Coll., 1978; postgrad. U. Tex., 1980-82. Caseworker Smithlawn Maternity Home, Lubbock, Tex., 1978-79; campus caseworker Christ's Haven for Children, Keller, Tex., 1979-82; VA, Temple, Tex., 1982—. Recipient Psychology/Sociology award, Lubbock Christian Coll., 1978-79. Mem. Nat. Assn. Social Workers. Mem. Ch. of Christ.

DUNCAN, MARGARET DUNSMORE (MRS. WILLIAM FOWLER DUNCAN), civic worker; b. Summit, N.J., Sept. 9, 1920; d. James and Margaret (Montgomery) Dunsmore; student Fresno State Coll., 1941; m. William Fowler Duncan, June 17, 1940; children—William Fowler, Laird Douglas, Fraser Scott. Gray lady A.R.C., Oahu, 1959—, chmn. vols. Langley AFB; active Heart Fund Dr., Neuromuscular Disease Dr.; mem. Los Ninos Guild, Childrens Hosp. Orange County. Mem. Fairfax Hosp. Aux., Clans of Scotland, U.S.A., Scribe, Internat. Platform Assn., Order of Diana, League Women Voters, Beta Sigma Phi (past chpt. pres.). Republican. Presbyterian. (chmn. missionary edn. women's assn., mariner, fellowship chmn. 1973, 74, deacon 1974-76). Clubs: Ikebana, Air Force Officers Wives (Washington); Neighborhood Garden; Wheeler AFB Officers Woman's (1st v.p. 1960) (Oahu, Hawaii); Langley Officers Wives, Langley Yacht, Langley Golf; San Clemente Women's; Am. Wives, Am. Officers' Wives, NATO Wives. Home: 502 Calle DeSoto San Clemente CA 92672

DUNCAN, MURIEL JEAN, corrections ofcl.; b. Evanston, Ill., Aug. 10, 1927; d. Thomas and Muriel Edena (Vaultz) Spence; student Wilberforce U., 1946-48; B.S., U. Phoenix, 1979, B.A., 1979; M.A., No. Ariz. U., 1981; m. Fred Emanuel Duncan, Apr. 10, 1960; children—Karen Jean, Doyle Ricardo, Lynn Louise. Legal sec. State Calif., Los Angeles, 1964-66, State Calif., Los Angeles Attys. Gen's Office, 1966-67; ct. reporter State Calif., Workman's Compensation Fund, 1967-71; correctional service officer State Ariz. Dept. Corrections, Phoenix, 1972-74, correctional program officer, 1974-77, delinquency prevention specialist, 1977-80, prevention unit dir. crime and delinquency prevention, 1980—; instr. techniques parenting classes throughout Ariz., 1977-80; dir. Ariz. Black Youth Recognition Confs., 1980—. Chmn Univ. Ariz. Cooperative Extension Service Parenting Adv. Bd., 1979-80; mem. Govs. Task Force Family and Marriage, 1978; mem. Urban Indian Adv. Bd., 1980—; active Arizonans for Prevention, 1980—; originator, creator, designer United Parents and Youth League, Inc., 1979—. Recipient Achievement award Nat. Assn. Counties, 1981. Mem. Nat. Assn. Blacks in Criminal Justice, City Phoenix Community Services Commn. (vice chmn.), Mesa-Tempe Mezona Bd. Found. (v.p.), Justice for Children Coalition, Am. Correctional Assn. Office: 821 W Indian School Rd Phoenix AZ 85013

DUNCAN, RUTH, artist; b. Greeley, Colo., Feb. 19, 1908; d. Edwin and Dukie (Rugh) Starkey; A.A., Stephens Coll., Mo.; B.F.A., U. Okla., Norman, 1930; studied with Harold A. Roney, Warren Hunter, Simon Michael; m. Robert Duncan, Sept. 20, 1933; children—Dean, William (dec.). Painter in oils and watercolor, also lectr. oil painting and design; over 50 one-woman exhbns. including: San Antonio Public Library, St. Mary's U., San Antonio, Stephens College, Columbia, Mo., Midland (Tex.) Coll., Bee County Coll., Beeville, Tex., San Antonio Westfall Library, McDowell Club Allied Arts, Oklahoma City, Nita S. Haley Meml. Library, Midland, Tex.; group exhbns. include: Smithsonian Instn., Washington, Coppini Acad. Fine Arts Gallery, San Antonio, Witte Meml. Mus., San Antonio, U. Tex., Austin, Panhandle Plains Hist. Mus., Canyon, Tex.; represented in permanent collections: Royal Bldg., Dallas, Nita Haley Library, Bexar County Ct. House, San Antonio, San Antonio Coll. Library, Stephens Coll.; lectr., demonstrator oil painting. Bd. dirs. Coppini Acad. Fine Arts, 1959-65, 76-77. Soprano soloist, dir. ch. choirs. Recipient Coppini award, 1971; Wonderland Gallery award realistic painting; medal of honor Coppini Acad. Fine Arts, 1979. Fellow Am. Artists Profl. League; mem. PEO (past chpt. pres.), Soc. Western Artists, River Art Group, Delta Gamma (past rec. sec.; Order Rose award 1973). Address: 1511 Fulton Ave San Antonio TX 78201

DUNCAN, VIRGINIA BAUER, television producer, dir., power corp. exec.; b. Lansing, Mich., June 9, 1929; d. Theodore Irving and Maurine Virginia (Foote) Bauer; B.A., U. Mich., 1951; m. Bruce G. Duncan, Oct. 27, 1956; children—John C., Michael G., Timothy B. Producer, dir. KQED-TV, San Francisco, 1960-75; pres. Candide Prodns., Inc., San Francisco, 1966—; corp. exec. Bechtel Power Corp.; dir. Corp. for Public Broadcasting, Washington, 1975-79, First Interstate Bank, 1979—. Bd. dirs. Town Sch. for Boys, San Francisco, 1966-70; pres., Parents Assn. Marin Parents Assn. Marin County Day Sch., Corte Madera, Calif., 1971-72; mem. public media panel Nat. Endowment for Arts, Washington, 1973-79; chmn. bd. dirs. Yosemite Inst., 1974—; trustee Katharine Branson/Mt. Tamalpais High Sch., Ross, Calif., 1975—; asso. council Mills Coll., Oakland, Calif., 1975—; mem. Carnegie Commn. on Future of Public Broadcasting, 1977-79; mem. Council for Arts, M.I.T., 1977-80; bd. dirs. James Irvine Found., 1979—. Recipient Edward W McQuade award for disting. programming in field of social justice, 1964; NET award for excellence for individual contbn. to outstanding television programming, 1966; Readers Digest Found. award, 1969; CINE Golden Eagle award, 1970; Emmy award Nat. Acad., TV Arts and Scis., 1971. Office: Box 18222 San Francisco CA 94118

DUNEGAN, LOIS JEAN, surgeon; b. Pitts., June 2, 1944; d. Leonard Paul and Martha Elenor (Roberts) Dunegan; B.S. with distinction, Pa. State U. 1966; M.D., U. Pitts., 1970. Intern in surgery Presbyterian U. Hosp., U. Pitts., 1970-71, resident in surgery, 1971-73, resident and sr. resident in surgery, 1974-76; research fellow Harvard Med. Sch., Peter Bent Brigham Hosp., Boston, 1973-74; asst. prof. gen. and vascular surgery Mich. State U., East Lansing 1976—, instr. surgery, 1976—, dir. surg. resident tng., 1977—; researcher quantitative measurements of extravascular lung water; cons. in field of shock. Recipient award DAR, 1962, scientific forum award Student AMA, U. Tex., 1969, residents' day award SW Pa. chpt. A.C.S., 1974, Charles C. Moore Surg. Teaching award, 1975, resident research award Pitts. Acad. Medicine, 1975; Harvard Med. Sch. fellow in surgery, 1973-74; Mich. State U. grantee, 1977—; Mich. Heart Assn. research grantee, 1977—. Mem. AMA, Pa. State U., Harvard Med. alumni assns., Iota Sigma Pi, Alpha Epsilon Delta. Roman Catholic. Contbr. numerous articles to profl. jours. Home: 692 Moorland Dr East Lansing MI 48823 Office: Dept Surgery B-437 Clin Center Mich State U East Lansing MI 48824

DUNEIER, DEBRA HOPE, gemologist; b. N.Y.C., Aug. 30, 1954; d. Jacob and Anita Arkow; student Queens Coll., 1976; grad. Gemological Inst. Am., 1980; m. Dana Brad Duneier, Sept. 2, 1971. With Clyde Duneier Inc., N.Y.C., 1975—, v.p. loose stone div., 1980—; lectr., seminar leader in field. Mem. Am. Gem Soc., So. Jewelers Travelers Assn., Retail Jewelers Am. Address: 1212 Ave Americas New York NY 10036

DUNGAN, MARY, banker; b. Phila., June 2, 1949; d. W. R. J. and Elizabeth (West) D.; B.A., U. Pa., 1975, M.B.A., 1977; 1 son by former marriage, Peter. Teaching fellow Wharton Grad. Div., U. Pa., Phila., 1976-77; investment banker Paine Webber Jackson & Curtis, N.Y.C., 1977-79; banker Crocker Nat. Bank, San Francisco, from 1979; now internat. banker Bankers Trust Co., N.Y.C.; mgmt. cons. Mem. Religious Soc. Friends. Home: 173 E 74th St Apt 1-C New York NY 10021

DUNHAM, ANEVA JO, educator; b. Portsmouth, Va., Mar. 20, 1938; d. Joseph William and Rachel Lorraine (Kight) D.; B.S. in Edn. cum laude, S.E. Mo. State Coll., 1960; M.Ed. in Elem. Edn., St. Louis U., 1972; postgrad. in mgmt. Webster Coll., 1981—. Tchr., Ritenour Consol. Sch. Dist., St. Louis, 1960—; Tri-Hi-Y coordinator YMCA, Overland, Mo., 1963-68; mem. nominating com. Ednl. Employees Credit Union, 1976-77, bldg. rep., 1975—. Mem. NEA, Kappa Delta Pi, Phi Alpha Theta. Democrat. Presbyterian. Home: 16 Coach Ct Saint Peters MO 63376 Office: 4301 Edmundson Rd Saint Louis MO 63134

DUNHAM, FADRA JOSEPHINE, civic worker; b. Lebanon, Mo., July 11, 1922; d. George Washington and Cora Anne (Chambers) Roberts; student Central Bus. Coll., Kansas City, 1941, Kansas City Jr. Coll., 1944; m. Robert Victor Dunham, Nov. 10, 1950. Sec., U.S. Treasury Dept., Kansas City, Mo., 1942-53; legal sec. Hoskins, King, McGannon, Hahn & Hurwitz, law firm, Kansas City, Mo., 1953-73. Sec., treas. Cowgill Community Housing Corp., 1978—, Cowgill Booster Club, 1970-74, 77—; mem. Antioch Community Ch., Kansas City, Mo. Club: Order Eastern Star. Collector, owner extensive prehistoric Hopewell Indian figurine sculptures. Home: Route 1 Cowgill MO 64637

DUNHAM, MENEVE, coll. pres.; b. Dubuque, Iowa, Dec. 28, 1930; d. Walter Edgar and Kathryn Mae (Babcock) D.; B.A., Clarke Coll., 1955; Mus.M., DePaul U., 1963; Ph.D., U. Mich., 1969. Mem. faculty Clarke Coll., Dubuque, 1962-71, asst. to pres., 1972-73, pres., 1977—; Am. Council Edn. fellow Claremont (Calif.) Colls., 1971-72, asst. dean Newcomb Coll., Tulane U., New Orleans, 1973-76, acting assoc. dean, 1976-77. Nat. Endowment for Humanities grantee, summer 1970. Mem. Am. Musicol. Soc., NOW, AAUW, Phi Delta Kappa. Editor: Vivaldi Cantatas, 2 vols., 1979. Office: Clarke Coll Dubuque IA 52001 *

DUNIHUE, ANNE WUNDUKE, city ofcl., steel co. ofcl.; b. Slovan, Pa., Sept. 22, 1924; d. George and Katherine (Yanchiak) Wunduke; Asso. Sci., Chaffey Coll., 1978; B.S., U. Redlands, 1979; m. George Van Sotraidis, Oct. 9, 1942; children—George Thomas, Steven Barry; m. 2d, Donald Wallace Dunihue, Nov. 5, 1952; 1 son, David Brian. With Kaiser Steel Corp., Fontana, Calif., 1951—, acctg. clk., 1968—; city councilwoman Fontana, 1976—, mayor pro-tem, 1977-79; chmn. bd. dirs. Omnitrans, 1979-80; chmn. Fontana Redevel. Agy., 1979-80; bd. dirs. San Bernardino County Transp. Commn., 1977—, East Valley Transit Service Authority, 1976—, Steelworkers Oldtimers Found., 1965—, YWCA, 1977—, United Way, 1979—; mem. Fontana adv. council Chaffey Coll., 1979—. Mem. Calif. Elected Women's Assn. for Edn. and Research, AAUW, United Steelworkers Am., Fontana C. of C., San Bernardino Asso. Govts. (dir.), So. Calif. Assn. Govts. (energy and environment com. 1977-80). Democrat. Baptist. Clubs: Fontana Bus. and Profl. and Women's (Woman of Yr. 1965, Woman of Achievement 1978), Zonta. Home: 9395 Mango Ave Fontana CA 92335 Office: PO Box 217 Fontana CA 92335

DUNKLE, MARIE KLEIN, assn. exec.; b. Pitts., May 17, 1952; d. Victor George and Gertrude Jane (Baldwin) K.; B.A., Pa. State U., 1973; m. Thomas A. Dunkle, Aug. 31, 1973. News writer, announcer WDFM Radio, State College, Pa., 1973-74; pub. affairs asst. C. of C. U.S., Washington, 1975-76; women's program coordinator Atomic Indsl. Forum, Washington, 1976-79, nuclear info. services mgr., 1979-80; mgr. industry relations Inst. Nuclear Power Ops., Atlanta, 1980—; lectr. in field. Mem. Nuclear Energy Women, Women in Communications, Am. Nuclear Soc., Nat. Assn. for Female Execs., Public Utilities Communicators Assn., Cobb County Symphony Orch. Producer, author: Women and Energy: The Vital Link, 1979 (slide-tape show), 1979. Office: 1820 Water Pl Atlanta GA 30339

DUNLAP, MARY KATHERINE, editor, communications firm exec.; b. Denver, Sept. 7, 1944; d. Robert Addison and Mary M. (MacDonald) D.; B.S., U. Kans., 1966; m. Lawrence Bronstein, June 29, 1970 (div. Feb. 1974); m. 2d, Donald L. Stein, Aug. 19, 1982. Sr. editor Am. Family Physician mag., Kansas City, Mo., 1968-78; editor-in-chief Current Prescribing mag., Oradell, N.J., 1978-79; sr. editor Diagnosis mag., Oradell, 1979—; mng. editor Advances in Reproductive Medicine, Oradell, 1982—; editor Lynch Digest, Manchester, Conn., 1982—; pres. MD Communications, Vernon, Conn., 1982—; partner The Editing Bur., 1968-71. Nat. bd. dirs. Hospitalized Vets. Writing Project. Mem. Women in Communications, Inc. (pres. Greater Kansas City chpt. 1977-1978), Am. Med Writers Assn. Democrat. Lutheran. Poetry editor Vets. Voices mag., 1976-78; editor: Quality Control in Nuclear Medicine (Buck A. Rhodes), 1977. Home: 590 Centre St Apt 3 Oradell NJ 07649 Office: 680 Kinderkamack Rd Oradell NJ 07649

DUNLEAVY, JANET FRANK EGLESON, educator, writer; b. N.Y.C., Dec. 16, 1928; d. Christian Joseph and Evelyn Vivienne (Aaron) Frank; B.A., Hunter Coll., 1951; M.A., N.Y. U., 1962, Ph.D., 1966; m. James D. Egleson (div. 1962); m. 2d, Gareth W. Dunleavy, July 25, 1971; children—Karen, Gweneth, Stephen. Editor, writer, 1951-64; lectr. Hunter Coll., 1964-66; asst. prof. SUNY, Stony Brook, 1966-70, master Benedict Coll., 1969-70; asst. prof. U. Wis., Milw., 1970-71, asso. prof., 1971-76, prof. English, 1976—; vis. prof. U. Ill., 1978. Named to Hunter Coll. Hall of Fame, 1978; Am. Council Learned Socs. grantee, 1971, Am.-Irish Found. grantee, 1973-74; Am. Philos. Soc. grantee, 1980. Mem. MLA, Am. Com. Irish Studies (editor Newsletter 1971-78), Internat. Assn. Study Anglo-Irish Lit., N.E. MLA, Midwest MLA, Wis. Acad. Scis., Arts and Letters (v.p. 1977). Club: N.Y. Univ. Author: Daddies, 1953; Davy Crockett and the Indians, 1956; Happy Days, 1956; (with James D. Egleson) Parents Without Partners, 1960; Design for Writing, 1971; George Moore: The Artist's Vision, The Storyteller's Art, 1973; (with Gareth W. Dunleavy) The O'Conor Papers, 1977; editor: George Moore in Perspective: Essays on the 50th Anniversary of his Death, 1983. Office: English Dept U Wis Milwaukee WI 53201

DUNMORE, CHARLOTTE JEANETTE, educator; b. Phila., Nov. 16, 1926; d. Charles and Georgia (White) D.; B.S., U. Pa., 1949; M.S.W., Columbia U., 1954; Ph.D., Brandeis U., 1968. Social worker Ch. Home Soc., Boston, 1954-57; supr. foster care and adoption Boston Children's Aide Soc., 1957-62; research worker Episcopal Community Services, Phila., 1962-64; asso. prof. Simmons Coll. Sch. Social Work, Boston, 1967-76; prof. Sch. Social Work, U. Pitts., 1976—; cons. Atlanta U. Sch. Social Work, 1973-75, Boston Model Cities Program, 1970; vis. research scholar UCLA, 1975, Radcliffe Coll., 1972. NIMH fellow, 1964, Research Scientist award, 1971-76; recipient Cabot award, 1969. Mem. Council Social Work Edn. (accreditation commn.), Nat. Assn. Social Workers, Nat. Assn. Cert. Social Workers, Nat. Assn. Black Social Workers, AAUP. Author bibliographies: Black Americans, 1970; Black Children and Their Families, 1975. Office: 2317CL U Pitts Pittsburgh PA 15260

DUNN, ARLENE DAUGHERTY, chem. distbr.; b. McKeesport, Pa., Aug. 20, 1934; d. Hugh F. and Grace E. (Klotz) Daugherty; student Douglass Bus. Coll., McKeesport, 1953-54, spl. courses Pa. State U., 1977-78, McCarthy Inst. Profl. Sales Mgmt., 1977, Dale Carnegie, 1980; m. Dwight A. Dunn, May 27, 1955; children—Diane, Rand, Todd. Bookkeeper, J.P. Mooney Co., 1952-54; office mgr. chem. lab. Opalco Lab., 1954-58; office mgr. P.B. & S. Chem. Co., McKeesport, 1970-73, asst. br. mgr., 1973-74, br. mgr., 1974-75, dist. mgr. W.Va., Pa. and Ohio, 1975—; arrangements chmn. Pitts. Chem. Day, 1981, gen. chmn., 1983. Named Mgr. of Yr., P.B. & S. Chem. Co., 1981; Mem. Nat. Assn. Chem. Distbrs., Am. Water Works Assn., Water Pollution Control Assn., Wastewater Operators Assn., Cleve. Chem. assn., Pitts. Chem. Sales Assn. (v.p.), Mon Yough C. of C., Mon Yough Mgrs. Club, Am. Soc. Profl. and Exec. Women. Republican. Methodist. Home: 1157 Center Extension White Oak PA 15131 Office: 4200 Walnut St McKeesport PA 15134

DUNN, CATHERINE LYNN, child psychiatrist; b. Kearny, N.J., Sept. 30, 1950; d. Thomas James and Mary Ann (Cotter) D.; B.S. in Chemistry, St. Peter's Coll., Jersey City, 1972; M.D., N.Y. Med. Coll., 1975; m. Thaddeus Paprocki, June 6, 1975. Intern in pediatrics Lenox Hill Hosp., N.Y.C., 1975-76; resident in psychiatry U. Wash., Seattle, 1976-78, fellow in child psychiatry, 1978-80, mem. clin. faculty, psychiatry, 1980—; practice medicine specializing in child psychiatry, Seattle, 1980-81, Anchorage, Alaska, 1981—; cons. Ketchikan Mental Health Center, Asian Counseling and Referral Service, Anchorage Mental Health Center, McLaughlin Youth Center. Mem. Am. Psychiat. Assn., Am. Med. Women's Assn., Alpha Omega Alpha, Audubon Soc. Club: Sierra. Home: Spruce Ln Eagle River AK 99577 Office: 101 E 9th Ave Anchorage AK 99501

DUNN, CHARLETA JESSIE, psychologist; b. Clarendon, Tex., Jan. 18, 1927; d. James Arthur and Ruby Roberta (Burcham) Sisk; B.S., West Tex. U., Canyon, 1951; M.S., 1954; Ed.D., U. Houston, 1966; postgrad. U. Tex., Galveston, 1970; m. Roy E. Dunn, Sept. 13, 1947; children—Thomas Arthur, Roy E. III, Sharleta Elaine. Tchr., Amarillo (Tex.) Pub. Schs., 1951-62; asst. prof. U. Houston, 1964-70; pediatric psychologist U. Tex., Galveston, 1970-71; dir. appraisal Goose Creek Ind. Sch. Dist., Baytown, Tex., 1971-74; prof. psychology Tex. Woman's U., Houston, 1974—; cons. Baytown Pub. Schs., Vidor Pub. Schs.; mental health speaker to clubs and orgns.; research dir. Hogg Found. Mental Health, 1966-70, Gusreda, 1965-66, Gusreda Research grantee Alpha Chi, 1950-51; Hogg Found. grantee, 1966-70; Region Ednl. Service Center research grantee, 1978. Mem. Am. Psychol. Assn., Tex. Psychol. Assn., Southwestern Psychol. Assn., Houston Profl. Hypnotists Assn. Presbyterian. Author: World of Work, 1971; Songs of Sharleta, 1966; contbr. articles to profl. jours. Office: Room 719 MGJ Bldg Texas Womans University 1130 M D Anderson Blvd Houston TX 77030

DUNN, CHERYLL ANN, psychologist, univ. adminstr.; b. Cin., Apr. 22, 1945; d. Charles Gilbert and Precious Vanessa (Riley) D.; A.A.S., Ohio Coll. Applied Sci., 1966; B.S., U. Cin., 1968, M.Ed., 1969, Ed.D., 1977. Lab. technician Taft Sanitation & Engring. Center, Cin., 1966-67, Jewish Hosp., Cin., 1967-70; summer and tutorial tchr. Cin. Bd. Edn., 1966-68; resident advisor U. Cin., 1969-70, head counselor, asst. to dean of students, 1970-74, teaching asst., 1974-77; counselor Lighthouse Runaway Shelter, Cin., 1977-78, Cin. Inst. Justice, 1978; coordinator student life and counseling U. Cin., 1978-80, asst. dean, dir. prep. engring. tech., field service asst. prof. devel. edn. Coll. Applied Sci., 1980—; workshop leader. Disability allocation com. Community Chest; chief liaison Cerebral Palsy Service Center, 1981; bd. dirs. YWCA, sec., 1982; vol. United Appeal Campaign, 1981, New Life for Girls, 1978-79, Meals on Wheels, 1974-77, childhood immunization program, 1978, Rollmans Psychiat. Inst., 1966-68. Recipient Laura Lovelace award Alpha Kappa Alpha, 1968, recognition of service plaque Soc. Women Engrs., 1981. Mem. Am. Psychol. Assn., Assn. Women Adminstrs. (dir.; asst. editor Grapevine 1981-82); Nat. Assn. Student Personnel Adminstrs., Nat. Soc. Black Engrs. (cert. of appreciation 1979, 81), Kappa Delta Pi, Tau Alpha Pi, Alpha Kappa Alpha. Roman Catholic. Home: 6172 Joyce Ln Cincinnati OH 45237 Office: College of Applied Science 100 E Central Pkwy Cincinnati OH 45210

DUNN, DIANA RAE, educator, univ. dean; b. Dayton, Ohio, May 27, 1937; d. Joseph L. and Beatrice (Nason) D.; B.S., U. Dayton, 1959, M.S., 1963; Ph.D., Pa. State U., 1970. Supr. recreation City of Dayton, 1957-63, City of Anaheim (Calif.), 1963-66; dir. research Nat. Recreation and Park Assn., Washington, 1969-72; prof. dept. recreation and leisure studies Temple U., 1972-77; prof. phys. edn. U. Ariz., Tucson, 1977-82, coordinator recreation program, 1977-78, head dept. phys. edn., 1978-82; dean Coll. Health, Phys. Edn. and Recreation, Pa. State U., University Park, 1982—; cons. U.S. Dept. Interior. Office Edn., HEW. Bur. of Research trainee, 1966-69. Mem. AAHPERD, World Leisure and Recreation Assn., Nat. Recreation and Park Assn., Am. Acad. Parks and Recreation Adminstrs., Acad. Leisure Scis., Internat. Sociol. Assn. Office: Coll Health Physical Education and Recreation Pa State U Recreation Bldg Rm 276 University Park PA 16802

DUNN, ELIZABETH YATES, ins. broker; b. Albuquerque, Apr. 4, 1925; d. Owen Thomas and Bertha Eunice (Centers) Yates; student Western Ky. U., 1942-44, 67-68; secretarial diploma Bowling Green Bus. U., 1945; m. Floyd Dunn, Jan. 17, 1947; children—Gregory Yates, Jeffrey Spencer. Spl. agts. asst. Hartford Ins. Group, Bowling Green, 1959-76; agt. Chester M. Mock Agy., Bowling Green, 1976-77; broker Charles M. Moore Ins. Agy., Bowling Green, 1977—; dist. rep. Modern Woodmen Am. Mem. Bowling Green C. of C., Nat. Assn. Ins. Women, So. Ky. Ins. Women Assn., Nat. Life Underwriters Assn., So. Ky. Assn. Life Underwriters, Beta Sigma Phi. Democrat. Baptist. Club: Bowling Green Women's. Address: 1610 Glendale Ave Bowling Green KY 42101

DUNN, ELLEN CATHERINE, educator; b. Balt., July 30, 1916; d. William M. and Mary (Kailer) Dunn; A.B., Coll. Notre Dame of Md., 1938; M.A., Cath. U. Am., Washington, 1940, Ph.D., 1947. Lectr., Chevy Chase Jr. Coll., Washington, 1940-42; instr. Cath. U. Am., 1947-52, asst. prof., 1952-57, asso. prof., 1957-62, prof., 1963-81, prof. emeritus, Sr. lectr., 1982—, chmn. English dept., 1969-78. Mem. Modern Lang. Assn., South Atlantic Assn. Depts. English (pres. 1972-73). Contbr. articles profl. jours. Home: 8419D Loch Raven Blvd Baltimore MD 21204 Office: Dept English Cath U Am Washington DC 20064

DUNN, ERAINA BURKE, sch. ofcl.; b. Chgo., Oct. 4, 1945; d. Marion H. and Lolita D. (Ward) Burke; B.A., Wilberforce U., 1968; m. James Dunn, July 23, 1981; children—Kyle T., Jamison L. Programmer, analyst Blue Cross/Blue Shield, Chgo., 1968-74, membership cons. Blue Cross Assn., 1975; personnel, benefits specialist Kimberly-Clark Corp., Atlanta, 1976-78; community coordinator Sch. Dist. 147, Harvey, Ill., 1980—. Active community-based edn., tng. workshops, voter registration, mgmt. tng., 1971—; coordinator Tchr. Corps. Project, Community Council, 1980—; vol. After sch. Tutorial Program, 1981—, United Family Found., 1981—. Recipient Outstanding Vol. Service award B.U.I.L.D., 1971, Outstanding Community Service award Dist. 147, 1981, Vol. After sch. Tutorial Program award, 1981. Mem. Ill. Community Edn. Assn., Delta Sigma Theta. Methodist. Home: 15221 Lincoln St Harvey IL 60426 Office: Sch Dist 147 Washington Sch 153d St and Lincoln Ave Harvey IL 60426

DUNN, HEDY GRACE MANNHEIMER, museum dir.; b. San Antonio, Mar. 4, 1943; d. Walter Herbert and Ilse (Holz) Mannheimer; B.F.A., Sophie Newcomb Coll., New Orleans, 1965; M.A. in Teaching, Wesleyan U., Middletown, Conn., 1968; m. Richard Byam Dunn, Jr.; children—Mark Edward, Lara Kristin. Art dir. Stony Hill Day Camp, Sharon, Mass., summer 1968; tchr. art Walpole (Mass.) Public Schs., 1967-70; asst. to dir. Los Alamos Hist. Mus., 1977-78, dir., 1978—. Mem. Los Alamos Lodger's Tax Adv. Bd., 1978—; mem. council Los Alamos Unitarian Ch., 1979-80; bd. dirs. Los Alamos Art Center, 1978. Tex. Hist. Commn. Winedale fellow, 1978; North Tex. State U. fellow, 1979. Mem. LWV (pres. Los Alamos 1975-76), Am. Assn. State and Local History, N.Mex. Hist. Soc. (sec. 1981—), Los Alamos Hist. Soc., N.Mex. Assn. Mus., Los Alamos Arts Council, No. N.Mex. Tourist Council. Club: Los Alamos Gymnastics (dir. 1980-82, pres. 1981-82). Office: PO Box 43 1921 Juniper St Los Alamos NM 87544

DUNN, HELEN ELIZABETH, counselor, educator; b. Peoria, Ill., July, 14, 1930; d. Albert Edward and Corinne Ada (Rudel) Joos; B.S., Bradley U., Peoria, 1951, M.A., 1970; m. Harry Christie Dunn, Feb. 4, 1951; children—Pamela Elizabeth, Patricia Louise. Tchr. public schs. in Hawaii and Ill., 1951-70; counselor, tchr. Peru (Ill.) Public Schs., 1970—. Bd. dirs. United Way Ill.; pres. Am. Field Service, 1977-78. Mem. NEA (life), Hawaii, Peoria (sec.), Peru edn. assns., LWV, Delta Kappa Gamma (pres. 1978—, state nominating com. 1979—, state expansion com. 1980-82), Epsilon Sigma Alpha (past pres.), Pi Lambda Theta. Office: Northview School Shooting Park Rd Peru IL 61354

DUNN, JOHANNA ALEXANDRA READ, fin. exec.; b. N.Y.C., Mar. 7, 1946; B.A. summa cum laude, Barnard Coll., 1965; M.A. summa cum laude, Columbia U., 1967, Ph.D. magna cum laude, 1970; postgrad. The Sorbonne, U. Paris, 1969-70. Editor, McKinsey & Co., Inc., N.Y.C., 1967; mng. editor European Bus., Paris, 1969-70; co-founder, chief bus. editor Tempo Economico, Lisbon, Portugal, 1970-74; chief fin. writer for Expresso Lisbon, 1970-74; fgn. correspondent The Guardian, Portugal, 1973-74; communications cons. Citicorp, 1975-76, Norton Simon Inc., 1975-76, Council of Americas, 1975-76; communications specialist N.Y. Stock Exchange, Inc., 1976-78; exec. asst. to office of chmn. N.Y. Stock Exchange, 1978-79, asst. v.p. corp. planning, 1979-80; v.p. market planning and support N.Y. Futures Exchange, 1980-81; asst. v.p. mktg. ops. N.Y. Stock Exchange, 1981—; cons. State Edn. Dept., State U. N.Y., 1975-81. Mem. Pres.'s Council Marymount Manhattan Coll., 1981—. Woodrow Wilson vis. fellow, 1979-81. Mem. Fin. Women's Assn., Investment Assn. N.Y., Bond Club, Wall St. Planning Group (v.p.), Phi Beta Kappa. Democrat. Presbyterian. Author: Counterpoint: A Book of Poetry, 1966; contbr. numerous poems to lit. publs. Home: 14 Sutton Pl S New York NY 10022 Office: NY Stock Exchange Inc 11 Wall St New York NY 10005

DUNN, LORETTA LYNN, lawyer; b. Owensboro, Ky., Dec. 3, 1955; d. John Edwin and Arnetta Mae (Trunnell) D.; B.A., U. Ky., 1976, J.D., 1979; LL.M., Georgetown U. Admitted to Ky. bar, 1979; staff atty. U.S. Senate, Com. Commerce, Sci. and Transp., Washington, 1979—. Mem. Am. Bar Assn., Ky. Bar Assn., U. Ky. Alumni Assn., Phi Beta Kappa, Order of Coif. Baptist. Office: 5102 Dirksen Washington DC 20510

DUNN, MADALINE JANE, real estate broker; b. Cushing, Okla., Aug. 26, 1944; d. Jason Homer and Evelyn Margaret (Lewis) Rosson; student Amarillo Coll. Hair Dressing, 1960-61, Amarillo Coll., 1973-76, Frank Phillips Coll., 1977-78; m. Troy Lynn Dunn, July 20, 1960; children—Dwayne, Deral. Beauty operator, instr., shop mgr. The Wig Shoppe, Pampa, Tex. 1969-79, owner, 1972-79; salesman Joe Fischer Realty, Pampa, 1975-78, now partner; sec. J.R. Devel. Co., Pampa, 1978; owner, broker Corral Real Estate, Pampa, from 1978; substitute tchr., 1975—; chmn. Pvt. Property Week, 1979-80. Active local Democratic Party, Meals on Wheels; vol. hair dresser sr. citizens, Pampa and Amarillo, Tex. Mem. Tex. Cosmetology Assn., Pampa Bd. Realtors, Nat. Bd. Realtors, Nat. Assn. Female Execs. Baptist. Home: 1817 Lynn Pampa TX 79065 Office: Joe Fischer Realty Inc Coronado Inn Pampa TX 79065

DUNN, MARY MAPLES, historian; b. Sturgeon Bay, Wis., Apr. 6, 1931; d. Frederic Arthur and Eva (Moore) Maples; B.A., Coll. William and Mary, Williamsburg, Va., 1954; M.A., Bryn Mawr Coll., 1956, Ph.D., 1959; m. Richard S. Dunn, Sept. 3, 1960; children—Rebecca Cofrin, Cecilia Elizabeth. Mem. faculty Bryn Mawr (Pa.) Coll., 1958—, prof. history, 1974—, acting dean Undergrad. Coll., 1978-79, dean, 1980—. Recipient Lindbeck Found. award for disting. teaching, 1969; fellow Inst. Advanced Study, Princeton U., 1974. Mem. Berkshire Conf. Women Historians (pres. 1973-75), Coordinating Com. Women Hist. Profession (pres. 1975-77), Am. Hist. Assn., Inst. Early Am. History and Culture (chmn. adv. council 1977—), Phi Beta Kappa. Author: William Penn: Politics and Conscience, 1967. Editor: Political Essay on The Kingdom of New Spain (Alexander von Humboldt), 1972; Papers of William Penn, 1979-80. Office: Taylor Hall Bryn Mawr Coll Bryn Mawr PA 19010

DUNN, MAUREEN M., social worker; b. Pasadena, Calif., Jan. 31, 1948; d. Robert L. and Grace M. (Curren) D.; B.A. in Psychology, Holy Names Coll., 1970; M.S.W. in Gerontology, U. Calif., Berkeley, 1975. Mental health aide E. A. Gladman Meml. Hosp., Oakland, Calif., 1970-76; coordinator patient and family services Los Medanos Community Hosp., Pittsburg, Calif., 1975-76; dir. social services Samuel Merritt Hosp., Oakland, 1976—; field work cons. U. Calif., Berkeley. Mem. steering com. East Bay Cancer Program, Head and Neck Pre-treatment Conf. Alameda County Am. Cancer Soc. Service and Rehab. Com.; field work cons. Holy Names Coll. U. Calif. regents fellow, 1973-74, Adminstrn. Aging trainee, 1974-75. Mem. Soc. Hosp. Social Work Dirs. (sec. No. Calif. chpt.), Nat. Assn. Social Workers (chpt. dir. 1981-83), Gerontol. Soc., Acad. Cert. Social Workers. Office: 350 Hawthorne Ave Oakland CA 94609

DUNN, MILDRED ELAINE, home economist, educator; b. Troy, Tex., Sept. 27, 1930; d. Fletcher Lafayette and Mildred Caroline Meredith Pool; B.S., Sam Houston State Tchrs. Coll., 1951; M.Ed., U. Houston, 1968; M.A., Sam Houston State U., 1977; m. David Eugene Dunn, June 23, 1957 (dec.). Tchr. home econs. Tex. sch. dists including Clear Lake, Aldine, Houston, Galveston, 1951-68; mktg. research asst. La. State U., 1964; cons. home and family living edn. Galveston Ind. Sch. Dist., 1968-80; tchr. spl. high sch. program in food service for disadvanted, 1980—; mem. Children's Council Galveston County; sec. Galveston's Occupational Tech. Adv. Council. Mem. Am. Home Econs. Assn., Tex. Home Econs. Assn., Houston Home Econs. Assn., Tex. Vocat. Assn., Am. Vocat. Assn., Tex. State Tchrs. Assn., Home Econs. Edn. Assn., Galveston Classroom Tchrs. Assn. (sec.), Galveston Hist. Found., Galveston Arts Council, Friends of Rosenberg Library, Cedar Lawn Assn., Galveston Ecumenical Choir, Vocat. Homemaking Tchrs. Tex., Galveston Profl. Educators. Methodist. Clubs: Galveston Garden, Galveston Musical. Home: 64 Cedar Lawn Circle Galveston TX 77550 Office: Ball High Sch 4115 Ave O Galveston TX 77550

DUNN, WENDY LYNN SCHRECK, psychologist, educator; b. Hampton, Iowa, Nov. 13, 1951; d. Gerald Peter and Doris Irma (Blom) Schreck; B.S. in Biology and Psychology, Iowa State U., 1974, M.S. in Exptl. Psychology (Iowa Women's Golf Assn. scholar), 1975; Ph.D. in Ednl. Psychology, U. Iowa, 1979; m. Gregory F. Dunn, Aug. 30, 1975. Dir. internal ops. Frank N. Magid & Assos., Marion, Iowa, 1975-76; lectr. Cornell Coll., Mt. Vernon, Iowa, Mt. Mercy Coll., Cedar Rapids, Iowa, and Kirkwood Community Coll., Cedar Rapids, 1976-80; asst. prof. psychology Coe Coll., Cedar Rapids, 1980—; instructional cons. Kirkwood Community Coll., 1979; cons. in testing and instructional design Random House, Inc., N.Y.C. and Holt, Rinehart & Winston, N.Y.C., 1979-82. Mem. Midwestern Psychol. Assn., Phi Beta Kappa, Phi Kappa Phi, Alpha Lamda Delta, Psi Chi. Editor nat. newsletter Div. Instructional Devel., 1978-79; author: Test Items II for Psychology Today, An Introduction, 1979; (with Katzev & Bragdon) Instructor's Manual to Accompany Child Psychology, 3d edit., 1980; Study Guide and Test Items to Accompany Psychology, 1st edit., 1981, also articles. Home: 1556 Matterhorn Dr NE Cedar Rapids IA 52402 Office: 115 Stuart Hall Coe Coll Cedar Rapids IA 52402

DUNNE, JOANNA LUPINACCI, psychologist; b. Stamford, Conn., Jan. 6, 1950; d. Anthony and Helen (Sudol) Lupinacci; B.A., U. Conn., 1971; M.S., U. Bridgeport, 1974, cert. advanced study, 1976; m. James Dunne, Aug. 6, 1978. Asst. head tchr. SPRED Learning Center, sch. for autistic children, Wilton, Conn., 1971-73; psychologist Greenwich (Conn.) Public Schs., 1974—; pvt. practice psychology, Stamford, 1977—. Cert. sch. psychologist, Conn. Mem. Am. Psychol. Assn., Conn. Assn. Sch. Psychologists, Psi Chi. Democrat. Presbyterian. Home: 28 Apple Tree Dr Stamford CT 06906 Office: Greenwich Bd Edn Greenwich Ave Greenwich CT 06830

DUNNE, MARY MAGUIRE, lawyer, govt. ofcl.; b. N.Y.C., Nov. 16, 1941; d. John Aloysius and Agnes (Cullen) Maguire; B.A. in English, Coll. New Rochelle, 1963; J.D., St. John's U., Jamaica, N.Y., 1966; postgrad. N.Y. U. Sch. Law, 1975-76; m. Martin F. Dunne, Apr. 24, 1982. Admitted to N.Y. bar, U.S. Supreme Ct. bar, U.S. Ct. Appeals bar, U.S. Dist. Ct. bar so. and eastern dists. N.Y.; appointee Atty. Gen.'s Program for Honor Law Grads., Dept. Justice Immigration and Naturalization Service, N.Y.C., 1966-70; asst. U.S. atty. Eastern Dist. N.Y. State, 1970-74; spl. asst. U.S. atty. So. Dist. N.Y. State, 1974-76; exec. asst. Bd. Immigration Appeals, Dept. Justice, Falls Church, Va., 1977, mem. bd., 1977—. Mem. Nat. Assn. Women Judges. Roman Catholic. Office: 5203 Leesburg Pike Falls Church VA 22041

DUNNIGAN, MARY ANN, ednl. adminstr.; b. St. Maries, Idaho, Sept. 7, 1915; d. William Henry and Mary Ellen (Kelly) D.; B.A., Holy Names Coll., Spokane, 1942; M.A., Gonzaga U., Spokane, 1957; postgrad. U. Idaho, UCLA. Tchr. rural schs. Bonner County, 1936-41, elem. schs., 1941, 45-59, high sch., 1942, 45, coordinator elem. edn., 1959-78; prin. kindergarten sch. dist. 271, Coeur d'Alene, Idaho, 1978—; pres. bd. dirs., treas. Coeur d'Alene Tchrs. Credit Union; tchr. extension classes U. Idaho; curriculum chmn. Gov.'s Conf. on Edn.; adv. council Head Start. Adv. council Council for Aging; mem. North Idaho Mus., Community Council, Community Concerts, Community Theater, North Idaho Booster Club, Mayor's Com. on Handicapped; mem. task force Diocesan Bd. Cath. Edn. of Idaho, 1969-74. Named Citizen of Yr., North Idaho Coll., 1974, Idaho Cath. Dau. of Yr., 1968. Mem. Idaho Edn. Assn., NEA, Assn. Supervision and Curriculum Devel., Internat. Reading Assn., Nat. Council Tchrs. of Social Studies, Nat. Council Tchrs. of Math., Nat. Council Tchrs. of English, Cath. Daus. Am. (state regent 1956-62), Delta Kappa Gamma Soc. Home: 720 9th St Coeur d'Alene ID 83814 Office: 725 Hazel Ave Coeur d'Alene ID 83814

DUNNING, CLAIRE PRICE, Realtor; b. Bryn Mawr, Pa., June 10, 1927; d. John Walton and Elizabeth (Field) Price; cert. Taylor Bus. Sch., Phila., 1950; B.S., Ursinus Coll., Collegeville, Pa., 1949; m. John B. Dunning, Oct. 20, 1951; children—Terry Anne, John Barnard. Sec. to regional sales mgr. carbide and carbon chem. div. Union Carbide Corp., Phila., 1950-51; sec. personnel B. F. Goodrich Co., 1954; ch. office sec. Community Ch., Stow, Ohio, 1962-69; sec. to service dir. City of Stow, 1975; residential salesperson Roger Owen Realty, Inc., Cuyahoga Falls, Ohio, 1976-78, Wilmoth, Inc., Cuyahoga Falls, 1978; resdl. salesperson, office mgr. Mitchell Realty, Inc., Stow, 1978—; mem. St. Clair-Broadview Savs. & Loan Adv. Com., 1976-77. Mem. Summit County council, Stow council PTA; mem. Stow Citizens Com. for Edn., 1961-68; mem. Citizens Adv. Com. Stow Schs., 1971; mem. Stow Park and Recreation Bd., 1965-75, chmn., 1973-75; interviewer Vol. Service Bur., 1969-73; bd. dirs. Stow Family YMCA, 1963-65; asso. mem. Stow Parade Com., 1962—; mem. adv. com. State and Local Govt. Commn., State of Ohio, 1979-80. Recipient Disting. Service award Stow Jr. C. of C., 1972. Mem. LWV (pres. Stow 1970-74, state pres. 1979-81), Nat. Assn. Realtors, Women's Council Realtors (bd. mem. 1978—), Ohio Assn. Realtors (trustee 1979-80), Akron Area Bd. Realtors (legis. chmn. 1979), Stow C. of C. (dir. 1972-73, 78-79, 82—) Republican. Mem. United Ch. of Christ. Club: Woman's (Stow). Home: 3391 Charring Cross Dr Stow OH 44224 Office: 3390 Kent Rd Stow OH 44224

DUNNING, KATHERINE MORRELL, public relations exec.; b. Greensboro, N.C., May 22, 1947; d. James Howell and Ruth (Sloan) Morrell; B.S. in Journalism, U. S.C., 1969; m. Donald Lynn Dunning, Sept. 12, 1970; 1 son, Sloan Hardin. Account exec., copywriter Cook/Ruef & Assocs., Columbia, S.C., 1969-70, Kaufmann-Davis Assocs., St. Simons Island, Ga., 1970-71; Statewide public relations coordinator Bankers Trust of S.C., 1971; asst. public relations dir. Richland Meml. Hosp., Columbia, 1971-72; dir. public relations and advt. Columbia Office Supply Co., 1972-74; free lance copywriter, Columbia, 1974-75; dir. advt./public relations Palmetto Hardware & Supply Co., Columbia, 1975-77; public info. specialist II Midlands Tech. Coll., Columbia, 1978-79, dir. public info., 1979—. Recipient Award of Excellence, Outside N.Y. Communicating Arts Show, 1969; Addy award, 1980. Mem. Public Relations Soc. Am. (publicity chmn. 1971-72), Columbia Communicating Arts Soc. (founding mem., dir. 1975-77), Carolina Assn. Bus. Communicators, Nat. Council for Community Relations (sec.), Columbia Network for Female Execs., DAR. Clubs: Altrusa, Media. Home: Route 2 PO Box 142 Hopkins SC 29061 Office: PO Box 2408 Columbia SC 29202

DUNNO, JENNIFER ANN, health care exec.; b. Victoria, Tex., Jan. 14, 1952; d. James Robert and Jean Ruth (Schoener) Zak; student Victoria campus U. Houston, 1981—; m. Jerry Dunno; children—Laura Lynn, Leighton Allan. With John Buess, M.D., 1970-75; med. sec. Victoria (Tex.) Women's Clinic, 1975-78, clinic mgr., 1978—. Mem. Med. Group Mgmt. Assn., Am. Soc. Profl. and Exec. Women, Med. Adminstrs. of Tex., Nat. Assn. Female Execs. Roman Catholic. Home: Star Route PO Box 169 Inez TX 77968 Office: 4204 N Laurent St Victoria TX 77901

DUNNOCK, MILDRED, actress; b. Balt.; A.B., Goucher Coll.; M.A., Columbia. Made profl. debut in Life Begins, N.Y.C., 1932; toured with Katharine Cornell in Herod and Marianne, 1938, with George M. Cohan in Madam, Will You Walk?, 1941, in The Corn is Green, 1942; appeared in Richard III, N.Y.C., 1943, Only the Heart, 1944, Foolish Notion, 1945, Another Part of the Forest, 1946, The Hallams, 1948, The Leading Lady, 1948, Death of a Salesman, 1949, Pride's Crossing, 1950, film version The Corn is Green, 1945, Child of Fortune, Love Me Tender, 1956, Baby Doll, 1956; Nun's Story, 1959, Story on Page One, 1960, Farewell Eugene, Butterfield 8, 1960, Sweet Bird of Youth, 1962, Seven Women, 1965, Barefoot in The Park, 1967, What Ever Happened to Aunt Alice?, 1969, Dragonfly, 1976; N.Y. stage play The Cantilevered Terrace, 1962, Traveller Without Luggage, 1964. Recipient TV award, 1955. Address: STE Representation Ltd 211 S Beverly Dr Suite 201 Beverly Hills CA 90212 *

DUNWIDDIE, CHARLOTTE, sculptor; b. Strasbourg, France, June 19, 1907; student Acad. Fine Arts, Berlin; pupil of Mariano Beulliure, Alberto Lagos. Sculpture represented in Mus. of Brookgreen Gardens, S.C., Marine Corps Mus., Washington, Aquaduct Racetrack, N.Y.C., New Britain (Conn.) Mus. Am. Art, Madrid, Buenos Aires, Argentina, others; also represented in pvt. collections. Recipient 15 gold medals, 30 other awards. Fellow Nat. Sculpture Soc. (pres. 1982—), Royal Soc. Arts (London); mem. NAD (academician), Allied Artists Am., Nat. Arts Club, Hudson Valley Art Assn., Pen and Brush (past pres.). Club: Cosmopolitan (N.Y.C.).

DUPLAIX, NICOLE, zoologist; b. N.Y.C., Aug. 21, 1943; d. Georges and Lily (Wheeler) D.; student Manhattanville Coll., 1963-65; M.Sc. in Ecology, U. Paris, 1966, D.Sc., 1981. Editor, Internat. Zoo Yearbook, London, 1971-74; sci. asst. to gen. dir. N.Y. Zool. Soc., Bronx Zoo, 1975; vis. research scientist office zool. research Nat. Zoo, Smithsonian Instn., Washington, 1978-79; founder, dir. Trade Records Analysis of Fauna and Flora in Commerce, Washington, 1979—; cons. to planners zool. parks, 1972-78; exec. sec. Am. Com. Internat. Conservation, 1979—; hon. sec. Otter Trust, Eng., 1972-79; bd. dirs. Zool. Cons. Ltd., 1971-80, founder, 1971. Fellow Am. Soc. Mammalogists, Linnaen Soc., Royal

Geog. Soc., Am. Assn. Zool. Parks and Aquariums (conservation com. 1972-74), Zool. Soc. London; mem. Assn. Study of Animal Behavior, Mammal Soc., Primate Soc. Gt. Britain, Brit. Ornithologists Union, Am. Ornithologists Union, Royal Soc. Protection of Birds, Internat. Union Conservation of Nature and Natural Resources (regional vice-chmn. species survival commn.), N.Y. Acad. Scis. Translator: King's Ottokar's Scepter (Herge), 1959; author: (with Noel Simon) World Guide to Mammals, 1976; contbr. articles and book revs. on zoology to profl. jours.; editor: (with Janet Kear) Flamingos, 1975. Home: 1692 31st St NW Washington DC 20007

DUPONT, ANN MCGEATH, home economist; b. Houston, Aug. 29, 1944; d. Joseph Everett and Alice Graham (Bishop) McGeath; B.S. in Home Econs., U. Tex., 1966; M.B.A., S.W. Tex. State U., 1977; Ph.D., Tex. Tech. U., 1978, postgrad. Law Sch.; m. Lawrence E. DuPont, Jr., Apr. 25, 1970; 1 dau., Diane. With Federated Dept. Stores, 1966-70, Asso. Dry Goods, 1970-72; asst. prof. home econs., dir. mdsg. program S.W. Tex. State U., 1975-77; asst. prof. home econs., dir. mdsg. program U. Tex., Austin, 1978—; cons. in field. Mem. Am. Home Econs. Assn., Assn. Coll. Profs. Clothing and Textiles, Am. Council Consumer Interests, Fashion Group, Phi Alpha Delta, Omicron Nu, Phi Upsilon, Delta Gamma. Presbyterian. Home: Route 2 Box 315E San Marcos TX 78666 Office: GEA 204 Austin TX 78718

DU PONT, ELISE RAVENEL WOOD, govt. ofcl.; b. N.Y.C., Dec. 27, 1935; d. Richard D. and Margaretta (Duane) Wood; B.A., Temple U., 1976; J.D., U. Pa., 1979; m. Pierre S. du Pont IV, May 4, 1957; children—Elise R., Pierre V, Benjamin, Eleuthere Irenee II. Real estate developer, Washington, 1973—; assoc. corporate law dept. Montgomery, McCracken, Walker and Rhoads, Phila., 1978-80; asst. adminstr. Bur. Pvt. Enterprise, AID, 1981—; admitted to Pa. bar, 1981; leader U.S. Dept. Commerce State Trade Mission to People's Republic of China, 1980. Mem. Del. World Affairs Council, Del. Bd. Health, 1969-72; chmn. State Council on Public Health; founder, chmn. Women's Campaign Fund, Washington; bd. mgrs. Franklin Inst., Phila., 1976-81. Recipient Speiser award U. Pa. Law Sch., 1979. Republican. Home: Rockland Rd DE 19732 Office: AID Washington DC 20523

DUPRE, D'MICHELLE PERSONNÉ, utility exec.; b. Denver, Nov. 24, 1951; d. Jack Mitchell and Ann P. (Saylor) Personné; B.A., U. S.C., 1978; m. J. Paul DuPre, Dec. 30, 1978. Tng. coordinator, systems adviser Sears, Roebuck & Co., Ashville, N.C., 1974-76; ins. specialist Colonial Life & Accident, Columbia, S.C., 1978-80; pres. Internat. Trade Assocs., Columbia, 1980-81; account exec. So. Bell Telephone Co., Columbia, 1980—; dir. Internat. Trade Assocs., 1981—; cons. in field. Mem. C. of C., Speakers Bur. (chmn. 1981), Am. Bus. Women's Assn. (Woman of Yr. 1981 pres. 1982-83), Williamsburg Soc. (sec. 1981-82), Ind. Ins. Agts. of S.C., Nat. Assn. Female Execs. (network dir. 1980-82). Republican. Club: Toastmasters (treas. 1981, adminstrv. v.p. 1982). Home: 116 King George Way Columbia SC 29210 Office: 1555 Harden St Extension Columbia SC 29203

DUPREY, JANET MARIE, county ofcl.; b. Plattsburgh, N.Y., Nov. 27, 1945; d. Peter Joseph and Edna Mae Lacy; student Empire State Coll., 1979—; m. Elmer C. Duprey, Sept. 9, 1967; children—John, Michelle. Exec. sec. Eastman Kodak Co., Rochester, N.Y., 1965-66; legal sec. John L. Bell, Plattsburgh, 1966-68; legis. asst. to Sen. Ronald B. Stafford, Plattsburgh, 1968-70; co-owner Rustic Restaurant, Peru, 1967—; mem. Clinton County Legislature, 1976 chairperson, 1981-82. Sec. bd. dirs. Apple Valley Sr. Housing Corp., Inc., 1977—; mem. N.Y. State Dept. Social Services Statewide Adv. Council, 1979—, Clinton County Social Services Adv. Council, 1976—, Office Aging Adv. Council, Child Abuse Task Force. Mem. LWV, N.Y. State Suprs. and Legislators Assn., Clinton County Hotel, Restaurant and Liquor Dealers Assn. (past pres.), Delta Kappa Gamma. Republican. Roman Catholic. Club: Plattsburgh AFB Officers (hon.). Home: Telegraph St Peru NY 12972 Office: 137 Margaret St Plattsburgh NY 12901

DURAN, ELVA, educator; b. Canutillo, Tex., July 12, 1946; d. Juan Provencio and Petra (Morales) D.; B.S., U. Tex., 1969, M.Ed., 1972; Ph.D., U. Oreg., 1978. Asst. prof. dept. ednl. psychology and guidance U. Tex., El Paso. Mem. Nat. Soc. Autistic Citizens and Adults, Internat. Reading Assn., Am. Ednl. Research Assn., Council for Exceptional Children, Tex. Soc. Autistic Citizens, Assn. for Children with Learning Disabilities. Roman Catholic. Contbr. articles to profl. jours. Home: 6705 Escondido St Apt C El Paso TX 79912 Office: Dept Educational Psychology and Guidance University of Texas El Paso TX 79968

DURAN, RITA PELL, public relations exec.; b. N.Y.C., Jan. 13, 1939; d. Charles Ford and Emma Mary (Koss) Holmes; B.A. summa cum laude in English, Boston U., 1962; m. Martin Gitlin, June 13, 1981; 1 son by previous marriage, Charles David Pell. Dir. adminstrv. services Schless & Co., N.Y.C., 1966-68; dir. adminstrv. services Richard Weiner, Inc., N.Y.C., 1968-75, v.p. adminstrn., 1975-79, sr. v.p. adminstrn. and fin., 1979-81; pres. Duran/Gitlin Group, 1982—. Mem. Public Relations Soc. Am., Publicity Club N.Y., Advt. Agys. Employees Assn. Home: 1653 Morningview Dr Yorktown Heights NY 10598

DURAND, BERNICE, physicist; b. Clarion, Iowa, Dec. 28, 1942; d. Henry Montgomery and Bernice (Bernard) Black; student Radcliffe Coll., 1959-61, 62); B.S., Iowa State U., 1965, Ph.D., 1971; m. Loyal Durand, Oct. 18, 1970. Lectr., research assoc. U. Wis., Madison, 1970-77; mem. Inst. Advanced Study, Princeton, N.J., 1975-76; asst. prof. physics U. Wis., Madison, 1977—; trustee Aspen Center for Physics, 1980—; cons. Los Alamos Nat. Lab., 1975—; vis. staff, 1975. Dept. Energy grantee; U. Wis. grantee. Mem. Am. Phys. Soc., AAUP, AAAS, Wis. Acad. Arts, Letters and Sci., Sigma Xi, Sigma Delta Epsilon. Contbr. articles to profl. jours. Office: Dept Physics U Wis Madison WI 53706

DURBIN, BETTY ANN, electronics co. ofcl.; b. San Mateo, Calif., May 27, 1939; 1 son, Arthur Dean. Assembler, Litton Industries, San Carolos, Calif., 1959. Advanced Tech. Labs., Mountain View, Calif., 1961-63, Daytron Inc., Mountain View, 1963-69; coil winder Stanford Applied Engring. Co., Santa Clara, Calif., 1969-71, Teledyne Co., Palo Alto, Calif., 1971-72; supr. coil winding Fall River Mills (Calif.) br. Mini-Magnetics Co., Inc., 1979—. Home and Office: 3939 Bidwell Dr 502-22 Fremont CA 94538

DURBROW, BARBARA HELEN, mgmt. cons.; b. Washington Court House, Ohio, Mar. 29, 1936; d. Roy Lee and Esta Pearl (Sword) Mustain; attended U. Cinn., Central Mich. U., U. Ala.; m. Brian Durbrow; children—Robert E., William D. Sr. cons. B.R. Durbrow & Assos., Cin., 1969-72; v.p., sec., treas., dir. Barbrisons Mgmts. Systems, Inc., Cin., 1972—; v.p. Mgmt. Research and Devel., Inc., Cin., 1975-80; v.p., dir. IE, Inc., 1980—. Mem. Nat. Mgmt. Assn., Acad. Mgmt., Commerce Execs. Soc., —co-developer of Accutrac Evaluation Systems— Republican. Co-author: Modern Research on Accident Proneness; contbr. articles to profl. jours. Office: 2957 Annwood St Cincinnati OH 45206

DURFLINGER, HELEN MARGARET, social worker; b. Elgin, Ill., Aug. 1, 1918; d. George Harold and Ruth Olive (Wills) Anderson; B.S., U. Ill., 1940; children—Gwendolyn Louise Wilson, Carol Elaine Skinner. Child welfare caseworker Allen County Dept. Public Welfare, Ft. Wayne, Ind., 1963-70; casework supr. social services div., 1970-81; ret., 1981. Pres., PTA, 1961-63. Recipient award Purdue U.-Fort Wayne, 1973. Mem. Bus. and Profl. Women's Club (pres. Ft. Wayne 1977-79), Internat. Platform Assn. Methodist (officer, ch. group leader). Clubs: Women of Moose (chpt. jr. regent); Toastmistress (past club pres., past council pres.; Woman of Influence 1975). Home: 1804 Hobson Rd Fort Wayne IN 46805

DURHAM, DIANE ELIZABETH NELSON, aerospace co. exec.; b. White Plains, N.Y., Oct. 25, 1953; d. George and Frances Nelson (Connor) Rentoumis; B.A., U. Denver, 1975; m. Michael Oakley Durham, Sept. 18, 1976. Sr. sci. programmer, asso. engr. Lockheed Missiles and Space Co., Sunnyvale, Calif., 1975—. Recipient commendation Lockheed Missiles and Space Co. Mem. U. Denver Alumni Assn. (recuitment chmn. Bay Area), Mortar Board Alumnae Assn., Kappa Delta Alumnae Assn. (pledge adv., house corp. fin. adv., house corp. pres.). Home: 5172 Bela Dr San Jose CA 95129 Office: 1111 Lockheed Way Bldg 152 Org 62-85 Sunnyvale CA 94086

DURHAM, KATHRYNANN WALRATH, state legislator; b. Chester, Pa., July 29, 1951; d. Glenn Smith and Catherine Mary (Talarico) Walrath; grad. Widener U., 1973, postgrad. Law Sch., 1982; m. Stephen A. Durham, July 14, 1973; 1 son, Stephen A. Tchr., 1973-78; mem. Pa. Ho. of Reps., 1979—. Mem. Bus. and Profl. Women, Order Women Legislators. Republican. Episcopalian. Office: Brookhaven and Edgmont Aves Brookhaven PA 19015

DURHAM, LINDA THEUNE, info. exec.; b. Ft. Leavenworth, Kan., Nov. 11, 1951; d. Stanley William and Carol Ann (Feld) Theune; student U. Ga., 1969-70; B.A., West Ga. Coll., 1973; m. Michael Bryan Durham, Aug. 4, 1973. Sec. The Coca-Cola Co., Atlanta, 1973-75, research asst., 1975-76, research specialist, 1976-77, supr. editorial services, 1977-79, editor internal. publs., 1979-81, mgr. consumer info. center, 1981—. Mem. Assn. to Revive Grant Park, 1980—. Nat. Merit scholar, 1969-73. Mem. Internat. Assn. Bus. Communicators, Soc. of Consumer Affairs Profls. Roman Catholic. Home: 366 Oakland Ave Atlanta GA 30312 Office: PO Drawer 1734 Atlanta GA 30301

DURHAM, PEGGY J., advt. exec.; b. Boise City, Okla., Aug. 19, 1941; d. John M. and Mildred C. (Phillips) D.; B.A. in Journalism, U. Okla., 1963. Dir. public info. U. Tulsa, 1967-70; mgr. communications Honeywell Info. Systems, Oklahoma City, 1970-75; dir. public info. Okla. Bar Assn., Oklahoma City, 1975-77; chmn. bd., partner Metro Media Ltd. Advt. Agy., Oklahoma City, 1977-78; pres. The Word Place Advt. Agy., Oklahoma City, 1978—; pres. Okla. Feminist Enterprises, Inc., Oklahoma City, 1977-80. Bd. dirs. PASEO Drug Counseling Center, Oklahoma City, 1970-73; bd. dirs., co-founder Okla. Women's Center, 1973-74; mem. ERA coalition NOW, 1973—. Named one of Okla.'s ten "movers and shakers" in women's movement Okla. Monthly Mag., 1976. Mem. Internat. Assn. Bus. Communicators, Oklahoma City Press Club, ACLU, Okla. Press Assn. Democrat. Editor Okla. Halfway House newsletter ALTERNATIVES, 1973; founder, editor Sister Advocate newspaper, Okla.'s only feminist newspaper, 1975-80. Home and Office: 1308 NW 10th Oklahoma City OK 73106

DURKA, GLORIA, educator; b. Buffalo, Oct. 12, 1939; d. Chester and Estelle Szustak (Godlewski) D.; B.A., Medaille Coll., 1968; M.A., Fordham U., 1969; Ph.D., N.Y. U., 1973; m. Paul E. Bumbar, Aug. 3, 1974. Acad. dir. Inst. Study of Religious Edn. and Service, asst. prof. religious edn. Boston Coll., 1973-76; asso. prof. religious edn., chairperson dept. religious studies and philosophy Barry Coll., Miami, Fla., 1977-78; asso. prof. religious edn. Fordham U., Bronx, N.Y., 1978—. Recipient Founder's Day award N.Y. U., 1974. Mem. Am. Acad. Religion, AAUP, Religious Research Assn., Religious Edn. Assn., Pi Lambda Theta. Democrat. Roman Catholic. Author: Modeling God, 1976; Basic Guidelines for Creative Teaching, 1975; Faith: Becoming True and Free, 1981; editor: Emerging Issues in Religious Education, 1976; The Aesthetic Dimensions of Religious Education, 1979; Family Ministry, 1980. Home: 153 Fawn Hill Rd Tuxedo Park NY 10987 Office: Keating Hall Fordham Univ Bronx NY 10458

DURKEE, JEAN KELLNER, mfg. corp. exec.; b. Chgo., Feb. 7, 1932; d. Herbert Ernest and Lucy (Stevens) Kellner; B.S. in Home Econs., U. Tex., Austin, 1953; m. Robert Rosswell Durkee, Jr., Oct. 3, 1953; children—Robert III, Mark, Todd. Dir., First Presbyn. Nursery Sch. and Kindergarten, Lafayette, La., 1954-56; dir. Grace Presbyn. Nursery Sch. and Kindergarten, Lafayette, 1965-67; pres. Tout de Suite, Inc., Lafayette, 1978—; tchr. microwave cooking. Pres., Lafayette Natural History Mus. Mem. Am. Home Econs. Assn., Home Economists in Bus., La. Home Econs. Assn. Internat. Microwave Power Inst., P.E.O. (pres. chpt. 1961-62). Republican. Methodist. Clubs: Jr. League (pres. club 1959-60) (Lafayette); Chez Amis Women's (pres. 1957-58). Author, pub.: Tout de Suite a la Microwave, I, 1977, II, 1980; co-author Blades and Waves column 1978—. Office: PO Box 30121 Lafayette LA 70503

DURKIN, DOROTHY ANGELA, univ. adminstr.; b. Glen Cove, N.Y., June 23, 1945; d. Frank Vincent and Rose Marie D.; B.A., SUNY, Stony Brook, 1968; M.A., N.Y. U., 1974; m. David Lawrence Hawthorne, July 13, 1975; 1 son, David Francis. Adminstrv. asst. State U. N.Y., Stony Brook, 1965-67; prodn. editor Holt, Rhinehart & Winston, Inc., 1967-69; editor Hill & Wang Pub., Inc., N.Y.C., 1969-70; asst. dir. public info. N.Y.U. Sch. Continuing Edn., N.Y.C., 1970-72, dir. public info., 1972—; cons. N.Y.C. Center for Lifelong Learning, 1974. Recipient Andy Advt. award of merit, 1972, Direct Mktg. Leadership award, 1977, 80, Nat. U. Extension Assn. award, 1978. Mem. Am. Coll. Public Relations Assn. (nat. award 1973), Council for Advancement and Support of Edn., Women in Communications (chmn. job info. N.Y.C. chpt. 1981-82), Nat. Univ. Extension Assn. (cons. 1977-78, chmn. info. services div. 1980), Public Relations Soc., Direct Mail/Mktg. Assn. Clubs: Scuba Diving, Community Sing. Producer TV series Continuum, WNYC, 1974; editor NSF student mag., 1961. Home: 200 Mercer St New York NY 10012 Office: NYU Sch Continuing Edn 126 Shimkin Hall New York NY 10003

DURLAND, DORA MAE, savs. and loan assn. exec.; b. Tulsa, Nov. 4, 1955; d. Raymond LeVarne and Vivian Lee (Caskey) Moreland; B.S. in Speech Communications and Bus., Tulsa U., 1977; m. Gary Alan Durland, Mar. 4, 1978. From adminstrv. asst. to supr. lease adminstrn. Telex Computer Products Co., Tulsa, 1978-80; corp. sec. Service Corp. Tulsa, Inc., subs. Mid-Am. Fed. Savs. & Loan Assn., 1980—. Mem. Exec. Women Internat., U. Tulsa Alumni Assn., Chi Omega. Home: 7925 South 86th East Pl Tulsa OK 74133

DURNING, KATHLEEN PHYLLIS, psychologist; b. South Bend, Ind., Jan. 28, 1945; d. Gordon Daniel and Phyllis Louise (Underwood) Skeoch; B.A., Wheaton Coll., 1965; M.A., San Diego State U., 1969; Ph.D., U. Ariz., 1973; 1 son, Blake G. Project dir. Head Start evaluation, Ariz. Center for Early Childhood Research and Devel., U. Ariz., Tucson, 1971-72, project dir. Ariz. regional med. program Coll. Medicine, 1972-73; research psychologist, project dir. Navy Personnel Research and Devel. Center, San Diego, 1973—; prin. investigator Equal Opportunity for Women, 1976—; instr. San Diego State U., 1976—; pvt. practice clin. psychology specializing in psychology of women, San Diego, 1978—; facilitor assertion tng. groups for women; cons. Navy Family Program. Mem. Am. Psychol. Assn. (div. psychology of women), Inter-Univ. Seminar on Armed Forces and Soc., Acad. San Diego Psychologists, Assn. Women in Sci., NOW, Sigma Xi, Psi Chi. Mem. United Ch. of Christ. Contbr. articles to profl. jours. Home: 7690 Volclay Dr San Diego CA 92119 Office: 1335 Hotel Circle S Suite 316 San Diego CA 92108

DUROSS, ANN THERESA, assn. exec.; b. Jersey City, Oct. 24, 1918; d. Joseph Benedict and Josephine Anna (Mollek) Stucky; B.A., Coll. of New Rochelle, 1940; m. Charles Edward Duross, June 26, 1941; children—Ann Celeste, Charles, Cornelia. Bd. dirs., pres. Camp Fire Council, Larchmont, N.Y., 1963-69, regional chmn./com. chmn. nat. bd. Camp Fire, Inc., 1968-75, council mgmt. cons.-staff vol., 1976—, pres. Westchester council, 1977—. Chmn., Larchmont Cath. Library, 1973—. Recipient Luther Gulik award Camp Fire, Inc., 1967. Club: Larchmont Ladies of Charity. Address: 1 Circle Ave Larchmont NY 10538

DUSKIN, MARGARET, real estate co. exec.; b. N.Y.; d. Stephen J. and Diana H. Duskin; student Hunter Coll., 1966-68; B.A., U. San Francisco, 1972; postgrad. Golden Gate U. Investment officer Singapore Econ. Devel. Bd., 1968-73; real estate broker Cushman Wakefield Co., San Francisco, 1973—. Lic. real estate broker, Calif. Mem. San Francisco Bd. Realtors, (dir. 1978-81), San Francisco C. of C., U. San Francisco Alumni Assn. (gov. 1975-77), Downtown Forum (exec. com.). Club: Commonwealth (San Francisco). Office: 555 California St Suite 2700 San Francisco CA 94104

DUTTON, NANCY EILEEN (SANDERS), real estate co. exec.; b. Pine Bluff, Ark., Oct. 22, 1948; d. Carl Wesley and Virginia Adelle (Lovan) Sanders; student U. Ark., 1966-67, Pensacola (Fla.) Jr. Coll., 1968, 70; m. Vernon L. Dutton, Nov. 17, 1967. Receptionist to adminstrv. asst. to pres. C.A. Hobbs Jr. Inc., Pensacola, 1970-77; with DeSoto Realty, Inc., Hot Springs, 1978—, gen. mgr., 1981—. Mem. Hot Springs Home Bldrs. Assn. (dir. 1982—), Nat. Assn. Realtors, Nat. Assn. Home Builders, Ark. Home Builders Assn., Ark. Realtors Assn., Hot Springs Bd. Realtors, Hot Springs Village Real Estate Assn. Conservative Baptist. Club: Toastmasters. Home: 17 El Espinar Ln Hot Springs Village AR 71909 Office: Star Route 10 PO Box 490 Hot Springs AR 71909

DUTTON, PAULINE MAE, fine arts librarian; b. Detroit, July 15; d. Thoralf Andreas and Esther Ruth (Clyde) Tandberg; B.A. in Art, Calif. State U., Fullerton, 1967; M.S. in Library Sci., U. So. Calif., 1971; m. Richard Hawkins Dutton, June 21, 1969. Elem. tchr., Anaheim, Calif., 1967-68, Corona, Calif., 1968-69; fine arts librarian Pasadena (Calif.) Public Library, 1971-80; art cons., researcher, 1981—. Mem. Pasadena Librarians Assn. (sec. 1978, treas. 1979-80), Calif. Library Assn., Calif. Soc. Librarians, Art Librarians N.Am., Nat. Assn. Female Execs., Am. Film Inst., Am. Entrepreneurs Assn., Gilbert and Sullivan Soc., Alpha Sigma Phi. Club: Toastmistress (local pres. 1974). Office: 954 Arroyo Dr S Pasadena CA 91030

DUVAL, BETSYANN, advt. agy. exec.; b. Detroit, Aug. 25, 1943; d. Richard Thomas and Betsy Cooper Wigginton; student Kalamazoo Coll., 1961-62, U. Mich., 1962-64; m. Robert J. Clawson, Dec. 29, 1972. Copywriter, salesperson, Gale & Polden Design Studio, London, 1964-65; salesperson New Homes Press, London, 1965; adminstrv. asst., sales dept. Cahners Pub. Co., Boston, 1965-66; copywriter Impact Advt., Inc., Boston, 1966-67, account exec., 1967-68, v.p., treas., 1968-72, pres., 1972—. Mem. Bus. Profl. Advt. Assn. New Eng., Boston Advt. Club. Office: Impact Advt Inc 143 Newbury St Boston MA 02116

DUVALL, CORINNE, nurse; b. Merriam, Ill., Nov. 17, 1928; d. Harrison and Carrie (Walters) Davis; R.N., St. Mary's Sch. Nursing, 1949; diploma St. Xavier Coll., 1978-81; B.S. in Nursing, Loyola Grad. Sch. Bus., 1982; children—Davee Anne Setzer, Melody Susan Duvall, John Harrison Duvall. Staff nurse St. Mary's Hosp., Evansville, Ind., 1949-56, relief house supr., 1956-62; staff nurse Roseland Community Hosp., Chgo., 1963-70, relief charge nurse, 1971-76, supr., 1976-78, asst. dir. nurses, 1978—. Mem. Ill. League Nursing, Nat. League Nursing, Emergency Dept. Nurses Assn., NOW, Sigma Theta Tau. Lutheran. Home: 12440 Benck Dr Apt 105 Alsip IL 60658 Office: 45 W 111th St Chicago IL 60658

DWIGHT, MARIA BURGEE, planner, gerontologist; b. Holyoke, Mass., Dec. 23, 1934; d. Henry Valle and Marcelle Marguerite (Melun) Burgee; B.A., Hampshire Coll., Amherst, Mass., 1975; M.S. in Gerontology, U. So. Calif., 1976; m. William Dwight, Jr., Sept. 25, 1954 (div. 1982); children—William Henry, Leslie Rathbun, Valle Elizabeth, Timothy Monk, Ryan Hamilton. Cons. in services and facilities for elderly, 1970—; dir. Eastern div. Geront. Planning Assos., Holyoke, Mass., 1972-75, v.p., Santa Monica, Calif., 1977—; chmn. bd. Geriatric Authority Holyoke, 1972-75; commnr. pub. welfare, Holyoke, 1966-69; chmn. bd. Mcpl. Nursing Home, Holyoke, 1966-72; v.p. Western Mass. Health Planning Council, 1972-76; bd. overseers Heller Grad. Sch., Brandeis U., 1972-76; adv. bd. Mass. Dept. Pub. Welfare, Mass. Housing Finance Agy., 1972-75. Pres. Holyoke Jr. League, 1964-66, Urban Ministry, Holyoke, 1967-70; del. Republican Nat. Conv., 1968; mem. Mass. Rep. State Com., 1968-75. Named Woman of Yr., Jr. C. of C., 1963. Mem. Geront. Soc., Am. Assn. Homes Aging (ho. of dels. 1974-76; Presdl. citation 1972), Nat. Council Aging. Episcopalian. Home: 847 19th St Santa Monica CA 90403 Office: 1448 15th St Suite 205 Santa Monica CA 90404

DWORKIN, JUDITH MARCIA, geographer; b. Worcester, Mass., July 14, 1949; d. Daniel Martin and Dorothea Barbara (Kumin) Dworkin; M.A., Clark U., 1975, Ph.D., 1978; m. Kalman David Pijawka, May 26, 1974; 1 son, Benjamin Michael. Geographer, U.S. Army C.E., New England div., Waltham, Mass., 1975-76; instr. U. Toronto (Ont., Can.), 1976-78; asst. prof. hydrology and water resources U. Ariz., Tucson, 1978—; cons. AID, Water Resources Council, Inst. Water Resources. Grantee NSF, Office Water Research and Tech.; NSF and C.E. dissertation fellow, 1975-76. Mem. Assn. Am. Geographers (dir. water resources specialty group 1980—), AAAS, Am. Geophys. Union. Asso. editor geog. jour. The Monadnock, 1975. Home: 4250 N Bear Claw Way Tucson AZ 85715 Office: Dept Hydrology and Water Resources U Ariz Tucson AZ 85721

DWORSKI, SYLVIA, emeritus educator; b. New Haven, Apr. 10, 1915; d. Louis and Ida (Miller) D.; student Conn. State Tchrs. Summer Normal Sch., 1933-35; B.A. with highest honors (Winthrop scholar), Conn. Coll., 1935; M.A., Yale U., 1937, Ph.D., 1941; Certificat d'études pratiques de prononiciaion française (Yale traveling fellow), Institut de Phonétique, U. Paris, 1939; U.S. grantee Spanish Lang. Inst. for Tchrs. Spanish, U. Mex., summer 1944; postgrad. in modern French theater, France, spring 1969-70; vis. fellow Romance langs. Yale U., 1941-42; tchr. French, Spanish and English, East Haven High Sch., 1942-44; instr. Spanish, New Haven State Tchrs. Evening Coll., 1941-44; instr. Romance langs. Sweet Briar Coll., 1944-46, St. Helena Extension, Coll. William and Mary, 1946-48; asst. prof. Wilkes Coll., 1948-54, asso. prof. modern langs., 1954-63; asso. prof. modern langs. St. Mary's Coll., Notre Dame, Ind., 1963-64, prof., 1964-80, prof. emeritus, 1980—, co-chmn. dept. modern langs., 1963-65, chmn. dept. French, 1965-67; vis. faculty mem. U. Notre Dame Grad. Sch., summers 1967-68. Mem. AAUP (sec.-treas. St. Mary's Coll. chpt. 1965-66, 78-79, exec. com. 1979-80), Am. Assn. Tchrs. of French, Common Cause, Public Citizen, Jewish Residents of Rossmoor, Phi Beta Kappa. Jewish. Home: 15300 Wallbrook Ct Unit 3-E Silver Spring MD 20906

DWYER, DORIOT ANTHONY, flutist; d. William C. and Edith (Maurer) Anthony; B.Music, Eastman Sch. Music, 1943; 1 child, Arienne. Second flutist Nat. Symphony, Washington, 1943, Los Angeles Philharm., 1945-52; 1st flutist Boston Symphony Orch., 1952—; flutist numerous chamber groups including: Boston Symphony Chamber Players, Doriot Anthony Dwyer and Friends; appeared at numerous music festivals including: Camel Back Festival, Berkshire Festival at Tangelwood, Rocky Mountain Music Festival; mem. faculty Pomona Coll., New Eng. Conservatory Music, Boston U.; Mem. Nat. Council of Women, Audubon Soc. Home: 3 Cleveland Rd Brookline MA 02146 Office: Am Internat Artists 275 Madison Ave New York NY 10016 *

DWYER, ETHEL THERESA, psychologist; b. Manchester, N.H., July 30, 1931; d. Joseph George and Florence Theresa (Kittredge) Thibodeau; Mus.B., Boston U., 1953, Ed.M., 1962, cert. advanced grad. study, 1965, Ed.D., 1968; m. John Philip Dwyer, June 22, 1957. Tchr., Miss Jacques Pvt. Sch., Manchester, 1953-54; asst. dir. Girls Club, Manchester, 1954-57; tchr. Manchester Public Schs., 1957-65; instr. edn. Boston U. Sch. Edn., 1965-66; asst. prof. psychology New Eng. Coll., Henniker, N.H., 1965-67; asso. prof. Mt. St. Mary Coll., Hooksett, N.H., 1968-70; staff psychologist N.H. Hosp., Concord, 1968-71; ind. practice child psychology, 1970—; mem. N.H. Bd. Examiners Psychologists, 1976-77, chmn., 1977-79; profl. adv. bd. N. River Sch., 1978-80, chmn., 1977; mem. teen age pregnancy/mothet adv. bd. Vis. Nurse Assn. Manchester, 1978—; research asst. Boston U. Center Exceptional Children, 1962-63; curriculum cons. Concord Public Schs., 1967-68; psychologist, cons. Easter Seal Rehab. Center, 1971-72. Diplomate sch. psychology Am. Bd. Profl. Psychology. Mem. Am. Psychol. Assn., NEA, Am. Ednl. Research Assn., Music Educators Nat. Conf., Eastern Psychol. Assn., New Eng. Psychol. Assn., Mass. Psychol. Assn., N.H. Dental Assn. Women's Aux., Hillsboro County Kennel Club (dir. 1980). Republican. Roman Catholic. Home: 2071 N River Rd Manchester NH 03104 Office: 1480 Elm St Manchester NH 03101

DWYER, MARIE RITA ROZELLE (MRS. JOHN D. DWYER), educator; b. N.Y.C., Sept. 4, 1915; d. Charles W. and Agnes (Coyle) Rozelle; student L'Assomption, Paris, France, 1932-33; B.A., Notre Dame Coll., 1936; M.A., Fordham U., 1938; postgrad. St. Louis U.; student Sorbonne, Paris, summers 1933-37, 52; m. John D. Dwyer, Sept. 8, 1942; children—John Duncan, Joseph Charles, James Gerard, Jerome Valentine. Tchr. French, Sch. of Edn., Fordham U., N.Y.C., 1938-42, Notre Dame Coll., N.Y.C., 1939-40, Coll. of St. Rose, Albany, N.Y., 1949-53, Washington U., St. Louis, 1959-60; faculty French dept. Webster Coll., 1966-74; dir. community services Internat. Students Program, St. Louis U., 1974—; faculty Meramec Community Coll., St. Louis, 1968-70. Active community fund drives, including Greater St. Louis Fund for Arts and Edn.; bd. dirs. St. Louis Christmas Carols Assn., 1962-64, Parish Council, 1966-67; adult adviser cultural program for young adults Archdiocesan Council Cath. Youth, 1961-67; mem. Archdiocesan Council Laity. Mem. Am. Assn. Tchrs. French (pres. St. Louis chpt. 1955-56), Mo. Acad. Sci. (life mem., chmn. linguistics sect. 1970-76, past mem. exec. bd.), Alliance Francaise, Société Française (past sec.), K. C. Aux. (past pres.), AAAS (rep. Mo. Acad. Sci. at conv. in Mexico City 1973), Notre Dame Coll. Alumnae Assn. (past pres.), Internat. Fedn. Cath. Alumnae (past pres. Albany), Jesuit Mothers Guild (pres. 1963-65), Cath. Women's League (pres. 1964-66), Archdiocean Council Cath. Women (mem. coms. family life teen-age code, corr. sec. 1963-64, pres. 1964-66 South Central dist.), Nat. French Honor Soc., AAUP, MLA, Mo. Modern Lang. Assn. (pres. 1961-63), Central States Conf. on Teaching Fgn. Langs., Société International de la Linguistique, Linguistic Soc. Am., Fgn. Lang. Assn. Mo. (past v.p.), 4-Coll. Consortium (Webster, Fontbonne, Maryville and Lindenwood) (sec. 1972-73), Centro Studie Scambi Internazionali (mem. internat. com.), Smithsonian Instn. Nat. Assos., Internat. Platform Assn., Pi Delta Phi. Club: St. Louis University Faculty Women's (pres. 1956-58, dir. 1959—). Extensive travel for ednl. and linguistic research. Home: 526 Oakwood Ave Webster Groves MO 63119

DYCHES, HILDA GUNTER, educator; b. Moultrie Ga., Feb. 23, 1918; d. William Van and Cora Mae (Young) Gunter; B.S. in Edn., U. Ga., 1950, M.S., 1966; m. Clinton Dyches, Mar. 31, 1945; 1 son, Hugh Tankersley. Instr., U. Ga., 1950-52, Avondale (Ga.) High Sch., 1952-54; asso. prof. English, Ga. State U., chmn. dept. speech and drama, 1954—, asso. prof. emerita GA State U. 1981, dir. ann. spring festival, 1954-65, dir. univ. players, 1954-58; judge forensics. Pres. Rowland Hills Civic Club, 1963-65. Mem. So., Ga. speech assns., Speech Communication Assn. Am., Internat. Communication Assn., Thalian Blackfriars, Mortar Bd., Phi Beta Kappa, Phi Kappa Phi, Kappa Delta Pi, Zeta Phi Eta, Alpha Psi Omega, Alpha Lambda Delta, Omicron Delta Kappa. Clubs: Ga. State Coll. Women's, Rowland Hills Garden. Home: 4233 Durham Circle Stone Mountain GA 30083 Office: University Plaza Atlanta GA 30303

DYER, CHARLOTTE LEAVITT (MRS. GEORGE BELL DYER), author, educator; b. N.Y.C.; d. Charles Wellford and Clara Gordon (White) Leavitt; student Scarborough Sch., 1918-19, Rosemary Hall, 1920-22, Wykeham Rise, 1923-24, Finch Sch., 1924-25, U. N.Mex., 1928; B.A. Barnard Coll., 1931; postgrad. Columbia U., 1932; A.M., U. Pa., 1948, Ph.D., 1950; m. George Bell Dyer, June 26, 1930. Instr. anthropology Barnard Coll., N.Y.C., field trips to Kutenai Indians, B.C. (Can.), 1928, 31; one of founders Farmers Digest mag., asst. editor, 1937-51; instr. Sch. of Horticulture, Ambler, Pa., 1937-38; instr. Army Gen. Sch., 1950-52, U. Pa., 1947-50, 53-67, Yale U., 1957-58; supr. Upper Makefield Twp., Bucks County, Pa., 1971-77, chmn., 1974-76. Pres. sch. bd. Upper Makefield Twp. Bucks County, Pa., 1957-58; founder (with George Bell Dyer), asso. dir. The Dyer Inst. of Interdisciplinary Studies, New Hope, Pa., 1952. Mem. Pa. Citizens Council Better Schs., 1959; mem. council Rock High Sch. Bd., 1955-67; mem. Gov.'s Council on Rural Devel., 1971. Served with WAAC, 1942; maj. WAC, AUS: U.S. and ETO, 1942-46; at Ft. Riley, 1950-52. Fellow Co. Mil. Historians; mem. Alumni Assn. Grad. Sch. Arts and Scis. U. Pa. (co-pres. 1959-62), Acad. Polit. Sci., Am. Acad. Polit. and Social Sci., Colonial Dames Am. (chpt. II chmn. new citizens com. 1968-75, pres. 1975-78), Bucks County Conservation Fedn. and Open Space (a founder 1969, 1st pres. 1970-82), Huntingdon Valley Hunt (dir. 1975); Lenape Hunt (joint master 1976-78), Pi Gamma Mu. Club: Faculty (U. Pa.). Author: (with George Bell Dyer) The Beginnings of a U.S. Strategic Intelligence System in Latin America, 1950; A Century of Strategic Intelligence Reporting, 1954; A Strategic Intelligence Lesson, 1956; The World Analyst, 1958; Exercises on an Assumption of Violence, 1962; The Cruelest War, 1965; Second Battle of Valcour Island, 1969; Great March to Quebec, 1975; co-author numerous monographs in profl. jours. including A Ritualization of War, 1975; The Bicentennial in a Different Drum, 1976. Home: Diabase Farm Box 109 RD 2 New Hope PA 18938

DYER, JANICE RAE MOSER, mfg. co. exec.; b. Lynwood, Calif., Sept. 14, 1946; d. Raymond Paul and Verena Clara (Wemhoff) Moser; B.S., U. So. Calif., 1968; m. John Lockwood Dyer, Dec. 15, 1973. In charge staff auditor Price Waterhouse & Co., Los Angeles, 1968-72; controller Mor-Win Products, Inc., Los Angeles, 1972-73, Monogram/Custom Craft, Culver City, Calif., 1973-76; chief fin. officer, corp. sec. Photo-Sonic's, Inc., Burbank, Calif., 1976—, Instrumentation Mktg. Corp., Burbank, 1976—, Photo Digesting Systems, Inc., 1979—. C.P.A., Calif. Mem. Am. Inst. Corp. Controllers, Calif. Soc. C.P.A.s, Am. Mgmt. Assn., Nat. Assn. Accts., U. So. Calif. Alumni Assn., Alpha Chi Omega, Beta Alpha Psi, Phi Chi Theta. Office: Photo-Sonic's Inc 820 S Mariposa St Burbank CA 91506

DYER, MELBA KATHLEEN, credit union exec.; b. St. Clair County, Mo., July 30, 1927; d. Willis Harrison and Rhoda Marie (McKinley) Weant; student S.W. Baptist Coll., 1945-46, Williams Wood Coll., 1963-64; also various continuing edn. courses; children—Harold, David. Clk., Sears Kansas City Fed. Credit Union (Mo.), 1954-58, clk.-teller, 1958-60, asst. mgr., 1963-68; chief loan officer Richards-Gebaur AFB Credit Union, Grandview, Mo., 1960-63; pres. Carpenters Local Credit Union, Kansas City, 1968-72; mgr. Chgo. Coll. Osteo. Medicine Credit Union, 1972-73; pres. U. Wis. at Milw. Credit Union, 1974—. Pres., U. Wis.-Milw. Women's Service Club, 1975-76, treas., 1982-83. Mem. Wis. Credit Union League, Internat. Consumer Credit Assn., Milw. Consumer Credit Assn., Nat. Assn. Female Execs. Democrat. Club: Ind. Order Foresters. Home: 2215 W Hampton Milwaukee WI 53209 Office: U Wis Garland Hall 102 Box 413 Milwaukee WI 53209

DYER, VICKI SUE, contract specialist; b. Wheeling, W.Va., Jan. 16, 1953; d. Charles Thomas and Margaret Lou (Piatt) D.; grad. Eaton Sch. Bus., 1976; student Grossmont Coll., SUNY; children—David Allen Clapp, Steven Corderey Clapp. Income tax cons., H&R Block, Ewa Beach, Hawaii, San Diego, 1972-75; real estate agt. Century 21, San Diego, 1976-77; mgmt. analyst Naval Aviation Logistics Center, San Diego, 1977-81; contract specialist, engr. Gen. Mgmt. Systems, Inc., San Diego, 1982—; cons. in field. Vol. Armed Services Recreation YMCA; chmn. awards com. Grossmont council Boy Scouts Am.; active Boys Club Athletic Assn. Mem. Nat. Assn. Female Execs., Am. Mgmt. Assn. ACLU, NOW, LWV, Sierra Club. Democrat. Office: 3737 Camino del Rio S Suite 309 San Diego CA 92108

DYKE, NANCY BEARG, U.S. govt. ofcl; b. Mpls., Feb. 11, 1947; d. Richard W. and Hildegarde V. Bearg; B.A., Williamette U. 1969, M.P.A. Harvard U. 1978; m. Charles W. Dyke, June 22, 1980. With U.S. Dept. State, 1969; with NSC, 1969-70; mem. profl. staff com. on armed services U.S. Senate 1970-75; analyst Congressional Budget Office 1975-77; dir. policy analysis for N. East, Africa and South Asia, U.S. Dept. Def. 1978-79; dep. asst. sec. of air force 1980; asst. to v.p. for nat. security affairs The White House, Washington 1981-82. Recipient Sec. Def. Meritorious Civilian Service medal 1979, Air Force Exceptional Civilian Service award 1980. Contbr. in field.

DYKEMAN, WILMA, author, educator; b. Asheville, N.C., May 20, 1920; d. Willard J. and Bonnie (Cole) Dykeman; B.S. in Speech, Northwestern U., 1940; Litt.D., Maryville Coll., 1974; L.H.D., Tenn. Wesleyan Coll., 1978; m. James R. Stokely Jr., Oct. 12, 1940; children—Dykeman Cole, James R. III. Lectr. English dept. U. Tenn., Knoxville, 1975—; columnist Knoxville News-Sentinel, 1962—; author: The French Broad, 1955, The Tall Woman, 1962, The Far Family, 1966, Return the Innocent Earth, 1973, others; co-author: Neither Black Nor White, 1957; contbr. articles to nat. mags.; nat. lectr. in field; dir. Merchants & Planters Bank. Bd. dirs. Appalachian Community Services Cable Network, Washington, 1980—; trustee Berea Coll., 1971—, Phelps Stokes Fund, 1981—. Guggenheim fellow, 1956-57, NEH fellow, 1976-77; recipient Hillman award, 1957. Mem. PEN, Authors Guild, So. Hist. Assn., Phi Beta Kappa. Home: 405 Clifton Heights Newport TN 37821

DYLAG, HELEN MARIE, psychiat. clin. nurse specialist; b. Cleve., Oct. 14, 1950; d. Stanley John and Helen Agnes (Jarkiewicz) D.; B.S. in Nursing summa cum laude, St. John Coll. of Cleve., 1971; M.S. in Nursing (NIMH trainee), Ohio State U., 1973. Registered nurse drug dependency unit VA Hosp., Brecksville, Ohio, 1971-72; psychiat. clin. nurse specialist consultation and edn. dept. Marymount Hosp. Mental Health Center, Garfield Heights, Ohio, 1973-78, dir. consultation and edn. dept., 1978—; faculty continuing edn. in nursing Cleve. State U. Mem. Am. Nurses Assn and Council of Advanced Practitioners in Psychiat.-Mental Health Nursing, Sigma Theta Tau. Contbr. chpts. to books in field. Home: 5709 Onaway Oval Parma OH 44130 Office: 12300 McCracken Rd Garfield Heights OH 44125

DYLAN, EDITH WUERGLER, former investment banker, govt. ofcl.; b. Franklin County, Va., Mar. 25, 1937; d. Ray William and Janie Hazel (Robertson) Wuergler; B.A. in Public Adminstrn., Upper Iowa U., Fayette, 1976; presently student U. So. Calif. Mgr. draft collection dept. Mountain Trust Bank, Roanoke, Va., 1957-65; public relations and research asst. Roanoke Valley C. of C., 1966-67; confidential asst. to pres. Va. Western Community Coll., Roanoke, 1967-68; adminstrv. asst. to v.p. internat. Genesco, Inc., Washington, 1968-70; congl. asst., 1970-71; asst. to v.p. Merrill Lynch, Pierce, Fenner & Smith Inc., Washington, 1971-79, mgr. legis. affairs Office Govt. Relations, 1979—. Mem. Women in Housing and Fin., Am. Mgmt. Assn., Women in Govt. Relations, Am. League of Lobbyists (com. mem.), Nat. Mus. of Women's Art. Republican. Methodist. Club: Internat. (Washington). Home: 2301 E St NW Washington DC 20037 Office: 1828 L St NW Suite 906 Washington DC 20036

DYNER, PATRICIA BRIDGET, speech pathologist; b. Bklyn., Sept. 7, 1951; d. Edward J. and Joan M. (Cleary) D.; A.A., Kingsborough Community Coll., 1971; B.A., Bklyn. Coll., 1974, M.S. cum laude, 1976. Speech pathologist Willowbrook Devel. Center, S.I., N.Y., 1976-77, United Cerebral Palsy of N.Y.C., Bklyn., part-time, 1976-79; devel. therapist United Cerebral Palsy N.Y. State, S.I., 1977-79, program coordinator, 1979-80, N.E. dist. program rep. nat. orgn., 1980—. Social Rehab. Services grantee, 1974-76; lic. speech pathologist N.Y. State. Mem. N.Y. State Speech and Hearing Assn. (pres. 1973-74), Am. Speech and Hearing Assn. (cert. of clin. competence), Phi Beta Kappa.

DY-RAGOS, LYDIA SY, investment co. exec.; b. Manila, Apr. 17, 1946; came to U.S., 1969; d. Thomas Tan and Maxima Co (Uy) Syling; B.S. in Bus. Adminstrn., St. Scholastica Coll., 1968; m. Ramon R. Dy-Ragos, June 28, 1969; children—R. Leonard, Julian B., Phillip L., Mark J. Credit/collection Sy Ling Chong Sons, Manila, part-time 1965-68, controller, 1968-69; mktg. researcher Va. Nat. Bank, Charlottesville, 1969-70; bus. mgr., corp. sec. Ramon R. Dy-Ragos M.D., Inc., Kansas City, Mo., 1977—; mng. partner D.T.K. Investment Co., Kansas City, Mo., 1978—, H.D.H. Investment Co., 1980—. Charter mem. Nat. Bank in N. Kansas City Women's Adv. Council, 1978; mem. N. Kansas City Meml. Hosp. Aux., 1981—; council mem. St. Therese Roman Cath. Ch., 1978-79, social chmn., 1978-79. Recipient Recognition cert. Bicentennial Ethnic Heritage Community Plan, 1976, Appreciation cert. St. Therese Ch., 1979. Mem. Filipino Assn. Greater Kansas City (social chmn. 1975, ways and means chmn. 1981, Appreciation award 1981), Clay County Med. Assn. Aux. (pres. 1982, county rep. to AMA Aux. 1981). Office: D T K Investment Co Suite 2 5601 N Antioch Rd Kansas City MO 64119

DYSART (VAGANKA), PATRICIA LOUISE, water treatment cons.; b. McKeesport, Pa., July 16, 1947; d. Duane Bernard and Louise Irene (Gergely) Gorecki; A.S. in Biology and Chemistry, Community Coll. Allegheny County, 1974; B.S. in Chem. Engring. and Public Policy Analysis, Carnegie-Mellon U., 1978; m. J. Kenneth Dysart, Apr. 19, 1980; 1 son by previous marriage, Bryan Christopher Vaganka. Student engr. Westinghouse Elec. Co., Pitts., 1974-77; policy analyst Brookhaven Nat. Lab., Upton, L.I., N.Y., 1977; paper product devel. engr. Procter & Gamble, Cin., 1978-81; tech. specialist water treatment Betz Labs., Cin., 1982—. Mem. Am. Inst. Chem. Engrs., Nat. Assn. Female Execs., Soc. Women Engrs., NOW, Career Exchange Network, Womways. Libertarian. Club: Finney Town Women and Soccer. Home: 959 Finney Trail Cincinnati OH 45224 Office: Betz Labs 260 Northland Blvd Suite 199 Cincinnati OH 45246

DYSERT, FREDA M., ednl. cons.; b. Greenwood, Ind., Feb. 21, 1917; d. John and Dora Jane (Surface) Mullinix; B.S., Ind. State U., 1951, M.S., 1955, ednl. specialist cert., 1963, postgrad., 1964-65; m. Milford Robert Dysert, July 31, 1943; 1 son, Stephen. Tchr. elem. public schs., Ind., 1936-64; elem. supr. Met. Sch. Dist. of Pike Twp., Marion County, 1964-68; reading specialist, Richmond, Ind., 1973-74; ednl. cons. Ginn and Co. ednl. group Xerox Corp., Lexington, Mass., 1968-79. Elder, vice chmn. bd. 7th and 8th United Christian Ch. Mem. NEA, Nat. Ret. Tchrs. Assn., Ind. Ret. Tchrs. Assn., Indpls. Ret. Tchrs. Assn. Republican. Home and office: 5110 Kessler Blvd N Dr Indianapolis IN 46208

DYSON, RUTH BERRY, govt. ofcl.; b. Washington, Apr. 22, 1927; d. Sherman Lee and Edith Louise (Jackson) Berry; B.C.S., Southeastern U., Washington, 1960; postgrad. Howard U. Without Walls; m. James Dyson, Apr. 6, 1957; 1 son by previous marriage, Michael Augustus Locksley. With Census Bur., Washington, 1942-52, Dept. Def., 1952-62; supervisory statis. asst. Dept. Labor, 1962-72, supervisory program analysis officer, 1972—; trainer nat. and field staff State and Nat. Apprenticeship Reporting System. Auditor, Fort DuPont Civic Assn., 1959—; mem. Minn.-Benning Econ. Revitalization Com., 1978—. Recipient Disting. Career Service award Dept. Labor, 1974, Superior Performance award, 1977, Spl. Achievement award, 1979; Appreciation award Boy Scouts Am., 1975; Fed. Women's Program Personal Achievement award, 1980. Mem. Nat. Employment and Tng. Workers, Blacks in Government, Southeastern U. Alumni Assn. (treas. 1979, v.p.), 900th Vets. Assn. (treas.). Democrat. Baptist. Club: Les Jolissantes (treas. 1970—). Home: 301 40th St NE Washington DC 20019 Office: 601 D St NW Rm 4006 Washington DC 20213

DZAMAN, FERN LORETTA, publishing co. exec.; b. Decker, Man., Can., Apr. 25, 1932; came to U.S., 1968, resident, 1968; d. Alfred Ernest and Euretta Jane (Doupe) Lints; grad. Man. Tchrs. Coll., 1952; postgrad U. Man., 1953-54, U. Sask, 1958; m. Russell Dzaman, July 2, 1953; children—Randall, Julie, Lesa, Kenneth, Grant.; Tchr. schs. Winnipeg and Flin Flon, Man. and Estevan, Sask., Can., 1952-62; co-pub. Estevan Sun, 1962-68; exec. dir. public relations Spears Chiropractic Hosp., Denver, 1973—; founder, pres. WWIC Internat. Pub. Co., Littleton, Colo., 1976—. Active PTA. Mem. Chiropractic Editors Guild, Assn. History of Chiropractic (founding). Clubs: Lions Women's Aux. Home: 3152 E Weaver Ave Littleton CO 80121 Office: PO Box 2615 Littleton CO 80161

DZIEPAK, FRANCES DOROTHY, psychotherapist; b. Dearborn, Mich., Oct. 2, 1926; d. John S. and Martha M. Bartos; B.A., Mercy Coll., 1973; M.A., U. Detroit, 1978; m. Harry Peter Dziepak, June 28, 1947; children—Shelley, David, Claudia, Christopher, Peter, Paul, Damien, Sara. Social worker Cath. Social Services, Detroit, 1964-69, St. Francis Home for Boys, Detroit, 1973-78, Cath. Social Services, Highland Park, Mich., 1977; psychotherapist Comprehensive Med. Clinics, Southfield, Mich., 1978—, asst. adminstr., 1979—. Mem. Am. Assn. Marriage and Family Therapists, Mich. Inter- Profl. Assn., Nat. Council on Family Relations, Am. Psychol. Assn. Democrat. Roman Catholic. Home: 23070 Manistee St Oak Park MI 48237 Office: 28165 Greenfield Rd Southfield MI 48076

DZINDZELETA, MERCEDES RAMONA, energy and environ. corp. exec.; b. South Milwaukee, Wis., Apr. 10, 1942; d. Gerhardt J. and Isabelle A. (Kujawa) Skibba; student U. Wis., Parkside, 1979; A.A.S., Milw. Area Tech. Coll., 1978; 1 dau., Ramona Marie. Health educator Kenosha (Wis.) City Health Dept., 1976-77; specialist recycling oil U. Wis. Extension, Milw., 1977-78; indsl. lab. technician Enviro-Analysts, Inc., Racine, Wis., 1978-79; pres., cons. Energy & Environ. Mgmt., Inc., Racine, 1979—; directing cons., dir./coordinator Wis. Oil Recycling Program, Racine, 1978-80; directing cons., environ. coordinator U.S. Dept. Energy Indsl. Petroleum Recycling Project, Racine, 1980-81. Counselor/lectr. Young Wis. Conservationist, 1979-81. Grantee, Wis. Div. State Energy, 1977-80, U.S. EPA, 1980, U.S. Dept. Energy, 1980-81, State of Alaska, 1981; lic. wastewater treatment plant operator, Wis. Mem. Soc. Mfg. Engrs., Central States Water Pollution Control Fedn., Nat. Water Pollution Control Fedn., Wis. Waste-water Works Operators Conf., Nat. Fedn. Ind. Bus., Racine Women's Network, Izaak Walton League Am. (pres. Milw. chpt. 1979-80), Racine Area C. of C. (spl. water and waste-water utilities rate com. 1979-81). Office: Energy & Environ Mgmt Inc 1509 Rapids Dr Racine WI 53404

EADIE, MARGARET LOUISE, ednl. and bus. services cons.; b. Johnsonburg, Pa.; d. Samuel John and Elsa (Fredrickson) Larson; A.B., Miami U., Oxford, Ohio; M.A. in Counseling and Psychometry, Chapman Coll.; Advanced M.Ed., U. So. Calif.; m. Robert J. Eadie; children—William F. II, Janet Eadie Cohen, Lynne Eadie Oddo, Craig Alan. Tchr., Tustin (Calif.) High Sch., 1965-70; lectr., supr. student tchrs. Calif. State U., Fullerton, 1971-73, program coordinator continuing edn., 1973-74; cons. ednl. and bus. services, Solano Beach, Calif., 1974—. Mem. Am. Psychol. Assn. (asso.), Western Psychol. Assn., Calif. Psychol. Assn., P.E.O. Panhellenic Assn. (two Athena awards 1973), Delta Delta Delta. Republican. Office: 652 Santa Helena St Solana Beach CA 92075

EAGAN, GLEN DERBES, antique dealer; b. New Orleans, July 10, 1925; d. Max J. and Mina (Delery) Derbes; B.B.A., Tulane U., 1946; m. Lloyd E. Eagan, Dec. 27, 1945; children—Duane Couch, Jean Perriliat, Lloyd E., Mina Meric, Charles II. Asst. mktg. dept. Tulane U., 1945-52; pres. Sixpence, Inc., New Orleans, 1972—. Past pres. Acad. Sacred Heart Mothers Club; trustee Acad. Sacred Heart; mem. bd. Speech and Hearing Center New Orleans; mem. chaplains team Touro Infirmary, New Orleans. Mem. La. Colonials, Enfant de Marie, Beta Gamma Sigma (past pres.). Democrat. Roman Catholic. Home: 1648 Joseph St New Orleans LA 70115 Office: 4904 Magazine St New Orleans LA 70115

EAKIN, LAURABELLE, med. librarian; b. New Castle, Pa., Nov. 9, 1916; d. Herbert Victor and Margaret Sarah (Badger) E.; A.B., Grove City (Pa.) Coll., 1938; B.S. in L.S., Western Res. U., 1946. Sch. librarian, Pa., 1941-49; librarian VA Hosp., Pitts., 1949-57; reference librarian Falk Library Health Scis., U. Pitts., 1958-75, dir., 1975—, instr. med. lit. Sch. Library Info. Scis., 1968—. Mem. Med. Library Assn., Spl. Libraries Assn., Bibliophiles. Republican. Presbyterian. Address: Falk Library Health Scis U Pitts Pittsburgh PA 15261

EAMES, MARY A., adminstrv. asst.; b. Worcester, Mass., Sept. 10, 1944; d. Alfred H. and Marguerite (Coffill) Heath; A.A. in Bus. Adminstrn., Quinebaug Valley Community Coll.; m. Walter R. Eames, Feb. 24, 1962; 1 dau., Anastasia. Sec., office mgr. Peter Drob, Worcester, 1973-74; sec. to dir. personnel Worcester Found. Exptl. Biology, Shrewsbury, Mass., 1974; exec. sec. Rogers Corp. Research & Devel. (Conn.), 1974-77; adminstrv. asst. office of dir. group claims Phoenix Ins. Co., Hartford, Conn., 1978-81; adminstrv. asst. Phoenix Gen. Ins. Co., Hartford, 1981—. Dir. East Thompson Vol. Fire Dept., 1976, 80; firefighter, 1975—; mem. Democratic Town Com., 1973-79, sec., 1976-78; mem. Thompson Bd. Fin., 1975-77; co-chmn. Thompson Bicentennial Com., 1975-76. Mem. Nat. Secs. Assn., Bus. and Profl. Women (chpt. pres. 1980—), Internat. Soc. Fire Service Instrs., Conn. Fire Dept. Instrs. Assn. Roman Catholic.

EARGLE, MARTHA LOIS, state legislator; b. Sumter, S.C., June 24, 1936; d. Manson and Retus (Grooms) Jackson; m. Jack Irvin Eargle; children—Stephen, Gwyn, Lynn, Susan. Co-owner, Eargle's Bus. Machines; mem. S.C. Ho. of Reps., 1977—; public relations cons.; mem. staff Citizen's Confs. on Justice; mem. Criminal Justice Commn., Crime/Juvenile Delinquent Commn., Court Reform Commn.; pres. Court Update, Inc., 1974-76. Bd. dirs. Horry Shelter Home, 1975; mem. ch. choir North Conway Bapt. Ch.; mem. S.C. Jud. Nominating Commn.; mem. Gov.'s Com. to Hire the Handicapped. Mem. Am. Judicature Soc. (dir. 1974-77), S.C. Fedn. Bus. and Profl. Women's Clubs (dir. dist. 3, 1970-71), Conway Bus. and Profl. Women's Club (pres. 1968-70), Conway C. of C., LWV. Office: 422D Blatt Bldg Columbia SC 29211 *

EARHART, EILEEN MAGIE, educator; b. Hamilton, Ohio, Oct. 21, 1928; d. Andrew J. and Martha (Waldorf) Magie; B.S., Miami U., Oxford, Ohio, 1950, H.H.D. (hon.), 1980; M.Ed. in Elem. Edn. and Adminstrn., Mich. State U., East Lansing, 1962, Ph.D. in Edn., 1969; m. Paul G. Earhart; children—Anthony G., Bruce P., Daniel T. Tchr. home econs. West Alexandria Schs., 1950-51; elementary tchr. Waterford Twp. Schs., Pontiac, Mich., 1958-65, reading specialist, 1965-67; prof., chmn. family and child ecology dept. Mich. State U., 1968—. Mem. adv. bd. Lansing Com. on Children's TV; bd. dirs. Women's Resource Center, Grand Rapids, Mich. Mem. Soc. Research in Child Devel., AAUW, Nat. Assn. Edn. Young Children, Assn. Childhood Edn. Internat., Am. Home Econs. Assn., Am. Ednl. Research Assn., Internat. Reading Assn., Am. Vocat. Assn., Nat. Council Family Relations, Mich. Home Econs. Assn. (pres. 1980-82), Assn. Supervision and Curriculum Devel. Author: Building the Child's Learning Skills; Attention and Classification Training Curriculum; many others. Asso. editor Family Relations, 1980—. Home: 2030 Tamarack St Okemos MI 48864 Office: Family and Child Ecology Dept Coll Human Ecology Mich State U East Lansing MI 48824

EARL, LOVELENE LORETTA, social worker; b. Bristow, Va., Mar. 19, 1942; d. Clifford Wilson and Bessie Lee (Champ) Thornton; B.A., Fisk U., Nashville, 1967; M.S.W., U. Tenn., Nashville, 1976; m. Riggins R. Earl, Jr., July 13, 1964; children—Renal, Nathan, Regina. Caseworker, Tenn. Dept. Public Welfare, Nashville, 1967-74; social worker Birth Defects Evaluation Center, U. Tenn. Hosp., Knoxville, 1976—, mem. bd. continuing edn. Sch. Social Work, 1979—. Bd. dirs. Monroe County Parents Group for Handicapped. Recipient Mary Beasely award Tenn. Dept. Public Welfare, 1971. Mem. Nat. Assn. Social Workers, Acad. Cert. Social Workers. Baptist. Home: 115 Morningside Dr Knoxville TN 37915 Office: 1924 Alcoa Hwy Knoxville TN 37920

EARLE, SYLVIA ALICE, oceanographer; b. Gibbstown, N.J., Aug. 30, 1935; d. Lewis Reade and Alice Freas (Richie) Earle; B.S., Fla. State U., 1955; M.A., Duke U., 1956, Ph.D., 1966. Resident dir. Cape Haze Marine Lab., Sarasota, Fla., 1966-67; research scholar Radcliffe Inst., 1967-69; research fellow Farlow Herbarium Harvard U., Cambridge, Mass., 1967-75, research asso., 1975—; research asso. botany Natural History Mus. Los Angeles County, 1970-75; research biologist, curator Calif. Acad. Scis., San Francisco, 1976—; research asso. U. Calif., Berkeley, 1969—; v.p., dir. Deep Ocean Tech., Inc., Oakland, Calif. Trustee World Wildlife Fund U.S. and World Wildlife Fund Internat., Charles A. Lindbergh Fund, Ocean Trust Found.; council mem. Internat. Union Conservation Nature; corp. mem. Woods Hole Oceanographic Inst.; mem. Nat. Adv. Com. Oceans and Atmosphere. Recipient Conservation Service award U.S. Dept. Interior, 1970, Boston Sea Rovers award, 1972, 79, Nogi award Underwater Soc. Am., 1976, Conservation service award Calif. Acad. Sci., 1979, Lowell Thomas award Explorer's Club, 1980, Order of Golden Ark, Prince Netherlands, 1980; named Woman of Year, Los Angeles Times, 1970, Scientist of Year, Calif. Mus. Sci. and Industry, 1981. Mem. Internat. Phycological Soc. (sec. 1974-80), Phycological Soc. Am., Am. Soc. Ichthyologists and Herpetologists, Am. Inst. Biol. Scis., AAAS, Brit. Phycological Soc., Marine Tech. Soc., Ecol. Soc. Am. Internat. Soc. Plant Taxonomists. Author: Exploring the Deep Frontier, 1980; contbr. articles on oceanographer to profl. jours. Office: Calif Acad Scis Golden Gate Park San Francisco CA 94118

EARLEY, JOIE HILL, educator; b. Whitley County, Ky., July 24, 1928; d. Joseph Samuel and Sarah Catherine (Powers) Hill; B.A., Union Coll., 1961, M.A., 1967; m. Wilbert Harold Earley, Jan. 7, 1951; children—Dennis Howard, Ronald Lee. Elem. tchr., Whitley County, 1947-53, Knox County Schs., 1961-73; elem. tchr. Barbourville (Ky.) City Sch., 1974—, remedial reading tchr., 1977-79. Mem. NEA, Ky. Edn. Assn., Barbourville Tchrs. Orgn., AAUW, Barbourville Bus. and Profl. Woman's Club. Republican. Baptist. Clubs: Barbourville Garden, Barbourville, Younger Woman's, Order Eastern Star. Home: 183 School St Barbourville KY 40906

EARLY, LYNN DIANE, sales exec.; b. Alexandria, Va., Jan. 16, 1954; d. Harry Alvin and Ruth Jean (Seder) E.; dental asst. cert. cum laude, No. Va. Community Coll., 1973; B.A., George Mason U., 1977; M.B.A., Southeastern U. Asst. personnel mgr. Burns Internat. Security Services, Washington, 1977-78; asst. dir. public relations Am. Apparel Mfrs. Assn., Rosslyn, Va., 1978-79; sr. corporate adminstrv. asst. Shannon & Luchs, Washington, 1979-80; customer sales rep. J. B. Temps, Alexandria, Va., 1980-81; account exec. ASC Assos., Alexandria, 1981—. Marshall, Cherry Blossom Parade. Notary public. Mem. Am. Dental Assts. Assn., Nat. Assn. Female Execs., Alexandria C. of C., George Mason Alumni Assn. Republican. Home: 8819 Camfield Dr Alexandria VA 22308 Office: 5641-L General Washington Dr Alexandria VA 22312

EARP, BRENDA CAROL, med. technologist; b. Lafe, Ark., Aug. 25, 1946; d. A.G. Harrison and Clarice Beatrice (Harris) Earp; A.S., Mott Community Coll., 1966; A.B., U. Mich., 1969; cert. Hurley Med. Center Sch. Med. Technology, 1970. Lab. asst. Dr. F.W. Baske, Flint, Mich., 1966-68; substitute tchr. Flint Community Schs., 1969; med. technologist microchemistry lab. Hurley Med. Center, Flint, 1970—; lectr. in field. Vol. ARC. Named Hurley Med. Center Employee of Month, 1976, of Yr., 1977; Brenda Earp Day proclaimed by mayor of Flint, 1977. Mem. U. Mich. Alumni Assn., Hurley Med. Center Med. Technologist Orgn., Am. Soc. Clin. Pathologists. Democrat. Baptist. Contbr. articles to profl. jours. Home: 652 Vermilya Ave Flint MI 48507 Office: 1 Hurley Plaza Flint MI 48502

EARTHY, LINDA SUSAN, business exec.; b. Newport, R.I., June 30, 1950; d. Robert Henry and C. Carole (Soldo) Richard; student Pa. State U., 1968-69. Various secretarial positions, Washington, San Francisco, 1969-72; flight attendant Trans Internat. Airlines, Oakland, Calif., 1972-77; steamship cargo sales rep. Matson Nav. Co., Oakland, 1977-79; dist. sales mgr. Moram Agys., Oakland, 1979; West Coast sales mgr. Philippines, Micronesia & Orient Nav. Co., San Francisco, 1979-81; regional sales mgr. Bekins Wide World, Oakland, 1981—. Mem. Oakland World Trade Assn. (dir. 1979). Clubs: San Francisco Traffic, Commonwealth of San Francisco. Home: 348 Pacheco St San Francisco CA 94116 Office: 2227 San Pablo Ave Oakland CA 94612

EASBEY, MARION MORIARTY, telephone co. mgr.; b. New Bedford, Mass., Apr. 8, 1930; d. Walter Vincent and Marion Elizabeth (Rigby) Moriarty; B.S., U. R.I., 1947-51; student Bell System Center for Tech. Edn., 1973—. Service rep. N.E. Telephone & Northwestern Bell, Providence and St. Paul, 1952-58; office supr. Northwestern Bell, St. Paul, 1958-63, engring. staff asst., 1963-64; engring. technician, asso. engr. and engr. Northwestern Bell, St. Paul and N.E. Telephone, Providence, 1967-79, project mgr. N.E. Telephone, Framingham, Mass., 1979—; engr. chief clk. Northwestern Bell, 1964-67. Practical politics instr. St. Paul C. of C., 1970; Lake Elmo Precinct chmn. and county conv. del., 1973. Recipient cert. of Accomplishment, CAP, 1968, cert. of Merit, 1968. Mem. Common Cause (state network chmn. 1976-79), Assn. Mgmt. Women, AAUW, ACLU, NOW. Democrat Unitarian. Club: Appalachian Mountain. Home: 100 Girard Rd Cumberland RI 02864 Office: 350 Cochituate Rd Framingham MA 01701

EASLEY, BETTY, state legislator; b. Victoria, Tex., Aug. 5, 1929; d. Clifford Pennington and Inez (Cary) Chapman; student U. Tex., 1947-49; m. Kenneth E. Easley, Nov. 11, 1966; children—Cary, Barbara, Katherine, Virginia, William (dec.). Med. illustrator Walter Reed Med. Center, Washington, 1952-55; owner B&K Acctg. System, Tampa, Fla., 1962-66; newspaper columnist, Clearwater, Fla., 1969-72; mem. Fla. Ho. of Reps., 1972—, mem. subcom. on edn. and transp. Appropriations Com., Fin. and Taxation Com., K-12 Edn. Com., Select Com. on Juvenile Justice, Select Com. on Mining and Reclamation, chmn. fin. instns. subcom. Fin. and Taxation Com., chmn. severence tax subcom. Mining and Reclamation Select Com. Vice chmn. Fla. Human Relations Commn., 1974-75; women's chmn. United Cerebral Palsy of Fla., 1973-75; mem. Fla. State Adv. Com. on U.S. Commn. Civil Rights, 1972-74, Pinellas County Met. Criminal Justice Planning Unit, 1972-80; del. Republican nat. conv., 1976; chmn. Pinellas Legis. Del., 1978-79; mem. Dist. V Mental Health Bd., 1974-78; bd. mem. Upper Pinellas Assn. for Retarded Citizens; mem. Women's Living and Learning Program Adv. Council, Fla. State Panel Am. Council on Edn., Fed. Edn. Data Acquisition Council. Recipient legis. award, Property Appraiser's Assn. Fla., 1981, presdl. award, 1981, legis. awards Fla. Phosphate Council, 1982, Juvenile Welfare Bd., 1976, Commn. on Human Rights, 1977, Fla. Assn. Community Colls., 1977, TIGER award, 1977, 79, 80, 81, Fla. Sch. Bd. Assn. 67baward, 1979, 80, 81, Friend of Edn. award, Pinellas Classroom Tchrs. Assn., 1980, Gavel of Authority award, Fla. Assn. Sch. Adminstrs., 1981, Allen Morris Award, 1981; named rep. of year Fla. Assn. Community Colls., 1979; nominated Most Valuable Mem. of the House, St. Petersburg Times, 1979, 80. Mem. Bus. and Profl. Women's Club, Fla. Fedn. Rep. Women's Clubs, Nat. Order Women Legislators (pres.), Beta Sigma Phi (hon.). Episcopalian. Club: Zonta. Office: 12800 Indian Rocks Rd Largo FL 33540

EASLEY, ELEANOR LUCIE, educator; b. Atmore, Ala., Feb. 14, 1950; d. Anselm Thedford and Sara Ella (Stewart) Easley; B.S., Judson Coll., 1971; M.R.E., So. Bapt. Theol. Sem., 1974; M.S.W., U. Louisville, Kent Sch. Social Work, 1975. Asst. social worker Norton Psychiat. Clinic, Louisville, 1973-75; mem. faculty So. Bapt. Theol. Sem., Louisville, 1975—, asst. prof. social work edn., 1976—. Bd. dirs. Hospice of Louisville, Inc.; mem. adv. com. Can Surmount; mem. allocation com. Metro United Way. Recipient Kentuckiana Metroversity Instructional Devel. award, 1979. Mem. Nat. Assn. Social Workers, Acad. Cert. Social Workers, So. Bapt. Social Services Assn. Democrat. Baptist. Home: 9601 Somerford Ct Louisville KY 40222 Office: 2825 Lexington Rd Louisville KY 40206

EASTERBROOK, HELEN LOUISE, banker; b. Cowles, Nebr., Feb. 2, 1917; d. Jesse M. and Lora Belle (Holland) Marsh; A.B., Hastings (Nebr.) Coll., 1938; M.S. in Edn., Kearney (Nebr.) State Coll., 1961; m. Carl W. Easterbrook, May 25, 1940; 1 dau., Leslie Eileen Easterbrook Holchak. Tchr. English, Nebr. high schs., 1939-58, Lab. Sch., U. No. Colo., Greeley, 1963-65; instr. English, Kearney State Coll., 1960-72; trust adminstrn. officer Platte Valley State Bank & Trust Co., Kearney, 1973—. Mem. Nat. Assn. Bank Women (pres. Central Nebr. Group 1980-81), Am. Inst. Banking. Presbyterian. Home: 3117 10th Ave Kearney NE 68847

EASTERLING, RUTH M., N.C. state legislator; b. Gaffney, S.C., Dec. 26; d. Benjamin Harrison and Lillie Mae (Crawley) Moss; B.A., Limestone Coll., 1932; student Queens Coll., Charlotte, N.C.; married. Exec. asst. to pres. Radiator Specialty Co., Charlotte, N.C. also Toronto, Ont., Can.; mem. Gov.'s Advocacy Council for Persons with Disabilities; mem. adv. council on OSHA; mem. Gov.'s Commn. on Status of Women, 1964; mem. Charlotte City Council, 1972-73; mem. N.C. Ho. of Reps., 1977-78, 79-80, 81—, vice-chmn. appropriations base budget com. on natural and econ. resources, appropriations expansion budget com. on natural and econ. resources, others. N.C. pres. Women's Polit. Caucus, 1974; mem. research and edn. com. Nat. Bus. and Profl. Women's Found., 1978-81; trustee Wildacres Retreat. Mem. AAUW, LWV, Bus. and Profl. Women's Club (nat. pres. 1970-71), Nat. Secs. Assn. (internat. chmn. pub. and world affairs 1975-76), Women's Polit. Caucus, Women's Equity Action League, Women Execs. Charlotte, Women's Forum N.C. Baptist (assoc. supt. tng., assoc. supt. intermediate dept. Sunday Sch., mem. library, fin. planning and personnel coms., pres. Baptist Bus. Women). Office: NC Ho Reps State Capitol Raleigh NC 27602

EASTLAND, MARY LOU, educator, publisher; b. McComb, Miss., July 3, 1939; d. James DeWitt and Mary Belle (Barnes) White; B.S.E., Delta State U., 1961; postgrad. U. So. Miss., 1978; m. Charles Lamar Eastland, Sr., Dec. 25, 1961; children—Charles Lamar, James Denson, Laura Lynette. Instr. phys. edn. and health El Paso (Tex.) Pub. Sch. System, 1961-62; accounts researcher, clk.-typist IRS, Jackson, Miss., 1963-65; co-owner, operator Bresler's 33 Flavors, Gulfport, Miss., 1974-76; instr. sci. Harrison County (Miss.) Sch. System, 1977—; owner Top-Flite Publs., Gulfport. Active YWCA, Girl Scouts U.S., baseball and softball programs of Orange Grove Youth Assn., youth basketball program of Orange Grove C. of C. Mem. Am. Entrepreneurs Assn., Beta Sigma Phi. Club: Orange Grove Opti-Mrs. Home: Route 2 Box 358-E Gulfport MS 39503

EASTMAN, ADALINE JONES, educator; b. Phila., Apr. 9, 1924; d. Harry Elmer and Mary Elizabeth (Saul) Seitz; B.S. in Edn., Shippensburg State Coll., 1945; M.A., Ohio State U., 1957, Ph.D., 1964; m. Herschel Frederick Eastman, Mar. 1, 1975; 1 son by previous marriage, William Russell Jones; 1 stepson, Michael Hall. Sec. to pres. Shippensburg (Pa.) State Coll., 1943-45; head bus. dept. Blacklick Twp. High Sch., Twin Rocks, Pa., 1945-51; sec. to mgr. dept. engring. econs. Battelle Meml. Inst., Columbus, Ohio, 1951-52; tchr. English and bus. Reynoldsburg (Ohio) High Sch., 1953-56; chmn. bus. dept. Capital U., Columbus, 1956-64; prof., coordinator vocat. tchr. edn. programs Ball State U. Coll. Bus., Muncie, Ind., 1964—. Recipient Jessie S. Heiges Disting. Alumnus award, 1978. Mem. Future Bus. Leaders Am./Phi Beta Lambda (state chmn. 1965-72), Nat. Bus. Edn. Assn. (Outstanding Coll. Tchr. of Yr. award), North Central Bus. Edn. Assn. (pres. 1979-80), Am. Vocat. Assn. (Disting. Service award), Nat. Assn. Distributive Edn. Tchrs., Council for Distributive Tchr. Edn., Ind. Vocat. Assn., Ind. Bus. Edn. Assn. (Outstanding Service award 1977), Ind. Mktg. and Distributive Edn. Assn., Ind. Bus. Educators' Club (pres. 1968-69), Ind. Council Vocat. Adminstrs., Delta Pi Epsilon, Pi Lambda Theta, Delta Kappa Gamma. Lutheran. Clubs: Twin Rocks Garden (pres. 1951), Toastmistress (treas. Muncie chpt.). Contbr. articles to profl. jours.; assoc. editor The Delta Pi Epsilon Jour., 1974-78. Home: 401 Winthrop Rd Muncie IN 47304 Office: PO Box 76 Whitinger Coll Bus Bldg Ball State U Muncie IN 47306

EASTMAN, BRENDA GAY, clin. psychologist, educator; b. Hardwick, Vt., Mar. 15, 1951; s. Howard Norcross and Evelyn (Gadapee) E.; B.A. summa cum laude (Honor scholar), U. Vt., 1973; M.A., U. Fla., 1976, Ph.D., 1979. Postdoctoral fellow in behavioral medicine U. Fla., 1979-81, vis. asst. prof. clin. psychology 1981-82; asst. prof. psychology U. Toledo, 1982—. Mem. Am. Psychol. Assn., Southeastern Psychol. Assn., Phi Beta Kappa, Phi Kappa Phi. Contbr. articles in pediatric psychology to profl. jours. Office: Dept Psychology U Toledo 2801 W Bancroft St Toledo OH 43606

EASTMAN, MARILYN MARIE, record and film producer; b. Davenport, Iowa, Dec. 17, 1933; d. Verne M. and Helen M. (Gedye) Johnson; degree in drama U. Iowa, 1955; children—John B., Michael E. Former child actress and dancer, writer, performer children's TV shows; exec. v.p. Hardman Assos. Inc., Pitts., 1963-81; pres. Hardman Eastman Studios, Inc., Pitts., 1982—; co-producer film Night of the Living Dead, 1969; actress Pitts. Civic Light Opera Assn., 1979; speaker in field. Recipient Cine-Golden Eagle award for film script The Catalyst, 1973. Mem. AFTRA, Actors Equity Assn., Pitts. Advt. Club. Author songs, short stories. Office: 1400 E Carson St Pittsburgh PA 15203

EASTMAN, PATRICIA KEARNEY, communications cons.; b. Bennington, Vt., May 30, 1950; d. Franklin Patrick and Sally (Skinner) Kearney; B.A., Annenberg Sch. Communications, U. Pa., 1971; postgrad. in bus. adminstrn. N.Y. U.; m. Aug. 7, 1976. Editor coll. div. Holt, Rinehart & Winston, N.Y.C., 1972-75; planning analyst CBS/Pub. Group, N.Y.C., 1975-77; pub. CBS Venture Pub., N.Y.C., 1977-79; dir. adminstrn. CBS Sch. Mgmt., N.Y.C., 1979-80; producer CBS Sports, 1980-81; communications cons., 1981—. Mem. Nat. Acad. TV Arts and Scis., Am. Mgmt. Assn.

EASTON, LAGENIA ANN, nurse; b. Olney, Ill., Nov. 17, 1954; d. James Henry and Wanda L. King; R.N., St. John's Sch. Nursing, 1975; A.A., Springfield Coll., 1975; postgrad. Sangamon State Coll., 1978—; m. Roy Easton, Aug. 9, 1975; children—Jeremy Bryce, Jason Brian. Staff nurse Pana (Ill.) Community Hosp., 1975-79, infection control nurse, 1977-79, utilization rev. nurse, 1977-78, dir. operating room dept., 1979—; vol. ARC, 1975-77. Mem. Assn. Operating Room Nurses, Delta Theta Tau. Democrat. Presbyterian. Home: 1 Huber St Pana IL 62557 Office: Pana Community Hosp S Locust St Pana IL 62557

EASTON, LOUISE LUMINO, newspaper publisher, editor; b. Jersey City, Dec. 27, 1931; d. Frank Charles and Philomena Ann (Sciarra) Lumino; B.A. in Journalism, Bowling Green State U., 1952; m. William Easton, Nov. 3, 1962; children—Philip, Peter, Russell (dec. 1978). Account supr. advt. dept. Worthington Corp., Harrison, N.J., 1955-64; editor Ind. Press, Summit, N.J., 1969-73; pub., editor Madison Eagle-Chatham Courier, Madison, N.J., 1973—. Pres., Jersey City Jr. Woman's Club, 1959-63; bd. dirs. Madison Eagle Christmas Fund; bd. mgrs. Vis. Homemakers Service; mem. exec. bd., jr. membership dept. N.J. Fedn. Women's Clubs, 1960-65; mem. New Providence Citizens Adv. Commn., Master Plan Rev., 1977. Named Suburban Journalist of Year, Suburban Newspapers Am., 1972, Woman of Year, Summit Area YWCA, 1975. Mem. Nat. Newspaper Assn. (McKinney award 1978), N.J. Press Assn. (cert. of excellence for editorial, for column), Suburban Newspapers Am. (cert. of excellence for feature writing 1976, 1st Place Nat. award for best continuing column 1977), AAUW, Madison Area C. of C. (Christmas com. 1975—). Club: Zonta. Home: 190 Sagamore Dr Murray Hill NJ 07974

EATON, ANTOINETTE JOAN, physician; b. Youngstown, Ohio, Jan. 11, 1931; d. Carmen and Rose Parisi; B.S. cum laude, Geneva Coll., Beaver Falls, Pa., 1952; M.D., Med. Coll. Pa., Phila., 1956; m. Samuel Eaton, 1959; children—Gregory, Lynne, Jeffrey, Anne. Rotating intern Youngstown Hosp., 1956-57; jr. asst. resident, then chief resident ambulatory pediatrics Children's Hosp., Columbus, Ohio, 1957-60, chief handicapped child sect., 1967-74, dir. Birth Defects Center, 1967-74, asso. med. dir. ambulatory services, 1980—; staff pediatrician, then chief pediatrics, dir. diagnostic center Columbus State Sch., 1961-66; mem. faculty Ohio State U. Med. Sch., 1960—, prof. pediatrics, 1980—; chief div. maternal and child health Ohio Dept. Health, 1974-80. Diplomate Am. Bd. Pediatrics. Mem. Am. Med. Women's Assn., Ambulatory Pediatric Soc., Am. Acad. Pediatrics, Central Ohio Pediatric Soc., Ohio Med. Assn., Ohio Perinatal Assn. (dir.), Ohio Pub. Health Assn., Franklin County Acad. Medicine, Ohio Soc. Pedodontists (hon.), Alpha Omega Alpha. Contbr. articles to med. jours. Home: 5668 Indian Mound Ct Columbus OH 43213 Office: 700 Children's Dr Columbus OH 43205

EATON, LYNDA LOU, med. diagnostic co. exec.; b. Nevada, Mo., Aug. 31, 1946; d. Ira and Anna Mae (Welch) E.; B.S. in Chemistry, Central Mo. State U., Warrensburg, 1967; M.B.A., Pepperdine U., 1981; m. John C. Carlisle, Dec. 1980. Blood bank supr. St. Luke's Hosp., Kansas City, Mo., 1968-71; acting blood bank supr. Hoag Meml. Hosp., Newport Beach, Calif., 1971-72; blood bank supr. City of Hope Nat. Med. Center, Duarte, Calif., 1975-77; mgr. Immuno-Science, Inc., Los Angeles, 1977—. Mem. Am. Soc. Clin. Pathology (med. technologist, specialist in blood banking), Am. Assn. Blood Banks. Republican. Home: 6 Palos Irvine CA 92715 Office: Immuno-Science Inc 845 W Laveta Ave Orange CA 92668

EATON, MARY ANN CECELIA, speech and lang. pathologist; b. Youngsville, N.Y., May 11, 1949; d. Charles John and Gertrude Marie (Kalbfleisch) Menges; B.A., SUNY, Albany, 1971, M.S., 1972, postgrad., 1973; m. Bryan Lynn Eaton, June 5, 1971; children—Tara Lynn, Lisa Ann, Thomas Bryan. Asst. tchr. Sullivan County Assn. Retarded Children, Liberty, N.Y., summer 1970; acad. advisor SUNY, Albany, 1971-73; speech and lang. therapist Pinewoods Center for Retarded, Troy, N.Y., 1973-74; speech and lang. pathologist Albany-Schenectady-Schoharie County BOCES, Maywood Sch., 1974—; guest lectr. Coll. St. Rose, Albany; participant, panel discussion on teaching children with special needs, tchr. edn. series, Public TV Sta. WMHT, 1974; script writer for film on deafness, 1979-80. Lic. speech pathologist, N.Y. Mem. Am. Speech-Lang. and Hearing Assn. (cert. clin. competence), N.Y. State Speech and Hearing Assn.

EATON, MARY JAYNE, psychologist; b. St. Louis, Nov. 14, 1921; d. Guy W. and Olivia E.; B.A., Washington U., St. Louis, 1949; M.A., U. Toledo, 1952; Ph.D., U. Ala., 1968. Dir. psychol. services Madison County Bd. Edn., Huntsville, Ala., 1960-68; chmn. dept. psychology and spl. edn. Athens (Ala.) Coll., 1968-75; psychologist Regional Edn. Service Center, Stillwater, Okla., 1978—; vol. counselor Payne County Program for Misdemeanants, Stillwater, 1978—. Mem. Southwestern Psychol. Assn., NOW, Am. Psychol. Assn., Okla. Sch. Psychologists Assn., Okla. Psychol. Assn., Cat Fanciers Assn., Burmese Breeders. Home: Route 5 Box 99 Stillwater OK 74074 Office: 215 E 12th St Stillwater OK 74074

EATON, PENELOPE ANNE, home bldg. co. exec.; b. Yorkshire, Eng., Aug. 17, 1951; came to U.S., 1973; d. Cedric Nigel and Doreen (Cook) Teather; B.A. in Philosophy with honors, U. Sussex (Eng.), 1973. Retirement plan saleswoman, Ft. Lauderdale, Fla., 1974-76; project mgr. Spring Run Condominiums, Sunrise, Fla., 1976-78; sales and mktg. mgr. Wilshire Diversified, Inc., Glendale, Calif., 1978-80; dir. land acquisition Ponderosa Homes, Irvine, Calif., 1980—; cons. on land use. Mem. Bldg. Industry Assn. (local govtl. affairs com.), Home Builders Council. Office: Ponderosa Homes 2082 Business Center Dr Suite 225 Irvine CA 92715

EATON, STEPHANIE, state ofcl.; b. Littleton, N.H., July 22, 1936; d. Stephen Ladd and Christie Margaret (Gordon) E.; B.A. in Sociology, Middlebury Coll., 1958; postgrad., U. Colo., 1960; M.A. in English, U. N.H., 1963; M.L.T., Norwich U., 1973; 1 child, Michels. Spl. edn. tchr. elem. and high sch. Crotched Mountain Rehab. Center, Greenfield, N.H., 1962-64; high sch. English tchr. and ski team coach, White Mountain Supervisory Union, Lancaster and Littleton, N.H., 1965-67; exec. sec. No. N.H. Mental Health System, Littleton, 1971-72; Region I Area Program dir. N.H. State Council on Aging, Littleton, 1972-73; med. lab. technician Littleton Hosp. Lab., 1974-75; dir. N.H. Sr. Health Screening, Littleton, Berlin, and Concord, N.H., 1975-79; dir. N.H. Div. Human Resources, Concord, 1979-81; dir. N.H. State Council on Aging, Concord, 1981—. Officer Littleton Planning Bd., 1968-72, Littleton Library bd. trustees, 1965-72, N.H. Library Trustee Assn., 1970-72, Littleton Hosp. Women's Aux., 1967; mem. Littleton Community Devel. Planning, 1979, Littleton Town Hall Study Com., 1971, Area Cons. Library Assn.; active March of Dimes, LWV; mem. Littleton Republican Com. Congregationalist. Club: Profile Women's. Office: 14 Depot St Concord NH 04301

EATON, SUSAN HELEN DRATCH, educator, bus. exec.; b. Yonkers, N.Y., July 19, 1947; d. Michael Stephen and Ann Helen (Palica) Dratch; B.S. summa cum laude, U. Bridgeport, 1969, postgrad., 1973—; M.A., Columbia U., 1970; m. Norman Clyde Eaton, July 3, 1971. Sec., Gen. Foods Corp., White Plains, N.Y., 1966-70; bus. educator White Plains High Sch., 1970-72; instr. secretarial adminstrn. U. Bridgeport (Conn.), 1972-75, asst. prof., 1975—, acting dir. Weylister Sch. of U. Bridgeport, 1978-79, dir., 1979—; owner, cons., corp. trainer Eaton Assn., Westport, Conn., 1981—; speaker, panelist, participant confs.; corp. cons., on-site trainer office adminstrn., secretarial adminstrn. and word processing, 1978—. Named Outstanding Bus. Student Westchester chpt. Adminstrv. Mgmt. Soc., 1965; recipient award of merit Nat. Bus. Edn. Assn., 1970. Mem. AAUP, Conn. Bus. Educators Assn., Coll. and Univ. Bus. Instrs. in Conn. (bd. dirs., sec. 1974-76), Eastern Bus. Edn. Assn., Internat. Info./Word Processing Assn., Nat. Assn. Female Execs., Nat. Bus. Edn. Assn., New Eng. Bus. Educators Assn., Bus. Edn. Alumni Assn. Tchrs. Coll., Craft Connection, Norwalk Newcomers, Nutmeg Quilters Guild, Delta Pi Epsilon, Kappa Delta Pi. Contbg. cons. Readers Digest Back to Basics, 1981. Home and Office: Lisa Ct Westport CT 06880 Office: University of Bridgeport Bridgeport CT 06601

EAVES, MARY MARIE, gas utility ofcl.; b. Wichita Falls, Tex., June 30, 1939; d. James Pinckney and Mary Edna (Hughes) Hines; student N.Mex. State U., San Juan, 1973-74; spl. course U. Colo., 1979; Public Utility Exec. Program, U. Mich., summer 1980; children—Christie Jo, Lea Ann. Sec., So. Union Gas Co., 1957-60; v.p. Chaparral Oil & Gas Co., Santa Fe, 1970—; pres. M.E.D. Tankers, Inc., 1971-78; co-owner The Linen Closet, 1972-74; adminstrv. asst. govt. relations Gas Co. N.Mex., 1975—; exec. on loan Interior Com., U.S. Ho. of Reps., fall 1981. Chmn., San Juan County Democratic Party, 1966-67; mem. N.Mex. Dem. State Central Com., 1966-73, Dem. Nat. Com., 1967-73; vice chmn. N.Mex. Dem. Party, 1967-73; mem. Nat. Dem. Charter Commn., 1972-74; del. Dem. Nat. Conv., 1968, alt. del., 1972, mem. platform com., 1968, rules com., 1972; adv. com. N.Mex. Commn. for Post-Secondary Edn.; mem. nominating com. bd. trustees St. Vincent's Hosp.; mem. N.Mex. adv. com. Mountain States Legal Found. Recipient Cert. of Appreciation adv. bd. Salvation Army, 1969-75, N.Mex. Dem. Party, 1974, N.Mex. Dem. Women, 1974. Mem. Ind. Producers Assn. N.Mex., New Mexicans for Jobs and Energy, N.Mex. Oil and Gas Assn., Am. Gas Assn. (gov.), N.Mex. Utility Attys. Group. Presbyterian. Clubs: Daus. of the Nile, Santa Fe Girls, Eastern Star. Home: 1345 Don Gaspar Ave Santa Fe NM 87501 Office: PO Box 1448 Santa Fe NM 87501

EBAUGH, ELIZABETH BROWN (MRS. FRANK WRIGHT EBAUGH), civic worker; b. Jacksonville, Tex.; d. John Lemuel and Jewel (Newton) Brown; B.A., U. Colo., 1925; M.A., Tchrs. Coll., Columbia U., 1927; m. Frank Wright Ebaugh, Feb. 22, 1930; 1 dau., Betty Jane (Mrs. Gordon B. McFarland, Jr.). Kindergarten tchr., Port Arthur, Tex., 1927-30. Bd. dirs. Jacksonville Pub. Library, 1944-77, pres., 1944-46, hon. mem. bd., 1977—, curator, organizer Vanishing Texana Mus., 1965-79. Mem. Cherokee County Hist. Commn., 1964—. Recipient Appreciation plaque Jacksonville Library, 1969. Mem. D.A.R. (charter; registrar 1965—), Chi Omega. Presbyn. (historian 1965-66). Home: 428 S Patton St Jacksonville TX 75766

EBBITT, WILMA ROBB, educator; b. Moose Jaw, Sask., Can., June 29, 1918; came to U.S., 1940, naturalized, 1949; d. William Alexander and Annie (Archer) Robb; B.A., U. Sask., 1938, M.A., 1940; Ph.D. (fellow), Brown U., 1943; m. David R. Ebbitt, Dec. 28, 1942; Instr., Brown U., 1943-45; mem. faculty U. Chgo., 1945-68, prof. English, 1966-68; freelance editor, 1968-73; lectr. U. Colo., 1968-69; vis. prof. U. Tex., Austin, 1973-74; prof. English, Pa. State U., University Park, 1974—. Mem. MLA, Nat. Council Tchrs. English, Rhetoric Soc. Am., Phi Beta Kappa. Democrat. Episcopalian. Author: (with Russel Nye) Structure in Reading and Writing, 1961; (with James Sledd) Dictionaries and THAT Dictionary, 1962; (with William T. Lenehan) The Writer's Reader, 1968; Writer's Guide and Index to English, 7th edit., 1982. Office: Dept English Pa State U University Park PA 16802

EBERHART, MARY ANN PETESIE, wholesale co. exec.; b. Baton Rouge, Aug. 20, 1940; d. Wilford Malvern and Mary Gordon (Davidson) E.; B.S., McNeese State U., 1963. With United Service Warehouse, Inc., Baton Rouge, 1963—, v.p., 1974—, sales mgr., 1979—; v.p. United Engine Service, Baton Rouge, 1980—, gen. mgr., 1981—. Recipient Worlds Champion Cutting Horse award Womens Profl. Rodeo Assn., 1971. Mem. Womens Profl. Rodeo Assn. (v.p. 1978—), McNeese State U. Alumni Assn., Delta Zeta. Democrat. Episcopalian. Home: 3770 Stumberg Ln Baton Rouge LA 70816 Office: 440 N 12th St PO Box 3076 Baton Rouge LA 70821 also 13521 S Choctaw St Baton Rouge LA 70815

EBERT, GLADYS EILEEN MEYER, home economist; b. Wellsburg, Iowa, Jan. 16, 1921; d. Eilert J. and Juliet O'Ressa (Thompson) Meyer; B.A., U. No. Iowa, 1942; M.S., Iowa State U., 1967, M.S., 1968, Ph.D., 1978; m. George Henry Ebert, Sept. 16, 1950; children—George Meyer, Ann Louise, Barbara Eileen. Tchr., McGregory (Iowa) High Sch., 1942-43, Sigourney (Iowa) High Sch., 1943-44, Wellsburg (Iowa) High Sch., 1944-46, Nevada (Iowa) High Sch., 1946-52, Freeborn (Minn.) High Sch., 1952-53, Westmarshall Community Sch., State Center, Iowa, 1962-65; research asst. home econs. Iowa State U., Ames, 1965-67, instr. home econs., 1967-78, asst. prof., 1979—; vis. prof. S.D. State U., summer 1977; mem. Iowa Task Force on Needs of Incarcerated Mothers, 1981-82; participant profl. confs. Mem. Am. Home Econs. Assn., Iowa Home Econs. Assn., Am. Vocat. Edn. Research Assn., Am. Ednl. Research Assn., Adult Edn. Research Assn., Assn. Tchr. Edn., Nat. Assn. Tchr. Educators for Home Econs., AAUW, Phi Delta Kappa, Omicron Nu, Phi Delta Gamma, Alpha Chi Omega. Republican. Presbyterian. Contbr. articles to profl. jours. Home: 2114 Greenbriar Circle Ames IA 50010 Office: Coll Home Econs Iowa State U Ames IA 50010

EBERT, TRUDY MARY, civic worker; b. St. Paul, Feb. 15, 1925; d. Edward M. and Gertrude C. (Connell) O'Leary; student U. Minn., 1948-49, St. Catherines Coll., 1967-68; m. Robert A. Ebert, Feb. 8, 1947; children—Kathryn Ebert-Hilger, Richard Friess. Disaster driver unit Ramsey County (Minn.) chpt. ARC, 1947-58; active PTA, Nativity, Derham Hall, St. Thomas Mil. Acad., St. Paul, 1957-71; nat. bd. dirs., pres. St. Croix Valley council Camp Fire Girls Am., 1956-82; chairperson Community Chest, St. Paul, 1958; pres., bd. dirs. Ramsey County Bar Assn. Aux., 1961-82; bd. dirs., pres. Inter Club Council, St. Paul, 1966-81; treas. Lawyers Wives Minn., St. Paul, 1968-70; pres. Women's Orgn. of Decathalon Athletic Club, Bloomington, Minn., 1969; pres. Nat. Lawyers Wives aux. Am. Bar Assn., 1974; mem. Minn. Gov.'s Vol. Task Force, 1975-79; pres. Minn. Hist. Soc. Women's Orgn., 1977-80; organizer Children and Law, Minn., 1968, nat., 1970; chairperson Republican Precinct, St. Paul. Recipient Outstanding Community Service award St. Paul Community Chest, 1959, Ernest Thomas Seton award Nat. Camp Fire Girls, 1966, Vol. Service award Minn. Gov., 1979, and other service awards. Mem. Minn. Hist. Soc., Ramsey County Hist. Soc., Good Old Girls Minn. Roman Catholic. Clubs: Univ. of St. Paul, St. Paul Athletic (aux. pres. 1970), St. Paul Women's, St. Paul Pool and Yacht. Home: 534 S Mississippi River Blvd Saint Paul MN 55116

EBLING, SALLY KLAAR, home economist county adminstr.; b. Lakewood, Ohio, Aug. 7, 1934; d. John A. Klaar and Katheryn Klaar Edmonds; B.S., Iowa State U., 1956; m. John K. Ebling, Apr. 4, 1959. Home service rep. Mich. Consol. Gas., Grand Rapids, 1956-58; county extension agt. in home econs. Akron County (Ohio), 1958-59 Baltimore County (Md.), 1959-60, Cuyahoga County (Ohio), 1960-77; chmn. Cuyahoga County Coop. Extension Service, 1978—; trustee Community Info. and Vol. Service. Trustee, Gt. Lakes Shakespeare Festival, Lakewood, 1976-79; county coordinator for Cuyahoga County, Internat. Yr. of Child, 1979. Recipient Superior Service award Dept. Agr., 1968; Emmy award Cleve. Radio and TV Council, 1974. Mem. Am. Home Econs. Assn. (sec. extension sect. 1976-77, chmn. publs. com. 1977-80), Nat. Assn. Extension Home Economists (Florence Hall award 1973), Ohio County Extension Agts. Assn., Adult Edn. Council, Phillis Wheatley Assn., Cleve. Council World Affairs, Cleve. Home Econs. Assn. (pres. 1962). Presbyterian. Clubs: Acad. of Medicine Women's Aux., Womanspace; Women's City (pres. 1974-76, v.p. Found. 1981—) (Cleve.). Local TV appearances. Home: 19032 Colahan Dr Rocky River OH 44116 Office: 3200 W 65th St Cleveland OH 44102

ECHOLS, IVOR TATUM (MRS. SYLVESTER J. ECHOLS), educator; b. Oklahoma City, Dec. 28, 1919; d. Israel E. and Katie (Bingley) Tatum; A.B., U. Kans., 1942; postgrad. (A.R.C. scholar) U. Nebr., 1945-46; M.S. in Social Work (Nat. Urban League fellow, Porter R. Lee fellow), Columbia, 1952, postgrad. (NIMH fellow), U. So. Calif., 1961-62, D.S.W., 1968; m. Kenneth Johnston, Dec. 28, 1943 (div. June 1951); 1 dau., Kalu Helene; m. 2d, Sylvester J. Echols, June 13, 1954 (div. 1976); 1 son, Kim Arnett. Tchr. social studies high sch., Holdenville, Okla., 1942-43, Geary, Okla., 1943-45; caseworker A.R.C., Chgo., 1946-47; resident group worker, Dosoris House for Teen-Age Girls, Community Services Soc., N.Y.C., 1950-51; supr. group work Walnut Grove Center Neighborhood Clubs, Oklahoma City, 1948-51; program dir. Camp Lookout YWCA, Denver, 1951; dir. program services Presbyn. Neighborhood Services, Detroit, summer 1960, supr. group work Merrill-Palmer Inst., Detroit, 1951-70; asst. dir. Merrill-Palmer Camp, Dryden, Mich., 1951-59; prof. Sch. Social Work, U. Conn., West Hartford, 1970—; del. Inter-Univ. Consortium of Social Devel., Hong Kong, 1980; mem. Conn. adv. com. U.S. Commn. Civil Rights. Mem. Ad Hoc Com. Citizens Concerned with Equal Ednl. Opportunity, Detroit, 1964—; cons. to N.E.A. Conf. Family Camping Washington, 1959, ednl. film Scott Paper Co., Phila., 1963, 64; summer study skills project Presbyn. Ch. Bd. Nat. Missions, Knoxville, Tenn., 1965—; sec. United Neighborhood Centers Am.; pres. Protestant Community Services, Detroit, 1969-70. Recipient Sojourner Truth award Detroit chpt. Nat. Assn. Negro Bus. and Profl. Women, 1969; Conn. Social Worker of Year, 1979. Mem. Nat. Assn. Colored Women's Clubs (participant White House Conf. on Children and Youth 1960), A.M.E. Ministers Wives, Acad. Certified Social Workers, Delta Sigma Theta. Mem. A.M.E. Ch. Home: 51 Chestnut Dr Windsor CT 06095 Office: U Conn 1800 Asylum Ave West Hartford CT 06007

ECK, DOROTHY FRITZ, state senator; b. Sequim, Wash., Jan. 23, 1924; d. Ira Edward and Ida (Hokanson) Fritz; B.S. in Secondary Edn., Mont. State U., 1961, M.S. in Applied Sci., 1966; m. Hugo Eck, Dec. 16, 1942; children—Lauvrence, Diana. Co-mgr. archtl. and property mgmt. bus., 1955—; conf. coordinator Am. Agrl. Econs. Assn., 1967-68; state-local coordinator Office of Gov. Mont., Helena, 1972-77; mem. Mont. State Senate, 1981—; mem. Mont. Environ. Quality Council, 1981—. Bd. dirs. Methodist Youth Fellowship, 1960-64, Mont. Council for Effective Legislature, 1977-78, Rocky Mountain Environ. Council, 1982—; del., Western v.p. Mont. Constl. Conv., 1971-72; chmn. Gov.'s Task Force on Citizen Participation, 1976-77; mem. adv. com. No. Rockies Resource and Tng. Center (now No. Lights Inst.), 1979-81. Recipient Outstanding Alumna award Mont. State U., 1981. Mem. LWV (state pres. 1967-70), Common Cause, Nat. Women's Polit. Caucus. Democrat.

ECKARDT, GLADYS EVANGELINE (MRS. KARL PAUL KONRAD ECKARDT), librarian; b. Hartland, N.Y., Sept. 7, 1912; d. Isaac John and Flora Caroline (Hofmeister) Beach; student U. Buffalo, 1930-32; B.A., U. Rochester, 1934; M.L.S., Rutgers State U., 1958; m. Karl Paul Konrad Eckardt, Oct. 19, 1940; 1 dau., Susan (Mrs. Edward Misiewicz). Dir. Wood-Ridge (N.J.) Pub. Library, 1956-59, Rutherford (N.J.) Pub. Library, 1959—. Trustee Wood-Ridge Pub. Library, 1954-56. Mem. Am., N.J. (sec. 1964-65, chmn. N.J. insts. 1968), Bergen-Passaic (pres. 1964-66), N.Y. library assn., Pub. Relations Council, Bergen County Small Libraries (v.p. 1963), Rutgers Alumni Assn. Club: Rutherford Women's College. Home: 537 Moonachie Ave Wood Ridge NJ 07075 Office: Park Ave Rutherford NJ 07070

ECKER, BARBARA HELENE, nutritionist; b. N.Y.C., Feb. 26, 1949; d. Seymour Martin and Miriam L. E., B.S., Sch. Human Ecology, Cornell U., 1970; M.S., Inst. Human Nutrition, Coll. Physicians and Surgeons, Columbia U., 1971. Therapeutic dietitian Harvard med. service Boston City Hosp., 1971-73; nutritionist Weight Watchers Internat., Manhassett, N.Y., 1973-78, supr. nutrition services, 1978-82, dir. nutrition services, 1982—; lectr. Coll. U., Columbia U. Mem. Am. Dietetic Assn., Soc. for Nutrition Edn., Am. Home Econs. Assn., Home Economists in Bus., Dietitians in Bus., Alumni Assn. Inst. Human Nutrition Columbia U., Omicron Nu, Phi Tau Sigma. Jewish. Office: Weight Watchers Internat 800 Community Dr Manhassett NY 11030

ECKHOFF, ROSALEE, nurse; b. Falls City, Nebr., Apr. 24, 1930; d. George and Blanche (Montague) Rieger; R.N., Nebr. Meth. Sch. Nursing, 1951; m. Robert Dale Eckhoff, Feb. 21, 1954; children—Dixie Dee, Monte Ray. Dir. nursing Sutherland (Nebr.) Hosp., 1952-55; head nurse med. ward Hastings (Nebr.) Regional Center, 1957-61; night supr. Good Samaritan Village, Hastings, 1962; charge nurse pediatrics Mary Lanning Hosp., Hastings, 1962-65; night supr. Broken Bow (Nebr.) Hosp., 1965-66; dir. nursing Bethel Nursing Home, Ainsworth, Nebr., 1966-67, adminstr., 1967-69; part-time staff nurse Ainsworth Hosp., 1969-70; nursing home counselor Norfolk (Nebr.) Regional Center, 1970-72; night supr. Albion (Nebr.) Boone County Hosp., 1970-75; adminstrv. dir. Mideast Nebr., Albion and Columbus Mental Health Clinic, 1975-76; dir. nursing Phelps Meml. Health Center, Holdrege, Nebr., 1976—. Mem. Region 4 Mental Health Assn., Am. Nurses Assn., Nebr. Mental Health Assn., Luth. Ch. Women, Dist. 4 Hosp. Assn. (dir. nurses). Home: 207 8th Ave Holdrege NE 68949 Office: 1220 Miller St Holdrege NE 68949

ECKLEY, GRACE ESTER, educator; b. Alliance, Ohio, Nov. 30, 1932; d. Clyde L. and Wilma Agnes (Hahn) Williamson; B.A., Mount Union Coll., 1955; M.A., Case Western Res. U., 1964; Ph.D., Kent State U., 1970; m. Wilton Eckley, Sept. 12, 1954; children—Douglas, Stephen, Timothy. Instr. English, Simpson Coll., Indianola, Iowa, 1965-68; prof. dept. English, Drake U., Des Moines, 1968—. Mem. AAUW. Author: Benedict Kiely, 1972; Edna O'Brien, 1974; (with Michael Begnal) Narrator and Character in Finnegans Wake, 1974; Finley Peter Dunne, 1981; contbr. articles to profl. jours. Home: 529 Waterbury Circle Des Moines IA 50312 Office: Drake U Des Moines IA 50311

ECKMAN, BERTHA ELIZABETH, educator; b. Berlin, Pa.; d. Frank and Augusta (Olson) Eckman; student Calif. Tchrs. Coll., 1929-31; B.S., U. Pitts., 1940, postgrad., 1950-61; in service tng. Ind. Tchrs. Coll., 1959-61. Tchr., Brothers Valley Twp. Sch., Berlin, Pa., 1931-33, Lincoln Twp., Somerset, Pa., 1934, Garrett, Pa., 1934-44, Maple Ridge Sch., 1944—; supervising tchr. California (Pa.) State Tchrs. Coll. Exec. sec. Somerset County Council Christian Edn., 1956—, editor yearbooks, 1958-82; youth counselor Somerset County Youth Camp, 1954—, tchr. young people's class; campaign chmn. ARC, Somerset, 1954-57; promotional sec. Somerset Council Sunday Sch. Convs., 1957—; mem. synodical affairs com. Fgn. Missions West Allegheny Conf. Central Pa.; campaign chmn. Allegheny Luth. Homes Aux., Johnstown, Pa.; pres. Garrett Parish Joint Council Luth. Ch. Am.; exec. sec. Garrett Parish Luth. Ch. Am.; pres. Somerset County aux. Allegheny Luth. Home for the Aged, Johnstown, Pa. Mem. NEA (del. to centennial conv. 1957, del. to classroom tchrs. conf.), Pa. Edn. Assn. (pres. Somerset County), United Ch. Women, Nat. Geog. Soc. Educators Beneficial Assn., Delta Kappa Gamma (chpt. pres., dir. work program), Internat. Platform Assn., Marquis Biog. Library Soc. Republican. Lutheran (program coordinator spl. spiritual programs 1936-82). Home: RD 3 Berlin PA 15530

ECKSTEIN, MARLENE R., vascular radiologist; b. Poughkeepsie, N.Y., Sept. 6, 1948; d. Marc and Lola (Charm) E.; A.B., Vassar Coll., 1970; M.D., Albert Einstein Coll. Medicine, 1973. Intern in medicine Yale-New Haven Med. Center, 1973-74, resident in diagnostic radiology, 1974-77; asst. radiologist, chief vascular radiology sect. South Nassau Communities Hosp., Oceanside, N.Y., 1977-78, asso. radiologist, chief vascular radiology sect., 1978-81, asst. dir. dept. radiology, chief vascular radiology sect., 1981—; asst. prof. clin. radiology SUNY-Stony Brook Med. Sch., 1980—. Mem. exec. com. and hosp. chmn. United Jewish Appeal of Physicians and Dentists of Nassau County (N.Y.), 1981—. Diplomate Am. Bd. Radiology. Fellow Am. Coll. Angiology; mem. Am. Coll. Radiology, Am. Inst. Ultrasound in Medicine, N.Y. State Med. Soc., Nassau County Med. Soc. and Acad., Medicine, Radiol. Soc. N.Am., L.I. Radiol. Soc. Designer and developer line of vascular catheters. Office: 2445 Oceanside Rd Oceanside NY 11572

ECONOMIDES, ELAINE, lawyer; b. N.Y.C., Sept. 14, 1948; d. Basil and Anastasia (Pavlakis) E.; B.A. cum laude (Granite State Merit scholar, Elks Assn. scholar), U. N.H., 1970; postgrad. London Sch. Econs., 1970-71; J.D., Suffolk U., 1977. Civil rights specialist GSA, Boston, 1972-73; contract negotiator Transp. Systems Center, Cambridge, Mass., 1973-78, spl. asst. to dir., 1978-79; spl. asst. to dir. Materials Transp. Bur., Washington, 1979-80, exec. officer, 1980-82; atty.-adv. RSPA, Dept. Transp., Washington, 1982—; fed. women's program coordinator GSA, 1972-73, Transp. Systems Center, 1973-74; bd. dirs. Kendall Sq. Fed. Credit Union, 1979; admitted to Mass. bar, 1977, Fed. bar, 1978. Mem. Am. Bar Assn., Mass. Bar Assn., English-Speaking Union, Pi Sigma Alpha, Phi Kappa Phi, Pi Gamma Mu. Greek Orthodox.

ECONOMOS, PATRICIA KAY, trade assn. exec.; b. Mitchell, S.D., May 30, 1943; d. Peter George and Maria K. Economos; student U. S.D., 1961-62; B.A., Dakota Wesleyan U., 1965; postgrad. Georgetown U., 1977-78. Tchr., Anoka (Minn.) Hennepin Sch. Dist. 11, 1965-68, Fairfax County (Va.) Sch. Bd., 1968-70; sr. staff researcher Office Vice-Pres. U.S., Washington, 1970-73; asst. to senator U.S. Congress, Washington, 1976; asst. dir. house liaison/govt. affairs Nat. Assn. Home Builders, Washington, 1977—. Mem. Women in Housing and Fin., Quill and Scroll. Club: Job's Daus. Home: 3051 Idaho Ave NW Washington DC 20016 Office: 15th and M Sts NW Washington DC 20005

EDDINGS, ALICE FAYE, retail ofcl.; b. Sherman, Tex., July 30, 1939; d. Allen and Ethel Aline (Tumey) Tatum; student N. Tex. Bus. Coll., 1954, LaSalle Extension U.; children by previous marriage—Lori Driggers, Donald Driggers, David Driggers. Employed in various credit, accounting and mgmt. positions, Tex., Fla., Ala. and Germany, 1954-71; office, credit mgr. Pioneer Logging Machinery, Inc., Columbia, S.C., 1971-74; office mgr. Camden Lugoff Chrysler-Plymouth-Dodge, Inc., Lugoff, S.C., 1974-76; dep. clk. in bankruptcy ct., clks. office U.S. Dist. Ct., Columbia, S.C., 1976-77; credit mgr. Salem Carpets, Inc., Columbia, 1977-78, officer, credit mgr., 1978—. Founder, exec. dir. Friendly Faces, Columbia, 1977—; bd. dirs. Columbia YWCA, 1981-82. Mem. Nat. Assn. Credit Mgrs., Am. Soc. Profl. and Exec. Women, Am. Bus. Womens Assn., Nat. Assn. Female Execs., Columbia Credit Mgrs. Assn., NOW, Credit Women Internat. (chpt. pres. 1981-82), Columbia Area LWV (dir. 1978-82), Soc. Cert. Consumer Credit Execs. Republican. Roman Catholic. Home: PO Box 11531 Columbia SC 29211 Office: Cogdill Carpets Inc PO Box 21306 Columbia SC 29221

EDDY, DARLENE MATHIS, educator, poet; b. Elkhart, Ind., Mar. 19, 1937; d. William Eugene and Fern (Paulmer) Mathis; B.A., Goshen Coll., 1959; M.A., Rutgers U., 1961, Ph.D., 1967; m. Spencer Livingston Eddy, Jr., May 23, 1964 (dec. May 1971). Instr., lectr. Douglass Coll. and Rutgers U., 1962-64, 66-67; asst. prof. English, Ball State U., Muncie, Ind., 1967-70, asso. prof., 1971-75, prof., 1975—. Recipient numerous research, creative teaching and creative arts grants; Woodrow Wilson Nat. fellow, 1959-62; Rutgers U. Grad. Honors fellow, 1964-65. Mem. Nat. Council Tchrs. of English, MLA, AAUP, Melville Soc., Shakespeare Assn., NOW, Nat. Women's Studies Assn., DAR. Author: The Worlds of King Lear, 1968; Leaf Threads, Wind Rhymes, 1982; contbr. articles to Am. Lit., English Lang. Notes and others, poetry to Green River Rev., Calyx, Bitterroot, Pebble, Hiram Poetry Rev., Forum, Rendezvous, others. Home: 1409 W Cardinal St Muncie IN 47303 Office: 207B English Ball State Muncie IN 47303

EDELSON, JEANNE, city ofcl.; b. Bronx, N.Y., Apr. 18, 1950; d. Doug and Frances (Fischer) Edelson; student SUNY, 1969, Legis. Inst. Baruch Coll., 1980. Dep. press officer N.Y.C. Parks, Recreation and Cultural Affairs Adminstrn.; asst. dir. community relations N.Y.C. Patrolmen's Benevolent Assn.; dir. public relations Nat. Council Jewish Women, N.Y.C.; account exec. Paul Bular Assos., Inc.; now dir. public affairs N.Y.C. Transit Authority. Legis. mcpl. adv., N.Y.C., 1979-82; dir. public relations Murray Hills Com., 1980-81; mem. Manhattan Community Bd., 1981; cons. Democratic Nat. Conv. Host Com., 1980, N.Y. Festival Salute to Congress, 1980; press rep. Congressman Robert Garcia, 1979-81. Mem. Public Relations Officers Soc., Women in Transp. Clubs: N.Y. Press, Publicity N.Y. Office: 370 Jay St Brooklyn NY 11201

EDELSON, MARY BETH, artist; b. East Chicago, Ind.; d. Albert Melvin and Mary Lou (Young) Johnson; student Art Inst. Chgo., 1953-54; B.A., DePauw U., 1955; M.A., N.Y. U., 1959; children—Lynn Strauss, Nick. One-woman shows: Indpls. Mus. Art, 1968, Corcoran Gallery Art, Washington, 1973, A.I.R. Gallery, N.Y.C., 1975, 77, 79, 81,

Franklin Furnace, N.Y.C., 1978, U. Iowa, 1978, Henri Gallery, Washington, 1971, 73, 75, 79, Reykjavik, Iceland, 1979, Albright-Knox Mus., Buffalo, 1980, Elise Meyer Gallery, N.Y.C., 1981, Survey of Photog. Works travelling exhbn., 1981, 82, Max Hutchinson Gallery, N.Y.C., 1981; group shows include: Internat. Feministische Kunst, Stichting de Appel, Amsterdam, 1979, Contemporary Art Center, New Orleans, 1979, Whitney Mus. Am. Art, N.Y.C., 1979, 82, Bronx Mus., 1979, N.A.M.E. Gallery, Chgo., 1980, Mus. Contemporary Art, Sao Paulo, Brazil, 1980, Aldrich Mus. Contemporary Art, Ridgefield, Conn., 1981; mem. A.I.R. Gallery, N.Y.C., 1975—; vis. lectr.-artist colls and univs. including Northwestern U., Chgo., St. Paul Sch. Art and Design, U. Mich., U. Iowa, San Francisco Art Inst., Reykjavic, Iceland, Hope Coll., Mich., U. Mass., Pratt Inst.; founding mem. Heresies, N.Y.C.; organizer Conf. for Women in the Visual Arts, Washington, 1972. Author: Seven Cycles: Public Rituals, 1980; also chpts. in books. Contbr. articles to profl. jours. Home: 110 Mercer St New York NY 10012

EDELSTEIN, ADRIENNE LYNN, employment agy. exec.; b. Phila., Jan. 24, 1950; d. Harold and Barbara Jane (Alkus) Milgrom; B.A. in English Edn., Temple U., Phila., 1971; m. William Steven Edelstein, June 18, 1972; 1 son, Marc Todd. Employment counselor Enwood Personnel, N.Y.C., 1972-73, Al-Dor Personnel, N.Y.C., 1973-74, Frank Leonard Personnel, Oakland Park, Fla., 1978, J.P. Internat., Ft. Lauderdale, Fla., 1978-79; pres. Marc Todd Career Cons., Inc., Ft. Lauderdale, 1979—, also chmn. bd., dir.; chmn. bd., dir. Marc Todd Career Cons. Miami, Inc. Program dir. Plainview (N.Y.) Nursery Sch., 1977. Mem. Nat. Assn. Female Execs., NOW, South Fla. Mfrs. Assn. Home: 8025 NW 28th St Sunrise FL 33322 Office: 1150 N Federal Hwy Fort Lauderdale FL 33304

EDELSTEIN, ROSEMARIE, nurse, educator, cons.; b. Drake, N.D., Mar. 3, 1935; d. Francis Jerome and Myrtle Josephine (Merbach) Hublou; B.S. in Nursing, St. Teresa's Coll., 1956; M.A. in Edn., Holy Names Coll., 1977; Ed.D., U. San Francisco, 1982; cert. public health nurse U. Calif., Berkeley, 1972; m. Harry Georg Edelstein, June 22, 1957 (div.); children—Julie, Lori, Lynn, Toni Anne. Dir., clin. supr. San Francisco Sch. for Health Professions, 1971-74, Rancho Arroyo Sch. Vocat. Nursing, Sacramento, 1974-75; intensive care nurse Kaiser-Permanente Hosp., San Rafael, Calif., 1976-77; dir. inservice edn. Ross (Calif.) Hosp., 1977-78; assoc. dir. nursing edn. St. Francis Meml. Hosp., San Francisco, 1978—; cons. in field; instr. CPR. Served to maj. Nurse Corps. USAR. Mem. Calif. Nurses Assn., Am. Heart Assn., Sigma Theta Tau. Roman Catholic. Author: (with Jane F. Lee) Acupuncture Atlas, 1974; The Influence of Motivator and Hygiene Factors in Job Changes by Graduate Registered Nurses, 1977; Effects of Two Educational Methods Upon Retention of Knowledge in Pharmacology, 1981. Home: 10 Grande Paseo San Rafael CA 94903 Office: 900 Hyde St San Francisco CA 94109

EDEN, JANET JONES, educator; b. Cordell, Okla., Sept. 30, 1938; d. Ray Lockwood and Ellen (Jones) Jones; student Am. U., 1956-57; B.S., U. Okla., 1960; M.Ed., Southwestern Okla. State U., Weatherford, 1965; m. Jimmie W. Eden, Jan. 23, 1964; children—Angela, Jimmie W. Clk.-typist, SBA, Washington, summers 1957-59; asst. counselor pilot program in dormitories U. Okla., 1959-60; tchr. Perryton (Tex.) High Sch., 1960-62, Sentinal (Okla.) High Sch., 1964—, European campus counselor Fgn. Study League, summers 1974, 79, advisor to newspaper and yearbook staffs, 4-H leader. Vice pres. bd. dirs. Okla. 4-H Leaders Orgn., judge speech tournaments; mem. Washita County Devel. Council, Senator Dewey Bartlett's Rural Devel. Adv. Council, 1974-76; Okla. Farm Bur. Farm Family of Year, 1974; Republican county chmn., 1972—, state com. woman, 1969-70, county coordinator elections, 1970, 72, 6th dist. coordinator, 1976, 80; mem. Okla. Rep. Task Force, 1982. Mem. NEA, Okla. Edn. Assn. (local rep. 1970-81), Washita County Okla. Edn. Assn. (pres. 1974-76, NEA del. 1976-78), Nat. Council Tchrs. of English, Okla. Council Tchrs. of English (local sch. accreditibility com., local staff devel. com. 1980—), Delta Kappa Gamma. Baptist. Home: Route 1 Rocky OK 73661 Office: 7th and Washington Sentinel OK 83664

EDER, MARI KAYE, army officer; b. Grove City, Pa.; d. Charles Leo and Helen Mae (Greer) E.; B.A. cum laude, Edinboro State Coll., 1975, M.A., 1976. Grad. asst. in pub. relations Edinboro State Coll., 1975-76; newspaper reporter, photographer, 1976-77; commd. 2d lt. U.S. Army, 1977, advanced to 1st lt., 1979; tng. officer Fort McClellan, Anniston, Ala., 1977-78; exec. officer U.S. Army Mil. Police Sch., 1978—, subject area action officer Officer Edn. Br., Tng. Devel. Bd. dirs. Women's Army Corps Found. Decorated Army Commendation medal. Mem. Armed Forces Communication Electronics Assn., Am. Taekwondo Assn., Nat. Council Tchrs. English, MLA, NOW, Assn. U.S. Army, Alumni Zeta Tau Alpha. Contbr. poems to ednl., lit. jours. Home: Franklin St Stoneboro PA 16153 Office: HHD 519th MP BN Fort Meade MD 20755

EDERER-SCHWARTZ, JANE, dance therapist; b. N.Y.C., Dec. 1, 1939; d. Abel and Gertrude (Glass) Ederer; A.B., Queen's Coll., City U. N.Y., 1961; M.S.W., Columbia U., 1966, M.A., 1975. Movement therapist Day Hosp., St. Luke's Hosp., N.Y.C., 1975-79; program dir. Shellbank Jewish Center, Bklyn., 1978—; movement therapist Shaaray Tefila, N.Y.C., 1978—, Creative Arts Rehab. Center, N.Y.C., 1980—; faculty dept. dance N.Y.U., 1980—; pvt. practice, supr. dance therapy. founding bd. dirs. Laban Inst. Movement Studies, N.Y.C., 1977—. Grantee, NIMH, 1964-66; cert. movement analyst Laban Inst. Movement Studies; cert. social worker, N.Y. State. Mem. Nat. Assn. Social Workers, Am. Dance Therapy Assn. (chmn. edn. N.Y. State 1980—), Dance Therapy Registry. Home: 544 E 86th St New York NY 10028 Office: 251 W 51st St New York NY

EDESON, BARBARA MAE, speech and lang. pathologist; b. Pitts., Dec. 29, 1955; d. Samuel and Ann Clare (Opachevsky) Edeson; B.S., Pa. State U., 1976; M.A., Kent State U., 1978. Speech-lang. pathologist Youngstown (Ohio) Hearing and Speech Center, 1979, South Hills Health System, Home Health Agy., Pitts., 1980—. Mem. Am. Speech, Lang. and Hearing Assn., Pa. Speech, Lang. and Hearing Assn., Southwestern Pa. Speech, Lang. and Hearing Assn., Hadassah (treas. Ziona group). Democrat. Jewish. Office: South Hills Health System Home Health Agy Mercy Hosp 1425 Forbes Ave Pittsburgh PA 15219

EDGAR, JUDITH STOREY, community found. exec.; b. East Orange, N.J., July 21, 1936; d. Matthew J. and Helen (Huntsberger) Storey; student Wellesley Coll., 1954-56; B.A., Cornell U., 1958; M.P.A., Golden Gate U., 1981; m. James Macmilland Edgar, June 28, 1958; children—Suzanne Lynn, James III, Gordon Stuart. Tchr. secondary sch., Ithaca, N.Y., 1958-60; community vol., 1960-76; elected ofcl., 1976-81; program exec. Marin Community Affairs, San Francisco Found., 1981—. Governing bd. Marin Community Coll. Dist., 1976-81. Recipient Assos. award Golden Gate U., 1981. Mem. Am. Soc. Public Adminstrn., No. Calif. Grantmakers, Nat. Women's Polit. Caucus, Jr. League San Francisco. Club: Wednesday Dialogue of Marin. Home: 10 Buckeye Way Kentfield CA 94904 Office: 500 Washington St San Francisco CA 94111

EDGE, DELIA L., lawyer; b. Mendenhall, Miss., June 30, 1906; d. Frank Stacey and Claudia (Nicholson) Ledbetter; student Fla. So. Coll., 1925-26; J.D., San Francisco Law Sch., 1952; m. Willis Graham Edge, Nov. 19, 1932; 1 dau., Phyllis Ann (Mrs. Verne Goram Koeppe). Admitted to Calif. bar, 1953; practiced in Oakland, Calif. until 1962; asso. firm Bledsoe, Smith, Cathcart, Johnson & Rogers, San Francisco, 1962-71. Pres. Phoenix unit Mt. Diablo Therapy Center, 1974, Mem. Am. Bar Assn., State Bar Calif., Queen's Bench (pres. 1965), Iota Tau Tau. Club: San Jose Woman's. Home: 1479 Kimberly Ct San Jose CA 95118

EDGERTON, MARY ALICE, broadcasting exec.; b. Atlanta, Tex., Dec. 9, 1920; d. Raymond William and Ada Lou (Blades) Riley; student Pasadena Community Playhouse, 1939-41; m. James E. Edgerton, Feb. 8, 1942; 1 dau., Sarah Jane. City clk. Hermosa Beach, Calif., 1967-71; election cons. Computer Election Systems, Berkeley, Calif., 1970-73, legis. agt., 1973-77, project dir., 1975-77; Calif. state mgr. News Election Service, Los Angeles, 1978; founder, dir. Creative Services Network, Public Network News, San Pedro, Calif., 1980—; writer, lectr. on networking, 1980—. Life mem. PTA; pres. Friends of Library, 1962-63. Named Hermosa Beach Woman of Yr., 1968; recipient Disting. Service award City of Hermosa Beach, 1971. Deomcrat. Mem. United Ch. Religious Sci. Pub., Point of You, 1979-81. Home: 1630 Stonewood Ct San Pedro CA 90732

EDGERTON, MISHEW ELLEN ROGERS, business exec.; b. Raleigh, N.C., Sept. 4, 1904; d. James Rufus and Ellen Mishew (Crudup) Rogers; grad. Nat. Park Sem., 1924; m. Norman Edward Edgerton, Feb. 9, 1929; 1 dau., Mishew Ellen Edgerton Smith. Pres., Rogers Realty & Ins. Co., 1961—; sec. Raleigh Bonded Warehouse, Inc., 1934—. Mem. D.R., DAR, Raleigh Jr. League, Order Crown in Am., Nat. Soc. Colonial Dames Am., N.C. Antiquities Soc. (life), N.C. State Art Soc., Am. Camellia Soc. (charter mem., former judge), Internat. Oceanographic Found., Nat. Trust Hist. Preservation. Methodist. Home: Tatton Hall 1625 Oberlin Rd Raleigh NC 27608

EDGMON, JOYCE ANN, cosmetics co. exec.; b. Tuttle, Okla., Sept. 6, 1939; d. Leroy A. and Sarah Alice (Mc Bride) Mc Clure; B.A. in Bus., Okla. U., 1957; student Okla. Real Estate Coll., 1975-76; children—Ricky Joe, Vicki Diane. Owner, operator beauty shop Blanchard, Okla., 1968-70; spl. agt. Gt. So. Life, Oklahoma City, 1971-75; sales agt. Employers of Wausau, Oklahoma City, 1976-78; field rep. Redken Labs., Inc., Oklahoma City, 1978, dist. mgr., St. Louis, 1978—; hon. dep. ins. commr. State Okla., 1973-74. Pres. PTA, Blanchard Sch. System, 1970-78; state v.p. Okla. Dairy Assn., 1968-72; v.p., sec. Blanchard Rodeo Assn. Mem. Am. Bus. Women's Assn., Beta Sigma Phi. Republican. Baptist. Home: 7752 Grant Ln Overland Park KS 66204 Office: 6625 Variel Ave Canoga Park CA 91303

EDINGER, MILDRED SINCLEAR, (MRS. FOSTER PARMELEE), artist; b. Wilmington, Del., May 27, 1903; d. John Curtis and Dorinda Irene (Sinex) Sinclear; grad. Darlington Sem., 1921; student Phila. Sch. Design, 1922-24; also pvt. study; m. Earl Eugene Edinger, Oct. 10, 1925 (dec.); children—John Sinclear, William Goodlander (dec.); m. 2d, Foster Parmelee, Oct. 31, 1970. Treas., organizer The Studio Group, Wilmington, also The East Coast Gallery, Provincetown, Mass.; art dir. Nat. League Am. Pen Women; lectr. on collage Palm Beaches and Lake Worth, Fla., 1966-67; artist; works rep. group exhibits Eastern and So. U.S., Am. Watercolor Soc., others; several one-, two-, and three-man shows, traveling shows, nat. jury shows, Chautauqua. Participant, del. World Constituent Assembly, Innsbruck, Austria, and Paris, 1977. Recipient award of merit Palm Beach Inst., 1966, Artists Guild, Palm Beach Art Inst., 1967, Lake Worth Art League, 1963, 65, 66, 68, 75, Nat. League Am. Pen Women of Palm Beaches, 1966, 67, Miami State award, 1967. Mem. Va. Mus. Art, Wilmington Soc. Fine Arts, Nat. League Am. Pen Women (2d v.p., art dir. 1971-72), Lake Worth Art League, Met. Mus. Art (Miami), Am. Watercolor Soc. Republican. Lutheran. Clubs: Wilmington Country; Gulf Stream Bath and Tennis (Delray Beach); Zonta (dir. Delray Beach 1968). Creator 8 collages for Bicentennial Year. Home: PO Box 665 14 NE 8th St Delray Beach FL 33444

EDLOW, ESTHER, food services exec.; b. Newark, July 14, 1925; d. Harry and Yetta (Leibel) Blonsky; B.S., Pratt Inst., 1947; student Rutgers U., 1950; m. Harold Edlow, Nov. 28, 1954; children—Jeremy, Helen. With Elizabeth (N.J.) Gen. Hosp., 1947-50; with Interstate United, Pa., N.J. and N.Y., 1950-60; regional v.p. Service Systems Corp., N.Y.C., 1966—. Mem. Am. Dietetic Assn., Nat. Restaurant Assn., Dietitians in Bus. and Industry, Nat. Automatic Merchandising Assn. Jewish. Office: 140 West St New York NY 10007

EDMISON, GWENDOLYN MARIE, restaurant exec.; b. Okla., Sept. 1, 1927; d. Delos and Alam (Allen) E.; student Langston U., 1948-49, U. So. Calif., 1956, N.Am. Sch. Acctg., 1972-73; children by previous marriage—Donald K. Brown, Cynthia Ann Evans, Charles E. DeWitt. Statis. clk. County Los Angeles Adminstrv. Office, 1950-61; owner mgr. Ed Kelco Discount Furniture Co., Los Angeles, 1969-74; funeral dir. Mortuary Mgmt. Inc., Los Angeles, 1974-81; owner, mgr. Pioneer Take Out 65, Studio City, Calif., 1980—. Bookkeeper, clk. Mt. Calvary Bapt. Ch., ch. rep. to Los Angeles Adv. Bd. Schs., 1968—. Notary public. Mem. Calif. Restaurant Owners Assn., Calif. Funeral Dirs. Assn., Nat. Assn. Female Execs. Democrat. Baptist. Home: 5631 Aladdin St Los Angeles CA 90008 Office: 12048 Ventura Blvd Studio City CA 91604

EDMISTEN, JANE MORET, lawyer; b. Boone, N.C., Oct. 25, 1938; d. Ralph D. and Lola (Thompson) Morely; B.A. with honors, U.N.C., 1960, M.A., 1962; J.D., George Washington U., 1967; 1 dau., Martha. Research analyst Georgetown (Ky.) U., 1962-63, Herner & Co., Washington, 1964; mil. assistance analyst USAF, Washington, 1964-66; chief, legis. reference sect. NASA, 1966-69; admitted to N.C. bar, 1967, D.C. bar, 1967, U.S. Supreme Ct. bar, 1972; faculty N.C. Central Law Sch., Durham, 1975-76; individual practice law, 1975-76; trial atty. tax div., appellate sect. U.S. Dept. Justice, Washington, 1970-74, 76-77; asst. gen. counsel HUD, 1977-79; dep. gen. counsel Merit Systems Protection Bd., 1979-81; mem. firm Moore & Foster, Washington, 1981—. Recipient Tom C. Clark award, 1980. Mem. Am. Bar Assn., D.C. Bar Assn., Fed. Bar Assn., Kappa Beta Pi, Phi Delta Delta. Office: Moore & Foster 1625 K St NW #500 Washington DC 20006

EDMISTON, MARILYN, clin. psychologist; b. Lewiston, Maine, Dec. 9, 1934; d. Lewis Walter and Anne Burgess; B.A. summa cum laude, Fla. Atlantic U., 1967, M.A., 1969; Ph.D., U. Ga., 1973; children—John Laing III, Eric James. Clin. psychologist, children's and adolescent unit Central Ga. Regional Hosp., Milledgeville, 1973-74, chief psychologist, 1974-75; clin. psychologist Psychol. and Guidance Center, San Diego, 1975, adolescent unit South Fla. State Hosp., Pembroke Pines, 1976-77; state psychol. cons. Office Vocat. Rehab., Fla. Dept. Health and Rehab. Services, Tallahassee, 1977—. Mem. Nat. Register Health Service Providers in Psychology, Am. Psychol. Assn., Capitol Area Psychol. Assn., Psi Chi. Home: 280 John Knox Rd Apt 206 Tallahassee FL 32303 Office: 1309 Winewood Blvd Tallahassee FL 32301

EDMOND, DOROTHY COLEY, nursing edn. adminstr.; b. Phila., Dec. 27, 1927; d. Warren J. and Lottie A. Coley; B.S., Fisk U., 1952; B.S. in Nursing, Meharry Med. Coll., 1952; M.A., Columbia U., 1959; Ed.D., George Peabody Coll., Vanderbilt U., 1977-81; m. Joel B. Edmond, Aug. 21, 1970. Gen. staff nurse Episcopal Hosp., Phila., 1952-53; sr. staff nurse Vis. Nurse Soc. Phila., 1953-55, Starr Centre Assn., Phila., 1955-59; instr. Tuskegee (Ala.) Inst. Sch. Nursing, 1959-60, Meharry Med. Coll., Sch. Nursing, Nashville, 1960-62, asst. dir. nursing service, 1962; instr. Tenn. State U., Nashville, 1962-66, asst. prof. Sch. Home Econs., 1966, dir. nursing edn., 1966-74, dir. Baccalaureate nursing program, 1979—, asso. prof., 1981—; asst. prof. div. nursing U. Tenn., Nashville, 1974-79. Mem. nursing service com. ARC, 1964-70. Recipient Profl. Women award Nat. Assn. Negro Bus. and Profl. Women's Club, 1968, Mid-South Regional Med. Service award, 1974. Mem. Tenn. Nurses Assn. (spl. com. edn. 1970-72, v.p. 2d dist. 1966-70), Am. Nurses Assn., Nat. League Nursing, Tenn. League Nursing (chmn. Mid-Cumberland chpt. 1975—), AAUW, Air Force Sgt. Assn. Aux., Tenn. Student Nurses Assn. (student adv. 1975—), Delta Sigma Theta, Chi Eta Phi (pres. 1969-71). Club: Enchanted Hills Community. Home: 4210 Eaton Creek Rd Nashville TN 37218 Office: 3500 John Merrit Blvd Nashville TN 37203

EDMOND, PATRICIA DUFFUS, mortgage banker; b. Nacozari, Senora, Mexico, Mar. 23, 1928 (parents Am. citizens); d. John Trent and Glynton (Small) Duffus; student U. Tex., El Paso, 1946-47; m. Robert D. Edmond, Jan. 31, 1963; children—Patricia, Michael, Trent. Clk. typist Mortgage Investment Co., El Paso, 1965-70, br. mgr., 1970-78, v.p., chief underwriter, 1978—. Mem. women's aux. U. Tex., El Paso. Mem. El Paso Bd. Realtors (women's council), Nat. Assn. Home Builders (past dir.), Women's Aux., Am. Bus. Women's Assn. Republican. Episcopalian. Club: Ladies Shrine. Home: 94 Sutton Pl El Paso TX 79912 Office: 420 Texas El Paso TX 79901

EDMONDSON, JEANNETTE B., sec. state Okla.; b. Muskogee, Okla., June 6, 1925; d. A. Chapman and Georgia (Shutt) Bartleson; B.A., U. Okla., 1946; m. J. Howard Edmondson, May 15, 1946 (dec.); children—James H. (dec.), Jeanne E. Watkins, Patricia E. Zimmer. Sec. of state State of Okla., Oklahoma City, 1979—. Chmn. bd. Okla. affiliate Am. Heart Assn., 1979. Democrat. Methodist. Office: Office of Sec of State 101 State Capitol Oklahoma City OK 73105 *

EDMONSON, BARBARA ANN TURNER, psychologist, educator; b. Kansas City, Mo., Oct. 15, 1912; d. James Ernest and Hortense Aileen (Taylor) Turner; B.A., U. Kansas City, 1951, M.A., 1953; Ed.D., U. Kans., 1970. Dir., Elmhurst Presch. for Retarded Children, Kansas City, Kans., 1954-60; research asst. U. Kans. Med. Center, Kansas City, 1961-64, NIMH grantee, 1961-63, research assoc., co-dir. Office of HEW SRS Grant, 1964-68, 1969-70; research assoc. U. Oreg., Eugene, 1969-71; dir. psychology tng. Herschel Nisonger Center for Devel. Disabilities, adj. assoc. prof. psychology Ohio State U., Columbus, 1971-79, adj. assoc. prof., 1980—; cons. mental health. Mem. Am. Assn. on Mental Deficiency, Am. Psychol. Assn., Ohio Psychol. Assn., Ohio Assn. on Mental Deficiency. Unitarian. Author: Social Perceptual Training for Community Living: Pre-Vocational Units for Retarded Youth, 1969; Manual and Scoring Guide: A Test of Social Inference, 1974; Socio-Sexual Knowledge and Attitudes Test, 1978; Socialization Games for Retarded Adolescents and Adults, 1981; Developing Prosocial Behavior in the Retarded, 1982. Home: 3043 Valley Creek Dr Columbus OH 43223 Office: The Nisonger Center 1580 Cannon Dr Columbus OH 43210

EDMUNDS, BETTY JANE, broadcaster; b. Atlanta, Jan. 7, 1926; d. Louie George and Annie Mae (Cooke) Sewell; student Bob Jones Coll., 1945-46; m. Arthur Walter Edmunds, June 4, 1947; children—William, Edwin, Elizabeth, Neva. With Rolla (Mo.) Daily News, 1948, Schenectady Gazette, 1949-51; columnist Grandview (Mo.) Weekly, 1953-54; choir dir. Long Grove (Ill.) Ch., 1962-72, Calvary Baptist Ch., Pueblo, Colo., 1973—; hostess daily radio show Sta. KFEL, Pueblo, 1977—, account exec., 1981—. Republican. Home: 3322 St Clair Ave Pueblo CO 81005 Office: 4411 Goodnight Ave Pueblo CO 81005

EDMUNDS, FRANCES RAVENEL, hist. found. exec.; b. Charleston, S.C., Dec. 11, 1916; d. Augustine T. and Harriott (Buist) Smythe; grad. Coll. of Charleston, 1937, hon. degree, 1972; m. S. Henry Edmunds, Dec. 23, 1943; children—Harriott, Eliza, Langdon. With Hist. Charleston Found., 1947—, dir. Ann. Festival of Houses, 1948, dir. Nathaniel Russell House Mus., 1956, dir. Ansonborough Rehab. Project, 1958-77, exec. dir. found., 1977—; radio and TV appearances; speaker on preservation. Recipient Historic Savannah Preservation award; Charleston Realtor Appreciation award; citation Preservation Soc. Charleston. Mem. Nat. Trust Historic Preservation (citation 1968, Louise duPont Crowninshield award 1971). Home: 10 Bedon's Alley Charleston SC 29401 Office: 51 Meeting St Charleston SC 29401

EDMUNDS, JANE CLARA, editor; b. Chgo., Mar. 16, 1922; d. John Carson and Clara (Kummerow) Carrigan; B.Ph. in Chemistry, Northwestern U., 1947; m. William T. Dean, Aug. 30, 1947 (div. 1953); 1 son, John Charles; m. Edmund S. Kopacz, Sept. 24, 1955 (div. 1973); children—Christine Ellen, Jan Carson. Chemist, Mars, Inc., Oak Park, Ill., 1942-47; with Maujer Pub. Co., St. Joseph, Mich., 1953-58, 69-74; asst. editor women's pages rewrite desk News-Palladium, Benton Harbor, Mich., 1967-68; free lance journalist, St. Joseph, 1959-68; sr. editor Cons. Engr. mag. Tech. Pub. Co., Barrington, Ill., 1975-77, exec. editor, 1977—. Chmn., Berrien County (Mich.) Nat. Found. March of Dimes, 1968; mem. campaign com. Republican party, 1954. Recipient award Bausch & Lomb, 1940, Nat. Found. Service award, 1969; AID grantee, 1979. Mem. Soc. Tech. Communication (Disting. Tech. Communication awards, chmn. St. Joseph chpt. 1972), Am. Soc. Bus. Press Editors (past bd. mem.), Nat. Press Club, Constrn. Writers Assn. (past bd. mem.), Smithsonian Instn., St. Joseph Art Assn., Barrington Assos., Field Mus. Assos. Republican. Episcopalian. Office: 1301 S Grove Ave Barrington IL 60010

EDMUNDSON, MARGARET ANN, nurse-midwife; b. Shawnee, Okla., Mar. 24, 1947; d. James Alfred and Mabel Irene (Stroud) E.; B.S. in Nursing, U. Nev., 1969; M.Nursing (USPHS trainee 1970-71), Emory U., 1972; cert. in nurse-midwifer (USPHS trainee 1976-77), SUNY, Bklyn., 1977. Nurse, Johns Hopkins Hosp., 1969-70; clin. nurse leader U. Ariz. Med. Center, Tucson, 1971-73; instr. Ariz. State U. Sch. Nursing, Tempe, 1973-76; asst. prof. U. Colo. Health Scis. Center, Denver, 1977-79; nurse-midwife Ob-Gyn Assos., Denver, 1979—; condr. childbirth edn. classes. Mem. Am. Coll. Nurse-Midwives, Am. Nurses Assn., Nurses Assn. of Am. Coll. Ob-Gyn, Colo. Nurses Assn., Sigma Theta Tau. Republican. Baptist. Author papers, reports in field. Office: 11175 E Mississippi St Aurora CO 80012

EDSON, CHARLOTTE PORTER BAYLISS, educator; civic worker; b. Melrose, Mass., May 8, 1936; d. Willard Clayton and Violet (Porter) Bayliss; B.A., Western Md. Coll., 1959 (div. 1971); 1 dau., Page Porter Scheuren; m. Charles Thomas Edson, Aug. 13, 1977; children—Kimberly Ann, Eric Charles. With Reader's Digest, Pleasantville, N.Y., 1954-56; tchr. English, Collegeville (Pa.) High Sch., 1959; personnel adminstr. N.J. Dept. Transp., Trenton, 1971-77; tchr. English, Mercer Christian Acad., Trenton, 1980—. Flag chmn. Gen. David Forman chpt. DAR, Trenton, 1962-65, 68-70, jr. membership chmn., 1961-62, publicity chmn., 1965-68, program chmn., 1968-70, 2d vice regent, 1965-68, 1st vice regent, 1968-70, page N.J. State confs., 1960-71, personal page state regents, 1961-70, pres. gen., 1965-68, state jr. membership chmn., 1965-68, state page chmn., 1968-71, state mag. chmn., 1971-74, page Nat. Continental Congresses, 1961-68, chief lobby pages, 1962, 64, 65, personal page to pres. gen., 1965-68, page marshal, 1964-65, nat. vice chmn. page com., 1968-77, nat. vice chmn. platform com. 1977—, nat. vice chmn. jr. membership, 1965-68, speakers staff, 1971-74, 80—, nat. def. chmn. Valley Forge (Pa.) chpt., 1962-65, Christmas hostess, program chmn., 1964-65, vice chmn. ann. jr. tea, 1964; escort for Princess Christina of Sweden on tour of Trenton, 1965; vol. worker Trent House Assn., 1966-71, bd. dirs., 1970, 80-81; vol. Old Barracks Assn.; cart chmn. Helene Fuld Hosp. Aux., Trenton, 1967-69; youth worker, Sunday Sch. tchr. Bapt. Ch., v.p., 1978-79; pres. Women's Gospel

Fellowship, 1979-81, dir., 1981—. Mem. Republican Women of Pa. Mem. Montgomery County Fedn. Women's Clubs (past county rec. sec.), Freedoms Found. at Valley Forge (women's com.), Trenton Hist. Soc., Nat. Assn. Parliamentarians, Americans for Patriotism (nat. jr. chmn. nat. insignia com.), Colonial Daus. 17th Century (jr. chmn. Pa. chpt.), New Eng. Women, Daus. of Founders and Patriots, Daus. Colonial Wars (N.J. rec. sec. 1968-71), Sons and Daus. of Pilgrims, Ancient and Hon. Arty. Co., Daus. Am. Colonists, Internat. Platform Assn., Questers, Germantown Hist. Assn., AAUW, Phila. Art Mus., Eastern Amateur Ski Assn., Jr. League (edn. sec., arts com.). Clubs: Collegeville Community Women's (past pres., dir.), Union League; Aronimink Golf (Newton Square, Pa.); Trenton Country. Home: 274 Westcott Blvd Pennington NJ 08534

EDWARDS, BERNYCE ROSE, ednl. adminstr.; b. Detroit, May 19, 1926; d. Steve and Julia (Allen) Edwards; B.S., Nazareth Coll., 1949; M.Ed., Wayne State U., 1958. Tchr., Webster Elem. Sch., Detroit, Mich., 1954-58; demonstration tchr. area lang. arts Detroit Public Schs., 1967-69, curriculum leader, 1969-70, asst. prin. Bell Elem. Sch., 1970-75, adminstr., 1972-75, prin. Charles R. Drew Middle Sch., 1975-80, Stark Elem. Sch., 1980—; spl. lectr. Wayne State U., Detroit, 1968-70; spl. cons. middle sch. programs Detroit Public Schs., 1970-72. Sec., North Woodward Inter-Faith Council, 1979; speaker Women's Conf. Concerns, 1982; treas. Friends of Cathedral, 1982. Mem. Detroit Women Adminstrs. Suprs., Orgn. Sch. Adminstrs. and Suprs., Assn. Supervision and Curriculum Devel., Mich. Elem. and Middle Sch. Prins. Assn., Wayne County Prins. Assn. Roman Catholic. Author: A Guide To Reading Readiness, 1977. Home: 9000 E Jefferson St Detroit MI 48214 Office: 12611 Avondale St Detroit MI 48215

EDWARDS, BETTY, artist, educator; b. San Francisco, Apr. 18, 1926; d. Orson McArthur and Winifred Lon Wasden; B.A. in Art, UCLA, 1947, Ed.D., 1977; M.A. in Art, Calif. State U., Northridge, 1968; children—Anne, Brian. Tchr., Venice (Calif.) High Sch., 1959-64; faculty Community Coll. Los Angeles, 1965-76; prof. art Calif. State U., Long Beach, 1977—. Mem. Phi Kappa Delta. Author: Drawing on the Right Side of the Brain, 1979. Office: Art Dept Calif State U Long Beach CA 90840

EDWARDS, BEVERLYE WRIGHT, plastics co. exec.; b. Baton Rouge, Feb. 14, 1935; d. John Dalton and Rachel (Gunter) Brown; student La. State U., 1955-57; m. William R. Wright, Apr. 6, 1957 (dec. 1961); children—William R., Whitney L.; m. 2d, Lee Edwards, Dec. 24, 1978 (dec. 1980). With Dow Chem. Corp., Plaquemine, La., 1957-58; with Wright Plastics Co., Chamblee, Ga., 1961—, dir., 1982—. Bd. govs. Baton Rouge Little Theatre, 1976-78.

EDWARDS, BILLIE MARCELLE, systems engr.; b. Morrison, Tenn., Jan. 12, 1935; d. William Jackson and Mary Eloise (Gilley) E.; student U. Tenn., 1955-56; B.S., Middle Tenn. State U., 1959; postgrad. UCLA, 1969-70. Mem. tech. staff semicondr. div. Hughes Aircraft Co., Newport Beach, Calif., 1959-60; sr. applications engr. Western Semicondrs., Inc., Sana Ana, Calif., 1960-65; electronic engr. Naval Ship Weapon Systems Engring. Sta., Port Hueneme, Calif., 1965-77, br. mgr. advances systems reliability/maintainability, 1972-77, dept. mgr. systems assurance, 1977—; cons. engring. students. Active Humane Soc., Spl. Olympics, Homeowners Assn., Ventura County Symphony. Named Woman of Yr., Naval Ship Weapons Systems Engring. Sta., 1972, Supr. of Yr., 1976, recipient performance awards, 1971, 72; registered profl. engr., Calif. Mem. Am. Soc. Quality Control. Club: Altrusa. Office: Code 0700 NSWSES Port Hueneme CA 93043

EDWARDS, CORDELIA MAE (CORDELIA MCFARLAND), writer; b. Runnels County, Tex., Feb. 11, 1917; d. Wilburn Jones and Cynthia Cordelia (Dowdy) McFarland; student So. Meth. U., 1935-38, Okla. State U., 1951-52; m. Carl S. Edwards, Dec. 16, 1939; children—Gregg Stanley, Cholly Clayton, Carolyn Diane, Jean (dec.). Sec., So. Meth. U., Dallas, 1937-38; sec., contbr. stories Oak Clice Tribune, Dallas, 1939-54; contbr. Dallas Library Anthology Dallas Families, 1979-80, 81-82; mktg. researcher, pollster T.O.P.S., Dallas; mktg. researcher, pollster Bauman Research and Elrick and Lavidge, 1980—. contbr. Historic Dallas Jour., Historic Preservation League, Dallas, 1982. Chmn. resource com. LWV, 1963-65. Mem. Women's Equity Action League, Women's S.W. Fed. Credit Union, Nat. Historic Preservation Assn.; Daus. Republic Tex. Methodist. Clubs: Spa and Racquet (pres.); Old Oak Cliff Conservation League. Author: Happiness is Struggle, 19 . Office: 1707 Rio Vista Dallas TX

EDWARDS, DONNA O'STEEN, pianist, educator; b. Dallas, June 2, 1932; d. George Daniel O'Steen and Gladys (Sears) O'Steen Mealer; B.Mus., So. Meth. U., 1953, M.Mus., 1954; postgrad. Conservatorio de Santa Cecilia and Accademia di Santa Cecilia, Rome, 1976-77; D. Musical arts, N. Tex. State U., 1980; m. Harold Hugh Edwards, Jr., Oct. 14, 1966; children—Richard, Margaret, Marianne. Solo appearances: Dallas Symphony Orch., 1951, 53, Dallas-So. Meth. U. Symphony, 1950, 51, 52, 53, Houston Symphony Orch., 1969, Symphony Orch. of Music Acad. West, 1957, Youth Orch. Ft. Worth, 1978; owner piano studio, Dallas, 1958-64, 66—; tchr. Highland Park Ind. Sch. Dist., 1964-66; asst. prof. piano, music lit. Tex. Christian U., 1975-81, assoc. prof., 1981—, chmn. piano pedagogy dept., 1975—, coordinator pedagogy prep. dept., 1982—, asst. to artist in residence, 1978—; vis. prof. Brookhaven Coll., Dallas, fall 1978. Fulbright fellow, 1956-57; recipient 1st place award G.B. Dealey Young Artists Competition, 1953. Mem. Dallas Music Tchrs. Assn., Tex. Music Tchrs. Assn., Nat. Music Tchrs. Assn., Nat. Piano Guild, Coll. Music Soc., Mu Phi Epsilon, Pi Kappa Lambda. Home: 3229 Regent St Dallas TX 75229 Office: Ed Landreth Auditorium University Blvd and Cantey St Tex Christian U Fort Worth TX 76129

EDWARDS, DOROTHY ANNE, med. technologist; b. Wichita Falls, Tex., Feb. 23, 1929; d. Alvin Owsley and Bess Irene (Waters) Hall; student Midwestern State U., 1946-48; B.S., N. Tex. State U., 1950; student med. tech., Baylor Hosp., Dallas, 1950; m. Harrold Edwards, Dec. 14, 1956 (dec. 1960); 1 son, Dewitt Hall. Chief technologist, lab. supr. Wichita Gen. Hosp., Wichita Falls, 1950-60; med. technologist Bio-Med. Labs., Wichita Falls, 1960-61; adminstrv. lab. supr., organizer Sch. Med. Tech., Wichita Gen. Hosp., 1961—. Active Boy Scouts Am. Mem. Am. Soc. Clin. Pathologists (cert. med. technologist), Tex. Soc. Med. Technologists, Am. Soc. Med. Technologists, Am. Assn. Blood Banks, S.Central Assn. Blood Banks, Beta Sigma Phi (Outstanding Girl of Yr. 1954-55, past pres. Rictual of Jewels chpt., Exemplar chpt.). Baptist. Home: 4941 S Lake Park Dr Wichita Falls TX 76302 Office: Wichita General Hospital 1600 8th St Wichita Falls TX 76301

EDWARDS, ELSIE BIGGS, home economist; b. Martin County, N.C., Nov. 11, 1925; d. Eason Fletcher and Sallie (Roberson) Biggs; A.B. in Home Econs. and Sci., E. Carolina U., Greenville, N.C., 1946; M.Ed., N.C. State U., 1980; m. Charles Vernon Edwards, Dec. 27, 1944 (dec.); children—Charlene Edwards Hayes, Julia Edwards DeRoy. Tchr. home econs. Pitt County Bd. Edn., Ayden, N.C., 1946-51; asst. home agt. Tyrrell County Agrl. Extension Service, Columbia, N.C., 1955-61; home econs. agt. Pasquatank County Agrl. Extension Service, 1961-70; area home econs. agt. N.C. Agrl. Extension Service, Edenton, 1970-80, area specialized agt.-crafts, 1980—; adv. Albemarle Craftsmans Fair and Guild, 1970—; mem. adult edn. adv. com. Coll. of Albemarle, 1971-72. Mem. Nat. Assn. Extension Home Economists (Disting. Service award 1968), Am. Home Econs. Assn., N.C. Assn. Extension Home Economists (sec. 1968), N.C. Crafts Assn. (dir.), N.C. Home Econs. Assn., N.C. Fedn. Extension Workers, Watermark Assn. Artisans, Epsilon Sigma Phi. Democrat. Baptist. Home: 1701 Crescent Dr Elizabeth City NC 27909 Office: PO Box 519 Edenton NC 27932

EDWARDS, HELEN HEY HARSHMAN, home economist; b. DeKalb, Ill., Mar. 20, 1952; d. Dale Lowell Harshman and Margaret Emma (Templeton) Harshman McEvoy; B.S. with honors, U. Ill., 1974, postgrad., 1977—; m. William S. Edwards, Aug. 25, 1973; children—Andrew Chester (dec.), Nancy Abigail. Asst. adv. U. Ill. Coop. Extension Service, Peoria, 1974-77, asso. adv., 1977-79, extension adv. home econs., 1979-82, staff leader, energy edn. coordinator, 1978-82; project cordinator Tri County Parents Anonymous, 1982—. Bd. dirs., patient relations com. Planned Parenthood Assn. Peoria; mem. adv. council Retired Sr. Vol. Program. Recipient Communication award Ill. Assn. Extension Advs., 1977; Laura A. Weber fellow, 1978-80. Mem. Nat. Assn. Extension Home Economists, Am. Mgmt. Assn., Am. Home Econs. Assn., Ill. Assn. Extension Home Economists, Ill. Assn. Home Econs., Hypertension Council, Peoria Friends of Internat. Students. Omicron Nu, Phi Upsilon Omicron. Home: 1634 W Columbia Terr Peoria IL 61606

EDWARDS, LILIAN MARY, educator; b. Oswestry, Wales, Eng., Feb. 6, 1932; came to U.S., 1958, naturalized, 1972; d. Herbert Arthur and Lilian Amelia (Roberts) E.; art tchrs. degree Liverpool U., 1954, diploma in design, 1955; B.A., Columbia U., 1960; M. Profl. Studies, Pratt Inst., 1976; postgrad. Center Expressive Psychotherapy, 1975-77; m. George M. Simpson, 1951 (div. 1961). Tchr. art, Selby Art Sch., Leeds, Eng., 1955-56, Baron Byng High Sch., Montreal, Que., Can., 1956-57, Rockland (N.Y.) State Hosp., 1958-61; freelance designer, Ascot, London, 1961-63; tchr. The Children's Village, Dobbs Ferry, N.Y., 1963-64; tchr. Roman Cath. elem. schs., Rockland, part-time 1965-68; freelance textile artist, Tappan, N.Y., 1965-70; art tchr., art therapist Rockland Children's Psychiat. Center, 1968—. Liverpool U. travelling scholar, 1954; recipient Employee Recognition award for outstanding service Rockland Children's Psychiat. Center, 1982. Mem. Inter-Agy. Creative Arts Group, Am. Art Therapy Assn. One-woman shows stitchery and silkscreens: Liverpool, Eng., 1955, Rockland Found. for Arts, Nyack, N.Y., 1970, Blauvelt Public Library, Rockland County, 1972; exhibited in group shows: Orangeburg (N.Y.) Town Hall, 1971, Bklyn. Mus. Art, 1977, Washington Psychiat. Mus., 1978; executed wall hangings for Lycoming Coll., Williamsport, Pa., Loyola U., Johns Hopkins U., U. Tenn. Home: 57 Tweed Blvd Grandview NY 10960 Office: Rockland Children's Psychiat Center Convent Rd Orangeburg NY 10962

EDWARDS, MARIE BABARE, psychologist; b. Tacoma; d. Nick and Mary (Mardesich) Babare; B.A., Stanford, 1948, M.A., 1949; m. Tilden Hampton Edwards (div.); 1 son, Tilden Hampton Edwards III. Counselor guidance center U. So. Calif., Los Angeles, 1950-52; project coordinator So. Calif. Soc. Mental Hygiene, 1952-54; pub. speaker Welfare Fedn. Los Angeles, 1953-57; field rep. Los Angeles County Assn. Mental Health, 1957-58; intern psychologist UCLA, 1958-60; pvt. practice, human relations tng., counselor tng., teaching U. So. Calif., U. Calif. at San Diego, Irvine, Santa Barbara. Mem. Calif., Am., Western, Los Angeles psychol. assns., A.A.A.S., Nat. Acad. Religion and Mental Health, Soc. Advancement Mgmt., So. Calif. Soc. Clin. Hypnosis, Internat. Platform Assn. Author: (with Eleanor Hoover) The Challenge of Being Single, 1974, paperback edit., 1975. Office: 6100 Buckingham Pkwy Culver City CA 90230

EDWARDS, MARY ALICE DOUTY, educator; b. Rochester, N.Y., Oct. 26, 1913; d. James Frederick and Mary Anna (Furlong) Douty; A.B., Goucher Coll., Balt., 1935; M.A., Union Theol. Sem., N.Y.C., 1936; Tchrs. Coll., Columbia U., Ed.D., 1955; m. Philip Corin Edwards, May 30, 1960. Dir. Christian edn. 1st Presbyn. Ch., Evansville, Ind., 1936-39; mem. staff Balt. conf. bd. edn. Methodist Ch., 1939-48, 54-56; tchr. Anne Arundel County (Md.), 1948-53; exec. sec. Balt. conf. bd. Meth. Ch., 1956-59; mem. faculty Wesley Theol. Sem., Washington, 1957—, prof. Christian edn., 1962—; trustee Morgan Christian Center, Morgan State U., Balt., 1956—, pres., 1973—; with chaplain's tng. program U.S. Navy, Europe, 1963; vis. lectr. Drew, Union and Garrett-Evang. sems. Lay mem. Balt. ann. conf. United Meth. Ch. Grantee Adminstrn. Aging, 1972. Mem. Christian Educators Fellowship United Meth. Ch., Assn. Profs. and Researchers Religious Edn., Religious Edn. Assn., United Meth. Assn. Profs. Christian Edn., Arena Stage Assocs., Common Cause, ACLU. Democrat. Author: How To Work with Church Groups, 1957; Leadership Development and the Workers Conference, 1967; Junior Teachers Guide, 1968; also articles, curriculum materials. Office: 4500 Massachusetts Ave NW Washington DC 20016

EDWARDS, RITA LILLIAN, library adminstr.; b. Toronto, Ont., Can., Apr. 5, 1928; d. Gordon Denis and Kathleen Constance (Bromley) Danby; B.A., U. Toronto, 1951, B.E., 1964, M.Ed., 1969, M.L.S., 1971; postgrad. Ont. Coll. Edn., 1952-53; B.Sc.B. magna cum laude, U. Ottawa, 1962, cert. med. librarianship, 1975; m. John Edwards, Dec. 19, 1958. Tchr., Loretto Coll. Sch., Toronto, 1951-52, Ledbury Park Elem. Sch., North York, Ont., 1953-54, Cobden (Ont.) Dist. High Sch., 1954-55, Nickle Dist. Collegiate Vocat. Inst., Sudbury, Ont., 1955-57; tchr. North Toronto Collegiate Inst., 1960-61; tchr.-librarian Laurentian High Sch., Ottawa, 1961-63; head librarian Bathurst Heights Secondary Sch., Toronto, 1963-68; dir. library services George Brown Coll. Applied Arts and Tech., Toronto, 1968-80, dir. library and audiovisual services, 1980—; tchr. classification Ryerson Poly. Inst., Toronto, 1968-69; mem. Standards Com. for Secondary Sch. Libraries in North York, 1967-68; mem. community coll. com. Ont. Assn. Continuing Edn., 1969-70; mem. user's adv. com. Coll. Bibliocentre, 1972-74, 79—; mem. exec. com. librarians Colls. Applied Arts and Tech. Ont., 1982—. Mem. Ont. Assn. Coll. and Univ. Librarians (chmn. 1973-75, rep. to Focus, news bull. Ont. Library Assn. 1976-78), Toronto Area Archivist Group, Can. Health Librarians Assn., Med., Can., Ont. library assns. Editor: Com-O-Lib newsletter, 1979—, Harbour Sq. newsletter, 1980-82; Ont. corr. CTCL Communiqué, newsletter community and tech. colls. sect. Can. Assn. Coll. and Univ. Libraries, 1982—; contbr. articles to profl. jours. Home: 33 Harbour Sq Apt 1811 Toronto ON M5J 2G2 Canada Office: PO Box 1015 Station B Toronto ON M5T 2T9 Canada

EDWARDS, ROXANNE FISHER, picture editor; b. White Plains, N.Y., Sept. 21, 1946; d. Sidney G. and Juanita B. Edwards; B.A., Lake Erie Coll., 1968; student U. Nancy (France), winter 1967. Picture researcher Newsweek Mag., N.Y.C., 1970-72; picture editor Grolier Ency., 1973, Am. Broadcasting Co., N.Y.C., 1974-77, Bus. Week Mag., 1977—; judge photo contests. Mem. Am. Soc. Picture Profls., Am. Soc. Mag. Photographers (sustaining). Libertarian. Office: 1221 Ave of Americas New York NY 10024

EDWARDS, RUTH ELLEN CHARLES, social worker; b. Boston, May 24, 1945; d. Jacob and Anne (Rosenfelt) Charles; A.B., Boston U., 1967; A.M. (VA grantee), U. Chgo., 1969; m. William H. Edwards, Dec. 22, 1973. Faculty, Morraine Valley Community Coll., Palos Hills, Ill., 1972-73; clin. social work adminstr. Pilsen-Little Village Mental Health Center, Chgo., 1969-76; adminstr. admissions Tinley Park (Ill.) Mental Health Center, 1976-78; aftercare program coordinator Beverly-Morgan Park Mental Health Center, Chgo., 1978—; partner, pres. corp. Chgo. Women's Counselling Collective, 1976—. Mem. Nat. Assn. Social Workers, Council on Women's Programs, Acad. Cert. Social Workers, State Street Bus. and Profl. Women's Club. Home: 10106 S Prospect Ave Chicago IL 60643 Office: Chgo Women's Counselling Collective Suite 1934 55 E Washington St Chicago IL 60602

EDWARDS, SARAH ANNE, clin. social worker; b. Tulsa, Jan. 7, 1943; d. Clyde Elton and Virginia Elizabeth Glandon; B.A. with distinction, U. Mo., Kansas City, 1965; M.S.W., U. Kans., 1974; m. Paul Robert Edwards, Apr. 24, 1965; 1 son, Jon Scott. Community rep. OEO, Kansas City Regional Office, 1966-68; social service/parent involvement specialist, program rev. and resource specialist Office Child Devel., HEW, Kansas City, Kans., 1968-73; dir. tng. social services dept., children's rehab. unit U. Affiliated Facility, U. Kans. Med. Center, Kansas City, 1975-76; co-dir. Cathexis Inst. S., Glendale, Calif., 1976-77; pvt. practice psychotherapy, tng. and cons. personal, interpersonal, organizational behavior, Sierra Madre, Calif, 1973—; founder, dir. tng., lead therapist Matrix, Kansas City, Mo., 1975-76; founder, sponsor Creative Transactions, Kansas City, Mo., 1977—; dir. tng. Public Affairs Assistance, Kansas City, Mo., 1974-76; staff therapist Las Virgines Med. Center, Woodland Hills, Calif., 1977-78, Rockhurst Coll. Counselling Center, Kansas City, Mo., 1975, U. Kans. Psychol. Clinic, Lawrence, 1973; lectr. Project Head Start, Kans. State Tchrs. Coll., Pittsburg, 1972; teaching asst. undergrad. social work U. Kans. Sch. Social Welfare, 1973-74; instr. psychology dept. Pepperdine U., 1978. Mem. Am. Soc. Tng. and Devel. (dir. Los Angeles chpt. 1980-81), Internat. Transactional Analysis Assn., Nat. Assn. Social Workers, Acad. Cert. Social Workers, Nat. Conf. Family Relations. Contbr. articles to profl. jours. Office: 677 Canyon Crest Dr Sierra Madre CA 91024

EDWARDS, VIRGINIA ANNE, nurse recruiter; b. Norfolk, Va., Mar. 29, 1925; d. James Preston and Virginia Dare (Sterling) Edwards; R.N., DePaul Hosp., Sch. Nursing, 1948; grad. Barnes Hosp. Sch. Anesthesia, St. Louis, 1950; B.S.N., Med. Coll. Ga., 1975; Head nurse med. floor DePaul Hosp., Norfolk, Va., 1948-49; staff nurse anesthetist Danville (Va.) Meml. Hosp., 1950-53; staff nurse anesthesia Mary Immaculate Hosp., Newport News, 1953-54, Kennestone Hosp., Marietta, Ga., 1954-60, Ga. Bapt. Hosp., Atlanta, 1960-63; chief nurse anesthetist Athens (Ga.) Gen. Hosp., 1963-75, asst. adminstr. nursing, 1975-81, nurse recruiter, 1981—. Mem. Bd. Regents Com. on Statewide Assessment of Nursing Edn., 1980—. Named Outstanding Nurse - DePaul Silver Loving Cup, 1948; named Bus. and Profl. Woman of Yr., 1979; Ga. Nurses Assn. Dist. 11 honoree, 1981. Mem. Ga. Assn. Nurse Anesthetists (pres. 1959-61), Am. Assn. Nurse Anesthetists (trustee 1965-67), Ga. Hosp. Nursing Service Adminstrs. (sec. 1977-78, pres. 1980-81), Ga. Hosp. Assn. (council on nursing 1979-80), Am. Nurses Assn., Ga. Nurses Assn., Am. Assn. Critical Care Nurses, Am. Heart Assn., Ga. Soc. Hosp. Nursing Service Adminstrs., Sigma Theta Tau. Democrat. Club: Pilot. Home: 150 Davis Pl Athens GA 30606 Office: 1199 Prince Ave Athens GA 30613

EELLS, MARY ANN, family therapist, educator; b. Sayre, Pa., June 2, 1933; d. Edward P. and Violet I. (Walters) Walsh; B.S., SUNY, Plattsburgh, 1955, cum laude; M.S., U. Rochester, 1968, Ed.D. (fellow), 1970; cert. P.H.S.M., Harvard U., 1974; postgrad. U. Md., 1981; m. Robert Curtis Eells, July 2, 1955 (div. 1968); children—John Robert, Peter Curtis. Staff nurse Clinton County Health Dept., Plattsburgh, N.Y., 1955-56; instr., dir. Sch. Nursing Bd. of Co-op Ednl. Services, Ellenburgh Depot, N.Y. 1963-66; staff nurse Rochester Gen. Hosp., N.Y., 1967-69; asso. prof. nursing U. Maine, Portland, 1969-75, dean Sch. Nursing, 1971-75; asso. prof. Rush Coll. Nursing, Chgo., 1975-77, asst. dean, 1975-77; asso. prof. Sch. Nursing, U. Md., Balt., 1977—, asso. dean, 1977-79; family therapist Howard County Health Dept., Md., 1980; pvt. practice family therapy, Columbia, Md., 1980—; mem. nurse adv. panel Nat. Commn. for Study of Nursing, 1969. Chmn. adv. com. Howard County Health Dept., Md., 1978-80. Mem. Am. Nurses Assn., Md. Nurses Assn., Soc. for Gen. Systems Research, Am. Soc. for Cybernetics, Drug and Alcohol Nursing Assn. Roman Catholic. Contbr. articles on time, families and alcoholism to profl. publs.; contbr. chpts. in field to books on nursing research. Home: 6302 Dewey Dr Columbia MD 21044 Office: Sch Nursing Univ Maryland Baltimore MD 21201

EFFINGER, KATHARINA VIOLA, hosp. exec.; b. Milw., June 15, 1941; d. Charles William and Eleanora (Hauer) E.; student Ft. Wayne (Ind.) Luth. Sch. Nursing, 1959-61; B.A. in Behavior Scis., Nat. Coll. Edn., Evanston, Ill., 1981. Reservation supr. Braniff Internat., 1961-69; sales rep. United Gasket Corp., 1969-70; admitting mgr. MacNeal Meml. Hosp., Berwyn, Ill., 1970-73; bus. office mgr. Lake Forest (Ill.) Hosp., 1974-77; asst. v.p. fin. Victory Meml. Hosp., Waukegan, Ill., 1978—; adv. bd. Lake County Vocat. Center. Mem. Hosp. Fin. Mgmt. Assn., Nat. Assn. Patient Accounts Mgrs. Office: 1324 N Sheridan Rd Waukegan IL 60085

EGAN, LINDA LEE, nurse; b. Daretown, N.J., Mar. 25, 1947; d. John Joseph and Mary Elizabeth (Woodruff) Egan; A.S. in Nursing, Cumberland County Coll., 1972; B.S.N., Stockton State Coll., 1978. Cottage attendant Vineland (N.J.) State Sch., 1965-69, cottage supr., 1969-72, staff nurse, 1972-74, head nurse intensive care, 1974-75; staff nurse intensive care Cooper Med. Center, Camden, N.J., 1975-77, inservice clinician, 1977-78; dir. nursing Vineland (N.J.) State Sch. Hosp., 1978-79, instr. nursing inservice, 1979-82; rehab. specialist Staff Builders, San Diego, 1982—; nursing care cons. (part-time) Am. Inst. for Mental Studies, 1980. Respiratory/circulatory emergency instr./multimedia first aide instr. ARC, Vineland, 1975—. Recipient Instl. award N.J. Assn. for Retarded Children, 1969. Mem. Profl. Traveling Nurses Assn., S.Jersey Inservice Exchange, Am. Nurses Assn., N.J. Nurses Assn., Am. Assn. Critical Care Nurses. Roman Catholic.

EGAN, LORRAINE ANNA MARIE, educator, civic worker; b. Albany, N.Y., June 20, 1938; d. Erwin Heinz and Anna (Britsch) Hummel; B.A., SUNY, Albany, 1960; m. Richard T. Egan; 1 son, Randolph. Tchr. Dolgeville (N.Y.) High Sch., 1960-61; interviewer Market Trends, 1964-71; substitute tchr. Montgomery County, Md., 1969-80; media coordinator Media Trend, 1980-81; office mgr. periodontist's office, 1981-82; telephone solicitor for DAV, 1967-72; advt. mgr. Burtonsville (Md.) Shopper, 1977. Founding pres. Dist. 14-A Democratic Club Montgomery County, 1976-78; mem. Md. State Dem. Central Com.; mem. Montgomery County Dem. Central Com., 1978-81; active Tamarack Triangle Civic Assn.; bus. mgr. Bark (newspaper), 1970, 74-76, mng. editor, 1974-76; mem. Springbrook Sr. High Sch. PTA, Page Elem. Sch. PTA; membership chmn. White Oak Jr. High Sch. PTA, 1974; mem. Women's Soc. Colesville United Meth. Ch.; active Triangle Theater; vol. fund drives for cancer, heart fund, cystic fibrosis, multiple sclerosis. Mem. Montgomery Assn. Substitute Tchrs. Clubs: Order Eastern Star, Women's Dem. Caucus, Albany State Alumni Assn. (social chmn. local chpt.). Home: 17537 Roseland Blvd Lathrup Village MI 48076

EGAN, SHIRLEY ANNE, nursing educator; b. Haverhill, Mass.; d. Rush B. and Beatrice (Bengle) Willard; diploma St. Joseph's Hosp. Sch. Nursing, Nashua, N.H., 1945; B.S. in Nursing Edn., Boston U., 1949, M.S., 1956. Instr. sci. Sturdy Meml. Hosp. Sch. Nursing, Attleboro, Mass., 1949-51; instr. sci. Peter Bent Brigham Sch. Nursing, Boston, 1951-53, ednl. dir., 1953-55, asso. dir. Sch. Nursing, 1955-59; nurse edn. adviser AID (formerly ICA), Karachi, Pakistan, 1959-67; prin. Coll. Nursing, Karachi, 1959-67; dir. Vis. Nurse Service, Nashua, 1967-70; exec. dir. Lowell (Mass.) Vis. Nurse Assn., 1970-71; cons. nursing edn. Pan Am. Health Orgn./WHO to faculty of medicine U. W.I., Jamaica, 1971-72; med.-surg. coordinator Peter Bent Brigham Sch. Nursing,

Boston, 1971-73, asso. dir., 1973-79, dir., 1979—; cons. nursing edn. Pakistan Ministry of Health, Labour and Social Welfare, 1959-67; adviser to editor Pakistan Nursing and Health Rev., 1959-67; mem. exec. bd. Nat. Health Edn. Com., Pakistan. Mem. Nashua Service League, 1970-81, pres., 1973-75; bd. dirs. Nashua Child Care Center, 1968-71; bd. dirs. Matthew Thornton Health Center, Nashua, 1971-81, sec. bd. dirs., 1971-75. Served as 1st lt. Army Nurse Corps, 1945-47. Mem. Nat. League Nursing, Diploma Nurses Assn. (treas. 1981—), Trained Nurses Assn. Pakistan, St. Joseph's Sch. Nursing Alumnae Assn., Boston U. Alumnae Assn., Brit. Soc. Health Edn., Sigma Theta Tau. Contbr. articles to profl. publs. Home: 20 Tinker Rd Nashua NH 03060 Office: 721 Huntington Ave Boston MA 02115

EGDORF, LINDA LEE, nurse; b. Hartley, Iowa, Aug. 27, 1941; d. George Harry and Pearl Amanda (Broesch) Lettengarver; diploma Lutheran Hosp. Sch. Nursing, Sioux City, Iowa, 1966; m. Arlan Dean Egdorf, Oct. 16, 1966. Nurse, Lutheran Hosp., 1966; staff nurse Orange City (Iowa) Mcpl. Hosp., 1966-70, dir. nurses, 1970—; instr. NW Iowa Tech. Coll., Sheldon. Cert. emergency med. technician. Mem. Iowa Hosp. Assn. Republican. Lutheran. Home: 604 Albany Ave NE Orange City IA 51041 Office: 115 4th St NW Orange City IA 51041

EGENES, SONJA CARLSEN, state legislator; b. St. Paul, Oct. 19, 1930; s. Samuel and Lillian Mildred (Querna) Carlsen; student St. Olaf Coll., 1947-48, State U. Iowa, 1948-50; B.S. in Home Econs. Edn., Iowa State U., 1951, postgrad. history and govt., 1957-59; m. John Stark Egenes, Aug. 15, 1948; 1 son, Jay Carlton. Tchr. high sch., Randall and Story City, Iowa, 1951-57; mem. faculty govt. Iowa State U., 1960-62, mem. indsl. engrng. adv. council, 1978; mem. Iowa Ho. of Reps., 1970—; mem. transp. com. Nat. Council State Legislatures; mem. Edn. Comm. of the States; convenor, vice-chmn. Iowa Women's Polit. Caucus, 1973-74. Dir. music Immanuel Luth. Ch., Story City, 1952-59; mem. adv. com. on curriculum and ednl. programming Iowa Ednl. Broadcasting Network; mem. program adv. com. for continuing edn. for women div. extension State U. Iowa. Republican candidate for U.S. Congress from 5th Dist. Iowa, 1962; vice chmn. Iowans for Rockefeller Com., 1964; alt. del. Rep. Nat. Conv., 1968; dist. pres. Iowa Fedn. Rep. Women, 1967-69, state v.p., 1970-71; bd. dirs. Ames Choral Soc. Fulbright scholar U. Oslo, 1959. Named Iowa Woman of Year, UPI, 1962. Mem. Iowa Council Cert. Landscape Critics, Iowa UN Assn. (co-chmn. congressional info. exchange), Omicron Nu, Phi Kappa Phi. Club: Federated Women's. Home: 905 Lafayette St Story City IA 50248 Office: Iowa State Capitol Des Moines IA 50319

EGER, ERNESTINA NANETTA, educator; b. Phila., Nov. 24, 1942; d. Urban Franz and Dorothy Lucille (Oblender) Eger; A.B., Muhlenberg Coll., 1963; A.M. (fellow), Emory U., 1965; Ph.D., U. Jaime Balmes, 1975. Tchr., Spanish and French, Haddonfield (N.J.) Jr. High Sch., 1964-65; assoc. prof. Spanish lang. and lit. Carthage Coll., Kenosha, Wis., 1965—. Sec. United Migrant Opportunity Services Bd., 1976-78, mem. bd., 1978-79; mem. Racine-Kenosha-Walworth Spanish Centers Bd., 1976-78. Lutheran Ch. in Am. grantee, 1969-73. Mem. MLA, Am. Assn. Tchrs. of Spanish and Portuguese, Nat. Assn. Interdisciplinary Ethnic Studies, Soc. for Multi-Ethnic Lit. in the U.S., Nat. Assn. Chicano Studies. Author: Bibliography of Criticism of Contemporary Chicano Literature, 1982; contbr. articles to profl. jours.; mem. editorial bd. La Palabra, 1979—; bibliog. cons. Bilingual Rev./Revista Bilingüe, Bilingual Press, 1981—. Home: 614A-15th Pl Apt 2 Kenosha WI 53140 Office: Fgn Langs Carthage Coll Kenosha WI 53141

EGERT, SARAH INGRID, city ofcl.; b. Graceville, Minn., Oct. 12, 1935; d. Leroy Alfred and Emma Spencer (Bailey) Sorenson; student U. Minn., 1953-54; B.S. in Nursing, Hamline U., 1958; m. Donald Plumer Egert, Jan. 30, 1960; children—Steven, James. Surg. nurse Holy Trinity Hosp., Graceville, 1958-60; mayor City of Ortonville (Minn.), 1976-80, mem. City Council, 1982—, Planning Commn., 1982—; bd. dirs. KWCM-TV. Mem. Ortonville Area C. of C. (dir. 1978-80), Minn. Assn. Mayors, Soc. of Lees of Va., Huguenot Soc., Daus. Am. Colonists, U.S. Daus. of 1812, DAR (vice-chmn., state officer, nat. chmn. Congress Housing 1981—). Republican. Lutheran. Mem. Order Eastern Star (worthy matron Laurel Crown chpt. 1979-80). Home: 542 Park Ave N Ortonville MN 56278

EGGERT, LUCILLE D., service co. exec.; b. Chgo.; d. Louis B. and Betty M. Duckmann; B.S., Northwestern U.; m. Warren C. Eggert; children—Kenneth, Jeffrey, Gerald. Exec., Capital Bus. Service, Chgo., 1958-63; co-founder, co-owner, exec. Certified Bus. Service, San Francisco, 1963—; exec. dir. Cert. Career Adv. Service div. CBS Inc., San Rafael, Calif., 1977—. Mem. adv. bd., work readiness instr. Regional Occupational Program, 1975—; mem. indsl. adv. bd. Goodwill Industries, San Francisco. pres. bd. dirs. Christian Sci. Ch., 1975-78. Mem. Am. Soc. Tng. and Devel., Bus. and Profl. Women (pres. 1972), San Rafael C. of C., Profl. Secs. Internat., Exec. Women Internat., San Francisco C. of C. (women's council), Delta Zeta. Club: Commonwealth Calif. Office: 1299 4th St Suite 207-C San Rafael CA 94901

EGGERTS, LAIMA MUDITE (MRS. ARTHUR H. EGGERTS), med. social worker; b. Latvia; d. Eduards V. and Rosalie (Grinvald) Zvaigzne; D.D.S., State U. Latvia, 1936; M.S. in Social Work, State U. Tenn., 1962; m. Arthur H. Eggerts, Dec. 16, 1930; 1 son, Ragnar Martin; came to U.S., 1959, naturalized, 1964. Pvt. practice dentistry, Latvia and Germany, 1936-49; organizer, head dental dept. United Christian Hosp., Lahore, Pakistan, 1957-59; psychiat. social worker Overbrook Hosp., Cedar Grove, N.J., 1962-65; med. social worker in geriatrics Lutheran Social Services N.J., Jersey City, 1965-74; cons. social work Luth. Homes of N.J.; lectr. inservice tng. nursing personnel, 1965—; psychiat. social worker in consultation and edn. Mental Health Center, Neptune, N.J., 1979—. Served as capt. Pakistan Army Dental Corps, 1950-57. Decorated Republic Commemoration medal (Pakistan). Mem. Nat. Assn. Social Workers, Latvian Med. and Dental Assn. in U.S.A., Acad. Cert. Social Workers, U. Tenn. Sch. Social Work Alumni Assn., Nat. Assn. Christians in Social Work, Gerontol. Soc. Inc., N.J. Gerontol. Soc. (charter), Daugaviete Sorority. Lutheran. Home: 115A Lowens Strasse Freehold NJ 07728 Office: 93 Nelson Ave Jersey City NJ 07307

EGGINTON, MARGARET LOUISE, lawyer, govt. ofcl.; b. Bklyn., Oct. 31, 1944; d. William L. and Elizabeth L. (Steinbugler) Maguire; B.A., Marymount Coll., 1965; M.A., Colgate U., 1969; J.D., U. Louisville, 1977; m. Everett Egginton, June 6, 1965; 1 son, William. Teaching, translation and interpretation of Spanish and English various schs. in U.S. and Colombia, 1968-74; admitted Ky. bar, 1977; counsel First Ky. Nat. Corp., Louisville, 1977-79; atty. Fed. Res. Bd., Washington, 1979-80; asst. to the dir. Fed. Deposit Ins. Corp., 1980-81, dep. to the chmn., 1981—. Served with Peace Corps, 1965-67. N.Y. State Regents scholar, 1961-65, Higher Edn. Act fellow, 1967-69. Mem. Am. Bar Assn. Office: Federal Deposit Insurance Corp 550 17th St NW Washington DC 20429

EGGLESTON, CLAIRE LYNN MASON, occupational therapist; b. E. Stroudsberg, Pa., Sept. 14, 1952; d. David Julius and Frances Lillian (Zacher) Mason; B.S. with honors, U. Fla., 1974; m. Ronnie Eggleston, Sept. 2, 1978; 1 dau., Michelle Lyn Mason. Occupational therapist Infant Stimulation and Children's Programs, United Cerebral Palsy Center of Miami (Fla.), 1974-75; dir. occupational therapy Parkway Gen. Hosp., North Miami, Fla., 1975-76; dir. occupational therapy Baytown (Tex.) Cerebral Palsy Center, 1976-77; dir. occupational therapy/hosp. risk mgr. Rosewood Gen. Hosp., Houston, 1977—; adj. faculty U. Tex. Med. Br., 1977—; ins. liaison for Tex. Occupational Therapists, 1979—. Chmn., Houston Occupational Therapists Dirs. Forum, 1978-79. Lic. occupational therapist, Fla. Mem. Nat. Assn. Female Execs., Am. Occupational Therapy Assn., Tex. Occupational Therapy Assn., (bd. dirs. 1979—), Tex. Soc. Allied Health Professions, Tex. Hosp. Safety Assn., Nat. Assn. Scuba Divers. Democrat. Jewish. Contbr. articles to profl. jours. Home: 7442 Water Park Ln Houston TX 77086 Office: 9200 Westheimer Rd Houston TX 77063

EGLITIS, IRMA, physician, educator; b. Riga, Latvia, Oct. 13, 1907; came to U.S., 1950, naturalized, 1956; d. Juris Georgs and Elizabete (Kronenberg) Liepinsh; M.D. maximum cum laude, U. Latvia, 1931; postgrad. Creative Problem Solving Inst., SUNY, Buffalo, 1968; m. John Arnold Eglitis, Apr. 17, 1938; Intern, Univ. Hosp., Riga, 1930-31, resident Dermatology and Venereal Diseases Clinic, 1932, 42-44; asst. instr. U. Latvia Faculty Medicine, 1932-36, jr. instr., 1936-37, instr., 1937-44; instr. Ernst Moritz Arndt U. Faculty Medicine, Greifswald, Germany, 1944-45; cons. specialist for dermatology and venereal diseases Brit. Control Commn., Med. Service, W.Ger., 1945-49; practice medicine specializing in dermatology, Schleswig, W.Ger., 1945-50; instr. Ohio State U. Coll. Medicine, Columbus, 1952-56, asst. prof., 1956-62, assoc. prof., 1962-67, prof., 1967-78, prof. emeritus, 1978—, prof. Coll. Dentistry and Grad. Sch. Recipient numerous awards Ohio State U., including Disting. Service Award Coll. Dentistry, 1978, Coll. Medicine, 1978, recognition and appreciation medallion Bd. Trustees, 1979; Golden Key and cert., Omicron Kappa Upsilon, 1979; diplomate state bd. dermatology and venereal diseases, Latvia, 1944. Fellow Ohio Acad. Sci.; mem. Am. Med. Women's Assn. (nat. exec. bd., nat. sec. 1969, nat. chmn. med. edn. and practice com. 1967, nat. chairman med. opportunities and practice com. 1968, nat. constn. and by-laws com. 1970, nat. chmn. resolutions com. 1972), Columbus Med. Women's Assn. (pres. 1961-63, 1968, v.p. 1959-60, sec. 1965-67, sec.-treas. 1958-59), Am. Assn. Anatomists, Med. Women's Internat. Assn., Council of Inst. for Research in Vision, Sigma Xi. Co-author: Anatomy and Histology of the Eye and Orbit in the Domestic Animals, 1960; (monograph) The Rabbit in Eye Research, 1964. Home: 123 E Lane Ave Columbus OH 43201 Office: Ohio State U Coll Medicine 333 W 10th Ave Columbus OH 43210

EHLERS, CAROL JEAN, coll. ofcl.; b. Milw., Mar. 14, 1937; d. William John and Edna Belle E.; A.A., Stephens Coll., 1955; B.A., U. Colo., 1957, M.A., 1960, Ph.D., 1975; postgrad. U. Innsbruck (Austria), 1961, (Fulbright fellow) Am. Classical Sch., Greece, 1964, (fellow) U. Erlangen-Nurnberg (W.Ger.), 1970-71. Tchr. fgn. langs. and English, Hudson's Bay High Sch., Vancouver, Wash., 1957-59; tchr. fgn. langs. and social studies Niagara Falls (N.Y.) Pub. Schs., 1960-61; instr. history and langs. Skagit Valley Coll., Mt. Vernon, Wash., 1961-66, 67-68, 71-72; Fulbright exchange tchr. Staatliches Symnasium Marquartstein, W.Ger., 1966-67; asst. prof. history Trenton State Coll., 1972-77, asst. to grad. Dean, 1976-78; asst. dean Montclair (N.J.) State Coll., 1978—, acting grad. dean, 1979—. Mem. Am. Hist. Assn., Conf. Group on German Politics, Phi Alpha Theta, Phi Delta Kappa, Kappa Delta Pi, Delta Kappa Gamma. Office: Graduate Office Montclair State Coll Upper Montclair NJ 07043

EHLERS, ELEANOR MAY COLLIER (MRS. FREDERICK BURTON EHLERS), civic worker; b. Klamath Falls, Oreg., Apr. 23, 1920; d. Alfred Douglas and Ethel (Foster) Collier; B.A., U. Oreg., 1941; secondary tchrs. credentials Stanford, 1942; m. Frederick Burton Ehlers, June 26, 1943; children—Frederick Douglas, Charles Collier. Tchr., Salinas Union High Sch., 1942-43; piano tchr. pvt. lessons, Klamath Falls, 1958—. Mem. Child Guidance Adv. Council, 1956-60; mem. adv. com. Boys and Girls Aid Soc., 1965—; mem. Gov.'s Adv. Com. Arts and Humanities, 1966-67; bd. mem. Friends of Mus. U. Oreg., 1966-69, Arts in Oreg., 1966-68, Klamath County Colls. for Oreg.'s Future, 1968—; chpt. pres. Am. Field Service, 1962-63; mem. Gov.'s Com. Governance of Community Colls., 1967; bd. dirs. Favell Mus. Western Art and Artifacts, 1971—, Community Concert Assn., 1950—, pres., 1966-74; established Women's Guild at Presbyn. Intercommunity Hosp., 1965, trustee hosp. sec. bd. trustees, 1962-65, 76—, mem. bldg. com. 1962-67, mem. planning com., chmn. edn. and research com. hosp. bd., 1967—. Named Woman of Month, Klamath Herald News, 1965; named grant to Oreg. Endowed Fellowship Fund, AAUW, 1971; recipient greatest Service award Oreg. Tech. Inst., 1970-71, Internat. Woman of Achievement award Quota Club, 1981, U. Oreg. Pioneer award, 1981. Mem. AAUW (local pres. 1955-56), Oreg. Music Tchrs. Assn. (pres. Klamath Basin dist. 1979—), P.E.O. (Oreg. dir. 1968-75, state pres. 1974-75, trustee internat. Continuing Edn. Fund 1977—), Pi Beta Phi, Mu Phi Epsilon, Pi Lambda Theta. Presbyterian. Address: 1338 Pacific Terr Klamath Falls OR 97601

EHLERS, SALLY MAE, physician; b. Marshall, Minn., July 25, 1945; d. Millard Earl and Doris (Wall) E.; B.A., Hamline U., 1967; M.D., U. Minn., 1971. Intern, W.Va. U. Med. Center, Morgantown, 1971-72; resident in internal medicine U. Minn. Hosps., Mpls., 1972-74, fellow in nephrology, 1974-76, instr., 1975-76, asst. prof., 1976—; chief sect. nephrology, dept. internal medicine St. Paul Ramsey Med. Center, 1976—, dir. dialysis, 1980—; practice medicine specializing in internal medicine and nephrology, St. Paul, 1975—; mem. staff St. Paul-Ramsey Med. Center, St. Joseph's Hosp., St. Paul; mem. faculty U. Minn., 1975—. Mem. task force on hypertension Minn. Heart Assn., 1980; mem. med. adv. bd. Minn. Kidney Found.; bd. dirs. Renal Network 7, 1981—. Mearf grantee, 1978-80; ednl. devel. grantee U. Minn., 1980-81; recipient Physician Recognition award AMA, 1981. Mem. Am. Soc. Nephrology, St. Paul Soc. Internal Medicine, Minn. Soc. Internal Medicine, Ramsey County Med. Soc., Minn. Kidney Found., Nat. Assn. Patients on Hemodialysis and Transplantation, Med. Soc. Minn. Mem. Universalist Ch. Contbr. articles to profl. jours. Home: 1125 Ivy Hill Dr St Paul MN 55118 Office: 640 Jackson St Saint Paul Ramsay Med Center St Paul MN 55101

EHLERT, BETTY JO (GILLARD), ednl. cons.; b. Charleston, W.Va., Dec. 12, 1942; d. Joseph Harold and Elizabeth Grace (Edwards) Gillard; B.S., Pa. State U., 1964; M.A., U. Iowa, 1966, Ph.D., 1970; 1 dau., Lisa Michelle. Dir. spl. edn., sch. psychologist Post Falls (Idaho) Sch. Dist. 273, 1973-79; regional cons. in spl. edn. Idaho Dept. Edn., Boise State U., 1979-81, cons. spl. edn., Boise, 1981—; pvt. practice psychology; occasional instr. U. Idaho. Mem. exec. bd. United Cerebral Palsy Idaho, 1978-82. Lic. psychologist, cert. sch. psychologist, cert. dir. spl. edn., Idaho. Mem. Nat. Assn. State Cons. for Sch. Psychol. Services, Nat. Assn. State Dirs. Spl. Edn., Idaho Sch. Psychologists Assn., Phi Beta Kappa, Phi Delta Kappa. Home: 4920 Parkwood Boise ID 83704 Office: Len B Jordan Bldg 650 W State St Boise ID 83704

EHRENBERG, DARLENE BREGMAN, psychoanalyst; b. N.Y.C., Aug. 15, 1942; d. Samuel and Pauline (Gellman) Bregman; B.A. magna cum laude, CCNY, 1963; M.S. (Harrison fellow), Yale U., 1965; Ph.D. (NIMH tng. fellow), N.Y. U., 1970; cert. William Alanson White Inst. Psychiatry, Psychoanalysis and Psychology, 1973; m. Bernard Ehrenberg, Nov. 26, 1970; children—Jonathan, Erica. Pvt. practice psychoanalysis and psychotherapy, N.Y.C., 1969—; supr. psychotherapy William Alanson White Inst. Psychiatry, Psychoanalysis and Psychology, N.Y.C., 1977—; supr. Inst. Contemporary Psychotherapy, 1974—; clin. instr. psychiatry Albert Einstein Coll. Medicine, 1968-69; conf. presenter. Carnegie Teaching fellow CCNY, 1964. Mem. Am. Psychol. Assn., William Alanson White Psychoanalytic Soc., Phi Beta Kappa. Asst. editor: Contemporary Psychoanalysis, 1979—, editorial bd., 1975-79; contbr. articles to profl. jours. Home and Office: 11 E 68th St New York NY 10021

EHRENKRANZ, SHIRLEY MALAKOFF, univ. dean, social work educator; b. N.Y.C., Nov. 9, 1920; d. Isidore and Diana Frances (Lewis) Malakoff; A.B., Hunter Coll., 1939; M.A., Bryn Mawr Coll., 1943; M.S.W., U. Pa., 1945; D.S.W., Columbia U., 1967; m. Gilbert Ehrenkranz, Mar. 29, 1946 (dec.); children—Jean, Joel, Pamela. Case worker Jewish Welfare Soc., Phila., 1943-44; case supr. S.I. Social Service, N.Y., 1945-48; case supr. United Family & Children's Service, Plainfield, N.J. 1949-53; field instr. Rutgers U., 1960-62; research asst. Columbia U., 1964-65; asst. prof. social work N.Y.U., 1966-68, asso. prof., 1968-73, prof., 1973—, asso. dean Grad. Sch. Social Work, 1969-76, acting dean, 1976-77, dean, 1977—. NIMH grantee, 1963-64, 65; recipient Disting. Alumna award U. Pa., 1979. Mem. N.Y. State Assn. Deans (v.p. 1979-80, pres. 1980-81), Nat. Assn. Social Workers, Acad. Cert. Social Workers. Contbr. book revs. and articles in field of social work to profl. jours. Office: NY Sch Social Work 3 Washington Sq N New York NY 10003

EHRHARDT, MARGARET WRIGHT, librarian; b. Orangeburg, S.C., Sept. 17, 1918; d. Harry Alison and Florence Olive (Black) Wright; B.A., Duke U., 1939; B.A.L.S., Emory U., 1949; postgrad. Furman U., 1970, U. S.C., 1978, U. Pitts., 1978; m. Benedict Groseclose Ehrhardt, Oct. 27, 1951; 1 son, Benedict Glen. High sch. librarian, library supr. Orangeburg (S.C.) Public Schs., 1945-51; children's librarian Richland County (S.C.) Public Library, Columbia, 1952-58; asst. order librarian U. S.C., Columbia, 1960-64; order librarian Wofford Coll., 1964-65; library cons. S.C. Dept. Edn., Columbia, 1965—. Mem. ALA, Southeastern Library Assn., S.C. Library Assn. (sec. 1971-72, pres. 1977), Delta Kappa Gamma. Lutheran. Editor: Media Services Newsletter, 1965-77; contbr. articles, revs. to S.C. Librarian, Media Center Messenger. Home: 227 Lawand Dr Columbia SC 29210 Office: 803 Rutledge Bldg Columbia SC 29201

EHRI, LINNEA CARLSON, psychologist, educator; b. Seattle, Jan. 7, 1941; d. Alden Carl and Lila Ruth (Weider) Carlson; B.S. in Psychology, U. Wash., 1963; M.A. in Psychology, Calif. State U., San Francisco, 1966; Ph.D. (Ednl. Research fellow), U. Calif., Berkeley, 1970; m. Walter William Ehri, June 18, 1963; 1 dau., Allison Ruth. Lectr. dept. edn. U. Calif., Davis, 1969-70, asst. prof., 1970-75, assoc. prof., 1975-80, prof., 1980—. Nat. Inst. Edn. grantee, 1974-76, 77-79; Nat. Inst. Child Health and Human Devel. grantee, 1979—. Fellow Am. Psychol. Assn.; mem. Am. Ednl. Research Assn., Internat. Reading Assn. (Jacobson award 1981), Nat. Reading Conf., Psychonomic Soc., Soc. for Research in Child Devel. Club: Woodland Chamber Singers. Contbr. numerous articles to profl. jours. Office: Dept Edn U Calif Davis CA 95616

EHRIG, LENORE GOODWIN, judge; b. N.Y.C., Feb. 26, 1924; d. Albert S. and Charlotte B. Goodwin; J.D., George Washington U., 1951; m. Leo J. Ehrig, Jr., Oct. 16, 1948; children—Charles, James. Admitted to D.C. bar, 1951; mem. firm Daly & Ehrig, Washington, 1952-63; atty. FCC, Washington, 1963-70, adminstrv. law judge, 1970-78, chief adminstrv. law judge, 1978—. Pres. bd. dirs. The Maret Sch. Mem. Nat. Assn. Women Judges (dir., pres. dist. 4), Conf. Adminstrv. Law Judges, Am. Bar Assn., Fed. Adminstrv. Law Judges Conf., D.C. Bar Assn., Women's Bar Assn. D.C. Office: FCC 1919 M St NW Washington DC 20554

EHRLICH, AVA, writer, TV producer; b. St. Louis, Aug. 14, 1950; d. Norman and Lillian (Gellman) E.; B.S.J., Northwestern U., 1972, M.S.J., 1973; M.A., Occidental Coll., 1976; m. Barry Freedman. Broadcast writer EPA, Chgo., 1973-74; reporter, asst. mng. editor Lerner Newspapers, Chgo., 1974-76; news editor, reporter, documentary writer CBS Radio, KMOX, St. Louis, 1976-79; producer news and documentaries Sta. WXYZ-TV, ABC, Detroit, 1979—; instr. Florissant Valley Community Coll., St. Louis, 1978-79; freelance writer, 1970—; guest editor Mademoiselle Mag., 1971; documentaries include: When Life Is Measured in Minutes 1977; The High Cost of Sanity, 1978. Trustee Coro Found., 1976-77; v.p. Coro Assos. of Midwest, 1977—; supporting mem. Hope and Home Family Services, Chgo., 1974-77. Recipient citation for community service Norridge (Ill.) Sch. Dist. 234, 1975; 1st place investigate reporting Mo. Broadcasters Assn., 1978; Media award Mo. Mental Health Assn., 1978; Media award Nat. Mental Health Assn., 1978, 79; Coro Found. fellow in pub. affairs, 1975-76; Danforth Found. met. leadership fellow, 1978-79; 1st pl. award Mich. AP, 1980. Mem. Women in Communications, AFTRA (chpt. dir. 1980-81), Soc. Profl. Journalists (dir.), Mo. Press Women, NOW, Kappa Tau Alpha. Democrat. Jewish. Home: 23741 Walden Ct Southfield MI 48034 Office: 20777 W 10 Mile Rd Southfield MI 48075

EHRLICH, ELEANOR ROSNER, mktg. and advt. exec.; b. N.Y.C., Aug. 3, 1945; d. Lothar and Gerda (Glaserfeld) Rosner; B.A., CCNY, 1966; M.A., U. Pa., 1968; m. Mel Ehrlich, May 6, 1979. Staff coordinator Univ. City Sci. Center, Phila., 1968-69; nat. customer service mgr. GAF Corp., N.Y.C., 1969-74, advt. mgr., 1974-78; nat. mktg. mgr. Phototron Corp., Rialto, Calif., 1978-80; dir. mktg. Berkey Photo, White Plains, N.Y. Mem. Nat. Assn. Female Execs., Direct Mail Mktg. Assn., Photo Mktg. Assn. Home: 30 Waterside Plaza New York NY 10010 Office: 1 Water St White Plains NY 10601

EHRLICH, ELLEN C., broadcast co. exec.; b. N.Y.C., Feb. 21, 1943; d. Morris and Beatrice E.; B.A., Wells Coll., 1964. Asst. to editor sch. div. Charles Scribner's Sons, N.Y.C., 1964-66; sr. copy editor Am. Heritage Pub. Co., N.Y.C., 1966-69; editor Frank Hiteshew & Assos., Los Angeles, 1969-70; copy editor Show Mag., Los Angeles, 1971; editor The Hollywood Reporter, Los Angeles, 1972; research Go Show, NBC, N.Y.C., 1972-73; east coast program coordinator Tomorrow Show, N.Y.C., 1972-73; research asso. CBS, N.Y.C., 1974-77, dir. info. services CBS News, 1977-80; dir. communications NBC News, N.Y.C., 1980—. Recipient Emmy cert. Nat. Acad. TV Arts and Scis.; named Outstanding Young Woman of Am., 1977. Mem. Am. Women in Radio and TV (dir. at large, dir. N.Y.C. chpt. 1976-78), Nat. Acad. TV Arts and Scis., Internat. Radio and TV Soc., Women in Communications, Inc. Copy editor: Eugene McCarthy: A Man of Courage, 1968; researcher: RFK: His Life and Death, 1968; editor: Don't Just Hear, Listen!, 1971. Office: 30 Rockefeller Plaza New York NY 10020

EHRLICH, KATHY FAYE, mfg. co. fin. exec.; b. Higgins, Tex., Apr. 23, 1953; d. George Burke and Zella Mae Hennigh; B.B.A. in Accounting, Tex. Technol. U., 1974; m. Mitchell Gene Ehrlich, May 6, 1972. Jr. mem. audit staff Touche Ross & Co., Houston, 1974-75, sr. auditor, 1975-77; dept. mgr. fin. analysis and subs. accounting Hughes Tool Co., Houston, 1977—. C.P.A., Tex. Mem. Tex. Soc. C.P.A.'s, Am. Inst. C.P.A.'s, Nat. Assn. Accountants (officer Houston chpt.), Am. Woman's Soc. C.P.A.'s. Methodist. Home: 7947 Fawn Terr Houston TX 77071 Office: PO Box 2539 Houston TX 77001

EHRLICH, WILLA KAY WIENER, research psychologist; b. N.Y.C., Dec. 17, 1948; d. Solomon Jack and Gertrude (Klings) Wiener; B.A. with honors in psychology SUNY, Stony Brook, 1970; Ph.D., U. Minn., 1974; m. Paul Harold Ehrlich, July 30, 1972; children—Samantha Frances, Mark Andrew Ross. NIMH postdoctoral research fellow, Brown U., 1974-76, research asso. dept. psychology, 1976-77, instr. sect. psychiatry and human behavior, div. biol. and med. scis., 1978-79; quantitative analyst dept. research and evaluation Butler Hosp., Providence, R.I., 1976-78; cons. Bankers Trust Co., N.Y.C., 1980—. NDEA fellow,

1970-73; NIMH Postdoctoral Research fellow, 1974-76. Mem. AAAS, Am. Statis. Assn., Am. Psychol. Assn., Soc. Math. Psychology, N.Y. Acad. Sci., Classification Soc. Address: 100 Haven Ave New York NY 10032

EICHEL, GLORIA LILLIAN, guidance counselor; b. Bklyn., Apr. 13, 1914; d. Meyer and Anna Rita (Housman) Jacobs; B.A., Hunter Coll., 1936; M.S. in Guidance, Bklyn. Coll., 1969; m. Arthur Eichel, Sept. 9, 1936 (dec. Aug. 1969); children—Alan Charles, Diane Sara, Martin Alexander. Caseworker home relief div. Dept. Welfare, Bklyn., 1938-42; tchr. Bklyn. Bd. Edn., 1950-65, guidance counselor, 1965-80; Supporting Services-Careers cons. Bur. Edn. and Vocat. Guidance N.Y.C., 1981—; condr. workshops on careers at profl. convs. Active Boy Scouts Am., 1950-81. Recipient plaque for services to parents and students Parents Assn. Public Sch. 181, Bklyn., 1979; Counselor of Yr. award Community Sch. Bd. 17, Bklyn., 1980. Mem. Bklyn. Coll. Guidance Assn. (pres. 1976-79), N.Y.C. Personnel and Guidance Assn. (sec. 1976-79), Nat. Vocat. Guidance Assn. (nat. chair career poetry contest 1979—, rep. nat. conv. 1979, 80, 81), N.Y. State Personnel and Guidance Assn. (chairperson membership 1980-81, chmn. ret. counselors 1982—), AAUW (chairperson chpt. edn.). Contbr. articles to N.Y. State Sch. Counselors Newsletters; columnist Ret. Counselors Network, 1978-81. Home: 1410 Ave L Brooklyn NY 11230

EICHER, JOANNE BUBOLZ, educator; b. Lansing, Mich., Sept. 18, 1930; d. George C. and Stella L. (Mangold) Bubolz; B.A., Mich. State U., 1952, M.A., 1956, Ph.D., 1959; m. Carl K. Eicher, June 8, 1952 (div. Dec. 1974); children—Cynthia, Carolyn, Diana. Instr., asst. prof. dept. social sci. Boston U., 1957-61; asst. prof. dept. human environment and design Coll. Human Ecology, Mich. State U., 1961-69, asso. prof., 1969-72, prof., 1972-77; prof. U. Minn., 1977—, head dept. textiles and clothing, 1977—; research asso. Econ. Devel. Inst., U. Nigeria, 1963-66; cons. Time-Life, Inc., Howard U., Prentice Hall, Inc. Research grantee Internat. Programs, Mich. State U., 1963-64, African Studies Center, 1965-66, 4-H Programs grantee Ethnic Heritage Program, 1974, research grantee Midwest U. Consortium for Internat. Affairs, 1968, Ford Found. individual grantee, 1973; resident scholar Rockefeller Found. Study and Conf. Center, Bellagio, Italy, 1973. Mem. Costume Soc. Am., Am. Home Econs. Assn., Am. Sociol. Assn., Assn. Coll. Profs. Textiles and Clothing, Costume Soc. (London, Eng.), Founders Soc. Detroit Inst. Arts and African Arts Com., Nigerian Nat. Mus. Soc., African Studies Assn., Phi Kappa Phi, Alpha Kappa Delta, Tau Sigma, Alpha Gamma Delta. Democrat. Lutheran. Author: (with Mary Ellen Roach) Dress, Adornment and the Social Order, 1965, The Visible Self: Perspectives on Dress, 1973; African Dress: A Select and Annotated Bibliography of Subsaharan Countries, 1970; (with Eleanor Kelley and Betty Wass) A Longitudinal Study of High School Girls' Friendship Patterns, Social Class and Clothing, 1974; Nigerian Handcrafted Textiles, 1976. Coordinator: African Textiles: An Outline of Handcrafted Sub-Saharan Fabrics, 1971. Contbr. articles to profl. jours. Home: 2179 Folwell St Saint Paul MN 55108

EICKHOFF, M. KATHRYN, economist; b. Sedalia, Mo., Apr. 11, 1939; s. Leo E. and Magdalene (Piatt) E.; B.A. with distinction, U. Mo., 1960; M.A., N.Y.U., 1971; m. A. James Smith, Jr., May 9, 1973. Contract writer Group Ins. Mut. of N.Y., N.Y.C., 1960-61; research asst. Van Alstyne, Neol & Co., N.Y.C., 1961-62; economist Townsend-Greenspan & Co., Inc., N.Y.C., 1962—, treas., 1966—, v.p., 1972-80, exec. v.p., 1980—; dir. Interpace Corp., Upjohn Co., ECONALYST; dir. N.Y. Futures Exchange, 1979-82; past sec., past dir. Quantitative Econ. Data Corp. Mem. alumni devel. council Coll. Bus. and Public Adminstrn., U. Mo., Columbia, 1976-78. Mem. Conf. Bus. Economists; fellow Nat. Assn. Bus. Economists (pres. 1980-81; exec. com. and governing council 1977-83); mem. Conf. Bus. Economists, Nat. Economists Club, Bus. Economists Council, Am. Fin. Assn., Am. Econ. Assn., Am. Statis. Assn., Women's Econ. Roundtable Contbr. to Ency. of Econs., also profl. jours. Office: Townsend-Greenspan & Co Inc 1 New York Plaza New York NY 10004

EICKMAN, JENNIFER LYNN, conf. center mgr., writer, artist; b. Urbana, Ill., Nov. 7, 1946; d. Marvin A. and Emma L. (Heartrick) Smith; B.F.A., U. Ill., 1967, postgrad. in Art History, 1967-70; m. Gary Edwin Eickman, June 9, 1968. Tchr., Univ. High Sch., Urbana, 1968, Champaign (Ill.) Public Schs., 1969-70; mem. faculty U. Ill., 1968-77, Richland Coll., Decatur, Ill., 1975-77; asst. to dir. of extension in visual arts U. Ill., 1969-70, asst. dir. Allerton House Conf. Center, 1974—; guest lectr., tchr. art workshops. Mem. Pacific Tropical Bot. Gardens, Defenders of Wildlife, Nat. Trust Hist. Preservation, Kappa Alpha Theta. Staff writer Champaign-Urbana mag.; author articles on art history, music, edn. and natural history. Home: Gate House Allerton Park Monticello IL 61856 Office: Allerton House Allerton Park Monticello IL 61856

EIDE, BARBY FAIRBANKS, author; b. Utica, N.Y., Aug. 26, 1938; d. Ben F. and Sally M. (Bawol) Swider; student City Coll. San Francisco, 1973-75; m. Leroy Michael Eide, Feb. 17, 1978. Asso. dir. public relations Ford Motor Co., San Francisco, 1971-73; dir. public relations and ednl. programs Unity Ch., Spokane, Wash., 1975-77; nat. speaker on nonverbal communication, stress mgmt., time mgmt., 1965—; instr. Wash. State Community Coll., Spokane YWCA; author cpts. books in field. Bd. dirs. City Coll. Spokane, 1977—. Mem. Am. Soc. Tng. and Devel. (chpt. program chmn. 1980), Nat. Speakers Assn., Spokane Area Conv. and Visitors Bur., Internat. Platform Assn. Republican. Office: PO Box 8524 Spokane WA 99203

EILBER, JANET SUSAN, dancer, singer, actress; b. Detroit, July 27, 1951; d. Charles Routledge and Carol Virginia (Brown) E.; B.F.A., Juilliard Sch., 1973. Tchr. dance Nat. Music Camp, 1970, 72; choreographer, performer Dance Mobile, 1969-72, Young Audiences, 1972; prin. dancer Martha Graham Dance Co., 1972-82; guest artist Joeffry Ballet, 1978, Am. Dance Machine, 1978—; leading role in Swing, Broadway musical, 1980. Roles created by Graham for Eilber: Hester Prynne in The Scarlet Letter, 1975, Night in Lucifer, Mary Queen of Scotts in Episodes, Young Love in Shadows, Cleopatra in Frescoes; roles performed with Graham: Joan of Arc in Seraphic Dialogue, Phadre, Cassandra, Frontier, Lamentation, Lilith, narrator in Owl and The Pussycat; invited to perform at White House, 1976, 79; featured in movie Whose Life Is It Anyway, 1981. Address: 550 Park Ave New York NY 10021 *

EINODER, CAMILLE ELIZABETH, educator; b. Chgo., June 15, 1937; d. Isadore and Elizabeth T. (Czerwinski) Popowski; student Fox Bus. Coll., 1954; B.Ed. in Biology, Chgo. Tchrs. Coll., 1964; M.A. in Analytical Chemistry, Gov.'s State U., 1977; m. Joseph X. Einoder, Aug. 5, 1978; children—Carl Frank, Mark Frank, Vivian Einoder, Joe Einoder, Tim Einoder, Sheila Einoder. Secretarial positions, Chgo., 1955-64; biology tchr. Chgo. Bd. Edn., 1964, biology-agr. tchr., 1975-81, chem. tchr., 1981—; human relations coordinator Morgan Park High Sch., 1980—; career devel. cons. for agr. related curriculum. Bds. dirs. Community Council, 1970, Neighborhood Council, 1974; rep. Chgo. Tchrs. Union, 1969. Sculptor bronze unicorn, 1971; contributed quilt sect. to Judy Chicago's Dinner Party, 1982; author research paper. Home: 10637 S Claremont St Chicago IL 60643 Office: 1744 W Pryor St Chicago IL 60643

EIPPER, ELIZABETH ANNE, biochemist; b. Elmira, N.Y., Nov. 11, 1945; d. Eugene Bretherton and Mary Elinor (Allen) E.; B.Sc., Brown U., 1968, M.S., 1968; Ph.D., Harvard U., 1973; m. Richard E. Mains, June 8, 1968; children—Marcie Alison, Jodi Elene. Postdoctoral fellow U. Oreg., 1973-75; mem. faculty U. Colo. Health Scis. Center, Denver, 1976-83, asso. prof. physiology, 1979-83; assoc. prof. neurosci. Johns Hopkins U. Sch. Medicine, Balt., 1983—. Me. Am. Soc. Biol. Chemists, Endocrine Soc. Author articles, revs. in field. Home: 363 Dahlia St Denver CO 80220 Office: Dept Neurosci 725 N Wolfe St Baltimore MD 21205

EISAN, FRANCES LUCILLE, sch. adminstr.; b. North Vernon, Ind., July 30, 1917; d. Charles Herbert and Golda Mae (Stearns) Kutchback; B.A. cum laude, La Verne Coll., 1939; M.A. in History, Claremont Coll., 1940; Specialist in Edn., Ind. U., 1966; m. Leslie Eisan, Apr. 5, 1941; children—Jonathan Andrew, Elisabeth Ann, Carol, Herbert Laurence, Jeannette Althea. Tchr. pub. schs., Bakersfield, Calif., 1940-41, Lynwood, Calif., 1941-42; faculty LaVerne (Calif.) Coll., 1942-43; tchr. pub. schs., Hanover, Ind., 1952-53; tchr., chmn. social sci. dept. Madison (Ind.) Consol. High Sch., 1957—; owner, operator Victorian Silver & Metalcrafts. Mem. State Textbook Screening Com. for Pub. Schs. in Ind., 1974; co-dir. Ind. History Day, 9th Congl. Dist., 1978; bd. dirs. Jefferson County Hist. Soc., 1976. Recipient Nat. Tchr. Educators award Freedom Found. of Valley Forge, Pa., 1977. Mem. Nat., Ind. councils for social studies, Nat. Trust for Historic Preservation, Ind. State Mus. Soc., League Women Voters, Jefferson County Hist. Soc., NEA, Ind. Tchrs. Assn., Historic Madison, Inc. Presbyterian. Author: River Village: Gateway to the West, 1977. Editor: The Way It Was: Glimpses Into the Past of Madison and Jefferson County, 1975. Home: Box 474 Hanover IN 47243

EISELE, PATRICIA O'LEARY, shopping center mgr.; b. Kansas City, Mo., Aug. 31, 1935; d. George Sexton and Dorothy Madeline (Stubbs) O'Leary; student Sarachon Hooley Bus. Sch., 1954-55, Rockhurst Coll., 1982-83; cert. Internat. Council Shopping Centers Mktg. Inst., 1978; m. John G. Eisele, July 16, 1955; children—Kathleen, Janice, Melissa, Patricia, John. Mktg. dir. Ward Pkwy. Center, Kansas City, Mo., 1974-79, mgr., 1979-80; mktg. counselor John Knox Village, Lee's Summit, Mo., 1981—; bd. dirs. local merchant's assn., 1977-80. Bd. dirs. Arthritis Found., Kansas City, Mo., 1980-82; bd. dirs., sec. Mid-Winter Art Fair Assn., Kansas City, 1980-82. Recipient award Heart Assn., 1979, 80, Easter Seal Soc., 1979, Muscular Dystrophy Assn., 1978, Ararat Shrine, 1980, Boy Scouts Am., 1979, 80. Mem. Chi Omega. Clubs: Altar Soc., Catholic Women's. Home: 2803 W 73d Terr Prairie Village KS 66208 Office: 500 N Murray Lee's Summit MO 64063

EISEN, HELGA SIMON, religious orgn. exec.; b. Frankfurt, Germany, Aug. 27, 1930; d. Walter A. and Erna (Marx) Simon; B.Sc., Ohio State U., 1952; m. Jesse Eisen, June 1, 1952; children—David Spencer, Marianne. Med. technician Hines (Ill.) VA Hosp., 1952-55; public relations rep. Blue Star Camps, 1960-68; mem. public relations staff B.R. Martin Co., Skokie, Ill., 1963-65; public relations dir. Glick's Furniture, Columbus, Ohio, 1965-71; owner, pres. Helga Eisen & Assos., Columbus, 1971—; founder, pres. Creative Conv. Services, Inc., 1973-75; adminstr. Temple Israel, Columbus, 1976—. Mem. women's bd. Columbus Symphony; mem. Community Relations Council. Mem. Nat. Assn. Temple Adminstrs. (dir.), LWV (v.p.), Columbus C. of C., Ohio Travel Council, Columbus Conv. Bur. Jewish. Club: Columbus Met. Home: 5099 Doral Ave Columbus OH 43213 Office: 5419 E Broad St Columbus OH 43213

EISEN, MARLENE RUTH, psychologist, educator; b. Chgo., Nov. 23, 1931; d. William and Sophia Maria (Brownwine) Friedlander; B.A., Roosevelt U., 1952; M.A., U. Chgo., 1967, Ph.D., 1977; m. Earl Price, Oct. 1951 (div. 1960); m. 2d, Lee Andalman Aug. 1962 (dec.); 1 son, Robert; m. Sydney B. Eisen, June 6, 1979; children—Martin Price, Daniel Price, Robert Andalman. Presch. tchr. Ravinia Nursery Sch., Highland Park, Ill., 1952-56, Country Schs., Los Angeles, 1959-62; kindergarten tchr., Evanston, Ill., 1962-72; coordinator, developer M.A. level early childhood program U. Chgo., 1973-74; coordinator child devel. program Harper Coll., Palatine, Ill., 1974—, developer new human services program, 1982; instr. hypnotherapy and devel. psychology Ill. Sch. Profl. Psychology; pvt. practice clin. psychology. Bd. dirs. LWV, Skokie, Ill., 1965-68; bd. NESPOA Community Assn., 1968-70. Mem. Am. Soc. Clin. Hypnosis, Nat. Assn. Edn. of Young Children, Am. Psychol. Assn., Soc. Clin. and Exptl. Hypnosis, Am. Soc. Clin. Hypnosis, Pi Lambda Theta. Author articles. Office: Harper Coll Algonquin and Roselle Palatime IL 60067

EISENBERG, SONJA MIRIAM, artist; b. Berlin, June 10, 1926; came to U.S., 1938, naturalized, 1947; d. Adolf and Meta Cecilie (Bettauer) Weinberger; student Queens Coll., 1943-46, Middlebury Coll., 1945; N.Y.U., 1952-54; B.A., N.Y.U., 1954; postgrad. Nat. Acad. Sch. Fine Arts, 1961; m. Jack Eisenberg, Mar. 31, 1946; children—Ralph, Lynn, Lauren. One-woman shows: Bodley Gallery, N.Y.C., 1970, 73, 75, 80, Galerie Art du Monde, Paris, 1973, Buyways Gallery, Sarasota, Fla., 1973, 74, Galerie de Sfinx, Amsterdam, Netherlands, 1974, Huntsville (Ala.) Mus. Art, 1974, Anglo-Am. Art Mus., Baton Rouge, 1974, comara Gallery, Los Angeles, 1974, Palm Spring (Calif.) Desert Mus., 1975, Fordham U., N.Y.C., 1976, Omega Inst., New Lebanon, N.Y.C., 1979, Am. Mus., Hayden Planetarium, N.Y.C., 1980, Avila Graphics, Ltd., 1981; group shows include: Mus. Fine Arts, St. Petersburg, Fla., 1973, Am. Watercolor Soc., 107th, 108th Exhbn., 1974, 75, Galerie Frederic Gollong, St. Paul de Vence, France, 1978, Betty Parson's Gallery, N.Y.C., 1981; represented in permanent collections: Archives Am. Art, Smithsonian Instn., Jewish Mus., N.Y.C., Fordham U. Mus., N.Y.C., Palm Springs Desert Mus. Designer, WFUNA cachet for UN Water Power Conf., 1977, UN Internat. Yr. of Disabled Persons, 1981. Mem. Academia Italia delle Arti e del Lavoro. Home and Office: 1020 Park Ave New York NY 10028

EISENBERG, SUSANNE, public relations cons.; b. Brookline, Mass., Mar. 20, 1953; d. Eugene Robert and Shirley (Helman) Eisenberg. B.A., Brown U., 1975. Account exec. Ruder and Finn/Public Internat Public Relations Inc., N.Y.C., 1975-77; press sec. City Council Pres. campaign, 1977; public relations cons., N.Y.C., 1977-78; public relations dir. N.Y. State Council Arts, N.Y.C., 1978; v.p. Jessica Dee Communications, N.Y.C., 1978-80; pres. Eisenberg Assocs., N.Y.C., 1980—; v.p. Brush Designs, Inc., Estate Documents Inc.; lectr. in field. Mem. N.Y. State Democratic Com., 1981-82. Contbr. articles to newspapers. Office: 888 7th Ave 19th Floor New York NY 10106

EISENMAN, TRUDY FOX, dermatologist; b. Chgo., Oct. 14, 1940; d. Nathan Henry and Bernice (Greenberg) Fox; student U. Ill. at Navy Pier, Chgo., 1958-60; M.D., U. Ill., 1964; m. Theodore S. Eisenman, Aug. 19, 1962; children—Lawrence, Robert. Rotating intern Milw. County Gen. Hosp., 1964-65, med. resident, 1965-66; resident in dermatology Northwestern U. Med. Sch., Chgo., 1970-73, instr., 1973—; practice medicine specializing in dermatology, Chgo., 1973—; attending dermatologist Louis A. Weiss Meml. Hosp., Chgo., 1973—. Diplomate Am. Bd. Dermatology. Fellow Am. Acad. Dermatology; mem. Chgo. Dermatol. Soc., Soc. for Investigative Dermatology, Am. Med. Women's Assn., AMA, Chgo. Med. Soc., Alpha Omega Alpha. Home: 2385 Castilian Circle Northbrook IL 60062 Office: 4640 N Marine Dr Chicago IL 60640

EISENSTADT, KAREN MARCIA, banker; b. Bklyn., Apr. 9, 1948; d. Nathan M. and Anne (Krugman) E.; B.A. cum laude, Bklyn. Coll., 1968; M.Regional Planning (NDEA fellow 1968-70), U. N.C., Chapel Hill, 1971. Mem. research staff Rand Corp., Santa Monica, Calif., 1970-72; with N.Y.C. Office Mgmt. and Budget, 1972-79, dep. asst. budget dir. for fin., 1977-79; asst. v.p. public fin. dept. Morgan Guaranty Trust Co., N.Y.C., 1979-82, v.p., 1982—; mem. adj. faculty New Sch., 1974, Columbia U., 1976. Mem. N.Y.C. Rent Guidelines Bd., 1981—; bd. dirs. Citizens Housing and Planning Council, 1982—. Mem. Phi Beta Kappa. Office: 23 Wall St New York NY 10015

EISENSTADT, MERRIE MADWAY, journalist; b. Phila., Apr. 25, 1957; d. Ralph K. and Bette Melba (Davis) Madway; B.J., U. Mo., Columbia, 1978; Isaac M. Wise program cert. Gratz Hebrew Coll., Phila., 1975; m. David Michael Eisenstadt, Nov. 19, 1978. Reporter, Sentinel Newspapers, Montgomery and Prince George's counties, Md., 1979-80, Balt. Jewish Times, 1980—. Exhbn. chmn. Balt. Jewish Am. Festival, 1981. Recipient Smolar award of excellence in N.Am. Jewish journalism, 1981. Mem. Sigma Delta Chi, Alpha Epsilon Phi (scholarship award 1976), Phi Eta Sigma, Kappa Epsilon Alpha. Jewish.

EISENSTADT, PAULINE DOREEN BAUMAN, politician; b. N.Y.C., Dec. 31, 1938; d. Morris and Anne (Lautenberg) Bauman; B.A., U. Fla., 1960; M.S. (NSF grantee), U. Ariz., 1965; postgrad. U. N.Mex.; m. Melvin M. Eisenstadt, Nov. 20, 1960; children—Todd Alan, Keith Mark. Tchr., Ariz., 1961-65, P.R., 1972-73; adminstrv. asst. Inst. Social Research U. N.Mex., 1973-74; founder, 1st exec. dir. Energy Consumers N.Mex., 1977-81; dir., host TV program Consumer Viewpoint, 1980-82; chmn. consumer affairs adv. com. Dept. Energy, 1979-80; v.p. tech. bd. Nat. Center Appropiate Tech., 1980—; vice chmn. Sandoval County (N.Mex.) Democratic Party, 1981—; mem. N.Mex. State Central Com., 1981—; pres. Sandoval County Dem. Women's Assn., 1979-81. Mem. NEA, LWV, NOW. Author: Corrales, Portrait of a Changing Village, 1980. Address: PO Box 658 Corrales NM 87048

EISNER, JANET, ednl. adminstr., nun; b. Boston, Oct. 10, 1940; d. Eldon and Ada (Martin) Eisner; A.B., Emmanuel Coll., 1963; M.A., Boston Coll., 1969; Ph.D., U. Mich., 1975. Joined Sisters of Notre Dame de Namur, Roman Catholic Ch., 1958; dir. admissions Emmanuel Coll., Boston, 1967-71, dir. Emmanuel Coll. and City of Boston Pairings, 1976-78, chmn. English Dept., 1977-78, acting pres., 1978-79, pres., 1979—; Trustee Trinity Coll.; dir. Regional Com. Colls.; mem. Mass. Bd. Regents, Ford fellow, 1971-73; Rockham Prize fellow, 1973-75. Mem. Assn. of Governing Bds. (pres.'s adv. council), Am. Council on Edn., Women's Coll. Coalition, Assn. of Cath. Colls. and Univs., New Eng. Enrollment Planning Council. Home: 37 Castleton St Jamaica Plain MA 02130 Office: 400 The Fenway Boston MA 02115

EISNER, RONA STEPHANIE, psychologist; b. Newark, Jan. 1, 1939; d. Ira Y. and Ethel Lenore (Whitfield) Copen; B.A. magna cum laude, Smith Coll., 1960; Ph.D., N.Y.U., 1967; m. Gilbert M. Eisner, Aug. 23, 1970; children—Eric Marshal, Mark Samuel. Psychologist dept. adolescent medicine Children's Hosp. D.C., 1966-71; chief psychologist Potomac Found. for Mental Health, Bethesda, Md., 1971-75; pvt. practice psychology, Kensington, Md., 1975—; clin. assoc. prof. Med. Sch., George Washington U., Washington, 1977—. Bd. dirs. Sisterhood Ohr Kodesh Congregation, Chevy Chase, Md., 1980—. Woodrow Wilson fellow, 1960-61, NIMH fellow, 1961-65. Mem. Am. Psychol. Assn., Sigma Xi, Phi Beta Kappa. Office: 3930 Knowles Ave Kensington MD 20895

EKIMOV, ROZA ELZBIETA, librarian; b. Warsaw, Poland, Nov. 11, 1932; d. Witold Eugeniusz and Janina Wanda (Boenisch) Pilsudski; came to U.S., 1963, naturalized, 1975; B.A., Calif. State U., Fullerton, 1968; m. Vassil Ekimov, Aug. 8, 1970. Tech. librarian Geodata Systems, Inc., Orange, Calif., 1970-71; exploration librarian in charge Exxon Co. U.S.A., Houston, 1971—. Charge welfare sect. Samopomoc, Polish fraternal orgn., Los Angeles, 1965-69. Grantee Samopomoc, 1965, Rotary Club, Bellflower, Calif., 1966, Whittier (Calif.) chpt. Am. Bus. Women's Assn., 1967. Mem. Spl. Libraries Assn. (chmn. petroleum div. 1974-75, pres. Colo. chpt. 1976-77), Geosci. Info. Soc. Roman Catholic. Contbr. articles to profl. jours. Home: 6515 Pebble Beach Dr Houston TX 77069 Office: Exxon Co USA PO Box 4279 Houston TX 77001

EKLUND, SUSAN JANE, psychologist, educator; b. San Antonio, June 2, 1939; d. Theodore Tilden and Jane (Kelley) E.; B.A., U. Tex., 1961; M.S., Trinity U., 1962; Ph.D., George Peabody Coll., 1970. Sch. psychologist Houston Ind. Sch. Dist., 1962-65; research asst. Demonstration and Research Center for Early Edn., George Peabody Coll., Nashville, 1965-68; instr. Tchrs. Coll., Columbia U., N.Y.C., 1968-69; asst. prof. ednl. psychology Ind. U., Bloomington, 1969-73, assoc. prof., 1973—, dir. sch. psychol. program, 1969—, chairperson dept. ednl. psychology, 1974-76, 80, dir. Inst. for Child Study. Cert. sch. psychologist, Ind. Mem. Am. Psychol. Assn., Am. Ednl. Research Assn., Gerontol. Soc., Nat. Assn. for Sch. Psychologists, Ind. Psychol. Assn. (Disting. Service award 1980). Home: 3617 Post Rd Bloomington IN 47401 Office: Inst for Child Study Ind U Bloomington IN 47405

EKSTROM, KATHERINE (KAY) VIRGINIA, sch. adminstr.; b. Chgo., Oct. 6, 1934; d. Carnie Ovis and Julia Augusta (Little) Grugett; student Prairie State Coll., Chicago Heights, Ill., 1978-79; cert. Kennedy Sinclaire Planned Gifts Tng. Program, 1981; certs. Inst. Orgn. Mgmt., 1973, 74, 75; m. Walter E. Ekstrom, Feb. 2, 1973; 1 dau. by previous marriage, Cindy Ivarson Fallick; stepchildren—John, Allison. Public relations asso. Wyman-Gordon Co., Harvey, Ill., 1968-72; exec. dir. South Suburban C. of C. and Industry, Harvey, 1972-76; account exec. Sheraton Inn, Homewood, Ill., 1976-77; dir. public relations Glenwood (Ill.) Sch. for Boys, 1977-81, dir. planned giving, 1981—; lectr. Estate Planning for Women. Mem. Com. to Elect George Marovich Circuit Ct. Judge, Cook County, Ill., 1975; mem. Bicentennial Commn. and Paramedic Fund, Harvey, 1975-76; bd. dirs. South Suburban Council Aging and Sr. Center, 1st v.p., 1980—. Mem. Chgo. Planned Giving Officers Roundtable (steering com.), Nat. Soc. Fund Raisers, South Suburban Network Bus. and Profl. Women. Office: Glenwood Sch for Boys 187th and Halsted St Glenwood IL 60425

EKSTROM, RUTH BURT (MRS. LINCOLN EKSTROM), psychologist; b. Bennington, Vt., July 2, 1931; d. Ralph Amos and Bertha Paisley (Lambert) Burt; A.B., Brown U., 1953; M.Ed., Boston U., 1956; Ed.D., Rutgers U., 1967; m. Lincoln Ekstrom, Nov. 9, 1957. Tchr. pub. schs., Beverly, Mass., 1953-57; research asst. Ednl. Testing Service, 1957-64, profl. asso., 1964-66, dir. documentation services, 1966-68, research scientist, 1968-80, sr. research scientist, 1980—; vis. lectr. Grad. Sch. Edn., Rutgers U., 1958-60. Trustee, Brown U., 1972-77, Fellow, 1977—, sec. corp., 1982—. Fellow Am. Psychol. Assn.; mem. Am. Assn. Higher Edn., Am. Ednl. Research Assn., Am. Personnel and Guidance Assn., Nat. Council for Measurement in Edn., Pi Lambda Theta. Co-editor: Kit of Factor Referenced Cognitive Tests, 1963, 76; contbr. articles to profl. publs. Home: 78 Westerly Rd Princeton NJ 08540 Office: Educational Testing Service Princeton NJ 08541

ELAM, PAMELA LYNN, legis. aide; b. Ashland, Ky., Apr. 28, 1950; d. James Harve, Jr. and Mildred (Hayes) E.; B.A. in Polit. Sci., U. Ky., 1972, J.D., 1975; M.A. in Women's History, Sarah Lawrence Coll., 1980. Staff asst. Ky. Commn. on Women, Frankfort, 1973-74; asst. Mcpl. Statute Revision, Ky. Gen. Assembly, Lexington, 1975; exec. dir. Ky. Civil Liberties Union, Louisville, 1976-77; teaching asst. Sarah Lawrence Coll., Bronxville, N.Y., 1979; clk. SLC Bookstore, Bronxville, 1978-80; legis. aide N.Y.C. Council, 1980—. Exec. com. Congressional Union Inc., 1980—; organizer Nat. Women's History Week activities, 1979—; lobbyist, lectr. women's issues, 1971—; del. Nat. Internat. Women's Yr.

Conf., 1977; exec. com., program chmn. Ky. Internat. Women's Yr. Com., 1977; chmn. Ky. Women's Agenda Coalition, 1976-78; coordinator Women's Center of Lexington, Inc., 1974; mem. state policy council Ky. Women's Polit. Caucus, 1971-78; chairwoman U. Ky. Council on Women's Concerns, 1973; alt. del. Democratic Nat. Conv., 1972. Recipient award, Ky. Women's Agenda Coalition, 1978. Mem. Orgn. Am. Historians. Author: How Long Must Women Wait for Liberty?: Perceptions of the Militant Woman Suffrage Movement in the United States, 1916-1920, 1980. Home: 1160 Midland Ave Bronxville NY 10708 Office: City Council City Hall New York NY 10007

ELAND, MARY CAROLYN, ednl. media specialist; b. Lexington, Ky., Jan. 10, 1942; d. Simon C. and Jane Isabel (Elam) Gilliam; B.A., Rollins Coll., 1964; M.Ed., Fla. Atlantic U., 1972; m. Kenneth Patrick Eland, June 9, 1966. Tchr., English, Sunrise Jr. High Sch., Ft. Lauderdale, Fla., 1964-65; tchr. English and social studies Merritt Island (Fla.) Jr. High Sch., 1965-66; tchr. English Seabreeze Jr. High Sch., Daytona Beach, Fla., 1966-69; tchr. French and math. Jefferson Davis Jr. High Sch., West Palm Beach, Fla., 1969-70; media specialist Jefferson Davis Jr./Middle Sch., West Palm Beach, 1970—; rep. Sch. Plant Planning Com.; mem. supt.'s com. on excellence in media. Sr. squadron procurement officer CAP, West Palm Beach, 1973. Mem. NEA, Fla. Teaching Profession, Palm Beach County Classroom Tchrs.'s Assn., Fla. Assn. Media in Edn., Palm Beach County Ednl. Media Assn. (sec. 1977-78, pres. 1979-80), ARC, Palm Beach County Hist. Soc., Collegiate and Internat. Panhellenic Assn., Alpha Phi (v.p. 1963, nat. conv. del. 1962), Alpha Delta Kappa (v.p. 1976-78, pres. 1978-80). Home: 1621 16th Ln Garden Lakes Palm Beach Gardens FL 33410 Office: Jefferson Davis Middle Sch 1560 Kirk Rd West Palm Beach FL 33406

ELASARIAN, ANNA, public housing authority exec.; b. Waukegan, Ill., Sept. 18; d. Ohan and Siranoush (Garabedian) Elasarian; student Carthage Coll., 1964, Coll. Lake County, Grayslake, Ill., 1974-76. Stenographer, Fansteel Metall. Corp., North Chgo., 1958-60; legal sec. Dixon and Seidenfeld, Waukegan, Ill., 1961-62; sec., acct. Waukegan Housing Authority, 1962-67, asst. exec. dir. to part-time dir., 1962-67, exec. dir., 1977—. Mem. task force com. United Way; mem. bd. Lake County Community Action Project, 1977—, sec., 1979—; bd. dirs., mem. Cardiac Charities Lake County, 1977-80. Mem. NAACP, Lake County Urban League, Nat. Assn. Housing and Redevel. Ofcls. (cert. public housing mgr.), Public Housing Authorities Dirs. Assn., Ill. Assn. Redevelopment Authorities, No. Ill. Council Housing Adminstrs., Am. Soc. Profl. and Exec. Women, Friends Am. Ballet Theatre, Nat. Assn. Female Execs., Chgo. Council Fgn. Relations, Phi Theta Kappa. Episcopalian. Club: Altrusa Internat. Office: 200 S Utica St Waukegan IL 60085

ELBERT, ROSEMARY RUDSTROM, lawyer; b. Two Harbors, Minn., Mar. 7, 1938; d. Leonard Gustav and Evelyn (Ryan) Rudstrom; student U. Minn., Duluth, 1951-53; A.B., Bryn Mawr Coll., 1955; M.S., U. Miami, 1957, postgrad. Law Sch., 1956-59; J.D., Marquette U., 1961; m. Thomas E. Elbert, Oct. 18, 1959; children—Catherine, Thomas E., Mary. Admitted to Wis. bar, 1961; title examiner Chgo. Title Ins. Co., Milw., 1965-67; asso. firm Laikin, Swietlik & Larkin, Milw., 1968-71; asst. corp. counsel. Milwaukee County, Milw., 1971-74; asso. firm James T. Rogers, Merrill, Wis., 1975-76; asso. firm Stevens & Drach, Wausau, Wis., 1976-77; individual practice law, Wausau, 1977—; dir. Wausau Transitions; instr. evening div. Milw. Area Tech. Coll., 1972-74, North Central Tech. Inst., Wausau. Mem. State of Wis. Legal Services Adv. Council, 1977. Mem. AAUW. Home: Route 1 Ringle WI 54471 Office: 512 Division St Wausau WI 54401 *

ELBERTH, MARYANN CATHERINE, psychiat. social worker; b. Bklyn., Dec. 3, 1950; d. John Blair and Mary (Lombardo) E.; B.A. in Sociology, Molloy Coll., 1972; M.S.W., Adelphi U., 1975. Recreation specialist Nassau County (N.Y.) Dept. Recreation and Parks, 1969-75; dir. social services Resort Nursing Home, Far Rockaway, N.Y., 1975-79; unit chief drug and alcohol detoxification unit St. John's Episcopal Hosp., Far Rockaway, 1980—; pvt. practice; adj. prof. Molloy Coll. Co-chairperson community adv. bd. Legal Aid Soc., Far Rockaway, 1978-80. Cert. social worker, N.Y. Mem. Acad. Cert. Social Workers, Nat. Assn. Social Workers, Coalition Rockaway Social Workers (chairperson 1978-79). Home: 6A Gianelli Ave Merrick NY 11566 Office: 327B 19th St Far Rockaway NY 11691

ELDER, CAROL RUTH, accountant; b. Cin., Dec. 11, 1944; d. Carl Albert and Dorothy Louise (Hance) Holley; B.A., Coll. Wooster, 1966; M.A., Northwestern U., 1967; m. Richard Bly Elder, June 17, 1967; children—Kristen, Laurel. Tchr. math. Glenview (Ill.) Jr. High Sch., 1966-68, Minnetonka (Minn.) High Sch., 1968-69; staff H & R Block, Danbury, Conn., 1979, tax preparer, 1980; acct. Jovil Mfg. Co., Danbury, 1979-81; staff acct. Joseph Fiorita, C.P.A.s, Danbury, 1981—. Treas., King St. Sch. Parent-Tchr. Orgn., 1976-78; mem. Citizen's Com. on Danbury's Future, 1979-80; mem. policy adv. com. for 208 Program, Danbury, 1977-80. Mem. LWV (pres. 1977-80). Democrat. Author: A Citizen's Guide to the Danbury Public School System, 1978. Home: 9 Centennial Dr Danbury CT 06810 Office: 146 Deer Hill Ave Danbury CT 06810

ELDER, GLORIA JORDAN, court reporter co. exec.; b. Columbus, Ga., Mar. 28, 1923; d. Charles A. and Billie Jo (Trice) Jordan; student Stenotype Inst., 1973-75; m. Merrill John Elder, Dec. 24, 1941; children—Don, Michael, Marie, John, Terrell. Various legal secretarial positions, 1941-69; owner, mgr. Gloria J. Elder & Assos., Jacksonville, Fla., 1969—; v.p. Fantasies by Glynn-oria, Inc., Ponte Vedra Beach, Fla.; court reporter Augusta (Ga.) Superior Ct., 1976-79. Mem. Nat. Shorthand Reporters Assn., Am. Bus. Women's Assn., Fla. Shorthand Reporters, Ga. Shorthand Reporters. Democrat. Roman Catholic. Club: Order of Eastern Star. Home: 6 Mackeral St Ponte Vedra FL 32082 Office: PO Box 28 Ponte Vedra Beach FL 32082

ELDER, JEAN KATHERINE, educator; b. Virginia, Minn., May 30, 1941; d. Clarence Adrian and Katherine C. (Miltich) Samuelson; B.S., U. Mich., 1963, A.M., 1966, Ph.D., 1969. Tchr. 5th grade Ypsilanti (Mich.) pub. schs., 1963-64; tchr. educable mentally retarded Quantico (Va.) Marine Corps Dependent Sch., 1964-65; dir. remedial reading program Iron Mountain (Mich.) pub. schs., 1966; research asst. U. Mich., 1966-69; asst. prof. spl. edn. Ind. U., Bloomington, 1969-70, cons. lab. ednl. devel., 1970-71; research asso. Center Ednl. Research and Devel. Mental Retardation, Bloomington, 1969-71; dir. delinquency modification through edn. project Marquette (Mich.)-Alger Intermediate Sch. Dist.-Marquette County Probate Ct., 1971-72; asst. prof. edn. No. Mich. U., Marquette, 1972-76, asso. prof., 1977-78, coordinator Title IX, 1975-76; project dir., asso. scientist Specialist Office Three, Wis. Research and Devel. Center Cognitive Learning, U. Wis., Madison, 1976-77; assoc. prof. med. edn. Coll. Human Medicine, Mich. State U., 1978-81, commr., 1981—; cons. in field. Mem. bd. Child and Family Service Upper Peninsula Mich.; mem. Pres.'s Com. on Mental Retardation, 1976—. U.S. Office Edn. fellow, 1966-69. Fellow Am. Assn. Mental Deficiency; mem. Am. Assn. Edn. Severely/Profoundly Handicapped, Nat., Mich. (dir.) assns. retarded citizens, Council Exceptional Children, AAUW (del. Mich.), Mich. Assn. Educators Learning Disabled, Pi Lambda Theta, Phi Delta Kappa, Delta Kappa Gamma. Lutheran. Club: Zonta. Author: (with others) Planning Individualized Education Program in Special Education, 1977. Contbr. articles to profl. jours. Home: 3803 Sandlewood Okemos MI 48864 Office: 200 Independence Ave SW Washington DC 20201

ELDER-JUCKER, PATRICIA LOUISA, psychologist; b. Trinidad, W.I., Dec. 10, 1945; came to U.S., 1967, naturalized, 1978; d. Jacob Delworth and Nevada Lenora Elder; B.A., Temple U., 1972, M.Ed., 1974, Ph.D., 1979; m. Walter Jucker, May 27, 1978. Staff psychologist Northwestern Inst. of Psychiatry, Phila., 1978-80, adj. profl. staff mem., 1980—; clin. psychologist ACORN, Phila., 1980-82; cons. Pastoral Care Program, Phila., 1980—; pvt. practice psychology, Phila., 1980—; clin. dir. The Bridge, Phila., 1981—; partner, asso. Miller-Rutman Assos., 1982—. Participant Winner project, Community Coll. Phila., 1982. Mem. Am. Personnel and Guidance Assn., Am. Psychol. Assn., Delaware Valley Assn. Black Psychologists, Phila. Soc. Clin. Psychologists, Yardley-Makefield Bus. and Profl. Women's Club. Contbr. writings to ACORN. Office: 10890 Bustleton Ave Suite 207 Philadelphia PA 19116

ELDREDGE, JANE MACDOUGAL, lawyer, state senator; b. Norwalk, Conn., Feb. 8, 1944; d. William Wallace, Jr. and Janann (Moeller) MacDougal; B.A., Smith Coll., 1965; J.D., U. Kans., 1977; m. Charles Child Eldredge, III, Apr. 12, 1944; children—Henry Gifford, Janann Bateson. Research asst. Psychol. Corp., N.Y.C., 1965-66; programmer Minn. Mut. Life Ins., 1966-68; programmer/analyst Analyst's Internat., 1968-70; systems analyst U. Kans., Lawrence, 1971-74; admitted to Kans. bar, 1977; individual practice law, Lawrence, 1978—; mem. Kans. Senate, 1981—. Bds. dirs. Lawrence LWV, Trinity Foster Home, Achievement Place for Boys, Douglas County Day Care Assn., Pinckney PTA pres. Pinckney Neighborhood Assn.; apptd. to Citizens Adv. Council Minimum Housing Code Bd. Appeals. Recipient various public service awards Kans. Bar Assn., Lawrence Edn. Assn., Lawrence Breakfast Cosmopolitan Club. Mem. Am. Bar Assn., Kans. Bar Assn., Douglas County Bar Assn., Lawrence C. of C., Lawrence Downtown Assn. Republican. Episcopalian. Office: 839 1/2 Massachusetts St Lawrence KS 66044

ELDRIDGE, MARIE DELANEY, statistician, govt. adminstr.; b. Balt., June 1, 1926; d. James Howard and Mathilda (Belz) Delaney; A.B. in Math., Coll. Notre Dame Md., 1948; Sc.M. in Johns Hopkins U., 1953; m. Paul Eldridge, Apr. 3, 1961; children—Julia Delaney, Dan Pattengill. Statistician, indsl. quality control Revere Copper and Brass, Balt., 1943-49; statistician Ralph Parsons & Co., Frederick, Md., 1953-54, U.S. Govt., 1954-60; instr. U. Balt., 1958-60; supr. statistician HEW, Washington, 1960-65; with Office Statis. Programs and Standards, U.S. Postal Service, Washington, 1965-72, dep. dir., 1968-70, dir., 1970-72; dir. math. analysis div. Nat. Hwy. Traffic Safety Adminstrn., Dept. Transp., 1972-73, dir. office stats. and analysis, 1973-75; adminstr. Nat. Center Edn. Stats., Dept. Edn., Washington, 1976—; mem. Edn. Commn. of States, 1976—; mem. tech. adv. com. Calif. Assessment Program, 1978—; mem. nat. accident sample adv. com. Dept. Transp. Recipient Superior Accomplishment award U.S. Postal Service, 1970; Outstanding Performance award Dept. Transp., 1975; cert. recognition HEW, 1976, 80. Fellow Am. Statis. Assn. (exec. council 1975-79, co-chmn. subcom. tng. statisticians for govt. 1979-81, com. fellows 1978-80); mem. Am. Edn. Research Assn., Internat. Assn. Survey Statisticians, Fed. Exec. Inst., Washington Statis. Soc. (pres. 1976-77), Phi Delta Kappa. Republican. Episcopalian. Office: 400 Maryland Ave SW Presdl Bldg Room 205 Washington DC 20202

ELDRIDGE, PATRICIA DARLENE, social worker; b. Mpls., June 11, 1937; d. George B. and Rhoda E. (Holmes) E.; B.A., Augsburg Coll., 1959; M.S.W., U. Minn., 1961. Social worker Travelers Aid Soc., Mpls., 1961, supr., 1961-63; social worker Lutheran Social Services, Mpls., 1963-68, supr. unmarried parent unit, 1968-73, dir. adoption counseling services, 1973—. Mem. Acad. Cert. Social Workers, Minn. Social Service Assn., Md. Adoption Council, Nat. Assn. Social Workers. Lutheran. Office: 2414 Park Ave Minneapolis MN 55404

ELENEWSKI, ROSLYN PASS, psychologist; b. Plainfield, N.J., June 18, 1936; d. Meyer Abraham and Naomi (Pisetzner) Pass; B.A., U. Pa., 1959; M.A., U. Miami, 1968, Ph.D., 1974; m. Jeffrey John Elenewski, July 28, 1972; children—Susan, Mark, Randy. Psychometrist Div. Psychol. Services, Dade County Dept. Youth Services, Miami, Fla., 1972-74; clin. psychologist Maxine Baker Clinic Community Mental Health Services, Inc., Miami, part-time 1974-76; pvt. practice cons. psychology, Coral Gables, Fla., 1974—; partner Synergistic Assos., Miami, 1975-77, Contemporary Family Cons., Miami, 1976—, Pan Am. Center for Personal Growth and Devel., Miami, 1977—, Psychdata, Inc., Miami, 1981—; cons. to child abuse treatment project Fla. State Protective Services; condr. seminars and workshops. Mem. Health Service Agy. Plan Devel. Com., 1978-80. Cert. practitioner neurolinguistic programming. Mem. Am. Psychol. Assn., Fla. Psychol. Assn., Dade County Psychol. Assn. Office: 1320 S Dixie Hwy Suite 860 Coral Gables FL 33146

ELFSTROM, DOROTHY LILLIAN BETTENCOURT (MRS. WALTER WILLIAM ELFSTROM), author; b. Galveston, Tex.; d. Henry Joseph and Margaret (Rowan) Bettencourt; grad. Draughon's Bus. Coll.; m. Walter William Elfstrom (dec.); children—Dorothy Elfstrom Bailey, Bill, Henry. Weekly columnist Texas City Daily Sun; poet laureate Galveston County; former poet laureate State of Tex. Recipient 1st pl. awards Nat. Fedn. Press Women, 1963, Tex. Press Women, 1963. Author: Challenge of the Seasons, 1963; Fireside Fancies, 1960; Voyager on the Sea of Life, 1971; Seeker, 1974. Writer various songs including But I Just Can't Say Goodbye; You're Way Behind the Beat, Lovely Galveston; What Are you Trying to Find; At Taps Time I Have a Date With You; Not for Keeps; You Have Shaken Up My World; I Know You've Got to Go; Now You Won't Let Me Be; No Plastic Heart for Me. Contbr. to numerous mags., newspapers. Home: 3815 Ave S Galveston TX 77550

ELGUIN-BÖDY, GITA, psychologist; b. Santiago, Chile; came to U.S., 1968; d. Serafín and Regina (Urízar) Elguin; B.S. in Biology, U. Chile, Santiago, Psy.D., 1964; Ph.D. in Counseling Psychology (Chancellor's fellow, NIMH fellow), U. Calif., Berkeley, 1976; m. Bart Bödy, Oct. 23, 1971. Clin. psychologist Barros Luco-Trudeau Gen. Hosp., Santiago, 1964-65; co-founder, co-dir. Lab. for Parapsychol. Research, Psychiat. Clinic, U. Chile, Santiago, 1965-68; research fellow Found. Research on Nature of Man, Durham, N.C., 1968; researcher psychol. correlates of EEG-Alpha waves U. Calif., Berkeley, 1972-76; originator holistic method of psychotherapy Psychotherapy for a Crowd of One, 1978; co-founder, exec. dir. Holistic Health Assos., Montclair, Oakland, Calif., 1979—; lectr. holistic health Piedmont (Calif.) Adult Sch., 1979-80; hostess Holistic Perspective, Sta. KALW-FM, Nat. Public Radio, 1980. Lic. psychologist, Chile, Calif. Mem. Am. Psychol. Assn., Alameda County Psychol. Assn., Assn. Advancement Psychology, Sierra Club, U. Calif. Alumni Assn. Contbr. articles in clin. psychology and holistic health to profl. jours. Office: Montclair Profl Bldg 2080 Mountain Blvd Suite 203 Oakland CA 94611

ELHASSANI, JOYCE NADINE, social worker; b. Burwell, Nebr., July 23, 1938; d. Glen Franklin and Ellen Lavina (Cook) Wiley; B.A., Calif. State U., Fullerton, 1963; M.S.W., Catholic U. Am., 1965; m. S.B. Elhassani, July 13, 1965; children—Layth, Camille. Clin. social worker D.C. Gen. Hosp., 1965-66; child welfare worker Los Angeles County, 1966-67; lectr. Univ. Coll., Baghdad (Iraq), 1967-68; tchr. Am. Consulate Sch., Dhahran, Saudi Arabia, 1968-70; adoptions worker Orange County, Santa Ana, Calif., 1970-71; tchr. Girls Secondary Sch., Baghdad, 1971-72; vol. worker, 1975—. Mem. LWV (dir. S.C. 1980—, pres. Spartanburg County chpt. 1979-81), Nat. Assn. Social Workers, AMA Aux., Alston-Wilkes Soc. Democrat. Editor: Polit. Directory Spartanburg County, 1979-80, 81-82; contbg. author: The Lives They Lived, 1981. Address: 1020 Eastwood Dr Spartanburg SC 29302

ELIAS, ROSALIND, mezzo-soprano; b. Lowell, Mass., Mar. 13, 1931; d. Salem and Shelahuy Rose (Namy) Elias; student New Eng. Conservatory Music, also in Italy; m. Zuhayr Moghrabi. Debut with Boris Goldowsky, Boston, 1948; appeared San Carlo Opera, Naples, Italy; debut Metropolitan Opera Co., 1954; originated role of Erika in Samuel Barber's opera, Vanessa; TV and concert artist; recs. for RCA, Columbia records. Mem. Sigma Alpha Iota. Office: care Columbia Artists Mgmt Inc 165 W 57th St New York NY 10019 *

ELIAS, SANDRA CHIAVARAS, educator; b. Clinton, Mass., Apr. 8, 1949; B.S. in Spl. Edn., Fitchburg (Mass.) State Coll., 1970, M.Ed. in Reading, 1976; postgrad. (fellow) Clark U., 1981-82; married; 1 child. Tchr. spl. class Webster (Mass.) Schs., 1970-73, asst. coordinator program materials, resource room, 1974, tchr./coordinator primary spl. needs program, 1975—, tchr. jr. high English, 1978-79, reading tchr. jr. high, 1979-80 adminstrv. asst. intern Shepherd Hill Regional Sch., Dudley, Mass., 1980-81. Mem. NEA, Mass., Webster (pres.-elect) tchrs. assns., AAUW, Nat. Council Tchrs. English. Cert. in elem. and spl. edn., reading, reading supervision, learning disabilities, Mass. Home: RD 2 Wayne Ave Dudley MA 01570

ELIASON, PHYLLIS MARIE, missionary; b. Greenacres, Fla., Dec. 21, 1925; d. John Sylvester and Catherine Marie (Graef) Underhill; B.A. in Psychology, U. Guam, 1971, M.Ed., 1974; m. Albert Augustus Eliason, Oct. 22, 1952 (dec. 1955); children—Phyllis Ann (Mrs. John Worthen), Nancy Louise (Mrs. William Wilkins), James Edward, Albert Augustus. Dir. Child Evangelism Fellowship Palm Beach County Fla., 1957-62; missionary dir. Child Evangelism Fellow, Guam, 1962—; traveling lectr. in U.S., 1966-67, 71-72, 73-74; tchr. trainer Leibenzell Missions Schs., Truk Island, 1968, 70, Bethania Girls Sch., Koror, Palau, 1965, 68; counselor, tchr. Marshalls Christian High Sch., Marshall Islands, 1975-76; counselor Reach to Recovery unit and ostomy group Am. Cancer Soc.; instr., bd. dirs. Extension Sch., Simpson Coll., Guam, 1977-78. Pres., Guam council Girl Scouts U.S.A., 1964-65, bd. dirs., 1978-79; sec. Guam Shell Club, 1964-65; bd. govs. Internat. Yr. of Child, 1979. Named hon. citizen, Huntsville, Ala., 1966. Mem. Council Exceptional Children, Christian Edn. Fellowship of Evang. Tchr. Tng. Assn., Am. Personnel and Guidance Assn., Calif., Hawaiian malacological assns., AAUW, Am. Orchid Soc., Underhill Soc. Am., Christian Women's Clubs (prayer adviser 1973), Chi Omicron Gamma. Address: PO Box 20217 GMF GU 96921

ELINE, CLAUDIA ANN, printing co. exec.; b. Providence, July 18, 1935; d. George Elmer and Lillian Alicia (Belmore) Dyer; student public schs., Warren, R.I.; m. Earl James Eline, Mar. 23, 1973. Mem. advt. dept. staff Gulf Am. Land Corp., Miami, Fla., 1965-66; clk. typist Universal Press, Inc., East Providence, R.I., 1966-71; sec. to Drs. England, Holton & Carlotti, oral surgeons, Providence, 1971-72; asst. to pres. Universal Press, Inc., East Providence, 1972-79, v.p. ops. Universal Press div. A&H Printing, 1979—. Mem. Nat. Assn. Exec. Secs., Bristol Women's Golf Assn. Roman Catholic. Home: 45 Division St Bristol RI 02809 Office: 5 Almeida Ave East Providence RI 02914

ELION, GERTRUDE BELLE, chemist; b. N.Y.C., Jan. 23, 1918; d. Robert and Bertha (Cohen) Elion; A.B., Hunter Coll., 1937; M.S., N.Y.U., 1941; D.Sc. (hon.), George Washington U., 1969; D.M.S. (hon.), Brown U., 1969. Lab. asst. biochemistry N.Y. Hosp. Sch. Nursing, 1937; research asst. Denver Chem. Mfg. Co., N.Y.C., 1938-39; tchr. chemistry and physics N.Y.C. secondary pub. schs., 1940-42; food analyst Quaker Maid Co., N.Y.C., 1942-43; research asst. Johnson & Johnson, New Brunswick, N.J., 1943-44; biochemist Wellcome Research Labs., Burroughs Wellcome Co., 1944-50; sr. research chemist Burroughs Wellcome Co., Research Triangle Park, N.C., 1950-55, asst. to assoc. research dir., 1955-63, asst. to research dir., 1963-67, head dept. exptl. therapy, 1967—; adj. prof. pharmacology and exptl. medicine Duke U., 1970—; adj. prof. pharmacology U. N.C., 1973; mem. bd. sci. counselors Nat. Cancer Inst., 1980. Recipient Pres.'s medal Hunter Coll., 1970; Disting. Chemist award N.C. Inst. Chemists, 1981. Mem. Am. Chem. Soc. (Garvan medal 1968), Am. Soc. Biol. Chemists, Am. Soc. Pharmacology and Exptl. Therapeutics, Am. Assn. Cancer Research, N.Y. Acad. Scis., Transplantation Soc., Chem. Soc. London. Contbr. articles to profl. jours.; assoc. editor Cancer Research, 1981—. Home: 1 Banbury Ln Chapel Hill NC 27514 Office: 3030 Cornwallis Rd Research Triangle Park NC 27709

ELIOT, LUCY CARTER, painter; b. N.Y.C., May 8, 1913; d. Ellsworth, Jr., and Lucy Carter (Byrd) E.; B.A., Vassar Coll., 1935; student Art Students League, N.Y.C., 1935-40. One-woman shows include: Cazenovia Coll., 1941, 62, Rochester Meml. Art Gallery, 1946, Syracuse (N.Y.) Mus. Fine Arts, 1947, Wells Coll., 1953, Ft. Schuyler Club, Utica, N.Y., 1971; works exhibited many nat. and regional exhbns., including Silvermine Guild; represented in permanent collections: Munson-Williams-Proctor Inst., Utica, Rochester Meml. Art Gallery. Recipient 1st prize Rochester Meml. Art Gallery, 1946; prize for painting Silvermine Guild, 1957; 1st prize in painting, Cooperstown (N.Y.) Art Assn., 1978. Mem. N.Y. Soc. Women Artists (pres. 1973-75), Artists Tech. Research Inst. (dir. 1975-79), Audubon Artists (dir. oils). Democrat. Episcopalian. Clubs: Cosmopolitan (N.Y.C.), Cazenovia (N.Y.). Home: 131 E 66th St New York NY 10021 also Cazenovia NY 13035

ELISSALDE, GWENDOLYN SCHEUERMANN, vet. microbiologist; b. Suyoc, Luzon, Philippines, Oct. 7, 1939; d. Gustav John and Helen Grace (Friday) Scheuermann; B.S., S.W. Tex. State U., 1973; B.S.Vet.Sci., Tex. A&M U., 1976, D.V.M., 1977, Ph.D., 1980; m. Marcel Howell Elissalde, Jr., Dec. 19, 1967; children—Kitty Lynette, Daniel Paul, Nora Elena. Electronics technician Tex. A&M U., 1964, lab. mechanic, 1964-66, marine geophysics technician, 1967-69, parasitology student worker, 1975-77, vet. clin. asso., 1977-80, asst. prof. dept. vet. microbiology-parasitology Coll. Vet. Medicine, 1980—. Faculty adv. women's service orgn., 1980—. Served in USN, 1958-59. Recipient Charles Spurgeon Smith award in Biology, 1974. Mem. AVMA, Am. Soc. Microbiology, AAUP, Am. Assn. Women in Sci., Am. Assn. Vet. Parasitologists, Am. Assn. Vet. Med. Colls. Council Educators, Alpha Chi, Beta Beta Beta, Phi Sigma. Unitarian. Contbr. articles to sci. jours. Home: 1507 Medina College Station TX 77840 Office: Coll Vet Medicine Tex A&M U College Station TX 77843

ELKHANIALY, HEKMAT ABDUL RAZEK, demographic cons.; b. Egypt, Dec. 17, 1935; came to U.S., 1961, naturalized, 1975; d. Abdul Razek Hussein and Nabiha Mursi (Kutb) E.; B. Commerce/Econs., Cairo U., 1959; Ph.D. in Sociology, U. Chgo., 1968; m. Chandra Kant Jha, Dec. 20, 1969; 1 dau., Lakshmi. Mem. faculty Roosevelt U., Chgo., 1968-75, asso. prof. sociology, 1973-75; demographic cons., Chgo., 1975—; sec. PSM Internat. Mem. Population Assn. Am., Am. Sociol. Assn., Chgo. Council Fgn. Relations. Contbr. articles to profl. jours. Home and Office: 2800 N Lake Shore Dr Chicago IL 60657

ELKIN, ANN JOYCE, psychologist; b. Chgo.; grad. Calif. State Coll., 1970; M.S., U. So. Calif., 1971; Ph.D., U.S. Internat. U., 1973. With Suicide Prevention Center, 1969-72; intern VA Hosp., Brentwood, Calif., 1972-73; postdoctoral intern Hacker Clinic, 1973-74; pvt. practice psychology specializing in eating disorders, psychosomatic medicine and hypnosis, Los Angeles, 1973—; cons. Naval Weapons Base, 1974; cons. alcohol programs Comprehensive Care Corp., 1979-81; supr. Wright Inst.; tutor, bd. dirs. Internat. Coll., vice chmn. bd., 1978-79. Mem. Am. Psychol. Assn., Acad. Psychosomatic Medicine, Am. Orthopsychiat. Assn., Am. Soc. Clin. Hypnosis, Soc. Clin. and Exptl. Hypnosis, Internat. Soc. Hypnosis. Research on early recollections of homosexuals. Office: 12301 Wilshire Blvd 413 Los Angeles CA 90025

ELKIN, BEVERLY DAWN DALTON, art dealer; b. Chgo., Apr. 23, 1933; d. James Manuel and Letha Alice (Will) Dalton; B.A., U. Ill., 1955, M.A., 1965; m. Richard H. Elkin, June 2, 1956; children—Theresa Gail, Richard Paul. Tchr. high sch. English and drama in Ill., 1955-70; art dealer, dir. House of Art Gallery, Champaign, Ill., 1971—. Mem. Profl. Picture Framers Assn. Home: 1103 W Green St Champaign IL 61820 Office: 108 N Walnut St Champaign IL 61820

ELKIND-TOURRE, RACHEL, composer, singer, producer records; b. Hong Kong, Sept. 22, 1937; came to U.S., 1946, naturalized, 1955; d. Gregory and Florence Joseph (Moalem-Elkind) Pissarevsky; B.A., U. Calif., Berkeley, 1959; m. Yves Marcel Tourre, June 22, 1979. Compositions include: Switched-on-Bach (Nat. Acad. Rec. Arts and Scis. Grammy for classical record of yr. 1969, Nat. Assn. Record Merchandisers award for best-selling classical record 1969, 72, Schwann Readers Poll winner 1969, 70); co-composer, producer: Remember Me for UNESCO Yr. of Child film, 1979; co-composer, producer film scores: A Clockwork Orange, 1971, The Shining, 1980; v.p. prin. Trans-Electronic Music Prodns., Inc., N.Y.C., 1968—. Pres., W. 87th St. Block Assn., N.Y.C., 1968. Mem. Nat. Acad. Rec. Arts and Scis., Broadcast Music, Inc. Republican. *

ELKINS, CAROL MAGDALENE, med. technologist; b. Phila., Jan. 30, 1939; d. Samuel Edward and Magdalene Gene (Brennecke) E.; B.S., Beaver Coll., 1960; M.Ed., Temple U., 1970. Chemistry technologist Abington (Pa.) Meml. Hosp., 1960-63, edn. coordinator Sch. of Med. Tech., 1963-70, lab. supr., 1967-70; cons. Medi Visuals, Inc., N.Y.C., 1969—; chmn. dept. med. tech. Sch. of Health Related Professions U. Pitts., 1970-75, asst. prof., 1970-75, asso. prof., 1975; exec. dir. Nat. Accrediting Agy. for Clin. Lab. Scis., Chgo., 1976—. Mem. Am. Soc. Assn. Execs., Nat. Assn. Female Execs., Am. Soc. Allied Health Professions, Am. Soc. Med. Tech., Council Postsecondary Accreditation (dir.), Council Specialized Accrediting Agys. (chmn. 1979-81). Office: Suite 608 547 W Jackson Blvd Chicago IL 60606

ELKINS, EVANGELINE CANONIZADO, consumer coop. ofcl.; b. San Pedro, Calif., Aug. 28, 1932; d. Estanislao C. and Felicia (Stokes) Canonizado; student San Jose State Coll., 1952-53; grad. U. San Francisco, 1978; m. Robert Alexander Elkins, July 1, 1961; children—Nikki Isaacs, Stacey Vilas, Danni Vilas. With Consumers Coop. of Berkeley (Calif.) Inc., 1958—, edn. asst. for community relations, 1964-73, supr. edn. dept., 1973-76, asst. to edn. dir., 1976-78, program coordinator edn. dept., 1980-81, personnel tng. coordinator, 1981—; also guitar tchr. Mem. Community Adv. Com., Bonita House, Berkeley, 1974; mem. steering com. for cultural and ethnic affairs Guild of Oakland Mus., 1973-74; dir. various activities YMCA, YWCA, Oakland City Recreation Dept., 1959-73. Recipient Honor award U. Calif. Student Coop., 1965, other awards. Mem. Coop. Educators Network Calif. Democrat. Unitarian. Columnist Coop. News, 1964—. Home: 516 Santa Barbara Rd Berkeley CA 94707 Office: 4805 Central Ave Richmond CA 94804

ELKINS, THELMA LOUISE, librarian; b. Crayne, Ky., Dec. 21, 1926; d. Pressley Odell and Mary Dee Elkins; B.A., Union U., Jackson, Tenn., 1951; M.R.E., Southwestern Baptist. Theol. Sem., Ft. Worth, 1954; M.S. in L.S., U. So. Calif., 1963; postgrad. Fla. State U. Reference librarian Calif. Bapt. Coll., Riverside, 1960-65, Calif. Wesleyan U., San Diego, 1965-66, Colo. State Coll., Greeley, 1966-68; library dir. Bapt. Coll. Charleston (S.C.), 1968—. Mem. ALA, S.C. Library Assn. Home: 2604 Cameron St Isle of Palms SC 29451 Office: Bapt Coll Library Charleston SC 29411

EL KOURY, ALICE FRANCISCO (MRS. JORGE P. EL KOURY), microbiologist, civic worker, educator; b. San Juan, P.R., Oct. 12, 1919; d. Miguel Francisco and Matilde Azize (Frangle) Assanna; B.S., Notre Dame Coll., Balt., 1939; M.T., Sch. Tropical Medicine, San Juan, 1940; M.S., U. Pa., 1941; m. Jorge P. El Koury, Nov. 11, 1942; children—Jorge Miguel, Jaime Antonio. Lab. technician Sch. Tropical Medicine, San Juan, 1940; prof. U. P.R., 1943-47, asso. prof. biology dept., 1957-76, prof., 1976—; head lab. San Juan Diagnostic Clinic, 1948-51. Bd. dirs. P.R. chpt. ARC, 1951-58, Assn. Infantile Paralysis, 1943-45; bd. regents Colegio Puertoriqueno de Ninas; bd. academia Perpetuo Socorro. Recipient merit pin Boy Scouts Am., 1953, award for meritorious vol. work ARC, 1962. Mem. AAAS, Am. Pub. Health Assn., Soc. Am. Microbiologists, Soc. Microbiologists P.R. (pres. 1964-66, 75—), Am. Soc. for Microbiology (edn. com., internat. activities com. 1975-78, membership com. 1976-77), Latin Am. Assn. for Microbiology, Soc. Med. Technologists of P.R., Tissue Culture Assn., Cath. Daus. Am., U. Pa. Alumnae Soc., Union Mujeres Americanas, Royal Soc. for Promotion Health (Eng.), Soc. Cath. U. Women, Corte de Lourdes de P.R., Hermandad del Santo Cristo, Nuestra Senora de la Providencia Soc., Asociacion Salud Publica de P.R., Navy League, Beta Beta Beta, Nu Sigma Chi. Roman Catholic. Clubs: Pa. Cornell, Swimming and Tennis, U.S. Travel (San Juan); Caseno de P.R., Civicos de Damas. Contbr. articles to profl. jours. Home: Magnolia 2009 Montefiores Santurce PR 00915 Office: PO Box 1105 San Juan PR 00902

ELLEDGE-HEIMER, MURIEL KAY, coll. adminstr.; b. Palatka, Fla., Nov. 23, 1933; d. Carl Parmerly and Muriel Ernestine (Wells) Arant; B.A. summa cum laude, Wake Forest U., 1955; M.A.T., Rollins Coll., 1964; Ed.D., Nova U., 1978; m. William Heimer, Jan. 1, 1979; children—Carolyn Ann, James Eugene. Asst. prof. English, Brevard Community Coll., Cocoa, Fla., 1964-74, dir. continuing edn. for women, 1974-78, dean spl. programs, 1978-80, provost Cocoa campus, 1980—. Grantee in field of edn. Mem. Am. Assn. of Women in Community and Jr. Colls. (pres., cons.), Assn. Communtiy Coll. Trustees, Fla. Assn. Community Colls., Phi Kappa Delta. Democrat. Presbyterian. Home: 3799 S Banana River Blvd Cocoa Beach FL 32931 Office: 1519 Clearlake Rd Cocoa FL 32922

ELLENBERGER, DIANE MARIE, nurse; b. St. Louis, Oct. 5, 1946; d. Charles Ernst and Celeste Loraine (Neudecker) E.; R.N., Barnes Hosp., St. Louis, 1970; B.S. in Nursing St. Louis U., 1976; M.S., U. Colo., 1977. Staff nurse hosps., clin. nurse, St. Louis, 1973-76; nurse clinician, Sedalia, Mo., 1977-78; nurse clinician, educator Bothwell Hosp., Sedalia, 1977-78; clin. nurse specialist, coordinator perinatal outreach edn. Cardinal Glennon Meml. Hosp. Children, St. Louis, 1978-80; instr. McKendree Coll., Lebanon, Ill., 1980; asst. prof. Maryville Coll., St. Louis, 1982—; owner, operator Diane Designs Needlepoint, St. Louis, 1981—. Served with Nurse Corps, USAF, 1970-72. Mem. Am. Nurses Assn., Nurses Assn. Am. Coll. Ob-Gyn, Nat. Perinatal Assn., Mo. Nurses Assn., Mo. Perinatal Assn. (v.p. 1980), Sigma Theta Tau. Mem. Divine Sci. Ch. Contbr. articles profl. jours. Home: 3929 Utah St Saint Louis MO 63116 Office: Maryville Coll Saint Louis MO 63141

ELLERT, JOANN CRISP, artist, educator; b. Syracuse, N.Y., Jan. 31, 1930; d. Wilbur C. and Leona (Weaver) Crisp; B.F.A., Syracuse U., 1948; diploma Royal Coll. Art, London, 1957; M.A., Am. U., 1962, Ph.D., 1970; postdoctoral fellow Yale U., 1971; diploma Sorbonne, Paris, 1964; m. Robert B. Ellert, May 29, 1950. Curator, Colonial Williamsburg, 1946-49; mus. art specialist Nat. Gallery Art, Washington, 1950; art specialist Arlington County (Va.) Schs., 1950—; asso. prof. art U. Md., Heidelburg, Ger., 1960-62, U. Va., Charlottesville, 1970-73; art edn. specialist Hirshhorn Mus. and Sculpture Garden, Washington, 1973; cons. Renwick Gallery, Washington, 1974, Grand Chaumiere, Paris, 1964; one-woman shows include: Williamsburg Lodge (Va.), 1949, So. Pines Gallery, Pinehurst, N.C., 1950, Columbia Club, London, 1956, Utica-Munson Proctor Inst., 1958, Rue de Sienne, Paris, 1964, Amerikhaus, Heidelberg, 1965, Arlington (Va.) Edn. Center, 1970-76, Fenwick Library, George Mason U., Va., 1973, Mt. Vernon Coll., Washington, 1973, Emerson Gallery, Washington, 1974, Washington Project for the Arts, 1975, Bridge Gallery, Washington, 1976, Artel Gallery, Washington, 1978, Nourse Gallery, Washington, 1980; group shows in N.Y.C., Washington, N.C., Chgo., San Francisco, Paris, London, Munich; represented in permanent collections: Syracuse U., Dura Co., So. Pines Community Center, George Mason U., Mt. Vernon Jr. Coll., Emerson Gallery, Fairfax, Va.; cataloguer Anni Albers Textile Collection, Yale U., 1970; bd. officers Artist's Equity, 1974-78. Recipient first prize in oil painting So. Pines Art Exhbt., 1950, Amerikhaus Exhbn., Heidelberg, 1965, Md. Fedn. Women's Clubs, 1974, others. Mem. Nat. Coll. Art Assn., Art League, Nat. Trust Hist. Preservation, Smithsonian Assos., Nat. Assn. Humanities Edn., Artists Equity Assn. (chpt. pres. 1981—), Friends of Corcoran Art Gallery, Phi Beta Kappa, Phi Kappa Delta. Contbr. articles to art and archtl. jours. Address: 3099 Q St NW Washington DC 20007 also Stone House Cape Vincent NY 13618

ELLINGTON, MARTHA BARA, psychologist; b. N.Y.C., Sept. 3, 1922; d. Augustus A. and Emily (Quintana) Bara; B.A., Hunter Coll., 1948, M.A., 1949; M.S., 1959; postgrad. N.Y.U.; m. Thomas W. Ellington, May 11, 1945; children—Stephanie M. (Mrs. Theodore Goetzinger), Katharine C. (Mrs. Arthur F. Custer), Deborah A., Candice J. Fgn. dept. translator Swiss Bank Corp., Co., N.Y.C., 1946-48; instr. Gifu U., Japan, summer 1956; instr., psychoanalyst U. Md., 1955-57; cons. Mental Health Center, Gifu, summer 1957; asst. to dir. profl. edn., instr. Indsl. Home for Blind, Bklyn., 1958-59; psychologist, rehab. counselor, student supr. Fountain House Found., N.Y.C., 1959-61, 64-66; supervising probation officer Los Angeles County Probation Dept., Torrance, Calif., 1961-64; research psychologist, rehab. counselor Research Facility, Orangeburg, N.Y., 1966-68; rehab. counselor, student supr. N.Y. State Dept. Edn., 1968—; cons. Bklyn. Assn. Mental Health, 1968—. Troop leader Girl Scouts U.S.A., 1955-59. Mem. Am. Personnel and Guidance Assn., Nat. Rehab. Counseling Assn., AAUW, Alpha Delta Pi, Kappa Delta Pi. Home: 900 W 190th St New York NY 10040 Office: 225 Park Ave S New York NY 10003

ELLIOT, GLADYS CRISLER, oboist; b. Macon, Ga., Sept. 5, 1929; d. George Edwin and Celeste (Rhyne) Crisler; B.Mus., N.Tex. State U., Denton, 1951; m. Willard Elliot, Sept. 3, 1951 (div. June 1976). Oboist, Dallas Symphony Orch., 1951-64; Contemporary Chamber Players, U. Chgo., 1964-81, WGN Staff Orch., 1966-69; prin. oboist Lyric Opera Chgo., 1964—, Chgo. Grant Park Summer Symphony, 1966—, Orch. of Ill., 1979—; instr. DePaul U. Sch. Music, Chgo. Mem. Internat. Double Reed Soc.

ELLIOT, JEANN NIELSEN, advt. and public relations exec.; b. Chgo., Dec. 30, 1924; d. William August and Grace Estella Juliet (Ottow) Ninneman; grad. Layton Art Sch., 1944; student Ind. U., 1950, Butler U., 1952; m. George Elliot, Apr. 18, 1964; 1 son, Robert James Becker. Successively office mgr., asst. distbr. sales mgr., advt. mgr. Regency Electronics, Indpls., 1949-54; account exec. Burton Browne Advt., Chgo., 1954-56; partner Cody Advt., Chgo., 1956-60; advt. mgr. ITT Distbr. Products, Lodi, N.J., 1960-62; sales promotion mgr. Triad Transformer div. Litton Industries, Inc., Venice, Calif., Huntington, Ind., 1962-65; advt. mgr. Fairchild DuMont Labs., Clifton, N.J., 1965-69; editor/writer The Advt., Monroe Calculator div. Litton Industries, Inc., Morris Plains, N.J., 1975; mktg. services adminstr. ITT Decca Marine, Inc., Palm Coast, Fla., 1978—. Pres., Syracuse Operetta Co.; sec. Young Republicans; active Palm Coast Chorus, Red Cross Motor Corps. Mem. Am. Mgmt. Assn., Nat. Office Mgmt. Assn., LWV (dir.), Los Angeles Advt. Women. Republican. Presbyterian. Clubs: Palm Coast Golf Assn., Palm Coast Bridge. Home: 55 Federal Ln Palm Coast FL 32037

ELLIOT, SONDRA RENÉ, bus. devel. and pub. relations ofcl.; b. N.Y.C., Feb. 22, 1929; d. Albert and Etta (Levy) Ross; B.S., George Washington U., 1948; M.A., N.Y. U., 1960; m. Chester Elliot, Dec. 20, 1947 (div. 1974); children—Denise Lori (dec.), Scott Martin. Tchr., guidance counselor N.Y.C. pub. schs., 1948-53; tchr. South Huntington (N.Y.) Pub. Schs., 1962-68; adminstr., personnel counselor, pub. relations dir. Amherst Employment Inc., Hicksville, N.Y., 1972-76; exec. search cons. maj. pharm. cos., 1972-76; mktg. and pub. relations exec. First Am. Bank, 1980—; pvt. practice psychology, 1979—; editor Temple Emanuel Topics, Palm Beach, Fla., 1978-80; pres. sisterhood, 1978-80; founder Meml. Denise Lori Elliot Fund, 1974. Recipient cert. honor Jewish Fedn., 1979; also honoree Temple Emanuel, 1978—; awards Rotary, Kiwanis and Lions clubs. Home: 2800 N Flagler Dr West Palm Beach FL 33407

ELLIOTT, BETTE SMITH, news service exec.; b. Coblentz, Germany, Sept. 14, 1921; (parents Am. citizens); d. William Alexander and Carmen Emily (Kellner) Smith; B.A., Coll. of William and Mary, 1942; children—Carmen Elliott, Lee Elliott. Reporter, women's editor The Raleigh (N.C.) Times, 1952-63; women's news dir. WRAL-TV, Raleigh, 1963-76; pres. Bill Kiser News Service, Inc., Raleigh, 1978—. Mem. N.C. Council of Hearing Impaired, 1981—; mem. spl. populations com. Raleigh Arts Commn., 1981-82; ex-officio mem. Gov.'s Council, Internat. Yr. of Disabled Persons, 1981—. Recipient Headliner award Women in Communications, 1980. Mem. N.C. Press Women, Raleigh Public Relations Soc., Women in Communications, DAR. Democrat. Roman Catholic. Writer, syndicated column, The Handicapped Mailbag, 1978—; contbr. articles to profl. jours. Home: 2310 White Oak Rd Raleigh NC 27608 Office: 5 W Hargett St Raleigh NC 27601

ELLIOTT, CAROL GEANNE, nursing educator; b. Sedalia, Mo., Nov. 2, 1938; d. James R. and Helen C. (Workover) Scott; grad. Penn Valley Coll., 1968; nurse anesthesia diploma U. Kans., 1973; B.A., Ottawa (Kans.) U., 1975; M.P.A., U. Kans., 1982, postgrad., 1982—; m. Robert Lee Elliott, Mar. 23, 1957; children—Kelly Ann, Michael, Kimberly Karol, Karen Kathleen. Asst. prof. Sch. Allied Health, U. Kans. Med. Center Campus, Kansas City, 1973—, chmn. dept. postgrad. edn. nurse anesthesia, 1973—; lectr. in field. Mem. Am. Nurses Assn., Am. Hosp. Assn., Am. Assn. Nurse Anesthetists, Mo. Assn. Nurse Anesthetists, Kans. Assn. Nurse Anesthetists, Internat. Anesthesia Research Soc., Assn. Operating Room Nurses, Allied Health Profls. Assn., Phi Theta Kappa. Contbr. articles on nurse anesthesia to profl. jours. Home: 14901 Rosehill Rd Olathe KS 66062 Office: Univ of Kansas 39th and Rainbow Kansas City KS 66103

ELLIOTT, CONSTANCE WATKINS, coll. ofcl.; b. Nashville, June 12, 1934; d. Church, Sr., and Ethel (Tarkington) Watkins; B.S., Tenn. State U., 1955; m. Riley William Elliott, Nov. 27, 1957; 1 dau., Jill Denise. Partner retail grocery, 1955-79; adminstrv. asst. Meharry Med. Coll. Sch. Nursing, 1955-62, cons. clerical staff dept. psychiatry, 1962; sec. Am. Bapt. Coll., Nashville, 1968-69, bursar, 1969—, dir. fin. aid, 1969-82. Pres. Met. Nashville Council PTAs, 1977-78; Mid-Cumberland regional dir., state pres., hon. life mem. Tenn. Congress Parents and Tchrs.; bd. dirs. Nashville Public TV Council; alumnus Leadership Nashville; public health council State of Tenn; mem. Spl. Task Force to Study Public Edn. in Tenn. Mem. Tenn. Assn. Student Fin. Aid Adminstrs., So. Assn. Student Fin. Aid Adminstrs., Assn. Bus. Adminstrs. Christian Colls. (dir.), Nat. PTA (hon. life). Mem. Ch. of Christ. Office: 1800 Whites Creek Pike Nashville TN 37207

ELLIOTT, DAISY, state legislator; b. Filbert, W.Va.; grad. Detroit Inst. Commerce; student Wayne State U., U. Detroit; 3 children. Del. Mich. Democratic Constnl. Conv., 1961-62; mem. Mich. Ho. of Reps., 1962—. Alt. del. Dem. Nat. Conv., 1972, 76; mem. Council Postsecondary Edn. and Joint Legis. Liaison Com., Govs. Commn. Higher Edn.; trustee Peoples Community Ch. Named One of Most Outstanding Black Women in Politics, Alpha Kappa Heritage Series, 1970; recipient Community Service award Peoples Community Ch., Meritorious Service award, Most Worshipful Prince Hall Lodge; named Woman of Yr., Mich. Fed. Dem. Club; recipient Disting. Service award Black Legislators Clearing House. Mem. Order Women Legislators, Nat. Soc. State Legislators, Mich. Dem. Black Caucus (sec.), United Black Coalition (sec.). Home: 8701 LaSalle Blvd Detroit MI 48206 Office: Michigan House of Representatives State Capitol Bldg Lansing MI 48909 *

ELLIOTT, ELEANOR THOMAS, chem. co. exec.; b. N.Y.C., Apr. 26, 1926; d. James A. and Dorothy Q. (Read) Thomas; B.A., Barnard Coll., 1948; m. John Elliott, Jr., July 26, 1956. Staff writer Vogue Mag., N.Y.C., 1948, asso. editor, to 1952; asst. dir. research and speech writing div. N.Y. State Republican Com., 1952, 53-56; social sec. to Sec. of State and Mrs. John Foster Dulles, Washington, 1953-56; dir. Celanese Corp., N.Y.C., 1974—, C.I.T. Fin. Corp., 1978-81. Trustee, Barnard Coll., 1959—, chmn., 1973-76; chmn. bd. dirs. Found. for Child Devel., 1972-79; bd. govs. N.Y. Hosp., 1970—; bd. dirs. United Way of Greater N.Y., 1977—, Catalyst Inc., 1978—, Am. Women's Econ. Devel. Corp., 1978—. Recipient Columbia U. medal, 1977, Barnard Coll. medal, 1979; named Extraordinary Woman of Achievement, NCCJ, 1978. Mem. Nat. Assn. Women, Nat. Women's Polit. Caucus. Republican. Episcopalian. Club: Colony. Author: Glamour Magazine Party Book, 1966. Address: 1035 Fifth Ave New York NY 10028

ELLIOTT, ELIZABETH M., assn. exec.; b. Mpls., Jan. 15, 1946; B.A. in English cum laude, U. Minn., 1970; M.A. (teaching fellow), Am. U., 1972; m. Robert L. Norris, Sept. 1, 1973. Copy editor Am. Soc. Microbiology, Washington, 1972-74; dir. public info. Nat. Assn. Hearing and Speech Action, Silver Spring, Md., 1974-75; editor Solar Energy Industries Assn., Washington, 1975; asso. dir. Better Hearing Inst., Washington, 1975-79; exec. dir., editor-in-chief Am. Running and Fitness Assn., Washington, 1978—; adj. instr. Am. U., 1971-72, 75. Mem. Am. Soc. Assn. Execs., Direct Mail/Mktg. Assn., Public Relations Soc. Am., Women in Communications. Office: 2420 K St NW Washington DC 20037

ELLIOTT, INGER MCCABE (MRS. OSBORN ELLIOTT), designer, textile co. exec.; b. Oslo, Norway, Feb. 23, 1933; d. David and Lova (Katz) Abrahamsen; came to U.S., 1941, naturalized, 1946; A.B. in History with honors, Cornell U., 1954; postgrad. Harvard U., 1955; A.M. (Jean Birdsall fellow), Radcliffe Coll., 1957; m. Osborn Elliott, Oct. 20, 1973; children by previous marriage-Kari McCabe, Alexander McCabe, Molly McCabe. Editor, East European Student and Youth Service, N.Y.C., 1957-60; photographer Rapho-Guillumette, U.S. and fgn. countries, 1960-73; pres. China Seas, Inc., N.Y.C., 1972—; tchr. Newton (Mass.) Public Schs., 1955-56. Recipient award Resources Council, 1977-81. Mem. Am. Soc. Mag. Photographers, Phi Beta Kappa. Author: Women Photographers, 1970; A Week in Amy's World, 1970; A Week in Henry's World, 1971; also portfolio in Infinity mag., 1969. Home: 10 Gracie Sq New York NY 10028 Office: China Seas Inc 21 E 4th St New York NY 10003

ELLIOTT, LEE ANN LAYTON, govt. ofcl.; b. St. Louis, June 26, 1927; d. Ernest Sylvester and Ida May (Davis) Layton; B.A., U. Ill., 1949; m. William Jerome Elliott, Sept. 22, 1956; 1 son, William Jay. Asso. exec. dir. Am. Med. Polit. Action Com., 1961-79; v.p. Bishop, Bryant & Assos., Inc., Chgo., 1979-81; commnr. Fed. Election Commn., 1982. Active numerous local Republican campaign coms.; v.p. polit. action com., co-campaign mgr. Skokie (Ill.) Caucus Party, 1968-82; trustee Skokie Mass Transit Dist., 1971; mem. Skokie Blood Commn., 1972-77. Recipient award excellence corp. public affairs NAM, 1979. Cert. assn. exec. Mem. Am. Soc. Assn. Execs., Am. Assn. Polit. Cons., Chgo. Area Public Affairs Group, Chgo. Women in Govt. Relations, Alpha Delta Pi. Office: 1325 K St NW Washington DC 20463

ELLIOTT, LINNEÁ CONSTANCE, publisher; b. N.Y.C., Feb. 23, 1948; d. Samuel and Edith Anna (Peterson) Whyte, Jr.; m. Peter Thomas Elliott, Aug. 31, 1969. Ground hostess Japan Airlines, N.Y.C., 1967-68; asst. to mng. editor Southmayd Corp., Yonkers, N.Y., 1968; public relations model Seagrams Corp., N.Y.C., 1968; prodn. editor, mgr. jours., editorial dept. Pergamon Press, Elmsford, N.Y., 1968-74; asso. pub. Appleton Century-Crofts div. Prentice-Hall, East Norwalk, Conn., 1974—; cons. in field. Mem. Healthcare Businesswomen's Assn., Pharm. Advt. Council, Assn. Ind. Clin. Pubs. (treas. 1981-82), Nat. Assn. Female Execs. Episcopalian. Mng. editor Jour. Family Practice, 1974—, Jour. Nat. Med. Assn., 1975-79. Home: 756 Sleepy Hollow Rd Briarcliff Manor NY 10510 Office: 25 Van Zant St East Norwalk CT 06855

ELLIOTT, MYRTLE EVELYN KEENER, educator; b. Annawan, Ill., Apr. 11, 1898; d. John William and Mary (Baldwin) Keener; A.B., Cornell Coll., 1921; M.A., Columbia, 1926; postgrad. summers U. Iowa, 1928, Ohio State U., 1930, 31, U. Chgo., 1933, San Francisco State Coll., 1949, Fresno State Coll., 1958, 59, 60; m. Leo Louis Elliott, Aug. 10, 1935 (dec. 1948); children—Mary Ellen (Mrs. Jack Agan), Winona (Mrs. Herbert C. Sample), James, Joan. Tchr. pub. high schs., Panora, Iowa, 1921-23, Dewitt, Iowa, 1923-25; head English dept., dean girls, Kemmerer, Wyo., 1926-29; dean girls and English, Pendelton, Oreg., 1929-30; tchr., Ely, Nev., 1930-31; girls' adviser boarding schs. U.S. Indian Service, 1931-35; tchr. Latin and English, Cut Bank, Mont., 1944-46; tchr. older educable retarded children for Kern County Supt. Schs., Bakersfield, Calif., 1949-68; pvt. work with children with learning disabilities. Recipient Alumni Merit award Cornell Coll., 1977. Fellow Am. Assn. Mental Deficiency; mem. Council for Exceptional Children, Calif. Tchrs. Assn., Nat. (hon. life), Calif. (hon. life) congresses parents and tchrs., Catholic Daus. Am., Columbia Tchrs. Coll. Alumni Assn. (past local chmn.), Cornell Coll. Alumni Assn., AAUW, Internat. Reading Assn., Phi Beta Kappa. Home: 2709 4th St Bakersfield CA 93304

ELLIOTT, ROSALIE CONN (MRS. F. SCOTT ELLIOTT), educator, club woman; b. Kosciusko, Miss.; d. Jefferson P. and Ada (Russell) Conn.; B.S., George Peabody Coll. Tchrs., 1924; M.A., U. N.C., 1935; postgrad. U. Chgo., several summers; m. F. Scott Elliott, Dec. 22, 1933; 1 son, F. Scott, Jr. Tchr. Columbia (S.C.) High Sch., 1924-26; tchr. head math. dept. Lee H. Edwards High Sch., Asheville, N.C., 1926-39; math. tchr. Durham (N.C.) High Sch., 1939-46; tchr. English and French, Whitmire (S.C.) High Sch., 1957-65. Past exec. bd., past sec. Newberry Civic League; active Crippled Children Soc.; sec. United Meth. Ch. Central, United Meth. Women. Mem. AAUW (chmn. local lit. div., past pres. Newberry br. 1958-60, 70-72, mass media chmn. state div. 1960-62), N.E.A., Newberry County Classroom Tchrs. (pres. 1959), Newberry Hist. Soc. (publicity chmn.), NEA (pres. math. div.), S.C.

Edn. Assn., S.C. Fedn. Women's Clubs (div. chmn. 1951-72, dir. N. dist. 1952-55, chmn. library services 1968-72), Nat. League Am. Pen Women (chmn. Piedmont poetry div.), Am. Legion Aux. (local pres. 1948-50), Women's Soc. Christian Service (local pres. 1952-56; dist. pres. 1956-60), U.D.C. (chpt. pres., recorder crosses S.C. div.), D.A.R. (past regent Jasper, state motion picture chmn., S.C. arts com.), S.C. Soc. Poets, Delta Kappa Gamma (chpt. pres. 1970-72), Epsilon Sigma Omicron (past chpt. pres,). Methodist (circle leader, Sunday sch. tchr.). Club: Woman's (pres. 1948-50). Poems included in Nat. Poetry Anthology, 1958-81, S.C. Mag. Home: 718 Glenn St Newberry SC 29108

ELLIOTT, ROSEMARY THERESA, pharm. co. exec.; b. Ridley Park, Pa., June 20, 1944; d. John Francis and Rose (Fizzano) Martin; B.A., West Chester State Coll., 1966. Personnel specialist Army Electronics Command, Phila., 1966-69; account exec. Alstin Advt. Agy., Phila., 1969-73; personnel positions Johnson & Johnson Cos., New Brunswick, N.J., 1973—, dir. selection and devel. Ortho Pharm. Corp., Raritan, N.J., 1978—. Mem. Am. Soc. Personnel Adminstrs., Employment Mgrs. Assn. Democrat. Roman Catholic. Office: Ortho Pharmaceutical Corp Route 202 Raritan NJ 08869

ELLIOTT, SHIRLEY RAE, med. technologist; b. Binghamton, N.Y., Oct. 21, 1922; d. John Rook and Carrie Marie (Keeney) Reynolds; student Duke U., 1940-42; student U. Tex., 1942-43, Sch. Med. Tech. Va., 1955-56; m. Floyd Strother Elliott, Nov. 13, 1943; children—Linda Rae, Teresa Marie, Rita Kay, Susan Irene, John Roger, Katherine Claire, Floyd Strother. Research technologist VA Med. Center, Nashville, 1956, med. technologist microbiology, chemistry, 1956-59, med. technologist, generalist, 1959-66, coagulation/parasitology, technologist, 1966-72, supr. med. technology, 1972—. Named Mother of the Yr., (Gallatin) Jaycettes, 1976, others. Mem. Nat. Geographic Soc., Cousteau Soc., Duke Alumni Assn., Met. Opera Guild, Am. Soc. Med. Technologists, Internat. Soc. Med. Technologists, Tenn. Soc. Microbiology, Am. Soc. Clin. Pathologists. Methodist. Clubs: Toastmasters, Nat. Commodore, Iron Dukes. Home: 1007 Bentley Cir Gallatin TN 37066 Office: 1310 24th Ave S Nashville TN 37203

ELLIOTT, SUSAN ALBERTA, lawyer, govt. ofcl.; b. Palm Springs, Calif., Mar. 28, 1948; d. William Henry and Ruth Elizabeth (Schureman) Elliott; B.A. magna cum laude, Harvard U., 1970; J.D., Boston U., 1974; m. Jean Pierre Swennen, Oct. 18, 1975; children—Tara, Kimberly. Admitted to D.C. bar, 1975, U.S. Supreme Ct. bar, 1978; asso. Jones, Day, Reavis & Pogue, Washington, 1974-76, Cadwallader, Wickersham & Taft, 1976-78; staff atty. div. advt. practices FTC, 1978-80, dep. asst., 1980-82, asst. dir., 1982—. Mem. Womens Legal Def. Fund, 1974—. Mem. D.C. Bar Assn. Methodist. Office: FTC 1101 Pennsylvania Ave Suite 6117 Washington DC 20580

ELLIS, ALICE MARIE, social worker; b. Mpls., Aug. 12, 1938; d. Walter C. and Jeanette O. Hogenson; student St. Olaf Coll., 1956-59; B.A. in Sociology, Luther Coll., Decorah, Iowa, 1960; m. Thomas K. Ellis, May 25, 1968; children—Lisa, Christian. Social worker Ramsey County Welfare Dept., St. Paul, 1960-62, Children's Home Soc., Montreal, 1963-64, Rochester State Hosp., 1965-69, Manitowoc County Social Services (Wis.), 1969-70; dir. social services Two Rivers (Wis.) Hosp., 1970-72; dir. social services St. John's Hosp., Red Wing, Minn., 1972—. Mem. Battered Women Task Force of Goodhue County (Minn.), 1977—, chairwoman, 1979; vol. adv. battered women, 1977—. Mem. AAUW (pres. Red Wing br. 1978—), Nat. Assn. Hosp. Social Work Dirs., Minn. Council Unmarried Parents (membership chairwoman 1973). Lutheran. Home: 1210 Foursome Red Wing MN 55066 Office: St John's Hosp Red Wing MN 55066

ELLIS, ALICIA ROLLINS, property mgmt. co. exec.; b. Jackson, Miss., Mar. 9, 1926; d. John Russell and Alicia (Farragut) Rollins; B.A., U. Miss., 1949; m. John Connell Ellis, Jr., Feb. 27, 1951; children—Janet, John, Russell, Elizabeth. Tchr., Pass Christian, Miss., 1949-50; researcher New Orleans Port Embarcation, 1950; with Hancock Bank, Bay St. Louis, Miss., 1951-52; contractor Lake Villa Builders, Biloxi and Pass Christian, 1971-73; with Ellis Property Mgmt. Co., Gulfport, Miss., 1973—, v.p., dir. ops., 1975-81, v.p. (semi-ret.), 1981—. Pres., Women's Guild, Trinity Episcopal Ch., Pass Christian, 1977; bd. dirs. Gulf Coast Crime Commn., 1979-81. Mem. Gulf Coast Apts. Assn. (pres. 1979-80), Kappa Delta. Democrat. Clubs: Yacht, Garden. Home: PO Box 34A Pass Christian MS 39571 Office: PO Box 967 Gulfport MS 39501

ELLIS, ANNE LOUISE NOLL (MRS. JOHN THOMAS ELLIS), club woman; b. Wahatchee, Tenn., Apr. 1, 1906; d. William Louis and Annie (Thomas) Noll; A.B., Randolph-Macon Woman's Coll., 1927; cert. Master Sch. Interior Decorating, 1932; m. Joseph Ramer Sawyer, Dec. 31, 1927 (dec. Jan. 1939); children—Joanne Noll (Mrs. Frank Tilden Hayes, Jr.), Mary ELizabeth (Mrs. Frank Alexander Knowles, Jr.); m. 2d, John Thomas Ellis, Feb. 9, 1949. English tchr. Cloverdale High Sch., Montgomery, Ala., 1927; sec. to pres. Huntingdon Coll., Montgomery, 1943-50; part-time interior decorator, Montgomery, 1934-79. Mem. DAR (chpt. regent, 1950-51; state historian, 1962-67; state chmn. motion pictures, 1967-70, state chaplain 1970-73), Daus. Am. Colonists (chpt. regent 1966-69, state chaplain 1967-70, state regent 1970-73, state parliamentarian 1973-76, nat. treas. 1978-82), Colonial Dames Seventeenth Century (state 3d v.p. 1973-75, state 2d v.p. 1975-77, pres. Maj. John Stith chpt. 1975-77), Daus. Colonial Wars (state treas. 1977-80), Magna Charta Dames (corr. sec. 1973-75, 4th v.p. 1976-77, 1st vice regent 1977-79, regent Ala. div. 1979-81), Order First Families of Va., Ala. Hist. Research Soc., Old South Hist. Soc., U.S. Daus. 1812, United Daus. of Confederacy, Ala. Geneal. Soc., Montgomery Geneal. Assn., Randolph-Macon Women's Alumnae (v.p. chpt. 1967-68, pres. 1968-69), Kappa Delta. Address: 3151 Southview Ave Montgomery AL 36106

ELLIS, BETTY LOUISE, credit union exec.; b. Clothier, W.Va., Feb. 21, 1936; d. Floyd Earl and Gladys Alta (Zornes) Reed; diploma gen. bus. Whiting Bus. Coll., Cleve., 1954; m. Roy Monroe Ellis, June 19, 1951; children—Roy Michael. Drema Anne Ellis Allegier. Credit investigator Beneficial Fin. Co., Cleve., 1954-57; clk.-typist Cadillac Glass Co., Cleve., 1959-64; office mgr. Uncle Bill's div. Cook United, Inc., Cleve., 1964-66; treas., mgr. Berea Sch. Employees Credit Union, Middleburgh Heights, Ohio, 1966—, also sec.-treas. bd. dirs. Mem. Credit Union Exec. Soc. Democrat. Club: Order Eastern Stars. Office: 19249 E Bagley Rd Middleburg Heights OH 44130

ELLIS, CAROLYN FAYE, mfg. co. exec.; b. Simpsonville, S.C., Aug. 25, 1935; d. Alvin O. and Eunice M. (Finley) Medlock; student public schs.; m. Donald C. Ellis, July 5, 1957; children—Catherine Denise, Mary Susan. Clk. typist Consol. Electrodynamics Co., Pasadena, Calif., 1957-61; personnel clk. Consol. Systems Corp., Pomona, Calif., 1961-64; personnel asst. SDS Data Systems Corp., Pomona, 1964-67; mgr. human resources aerospace div. Perkin Elmer Corp., Pomona, 1967—. Mem. Nat. Assn. Female Execs., Nat. Notary Assn., San Gabriel Valley Compensation Assn., Pomona Valley Personnel Assn. Office: 2771 N Garey Ave Pomona CA 91767

ELLIS, DOROTHY J. CARPENTER (MRS. GENE GREGORY ELLIS), Realtor; b. Phila., Aug. 20, 1938; d. Alfred Barrett and Dorothy Aiken (Buzby) Carpenter; student Northwestern U., 1956, U. Miami, 1963, DePaul U., 1981—, Harper Jr. Coll., 1979; grad. Realtor Inst., 1970; m. Gene Gregory Ellis, Jan. 24, 1959 (dec. May 1962); children—Theresa, Laura, Kathleen. Saleswoman, Boehmer & Hedlund, Park Ridge, Ill., 1966-68, Baird & Warner, Inc., Des Plaines, Ill., 1968-70; v.p. Rich Port, Realtor, Arlington Heights, Ill., 1970—. Sec. Einstein Elem. Sch. PTA, 1969-71; bd. dirs. Park Ridge YMCA, 1979-81, chmn. resource devel. com., 1979-80; precinct capt., dep. committeeman Elk Grove Twp. Republican Orgn. Cert. residential specialist, real estate brokerage mgr. Mem. Nat. Assn. Realtors (chmn. polit. and local govt. affairs com. of N.W. suburban bd., speaker ann. conv. 1975-80), Ill. Assn. Realtors (chmn. polit. involvement com., chmn. legis. steering com.), Realtors Nat. Mktg. Inst., DAR, Park Ridge, Des Plaines chambers commerce. Episcopalian. Office: 210 W Northwest Hwy Arlington Heights IL 60004

ELLIS, ELIZABETH MUELLER, psychologist; b. Milw.; d. Louis John and Jean (Cunliffe) Mueller; B.A., U. Chgo.; M.A., George Washington U., 1963; Ph.D., U. Md., 1972; m. Daniel M. Friedman, Oct. 18, 1975; children by previous marriage—Elizabeth Ellis, Jonathan Ellis, Benjamin Ellis, Nancy Ellis. Staff psychologist Alexandria (Va.) Community Mental Health Center, 1963-70; pvt. practice clin. psychology, Washington, 1972—; cons. Community Psychiat. Clinic, Bethesda, Md., 1973—. Mem. Am. Psychol. Assn., D.C . Psychol. Assn., Psi Chi.

ELLIS, EVA LILLIAN, artist; b. Seattle, June 4, 1920; d. Carl Martin and Hilda (Persson) Johnson; B.A., U. Wash., 1941; M.A., U. Idaho, 1950; m. Everett Lincoln Ellis, May 1, 1943; children—Karin, Kristy, Hildy, Erik. Asso. dir. art Best & Co., Seattle, 1943; dir. Am. Art Week, Idaho, 1949-55; mem. faculty dept. art U. Idaho, 1946-48; dir., tchr. Children's Art Oreg., 1966-71; exhibitions include: Henry Gallery, U. Wash., 1941, Immanuel Gallery, N.Y.C., 1943-46, U. Mich., 1956-65, Detroit Inst. Art, 1959, Kresge Gallery, 1959-64, Portland Art Mus., 1967, Corvallis Art Center, Oreg., 1966, U. Idaho, 1946-56, U. Canterbury, New Zealand, 1979, Boise Mus., 1949-55, CSA, 1972, 79, Surrey of New Zealand Art, 1979, Shoreline Mus., Seattle, 1981, New Zealand Embassy, London, 1979, Karlshamn Art Soc., Sweden, 1979; represented in permanent collections: U. Calif., Berkeley, U. Wash.; Counselor Cancer Soc.; active Girl Scouts U.S.A. Recipient awards Acad. Art and Sci., 1958-66, Ann Arbor Women Painters, diploma with gold medal, Italian Acad. Art, 1980. Mem. Nat. League Am. Pen Women, Fine Arts Soc. Idaho, Canterbury Soc. Art New Zealand, Alpha Omicron Pi. Clubs: Scandinavian (pres. 1977—), Faculty Wives (pres. 1979). Address: 71 Clifton Terr Christchurch New Zealand

ELLIS, GLORIA BURROW, library dir.; b. Long Branch, N.J., Oct. 30, 1930; d. Robert and Mary Celia (Katz) Burrow; B.A., Rutgers U., 1951; tchr. cert. Wayne State U., 1967, M.S.L.S., 1972; m. Robert Lowell Ellis, Feb. 5, 1956; children—Wendy Lee, Jeffrey B., Richard C. Newspaper reporter, 1951-55; tchr. Hillel Day Sch., Farmington, Mich., 1968-71; librarian Walsh Coll. Accountancy and Bus. Adminstrn., Troy, Mich., 1973—, library dir., 1974—. Mem. ALA, Spl. Libraries Assn., Mich. Library Assn. Club: B'nai B'rith Women (chmn. Midwest region 1978-80, mem. nat. exec. bd. 1982—). Home: 18747 Jeanette Southfield MI 48075 Office: 3838 Livernois Troy MI 48084

ELLIS, MADELEINE BLANCHE, educator; b. North Vancouver, B.C., Can., Mar. 10, 1915; d. George Porter and Lilian (Fitzmaurice) E.; B.A. with honors, U. B.C., 1936, M.A., 1937; postgrad. (French scholar) Bryn Mawr (Pa.) Coll., 1937-38; Ph.D. (French fellow 1938-40), U. Toronto, 1944; Lectr. French, U. Toronto, 1944-46; prof. French, fine arts, humanities Marianopolis Coll., Montreal, Que., Can., 1946—, chmn. modern lang. and lit., 1964-72; prof., chargée de cours Universite de Laval, Que., 1949; lectr. U. Orange Free State, Bloemfontein, South Africa, 1964; lectr. internat. congress McGill U., 1978. Carnegie Found. scholar, 1936-38; Humanities Research Council Can. grantee, 1949. Mem. Société J. J. Rousseau, Société française d'etude du XVIII e siècle, Comité du Montlouis, Am. Soc. Eighteenth-Century Studies, Société Canadienne d'étude du XVIIIe siècle. Roman Catholic. Author: Robert Charbonneau et la creation romanesque, 1948; St-Denys-Garneau: art et realisme, 1949; Julie or La Nouvelle Heloise: A Synthesis of Rousseau's Thought 1749-59, 1949; Rousseau's Venetian Story: An Essay Upon Art and Truth in the Confessions, 1966; Rousseau's Socratic Aemilian Myths: A Literary Collation of Emile and the Social Contract, 1977; Le Nouveau Socrate in Diderot Studies XXI, 1983; collaborator Dictionnaire international des termes littéraires, 1970—; contbr. articles to profl. jours. Office: 3880 Cote-des-Neiges Montreal PQ H3H 1W1 Canada

ELLIS, SUSAN GOTTENBERG, psychologist; b. N.Y.C., Jan. 24, 1949; d. Sam and Sally (Hirschman) Gottenberg; B.S., Cornell U., 1970; M.A., Columbia U., 1971; M.A., Hofstra U., 1975, Ph.D., 1976; m. David Roy Ellis, July 23, 1972; 1 dau., Shanon Rachel. Instr. health edn. Nassau Community Coll., Garden City, N.Y., 1971-73; sch. psychologist public schs., Somerville, N.J., 1976-77; clin. psychologist Somerset County Community Mental Health Center, Somerville, 1976-77; sch. psychologist, Pinellas County, Fla., 1977-78; instr. St. Petersburg (Fla.) Jr. Coll., 1978; clin. psychologist, Largo, Fla., 1977—; cons. Fla. Dept. Health and Rehab. Services, Gables Acad., Fla., Med. Center Hosp., Largo, Morton Plant Hosp., Clearwater, Fla., Health Maintenance Orgn., Fla. N.Y. State Regents scholar, 1966-71. Mem. Am. Psychol. Assn., Fla. Psychol. Assn., Pinellas Psychol. Assn. (treas. 1978, polit. action chairperson 1979), Mental Health Assn. Pinellas County, Kappa Delta Pi. Club: Cornell U. Suncoast (v.p. 1979-80). Home: 1904 Oakdale Ln North Clearwater FL 33516 Office: 2499 East Bay Drive Suite 103 Largo FL 33541

ELLIS, ZENA SAYLOR, reading specialist; b. Molus, Ky., Mar. 12, 1922; d. John P. and Flora (Howard) Saylor; A.B., Union Coll., 1957; m. Joseph J. Ellis, Mar. 16, 1946; 1 dau., Linda Jo. Tchr., Harlan (Ky.) Ind. Sch., 1956, Pontiac (Mich.) Schs., 1957, Harlan County (Ky.) Sch. System, 1958—. Mem. NEA, Ky. Edn. Assn., Upper Cumberland Edn. Assn., Harlan County Edn. Assn.

ELLISON, MARCIA MANSFIELD, interior designer, photographer; b. Chgo., Jan. 24, 1946; d. Sheldon E. and Marcia E. (Segal) Berkson; A.A., Stephens Coll., Columbia, Mo., 1965; B.Ed., Nat. Coll. Edn., Evanston, Ill., 1967; M.A., Northwestern U., 1967; grad. Chgo. Real Estate Sch., 1973; m. Stuart H. Ellison, May 26, 1977; children—Robert, Jon, Adam. Tchr. schs. in Ill., 1967-75; saleswoman Ringer Realty, Highland Park, Ill., 1973; with Lord & Taylor, Northbrook, Ill., 1976-77; lic. practical nurse to doctor, Highland Park, 1977-78; model, actress, 1967-78; owner Pandy Enterprises, Ltd., Glencoe, Ill., 1978—. Mem. jr. bd. Highland Park Hosp., 1979-81; mem. jr. com. Michael Reese Hosp., Chgo., 1979-82. Jewish. Address: 537 Greenleaf Ave Glencoe IL 60022

ELLISTON, LURA DUFF, II, designer, poet; b. Ft. Worth, July 20, 1933; d. Fred Addison and Lura Duff (Elliston) M.; student Duke, 1951-52, U. Tex., 1952-54; children—Edward Duff Nowotny, George Edward Nowotny, III, Addison Dance Nowotny. Owner, Interiors, Ltd., Ft. Smith, Ark., 1975—; pres. Elliston Investments, 1974—, The Mulberry Bush Inc., 1979-82, Duff Devel., 1982—. Dir. Sebastian County Mental Health Assn., 1963-69, Ark. Assn. Mental Health, 1966-72; gov. Western Ark. Counseling and Guidance Center, 1969-74; bd. dirs. Spark's Hosp. Guild, 1964-70, 71-73, pres., 1973; bd. dirs. Concert Assn., 1968-72; pres. Ft. Smith Affiliation of the Arts, 1968; co-founder J.E. Duff Scholarship Fund, Tex. A. and M. U., 1960—; co-chmn. arts festivals, 1964, 65, 70; leadership cons. Nat. Assn. Retarded Children, 1968-69; mem. Retardation Com. State Health Planning, 1968-69, Human Relations Council, 1967-69; area chmn. Council on Children's Emotional Health, 1974. Committeewoman Republican 3d Congl. Dist., 1962-64, 68-70, vice chmn., 1976-78; charter mem. County Rep. Women, 1961-72; co-chmn. Rep. United Campaign, 1962; sec. Rep. State Conv., 1968; justice of peace, 1973-74. Life trustee Old Fort Museum, 1968, pres., 1970-72; mem. adv. bd. St. Edward's Mercy Hosp., 1967-69; trustee, v.p., treas. St. John's Sch. for Children with Learning Disabilities, 1971-75; bd. govs. Juvenile Detention Center of Sebastian County, 1974-75; chmn. Ft. Smith Art Center Antique Show, 1978; art juror Ft. Chaffee Cuban Art Competition, 1980. Recipient first place lyric poetry award Ark. Arts Festival, 1968, Orchid award Ft. Smith Pride, 1981; Hon. Girl award Ft. Smith Girl's Club, 1978; named One of Outstanding Young Women of Am., 1966. One of 100 Women of Achievement, Ark. Presswomen, 1980; Ark. finalist Good Housekeeping's Gt. Quilts of Am., 1978; designer Award-Winning Stores, Retail Mchts. Assn., 1981. Mem. La. Ind. Producers and Royalty Owners, Jr. League Ft. Smith, D.A.R., C. of C., Delta Delta Delta. Episcopalian (chmn. altar guild 1967, 70, pres. ch. women 1961-62). Clubs: Ft. Smith, Ft. Smith Town, Hardscrabble Country. Founder, designer Ft. Smith Children's Museumobile, 1965; author vol. art enrichment program Ft. Smith Pub. Schs., 1969, design concept miniparks City of Ft. Smith, 1972; author: New Look Trio, 1970. Home: 4106 S 25th St Fort Smith AR 72903 Office: 1 Old Town Fort Smith AR 72913

ELLMANN, SHEILA FRENKEL, investment co. exec.; b. Detroit, June 8, 1931; d. Joseph and Rose (Neback) Frenkel; B.A. in English, U. Mich., 1953; m. William M. Ellmann, Nov. 1, 1953; children—Douglas Stanley, Carol Elizabeth, Robert Lawrence. Dir. Advance Glove Mfg. Co., Detroit, 1954-78; v.p. Frome Investment Co., Detroit, 1980—. Mem. U. Mich. Alumni Assn. Home: 28000 Weymouth St Farmington Hills MI 48018

ELLNER, CORNELIA JOHNS, clin. microbiologist; b. New Haven, July 26, 1941; d. Cornelius R. and Pauline (Korn) Johns; B.A. in Biology with honors (scholar), Wheaton Coll., 1963; M.S. in Clin. Microbiology, Columbia U. Coll. Physicians and Surgeons, 1976; m. Paul D. Ellner, Jan. 15, 1965; children—David Charles, Jonathan Bennett. Technologist diagnostic microbiology service Presbyn. Hosp., N.Y.C., 1964-65, supr. diagnostic microbiology service, 1967-68; supr. microbiology lab. Columbus Hosp., N.Y.C., 1966-67; asst. dir. microbiology lab. Roosevelt Hosp., N.Y.C., 1968-69; supr. microbiology lab. St. Agnes Hosp., White Plains, N.Y., 1970—; mem. infection com. Roosevelt Hosp., 1968, St. Agnes Hosp., 1970; lectr. clin. microbiology to pathology residents, 1972. USPHS grad. fellow, 1963-66. Mem. Am. Soc. Microbiology. Republican. Home: 4 Little Ln White Plains NY 10605 Office: St Agnes Hosp 311 North St White Plains NY 10605

ELLSWEIG, PHYLLIS LEAH, psychotherapist; b. Irvington, N.J., Apr. 19, 1927; d. Sumar and Jeanette (Geffner) Schwartz; B.S., East Stroudsburg (Pa.) State Coll., 1947; Ed.M., Lehigh U., 1966, Ed.D., 1972; m. Martin Richard Ellsweig, Dec. 25, 1947; children—Bruce, Steven. Tchr., Stroud Union High Sch., 1963-66; guidance counselor East Stroudsburg Schs., 1966-68; asst. prof. edn. East Stroudsburg State Coll., 1968; staff psychologist, outpatient supr. Mental Health Center Carbon, Monroe and Pike Counties, Stroudsburg, 1968—; pvt. practice, 1969—. Pub. speaker, cons. to schs., orgns.; mem. staff Gen. Hosp. Monroe County, East Stroudsburg. Mem. Am., Eastern, Pa. psychol. assns., Am. Acad. Psychotherapists, Am. Group Psychotherapy Assn., Am. Soc. Clin. Hypnosis, Internat. Soc. Hypnosis, NOW (profl. cons. 1973—), Internat. Assn. Group Psychotherapy. Home: 58 S Green St East Stroudsburg PA 18301 Office: 322 Park Ave Stroudsburg PA 18360

ELLZEY, JOANNE TONTZ, biologist; b. Balt., Mar. 23, 1931; d. E. Logan and Charlotte (Mullikin) Tontz; B.A., Randolph-Macon Woman's Coll., 1959; M.A. in Zoology, U. N.C., 1963; Ph.D. in Botany and Cell Biology, U. Tex., 1969; m. M. Lawrence Ellzey, Jr., Jan. 25, 1969. Teaching asst. Randolph-Macon Woman's Coll., 1956-59, U. N.C., Chapel Hill, 1959-62; instr. U. N.C., Greensboro, 1962-64;. NIH trainee Cell Research Inst., U. Tex., Austin, 1964-69; asst. prof. biol. scis. U. Tex., El Paso, 1969-75, assoc. prof., 1975—, dir. Ultrastructure Lab., 1973—, chmn. biol. scis. honor program, 1981, adv. provisional students, 1981—. Mem. adminstrv. bd. Western Hills United Meth. Ch., 1972—, adult church sch. tchr., 1972-81; chmn. Wesley Found. Adminstrv. Bd., 1979-82. Mem. Mycol. Soc. Am., Microbiol. Soc. Am., Electron Microscopy Soc. Am., Tex. Soc. Electron Microscopy, AAAS, Sigma Xi (treas. U. Tex. El Paso chpt. 1980—), Beta Beta Beta. Democrat. Contbr. articles on electron microscopy to profl. jours. Home: 310 Olivia Circle El Paso TX 79912 Office: Biological Sciences Univ Texas El Paso TX 79968

ELMORE, ANNIE SUE, home economist; b. Elba, Ala., June 7, 1928; d. Robert Walton and Annie Mae (White) E.; B.S., Ala. Coll., 1950; M.S., U. Tenn., 1959. Tchr. home econs. and supr. lunchroom Lauderdale County (Ala.) Public Schs., 1950-52; tchr. sci. Hawkinsville (Ga.) Public Schs., 1952-53; asst. home agt., Gadsden, Ala., 1953-55, Florence, Ala., 1955-57, Guntersville, Ala., 1957, Dothan, Ala., 1957-60; home agt. and dir. home econs. program Coop. Extension Service, Wauchula, Fla., 1960-61, extension home econs. agt., Chipley, 1961—. Chmn., Heart Fund Drive, Chipley, 1970-72; info. officer Am. Cancer Soc., Chipley, 1978-79; chmn. Fla. Heart Assn., 1970-73, co-chmn., 1973-74. Mem. Nat. Assn. Extension Home Economists, Fla. Assn. Extension Home Econs. Agts. (dist. dir. 1964-66, 81-82), Epsilon Sigma Phi. Baptist. Contbr. articles on home econs. to profl. publs. Home: 106 Forrest Chipley FL 32428 Office: 800 Hwy 90 Chipley FL 32428

ELNICKI, JUDITH SHANNON, pay TV co. exec.; b. Omaha, Nov. 14, 1942; d. Lewis Raymond and Grace Helen (Connell) Shannon; A.A., U. Detroit, 1963, postgrad. 1964-66; B.S. B.A., Am. U., 1975; 1 son, Eric Shannon. Mgr. shareholder relations COMSAT, Washington, 1975-77, mgr. media relations, 1977-79, dir. public relations, 1979-80; v.p. public affairs Satellite TV Corp., Washington, 1980—. Mem. Public Relations Soc. Am., Am. Women in Radio and TV, Women in Cable, Washington Women in Public Relations. Roman Catholic. Club: Washington Cable, Nat. Press. Office: 1301 Pennsylvania Ave NW Suite 1201 Washington DC 20004

ELROD, LINDA DIANE HENRY, lawyer; b. Topeka, Kans., Mar. 6, 1947; d. Lyndus Arthur Henry and Marjorie Jane (Hammel Allen; student U. Copenhagen, 1967; B.A. with departmental honors, Washburn U., 1969, J.D. cum laude, 1971; m. Mark Douglas Elrod, June 5, 1971; children—Carson Douglas, Bree Elizabeth. Tchr. English, Topeka, Kans., 1969-71; research asst. for city atty., Topeka, 1970; admitted to Kans. bar, 1972; research asst. for Kans. Jud. Council, 1972-74; prof. law Washburn U., Topeka, 1974—, William O. Douglas disting. prof., 1978-79; practice law, Topeka. Republican precinct committeewoman, Topeka, 1972-73; bd. dirs. YWCA, 1978—, chmn. health, phys. edn. and recreation com., 1979—, exec. bd., 1981-82, pres., 1982—; bd. dirs. Colonial Park Townhouses, Inc., 1972-73, Univ. Child Devel., 1976-78. Mem. Am., Kans., Topeka (mem. exec. bd., 1977—, sec. 1980—, chmn. title standards com., program com.) bar assns., Washburn Alumni Assn. Women Lawyers Assn., Washburn Law Sch. Assn. (exec. sec. 1978—, editor The Circuit Rider), Shawnee County Hist. Soc., Friends of Topeka Zoo, Kappa Alpha Theta (adv. bd.), Phi Alpha Delta (pres. 1974-75, bd. dirs. 1975—), Phi Kappa Phi. Presbyterian. Clubs: Bridge, Channel 11. Contbr. articles to legal jours. Home: 231 Edgewood St Topeka KS 66606 Office: Washburn Univ of Topeka Topeka KS 66621

EL SAFFAR, RUTH SNODGRASS, educator; b. N.Y.C., June 12, 1941; d. John Tabb and Ruth (Wheelwright) Snodgrass; B.A., Colo. Coll., 1962; Ph.D., Johns Hopkins U., 1966; m. Zuhair M. El Saffar, Apr. 11, 1965; children—Ali, Dena, Amir. Instr. Spanish, Johns Hopkins U., 1963-65; instr. English, Univ. Coll. Baghdad, 1966-67; asst. prof. Spanish, U. Md., Balt. County, 1967-68; asst. prof. U. Ill., Chgo. Circle, 1968-73, asso. prof., 1973-78, prof., 1978—; Nat. Endowment for Humanities summer seminar dir., 1979, 82. Woodrow Wilson fellow, 1962; Nat. Endowment for Humanities fellow, 1970-71; Guggenheim fellow, 1975-76; Am. Council Learned Socs. grantee, 1978; Newberry Library fellow, 1982. Mem. MLA (exec. council 1974-78), Am. Assn. Tchrs. Spanish and Portuguese, Midwest MLA. Author: Novel to Romance: A Study of Cervantes' Novelas Ejemplares, 1974; Distance and Control in Don Quixote, 1975; Cervantes' Casamiento engañoso and Coloquio de los perros, 1976. Home: 7811 Greenfield River Forest IL 60305 Office: Dept Spanish U Ill Chicago IL 60680

ELSBURY, ELLEN MARIE, hosp. exec.; b. Osage, Iowa, Sept. 4, 1944; d. Jack Matthew and Ruth Ellen (Cordes) Conklin; R.N., St. Joseph Mercy Sch. Nursing, Mason City, Iowa, 1965; B.A. with distinction, U. Redlands (Calif.), 1977; M.B.A., U. Calif., Riverside, 1979; 1 dau., Tanya Marie. Adminstrv. cons. Sunlite Med. Centers, Inc., 1966-70; dir. nurses Am. West, 1970-72, Loma Linda (Calif.) Community Hosp., 1972-74; dir. dept. infection control San Bernadino County (Calif.) Med. Center, 1974-78; self-employed cons., lectr., 1978-79; v.p. Allen Meml. Hosp., Waterloo, Iowa, 1979—; mem. nursing program, emergency med. services adv. coms. Hawkeye Inst. Tech., Waterloo; adv. com. Allem Meml. Hosp. Sch. Nursing; cons. in field. Mem. Am. Nurses Assn., Am. Soc. Nursing Services Adminstrs., Nat. Assn. Female Execs., Assn. Practitioners Infection Control, Iowa Nurses Assn., Iowa Hosp. Assn., Nursing Alumnae Assn. St. Joseph Mercy Sch. Nursing. Republican. Lutheran. Office: 1825 Logan Ave Waterloo IA 50703

ELSEA, PAULINE SAPPINGTON, civic worker, clubwoman; b. Arrow Rock, Mo., Aug. 5, 1906; d. Cardwell Wyan and May (Hupp) Sappington; A.A., Columbia Coll., 1926; student piano Missouri Valley Coll., 1922-24; m. Charles Wayne Elsea, June 19, 1926; children—Kathryn May Elsea Pile, Charles Wayne (dec.). Trustee, Columbia Coll., 1971-73, nat. fund chmn., 1965-71, bd. nat. alumnae assn., 1965-73; reporter Friends of Arrow Rock, 1960-73; tour chmn. Frontier Nursing Service, Nat. Soc. Daus. Colonial Wars, 1972, 78; mem. bd. Arrow Rock Lyceum; vice commr. Marshall council Girl Scouts U.S.A., 1946-52; mem. bldg. com. Covenant Presbyn. Ch., Marshall, Mo., 1965-70. Mem. Mo. Hist. Soc., Saline County Hist. Soc., Magna Charta Dames, Order Ams. Armorial Ancestory, Order Physicians and Chirurgeons, Colonial Dames Am. (past treas. chpt. XIII), Daus. Colonial Wars (Mo. sec. 1965-68, pres. 1968-71, 1st v.p. nat. soc. 1971-74, nat. pres. 1974-77, pres. Nat. Officers Club 1980—), Nat. Gavel Soc., DAR (regent Marshall chpt. 1954-56, state historian Mo. 1950-52, 78-80, pres. state officers club 1962-65, organising sec. 1980-82, nat. vice chmn. Am. heritage South Central div. 1971-74, nat. vice chmn. South Central div. DAR Friends of Mus. 1977-80), Children Am. Revolution (sr. state pres. Mo. 1946-48, nat. promoter, investor state prom, mem. Nat. Officers Club), PEO (vice chmn. state conv. 1966). Democrat. Clubs: Monday (pres. 1950-51). Home: 1904 S Odell Ave Marshall MO 65340

ELSON, CAROLYN ANDERSON, hosp. adminstr.; b. Ray, Ariz., Aug. 13, 1949; d. John Reginald and Lucille Annette (Steinke) A.; B.S., Baylor U., 1971; M.S., Ariz. State U., 1976; m. James Robert Elson, June 26, 1971. Asst. v.p. outpatient services. Phoenix Baptist Hosp., 1976-77, v.p. ops., 1978-80, exec. v.p. corp. planning mktg. and edn., 1980-81, exec. v.p., chief operating officer, 1981—. Mem. Am. Acad. Med. Adminstrs., Am. Coll. Hosp. Adminstrs., Phoenix Regional Hosp. Council, Ariz. Hosp. Assn., Beta Gamma Sigma. Home: 12599 E Silver Spur Scottsdale AZ 85259 Office: 6025 N 20th Ave Phoenix AZ 85015

ELSTON, JEANNINE NEWTON, banker; b. Shreveport, La., Oct. 1, 1930; d. Chester Arthur and Edith Cecile (Shelby) Newton; student Northwestern State U., 1946-48, Norton Bus. Coll., 1949-50; m. Raymond Lee Elston, May 12, 1951. Consumer credit investigator First Nat. Bank, Shreveport, 1950-52; with Tex. A&M Engring. Sch., 1953-54; with First National Bank, Shreveport, 1955—, sr. fin. analyst, 1975-77, asst. vice-pres., 1978—, asst. mgr. comml. credit, 1978-81, mgr. consumer credit div., 1981—. Active Shreveport Symphony Fund Drive, 1979. Mem. Am. Inst. Banking, Nat. Assn. Bank Women, Robert Morris Assos., Shreveport C. of C. Clubs: Quarter Century (pres.), Shreveport Wholesale Credit. Office: 400 Texas St Shreveport LA 71154

ELVEBACK, LILLIAN ROSE, statistician; b. Sidney, Mont., Dec. 5, 1915; d. Jay Nelson and Rose Agnes (Dame) E.; B.A., U. Minn., 1941, Ph.D. (Mayo Found. fellow), 1955; M.A., Columbia U., 1948. Instr. math. U. Minn., 1943-44; tech. aide Nat. Def. Research Council, 1944-45; instr. biostats. Columbia U., 1946-50; lectr. biostats. U. Minn., 1950-55, assoc. prof., 1955-58; head, stats. sect. Pub. Health Research Inst., N.Y.C., 1960-65; lectr. preventive medicine N.Y. U. Med. Sch., N.Y.C., 1960-65; prof. biostats. Mayo Med. Sch., Rochester, Minn., 1965—; cons. sect. med. research stats. Mayo Clinic, 1965—. Fellow Am. Pub. Health Assn., Am. Statis. Assn.; mem. Biometric Soc., Inst. Math. Stats., Am. Statis. Assn., AAAS, Am. Epidemiologic Soc., Am. Coll. Epidemiology (dir. 1981—), Soc. Epidemiologic Research. Author: (with J. P. Fox and C. R. Hall) Epidemiology: Man and Disease, 1970; mem. editorial bd. Am. Jour. Epidemiology, 1976-79. Home: 512 13th St NE Rochester MN 55901 Office: 200 1st St SW Rochester MN 55905

ELVIDGE, VIVIAN PATRICIA, mus. dir.; b. Okanogan, Wash., Jan. 6, 1940; d. Floyd Kenneth and Martha Grace (Hinshaw) Byrd; A.B., Bellevue Community Coll., 1974; B.A. cum laude in Anthropology, U. Wash., 1977, M.A. cum laude in Anthropology, 1980; m. Robert Fred Elvidge, Dec. 26, 1962; 1 dau., Janice April. Vol. coordinator Marymoor Mus., Redmond, Wash., 1979, curator, 1978-80, dir., 1980—. Mem. Am. Assn. of Mus., Wash. Mus. Assn., Am. Assn. for State and Local History, Phi Beta Kappa. Methodist. Author: Redmond Historic Tour Guide, 1981; Report on Collections, Marymoor Mus.: Lace Collection, 1979, Indian Artifacts, 1978. Home: 17511 Avondale Rd Woodinville WA 98072 Office: PO Box 162 6046 W Lake Sammamish Pkwy Redmond WA 98052

ELWELL, ELLEN C., sales tng. co. exec.; b. Jacksonville, Fla., July 7, 1945; d. Merrill K. and Hermine (Chalfin) Cohen; B.A., U. Mich., 1967; M.A., N.Y.U., U. Ill., 1968; m. John Lee Elwell, Feb. 10, 1968; 1 dau., Melissa Mae. Advanced mktg. support rep. IBM, Oklahoma City, 1969-73, program planner/designer sales tng. programs, Dallas, 1973-79; owner, operator Elwell Assos., Inc., Dallas, 1979—; dir. Indsl. Catering Co., Indpls. Recipient Outstanding Contbn. award IBM, 1976. Mem. Am. Soc. Tng. and Devel., Am. Soc. Profl. Cons., Am. Mgmt. Assn. Club: 2001 (Dallas). Author numerous corp. tng. books, 1976—. Home and Office: 7230 Briarmeadow St Dallas TX 75230

ELWES, POLLY, journalist; b. London, Feb. 29, 1928; d. Richard and (Mary) Freya (Sykes) E.; student Central Sch. Drama, London, 1948-51; m. Peter Dimmock, Dec. 3, 1960; children—Amanda, Christina, Freya. Actress, BBC-TV dramas, 1951, Windsor Repertory Co., 1952-54; appeared in For Better, For Worse, London, 1954; hostess, presenter, journalist BBC-TV, 1956—; reporter news mag. Tonight, 1960-77; weekly columnist London Evening News, 1974-75; panelist What's My Line, Face The Music, others; producer, presenter Internat. Brit. Hour, Tele-Monte Carlo Monaco, 1980; lectr. on TV, beauty care, poetry. Recipient Silver cup poetry reading Central Sch. Speech and Drama, 1949. Mem. Nat. Union Journalists, Actors Equity. Conservative. Roman Catholic. Author: Lets Fact It, Vol. 1, 1974, Vol. 2, 1975; also articles. Home: 40 Central Park S New York NY 10019 Office: care ABC Le Mirabeau 1307 Monte Carlo Monaco

ELWOOD, NANCY C., lawyer; b. Annapolis, Md., Feb. 21, 1952; d. Hugh McJunkin and Harriet Mildred (Theobald) Elwood; student U. Denver, 1970-71; B.A., George Washington U., 1975; J.D., Cath. U. Am., 1980; postgrad. Georgetown U., 1980—. Bilingual paralegal asst. Joel H. Skirble, Washington, 1975; caseworker Hon. Thomas E. Morgan, U.S. Ho. of Reps., 1975-76; legis. asst., corr. Hon. George E. Danielson, U.S. Ho. of Reps., 1977-79; legis. asst. Hon. James T. Broyhill, U.S. Ho. of Reps., 1979-81; admitted to D.C. bar; legis. dir., counsel Hon. W. Eugene Johnston, U.S. Ho. of Reps., 1981—. Mem. Am. Bar Assn., D.C. Bar Assn., D.C. Womens Bar Assn. Club: Capitol Hill Equestrian. Office: W Eugene Johnston US House of Representives 128 Cannon Washington DC 20003

EMAN, EVELYN KAY, communications co. exec.; b. N.Y.C., Dec. 31, 1949; d. John and Gay (Simon) Eman; student HB Studio, N.Y.C., 1967-68, N.Y.U., 1975-76, Baruch Coll., 1981-82. Asst. mgr. Vanderbilt Athletic Club, N.Y.C., 1967-68; public relations mgr. DEC Enterprises, Inc., N.Y.C., 1968-73; exec. interviewer Dun & Bradstreet, Inc., N.Y.C., 1974; public relations rep. Parsons & Whittemore, Inc., N.Y.C., 1974-77; corp. mgr. public relations NEC Am., Inc., Melville, N.Y., 1977—. Mem. Huntington Twp. C. of C., Internat. Assn. Bus. Communicators, Japan Soc., Long Island Assn., Public Relations Soc. Am., Publicity Club of N.Y. (cert. of merit 1976-77), Internat. Platform Assn., Women in Communications. Composer: Face Another Day, 1973, Songbird, 1973; Hey Mister, 1974, There's the Man, 1973, In the Morning, 1974, It's Never Been Like This, 1974. Contbg. editor PR Essay, 1976-77; contbr. articles to profl. jours. Office: 532 Broad Hollow Rd Melville NY 11747

EMANAVIN, DIANA CHRISTENE, state ofcl.; b. Chgo., Dec. 9, 1947; d. Forrest and Elizabeth Modesta (Panalle) McCool; B.S. in Ops. Research, U. So. Calif., 1975; M.B.A. (Dean's scholar), Golden Gate U., San Francisco, 1980; m. Chaiyuth Emanavin, Apr. 7, 1969; children—Darrine, Chaeny. Mgmt. analyst Calif. Dept. Transp., 1969-75; dir. strategic planning Calif. Franchise Tax Bd., 1975—. Mem. Folsom-Cordova Adult Sch. Adv. Com., 1981. Mem. Corp. Planners Assn., Planning Execs. Inst. Home: 10407 Ambassador Dr Rancho Cordova CA 95670 Office: Franchise Tax Bd PO Box 1468 Sacramento CA 95807

EMANUEL, HELENE RICH, musician, educator; b. N.Y.C., Mar. 31, 1926; d. Irving Wolf and Annette (Moskowitz) Rich; B.A., U. Mich., 1947; J.D., Cardozo Schl. of Law, Yeshiva U., 1982; m. Paul Emanuel, 1950; children—Irene, Carol, Ruth. Chmn. bd. N.J. Fedn. Music Clubs, mem. legis. action com.; trustee Bergen Philharm.; adjudicator N.J. Fed. Festivals; French horn player U. Mich. Concert Band, 1945-47, Bklyn. Philharm., 1948; pvt. tchr. of piano, 1948—; jud. clerkship Morris Malech, Superior Ct., Bergen City, N.J.; tchr. folk dance Bklyn. youth groups, 1948-50; composer, dir. confirmation programs, North Bergen, N.J., 1954-59; choir dir. Temple Israel, Cliffside Park, N.J., 1954-57, Bergenfield (N.J.) Jewish Center, 1960-62. Chmn. Bklyn Jewish Music Festival, 1949; children's concerts Bergen County YMHA, 1977. Recipient award Music Edn. League, 1936; Founder's medal Theodore Roosevelt Soc., 1938; scholar Brandeis Camp Inst., 1949. Mem. Bklyn. Music Tchrs. Guild, Profl. Music Tchrs. Assn., Interstate Music Tchrs. Assn. Co-author: Tercentenary History of Jews, 1954. Address: 468 Churchill Rd Teaneck NJ 07666

EMBRY, JUDY KAY, cons./researcher; b. Polk County, Ark., Jan. 30, 1951; d. George R. and Irene K. (Brewer) E.; B.A., Ark. Tech. U., 1973; M.S. in Psychology, Tex. A&M U., 1975; m. Robert Nininger, Dec. 21, lectr. in psychology Tex. A&M U., 1975-76; instr. in psychology Francis Marion Coll., 1976-77; head dept. human services Florence (S.C.)-Darlington Tech. Coll., 1977-79; head dept. gen. studies Wilson County Tech. Inst., 1979-80, researcher, 1980—; asso. Center for Stress Mgmt. and Personal Assessment, Raleigh, N.C., 1980. Mem. AAUP, Psi Chi (past chpt. pres.). Club: YWCA (Raleigh). Home: 4670 Grinding Stone Dr Raleigh NC 27604

EMBRY, SANDRA WALTERS, radio supply co. exec.; b. Independence, Mo., June 25, 1938; d. William J. and Elizabeth Louise (Owen) Walters; B.S., U. Kans., 1958; postgrad. U. Mo., Kansas City, 1958-61; m. Ben T. Embry, Jr., Feb. 2, 1963; children—Elizabeth, Ellen, William, Benjamin. Head technician Open Heart Surgery Lab., St. Luke's Hosp., Kansas City, 1961-63; with Walters Radio Supply, Inc., Kansas City, Mo., 1963—, exec. v.p., sec.-treas., 1965—. Treas., Kansas City (Mo.) Jr. League, 1973-74, bd. dirs., 1972-74; bd. dirs. Kansas City Philharm., 1970-74; pres. Alumni Assn. of Barstow Sch., 1971-72, Jr. Women's Philharm., 1972-73; bd. govs. Am. Heart Assn., 1978-79. Mem. Nat. Electronic Distbrs. Assn. Republican. Episcopalian. Clubs: The River, Kansas City Country, Minnesouri. Home: 5406 State Line Rd Mission Hills KS 66208 Office: 3635 Main St Kansas City MO 64111

EMBURY, SHEILA BARBARA, Canadian provincial legislator, nurse; b. Calgary, Alta., Can., June 6, 1931; d. Herbert Leonard and Beatrice Mary (Taffler) Pease; R.N. diploma Calgary Gen. Hosp. Sch. Nursing, 1953; diploma in teaching and supervision U. Alta. Sch. Nursing, Edmonton, 1955, B.Sc. in Nursing, 1971; postgrad. in ednl. psychology U. Calgary, 1974-75; m. David Edward Embury, June 4, 1955; children—Barbara Lynn, James Edward. Mem. faculty Calgary Gen. Hosp. Sch. Nursing, 1953-54, 55-56; gen. staff nurse med. ward Vancouver (B.C., Can.) Gen. Hosp., 1954; gen. staff nurse, emergency dept. Peace River (Alta.) Mcpl. Hosp., 1964-66; gen. staff nurse, med. ward Royal Alexandra Hosp., Edmonton, 1967; mem. nursing res. Foothills Hosp., Calgary, 1969-71; clin. instr. Sch. Nursing, U. Calgary, 1971-72, profl. asso., 1972-73, asst. prof. nursing, 1973-74, asst. prof. Faculty Nursing, 1974-79, research asso., 1980-81; mem. Legis. Assembly Alta., Edmonton, 1979—, chmn. health and social services; lectr. on politics and health issues. Pres., Calgary West Progressive Conservative Provincial Constituency Assn., 1977-78; bd. dirs. Alta. Housing Corp. Mem. Internat. Council Nurses, Can. Nurses' Assn., Alta. Assn. RNs (v.p. North Dist. 1966-67, mem. South Central Exec. 1970-71, 78-79), Can. Assn. Univ. Schs. Nursing, Can. Nurses' Found. Home: 1204 Varsity Estates Rd NW Calgary AB T3B 2X2 Canada

EMERLING, CAROL G., mfg. co. exec.; b. Cleve., Sept. 13, 1930; d. Bernard and Florence A. Greenbaum; student Vassar Coll., 1948-49; student Case Western Res. U., 1949-50; LL.B. summa cum laude, Cleve. State U., 1955; m. Norton H. Noll, 1950 (dec.); m. 2d, Stanley J. Emerling, 1953 (div. 1971); children—Keith S., Susan C.; m. 3d, Jerrold A. Fadem, 1974 (dissolved 1978). Admitted to Ohio bar, 1955, Calif. bar, 1975, N.Y. bar, 1982; staff atty. Legal Aid Defenders Office, Cleve., 1962-69, atty. in charge, 1969-70; regional dir. FTC, Cleve., 1970-74, Los Angeles, 1974-78; corp. sec. Am. Home Products Corp., N.Y.C., 1978—; mem. adv. com. on rules of criminal procedure Supreme Ct. Ohio, 1970-73. Sec., Pepper Pike (Ohio) Charter Commn., 1966. Recipient Legal Aid Soc. Claude E. Clarke award, 1967; FTC Disting. Service award, 1972. Mem. Assn. Bar City N.Y., Am. Bar Assn., Women's Forum Inc. Republican. Jewish. Author: (with Eugene O. Jonckers) The Allergy Cookbook, 1969; contbr. articles to legal jours. Office: 685 3d Ave New York NY 10017

EMERS, SANDRA LAVERNE, computer software engr.; b. L.I., N.Y., Nov. 13, 1952; d. Thomas Oscar and Agnes (Kuntz) Emers; A.S. in Computer Programming, Brevard Community Coll., 1973; B.S. in Computer Sci., Fla. Technol. U., 1977. Asso. programmer Sperry Univac Tech. Services Div., Orlando, Fla., 1977-78; sr. software engr. Harris Corp. Controls Div., Melbourne, Fla., 1979—. Mem. Assn. Computing Machinery, Audubon Soc. Democrat. Roman Catholic. Home: 1500 Virginia Dr Melbourne FL 32935 Office: Controls Div Harris Corp PO Box 430 Melbourne FL 32901

EMERSON, ALICE FREY, coll. pres.; b. Durham, N.C., Oct. 26, 1931; d. Alexander Hamilton and Alice (Hubbard) Frey; A.B., Vassar Coll., 1953; Ph.D., Bryn Mawr Coll., 1964; div.; children—Rebecca, Peter. Tchr., Newton (Mass.) High Sch., 1956-58; mem. faculty Bryn Mawr (Pa.) Coll., 1961-64; mem. faculty U. Pa., Phila., 1966-75, asst. prof. polit. sci., 1967-75, dean women, 1966-69, dean students, 1969-75; pres. Wheaton Coll., Norton, Mass., 1975—; dir. 1st Nat. Boston Corp., 1st Nat. Bank Boston; trustee Penn Mut. Life Ins. Co.; adv. bd. HERS Mid Atlantic. Mem. vis. com. on athletics Harvard U., 1975-79; mem. com. on coll. athletics Am. Council on Edn., 1979—, mem. nominating com., 1980-81; pres. New Eng. Colls. Fund, 1978-80; trustee Vassar Coll., 1978—, Sturdy Meml. Hosp. Mem. New Eng. Concerns Group, Am. Polit. Sci. Assn., AAUP, Americal Council Edn., Women's Coll. Coalition (exec. com. 1980—). Mem. adv. bd. Ednl. Record, 1980—, Wharton mag., 1980—. Office: Office of Pres Wheaton Coll Norton MA 02766 *

EMERSON, ANDI (MRS. EMERSON WEEKS), sales and advt. exec.; b. N.Y.C.; d. Willard Ingham and Ethel (Mole) E.; student Barnard Coll.; m. George G. Fawcett, Jr. (div.); children—Ann Emerson II, George Gifford III, Christopher Babcock; m. 2d, Kenneth E. Weeks; 1 dau., Electra Ingham. Pres., Emerson Assos., Inc., N.Y.C.; exec. v.p., partner Eugene Stevens, Inc., N.Y.C.; pres. Emerson-Weeks, Inc., N.Y.C., 1960-74; pres., dir. Emerson-Weeks & Fawcett Corp., 1974-78, Mail Order Operating Co. Ltd., London and N.Y.C., Ingham Hall Ltd., 1977—, Emerson Mktg. Agy. Inc., N.Y.C., 1979—; dir. House of Stewart, Inc.; instr. N.Y. U., 1960-65. Block chmn. fund raising ARC, Multiple Sclerosis, Nat. Found., Crippled Children, Found. for Blind, 1954-63; vol. worker Children's Ward, Meml. Hosp., 1964-66, Hosp. Spl. Surgery, 1967; mem. adv. com. African Students League, 1965-67; bd. dirs. Violet Oakley Meml. Found., Phila., 1964—. Mem. Direct Mail Mktg. Assn., Sales Promotion Execs., Direct Mktg. Creative Guild (pres. 1975—), Mktg. Execs. Club, Mail Order Profls. Group, Soc. Profl. Writers, N.Y.C. Advt. Club, Hundred Million Club (treas. 1960-61). Clubs: N.Y. Jr. League, Barnard. Home: 16 E 96th St New York NY 10028 Office: 4 E 29th St New York NY 10016

EMERSON, ANN PARKER, dietitian; b. Twin Lakes, Fla., Dec. 3, 1925; d. Charles Dendy and Gladys Agnes (Chalker) Parker; B.S., Fla. State U., 1947; M.S., U. Fla., 1968; m. Donald McGeachy Emerson, Sept. 22, 1950; children—Mary Ann, Donald McGeachy, Charles Parker, William John. Research dietitian U. Chgo., 1948-50; adminstrv. research dietitian U. Fla. Coll. Medicine, Gainesville, 1962-68, dir. dietetic edn., 1968-74, dir. dietetic internship program, 1968-75, dir. program in clin. and community dietetics, 1974—; mem. Commn. on Dietetic Registration, 1974-77, Commn. on Accreditation, 1980—. Pres., Gainesville chpt. Altrusa, Internat., 1977-78. VA Allied Health Manpower grantee, 1974-81; HEW Allied Health Manpower grantee, 1975-78, 78-81. Mem. Am., Fla. dietetic assns. Democrat. Roman Catholic. Club: Jr. League (Gainesville). Office: PO Box J-184 JHMHC Gainesville FL 32610

EMERSON, DOROTHY, home economist; b. Waltham, Mass.; d. Philip and M. Evelyn (Dewey) E.; grad. in home econs. Framingham State Tchrs. Coll.; summer study Dartmouth Coll., Columbia U., Amherst. Tchr., Boston Public Schs., Kimball Union Acad. Urban home demonstration agt., Portsmouth, N.H.; county club agt. Sussex County, Del.; prof., asso. state 4-H Club agt. Md. Extension Service, 1923-61, now extension prof. emeritus; now cons. citizenship-leadership div. Nat. 4-H Council, also lectr. on 4-H Club work. Mem. Pen Women, Delta Kappa Gamma (hon.), Epsilon Sigma Phi (Ruby award 1975) Phi Kappa Phi. Author: Scrapbook, 1966; also articles. Home: 3445 S Leisure World Blvd Silver Spring MD 20906 Office: 7100 Connecticut Ave Chevy Chase MD 20815

EMERSON, ROSA-LEE, clin. psychologist; b. N.Y.C., B.A., CUNY; M.A., Yeshiva U., 1976, Ph.D., 1979. Crisis intervention unit dir. Westchester County Med. Center, Valhalla, N.Y.; pvt. practice psychol. counseling, N.Y.C. and Westchester, N.Y.; adj. asst. prof. L.I.U., Dobbs Ferry; clin. asst. prof. psychiatry N.Y. Med. Coll., Valhalla. Mem. Am. Psychol. Assn.

EMERSON, SUZANNE MICHEL, marriage, family and child counselor; b. Marion, Ohio, Mar. 13, 1934; d. Paul Devere and Esther (Kent) Michel; student U. Dayton, 1952-53; B.S., Ohio State U., 1953-56; M.A., Loyola U., Los Angeles, 1974; Ph.D., U.S. Internat. U., San Diego, 1981; 1 son, Dane E.M. Little. Staff occupational therapist Ohio State U. Hosp., Columbus, 1956-60; sr. psychiat. therapist VA Hosp., Brentwood, Calif., 1960-61; coordinator adjunctive therapy and adult treatment program Westwood Hosp., Los Angeles, 1961-73; pvt. practice as therapist, also cons., Los Angeles, 1966-74; pvt. practice marriage, family and child counselor, La Jolla, Calif., 1975—; research coordinator U. Calif. Hosp., San Diego, 1975-77; instr. U. Calif., San Diego; cons. Calif. Assn. Mental Health, 1968-69; lectr. in field. HEW grantee, 1958-1962. Mem. So. Calif. Occupational Therapy Assn. (office chmn. 1968-69), Psi Chi, Kappa Alpha Theta. Democrat.

EMERY, MARGARET HENCKEL, lawyer; b. Cleve., Sept. 23, 1904; d. Edward V. and Anna C. (Patton) Henckel; student Western Res. U., 1922-24; A.B. cum laude, U. Mich., 1926, J.D. with distinction, 1931; m. William Marshall Emery, Sept. 23, 1932; children—John Henckel, Henry McLachlin. Admitted to Ill. bar, 1933; resident property mgr. Title & Trust Co., Chgo., 1932-34; clk. E.H. McDermott, Chgo., 1934; hearing officer Open Housing Ordinance, Winnetka, Ill., 1971-74; legal cons., 1967—; lectr. on constl. history and law, 1961—. Bd. govs. United Republican Fund of Ill., 1961-75; mem. bd. Devel. Council, U. Mich. Law Sch., 1971—; bd. dirs. New Trier Citizens League, 1963-72; trustee Village of Winnetka, 1967-71. Mem. Fed., Ill. bar assns., Nat. Assn. Women Lawyers, Kappa Beta Pi, Delta Sigma Rho, Pi Lambda Theta. Republican. Christian. Clubs: Union League (Chgo.); Sunset Ridge Country, Winnetka Woman's. Home: 680 Green Bay Rd Winnetka IL 60093

EMETT, SHARON ELIZABETH, educator; b. Gt. Falls, Mont., June 12, 1938; d. Truce William and Isabel Virginia (Rogers) Emett; B.A., Mont. State U., 1960, U. Colo., 1974-75. Tchr., Meadow Lark Sch., Gt. Falls, 1960—. Mem. Gt. Falls Edn. Assn. (sec. 1966-70), Assn. Supervision and Curriculum Devel., Delta Kappa Gamma. Republican. Clubs: Eastern Star, Daus. of the Nile, White Shrine of Jerusalem. Home: 700 3d Ave S Great Falls MT 59405 Office: 2204 Fox Farm Rd Great Falls MT 59404

EMIG, LOIS IRENE MYERS, composer; b. Roseville, Ohio, Oct. 12, 1925; d. Earl Francis and Margaret Byrd (Weaver) Myers; B.S. with distinction, Ohio State U., 1946; postgrad. Ohio State U., Queens Coll.; m. Jack Wayne Emig, June 7, 1947; children—Sandra Jill, Keith Jack. Public sch. vocal and instrumental music tchr., Ohio and N.Y., 1946-65;

pvt. tchr. piano and theory, 1954—; composer and librettist for adult and children's choirs; church organist; pub. works include 9 cantatas, 2 piano books, over 162 varied choral works. Recipient 1st prize, W.Va. Women's Clubs, 1954, winner Lorenz Anniversary Contest, 1954, 1st prize Lorenz Children's Anthem contest, 1964. Mem. ASCAP, Delta Omicron. Contbr. music to profl. jours. Home and Studio: 2149 N Hampton Circle Winter Park FL 32792

EMMETT, CYNTHIA JOAN, nurse; b. Weisbaden, Germany, Nov. 1, 1953; d. Jewell Von and Dartha Joan (Swope) E.; student U. South Ala., 1971; grad. Mastin Sch. Nursing, 1974; student Hill Jr. Coll., 1981—. Psychiat. nurse Fort Walton Beach (Fla.) Gen. Hosp., 1974-75; charge nurse Timberlawn Psychiat. Hosp., Dallas, 1975-77, asst. supt., 1977-78; counselor Dallas County DARCO Drug Free and Methadone Center, 1978-81; labor and delivery nurse Johnson County Meml. Hosp., 1981-82; labor and delivery nurse Ft. Walton Beach (Fla.) Gen. Hosp., 1982—. Home: 136 Ferry Rd NE Fort Walton Beach FL 32548 Office: 1000 Mar Walt Dr Fort Walton Beach FL 32548

EMMONS, CAROL ANN, mortgage banker; b. Jersey City, Jan. 26, 1936; d. Max and Dorothy (Peters) Leuck; student El Camino Jr. Coll., Torrance, Calif., 1960-61, Dutchess Community Coll., 1974-75, D'Youville Coll., 1977-81, various courses SUNY, Buffalo, and Dale Carnegie; children—Linda, Conrad, Rodney. Mortgage adminstr., asst. br. mgr. Soc. for Savs., Hartford, Conn., 1965-75; asst. br. mgr. Reliance Equities, Inc., Poughkeepsie, N.Y., 1975-76, br. mgr., Buffalo, 1976-80, asst. v.p., 1980, pres., dir., Buffalo, 1981—; pres. Nat. Mortgage Banking Corp. Bus. adv. bd. High Sch. Students. Notary public. Mem. Mortgage Bankers Assn. Western N.Y. (pres. 1981), Greater Buffalo Bd. Realtors, Nat. Assn. Female Execs., Council Small Bus. Enterprises, Better Bus. Bur., Buffalo C. of C., Center for Women in Mgmt. of D'Youville Coll., Women for Downtown Buffalo. Office: 1700 Statler Bldg Buffalo NY 14202

EMMONS, LINDA NYE, state legislator; b. Ridgewood, N.J., July 8, 1937; d. Drake and Helen N. Pinkney; A.A., Centenary Coll. Women, Hackettstown, N.J., 1957; B.A., Conn. Coll., 1972; m. Richard L. Emmons, Dec. 13, 1958; children—Mark Richard, Dwight Nye. Staff asst. AT&T Co., 1957-61; self-employed accountant, 1975—; mem. Conn. Ho. of Reps. from 101st Dist., 1977—, mem. Gen. Assembly com. on revenue, bonding and fin., 1977-81, com. on appropriations, 1981—, ranking mem., 1981—, asst. minority leader for fiscal affairs, 1981—; mem. Conn. Bond Commn. Mem. Madison (Conn.) Charter Commn., 1967-69, Madison Republican Town Com., 1970-77; chmn. Madison Bd. Fin., 1977-79; bd. dirs. E.C. Scranton Meml. Library, 1973—. Mem. Order Women Legislators, LWV (voters service chmn. 1968-69). Address: 111 Yankee Peddler Path Madison CT 06443

EMORY, ANNA L., real estate broker; b. Clymer, N.Y., Sept. 17, 1940; d. Leon F. and Florence U. (Daniels) Barringer; student Boston Inst., 1965; student Jamestown Community Coll., 1977, 82—; m. Dallas G. Emory, July 18, 1958; children—Denise G., Diane M. Med. asst., Clymer, N.Y., 1963-72; real estate sales rep. Eagle Realty, Jamestown, N.Y., 1977-80; owner, broker Emory Real Estate, Mayville, N.Y., 1980—; partner Eaton & Emoty Bldg. Contractors, 1970—. Supr. Town of French Creek, 1975-77. Mem. N.Y. State Bd. Realtors, No. Chautauqua County Bd. Realtors, Am. Assn. Bd. Realtors, Nat. Honor Soc. Methodist. Club: Zonta. Office: 26 N Erie St Mayville NY 14757

EMORY, CAROL ANNE, lawyer; b. Petersburg, Va., Jan. 5, 1944; d. Warden Tyrus and Helen Drew (Davis) E.; B.A., Mary Baldwin Coll., 1965; J.D., U. Calif., Berkeley, 1971; m. Arthur Gustave Kroos, III, Mar. 28, 1980. Admitted to Calif. bar, 1972, U.S. Supreme Ct. bar, 1977, D.C. Ct. Appeals bar, 1978; asso. instr. law U. Calif., 1971-73; asso. firm Crosby, Heafey, Roach & May, Oakland, Calif., 1972-73; legal counsel Bechtel Corp., San Francisco, 1973-75, Washington, 1976-78, Bechtel Power Corp., Gaithersburg, Md., 1975-76; div. legal counsel Bechtel Inc., San Francisco, 1978-79; editor, co-pub. Internat. Lawyers Newsletter, Washington and Amsterdam, Netherlands, 1979—; individual practice law, Malibu, Calif., 1979—. Chmn. nat. devel. com. Mary Baldwin Coll., 1979-80, sec. adv. bd. visitors, 1978—. Mem. State Bar Calif., Bar D.C., Am. Bar Assn., Calif. Women Lawyers Assn. Episcopalian. Home and Office: 21609 Rambla Vista Malibu CA 90265 also De Lairesse St 163 Amsterdam Netherlands

ENG, DONNA MAI, hotel exec.; b. N.Y.C., Sept. 29, 1952; d. Edward Kwock and Ann Eng; B.A., U. Hawaii, 1974. Sr. Client rep. Wardair/Internat. Vacations, Honolulu, 1978-79; restaurant and room service mgr./hotel asst. mgr. Sheraton Maui Hotel, Hawaii, 1979-80; sr. asst. front office mgr./sales mgr. Hyatt on Union Sq., San Francisco, 1980-82; sales mgr. Hotel Meridien, San Francisco, 1982—. Fund raiser Child Abuse Council; mem. Vol. Bur. Mem. Hotel Sales Mgrs. Assn., Bay Area Traffic Assn. Democrat. Methodist. Office: care 300 Montgomery St San Francisco CA 94133

ENG, GLORIA, broadcasting exec.; b. Newark, Jan. 13, 1951; d. Ng Kim Lun and Kim Har Lee; student Amherst Coll., 1971-72; B.A. cum laude with honors in Econs., Smith Coll., 1973; M.B.A. (Smith Coll. Alumnae fellow 1973-74, Council Opportunity for Grad. Mgmt. Edn. fellow 1973-75), Wharton Sch., U. Pa., 1975. With CBS Inc., N.Y.C., 1975—, sr. fin. planning analyst corp. tech. and CBS Broadcast Group, 1977—, dir. fin. planning, reports and consolidations CBS News, dir. planning, capital and sales analysis Sta. WCBS-TV, 1979-81; dir. sales and profitability CBS TV Stas., 1981—. Mem. Internat. Radio and TV Soc., Gotham Club of Bus. Profl. Women. Clubs: St. Bartholomew's, Fifth Ave Racquet (N.Y.C.). Home: RD 2 Box 128 Englishtown NJ 07726 Office: CBS 51 W 52d St New York NY 10019

ENG, JOYCE FRANCES, govt. ofcl.; b. East Orange, N.J., Aug. 16, 1946; d. Walter K. and Caroline C. (Young) E.; B.S. in Med. Tech., Fairleigh Dickinson U., 1969; M.S., C.W. Post Center of L.I. U., 1972; M.A. in Theology, Ecumenical Inst. Theology, St. Mary's Sem. and U., 1980. Med. tech. intern Sch. Med. Tech., Morristown (N.J.) Hosp., 1968-69, med. technologist, 1969-70; blood bank technologist Dover (N.J.) Gen. Hosp., 1971; med. technologist Glenridge Labs., Bklyn., part-time 1972; instr. dept. clin. pathology U. Md. Sch. Medicine, Balt., 1972-73, asst. prof. dept. med. tech., 1972-73; chief bacteriologist Howard County Gen. Hosp., Columbia, Md., 1973-74; instr. anatomy and physiology div. biology Catonsville (Md.) Community Coll., 1975; health care specialist Bur. Health Ins., Social Security Adminstrn., HEW, Balt., 1975-78, standards and cert. analyst Health Care Financing Adminstrn., Health Standards and Quality Bur., Dept. Health and Human Services, Balt., 1978—. Recipient cert. of appreciation Health Care Financing Adminstrn., 1981; Spl. Achievement award Health Care Financing Adminstrn., 1980; USPHS Allied Health trainee, 1971-72; AAUW award, 1968-69. Mem. Am. Soc. Med. Tech. (ho. of dels. 1981-82), Md. Soc. Med. Tech. (chmn. civil service subcom. 1981-82), Am. Soc. Clin. Pathologists, Am. Soc. Microbiology, Nat. Registry Microbiologists, Assn. Mil. Surgeons U.S.

ENGE, SUSAN RADOVICH, mktg. systems engr.; b. Thermopolis, Wyo., May 17, 1949; d. Kenneth Allen and Evelyn Mae (Grubbs) Radovich; B.A. cum laude (tuition scholar 1967-71), Washington U., St. Louis, 1971; m. Roby D. Enge, June 13, 1971; 1 son, K. Mark. With IBM Corp., 1971—, regional mktg. programs adminstr., 1979-81, systems engring. mgr. nat. fed. mktg., Rosslyn, Va., 1981-82, systems engring. mgr. Nat. Accounts div., Washington, 1982—. Home: 1104 Artic Quill Rd Herndon VA 22070 Office: 4301 Connecticut Ave NW Washington DC 20008

ENGEBRETSON, MARY EVONE, librarian; b. Albert Lea, Minn., Apr. 9, 1947; d. Merel Harlan and Darlyne Geneva (Johnson) E.; B.A., Luther Coll., 1969; M.A., U. Denver, 1971; M.B.A., Ariz. State U., 1977. Head, bookmobile dept. Whatcom County Library, Bellingham, Wash., 1971-75; market research analyst Helene Curtis, Inc., Chgo., 1977-78; assoc. librarian U. Fla., Gainesville, 1978—. Mem. Fla. Library Assn., Spl. Library Assn. Home: 2022 SW 37th Way Apt 2 Gainesville FL 32607 Office: U Fla 148 Library W Gainesville FL 32611

ENGEL, JOANNE BOYER, ednl. psychologist; b. Meadville, Pa., Mar. 15, 1944; d. Edward Charles and Wanda Ann (Chasco) Boyer; B.S., Pa. State U., 1965; M.Ed., U. Sydney (Australia), 1972; M.S., Iowa State U., 1967, Ph.D., 1979; m. Harold Nicholas Engel, Mar. 12, 1971; children—Cynthia, Keith. Tchr. pub. schs., Broomall and Wallingford, Pa., 1966-68, Sydney, Australia, 1968-70; instr. and program dir. child devel. and family relations dept. child study center Sch. Home Econs., Auburn (Ala.) U., 1972-75; instr. child devel. and psychology dept. Iowa State U., Ames, 1975-79; chmn. edn. dept. Willamette U., Salem, Oreg., 1981—; cons. in field. Leader Jr. High Church, Cub Scouts; referee Am. Youth Soccer; mem. Oreg. Women's Polit. Caucus. Mem. Am. Psychol. Assn., Am. Ednl. Research Assn., Oreg. Assn. for Curriculum Devel., Oreg. Talented and Gifted Assn., Confederation of Oreg. Sch. Adminstrs., N.W. Women in Ednl. Adminstrn., Oreg. Psychol. Assn. (state officer), Phi Delta Kappa (officer), Kappa Delta Pi (nat. officer), Psi Chi. Presbyterian. Contbr. articles to profl. jours.; editor: Kaliadescoper: The Way We Work, Vol. 2 and Kaliadescoper: Women and Technology, Vol. 3, 1981, 82. Home: 2855 NW Skyline Dr Corvallis OR 97330 Office: Willamette U 900 State St Salem OR 97301

ENGELEITER, SUSAN SHANNON, state senator; b. Milw., Mar. 18, 1952; d. Arthur W. and Helen J. (Hildebrandt) Shannon; B.S., U. Wis., 1974, J.D., 1981; m. Gerald Engeleiter, Nov. 27, 1976. State rep. Wis. 99th Assembly Dist., Madison, 1974-79; legis. asst. Gov. Lee Sherman Dreyfus, Madison, 1979-80; mem. Wis. Senate from 33rd Dist., 1980—. Bd. dirs. St. Luke's Hosp.; mem. adv. bd. Waukesha County Tech. Inst. Mem. AAUW, Mortar Bd. Republican. Lutheran. Office: State Capitol Room 408-S Madison WI 53702

ENGELHARDT, MARY VERONICE, ednl. psychologist; b. Syracuse, N.Y., Mar. 29, 1912; b. Herman J. and Ella (Collins) E.; B.S. in Edn., Catholic U. Am., 1937, M.A. in Ednl. Psychology, M.A. in Psychology, 1938, Ph.D. in Edn. and Psychology, 1962. Joined Sisters of St. Francis, Roman Cath. Ch., 1929; demonstration tchr. Campus Sch., Cath. U. Am., 1935-36; tchr. edn. and psychology St. Francis Normal Sch., Syracuse, 1938-52; diocesan and community sch. supr., Syracuse, 1952-56; dean women, head dept. edn. and psychology Chaminade Coll., Honolulu, 1957-60; clin. instr. Child Center, Cath. U. Am., 1960-61, supr. student teaching, 1961-62; head dept. edn. and psychology Maria Regina Coll., Syracuse, 1962-68, founding, dir. reading and speech clinics, 1962-68; dir. Franciscan Learning Center, Syracuse, 1968—; asst. mother gen. order 3d Franciscan, 1965-71, chmn. personnel bd., 1972-75, chmn. communications bd., 1972-82, editor newsletter Catalyst, 1972-82; cons., lectr., evaluator in field. Mem. Am. Psychol. Assn., Am. Ednl. Research Assn., Internat. Reading Assn., Nat. League Am. Pen Women (1st v.p., editor newsletter Central N.Y. br. 1981-82). Author: God's World, 1950; co-author: Songs About God's World, 1951. Address: 1024 Court St Syracuse NY 13208

ENGELHARDT, SARA LAWRENCE, found. exec.; b. Phila., Aug. 23, 1943; d. Ruddick Carpenter and Barbara (Dole) Lawrence; B.A., Wellesley Coll., 1965; M.A., Tchrs. Coll., Columbia U., 1970; m. Dean Lee Engelhardt, June 20, 1970; children—Barbara Elizabeth, Margaret Ann. Staff asst. Carnegie Corp., N.Y.C., 1966-70, asst. sec., 1972-74, asso. sec., 1974-75, sec., 1975—; free-lance editor and writer, Storrs, Conn., 1970-72. Home: 173 Riverside Dr New York NY 10024 Office: Carnegie Corp 437 Madison Ave New York NY 10022

ENGELKEN, DIANE MARGARET, profl. sports exec.; b. Seneca, Kan., Apr. 21, 1954; d. Benedict H. and Myrtle Ione (Graham) Engelken; B.A. in Phys. Edn., Benedictine Coll., 1976; M. Sports Adminstrn., Ohio U., 1977. Vice pres. student govt. Benedictine Coll., 1975-76, asst. to dir. women's athletics, 1975-76; student originated studies project dir. NSF, 1973-74; with Washington Diplomats Soccer div. Madison Sq. Garden, Washington, 1977—, exec. dir., 1977-79; asst. gen. mgr. Detroit Lightning, profl. soccer, 1979-80, San Jose Earthquakes, profl. soccer, 1980—. Bd. dirs. Ohio U. Sports Adminstrn. Program, 1979; speaker Ohio Univ. Sports Symposium, 1979; mem. Student Rep. to Coll. Athletic Bd., 1975. Recipient Certificate for Service Spl. Olympics, 1979; named Outstanding Phys. Educator Benedictine Coll., 1976. Mem. Am. Alliance for Health, Phys. Edn. and Recreation, Nat. Assn. for Sport and Phys. Edn., Nat. Assn. for Girls and Women in Sports. Roman Catholic. Clubs: Women's Physical Education; Women's Recreation; Soccer.

ENGELMAN, MARGE ANN, univ. adminstr.; b. Delavan, Ill., Oct. 9, 1927; d. John B. and Reka M. (Hellmann) Jeckel; B.A. in Sociology, Ill. Wesleyan U., 1949; M.A. in Religious Edn., Northwestern U., 1953; M.S., U. Wis., Madison, 1965, Ph.D., 1977; m. Kenneth L. Engelman, Mar. 26, 1949; children—Ann, Barth. Instr., U. Wis. Extension, Madison, 1963-65, U. Wis., Fox Valley, Green Bay, 1966-68; asst. to asst. chancellor U. Wis., Green Bay, 1969-72, dir. equal opportunity, 1974-79, dir. outreach, 1973—, instr., 1981—. Trustee, Garrett Theol. Sem., Northwestern U., 1975—; mem. Wis. Humanities Com., 1976-79; mem. corp. bd. Bellin Hosp., Green Bay, 1978—; mem. State Adv. Council Community Edn., 1979—; mem. univ. senate United Methodist Hosp. Recipient Elmer Winter award Wis. Designer Craftsman Show, Milw., 1970. Mem. Am. Council Edn. (mem. Wis. planning com. nat. identification women in higher edn. adminstrn. program), Am. Assn. Higher Edn., Adult Edn. Assn. U.S.A., Am. Craftsmen Council, Gerontol. Soc., Adult Edn. Assn. Wis., AAUW. Club: Univ. League. Contbr. articles in field to profl. jours. Home: 1164 Emilie St Green Bay WI 54301 Office: Office Outreach U Wis Green Bay WI 54302

ENGELMAN, SUSAN PHYLLIS, lawyer; b. Trenton, N.J., Oct. 18, 1948; d. Jacob and Anita (Sklar) Feinsilber; B.A. cum laude, U. Pa., 1969; LL.B. cum laude, U. Toledo, 1972. Admitted to Md. bar, 1973; with civil div. honors program Dept. Justice, Washington, 1973-75, asst. br. dir. torts br., civil div., 1981—; with U.S. Atty.'s Office, Newark, 1975-80, dep. chief civil div., 1978-80; tchr. Advocacy Inst., 1979-82. Recipient award Ford Found., 1971, awards Dept. Justice, 1979, 80. Mem. Women's Bar D.C. Office: 521 12th St Washington DC 20530

ENGERRAND, DORIS DIESKOW, educator; b. Chgo., Aug. 7, 1925; d. William Jacob and Alma Willhelmina (Cords) D.; B.S. in Bus. Adminstrn., N. Ga. Coll., 1958, B.S. in Elementary Edn., 1959; M. Bus. Edn., Ga. State U., 1966, Ph.D., 1970; m. Gabriel H. Engerrand, Oct. 26, 1946; children—Steven, Kenneth, Jeannine. Tchr., dept. chmn. Lumpkin County High Sch., Dahlonega, Ga., 1960-63, 65-68; tchr., Gainesville, Ga., 1965; asst. prof. Troy (Ala.) State U., 1969-71; asst. prof. bus. Ga. Coll., Milledgeville, 1971-74, asso. prof., 1974-78, prof., 1978—, chmn. dept. bus. edn. and office adminstrn., 1978—; cons. Named Outstanding Tchr. Lumpkin County Pub. Schs., 1963, 66, Outstanding Educator bus. faculty Ga. Coll., 1975. Mem. Am. Bus. Communication Assn. (nat. dir.; v.p. S.E. 1978-80), Internat. Communication Assn., Soc. Tech. Communication, Acad. Mgmt., So. Mgmt. Assn., Nat., Ga. bus. edn. assns., Am., Ga. vocat. assns., Nat. Secs. Assn., Ninety-nines Internat. (chmn. N. Ga. chpt. 1975-76, named Pilot of Year N. Ga. chpt. 1973). Methodist. Contbr. articles on bus. edn. to profl. publs. Home: 1674 Pine Valley Rd Milledgeville GA 31061 Office: Ga Coll Milledgeville GA 31061

ENGLAND, MARY JANE, state govt. ofcl.; b. Brighton, Mass., July 22, 1938; d. Thomas J. and Anna Elizabeth Fahey; A.B., Regis Coll., Weston, Mass., 1959; M.D., Boston U., 1965; m. Robert A. England, July 8, 1962; children—Alexandra, Kara, Thomas. Rotating intern Framingham (Mass.) Union Hosp., 1964-65; resident in psychiatry Boston U. Hosp., 1965-66, also teaching fellow Med. Sch.; resident in psychiatry, cons. adolescent med. clinic Mt. Zion Hosp., San Francisco, 1966-67; fellow child and adolescent psychiatry Boston U.-Boston City Hosp. Child Guidance Clinic, 1967-69; dir. child psychiatry St. Elizabeth's Hosp., Brighton, 1969-72; dir. clin. psychiatry Brighton-Alliston Mental Health Clinic, 1972-74; with Mass. Dept. Mental Health, 1974-79, asso. commnr., 1976-79; commr. Mass. Dept. Social Services, 1979—; mem. manpower policy com. NIMH, 1977—. Pres. Action for Boston Community Devel., 1973-75; Bd. dirs. United Way Boston, 1980—, Mass. Children's Lobby, 1972-73; chmn. regional subpanel United Community Planning Corp., 1971-73; exec. bd. Mass. Com. Children and Youth, 1973-76; chmn. policy com., bd. dirs. Boston-Brookline Collaborative Center, 1971-75; pres. bd. dirs. Brighton-Allston Mental Health Assn., 1969-71; mem. Mass. Mental Health Center Area Bd., 1970-72. Mem. Am. Acad. Child Psychiatry, Am. Assn. Psychiat. Services to Children, Am. Orthopsychiat. Assn., Am. Psychiat. Assn., Am. Med. Women's Assn. (chair legis. com.), Assn. Psychiat. Treatment Offenders, Am. Coll. Mental Health Adminstrs., Mass. Psychiat. Soc., New Eng. Council Child Psychiatry (co-chmn. legis. com. 1973-75, dir. 1975—). Office: 150 Causeway Boston MA 02114

ENGLANDER, ANN, hosp. adminstr., editor, writer; b. Cin., July 13, 1932; d. Henry Stanley and Adele (Covy) Englander; student U. Mich., 1950-52; B.S., Northwestern U., 1954, M.A., 1956, Ph.D., 1966. Asst. editor lang. arts dept. Sci. Research Assos., Chgo., 1966-69; sr. editor lit. and arts Brit. Jr. Ency., 1969-72; asso. editor lit. and arts Ency. Brit., 1972-73; vis. lectr. Medill Sch. Journalism, Northwestern U., 1974; adminstrv. coordinator alcoholism treatment program Inst. Psychiatry, Northwestern Meml. Hosp., Chgo., 1975-80, adminstrv. coordinator chem. dependence program, 1980-82; dep. dir. adminstrn. alcoholism treatment center Martha Washington Hosp., Chgo., 1982—; instr. clin. psychiatry Northwestern U. Med. Sch., Chgo., 1975—; freelance editor, 1966—. Mem. MLA. Office: Martha Washington Hosp Chicago IL

ENGLE, JESSIE ANN, mathematician; b. Chgo., Sept. 17, 1918; d. Jesse Ward and Natalia (Carson) Nelson; B.A., Bennington Coll., 1940; M.S., Ohio State U., 1964, Ph.D., 1971; children—Lars David, Sarah Nelson, Elizabeth Carson. Instr. music Black Mountain Coll., N.C., 1940-42; engr. Columbia Broadcasting Corp., 1942-44; research assoc. Radio Research Lab., Harvard U., 1944-46; engr. Airborne Instrs. Lab., 1946-48; recording engr. Juilliard Sch. Music, 1949-53; violist Columbus Symphony (Ohio), 1958-62; vis. asst. prof. math. Ohio State U., Columbus, 1971-72, asst. prof., 1972-77, assoc. prof., 1977—. Mem. Am. Math. Soc., Math. Assn. Am., Assn. Women in Math, Nat. Council Tchrs. Math, Ohio Council Tchrs. Math, AAAS, Assn. Women in Sci. Central Ohio. Patentee in microwave antennas and components; contbr. articles to profl. jours. Home: 153 E Lane Ave Columbus OH 43201 Office: Dept Math Ohio State U Columbus OH 43302

ENGLEBERT, JACQUELINE GORKA, nurse; b. Pitts.; d. Norbert Joseph and Emelia Mary (McCluske) Gorka; R.N., Mercy Hosp., Pitts., 1952; B.S. in Nursing Duquesne, U., Pitts., 1956; M.S., U. Ala., 1962; m. Searcy E. Englebert, Jr.; children—Richard Joseph, Katherine Marie. Mem. nursing staff Mercy Hosp., 1952-55, instr. Sch. Nursing, 1955-61; instr., then asst. prof., head fundamental dept. Sch. Nursing U. Ala., 1962-66; mem. nursing staff Providence Sch. Nursing, Mobile, 1967—, dir., 1978—. Mem. Nat. League Nursing, Alpha Tau Delta (nat. award 1964, 66), Sigma Theta Tau. Home: 4252 Regulus Dr Mobile AL 36609 Office: PO Box 208 Mobile AL 36601

ENGLER, CAROL KEHL, real estate agt.; b. N.Y.C., Apr. 28, 1953; d. David and Arline Gloria (Myers) Levenson; student No. Ariz. U., Flagstaff, 1971-73; m. Don B. Engler, May 20, 1978. Reporter, Yuma (Ariz.) Daily Sun, 1974-79, police beat reporter, 1974-75, AP wire editor, 1975-76, city-county govt. court beat reporter, 1977-79; asso. Stephenson Realty, Yuma, 1979-81; founder Realty Execs. of Yuma, 1981; lectr. Ariz. Western Coll. Active movement to bring kidney dialysis unit to Yuma; bd. dirs. Yuma Kidney Found.; mem. Ariz. Lang. Arts Com.; candidate Ariz. Ho. of Reps.; apptd. mem. Ariz. Women's Commn., 1978-80, sec., 1980; chmn. county campaign Bill Schulz for U.S. Senate, 1980. Recipient cert. of appreciation Salvation Army, 1976; lic. Realtor, Ariz. Mem. Ariz. Press Women (pres. western dist. 1976-80), LWV, Yuma Democratic Women, Dem. Nucleus (sec.). Home: 1327 18th St Yuma AZ 85364 Office: 1910 S 4th Ave Yuma AZ 85364

ENGLISH, DOROTHY LOUISE, med. technologist; b. Rosiclare, Ill., June 14, 1927; d. Walter Pierce and Nina Mae (Lynch) Coram; A.S., Paducah Jr. Coll., 1960; B.S. in Med. Tech., U. Tenn., 1961; m. Ardell English, June 24, 1943 (dec.); 1 dau., Carolyn Sue. Med. technologist Western Bapt. Hosp., Paducah, Ky., 1961-63; asst. chief technologist Med. Center Hosp., Punta Gorda, Fla., 1963-71; chief med. technologist, lab. mgr. St. Joseph Hosp., Port Charlotte, Fla., 1971—. Lic. lab. supr., Fla., cert. bioanalyst lab. dir. Mem. Am. Soc. Clin. Pathologists, Am. Soc. Med. Technologists, Am. Assn. Blood Banks (dir.), Fla. Assn. Blood Banks, Nat. Crediting Agy. Republican. Mem. Ch. of Christ. Home: 102 NW Harbor Blvd Port Charlotte FL 33952 Office: 601 NE Harbor Blvd Port Charlotte FL 33952

ENGLISH, EVA UBER, vol. arts council exec.; b. Neumarkt, Silesia, Apr. 20, 1925; came to U.S., 1954, naturalized, 1957; d. Konrad and Margarete (Reimann) Uber; Lab. Asst. Dipl., Fachschule for Chemistry and Physics, 1943; m. Charles B. English, Oct. 3, 1954; children—Gwendolyn, Carolyn (dec.). Lab. asst. Bosch GmbH., Reichenbach, Silesia, 1944; cons. edn. br. Am. Consulate, Frankfurt, W. Ger., 1947-54; pres. Champaign County Mental Health Assn., Urbana, Ohio, 1967-69; mem. Logan-Champaign County 648 Bd. Mental Health and Retardation, 1970-77, v.p., 1970-72; bd. dirs. Springfield (Ohio) Symphony Orchestra Assn., 1968-80; founder, pres. vol. exec. dir. Champaign County Arts Council, 1974-79, also trustee, chmn. arts-in-schs. program, 1979—. Home: 5185 Waldenbergland Rural Route Cable OH 43009 Office: PO Box 271 Urbana OH 43078

ENGLISH, RUTH HILL, artist, educator, art cons.; b. Andover, Mass., Feb. 7, 1904; d. Herbert Hudson and Ada Jane (Wells) Hill; grad. Abbot Acad., Andover; m. A. Evans Kephart, June 28, 1929; children—Susan K. (Mrs. Howard K. Simpson), Katharine K. (Mrs. Christopher R. Barnes); m. 2d, E. Schuyler English, July 4, 1959. Mem. faculty Bryn Mawr Art Center (later Main Line Center of Arts), 1945-65, Wayne Art Center, 1947-49; dir. Hedgeabout Studio, Wynnewood, Pa., 1965—; lectr. throughout East, 1960-70. Past mem. womens bd. Pa. Hosp.; mem. womens bd. Babies Hosp., 1934-39. Mem. Hist. Soc. Early Am. Decoration (pres. William Penn chpt. 1950-51), Pa. Craftsmans Guild (dir. 1952-54). Republican. Episcopalian. Club: Acorn. Home: 47 E

Wynnewood Rd Merion PA 19066 also Skytop PA 18357 Studio: 306 Gypsy Ln Wynnewood PA 19036

ENGLUND, GAGE BUSH, dancer, educator; b. Birmingham, Ala., Sept. 7, 1931; d. Morris Williams and Margaret Wallace (Gagé) Bush; student Sweet Briar Coll.; student (Ford Found. scholar) Sch. Am. Ballet, 1960; m. Richard Bernard Englund, Dec. 1, 1959; children—Alixandra, Rachel Rutherford. Founder, Birmingham Civic Ballet, 1952; mem. Robert Joffrey Ballet, N.Y.C., 1957-60, soloist, 1959-60; mem. Am. Ballet Theatre, N.Y.C., 1960-63, Huntington Dance Ensemble, L.I., N.Y., 1968-69; soloist Dance Repertory Co., 1969-72; tchr. ballet, asso. chmn. Friends of Am. Ballet Theatre, N.Y.C., 1972—; mem. scholarship com. Am. Ballet Theatre Sch., N.Y.C., 1974—; dir. Ala. By-products Corp., 1971-77. Bd. dirs. Children's Hosp. Clinic, Birmingham, 1955-57, Spoleto Festival, U.S.A., 1980, Ala. State Ballet, 1967——, Birmingham Civic Ballet, 1952-67; trustee Ballet Theatre Found., 1974—, v.p., 1980-81; trustee Episcopal Sch. of N.Y., 1979—, Animal Med. Center, N.Y.C., 1982—. Recipient Silver Bowl award Birmingham Festival of Arts, 1955; named Queen of Birmingham Festival of Arts, 1957. Mem. Am. Guild Mus. Artists, Colonial Dames Ala., Jr. League N.Y.C. Episcopalian. Club: Lakewood Country. Home: PO Box 469 Point Clear AL 36564 Office: 322 W 78th St New York NY 10024

ENLOE, IRENE MARGARET, plumbing co. exec.; b. South El Monte, Calif., Jan. 21, 1936; d. William Brown and Gladys Irene (McWilliams) Van Fossen; student public schs., Los Angeles; m. James Lee Enloe, June 19, 1954; children--William Lee, Laurel Irene. Clk. So. Calif. Gas Co., Los Angeles, 1954-55; v.p., office mgr. Lee's Plumbing, South El Monte, Calif., 1967—. Campaign treas. local elections, 1977, 81. Republican. Baptist. Club: Colima-Hacienda Rep. Women's. Office: Lee's Plumbing 2407 N Lee Ave South El Monte CA 91733

ENNIS, MILDRED MCINTOSH, home economist; b. Obion, Tenn., Dec. 7, 1920; d. Odie B. and Prudence (Wright) McIntosh; B.S. in Home Econs., U. Tenn., 1942; M.Continuing Edn., Livingston (Ala.) U., 1972; m. Robert W. Ennis, Mar. 31, 1945; children—Elizabeth Lea, Mildred M., Robert W., Julian. Extension home economist Tenn. Extension Service, Savannah, 1942-45; tchr. vocat. home econs. Livingston High Sch., 1957-58; extension home economist Ala. Extension Service, Livingston, 1958-80; prof. home econs. Livingston U., 1957. Vice pres. Presbyn. Exec. Women's Council; deacon Livingston Presbyn. Ch., 1979. Mem. Nat. Assn. Extension Home Economists (Outstanding Service award, Disting. Service award 1968), Ala. Assn. Extension Home Economists, AAUW (chpt. v.p. 1954), Federated Civic Club (chpt. pres. 1957), Epsilon Sigma Phi, Omicron Nu. Author weekly news column, also radio broadcasts. Home: PO Box 216 Livingston AL 35490

ENNIS, PAMELA ANN, cons. indsl. psychologist; b. Toronto, Can., Mar. 29, 1951; d. Louis and Claire Koza; B.Sc., U. Toronto, 1973, M.A., 1974; Ph.D. (Can. Council fellow), York U., 1976; m. Roger Bryson Billings, Mar. 19, 1981. Scientist, Addiction Research Found., Toronto, 1976-78; psychologist Beech Shepell & Partners, Toronto, 1978-79; pres. Ennis Shepell Indsl. Psychologists, Toronto, 1979-80, Pamela Ennis & Assos., Inc., Toronto, 1980—; spl. lectr. U. Toronto. Mem. Am. Psychol. Assn., Ont. Psychol. Assn. Club: Twenty-One McGill. Contbr. articles to profl. jours. Office: 1075 Bay St Toronto M5S 2W5 Canada

ENNIS, RUTH M. DETWILER, realtor; b. Toledo, Feb. 27, 1913; d. Charles Newton and Ethel J. (Wagoner) Detwiler; student pub. schs., Toledo; m. Arthur Waldo Holly, Jan. 19, 1935 (div.); 1 dau., Barbara Ann (Mrs. Lawrence J. Novak); m. 2d, Harry E. Beddoe, Sept. 29, 1948 (div. 1967); 1 son, Thomas Weston; m. 3d, Wilbur John Ennis, Feb. 14, 1974. Real estate broker Chas. N. Detwiler, realtor, Huntington Park, Calif., 1942-48, Harry E. Beddoe, realtor, Huntington Park and Downey, Calif., 1948-68; pres. Golden State Hawaiian Corp.; pres., dir. Land, Inc., Hilo, Hawaii; v.p., dir. Hawaii Home Developers, Inc.; sec., dir. Hale Moana and Hale Kahakai; escrow officer Universal Escrow Co., Huntington Park, 1944, Advance Escrow Co., 1945-47. Treas., bd. dirs. Ainaloa Community Assn.; Republican precinct capt., Buena Park, Calif., 1960, area chmn., 1962-70. Mem. Downey Bd. Realtors, Calif. Real Estate Assn., Hawaii Bd. Realtors. Clubs: Woman's (Downey); Hilo Yacht; Golden Hills Country (Tehachapi, Calif.). Author (song): Aloha, Ainaloa. Designer residence plans. Home: Apt 506 2405 Kalanianaole Ave Hilo HI 96720 also 20864 Old Town Rd Tehachapi CA 93561 Office: Suite 308 120 Pauahi St Hilo HI 96720

ENRIGHT, JANICE MARIE, med. clinic ofcl.; b. San Jose, Calif., Jan. 2, 1951; d. John George and Antoinette H. (Burgos) Lesch; student West Valley Jr. Coll., 1969-71; m. David Enright, Nov. 18, 1980. 1 son, Jason Aaron Baca. Emergency room clk. O'Connor Hosp., San Jose, 1967-73; auditing sec. Ernst & Whinney, San Jose, 1974-76; exec. sec. San Jose Med. Clinic, 1976—. Vol. worker Muscular Dystrophy Telethon, San Jose, 1974-76, O'Connor Hosp., 1965-66, San Jose Bicentennial Celebration, No. Calif. chpt. Hosp. Fin. Mgmt. Assn., 1976-78; sec. Econ. Opportunity Commn., 1965-66. Notary public, Calif. Mem. Exec. Women Internat., Nat. Assn. Exec. Secs. Address: 17781 Cherokee Trail Los Gatos CA 95030

ENSLIN-WILLIS, ELLEN DEBORA, psychiatric nurse; b. Carbondale, Pa., Feb. 21, 1941; d. Niles John and Ruth Elizabeth (Farrell) Kiefer; R.N., Kings County Hosp. Sch. Nursing, 1960; postgrad. St. Joseph's Coll.; m. Bernard J. Willis; 1 son, Edward John Enslin III. Staff nurse Kings County Hosp. Center, Bklyn., 1960-61; research asst. dept. cardiology Downstate Med. Center, U. Bklyn., 1961-63; pvt. duty nurse, N.Y.C., 1963; operating room nurse Scranton (Pa.) Gen. Hosp., 1963-64; asst. operating room supr. Carbondale (Pa.) Gen. Hosp., 1964-65, staff nurse, 1969-70; head nurse St. Joseph's Hosp., Carbondale, 1965-66, Horton Hosp., Middletown, N.Y., 1966-67, Middletown State Hosp., 1967-68; nursing supr. Farview State Hosp., Waymart, Pa., 1970-74, patient care coordinator, 1974—. Commr., Econ. and Gen. Welfare Commn.; trustee Pa. Nurses Assn. Health and Welfare Fund. Cert. psychiat. mental health nurse. Mem. Am. Nurses Assn., Pa. Nurses Assn. (chmn. occupational unit state employees), Pa. Assn. Patient-Care Coordinators, Nat. Assn. Forensic Psychiatric Nurses. Home: 26 Old Gravity Rd Carbondale PA 18407 Office: Farview State Hospital PO Box 128 Waymart PA 18472

ENSMINGER, AUDREY HELEN, publishing co. exec.; b. Winnipeg, Can., Dec. 30, 1919; came to U.S., 1940, naturalized, 1944; d. Ernest William and Helen Myra (Greaves) Watts; B.Sc., U. Manitoba, 1940; M.A., Wash. State U., 1943; m. Marion Eugene Ensminger, June 11, 1941; 1 son, John Jacob. Teaching asst. dept. chemistry U. Manitoba, 1939-40, tutor dept. home econs., 1937-40; teaching asst. U. Minn., 1940-41; instr. Wash. State U., 1945-46; office mgr. Cons.-Agriservices Found., Clovis, Calif., 1962-77, asst. dir., 1977—; sec. treas. Pegus Co., Inc., Clovis, 1965—; co-owner Ensminger Pub. Inc., Clovis, 1978—; asst. leader Tour-Study Dels., 1966—. Trustee, Pullman (Wash.) Presbyterian Ch., 1958-62; sec. Lincoln Jr. High Sch. PTA, Pullman, Wash. Mem. Can. Home Econs. Assn. Author: (with others) China-The Impossible Dream, 1973; Foods and Nutrition Encyclopedia, 1983. Home and office: 648 W Sierra Ave Clovis CA 93612

ENSTROM, DALY HIRSCH, speech and lang. pathologist; b. Mariampole, Lithuania, Jan. 7, 1937; came to U.S., 1950, naturalized, 1957; d. John and Lydia Emelie (Wirbeleit) Hirsch; B.A. with high honors, Emerson Coll., 1960, M.A. (Vocat. Rehab. fellow), 1964; Ph.D., U. Zürich (Switzerland), 1976; m. Ronald E. Enstrom, Sept. 6, 1958; children—Lars H., Birgit H. Tchr., Watertown (Mass.) High Sch., 1960-61; instr. speech and hearing Douglas Coll.-Rutgers U., New Brunswick, N.J., 1971-73, co-adj. grad. sch., 1978-80; dir. speech and lang. pathology and audiology N.J. Dept. Human Services, Trenton, 1978—. Teenage co-chmn. R.I. March Dimes, 1957; pres. Princeton YMCA Newcomers Club, 1965; bd. dirs., membership chmn. Princeton YMCA, 1966-70, v.p., exec. com., 1968-70. Mem. Am. Speech-Lang.-Hearing Assn. (com. on mental retardation and developmental disabilities), Internat. Assn. Logopedics and Phoniatrics, N.J. Speech-Lang.-Hearing Assn., LWV. Lutheran. Contbr. articles to profl. jours. Home: 81 Sycamore Ln RD Skillman NJ 08558 Office: 222 S Warren St Trenton NJ 08625

ENTERLINE, ESTHER GOLDSTEIN, psychologist; b. N.Y.C.; d. Mack B. and Ray L. (Moskowitz) Goldstein; B.A., Coll. City N.Y., 1961; M.A., Columbia U. Tchrs. Coll., 1966; Ph.D., Columbia U., 1969; m. James Robert Enterline, Mar. 28, 1965. Asso. research psychologist Creativity Research Inst., Fordham U., 1969-70; postdoctoral fellow clin. psychology N.Y. U. Med. Center, 1970-71; staff psychologist S.I. Mental Health Soc., 1971-72; psychotherapist Fifth Ave. Center for Counseling and Psychotherapy, 1971—; chief psychologist Neuropsychiat. Outpatient Clinic, St. Joseph's Med. Center, Paterson, N.J., 1973-74; asst. prof. Montclair State Coll., 1972-73; pvt. practice, N.Y.C., 1974—; chief psychologist Child Devel. Center, Fordham Hosp., N.Y.C., 1973-75; sr. psychologist Bur. Child Guidance, N.Y.C., 1975; supervising psychologist L.I. Jewish-Hillside Med. Center, N.Y.C., 1975-76; chief psychologist, chief children's services Washington Heights-West Harlem-Inwood Mental Health Council, N.Y.C., 1976-78; supr. psychotherapists Whitman Inst., N.Y.C., 1978—; clin. asso. Psychol. Service Center, N.Y. Soc. Clin. Psychologists, 1978—. N.Y. State Regents scholar; NDEA fellow; grantee Columbia U. Tchrs. Coll.; cert. master practitioner art of neuro-linguistic programming. Mem. Internat. Transactional Analysis Assn., Am. Assn. Marriage and Famliy Therapists (clin. mem.), Am., N.Y. State psychol. assns., Am. Acad. Psychotherapists, Acad. Psychologists in Marital, Sex and Family Therapy. Psi Chi. Address: 144 W 95th St New York NY 10025

ENVALL, JANIECE TOWERS, interior designer, design group exec.; b. Olathe, Kans., Feb. 12, 1936; d. Guy McKinley and Mable Daisy Towers; student San Bernardino Coll., 1960, U. Denver, 1963; student Tex. A. and M. U., 1974-77; m. Robert W. Envall, Jan. 19, 1981; children—Joseph C. Hutchinson, Jennifer A. Hutchinson, Jeffrey W. Hutchinson. Free-lance design cons., Colo., Kans., Tex., 1967-75; interior designer Tex. A. and M. U., 1975-79; interior designer, dir. design hpi Design Group, Dallas, 1979—. Chmn. performing arts area Humanities and Fine Arts Commn., Colo. N.E. Dist., 1966-67. Design projects include: Prestonwood Tower, Dallas, Thanksgiving Tower, Dallas, Plasades Central, Dallas, Penrod Bldg., Lafayette, La.; restoration designer for Council Grove Nat. Bank (Kans.). Home: 4423 Southcrest Rd Dallas TX 75202 Office: 1407 Main Suite 1600 Dallas TX 75202

ENWALL, BEVERLY MOEN, state dept. adminstr.; b. Seattle; d. James O. and Dorothy O. (Singer) Moen; B.A., Pomona Coll.; M.A., Ph.D., Stanford U.; children—James, Henry, Laura, Lefric, Gillian. Tchr., San Juan High Sch. San Jose City Coll., Am. River City Coll.; teaching asst. Stanford U.; asst. prof. Sacramento State U.; state fgn. lang. cons. Dept. Edn. State of S.C., Columbia, now chief supr. curriculum. Mem. Am. Assn. Sch. Supts., Assn. Supervision and Curriculum Devel., Phi Beta Kappa. Contbr. in field. Office: Rutledge Bldg 1429 Senate St Columbia SC 29201

EPHRON, NORA, author; b. N.Y.C., May 19, 1941; d. Henry and Phoebe (Wolkind) Ephron; B.A., Wellesley Coll., 1962; L.H.D. (hon.), Briarcliffe (N.Y.) Coll., 1975; m. Carl Bernstein, Apr. 14, 1976; children—Jacob, Max. Reporter, N.Y. Post, 1963-68; freelance writer, 1968—; contbg. editor, columnist Esquire mag., 1972-73, sr. editor, columnist, 1974-78; contbg. editor N.Y. mag., 1973-74. Mem. Writers Guild Am., AFTRA, Authors Guild. Author: Wallflower at the Orgy, 1970; Crazy Salad, 1975; Scribble Scribble, 1978; Heartburn, 1983. Address: care Lynn Nesbit ICM 40 W 57th St New York NY 10019

EPLEY, LINDA MORRISON, educator; b. Fort Deposit, Ala., June 19, 1939; d. Clarence Alexander and Buena Ethyl (Murray) Morrison; Mus.B., Samford U., 1961; Mus.M., So. Bapt. Theol. Sem., 1965; postgrad. N. Tex. State U., 1983—; m. William Arnold Epley, June 11, 1960; children—Eric, Allen. Pvt. piano and organ tchr., 1963—; minister of music Crescent Hill Baptist Ch., Louisville, 1973-76; faculty La. Coll., Pineville, 1976—, asst. prof. music, 1979—. Mem. Am. Guild Organists. Baptist. Home: 1824 Bryn Mawr St Alexandria LA 71301

EPP, JANET BESS, career planning cons.; b. Pasadena, Calif., Nov. 12, 1945; d. William and Lily (Rappaport) Goldberg; B.A., U. Calif., Berkeley, 1967, M.A., 1968; M.A., San Francisco State U., 1971; m. Elliot G. Steinberg; 1 son, Scott. Outpatient specialist San Francisco Gen. Hosp., 1968-69; counseling supr. Planned Parenthood, San Rafael, Calif., 1970-72; dean spl. services, dir. strategic planning, dir. women's program Title IX Coll. of Marin, Kentfield, Calif., 1973-82; dir. Career Planning Group, Tiburon, Calif., 1981—; founder New Horizons Savs. and Loan; cons. various orgns. and edn!. instns. Active San Francisco Conservatory of Music; past pres. bd. Woman's Way, 1978-79; co-pres. Reed Dist. Sch. Bd. Found. Dr., 1982-83; active San Francisco Art Inst. Mem. Wednesday Morning Dialogue, AAUW, Nat. Women's Polit. Assn., Nat. Assn. Women Deans, Adminstrs., and Counselors, Tiburon C. of C. Home: 17 Tara Hill Rd Tiburon CA 94920 Office: 1610 Tiburon Blvd Tiburon CA 94920

EPP, MARGARET (AGNES), author; b. Waldheim, Sask., Can., Aug. 1, 1913; d. Henry M. and Aganetta (Goossen) E.; grad. Bethany Bible Inst., Hepburn, Sask., Prairie Bible Inst., Three Hills, Alta., Can.; student Sask. U. Freelance writer, 1949—; author weekly column Sask. Valley News, 1980—; latest books include (for teens) The Call of Wahoa, 1971, The Great Frederick, 1972, Runnaway at the Running K, 1972; (adult non-fiction) Into All The World, 1973, The Earth is Round, 1974, Proclaim Jubilee, 1976, 8 Tulpengasse, 1978, also Sarah Scott series, 1967—. Mem. Evang. Mennonite Ch. Address: Box 178 Waldheim SK S0K 4R0 Canada

EPPINETTE, SHIRLEY LYNN, educator, journalist; b. New Orleans; d. Woodie Trevillion and Thelma Elizabeth (Axline) E.; A.A. (Journalism Alumni Assn. scholar), East Los Angeles Coll., 1967; B.A. (Arthur J. Baum journalism scholar), Calif. State U., Los Angeles, 1969, postgrad., 1969-70; postgrad. U. Santa Clara, 1981, U. So. Calif., 1982. Elementary tchr. Covina-Valley Unified Sch. Dist., 1970-74, San Gabriel (Calif.) Sch. Dist., 1974-75, Alhambra (Calif.) City Sch. Dist., 1976-78, Los Angeles City Unified Sch. Dist., 1978—; rewrite editor, staff writer San Gabriel Valley Newspaper Publs., 1975-76; mem. membership adv. group Automobile Club So. Calif. Recipient TAP award Alhambra-San Gabriel dist. Soroptimist Club, 1975; Calif. State PTA scholar, 1981. Mem. NEA, Calif. Tchrs. Assn., United Tchrs. Los Angeles, Women in Communications, Alhambra, San Gabriel Tchrs. bowling leagues, Nat. Press Women, AAUW (com. internat. relations 1977-78, chmn. ednl. com. 1978-79), Sigma Delta Chi. Club: Pacific Coast Press. Home: 1717 S 8th St Alhambra CA 91803

EPPLE, ANNE YVONNE (MRS. LEWIS EDWIN EPPLE), author; b. Tuckahoe, N.Y., Feb. 9, 1927; d. Albert and Anna Marie (Ritter) Orth; certificate Famous Writers Sch., 1967; m. Lewis Edwin Epple, July 17, 1949; children—Lee Scott, Douglas Craig. Sch. lectr., asst. edn. dept. N.Y. Zool. Park, Bronx, 1946-52. Mem. Nat. Geog. Soc., Nat. Wildlife Fedn., Britannica Soc., Nat. Council State Garden Clubs (accredited judge flower shows). Club: Evergreen Garden (pres. 1981—). Author: Nature Quiz Book, 1955; Modern Science Quiz Book, 1958; The Beginning Knowledge Book of Ants, 1969; The Beginning Knowledge Book of Fossils, 1969; The Lookalikes, 1971; Nature Crafts, 1974; Something from Nothing Crafts, 1976. Home: 336 Wickham Rd Glastonbury CT 06033

EPPS, BARBARA ANNE, retail co. exec.; b. Englewood, N.J., July 17, 1941; d. Roy Sherman and Lillian Grace (McCloud) Watson; student U. Ill., Navy Pier, 1959, Roosevelt U., 1967. Adminstrv. asst., labs. applied scis., lab. astrophysics and space research U. Chgo., 1959-69, asst. compensation mgr., personnel office, 1969-76; salary adminstrn. specialist Montgomery Ward and Co., Chgo., 1976-79, corp. wage adminstrn. mgr., 1979—; asst. developer compensation plan Provident Hosp., 1970. Recipient HEW award, 1977. Mem. Coll. and Univ. Personnel Assn., Am. Soc. Profl. and Exec. Women, Delta Sigma Theta. Episcopalian. Home: 4800 S Chicago Beach Dr #1111N Chicago IL 60615 Office: 1 Montgomery Ward Plaza Chicago IL 60671

EPSTEIN, BEE J., cons.; b. Tubingen, Germany, July 14, 1937; came to U.S., 1940, naturalized, 1945; d. Paul and Milly (Stern) Singer; student Reed Coll., 1954-57; B.A., U. Calif., Berkeley, 1958; M.A., Goddard Coll., 1976; Ph.D., Internat. Coll., 1982; m. Leonard Epstein, June 14, 1959 (div. 1982); children—Bettina, Nicole, Seth. Bus. instr. Monterey Peninsula Coll., 1975—; owner, mgr. Bee Epstein Assos., Cons. to Mgmt., Carmel, Calif., 1977—; pres. Success Tours Inc., Carmel, 1981—; founder, prin. Monterey Profl. speakers, 1982; instr. Monterey Peninsula Coll., Golden Gate U., U. Calif., Santa Cruz, Am. Inst. Banking, Inst. Ednl. Leadership, Calif. State Fire Acad. Monterey Peninsula Coll. Research grantee, 1976. Mem. Am. Mgmt. Assn., Nat. Speakers' Assn., Am. Soc. Tng. and Devel., Nat. Assn. Female Execs., Peninsula Profl. Women's Network, Calif. Tchrs. Assn. Democrat. Jewish. Office: PO Box 221383 Carmel CA 93922

EPSTEIN, DIANA, retail exec.; b. N.Y.C., June 17, 1936; d. Samuel H. and Pearl (Barnett) E.; student U. Chgo., 1954-57. Owner, operator Tender Buttons, contemporary and antique button shop, N.Y.C., 1964—; designer greeting cards Caspari & Co., 1973-76; designer fabrics Carol Horn, Inc., 1974-75; designer dresses Ashanti Boutique, 1981; guest lectr. Parsons Sch. Design, 1979-80; freelance designer, 1970—. Life mem. Nat. Button Soc. Author: Buttons, 1968; also articles. Address: 143 E 62d St New York NY 10021

EPSTEIN, DOREEN SHARIN, apparel mfg. co. exec.; b. N.Y.C.; d. Leo and Eva (Karp) Sharin; student Hunter Coll., 1948, CCNY, 1949-51; m. Kenneth J. Epstein, Oct. 9, 1964; 1 dau., Amy. Buyer, Steinberg-Kass Co., N.Y.C., 1960-65; with exec. sales Rousso Sportswear Co., N.Y.C., 1965-67; v.p., fashion dir. Omnico div. U.S. Industries, N.Y.C., 1957-81, mem. exec. bd., 1969-81; v.p. fashion and merchandising Happy Legs div. Spencer Co., 1976-81; exec. dir. VF Design div. VF Corp., Wyomissing, Pa., 1981—. Mem. N.Y. Assn. Brain Injured Children, Nat. Assn. Ileitis and Colitis. Home: 70 E 10th St New York NY 10003 Office: VF Design Inc 209 W 38th St New York NY

EPSTEIN, DORIS WRIGHT, psychotherapist; b. Wis., Aug. 4, 1924; d. Leo G. and Gertrude H. (Hornbach) Wright; B.S., U. Wis., 1944; M.S., Case-Western Res. U., 1946; m. Herman T. Epstein, May 30, 1947; children—Becky S., Karen A., Erika B., David A. Dir., cons. vols. in schs. Social Welfare Dept., Tel Aviv, 1969-70; dir. social services Tech. Devel. Corp., Boston, 1970-76; dir. social work asso. program Middlesex Community Coll., Bedford, Mass., 1971-81; psychotherapist, partner Counseling Collaborative, Lexington, Mass., 1976—. Mem. Acad. Cert. Social Worker, Nat. Assn. Social Workers. Author articles in field. Office: 789 Massachusetts Ave Lexington MA 02173

EPSTEIN, EDNA SELAN, lawyer; b. Yugoslavia, July 26, d. Carl and Lotte (Eisner) Selan; came to U.S., 1944, naturalized, 1951; A.B. cum laude, Barnard Coll., 1960; M.A. (AAUW fellow), Johns Hopkins U., 1961; Ph.D., Harvard U., 1967; J.D. cum laude (Law Rev.), U. Chgo., 1973; m. Wolfgang Epstein, June 12, 1961; children—Matthew, Ezra, Tanya. Asst. prof. French, U. Ill., Chgo. Circle, 1967-70; admitted to Ill. bar, 1973; with Cook County State's Atty., 1973-75; with firm Sidley & Austin, Chgo., 1976—; mem. faculty Mich. Inst. Continuing Legal Edn., 1977, Nat. Inst. Trial Advocacy, 1979; vis. lectr. U. Chgo. Sch. Law, 1980-81; vis. lectr. NITA programs Hofstra U., Emory U., 1980-82. Bd. govs. Hyde Park-Kenwood Community Conf., 1974-77; bd. dirs. Friends of Parks, 1978—; mem. Citizens Com. for Victim Assistance, 1976-78, Cook County State's Atty.'s Profl. Adv. Com., 1981-82, Mayor Byrne's Transition Task Force, 1979; del. Dem. Nat. Conv., 1980, also chmn. rules com. Mem. Am., Chgo. bar assns., Chgo. Council Lawyers (bd. govs. 1975-77), Phi Beta Kappa, Order of Coif. Contbr. articles to learned jours. Office: Suite 4800 One First Nat Plaza Chicago IL 60603

EPSTEIN, HARRIET MOSKOWITZ, social worker; b. N.Y.C., Oct. 1, 1936; d. Sol and Frieda (Scharf) Moskowitz; B.S., Barry Coll., 1973, M.S.W., 1975; m. Lester Epstein, Oct. 6, 1956; children—Bryce, Jeff, Julie. Clin. social worker Family Service Agy., Fort Lauderdale, Fla., 1976—; clin. faculty mem. Barry Coll., 1978-79, Fla. State U., 1980—. Mem. Nat. Assn. Social Workers, Acad. Cert. Social Workers. Home: 19001 NE 21st Ave North Miami Beach FL 33179 Office: 1300 S Andrews Ave Fort Lauderdale FL 33316

EPSTEIN, SARAH GUNY, library media specialist; b. Providence; d. Maurice and May (Guny) Epstein; student R.I. Coll. Edn., 1943-45, U. Miami, Coral Gables, 1955; B.A., U. R.I., 1957; M.L.S., Pratt Inst., 1958. Asst. catalog dept. Providence Pub. Library, 1946-55; library media specialist George J. West Elem. Sch., Providence, 1958—. Mem. ALA, Am. Assn. Sch. Librarians, (state assembly del. 1974-75), New Eng. Ednl. Media Assn., R.I. Sch. Media Assn. (treas. 1963-65), R.I. Library Assn., Pratt Inst. Grad. Library Sch. Alumni Assn. Jewish. Home: 36 Lincoln Ave Providence RI 02906 Office: 145 Beaufort St Providence RI 02908

EPSTEIN, WILMA M. GELLER, advt. agy. exec.; b. N.Y.C., Jan. 6, 1946; d. Jack R. and Dorothy B. Geller; student Bernard Baruch Sch. Bus., 1963-65, New Sch. Social Research, 1964-66; m. Jeffrey Epstein, Oct. 27, 1969; 1 dau., Jill. Asst. media planner B.B.D. & O., N.Y.C., 1965; media planner West, Weis & Bartel, N.Y.C., 1966-68; planner Ogilvy & Mather Inc., N.Y.C., 1968-75, v.p., 1975-79, sr. v.p., asso. media dir., 1979—; dir. Bus. Pubs. Audits, 1983-86. Office: 2 E 48th St New York NY 10017

ERB, PHYLLIS, chem. engr.; b. Milw., Aug. 7, 1941; d. Ernest Wilhelm and Mary (Anderson) Erb; B.S. in Chem. Engring., U. Wis., Madison, 1964. Research engr. DuPont Co., Wilmington, Del., 1964-70, advt. rep. for indsl. chem., synthetic films, x-ray testing products, 1970-74; tech. rep. x-ray products, N.Y.C., 1975-76; sales mgr. Celanese Corp., Charlotte, N.C., 1977-80; advt. mgr. Ga.-Pacific Corp., Portland, Oreg., 1980—. Active campaigns for gov. Del. R. Peterson and P.S. DuPont; active Young Republicans N.C.; sec. Carriage Post Condominium, N.J., 1975, 76; controller Sir Johns Hill Condominium, N.C., 1977-80; bd.

dirs. Chamber Music Soc., Charlotte, 1979. Mem. Portland Art Assn., Japanese Garden Soc., Portland Ad Fedn., Internat. Assn. Bus. Communicators. Home: 4 Pointe Terr Atlanta GA 30339 Office: 133 Peachtree St Atlanta GA 30303

ERBLICH, JOANNE EVE MONTELL, psychiat. social worker; b. St. Louis, Jan. 4, 1940; d. Louis Albert and Charlotte (Sparberg) Montell; A.B., Washington U., St. Louis, 1960; M.A., 1963; M.S.W., 1976; m. Allan Erblich, Apr. 3, 1957; children—Jonathon, Timothy, Peter, Christopher. Formerly lectr. English Washington U., St. Louis; with Barnes Hosp./Renard Psychiat. Hosp., St. Louis; now chmn., social worker, diagnostician Spl. Sch. Dist. St. Louis County, Mo. Fellow Am. Orthopsychiat. Assn.; mem. Acad. Cert. Social Workers, Mo. Hist. Soc., Friends of City Art Mus., Symphony Soc., AAUW, Nat. Assn. Social Workers, Am. Psychiat. Assn., NEA. Republican. Unitarian. Clubs: Jr. League, Washington U. Women's. Home: 7739 Davis Dr Clayton MO 63105 Office: 12110 Clayton Rd St Louis MO 63131

ERB-PAPPAS, BARBARA LOUISE, communications co. exec.; b. Jersey City, Apr. 16, 1938; d. Charles Gottlieb and Louise Agnes (Merz) Erb; student public schs.; m. James Peter Pappas, Aug. 30, 1981. Asst. to guidance counselor Summit (N.J.) High Sch., 1956-61; adminstrv. asst. to exec. v.p. Gen. Artists Corp., N.Y.C., 1961-63; asst. to chmn. bd. Chris-Craft Industries, Inc., N.Y.C., 1963—, asst. corp. sec., 1973—. Address: 440 E 62d St New York NY 10021

ERCIUS, HELEN LOUISE, city ofcl.; b. Knoxville, Tenn., Aug. 20, 1919; d. Walter Thurman and Christine (Godfrey) Lay; B.S. in Edn. cum laude, U. Tenn., 1940; m. Richard Ercius, Nov. 16, 1940; children—Chris Ann Elliott, Walter Richard. Sec., Pass-A-Grille Woman's Club, St. Petersburg Beach, Fla., 1960-61, 2nd v.p., 1961-62; city commr. Dist. #4, St. Petersburg Beach, 1975—, vice mayor, 1976-80. Pres., Friends of St. Petersburg Beach Library, 1968-72, mem. organizing bd., 1966-68; charter revision com. mem. City of St. Petersburg Beach, 1974-75; alternate mem. Tampa Bay/Regional Planning Council, 1976-77, ofcl. mem. representing City of St. Petersburg Beach, 1980—, mem. A-95 com.; chmn. St. Petersburg Beach Waste Water Treatment Commn., 1975-79; mem. Pinellas County Planning Council. Mem. Suncoast League Cities (pres.), Fla. League Cities, Viña del Mar Assn., U. Tenn. Alumni Assn., LWV. Republican. Clubs: Pass-A-Grille Community Assn., St. Petersburg Beach Community (pres. 1977-79). Home: PO Box 46434 St Petersburg FL 33741 Office: 7701 Boca Ciega Dr Saint Petersburg Beach FL 33706

ERDMAN, JOYCE MICKEY, coll. exec.; b. Washington, July 5, 1924; d. William Earle and Louise (Doocy) Mickey; student Middlebury Coll., 1942-44; B.A., U. Wis., Madison, 1946, M.A. in Econs., 1947; m. Marshall Erdman, Aug. 17, 1946; children—Deborah, Timothy, Rustin, Daniel. Staff assoc. Govs. Commn. Human Rights, Madison, Wis., 1948-53; research asst. Office Internat. Studies and Program, U. Wis., Madison, 1962-67, regent U. Wis. System, 1975—, v.p. bd. regents 1979-80, pres., 1980-82. Trustee Village of Shorewood Hills, Wis., 1971-73; pres., 1973-77; pres. Alliance for Children and Youth, Madison, 1973—; sec. rustic rds. bd. Wis. Dept. Transp., 1972-82; regional dir. Wis. Conf. Christians and Jews, 1977—. Mem. Wis. Bd. Vocat. Tech. and Adult Edn. Author: Wisconsin Indians, 1952, rev., 1967; Non-White Housing in Wisconsin, 1953. Home: 3408 Circle Close Madison WI 53705 Office: 1220 Linden Dr Madison WI 53706

EREL, SHARON LEE PERKINS, internist; b. Toledo, July 14, 1935; d. Ernest and Mae (Henry) Perkins; B.S., U. Toledo, 1957; M.D., U. Istanbul, 1968; m. Sahabettin Erel, Jan. 18, 1957; children—Robert Huseyin, Murad Richard. Intern, Toledo Hosp., 1969-70, asst. dir. med. edn., 1973-74; resident Med. Coll. Ohio at Toledo, 1970-73, active staff, clin. instr. internal medicine, 1973—, Am. Cancer Soc. grantee, 1972-73; practice medicine specializing in internal medicine, Sylvania, Ohio, 1973—; mem. staffs Flower, Toledo, Med. Coll. hosps. Med. dir. N.W. Ohio Hospice Assn., 1981—; former mem. exec. com. of med. adv. bd. Kidney Found.; mem. med. adv. bd. Planned Parenthood, Community Nursing Service; mem. chemotherapy subcom N.W. Ohio Cancer Network. Mem. AMA, Ohio Med. Assn., Assn. Practitioners of Infection Control, Am. Soc. Internal Medicine, Nat. Hospice Orgn., Toledo Acad. Medicine. Office: 6465 Monroe St Sylvania OH 43560

ERENS, PATRICIA BRETT, educator; b. Washington, May 31, 1938; d. Benjamin and Nettie (Norman) Brett; B.A., George Washington U., 1959; M.A., U. Chgo., 1963; Ph.D., Northwestern U., 1981; m. Jay Allan Erens, Aug. 21, 1960; children—Pamela, Bradley. Lectr., U. Chgo., 1965-66, 74, U. Ill., 1963-64, Northwestern U., 1975; instr. communications Rosary Coll., River Forest, Ill., 1976-80, asst. prof., 1981—; instr. Hebrew U., Jerusalem, 1979; staff asst. Art Inst. Chgo., 1963-70. Mem. exec. bd. Am. Jewish Com., 1968—; bd. dirs. Internat. Visitors Center, 1965-68, Film Center of Art Inst. Chgo., 1972—, Midwest Women's Center, 1980—, Zero Population Growth, 1977; active local Planned Parenthood Assn., LWV. Internat. Communications Agy. travel grantee, Japan, 1978, Israel, 1979. Mem. Soc. Cinema Studies, Univ. Film Assn., Popular Culture Assn. Jewish. Club: Arts (Chgo.). Author: The Films of Shirley MacLaine, 1978; Akira Kurosawa: A Guide to References and Resources, 1979; Masterpieces: Famous Chicagoans and Their Paintings, 1979; editor: Sexual Stratagems: The World of Women in Film, 1979; Film Reader; Quar. Rev. Film Studies. Office: 7900 W Division St River Forest IL 60305

ERES, EUGENIA, artist; b. Ukraine, Apr. 28, 1928; came to U.S., 1960, naturalized, 1975; d. Vasily and Maria (Nosikow) Kutusow; ed. Fine Arts Sch., São Paulo, Brazil, 1954-58, Famous Artists Sch., Westport, Conn., 1966-69, Nat. Acad. Fine Arts, N.Y.C., 1970-71; m. Ivan Eres, Nov. 24, 1945; children—Ari, Walter, Luba. Exhibited in one-woman shows at Gall. de Artes IV Centenario, São Paulo, Ukrainian Art and Lit. Club, N.Y.C., Panoras Gallery, N.Y.C., Bronxville (N.Y.) Library; exhibited in group shows at Nat. Acad. Galleries, Exposition Intercontinentale, Monaco, Nat. Arts Club, World Trade Center Gallery, N.Y.C., Hammond Mus., N.Y., others; works in numerous pvt. and public collections, including Russian Am. Mus., Lakewood, N.J., collection of Jacqueline Kennedy Onassis. Recipient 1st prize Irvington Art Assn., 1963, Russian Am. Art Assn, 1975-78, Pen and Brush, 1977-78; Gold medal of honor Nat. Art League, 1977; Oscar, São Paulo, 1958; Academician of Italy with Gold Medal, 1979; Master of Painting award Internat. Seminar of Modern and Contemporary Art, 1982; numerous others. Fellow Am. Artists Profl. League (life); mem. Knickerbocker Artists, Nat. Art League, Hudson Valley Art Assn., Accademia Italia delle Arti (Golden Centaur award 1982), Internat. Platform Assn. Address: 86-10 109th St Richmond Hill NY 11418

ERICH, DOROTHY BEATRICE, nurse; b. Chillicothe, Ohio, Oct. 4, 1915; d. Oliver Gustave and Daisy Mae (Orr) Erich; R.N., Bethesda Hosp., 1941; B.Th., Olivet Nazarene Coll., 1953. Nurse, Ft. Hamilton Hosp., Hamilton, Ohio, 1953-55, Chillicothe Hosp., 1955-60; orthopedic nurse Mt. Logan Sanitorium, Chillicothe, 1960-70; nurse surgery Greenfield (Ohio) Hosp., 1970-73; nursing cons. Gospel Light Nursing Home, Kingston, Ohio, 1980—; part-time preacher in youth work. Mem. Am. Nurses Assn. Mem. Nazarene Ch. Republican.

ERICKSEN, ANNA MAE, nursing adminstr.; b. Moose Jaw, Sask., Can., Nov. 1, 1919; d. Eric Andrew and Evelyn (Kyle) E.; R.N., Deaconess Hosp., Spokane, Wash., 1943. Night charge nurse Deaconess Hosp., Spokane, 1943, pvt. duty nurse, 1946, staff nurse, 1947, head nurse emergency dept., outpatient dept. Spokane Poison Center, 1948-57, supr., 1957-70, asst. dir., 1970-73, asso. dir. nursing service, 1973-78, adminstrv. asst. regional out research services, physician liaison, 1978, asst. to adminstr., dir. outreach program, coordinator continuing edn., dir. Spokane Poison Center, dir. physician liaison, 1979—; founder, asso. dir. Spokane Poison Center, 1957—, chmn. disaster com., mem. safety com.; advisor to State of Wash. Asso. Nursing Students, 1956-60; bd. dirs. Regional Emergency Med. Services Council, 1975—, 1st v.p., 1978-79, chmn., 1979—; mem. N.E. Hosp. Disaster Com.; mem. Gov.'s ad hoc com. Emergency Med. Services, Emergency Med. Ambulance Pier Com., Emergency Med. and Ambulance Review Com., Review Com. for Tng. Emergency Med. and Paramed. Technicians; bd. dirs. Nat. Poison Center Network. Mem. Spokane Health Assn.; v.p. NE Heart Assn.; recruitment nurse for ARC in Inland Empire, 1960-68; bd. dirs. Spokane Area Safety Council, 1963-67, vice chmn., 1966-67; bd. govs. Home Safety Council Wash. State, 1966-69, v.p., 1969-70; bd. dirs. NE chpt. Wash. State Heart Assn., 1966—, v.p., 1974-75; polio fund com. Spokane County Med. Soc.; program chmn. Spokane Youth Health Council; bd. dirs. Human Tng. Services Inst., Spokane, 1974-80, sec.-treas., 1976-77; mem. panels United Crusade; panel mem. campaign com. United Way, 1978—; active Polio Program, 1962-69. Served to capt. Nurse Corps, U.S. Army, 1943-46. Named Spokane Woman of Achievement, Am. Bus. and Profl. Women, 1961, Theta Sigma Phi, 1968, Wash. State's Most Involved Nurse, 1970, Outstanding Lady of Year, Spokane, 1972; recipient Key award Inland Empire chpt. Safety Council, 1976. Mem. Inland Empire (bd. 1956-60), Wash. State (bd. dirs. 1959-63, pres. 1960-64, chmn. careers com. 1970-72), Am. (del. 1960-62, 64), Emergency Dept. (founder Inland Empire chpt., pres. 1971, region X rep., 1970-77, asst. exec. dir. 1972, nat. pres. 1975-76, nat. bd. dirs. 1970-77) nurses assns. Presbyterian. Clubs: Altrusa (pres. 1965-67), Epsilon Sigma Alpha (pres. Spokane chpt. 1960-62, treas. 1958-59, mem. state coms.). Home: 2311 W 16th Ave Apt 70 Spokane WA 99204

ERICKSON, NANCY SALOME, lawyer; b. Orange, N.J., Sept. 26, 1945; d. George Hugh and Salome Celestia (Brennesholtz) E.; B.A., Vassar Coll., 1967; J.D. (editor-in-chief law rev. 1972-73), Bklyn. Law Sch., 1973; LL.M., Yale U., 1979; 1 dau., Laura. Admitted to N.Y. bar, 1974; asso. atty. firm Botein, Hays, Sklar & Herzberg, N.Y.C., 1973-75; asst. prof., then asso. prof. N.Y. Law Sch., 1975-80; vis. asso. prof. law Cornell U. Law Sch., spring 1980; asso. prof., then prof. law Ohio State U. Coll. Law, Columbus, 1980—. Mem. Soc. Study Women in Legal History (founder, coordinator 1980), Assn. Am. Law Schs. (newsletter editor sect. women in legal edn. 1978—), Am. Soc. Legal History, Orgn. Am. Historians, Soc. Am. Law Tchrs., Met. Women Law Tchrs. Assn. N.Y.C. (a founder). Author articles on sex discrimination, family law, constl. law. Address: 1659 N High St Columbus OH 43210

ERICSON, RUTH ANN, psychiatrist; b. Assaria, Kans., May 15; d. William Albert and Anna Mathilda (Almquist) E.; student So. Meth. U., 1945-47; B.S., Bethany Coll.; M.D., U. Tex., 1951. Intern, Calif. Hosp., Los Angeles, 1951-52; resident in psychiatry U. Tex. Med. Br., Galveston, 1952-55; psychiatrist Child Guidance Clinic, Dallas, 1955-63; clin. instr. Southwestern Med. Sch., Dallas, 1955-72; practice medicine specializing in psychiatry, Dallas, 1955—; cons. Dallas Intertribal Council Clinic, 1974-81, Dallas Ind. Sch. Dist., U.S. Army, Welfare Dept., Tribal Concerns, alcoholism, Adv. Bd. Intertribal Council. Mem. So., Tex., Dallas med. assns., Am., Tex., N. Tex. psychiat. assns., Am. Geriatric Soc., Am. Med. Women's Assn., Dallas Area Women Psychiatrists, Alumni Assn. U. Tex. (Med. Br.), Navy League (life), Air Force Assn., Tex., Dallas (pres. 1972-73, 82—) archaeol. socs., Dallas C. of C., Alpha Omega Alpha, Delta Psi Omega, Alpha Psi Omega, Pi Gamma Mu, Lambda Sigma, Alpha Epsilon Iota. Lutheran. Home: 4007 Shady Hill Dr Dallas TX 75229 Office: 2339 Inwood Rd #22 Dallas TX 75235

ERIKSSON, SANDRA HOPE, sports found. research exec.; b. Bridgeport, Conn., Jan. 26, 1944; d. Erik A. Eriksson and Madelyn L. Eriksson Sheping Mulcahy; A.A., Norwalk Community Coll., 1974; B.A., Western Conn. State Coll., 1976; postgrad. Pa. State U., 1983—. Asst. mgr. salary adminstrn. Pa. State U., 1976-81; dir. research Nat. Golf Found., North Palm Beach, Fla., 1981—; facility cons. Nat. Golf Found. Pres. D. Fairchild Wheeler-Women's Golf Assn., Fairfield, Conn., 1974. Mem. Phi Alpha Theta (pres. chpt. 1975-76). Roman Catholic. Editor: Golf Instructor's Guide, 1979; Golf Facilities in the United States, 1982. Office: 200 Castlewood Dr North Palm Beach FL 33408

ERKKILA, BARBARA LOUISE, newspaper writer; b. Boston, July 11, 1918; d. John William and Adelia Parsons (Jones) Howell; student Boston U. Evening Coll., 1959; m. Onni R. Erkkila, Apr. 27, 1941 (dec. 1981); children—John W., Kathleen L., Marjorie A. Corr., Gloucester (Mass.) Daily Times, 1936-53, feature writer, 1953—, women's editor, 1967-74, community news editor, 1972-74; freelance article writer for mags., 1953—; editor weekly mag. Essex County Newspapers, Gloucester, 1973, editorial asst., 1974—, writer, photographer, 1970—; tchr. Russian, Ipswich (Mass.) Public Schs., evenings, 1962-63; mem. Boston U. study group to USSR, 1960. Mem. price panel Office Price Adminstrn., 1940's; mem. ARC nurse's aide class Addison Gilbert Hosp., Gloucester, 1942-43; formerly active Girl Scouts U.S.A. Recipient historian award Town of Rockport, 1978. Mem. Sandy Bay Hist. Soc. Republican. Conglist. Club: North Shore Button. Author: Hammers on Stone, 1981; editor: Lane's Cove Cook Book, 1954. Home: 330 High St Gloucester MA 01930 Office: Essex County Newspapers Whittemore St Gloucester MA 01930

ERKSON, PAMELA, Vt. state legislator; b. Rutland, Vt., July 22, 1957; student U. Vt. Mem. Burlington Democratic Com., Chittenden County Dem. Com.; mem. Vt. Ho. Reps., 1979-80, 81—. Bd. dirs. Vt. Children's Aid Soc.; A Burlington for Better Alternatives. Roman Catholic. Office: Vt Ho of Reps State House Montpelier VT 05602

EROLA, JUDITH A., Canadian govt. ofcl.; b. Sudbury, Ont., Can., Jan. 16, 1934; d. Niilo M. and Laura (Rauhala) Jacobsen; m. Aug. 27, 1955; children—Laura Elizabeth, Kelly Ann. Interviewer, commentator, performer stas. CKSO and CKNC-TV, 1950—; account exec. Sta. CHNO prior to election to House of Commons; co-owner, operator Marina & Tourist Outfitting Bus., 1971-72; elected to Ho. of Commons, 1980, minister of state for mines, 1980—, minister responsible for status of women, 1981—. Former bd. dirs. Meml. Hosp. Sudbury; mem. advt. com. Sudbury Dist. C. of C.; mem. Sudbury Folk Art Council; founding mem. Sudbury Little Theatre. Liberal. Lutheran. Office: 707 Confederation Bldg Ottawa ON K1A 0X2 Canada *

ERTLE, NANCY LOUISE, chem. co. exec.; b. Harvey, Ill., July 5, 1935; d. Louis Robert and Mary Loretta (O'Boyle) E.; B.S., U. Ariz., 1957; M.B.A., Northwestern U., 1968. Asst. chemist films-packaging div. Union Carbide Corp., Chgo., 1957-70, research chemist, 1970-76, planning mgr., 1976, dir. mktg., 1976-79, v.p. mktg., 1979—. Mem. Inst. Food Technologists, Am. Mktg. Assn., Chem. Mktg. Research Assn. Office: 6733 W 65th St Chicago IL 60638

ERVIN, ANNE, nurse; A.A.S., City U. N.Y.; B.A. in Sociology, Fordham U.; L.P.N., Ft. Lauderdale Sch. Vocat. Nursing; children—Michelle, L'Tanya, Earl, Marcus. Nurse outpatient dept., maternal and child care counselor North Central Bronx Hosp., 1978—, chmn. ambulatory care; staff nurse Fordham Hosp., Bronx. Vice pres. Black Nurses for Polit. Action in Bronx County, 1977, chmn. exec. bd., 1977-78, now pres.; bd. dirs. Twin Park Day Care Center, 1978—. Registered nurse, N.Y. Mem. Am., N.Y. State (quality assurance nursing practice com.) Dist. 13 (membership com.), North Central Bronx (chpt. chmn.), N.Y. County (chmn. membership com.) nurses assns., N.Y. State Nurses for Polit. Action. Democrat. Lutheran. Club: Order of Eastern Star. Home: 2311 Southern Blvd Bronx NY 10460

ERVIN, BONNIE BUCK, radio sta. ofcl.; b. Lebanon, Mo., Oct. 12, 1931; d. John Charles and Vada Beatrice (Henson) Buck; student public schs., Phillipsburg, Mo.; m. C. Lee Ervin, May 1, 1952; children—Michael Lee, Teresa Ann Ervin King. Asst. personnel dir. Rice-Stix Mfg. Co., Lebanon, 1949-52; clk. ins. dept. Black, Sivall & Bryson Inc., Kansas City, Mo., 1953; women's program dir. Sta. KLWT, Lebanon, 1964—, host Coffee Time, women's talk show, 1964—; sec. to agy. mgr., agt. State Farm Ins. Co., Lebanon, 1978—; master of ceremonies for fashion shows, 1964—. Pres., Laclede County Council Garden Clubs, 1965, Rainbow Garden Club, 1964; treas. Libra Club, 1979; asst. to chmn. Miss Merry Christmas Contest and Christmas Parade, 1978; judge oratorical contest Optimist Club, Lebanon, 1980; mem. Am. Shappers Panel, 1977—; hon. band dir. Lebanon High Sch. Marching 100, 1974. Recipient Avon Bearer of Royal Pen award, 1974. Republican. Mem. Ch. of Christ. Home: 1314 Prosser Dr Lebanon MO 65536 Office: State Farm Ins Co W Business Route 66 Lebanon MO 65536 also Sta KLWT Radio Park Lebanon MO 65536

ERVIN, MARSHENELL, social worker; b. East Chicago, Ind., Mar. 6, 1949; d. John and Geniece (Bailey) Miller; B.S., Purdue U., 1971; M.S.W., U. Houston, 1977; m. Kenneth L. Ervin, Oct. 1, 1977; children—Daryl Lamonte, Brian Keith. Caseworker Ben Taub Gen. Hosp., Houston, 1971-73; counselor Mental Health Mental Retardation Authority Harris County, Houston, 1973-75, counselor liaison, 1977-78; supr., counselor Gulf Coast Community Services Assn., Houston, 1976; teaching asst. U. Houston, 1976-77; dir. Upward Bound, Tex. Coll., Tyler, 1978—, chmn. admissions/recruitment com., 1981-82, yearbook sponsor, 1981-82; mem. adv. bd. East Tex. Ednl. Opportunity Center, Longview, 1980—. Active Big Sisters Greater Houston, 1973-75; vol. Ann. United Negro Coll. Fund, 1974-80; mem. Black Orgn. for Leadership Devel., 1976-78; adv. Explorer Scouts, Boy Scouts Am., 1980—. Inland Steel-Ryerson scholar, 1967-71; recipient Tex. Assn. Student Spl. Services Programs Outstanding Service award, 1981. Mem. Southwest Assn. Student Assistance Programs (exec. bd.), Nat. Assn. Black Social Workers (nat. steering com. 1976-77), Tex. Assn. Student Spl. Services Programs (pres.), Alpha Kappa Alpha (sec.). Clubs: Civitan, Rosette. Office: 2404 N Grand Ave Tyler TX 75702

ERVIN-CARR, CHARLESETTA YVONNE, educator; b. Seattle, June 10, 1946; d. Charles Woodrow and Christene Rosetta (Griffin) Ervin; B.A. in Speech and English, U. Wash., 1969, M.Ed., 1971; 1 son, David Anthony Carr. Tchr. Seattle Public Schs. Dist. 1, 1971—; instr. Seattle Central Community Coll., part-time 1977—; instr. U. Wash., Seattle, 1979—; tng. and employee devel. cons. City of Seattle, 1981—; owner, cons. Effective Communication Skills, Seattle, 1980—. Bd. dirs. Shades of Beauty, Seattle, 1979—. Mem. Am. Soc. Tng. and Devel., AAUW, Black Profl. Educators of Greater Puget Sound, Council on Black Am. Affairs, Women's Profl. and Managerial Network, Nat. Assn. Female Execs., Delta Kappa Gamma. Office: PO Box 18965 Seattle WA 98118

ERWIN, JACQUELINE ANNMARY, mgmt. cons.; b. Toledo, Dec. 21, 1943; d. Elwood Jack and Marie Erwin; B.S. in Indsl. Relations and Humanities, U. Toledo, 1980; grad. Am. Bankers Assn. Sch. Bookkeeper, Toledo Automobile Club, 1965-69; compensation specialist Questor Corp., Toledo, 1976-79; personnel dir. People's Jewelry Co., Toledo, 1976-79; asst. dir. tng. Toledo Trust Co., 1979-82; owner, cons. Comprehensive Profl. Services, Toledo, 1982—; facilitator U. Toledo seminars. Bd. govs. Rescue/Crises Services. Mem. Internat. Assn. Personnel Women (nat. dir., past pres. Toledo chpt.), Am. Soc. Tng. and Devel., Am. Soc. Personnel Adminstrn., Am. Compensation Assn., Toledo Indsl. Recreation and Employee Services Council (past pres.), Toledo Personnel Mgmt. Assn. (dir.). Republican. Lutheran. Contbr. articles to profl. jours. Office: 800 Washington Toledo OH 43624

ESCASA-BRAVO, LETICIA ASUNCION SANTOS, physician; b. Manila, Philippines, Aug. 15, 1945; came to U.S., 1969; d. Vicente L. and Magnifia R. (Santos) Escasa; A.A., U. Santo Tomas, 1960-63, M.D., 1968; m. Mario S. Bravo; children—Maria-Felicia, Mario Melvin. Rotating intern Marion County Gen. Hosp., Indpls., 1970-71; resident in pediatrics Fordham Hosp., Bronx, N.Y., 1971-73; practice medicine specializing in pediatrics, Bedford, Ind., 1973-74, Bloomington, Ind., 1974-76; med. staff Dunn Meml. Hosp., Bedford, 1973-74; asso. staff dept. pediatrics Bloomington Hosp., 1974-76, active staff, 1976; fellow ambulatory pediatrics and community medicine Nassau County Med. Center, E. Meadow, N.Y., 1976-77; pediatric house staff physician St. John's Hosp., Queens, N.Y., 1977-79; attending physician dept. pediatrics Kings County Hosp. Center, Bklyn., 1978—, Lincoln Hosp.-N.Y. Med. Coll., Bronx and Brookdale Hosp. Med. Center, Bklyn., 1979—; asst. prof. N.Y. Med. Coll. Mem. AMA (Physician's Recognition award 1973, 81), Am. Acad. Pediatrics, Lawrence County, Monroe-Owen County med. socs., Pediatric Soc. N.Y. Med. Coll. Address: 9905 Flatlands Ave Brooklyn NY 11236

ESCHER, DORIS JANE WOLF, physician, educator; b. N.Y.C., July 1, 1917; d. Morris and S. Jean (Horowitz) Wolf; B.A., Barnard Coll., Columbia, 1938; M.D., N.Y. U., 1942; m. George Charles Escher, June 30, 1938; children—Jeffrey Ethan, Daralynn Escher Gordon. Intern, Montefiore Hosp. and Med. Center, N.Y.C., 1942-43; resident Jewish Hosp., Bklyn., 1943-44; practice medicine specializing in cardiology, N.Y.C., 1946—; asst. physician Bellevue Hosp. Cardiac Clinic, N.Y.C., 1945-48; clin. asst. Mt. Sinai Hosp., N.Y.C., 1946-48; head cardiac catheterization lab. Montefiore Hosp. and Med. Center, Bronx, N.Y., 1950—, adj. medicine, 1951-57, asso. diagnostic radiology, 1957—, asso. physician, 1957-67, attending physician, med. div., 1967—; lectr. medicine Columbia, N.Y.C., 1957-64; asso. prof. medicine Albert Einstein Coll. Medicine, Bronx, 1970-75, prof., 1975—. Cons. cardiologist Lawrence Hosp., Bronxville, N.Y., 1973—. Bd. dirs. Escher Found. NIH grantee, 1959—. Fellow Am. Coll. Cardiology, N.Y. Cardiological Soc. (dir. 1977—); mem. Am. Heart Assn., Assn. Advancement Med. Instrumentation, Am. Fedn. Clin. Research, N.Am. Soc. for Pacing and Electrophysiology (dir. 1980), Internat. Cardiovascular Soc., Am. Soc. Artificial Internal Organs, N.Y. Acad. Sci., N.Y. State and County Med. Soc. Author: (with Seymour Furman) Principles and Techniques of Cardiac Pacing, 1970, Modern Cardiac Pacing, 1975; contbr. articles on cardiovascular medicine to profl. jours. Office: Montefiore Hosp and Med Center 111 East 210th St Bronx NY 10467 *

ESCHUK, MARY ELIZABETH, ednl. adminstr.; b. Daytona Beach, Fla.; d. Lloyd James and Annie (Coleman) Appleby; B.A. in English, Cleve. State U., 1969, M.Ed., 1972, Ed.S., 1979; m. Steven Eschuk, Oct. 22, 1949; children—Holly, Lauren, Steven. Tchr. English public schs., Cleve., Parma, Ohio, 1969-74; dept. head English Normandy High Sch., Parma, 1972-74; asst. prin. Hillside Jr. High Sch., Parma, 1974-76; prin. Schaaf Jr. High Sch., Parma, 1976-82; prin. Parma High Sch., 1982—. Nat. Endowment Humanities grantee, 1981; named Outstanding Educator Ohio PTA, 1981. Mem. Nat. Assn. Secondary Sch. Adminstrs., Ohio Assn. Secondary Sch. Adminstrs. (dir.), Assn. Parma Adminstrs. Home: 7195 Glencairn Dr Parma OH 44134 Office: 5983 W 54th St Parma OH 44129

ESCOBAR, HILDA LOPEZ, nurse; b. N.Y.C., Aug. 6, 1929; d. Eladio and Josephine (Justiniano) Lopez; A.A.S., Nassau Community Coll., 1967; B.S.N., C.W. Post U., 1975; Adult nurse practitioner, SUNY, 1978; m. John Louis Escobar, Sept. 10, 1949; children—Linda, Michael, Jean. Staff nurse, South Nassau Community Hosp., Oceanside, N.Y., 1967-68; staff nurse Nassau Hosp., Mineola, N.Y., 1968-78, head nurse hemodialysis unit, 1976-78. Certified hemodialysis nurse, 1978; adult health practicioner, 1978. Mem. Am. Assn. Nephrology Nurses and Technicians, 1976, Sigma Theta Tau. Home: New Hyde Park

ESCOT, POZZI, educator, composer; b. Cambridge, Mass., Oct. 1, 1933; d. M. Emm and Lucie (Pozzi) Escot; student Juilliard Sch., 1954-57, Statliche Hochschule Jur Musik und Darstellende Kunst, Hamburg, W.Ger., 1957-61. Prof. music Wheaton Coll., Norton, Mass., 1972—; mem. faculty Grad. Theoretical Studies Faculty, New Eng. Conservatory Music, Boston, 1980—. Mem. Internat. Yr. of Woman, 1975; selected by N.Y. Philharm. Orch. as one of 5 leading women composers of 20th Century, 1975; Radcliffe Inst. fellow, 1970; Ford Found. grantee, 1966. Author: Sonic Design: The Nature of Sound and Music, 1976; Sonic Design: Practice and Problems; composer: Sands, 1965; Interra I, 1968, II, 1980; Fergus Are, 1975; Neyrac Lux, 1978; Eure Pax, 1980. Address: 24 Avon Hill Cambridge MA 02140

ESFELD, FRANCES AGNES, mfg. co. exec.; b. Topeka, Aug. 17, 1917; d. Charles Henry and Catherine Ellen (Birmingham) Dale; m. William Englebert Esfeld, Aug. 28, 1939; children—John W., Mary Ann, Charles E., Jane F., Anthony G. (dec.). Vice pres. Esfeld Trucking Co., Gt. Bend, Kans., 1954-82; pres. Epox-Poly Fittings, Gt. Bend, 1976-82, also personnel dir. Leader, 4-H, 1948-50, Girl Scouts U.S.A., 1955-56; asso. mem. 3d Order Dominican Sisters, Gt. Bend, 1982—; crusader Blue Army of Our Lady of Fatima, Washington, N.J. Fellow Am. Council Applied Clin. Nutrition Found., 1976. Mem. Internat. Graphoanalysis Soc. Chgo. (presdl. excellence citation 1972), Nat. Assn. Document Examiners. Republican. Clubs: Portia, Daughters of Isabella.

ESIBILL, NANCY LYNNE, educator; b. N.Y.C., Sept. 26, 1938; d. Francis Eugene and Elizabeth Moore (Craig) E.; B.A., Beaver Coll., 1959; M.S. in Edn. (HEW grantee), Hunter Coll., 1966; Ph.D., N.Y.U., 1976. Statis. analyst Met. Life Ins., N.Y.C., 1959-64; sr. rehab. counselor Inst. Rehab. Medicine, N.Y.U., N.Y.C., 1966-74, asst. prof. Dept. Rehab. Counseling, 1974—. Adv. com. Planned Parenthood N.Y.C., 1980. Cert. rehab. counselor. Mem. Am. Psychol. Assn., Nat. Rehab. Assn. (named Outstanding Rehab. Profl. 1969, pres. met. N.Y. chpt. 1980), Nat. Rehab. Counseling Assn., Am. Personnel and Guidance Assn., Am. Rehab. Counseling Assn., Coalition on Sexuality and Disability (dir. 1980), Sex Info. and Edn. Council U.S. (dir. 1980—). Author: Sex and Disability: A Model for Short Term Training, 1980, co-author: Factors in the Vocational Success of Hemiplegic Patients, 1971. Home: 2 Washington Square Village New York NY 10012 Office: 25 W 4th St New York NY 10012

ESKENS, ESTHER PAULINE, nurse, state legislator; b. Manhattan, Kans., Nov. 30, 1924; d. Paul George and Viola Rose (McDowell) Brown; R.N., St. Mary's Sch. Nursing, Manhattan, Kans., 1945; m. Henry R. Eskens, June 4, 1954; children—Joan Eskens Fagnant, Henry R. Staff nurse St. Luke's Hosp., Kansas City, Mo., 1948-50, head nurse, 1950-51, clin. med.-surg. instr., 1951-56; office mgr. for physician, Casper, Wyo., 1979—; mem. Wyo. Ho. of Reps., 1975—, chmn. travel, recreation and wildlife com., 1981-82. Recipient award Gov.'s Commn. on Aging, 1979, Beautification award Casper C. of C., 1980. Mem. Am. Nurses Assn., AMA Aux., Nat. Orgn. Women Legislators, Wyo. Bus. and Profl. Women's Club (Woman of Year 1974-75, chmn. 1980-81), Wyo. Med. Soc. Aux. (pres. 1971-72), Natrona County Med. Soc. Aux. Republican. Office: 1045 S Ash St Casper WY 82601

ESKRIDGE, ANN ELIZABETH, state ofcl.; b. Chgo., July 17, 1949; d. Arnett E.V. and Marguerite Marie (Hinds) Eskridge; B.A. in Journalism, U. Okla., 1971; postgrad. Mich. State U., 1979—. News reporter-writer Chgo. Daily Defender, 1969; feature editor Okla. Daily, Norman, 1970, reporter Okla. Jour., Oklahoma City, 1970; news reporter KWTV, Oklahoma City, 1970-71, WBEN-TV, Buffalo, 1971-72, WXYZ-TV, Southfield, Mich., 1972-76; public relations cons. Citizens's Com. for Sch. Millage, Detroit, 1976; public relations and media cons., 1976-78; exec. asst. Office of Lt. Gov., State of Mich., Lansing, 1978, adminstrv. asst. Office of State Treas., 1979-81; exec. asst. Statewide Nutrition Commn., 1982—. Publicity adv. Detroit City Dance Center, 1976-78; bd. dirs. Chief Okemos council Boy Scouts Am., 1979—; sec. Greater Lansing Area Black Reps., 1979—; adv. council on promotion and publicity Mich. Council Arts, 1979—. Recipient Disting. Service award Detroit City Council, 1974; Mayor's award of merit, Detroit, 1975; award Alpha Kappa Alpha; Key to City of Pontiac (Mich.); Mich. Senate honoree, 1976. Mem. Mich. Cable TV Assn., Nat. Fedn. Local Cable Programmers. Club: Detroit Girlfriends. Home: 17217 Fairfield St Detroit MI 48221 Office: PO Box 15128 Lansing MI 48901

ESKRIDGE, THELMA LEONA, savs. and loan assn. exec.; b. Muskogee, Okla., Jan. 17, 1921; d. George Albert and Myrtle Alma (Orr) Hunt; student public schs.; m. Nathan Thomas Eskridge, July 10, 1945; children—Paul Nathan, Carolyn Joyce. With Phoenix Fed. Savs. & Loan Assn., Muskogee, 1944—, teller, 1944-47 acct., 1947-74, controller, 1974-77, v.p., auditor, 1977—. Recipient Achievement award Am. Savs. & Loan Inst., 1962. Mem. Fin. Mgrs. Soc. for Savs. Instns. (internal auditors dir.), Muskogee Bus. and Profl. Women's Club, Phi Sigma Alpha. Democrat. Presbyterian. Clubs: Knife and Fork, Soroptomist (Muskogee). Office: 1111 W Broadway Muskogee OK 74401

ESKRIDGE, VERONICA LUCIA, educator; b. Weatherford, Tex., May 5, 1944; d. Verne V. and Dorothy Jane McCarty; B.A. in Phys. Edn., U. Ky., 1966; M.S. (Sigma Delta scholar 1969), Western Ky. U., 1969; Ph.D., U. Oreg., 1972. Instr., coach high schs. in Va., 1966-68; grad. teaching asst. Western Ky. U., 1968-69; grad. teaching fellow U. Oreg., 1969-72; asst. prof. health and phys. edn. Sam Houston State U., Huntsville, Tex., 1972-76; asso. prof. phys. edn. Ithaca (N.Y.) Coll., 1976—. Nat. Assn. Phys. Edn. for Coll. Women grantee, 1977; Ithaca Coll. grantee, 1978. Mem. AAHPER, Am. Psychol. Assn., Assn. Women in Psychology, Biofeedback Soc. Am., Eastern Dist. Assn. Health, Phys. Edn. and Recreation, N.Y. Acad. Scis., N.Y. Assn. Health, Phys. Edn. and Recreation, N.Am. Soc. Psychology Sport and Phys. Activity, Soc. Psychophysiol. Research, NOW, Audubon Soc. (charter, chmn. edn. com. Huntsville chpt. 1973-76), Sierra Club. Author papers in field. Office: Sch HPER Ithaca Coll Ithaca NY 14850

ESPENAK, LILJAN WINIFRED, dance therapist, educator; b. Bergen, Norway; d. New Ragnvald and Margaret Anne (Porter) E.; came to U.S., 1941, naturalized, 1948; B.A., U. Dresden (Germany), 1936; M.A. in Dance Edn., U. Berlin, 1939; cert. Inst. Individual Psychology, 1955. Mem. Mary Wigman Dance Co., Dresden, 1934-38; asst. tchr. Mary Wigman Sch., Berlin, 1937; tchr. Volkschochschule für Leibesubungen, Berlin, 1938; mem. Modern Dance Group, Mask Theatre, London, 1938; choreographer West End prodns., London, 1938-39; choreographer, dancer, tchr., Broadway, 1942; dance therapist Alfred Adler Clinic and Flower and Fifth Ave. Hosp., N.Y.C., 1958; pioneer 1st postgrad. course in dance therapy in U.S.A., N.Y. Med. Coll., 1965, asst. prof. rehab. medicine, 1975—; lectr. Alfred Adler Inst., N.Y. U., York U., Toronto, also confs. and symposia, U.S. and abroad. Fellow Am. Assn. Mental Deficiency; charter mem., hon. life mem. Am. Dance Therapy Assn. (registered); mem. Individual Psychology Assn., Bioenergetic Analysis Inst. Author articles, books, records, papers in field. Home: 45-36 39th Pl Long Island City NY 11104 Office: 2121 Broadway Room 404 York NY 10023

ESPINAS, GLENDA ZAMUDIO, trade assn. fin. adminstr.; b. Daraga, Albay, Philippines, Oct. 7, 1939; came to U.S., 1974, naturalized, 1980; d. Beato Mayores and Purita Amaranto (Zamudio) E.; student in elem. edn. Albay Normal Coll., Legaspi City, Philippines, 1955-56; student in secretarial sci. U. of East, Manila, 1956-57, B.B.A. in Acctg., 1964; 1 dau., Glendalie Espinas Fabia. Personal sec. to project dir. UN Devel. Program, Laguna de Bay Feasibility Study, Manila, 1968-70; sec. Laguna Lake Devel. Authority, Pasig, Rizal, Philippines, 1970-71; sec. Internat. Rice Research Inst., Laguna, Philippines, 1971-74; acct. Kramer Assos., Inc., Washington, 1974-77, also dir. and sec. bd. dirs.; acct. Found. for Applied Research, Inc., 1974-77; acct. Washington Bd. Realtors, 1977-78, dir. fin., 1979—; acct. Washington Realtors Polit. Action Com., Inc., 1978—, Washington Home Ownership Council, 1979—. Vol. telethon, art shows, fund-raising drives Leukemia Soc. Am., Washington, 1979—. Recipient Most Outstanding Betan award Sigma Beta Lambda, 1964. Mem. Am. Soc. Women Accts. (editor D.C. chpt. Capitol Accounts 1979-80, sec. and dir. D.C. chpt. 1981-82, chmn. registration com. Nat. Spring Conf. 1982, v.p. and dir. D.C. chpt. 1982-83), Inst. Mgmt. Acctg., Nat. Assn. Accts. (asso. dir. membership D.C. chpt. 1981-83). Home: 1414 17th St NW Washington DC 20036 Office: 777 14th St NW Washington DC 20005

ESPOSITO, PATRICIA, assn. exec.; b. Bklyn., Nov. 28, 1944; d. Charles and Camille (D'Andrea) Butindaro; B.S., L.I. U., 1968; m. Ralph Esposito, July 9, 1966; children—Vincent, Matthew. Bus. edn. instr. N.Y.C. Bd. Edn., 1968-73; free-lance corp. tng. cons., Westchester and N.Y.C., 1973-78; asst. dir. DETO, Scarsdale, N.Y., 1978-80; exec. dir. Plumbing Industry Promotion Fund, Hartsdale, N.Y., 1980—. Mem. Westchester County Pvt. Indsl. Council, 1981—; Westchester County Drought Emergency Task Force, 1981—; chmn. Yorktown Community Devel. Adv. Council, 1980—; co-chmn. Yorktown Youth Council, 1980—; dir. Youth Employment Service, 1974-75. Mem. Am. Soc. Assn. Execs., Nat. Assn. Female Execs. Home: 435 Yorkhill Rd Yorktown Heights NY 10598 Office: 250 E Hartsdale Ave Hartsdale NY 10530

ESSLINGER, SANDRA LEE BRADLEY, corp. supr., civic worker; b. Birmingham, Ala., May 21, 1941; d. Fredrick Leslie and Ina Elizabeth (Morrow) Bradley; student LaSalle U. Corr. Sch., 1971, Huntsville (Ala.) Tech. Center, 1976; m. Sherrill Haden Esslinger, Mar. 5, 1960; children—Teresa Lee, Catherine Elizabeth, Cheryl Ann. Bookkeeper, clk., PBX operator Edwards Chevrolet Co., Inc., Birmingham, 1957-60; typist, clk. Watland, Inc., Redstone Arsenal, Ala., 1960-61; sr. file clk. Rocketdyne div. N. Am. Rockwell, Inc., Huntsville, 1960-70; sec., security officer LTV Aerospace Corp., Huntsville, 1972-73; successively adminstrv. procurement asst., adminstrv. clerical aide, adminstrv. asst., adminstrv. clk., sec. Kentron Hawaii, Ltd., Huntsville, 1973-77; procurement services supr., expediter United Space Boosters, Inc., Huntsville, 1977—. Vol. ARC; chmn. first aid room sch. in Gurley, Ala., 1970-72; pres. Chestnut Grove United Methodist Women, 1968-79; sec. ch. charge conf., 1972-73, 78—, bd. trustees, 1976-79; sec.-treas. Madison County High Sch. PTA, 1973-75; pres. Madison County High Sch. Band Parents Assn., 1973-74, treas., 1974-80. Mem. Am. Bus. Women's Assn. (pres. Ala-Hunt chpt. 1977-78, treas. Val-Mont chpt. 1975-76). Clubs: Gurley Saddle Lioness (pres. 1982-83). Home: 1614 McMullen Rd Gurley AL 35748 Office: PO Box 1626 Huntsville AL 35807

ESTA, OFELIA CURAMMENG, educator; b. Pasuquin, Ilocos Norte, Philippines, Feb. 12, 1941; d. Vito Segundo and Adelaida Aguda Curammeng; M.A. in Bilingual Edn., San Francisco State U., 1982; m. Valerio M. Esta, June 6, 1966; children—Marcia Adelene, Val Mark. Jr. and sr. high sch. tchr. Benton County (R.I.) Sch., Cole Camp, Mo., 1963-64, Ozark (Mo.) Sch., 1964-65; high sch. tchr. Orestimba Unified Sch., Newman, Calif., 1965-66; pre-kindergarten tchr. Bessie Carmichael, San Francisco, 1966—. ESEA grantee, 1963-64. Baptist. Home: 2155 34th Ave San Francisco CA 94116 Office: 55 Sherman St San Francisco CA 94103

ESTER, MARY ELLEN, cosmetologist, cosmetician, esthetician; b. Carey, Ohio, Apr. 26, 1926; d. John Cleveland and Flora Effie Ellen (Snider) Leasure; lic. Cleve. Acad. Cosmetology, 1945; grad. Realtors Inst., U. Mich., 1975; cert. Newspaper Inst. Am., 1980; m. Henry Ester, Aug. 25, 1946; 1 dau., Barbara Rosanne Ester Christensen. Tchr. cosmetology Am. Beauty Sch., Cleve., 1969-70; owner, mgr. Fair Lady Beauty Salon, Fairview Park, Ohio, 1960-70; staff Martin, Ketchum & Martin Inc., Realtors, Livonia, Mich., 1972-76; esthetician, rep. Adrien Arpel Skin Care and Cosmetics, Directives Hair Design, Rocky River, Ohio, 1977—; tchr. adult edn., cons. adult classes Lakewood High Sch. Campaign mgr. local polit. elections, 1959, 63, 71. Mem. Women's Council of Realtors, Bus. and Profl. Women, Nat. Hairdressers and Cosmetologists Assn. Home: 18849 Timber Ln Fairview Park OH 44126 Office: 20629 Center Ridge Rd Rocky River OH 44116

ESTES, EDITH LEE, income tax cons.; b. Wood River, Ill., Jan. 14, 1942; d. Lee W. and Vaunda Maude (Edmister) Estes; licence Central Beauty Sch., 1963; student So. Ill. U., 1967, U. Tex. Real Estate Sch., 1978. Clk., purchaser, East Alton (Ill.) Dairy Co., 1959-66; cashier White Front Store, Sacramento, Calif., 1969; with McDonnel Douglas Co., 1970-73; with H&R Block Co., various locations, 1968—, adminstrv. asst., McAllen, Tex., 1973-79, dist. mgr., Charleston, W.Va., 1979—. Democrat. Club: Order Eastern Star. Office: 4410 MacCorkle Ave South Charleston WV 25309

ESTES, EDNA EVA, ret. educator; b. Jasper, Ala., Nov. 23, 1921; d. F. E. and Ethel Etta (Ford) E.; student Birmingham So. Coll., 1946-47; B.S., U. Ala., 1948, M.S., 1949, Ph.D., 1957. Asst. prof. biology Flora Macdonald Coll., Red Springs, N.C., 1949-53; instr. U. Ala., Mobile, 1953-54, St. Mary's Jr. Coll., St. Mary's City, Md., 1957-59; asst. prof. Del Mar Coll., Corpus Christi, Tex., 1959-60, State Tchrs. Coll., Salisbury, Md., 1960-64; asso. prof. biology Salisbury State Coll., 1964-65, prof. biology, 1965-78. Served with WAC, AUS, 1943-45; PTO. Recipient Graham award U. Ala., 1956; So. Fellowship Fund fellow, 1956-57. Mem. AAAS, AAUW (pres. Salisbury br. 1966—), Bot. Soc. Am., Am. Assn. Plant Physiologists, Southeastern Assn. Biologists, Ala. Acad. Scis., Sigma Xi, Delta Kappa Gamma. Research in phosphorus 32 uptake and localization correlated with photosynthetic factors in higher plants. Home: 1177 S Division St Salisbury MD 21801

ESTES, ELAINE ROSE GRAHAM, librarian; b. Springfield, Mo., Nov. 24, 1931; d. James McKinley and Zelma Mae (Smith) Graham; B.S., Drake U., 1953, teaching certificate, 1956; M.L.S., U. Ill., 1960; m. John M. Estes, Jr., Dec. 29, 1953. With Pub. Library Des Moines, 1956—, head Franklin Ave. library, 1970-78, dir., 1978—; furniture adv. Living History Farms. Bd. dirs. Des Moines Community Playhouse, 1965-71; trustee Des Moines Art Center, Civic Center. Recipient Drake U. Disting. Alumni Service award, 1979; Des Moines Architects Council reward, 1981; YWCA award, 1982. Mem. ALA, Iowa Library Assn. (pres. 1978-79), Met. Library Assn. Greater Des Moines (past pres.), Iowa Soc. Preservation of Historic Landmarks (dir.), Polk County Hist. Soc., Nat. Trust Historic Preservation (bd. advs. 1971-78), Terrace Hill Soc. (dir.), Iowa Historic Materials Preservation Soc. (v.p. 1982), Questers (1st v.p. chpt.), Beta Phi Mu. Republican. Methodist. Contbr. articles to profl. publs. Home: Des Moines IA 50309 Office: 100 Locust St Des Moines IA 50309

ESTES, ELEANOR, author; b. West Haven, Conn., May 9, 1906; d. Louis and Caroline (Gewecke) Rosenfeld; grad. (Caroline M. Hewins scholar) Pratt Inst. Sch. Library Sci., 1932; m. Rice Estes, Dec. 8, 1932; 1 dau., Helena Estes Haeseler. Children's librarian Free Public Library, New Haven, 1924-31, N.Y.C. Public Library, 1932-40; lectr. on writing for children; author: The Moffats, 1941, The Middle Moffat, 1942, The Sun and the Wind and Mr. Todd, 1943, Rufus M., 1943, The Hundred Dresses, 1944, The Echoing Green, 1947, The Sleeping Giant, 1948, Ginger Pye (Newbery medal, Herald Tribune Spring Book Festival) 1951, A Little Oven, 1955, Pinky Pye, 1958, The Witch Family, 1960, The Alley, 1964, Miranda The Great, 1967, The Lollipop Princess, 1967, The Tunnel of Hugsy Goode, 1972, The Coat-Hanger Christmas Tree, 1973; The Lost Umbrella of Kim Chu, 1978; contbr. articles to profl. mags., stories to children's mags. Recipient Newbery medal, 1951; Ann. Alumni award Pratt Inst., 1957. Mem. PEN, Authors League, Authors Guild. Episcopalian.

ESTES, MARGARET TURNER, univ. adminstr.; b. Caldwell, Kans., July 1, 1924; d. William Jennings Bryant and Margaret Violet (Kern) Turner; B.A., U. Kans., 1965, M.A., 1967, Ph.D. in Sociology, 1972; m. John King Estes, Jan. 13, 1943; (dec.), children—John, Greg, David, Jennifer. Instr., U. Kans., 1965-68; asst. prof. sociology Millersville (Pa.) State U., 1968-70; asst. prof. anthropology/sociology Haskell Indian Coll., Lawrence, Kans., 1970-71; prof. sociology, chmn. dept. No. Ariz. U., Flagstaff, 1972-78; asso. v.p. acad. affairs, prof. sociology Miss. State U., Starkville, 1978—. Mem. Gov. Ariz. Commn. Women, 1976, Gov. Ariz. Task Force Marriage and Family, 1976-78. Named Faculty Woman of Year, No. Ariz. U., 1973; Margaret Turner Estes scholarship established, 1978. Mem. Am. Assn. Higher Edn., N.Am. Assn. Summer Sessions, So. Sociol. Assn., AAAS (past dir.), Am. Sociol. Assn., Phi Kappa Phi, Phi Delta Kappa. Democrat. Congregationalist. Office: Drawer BQ Miss State U Mississippi State MS 39762

ESTEY, AUDREE, exec., cons. ballet soc.; b. Winnipeg, Man., Can., Jan. 7, 1910; d. Robert and Anna (Harrington) Phipps; student Immaculate Heart Coll., 1927-29; m. L. Wendell Estey, Sept. 18, 1933; children—Lawrence Mitchell, Carol. Ballet tchr. Lawrenceville and Princeton, N.J., 1938-80, Perry Mansfield Camp, Steamboat Springs Colo., summers 1949-50; head dance dept. Les Chalets Francais, Deer Isle, Maine, 1951-73; founder non-profit Princeton (N.J.) Ballet Soc., 1954, dir., cons.; founder Princeton Regional Ballet Co., 1963; founder profl. co., Princeton Ballet, 1979. Apptd. by gov. N.J. State Commn. to Study Arts, 1968, trustee N.J. Sch. of the Arts, 1980. Mem. N.E. Regional Ballet Assn. (pres., 1967-68, exec. v.p., 1968-71). Episcopalian. Choreographer over 20 ballets for children and young dancers including: Festival of the Gnomes, Pastels, Peter and the Wolf, Sleeping Beauty, Cinderella, Pied Piper, The Nutcracker (choreography for Act I currently used by Princeton Ballet), Chanson Innocente, Graduation Ball, Coppelia. Office: 262 Alexander St Princeton NJ 08540

ESTRADA, ISABEL VICTORIA, obstetrician, gynecologist; b. San Juan, P.R., Nov. 17, 1918; d. Serafin and Elisa (Molinari) Estrada; student, U. P.R., 1938; M.D., Marquette U.; children—Kenneth Wayne, Lisa Darlene. Intern St. Joseph's Hosp., Milw.; gen. practice medicine Santurce, P.R., 1943-50; resident St. Luke's Hosp., New Bedford, Mass., 1950-51; fellow in ob-gyn pathology Free Hosp. Med. Women, Brookline, Mass., 1952; resident Mt. Sinai Hosp., Milw., 1952-54; USPHS fellow, Rio Piedras, P.R., 1956-62; practice medicine specializing in ob-gyn, Whittier, Calif. Pres. pro tem Hispanic Republican Women Los Angeles County. Recipient Los Angeles Med. Woman of Yr. award Am. Med. Women's Assn., 1966; Cert. of Appreciation of Vol. Service Am. Coll. Obstetricians and Gynecologists and Indian Health Service, 1981; Pope John XXIII award Italian Cath. Fedn., Shiprock, N.Mex., 1982; diplomate Am. Bd. Ob-Gyn Fellow Am. Coll. Obstetricians and Gynecologists, ACS, Los Angeles Ob-Gyn Soc.; mem. Gynecol. Urological Soc., Los Angeles County Med. Women (pres. 1968), Calif. Hispanic Drs. Assn., P.R. Med. Soc., P.R. Ob-Gyn Soc., Assn. Marquette Univ. Women (dir. 1954-56), Flying Drs. of Mercy, Am. Med. Women's Assn., N.Y. Acad. Scis., AAAS, Women's Overseas Service League, Marquette U. Med. Alumni Assn. (bd. dirs. Los Angeles County), La Mirada Bus. and Profl. Women, Baker-Channing Soc., Alpha Sigma Nu, Gamma Pi Epsilon. Office: 12464 E Washington Blvd PO Box 1487 Whittier CA 90609

ESTRADA, NORMA RUTH, psychologist; b. Oakland, Calif., Oct. 29, 1926; d. Fred and Evelyn (Costa) Cambra; student Calif. Coll. Arts and Crafts, 1946-47; B.A., Antioch Coll. West, 1975; Ph.D., Union Grad. Sch. West, 1978; m. Marce Estrada, Aug. 22, 1959; children—Jeffrey, Jamie. Adminstrv. asst. research and devel. Gladman Meml. Hosp., Oakland, 1966—, also exec. dir. The Gladman Center, 1975—; co-therapist in pvt. practice Hotel Claremont, Berkeley, Calif., 1972—; bd. dirs. Health Research Found., 1977—. Fellow Menninger Found.; mem. Am. Psychol. Assn., Biofeedback Soc. Am., Am. Assn. Biofeedback Clinicians, Biofeedback Soc. Calif. (dir. 1979-80), AAAS. Democrat. Roman Catholic. Contbg. author: Psychiatry and Mysticism (Stanley Dean, editor), 1975. Office: 2633 E 27th St Oakland CA 94601

ESTRERA, LEONOR OTADOY, physician; b. Poro, Cebu, Philippines, Mar. 1, 1936; d. Eugenio Ylaida and Rosario Garciano (Otadoy) Estrera; B.S., U. San Carlos, 1955; M.D., U. Philippines, 1960. Intern, Youngstown (Ohio) Hosp. Assn., 1961; pediatric resident Childrens Hosp. of D.C. and Georgetown U., 1962-64; asst. prof. pediatrics Southwestern U., Cebu City, Philippines, 1967-73; chief of clinics Sacred Heart Hosp., Cebu City, Philippines, 1971-73; practice medicine, specializing in pediatrics, Princeton, W.Va., 1974—; chmn. dept. pediatrics Princeton Community Hosp., 1980—. Josiah Macy Found. fellow, 1971-73; diplomate Am. Bd. Pediatrics. Fellow Am. Acad. Pediatrics; mem. AMA (Physicians Recognition award 1978), W.Va. Med. Assn., Mercer County Med. Soc., Princeton Mercer C. of C. Roman Catholic. Home: 21 Crestview Dr Princeton WV 24740 Office: Med Arts Clinic Suite 15 Princeton WV 24740

ETCHESON, DENISE ELENE, architect; b. Iowa City, Iowa, May 17, 1950; s. Warren Wade and Marianne (Newgent) E.; B.A. in Environ. Design, U. Washington, 1974, cert. in Urban Design, 1977, M.Arch., 1977. Planner, designer Temel Muhendislik A.S., Istanbul, Turkey, 1974; project designer Astra Zarina Assos., Seattle, 1973-74, 76-77; project designer, constrn. coordinator G.R. Bartholick Architect/Planner, Seattle, 1975, 78; project mgr. TRA Airport Cons., Seattle, 1978—; lectr. U. Wash., 1977. Mem. City of Seattle Pike Pl. Market Hist. Commn., 1975—, vice chmn., 1977-79, chmn., 1979-81, mem. Landmarks Preservation Bd., 1976-77. Recipient U. Wash. Archtl. Found. award, 1975. Mem. Am. Planning Assn., Historic Seattle Preservation and Devel. Authority, Nat. Trust Historic Preservation, Internat. Council Monuments and Sites. Home: 3146 Portage Bay Pl E Seattle WA 98102 Office: 215 Columbia St Seattle WA 98104

ETELSON, DORIS C., restaurant chain exec.; b. 1930; B.S., SUNY, 1975. With Joseph Dixon Pencil Co., 1950-57; mgr. exec. dining rm. St. Regis Paper Co., 1960-61; with Howard Johnson Co., Dorchester, Mass., 1965—, mgr. adminstrn. and maintenance, 1972-77, v.p. service standards restaurant group, 1977-82, v.p. service standards, 1982—. Office: Howard Johnson Co Howard Johnson Plaza Dorchester MA 02119

ETESS, ELAINE GROSSINGER, hotel exec.; b. N.Y.C., Dec. 9, 1927; d. Harry and Jennie Grossinger; student Russell Sage Coll., Troy, N.Y., Syracuse (N.Y.) U.; m. David Etess, Aug. 10, 1947; children—Susan, Mark, Mitchell. Co-owner, exec. v.p. Grossinger (N.Y.) Hotel. Mem. Community Gen. Hosp. Aux., Sullivan County; life mem. PTA. Recipient Career award N.Y. State Bus. & Profl. Women's Clubs, 1977; Doris L. Crockett Disting. Service award Russell Sage Coll., 1979. Mem. N.Y. State Hotel & Motel Assn. (past chmn. bd. 1979-80), Am. Hotel and Motel Assn. (dir. mem. exec. com. and long-range planning com., trustee ednl. inst.), Sullivan County Bus. and Profl. Women. Home and Office: Grossinger's Grossinger NY 12734

ETHAN, CAROL BAEHR, psychotherapist; b. N.Y.C., May 30, 1920; d. Irving and Susan (Goldman) Baehr; trained at Met. Inst. Psychoanalytic Studies, N.Y.C., 1965-70; B.A. in Psychology (Univ. honors scholar 1978), N.Y. U., 1978; M.A. in Psychology, New Sch., 1981; m. 2d, Sy Ethan, Mar. 18, 1955; children—Willa Capraro, Barbara Ethan. Writer, Irvington (N.J.) Herald, 1946; staff writer Walt Framer Prodns., N.Y.C., 1949-50; cons., researcher consumer psychology, N.Y.C., 1950-70; instr. tech. writing Queens Coll., 1956-57; consumer research Dancer Fitzgerald Sample, Ogilvy & Mather; staff psychotherapist Fifth Ave. Center Counseling and psychotherapy, N.Y.C., 1965-70; motivation analyst J. Walter Thompson, N.Y.C., 1966-67; asso. research dir. Papert, Koenig, Lois, N.Y.C., 1967-68; pvt. practice psychoanalytic psychotherapy, N.Y.C., 1967—; human relations columnist Taconic Press, 1981—. Committeewoman Queens County Democratic Party, 1960; vol. social rehab. program Queens County Mental Health Soc., 1965-66. Mem. Am. Orthopsychiat. Assn., N.Y. State Assn. Practicing Psychotherapists, AAUW, Nat. Accreditation Assn. Psychoanalysts (affiliate), Am. Psychol. Assn. (assoc.), Family Mediation Assn., Am. Personnel and Guidance Assn.

ETHIER, PATRICIA KELLEHER, ins. co. exec.; b. Montague, Mass., June 28, 1951; d. Edward Patterson and Mary Elizabeth (Masterson) Kelleher; A.A., Greenfield Community Coll., 1971; student Am. Coll., 1979-82; m. Gerard R. Ethier, Aug. 3, 1973. Titlist policy title Phoenix Mut. Life Ins. Co., Greenfield, Mass., 1971-76, supr. group major med. claims, 1976-78, asso. mgr. group claims, 1978-79, mgr. policy title, 1979—. Allocations chmn. Franklin County United Way, 1980-81, bd. dirs., 1980-82; mem. adv. bd. Dept. Social Services, Franklin County, 1981—; bd. dirs. New England Learning Center Women in Transition, 1981—. Fellow Life Office Mgmt. Assn., Western Mass. Assn. Female Execs., Nat. Assn. Female Execs. Roman Catholic. Home: 205 Fairview West Greenfield MA 01301 Office: 101 Munson St Greenfield MA 01301

ETHRIDGE, BETTY S., cosmetics co. sales ofcl.; b. Birmingham, Ala., Mar. 4, 1941; d. Gordon and Pauline J. (Isbell) Reed; student schs. Trussville, Ala.; m. Gary J. Ethridge, Nov. 27, 1957; children—Barry, Elisa. Exec. sec., Hayes Internat. Corp., Birmingham, Ala., 1961-70; legal sec. firm Atwell & Caton, Pensacola, Fla., 1971-72, firm McGraw, Pensacola, 1972-73; sr. sales dir. Mary Kay Cosmetics, Dallas, 1973—, also tchr. direct sales, seminars. Recipient award Dale Carnegie mgmt. seminar, 1980, sales awards, Mary Kay Cosmetics, 1978—. Mem. Nat. Assn. Female Execs., Bus. and Profl. Women's Club, Mary Kay Pink Cadillac Club. Republican. Baptist. Address: 8135 Fordham Dr Pensacola FL 32504

ETHRIDGE, DEBORAH JANE, lawyer; b. Midland, Tex., Sept. 14, 1951; d. Morris and Marie E. (Raiford) E.; student U. Tex., 1971; B.A., Baylor U., 1972, J.D., 1975. Admitted to Tex. bar, 1975; briefing atty. 5th Supreme Judl. Dist., Ct. of Civil Appeals, State of Tex., Dallas, 1975-76; atty. Braniff Airways, Dallas, 1976—, corporate sec., 1979—. Mem. Am. Bar Assn., Tex. Bar Assn., Dallas Bar Assn., Am. Soc. Corporate Sec., Dallas Assn. Young Lawyers, Assn. Women Execs. Baptist. Clubs: Cimarron (pres. 1982-83), Slipper, Altrusa, 500 Inc., Innovators. Office: Braniff Airways PO Box 61747 Dallas TX 75261

ETKIND, POLLY ROSE, virologist, molecular biologist; b. Elmira, N.Y., Apr. 26, 1944; d. Max and Anna Mae (Botnick) Etkind; B.A., Goucher Coll., 1966; Ph.D. in Biology, Cornell U. Grad. Sch. Med. Scis., 1976; m. Herman Hochberg, Sept. 6, 1981. Sr. research technician Sloan-Kettering Inst., N.Y.C., 1966-70; predoctoral fellow Cornell U. Grad. Sch. Med. Scis., 1970-76; Arthritis Found. postdoctoral fellow Rockefeller U., N.Y.C., 1976-79; research asso. Sloan-Kettering Inst., N.Y.C., 1979—. Recipient Vol. award United Hosp. Assn., 1968. Mem. Am. Soc. Microbiologists. Republican. Jewish. Contbr. articles to profl. jours. Home: 405 E 63rd St New York NY 10021 Office: Meml Sloan-Kettering Cancer Center 1275 York Ave New York NY 10021

ETSCOVITZ, ANITA GROSS, social worker; b. Manchester, N.H., Nov. 24, 1937; d. Hyman and Ruth (Wexler) Gross; B.A., U. N.H., 1959; M.S.W., Boston U., 1961; m. Lionel Etscovitz, Aug. 20, 1961 (div.); children—Hyman, Barry, Marcie. Student placement caseworker Jewish Family and Children's Services, Worcester, Mass., 1959-60, VA Hosp., Jamaica Plains, Mass., 1960-61; social worker Beth Israel Hosp., Boston, 1961-63; now social worker Haverford Dialysis Unit, Bryn Mawr, Pa. Mem. Council Nephrology Social Workers (group sec.-treas.), Acad. Cert. Social Workers, Nat. Assn. Social Workers, Nat. Kidney Found. Home: 408 Penwyn Rd Wynnewood PA 19096

ETTINGER, SUSI STEINITZ, artist; b. Berlin, July 29, 1922; came to U.S., 1939, naturalized, 1944; d. Otto and Grethe Steinitz; B.F.A. cum laude, U. Louisville, 1943; m. Manford F. Ettinger, June 2, 1944; children—Linda, Daniel. Staff lectr. Met. Mus. Art, N.Y.C., 1944-45; staff instr., dir. children's classes Springfield (Mo.) Art Mus., 1960-66; instr. and lectr. art S.W. Mo. State U., Springfield, 1964—, also area head found. art program; one-woman shows include: Ft. Smith (Ark.) Art Mus., 1968, Sch. of Ozarks, 1972, Park Central Gallery, Springfield, 1974, Springfield Art Mus., 1976; exhibited group shows in Mo., 1966, 67, 75, 79, Omaha, 1970; represented in permanent collections: Mo. Hist. Soc., Springfield Art Mus. Recipient Appreciation cert. Mo. Women in Arts, 1974. Home: 2020 Ventura Ave Springfield MO 65804 Office: SW Mo State U Springfield MO 65806

ETZEL, BARBARA COLEMAN, psychologist, educator; b. Pitts., Sept. 19, 1926; d. Walter T. and Ruth (Coleman) E.; A.A., Stephens Coll., 1946; B.S. in Psychology, Denison U., 1948; M.S., U. Miami (Fla.), 1950; Ph.D. in Exptl. Child Psychology, State U. Iowa, 1953. Staff psychologist Ohio State Bur. Juvenile Research, Columbus, 1953-54; asst. prof. psychology Fla. State U., Tallahassee, 1954-56; chief psychologist, child psychiatry U. Wash. Med. Sch., Seattle, 1956-61; asso. prof. psychology Western Wash. State U., Bellingham, 1961-65, dir. grad. program in psychology, 1963-65; spl. fellow sect. early learning and devel. NIMH, Bethesda, Md., 1965-66; asso. prof. dept. human devel. U. Kans., Lawrence, 1965-69, mem. grad. faculty, 1965—, prof. dept. human devel., 1969—, dir. Edna A. Hill Child Devel. Lab., 1965-72, dir. Kansas Center for Research in Early Childhood Edn., 1968-71, asso. dean Office of Research Adminstrn. and Grad. Sch., 1972-74, dir. John T. Stewart Children's Center, 1975—; vis. prof. Universidad Central de Venezuela, Caracas, 1981-82; cons. Manchester Sch. Presch. Program, U. Mex., Mexico City, 1973-75, George Peabody Tchrs. Coll., 1978, St. Luke's Hosp., Kansas City, Mo., 1981—. Bd. dirs. Community Children's Center, Inc., 1968-71; trustee Center for Research, Inc., U. Kans., 1975—. Elected to U. Kans. Women's Hall of Fame, 1975; Japan Soc. for Promotion for Sci. fellow, 1981. Fellow Am. Psychol. Assn.; mem. Soc. for Research in Child Devel., Midwestern Psychol. Assn., Am. Ednl. Research Assn., AAAS, AAUP, Southwestern Soc. for Research in Human Devel., Sigma Xi, Psi Chi, Pi Lambda Theta. Author: (with J.M. LeBlanc and D.M. Baer) New Developments in Behavioral Research, 1977; contbr. numerous articles on learning and human devel. to profl. publs.; editorial bd. Behavior Analyst, 1979—. Home: Woodsong at JB Ranch Rt 1 PO Box 82-E Oskaloosa KS 66066 Office: Dept of Human Development U Kans Lawrence KS 66045

ETZLER, LOIS RUTH, med. technologist; b. Lancaster, Ohio, Jan. 27, 1941; d. Edward Ferdinand and Ruth Faye (Cofman) Walter; B.S. in Med. Tech., Ohio State U., 1963; postgrad. Central Mich. U.; m. Alvin Lorenz Etzler, May 4, 1963; children—Paul, Janice. Med. technologist Ohio State U. Hosp., 1962-63; blood bank technologist OB Hunter Lab., Washington, 1963-65; blood bank supr. Jewish Hosp., Louisville, 1965-66; mem. lab. staff Southeast Community Hosp., Washington, 1969—, dcb. and quality control supr., 1975-81, computer system and edn. coordinator, quality control supr., 1981—. Fin. sec. Chesapeake dist. Lutheran Women's Missionary League, 1978-82, pres. zone, 1976-78; del. Nat. Capitol area Luth. High Sch. Assn., 1978—. Mem. Am. Soc. Clin. Pathologists, Echo. Home: 2211 Green Valley Dr Sunderland MD 20689 Office: Dept Pathology 1310 Southern Ave Washington DC 20032

EU, MARCH KONG FONG, state ofcl.; b. Oakdale, Calif., Mar. 29, 1927; d. Yuen and Shiu (Shee) Kong; student Salinas Jr. Coll.; B.S., U. Calif., Berkeley; M.Ed., Mills Coll., 1951; Ed.D., Stanford U., 1956; postgrad. Columbia U., Calif. State Coll., Hayward; children by previous marriage—Matthew Kipling, Marchesa Suyin; m. Henry Eu, July 30, 1973; stepchildren—Henry, Adeline, Yvonne, Conroy, Alaric. Chmn. div. dental hygiene U. Calif. Med. Center, San Francisco, dental hygienist Oakland (Calif.) Pub. Schs.; supr. dental health edn. Alameda County (Calif.) Schs.; lectr. health edn. Mills Coll., Oakland; mem. Calif. Legislature, 1966-74, chmn. select com. on agr., foods and nutrition, 1973-74, mem. com. natural resources and conservation, com. commerce and pub. utilities, select com. med. malpractice; sec. state State of Calif., 1975—. Spl. cons. Bur. Intergroup Relations Calif. Dept. Edn.; ednl., legis. cons. Sausalito (Calif.) Pub. Schs., Santa Clara County Office Edn., Jefferson Elem. Union Sch. Dist., Santa Clara High Sch. Dist., Santa Clara Elem. Sch. Dist., Live Oak Union High Sch. Dist. Mem. Alameda County Bd. Edn., 1956-66, pres., 1961-62, legis. adv., 1963; mem. budget panel Bay Area United Fund Crusade; mem. Oakland Econ. Devel. Council; mem. tourism devel. com. Calif. Econ. Devel. Commn., mem. citizens com. on housing Council Social Planning; mem. Calif. Interagy. Council Family Planning; edn. chmn., mem. council social planning, dir. Oakland Area Baymont Dist. Community Council; charter pres. hon. life mem. Howard Elementary Sch. PTA; charter pres. Chinese Young Ladies Soc., Oakland; mem., vice chmn. adv. com. Youth Study Centers and Ford Found. Interagy. Project, 1962-63; chmn. Alameda County Mothers' March, 1971-72. Mem. exec. com. Calif. Democratic Central Com., mem. central com., 1963-70; asst. sec., del. Dem. Nat. Conv., 1968; dir. 8th Congl. Dist. Dem. Council, 1963; v.p. Dems. of 8th Congl. Dist., 1963; dir. Key Women for Kennedy, 1963; women's vice chmn. No. Calif. Johnson for Pres., 1964. Bd. dirs. Oakland YMCA, 1965. Recipient ann. award for outstanding achievement Eastbay Intercultural Fellowship, 1959, Phoebe Apperson Hearst Distinguished Bay Area Women of Year award, Woman of Year award Calif. Retail Liquor Dealers Inst., 1969, Merit citation Calif. Assn. Adult Edn. Adminstrs., 1970, Art Edn. award. Mem. Am. (life, pres. 1956-57), No. Calif. (life) dental hygienists assns., Oakland LWV, AAUW (area rep. in edn. Oakland br.), Calif. Tchrs. Assn., Calif., Alameda County (pres. 1965) sch. bds. assns., So. Calif. Dental Assn. (hon.). Bus. and Profl. Women's Club, Delta Kappa Gamma. Office: 1230 J St Suite 605 Sacramento CA 95814

EUBANKS, FRANCES OLIVE DOWELL (MRS. ELI T. EUBANKS), oil co. mgr.; b. Wellsford, Kans.; d. Frank E. and Eva (Thomas) Dowell; student U. Kans., 1945-46; B.S., Kans. State U., 1949, M.S., 1950; m. Eli T. Eubanks, Dec. 23, 1940. Teaching fellow dept. home mgmt. Kans. State Coll., Manhattan, 1949-50; instr. U. Louisville, 1950-51, U. Wash., Seattle, 1951-52; mgr. records dept. Adair Oil Co., Wichita, Kans., 1955—. Sec. Young Democrats Club, U. Kans., 1945-46. Mem. Omicron Nu, Phi Kappa Phi. Home: Route 1 Viola KS 67149 Office: POB 2823 Wichita KS 67201

EUTSLER, BRENDA LEE, paralegal; b. Phila., Nov. 11, 1953; d. Herbert Paul and Angeline Eleanor (Palmieri) E.; grad. Ryder Bus. Sch., 1972; cert. paralegal Inst. Paralegal Tng., 1976. Office mgr./paralegal Bruce MacNaul, Esq., Haddon Heights, N.J., 1972-77; paralegal/sec. Henry S. Hilles, Jr., Esq., Drinker, Biddle & Reath, Phila., 1977-78; dep. surrogate Camden County, Camden, N.J., 1978-81; freelance paralegal, Haddonfield, N.J., 1981—; instr. Paralegal Inst., 1981—; lectr. in field. Co-chmn., Camden County Adv. Council for Juvenile Conf. Coms., 1979—; sec. Oaklyn Juvenile Conf. Com., 1977—; co-founder, trustee, exec. dir. endl., counseling and support program for widows and widowers, Camden, 1978; pres. Camden County chpt. Sunshine Found., 1981—. Mem. Nat. Assn. Female Execs., Bus. and Profl. Women. Democrat. Roman Catholic. Contbr. articles to profl. jours. Home: 116 E Clinton Ave Haddon Twp NJ 08107 Office: 76 Euclid Ave Haddonfield NJ 08033

EVANS, ANN PRATT, arts adminstr.; b. Kansas City, Mo., Dec. 22, 1946; d. Richard Clifford and Mary Ruth (McDade) Kaiser; B.S., U. Kans., 1969; m. David C. Evans, Aug. 9, 1969; 1 dau., Whitney Ann. Tchr., Shawnee Mission Sch. Dist., Overland Park, Kans., 1969-70; supr. Avis Rent-a-Car, Boston, 1970-71; visual arts coordinator, asst. to dir. Arts Center, Albany, N.Y., 1972-74; dir. Lawrence (Kans.) Arts Center, 1974—. Bd. dirs. Seem-to-be-Players, Douglas County Planning Council on Services for Aging, 1974-82; adv. Lawrence Community Theatre, U. Kans. Arts Council, Lawrence Art Commn., fine arts program Unified Sch. Dist. 497. Recipient grants Kans. Arts Commn., 1974-79, Nat. Endowment Arts, 1979, 80, 81, 82. Mem. Lawrence Art Guild (dir.), Kaw Valley Weavers Guild, Kans. Designer Craftsmen Assn., Am. Crafts Council, Surface Design Assn., Kaw Valley Quilters Guild, LWV, Alpha Gamma Delta (dir., v.p.). Club: Daffodil (pres. 1980—). Home: 1636 Louisiana St Lawrence KS 66044 Office: 9th and Vermont Sts Lawrence KS 66044

EVANS, BARBARA FRANKILEE COMER, security services co. mgr.; b. Phoenix, Oct. 7, 1928; d. Lee Martin and Catherine Diana Jenkins Comer Beazell; student Brigham Young U., 1947-48, Utah Tech. Coll., 1968, Wharton Sch. U. Pa., 1977; m. Ross T. Evans, Jan. 18, 1953 (dec. Apr. 1967); children—Catherine Lynn Evans Wardle, Richard Lee, Robert Ross. Sec., Grand Junction (Colo.) Public Sch., 1948-52; sec. Arden Sunfreze, 1952-53; with Burns Internat. Security Services, various locations, 1963—, group acctg. mgr. Mid-West, Chgo., 1978-80, group ops. services mgr., 1980-82, corp. field services mgr., 1982—. Recipient Silver Beehive award Salt Lake Greater council Boy Scouts Am., 1968; named Woman of Yr., Am. Bus. Women's Assn. Salt Lake City, 1972. Mem. Am. Soc. Indsl. Security, Nat. Assn. Fleet Adminstrs., Am. Bus. Women's Assn. Club: Zonta. Home: 47 C Jefferson Oval Yorktown Heights NY 10598 Office: 320 Old Briarcliff Rd Briarcliff Manor NY 10510

EVANS, CAROLYN MARGARET, jud. edn. profl.; b. Camden, N.J., Jan. 19, 1946; d. Philip Louis and Margaret Caroline (Henry) Iuliucci; B.A., Rutgers U., 1968; postgrad. LaSalle Coll., 1981—. Probation officer Camden (N.J.) County Probation Dept., 1968-70, sr. probation officer, dir. vols., 1970-74; dir. vol. services Adminstrv. Office of Cts., Trenton, N.J., 1974-81, asst. chief jud. edn., 1981—; mem. adj. faculty tng. for vol. mgrs. Rutgers U. Mem. Nat. Assn. for Female Execs., Am. Soc. for Tng. and Devel., Vols. in Cts. and Corrections Assn. of N.J. (pres. 1980-82), Nat. Assn. on Vols. in Criminal Justice (sec. 1977-79, adv. bd., chmn. com. on adult cts. and probation Nat. Guidelines Project 1980-82). Home: 4 Randolph Pl Willingboro NJ 08046 Office: Justice Complex CN 037 Trenton NJ 08625

EVANS, CAROLYN MARIE, employment agy. exec.; b. Phila., Oct. 8, 1933; d. Robert Wayne and Gertrude Marie (Oelschlager) Clark; B.S. in Edn., Temple U., 1962, postgrad., 1972; m. Virgil Lang Evans, Dec. 19, 1953; children—Morgan Lang, Stephanie Marie, Mark Harris, Kathryn Elizabeth. Owner, mgr. comml. orchard Evans Orchards, Duncannon, Pa., 1968-78; personnel cons. Jobs Inc., Harrisburg, Pa., 1976-77; owner, sec.-treas. Phoenix Personnel Services Inc., Lemoyne, Pa., 1977—; pres. Carolyn Evans Assos., Inc., tech. and profl. recruiters, Plymouth Meeting, Pa., 1980—. Bd. dirs. Mid-Susquehanna Arts in Edn. Council, 1979—. Mem. Nat. Assn. Personnel Cons. (cert. personnel cons.), Pa. Assn. Personnel Cons., Adminstrv. Mgmt. Soc. (sec., v.p. membership). Quaker. Club: Monday. Home: 4104 McIntosh Rd Harrisburg PA 17112 Office: Carolyn Evans Assos Inc Plymouth Plaza Suite 101 580 W Germantown Pike Plymouth Meeting PA 19462

EVANS, CHARLOTTE PFAU (MRS. G. ROBERT EVANS), writer, communications cons.; b. Newton, N.J., Nov. 26, 1933; d. Karl Otto and Wilhelmina (Otterbach) Pfau; student Douglass Coll., 1952-54; B.S., R.N., Columbia U. Presbyn. Hosp., 1957, postgrad., 1957-59; postgrad. N.Y.U., 1959-60; M.P.A., Coll. of Notre Dame, 1979; m. John Atterbury Mortimer, Nov. 20, 1964; children—Meredith Elizabeth, Mandy Leigh; m. 2d, G. Robert Evans, Sept. 4, 1982. Spl. assignment nurse Columbia-Presbyn. Med. Center, N.Y.C., 1957-59; med. advt. copywriter Paul Klemtner & Co., N.Y.C., 1959-61, William Douglas McAdams Agy., N.Y.C., 1961-62; account exec. Arndt, Preston, Chapin, Lamb & Keen, N.Y.C., 1962-63; Rocky Mountain corr. Med. World News, Denver, 1963-64; owner Publicite, Denver; gen. mgr. Center Mktg. Asso., Palo Alto, Calif., 1964-66; free lance writer, pub. relations and mgmt. cons., Woodside, Calif., 1966—; pres. Communications for Youth, 1979—. Mem. Palo Alto-Stanford Hosp. Aux., 1968-72; pub. relations assistance Peninsula Children's Center, Palo Alto, 1968-73, Triton Mus. Art, San Jose, Calif., 1966-70; chmn. citizens adv. com. San Mateo County Juvenile Social Services; health component Early Childhood Com., Woodside Elem. Sch. Dist.; mem. adv. com. South County Youth and Family Services Program; bd. dirs. N.J. Jr. C. of C./UNICEF/ African Project, 1960-61. Home: 700 Kings Mountain Rd Woodside CA 94062 Office: PO Box 4136 Woodside CA 94062

EVANS, ELEANOR JUANITA, mfg. and bus. cons. co. exec.; b. Annapolis, Md., Nov. 8, 1944; d. Simon Theodor and Ernestine (Hayes) Evans; A.B. in Social Sci., San Diego State U., 1967, postgrad. in Edn. Adminstrn., 1974, M.S. in Counseling, 1974. Tchr., San Diego Unified Schs., 1968-77, substitute prin. Johnson Elementary Sch., 1974-76; instr. dept. psychology Ednl. Cultural Complex San Diego Community Coll. Dist., 1977; owner, operator Zucchini Prodns., San Diego, 1977—; dir. San Diego County Youth Conservation Corps., 1974-75; cons. in field. Bd. dirs. San Diego Urban League, 1970—, sec., 1974, chmn. com. to select exec. dir., 1975, also life mem.; den leader Cub Scouts Golden Hills council Boy Scouts Am., 1976; bd. dirs. Headstart Program, Golden Hills United Presbyn. Ch., San Diego, 1976; rep. from 79th Assembly Dist. to Republican County Central Com. of San Diego County, 1972—; asso. mem. Republican Central Com. of Calif., 1974—; precinct chmn. 79th Assembly Dist., 1976. Recipient certificate of achievement San Diego Urban League Ednl. Service, 1976. Mem. Delta Sigma Theta. Club: Mt. View Tennis. Author curriculum guide for teaching reading to students who speak with cultural dialects, 1972—. Home: 651 Bollenbacher St San Diego CA 92114

EVANS, ELLEN LOVELL, historian, educator; b. Paris, Nov. 17, 1930 (parents Am. citizens); d. Leander Bell and Enid (Baird) Lovell; B.A., Swarthmore Coll., 1951; M.A., U. Wis., 1952; Ph.D., Columbia U., 1956; m. Trevor Evans, Dec. 26, 1953; children—Judith Ann, Susan Enid, Martha Lillian. Instr. U. Ga., Atlanta, 1954-58; asst. prof. history Ga. State U., Atlanta, 1963-68, assoc. prof., 1968—. Mem. Am. Hist. Assn., So. Hist. Assn., Conf. Group Central European History, Ga. Assn. Historians, Phi Alpha Theta. Author: The German CenterParty 1870-1933: A study in Political Catholicism, 1981. Office: Dept History Ga State U Atlanta GA 30303

EVANS, FAITH PATRICIA, govt. ofcl.; b. Honolulu, May 11, 1937; d. Freeman G. and Marie C. (Rodrigues) Ernesto; R.N. with honors, St. Francis Sch. Nursing, 1958; m. Noel D. Evans, Jan. 27, 1962; children—Tricia, Kathleen, John. Nurse, St. Francis Hosp., 1958-60, Kaiser Permanente Clinic, 1961-62, Windward Med. Center, 1965-66; office mgr. Hawaii State PTA, 1974; mem. Hawaii Ho. of Reps., Honolulu, 1974-80, house minority floor leader, 1978-80, asst. minority floor leader, 1976-78; U.S. marshal Dist. Hawaii, 1982—. 3d v.p. Hawaii PTA, 1976, chmn. state legis. com., 1974, chmn. state publicity com., 1971-72, pres. Windward Dist., 1972-74, Maunawili Sch., 1973-74; mem. Maryknoll PTG Bd., 1974-76; bd. dirs. Spl. Edn. Center Oahu, Olomama Community Assn., 1973-82, Kailua Community Council, 1973-82; mem. Windward Mental Health Adv. Council; bd. dirs. Windward Health Planning Council, 1974-76; pres. women's aux. Hawaii Pharm. Assn., 1967; mem. Nurses Coalition for Action in Politics, 1975-78; bd. dirs. Kailua Nat. Little League, 1975-78; mem. Farrington Alumni Found.; bd. dirs. Kekuaanaui (Hawaii) Big Sisters, Inc., 1976-78, Am. Cancer Soc.; mem. public relations com. Pacific council Girl Scouts U.S.A., 1973-76; mem. adv. bd. Liberty House, 1972-73; pres. Hui O' Pohakupu, 1969, Hui Hauoli, 1970; mem. Immunization Action Com., 1976-78; mem. Windward Sub-Area Health Planning Council, 1978-79; mem. State Hosp. Adv. Com.; mem. Castle Hosp. Citizen's Adv. Council; mem. Oahuwide Certificate of Need Com.; bd. dirs. Hawaii Epilepsy Soc.; exec. v.p. Scoliosis Club Hawaii; 1st vice-chmn. Hawaii Republican Com., 1977-79. Mem. Kaneohe Bus. and Profl. Women's Club. Office: 300 Ala Moana Blvd Room C103 Honolulu HI 96850

EVANS, GRACE TROUT, Realtor asso.; b. Jacksonville, Fla., Nov. 14, 1920; d. Philip Wilbur and Leona M. (Mahin) Trout; student Fla. State U., 1938-39, U. Miami, 1939-40, U. N.C., 1940-41; m. Raymond G. Sage, Mar. 21, 1942; children—Raymond G., Mary Lee Sage Sole; m. 2d, Samuel F. Evans, Aug. 19, 1964. Realtor, Grand Bahama Devel. Corp., Ltd., Jacksonville, also Eleuthera Island Club Ltd., 1965-68; owner, mgr. Grace T. Evans Realtors, 1975-80; asso. Nautilus Realty & Mgmt. Co. Patron, Walaka Vol. Fire Dept.; sec. Putnam County Republican exec. com., 1980, v.p., 1982—; mem. Welaka City Council; chmn. Welaka Zoning Commn. Recipient emerald and diamond pin award Woman's council Nat. Assn. Realtors, 1973-74. Mem. Nat., Fla. assns. Realtors, Nat., Fla., Jacksonville (v.p.) women's councils Realtors, Jacksonville Real Estate Exchangors, Jacksonville Area Mortgage Brokers Assn. (dir. 1971-73), Putnam County Bd. Realtors, Nat. (state v.p. 1973-75), Fla. mortgage brokers assns., Brokers Co-op Jacksonville, Inc. (v.p. 1975-76), DAR, Delta Delta Delta. Episcopalian. Clubs: Palatka Yacht, Welaka Women's (1st v.p. 1978-80), Garden of Welaka. Corr. Courier Jour., Crescent City, Fla. Home: Thevans PO Box 255 Welaka FL 32093

EVANS, HANNAH IMOGENE, psychologist; b. Richmond, Va., Nov. 6, 1945; d. Charles and Ruth (Powell) E.; B.A., U. Vt., 1967; M.S., Pa.

State U., 1970, Ph.D., 1972; M.P.A., U. Colo., Denver, 1981; m. Robert F. McKenzie, July 12, 1975. Clin. psychology intern, psychol. cons. II, Denver Dept. Health and Hosps., 1972-77; adj. faculty U. Colo., Denver, summer 1978; resource counselor Regional Transp. Dist., 1978-79; pvt. practice psychotherapy, Denver, 1976—. Mem. community adv. bd. Sch. Profl. Psychology, U. Denver; mem. grievance com. Colo. Supreme Ct., 1982—; mem. transp. group Project Colo., 1982—; mem. Gov.'s Front Range Task Force, 1980-81; bd. dirs. Denver Sexual Assault Council, 1974-80; founding bd. Colo. Center Women and Work, 1979-81; mem. Women's Forum of Colo., 1979—, selection com., 1980—. USPHS fellow, 1968-70; named one of Faces of Colo., Colo. mag., 1976. Mem. Am. Psychol. Assn., Colo. Psychol. Assn., Colo. Women Psychologists, Rocky Mountain Road Runners. Club: Phiddipides Track. Contbr. articles to profl. jours. and popular mags. Office: 60 Kearney St Denver CO 80220

EVANS, HELEN WITTEN, state govt. ofcl.; b. Tazewell, Va., Aug. 5, 1905; d. Joseph and Sallie (Witten) Witten; grad. in secondary edn. Va. State Coll., 1927; postgrad. Coll. Social Adminstrn. Ohio State U., 1948; m. John C. Evans, Dec., 1927 (dec.); 1 son, John R. Tchr. Tazewell (Va.) Public Schs., 1924-27; with Div. of Aid for the Aged, Dept. Public Welfare, State of Ohio, Columbus, 1939-51, asst. cashier and public relations, treas. State of Ohio, 1952-58, auditor of state, welfare audits, 1958-62, dep. dir. State Dept. Indsl. Relations, 1962-70, dir. Ohio Dept. Indsl. Relations, 1975—; staff mem. Ohio Republican Com., 1970-74; Co-founder Ohio Rep. Council, 1952, exec. sec., 1952—; alt.-at-large Rep. nav. conv., 1972, del.-at-large, 1976; apptd. nat. del. White House Conf. on Aging, 1981, bd. trustees Central State U., 1982—. Recipient gov.'s award for Excellence of Achievement, 1980, Carnegie award, 1981; citation Ohio Women's Adv. Council, 1982. Mem. Internat. Assn. Govt. Labor Ofcls., Ohio Commodores. Methodist. Only black woman in U.S. to sit in gov.'s cabinet. Office: 2323 W 5th Ave Columbus OH 43216

EVANS, JANE G., home economist; b. Olney, Md., June 15, 1951; d. Ulysses, IV and Marion Margaret (Taylor) G.; B.Sc. in Human Ecology, U. Md., 1973 postgrad. in adminstrv. Sci. Johns Hopkins U. Tchr. home econs. Berlin (Md.) Middle Sch., 1973-75; youth program developer, Swaziland, 1975-76; vis. lectr. Md. Coop. Extension Service, 1977, 4-H and youth agt. Howard County, 1977—; mem. faculty U. Md., 1977—; asst. supt. 4-H foods dept. Md. State Fair, 1978-81; tchr. home econs. Jessup Correctional Inst. Women, 1972. Mary Faulkner scholar, 1969; Md. Senatorial scholar, 1969; Johns Hopkins U. fellow in Orgnl. and Community Systems, 1980-81. Mem. Am. Home Econs. Assn., Md. Home Econs. Assn. (chmn. by-laws com. 1979, v.p. for programs 1980-82), Nat. Assn. 4-H Agts. (N.E. regional contact for public relations and info. com. 1981-82), Md. Assn. 4-H Agts. (chmn. nominating com. 1980-81), Md. Internat. 4-H Youth Exchange Assn., Md. 4-H All Stars, Mortar Board, Omicron Nu. Author newsletters in field. Home: 21512 Montgomery Ave Laytonsville MD 20879 Office: 8306 Forrest St Ellicott City MD 21043

EVANS, JO BURT, TV translator co. exec.; b. Kimble County, Tex., Dec. 18, 1928; d. John Fred and Sadie (Oliver) Burt; B.A., Mary Hardin-Baylor Coll., 1948; M.A., Trinity U., 1967; m. Charles Wayne Evans II, Apr. 17, 1949; children—Charles Wayne III, John Burt, Elizabeth Wisart. Owner, mgr. Sta. KMBL, Junction, Tex., 1959-61; real estate broker, Junction, 1965-74; staff economist, adv. on 21st Congl. Dist., polit. campaign Nelson Wolff, 1974-75; asst. mgr., bookkeeper family owned ranches and rent property, Junction, 1948—; gen. mgr. TV Translator Corp., Junction, 1968—, sec.-treas., 1980—. Treas., asst. to coordinator Citizens for Tex., 1972; historian Kimble Hist. Soc.; mem. Com. of Conservation Soc. to Save the Edwards Aquifer, San Antonio, 1973; treas., asst. coordinator New Constitution, San Antonio, 1974. AAUW scholarship named in honor, 1973; named an outstanding Texan, Tex. Senate, 1973. Mem. Nat. Translator Assn., AAUW, Daus. Republic Tex., Tex. Sheriffs Assn., Internat. Platform Assn., Bus. and Profl. Women (pres. 1981-82). Democrat. Mem. Unity Ch. Home: PO Box 283 Junction TX 76849 Office: 618 Main St Junction TX 76849

EVANS, LOIS MARJORIE, philatelist; b. Providence, May 25, 1932; d. Leslie George and Lottie Emma (Bourne) Yuill; B.A., Boston U., 1954, M.B.A., 1956; m. William Lane Evans, July 11, 1959; children—Mark Yuill, Peter Lane, David William. Tchr., public schs., Needham, Belmont and Brookline, Mass., 1969-74; instr. econs. Boston U., evenings; adminstr. Am. Philatelic Research Library, State College, Pa., 1974-79; philatelic judge and chmn. Expert Com. for Japanese Stamps, 1969—; sec.-treas., dir. Am. Philatelic Soc., 1965—, v.p., 1981—; sec.-treas. Internat. Soc. Japanese Philately, 1965—; dir. Combined Philatelic Orgns.; sales mgr. R & R Cover Co. div. H.E. Harris Inc., Boston, 1980-81, asso. sales mgr. H.E. Harris div. Gen. Mills Co., 1981—. Fin. officer Centre County (Pa.) Rape Crisis Center, 1978-79, vol., 1977-79. Recipient Anna Marie Chemi award Am. Philatelic Soc., 1972. Mem. Am. Arbitration Assn. (panelist), Am. Philatelic Research Library, Soc. Philatelic Americans, Am. Philatelic Congress, German Philatelic Soc. Contbr. articles to profl. jours. Home: PO Box 752 Quincy MA 02169

EVANS, LOUISE, psychologist; b. San Antonio; d. Henry Daniel and Adela (Pariser) E.; B.S., Northwestern U., 1949; M.S. in Psychology, Purdue U., 1952, Ph.D. in Clin. Psychology, 1953; m. Thomas Ross Cambrell, Feb. 23, 1960. Intern clin. psychology Menninger Found., Topeka (Kans.) State Hosp., 1952-53, USPHS-Menninger Found. fellow clin. child psychology, 1955-56; staff psychologist Kankakee (Ill.) State Hosp., 1954; head staff psychologist child guidance clinic Kings County Hosp., Bklyn., 1957-58; dir. psychology clinic, instr. med. psychology Washington U. Sch. Mission, 1959; clin. research cons. Episcopal City Mission, St. Louis, 1959; pvt. practice clin. psychology, 1960—; psychol. cons. Fullerton (Calif.) Community Hosp., 1961—; staff cons. clin. psychology Martin Luther Hosp., Anaheim, Calif., 1963-70; lectr. clin. psychology schs. and profl. groups, 1950—; participant psychol. symposiums, 1956—; guest speaker clin. psychology civic and community orgns., 1950—. Elected to Hall of Fame, Central High Sch., Ind., 1966; recipient Service award Yuma County Head Start Program, 1972; named Miss Heritage, Heritage Publs., 1965; lic. psychologist N.Y., Calif.; diplomate Clin. Psychology. Fellow Am. Psychol. Assn., Royal Soc. Health of England, Internat. Council of Psychologists (dir. 1977-79, sec. 1962-64, 73-76), AAAS, Am. Orthopsychiat. Assn., World Wide Acad. of Scholars of N.Z.; mem. AAUP, Los Angeles Soc. Clin. Psychologists (exec. bd. 1966-67), Calif. State Psychol. Assn., Los Angeles County Psychol. Assn., Orange County Psychol. Assn. (exec. bd. 1963-65, pres. 1964-65), Am. Public Health Assn., Rehab. Internat., Internat. Platform Assn., Am. Acad. Polit. and Social Scis., N.Y. Acad. Scis., Purdue U. Alumni Assn. (Citizenship award 1975), Am. Judicature Soc., Center for Study of Presidency, Alumni Assn. Menninger Sch. Psychiatry, Sigma Xi, Pi Sigma Pi. Contbr. articles on clin. psychology to profl. publs. Home: 727 S Beverly Glen Blvd Los Angeles CA 90024 Office: 127 W Commonwealth Ave Fullerton CA 92632

EVANS, LYNETTE EILEEN, newspaper pub.; b. Everett, Wash., Apr. 26, 1941; d. Delmer H. and Georgia Mary (Johnson) Buse; B.A., U. Wash., 1963; postgrad. U. Nev., Las Vegas, 1967-68; m. John Basil Evans, Nov. 10, 1962. Sch. tchr., Everett, Wash., 1963-64; police officer, Everett, Wash., 1964-65; teaching asst. U. Nev., Las Vegas, 1967-68; reporter, women's news editor Everett (Wash.) Herald, 1969-74; dir. Learning Center Tulalip Indian Tribes, 1974-75; Sunday mag. editor Las Vegas (Nev.) Sun, 1976; news dir. Foster's Dailey Democrat, Dover, N.H., 1977-79; pub. Lake Tahoe News, South Lake Tahoe, Calif., 1979—; v.p. Buse Media, Inc., Everett, Wash. Mem. South Lake Tahoe Theatre Co. Guild, 1980—. Recipient State Writing awards Wash. Press Women, 1972. Mem. NOW, Nat. Newspaper Assn., Sigma Delta Chi, South Lake Tahoe C. of C. (dir. 1981-85). Author: (with George Burley) Roche Harbor: A Saga in the San Juans, 1972. Home: 3406 Warr Rd PO Box 658 South Lake Tahoe CA 95705 Office: 2095 James St PO Box 658 South Lake Tahoe CA 95705

EVANS, LYNN S(USAN), fin. planner, ins. cons.; b. Scranton, Pa., Sept. 15, 1951; d. William P. and Shirley R. (Zenker) E.; B.A., Cedar Crest Coll., 1973. Field underwriter Mut. N.Y., Scranton, 1975-79; sales asso. Alden-Levine Assos., Allentown, Pa., 1979; fin. planner Profl. Econs., Inc., Bethlehem, Pa., 1979—; pres., fin. planner Assoc. Fin. Planners, Inc., Scranton, 1980—; ins. cons. Creative Planning, Scranton, 1980—. Panelist, allocations com. United Way of Lackawanna County (Pa.), 1980—; chairperson adv. com. Women's Resource Center, Inc., Scranton, 1981—. Mem. Inst. Cert. Fin. Planners, Internat. Assn. Fin. Planners. Office: 405 Miller Bldg Scranton PA 18503

EVANS, MALINDA MURPHEY, librarian; b. Bloomington, Ill., Sept. 11, 1935; d. Earl C. and Imogene (Swigart) Murphey; B.S. in L.S., Ill. State U., Normal, 1973; m. Donald Lee Evans, Apr. 25, 1976; children by previous marriage—Melanie, Laurie, Patrick. Librarian, Vespasian Warner Public Library, Clinton, Ill., 1973—; author weekly column Bookmarks, Clinton Daily Jour.; pub. sec. Jr. Mens Round Table, 1977. Mem. Am., Ill. (dir.-at-large jr. mems. round table), Am. Bus. Women's Assn. (sec. 1976, pres. 1977, Woman of Yr. 1977). Methodist. Home: 40 Park Ln Clinton IL 61727 Office: 120 W Johnson St Clinton IL 61727

EVANS, MARGARET A., civic worker; b. N.Y.C., Jan. 20, 1924; d. Bernard J. and Katherine (Walsh) Markey; B.A., Coll. Mt. St. Vincent, Mt. St. Vincent-on-Hudson, N.Y., 1944; evening student Columbia U.; m. John Cullen Evans, Jr., Nov. 24, 1951. Rep. N.Y. Telephone Co., 1944; personnel office Sak's 34th, N.Y.C., 1944-45, tng. supr., selling and non-selling depts., 1945-49, spl. assignment for store mgr. 1949-50; non-selling tng. supr. Gimbel Bros., 1950-51; rep. Gimbels and Sak's 34th at NCCJ Retail Group meeting, 1949-50. Instr. textile painting for ARC, Chelsea Navy Hosp., 1952-54, ARC vol., 1980—; bd. dirs. Marblehead Hosp. Aid Assn., 1954, pres., 1955-58; sec. Mass. Hosp. Assn. Council of Hosp. Auxiliaries, 1957-59, chmn. North Shore region, 1959-61, chmn.-elect, 1961-62, chmn., 1962-64; exofficio trustee Salem Hosp.; trustee Mary A. Alley Hosp., 1956-79, chmn. bd., 1974-79; mem. Welcome Wagon of Fairfield/Easton (Conn.); chmn. Fairfield/Easton Theater Group. Mem. Alumnae Assn. Coll. Mt. Saint Vincent, Arrangers of Marblehead (chmn. garden therapy 1967-79). Clubs: Marblehead Women's Newcomers (pres. 1953). Home: 108 Cedarwoods Ln Fairfield CT 06430

EVANS, MARGARET MARY, sales exec.; b. Annapolis, Md., Oct. 6, 1938; d. Frank Joseph and Margaret Mary (Ruzicka) Wanex; B.A., Newcomb Coll., 1960; student Sorbonne, 1958-59; m. Glen Evans, Jan 2, 1962; 1 dau., Lisa Glyn. Systems analyst IBM Corp., Balt., 1961-62; systems supr. U.S. Naval Acad., Annapolis, Md., 1963-67; mktg. dir. Fawcett Pubs., Inc., Greenwich, Conn., 1967-77; sales v.p. Neodata Services/A.C. Nielsen Co., N.Y.C., 1977—; Co-chmn. Parent's Assn., White Mt. Sch., Littleton, N.H., 1979-80; bd. dirs. White Mt. Sch., 1979-80. Recipient Spl. Service award, Fulfillment Mgmt. Assn., 1980. Mem. Fulfillment Mgmt. Assn. (program chmn. 1978-80, dir. 1980-82), Am. Mgmt. Assn., Data Processing Mgmt. Assn., Women's Direct Response Group. Democrat. Clubs: Sales Execs. of N.Y., Direct Mktg. Club N.Y. Home: 76 Rock Spring Rd Stamford CT 06906 Office: 1290 Ave of the Americas New York NY 10104

EVANS, MARY CAROLE, ednl. adminstr.; b. Pasadena, Calif., Oct. 7, 1940; d. James S. and Louise (Winters) Evans; B.A., Calif. State U., San Jose, 1962; M.A., U. San Francisco, 1978; postgrad. U. Calif., Berkeley, 1966-68, Calif. State U., 1970-72. Tchr., Marlborough Sch., Los Angeles, 1962-65, Harry Ells High Sch., Richmond, Calif., 1965-67; tchr. Oakland (Calif.) Tech. High Sch., 1967—, dir. student activities, 1969-79, dean students, 1979—; driver training instr. Albany Unified Schs., 1968-69, Oakland public schs., 1968—; instr. Cal-Poly. Women's Secondary Schs. phys. edn. workshop, summer 1974, asst. dir. summer 1979, Calif. state chmn. Girls' and Women in Sport, 1973-74. Liaison officer Calif. Women Coaches Acad., 1974-75; treas. Nat. Volleyball Coaches Acad., 1974—. Served with USNR, 1975—. Recipient Calif. Girls and Women in Sport service award, 1980; Bay Area Image Builder award, 1980. Mem. Calif. Assn. Dir. Activities, Calif. Assn. Health, Phys. Edn. and Recreation. Republican. Nat. adv. bd. Pep mag., 1973. Office: 765 58th St Oakland CA 94609

EVANS, MAUDE JEAN, nurse; b. Quitman, Miss., Sept. 19, 1931; d. Jesse Morgan and Mary Gertrude (Banks) Gage; R.N., Malcolm X Coll., 1970; B.S. with highest honors, Coll. St. Francis, 1981; postgrad. Nat. Coll. Edn., 1982—, Ethical Hypnosis Tng. Center, 1977, Internat. Guild Hypnosis, 1975, Decaran Inst. Hypnosis, 1978; m. Albert Evans, Aug. 8, 1952; children—Cassandra, Mitchell, Dennis, Celia, Carl. Lic. practical nurse Hines VA Hosp., Chgo., 1959-60, U. Ill. Hosp., Chgo., 1960-67; head nurse Rosewood Terr. Nursing, Chgo., 1967-68; R.N., U. Ill. Hosp., 1970-79, personnel vis. nurse, 1979—; profl. instr., cons. Dacaran Inst. Applied Hypnosis and Internat. Guild Hypnosis. Mem. Ill. Nurses Assn., Assn. Advancement of Ethical Hypnosis, Assn. Research and Enlightenment. Home: 1837 S Kildare Ave Chicago IL 60623

EVANS, NORMA KAY, hotel exec.; b. Brainerd, Minn., Oct. 25, 1946; d. Lloyd Arthur and Naomi (Kay) Arthur; student public schs., Indpls.; m. Robert B. Evans, Mar. 31, 1976. Conv. service mgr. Indpls. Hilton Hotel, 1973-75, sales mgr. Nat. Conf. Center/Hilton, East Windsor, N.J., 1975; sales mgr. Sheraton Poste, Cherry Hill, N.J., 1975-76; dir. sales and mktg. Sheraton Newport Hotel, Newport Beach, Calif., 1976—. Mem. Newport Beach C. of C., Orange County C. of C., Newport Beach Conv. and Visitors Bur. (v.p.), Internat. Hotel Sales Mgmt. Assn., Am. Soc. Assn. Execs., Orange County Hotel Sales Mgmt. Assn. Office: 4545 MacArthur Blvd Newport Beach CA 92660

EVANS, ORINDA DALE, fed. judge; b. Savannah, Ga., Apr. 23, 1943; d. Thomas and Virginia G. Evans; A.B., Duke U., 1965; J.D. with distinction, Emory U., 1968; m. Roberts O. Bennett, Apr. 12, 1975; 1 son, Wells Cooper. Admitted to Ga. bar, 1968; asso. firm Fisher & Phillips, Atlanta, 1968-69; partner firm Alston, Miller & Gaines, 1969-79; U.S. judge No. Dist. Ga., 1979—. Mem. Atlanta Bar Assn. Democrat. Episcopalian. Office: 1988 US Courthouse 75 Spring St SW Atlanta GA 30303

EVANS, PAULA LORRAINE, bus. exec.; b. Hot Springs, Ark., May 10, 1941; d. Paul Carter and Susie (Rixie) Wright; student Ark. schs.; m. William R. Evans, Feb. 10, 1973; children—Christopher C., Kelly Ann. Office mgr. Hot Springs Conv. Bur., 1970-71; bus. mgr. Therapy Services, Inc., 1971-73; partner The Crystal House, 1974-76; dir., bus. and fin. adminstr. Evans Art Gallery, Inc., Hot Springs, 1976—, also co-owner House of Diamonds and Park Central Art Gallery. Lic. nursing home adminstr., Ark. Democrat. Roman Catholic. Club: Hot Springs Altrusa (pres.). Office: 308 Central Ave Hot Springs AR 71901

EVANS, PEGGY JOE, real estate broker; b. Wichita Flls, Tex., July 30, 1934; d. Allen Rolland and Wanda (Smallwood) Hurst; ed. Eastfield Coll.; m. Burl Joe Evans, Nov. 17, 1951; children—Burl Jr., Jefferson Allen, Becky Sue, Garry and Larry (twins), Debra. Realtor asso. Patti Monore Realty, Dallas, 1968-73; broker asso. Jim Turner Realty, Lewisville, Tex., 1973-76; broker asso. Maner Co., Nacogdoches, Tex., 1977-78; realtor, broker owner Lamplighter Realty, Nacogdoches, 1978—; artist. Mem. Nacogdoches C. of C., Fedn. Women's Clubs (sec. 1980), Nacogdoches County Bd. Realtors (v.p. 1982-83), Tex. Fine Arts Assn. Baptist. Home: 2611 Dogwood Nacogdoches TX 75961 Office: 3211 Appleby Sand Rd Nacogdoches TX 75961

EVANS, POLLY WILLIAMS, constrn. co. exec.; b. Annapolis, Md., May 18, 1943; d. Jack Bercaw and Polly Trenholm (Ferguson) Williams; diploma, Washington Sch. for Secs., 1962; m. Haydn Barry Evans, Apr. 11, 1964; children—Michael Haydn, Lauren Trenholm. Sec. to v.p. Alexandria Nat. Bank (Va.), 1962-64; sch. mgr. Head Start Project, Washington, 1964-66; sec. Case Constrn. Co., Washington, 1970-71, estimator, designer, 1971—, v.p., 1975—, head design and estimating dept., 1976—. Mem. D.C. Bd. Elections. Mem. Soc. Cert. Kitchen Designers, Nat. Assn. Female Execs. Inc., Nat. Remodelers Assn. Episcopalian. Home: 3805 Warren St NW Washington DC 20016 Office: 5135 MacArthur Blvd NW Washngton DC 20016

EVANS, SARAH FRANCES HINTON, nurse; b. Athens, Clark County, Ga., July 19, 1924; d. Charles Jackson and Bessie Marie (Hickman) Hinton; R.N., Macon Hosp. Sch. Nursing, 1945; B.S. in Nursing, Med. Coll. Ga., 1975; m. Omer Fountain, Oct. 9, 1948 (div. 1964); children—Anita Francine, Sarah Alice; m. John Duggan Evans, Feb. 14, 1969 (dec. Apr. 1971). Night supr. Ware County Hosp., Waycross, Ga., 1946-47; staff nurse nursery and obstetrics Mercy Hosp., Macon, Ga., 1947-48; staff nurse obstetrics Macon (Ga.) Hosp., 1952-54, 55-56, head nurse colored labor and delivery, 1956-64, obstet. staff nurse, 1964-65; head nurse newborn nursery Med. Center Central Ga., Macon, 1965-74, infection control nurse, 1974—; mem. Ga. Bd. Nursing, 1977-80. Mem. Am. Nurses Assn. (del. from Ga. 1976, 78), Assn. Practitioners in Infection Control, Ga. Heart Assn., Ga. Public Health Assn., Sixth Dist. Ga. Nurses Assn., Med. Center Central Ga. Alumnae, Med. Coll. Ga. Alumnae Assn. Baptist. Home: 6375 Houston Rd Macon GA 31206 Office: Med Center Central GA Box 6000 Macon GA 31208

EVANS-JONES, MARILYN BAILEY, state legislator; b. Deland, Fla., Nov. 19, 1928; d. Cecil Cabanis and Augusta Davis (Mann) Bailey; B.A., Duke U., 1950; m. Edward E. Jones, Jr., Jan. 10, 1981; children from previous marriage—Hugh M., Daniel, Cecile, Mary Louise. Substitute tchr. schs. in Fla., 1970-75; real estate salesperson Evans-Butler Realty, Melbourne, Fla., 1973—; mem. Fla. Ho. of Reps. from 33d Dist., 1975—, Republican caucus chmn., 1978-80; sec. Pinewell Corp. Sec. legis. affairs Fla. conf. United Methodist Women; bd. dirs. Big Bros. and Big Sisters Fla.; mem. adv. council Continuing Edn. Women, Eau Gallie High Sch.; mem. Fla. State Republican Com. Recipient Woman of Year award Melbourne C. of C., 1976; Good Govt. award Melbourne Jaycees, 1977-78; Rep. of Yr. award Fla. Assn. Retarded Citizens, 1979; Service award Fla. Assn. Community Colls., 1979; Juvenile Guidance award Brevard County PTA Council; Susan B. Anthony award NOW, 1979. Mem. AAUW (chpt. legis. chmn.), Nat. Rep. Legislators Assn., Am. Legis. Exchange Council, Melbourne Area Bd. Realtors, United Meth. Women (life). Office: 1495 N Harbor City Blvd Melbourne FL 32935

EVANSON, JANE LOUISE, educator, univ. dean; b. San Francisco, July 20, 1944; d. Charles William and Margaret (Bull) Evanson; B.S., Calif. Poly. State U., 1965; M.Ed., U. Va., 1972; Ph.D., Fla. State U., 1974. Asso. dir. Adult Edn. Resource Center, Montclair (N.J.) State Coll., 1974-75; asst. prof., asso. prof. Worcester (Mass.) State Coll., 1975-79; asso. prof. Alaska Pacific U., Anchorage, 1979-80, prof., 1980—, dean of students 1980—; editorial cons. Contemporary Books, Inc., Chgo. Bd. dirs. Alaska Native Social and Recreation Center. Recipient Outstanding Service Award, Adult Edn. Assn. U.S.A., 1981. Mem. Nat. Assn. Women Deans, Adminstrs. and Counselors, Internat. Reading Assn., Western Coll. Reading Assn., Phi Delta Kappa. Presbyterian. Club: Soroptomist Internat. (Cook Inlet, Anchorage). Author: From Pictures to Passages: Building Skills in Reading Comprehension, 1976; contbr. articles to profl. jours. Home: Faculty Row L-1 Alaska Pacific U 3500 University Dr Anchorage AK 99504 Office: 119 Campus Center Alaska Pacific U 3500 University Dr Anchorage AK 99504

EVELTI, MARY MARLOW, Vt. state legislator; b. Boston, May 16, 1920; ed. Burdett Coll., Boston. Former real estate broker; mem. Burlington Democratic City Com., Ward 5 Democratic Com., Chittenden County Dem. Com.; mem. Vt. Ho. of Reps., 1975-76, 77-78, 79-80, 81—. Bd. dirs. Burlington Emergency Shelter Services. Roman Catholic. Office: Vt Ho Reps State House Montpelier VT 05602

EVENSEN, BARBARA ANN, bank data processing exec.; b. Yonkers, N.Y., July 12, 1942; d. Albert and Hazel Christina (Jorgensen) E.; B.B.A., Pace U., 1974. Computer programmer Chem. Bank, N.Y.C., 1967-70, coordinator tech. tng., 1971-75, asst. mgr. long range automation planning, 1976-78, asst. treas. Mini-Computer Services, 1978-79, dir. acad. computing on spl. assignment to Pace U., 1979-80, cons. internat. div., 1980—; sec. GUIDE Internat. Corp. Users Group, 1975-79, dir., 1973-75; nat. sec. Video Users Edn. Group, 1972, 73, pres. N.Y. group 1972, 73. Trustee Pace U., 1981—. Trustee Pace U., 1981—. Mem. Pace U. Alumni Assn. (sec. 1978-79, v.p. 1979-81, pres. 1981-83, dir. 1975—), Data Processing Mgmt. Assn. Editorial adv. bd. Computer Educator, 1974; cons., lectr. in field. Office: Chem Bank 20 Pine St New York NY 10005

EVENSEN, LYNDHA ELAYNE, TV broadcast engr.; b. Pasadena, Calif., Feb. 28, 1951; d. Celdon Nils and Lillie Christina (Brott) E.; B.A. in Public Adminstrn., Calif. State Poly. U., 1971. Videotape tng. engr. Sony Corp., Compton, Calif., 1978-79; engr. Vidtronics Inc., Los Angeles, 1979-80; technician CBS-TV Network, Los Angeles, 1980—. Mem. Internat. Alliance Theater and Stage Employees (conv. del. 1980). Democrat. Jewish. Only woman broadcasting technician in Los Angeles who repairs and troubleshoots equipment at major TV network facility. Home: 12358 Moorpark St Apt 9 Studio City CA 91604 Office: 7800 Beverly Blvd Los Angeles CA 90036

EVENSTEIN, JOSEPHINE JIHRLL, apparel mfg. co. exec.; b. Chgo.; d. Louis Benjamin and Fannie (Gluckman) Evenstein; B.S., Ill. Inst. Tech., 1944. Credit mgr. Catalina, Inc., Los Angeles, 1946-52, Jerry Mann of Calif., Los Angeles, 1953-63; controller Hartog of Calif., Los Angeles, 1964-73; controller Lucie Ann, Beverly Hills, Calif., 1973—. Mem. Greater Los Angeles Zoo Assn., Brentwood-Westwood Symphony Assn., Concern Found. for Cancer Research, Los Angeles County Mus. Art and Natural History. Democrat. Jewish. Clubs: Hadassah (fin. sec. 1977-78), B'nai B'rith. Home: 350 S Fuller Ave Apt 7-E Los Angeles CA 90036 Office: 1 Lucie Ann Ln Beverly Hills CA 90210

EVERETT, CAROLYN WOOD, banker; b. Benton, Ark., May 13, 1939; d. James A. and Mary K. (Hearnsberger) Wood; student Kilgore Coll., 1958; m. Kenneth W. Everett, Aug. 6, 1960; 1 son, Wayne. Bookkeeper, Kilgore First Nat. Bank (Tex.), 1958-59, proof operator, 1959-67, teller, 1967-70, exchange teller, 1970-76, asst. cashier, 1976—. Mem. Nat. Assn. Bank Women. Presbyterian. Home: 314 Erskine Dr Longview TX 75601 Office: 910 N Kilgore TX 75662

EVERNDEN, MARGERY ELIZABETH, English language educator, writer; b. Okeechobee, Fla., June 6, 1916; d. Hans Foord and Rose (Wagner) E.; B.A., U. Calif.-Berkeley, 1938; M.A., U. Pitts., 1967; m. Earl Alfred Gulbransen, July 2, 1938; children—Karen Elizabeth, Kristin Ellen, David Erling. Assoc. prof. dept. English, U. Pitts., 1978—; books include: Secret of the Porcelain Fish, 1947; Knight of Florence, 1950; Simon's Way, 1970; Lyncoya, 1973; contbr. short stories, articles to mags; authored plays for children. Mem. Phi Beta Kappa. Democrat. Unitarian. Home: 63 Hathaway Ct Pittsburgh PA 15235 Office: Dept English U Pitts Pittsburg PA 15213

EVERS, BARBARA JO, savs. and loan ofcl.; b. Portland, Oreg., Jan. 22, 1949; d. Marvin Allen and Dorothy Geneva (Berry) Emerson; student Mills Coll., 1967-69; B.S. in Mgmt. summa cum laude, Woodbury U., Los Angeles, 1979; cert. in real estate Fullerton (Calif.) Coll., 1980, cert. in escrow, 1982; cert. in mortgage banking Cypress Coll., 1980. Service rep. Pacific Telephone Co., 1969-76; loan servicing analyst to loan adminstrn. supr., Coldwell Banker Mgmt. Corp., Los Angeles, 1976-78; mktg. services mgr., document control mgr., systems devel. mgr. Standard Precision, Inc., Santa Fe Springs, Calif., 1978-80; project adminstr. to procedures design and publs. mgr. Home Fed. Savs. & Loan Assn., San Diego, 1980—; tchr. resume writing, interview techniques; cons. organizational systems. Recipient Grand Cross of Color, Internat. Order Rainbow for Girls, 1967. Mem. Women in Mgmt., Nat. Assn. Female Execs., Am. Soc. Profl. and Exec. Women, Project Mgmt. Inst., Ops. Research Soc. Am., Inst. Mgmt. Scis., Calif. State Scholarship Fedn., Phi Gamma Kappa, Alpha Gamma Sigma. Home: 1650 8th Ave San Diego CA 92101 Office: 701 Broadway San Diego CA 92101

EVERS, JEAN GRAF (MRS. CARL G. EVERS), editor, writer; b. Columbus, Ohio, Dec. 27, 1917; d. Ray W. and Marie A. (Dooley) Arms; B.A. magna cum laude, Northwestern U., 1940; m. Don Graf, May 15, 1947 (dec. Nov. 1962); m. 2d, Carl G. Evers, Jan. 22, 1964. Asso. editor House and Garden Mag., N.Y.C., 1942-45, Life Mag., N.Y.C., 1945-47; partner Graf & Graf, public relations, N.Y.C., 1947-63; staff public relations Am. Carpet Inst., N.Y.C., 1955-57; public relations dir. Galbraith-Hoffman, N.Y.C., 1958-60; guest home furniture editor Modern Bride, 1955; guest editor Decorating Supplements and Herald Tribune Sun. mag. Today's Living, N.Y.C., 1960-61; dir. interior furnishings Mohair Council at Kairalla Agy., N.Y.C., 1966-68; asst. editor Voices, regional newspaper, Southbury, Conn., 1973-74, editor, 1974—. Press chmn. Tercentennial Celebration, Southbury, Conn., 1972. Recipient Vogue Prix de Paris, 1940. Mem. Nat. Home Fashions League (nat. dir. N.Y. chpt. 1972-73, nat. 1st v.p. 1973-74, nat. pres. 1975-76), Am. Soc. Interior Designers, Phi Beta Kappa, Sigma Delta Chi, Delta Gamma. Author: Practical Houses for Contemporary Living, 1954; Doubleday Decorating Books, 1972. Contbr. numerous articles to various women's and home mags. Home: 738 B Heritage Village Southbury CT 06488

EVERSON, SUSAN TOFT, research and devel. project dir.; b. St. Louis, Nov. 22, 1944; d. Martin John and Edna Ann (Mortensen) Toft; B.S., U. Mo., 1966; M.A., Peabody Coll., 1974; postgrad. U. Wis., 1977-78; m. David E. Everson, Jr., June 11, 1966; 1 dau., Courtney Anne. Tchr., Webster Groves (Mo.) Schs., 1966-67; resident dir. U. Mich., Ypsilanti, 1968-69; dir. child devel. program, Cape Elizabeth, Maine, 1972-73; instr. U. Ga., 1974-77; program asso. Mid-Continent Regional Ednl. Lab., Kansas City, Mo., 1978-79, project dir., 1979—; coordinator Mo. Sch. Improvement Project, 1981-82. Mem. Adult Basic Edn. Bd., Kansas City, Mo., 1981-82. Mem. Kansas City Women's Ednl. Network, Am. Ednl. Research Assn., Nat. Assn. Exec. Women, Nat. Assn. Edn. Young Children, Phi Delta Kappa. Democrat. Clubs: Sierra, Internat. Relations, Audubon Soc. Home: 831 Westover Rd Kansas City MO 64113 Office: 4709 Belleview Kansas City MO 64112

EVERT, CHRISTINE MARIE (CHRIS), profl. tennis player; b. Ft. Lauderdale, Fla., Dec. 21, 1954; d. James and Colette Evert; ed. pvt. schs. Ft. Lauderdale; m. John Lloyd, Apr. 17, 1979. Amateur tennis player until Dec., 1972; now profl. player, mem. Women's Pro Tennis Tour; U.S. jr. champion, 1970-71; singles titlist U.S. Clay Ct. Championship, 1972, 73, 74, 75, 79, 80, U.S. Lawn Tennis Assn. tournament, 1973, South African Open, 1973, Wimbledon, 1974, 76, 81, Italian Open, 1974, 75, 79, 80, French Open, 1974, 75, 79, 80, Canadian Open, 1974, 80, Family Circle Mag. Cup tournament, 1974, 75, 77, 78, U.S. Open, 1975, 76, 77, 78, 80, 82, Va. Slims Championship, 1975, 77, numerous others. Mem. Wightmen Cup team, 1971, 72, 73, 75, 76, 79, Bell Cup team, 1972, 73. Recipient Most Valuable Player trophy Wightman Cup Championship 1971; Lebair Sportsmanship trophy, 1971, named Female Athlete of Year AP, 1974, 75. Mem. U.S. Lawn Tennis Assn. (named top Women's Singles Player 1974), Nat. Honor Soc. Address: 1628 7th Pl NE Fort Lauderdale FL 33304 *

EVERTON, MARTA VE, ophthalmologist; b. Luling, Tex., Nov. 12, 1926; d. T.W. and Nora E. (Eckols) O'Leavy; B.A., Hardin-Simmons U., 1945; M.A., Stanford U., 1947; M.D., Baylor U., 1955; postgrad. N.Y.U.-Bellevue Hosp., 1956-57; m. Robert K. Graham, Oct. 15, 1960; children—Marcia, Christie, Leslie Fox. Intern, Meth. Hosp., Houston, 1955-56; resident in ophthalmology Baylor Affiliated Hosps., Houston, 1957-59; clin. instr. ophthalmology Baylor U., 1959-60; asst. clin. prof. ophthalmology Loma Linda U., 1962-73; practice medicine specializing in ophthalmology, Houston, 1959-60, Pasadena, Calif., 1961-74, Escondido, Calif., 1974—. Mem. AMA, Am. Acad. Ophthalmology, Am. Med. Women's Assn., Alpha Omega Alpha. Home: 3024 Sycamore Ln Escondido CA 92025 Office: 810 E Ohio Ave Escondido CA 92025

EVESONG, SARIBENNE, artist; b. Jackson, Miss., Jan. 30, 1931; d. Benjamin William and Delphia (Chesteen) Thomas; B.S. in Art, U. Wis., 1958, M.S. in Art, 1961, M.F.A., 1962, M.S. in Behavioral Disabilities, 1969; m. Vernon A. Stone, June 11, 1966; children—Hallie Maureen, Adam Edward. One-man shows: U. Ga., 1975, Heath Gallery, Atlanta, 1978, Franklin Furnace, N.Y.C., 1980, Univ. Mus., So. Ill. U., Carbondale, 1981; group shows include: Watercolor U.S.A., Springfield, Mo., 1973, 78 (award), Works on Paper Montgomery (Ala.) Mus. Fine Arts, 1975, Ball State U., 1975, Kvindeudstillingen XX, Copenhagen, 1975, Laguna Gloria Mus., Austin, Tex., 1977, Smithsonian Instn. Traveling Exhbn., 1978—, 82—, Wildeliff Mus., New Rochelle, N.Y., 1979, Powerhouse Gallery, Montreal, Que., Can., 1979, Peter M. David Gallery Inc., Mpls., 1979, Fendrick Gallery, Washington, 1979, Seibu Mus., Tokyo, 1979, Walker Art Center, Mpls., 1981, Eaton/Shoen Gallery, San Francisco, 1981, Atkins Mus. Fine Arts, 1980; works include hand formed paper art, acrylic and canvas wall books; co-founder Moving Women Art Center, Madison, 1975; lectr., workshop condr. in field. Chmn. social services Unitarian Soc. Madison, 1964, membership and pub. relations NAACP., Madison, 1973-74, Friends of Ga. Mus. Programs, 1976; sec. Madison Meml. Soc. chpt. Wis. Planned Funeral Soc., 1964. Mem. Atlanta Art Workers Coalition Ltd., Atlanta Women's Art Collective Inc. Home and office: 107 Lynne Ln Carterville IL 62918

EVON, CARMELA NATALIE, tool mfg. co. exec.; b. Waterbury, Conn., June 15, 1920; d. Joseph and Linda (Immella) Falzone; m. Louis J. Evon, Jan. 4, 1941. Adminstrv. asst. to v.p. Mattatuck Mfg. Co., 1950-57; liaison Springfield Ordance, 1952-57; systems analyst Metal Fabrications, Waterbury, 1959-61; sec.-treas. Enterprise Carbide Tool Co., Inc., Watertown, Conn., 1968—, now owner, adminstr., also dir. Commr., vice-chmn. Naugatuck Valley Loan Com. Mem. Nat. Assn. Female Execs., Conn. Bus. and Industry. Democrat. Roman Catholic. Home: 120 Sabal Dr Waterbury CT 06708 Office: PO Box 4 Knight St Watertown CT 06795

EWALD, ROBERTA GRANT, 11 art gallery exec.; b. Mpls., Aug. 25; d. and Hannah Theolinda (Johannson) Grant; student Calif. Sch. of Arts, m. Henry C. Ewald, Sept. 7, 1946; 1 son, Grant. Public acct. Ernst & Ernst, San Francisco, 1943-44, Harris Kerr Forster, San Francisco, 1944-46; owner, operator Travelers' Art Gallery, Roberta's Art Gallery, 1973—, Travel Services, South San Francisco, Calif. Bd. dirs. Art Guild Pacifica (Calif.), 1960-64, pres., 1963-64; bd. dirs. Pacifica Spindrift Players, 1978—, pres., 1979, dir. children's choirs, 1968-73. Recipient various art exhibit awards. Mem. Pacific Area Travel Assn., Am. Soc. Travel Agts., San Francisco Conservatory Music. Author, lead, producer musical The Wanderers, 1979; sponsor various art functions; numerous appearances with local theatrical groups, 1938—. Office: 757 Kains St San Bruno CA 94066 also 345-9 Baden St San Francisco CA 94080

EWERSEN, MARY VIRGINIA, educator; b. Von Wert County, Ohio, June 7, 1922; B.S. in Elem. Edn., Bowling Green (Ohio) State U., 1966, now postgrad.; m. Herbert Ewersen (dec.); 2 children. Remedial reading tchr. Port Clinton (Ohio) City Schs., 1966-70, reading tchr./coordinator, 1970—. Mem. bd. trustees and advisers Erie-Ottawa Guidance Center, Sandusky, Ohio, 1972—. Cert., Ohio. Mem. NEA, Ohio, N.W. Ohio, Port Clinton edn. assns., Internat. Reading Assn., Kappa Delta Pi. Author activity card set: From Hyperactive to Happy-Active in Limited Spaces, 1979. Home: 1786 S Hickory Grove Rd Port Clinton OH 43452 Office: 431 Portage Dr Port Clinton OH 43452

EWERT, KARLA RUTH, telephone co. ofcl.; b. Des Moines, Aug. 16, 1949; d. Lowell E. and Martha H. (Henry) Strahan; B.S. in Christian Edn. and Music, Grace Coll. Bible, Omaha, 1971; m. Stanley B. Ewert, June 19, 1971; 1 dau., Lisa Renae. With Northwestern Bell Telephone Co., Omaha, 1971-72, 73—, staff supr. ednl. relations, 1977-78, mgr. community relations, 1978—; speaker in field. Coordinator, Wintertainment Festival, 1981; bd. dirs. Omaha Summer Arts Festival, 1981; coordinator Sundae Sunday, Omaha Children's Museum Festival, 1982; mem. River City Roundup Com., 1982. Mem. Soc. Consumer Affairs Profls., Jr. League Omaha. Home: Route 2 Surrey Hills Dr Omaha NE 68122 Office: 100 S 19th St Room 1240 Dodge Omaha NE 68102

EWING, MARY ARNOLD, lawyer; b. Shreveport, La., Feb. 21, 1948; d. George and Christine (Cocek) Hengy; B.A., U. Colo., 1972; J.D., U. Denver, 1975; m. Robert Craig Ewing, Aug. 30, 1981. Admitted to Colo. bar, 1975, U.S. Supreme Ct. bar, 1979; law clk. Johnson and Mahoney, P.C., Denver, 1972-75, asso., 1975-80; partner firm Branney, Hillyard, Ewing and Barnes, Englewood, Colo., 1980-81, firm Branney, Hillyard, Ewing and Barnes, 1981—; asst. prof. law U. Denver Coll. Law, 1977-78, part-time prof., 1978—; judge continuing legal edn. Course in Trial Advocacy, 1979, 80; guest lectr. local colls. and univs. Chmn., Denver County Task Force, Health and Hosp., 1976-77; treas. 1st. Congressional Dist. Central Com., 1976-77; v.p. Young Republican League of Denver, 1975, pres., 1976; mem. govt. relations com. Jr. Symphony Guild, 1978—. Mem. Am. Bar Assn., Colo. Bar Assn. (ethics com.), Denver Bar Assn. (vice chmn. new lawyers assistance com. 1977), Colo. Women's Bar Assn., Internat. Platform Assn., Mountain States Combined Tng. Assn., Rocky Mountain Dressage Soc. (sec. High Plains chpt. 1979, 80), Am. Trial Lawyers Assn., Colo. Trial Lawyers Assn. (bd. govs., chmn. interprofl. com. 1980, dir. 1981—), Am. Arbitration Assn., U. Denver Coll. Law Alumni Council, Kappa Beta Pi (pres. 1977-78). Club: Toastmasters Internat. Home: 816 W Quarry Rd Littleton CO 80124 Office: 3333 S Bannock St 10th Floor Englewood CO 80110

EWING, TERRY LYNN GARDNER, graphic arts co. exec.; b. Indpls., Aug. 18, 1950; d. William Clyde and Donna Louise (Lain) Gardner; student Ind. U., Indpls., 1971-76; m. Michael Paul Ewing, June 27, 1980; 1 dau., Lauren Noel. Graphic artist, typesetter, Indpls., 1968-70; corp. artist Am. Monitor Corp., Indpls., 1970-71, 73-74; adminstrv. asst. Campaign Communicators, Inc., Indpls., 1972; customer coordinator Universal Printing Co., Indpls., 1974; prodn. mgr. Plywood & Panel Mag., Indpls., 1974-75; prodn. mgr. Indytype, Inc., Indpls., 1975-79, v.p. prodn. div., 1979—, editor-in-chief Art Product News, bd. dirs. Indytype, Inc., exec. editorial bd. Art Product News Mag., Mimar Corp.; pvt. tutor, tchr. migrant children. Mem. Women in Communications, Ind. Bus. Communicators. Home: 4923 W 14th St Speedway IN 46224 Office: 4040 W 10th St Indianapolis IN 46222

EXUM, FRANCES BELL, educator; b. Birmingham, Ala., May 11, 1940; d. Frank Kinney and Frances Henrietta (Bell) E.; B.A. in Spanish cum laude, Fla. State U., 1962, M.A. in Spanish, 1963, Ph.D. in Spanish, 1970. Instr. Spanish, N.C. Wesleyan Coll., 1963-65, Greensboro Coll., 1965-67; asst. prof. Spanish, Winthrop Coll., 1970-74, asso. prof., 1974-77, prof., 1977—. Mem. MLA, Asociación Internacional de Hispanistas, Am. Assn. Tchrs. Spanish and Portuguese (pres. S.C. chpt. 1979-80), AAUP (pres. chpt. 1976-77), Renaissance Soc. Am., Phi Beta Kappa, Phi Kappa Phi, Pi Beta Phi. Author: The Metamorphosis of Lope de Vega's King Pedro, 1974; contbr. articles and book revs. to profl. publs. Home: 4000 Colony Pkwy Charlotte NC 28211 Office: Dept Modern and Classical Langs Winthrop Coll Rock Hill SC 29733

EYBERG, SHEILA MAXINE, clin. psychologist; b. Omaha, Dec. 31, 1944; d. Clarence George and Geraldine Elizabeth (Gilbert) E.; B.A., U. Omaha, 1967; M.A., U. Oreg., 1970, Ph.D., 1972. Intern in med. psychology U. Oreg. Health Scis. Center, Portland, 1971-72, postdoctoral resident, 1972-74, asst. prof. med. psychology, 1974-81, asso. prof., 1981—; cons., workshop leader psychol. assessment and treatment of children Curry County Mental Health Clinic, Gold Beach, Oreg., 1973; psychol. cons. North Clackamas Sch. Dist., Portland, 1974-75; psychol. cons. Summer Speech and Lang. Clinic, Portland Center for Hearing and Speech, 1974-75; psychol. cons. Parent-Child Services, Inc., Portland, 1976; mem. asso. profl. staff Woodland Park Psychiat. Hosp., Portland, 1977-81, mem. neuropsychiat. com., 1977-81; workshop leader Parent-Child Interaction Tng. for Therapists, U. Wash., 1980, 81. Lic. psychologist, Oreg. Mem. Am. Psychol. Assn., Soc. Pediatric Psychology, Western Psychol. Assn., Oreg. Psychol. Assn., Assn. Advancement of Behavior Therapy, Oreg. Acad. Profl. Psychologists, Nat. Register of Health Service Providers, Alpha Lambda Delta, Phi Kappa Phi, Psi Chi. Contbr. numerous articles to profl. jours. Cons. editor: Journal of Pediatric Psychology, 1977—; cons. editor Jour. Clin. Child Psychology, 1982—; editorial cons. Behavior Therapy, 1978; Jour. of Consulting and Clinical Psychology, 1979—, Behavior Modification, 1981, Child Devel., 1981—. Home: 31 Greenridge Ct Lake Oswego OR 97034 Office: 3181 SW Sam Jackson Park Rd Portland OR 97201

EYLES, HEBERLE HELEN JONES, mfg. co. exec.; b. Wheeling, W.Va., Mar. 9, 1943; d. Clyde Calvin and Jean Louise Beatrice (Eyles) Jones; B.S., West Liberty State Coll., 1963; postgrad. Ohio State U., 1963-64; M.S. in L.S., Case Western Res. U., 1969; m. Robert R. McCoy, Dec. 1, 1976. Tchr. physics, math., sci. New Albany (Ohio) High Sch., 1964-66; asst. editor Chem. Abstracts Service, Columbus, Ohio, 1966-68; mem. research and devel. dept. Procter & Gamble Co., Cin., 1969—, systems designer Tech. Info. Service, 1969-73, sect. head, 1973-74, sect. head math. and tech. info. services, 1974—. Mem. Am. Soc. Info. Sci. (pres. So. Ohio chpt.), Spl. Libraries Assn., Pi Beta Mu, Alpha Psi Omega. Home: 5418 Winton Rd Fairfield OH 45014 Office: PO Box 39175 Cincinnati OH 45239

EYSTER, NINA LARAINE, window and door mfg. exec.; b. Nora Springs, Iowa, Feb. 24, 1928; d. Harry G. and Lila E. (Dean) Hedden; student public schs.; m. W.J. Eyster, Feb. 5, 1962; children by previous marriage—Patrick, Candice, Tralee McKiness. Head sportswear dept. Montgomery Ward, 1946-48; with McKiness Nursery and Landscape Service, 1948-69, propr., 1963-69; pres. Retsye Industries, Inc., Des Moines, 1969—. Former pres. Migrant Action Program, St. Helean's Roman Catholic Ch. Group, Am. Field Service. Mem. Nat. Home Improvement Council (nat. dir., past pres. Iowa chpt.), Assn. Vinyl Mfrs. Republican. Clubs: Des Moines, Pilot Internat. (past pres.). Home: 1701 SW Evans St Des Moines IA 50315 Office: 5387 2d Ave Des Moines IA 50313

EYTAN, RACHEL, novelist, educator; b. Israel, May 4, 1932; came to U.S., 1967, naturalized, 1979; d. Yaacov Litai and Sara Zweig; B.A., Hakibutzim Tchrs. Coll., Israel, 1950; B.A., N.Y.U., 1973, M.A., 1975, doctoral student, 1976-79; m. Jerry H. Fishman, Oct., 1967; children—Omry, Hamutal, Yonatan. Tchr., Israeli Kibbutz, Tel Aviv, 1950-53; novelist; books include: The Fifth Heaven, 1963; Shida Veshidot, 1973 (published in U.S. 1983); contbr. short stories and articles to Am. lit. mags.; editor, contbr. to Israeli and Am. lit. mags. and newspapers; prof. Israeli lit. Gratz Coll., Phila., 1967-68; prof. Israeli, Hebrew and Yiddish lit. Hofstra U., 1968—; lectr. Am., European and Israeli univs., TV and radio. Active Israeli-Arab Peace Movement, NOW, Women Ink Writers. Recipient Brenner prize for lit., Israel, 1966, Founders Day award N.Y.U., 1973. Mem. MLA, AAUP, Israeli Pen Club, Israeli Writers Assn. Home: 227 Central Park W New York NY 10024 Office: Hofstra U Hempstead NY 11550

EZELL, ANNETTE SCHRAM, educator; b. West Frankfort, Ill., June 19, 1940; d. Woodrow C. and Rosa (Franich) Schram; student Evansville Coll., 1957, Protestant Deaconess Hosp. Sch. Nursing, 1957-59, Ind. U., 1959; B.S. in Nursing, U. Nev., 1962, M.S. in Physiology, 1967, postgrad., 1969; Ed.D., Brigham Young U., 1977; children—Michael L., Rona Maria. Staff nurse Washoe Med. Center, Reno, 1962; teaching asst. U. Nev., Reno, 1962-63, instr., 1963-64, 1965-67, asst. prof. nursing, 1967-71; curriculum specialist U. Nev. Med. Sch., 1971-72, project mgr. Fed. Grant Intercampus Nursing Edn. Project, 1969-71, asso. prof. nursing, curriculum specialist rural nurse practitioner program, 1971-73, staff asso. Mountain States Regional Med. Program, 1974-75; cons. Nev. Dept. Edn., 1975-77; asst. dean acad. affairs Coll. Nursing, U. Utah, Salt Lake City, 1977-80; acting Dean, 1981, dir., prof. doctoral program Nursing Edn. Adminstrn.; prof., dept. head for nursing, Coll. Human Development, Penn. State U., 1982—; cons. nursing edn., TV edn., research methodology; adviser to various research, polit. and ednl. bds. Mem. Am., Nev. nurses assns., AAAS, Am. Acad. Arts and Scis., AAUP, Am., Penn. Nurses Found., Nat. League of Nursing, Nev. Pub. Health Assn., Western Ednl. Soc. for Telecommunications, Phi Kappa Phi. Home: 603 Old Farm Ln State College PA 16801 Office: Coll Human Devel Penn State U University Park PA 16802

EZZARD, MARTHA MCELVEEN, state senator; b. Atlanta, Nov. 8, 1938; d. George Davant and Gladys Caroline (Lewis) McElveen; A.B. in Journalism, U. Ga., 1960; M.A., U. Mo., 1968; J.D., U. Denver, 1982; m. John A. Ezzard, Dec. 27, 1960; children—Shelly Lynne, Lisa Annette, John A. With Atlanta Jour., 1959-60, Sta. WSB-TV, Atlanta, 1960; tchr. Littleton (Colo.) High Sch., 1961-62; with Sta. KOMU-TV, Columbia, Mo., 1965-68; polit. press aide, 1973-75; polit. columnist Rocky Mountain Jour., Denver, 1976-77; mem. Colo. Ho. of Reps. from 37th Dist., 1978-80, Colo. Senate from 20th Dist., 1980—; dir. United Bank Littleton. Bd. dirs. Arapahoe Mental Health Bd., Arapahoe Community Coll. Named Outstanding Republican Legislator, 1980, 81. Mem. Colo. Press Women (Feature and Editorial Writing awards), Colo. Edn. Accountability, Women's Forum. Episcopalian. Clubs: Cherry Hills Country, Petroleum. Office: Colo Senate State Capitol Denver CO 80203

FAATZ, JEANNE RYAN, state legislator; b. Cumberland, Md., July 30, 1941; d. Charles Keith and Myrtle Elizabeth (McIntyre) Ryan; B.S., U. Ill., 1962; postgrad. U. No. Colo., Greeley; children—Kristin, Susan. Tchr., English and speech, Ill. and Colo., 1963-67; sec. to majority leader Colo. Senate, 1976-78; mem. Colo. Ho. Reps. from Dist. 1, 1978—, chmn. transp. and energy com., chmn. regional transp. dist. legis. oversight com., mem. judiciary com. Past pres. Harvey Park (Colo.) Homeowners Assn., S.W. Denver YWCA Adult Edn. Club; S.W. met. coordinator UN Children's Fund, 1969-74; mem. citizens adv. council Ft. Logan Mental Health Center; bd. mgrs. S.W. Denver YMCA; bd. dirs. S.W. Denver Community Health Services. Mem. Bear Creek Republican Women's Club. Home: 2903 S Quitman St Denver CO 80236 Office: State Capitol Denver CO 80203

FABER, EMMY-LOU EATON, nurse, educator; b. Utica, N.Y., May 19, 1930; d. Tom and Agnes (Barker) Eaton; student Paterson State Tchrs. Coll., 1947-49, Middle Tenn. State U., 1963; R.N., Oglethorpe U., 1970; M.Community Health, Emory U., 1977; m. Theodore Faber, Dec. 10, 1949; children—Christopher Jay, Theodore Tom, Timothy Andrew. Nurse, Emory U. Hosp., Atlanta, 1967-70; nurse recruiter Northside Hosp., Atlanta, 1970—, dir. edn. dept., 1971—; clin. asst. prof. Sch. Nursing, Ga. State U.; sch. cons. DeKalb County Bd. Edn. Mem. Am., Ga. nurses assns., Nat., Ga. leagues nursing, Am., Ga. (sec. 1982-83) socs. health manpower edn. and teaching, Ga. Heart Assn., Ga. Adult Edn. Assn., Am. Cancer Soc., Sigma Theta Tau. Episcopalian. Club: Toastmasters. Home: 14155 Hopewell Rd Alpharetta GA 30201 Office: 1000 Johnsons Ferry Rd Atlanta GA 30042

FABER, SANDRA MOORE, astronomer, educator; b. Boston, Dec. 28, 1944; d. Donald Edwin and Elizabeth Mackenzie (Borwick) Moore; B.A., Swarthmore Coll., 1966; Ph.D., Harvard U., 1972; m. Andrew L. Faber, June 9, 1967; children—Robin, Holly. Asst. prof., astromomer Lick Obs., U. Calif. Santa Cruz, 1972-77, assoc. prof., astronomer 1977-79, prof., astronomer 1979—; mem. NSF astronomy adv. panel. NSF fellow; Woodrow Wilson fellow; Alfred P. Sloan fellow. Mem. Am. Astron. Soc., Internat. Astron. Union, Phi Beta Kappa. Contbr. articles to profl. jours. Office: Lick Observatory University of California Santa Cruz CA 95060

FABIAN, DEBRA KERSTETTER, univ. exec.; b. Fairbanks, Alaska, June 2, 1955; d. William Harris and Carolyn Marie (Walb) Kerstetter; B.A. cum laude, Miss. U. for Women, 1977; postgrad. U. Miss., 1977-78; m. Leonard William Fabian, Oct. 20, 1979. Staff writer Office Public Relations, U. Miss., Oxford, 1977-78, sr. staff writer, 1978-79, asst. news dir., 1979-82; coordinator med. news and info. Washington U. Sch. Medicine, St. Louis, 1982—. Named an Outstanding Young Woman of Am., 1980. Mem. Women in Communications, Council for Advancement and Support Edn., AAUW, Sigma Delta Chi. Home: 1570 Foxleigh Ct Saint Louis MO 63131 Office: 660 S Euclid Saint Louis MO 63110

FABIAN, ELISSA ANN, nurse; b. N.Y.C., Dec. 9, 1937; d. Julius and Betty (Tischelman) Rothholz; L.P.N., Montefiore Hosp., N.Y.C., 1965; A.A.S., County Coll. of Morris, 1974; student Fla. Internat. U., 1976-79; grad. with honors County Coll. of Morris, 1974; m. Herbert Fabian, Dec. 18, 1977; children by previous marriage—Jodi Zackowitz Sohl, Corey Bruce Zackowitz; stepchildren—Michael Allen, Cheryl Fabian Styck. Staff nurse St. Barnabas Med. Center, West Orange, N.J., 1974-76; charge nurse, relief supr., and critical care coordinator Coral Gables (Fla.) Hosp., 1976-79; dir. admission preplanning Victoria Hosp., Miami, Fla., 1979; asst. dir. nursing Hanover Nursing Center, Miami, 1979-80; dir. nursing LaPosada Nursing Home, Miami, 1980-81, Jackson Heights Nursing Home, Miami, 1981—. Active March of

Dimes, Multiple Sclerosis Assn. Recipient Employee of Yr. award Jackson Heights Nursing Home, 1981; County Coll. Morris scholar, 1972-74; Fla. Internat. U. scholar, 1976-79. Mem. Am. Nurses Assn., N.J. Nurses Assn., S. Fla. Nursing Home Dirs., Fla. Nursing Assn. Democrat. Jewish. Home: 11820 SW 170 Terr Miami FL 33177 Office: 1404 NW 22 St Miami FL 33142

FABITORE, JACQUELINE EDITH, securities co. exec.; b. Camden, N.J., Oct. 3, 1946; d. John and Nancy Katherine (Terrachone) F.; B.S., Empire State Coll., 1975; postgrad. Pacific Oaks Coll., 1977-79. Model, Miami, Fla., 1963-67; ednl. therapist Marianne Frostig Center, Los Angeles, 1967-68; ednl. therapist Irwin Lehrhoff, & Assos., Los Angeles, 1968-70; pvt. practice ednl. therapist, Los Angeles and Gstaad, Switzerland, 1970-77; adminstrv. dir. Beverly Center Sch., Los Angeles, 1977-78; tchr. high sch., Los Angeles, 1976-77; account rep. Security First Group, Los Angeles, 1978-79, sr. account rep., 1979-82, regional sales dir., 1982—. Advance worker, Pete Wilson for Gov., 1977, Vice Pres. Walter Mondale, 1979-81. Mem. Nat. Assn. Security Dealers, LWV, NOW, Am. Soc. Profl. and Exec. Women, Nat. Head Injury Found., Washington Womans Network, Cousteau Soc. Home: 2316 S Quincy St Arlington VA 22204 Office: 1800 Ave of Stars Los Angeles CA 90067

FABRAY, NANETTE, actress; b. San Diego, Oct. 27; d. Racul Bernard and Lillian (McGovern) Fabares; student Los Angeles City Coll.; D.H.L., (hon.), Gallaudet Coll., 1970; D.F.A. (hon.), Md. Coll., 1972; m. David Tebet, Oct. 26, 1947 (div. July 1951); m. 2d, Ronald MacDougall, 1957 (dec. Dec. 1973); 1 son, Jamie. Appeared as actress in Broadway shows Let's Face It, 1941, Meet the People, 1940, By Jupiter, 1943, Bloomer Girl, 1944, High Button Shoes, 1947, Arms and the Girls, 1950, Love Life, 1948, Make A Wish, 1951, Mr. President, 1962, Jackpot, No Hard Feelings, 1973, Applause, 1973-74, Plaza Suite, 1973-74, The Secret Affairs of Mildred Wild, 1977; co-star with Sid Caesar on Caesar's Hour, CBS-TV, 1954-56; star TV series Yes, Yes Nanette, 1961-62, spls. Happy Birthday & Goodby, 1974, George M!, 1970; motion pictures include Private Lives of Elizabeth and Essex, 1939, The Bandwagon, 1952, The Happy Ending, 1969, A Child is Born, 1940, Cockeyed Cowboys of Calico County, 1970, That's Entertainment, Part 2, 1976, Harper Valley PTA, 1978, Trustee Eugene O'Neill Meml. Found., Nat. Theatre of Deaf; bd. dirs., v.p. Nat. Assn. Hearing and Speech Agys.; bd. dirs. Pres.'s Nat. Adv. Com. on Edn. Deaf, Pres.'s Com. on Employment Handicapped, Muses of Calif. Mus. Found. Recipient 2 Donaldson awards for High Button Shoes, 1947; Tony award for Love Life, 1949; Emmy award as best comedienne, 1955, 56, best supporting performer Caesar's Hour, 1955; Eleanor Roosevelt Humanitarian award, 1964; Human Relations award Anti-Defamation League, 1969; 1st ann. Cogswell award Gallaudet Coll., 1970; Pres.'s Disting. Service award, 1970; named Woman of yr., Radio and TV Editors, 1963, Jewish War Vets. Am., 1969. Office: care Talent Mgmt Internat 6380 Wilshire Blvd Suite 910 Los Angeles CA 90048 *

FABRIZIO, ANGELINA MARIA, educator, med. researcher, microbiologist; b. Montenero Valcocchiaro, Italy (parents Am. citizens); d. Amico Gaetano and Felicita Francesca (Danese) F.; B.S., Villa Maria Coll., Erie, Pa., 1944; M.S. (fellow 1944-45), U. Ky., 1947; Ph.D., U. Pa., 1952; cert. Hahnemann Med. Coll. and Hosp., Phila., 1955. Asst. bacteriology U. Ky., 1945-46, instr. Italian, 1946-47; research bacteriologist antibiotics U. Cin. Coll. Medicine, Cin. Gen. Hosp., 1947-48; research asso. exptl. cancer and tissue culture Presbyn. Hosp., Phila., 1951-65; research asso. exptl. cancer and tissue culture Jefferson Med. Coll., Phila., 1965-67, asst. prof. pathology, 1967—; mem. faculty Coll. Grad. Studies, 1971—; instr. U. Pa. Sch. Medicine, 1960; cons. VA Hosp., Coatesville, Pa., 1968—. Recipient Career award Villa Maria Coll. Alumnae, 1974; Nat. Tb Assn. fellow, 1948-51. Fellow AAAS; mem. Tissue Culture Assn., Am. Soc. Microbiology, N.Y. Acad. Sci., Am. Assn. Pathologists, Sigma Xi, Sigma Delta Epsilon (chpt. pres. 1959-60, nat. pres. 1973-74, dir. 1975-80). Home: 2045 Spruce St Philadelphia PA 19103

FADER, SHIRLEY SLOAN, writer; b. Paterson, N.J.; d. Samuel Louis and Miriam (Marcus) Sloan; B.S., M.S., U. Pa.; m. Seymour J. Fader, June 26, 1951; children—Susan Deborah, Steven Micah Kimchi. Writer, journalist, author, Paramus, N.J., 1956—; writer of People and You, Jobmanship columns Family Weekly, 1971-81, contbg. writer, 1977—; columnist, writer How To Get More From Your Job column, contbg. editor Glamour mag., 1978-81; columnist, writer Start Here column Working Woman mag., 1980—, contbg. editor, 1982—; writer Women Getting Ahead column Ladies' Home Jour., 1981—; contbr. articles to numerous nat. mags.; coordinator ann. writers' seminar Bergen Community Coll., 1973-75. Mem. Authors Guild, Am. Soc. Journalists and Authors (nat. v.p. 1976-77, nat. exec. council 1976-78), Nat. Press Club. Author: The Princess Who Grew Down, 1968; From Kitchen to Career, 1977; Jobmanship, 1978; Successfully Ever After; A Young Woman's Guide to Career Happiness, 1982. Address: 377 McKinley Blvd Paramus NJ 07652

FAEGENBURG, BERNICE, artist; b. Phila.; d. Simon and Dora (Rudnick) Kaufman; B.S., Tyler Sch. Fine Arts, Temple U.; postgrad. Art Students League, Nat. Acad. Design; M.S. in Art Edn., C.W. Post Coll., 1972; m. David Faegenberg; children—Nancy, Glenn, Russell. Tchr. children's classes Phila. Art Mus.; tchr. art Phila. Public Schs., Westbury (N.Y.) Schs.; tchr. art to emotionally disturbed children Roslyn (N.Y.) Jr. High Sch., 1972, silk screen printing to adults Roslyn, 1975—, tchr. creative arts workshop, 1977—; exhibited numerous one-person shows including: C.W. Post Coll., 1972, Syosset Library, 1973, Locust Valley (N.Y.) Library, 1973, Shelter Rock Library, 1976, B.J. Spoke Gallery, 1977, 80, Viridian Gallery, 1978, 80, Country Art Gallery, Locust Valley, 1982; exhibited numerous group shows including: Firehouse Gallery Nassau Community Coll., 1975, Long Beach Art Assn., 1976, Nat. Assn. Women Artists, 1976, 77, Locust Valley Art Show, 1976, 77, Huntington Township Art League, 1977, Nat. Soc. Painters in Casein & Acrylic, 1977, Avery Fisher Hall at Lincoln Center, 1978, Concordia Coll., 1979, Silvermine Guild of Artists, 1979, Gracie Sq. Art Show, 1979 Parrish Art Mus., 1981, City Gallery, N.Y.C., 1982, travelling graphics show, Egypt and Israel, 1981-82; also represented in permanent collections. Pres. East Hills PTA, 1970; co-pres. L.I. Artists Alliance, 1975. Recipient award excellence Long Beach Art Assn., 1976; Henningsen Meml. prize, 1980. Mem. Internat. Assn. Art, Nat. Assn. Women Artists (Grumbacher award of merit 1978, co-chmn. program com.). Treas., B.J. Spoke Gallery, Port Washington, N.Y., 1976—; membership chmn. Viridian Gallery, N.Y.C., 1977—, treas., 1981. Home and Studio: 31 Canterbury Ln Roslyn Heights NY 11577

FAGAN, BETTY MAHON, fin. exec.; b. Jackson, Tenn., Apr. 25, 1932; d. Robert Perry and Claire (Rogers) Mahon; B.A. cum laude, Vanderbilt U., 1953; m. Arthur Lawrence Fagan, Jr., Dec. 27, 1962; children—Perry Lawrence, Mark Malone, Anthony Rogers. Jr. analyst Smith Barney & Co., N.Y.C., 1960-65; v.p., sr. analyst White, Weld & Co., Inc., N.Y.C., 1972-78, Merrill Lynch, N.Y.C., 1978-80, First Boston Corp., N.Y.C., 1980-82; portfolio strategist Ford Found., N.Y.C., 1982—. Trustee, chmn. fin. com. Greenfield Hill Congregational Ch. Mem. Fin. Women's Assn., Fin. Analysts Fedn., N.Y. Soc. Security Analysts. Club: Cosmopolitan (gov., chmn. fin. com.) (N.Y.C.).

FAGIN, CLAIRE MINTZER, nurse, univ. dean; b. N.Y.C., Nov. 25, 1926; d. Harry and Mae (Slatin) Mintzer; B.S., Wagner Coll., 1948; M.A., Columbia U., 1951; Ph.D., N.Y.U., 1964; m. Samuel Fagin, Feb. 17, 1952; children—Joshua, Charles. Dir. grad. programs psychiat. mental health nursing N.Y.U., 1965-69, assoc. prof., 1967-69; chmn., prof. nursing Herbert H. Lehman Coll., City U. N.Y., 1969-77; dir. health professions inst. Herbert H. Lehman Coll.-Montefiore Hosp. and Med. Center, 1975-77; dean, prof. Sch. Nursing, U. Pa., 1977—; speaker; dir. Provident Mut. Ins. Co. (audit com. 1978—, chmn. 1982—); expert adv. panel on nursing WHO. Bd. trustees United Way of Southeastern Pa., 1981—. Recipient Founders Day award N.Y.U., 1964, Disting. Alumna award, 1979, Spl. Disting. Alumnus award, 1982, Alumni Achievement award Wagner Coll. Nursing Sch., 1973, Alumni award for disting. achievement in nursing practice Tchrs. Coll., Columbia U., 1975, Mary Tolle Wright Founder's award Sigma Theta Tau, 1981. Mem. Nat. Acad. Scis. (governing council Inst. Medicine 1981-83), Am. Acad. Nursing, Nat. Bd. Med. Examiners (mem. at large). Author: Desirable Functions and Qualifications of Psychiatric Nurses, 1953; The Effects of Maternal Attendance During Hospitalization on the Behavior of Young Children, 1966; (with B. Starrett, B. Goodwin, D. McGivern and S. Stokes) Physical Assessment Lecture Series, 1974; editor: Family Centered Nursing in Community Psychiatry: Treatment in the Home (Book of Yr. award Am. Jour. Nursing), 1970; Nursing in Child Psychiatry (Book of the Yr. award Am. Jour. Nursing), 1972; Readings in Child and Adolescent Psychiatric Nursing, 1974; editorial bd. Cancer Nursing: An Internat. Jour. Cancer Care, 1977—, Jour. Nursing Leadership, 1978-81, Jour. Pub. Health Policy, Inc., Am. Jour. Orthopsychiatry, 1981-83; contbr. articles to profl. jours. Office: Nursing Education Bldg Univ Pa Philadelphia PA 19104

FAHEY, MARCELLA FAHEY, state senator; b. Hartford, Conn., July 23, 1934; d. James and Mary (Cafferty) Clifford; A.A., Manchester Community Coll., 1975; B.A., Central Conn. State Coll., 1977; m. John Palmer Fahey, 1956; children—Mary-Beth, Jeffrey. Statis. clk. Aetna Life & Casualty, 1950-57; sales rep. Avon Products Inc., 1956-71; exec. sec./bookkeeper St. Rose Ch., East Hartford, Conn., 1972-76; bookkeeper Display Workshop, 1975-76; freelance program cons., 1977-78; mem. Conn. Senate, 1979—. Commr., East Hartford Human Rights Commn., 1975-78, Conn. Human Rights and Opportunities Commn., 1976-78; del. Democratic Nat. Conv., 1980; bd. dirs. Capitol Region Conf. of Chs.; mem. adv. bd. Sta. WFSB-TV; bd. dirs. Greater Hartford Process. Roman Catholic. Office: Connecticut Senate Hartford CT 06115 *

FAHR, LINDA MEYERS, radiologist; b. N.Y.C., Sept. 20, 1942; d. Paul Tabor and Jessie V. (Jones) Meyers; B.A., Barnard Coll., 1964; M.D., U. Iowa, 1968; m. James Dwight Watson, Mar. 29, 1980; children—John Pearson Fahr, Bruce Tabor Fahr. Resident in radiology U. Iowa, Iowa City, 1971-74; staff radiologist VA Hosp., Houston, 1974-77, chief dept. radiology, 1977-79; chief radiologist MacGregor Med. Clinic, Houston, 1980—; clin. asst. prof. Baylor Coll. Medicine, Houston, 1974-79. Mem. Am. Assn. Women Radiologists (pres.-elect 1982), Am. Coll. Radiology, Radiol. Soc. N.Am., Tex. Radiol. Soc., Houston Radiol. Soc. (treas. 1982), Tex. Med. Assn., Harris County Med. Assn., Women's Profl. Assn. Office: 8100 Greenbriar Houston TX 77054

FAHRENKAMP, BETTYE, state senator; b. Wilder, Tenn., Sept. 6; B.S. in Math. and Music, U. Tenn.; M.S. in Adminstrn. and Supervision, U. Alaska. Former civil engr., Oak Ridge; tchr. North Star Borough Sch. Dist., 1957-73; spl. asst. to U.S. Senator Mike Gravel, 1975-78; mem. Alaska Senate, 1978—. Mem. Democratic Nat. Com., 1972-79. Office: Pouch V Juneau AK 99811 *

FAHRER, ALISON CLARK (MRS. G. WILLIAM FAHRER, JR.), music publisher, composer, ednl. adminstr.; b. Spokane, Wash., Mar. 29, 1923; d. Levi and Josephine (Forrest) Clark; student U. Wash., Seattle, 1939-40; m. David Demarest, July 22, 1940 (div. Nov. 1965); children—Martha, Charles, Ellen D. (Mrs. Stephen Beers), Jean D. (Mrs. Dean Thresher), David; m. 2d, G. William Fahrer, Jr., Jan. 13, 1967. Pianist, composer, tchr., 1945—; founder Canyon Press, Inc., East Orange, N.J., 1951, pres., 1972—; cons. music edn. Baldwin United, Cin., 1966—, dir. edn. div., 1973-77. Mem. arts council Cin. Recreation Commn., 1969-77; commr. Monroe County, 1982—. Mem. Music Educators Nat. Conf., Music Pubs. Assn. (dir. 1958-62, 77—), Music Industry Council, Izaak Walton League (pres. Fla. Keys chpt. 1981—, v.p. Fla. div. 1982—), Islamorada C. of C., Internat. Soc. Music Edn. Author: Elements of Music, 1970. Editor: Canyon Hymnal for Boys and Girls, 1958. Contbr. articles on music to profl. publs. Composer various piano and choral works, 1952—.

FAHRINGER, CATHERINE HEWSON, savs. and loan assn. exec.; b. Phila., Aug. 1, 1922; d. George Francis and Catherine Gertrude (Magee) Hewson; m. Edward F. Fahringer, July 8, 1961; 1 son, Francis George Beckett. With Dade Savs. and Loan Assn., Miami, Fla., 1958—, v.p., 1967-74, sr. v.p., 1974, sr. v.p., sec., 1975-79, sr. v.p., head savs., personnel and mktg. div., 1979-81, exec. v.p., dir., 1981—. Co-chmn. Panel C, United Way of Dade County (Fla.), 1978-80, trustee, 1980; vice-chmn. Public Health Trust Dade County, 1977-78, chmn. bd. dirs., 1979-81, chmn. joint conf. com., 1982; pres. Center for Continuing Edn. of Women Dade County, 1974-76; bd. dirs. Downtown Miami Bus. Assn., 1979-80; trustee Dade County Vocat. Found., Internat. Univ. Found.; vice-chmn. S. Fla. Blood Services, 1981. Mem. U.S. League of Savs. Assns., Nat. League Savs. Assns., Fla. Savs. and Loan League, Savs. and Loan Personnel Soc. So. Fla., Savs. and Loan Mktg. Soc. So. Fla. (pres. 1968), Dade Bus. and Profl. Women's Club (pres. 1966-67, named woman of year 1974), Inst. Fin. Edn. (nat. dir. 1974-77), Bankers Club. Democrat. Congregationalist. Club: Coral Gables County. Office: 101 E Flagler St Miami FL 33131

FAIN, DEBORAH, mktg. exec.; b. Waterbury, Conn., Oct. 27, 1947; d. Mitchell Selig and Mildred Elizabeth (Carlson) Fain; B.A., Duke U., 1969; M.B.A., Columbia U., 1972; m. William Friedlich, Dec. 15, 1974. Mgr. advt. Doubleday & Co., N.Y.C., 1972-74; prin., Deborah Cons. Co., N.Y.C., 1974-76; product mgr. Am. Express Co., N.Y.C., 1976-79; pres. F & F Mktg. Corp., N.Y.C., 1979—. Vol., Urban Cons. Group, 1973—, recipient super vol. award, 1979; chmn. Arts Roundtable, 1981—. Mem. Women Bus. Owners of N.Y. Home and Office: 143 W 20th St New York NY 10011

FAIRBANKS, MARY JOANNE, edn. ofcl.; b. Massena, N.Y., Dec. 21, 1939; d. James William and Inez (Cappiello) Phillips; Asso. in Bus. Adminstrn., Central City Bus. Inst., Syracuse, N.Y. 1959; student in accounting LaSalle Extension U., 1974—; student in mgmt., Syracuse U., 1974—. Sec. elec. and computer engring. dept. Syracuse U., 1959-65, asst. to adminstrv. asst., 1965-72, publs. mgr. Assembly on U. Governance, 1970-72, coordinator computer confs., 1972-81, adminstr. short course Air Force intrasystem analysis program, 1974-78, supervisory asst. to chmn. dept. elec. and computer engring. and mgr. Air Force Post-Doctoral Program, Rome Air Devel. Center, 1972-78, adminstrv. asst. to chmn. dept. indsl. engring. and ops. research 1978-82, dir. Engring. Coop. Edn. program, 1982—; mgr. electromagnetic compatibility analysis techniques advancement program, 1978-82; coordinator workshops on computer architecture, 1977-79; ofcl. stenographer 1985 Project, USMC, 1963; mem. computer scoring team XIII Olympic Winter Games, Lake Placid, N.Y., 1980; Alpine ofcl. U.S. Ski Assn., 1980—. Pres. LWV Met. Syracuse, 1981—; mgr., editor publs. Onondaga County Bicentennial Quilt, 1976; editor 7 elec. engring. textbooks, 1960-78; co-author: Career Portfolio for Volunteers, 1980, Patterns of Government in Onondaga County, 1981. Home: 140 Edgehill Rd Syracuse NY 13224 Office: 359 Link Hall Syracuse U Syracuse NY 13210

FAIRCLOUGH, ELLEN LOUKS, Can. politician, mem. Privy Council; b. Hamilton, Ont., Can., Jan. 28, 1905; d. Norman Ellsworth and Nellie Bell (Louks) Cook; student schs. Hamilton, Ont.; LL.D., McMaster U., 1975; m. David Henry Gordon Fairclough, Jan. 28, 1931; 1 son, Howard Gordon. Founder, prin. acctg. practice, 1935-57; mem. Ho. of Commons Can., 1950-63, sec. of state, 1957-58, minister citizenship and immigration, 1958-62, mem. Privy Council, 1957—, postmaster gen., 1962-63; adv. mem. Can. del. to UN, 1950; del. to Conf. of Parliamentarians from NATO Countries, Paris, 1955; ambassador extraordinary to Argentina for presdl. inauguration, 1958; apptd. sec. Hamilton Trust & Savs. Corp., 1963-77 (amalgamated with Can. Permanent Trust); chmn. Hamilton Hydro Electric Commn. Past v.p. Young Conservatives Ont.; alderman Hamilton City Council, 1946-50, controller, 1950; bd. dirs. Can. Council Christians and Jews; patron Huguenot Soc. Can. Decorated officer Order of Can.; govt. bldg. named in her honor, 1982. Fellow Chartered Accts.; mem. Gen. Accts. Assn. Can. (life), United Empire Loyalist Assn. (dominion sec. 1935-40), Imperial Order Daus. of Empire (officer provincial and nat. chpts. 1935-48), Hamilton C. of C. Anglican. Club: Zonta Internat. (pres., Hamilton 1940-42, dist. gov. 1948-49, internat. treas. 1972-76). Office: Hamilton Hydro Electric Commn 55 John St N Hamilton ON L8N 3E4 Canada

FAIRLEY, WILMA K., ednl. adminstr.; b. Washington, Apr. 25, 1933; d. Elton F. and Edith King; B.A., D.C. Tchrs. Coll., 1956; M.A., Stanford U., 1970; children—Ricki F. Sharon R. Tchr. various sch. systems, 1960-69; lang. arts tchr.-specialist Montgomery County Public Schs., Rockville, Md., 1969-70, coordinator human relations tng., 1970-71, dir. human relations, 1971—, EEO officer, 1973—. Second v.p. Nat. Tots and Teens, 1972-73; bd. dirs. YWCA, 1974-75; mem. nat. bd. dirs. Girl Scouts U.S.A., 1974-75. Named Woman of Yr., Montgomery County chpt. NAACP, 1978. Mem. Am. Assn. Sch. Adminstrs., Nat. Assn. Elem. Prins., Nat. Alliance Black Sch. Educators, NAACP (life) NCCJ (bd. dirs. 1982—), Delta Sigma Theta, Phi Delta Kappa. Home: 1925 Lyttonsville Rd Silver Spring MD 20910 Office: Dept Human Relations Montgomery County Public Schs 850 Hungerford Dr Rockville MD 20850

FAIRWELL, KAY LORRAINE, editor; b. Waukegan, Ill., Aug. 20, 1947; d. Edwin Henry and Doris Lorraine (Warren) Siemons; B.A. in Communications and Public Policy, U. Calif., Berkeley, 1969. Asst. to ops. officer Am. Savs. Assn., Oakland, Calif., 1971-72; sr. editor Lawrence Hall Sci., U. Calif., Berkeley, 1972—; editor sci. edn. publs., Berkeley, 1972—. Recipient Outstanding Service award U. Calif., Berkeley, 1979. Mem. Nat. Assn. Female Execs., Am. Film Inst., Smithsonian Inst. Democrat. Office: Lawrence Hall Sci Univ Calif Berkeley CA 94720

FAIT, JAMI LUCILLE, constrn./comml. real estate co. mgr.; b. Inglewood, Calif., Mar. 18, 1950; d. Benjamin Raul and Lillian Sophia (Aquino) Ybarra; B.B.A., Calif. State U., 1972; student Cypress Jr. Coll., 1979-80. Asst. to pres. Constrn. Restaurant Adventures, Garden Grove, Calif., 1971-73; mgmt. cons. Thomas Temporaries, Newport Beach, Calif., 1973-77; adminstrv. asst. property mgmt. Pacific Mut. Life Ins. Co., Newport Beach, Calif., 1977-78; property mgmt. and devel. Hughes Investments, Inc., Newport Beach, 1977-81; acting regional v.p. The Heritage Group, Beverly Hills, Calif., 1981-82; propr. The Property Doctor, 1982—. Mem. Apt. Owners and Mgrs. Assn., Internat. Council Shopping Centers, Nat. Assn. Female Execs., Long Beach Civic Light Opera Club, South Coast Repertory Theater. Office: 1963L W Greenleaf Ave Anaheim CA 92803

FALCO, MARIA JOSEPHINE, polit. scientist, educator; b. Wildwood, N.J., July 7, 1932; d. John J. and Mafalda M. (Barbieri) Falco; A.B., Immaculata (Pa.) Coll., 1954; Fulbright scholar, U. Florence, Italy, 1954-55; M.A. in Polit. Philosophy, Fordham U., 1958; Ph.D., Bryn Mawr (Pa.) Coll., 1963; postdoctoral research fellow, Yale U., 1965-66; NSF grantee, U. Mich., summer 1968. Instr., asst. prof. history and polit. sci. Immaculata Coll., Pa., 1957-63; asst. prof. polit. sci. Washington Coll., Chestertown, Md., 1963-64; research asst. to Genevieve Blatt, candidate for U.S. Senator from Pa., 1964-65; asst. prof., asso. prof. polit. sci. LeMoyne Coll., Syracuse, N.Y., 1966-73, chmn. polit. sci. dept., 1967-73; prof. polit. sci. Stockton State Coll., Pomona, N.J., 1973-76; chmn. social and behavioral scis. faculty U. Tulsa, 1976-79; dean Coll. Arts and Scis., Loyola U., New Orleans, 1979—; pres. Womens Caucus for Polit. Sci., 1976. Pres., Syracuse chpt. New Democratic Coalition, 1970-71. Named Outstanding Educator in U.S., 1975. Faculty fellow in state and local politics Nat. Center for Edn. in Politics, 1964. Mem. Am. Polit. Sci. Assn. (mem. Benjamin Evans Lippincott award com. 1976, chmn. sect. program com. 1975, mem. profl. ethics and acad. freedom com. 1977-80), Midwest Polit. Sci. Assn. (com. on status of women), S.W. Polit. Sci. Assn. (outstanding conv. paper award com.), Northeastern Polit. Sci. Assn., AAUP (v.p. LeMoyne chpt. 1971-72), Founds. Polit. Theory Group. Roman Catholic. Author: Truth and Meaning in Political Science: An Introduction to Political Inquiry, 1973; Through the Looking Glass: Epistemology and the Conduct of Political Inquiry, 1979; —Bigotry—!: Ethnic, Machine and Sexual Politics in a Senatorial Election, 1980; contbr. articles to profl. publs. Office: Coll Arts and Scis Loyola U New Orleans LA 70118

FALCON, THERESA MACALALAG, physician; b. Philippines, Aug. 7, 1945; d. Francisco Z. and Juanita E. Macalalag; M.D., U. Santo Tomas, Manila, 1969; m. Iraj Azizpour, Dec. 29, 1980; children—Mary Jo, Belinda, Elizabeth, Zenaida. Resident in ob-gyn, Philippines, 1969-73, U. Ill. Affiliated Hosp., Chgo., 1973-77; cons. Mt. Sinai Hosp., Chgo., 1977-78; adj. prof. Rush Med. Sch., Chgo., 1977-78; practice medicine specializing in ob-gyn, Pekin, Ill.; cons., attending physician Pekin Meml. Hosp., St. Francis Hosp., Peoria, Ill. Diplomate Am. Bd. Ob-Gyn. Fellow Am. Coll. Ob-Gyn; mem. AMA, Am. Assn. Gynecologic Laparoscopists. Roman Catholic. Club: Pekin Country. Office: 3223 Griffin Ave Pekin IL 62554

FALK, ALMA MARTHA (MRS. BYRON A. FALK), former educator; b. Chgo., Apr. 18, 1910; d. Henry and Alma (Wolowski) Weihofen; cert. Chgo. Tchrs. Coll., 1932; B.A., George Washington U., 1937, M.A., 1957; postgrad. Howard U.; m. James E. Curry, Apr. 28, 1934 (dec. Aug. 1972); 1 dau., Aileen Curry-Cloonan; m. 2d, Byron A. Falk, Nov. 22, 1966. Tchr., Hull House, Chgo., 1930-32; social worker Ill. Relief Commn., 1932-35; tchr. elem. sch., Chgo., 1937-38, 46-47; office mgr. law firms in P.R. and Washington, 1948-53; elem. tchr. Jr. Village Sch., Washington, 1953-57; reading coordinator Washington Public Schs., 1957-72; instr. George Washington Reading Clinic, 1957-66; pres. Greater Washington Reading Council, 1966-67. Vol. asst. CD Milk Sta. Program, San Juan, P.R., 1942-46; instr. Urban Service Corps. of Vols., 1952-56; bd. dirs. Internat. Student House, 1980—, Washington. Recipient citation White House Conf. on Children, 1962. Mem. AAUW (chmn. edn. com. Washington br. 1959-61, dir. 1976-80), Nat. Mil. Wives, Internat. Reading Assn., Am. Fedn. Tchrs., Women's Internat. League for Peace and Freedom, Washington Tchrs. Union (rep. reading specialists 1968-70), Am. Humanist Assn., UN Assn., Phi Delta Gamma. Club: George Washington U. (charter). Home: 922 24th St NW Washington DC 20037

FALK, BARBARA ANN, acctg. exec.; b. Eugene, Oreg., Feb. 1, 1944; d. Everett Henry and Phyllis Ruth (Wetgen) F.; student So. Oreg. State Coll., 1962-63; A.S., Lane Community Coll., 1971. Accounts receivable bookkeeper Junction City Implement Co. (Oreg.), 1963-64, Eugene Farmers' Co-op, 1964-65; bookkeeper Chef Francisco, Inc., Eugene, 1978-79, sr. acct., 1979, acctg. supr., 1980—. Mem. Nat. Assn. Female Execs., Nat. Assn. Accts. (dir. chpt. 1971-79, pres. chpt. 1979-80, nat. dir. 1981-83, Eugene-Springfield chpt. Most Valuable Mem. 1979, 82), Eugene-Springfield Credit Women (dir. 1978-82), Am. Mgmt. Soc. Republican. Baptist. Home: 140 Tatum Ln Eugene OR 97404 Office: 1500 Valley River Dr Eugene OR 97401

FALK, DIANE SENA, psychiat. social worker; b. Oak Park, Ill., Mar. 15, 1941; d. Philip and Leta Jessie (Edgecombe) Miller; B.A., U. Chgo., 1963, M.A., 1966; M.S.W., U. Pa., 1971; m. Charles D. Falk, July 16, 1965 (div. Oct. 1980); 1 son, David Andrew. Social worker Del. Dept. Pub. Welfare, Wilmington, 1967-69; staff social worker Children's Psychiat. Center, Eatontown, N.J., 1971; dir. transitional services Raritan Bay Mental Health Center, Perth Amboy, N.J., 1972-80, dir. adult outpatient services, 1980—; field work instr. Sch. Social Work, Rutgers U., 1976—. Bd. dirs. ACLU Monmouth County, 1973-76. Mem. Nat. Assn. Social Workers (sec. to bd. dirs. N.J. chpt. 1978-80), Acad. Cert. Social Workers, Am. Orthopsychiat. Assn., Otto Rank Assn. Episcopalian. Contbr. articles to profl. jours. Home: 94 Conover Rd Marlboro NJ 07746 Office: 570 Lee St Perth Amboy NJ 08861

FALK-DICKLER, FLORENCE, human devel. specialist, govt. ofcl.; b. Bklyn., July 27, 1931; d. Maxwell and Minnie (Orshan) Falk; student (Sidney Hillman scholar) Cornell U., 1948-50; B.A. (Dean Bacon scholar), U. Mich., 1952; postgrad. (Inst. Internat. Edn. scholar) Oxford (Eng.) U., 1952; M.S., City U. N.Y., 1962; Ed.D., Columbia U., 1981; m. J. Martin Dickler, June 14, 1953; children—Lisa Suzanne, Maura Nan. Personal and career educator, counselor, Bergen County, N.J., 1962-64; child study team sch. social worker, 1969-72; personal and career counselor, career educator, lectr. Bergen Community Coll., 1972-75; pvt. practice career and personal adjustment counseling, 1972-75; human resources/program devel. specialist Region II, Women's Bur., Dept. Labor, N.Y.C., 1975—. Mem. Nat. Assn. Women Adminstrs., Deans and Counselors, Am. Personnel and Guidance Assn., Am. Soc. Tng. and Devel., N.Y. Orgn. Devel. Network, Orgn. Devel. Network, Women in Cable, Networks Unltd., NOW (nat. coordinator child care, founder No. N.J. chpt.), Phi Sigma Alpha, Phi Delta Kappa, Kappa Delta Pi. Club: River View Racquetball (River Edge, N.J.). Contbr. to profl. jours. Home: 1321 Trafalgar St Teaneck NJ 07666 Office: Women's Bur Dept Labor 1515 Broadway New York NY 10036

FALKENBERG, MARY ANN THERESA, realtor; b. Chgo., Dec. 8, 1931; d. Joseph and Catherine (Bausch) Haselsteiner; student Barat Coll., 1953; m. Charles V. Falkenberg, Jr., Apr. 9, 1955; children—Catherine, Grace Ann, Susan Marie, Charles V., Robert, Thomas, Martin, Mary, Elizabeth, Joseph. Tchr. piano, 1946-73; organist St. Thomas of Villanova Ch., 1960—, choir dir., 1960—; sales staff Quinlan & Tyson, Realtors, Inc., Palatine, Ill., 1970-77; broker, mgr., co-owner Assos. Realty Corp., Palatine, 1978—. Named Palatine Woman of Yr., Surburban Press Found., 1962; cert. home protection cons. Mem. Women in Mgmt., Ill. Assn. Realtors (life mem. two million dollar club), Nat. Assn. Realtors, Nat. Assn. Female Execs., N.W. Suburban Bd. Realtors (edn. com. 1977-78, non-resident com. 1982), Women in Sales, Barat Coll. Alumni Assn. Club: Women's. Republican. Roman Catholic. Home: 517 Warwick St Palatine IL 60067 Office: 630 N Court St Palatine IL 60067

FALKNER, PAMELA POLLARD, acct., realtor; b. Helena, Ark., Sept. 29, 1949; d. Robert Edward and Doris Marie (Carlton) Pollard; B.S. U. Tenn., Knoxville, 1970; M.S., Memphis State U., 1977; m. Terrell Manning Falkner, Dec. 19, 1970. Broker, Falkner Realty, Hughes, Ark., 1973—; dir. tax services Agro Systems Corp., Memphis, 1977-78; partner Hickman, Falkner & Assos., Memphis, 1979-80; owner, operator Pam Falkner, CMA, CPA, West Memphis, Ark., 1980—. Mem. Am. Inst. C.P.A.s, Ark. Soc. C.P.A.s, Beta Gamma Sigma, Beta Alpha Psi, Phi Kappa Phi. Methodist. Club: Town and Country Garden (pres.). Home: 201 Tournament West Memphis AR 72301 Office: 1310 S Avalon West Memphis AR 72301

FALLEY, MARGARET DICKSON (MRS. GEORGE FREDERICK FALLEY), author, genealogist; b. Mpls., Nov. 8, 1898; d. George E. and Edith (Baker) Dickson; B.S., Northwestern U., 1920; m. George Frederick Falley, Mar. 10, 1921 (dec. 1962); children—Katharine (Mrs. Edward H. Bennett, Jr.), Margaret Jane (Mrs. Raymond M. Galt), Carol (Mrs. Warner G. Baird, Jr.), Priscilla (Mrs. Henry W. Apfelbach). Ann. lectr. to Am. Inst. Genealogy at Nat. Archives, Washington, 1955-60, Geneal. Inst. Samford U., Birmingham, Ala., 1967; participant Inst. Humanistic Studies, Aspen, Colo., 1967; lectr. Bicentennial Conf. Am. Genealogy, Cleve., 1976; founding mem. John Evans Club, Northwestern U., 1954—; geneal. lectr. state, tchr. hist. socs., clubs, orgns. Mem. exec. bd. library council Northwestern U., 1979—. Recipient Merit award Nat. Geneal. Soc., 1963. Fellow Am. Soc. Genealogists (v.p. 1962-63); Am. rep. council Harleian Soc., London, Eng.; colonial mem. New Eng. Historic Geneal. Soc.; mem. Northwestern U. Alumni Assn. (v.p. 1935-36), Northwestern U. Settlement Sr. Bd. (pres. 1945-46), Colonial Dames Am., D.A.R., Nat. Soc. Descs. Lords of Md. Manors, Daus. of Barons of Runnymeade, Kappa Kappa Gamma (Outstanding Alumnae award 1970). Methodist. Clubs: Union League (Chgo.); Glen View (Golf, Ill.). Author: Richard Falley and Some of His Descendants Including Grover Cleveland, 1952; Palmer Genealogy, Part I (English and Irish Ancestry of George Palmer), 1957; Irish and Scotch-Irish Ancestral Research, 2 vols., 1962; Baird-Green and Allied Families, Part II, 1976. Contbr. articles to geneal. jours. Address: 1500 Sheridan Rd Wilmette IL 60091

FALLIS, ELIZABETH ANN, corp. exec.; b. Shelbyville, Ind., Jan. 31, 1944; d. James Herbert and Elizabeth Justine (Piper) Wisker; B.A., Butler U., 1967; postgrad. G.E. Fin. Mgmt. program, 1975-77, Acctg. Edn. Assn., 1980; m. Kenneth C. Fallis, Aug. 22, 1964; children—James Dennis, Thomas Allen. Cost estimating specialist Gen. Electric Co., Shelbyville, Ind., 1974-75, bus. analysis and planning specialist, 1975-76, sales acctg. specialist, 1977-77, gen. and tax acctg. specialist, 1977-78, specialist of disbursements, 1978-79; mgr. profit planning frozen foods div. Stokely-Van Camp, Inc., Indpls., 1979-80, mgr. gen. acctg. and fin. statements canned foods div., 1980-81, mgr. gen. acctg. and fin. statements U.S. Grocery Products Group, 1981—. Mem. exec. com. March of Dimes Birth Defects Found., Shelby County, Ind., 1967—, treas., 1970-72, chpt. chmn., 1972—, 15 Yr. Service award, 1982; Stokely-Van Camp chmn. United Way. Cert. mgmt. acct. Mem. AAUW (v.p. programs 1970-72), Nat. Assn. Accts. dir. community programs 1980-81, dir. profl. devel. 1981-82, dir. manuscripts 1982-83, mem. Lincoln Trails Council), Nat. Assn. Female Execs., Am. Soc. Profl. and Exec. Women, Delta Theta Tau (past v.p., sec., historian). Roman Catholic. Club: Shelbyville Girls (mem. women's council 1973-75, chmn. book drive 1973). Office: 941 N Meridian St Indianapolis IN 46206

FALLON, KILTON (TINA) PEELE, state legislator; b. Dudley, N.C., Sept. 16, 1917; d. George and Lillain (Langston) Peele; A.B., Meredith Coll., 1938; M.Ed., U. Del., 1956; m. James D. Fallon, Jr., July 30, 1938; children—George Peele, James D., William Norwood, Howard F. Tchr., N.C., Preston, Md., Federalsburg, Md., Istanbul, Turkey, Seaford, Del., 1948-77; mem. Del. Ho. of Reps., 1979—, chmn. agr. com., vice chmn. natural resources com., mem. environ. control and edn. com.; mem. gov.'s advisory com. on farmland preservation and gov.'s library task force. Active Hosp. Aux., local, county, state Rep. orgns. NSF grantee in marine biology U. Del., 1961, in astronomy Northeastern U., 1973. Mem. Nat. Conf. State Legislators, C. of C., Bus. and Profl. Women, AAUW, Nat. Ret. Tchrs. Assn. (del.), Alpha Beta Phi, Beta Sigma Phi. Episcopalian. Clubs: Acorn, Kiwives. Office: Room 104 Legislative Hall Dover DE 19901 *

FALLS, HELEN EMERY, educator; b. Bay City, Tex., Apr. 17, 1916; d. Oswald Benjamin and Glennie Agusta (Parker) Falls; A.B., U. Richmond, 1936; M.R.E., So. Bapt. Theol. Sem., 1941; M.A., Columbia U., 1953, Ed.D., 1964; D.D. (hon.), U. Richmond, 1976. Tchr. pub. schs., Va., 1936-39; State Young People's leader, Balt., 1941-43, Louisville, 1943-45; dean women and prof. missions New Orleans Bapt. Theol. Sem., 1945—, prof. missions, 1953—, counselor for women, 1947—. Lilly Found. grantee, 1963-64; named Disting. Alumna, U. Richmond, 1976. Mem. AAUW, Am. Personnel and Guidance Assn., Mortar Bd., Kappa Delta Pi. Republican. Baptist. Club: As You Like It Lit. Author: History of Christian Missions, 1975; A Survey of Contemporary Southern Baptist World Missions, 1969, 2nd edit. 1977; contbr. articles to profl. jours. Office: 3939 Gentilly Blvd New Orleans LA 70126

FALLS, WALDTRAUT MARGRETE GOETZE, med. librarian; b. N.Y.C., June 28, 1941; d. Otto Paul and Anna Irma (Zander) Goetze; A.B., State U. N.Y. at Albany, 1963, M.A. (scholar), 1964; M.S., Columbia U., 1967; m. John Allen Falls, Jr.; children—John Francis, Michael Gregory. Asst. advt. librarian Curtis Pub. Co., N.Y.C., 1964-65; library asso. N.Y. U. Commerce Library, N.Y.C., 1965-67; librarian, instr. N.Y.C. Community Coll., Bklyn., 1967-69, 70, 73-75; med. librarian Victory Meml. Hosp., Bklyn., 1975—. Mem. ALA, Med. Library Assn., N.Y. Library Club (life). Home: 328 78th St Brooklyn NY 11209 Office: Victory Meml Hosp 9036 7th Ave Brooklyn NY 11228

FALSONE, ANNE MARIE MCMAHON, state ofcl.; b. N.Y.C., May 20, 1937; d. Thomas Henry and Betty May (Stansel) McMahon; B.S., Memphis State U., 1956; M.A., 1968; M.L.S., George Peabody Coll., 1969; m. James H. Kennedy. Head librarian White Sta. Jr./Sr. High Sch., Memphis, 1966-71; asst. head history dept. Memphis Public Library, 1971-72; cons. sch. libraries Colo. State Library, Denver, 1972-75; supr. state sch. library programs Colo. Dept. Edn., Denver, 1975-76, asst. commr. Office Library Services, 1976—; trustee Bibliog. Center Research; mem. Western Council State Libraries; mem. network adv. com. Library Congress; mem. Colo. Gov.'s Commn. on Public Telecommunications. Mem. ALA, Colo. Library Assn., Colo. Ednl. Media Assn., Chief Officers State Library Agys., Assn. Specialized and Coop. Library Agys. (pres.-elect), Colo. Assn. Sch. Execs., Phi Alpha Theta, Beta Phi Mu, Alpha Lambda Delta, Alpha Delta Pi. Office: 1362 Lincoln St Denver CO 80203 *

FALSTAD, JAN BETH, radio polit. reporter; b. Williston, N.D., Jan. 4, 1952; d. Robert Coleman and Beverly Mae (Weberg) Falstad; B.A., U. Minn., 1977; student Brown Inst. Broadcasting, 1974; m. Greg Pratt, Sept. 18, 1981. Announcer, reporter Sta. KDAN-AM, Newport, Minn., 1974-75, Sta. KUOM-AM (NPR), Minn. U., Mpls., 1976-77; govt. corr., reporter, announcer Sta. WWTC-AM, Mpls., 1976-77, KSJN-FM (NPR), St. Paul, 1977-78; programming asst. Sta. KTCA-KTCI-TV, St. Paul, 1979-80; govt. corr. Sta. WCCO-AM, Mpls., 1980—. Recipient 1st place radio documentary award Sigma Delta Chi, 1976; Radio and TV News Dirs. Assn. scholar, 1976; KSTP-TV scholar, 1976; Rotary Internat. fellow, Sweden, 1977. France, 1978, 79; Mem. Nat. Assn. Female Execs., Press Women Minn., Sigma Delta Chi. Home: 3209 Park Ave S Minneapolis MN 55407 Office: 625 2d Ave Minneapolis MN

FALVEY, BARBARA JOANNE, stockbroker; b. San Francisco, June 21, 1958; d. Raymond Joseph and Beverly Joan Falvey; student West Valley Coll., Saratoga, Calif., 1976-78, Mesa Jr. Coll., San Diego, 1978-79, Orange Coast Coll., Costa Mesa, Calif. Stockbroker Montano Securities Corp., Los Angeles, 1979-80, Smith, Barney Harris Upham & Co., Newport Beach, Calif., 1980—. Mem. Am. Bus. Women Assn., We Can Women's Network, Women in Mgmt. Republican. Roman Catholic. Home: 90 Lakepines St Irvine CA 92714 Office: 4000 MacArthur Blvd Suite 110 Newport Beach CA 92660

FALVO, DONNA ROSE, behavioral scientist; b. Douglas County, Ill., Mar. 17, 1945; d. Harry Johan and Christina Katherine (Stortzum) Schmohe; R.N., Mercy Sch. Nursing, 1966; M.S., So. Ill. U., 1975, Ph.D., 1978. Nurse, McKinley Hosp., Urbana, Ill., Wahiawa (Hawaii) Hosp., Doctor's Meml. Hosp., Cardondale, Ill., 1966-70; instr. Vocat. Tech. Inst., So. Ill. U., Carbondale, 1970-72, instr. dept. family practice Sch. Medicine, 1974—, researcher, 1973-74, dir. behavioral sci., 1977—; bd. dirs. Quality of Life Geriatric Program; coordinator regional So. Ill. Genetic Counseling Program. Mem. Am. Psychol. Assn., Soc. of Tchrs. Family Medicine, Psychologists in Family Medicine and Primary Health Care, Assn. Behavioral Sci. and Med. Edn., Ill. Assn. Maternal and Child Health (dir.). Lutheran. Office: 404 W Main St Carbondale IL 62901

FANCHER, HELEN IRENE, state legislator; b. Seattle, Mar. 1, 1931; d. Robert Warren and Mary Caroline (Foy) Walker; student U. Wash., 1948, Eastern Wash. U., 1949-50; m. John T. Fancher, Aug. 14, 1950; children—Scott, Donald, Nancy Connelly. Profl. musician, Seattle, Spokane, Wash., 1947; sec.-treas., dir. Pilot Wheel Ranch, Inc., Tonaska, Wash., Three Toed Feedlot, Inc., Quincy, Wash., 1971—; mem. Tri-County Law and Justice Commn., 1970, Okanogan County Planning Commn., 1974; mem. Wash. Ho. of Reps., 1976—. Precinct committeeman Republican party; dir. Agr.-Forestry Leadership Found., 1982; pres. Okanogan County Cow Belles, 1972-73; v.p. Wash. State Cow Belles, 1975-76; mem. Wash. State Timber Tax Adv. Com.; asst. majority leader Ho. of Reps. Named Hon. State Farmer, Future Farmers Am., 1982. Mem. Nat. Cow Belles and Cattlemen's Assn., Musicians Union, Am. Legis. Exchange Council, Mu Phi Epsilon.

FANDEL, NANCY ANN, publishing cons.; b. Newport, R.I., Sept. 10, 1948; d. Ralph, Jr., and Mabel (Bishop) F.; student U. No. Iowa, 1966-69; B.Gen. Sci., U. Iowa, 1974. Asst. mgr. single copy sales Meredith Corp., Des Moines, 1976-79; dir. mktg. ARA Periodicals, Washington, 1980-81; pres. N.A. Fandel, Ltd., Washington, 1981—; instr. women's studies Peninsula Coll., Port Angeles, Wash., 1975-76. Mem. Nat. Assn. Female Execs., Washington Women in Advt. and Mktg. Democrat. Office: 5803 Gloster Rd Bethesda MD 20816

FANG, DONNA MARIE, govt. adminstr., accountant; b. Washington, July 31, 1942; d. William Henry and Angela Foreman (Myers) Miller; B.S. in Acctg., U. Md., 1971; M.B.A. in Fin., Southeastern U., 1982; m. David Fang, Sept. 16, 1977; children—Jason Brian, Angela Beth. Agt./tax instr. IRS, Washington, 1971-76; br. mgr. GSA, Washington, 1977—; mem. faculty No. Va. Coll. Mem. Assn. Govt. Accts., Am. Inst. C.P.A.s. Home: 1221 N George Mason Dr Arlington VA 22205 Office: GSA 19th and F St NW Washington DC 20405

FANNALY, VERONICA LOUISE, hotel fin. exec.; b. Hammond, La., Oct. 17, 1944; d. Lawrence Herman and Frances Louise (Harden) F.; student Southeastern La. Coll., 1962-64; children—Deborah, Seth. Clk., Royal Sonesta Hotel, New Orleans, 1970-71, Royal Orleans Hotel, New Orleans, 1971-72; sr. auditor Marriott Hotel, New Orleans, 1972-74; comptroller Bourbon Orleans Hotel, New Orleans, 1981-82; v.p. L.H. Fannaly Inc., 1982—. Historian, publicist Ponchatoula Jaycee Jaynes, 1979. Mem. Am. Businesswomen's Assn. (rec. sec. 1972), Nat. Assn. Female Execs. Republican. Roman Catholic. Home: PO Box 1012 Ponchatoula LA 70454

FANNING, KAY EILENE, retail cosmetics co. exec.; b. Springfield, Ohio, Sept. 4, 1942; d. Wilbur J. and Ethel Waddle; B.S., Wittenberg U., 1964; student U. Dayton, summer 1965, Bowling Green U., summer 1966; m. Robert H. Fanning, Feb. 1, 1964; children—Leann Kay, (Robert) Shane, Aaron Carter. Tchr., Shawnee High Sch., Springfield, Ohio, 1964-67; tchr. Clark Tech. Coll., 1967-70; beauty cons. Fashion Two Twenty Cosmetics, Springfield, 1969-70, mgr., 1970- , asso. dir., 1970-78, dir., 1978; pres. Mic-Kay, Inc., Springfield, 1979—; regional mgr. Cher-Beli Creations, Inc., Memphis, 1981-82, area v.p., 1982—. Mem. Clark County Bd. Edn., 1974—, v.p., 1978, pres., 1979; mem. Springfield-Clark County Joint Vocat. Sch. Bd. Edn., 1979—, v.p., 1981-82, pres., 1982—; mem. Clark County Republican Women. Mem. Nat. Assn. Female Execs., Springfield Area C. of C., Alpha Delta Pi. Republican. Baptist. Address: 364 W Jackson Rd Springfield OH 45502

FANNING, LUCRETIA PICCIONE, speech and lang. pathologist; b. Bklyn., Oct. 8, 1953; d. Luciano Joseph and Laura Rose (Colonna) Piccione; B.A. cum laude, U. Conn., 1975; M.A., George Washington U., 1976; m. Philip John Fanning, July 9, 1977. Speech and lang. pathologist Glastonbury (Conn.) Public Schs., 1976—, also Mt. Sinai and New Britain Gen. hosps.; cons. in field. Mem. Am. Speech and Hearing Assn. Roman Catholic. Patentee computerized lang. program.

FANSLER, LOTTIE ELAINE, tire dealership exec.; b. Caldwell, Kans., Apr. 12, 1937; d. Otto Jayce and Alta Grace (Terry) Cash; student public schs., Caldwell; m. Harold Fansler, July 13, 1970; children—Shawna, Betrice, Scott. Med. clk. Wichita (Kans.) Clinic, 1956-57, drs. offices Pratt, Kans., 1960-62 and Lyons, Kans., 1966-68; Medicare dir. St. Catherine Hosp., Garden City, Kans., 1968-70; exec. v.p. Fansler Tires, Inc., Garden City, Liberal and Dodge City, Kans., 1977—, also dir. Notary public, Kans. Republican. Mem. Assemblies of God Ch. Home: 911 3d St Garden City KS 67846 Office: 120 N Main St Garden City KS 67846

FANSLOW, ALYCE MUCK, home economist; b. Buhl, Minn., Feb. 28, 1935; d. Roy Howard and Mary A. Muck; B.S., U. Minn., 1957; M.S., Iowa State U., 1960, Ph.D., 1966; m. Glenn E. Fanslow, May 28, 1960; children—Kathryn M., Janet L. Tchr. home econs. Owatonna (Minn.) Pub. Schs., 1957-58; mem. faculty Iowa State U., Ames, 1966—, prof. home econs. edn., 1979—, disting. prof. in home econs., 1982—. Gen. Foods Fund fellow, 1958-59; Julie Kiene fellow, 1959-60; Omicron Nu fellow, 1963-64. Mem. Am. Home Econs. Assn. (chmn. membership survey com. 1979—), Am. Vocat. Assn., Am. Vocat. Edn. Research Assn., Am. Ednl. Research Assn., Phi Delta Kappa. Presbyterian. Club: Altrusa. Author articles in field; mem. editorial bd. Home Econs. Research Jour. Office: 219 MacKay Hall Iowa State U Ames IA 50011

FANTARELLA, ANNA MARY FRIONE, concrete co. exec.; b. New Haven, Jan. 21, 1925; d. Domenic Victor and Mary Ella (Velleca) Frione; student summers Albertus Magnus Coll., 1943, U. Vt., 1944; B.A. in Econs., Trinity Coll., 1945; m. Louis A. Fantarella, June 26, 1948 (div. 1956); 1 son, Richard. With payroll and personnel depts. D.V. Frione & Co., Inc., hwy. constrn. co., New Haven, 1956-60, corporate sec., 1960-71, treas., 1971-76, also dir.; sec., dir. Foxon Concrete Corp., New Haven, 1960-78, treas., 1974—, pres., 1978—, also dir.; sec., dir. Frione Real Estate Corp., New Haven, 1963-72, treas., 1971-77; sec.-treas., dir. Morgan-Essex Corp., Amdon Corp.; real estate sales rep. Fla. Futures, Milford, Conn. Mem. exec. bd. Cub Scouts, Orange council Boy Scouts Am., 1962-64; mem. exec. bd. P.T.A., Orange, 1965-66. Bd. dirs. Benhaven Sch. Autistic Children, 1973—. Mem. Conn. Constrn. Industries Assn. (bd. dirs. 1977-78), AAUW (pres. 1970-72), Trinity Coll. Alumnae Assn. (pres. 1961). Roman Catholic. Club: New Haven Women's. Home: 411 Prudden Ln Orange CT 06477 Office: 135 Cherry St Milford CT 06460

FANTZ, RAINETTE EDEN, clin. psychologist; b. Cleve., Dec. 13, 1922; d. Dimitri Dimiter and Anna (Asher) Dobreff; student Cleve. Inst. Art, 1941-43, Flora Stone Mather Coll., 1941-43; B.S., Western Res. U., 1951, Ph.D., 1962; m. Robert L. Fantz, Nov. 2, 1960; 1 dau., Lorian. Comml. artist Bailey's, Cleve., 1943-48; free-lance artist, 1943-48; actress leading roles Repertory Theatre, Washington, 1952-53; cons. Cleve. Diabetes Assn., 1955; asst. psychologist Fairview Park (Ohio) Public Schs., 1956-57; asst. psychologist Highland View Hosp., Cleve., 1957-62; psychologist James R. Hodge, M.D., Akron, Ohio, 1958-63; pvt. practice clin. psychology, Cleve., 1962—; mem. faculty Gestalt Inst. of Cleve., 1968—, chmn. intensive postgrad. program, 1973—. Mem. Am. Psychol. Assn., Ohio Psychol. Assn., Cleve. Psychol. Assn., Am. Acad. Psychotherapists, Cleve. Acad. Cons. Psychologists (past pres.), Assn. for Advancement of Psychology, Cleve. Inst. Music, Cleve. Inst. Art, Cleve. Mus. Art, Supporters of Cleve. Orchestra, ACLU, Common Cause, Phi Beta Kappa. Contbr. chpts. to books; editor publs. in field. Home: 11 Mornington Ln Cleveland Heights OH 44106 Office: 1588 Hazel Dr Cleveland OH 44106

FARAH, MADELAIN MARY, educator, author; b. Portland, Oreg., Dec. 20, 1934; d. Sam and Laurice (Nasrallah) F.; student U. Oreg., 1955; B.A., Portland State U., 1959, M.A.T., 1967; postgrad. Am. U., Cairo, 1961-62, U. Tehran, summer 1970; Ph.D., U. Utah, 1976; 1 dau., Leila Habib. Buyer, mgr., sales Farah's Dept. Store, Portland, Oreg., 1946-59; profl. free-lance model, Portland, 1951-59; sec., translator U.S. Dept. State, Washington, 1956-60; instr. Arabic, Portland (Oreg.) State U., 1966; French tchr. Lincoln High Sch., Portland, 1972—; cooking instr. Portland Community Coll., 1976-77; area adminstr. Am. Inst. Fgn. Study, Portland, 1979—; author: Lebanese Cuisine, 1972, 5th edit., 1981; corrs. Word Mag., Portland, 1973-75; columnist News Circle, Los Angeles, 1973-74. Del. to Nat. Conf. on Citizenship, 1956; bd. dirs. local chpt. UN, 1958-62; co-chmn. Mayor Goldschmidt's adv. com. for Urban Devel. of Lents, 1977. Fulbright fellow, Cairo, 1961-62; Nat. Def. Fgn. Lang. fellow, 1969-71; Am.-Iranian cultural exchange fellow, 1970. Mem. Am. Assn. Tchrs. French (Professeur du Laureat award), Confedn. Oreg. Fgn. Lang. Tchrs., NEA, Oreg. Edn. Assn., Portland Assn. Tchrs., Smithsonian Inst. Antiochian Orthodox (v.p. western region 1975, parish council pres. 1976, Sunday sch. supt.). Clubs: Greek Civic, . George Ladies Guild, Oreg. Grange. Office: PO Box 66395 Portland OR 97266

FARBER, NORMA (MRS. SIDNEY FARBER), musician, poet; b. Boston, Aug. 6, 1909; d. G. Augustus and Augusta (Schon) Holzman; A.B., Wellesley Coll., 1931; M.A., Radcliffe Coll., 1932; m. Sidney Farber, July 3, 1928; children—Ellen, Stephen, Thomas, Miriam. Singer, soprano, solo recitals, appearances with small ensemble groups and orchs., 1940—. Recipient premier prix in singing, Jury Central des Etudes Musicales, Belgium, 1936, prizes for poetry Poetry Soc. Am.; Golden Rose award for poetry, N.E. Poetry Club. Mem. Phi Beta Kappa. Author: (poetry) The Hatch 1955, Look to the Rose, 1958, A Desperate Thing, 1973, Household Poems, 1975; Something Further, 1979; (juvenile) Did You Know It Was the Narwhale; 1967, I Found Them in the Yellow Pages, 1973, Where's Gomer?, 1974, This Is the Ambulance Leaving the Zoo, 1975, As I Was Crossing Boston Common, 1975 (nominated for Nat. Book award), Six Impossible Things Before Breakfast, 1977, A Ship in a Storm on The Way To Tarshish, 1978, Three

Wanderers from Wapping, 1978, How The Left-Behind Beasts Built Ararat, 1978, There Once Was a Woman Who Married a Man, 1978, Never Say Ugh! to a Bug, 1979, Small Wonders, 1979, Up the Down Elevator, 1979, How Does It Feel to be Old?, 1979, How the Hibernators Came to Bethlehem, 1980, A Night on Gars Mountain, 1981; (novel) Mercy Short, A Winter Journal, North Boston, 1692-93, 1982, others; co—translator: To Live in Pronouns, 1974; (record) Love Can Be Still: Music on Verses of Norma Farber, 1981. Address: 1010 Memorial Dr Cambridge MA 02138

FARBER, SARAH R., psychotherapist; b. Terre Haute, Ind., Nov. 22, 1928; d. Max and Rose (Goldberg) Sussman; B.S. in Social Work, U. Chgo., 1950, M.S.W., 1952; m. Bernard E. Farber, June 26, 1957; children—Miriam Daphne, Sharon Lee, Rena Mindy. Social worker children's div. Chgo. Welfare Dept., 1950-51; psychiat. social worker Lasker Mental Hygiene Clinic Hadassah, Jerusalem, Israel, 1952-56, Jewish Family Service, N.Y.C., 1956-59; psychotherapist Rockland County Mental Health Clinic, Pomona and Orangeburg, N.Y., 1972—; pvt. practice psychotherapy, Pomona, N.Y., 1973—; mental health assn. speaker, educator, 1974—; tchr. workshops Rockland Community Coll., Suffern, N.Y., 1975—; counselor, supr. paraprofls. Vol. Family Counseling Service, New City, N.Y., 1971—; field instr. social work interns Fordham U., N.Y.C.; supr. psychiat. resident N.Y.C. Cert. social worker, N.Y.; cert. sch. counselor, N.J.; lic. marriage counselor, N.J. Fellow Soc. Clin. Work Psychotherapists; mem. Acad. Cert. Social Workers of Nat. Assn. Social Workers, Hadassah (v.p. membership 1965-66, v.p. edn. 1967-69, 71-72, award 1968). Home: 392 Chelsea St Paramus NJ 07652 Office: Mental Health Clinic 63 Staff Rd Orangeburg NY 10962

FARCUS, JOAN IRAYNA, lawyer; b. Bridgeport, Conn., Aug. 8, 1944; d. Joseph M. and Dorothy Sayre (Meyers) Farcus; B.A. in English, U. Bridgeport, 1966; J.D., Suffolk U. Law Sch., 1969. Admitted to Conn. bar, 1972, Fla. bar, 1977, N.Y. State bar, 1981, D.C. bar, 1982; practice law, Miami, Fla., 1977—; mem. firm DePiano & Palmesi, P.C., Bridgeport, 1971—; adj. prof. law Coll. Bus. Adminstrn., Sacred Heart U., Bridgeport, 1971—, founder, dir. legal assts. program, 1974-76; dir. Technographics Inc., Fairfield, Conn. Bd. dirs. Conn. Assn. Paralegals, 1975—; co-founder, bd. dirs. Magyar Studies, Inc., Bridgeport, 1977—; chmn., bd. dirs. Trans Nat., N.A., Ltd., 1981—; mem. bd. Technology Exports, Inc., Cheshire, Conn., 1981—. Co-founder Magyar Studies, Inc., 1977—. Mem. Conn. Assn. Paralegals (legal advisor), Am. Bar Assn., Am. Judicature Soc., Am. Soc. Law and Medicine, Assn. Trial Lawyers Am., Conn. Bar Assn., Conn. Bar Assn., Fla. Bar Assn., Greater Bridgeport Bar Assn., N.Y. Bar, Fed. Bar U.S., Alumni Assn. U. Bridgeport, Suffolk U. Law Sch. Alumni. Home: 202 Washington Ave Bridgeport CT 06604

FARDEN, MARCY JOANNE KAILIKEA, lawyer; b. Newport, R.I., Aug. 11, 1952; d. Carl Alexander and Joanne Marie (Gaffney) F.; B.A., Manhattanville Coll., 1974; J.D., U. Hawaii, 1977. Legis. dir., counsel Rep. Daniel K. Akaka, Washington; admitted to Md. bar. Mem. ed. Bar Assn., D.C. Women's Bar Assn. Roman Catholic. Office: 1510 Longworth House Office Bldg US Ho of Reps Washington DC 20515

FARENTHOLD, FRANCES TARLTON, lawyer, former coll. pres.; b. Corpus Christi, Tex., Oct. 2, 1926; d. Benjamin Dudley and Catherine (Bluntzer) Tarlton; A.B., Vassar Coll., 1946; J.D., U. Tex., 1949; LL.D., Hood Coll., 1973, Boston U., 1973, Regis Coll., 1976, Lake Erie Coll., 1979, Elmira Coll., 1981; m. George E. Farenthold, Oct. 6, 1950; children—Dudley Tarlton, George Edward, Emilie, James Dougherty, Vincent Bluntzer (dec.). Admitted to Tex. bar, 1949; mem. Tex. Ho. of Reps., 1968-72; dir. legal aide Nueces County, 1965-67; asst. prof. law Tex. So. U., Houston; pres. Wells Coll., Aurora, N.Y., 1976-80. Mem. Human Relations Com., Corpus Christi, 1963-68, Corpus Christi Citizen's Com. Community Improvement, 1966-68. Mem. Tex. adv. com. to U.S. Commn. on Civil Rights, 1968-76; mem. nat. adv. council ACLU. Mem. Orgn. for Preservation Unblemished Shoreline, 1964—. Democratic candidate Gov. Tex., 1972; del. Dem. nat. conv., 1972, 1st woman nominated to be candidate v.p. U.S., 1972; nat. co-chmn. Citizens to Elect McGovern-Shriver, 1972; chairperson Nat. Women's Polit. Caucus, 1973-75. Trustee Vassar Coll., 19 Recipient Lyndon B. Johnson Woman of Year award, 1973. Mem. State Bar Tex. Office: 3303 Main St Suite 332 Houston TX 77002

FARIAN, BABETTE SOMMERICH, artist; b. N.Y.C., June 6, 1916; d. Hugo Joseph and Clara Julia (Hart) Sommerich; student Parsons-N.Y. Sch. Fine and Applied Art, 1933-35, Cooper Union Sch. Art, 1939-42, Modern Mus. Art Sch., 1965-68; pvt. student Morris Kantor, 1941, Joseph Margulies, 1947-49, Donald Stacy, 1969-79; m. Robert A. Farian, Sept. 27, 1942; 1 son, Robert A. Asst. head studio Manhattan Shirt Co., N.Y.C., 1960-64; instr. color and design Cooper Union, N.Y.C., 1941-42; designer Hanscom Fabrics, Krasom Co., N.Y.C., 1955-57; free lance textile and greeting card designer, 1958-59; one woman shows at Serial Fed. Savs. Bank, N.Y.C., 1976, Walter Reade Theatres, N.Y.C., 1977, 81; exhibited in group shows at Atelier Gallery of Contemporary Art, N.Y.C., 1967, 68, Am. Artist Profl. League, N.Y.C., 1958-59, Impulse Gallery, Martha's Vineyard, 1968, U.S. Fine Arts Registry, 1968, L.I. Art League, 1965, 1st Unitarian Ch. of Flushing (N.Y.), Art Group AAUW of Rochester (N.Y.), 1969, Westchester Art League, Barnard Club Art Exhbn., Nat. Art League, 1974, Northwestern Conn. Art Assn., 1976, Sherman (Conn.) Benefit Art Show, 1976, Rowayton (Conn.) Art Club, 1976, The Gallery, N.J., 1981, others; represented in permanent collections Tamassee (S.C.) DAR Sch., Women's Fine Arts Mus., N.Y.C., 1st Unitarian Ch., Flushing. Sunday sch. tchr. 1st Unitarian-Universalist Ch. of Flushing, 1950-55. Recipient prize News World, 1978, Pendulum mag., 1978; Grumbacher award Jackson Heights Art Club, 1974; Internat. Women's Yr. award, 1976; Winsor-Newton prize Golden Age Art Exhibit, 1978; Shiva prize Nat. Art League, 1978; Award of Merit, Nat. League Am. Pen Women, 1979; 1st prize Nat. Art League Sr. Artists, 1979; contest award Internat. Soc. Artists, others. Mem. Burr Artists (catalogue chmn.), Gotham Painters, Composers, Authors and Artists Am. (nat. art membership chmn. 1973-80, 3d prize for watercolor 1980, 1st prize for short story 1981), Artist's Equity Assn. N.Y., Nat. League Am. Pen Women (corr. sec. 1980—), Internat. Soc. Artists, Internat. Beaux Art, Cath. Artists of the 1980's.

FARINHOLT, (MARY) KATHARINE WOLTZ (MRS. WILLIAM WORTHAM FARINHOLT), ednl. cons.; b. Chapel Hill, N.C., Feb. 5, 1912; d. Albert Edgar and Daisy (Mackie) Woltz; B.A. with honors, Agnes Scott Coll., 1933; M.Ed., Emory U., 1964; m. Holcombe Tucker Green, Oct. 16, 1934; children—Caroline Tucker, Holcombe Tucker; m. 2d, William Wortham Farinholt, July 18, 1959; 1 stepson, Lewis Sharp. Tchr. English, Belmont (N.C.) High Sch., 1933-34; tchr. English, Westminster Schs., Atlanta, 1958-59, 64-74, prin. Girls' Jr. High Sch., 1964-74; now cons. Pres. Atlanta council Girl Scouts U.S.A., 1953, bd. dirs., 1950-53; pres. Child Service Assn. Atlanta, 1956-58; mem. exec. bd. Atlanta Music Club, 1951-59; hon. dir. Met. Atlanta Child Service and Family Counseling Center, 1975—; trustee Agnes Scott Coll., 1944-45, Appleton Ch. Home, Macon, Ga., 1962-65. Named One of 10 Leading Ladies of Atlanta, 1975. Mem. Nat. (jr. high sect. chmn. 1969-70, mem. exec. bd. 1969-70, editorial bd. jour. 1972-74, adv. com. 1975, treas. 1975-77, citation 1982), Ga. assns. women deans, adminstrs. and counselors, Ga. Assn. Middle Sch. Prins. (sec.), Mortar Bd. (nat. treas. 1945-47, fellowship chair 1950-52), Nat. Soc. Colonial Dames, Agnes Scott Coll. Alumnae Assn. (pres. 1944-45, citation 1975), Nat. League Am. Pen Women, AAUW, Phi Beta Kappa, Delta Kappa Gamma. Episcopalian (pres. women's group). Address: 567 Peachtree Battle Ave Atlanta GA 30305

FARIS, JULIA GREGORY, metal co. exec.; b. Louisville, June 29, 1951; d. Clark Royster and Dorothy (Ferguson) Gregory; student Wharton Sch. of Fin., U. Pa., 1976-77; 1 son, Peter Ferguson. Admissions asst. to asso. dean Coll. of Engring., U. Pa., 1976-78; publ. asst. to pres. No. Community Investment Corp., St. Johnsbury, Vt., 1978; exec. dir. St. Johnsbury C. of C., 1978-80, Assn. to Boost Lamoille Enterprises, Morrisville, Vt., 1980-81, Small Bus. Devel. Center of Vt., 1981-82; plant mgr. Am. Metal Fibers, Inc., 1982—. Mem. Am. Indsl. Devel. Council, Northeastern Indsl. Developers Assn., Vt. Indsl. Profls., Bus. and Profl. Women. Congregationalist. Home: PO Box 591 Morrisville VT 05661 Office: PO Box 455 Morrisville VT 05661

FARKAS, ANN ELIZABETH, archaeologist, educator; b. New Brighton, Pa., Mar. 7, 1931; d. Eli and Rebecca (Balter) Rosenberg; B.A., U. Chgo., 1950; M.A., Columbia U., 1963; Ph.D., (Woodbridge Hon. fellow), 1967; m. Alexander Farkas, Apr. 22, 1950 (div. 1961); 1 son, Allister. Instr. dept. art history and archaeology Columbia, 1967-68, asst. prof., 1968-73; asso. prof. New Sch. Liberal Arts, Bklyn. Coll., City U. N.Y., 1973-78, prof., 1979—; mem. Inst. for Advanced Study, 1979-80. Columbia U. Council for Research in Humanities summer grantee, 1968, 69. Mem. Coll. Art Assn., Archeol. Inst. Am. Am. Schs. Oriental Research, Columbia U. Seminar on Archeology of Eastern Mediterranean, Eastern Europe and Nr. East. Democrat. Clubs: Princeton; Washington. Author: Achaemenid Sculpture, 1974; (introduction) From the Lands of the Scythians, 1975; also articles. Home: New Preston Hill Rd New Preston CT 06777 Office: Bklyn Coll Bedford Ave and Ave H Brooklyn NY 11210

FARLEE, CORALIE, health sci. adminstr.; b. Princeton, N.J., Aug. 13, 1929; d. William H. and Anna M. (Kunze) Graeber; B.A. Rutgers U., 1959, M.A., 1961, Ph.D., 1971. Asst. research prof. sociology dept. Rutgers U., New Brunswick, N.J., 1959-72; asst. dir. office of health professions edn. N.J. Dept. of Higher Edn., 1972-75; exec. dir. Assn. of U. Affiliated Facilities, 1975-76; dir. faculty roster system Assn. Am. Med. Colls., Washington, 1976-78; policy analyst EPA, Washington, 1978-80; cons. Nat. Center for Health Services Research, Hyattsville, Md., 1970-80, health sci. adminstr., 1980-81, asst. dir. for program ops. NIH, Bethesda, Md., 1981—; professorial lectr. George Washington U., 1976—; mem. Health Systems Agys., 1973; mem. council for continuing pharm. edn., N.J. Bd. Pharmacy, 1972-75; bd. dirs. Symposium for Computer Applications in Med. Care, Inc., also chmn. sponsorship com. Bd. dirs. Dr. Leslie Mintz Optometric Scholarship Found., 1973-75. Mem. Am. Public Health Assn., Am. Sociol. Assn., Soc. for Occupational and Environ. Health, Assn. for Health Records, Inst. Soc., Ethics and Life Scis., Evaluation Research Soc., World Future Soc., Assn. Instl. Researchers, Am. Statis. Assn., Assn. for Health Records. Author: (with Cohen and Farlee) Manual on Use of Computer Programs for Social Science Research, 1966; manuscript reviewer Growth and Change Jour., 1978; contbr. articles on health services and edn. to profl. jours. Home: 389 O St SW Washington DC 20024 Office: Fogarty Internat Center NIH Dept Health and Human Services Bethesda MD

FARLEY, BARBARA LORRAINE, nurse; b. Waukegan, Ill., Sept. 3, 1951; d. Charles Edward and Cleryce (Harrell) F.; B.S. in Nursing, U. Ala., Birmingham, 1975. Staff nurse Children's Hosp., Birmingham, 1972-79, head nurse med. nursing, 1978-79; staff nurse Univ. Hosp., Birmingham, 1972-75; clin. instr. U. Ala. Sch. Nursing, Birmingham, 1976-77; supr. maternal child health div. Carraway Methodist Med. Center, Birmingham, 1977-78; head nurse Tex. Children's Hosp., Houston, 1978-80; head nurse pediatrics M.D. Anderson Cancer and Tumor Instn., Houston, 1980-81; pvt. duty nurse, 1981—. Vol. swimming instr. ARC. Mem. Am. Nurses Assn., Nat. League Nursing, Ala. Nurses Assn., Tex. Nurses Assn., Sigma Theta Tau. Baptist. Author papers in field. Address: 4613 Briarbend Houston TX 77305

FARLEY, DONNA OETJEN, health services adminstr.; b. Westfield, N.J., Sept. 28, 1943; d. Donald V. and Grace (Simpson) Oetjen; B.A., Coe Coll., 1965; M.P.H., U. Ill., 1975, M.S., 1976; children—Kristina Lynn, William David. Environ. health asst. Northeastern Ill. Planning Commn., Chgo., 1972-74; tech. asst. Ill. Pollution Control Bd., Chgo., 1976-77; sr. planner Suburban Cook County-DuPage County Health Systems Agy., Inc., Oak Park, Ill., 1977-78, asso. dir. plan implementation dept., 1978-80; exec. dir. Dental Assisting Nat. Bd., Chgo., 1980—; mem. nominating com. Nat. Commn. Health Certifying Agys.; mem. Ill. Statewide Health Coordinating Council, 1976-77. Mem. Elk Grove (Ill.) Village Flood Control Commn., 1974-76, Elk Grove Village Plan Commn., 1979-80; mem. Elk Grove Village Bd. Health, 1970-76, chmn., 1975-76; bd. dirs. Northwest Cook County council Girl Scouts U.S., 1979—; chmn. Family Partnership, 1981; trustee Alexian Bros. Med. Center, Elk Grove Village, 1973-78, 80—, chmn., 1977-78. Named Elk Grove Citizen of Yr., 1972, Citizen of Month, Lerner Publs., Voice Newspaper, 1977; NSF grantee, 1965. Mem. Am. Public Health Assn., Ill. Public Health Assn. (resolutions com. 1979-80), Delta Omega. Author: Energy Utilization and Environmental Health, 1978. Home: 75 Walpole Rd Elk Grove Village IL 60007 Office: Dental Assisting Nat Bd Inc 666 N Lake Shore Dr Chicago IL 60611

FARLEY, DOROTHY ANNE, nursing educator; b. Orange, N.J., May 6, 1934; d. Howard McKinley and Lois Perry (Woods) F.; B.S., N.Y. U., 1957; M.A., Tchrs. Coll., Columbia U., 1963; D.N.Sc., Boston U., 1971. Instr. psychiat.-mental health nursing St. Michael's Hosp. Sch. Nursing, Newark, 1966-67; asst. prof. allied health div., dept. nursing Essex County Coll., Newark, 1970-73; chief psychiat. nursing N.J. Med. Sch. Community Mental Health Center and clin. asso. prof. dept. psychiatry N.J. Med. Sch., Newark, 1973-81; cons. Model Cities, Boston, 1968-70; mem. Nursing Archives, Boston U., 1973—. Bd. dirs. Episcopal Ch. Women, 1970—, Essex County Heart Assn., 1972-79, Louis Loesser Meml., 1975-81. NIMH scholar, 1961-63, 67-71; cert. clin. specialist mental health. Mem. NOW, C. of C., Am. Nurses Assn., N.J. Nurses Assn. (dir. 1974-77), N.J. League Nursing, Nat. League Nursing, LWV, Mental Health Assn. N.J., (dir. 1972-78), Chi Eta Phi. Home: 305 Olcott St Orange NJ 07050

FARLEY, DOROTHY BIEBER, artist, civic worker, educator; b. St. Louis, May 27, 1927; d. Ralph Paul and Ida (Parker) Bieber; B.F.A. in Art Edn., U. Ill., 1949; m. Donald Gene Farley, June 16, 1951; children—Dale Ellen, Ronald Wesley. Secondary sch. art tchr., Ferguson, Mo., 1949-51; secondary art tchr. Normandy, Mo., 1955-57; art gallery dir. Craft Alliance, St. Louis, 1970-81; exhbn. juror, lectr., cons., 1977—; treas. Craft Alliance, 1967-68; pres. Craft Alliance, 1968; enamel artist, tchr., 1955—. Community chmn. March of Dimes, Creve Coeur, Mo., 1963; mem. adv. commn. Univ. City Loop Spl. Bus. Dist., 1981; city clk., Crystal Lake Park, Mo., 1981—. Mem. Am. Crafts Council (sec. n. central region, 1973-80), World Crafts Council, Advocates for the Arts, Mo. Crafts Council, Craft Alliance Gallery (exhibiting mem.), Mo. City Clks. and Fin. Officers Assn., Art Coordinating Council, Soc. N.Am. Goldsmiths. Home: 2332 Putter Ln St Louis MO 63131

FARLEY, JENNIE TIFFANY TOWLE, sociologist, author; b. Fanwood, N.J., Nov. 2, 1932; d. Howard Albert and Dorothy Jane (Van Wagner) Towle; B.A., Cornell U., 1954, M.S., 1969, Ph.D. in Devel. Sociology 1970; m. Donald Thorn Farley, Jr., June 16, 1956; children—Claire Hamlin, Anne Tiffany, Peter Towle. Mem. editorial staff Mademoiselle mag., 1954-55; asst. to asso. editor Seventeen mag., 1955-56; news writer Cornell U. News Bur., 1956-59; free lance writer, Cambridge, Eng., 1959-60, Goteborg, Sweden, 1960-61, Chaclacayo, Peru, 1961-64; daily columnist La Prensa, Lima, Peru, 1964-67; research asso. Cornell U., Ithaca, N.Y., 1972, mem. faculty, 1971—, assoc. prof. indsl. and labor relations, 1982—, dir. Cornell's Women Studies Program, 1972-76. Mem. Seven Lakes Council Girls Scouts U.S.A., 1980—. Mem. Am. Sociol. Assn., Sociologists for Women in Soc., Acad. Mgmt. AAUP, AAUW, NOW. Author: Affirmative Action and The Woman Worker: Guidelines for Personnel Management, 1979; Academic Women and Employment Discrimination: A Critical Annotated Bibliography, 1982; editor: Sex Discrimination in Higher Education: Strategies for Equality, 1981; contbr. articles to profl. jours. Home: 711 Triphammer Rd Ithaca NY 14850 Office: 112 ILR Extension Cornell U Ithaca NY 14853

FARLEY, NORMA SUE, educator; b. Kansas City, Mo., Nov. 15, 1936; d. Leroy James and A. Ione (Thompson) Markwell; student Northwestern U., 1954-55; B.S. in Edn., U. Kans., 1958, M.A., 1968; m. James W. Farley, June 27, 1981; children—R. Michael Murphy, Kathleen A. Murphy, James Mark Murphy. Tchr. social sci. dept. Park Hill Sr. High Sch., Kansas City, Mo., 1963—. Twp. committeewoman Kickapoo Twp., treas. Platte County Dem. Women's Club, chmn. Platte County Central Com., del. Dem. nat. conv., 1980. Recipient award Young Democrats of Mo., 1981. Mem. NEA, Mo. Edn. Assn., Park Hill Edn. Assn., Mo. State Tchrs. Assn., Nat. Council Social Studies, Mo. Council Social Studies, Platte County Hist. Soc., Delta Kappa Gamma, Sigma Alpha Iota, Pi Lambda Theta, Alpha Delta Pi. Methodist. Pianist; solo performance with Kansas City Philharm. Orch., 1951. Home: 6514 Fairway Dr Kansas City MO 64152

FARLEY, URSULA PATRICIA, copywriter/cons.; b. Bklyn., July 31, 1942; d. Walter Howard and Ursula Michaela (Kirsten) F.; student Marywood Coll., 1960-61, Columbia U., 1961-64. Asst. bus. mgr. book div. The Conde Nast Publs., Inc., 1966-68; mgr. client services, sr. copywriter Response Scis. Corp., 1968-70; creative dir. Throckmorton/Satin Assos., Inc., N.Y.C., 1970-73; free-lance copywriter/cons. direct mktg., N.Y.C., 1973—. N.Y. County com. mem. Republican party, 1967, 68; dist. capt. Village Rep. Club, 1967-68; mem. bd. elections, 1967-68. Recipient award Lynchburg (Va.) Advt. Club, 1975; award Am. Printers Council, 1975. Mem. Nat. Assn. Female Execs. (past dir.), Direct Mktg. Creative Guild (dir.), Women's Direct Response Group. Club: 100 Million (N.Y.C.). Author: Kenneth Beauty Consultation, 1974; The Advertising Trivia Book, 1978; Resume Preparation Guide, 1977; co-author: Getting Your Own Through Powertalk, 1983.

FARLIE, BARBARA LEITZOW, writer, cons. in handicraft and interior design; b. St. Paul, June 11, 1936; d. Herman Wilhelm and Blanche (Czarnowski) Leitzow; B.A., Smith Coll., 1958; m. William Newman Farlie, Jr., Jan. 30, 1960; children—Elisabeth Anne, William Newman, III, Craig Leitzow, Matthew Bradford. Co-hostess TV series All About Crafts, 1973; free lance writer, 1971—; partner The Finders, 1978—; tchr. Montclair (N.J.) Adult Sch., 1969-73; TV guest appearances; lectr. on handicrafts; interior design cons. Sustaining mem. Jr. League Montclair-Newark. Mem. Am. Soc. Interior Designers. Roman Catholic. Clubs: Montclair Golf; Smith Coll. of Montclair. Author: Beading: Basic and Boutique, 1971; Pennywise Boutique, 1974; (with Charlotte Clarke) All About Doll Houses, 1975; (with Constance Sloan) Your House in Needlepoint, 1976; (with Vivian M. Abell) Flower Craft, 1979; contbr. articles to mags. Home: 155 Wildwood Ave Upper Montclair NJ 07043 Office: The Finders 15 Prospect Ave Montclair NJ 07042

FARLOW, MELISSA KAY, photojournalist; b. Washington County, Ind., Oct. 10, 1951; d. James Joseph and Gertrude Miriam (Luostari) F.; A.B. in Photojournalism, Ind. U., 1974. Editor-in-chief, staff photographer Arbutus, Ind. U. yearbook, 1972-73; photographer, then chief photographer Ind. Daily Student, 1972-74; staff photographer Courier Jour. and Louisville Times, 1974—. Recipient 3d Pl. award William Randolph Hearst Contest, 1973, 1st Pictorial award and other awards Atlanta Press Photographers Assn., 1977, numerous awards from AP and Ind. News Photography contests. Mem. Nat. Press Photographers Assn. (3d prize for sports feature 1977). Contbr. photographs to books; mem. photog. team covering busing in Louisville (Pulitzer prize 1975). Office: 525 W Broadway Louisville KY 40202

FARMANN, KATHLEEN ELIZABETH, law librarian; b. Addison, N.Y., Aug. 21, 1920; d. Michael Francis and Elizabeth Lee (McClintock) Godfrey; A.B., Trinity Coll., Washington, 1941; J.D., Cath. U., 1945; M.L.L., U. Wash., Seattle, 1957; m. Stanley L. Farmann, June 14, 1958. Admitted to D.C. bar, 1945; asso. firm Covington & Burling, 1945-53; asst. law librarian Ohio State U., 1957-61, asst. dir. research services, 1962-66; law librarian Hawaii Supreme Ct., 1961-62; law librarian U. Notre Dame, 1966—, asst. to dean Law Sch., 1975-77. Exchange student Dept. of State, 1942. Mem. Bar Assn. D.C., Ohio Regional Assn. Law Libraries (past pres.), Am. Assn. Law Libraries. Democrat. Roman Catholic. Home: 19053 Summers Dr South Bend IN 46637 Office: Box 535 Notre Dame IN 46556

FARMER, ANNETTE, state legislator; b. Sofia, Bulgaria, Nov. 2, 1921; d. Vangel and Luba Pishmanova Georgiev; student drama and theatre arts sch., Bulgaris, 1942-44; m. James Melvin Farmer, 1946; children—Gerald Allan. Adult edn. instr. Portland Community Coll., 1972-73, Clackamas Community Coll., 1978-80; mem. Oreg. Ho. of Reps., 1980—. Mem. precinct com. Democratic Party, Oreg., 1973—, dist. leader, 1976-80; mem. rulaes and budget coms. Oreg. Dem. Central Com., 1980—; mem. Met. Arts Commn., 1980—; pres. Portland Opera Guild, 1971-73, Mt. Hood Community Arts Council, 1975-77. Mem. Women's Polit. Caucus. Club: Elks. Editor, Portland Opera Guild Paper, 1977-79. Office: Oreg Ho Reps State Capitol Salem OR 97310*

FARMER, BONNITA MAY, educator; b. Bloomington, Ind., May 26, 1939; d. Winfield Scott and Mary Audrey (Capshew) Richards; B.S. with distinction, Ind. U., 1961; M.S., U. Ill., 1962; M.A., U. Calif., Riverside, 1977, Ph.D., 1979; m. Walter J. Farmer, June 24, 1962; children—Margaret Rose, Melissa Marie. Extension clothing and textiles specialist

State of Ind., Purdue U., Lafayette, Ind., 1962-66; mem. faculty U. Calif. Extension, Riverside, 1966-76; asst. prof. consumer scis. Loma Linda U., Riverside, 1968-80; asst. prof. Calif. Poly. State U., Pomona, 1979—; instr. home econs. San Bernardino Valley Coll., Calif., 1966-69; mem. faculty Calif. State Poly. U., Pomona, 1979, Riverside City Coll., 1976—. Mem. Am. Home Econs. Assn., ASTM, Calif. Home Econs. Assn., Calif. Tchrs. Assn., Delta Zeta, Omicron Nu. Congregationalist. Home: 5086 Berryhill Pl Riverside CA 92507

FARMER, DOROTHA F., adminstrv. asso.; b. New Bloomfield, Mo., Nov. 8, 1942; d. James B. and Bertha E. (Vaughan) Gray; student U. Mo., 1971—; m. John C. Farmer, Sept. 2, 1961; stepchildren—John C. (dec.), Michael A. Clinic sec. Ellis Fischel State Cancer Hosp., Columbia, Mo., 1961-64; sec. to dir. Mo. Div. Employment Security, Columbia, 1965-66; departmental sec., dept. indsl. engring. U. Mo., Columbia, 1966-71, office mgr. bioengring./advanced automation program, 1974-78, adminstrv. asso., radiology computer research center, Mid-Am. Bone Diagnostic Center, 1978—; cons. NIH, 1980-82. Mem. Bus. and Profl. Women, Mo. Farmers Assn., Women's Progressive Farmers Assn. Roman Catholic. Contbr. articles to profl. jours. Home: RR 2 Huntsville MO 65259 Office: U Mo 410 Lewis Hall Columbia MO 65211

FARMER, HELEN SWEENEY, psychologist; b. Ottawa, Can., Dec. 23, 1929; d. Henry Bertrum and Mabel Sarah (Switzer) Sweeney; B.A., Queens U., Can., 1952; B.D., Union Theol. Sem., 1955; M.A., Columbia U., 1969; Ph.D., UCLA, 1972; m. James A. Farmer, Jan. 25, 1955; children—James Sweeney, David Sargent, Paul Alexander. Dir. evaluation services INSGROUP, Long Beach, Calif., 1971-74; asst. prof. counseling psychology U. Ill., Urbana, 1974-81, assoc. prof., 1981—. Queens U. scholar, 1949; Can. Govt. scholar, 1949-52; recipient Tchr. of Yr. award dept. ednl. psychology U. Ill., 1977, 78, 80; recipient Nat. Inst. Edn. grantee, 1974, 76, 78. Mem. Am. Psychol. Assn., Am. Ednl. and Research Assn., Am. Personnel and Guidance Assn. Author: (with Tom Backer) New Career Options for Women: Counselor's Sourcebook, 1977, New Career Options for Women: A Woman's Guide, 1977; contbr. articles to profl. jours. Home: 2204 S Staley Rd Champaign IL 61820 Office: Sch Edn U Ill Champaign IL 61820

FARMER, HELENE FRANKLIN, psychotherapist, mgmt. cons.; b. N.Y.C., Mar. 4, 1928; d. Joseph and Elsie (Wolpow) Feldhun; B.A., City U. N.Y., 1965, M.S., 1969; m. Anthony X. Farmer, May 23, 1976; 1 son, Joel Franklin. Tchr., N.Y.C. Bd. Edn., Bklyn., 1966-67; psychometrist N.Y. U., 1967-68; psychotherapist Counseling and Psychotherapy Center, Fairlawn, N.J., 1968-70, Center for Counseling, Ridgewood, N.J., 1970-74; exec. dir., asst. dir. psychotherapeutic services North Jersey Center for Counseling and Psychotherapy, Fort Lee, N.J., 1974—; asso. dir. North Jersey Center for Mgmt. Cons., 1978—; v.p., treas. North Jersey Center, Inc., Ft. Lee, 1979—. Lectr., Bergen Community Coll., Paramus, N.J., 1969-70. Mem. Am., N.J. psychol. assns., Am. Personnel and Guidance Assn. Home: 4 Horizon Rd Fort Lee NJ 07024 Office: 444 Main St Fort Lee NJ 07024

FARMER, MARJORIE ELIZABETH, electrochemist; b. Detroit; d. Henry and Jessie (Lodewyck) F.; B.A., Mt. Holyoke Coll. Research electrochemist Pratt & Whitney div. United Techs. Corp., East Hartford, Conn., 1942-51; electrochemist Chem. Corp., Springfield, Mass., 1953; research electrochemist Convair div. Gen. Dynamics Corp., Pomona, Calif., 1953; electrochemist U.S. Navy Shipyard, Long Beach, Calif., 1954-55; mem. tech. staff Rockwell Internat. Corp., Anaheim, Calif., 1957—, lead instr. in advanced career tng. program for high sch. students in coordination with Regional Occupation Program. Registered profl. engr., Calif. Fellow Inst. Metal Finishing (Gt. Britain); mem. Am. Electroplaters Soc. (certified electroplater-finisher), New Eng. Anti-Vivisection Soc. Humane Soc. U.S., Nat. Assn. Corrosion Engrs., Def. Preparedness Assn., Am. Soc. Metals (officer), Am. Horse Protection Assn., Animal Protection Inst. Am., Mercy League, Amnesty Internat. Club: Mt. Holyoke. Contbr. articles to profl. jours.

FARMER, MARY MARGARET WILSON, med. technologist; b. Asheville, N.C., July 5, 1933; d. Roeby Bryant and Flossie Aurora (Montieth) Wilson; B.S., Wake Forest Coll., 1954; B.S. in Med. Tech., Bowman Gray Sch. Med. Tech., 1954; m. Gary Clayton Farmer, Apr. 28, 1962; children—Mary Elizabeth, Melissa Margaret. Med. technologist Aston Park Hosp., Asheville, 1954-56, Occupational Health Services, Asheville, 1956-58; med. technologist, asst. lab. supr. Meml. Mission Hosp., Asheville, 1958-62; med. technologist, lab. dir. Joseph E. Seagram & Co., N.Y.C., 1962-65; dir. blood collections and phlebotomy Richmond (Va.) Met. Blood Bank, 1974-77; lab. mgr., med. technologist Thoms Rehab. Hosp., Asheville, 1980—; sec./treas. Assos. for Human Devel., Asheville. Chmn. fund raising Biltmore PTA, Asheville, 1978-79, chmn. membership, 1979-80; v.p. Valley Springs PTA, Skyland, N.C., 1980-81, pres., 1981-82; mem. Roberson dist. Buncombe County (N.C.) Schs. Adv. Council, 1981-82; mem. outreach, youth and worship commns. All Souls Episc. Ch., co-dir. acolyte program; v.p. Women of Gen. Theol. Sem., 1963-64. Recipient Citizenship award United Daus. of Confederacy. Mem. Am. Soc. Med. Technologists, Am. Soc. Clin. Pathologists (med. technologist), AAUW, N.Am. Benefit Assn., Episcopal Church Women, Beta Sigma Phi (pres. Beta Tau chpt. 1961-62). Democrat. Clubs: Mahjong, Bridge. Home: 8 Busbee Rd Asheville NC 28803 Office: 1 Rotary Dr Asheville NC 28803

FARMER, MILDRED LAVERNE, educator; b. Townsend, Tenn., July 12, 1931; d. Clark and Lou Ella (Abbott) Farmer; B.S., U. Tenn., 1953, M.S., 1959. County extension home economist Unicoi County, Tenn., 1953-58; prof. family econs. and mgmt. U. Tenn., Knoxville, 1959—. Bd. dirs. Smoky Mountain Passion Play, 1972—; chmn. bd. trustees Bapt. Ch. and Cemetery, 1975—. Mem. Am. Home Econs. Assn., Tenn. Home Econs. Assn., Am. Council on Consumer Interests, Electric Women's Roundtable, Nat. Assn. Extension 4-H Agts., Tenn. Assn. Extension 4-H Agts., Gamma Sigma Delta, Omicron Nu, Epsilon Sigma Phi. Contbr. articles to profl. jours. Home: 3113 Ginn Rd Knoxville TN 37920 Office: PO Box 1071 Knoxville TN 37901

FARMER, PENELOPE BROWN, real estate broker; b. San Diego, May 6, 1945; d. A. Earle and Ruth Brown; A.A., Stephens Coll., 1963; B.A., San Diego State U., 1968; postgrad. lawyers asst. program U. San Diego, 1981; m. Rudolph D. Farmer, Sept. 28, 1974. Broker, owner Century 21, Gold Star Properties, San Diego, 1976—; corp. sec., dir. Am. Heritage Home Loans, Inc., San Diego, 1980—. Mem. Nat. Assn. Female Execs., San Diego C. of C., Calif. Assn. Realtors, Nat. Assn. Realtors, Am. Mgmt. Assn. Home: 6030 Bernadette Ln San Diego CA 92120 Office: 6975 Navajo Rd San Diego CA 92119

FARNES, MARY PATRICIA, physician, educator; b. Portland, May 16, 1931; d. Cecil Julian and Lucile Augusta (Menges) F.; B.A., Willamette U., Salem, Oreg., 1953; M.S., U. Oreg., 1956, M.D., 1956. Intern, Presbyterian Hosp., Chgo., 1956-57; fellow in Hematology Presbyn.-St. Luke's Hosp., Chgo., 1959-60; research asso. dept. pathology R.I. Hosp., 1960-68, hematologist, 1971—, dir. hematology div., 1979—; asst. prof. medicine Brown U., 1968-74, asso. prof. med. sci., 1974—; adj. asso. prof. Women's studies U. R.I., 1981—; vol. vis. specialist Care-Medico, Hosp. Civil de Beni Messons, Algiers, 1962, Avicenna and Jambouriat Hosps., Kabul, Afghanistan, 1972, 74, 76, 78. NIH grantee, 1966-70; Am. Cancer Soc. Research grantee, 1961-65. Mem. Am. Hematology Soc., Internat. Soc. Exptl. Hematology, Nat. Women's Studies Assn., Haiku Soc. Am., Audubon Soc., Am. Soc. Cell Biology, NOW, Women for Non-Nuclear Future, Alpha Omega Alpha. Editor: Haemic Cells in Vitro, 1969; contbr. articles to profl. jours. Home: 62 Auburn Rd Wakefield RI 02879 Office: 593 Eddy St Providence RI 02902

FARNHAM, MARJORIE JEAN, civic worker; b. Cin., Aug. 17, 1927; d. Gilbert Henry and Helen Cora (Fell) Holocher; student public schs., Cin.; m. Arthur E. Farnham, Aug. 31, 1945; children—Marcie, Claire, Arthur E., Mitchell. Co-chmn. 1976 Manatee County (Fla.) campaign Reagan for Pres.; chmn. Manatee County campaign Pres. Ford, 1976; chmn. Republican Hdqrs., Manatee County, 1976; mem. adv. com. Reagan/Bush Presdl. Campaign, 1980; adv. to state Senator Paula Hawkins campaign, Fla., 1980; charter mem. legis. campaign com. Rep. Party Fla., 1980; 2d v.p. Fla. Fedn. Rep. Women, 1979-80, 81-83; pres. Manasota Rep. Women's Club, 1978-82; vice chmn. Manatee County Rep. Exec. Com., 1977-79; precinct committeewoman Rep. Exec. Com., Manatee County, 1974-79; attended 1981 Presdl. Inauguration; pres. Manatee Assn. Retarded Citizens, 1978-82; mem. Whitfield Estates-Ballentine Manor Estates Assn. (dir. 1981—, sec. 1982-83); bd. dirs. Selective Service System, Airport Expansion Adversaries Whitfield-Ballentine, 1982. Recipient Outstanding Service award Manatee County Rep. Exec. Com., 1976, plaque for devoted service, 1979, citation of recognition Rep. Party Fla., 1975-79. Mem. Gulf Coast Parliamentarians (pres. 1980—), Am. Inst. Parliamentarians (regional lt. gov. 1982, dist. dir. 1981-82). Lutheran. Home: 8163 Westmoreland Dr Sarasota FL 33580

FARNSWORTH, BEATRICE, historian, educator; b. Bklyn., Feb. 3, 1935; d. Max O. and Letty (Olshansky) Brodsky; B.A., Ind. U., 1955; M.A., Yale U., 1956, Ph.D., 1959; m. John Farnsworth, July 31, 1965; children—David, Daniel, Peter. Instr., Hobart and William Smith Colls., 1961-64; asst. prof. history Wells Coll., Aurora, N.Y., 1965-66, assoc. prof., 1968—; assoc. Russian Research Center, Harvard U., 1964-65; fellow Radcliffe Inst. Ind. Study, 1964-65, 66-67; Social Sci. Research Council fellow, 1955-56; Am. Philos. Soc. grantee, 1974. Mem. Am. Hist. Assn., Am. Assn. Advancement Slavic Studies. Author: William C. Bullitt and the Soviet Union, 1967; Aleksandra Kollontai: Socialism, Feminism and the Bolshevik Revolution, 1980. Home: 410 Brampton Dr Syracuse NY 13214 Office: Dept History Wells Coll Aurora NY 13026

FARNSWORTH, SUSAN STEELE HIGGINS, writer; b. New Braunfels, Tex., Sept. 8, 1949; d. Walter Sayers and Marian Louise (Schumann) Higgins; B.J., U. Tex., Austin, 1971; m. Dan Collins Farnsworth, Jan. 26, 1974; 1 son, Christopher Sayers. Editor, The Greater Houston Tchrs. Jour., Media Am. Inc., 1973; tax editor/editorial supr. Peat, Marwick, Mitchell & Co., N.Y.C., 1974-77; copywriter Cannon Advt. Agy., N.Y.C., 1977; columnist The News Tribune, Woodbridge, N.J., 1977-79; writer Peat, Marwick, Mitchell & Co., N.Y.C., 1977-78, Alden & Assocs., N.Y.C., 1979-80; writer/communications cons. Peat, Marwick, Mitchell & Co., Dallas, 1979-82; dir. profl. services unit Hill and Knowlton, Inc., Dallas, 1982; owner Farnsworth & Assocs., Dallas, 1981—. Named Outstanding Advt. Student, U. Tex., Austin, 1970-71. John E. McGary scholar. Mem. Nat. Assn. Female Execs. Episcopalian. Contbr. articles to profl. jours. Address: 518 Chaffee Dr Arlington TX 76011

FARNUM, JANET ELIZABETH, psychologist; b. Buffalo, Dec. 28, 1927; d. Reginald M. and Frances V. (McGill) Barker; B.A., State U. Coll., Brockport, 1971; Ph.D., U. Rochester, 1975; m. Bernard L. Farnum, Nov. 8, 1946; children—Susan Elizabeth, Christopher Barker, Gretchen Jane, Timothy Michael. Asst. prof. psychology LeMoyne Coll., Syracuse, N.Y., 1975-78; adj. faculty mem. Empire State Coll., Genesee Valley Learning Center, Rochester, N.Y., 1978—; adj. asst. prof. LeMoyne Coll., Syracuse, N.Y., 1979; vis. asst. prof. Rochester (N.Y.) Inst. Tech.; cons. Christian Edn. Commn., Episcopal Diocese of Rochester. Bd. dirs. Episcopal Ch. Home; mem., vice-moderator Diocesan Council, Episcopal Diocese of Rochester. Mem. Am. Psychol. Assn., Soc. Research in Child Devel., AAUP, Piaget Soc. Home: 16 4th Ave Fairport NY 14450 Office: 1 Lomb Memorial Dr Rochester NY 14623

FARONE, LOIS LORRAINE PENNINGTON, home economist; b. Wichita, Kans., June 11, 1912; d. John Wesley and Olive Lily (Kelsey) Pennington; student Friends U., 1930-32; B.A., Park Coll., 1934; M.A., Ariz. State U., 1956, Ed.D., 1971; m. Alphonse E. Farone, July 25, 1938 (dec.); children—Barbara, Margaret, John, Ronald. Home economist Schrafts Restaurants, N.Y.C., Boston, 1934-39; dietitian Wichita (Kans.) Hosp., 1944-45; chmn. home econs. dept. South Mountain High Sch., Phoenix, 1956-62; adult tchr. Phoenix Union High Sch. System, 1963-65; chmn. dept. home econs. Phoenix Coll., 1965-77, prof., 1965—. Bd. dirs. Save A Child League, Women's Equity Action League, YWCA; mem. state adv. com. Home Econs. Related Occupations, Future Homemakers Am. Mem. NEA, Nat. Council Family Relations, Am. Vocat. Assn., Am. Home Econs. Assn., Ariz. Home Econs. Assn. (Hall of Fame award, Higher Edn. Profl. Recognition award), Adult Edn. Assn. U.S.A., Nat. Assn. Edn. Young Children, Mental Health Assn. Ariz., Am. Assn. Women in Community and Jr. Colls., Nutrition Today Soc., Kappa Delta Pi, Delta Kappa Gamma. Republican. Home: 3413 N 16th Dr Phoenix AZ 85015 Office: Dept Home Econs Phoenix Coll Phoenix AZ 85013

FARR, KATHERINE LUCILE, forester; b. Oregon City, Oreg., Nov. 16, 1951; d. William Edgar and Emma Lucille (Anderson) F.; B.S. in Forest Mgmt., Oreg. State U., 1975. Forestry aide U.S. Forest Service, 1972, forestry technician, Corvallis, Oreg., 1973-77, forester, Hines, Oreg., 1977-80, land. mgmt. planner, Flagstaff, Ariz., 1980—. Mem. Soc. Am. Foresters, Nat. Assn. Female Execs., Xi Sigma Pi. Office: US Forest Service Flagstaff AZ 86001

FARR, MARY ELIZABETH, hosp. adminstr.; b. Topeka, Kans., Aug. 6, 1931; d. James Anderson and Minnie Emma (Lewis) White; B.Ed., Washburn U., 1954; M.S., Kans. State U., 1981; m. Jarvie Elester Farr, Dec. 11, 1955; children—Tami Elizabeth, Kent Lee, Lisa Carol. Dir. girls and women program Carver br. Topeka YMCA, 1953-55; with dept. recreation Topeka State Hosp., 1955—, dir. recreational therapy, 1959—. Sec. bd. dirs. Shawnee council Camp Fire Inc., 1976-80, pres., 1980-82. Cert. phys. edn. tchr., Kans. Mem. Nat. Assn. Recreational Therapy (sec.), Kans. Activity Therapy Assn. (dir. 1980-81), Kans. Recreation and Parks Assn., Nat. Recreation Assn., Adult Edn. Assn., Topeka Black Pan-Hellenic Council, Delta Sigma Theta. Episcopalian. Home: 1012 W 22d St Topeka KS 66611 Office: 2700 W 6th St Topeka KS 66606

FARRAR, ELAINE WILLARDSON, artist; b. Los Angeles, Feb. 27, 1929; d. Eldon and Gladys Elsie (Larsen) Willardson; B.A., Ariz. State U., 1967, M.A., 1969; children—Steve, Mark, Gregory, Leslie Jean, Monty, Susan. Tchr., Camelback Desert Sch., Paradise Valley, Ariz., 1966-69; mem. faculty Yavapai Coll., Prescott, Ariz., 1970—, chmn. dept. art, 1973-78, instr. art in watercolor and oil and acrylic painting and intaglio, 1971—; one-man shows include: R.P. Moffat's, Scottsdale, Ariz., 1969, Art Center, Battle Creek, Mich., 1969, The Woodpeddler, Costa Mesa, Calif., 1979; group show Prescott (Ariz.) Fine Arts Assn., 1982, N.Y. Nat. Am. Watercolorists, 1982; works rep. local and state exhibits; supt. fine arts dept. County Fair; com. mem., hanging chmn. Scholastic Art Awards. Mem. Mountain Artists Guild (past pres.), Nat. League Am. Pen Women (treas. Prescott br.), NEA, Ariz. Edn. Assn., Nat. Art Edn. Assn., Ariz. Coll. and Univ. Faculty Assn., AAUW, Verde Valley Art Assn., Kappa Delta Pi. Republican. Mormon. Home: 635 Copper Basin Rd Prescott AZ 86301 Office: Yavapai College Art Dept 1100 E Sheldon Rd Prescott AZ 86301

FARRAR, MARGARET FOSTER, home economist; b. Natchitoches, La., Nov. 4, 1950; d. Orin Felix and Anna Fern (Wood) Foster; B.S., Northwestern State U., 1971, M.S., 1976; m. Glenn Aaron Farrar, Sept. 9, 1972; children—Kathryn Nicole, Kristopher Aaron. 4-H home economist Rapides Parish Extension Services, 1971-72; tchr. sci., high sch., Baton Rouge, 1972-73; tchr. kindergarten, Natchitoches, 1973-76; 4-H home economist Tangipahoa Parish Extension Service, Amite, La., 1977—; tchr. Bapt. Women's Missionary Union, 1978—. Recipient Citizenship in Action grant Readers Digest, 1978. Mem. La. Assn. Extension 4-H Agts. (dir., co-chmn. state conv. com. 1982; Outstanding Agt. 1980), Assn. Preservation Hist. Natchitoches, Family Life Council La., La. Assn. Extension Home Economists, La. Assn. Children Under Six, Epsilon Sigma Phi. Baptist. Club: Les Amies. Home: PO Box 226 Amite LA 70422 Office: PO Box 725 Amite LA 70422

FARRAR, MARGARET MARION, educator, former sch. ofcl.; b. Schriever, La., Feb. 8, 1911; d. Louis James and Lillian Gertrude (Smith) F.; B.A. cum laude, Dillard U., 1941; M.Ed., Boston U., 1953; Ph.D., Laurence U., 1975. Tchr. kindergarten New Orleans Public Schs., 1931-60; kindergarten tchr. D.C. Public Schs., 1960-67, reading specialist, 1967-71, reading cons., 1971-81. Mem. Nat. Council Tchrs. Math., Nat. Council Tchrs. English, Nat. Assn. Univ. Women, AAUW, Nat. Council Negro Women, D.C. Reading Council (pres.) Internat. Reading Assn., NEA, Pi Lambda Theta. Democrat. Home: 5162 34th St NW Washington DC 20008

FARRELL, DIANNE KAY, mfg. co. exec.; b. Hibbing, Minn., July 20, 1950; d. Louis L. Ivanca and Irene L. (Reitmeier) Ivanca Grahek; B.S., St. Cloud (Minn.) State Coll., 1973; m. Timothy J. Farrell, June 23, 1973. Controller, No. Ductile Castings, Inc., Hibbing, 1973—; adv. bd. dirs. First Bank Hibbing. Mem. Am. Foundrymen's Soc., Am. Mgmt. Assn., Gray and Ductile Iron Foundry Soc., Am. Inst. Corporate Controllers. Home: 217 NW 10th St Chisholm MN 55719 Office: 555 W 25th St Hibbing MN 55746

FARRELL, EILEEN, singer, soprano; b. Williamantic, Conn., Feb. 13, 1920; d. Michael John and Catherine (Kennedy) Farrell; hon. degrees U. R.I., Loyola U., U. Hartford, Notre Dame Coll. (N.H.), Wagner Coll., Cin. Conservatory; m. Robert V. Reagan, Apr. 4, 1946; children—Robert V., Kathleen. Made debut as singer Columbia Broadcasting Co., 1941; singer, own program, CBS, 6 yrs.; made opera debut in Il Trovatore with San Francisco Opera; singer with major symphony orchs. in U.S., toured throughout U.S. and in S.Am.; performer pops, blues and jazz with symphony orchs.; vis. prof. Hartford U.; rec. artist ABC Dunhill, Columbia, RCA, London, Angel records. Recipient Grammy award. Address: ICM Artists Ltd 40 W 57th St New York NY 10019 *

FARRELL, EILEEN MARIE, nurse; b. N.Y.C., Oct. 8, 1950; d. William James and Ann Marie (Hogan) F.; B.S. in Nursing, Columbia U., 1972, M.P.H. candidate. Staff nurse Vanderbilt Clinic, Columbia Presbyn. Med. Center, N.Y.C., 1972-74, sr. supr. evenings Emergency Services, Vanderbilt Clinic, 1974-78, sr. supr. days, 1978-80, adminstrv. nurse clinician emergency services, 1980—, nursing liaison ambulatory care, 1982—; preceptor, cons. Edna McConnell Clark and Columbia U. Sch. Nursing, 1978—, preceptor ambulatory care Columbia U. Sch. Public Health, 1980—; tchr. seminars in field. Registered nurse. Mem. Emergency Dept. Nurses Assn., Nat. Assn. Female Execs., Columbia U. Presbyn. Hosp. Alumnae Assn. Office: 622 W 168th St New York NY 10032

FARRELL, JUNE MARTINICK, public relations exec.; b. New Brunswick, N.J., June 30, 1940; d. Ivan and Mary (Tomkovich) M.; B.S. in Journalism, Ohio U., 1962; M.S. in Public Relations, Am. U., Washington, 1977; m. Duncan G. Farrell, July 31, 1971. Public relations asst. Corning Glass Works, N.Y.C., 1963-65; assoc. beauty editor Good Housekeeping mag., N.Y.C., 1966; public relations specialist Gt. Am. Ins. Co., N.Y.C., 1967-68; assoc. editor Eastern Airlines, N.Y.C., 1968-82, regional public relations mgr., Washington, 1976-82; public relations dir. Nat. Captioning Inst., Falls Church, Va., 1982—; adj. instr. Montgomery County Community Coll., also mem. hotel/tourism adv. bd., 1980—; staff cons. Office of Public Liaison, White House, 1981-82. Creator, condr. spl. career awareness program for inner city youth, Washington, 1979-80; mem. public relations com. Jr. Achievement, 1979; motivational counselor for youth Nat. Alliance of Businessmen, 1979. Mem. Internat. Orgn. Women Execs., Washington Exec. Women in Travel, Washington Women's Network, Phi Mu. Republican. Clubs: Zonta, Internat. Aviation. Home: 6630 Lybrook Ct Bethesda MD 20817 Office: Nat Captioning Inst 5203 Leesburg Pike Suite 1500 Falls Church VA 22041

FARRELL, KATHY, search co. exec.; b. Washington, Sept. 11, 1943; d. Jack M. and Maxine (Bascue) Kimbell; B.A., U. Va., 1965; postgrad. Pepperdine U.; m. Frank Farrell, Sept. 16, 1978. Tech. writer Wang, Boston, 1969; systems analyst Fin. Info. Co., Los Angeles, 1970; product cons., trainer, field cons., project mgr., mktg. staff specialist Xerox Computer Services, Los Angeles, 1971-77; mktg. staff specialist Computer Scis. Corp., El Segundo, Calif., 1977-78; pres., owner Farrell Assos., Marina Del Rey, Calif., 1978—. Mem. Am. Soc. Tng. and Devel., Am. Mktg. Assn., Am. Mgmt. Assn., Women in Bus. (dir.). Home: 4324 Promenade Way Suite 114 Marina del Rey CA 90291 Office: 4314 Marina City Dr Suite 122 Marina del Rey CA 90291

FARRELL, PATRICIA ANN, psychologist; b. N.Y.C., Mar. 11, 1945; d. Joseph Alexander and Pauline (Loth) F.; B.A., Queens Coll., 1976; M.A., N.Y. U., 1978, postgrad., 1980—. Asso. editor Pubs. Weekly Mag., N.Y.C., 1968-72; editor Bestsellers Mag., N.Y.C., 1972-73; asso. editor King Features Syndicate, N.Y.C., 1973-78; staff psychologist, intake coordinator Mid-Bergen Community Mental Health Center, Paramus, N.J., 1978—; pres. Discovery, Paramus; instr. Bergen Community Coll., Paramus, 1978—; appeared on radio shows Sta. WWDJ, Hackensack, N.J. Recipient Social Scis. award Queens Coll., 1976. Mem. Am. Psychol. Assn. (asso.), N.J. Psychol. Assn. (asso.), Assn. Women in Psychology. Office: Mid-Bergen Community Mental Health Clinic 11 Park Pl Paramus NJ 07652

FARRELL, SUZANNE, ballerina; b. Cin.; began study ballet Cin. Conservatory Music with Marian LaCour; became Ford Found. scholar Sch. Am. Ballet, 1960; m. Paul Mejia, Feb. 1969. With N.Y. City Ballet, 1961-69, 75—, became featured dancer, 1962, prin. dancer, 1965-69, roles include Arcade, Movements for Piano and Orchestra, Apollo, Bugaku, Meditation, Clarinade, Episodes, Stars and Stripes, Glinkaiana, Chaconne, Metastaseis and Pithoprakta, Western Symphony, Symphony in C, Concerto Barocco, A Midsummer Night's Dream, Agon, Ballet Imperial, Irish Fantasy, The Nutcracker, Don Quixote, La Sonnambula, Raymonda Variations, Mozartiana, Brahms-Schoenberg Quartet, Variations, Swan Lake, Jewels, Prodigal Son, Divertimento 15, Slaughter on 10th Ave., (film version) Midsummer Night' Dream; with Bejart Ballet of 20th Century, Brussels, Belgium, 1971-75; created role in Bach Sonate #5; other ballets include Beethoven's 9th Symphony, Messe pour le temps present, Bhakti, Erotica pas de deux, Marteau Sans Maitre, Ah, Vous Dirais Je, Maman?, Juliet in Romeo and Juliet; created The Young Girl in Rose in Nijinsky . . . Clown of God, 1971, Bolero, The Rite of

Spring, Laura in I Trionfi; created roles with N.Y.C. Ballet in New Ravel Festival, Tzigane, In G Major. 1976, Hon. lectr. dance U. Cin.; mem. faculty Sch. Am. Ballet. Recipient Spl. award of merit in creative and performing arts, U. Cin., 1965; Merit award Mademoiselle mag., 1965; Dance Mag. award, 1976; Creative Arts award in dance Brandeis U., 1980; award of honor for arts and culture N.Y.C., 1980; featured in Sta. WNET-TV Dance in Am., Balanchine, Parts I-IV. Address: care New York City Ballet Lincoln Center Plaza New York NY 10023

FARRELLY, JANET, ins. co. mgr.; b. Arlington, Mass., Oct. 11, 1928; d. Philip and Constance Franklin; B.A., Radcliffe Coll., 1950; postgrad. Smith Coll., Harvard U., Princeton U., ins. courses; m. Richard Lloyd Farrelly, II, Apr. 29, 1972; children by previous marriage—Andrea Benes, Nicholas E. Benes. Head art dept. Northampton Sch. for Girls, 1950-51; agt. Mut. of Omaha, Succusunna, N.J., 1975-77, unit mgr., 1977-79, unit mgr., Greeley, Colo., 1979—; speaker. Higher edn. chmn. Mendham-Chester LWV, 1960-61; chmn. Chester Community Chest, 1963; com. mem. Morris Mus. Concerts, 1971-74. Recipient numerous ins. awards; lic. ins. broker, security dealer. Mem. Nat. Assn. Life Underwriters, Nat. Assn. Female Execs. Republican. Episcopalian. Club: Radcliffe of N.J. (past pres.). Home: 3010 S Lincoln St Loveland CO 80537 Office: Suite 660 Greeley National Plaza Greeley CO 80631

FARREN, CAROL ELESE, communications co. ofcl.; b. Montclair, N.J., Dec. 10, 1944; d. Merritt Freeman and Katherine Elizabeth (Broadbent) F.; B.S. (Montclair Women's Club scholar, Univ. scholar), Cornell U., 1966; spl. student Parsons Sch. Design, 1966-67; M.B.A., N.Y. U., 1979; m. Steven Charles Bagdan, May 17, 1969 (div. Jan. 1976). Asst. project coordinator Maria Bergson Assos., N.Y.C., 1967-69; project coordinator J. Gordon Carr & Assos., N.Y.C., 1969-70; adminstrv. dir. interior design dept. Carson, Lundin & Thorson, N.Y.C., 1970-73; purchasing agt., corp. designer Warner Communications, Inc., N.Y.C., 1973-75, facilities planning mgr., 1979—; pres., founder CD/3 Design, N.Y.C., 1976-80; speaker Designer's Saturday, 1978, Cornell U., 1979; guest lectr. Parsons Sch. Design, 1978. Mem. Am. Inst. Interior Designers, N.Y. Assn. Women Bus. Owners, Nat. Small Bus. Assn., Beta Gamma Sigma, Omicron Nu, Kappa Delta. Republican. Club: N.Y.C. Cornell Women's. Home: 301 E 48th St New York NY 10017 Office: Warner Communications Inc 75 Rockefeller Plaza New York NY 10019

FARRIER, SHIRLEY ELIZABETH COPENHAVER, educator; b. Glade Spring, Va., Dec. 6, 1923; d. John Franklin and Mary Loucile (Mock) Copenhaver; student Hiwassee Coll., 1940-42; B.S., Radford (Va.) Coll., 1944; M.S., Va. Poly. Inst. and State U., 1960; Ed.D., U. Va., 1968; m. Robert Henry Farrier, May 9, 1946; children—Helen Elizabeth Farrier Helve, Robert Henry. Tchr. home econs. Giles County (Va.) Schs., 1944-48, 53-55; research asst. Va. Poly. Inst. and State U., Blacksburg, 1959-60; instr., dir. Univ. Lab. Sch., Va. Poly. Inst. and State U., 1960-65, asst. prof., dir., 1965-70, asso. prof., dir. 1970-79, asso. prof. mgmt., housing and family devel., 1979—; participant, co-dir. Study Abroad programs. Recipient Wine award for excellence in teaching, 1966. Mem. Am. Home Econs. Assn., Va. Home Econs. Assn., Nat. Assn. Edn. of Young Children, Va. Assn. Early Childhood Edn., So. Assn. Children Under Six, Soc. Research in Child Devel., Council Exceptional Children, Southeastern Council Family Relations, Orgn. Mondiale pour l'Edn. Préscolaire, Phi Upsilon Omicron, Kappa Delta Pi, Phi Delta Kappa. Methodist. Club: Newport Woman's. Research on rural and low-income youth. Home: Box 85 Newport VA 24128 Office: Virginia Polytechnic Institute and State University Blacksburg VA 24061

FARRINGTON, ELIZABETH PRUETT, former congresswoman; b. Tokyo, May 30, 1898; d. Robert Lee and Josie (Baugh) Pruett; grad. Belmont Jr. Coll., Nashville, 1916; B.A. in Journalism, U. Wis., 1918; M. U. Hawaii, 1931; m. Joseph Rider Farrington, May 17, 1920; children—Beverly Farrington Richardson, John. Reporter, Wis. State Jour., Madison, 1918-20; congl. corr. numerous newspapers, Washington, 1920-24; founder Washington Press Service, 1920; originator, editor Washington Newsletter, from 1948; mem. Congress from Hawaii, 1954-57; pres., dir. Honolulu Star Bull., Ltd., 1957-62, Star Bull. Printing Co., Ltd., Hilo Tribune-Herald, Ltd., Hawaiian Broadcasting Co.; chmn. bd. Honolulu Lithograph Co. Ltd., 1957-62; adv. Japanese Student's Assn., Honolulu, Chinese Students Alliance, Honolulu; active Honolulu Acad. Arts. Pres. Republican Women, Washington, 1946-48; chmn. public relations Nat. Fedn. Rep. Women, 1946-48, pres. 1947-63; nat. bd. dirs. N.Y. World's Fair, 1964-65, mem. Hawaii state commn., 1964-65. Mem. AAUW, Nat. Fedn. Bus. and Profl. Womens Club, Pan-Pacific Union, Theta Sigma Phi, Alpha Omicron Pi. Clubs: Congressional, Capitol Hill. Address: 1010 Wilder Ave Honolulu HI 96822

FARRIS, CHARLOTTE JOHNSTON, ednl. adminstr.; b. Evanston, Ill., Apr. 20, 1934; d. William Charles and Marie (McCambridge) Johnston; B.S., Western Ill. State U., 1956, M.S., 1957; Ph.D., Pa. State U., 1972; m. Dan Curry, Aug. 27, 1955; children—Marie Margaret, Laura Lynn, Daniel Scott. Asst. prof. Mansfield (Pa.) State Coll., 1971-74, Coll. of Human Ecology, Cornell U., Ithaca, N.Y., 1974-79; project dir., adj. grad. faculty mem. SUNY Coll. Tech., Utica, 1979—; cons. Mem. N.Y. State Commr.'s Adv. Council on Status of Women, 1981—; pres. Nat. Assn. Tchr. Educators for Vocat. Home Econs., Am. Vocat. Assn., 1980-81. NSF fellow, summer 1972. Mem. Am. Home Econs. Assn., N.Y. State Home Econs. Assn. (pres. 1983—), Am. Vocat. Assn., Am. Soc. Tng. and Devel., AAUW, NOW, Phi Delta Kappa, Phi Lambda Theta, Omicron Nu. Author: Incorporating Leadership Development into Undergraduate Home Economics Education, 1979; (with others) Pioneering Programs in Sex Equity, 1980, Expanding Adolescent Role Expectations, 1978; contbr. articles to profl. publs. Home: 35 James St Cortland NY 13045 Office: Project MOVE SUNY Coll Technology Utica NY 13502

FARRIS, DOROTHY COLE, office systems co. ofcl.; b. Binghamton, N.Y., June 1, 1951; d. Eudelmar Edgar and Arlouine Louise (Dunham) Cole; B.S. in Bus. Adminstrn., Rochester (N.Y.) Inst. Tech., 1973; m. William H. Farris, Oct. 13, 1979. With IBM Corp., 1973-80, account mgr., Orange, Calif., 1979-80; mgr. QYX, Exxon Office Systems Co., Los Angeles, 1980-81, regional sales program mgr., 1982—. Mem. Nat. Assn. Female Execs., Huntington Beach C. of C. Home: 3505 Alma Ave Manhattan Beach CA 90266 Office: 695 Town Center Dr Suite 1440 Costa Mesa CA 92626

FARROW, MIA VILLIERS, actress; b. Los Angeles, Feb. 9, 1945; d. John Villiers and Maureen Paula (O'Sullivan) Farrow; student pub., pvt. schs.; m. 2d, Andre Previn, Sept. 10, 1970 (div. Feb. 1979); children—Matthew Phineas and Sascha Villiers (twins), Lark Song, Fletcher Farrow, Summer Song, Gigi Soon Mi, Misha. Actress appearing in TV and films; debut The Importance of Being Earnest, N.Y.C. 1964; starred in TV series Peyton Place; films include Guns at Batasi, A Dandy in Aspic, Rosemary's Baby, Secret Ceremony, John and Mary, Blind Terror, Doctor Paupul, See No Evil, The Public Eye, Goodbye Raggedy Ann, The Great Gatsby, Full Circle, Peter Pan, The Wedding, Death on the Nile, Hurricane; appeared in stage plays Mary Rose, The Three Sisters, The House of Bernarda Alba, Romantic Comedy; joined Royal Shakespeare Co., London, 1974, appeared in the Marrying of Ann Leete, A Midsummer Nights Dream, The Zykovs, Ivanov. Recipient best actress award French Acad., 1969, Golden Globe award, 1967, Rio de Janero Film Festival award, 1969, Italian Acad. Award, 1970. Address: care Lionel Larner Ltd 850 7th Ave New York NY 10019 *

FARROW, SHIRLEY JEANNE SILLIMAN, coll. adminstr.; b. Sioux City, Iowa, Mar. 14, 1930; d. Eugene Lincoln and Marion (Gleason) Silliman; student Lawrence U., 1948-49; B.A., N. Tex. State U., 1951; M.Ed., Stephen F. Austin U., 1978; m. George R. Farrow, Sept. 1, 1949; children—Scott, Debra, Douglas, Sherry. Copy-writer, announcer KORK Radio, Las Vegas, Nev., 1951-52; secondary tchr. Las Vegas Ind. Sch. Dist., 1952-53; distributive edn. coordinator Cedar Hill (Tex.) Ind. Sch. Dist., 1970-75; job placement dir. Duncanville (Tex.) Ind. Sch. Dist., 1975-78; dir. coop. edn. North Lake Coll., Irving, Tex., 1978—. Mem. Tex. Coop. Edn. Assn. (pres. 1981-82), Irving Women's C. of C. (bd. dirs. 1980-82). Republican. Presbyterian. Club: Eastern Star. Author: Looking for a Job?, 1979; Actions Speak Louder than Words, 1981. Office: 5001 N MacArthur Blvd Irving TX 75062

FARWELL, SIGRID OLAFSON, cons. co. exec.; b. Ithaca, N.Y., June 4, 1933; d. Peter and Harriette (Smith) O.; B.A., Cornell U., 1955; tchr. cert. U. Colo., 1972, M.A., 1978; m. Theodore Austin Farwell, Jr., July 11, 1954; children—Karin, Peter, Eric Edward. Owner, tchr. Farwell Ballet Sch., Littleton, N.H., 1960-68; inservice coordinator nine sch. dists. Northwest Colo., 1974-75; head theatre dept. Platt Jr. High Sch., Boulder, Colo., 1976-79, Fairview High Sch., Boulder, 1979-80; pres. Sigrid Farwell & Assos., Inc., Boulder, 1980—, BDF Reflections, Inc., 1982—. Founder Evergreen Jr. Theatre, 1970, Storybook Players, 1973; mem. Council Arts and Humanities, Steamboat Springs, 1973-75; vol. horseback riding and skiing programs Fitzsimmons Army Hosp. Amputee programs, 1970-73. Recipient Internat. Yr. of Child award for service and dedication, Family Acad. Internat. Children's Center, Stravanger, Norway and San Francisco, 1979. Mem. Colo. Drama and Speech Assn. (pres.), Am. Soc. Tng. and Devel., Nat. Assn. Female Execs., Nat. Speakers Assn. Pub. play The Child of Fear, 1978. Home and Office: 7363 Cortez Ln Boulder CO 80303

FASANO, CLARA, sculptor; b. Castellaneta, Italy, Dec. 14, 1900; d. Pasquale and Julia (de Feudis) Fasano; came to U.S., 1907, naturalized, 1939; student Cooper Union Art Inst., Art Students League, N.Y.C., 1917-21, Julien Academie and Colarossi Academie, Paris, 1924-26; scholar, Rome, Italy, 1922-24; m. Jean de Marco, July 8, 1936. Exhibited at Salon d'Automne, Paris, 1925; worked in own studio, exhibited in Rome, 1926-32; tchr. sculpture adult edn. Bd. Edn. N.Y., 1948-58; exhibited in numerous shows, including Worlds Fair, N.Y.C., 1939, Whitney Mus., NAD, Pa. Acad., Art Inst. Chgo., Met. Mus. Art, Am.-Brit. Center, N.Y.C., Ferragil, Buckholz galleries; works represented in permanent collections at Met. Mus. Art, N.Y.C., Manhattanville Coll. Sacred Heart, Purchase, N.Y., Norfolk Mus. Arts and Scis., Smithsonian Instn., Washington, Syracuse U., also pvt. collections U.S., abroad; important works include series of 12 portraits in bronze, the last being of His Excellency Giuseppe Cataldi, pres. Corte dei Conti of Italy; tchr. Manhattanville Coll. Grantee, recipient citation Nat. Inst. Arts and Letters, 1952; recipient medal of Honor with citation Am. Artists Mag., Audubon Annual Exhbn., 1956, hon. mention Archtl. League N.Y., Gold Medals Exhbn., 1956, Daniel Chester French medal NAD, 1965, Peter Caesar Alberti award Italian Execs. Am. Inc., 1967, Dessie Greer award for sculpture NAD, 1968, 2d pl. sculpture competitions for entrance Supreme Ct. of Bklyn., for fountain sculpture for lobby 100 Church St. bldg., N.Y.C., sculpture commn. for relief Middleport (Ohio) Post Office U.S. Treasury Dept. competition for Apex Bldg. in Washington. Academician, NAD. Fellow Nat. Sculpture Soc. (hon. mention 1956); mem. Audubon Artists (M. Grumbacher prize 1954), Sculptors Guild, Nat. Assn. Women Artists (Anonymous prize 1945, Marcia Brady Tucker prize 1950, medal of Honor for sculpture 63d ann. exhbn. 1955). Subject of articles, works reproduced in Am. Artist mag., Nat. Sculpture Rev., also books Sculpture in Modern America, Contemporary American Sculpture, The Materials and Methods of Sculpture. Home: Cervaro-Prov Frosinone Italy Office: 1083 Fifth Ave New York NY 10028 *

FASCIA, DOMENICA MARY, med. technologist; b. Mechanicsville, N.Y.; d. Anthony and Assunta (Dinardo) F.; B.S., Calif. State U., Los Angeles, 1970, M.A., 1974. Chief med. technologist St. Mary's Hosp., Troy, N.Y., 1951-56, Santa Teresita Hosp., Duarte, Calif., 1956—; cons. Sierra Madre (Calif.) Community Hosp., 1972—. Registered sanitarian; profl. entomologist; hazard control mgr. Mem. Am. Soc. Clin. Pathologists, Am. Registry Profl. Etomologists, Internat. Soc. Clin. Lab. Tech., Calif. Assn. Med. Tech., Am. Soc. Microbiology, Am. Assn. Blood Banks, Assn. of Practitioners in Infection Control, Healthcare Safety Profls., Am. Philatelic Soc. Democrat. Roman Catholic. Clubs: Am. Contract Bridge League, Federated Women's Am. Address: 403 N Grand Ave Monrovia CA 91016

FASEL, IDA, author; b. Portland, Maine, May 9, 1909; d. I. E. and Lilian (Harwich) Drapkin; B.A. cum laude, Boston U., 1931, M.A., 1945; Ph.D., U. Denver, 1963; postgrad. Tex. Woman's U., Denton, 1957-59; m. Oscar A. Fasel, Dec. 24, 1946. Instr., U. Conn., New London, 1946-50, Midwestern U., Wichita Falls, Tex., 1957-59, Colo. Women's Coll., Denver, 1959-62; prof. English, U. Colo., Denver, 1962-77, prof. emeritus, 1977—. Council on Research and Creative Work, U. Colo. faculty fellow, 1967, travel grantee, 1965, 67. Mem. Milton Soc. Am., Poetry Soc. Tex., Poetry Soc. Am., Collegium Disting. Alumni Boston U., Phi Beta Kappa. Club: Friends of Milton's Cottage. Author: On the Meanings of Cleave, 1979; Thanking the Flowers, 1981; contbr. articles and poetry to profl. jours.

FASNACHT, MARY JEAN (MRS. DAVID A. SKIDMORE), chem. co. exec.; b. Phila., Oct. 9, 1955; d. Richard Sharp and Betty (Beegle) F.; B.S., U. Pitts., 1977; m. David Allen Skidmore, Jan. 6, 1979; 1 dau., Dawn F. Proofreader, writer, photographer The Bradford Era, daily, (Pa.), 1973-75; engr., cigarette tow devel. Celanese Fibers Co., Narrows, Va., 1977-78, engr. cigarette tow quality assurance, 1978-79, cigarette tow product performance engr., 1979-80, filament quality assurance engr., 1980-82, area supr. filament quality assurance and tech support, 1982—. Mem. Giles Little Theater, 1977-79. Mem. Nat. Assn. Female Execs., Am. Assn. Profl. and Exec. Women. Republican. Home: Route 3 Box 219 Bluefield VA 24605 Office: PO Box 1000 Narrows VA 24124

FAST, RACHEL ANN, clin. psychologist; b. N.Y.C., May 26, 1944; d. Howard and Bette (Cohen) Fast; student Wellesley Coll., 1962-65, Columbia U., 1967-68; B.A. summa cum laude in Psychology, Hunter Coll., 1972; M.A., L.I. U., 1974, Ph.D., 1976. Teaching fellow L.I. U., 1974-75; sr. psychologist Inst. Rehab. Medicine, N.Y. U. Med. Center, N.Y.C., 1975-81; pvt. practice clin. psychology, N.Y.C., 1975—; lectr. on stroke effects N.Y.C. Dept. Motor Vehicles, 1978-81; speaker on psychol. aspects of stroke and disability, 1976-81. Mem. Am. Psychol. Assn. Home: 43 Fifth Ave New York NY 10003

FAUL, ALENE, educator; b. Mascoutah, Ill., Dec. 20; d. James Patrick and Georgiana Lily of the Valley (Beatty) F.; A.B., St. Louis U., 1945, M.A., 1951, Ph.D., 1980; M.A., U. Notre Dame, 1971. Joined Congregation of Sisters of Notre Dame, 1941; chmn. depts. English and speech theatre Notre Dame High Sch., 1953; reader in English composition Ednl. Testing Service, 1962-81; chmn. dept. communication, instr. theology Notre Dame Coll., 1972-76; prof. communication, exec. council St. Louis U., 1977—; public speaker; condr. adult edn. seminars. Speaker, United Way campaigns, 1981. Fellow Oxford U., 1962; Tchr. Exchange fellow to Japan, 1963. Mem. Soc. Scholarly Pub., Internat. Platform Assn., Smithsonian Assos., Speech Assn. Am., Mariological Soc. Am., Planetary Soc., Internat. Communication Assn., E.S.P. Sci. Research Assos. Found., World Futures Soc., Speech Theatre Assn. Mo. Roman Catholic. Author: A Rhetoric and a Word, 1980; Leadership, 1974; The Prophets Say: He Comes, 1967; Parables for Public Speaking, 1982. Home: 320 E Ripa Ave Saint Louis MO 63125 Office: Dept of Communication 3733 W Pine Blvd Saint Louis MO 63108

FAULCONER, KAY ANNE, mgmt. cons., educator; b. Shelbyville, Ind., Aug. 19, 1945; d. Clark J. and Charlotte Keenan; B.A. in English, Calif. State U., Northridge, 1968; M.B.A., Pepperdine U., 1975, M.A. in Public Communications, 1976; m. James R. Faulconer; children—Kevin Lee, Melissa Lynne. Personnel mgr. Uni-Systems, Inc., Ventura, Calif., 1977; pres. Kay Faulconer & Assos., mgmt. cons., Oxnard, Calif., 1977—; instr. U. LaVerne, 1978—, Oxnard Coll., 1978—. Founder, past pres., sec. Oxnard Friends of Library, 1975-81; bd. dirs., sec. Girls Club Oxnard, 1980—; bd. dirs Oxnard Boys Club, 1981. Recipient Clubwoman of Year award Oxnard Jr. Women's Club, 1975, Bus. Woman of Year award Oxnard Bus. and Profl. Women's Club, 1977, Young Career Woman award; Mark Hopkins award Oxnard Coll., 1981-82. Mem. Am. Soc. Tng. and Devel. (dir. Los Padres chpt.), Am. Soc. Profl. Cons., Ventura County Profl. Women's Network, Am. Assn. Women in Community and Jr. Colls. Home and Office: 601 Janetwood Oxnard CA 93030

FAULKNER, CHARLA REID, educator; b. Las Cruces, N.M., Mar. 14, 1950; d. Lloyd Reid and Emily Meek (Kittle) F.; B.A., Hendrix Coll., 1972; M.Ed., U. Ark., 1979; div.; 1 son, Andrew Christopher Hunter. Tchr. math., biology Little Rock (Ark.) Central High Sch., 1976-80; instr. math. Governor's Sch. of Ark. for Gifted and Talented, summer 1981; instr. math. Hendrix Coll., 1981-82; pvt. math. tutor. Mem. Ark. Council Tchrs. Math. (exec. bd. 1981—), Nat. Edn. Assn., Ark. Edn. Assn., Nat. Council Tchrs. Math., Am. Math. Soc., Pi Mu Epsilon, Mu Alpha Theta. Methodist.

FAULKNER, RUTH RENAUD, utility co. exec.; b. New Haven, July 21, 1930; d. Howard Ellsworth and Elizabeth Lillian (Wilson) Renaud; student Ariz. State U., 1976; B.S., U. Phoenix, 1979; 1 son, Joe S. Exec. sec. Salt River Project, Phoenix, 1955-63, sr. exec. sec., 1963-76, asst. to pres., 1976—; del. elec. utilities to People's Republic of China, 1976. Mem. Gov's. Voc-Tech. Adv. Council, 1978—; bd. dirs. Arizonans for Jobs and Energy, 1980-82, Valley Big Bros., NCCJ, Phoenix Zoo; nat. chmn. Nuclear Energy Women, 1978-81; mem. Ariz. Mex. Commn.; mem. adv. council Coll. Bus., Ariz. State U.; mem. exec. com. Phoenix Charter 100, 1981-82; mem. internat. bd. United Ch. of Religious Sci., 1978-83; mem. corporate bd. YMCA, 1980—, bd. dirs. Valley of Sun United Way, 1981—, Found. Sr. Adult Living, 1980—, Phoenix Together, 1981—. Recipient Golden Torch award Ariz. Fedn. Bus. Mem. Nat. Assn. Female Execs., Colo. River Water Users Assn., Central Ariz. Project Assn., Ariz. Acad., Am. Nuclear Soc., Am. Public Power Assn., Elec. Assn. for Women (hon.) (London). Republican. Club: Soroptimist. Office: PO Box 1980 Phoenix AZ 85001

FAUR, YVONNE CONSTANCE, microbiologist; b. Romania, Sept. 11, 1916; came to U.S., 1963, naturalized, 1968; d. Alexander S. and Clara I. (Abra) Afdan; M.D., U. Bucharest, 1940; m. Aurel Sebastian Faur, Nov. 20, 1943. Chief microbiology lab. Cantacuzino State Inst., Bucharest, 1948-62; research scientist immunohematology dept. N.Y.U., 1963-66; cons. microbiologist Bur. Labs., N.Y. State Dept. Health, 1966-73, sr. research scientist, 1973—, lectr. microbiology, 1967—. Recipient Sci. Paper award Am. Public Health Assn., 1979. Fellow Am. Acad. Microbiology; mem. Am. Soc. Microbiology. Author manual, 60 papers in field. Patentee medium for pathogenic neisseria. Office: 455 1st Ave New York NY 10016

FAUROT, JEANNETTE LOUISE, linguist; b. St. Lambert, Que., Can., Mar. 1, 1943; d. Jean Hiatt and Louise (Johnson) F.; B.A., Harvard U., 1964; M.A., U. Calif., 1967, Ph.D., 1972. Mem. faculty U. Tex., Austin, 1971—, asst. prof. Chinese, 1973-77, assoc. prof., 1977—. Recipient Harry H. Ransom Teaching Effectiveness award U. Tex., 1974-75. Editor: Chinese Fiction from Taiwan: Critical Perspectives, 1980. Office: Dept Oriental and African Langs U Tex Austin TX 78712

FAUSETT, PATRICIA LEE, electronics co. exec.; b. Washington, Feb. 8, 1944; d. Gerald LeRoy and Bernice Kennedy; B.S., Purdue U., 1965; M.B.A. candidate Golden Gate U., 1979—; m. Richard Orlin Fausett, Sept. 15, 1979; children—Stephen Johnson, Jr., Michael Lee Johnson. Tchr., Franklin Sch., Burlingame, Calif., Peter Hoy Sch., Lombard, Ill., 1966-71; acct. Hewlett-Packard, Sunnyvale, Calif., 1978-81, buyer, 1981—. Treas., Almond Sch. PTA, Los Altos, Calif., 1978-79. Mem. Alpha Chi Omega, Alpha Delta Kappa. Democrat. Roman Catholic. Home: Los Altos CA 94002 Office: 1330 Kifer Rd Sunnyvale CA 94086

FAUST, ELIZABETH JEANETTE, nurse; b. Kansas City, Kans., Apr. 13, 1940; d. Leon and Alida Marie (Millert) DeNolf; student Sisters of Charity Sch. Nursing, Kansas City, Kans., 1958-61; B.S.N., St. Louis U., 1977; M.A.Ed., Washington U., St. Louis; m. Paul Anthony Faust, June 20, 1964; 1 son, Paul Stefen. Nurse, St. Mary's Health Center, St. Louis, 1962-63, St. Joseph's Hosp., Louisville, 1963-64, Deaconess Hosp., St. Louis, 1964-66; head nurse surg. div. City Hosp., St. Louis, 1977-78; asst. dir. staff devel. Deaconess Hosp., St. Louis, 1978—, also coordinator continuing edn. Mem. Mo. 3d Dist. Continuing Edn. Com., Adult Edn. Council Greater St. Louis. Am. Cancer Soc. scholar, 1958-61. Mem. Am., Mo. nurses assns., Nursing Oncology Soc. Roman Catholic. Home: 26 Grantwood Ln St Louis MO 63123 Office: 6150 Oakland Ave St Louis MO 63139

FAUST, NAOMI FLOWE, educator, poet; b. Salisbury, N.C.; d. Christopher Leroy and Ada Luella (Graham) Flowe; A.B., Bennett Coll.; M.A., U. Mich., 1945; Ph.D., N.Y. U., 1963; m. Roy Malcolm Faust, Aug. 16, 1948. Elem. tchr. Public Schs. Gaffney (S.C.); tchr. English, French, phys. edn. Atkins High Sch., Winston-Salem; instr. English, Bennett Coll. and So. U., Scotlandville, La., 1944-46; prof. English, Morgan State Coll., Balt., 1946-48; tchr. English, Greensboro (N.C.) Public Schs., 1948-51, N.Y.C. Public Schs., 1954-63; prof. edn. Queens Coll. of City U. N.Y., Flushing, 1964-82; lectr. in field; writer, lectr., poetry readings, 1982—. Named Tchr.-Author of 1979, Tchr.-Writer; cert. of Merit for poem Cooper Hill Writers Conf., 1970. Mem. AAUP, Nat. Council Tchrs. English, Nat. Women's Book Assn., World Poetry Soc. Intercontinental, N.Y. Poetry Forum, NAACP, United Negro Coll. Fund, Alpha Kappa Alpha, Alpha Kappa Mu, Alpha Epsilon. Author: Discipline and the Classroom Teacher, 1977; (poetry) Speaking in Verse, 1974; All Beautiful Things, 1983; contbr. poetry to jours. Home: 112-01 175th St Jamaica NY 11433

FAUST-LÉVY, ELIE (ELEANOR SARAH), editor, journalist; b. Newark, Jan. 10; d. Jacob and Hedda Krieg (Waldinger) Faust; B.S., Simmons Coll., Boston, 1960; postgrad. Harvard U., Columbia U.; m. John Corcos Lévy, June 3, 1973. Reporter, Jewish News, Newark, 1961-63; freelance journalist, Israel, 1963-66; staff writer Amalgamated Clothing Workers Am., 1967; editorial asst. Midstream mag., 1967; editor Ort Reporter, N.Y.C., 1968—; founder Lilith mag., 1973, mem. editorial adv. bd., 1979—; 1st pres. Lilith Publs. Inc., 1974. Mem. task force changing role of women Fedn. Jewish Philanthropies, N.Y.C., 1979—. Mem. Nat. Assn. Female Execs., Am. Jewish Press Assn., Fgn. Press Assn. Israel, Internat. Labor Press, N.Y. League Bus. and Profl. Women, Alpha Lambda Delta. Clubs: Simmons, Met. (N.Y.C.). Contbr. numerous articles, revs. to mags., newspapers. Office: 1250 Broadway New York NY 10001

FAUSTO-STERLING, ANNE, educator; b. N.Y.C., July 30, 1944; d. Philip and Dorothy Ruth (Dannenberg) Sterling; B.A., U. Wis., 1965; Ph.D., Brown U., 1970; m. Nelson Fausto, Dec. 3, 1966. Asst. prof. Brown U., Providence, 1971-76, asso. prof. biology, 1976—; NSF grant reviewer devel. biology. Mellon fellow Wellesley Center for Research on Women, 1980-81; fellow Pembroke Center Research and Teaching on Women, 1982-83. Mem. AAAS, Soc. Developmental Biology, Genetics Soc. Am., Nat. Women's Studies Assn., Internat. Soc. Developmental Biology. Contbr. articles to publs. sci. and women's studies. Office: Box G Brown Univ Providence RI 02912

FAVA, SYLVIA FLEIS, educator; b. N.Y.C., June 1, 1927; d. Joseph and Anna (Karner) Fleis; B.A., Queens Coll., 1948; Ph.D., Northwestern U., 1956; m. John L. Fava, Aug. 12, 1951. Lectr. to asso. prof. Bklyn. Coll., City U. N.Y., 1951-72, prof. sociology, 1972—. Mem. Am. Sociol. Assn., Eastern Sociol. Soc., Soc. Study of Social Problems. Author: Sexual Behavior in American Society: First Two Kinsey Reports, 1955; Urban Society, 5th edit., 1964, 6th edit., 1974; Urbanism in World Perspective, 1968. Office: Sociology Dept Brooklyn College Bedford Ave and Ave H Brooklyn NY 11210

FAVARO, MARY KAYE ASPERHEIM, physician, author; b. Edgerton, Wis., Sept. 30, 1934; d. Harold Wilbur and Genevieve Catherine (Hyland) Asperheim; B.S. in Pharmacy, U. Wis., 1956, M.D., 1969; M.S. in Pharmacy, St. Louis Coll. Pharmacy, 1965; m. Biagino Philip Favaro, May 31, 1969; children—Justin Peter, Gina Sue. Instr. pharmacology St. Louis U. and St. Mary's Hosp., St. Louis, 1959-63; intern Albany Med. Coll., 1969-70; resident in pediatrics Albany Med. Coll., 1970-71, Med. U. S.C., 1972-73; asst. prof. pediatrics Med. U. S.C., 1973—; practice medicine specializing in pediatrics and family practice, Charleston, S.C., 1974—; books include: Pharmacology for Practical Nurses, 1976; The Pharmacologic Basis of Patient Care, 1977. Mem. AMA, S.C. Med. Assn., Charleston County Med. Assn., Charleston County Pediatric Soc. Home: 1866 Capri Dr Charleston SC 29407 Office: 5060 Dorchester Rd Charleston Heights SC 29405

FAWCETT, MARIE ANN FORMANEK, civic worker; b. Mpls., Mar. 6, 1914; d. Peter Paul and Mary Ann (Stepanek) Formanek; grad. high sch., Mpls.; certs. Harvard U., 1976-82; m. Roscoe Kent Fawcett, Mar. 16, 1935; children—Roscoe Kent, Jr., Peter Formanek, Roger Knowlton II, Stephen Hart. Vol. chmn. Nathaniel Witherell Hosp., Greenwich, 1952-56, chmn. vols., 1956—, now bd. dirs. aux.; chmn. vols. Greenwich Hosp., 1953-54; dist. chmn. ARC, Community Chest, Mental Health, 1946-50; vol. mentally retarded children Milbank Sch., Greenwich, 1958-59; participating mem. Huxley Inst. for Biol. Research; vol. numerous charity drives. Bd. dirs. Merry Go Round for Aged, Greenwich, Putnam Sch.; bd. dirs., recreation chmn. Merry Go Round Mews for Elderly; bd. dirs. Nathaniel Witherell Hosp. Aux., Cerebral Palsy, Greenwich Philharmonia; bd. dirs. Multiple Sclerosis Soc., 1948—, corr. sec., 1958—. Named Woman of Year, Soroptomist Club, 1967; recipient Fairfield County Community Service award; reference service Am. Bicentennial Research Inst.; award for service to Sr. Citizens; Vol. in Limelight citation for vol. work Greenwich Hosp.; citation and certs. for work at Witherell Hosp. from Conn. Dept. Health. Mem. Internat. Platform Assn., Marquis Biog. Library Soc. (adv.). Clubs: Woman's of Greenwich (various coms.); Old York (N.Y.C.). Address: North St and Hawkwood Ln Greenwich CT 06830

FAWCETT-HOOVER, JANE, lobbyist; b. Defiance, Ohio, June 10, 1943; d. Novice G. and Marjorie (Keener) Fawcett; B.S., Ohio State U., 1965, postgrad., 1965-68; m. William Hoover, Jr., July 15, 1978. Consumer specialist Procter & Gamble Co., Cin., 1968-74; dir. info. services Grocery Mfrs. of Am., Washington, 1974-77; nat. govt. relations specialist Procter & Gamble, Washington, 1977—. Mem. at large Nat. Safety Council, 1976-78. Recipient cert. of appreciation Pres. Richard Nixon, 1972. Mem. Women in Govt. Relations, Pharm. Industry Washington Adv. Com., Ohio State Alumni Assn., Jr. Friends Alexandria Community Y. Republican. Methodist. Clubs: Capital Hill, Internat., Woodlawn Country. Office: 1801 K St NW Suite 230 Washington DC 20006 *

FAY, CATHERINE ANN, speech-lang. pathologist; b. Bklyn., July 7, 1951; d. Thomas Joseph and Catherine Margaret (Ridge) F.; B.A., St. Joseph's Coll., Bklyn., 1972; M.A., N.Y.U., 1974. Tchr., Yeshiva Rambam, Bklyn., 1974; speech lang. pathologist Chama Child Devel. Center, N.Y.C., 1974-77; dir. speech-lang. pathology Community Life Centers, N.Y.C., 1977-82; cons. Ft. George Community Enrichment Center, N.Y.C., 1982—; pvt. practice speech pathology, Bklyn., 1977—; cons. Mennonite Head Start programs, N.Y.C. Cert. tchr., N.Y. State. Mem. Internat. Assn. Logopedics and Phoniatrics, Am. Speech-Lang. and Hearing Assn. (cert. clin. competence), N.Y. State Speech-Lang. and Hearing Assn., Biofeedback Soc. Am., Sigma Iota Chi. Republican. Home and Office: 348 4th St Brooklyn NY 11215

FAY, CYNTHIA STEIL, ins. co. exec.; b. Miami, Fla., June 25, 1951; d. Robert Joseph and Mary Louise (Eustice) Steil; B.S., Nicholls State U., 1973; m. Gary Michael Fay, May 12, 1973; children—Shane, Shannan. With First Nat. Bank of Commerce, New Orleans, 1973-74; with Pan-Am. Life Ins. Co., New Orleans, 1974—, sr. auditor, 1975—. Advisor, Jr. Achievement, 1974-77. Cert. internal auditor. Mem. Inst. Internal Auditors (sec.), Health Ins. Assn. Am. Office: PO Box 60219 New Orleans LA 70053

FAY, FRANCESCA CASTRONOVO, nurse, educator; b. Norwalk, Conn., Sept. 14, 1943; d. Angelo M. and Anne (Archbold) Castronovo; B.S. in Nursing, Cornell U., 1967; M.A., N.Y.U., 1970; M.A., Columbia U., 1974, Ed.D., 1977; m. Leon Fay, June 10, 1978; 1 son, Ashley. Instr. nursing Columbia U., 1970-74; asst. prof. Cornell U., 1974-77; asst. prof. Boston Coll., 1977-78; asst. prof. nursing Va. Commonwealth U., Charlottesville, 1978-80; asst. prof. U. Va., 1980-82; with Valley Health Center, East Corinth, Vt., 1982—. Mem. Am. Heart Assn., Nat. Assn. Pediatric Nurse assos. and Practitioners, Nat. League Nursing. Democrat. Contbr. in field. Home: East Corinth VT 05040 Office: Valley Health Center East Corinth VT 05040

FAY, TONI GEORGETTE, publishing co. ofcl.; b. N.Y.C., Apr. 25, 1947; d. George E. and Allie C. (Smith) F.; B.A., Duquesne U., Pitts., 1968; M.S.W. (NIMH fellow 1970-72), U. Pitts., 1972, M.Ed., 1973; cert. Yale U. Drug Dependence Inst., 1973. Caseworker, N.Y.C. Dept. Welfare, 1968-70; regional commr. Gov. Pa. Council Drugs and Alcohol, 1973-76; dir. social services Pitts. Black Action Against Drug Abuse, 1972-73; dir. planning and devel. Nat. Council Negro Women, 1977-79; exec. v.p. D. Parke Gibson Assos., 1979-82; mgr. community relations Time Inc., N.Y.C., 1982—. Bd. dirs. Alliance for Volunteerism; mem. steering com. Pa. Gov.'s Task Force on Health Planning, 1976; mem. trustee com. U. Pitts., 1972-73; mem. com. Rosalynn Carter's Communities Plan, 1978. Named Woman of Yr., Pitts. YWCA, 1975. Mem. Nat. Assn. Black Social Workers, Coalition of 100 Black Women, Nat. Council Negro Women (life), Alpha Kappa Alpha. Office: Time Life Bldg Rockefeller Center New York NY 10020

FAYLE, FLORANCE IRENE HOLLAND, travel agt.; b. Wakefield, Mass., Dec. 29, 1932; d. William Henry and Irene Frances (Holland) F.; A.A., Colby-Sawyer Coll., 1953; B.A., U. Colo., 1957; postgrad. langs. Harvard U., 1964-66. Mgr., Coll. Sport Shop, New London, N.H., 1955-57; rep. Advt. Research Found., N.Y.C., 1953-55; office mgr. U.S. Freight Co., San Francisco and Boston, 1960-66; mgr. Alert Telephone Communications, Honolulu, 1967-75; pres. Travel Express Ltd., Honolulu, 1975—; cons. in field. Mem. Assn. Retail Travel Agts. (chpt. membership chmn. 1980—, treas., dir. 1982—). Republican. Roman Catholic. Clubs: Honolulu (a founder), Fgn. Travel (Honolulu). Office: 98-1247 Kaahumanu St Suite 306 AIEA HI 96701

FAZIO, CAROLYN RAFFA, fin. cons.; b. Colorado Springs, Colo., June 3, 1947; d. Joseph L. and Mildred S. (Olleia) Raffa; B. Music, Manhattanville Coll., 1969; M. Music (Teaching fellow 1969-70), U. Mass., 1970; postgrad. U. Chgo., 1973; m. Charles R. Fazio, II, June 25, 1973; children—Francesca Pilar, Victoria Felice. Publs. editor Nat. Auto Dealers Assn., Washington, 1970; research analyst Nat. Adv. Council Extension and Continuing Edn., Washington, 1971-72; devel. officer Nat. Symphony Orch., Washington, 1972; dir. devel. Pa. Ballet Assn., Phila., 1973-75; dir. alumni and research St. Mary's Jr. Coll., Mpls., 1975-77; philanthropic cons. McManis Assos., Inc., Washington, 1977—. Mem. Public Relations Soc. Am., Women in Communications, Washington Women in Public Relations, Choral Arts Soc. Washington (dir.), Manhattanville Alumnae Assn., Council for Advancement and Support of Edn. (ann. award for alumni programming 1976). Roman Catholic. Home: 1843 Mintwood Pl NW Washington DC 20009 Office: 1201 Connecticut Ave NW Suite 300 Washington DC 20036

FEDDOES, SADIE CLOTHIL, banking exec.; b. St. Vincent, West Indies, Sept. 30; d. Jane (Crick) Feddoes; came to U.S., 1952, naturalized, 1957; B. Profl. Studies in Bus., Pace U., N.Y., 1977. Dir. community and govt. relations Citibank N.A., Bklyn. and S.I. region, 1976—; asso. Caribbean Cable TV Co., Ltd.; appeared in Today Show program Sta. WNBC-TV, 1975. Fund raising vol. YMCA, Bklyn., 1973-74; mem. exec. com. Bklyn. chpt. ARC, 1975—; bd. dirs. Bedford Stuyvesant Restoration Corp.; bd. dirs. Overall Econ. Devel. Program Bklyn.; mem. Mayor's Council on Inergroup Relations; chmn. bd. dirs. Billie Holiday Theatre, Bklyn., 1974—. Recipient Community Service award Nat. Assn. of Negro Bus. and Profl. Women's Clubs, 1975, Personal Banking Achievement Council award, 1970; numerous other awards from chs., civic orgns. Mem. Am. Mgmt. Assn., Nat. Fedn. Press Women, N.Y. Women in Communications, Nat. Women in Communications, N.Y. Press Women, Empire State Fedn. of Women's Clubs (Journalism award 1976). Club: Ta-Wa-ses. Columnist N.Y. Amsterdam News, 1972—. Office: 885 Flatbush Ave Brooklyn NY 11226

FEDELLE, ESTELLE, artist; b. Chgo.; d. John and Julia (Porebski) Szymanski; student Am. Acad., 1944-47, Northwestern U., 1949-51, Inst. Design, Art Inst. Chgo.; also pvt. study. Exhibited in 47 one-man shows including Wheaton (Ill.) Pub. Library, Libertyville (Ill.) Art League; exhibited in group shows Visual Arts Center, Chgo., Chgo. Pub. Library, Ill. State Fair, Baron Galleries of Chgo. and Las Vegas, Grand Central Gallery, N.Y.C., numerous others; painted portraits; pvt. art tchr., 1950—; dir. Fedelle Sch. Art, Chgo.; newspaper columnist Art and You, 1974—. Recipient 75 awards for painting including Margaret R. Dingle award, 1953; Cert. of Merit Disting. Service in Art, 1967. Fellow Royal Soc. Art London (hon.); mem. Austin-Oak Park-River Forest Art League, Nat. League Am. Pen Women, Park Ridge, Mcpl., Art League (dir.), Regent Art League. Author: How To Begin Painting for Fun, 1964; contbg. author: Fun Book on Painting, How to Paint from your Color Slides. Home: 1500 S Cumberland St Park Ridge IL 60068 Office: Fedelle Studio 6733 N Olmsted St Chicago IL 60631

FEDERROLL, SUSAN WEDEMEYER, psychiat. social worker; b. Columbus, Ohio, July 10, 1940; s. Norman George and Virginia Marion (Hawkins) Wedemeyer; B.A. cum laude, U. Md., 1972; M.S.W., U. Md., 1976; m. Donald J. Federroll, July 30, 1960; children—D. Craig, D. Keith. Social worker Anne Arundel County (Md.) Dept. Social Services, 1972-78, supr., 1979—; psychiat. social worker Crownsville (Md.) Hosp. Center, 1978-79; cons., family therapist Charles County Mental Health, Glen Burnie, Md., 1976—; field instr. U. Md.; mem. adv. bd. Sexual Offense Crisis Center; pvt. practice. Bd. dirs., central admissions com. Anne Arundel County Assn. Retarded Citizens. Lic., cert. social worker, Md. Mem. Nat. Assn. Social Workers, U. Md. Sch. Social Work Alumni Assn., Phi Kappa Phi, Chi Omega. Republican. Episcopalian. Home: 422 Park Creek Rd Pasadena MD 21122 Office: 120 N Langley Rd Glen Burnie MD 21061

FEDOROFF, BARBARA ANNE LIMING, communications and fund devel. exec.; b. Jersey City; d. Ambrose E. and Harriet E. (Hicks) Liming; student N.Y. U., 1953-54; m. Serge M. Fedoroff; children—Nadine Fedoroff Noel, Beth, Brenda, Meg. Account supr. Cherenson/Carroll Assos., Livingston, N.J., 1968-70; public relations mgr. Congoleum Industries, Kearny, N.J., 1970-71; account supr. Media Methods, Montville, N.J., 1971-73; mktg. cons. Newark Broadcasting, Livingston, N.J., 1973-75; advt. dir. Mall, Short Hills, N.J., 1975-77; asso. dir. devel. Archdiocese Newark, 1977-79; dir. nat. council fund devel. Girl Scouts U.S.A., N.Y.C., 1980—; communications cons. Nat. Assn. Children with Learning Disabilities, 1972-73. Campaign dir. sch. bds., freeholders Morris and Sussex Counties, 1971-74; mem. Communications Council, Archdiocese Newark, 1976-77; chmn. Internat. Service Agys., Overseas; chmn. campaign com. Nat. Vol. Orgns. Mem. Nat. Assn. Female Execs., Nat. Soc. Fund Raising Execs. (dir. N.Y. Chpt.). Clubs: Essex Racquet and Health. Offshore Sailing (City Island, N.Y.). Home: 10 Carriage Way Montclair NJ 07042 Office: 830 3d Ave New York NY 10022

FEELEY, THERESA GOUVIN, state legislator; b. Westerly, R.I., May 9, 1947; d. Paul Henry and Lumina Rose (Cayer) Gouvin; B.S. in Biology, Trinity Coll., Burlington, Vt., 1969; M.Ed., St. Michael's Coll., 1980; m. Richard Todd Feeley, Sept. 9, 1967; children—Bradford Michael, Seth Todd. Med. technologist U. Vt., 1966-70; mem. Vt. Ho. of Reps., 1976—, mem. edn. com., appropriations com. Vice chmn. Vt. Higher Edn. Planning Commn.; trustee Vt. State Colls., 1980-82; trustee Burnham Meml. Library, Colchester, Vt., 1974-76; pres. Chittenden County Democratic Women, 1976-78; bd. dirs., pres. Essex Meals on Wheels. Mem. Vt. Bd. Realtors. Roman Catholic. Club: Burlington Tennis.

FEENEY, MARY ELIZABETH, librarian; b. Kansas City, Mo., Sept. 18, 1918; d. Joseph Francis and Mary Eleanor (O'Neill) F.; A.B., U. Pa., 1947, postgrad. In-service Library Program, 1949. Asst. librarian Coll. Physicians, Phila., 1962-64; asso. librarian N.Y. Acad. Medicine, N.Y.C., 1964-70, dir. New Eng. Regional Med. Library Service, Harvard U. Med. Sch., 1970-77; librarian Yale U. Med. Library, 1977—. Served to lt. USNR, 1943-45. Mem. Med. Library Assn., Spl. Libraries Assn. Roman Catholic. Office: Yale U Med Library 333 Cedar St New Haven CT 06510

FEENEY, RENA LUCIA, record producer-pub., rec. artist; b. Bayonne, N.J., July 12, 1931; d. Salvatore and Josephine Carmelina (Ferro) Romano; student public schs., N.J.; m. William Francis Feeney, June 17, 1949; children—William Anthony, Maureen Grace, Christopher Salvatore. Founder, pres. R.R. Music Pub. Co., N.Y.C., 1966—, R&R Records, Inc./Ren-Maur Music Corp., N.Y.C., 1968-75, Can-Scor Prodns., Inc., N.Y.C., 1975—, Factory Beat Records, Inc., N.Y.C., 1979—; recs. include Do It To Me, Love a Little Longer, Dance It Off, I Love Your Beat, Once You Fall in Love; producer Sounds of the Future on Manhattan cable TV show The Rena Romano Show, 1975-80. Mem. AGVA, AFTRA, Am. Guild Authors and Composers, Broadcast Music Inc., Am. Fedn. Musicians, Nat. Acad. Rec. Arts and Scis., Nat. Assn. Cable Programmers, Nat. Assn. Female Execs. Roman Catholic. Clubs: Spaulding Raquetball, Lucaya Beach Country. Home: 31 Engleside St Cresskill NJ 07626 Office: 663 Fifth Ave New York NY 10022

FEERICK, JO ANN MILLER, mfg. co. exec.; b. Milw., Nov. 18, 1953; d. James Richard and Helen Marie (Schwemer) Miller; A.A. in Bus., U. Wis., Milw., 1973; m. Patrick Henry Feerick, May 19, 1974. Mail clk. U.S. Postal Service, Milw., 1973-74; parts warehouse sales clk., then inside sales rep. Taylor Electric Co., Mequon, Wis., 1976-79, dist. sales mgr. electronic consumer goods, 1979—; tchr. Dale Carnegie courses. Vol. probation counselor Salvation Army, 1975. Mem. Nar. Assn. Female Execs., Soc. Audio Cons. Democrat. Roman Catholic. Club: Port Washington Jr. Women's. Home: 2550 Hwy 33 Saukville WI 53080 Office: 1000 W Donges Bay Rd Mequon WI 53092

FEGAN, MAUREEN WELDON, retail co. ofcl.; b. River Forest, Ill., Oct. 1, 1951; d. William Glynn and Mary Patricia (Butler) Weldon; B.A. in Psychology, Northwestern U., 1973; M.A. in Psychology, Roosevelt U., 1977; m. John Joseph Fegan, Sept. 7, 1979. Staff asst psychol. testing Sears Roebuck & Co., Chgo., 1973-77, divisional asst. retail mdse. info., 1977-78, staff asst. nat. retail promotions, 1978, mktg. staff mdse. adminstrv., 1978-79, buyer gourmet foods, 1979-81, asst. mgr. market devel., 1981—, also dept. reporter hdqrs. newsletter. Vice-pres. membership Santa Clause Anonymous, 1979-80. Mem. Am. Psychol. Assn. Roman Catholic. Office: Sears Tower 40th Floor Chicago IL 60684

FEHER, LESLIE, psychotherapist; b. N.Y.C., Mar. 6, 1944; d. Alexander and Elizabeth F.; B.A., Pace U., 1967; M.A., New Sch. Social Research, N.Y.C., 1970; m. Ralph Ferney, Nov. 3, 1967; 1 dau., Vanessa. Co-dir., Analytic Inst. Motivational Edn., 1968-74; founder, dir. Elizabeth Fehr Natal Therapy Inst., N.Y.C., 1974—; founder, pres., dir. Assn. for Birth Psychology, N.Y.C., 1978—; founder, editor Birth Psychology Bull., 1979—. Mem. Am. Psychol. Assn., Women in Sci., Assn. Poetry Therapy, Assn. Birth Psychology, Am. Personnel And Guidance Assn. Author: The Psychology of Birth: The Foundation of Human Personality, 1980. Home: 444 E 82d St New York NY 10028

FEHRENBACH, ALICE R. O'SULLIVAN, psychologist; b. Denver, Nov. 14, 1910; d. John Alexander and Gertrude (Gaffney) McTammany; A.B., Barnard Coll., 1931; M.A., U. Denver, 1944, Ph.D., 1955; m. Frank O'Sullivan, July 6, 1940 (dec. Feb. 1941); m. 2d, Carl E. Fehrenbach, June 8, 1953 (dec. 1961). Tchr., Denver public schs., 1935-47, psychologist, 1948-68; pvt. practice psychology, Denver, 1948—; prof. psychology Regis Coll., 1968-76, prof. emeritus, 1976—, faculty lectr., 1972, acting dir. counseling service, 1971-73, dir. counseling services, 1974-76; staff Mt. Airy Psychiat. Center, 1976—; vis. lectr. U. Nev., Stanford U.; guest appearances radio, TV series, Denver; mem. Intermountain bd. Am. Bd. Profl. Psychology, 1978—; mem. Colo. Bd. Psychologist Examiners. Bd. dirs. Camp Fire Girls, 1949-55. Recipient Alumnae Recognition award Barnard Coll., 1975; Dir.'s award Regis Coll., 1975; Outstanding Social Action award Colo. Mental Health Assn., 1975. Diplomate in sch. psychology Am. Bd. Profl. Psychologists. Fellow Am. Psychol. Assn.; mem. Colo. Psychol. Assn. (dir.; pres. 1973-74; Disting. Service award 1969), Rocky Mountain Psychol. Assn. (exec. bd.), English-Speaking Union, Assn. Specialized Services (pres. 1953-54), Denver Mental Health Assn. (profl. adv. bd.), Columbia U. Women's Club Colo. (founder 1948, pres. 1948-50), Denver Women's Press Club, Women's Forum Colo., Delta Kappa Gamma. Author personality test; contbr. articles to profl. jours. Office: 3232 S Josephine St Denver CO 80210

FEIG, BARBARA KRANE, author; b. Mitchell, S.D., Nov. 8, 1937; d. Peter Abraham and Sally (Gorchow) Krane; student Washington U., 1955-58; B.Edn., Nat. Coll. Edn., 1960; postgrad. Northeastern U.; m. Jerome Feig, June 8, 1963; children—Patricia Lynn, Lizabeth Ann. Tchr., Ridge Sch., Elk Grove Village, Ill., 1960-63, Cleveland Sch., Skokie, Ill., 1963-66, Anshe Emet Day Sch., Chgo., 1966-68, now at Anshe Emet and Sacred Heart schs.; author: Now You're Cooking, A Guide to Cooking for Boys and Girls, 1975; The Parents' Guide to Weight Control for Children, 1980; dir. Media Merchandising, Inc., Barclee Cosmetics, Inc., J.B. Pal & Co., Inc. Trustee Chgo. Inst. Psychoanalysis; bd. dirs. Juvenile Diabetes Found.; mem. women's bd. Francis Parker Sch. Jewish. Address: 904 Castlewood Terr Chicago IL 60640

FEIGEN, BRENDA F., lawyer; b. Chgo., July 7, 1944; d. Arthur Paul Feigen and Shirley (Bierman) Feigen Kadison; B.A. cum laude in Math., Vassar Coll., 1966; J.D., Harvard U., 1969; m. Marc S. Fasteau, Dec. 21, 1968; 1 dau., Alexis Feigen-Fasteau. Admitted to Mass. bar, 1970, N.Y. bar, 1971; chief analyst Boston Redevel. Authority, 1969; asso. firm Rosenman, Colin, Kaye, Petschek, Freund & Emil, N.Y.C., 1970; coordinating dir. Women's Action Alliance, N.Y.C., 1970-72; dir. nat. women's rights project ACLU, N.Y.C., 1972-74; partner firm Fasteau and Feigen, N.Y.C., 1974-80; asso. firm Hess, Segall, Guterman, Pelz & Steiner, N.Y.C., 1980-81; agt., atty. William Morris Agy., N.Y.C., 1982—; adj. instr. law Coll. of New Rochelle, 1976. Hon. pres.'s fellow Columbia U., 1977-78, also mem. program social sci. research on sex roles and social change; participant Exec. Seminar, Aspen Inst., 1979. Adv. bd. Working Women United; candidate for N.Y. State Senate, 1978. Mem. NOW (nat. legis. v.p. 1970-71), ACLU (equality com.), Assn. Bar City N.Y. (jud. observation com.), Women's Action Alliance (co-founder, dir.), Nat., Manhattan (nat. adv. com.) women's polit. caucuses. Democrat. Contbr. articles to mags., chpt. to book. Address: 944 Park Ave New York NY 10028

FEIGIN, BARBARA SOMMER, advt. exec.; b. Berlin, Nov. 16, 1937; came to U.S., 1940, naturalized, 1949; d. Eric Daniel and Charlotte Martha (Demmer) S.; B.A., Whitman Coll., Walla Walla, Wash., 1959; cert. bus. adminstrn. Harvard U.-Radcliffe Coll., 1960; m. James Feigin, Sept. 17, 1961; children—Michael, Peter, Daniel. Mktg. research asst. Richardson-Merrell Co., 1960-61; market research analyst SCM Corp., 1961-62; group research supr. Benton & Bowles, Inc., 1962-68; asso. research dir. Marplan Research Co., 1968-69; sr. v.p., dir. mktg. and research Grey Advt., N.Y.C., 1969—. Bd. overseers Whitman Coll. Mem. Advt. Research Found., Am. Mktg. Assn., Copy Research Council, Agy. Research Dirs. Council. Contbr. articles to profl. jours. Office: 777 3d Ave New York NY 10017

FEIL, NAOMI WEIL, script writer, gerontologist; b. Munich, Germany, July 22, 1932; came to U.S., 1937, naturalized, 1944; d. Julius and Helen (Kahn) Weil; student Oberlin Coll., 1950-51, Western Res. U., 1950-51, Columbia U., 1951-54; B.S. cum laude, Columbia U., 1954, M.S.W., 1956; m. Edward Feil, Dec. 29, 1963; children by previous marriage—Victoria, Beth; children—Edward G., Kenneth J. Dir. group work William Hodson Center, 1960-62, Bird S. Coler Hosp., Welfare Island, N.Y., 1962-63, Montefiore Home for Aged, 1963-80; script writer, actress documentary films Edward Feil Prodns., 1963—; cons. Case Western Res. U., also adj. field instr.; workshop leader; group worker, cons. Amasa Stone; writer books on gerontology, documentary films; films awarded internat. awards include: Where Life Still Means Living, 1965; The Inner World of Aphasia, 1967; Looking for Yesterday: 100 Years to Live, 1981; contbr. articles to Gerontology, Humanistic Jour., Pilgrimmage. Recipient award for human relations in pub. service, Cleve., 1974, Cine award for documentary films, 1965, 68. Mem. Nat. Assn. Social Workers, Transpersonal Psychology Assn., Humanistic Psychology Assn., Univ. Film Assn., Gerontology Assn. Democrat. Jewish. Home: 21987 Byron Rd Cleveland OH 44122 Office: 4614 Prospect Ave Cleveland OH 44103

FEILD, RACHEL NANNEY, printing co. exec.; b. Spindale, N.C., Nov. 11, 1927; d. Roy and Cora Lillian (Beam) Nanney; B.S., Queens Coll., Charlotte, N.C., 1947; m. George Feild, Jr., May 26, 1951 (div. 1957); children—John Anthony, Kathryn Elizabeth. With Aerospace Industries Assn. Am., Inc., Washington, 1956-69, com. exec. procurement and finance, 1961-69; part-owner, sec.-treas. Taylor Printing Co., Inc., Hyattsville, Md., 1969—. Mem. Nat. Assn. Female Execs. Episcopalian. Office: 5206 46th Ave Hyattsville MD 20772

FEIN, LEAH GOLD (MRS. ALFRED G. FEIN), psychologist; b. Minsk, Russia; d. Jacob Lyon and Sarah Freda (Meltzer) Gold; B.S., Albertus Magnus Coll., 1939; M.A., Yale U., 1942, Ph.D. (Marion Talbot fellow), 1944; m. Alfred Gustave Fein, June 10, 1944; 1 son, Ira Hirsh. Health educator New Haven Schs., 1930-43; instr. psychology Carleton Coll., 1944-45; research asso. Conn. Interracial Commn., 1946; chief psychologist Seattle Psychiat. Clinic, 1947-48; prof. U. Bridgeport, 1946-47, 52-58; ind. clin. practice, specializing in clin., child consultation, Seattle, 1948-52, Stamford, Conn., 1952-64, N.Y.C., 1967-81, West Palm Beach, Fla., 1982—; clin. cons. Conn. Commn. on Alcoholism Clinic, 1952-60; research asso. Soc. for Investigation Human Ecology; therapist Norwalk Psychiat. Clinic, 1952-64; cons. Child Edn. Found., 1953-56; dir. research Sch. Nursing Norwalk Hosp., 1961-64; dir. clin. services cerebral palsy and mental retardation, Waterbury, Conn., 1964-65; asso. prof. Quinnipiac Coll., Hamden, Conn., 1965-66; cons., instr., med. staff N.Y. Hosp.-Cornell Med. Center, White Plains, 1966-67; dir. psychology Psychiat. Treatment Center, N.Y., 1967-68; research asso. Roosevelt Hosp. Child Psychiatry, 1968-69; supr., cons. research psychologist Bur. Child Guidance, N.Y.C. Board Edn., 1969-72; faculty Greenwich Inst. Psychoanalytic Studies, 1971-79; sr. research scientist Postgrad. Center for Mental Health, N.Y.C., 1980-82; mem. program com. Internat. Congress Social Psychiatry, 1974; research cons. N.Y.C. Mayor's Vol. Action Com., Human Resources Adminstrn., N.Y.C. Study of Delinquency and Study Abused and Neglected Children; cons., inservice trainer Center Group Counseling, Boca Raton, Fla., 1982—; manuscript reviewer Perceptual Motor Skills, Profl. Psychology. Diplomate clin. psychology Am. Bd. Profl. Psychology. Fellow Soc. Personality Assessment, Am. Psychol. Assn., Am. Acad. Psychotherapists, Internat. Council Psychologists (v.p. 1961-62, 71-73, pres. 1973-75), Am. Orthopsychiat. Assn., N.Y. Acad. Sci.; mem. Nat. Assn. Gifted (v.p. 1961-62), Internat. Council Women Psychologists (chmn. profl. relations among psychologists), Psychologists in Pvt. Practice (treas. 1972-78), Am. Psychol. Assn. (sec. div. psychotherapy 1966-69; council of reps.), N.Y. State, Fla., psychol. assns., Am. Assn. Group Psychotherapy and Psychodrama (council 1973-75), World Fedn. Mental Health, Nat. Council Jewish Women, Hadassah. Club: Yale (N.Y.C.). Author: The Three Dimensional Personality Test—Reliability, Validity and Clinical Implications, 1960; The Changing School Scene: Challenge to Psychology, 1974; editor Jour. Internat. Understanding, vol. 9-10, 1974; Jour. Psychology Div. Am. Friends Hebrew U.; guest editor Jour. Clin. Child Psychology, 1975; cons. editor Jour. Psychotherapy in Pvt. Practice; others; contbr. Jour. Clin. Psychology, other profl. jours. Address: 213 29th St West Palm Beach FL 33407

FEIN, SYLVIA, author, painter; b. Milw., Nov. 20, 1919; d. Alfred E. and Elizabeth (Routt) F.; B.S., U. Wis., Madison, 1942; M.A., U. Calif., Berkeley, 1951; m. William K. Scheuber, May 30, 1942; 1 dau., Heidi. One-woman exhbns. include: U. Wis. Meml. Union Gallery, 1942, Milw. Art Inst., 1942, Perls Galleries, N.Y.C., 1946, Feingarten Galleries, San Francisco, 1957, 59, Carmel, Calif., 1959, N.Y.C., 1961, Sagittarius Gallery, N.Y.C., 1958, St. Mary's Coll., Moraga, Calif., 1960, Kunstkabinett, Frankfurt, W.Ger., 1960, Mills Coll. Art Gallery, Oakland, Calif., 1962, Ruthermore Galleries, Oakland, 1962, Maxwell Galleries, San Francisco, 1963, Nicole of Berkeley (Calif.), 1965, Bresler Galleries, Milw., 1966, Oshkosh (Wis.) Pub. Mus., 1967; numerous group exhbns., 1941—, latest being 5th Winter invitational Calif. Palace Legion of Honor, 1964, Art of Landscape, San Francisco Art Inst. travelling exhibit, 1964-65, Three Painters, St. Mary's Coll., 1964, Magic and Fantastic Art, Walnut Creek (Calif.) Library, 1968; author: Heidi's Horse, 1976; owner, pub. Exelrod Press, 1975—; chmn. Archtl. Rev. Comm., Pleasant Hill, Calif., 1975. Recipient Elizabeth Water's Purchase prize U. Wis., 1941, John Steuart Curry award, 1942; Joseph E. Davies Purchase award Wis. Salon Art, 1941, Wis. Union Purchase prize, 1942. Home: 341 Strand Ave Pleasant Hill CA 94523 Office: PO Box 2303 Pleasant Hill CA 94523

FEINBERG, GLORIA GRANDITER, psychologist; b. N.Y.C., Dec. 18, 1923; d. David and Ray (Davis) Granditer; A.B., U. Pa., 1944; M.A., N.Y. U., 1947; m. Mortimer R. Feinberg, June 22, 1947; children—Stuart Andrew, Todd E. Asst. psychologist Grasslands Hosp., Valhalla, N.Y., 1948-51; cons. BFS Psychol. Assos., N.Y.C., 1960-77, pres., 1977—. Certified Psychologist, N.Y. Mem. Am. Psychol. Assn., Phi Beta Kappa, Pi Gamma Mu. Author: Leavetaking, 1978. Home: 34 Brook Ln Peekskill NY 10566 Office: 666 5th Ave New York NY 10103

FEINBERG, MILDRED, artist, ret. advt. exec.; b. N.Y.C.; d. Joseph and Bessie (Atkin) Feinberg; student Parson's Sch. Design, 1917; grad. Pratt Inst. Fine Arts, 1920; pupil George E. Brown, Joseph Newman, Alex Rodein, Umberto Romano, others; m. Samuel Blumgarten, Dec. 18, 1938 (div. 1941). Partner with twin sister of Twins Advt. Art Service, N.Y.C., 1923-65; illus. children's books, also fashions, 1923-65; exhbns. with sister Town House Gallery, Woodstock, N.Y., 1952, Charles Barzansky Galleries, N.Y.C., 1957; group exhbns. Ward Eggleston Galleries, 1953-55, anns. Nat. Assn. Women Artists, 1957—, Tokyo Municipal Art Mus., 1960, Riverside Mus., N.Y.C., 1960, Royal Acad. Galleries, Edinburgh, Scotland, 1963, Royal Soc., Birmingham, Eng., 1964, Nat. Acad. Design anns., 1963, Allied Artists anns., 1961-63; paintings exhibited Lever House, N.Y.C., 1965-68, 72, Palazzo Vecchio, Florence, Italy, 1972, Salvator Rosa Pub. Garden, Naples, Italy, 1972; represented in permanent collections Rose Art Mus., Brandeis U., Norfolk (Va.) Mus. Arts and Scis., Evansville (Ind.) Mus. Arts and Scis. Recipient medal honor for painting Nat. Arts Club, 1968; Woman art award honorable mention, 1978, 79; Ziuta and Joseph James Akston Found. prize for painting of Whitney Mus., 1979. Mem. Nat. Assn. Women Artists (Lillian Cotton Meml. prize 1965), Artists Equity Assn. N.Y., Woodstock Artists Assn. Address: 239 E 79th St New York NY 10021

FEINBERG-FOX, FELISE NAN, social worker; b. N.Y.C., Oct. 24, 1952; d. Jerome and Dorothy Inez (Lunine) Feinberg; B.A., George Washington U., 1974; M.S.W., Adelphi U., 1976, post-master's degree in Gerontol. Practice, 1979; m. Jeffrey William Fox, Dec. 3, 1978. Caseworker, group worker L.I.-Jewish Hillside Med. Center, New Hyde Park, N.Y., 1975-76; outreach social worker community sr. center Central Queens YM & YWHA, Forest Hills, 1976; acting dir. social work with Holocaust clients Margaret Tietz Center for Nursing Care, Jamaica, N.Y., 1976—. Mem. Acad. Cert. Social Workers, Nat. Assn. Social Workers. Jewish. Office: 164-11 Chapin Pkwy Jamaica NY 11432

FEINSTEIN, BARBARA BAROFF, social worker; b. New Brunswick, N.J., Mar. 3, 1940; d. Louis and Frieda Lee (Berlant) Baroff; B.A., Duke U., 1961; M.S.W. with honors (NIH fellow, NIMH grantee), Boston U., 1963; m. Herbert William Feinstein, June 17, children—Lisa Beth, Debra Lyn. Med. social worker New Eng. Med. Center, Boston, 1963-64; dir. case-aide unit Mass. Dept. Mental Health, Waltham, 1966-73; program dir. Title 1, Mass. Dept. Edn., Watertown, 1974-75; asst. prof., clin. supr. Boston Coll. Sch. Social Work, 1975-77; adj. faculty R.I. Coll. Social Work, 1981—; exec. dir., owner People to People Assos., human services agy., Waltham, 1977—; trainer Nat. Center Alcohol Edn., Mass. Criminal Justice Tng. Council, Am. Soc. Tng. and Devel.; mem. Mystic Valley Mental Health and Retardation Area Bd., 1975-78; mem. program com. New Eng. Women Bus. Owners, 1980—. Grantee Nat. Inst. Alcohol and Alcohol Abuse, 1975-77. Mem. Assn. Labor-Mgmt. Cons. and Adminstrns. Alcoholism (exec. bd. Mass. chpt. 1978-80), Nat. Assn. Social Workers, Am. Soc. Tng. and Devel., Nat. Council Alcoholism, Mass. Assn. Mental Health, LWV, Boston C. of C. Democrat. Jewish. Author: The New Volunteerism: A Community Connection, 1978; The New Partnership: Human Services, Business and Industry, 1981. Home: 5 Young St Lexington MA 02173 Office: 181 West St Suite 16 Waltham MA 02154

FEINSTEIN, DIANNE, mayor San Francisco; b. San Francisco, June 22, 1933; d. Leon and Betty (Rosenburg) Goldman; B.S., Stanford U., 1955; D.Public Adminstrn. (hon.), U. Manila, 1981; H.H.D. (hon.), Philippine Women's U., 1981; m. Bertram Feinstein, Nov. 11, 1962; 1 dau., Katherine Anne; m. 2d, Richard Blum, Jan. 20, 1980. Intern public affairs Coro Found., San Francisco, 1955-56; asst. to Calif. Indsl. Welfare Commn., Los Angeles, also San Francisco, 1956-57; vice-chmn. Calif. Women's Bd. Terms and Parole, Los Angeles, also San Francisco, 1962-66; chmn. San Francisco City and County Adv. Com. for Adult Detention, also mem. Mayor's Com. on Crime, 1968-69; mem. Bd. Suprs. City and County of San Francisco, 1970-73, 74-77, 78, pres. bd., 1970-71, 74-75, 78; mayor of San Francisco, 1978—; mem. exec. com., del. gen. assembly Assn. Bay Area Govts., 1970-74, 76-78, chmn. Environ. Mgmt. Task Force, 1976-78; bd. govs. Bay Area Council, 1972-73; mem. Bay Conservation and Devel. Commn., 1973-78. Chmn. bd. regents Lone Mountain Coll., 1972-75. Recipient Women Achievement award Bus. and Profl. Women's Clubs San Francisco, 1970, Distinguished Woman award San Francisco Examiner, 1970; CORO award, 1979; SCOPUS award, 1981. Mem. Multi-Culture Inst. (dir.), Calif. Tomorrow, Bay Area Urban League, Planning and Conservation League, Friends of Earth, Chinese Culture Found., Sierra Club. Clubs: Propeller, Commonwealth. Home: 2030 Lyon St San Francisco CA 94115 Office: City Hall San Francisco CA 94102

FEIR, DOROTHY JEAN, entomologist; b. St. Louis, Jan. 29, 1929; d. Alex R. and Lillian (Smith) F.; B.S., U. Mich., 1950; M.S., U. Wyo., 1956; Ph.D., U. Wis., 1960. Instr. biology U. Buffalo, 1960-61; mem. faculty St. Louis U., 1961—, prof. biology, 1967—; mem. tropical medicine and parasitology study sect. NIH, 1980—. Mem. Emtomol. Soc. Am., AAAS, Am. Physiol. Soc., N.Y. Acad. Sci., Mo. Acad. Sci., Sigma Xi. Editor Environ. Entomology, 1977—. Office: Biology Dept St Louis U Saint Louis MO 63103

FEIST, BERNADETTE, air force officer; b. Linton, N.D., Sept. 28, 1945; d. John K. and Cecilia (Nagel) F.; B.S. in Dietetics, U. N.D., Grand Forks, 1967; M.S. in Edn., Troy (Ala.) State U., 1973; Ed.D. candidate U. So. Calif. Commd. officer USAF, 1971, advanced through grades to maj.; chief clin. dietetics and clin. dietitian Andrews AFB, D.C., 1976—; speaker, lectr.; instr. USAF dietetic internship. Mgr. coffee house Unitarian Ch., 1972-74; mem. Alexandria Little Theatre, 1977-78. Decorated Air Force Commendation medal. Mem. Soc. Internat. Edn., Tng. and Research, Am. Dietetic Assn., Internat. Food Service Execs. Assn., VFW, Assn. Mil. Surgeons U.S., Exec. Female, Air Force Assn., Soc. Nutrition Edn., Dietitians in Bus. and Industry, Am. Soc. Profl. and Exec. Women. Roman Catholic. Clubs: Woodlawn Country, Andrews Officers. Home: 2000 Huntington Ave Apt 1425 Alexandria VA 22303

FELCHLIN, MARY KATHLEEN CONROY, financial exec.; b. Cleve., Feb. 16, 1951; d. Ernest J. and Margaret Jane Conroy; B.A., U. Calif., Berkeley, 1973; M.B.A., U. So. Calif., 1977. Adminstrv. asst. Mason McDuffie Investment Co., Berkeley, 1974-75; mortage mktg. staff Gibraltar Savs. & Loan, Beverly Hills, summer 1976; account officer Wells Fargo Bank, Los Angeles, 1977-79; sr. account officer Citicorp Real Estate, Inc., Los Angeles, 1979-80, asst. v.p., 1981-82, v.p., 1982—. Wittenberg fellow, 1975-76; Commerce Assos. fellow, 1976-77. Mem. Am. Mgmt. Assn. Home: 8960 Wonderland Ave Los Angeles CA 90046 Office: 444 S Flower St Los Angeles CA 90071

FELDER-HOEHNE, FELICIA VAUGHAN, librarian; b. Knoxville, Tenn.; d. Geraldine C. Harris-Ivey; B.S., Knoxville Coll., 1960; M.S.L.S., Atlanta U., 1966; postgrad. U. Tenn., 1972-81; m. Paul A. Hoehne, Jan. 2, 1979. Sec., SCLC, Atlanta, 1958-59; tchr. J.L. Cook High Sch., Athens, Tenn., 1960-61; receptionist Office of Pres., Knoxville Coll., 1961-63, asst. to dir. pub. relations, 1963-65, head circulation dept., 1966-69; asso. prof., reference librarian U. Tenn., Knoxville, 1969—; del. Tenn. Conf. Libraries and Info. Services, 1978. Sec. Knoxville-Knox County Library Bd. Trustees, 1971-77; bd. dirs. Knoxville Roundtable of NCCJ, 1971—, chmn. Brotherhood Week Commn., 1979-82; mem. Knoxville Nativity Pageant Choir, 1975—; mem. Knoxville Black Ofcls. Coalition, 1976-79; mem. Interdenominational Concert Choir, 1970—; pres. Spring Place Community Club, 1980—. Recipient Religious Service award NCCJ, 1976; cert. for outstanding contbns. to library and info. sci. and edn. Jack and Jill of Am., Inc., 1976; cert. of appreciation Sta. WJBE, 1978; cited by Chancellor of U. Tenn. for Extraordinary Community Service, 1978; Citizen of Yr. award Order Eastern Star, Prince Hall Masons, 1979. Mem. Southeastern Library Assn., Tenn. Library Assn. (pub. relations com., honors and awards com.), East Tenn. Library Assn. (nominations com.), NAACP, Knoxville Coll. Alumni Assn., Alpha Kappa Alpha. Baptist. Author: A Subject Guide to Basic Reference Books in Black Studies, 1977. Home: 5413 Spring Place Circle NE Knoxville TN 37914 Office: University of Tennessee 1015 Volunteer Blvd Knoxville TN 37996

FELDHAMER, THELMA LEE, architect; b. Bklyn., May 10, 1925; d. Frank and Anna Pearl (Shapiro) Sitzer; student Cooper Union, 1942-46, B.Arch. (hon.); student Bklyn. Coll., 1942; m. Carl Feldhamer, Aug. 27, 1950; children—Randi Judith Feldhamer Wathen, Mark David. Archtl. draftsman-designer Caleb Hornbostel, N.Y.C., 1946-47, John F. Milan, Denver, 1963-65, Lultcho Boduroff, Denver, 1965-66, Gerri Von Frellick, Denver, 1966-68; asso. architect Joseph E. MacMillan, Denver, 1968-81; prin. Feldhamer & Assos., P.C., Inc., Denver, 1981—. Democratic precinct committeewoman Dist. 13, 1977-78; 1st lt., personnel officer 76th sr. squadron CAP, Colo. Mem. AIA, Women in Architecture (co-founder), Bus. and Profl. Women's Club Denver (pres. 1974-76). Democrat. Clubs: Altrusa, Hadassah, Pres.'s Council Denver. Architect: Pine Haven Nursing Home, Morrison, Colo., Harris Gardens I and II office bldgs., Denver, Linden Lea House Devel., Denver, The Reserve, Green Oaks, Cherry Hills. Home: 748 Ivy St Denver CO 80220 Office: Feldhamer & Assos 1471 S Holly St Denver CO 80222

FELDHAUS, MARY ANN CATHERINE, printing products co. exec.; b. St. Louis, Mar. 9, 1951; d. Darvin Lambert and Lucille Edna (Berghold) F.; B.S. summa cum laude in Mktg., St. Joseph's Coll., 1973; M.B.A., U. Pa., 1976. Procurement systems support analyst Re-entry and Environ. Systems div. Gen. Elec. Co., Phila., 1973-75; mktg. ops. analyst 3M Corp. Mktg. Analysis & Systems, St. Paul, 1976-78, mktg. planning supr. Printing Products div., 1978-81, mktg. services supr., 1981, mktg. services mgr., 1981—; tchr. Bus. and Econ. Edn. Found. Mem. exec. com. Careers Workshop Greater Mpls. council Girl Scouts U.S.A., 1980; vol. Ind.-Republican City Alderman campaign, 1979, mem. steering com. Mpls. Ind. Rep. City Alderman campaign, 1981, precinct chairwoman, 1982-83. Mem. Am. Mgmt. Assn. Club: Wharton Alumni of Minn. (dir.). Home: 408 Sheridan Ave S Minneapolis MN 55405 Office: 3M Co 3M Center Bldg 223-2N Saint Paul MN 55144

FELDMAN, BETTY SANDLER, real estate broker; b. Balt., Sept. 14, 1908; d. Abraham and Rebecca (Rosen) Sandler; B.A., George Washington U., 1930; grad. Dale Carnegie Inst. Human Relations, 1939; L.H.D. (hon.), Life Bible Crusade Coll., 1978; m. Samuel Feldman, Jan. 28, 1943 (dec.). Civil service employee, 1927-44; agt. Met. Life Ins. Co., Balt., 1944-45, Travelers Ins. Co., Balt., 1945-50; owner, operator Lady Lynn Shop, Arbutus, Md., 1950-58; real estate broker, Betty S. Feldman, Balt., 1958—; pres. Hope Enterprises, Balt., 1965—. Bd. dirs. Boys Homes of Md., Safety First Club, Md. Nursing Home Advocacy; bd. govs. Israel Bonds. Recipient James Swartz medallion, WBAL Radio Brotherhood award, 1972. Mem. Internat. Platform Assn., Broadcast Music Inc., Real Estate Bd. Greater Balt., Clowns of Am., Am. Jewish Congress (bd., charter and life mem.), Md. C. of C. (past pres.), Women's Internat. League for Peace and Freedom, Am. Legion Aux., U.S. China Friendship Assn. Baha'i Faith. Clubs: Variety, Order of Eastern Star.

FELDMAN, JANET MOSHINSKY, speech pathologist; b. Phila., Apr. 11, 1951; d. Samuel and Tybie (Marder) Moshinsky; B.A. in Speech Edn., U. Md., 1972; M.S. in Speech Pathology/Audiology, Loyola Coll., Balt., 1975; m. Stephen Marc Feldman, Sept. 3, 1972. Speech pathologist Carroll County (Md.) Bd. Edn., 1975; coordinator speech and hearing services Program Aux. Services for Students, Phila., 1976-78; chief speech and hearing therapist Woods Schs., Langhorne, Pa., 1978—; instr. sign lang., cons. in field. Mem. Am. Speech, Lang. and Hearing Assn. (cert.), Pa. Speech and Hearing Assn. Home: 366 Penncrest Dr Langhorne PA 19047 Office: Woods Schs Langhorne PA 19047

FELDMAN, JOANNE MARIE ZAGST, violinist; b. Shreveport, La., Feb. 26, 1934; d. Thomas Andrew and Margaret Edna (Nagle) Zagst; B.S., Juilliard Sch. Music, 1957, M.S., 1958; m. Leonard Feldman, Sept. 1, 1958; children—William, Sylvia, Stephen. Mem. violin faculty Bronx (N.Y.) House Music Sch., 1956-58; mem. 1st violin sect. Rochester (N.Y.) Philharm. Orch., 1958-59; mem. Dayton (Ohio) Philharm. Orch., also mem. music faculty Wilmington (Ohio) Coll., 1959-62; mem. Alard String Quartet, 1959—; mem. music faculty U. Canterbury, Christchurch, N.Z., 1962, 63, 81, 82, Pa. State U., 1964—; summer resident SUNY, Potsdam, 1961, 62. Mem. Chamber Music Am., Am. Fedn. Musicians. Office: 105 Music Bldg University Park PA 16802

FELDMAN, JUDITH ELLEN, banker; b. N.Y.C., Apr. 7, 1945; d. Carl Benjamin and Florence Siskind; B.A., Vassar Coll., 1966; M.S., Stevens Inst. Tech., 1969; m. Melvyn J. Feldman, Aug. 18, 1968. Mem. tech. staff Bell Telephone Labs., Holmdel, N.J., 1966-69; with Morgan Guaranty Trust Co. N.Y., N.Y.C., 1969—, now v.p. fin. analysis. Pres. 353 W. 29th St. Housing Corp., 1982—; mem. nat. devel. council Stevens Inst. Tech. Office: 23 Wall St New York NY 10015

FELDMAN, LILLIAN MALTZ, ednl. adminstr.; B.A. in Zoology, Geo. Washington U., 1937, M.A. in Ednl. Psychology, 1939; C.A.S. in Early Childhood Edn., Syracuse (N.Y.) U., 1977; married; 4 children. Tchr. pre-kindergarten pvt. sch., Cin., 1947-49; tchr. kindergarten Syracuse Sch. Dist., 1959-65, supr. early childhood edn., 1968—. Bd. dirs. Consortium Children's Service, 1973—, S.W. Area Day Care Center, 1972—. Cert. in adminstrn., N.Y.; named Woman of Achievement in Edn., Syracuse Post Standard, 1969. Mem. Nat. Assn. Edn. Young Children, Day Care, Child Devel. Council Am., N.Y. Council Jewish Women (Hannah B. Solomon award 1978), Sch. Adminstrs. Assn. N.Y. State, Delta Kappa Gamma. Home: 704 Crawford Ave Syracuse NY 13224 Office: Pre-Kindergarten Program 401 E Castle St Syracuse NY 13205

FELDMAN, LONA L., lawyer; b. Phila., Nov. 15, 1949; d. Myer and Beatrice (Konesky) F.; B.A., U. Pa., 1970; J.D., Boston Coll., 1974; m. Michael A. Mates, May 28, 1972. Admitted to Mass. bar, 1974, D.C. bar, 1975; with Office of Exceptions and Appeals, FEA, 1974-77; atty. interpretations and rulings div. Office Gen. Counsel, Dept. Energy, 1977-78, dep. asst. gen. counsel for enforcement, 1978-80, asst. gen. counsel interpretations and rulings, 1980-82, asst. gen. counsel conservation and renewable energy, 1982—. Mem. Women's Legal Def. Fund, Am. Bar Assn., D.C. Bar Assn., Mass. Bar Assn. Office: Forrestal Bldg 6B144 1000 Independence Ave SW Washington DC 20585

FELDMAN, MARY HELEN KEARNEY, librarian; b. Sapulpa, Okla., July 21, 1920; d. Fabian Earl and Doris Earl (Nave) Kearney; A.A., Monte Cassino Jr. Coll., 1939; student Cin. Conservatory Music, 1939-41; B.S. in Edn., U. Md., 1963; M.L.S., Cath. U. Am., 1965, postgrad. cert. in library sci., 1975; m. Leon Feldman, Aug. 29, 1945 (div. Mar. 1967); children—Jo Kathleen, Michael John, Judith Ellen, Stephen Robert. Tchr., Montgomery County Public Schs., Silver Spring, Md., 1963; cataloger U.S. Book Exchange, Washington, 1964; indexer New Cath. Ency., Washington, 1964-66; head tech. services Trinity Coll. Library, Washington, 1965-72; research asst. library sci. dept. Cath. U. Am., Washington, 1966-71; reference librarian Georgetown U. library, Washington, 1970-72; cataloger Dept. Transp., Washington, 1972-73, chief cataloging sect., 1973-79, chief Hdqrs. Service Br., 1979-82; info. dir. Clearinghouse on Family Policy, Clearinghouse on Families and Religion/Family Ministries, Nat. Center for Family Studies, Cath. U. Am., Washington, 1982—, instr. dept. library sci., 1978—, coordinator home study div., 1980—. Vice chmn. Democratic precinct, Montgomery County, 1962-64, chmn., 1958-61. Mem. Cath. (chmn. legislative com. 1969-72), Am. (chmn. memberships D.C. chpt. 1968-72), D.C. (sec. 1969-71) library assns., Spl. Libraries Assn. (sec.-treas. transp. div. D.C. chpt. 1973-74, pres. 1974-75, sec. documentation group D.C. chpt. 1975-77, chpt. corr. sec. 1977-78), Potomac Tech. Processing Librarians (sec. 1979-81), Am. Soc. Indexers (pres. Washington chpt. 1982-83), Phi Kappa Phi, Beta Phi Mu (pres. Iota chpt. 1973-74). Editor: Inter-Com, 1971—, CLENExchange, 1975-79; Alumni Forum, Cath. U. Am., 1973—. Home: 7117 Poplar Ave Takoma Park MD 20912 Office: St John's Hall Cath U Am Washington DC 20064

FELDMANN, SHIRLEY CLARK, educator; b. Niagara Falls, N.Y.; d. Franklin T. and Mildred L. (Payne) Clark; B.A., Barnard Coll., 1951, M.A., Columbia U., 1952; Ph.D., 1961; m. Robert Feldmann, June 1952 (dec.); m. 2d Horace S. Bush. Asst. prof. edn. SUNY, Fredonia, 1958-60; asst. research prof. psychiatry N.Y. Med. Coll., N.Y.C., 1960-63; prof. Sch. Edn., City Coll., City U. N.Y., N.Y.C., 1963—, prof., exec. officer Ph.D. program in ednl. psychology Grad. Sch., 1976—. Mem. Am. Psychol. Assn., Internat. Reading Assn., Am. Ednl. Research Assn., Soc. for Research in Child Devel. Contbr. articles to profl. jours. Home: 600 West End Ave New York NY 10024 Office: Grad Sch City U NY 33 W 42d St New York NY 10036

FELDSINE, FRANCES TERESA, nursing adminstr.; b. Schenectady, N.Y., Nov. 3, 1935; d. William and Mildred (Kellogg) Haley; diploma nursing St. Mary's Hosp., N.Y., 1956; B.S. in Nursing, Adelphi U., 1967; M.S. in Nursing, Case Western Res. U., 1969; m. John Feldsine, June 3, 1972; 1 dau., Deborah. Staff nurse VA Hosp., Albany, N.Y., 1956-57; asst. head nurse Meml. Hosp., Albany, 1957-59; supr. med.-surg. Mercy Hosp., Rockville Center, N.Y., 1962-67, dir. nursing, 1969-71; coordinator inservice dept. Berkshire Med. Center, Pittsfield, Mass., 1972; dir. nursing United Health Services, Binghamton (N.Y.) Gen. Hosp., 1972, v.p., 1981—; mem. N.Y. State Bd. Nursing, 1981—. Cert. advanced nursing adminstrn. Am. Nurses Assn., 1980. Mem. Am. Nurses Assn., N.Y. State Nurses Assn. (pres. dist. 5 1980—, chmn. edn. com. 1974-79),

Am. Hosp. Assn., Central N.Y. Hosp. Assn., Am. Cancer Soc. (adv. com.), Am. Heart Assn. (public health edn. com. 1980—, research com., program com.), Community Coalition Health Personnel Edn., Am. Soc. Nursing Service Adminstrs., Broome County C. of C. (edn. com.), Sigma Theta Tau (chpt. pres.). Roman Catholic. Home: One Crestmont Rd Binghamton NY 13905 Office: Binghamton General Hosp Mitchell Ave Binghamton NY 13903

FELIX, GERTRUDE ELAINE, civic worker, former YWCA exec.; b. Flandreau, S.D., Oct. 9, 1927; d. Isaac Ernest and Elsie Luella (Lyng) Locke; B.S., S.D. State U., 1949; m. Paul N. Felix, Sept. 1, 1950; children—Richard, David, Stanford, Bruce, Anthony, Kathryn. Medical sec., 1951, 56, 57-59; tchr., 1962-71; coordinator Greater Huron (S.D.) Area Athletic Club, 1972-73; exec. dir. Huron YWCA, 1973-80. Pres. Hayward Sch. PTA, Sioux Falls, S.D.; bd. dirs. Community Support Center, Huron, United Way of Huron. Mem. PEO. Mem. United Ch. Christ. Club: Order Eastern Star.

FELIX, MAUREEN ALICE, speech pathologist; b. N.Y.C., June 20, 1944; d. Kenneth and Ida Kopelson; A.B., Brandeis U., 1965; M.A., Brown U., 1967; M.S., William Paterson Coll., 1978; m. Arthur M. Felix, Oct. 28, 1967; children—Alison, Stephan. Mem. research dept. Radio Liberty Com., N.Y.C., 1966-67; tchr. Russian Summit (N.J.) High Sch., 1968-70; instr. Russian, West Caldwell (N.J.) Continuing Edn. Center, 1972—; speech pathologist Preakness Hosp., Wayne, N.J., 1978-80, Montville Twp. (N.J.) Public Schs., 1980-81, Caldwell-West Caldwell Public Schs., 1982—. Pres., Washington Home and Sch. Assn., West Caldwell, 1980-82; chmn. internat. affairs com. LWV, 1970. Mem. Am. Speech, Lang. and Hearing Assn., N.J. Speech and Hearing Assn. Home: 257 Central Ave West Caldwell NJ 07006

FELLER, MIMI A., legis. adminstrv. asst.; b. Omaha, Feb. 19, 1948; d. Lloyd L. and Millicent (Wagoun) Feller. B.A. cum laude, Creighton U., 1970; J.D., Georgetown U., 1981. Mgmt. intern, 1970-71; with pub. bldg. service GSA, Washington, 1971-73, senate legis. liaison officer, 1973-77; legis. asst. environ. and pub. works Sen. Chafee, R.I., 1977-79, legis. dir., 1979-80, adminstrv. asst., 1981—. Mem. Gamma Pi Epsilon, Delta Zeta. Roman Catholic. Office: Room 5229 Dirksen Senate Office Bldg Washington DC 20510

FELLS, AUDREY CAROL, med. technologist; b. Seattle, May 29, 1934; d. Glenn Donald and Edna Merle (Hollingsworth) Morgan; B.S. in Med. Tech., U. Wash., Seattle, 1957; M.A., Central Mich. U., 1979; m. Charles Dayton Fells, Sept. 29, 1962; 1 son, Donald Kevin. Med. technologist Gibb Lab., Bellingham, Wash., 1957-58, Everett (Wash.) Clinic, 1958-61, 63-65, Children's Orthopedic Hosp., Seattle, 1962; position control clk. European Exchange System, Stuttgart, W.Ger., 1966, Civilian Personnel Office, Stuttgart, 1966-67; med. technologist Gen. Hosp. Everett, 1968-70, adminstrv. technologist, 1970—; sec. lab. adminstrv. sect. Sci. Assembly N.W., 1982; mem. exam. council Nat. Cert. Agy. Med. Lab. Personnel, 1982. Mem. Am. Soc. Med. Tech., Seattle Soc. Med. Tech. Office: 1321 Colby Ave Everett WA 98201

FELMLEY, JENROSE WELDON, ednl. found. exec.; b. Abbeville, S.C., Oct. 3, 1935; d. William Heathly and Jenrose (Pressly) Weldon; B.A., U. S.C., 1956; postgrad. U. Chgo., 1965, Am. U., 1975-76; M.L.S., U. Md., 1973; m. Jerry John Felmley, Apr. 11, 1958; children—Melissa Scott, Jennifer Weldon, Amy Stephenson. Dir., Media Center, Miami Valley Sch., Dayton, Ohio, 1968-71; research librarian Ford Found. Energy Policy Project, Washington, 1972-74; library dir. Bus. and Profl. Women's Found., Washington, 1974-76; exec. dir. Bus. and Profl. Women's Found., Washington, 1977—; thesaurus cons. Women's History/Resource Data Bank, Am. Revolution Bicentennial Com.; cons. U. Md. Women's Info. Service Project. Fulbright fellow U. Waikato, Hamilton, N.Z., 1980. Mem. ALA (com. on status women), Women and Founds./Corp. Philanthropy (dir. 1979-82). Episcopalian. Mem. adv. bd. Comment, 1980-82. Home: 4509 Lowell St NW Washington DC 20016 Office: 2012 Massachusetts Ave NW Washington DC 20036

FELTNER, PAULA JO, educator; b. Rock Springs, Wyo., Nov. 29, 1946; d. Joseph and Joanne Frances (Marinoff) F.; B.A. in Polit. Sci., U. Wyo., 1969, M.A. (fellow), 1970; postgrad. U. Ky., 1971-75; m. Michael K. Eberle, Sept. 30, 1975. Teaching asst. U. Wyo., Laramie, 1969-70; asst. U. Ky., Lexington, 1970-74; prof. polit. sci. Luther Coll., Decorah, Iowa, 1975—; dir. House Republican Caucus, Iowa Gen. Assembly, Des Moines; public relations cons. firm Michael Goldstein Co., N.Y.C., summers 1968, 69, 73. Mem. Iowa Women's Polit. Caucus, Iowa Women's Polit. Task Force, LWV, NOW, AAUP, AAUW, Sierra Club, Audubon Soc., ACLU, Am., Midwest, So. polit. sci. assns., Iowa Fedn. Rep. Women, Pi Sigma Alpha. Republican. Home: 1212 64th St Des Moines IA 50311 Office: House Rep Caucus Iowa Gen Assembly State Capitol Bldg Des Moines IA 50320

FELTON, JUDITH R. KIRSHENBAUM, psychoanalyst, social worker; b. Phila., Aug. 21, 1942; d. Martin and Laura (Goldman) Kirshenbaum; A.B. in Govt., Wheaton (Mass.) Coll., 1963; M.S.W., Rutgers U., 1966, postgrad., 1974—; grad. N.Y. Center for Psychoanalytic Tng., 1978; m. Stephen Felton, Feb. 8, 1966; 1 dau., Jane Jennifer. Clin. social worker VA, Newark, 1967; psychotherapist Santa Barbara (Calif.) Mental Health Services, 1967-69; supr. Santa Barbara Counselling Center, 1967-69; pvt. practice psychoanalysis, 1969—; psychoanalyst, therapist Fifth Ave. Center for Psychotherapy, N.Y.C., 1969-72; instr. Marymount Manhattan Coll., 1971; psychotherapy supr. clin. faculty, dept. psychiatry Rutgers U. Med. Sch., New Brunswick, N.J., 1972-75, teaching asst. Grad. Sch. Social Work, 1974-76; vis. lectr. Bryn Mawr Coll. Sch. Social Work and Social Research, 1980; mem. faculty N.Y. Center for Psychoanalytic Tng., 1980—. NIMH fellow, 1965; diplomate Am. Bd. Psychotherapy. Fellow N.J. Soc. for Clin. Social Work; mem. Nat. Assn. Social Workers, Conf. Psychoanalytic Psychotherapists, Nat. Assn. for Advancement Psychoanalysis, Groves Conf. on Family, Acad. Cert. Social Workers, Soc. for Psychoanalytic Tng., AAUP. Home and office: 159 Valley Rd Princeton NJ 08540

FENG, LILLIAN WAN-MING LEI, nurse, nursing home adminstr.; b. Canton, China, May 5, 1923; came to U.S., 1968, naturalized, 1973; d. Chin Chang and Sui Ching (Chen) Lei; R.N., Turner Sch. Nursing, Canton, China, 1946; B.S. in Health Care Adminstrn., Central Mich. U., 1976, M.A., 1979; m. Ping Tien Feng, June 3, 1950; children—Paul, Lucy, May, Howard. Asst. head nurse, nursing instr. Turner Nursing Sch. of Hacket Hosp., Canton, China, 1946-47; head nurse, instr. Hoihow (China) Am. Presbyn. Hosp. and Nursing Sch., 1947-50; instr. Tb nursing, head nurse Taiwan Tb Control Center, 1950-56, supr., 1956-66; clin. head nurse U.S. Naval Med. Research Unit No. 2, Taiwan, China, 1966-67; asst. adminstr. Palolo Chinese Care Home, Honolulu, 1968—. U.S.A. Internat. Corp. Adminstrn. grantee, 1958. Mem. Hawaii Nurses Assn., Am. Nurses Assn., Nat. League for Nursing, Hawaii Pacific Gerontol. Soc., Am. Gerontol. Soc., Acupuncture Sci. Research Found. Hawaii, Am. Health Care Assn., Central Mich. U. Alumni Assn., Hawaii Long Term Care Assn. Address: 2459 10th Ave Honolulu HI 96816

FENNELL, MARY THERESE, textile co. exec.; b. Mt. Vernon, N.Y., July 13, 1934; d. Joseph F. and Helen B. (Grace) F.; A.A., Centenary Coll., 1954; B.A., Columbia U., 1970; M.B.A., Grad. Sch. Bus., Fairleigh Dickinson U., 1978; m. Andrew J. Gerber, Oct. 26, 1963; children—Carol Jean, James Joseph. Account exec. Lubar Assos., N.Y.C., 1957-60; asst. account exec. Hockaday Assos., Inc., Advt., N.Y.C., 1960-63; account exec. Johnstone, Inc., N.Y.C., 1963-65; dir. fashion mktg. services Lester Harrison, Inc., N.Y.C., 1965-66; account exec. Rea Lubar, Inc., Pub. Relations, 1967-72; pub. relations mgr. Monsanto Textiles Co., N.Y.C., 1972—. Mem. Chem. Mfg. Assn. (chmn. subcom. on consumers 1977-79), Nat. Home Fashions League (pres. N.Y. chpt. 1979-81), Am. Council Consumer Interests, Am. Women in Radio and TV, Fashion Group (chmn. Fashion Group Found. scholarship com. 1981—, trustee 1982—), Pub. Relations Soc. Am. Office: 1114 Ave of Americas New York NY 10036

FENNELL, SALLY ANN, mktg. communications exec., free-lance writer; b. Greensburg, Pa., Feb. 17, 1950; d. Clifford Seanor and Charlotte Louise (Hoffman) Fennell; B.S. in Journalism, Ohio U., 1972 cum laude; M.A. in Journalism, magna cum laude, Marshall U., 1974. Intern, reporter Tribune-Rev., Greensburg, Pa., 1972; prodn. asst. Harper's Bazaar, N.Y.C., 1972; reporter UPI, Birmingham, Ala., 1972-73; reporter, dept. editor HFD-Retailing Home Furnishings, Fairchild Pubs., N.Y.C., 1975-77; account exec., account supr. Burson-Marsteller, N.Y.C., 1977—, client service mgr., 1982—; grad. teaching asst. Sch. Journalism/Reporting, Marshall U., Huntington, W.Va., 1973-74. Mem. N.Y. Council Design and Interior Furnishings. Recipient Lasher award Ohio U. Sch. Journalism, 1972. Mem. Soc. Profl. Journalists/Sigma Delta Chi, Nat. Home Fashions League. Clubs: Deadline, N.Y. Press. Home: 74 Irving Pl Apt 3R New York NY 10003 Office: 866 3d Ave New York NY 10022

FENNER, JEANNE TUCKER, state legislator; b. Washington, Sept. 3, 1933; d. Herbert A. and Geraldine S. Tucker; student Atlantic Christian Coll., 1960-65; m. William Eaton Fenner, Mar. 15, 1953; children—William Eaton, Elizabeth, Edwin, Thomas, Ashley. Mem. N.C. Ho. of Reps., 19-. Vol. advocate mentally retarded, 1968-80; mem. N.C. Council Developmental Disabilities, 1977; pres. N.C. Assn. Retarded Citizens, 1977; pres. Wilson County Assn. Retarded Citizens, 1975-77; mem. Wilson County Democratic Women. Recipient Layman of Year award N.C. Assn. Retarded Citizens, 1976, Service to Mankind award Sertoma Club, 1978, Dybwad award Nat. Assn. Retarded Citizens, 1979, Mem. of Year, 1980; named Legislator of Year, N.C. Mental Health Centers Assn., 1981. Presbyterian. Club: Altrusa.

FENNER, JILL, railroad exec.; b. Boston, Feb. 7, 1947; d. Edward Joseph and Mary Jane (Bryce) Fenner; B.A., U. Mass., 1970; student U. Nebr., Omaha, 1977—; m. Stanley Paul Jaskolka, Jan. 10, 1970. Rape edn. coordinator City of Omaha, 1977-78; acting exec. coordinator Omaha Mayor's Commn. on Status of Women, 1978-79; program devel. specialist U. Nebr., Omaha, 1979-80; mgmt. trainee Union Pacific R.R., Omaha, 1980-81, human resources devel. and affirmative action officer, 1981—; cons. Greater Omaha Neighborhood Assn. Bd. dirs., chmn. program com. YWCA; program com. Girls Club of Omaha; mem. Omaha-Douglas County Crime Commn., 1978—; bd. dirs. KVNO-Public Radio, Vol. Bur.; sec. Omaha Connections. Named One of 10 Outstanding Young Omahans, 1979 80, 81. Law Enforcement Assistance Adminstrn. grantee, 1977-79; recipient Susan B. Anthony award, 1978. Mem. Am. Soc. Tng. and Devel., Nat. Assn. Female Execs., Joslyn Art Mus. Democrat. Roman Catholic. Office: Union Pacific RR Omaha NE 68179

FENNESSY, JEAN FRANCES, field ins. underwriter; b. Bklyn., Oct. 26, 1930; d. Michael John and Mary Anne (Maloney) McMahon; student Am. Coll., 1979-80; m. Jean Frances McMahon, Jan. 6, 1951; children—James, Michael, Mary, Jean, Kathleen, Carolyn, Ievin, Colleen. Real estate salesperson Harrison Realty, Sayreville, N.J., 1972-75; with N.Y. Life Ins. Co., Edison, N.J., 1975—, underwriter, 1975—. Democratic County committeewoman Old Bridge Twp., 1964-72, vice chmn., 1970-71, chmn., 1971-72. Recipient Nat. Quality Award N.Y. Life Ins. Co., 1975, 76, 77, also New Agt. Leader award, 1975. Mem. Nat. Assn. Life Underwriters, Metuchen Businessman's Assn. (dir. 1981-82), Women's Leader Roundtable. Roman Catholic. Clubs: Sayrewoods South Democratic (treas. 1970-71); South Madison Women's Democratic (treas. 1963-65). Home: 30 York St Old Bridge NJ 08857 Office: 10 Parsonage Rd Edison NJ 08817

FENTON, ELAINE REIMAN, speech pathologist; b. Cin., Apr. 13, 1937; d. E.J. and Claire (Dwyer) Reiman; B.A., Marymount Coll., 1959; M.A., Hunter Coll., 1962; Ph.D., N.Y. U., 1971; m. Bradford Donaldson Fenton, May 23, 1964; 1 son, Bradford William Kevin. Speech therapist St. Vincent's Hosp., N.Y.C., 1960-62; asst. prof. Marymount Manhattan Coll., 1962-69, John Jay Coll., City U. N.Y., 1970-72; asst. prof. speech pathology, mem. grad. faculty Rutgers U., New Brunswick, N.J., 1971-76; speech pathologist/voice therapist, N.Y.C., 1976—; dir. Manhattan Speech-Lang.-Voice Pathology Service, research asso. in neurology N.Y. Hosp., 1975—; cons. Jewish Guild for Blind, N.Y.C.; research asso. Haskins Labs., New Haven. Mem. social com. Sutton Area Community Assn., 1978—; chmn. youth com. St. John's Ch. Parish Council, 1978-81. VA fellow, 1965; Voice Found. grantee M.I.T., 1977, 79. Mem. Nat. Trust Hist. Preservation, N.Y. Acad. Sci. (linguistic adv. com. 1975—), Am. Speech, Lang. and Hearing Assn. (cert.), N.Y. State Speech and Hearing Assn. (chmn. public relations com. 1966), Am. Assn. Phonetic Scis., Internat. Soc. Phonetic Scis., Psycholinguistics Circle N.Y., Acoustical Soc. Am. Roman Catholic. Clubs: St. John's Tennis; Clean-and-Green of SAC. Contbr. articles to profl. jours. Home: 36 South Sutton Pl New York NY 10022 Office: 36 South Sutton Pl New York NY 10022

FENWICK, MARGARET EDINA, paper co. ofcl.; b. Sussex, N.B., Can., Dec. 10, 1946; d. Earle McLeod and Florence (Sinclair) F.; student Mt. Ida Jr. Coll., Augusta Sch. Bus., U. Maine. Office mgr. and service dir. Town & Country Equipment Co., Winthrop, Maine, 1967-73; service advisor Kennebec Volkswagen-Audi, Augusta, Maine, 1973-76, Clark Buick-Volkswagen, Augusta, 1976-79; service mgr. Blouin Chrysler-Plymouth-Jeep, Inc., Augusta, 1977; coordinator maintenance Internat. Paper Co., Augusta, 1979—; cost adminstr. N.E. region Internat. Paper Co., 1980-82; instr. nat. program Chrysler Women on Wheels. Mem. Chrysler Service Mgr. Guild. Home: 59 Highland Ave Lewiston ME 04240 Office: 9 Green St Augusta ME 04330

FENWICK, MILLICENT HAMMOND, congresswoman; b. N.Y.C., Feb. 25, 1910; d. Ogden Haggerty and Mary Picton (Stevens) Hammond; student Foxcroft Sch., Columbia Extension Sch., New Sch. for Social Research; div.; children—Mary Fenwick Reckford, Hugh. Asso. editor Conde Nast Publs., N.Y., 1938-52; mem. N.J. Gen. Assembly, 1970-73; dir. div. consumer affairs N.J. Dept. Law and Pub. Safety, 1973-74; mem. 94th-97th Congresses from 5th N.J. Dist. Vice chmn. N.J. adv. com. to U.S. Commn. on Civil Rights. Mem. Bd. Edn., Bernardsville, N.J., 1938-41; mem. Borough Council, 1958-64. Republican. Author: Vogue's Book of Etiquette, 1948; Speaking Up, 1982. Office: 1230 Longworth House Office Bldg Washington DC 20515

FERBER, MARIANNE ABELES, economist, educator; b. Czechoslovakia, Jan. 30, 1923; came to U.S., 1944, naturalized, 1947; d. Karl and Elsa (Ornstein) Abeles; B.A., McMaster U., Hamilton, Ont., Can., 1944; M.A., U. Chgo., 1946, Ph.D., 1954; m. Robert Ferber, Aug. 18, 1946 (dec. 1981); children—Don R., Ellen J. Economist, Standard Oil Co. N.J., 1946-48; lectr. Hunter Coll., N.Y.C., 1947-48; mem. faculty U. Ill., Champaign-Urbana, 1954—, prof. econs., 1979—, dir. women's studies, 1980—. Bd. dirs. LWV Champaign County, 1952-63, pres., 1959; bd. dirs. U. Ill. YWCA, 1964-68, chmn., 1966. Mem. Am. Econs. Assn., Am. Statis. Assn., NOW, Am. Profs. for Peace in Middle East. Jewish. Author articles in field. Home: 606 S Western St Champaign IL 61820 Office: 319 DKH U Ill Urbana IL 61801

FERDON, NONA STINSON, clin. psychologist; b. Homerville, Ga., Jan. 19, 1938; d. Haskell and Ilda Marie (Stinson) F.; B.A., U. Ga., 1958; D.O., U. Innsbruck (Austria), 1950; postgrad. U. Calif., Berkeley, 1964-65; Ph.D., U. Hawaii, Honolulu, 1971; m. Sheldon A. Davis, June 7, 1980; children—Steven, Sharon. Fgn. student guidance specialist Fulbright orientation, Honolulu, 1961-63; successively research asst. ednl. psychology, asst. dir. New Coll., asst. dir. Man in Soc. Program, instr. U. Hawaii, Honolulu, 1964-71; lectr. in psychology Clark U., 1971-72; asst. prof. U. Mass., 1972-73, Northeastern U., 1973-74; corp. psychologist Digital Equipment Corp., Maynard, Mass., 1973-81; founder, dir. Boston Psychol. Center for Women, 1974—; cons. to industry. Bd. dirs. Samaritans of Boston. NIMH grantee, 1967-69; Univ. Research Council grantee, 1968-69. Mem. Am. Psychol. Assn., Mass. Psychol. Assn., Soc. Psychol. Study of Social Issues, Assn. Women in Psychology, Psi Chi. Author: The Psychological Origins of a Public Life, in progress; contbr. articles to profl. jours. Office: Boston Psychol Center for Women Suite 902 Statler Office Bldg 20 Park Plaza Boston MA 02116

FERENS, MARCELLA (MRS. JOSEPH J. FERENS), educator; b. Pitts.; d. Ignatius and Marcella (Buzas) Slevinskas; student Greensburg Bus. Coll., 1934-35, Maison Frederic Cosmetology, 1936, Kree Inst. Electrolysis, N.Y., 1952; B.S., U. Pitts., 1957; postgrad. Mid-Western U., 1962; M.Ed., Duquesne U., 1964; m. Joseph J. Ferens, Nov. 27, 1937; children—Joseph Ferens, James. Cosmetologist and electrologist, Manor and Barrack, Pa., 1937—; research in hair regrowth, Darragh, 1954—; tchr. algebra, reading and drama dir. Harold Jr. High Sch., Greensburg, Pa., 1958—; tchr. cosmetology Uniontown (Pa.) Vocat. High 1954-55. Insp. Chem. Corps, Dept. of Army, N.Y., 1951. Mem. Nat. Council Tchrs. Math., Nat., Pa. edn. assns. Patentee in field. Home: Box 84 Daragh PA 15625 Office: Rural Free Delivery 6 Greensburg PA 15601

FERGUS, PATRICIA MARGUERITA, educator, writer; b. Mpls., Oct. 26, 1918; d. Golden Maughan and Mary Adella (Smith) F.; B.S., U. Minn., 1939, M.A., 1941, Ph.D., 1960. Various personnel and editing positions with U.S. Govt., 1943-59; mem. faculty U. Minn., 1964-79, asst. prof. English, 1972-79, coordinator writing program conf. on writing, 1975, dir. writing centre, 1975-77; prof. English and writing, asso. dean Coll., Mt. St. Mary's Coll., Emmitsburg, Md., 1979-81; dir. writing seminars Mack Truck, Inc., Hagerstown, Md., 1979-81; writer, 1981—; cons. in field; dir. 510 Groveland Assos.; bus. mgr. Eitel Hosp. Gift Shop. Recipient Outstanding Contbn. award U. Minn. Twin Cities Student Assembly, 1975, Horace T. Morse-Amoco Found. award, 1976; Ednl. Devel. grantee U. Minn., 1975-76; Mt. St. Mary's Coll. grantee, 1980. Mem. Internat. Biog. Centre Assn., Am. Biog. Research Assn., AAUW, Nat. (regional judge writing awards program 1974, 76-77, state coordinator 1977-79) Minn. (chmn. career and job opportunities com., mem. spl. com. on cert. and preparation of tchrs., sec. legis. com.) councils tchrs. English, AAUP, Pi Lambda Theta (records keeper). Roman Catholic. Author: Spelling Improvement, 3d edit., 1978; contbr. to Minn. English Jour., Downtown Cath. Voice, Mpls., Mountaineer Briefing. Home and Office: 510 Groveland Ave Minneapolis MN 55403

FERGUSON, CHARLOTTE BRAINARD, wholesale lumber exec.; b. Chicopee, Mass., June 18, 1929; d. Charles Duncan and Gladys (Hamilton) Brainard; B.A., Ohio Wesleyan U., 1950; M.Ed., Boston U., 1956; m. Albert D. Wood, 1957 (div. 1972); children—Jeffrey D., Maribeth L., Jennifer H.; m. 2d, Robert Bruce Ferguson, Dec. 28, 1973. Traffic mgr. sta. WHDH, Boston, 1951-52; sec. Harold Cabot Advt. Agy., Boston, 1953; copywriter Gabriel Stern Advt. Agy., Boston, 1954-55; tchr. Weston (Mass.) Elem. Sch., 1956-57; dir. Village Sch., Boxford, Mass., 1967-72; tchr. Tuftonboro (N.H.) Central Sch., Gov. Wentworth Regional Sch. Dist., 1973-80; v.p. Wood Dimensions Inc., Tuftonboro, 1980—. Mem. Pi Lambda Theta, Alpha Delta Pi, Alpha Epsilon Rho. Republican. Congregationalist. Address: RFD 1 Box 144 Tuftonboro Corner Ossipee NH 03864

FERGUSON, CYNTHIA RIDDLE, psychol. and rehab. counselor, educator; b. Sanford, N.C., Mar. 26, 1947; d. Luke Ralston and Mary Frances (Underwood) Riddle; B.A., Meth. Coll., 1970; M.A. in Edn., E. Carolina U., 1977; m. Thomas Neal Ferguson, Aug. 5, 1967. Pvt. practice psychol. and rehab. counselor, Fayetteville, N.C. 1978—; instr. Campbell U., Ft. Bragg, N.C., 1981—; crisis counselor Cumberland County, Fayetteville, 1980; cons. Nat. Center for Instns. and Alternatives, Fayetteville, 1982. Mem. Am. Psychol. Assn., Arthritis Found., Arthritis Health Profls. Fedn. Blind, Soc. for Psychol. Study of Social Issues. Democrat. Episcopalian. Club: Fayetteville Fedn. for Blind (dir. 1981-82). Text adv. bd. editors: Social Psychology, 1981-83; contbr. articles in field to profl. publs. Home: 545 Waterbury Dr Fayetteville NC 28301 Office: Campbell U PO Box 70618 Fort Bragg NC 28307 also 545 Waterbury Dr Fayetteville NC 28301

FERGUSON, ELIZABETH ADELE, dance educator, choreographer; b. Dallas, June 10, 1928; d. Fred Dillahunty and Nel Jennings (Ryan) Stewart; B.B.A., North Tex. State U., 1949; M.F.A. in Dance, Southern Meth. U., 1967; m. Joe Durwood, Mar. 31, 1950; children—Susan Adele, Joann Elizabeth. With So. Meth. U., Meadows Sch. of Arts, Dallas, 1968—, dir. Dance Preparatory, 1969-78, asst. prof., 1972, asso. prof., 1979, acting dir. Grad. Dance Program, 1979-81, dir. Grad. Dance Program, 1981, acting chmn. dance div., 1982—; lectr.; choreographer Dallas Jr. League Ball Shows, 1971—. Bd. dirs. Faculty Women's Research Group, 1982, Dallas Dance Council, 1980-82; mem. dance cert. com. Commn. Standards for Dance Edn., Tex. Edn. Agy., 1982. Recipient Outstanding Prof. award So. Meth. U., 1977. Mem. Nat. Assn. Dance Schs., AAUP, Am. Dance Guild, Dance History Scholars, Congress on Research in Dance, Dallas Dance Council. Episcopalian. Club: Southern Methodist University Faculty (dir.). Home: 11628 Colmar St Dallas TX 75218 Office: Meadows Sch Arts Dance Div Dallas TX 75275

FERGUSON, EMILY ROULETTE, newspaper editor-publisher; b. Cape Girardeau, Mo., Sept. 8, 1941; d. Leon Roulette and Mary Jane (Benjamin) Brennecke; B.S. in Secondary Edn., S.E. Mo. State Coll., Cape Girardeau, 1963; widow; children—Kathryn Ryan, Art supr. Sikeston (Mo.) High Sch., 1963-66; elem. art supr. Fredericktown (Mo.) R-1 Sch. System, 1966-69; advt. mgr. Democrat-News, Fredericktown, 1968-79, editor-pub., 1979—. Del., Mo. Democratic Conv., 1980. Mem. Nat. Newspaper Assn., U.S. C. of C., Mo. Press Assn. (sec. 1982—), Mo. Dem. Editors Assn. (2d v.p. 1982—), S.E. Mo. Press Assn. (dir. 1981-82), Fredericktown C. of C. (dir. 1981-82), Mo. C. of C., Fredericktown Retail Mchts. Assn., Ironton Retailers Assn., Farmington C. of C. Roman Catholic. Clubs: Friday, Federated Women's. Office: 148 E Main St Fredericktown MO 63645

FERGUSON, KAREN ROCHELLE, social worker; b. Lynchburg, Va., Mar. 11, 1950; d. William Bernard and Delores Mildred (Nichols) F.; B.A., N.C. A&T State U., 1972; M.A. (HEW fellow), U. Chgo., 1974, cert. mgmt. tng., 1979. Public health social worker Chgo. Dept. Health, 1974-77; dir. case mgmt. and licensing Afro-Youth Community Inc., Chgo., 1976-79; psychiat. social worker Mile Sq. Health Center, Chgo., 1979—; cons. in field. Mem. Acad. Cert. Social Workers, Nat. Assn. Social Workers, Nat. Assn. Black Social Workers. Democrat. Home: 5140 S Kenwood Ave Chicago IL 60615 Office: 2045 W Washington Blvd Chicago IL 60612

FERGUSON, LINDA, acctg. co. exec.; b. Cleve., Mar. 15, 1938; d. Stephen G. and Helen Gall Salay; student Northwestern U., 1955-56; A.B. in Chemistry, Western Res. U., 1959; B.S. in Acctg., U. Akron, 1975, M.S. in Acctg., 1977; m. Peter James Ferguson, Nov. 25, 1978; children—Wendy Lynne Wicks, Douglas Andrew Wicks, Bruce Matthew Wicks. Acting controller Cleve. Pro Basketball Co., Cleve., 1976-77; staff acct. Akron (Ohio) Beacon Jour., 1977; acct. Schlabig, Stanoch & Assos., Akron, 1977-79; tax and data processing mgr. Samuel

Bingham Co., Chgo., 1979-81; sr. acct. Harry F. Shea & Co., 1981—. Asst. treas. Congregational Ch., Hudson, Ohio, 1977-79, mem. fin. com., 1975-77; bd. dirs. Hudson Coop. Nursery Sch.; active Naperville Community Chorus. PEO grantee, 1977; C.P.A., Ohio, Ill. Mem. Nat. Assn. Accts., Ohio Soc. C.P.A.s, Ill. Soc. C.P.A.s, Am. Soc. Women C.P.A.s. Republican. Home: 504 Cassin Rd Naperville IL 60565 Office: Harry B Shea & Co 130 W Liberty Blvd Wheaton IL 60187

FERGUSON, LINDA FERRELL, coll. ofcl.; b. Baytown, Tex., May 17, 1949; d. Walter Monroe and Bonnie (Harrison) Ferrell; student Lee Coll., 1967-70; m. Wylie C. Ferguson, Jr., Oct. 6, 1976; children—Walter Wayne Cassity, Ferrell Jason, Bonnie Elizabeth. Reporter, teen editor, asst. women's editor, photographer Baytown (Tex.) Sun, 1967-72; editorial asst. public info. dept. Lee Coll., Baytown, 1972—; advt. mgr. Miss Baytown-Lee Coll. Scholarship Pageant. Mem. Council for Advancement and Support of Edn., Nat. Fedn. Press Women, Tex. Press Women, (various awards), Lee Coll. Ednl. Secs. Assn. (sec. 1974-76), Beta Sigma Phi (pres. Xi Gamma Chi Exemplar Chpt., 1978-79, Valentines Sweetheart, 1978, mem. city council). Mem. Christian Church (Disciples of Christ). Club: Order Rainbow Girls (Goose Creek chpt.). Office: PO Box 818 Baytown TX 77520

FERGUSON, MARILYN, publisher; b. Grand Junction, Colo., Apr. 5, 1938; d. Michael and Helen O. (Bauer) Grasso; student Mesa Coll., 1955-57, U. Colo., 1960-61; John F. Kennedy U., 1982; children—Eric, Ann Kristin, Lynn. Writer, founder Brain/Mind Bulletin, Los Angeles, 1975, Leading Edge Bulletin, 1980—; pres. Interface Press. Bd. dirs. Inst. Noetic Scis., Holmes Found. Mem. Assn. Humanistic Psychology, Assn. Transpersonal Psychology. Office: PO Box 42211 Los Angeles CA 90042

FERGUSON, REBECCA JEAN, lawyer; b. Dayton, Ohio, May 15, 1950; d. Bertice Earl and Lois Jean (Lally) F.; B.S., Ohio State U., 1972; J.D., Wake Forest U., 1975. Admitted to Ohio bar, 1975; asst. pros. atty. Preble County (Ohio), 1975—; individual practice, Eaton, Ohio, 1976—. Bd. dirs. Preble County Crisis Center, 1978-80. Mem. Am. Bar Assn., Assn. Trial Lawyers Am., Nat. Dist. Attys. Assn., Ohio Bar Assn., Ohio Acad. Trial Lawyers, Preble County Bar Assn., Bus. and Profl. Women's Club (Young Career Woman of Year award 1978). Republican. Home: 321 S Barron St Eaton OH 45320 Office: 104 W Main St Suite 100 Eaton OH 45320

FERGUSON, SHANNON, accountant; b. Chattanooga, Tenn., June 26, 1945; d. William Fleming and Grace Gwendolyn (Marshall) Cargo; student Mount San Antonio Coll., 1963-64; student UCLA, 1966; m. William Clark Ferguson III, Dec. 30, 1967; children—William Jeffrey, Jill. Jr. acct. United Geophys. Corp., Pasadena, Calif., 1964-67; controller, chief fin. officer, corp. sec. Presto-Tek Corp., Los Angeles, 1979-81; corp. sec., chief fin. officer Accessory Supply, Arcadia, Calif., 1981—, also dir. Asst. treas. Holiday Homes Tour, 1981, safety chmn., 1980; chmn. 20th Anniversary Ball Meth. Hosp., 1977; active Arcadia Tournament of Roses Assn.; mem. U.S. Bus. Adv. Bd., Washington, Republican Presdl. Task Force, Arcadia aux. Meth. Hosp.; sustaining mem. Rep. Nat. Com., Calif. Rep. Com. Mem. Internat. Div. Credit Mgrs., Exec. Female, Office Automation Mgmt. Adv. Bd., Credit Mgrs. So. Calif. Republican. Home: 1230 Oakglen Ave Arcadia CA 91006

FERGUSON, SHIRLEY MARTHA, physician, educator; b. Syracuse, N.Y., Mar. 9, 1923; A.B. magna cum laude, Syracuse U., 1945, M.D. magna cum laude, 1947; diploma in psychiatry McGill U., Montreal, Can., 1955; m. Mark Rayport, 1951; children—Stephen, Jeffrey, Jennifer. Intern, Jewish Hosp., Bklyn., 1947-48, N.Y. Infirmary, N.Y.C., 1948-49, resident in obstetrics, 1949-50; resident in medicine and neurology Goldwater Meml. Hosp., N.Y.C., 1950-51; resident in neuropsychiatry VA Hosp., Lexington, Ky., 1951-53; resident Allan Meml. Inst. Psychiatry, Montreal, 1953-54, clin. fellow, 1954-55; research fellow Montreal Neurol. Inst., 1957-58, psychiatrist Epilepsy Clinic, 1957-58; staff psychiatrist Montreal Children's Hosp., 1955-56; research asso. dept. psychiatry Queen Mary VA Hosp., Montreal, 1956-57; research asso. dept. neurol. surgery and neurology Columbia U., 1958-60; asst. neurologist Columbia-Presbyn. Med. Center, N.Y.C., 1959-63; research asso. dept. neurol. surgery Albert Einstein Coll. Medicine, 1960-65; asst. attending psychiatrist Montefiore Hosp., N.Y.C., 1965-68; adj. dept. psychiatry Mount Zion Hosp. and Med. Center, San Francisco, 1968-69; mem. staff dept. psychiatry Med. Coll. Ohio Hosp., Toledo, 1969—; asso. prof. psychiatry Med. Coll. Ohio, 1969—, asso. prof. neuropsychiatry, 1976—, head sect. behavioral neurology dept. neurosciences, 1976—; dir. inpatient teaching unit of adult psychiatry Toledo Mental Health Center, 1971—; attending staff dept. clin. neurosciences Mercy Hosp., Toledo, 1976—; asst. vis. psychiatrist Bronx Mcpl. Hosp. Center, N.Y.C., 1960-68. Trustee Creative Arts Community, Toledo, 1974-76. Fellow Am. Psychiat. Assn.; mem. Am. Epilepsy Soc., Soc. Biol. Psychiatry, Acad. Medicine Toledo and Lucas County, Ohio Psychiat. Assn., Ohio State Med. Assn., Internat. Assn Study Pain, Phi Beta Kappa, Alpha Omega Alpha. Contbr. articles to profl. jours. Office: Medical College of Ohio Toledo OH 43699

FERGUSON, SUSAN LILLIAN, modeling sch. exec.; b. Chgo., Feb. 17, 1927; d. Edward and Mabel E. (Erickson) Bakke; m. William Ferguson, Feb. 17, 1947. Sec. dr.'s office, 1949-60; teacher, modeling sch., 1960-62; owner Cinderella Sch., Salem, Oreg., 1962—. Chmn. hosp. flea market, 1963-64; chmn. county mother's marsh Muscular Dystrophy, 1965; active Heart Assn., 1963, Sch. for Blind, 1968-70; penitentiary tchr. personal devel., 1975-78. Named Tchr. of Year, Chemekta Coll., 1975. Mem. Oreg. Pvt. Sch. Assn., Nat. Assn. Public and Continuing Edn., Modeling Assn. Am. (Sch. of Year award 1962), Oreg. Fedn. Women's Clubs (pres. 1960-62, dist. pres. 1963-64, internat. hostess 1961). Democrat. Roman Catholic. Author: Charm and Charisma, 1977. Office: Cinderella Sch 317 NE Court St Salem OR 97301

FERGUSON, SUZANNE CAROL, educator; b. East Stroudsburg, Pa., Aug. 13, 1939; d. Edwin Roy and Edna Mabel (Reeves) Butts; A.A., Va. Intermont Coll., 1958; B.A., Converse Coll., 1960; M.A., Vanderbilt U., 1961; Ph.D., Stanford U., 1966; m. James H. Ferguson, May 29, 1960; 1 dau., Cynthia Katherine. Asst. prof. English, U. Calif., Santa Barbara, 1966-71; assoc. prof. English, Ohio State U., Columbus, 1971—; vis. assoc. prof. Kenyon Coll., Gambier, Ohio, 1977; edit. cons. pub. cos. Woodrow Wilson fellow, 1960; Stanford Wilson dissertation fellow, 1965-66; U. Calif. faculty fellow, 1970. Mem. MLA, Virginia Woolf Soc., Am. Recorder Soc. (dir., sec., 1980—). Democrat. Author: The Poetry of Randall Jarrell, 1971; editor: Critical Essays on Randall Jarrell, 1983; contbr. articles to profl. jours.; dir. Augustans Baroque Ensemble, 1979—. Home: 33 Erie Rd Columbus OH 43214 Office: Dept English Ohio State U Columbus OH 43210

FERGUSON, SYBIL RAE, franchise bus. exec.; b. Barnwell, Alta, Can., Feb. 7, 1934; came to U.S., 1938, naturalized, 1975; d. Alva John and Xarissa (Merkley) Clarke; student public schs.; m. Roger N. Ferguson, July 10, 1952; children—Debra Kay, Michael David, Wade Clarke, Lois Christine, Julie Xarissa. Founder, owner Diet Center, Inc., Rexburg, Idaho, 1970—; dir. Dietology Sch., Diet Center Inn, Ferguson's Pharm. Labs., Diet Center Shipping and Receiving Co., Diet Center Print Shop, Audio-Visual Studio, Sybils Inc., Ferguson and Assos. Charter mem. women's aux. Madison Meml. Hosp.; adv. bd. dept. of bus. Ricks Coll.; active Mormon Relief Soc. Recipient Bus. Leader of Yr. award Ricks Coll., 1980. Mem. Rexburg C. of C. (program dir. 1976). Clubs: Rexburg Civic, Soroptomists (v.p. Rexburg 1975, award 1979). Office: Diet Center Inc 220 W 2nd St S Rexburg ID 83440

FERGUSON, VERBENA SHOULTZ, educator; b. Phila., July 23, 1936; d. Otis and Octavia V. (Tooks) Shoultz; B.S., State Tchrs. Coll., Cheyney, Pa., 1955; M.Ed., Antioch Grad. Sch., 1975; Ph.D., Union for Experimenting Colls. and Univs., Cin., 1979; 1 son, Daryll M. Classroom tchr. Bd. Public Edn., Phila., 1958-64, reading cons., ednl. improvement program for disadvantaged, 1964-68, reading specialist, achievement for individual devel. program in middle and jr. high sch., 1977—, dir. tutoring service agy., Phila. Recipient Higgins Sci. award Chapel of Four Chaplains, 1970; merit cert. in reading/lang. arts Ednl. Improvement Program; NDEA grantee, 1968-69. Mem. Internat. Reading Assn., Del. Valley Reading Assn., Assn. Supervision and Curriculum Devel., Council Basic Edn., Phila. Fedn. Tchrs., Nat. Assn. Female Execs. (network dir.), Delta Sigma Theta. Designer reading program for deaf. Home: PO Box 14151 Philadelphia PA 19138 Office: Achievement for Individual Devel Office Adminstrn Bldg 21st and Parkway Philadelphia PA 19103

FERGUSSON, MURIEL MACQUEEN, lawyer Can. politician, mem. Privy Council; hom. degrees include: D.C.L., Mt. Allison Coll., 1953, Acadia Coll., 1974, St. Thomas U., 1974; LL.D., U. N.B., 1969, U. Western Ont., 1977. Called to N.B. bar; created Queen's Counsel, 1974; practice law, Grand Falls, N.B., Can.; mem. Senate of Can., 1953-75, apptd. 1st woman Speaker, 1975, ret., 1975; named to Privy Council; former dep. mayor Fredericton (N.B.); mem. Fredericton City Council; regional dir. N.B. Dept. Nat. Health and Welfare, 1947-53; dir. N.B. Safety Council. Pres., Provincial Council of Women; hon. pres. Canadian Council on Social Devel.; trustee Forum for Young Canadians; dir. du Maurier Council for Performing Arts; patron Lester B. Pearson Coll. of Pacific; patroness Women's Insts. N.B.; mem. N.B. Assn. Hosp. Auxs. Decorated officer Order of Can., 1976. Mem. Can. Bar Assn., N.B. Barristers Soc., Bus. and Profl. Women's Club, Can. Fedn. Bus. and Profl. Women's Clubs (chmn. internat. relations com.). . Office: 102 Waterloo Row Fredericton NB E3B 1Z1 Canada *

FERMAN, JOHANNA, psychiatrist; b. N.Y.C., Aug. 12, 1949; d. Harold Jack and Celia (Polonsky) F.; B.Sc. with honors in Physiology, U. London, 1971; M.D., Wayne State U., 1976. Resident in psychiatry Detroit Psychiat. Inst., 1976-78, N.Y. Hosp. Cornell Med. Center, Westchester div., 1978-79; attending psychiatrist and fellow Montefiore Hosp. and Med. Center, Bronx, N.Y., 1979-80; instr. psychiatry Albert Einstein Coll. Medicine, Bronx, 1979-80; attending psychiatrist N. Central Bronx Hosp., 1979-80; cons. psychiatrist prison health services Women's House of Detention, Rikers Island, Queens, N.Y., 1980; cons. psychiatrist N.Y.C. Dept. Mental Health, Mental Retardation and Alcoholism Services, 1980—. Co-chmn. N.Y.C. region Gov.'s Temporary Com. on Discharge Planning, 1981-82; mem. Mayor's Task Force for Mental Health for the Prison System, N.Y.C., 1981-82; mem. State Office of Mental Health Forensic Task Force, 1982—. Diplomate Am. Bd. Psychiatry and Neurology. Mem. Am. Psychiat. Assn. (chairperson com. on legis. br., liaison to exec. council). Democrat. Home: 60 Gramercy Park New York NY 10010 Office: NYC Dept Mental Health 93 Worth St New York NY 10013

FERN, RUTH KANE (MRS. WALLACE EDWARD FERN), educator; b. Somerville, N.J., May 12, 1919; d. James Aloysius and Marguerite Anne (Carberry) Kane; B.S., Trenton State Coll., 1941; M.A., N.Y.U., 1944; M.A. in Adminstrn., Montclair State Coll., 1953; postgrad. Columbia U., 1957-69, New Coll., Oxford, Bedford Coll., U. London; m. Wallace Edward Fern, Sept. 3, 1960. Tchr. sr. English Flemington (N.J.) High Sch., 1941-44; dept. chmn., tchr. sr. English, Passaic Valley High Sch., Little Falls, 1944-51; instr. Newark State Coll., 1951-55, asst. prof., 1955-57, dir. pub. relations, 1952-57; asso. prof. English, edn., William Paterson Coll. of N.J., Wayne, 1958—. Cons., English Lang. Arts, Pequannock (N.J.) Pub. Schs., spring 1966, secondary sch. reading Pompton Lakes Pub. Schs., winter 1972. Vice-pres. Essex County (N.J.) Council State Employees, 1956-57; trustee, sec. bd. Passaic County Hist. Soc. Flemington (N.J.) Bd. Edn. grantee, 1942-43. Mem. NEA (life mem.), N.J. Edn. Assn. N.J. Assn. Tchrs. English (exec. bd. 1963—), Nat. Council Tchrs. English, Nat. Assn. Tchr. Educators, N.J. Hist. Soc., Delta Kappa Gamma (chpt. pres. 1970-72), Kappa Delta Pi, Pi Lambda Theta (adviser coll. chpt.). Contbr. articles to profl. publs. Home: 62 Alpine Dr Wayne NJ 07470 Office: 300 Pompton Rd Wayne NJ 07470

FERNANDEZ, ANNA G., fishery biologist; b. Chgo., Dec. 23, 1954; d. Ralph R. and Frances (Aparicio) F.; B.S., Mundelein Coll., 1980; M.S., N.E. La. U., 1982. Teaching asst. biology N.E. La. U., 1980-82, mus. asst. Mus. Zoology, 1981. Democrat. Roman Catholic. Home: 6115 N Seeley Ave Chicago IL 60659

FERRANTINO, JOYCE ANN, med. office mgr.; b. Berwyn, Ill., Sept. 20, 1946; d. Joseph and Mae Elfrieda (Nolting) F.; student Western Ill. U., Macomb, 1964-65, Coll. of DuPage, Glen Ellyn, Ill., 1970-72, U. Wis., Wausau, 1978. With retail and catalog sales dept. Sears Roebuck & Co., 1964-67, bookkeeper, 1966-67; teller loans Lisle Savs. & Loan (Ill.), 1967-68; payroll acct. Montgomery Ward & Co., 1968-69, sr. fin. analyst, 1969-78; bus. mgr. Smith, Cadwell, Witt & Kaupie Family Physicians, S.C., Wausau, Wis., 1978—; instr. transactional analysis; speaker bus. subjects. Mem. Wis. Clinic Mgrs. Assn., Med. Group Mgmt. Assn., Wis. Clinic Personnel Mgrs. Assn., Am. Assn. Med. Assts., Med. Adminstrn. Group of Wausau, Wausau Area Personnel Assn. Republican. Clubs: Altrusa, White Shrine. Home: 517 Remington Rd Mosinee WI 54455 Office: 212 Sturgeon Eddy Rd Wausau WI 54401

FERRARA, RUTH REIORDAN, assn. exec.; b. Ducktown, Tenn., Nov. 8, 1924; d. Robert Harrison and Lillian (Fralix) Reiordan; student public schs.; grad. Jones Bus. Coll.; m. Joseph James Ferrara, Oct. 10, 1946; children—James Michael, John Richard. Machinist, Jacksonville (Fla.) Naval Air Sta., 1942-44; with Greyhound Bus Co., Jacksonville, 1944-45; head cashier womens apparel Mangels Ladies Wear, Jacksonville, 1945-46; owner, operator restaurant, Jacksonville, 1946-47, Copperhill, Tenn., 1946-48; bookkeeper Henley & Beckwith, Inc., Jacksonville, 1949-50; mem. purchasing dept. Am. Hardware Corp., New Britain, Conn.. 1948-49; sec.-mgr. Greater Jacksonville Fair Assn., 1966-69, dir., 1959-69, exec. sec., 1965-69; pres. Fla. Fedn. Fairs and Livestock Shows, 1969-70, also dir. public relations; exec. sec. Fla. Fedn. Fairs, 1970—, S.C. State Fair, Greenville, 1972-77; exec. sec., mgr. North Fla. Fair, Tallahassee, 1977—. Mem. Fla. Council for Aged, 1966-70; mem. aging com. Community Planning Council, 1966-70. Bd. dirs. Jacksonville Fair, 1959-68, State and Provincial Assn. Fairs, 1976—; sec. Venetia Boys Club, 1958-62; bd. advisers Cathedral Towers, 1966-70. Democrat. Methodist. Clubs: Jacksonville Garden (dir. 1960-68), Order Eastern Star, Venetia Manor Garden Circle (pres. 1960-62). Home: 2795 Blair Stone Ct Tallahassee FL 32301 Office: 441 Paul Russell Rd Tallahassee FL 32301

FERRARI, EILEEN STEWART, hotel exec.; b. Fairfield, Calif., Apr. 27, 1950; d. Albert and Margaret (Mulroney) F.; B.A. in Fine Arts, U. Mont., 1973. Buyer, mgr. Farm Gift Shop, Vallejo, Calif., 1973-75; asst. food mgr. Red Top Coffee Shop, Vallejo, 1973-75; asst. food and beverage mgr. Holiday Hotel/Casino, Reno, 1975-77, dir. sales and mktg., 1977-82, gen. mgr. hotel ops. and sales, 1982—, also dir., sec.; founding mem. Mavericks; mem. Reno Ad Hoc Com. Devel. Tourism. Vice pres. Riverside Living Assn.; mem. Com. to Aid Abused Women; bd. dirs. Jr. League Reno. Mem. Hotel Sales Mgmt. Assn., Nat. Assn. Female Execs., No. Nev. Hotel/Motel Assn., NOW, Kappa Kappa Gamma. Republican. Episcopalian. Club: Virginia (dir.). Author bartender recipe books, also handbooks. Home: 1246 Riverside Dr Reno NV 89503 Office: PO Box 2700 Reno NV 89505

FERRARO, GERALDINE ANNE, congresswoman; b. Newburgh, N.Y., Aug. 26, 1935; d. Dominick and Antonetta L. (Corrieri) Ferraro; A.B., Marymount Coll., 1956; J.D., Fordham U., 1960; postgrad. N.Y. U. Law Sch., 1978; m. John A. Zaccaro, 1960; children—Donna Zaccaro, John Zaccaro, Laura Zaccaro. Tchr. public schs., N.Y.C., 1956-60; admitted to N.Y. bar, 1961, U.S. Ct. Appeals bar for 2d Circuit, 1975, U.S. Supreme Ct. bar, 1978; individual practice law, N.Y.C., 1961-74; asst. dist. atty. Queens County (N.Y.), 1974-78; mem. U.S. Ho. of Reps. from 9th dist. N.Y. State, 1978—; mem. adv. council for housing Civil Ct. City N.Y., 1978. Democrat. Roman Catholic. Office: 312 Cannon House Office Bldg Washington DC 20515

FERRELL, RUTH MORRIS (MRS. FRANK M. FERRELL), lawyer; b. Portsmouth, Va., Apr. 29, 1928; d. Francis Hubert and Ruth (Whitehead) Morris; B.A., Agnes Scott Coll., 1949; M.A., Emory U., 1952; J.D., U. Pa., 1960; m. Frank M. Ferrell, Apr. 7, 1958. Admitted to Del. bar, 1960, U.S. Supreme Ct. bar; practiced in Wilmington, Del., 1960—; law clk. judges Del. State Cts., 1961-62; dep. atty. gen. Del., 1963-70; head civil div. Del. Atty. Gen's Office, 1967-70; asst. regional atty. Phila. Regional Litigation Center, U.S. Equal Employment Opportunity Commn., 1973; mem. Gov.'s Commn. on Status Women, 1963-68; mem. European adv. council U.S. Dept. State, 1971-72. Pres., Women's Republican Club Wilmington, 1965-67; nat. trustee John Marshall House. Recipient award for outstanding pub. service Rep. Nat. Com. N.E. Regional Women's Conf., 1967. Mem. Am. (chmn. advt. specialization and law lists com., mem. council local govt. sect., ethics in pub. contract com.), Del. bar assns., Christina Bus. and Profl. Women's Club (pres.), Mortar Bd., Phi Beta Kappa. Presbyterian. Contbr. articles to profl. publs. Home: 17 Cragmere Rd Wilmington DE 19809 Office: 912 Market Tower Bldg 901 Market St Wilmington DE 19801

FERRIER, MICHELE MARIE, retail adminstr.; b. Oakland, Calif., Sept. 19, 1946; d. G. H. and Anne Bernice (Giambruno) F.; student U. San Francisco, 1964-66, U. Calif., Berkeley, 1966-68; B.A., San Francisco State U., 1972, postgrad., 1973-75. Tchr., Oakland (Calif.) Public Schs., 1971-79; retail area supr. Richardson Vicks, Inc., Wilton, Conn., 1979-80, retail adminstrn. mgr., 1980—. Mem. World Affairs Council. Democrat. Roman Catholic. Office: CO Richardson Vicks 10 Westport Rd Wilton CT 06897

FERRIS, DIXIE CALDER, legal sec.; b. Hemingway, S.C., June 29, 1951; d. Leroy Alfred and Jessie Frances (Rhinehart) C.; B.A., U. N.C., Chapel Hill, 1973; postgrad. N.C. State U., 1977, 80; diploma Fonville-Morisey Center for Real Estate Studies, 1979; m. Richard B. Ferris, May 16, 1981. Miscellaneous steel detailer Constrn. Dynamics, Inc., Charlotte, N.C., 1973-76; legal asso. N.C. Dept. Justice, Raleigh, 1976-79; fabricator Machine Tool and Heat Treat Service, Inc., Raleigh, 1979; elec./instrumentation detailer J. E. Sirrine Co., Research Triangle Park, N.C., 1979-81; legal sec. firm Ragsdale & Kirschbaum, P.A., 1981—. Precinct sec. Wake and Mecklenburg Counties, N.C. Notary public, N.C. Mem. Am. Soc. Metals, Am. Soc. Notaries, Am. Soc. Tng. and Devel., Instrument Soc. Am., Nat. Assn. Female Execs. (network dir.), Greater Raleigh C. of C., Sports Car Club Am. (nat. flagging and communications lic., bus. mgr. Bull.), Sir Walter Jaycees. Club: N.C. Young Democrats. Home: PO Box 18952 Raleigh NC 27619 Office: PO Box 19766 Raleigh NC 27619

FERRIS, ELLEN LINDA, home economist; b. Coshocton, Ohio, May 4, 1947; d. Glenn H. and Lucy I. (Casey) Wells; B.S. in Home Econs. Edn., Ohio State U., 1969, M.S. in Agrl. Edn., 1979; m. Steven P. Ferris, Aug. 23, 1969; children—Stephanie, Jacqueline. Foods service tchr. Riverview Sch. for Girls, Powell, Ohio, 1969-70; vocat. home econs. tchr. Fremont (Ohio) Ross High Sch., 1970-72; county extension agt. home econs. Ohio Coop. Extension Service, Sandusky County, Fremont, 1972-73, Brown County, Georgetown, 1973-80, Warren County, Lebanon, 1980—; speaker civic, religious, social groups. Sunday sch. tchr. Georgetown (Ohio) Presbyn. Ch., 1979-80, choir, 1973-75, ch. trustee, 1979-80; active Lebanon United Meth. Ch., 1981—; mem. adv. bd., dept. agrl. edn. Ohio State U. Mem. Nat. Assn. Extension Home Economists, Ohio Coop. Extension Agts. Assn., Am., Ohio, Tri-County (v.p. 1982-83) home econs. assns., Ohio State U. Coll. of Agr. Home Econs. and Natural Resources Alumni Bd. (v.p. 1980-82), Shawnee Forest Area Coll. of Agrl. Home Econs., Natural Resources Alumni Club (co-chmn.), Brown County Farm Bur., Ohio Valley Arabian Horse Assn., Internat. Arabian Horse Assn., Georgetown Women's Club (pres., 1977), Brown County Bus. and Profl. Women, Am. Bus. Women's Assn., Epsilon Sigma Phi, Phi Epsilon Omicron (scholar 1969). Club: Lebanon Garden. Home: 200 B Northwood Dr Lebanon OH 45036 Office: 777 Columbus Ave Lebanon OH 45036

FERRY, DIANE LOUISE, educator; b. Ligonier, Pa. Apr. 24, 1947; d. William Glenn and Marjorie (Houpt) F.; B.A., Gettysburg Coll., 1969; M.B.A., Shippensburg State Coll., 1974; Ph.D., U. Pa., 1978. Computer systems analyst Dept. Army, Chambersburg, Pa., 1970-74; research asso. U. Pa., Phila., 1975-78; instr. Temple U., Phila., 1977-78; asst. prof. bus. adminstrn. U. Del., Newark, 1979—; cons. Kappa Systems, Inc., Rosslyn, Va., 1981—, Urban Inst., Washington, 1980—. Mem. Nat. Acad. Mgmt., Am. Mgmt. Assn., Am. Psychol. Assn., Phi Beta Kappa. Author: (with A.H. VandeVen) Measuring and Assessing Organizations, 1980. Address: Dept Bus Adminstrn Univ Del Newark DE 19711

FESAK, MARY KELLY, govt. agy. adminstr.; b. Little Rock, Apr. 20, 1939; d. William Joseph and Bertha Maria (Dehmer) Kelly; B.S. in Natural Sci. and Edn., Marillac Coll., Normandy, Mo., 1964; postgrad. U. Ark. Med. Sch.; m. Frank M. Fesak, Oct. 12, 1973 (dec.). With VA, 1972—, program analyst, office dir., Little Rock, 1980-82, exec. asst. to dir., 1981—; co-chmn. vets. affairs subcom. Gov. Ark. Com. Employment People with Disabilities, 1980-81; mem. Gov. Ark. Commn. People with Disabilities, 1981—. Adv., Ark. chpt. NCCJ, 1981—. Recipient Superior Performance award VA Med. Center, Little Rock, 1971; Outstanding Service to Disabled People award Ark. Rehab. Assn., 1980; NIH fellow, 1968-70; named Ark. Fed. Employee of Yr., 1980. Mem. Nat. Assn. Exec. Females, Ark. Quality Assurance Profls. Republican. Roman Catholic. Contbr. articles profl. jours. Home: 1106 Abercorn St Sherwood AR 72216 Office: 300 E Roosevelt St Little Rock AR 72206

FESHBACH, NORMA DEITCH, educator; b. N.Y.C., Sept. 5, 1926; Samuel and Lena (Katz) Deitch; B.S. cum laude, CCNY, 1947, M.S. in Ednl. Psychology, 1949; Ph.D. (USPHS fellow) U. Pa., 1956; m. Seymour Feshbach, Aug. 16, 1947; children—Jonathan Stephan, Laura Elizabeth, Andrew David. Research psychologist UCLA, 1964-65, prof. Grad. Sch. Edn. and dept. psychology, 1965—, head program in early childhood devel. studies, 1968-80, dir. NIMH tng. program in early childhood and devel. studies, 1972—, co-dir. Bush Found. Tng. program in child devel. and social policy, 1978—. Mem. Delta Phi Upsilon. Contbr. articles to profl. jours. Office: Grad Sch Edn UCLA 405 Hilgard Ave Los Angeles CA 90024

FESLER, ELIZABETH, educator, psychologist; b. Youngstown, Ohio, Nov. 5, 1930; d. Raymond and Mary (Theodore) Cosetti; B.S., Kent State U., 1952, M.S., 1961, Ph.D., 1974; m. July 8, 1953; children—Kim. Tchr., Buchtel High Sch., Perkins Jr. High Sch., 1952-62; counselor, Akron, Ohio, 1962-70; psychologist Akron Public Schs., 1970-76, coordinator spl. needs, 1976-78, dir. spl. edn., 1978-80, prin. Goodrich Jr. High Sch., 1978-80, dir. spl. edn., 1980—. Pres., Support Inc., suicide prevention; bd. dirs., chmn. edn. div. Planned Parenthood Assn.; v.p. bd. dirs. Mental Health Assn.; mem. women's aux. bd. Summit County Juvenile Ct.; mem. Children's Transitionals Services Bd. Kent State U.

scholar. Mem. Am. Assn. Psychologists, Ohio Assn. Psychologists, Akron Assn. Psychologists, Am. Assn. Secondary Sch. Prins., Ohio Assn. Secondary Sch. Prins., Akron Assn. Secondary Sch. Prins., Nat. Assn. Sch. Psychologists, Alpha Xi Delta. Home: 65 N Wheaton Rd Akron OH 44313 Office: 65 Steiner Ave Akron OH 44301

FESSELMEYER, DONNA LOUISE BUTZOW, bus. forms mfg. co. exec.; b. Watseka, Ill., July 3, 1941; d. William Donald and Norma Louise (Zumwalt) Butzow; m. Robert John Fesselmeyer, Oct. 25, 1975. With UARCO, Inc., Watseka, 1959-80, corp. buyer, Barrington, Ill., 1980—. Bd. dirs. Belmont-Middleport United Way Fund.; mem. Welcome Wagon of Barrington. Mem. Am. Mgmt. Assn., DAR, Iroquois County Hist. Soc. Republican. Mem. Disciples of Christ. Office: UARCO Inc W County Line Rd Barrington IL 60010

FETHEROLF, MIRIAM MARKHAM (MRS. RICHMOND D. FETHEROLF), ret. newspaper editor; b. Baldwin, Kans., Sept. 28, 1901; d. William Colfax and Carrie (Hoover) Markham; music supr. certificate Baker U., 1922; A.B., Bucknell U., 1923; m. Richmond D. Fetherolf, June 24, 1927 (dec. Oct. 1954); 1 son, Donald Markham. Supr. music Mt. Holly (N.J.) Pub. Schs., 1923-31; food editor Van Nuys (Calif.) News, 1954-76, Los Angeles Suburban Newspapers, 1957-65. Vice pres. Van Nuys Pub. Co., 1956-58, treas., 1958-76. Chmn. mothers group Home and Sch., 1945-46, 49-50, chmn. of chairmen, 1947-48. Bd. dirs. ARC, Swarthmore, 1950-52. Recipient Disting. Service award Baker U., 1976. Mem. Nat. Fedn. Press Women (affiliate), P.E.O., Delta Delta Delta (pres. West Phila. 1947-50). Republican. Presbyn. Club: Old Treasures (pres. 1965-67) (Van Nuys). Home: 17225 Gault St Van Nuys CA 91406

FETRIDGE, BONNIE-JEAN CLARK, civic worker; b. Chgo., Feb. 3, 1915; d. Sheldon and Bonnie (Carrington) Clark; student Finch Coll., N.Y.C.; m. William Harrison Fetridge, June 27, 1941; children—Blakely (Mrs. Harvey Hollister Bundy III), Clark Worthington. Asst. sec. The Dartnell Corp., Chgo., 1981—. Bd. dirs. region VII, Girl Scouts U.S.A., 1939-43, dir. Chgo. Council, 1936-51, 59-69, sec., 1936-38, v.p. 1946-49, 61-65, mem. Juliette Low world friendship com., 1959-77, chmn., 1959-67, 71-72, mem. nat. program com., 1967-70, mem. Nat. Juliette Low Birthplace Com., 1967-69, mem. nat. adv. bd., 1972—; mem. Internat. Commrs. Adv. Panel, 1973-75; mem. women's bd. Chgo. Area council Boy Scouts Am., 1964-69; mem. nat. exploring com. Boy Scouts Am., 1973-75, nat. council, 1973-76; mem. Our Cabana Friends com. World Assn. Girl Guides and Girl Scouts, 1969—, membership com., 1975—, vice chmn., 1982—; bd. dirs. Jr. League Chgo., 1937-40, Vis. Nurse Assn. Chgo., 1951-58, 61-66, also asst. treas.; women's bd. dirs. Children's Meml. Hosp., 1946-50; bd. dirs., v.p. Latin Sch. Chgo. Alumni Assn., 1964-69 v.p. Parents Council, 1952-54, Fidelitas Soc., 1979; mem. women's bd. USO, 1965-75, treas., 1969-70, v.p., 1970-74; staff aide ARC, mem. Motor Corps, World War II. Recipient Community Service award Sta. WAIT, Chgo., 1971. Mem. Nat. Soc. Colonial Dames Am. (Ill. bd. mgrs. 1962-65, 69-76, 78-82, historian 1964-66, v.p. 1970-72, 1st v.p. 1980-82, state chmn. geneal. info. services com. 1972-76, corr. sec. 1978-80, hist. activities com. 1979—, mus. house com. 1979—), Chgo. Dobbs Alumnae Assn. (past pres.), Nat. Soc. DAR, English Speaking Union, N.Y. Geneal. and Biog. Soc., New Eng. Historic Geneal. Soc., Conn. Soc. Genealogists, Nat. Geneal. Soc., Newberry Library Assos., Nat. Archives (asso.), Guild Chgo. Hist. Soc., Youth for Understanding, Couriers Bicentennial Project, Anti-Cruelty Soc. Chgo. (governing mem.). Episcopalian. Clubs: Casino, Saddle and Cycle, Woman's Athletic. Home: 2430 N Lakeview Ave Chicago IL 60614

FETSKE, RUTH BETTY, advt. agy. exec.; b. Rahway, N.J., Sept. 24, 1922; d. Plato Settle and Mitzie (Mihalovics) Bumgarner; student public and pvt. schs., Rahway, N.J., N.Y.C.; m. William A. Fetske, Jan. 29, 1944. Editorial asst. Woman's Home Companion mag., N.Y.C., 1941-44; photog. stylist Anton Bruehl Studios, N.Y.C., 1944-45; fashion copywriter West-Marquis Advt. Agy., Los Angeles, 1945-46; copywriter Lerner Shops, N.Y.C., 1946-47; copywriter, account exec. Dorland Internat. Advt. Agy., N.Y.C., 1947-48; advt. mgr. Marcus Breier Sons, Inc., men's outerwear, N.Y.C., 1951-53; account exec. Lester Harrison Advt. Agy., N.Y.C., 1953-60, Mervin & Jesse Levine Advt. Agy., N.Y.C., 1960-68; pres., owner Ruth B. Fetske Assos., Inc., N.Y.C. and Conn., 1969—. Mem. Fashion Group, Inc., Nat. Assn. Female Execs. Contbg. writer/photographer to profl. publs. Office: PO Box 248 Cobalt CT 06414

FETTERMAN, NELMA IRENE, home economist; b. Starbuck, Man., Can., Feb. 21, 1938; d. Laude and Hesper Orpha (Olsen) F.; B.Ed., U. Alta., 1965; M.A., Mich. State U., 1968; Ph.D., Ohio State U., 1977. Elem. sch. tchr., Domain, Man., Can., 1958-60; jr. high sch. English tchr., Lethbridge, Alta., Can., 1960-62; high sch. tchr., Nanton, Alta., 1965-66; jr. high sch. home econs. tchr., Edmonton, Alta., 1966-67; asso. prof. home econs. U. Alta., Edmonton, 1968—. Mary A. Clarke scholar, 1974-75; Marion K. Piper internat. fellow, 1975-76. Mem. Am. Home Econs. Assn., Assn. Coll. Profs. Textiles and Clothing, Am. Soc. Info. Sci., Can. Home Econs. Assn., Alta. Home Econs. Assn. Mem. United Ch. Can. Home: 247 Surrey Gardens Edmonton AB T5T 1Z3 Canada Office: 206B Home Econs Bldg U Alta Edmonton AB T6G 2M8 Canada

FETTY, LORA DELL, mfg. co. exec.; b. Huntington, W.Va., Feb. 28, 1920; d. Ralph William and Ethel Lovesta (Hesson) Brafford; student public schs., Huntington, W.Va.; m. John Wesley Fetty, Mar. 23, 1940; 1 dau., Sheila Kay. Sec., Hopstetter's Bakery, Huntington, 1937-40; mgr. Sharps Variety Stores, 1949-51, Ferne's Variety Store, 1951-64; office mgr. Chapman Printing Co., 1964—; sec., dir. Harrah & Reynolds Corp., 1966—. Home: 213 Buffington St Huntington WV 25702 Office: Chapman Printing Co 625 8th Ave Huntington WV 25701

FETZER, PATRICIA NASSIF, lawyer, educator; b. Cedar Rapids, Iowa, June 7, 1949; d. M. Morey and Barbara (Lindsey) Nassif; B.A. in history with honors, U. Iowa, 1971, J.D., 1974; m. William E. Fetzer, Aug. 29, 1970. Admitted to Iowa bar, 1974; assoc. atty. Simmons, Perrine, Albright & Ellwood, Cedar Rapids, 1974-78; sole practice, Cedar Rapids 1978-80; Bigelow teaching fellow, lectr. law U. Chgo., 1980-81; vis. assoc. prof. Coll. Law U. Iowa, 1981—. Mem. ABA, Iowa Bar Assn., Order of Coif, Phi Beta Kappa. Christian Scientist. Editor notes and comments The Iowa Law Rev. 1973-74; contbr. articles in field. Office: University of Iowa College of Law Iowa City IA 52242

FEUERMAN, CAROLE JEANE, sculptor; b. Hartford, Conn., Sept. 21, 1945; d. Milton J. and Doris Sye (Molbegat) Ackerman; children—Lauren, Sari, Craig. One-person shows MJS Internat. Gallery, Ft. Worth, 1978, 81, Art Expo, 1978, Hansen Gallery, N.Y.C., 1980, Elzine Horwitch Gallery, Sante Fe, N.Mex., 1981, Gallerie Ninety-Nine, Bay Harbor, Fla., 1982, Sindin Gallery, N.Y.C., 1982, R.K. Parker, 1982, O.K. Harris West, Ariz., 1982; numerous group shows; represented in numerous bus. and pvt. collections; lectr. in field. Mem. Am. Inst. Graph Arts, Nat. Orgn. Women Artists. Jewish. Home: 45 Oriole Dr Roslyn NY 11576 Office 371 Sycamore Ave Mineola NY 11501

FEUERSTEIN, KATHLEEN W., auditor; b. Gill, Colo., Dec. 16, 1925; d. Emanuel and Anna Elizabeth (Weibert) student Central Bus. Coll., Denver; m. Clyde W. Feuerstein, Nov. 16, 1947; children—Randall John, Larry Dean. Office mgr. Wheeler Realty Co., 1950-57; controller Monfort Packing Co., 1960-68; corporate controller, sec. Monfort Colo., Greeley, 1968-80, v.p. internal audit, 1980—. Mem. EDP Auditor's Assn. Congregationalist. Office: PO Box G Greeley CO 80632

FIASCO, CAROLYN LEE, counselor; b. Wayne, Mich., Oct. 16, 1944; d. Manuel Maurice and Virginia Lee (Tapp) Graddy; B.S., Murray (Ky.) State U., 1966; M.A. in Communications, Purdue U., 1969, Ed.S. in Counseling and Personnel, 1971; m. John Mirrell Fiasco, May 1, 1981. Family living editor, agrl. info. dept. Purdue U., 1969-72; tech. assoc. Center Vocat. and Tech. Edn., Ohio State U., Columbus, 1972, residence complex dir., 1972-74; dir. residence life Capital U., Columbus, 1975-78; counselor, faculty mem. Manatee Jr. Coll., Bradenton, Fla., 1978—; workshop dir., cons. in field. Bd. dirs. Cordova Lakes Homeowners Assn., 1982; chmn. Circle 12, Palma Sola Presbyn. Ch., Bradenton, 1982-83. Mem. Am. Personnel and Guidance Assn., Am. Coll. Personnel Assn., Nat. Assn. Student Personnel Adminstrs., Nat. Assn. Women Deans, Adminstrs. and Counselors, Speech Communication Assn., Alphecca, Alpha Omicron Pi, Chi Delta Phi, Lambda Iota Tau. Author articles in field. Home: 6106 37th Ave W Bradenton FL 33529 Office: 5840 26th St W Bradenton FL 33507

FICK, BESSIE DAVEY, educator; b. Detroit, Nov. 8, 1920; d. Edwin John and Lilian Ada (Spurr) Davey; B.S., Wayne State U., 1943; M.S., Oreg. State U., 1945, Ph.D., 1949; m. Reuel LeRoi Fick, Dec. 18, 1964. Asso. prof. U. Ala., Tuscaloosa, 1949-53, prof., head dept. foods and nutrition, 1953-61; prof., head dept. home econs. N.Mex. State U., Las Cruces, 1961-66; head dept. home econs. Eastern Ariz. Coll., Thatcher, 1966-70; prof. nutrition and foods Auburn (Ala.) U., 1970—, head dept. nutrition and foods, 1977—. Oreg. State U. Expt. Sta. fellow, 1948-49. Mem. Am. Dietetic Assn., Am. Home Econs. Assn., Am. Inst. Nutrition, Sigma Xi, Omicron Nu, Phi Upsilon Omicron, Alpha Delta Kappa. Methodist. Mem. jour. bd. Am. Dietetic Assn., 1974-77. Home: Wesley Terr Apt 201 Auburn AL 36830 Office: Sch Home Econs Auburn University AL 36849

FICKLING, JUDITH ANN, risk mgmt. services exec.; b. Lewiston, Maine, May 22, 1950; d. Howard Daniel and Sylvia Margaret (Anderson) Whiting; A.B., Coll. Charleston, 1972; M.S.W., U. S.C., 1976; m. Elliott Reed Fickling, Aug. 24, 1974; 1 dau., Patricia Katherine. With S.C. Med. Care Found., Columbia, 1976-80, long-term care program mgr., 1977-78, asso. exec. dir., 1978-80; v.p. So. Risk Mgmt. Services, Inc., 1981—. cons. HEW. Dir. patient services Multiple Sclerosis Soc.; dir. Women's Symphony Assn., 1976-77, 80-81. Mem. Nat. Assn. Social Workers (dir. S.C. chpt. 1977-78), Am. Mgmt. Assn. Presbyterian. Club: Summit. Home: 1429 Berkeley Rd Columbia SC 29205 Office: 3325 Medical Park Rd Columbia SC 29203

FIDLER, DEBRA DENISE, ednl. adminstr.; b. Dothan, Ala., Oct. 31, 1952; d. Lamar Melvin and Rose Marie (Hardon) F.; A.A., Chaffey Coll., 1972; B.A., Calif. State U., Los Angeles, 1974. Sr. event attendant Music Center of Los Angeles County, 1974-79; student acad. governance coordinator Calif. State U., Los Angeles, 1976-78, adminstrv. trainee Affirmative Action Office, 1978-79, fin. aid counselor, 1979—, chair Univ. Affirmative Action Com., 1976-79; chair Women's Resource Center Com., 1976-78, Women's Week Planning Com., 1975-79. Active Women's Rights Project, ACLU, 1976—; liaison to County Commn. on Status of Women, 1977-78; active NOW, Nat. Abortion Rights Action League. Recipient cert. of appreciation Los Angeles County Commn. on Status of Women, Calif. State U., Los Angeles, 1977, acad. governance award, grad. recognition program, 1977, 78, associated students hon. life award, 1977. Mem. Calif. Women in Higher Edn. (state rep. alt. region 13). Club: Women's Sports Found. Home: 1500 S 9th St Apt B Alhambra CA 91803 Office: Financial Aid Office Calif Poly State U Pomona 3801 W Temple Ave Pomona CA 91768

FIE, JACQUELYN JOYCE, educator; b. Chgo., July 11, 1937; d. Peter Carl Klein and Dorothy Marjorie (Berndt) Klein Rothe; B.S. magna cum laude, Northwestern U., 1959; m. John J. Uphues, June 18, 1960; children—Jeffrey S., Christopher J.; m. 2d, Larry E. Fie, July 24, 1971. Tchr. phys. edn., gymnastic coach Evanston (Ill.) Twp. High Sch., 1959-62, Evanston Parks and Recreation Commn., 1963-68, Niles West High Sch., Chgo., 1970-71; nat. tech. dir. women's program U.S. Gymnastic Fedn., 1965-78, internat. tech. dir., women's program, 1976—; mem. women's tech. com. Internat. Fedn. Gymnastics, 1976-80, 81-84; head judge World Championships, 1978, 79, 81, 83, World Cup, 1977-80, 82, Olympic Games, 1968, 72, 76, 84, European Championships, 1977, 79-81; tchr. numerous grad. and spl. courses colls. and univs.; mem. U.S. Olympic Gymnastic Team, 1956; tech. advisor Joint Cert. Com. for Gymnastic Judges; mem. adv. bd. Women's Sport Found. Recipient expert award gymnastics Internat. Olympic Com., 1980; named to Citizens Savs. Athletic Found. Hall of Fame, 1979. Mem. AAHPER, Nat. Assn. Girls and Women in Sports, U.S. Gymnastic Fedn. (exec. com., honor award for service 1978, Master of Sport award 1980), Nat. Assn. Women Gymnastic Judges (life; named to Hall of Fame 1979), Nat. Assn. Girls and Women in Sports, Am. Turners. Republican. Roman Catholic. Clubs: Soroptomist, Greene County Golf and Country. Co-author: Judging and Coaching Women's Gymnastics, rev. edn. edit., 1981; Judges Training Course Outline, rev. 2d edit., 1982. Address: 1205 Southfield Dr Jefferson IA 50129

FIEDLER, BOBBI, congresswoman; b. Santa Monica, Calif., Apr. 22, 1937; student Santa Monica City Coll., Santa Monica Tech. Sch.; LL.D. (hon.), West Coast Coll. Law, 1979; children—Lisa, Randy. Owner, mgr. pharmacies; mem. Los Angeles Bd. Edn., 1977; co-founder BUSTOP antibusing orgn.; mem. 97th Congress from 21st Dist. Calif. Bd. dirs. Com. Investigating Valley Ind. City/County; mem. sponsors bd. B'nai B'rith Youth Orgn. Mem. Bus. and Profl. Women's Assn. Republican. Office: 1607 Longworth House Office Bldg Washington DC 20515

FIEDOR, GENEVIEVE EILEEN, nurse; b. Big Goose Creek, Wyo., Nov. 22, 1919; d. John and Magdaline (Sefczyk) Kopchia; R.N., Providence Sch. Nursing, Detroit, 1944; B.A. with distinction, U. Redlands, 1976, M.A., 1979; m. Adolph J. Fiedor, Aug. 25, 1944; children—Jeanette M., Alan J., Diane L., John C. Nurse, Providence Hosp., Detroit, 1944, St. Mary's Hosp., San Francisco, 1944-46; office nurse Dr. Clyde Kennedy, San Diego, 1946-54; with Stanford U. Hosp., 1965—, adminstrv. clin. nursing supr., 1968—. Active, Girl Scouts U.S.A., 1956-67, Boy Scouts Am., 1959-61, Palo Alto PTA, 1956-77, Palo Alto Little League, 1959-63, 68-71, ARC, 1981-82. Mem. Am. Assn. Critical Care Nurses, Am. Assn. Evening and Night Suprs., Providence Hosp. Nurses Assn. Republican. Roman Catholic. Contbr. in field. Home: 16 Tulip Ln Palo Alto CA 94303 Office: Nursing Service Stanford U Hosp Stanford CA 94305

FIELD, CHARLOTTE, ret. assn. exec.; b. Seattle, June 9, 1915; d. Charles Henry and Evelyn Maude (Westcott) F.; B.A., U. Wash., 1936. Fashion coordinator Bon Marche Dept. Store, Seattle, 1940-41, display coordinator, 1941-44, asst. merchandising mgr., 1944-45, asst. rep., N.Y.C., 1945-46; asst. dir. publicity Lord & Taylor Dept. Store, N.Y.C., 1946-47; merchandising coordinator, design cons., asst. to pres. Gump's Dept. Store, San Francisco, 1949-50; account exec. Abbott Kimball Agy., San Francisco, 1951-54; dir. nat. food publicity Wash. State Apple Commn., Seattle, 1957-75. Mem. Fashion Group, Am. Women in Radio and TV (pres. Evergreen chpt. 1966-67), Nat. Edn. Found. (rep. Am. Women in Radio and TV 1967-68), Elec. Women's Round Table. Club: Wash. Athletic. Home: 10624 Woodhaven Ln Bellevue WA 98004

FIELD, ELIZABETH ASHLOCK, former govt. ofcl.; b. Little Rock, Nov. 27, 1915; d. Jesse Vernon and Felecia Irene (Bruner) Ashlock; grad. Little Rock Jr. Coll., 1934; student Washington U., St. Louis, 1934-35, U. Ark., 1962-63; m. Henry Lamar Field, Sept. 8, 1938 (dec. Nov. 1960); 1 dau., Elizabeth Field Wassell. Dir. historic house mus. Angelo Marre House, 1965-71; dir. Ark. Commemorative Commn., Little Rock, 1972-74. Spl. advisor Coral Gables House-Home of George Merrick, founder of Coral Gables; vol. council bd. Hist. Assn. So. Fla.; chmn. St. Joan's chpt. St. Thomas Ch., also mem. women's bd. Mem. Nat. Trust for Historic Preservation, Decorative Arts Trust, Lowe Art Mus., Am. Clan Gregor Soc., Dade Heritage Trust (trustee 1975-76), Vizcayans, Hist. Soc. So. Fla. (sec. 1980-81), Quapaw Quarter Assn. (pres. 1972-74), Phi Theta Kappa. Episcopalian. Home: 5520 Maggiore Coral Gables FL 33146

FIELD, JOAN ROBERTS, psychologist; b. N.Y.C., Apr. 12, 1942; d. Frank H. and Reta Althea (Publicover) Roberts; B.A., N.Y.U., 1963; M.Ed., Columbia U., 1969; M.A., U. Md., 1970, Ph.D., 1973; m. Peter Benjamin Field, Feb. 17, 1980. Staff psychologist and treatment team leader Walter P. Carter Center, Balt., 1973-75, chief psychologist, 1975-80; cons. psychologist Clifton Perkins Hosp., Jessup, Md., 1980-81; pvt. practice psychologist, Columbia, Md., 1974—; cons. bus. and mental health facilities in stress reduction. Mem. Am. Psychol. Assn., Md. Psychol. Assn. (pres. 1982-83), Soc. Clin. and Exptl. Hypnosis, Am. Soc. Clin. Hypnosis, Md. Soc. Clin. Hypnosis. Home: 2401 Hillhouse Rd Baltimore MD 21207 Office: 2000 Century Plaza Suite 221 Columbia MD 21044

FIELD, SUSAN INGEBORG, biologist; b. Providence, R.I., Nov. 20, 1953; d. Robert Eugene and Ellen Louise (Lewis) F.; B.S. in Biology, B.A. in Sociology, Providence Coll., 1976; M.B.A., 1980. Research biologist R.I. Hosp., Providence, 1977—, adminstrv. intern, 1978-81; spl. lectr. Community Coll. R.I., 1979-81; dir. Nutri Sea Foods, Inc. Rep. U.S. Congressional Adv. Bd., 1982-83; researcher/canvasser People Acting Through Community Effort, 1970, 73; social worker Catholic Inner City Center, 1968-69. Officer candidate Army N.G., 1981—. Mem. Assn. M.B.A. Execs., Nat. Assn. Female Execs., Am. Hosp. Assn., AAUW, Club: Toastmasters. Home: 114 Veazie St Providence RI 02908 Office: 293 Eddy St Providence RI 02902

FIELDEN, GEORGIA FREEMAN (MRS. C. FRANKLIN FIELDEN, JR.), interior designer, residential and comml. cons.; b. Alexandria, La., Aug. 3, 1919; d. John D. and Landis (Barton) Freeman; student fine arts Ward-Belmont, 1932-37, Blue Mountain Coll., 1937-38; B.S., George Peabody Coll., 1941; postgrad. N.Y. Sch. Interior Design, 1953; m. Clarence Franklin Fielden, Jr., July 16, 1942; children—Clarence Franklin III, Landis Michaux. Head dept. arts and crafts Camp Bon Air, Sparta, Tenn., 1939-42; asst. instr. fine arts demonstration sch. Peabody Coll., 1940-41; instr. fine arts Jackson (Miss.) Pub. Schs., 1941-42; lectr., interior designer, Colorado Springs, Colo., 1952-67; design cons., Denver, 1968—. Local pres. PTA, 1954-56. Mem. AAUW, Am. Inst. Interior Designers (Rocky Mountain publicity dir. 1957-58, sec. 1959-60, nat. com. public relations 1959-61), Am. Soc. Interior Designers, English Speaking Union, Huguenot Soc. London, Constrn. Specifications Inst., DAR, Illuminating Engring. Soc. (asso.), Nat. Trust Hist. Preservation, Nat. Soc. Lit. and the Arts, Internat. Platform Assn., Nat. Geneal. Soc., Huguenot Soc. Founders Manakin in Colony Va., Smithsonian Assos., Inner Wheel, Assn. Preservation Va. Antiquities. Presbyterian. Clubs: Rotary Ann (local v.p. 1959-60), Soroptimists. Contbr. articles to profl. jours. Home and Office: 518 17th St #260 Denver CO 80202

FIELDING, DIANTHA JUNE, designer; b. Long Beach, Calif., Nov. 7, 1931; d. James Elmo and Marybelle (Hendrickson) F.; B.A., UCLA, 1955; A.A., Long Beach City Coll., 1949-51; student Long Beach State U., 1951-53. Draftsman, Art Services, Hughes Aircraft Co., Culver City, 1955-57, animator, cameraman, film unit, 1957-68; prodn. mgr. Bosustow Prodns., Los Angeles, 1968-70; prodn. coordinator BFA Ednl. Media, Santa Monica, 1970-78, art dir., 1978-80; pres. Fielding Enterprises, Los Angeles, 1980—; cons., designer Paragon Art & Linen Co., 1966-75. Recipient Cindy award Informational Film Prodn. Assn., 1962, 64. Mem. UCLA Art Council, Embroiderers Guild, World Craft Council. Democrat. Author: Applique, 1972; Diantha Fielding design line embroidery and applique kits, 1965. Home: 3022 A Colorado Ave Santa Monica CA 90404 Office: 1848 1/2 Sawtelle Blvd Los Angeles CA 90025

FIELDING, ELIZABETH MAY, editor, writer, public relations exec.; b. New London, Conn., May 16, 1917; d. Frederick James and Elizabeth (Martin) F.; A.B., Conn. Coll. for Women, 1938; M.A., Am. U., 1944. Research writer Republican Nat. Com., Washington, 1940, 42-48, acting dir. research, 1944, asst. dir. research, 1948-53; govt. statistician, personnel clk., economist, 42, staff writer, spl. cons. to several U.S. congressmen, 1944-52; exec. sec. legis. asst. to Senator Alexander Wiley of Wis., 1953-54, asso. dir. research Rep. Nat. Com., 1954-57; researcher, speech writer, 1960-61; legis. analyst, newsletter editor Nat. Assn. Electric Cos., 1957-60; public relations dir. Nat. Fedn. Rep. Women, 1961-68; spl. asst. to asst. postmaster gen. U.S. Post Office Dept., 1969-71; public affairs dir. Pres.'s Council on Youth Opportunity, 1970-71; asst. adminstr. for public affairs Nat. Credit Union Adminstrn., 1971-75; pres. Profl. Enterprises, 1975—; editorial asst. U.S. Ho. of Reps., 1976-82. Editor Rep. Clubwoman, 1961-68; dir. spl. activities women's div. United Citizens for Nixon-Agnew, 1968; fin. coordinator Inaugural Com., 1968-69; citizen mem. rev. panel Atty. Grievance Commn., State of Md., 1980—. Recipient medal of achievement for outstanding govt. service Conn. Coll., 1971; Disting. Service award Nat. Fedn. Rep. Women, 1964, 67. Mem. Am. Polit. Sci. Assn., Am. Acad. Polit. and Social Sci., AAAS, Soc. Scholarly Pub., Nat. Assn. Govt. Communicators, Nat. Assn. Women Bus. Owners, Nat. Assn. Female Execs., Exec. Link, Rep. Women of Capitol Hill, Rep. Women's Fed. Forum, Internat. Biog. Assn., Internat. Platform Assn., Soc. Tech. Communication, Am. Soc. Dowsers, Senate Toastmasters, Nat. Fedn. Press Women, Phi Beta Kappa. Methodist. Clubs: Nat. Press, Washington Press, Am. News Women's, Capital Press Women, Capitol Hill, Capital Yacht, Congressional Flying, U.S. Senate Staff, U.S. Congressional Staff, Antique Auto Am. Author: A History of the Republican Party, 1854-1954. Home: 1312 Thornton Pkwy Fort Washington MD 20744 also McFarland Shores New Harbor ME 04554

FIELDING, PEGGY LOU MOSS, pub. co. exec.; b. Davenport, Okla., Oct. 28, 1928; d. John Richard and Hazel (Matlock) Moss; B.S., Central State U., 1949, M.A., U. Santo Tomás, 1971. Tchr. various U.S. govt. overseas schs., Japan, Cuba and Philippines, 1955-71; owner Partners in Pub., Tulsa, 1975—; instr. writing Tulsa Jr. Coll., 1976—. Mem. Okla. Writers Fedn., Southwest Writers Assn., Tulsa Night Writers Club, Nat. Assn. Female Execs, Inc., Small Pubs. Alliance, COSMEP. Democrat. Baptist. Office: 415 W Brady St Tulsa OK 74103

FIELDS, BARBARA JEAN, engring. co. exec.; b. Franklin, Ky., July 4, 1943; d. Jesse Jewell Shaw and Ruby Mae (Perdue) Shaw Hunter; student Columbus Tech. Inst., 1974; m. David Ralph Fields, Nov. 8, 1964; children—David Allen, Debra Ann, Lorrie Anne. With Indsl. Nucleonics Co., Columbus, Ohio, 1965-73; secretarial coordinator R.S. Fling & Partners, Inc., Columbus, 1975-76, asst. mktg. services coordinator, 1976-78, mktg. services coordinator, 1978-80, public relations dir., 1980—. Chpt. v.p. Childhood Conservation League. Lic. realtor, Ohio. Mem. Soc. Mktg. Profl. Services, Grain Elevator and Processing Soc. (asso. v.p., chpt. dir. internat. assos. 1982), Columbus Advt. Fedn. (Bronze Addy 1977, 80). Home: 2247 Severhill Dr Dublin OH 43017 Office: RS Fling & Partners Inc 999 Crupper Ave Columbus OH 43229

FIELDS, BARBARA P. LINDER, mktg. exec.; b. Bklyn., Jan. 29, 1950; d. Philip J. and Doris S. (Wander) Goldin; m. Nolan I. Fields; children—Adam Wayne, Brittany Leigh. Showroom and sales dir. Faded Glory Jeans, N.Y.C., 1974-75; owner, pres. Blazing Sadie, N.Y.C., 1975-78; owner, pres. Personal Connections, 1979—; internat. sales and mktg. dir. Multilite, Inc., N.Y.C., 1979—. Home: 46 Schenck Ave Apt 2J Great Neck NY 11021 Office: 230 5th Ave New York NY 10001

FIELDS, CHERYL ALICE, librarian; b. Montgomery, W.Va., Dec. 15, 1954; d. Herbert Wilson and Mary Elizabeth (Garland) F.; B.A. in Secondary Edn., W.Va. Wesleyan Coll., 1977; M.S., U. Ky., 1980. Tchr., W.Va., 1977-78; library asst. Vining Library, W.Va. Inst. Tech., Montgomery, 1978-79; grad. asst. Engring. Library, U. Ky., 1979-80; serial record librarian La. State U., Baton Rouge, 1980—. Scholarship student W.Va. United Methodist Conf., 1973-77. Mem. ALA, La. Library Assn., Assn. Coll. and Research Libraries, U. Ky. Coll. Library and Info. Sci. Alumni Assn. Democrat. Home: 5150 Capital Heights Apt 105 Baton Rouge LA 70806 Office: Serials Dept La State U Library Baton Rouge LA 70803

FIELDS, DAISY BRESLEY, cons. human resource devel.; b. Bklyn.; student Hunter Coll., 1932-35, Am. U., 1949-53; m. Victor Fields, Aug. 2, 1936; 1 dau., Barbara Fields Ochsman. Personnel officer USAF Base, Norfolk, Va., 1942-45; asst. personnel officer Dept. Agr., Phila., 1945-47; asst. dir. personnel Smithsonian Instn., Washington, 1954-60; chief spl. programs NASA, Washington, 1960-67; spl. asst. Fed. Women's Program, VA, Washington, 1967-70; sr. program asso. Nat. Civil Service League, 1971-72; cons. Equal Employment Opportunity/Affirmative Action, 1972-75, 78—; exec. dir. Federally Employed Women, Washington, 1975-77; pres. Fields Assos., Silver Spring, Md., 1978—; exec. dir. The Women's Inst., Am. U.; instr. Mt. Vernon Coll., 1979-80, Am. U., 1982. Chmn., Montgomery County (Md.) Personnel Bd., 1972-78; chmn. legis. com. Comm. for Women in Public Adminstrn., 1976-79; mem. Montgomery County Commn. for Women, 1979-82; vice chmn. Clearinghouse on Women's Issues; bd. dirs. Women's Inst./Am. U. Recipient award Federally Employed Women, 1974, 78, UN Assn. U.S.A., 1980. Mem. Am. Soc. Tng. and Devel., Am. Soc. Public Adminstrn., Internat. Assn. Personnel Women, Internat. Personnel Mgmt. Assn., Nat. Council Career Women, Women's Equity Action League (pres. Md. 1972-74; award 1978), Federally Employed Women (pres. 1969-71), Nat. Press Club, Am. News Women's Club, Capital Press Women, Fedn. Orgns. Profl. Women (exec. council), Nat. Assn. Women Bus. Owners. Author: A Woman's Guide to Moving Up in Business and Government, 1983; contbr. articles to profl. jours.; editor-at-large IAPW Jour., 1972-76; editor FEW News and Views, 1972-77, Washington Ind. Writers. Home and Office: 13905 N Gate Dr Silver Spring MD 20906

FIELDS, EVA LOU, business exec.; b. Cordele, Ga., Sept. 7, 1927; d. Tommy and Bertha Pearl (Musselwhite) Chandler; student public schs., Jacksonville, Fla.; m. Richard L. Fields, June 29, 1972; children—Ross D Bruner, Jay C. Bruner. Partner, Bruner Constrn. Co., Madison, Wis., 1954-66; asst. to dir. tng. Blue Cross Blue Shield, Dallas, 1967-70; ter. mgr. Southern Ill., Hollister Inc., Chgo., 1971-74, sales edn. mgr., 1974-80; dir. sales devel. Sween Corp., Lake Crystal, Minn., 1981—. Mem. Nat. Soc. Sales Tng. Execs., Am. Soc. Tng. and Devel. (past mem. exec. com. sales tng. div.), Minn. Tng. Dirs. Assn. Presbyterian. Home: 30 Hilltop Ln Mankato MN 56001 Office: PO Box 3485 Mankato MN 56001

FIELDS, FREDRICA HASTINGS, designer, craftsman; b. Phila., Jan. 10, 1912; d. Theodore Mitchell and Carolyn Corlies (Baily) Hastings; student Wellesley Coll., 1930-32, Art Students League, 1933; m. Kenneth E. Fields, July 10, 1934; children—David Edward (dec.), Luellen, Stephen Francis. Designer craftsman in stained glass, 1948—; exhibited in one man show Artists Mart, Washington, 1955, First Presbyn. Ch., Stamford, Conn., 1976, Concordia Coll., Bronxville, N.Y., 1982, Greenwich (Conn.) YWCA, 1982; exhibited in group shows Nat. Soc. Arts and Letters, Washington, 1951, Smithsonian Instn., 1951, 53, 54, 57, 58, Corcoran Gallery Art, 1955, 56, Nat. Conf. on Religious Architecture, N.Y.C., 1967, Washington, 1970, Greenwich (Conn.) Art Soc. Ann. Exhbns., 1968-78, Stamford (Conn.) Art Soc., 1972, Danbury (Conn.) Public Library, 1974, Stained Glass Internat., N.Y.C., 1982; represented in permanent installations at Washington Cathedral, Marie Cole Auditorium, Greenwich Library, YWCA, Greenwich, Assn. for Research and Enlightenment Meditation/Prayer Center, Virginia Beach, Va., Conn. Hospice Inc., Branford, Concordia Coll., Bronxville, N.Y., many pvt. collections; tchr. classes in stained glass, Washington, 1950, YWCA, Greenwich, 1966, at studio, 1968-71. Recipient awards in stained glass Corcoran Gallery Art, 1955, 56, B.F. Drakenfeld award 6th Internat. Exhbn. of Ceramic Arts, Nat. Collections Fine Arts, Smithsonian Instn., 1957. Mem. Stained Glass Assn. Am., Greenwich Art Soc. Address: 561 Lake Ave Greenwich CT 06830

FIELDS, JOAN R., chem. co. exec.; b. N.Y.C., Jan. 18, 1930; d. Albert and Etta (Levy) Ross; B.S., Adelphi U., 1951; certified early childhood edn. Ann Reno Inst., 1951; children—Larry M., Paul B. Tchr., Woodward Sch., Bklyn., 1951-52, Syosset Sch. Dist., 1959-65; corp. sec. Albatross Chem. Co., Long Island City, N.Y., 1966-69, pres., chmn. bd., 1969—; chmn. bd., pres. Etro Realty Corp., 1969—, Apparel Innovations Inc., 1978—; pres. J.R.F. Properties Inc., 1980—. Mem. young profl. com. United Jewish Appeal; mem. Sutton Pl. Synagogue. Mem. N.Y. Assn. Women Bus. Owners, Internat. Platform Assn., Phi Sigma Sigma. Clubs: B'nai B'rith, Atrium. Home: 303 E 57th St New York NY 10022 Office: 36-55 36th St Long Island City 11106

FIELDS, KAREN KAY, nurse; b. Columbus, Ohio, Sept. 8, 1942; d. James Wilson and Leuara Jane (Fout) F.; cert. med. tech. Brown's Sch., Columbus, 1964; R.N., Los Angeles City Coll., 1974; B.S. in Nursing, Calif. State U., Los Angeles, 1978. Med. technologist Ohio State U. Hosps., Columbus, 1965-67; med. instr., cons. Career Acad., Columbus and Los Angeles, 1967-71; nurse, nurse recruiter Cedars Sinai Med. Center, Los Angeles, 1974-79; asst. dir. nursing, nurse recruiter Los Angeles New Hosp., 1979-80; dir. nursing services Nursing Services Internat., Los Angeles, 1980—. Mem. Nat. Assn. Female Execs., So. Calif. Assn. Nurse Recruiters, Van Nuys C. of C., Los Angeles County Mus., Am. Film Inst. Office: 8383 Wilshire Blvd Suite 260 Beverly Hills CA 90211

FIELDS, KAY LOUISE, scientist, educator; b. Palo Alto, Calif., July 22, 1941; d. Ralph R. and Catherine Julia (Tinker) F.; A.B., Radcliffe Coll. Harvard U., 1963; Ph.D. (NIH fellow), M.I.T., 1968. Fellow, research assoc. Inst. Molecular Biology, U. Geneva (Switzerland), 1968-71; Med. Research Council scientist Univ. Coll., London, 1971-77; asst. prof. neurology and neurosci. Albert Einstein Coll. Medicine, Bronx, N.Y., 1977-81, assoc. prof., 1981—. Am. Cancer Soc. fellow, 1968-70. Mem. Internat. Soc. Neurochemistry, Am. Soc. Neurochemistry, Assn. Women in Sci., N.Y. Acad. Scis., Common Cause, Sierra Club, Council Livable World, ACLU. Democrat. Mem. editorial bd. Jour. Neuroimmunology, 1981—; contbr. articles in field. Home: 671 N Highland Ave Upper Nyack NY 10960 Office: Albert Einstein College Medicine Bronx NY 10461

FIELDS, LULA, business exec.; b. Farmville, N.C., May 6; d. Claude and Hulda (Darden) F.; A.A., Cortez Peters Bus. Coll., Washington; grad. Vogue Modeling and Charm Sch., Los Angeles; cert. Bevans Sch. Speech and Drama, Los Angeles; student Howard U.; teaching cert. UCLA; m. Klovis Z. Walker. Pres., dir. Lula Fields Sch. Modeling and Self-Improvement, Los Angeles, 1967—; former fashion and photog. model; former fashion coordinator Sears, Roebuck & Co.; instr. Los Angeles City Coll., 1978-80, Central City Occupational Center, 1976-77; lectr. community colls.; fashion columnist Wave Newspapers, 1970—, Lyric mag., 1974-79; charm cons. to bus. firms and pvt. schs. Recipient Merit award Youth-on-Stage, 1970, Achievement award Calif. Associated Designers, 1978, resolution Los Angeles City Council, 1970, 81, Calif. State Senate, 1981. others; cert. vocat. studies tchr., Calif. Mem. Nat. Assn. Female Execs., Nat. Assn. Media Women, NAACP, Black Women's Forum Los Angeles, Tau Gamma Delta. Episcopalian. Author: (juvenile fiction) Lyla, The Little Charmer, 1978. Office: 9348 Santa Monica Blvd Beverly Hills CA 90210

FIELDS, NATALIE G., speech pathologist; b. Leningrad, Russia, July 7, 1915; came to U.S., 1938, naturalized, 1944; d. Simon and Anna Stein; B.A., CCNY, 1957; M.A. (Augusta Learned scholar), Teachers Coll., Columbia U., 1960; m. Jacob Barosin, Dec. 27, 1976; children—Katherine, Peter. Asst. to dir. Children's Speech Clinic, CCNY, N.Y.C., 1957; fellow St. Barnabas Hosp., Bronx, N.Y., 1960; research asst. Columbia U., N.Y.C., 1960-65; speech, lang., and remedial reading therapist Pediatric Lang. Disorder Clinic, Presbyn. Hosp., Columbia Med. Center, N.Y.C., 1962-68, pvt. practice speech and lang. pathologist, Kew Gardens, N.Y., 1968—; speech and lang. pathologist pre-sch. children Learning Diagnostic Center, L.I. Jewish Hosp., 1980-81; speech cons. Child Devel. Center, 1969-76. Recipient Gustav F. Schulz prize, CCNY, 1957. Lic. speech pathologist, N.Y. State Edn. Dept. Mem. Am. Speech, Lang. and Hearing Assn. (cert.), Orton Soc., Phi Beta Kappa. Co-researcher for book by Katrina de Hirsch, 1961-65.

FIELDS, NORA JANET, artist, educator; b. N.Y.C.; d. Alexander and Sara Soling; B.S., N.Y. U., 1942; M.A., Columbia, 1943; m. Samuel B. Fields, Aug. 8, 1948; children—Melinda Sue, Nanette Gail. Tchr. art high schs.; tchr. Westchester Art Workshop, White Plains, N.Y., 1963-78; prof. Ikebana Ikenobo Art Center, Kyoto, Japan, 1963—; flower show master judge; accredited instr. Nat. Council State Garden Clubs; lectr. gardening, arranging, art; garden and art coordinator Muscoot Park, 1977-78; tchr. and coordinator N.Y. Bot. Garden, 1978—; tchr. Fairfield U., 1978—, Pace U., 1979—; lectr.; exhibited sculpture, mosaics, watercolors in group shows, N.Y.C., Westchester, N.Y., Conn. Mem. Art Students League (life), Federated Garden Clubs N.Y. State, Ikebana Internat. (pres. Hudson Valley chpt. 1969-72), LWV (treas. 1960-62). Republican. Mem. United Ch. of Christ. Author: New Ideas for Christmas Decoration, 1967; Flowers and Foliage-Creative Compositions, 1973; Flower Arranging for Parties, 1975; contbr. numerous articles on flower arranging and indoor gardening to various mags. Address: 1251 Pleasantville Rd Briarcliff Manor NY 10510

FIELDS, PAULA JANE, dental lab. technician; b. Catskill, N.Y., Apr. 20, 1944; d. A. Earl and Pauline B. Carde; A.A. with honors, Brevard Community Coll., Fla., 1975; B.A., U. Central Fla., 1981; children—Laura Jeanne, Katharine Paulette. Dental lab. technician Dr. D.J. Scalera, Cocoa, Fla., 1968-74, Dr. B. Chodorov, Rockledge, Fla., 1974-75, Creare Dental Lab., Cocoa, 1975-77, Dr. D.J. Scalera, 1977-81; owner, pres. Creative Dental Designs Dental Lab. Cert. dental technician. Mem. Fla. Dental Lab. Assn. (dist. del.), Indian River Anthrop. Soc. (past pres.), Fla. Anthrop. Assn. (past 2d v.p.), BCC Anthrop. Club (past sec.), Phi Theta Kappa, Omicron Delta Kappa. Clubs: Scuba (past sec.), Surfside Players, Mus. Theatre Brevard, Arlan Ropps Follies and Theatrical Troupe, Brevard Chorale. Home: 1160 King St Merritt Island FL 32952 Office: 111 Olive St Cocoa FL 32922

FIELDS, RONA MARCIA, psychologist; b. Chgo., Oct. 27, 1934; d. William Samuel and Kate Darcy (Goldman) Katz; B.A., Lake Forest Coll., 1953; M.S., U. Ill., 1955; M.A., Loyola U., Chgo., 1964; Ph.D., U. So. Calif., 1970; m. Armond Fields, June 9, 1953 (div. 1967); children—Louis Marc, Sean Steven, Cathy Nikema, Miriam Star. Community psychologist Chgo. Bd. Health, 1963-64; psychologist NDEA program Monrovia (Calif.) Guidance Center, 1964-67; asst. prof. psychology Pasadena (Calif.) City Coll., 1966-69; prof. human devel. Calif. State U., Los Angeles, 1967-72. Pacific Oaks Coll., Pasadena, 1969-71; vis. prof. edn. Calif. State U., Northridge, 1971-72; asso. prof. sociology Clark U., Worcester, Mass., 1972-76; founding mem. Sozialwissenschaftliches Institut fur Katastrophenund Umgallforschung, Kiel, W.Ger., 19-; asso. Transnational Family Research Inst., Bethesda, Md., 19-; sr. partner Assos. in Counseling Psychology and Barrier Free Environments, 19-. Co-chmn. campaign for Betty McCann candidate for Va. State Legislature, 1979; sec. Alexandria (Va.) Mayor's Com. for the Handicapped, 1980-82. Recipient Phila. Mayor's Award for Outstanding Service in Human Rights, 1978. Mem. Am. Psychol. Assn. (mem. taskforce on the status of women 1970-73, bd. social ant ethical responsibility 1971-73), Am. Sociol. Assn., Internat. Studies Assn., Sociologists for Women in Soc., Soc. for Psychol. Study of Social Issues, Gaelic League, Irish Am. Cultural Inst., Psychologists for Social Action (nat. coordinator 1969-72), So. Calif. Peace Action Council (leadership collective 1969-72), Assn. for Women in Psychology. Author: Society on the Run, 1973; The Armed Forces Movement and the Portuguese Revolution, 1976; Society Under Siege, 1976; Northern Ireland, 1979; The Future of Women, 1982; contbr. articles in field to profl. jours. Home and office: 222 E Del Ray Ave Alexandria VA 22301

FIELDS-BOOK, SUSAN TERRI, speech pathologist; b. Phila., Nov. 5, 1948; d. Bernard and Evelyn Mildred (Simon) Fields; B.A., George Washington U., 1970; M.A., Howard U., 1972; m. Martin Howard Book, July 19, 1970; children—Blair M., Brett H. Speech-lang. pathologist Prince George's County (Md.) Public Schs., Bowie, later Lanham, 1970— ; research asst. Social Ednl. Research Devel., Washington and Bethesda, Md., 1973-74. Rec. sec. B'nai B'rith Women, 1976-77. Mem. Am. Speech and Hearing Assn., Md. Speech and Hearing Assn., NEA, Md. Teaching Assn., Prince Georges County Educators Assn. Jewish. Home: 9602 Shadow Oak Dr Gaithersburg MD 20879

FIELEKE, CATHARINE NICHOLSON (MRS. LESSLY C.A. FIELEKE), author, reader, lectr., columnist; b. Ash Grove, Mo., Sept. 27, 1909; d. John Warren and Mattie (Duncan) Nicholson; student Drury Coll., Olivet Coll., U. Chgo.; m. Lessly C.A. Fieleke, Dec. 24, 1929; children—Norman, Sharon Fieleke Cohly, Cathy Fieleke Butterfield, Lessly, Laurel Fieleke Shoshani, Curtis, Teresa Fieleke Brooks. Pres., Fieleke Implement Co., 1965-67. Recipient awards Woman's Club, Am. Pen Women, others. Mem. World Soc. Poets Intercontinental, Pen Women (pres. Chgo. br. 1974-76, chmn. Nat. Mid.-Adminstrn. Congress 1977), Nat. Writers Club, Internat. Platform Assn., Internat., Ill. (v.p.) poetry socs., Am. Acad. Poets, Internat. Biog. Assn., Friends Am. Writers, Children's Reading Round Table, Chgo. Poets and Patrons, Poets Club of Chgo., Kankakee Area Writers Group. Baptist. Club: Women's. Author: (poetry) Run-off from Northern Springs; Summer Solstices; Aspects of Autumn; The White Fields of Winter; author, prodn. asst. American Poetry Series, 1965; scripts for ednl. tapes Imperial Internat. Learning, Kankakee, Ill.; lectures and poetry editor Pen Woman mag.; contbr. articles and poems to newspapers and mags., column to area newspapers. Home: 312 Ohio St Momence IL 60954

FIELO, MURIEL BRYANT, interior designer; b. Bklyn., Dec. 11, 1921; d. Harry and Minnie (Dick) Bryant; student CCNY, evenings 1938-41, Rutgers U., evenings 1965-69; cert. N.Y. Sch. Interior Design, 1970; m. Julius Fielo, June 17, 1937; 1 son, Michael Kenneth. Gen. mgr. Fidelity Discount Corp., Irvington, N.J., adv. supr. Lincoln Loan Co., Essex County, N.J., 1941-49; interior designer Alex Fielo Interior Decorators, Newark, part-time 1942-49, prin., 1949-69, owner, 1969—; owner MUDGE, Interior Designer, cons. space engr., East Orange, N.J., 1969—. Essex County freeholder clk. Bd. Freeholders, part-time 1972-76; commr. East Orange Bus. Devel. Authority, 1977—; mem. U.S. adv. council SBA-Region II, 1980-81; active LWV, 1950-55; organizer, 1st pres. Women's Am. ORT, 1952-54, mem. nat. speakers bur., 1952-65, parliamentarian No. N.J. council, 1955-65; pres. Amity chpt. B'nai B'rith, Newark, 1946-48, v.p. No. N.J. council, 1948-49, mem. nat. speakers bur., 1948-68, dep. Dist. 3, 1948-62, bd. dirs. Untermann chpt., 1978-80; mem. nat. com. on sect. fund raising Nat. Council Jewish Women, 1979-81, nat. tour. chmn., 1979-81, v.p. Maplewood div., 1977-79, nominating chmn. div., 1979—, Essex County sect., 1979—, mem. sect. long range planning com., 1976—; trustee community services council Oranges and Maplewood, United Way of Essex and West Hudson, 1981—; bd. dirs. East Orange Central Ave. Mall Assn., 1979—, Fight for Sight League, 1949-70, United Community Fund drive, 1950-60; chmn. new voter registration drive East Orange 2d Ward, 1955—, entire city, 1969; pres. East Orange Democratic Club, 1957-58, campaign coordinator for Dem. mayoral candidate, 1969, calendar coordinator Essex County Dem. party, 1970-76; mem. N.J. Bipartisan Coalition for Women's Appts., 1981—. Recipient various awards for civic service. Mem. Internat. Soc. Interior Designers (cert., dir. 1981—), Am. Soc. Interior Designers, Nat. Home Fashions League, Nat. Home Furnishings Assn., Gift and Decorative Accessories Assn. Am., Internat. Soc. Artists, Interior Design Soc., N.J. Assn. Women Bus. Owners (state bd. 1979-81), Women Entrepreneurs N.J. (pres. 1981—), N.J. Furniture Assn. (dir. 1982—), N.J. Bus. and Industry Assn., N.J. Network Bus. and Profl. Women, East Orange C. of C. (dir. 1977-81, v.p. 1981—), Bus. and Profl. Women's Club of Oranges (dir. 1958-66). Jewish. Mem. adv. panel Interior Design Mag., 1977—. Office: Mudge Interior Design and Gift Studio 185 S Clinton St East Orange NJ 07018

FIELSTRA, HELEN ADAMS (MRS. CLARENCE FIELSTRA), educator; b. Elkhorn, W.Va., Feb. 26, 1921; d. Fred Russell and Clara Sue (Williams) Adams; A.B., UCLA, 1950; M.A., Stanford U., 1954, Ed.D., 1967; m. Edmond T. Dooley, Jr., Nov. 15, 1941 (div. 1948); 1 dau., Dereth Dooley Pendleton; m. 2d, Clarence Fielstra, Jan. 1, 1956. Tchr., Santa Monica (Calif.) Unified Sch. Dist., 1947-50; supr. elem. sch. San Diego County Schs., 1950-52; lectr. edn. Stanford U., 1953-54, UCLA, 1957-58; gen. elem. supr. Burbank (Calif.) Unified Sch. Dist., 1954-56, Beverly Hills (Calif.) Unified Sch. Dist., 1959-61; asst. prof., asso. prof., prof. edn. Calif. State U., Northridge, 1961—; tng. coordinator Office Econ. Opportunity Tng. and Devel. Center for So. Calif., 1965-66; cons., speaker curriculum devel. and instructional supervision, 1952—; prin. investigator prospective tchr. grad. fellowship project U.S. Office Edn., 1968-70; dir., prin. investigator NSF Interdisciplinary Social Sci. Projects, 1972-82; sec.-treas. Hadco, Inc., Los Angeles, Fielstra Publs., Inc., Pacific Palisades. Recipient Disting. Teaching award Calif. State Univ. and Colls., 1969, Associated Students' cert. of service Calif. State U., Northridge, 1970. Mem. Am. Ednl. Research Assn., Nat. Soc. for Study Edn., Nat. Council Social Studies (publs. bd.), NEA (life), Assn. Supervision and Curriculum Devel., Calif. Assn. Supervision and Curriculum Devel. (chmn. com. supervision in structure public edn.), AAUP, Calif. Higher Edn. Assn. (dir. 1970-75, pres. 1973-74), Calif. Coll. and Univ. Faculty Assn. (pres. Calif. State U., Northridge chpt. 1969-70, state v.p. 1970-71, state pres. 1972-73), Am. Film Inst., Delta Kappa Gamma (life; chpt. pres. 1960-62). Democrat. Clubs: Stanford, Town Hall Calif. (Los Angeles); Palisadian Woman's. Author: (with L.G. Thomas, A. Coladarci, Lucien Kinney) Perspective on Teaching, 1961; (with Clarence Fielstra) Africa-With Focus on Nigeria, 1963; author numerous curriculum guides, 6 ednl. films; editorial bd. Calif. Jour. Instructional Improvement, 1967-70; editor Reading Monograph, 1970; Social Studies in the Elementary School, 1972. Home: 14177 Sunset Blvd Pacific Palisades CA 90272 Office: Calif State U Northridge CA 91330

FIENBERG, LINDA DORIS, lawyer; b. Albany, N.Y., July 7, 1942; d. Chester Leonard F. and Marcia Doris Kartzman; B.A. with distinction, Cornell U., 1964; M.A.T. with honors, Wesleyan U., 1966; J.D., Georgetown U., 1973; m. Jeffrey D. Bauman, Mar. 2, 1980; children—Amy Bauman, Lane Blumenfeld, Jessica Bauman, Shawn Blumenfeld. Instr., Huntingdon Coll., Montgomery, Ala., 1966-67; research analyst U.S. EEO Commn., 1967-68, U.S. Civil Rights Commn., 1968-70; asso. Arnold & Porter, Washington, 1973-78; spl. counsel. SEC, 1979-80, asst. gen. counsel, 1980-82, asso. gen. counsel, 1982—; admitted to D.C. bar, 1973. Mem. Am. Bar Assn., Women's Legal Defense Fund, Phi Beta Kappa. Office: 405 5th St NW Washington DC 20549

FIFIELD, JULIA MENTZER (MRS. CLIFFORD CRANE FIFIELD), civic worker; environmentalist; b. Somerville, Mass., Dec. 4, 1905; d. Charles Almon and Gertrude (Vinton) Mentzer; grad. high sch.; m. Charles Paget Golding, Aug. 23, 1930 (dec. 1947); children—Ann, Charles Paget; m. 2d, Clifford Crane Fifield, Apr. 2, 1960 (dec. 1978). Tchr., Melrose (Mass.) Elem. Sch., 1926-30; owner Old House Yarns, 1948-58; social sec., 1955-58; contract gardener, 1954-63; owner Fifield Farm, Orford, N.H., 1966—, Hanover Inn (N.H.), 1980—; corporator, trustee Canterbury Shaker Village, Inc. (N.H.), 1980—, v.p., 1982—; bd. dirs. Conn. River Watershed Corp., 1970—; bd. dirs. Hopkins Center for Arts, Dartmouth Coll., 1966—, v.p., 1979-80; trustee Friends Acad., South Dartmouth, Mass., 1941-55; corporator Hitchcock Found., 1977—, trustee, 1977-79; active Jr. League Springfield (Mass.), 1932-55; trustee Mary Hitchcock Meml. Hosp, Hanover; bd. dirs. New Bedford (Mass.) Day Nursery, 1940—, hon. mem., 1963—; mem. women's br. New Bedford Port Soc., 1938-63; mem. Orford Sch. Com., 1964-65; chmn. Orford Conservation Commn., 1979—, Orford Cemetery Commn., 1978—; capt. ARC Motor Corps, New Bedford, 1940-48; sr. warden and lay reader St. Martin's Episcopal Chapel, Fairlee, Vt., 1976—; mem. rev. bd. N.H. Gov.'s Com. Hist. Preservation, 1972—, vice-chmn., 1972-80, chmn., 1980—. Mem. Garden Club Am. (lectr. 1960—, nat. judge 1963—, nat. chmn. horticulture com. 1973-74, nat. chmn. flower show com. 1975, nat. chmn. conservation com. 1976-77, dir. 1979-80, mem.-at-large 1981—; Bulkley medal 1970, Consrvation Com. Testimonial 1977), Garden Club Buzzard's Bay (sec. 1956, v.p. 1958, pres. 1960-61, hon. mem. 1981—), Hanover Garden Club, Woodstock Garden Club. Republican. Clubs: Chilton (Boston); Colony (N.Y.C.); Rondo (pres. 1979) (Orford). Author mag. articles. Home: The Ridge Orford NH 03777

FIFIELD, LILLENE HENRIETTA, social worker, psychotherapist, lesbian activist; b. Los Angeles, Oct. 28, 1941; d. Howard Charles and Esther Shana (Goldstein) F.; B.A. with honors, Calif. State U., Los Angeles, 1971; M.S.W. with honors, U. So. Calif., 1973. Lectr. and cons. lesbian and feminist issues and mental health concerns; research asso. Regional Research Inst. in Social Welfare, Sch. Social Work, U. So. Calif., Los Angeles, 1972-75; pvt. practice clin. social work, Los Angeles, 1976-79; psychiat. social worker Douglas County Mental Health, Roseburg, Oreg., 1980-81. Past bd. dirs., 1st co-chairwoman Calif. Women's Commn. on Alcoholism; past bd. dirs. Los Angeles County Alcoholism Adv. Bd., Calif. Inst. for Human Sexuality, Calif. Alcoholism Found.; dir. emeritus Gay Community Services Center, Los Angeles; Calif. del. Internat. Women's Yr. Conf., 1977. Named Woman of Yr., Los Angeles Gay Community, 1978. Mem. Nat. Assn. Social Workers, Acad. Cert. Social Workers, NOW, Nat. Gay Task Force, Los Amigos de la Humanidad U So Calif., Gay and Lesbian Alliance Roseburg (co-chairperson), Umpqua Rivers NOW (founding). Democrat. Jewish.

FIGNAR, ROSEMARY CASEY, business cons.; b. Pottsville, Pa., July 6, 1945; d. Joseph Edward and Marie (Burns) Casey; B.S. in Home Econs. Edn., Coll. Misericordia, Dallas, Pa., 1967; postgrad. U. Puget Sound, Robert Morris Coll.; m. Eugene Michael Fignar, June 15, 1968. Tchr. home econs. Pitts. Bd. Edn., 1968-70; dietician Kaufmann's Dept. Store, Pitts., 1971-73; consumer specialist Better Bus. Bur. Pitts., 1973-74; supr. consumer and public affairs Beecham Products, Pitts., 1974-79; mgr. consumer affairs Pepsi-Cola Bottling Group, Purchase, N.Y., 1979-81; ind. bus. cons., Old Greenwich, Conn., 1982—. Mem. Literacy Vols. Am., Stamford, Conn., 1982—. Mem. Soc. Consumer Affairs Profls. Grocery Mfrs. Am., Elec. Women's Round Table (nat. dir.), Home Economists in Bus., Am. Home Econs. Assn.

FIGURELLI, JENNIFER CONSTANCE, psychologist; b. Jersey City, May 11, 1945; d. Francesco Antonio and Jean (Bigler) F.; B.S., St. Lawrence U., 1966; M.A., U. S.C., 1970; Ph.D., Fordham U., 1977; postgrad. U. Calgary, Jersey City State Coll. Research psychologist Alta. (Can.) Mental Hosp., Ponoka, 1967; psychol. research asst. U. Calgary (Alta.), 1968-69; psychologist Columbia (S.C.) Public Schs., 1969-70; psychologist Jersey City Public Schs., 1970-82, dir. bur. spl. services, 1982—; asst. prof. psychology St. Peter's Coll., Jersey City, 1970—. Mem. S.C. State Com. on Legalization Abortion, 1970. Mem. NEA, N.J., Jersey City edn. assns., Nat. Assn. Sch. Psychologists (chmn. ad hoc com. 1972-73), Am., N.J., Inter-Am., Southeastern psychol. assns., Internat. Assn. Applied Psychology, N.J. Assn. Sch. Psychologists, Soc. Research in Child Devel., Am. Ednl. Research Assn. Editorial bd. Sch. Psychology Digest. Home: 88 Highland Ave Jersey City NJ 07306 Office: 88 Clifton Pl Jersey City NJ 07305

FILE, KAREN NOVICK, mgmt. cons.; b. Bryn Mawr, Pa., Dec. 4, 1947; d. Jerome F. and Mary S. (Shea) Novick; B.A., Cornell U., 1969; M.Urban Affairs, Boston U., 1973; Ph.D. in Sociology, Temple U., Phila., 1978; m. Joseph C. File, May 1971; children—Charles Francis, Michael McNerney. With Booz, Allen & Hamilton, Phila., 1975—, v.p., 1979—. Mem. Am. Sociol. Assn., Am. Mktg. Assn., Internat. Communications Assn. Author articles in field. Office: 400 Market St Philadelphia PA 19106

FILKINS, MARYELLEN BRYANT, ednl. adminstr.; b. Honolulu, Dec. 18, 1928; d. Paul Kenneth and Eleanor Lillian Bryant; student U. Hawaii, 1946-47; B.S.B.A., Northwestern U., 1951; M.A. in Bus. Edn., U. Wis., Eau Claire, 1970; m. Dwaine Wiley Filkins, May 17, 1952; children—Judith H. Filkins Haight, Mark Bryant, Martha Elizabeth, Suzanne Louise. Asst. sect. mgr. Marshall Field & Co., Oak Park, Ill., 1947-52; substitute tchr. public schs., Menominee, Mich., 1962-64, Rice Lake, Wis., 1964-65; instr. in bus. Wis. Indianhead Tech. Inst., 1965-78, supr. Evening Sch., 1975-78, adult edn. adminstr., 1978—. Pres. chpt. Am. Field Service, Petoskey, Mich., 1963-64; mem. vestry, parish treas. Grace Episcopal Ch., Rice Lake, 1972—; mem. edn. com. Rice Lake C. of C., 1978-79. Mem. AAUW (Wis. dir. 1967—, Wis. pres. 1977-79), Am. Vocat. Assn., Wis. Assn. Vocat. and Adult Edn., Wis. Bus. Edn. Assn., Wis. Vocat. Bus. Edn. Assn. (state sec.-treas. 1967-68), Delta Kappa Gamma (1st v.p. Psi chpt. 1978), Delta Pi Epsilon. Office: 1900 College Dr Rice Lake WI 54868

FILLINGHAM, LINDA JOYCE, savs. and loan exec.; b. Niagara Falls, N.Y., June 25, 1941; d. Kenneth Edward and Marian Georgina (Cooper) F.; m. Bill Shanhouse, Dec. 29, 1980. Asst. to v.p. Riggs Nat. Bank, Washington, 1965-73; exec. v.p., chief operating officer, dir. Friendship Savs. & Loan Assn., Chevy Chase, Md., 1973—. Trustee Studio Theatre (Washington). Mem. Mortgage Bankers Assn., U.S. League Savs. Assns., Md. Savs. and Loan League, Washington Women's Network, Women in Housing and Fin., Fin. Mktg. Council of Greater Washington. Republican. Home: 10708 Great Arbor Dr Potomac MD 20854 Office: 5415 Friendship Blvd Chevy Chase MD 20015

FILSINGER, JOAN DURRANT, real estate sales mgr.; b. Elmira Heights, N.Y., Mar. 23, 1931; d. Arthur John and Erma Belle (Abbott) Bensley; cert. med. office practice, Erie Community Coll., Williamsville, N.Y., 1966; A.S. in Bus. Adminstrn. summa cum laude, Quinsigamond Community Coll., Worcester, Mass., 1981; postgrad. Worcester State Coll., 1981—; m. Raymond K. Filsinger, June 15, 1949 (div. Jan. 1971); children—Linda M. Filsinger Richey, Edward M., Pamela A. Filsinger Revezzo, Victoria M. Filsinger Pires, William A. Med. sec., then med. asst., Buffalo, 1966-68; med. technician Buffalo Gen. Hosp., 1968-70; pharm. sales rep. Milex Products Co., Chgo., 1970-73; profl. rep. Purdue Frederick Co., Norwalk, Conn., 1973-78; applications engr. Life-Tech Instruments Co., Houston, 1978-80; sales mgr. Hearthstone Realty, Inc., 1980—. Active local girl Scouts, Cub Scouts; notary public. Recipient various sales awards. Mem. NOW (chpt. v.p. 1976-77), Nat. Assn. Female Execs. Address: 65 Janet Circle PO Box 184 Shrewsbury MA 01545

FILTER, JEANNE MARIE FINCH, educator; b. Des Moines, July 2, 1926; d. Everett Dale and Alice Evalyn (Rudkin) Finch; B.A. in Psychology, U. Nebr. at Omaha, 1948; m. Kenneth C. Filter, June 24, 1949; children—Douglas C., Daniel C., Julia M. Davison, Joan C., Mary Jane. Tchr., Bloomfield (Nebr.) High Sch., 1948-49; tchr. Littleton (Colo.) Schs., 1955-60; instr. piano, organ Jeanne Filter Studio, Littleton, 1961—; pottery maker, Littleton, 1959—, winner various awards; dir. 1st Nat. Space Art Show, Denver, 1969—. Pres., Keep Littleton Beautiful Assn., 1975—, recipient 1st Place in Colo. prize, 1975; pres. Ladies Guild, Ascension Lutheran Ch., Mo. Synod, Littleton, 1955-57, organist, 1950—; bd. dirs. Community Arts Symphony, Littleton, 1969—; bd. dirs. Bemis Pub. Library, Littleton, 1969-77, chmn., 1972-76; active Republican Party, Littleton, 1949—; rep. of Am. Coll. Musicians in People to People Ambassador Tour to Austria, Poland, U.S.S.R., Rumania, Italy, 1976. Recipient ForeMost Mother award City of Littleton, 1975. Mem. Tchr. for Art Publs. Soc. of St. Louis Inst. Music, Music Tchrs. Nat. Assn., Colo. State Music Tchrs. Assn., Am. Coll. Musicians (judge 1978—), Suburban Music Tchrs. Assn., Nat. Guild Piano Tchrs. (chmn. Littleton-Englewood center 1974—), Community Arts Symphony Guild of Littleton (pres. 1971-72), Monday Musicale of Littleton, Littleton Jaycee Jaynes (pres. 1953-54), Mother's Study Club of Littleton (pres. 1952-53). Home and studio: 742 W Caley Ave Littleton CO 80120

FIMIANI, BETTY JANE, info. source specialist; b. Bassett, Va.; d. William McKinley and Edith Mae (Perdue) Maxey; m. Zane Patrick Hall, Nov. 20, 1956 (div.); 1 dau., Becky Jane Hall; m. 2d, Joseph E. Fimiani, Jr., Sept. 7, 1980. With Battelle Meml. Inst., Washington, 1963—, now corp. rep.; judge U.S. Fed. Paperwork awards, 1974, mistress of ceremonies, 1976. Co-leader troop Girl Scouts U.S.A., 1971. Mem. Nat. League Am. Pen Women (nat. auditor 1976-78, pres. Washington Capitol br. 1976-78, br. auditor 1980—, nat. asst. treas. 1980-82), Assn. Records Execs. and Adminstrs. (nat. conf. treas. 1970, nat. treas. 1973-75) Assn. Records Mgrs. and Adminstrs. (v.p. Nat. Capitol chpt. 1975-76, pres. 1976-77, trustee 1977-80; chpt. Mother of Yr. 1977), Spl. Libraries Assn., W.Va. State Soc., Washington Women's Network. Home: 14115 Chelmsford Rd Rockville MD 20853 Office: Battelle Meml Inst 2030 M St NW Washington DC 20036

FINBERG, BARBARA DENNING, found. exec.; b. Pueblo, Colo., Feb. 26, 1929; d. Rufus Raymond and Velma Aileen (Hopper) Denning; B.A., Stanford U., 1949; M.A., American U. of Beirut (Lebanon), 1951; m. Alan R. Finberg, June 21, 1953. Intern, U.S. Dept. State, Washington, 1949-50, fgn. affairs officer Tech. Coop. Adminstrn., 1952-53; program specialist, area chief, Inst. of Internat. Edn., N.Y.C., 1953-59; editorial asso., program officer, 1965-80, v.p. program Carnegie Corp. of N.Y., N.Y.C., 1980—; trustee N.Y. Found., 1979—. Trustee Stanford U., 1976, v.p. bd., 1980—; mem. N.C. Central U. Sch. Library Sci. adv. council, 1973—. Mem. Am. Ednl. Research Assn., Soc. for Research in Child Devel. Democrat. Home: 165 E 72nd St New York NY 10021 Office: 437 Madison Ave New York NY 10022

FINCH, COLETTE ANTOINETTE LESSUISE, social worker; b. Green Bay, Wis., Feb. 12, 1942; d. Winfred George and Antoinette Mary Lessuise; B.A., St. Norbert Coll., 1964; M.S.W., Loyola U., 1969; m. John Joseph Finch, June 17, 1972. Tchr., St. Joseph's Children's Home, Oklahoma City, 1964-65; social worker Cath. Social Services, Green Bay, 1965-67, summer Head Start, Chgo., 1968; day camp dir., social worker Jane Addams Settlement House, Chgo., summer 1969; social worker Green Bay (Wis.) Pub. Schs., 1969—, dept. co-chairperson, 1977-79; exec. bd. Spl. Ednl. Needs, 1975-78, Child Find, 1977-78. Mem. adv. bd. Big Bros., 1973-79, co chmn. screening com., 1977-79; sec. bd. dirs., prodn. mgr. People's Ballet Co. Ltd., 1979—. Recipient vol. of year award Big Bros., 1977; NIMH grantee, 1967-69. Mem. Acad. Certified Social Workers, Nat. Assn. Social Workers (register of clin. social workers), Wis. Sch. Social Workers Assn., Wis. Alliance Concerned with School Age Parents, Green Bay, Wis. edn. assns., NEA, Behavioral Sci. Book Service. Roman Catholic. Co-founder Green Bay Adventures in Movement for disabled students, 1970. Home: 1122 Garland St Green Bay WI 54301 Office: 200 S Broadway Green Bay WI 54303

FINCH, LINDA MARTIN, architect; b. Phila., Apr. 30, 1948; d. Thomas Vernon and Roma Northcutt (Morgan) F.; B.Arch., U. Fla., 1971. Asso., Oscar Vagi & Assos., Ft. Lauderdale, Fla., 1978-79; prin. Linda Finch, Architect, Ft. Lauderdale, 1978—; dir. design Michael A. Shiff & Assos., Ft. Lauderdale, 1980—; works include: Margate Mcpl. Complex, Lauderhill Mcpl. Complex, rural housing rehab. No. Fla. county. Advisor Greater Victoria Park Civic Assn.; mem. Nat. Sex Equity Demonstration Project. Recipient design award for hdqrs. bldg. Internat. Union Operating Engrs., 1981. Mem. AIA, Assn. Women in Architecture, Union Internationale des Femmes Architects, Nat. Assn. Female Execs. Research on modern European architecture. Office: 1061 W Oakland Park Blvd Oakland Park FL 33311

FINCH, MERRILLEE ANN, automotive leasing co. exec.; b. Chgo., Oct. 31, 1942; d. Bernard James and Margaret Catherine (Walsh) F. Tng. supr Ill. Bell Telephone, Chgo., 1961-72; gen. mgr. Sandpiper Builders, Chgo., 1972-75, Hold & Hooker Property Mgmt., Orlando, Fla., 1975-77; v.p. Don Mealey Chevrolet Leasing Co., Orlando, 1977—; Mem. planning and zoning bd. City of Crestwood (Ill.). Named Saleswoman of Yr. in U.S. U.S. C. of C., 1977. Mem. Orlando Area C. of C. (dir.). Office: 3707 W Colonial Dr Orlando FL 32808

FINCH, SALLY JO, educator; b. Galesburg, Ill., July 7, 1943; d. E.A. and Alice L. (Hartman) Pople; B.S., Ill. State U., 1965; m. Robert E. Finch, June 12, 1966; 1 son, Mark Paul. Tchr., Springfield (Ill.) Public Schs., 1965-66; tchr. Knoxville (Ill.) Sch. Dist., 1966-71, title I reading tchr., 1977—; tchr. Knox-Warren Spl. Edn. Co-op., Galesburg, 1971-74; office mgr. Dr. Donald L. Grieme, Galesburg, 1974-77; part-time prof. edn. Monmouth (Ill.) Coll., 1970—, Carl Sandburg Jr. Coll., Galesburg, 1981—. Treas., John Ericsson Republican League of Knox County, 1981—; Henderson Twp. precinct committeewoman, 1980—. Mem. Ill. Reading Council, Beta Sigma Phi. Methodist. Club: Carl Sandburg Coll. Booster. Home: 560 Kenwick Dr Galesburg IL 61401 Office: Knoxville Sch Dist Mill St Knoxville IL 61448

FINCHER, MARGARET ANN, educator; b. Harrodsburg, Ky., June 2, 1934; d. Henry Alexander and Minnie Bee (White) Cathey; B.S. in Bus. Edn., Auburn U., 1955; M.Ed., U. New Orleans, 1978; m. Willie John Fincher, Jr., Apr. 1, 1955; children—John Richard, Joseph Michael, Judy Darlene, James Andrew. Bookkeeper, Markle's Drug Store, Auburn, Ala., 1952-54; asst. to dir. Auburn U. Library, 1955; elem. tchr., Birmingham, Ala., 1959-62; bus. edn. tchr. Abramson High Sch., New Orleans, 1964—; owner, mgr. craft shop Fanci Krafts, New Orleans, 1977-78; asst. supr. Shaklee Corp., 1979—. Supr. adult Bible tng. dept. Word of Faith Temple, 1982, cons. library devel., 1982, tchr., 1975-80; bd. dirs. Lamb Day Care Center, 1979-81; sustaining mem. Meth. Hosp. Aux., 1967—; adv./sponsor Christian Life on Campus Club. Recipient Am. Legion citation of appreciation, 1981; Future Bus. Leaders Am., award of Appreciation, 1976. Mem. Donna Villa Improvement Assn., Metro. Ednl. Media Orgn., Ch. and Synagogue Library Assn. So. Bus. Edn. Assn., Nat. Bus. Edn. Assn., La. Assn. Bus. Edn., La. Vocat. Assn., United Tchrs. New Orleans, Policemen's Assn. New Orleans (hon.). Democrat. Christian Ch. Office: 5553 Read Blvd New Orleans LA 70127

FINDLATER, (EVELYN) JEANNE, TV sta. exec.; b. Detroit, Sept. 17, 1930; d. Herbert Luke and Gertrude Lennie (Hosking) Sullivan; B.S., Wayne State U., 1963; m. Richard Peter Findlater, Apr. 26, 1969; children by previous marriage—Christopher Grant Osborn, Claudia Lynn Osborn. Tchr. public schs., Detroit, 1963-65; researcher/reporter Detroit Free Press, 1965-67, asso. editor Detroit Mag., 1969-71; producer Sta. WTVS, Detroit, 1967-68, Sta. WKBD-TV, Detroit, 1968-69; producer Sta. WXYZ-TV (ABC), Southfield, Mich., 1969-73, exec. producer, asst. program dir., 1973-75, program dir., 1975-79, v.p., gen. mgr., 1979—. Bd. dirs. Detroit Orch. Hall, Conv. and Visitors Bur. Recipient awards San Francisco State Coll., 1974, 78, Action for Children's TV, 1977, Detroit Women Lawyers, 1978; named Woman of Yr., Am. Women in Radio and TV, 1978. Mem. Nat. Assn. TV Program Execs., Detroit Acad. TV Arts and Scis. (dir.), Greater Detroit C. of C. Episcopalian. Clubs: Detroit Press, Detroit Econ., Adcraft. Office: WXYZ-TV Box 789 Southfield MI 48075 *

FINDLEY, MARY BAKER, violinist; b. Norfolk, Va., May 9, 1943; d. Henry Givens and Virginia Marie (Bredenfoerder) Baker; B.Mus. (Outstanding Sr. Woman in Music), U. Cin., 1965, M.Mus., 1966, D.M.A., 1974; student Staatlich Hochschule Musik, Frankfurt/Main, W. Ger., 1966-68; m. David Francis Findley, Mar. 3, 1966. Pvt. studio, Cin., 1972-75, Tulsa, 1976-80; adj. asst. prof. violin Oral Roberts U., Tulsa, 1976-80; Arts Council Okla. artist-in-residence, 1977-81; concertmaster, soloist, founding mem., bd. dirs. Tulsa Little Symphony Orch., 1978-80; founder Tulsa Chamber Music Festival, 1980; founding mem. Washington Music Ensemble, 1981—; instr. violin George Washington U. and Selma M. Levine Sch. Music (both Washington), 1981—; founder All-Okla. String Symposium, 1977. Mem. Am. String Tchrs. Assn., Music Educators Nat. Conf., Nat. Sch. Orch. Assn., Music Tchrs. Nat. Assn., Mortar Board, Sigma Alpha Iota (Performance award 1972). Office: Music Dept George Washington U Washington DC 20006

FINE, EUNICE WHARTON, state legislator; b. Weld County, Colo., Sept. 28, 1923; grad. summa cum laude David Lipscomb Coll.; m. Donald Fine; children—Cappie, Elissa, Todd. Election coordinator City of Greeley; v.p. Greeley (Colo.) Coca-Cola Bottling Co., now mem. Colo. Ho. of Reps., mem. edn. com., bus. affairs and labor com.; mem. Majority Party Adv. Council on Career Edn. Mem. adv. bd. Greeley Pub. Library; mem. adv. bd. home econs. dept. U. No. Colo.; mem. Edn. Commn. of the States; mem. cabinet, bd. dirs., tchr. Sunday Sch., First Christian Ch., Greeley. Recipient cert. of appreciation in vocat. edn. State of Colo.; named Outstanding Businesswoman, Bus. and Profl. Women's Club, 1979. Mem. P.E.O., Greeley Area C. of C. Republican. Club: Greeley Excelsis Women's. Office: Colorado Ho of Reps State Capitol Denver CO 80203 *

FINE, EVELYN COHEN, coll. adminstr.; b. N.Y.C., Oct. 4, 1945; d. Israel and Louise (Canter) Cohen; B.A. in Journalism and English, L.I. U., 1961; postgrad U. Central Fla., 1979-80; m. Bernard Fine, Mar. 12, 1961; children—Mark, Joanne. Staff mem. Sidney J. Wain Public Relations Agy., N.Y.C., 1961-65; staff writer Daytona Beach (Fla.) News Jour., 1974-75; coordinator employment relations Coop. Career Center, Daytona Beach Community Coll., 1976-79, coordinator public service employees tng. program, 1979—; host show Spectrum Stas. WNDB and WWLV. Vice pres. Temple Beth El, Daytona Beach. Mem. Fla. Coll. Placement Assn., Fla. Assn. Community Colls. (pres.-elect 1982), Volusia Assn. Retarded Citizens, Orgn. Rehab. Tng. Democrat. Club: Greater Daytona Beach Press (v.p. 1974-76). Home: 215 Brookline Ave Daytona Beach FL 32018 Office: PO Box 1111 Daytona Beach FL 32015

FINE, JO RENÉE, audio-visual prodn. co. exec.; b. Norfolk, Va., June 19, 1943; d. Ruby Arthur and Tillie Fern (Goldman) F.; B.A., Smith Coll., 1965; M.A., N.Y.U., 1968, Ph.D., 1973; m. Edward Trieber, Apr. 12, 1981. Probation officer N.Y.C. Office Probation, 1966; research asst. N.Y.U., N.Y.C., 1966-68, asso. research scientist Inst. Developmental Studies, 1968-73, research scientist, 1973-77, adj. asst. prof. dept. ednl. psychology, 1973-76; program analyst N.Y. State Dept. Mental Hygiene, N.Y.C., 1977-78; pvt. practice psychotherapy, N.Y.C., 1978-81; pres. CVM Prodns., Inc., N.Y.C., 1978—; cons. to bds. edn., N.Y.C., also greater met. area, 1973—. Mem. Am. Psychol. Assn., Soc. Psychol. Study of Social Issues, Assn. for Multi-Image (sec.), Am. Women in Radio and TV. Co-author: The Synagogues of New York's Lower East Side, 1978. Home and office: 55 W 16th St New York NY 10011

FINE, MARCIA JEANNE, self improvement and modeling sch. exec.; b. Salt Lake City, Dec. 2, 1945; d. George and Regina (Dines) Blumenthal; B.Ed., Fla. State U., 1966; M.Ed., cert. concentration in women's studies, Ariz. State U., 1979; m. Samuel M. Feinstein, June 23, 1967; children—Jessica Leigh, Ara Jorden. Tchr. English, public high schs., Miami Beach, Fla., Camden, N.J., 1966-71; instr. John Robert Powers Modeling Sch., Phila., 1966-67; teaching asst. Ariz. State U., 1977-79; owner, dir. L'Image Sch. of Self Improvement and Modeling, Scottsdale, Ariz., 1979—; owner, operator L'Image Modeling Agy.; image cons.; lectr. in field. Mem. Today Award com. Scottsdale C. of C. Mem. Bus. and Profl. Women (1st v.p. chpt.), Jewish Bus. and Profl. Women, Am. Modeling Assn. Internat., Nat. Speakers Assn., Costume Inst., Women Emerging, Better Bus. Bur. Democrat. Contbg. editor Women Image Now, 1980. Office: 7220 Stetson Dr Scottsdale AZ 85251

FINE, VIVIAN, composer; b. Chgo., Sept. 28, 1913; d. David and Rose (Finder) F.; privately ed.; m. Benjamin Karp, Apr. 5, 1935; children—Margaret, Nina. Faculty, N.Y. U., 1945-48, Julliard Sch. Music, 1948, State U. N.Y. at Potsdam, 1951, Conn. Coll. Sch. Dance, 1963; music dir. B. deRothschild Found., 1954-60; faculty music div. Bennington (Vt.) Coll., 1964—. Recipient award Am. Acad. and Inst. Arts and Letters, 1979; Rockefeller Found. grantee, 1964, Ford Found. grantee, 1969, Nat. Endowment of Arts grantee, 1974, Woolley Fund grantee, 1973, Martha Baird Rockefeller Fund for Music grantee, 1981. Mem. ASCAP, Inst. of Am. Acad./Inst. Arts and Letters Composer: Two Neruda Poems, 1971, Teisho, 1975, The Women in the Garden, 1977, Romantic Ode, 1976, Brass Quartet, 1977, Momenti, 1978, Missa Brevis, 1972, Sonnets for Baritone and Orch., 1976. Home: RFD 2 Box 630 Hoosick Falls NY 12090 Office: Bennington Coll Bennington VT 05201

FINES, ADA MARIE, sales exec.; b. Pope County, Ill., Mar. 5, 1924; d. Frank and June Belle (McElmurrey) Shetler; student Drake U., 1969; m. James Robert Fines, Sept. 11, 1946; children—James Robert, Frank David. With L.L. Parker Furniture Store, Harrisburg, Ill., 1940-41, Mo. Valley Bridge & Iron Co., Evansville, Ind., 1942-46, Pittsburg-Des Moines Steel Co., 1947-60, Kaiser Engrs., Mountain Home, Idaho, 1961-62; sec., asst. sales mgr. Capp Homes, Des Moines, 1963-73; sales coordinator U.S. Homes, Des Moines, 1973-78, sales mgr., 1978—. Mem. Home Builders Assn. Democrat. Baptist. Club: Order Eastern Star. Contbr. articles to profl. jours.; author short stories appearing in Travel, Redbook, McCalls. Home: 2736 Norwood Dr Des Moines IA 50317 Office: 5390 Second Ave Des Moines IA 50313

FINIZZI, MARGUERITE H(ELENE), educator; b. Allentown, Pa., Nov. 16, 1934; d. John Michael and Margaret Mary (Havrilla) Martin; B.S. in Secondary Edn., Kutztown State Coll., 1956; M.A. in English, Lehigh U., 1973; m. Joseph Anthony Finizzi, Nov. 19, 1954. Tchr. English, Harrison-Morton Jr. High Sch., Allentown, 1956-64, Louis E. Dieruff High Sch., Allentown, 1964-76, Allen High Sch., Allentown, 1976—; instr. to develop. drug edn. competency for tchrs.; mem. in-service council Allentown Sch. Dist., 1973—; discussion leader for jr. classes Jewish Day Sch., 1969-71; seminar discussion leader Council of Youth, 1980; co-owner Parkland Dairy Mart, 1967—. Pres. Lehigh County (Pa.) Coordinating Council, 1967-71. Recipient Meritorious award Kutztown State Coll., 1956; Newspaper Fund fellow, 1981. Mem. Nat. Council Tchrs. English, Pa. Council Tchrs. English, NEA, Pa. State Edn. Assn. (editor eastern region constn.), Allentown Edn. Assn. (social chairperson 1964-79, exec. sec. 1964-69), AAUW, Allentown Women Tchrs. Club (editor constn. and by-laws), Lehigh U. Alumni, Kutztown State Coll. Alumni (pres. Lehigh County 1969-72), Young Democratic Women, Women's Alliance, Women's Benefit, Columbia Scholastic Press Assn. Assn. Adv., Reflector Sci. newsletter, 1979-80. Home: 3025 Pearl Ave Allentown PA 18103 Office: 2387 Main St Schnecksville PA 18078

FINK, RUTH GARVEY, grain co. exec.; b. Colby, Kans., Apr. 26, 1917; d. Ray Hugh and Olive (White) Garvey; student U. Wichita, 1934-37, U. Kans., 1940-41; B.A., U. Ill., 1938; H.H.D. (hon.), Washburn U., 1981; m. Richard L. Cochener, Feb. 17, 1942 (dec. 1954); children—Bruce G., Diana Cochener Broze, Caroline Cochener Bolene; m. 2d, H. Bernard in Mar. 31, 1955. Vice pres., dir. C-G-F Grain Co., Inc., 1957—; pres., dir. Midwest Industries, Inc., 1972—; dir. Garvey, Inc., Stauffer Communications, Inc. Trustee, Garvey Found., Garvey Family Found.; pres. Fink Found., 1962—; bd. dirs. Topeka YWCA, ARC; trustee Washburn Coll., 1960—, Alumni award, 1968; chmn. Bible com. Washburn Coll. Bible, 1977—; Kans. regent Gunston Hall, Lorton, Va., 1966-79. Mem. Nat. Soc. Colonial Dames of Kans. (Roll of Honor 1980), Delta Gamma (Cable award 1965, Shield award 1970), PEO. Republican. Congregationalist. Office: 800 First National Bank Tower Topeka KS 66603

FINLEY, BARBARA SUE, social worker, educator; b. Syracuse, N.Y., Feb. 12, 1935; d. Harold H. and Shirley E. (Abelson) F.; student Syracuse U., 1952-54, M.S.W., 1966; B.A. in Sociology, U. Miami, Fla., 1956. Med. caseworker Onondaga County (N.Y.) Welfare Dept., 1956; med. social worker Syracuse Dispensary, Out Patient Clinic, 1957-60, 62-63, Syracuse Meml. Hosp., 1960-62; social work therapist Jewish Family Service, Syracuse, 1964-65; social work cons. Fountainhead Convalescent Home, N. Miami, Fla., 1968-70; med. social worker Mt. Sinai Hosp., Miami Beach, Fla., 1966-70, State U. Hosp., Upstate Med. Center, Syracuse, 1970-73; field work supr. undergrad. program U. Miami, Fla., 1973-75; clin. asst. prof. dept. pediatrics U. Miami, 1973-75; mem. adj. faculty Onondaga Community Coll., Syracuse, N.Y., 1975-76; field instr. Grad. Sch. Social Work, Syracuse U., 1975—; supr. and direct worker dept. social work State U. Hosp., Syracuse, 1975—; clin. asst.

prof. dept. pediatrics Upstate Med. Center, 1981—. Mem. service com. Am. Cancer Soc., Onondaga County unit, 1970-73, chmn. social work com. edn. div. N.Y. State, 1980-82; bd. dirs. Ronald McDonald House, Central N.Y., 1981—, Consortium Children's Services, 1981—. Cert. social worker, N.Y. Mem. Nat. Assn. Social Workers. Home: 241 Lafayette Rd #402 Syracuse NY 13203 Office: Social Work Dept State University Hosp 750 E Adams St Syracuse NY

FINLEY, GLENNA, author; b. Puyallup, Wash., June 12, 1925; d. John Ford and Gladys De Ferris (Winters) F.; B.A. cum laude, Stanford U., 1945; m. Donald MacLeod Witte, May 19, 1951; 1 son, Duncan MacLeod. Producer internat. div. NBC, 1945-49; film librarian March of Time, 1949; writer Life mag., 1950; publicity and radio writer, Seattle, 1950-51; freelance writer, 1951-57; contract writer New Am. Library, Inc., N.Y.C., 1970—; author numerous books, 1957—; latest being Master of Love, 1978; Beware My Heart, 1978; The Marriage Merger, 1978; Wildfire of Love, 1979; Timed for Love, 1979; Love's Temptation, 1979; Stateroom for Two, 1980; Affairs of Love, 1980; Midnight Encounter, 1981; Return Engagement, 1981; One Way to Love, 1982. Named Matrix Table Woman of Achievement, 1976. Mem. Free-lances, Mystery Writers Am., Romance Writers Am. Republican. Anglican. Club: Women's Univ. (Seattle). Address: 2645 34th Ave W Seattle WA 98199

FINLEY, JOANNE ELIZABETH, state govt. ofcl.; b. Brockport, N.Y., Dec. 28, 1922; d. Frank Robert and Margaret (Matthews) Otte; B.A. with highest honors, Antioch Coll., Yellow Springs, Ohio, 1944; M.P.H. with highest honors, Yale U., 1951; M.D., Case Western Res. U., 1962; m. Joseph E. Finley, July 19, 1950; children—Scott M., Ethan C., Lucinda M., William N. Health edn. dir. Montgomery County (Md.) Tb and Heart Assn., 1952-55; exec. dir. Montgomery County Planned Parenthood League, 1955-56; founder, dir. Parent and Child, Inc., 1956-57; research dir. Cleve. Health Goals Project, 1963-66; dep. commr. med. acting health commr. Cleve. Div. Public Health, 1966-68; pediatric adolescent medicine intern Hosp. Med. Coll. Pa., 1971; dir. health planning Phila. Dept. Public Health, 1968-72; v.p. med. affairs Blue Cross Greater Phila., 1972-73; dir. public health New Haven Dept. Health, also instr. health adminstrn. Yale U. Med. Sch., 1973-74; commr. health State of N.J., 1974—; asst. clin. prof. Med. Coll. Pa., 1969—; vis. lectr. N.J. Coll. Medicine and Dentistry, 1974—; commr. Kellogg Found. commn. edn. health adminstrn., 1972-74. Diplomate Am. Bd. Preventive Medicine. Mem. Am. Assn. State and Territorial Health Officers, Am. Public Health Assn., Am. Soc. Public Adminstrn., Assn. State Ofcls. Author papers. Office: CN360 Trenton NJ 08625

FINLEY, TARA ANA, fine arts auctioneer; b. Portland, Oreg., July 23, 1948; d. A. Craig and Charlotte (Welsh) F.; B.A. in Art History, Finch Coll., N.Y.C., 1973. Cataloguer antiquities and ethnographic arts, dir. customer service and bids and reserves dept. Sotheby Parke Bernet, N.Y.C., 1973-78; v.p., auctioneer, cataloguer, gallery dir. Phillips Auctioneers, N.Y.C., 1978-81; auctioneer, lead soldier and military miniature, antiquities and ethnographic art specialist Christie's, N.Y.C., 1981—. Mem. Model Figure Collector's Assn., N.Y. Jr. League. Republican. Episcopalian. Club: St. Bartholomew Community. Home: 110 E 87th St New York NY 10028 Office: 219 E 67th St New York NY 10021

FINN, BARBARA JUNE, nurse, educator; b. Evansville, Ind., Dec. 18, 1938; d. Roscoe F. and Doris J. (Lehmann) Norris; diploma Protestant Deaconess Hosp. Sch. Nursing, 1959; student U. Evansville, 1956-57, St. Petersburg Jr. Coll., 1968, U. South Fla., 1976-78; 1 dau., Melissa Ann. Nurse physician's office, Clearwater, Fla., 1959-63; gen. med. nurse Morton F. Plant Hosp., Clearwater, 1963-66; nurse physician's office, Clearwater, 1966-68; head nurse emergency dept. Clearwater Community Hosp., 1968-72; adminstrv. coordinator to emergency physicians, Clearwater, 1972-76; chairperson emergency med. tech. program St. Petersburg (Fla.) Jr. Coll., 1976—; cons. to Fla. Dept. Edn., 1980-81, Tampa Bay Med. Center (Fla.), 1974-75; chmn. edn. com. Tampa Bay Regional Health Planning Council, 1979-80. Mem. Pinellas County Emergency Med. Services Adv. Council, vice-chmn., 1979-80, chmn. edn. and tng. com., 1981-82, chmn. subcom. C.P.R., 1982; mem. adv. council Fla. Gulf Health Systems Agy., 1981-82; instr.-trainer Am. Heart Assn., 1978—. Mem. Fla. Nurses Assn. (dir. 1968-70, v.p. 1968-69), Nat. Assn. Emergency Med. Technicians and Paramedics, Fla. Emergency Med. Technician Assn., Emergency Med. Service Educators Fla. (rec. sec. 1982), Fla. Assn. Community Colls. Republican. Presbyterian. Home: 1316 S Evergreen Dr Clearwater FL 33516 Office: PO Box 13489 St Petersburg FL 33733

FINN, JOAN LOCKWOOD, writer; b. Plainfield, N.J., June 6, 1929; d. William Albert and Ada Louise (Dayton) F.; B.A. in Am. History, Radcliffe Coll., 1951; certificate d'attendance U. Paris Sorbonne Coll., 1952; M.A. in Lang. and Communications, Columbia U., 1979, Ed.M. in Communications, 1981, also postgrad.; Copywriter, J.C. Penney Co., Inc., 1957-58; jr. account exec. Dudley-Anderson-Yutzey, 1958-61; account exec. Theodore R. Sills & Co., 1961-63, Ted Bates & Co., 1963-67; account supr. Henderson & Roll, 1967-69; dir. press relations Motion Picture Assn. Am., N.Y.C., 1969-70; freelance writer, N.Y.C., 1971-73; communications specialist Coopers & Lybrand, 1973-78; communications specialist Urban Acad. for Mgmt., Inc., 1979—. Mem. Public Relations Soc. Am. (accredited), Nat. Council Tchrs. English, Am. Assn. Applied Linguistics. Club: Harvard (N.Y.C.). Author: Heritage of Evil, 1968; Kiss More or How to Get Across in Writing, 1977; librettist Chicken Little; editor Diet Ann., 1973, Diet Yearbook, 1973; contbr. articles to Motor Boating, Ideal Romances, Am. Mercury, Jack O'Dwyer's Newsletters, New Ideas for Figure and Diet, Modern Maturity mags., others. Home: 17 W 54th St New York NY 10019

FINN, PAULA ANNE, rehab. services adminstr.; b. Butte, Mont., Nov. 7, 1949; d. John D. and Lucille T. (Martinesso) Sheehan; B.A. in Sociology, St. Mary Coll., 1971; M.S.W., U. Ill., 1973; m. James W. Finn, Dec. 29, 1970. Mental health technician Kans. Neurol. Inst., Topeka, 1970; community living specialist Macon County Rehab. Facilities, Inc., Decatur, Ill., 1972-73, dir. client services, 1973-75, adminstrv. asst., 1975-77, exec. dir., 1977—; cons. various rehab. facilities in Ill., 1972—, Kans. Dept. Vocat. Rehab., 1981; mem. exec. com. Social Services Agy., 1977—. Cert. rehab. counselor, 1975. Mem. Nat. Assn. Social Workers, Ill. Rehab. Assn. (pres. 1979-80), Ill. Assn. Rehab. Facilities (dir. 1979—), Macon County Assn. Developmentally Disabled, Decatur C. of C. Club: Zonta (dir. 1979-81). Office: 904 E Locust Decatur IL 62526

FINN, SUSAN KUDLA, govt. relations specialist; b. Chicopee, Mass., Nov. 8, 1952; d. Robert F. and Phyllis T. (Swol) Kudla; student Springfield Coll., 1970-71; A.B., Georgetown U., 1974; M.A., George Washington U., 1978; m. Peter C. Finn, May 31, 1975; 1 son, Robert Peter. Intern, Office of Congresswoman Margaret Heckler, 1971-72; correctional intern U.S. Dept. Justice, 1973; intern, editor U.S. Dept. Justice, 1972-74; adminstrv. asst. to mgr. fed. public affairs R. J. Reynolds Industries, Winston-Salem, N.C., 1974-76, fed. public affairs asst., 1976-77, fed. public affairs asso., 1977-78; govt. relations specialist Smith, Bucklin & Assos., 1978—; dir. regulatory affairs Pet Food Inst., Washington, 1978—; guest lectr. Georgetown U., 1975; career adv. Georgetown U., 1980—. Youth coordinator Gov's campaign in Mass. Recipient Spl. Performance award U.S. Dept. Justice, 1973. Mem. Women in Govtl. Relations, Inc. (past pres.), Food Group, Fourth Friday Group. Roman Catholic. Home: 2601 Valley Dr Alexandria VA 22302 Office: 1101 Connecticut Ave Suite 700 Washington DC 20036

FINNEGAN, SARA ANNE, publishing co. exec.; b. Balt., Aug. 1, 1939; d. Lawrence Winfield and Rosina Elva (Huber) F.; B.A., Sweet Briar Coll., 1961; M.L.A., Johns Hopkins U., 1965; m. Isaac C. Lycett, Jr., Aug. 31, 1974. Tchr., chmn. history dept. Hannah More Acad., Reisterstown, Md., 1961-65; redactor Williams & Wilkins Co., Balt., 1965-66, asst. head redactory, 1966-71, editor book div., 1971-76, asso. editor-in-chief, 1976-77, v.p., editor-in-chief, 1977-81, pres., 1981—; editor Kalends, 1973-79, exec. sponsor jour. Histochemistry and Cytochemistry, 1973-77. Trustee St. Timothy's Sch., Stevenson, Md., 1974—, sec. bd., 1974-78; adv. bd. Balt. Ind. Schs. Scholarship Fund, 1977—. Republican. Lutheran. Home: Ross House Delta PA 17314 Office: Williams & Wilkins Co 428 E Preston St Baltimore MD 21202

FINNEY, JOAN MARIE MCINROY, state ofcl.; b. Topeka, Feb. 12, 1925; d. Leonard L. and Mary M. (Sands) McInroy; B.A., Washburn U., 1974; m. Spencer W. Finney, Jr., July 24, 1957; children—Sally, Dick, Mary. Asst., Washington and Topeka offices U.S. Senator Frank Carlson, 1953-69; commr. elections Shawnee County, Kans., 1970-72; adminstrv. asst. to mayor of Topeka, 1973-74; treas. State of Kans., Topeka, 1974—. Candidate for U.S. Ho. of Reps., 1972. Mem. Nat. Assn. State Treasurers (Midwest v.p.), Nat. Assn. Unclaimed Property Assn., Nat. Assn. Auditors, Comptrollers and Treas. (dir.), Kans. Women's Polit. Caucus, Bus. and Profl. Women's Club, Sigma Alpha Iota. Democrat. Roman Catholic. Home: 4600 W 19th St Topeka KS 66604 Office: Office of State Treasurer 535 Kansas Topeka KS 66612

FINNEY, LYNNE DRATLER, lawyer; b. June 29, 1941; B.A. cum laude, U. Calif., Berkeley, 1962; J.D. magna cum laude, Loyola U., Los Angeles, 1967. Admitted to Calif. bar, 1968, D.C. bar, 1975; with firm Loeb & Loeb, Los Angeles, 1967-70; asst. county counsel County of Santa Cruz, Calif., 1970-71; counsel U.S. Senator Mike Gravel, Washington, 1973-75; atty. spl. subcom. on investigations of house interstate and fgn. commerce com. U.S. Ho. of Reps., Washington, 1973-75; partner firm Gailor & Elias, Washington, 1975-77; dir. Office of Industry Devel., Fed. Home Loan Bank Bd., Washington, 1977-79; pres. Internat. Fin. Services, 1980—; atty.-adv. AID, 1981—; adj. prof. Loyola U., Los Angeles, 1969-70; asst. prof. U. Santa Clara, 1971-73, dir. Law Clinic, 1971-73; adj. prof. Washington Coll. Law Am. U., 1974-75; cons. in field. Bd. dirs. Mexican-Am. Legal Def. Fund, Los Angeles, 1969-70; mem. Pres.'s Task Force on Women, Pres.'s Task Force on Small Bus., 1977-79; bd. dirs. Legal Aid Soc. Santa Clara County, Calif., 1971-73; chairperson The Network, 1975-80; sponsor Women's Campaign Fund, 1979-80. Mem. Am. Judicature Soc., D.C. Bar Assn., Calif. Bar Assn., U.S. Supreme Ct. Bar Assn., Am. Bar Assn., Fed. Bar Assn. Address: 11018 Oakwood St Silver Spring MD 20901 *

FINTZY, NANCY ARO, bank exec.; b. Pitts., June 10, 1943; d. Herbert Andrew and Ellenrosan Gretchen (Peters) Grosick; B.S. (Nat. Merit scholar), Denison U., 1965; M.S. (NASA fellow), Carnegie-Mellon U., 1967; M.B.A. with distinction, N.Y. U., 1978; m. Richard Albert Fintzy, Sept. 16, 1978. With Fed. Res. Bank N.Y., N.Y.C., 1969-75, sr. tech. systems analyst, 1973-74, tech. dir., 1974-75; 2d v.p. Chase Manhattan Bank, N.A., N.Y.C., 1975—. Mem. Soc. Mgmt. Info. Systems, Phi Beta Kappa. Lutheran. Office: One Chase Manhattan Plaza New York NY 10081

FIORATTI, HELEN ELIZABETH, designer, antique dealer; b. N.Y.C., Mar. 16, 1931; d. Arturo and Ruth (Teschner) Costantinio; B.S., Parsons Sch. Design; m. Nereo Fioratti, Nov. 19, 1963; 1 dau., Arianna. Jewelry, furniture designer; v.p. L'Antiquaire, Inc., N.Y.C. Republican. Club: Tennis (Firenzo, Italy). Author: How to Know French Antiques. Home: 555 Park Ave New York NY 10021 Office: 717 Madison Ave New York NY 10021

FIORAVANTI, NANCY ELEANOR, bank ofcl.; b. Gloucester, Mass., Apr. 10, 1935; d. Richard Joseph and Evelyn Grace (Souza) Fioravanti; grad. high sch. Various positions and depts. Cape Ann Bank and Trust Co. (successor to Gloucester Safe Deposit & Trust Co.), Gloucester, 1953—, with trust dept., 1959—, asst. trust officer, 1970—. Treas. art adv. com. Gloucester Lyceum and Sawyer Free Library. Mem. Nat. Assn. Bank Women. Home: 19 Harvard St Gloucester MA 01930 Office: 154 Main St Gloucester MA 01930

FIORE, JOAN, psychologist; b. Englewood, N.J., May 26, 1951; d. Romeo and Helen (Unites) F.; B.A. summa cum laude, Duke U., 1972; M.A. (NIMH fellow), Emory U., 1975, Ph.D., 1977; m. Roger Silfvast, July 14, 1979; 1 dau., Brittany. Psychologist, Providence Med. Center, Seattle, 1977; lectr. Seattle U., 1977; staff psychologist family treatment program, med. cons. suicide and assault team VA Med. Center, Seattle, 1978-82; instr. U. Wash. Sch. Medicine, Seattle, 1978-82, clin. asst. prof., 1982—. Cert. sex therapist, Wash.; lic. clin. psychologist, Wash. Mem. Am. Psychol. Assn., Western Psychol. Assn., Wash. State Psychol. Assn. Home: 1911 31st Ave S Seattle WA 98144 Office: Dept Psychiatry and Behavioral Sci U Wash Sch Medicine RP-10 Seattle WA 98195

FIORELLA, BEVERLY JEAN, med. lab. scientist; b. Owensboro, Ky., Oct. 29, 1930; d. Gabriel and Agnes Loretta (Kurz) F.; B.S., Webster Coll., 1952; M.A., Central Mich. U., 1976. Chief microbiology and blood bank St. Mary's Hosp., Kansas City, Mo., 1956-67; instr., asst. prof. med. lab. scis. dept. Coll. Assoc. Health Professions, U. Ill., Chgo., 1967-74, assoc. prof., 1974-80, prof., 1980—, assoc. head dept. med. lab. scis., 1977—, grad. program coordinator, 1977-81; mem. adv. panel on health ins. Subcom. Health of Com. on Ways and Means, Ho. of Reps., 1975-80. cons. lab. improvement sect. immunohematology divs. labs. Dept. Public Health State of Ill., 1975—. Mem. Am. Soc. Med. Tech. (pres. 1976-77), Am. Assn. Blood Banks, Ill. Assn. Med. Technologists (named Ill. Med. Technologist of Yr. 1976), Chgo. Soc. Med. Technologists (treas., dir. 1969-70), Chicagoland Blood Bank Soc. (v.p. 1975-76), Acad. Clin. Lab. Physicians and Scientists, Am. Soc. Allied Health Professions, Internat. Soc. Blood Transfusion, Alpha Mu Tau. Mem. bd. editors Med. Tech.- A Series, 1970-74. Office: Dept Med Scis Coll Assoc Health Professions U Ill at Chgo 808 S Wood St 690 CME Chicago IL 60612

FIORI, PAMELA, editor; b. Newark, Feb. 26, 1944; d. Edward and Ruth (Rascati) Fiori; B.A. cum laude, Jersey City State Coll., 1966; m. Colton Gioner. Research assoc. Holiday mag., N.Y.C., 1968-69, assoc. editor 1970-71; assoc. editor Travel & Leisure, N.Y.C., 1971-74, sr. editor, 1974-75, editor-in-chief, 1975—; exec. v.p. Am. Express Pub. Corp. Mem. Am. Soc. Mag. Editors, Women's Forum, N.Y. Travel Writers. Office: 1350 Ave of Americas New York NY 10019

FIPPINGER, GRACE J., telephone co. exec.; b. N.Y.C., Nov. 24, 1927; d. Fred Herman and Johanna Rose (Tesio) F.; B.A., St. Lawrence U., Canton, N.Y., 1948; LL.D. (hon.), Marymount Manhattan Coll., 1980. With N.Y. Telephone Co., N.Y.C., 1948—, div. mgr., Nassau, 1966-71, gen. comml. mgr., Queens, 1971-74, Bklyn., 1973-74, v.p., sec.-treas., 1974—; dir. Conn. Mut. Life Ins. Co., Pfizer, Inc., Gulf & Western Industries, Inc., L.I. Trust; mem. adv. bd. Manhattan East, Mfrs. Hanover Trust Co. Hon. bd. dirs. L.I. div. Am. Cancer Soc.; bd. dirs. Greater N.Y. Fund; trustee Citizens Budget Commn. Recipient John Peter Zenger award Nassau County Press Assn., 1975; named Woman of Year, Bus. and Profl. Women Nassau County, 1969, Woman of Achievement, Flatbush Bus. and Profl. Women's Assn., 1974; Outstanding Bus. Woman award Marymount Manhattan Coll., 1978. Mem. Am. Soc. Corp. Secs., Fin. Execs. Inst., N.Y. C. of C. and Industry, Ladies Profl. Golf Assn. (hon.). Clubs: St. Lawrence of L.I.; Soroptimist (Woman of Year, Central Nassau 1974); Board Room. Home: 31 Meadow Ln Hicksville NY 11801 Office: 1095 Ave of Americas New York NY 10036

FIRCHOW, EVELYN SCHERABON, educator; b. Vienna, Austria; came to U.S., 1951, naturalized, 1964; d. Raimund and Hildegard (Nickl) Scherabon; B.A. (Fulbright scholar), U. Tex., 1956; M.A., U. Man. (Can.), 1957; postgrad. U. Munich (W.Ger.), 1960-61; Ph.D., Harvard U., 1963; m. Peter E. Firchow, 1969; 2 children. Instr. coll. math. Balmoral Hall Sch., Winnipeg, Man., 1953-55; teaching fellow in German, Harvard U., Cambridge, Mass., 1957-58, 61-62; lectr. in German, U. Md. in Munich, 1961; instr. dept. German U. Wis., Madison, 1962-64, asst. prof., 1964-65; assoc. prof. German U. Minn., Mpls., 1965-69, prof. German and Germanic philology, 1969—; vis. prof. U. Fla., Gainesville, 1973; vis. research prof. Nat. Cheng Kung U., Tainan, Taiwan, 1982-83. Alexander von Humboldt fellow, 1960-61, 74, 81; Fulbright fellow, Iceland, 1967-68, research prof., 1980; McMillan travel grantee, 1969, 77; Austrian govt. grantee, 1977; Nat. Endowment Humanities fellow, 1980-81. Mem. MLA (chmn. div. German lit. to 1700 1979-80, exec. com. 1976-81), Medieval Acad. Am., Soc. German-Am. Studies, Internat. Comparative Lit. Assn., Soc. Advancement Scandinavian Studies, Assn. Lang. and Lit. Comparison (founding), Am. Comparative Lit. Assn., Midwest Modern Lang. Assn. (chmn. Scandinavian sect. 1979), Internationale Vereinigung der Germanizten, Am. Assn. Tchrs. of German, Modern Humanities Research Assn., AAUP. Editor: (pseudonym E.S. Coleman) Taylor Starck-Festschrift, 1964; Stimmen aus dem Stundenglas, 1968; Studies by Einar Haugen, 1972; Studies for Einar Haugen, 1972; Was Deutsche lesen, 1973; Rentunj und Bedentunj, 1973. Translator: Einhard: Vita Caroli Magni, Das Leben Karl ds Goonen, 1968; Einhard: Vita Caroli Magni, The Life of Charlemagne, 1972; Icelandic Short Stories, 1974; East German Short Stories, 1979. Contbr. articles and book revs. to Am. and internat. scholarly jours. Office: Dept German U Minn Minneapolis MN 55455

FIREBAUGH, FRANCILLE MALOCH, educator, adminstr.; b. El Dorado, Ark., July 15, 1933; d. Delton Verdis and Dorothy Lucille (Measeles) Maloch; B.S., U. Ark., 1955; M.S., U. Tenn., 1956; Ph.D., Cornell U., 1962; m. John David Firebaugh, Dec. 28, 1970. Instr., U. Tex., Austin, 1956-58; asst. prof. home econs. Ohio State U., Columbus, 1962-65, asso. prof., 1965-69, prof., 1969—, dir. Sch. Home Econs., 1973—, acting v.p. agrl. adminstrn., exec. dean of agr., home econs., natural resources, 1982—. Mem. joint com. on agrl. devel. Bd. Internat. Food and Agr., 1981-82; moderator First Baptist Ch., 1981—. Mem. Nat. Council Family Relations, AAAS, Am. Home Econs. Assn., Ohio Home Econs. Assn., Assn. Adminstrs. Home Econs., Sigma Xi, Sigma Delta Epsilon, Omicron Nu, Phi Upsilon Omicron, Gammas Sigma Delta, Phi Kappa Phi, Epsilon Sigma Phi. Club: Columbus Met. Author: Home Management: Context and Concepts, 1975; Family Resource Management, 1981. Office: Ohio State Univ 1787 Neil Ave Columbus OH 43210

FIREOVED, OPAL MAY, brass and copper co. exec.; b. Aloyansie, Mich., Nov. 12, 1906; d. Fred August and Nessie May (Brown) Eichler; student public schs., Reading, Mich.; m. Donald Gale Fireoved, Sept. 6, 1926; 1 dau., Shirley Ann. Vice pres. Reading Brass Co., Inc., Hillsdale, Mich., 1945-59, owner, pres., 1959—. Methodist. Clubs: Hillsdale Golf and Country, Order of Eastern Star, Lady Elks. Home: 47 S Broad St Hillsdale MI 49242 Office: Reading Brass Co Inc 37 Carleton Rd Hillsdale MI 49242

FIRESTONE, (REBECCA) DARLENE, relocation exec.; b. Norman, Okla., Nov. 4, 1946; d. Jesse Gerald and Dorothy Charlene F.; student Mt. San Antonio Coll., 1964-66; B.A., Pasadena Coll., 1969; postgrad. Iona Coll., 1979—. With Merrill Lynch Relocation Mgmt., White Plains, N.Y., 1970—, successively receptionist, sec., admistv. asst., research analyst, Los Angeles, 1970-74, successively homefinding cons., mgr. homefinding ops., asst. v.p., v.p. homefinding and property mgmt. services, v.p. corp. services, N.Y.C., 1974-80, v.p. homesale services, 1982—cons. relocation Fed. Res.; Bank of N.Y. Bd. dirs. Homeowners Assn., 1979-81. Mem. Internat. Word Processing Assn. (sec.), Nat. Assn. Female Execs., Indsl. League Orange County. Republican. Contbr. articles to profl. jours., newspapers. Office: 4100 Mac Arthur Blvd Newport Beach CA 92660

FIRESTONE, RUTH HARTZELL, educator; b. Balt., Aug. 19, 1936; d. John W. and Ruth Insley (Roberts) Hartzell; B.A., U. Pa., 1959; M.A., U. Colo., 1965, Ph.D., 1972; m. Robert T. Firestone, June 12, 1970; children—Susan, Andrew. Asst. prof. German, Otterbein Coll., Westerville, Ohio, 1969-70; sec. Jim Claus Constrn. Co., Boulder, Colo., 1971-72; sec. to pres. Gerico Inc., Boulder, 1973; asst. prof. German, U. Mo., Columbia, 1973-78, assoc. prof., 1978—, chmn. dept. Germanic and Slavic studies, 1981—. Lector, cantor Our Lady of Lourdes Ch., 1973—, mem. fin. com., 1981—. Summer grantee U. Mo., 1976; Fulbright summer grantee, 1977. Mem. Am. Assn. Tchrs. German, MLA, Western Assn. German Studies. Democrat. Roman Catholic. Author: Elements of Traditional Structure in the Couplet Epics of the Late Middle High German Dietrich Cycle, 1975. Home: Route 3 122 Gateway S Columbia MO 65201 Office: Dept German and Slavic Studies U Mo Columbia MO 65211

FIRSTENBERG-GROSSMAN, IRIS ZAIDELL, archtl. planner and designer; b. Bklyn., May 30, 1945; d. Sol Louis and Rosa Edith (Miller) Firstenberg; B.F.A., Pratt Inst., 1967; postgrad. Sch. Visual Arts, 1972-74; m. Richard Philip Grossman, May 26, 1975. Designer, Pomerance and Brienes, N.Y.C., 1967-69; dir. interior planning, Shreve Lamb and Harmon Architects, N.Y.C., 1971-75; project designer, Kuhn Drake Hessberger Architects, Summit, N.J., 1975-76; project dir., Bonsignore Brignati and Mazzotta Architects, N.Y.C., 1976-79; project designer Swanke Hayden Connell & Partners, N.Y.C., 1979—; cons. in field. VISTA vol. with Sioux Indians, Pineridge Reservation and Rapid City, S.D., 1969-71; active presdl. campaigns Eugene McCarthy and George McGovern; local area leader Al Blumenthal's N.Y.C. mayoralty campaign, 1973. Democrat. Exhibitor Women in Architecture show, 1974; designer bank renovations Irving Trust Co. and Bankers Trust Co., 1972-75, Shearson Loeb Rhoades Inc.; planner N.Y. Stock Exchange, 1978; designer Shearson/Am. Express, 1980-82. Home: 320 W 89th St New York NY 10024 Office: 400 Park Ave New York NY 10022

FISCHER, ASMA QURESHI, pediatric neurologist; b. Pakistan, Apr. 8, 1950; came to U.S., 1975; d. Muhammad Siddique and Mahmudah Qureshi; M.B., B.S., U. Karachi, 1973; m. Paul Mehdi Fischer, Dec. 30, 1977. Resident in pediatrics Waterbury (Conn.) Regional Hosp.-U. Conn., 1975-77, Brookdale Hosp. Med. Center, Bklyn., 1977-78; fellow in pediatric neurology Bowman-Gray Med. Sch., Winston-Salem, N.C., 1978-81; instr. pediatric neurology U. Nebr.-Creighton U. med. schs., Omaha, 1981—; cons. in field. Mem. Am. Acad. Neurology, Child Neurology Soc., Assn. Pakistan Physicians, Internat. Assn. Child Neurology, Nat. Assn. Female Execs. Muslim. Author papers in field. Office: Dept Neurology 42d and Dewey Ave Omaha NE 68105

FISCHER, BARBARA JEAN, food processing co. exec.; b. Onawa, Iowa, Sept. 4, 1950; d. R. W. and J. Noreen (Greenawalt) F.; B.A. cum laude, Colo. Coll., 1972; M.B.A., U. Pa., 1974. Mgmt. research analyst Busch Center U. Pa., 1973-74; fin. analyst corp. fin. staff Xerox, Rochester, N.Y., 1974-77; v.p. Internat. Bus. Assos., Cedar Falls, Iowa,

1977-80; comptroller Soypro of Iowa, Cedar Falls, 1977-80; mgmt. cons. Frito-Lay, Inc., Dallas, 1980-81, distbn. exec., 1981—; mem. adv. bd. Burst Products, Inc.; Iowa del. White House Conf. on Small Bus., 1980. Mem. adv. bd. Kirkwood Community Coll., 1978-79. Mem. Exec. Women, Dallas, Internat. Trade Assn. Dallas, Dallas Opera Guild, World Future Soc., Phi Beta Kappa, Pi Gamma Mu. Republican. Mem. Unity Ch. Club: P.E.O. (treas. 1975-77). Contbr. articles to profl. jours. Home: 2201 Nolan Dr Carrollton TX 75006 Office: Frito-Lay Hdqrs PO Box 35034 Dallas TX 75235

FISCHER, CONSTANCE TAYLOR, psychologist; b. Oahu, Hawaii, July 29, 1938; d. Milton Clay and Irene Elsie (Nelson) Taylor; Ph.D., U. Ky., 1966; m. William Frank Fischer, Apr. 16, 1964; 1 son, Michael Allen. Psychology trainee VA Hosps., Lexington and Louisville, Ky., 1961-65, Pitts., 1965-66; asst. prof. psychology dept. Duquesne U., Pitts., 1966-70, asso. prof., 1970-82, prof., 1982—; parttime pvt. practice clin. and cons. psychology, 1968—; cons. Hay Assos., 1980—, Somerset Hosp., 1970—. Bd. dirs. Allegheny Children and Youth Services Council, 1978—. Cert. sch. psychologist, lic. clin. psychologist. Fellow Soc. Personality Assessment; mem. Am. (chmn. tng. com., sect. 1, div. 12, 1975-80), Eastern, Pa. (pres. clin. div. 1980-81, treas. 1981-83), Greater Pitts. (dir. 1973-79) psychol. assns. Author: Individualized Assessment, 1982. Editor: (with Giorgi and Murray) Duquesne Studies in Phenomonological Psychology, Vol. II, 1975; (with Brodsky) Client Participation in Human Services, 1978. Contbr. articles to profl. jours. Home: 319 Garlow Dr Pittsburgh PA 15235 Office: Psychology Dept Duquesne U Pittsburgh PA 15282

FISCHER, JEANETTE LUCILLE STOCKETT (MRS. RICHARD ALLEN FISCHER), occupational therapist; b. Albert Lea, Minn., Nov. 13, 1937; d. Stewart Joseph and Bessie Lucille (Junk) Stockett; B.S. in Occupational Therapy, Washington U., St. Louis, 1960; postgrad. Webster Coll.; m. Richard Allen Fischer, Oct. 22, 1960; children—Richard Arnold, Robert Andrew. Occupational therapy aide St. Louis State Hosp., 1958-59; dir. occupational therapy Alexian Bros. Hosp., St. Louis, 1960-62, Americana Healthcare Center, Florissant, Mo., 1975-80; coordinator occupational therapy, phys. medicine dept. St. Mary's Health Center, 1980-81; dir. occupational therapy dept. Fullerton (Calif.) Care Convalescent Hosp., 1981—. Clinic vol. aide ARC, 1971-73; treas. Midland Valley Estates Improvement Assn., 1966-68, 69-70, v.p., 1971-72, pres., 1972-73, bd. dirs., 1974-81, treas., 1972-73; treas., Marion PTA, 1967-68, carnival chmn., 1968-69, v.p., 1969-71, picnic chmn., 1969-73; sch. talent show dir. Boy Scouts Am., 1971-72; mem. St. Louis Civic Ballet, 1973-78; mem. Sta. KETC-TV Ednl. TV, 1971-78; sec.-receptionist Michael Simms Acad. Dance, St. Louis, 1974-76. Mem. Am., Mo. (public relations chmn. 1965, program chmn. 1979, pres. 1980-81), Calif. occupational therapy assns., World Fedn. Occupational Therapy, Los Angeles Occupational Therapy Dirs. Forum, Internat. Platform Assn., Met. Ballet St. Louis, St. Louis Dance Concert Soc., Humane Soc. Mo., Alpha Xi Delta. Lutheran. Home: 4217 Elder Ave Seal Beach CA 90740 Office 2222 N Harbor Blvd Fullerton CA 92635

FISCHER, MARGARET ELEANOR, psychologist, educator; b. Newark, Dec. 4, 1927; d. John T. and Mary (Worden) F.; B.S. cum laude in Psychology, Seton Hall U., 1958; postgrad. U. Paris, 1958, Carl G. Jung Inst., Switzerland, 1958-59, N.Y. U., 1959-60, U. Md., 1960-63; M.A. magna cum laude in Ednl. Psychology, San Diego State U., 1966; postgrad. (NDEA grantee), U. Alaska, 1965; Ph.D. cum laude in Psychology, U. Wash., 1970. Resident counselor Children's Center, N.Y.C., 1959-60; tchr. Am. Dependents' Schs., Okinawa, Germany, Turkey, France, 1960-64; tchr. English as fgn. lang. Jean Giraudoux Lycée, Chateauroux, France, 1963-64; tchr. English and French, Sweetwater Sch. Dist., Chula Vista, Calif., 1964-66; asst. to editor Rev. of Ednl. Research Jour., Seattle, 1967-68; psychologist vocat. rehab. program Edmonds Sch. Dist., Lynnwood, Wash., 1968-70, Charles Denny Youth Center, Everett, Wash., 1969-71; instr. psychology Seattle Community Coll., 1971; asst. prof. dept. social scis., humanities and edn. Purdue U., Lafayette, Ind., 1971-72; lang. evaluation specialist Def. Lang. Inst., Monterey, Calif., 1972; research psychologist U. Calif., San Francisco, 1972; asst. prof. psychology U. Calif., Santa Cruz, 1973, Mass. State Colls., 1973-76; pvt. practice psychology, Mass., 1976-78; psychologist N.Y. State Dept. Mental Hygiene, 1978, Alaska div. mental health Harborview Devel. Center, Valdez, 1978-79; psychologist Alaska Psychiat. Inst., Anchorage, 1979—. Recipient internat. travel award Purdue U., 1972, scholarly support award Mass. State Coll., 1974, 75, 76; lic. psychologist, Alaska. Mem. Am. Psychol. Assn., Internat. Council Psychologists (area chmn. Alaska 1979-80), Interam. Soc. Psychologists, DAR, Mensa. Contbr. articles to psychol. jours. Home: PO Box 10-1222 Anchorage AK 99511 Office: Alaska Psychiat Inst 2900 Providence Dr Anchorage AK 99504

FISCHER, RUTH, editor, author, critic; b. Cleve., Nov. 4, 1918; d. Hyman Joseph and Lillian (Hirsch) J.; B.A., Ohio State U., 1942; m. Robert W. Fischer, June 15, 1942 (div. 1970); children—Jeffrey, Kathleen, Julie; m. 2d, Morris Kaplan, 1971 (dec. 1971); m. 3d, Louis Bernstein, 1972. Editor, The AP, Columbus, Ohio, 1942-45; editor publications The Cleve. Play House, 1957-70; book reviewer The Cleve. Plain Dealer, 1958—; drama critic Sun Papers of Ohio, 1966-70; asso. editor Change Mag., 1973-75; mng. editor Civil Liberties Rev., 1975-78; sr. editor World Press Rev., N.Y.C., 1978—; contbr. articles to mags. including The Nation, New Republic, Playboy, Consumer Reports, N.Y. Times; contbr. chpts. to books; adj. asso. prof. Case Western Reserve U., 1965-70. Fellow Theatre Critics Inst.; mem. Nat. Book Critics Circle, Sigma Delta Chi. Home: 44 Old Country Rd New Rochelle NY 10804 Office: 230 Park Ave New York NY 10017

FISCHLER, PAMELA FRAN, advt. exec.; b. Bklyn., Sept. 25, 1951; d. Martin Lee and Gilda Augusta (Gerber) Greenfield; student Stephens Coll., 1969-71; B.A., Hofstra U., 1973; m. Burton Fischler, July 3, 1973. New account exec. Unique Security Agy., Great Neck, N.Y., 1973-75; career counsellor, account exec. Dartmouth Consultants, recruiting agy. personnel, N.Y.C., 1975; account liaison MGA Inc. advt., Great Neck, 1975-76, v.p. public relations and media, 1977-80, exec. v.p., 1980—. Home: 1495 Cleveland Ave East Meadow NY 11554 Office: 525 Northern Blvd Great Neck NY 11021

FISH, (CHARLOTTE) RUTH GOODALL, journalist, social worker; b. Alamosa, Colo., Nov. 11, 1892; d. Alfred Alexander and Lavina Jane (Dorris) Goodall; M.S.W., Smith Coll., 1923; postgrad. U. Mich., 1923-24; m. John Clayton Fish, Sept. 24, 1911 (dec. 1929); 1 dau., Dorris F. (Mrs. Leonard J. Coyne). Soc. editor, feature writer Alamosa Courier, 1910-14; news editor Alamosa Jour., AP reporter, feature writer Denver Post, Pueblo (Colo.) Star-Jour., 1918-21; disaster relief worker ARC, Pueblo, Tulsa, 1921-22; child welfare worker, Pontiac, Mich., 1922-23; med. social worker U. Mich. Hosp., Ann Arbor, 1923-30; dir. med. Clinics St. Luke Hosp., Chgo., 1930-34; dir. emergency relief Taos County, N.Mex., 1934-36; editor Taos Valley News, 1936; AP reporter, Taos County and Santa Fe New Mexican, 1937-46; editor column Wiesbaden (Germany) Post, USAF Hdqrs., 1947-49; dir. visitors' service, sec. Taos County C. of C., 1950-58; AP reporter Taos County, 1951-55, UPI reporter, 1955-60; county editor El Crepusculo de Liberdad, Taos, 1958-60; free-lance writer. Substitute tchr. Taos Indian Day Sch., 1938, Taos Municipal Schs., 1942-46; sec. Taos Fiesta Corp., 1935-46, 50-61; chmn. Taos County chpt. N.Mex. Com. on Aging, 1964-74; Social Service cons. County Project on Aging. Mem. Taos Little Theater, Play Readers' Club, 1951-75; pres. Holy Cross Hosp. Aux., 1940-44, admissions officer, 1961-66. Recipient Civilian Service Cross ARC, World War I. Mem. Taos County Hist. Soc. (v.p. 1962—), Am. Assn. Social Workers (charter, Golden Membership award 1966). Democrat. Episcopalian. Clubs: Taos Garden (pres. 1951-53), Playreaders. Home: La Casita Santa Fe Rd Taos NM 87571

FISH, KATHLEEN ANN, assn. exec.; b. Milw., Apr. 6, 1943; d. Ralph Eugene and Aurelia Mary (Armbruster) F.; student U. Wis., 1961-62; m. Michael Kessenich, May 3, 1974. Office mgr. Karan, Roth, Frank & Co., C.P.A.'s, Milw., 1963-73; treas. Maggie's Travel Shoppe, Milw., 1971-74, also dir.; with customer relations dept. Italian Line Cruises, N.Y.C., 1978-79; communications mgr. U.S. C. of C., N.Y.C., 1979-81, pub. affairs mgr., 1981—. Mem. Pub. Relations Soc. Am., Women in Communications Inc., N.Y. Soc. Assn. Execs. Republican. Congregationalist. Home: 20 Waterside Plaza 8F New York NY 10010 Office: 711 3d Ave New York NY 10017

FISH, SALLY R., mktg. exec.; b. Albuquerque, Dec. 3, 1936; d. Jackson Cooper and Virginia (Weldey) Fish; B.A. with distinction in journalism, San Diego State U., 1961, postgrad., 1977—; M.B.A. with honors in mktg., Nat. U., San Diego, 1980. Airline hostess various airlines, Los Angeles, 1955-59; data processor Douglas Aircrft El Segundo, Calif., 1957-58; statistician aide San Diego State U., 1958; editor, writer Splty. Mags., San Diego, 1959-62; public relations writer, coordinator Melvin Agy., Las Vegas, Nev., also Phillips-Ramsey Agy., San Diego, 1962-63; coordinator, adminstr., tchr. Lakeside (Calif.) Sch. Dist., 1965-77, 78-80; cons. sales Joan Bodin Fashions UTA, Los Angeles, Tanners Indian Arts, La Jolla, Calif., 1970—; cons. mktg. Grossmont Coll. and Dist., 1978; partner, cons. PR Assos. Agy., San Diego, 1977-78; market adminstr. Pacific Telephone, Orange, Calif., 1981-82, AT&T Long Lines, Santa Clara, Calif., 1982—; cons. in field. Recipient Outstanding Cert. for Service and Achievement in Journalism, San Diego State U., 1961. Edith R. Allen Meml. scholar, 1959-60. Mem. AAUW, Career Women's Assn., Women in Sales, Sigma Delta Chi. Contbr. articles to profl. jours. Home: 3500 Granada Santa Clara CA 95051 Office: 3970 Freedom Circle Dr Santa Clara CA 95050

FISHEL, BARBARA LOUISE, med. orgn. exec.; b. Pa., June 1, 1948; d. Vernon Delmar and Geneva Jane (Simpkins) F.; B.S., U. Del., 1970. Tchr., Brainard Jr. High Sch., Cherry Hill, N.J., 1970-72; tchr., Dickinson High Sch., Wilmington, Del., 1972-74; regional dir. Ortho Pharm. Co., Raritan, N.J., 1974-75; v.p. Nat. Women's Health Orgn., N.Y.C., 1976-79; dir. health services Singer Ednl. Div., Pt. Deposit, Md., 1979-82, div. mgr. edn. div. E.A. Singer, 1982—. Sec.-treas., Suburban Conf. for Women's Athletics, 1972-74; umpire Little League Softball, 1979-80; instr. swimming ARC. Mem. Nat. Assn. Female Execs., AAHPER and Dance, Nat. Assn. Bus. and Profl. Women, New Castle Realtors Assn., NOW, U. Del. Alumni Assn. Address: 4910 Raintree Ct Wilmington DE 19808

FISHER, AILEEN LUCIA, author; b. Iron River, Mich., Sept. 9, 1906; d. Nelson E. and Lucia (Milker) F.; B.J., U. Mo., 1927. Reporter, Nat. Journalistic Register, Chgo., 1929-32; freelance author over 70 books of juvenile verse, plays, stories and biography, 1932—; prin. works include That's Why, 1946; Up the Windy Hill, 1953; Holiday Programs for Boys and Girls, 1953; Runny Days, Sunny Days, 1958; Christmas Plays and Programs, 1960; Going Barefoot, 1960; Where Does Everyone Go?, 1961; Cricket in a Thicket, 1963; Listen, Rabbit, 1964; In the Woods, In the Meadow, In the Sky, 1965; Valley of Smallest, 1966; Feathered Ones and Furry, 1971; I Stood on a Mountain, 1979; Out in the Dark and Daylight, 1980. Recipient Silver medal Treasury Dept., 1978, Poetry award for children Nat. Council Tchrs. English, 1978. Mem. Women in Communications. Democrat. Address: 505 College Ave Boulder CO 80302

FISHER, ALICE POINDEXTER, assn. exec.; b. Durant, Okla., Nov. 27, 1941; d. Charles Jack and Mary Lucyle (Cox) Fisher; B.A., San Diego State U., 1963, M.A., 1969; Ph..D., CUNY, 1979; m. Dennis P. Cirillo, Jan. 25, 1978. Tchr. English, Laguna Beach (Calif.) High Sch., 1964-65; Peace Corps vol., Colombia, S.Am., 1965-67; instr. English San Diego State U., 1967-69; instr. Expt. in Internat. Living, Patzcuaro, Mex., 1969; instr. Sch. Internat. Tng., Murcia, Spain, 1970; asst. prof. Hostos Community Coll., CUNY, Bronx, 1970-74; program coordinator Com. on Minority Groups and the Study of Lang. and Lit., MLA, N.Y.C., 1974-78, dir. English programs, 1979-81, spl. cons. minority lit., 1974—; spl. cons. minority lit. various colls. and univs., 1974—. Mem. Assn. Depts. English (dir., editor bull. 1979-81), Modern Lang. Assn., Assn. Studies Am. Indian Lit., Soc. for Study of Multiethnic Lit. of U.S., Nat. Women's Book Assn., AAUW. Editor: Minority Language and Literature: Retrospective and Perspective, 1977; (with Robert B. Stepo) Afro-American Literature: The Reconstruction of Instruction, 1979; The Third Woman: Minority Women Writers of the United States, 1980; Critical Introduction to Cogewea, 1981. Contbr. articles to profl. jours. Home: 301 E 73d St New York NY 10021

FISHER, CARRIE FRANCES, actress; b. Oct. 21, 1956; d. Eddie Fisher and Debbie Reynolds; ed. high sch., Beverly Hills, Calif. Mem. chorus in Broadway musical Irene, 1972; appeared motion pictures Shampoo, 1975, Star Wars, 1977, The Empire Strikes Back, 1980, TV movie Come Back, Little Sheba, 1977, Mr. Mike's Mondo Video, 1979, The Blues Brothers, 1980, Under the Rainbow, 1981. Office: William Morris Agency Inc 151 El Camino Beverly Hills CA 90212 *

FISHER, COLLEEN M., mem. congl. staff; b. Pitts., Sept. 29, 1954; d. C. Francis and Dolores Rida (Darby) Fisher; B.A. with honors in govt., Georgetown U., 1976; M.A., George Washington U., 1980. Constituent asst. to Sen. Richard Schweiker of Pa., 1977-79, legis. asst., 1979-81; profl. staff mem. subcom. on HUD-Ind. Agys., Senate Com. on Appropriations, Washington, 1981—. Mem. Georgetown Alumni Orientation Com. Republican. Office: Room 1241 Dirksen Senate Office Bldg Washington DC 20510

FISHER, DANNA LOUISE, ins. co. sales rep.; b. Stillwater, Okla., Apr. 25, 1954; d. Raymond Wilson and Helen Louise (Ramey) F.; student Hendrix Coll., Conway, Ark., 1972-73. Sec., Steele Canning Co., Inc., Springdale, Ark., 1973-74; legal sec. Cooper Communities, Inc., Bella Vista, Ark., 1974-75; sec. Blue Cross Blue Shield, Little Rock, 1975-77; sales rep. Aetna Life & Casualty, Little Rock and Washington, 1977—. Area rep. Youth for Understanding, Little Rock. Named to Pres.'s Club, 1979, Leader's Seminar, 1979, Corp. of Regionnaires, 1978, 79, 80, Group Leaders' Club, 1979, Women Leaders' Round Table, 1980; named Outstanding New Agt. of Yr., Gen. Agts. and Mgrs. Assn., 1978, Tigress of Yr., 1979. Mem. Nat. Assn. Life Underwriters, Ark. Life Underwriters Assn., Little Rock Assn. Life Underwriters, Am. Bus. Women's Assn., Nat. Assn. Female Execs., ANEW (exec. dir., founder), Annapolis Women's Network. Republican. Methodist. Home: 203 Dreams Landing Way Annapolis MD 21401 Office: 8401 Connecticut Ave Suite 800 Washington DC 20015

FISHER, ELIZABETH CHRISTENSEN (BETTY), photojournalist; b. Salt Lake City, May 9, 1919; d. Orsen Reuben and Anna Katherine (Felix) Christensen; student U. Utah, 1938-39; m. Etsil Robert Fisher, Apr. 23, 1943 (dec. June 1981); children—Edward Robert, Ellen Fisher Trickler, Colleen Fisher Newey, Randall Etsil, Garth Newell (sec.). Corr., Deseret News, Salt Lake City, 1951-60; asst. editor, photographer Weekly Reflex, Kaysville, Utah, 1961-63; asst. editor Br. Clearings, First Security Bank, Salt Lake City, 1962-64; corr. Salt Lake Tribune, 1963-64; photo-journalist Magna (Utah) Times, 1963-64; courthouse reporter Davis County Clipper, 1961-64; editor Weekley Reflex, 1964-69; freelance photo-journalist, public relations exec., editor, 1969—; editor Utah Women Speak, 1979—; condr. workshops, lectr. in field. Mem. Davis County Fair Bd., 1952-80, Davis County Indsl. Commn., 1958-61; publicity and promotion chmn. Davis County Fair, 1975-81; public info. chmn. Davis S. unit Am. Cancer Soc., 1974-80, mem. public info. bd. Utah div., 1976-80. Recipient 4 public info. awards Am. Cancer Soc., 18 awards Utah Press Assn. Mem. Nat. Fedn. Press Women (7 press awards), Utah Press Women (pres. 1958-60, now historian; Utah Woman of Achievement 1981; 63 press awards), Utah Assn. Indsl. Editors (2 awards), Internat. Platform Assn. Utah Assn. Women. Mem. Ch. Jesus Christ of Latter-Day Saints. Asst. editor: My Farmington, 1975; editor Utah Women Speak, 1979—; editor indsl. brochures, jours.; contbr. articles, features to mags. Address: 375 North 200 East Farmington UT 84025

FISHER, GLADYS SANDRA, govt. ofcl.; b. Clinton, N.C., May 3, 1941; d. Millard R. and Gladys I. (Bryant) F.; A.B., Meredith Coll., 1963; M.A. in Teaching, U. N.C., 1964; postgrad. Grad. Sch. Bus. Adminstrn., Harvard U., 1981; m. Robert M. Sprinkle, Mar. 31, 1967. Coordinator adult edn. program Craven Operation Progress, Inc., N.C., 1965-66; program officer VISTA/OEO, Washington and N.Y.C., 1966-69; asso. Leo Kramer, Inc., mgmt. cons., Washington, 1970-71; program devel. specialist Adminstrn. on Aging, HEW, 1971; sr. program specialist Ret. Sr. Vol. Program, ACTION, 1971-74; program mgr. div. research applications and demonstrations Adminstrn. on Aging, Dept. Health and Human Services, 1974-79, dir. div. continuing edn. and tng., 1979—; mem. Howard County Commn. Aging, 1975-80; cons. in adult edn. Scholar N.C. Bd. Edn., 1959-63, James E. and Mary Z. Bryan Found., 1962; Ford Found. grantee, 1963-64. Mem. Am. Soc. Tng. and Devel., Geront. Soc., Am. Assn. Higher Edn., Am. Soc. Public Adminstrn. Baptist. Office: Adminstrn Aging HHS Washington DC 20201

FISHER, HARRIET HAYES (MRS. WILLIAM S. FISHER), clothing designer; b. Toledo, Feb. 25, 1919; d. Ernest Eugene and Gertrude (Bradley) Hayes; student Ohio State U., 1938; B.A. cum laude, U. Toledo, 1940; postgrad. Parsons Sch. Design, 1940-41; m. Robert H. Raymond, Apr. 6, 1943 (dec. June 1943); m. 2d, William S. Fisher, Sept. 22, 1945 (dec. Jan. 1958); children—William S. II, Nancy Jane, John Hayes. Sportswear designer Patti, Glen Mfg. Co., Milw., 1942-45; sportswear designer Jr. House of Milw., 1945-60, v.p., 1958-60; head designer Jack Winter, Inc., Milw., 1960-72; designer Arthur Jay, 1972-73; cons., freelance designer, 1973—. Mem. Friends of Art, Pi Beta Phi. Republican. Congregationalist. Address: 1074 E Circle Dr Milwaukee WI 53217

FISHER, JANET ELIZABETH, govt. ofcl., computer systems specialist; b. Green Creek Twp., N.C., Dec. 1, 1928; d. William Mack and Venona Lee (Cole) Fisher; B.A., George Washington U., 1964; postgrad. Cath. U., 1965-70, George Washington U., 1971—. Mem. staff identification div. FBI, Washington, 1945-62; mathematician, crystallographer U.S. Naval Research Lab., Washington, 1963-70; mathematician, computer systems analyst, nonexpendable ordnance div. Central Naval Ordnance Mgmt. Info. Systems Office, Naval Ordnance Sta., Indian Head, Md., 1970-73; computer systems specialist, mgmt. info. and data systems div. Naval Sea Systems Command, Washington, 1973-77, policy, planning and programming directorate Automatic Data Processing Plans div. Naval Data Automation Command, Washington, 1977—. Mem. Sci. Research Soc. Am., Am. Math. Soc., Am. Crystallographic Assn., Philos. Soc. Washington, AAAS, IEEE, Assn. Sr. Engrs., Sigma Xi. Home: 6117 Greeley Blvd Springfield VA 22152 Office: Policy Planning and Programming Directorate Automatic Data Processing Plans Div Naval Data Automation Command Washington DC 20374

FISHER, JOANNE LOUISE, lawyer; b. Detroit, Dec. 13, 1949; d. Charles Eugene and Helen Ruth (Bluhm) F.; B.A., Oberlin Coll., 1972; J.D., Wayne State U., 1975. Admitted to Mich. bar, 1975; mem. firm Leonard C. Jaques, Detroit, 1976-78; asst. cashier, legal counsel Bank of Commonwealth, Detroit, 1978-79, asst. v.p., legal counsel, 1979-80; legal officer Mich. Nat. Bank Detroit, Clawson, 1980—. Mem. Women Lawyers Assn. Mich. (corr. sec. 1981-82, treas. 1982-83), Am. Bar Assn., State Bar Mich., Detroit Bar Assn. Lutheran. Office: 1400 W Fourteen Mile Rd Clawson MI 48017

FISHER, JULIANNE, educator; b. Walla Walla, Wash., July 20, 1951; d. William L. and Dorothy (Foley) F.; B.A., Walla Walla Coll., 1976. Adminstrv. asst. to dir. mktg., public relations and devel. St. Helena Hosp. and Health Center, Deer Park, Calif., 1976-79; instr. voice, exec. sec. to chmn. dept. music Walla Walla Coll., 1980—. Mem. Am. Choral Dirs. Assn.

FISHER, LAURA MAGDALYNE, guidance counselor; b. Franklinton, N.C., Aug. 11, 1941; student Drakes Bus. Col., 1958-60; A.A., Essex County Coll., 1970; B.A. in Spl. Edn., Jersey City State Coll., 1972, M.A. in Guidance and Student Personnel Services, 1974. Clk.-typist Dept. Agr. FDA, 1967; tchr. handicapped Newark Bd. Edn., 1972-75; guidance counselor Dayton St. Sch., Broadway Jr. High Sch., Weequahic High Sch., 1975—; head tchr. Seton Hall U. Neighborhood Adult Edn. Center, 1976; adv., founder Career Devel. Club, Weequahic High Sch., sec. curriculum com. on spl. edn. Newark Bd. Edn. Recipient award for work with juvenile delinquents Essex County Youth House, 1977, for work with elderly Newark Extended Care Facility, 1981. Mem. Essex County Guidance Assn., Am. Personnel and Guidance Assn., Assn. Non-White Concerns, Urban Council on Adolescents (affiliate), Planned Parenthood. Baptist. Home: 291 Pomona Ave Newark NJ 07112 Office: 279 Chancellor Ave Newark NJ 07112

FISHER, (LOIS) BARBARA, violinist; b. Lima, Ohio, Sept. 20, 1950; d. Lynn Adrian and Lois Mae (Wisener) F.; B.Mus. (scholar), U. N.Mex., 1972; M.Mus., Ind. U., 1974; fellow N.C. Sch. Arts, 1974-75. Violinist, Piedmont Chamber Orch., 1974-75; 1st violinist Indpls. Symphony Orch., 1975—; 2d violinist Thouvenel String Quartet, 1975-76; pvt. violin tchr., dir. jr. high sch. orchs., solo and chamber music recitalist. Mem. Am. Fedn. Musicians, Delta Gamma, Sigma Alpha Iota. Lutheran. Office: Clowes Hall 4600 Sunset St Indianapolis IN 46208

FISHER, MARILYN, communication prodn. co. exec., ins. underwriter; b. New Rochelle, N.Y., May 30, 1922; d. Charles D. and Lucile (Rockwell) F.; illustration and indsl. design cert. Pratt Inst., 1943; student Hofstra U., 1958-59; 1 dau., Sharon Kathleen Neilland Hanna. Comml. artist, illustrator Harcourt Brace, 1943-45; art dir. Depicto Films, Inc., N.Y.C., 1946-56; ind. ednl. film producer, N.Y.C., 1956-62; v.p., art dir. Bear Films, Inc., Baldwin, N.Y., 1962-72; pres. Communica-Vision Prodns., Princeton, N.J., 1972-81; registered rep. John Hancock Family of Cos.; fin. seminars, tax-favored retirement planning, 1981—; seminars in film prodn., color coordinating, organizational techniques and sales methods; color cons. Am. Standard Corp. Recipient Gold medal Internat. Film and TV Festival of N.Y., 1970, Silver medal, 1974, Bronze medal, 1975; Silver medal V.I. Internat. Film Festival, 1978; U.S. Indsl. Film Festival award for creative excellence, 1979; Mem. Nat. Assn. Life Underwriters, Women's Life Underwriters Council, Nassau Assn. Life Underwriters, Internat. Women in Communications, Info. Film Producers Am., Internat. Indsl. TV Assn. Clubs: Princeton Ski, Armand Sodero Chorale (publicity cons.). Home: 150 S Forest Ave

Rockville Centre NY 11570 Office: 3601 Hempstead Turnpike Suite 306 Levittown NY 11756

FISHER, MARJORIE HELEN, librarian; b. Losantville, Ind., Nov. 27, 1924; d. James Cleo and Isie May (Sutton) Hardwick; student Olivet Nazarene Coll., 1943-45; A.B., Ball State U., 1947; postgrad Ariz. State Tchrs. Coll., 1949, Ind. U., 1955, Ind. State U., 1957, Butler U., 1958; m. Delmar Fisher, Sept. 29, 1950; children—Deljon Ray, Madge Denise Fisher Gaines. Tchr., Superior (Ariz.) Elem. Schs., 1947-48, Yuma (Ariz.) schs., 1949-51; tchr. English, librarian Hamlet (Ind.) High Sch., 1952-56; dir. library services Plymouth (Ind.) Community Sch. Corp., 1957—; organizer Divine Heart Sem. Library, Donaldson, Ind., 1960. Mem. AAUW (sec. 1979-80), NEA, Ind. State Tchrs. Assn., Assn. Ind. Media Educators. Home: 917 N Walnut St Plymouth IN 46563 Office: 810 N Randolph Plymouth IN 46563

FISHER, MARTHA ANN, ret. clin. psychologist; b. Susquehanna, Pa., Oct. 28, 1900; d. Charles Ithura and Verna O. (Cook) F.; diploma Bloomsburg State Normal, 1925; Mus.B., Susquehanna U., 1933, B.A., 1937; M.A., Bucknell U., 1943; postgrad. Pa. State U., summers 1943-46, 51, 52, 56. Tchr. rural sch., Snyder County, Pa., 1923-24; tchr. elem. schs., Sunbury, Pa., 1925-38, tchr. jr. high sch. music, 1938-40, tchr. classes mentally retarded, 1940-47; clin. psychologist, Danville State Hosp., 1943-44; dir. guidance Sunbury Area Schs., 1947-59, sch. psychologist, 1947-59; clin. psychologist, dir. treatment, conductor in-service tng. State Correctional Instn., Muncy, Pa., 1947-72; tchr. advanced psychology Susquehanna U., nights, 1954. Sec. adv. bd. Sunbury Salvation Army, 1930—. Award for outstanding contribns. to human welfare, Pa. Psychol. Assn., 1981. Mem. AAUW, Am., Pa. assns. ret. persons, Internat. Council for Exceptional Children (Pa. pres. 1946), Am., Pa. psychol. assns., Pa. Assn. Ret. Pub. Sch. and State Employees, Am. Correctional Psychologists, Bus. and Profl. Women's Club (pres. 1948), Northumberland-Snyder County Hist. Soc., Delta Kappa Gamma (chpt. pres. 1950). Methodist. Clubs: Order Eastern Star, Soroptimist, Triangle-Civic. Home: Park Rd Hummel's Wharf PA 17831

FISHER, MARY HANNAH FAHRINGER, artist, illustrator; b. Wilksbarre, Pa., Jan. 29, 1910; d. Wallace E. and Ella Mabel (Horton) Fahringer; student Pa. Sch. Design for Women (later named Moore Art Inst.), 1930; also student arts and crafts, art with pvt. instrs.; m. John Edward Fisher, Feb. 29, 1936 (dec.); children—Jane, John. Exhibited watercolors, oils in two-person show: Dr. Marthann Wilson Gallery, 1979; group shows include: St. Philip's Gallery-Two Flags, 1977, Nat. League Am. Pen Women, 1978; represented in numerous permanent collections, illustrator for books and mags.; graphics artist for local businesses; mem. arts and crafts faculty Montgomery County Valley Forge Hosp., 1946-49; developed marionette theatres. Pa. rep. Internat. Conf. on Scouting, Santa Fe, N. Mex., 1954; mem. Republican Presdl. Task Force, 1980-81. Recipient Medalion award Two Flags Festival, 1976. Mem. Nat. League Am. Pen Women, Ariz. State Poetry Soc., Nat. Rifle Assn., Am. Security Council, Nat. Writers Club, Nat. Audubon Soc. Quaker. Club: Toastmistresses. Contbr. poetry, short stories to various publs. Home and Office: 831 N Venice Ave Tucson AZ 85711

FISHER, (MARY) JEWEL TANNER, constrn. co. exec.; b. Port Lavaca, Tex., Oct. 31, 1918; d. Thomas M. and Minnie Frances (Dunks) Tanner; grad. Tex. Lutheran Coll., 1937; m. King Fisher, Aug. 13, 1937; children—Ann Fisher Boyd, Linda Fisher LaQuay. Sec. treas. King Fisher Marine Service, Inc., Port Lavaca, 1959—; dir., cons. King Fisher Marine Service; artist. Trustee Champ Traylor Hosp., 1976-81, Golden Crescent Council Govts., 1980-81. Lic. pvt. pilot. Mem. DAR. Home: Box 183 Port Lavaca TX 77979 Office: Box 108 Port Lavaca TX 77979

FISHER, MAULFREY STEWART, public relations and advt. agy. exec.; b. Omaha, Mar. 11, 1933; d. Roland Augustus and Marian Youel (Thompson) Stewart; B.Sc. in Edn., U. Nebr., Omaha, 1953; m. Laird B. Fisher, Aug. 7, 1958; children—Stephen Laird, Andrew Scott, Pamela Jane; m. 2nd Theodore W. Vrana, Nov. 27, 1982. Editor Exec. mag., Omaha, 1978-81; communications dir. Century 21, 1976-78; public relations exec. Easter Seal Soc., 1981-82; owner Muffy Fisher Assos., Omaha, 1976—. Mem. Nat. League Am. Pen Women, Public Relations Soc. Am., Am. Soc. Tng. and Devel., Nat. Assn. Female Execs., Profl. Women's Assn., Bus. and Profl. Women's Assn., Nat. Assn. Women Bus. Owners, Nat. Speakers Assn., PEO. Republican. Episcopalian. Address: 10024 Seward St Omaha NE 68114 also 3260 Van Dorn Lincoln NE 68502

FISHER, PEG JEAN, mktg. and tng. cons.; b. Kenosha, Wis., Oct. 15, 1940; d. Edwin and Lucille (Grimm) Reuter; B.S., U. Wis., Milw., 1964, M.S., 1969. Curriculum officer Nat. Assn. Housing and Redevel. Ofcls., Washington, 1971-72; dir. tng. and mgmt. devel. N. Am. ops. Manpower Temporary Services, Milw., 1973-76; cons., trainer Manpower Temporary Services, Milw. also Universal Tng. Systems Co., Northbrook, Ill., 1976-77; gen. mgr. Universal Tng. Systems, 1977-80; pres. Peg Fisher & Assos., Racine, Wis., 1980—; internat. mktg. cons. CREACTIVE, internat. cons. and mktg. firm, Belgium, 1981—; profl. asso., mem. adv. bd. communication program U. Wis., Parkside, 1982—. Sec., Preservation-Racine Inc., 1981-82; chmn. Starving Artists Outdoor Art Fair, Racine Art Guild, 1981. Mem Wis. Women Execs. Contbg. editor Supply House Times, Elec. Distbr. Mag. Home: 1201 S Wisconsin Ave Racine WI 53403

FISHER, SHEILA ABUGOV, psychologist; b. Cornwall, Ont., Can., July 20, 1932; d. Philip and Ada (Cohen) Abugov; B.A. magna cum laude, Case Western Res. U., 1970, M.A., 1971, Ph.D., 1972; m. Jack B. Fisher, June 3, 1952; children—Jeffry A., Barbara L., Pamela S. Cons. drug outreach tng. program Cath. Community League, Canton, Ohio, 1970-71; cons., trainer Suicide and Crisis Help Service of Stark County (Ohio), 1969-75; psychologist Cath. Community League, Canton, 1970-72; psychologist Psychol. Services, Canton, 1972-73; pvt. practice psychology, Canton, 1973—; bd. dirs. Acad. Research in Ednl. Devel., Wright State Sch. Profl. Psychology, 1977-80; cons. befriender tng. program Massilon State Hosp., 1973. Pres., founder Suicide and Crisis Help Service Stark County, 1969-74; bd. mem. Mental Health Assn. Stark County, 1969-75; pres. Human Effectiveness Cons., Inc., 1979-80. Recipient Virda Laura Stewart award Case Western Res. U., 1970; named Vol. of Year, Mental Health Assn., 1970. Mem. Am. Psychol. Assn., Am. Assn. Marriage and Family Therapists (clin. mem. 1972—), Ohio Psychol. Assn. (dir. 1972-76), Soc. Clin. and Exptl. Hypnosis, Fla. Psychol. Assn., Cleve. Acad. Cons. Psychologists, Delta Kappa Gamma (hon.). Author: Suicide and Crisis Intervention: A Guide to Services, 1974. Office: 2121 Fulton Rd Canton OH 44709

FISHER, SUSAN GROSSMAN, banker; b. N.Y.C., July 27, 1946; d. Bernard and Leah Irene (Gordon) Grossman; B.A. in Math. with honors, U. Wis.; M.A., Columbia U., 1968, M.B.A. with honors, 1976; m. Yale L. Fisher, June 17, 1968; children— Douglas Carl, Robin Leah. Asst. trust officer Mfrs. Hanover Trust Co., N.Y.C., 1971-73, asst. v.p., 1973-76, v.p. trust div., 1977-79; v.p. Wells, Rich, Greene, Inc., N.Y.C., 1979-80; v.p. Met. div. Chem. Bank, N.Y.C., 1980—; mem. leadership devel. group for execs. Brandeis U., 1974—. Bd. dirs. Emanuel Midtown YM-YWHA, YWCA of City of N.Y., 1979-82, Manhattan Community Bd. #5, 1981—, Dance Notation Bur.; mem. women's bd. Jewish Guild for Blind; mem. Nat. Choral Council, 1981—. Mem. Inst. Quantitative Research in Fin. (dir. 1975-79), N.Y. State Bankers Assn. (com. communications policy 1981—), Fin. Women's Assn. (dir., chmn. corp. bd. com.; pres. 1978-80), Investment Tech. Symposium (dir. 1974-78), Council Mcpl. Performance (dir.), Communications Industry Council (steering com.), Columbia Grad. Sch. Bus. Alumni Assn. (dir. 1981—), Beta Gamma Sigma. Club: Econ. (N.Y.C.).

FISHER, ZEORA DOT HESSELTINE, former city ofcl.; b. nr. Promise City, Iowa, June 7, 1903; d. Henry Elmor and Arminda Alice (Close) Hesseltine; B.A., Chillicofhe (Mo.) Bus. Coll., 1934; student Drake U., 1942-43; m. Theodore N. Walmer, Mar. 30, 1921; children—Mickey Ahlin Walmer Burrell, Clara Denise Walmer Came; m. 2d, Darwin E. Fisher, Feb. 6, 1937. Sales clk., gen. store, 1920-21; legal sec., Chariton, Iowa, 1934-35; bookkeeper Ford Garage, Rockwell City, Iowa, 1935-36; bookkeeper Cutchell Motor Co., Newton, Iowa, 1936-37; with Nat. Seed Corn Co., Anamosa, Iowa, 1938-39; timekeeper, gen. ledger acct. Gen. Tire Def. Plant, Des Moines, 1941-43; acct., owner automobile and machinery co., Palmer, Iowa, 1945-57; with Davis Ford Agy., Covina, Calif., 1957-58, Aero-Jet Gen. Corp., Covina, 1958-68; secretarial position, 1971-77; sec., acctg. officer Union Carbide Credit Union, Centerville, Iowa, 1972-78. Mem. Centerville City Council, 1974-82; ward chmn. Cancer Drive, 1979; com. mem. Agy. for the Aging; mem. St. Joseph Mercy Hosp. Aux. Com. Mem. Hist. Soc. (dir.), Am. Legion Aux. Republican. Clubs: Order of Eastern Star (past matron), White Shrine of Jerusalem. Home: 511 Haynes Ave Centerville IA 52544

FISHMAN, HELENE BETH, social worker; b. Portchester, N.Y., Oct. 23, 1937; d. Henry William and Hortense (Baumblatt) Sandground; B.A., Mt. Holyoke Coll., 1959; M.S. in Social Work, Columbia U., 1961; m. Bernard Fishman, Feb. 14, 1959; children—Kara Jo, Charles Lee. Psychiat. social worker Children's Village, Dobbs Ferry, N.Y., 1961, 1965-66; asst. dir. Afro-Am. Cultural Found., White Plains, N.Y., 1968-78; mental health technician tchr., White Plains, 1970-71; cons. social worker, Hartsdale, N.Y., 1978—. Chmn. cottage program Greenburgh Dist. 7; active PTA. Mem. Assn. for Children with Learning Disabilities (chmn. dist. 7). Jewish. Home: 6 Old Farm Ln Hartsdale NY 10530

FISHMAN, RITA PAULETTE, banker; b. N.Y.C., Aug. 25, 1949; d. Alvin and Shirley (Stein) F.; B.A., SUNY, Binghamton, 1971; M.A., Ind. U., 1973. Grants adminstr. Inst. Internat. Edn., N.Y.C., 1975-76; seminar leader telecommunications MCI Communications, N.Y.C., 1977-81; asst. v.p. telecommunications Bankers Trust Co., N.Y.C., 1981—. NDEA grantee, 1969, 73, USSR, Yugoslavia. Mem. Am. Bankers Assn., Internt. Communications Assn. Home: 350 E 30th St New York NY 10016 Office: 1 Bankers Trust Plaza New York NY 10015

FISK, JEAN A., child devel. clinic adminstr.; b. Aberdeen, S.D., June 11, 1946; d. Darwin A. and Ardith (Severance) F.; B.S., U. Wis., Oshkosh, 1972; M.S.Ed., U. Wis., Whitewater, 1974; postgrad. Nat. Coll. Edn., Evanston, Ill., 1975, No. Colo. U., 1979. Supr., N.W. Spl. Edn. Dist., Freeport, Ill., 1972-73; cons. Racine County Spl. Edn., Union Grove, Wis., 1973-74; instr. Nat. Coll. Edn., 1974-77; exec. dir. Chgo. Clinic for Child Devel., 1976—; in-service dir., cons. to schs. Recipient Title VI-D fellowship award, 1972. Mem. Assn. for Children with Learning Disabilities, Exec. Female Assn., Hyde Park Businessmen's Assn., Council for Exceptional Children. Christian. Club: Zonta. Author: EmH-SLD????, 1972; Handbook for Parents of Children with Learning Disabilities, 1973; Nonsense Syllables as an Aide to Teaching Reading, 1973. Office: 1525 E 53d St Chicago IL 60615

FISK, LORETTA FAYE, newspaper editor; b. Astoria, Ill., July 4, 1926; d. Jesse William and Fannie Elizabeth (Loucht) Utsinger; student Western Ill. U.; m. George Allen Fisk, Jan. 19, 1947; children—Sharon Elizabeth Fisk Miller, Charles William, Georgia Faye. Bookkeeper, Alexander Lumber Co., Astoria, summer 1943; with Stevens Pub. Co., Astoria, 1960—, soc. editor Astoria South Fulton Argus, 1960-67, editor, 1967—. Mem. Vt. Women's Bowling Assn. Republican. Methodist. Clubs: Order Eastern Star (worthy matron 1955, 70), Rolling River Ramblers Travel Trailer (sec., past treas.), Pythian Sisters Order (past chief), Shooting Stars Square Dance (pres.). Home: PO Box 685 Astoria IL 61501 Office: PO Box 427 Astoria IL 61501

FISKE, SANDRA JOYCE RAPPAPORT (MRS. JORDAN J. FISKE), psychologist, educator; b. Syracuse, N.Y., Sept. 25, 1946; d. Sidney Saul and Helen (Lapides) Rappaport; B.S., Cornell U., 1968; M.Ed., Tufts U., 1969; M.A., Columbia U., 1971, Ph.D., 1974; m. Jordan J. Fiske, June 22, 1974. Supervising sch. psychologist St. Elizabeth's Sch., N.Y.C., 1971-76; clin. asso. dept. psychology, schooling Columbia U., 1975-76, instr. clin. psychology, 1973; adj. prof. Syracuse U., 1976; sch. psychologist Syracuse Bd. Edn., 1976-77; adj. prof. Onondaga Community Coll., 1976, asso. prof., 1977—. NIMH fellow, 1969-72. Mem. Am. Psychol. Assn., Sigma Xi, Psi Chi, Omicron Nu. Home: 241 Lafayette Rd #442 Syracuse NY 13205

FITCH, MARGARET EDSEL, home economist; b. Seiling, Okla., Dec. 16, 1919; d. Alpha and Dora Almeda (Hogue) Edsel; B.S., Okla. State U., 1942, M.S., 1960; m. Eugene E. Fitch, Oct. 12, 1952 (dec. Jan. 1966). Tchr. vocat. homemaking Waynoka (Okla.) High Sch., 1942-43; extension home economist Okla. State U., 1943-70; state leader home econs. Coop. Extension Service, U. Ariz., Tucson, 1970-75; asst. dir. human resource devel. Coop. Extension Service, U. Hawaii, Honolulu, 1975-77, acting asso. dir., 1977-82; adj. asst. prof. home econs. Okla. State U., Stillwater, 1982—. Recipient Profl. award Okla. Home Econs. Assn., 1970; named El Reno (Okla.) Bus. Woman of Yr., Bus. and Profl. Women's club, 1954. Mem. Am. Home Econs. Assn. (pres. 1974), Nat. Assn. Extension Home Economists (sec. 1969-70, Disting. Service award 1958), Assn. Home Econs. Adminstrs. (sec. 1971-73), Internat. Fedn. Home Econs. (pres. 1980—), Am. Council Consumer Interests, Am. Soc. Tng. and Devel., Adult Edn. Assn. U.S., Okla. State U. Alumni Assn., Bus. and Profl. Women's Club (Woman of Achievement award U. Ariz. 1973), AAUW (v.p. El Reno 1966), Delta Zeta (Alumnae award 1968, Nat. Woman of Yr. award 1975). Club: Zonta (chmn. internat. com. Honolulu 1978-79). Home: 902 Amity Ln Reno OK 73036

FITCH, RACHEL, nurse; b. Deering, Mo., July 27, 1933; d. Allen Edward and Rosie Leola (Jones) Farr; R.N., St. Vincent Hosp., 1954; student Little Rock U., 1965-67; B.S., St. Louis U., 1974, M.S., 1976, doctoral candidate, 1976—; m. Coy Dean Fitch, Mar. 31, 1956; children—Julia Anne, Jaquelyn Kay. Psychiat. staff nurse VA Ft. Root Hosp., North Little Rock, Ark., 1954-57; surg.-med. staff nurse St. Vincent Infirmary, Little Rock, 1957-65; acute care nurse Georgetown U. Hosp., Washington, 1968-69; public health nurse to adminstr. South office Vis. Nurse Assn. Greater St. Louis, 1970-73; cons. in edn. St. Louis City Health Dept., 1977-80; research specialist Sen. John C. Danforth, St. Louis, 1980; project dir. study of infant mortality in city of St. Louis, 1978. Vol. cert. instr. CPR, mem. community health edn. com. Am. Heart Assn., 1977—; vol. ARC, 1974—; vol. speaker Am. Cancer Soc., 1977—. Mem. Am. Nurses Assn., Mo. Nurses Assn. (Nurse of Yr. 3d Dist. 1980), Am. Public Health Assn., Mo. Council Nursing Research, Acad. Polit. Sci., AAAS, Sigma Theta Tau.

FITE, BARBARA ALICE, home economist; b. Weaver, Ala.; d. Howard Wester and Edith (Williamson) F.; B.S., Ala. Coll., 1955; M.A., U. Ala., 1966, Ed.D., 1973. Home econs. tchr. West Point (Ala.) High Sch., 1955-56; extension home demonstration agt. Ala. Extension Service, Birmingham, 1956-66; specialist in human devel. Ala. Extension Service, Auburn U., 1966-74; asso. prof. and staff devel. specialist Va. Poly. Inst. and State U., Blacksburg, 1974-79, interim dir. family resources, 1979-81, dir. family resources, 1981—; adv. Va. Assn. Extension Home Economists, 1979—. Mem. Ala. State Adv. Com. Children and Youth; Ala. planning com. sec. White House Conf. Children and Youth; del. White House Conf. on Children, 1970, White House Conf. on Youth, 1971. Mem. AAUW, AAUP, Ala. Coll. Home Econs. Alumni Adv. Council, Am. Soc. Tng. and Devel., Am., Ala. (liaison to nat. assn. family planning com. 1973, v.p. 1974) home econs. assns., Ala. Coll., U. Ala. alumni assns., Va. Adult Edn. Assn., Internat. Fedn. Home Econs., Kappa Delta Pi, Delta Kappa Gamma (1st v.p. chpt. 1978-80, pres. 1980—), Phi Delta Kappa, Epsilon Sigma Phi. Home: PO Box 745 Blacksburg VA 24060

FITE, GLENDA LOUISE, personnel specialist; b. Henryetta, Okla., Oct. 14, 1946; d. Elvin Glenn and Bettie Louise (Carlton) F.; B.S. in Elem. Edn., Okla. State U., 1968. Sec. to v.p. City Bank & Trust Co., Tulsa, 1968-71; adminstrv. asst. to new accounts supr. Cities Service Oil Co., Tulsa, 1971-72, sec. to asst. mgr., legis. coordinator, systems and programming coordinator, 1972-74; bookkeeper and receptionist, sec. to pres. and owner WRP Lumber Corp., Sedro Woolley, Wash., 1974-75; personnel asst. Homequity, Inc., Wilton, Conn., 1975-76, personnel adminstr., 1976-77, mgr. adminstrn., San Mateo, Calif., 1977-82. Mem. Bay Area Personnel Assn., Am. Soc. Personnel Adminstrs., Adminstrv. Mgmt. Soc., Internat. Assn. Personnel Women, Nat. Assn. Female Execs. Republican.

FITSCHER, TAMA CROWELL, educator; b. Cin., June 1, 1952; d. Donald J. and Claire (Montgomery) Crowell; B.S., Syracuse U., 1974; postgrad. U. Buffalo, 1976-79; M.S., Buffalo State Coll., 1976; m. Dennis R. Fitscher, Aug. 19, 1978. Speech therapist West Seneca (N.Y.) Devel. & Psychiatric Center, summer 1976; speech and lang. therapist Buffalo State Summer Lang. Clinic, 1977; speech therapist Springville (N.Y.) League for Handicapped, summer 1979, 80; primary hearing handicapped tchr. Bd. Coop. Ednl. Services #2, Eden, N.Y., 1974—, mem. speech and lang. evaluation com. 1977-78; mem. Buffalo Philharm. phonic ear research com. 1979-80. Cert. speech and hearing handicapped tchr., tchr. of deaf, N.Y. State. Mem. Am. Speech and Hearing Assn. (cert.), Alexander Graham Bell Assn., Kappa Alpha Theta. Home: 404 North St East Aurora NY 14052 Office: 4071 Hardt Rd Eden NY 14057

FITZGERALD, BARBARA MULLIN, fin. planner; b. Harrisburg, Pa., Nov. 30, 1954; d. John and Joyce Mullin; B.A., Pa. State U., 1976. Mktg. rep. Armstrong World Industries, 1976-79; agt. Conn. Gen. Life Ins. Co., N.Y.C., 1980-81; asso. Corporate Planning Assos., N.Y.C., 1981—. Active blood donor Lenox Hill Hosp. Mem. N.Y. Police Athletic League, Nature Conservancy, Fresh Air Fund, Pa. State Alumni Assn. Club: N.Y. Road Runners. Office: 555 Fifth Ave New York NY 10017

FITZGERALD, ELLA, singer; b. Newport News, Va., Apr. 25, 1918; m. Ray Brown (div. 1953); 1 son, Ray. Began singing with Chick Webb Orch., 1934-39; tours throughout U.S., Japan, Europe with Jazz at the Philharm. troupe, 1948-57; rec. artist for Decca, 1936-55, Verve, from 1956, now Pablo Records; appeared in motion picture Pete Kelly's Blues, 1955; nightclub appearances include Sahara Hotel, Caesar's Palace (both Las Vegas), Fairmont Hotel, San Francisco, Ronnie Scott's Club, London; appeared on TV in spls. with Frank Sinatra, also on Screen Gems hours with Duke Ellington, All Star Swing Festival, 1972; concert with Boston Pops, 1972, later with more than 40 Symphony orchs. throughout U.S. Recipient numerous popularity awards from Down Beat mag., Metronome mag., Musicians Poll. JAY Award Poll; 8 Grammy awards, Am. Music award, 1978; named number 1 female singer 16th Internat. Jazz Critics Poll, 1968; Kennedy Center honor, 1979. Records include: At Duke's Place, 1966; Best, 1967; Clap Hands, 1961; Cote d' Azur (with Ellington), 1967; Ella; Ella Fitzgerald; In Hamburg, 1965; Mack the Knife. Ella in Berlin, 1960; Sunshine of Your Love; Things Ain't What They Used to Be; Tribute to Porter, 1965; Whisper Not, 1966; Watch What Happens, 1972; Take Love Easy, 1975; Ella in London, 1975; Montreux Ella. Address: care Norman Granz 451 N Canon Dr Beverly Hills CA 90210 *

FITZGERALD, FRANCES, author; b. 1940; d. Desmond and Marietta Peabody FitzGerald Tree; grad. magna cum laude Radcliffe Coll., 1962; studied Chinese and Vietnamese history, religion and culture informally with Paul Mus. Writer series of profiles Herald Tribune mag.; freelance writer, Vietnam, 1966. Recipient Overseas Press Club award for interpretative reporting, 1967; Nat. Inst. Arts and Letters award, 1973; Pulitzer prize, 1973; Nat. Book award, 1973; Sydney Hillman award, 1973; George Polk award, 1973; Bancroft award for history, 1973. Author: Fire in the Lake: The Vietnamese and the Americans in Vietnam, 1972; America Revised, 1979. Contbr. articles to mags. Address: care Random House Inc 201 E 50th St New York NY 10022 *

FITZGERALD, HARRIET, artist, lectr.; b. Danville, Va., Sept. 14, 1904; d. Harrison Robertson and Ida Lee (Flippin) Fitzgerald; A.B., Randolph-Macon Woman's Coll., 1926, H.H.D., Randolph-Mason Coll., 1977; student Art Students League, N.Y.C., 1927-29. Tchr. pvt. studio, N.Y.C., 1939-47; dir. Abingdon Sq. Painters, N.Y.C., 1948—; lectr. arts program Assn. Am. Colls., 1955-64, 66-68; vis. lectr. Stratford Coll., Danville, 1957-74; one-man shows Va. Mus. Fine Arts, 1942, Charles Barzansky Gallery, N.Y.C., 1944, 46, 47, 50, 58, 64, Danville Mus. Fine Art and History, 1975, 79, Yale U. Div. Sch., 1980; exhibited in group shows at Milch, and Macbeth Galleries, N.Y.C., Butler Art Inst., Youngstown, Ohio, Daton Mus., Gallery Birmingham Pub. Library, Milch and Macbeth Galleries, ACA Gallery, Norfolk Mus. Art., others; represented in permanent collections Randolph-Macon Woman's Coll., Lynchburg, Va., Lincoln U., Oxford, Pa., Sheldon Swope Gallery, Terre Haute, Ind., S.I. Mus., Bluffton (Ohio) Coll., Lawrence Coll., Appleton, Wis., Westminster Coll., Fulton, Mo., Randolph-Macon Coll., Ashland, Va., Stratford Coll., Meml. Hosp., Danville, Danville Community Coll., Danville Mus., Hines Gallery of Rocky Mount Arts Center, U. Ala., Birmingham. Trustee emerita Randolph-Macon Coll., Randolph-Macon Woman's Coll. Recipient award Am. Artists Congress, 1939; citation for disting. work in arts Randolph-Macon Woman's Coll., 1960. Mem. Artists Equity Assn., Phi Beta Kappa, Pi Gamma Mu, Phi Mu. Home: 720 Greenwich St New York NY 10014 also Meadows of Danville VA 24120

FITZGERALD, JANET ANNE, coll. pres.; b. Woodside, N.Y., Sept. 4, 1935; d. Robert William and Lillian (Shannon) F.; B.A. in Math. magna cum laude, St. John's U., 1965, M.A. in Philosophy of Sci., 1967, Ph.D. in Philosophy, 1971, LL.D. (hon.), 1982. Joined Sisters of St. Dominic, Roman Catholic Ch., 1953; elem. tchr. St. Ignatius Sch., 1955-56, St. Thomas Apostle Sch., 1956-65; math. tchr. Bishop McDonnell High Sch., 1965-69; prof. philosophy Molloy Coll., Rockville Centre, N.Y., 1969—, pres., 1972—; chmn. L.I. Regional Adv. Council on Higher Edn.; trustee Commn. Ind. Colls. and Univs.; mem. instl. rev. bd. St. John's U., Jamaica, N.Y.; bd. advisors Sem. Immaculate Conception, 1975-80; Cath. del. Nat. Congress Church-Related Colls. and Univs., 1979. Trustee, Cath. Charities, Diocese of Rockville Centre, 1979-82; mem. edn. com. of adv. com. bd. dirs. St. Francis Hosp., Roslyn, N.Y. Named Educator of Year, Assn. Tchrs. N.Y., 1980; cited Achiever in Edn., Bus. and Profl. Women, L.I. Center of Poly. Inst. N.Y., 1977; cited Fall Gal (lifetime governship) L.I. Sky Club, 1980. Mem. Assn. Am. Colls., Assn. Colls. and Univs. State of N.Y., Assn. Governing Bds. Univs. and Colls., Council Ind. Colls., Small Coll. Consortium, Nat. Assn. Ind. Colls. and Univs., Fellowship Cath. Scholars (trustee 1977, v.p. 1977-80). Author: Alfred North Whitehead's

Early Philosophy of Space and Time, 1979; contbr. article to L.I. Bus. Rev. Home and Office: 1000 Hempstead Ave Rockville Centre NY 11570

FITZGERALD, JOANNE KAY, med. technologist; b. Chgo., June 7, 1951; d. John Daniel and Elise Ann (Kuehn) Stueland; B.S. in German and Chemistry, Pacific Lutheran U., Tacoma, 1973; B.S. in Med. Tech., Holy Cross Hosp., Chgo., 1974; m. Robert Joseph Fitzgerald, Apr. 29, 1978; 1 son, John Robert. Staff med. technologist Martha Washington Hosp. Lab. Assocs., Chgo., 1974-75, Northwestern Meml. Hosp., Chgo., 1975—. Med. technologist scholar, 1973. Mem. Am. Soc. Clin. Pathologists, Am. Chem. Soc., Am. Soc. Med. Tech., Le Leche League. Lutheran. Home: 3930 Oak Ave Brookfield IL 60513

FITZGERALD, JOYCE LUCILLE, biologist, coal co. ofcl.; b. Coshocton, Ohio, Mar. 9, 1947; d. Earl Lester and Doris Lucille (Lapp) F.; B.S. in Edn. and Biol. Scis., Ohio U., 1970, postgrad., 1971; postgrad. Ohio State U., 1972. Instr. biol. sci. Zanesville (Ohio) Public Schs., 1970-72; adminstrv. asst. Ohio Dept. Natural Resources, Columbus, 1972-73; adminstrv. dir. Boys, Inc., Columbus, 1973-74; biologist Skelly & Loy, Cons. Engrs., Harrisburg, Pa., 1975-76; adminstrv. chief Ohio EPA, Columbus, 1976-78; mgr. environ. affairs Ind. div. Peabody Coal Co., Evansville, 1978—. Named Ohio Wildlife Conservationist of Yr., 1977; cert. wastewater operator, Ind.; cert. biologist U.S. Fish and Wildlife Service; lic. pvt. pilot FAA. Mem. Ind. Wildlife Soc., Ind. Water Resources Assn., Nat. Wildlife Fedn., Ind. Coal Inst., Ind. Sportsman Alliance. Office: Peabody Coal Co 1314 Burch Dr Box 4331 Evansville IN 47711

FITZGERALD, LAURINE ELISABETH, educator; b. New London, Wis., Aug. 24, 1930; d. Thomas F. and Laurine (Branchflower) F.; B.S., Northwestern U., 1952, M.A., 1953; Ph.D., Mich. State U., 1959. Instr. English, dir. devel. reading lab., head resident-dir. Wis. State Coll., Whitewater, 1953-55; area dir. residence and counseling Ind. U., 1955-57; teaching grad. asst. guidance and counseling, then instr., counselor Mich. State U., East Lansing, 1957-59; asst. prof. psychology and edn., asso. dean students U. Denver, 1959-62; asst. prof. counseling psychology, staff counselor for Carnegie Found. project U. Minn., 1962-63; asst. dean, asst. prof. Mich. State U., 1963-70, asso. dean students, prof. adminstrn. and higher edn., dir. div. edn. and research, 1970-74; dean Grad. Sch., prof. counselor edn., dir. NE Wis. Coop. Regional Grad. Center, U. Wis., Oshkosh, 1974—; vis. lectr. U. Okla., Norman, 1961; vis. prof. Oreg. State U., 1977; cons. in field. Recipient Higher Edn. award Rocky Mountain council Girl Scouts, 1961; Evelyn Hosmer award U. Denver, 1962; fellow Elin Wagner Found., 1963-64. Mem. Am., Mich. psychol. assns., Am. Personnel and Guidance Assn., Am. Coll. Personnel Assn. (sec. 1965-67, exec. bd. 1968-70, chmn. women's task force 1970-71, editor jour. 1976-82), Assn. Counselor Edn. and Supervision, Am. Assn. Higher Edn., Nat. Assn. Women Deans, Adminstrs. and Counselors (pres. 1980-81), AAUP (chpt. treas. 1955-56), NEA, Mich. Assn. Women Deans, Adminstrs. and Counselors (pres. 1967-69), Mich., Wis. coll. personnel assns., Midwest Assn. Grad. Schs. (pres. 1980-81), Intercollegiate Assn. Women Students (editorial bd., nat. adviser), AAUW, Women's Equity Action League (past pres. Mich.; nat. sec.-treas. legal and edn. def. fund), Bus. and Profl. Women's Club (Lena Lake Forrest fellow 1966-67; named Most Disting. Woman in Edn., Mich. 1973, Harriet Meyer award 1977, pres. Oshkosh 1980-81), Mortar Bd., Beta Beta Beta, Psi Chi, Alpha Lambda Delta, Delta Kappa Gamma. Club: Zonta Internat. (pres. Lansing; chmn. internat. status of women). Author numerous articles in field; co-author monograms, texts. Home: 3715 Pau Ko Tuk Ln Oshkosh WI 54901 Office: Grad Sch Wis Oshkosh WI 54901

FITZGERALD, MARCIA ANN, bank exec.; b. Pueblo, Colo., Apr. 14, 1932; d. Robert Russell and Beulah Elizabeth (Coe) Atchison; student Met. State Coll., Denver, 1973-81, Regis Coll., 1981—; m. William R. John, Feb. 7, 1949 (dec.); m. 2d, Robert Russell Fitzgerald, June 1, 1974; children—Linda Lee John, Laura Lynn John Egan, Lisa C. John Wilkerson, Daniel R. John. Indsl. relations rep. Sun Oil Co., Denver, 1968-73; personnel dir. Sturgeon Electric Co., Denver, 1974-75; adminstrv. mgr. Nat. Controls Inc., Denver, 1975-79; asst. v.p. human resources Central Bank Denver, 1980—. Mem. Denver C. of C., Colo. Soc. Personnel Adminstrs., Am. Soc. Personnel Adminstrs., Nat. Assn. Bank Women. Republican. Baptist. Home: 7141 S Vine Circle W Littleton CO 80122 Office: PO Box 5548 TA Denver CO 80217

FITZGERALD, MARY IRENE, psychologist; b. Hartford, Conn., Dec. 11, 1929; d. Daniel Thomas and Margaret Elinor (Queenin) Fitzgerald; student U. Hartford, 1947-49; A.B., Smith Coll., 1951; M.A., U. Conn., 1960, certificate in sch. psychology, 1962. Underwriting asst. Travelers Ins. Co., Hartford, 1951-52; tchr. elementary and secondary schs., East Hartford, 1952-55, 57-61; guidance counselor Old Saybrook (Conn.) Jr.-Sr. High Sch., 1961-62, Staples High Sch., Westport, Conn., 1962-64; sch. psychologist Windham Bd. Edn., Willimantic, Conn., 1964—. Co-founder, asst. dir. Family Counseling Service, Willimantic, 1973—; active fund raising drives various local charitable orgns. Mem. Nat., Conn. assns. sch. psychologists, Alumnae Assn. Smith Coll., U. Hartford Enlightenment Soc., Mensa, Delta Kappa Gamma. Clubs: Smith College (Hartford), Manchester (Conn.) Country. Home: 12 Garth Rd Manchester CT 06040 Office: 322 Prospect St Willimantic CT 06226

FITZGERALD, RITA LOUISE, author; b. Boston, Feb. 8, 1925; d. Joseph Patrick and Agnes (Coyne) Howley; grad. Boston Tchrs. Coll., 1947; postgrad. U. Calif., Berkeley, 1971-74, Hayward State U., 1974, U. Calif., Santa Clara, 1972, St. Mary's of Notre Dame, Belmont, Calif., 1975, San Jose State U., 1967-68; m. John Gerald Fitzgerald, Aug. 9, 1947 (dec.); children—John Joseph, Robert Vincent. Tchr., Boston Public Schs., 1947-56, Richmond (Calif.) Unified Sch. Dist., 1956-76, ret., 1976; West Coast rep. Louise Downey McNamara and Assos., Quincy, Mass., 1979—; asso. author edn. div. World Almanac, Cleve., 1980—; tutor; ednl. cons., scholarship advisor, public speaker, reading asso. Marlborough Sch., London, 1975-76. Active Mt. Diablo Hosp. Vols. Assn., Mt. Diablo Host. Found. Assn., Roundtree Homeowners Assn., Concord High Sch. Boosters Club. Served with USN, 1945-46. Cert. in hosp. ministry tng.; reading specialist and elem. edn. lifetime teaching credentials, Mass., Calif. Life mem. NEA, Calif. Tchrs. Assn.; mem. Fairmede Tchrs. Assn., Boston Tchrs. Coll. Alumnae Assn., U. Calif. Alumnae Assn., AAUW, Internat. Assn. Childhood Edn. Democrat. Roman Catholic. Author: Amanda Panda, 1981 (ednl. program); author 9 books on phonics, numbers, vocabulary, art. Home and Office: 1722 D Sapling Ct Concord CA 94520

FITZGERALD, SARA JEAN, journalist; b. Flint, Mich., Aug. 22, 1951; d. Glen Ray and Mary Louise (Ellis) F.; B.A., U. Mich., 1973; m. Walter W. Wurfel, Aug. 30, 1975; 1 son, Stephen Fitzgerald. Reporter, copy editor St. Petersburg Times, 1973-75; asso. editor Nat. Jour. mag., Washington, 1975-79; CompuServe editor, asst. city editor Washington Post, 1979—, editor Fed. Report, 1979—. Recipient Mark of Excellence award Sigma Delta Chi, 1973. Mem. Women in Communications, Inc., Phi Beta Kappa. Office: 1150 15th St NW Washington DC 20071

FITZGERALD, SARAH SUSAN, business ofcl.; b. Boston, Sept. 26, 1947; d. Nicholas Howard and Helen Louise (McCauley) F.; A.A., Dean Jr. Coll., Franklin, Mass., 1967; student Chandler Sch. Women, 1968; student in orgnl. behavior Lesley Coll., Cambridge, Mass. Sec., EG&G, Inc., Bedford, Mass., 1968-70; sec., adminstrv. asst. Sloan Sch. Mgmt., M.I.T., 1970-79; pres. Sarah Susan Fitzgerald & Assos., Wakefield, Mass., 1978-81; asst. dir. adminstrn. Center for Info. Systems Research M.I.T., 1979-81; adminstrv. asst. to pres. Analysis & Inference, Inc., Boston, 1981—; cons. Citibank, Decision Support Services, Inc. Mem. Nat. Assn. Female Execs., Women Entrepreneurs. Home: 98 Cedar St Wakefield MA 01880

FITZPATRICK, CHRISTINE MORRIS, public broadcasting co. exec.; b. Steubenville, Ohio, June 10, 1920; d. Roy Elwood and Ruby Lorena (Mason) Morris; student U. Chgo., 1943-44; B.A., Roosevelt U., 1947; postgrad. Trinity Coll., Hartford, Conn., 1970; m. T. Mallary Fitzpatrick, Jr., Dec. 19, 1942; 1 son, Thomas Mallary III. Asso. dir. Joint Human Relations Project, City of Chgo., 1965-66; tchr. English, Austin Sch. for Girls, Hartford, 1966-70; promotion coordinator Conn. Public TV, Hartford, 1971-72, dir. community relations, 1972-73, v.p., 1973-77; public relations/public affairs cons. Commonwealth Edison Co., Chgo., 1977-79; dir. spl. events WTTW, Channel 11, Chgo., 1979—. Pres. Chgo. chpt. LWV, 1962-64, v.p. Hartford chpt., 1971-73; bd. advisers Greater Hartford Mag., 1975-77; bd. dirs. World Affairs Center, Hartford, 1975-77; mem. adv. council Am. Revolution Bicentennial Commn. Conn., 1975-77. Mem. Am. Women in Radio and TV (pres. New Eng. chpt. 1976-77), Public Relations Soc. Am. (dir. Conn. Valley chpt. 1976-77), Chgo. Architecture Found., Art Inst. Chgo., Chgo. Council on Fgn. Relations. Mem. United Ch. Christ. Clubs: Chgo. Press, Arts (Chgo.). Home: 2500 N Talman Ave Chicago IL 60647 Office: WTTW 5400 N St Louis Ave Chicago IL 60625

FITZPATRICK, JANE MARIE, mail order co. exec.; b. Los Angeles, June 11, 1940; d. Thomas Harold and Marie (Maxcy) F.; B.S.B.A., Calif. State Poly. Coll., 1962. Buyer, Venberg's, Glendora, Calif., 1955-59; asst. buyer costume jewelry Broadway Stores, Los Angeles, 1962-69; buyer accessories Desmonds, Los Angeles, 1969; buyer costume jewelry and handbags Weinstock Stores, Sacramento, 1969-73; divisional group mdse. mgr., br. store Donaldsons, Mpls., 1974; buyer jewelry H. C. Prange's, Green Bay, Wis., 1974-77; exec. v.p. Jhirmack of N.E. Wis., Green Bay, 1979; owner Jane Elff Enterprises, Green Bay, 1982—; artist in watercolor and acrylic painting. Bd. dirs. Family Life and Growth Center. Creator board game Ricochet, 1978; author: Pop-Cubes Plus, 1980.

FITZPATRICK, MARY BLANCHE, economist, educator; b. Medford, Mass.; d. Joseph Leo and Elizabeth Dorothy (Bresnahan) F.; A.B. summa cum laude, Tufts U., 1945; A.M., Stanford U., 1950; Ph.D., Harvard U., 1966. Labor relations analyst Raytheon, Boston, 1949; price economist Dept. Labor, Boston, 1949-53; dir. sales analysis Polaroid, Cambridge, Mass., 1953-58; faculty econs. Lesley Coll., 1958-64; asst. prof. Calif. State U., Fullerton, 1964-65; asst. prof. Boston U., 1965-66, assoc. prof, 1966-71, prof., 1971—; chair, econ., Goucher Coll., 1980-82; lecturer Harvard U. Extension, 1971-77; mem. faculty adv. com. Md. Bd. Higher Edn., 1981-82; cons. in field. Mem. Mass. Gov.'s Commn. on Status of Women, 1971-74; mem. Mass. Bd. Higher Edn., 1975-76; trustee U. Lowell, 1975-78. Mem. Am. Econ. Assn., Eastern Econ. Assn., Indsl. Relations and Research Assn., Chesapeake Assn. Econ. Educators, Phi Beta Kappa. Author: Women's Inferior Education: An Economic Analysis, 1976. Office: 270 Bay State Rd Boston MA 02215

FITZPATRICK, MARY THERESE, educator; b. Bklyn.; d. John and Elizabeth Fitzpatrick; Ph.D., Fordham U., 1966. Tchr. high sch., Diocese of Bklyn., 1957-59, jr. high counselor, 1961-64; prof. Molloy Coll., Rockville Centre, N.Y., also chmn. dept.; cons. in field. Recipient Disting. Service medal Molloy Coll. Mem. Am. Psychol. Assn., Eastern Psychol. Assn., Internat. Transactional Analysis Assn., Fordham Counseling Assn., Assn. Advancement Higher Edn., Nassau County Psychol. Assn. Author: Getting to Know Me, 1967; Understanding Death, 1976. Office: Molloy Center Rockville Centre NY 11570

FITZPATRICK, NANCY HECHT, corp. exec.; b. East Orange, N.J., Dec. 29, 1942; d. Ira Youngwood and Bettie Jane (Van Cleave) Hecht; student Upsala Coll., 1960-62, New Sch. Social Research, 1962-64; m. Alan Rush Fitzpatrick, Dec. 15, 1973. Copy trainee Am. Home mag., N.Y.C., 1962-64, asst. copy editor, 1964-68; v.p. Creative Communications Assos., Newark, 1968-70; sr. editor Family Circle mag., N.Y.C., 1970-77; corp. sec., v.p. Alternative Telecommunications Corp., N.Y.C., 1977—. Mem. N.Y. Women in Communications (screening com. Matrix Awards 1977). Editor various publs. Office: 80 8th Ave New York NY 10011

FITZSIMMONS, KATHLEEN MARION, consumer affairs exec.; b. Bklyn., June 13; d. James W. and Helena A. (Ritter) F.; B.S., U. Dayton, 1968; M.S., Purdue U., 1971. Supr., Practical Evaluations Lab., Colgate-Palmolive, Piscataway, N.J., 1971-73, supr. consumer relations, N.Y.C., 1973-77, mgr. consumer affairs, 1978—. Vol. English-in-Action Partner; vol. Bellevue Hosp., N.Y. Hosp.; officer Knickerbocker Republican Club, 1979-81. Recipient Silver Trivet award Stokely Van Camp, 1968, TWIN Tribute to Women in Industry, YWCA, 1981. Mem. Soap and Detergent Assn. (chmn. consumer affairs com. 1981-83), Home Economists in Bus. (chmn. N.Y.C. 1980-81), Soc. Consumer Affairs Profls., Am. Home Econs. Assn. Office: 300 Park Ave New York NY 10022

FITZSIMONS, SHARON RUSSELL, fin. exec.; b. Toronto, Ont., Can., June 25, 1945; d. Leslie Alfred and Winifred Marjorie (Williston) Russell; B.A., U. So. Calif., 1968; M.A., Calif. State U., 1971; M.S. in B.A., U. Calif., Irvine, 1978; m. John Henry Fitzsimons, Jan. 4, 1969; children—Luke Edward, Michael Russell. Mgr. research William Pereira Assos., Newport Beach, Calif., 1970-71; asst. mgr. interior design Concept Environment Inc. subs. Ford Motor Co., Long Beach, Calif., 1971-72; v.p. Urban Interface Group, Laguna Beach, Calif., 1972-74; v.p. community devel., 1977; mgr. strategic planning Mission Viejo cons. Co., Orange County, Calif., 1980-82; mgr. fin. Philip Morris Internat., N.Y.C., 1980—, asst. treas., 1982—; cons. in field. Bd. dirs. Retinits Pigmentosa Found. Office: 120 Park Ave New York NY 10017 *

FITZWATER, JUANETTE KITTEN, med. cons., med. loan broker; b. Austin, Tex., Aug. 19, 1945; d. Robert Vane and Lola Irene (Wisenbaker) Helms; M.B.A., U. Tex., 1965; m. Richard Alan Fitzwater, Nov. 11, 1974; 1 son, Samuel Dewey. Mgr., Tinker & Toter Nursery Sch., Houston, 1958-63; owner, operator Kitten's Kreations, Pasadena, Tex., 1966-69; designer Spinnerin Yarns, N.Y.C., 1966-69; owner, driver Ellis Racing Enterprises, Santa Ana, Calif., 1970-74; v.p. Cos Profl. Services, Inc., Costa Mesa, Calif., 1976-80; prin. Fitzwater, Inc., Sunnymead, Calif., 1980—. Judge Youth for Talent, Santa Ana; pres. Young Republicans of Am. Recipient Appreciation award Exchange Clubs Am., 1978, Speaker award, 1980. Mem. Moreno Valley Equestrian Assn. (dir.), Moreno Valley Vaqueros, Lake Elsinore Valley Riders, Sports Car Clubs Am., Am. Quarter Horse Assn., Appoloosa Horses Am. Patentee auto aerodynamics, 1960-72; author instrl. booklets for med. office procedures, 1976-78. Home and Office: 11390 Carrie Ln Sunnymead CA 92388

FIX, HELEN HERRINK, state legislator; b. Richmond, Va., Sept. 21, 1922; d. Louis Shepard and Virginia (Wardwell) Herrink; B.A., U. Richmond; m. John C. Fix, 1944; children—John C., Carol (Mrs. Thomas Brown), Marian (Mrs. Charles Van Slaars). Mem. council Amberley Village, Ohio, 1967-75; mem. Ohio Ho. of Reps. from 26th Dist., 1975—. Editor, reporter, Cin., 1955-57; editor Northeastern Suburban Life, Cin., 1961-71. Mem. Women in Communications, Ohio Newspaper Women's Assn., Cin. Women's Polit. Caucus, U. Cin. Alumni (mem. coll. adv. bd.), Hamilton County Police Assn. Methodist. Office: Ohio Ho of Reps State Capitol Columbus OH 43215

FLACK, AUDREY, artist, educator; b. Bklyn., May 30, 1931; d. Morris and Jeannette (Flack) F.; grad. Cooper Union U., 1951; B.F.A., Yale U., 1952; m. H. Robert Marcus, June 7, 1970; children—Melissa, Hannah. Instr. anatomy N.Y.U., 1964-70; instr. drawing and painting Pratt Inst., 1963-70; instr. drawing, painting Sch. of Visual Arts, 1969-72; prof. art U. Bridgeport, 1975—; one-woman shows include Roko Gallery, 1959-63, French and Co., N.Y.C., 1972, Louis K. Meisel Gallery, N.Y.C., 1974, 76-78, Joseloff Gallery, U. Hartford (Conn.), 1974, Carlson Gallery, U. Bridgeport, 1975; group exhibitions include Riverside Mus., 1969, Whitney Mus., 1970, 78, Wadsworth Athaneum, Hartford, 1974, Nat. Gallery Australia, Canberra, 1977-78; represented in permanent collections including Met. Mus. Art, N.Y.C., Mus. Modern Art, N.Y.C., Guggenheim Mus., N.Y.C., Whitney Mus. Am. Art, St. Louis Mus. Art, Allen Meml. Art Mus., Oberlin, Ohio, Nat. Gallery, Canberra, Australia, Melbourne (Australia) Mus.; represented by Louis K. Meisel Gallery, N.Y.C. Address: care Louis K Meisel Gallery 141 Prince St New York NY 10012 *

FLACK, DORA DUTSON, writer, performing artist, lectr.; b. Kimberly, Idaho, July 9, 1919; d. Alonzo Edmund and Iona (James) Dutson; student Brigham Young U., U. Utah, Utah State U.; m. A. LeGrand Flack, Jan. 7, 1946; children—Marc Douglas, Lane LeGrand, Kent Dutson, Marlane, Karen, Marie. Exec. sec. Utah State Nat. Bank, Salt Lake City, 1938-46; author: Wheat for Man...Why and How, 1952; England's First Mormon Convert, 1957; Dutson Family History, 1957; What About Christmas?, 1971; Fun with Fruit Preservation, 1972; (with others) The Joy of Being a Woman, 1972; (with Lula P. Betenson) Butch Cassidy, My Brother, 1975; Dry and Save, 1976 (U.S. Info. Service selection for Internat. Book Fair, Cairo, 1978); (with Janice T. Dixon) Preserving Your Past, 1977; Christmas Magic, 1977; Testimony in Bronze, 1980; contbr. numerous articles, stories to hist., religious and homemaking mags.; performing artist western U.S.; TV and radio appearances; mem. lit. panel Utah Arts Council, 1979-81; mem. faculty Brigham Young U. Edn. Week, 1976—; mem. faculty World Conf. on Records, Salt Lake City, 1980. Mem. Utah Gov.'s Com. on Employment Handicapped, 1975-81. Recipient numerous state and nat. writing awards, including Utah State Inst. Fine Arts, 1969, League Utah Writers, 1980, Nat. League Am. Pen Women, 1980. Mem. League Utah Writers, Nat. League Am. Pen Women, Daus. Utah Pioneers. Republican. Mormon. Club: Soroptimists. Home and Office: 448 E 775 N Bountiful UT 84010

FLACK, ROBERTA, singer; b. Feb. 10, 1939; d. Laron and Irene Flack; B.A. in Music Edn., 1958; m. Stephen Novosel, 1966 (div. 1972). Tchr. music and English lit. pub. schs., Farmville, N.C. and Washington, 1959-67; rec. artist Atlantic Records, 1968—; star ABC TV spl. The First Time Ever, 1973. Recipient Gold Record for The First Time Ever I Saw Your Face, 1972, Grammy award for song and record of year, 1972; winner Downbeat's reader poll as best female vocalist, 1971-73; Grammy award best popular female vocal for Killing Me Softly with His Song, 1973. City of Washington celebrated Roberta Flack Human Kindness Day, 1972. Mem. Sigma Delta Chi. Composer: (with Jesse Jackson and Joel Dorn) Go Up, Moses. Address: care Atlantic Records Inc 75 Rockefeller Plaza New York NY 10019 *

FLACK-DARKO, BARBARA JEAN, TV news exec; b. Charlotte, N.C., Nov. 5, 1946; d. Peter R. and Juanita (Alford) Preston; B.A. in English, Johnson C. Smith U., 1968; M.S., Columbia U., 1971; m. Ohene Darko, Oct. 2, 1980. Researcher, CBS-NEWS, N.Y.C., 1972-76, producer, 1977-80; producer WCBS-TV, N.Y.C., 1976-77; exec. producer Cable News Network, Atlanta, 1980—; tchr. Inst. of New Cinema Artists, 1979-80; cons. TV News Writers Guild of Am., 1972—, Women in Communications, others. Mem Nat. Assn. Black Journalists, Soc. Journalists, Women in Communications, Writers Guild Am., Producers Guild. Methodist. Clubs: Women's Commerce, Women's Forum. Office: 1050 Techwood Dr NW Atlanta GA 30318

FLADELAND, BETTY, historian, educator; b. Grygla, Minn., Jan. 18, 1919; d. Arne O. and Bertha (Nygaard) F.; B.S., Duluth State Coll., 1940; M.A., U. Minn., 1944; Ph.D. (Rackham fellow), U. Mich., 1952. Mem. faculty Wells Coll., Aurora, N.Y., 1952-55, Central Mich. U., 1956-59, Central Mo. State Coll., 1959-62; mem. faculty So. Ill. U., Carbondale, 1962—, prof. history, 1968—; vis. prof. U. Ill., summer 1966. Recipient Anisfield-Wolf award in race relations, 1972; grantee Am. Philos. Soc., 1963, 75, Lilly Found., 1962. Mem. Am. Hist. Assn., So. Hist. Assn., Orgn. Am. Historians (exec. bd.), Assn. Study Afro-Am. Life and History, Norwegian-Am. Hist. Soc., Soc. Historians Early Am. Republic (adv. bd., bd. editors), ACLU, Phi Beta Kappa, Phi Kappa Phi. Author: James Gillespie Birney: Slaveholder to Abolitionist, 1955; Men and Brothers: Anglo-American Antislavery Cooperation, 1972; also articles. Home: Route 2 Carbondale IL 62901 Office: Dept of History Southern Illinois University Carbondale IL 62901

FLAGG, JANICE KOEPPE, writer, editor; b. Oakwood, Ohio, Sept. 11, 1929; d. Paul Dunbar and Laura May (Boston) Koeppe; scholar in journalism Kent State U., 1948-49; m. Donald C. Flagg, June 5, 1948 (div. 1954). Copywriter, WTVJ-TV, Miami, Fla., 1959-61; public info. dir. Aloe Creme Labs., Inc., Ft. Lauderdale, Fla., 1964-67; press aide, legis. aide to Congressman Jerry L. Pettis, 1967-68; press aide to Congressman G. Elliott Hagan, 1968-69; public info. dir. Nat. Recreation and Park Assn., Washington, 1969-71; advt. copywriter U.S. News and World Report, 1971-72; communications dir. Internat. Eye Found., Washington, 1972-73; public info. dir. Bur. Land Mgmt., Dept. Interior, Washington, 1974-75; tech. info. specialist Nat. Fire Adminstrn., Dept. Commerce, Washington, 1975-76, writer, editor Nat. Ocean Survey, NOAA, Washington, 1976-80. Recipient citation for creativity WTVJ-TV, Miami, 1961. Mem. Nat. Capital Press Women, Nat. Fedn. Press Women. Author: Public Relations Guidelines, 1971; contbr. articles mags. Home: 77 Fall Dr Port Orange FL 32019

FLAHERTY, ROSE IZZO, educator; b. Brookville, N.Y., Feb. 9, 1929; d. P. A. and Mary Nancy (D'Andre) Izzo; B.S.Ed., SUNY, Potsdam, 1951; M.S.Ed., St. Lawrence U., 1954; profl. diploma in reading Hofstra U., 1965, Ed.D. in Reading, 1974; m. Joseph A. Flaherty, July 20, 1957. Tchr., Congdon Campus Sch., SUNY, Potsdam, 1951-56, Plandome Rd. Sch., Manhasset (N.Y.) Pub. Schs., 1956-66, Munsey Park Sch., 1966-70; head reading cons. Manhasset Elem. Schs., 1970-73; diagnostic reading specialist Shelter Rock Sch., Manhasset, 1973-79, Manhasset Elem. Schs., 1979-80, dist. reading specialist Manhasset Pub. Schs., 1980—; speaker in field. Recipient Profl. awards. Mem. N.Y. State Reading Assn., Nassau Reading Council (past pres., hon. life), Internat. Reading Assn., NEA (life), Musical Box Assn. Cert. elem. edn., prin., supr., reading specialist, spl. educator, N.Y. State. Roman Catholic. Author articles. Home: 10 Orchard St Glen Head NY 11545 Office: Shelter Rock School Manhasset NY 11030

FLAHERTY, TINA SANTI, corp. exec.; b. Memphis; d. Clement and Dale (Pendergrast) S.; B.A., Memphis State U., 1961; hon. doctorate St. John's U., 1978; m. William Edward Flaherty, Feb. 22, 1976. Daily commentator interview program Sta. WMC-TV, Memphis, 1959-61; newscaster, commentator Sta. WHER, Memphis, 1961-62; community relations specialist Western Electric Co., 1964-65; v.p. Grey Advt., N.Y.C., 1966-71; corp. v.p., officer Colgate-Palmolive Co., N.Y.C.,

1972—. Chmn., Salute to Women in Bus., YWCA, 1979; mem. nat. bd. Jr. Achievement, 1978; chmn. Bus. Council UN Decade for Women, 1977—; bd. dirs. Hugh O'Brian Youth Found., 1982—; v.p. Girls Clubs Am., 1978, Women's Forum, 1979; mem. Com. of 200, 1982—. Named One of Top Corp. Women's Bus. Week, 1976; Extraordinary Woman of Achievement NCCJ, 1978; One of 8 Outstanding Women in Bus. and Labor, Women's Equity Action League, 1978; recipient Equal People award UN Decade for Women, 1979. Home: 50 E 89th St New York NY 10028 Office: 300 Park Ave New York NY 10022

FLAKE, JUDY CAROL JONES, adminstrv. asst.; b. New Ulm, Tex., Nov. 27, 1946; d. Roy McKinley and Viola Mae Jones; A.A., Austin Community Coll., 1977; B.A. with high honors, U. Tex., Austin, 1979, M.A., 1980. Exec. sec. Tex. So. U., Houston, 1964-66; sr. bookkeeper, gen. clk. Tex. Commerce Bank, Houston, 1966-73, adminstrv. technician Tex. Senate, Austin, 1973-76; adminstrv. asst. Tex. Ho. of Reps., Austin, 1976—; guest lectr. Austin Community Coll., 1973—; legis. liaison Afro-Am. Center, 1976-77. Bd. chmn. Miss Black Austin Pageant, 1976; publicity dir. for activities in Austin Project Able, 1974. Recipient Community Outreach award Austin Women Center, 1979, Orgn. Mgmt. Spl. Project award U. Tex./Austin Coll. Bus. Adminstrn., 1979. Mem. Pi Sigma Alpha. Home: 3469 North Hills Dr Austin TX 78731 Office: PO Box 2910 Austin TX 78758

FLAMM, LOIS ELLEN, psychologist; b. Springfield, Mass., Oct. 1, 1944; d. Bernard and Henrietta Canter; B.A., Skidmore Coll., 1966; M.A., Northeastern U., Boston, 1968, Ph.D. in Exptl. Psychology, 1971; m. Daniel L. Flamm, Oct. 30, 1965; children—Jonathan, Stephen. Asst. prof. psychology Tex. A&M U., 1972-76; mem. tech. staff Bell Labs., Whippany, N.J., 1977—. USPHS predoctoral fellow, 1969-71; NASA-Am. Soc. Engring. Edn. summer faculty fellow, 1974, 75. Mem. Optical Soc. Am., Assn. Research in Vision and Ophthalmology, Human Factors Soc., Sigma Xi, Phi Kappa Phi. Contbr. articles to profl. jours. Office: Bell Labs Whippany NJ 07981

FLAMMER, MAUREEN FRANCES, chiropractor; b. Bklyn., Mar. 27, 1948; d. George and Helen (Giff) F.; B.A., SUNY, 1970; D.Chiropractic (King Koil chiropractic scholar), N.Y. Chiropractic Coll., 1977. Pvt. practice chiropractic medicine, Cambridge, Mass., 1978—; tchr. Cambridge Center for Natural Healing; chiropractic cons. Boston U. Pub. Health Inst., 1982, Our Bodies Ourselves. Mem. Am. Chiropractic Assn., Mass. Chiropractic Soc., Greater Boston Chiropractic Soc. (pres. 1982). Office: 678 Massachusetts Ave Cambridge MA 02139

FLANAGAN, ALICE PATRICIA, legal assn. ofcl.; b. Albany, N.Y., July 7, 1942; d. Patrick J. and Alice M. (Gannon) F. Sec., Mchts. Mut. Ins. Co., Albany, 1960-64; with N.Y. State Bar Assn., Albany, 1964—, asst. to counsel, 1980-82, adminstrv. liaison, 1982—. Mem. Nat. Assn. Female Execs., N.Y. State Defenders Assn. (aux. mem.). Home: 42 Wilkins Ave West Albany NY 12205 Office: One Elk St Albany NY 12207

FLANAGAN, BARBARA MALLON, speech pathologist; b. Arlington, Mass., Oct. 17, 1945; d. Hugh Augustus and Geraldine (McCarthy) Mallon; B.S., Towson State U., 1971; M.A., U. Mich., 1974; M.Ed., Harvard U., 1982; m. Henry E. Flanagan Dec. 16, 1966; children—Amber Leigh, Heather Brandeis. Speech pathologist Project Head-Start, Wayne-Westland Schs., Detroit, 1969-71, Speech Clinic, U. Mich., 1971-73, pre-sch. program Squadron Line Sch., Simsbury, Conn., 1972-82; exec. dir., speech pathologist Avon (Conn.) Speech Assos., 1975—; co-dir. pre-sch. diagnostics Town of Simsbury, 1978-82; asst. admissions officer Miss Porter's Sch., Farmington, Conn., 1981-82. Mem. service com. PTO, Towpath Elem. Sch., Avon; chmn. Avon Ways and Means Com.; mem. adv. bd. Farmington Valley Vis. Nurses Assn., Torrington (Conn.) Vis. Nurses Assn., 1979-82. Mem. Am. Speech and Hearing Assn., Conn. Speech and Hearing Assn., Phi Delta Kappa. Club: Jr. League West Hartford. Home: 223 College St Hudson OH 44236 Office: Western Res Acad Hudson OH 44236

FLANAGAN, FIONNULA MANON, actress, writer, producer; b. Dublin, Ireland, Dec. 10, 1941; d. Terence Niall and Rosanna (McGuirk) F.; ed. U. Fribourg (Switzerland); student Abbey Theatre Sch., Dublin, 1964-66; m. Garrett O'Connor, Nov. 26, 1972. Appeared in film: In The Region of Ice, 1977; plays include: Ulysses in Nighttown, N.Y.C., 1974; TV appearances include: Rich Man Poor Man, 1976 (Emmy award for most outstanding support role), How The West Was Won, ABC TV series; author, performer stage show: James Joyce's Women (Drama League award 1978, Los Angeles Drama Critics award 1979, San Francisco Bay Area Theatre Critics Circle award 1979); pres. prodn. co. Rejoycing Co.; fellow Study Center for Orgn. and Leadership Authority; Recipient Jacob's award for most outstanding performance in Irish TV, 1967. Mem. Actors Equity, Screen Actors Guild, AFTRA.

FLANAGAN, MARTHA LANG, newspaper exec.; b. Cin., Mar. 23, 1942; d. Gordon Walter and Alma Marie (Strobl) L.; B.S. in Fine Arts, U. Cin., 1978; m. John A. Flanagan. Various exec. secretarial positions, 1960-75; corp. sec., asst. to pres. Cin. Enquirer, 1973—. Mem. Cin. Police Chief's Communications Adv. Com., 1976—, Cin. Music Hall Centennial Com., 1976-78. Roman Catholic. Office: 617 Vine St Cincinnati OH 45202

FLANAGAN, MAUREEN ANNE, freight co. exec.; b. Elizabeth, N.J., Oct. 13, 1953; d. Samuel Patrick and Helen Marie (Ferguson) Flanagan; B.A., Kean Coll., 1975. With REA, Rahway, N.J., 1977—, now product mgr. Active Union County Women's Polit. Caucus, Union County Women's Democratic Club, Young Dems. of Union County, 9th Ward Dem. Club. Mem. Women in Electronics, Nat. Assn. Female Execs., Central N.J. Women's Network, AAUW, Linden Bus. and Profl. Women (found. chmn.). Democrat. Episcopalian. Clubs: Plainfield Ski, Bowling. Home: 229 Rosewood Terr Linden NJ 07036 Office: 937 E Hazelwood Ave Rahway NJ 07065

FLANAGAN, NATALIE ROBBINS-SMITH, state legislator; b. Haverhill, Mass., Aug. 6; d. Forrest Van Zandt and Blanche Matella (Robbins) Smith; m. John F. Flanagan, Sept. 20, 1943. Mem. N.H. Ho. of Reps., 1974—, chmn. com. county human services, 1976—; chmn. N.H. Statutory Revisions Com., 1977-78, 79-82. Trustee Kimball Public Library, 1972—. Republican. Address: Maple Ave Atkinson NH 03811

FLANAGAN, NORMA ANN, mfg. co. exec.; b. Pawtucket, R.I., Dec. 1, 1952; d. Norman Earl and Anne Veronica (Halpin) F.; grad. Bauder Fashion Coll., 1973. Asst. designer Sting Bee Inc., N.Y.C., 1973-75; co-designer, asst. prodn. Thumbs Up, N.Y.C., 1975-76; prodn. mgr., trimming and price goods buyer When I Grow Up, N.Y.C., 1976-78; designer, prodn. mgr. children's sportswear Sting Bee, Inc., N.Y.C., 1978-82; design coordinator childrens Calvin Klein jeans Puritan Fashions Inc., N.Y.C., 1982—; v.p. merchandising and design Complements Sportswear for Children, N.Y.C., 1982—; lectr. Recipient Spl. Achievement award Bauder Fashion Coll., 1975. Mem. Fashion Group. Designs pub. in Women's Wear Daily and Earnshaw's mag. Home: 126 W 86 St Apt 1A New York NY 10034 Office: 112 W 34 St New York NY 10001

FLANAGAN, SUSAN ANN, bank exec.; b. N.Y.C., Nov. 20, 1941; d. Frank Vincent and Dorothy Augusta (Ruff) F.; B.A. in Econs., U. Vt. 1962. With Morgan Guaranty Trust Co. N.Y., N.Y.C. 1962—, now v.p. Office: 23 Wall St New York NY 10015

FLANINGAM, DONA LEE, educator; b. Ligonier, Pa., Sept. 24, 1938; d. J. Cecil and Ruth V. (Dahlmann) Graham; B.S. in Physics, Mich. Tech. U., 1960, B.S. in Math., 1960; M.S. in Computer Sci., Central Mich. U., 1982; m. Ora Ley Flaningam, Apr. 13, 1963; 1 dau., Lian Marie; 1 foster son, Raymond C. Graham. Chemist, Dow Chem. Co., Midland, Mich., 1960-68, systems analyst, 1966-68; instr. basic physics Delta Coll., Midland, 1979; instr. bus. math. and data processing Northwood Inst., Midland, 1979; instr. programming langs. Central Mich. U., Mt. Pleasant, 1980—. Mem. Vols. in Tech. Assistance, 1965—; active Theatre Guild of Midland Center for Arts, 1960—, vice chmn. bd., 1977, chmn. bd., 1977-78, mgr. bd., 1978-79; chmn. Peanut Gallery, children's theatre orgn., Midland, 1972-73; vol. tutor to children with learning disabilities, 1973-79. Recipient Stagecrafter award Theatre Guild, 1974. Home: 3227 E Stewart Rd Midland MI 48640

FLARIS, KATHRYN GEORGIA, public sch. tchr.; b. East Chicago, Ind., Dec. 28, 1947; d. George and Georgia Jean (Floros) F.; B.S. in English, Ind. U., 1969; M.A., Purdue U., 1976; m. James E. Blair, Apr. 12, 1982. Tchr., English, Whiting (Ind.) schs., 1969—, chmn. reorganizing scope and sequence in English, 1982—; guest lectr. English, Purdue U., Hammond, Ind., 1975—, mem. com. restructuring English courses, 1982—. Grantee, Shakespeare Inst., 1977. Mem. Nat. Council Tchrs. English, MLA, NEA, Ind. Tchrs. Assn., Women in Action!, Alliance of Women. Mem. Greek Orthodox Ch. Club: Maids of Athena. Author book revs. Home: 1030 N State St Chicago IL 60610

FLATT, JANE DEE, publishing co. ofcl.; b. Chgo., Aug. 8, 1945; d. Oscar and Marion (Dietler) Dystel; student Jackson Coll. for Women, Tufts U., 1963-65, U. Grenoble (France), 1964, New Sch. for Social Research, 1965; B.A. in Polit. Sci. cum laude, Washington Sq. Coll., 1967; postgrad. Georgetown U. Law Center, 1967-68; m. S. Thomas Flatt; 1 dau., Jessica Fanny. Research asst. contracts dept. Bantam Books, summer 1967, editorial asst., 1968-69, permissions editor, 1969-70, permissions editor, legal asst., 1970-73; adminstrv. editor Grosset & Dunlap, 1973-74, editor, 1974-76; sr. editor A & W Pubs., Inc., N.Y.C., 1976-77; dir. publs. Enterprise Publs., Newspaper Enterprise Assn., pub. of World Almanac, N.Y.C., 1977—; v.p. United Features Syndicate, Newspaper Enterprise Assn. Mem. Pubs. for McGovern Com., 1972. Mem. Assn. Am. Pubs. (copyright com. 1971-74), Coat of Arms Soc., Phi Beta Kappa. Home: 1172 Park Ave New York NY 10028 Office: 200 Park Ave New York NY 10166

FLATT, MARGARET NICHOLS, nurse; b. Wilmington, Del., Oct. 13, 1933; d. Daniel John and Julia Bell (Harper) Nichols; R.N., Fla. So. Coll., 1963; m. Harvey Wayne Flatt, Aug. 11, 1957; children—Rodney Glenn, Kevin Sean. Sec., Fla. Dept. Transportation, Bartow, 1958-68; charge nurse Lakeland (Fla.) Gen. Hosp., 1976-78, Fla. United Presbyterian Nursing Center, Lakeland, 1978—; health lectr.; first aid counselor Boy Scouts Am. Mem. Churches of Christ. Home: 2 Greywicke Way Lakeland FL 33803 Office: 1919 Lakeland Hills Blvd Lakeland FL 33805

FLECK, GLORIA KENNEDY, newspaper exec.; b. Providence; d. Charles R. and Anna (Oneppo) Kennedy; grad. in public adminstrn./polit. sci., R.I. Coll., 1978; children—Donald Kennedy, Karyn Ann Kennedy. Union organizer USWA Steelworks, 1978; pvt. practice advt. consulting, 1980-81; newspaper advt. exec., 1981—. Democrat. Address: 5 Spofford Dr Warwick RI 02888

FLEENER, ANN MULL, educator; b. Iowa City, Feb. 28, 1947; d. William Louis III and Dorothy Carolyn (Jensen) Mull; A.A., Eastern Iowa Community Coll., Muscatine, 1967; B.S., U. Minn., Mpls., 1969, M.A., 1976, postgrad., 1982—; m. Theodore William Fleener, May 30, 1970; children—Catherine, Matthew. Tchr. 12th grade social studies Henry Sibley High Sch., West St. Paul, Minn., 1969-73; substitute tchr. Mounds View (Minn.) Sch. Dist. 162, 1974-77; instr. in curriculum and instrn. U. Minn., 1977—, supr. secondary edn. social studies student tchrs., 1977—; co-dir. Camp Lael, Grand Rapids, Minn., summers 1970-71. Bd. dirs., group home chmn., exec. officer The City, Inc., Mpls., 1977-80; bd. dirs. Jr. League Mpls., Inc., 1980-82, exec. officer, 1981-82; pres. Parent Tchr. Orgn., Excelsior (Minn.) Elem. Sch., 1981-82; mem. dist. adv. com. Minnetonka (Minn.) Sch. Dist. 276, 1981-82; mem. Community Pres.'s Gavel Club, Excelsior, 1981-82. Mem. DAR, Alpha Delta Kappa. Home: 385 Lakeview Ave Excelsior MN 55331 Office: 152 Peik Hall 159 Pillsbury Dr SE Minneapolis MN 55455

FLEGLE, JANICE MARIE, nurse, health service adminstr.; b. Aberdeen, Miss., Feb. 26, 1948; d. Lonnie Ervin and Ruth Imogene (Randle) Bell; grad. Baptist Meml. Hosp. Sch. Nursing, Memphis, 1969; student Memphis State U., 1966-67, U.S. Fla., 1973-75, Miami Dade Community Coll., 1975; m. Larry Vernon Flegle, Sept. 6, 1969; 1 dau., Krista Leann. Charge nurse pediatric surgery unit Norfolk (Va.) Gen. Hosp., 1970-73; charge nurse self dialysis unit VA Hosp., Tampa, Fla., 1973-75, VA Hosp., Miami, Fla., 1975-77; unit adminstr. Community Dialysis Center of N.W. Ala., Sheffield, 1977-79; asst. regional adminstr. Community Dialysis Centers, Norcross, Ga., 1979-80, regional adminstr., 1980-81, asst. v.p., Atlanta, 1981—. Mem. Am. Assn. Nephrology Nurses and Technicians, Am. Assn. Nurses. Democrat. Baptist. Office: 5117 New Peachtree Rd Suite 302 Atlanta GA 30391

FLEISCHER, RUTH FRANCES, legis. asst.; b. Yonkers, N.Y., Sept. 12, 1947; d. William F. and Doris Hulda (Linder) F.; B.A., U. Mich., 1969, M.A., 1970, J.D., Boston U., 1973; m. Gordon Gregory Young, June 29, 1975. Bar: N.Y. bar, D.C. bar. Atty., U.S. EPA, N.Y.C., 1973-75; sole practice, Syracuse, N.Y., 1975-79; pvt. practice environ. and energy cons., 1979-80; legis. asst. Office of William Proxmire, U.S. Senate, 1980—; adj. faculty SUNY, Syracuse 1979. Mem. ABA. Office: 5241 Dirksen Senate Office Bldg Washington DC 20510

FLEISCHMAN, BARBARA GREENBERG, public relations cons.; b. Detroit, Mar. 20, 1924; d. Samuel J. and Theresa (Keil) Greenberg; B.A., U. Mich., 1944; m. Lawrence A. Fleischman, Dec. 18, 1948; children—Rebecca, Arthur, Martha. Tchr., Detroit Public Schs., 1944-45, psychoanalyst's sec., Detroit, 1947-49; sec. Greenberg Ins. Agy., Detroit, 1947-49; customer/public relations cons. Kennedy Galleries, N.Y.C., 1976—. Bd. dirs. Detroit Artists Market, 1958-66; mem. women's com. Detroit Inst. Arts, 1957-66, founder, pres. vol. com., 1961-66; bd. dirs. Friends of Channel 13, 1968-80, pres., N.Y.C., 1975-79, chmn. auction, 1975, trustee, 1975—; pres. Friends of N.Y. Public Library, 1979—, trustee, 1980—; governing bd. Off the Record Luncheons, Fgn. Policy Assn., 1978—; asso. producer Channel 13 Auction, 1978-80. Jewish. Club: Cosmopolitan. Home: 870 United Nations Plaza New York NY 10017 Office: 40 W 57 St New York NY 10019

FLEISCHMANN, SHIRLEY ETTA, pianist; b. Birmingham, Ala., Feb. 17, 1926; d. Morris Herman and Frances (Wacholder) Cohen; B.A., Rice U., 1947; student Oberlin Coll. Conservatory of Music, 1945-46; m. Stanley G. Fleischmann, Nov. 8, 1947; children—Rosanne Fleischmann Lapan, Marilyn Fleischmann Arensberg, Adrienne Fleischmann Laws, Steven. Performing pianist, Houston and Seattle, 1942—; tchr. piano, Bellevue, Wash., 1960—; music chmn. Women's Univ. Club, 1976—. Accredited piano tchr. Mem. Wash. State Music Tchrs. Assn. (v.p. NW sect. 1974-76, pres. Eastside chpt. 1974-76). Democrat. Jewish. Research on art of practicing. Home: 1615 90th St NE Bellevue WA 98004

FLEISS, KAREN MANDELL, banker; b. N.Y.C.; d. Sol S. and Pauline V. (Varon) Mandell; B.A., Barnard Coll., 1968; M.B.A., Columbia U., 1971; m. David J. Fleiss, June 29, 1968; children—Eric, Andrew, Peter. With Fed. Res. Bd., Washington, 1970-71, U.S. Trust Co., N.Y.C., 1971-74; with Bankers Trust Co., N.Y.C., 1974—, now v.p., investment analyst. Mem. Fin. Analysts Assn., N.Y. State Soc. Security Analysts. Office: 280 Park Ave New York NY 10017

FLEMING, ALICE CAREW MULCAHEY (MRS. THOMAS J. FLEMING), author; b. New Haven, Dec. 21, 1928; d. Albert Leo and Agnes (Foley) Mulcahey; A.B., Trinity Coll., 1950; M.A., Columbia, 1951; m. Thomas J. Fleming, Jan. 19, 1951; children—Alice, Thomas, David, Richard. Trustee, St. Vincent's Hosp. and Med. Center, N.Y.C. Recipient Nat. Media award Family Service Assn. Am., 1973. Mem. P.E.N., Authors Guild. Author: The Key to New York, 1960; Wheels, 1960; A Son of Liberty, 1961; Doctors in Petticoats, 1964; Great Women Teachers, 1965; The Senator from Maine: Margaret Chase Smith, 1969; Alice Freeman Palmer: Pioneer College President, 1970; Reporters At War, 1970; General's Lady, 1971; Highways into History, 1971; Pioneers in Print, 1971; Ida Tarbell, The First of the Muckrakers, 1971; Nine Months, 1972; Psychiatry, What's it All About?, 1972; The Moviemakers, 1973; Trials that Made Headlines, 1974; Contraception, Abortion, Pregnancy, 1974; New on the Beat, 1975; Alcohol: The Delightful Poison, 1975; Something for Nothing, 1978, The Mysteries of ESP, 1980; What to Say When You Don't Know What to Say, 1982. 1978. Editor: Hosannah the Home Run!, 1972; America Is Not All Traffic Lights, 1976. Contbr. articles to mags. Address: 315 E 72d St New York City NY 10021

FLEMING, ALICE MAY, psychiatrist; b. Boston; d. Michael J. and Julia M. (Penney) F.; B.A., Radcliffe Coll., 1933; Ed.M., Harvard U., 1938; M.D., Boston U. Sch. Medicine, 1950. Intern, St. Vincent Hosp., N.Y.C., 1950-51; resident Boston State Hosp., 1951-52, Univ. Hosp., 1952-53, Putnam Children's Center, 1953-55, Judge Baker Guidance Center, 1955—; pvt. practice, dir. Boston unit Judge Baker Pilot Tng. Program in Delinquency, 1956-61; dir. Cape Cod Child Guidance Clinic, Barnstable, Mass., 1954-65, Boston Juvenile Ct. Clinic, 1965-81; mem. staff Children's Hosp. Med. Center and Judge Baker Guidance Center, Boston, 1955-81; mem. faculty Harvard Med. Sch., Boston, 1955—, vis. lectr. psychiatry, 1981—; pvt. practice specializing in child psychiatry, Boston, 1953—; cons. psychiatrist May Sch. for Autistic Children, Chatham, Mass., 1957-78; mem. corp. Boston Children's Services, 1981—; mem. staff Children's Hosp. and Med. Center. Served to lt. (j.g.) USNR, 1943-46. Recipient Marsalin award, 1966; John F. Pelsius award Boston Juvenile Ct., 1982. Mem. AMA, New Eng. Council Child Psychiatry, Am. Psychiat. Assn. Home: Box 353 East Wareham MA 02538 Office: 295 Longwood Ave Boston MA 02115

FLEMING, ANNE VERNON ROLAND, banker; b. Lincoln, Nebr., Mar. 29, 1945; d. Aulton E. and Doris (Vernon) Roland; student U. N.Mex., 1963-64; student banking and fin., Santa Barbara City Coll., 1975-77, U. Calif., Santa Barbara, 1978; 1 dau., Lisa Sue. Communications cons. Pacific Telephone Co., Alhambra, Calif., 1969-74; asst. mgr. Barclays Bank of Calif., Goleta, 1974-80, mgr., 1980-82, asst. v.p., mgr., 1982—. Active worker Am. Field Service; mem. adv. bd. Regional Occupational Program, 1979-80; mem. Goleta Incorporation Com. Mem. C. of C., Inst. Am. Research (dir.), Goleta Downtown Bus. Assn. (pres.). Republican Congregationalist. Office: Barclays Bank of Calif 5827 Hollister Ave Goleta CA 93017

FLEMING, (BEVERLY) JEANNE, psychologist; b. Chattanooga, Apr. 3, 1949; d. Delbert and Gladys Marie (Hicks) Swanson; B.S., U. Fla., 1971; M.S. in Marriage and Family Counseling, Loma Linda (Calif.) U., 1975; Ph.D., U.S. Internat. U., San Diego, 1979; m. John Richard Fleming, Sept. 6, 1973. Ind. practice marriage-family counseling, Calif., 1975-78; custody investigator Cowlitz County (Wash.) Family Ct., 1979-81; psychology resident Dean V. Harris & Assocs., Vancouver, Wash., 1981-82; pvt. practice psychology, Vancouver, 1982—; mem. family life com. Oreg. conf. Seventh-day Adventists; bd. dirs. Children's Home Soc. Wash.; cons. in field. Mem. Am. Psychol. Assn., Am. Assn. Marriage and Family Therapists, Western Psychol. Assn., Wash. Psychol. Assn. (exec. bd. 1981-82), S.W. Wash. Assn. Psychologist (sec.-treas. 1981-82). Author articles in field. Office: 2011 St Johns Blvd Vancouver WA 98661

FLEMING, ROSE ANN, coll. pres.; b. Cin., Aug. 23, 1932; d. Thomas John and Mary Gertrude F.; B.A., Mt. St. Joseph-on-the-Ohio, 1954; M.A. in English, U. Detroit, 1964; M.Ed., Xavier U., Cin. 1969; Ph.D., Miami U., Oxford, Ohio, 1973. Joined Sisters of Notre Dame de Namur, 1952; tchr. Latin, social studies, and English Mt. Notre Dame High Sch., Reading, Ohio, 1954-60; mem. faculty Summit Country Day Sch., Cin., 1960-75; supr., 1967-75; pres. Trinity Coll., Washington, 1975—; mem. Washington Commn. Post Secondary Edn., 1975—; assoc. mem. Consortium Univs. and Colls., Washington, 1975—. Trustee, Washington Ednl. TV Assn. Mem. Kappa Gamma Pi. Office: Trinity College Michigan Ave and Franklin St SE Washington DC 20017 *

FLEMING, SIDNEY HOWELL, psychiatrist, med. educator; b. Lubbock, Tex., May 22, 1938; d. McKinley and Wilna Adrian (Simer) Howell; B.A., Agnes Scott Coll., Decatur, Ga., 1959; M.D., Emory U., 1964; m. J.D. Fleming, Jr., June 28, 1960; 1 dau., Julie Adrianne. Intern, Emory U./Va. Hosp., Atlanta, 1964-65, resident in psychiatry, 1965-68; mem. faculty Emory U. Med. Sch., 1968—, assoc. prof. psychiatry, 1979—. Grantee, NIMH, 1969-71; diplomate Am. Bd. Psychiatry and Neurology. Mem. Am. Psychiat. Assn. (editorial bd. on curriculum on psychiatry of women and men 1979-81), AMA, Assn. Acad. Psychiatrists, Ga. Psychiat. Assn., Med. Assn. Ga. Republican. Club: Druid Hills. Address: 2238 Hill Park Ct Decatur GA 30033

FLEMING, SUSAN L., journalist; b. Detroit, Aug. 20, 1947; d. Charles E. and Lillian V. (Burns) F.; B.S. in Journalism, Wayne State U., 1972. Reporter, Community News, Detroit, 1966-69; reporter, edn. writer, politics writer, county bur. chief, life style editor Macomb Daily, Mt. Clemens, Mich., 1969-73; reporter, asst. city editor, night city editor, asst. state and met. editor, Sunday editor Detroit News, 1973-78, mem. Page One team, 1978-79, asst. Page One editor, 1979-80, asst. to editor, 1980-81, mem. Nat. Desk staff, 1981—. Recipient numerous news writing and feature writing awards. Mem. Women in Communications (program chmn., 1st v.p. Detroit chpt.), Mich. Women's, Detroit press clubs, Sigma Delta Chi (dir. Detroit chpt.) Home: 18143 Juliana St East Detroit MI 48021 Office: 615 W Lafayette Blvd Detroit MI 48231

FLETCHER, ANNA LOU, high tech. co. exec.; b Kansas City, Mo., Oct. 4 1944; d. George Richard and Mary Louise (Williams) Rodelander; B.A., U. Kans., 1965; M.S., Iowa State U., 1973; M.A., U. Md., 1977; children—Ethan H. Haggard, Frederick C. Haggard. Dir., Office Strategic Res. and Internat. Ops., Fed. Energy Adminstrn., Washington, 1974-77; sr. asso. energy div., Booz-Allen & Hamilton, Bethesda, Md., 1977-80; dir. bus. devel. alt. energy group EG & G, Inc., Wellesley, Mass., 1980—. Recipient Superior Service award Fed. Energy Adminstrn., 1976. Mem. Internat. Assn. Energy Economists, Am. Econ. Assn., Nat. Assn. Bus. Economists, Kappa Kappa Gamma, Sigma Delta Pi, Phi Kappa Phi. Office: 20 William St Wellesley MA 02181

FLETCHER, BETTY BINNS, judge; b. Tacoma, Mar. 29, 1923; d. John Howard and Caroline (Hammond) Binns; B.A., Stanford U., 1943; LL.B., U. Wash., 1956; m. Robert L. Fletcher, June 13, 1942; children—Susan Fletcher French, William Alan, Katherine, Paul Robert. Admitted to Wash. bar, 1956, U.S. Sup. Ct., 1972; ptnr. Preston,

Thorgrimson, Ellis, Holman & Fletcher, Seattle, 1963-79; judge U.S. Cir. Ct. Appeals 9th Circuit Wash.; 1979—; chmn. judges adv. com. to Com. on Ethics and Profl. Responsibility, 1981—. Mem. adv. bd. Children's Home Soc. Wash.; trustee Seattle Symphony; bd. visitors Stanford U. Law Sch.; mem. State Selection Com. for Rhodes Scholars, 1980, 81. Named Woman of Year, Quota Club, 1971. Mem. Am. Bar Assn. (cons. commn. on evaluation profl. standards), Nat. Conf. Bar Pres., Am. Bar Found., Am. Judicature Soc. (dir.). Home: 1010 5th Ave Seattle WA 98104

FLETCHER, DENISE KOEN, publishing and communication co. exec.; b. Istanbul, Turkey, Aug. 31, 1948; d. Moris and Kety (Barkey) Koen; came to U.S., 1967, naturalized, 1976; A.B. (Coll. scholar), Wellesley Coll., 1969; M. City Planning, Harvard U., 1972; m. Robert B. Fletcher, Nov. 11, 1969; children—David, Kate. Analyst, Getty Oil Co., N.Y.C., 1972-73, sr. analyst, 1973-74, cash mgmt. and bldg. supr., 1974-76, asst. treas., 1976; asst. treas. The N.Y. Times Co., N.Y.C., 1976-80, treas., 1980—. Mem. Larchmont (N.Y.) Budget Com. Mellon scholar, 1970. Mem. Fin. Women's Assn., Phi Beta Kappa. Club: Harvard (N.Y.C.).

FLETCHER, DIXIE CHAFIN, nurse; b. Waynesboro, Va., May 11, 1950; d. Richard Dix and Ann (Fainter) Chafin; student Med. U. S.C., 1968-70; B.S. in Nursing Northwestern State U., 1972; m. Oliver Fletcher, Dec. 29, 1970. Night supr. Confederate Meml. Med. Center, Shreveport, La., 1973; dir.-inservice edn. Tri-Ward Hosp., Bernice, La., 1976-78; med. coordinator Med. Personnel Pool of Birmingham (Ala.), 1981—. Mem. Am., Ala. nurses assns. Republican. Methodist. Home: 2525 Brookwater Circle Country Brook Birmingham AL 35243

FLETCHER, M. JOSEPHINE, psychologist; b. Winlock, Wash., May 1, 1921; d. Wakefield P. and Mary Elizabeth (Marsh) F.; A.A., Pacific Luth. Coll., Tacoma, 1941, M.A. in Counseling, 1969; diploma Moody Bible Inst., Chgo., 1946; R.N., Swedish Covenant Hosp., Chgo., 1958; B.S. in Nursing, North Park Coll., Chgo., 1960; M.S. in Teaching Nursing, DePaul U., Chgo., 1963; Ph.D. in Counseling and Ednl. Psychology (Delta Kappa Gamma scholar), U. Wash., Seattle, 1972. Dir. Christian edn. Buena Presbyn. Ch., Chgo., 1946-47; field rep., camp dir. Pioneer Girls, Chgo., 1947-55; clin. instr. Swedish Covenant Hosp., 1958-63; instr. med. surg. nursing Pacific Luth. U., 1963-64, asst. prof., 1964-70, assoc. prof. counseling and guidance, 1972-77, prof., 1977—; cons. King County Head Start Program, 1969-71, Oreg., 1970-72; counselor parochial schs., 1973-75; condr. workshops; mem. policy bd. Tacoma-Pacific Luth. U. Counselor Consortium; mem. Rev. Bd. Counselor Cert. Recipient Faculty Growth award, Am. Luth Ch., 1969. Mem. Am. Personnel and Guidance Assn., Wash. State Personnel and Guidance Assn., Wash. State Assn. Counselor Educators and Suprs. (pres. 1976), Puget Sound Adlerian Soc. (governing bd. 1973), Am. Psychol. Assn., Wash. State Psychol. Assn., Delta Kappa Gamma, Pi Delta Kappa. Office: Pacific Lutheran University Tacoma WA 98447

FLETCHER, MARILYN PENDLETON, librarian; b. El Dorado, Ark., Aug. 3, 1940; d. J.C. and Helen (Spires) Pendleton; A.A., Gulf Park Coll., 1960; B.S. in Bus., Centenary Coll., 1962; M.L.S., La. State U., Baton Rouge, 1965; m. Tom Cole Fletcher, Dec. 28, 1971; children—Elizabeth Cole, Catherine Pendleton. Bookkeeper, Ark. Democrat, Little Rock, 1962-63; asst. acquisitions librarian U. N.Mex., Albuquerque, 1965-66, acquisitions librarian, 1966-68, serials librarian, 1970-73, head serials cataloging team, 1973-77, acting head Parish Bus. Library, 1975; monograph and tech. reports cataloger Sandia Labs., Albuquerqe, 1968-70; serials cataloger U. Southwestern La., Lafayette, 1977-79; serials cataloger U. N.Mex., 1980-81, serials acquisitions librarians, 1981—; chmn., organizer Workshop on Serials Automation, Albuquerque, 1973. Vol. Planned Parenthood of Albuquerque, 1975-76 Brownie troop leader Girl Scouts U.S. Mem. Am., Southwestern, N.Mex. (treas. 1973-74, chmn. coll., univ. and spl. libraries div. 1969-70, chmn. scholarship com. 1968-71) library assns., AAUP, AAUW, Friends of Albuquerque Public Library, Civitan Internat., Beta Phi Mu. Democrat. Episcopalian. Editor: Science Fiction Story Index 1950-1979, 1980; contbr. to profl. lit. Home: 10429 Karen NE Albuquerque NM 87111

FLETCHER, MARJORIE AMOS, librarian; b. Easton, Pa., July 10, 1923; d. Alexander Robert and Margaret Ashton (Arnold) Amos; A.B., Bryn Mawr Coll., 1946; m. Charles Mann Fletcher, May 14, 1949; children—Robert Amos, Elizabeth Ashton, Anne Kennard. Asst. to dir. research, then research asst. to pres. Pa. Mut. Life Ins. Co., 1946-49; officer A.R. Amos Co., Phila., 1949-66; part-time tchr., 1965-68; librarian Am. Coll., Bryn Mawr, Pa., 1968-77, archivist, 1973—, dir. oral history collection, 1975—, lectr. on archives, 1975—, asst. prof. edn., 1973—, dir. archives and oral history, 1977—. Recipient awards Phila. Flower Show, 1965—. Mem. Spl. Libraries Assn. (pres. Phila. 1977-78), Soc. Am. Archivists, Oral History Assn., Hist. Soc. Pa., U.S. Pony Club, D.A.R., Nat. Soc. Colonial Dames. Republican. Presbyterian. Clubs: Phila. Skating; Bridlewild Pony (sponsor), Bridlewild Trails (Gladwyne). Author articles in field. Home: 1135 Norsam Rd Gladwyne PA 19035 Office: American Coll Bryn Mawr PA 19010

FLETCHER, MARJORIE R. PALMER, trade exchange exec.; b. Peoria, Ill., Apr. 13, 1928; d. Walter Edward and Marguerite Romana (Cain) Palmer; student Ward-Belmont Coll. for Women, 1946-48, U. Okla., 1948-50; m. Charles F. Fletcher, Dec. 27, 1949; children—Frederick R., Charles Walter. Interior designer Fletcher Interiors, Oklahoma City, 1953-69; designer Dore de Mardi, Oklahoma City, 1957-65; public relations and advt. officer Globe Houston Corp., 1969-75; interior designer Design Focal Points, Houston, 1976-79; pres. Trade Exchange, Santa Fe, 1979—, Gran Quivira Trade Exchange, Inc., Santa Fe, 1980—; nat. bd. dirs. Inter-Trade System, San Antonio, 1981-83. Mem. Santa Fe C. of C., Nat. Assn. Female Execs., Internat. Assn. Trade Exchanges. Republican. Roman Catholic. Office: 314 Guadalupe St Santa Fe NM 87502

FLETCHER, NANCY LOUISE, clin. social worker; b. Princeton, N.J., Apr. 27, 1931; d. Francis Summers and Margaret (Fish) F.; student Bloomsburg State Tchrs. Coll., 1949-50; B.S., Schauffler Coll., Cleve., 1954; M.S.S.A., Western Res. U., 1965; cert. introductory family therapy Phila. Child Guidance Clinic, 1973. Caseworker, Cuyahoga County Welfare Dept., Cleve., 1960-67; caseworker, outpatient coordinator Florence Crittenton Home, Cleve., 1967-71; outpatient coordinator, casework supr., therapist Community Counseling Services, Pottstown, Pa., 1971-78, fee-for-service psychotherapist, 1978—. Mem. Nat. Assn. Social Workers, Acad. Cert. Social Workers. Home: 907 N 32d St Allentown PA 18104 Office: 1314 High St Pottstown PA 19464

FLETCHER, RAMONA NEAL, textile co. supr.; b. Danville, Va., Aug. 12, 1943; d. J. Edward and Mattie Sue (Guill) Neal; student Danville Community Coll., 1980—; m. Floyd Fletcher, Jr., Sept. 27, 1980; 1 stepson, James Christopher; 1 dau., Deborah. Office cashier G.C. Murphy Co., 1964-70; sec. to supt. yarn dyeing Dan River, Inc., Danville, 1970-80, dyeing supr., 1980—. Chmn. safety com. and waste com. March of Dimes, 1975-80; active Spl. Olympics, 1978. Mem. Am. Bus. Women's Assn., Beta Sigma Phi. Republican. Baptist. Home: 130 D2 Navajo Ct Danville VA 24540 Office: Dan River Inc W Main St Danville VA 24541

FLETCHER, WENDY SCOTT, educator; b. White Plains, N.Y., Dec. 13, 1945; d. Cyril Scott and Olga Noreen (Brigg) F.; B.A., U. South Fla., 1968; postgrad. UCLA, 1972-74. Tutor autistic children Child Guidance Center, Tampa, Fla., 1968-69; art tchr. Summer Gifted Program, U. South Fla., Tampa, 1968; tchr. Hillsborough County, Fla., 1968-69, Sydney (Australia) Ch. of Eng. Girls Grammar Sch., 1970; tchr. remedial reading Garvey Jr. High Sch., Rosemead, Calif., 1971-72; Title I math specialist Garvey Sch. Dist., Rosemead, Calif., 1972-75; tchr. Lexington (Mass.) Public Schs., 1976—. Mem. Internat. Reading Assn., Mass. Marine Educators. Club: New Eng. Aquarium Dive. Author and illustrator: My Ancestors Are From Australia and Canada, 1975. Home: 276 Chestnut W Randolph MA 02368

FLEY, JOANN, educator; b. Hamilton, Ohio, May 10, 1930; d. James Herman and Geneva Kathryn (Boehm) F.; B.A., Western Coll. for Women, 1952; M.A., U. Wyo., 1953; Ed.D., Tchrs. Coll., Columbia U., 1963. Asst. to dean women U. Wyo., 1954-56; asst. to dean women Ohio State U., 1956-58; asst. prof. edn. Tchrs. Coll., Columbia U., N.Y.C., 1964-65; asst. dean women U. Ill., Urbana, 1960-64, asst. prof. higher edn., 1965-69, assoc. prof., 1969—. Mem. Nat. Assn. Women Deans, Adminstrs. and Counselors (v.p. 1974-76), AAUP (local v.p.), NOW, AAUW, Am. Assn. Higher Edn., Assn. Study Higher Edn. Mem. United Ch. Christ. Home: 1517 Grandview Champaign IL 61820 Office: Coll Edn U Ill Champaign IL 61820

FLIEGELMAN, AVRA LEAH, editor; b. Hartford, Conn., Mar. 5; d. Irving and Rose (Bason) F.; student public schs. With publicity dept. Columbia Pictures Corp., N.Y.C., 1949; with Asso. Artists Prodns., and successor UA-TV, N.Y.C., 1955-58; with Broadcast Info. Bur. Inc., N.Y.C., 1958—, editor-in-chief, 1969—, exec. v.p., 1979—. Mem. Am. Women in Radio and TV. Democrat. Jewish. Home: 205 3d Ave New York NY 10003 Office: 100 Lafayette Dr Syosset NY 11791

FLIESSER, ELAINE RUTH, social worker; b. Danville, Ill., Aug. 4, 1942; d. Werner and Ilse Johanna (Jacob) F.; B.S., U. Ill., 1964, M.S.W., 1967. Social worker Children's Clin. Services, Springfield, Ill., 1966-67; social worker Public Schs. Dist. U-46, Elgin, Ill., 1967-80; sch. social work supr. 4 Rivers Spl. Edn. Dist., Jacksonville, Ill., 1980-81; sch. social worker Kendall County Spl. Edn. Coop., Plano, Ill., 1981—; mem. Pupil Personnel Services Adv. Bd., Ill. Bd. Edn., 1977-78; mem. Pupil Personnel Services Consortium, 1977-80; mem. sch. social work splty. adv. bd. U. Ill. Sch. Social Work, 1981—. Mem. Ill. Assn. Sch. Social Workers (pres., dir.), Nat. Assn. Social Workers (nat. sch. social work conf. planning task force), Acad. Cert. Social Workers. Council Exceptional Children. Jewish. Home: 1248 California Ave Aurora IL 60506

FLINDT, ELFRIEDE E., social worker; b. Bremerhaven, Germany, Jan. 4, 1921; came to U.S., 1921, naturalized, 1932; d. Albert Christian and Elfriede Marie (Galley) Angermayer; B.A., U. Calif., 1947; M.S.W., U. Calif., Berkeley, 1965; m. Max H. Flindt, May 31, 1958; social worker Nevada County Welfare Dept., Nevada City, Calif., 1945-51, Alameda County Welfare Commn., Oakland, Calif., 1952, Contra Costa County Dept. Social Services, Richmond, Calif., 1952-58; social worker Santa Clara County Dept. Social Services, San Jose, Calif., 1961-63, 71—, adoption unit, 1965-66, spl. adminstrv. unit, 1971-82, children's services, 1982—; in-service career trainee in crisis intervention and human sexuality Dept. Social Services and San Jose State U., 1966, 78; pvt. practice psychiat. social work, 1966-70. Lic. clin. social worker; lic. marriage, family and child counselor. Mem. Vocat. Counselors Assn. Calif. (Santa Clara chpt.), Nat. Assn. Social Workers. Democrat. Club: AAUW (piano and instrumental sec.). Contbr. poetry to Involvement, 1979. Home: 344 San Luis Ave Los Altos CA 94022

FLINK, JANE DUNCAN, newspaper editor; b. Atlanta, Feb. 17, 1929; d. James Archibald and Frances (Watkins) Duncan; student Carleton Coll., 1948-49, U. Mo., 1967, Columbia (Mo.) Coll., 1974-75; m. Richard Albert Flink, Nov. 20, 1954; children—Jennifer, Elizabeth, Caroline, Charles Albert, James Duncan. Reporter, Tri-Town News, Greendale, Wis., 1958-61; reporter, photographer, feature writer, editor Central Mo. Rural and Farm Life Mag., Centralia (Mo.) Fireside Guard, 1973-78; briefly editor Bus. Briefs, MFA Oil Co., Columbia, Mo., 1977; editor Lifestyles, Kingdom Daily News, Fulton, Mo., 1978-82; asst. editor Centralia Fireside Guard, 1982—. Republican committeewoman Ward I, Centralia, 1972, 74, 76; mem. exec. bd. Friends of Churchill Meml., Fulton; mem. Boone County Commn. on Child Abuse, 1978-81. Recipient numerous editorial awards. Mem. Nat. Fedn. Press Women (nat. achievement award 1982), Mo. Press Women (dist. v.p. 1978-79; chmn. honors, awards 1979-81), Mo. Press Assn., Sigma Delta Chi, Centralia C. of C., Centralia Hist. Soc. Clubs: Centralia Country, Centralia Women's. Home: The Clearing Route 4 Centralia MO 65240 Office: Centralia Fireside Guard 118 W Sneed St Centralia MO 65240

FLINN, CHARLOTTE S., human resources cons.; b. N.Y.C., Dec. 13, 1933; d. Oscar Abraham and Sophie (Leff) Stiglitz; B.A., Queens Coll., City U. N.Y., 1963; postgrad. Nat. Coll. of Edn.; m. Robert D. Flinn, Sept. 7, 1975; 1 dau., Thea Lisa. Tchr. academically talented Morris Twp., N.J., 1963-65; tchr. behavioral and learning disabled Starling Jr. High Sch., Columbus, Ohio, 1965-66; fgn. policy leader, local, state, and nat. LWV, Columbus, 1966-72; tchr. accelerated and devel. reading Shepard Jr. High Sch., Deerfield, Ill., 1972-73; group leader, trainer Effectiveness Tng. Assos., Pasadena, Calif., 1972-76; tchr., tchr. staff trainer LASS modular and affective edn. Fairview South Jr. High Sch., Skokie, Ill., 1974-76; v.p., prin. Flinn Consultants, Inc., Highland Park, Ill., 1976—; prin. Job Search Network, Lake Bluff, Ill.; speaker in field of careers for women; founder Moving Up career devel. seminars. Candidate for County Bd. Suprs., Lake County, Ill., 1972; co-chmn. polit. campaign Lake County, 1974; planner, chmn. LWV confs. on Mil. Spending and Nat. Security, 1969; LWV del. to internat. econ. devel. aid conf., 1970, del. to first convocation of Nat. Com. on U.S. China Relations, 1969; active NOW, Nat. Women's Polit. Caucus, ACLU, Unitarian-Universalist Service Com.; vice chmn. adminstrn. North Shore Unitarian Ch., Deerfield, Ill. Mem. Internat. Orgn. Women Execs., Nat. Assn. Female Execs., Women in Mgmt., Women in Communications, Mensa, United Chpts. of Phi Beta Kappa. Researcher, designer, author curricula: Academically Talented Learners, Morristown, 1965; Behavioral and Learning Disabled, Columbus, 1966; Language Arts and Social Studies Modules, Skokie, 1974-76, Affective Education Program, Skokie, 1974-76.

FLINT, SHIRLEY HAWLEY, pianist, organist, tchr.; b. San Jon, N.Mex., Jan. 27, 1935; d. James Carlyle and Anne Mae (Gordon) Hawley; Mus.B. cum laude, U. Tulsa, 1957; m. Quinnie Marinea Flint, July 13, 1957; children—Clifford, Stephen, Franklin. Mem. faculty piano prep. dept. Ul Tulsa, 1956-57; pvt. piano tchr., 1960-68; organist Brookside Baptist Ch., Tulsa, 1956-57, First Bapt. Ch., Las Cruces, N.Mex., 1961, 64—; piano soloist Amarillo (Tex.) Symphony, 1953, U. Tulsa Symphony, 1957; piano accompanist High Sch. Music Festival, Las Cruses, 1973; accompanist for instrumental soloists N.Mex. State U., 1973-81; judge piano sect. Fine Arts Festival, Temple, Tex., 1962; co-chmn. Frances Clark Piano Tchrs. Workshops, N.Mex. State U., 1966; bd. dirs. Las Cruces Community Concerts Assn.; mem. Las Cruces Civic Symphony Soc. Den mother Boy Scouts Am., 1968-70, 71-73, 75—; bd. dirs. Las Cruces Jr. Cotillion, 1974-75; mem. organ acquisition com. Performing Arts Center, N.Mex. State U.; pres. Las Cruces Band Parents, 1980-81, Mesilla Park Elem. Sch. PTA, 1978-79. Mem. Nat. Guild Piano Tchrs. (mem. faculty, judge), Music Tchrs. Nat. Assn.) N.Mex. (v.p. 1965-66, adjudicator state auditions 1974), Nat. (certificate), Las Cruces (charter, 1st pres. 1964-66) music tchrs. assns., Mortar Bd. (pres. Las Cruses 1968-69), Sigma Alpha Iota (Sword of Honor award 1957), Chi Omega. Baptist. Club: Las Cruces Christian Woman's (v.p. 1971-72). Address: 1809 Halfmoon Dr Las Cruces NM 88001

FLOOD, CARLA MERNER, interior designer; b. Toronto, Ont., Can., June 12, 1931; came to U.S., 1939, naturalized, 1953; d. F. Carl and Dorothy M. (Welch) Merner; B.F.A., U. Calif., Berkeley, 1953; postgrad. Calif. Sch. Fine Arts, 1954-56; children—Kirk N., Jennifer M., Kathleen S., Keith C. Owner, prin. designer Carla M. Flood, interior design, Ross, Calif., 1961—, Interiors Pacific, Kihei, Maui, Hawaii, 1976—. Founder, trustee Jose Moya del Pino Art and Garden Library, Ross, 1970—; past bd. dirs. Marin Art and Garden Center, Ross. Recipient Anne B. McDonald award for excellence in design Marin Designers Showcase, 1977; Ford Found. grantee, India, Pakistan and Ceylon, 1953. Mem. Am. Soc. Interior Designers (past bd. govs. No. Calif. chpt.), Design Found., Marin Arts Council, Marin Soc. Artists (pres. 1961). Republican. Club: Commonwealth. Home and Office: 8 Redwood Dr PO Box 527 Ross CA 94957 also Island Surf Bldg Suite 212 Kihei Maui HI 96753

FLOOD, FREDA PHOEBE, TV exec., astrologer cons.; b. Bklyn.; d. Joseph and Rose (Bauman) Roberts; A.A. cum laude, Morris County Coll., 1973; B.A. magna cum laude, William Paterson Coll., 1976; m. Jim Flood, May 29, 1963. Asst. to pres. Spanish Internat. Network, N.Y.C., 1962; ops. mgr. Channel 41, Secaucus, N.J., 1976—; pres. Astro Greetings, Inc., 1982—; astrological cons. World Fragrances Ltd.; astrologer cons., lectr., 1962—; astrology tchr. Adult div. N.J. Bd. Edn., 1970—; Mem. Am. Women in Radio-TV, Nat. Soc. Geocosmic Research (pres. N.J. div. 1974), Nat. Assn. Female Execs., Astrol. Assn. Am., Psi Chi. Columnist, Lincoln Herald, Lincoln Park, N.J., 1974—. Address: 15 Pine Brook Rd Lincoln Park NJ 07035

FLORA, PATRICIA LEE, personnel exec., cons.; b. Litchfield, Ill., Sept. 18, 1934; d. Fred L. and Ruby O. (Martin) Dively; student public schs., Litchfield; m. Anthony G. Flora, June 21, 1979; children—Michael Meyer, Kim DuPont, Todd Meyer, Shanna Meyer. Exec. sec. Internat. Paper Co., Litchfield, 1958-68, adminstr. asst. in research and devel., 1968-74; personnel mgr. Hecon Corp., Tinton Falls, N.J., 1974—; cons. flexible work hours, total woman. Mem. Am. Mgmt. Assn., Am. Compensation Assn., Am. Soc. Personnel Adminstrn., Nat. Assn. Female Execs., Work in Am. Inst. Lutheran. Home: RD 4 125 A Jackson Mills Rd Freehold NJ 07728 Office: 31 Park Rd Tinton Falls NJ 07724

FLORES, OLGA ELISA, social worker; b. N.Y.C., Feb. 25, 1945; d. Hector Andres and Olga (Segurola) F.; B.A., U. Tex. at Austin, 1967; M.S.W., U. Houston, 1974; m. Richard Lucas Petronella. Microbiologist Baylor Coll. Medicine, Houston, 1967-72; psychiat. social worker Tex. Research Inst. Mental Scis., Houston, 1974-81, pvt. practice, 1981—; adj. faculty U. Houston, 1978-81. Bd. dirs. San Jacinto council Girl Scouts U.S.A., 1980-83; mem. allocations panel United Way, 1981-82. Mem. Nat. Assn. Social Workers, Acad. Cert. Social Workers, Am. Assn. Marriage and Family Therapy, Phi Kappa Phi. Address: 3101 Richmond Ave Suite 270 Houston TX 77098

FLORIAN, MARIANNA BOLOGNESI, civic worker; b. Chgo.; d. Giulio and Rose (Garibaldi) Bolognesi; B.A. cum laude, Barat Coll., 1940; postgrad. Moser Bus. Sch., 1941-42; m. Paul A. Florian III, June 4, 1949; children—Paul, Marina, Peter, Mark. Asst. credit mgr. Stella Cheese Co., Chgo., 1942-45; With ARC ETO Clubmobile Unit, 1945-47; mgr. Passavant Hosp. Gift Shop, 1947-49; pres., Jr. League Chgo., Inc., 1957-59; pres. woman's bd. Passavant Hosp., 1966-68; bd. dirs. Northwestern Meml. Hosp., 1974—; pres. Women's Assn., Chgo. Symphony Orch., 1974-77; v.p. Guild Chgo. Hist. Soc., 1977-81, chmn., 1981—, v.p., exec. com. Orchestral Assn., 1978—; mem. women's bd. Northwestern U. Recipient Citizen Fellowship, Inst. Medicine Chgo., 1975. Clubs: Friday (pres. 1972-74), Contemporary; Winnetka Garden.

FLOURNOY, CAROLYN CLAY, food columnist, cooking tchr.; b. Pine Bluff, Ark., July 1, 1924; d. Paul Eugene and Ruth (Elmer) Clay; B.S. in Bus. Adminstrn., Centenary Coll., 1945; M.S. in Journalism, Northwestern U., 1947; m. Camp Rogers Flournoy, May 14, 1947; children—Clay McAfee, John Craig, Kathryn, Charles Rogers. Advt. copywriter Bozell & Jacobs, Shreveport, La., 1947-48; asst. prof. Centenary Coll., Shreveport, 1951-54, alumni and public relations dir., 1954-56; feature writer Shreveport Times, 1968, women's editor, 1968-69, cooking columnist, 1974—, also weekly restaurant reviewer; cooking tchr., lectr., demonstrator; public relations and advt. Bevery Barn Playhouse, 1974-75; public relations dir. Woman's Dept. Club, 1965-76; tchr. Creole cooking Venice and Rome, Italy, summer 1977. Del. Rep. conv., 1968, vice chmn. exec. com. Caddo Parish Rep. party, 1968—, state chmn. Women for Nixon, 1968, 72; officer Goodwill Industries, YWCA, Mental Health Assn., 1964-74; sec. St. Paul's Day Sch., 1954-60. Named Jr. League sustainer of year, 1979. Mem. Nat. Assn. Press Women (nat. and state awards 1967-69). Episcopalian. Clubs: Shreveport Country, Demoiselle, Royal, Woman's Dept., Chi Omega Alumnae (pres. 1947-48). Writer scripts Public TV series Bridge with the Experts, 1968 (nat. award U.S. Press Women); author: Cajun Cooker - Water Smoking Cooking, 1978; Shreveport Times cooking column pub. nationally, 1979—; nat. champion Am. Contract Bridge League, 1972. Home: 818 Erie Shreveport LA 71106 Office: 222 Lake Shreveport LA 71101

FLOURNOY, MARY FRANCES, educator; b. Snyder, Ark., Feb. 6, 1921; d. George Robert and Emma Harrell F.; B.A., Northwestern State Coll. La., 1942; M.A., George Peabody Coll., 1946; Ph.D., U. Iowa, 1953. Asst. prof. U. Ariz., 1953-55; asst. prof. U. Tex., Austin, 1955-59, asso. prof., 1959-69, prof. dept. curriculum and instrn., 1969—, in-service tchr. workshops on teaching elem. math.; vis. prof. U. Md., summer 1966. U. Tex. Univ. Research grantee, 1969-70. Mem. Nat. Council Tchrs. Math., Tex. Council Tchrs. Math., Am. Ednl. Research Assn., Pi Lambda Theta, Delta Kappa Gamma, Phi Kappa Phi. Contbr. articles to profl. jours. Author: Elementary School Mathematics, 1966; Mathematics Textbook Series, Kindergarten to Grade 8, 1966, 74, 78, 81. Office: Edn Bldg 406 Dept Curriculum and Instrn U Tex Austin TX 78712

FLOWER, ANNETTE CHAPPELL, univ. dean; b. Washington, Oct. 31, 1939; d. Joseph John and Annette B. (Harley) Chappell; A.B., U. Md., 1962, M.A., 1964, Ph.D., 1970; m. Brian Flower, Sept. 3, 1960. Lectr., European div. U. Md., 1965-66, instr. English, College Park, 1966-69; mem. faculty Towson (Md.) State U., 1969—, prof. English, 1979—, dean Humanities div. 1977-82, dean Humanities/Social Scis., 1977-82, dean Coll. Liberal Arts, 1982—. Pres. Balt. County Commn. Women, 1977-79; bd. dirs. Balt. County Sexual Assault and Domestic Violence Center, 1978—, pres., 1980-82; adv. bd. Md. Center Public Broadcasting Co., 1980—; lay reader, chalicist All Saints Episcopal Ch., Reisterstown, Md., 1972—. Mem. AAUP, MLA, Shakespeare Assn., Am. Assn. Higher Edn., Exec. Women's Council Md. (pres. 1981). Author articles, revs. in field. Address: Towson State U Towson MD 21204

FLOWERS, DAISY MAE, state ofcl.; b. Elba, Ala., Dec. 14, 1916; d. Cleveland W. and Melzia (Carpenter) Warren; student (spl. project) Ohio State U., 1967-69; m. William B. Flowers, Sept. 4, 1942; children—Melzia, Hazel, William, Beverly and Robert (twins), Alice. Owner, operator Tootie's Sandwich Shop and Variety Store, Columbus, Ohio, 1947-63, Flowers Housecleaning Co., Columbus, 1945-50; with

Ohio Bur. Motor Vehicles, 1963-64, Ohio Dept. Hwys., Columbus, 1964-66; community organizer, housing specialist Columbus Met. Community Action Orgn., 1966-70; with Model Cities Program, HUD, 1970-75; with Public Utilities Commn. Ohio, Columbus, 1977-81, investigator, to 1981; mem. Ohio Civil Rights Commn., 1981—. Sec., trustee Neighborhood Devel. Corp., Inc., Columbus, 1975—; bd. dirs. Columbus Service System, 1974—. Mem. NAACP (pres. br. 1976—), Nat. Council Afro-Am. History and Culture, Columbus Urban League, LWV, Civil Rights Council, Epilepsy Assn., Ohio Hist. Soc. Baptist. Home: 46 N Ohio Ave Columbus OH 43203 Office: 220 Parsons Ave Columbus OH 43215

FLOWERS, JACQUELINE BROADBENT, nurse, flutist; b. Kingston, Pa., Mar. 13, 1939; d. Clyde E. and Mary (Kalina) Broadbent; R.N., McKeesport (Pa.) Hosp., 1960; A.A., Santa Rosa Jr. Coll., 1973; B.A., St. Marys Coll., 1978; M.A. in Counseling, Sonoma State U., 1981; Ph.D. in Nursing Adminstrn. and Gerontology, Columbia Pacific U., 1981, M.A. in Music candidate, 1982—; m. James Flowers, Jan. 14, 1971; children—Terry, Amy; stepchildren—James, Jeffrey. Staff nurse McKeesport Hosp., 1960-62; office nurse and dr.'s office mgr., Garden Grove, Calif., 1962-71; staff nurse Warrack Hosp., Santa Rosa, Calif., 1971-73; R.N. team leader Palm Drive Hosp., Sebastopol, Calif., 1973-77; dir. nursing Manzanita Convalescent Hosp., Cloverdale, Calif., 1977-79; dir. nursing Driftwood Convalescent Hosp., Santa Rosa, 1979—; flutist Baroque Sinfonia of Santa Rosa, 1971—, Santa Rosa Baroque Ensemble, 1971—; participant Bath Sch. Baroque Music, 1979; pvt. instr. modern and baroque flute; harpsichordist; flute soloist Los Angeles Doctors Symphony, Middle East tour, 1970. Elder, Knox Presbyterian Ch., Santa Rosa; founder, trustee Baroque Sinfonia of Santa Rosa, 1971—; personnel mgr. Long Beach and Orange County Doctors' Symphony, 1968-71. Mem. Am., Calif. nurses assns., Nat. Flute Assn., Calif. Music Tchrs. Assn. Republican. Past prin. flutist, Bell Flower Symphony, Calif., Long Beach and Orange County Doctors Symphony, Vallejo Symphony, Napa (Calif.) Symphony; past mem. Santa Rosa Symphony; decorator harpsichords in hist. patterns. Home: 1006 Leonard Ave Hot Springs AR 71901 Office: 850 Sonoma Ave Santa Rosa CA 95404

FLOWERS, KATHRYN, writer; b. Cass City, Mich., Sept. 23, 1939; d. John Claud Lakin Zemke and Madeline Mary Zemke Beaudry; B.A., Mich. State U., 1961; M.A., San Francisco State U., 1972; divorced; children—John Lakin, David Brandon. News editor, editorial writer Sta. KCBS, San Francisco, 1972-77; anchor reporter, dir. ops. AMI Radio News Bur., San Francisco, 1977-80; contbg. editor Nat. Opinion Mag., San Rafael, Calif., 1978; self-employed writer, 1981—; dir., founding partner Video Experience, Inc., Santa Rosa, Calif., 1981—. Mem. Tiburon (Calif.) Parks Commn., 1977-82, chmn., 1978; mem. Joint Belvedere Tiburon Commn., 1978-79, Tiburon Downtown Com., 1981; commr., founder, dir. San Anslemo Youth Soccer Assn., 1973. Mem. Nat. Assn. Press Women, AFTRA, Calif. Press Women, World Affairs Council, Sierra Club, Marin Arts Council, Alpha Epsilon Rho, Gamma Alpha Chi. Clubs: Marin Cyclists, Tamalpa Runners, Mt. Tam Racquet. Address: PO Box 682 Tiburon CA 94920

FLOWERS, MAXINE ROGERS, psychiat. social worker; b. South Pittsburg, Tenn., Jan. 7, 1935; d. Omer Leighton and Mamie Gertrude (Parker) Rogers; A.B., Birmingham So. Coll., 1956; M.S., Columbia U., 1964; postgrad. Menninger Found., 1965; m. John Baxton Flowers, III, Oct. 4, 1969; 1 son, Bryan. Child welfare worker Dept. Public Welfare, Nashville, 1956-59; caseworker Children's Home Soc., Miami, Fla., 1959-63; caseworker Menninger Found. Children's Service, 1965-69; supr. adult services Pitt County Mental Health Center, 1969-71; staff social worker div. child psychiatry Duke U. Med. Center, Durham, N.C., 1971-76, chief social worker div. child psychiatry 1976—; cons. day care centers; bd. dirs. Durham Nurses Assn., Family Counseling Services Durham; mem. profl. adv. com. Mental Health Assn. Trustee, Hist. Preservation Soc. Durham; mem. Assn. Preservation of Eno Valley, Mus. Life and Sci. Mem. Acad. Cert. Social Workers, Nat. Assn. Social Workers, N.C. Soc. Clin. Social Work (ethics chmn.), N.C. Soc. Colonial Dames Am. (chmn. hist. activities com., mem. Durham-Orange com.). Democrat. Methodist. Home: 128 Pinecrest Rd Durham NC 27705 Office: Duke U Medical Center Trent and Elba Sts Durham NC 27705

FLOWERS, THELMA, educator; b. Shreveport, La., Jan. 31, 1922; d. William H. and Irene (Colding) Deloney; B.S. in Edn., Wayne State U., Detroit, 1971, M.Ed., 1973, Ed.S. in Ednl. Adminstrn., 1980; m. Lucious Flowers, June 2, 1954; children—Carolyn, Sonja, Rasberry. Tchr., Detroit Public Schs., 1971—; prescription learning reading lab. tchr., 1974—; workshop leader, 1974—. Mem. Am. Fedn. Tchrs., Mich. Reading Assn., Am. Bridge Assn., Am. Fedn. Tchrs., Phi Delta Kappa, Sigma Gamma Rho, Pi Lambda Theta. Clubs: Pilot, Wash-O-Com Block. Home: 19312 Washburn St Detroit MI 48221 Office: 15325 Pinehurst St Detroit MI 48235

FLOWERS, VIRGINIA ANNE, univ. adminstr.; b. Dothan, Ala.; d. Kyrie Neal and Annie Laurie (Stewart) Flowers; B.A., Fla. State U., 1949; M.Ed., Auburn U., 1958; Ed.D., Duke, 1963. Elementary tchr. Minnie T. Heard Sch., Dothan, Ala., 1949-52; secondary tchr. Dalton (Ga.) High Sch., 1952-55, personnel dir., asst. prin., 1955-61; instr. U.S. history U. Ga. Extension, Dalton, 1960-61; part-time instr. Duke, Durham, N.C., 1961-62, vis. prof., summers 1966, 67, 69, 70, asst. provost, asso. dean Trinity Coll. Arts and Scis. Duke, 1972—, acting vice provost, acting dean, 1973-74, chmn. dept. edn., asst. provost ednl. program devel., Duke, 1974-80; asso. prof. edn. Columbia (S.C.) Coll., 1962-66, prof. edn., 1966-68, head dept. edn., 1966-68, asso. dean, 1969-71, dean, 1971-72; prof. elementary edn. Va. Commonwealth U., Richmond, Va., 1968-69, asso. dean Columbia Coll., 1969-71, dean, 1971-72; dean Sch. Edn., Ga. So. Coll., Statesboro, 1980—; mem. Commn. on Colls., So. Assn. Colls. and Schs., 1979—, Ga. Profl. Standards Commn. Mem. NEA, Nat. Orgn. Legal Problems in Edn., Am. Ednl. Research Assn., Nat. Soc. for Study Edn., Am. Assn. Colls. Tchr. Edn. (dir. 1979—, pres.-elect), AAUP, Am. Assn. Higher Edn., Kappa Delta Epsilon, Kappa Delta Pi, Delta Kappa Gamma, Alpha Kappa Gamma. Research and publs. in field. Home: Box 4148 Statesboro GA 30458

FLOYD, ANGELEITA STEVENS, flutist; b. Concord, N.C., Aug. 6, 1952; d. William Russel and Elizabeth (Hopkins) F.; B.Mus., Stetson U., 1974; M.Mus., Fla. State U., 1979, M.Mus. Edn., 1981, D.Mus., 1982. Music tchr., Rockhill, S.C., Charlotte and Concord, N.C., 1974-77; appearances with Charlotte Opera Assn., Charlotte Summer Pops Orch., Ice Capades, Oratorio Singers; concert tours as soloist and with chamber groups in S.E., 1977-82; mem. faculty Valdosta (Ga.) State Coll., 1977-82; grad. asst. Fla. State U., Tallahassee, 1980—. Mem. NOW, Nat. Flute Assn., Charlotte Flute Assn., Music Educators Nat. Conf. Presbyterian. Home and Office: 1010 San Luis Rd Tallahassee FL 32304

FLOYD, JANE BIGGERSTAFF, nurse, educator; b. Rutherfordton, N.C., Feb. 15, 1943; d. James Garland and Katie (Earley) Biggerstaff; B.S. in Nursing, Lenoir Rhyne Coll., Hickory, N.C., 1965; M.Nursing (HEW grantee), Emory U., Atlanta, 1967; m. John G. Floyd, June 18, 1967; children—Kelly Jane, John Robert II. Instr., Lenoir Rhyne Coll., Hickory, N.C., 1966, 67-71, Druid City Hosp., Tuscaloosa, Ala., 1972-75; asst. prof. Samford U., Birmingham, 1977-79; asst. prof. U. South Fla., Tampa, 1980—; cons. Sch. Bd. Hillsborough County (Fla.), Women's Hosp. Mem. adv. bd. Crippled Children's Assn.; chmn. public edn. Am. Heart Assn.; active Girl Scouts U.S.A.; chmn. bd. Wee World Day Sch.; bd. cons. Childbirth Edn. Assn. Mem. Am. Nurses Assn., Nurses Assn. Am. Coll. Obstetricians and Gynecologists, Sigma Theta Tau. Baptist. Clubs: Friendship of Temple Terrace, U. South Fla. Women's. Home: 6615 Whiteway Dr Temple Terrace FL 33617 Office: U South Fla Med Center Coll Nursing Box 22 12901 N 30th St Tampa FL 33612

FLOYD, LINDA LOU ADAMS, banker; b. Williamsburg County, S.C., Dec. 14, 1935; d. Charlie Wilmot and Ella Louise (Gibbons) Adams; student Lee's McRae Coll., 1955-56, U. S.C., S.C. Bankers Sch., 1978-80; m. Henry Benjamin Floyd, June 9, 1957; 1 dau., Sherrian Angela. Bookkeeper, S.C. Nat. Bank, Charleston, 1956-57, comml. teller, Sumter, S.C., 1957-70, head teller, 1971-72, mgr. tellers, 1972-76, br. mgr., 1976-77, asst. v.p., br. mgr., 1977—. Bd. dirs., coach Sumter YMCA; exec. bd., fin. com. Aldersgate Methodist Ch., Sumter. Mem Am. Inst. Banking, S.C. Bankers Assn., Bankers Adminstrn. Inst., Nat. Assn. Bank Women, Nat. Assn. Accredited Talent and Beauty Pageant Judges, Sumter Credit Women (past pres.), Sumter C. of C. (membership com. 1980-82), Sumter YWCA. Club: Sumter Altrusa (past sec.). Home: Route 4 PO Box 141 Sumter SC 29150 Office: 1119 Broad St Sumter SC 29150

FLOYD, LINDA MARIE, psychologist; b. New Orleans, Apr. 22, 1949; d. Henry James and Joyce Mary (Adams) F.; B.S., La. State U., 1970, M.A. (NIMH fellow), 1972, Ph.D., 1975; m. William Henry Costelloe, Mar. 5, 1977. Organizational cons. Lane Costelloe and Floyd, Baton Rouge, 1974-78; clin. asst. prof. La. State U. Med. Center, Baton Rouge, 1976-78; tng. cons. East Baton Rouge (La.) Family Ct., 1976-78; pvt. practice psychology, Baton Rouge and Opelouses, La., 1977-78, New Orleans, 1979—; staff psychologist Smith Mental Health Centre, Mandeville, La., 1979-80; clin. asst. prof. La. State U. Med. Center, New Orleans, 1980—; supervising psychologist Jefferson (La.) Parish Sch. Bd., 1980-81; cons. psychologist Orleans (La.) Parish Sch. Bd., 1980—, Sch. Life Ins. Mktg., Lafayette, La., 1975-81; tng. specialist La. Community Lab. Learning Insts., Baton Rouge, 1971-73; bd. advisors Women's Correctional Facility, Baton Rouge, 1978. Bd. dirs. Big Sisters Greater New Orleans, Inc., 1981—. Lic. psychologist, La. Mem. Am. Psychol. Assn., Orleans Soc. Applied Psychologists. Democrat. Home: 7508 Burthe St New Orleans LA 70118 Office: 3440 Coliseum St New Orleans LA 70115

FLOYD, MARIA KETTLE, interior designer, fashion coll. adminstr.; b. Phila., Feb. 4, 1944; d. Anthony and Margaret (Patrone) Fraietta; grad. U. Pa., 1964; m. Raymond Loran Floyd, Dec. 8, 1973; children—Raymond Loran, Robert Loran, Christina. Dir. Bauder Fashion Coll., Miami, Fla., 1967—; interior designer, Miami, 1970—. Mem. Fashion Group Am., Greater Miami C. of C. (chmn. pres.'s assn.). Clubs: Palm Bay, Indian Creek Country, La Gorce Country. Home: 1 Palm Bay Ct Miami FL 33138 Office: 1140 Hane Concourse Miami Beach FL 33154

FLUD, VIRGINIA L., banker; b. Sargent, Ga., Apr. 13, 1942; d. Vancie Lee and Martha Lou Cynthia (Cole) Stapler; m. Clifford Wayne Flud, Apr. 15, 1961; children—Cynthia Ann, Troy Wayne. Head teller First Nat. Bank in Newnan (Ga.), 1960-72; asst. cashier Bank of Coweta, Newnan, 1972-74, asst. v.p., 1974-75, v.p., 1975—; mem. steering com. Fin. Data Services Inc. Sec., Newnan Coweta Little League, 1978; mem. Newnan Council on Aging, Newnan Civic Council. Mem. Bank Adminstrn. Inst., Newnan Coweta C. of C. Club: Pilot of Newnan (dir. 1973-75, pres. 1976-77), Newnan Coweta Little League Booster (v.p.). Home: Route 6 Box 165 Lakewood Dr Newnan GA 30263 Office: 110 Jefferson St Newnan GA 30263

FLUKE, LYLA ADAIR, publisher; b. Maddock, N.D.; d. Olaf John and Anne Marie (Rodberg) Schram; B.S. in Zoology and Physiology, U. Wash., Seattle, 1934, teaching diploma, 1935; m. John M. Fluke, June 5, 1937; children—Virginia Fluke Gabelein, John M., David Lynd. High sch. tchr., 1935-37; tutor Seattle schs., 1974-75; pub. Portage quar. jour. Hist. Soc. Seattle-King County, 1980—. Founder, N.W. chpt. Myasthenia Gravis Found., 1953-63; obtained N.W. artifacts for destroyer tender Puget Sound, 1966; mem. Seattle Mayor's Com. for Seattle Beautiful, 1968-69; sponsor Seattle World's Fair, 1962; charter mem. Seattle Youth Symphony Aux., 1974. Fellow Seattle Pacific U., 1972—. Mem. Nat. Assn. Parliamentarians (charter mem., pres. N.W. unit 1961), Wash. Parliamentarians Assn. (charter), IEEE Aux. (chpt. charter mem., past pres.), Seattle C. of C. (women's div.), Seattle Symphony Women's Assn. (life mem.; sec. 1970), Hist. Soc. Seattle and King County (exec. com. 1975-78), pres. women's mus. league 1975-78, pres. Moritz Thomsen Guild of Hist. Soc., 1978-80. Republican. Lutheran. Clubs: Women's U., Rainier, Seattle Golf. Author articles on history. Address: 1206 NW Culbertson Dr Seattle WA 98177

FLUME, VIOLET BRUCE SIGOLOFF, artist; b. Huntington, W.Va.; d. Rufus Otho and Rachel (Witt) Bruce; student Huntington Coll., Trinity U., 1964-65; studied with portrait artist David Philip Wilson, 1963-64; m. Samuel Sigoloff, Oct. 20, 1945 (dec.); children—Bruce Myron, Nelson Witt; m. 2d, Lawrence Flume, Jr., Feb. 1, 1979. Owner, Wonderland Gallery, 1966—, Sigoloff Fine Art Galleries, San Antonio, 1972—; exhibited one-man shows St. Mary's U., 1966, Southwestern Fine Arts Inst., U. Tex., 1967, HemisFair, 1968, Trinity U., 1968; exhibited in group shows at River Art, 1964-68, San Antonio Art League, 1964-70; represented in pvt. collections. Chmn. edn. for family living PTA, 1962, v.p., 1964-65; art judge Hallmark Contest, 1969. Recipient 1st Pl. award in miniatures Composers Authors and Artists Am. Nat. Exhibit, N.Y.C., 1965; named San Antonio's Outstanding Woman in Art, San Antonio Express and San Antonio Evening News, 1967. Mem. Tex. Fine Art Assn., San Antonio Art League, San Antonio River Art Group. Clubs: Acacia (pres. 1961, 64), Zonta (San Antonio). Home: 8410 Tiffany Dr San Antonio TX 78230 Office: Sigoloff Gallery St Anthony Hotel San Antonio TX 78205 also Sigoloff Gallery 7700 Broadway San Antonio TX 78209

FLUOR, MARJORIE LETHA WADE, author; b. Christiansburg, Va., May 6, 1926; d. Hubert Dodd and Ida (Sowers) Wade; m. John Simon Fluor, Aug. 17, 1956. Author prose and poetry; co-author: Alfred Nobel, The Loneliest Millionaire, 1969. Chmn. vols. ARC, 1960-62; adv. bd. Children's Hosp. Orange County, 1965-68; bd. dirs. Orange County Symphony Assn., 1964-69, Orange County Community Chest, 1962-66, Salvation Army, 1963-68, YWCA, 1963-68, World Affairs Council Orange County, 1975—; mem. exec. bd. Holmes Research Center, Los Angeles, 1975—; spl. rep. Calif. Bicentennial Celebration Commn., 1967-69; nat. trustee United Ch. of Religious Sci., Los Angeles; trustee Friends of Girl Scouts Trust, Orange County, Calif., 1977—. Recipient Headliner award Orange County Press County, 1966; Heart to God, Hand to Man award Salvation Army, 1968; award Disneyland Community Service Program, 1967. Mem. DAR (past regent, state asst. chaplain), Freedoms Found. (life), Assistance League, Federated Republican Women, Les Dames de Champagne (chmn. 1970-74), PEO (chpt. chaplain). Club: Order Eastern Star. Address: 1920 Heliotrope Dr Santa Ana CA 92706

FLY, CELIA PATTERSON, research co. exec.; b. Direct, Tex., Aug. 15, 1928; d. Martin and Laura (Hollingshead) Patterson; B.S., Tex. Tech. U., 1951; m. A.B. Fly, July 6, 1947; children—Charles Bruce, Gerald Wayne. Adminstrv. dietitian St. Anthony's Hosp., Amarillo, Tex., 1955-57, Calif. Hosp., Los Angeles, 1967-68; office mgr. Hydro-Jet Service, Inc., Hydro-Torq Pump Co., Amarillo, 1959—; also dir.; dir., sec. treas. Marine Metals Inc., Fly Enterprises, Inc., Aero-Span, Inc., Amarillo; controller Aero-Span Research Ltd., Hi-Plaines Minerals Ltd., Amarillo, 1980—; sec., treas., office mgr. Tuff-N-Lite Inc., 1980—. Mem. Aircraft Owners and Pilots Assn. Republican. Inventor vapor suppression solar collector film system. Office: 500 W Farmers Ave Box 30400 Amarillo TX 79120

FLYNN, ANITA ABEL, ret. bus. exec., civic worker; b. Otterbein, Ind., Sept. 20, 1916; d. Ernest Andrew and Jessie Sara (Foster) Abel; student Ball State Tchrs. Coll., 1934-38; m. Edward J. Flynn, Nov. 24, 1945. Tchr., Shelbyville, Ind., until 1941; optician, Indpls., 1941-44, also Optical Am. Co., Terra Haute, Ind.; substitute tchr., Somersworth, Ind., 1953-60; bus. adminstr. Tri-Area Vis. Nurse Assn., 1965-80. Mem. Somersworth Planning Bd., 1966-74; sec. Planning Bd. and Bd. Adjustment, 1969-74; library trustee, 1972—; candidate for Ind. Ho. of Reps. Democrat. Episcopalian. Club: Women's. Home: 12 Pine Grove Terr Somersworth NH 03878

FLYNN, JANICE FITZGERALD, glass mfg. co. exec.; b. Cleve., May 15, 1955; d. Robert A. and Janice P. (Argraves) Fitzgerald; B.A. in Econs., U. Pitts., 1978; m. Robert H. Flynn, Jan. 26, 1980. Mgmt. trainee Anchor Hocking, Lancaster, Ohio and Jacksonville, Fla., 1979, mgmt. coordinator, Jacksonville, 1980-81, dept. supr., 1981-82, Impac coordinator, 1982—. Asst. to chmn. Mayor's Licencing and Permitting com. City of Jacksonville, 1981; mem. steering com. Transient Youth Center, Jacksonville, 1981. Republican. Roman Catholic. Club: Park Ave Racket. Contbr. in field. Home: 12268 Mayors Dr Jacksonville FL 32223 Office: PO Box 6932 2121 Huron St Jacksonville FL 32205

FLYNN, JUDITH C. S., business exec.; b. Wichita Falls, Tex., Nov. 27, 1945; d. W.H. and Teena H. Chittum; B.A., Grove City (Pa.) Coll., 1966; M.A. in Teaching (teaching fellow 1967), Brown U., 1967; m. Harold F. Flynn, Jr.; children—Harold F., III, Peter Craig, Alison J. Tchr., Franklin (N.H.) High Sch., 1967-68; internat. advt. coordinator Franklin Mint, Franklin Center, Pa., 1969-72; fin. mgr. Fire Service Agy., Annapolis, Md., 1972-74; asst. to comptroller Alcoa Marine Corp., Washington, 1974-76; v.p. fin., dir. Martel Labs., Inc., Balt., 1977-80, exec. v.p., 1982—; pres., dir. Martel Lab. Services, St. Petersburg, Fla., 1982—; dir. Leartek Corp., 1977—, Chgo. Aerial Survey, Inc., 1982—. Mem. Engring. Soc. Balt., Nat. Assn. Female Execs., Internat. Oceanographic Found., Nat. Assn. Women Bus. Owners, Com. of 200, Assn. Women Govt. Contractors. Republican. Episcopalian. Home: 7450 14th St NE Saint Petersburg FL 33702 Office: 7100 30th Ave N Saint Petersburg FL 33710

FLYNN, KATHLEEN DOROTHY, architect; b. Washington, June 21, 1948; d. Charles Lenean and Winifred Judith (Carocari) F.; A.B., Manhattanville Coll., 1970; student So. Conn. State Coll., 1973-74; M.A., St. John's Coll., Santa Fe, N.Mex., 1979; postgrad. U. Wash., 1978—. Art tchr. Found. Sch., Orange, Conn., 1970-72; art tchr. Milford (Conn.) Public Schs., 1974-78; housing intern Office of Housing Devel., Dept. Community Devel., City of Seattle, 1980; intern architect Olson Walker Partners, Architects, Seattle, 1981—. NEA grantee, 1981.

FLYNN, MARGARET ALBERI, nutritionist; b. Hurley, Wis., Nov. 22, 1915; d. Bernard and Anna (Chiado) Alberi; B.S., Coll. of St. Catherine, St. Paul, 1937; M.S., U. Iowa, 1938; Ph.D., U. Mo., 1966; m. Joseph E. Flynn, May 1938; children—Phoebe, Timothy. Mem. faculty U. Mo., Columbia, 1966—, prof. family and community medicine, 1969—. Diplomate Am. Bd. Nutrition. Mem. Am. Soc. Clin. Nutrition, Am. Inst. Nutrition, Phi Beta Kappa, Sigma Xi, Omega Delta Kappa, Iota Sigma Pi. Author articles in field. Address: M304 Medical Center Stadium Rd Columbia MO 65201

FLYNN, MARIE COSGROVE, mgmt. co. exec.; b. Honolulu, Jan. 1, 1945; d. John Aloysius and Emeline Frances (Cael) Cosgrove; B.A., Trinity Coll., 1966; student U. Fribourg (Switzerland), 1964-65; m. John Thomas Flynn, Jr., June 3, 1968; children—Jamie Marie, Jacqueline Elizabeth. Mgmt. trainee, analyst U.S. Govt., Washington, 1967-70; coordinator nat. reading council F.X. Doherty Assos., N.Y.C., 1970-71; security analyst Corinthian Capital Co., N.Y.C., 1971-73; portfolio mgr. Clark Mgmt. Co., Inc., N.Y.C., 1973-78; v.p., sr. portfolio mgr. Lexington Mgmt. Corp., Englewood Cliffs, N.J., 1978—. Mem. Fin. Analysts Fedn., Inst. Chartered Fin. Analysts, Fin. Women's Assn., N.Y. Soc. Security Analysts, Bus. and Profl. Women's Club, Profl. Women's Network. Home: 70 Evergreen Dr Berkeley Heights NJ 07922 Office: 580 Sylvan Ave Englewood Cliffs NJ 07632

FLYNN, MARYELLEN, advt. agy. exec.; b. Boston, Aug. 22; d. Cornelius and Helen G. Flynn; student Fordham U., 1957-60, Am. Acad. Dramatic Arts, 1960-62. Creative supr. Young & Rubicam, N.Y.C., 1970-73; creative dir. Revlon Inc., N.Y.C., 1973-75; founding partner, v.p., creative dir. Renning, Kuryla, Lieberman, Flynn Inc., N.Y.C., 1975-78; v.p., creative dir. Grey Advt., N.Y.C., 1979—. Founder, producing dir. Gryphon Theatricals, Inc., 1979; producer off-Broadway play A Coupla White Chicks Sitting Around Talking, 1980. Recipient Clio award, 1969, 74, Anny award, 1965, IBA award, 1963, Venice Grand Prix award, 1962. Mem. Nat. Assn. TV Arts and Scis., Actors Equity. Office: Grey Advt 777 3d Ave New York NY 10017

FLYNT, ALTHEA SUE, publisher, editor; b. Marietta, Ohio, Nov. 6, 1953; d. Richard Earl and June Avonelle (Osbourne) Leasure; m. Aug. 21, 1976. Pres., Mini Clubs Am., Ohio nightclub chain, 1971-74; pub., editor, chmn. bd., chief exec. officer Hustler Mag., Inc., Chic Mag., Inc., and Gentleman's Companion Mag., Inc., 1974—; pres. Larry Flynt Publs., Inc., 1980—; pres., chmn. bd. Flynt Distbg. Co., Inc., Flynt Subscription Co., Inc., and Flynt Domestic Internat. Sale Corp., 1974—. Office: 2029 Century Park E Suite 3800 Los Angeles CA 90067

FOCH, NINA, actress, educator; b. Leyden, Netherlands, Apr. 20, 1924; d. Dirk and Consuelo (Flowerton) F.; came to U.S., 1928, naturalized, 1933; grad. Lincoln Sch., N.Y.C., 1939; m. James Lipton, June 6, 1954; m. 2d, Dennis R. Brite, Nov. 27, 1959; 1 son, Schuyler Dirk; m. 3d, Michael Dewell, Oct. 31, 1967. Appeared in motion pictures: Nine Girls, 1944, Return of the Vampire, 1944, She's A Sweetheart, 1944, Shadows in the Night, 1944, Cry of the Werewolf, 1944, Escape in the Fog, 1945, A Song to Remember, 1945, My Name is Julia Ross, 1945, I Love A Mystery, 1945, Johnny O'Clock, 1947, The Guilt of Janet Ames, 1947, The Dark Past, 1948, The Undercover Man, 1949, Johnny Allegro, 1949, An American in Paris, 1951, Scaramouche, 1952, Young Man with Ideas, 1952, Sombrero, 1953, Fast Company, 1953, Executive Suite, 1954 (Acad. award nominee for supporting performance 1954), Four Guns to the Border, 1954, You're Never Too Young, 1955, Illegal, 1955, The Ten Commandments, 1956, Three Brave Men, 1957, Cash McCall, 1959, Spartacus, 1960, Such Good Friends, 1971, Salty, 1973, Mahogany, 1976, Jennifer, 1978; Broadway plays include: John Loves Mary, 1947, Twelfth Night, 1949, A Phoenix Too Frequent, 1950, King Lear, 1950, Second String, 1960; appeared with Am. Shakespeare Festival in Taming of the Shrew and Measure for Measure, 1956; appeared with San Francisco Ballet and Opera in The Seven Deadly Sins, 1966, also many regional theatre productions, including Seattle Repertory Theatre in All Over, 1972, The Seagull, 1973; actress TV, 1947—, including Playhouse 90, Studio One, Pulitzer Playhouse, Playwrights 56, Producers Show Case, Naked City, Kraft Suspense Theatre, Route 66, Arrest and Trial, Burke's Law, The Trailmaster, Dr. Kildare, The Outer Limits, The Steve Allen Show, Gunsmoke, McCloud, Mod Squad, I Spy, Columbo, Barnaby Jones,

Hawaii Five-O, The Name of the Game, The Wonderful World of Disney, Lou Grant, also many other series, network spls. and films for TV; TV panelist and guest on numerous shows, including The Tonight Show, Dick Cavett Show, Merv Griffin Show, Mike Douglas Show, Dinah Shore Show; TV moderator Let's Take Sides, 1957-59; asso. dir. film The Diary of Anne Frank, 1959; dir. nat. tour and Broadway production Tonight at 8:30, 1966-67; asso. producer re-opening Ford's Theatre, Washington, 1968; adj. prof. U. So. Calif., 1966-68; artist-in-residence U. N.C., 1966, Ohio State U., 1967, Calif. Tech. Inst., 1969-70; mem. sr. faculty Am. Film Inst., 1973-77; founder, tchr. Nina Foch Studio, Hollywood, Calif., 1973—; adj. prof. U. So. Calif., 1978-80; a founder, actress Los Angeles Theatre Group, 1960-65; bd. dirs. Nat. Repertory Theatre, 1967-75. Hon. chmn. Los Angeles chpt. Am. Cancer Soc., 1970. Mem. Acad. Motion Picture Arts and Scis. (exec. com. for fgn. film award 1973—), Hollywood Acad. TV Arts and Scis. (gov. 1976-77). Address: PO Box 1884 Beverly Hills CA 90213

FOGEL, MARJORIE, public relations exec.; b. Port Chester, N.Y., Dec. 14, 1931; d. Maurice and Betty Schneider; student Pembroke Coll. of Brown U., 1949-50, N.Y.U., 1951-52, 78; m. Harold V. Fogel, June 12, 1954; children—Jonathan, Glenn. Prodn. asst., then prodn. mgr., copywriter, editor Jack Danowitz Advt., Inc., N.Y.C., 1951-52; community/public relations coordinator Planned Communities, Inc., Rye, N.Y., Washington, 1975-76; free-lance public relations, 1977; exec. dir. Energy Resources Devel. Inst., also exec. dir. Apt. Owners Adv. Council, White Plains, N.Y., 1978-79; founder, prin. Marje Fogel Communications, Rye Brook, N.Y., 1980—. Vol. ARC, 1955-59, United Hosp., 1968-77; mem. Westchester County Democratic Com., 1972-81; mem. exec. com. Port Chester-Town of Rye Voter Registration Dr., 1972-76; coordinator fund-raising, community relations Mental Health Assn. Westchester County, 1975; mem. steering com. Port Chester-Town of Rye Bicentennial, 1975-76; bd. dirs. Port Chester-Town of Rye Community Action Program, 1976-77; publicity coordinator Dem. candidates, 1975-77; mem. Rye Town Planning Bd., 1980—. Recipient ARC service award; United Hosp. service award; Westchester Mental Health Vol. Service award. Mem. Advt. Club. Westchester. Jewish. Club: Hampshire County (Mamaroneck, N.Y.). Address: 201 Country Ridge Dr Rye Brook NY 10573

FOGERTY, RAMONA ODESSA, naprapath, sch. dir.; b. Chgo., Aug. 6, 1928; d. Alvin Chris and Lillian Odessa (Tillman) Fogerty; B.Ed., Chgo. Tchrs. Coll., 1956; M.A., U. Chgo., 1961; D.N., Chgo. Nat. Coll. of Naprapathy, 1976. Dir., Potential Sch. for Exceptional Children, Chgo. Founder 2 elem. schs. for destitute children in Petite Riviere des Nippes, Haiti, 1980; instituted self-help bakery and chicken farm projects in St. Marc and Petite Riviere des Nippes, 1982. Home: 5807 S Dorchester Ave Chicago IL 60637 Office: 7222 S Exchange St Chicago IL 60649

FOLEY, ANNA BERNICE WILLIAMS (MRS. WARREN MASSEY FOLEY), author; b. Wigginsville, Ohio, Nov. 20, 1902; d. Karl Howland and Bertye (Young) Williams; B.A., U. Cin., 1924; postgrad. Nanking (China) Lang. Coll., 1926, Columbia U., 1931; grad. cert. Jesus Coll., Oxford (Eng.) U., 1969; m. Warren Massey Foley, Feb. 25, 1924; children—Williams Massey, Karlanne Foley Hauer. Commentator, Sta. WKRC, Cin., 1934, Sta. WSAI, Cin., 1938, Sta. WCPO-TV, Cin., 1939-44; spl. events coordinator Mabley & Carew Dept. Store, Cin., 1951-66; dir. Martha Kinney Cooper Ohioana Library Assn., Columbus, Ohio, 1966-77, also editor Quar. mag., Yearbook, 1966-77; lectr. creative writing; lectr. U. Cin. Evening Coll., 1941-44; book reviewer Sunday Columbus Dispatch, 1967-77, Asia Mail, 1976-77. Bd. dirs. Ohio Poetry Day, 1968-77. Recipient Valley Forge Honor certificate Freedoms Found., 1976, certificate Columbus Art League, 1976; named to Ohio Women's Hall of Fame, 1982. Mem. English Speaking Union (br. pres. 1966-69), Ohio Arts Council (lit. panel 1966-70), Ohio Press Women, Women in Communication (pres. Columbus 1973), World Assn. Women Journalists and Writers, MacDowell Soc., Overseas Press Club, Sigma Delta Chi, Kappa Kappa Gamma (Woman of Achievement 1974). Author: (juvenile) Star Stories, 1970; Spaceships of the Ancients, 1978; Korean Legends, 1979; A Walk Among Clouds, 1980; Why the Cock Crows Three Times, 1980; The Gazelle and the Hunter, 1980; also weekly newspaper column. Home: 10224 Linden Ln Overland Park KS 66207

FOLEY, CAROL ANN, educator; b. Youngstown, Ohio, Jan. 8, 1935; d. Bert E. and Gertrude F. (Hagberg) Olsen; A.A., Stephens Coll., Columbia, Mo., 1955; m. James N. Foley, June 9, 1956; children—Jon, Karla. Designer, patternmaker Kerr-McFall Garment Co., Iola, Kans., 1955-57, Kamahamaha Garment Co., Honolulu, 1958-59; instr. fashion design Stephens Coll., 1959--, coordinator intermediate design search com., 1973, 77, 79; instr. fashion design Columbia Coll., 1980. Vice pres. Macon (Mo.) PTA, 1964. Mem. Fashion Group. Republican. Office: Sampson Hall Stephens Coll Columbia MO 65201

FOLEY, HELEN ANN, state legislator; b. Las Vegas, Nev., Oct. 20, 1953; student U. Nev., Reno, 1971-73; B.A. in Polit. Sci., U. Nev., Las Vegas, postgrad., 1982—. Mem. staff U.S. Senate Com. on Rules and Adminstrn., Washington, 1975-76; aide to Senator Howard W. Cannon, Washington, 1974-75, Congressman James Santini, Las Vegas, 1976-78; dir. devel. Opportunity Village for Retarded Citizens, Las Vegas, 1978-81; mem. Nev. Assembly, 1981-82; mem. Nev. Senate, 1983—. Bd. dirs. Aid to Adoption of Spl. Kids; past v.p. Nev. Young Democrats; mem. Clark County Dem. Central Com. Roman Catholic. Club: Jr. League. Office: Legislative Bldg 401 S Carson St Carson City NV 89710 *

FOLEY, HELEN LUCILLE GORDON, accountant, travel agy. exec.; b. St. Joseph, Mo., Oct. 27, 1918; d. Claude Cecil and Roberta May (Berry) Gordon; student Platt-Gard Bus. Coll., St. Joseph, 1936-37; m. Joseph John Foley, June 18, 1946. Clk.-typist Universal Motor Fuels Co., Wichita, Kans., 1941-42; supr. typist pool U.S. Army Air Force, Wichita, 1943-44; with J.A. Folger Co., Kansas City, Mo., 1944-46; secretarial positions Sprague Electric Co., North Adams, Mass., 1948-50, Mine & Smelter Supply Co., Denver, 1951-59, Belshe Realty Co., Denver, 1960-62; acct., sec.-treas. Woodruff World Travel, Inc., Denver, 1963—; instr. Met. State Coll., Denver, 1980-81. Home: 2019 S Osceola Way Denver CO 80219 Office: Woodruff World Travel Inc 201 University Blvd Denver CO 80206

FOLEY, KATHLEEN A., advt. agy. exec.; b. Fresh Meadows, N.Y., Oct. 15, 1952; d. Thomas and Audrey Foley; grad. Marymount Coll., 1974; student Inst. European Studies, Vienna, Austria, 1973-74. With Ogilvy & Mather, Inc., N.Y.C., 1974—, account exec., 1981-82, account supr., 1982—. Class rep. Marymount Coll. Alumnae Assn., 1974—. Roman Catholic. Club: Uptown Racquet (N.Y.C.). Office: 2 E 48th St New York NY 10017

FOLEY, LOUISE HELEN, research chemist; b. Washington, Oct. 23, 1943; d. John Dennis and Helen Mathilde (Lockwood) F.; B.S. in Chemistry, U. Vt., 1965; Ph.D. (NIH fellow), M.I.T., 1970. Sr. scientist Hoffmann-La Roche, Inc., Nutley, N.J., 1970-78, asst. research group chief, 1978-82; asst. prof. chemistry Fordham U., 1978-79, adj. asst. prof., 1979-82; ednl. counselor M.I.T., 1976—, vis. scientist, 1981—. Mem. Am. Chem. Soc., Am. Women in Sci., N.Y. Acad. Scis., Sigma Xi. Contbr. articles to profl. jours. Home: 244 Kennedy Dr Apt 306 Malden MA 02148 Office: 18-230 Dept Chemistry MIT Cambridge MA 02139

FOLEY, MARY ALICE DODD (MRS. LAWSON EDGAR FOLEY), piano tchr., civic worker; b. Roanoke, Va., Dec. 24, 1912; d. Cubert Bosworth and Fannie (Hale) Dodd; student St. Louis Inst. Music, 1932, 37, U. Va., 1939-53, Hollins Coll., 1953-55, U. Richmond, 1960-62, U. N.C., summers 1965-67; m. Lawson Edgar Foley, Apr. 12, 1933. Tchr. piano, Roanoke, 1933—. Del., People to People Travel Program. Mem. Roanoke Music Tchrs. Assn. (parliamentarian 1969-71, 75-77), Nat. Guild Piano Tchrs. (Hall of Fame), Music Tchrs. Nat. Assn. (nat. cert. bd., chmn. So. div. 1977-80), Va. Music Tchrs. Assn. (historian 1977-79, state parliamentarian 1969-71, 73-75; 1st v.p. 1968-70, chmn. bd. cert. 1971-77), Nat. Geneal. Soc. Daus. of Confederacy (pres. 1966-68), Wythe County, New River (charter mem. drama com.) hist. socs., Historic Fincastle, Magna Charta Dames, Soc. Descs. Knights Most Noble Order Garter, Nat., Va. (councilor 1971-74) socs. daus. colonial wars, Huguenot Soc. Va. (rec. sec. 1971-73), Roanoke Hist. Soc., Colonial Dames XVII Century (chpt. pres. 1971-73, chmn. nat. def. 1977-80), DAR (chpt. regent 1968-71, dist. dir. 1971-74, chmn. state friends of mus. com. 1974-77, dist. parliamentarian 1974-77, chpt. historian 1980-83), SW Va. Geneal. Soc., Alpha Pi Mu (past pres.). Methodist. Home: 6576 Laban Rd Roanoke VA 24019

FOLEY, MARY REGINA RYAN, mgmt. cons.; b. Madison, Wis., Sept. 26, 1941; d. Louis August and Marian Jane (O'Connell) Maier; A.B., Marquette U., 1963; M.S.W. (U.S. Children's Bur. scholar), St. Louis U., 1965; m. Henry A. Foley, Aug. 21, 1982; children from previous marriage—Christopher John Matek, Monica Marie Matek, Maria Regina Matek. Med. social worker Milwaukee County Gen. Hosp., 1965-67; cons. dept. sociology Marquette U., 1969-71; research asst. Mental Health Planning Com. Milwaukee County, 1971-73; field rep. Nat. Found. March of Dimes, 1976-77; dir. community services Orange County Health Planning Council, Tustin, Calif., 1977-82; cons. Western Center Health Planning, San Francisco, 1978—; Los Angeles Health Planning and Devel. Agy., 1981—, Orange County Health Planning Council, 1982—. Chmn., Tustin Traffic Commn., 1976-77; del. Wis. Democratic Conf., 1971; bd. dirs. Orange County Employee Benefits Council; mem. citizens' adv. council KOCE-TV; mem. adv. com. Calif. Health Tng. Center, Family Service Assn. Orange County. mem. coms. United Way, Family Service Assn., Am. Cancer Soc., March of Dimes Birth Defects Found., 1978—; host, interviewer KOCM Community Forum Program, 1979—. Mem. Am. Public Health Assn. (governing council 1981—), Am. Health Planning Assn., Roman Catholic. Club: Jr. League Phoenix. Home: 4605 E Palo Verde Dr Phoenix AZ 85018 Office: 14412 Acacia Dr Tustin CA 92680

FOLK, SHARON LYNN, printing co. exec.; b. Bellefontaine, Ohio, June 13, 1945; d. Emerson D. and Berdena Isabelle (Brown) F.; A.B., Belmont Abbey Coll., 1968. Exec. v.p. Nat. Bus. Forms, Inc., Greeneville, Tenn., 1968-73, pres., chmn. bd., 1973—; chmn. bd., pres. Nat. Forms Co., Inc., Gastonia, N.C., 1973-79; dir. Andrew Johnson Bank, Greenville, 1981—. Mem. Presdl. steering com. Senator Howard Baker, 1979-80; mem. Rep. Presdl. steering com., 1981—; life mem. Rep. Nat. Com., 1981—; bd. dirs. Greeneville YMCA, 1977-80, Greeneville United Way, 1980—. Mem. Internat. Bus. Forms Industry Assn. (dir. 1982—, chmn. employee relations com. 1978—), Nat. Bus. Forms Assn., Nat. Assn. Women Bus. Owners (com. of 200, 1982—), U.S. Tennis Assn. (life). Roman Catholic. Home: 1131 Hixon Ave Greeneville TN 37743 Office: 100 Pennsylvania Ave Greeneville TN 37743

FOLLANSBEE, DOROTHY L. (DOROTHY L. LELAND), publisher; b. St. Louis, Mar. 24, 1911; d. Robert Leathan and Minnie Cowden (Yowell) Lund; grad. Sarah Lawrence Coll., 1931; m. Austin Porter Leland, Apr. 24, 1935 (dec. 1975); children—Mary Talbot Leland MacCarthy, Austin Porter Jr. (dec.), Irene Austin Leland Barzantny; m. 2d, Robert Kerr Follansbee, Oct. 20, 1979. Pres., Station List Publ. Co., St. Louis, 1975—; dir. Downtown St. Louis Inc. Hon. chmn. Old Post Office Landmark Com., 1975—; bd. dirs. Services Bur. St. Louis, 1943, pres., 1951; bd. dirs. Robert E. Lee Meml. Assn.; mem. St. Louis County Parks and Recreation Dept., 1969; bd. dirs. Stratford Hall, Va., 1953—, pres., 1967-70, treas., 1970—; bd. dirs. Historic Bldgs. Commn. St. Louis County, 1959—, Mo. Hist. Soc., 1960-82, Mo. Mansion Preservation Com., 1975—, Chatillon DeMenil House, 1977-79. Recipient Landmarks award Landmarks Assn. St. Louis, 1974; Pub. Service award GSA, 1978; Crownenshield award Nat. Trust for Hist Preservation, 1979. Mem. Colonial Dames Am., Episcopalian. Clubs: St. Louis Country, Princeton of N.Y., St. Louis Jr. League. Home: 35 Pointer Ln Saint Louis MO 63124 also 1001 River Oaks Dr Pittsburgh PA 15215 Office: Station List Co 818 Olive St Saint Louis MO 63101

FOLLETT, MARY VIERLING, artist, conservator, art gallery exec.; b. Chgo., Feb. 9, 1917; d. Arthur Garfield and Grace May (Cummings) Vierling; student U. So. Calif., 1932-34; m. Garth Benepe Follett, Feb. 16, 1945; 1 dau., Dawn Valerie Follett Goshorn. Owner, operator Paintin' Place, Oak Park, Ill., 1973—; dir. Palette and Chisel Acad. Fine Arts, Chgo., 1975, 76. Vice pres. Oak Park LWV, 1952-54, welfare chmn., Ill., 1956-58; treas. Oak Park Council Internat. Affairs, 1962-74. Recipient numerous awards including Gold medal Palette and Chisel Acad. Fine Arts; 1st award Union League Civic Assn., 1977. Mem. Pen Women Am., Palette and Chisel Acad. Fine Arts (dir.), Mcpl. Art League Chgo., Art League Oak Park and River Forest (v.p.), Am. Soc. Artists, Art Inst. Chgo. (women's bd. assos. 1967—), 19th Century Woman's Club. Home: 1440 Park Ave River Forest IL 60305 Gallery: 820 North Blvd Oak Park IL 60301

FOLSOM, RODDELLE BRANTLEY, librarian; b. Washington County, Ga., Mar. 8, 1925; d. Roger Tennyson and Evona (Smith) Brantley; student South Ga. Coll., 1941-42, 43-44; B.S. in Edn., U. Ga., 1955; M.L.S., Fla. State U., 1973; m. Elton Brown Folsom, May 30, 1946; 1 dau., Kathryn Yvonne. Tchr. elem. and high schs., Ga., 1944-51; extension librarian S. Ga. Regional Library, Valdosta, 1952-71, acting dir., 1971-73, dir., 1973—. Bd. dirs. Valdosta Girl's Club, 1977-79, sec., 1978-79; bd. dirs. Adult Edn. dir. Valdosta Tech. Sch., 1982-83. Mem. AAUW (editor newsletter 1975), Southeastern Library Assn., Ga. Library Assn., Lowndes Adult Edn. Assn. (pres. 1977-78), Valdosta and Lowndes County Library Assn. (pres. 1981-82), S. Ga. Associated Libraries, Tri-State Library Assn. Democrat. Baptist. Clubs: Wymodausis (1st v.p. 1982—), Quota (1st v.p. 1978-79, pres. 1979-80). Home: 1110 Dellwood Dr Valdosta GA 31601 Office: 300 Woodrow Wilson Dr Valdosta GA 31601

FOLTZ, VIRGINIA CAMPBELL (MRS. DANIEL SHANNON FOLTZ), educator; b. Ashtabula, Ohio, Aug. 3, 1911; d. Hosea William and Grace Evelyn (Griffey) Campbell; B.S., Baldwin Wallace Coll., 1933; M.S., U. Houston, 1966; Ph.D., Tex. Woman's U., 1969; m. Daniel Shannon Foltz, June 12, 1933; children—Richard Campbell, James Lance. Instr., U. Houston, 1963-64; teaching fellow Tex. Woman's U., Denton, 1965; asst. prof. La. Tech. U., Ruston, 1969-70; asst. prof. dept. biology Pan Am. U., Edinburg, Tex., 1970-73, asso. prof., 1973-81. Welch Found. fellow, 1968. Mem. AAAS, Genetics Soc. Am., Tex. Assn. Radiation Research, Tex. Acad. Sci., Sigma Xi, Beta Beta Beta. Home: 909 McKee Dr Edinburg TX 78539 Office: Dept Biology Pan Am U Edinburg TX 78539

FONDA, JANE, actress; b. N.Y.C., Dec. 21, 1937; d. Henry and Frances (Seymour) Fonda; student Vassar Coll., 2 years Art Students League, N.Y.C.; pupil acting with Lee Strasberg; m. Roger Vadim, 1966 (div.); 1 dau.; m. 2d, Tom Hayden, Jan. 20, 1973; 1 son. Appeared with father in summer stocks in The Country Girl, Omaha; actress on Broadway stage in There Was A Little Girl, 1960, The Fun Couple, 1962; in Actor's Studio prodn. Strange Interlude, 1963; appeared in films including: Tall Story, 1960, A Walk on the Wild Side, 1962, Period of Adjustment, 1962, Sunday In New York, 1963, In the Cool of the Day, 1963, The Love Cage, 1963, La Ronde, 1964, Barbarella, They Shoot Horses, Don't They?, 1969, Klute (Acad. award best actress), 1971, Steelyard Blues, 1973, A Doll's House, 1973, The Blue Bird, 1976, Fun With Dick and Jane, 1977, Julia, 1977, Coming Home, 1978 (Acad. award), Comes A Horseman, 1978, California Suite, 1978, The China Syndrome, 1979, The Electric Horseman, 1979, Nine to Five, 1980, Roll Over, 1981, On Golden Pond, 1982. Recipient Golden Globe award, 1978; N.Y. Film Critics award, 1969, 71. Address: PO Box 900 Beverly Hills CA 90213 *

FONDILLER, SHIRLEY HOPE ALPERIN, nurse, journalist, educator; b. Holyoke, Mass.; d. Samuel and Rose (Sobiloff) Alperin; grad. Beth Israel Hosp. Sch. Nursing, Boston; B.S., Tchrs. Coll. Columbia U., 1962, M.A., 1963, M.Ed., 1971, Ed.D., 1979; m. Harvey V. Fondiller, Dec. 27, 1957; 1 son, David Stewart. Staff asst. Am. Nurses Assn., N.Y.C., 1963-64, dir. ednl. adminstrs., cons. and tchrs. sect., 1964-66, coordinator Am. Nurses Assn.-Nat. League for Nursing careers program, 1967-70; coordinator clin. sessions Am. Nurses Assn., 1971-72, editor Am. Nurse, Kansas City, Mo., 1975-79; asso. prof., asst. to dean for spl. projects Rush-Presbyn.-St. Luke's Med. Center, Chgo., 1979—. Mem. Kappa Delta Pi, Sigma Theta Tau. Writer, columnist Nursing World, 1955-60; film reviewer Am. Jour. Nursing, 1963-64, Film News, 1963-66; writer, dir. The Open Door, radio documentary, 1960; contbg. editor Am. Jour. Nursing, 1971-75; author books and articles on nursing, health care, edn. Home: 1550 N Lake Shore Dr Chicago IL 60610

FONES, BEATRICE DE HART WILLIAMS, govt. auditor; b. Swain County, N.C., Aug. 5, 1936; d. Arthur A. and Lexie I. (McMahan) DeH.; B.S.B.A., U. N.C., Chapel Hill, 1958; m. Robert W. Fones, Aug. 3, 1973; children—Roger David, Tina Marie. Staff auditor Hoffmann and Rink, C.P.A.s, summer 1957; traffic clk. DeHart Motor Lines, Inc., Hickory, N.C., 1958-59, personnel and safety dir., 1959-60; auditor Library of Congress, Washington, 1962-63, 68-70; owner, operator Hickory Custom Finishing Co. (N.C.), 1963-65; customer service rep. Nat. Cash Register Co., Hickory, 1965-66, Greensboro, N.C., 1966-67; cost acct. Western Electric Co., Greensboro, 1967; auditor D.C. Govt. Office Mcpl. Audit, 1970-73; sr. auditor Capital region Naval Audit Service, Washington, 1973-80, fed. women's program mgr., 1977-80; supervisory auditor office audits EEO, Washington, 1980—; chairwoman supervisory com. D.C. Govt. Employee Credit Union; auditor Library of Congress Credit Union. Recipient Unit Meritorious award Sec. Navy, 1977, letter of appreciation Comptroller Gen. Navy, 1979, Audit of Quarter award Navy Audit, 1979, 80. Mem. Assn. Govt. Accts. (chpt. exec. com. 1971-73, 2d pl. in research competition 1972, cert. appreciation chpt. 1972, 73), Am. Soc. Mil. Comptrollers, Federally Employed Women, U. N.C. Alumni Assn. (life). Developed programmed text on appropriation acctg. for Navy Audit trainees. Home: PO Box 224 Annandale VA 22003 Office: 2401 E St NW Washington DC

FONSECA, EMMA HAIDEE, histotechnologist; b. Oriente, Cuba, Dec. 31, 1917; came to U.S., 1964, naturalized, 1971; d. Dalmiro Abel and Ana Marie (Zayas) Sanchez; B.A., B.S., Immaculada Coll., Havana, Cuba, 1936; D.Pharmacy, Havana U., 1939; m. German E. Fonseca, Dec. 25, 1939; children—Emma Julia, Enid. Asst. dir., then tech. dir. Linner Labs., Inc., Havana, 1939-62; with Miles Labs., Inc., Elkhart, Ind., 1964—, asso. research toxicologist, 1970-75, supr. histology and toxicology dept., 1975—. Mem. AAUW, Nat. Assn. Female Execs., Nat. Soc. Histotechnologists, Am. Soc. Med. Technologists. Roman Catholic. Home: 54637 Michael Dr Elkhart IN 46516 1127 Myrtle St Elkhart IN 46515

FONSECA, OTILIA ENRIQUETA, sch. psychologist; b. Bayamo, Cuba, Oct. 16, 1945; came to U.S., 1961, naturalized, 1972; d. Olimpo Fonseca and Otilia Hilda Aguirre de Fonseca; B.A., Columbia U., 1970; M.A., Montclair (N.J.) State Coll., 1971, postgrad., 1979—. Teaching asst. dept. psychology Montclair State Coll., 1970-71, instr. Spanish, counselors tng. program, 1971-72; sch. psychologist Elizabeth (N.J.) Bd. Edn., 1972—. Cert. sch. psychologist, N.J. Mem. Am. Psychol. Assn. (asso.), Nat. Assn. Sch. Psychologists, N.J. Assn. Sch. Psychologists, Union County Assn. Sch. Psychologists, Psi Chi. Roman Catholic. Club: Lioness. Home: 347 Elmora Ave Elizabeth NJ 07208 Office: Elizabeth Bd Edn 500 N Broad St Elizabeth NJ 07207

FONTAINE, JOAN, (born de Havilland), actress; b. Tokyo, Oct. 22, 1917; d. Walter and Lilian (Ruse) de Havilland; m. Brian Aherne, Aug. 20, 1939 (div. 1944); m. 2d, William Dozier, May 2, 1946; 1 dau., Deborah Leslie, 1 adopted dau., Martita Valentina Caideron; m. 3d, Collier Young, Nov. 10, 1952 (div. 1961); m. 4th, Alfred Wright, Jr. Feb. 1964. Has appeared in numerous motion pictures since 1937; pictures include: Rebecca, 1939 (N.Y. Critics award, Can. Film Critics award); Suspicion, 1940 (Acad. award); Constant Nymph, 1943; Jane Eyre, 1944; Frenchman's Creek, 1944; Ivy, 1947; You Gotta Stay Happy, 1948; September Affair, 1949; Born to be Bad, 1949; Something to Live For, 1950; Darling How Could You, 1950; Ivanhoe, 1951; Decameron Nights, 1952; Casanova, 1953; Beyond a Reasonable Doubt, 1956; Island in the Sun, 1957; Until We Sail, 1957; A Certain Smile, 1958; Voyage To The Bottom of The Sea, 1961; Tender Is the Night, 1962; The Devils Own, 1966; broadway debut in Tea and Sympathy, 1954; other theatre prodns. include Private Lives, The Marriage-Go-Round, Dial —M— for Murder, Forty Carats, Cactus Flower; TV panelist, lectr. univs., women's clubs. Bd. dirs. Motion Picture Welfare Trust Fund. Recipient Eleanor Roosevelt award, 1966; nominated for Emmy award for role in Ryan's Hope, 1980. Mem. Motion Picture Acad. Author: No Bed of Roses, 1978. Address: care Gage Group 8732 Sunset Blvd Los Angeles CA 90069 *

FONTAINE, SUE (JEANE), public relations practitioner; b. Rolfe, Iowa, June 28, 1928; d. Vernette M. and Dorothy (Messinger) Gaskins; B.A. in Journalism, U. Iowa, 1947; M.A. in L.S., U. Mo., 1977; m. Henry A. Fontaine, Jr., July 1, 1948 (div. 1970); children—Eva Joel, Jeffrey David. Radio and TV dir. Swigart Advt., Inc., New Orleans, 1948-54, 1962-65; producer Sta. WDSU-TV, New Orleans, 1954-60; dir. public relations La. State Library, Baton Rouge, 1960-62; Tulsa City-County Library, 1965-67, 70-76; spl. projects asst. U. Mo. Sch. Library/Info. Sci., Columbia, 1976-77; public info. officer Wash. State Library, Olympia, 1977-81; assoc. chief public relations N.Y. Public Library, N.Y.C., 1981—; audio-visual, public relations cons. to various libraries and comml. clients, 1960—. Recipient 5 John Cotton Dana Public Relations award, 1965-75. Mem. Public Relations Soc., ALA (sect. and com. chmn., chmn. bd.), Women in Communications (chpt. pres.), N.Y. Library Assn., Alpha Xi Delta, Episcopalian. Editor: (with Susan Phelps) Communications for the Humanities, 1975; Public Relations: Tick/Click, 1975; contbr. articles to profl. jours. Home: 235 E 13th St New York NY 10003 Office: New York Public Library Fifth Ave at 42nd St New York NY 10018

FONTANNE, LYNN, actress; b. London, Eng.; d. Jules Pierre Antoine and Frances Ellen (Thornley) Fontanne; L.H.D., Dartmouth, 1954; m. Alfred Lunt. Made first stage appearance as a child at the Drury Lane Pantomine; first London appearance, 1909; first N.Y.C. appearance as Harriet Bludgeon in Mr. Preedy and the Countess, 1910; played Gertrude in Milestones on tour and later in the revival; small parts in

My Lady's Dress, London; then followed, in N.Y. in The Wooing of Eve, Harp of Life, Out There, Happiness, Dulcy, In Love With Love, The Guardsman, Queen Elizabeth, Design for Living, Reunion in Vienna, Point Valaine, Idiot's Delight, Amphitryon, The Sea Gull, Taming of the Shrew, There Shall Be No Night, The Pirate, O Mistress Mine, I Know My Love, Quadrille, 1954, The Great Sebastians, 1956, others. Played in motion picture The Guardsman with Alfred Lunt.

FONTENAY, MARTHA HOWARD, social worker; b. Chattanooga, May 19, 1937; d. Dave Burton and Nora (Eaves) Howard; B.S., U. Chattanooga, 1959; M.S. in Social Work, U. Tenn., 1961; m. Charles L. Fontenay, Sept. 29, 1962; children—Margarethe Louise, Blake. Clk., Hamilton County Election Commn., Chattanooga, 1957; tchr. secondary grades Chattanooga City Schs., 1959; caseworker Travelers Aid of Chattanooga, 1959-62; intake supr. Knox County Juvenile Ct., Knoxville, Tenn., 1962-63; dir. casework Travelers Aid of Nashville Area, 1966—; field instr. U. Tenn. Sch. Social Work, 1974-77. Chmn. bd. St. Ann's Day Care Center, 1977-80; mem. County Wide Citizens Adv. Com. on Community Devel., 1978-80, Met. Planning Commn., 1981—. Mem. Nat. Assn. Social Workers, Acad. Cert. Social Workers, Tenn. Conf. Social Welfare, Nat. Women's Polit. Caucus. Democrat. Episcopalian. Club: Order Eastern Star. Home: 405 Scott Ave Nashville TN 37206 Office: 122 7th Ave N Nashville TN 37203

FOOTE, BARBARA AUSTIN, civic found. exec.; b. Seattle, Mar. 26, 1918; d. Edwin Charles and Marion Roberts A.; A.B., Vassar Coll., 1940; m. Robert Lake Foote, June 14, 1941; children—Markell Foote Kaiser, Marion Roberts, Helen Foote Schloerb. Tchr., Shady Hill Sch., Cambridge, Mass., 1942-43, Madeira Sch., Greenway, Va., 1943-44, North Shore Country Day Sch., Winnetka, Ill., 1960-71; mem. exec. com. Chgo. Community Trust, 1970—, chmn. exec. com., 1978—; dir. Glencoe Nat. Bank (Ill.), New Eng. Mut. Life Ins. Co., Boston. Pres., Jr. League Chgo., 1947-49, Assn. Jr. Leagues Am., 1954-56, Glencoe Bd. Edn., 1957-63; trustee Vassar Coll., 1966-74. Mem. Vassar Alumni Assn. (nat. pres. 1975-78), Phi Beta Kappa. Congregationalist. Clubs: Fortnightly of Chgo.; Cosmopolitan (N.Y.C.). Author book of verse, 1948. Home: 587 Longwood Ave Glencoe IL 60022 *

FOOTE, EVELYN PATRICIA, army officer; b. Durham, N.C., May 19, 1930; d. Henry and Evelyn (Womack) Foote; B.A., Wake Forest U., 1953; M.S., Shippensburg State Coll., 1977; postgrad. U.S. Army Command and Gen. Staff Coll., 1972, U.S. Army War Coll., 1977, U. Va., 1980. Commd. Capt. U.S. Army, 1960, advanced through grades to col., 1980—, co. comdr. Engr. Center, Ft. Belvoir, Va., 1964-66, exec. officer Public Affairs Office, Vietnam, 1967, WAC br. Office of Personnel Ops., Washington, 1968-71, plans officer Office of Dir. WAC, Washington, 1972-74, exec. officer Human Resources Div., dep. chief of staff for personnel, Ft. McPherson, Ga., 1974-76, comdr. 2d Basic Tng., Ft. McClellan, Ala., 1977-79, dir. personnel mgmt. system Dept. Command and Mgmt., Carlisle Barracks Pa., 1979-82; German lang. trainee, 1982-83; comdr. 42d Mil. Police Group, Mannheim, W.Ger., 1983—; del. Inter-Univ. Seminar on Armed Forces and Soc. lectr. in field. Decorated Legion of Merit, Bronze Star medal, Meritorious Service medal with two oak leaf clusters, Army Commendation medal with oak leaf cluster, Vietnam Gallantry Cross. Mem. AAUW, NOW, Nat. Assn. Female Execs., Am. Soc. Public Adminstrn., WAC Vets Assn., Assn. U.S. Army, Phi Beta Kappa, Sigma Phi Alpha. Contbr. articles to profl. jours. Home: 1121 Arlington Blvd Apt 245N Arlington VA 22209 also 1327 Arlene Ct Lilburn GA 30247 Office: Hdqrs 42d Military Police Group (Customs) APO New York NY 09086

FOOTE, MARGIE ELLEN, retail merchant; b. Reno, Dec. 23, 1929; d. Harry Stephen and Marie Alice (Williams) F.; A.A., Cottey Coll., 1949; B.A., U. Nev., 1951. Tchr. pub. schs., Sparks, Nev., Santa Maria, Calif. and Sacramento, 1951-55; owner children's apparel shop, Sparks, 1955-79; mem. Nev. State Assembly, 1967-74; mem. Nev. Senate, 1975-78; v.p., dir. Harry's Bus. Machines Inc., Reno, mgr. Sparks br., 1979—. Trustee, Sierra Sage council Campfire Girls, 1978-80; chmn. bd. trustees Emmanuel 1st Baptist Ch., 1979. Named Outstanding Nevadan, Asso. Gen. Contractors, 1979. Democrat. Home: 5585 Wedekind Rd Sparks NV 89431

FORBES, MARIE VONGUNTEN, free-lance journalist; b. Balt., June 9, 1928; d. Carl A. and Bessie (Moser) vonGunten; student Md. State Tchrs. Coll., 1945-46, McCoy Coll., Johns Hopkins U., 1946-52, Coll. Notre Dame Md., 1971-72; m. James E. Forbes, Apr. 3, 1971; children by previous marriage—Jean, Hollace, Douglas, Roger, Priscilla and Patricia Wisner. Emergency tchr. Balt. County Public Schs., 1945-46; tchr. Rosewood State Hosp. for Retarded Children, Owings Mills, Md., 1948-52; wood-carver, Owings Mills, 1968-74; freelance journalist, Owings Mills, 1974—; conductor writing workshops, 1978-80. Co-founder Balt. Writers' Alliance, 1980; pres. Owings Mills History Council, 1980-82; v.p. Woman's Club Glyndon, 1968-69; bd. dirs. Pleasant Hill Church, 1958-64. Mem. Author's Guild, Washington Ind. Writers, Md. Writers Council, Balt. Writers Assn. Contbr. articles to mags. and newspapers. Home and Office: 9709 Sherwood Rd Owings Mills MD 21117

FORD, ALMA REGINA, union ofcl.; b. Owings, W.Va., Oct. 4, 1939; d. Charles Feathers and Pearl (Costello) F.; A.B., Fairmont (W.Va.) State Coll., 1960; M.A., W.Va. U., 1964. Tchr. in Ohio, W.Va., Turkey, Eng., France, Italy and W. Ger., 1961-79; v.p., dep. rep. for Dodds-Europe, negotiator Overseas Fedn. Tchrs., 1979—; del. various internat. meetings. Recipient Sustained Superior Commendation award Dept. Army, 1972-76; NDEA fellow, 1968. Mem. AAUW, Nat. Council Tchrs. English, Speech Assn. Am., Am. Fedn. Tchrs., Overseas Fedn. Tchrs., Phi Delta Kappa, Alpha Psi Omega. Home: 724 Locust Ave Fairmont WV 26554 Office: 6 Sachsenstrasse Zweibrucken 6660 Federal Republic Germany

FORD, BARBARA GAY, ednl. cons.; b. Blackwell, Okla., Aug. 1, 1947; d. Bert William and Velma Loye (Burgess) Baumgartner; B.S., U. Mo., 1969; M.Ed., 1971; Ph.D., U. Conn., 1975; m. Ronald David Ford, June 5, 1971; children—Vanessa Meghan, Hadley Morgan. Tchr. spl. edn. Columbia (Mo.) Public Schs., 1971-72, Ironton (Mo.) Public Schs., 1972-73; co-evaluator movement edn. for handicapped program Conn. Public Schs., 1974-75; dir. Area Service Center for the Gifted, No. Ill. U., DeKalb, 1975-78, prof. dept. spl. edn., 1975-82; ednl. and mgmt. cons., partner Ford & Ford Assos., St. Charles, Ill., 1982—. Recipient Mo. Curator's Award, 1965. Mem. Council for Exceptional Children, Nat. Assn. Gifted children, Assn. for Gifted (pres.-elect), Nat. Soc. for Performance and Instrn., Phi Delta Kappa. Episcopalian. Author: New Directions in Creativity, Mark A, 1976, Mark B, 1976; contbr. articles on spl. edn. to profl. jours.; editor: Roeper Review, 1978-81; asso. editor: Exceptional children, 1982—. Home: 1415 S 9th St Saint Charles IL 60174 Office: 203 W Main St Saint Charles IL 60174

FORD, CARLA A., social services adminstr.; b. N.Y.C., July 4, 1945; d. Theodosius Demosthenes and Augusta Louise (Bell) Fagan; B.S., City Coll., City U. N.Y., 1967; M.S.W., Fordham U., 1979; m. Joudon Major Ford, July 6, 1968. Research asst. Psychol. Corp., N.Y.C., 1966-68; caseworker N.Y.C. Dept. Social Services, 1968-71; investigating probation officer N.Y.C. Dept. Probation, 1971-72, supervising probation officer, 1972-73, dir. Alternatives to Detention, 1973-76; asst. dir. Hegeman Diagnostic Reception Center, Bklyn., 1976-77, dir., 1977-79; dir. Baychester Diagnostic Reception Center, Bronx, N.Y., 1979—. Corr. sec. Parkway Ind. Democrats, 1976-79; Dem. County committeewoman, 1978-80; bd. dirs. Protestant Bd. Guardians, pres., 1980—; v.p. bd. dirs. Turner Towers Tenant Corp., 1980-81. Mem. Nat. Assn. Black Social Workers, Nat. Assn. Social Workers, Am. Public Welfare Assn., Nat. Assn. Female Execs., NAACP. Home: 135 Eastern Pkwy Brooklyn NY 11238 Office: 1250 E 229th St Bronx NY 10466

FORD, E. DIANE, artist; b. Ruston, La., Mar. 28, 1934; d. Amos Weeks and Elizabeth M. (Clark) F.; B.A., La. Tech. U., 1956; M.A., Tex. Women's U., 1961; Ed.D., North Tex. State U., 1967; m. Robert William Gruebel, July 22, 1978. Tchr., Dallas schs., 1956-65; mem. faculty Stephen F. Austin State U., Nacogdoches, Tex., 1965—, asso. prof. art, 1972—. Mem. Nat. Art Edn. Assn., Handweavers Guild Am., Tex. Art Edn. Assn., Contemporary Handweavers Tex., Daus. Republic Tex., Colonial Dames 17th Century, Phi Delta Kappa. Home: 2408 Pinecrest Dr Nacogdoches TX 75961 Office: Stephen F Austin State U Box 13001 Nacogdoches TX 75962

FORD, EILEEN OTTE (MRS. GERARD W. FORD), modeling agy. exec.; b. N.Y.C., Mar. 25, 1922; d. Nathaniel and Loretta Marie (Laine) Otte; B.S., Barnard Coll., 1943; m. Gerard William Ford, Nov. 20, 1944; children—Margaret (Mrs. Robert Craft), Gerard William, M. Katie, A. Lacey. Stylist, Elliot Clarke Studio, N.Y.C., 1943-44, William Becker Studio, 1945; copywriter Arnold Constable, N.Y.C., 1945-46; reporter Tobe Coburn, 1946; v.p. Ford Model Agy., N.Y.C., 1946—. Bd. dirs. London Philharmonic, 1948—. Recipient Harpers Bazaar award for promotion internat. understanding. Author: Eileen Ford's Book of Model Beauty; Eileen Ford's Secrets of the Model World; A More Beautiful You in 21 Days; You Can Be Beautiful, 1977. Office: 344 E 59th St New York NY 10022 *

FORD, ELIZABETH BLOOMER (MRS. GERALD R. FORD), wife of former Pres. of U.S.; b. Chgo., Apr. 8, 1918; d. William Stephenson and Hortence (Neahr) Bloomer; student Bennington Sch. Dance, 1936-38; m. William Warren, 1942 (div. 1947); m. 2d, Gerald R. Ford (38th Pres. U.S.), Oct. 15, 1948; children—Michael Gerald, John Gardner, Steven Meigs, Susan Elizabeth. Dancer, Martha Graham Concert Group, N.Y.C., 1939-41; model John Powers Agy., N.Y.C., 1939-41; fashion dir. Herpolsheimer's Dept. Store, Grand Rapids, Mich., 1943-48; dance instr., Grand Rapids, 1932-1948. Chmn., Heart Sunday, Washington Heart Assn., 1974; pres. Red Cross Senate Wives Club; patron Salvation Army Aux. Ann. Fashion Show Luncheon; active benefits Hosp. for Sick Children, Washington; hon. chmn. crusade Am. Cancer Soc., 1975; trustee Eisenhower Med. Center, also chmn. adv. com. Betty Ford Center; trustee Martha Graham Center Contemporary Dance. Named Woman of Yr., Ladies Home Jour. Episcopalian (Sunday sch. tchr. 1961-64). Author: (autobiography) The Times of My Life, 1979. *

FORD, EUGENIA MAUDE, educator; b. Fayette, Miss., Feb. 21, 1912; d. Marvin Whitfield and Bessie (Beam) Corban; B.A., La. State U., 1956; M.A., U. Ala., 1957; m. Warwick Swift Ford, June 2, 1949. Tchr., Miss. Sch. for Deaf, Jackson, 1933-36, Okla. Sch. for Deaf, Sulphur, 1936-39, La. Sch. for Deaf, Baton Rouge, 1939-44, 46-71, 72-74, Colo. Sch. for Deaf, Colorado Springs, 1945-46; data clk. Standard Oil Co., Baton Rouge, 1944-45, Miss. Health Dept., Jackson, 1946, 47; tutor deaf children, 1941-43; tchr. lip reading, speech, auditory training to deafened adults, tchr. vocational edn. State Dept. Edn., Baton Rouge, 1952-67; instr. spl. edn. dept. La. State U., Baton Rouge, 1972, 73, 74, U. So. Miss., Jackson, 1974, Jackson State U., 1975, summer 1977; supr. acad. instrn. Elem. Dept., La. Sch. Deaf, 1966-74; coordinator/supr. speech and hearing program Miss. Sch. Deaf, Jackson, 1975-82; cons., lectr. in field. Mem. Council on Edn. Deaf, Am. Instructors of the Deaf, A. G. Bell Assn. Educators of Deaf, Miss. Educators Assn., NEA, Nat. Ret. Tchrs. Assn., La. Ret. Tchrs. Assn., Am. Assn. Ret. Persons, Miss. Speech and Hearing Assn., La. Tchrs. Assn., PEO, Beta Sigma Phi. Methodist. Club: Quota. Home: 518 Alta Woods Blvd Jackson MS 39204 Office: 1253 Eastover Dr Jackson MS 39211

FORD, JUDITH, social worker; b. Washington, Sept. 11, 1937; d. Robert Henry Onstott and Wilma (James) Onstott Frederick; B.S., U. Md., 1959; M.S.W., Catholic U. Am., 1976; m. James Altmeyer Ford, Aug. 8, 1959 (div. 1973); children—Kathleen Marie, James Frederick, Kelly Lynn. Tchr., Montgomery County (Md.), 1959-61; asst. to adminstr. A.K. Rice Inst., Washington Sch. Psychiatry, 1971-73; social worker Met. Washington Renal Dialysis Center, 1976-81; co-dir. Bethesda (Md.) Counseling Assos., 1981—; staff psychotherapist Md. Found., 1978—; part-time pvt. practice psychotherapy, 1980—. Sec. Montgomery County Republican Central Com., 1970-74. Lic. cert. social worker, Md. Mem. Nat. Assn. Social Workers, Acad. Cert. Social Workers, Council Nephrology Social Workers, Am. Orthopsychiat. Assn., Montgomery County Mental Health Assn., Folklore Soc. Washington. Episcopalian. Author papers in field. Home and Office: 5501 Huntington Pkwy Bethesda MD 20014

FORD, KATHLEEN, artist, designer, writer; b. San Francisco, Mar. 3, 1932; d. Edward Francis and Mary Catherine (Donnelly) Dowd; student San Francisco Coll. for Women. 1950-53; B.A. in Design, Salinger Sch. Design, San Francisco, 1954. Head designer swimwear Gantner of Calif., San Francisco, 1954-55; asst. designer Jantzen, Inc., Seattle, 1955-56; owner, mgr. Kathleen Dowd Boutique, Sausalito, Calif., 1956-62; designer Constructions For Sound and Video, objects for manufacture, 1976—; author: The Three-Cornered House, 1968; The End (film); Last And 1/2 (film); author, designer Star Rings (film); authored kits for making miniature prodns.; dir. The Loyola Internat. Art Consortium. Mem. Contemporary Authors, Writers Guild of Am. Home: 425 Castenada Ave San Francisco CA 94116

FORD, LEE ELLEN, lawyer; b. Auburn, Ind., June 16, 1917; d. Arthur Whitten and Geneva Myrtle (Muhn) F.; B.S., Wittenberg U., Springfield, Ohio, 1947; M.S. in Cytogenetics, U. Minn., 1949; Ph.D. in Cytogenetics, Iowa State Coll., Ames, 1952; J.D., U. Notre Dame, 1972. Engaged in bus. and acctg., 1934-44; asso. prof. Gustavus Adolphus Coll., St. Peter, Minn., 1950-51; asso. prof. and prof. biology and cytogenetics various colls., 1952-69; admitted to Ind. bar, 1972; ind. practice, Auburn, 1972—; aide to gov. Ind., 1972-75; cons. in field. Mem. Presdl. Com. Drug Abuse, 1974-76. Mem. Am. Bar Assn., Ind. Bar Assn., DeKalb County Bar Assn., AAUW. Republican. Lutheran. Author papers in field. Address: 824 E 7th St Auburn IN 46706

FORD, LORETTA C., univ. dean; b. N.Y.C., Dec. 28, 1920; d. Joseph F. and Nellie A. (Williams) Pfingstel; R.N., Middlesex Gen. Hosp., New Brunswick, N.J., 1941; B.S. in Nursing, U. Colo., 1949, M.S., 1951, Ed.D., 1961; m. William J. Ford, May 2, 1947; 1 dau., Valerie. Staff nurse New Brunswick Vis. Nurse Service, 1941-42; supr., dir. Boulder County (Colo.) Health Dept., 1947-58; asst. prof., then prof. U. Colo. Sch. Nursing, 1960-72; dean Sch. Nursing, dir. nursing, prof. U. Rochester (N.Y.), 1972—; vis. prof. U. Fla., summer 1968, U. Wash., Seattle, 1974; mem. educators adv. panel GAO; dir. Security Trust Co., Rochester, Rochester Telephone Co. Bd. dirs. Threshold Alte. Youth Services, Easter Seal Soc. Served with Nurse Corps, U.S. Army, 1942-46. Named Colo. Nurse of Year. Fellow Am. Acad. Nursing; mem. Nat. League Nursing (fellowship, Linda Richards award), Am. Coll. Health Assn. (Boynton award), Am. Nurses Assn., Am. Public Health Assn., Inst. Medicine. Author articles in field, chpts. in books. Office: 601 Elmwood Ave Rochester NY 14618

FORD, LUCILLE GARBER, coll. dean; b. Ashland, Ohio, Dec. 31, 1921; d. Ora Myers and Edna Lucille (Armstrong) Garber; A.A., Stephens Coll., 1942; B.S. in Commerce, Northwestern U., 1944, M.B.A., 1945; Ph.D., Case Western Res. U., 1967; m. Laurence Welsey Ford, Sept. 1, 1946; children—Karen Elizabeth, JoAnn Christine. Asst. sec. corp., personnel dir. A.L. Garber Co., Ashland, 1947-67; chmn. econs. dept., prof. econs. Ashland Coll., 1970, dir. Gill Center for Bus. and Econs. Edn., 1974—, dean spl. program, 1977-79, dean, 1979-80, v.p., dean Sch. Bus., 1980—; dir. Ohio Edison, Nat. City Bank, Nat. City Corp., Shelby Mut. Ins. Co.; instr. Allegheny Coll., Meadville, Pa., U. Ala. Past chmn. ARC Mobile, pres. Tb Assn., 1950's; bd. curators Stephens Coll., 1976-80; candidate for lt. gov. State of Ohio, 1978; elder Presbyn. Ch., 1960—; mem. nat. Presbyn. Found. Bd., 1981—. Recipient Disting. Alumni award Stephens Coll., NSF grantee; Martha Holden Jennings Found grantee. Mem. Am. Arbitration Assn. (nat. labor panel), Am. Econs. Assn., Indsl. Relations Research Assn., Nat. Platform Assn., Am. Acad. Sci., Ohio Assn. Economists and Polit. Scientists, Social Econs. Assn., AAUW. Club: Altrusa (hon.). Author: University Economics for Education Majors, 1979; Economics: Learning and Instruction, 1981; lectr. in field. Office: Gill Center Ashland Coll Ashland OH 44805 *

FORD, MARTHA ELIZABETH, assn. exec.; b. Greensboro, N.C., July 22, 1953; d. Robert Charles and Elizabeth Sarah (Linson) F.; B.A. with distinction, U. Va., 1975; M.S. in Communications Design, Pratt Inst., 1977; postgrad. Nat. Law Center, George Washington U., 1979—. Art dir. Oberly & Newell, Inc., N.Y.C., 1975-77; pub. relations and program coordinator D.C. Spl. Olympics, Inc., Washington, 1977-79; membership and youth services coordinator D.C. Assn. for Retarded Citizens, Washington, 1979—. Active vol. D.C. Spl. Olympics Program. Mem. Nat. Conf. Execs. of Assns. for Retarded Citizens (editor The Exec. 1981—), Nat. Assn. for Retarded Citizens, D.C. Assn. for Retarded Citizens. Home: 916 East Capitol St NE Washington DC 20003

FORD, MARY ALICE, state legislator; b. Los Angeles, Apr. 23, 1935; d. John Hiram and Frances Alasan (Epinette) Hood; B.A., Stanford U., 1956; children—Sherilyn Dian, Thomas Taylor, John Hiram Hood. Tchr., Cherry Park Sch., Portland, Oreg., 1957-58, Central Sch., LaGrande, Oreg., 1958-59; attache Idaho State Senate, Boise, 1961, 65-66; mem. Oreg. Ho. of Reps., 1979—. Bd. dirs. Tualatin Valley Mental Health Center, 1980—; mem. Architecture and Transp. Barriers Compliance Bd., Washington, 1982—; bd. dirs., sec. Council on Aging, 1979—. Mem. Nat. Council State Legislators. Republican. Episcopalian.

FORD, MAUREEN MORRISSEY, civic worker; b. St. Joseph, Mo., July 1, 1936; d. Albert Joseph and Rosemary Kathryne (FitzSimons) Morrissey; student U. N.Mex., 1953-54, U. Bridgeport (Conn.), 1966-68, Fairfield (Conn.) U., 1976—; m. James Henry Lee Ford, Jr., Feb. 12, 1954; children—Kathryne Elizabeth, Maryellen, James Henry Lee III, William Charles, Maureen Lee. Charity and sch. vol., 1959—; fundraiser for community causes, mus., agys., 1964—; active presdl. campaign Barry Goldwater, 1963-64, congressional campaign Senator Lowell Weiker, 1968; pre-sch. tchr. Nature Center Environ. Activities, 1966-68, trustee, v.p. bd. dirs., 1968-75; v.p. Women's League, 1966-70; mem. exec. com. Republican Women's Club, Westport, 1967-68; leader, trainer Troops on Fgn. Soil br. Girl Scouts USA, Caracas, Venezuela, 1971-72; founding trustee, treas. Kara Mus., Norwalk, Conn.; mem. adv. council Fairfield County (Conn.) for spl. edn. Staples High Sch.; bd. dirs. CLASP; mem. exec. com. Group Home Search; cons., facilitator life planning workshops Merideth Assos., Westport; mem. 1st selectmen's com. on recycling, 1974-75; bd. dirs. PTA, 1976-79; mem. YWCA of Bridgeport Com. of 100 and Task Force; v.p. bd. dirs. YWCA, 1980-83; founding mem. Concerned Women Colleagues of Bridgeport; pres. Jr. League Greater Bridgeport, Inc., 1977-78; v.p., sec. J.H.L.F. Inc., Westport. Mem. Assn. Jr. League Am., Westport YMCA, Westport Tennis Assn. Roman Catholic. Home: 299 Sturges Hwy Westport CT 06880

FORD, PATRICIA, interior designer; b. Warsaw, N.Y., Feb. 17, 1947; d. Homer James and Ellen Louise (Dixon) F.; B.A. in Fine Arts, UCLA, 1969, M.A. in Fine Arts, 1971; m. Dale Andrew Thrush, Dec. 18, 1976. Designer, Herb Rosenthal & Assos., Los Angeles, 1973; sr. designer Charles Kratka Planning and Design, Los Angeles, 1973-75; partner The Ford Wilson Partnership, Los Angeles, 1975-78; pres. Ford Design Group Inc., Los Angeles, 1978-82; dir. interior design Bobrow Thomas & Assocs., architects, Los Angeles, 1982—. Mem citizens adv. council Los Angeles Olympics of 1984, 1980—; mem. Los Angeles Hdqrs. City Assn. 1980—. Mem. Assn. Women in Architeture (v.p.), Am. Soc. Interior Designers, AIA. Episcopalian. Contbr. articles to profl. jours. Office: 1001 Westwood Blvd Los Angeles CA 90024

FORD, RUTH VAN SICKLE, artist, educator; b. Aurora, Ill., Aug. 8, 1897; d. Charles P. and Anna (Miller) Van Sickle; student Chgo. Acad. Fine Arts, 1915-18, Art Students League, summers 1916-17; D.F.A. (hon.), Aurora Coll., 1974; m. Albert G. Ford, Feb. 7, 1917; 1 dau., Barbara Ford Turner. One-woman shows: Chgo. Art Inst., Grand Central Galleries, N.Y.C., 1947, Mexico City Country Club, Oklahoma City Art Center, 1948, Pomona Coll., Claremont, Calif., Hickory Mus. Art, N.C., 1948, Laguna Beach (Calif.) Art Assn., Centre D'Art, Port-au-Prince, Haiti, 1949, Palmer House Galleries, Chgo., 1949; exhibited in group shows: NAD, N.Y.C., Chgo. and Vicinity Artists Show at Chgo. Art Inst., Internat. Water Color Shows, Am. Artists Show at Art Inst., Pa. Acad. Ann. Water Color Show, Nat. Assn. Women Artists, 1949, Traveling Water Color Show, Oakland (Calif.) Art Gallery, 1949, Argent Gallery, N.Y.C., 1949, Miami Beach (Fla.) Art Center, Chgo. Painter and Sculptors Shows, Am. Water Color Soc., N.Y.C., Water Color, U.S.A.; pres., dir. Chgo. Acad. Fine Arts, 1937-60; instr. art Aurora Coll., 1964-72. Recipient numerous art awards. Mem. Conn. Acad., Grand Central Galleries, Chgo. Painters and Sculptors Assn., Salon Women Painters, Nat. Assn. Women Artists N.Y., Artists Guild Chgo. (hon.), Palette and Chisel Acad., Am. Artist Profl. League, Rockport (Mass.) Art Assn., Am. Watercolor Soc., Clinton Art Assn. (asso.), Palette and Chisel (hon.). Home and Studio: 69 Central Ave Aurora IL 60506

FORD, SALLY LEE, investment co. rep.; b. Seneca, Mo., Dec. 10, 1938; d. Roy Newton and Alene Chloe (Rakes) Lowrey. B.S. in Bus. Adminstrn., Rockhurst Coll., Kansas City, Mo., 1978, postgrad. in bus; m. Jack M. Ford, June 9, 1968. Hourly personnel adminstr. Ford Motor Co., Kansas City, Mo., 1965-68; employment rep. Chemagro div. Mobay Co., Kansas City, Mo., 1969-74; office mgr. Farmland Industries, Kansas City, Mo., 1975-79; personnel specialist KW-Dart Truck Co., div. Paccar Corp., Kansas City, Mo., 1979-80; personnel mgr. AOC Internat. Am., Inc., Kansas City, Mo., 1980-81; registered rep. Investors Diversified Services, Mission, Kans., 1982—. Mem. Kansas City Met. Regional Commn. on Status of Women. Mem. Dimensions Unltd., Central Exchange, Nat. Assn. Female Execs. Baptist. Home: 9905 NW 75th St Parkville MO 64152 Office: 5700 Broadmoor St Mission KS 66202

FORD, W. ANTOINETTE, govt. ofcl.; d. James F. and Rosemary E. Taylor; student in French, Laval U., Quebec, Que., Can., 1960; B.S. in Biology, Chestnut Hill Coll., 1963; M.S. in Biology, Am. U., 1966; postgrad. (NSF fellow) Stanford U., 1967; oceanography cert. Dept. Navy, 1968; postgrad. (Inst. Politics fellow) Harvard U., 1975; mgmt. cert. Fed. Exec. Inst., 1976; m. Melvin W. Ford, Nov. 12, 1966; 1 dau., Regan. Oceanographer, Bur. Comml. Fisheries, Washington, 1964-65, Smithsonian Oceanographic Center, Washington, 1965-66. Nat. Oceanog. Data Center, Washington, 1966-68; with Ogden Corp., 1968-71; spl. asst. to Dir. Office Minority Bus. Enterprise, Dept. Commerce, Washington, 1972-73, mktg. specialist Bur. Internat. Commerce, 1973-75; cons. govt. relations, regulatory analysis, personnel mgmt. and public affairs, Washington, 1975-77; mgr. mfg. Gen. Motors Corp., Detroit, 1978-81; asst. adminstr. Bur. for Nr. East, AID, Washington, 1981—; White House fellow, asst. to Sec. Treasury, Washington, 1971-72; mem. Presdl. Clemency Bd., 1975-76; dep. dir. Office Fed. Contract Compoiance Programs, Dept. Labor, Washington, 1976-77. U.S. del. Internat. Peace Acad., Helsinki, 1972; rep. to Soviet Union, Am. Council Young Polit. Leaders, 1974; mem. D.C. City Council, 1973-75. Recipient Outstanding Service award Smithsonian Instn., 1966, UN Assn., 1977, Nat. Hook-Up of Black Women, 1979; named Most Successful Under-30 Woman, New Woman, 1971. Office: AID 22d and C St Washington DC 20523

FORD-CARR, KATHRYNE ELIZABETH, energy resource cons.; b. Albuquerque, Jan. 31, 1955; d. James Henry Lee and Maureen (Morrissey) Ford, Jr.; B.A. in Latin Am. Studies, Allegheny Coll., 1979; m. David Wilkinson Carr, Jr., Aug. 29, 1981. Intern energy program Mercer County Consortium Inc., Meadville Pa., 1978; energy market analyst Mktg. Corp. Am., Westport, Conn., 1979; mem. tech. staff MITRE Corp., McLean, Va., 1980—; cons. to cos. mfg. energy techs.; speaker on energy planning, policy and techs. to local orgns.; energy market advisor to U.S. govt. for Internat. Conf., Nairobi, Kenya, 1981. Mem. Internat. Solar Energy Soc. (planning com. for 1980 ann. meeting and conf.). Roman Catholic. Author: (with Abu Talib) The Bio-Energy Handbook for Developing Countries, 1981. Home: Route 5 Barractside Charlottesville VA 22901 Office: 1820 Dolly Madison Blvd Suite W250 McLean Va 22102

FORDNEY, MARILYN TAKAHASHI, educator; b. Los Angeles, Dec. 22, 1936; d. James Toshio and Margaret O'Brien (Uchiyamada) Takahashi; student U. Calif., Santa Barbara, UCLA, U. So. Calif., Los Angeles City Coll., Pierce Coll.; cert. med. asst., 1975; m. Alan Fordney, Aug. 30, 1970. Med. sec., 1954-68; tchr. med. subjects, 1968—; med. instr. Ventura (Calif.) Coll., 1971—; pres. Channel Island Artisans, 1974-75. Named Outstanding Woman of Year, Bus. and Profl. Women's Club, Oxnard, Calif., 1977. Mem. Am. Assn. Med. Assts. (chpt. certification chmn. 1976-79), Calif. Assn. Med. Asst. Instrs. (v.p. 1976-78, membership chmn. 1974-76), Ventura County Med. Secs. and Assts. Assn. (publicity chmn. 1973). Roman Catholic. Author: Medical Transcribing: Techniques and Procedures, 1979; Insurance Handbook for the Medical Office, 1977, 2d edit., 1981; Administrative Medical Assisting, 1982. Address: 3821 Ocean Dr Oxnard CA 93030

FORDYCE, VERA CRISTINE, nurse; b. St. Joseph, Mo., Apr. 2, 1925; d. Christopher Lewis and Rachel Mae (Orr) Vanderau; R.N., St. Joseph (Mo.) Hosp., 1946; m. Darryl Carlyle Fordyce, May 24, 1949; children—Regina Adell, Morris Carlyle, Gordon Duane, Harold Dean. Mem. nursing staff hosps. in Mo., 1945—; mem. nursing staff Crestview Home, Inc., Bethany, Mo., 1968-69, 70—, dir. nursing, 1970—; tchr., cons. in field; mem. adv. bd. Harrison County Health Dept., Vocat.-Tech. Sch., Bethany. Mem. Community Ch. Home: Rural Route 3 Bethany MO 64424 Office: PO Box 430 Bethany MO 64424

FOREHAND, JENNIE MEADOR, state legislator; b. Nashville, Dec. 17, 1935; d. James T. and Estelle (Woodall) Meador; student Woman's Coll. of U. N.C., Greensboro, 1954-56; B.S. in Indsl. Relations, U. N.C., Chapel Hill, 1958; m. William E. Forehand, Jr., July 19, 1958; children—Mary Virginia, John Bentley. Reporter, Charlotte (N.C.) News, 1954-56; probation counselor Juvenile Ct., Charlotte, 1958; tchr. Anne Arundel County (Md.), 1958-60; statis. analyst NIH, Bethesda, Md., 1961-62; edn. research project evaluator Montgomery County (Md.) Bd. Edn., 1973-74; interior designer, owner Antiques and Interiors, Rockville, Md., 1971—; mem. Md. Ho. of Dels., 1978—; mem. appropriations com., joint capital budget com., health and environ. subcom.; adv. bd. First Women's Bank of Md. Planning bd. Montgomery County Health Systems Agy. chmn. edn. and community involvement; past chmn. Rockville Civic Improvement Adv. Commn.; consumer rep. Rockville Econ. Devel. Council; mem. Montgomery County Bd. of Edn. Med. Adv. Com.; mem. Md. Community Mental Health Adv. Bd.; pres. local civic assn.; bd. dirs. Mid-Md. Lung Assn.; bd. dirs. local sch. Parent Tchr. Student Assn.; mem. Peerless Rockville Hist. Preservation, Ltd., Questers. Mem. Women's Caucus of Md. Gen. Assembly, AAUW, Nat. Order Women Legislators, Md. Assn. Elected Women, Women's Polit. Caucus. Democrat. Methodist. Office: 224B House Office Bldg State House Annapolis MD 21401

FOREMAN, CAROL LEE TUCKER, bus. exec.; b. Little Rock, May 3, 1938; d. James Guy and Willie Maude (White) Tucker; A.A., William Woods Coll., Fulton, Mo., 1958; A.B., Washington U., St. Louis, 1960; postgrad. Am. U.; LL.D. (hon.), William Woods Coll., Fulton, Mo., 1976; m. Jay Howell Foreman, June 13, 1964; children—Guy Tucker, Rachel Marian. Research asst. Com. on Govt. Ops., U.S. Senate, 1961; asso. Fed. Counsel Assos., 1961-63; instr. Am. govt. William Woods Coll., Fulton, 1963-64; press officer So. Calif. Com. to Elect Johnson and Humphrey, 1964; exec. asst. to Rep. James Roosevelt, 1964; writer-researcher Nat. Ednl. TV, 1965; dir. research and publs. Democratic Nat. Com., 1965-66; Congressional liaison aide HUD, 1967-69; chief info. liaison Center for Family Planning Program Devel., Planned Parenthood-World Population, 1969-71; dir. policy coordination Commn. on Population and Am. Future, 1971-72; exec. dir. Citizens Com. on Population and Am. Future, 1972-73, Paul Douglas Consumer Research Center, 1973-77, Consumer Fedn. Am., 1973-77; asst. sec. food and consumer services Dept. Agr., Washington, 1977-81; cons. Pioneer Systems, Inc., N.Y.C., 1981—; exec. com. Regulatory Council, 1979-81; mem. Interagy. Regulatory Liaison Group, Interdeptl. Task Force on Women; mem. gen. adminstrn. bd. Grad. Sch., Dept. Agr., 1977-81; mem. adv. com. on nat. growth policy Commn. on Supplies and Shortages; mem. D.C. Commn. on Status Women, 1973-74; adviser food policy Consumer Fedn. Am.; co-chmn. Network Better Nutrition; dir. Commodity Credit Corp., 1977-81, Nat. Consumer Coop. Bank, 1979-81; vice-chair Center Nat. Policy, Center Population Options; mem. Task Force Econs. and Indsl. Policy, Dem. Nat. Com., co-chair Women's Council. Recipient Disting. Alumni award Washington U., 1979. Mem. Women's Equity Action League (past pres. local chpt.), Woman's Nat. Dem. Club, Pi Beta Phi. Home: 5408 Trent St Chevy Chase MD 20015 Office: Room 700 11 Dupont Circle NW Washington DC 20036

FOREMAN, LISA LOUISE COOK, florist; b. Tucson, Ariz., July 7, 1952; d. Harlin Maurice and Patricia Lou (Cochran) Cook; student Phoenix Coll., 1971-73; m. Marvin Eugene Foreman, Jr., Nov. 15, 1975; 1 son, Christopher Mark. Jr. account exec. COMCO Public Relations, Phoenix, 1969-75; owner Maryvale Floral, Phoenix, 1976-78; v.p. SAGE IV Enterprises, Inc., Phoenix, 1978—. Mem. Nat. Thespian Soc., Nat. Fedn. Press Women, Florist Transworld Delivery Assn., Internat. Entrepreneurs Assn., Nat. Assn. Female Execs., Inc., Ariz. Press Women, Phi Theta Kappa. Editor, Montage, 1971-72, The Owl, 1972-73. Home and Office: PO Box 461 Munds Park AZ 86017

FORER, MARGERY PATRICIA, greeting card co. exec.; b. N.Y.C., Mar. 17, 1922; d. David and Hattie Bregman; B.S., Skidmore Coll., Saratoga Springs, N.Y., 1943; m. David Forer, Dec. 17, 1948; children—David Brett, Katherine Ellen. Asst. testing dept. Manhattan Project, Columbia U., 1943-44; fashion reporter Women's Wear Daily, 1944-47; 1st fashion editor Footwear News, 1947-49; co-founder, 1949, since sec.-treas. D. Forer & Co., Inc., N.Y.C., also stylist-designer Brett-Forer Co. div.; mem. adv. bd. greeting card com. UNICEF. Speaker, cons. in field. Mem. Nat. Assn. Greeting Card Pubs. (pres. 1982), Fedn. Nat. Assn. (dir.). Office: 105 E 73d St New York NY 10021

FOREST, SUZANNE ELISABETH, psychologist, lawyer; b. Magog, Que., Can., Aug. 5, 1948; d. Yves Lionel and Elizabeth Margaret (St. Martin) F.; B.A., U. Sherbrooke, 1968, B.Ps., 1970; M.Ps., U. Montreal, 1972, D.Ps., 1977; B.C.L., McGill U., Montreal, 1981. Counseling psychologist U. Montreal, 1973-74; child and family therapist Marie-Enfant Hosp., Montreal, 1974-75; expert psychologist family div. Superior Ct. Montreal, 1976-81; ind. practice psychotherapy, part-time 1976-81; articling atty. firm Robinson, Cutler, Sheppard & Assos., Montreal, 1981-82. Mem. Am. Psychol. Assn., Can. Bar Assn., Am. Psychology-Law Soc. Address: 3475 Mountain St Apt 910 Montreal PQ H3G 2A4 Canada

FORESTER, JEAN MARTHA BROUILLETTE (MRS. JAMES LAWRENCE FORESTER), librarian; b. Port Barre, La., Sept. 7, 1934; d. Joseph Walter and Thelma (Brown) Brouillette; B.S., La. State U., 1955; M.A. (Carnegie fellow), George Peabody Coll. Tchrs., 1956; m. James Lawrence Forester, June 2, 1957; children—Jean Martha, James Lawrence. Librarian, Howell Elem. Sch., Springhill, La., 1956-58; asst. post librarian Fort Chaffee, Ark., 1958; command librarian Orleans Area Command, U.S. Army, Orleans, France, 1958-59; acquisitions librarian Northwestern State U., Natchitoches, La., 1960; serials librarian La. State U., New Orleans, 1960-66; mem. faculty La. State U., Eunice, 1966—, asst. librarian, asst. prof., 1972—. Active Eunice Assn. Retarded Children. Mem. La. Library Assn. (sect. sec. 1971-72), UDC, Delta Kappa Gamma (chpt. parliamentarian 1972-74), Alpha Beta Alpha, Phi Gamma Mu, Phi Mu. Democrat. Baptist. Club: Order Eastern Star. Contbr. articles to profl. jours. Home: 1351 Gregg Ave Eunice LA 70535

FORKAN, PATRICIA ANN, assn. exec.; b. N.Y.C., June 13, 1944; d. Robert James and Elaine May (Van Horn) F.; B.A. in Polit. Sci., Pa. State U., 1966; postgrad. Am. U., 1968-69; m. Robert Eugene Eisenbud, Apr. 16, 1977. Manpower analyst Dept. Labor, Washington, 1967-69; nat. coordinator Fund for Animals, N.Y.C., 1970-76; v.p. program and communications Humane Soc. of U.S., Washington, 1976—; mem. U.S. del. Internat. Whaling Commn., 1978, Re-negotiation of Conv. for Regulation of Whaling, 1978; mem. U.S. Public Adv. Com. to Law of the Sea; vice chmn. bd. Citizens for Ocean Law; host, producer weekly radio call-in show. Contbr. articles to environ. and animal welfare publs. Office: Humane Soc of US 2100 L St Washington DC 20037

FORKER, BARBARA ALLEN, educator; b. Kendalville, Ind., Aug. 28, 1920; d. Bessie O. F.; B.S., Eastern Mich. U., 1942; M.S., Iowa State U., 1950; Ph.D., U. Mich., 1957. Instr. phys. edn., Wyandotte, Mich., 1942-45; served with ARC, ETO, 1945-47; instr. phys. edn. Iowa State U., Ames, 1948-58, prof., head dept. phys. edn. for women, 1958-74, prof., head dept. phys. edn., 1974-78, disting. prof., head dept. phys. edn. and leisure studies, 1978—; mem. President's Commn. on Olympic Sports, 1975-77; mem. U.S. Olympic Com. and exec. bd., 1979—. Named Prof. of Yr., Iowa State U., 1963; recipient honor award Central Dist. Assn. Health, Phys. edn. and Recreation, 1964, faculty citation Iowa State U. Alumni, 1966, Women Helping Women award Ames Soroptimist Club, 1976. Fellow Am. Acad. Phys. Edn.; mem. Iowa Assn. Health, Phys. Edn., Recreation and Dance (honor award 1961), AAHPER (nat. honor award 1971), Central Assn. Phys. Edn. in Higher Edn., Nat. Assn. Phys. Edn. in Higher Edn., Am. Coll. Sports Medicine, AAUP, Internat. Assn. Phys. Edn. and Sport for Girls and Women, Internat. Council Health, Phys. Edn. and Recreation. Home: 1108 Wisconsin Ave Ames IA 50010 Office: Iowa State University Ames IA 50011

FORMAN, JEANNE LEACH, piano tchr.; b. Los Angeles, Mar. 3, 1916; d. Rowland E. and Charlotte F. (Van Wickle) Leach; student U. Redlands, 1934-36, UCLA, 1937; m. Edward S. Forman, July 28, 1945; children—Bonnie Jeanne (Mrs. James Field Ottinger), Karen Lynn (Mrs. Patrick Maginnis), Wendy K. Forman (Mrs. Michael Bolduc). Pvt. tchr. piano, Pasadena, Calif., 1945-52, Tucson, 1952-58, Sunnyvale, Calif., 1958-75, Santa Barbara, Calif., 1976—; owner, dir. Jeanne Forman Studios, Sunnyvale; owner/dir. Jeanne Forman Enterprises (Music to Write By), 1982—; owner J. Forman Advt. Agy.; propr. Jeanne Forman Advt. and Enterprises; writer Los Angeles Times, 1978-80; columnist The Galeria Santa Barbara News Press, 1978—; publicity writer Music Tchrs. Assn.; tchr. of blind Santa Clara County Assistance League; lectr. on blind techniques; freelance writer; gen. edn. staff Brooks Inst. Photography Santa Barbara. Active Santa Clara Assistance League. Mem. Calif. Assn. Profl. Music Tchrs., Music Tchrs. Nat. Assn., Compositions performed by U. Calif., Santa Barbara, 1971. Home: 1119 Alameda Padre Serra Santa Barbara CA 93105

FORMAN, MONA VAE (CUNNINGHAM), bank mktg. exec.; b. Keokuk, Iowa, May 16, 1947; d. Richard L. and Ollie Elizabeth (McHone) Cunningham; cert. Am. Inst. Banking, 1976, Am. Bankers Assn., 1978; student Western Ill. U., 1979—; m. Charles V. Forman, Oct. 2, 1976; 1 dau., Von Maree. Bookkeeper, Union Nat. Bank, Macomb Ill., 1973-75, teller, 1975, mktg. asso., 1975—, mktg. supr., 1977-80, advt. dir., 1980—. Mem. McDonough County (Ill.) Arts Council, 1980; bd. dirs. McDonough County United Way, 1980. Mem. Am. Inst. Banking (dir. chpt.), Bank Adminstrn. Inst. (dir. chpt.), Nat. Assn. Bank Women, Macomb Retail Assn., Union Nat. Bank Employees Club (pres. 1980). Republican. Mem. Christian Ch. (Disciples of Christ). Clubs: Bus. and Profl. Women's (club pres. 1979-79, club corr. sec. 1979-80), Industry Booster. Home: PO Box 271 Industry IL 61440 Office: PO Box 417 N Randolph Macomb IL 61455

FORONDA, ELENA ISABEL, educator; b. N.Y.C., Jan. 15, 1947; d. Severino Deliso and LaVerne (Ibanez) F.; B.S. in Music, Hunter Coll., City U. N.Y., 1969, M.A. in Music Edn., 1971. Tchr. vocal music N.Y.C. Public Sch. System, 1970—; asst. dir. tchr. placement Hunter Coll., City U. N.Y., summers 1971-72. Sponsor children in Philippines and El Salvador, World Vision Internat.; del. Asian Am. Women's Caucus, 1977. Dist. winner Nat. Piano Playing Auditions, 1965; recipient N.Y. State permanent cert. Dept. Edn., 1971. Mem. Music Educators Nat. Conf., N.Y. State Sch. Music Assn., Amateur Chamber Players (Vienna, Va.), Internat. Platform Assn. Democrat. Episcopalian. Mem. choirs Hunter Coll., 1968-69, 71.

FORREST, KAY FRANCES, curriculum cons.; b. Balt.; d. Wilbur Coleman and Edna Earle (Johnson) F.; B.A., Goucher Coll., 1956; M.A., Northwestern U., 1978. Former tchr. public schs., Balt., Houston, Jackson, Miss.; lang. arts coordinator Glencoe (Ill.) Public Schs.; freelance writer, editor Follet Publ. Co., McDougal Littell Pub. Co., A.B. Dick, Bell & Howell, Internat. Minerals Co., Trans-World Exhibits. Mem. ednl. com. Ill. Commn. on Status of Women, 1979. Mem. Nat. Council Tchrs. English, Nat. Council Social Studies, Am. Assn. Supervision and Curriculum Devel. Democrat. Home: 1700 F Northfield Sq Northfield IL 60093 Office: 620 Greenwood Ave Glencoe IL 60022

FORREST, VIRGINIA OGDEN RANSON (MRS. WILBUR STUDLEY FORREST), civic leader; b. Balt., June 24, 1896; d. Henry Warfield and Nannie Deaver (Cooper) Ranson; ed. Calvert Sch., Arundell Sch.; m. Frederick Beasley Williamson, Jr., July 5, 1917 (dec. July 1957); children—Virginia Williamson Hutton, Beverley Williamson Magill, Frederick Beasley III; m. 2d, Wilbur Studley Forrest, Apr. 20, 1960. Dir., Goodall Rubber Co., hon. dir., 1973—. Pres. Jr. League, Elizabeth, N.J., 1924-26, hon. mem., 1944; mem. hostess com. Franklin Inst., Phila., 1941; mem. N.J. Recreation Soc., Elizabeth, 1934-35, rep. N.J. to nat. conv., Chgo., 1935; chmn. New Hope (Pa.) chpt. ARC, 1939-43, head flood disaster chpt., 1955, chmn. home service, 1943-45; hon. v.p. New Hope Art Assos., 1940; mem. adv. com. Jonathan Dickinson State Park, Martin County, Fla., 1970—; organizer adviser Bucks County Conservation Alliance; mem. New Hope Centennial Com., 1976; bd. dirs. Martin County Conservation Alliance, 1966-74, Honey Hollow Watershed Assn., 1969—, Soc. Prevention Cruelty to Children Family Welfare Bd., Elizabeth, 1928, YWCA, Elizabeth, 1928, Abington (Pa.) Meml. Hosp. Women's Bd., 1941, Vis. Nurse Assn., New Hope, 1941-49; bd. dirs., 2d v.p. Garden Club, Stuart, Fla., 1951-60; trustee Egnolf Day Nursery, Elizabeth, 1923-36, Holmquist Sch. for Girls, New Hope, Martin County Public Library, Stuart, 1958-61; bd. dirs. Free Public Library Elizabeth, 1926-39, sec., 1927-36; bd. dirs. Keep Fla. Beautiful Com.; mem. founder's bd. Transylvania U., Lexington, Ky., 1979—. Recipient award Fla. Fedn. Garden Clubs, 1961; Gov.'s gold medal conservation award (1st woman recipient), 1961; Gov. Kirk's Conservation award, 1970; Conservation Heritage award U.S. Dept. Interior, 1979; Virginia Forrest Day observed by Martin County (Fla.) Audubon Soc., 1976; Virginia Forrest Beach dedicated, Hutchinson Island, Fla., 1976; Allan D. Cruickshank award Fla. Audubon Soc., 1981; Community Service award Commonwealth of Pa.; Delaware Canal Sesquicentennial award Pa. Dept. Environ. Resources, 1982. Mem. Fla. (recipient award 1960, chmn. Bald Eagle project 1959—, mem. wildlife com. 1959—, v.p. 1962-69, hon. v.p. 1970—), Martin County (dir. 1957—, chmn. exec. com. 1973-74), Bucks County (dir., adviser, citation for conservation 1972) Audubon socs., New Hope Hist. Soc. (dir. 1959-60, 67—, v.p. 1977-80), Fla. Fedn. Garden Clubs (hon. life), Colonial Dames N.J., Woman Fly Fishers Am. Clubs: Mt. Vernon (Balt.); Hartwood (Monticello, N.Y.); Martin County Anglers (dir. 1966—). Home: Pennswood Village D105 Newtown PA 18970

FORRESTER, MAUREEN KATHERINE STEWART, contralto; b. Montreal, Que., Can., July 25, 1930; d. Thomas and Mae (Arnold) F.; student of Sally Martin, Frank Rowe, Bernard Diamant; D.Mus. (hon.), St. George William U., St. Mary's U., Toronto U., McMaster U., Victoria U., Bishop's U., York U., Western U., Mt. Allison U., Wilfred Pelletier U.; m. Eugene J. Kash, July 1954; children—Paula, Gina, Daniel, Linda, Susanna. Debut in Can., 1953, at Town Hall, N.Y.C., 1956; concert appearances maj. orchs. and festivals throughout world, with various cos. N. Am.; rec. artist for RCA Victor, Decca, Westminster, Philips, Columbia, DGG, Vanguard. Decorated companion Order of Can.; recipient Molson prize. Address: care Shaw Concerts Inc 1995 Broadway New York NY 10023 *

FORRESTER, NANCY GALE, psychologist; b. Parma, Mo., Dec. 7, 1936; d. Floyd Benton and Grace Elizabeth (Meek) Gale; B.A., Ariz. State U., 1958, M.S., 1973, Ph.D., 1980. Psychologist, Interfaith Counseling Service, Phoenix, 1974—; vis. staff, instr. Phoenix Coll. Mem. Am. Psychol. Assn., Am. Assn. Marriage and Family Therapists. Democrat. Office: 555 W Glendale Ave Phoenix AZ 85021

FORSETH, LUISE K., legislative asst.; b. Menomonee, Mich., June 16, 1947; d. Bernard and Marion (Dahlstrom) Forseth; student U. Wis., Milw., 1965-67; B.A., U. Wis., Eau Claire, 1970; M.A., U. Minn., 1972. Trainer, cons. human relations, Mpls., 1972-75; research specialist, Mpls., 1975-77; exec. dir. Chrysalis Center for Women, Mpls., 1977-79; legis. asst. to U.S. Sen. Durenberger from Minn., 1979—. Office: Room 353 Russell Senate Office Bldg Washington DC 20510

FORST, ELLEN GAIL, speech pathologist; b. Boston, July 21, 1948; d. Julius and Norma (Rivkind) F.; B.S., Boston U., 1970; M.A., U. So. Calif., 1972. Speech, hearing and lang. pathologist Met. Centers Speech and Hearing Therapy, West Newton, Mass., 1972-76; speech and lang. pathologist Needham (Mass.) public schs., 1976—; in-service instr., cons. in field. Mem. nat. alumni council Boston U., 1977; mem. young profl. div. and upgrade coms., mem. young profls. exec. bd. Combined Jewish Philanthropies. Mem. Am. Speech, Hearing and Lang. Assn., Mass. Speech, Hearing and Lang. Assn., Boston U. Sch. Edn. Alumni Assn. (pres. 1978-80), Pi Lambda Theta. Club: Boston U. Woman's Grad. (dir. 1980—, v.p. 1981). Office: 1330 Highland Ave Needham MA 02192

FORSTER, HARRIET HERTA, educator; b. Vienna, Austria; came to U.S. 1940, naturalized 1945; d. Karl and Olga (Frankfurter) F.; student U. Vienna; M.A., U. Calif., 1947, Ph.D. 1948; m. G.F.J. Gerlick, Jan. 6, 1977. Instr. physics U. So. Calif. 1948-51, asst. prof. 1951-56, assoc. prof. 1956-64, prof. 1964—, chmn. dept. physics 1962-64, dep. chief investigator Nuclear Physics Lab., 1965-70, prin. investigator, 1970-72, chmn. nuclear consortium, 1971-72. AAUW fellow 1956-57; recipient Women of Achievement award Bus. and Profl. Women, 1981. Fellow Am. Phys. Soc. Contbr. articles to profl. jours. Office: SH5371 U So Calif Los Angeles CA 90089

FORSYTH, JANE L(OUISE), geologist; b. Hanover, N.H., Nov. 9, 1921; d. Chester Hume and Louise Ann (James) F.; A.B., Smith Coll., 1943; M.A., U. Cin., 1946; Ph.D., Ohio State U., 1956. Pleistocene geologist Ohio Geol. Survey, 1955-65; mem. faculty Bowling Green (Ohio) State U., 1965—, prof. geology, 1974—; mem. Ohio Natural Areas Council, 1975—. Recipient Ohioana Library citation award, 1976. Fellow Geol. Soc. Am., Ohio Acad. Sci. (past v.p. geology, editor-in-chief Ohio Jour. Sci.); mem. Ecol. Soc. Am., Nat. Assn. Geology Tchrs. (councilor 1981—), Am. Assn. Quarternary Environ., Mortar Bd. Author: Physical Features for the Toledo Regional Area, 1968; Elementary Geology Laboratory Manual, 1969; Geology of the Lake Erie Islands and Adjacent Shores, 1971; contbr. numerous articles to profl. jours. Address: Geology Dept Bowling Green State U Bowling Green OH 43403

FORSYTHE, MARY MACCORNACK, state legislator; b. Whitehall, Wis., May 23, 1920; d. Robert Lee and Gladys Fry MacCornack; B.Mus., St. Olaf Coll., 1942; m. Robert A. Forsythe, July 18, 1942; children—Robert A., Polly Forsythe Johnson, Jean Forsythe Peterson, Ann Forsythe Smith, Joan. Tchr., Viroqua, Wis., 1942-43, Whitehall, Wis., 1944-46; mem. Minn. Ho. of Reps., St. Paul, 1972—. Mem. Guthrie Theater Found., 1973-80; mem. Minn. Commn. on Econ. Status of Women, 1976-79, Minn. News Council, 1979—; bd. dirs. Fairview Hosp., 1980—. Recipient Disting. Alumna award St. Olaf Coll., 1974; Dr. I. Michael Kuhn award Nat. Hemophilia Found., 1978; Outstanding Woman of Edina Bicentennial award, 1978; Community Service award Edina Optimists, 1982. Mem. Nat. Conf. State Legislators (vice chmn. human resources com. 1977-78). Republican. Lutheran. Home: 5308 Brookview Ave Edina MN 55424 Office: Room 368 State Office Bldg Saint Paul MN 55155

FORT, MARY ELIZABETH, insurance agt.; b. San Francisco, June 28, 1919; d. Homer Garfield and Florence Merle (Simmons) Rosebaum; A.A., William Woods Coll., 1938; student U. Mo., 1938-39; M.S.F.S., American Coll., 1980; m. Victor E. Brandrup, Feb. 14, 1980; children—John Richard Fort, Sandra Irene Fort Clapp. Insurance agt. various cos., 1942-62; with American Nat. Ins. Co., Chevy Chase, Md., 1962—, named to Pres.'s club, 16 yrs. Leader Camp Fire Cub Scouts Am., 1953-56; active Boy Scouts Am., 1956-58; mem. spl. gifts com. local Am. Cancer Soc., 1958-62. Recipient Bernard L. Wilner award D.C. Life Underwriters Assn., 1975. C.L.U. Mem. Nat. Assn. Life Underwriters (trustee), Md. Life Underwriters Assn., Suburban Md. Life Underwriters Assn. (Harry L. Meyer award 1972), Suburban Md. Estate Planning Council, Am. Soc. C.L.U.s, Golden Key Soc., Bus. and Profl. Women, Nat. Congress Career Women. Republican. Club: Maryland Lupac Century. Contbr. articles to various publs. Home: 2100 Washington Ave Silver Spring MD 20910 Office: 35 Wisconsin Circle Chevy Chase MD 20815

FORTALEZA, JUDITH ANN, ednl. adminstr.; b. Dayton, Ohio, Sept. 10, 1936; d. Jesse Beldon and Vivian (Bussertt) Moore; B.S., Wright State U., 1971, M.S., 1976; postgrad. U. Dayton, 1978; Ed.D., U. Sarasota; children—Allen Dale Little, Jeffrey Kent Little, Stewart Elliott Little. Tchr. educable mentally retarded and learning disabilities/behavior disorders Sugarcreek Elem. Sch., Bellbrook, Ohio, 1969-73; tchr. educable mentally retarded Greene Joint Vocat. Sch., Xenia, Ohio, 1973-74, London (Ohio) High Sch., 1974-75; cons. Central Ohio Spl. Edn. Regional Resource Center, Columbus, 1975-79, now coordinator; coordinator instrnl. resource project Hopewell Spl. Edn. Regional Resource Center, Hillsboro, Ohio, from 1979. Cert. spl. edn. tchr., elem. tchr., supr., elem. and secondary prin., Ohio. Mem. Council Exceptional Children (pres. chpt. 933 1977-79), Ohio Fedn. Council Exceptional Children (program chairperson 1979), Assn. Children With Learning Disabilities, Council Adminstrs. Spl. Edn., Ohio Assn. Regional Resource Center Spl. Edn., Wright State Alumni Assn., Nat. Assn. Female Execs., Kappa Delta Phi. Club: Altrusa. Research on job placement for educable mentally retarded. Home: 4636 Northtowne Blvd Columbus OH Office: 133 Willow St Hillsboro OH 45311

FORTI, CORINNE ANN, chem. co. communications ofcl.; b. N.Y.C., July 26, 1941; d. Wilbur Walter and Sylvia Joan (Charap) Bastian; B.A., Hunter Coll., 1963; m. Joseph Donald Forti, Aug. 18, 1962 (dec.); 1 dau., Raina. Adminstrv. asst. Ednl. Broadcasting Corp., 1963-65; adminstrv. asst. W.R. Grace & Co., N.Y.C., 1965-67, public relations rep., 1967-70, mgr. info. services, 1970-79, div. info. services, 1980—; lectr. photography and graphics Am. Mgmt. Assn. Named to Acad. Women Achievers, YWCA, 1979; recipient citation award in communications Nat. Council of Women, 1979. Mem. Am. Women in Radio and TV, Women Execs. in Public Relations, Chem. Mfrs. Assn., Soc. Consumer Affairs Profls. Republican. Roman Catholic. Home: 10 E 85th St New York NY 10028 Office: 1114 Ave of Americas New York NY 10036

FORTIN, DENISE HELEN, hosp. adminstrv. ofcl.; b. Attleboro, Mass., Feb. 9, 1953; d. Frederick Louis, Jr. and Lucille Marie (Hetu) F.; A.S. in Cytotech., Quinnipiac Coll., Hamden, Conn., 1974; student Our Lady of Fatima Sch. Cytotech., North Providence, 1973-74; B.S. in Health Services Adminstrn., Providence Coll., 1978, cert. in labor relations, 1981; M.B.A. candidate Bryant Coll., Smithfield, R.I., 1979—. Cytotechnologist, Morton Hosp., Taunton, Mass., 1974-79, employee relations specialist, 1979-81; personnel supr. Meml. Hosp., Pawtucket, R.I., 1981-82, asst. dir. personnel, 1982—. Chmn., R.I. div. Am. Cancer Soc. meeting, 1976, 78, co-chmn., 1977; vol. United Fund, Heart Fund, Cath. Charity Appeal Campaign. Mem. Am. Soc. Clin. Pathologists (registered), Assn. M.B.A. Execs., Soc. Advancement Mgmt. (asso.), Mass. Hosp. Personnel Dirs. Assn., Am. Soc. Tng. and Devel., Quinnipiac Coll. Alumni Assn., Providence Coll. Alumni Assn. Home: PO Box 703 108 Holmes Rd North Attleboro MA 02760 Office: Memorial Hosp Prospect St Pawtucket RI 02860

FORTIN, DIANE DEBORAH, tng. exec.; b. Providence, R.I., Oct. 31, 1952; d. Robert G. and Virginia M. (Bessette) F.; B.A., U. R.I., 1974; M.A., U. Mass, 1977. Speech-lang. pathologist Community Options, Inc., Belchertown, Mass., 1977, Hampshire Ednl. Collaborative, Hadley, Mass., 1978, Fort River Elem. Sch., Amherst, Mass., 1978-79, The Therapeutic Center, Brookline, Mass., 1979-81; course mgr. Internat. Tng. and Edn. Co., Framingham, Mass., 1982—; radio news announcer U. R.I., 1973-74; instructional aide Northwestern Elem. Sch., Storrs, Conn., 1973-75. Cert. tchr. speech and hearing handicapped, Mass. Democrat. Roman Catholic. Office: Speen St Framingham MA 01701

FORTIN, GERTRUDE LOUISE, educator; b. South Bend, Ind., June 28, 1915; d. Frank and Henrietta F.; B.A., St. Mary's Coll., 1936; cert. in library sci. Ind. U., 1938; M.A., Northwestern U., 1955; cert. in guidance and adminstrn. U. Notre Dame, 1958. Tchr., English and speech Washington High Sch., South Bend, Ind., 1939-56; English tchr. Riley High Sch., South Bend, 1956-58; part-time asso. instr. speech edn. dept. Ind. U., South Bend, 1958-64, asso. staff supr., counselor student tchrs., 1979—; guidance counselor Thomas Edison Elem. Sch., South Bend, 1958-72, prin., 1972-79. Mem. exec. bd. South Bend chpt. Nat. Found. March of Dimes; mem. ladies div. South Bend Symphony. Mem. Nat. Assn. Elem. Sch. Prins., Ind. Assn. Elem. Sch. Prins., Nat. Ret. Tchrs. Assn., Ind. Ret. Tchrs. Assn., Phi Delta Kappa, Delta Kappa Gamma, Psi Iota Xi. Republican. Methodist. Developer ungraded primary program Edison Sch., South Bend, 1974. Home: 2828 Erskine Blvd South Bend IN 46614

FORTNEY, ANNE PRICE, lawyer; b. Miami Beach, Fla., June 9, 1944; d. Camden Page and Margery (Shaut) F.; B.A., Mary Washington Coll., 1966; J.D., Georgetown U., 1969. Admitted to D.C. bar, 1969; asso. Cleary, Gottlieb, Steen & Hamilton, Washington, 1969-71; atty. FTC, Washington, 1971-76, adv. to commr., 1972-73; atty. Bur. Consumer Protection, 1972-76; atty. Washington Legal Office, J.C. Penney Co., Inc., 1976-82; asso. dir. credit practices Bur. Consumer Protection, FTC, Washington, 1982—. Bd. visitors Mary Washington Coll., 1982—, alumni bd. dirs., 1980-82, mem. regional scholarship com., 1974-78, chmn., 1974-76, 1st v.p. alumni bd. dirs., 1972-74. Mem. Am. Bar Assn., D.C. Bar Assn., Women's Bar Assn. D.C. Home: 1401 44th St NW Washington DC 20007 Office: Bur Consumer Protection FTC Washington DC 20580

FORTUNATO, BARBARA SHOPLACK, data processing co. exec.; b. Edwardsville, Pa., Feb. 20, 1939; d. Metro and Eleanor Mary (Durachansky) Shoplack; student Kean Coll., 1976—; div.; children—Michael, Eileen. Legal sec. Leonard & Leonard, Linden, N.J., 1955-57; tech. staff sec. Exxon Research & Engring. Co., Florham Park, N.J., 1957-60; asst. plant mgr. Magnus Organ Corp., Linden, N.J., 1962-67; adminstrv. asst. to bd. dirs. Automated Data Assos., Rahway, N.J., 1967—, controller, 1976—; fin. cons. Diane Nolan Design Studios, Inc., Middletown, N.J., Massa Computer Service, Red Bank, N.J.; corp. liaison officer young women's bus. entry program Middlesex (N.J.) High Sch. System. Mem. Nat. Trust for Hist. Preservation, Baker Street Irregulars (N.J. div.), Sherlock Holmes Soc. (London). Roman Catholic. Home: 269 Morton Ave Rahway NJ 07065 Office: Automated Data Assos 1333 Lawrence St Rahway NJ 07065

FORTUNE, MARY K., mgmt. cons. co. exec.; b. Mechanicville, N.Y.; B.S. in Psychology, Union Coll., Schenectady. Mgr. personnel and adminstrn., corp. research and devel. Gen. Electric Co., Schenectady, 1955-73; cons. Nat. Bur. Standards, Gaithersburg, Md., 1974-75; mgr. orgn. and manpower computer services Gen. Electric Co., Rockville, Md., 1975; dir. Office Profl. Devel., NASA, Washington, 1975-78; pres. Mary K. Fortune Cons., Bethesda, Md., 1978—; Recipient plaque NASA, 1977. Mem. IEEE, Assn. for Computing Machinery, Am. Mgmt. Assn., Data Processing Mgmt. Assn., Lic. Employment Agts. Assn. Md., Nat. Personnel Consultants, Capital Speakers. Home: 5225 Pooks Hill Rd Apt 925N Bethesda MD 20814 Office: 4330 East-West Hwy Bethesda MD 20814

FORWARD, DOROTHY ELIZABETH, probate legal asst.; b. Medford, Mass., Oct. 12, 1919; d. Roy Clifford and Julia (Lane) Hurd; student UCLA, 1964; m. Winston W. Forward, Sept. 29, 1942. Sec. nat. dir. fund raising ARC, Washington, 1943-46; legal sec. William W. Waters, Esq., Los Angeles, 1953-56; office mgr. Winston W. Forward, Ins. Adjuster, Arcadia, Calif., 1956-64; legal asst. John M. Podlech, Esq., Pasadena, 1964-79; dir. Calif. Probate Insts., Arcadia, 1970—; ind. probate legal asst., 1979—; condr. workshops in probate procedures, 1969—. Recipient ARC Meritorious Service award, 1945; named Legal Sec. of Yr., Pasadena Legal Secs. Assn., 1974, 75, 77; Freedom Through Edn. award, Pasadena Legal Secs. Assn., 1975. Mem. Nat. Assn. Legal Secs., Legal Secs. Inc., Calif. Legal Secs. Assn. (parliamentarian 1982-83), Pasadena Legal Secs. Assn. (pres. 1976-78), Los Angeles County Forum of Legal Secs. (chmn. 1978-80), Nat. Assn. Legal Assts. (charter). Office: PO Box 311 Arcadia CA 91006

FORYST, CAROLE, govt. ofcl.; b. Chgo., Apr. 8, d. James M. and Marie V. (Votruba) F.; student Rosary Coll., 1958-61, Cite Universite de Grenoble, France, 1961, Hunter Coll., 1964-67, Roosevelt U., 1970-71; m. Anthony H. Cordesman, Feb. 14, 1976; children—Justin Galen Foryst, Alexander Scott Foryst. Fin. reporter Chgo. Sun-Times, 1969-72, Los Angeles Times, 1972; staff asst. to sec. U.S. Dept. Treasury, Washington, 1973-76; dep. dir. public affairs U.S. Dept. Interior, Washington, 1976; asst. v.p. Assn. Am. Railroads, Washington, 1977-78; v.p. AMTRAK, Washington, 1979-81; asso. adminstr. budget and policy Urban Mass Transp. Adminstrn., Washington, 1981—. Republican. Home: 1407 S 21st St Arlington VA 22202

FOSHAY, MAXINE VALENTINE SHOTTLAND (MRS. ROBERT LETHBRIDGE FOSHAY), civic worker; b. N.Y.C., Feb. 14, 1921; d. Maximillian Stanford and Violet Gertrude (Turner) Shottland; B.A., Royal Acad. Dramatic Arts, London, 1943; m. Robert Lethbridge Foshay, Mar. 16, 1956. Field rep. Am. Cancer Soc., N.Y.C. div., 1967-68; dir. fund raising and pub. relations Preventive Medicine Inst., Strang Clinic, 1969-71; dir. fund raising and pub. relations Fedn. Handicapped, N.Y.C., 1971-72; exec. dir. Irvington House, 1972-73; chmn. group affiliates Meml. Sloan Kettering, 1960-66; v.p. Meml. Sloan Kettering Soc., 1966-67; vol. Meml. Sloan Kettering Cancer Soc., 1956-77; propr. Maxine V. Foshay & Assocs., N.Y.C.; dir. vols. Children's Found. N.Y. Bd. dirs. Elder Craftsmen N.Y.C. Mem. Nat. Soc. Fund Raisers, Daus. of Brit. Empire in State of N.Y. (dir., 1st v.p.). Home: 215 E 68th St New York NY 10021

FOSS, LINDA LOUISE, nurse; b. Pierre, S.D., July 28, 1947; d. Francis Eugene and Josephine Frances (Donahue) F.; B.S. in Nursing, Tex. Women's U., 1969; postgrad. Metro State Coll., Denver, 1976-79; M.P.A., U. Colo., Denver, 1982. Intensive care nurse Diagnostic Hosp., Houston, 1970-71; sch. nurse Overseas Sch. System, U.S. Dept. of Def., Okinawa, Japan and Gelnhausen, W.Ger., 1971-75; public health nurse Vis. Nurse Service, Denver, 1975-79; public health supr. La Casa Health Sta., Denver, 1979-80; asst. dir. nursing Denver Gen. Hosp., 1980—. Co-chmn. Human Resource Task Force, Glendale, Colo., 1976-77; citizen rep. Denver Regional Council of Govts., 1976-77. Recipient Outstanding Employee award for Denver Health and Hosps., 1979. Mem. Am. Soc. Public Adminstrn., Colo. Nursing Assn. (pres. 1981-83), Am. Nurses Assn., Sigma Theta Tau. Democrat. Roman Catholic. Home: 601 S Forest St Denver CO 80222 Office: W 8th Ave and Cherokee St Denver CO 80204

FOSSETT, CAROL, educator; b. Toledo, Ohio, Mar. 19, 1931; d. George Russell and Margaret Ann (Dolan) Graff; B.A., Mary Manse Coll., 1953; M.A., U. Mich., 1955; m. John J. Fossett, Jan. 4, 1958; children—John, Mary, Anthony, Andrew, Joseph, James. Tchr. elem. schs., 1960-68, part time, 1968—. Vol. worker for mental health action groups. Mem. Nat. Autistic Soc., Assn. Advancement Elm. Edn. Roman Catholic. Office: Rose Hulman Inst Tech Terre Haute IN 47803

FOSTER, CAROLINE ROBINSON, personnel dir.; b. Mobile, Ala., Oct. 2, 1937; s. Lucius Waite and Vassar Austill (Bowling) Robinson; student Troy State U., 1956-57; student bus. mgmt., indsl. relations U. South Ala., 1972—; m. Edward Eugene Foster, May 23, 1964; children—Robin Caroline, Edward Eugene. Sec., Pacific Fin. Corp., Yuma, Ariz., 1957-58; sec. Univ. Hosp., Mobile, 1962-64, sec. to dir., asst. dir. social service, 1966-68; asst. to pres., dir. personnel Goodwill Industries, Inc., Mobile, 1968—; regional personnel dir. Retail Mchts. Service/Citicorp.; chmn. program com. Personnel and Indsl. Relations Conf., Ala. Dept. Continuing Ed., 1977, conf. chmn., 1978. Mem. exec. com. Mobile County Republicans; regional rep. ARC, 1979; area rep. Am. Intercultural Student Exchange. Mem. Internat. Mgmt. Council (del. to USSR, Council-YMCA mgmt. exchange program; named Key Person 1977), Am. Soc. Personnel Adminstrs. (dist. dir. 1979-80, mem. leadership tng. com. 1979-80, mem. coll. relations com. 1981—), Nat. Rehab. Assn. (mem. state conf. planning com.), Women in Mgmt., Mobile Personnel Assn. (dir. 1972-74, sec.-treas. 1975-76, v.p. 1976-77, pres. 1977-78). Baptist. Club: Gayfers Career Women. Home: 5778 Honor St Mobile AL 36608

FOSTER, CHERYL ANN, social worker; b. Pawtucket, R.I., Nov. 19, 1943; d. Edward Francis and Vivian Adrienne (Davagne) F.; A.B., Salve Regina Coll., 1966; postgrad. Providence Coll., 1965-74, U. R.I., 1967, 74, Northeastern U., 1967-68, Boston U., 1972-73. Mathematician, Raytheon Corp., 1965-68; social caseworker R.I. Social and Rehab. Services, Newport, 1969-70, Pawtucket, 1970-73, Newport, 1973—; specialist U.S. Army Res., 1973-76, RING, 1976-81; chmn. Newport County Task Force on Child Abuse and Neglect, 1981; mem. Newport County Council Community Services, 1980—. Mem. Middletown Food Coop., 1981—. Recipient Donor award Am. Assn. Blood Banks, 1972, Plywood Innovator award Am. Plywood Assn., 1967. Mem. Am. Math. Soc., Nat. Assn. Social Workers, AAUW. Republican. Roman Catholic. Contbr. poetry to various anthologies. Home: 18 Gunning Ct Middletown RI 02840 Office: RI Social and Rehab Services 12 Elm St Newport RI 02840

FOSTER, CLARA HODNETTE, educator; b. Chatom, Ala., Oct. 30, 1921; d. Robert Edward and Clara Martha (Brooks) Hodnette; A.B., Huntingdon Coll., 1951; M.S., Auburn U., 1969; postgrad. Troy State U., 1974-75; m. Ralph Shell Foster, July 5, 1954; children—Edward Frank, Ralph Shell. Med. technologist Communicable Disease Center, USPHS, Montgomery, Ala., 1952-56; instr. biology Huntingdon Coll., Montgomery, 1957-72; chmn. dept. sci. St. James Sch., Montgomery, 1971-75; instr. sci. Troy State U., Montgomery, 1973—. Recipient G. Stanley Frazer Meml. award St. James Sch., 1974. Mem. Am. Soc. Clin. Pathologists (certified med. technologist, affiliate), Am. Soc. Parasitologists, Sigma Xi, Gamma Sigma Delta, Women's Aux. Ala. Dental Assn. (past pres., adv. bd. 1969-71). Baptist. Home: 3131 Whitney Dr Montgomery AL 36106 Office: Troy State U Montgomery AL 36104

FOSTER, F. BLANCHE, writer; b. Centerville, Tenn., Jan. 6, 1919; d. L. George and F. Blanche F.; B.S., Tenn. State U., 1940; B.L.S., Atlanta U., 1947; A.M.L.S., U. Mich., 1953. Librarian, Sam Houston Coll., 1947-50; librarian, lectr. Detroit Public Schs., 1951-70; lectr. U. Ibadan (Nigeria), 1971-73; librarian South Vigo High Sch., Terre Haute, Ind., 1974-81; author books, most recent being: Dahomey, 1971, West Indies, 1976, East Central Africa, 1981. Co-chmn., Terre Haute chpt. Women's Internat. League for Peace and Freedom, 1979—; active NAACP, YWCA, African-Am. Mus., Detroit, Your Heritage House, Detroit. Named Outstanding Woman Ind., Ind. Black Caucus, 1975; recipient Outstanding Community Achievement award Alpha Kappa Alpha, 1976. Mem. ALA, Vigo County Ret. Tchrs. Assn., People to People, Alpha Kappa Alpha. Home: 2239 Spruce Terre Haute IN 47807

FOSTER, FLORENCE PEREY, ednl. adminstr.; b. Hollis, N.Y., Jan. 26, 1924; d. John Francis and Florence Louise (Spilbor) Perey; B.S. in Foods and Nutrition, Beaver Coll., 1946; M.A. in Early Childhood Edn., Kean Coll. N.J., 1964; postgrad. Bank Street Coll. Edn., 1965, Rider Coll., 1968, Glassboro State Coll., 1972, Trenton State Coll., 1979; m. Gerald R. Foster, July 27, 1943; 1 son, Brian Gerald. Social worker Dept. Public Welfare, Long Island, N.Y., 1947-48; nutritionist Beechnut Co., N.Y.C., 1948-49; head tchr. Wesley Hall, Westfield, N.J., 1958-62; dir. Bound Brook (N.J.) Coop., 1962-63; head tchr. Pickwick Nursery East Orange, N.J., 1963-64; edn. dir. Child Service Assn., Newark, 1964-66; asst. in early childhood N.J. State Dept. Edn., Trenton, 1966-68, coordinator fed. early children programs, 1968-69, dir. early childhood and state follow through coordinator, 1969-70, dir. early childhood edn., 1971-72; asso. dir. Follow Through and Head Start Bank Street Coll. Edn., N.Y.C., 1970-71; dir. Bainbridge Nursery Sch. and Crosswicks (N.J.) Country Day Sch., 1972-73; N.J. head start regional tng. officer Region 2 Office Child Devel., HEW, Rider Coll., Lawrence, N.J., 1973-75; exec. dir. Egenolf Day Nursery Assn., Elizabeth, N.J., 1975-77; N.J. Head Start Regional tng. officer, Region 2 Adminstrn. for Children, Youth and Families, Dept. Health and Human Services, Rutgers U., New Brunswick, N.J., 1977-78; dir. child devel. asso., head start supplementary tng. program dept. elem. early childhood and reading Trenton State Coll., 1978—. NDEA fellow for Early Childhood Adminstrs., 1965. Mem. Nat. Assn. Edn. Young Children, Organization Mondiali pour l'Education Prescolaire, N.J. Assn. Edn. Young Children (edn. and research chmn. 1962—, chpt. pres. 1968-70), Assn. Childhood Edn. Internat. Congregationalist. Editor Young World, 1962—; contbr. articles to profl. jours. Home: 810 Harding St Westfield NJ 07090 Office: Trenton State Coll Dept Elem Early Childhood and Reading Hillwood Lakes CN 550 Trenton NJ 08625

FOSTER, GEORGIA SNUDDEN, fin. instn. exec.; b. Elkhorn, Wis., June 14, 1944; d. Donald Clifford and Mary Alice (Dickson) Snudden; cert. Am. Inst. Banking, 1969; m. Louis Leon Foster, Mar. 17, 1973. Cashier, asst. trust officer Citizens Nat. Bank, Lake Geneva, Wis., 1962-73; adminstv. asst. employee benefits Trust Co. of Fla., Orlando, 1973-78, asst. v.p., asst. sec. employee benefits, 1978-80, v.p., trust officer, 1980—. Vice chmn. Central Fla. Women's Exec. Council, Orlando, 1977-78; treas. Employee Benefits Council Central Fla., 1982; treas. Am. Cancer Soc., Walworth County, Wis., 1968-72. Recipient Outstanding Woman in Bus. award, Orlando, 1976, Disting. Service award Fla. Savings and Loan League, 1977-79, Outstanding Service award U. Central Fla., 1981. Mem Bus. and Profl. Women, Nat. Assn. Bank Women, Safe Deposit Assn. Clubs: Order Eastern Star, Job's Daus. Home: 102 Sweetwater Blvd N Longwood FL 32750 Office: 200 E Robinson St Orlando FL 32802

FOSTER, JODIE, actress; b. Los Angeles, Nov. 1962. Acting debut TV show Mayberry, R.F.D.; numerous other TV appearances, including My Three Sons, The Courtship of Eddie's Father, Paper Moon, 1974-75; TV spl. The Secret Life of T.K. Dearing, 1975; TV movies; Smile, Jenny, You're Dead, Rookie of the Year; motion picture appearances: Napoleon and Samantha, 1972, Menace of the Mountain, One Little Indian, 1973, Tom Sawyer, 1973, Kansas City Bomber, 1972, Alice Doesn't Live Here Any More, 1975, Taxi Driver (Acad. award nominee Best Supporting Actress), 1976, Echoes of a Summer, 1976, Bugsy Malone, 1976, Freaky Friday, 1976, The Little Girl Who Lives Down the Lane, 1977, Candleshoe, 1977, Foxes, 1980, Carny, 1980. Office: care Internat Creative Mgmt Inc 8899 Beverly Blvd Los Angeles CA 90212 *

FOSTER, JOYCE ANN, tech. writer; b. Louisiana, Mo., Dec. 8, 1942; d. Ralph Pendleton and Sybil Bernice (Creech) Norton; cert. bus. mgmt. Internat. Corr. Schs., 1976; postgrad. U. Mo., 1976, Washington U., St. Louis, 1979; divorced; children—Tina Louise, Terry Lee. Sec., Sverdrup & Parcel, Engrs., Architects, Planners, Constrn. Mgmt., St. Louis, 1960-68, project asst., document coordinator 1971—; writer Delta Junction (Alaska) Midnight Sun, 1969-71; writer, research asst. The Way of Alaska, Delta Junction, 1969-71. Mem. Nat. Assn. Female Execs., Am. Mgmt. Assn., Am. Legion Aux. (past post pres.). Republican. Methodist. Home: 12462 Horizon Village Dr Apt C St Louis MO 63138 Office: 801 N 11th Blvd St Louis MO 63101

FOSTER, KAY FRANCES DAILEY, home economist; b. Haleyville, Ala., Aug. 13, 1944; d. Harold and Kate (Peak) Dailey; B.S. in Home Econs., Auburn U., 1967; m. Albert Russell Foster, June 16, 1967; 1 son, Harold Allen. Tchr., Dallas County (Ala.) Bd. Edn., Selma, 1967-70; residential energy adv. Ala. Power Co., Selma, 1970—; mem. adv. bd. Ala. Coop. Extension Service Impact '80. Mem. adv. bd. Dallas County Juvenile Ct., 1978—. Mem. Ala. Home Econs. Assn., Am. Home Econs. Assn., Home Economists in Bus., Nat. Mgmt. Assn. Methodist. Clubs: Emblem, Order Eastern Star, Daus. of Nile, Altrusa. Home: Route 1 Box 34 Safford AL 36773 Office: 217 Church St Selma AL 36701

FOSTER, MARCIA LEA, bus. exec.; b. Fitchburg, Mass., Nov. 5, 1951; d. Robert Nathan and Constance Louise (Stevenson) F.; B.A., Elmira (N.Y.) Coll., 1973. Tchr., Sandwich (Mass.) Public Schs., 1973; sec. Provident Mut. Life Ins. Co., Boston, 1974-75; office mgr. McCarthy Assos., Boston, 1975-77; owner, mgr. M.L. Foster Ins. Agy., Inc., Lexington, Mass., 1977-80; procurement and distbn. mgr., import specialist/inventory coordinator BAADER N. Am. Corp., Woburn, Mass., 1980—. Import traffic and documentation specialist Conn. Inst. Internat. Traffic. Mem. Women West, Nat. Assn. Female Execs. (network dir. 1978—). Home: 5 Summit Rd Lexington MA 02173

FOSTER, MARGERY SOMERS, educator; b. Boston, Mar. 27, 1914; d. L. Brent and Grace (Butler) F.; B.A., Wellesley Coll., 1934; Ph.D.,

Radcliffe Coll., 1958; Litt.D., Russell Sage Coll., 1968. Asst. to actuary New Eng. Mut. Life Ins. Co., 1934-43; dep. comptroller and dir. devel. Wellesley Coll., 1946-54; lectr. econs. Harvard U. Sch. Bus. Administrn., 1956-58; lectr. econs., sec. coll. Mt. Holyoke Coll., 1958-64; prof. econs., dean coll. Hollins Coll., 1964-67; prof. econs., dean coll. Douglass Coll. of Rutgers U., 1967-75. Univ. prof. econs. Rutgers, 1975—. Dir. Prudential Ins. Co. Am., Pub. Service Electric & Gas Co. N.J. Mem. commn. on tests Coll. Entrance Exam. Bd., 1966-70, trustee, 1969-72; mem. commn. on instl. affairs Assn. Am. Colls., 1971-74; mem. Harvard U. overseer's vis. com. for Warren Center in Am. History; trustee Middle States Assn. Colls. and Schs. Served to lt. Women's Res., USNR, 1943-46. Mem. Am. Econ. Assn., Econ. History Assn., Econ. History Soc., Nat. Tax Assn. Clubs: Appalachian Mountain, Cosmopolitan. Author: Out of Smalle Beginnings, An Economic History of Harvard College in the Puritan Period, 1962. Spl. research on Am. colonial econ. history, history of edn., pub. fin. Address: Francestown NH 03043

FOSTER, MARY CHRISTINE, TV prodn. co. exec.; b. Los Angeles, Mar. 19, 1943; d. Ernest A. and Mary (Quilici) F.; B.A. magna cum laude, Immaculate Heart Coll., 1967; M. Journalism in TV News Documentary, U. Calif., Los Angeles, 1968. Tchr. parochial schs., Piedmont, Santa Barbara and La Puente, Calif., 1963-65; dir. tchrs. Pacific U., 1968; dir. research Metromedia Producers Corp., Los Angeles, 1968-71; dir. prodn. services and devel. Wolper Orgn., Los Angeles, 1971-76; mgr. film programs NBC TV Network, Burbank, Calif., 1976-77; dir. movies and longforms Columbia Pictures TV, Burbank, 1977-79, v.p. movies for TV, 1979-81, v.p. series programming, 1981; v.p. program devel. Group W Prodns., Westinghouse Broadcasting Corp., Universal City, Calif., 1981—. Bd. dirs. Archdiocesan Communications Commn., 1977-80; student body v.p. Immaculate Heart Coll., 1966-67; alumnae pres., bd. dirs. Immaculate Heart High Sch., 1971-72, trustee, 1977—. Recipient Archbishop Cantwell award for gen. scholastic and service excellence, 1967, Distinguished Student award Kappa Tau Alpha, 1968; named Outstanding Student of Year, Sigma Delta Chi, 1968. Mem. Women in Film (dir. 1976-77), Catholic Press Council So. Calif., Acad. TV Arts and Scis., Kappa Gamma Phi, Delta Epsilon Sigma. Democrat. Home: 2367 W Silver Lake Dr Los Angeles CA 90039

FOSTER, NANCY DANA, social services cons.; b. Cambridge, Mass., Mar. 18, 1934; ed. Colby Coll., Wellesley Coll., Hitchins Sch. of Ballet, N.Y.C., Harvard U. Sch. Psychomotor Therapy; 3 children. Owner, tchr. McPhail Sch. of Ballet, Marshall, Tex., 1950-76; intern, preceptor Rusk (Tex.) State Hosp., 1969-70; psychiat. therapist Gregg-Harrison Mental Health-Mental Retardation Center, 1969-73; social services cons. Marshall Manor Nursing Home, Harrison County Nursing Home, Merritt Plaza Nursing Home, 1973; social services dir. Marshall Manor Nursing Home, 1973-76; ombudsman dir. Parkland Hosp., Dallas County Hosp. Dist., Dallas, 1976-81; adminstr. social rehab. activities central div. Beverly Enterprises, Ft. Smith, Ark., 1981—; former choreographer drama dept. E. Tex. Baptist Coll.; cons. choreographer Shreveport Little Theatre, Kilgore Coll.; ednl. cons. various schools including Tyler State Coll., Tyler Jr. Coll., Austin State Hosp., N.Tex. State U. Continuing Edn. System, Paris Jr. Coll., Dept. Pub. Welfare, Tex. Edn. Agy, Southwestern Med. Sch., U. Tex. Health Sci. Center, Grad. Sch. Mgmt. U. Dallas; cons. orgns. including Gov.'s Com. on Aging, Archtl. Barriers Com. E. Tex., E.Tex. Council Govts., HEW, Tex. Edn. Agy., Tex. Assn. Homes for the Aging, Home Health Services of Dallas, Dallas Rehab. Inst.; participant, student various confs. and tng. sessions in dance and adminstrn. in field. Founding pres. Marshall Symphony League; bds. Ret. Sr. Vol. Program, Home Health Services of Dallas, Am. Cancer Soc.; trustee, adv. com. Dallas Ballet; mem. com. on aging, bd. mem. urban concern Dallas Community of Churches; mem. Gov.'s Task Force Resettlement Indochinese; mem. Greater Dallas Community of Churches. Notary public, Tex.; recipient award Kansas City Art Guild; spl. commendations Gov. Price Daniel, Lady Bird Johnson; Am. Bus. Women speaker of year award. Mem. Tex. Hosp. Assn. (past state pres.), Tex. Nursing Home Social and Rehabilitative Dirs. Council (past state pres.), Am. Dance Therapy Assn., Dallas Hosp. Council, Am. Hosp. Assn. Soc. for Patient Reps., Am. Psychiat. Assn., Home Health Services of Dallas (bd.), Am. Soc. Law and Medicine. Episcopalian. Author audiovisual presentation An Act of Caring. Address: 2910 Jenny Lind PO Box 1628 Fort Smith AR 72902

FOSTER, PHYLLIS MARIE-ANNE, therapeutic activities cons.; b. Yonkers, N.Y., May 27, 1930; d. Charles Silas and Anna Florence (Bloom) Perry; m. Wilson Brooks Foster, Feb. 5, 1949; children—William Patrick, Kenneth John, Barbara Anne, Patricia Lee, Leslie Rae. Activity coordinator nursing homes, Denver, 1962-72; activity cons., educator Colo. Health Care Assn., Denver, 1972-74; pvt. practice activities cons., Littleton, Colo., 1974-76; coordinator/cons. Swedish Gerontology Health Resources, Littleton, 1976-79; course dir., curriculum coordinator Colo. Activity Dir. Tng. Program, 1972-79, HEW Regional VIII Suveyors Tng. Program, 1974, 78; speaker Am. Health Congress, Chgo., 1974; condr. workshops for activities personnel, 1972—; pvt. activities cons. to long term care facilities, 1978—; pvt. geriatric counsellor, 1979—. Mem. Long Term Care Criteria Devel. com. for PSRO, Colo. Found. for Med. Care., 1979—; participant, group leader White House Conf. on Aging, Colo., 1970; mem. Arapahoe County Council Sr. Citizens, 1974—. Recipient Better Life award for humanitarian services for outstanding achievement in caring for needs of elderly Am. Health Care Assn., 1978. Mem. Colo. Med. Soc. (long term care com. 1974-77), Nat. Assn. Activity Profls. (charter mem., steering com., chmn. membership com. 1981—), Colo. Assn. Activity Dirs., Am. Health Care Assn., Council Activity Coordinators (chmn. 1975-78), Western Gerontol. Soc., Nat. Assn. Female Execs. Founding editor Activities, Adaptation and Aging, 1980—. Address: 6549 S Lincoln St Littleton CO 80121

FOSTER, RUTH SULLIVAN, real estate co. exec., state legislator; b. Machias, Maine, Apr. 18, 1929; d. John Francis and Edith (Meserve) Sullivan; student U. Maine; children—Jennifer, Jacquelyn. Owner, mgr. real estate firm, Ellsworth, Maine; mem. Maine Ho. of Reps., 1981—. Republican. Roman Catholic.

FOSTER, SARA ANN, educator; b. Greencastle, Ind., Feb. 19, 1927; d. Harold and Anne May (Kemp) Zink; student DePauw U., 1944-47; B.A., U. N.Mex., 1948; M.A., Ohio State U., 1952; postgrad. U. Wis., 1972-74; m. John Ferguson, May 20, 1974; 1 dau., Anne Claire Foster. Psychiat. social worker Div. Mental Hygiene, State of Ohio, 1952-53; research analyst High Commn. for Germany, Frankfort, 1950-51; social work researcher Westside Day Nursery, Northside Day Nursery, Columbus, 1954-55; caseworker, supr. Children's Services County of Franklin, Columbus, 1956-62; instr. dept. sociology Ohio Wesleyan U., 1963-69; asst. prof. social work Ohio State U., 1963—. NIMH grantee, 1972-74. Mem. Ohio Women Inc., Council on Social Work Edn. (ho. of dels. 1976-79, 81—), Nat. Assn. Social Workers (state bd. dirs. 1976-77), Acad. Cert. Social Workers, Ohio Coll. Assn. Social Service Educators, AAUP. Democrat. Methodist. Home: 5812 Olentangy Blvd Worthington OH 43085 Office: 1947 N College Rd Ohio State U Columbus OH 43210

FOTO, MARY ELIZABETH SMITH (MRS. STEPHEN ANTHONY FOTO), health cons.; b. Iowa Falls, Iowa, Sept. 1, 1941; d. Roy D. and Margaret Grace (Binnie) Smith; B.S., U. So. Calif., 1966; m. Stephen Anthony Foto, Aug. 29, 1964; 1 dau., Alison Marie. Clin. affiliate U. So. Calif.-Los Angeles County Med. Center, Rancho Los Amigos, Brentwood VA Hosp., 1966-67; staff therapist Crippled Children's Services Los Angeles County, 1967-68; staff therapist Coll. Vista Convalescent Hosp.; pvt. practice as occupational therapist, Eagle Rock, Calif., 1968-70; head therapist Glen Wheeler Assos., San Gabriel, Calif., 1970-73; cons. Hillhaven Convalescent Hosp., Inc., Tacoma, 1972-74; occupational therapy cons. Blue Cross So. Calif., Los Angeles, 1972—; tchr. restorative services sect. Western Center Continuing Edn. in Adminstrn. of Health Core Facilities, UCLA, 1971-74; lectr. Loma Linda U. Allied Health Sch., 1973, instr., 1978-81, asso. prof., 1981—; preclin. instr. U. So. Calif. Sch. Occupational Therapy, 1973, 74; tchr. restorative services Calif. Nursing Home Assn., 1973; lectr. Acad. Speech Pathology, 1974. Cons. Health Programs Evaluation Services, Inc., Los Angeles, 1973—, Westchester Phys. Therapy, Bakersfield, Calif., 1972-74. Mem. Parent involvement Com. All Saints Day Care Center, 1971-74, bd. dirs., 1978—. Mem. Am. (spl. adviser on pvt. practice-nat. legislative com. 1973, commn. on practice 1977—), So. Calif. (legislative chmn. 1972) occupational therapy assns., Alpha Chi Omega. Republican. Episcopalian. Home: 445 Pilgrim Pl San Marino CA 91108 Office: PO Box 70000 Van Nuys CA 91470

FOUCH, ROSA LEE, educator; b. Union City, Ga., June 3, 1936; d. Wilson and Donnie Mae (McCrory) Hickson; grad. Atlanta Sch. Tailoring, 1958; student Atlanta U., 1968-69; m. Romeo Costello Fouch, Feb. 4, 1964; children—Demetrius Leo, Ninortchaka. Seamstress, Saul's Reweavers, Atlanta, 1956-59, Kleinmaier Tailoring Co., Atlanta, 1961-63; sales clk., designer Fashion Fabrics, Inc., Atlanta, 1964-67; co-owner Lee's Reweavers, Atlanta, 1969-71; beauty cons. Mary Kay Cosmetics, Inc., Atlanta, 1971—; tchr. Atlanta Area Tech. Sch., Atlanta, 1976—. Democrat Mem. Ch. of Christ. Home: 4534 Santa Fe Trail SW Atlanta GA 30331

FOUCH, STEPHANIE SAUNDERS, advt. agy. exec.; b. Yonkers, N.Y., Apr. 22, 1947; d. Stephan L. and Rosetta J. (Arvonio) Saunders; B.A., Vassar Coll., 1968; m. Gregory G. Fouch, Mar. 6, 1976. Asst. account exec. Chirurg & Cairns, Inc., N.Y.C., 1968-70; account exec. Benton & Bowles, Inc., N.Y.C., 1971-75; pub. cons., N.Y.C. and Washington, 1975-77; v.p. Weitzman, Dym & Assos., Inc., Washington, 1978-82; v.p., client services dir. Abramson Assos., Washington, 1982—; speaker, adv. in field. Bd. dirs. Henry St. Settlement, N.Y.C., 1971-73. Recipient Merit award United Fund Greater N.Y., 1972. Mem. Am. Advt. Fedn., Washington Media Mgmt. Network, Advt. Club Washington. Club: Vassar (dir. N.Y.C. 1972-74). Office: 1133 15th St NW Washington DC 20005

FOULKES, MARTHA LEE ELLIOTT, broadcasting exec.; b. Terre Haute, Ind., Oct. 4, 1925; d. Ross Edward and Norma Maybelle (Reichert) Elliott; student Ind. State U., Terre Haute, 1943-45; m. George Arthur Foulkes, Mar. 21, 1948 (dec. May 1977); children—Merrilee, Kathleen, Elizabeth, Jennifer, Arthur. Messenger, bookkeeper Ind. State Bank, Terre Haute, 1943-45; exec. sec. Mchts. Nat. Bank, Terre Haute, 1945-48; sec.-treas. Sta. WAAC, Terre Haute, 1963-77, pres., 1977—; cons., speaker in field. Bd. dirs. Jr. Achievement Wabash Valley, Wabash Valley chpt. ARC, Terre Haute Area Clean Community; pres. Inactive League Terre Haute, 1975-76. Mem. Terre Haute Area C. of C., Terre Haute Downtown Bus. Council, Kappa Kappa Kappa, Delta Gamma (alumnae pres. 1965-66). Republican. Christian Scientist. Club: Terre Haute Country. Home: 80 Allendale Terre Haute IN 47802 Office: 643 Ohio St Terre Haute IN 47808

FOUNTAIN, HELEN SMITH, home economist; b. Fillmore, N.Y., May 3, 1926; d. Chris H. and Mabel J. (Kellogg) Smith; B.S. in Home Econs., SUNY, Buffalo, 1948; M.S., Syracuse (N.Y.) U., 1952; m. John H. Fountain, Oct. 21, 1978. Tchr. home econs. schs. in N.Y. and Pa., 1948-59; supr. secondary testing and instrn. Palmyra-Macedon (N.Y.) schs., 1959-63; mgr. women's div., then mgr. family program Dairylea Coop., Syracuse, 1962-76, mgr. mem. devel. program, 1976—; chmn. nat. com. women's involvement coops. Am. Inst. Coop., 1975-79; chmn. young farm couples seminar N.Y. State Council Farmer Coops., 1975—; adv. N.Y. State Council Rural Women, 1963—. Mem. Am. Home Econs. Assn., Home Economists in Bus., N.Y. State Agrl. Soc. Club: Syracuse Zonta. Author manuals, articles in field. Home: 103 Vollmer Rd Fayetteville NY 13066 Office: 810 Burnet Ave Syracuse NY 13217

FOUNTAIN, SHARON (ELIZABETH) SLACK, mgmt. co. adminstr.; b. Dallas, Apr. 21, 1947; d. Richard A. and Nancy L. (Witt) Slack; student Montgomery Coll., 1965-67, 70, 76-78, Johns Hopkins U., 1982; m. Glen Harold Fountain, June 14, 1969. Market research asst. Resource Mgmt. Corp., Bethesda, Md., 1968-69; spl. edn. asst. Pleasant View Elem. Sch., Kensington, Md., 1969-70; sec. U. Md., College Park, 1970-72; adminstrv. asst. Hydronautics, Inc., Laurel, Md., 1972-73; orgn. mgr. Fashion Two Twenty Cosmetics Silver Spring, Md., 1972-74; indsl. security adminstr. Technology Service Corp., Silver Spring, 1974-79; sr. corp. staff mem. Life Dynamics, Inc., Columbia, Md., 1979-80; pres., propr. Performance Devel. Corp., Silver Spring 1980—; mem. faculty Westinghouse Sch. Applied Engring. Sci., 1980—, Howard Community Coll., 1979—, Montgomery Coll., 1981—; condr. tng. programs U.S. Office Personnel Mgmt., 1981—; mgmt. cons., 179—; freelance writer. Republican county election judge, 1976—. Mem. Am. Soc. Tng. and Devel. (dir. Md. chpt. 1980-82, treas. 1982—; 2 chpt. awards 1981, regional award 1981). Republican. Methodist. Address: 15323 Valencia St Silver Spring MD 20904

FOUNTAINE, BEECHER CASSELLS, real estate co. exec.; b. Atlanta, Feb. 28, 1927; d. Thomas Beecher and Bertha M. (Jackson) Travis; cert. Aristo Bus. Coll., N.Y.C., 1950; student Freedman's Hosp. Sch. Nursing, 1961-63; B.S., D.C. Tchrs. Coll., 1968, postgrad. 1969—; m. Shepard Fountaine, Jr., May 20, 1972. Ednl. media specialist D.C. Public Schs., 1968-69; dir. health careers program Nat. Med. Assn., 1969-72; cons. Office of Health Manpower HEW, NIH, 1972-74; realtor asso., pres. Bee Tee Enterprises, Sacramento, 1974—; del. White House Conf. on Poverty; mem. Pres. Com. on Health Edn., White House Conf. on the Aged. Mem. AAUW, Council Adminstrv. Women in Edn., Calif. Assn. Realtors, Sacramento Bd. Realtors, Nat. Urban League, NAACP, Nat. Med. Assn., A-Capitol Med. Soc., Nat. Council Negro Women, Sacramento Symphony League, Alpha Kappa Alpha. Author: Health Careers Guide. Democrat. Methodist. Clubs: Sacramento Democratics Womens, Nat. Democratic Womens, Links, Comstock. Office: 2720 Capitol Ave Suite 200 Sacramento CA 95816

FOUR, MARY ANN, business exec.; b. Queens, N.Y., June 26, 1952; d. Caroline M. Four; student Dunbarton Coll., 1970-72, Marymount Manhattan Coll., 1976-79; m. Stephan L. Rosenbaum, June 26, 1976. With Travel Dynamics Inc., N.Y.C., 1973-81, asst. to pres., 1975-77, ops. mgr., 1977-79, v.p. ops., 1980-81; mgr. travel services ABC, N.Y.C., 1981—. Mem. Nat. Assn. Female Execs. (charter), Nat. Passenger Traffic Assn. Home: 115-10 84th Ave Kew Gardens NY 11418

FOURCARD, INEZ GAREY, found. exec.; b. Bklyn., Sept. 26, 1930; d. George W. and Frances E. (MacDonald) Garey; student Pratt Inst., 1946-48; B.F.A., McNeese State U., 1963; m. Waldren Arthur Fourcard, Aug. 7, 1948; children—Chrystal Frances, Sharon Lynn, Waldren Arthur, Andrea Renee, David Marquard, Anita Lynn. Exhibited in numerous one man shows throughout U.S., also in Eng., France and Spain; mem. gifted and talented sect. of Spl. Edn. State of La., 1971-73; mem. adv. council Child Centered/Parent Tutored Kindergarden Program, 1974—; mem. La. Task Force for Community Edn., 1974-75; v.p. La. Assn. for Sickle Cell Anemia, 1974—, named best statewide vol.; mem. Calcasieu Parish Bicentennial Com., 1974—; exec. dir. Southwestern Sickle Cell Anemia Found., Lake Charles, La., 1973—. Named Hon. Citizen of Fort Worth, 1977; recipient Award of Merit, Human Relations Council of Lake Charles Deanery, award for services to sickle cell disease Sigma Gamma Rho, award for community service Phi Beta Sigma. Democrat. Roman Catholic. Important works include The Widow in pvt. collection Bertrand Russell Peace Found., London. Home: 1414 St John St Lake Charles LA 70601 Office: PO Box 3254 118 Enterprise Blvd Lake Charles LA 70601

FOUSHEE, OLA MAIE SUTTENFIELD (MRS. JOHN MCIVER FOUSHEE), painter, author, lectr.; b. Avalon, N.C.; d. Emmett R. and Callie Jane (Keaton) Suttenfield; student U. N.C., intermittently 1953-57, pvt. tchrs.; m. John McIver Foushee, Sept. 5, 1931; children—John McIver, June Keaton. Tchr. arts and crafts Army Convalescent Hosp., 1945, U. N.C., 1946; tchr. art Allied Arts, Durham, N.C., 1955-56; now v.p., adv. mgr. Foushee Realty and Ins. Co., Chapel Hill, N.C.; one-woman shows in N.C., S.C.; exhibited in group shows, N.C., S.C., Pa., Va., also Rowan Art Gallery, Salisbury, N.C., Center Gallery, Carrboro, N.C., 1981, Meredith Coll., Raleigh, N.C., 1981, Atlantic Christian Coll., 1982, Salem Coll., 1982, Appalachian U., 1982, also others; lectr. on art; mem. art juries. Recipient citation N.C. State Art Soc., 1962. Charter mem. Durham Art Guild; Chapel Hill Jr. Service League; founder Chapel Hill Sch. Art Guild, co-founder Asso. Artists of N.C.; mem. Alliance Francaise, Am. Fedn. Arts, State Art Soc. N.C. (life), Internat. Platform Assn., Phi Mu. Author: Art in North Carolina: Episodes and Developments 1585-1970, 1972; History of the Suttenfield Family, 1974; Avalon: A North Carolina Town of Joy and Tragedy, 1977; art columnist Greensboro Daily News, Durham Morning Herald, Rocky Mount Evening Telegram, High Point Enterprise, Charlotte Observer, Wilmington Star and others, 1958-63, Chapel Hill Weekly, 1963—; also TV series on N.C. Artists, 1975; TV Spl. on Outdoor Sculpture and Murals in N.C., 1978, 79. Home: Chapel Hill NC 27514

FOUST, JO ROBERSON, county ofcl.; b. Almance County, N.C., Sept. 25, 1937; d. Robert E. and Emma L. (Holt) Roberson; grad. Burlington (N.C.) Bus. Coll., 1960; student Inst. Govt., U. N.C., Chapel Hill, 1960-62; m. Robert A. Foust, Apr. 15, 1979; 1 son by previous marriage—Dale. Dep. register of deeds Alamance County Govt., Graham, N.C., 1958-71, adminstrv. asst. to county mgr., 1971-73, personnel dir., 1973—; v.p. Holt Constrn. Co., Graham, N.C.; dir. Nu-Med Ins. Co.; EEOC officer. Bd. dirs. United Way, Am. Heart Assn.; adv. council Employment Security Commn. Mem. Am. Soc. Personnel Adminstrs., Am. Soc. Public Adminstrs., Alamance County Personnel Assn., N.C. Heart Assn., Nat. Assn. County Ofcls. Democrat. Methodist. Club: Moose. Home: 520 Ward St Graham NC 27253 Office: 124 W Elm St Graham NC 27253

FOWKE, EDITH MARGARET FULTON, author, educator; b. Lumsden, Sask., Can., Apr. 30, 1913; d. William Marshall and Margaret (Fyffe) Fulton; student Regina Coll., 1929-31; B.A. with high honours in English and history, U. Sask., 1933, M.A. in English, 1938; LL.D. (hon.), Brock U., 1974; D.Litt., Trent U., 1975, York U., 1982; m. Franklin George Fowke, Oct. 1, 1938. Editor, Western Tchr., Saskatoon, Sask., 1937-45; asso. editor Mag. Digest, Toronto, Ont., Can., 1945-50; asso. prof. English dept. York U., Downsview, Ont., 1971-77, prof., 1977—. Decorated Order of Can. Fellow Am. Folklore Soc.; mem. English Folk Dance and Song Soc., Assn. Canadian Univ. Tchrs. English, Folklore Studies Assn. Can., Canadian Folk Music Soc. (v.p.), Mensa. Author: Folk Songs of Canada, 1954; Folk Songs of Quebec, 1957; Songs of Work and Freedom, 1960; Canada's Story in Song, 1960; Traditional Singers and Songs from Ontario, 1965; More Folk Songs of Canada, 1967; Lumbering Songs from the Northern Woods, 1970; Sally Go Round the Sun, 1969; Penguin Book of Canadian Folk Songs, 1974; Folklore of Canada, 1976; Ring Around the Moon, 1977; Folktales of French Canada, 1979; A Bibliography of Canadian Folklore in English, 1981; Sea Songs and Ballads from 19th Century Nova Scotia, 1982. Editor Canadian Folk Music Jour., 1973—. Office: Winters College York U 4700 Keele St Downsview ON M3J IP3 Canada

FOWLER, BARBARA HUGHES, educator; b. Lake Forest, Ill., Aug. 23, 1926; d. Fay Orville and Clara Emily (Reber) Hughes; B.A., U. Wis., 1949; M.A., Bryn Mawr Coll., 1950, Ph.D., 1955; m. Alexander Murray Fowler, July 14, 1956; children—Jane Alexandra, Emily Hughes. Instr. classics Middlebury Coll., 1954-56; asst. prof. Latin, Edgewood Coll., 1961-63; lectr. classics, John Bascom prof. classics, U. Wis., Madison, 1963—. Mem. Am. Philol. Assn., Archaeol. Inst. Am., Classical Assn. Midwest and South. Contbr. articles to profl. jours. Home: 1102 Sherman Ave Madison WI 53703 Office: 902 Van Hise Hall Univ of Wis Madison WI 53706

FOWLER, BETTY JANMAE, dance co. dir., editor; b. Chgo., May 23, 1925; d. Harry and Mary (Jacques) Markin; student Art Inst., Chgo., 1937-39, Stratton Bus. Coll., Chgo., 1942-43, Columbia U., 1945-47; 1 dau., Sherry Fowler Connors. Mem. public relations dept. Girl Scouts U.S.A., N.Y.C., 1961-63; adminstrv. asst. to editor-in-chief Scholastic Mags., N.Y.C., 1963-68; adminstrv. dir. Leonard Fowler Dancers, Fowler Sch. Classical Ballet, Inc., N.Y.C., 1959-78, tchr. ballet, 1959-61; editor Bulletin, Kiwanis weekly publ., Spokane, Wash., 1978-82, also adminstrv. sec. Kiwanis Club; instr. Spokane Falls Community Coll., 1978. Cert. metabolic technician Internat. Health Inst. Address: N 7105 G St Spokane WA 99208

FOWLER, CAMELLIA SMITH MULLINS, mfg. co. exec.; b. Holden, W.Va., Dec. 1, 1941; d. Frank and Clara Isabelle (Mannich) Smith; student Beckley (W.Va.) Jr. Coll., 1964, Ohio U., Lancaster, U., Cin.; divorced; children—Kelly Rene, Donald, Angela; m. 2d, Jonathan Peters Fowler, May 15, 1982. Personnel asst. Lancaster Glass Corp., 1967-68; adminstrv. asst. to v.p. internat. div. Anchor Hocking Glass Corp., Lancaster, 1968-70; asst. personnel mgr. Randall div. Textron, Inc., Cin., 1970-72; adminstrv. asst. to pres. Reading C/M Concrete, Inc., Cin., 1972-76; part-time sales asso. Berkley Realty, Cin., 1974-76; sales, adminstrv. and customer relations mgr. Pease Corp., Hamilton, Ohio and Denver, 1976-78; sales mgr. comml. microwaves Litton Industries, Inc., Denver, 1978-82, Los Angeles, 1982—; speaker in field. Lic. real estate broker. Mem. Nat. Restaurant Assn., Colo.-Wyo Restaurant Assn., Utah Restaurant Assn., N.Mex. Restaurant Assn. Republican. Lutheran. Address: 34647 Hwy 103 Evergreen CO 80439

FOWLER, ELAINE DANIELSON, educator; b. Concordia, Kans., Oct. 25, 1938; d. Clarence Frederick and Blanche Vendla (Magnus) Danielson; B.S., Kans. State U., 1960; M.S., U. Kans., 1964; Ph.D., U. Tex., Austin, 1969; m. Donald Fowler, Aug. 25, 1968; children—James, Thomas. Tchr. pub. schs., Topeka, 1960-63, Center Sch. Dist., Kansas City, Mo., 1964-66; teaching asst. U. Tex., Austin, 1966-69, asst. prof., 1969-75, asso. prof. 1975—; cons. Pullman-Kellogg Project, Algeria, Africa, 1978. Vice pres. Austin Assn. Retarded Citizens, 1980-82. Mem. Nat. Council Tchrs. English, Internat. Reading Assn., Delta Kappa Gamma, Phi Kappa Phi, Phi Delta Kappa, Phi Lambda Theta. Methodist. Author: Banner English Series, 1981; contbr. articles to profl. jours. Home: 4801 Crestway Dr Austin TX 78731 Office: EDB 406 U Tex Austin TX 78712

FOWLER, ELIZABETH MILTON, real estate exec.; b. Watertown, Fla., Jan. 11, 1919; d. Arthur Wellington and Mattie Jean (Hodges) Milton; student Bowling Green Bus. U., 1938-39; m. Albert L. Fowler, Jr., Aug. 6, 1948; children—Patricia Dawn Cecilia, Richard Gordon Sean. Sec. to dir. Workmen's Compensation Div., Fla. Indsl. Commn., Tallahassee, 1940-41; sec. to supt. div. Gibbs Ship Yard Repair, 1942-44; sec. to elec. engrs. Reynolds, Smith & Hills, Architects and Engrs., 1946-49; sec. to pres. Aichel Steel Corp., Jacksonville, Fla., 1949-50; adminstr. office mgr. for prin., vice-prin. Am. Dependent Sch., Moron Air Base, Spain, 1961-63; owner, mgr. Elizabeth Properties, Jacksonville, 1956—. Chmn. ways and means com. Chattanooga High Sch. PTA, 1956-57; asst. den mother Cub Scout Troop, 1970; block worker Gov.

Reagan's Presdl. Campaign. Recipient Spl. Appreciation award Eglin AFB, Fla., 1969. Mem. Nat. Assn. Female Execs., Am. Security Council (nat. adv. bd.), Dade County Crimewatch Orgn. Republican. Home and Office: 20101 SW 92d Ave Miami FL 33189

FOWLER, SAMANTHA NELSON, dental mgmt. cons.; b. South Bend, Ind., July 16, 1949; d. Alan and Shirley Clark (Pipher-Spring) Nelson; A.A.S. in Mdsg., Fashion Inst. Tech., N.Y.C., 1969; C.D.A., Toledo Med.-Ednl. Center, 1971; m. William R. Fowler, III, May 30, 1974. Engaged in retailing, 1965-70; office mgr. dental specialists, N.Y.C., 1970-78; dental mgmt. cons., 1978—; editorial cons. Dental Practice mag., 1980—; exec. editor Dental Assisting mag., 1981—; partner Profl. Practice Sales, Inc.; lectr. in field, vol. N.Y. Exchange Women's Work. Mem. Am. Mgmt. Assn., Nat. Dental Assts. Assn., N.Y. Dental Mgmt. Assn. (founder, pres. 1978). Address: 253 E 77th St Suite 2G New York NY 10021

FOWLER, SUSAN ANN, restaurant exec.; b. New Castle, Ind., Dec. 30, 1954; d. Eugene W. and Margaret E. (Shelton) F.; B.S. in Mgmt. and Fin., Ball State U., Muncie, Ind., 1977. Fin. advisor to mayor City of Muncie, 1977-78; head ops. mgr. RAX of Ind. and Ill., Inc., Ft. Wayne, Ind., 1978—. Bd. dirs. New Haven (Ind.) Festival Com. Recipient award for outstanding community involvement New Haven C. of C., 1980. Mem. Nat. Assn. Female Execs., Am. Bus. Women's Assn., New Haven C. of C. (2d v.p.), Allen County Democrats Assn., YWCA, VFW Aux. Roman Catholic. Club: Moose. Home: 3728 Oaklawn Dr Anderson IN 46014 Office: 2820 N Broadway Dr Anderson IN 46012

FOWLKES, NANCY LANETTA PINKARD (MRS. VESTER GUY FOWLKES), social worker; b. Athens, Ga.; d. Amos Malone and Nettie (Barnett) Pinkard; B.A., Bennett Coll., 1946; M.A., Syracuse U., 1952; M.S.W., Smith Coll., 1963; M.P.A., Pace U., 1982; m. Vester Guy Fowlkes, June 4, 1955 (dec. May 1965); 1 dau., Wendy Denise. Dir. publicity Bennett Coll., Greensboro, N.C., 1946-47, 49-50; asst. editor Va. Edn. Bull. ofcl. organ Va. Tchrs. Assn., Richmond, 1950-52; asst. office mgr. Community Service Soc., N.Y.C., 1952-55; social caseworker, asst. supr. Dept. Social Services, Westchester County, White Plains, N.Y., 1959-67, supr. adoption services, 1967-77, supr. adoption and foster care, 1977—; mem. adv. bd. White Plains Adult Edn. Sch. First v.p. Eastview Jr. High Sch., 1970-71; area chmn. White Plains Community Chest, 1964; sec. Mt. Vernon Concert Group, 1952-54; fund raising co-chmn. Urban League Guild of Westchester, 1967; pres. White Plains Interfaith Council, 1972-74; bd. dirs. Family Service of Westchester, Bethel Meth. Home, Ossining, N.Y.; trustee N.Y. Conf., United Meth. Ch., 1982—. Mem. Nat. Assn. Social Workers, Acad. Cert. Social Workers, Jack and Jill Am. (chpt. pres. 1965-67, regional sec.-treas. 1967-71), Nat. Bus. and Profl. Women's Club (chpt. sec. 1954-56), Internat. Platform Assn., Theta Sigma Phi (treas. 1975—), Zeta Nu Omega, Alpha Kappa Alpha (pres. 1960-64, treas. 1975-78). Methodist (chmn. adminstrv. bd. 1970-72, vice chmn. 1978-80, vice chmn. trustees 1973-77, treas. 1978—, lay speaker, lay leader 1980-81, chmn. adminstrv. bd. 1982; v.p. Met. dist. United Meth. Women 1977—, exec. bd. N.Y. conf.). Club: Regency Bridge (pres. 1963-65, v.p. 1965-67). Home: 107 Valley Rd White Plains NY 10604 Office: County Office Bldg White Plains NY 10601

FOX, ALICE, educator; b. Trenton, N.J., July 29, 1928; d. Fred and Molly Fox; B.A., U. Mo., 1950; M.A., U. Tenn., 1957; Ph.D., Mich. State U., 1965; children—Genevra, Christine. Instr. English, Wash. State U., 1959-60; with Western Coll. for Women, Oxford, Ohio, 1961-74, prof., 1968-74, chmn. dept. English, 1968-70; assoc. prof. English, Miami U., Oxford, 1974-79, prof., 1979—, asst. dir. grad. studies English, 1976-78, dir. grad. studies in English, 1982—; mem. nat. screening com. for Fulbright scholarships to U.K., 1977-80. Southeastern Inst. Medieval and Renaissance Studies fellow Duke U., 1968; Nat. Endowment for Humanities fellow U. Calif., Santa Cruz, 1973. Mem. MLA, Shakespeare Assn. Am., Spenser Soc., Virginia Woolf Soc., Porlock Soc. (pres. 1975—). Author: Suicidal Ending in Virginia Woolf, 1960. Contbr. articles to profl. jours. Home: 22 E Rose Ave Oxford OH 45056 Office: Dept English Bachelor Hall Miami U Oxford OH 45056

FOX, CAROL CAMPBELL, ednl. cons.; b. Albuquerque, N.Mex., June 26; d. Smith Keith and Gwynne Orba (Powell) Campbell; B.S., Pepperdine U.; M.S., U. So. Calif., 1962, postgrad., 1962-70; 1 son, Christian. Tchr., Torrance (Calif.) Unified Sch. Dist., 1957-61; tchr. Centralia Sch. Dist., Buena Park, Calif., 1961-63; cons. Redondo Beach (Calif.) Sch. Dist., 1963-64; coordinator El Segundo (Calif.) Unified Sch. Dist., 1964-65; cons., Office of Los Angeles County Supt. of Schs., 1965-68, cons. individual instrn. and staff devel., 1974—; dir. Edn. Center, Tustin (Calif.) Unified Sch. Dist., 1968-69; asst. prof. Calif. State U., Los Angeles, 1970-74; tchr. Pepperdine U., Loyola U., U. So. Calif.; regional cons. Assn. for Individually Guided Edn; cons. to various schs. dists. Bd. dirs. South Bay Children's Hosp., Educare; mem. Peninsula Com. for Philharm. Orch. Mem. Assn. for Calif. Sch. Adminstrs., Women in Ednl. Leadership, Assn. for Supervision and Curriculum Devel. (pres. So. Calif. sect.), Bus. and Profl. Women's Club (pres. 1965-66). Club: Order of Eastern Star. Office: 9300 E Imperial Hwy Downey CA 90742

FOX, DANIELLE DALEY, floral designer; b. Newark, Nov. 17, 1949; d. Daniel Daley and Clara (Reheis) Fox; student Centenary Coll. for Women, 1967-68; B.A., Finch Coll., 1973. Sec., Flavia's Creations, Summit, N.J., 1973-76, floral designer, 1976-79; freelance designer, 1979—. Mem. Jaguar Club Am., Finch Alumni Assn. Author: Extension - An Anthology of Modern Poetry, 1968. Home: 18 Cromwell Pkwy Summit NJ 07901

FOX, DAPHNE SHARON, lawyer, columnist; b. Austin, Tex., Apr. 30, 1946; d. Charles and Earline F.; B.A., Calif. State U., Long Beach, 1968; J.D., Golden Gate U., 1975. Negotiator, U.S. Navy, Oakland, Calif., 1969-74; admitted to Calif. bar, 1976; adminstr. Electric Power Research Inst., Palo Alto, Calif., 1976—; individual practice law, Pacifica, Calif., 1978—; columnist Lady Lawyer, San Francisco, 1978—; guest lectr. on women and the law. Mem. Calif. State Bar. Republican. Office: 1117 Grand Teton Dr Pacifica CA 94044

FOX, DEL FRANKLIN, counselor; b. Hartford, Conn., Oct. 11, 1923; d. Marcus Irving and Lee (Olshan) Franklin; B.A., N.Y. U., 1944; M.A., U. South Fla., 1968; m. Mark Edward Fox, Jan. 14, 1951; children—Andrew Eric, Steven Alan. Copywriter, WSRR, Stamford, Conn., 1945-48; pub. relations staff Sidney Ascher & Assos., 1949-51; feature writer Fla. Times Union, Jacksonville, 1952-59; feature writer Sarasota (Fla.) Mag., 1960-68; adult guidance counselor Sarasota County Vocat. Tech. Center, 1968—; weekly broadcast WSPB, 1969—. Mem. Sarasota Manatee Bi-County Commn. on Status of Women, 1975—; mem. Gov.'s Commn. on Status of Women, 1978—; bd. dirs. Women's Center of Sarasota, 1979—; mem. steering com. Fla. Women's Network, 1980—. Mem. Am. Personnel and Guidance Assn., Nat. Assn. Commns. for Women (dir. 1982—), Am. Vocat. Assn., Nat. League Am. Pen Women, Delta Kappa Gamma. Club: University. Home: 4634 Higel Ave Sarasota FL 33581 Office: 4748 Beneva Rd Sarasota FL 33581

FOX, ELLEN JOAN, psychotherapist; b. Bklyn., Sept. 24, 1941; d. George and Lucille Ruth (Finkelstein) Cooper; B.A., Bklyn. Coll., 1962; M.S.W., U. Calif., Berkeley, 1972. Exec. sec. project instl. racism Nat. Assn. Social Workers, 1972-73; cons. Pacific Mgmt. Sustems, San Francisco, 1972-73; community organizer, then dir. Office Community Liaison, E. Oakland Community Mental Health Center, Oakland, Calif., 1973-75; asst. prof. Coll. Santa Fe, 1975-76; pvt. practice psychotherapy, Santa Fe, 1976—; bd. dirs. S.W. Mgmt. Alternatives, Inc.; mem.-at-large N.Mex. council White House Conf. Families, 1980—; clin. cons. Santa Fe Group Homes, Inc., Suenos de Esperanza Program, Santa Fe Mountain Center. NIMH trainee, 1971-72. Mem. Nat. Assn. Social Workers, Am. Orthopsychiat. Assn., N.Mex. Council Community Mental Health Services, Santa Fe Mental Health Assn., Sierra Club, Hadassah. Democrat. Jewish. Office: 200 W De Vargas St Santa Fe NM 87501

FOX, ELLEN RANDI, business exec.; b. Cheyenne, Wyo., Nov. 24, 1949; d. Abraham Harvey and Edith (Wolinsky) Fox; student public schs., Cheyenne. Microfilmer, City and County of Denver, 1969-70; asst. buyer Randall's Formalwear, Denver, 1970-72; owner, mgr. Firebird Motel, Cheyenne, 1972—, Grandma Brindel's Waterbeds & Things, Cheyenne, 1979—, Craft Collection, 1981—; sec., treas. Fox Enterprises, Inc.; partner Lam-I-Dent Co. Active NOW, Wyo. Named Retailer of Yr., Am. Merchandising Enterprises Distributors, 1979. Mem. Bus. and Profl. Women. Jewish. Led demonstration against local newspapers for not inviting women on Treagle Train, 1979. Home: 5381 Kennedy Dr Cheyenne WY 82001 Office: 1607 Capitol Ave Cheyenne WY 82001

FOX, ELSIE HAZEL, educator; b. Hugoton, Kans., Dec. 11, 1929; d. Earl A. and Alta B. (Florence) Farmer; B.A., So. Colo. State Coll., Pueblo, 1974; m. Myron George Curtiss, Oct. 9, 1946 (div. 1951); children—Nancy, Allen, Edwin, Ronnie; m. 2d, Thomas Alvin Fox, June 9, 1959 (dec. Jan. 1977); 1 son, Terry Lee. With Pueblo Army Depot, 1952-55, Grove Drugs, Pueblo, 1955-74; tchr. Manzanola (Colo.) Public Schs., 1974—; tchr. migrant sch., summers 1974-75. Mem. Manzanola City Council, 1976—; precinct committeewoman Democratic Party; town rep. Manzanola Library Bd. Mem. Jane Jeffersons (pres.), Bus. and Profl. Women's Club. Home: 128 Canal St Manzanola CO 81058 Office: PO Box 148 Manzanola CO 81058

FOX, JOAN PHYLLIS, environ. engr.; b. Rockledge, Fla., July 16, 1945; d. John A. and Nonie L. (Knutson) F.; B.S. with high honors in Physics, U. Fla., 1971; Ph.D. in San. Engring., U. Calif., Berkeley, 1980. Engr., Bechtel, Inc., San Francisco, 1971-76; dir. and prin. investigator Lawrence Berkeley Lab., 1977-81; prin. engr., pres. Fox Cons., Berkeley, 1981—; guest lectr. dept. conservation and resource studies U. Calif., Berkeley, 1980—. EPA grantee, 1978-81; Dept. of Energy grantee, 1976-81. Mem. Am. Geo-phys. Union, Nat. Resources Def. Council, Am. Chem. Soc., ASTM, Water Pollution Control Fedn., Nat. Acad. Scis. (mem. com. oil shale of COSMAR 1977-79), AAAS, Audubon Soc., Phi Beta Kappa, Sigma Pi Sigma. Contbr. articles on oil shale and water quality control to profl. publs. Office: 1988 California St Berkeley CA 94703

FOX, JUDITH ELLEN, temporary services co. exec.; b. N.Y.C., Aug. 2, 1941; d. Murray A. and Harriette Schneider; student Pa. State U., 1959-60; m. Jerry Fox, Aug. 16, 1964; children—Brian Spencer, Jennifer Leslie. Asst. personnel dir. Miles Shoe Co., N.Y.C., 1961-63; freelance writer, photographer Coronet, The Progressive, U.S. Catholic, numerous local and state periodicals, 1962-77; asst. personnel dir. Wallachs, Inc., N.Y.C., 1963-64; co-owner, photographer J. Fox Photographers, Stony Brook, N.Y., 1968-72; mgr. Forbes Temporaries, Richmond, Va., 1975-78; pres., founding partner Fox Huber Temporaries, Inc., Richmond, 1978—; mem. adv. bd. Womensbank, 1981—; chmn. customer adv. bd. Va. Electric and Power Co., 1981—; personnel cons. pvt. industry and state govt., 1980—. Dist. chmn. Va. gubernatorial campaign, 1977; bd. dirs. Multiple Sclerosis Soc., Central Va. chpt., 1979-80, Met. YMCA, 1982—; mem. exec. bd. Gov.'s Adv. Com. on Small Bus., 1982—; mem. fundraising com. Hampton Inst., Mem. Nat. Assn. Temporary Services, Richmond C. of C. (chmn. small bus. council 1982, ex-officio bd. dirs. 1982, legis. affairs com.), Nat. Assn. Female Execs., Nat. Assn. Women Bus. Owners (exec. bd. 1982—), Va. Assn. Temporary Services (v.p. 1981—) Office: 5006 Monument Ave Richmond VA 23230

FOX, JULIA VAN DEUSEN, educator; b. Randolph, Vt., June 23, 1934; d. Arthur W. and Jessie D. (Hitchcock) Van Deusen; B.S. cum laude, U. N.H., 1957; M.A., U. So. Calif., 1963, Ph.D., 1971; m. Frank H. Fox, Dec. 28, 1958; children—Van Eric, Jeanelle Lee. Occupational therapist Pa. Rehab. Center, Johnstown, 1959-62; instr. occupational therapy Sch. Medicine, U. Wis., Madison, 1963-68; vis. asst. prof. U. So. Calif., Sch. Edn. European Grad. Programs, Los Angeles, 1973-75; asso. prof. occupational therapy Coll. Allied Scis., Howard U., Washington, 1977-80; asst. prof. occupational therapy Sch. Allied Health Professions, U. Wis., Madison, 1982—. Vocat. Rehab. Adminstrn. trainee, 1962; Rehab. Services Adminstrn. trainee, 1968. Mem. Am. Psychol. Assn., Am. Occupational Therapy Assn., Am. Assn. Higher Edn., Am. Ednl. Research Assn. Contbr. articles to profl. jours. Home: 12322 Chavers Av Downey CA 90242 Office Occupational Therapy Dept Sch Allied Health Professions U Wis Madison WI 53706

FOX, LEOLENE LANGFORD, state ofcl.; b. Opelousas, La., Apr. 21, 1927; d. James Nathaniel and Nanelle (Coney) Langford; with Dept. Public Welfare State of La., 1949-55, sec. Dept. Culture, Recreation & Tourism, Baton Rouge; with U.S. Army Corp Engrs. Army Maneuver Rights, Quachita Parish, La., 1954; substitute tchr. Monroe (La.) City Sch. System, 1969-70; supr. U.S. Dept. Commerce, Census Bur., Quachita Parish, 1970. Mem. Republican State Central Com., 1966-72, del. Nat. Conv., 1972; U.S.A. del. Internat. Encampment Girl Scouts and Girl Guides, Adelboden, Switzerland, 1946. Mem. DAR, Kappa Kappa Gamma. Republican. Presbyterian. Clubs: Bayou DeSiard Country, Ladies Tennis Assn., Chauvin Racquet, Jr. Charity League, Quachita Parish Women's Rep. Club. Office: 666 N Foster St Baton Rouge LA 70806

FOX, LYNN (ELLEN) HUSSEY, educator; b. Balt., Jan. 5, 1944; d. Harry and Gertrude (Leighs) F.; B.S. with honors, U. Fla., 1965, M.Ed., 1968; M.A. in Psychology, Johns Hopkins U., 1973, Ph.D., 1974; m. Harrison William Fox, Jr., Sept. 2, 1967; children—Harrison William III, Thomas Randolph and Leigh Lynn (twins). Tchr. math. Orange County Public Schs., Orlando, Fla., 1965-67; edn. specialist U.S. Office of Edn., 1969-71; research asst. dept. psychology Johns Hopkins U., Balt., 1972-73, asso. project dir. study of mathematically precocious youth, 1971-74, instr. evening div., 1974-75, asst. prof. edn. Evening Coll., 1975-78, asso. prof., 1978-81, prof., 1981—; instr. Towson State U., Balt., 1974; cons. to Ford Found., 1979-80; reviewer jours. in psychology and child devel., 1977—. Mem. adv. com. gifted and talented programs and services Balt. City Schs., 1977—; mem. Balt. Mayors Vol. Cadre on Edn., 1976-77. Nat. Inst. Edn. grantee, 1977-81; Md. Dept. Edn. grantee 1977-78; Spencer Found. grantee, 1974-77, 79-82. Mem. Nat. Assn. for Gifted Children (exec. bd. 1977—), Council for Exceptional Children Am. Ednl. Research Assn. (program com. 1975-76), Am. Psychol. Assn., AAAS, Sigma Xi, Phi Delta Kappa. Democrat. Methodist. Contbr. numerous articles to ednl. jours.; co-editor; Mathematical Talent, 1974, Women and the Mathematical Mystique, 1980. Home: 215 Ridgemede Rd Baltimore MD 21210 Office: 100 Whitehead Hall Johns Hopkins Univ Baltimore MD 21218

FOX, MARGARET BLAIR, personal services firm exec.; b. Dover, Del., Nov. 5, 1951; d. William Robert and Penelope Rodney (Layton) F.; B.A., Colby Coll., Waterville, Maine, 1974; diploma Katherine Gibbs Sch., Boston, 1974. Legal asst., Boston, 1974-76, Houston, 1977-78; placement cons. M. David Lowe Personnel, Houston, 1976; social sec. Plaza Club, Houston, 1977; corp. rep. McFaddin-Kendrick, Houston, 1978; sales rep. Dictaphone Corp., Houston, 1978-79; pres. Personal Assistance Plus, Houston, 1982—. Team capt. Houston Mus. Fine Arts, 1980—. Mem. English Speaking Union, Descs. of Signers Declaration of Independence, DAR. Republican. Episcopalian. Club: Houston Polo. Address: 5001 Woodway Suite 1006 Houston TX 77056

FOX, MARY ELIZABETH, pianist, lectr., journalist; b. Granger, Tex.; d. J. S. and Frances (West) F.; A.B., B.S., Southwestern U., also A.M.; postgrad. U. Tex. Prof. journalism Southwestern U., Georgetown, Tex., 1944—, dir. publicity, 1950—; corr. to UN, 1945—. Del. Williamson County, Tex., Nat. Democratic convs. Mem. Am. Assn. Profs. Journalism, Nat. Collegiate Players, LWV, Tex. Woman's Press Assn., Nat. Fedn. Press Women, AAUP, Am. Newspaper Women's Club, Am. Judicature Soc., Acad. Polit. Sci., Tex. Hist. Soc., AAUW, Brit. Horse Soc., Internat. Platform Assn., Marquis Biog. Library Soc. (adv. bd.), Women in Communication, PEO, Sigma Phi Alpha, Sigma Tau Delta, Delta Omicron, Pi Epsilon Delta, Pi Delta Epsilon, Delta Delta Delta. Methodist. Clubs: Mill Creek Country, Bell News Media, Stagecoach Country; Music, Writers and Press (London) Ltd. Address: 2411 S 61st St C-3 Temple TX 76501

FOX, MURIEL CORINNE, public relations exec.; b. Newark, Feb. 3, 1928; d. Morris and Anne L. (Rubinstein) F.; student Rollins Coll., 1944-46; B.A. summa cum laude, Barnard Coll., 1948; m. Shepard G. Aronson, July 1, 1955; children—Eric A., Lisa S. Reporter, UP, 1946-48; art critic and bridal editor Miami (Fla.) News, 1946; advt. copywriter Sears, Roebuck & Co., 1948-49; polit. speechwriter, publicist, 1949-50; with Carl Byoir & Assos., N.Y.C., 1950—, TV-radio writer, 1950-52, dir. TV-radio dept., 1952-57, v.p., 1957-74, group v.p., sr. cons., exec. com., 1974-76, exec. v.p., 1977—; pres. By/Media, Inc.; chmn. MediaCom Communicating Tng. (Byoir subs.), 1975—; dir. Harleysville Ins. Co., Rorer Group, 1979—. Co-chmn. Vice Presdl. Task Force on Women, 1968; bd. dirs. Women's Forum, 1974-78, pres., 1976-78; nat. adv. com. Nat. Women's Polit. Caucus; nat. adv. bd. Ethnic Woman; bd. dirs. N.Y. Diabetes Assn., 1956-66, Holy Land Conservation Fund, United Way of Tri State, Internat. Rescue Com., 1977—, Am. Arbitration Assn., 1982—; founder NOW, v.p., 1967-70, chmn. bd., 1971-73, chmn. nat. adv. com., 1973-74; bd. dirs. Legal Def. and Edn. Fund, 1974—, v.p., 1977, 78, pres., 1978—; mem. adv. council Democrats of the Senate, N.Y. State, 1979—. Winner ADA Bus. Leader of Yr. award, 1979, Women in Communications Matrix award, 1975; named to 100 Top Corp. Women, Bus. Week, top-rated P.R. Woman, 1974. Mem. Am. Women in Radio and TV (dir. 1959-61, chmn. nat. publicity com. 1955-57, chmn. nat. public relations com. 1957-59), Am. Arbitration Assn., Fin. Women's Assn. Office: Carl Byoir & Associates Inc 380 Madison Ave New York NY 10017

FOX, PEGGY ANN, telephone co. mgr.; b. LaCrosse, Wis., Mar. 19, 1946; d. John Lehr and Lorraine Elizabeth (Fink) F.; B.S. in Secondary Edn., U. Wis., LaCrosse, 1969; M.Ed. in Career and Vocat. Edn., Colo. State U., Ft. Collins, 1974. Instr., Cochrane-Fountain City (Wis.) High Sch., 1969-70; curriculum developer, instr. Western Wis. Tech. Inst., LaCrosse, 1970-73; asst. coordinator for state career edn. program Bur. Social and Ednl. Services, R.I. Coll., 1973-75; resource liaison O'Rourke's Children's Center, Providence, 1975-76; career and vocat. edn. cons., sales rep. Communications Cons., Inc., Oklahoma City, 1976-79; asst. dir., instr., curriculum developer Pikes Peak Inst. Med. Tech., Colorado Springs, Colo., 1978-79; account exec. Peak Health Plan, Colorado Springs, 1979-80; market adminstr. Mountain Bell Telephone Co., Colorado Springs, 1980-82, asst. mgr. small bus. dist., Denver, 1982—; cons. in field. EPDA fellow, 1973-74. Mem. AAUW, Internat. Assn. Personnel Women, Nat. Assn. Female Execs., NOW, Colorado Springs, C. of C. Office: Room 640 999 18th St Denver CO 80201

FOX, ROBERTA FULTON, lawyer; b. Phila., Nov. 25, 1943; d. Robert Fulton and Irmgard F.; B.A., U. Fla., 1964, J.D., 1967; m. Mike Gold; 1 stepdau., Shari Anna Gold. Admitted to Fla. bar, 1968; mem. Govt. Research Council, Miami-Dade C. of C., 1964-65; staff Goldin & Jones, Gainesville, Fla., 1968; atty. Migrant Legal Services, Miami, 1968-69, Legal Services Greater Miami, 1970-72; pvt. practice law, Coral Gables, Fla., 1972-80; partner firm Gold & Fox, P.A., 1972—; mem. Fla. Ho. Reps., 1976-82; mem. Gov.'s Commn. on Marriage and the Family Unit, 1974-76; chairperson Dade County Women's Polit. Caucus, 1971-74; counsel NOW, Women's Action Center, Inc.; chairperson sex-biased discrimination com. of minority affairs com. Democratic Issues Conv., 1976-78. Mem. affirmative action agy. adv. bd., treas. Transition, Inc.; mem. council, bd. dirs. Planned Parenthood of S. Fla.; bd. dirs. NOW Legal Def. and Edn. Fund.; hon. bd. dirs. Girls Clubs Greater Miami. Recipient Outstanding State Legislator award, 1979; Gov.'s award for Art, 1980. Mem. Bus. and Profl. Women, Fla. Women Lawyers Assn., Fla. Bar Assn., Voters Inc., Coral Gables C. of C., Nat. Women's Polit. Caucus, Fla. Women's Polit. Caucus, Dade County Women's Polit. Caucus, LWV, AAUW, Citizens League, Inc., ACLU, Panel of Am. Women, Common Cause, U. Fla. Law Center Assn., Zero Population Growth. Office: 4601 Ponce De Leon Suite 310 Coral Gables FL 33146*

FOX, TRICIA, ednl. adminstr., businesswoman; b. Madison, Wis., July 1, 1947; d. George Thomas and Beatrice (Sill) Fox; B.S. cum laude, U. Wis., 1970; student Calif. State U., Long Beach, 1974; m. Keith A. Gordon, Mar. 26, 1977; children—Teresa, Karin, Keith A. Tchr. German, Wis. Heights Sch., Mazomanie, Wis., 1968-70; mgr. Roland and Lynn Carol, Los Angeles, 1970-73; mem. mktg. staff IBM, Los Angeles, Australia, Wis., 1973-78; mem. mktg. staff Datapoint Computers, Chgo., 1978-80; pres. The Fox Day Schs., Inc., Northbrook, Ill., 1979—, The Fox Day Camps, Inc., 1979—; owner The Fox Corp. Child Care Services; cons. corps.; pres. bd. dirs. Second City Day Sch. Mem. Women in Mgmt. (vice-pres. 1981—), Nat. Assn. Women Bus. Owners, AAUW, Chgo. Assn. Edn. Young Children, Nat. Assn. Edn. Young Children, Nat. Assn. Female Execs. Roman Catholic. Office: 3323 Walters Ave Northbrook IL 60062

FOX-GENOVESE, ELIZABETH ANN, historian; b. Boston, May 28, 1941; d. Edward Whiting and Elizabeth Mary (Simon) Fox; B.A. in History with honors, Bryn Mawr Coll., 1963; M.A., Harvard U., 1966, Ph.D., 1974; m. Eugene Dominick Genovese, June 6, 1969. Teaching fellow Harvard U., 1965-66, 67-69; asst. editor Houghton Mifflin Co., 1966-67; asst. prof., then assoc. prof. history U. Rochester (N.Y.), 1973-80; prof. history SUNY, Binghamton, 1980—, vice chmn. grad. affairs, 1981—; instr. summer inst. quantitative methods for historian Newberry Library, 1980. Nat. Endowment Humanities fellow, 1976-77; Rockefeller Found. fellow, 1980; Eleutherian Mills Hist. Library grantee, 1972, 73. Mem. Orgn. Am. Historians (dir. project intergration materials on women into basic survey courses 1979—), Am. Hist. Assn., Am. Studies Assn., Berkshire Conf. Women Historians, Soc. 18th Century Studies, Econ. History Assn., So. MLA, Inst. Early Am. History and Culture (assoc.), So. Hist. Assn., Social Sci. History Assn., AAUW, NOW Women's Equity Action League. Democrat. Author: The Origins of Physiocracy, 1976; co-author: Fruits of Merchant Capital, 1982; assoc. editor Marxist Perspectives, 1976-80; asst. editor Partisan Rev., 1978—; mem. adv. bd. Women and History, 1982—; contbr. articles to profl. jours. Home: 115 E Upland Rd Ithaca NY 14850 Office: Dept History SUNY Binghamton NY 13901

FOXWORTH, FLORENCE GERALD, educator; b. Mullins, S.C., Aug. 20, 1931; d. McKinley and Rosa Gerald; A.B. in Elementary Edn., Benedict Coll., 1951; M.Ed. in Mental Retardation, N.C. Central U., 1974; m. Lamar Foxworth; children—Lamar, Cheryl. Tchr., Pleasant Grove Elementary Sch., Rains, S.C., 1951-57, Terrell's Bay Elementary Sch., Centenary, S.C., 1957-68, North Mullins Primary Sch., Mullins, S.C., 1968-75; spl. edn. tchr. Mullins Elementary Sch., 1975-77; tchr. Mullins High Sch., 1977—. Bd. dirs. Marion County Cancer Assn.; v.p. Assn. Retarded Citizens; mem. adminstrv. council Mental Retarded Pre-Sch. Center. Mem. Nat. Tchr's. Assn., S.C. Edn. Assn. Research on visual discrimination as an aid in teaching reading to mentally retarded.

Specialist in mental retardation, elementary edn., emotionally disturbed. Home: 801 Strawberry St Marion SC 29571 Office: Mullins High Sch Mullins SC 29574

FRACKMAN, NOEL, art critic; b. N.Y.C., May 27, 1930; d. Walter D. and Celeste (Barman) Stern; student (Sarah Williston scholar, 1950), Mt. Holyoke Coll., 1948-50; B.A., Sarah Lawrence Coll., 1952, M.A., 1953; postgrad. in art history Columbia U., 1964-67; M.A., Inst. Fine Arts, N.Y.U., 1976, now doctoral candidate; m. Richard B. Frackman, July 2, 1950; 1 dau., Noel Dru Frackman Pyne. Art critic Scarsdale (N.Y.) Inquirer, 1962-67; mus. lectr. Aldrich Mus. Contemporary Art, Ridgefield, Conn., 1967-75; lectr. Gallery Passport, Ltd., N.Y.C., 1968—; with Arts Mag., N.Y.C., 1968—, contbg. editor 1977—; curator of edn. Storm King Art Center, Mountainville, N.Y., 1973-75. Mem. Internat. Assn. Art Critics, Coll. Art Assn. Contbr. articles in field to various mags. Home: 3 Hadden Rd Scarsdale NY 10583

FRAICHE, DONNA DIMARTINO, lawyer; b. New Orleans, Dec. 8, 1951; d. Anthony and Rose Mary (Batchelona) DiMartino; student St. Mary's Dominican Coll., New Orleans, 1971, La. State U., 1972; J.D., Loyola U., New Orleans, 1975; m. John F. Fraiche, Dec. 27, 1974; 1 son, Geoffrey Michael. Admitted to La. bar, 1975, U.S. Ct. Claims bar, 1979, U.S. Tax Ct. bar, 1977, U.S. Supreme Ct. bar, 1979, since practiced in New Orleans, Baton Rouge; law clk., asso. firm Martzell & Montero, 1972-76; asso. firm McCollister, McCleary, Fazio, Mixon, Holliday and Jones, 1976-78; individual practice law, 1978-80; pres. Donna D. Fraiche, P.C., 1980—. Mem. pres.'s adv. com. to bd. Our Lady of Holy Cross Coll., New Orleans, 1979; mem. jr. women's com., Opus '81 com. New Orleans Symphony. Recipient cert. of merit Loyola U. Sch. Law, 1975. Mem. Am. Bar Assn. (mem. forum com. on health law, co-chmn. New Orleans forum com. on health law), Nat. Health Lawyers Assn. (dir. 1982-85), Am. Soc. Hosp. Attys., Am. Coll. Legal Medicine (asso.), Assn. Trial Lawyers Am., La. Trial Lawyers Assn., Am. Women Lawyers Assn., Mortar Bd., Phi Delta Phi. Past editor in chief Delta mag. La. State U. Democrat. Roman Catholic. Home: 3200 Saint Charles Ave New Orleans LA 70115 Office: 3715 Prytania St Suite 503 New Orleans LA 70115

FRALEY, MARY CLAUDICE, cellist; b. Oakland, Md., Feb. 20, 1928; d. Neil Claudice and Eleanor Curtis (Hindbaugh) F.; Mus.B., Oberlin Coll., 1950; postgrad. Juilliard Sch. Music, 1950-51; soloist diploma Longy Sch. Music, 1960; children from previous marriage—Bonnie C. Johnson, Mahlon D. Johnson. Instr. cello Oberlin (Ohio) Conservatory, 1964-65, asst. prof., 1965-66; asst. prof. music U. Tenn., Knoxville, 1966-69, assoc. prof., 1969—; concert artist. Recipient Nat. Alumni Outstanding Tchr. award U. Tenn., 1974. Mem. Women in Arts, Pi Kappa Lambda. Republican. Showcase artist, So. Artist exchange, So. Fedn. Arts, 1981. Home: 4025 Kingston Pike Knoxville TN 37919 Office: Music Dept U Tenn Knoxville TN 37919

FRALEY, RUTH ANN, librarian; b. Peekskill, N.Y., Oct. 16, 1942; d. Joseph Edward and Cora Marie (McEachern) Salerno; B.A., SUNY, Albany, 1964, M.S. in L.S., 1966; M.B.A., Union Coll. Schenectady, 1981; m. James M. Fraley, Sept. 26, 1964; children—Christine, Melissa, Heather. Library media specialist Schenectady Public Schs., part-time 1966-72; reference librarian, then head tech. services Library Resources Center, Schenectady County Community Coll., 1972-79, chmn. adv. com., 1981—; head Hawley Library, SUNY, Albany, 1979-81, head Grad. Library Public Affairs and Policy, 1981—. Recipient Chancellor's award Schenectady County Community Coll., 1979. Mem. ALA (chmn. publ. award jury resources and tech. services div. 1982—, chmn. circulation stats. com. library adminstrn. mgmt. div. 1982—), Am. Soc. Info. Scis., N.Y. Library Assn. (past pres. resources and tech. services sect.), Hudson-Mohawk Library Assn., Upstate N.Y. Labor History Assn., Albany Women's Forum. Roman Catholic. Author, editor in field. Home: 29 Roslyn Dr Ballston Lake NY 12019 Office: Hawley Library SUNY 1400 Washington Ave Albany NY 12222

FRALICK, JANETTE KAY, educator; b. Corning, N.Y., Apr. 25, 1930; d. Fred and Bernice (Bulkley) Bucher; B.A., Nazareth Coll., Rochester, N.Y., 1968, M.S., 1974; m. Roger M. Fralick, Dec. 17, 1948; children—Rebecca Lyn, Jean Ann. Tchr., Henrietta, N.Y., 1968-69, Palmyra, N.Y., 1969—. Cert. spl. edn. tchr. of handicapped. Home: 64 Garnsey Rd Pittsford NY 14534 Office: 120 Canandaigua St Palmyra NY 14522

FRAME, ADRIANNE MARIE, med. systems analyst; b. Stambaugh, Mich., Aug. 12, 1948; d. Blake Adrian and Lucy Ethel (Hickey) Jenkins; student public schs. Asheville, N.C.; m. Michael B. Frame, Nov. 16, 1968; children—Brian Blake, Eric Michael. Office mgr. Robert I. Brunton, M.D., Olympia, Wash., 1970-74; ophthalmic asst. St. Luke's Eye Clinic, New Port Richey, Fla., 1974-76; med. systems analyst Coherent, Inc., Palo Alto, Calif., 1976—. Served with U.S. Army, 1966-67. Mem. Am. Assn. Cert. Allied Health Personnel in Ophthalmology, Am. Assn. Med. Assts. (pres. 1974). Home: 130 Terry St Indian Harbour Beach FL 32937 Office: 3270 W Bayshore Rd Palo Alto CA 94303

FRAME, ANNE PARSONS (TOOTELL-BRADY), civic worker; b. Berkeley, Calif., Jan. 3, 1904; d. Reginald H. and Maude (Bemis) Parsons; B.A., Mills Coll., 1924; postgrad. Columbia U., 1924-25; m. Frederic D. Tootell, Apr. 3, 1926 (div. July 1935); children—Geoffrey Howland, Natalie Anne Tootell Oliver; m. 2d, Jasper Ewing Brady, (dec. Dec. 1944), 1 son, Hugh Parsons; m. 3d, Howard Andres Frame, Mar. 29, 1948. Dir. Parsons, Hart & Co., Parsons Investment Co., Hillcrest Orchard Corp. Mem. Park and Recreation Commn., Town of Atherton, 1972-82, vice chmn. 1972-74; bd. dirs. Wash. State Bataan Relief Soc., chmn., 1943-46; bd. dirs. Children's Health Council, Palo Alto, Calif., 1953-58, 59-76, pres., 1954-58; bd. dirs. Nat. Recreation Assn., 1949-66; bd. dirs. Nat. Recreation and Park Assn. (award 1974), 1966-73, sr. aux. to Stanford (Calif.) Convalescent Home, 1958-62, v.p., 1964-65; bd. dirs. Children's Hosp., Stanford, 1967-81; mem. bd. mgmt. Palo Alto br. ARC, 1955-61, chmn. home service com., 1950-55; mem. bd. govs. San Francisco Symphony Assn., 1963-79; trustee Children's Orthopedic Hosp. and Med. Center, Seattle, 1942-48, Mills Coll., 1952-62, chmn. student life com., 1953-58. Mem. Chgo., Seattle, Calif., San Mateo County hist. socs., Nat. Soc. of Colonial Dames, Mus. Soc. of San Francisco , Nat. Trust for Hist. Preservation. Republican. Episcopalian. Clubs: Seattle Tennis, Sunset Club of Seattle; Francisca Club of San Francisco, Woodside-Atherton Garden. Home: 587 Fletcher Dr Atherton CA 94025 Office: Parsons Hart & Co 1218 3d Ave Seattle WA 98101

FRAME, KATHRYN ALICIA, publ. exec.; b. Brewerton, N.Y., Oct. 1, 1930; d. Leonard Lionel and Kathryn Jane Ellis; B.A., Antioch Coll., Yellow Springs, Ohio, 1954; m. Norman Joseph Frame, June 29, 1956; children—David Ellsworth, Eric Norman. Asso. editor Harcourt Brace Jovanovich Publs., Duluth, Minn., 1974-79; asst. to pres. The Exec. Com., Milw., 1979—. Bd. dirs. Family Service Soc., Duluth, 1974-79. Recipient Am. Bus. Press Jesse Neal award, 1975, Melville H. Cane Scholarship Fund award, 1976. Mem. Nat. Assn. Female Execs., Am. Audiology Soc., Am. Bus. Press. Editor Hearing Instruments mag., 1974-79; contbr. articles to profl. jours. Home: 4832 N Shoreland Ave Whitefish Bay WI 53217 Office: 7101 N Green Bay Ave Milwaukee WI 53209

FRANCHINI, ROXANNE, employee benefits mgr.; b. N.Y.C., Mar. 20, 1951; d. Tullio and Jean (Brady) F.; ed. Emerson Coll., Ricker Coll., New Sch. Social Research. With Princess Marcella Borghese div. Revlon, N.Y.C., 1972-73; stewardess TWA Airlines, 1973-74; asst. to pres. N.Y. Shipping Assn., N.Y.C., 1974-79; benefits mgr. Kidde, Inc., Clifton, N.J., 1979—; coordinator community fund raising campaigns. Mem. Nat. Assn. Female Execs., Am. Mgmt. Assn., Internat. Founds. Employee Benefits. Office: 9 Brighton Rd Clifton NJ 07015

FRANCIS, FADRA SUE, collection and repossession co. exec.; b. Winnsboro, Tex., Dec. 12, 1926; Henry Sylvester and Sally Mae (Boone) Brown; grad. Fed. Inst. Bus. Sch., Tyler, Tex., 1946; m. Robert H. Francis, Jan. 28, 1949 (dec.); children—Bobbie Sue, Debbie Lou. Sec., M. Oliver Rose Farm, Tyler, 1946-47, Reilly Oil Co., Tyler, 1947-48; office mgr. Caruthers Jewelry Store and Sch. Horology, Tyler, 1948-51; co-owner R. H. Francis Co., Tyler, 1951-54, owner, San Antonio, 1954—. Leader, San Antonio council Girl Scouts U.S.A. Mem. Allied Fin. Adjusters Conf., Nat. Fin. Adjusters, Am. Recovery Assn., Nat. Fedn. Ind. Bus., Greater San Antonio C. of C. Baptist. Clubs: Sunridge, Daus. of Nile. Home: 1263 Bandera Rd San Antonio TX 78228 Office: 1263 Bandera Rd Sn Antonio TX 78228

FRANCISCO, ALICE NEPOMUCENO, physician; b. Manila, Nov. 17, 1937; d. Augusto Santos Nepomuceno and Mercedes (Balingit) Cuyugan Nepomuceno; M.D., U. Santo Tomas, 1961; m. Aris Francisco, Dec. 29, 1959; children—Christan, Armel, Aris II, Alice Regina. Intern U. Santo Tomas Hosp., 1960-61; practice gen. medicine Angeles City, Philippines, 1962-69; mem. med. staff United Med. Services, N.Y.C., 1969-72; staff physician Jewish Home & Hosp. N.Y.C., 1972-76; resident in diagnostic radiology St. Luke's Hosp., N.Y.C., 1976-79; asst. chief diagnostic radiology USPHS Hosp., S.I., 1979-81; practice medicine specializing in diagnostic radiology and imaging, West New York, N.J., 1981—; asst. clin. prof. diagnostic radiology Columbia U., N.Y.C., 1981—; sec. Golden Acres Corp.; dir. Philippine Am. Travel Services. Bd. dirs. Bergen County Congress Filipino-Am. Citizens, 1978—, N.J. Fedn. Filipino Socs., 1971-73. Diplomate Am. Bd. Radiology. Mem. N.J. Women's Med. Assn., N.Y. Gerontol. Soc., Philippines Am. Med. Assn., N.Y. Roentgen Soc., Am. Coll. Radiology, Radiol. Soc. N. Am., Am. Inst. Ultrasound in Medicine, Am. Roentgen Ray Soc., Philippine Am. Med. Soc. N.J., Assn. Filipino Practicing Physicians Am., Bergen County Med. Soc., Assn. Filipino-Ams. in Bergen County. Roman Catholic. Author: FLEX and ECFM6 Medical Reviewer, 1975; radiology text for physician asst. program, 1980. Home: 579 Teaneck Rd Ridgefield Park NJ 07660

FRANCISCO, JACQUELINE TUFARIELLO, psychologist; b. Newark, May 18, 1945; d. Domenick J. and Alice R. (Gesumaria) Tufariello; B.A. (sr. fellow), Jersey City State U., 1966; M.Ed. (grad. fellow), U. Miami, 1968; Psy.D., Rutgers U., 1979; m. David Francisco, July 4, 1974. Psychologist, East Hanover (N.J.) Bd. Edn., 1976, Florham Park (N.J.) Bd. Edn., 1977; coordinator spl. services dept. Denville (N.J.) Bd. Edn., 1978; psychologist Livingston (N.J.) Bd. Edn., 1979; pvt. practice psychology, East Hanover, N.J., 1979—; adj. prof. William Paterson Coll., 1975. Mem. Am. Psychol. Assn., N.J. Assn. Sch. Psychologists, Council Exceptional Children (pres.), Nat. Assn. Sch. Psychologists. Home and Office: 156 Overlook Ave East Hanover NJ 07936

FRANCKE, KATHARINE ELIZABETH, real estate and ins. co. exec.; b. Santa Rita, N.Mex., Sept. 24, 1942; d. Bronson Coxe and Juanita (Jackson) Lansing; grad. N.Y. Inst. Fin., 1976. Exec., Florida Realty, Inc., Indpls., 1967-71; v.p. Vista West Properties, Inc., Indpls., Chgo., 1971-75; account exec. E.F. Hutton and Co., Colorado Springs, Denver, 1975-76; v.p. sales and adminstrn. Conserv-Electric, Inc., Kansas City, Mo., 1976-78; exec. v.p. Mary Rae and Assos., Ltd., Denver, 1978-79; housing dir. Gen. Devel. Corp., Indpls., 1979-80, Chgo., 1980-81; v.p. Valley Vista Enterprises, Ltd., 1981—. Mem. LWV, Sales and Mktg. Execs., Am. Bus. Women's Assn. Republican. Episcopalian. Address: 11195 E Linvale Dr Aurora CO 80014

FRANCOVILLA, MARY ANN, banker; b. N.Y.C., Aug. 31, 1954; d. Anthony Peter and Josephine Genevieve (Presta) F.; student SUNY, Oswego, 1972-74, Fordham U., 1975-77. Prodn. control asst. CBS TV Network, N.Y.C., 1975-76; ops. coordinator CBS Radio Network, N.Y.C., 1976-77, asso. dir., 1977-78; account exec. Merrill Lynch, Pierce, Fenner & Smith, Inc., N.Y.C., 1978-79; sales rep. Barclays Visa travelers cheques div. Barclays Bank Internat., N.Y.C., 1979-80, asst. v.p., regional sales mgr., Dallas, 1980-82, v.p., sales mgr.-south, 1982—. Registered rep. N.Y. Stock Exchange, Am. Stock Exchange, Nat. Assn. Securities Dealers. Mem. Nat. Assn. Female Execs., Am. Mgmt. Assn. Home: 8110 Skillman Apt 2034 Dallas TX 75231 Office: Barclays Bank Internat 8200 Brookriver Dr Suite 502N Dallas TX 75247

FRANDELL-SPICER, CAROL JEAN, educator; b. Portland, Oreg., Aug. 27, 1940; B.A., San Diego State U., 1965. Elem. sch. tchr., 1965-75; spl. edn. tchr., 1975-77; program specialist spl. edn. San Diego city schs., 1978—. Guild chmn. San Diego Opera Assn., 1976; v.p. awards Freedoms Found., 1979-80. Mem. Council Exceptional Children (membership chmn. 1976-80), Assn. San Diego Educators Gifted (rec. sec. 1978, dir. 1978-80), Calif. Assn. Program Specialists, Feingold Assn., San Diego State U. Alumni Assn., Calif. Fedn. Women's Clubs (chmn. 1973-76). Club: San Diego Jr. Woman's (pres. 1970; Outstanding Citizen of Year award 1971). Address: 9864-C Apple Tree Dr San Diego CA 92124

FRANK, EDITH SINAIKO, civic worker; b. Madison, Wis., July 16, 1902; d. Isaac and Sarah (Goldberg) Sinaiko; B.A., U. Wis., 1924; postgrad. Wheeler Sch. Music, 1922, Cosmopolitan Sch. Music, 1926-42; m. David S. Frank, June 24, 1924 (dec. 1962); 1 dau., Suzanne Frank Freund. Pres., Toledo Friends of Library, 1949; mem. bd. Madison Friends of Library, 1973; mem. bd. Toledo Symphony Orch., 1951; mem. women's aux. Chgo. Symphony, 1951; mem. bd. Met. Housing and Planning Council Chgo.; pres. women's council City Renewal, Chgo.; mem. bd. Madison Civic Center Commn., 1973-82; mem. bd. Found. for Arts, 1974—; bd. curators Aux. State Hist. Soc. Wis., 1976, pres. aux., 1974-76; mem. bd. Madison Found., 1976—. Recipient Service award Municipal Defense Council, Charleston, W.Va., 1945, Outstanding Citizen award Toledo Newspaper Guild, 1951, Page I Citizenship award Madison Newspaper Guild, 1976, award Rotary Club, 1976. Mem. Women in Communications (pres. Madison chpt. 1966), Madison Press Club (sec. 1969-70), Wis. Acad. Scis., Arts and Letters, LWV, Theta Sigma Phi. Clubs: Arts (Chgo.); University (Madison, Wis.). Home: 1515 Vilas Ave Madison WI 53711

FRANK, ELAINE KOENIGSDORF, lawyer; b. Kansas City, Mo.; d. Henry and Dorothy Belle (Levin) Koenigsdorf; cert. Lindenwood Coll., 1937; student McKay's Bus. Coll., 1948; LL.B., Southwestern U., 1957; children—Babette Frank Naslund, Robert Nelson Frank, Jr. Legal sec., Los Angeles, 1948-57; admitted to Calif. bar, 1958; research atty. Los Angeles Superior Ct., 1958-59; atty. Belli, Ashe & Gerry, San Francisco, 1959; research atty. Calif. Supreme Ct.-Calif. Jud. Council, 1959-60; practiced in Los Altos, 1961—; atty.-editor Commerce Clearing House, San Francisco, 1961-62; staff atty. Continuing Edn. of Bar, U. Calif., Berkeley, 1963-75; corp. counsel, dir. legal econs. Capital Diversified Internat., Ltd., 1978—. Mem. curriculum guide com. Calif. Community Colls., 1973-74; mem. adv. com. legal forms Jud. Council, 1974-79. Mem. Am. Judicature Soc., State Bar Calif. (recorder com. on probate and trust law 1970-77), Santa Clara County Bar Assn., Am. Fedn. Tchrs., Alumni Assn. Southwestern U. Sch. Law, Themis Soc., Harry S. Truman Library Inst., Internat. Platform Assn., Iota Tau Tau. Author, editor: California Civil Court Forms, 1972; editor, co-author: California Civil Writs, 1970. Home and Office: 1405 Montclaire Pl Los Altos CA 94022

FRANK, FLORENCE MILDRED, pvt. vocat. sch. co. exec.; b. Irvington, N.J., June 5, 1931; d. William and Bertha Anne (Knull) F.; grad. Inst. Certified Travel Agts., 1977; m. Murray Goldberg, Mar. 6, 1971. Office mgr. Skil Corp., Hillside, N.J., 1950-56; corp. sec., real estate broker Nicolson, Porter and List, Inc., Chgo., 1956-71; pres. Internat. Travel Tng. Courses, Inc., Washington, 1971—, also dir.; cons. dept. adult edn. U. Md. Bd. dirs. Community Assns. Inst., Washington, 1976—. Mem. Inst. Certified Travel Agts., Bon Vivants, Pacific Area Travel Assn., Am. Soc. Travel Agts., Internat. Travel Soc. Club: Quota, Prost (Washington). Home: 2716 Unicorn Ln NW Washington DC 20015 Office: 5100 Wisconsin Ave NW Washington DC 20016

FRANK, LORAINE SERWIN, state ofcl., lawyer; b. Passaic, N.J.; d. John and Katherine Serwin; B.S., Okla. State U., 1951, M.S., 1952; J.D., U. Okla., 1973; m. Reginald Hull Frank, May 31, 1952; children—Liane Renee, Lisa Roanne. Mem. home econs. faculty Arkansas City (Kans.) Jr. Coll., 1960-63, Perkins (Okla.) High Sch., 1956-58, U. Tulsa, 1952-53; field rep. U.S. Census Bur., 1960; condr. various surveys, 1964-65; salesman Carousel Realty, Del City, Okla., 1968-69; admitted to Okla. bar, 1974; atty. Public Defender's Office, Mcpl. Ct., Oklahoma City, 1974-75; cons. atty. child support enforcement unit Okla. Dept. Instns., Social and Rehab. Services, Oklahoma City, 1975-77; adminstr. Okla. Bd. Property and Casualty Rates, Oklahoma City, 1977—; sec. bd. mgrs. Okla. State Ins. Fund. Mem. Okla. Bar Assn., Cleveland County Bar Assn., Bus. and Profl. Women's Club. Presbyterian. Office: 401 Will Rogers Bldg State Capitol Oklahoma City OK 73105

FRANK, MARION RUDIN, psychologist, organizational cons.; b. Phila., June 1, 1942; d. Bernard and Eve (Rochlin) Rudin; B.A., Pa. State U., 1963; student U. Strasbourg (France), spring 1962; M.A., Columbia U., 1967; Ed.D., Temple U., 1977; 1 dau., Jilian Beth. Instr., Temple U., 1972-79; tng. grantee Regional Tng. Inst. for Aging, 1979-80, Council on Drug and Alcohol Abuse, 1976-77; psychol. cons. on gerontology, chronic illness, stress, corp. mgmt., women's issues, Phila., 1971—, Kaslow Med. Self-Care Center, 1979—; seminar leader Ins. Co. N.Am., 1978-80, Epilepsy Commn. of Med. Coll. Pa., 1977—, Inst. of Awareness, 1975—; pvt. practice psychotherapy, Phila., 1976—; exec. dir. Eastern Cons. Assos., 1980—; pres. Health Resource Coalition of Del. Valley, 1980—; pres. Internat. Epilepsy Network; co-founder Women Assos., cons. firm, health resource network, Phila., 1975—; founder Progressive Epilepsy Network; cons. ACLU, 1970. Lic. psychologist, Pa. Mem. Nat. Assn. Humanistic Gerontology (regional coordinator), Am. Psychol. Assn., Pa. Psychol. Assn. (sec. community psychology div.), Assn. Humanistic Psychology (workshop leader), Center for Study Psychoednl. Processes (adv. bd.), Phila. Women's Network (dir.), Am. Soc. Tng. and Devel., NOW, Women's Internat. League for Peace and Freedom, West Mt. Airy Neighbors, Germantown Dance Theatre. Jewish. Home: 402 W Mt Airy Ave Philadelphia PA 19119 Office: Suite 624 1315 Walnut St Philadelphia PA 15218

FRANK, MARJORIE HOFHEIMER (MRS. CHRIS GABLE), city health ofcl., educator; b. N.Y.C., Feb. 25, 1906; d. Arthur and Helen (Milius) Hofheimer; student Columbia Sch. Bus. Adminstrn., 1924; m. Harry Frank, Jr., Oct. 14, 1926 (dec. Mar. 1963); m. 2d, Christopher Gable, Dec. 29, 1969. Dir. service in VA hosps., North Atlantic area ARC, 1945-49; asst. exec. dir. Nat. Assn. Mental Health, N.Y.C., 1949-59; asso. exec. sec. Nat. Family Life Found., 1959-61, asso. adminstrv. dir. Jewish Guild for Blind, N.Y.C., 1961-63; N.Y.C. regional planning rep. N.Y. Dept. Mental Hygiene, 1963-65, asst. to commr. N.Y.C. Community Mental Health Services, 1965-68; instr. adminstrv. sch. public health Columbia U., 1968-73, dept. psychiatry, 1968—, adminstrv. asso. to chmn. dept. psychiatry 1968-75; spl. cons. N.Y.C. Comprehensive Health Planning Agy., 1973-74; cons. New Sch. Social Research, N.Y.C., 1974-76, faculty, 1976—; spl. cons. N.Y.C. Comprehensive Health Planning Agy., 1973-74; asso. dir. mental health services Gouverneur Hosp., N.Y.C. Health and Hosp. Corp., 1973-76; rehab. cons. N.Y. Dept. Mental Hygiene, N.Y.C. Regional Office, 1976-78, N.Y.C. Health Systems Agy., 1978-79; dir. grants devel. and mgmt. Met. Hosp., N.Y.C. Health and Hosp. Corp., 1979—. Dep. comdr. Warren Twp. (N.J.) CD, 1940-45; bd. mem.-at-large Plainfield Council Social Agys., 1944-47; founder, pres. Union County Mental Hygiene Soc., 1944-49; adv. council on citizen participation Community Chests and Councils of Am., 1951-57; mem. bd. Psychoanalytic Research and Devel. Fund; alt. pres. Nathan Hofheimer Found., 1959-75. Fellow Am. Public Health Assn., Am. Orthopsychiat. Assn. Unitarian. Home: 1155 Park Ave New York NY 10028

FRANK, MARY ANNA, business exec.; b. Plainfield, N.J.; d. Jacob Alfred and Christine (Manhattan) Frank; student Rutgers U., Upsala Coll., certificate in advt. Tex. Christian U., 1967. With Liberty Mut. Ins. Co., 1941-47; advt. mgr. Am. Handicrafts Co. div. Tandy Corp., East Orange N.J., 1947-53, Tandy Leather Co., Ft. Worth, 1953-64, dir. marketing services Tandy Corp., Ft. Worth, 1964-67, dir. corporate relations, 1967-74; advt. mgr. Am. Handicrafts Co. div. Tandycrafts, Inc., 1974-76; gen. mgr. Telephone and Safehouse Retail Booth div. Tandy Corp., 1977-81. Chmn., Ft. Worth unit Postal Customer Council. Bd. dirs. YMCA, Tarrant County Easter Seal Soc., Ft. Worth Better Bus. Council, Am. Heart Assn., Tarrant County chpt. ARC. Named One of Top 10 Women in Advt., Am. Advt. Fedn., 1971; Exec. Woman of Year, Ft. Worth chpt. Zonta Internat., 1973. Mem. Ft. Worth Advt. Club, Ft. Worth Direct Mail Club (pres. 1969), Theta Sigma Phi (treas. 1966-67). Home: 3301 Bellaire Dr Apt 56 Fort Worth TX 76109

FRANK, PAULA FELDMAN (MRS. GORDON D. FRANK), business exec.; b. Tulsa; d. Maurice M. and Sarah (Bergman) Feldman; B.S., Northwestern U., 1954; m. Gordon D. Frank, Dec. 15, 1955; children—Cynthia Jan, Margaret Jill. Directed, wrote and appeared in TV films for Nat. Safety Council, Chgo., 1954-55; appeared in TV commls., 1955-56; asst. prodn. mgr. Kling Films, Chgo., 1956; now pres. Gaston Ave. Optical Inc., Dallas. Social chmn. Baylor Hosp. Vol. Corp., Dallas, 1962-—; asst. dir. Des Plaines (Ill.) Theater Guild, 1956-57, Pearl Chappell Playhouse, Dallas, 1962-63, Dallas Theater Center, 1964. Mem. Hockaday Alumni Assn., Idle Wives Book Rev. Club (treas.), Tau Gamma Epsilon, Phi Beta, Sigma Delta Tau. Home: 7123 Currin Dr Dallas TX 75230

FRANK, RUBY MERINDA, employment agy. exec.; b. McClusky, N.D., June 28, 1920; d. John J. and Olise (Stromme) Hanson; student in bus. adminstrn., coll., Mankato, Minn., also Aurora (Ill.) Coll.; m. Robert G. Frank, Jan. 14, 1944 (dec. 1973); children—Gary Frank, Craig. Exec. sec., office mgr. Nat. Container Corp., Chgo., 1943-50; owner, operator Frank's Office & Employment Service, St. Charles, Ill., 1957—; dir. St. Charles Savings & Loan Assn. Sec. bd. trustees Delnor Hosp., St. Charles, 1959—, also life mem. women's aux.; vice chairwoman Kane County (Ill.) Republican Com., 1968-77; pres. Women's Rep. Club, 1969-77; adv. council Dellora A. Norris Cultural Arts Center. Named Fox Valley Exec. of Yr., 1982. Mem. St. Charles C. of C. (pres., dir. 1976—), Kane-DuPage Personnel Assn. (v.p. 1971—), Nat., Ill. employment assns., Ill. Assn. Personnel Cons. (dir.). Lutheran. Clubs: St. Charles Country; Execs. of Chgo. Contbr. weekly broadcast Sta. WGSB, 1965-80. Home: 534 Longmeadow Circle Saint Charles IL 60174 Office: Arcada Theater Bldg 12 S 1st Ave Saint Charles IL 60174

FRANK, SELMA, civic worker; b. St. Louis, Apr. 20, 1907; d. Abraham Marcus and Rachel (Klein) Pachter; student Washington U., St. Louis, 1924-75; m. Maurice Frank, Jan. 17, 1932; 1 dau., Mrs. Ray Dobinsky. Mem. pub. relations com. St. Louis council Girl Scouts Am., 1942; mem. pub. relations com. Miriam Convalescent Hosp., 1946; active Women's Assn. St. Louis Symphony, 1953-82; editor Bear Facts, Washington U. Women's Assn., 1975-79; exec. dir., mgr. Little Symphony Concerts

Assn. Summer Concerts, Washington U., 1948-80; exec. sec. St. Louis sect. Nat. Council Jewish Women, 1955-71; mem. spl. com. Tapes for Blind Listeners of Radio Info. Source, Lady of Snows, Belleville, Ill., 1979—. Mem. Nat. Soc. Arts and Letters. Home: 404 Marford Dr Saint Louis MO 63141

FRANK, SHERAL LEE, sales exec.; b. Carbondale, Ill., Apr. 3, 1952; d. Finis Lee and Ruth Marie (Richardson) Frank; B.A. in Psychology and Social Work, U. Nebr., 1974; M.B.A., Pepperdine U., 1982. Patient care coordinator Jersey Shore Med. Center, Community Mental Health Center, Neptune, N.J., 1974-76; psychiat. social worker Project Anchor Liaison, Ocean County Mental Health Center, Toms River, N.J., 1976-78; lumber broker U.S. Forest Products, Inc., Phoenix, 1978-79; ter. mgr. operating room products div. The Kendall Co., Boston, 1979—; operating room systems analysis and design cons. med. centers and hosps. Vol. March of Dimes, United Way, Am. Heart Assn. Mem. Internat. Assn. Central Service Mgmt., Am. Soc. Group Psychotherapy and Psychodrama, Nat. Assn. Female Execs., Curity Club, Alpha Phi. Club: Westwood Ski. Home: 2923 Yale Ave Marina del Rey CA 90291 Office: 1 Federal St Boston MA 02101

FRANKEL, BETTY SOPHIA, writer, landscape designer; b. N.Y.C., Mar. 26, 1923; d. Harry B. and Estelle Ruth (Weil) Schwartz; B.S. in Botany, U. Mich., 1944; M.Landscape Architecture, U. Mich., 1973; m. Richard W. Frankel, Feb. 7, 1943; children—Martha, Barbara, Edward. Tchr., Elmira (N.Y.) Schs., 1945-46; tchr. English and art Farmington (Mich.) schs., 1962; asst. botanist Cranbrook Inst. Sci., Bloomfield Hills, Mich., 1964-65; garden writer Observer Newspapers, Mich., 1958-71, Detroit Free Press, 1969—; freelance garden and landscape designer, Farmington Hills, Mich., 1973—; lectr. in field. Mem. Farmington Hills Park Commn., 1971-80. Mem. Garden Writers Assn. Am., Mich. Assn. Landscape Architects, AAUW, Federated Garden Clubs Mich., Mich. Bot. Club, Mich. Nature Assn., Phi Sigma, Phi Kappa Phi. Democrat. Jewish. Author: Adventures in Landscaping, 1973. Home and office: 30300 Rockshire Rd Farmington Hills MI 48018

FRANKEL, DEXTRA LORENE, artist, educator; b. Los Angeles, Nov. 28, 1924; d. Melville and Lorene Leota (Radcliffe) Coakley; student John Muir Jr. Coll., Pasadena, Calif., 1950-52, Valley Jr. Coll., Van Nuys, Calif., 1955-56, Long Beach State Coll., 1957-60; cert. mus. mgmt., U. Calif., Berkeley, 1979; div.; 1 son, Kenneth. Exhibiting artist, 1956-70; organizer 24 major exhbns. mus. or galleries, also designer 13 exhbns. in Pasadena, Los Angeles, Laguna Beach, Long Beach, Calif., Honolulu, Phoenix, Albuquerque, and Tokyo; public lectr., 1957—; recipient archtl. commns. in metal sculpture, 1960-67; instr. art Calif. State U., Fullerton, 1965-67; dir. art gallery, prof. art Calif. State U., Fullerton, 1967—; partner Lax Design Studio 1976—; art exhbn. juror, 1958—; U.S. del. World Crafts Conf., Mex., 1976; mem. cultural and fine arts adv. com. Olympic Games, 1981-84; bd. dirs. Fine Arts Commn., Images and Issues mag., 1981-84; condr. exhbn. design workshops. Recipient design award for Print Casebooks, the Best in Exhn. Design, 1977, 79; design award For the Record: The West Coast Show, Western Art Dirs. Club, 1979; Silver Medallion award YWCA, 1981, design award The 1981 Chicago STA/100 Society of Typog. Arts, Union Bank History Mus., 1981; Nat. Endowment for Arts mus. profl. grantee, 1978; 13 individual and found. grants for spl. exhbns., 1970-81, 8 Nat. Endowment for Arts grants for spl. exhbns., 1975-83. Mem. Am. Assn. Mus., Am. Inst. Graphic Arts, Am. Craft Council (trustee 1975-78), Western Assn. Art Mus. Art Mus. Assn. (trustee 1978-81). Office: Calif State University 800 N State College Blvd Fullerton CA 92634

FRANKEL, KIMBERLY CONDE, judge; b. Jersey City, Feb. 9, 1945; d. Henry and Maria Philomena (Maiden) F.; student U. Oreg., 1961-63, B.A., 1965, J.D., 1969; student Portland State U., Pavia, Italy, 1963-64. Admitted to Oreg. bar, 1970; law clk. Oreg. Ct. Appeals, Salem, 1969-71; dep. dist. atty. Multnomah County, Portland, 1971-76; atty. Oreg. Traffic Safety Commn., Portland, 1976-78; tchr. Portland Police Bur., 1972-74, Multnomah County Sheriff's Dept., 1972-74, Oreg. Police Acad., 1976—, Nat. Inst. Trial Advocacy, 1977; faculty Nat. Jud. Coll., 1980—; lectr. N.W. Traffic Inst., 1979; instr. Wash. State Patrol Acad., Idaho State Patrol Acad.; mem. Jud. Conduct Com., 1978-79, Jud. Edn. Com., 1978; dir. negligent homicide project Dist. Atty.'s Office, 1973. Vol. worker Headstart, also Valley Migrant League, Salem; bd. dirs. Multnomah County Legal Aid, 1974-75. Mem. Am., Oreg., bar Multnomah County assns., Am. Judicature Soc., Oreg. Hist. Soc., Portland Art Assn., Kappa Tau Alpha. Co-author: Arraignment and Related Procedures. Office: 1021 SW 4th St Suite 322 Portland OR 97204

FRANKENTHALER, HELEN, painter; b. N.Y.C., Dec. 12, 1928; d. Alfred and Martha (Lowenstein) Frankenthaler; B.A., Bennington Coll., 1949; L.H.D., Skidmore Coll., 1969; D.F.A., Smith Coll., 1973, Moore Coll. Art, 1974, Bard Coll., 1976, Radcliffe Coll., 1978, Amherst Coll., 1979, N.Y.U., 1979, Phila. Coll. Art, 1980, Williams Coll., 1980, Harvard U., 1980, Yale U., 1981; m. Robert Motherwell, Apr. 6, 1958. One woman shows include: Tibor de Nagy Gallery, N.Y.C., 1951-58, Andre Emmerich Gallery, N.Y.C., 1959-63, 65, 66, 68, 69, 71-73, 75-77, 78, 79, 81, Jewish Mus., N.Y.C., 1960, Everett Ellin Gallery, Los Angeles, 1961, Galerie Lawrence, Paris, 1961-63, Bennington Coll., 1962, 78, Galleria dell'Ariete, Milan, 1962, Kasmin Gallery, London, 1964, David Mirvish Gallery, Toronto, 1965-71, 73, 75, Gertrude Kasle Gallery, Detroit, 1967, 71, Nicholas Wilder Gallery, Los Angeles, 1967, Andre Emmerich Gallery, Zurich, 1974, Swarthmore (Pa.) Coll., 1974, Solomon R. Guggenheim Mus., N.Y.C., 1975, Corcoran Gallery Art, Washington, 1975, Seattle Art Mus., 1975, Mus. Fine Arts, Houston, 1975, Ace Gallery, Vancouver, B.C., Can., 1975, Rosa Esman Gallery, N.Y.C., 1975, 3d Internat. Contemporary Art Fair, Paris, 1976, Gimpel-Hanover and Andre Emmerich Gallery, Zurich, 1980; retrospective Whitney Mus. Am. Art, 1969, Whitechapel Gallery, London, 1969, Kongresshalle, Berlin, Kunstverein, Hanover, 1969, Heath Gallery, Atlanta, 1971, Galerie Godard Lefort, Montreal, 1971, Fendrick Gallery, Washington, 1972, 74, 79, 80, Carl Solway, Cin., 1972, John Berggruen Gallery, San Francisco, 1972, 76, 79, 82, Portland (Oreg.) Art Mus., 1972, Waddington Galleries II, London, 1973, 74, Janie C. Lee Gallery, Dallas, 1973, Houston, 1975, 76, 78, 80, 82, Met. Mus. Art, N.Y.C., 1973, Cologne Art Fair, 1974, Gallery Diane Gilson, Seattle, 1976, Greenberg Gallery, St. Louis, 1977, Galerie Wentzel, Hamburg, Ger., 1977, Jacksonville (Fla.) Art Mus., 1977-78, Ft. Lauderdale (Fla.) Mus. Arts, 1978, Loch Haven Art Center, Orlando, Fla., 1978, Internat. Communications Agy. Exhbn., N.Y.C., 1978 (travelled to Japan, Taiwan, Phillipines, Singapore, Australia, Mex., Venezuela, Colombia, Brazil 1978-79), Knoedler Gallery, London, 1978, 81, Atkins Mus. Fine Art, William Rockhill Nelson Gallery Art, Kansas City, Mo., 1978, Saginaw (Mich.) Art Mus., 1980, U. Mich. Art Mus., Ann Arbor, 1980, Grand Rapids (Mich.) Art Mus., 1980, Kalamazoo (Mich.) Inst. Arts, 1980, Sterling and Francine Clark Art Inst., Williamstown, Mass., 1980 (travelled to Phillips Collection, Washington, 1980, Birmingham (Ala.) Mus. Art, 1981, Toledo Mus. Art, 1981, Palm Springs (Calif.) Desert Mus., 1981, Santa Barbara (Calif.) Mus. Art, 1981, Mus. Fine Arts, Boston, 1981), Galerie Ulysses, Vienna, 1980, Rose Art Mus., Brandeis U., 1981, Thomas Segal Gallery, Boston, 1981; exhibited in group shows including: Whitney Mus., 1958, 71, 77, 78, Carnegie Internat., Pitts., 1955, 58, 61, 64, Columbus Gallery Fine Arts, 1960, Guggenheim Mus., 1961, 76, 77, Seattle World's Fair, 1962, Art Inst. Chgo., 1963, 69, 72, 76, San Francisco Mus. Art, 1963, 68, Krannert Mus., U. Ill., 1959, 63, 65, 67, Washington Gallery Modern Art, 1963, Pa. Acad. Fine Arts, 1963, 68, 76, N.Y. World's Fair, 1964, Am. Fedn. Arts Circulating Exhbn., 1964, U. Austin Art Mus., 1964, Rose Art Mus. Circulating Exhbn., 1964, Detroit Inst. Arts, 1965, 67, U. Mich. Mus. Art, 1965, Md. Inst., 1966, Norfolk Mus. Arts and Scis., 1966, Venice Biennale, 1966, Smithsonian Instn., 1966, 78, 80, Expo '67, Montreal, 1967, Washington Gallery Modern Art, 1967, Ga. Mus. Art, Athens, 1967, U. Okla. Mus. Art, Norman, 1968, Philbrook Art Center, Tulsa, 1968, Cin. Mus., 1968, U. Calif., San Diego, 1968, Mus. Modern Art, N.Y.C., 1969-75, 80, Met. Mus., N.Y.C., 1969-70, 76, 79, Va. Mus., Richmond, 1970, 74, Balt. Mus. Art, 1970, 76, Boston U., 1970, Boston Mus. Fine Arts, 1972, Des Moines Art Center, 1973, Mus. Fine Arts, Houston, 1974, Smith Coll. Mus. Art, Northampton, Mass., 1974, El Instituto de Cultura Puertorriquena, San Juan, 1974, Basil Art Fair, Basel, Switzerland, 1974, 76, 78, Finch Coll. Mus. Art, N.Y.C., 1974, S.I. Mus., 1975, Denver Art Mus., 1975, 76, Visual Arts Mus., N.Y.C., 1975, 76, Mus. Modern Art, Belgrade, Yugoslavia, 1976, Galleria d'Arts Moderna, Rome, 1976, Am. Art since 1945 from the collection of Mus. Modern Art, Worcester (Mass.) Art Mus., 1976, Toledo Art Mus., 1976, Denver Art Mus., 1976, Fine Arts Gallery San Diego, 1976, Dallas Mus. Fine Arts, 1976, Joslyn Art Mus., Omaha, Greenville (S.C.) County Mus., 1977, Va. Mus. Fine Arts, Richmond, 1977, Bronx Mus. Arts, 1977, Everson Mus. Art, Syracuse, 1976, Chrysler Mus. Norfolk, Art Ins. Chgo., 1976, Seibu Mus., Tokyo, 1977, 78, Orangerie of Charlottenburg Palace, West Berlin, W.Ger., 1977, Tacoma Art Mus., 1977, Mus. Art Wash. State U., Pullman, 1977, Cheney Dowles Meml. State Mus., Spokane, Wash., 1977, Detroit Inst. Arts, 1977, San Francisco Mus. Modern Art, 1977, Cooper-Hewitt Mus., 1977, Fogg Art Mus., Cambridge, Mass., 1978, Cranbrook Acad. Art Mus., Bloomfield Hills, Mich., 1978, Newport Harbor Art Mus., Newport, R.I., 1979, Oakland Mus., Cin., 1979, Mus. S.Tex., Corpus Christi, 1979, Krannert Art Mus., Champaign, Ill., 1979-80, Art Gallery Ont., Toronto, 1979, Sierra Nev. Mus., Reno, 1979, Corcoran Gallery Art, Washington, 1979; represented in permanent collections: Met. Mus. Art, Bklyn. Mus., Solomon R. Guggenheim Mus., N.Y.U., Mus. Modern Art, Whitney Mus. (all N.Y.C.), Albright-Knox Art Gallery, Buffalo, Milw. Art Inst., Wadsworth Atheneum, Hartford, Newark Mus., Yale U. Art Gallery, U. Nebr. Art Gallery, Carnegie Inst., Pitts., Detroit Inst. Art, Balt., Mus. Art, Univ. Mus., Berkeley, Calif., Bennington (Vt.) Coll., Art Inst. Chgo., Cin. Art Mus., Cleve. Mus. Art, Honolulu Acad. Arts, Contemporary Arts Assn., Houston, Pasadena Art Mus., City Art Mus., St. Louis, Mus. Art, R.I. Sch. Design, Providence, San Francisco Mus. Art, Everson Mus., Syracuse, N.Y., Smithsonian Instn., Walker Art Inst., Mpls., Washington Gallery Modern Art, Nat. Gallery Victoria, Melbourne, Australia, Australian Nat. Gallery, Canberra, Victoria and Albert Mus., London, Tokyo Mus., Ulster Mus., Belfast, No. Ireland, Elvenhjem Art Center, U. Wis., Newark Mus., Phila. Mus. Art, Phoenix Art Mus., Corcoran Gallery Art, Washington, Boston Mus. Fine Arts, Springfield (Mass.) Mus. Fine Arts, Witte Mus., San Antonio, Abbott Hall Art Gallery, Kendal, Eng., Mus. Contemporary Art, Nagaoka, Japan, numerous others; mem. faculty Yale U., 1966, 67, 70, 78, Hunter Coll., 1970, Princeton U., 1971, Cooper Union, N.Y.C., 1972, Skidmore Coll., 1973, Swarthmore Coll., 1974, Drew U., 1975, Harvard U., 1976, Radcliffe Coll., 1976, also N.Y.U., U. Pa., Sch. Visual Arts Goucher Coll., Washington U., Yale Grad. Sch., Detroit Inst. Arts, 1977, Bard Coll., Annandale-on-Hudson, N.Y., 1977, U. Ariz., Tucson, 1978, Davenport Coll., 1978, others. U.S. rep. Venice Biennale, 1966. Trustee Bennington Coll., 1967. Fellow Calhoun Coll., Yale U., 1968. Recipient 1st prize for painting Paris Biennale, 1959; Gold medal Pa. Acad. Fine Arts, 1968; Great Ladies award Fordham U., Thomas Moore Coll., 1969; Spirit of Achievement award Albert Einstein Coll. Medicine, 1970; Gold medal Commune of Catania, III, Biennale della Grafica d'Arte, Florence, Italy, 1972; Garrett award 70th Am. Exhbn., Art Inst. Chgo., 1972; Creative Arts awards Nat. Women's div. Am. Jewish Congress, 1974; Art and Humanities award Yale Women's Forum, 1976; An Extraordinary Woman of Achievement award 50th Anniversary NCCJ, 1978; Outstanding Achievement award Bennington Coll. Alumni, 1979. Mem. Nat. Inst. Arts and Letters. Address: 173 E 94th St New York NY 10028 *

FRANKFORT, LILA, hosp. adminstr.; b. Uniontown, Pa., Apr. 11; d. Rudolph and Rose (Lebowitz) Fragner; cert. hosp. mgmt., Rutgers U., 1975; m. Leonard J. Frankfort, Jan. 9; children—Judith, Hollace, Michelle. Asst. public affairs dir. Hackensack (N.J.) Med. Center, 1967-69; community relations exec. Barnert Meml. Hosp. Center, Paterson, N.J., 1969—. Trustee Teaneck Community Blood Assn., 1965-74; pres. Am. Jewish Congress, 1968-69; chmn. fund raising Jewish Center, Teaneck, N.J., 1981. Mem. Am. Hosp. Assn., Am. Soc. Hosp. Public Relations, N.J. Hosp. Assn., N.J. Hosp. Public Relations Assn. (exec. com. 1978-81), Nat. Fedn. Press Women, N.J. Press Women, Bergen/Passaic Hosp. Public Relations Council (chmn. 1981). Clubs: Westmount Country, United Order True Sisters. Contbr. in field. Office: 680 Broadway Paterson NJ 07514

FRANKL, JEANNE SILVER, assn. exec.; A.B. in Lit. summa cum laude, Brown U., 1952; LL.B., Yale U., 1955; m. Kenneth R. Frankl; 1 dau., Kathryn. Admitted to Conn. bar, 1955, N.Y. bar, 1956; law sec. to Hon. Edmund L. Palmieri, 1955-56; atty. Port of N.Y. Authority, 1955-60; asso. firm Rosenman Colin Kaye Petschek Freund & Emil, N.Y.C., 1960-67; chief of program planning, office of edn. liaison, City Human Resources Adminstrn., 1967-69; spl. asst. to dep. adminstr. N.Y.C. Human Resources Adminstrn., 1969-70; asst. dir. Community Sch. System Project, N.Y. Lawyers Com. for Civil Rights under Law, 1970, dir., 1970-73; counsel and law project dir. Public Edn. Assn., N.Y.C., 1973-80, exec. dir., 1980—; lectr. Rutgers U. Law Sch. Edn. Law Seminar, 1972-73. Bd. dirs. Citizens Union City of N.Y., 1974—, local candidates com., 1971—, various coms. Mem. Assn. of Bar City of N.Y., Phi Beta Kappa. Home: 20 W 40th St New York NY 10018 Office: 45 Christopher St New York NY 10014

FRANKLIN, BARBARA HACKMAN, corp. cons., educator; b. Lancaster, Pa., Mar. 19, 1940; d. Arthur A. and Mayme M. (Haller) Hackman; B.A. with distinction, Pa. State U., 1962; M.B.A., Harvard U., 1964; D.Sc. (hon.), Bryant Coll., 1973. Mgr. environ. analysis Singer Co., N.Y.C., 1964-68; asst. v.p. Citibank, N.Y.C., 1969-71; mem. White House staff, Washington, 1971-73; vice chmn. U.S. Consumer Product Safety Commn., Washington, 1973-79; sr. fellow in public mgmt. Wharton Sch., U. Pa., Phila., 1979—; dir. Aetna Life and Casualty Co., Dow Chem. Co., Westinghouse Electric Corp., Am. Inst. C.P.A.s. Bd. trustees Pa. State U.; mem. State Bd. Edn., Commonwealth of Pa.; adv. councils to Nat. Fedn. Republican Women, Rep. Women's Fed. Forum; mem. Pres. Reagan's transition team, 1980. Recipient Disting. Alumni award Pa. State U., 1972, Catalyst Award to Women Corp. Dirs., 1981, Excellence in Mgmt. award Simmons Coll., 1981, ann. award Am. Assn. Poison Control Centers, 1979, cert. appreciation, Am. Acad. Pediatrics, 1978. Mem. Women's Forum Washington. Club: F Street (Washington). Contbr. articles to publs. Office: 107 Vance Hall CS Wharton Sch Univ Pa Philadelphia PA 19104

FRANKLIN, BEVERLY JEAN, artist; b. Los Angeles, Dec. 2, 1922; d. Harvey Franklin and Marian Ida (Cox) Keyse; student Baylor U., Waco, Tex., 1958-59; m. Charles Francis Franklin, Oct. 27, 1946; chidren—Christine Marie Franklin Carlin, Peter Charles, Kathleen Anne Franklin Watton. One-woman shows include La Jolla (Calif.) Art Assn., 1975, 76, Knowles Gallery, La Jolla, 1978, 80, 82. Mem. La Jolla Art Assn. (dir. 1973-76), San Diego Watercolor Soc. (dir. 1976-77), Am. Watercolor Soc. (asso.), Nat. League Am. Pen Women, Los Angeles Art Assn. Address: 7205 Via Capri La Jolla CA 92037

FRANKLIN, BEVERLY JOAN, mktg. resource exec.; b. Rockville Centre, N.Y., July 4, 1949; d. George Robert and Doris Elaine (Crossett) Franklin; B.A., Fla. Atlantic U., 1971; diplomate Grad. Sch. Sales and Mktg. Mgmt., Syracuse U., 1979. Tchr., St. Augustines Coll., Nassau, Bahamas, 1971-72; adminstrv. aide Walt Disney World, Lake Buena Vista, Fla., 1972-73; dir. communication skills lab. Academic Interamerica of Miami, Inc., Coral Gables, Fla., 1973; banquet sales mgr. Holiday Inn Oceanside, Fort Lauderdale, Fla., 1974-75; mktg. rep. Cook Cons., Inc., Fort Lauderdale, 1975-80; dir. ops. Jr. Achievement of Broward County, Ft. Lauderdale, 1980-81; prin. Periscope Inc., mktg. resources, Atlanta, 1982—; cons. Bell & Howell Co., Instructional Communications Tech., Inc. Judge of contests, speaker Distributive Edn. Clubs Am.; judge of contests, advisor Jr. Achievement Broward County. Mem. Sales and Marketing Execs. Internat. (sec. Fort Lauderdale, treas., bd. dirs.), DAR. Republican. Methodist. Club: Women's Exec. (Fort Lauderdale). Office: 2900 Chamblee-Tudor Rd Atlanta GA 30341

FRANKLIN, BONNIE GAIL, actress; b. Calif., Jan. 6, 1944; d. Samuel B. and Claire (Hersch) Franklin; student Smith Coll., 1961-63; B.A. in English, UCLA, 1966. Appeared in plays Your Own Thing, San Francisco, 1968, Los Angeles, 1968, N.Y.C., 1968-69, Dames at Sea, N.Y.C., 1969, Applause, 1970-72; star TV series One Day At A Time, CBS, 1975—; TV spl. Bonnie and the Franklins, 1982; appeared in TV movies The Law, 1974, Portrait of a Rebel: Margaret Sanger, 1980. Recipient Outer Critics Circle award for outstanding performance in Applause, 1969-70, Theatre World award, 1969-70; nominated Antoinette Perry award for best supporting actress-musical, 1969-70. Office: CBS-TV 51 W 52d St New York NY 10019

FRANKLIN, CAROL ANN, educator; b. Kokomo, Ind., Aug. 13, 1946; d. Charles William and Elizabeth (Bailor) F.; B.S., Ind. U., 1968, Ed.D. in Service Edn. and Curriculum and Instrn., 1981; M.A. (Edn. Profl. Devel. Act fellow), Western Mich. U., 1974. Tchr. sci. Niles North High Sch., Skokie, Ill., 1968-71; camp dir. Tribal Trs. council Girl Scouts U.S.A., Logansport, Ind., 1970-71; asso. instr. Ind. U., Bloomington, 1972-74; asst. prof. edn. U. Redlands (Calif.), 1974—; cons. secondary edn. Bd. dirs. Bloomington council Girl Scouts U.S.A.; v.p. YWCA, Redlands; active United Way of Redlands. Recipient Thanks Badge, Nat. Girl Scouts U.S.A., 1972; Outstanding Educator award Alpha chpt. Phi Delta Kappa, 1976. Mem. Nat. Sci. Tchr., Assn. Supervision and Curriculum Devel., World Future Soc., Calif. Council Tchr. Edn., Calif. Assn. Colls. Tchrs. Edn., NOW, Phi Lambda Theta, Phi Delta Kappa. Guest editor Calif. Jour. Tchr. Edn. Office: Sch Edn U Redland Redland CA 92373

FRANKLIN, COSTELLA MOONE, nurse; b. Durham, N.C., Mar. 14, 1932; d. Bennie Fred and Rosa Lee (Reaves) Moone; R.N., Hampton (Va.) Sch. Nursing, 1954; divorced; children—Saadia Ardisa, Kevin Leonard, Michael Bernard. Charge nurse Children's Hosp., Washington, 1955-56; asst. charge nurse Children's Hosp., Los Angeles, 1956-60, Daniel Freeman Hosp., Inglewood, Calif., 1960-65; staff nurse Long Beach (Calif.) Meml. Hosp., 1968-71; co-sponsor Blue Angels Sch. Retarded Children, Los Angeles, 1968—; citizen advocate Calif. Retarded Children, 1977—; pres. Exceptional Adult Center Retarded Citizens, 1979; sec. Ind. Center Exceptional Adults, 1980; spl. edn. commr. Los Angeles Unified Sch. Dist.; founder Blue Angels Charity Club, 1961. Recipient various service awards, certs. appreciation. Mem. Nat. Assn. for Retarded, Nat. League Nursing, Assn. West Indian/Am. Peoples (publicity and communications, dir.), Chi Eta Pi; asso. mem. Calif. Assn. Retarded, S.W. Assn. Retarded. Address: 1351 Bankers Dr Carson CA 90746

FRANKLIN, ELAINE A., communications specialist; b. N.Y.C., June 25, 1945; d. Abraham and Josephine (Epstein) Auerbach; B.A., Douglass Coll., 1967; M.B.A., Pace U., 1981; m. David Franklin, Aug. 28, 1966; children—Alisa, Daniel. Reporter Patterson (N.J.) Evening News, 1966; asso. editor Reader's Digest, Pleasantville, N.Y., 1967-80; mgr. corporate consumer affairs PepsiCo, Purchase, N.Y., 1980—. Leader Ossining Girl Scouts U.S. 1979. Mem. Women in Communications (mem. com.), Soc. Consumer Affairs Profls. in Bus., Internat. Assn. Bus. Communicators, Delta Mu Delta. Home: 65 Ganung Dr Ossining NY 10562 Office: Anderson Hill Rd Purchase NY 10577

FRANKLIN, FRANCES STARK, educator; b. Jonesboro, Ark., Nov. 19, 1930; d. Clyde and Mary (Stark) Carruthers; B.A., La. Tech. U., 1965, M.A., 1966; postgrad. N.E. State U., 1968-72; m. Alton Dale Franklin, Apr. 29, 1966; children—Merry Darlene, Carol Ann. Clk. Miss. Employment Security Div., Greenville, 1956-58, Miss. Dept. Public Health, Greenville, 1958-62; instr. speech Ark. A. and M. Coll. (now U. Ark.), Monticello, 1966-70, asst. prof., 1970—; tech. theatre cons. S.E. Ark. Public Schs., 1968—; theatre cons. S.E. Ark., 1970—. Bd. dirs. Drew County, 1980—, county film commr., 1982—. NIMH grantee, 1982; Ark. Endowment Humanities grantee, 1979—. Mem. Conf. Ark. Theatre (incorporator, sec. 1978—), Nat. Fedn. Press Women. Poet, playwright. Democrat. Baptist. Home: Box 2491 UAM Monticello AR 71655

FRANKLIN, JEAN, anthracite coal producing co. exec.; b. Hazleton, Pa., Mar. 11, 1935; d. Michael and Mary (Fedullo) Lauro; student Moravian Coll., 1952-53; diploma Am. Savs. and Loan Inst. Asst. sec. of assn. 1st Fed. Savs. and Loan Assn., Hazleton, 1953-60, Security Savs. Assn., Hazleton, 1961-75; sales mgr. In-Com, Inc., real estate, Hazleton, 1975-77; v.p. sales Beltrami Enterprises, Inc., Hazleton, 1977—. Sec. Philharm. Fund Raising Com., 1978—. Mem. Northeastern Pa. Shippers Coop., Wyoming Valley Traffic Club, Delta Nu Alpha. Clubs: Valley Country (Conyngham, Pa.); Kingston (Pa.) Tennis. Home: 218 N Wyoming St Hazleton PA 18201 Office: 109 E 1st St Hazleton PA 18201

FRANKLIN, LINDA CAMPBELL, writer, illustrator, editor; b. Memphis, Feb. 4, 1941; d. Robert Dumont and Mary McFarland (Wilson) F.; student U. Colo., 1958-60; B.A. in English and Fine Arts, U. Toledo, 1962. Librarian, Brooks Meml. Art Gallery, Memphis, 1962-65; dirs. asst. Internat. Film Found., N.Y.C., 1964-66; freelance illustrator, writer, N.Y., 1967-77; editor, writer Tree Communications, N.Y.C., 1977—, creative dir., 1981—; occasional lectr. on antiques to various mus. Mem. Early Am. Industries Assn., Am. Printing History Assn., Ephemera Soc. Am. (editor Ephemera News 1981—). Author: From Hearth to Cookstove, 1976; Antiques and Collectibles: A Bibliography of Works in English, 16th Century to 1976, 1978; Library Display Ideas, 1980; 300 Years of Kitchen Collectibles, 1981; series author/editor: An Old Fashioned Keepbook, 10 vols., 1979—. Home: 438 3d Ave New York NY 10016 Office: 250 Park Ave S New York NY 10003

FRANKLIN, LYNDA LONG, public relations agy. exec.; b. Macon, Ga., July 13, 1947; d. Hollis Alton and Lucile (Busbee) Long; B.S., U. South Fla., Tampa, 1969; m. Raymond Wesley Franklin, Feb. 10, 1979; 1 son, Jason Scott Foures. Tchr. English, drama and speech Leto High Sch., Tampa, 1976-78; chief copywriter Sta. WCTV, Tallahassee, 1978-80; account exec. First Mktg. Corp., Ft. Lauderdale, Fla., 1980-81; v.p. ops. and creative services Azen & Assos., Ft. Lauderdale, 1981—. Recipient local Addy award, Tallahassee, 1979. Mem. Fla. Bank Mktg. Assn. (past editor newsletter), Women's Exec. Club Ft. Lauderdale (pres. elect 1981). Office: 2929 E Commercial Blvd Suite 806 Fort Lauderdale FL 33308

FRANKLIN, MARGARET LAVONA BARNUM (MRS. C. BENJAMIN FRANKLIN), civic worker; b. Caldwell, Kans., June 19, 1905; d. LeGrand Husted and Elva (Biddinger) Barnum; student U. No. Iowa, 1923-25, U. Iowa, 1937-38; B.A., Washburn U., 1952; m. C. Benjamin Franklin, Jan. 20, 1940; children—Margaret Lee (Mrs. Michael John Felso), Benjamin Barnum. Tchr. pub. schs., Union, Iowa, 1925-27, Kearney, Nebr., 1927-28, Marshalltown, Iowa, 1928-40; advance rep. Chautauqua, summers 1926-30. Bd. dirs. state chpt. Nat. Multiple Sclerosis Soc., 1963-66; bd. dirs. Topeka Pub. Library, treas., 1962-65, chmn., 1965-67, sec., 1969-70, bd. rep. to N.E. Kans. Library System, 1968-71, awards for service, 1977, 80; mem. Mayor's Citizens Adv. Com., 1965-69; mem. Topeka Com. for Rescue Italian Art, 1966-67; bd. dirs. Friends of Library, 1960-79. Recipient Waldo B. Heywood award for cultural contbn. to Topeka, 1967; named Outstanding Mother of Kans., Alpha Delta Pi, 1971. Mem. Shawnee County Hist. Soc. (dir. 1963-75, sec. 1964-66), D.A.R. (state chmn. mus. 1968-71), AAUW, Topeka Art Guild, Topeka Civic Symphony (dir. 1952-57, service honor citation 1960), Doll Collectors Am., Stevengraph Collectors Assn., Marshalltown Community Theatre (pres. 1938-40), Topeka Geneal. Soc., Topeka Stamp Club, Nonoso, P.E.O. (chpt. pres. 1956-57, pres. coop. bd. 1964-65, chpt. honoree 1969), Alpha Beta Gamma. Republican. Mem. Christian Ch. Clubs: Western Sorosis (pres. 1960-61), Minerva, Woman's (1st v.p. 1952-54). Home: 4808 W Hills Dr Topeka KS 66606

FRANKLYN, AUDREY POZEN, public relations counselor; b. Detroit, Dec. 8, 1930; d. Sidney and Rachel (Slobasky) Pozen; A.A., Los Angeles City Coll., 1952; student UCLA, 1952-55. Founder Franklyn Agy., Los Angeles, 1959—, promoter Ella Fitzgerald, Mahalia Jackson, Tom Lehrer, Pearl Bailey; exclusive promoter Ella Fitzgerald, 1966—, Merrell Fankhauser, rock music writer, 1971—; promoter concerts U.S. and Can., also Pablo Records, Beverly Hills and Norman Granz; mgr. Jackie Vernon, 1980—; lectr. in field, numerous radio and TV appearances; hostess cable TV talk show, 1981—. Mem. Women in Communications. Democrat. Jewish. Club: Los Angeles Press. Address: 1010 Hammond St Suite 312 Los Angeles CA 90069

FRANKS, JOAN LOOPE, writer; b. New Tazewell, Tenn., June 2, 1935; d. G. Dewey and Eunice G. (Hopper) Loope; A.B., U. Tenn., 1962, M.Ed., 1964; postgrad. U. Edinburgh (Scotland), 1964, Am. U., 1966, U. Tenn., 1967, U. So. Ill., 1969; m. Herschel P. Franks, June 2, 1957; 1 dau., Ramona. With Knoxville (Tenn.) Utilities Bd., 1957-59, Electric Power Bd., Chattanooga, 1959-64; mem. faculty U. Tenn., Chattanooga, 1964-70. Mem. John Ross Park Adv. Bd., 1972-80, Hamilton County-Chattanooga Hist. Adv. Bd., 1977-80, French Store Adv. Bd., 1977-80. Mem. Chattanooga Audubon Soc. (pres. 1972, 77-78), Chattanooga Art Hist. Assn. (pres. 1970-72, 77-80), Tenn. Hist. Soc. v.p. 1977-79), Chattanooga Opera Assn. (dir. 1972-78), Chattanooga Opera Guild (dir. 1973), John Ross Assn. (dir. 1972-80), So. Hist. Assn., Tenn. Hist. Commn., Am. Acad. Polit. Sci., Ga. Hist. Assn., Hamblen County Hist. Assn., James County Hist. Assn., Sullivan County Hist. Assn., Nat. Hist. Assn., East Tenn. Hist. Soc., West Tenn. Hist. Soc., Rugby Hist. Soc., Freedoms Found. at Valley Forge (pres. Chattanooga chpt.), others. Democrat. Congregationalist. Editor: Walk with History, 2 edits., 1976, 77; editor publs. Opti-Mrs. News, 1963, Chattanews, 1973-75, Audubon Flyer, 1977; author: Holdings of the John Storrs Fletcher Library, 1968; contbr. articles to profl. jours.; preservationist Spring Frog's Cabin, circa 1754, John Browns Tavern, circa 1803. Address: 703 Browns Ferry Rd Chattanooga TN 37419

FRANKS, MELVERINE H., decorator, furniture salesperson; b. Independence, Kans., Apr. 10, 1934; d. Hope Montgomery and Gertrude (Dennis) Anderson; student Washington Sch. Art, 1966, Wichita Vocat. Tech. Coll., Wichita State U., 1976-77; grad. Chgo. Sch. Interior Decoration, 1972; m. James Allen Franks, Aug. 31, 1952; children—Troy Allen, James M., Tammy V., John C. Operator, S.W. Bell Telephone Co., Independence and Wichita, Kans., 1950-67; home and floor decorator Macy's, Wichita, 1968-72, jr. exec., 1977; selling specialist, J.C. Penney Co., St. Joseph, Mo., 1972-76, sales specialist home furnishings, 1978—; pvt. decorating cons. Co-chmn. People to People Orgn., Eldorado, Kans., 1964-66; vol. STOP Polio Program, 1962-63; asst. to chmn. United Fund Drive, 1967. Mem. Internat. Platform Assn., Nat. Hist. Soc., Smithsonian Assos. Clubs: Order Eastern Star, Nat. Writers. Author: Color Your Life Happy, 1979; contbr. articles on inter-city beautification and renovation to local newspapers. Home: Rural Route 2 Saint Joseph MO 64506

FRANTZ, BEVERLY EDWARDS, business exec.; b. Harrisburg, Pa., Nov. 10, 1942; d. Harry Jacob and Elizabeth (Moore) Maurer; cert. Thompson Inst., 1960; Student Harrisburg Area Community Coll., 1981-82; m. William Samuel Frantz, May 27, 1978; 1 son by previous marriage, Timothy Alan Edwards. Statis. clk. Nationwide Ins. Co., Harrisburg, 1960-63; file clk. Commonwealth of Pa., Harrisburg, 1964-66; keypunch-tab operator Penna Dutch Megs, Inc., Harrisburg, 1966-68; owner, v.p. MASCO, Harrisburg, 1968-78; owner, pres. BE Services, Inc., Harrisburg, 1979—. Mem. Am. Bus. Women's Assn. (chpt. pres. 1971-72, 76-77, 78-79). Mem. Grace Bible Fellowship. Club: Soroptimists (chpt. rec. sec. 1980-81). Home and Office: 1477 Quail Hollow Rd Harrisburg PA 17112

FRANZ, LYDIA MILLICENT TRUC (MRS. ROBERT FRANZ), real estate exec.; b. Chgo., Jan. 11, 1924; d. Walter and Lydia (Kralovec) Truc; Mus.B., Ill. Wesleyan U., 1944; Mus.M., Northwestern U., 1949; m. Robert Franz, Aug. 27, 1952. Tchr. music pub. schs., Muskegon, Mich., 1947-48; marketing research analyst Grant Advt. Agy., Chgo., 1949; asst. to dir. mktg. research Buchen Co., 1949-52; asst. dir. mktg. research Sherman Marquette Advt. Co., Chgo., 1952; asst. to pres., dir. media and research Andover Advt. Agy., 1952-55; salesman Boehmer & Hedlund, realty, Barrington, Ill., 1960-63; pres. Country Squire Real Estate, Inc., Barrington, 1963-74, Century 21-Country Squire, Inc., 1974—. Mem. real estate adv. com. William Rainey Harper Coll., Palatine, Ill., 1971—. Served with WAC, 1944-46. Mem. Women in Real Estate (pres. 1966-67), Barrington Bd. Realtors (pres. 1968-69), Ill. Assn. Real Estate Bds. (dir. 1972-75, gov. Realtor's Inst. of Ill. 1972-78, treas. 1981-82), Nat. Assn. Realtors (dir. 1982), Realtors Nat. Mktg. Inst. (bd. govs. 1978—), Barrington C. of C. (v.p. 1968-71, pres. 1974, dir. 1972-74), Am. Cryptogram Soc., Am. Contract Bridge League, Mensa, Barrington Bus. and Profl. Women's Club, Sigma Alpha Iota. Republican. Home: 76 Lakeview Pkwy Timberlake Barrington IL 60010 Office: 209 Park Ave Barrington IL 60010

FRANZEN, ANN MARIE, ednl., clin. cons.; b. Chgo., Jan. 16, 1941; d. John and Marie (Nemeth) F.; B.R.E., Bapt. Sem., 1964; M.A., U. N.C., Boone, 1972; Ed.D., U. Ga., 1974. Tchr. public schs., Rochester, N.Y., 1967-71; teaching asst. U. N.C., Boone, 1971-72, U. Ga., 1972-74; editorial reading cons. Oakland Schs., Pontiac, Mich., 1974-75; reading test editor Houghton Mifflin Co., Iowa City, Iowa, 1976-77; dir. Acad. Testing and Tutoring Service, Rochester, N.Y., 1977—; adj. asst. prof. Nazareth Coll., Rochester, 1977—; cons. N.Y. State Dept. Edn. Mem. Internat. Reading Assn., N.Y. State Reading Assn., Monroe County Learning Disabilities Assn., Coll. Reading Assn., Dreikurs Assn., Phi Kappa Phi, Kappa Delta Pi, Phi Delta Kappa. Office: 1157 Fairport Rd Fairport NY 14450

FRANZONI, JANET BRENNER, psychologist; b. New Haven, Apr. 10, 1934; d. Moses and Madelyn Agatha (McDermott) Brenner; B.A., Albertus Magnus Coll., New Haven, 1955; M.A., U. N.C., Greensboro, 1970; M.Ed., Ga. State U., Atlanta, 1975, Ed.S., 1976, Ph.D., 1978; m. Louis Mark Franzoni, June 22, 1957; children—Linda Franzoni Peretti, Lisa Franzoni Stilwell, Louis Mark, Brenda Kelley, Christopher Joseph. Tchr. English and social studies sr. and jr. high schs., Conn., N.Y. and N.C., 1955-68; instr. history U. N.C., Greensboro, 1970-72; sch. psychologist Fulton County (Ga.) Schs., 1977-79; asst. prof. counseling and psychol. services Ga. State U., 1980—, also curriculum coordinator Coll. Edn. for Gerontology Center; cons. in field. Research grantee Ga. State U. Coll. Edn., 1980. Am. Psychol. Assn., Am. Personnel and Guidance Assn., Nat. Assn. Sch. Psychologists, Council Exceptional Children, Southeastern Psychol. Assn. (student research award women's div. 1978), Ga. Psychol. Assn., Ga. Assn. Sch. Psychologists, So. Gerontol. Soc. Roman Catholic. Clubs: Georgetown Recreation (Dunwoody); Atlanta Lawn Tennis Assn. Author papers in field. Home: 4483 Kellogg Circle Dunwoody GA 30338 Office: Dept Counseling and Psychol Service Ga State U Atlanta GA 30303

FRARY, MARTHA PHYLLIS CODY, mgmt. cons.; b. El Paso, Tex., Nov. 7, 1931; d. Nicholas and Bernice (Taylor) Cody; student public schs., Phoenix; m. John Hoatson Frary, Aug. 5, 1951; children—Lydia Denise, Julia Bernice, Cynthia Louise, John Hoatson, Gregory Orin. Store mgr. Russell Stover Candy Stores, Phoenix, 1965-70; office coordinator Dr. Robert Gilbertson, Phoenix, 1970-75; office mgr. Monte Vista Med. Clinic, Phoenix, 1975-77; partner Leavitt, McCaleb & Frary, Phoenix, 1977—. Mem. Dental Group Mgmt. Assn., Nat. Speakers Assn., Am. Mgmt. Assn., Nat. Assn. Female Execs., Internat. Platform Assn. Mormon. Home: 4649 W Hayward Circle Glendale AZ 85301 Office: 4323 N 12th St Phoenix AZ 85014

FRASER, ALICE GORDON, educator; b. Hartford, Conn., Mar. 27, 1921; d. Thomas Gordon and Margaret Loretta (Lonergan) F.; Mus.B., Hartt Coll. Music, 1943; M.Ed., U. Hartford, 1962. First woman announcer Sta. WDRC, Hartford, 1943-44; programmer, librarian WOR Mut. Broadcasting Co., N.Y.C., 1944-47; artist-singer NBC-TV, Radio City Music Hall, Manhattan Opera Co., N.Y.C., 1946-56; stock broker Carter & Co., N.Y.C., 1956-60; tchr. pub. elementary schs., Hartford, 1960-65; editor curriculum publs., reading cons. Hartford Pub. Schs., 1965—; story lady specialist City of Hartford, 1965-66; adj. instr. U. Hartford, 1970—. Doris Doe voice scholar Met. Opera Co., 1951. Mem. Internat. Reading Assn., Conn. Assn. Reading Research. Club: Zonta. Author elementary reading textbook. Home: 100 Kane St West Hartford CT 06119

FRASER, BARBARA ANNE, violinist; b. Milw., Aug. 12, 1943; d. Allen M. and Mary K. (Nicol) F.; B.Mus., Wis. Conservatory; M.Mus., Eastman Sch. Mus. Violinist, Chgo. Symphony; tchr. violin Wis. Conservtory. Mem. Trio a Corde, Council Fgn. Relations Chgo. Office: 220 S Michigan Ave Chicago IL 60604

FRASER, JACQUELINE LILLIAN, nurse, educator; b. Bklyn., May 14, 1930; d. Andrew Jacob and Alice Viola (Tuerling) Schofer; Diploma, Flower-Fifth Ave. Sch. Nursing, 1951; B.S., Columbia U., 1954, M.A., 1955; postgrad. N.Y. U.; m. William Alexander Fraser Jr., Sept. 11, 1954 (dec. May 1964); 1 son, David Andrew. Staff nurse, head nurse Flower Fifth Ave. Hosp., N.Y.C., 1951-53, asst. dir. staff devel., 1960-62; instr. Hunter Coll., N.Y.C., 1956-61; asso. chief, chief clin. nursing program Center Chronic Disease, N.Y. Med. Coll., N.Y.C., 1968-71, asst. prof., 1969-73; asst. prof. Pace U., Pleasantville, N.Y., 1973-76; asst. prof., project dir. grad. program Gerontol. Nursing, Adelphi U., Garden City, N.Y., 1976-80; asso. dir. nursing services Met. Jewish Geriatric Center, Bklyn., 1981—. Mem. geriatric com. Queens Fedn. Mental Health and Mental Retardation, 1974—; apptd. to N.Y. State Gov.'s Conf. on Aging, 1981; chmn. adminstrv. bd. First United Meth. Ch., Flushing, 1971-72, sec. bd. trustees, 1973—. Johnson Found. grantee, 1953, USPHS trainee, 1962-66. Mem. Am. Nurses Assn., N.Y. State Nurses Assn. (council on cert. 1978—, chmn. gerontol. nursing practice group 1978—), N.Y. Heart Assn., Gerontol. Soc., Nat. Council Aging, Nat. League for Nursing, N.Y. Acad. Scis., N.Y. Assn. Gerontol. Educators, Kappa Delta Pi, Sigma Theta Tau. Office: 4915 10th Ave Brooklyn NY 11219

FRASER, LEILA, banker; b. Chgo., May 26, 1942; d. Paul and Emily (Dzierzyck) Hucko; A.B. with high distinction in Polit. Sci., U. Ill., 1964, M.A., 1966, Ph.D., 1971; 1 son, Alec. Teaching asst. Carleton U., Ottawa, Ont., Can., 1967-68; lectr. polit. sci. U. Ky., Lexington, 1970, asst. dir., then acting dir. Office Internat. Programs, 1970-72; staff asso., then asst. to vice chancellor U. Wis., Milw., 1972-76, asst. vice chancellor, 1976-77, asst. to chancellor, 1977; chief adminstr. to mayor City of Milw., 1977-82; v.p. for mktg. Marine Corp., Milw., 1982—. Mem. adv. com. on women and minorities Office Wis. Commr. Securities, 1976-80; bd. dirs. Milw. Exposition, Conv. Center and Arena, 1978-82, Milw. Symphony Orch., 1979—; bd. dirs., 1st v.p. Milw. Council Alcoholism, 1979—; mem. planning and allocation council United Way Greater Milw., 1978—; mem. Am. Council on Edn. Nat. Commn. on Higher Edn. Issues, 1981—. Recipient Outstanding Achievement cert. 4th Dist. Wis. Fedn. Women's Clubs, 1978; fellow Am. Council Edn., 1976-77. Mem. Am. Polit. Sci. Assn., Midwest Polit. Sci. Assn., Women's Caucus Polit. Sci., Phi Beta Kappa, Phi Delta Kappa. Author articles in field. Office: Marine Corp 111 E Wisconsin Ave Milwaukee WI 53202

FRASER, LESMAH JACQUELINE, health care adminstr.; b. Jamaica, Aug. 16, 1947; came to U.S., 1970, naturalized, 1980; d. Edward Victor and Pearline Linnette Fraser; B.A., Herbert H. Lehman Coll., 1975; M.P.S., New Sch. for Social Research, 1980; postgrad. in Public Adminstrn., N.Y. U. Tng. specialist M.I.N.D., Inc., Kingston, Jamaica, 1975-77; admissions supr. St. Barnabas Hosp., Bronx, N.Y., 1977-80; adminstrv. resident Met. Hosp. Center, N.Y.C., 1980-81, asst. dir. pre-admission, 1980, dir. enrollment and registration, 1981—. Cert. radio broadcaster. Mem. Nat. Assn. Health Execs., Nat. Assn. Hosp. Admitting Mgrs., Am. Mgmt. Assn., N.Y.C. Women's Adv. Com., Am. Hosp. Assn., Nat. Assn. Female Execs. Office: Metropolitan Hosp Center 1901 First Ave New York NY 10029

FRASER, MARYANN, social worker; b. Los Angeles, June 19, 1945; d. John M. and Martha B. Fraser; B.A., Calif. State U., Los Angeles, 1968; M.S.W. (Calif. Dept. Welfare grantee), UCLA, 1971, M.B.A., 1981. Psychiat. social worker, then clin. supr. Child, Youth and Parent Counseling, Los Angeles, 1971-78; dep. dir., dir. Family and Child Guidance Clinic, Didi Hirsch Community Mental Health Center, Culver City, Calif., 1978—; cons. in field. Sec., bd. dirs. Westside Child Trauma Council, 1979—; chmn. child and youth com. Los Angeles Council of Community Mental Health Centers, 1980—. Lic. clin. social worker, Calif. Mem. Soc. Clin. Social Work, Nat. Assn. Social Workers, Acad. Cert. Social Workers. Contbr. articles to profl. jours. Office: 4760 S Sepulveda Blvd Culver City CA 90230

FRASER, MONICA CONLEY, real estate exec.; b. Boston, Mar. 28, 1944; d. Walter V. and Kathryn M. (Ceurvels) Conley; R.N., A.Sc., No. Essex Community Coll., 1978; B.S., New Eng. Coll., 1982; m. John B. Fraser, May 17, 1969. Staff nurse Lemuel Shattuck Hosp., Boston, 1963-65; airline stewardess Northeast Airlines, 1965-71; broker Bassett Real Estate Co., Kingston, N.H., 1971-74, Gordon Brown Real Estate Co., Atkinson, N.H., 1974-79; propr. JBM Assos., Atkinson, 1979—. Recipient Splendid Am. award Thomas A. Dooley Found., Katmandu, Nepal, 1968. Mem. Am. Nurses Assn., Rockingham Bd. Realtors, Nat. Ski Patrol, Dooley Overseas Vols. (council). Republican. Roman Catholic. Clubs: Atkinson Garden, Arundel Yacht, Edgecomb Tennis. Home: 35 Meditation Ln Atkinson NH 03811 Office: Box 329 Atkinson NH 03811

FRASIER, MARY MACK, ednl. psychologist; b. Orangeburg, S.C., May 17, 1938; d. Fred and Mozelle (Agnew) Mack; B.S. in Music Edn., S.C. State Coll., 1958, M.Ed. in Guidance and Counseling, 1970; Ph.D., U. Conn., 1974; m. Richard Frasier, Dec. 23, 1963; children—Deirdre Richelle, Mariel Renee. Tchr. high sch., Orangeburg, 1958-70; summer instr. Upward Bound, 1968-70; dir. spl. services for students in instns. higher edn. S.C. State Coll., 1971-72; adminstrv. asst. Operation TACT, U. Conn., 1973-74; asst. prof. ednl. psychology, co-coordinator program gifted U. Ga., Athens, 1974-80, asso. prof., coordinator, 1980—; mem. Ga. Adv. Bd. Gifted, 1981-83; coordinator Nat. Placement Services Grads. in Gifted Edn., 1978—; adv. bd. Intermountain Center Gifted, 1978—; cons. in field. Pres. Hilsman Middle Sch. PTA, 1978-79. Ford Found. Early Entrant scholar, 1954-55; Am. Psychol. Assn.-Nat. Inst. Edn. fellow, 1981-82. Mem. Nat. Assn. Gifted (exec. bd. 1978—), Am. Assn. Gifted, Council Exceptional Children (pres. Ga. chpt. 1977-78), Phi Delta Kappa, Pi Lambda Theta, Delta Sigma Theta. Democrat. Presbyterian. Author articles in field. Co-editor Am. Middle Sch. Educators Jour., summer 1981. Referee Gifted Child Quar., 1978—, Teaching Exceptional Children, 1980—, Roeper Rev., 1981—, Exceptional Children, 1982—. Home: 505 Sandstone Dr Athens GA 30605 Office: 325 Aderhold Dept Ednl Psychology U Ga Athens GA 30602

FRATES, MRS., CLIFFORD LEROY, civic worker; b. Moweaqua, Ill., Jan 15, 1908; d. William James and Gertrude (Gunderson) Rodman; student Pine Manor Jr. Coll., 1924; B.A., U. Okla., 1929; m. Clifford L. Frates, Nov. 15, 1935; children—Rodman A., Kent F. Mem. bd. ARC, Oklahoma City; dir. Community Fund Bd.; trustee Jane Brooks Sch. Deaf, Okla. Art Center, Okla. Coll. for Women; chmn. adv. bd. Mercy Hosp., now also trustee; bd. dirs. Okla. State Library, League for Blind, dir. Jr. Leagues of Am.; mem. bd. Okla. Heritage Assn., Allied Arts of Oklahoma City, Oklahoma City Symphony, YWCA, Blood Inst., Better Bus. Bur.; mem. Children's Rehab. and Edn. Bd.; dir. chmn. Central Vol. Bur.; chmn. women's div. United Fund; chmn. Art Center drive; chmn. Oklahoma City Savs. Bond Com.; chmn. Episcopal Women's Conf. Okla.; div. chmn. for Christian social relations; mem. Episcopal Bishop and Council; mem. vestry All Souls Ch. chmn. Re-act campaign for Oklahoma City Vol. Action Center, 1971. Named to Okla. Hall of Fame, 1969; recipient award NCCJ; By-Liners award Women in Communication, 1979. Mem. Oklahoma City Art Assn., Phi Beta Kappa (pres. Oklahoma City alumnae 1964-66, alumna award 1978), Kappa Alpha Theta, Mortar Bd. Republican. Home: 2607 Warwick Dr Oklahoma City OK 73116

FRATTALI, ROSE ESTHER, ins. co. exec.; b. Watertown, N.Y., Apr. 5, 1931; d. Joseph and Angeline (Geglia) Oliverio; student public schs.; m. Vincent J. Frattali, Aug. 14, 1954; children—Steven, Lisa. Corp. sec. Agrl. Ins. Co., Watertown, 1973-76; v.p., then sr. v.p. N.Y. Casualty Ins. Co., Watertown, 1976-79, exec. v.p., 1979—. Vice pres., chmn. exec. com. Jefferson County (N.Y.) unit Am. Cancer Soc., 1977—; trustee bd. edn. Immaculate Heart Central High Sch., Watertown, 1974-77. Roman Catholic. Club: Watertown Zonta (past v.p.). Office: 120 Washington St Watertown NY 13601

FRAYER, DOROTHY ANN, univ. dean; b. Detroit, Nov. 1, 1938; d. Rudolph and Anna Jane (Funk) F.; B.A., Mich. State U., 1960, M.A., 1962; Ph.D., U. Wis., Madison, 1969. Freshman adv. Miami U., Oxford, Ohio, 1962-64; guidance counselor Lincoln-Way Community High Sch., New Lenox, Ill., 1964-66; asst. scientist Wis. Research and Devel. for Cognitive Learning, Madison, 1966-72; asso. prof. Hofstra U., Hempstead, N.Y., 1972-81, assoc. dean edn., 1973-75, dir. grants, 1976-81; dean Sch. Edn., Duquesne U., Pitts., 1981—. Recipient Disting. Alumni award Mich. State U., 1970. Mem. Am. Psychol. Assn., Am. Ednl. Research Assn., Am. Assn. Higher Edn., Am. Assn. Colls. for Tchr. Edn., Phi Delta Kappa, Kappa Delta Pi. Author: Conceptual Learning and Development: A Cognitive View, 1974. Home: 413 Allenberry Dr Pittsburgh PA 15237 Office: Canevin Hall Duquesne Univ Pittsburgh PA 15282

FRAZEE, PAMELA WALKER, ins. exec.; b. New Brighton, Pa., July 8, 1947; d. Ralph Wayne and Pearl Armour W.; B.S., Edinboro State Coll., 1969; M.Ed., Memphis State U., 1975; postgrad. San Antonio Coll., 1977, U. Mex., 1977, U. Tex., Austin, 1978-80, Trinity U., 1979; children—Tasha Jane, Nikki Mila. Tchr., Erie (Pa.) City Schs., 1969, Norton (Ohio) City Schs., 1969-73, Trenors Day Sch., Memphis, 1973-74; project dir. Stanford Research Inst., Menlo Park, Calif., 1978; ednl. cons. Learning About Learning, San Antonio, 1978-80; sales dir. Colonial Life & Accident, San Antonio, 1980—. Mem. NOW, Nat. Art Edn. Assn., Nat. Assn. Profl. Saleswomen, Nat. Assn. Exec. Females, Phi Mu Phi. Home: 1403 Ridgemeadow St San Antonio TX 78233 Office: Colonial Life and Accident 8546 Broadway Suite 212 San Antonio TX 78217

FRAZIER, CAROLYN MAE CASEY, nurse; b. Huntsville, Tex., July 26, 1946; d. Carl and Addie Mae (Shipper) Casey; A.A., San Jacinto Coll. Sch. Nursing, 1971; B.S. in Nursing, Tex. Woman's U., 1977; m. William Sumpter Frazier, Aug. 5, 1966; children—Casey Rene, Kelley Shea. Nurse intensive care Rockglen Hosp., Houston, 1973-74; supr. emergency room Gulf Coast Hosp., Baytown, Tex., 1974-75, nursing supr., 1975-77; supr. critical care N.E. Med. Plaza, Humble, Tex., 1977-79; instr. San Jacinto Coll. Vocat. Nursing Program, 1976-77; instr. Am. Heart Assn., 1973-78. Mem. Am. Assn. Critical Care, Emergency Dept. Nursing Assn., Am., Tex., Dist. 9 nursing assns. Democrat. Mem. Ch. of Christ. Home: 27127 Glencreek St Huffman TX 77336 Office: PO Box 1000 Humble TX 77338

FRAZIER, PEGGY KALUZ, pharmacist; b. Detroit, Apr. 9, 1943; d. Theodore and Tiami (Laeno) Kaluz; B.S. in Pharmacy, Ferris State Coll., 1965; postgrad. U. Pa.; m. Peter White Frazier, July 7, 1973; children—Patricia Evelyn, Peter White II. Staff pharmacist St. Lawrence Hosp., Lansing, Mich., 1965; pharmacy chief Edgewater/Holy Family Hosp., Chgo., 1966-67; pharmacy dir. health center No. Mich. U., Marquette, 1971—, equal opportunity coordinator 1976-77, licensure exam. rev. com. and instl. pharmacy com. Nat. Assn. Bds. Pharmacy; pres. Mich. Bd. Pharmacy, 1977-78; dir. Redman Ins. Agy. Co-founder, treas. Marquette V.D. Clinic, 1971—; chmn. Adv. Com. Substance Abuse, 1972-74; chmn. United Way, 1972-74; mem. Child Family Service Bd., 1973—, North Central Sub-Area Council, 1976-80, Upper Peninsula Health Systems Agy., 1977-80; active Planned Parenthood Teen Clinic, 1975—; co-chmn. Milliken govtl. campaign, 1978; mem. bd. control Ferris State Coll., 1979—, 2d vice-chmn., treas., 1982—; chmn. Marquette County Republican party, 1979—. Named Woman of Yr., Greek Woman of Yr., recipient Pharmacy Adminstrn. award Ferris State Coll., 1965; recipient Nat. award of merit Lambda Kappa Sigma, 1978; Disting. Alumna award Ferris State Coll., 1979. Mem. Am. Pharm. Assn., Mich. Pharm. Assn., Upper Peninsula Pharm. Assn., Am. Soc. Hosp. Pharmacists, Community Pharmacists Alliance (chmn.), AAUW (v.p. 1974-76, named Profl. Woman of Yr. 1975), Women's Equity Action League, LWV, Women's Polit. Caucus (treas.). Episcopalian. Clubs: PEO, Zonta (pres. Marquette Area chpt. 1977-78). Home: 3 Marquette Dr Marquette MI 49855 Office: No Mich U Health Center Pharmacy Marquette MI 49855

FRAZIER, PHEBE MORROW, banker; b. Evensville, Tenn., Aug. 26, 1941; d. Charles Chester and Eula Mae (Sneed) Morrow; student Tenn. Young Bankers Sch., Vanderbilt U., 1978-79; various courses Am. Inst. Banking; m. Roy Clyde Frazier, Aug. 28, 1960; 1 son, Roy Christopher. With Suburban Mfg. Co., Dayton, Tenn., 1959-60, 62-70; v.p., cashier Dayton Bank & Trust Co., 1970—, mem. mgmt. com., 1979—. Mem. Nat. Assn. Bank Women, Bank Adminstrn. Inst. (dir. Cherokee chpt. 1976-77), Dayton Bus. and Profl. Women's Club (2d v.p. 1977-78, treas., 1979-80). Baptist. Home: Lakeview Circle Dayton TN 37321 Office: Dayton Bank & Trust Co Market and 3d St Dayton TN 37321

FRAZIER, SELENA AGNES ADAMS, assn. exec.; b. N.Y.C., Feb. 23; Austin Hillgrove and Lucretia Ann (Berry) Adams; student Pace U., 1973-78; m. William A. Frazier, Aug. 31, 1938; children—Lucretia Ann, Judith Annette, Philip Anthony. Typist, then stenographer, 1960, 65-69; sec. N.Y. Telephone Co., 1969-71, dist. sec., 1971—; mem. Nat. Secretaries Assn. Internat., 1969—, edn. chmn., 1970—, chmn. other coms., 1969—; owner Selena's Secretarial Service, Inc., St. Albans, N.Y. Pres., Merrick-Marsden Neighbors Assn., 1973-77, 79-81, treas., 1977-79, chmn., 1975—, 3d v.p. Community Bd. 12, N.Y.C., 1979; county commr. of deeds; organizer, 1st pres. Merrick Blvd. Local Devel. Corp. of Bus. Mchts. Mem. Cert. Profl. Secs. Assn., Community Liaisons in Queens for United Enterprise (pres.), N.Y. Telephone Pioneers, Black Achievers Alumni. Democrat. Painter bldg. wall murals; design, creater Benson Meml. Parksite. Home: 170-02 118th Ave St Albans Queens NY 11434 Office: 88-11 165th St Jamaica Queens NY 11432

FRAZIER, WYNETTA ARTRICIA, public health ofcl.; b. Mounds, Ill., July 21, 1943; d. Willie J. and Anna L. Williams; B.A., DePaul U., 1965; M.S. (Gavin fellow), Gov.'s State U., 1976; children—Artricia, Tommie, Clifford. Exec. dir. Midsouth Health Planning Orgn., 1976; prof. health sci. Shimer Coll., Mt. Carroll, Ill., 1971-79; dean Daniel Hale Williams U., Chgo., 1976-77; asst. to Ill. Gov. James Thompson, 1976-77; health adminstr., spl. asst. to commr. Chgo. Dept. Health, 1981—. Pres., Aux. Cook County Hosp., Chgo., 1973-79; program dir. 3d Ward Democratic Party, Chgo., 1980—. Recipient Human Service award Search for Truth, Inc., 1980; Appleman award Chgo. Dental Soc., 1979; Nat. Assn. Health Scis. Execs. fellow, 1977-78. Mem. Nat. Assn. Health Services Execs., Southside Ind. Polit. Action Com., Nat. Hook-up of Black Women (pres. Chgo. 1982—), Renaissance Women, League Black Women. Contbr. articles in field to profl. publs. Office: 50 W Washington St Chicago IL 60602

FREDE, MARTHA CHAMBERS, clin. psychologist; b. Marvell, Ark., June 18, 1926; d. Landon Benjamin and Marie (Quinelly) Chambers; B.A. cum laude, U. Tex., Austin, 1945; Ph.D., U. Houston, 1970; m. Ralph Edward Frede, Dec. 25, 1946; children—Phyllis Frede Patrick, Bethann Frede Walmus Gretchen (dec.), Ellen Frede-Lynn, Sarah Jane Frede Jenkins. Diagnostic bacteriologist Tex. Health Dept., Austin, 1945-48; pre-sch. tchr. St. Francis Episcopal Day Sch., Houston, 1961-65; center program coordinator Parent-Child Devel. Center, U. Houston, 1970-72, psychologist Counseling Center, 1972-75; pvt. practice clin. psychology, Houston, 1974—; tchr. Houston Community Coll., 1973-74; cons. to community groups and agys. Bd. dirs. Can-Do-It, 1982—. Mem. Am. Psychol. Assn., Am. Assn. Sex Educators, Counselors, and Therapists (cert. sex therapist), Southwestern Psychol. Assn., Tex. Psychol. Assn., Houston Psychol. Assn. (sec.-treas. 1974-75), Houston Behavior Therapy Assn., Assn. for Advancement of Behavior Therapy, Houston Behavior Assn. (pres. 1976-77), Houston Zool. Soc., Houston Ballet Guild, Phi Kappa Phi. Episcopalian. Home: 849 Hickorywood St Houston TX 77024 Office: 9039 Katy Freeway Suite 414 Houston TX 77024

FREDERICK, AUDREY ANN, real estate and interval ownership sales exec.; b. Nanticoke, Pa., Oct. 5, 1932; d. Irene Mary Drake; student SUNY, 1963-65; grad. in bus. adminstrn. Lowell Sch. Bus., 1968; m. Richard A. Frederick, Dec. 9, 1974; chidren—Christopher, Joseph, Douglas, Jan Marie, Victoria, Richard. Research and devel. technician Gen. Electric Corp., Johnson City, N.Y., 1951-64; research and devel. staff asst. IBM, Owego, N.Y., 1965-68; office mgr. Sta. WLOD, Pompano Beach, Fla., 1968-71; gen. mgr. Sta. WSBR, Boca Raton, Fla., 1971-73; asst. to pres. Tennis Championship Inc., Ft. Lauderdale, Fla., 1973-76; bus. mgr. U. Sarasota, 1977-79; pres. Orlando Internat. Investors (Fla.), 1979—. Mem. Nat. Assn. Female Execs. Republican. Home: 829 Lowell Blvd #17B Orlando FL 32803

FREDERICK, ERICA SPITZ, assn. public relations exec.; b. N.Y.C., Feb. 13, 1947; d. David H. and Roslyn G. (Geshwind) Sonabend; student Dartmouth Coll., 1966-67; B.A. in English, Skidmore Coll., 1968; M.P.A., N.Y. U., 1980; 1 son by previous marriage—Benjamin J. Spitz; m. Martin Frederick, June 13, 1982; stepchildren—Shara, Jessica. Press sec., exec. asst. to N.Y.C. councilman, 1973-75; dir. public information Addiction Research and Treatment Corp., Bklyn., 1975-77; dir. pub. affairs resource center N.Y. Urban Coalition, N.Y.C., 1977-80, v.p. pub. affairs, 1981—; cons. on public relations to community orgns.; lobbyist; public Neighborhood: The Jour. for City Preservation, 1981—. Active polit. campaigns; nat. adv. bd. Women in Crisis Conf., 1979—; coordinator N.Y. State Gov.'s Adv. Council on Substance Abuse, 1980-82. Mem. N.Y. State Assn. Substance Abuse Programs, Women in Communication. Author: Economic Development in the Black Community, 1980.

FREDERICK, JANICE NELL, architect; b. Sheffield, Ala., Oct. 3, 1947; d. Robert Jay and Amy Ruth (Gaines) Ford; student U. North Ala., 1965-67, U. Cin., 1967-71; B.Arch., U. Ariz., 1974; m. Maynard Terry Frederick, June 12, 1971; children—Erica Koren, Alison Elizabeth. With Northington-Smith, Kranert, Tomblin & Assos., 1968-71, Tweddle, Wheeler, Strickland & Beumer, 1971; architect-in-tng. Gresham-Hockings, Architects, 1972-75; assoc. architect Barr & Tune Assos., P.C., Florence, Ala., 1978—; mus. room cons. Kennedy-Douglas Art Center. Vice-chmn. Florence Planning Commn., 1982; elder Presbyn. Ch. Mem. AIA. Democrat. Club: Turtle Point Yacht and Country. Home: 1617 Bridlewood Dr Florence AL 35630 Office: 454 N Pine St Florence AL 35630

FREDERICK, NANCY, govt. ofcl.; b. Lakewood, Ohio, Aug. 23, 1932; d. Howard Peter and Marian Bissell (Slater) F.; B.A., U. Colo., 1955; postgrad., George Washington U., 1962-63, U.S. Dept. Agr., 1964-65, Fgn. Service Inst., 1968, AID Devel. Studies Program, 1976; m. Francis Liell Wenger, Nov. 24, 1979. Reporter/photographer, city editor Robinson (Ill.) Daily News, 1956-61; area reporter UPI, 1956-61; spl. asst. to Congressman Peter Mack, Washington, 1961-62; with AID, 1962—, info. officer/photographer, 1962-65, editor Front Lines, 1966-68, program analyst devel. planning offices Latin Am. and Africa Burs., 1968-69, asst. desk officer Nigeria Relief and Rehab., 1969-71, Cameroon, Chad, Central African Republic (now Central African Empire), Gabon, Congo-Brazzaville and Equatorial Guinea, 1971-73, Sahelian Drought Emergency Unit, 1973-74, human resources devel. officer Central/West African Affairs, 1972-74, coordinator Women in Devel. AID, 1974-77, program analyst to dep. dir. Am. Schs. and Hosps. Abroad, 1978—; mem. AID Women's Adv. Com., 1973-75; AID adv., del. UN World Conf. Internat. Women's Yr., Mexico City, 1975; U.S. del. UN Conf. Status of Women, Geneva, Switzerland, OAS Inter. Am. Conf. for Women, 1976; asst. founding spl. offices for women devel. activities, Peace Corps, WHO, FAO, World Bank; agy. speaker, panelist various confs., 1975-77. Trustee Chesapeake Environ. Protection Assn., editor Chesapeake Environ. Protection Assn. Quar., 1979—. Recipient five awards Fed. Editors Assn., 1966-69, various awards and citations AID, cert. Nat. Council of Negro Women, 1975. Author, co-author plans and papers in field. Home: Route 1 Box 170 West River MD 20778 Office: FVA/ASHA AID Washington DC 20523

FREDERICK, PAULINE, broadcast news analyst; b. Gallitzin, Pa.; d. Matthew Phillip and Susan (Stanley) F.; A.B., Am. U., Washington, also A.M.; numerous hon. degrees; m. Charles Robbins. State Dept. corr. U.S. Daily; radio editorial asst. H.R. Baukhage, Blue Network and ABC; free-lance Western Newspaper Union, N.Am. Newspaper Alliance, also news commentator ABC, 1946-53; news corr. NBC, 1953-74, also UN corr. ABC, NBC; radio anchor Dem. and Rep. Convs., NBC, 1956; internat. affairs analyst Nat. Public Radio; moderator 2d debate Pres. Ford-Gov. Carter, Oct. 6, 1976. Bd. dirs. Am. U., Save the Children, UN Assn. U.S.A. Recipient Headliner award Theta Sigma Phi, Alfred I duPont award, George Foster Peabody award for contbn. to internat. understanding, Golden Mike award for outstanding woman in radio-TV, McCall's; Paul White award for contbn. to broadcast journalism Radio and TV News Dirs. Assn.; voted radio's woman of yr. Radio-TV Daily poll; U. Mo. Sch. Journalism medal; spl. citation for UN coverage Nat. Fedn. Women's Clubs, East-West Center award; Journalism Achievment award U. So. Calif.; 1st Pa. Journalism Achievment award; Carr Van Anda award Ohio U. Sch. Journalism; named to N.Y. Profl. Journalists Soc. Hall of Fame. Fellow Soc. Profl. Journalists; mem. UN Corrs. Assn. (pres.), Assn. Radio and TV Analysts, Council on Fgn. Relations.

FREDERICK, VIRGINIA FIESTER, state legislator; b. Rock Island, Ill., Dec. 24, 1916; d. John Henry and Myrtle (Montgomery) Heise; B.A., U. Iowa, 1938; postgrad. Lake Forest Coll., 1942-43; m. C. Donnan Fiester (dec. 1975); children—Sheryl Fiester Mestemaker, Alan R., James D.; m. 2d Kenneth Jacob Frederick, 1978. Free-lance fashion designer, Lake Forest, Ill., 1952-78; pres. Mid Am. China Exchange, Kenilworth, Ill., 1978—; mem. Ill. Ho. of Reps., Springfield, 1979—. Mem. fin. com. Lake Forest Caucus, 1974-75; alderman, first ward Lake Forest, 1974-78; mem. Ill. Commn. on Status of Women subcom. pensions and employment, 1976-79; co-chmn. Conf. Women Legislators. Named Chgo. Area Woman of Achievement, Internat. Orgn. Women Execs., 1978. Recipient Lottie Holman award, 1980, Jane Addams award, 1982. Mem. LWV (local pres. 1958-60, state dir. 1969-75, mem. nat. com. 1975-76), AAUW (local pres. 1968-70, state pres. 1975-77, state dir. 1963-69, mem. nat. commns. 1967-69), UN Assn. (dir.), Chgo. Assn. Commerce and Industry (dir.). Methodist. Address: 1540 Greenleaf Ave Lake Forest IL 60045

FREDERICK, VIRGINIA LEE HAMMER, clin. social worker; b. Rochester, N.Y., June 28, 1943; d. Edward and Madlyn (Kern) Hammer; B.A., Mercyhurst Coll., 1965; M.S.W. (NIMH fellow), Buffalo U., 1967; m. Kenneth Charles Frederick, May 23, 1970; children—Ryan Edward, Kara Anne. Clin. social worker social service dept., student supr. Simmons Coll. Grad. Sch. Social Work, Mass. Gen. Hosp., Boston, 1967-70; sr. clin. social worker Norwich (Conn.) Hosp., 1970-71; clin. coordinator youth treatment programs Greater Salem (N.H.) Mental Health Center, 1971-72; dir. social work dept. John F. Kennedy Center, Boston, 1972-73; sr. clin. social worker, mental health cons. Woodburn Center for Community Mental Health, Annandale, Va., 1974—; pvt. practice psychotherapy, Vienna, Va., 1974—; mem. faculty Smith Coll. Grad. Sch. Social Work, 1974-76; clin. instr. Cath. U. Am., 1977. Mem. bd. mental health in law project T.C. Williams Sch. Law, U. Richmond, 1976-80; sec. Westbriar Civic Assn. Mem. Nat. Assn. Social Workers, Acad. Cert. Social Workers, Am. Orthopsychiat. Assn., St. Lukes Assn. Contbr. articles to profl. jours. Home: 6606 Tina Ln McLean VA 22101 Office: 3340 Woodburn Rd Annandale VA 22030

FREDERICK-MAIRS, T(HYRA) JULIE, alcohol agy. ofcl.; b. Islip, N.Y., Jan. 4, 1941; d. Manuel and Thyra C. (Thorsen) Cajiao; B.A., Adelphi U., 1961; M.S.W., U. So. Calif., 1972. Social worker Los Angeles County Dept. Social Services, 1966-67, social work supr., 1967-70; planning cons. Los Angeles County Dept. Social Services and Los Angeles County Chief Adminstr.'s Office, 1972-76; dep. to supr. 4th Dist., Los Angeles County, 1976-80; asst. dir. Los Angeles County Office Alcohol Abuse and Alcoholism, 1980—. Mem. adv. bd. Los Angeles County Child Sexual Abuse Project; mem. Commn. for Sex Equity, Los Angeles Unified Sch. Dist.; mem. or former mem. Harbor Police Community Adv. Council, Los Angeles; mem. San Pedro and Peninsula Family Stress Task Force, Los Angeles; mem. ops. com. Interagy. Council on Child Abuse and Neglect; bd. dirs. Marshall High Sch. PTA, Los Angeles; adv. com. UCLA Alcohol Research Center; mem. Westside Child Trauma Council. Mem. Los Amigos de la Humanidad, Alpha Epsilon Delta, Beta Beta Beta. Clubs: Bus. and Profl. Women's, Soroptimists, Catholic Maritime (dir.). Author: (with others) Youth Program Planning, 1975. Office: 849 S Broadway Los Angeles CA 90014

FREDERICKS, CATHERINE CHOMICKI, speech and lang. pathologist; b. N.Y.C., Mar. 5, 1953; d. Michael Leo and Helen (Danielewska) Chomicki; B.S. magna cum laude in Elem. Edn. and Speech Correction, Seton Hall U., South Orange, N.J., 1975, M.A. summa cum laude in Speech Pathology, 1976; m. Glen R. Fredericks, Aug. 9, 1975; 1 son, Michael James Glen. Speech and lang. pathologist Mt. Carmel Guild, Newark, 1976-77, multiply handicapped program Bergen County (N.J.) Spl. Services, 1977-78, 79—; supr. speech/lang. program, intermediate care facility cottages North Jersey Tng. Sch., Totowa, 1978-79; pvt. practice speech/lang. pathology, 1976—. Mem. Am. Speech, Lang. and Hearing Assn. (cert. clin. competence), N.J. Speech and Hearing Assn. (asso. editor newsletter 1978), Kosciuszko Found., Kappa Delta Pi. Home: 109 E 1st St Clifton NJ 07011 Office: 333 E Ridgewood Ave Paramus NJ 07652

FREE, HELEN MAE, chemist; b. Pitts., Feb. 20, 1923; d. James Summerville and Daisy (Piper) Murray; A.B. in Chemistry with honors, Coll. of Wooster (Ohio), 1944; M.A. in Mgmt., Central Mich. U., Mt. Pleasant, 1978; m. Alfred H. Free, Oct. 18, 1947; children—Eric Scot, Penny Alene, Kurt Allen, James Jacob, Bonnie Anne, Nina Joann. Mem. staff Miles-Ames Research Lab., Elkhart, Ind., 1944-59; assoc. research biochemist, group leader Ames Research Lab., 1959-64, Ames Product Devel. Lab., 1964-66; assoc. research biochemist, group leader Ames Tech. Services Lab., 1966-69, new product mgr., clin. test systems/chem. test systems, 1969-74, sr. new product mgr. microbiol. test systems, 1974-76; dir. specialty test systems Ames Co., 1976-78; dir. clin. lab. reagts. research products div. Miles Labs., Inc., Elkhart, 1978-79, dir. mktg. services research products div., 1979—; mem. faculty Ind. U., South Bend, 1975—. Mem. Ind. Health Coordinating Council, 1977-79; bd. dirs. Elkhart YWCA, 1977-79; mem. steering com. to establish City Sch. award in Women's Athletics, Elkhart, 1978. Recipient Disting. Alumna award Coll. of Wooster Alumni Assn., 1980, Silver Bowl award YWCA Elkhart, 1981. Mem. Am. Chem. Soc. (Garvan medal 1980, Service St. Joseph Valley sect. award 1981), Am. Soc. Med. Tech. (Achievement award 1976), Am. Inst. Chemists (co-recipient Honor Scroll award Chgo. chpt. 1967), Am. Assn. Clin. Chemistry (membership chmn.), Assn. Clin. Scientists, AAAS, Chemists Club N.Y.C., Iota Sigma Pi (hon.), Alpha Mu Tau, Kappa Kappa Kappa. Republican. Presbyterian. Clubs: Ladies Elks, Elkhart Concert, Altrusa of Elkhart County. Co-author: Uro-dynamics, Concepts Relating to Urinalysis, 1972; Urinalysis in Clinical Laboratory Practice, 1976; contbr. articles profl. jours. Patentee in field. Home: 3764 E Jackson Blvd Elkhart IN 46516 Office: Research Products Div Miles Labs Inc Box 2000 Elkhart IN 46515

FREED, CATHERINE CAROL MOORE (MRS. DEBOW FREED), educator; b. Omaha, Dec. 27, 1925; d. Prentice Lauri and Henryetta (Banker) Moore; B.A., B.F.A., U. Tex., 1948; M.A., U. Kans., 1961; m. DeBow Freed, Sept. 10, 1949; 1 son, DeBow II. Mem. faculty St. Mary's Coll., Xavier, Kans., 1958-59, U. Kans., Lawrence, 1959-61, U. N.Mex., Albuquerque, 1961-65, Huntingdon Coll., Montgomery, Ala., 1965-67; lectr. in English, Ladycliff Coll., Highland Falls, N.Y., 1967-69. Adviser, Albuquerque Sch. System on Gifted Child Edn., 1962-64; writer, producer film on purposes and objectives of PTA, 1964; pres. Alliance Community Concert Assn., 1970-74; Alliance area chmn. Blossom women's com. Cleve. Symphony Orch., 1971-74; elder United Presbyn. Ch., U.S.A., 1976; commr. 189th Gen. Assembly, moderator Presbytery of Gt. Rivers, 1979. Mem. Speech Assn. Am., Nat. Council Tchrs. English, Daus. of U.S. Army (pres. chpt. Ft. Benning, Ga. 1954-55), Internat. Platform Assn., PEO, DAR, Mortar Bd., Phi Beta Kappa, Delta Sigma Rho, Pi Kappa Delta, Kappa Phi, Alpha Psi Omega, Alpha Delta Pi. Home: 115 W Lima Ave Ada OH 45810 Office: Office of Pres Ohio No U Ada OH 45810

FREED, MARILYNNE MAUD, mfg. co. exec.; b. Youngstown, Ohio, Sept. 18, 1949; d. Warren P. and Phyllis I. (Avery) Freed; B.S., Case-Western Res. U., 1971; m. William E. Pastor, Jr., May 20, 1978. Acctg. mgr. Sta. WFMJ-TV, Youngstown, Ohio, 1971-72; acctg. supr., Sta. WFLD-TV, Kaiser Industries, Chgo., 1973-74, chief acct., 1974-75; v.p., treas. Mahoning Culvert Co. Div. Youngstown Steel & Alloy Corp., Canfield, Ohio, 1975-82; pres. Life-Time Truck Products, Inc., Youngstown, Ohio, 1982—; v.p. Valley Truck & Trailer, Youngstown, 1979—. Chmn., Pvt. Industry Council of Mahoning County, 1981-82; mem. Small Bus. Mgmt. adv. bd. Mahoning County Joint Vocat. Sch., 1980—; bd. dirs. Family Bus. Assn. Northeastern Ohio, 1978-80. Mem. Youngstown Area C. of C. Republican. Methodist. Club: Canfield Businesswomen, Audubon Soc. Office: 4300 Simon Rd Youngstown OH 44512 also Life-Time Truck Products Inc PO Box 3346 Youngstown OH 44512

FREEDHEIM, GERDA KILIAN, community planner; b. Fulton, N.Y., Apr. 27, 1936; d. Rudolph Robert and Heddy Helen (Maehle) Kilian; B.S., Simmons Coll., 1958; M.S. in Social Adminstrn., Case Western Res. U., 1974; m. Donald Koperlik Freedheim, Aug. 31, 1958; children—Amy Jean, Julie Kay, Sara Beth. Exec. dir. Suburban Citizens for Open Housing, 1970-72; community organizer, urban devel. sec. Legal Aid Soc., 1972-74; project dir. Urban Research and Planning Corp., Cleve., 1974; project co-investigator Brookdale Inst., Jerusalem, 1974-75; sr. planning asso. Fedn. for Community Planning, Cleve., 1975-80, asso. dir., 1980—; field work instr. Cleve. State U., Case Western Res. U. Pres. Heights Citizens for Human Rights, 1970-71; mem. Cleveland Heights (Ohio) Planning Commn., 1975-81; trustee Parents Anonymous of Northeastern Ohio, 1978—, Am. Jewish Com., Cleve., 1972—, Ohio Protection and Advocacy Assn., 1979-80; mem. Cleveland Heights Democratic Com., 1981—, Cuyahoga County Women's Polit. Caucus, 1981—. Mem. Nat. Assn. Social Workers. Club: Cleve. City. Contbr. articles to profl. jours. Home: 2617 Dartmoor Rd Cleveland Heights OH 44118 Office: 1001 Huron Rd Cleveland OH 44115

FREEDMAN, ELAINE DOROTHY, psychiat. social worker; b. Boston, Oct. 11, 1931; d. Samuel and Rebecca (Close) Cohen; A.B., U. Mich., 1952; M.S. in Social Service, Boston U., 1955; m. Melvin Freedman, Mar. 8, 1959; children—Barry, Jill, Alan. Psychiat. social worker Washingtonian Center for Addictions, Jamaica Plain, Mass., 1955-59; supr. research interviewing Center for Community Studies, Boston, 1960; prin. clin. social worker Counseling Service, Mass. Correctional Instn., Concord, 1974-81, clin. dir., 1981—; family therapist, assertiveness tng. group leader Cutler Counseling Center, Norwood, Mass., 1980—; field work instr. Boston U. Sch. Social Work; pvt. practice psychiat. social work. Mem. Nat. Assn. Social Workers, Acad. Cert. Social Workers. Club: Hadassah (pres. Wellesley chpt. 1965-66). Home: 20 Bobolink Rd Wellesley MA 02181

FREEDMAN, MARION GLICKMAN, counselor; b. N.Y.C., Feb. 3, 1922; d. Edward and Minnie (Tokarsky) Glickman; B.S., N.Y. U., 1942, M.A. in Secondary Edn., 1964, M.A. in Guidance, 1967, postgrad., 1975-77; m. Bernard M. Freedman, Nov. 29, 1941; children—Rochelle Freedman Hassen, Diane Freedman Slatz. Tchr. high sch., guidance counselor Bushwick High Sch., Bklyn., 1965-74; guidance counselor James Monroe High Sch., Bronx, N.Y., 1974-76, 77—; career counselor Walton High Sch., Bronx, 1976-77. Mem. N.Y. U. Alumni Assn., Am., N.Y. State, N.Y.C. personnel and guidance assns., Delta Pi Epsilon. Jewish. Home: 6556 174th St Flushing NY 11365 Office: 1300 Boynton Ave Bronx NY 10472

FREEDMAN, RUTHE GOLDSTONE, communications cons.; b. Phila., Jan. 17, 1935; d. Jack Meyer and Betty (Rabinowitz) Goldstone; B.A. in Journalism cum laude, Temple U., Phila., 1977; m. Jay L. Freedman, Aug. 16, 1973; children—Gary, Trudy, Jamie; children by previous marriage—Steven, Sharon. Reporter, feature writer Montgomery Newspapers, Jenkintown, Pa., 1973; dir. Swedish-Am. exchange program Swedish Govt., Stockholm, 1975-77; public relations cons., 1976-77; public relations dir. Ambler (Pa.) Area Arts Alliance, 1977-79, Klein br. Jewish Ys and Centers, Phila., 1979-81; pres. RGF Assocs., Melrose Park, Pa., 1981—. Mem. Nat. Assn. Female Execs., NOW, Kappa Tau Alpha. Club: Toastmasters Internat. (past pres. Independence chpt.). Author newspaper, mag. articles. Home and Office: 932 Melrose Ave Melrose Park PA 19126

FREELAND, FRANCES JEANNETTE, alcoholism treatment center exec.; b. Danville, Ill., Apr. 11, 1938; d. John Terrence and Marie Amber (Iliff) F.; B.S. in Nursing, Coll. Mt. St. Joseph, Cin., 1960; M.S. in Extension Edn., Purdue U., Indpls., 1978, postgrad. in sch. supervision. Staff nurse in premature and critical care nursery Good Samaritan Hosp., Cin., 1960-61; joined Carmelite order, Roman Catholic Ch., 1961, with Carmelite Contemplative Community, Indpls., 1961-71; staff nurse VA Hosp., Indpsl., 1971-72; med./surg. staff nurse St. Francis Hosp., Beech Grove, Ind., 1972-74; dir. alcoholism detoxification unit Salvation Army, Indpls., 1974-79, program dir. Salvation Army Adult Rehab. Center, 1979—; tchr. alcoholism therapy; mem. Ind. Substance Abuse Task Force; v.p. Ind. Free Standing Addiction Agys. Coalition. Bd. dirs., mem. exec. bd. First Step Inc., half-way house for women, Indpls. Recipient award of appreciation Koala Center, Lebanon, Ind., 1978. Mem. Ind. Nurses Soc. on Alcoholism, Nat. Nurses Soc. on Alcoholism (planning com. 1982 Forum). Democrat. Home: 2335 Coyner Ave Indianapolis IN 46218 Office: 130 W Louisiana St Indianapolis IN 46218

FREEMAN, CATHERINE CORNELL, nurse; b. Norfolk, Va., July 15, 1932; d. Arsia Charles and Mamie Catherine (Seward) Butler; R.N., Phila. Gen. Hosp., 1958; B. Gen. Studies, Windsor U., 1973, M.S. in Behavioral Scis., 1975; m. William Walton Freeman, July 23, 1971. Evening staff nurse VA Hosp., Phila., 1958-60; head nurse gastroenterology service Wadsworth VA Hosp., Los Angeles, 1962—. Served with USAF, 1952-55; to lt. (j.g.) Nurse Corps, USN, 1960-62. Recipient Nurse Researcher of Yr. award, 1980. Mem. Am., Calif. nurses assns., Alumnae Assn. Phila. Gen. Hosp. Democrat. Methodist. Author patient info. booklet on hepatitis, VA Hosp. Home: 3500-369 W Manchester Blvd Inglewood CA 90305 Office: Wadsworth VA Hospital Wilshire and Sawtelle Blvd Los Angeles CA 90073

FREEMAN, CORINNE, mayor; b. N.Y.C., Nov. 9, 1926; d. Bernard Jonas Hirschfeld and Sidonie (Daxe) Lichtenstein; grad. Adelphi Coll. Sch. Nursing, 1947; m. Michael S. Freeman, Mar. 14, 1948; children—Michael L., Stephan J. Registered nurse various hosps., Boston and Salem, Mass., 1950-64; mayor St. Petersburg (Fla.), 1977—; mem. Pinellas Council Mayors; mem. subcom. internat. trade, urban econs. policy com., mem. community devel., housing and econ. devel. standing com. U.S. Conf. Mayors; pres. Fla. League Cities; mem. revenue and fin. task force, mem. fin. adminstrn. and intergovtl. relations policy com. Nat. League Cities; mem. mgmt. adv. group to mcpl. constrn. div. EPA; chmn. local govt. adv. com. So. Growth Policies Bd. Past chmn. Budget Rev. Com. St. Petersburg, Youth Service Systems Council Pinellas County, Social Service Allocation Com., St. Petersburg; past pres. St. Petersburg Area; bd. dirs. Bayfront Med. Center, Friends of Library, St. Petersburg. Club: St. Petersburg Women's Republican. Office: City Hall 2d Ave N and 5th St Saint Petersburg FL 33701

FREEMAN, JANET ELLIOTT, retail exec.; b. New Britain, Conn., Dec. 9, 1929; d. Roger Bolton and Mabel Topham (Elliott) F.; B.A., Conn. Coll., 1951; B.A. in Psychology, Hunter Coll., 1967. Asst. personnel dir. J.W. Robinson, 1958-60; corp. tng. dir. Allied Stores Corp., N.Y.C., 1960-63; div. v.p. personnel Asso. Merchandising Corp., N.Y.C., 1963-77; with Stop & Shop Cos. Inc., North Quincy, Mass., 1977—, corp. v.p. human resources and orgn. devel., 1982—; instr. Sch. Bus. N.Y. U., 1973-77. Facilitator project bus. Michaelangelo Public Sch., 1980-81. Mem. Nat. Retail Merchants Assn. (dir. 1982-83), Am. Soc. Tng. Devel., Human Resource Planning Soc. Club: Soroptimist Internat. (pres. 1981-82). Office: 1776 Heritage Dr North Quincy MA 02169

FREEMAN, JANICE FAY MONK, mgmt. analyst; b. Clinton, N.C., June 3, 1941; d. George Washington and Hesba Mae Catherine (Howard) Monk; student N.C. Agrl. and Tech. State U., 1961-64; B.S. in Bus. and Mgmt., U. Md., 1978; postgrad. Am. U., 1979—; m. Joe Kenneth Freeman, Nov. 1, 1969; children—Sheryl Janese, Wanda Michelle. Engring. writer Volt Info. Scis. Corp., Rockville, Md., 1968-70; documentation specialist Wolf Research and Devel. Corp., Riverdale, Md., 1970-73; sci. writer/editor Raytheon Service Co., Riverdale, 1974-77, configuration mgmt. coordinator, 1977-78; engring. adminstr. OAO Corp., Beltsville, Md., 1978—. Mem. Soc. Tech. Communications, Am. Soc. Tng. and Devel., Nat. Assn. Female Execs., Phi Chi Theta. Democrat. Lutheran. Home: 3737 Halloway N Upper Marlboro MD 20870 Office: 50/50 Powder Mill Rd Beltsville MD 20705

FREEMAN, JULIA DELORES, educator; b. Chattanooga, July 12, 1939; d. Neal C. and Jewell (Towns) F.; B.S. in Edn., Tenn. A&I State U., 1963; M.A. in Multicultural Edn., Pepperdine U., 1976. Tchr., Kansas City (Kans.) Sch. System, 1963-71, San Diego Sch. System, 1971—. Mem. Calif. Tchrs. Assn., San Diego Tchrs. Assn., Nat. Assn. Negro Bus. and Profl. Women's Clubs (rec. sec. Asha-Bonita chpt.). Baptist. Club: Toastmistress. Home: 458 Ridgeway Ct Spring Valley CA 92077

FREEMAN, LOIS INGELS, educator; b. Springfield, Ill., Sept. 26, 1927; d. Merl and Mabel (Zachary) Ingels; B.A., MacMurray Coll., Ill., 1960; M.Ed., U. Ill., 1970, doctoral candidate, 1982—; m. William E. Freeman, Apr. 26, 1947; children—Sheryl, William, John, Ronald. Elem. tchr., Jacksonville, Ill., 1960-73; asst. prof. elem. edn. Ill. Coll., Jacksonville, 1973-77; asst. prof. elem. edn. MacMurray Coll., Jacksonville, 1977-81, dir. programs for gifted, 1981—; cons. Life mem. Art Assn. Jacksonville, 1st v.p., 1974-80; mem. adminstrv. bd., trustee Methodist Ch., 1970 82; pvt. pilot; flew in Powder Puff Derby, 1977. Named Alumna of Yr., MacMurray Coll., 1974. Mem. Nat. Assn. for Gifted, Ill. Council for Gifted, Central Ill. Reading Council, Council Exceptional Children, Assn. Tchr. Educators, AAUW, Phi Delta Kappa. Home: Rural Route 3 Jacksonville IL 62650 Office: MacMurray College Jacksonville IL 62650

FREEMAN, MARINDA YERDA, corp. exec.; b. Chgo., Aug. 17, 1947; d. William Harrison and Esther Lillian (Jansson) F.; student Franklin (Ind.) Coll., 1965-67; diploma Tobe-Coburn Sch. Fashion Merchandising and Promotion, 1968. Exec. trainee, dept. mgr. handbags R.H. Macy Co., N.Y.C., 1968-69, asst. buyer, 1969-70; asst. floor mgr. Joseph Magnin U.S.A., San Francisco, 1970-71, asst. buyer, 1971-72, floor mgr., 1972-74, spl. assignment to fashion dir., 1975, buyer, 1975-78, spl. assignment Joseph Magnin Japan, Inc., Tokyo, 1974-75; buyer Diamond's, Tempe, Ariz., 1978-79, Bergdorf Goodman, N.Y.C., 1979-80; new product cons. Franklin Mint, Phila., 1980-81; founder, pres. Food Networks, div. Efficiency Networks, Inc., N.Y.C., 1981—; owner Fabric Networks, 1981—; cons. product devel., merchandising, packaging, kitchen orgn.; cooking instr. Mem. Nat. Assn. Female Execs. Home: 330 E 39th St New York NY 10016 Office: 225 W 34th St Suite 405 New York NY 10001

FREEMAN, SALLIJO ANN, advt. corp. exec.; b. Phila., Oct. 22, 1942; d. Oscar LaRoche and Nedra Vivian (Kellam) F.; A.B. (Academic scholar 1959-60), Queens Coll., 1966, postgrad. 1978—; children—James D. Smith, Oscar Smith, Michael Fakir. Founder, LaRoche Imports, N.Y.C., 1966—; founder, pres. Smith Advt. and Pub. Relations, Inc., Long Beach, N.Y., 1970—; founder, owner Fakir Maintenance Corp., Long Beach, 1978—; chmn. bd. LaRoche Imports and Mfg. Inc.; cons. various fgn. agencies. Active League Women Voters. Mem. Pub. Relations Soc., Am. Mgmt. Assn., Presidents Assn. Roman Catholic. Club: Downtown Athletic. Home: 162 W Penn St Long Beach NY 11561

FREEMAN, SARA CELESTE, banker; b. Tulsa, Mar. 24, 1948; d. Walter F. and Helen (Smith) F.; B.A., St. Louis U., 1970, M.A., 1974. Teller, Webster Groves Trust Co., St. Louis, 1970-73; grad. asst. St. Louis U., summer 1973, adminstrv. asst. Mental Health Inst., 1973-74; with Bank of Okla., N.A., Tulsa, 1974-82, asst. v.p., 1978-82, v.p., mgr. secured lending adminstrn. dept., 1979-82; v.p., mgr. credit and collateral ops. 1st Nat. Bank, Midland, Tex., 1982—; part-time instr. Tulsa Jr. Coll.; guest speaker. Mem. Nat. Assn. Bank Women, Phi Alpha Theta. Author manuals. Office: PO Box 1599 Midland TX 79702

FREEMAN, SHIRLEY JEAN, answering service co. exec.; b. Richmond, Calif., Feb. 11, 1949; d. John Joseph and Genevieve Laura (Muncy) Rubick; student Contra Costa Coll., Heald Bus. Coll.; m. Lake L. Freeman, Dec. 31, 1972; stepchildren—David, Daniel. Sr. service asst. Prudential Ins. Co., 1968-73; founder, 1971, since pres. Community Communications Corp., and predecessor, Concord, Calif.; sec.-treas., mem. exec. bd. Diablo Direct Mail & Printing Co. Mem. Concord Status of Women Com., 1980-81. Recipient various service awards. Mem. Nat. Women's Polit. Caucus, NOW, Todos Santos Bus. and Profl. Women (2d v.p. membership 1980-82, pres. 1982-83), Nat. Assn. Female Execs., Asso. Telephone Answering Exchanges, Concord C. of C., Direct Mail Media Assn. Office: 3112 Clayton Rd Concord CA 94519

FREEMAN, SYBIL, account exec.; b. Atlanta, Feb. 15, 1951; d. Isaac and Dorothy Louise (Howard) Freeman; B.A. in Sociology, Coll. of St. Mary, 1973. Editor, TV Guide Mag., Atlanta, 1973-74, sr. regional sec., 1974-76, promotion rep., 1976-79, account exec., 1979—. Vol., Big Bros./Big Sisters of Atlanta, 1978—; active John Anderson Presdl. Campaign, 1980; counselor Youth Assistance Program, DeKalb County, Ga., 1981—. Mem. Atlanta Assn. Black Journalists, Am. Women in Radio and TV (pres. elect 1981-82). Democrat. Lutheran. Club: Atlanta Advt. Office: 2600 Century Pkwy Suite 480 Atlanta GA 30345

FREETHY, MARY ELIZABETH, banker; b. Los Angeles, June 14, 1940; d. Walter Henry and Janice (Humason) Jonkey; B.A., San Jose State U., 1962; M.B.A., Hayward State U., 1978; children—James Lawrence, Sandra Renee, Jacqueline Ann. Mgmt. cons. Informatics Mgmt. Horizons, Marina Del Rey, Calif., 1979-81; liaison officer world banking div. Bank of Am., San Francisco, 1981—. Del., San Francisco-East Bay City Panhellenic Orgn., 1968-74, Woman of Yr. award, 1972. Mem. AAUW (br. pres. 1966-67, v.p. 1968-69), Chi Omega Alumnae (pres.). Republican. Episcopalian. Home: 974 Dolores Dr Lafayette CA 94549 Office: 5 Thomas Mellon Circle San Francisco CA 94134-2576

FREHNER, ELLEN, city ofcl.; b. Plano, Idaho; children—Dalby, Craig, Lezle Ann, Linden. Sec., State Dept. Public Assistance, Rexburg, Idaho, 1953; exec. sec. Beneficial Life Inst. Co., Idaho Falls, Idaho, 1954; sec. dept. entomology Ednl. Field Service Placement Bur., U. Idaho, 1954-56; sec. to prin. Basic High Sch., Henderson, Nev., 1956; telephone operator Henderson (Nev.) Telephone Co., 1957; publicity asst. Tropicana Hotel, Las Vegas, Nev., 1957-58; exec. dir. Henderson C. of C., 1958-72; exec. v.p. North Las Vegas (Nev.) C. of C., 1972—. State commr. EPA, 1973-76; bd. dirs., sec.-treas. So. Nev. Mus.; mem. Gov.'s Com. Fed. Landlaws Bd., 1971; sec. Nev. Indsl. Adv. Council, 1972; mem. State Energy Com., 1978-80; adv. bd. Regina Hall, Inc. Mem. Am. Bus. Woman's Assn., Am. C. of C. Execs. Assn., Nev. State C. of C. (dir.). Home: 1728 Arrowhead North Las Vegas NV 89030 Office: City of North Las Vegas Chamber of Commerce 1023 E Lake Mead Blvd North Las Vegas NV 89030

FREI, FAYE LOUISE, weaver; b. Bend, Oreg.; d. Gerald Roderick and Sarah Oliver (Perkins) Shearer; B.S. (Oreg. Bd. Edn. scholar 1958-62), So. Oreg. Coll., 1962; M.S. (NDEA grantee 1967), Oreg. Coll. Edn., 1968; m. John R. Frei, Dec. 17, 1966. Elem. sch. tchr., Bend, 1962-67; classroom tchr. Silverton (Oreg.) elementary schs., 1967-69, tchr. handicapped learner specialist, 1971-81 Title I coordinator, 1971-74; vol. tutor Oreg. literacy project, 1970—; owner, mgr. Spiderspun Handweaving, Dallas, Oreg., 1981—; mem. part-time faculty Chemeketa Community Coll., Salem, Oreg., 1974—. Dept. supt. Polk County Fair, 1974—. Mem. NEA, Oreg. Edn. Assn., Silverton Edn. Assn. (past pres.), Corvallis (Oreg.) Handweavers and Spinners Guild (past pres.), Salem Art Assn., Portland Handweavers Guild, Sigma Epsilon Pi. Republican. Mem. Open Bible Standard Ch. Home: 380 NW Douglas St Dallas OR 97338

FREIBURG, MARY WORKS, biologist; b. Humboldt, Kans., Dec. 5, 1926; d. Clark O. and Leota (Wilson) Works; B.S., Coll. Emporia (Kans.), 1948; M.A., U. Kans., 1950; Ph.D. (NSF fellow), U. Mo., 1971; m. Richard Freiburg, 1950; children—Ann, Stuart, Jeanne, Jane. Mem. faculty MacMurray Coll., Jacksonville, Ill., 1967—, prof. biology, 1980—. Mem. Malacologia, Phi Beta Kappa. Presbyterian. Home: 1909 Southview Ct Jacksonville IL 62650 Office: Biology Dept MacMurray Coll Jacksonville IL 62650

FREIDENBERGS, INGRID, psychologist; b. Latvia, Aug. 6, 1944; came to U.S., 1951, naturalized, 1961; d. Olgerts and Marta (Purvins) F.; B.A., CCNY, 1966, M.S. in Sch. Psychology, 1970; M.A. in Clin. Psychology, L.I. U., 1973, Ph.D. in Clin. Psychology, 1975. Sch. psychologist N.Y.C. Bd. Edn., 1971-73; grad. asst. L.I. U., Bklyn., 1971-72; intern in clin. psychology Bellevue Psychiat. Hosp., N.Y.C., 1973-74; staff psychologist Inst. Rehab. Medicine, N.Y. U. Med. Center, N.Y.C., 1974-75, sr. psychologist, 1974-78, clin. coordinator oncology rehab. service, 1979—, clin. instr. dept. psychiatry, 1981—; adj. asst. prof. dept. counselor edn. N.Y. U., 1978—. NSF fellow, 1966; certified sch. psychologist, N.Y. State; lic. psychologist, N.Y. State. Mem. Am. Psychol. Assn. Home: 29 W 9th St New York NY 10011 Office: Inst Rehab Medicine NY U Med Center 400 E 34th St New York NY 10016

FREILICHER, JANE, artist; b. N.Y.C., Nov. 29, 1924; B.A., Bklyn. Coll.; M.A., Columbia U.; studied Hans Hofmann Sch.; studied art history with Meyer Schapiro. One-woman shows include: Tibor de Nagy Gallery, N.Y.C. (14 exhbns.), 1952—, Fischbach Gallery, N.Y.C., 1975, 77, 79, 80, Utah Mus. Fine Arts, 1979, Lafayette Coll., 1981, Coll. of the Mainland, 1982; group shows include: Whitney Mus. Am. Art Ann., 1955—, Vassar Coll., 1968, Dept. Interior Traveling Show, 1976, Denver Mus. Art, 1979, Met. Mus. Art, N.Y.C., 1979; vis. critic and lectr. U. Pa. Grad. Sch. Fine Arts, Skowhegan Sch. Art, Carnegie-Mellon Inst., Sch. of Mus. Fine Arts, Boston, Coll. Creative Studies, U. Calif., Santa Barbara. Recipient Hallmark Internat. Art award, 1960; AAUW award, 1974; Nat. Endowment for Arts grantee, 1976. Illustrator: Turandot and Other Poems, 1953; Paris Review (portfolio of drawings), 1965; subject of articles and revs.

FREIRE, GLORIA MEDONIS, social worker; b. Pitts., Apr. 19, 1929; d. Vincent X. and Anastasia T. (Puida) Medonis; B.A. in Polit. Sci. and Econs., Carlow Coll., 1950; M.S.S.A., Case-Western Res. U., 1955; m. Luis Francis Freire, Aug. 30, 1958; children—Michael, Charles. Teenage dir. Merrick House, Cleve., 1955-62; group psychotherapist Cleve. Psychiat. Inst., 1966-73; lectr. Sch. Applied Social Scis., Case-Western Res. U., Cleve., 1973-75; cluster dir. Golden Age Centers, Cleve., 1975-76; specialist Community Guidance and Human Services (now Community Guidance, Inc.), Cleve., 1976—, staff tng. and devel. coordinator, 1977, dir. consultation and edn., 1978—. Chmn. steering com. East Community Task Force on Desegregation; chmn. Consultation and Edn. Council Cleve.; chmn. Ohio Consultation-Edn.-Prevention com. Ohio Council Community Health Centers, 1981—; coordinator Christian Formation Community of St. Malachi, 1975-77, coordinator liturgy commn., 1978-80; mem. Urban League Edn. Adv. and Task Force on Minimum Competency, 1978—. Mem. Nat. Assn. Social Workers (co-chmn. task force on desegregation 1981—, coordinator polit. action com. 1977, dir. Cleve. chpt. 1975-77, sec.-treas. Ohio council of chpts. 1975-76), Acad. Cert. Social Workers, Am. Group Psychotherapy Assn., Tri-State Group Psychotherapy Soc. Democrat. Roman Catholic. Editor: SASS mag., Case-Western Res. U. Alumni, 1973-79. Home: 5001 Tuxedo Ave Cleveland OH 44134 Office: 3740 Euclid Ave Cleveland OH 44115

FREITAS, ANTOINETTE JUNI, ins. co. exec.; b. Kansas City, Mo., Feb. 14, 1944; d. Anthony P. and Mariam L. Freitas; B.A., Calif. State U., Long Beach, 1966; M.A., U. So. Calif., 1974; m. Stephen R. Krajcar, July 4, 1980. Counselor, U. So. Calif., 1967-70, asso. dir. fin. aid, 1970-75; sales agt. Equitable Life Assurance Co., 1975-79, dist. mgr., San Francisco, 1979—. Recipient various sales and mgmt. awards; mem. Million Dollar Round Table. Mem. Nat. Assn. Life Underwriters, AAUW, U. So. Calif. Alumni Assn., Women Life Underwriters Conf. Republican. Episcopalian. Office: 5 Thomas Mellon Circle Suite 304 San Francisco CA 94134

FREIWALD, JOYCE GROSS, congl. staff, energy specialist; b. Fulton, Mo., June 22, 1944; d. Fred Alfred and Susan (Kist) Gross; B.S. in Math. (scholar), U. N.Mex., 1966; M.Arch., 1976, postgrad. in math. and physics, 1967-68; m. David Allen Freiwald, Apr. 3, 1976; children—Wesley, Todd, Christopher. Mathematician, Air Force Weapons Lab., Albuquerque, 1963-65, Sandia Nat. Lab., Albuquerque, 1966-69; owner, mgr. Costello Cons. Co., Albuquerque, 1970-72; scientist Sci. Applications, Inc., Albuquerque, 1973-75; pres. Phoenix Forth, Inc., Albuquerque, 1975-76; mem. staff Los Alamos Nat. Lab., 1976-81; Republican tech. cons. U.S. Ho. Reps. Com. on Sci. and Tech., Washington, 1981—. Candidate for Albuquerque City Commn., 1970, N.Mex. Senate, 1971; chairwoman N.Mex. Equal Rights Legis. Com., 1972, Citizen's Coalition for Land Use Planning, 1975; former mem. various state and county bds. and commns. Hydro-Conduit Corp. scholar, 1970. Mem. Assn. Women in Sci., N.Mex. Women in Sci. and Engring., AAAS, N.Mex. Acad. Sci., World Future Soc., Environ. Design Research Assn., Nat. Assn. Female Execs., Phi Kappa Pi, Kappa Mu Epsilon, Alpha Delta Pi. Republican. Contbr. numerous articles on energy, environ. and tech. issues to profl. jours. Home: 10401 LLoyd Rd Potomac MD 20854 Office: B374 Rayburn House Office Bldg Washington DC 20515

FRENCH, CANDACE ANN, ednl. adminstr.; b. Soldier, Kans., Apr. 18, 1927; d. Albert Osmond and Lula Marie (Stanley) F.; B.S., Emporia State U., 1949; M.A., Colo. Coll., 1965. Tchr., Lincoln (Kans.) High Sch., 1949-57; tchr. Widefield High Sch., Colorado Springs, Colo., 1957-58, counselor, 1958-64, dean, 1964-72, prin. summer session, 1969-73, asst. prin., 1972-82; prin. elem. sch., Colorado Springs, 1982—. Mem. NEA, Nat. Assn. Secondary Sch. Prins., Nat. Assn. Female Execs. Methodist.

FRENCH, CATHERINE, arts assn. exec.; b. Teaneck, N.J., Nov. 13, 1946; d. Lester John and Catherine M. (Doyle) F.; B.Mus., Manhattanville Coll., 1968. Exec. dir. Am. Symphony Orch., N.Y.C., 1970-72; mng. dir. N.J. Symphony, 1972-74; asst. dir. Am. Symphony Orch. League, from 1974, now exec. v.p., chief exec. officer. Bd. dirs. Nat. Music Council. Mem. Am. Soc. Assn. Execs., Chamber Music Soc. Am. Roman Catholic. Home: 2500 Q St NW Washington DC 20007 Office: care Am Symphony Orch League 1551 Trapp Rd Vienna VA 22180

FRENCH, ELIZABETH CHAMBERLAIN, harpsichordist, ednl. adminstr.; b. Altoona, Pa., Aug. 16, 1929; d. Alton Francis and Margaret (Griffith) Chamberlain; B.Mus. in Edn. with honors, Wheaton Coll., 1951; M.Mus., Coll. Conservatory of Music, U. Cin., 1963; postgrad. Peabody Conservatory of Music, 1967-70; Dr.Mus.Arts, Boston U., 1975; postgrad. U. Ariz., 1978; children—Eugene Thurman Vest, Jonathan Mark Vest, Harry Allan Vest, Michael Robert Vest. Dir. music Westminster Presbyn. Ch., Bluefield, W.Va., 1951-53, Bland St. Meth. Ch., Bluefield, 1959-70; instr. music Concord Coll., Athens, W.Va., 1964-66, asst. prof., 1966-70; mus. dir. Barter Theater, Abingdon, Va., 1968; dir. music Episcopal Ch. of St. Matthew, Tucson, 1973-76; organist Trinity Presbyn. Ch., Tucson, 1976-78; sr. staff asso. for acad. affairs Ala. Commn. on Higher Edn., Montgomery, 1978—; profl. appearances as harpsichord and organ recitalist in Ohio, Ky., W.Va., S.C., Mass., Ariz., Ala., 1951—; harpsichordist with chamber ensemble, Birmingham Musica Antiqua, 1980—; dir. music Temple Beth Or, Montgomery, 1980—. Mem. Episcopal Diocesan Music Commn., State of Ariz., 1973-78; mem. Gov.'s Study Commn. on Library Coop., State of Ala., 1979-81; bd. dirs. Friends of Temple of Music and Art, Tucson, 1975-78; mem. exec. bd. Pres.'s Council of Montgomery, 1981—; Montgomery bd. dirs. Ala. Symphony, 1980—; mem. Ala. Adv. Council on Libraries, 1981—. Mem. AAUW, Coll. Music Soc., Am. Musico. Soc., Am. Assn. Higher Edn., Assn. Study Higher Edn., Am. Guild Organists (Ala. state chmn. 1981—), Southeastern Hist. Keyboard Soc., Phi Kappa Phi. Club: Capital City. Contbr. articles to profl. jours. Home: 37 Tecumseh Dr Montgomery AL 36117 Office: Suite 221 One Court Sq Montgomery AL 36104

FRENCH, ELLA J., caseworker; b. Elkmont, Ala., Sept. 25, 1929; d. George and Lenton Hall (Martin) Jackson; A.B., Fisk U., 1950; student Ala. A&M U., 1950; m. Joe W. French, Sept. 26, 1953; children—Michael W., Deborah French Keys, Vincent K., Gregory M. Tchr., Limestone County Bd. Edn., Athens, Ala., 1950-54; tchr., counselor, sec. to prin. Trinity High Sch., Athens, Ala., 1956-62; caseworker V, Medicaid div., Marion County Dept. Public Welfare, Indpls., 1964—. Bd. trustees Buggs Temple Ch. of God in Christ, Indpls., dist. missionary, adult Sunday sch. tchr., lic. evangelist. Democrat. Home: 3333 Carrolton Ave Indianapolis IN 46205 Office: 141 S Meridian St Indianapolis IN 46225

FRENCH, IRENE BELLE, health care exec.; b. Wichita, Kans., Sept. 2, 1927; d. Merlin Neal and Thelma Lora (Hartley) Lahey; m. J. Calvin French, Oct. 11, 1946; children—Russell Neil, James Calvin, II. Vice pres., treas., dir. Medifax, Inc., Kansas City, Mo., 1978—. Mem. Merriam (Kans.) City Council, 1973-81, mayor, 1981—. Recipient Outstanding Citizens award City of Merriam, 1980. Mem. Merriam C. of C. (dir.), Am. Legion Aux. Republican. Episcopalian. Clubs: Elephant, Sunflower. Home: 10235 W 70th St Merriam KS 66203 Office: 3100 Broadway Suite 111 Kansas City MO 64111

FRENCH, JEANA TURNER, mental health agy. exec.; b. Tallahassee, Fla., Feb. 22, 1947; d. Cleveland Adelbert and Myra Alice (Hartsfield) Turner; B.S., Fla. State U., 1967, M.S., 1970, Ph.D., 1972; m. John H. French, Jr., Dec. 27, 1966. Tchr. 2d grade Leon County Sch. System, Tallahassee, 1967-69, tchr. Head Start program, 1968; instr. early childhood edn. Fla. State U., Tallahassee, 1969-71, program coordinator, academic advisor, 1971-72, asst. prof., 1974-78; mental health program analyst Dept. Health and Rehab. Services, 1978-79, tng. mgr., 1979-81, dir. staff devel. and tng., 1981—; curriculum specialist Wakulla County, Crawfordville, Fla., 1972-73; dir. evaluation and research Choctaw Reservation Project, Philadelphia, Miss., 1973-74; cons. Cherokee (N.C.) Reservation Evaluation and Research Project, 1973-74; cons. Metcor, Inc., Washington, 1973-74; mem. 25th anniversary commemoration com. Fla. State U., 1972; mem. Fla. Democratic Credentials Com., 1972; instr. Fla. Dem. Polit. Leadership Schs., 1974; mem. Leon County (Fla.) Dem. Com., 1979-81. Mem. Fla. State U. Coll. Edn. Alumni Assn. (dir. 1976-78), Nat. Assn. Edn. of Young Children, Fla. Assn. Children Under Six, Nat. Council Social Studies, Assn. Childhood Edn., Internat. Reading Assn., Phi Kappa Phi, Kappa Delta Pi, Phi Delta Kappa, Alpha Gamma Delta. Democrat. Methodist. Contbr. bibliography, research papers in field. Home: 3509 Turkey Run Ln Tallahassee FL 32312 Office: 1317 Winewood Blvd Bldg 3 Room 205 Tallahasse FL 32301

FRENCH, JOYCE NORTON, ednl. adminstr.; b. Buffalo, NY., Dec. 9, 1929; d. Thomas Lowell and Verna (Cutler) Norton; B.A., Wellesley Coll., 1951; M.S., U. Bridgeport, 1967; Ph.D., Columbia U., 1976; m. Donald F. French, June 11, 1951; children—Susan Linda French Falk, Richard Norton. Tchr., Greenwich (Conn.) Public Schs., 1965-70; head lower and middle schs. Greenwich Country Day Sch., 1970-76; dir. tchr. edn. Manhattanville Coll., Purchase, N.Y., 1977—; vis. prof. Columbia U., N.Y.C., 1980-81. Research Inst. for Study of Learning Disabilities research fellow Columbia U., 1978-80. Mem. Am. Psychol. Assn., Internat. Reading Assn., N.Y. State Learning Skills Assn., N.Y. Acad. Scis., Sigma Xi. Contbr. articles in field to profl. publs. Home: 185 Shore Rd Old Greenwich CT 06870 Office: Manhattanville Coll Purchase NY 10577

FRENCH, LENA GARRETT, banker; b. Lebanon, Va., May 25, 1919; d. Edmond Kenan and Daisy (Johnson) Garrett; secretarial sci. and acctg. diploma, W.Va. Bus. Coll., Bluefield, 1938; student langs. and lit. Bluefield Coll., 1939-40; cert. Am. Inst. Banking, 1948, W.Va. Sch. Banking, 1951; m. John Reid French, Aug. 25, 1942. With First Nat. Bank Bluefield, 1938—, asst. cashier, 1965-77, v.p. SBA loans and gen. banking, 1977-81, v.p. customer relations, 1981—; treas., dir. Bluefield Office Bldg. Com. Mem. Bluefield Beautification Commn., 1976-80, treas., 1978—; sponsor Craft Meml. Library, Bluefield, Assn. Better Reading; mem. Bluefield Com. Art in Pub. Bldgs.; bd. dirs. Bluefield chpt. ARC. Mem. Nat. Assn. Bank Women (chmn. W.Va. group 1964), Am. Inst. Banking (v.p. Bluefield chpt. 1947-48), Bluefield C. of C. Republican. Baptist. Clubs: Bluefield Travel (past pres.), Evening Primrose Garden. Office: 500 Federal St Bluefield WV 24701

FRENCH, MARILYN, author, critic; b. N.Y.C., Nov. 21, 1929; d. E.C. and Isabel (Hazz) Edwards; B.A., Hofstra Coll., 1951, M.A., 1964; Ph.D., Harvard U., 1972; children—Jamie, Robert. Secretarial, clerical worker, 1946-53; lectr. Hofstra Coll., 1964-68; asst. prof. Holy Cross Coll., Worcester, Mass., 1972-76; Mellon fellow Harvard U., 1976-77; writer, lectr., 1967—; author: (criticism) The Book as World - James Joyce's "Ulysses", 1976; Shakespeare's Division of Experience, 1981; Edith Wharton's Summer and The House of Mirth, 1981; novels: The Women's Room, 1977, The Bleeding Heart, 1980. Mem. MLA, James Joyce Soc., Virginia Woolf Soc., Soc. for Values in Higher Edn. Office: care Summit Books 1230 Ave of Americas New York NY 10020 *

FRENCH, MARY BLAKE, editor, writer, educator; b. Dallas, July 21, 1942; d. Harry Blake and Mary Virginia (Jones) French; B.A., Coll. William and Mary, 1965; M.A., U. Va., 1966; m. Richard Edelin Crouch, Feb. 6, 1965; children—John, Virginia. Columnist, reporter Va. Gazette, Williamsburg, 1961-65; mng. editor William and Mary Rev., Williamsburg, 1963-64; asst. editor Microfilm Publs., U. Va., Charlottesville, 1966-67; lectr. Am. lit. and women in lit. U. Va., Falls Church, 1968—; instr. English, No. Va. Community Coll., Annandale, 1968-69; instr. English composition George Washington U., Washington, 1970; cons. in lit. humanities project Arlington County Library, 1976; editor Spokeswoman mag., 1979-82, Washington Women's Representative Newsletter, 1979-82; mng. editor Women's News Service, Washington, 1979-82; assoc. editor Grad. Woman mag., AAUW, Washington, 1982—. Mem. Com. on Status of Women, Arlington, Va., 1976; mem. steering com. Coalition on Optimum Growth, 1970-73. Mem. MLA, AAUW (chmn. women's studies, dir. Arlington br. 1974-76), Women's Caucus of Modern Langs., Washington Women's Network, Nat. Women's Polit. Caucus, ACLU, English-Speaking Union, Edgar Allan Poe Found., Thoreau Soc., NOW (dir. Arlington chpt. 1975-76, v.p. 1976-77), AAUP, U.S. Congress Periodical Press Correspondents' Assn., Nat. Trust Historic Preservation, Sigma Delta Chi. Democrat. Episcopalian. Club: Nat. Press. Author: The State Slate: A Guide to Legislative Procedures and Lawmakers, 1977; compiler: Women in Literature: A Bibliography, 1973; editor (with J.L. Anderson) Microfilm Edition of the Papers of R.M.T. Hunter, 1817-1887, 1966. Home: 2624 N 18th St Arlington VA 22201 Office: AAUW Edn Center 2401 Virginia Ave NW Washington DC 20037

FRENCH, STEPHANIE TAYLOR, arts adminstr.; b. Newark; d. William Taylor and Connie V. F.; B.A., Wellesley Coll., 1972; M.B.A., Harvard U., 1978; m. Amory Houghton, III, Sept. 8, 1979. Traffic mgr. Radio Sta. KFRC, 1973-74; dir. European Gallery, San Francisco, 1974-75; acct. exec. Young & Rubican, N.Y.C., 1978-79; acct. supr. Rives Smith Baldwin & Carlberg, Houston, 1980-81; mgr. cultural affairs and spl. programs Philip Morris, Inc., N.Y.C., 1981—. Clubs: Harvard Bus. Sch., Wellesley. Home: 136 E 36th St Apt 9D New York NY 10016 Office: 100 Park Ave New York NY 10016

FRENGUT, RENEE HIRSCH, marketing research exec.; b. N.Y.C., May 14, 1945; d. Erich F. and Eleanore F. (Kaplan) Hirsch; B.A., CCNY, 1966; M.A., Yeshiva U., 1968, Ph.D. (NIMH fellow), 1977; m. Robert John Frengut, Mar. 3, 1973. Instr. (part-time) dept. psychology N.Y. Inst. Tech., N.Y.C., 1968-69; clin. intern N.Y. State Psychiat. Inst., Columbia U. Coll. Physicians and Surgeons, 1969-70; staff psychologist Westchester County Community Mental Health Bd., 1970-71; staff psychologist Abbott House for Children, Irvington, N.Y., 1971-72, supr. exptl. therapeutic group homes, 1971-72; mem. faculty dept. psychology Montgomery Coll., Rockville, Md., 1972-74; staff psychologist Potomac Found. for Mental Health, Rockville, Md., 1973-75; pvt. practice clin. psychology, 1974-77; research cons. social research div. NBC, N.Y.C., 1976; qualitative media research cons. R.H. Bruskin Assos., New Brunswick, N.J., 1976; lectr. (part-time) psychology Mercy Coll., Dobbs Ferry, N.Y., 1976-78; research group head The Nowland Orgn., Greenwich, Conn., 1977-78; pres. Qualitative Decisions Center, Inc., N.Y.C., 1978—. Cert. psychologist. Mem. Am. Psychol. Assn., Am. Mktg. Assn., AAUP, Assn. Psychophysiol. Study of Sleep. Office: 205 Lexington Ave New York NY 10016

FRENI, MIRELLA, soprano; b. Modena, Italy, Feb. 27, 1935; d. Ennio and Gianna F.; m. Leone Magiera, 1955; 1 dau., Micaela. Debut as Micaela in Carmen, Modena, 1955; since has appeared in major opera house throughout world, including La Scala, Royal Opera House, Covent Garden, Met. Opera, Vienna State Opera, Paris Opera, Salzburg Festival, Glyndebourne Festival: appeared in film Madame Butterfly and U.S. pub. TV broadcast of The Marriage of Figaro; major roles include: Nanetta in Falstaff, Mimi in La Boheme, Violetta in La Traviatta, Desdemona in Otello, Zerlina in Don Giovanni; appeared on numerous operatic recs., including Carmen (Grammy award for best opera rec. 1964). Office: care Hervert H Breslin Inc 119 W 57th St New York NY 10019 *

FREUDEN, PATRICIA, mfg. co. exec.; b. Arnold, Pa., Feb. 26, 1940; d. Joseph M. and Julie (Ference) Ratajczak; student U. Pitts., 1966, nights, 1978—; m. Donald F. Freuden, Aug. 17, 1970. Sec., technician Wesley Jessen Lens Labs., Pitts., 1962-70, sec., contact lens fitter, 1970-75; v.p. Payramid Plastics Ltd., Pitts., 1976—; partner Freuden Optical Co., Pitts., 1979—. Mem. Contact Lens Mfg. Assn. Am.

FREUND, ROYLE LAUNCEY, investment and mfg. co. exec.; b. Milw., June 14, 1930; d. Leroy and Anne (Edelman) Michel; children—Kim Glaser Selbert, Leslie Glaser Kanner. With Revell, Inc., Venice, Calif., 1958-82, pres., chief exec. officer, 1970-72, chairwoman bd., 1972-79, vice chairwoman bd., 1979-82; pres. R&M Investment Co.; v.p. mktg. Kryton Industries; dir. Merc. Nat. Bank, Los Angeles; video-tape participant UCLA mgmt. course, 1974. Mem. Toy Mfrs. Assn. (dir. 1975), Hobby Industry Assn. Am. (dir. 1974-75, sec. 1975, exec. com. 1975), Young Pres. Orgn. (exec. com. 1976-77), young Pres. Orgn.-Grads., World Bus. Council. Office: 330 Washington St Suite 330 Marina del Rey CA 90291

FREY, AUDREY ETHEL, pub. co. ofcl.; b. India, Feb. 27, 1926; came to U.S., 1948, naturalized, 1953; d. Louis Percival and Marguerita Isabel (D'Silva) Spencer; S.C. honors degree, Cambridge (Eng.) U., 1942; student Govt. Sch. Art, 1942-47, Art Students League, 1949-50, 51-52; m. Eric Konstantin Frey, Jan. 21, 1961. With McGraw-Hill Pub. Co., N.Y.C., 1955—, prodn. mgr. Coal Age, also Engring. and Mining Jour., 1955-66, bus. mgr. Internat. Mgmt., 1966-69, service ops. mgr. Internat. Publs., 1969-76, U.S. mktg. services mgr. Internat. Mgmt. Network of Publs., 1976—, dir. U.S. publ. services; speaker internat. mag. communications; panel mem. bus. seminars. Mem. Mus. Natural History, Nat. Wildlife Fedn., Art Students League. Recipient 3 first awards Printing Industries Met. N.Y. Home: 2860 Bailey Ave New York NY 10463 Office: 1221 Ave of the Americas New York NY 10020

FREY, BARBARA JEAN, state data processing adminstr.; b. Dansville, N.Y., Mar. 6, 1940; d. Martin Anthony and Helen (Bricks) Pfuntner; student parochial schs., Rochester, N.Y.; m. Kenneth Ronald Frey, Dec. 22, 1973; children—Everett Gary Garnsey, Bradley Scott Frey. Keypunch/tab operator Rochester Telephone Co. (N.Y.), 1958-60; key punch operator, computer analyst, programmer Monroe County (N.Y.) Dept. Social Services, Rochester, 1961-68, asst. to commr. for data processing methods and procedures, 1969-74; dir. ops. N.Y. State Dept. Social Services, Albany, 1974-80, asso. commr. for regional adminstrn., 1980-81, MA-EDP coordinator, 1981—; pvt. solar constrn. cons., 1980—. Tech. certs. IBM. Mem. Am. Soc. Pub. Adminstrs. Roman Catholic. Home: Route 1 Veeder Rd Slingerlands NY 12159 Office: 40 N Pearl St Albany NY 12243

FREY, CHERYL DIANNE, design co. exec.; b. Grafton, W.Va., Feb. 1, 1949; d. John Edwin and Audrey Louise (Reitelbach) Frey; student St. Augustine's Coll., Salem Coll.; m. Donald Furniss, Feb. 16, 1970; children— Chasen Telly, Cortney Cashton. Asst. sales trainer Creative Designs, Redland, Md., 1970, trainer, 1970, regional mgr., 1970-72, asso. dir. sales, 1972-73, dir. sales, 1973—; mng. dir. Washington Art Auction and Gallery, 1980—; ops. mgr./dir. Creativity Unltd. Fine Art, 1980—. Mem. Nat. Assn. Female Execs., NOW, Women U.S.A., Design League. Home: PO Box 163 Gaithersburg MD 20760

FREY, CHERYL MILLER, phys. chemist; b. Lorain, Ohio, Sept. 7, 1943; d. Louis Andrew and Margaret Louise (Metz) Miller; B.S. in Chemistry, Western Res. U., 1965; M.S. in Chemistry, Case-Western Res. U., 1968, Ph.D., 1971; m. Robert George Frey, Mar. 31, 1967. Sr. chemist B.F. Goodrich Chem. Co., Avon Lake, Ohio, 1974-78; asso. scientist Glidden Coatings & Resins, Strongsville, Ohio, 1978-81, scientist, 1981-82; tech. specialist 3M, St. Paul, 1982—; speaker women in sci. program Notre Dame Coll. Mem. Nat. Assn. Corrosion Engrs., Am. Chem. Soc., Cleve. Soc. Coatings Tech., Am. Paint Soc. Contbr. articles to Jour. Am. Chem. Soc., 1971-81. Home: 9650 Justen Trail White Bear Lake MN 55110 Office: 3M Center 236-2C Saint Paul MN 55144

FREY, DIANE ELIZABETH, psychologist, educator; b. Quakertown, Pa., Apr. 6, 1945; d. Norman L. and Helen Ruth (Snyder) F.; B.S., Shippensburg State Coll., 1966; M.Ed., U. Ill., 1967, Ph.D., 1970. Tchr., Upper Darby (Pa.) Sch. Dist., 1966; counselor St. Joseph (Ill.) Ogden High Sch., 1967-69; research asst. U. Ill., Champaign, 1969-70; asso. prof. counseling psychology Wright State U., Dayton, Ohio, 1970—; pvt. practice clin. psychology, Dayton, 1971—; chief psychol. cons. Ohio Bur. Vocat. Rehab., 1974-81; chmn. treatment of child abuse and neglect Greater Dayton Area, SCAN, 1977-80; nat. trainer Human Devel. Tng. Inst., 1978—; cons. Alcohol Safety and Prevention Program, 1982—. NDEA fellow, 1966-67. Mem. Am. Psychol. Assn. Research in conflict mgmt., self-esteem, child counseling. Home: 7431 Union School House Rd Dayton OH 45424 Office: 374-F Millett Hall Wright State U Dayton OH 45431

FREY, ELAINE MARILYN, township govt. ofcl.; b. Throggs Neck, N.Y., Aug. 1, 1925; d. Harry Arthur and Madeline Anna (Blum) Dalhauser; B.A., Hunter Coll., N.Y.C., 1947; m. Francis Robert Frey, July 30, 1949; children—Christopher Mitchell, Elyse Fidelis, Francis Scott. Bacteriologist, Vick Chem. Co., Flushing, N.Y., 1943-47; bacteriological technician Cornell U. Med. Sch., 1947-50; with transp. dept. Holmdel (N.J.) Bd. Edn., 1967—; mem. Holmdel Twp. Com., 1977—, mem. planning bd., 1979—; chmn. Holmdel Bd. Recreation Commrs., 1967-75. Bd. mgrs. YMCA-Camp Arrowhead, 1968-70; mem. Holmdel Juvenile Conf. Bd., 1971-76; mem. Holmdel Bicentennial com., 1977-78. Recipient Bicentennial Public Safety award, 1976. Mem. Holmdel Hist. Soc. (founder, pres. 1974-76). Republican. Roman Catholic. Author: Sketch Book of Historic Holmdel, 1976, Saint Catharine's Centennial History, 1979. Home: 4 Parkway Pl Holmdel NJ 07733 Office: Box 385 14 Crawford Corners Rd Holmdel NJ 07733

FREY, ELLEN THERESA, courier co. ofcl.; b. N.Y.C., Nov. 18, 1950; d. Samuel Vincent and Theresa Ann (Mahoney) Sabatino; student Coll. Notre Dame, S.I., 1969-70; B.A. in Sociology, St. Peter Coll., 1973; m. Anthony Lester Frey, Apr. 7, 1972. Tchr. parochial sch., Jersey City, 1973-75; with ops. dept. World Courier, N.Y.C., 1975-76, customer service dept., 1976-77, mgr. customer service, 1977-80, mgr. dept. met. sales and customer service, 1980—. Mem. Women's Traffic Club N.Y. Home: 480 Broadway Passaic NJ 07055 Office: 19 Rector St New York NY 10006

FREY, MARGARET CHARLENE, hotel/motel co. ofcl.; b. Flagstaff, Ariz., Nov. 21, 1925; d. Charles Edward and Myrtle Estelle (Williams) Monier; student U. Ariz., 1942-43; m. Harold Phil Frey, Sept. 15, 1946; children—Garldene Bobette, Harold Phil, Elizabeth Ann. Med. and ins. sec., 1956-70; ophthal. technician, 1960-71; media buyer, Phoenix, 1972-74; with Best Western, Inc., Phoenix, 1974—, mgr. media Road Atlas and Travel Guide, 1975-79, ednl. services mgr., 1979-81, account exec. in-house advt., 1981—, asso. B-W Advt. in-house agy.; adv. bd. U.S. Travel Data Center, Washington. Active Prisoners of War/Missing in Action. Served with M.C., USNR, 1943-45. Republican. Lutheran. Clubs: Toastmasters, USAF Officers Wives. Home: 7237 E Latham St Scottsdale AZ 85257 Office: Best Western Internat Best Western Way PO Box 10203 Phoenix AZ 85064

FREY, MARSHA LEE, historian; b. Toledo, Feb. 21, 1947; d. Henry and Dolores (Saionz) F.; B.S., B.A. summa cum laude, Ohio State U., 1967, M.A., 1968, Ph.D. (NDEA fellow), 1971. Lectr., Ohio State U., 1971-72; vis. asst. prof. U. Oreg., 1972-73; asst. prof. history Kans. State U., Manhattan, 1973-79, assoc. prof., 1979—. Folber Shakespeare Library fellow, 1974; grantee Nat. Endowment Humanities, 1977-78, Am. Council Learned Socs., 1981, U.S. Office Edn., 1982. Mem. Am. Hist. Assn., Western Soc. French History, Western Assn. German History, Conf. Salvic and East European History, Phi Beta Kappa, Phi Alpha Theta, Alpha Lambda Delta. Author: (with Frey and Rule) Observation from the Hague and Utrecht, 1978; co-translator: The Gods Are Athirst, 1979; contbr. articles to profl. jours. Home: 1729 Denholm Dr Manhattan KS 66502 Office: Dept History Kans State U Manhattan KS 66502

FREYBERGER, RUTH MATILDA, educator; b. Reading, Pa., Nov. 15, 1912; d. John Jacob and Hattie Matilda Freyberger; B.S. in Pub. Sch. Art, Kutztown State Coll., 1935; M.Ed. in Art Edn., Pa. State U., 1940, Ed.D. in Art Edn. and Fine Arts, 1951. Art tchr., supr. New Holland (Pa.) Borough Schs., 1935-41, Huntingdon (Pa.) Borough Schs., 1941-45, art tchr. jr. and sr. high schs., jr. coll., Derry Twp. High Sch., Hershey Jr. Coll., Hershey, Pa., 1945-50; prof. art Ill. State U., Normal, 1951—, also continuing edn. prof. in folk art. Mem. Nat. Art Edn. Assn., Ill. Art Edn. Assn., Phi Delta Kappa, Pi Lambda Theta, Delta Kappa Gamma. Republican. Lutheran. Contbr. articles to profl. jours. Home: 903 W Hovey Ave Normal IL 61761 Office: CVA-102 Ill State U Normal IL 61761

FREYN, BARBARA LYNN, indsl. designer; b. Newark, N.Y., Oct. 26, 1946; d. William Raymond and Eleanor Theora (Allen) F.; grad. public schs., N.Y. Engring. aide Stone & Webster Engring Corp., Boston, 1973-75; operator Sea-3, Inc., Newington, N.H., 1975-76; designer II, United Engrs. and Constructors Co., Boston, 1976-80, Daniel Internat. Corp., Greenville, S.C., 1981—. Served with USN, 1965-73. Mem. Instrument Soc. Am. (sect. sec.).

FRICK, DOROTHY MARY LES MONDE (MRS. RAY J. FRICK), artist, civic worker; b. Green Bay, Wis., Jan. 7, 1912; d. Desire Joseph and Olive Belle (Trask) Les Monde; pvt. study art; m. Ray J. Frick, Aug. 27, 1930 (dec. Aug. 1970); 1 son, William. One-man show at Rahr Civic Center, Manitowoc, Wis., 1963, 66; exhibited in group shows at Green Bay, Madison and Two Rivers, Wis.; sec. Little Gallery Inc., 1974-76, 79-80, pres., 1980-83, dir., 1974—. Active fund drives ARC, Am. Cancer Soc.; pres. Little Gallery, Inc., Manitowoc, 1946-47, 66-67, sec., 1967-70, exhibit chmn., 1968-69; mem. City Council of Arts, 1970—. Bd. dirs. Rahr Civic Center, Manitowoc, 1960-68, vice chmn. mus. bd., 1960-68; bd. deacons First Presbyterian Ch., 1980-83. Mem. Fedn. Women's Clubs, Manitowoc County Hist. Soc. (pres. 1961-63, v.p. 1966-68), Palettiers (sec. 1966-67). Home: 815 Park St Manitowoc WI 54220

FRICKE, ALMA BLAKE, clubwomen; b. Somerville, Tex., June 3, 1916; d. Edward Henry and Alice Mae (Warren) Lott; student Tex. Woman's U., 1938-39, N. Tex. State U., 1939-41; m. Frederick John Fricke, Apr. 16, 1941; children—Frederick John, Alice June Fricke Missall. Organizing regent Charles Dibrell chpt. DAR, 1963, chpt. regent, 1963-65, state librarian N.Mex., 1965-67, state treas., 1969-71, dist. dir., 1971-73, state vice-regent, 1971-73, state regent, 1973-75, v.p. gen., 1976-78. Mem. adv. bd. Kate Duncan Smith Sch., Grant, Ala., 1977-80. Recipient medal of appreciation, SAR, 1976. Mem. Soc. Lees of Va., Order First Families of Miss., Washington Family Descs., Colonial Dames XII Century, Daus. Am. Colonists (state vice regent), Jamestowne Soc. (life), Daus. Am. Revolution, Daus. Republic of Tex., United Daus. Confederacy, Nat. Huguenots Soc., Alumni Assn. Tex. Woman's U. Republican. Episcopalian. Home: 4214 Avenida La Resolana NE Albuquerque NM 87110

FRICON, TERRI MADELINE, music publisher, producer, cons.; b. Buffalo, July 19, 1944; d. Anthony Edward and Josephine Rose (D'Amico) F.; student San Jose (Calif.) State U., 1961; B.Mus., U. Miami (Fla.), 1963. Asst. to profl. mgr. Screen Gems Music, 1964; v.p., partner Wednesday's Child Prodns., 1967; pres. music group Filmways, also dir. music dept. Filmways TV and Filmways Motion Pictures, 1974-81; pres. Fricon Entertainment Co., Inc., Los Angeles, 1982—, Calif. Copyright Conf., 1980-81; chmn. Music Pubs. Forum, 1979-81. Recipient Golden Staff award Music and Arts Found. Am., 1975—, Profl. Achievement award Soroptimist Club Los Angeles, 1977. Mem. ASCAP (pubs. adv. com. 1977—), Assn. Ind. Music Pubs., Nat. Acad. Rec. Arts and Scis., Nashville Songwriters Assn., Acad. Country Music, Black Music Assn., Nat. Music Pubs. Assn., Broadcast Music, Inc. Address: 8825 Ashcroft Ave Los Angeles CA 90048

FRIDAY, SHARON HENDERSON, purchasing exec.; b. Monroe, N.C., Nov. 18, 1951; d. Truman Jesse and Gladys (Nash) Henderson; student Western Carolina U., 1970-71, Gaston Coll., summer, 1980, Queens Coll., 1980-81; student Limestone Coll., 1981—; m. Barry Ernest Friday, Mar. 17, 1974; 1 son, Craig Ernest. With Mill-Power Supply Co. subs. Duke Power Co., Charlotte, N.C., 1971—, purchasing specialist, 1979—, dir. adminstrn. Duke Power Task Force, 1979-82, buyer/expediter, 1982—. Recipient Am. Mgmt. Soc. award, 1970; Clyde A. Erwin scholar, 1970-71; N.C. Tuition grantee, 1970-71; Mem. Nat. Assn. Female Execs. Democrat. Baptist. Club: Lincoln County Democratic Women's. Home: Route 2 PO Box 775 Denver NC 28037 Office: PO Box 32307 Charlotte NC 28232

FRIED, DOROTHY MAXINE, social worker; b. Chgo., June 8, 1946; d. Fred Herman and Edith (Salomon) Nathan; B.A., Bradley U., 1968; M.S. in Social Work, U. Chgo., 1971; m. Michael Fried, Sept. 5, 1971; 1 son, Ian Nathan. Social work asst. United Charities of Chgo., 1968-69, social worker, 1971-72; social worker Jewish Family and Children's Services, New Orleans, 1972-74; social worker Summit County Children's Services Bd., Akron, Ohio, 1974-75; social worker cons. Social Work Cons, Inc., Huntington Beach, Calif., 1977—; pvt. practice social work, also tchr. Lic. clin. social worker, Calif. Mem. Nat. Assn. Social Workers. Home: 6034 Carpenter Ave North Hollywood CA 91606 Office: 4952 Warner Ave Suite 217 Huntington Beach CA 92649

FRIED, ELAINE JUNE, business exec.; b. Los Angeles, Oct. 19, 1943; grad. Pasadena (Calif.) High Sch., 1963; various coll. courses; m. Howard I. Fried, Aug. 7, 1966; children—Donna Marie, Randall Jay. Agt., office mgr. Howard I. Fried Agy., Alhambra, Calif., 1975—; v.p. Sea Hill, Inc., Pasadena, Calif., 1973—. Publicity chmn. San Gabriel Valley (Calif.) unit Am. Diabetes Assn.; publicity chmn. San Gabriel Valley sect. Nat. Council Jewish Women, also tribute chmn. San Gabriel Valley sect.; bd. dirs. Vis. Nurse Assn. Pasadena and San Gabriel Valley chmn. spl. events publicity Temple Beth Torah, Alhambra. Recipient Vol. award So. Calif. affiliate Am. Diabetes Assn., 1974-77. Clubs: B'nai B'rith Women, Hadassah. Speaker on psycho-social aspects of diabetes, life and health ins. for diabetics.

FRIED, ELEANOR REINGOLD, mental health cons.; b. Quantico, Va., Jan. 4, 1943; d. Morris and Eleanor (Wilson) Reingold; B.S. cum laude, Boston U., 1964; M.S., CCNY, 1971; postgrad. Fordham U., 1971-73; Ph.D., Fielding Inst., Santa Barbara, 1981; m. Albert M. Fried, July 16, 1967; children—Joshua Mark, Noah Seth, Adam Lawrence. Psychology intern, Roosevelt Hosp., N.Y.C., 1971-73; cons. Inwood House, N.Y.C., 1971—; staff therapist Univ. Cons. Center for Mental Hygiene, Bronx, 1974-79; clin. instr. Univ. Cons. Center for Mental Hygiene, 1976—; cons. Early Childhood Learning Center, Paramus, N.J., 1978—, Found. for Religion and Mental Health. Mem. Am. Psychol. Assn. (asso.), Kappa Tau Alpha. Address: 44 Afterglow Way Verona NJ 07044

FRIEDAN, BETTY, author, feminist leader; b. Peoria, Ill., Feb. 4, 1921; d. Harry and Miriam (Horwitz) Goldstein; B.A. summa cum laude, Smith Coll., 1942, D.H.L., 1975; m. Carl Friedan, June 1947 (div. May 1969); children—Daniel, Jonathan, Emily. Research fellow U. Calif. at Berkeley, 1943; lectr. feminism univs., bus. and profl. orgns., polit. groups in U.S. and Europe; founder NOW 1st pres., 1966-70, chairwoman adv. com., organizer Nat. Women's Polit. Caucas, 1971; organizer, dir. Womans First Woman's Bank. Bd. dirs. NOW Legal Def. and Edn. Fund, Girl Scouts U.S. Recipient Humanist of Year award, 1975. Mem. P.E.N., Soc. Mag. Writers, Am. Sociol. Assn., Phi Beta Kappa. Author: The Feminine Mystique, 1963; It Changed My Life, 1976; contbg. editor McCall's mag., 1971; contbr. Harper's, Social Policy, N.Y. Times mag.; editorial bd. Present Tense. Address: NOW 425 13th St NW Suite 1048 Washington DC 20004 *

FRIEDBERG, CHRISTINE CHURCH, banker; b. Des Moines, June 11, 1946; d. Harold Brownlee and Dorothy Ellen (Rhyne) Church; A.B., Wellesley Coll., 1968; cert. of completion Consumer Banker's Sch. Retail Bank Mgmt., 1977; m. William David Friedberg, Mar. 13, 1969; children—David Brownlee, Adam Church. Mgmt. trainee Shawmut Bank, Boston, 1968-72, loan officer/br. mgr., 1972-77, retail sales mgr., corp. sales mgr., 1977-78; adminstr. Econ. Devel. and Indsl. Corp., Boston, 1978-80; asst. v.p. First Nat. Bank, Boston, 1981—; thesis adviser Consumer Banker's Sch. Retail Bank Mgmt., 1980—. Bd. dirs. Action for Children's TV, 1978—; mem. adv. com. Town of Brookline, 1979-82. Club: Wellesley Coll. (Boston). Home: 133 Hyslop Rd Brookline MA 02046 Office: 100 Federal St Boston MA 02110

FRIEDEL, HARRIETT ANN, food mktg. cons.; b. Phila., July 1, 1940; d. Herman August and Harriett Martha (Singer) Friedel; B.S., Drexel U., 1962, M.B.A., 1978. Dir. home service Acme Markets, Inc., Phila., 1962-71; corp. new products staff McCormick & Co., Inc., Hunt Valley, Md., 1971-76; pres. Harriett A. Friedel, Ltd., Jenkintown, Pa., 1976—;

lectr. St. Joseph's U., Phila., 1978—. Mem. Am. Home Econs. Assn., Home Economists in Bus. (Phila. group chmn. 1970-71), Am. Mktg. Assn., Inst. Food Technologists, Packaging Inst. U.S. (Phila. bd. dirs. 1978—), AAUW, Phi Mu. Republican. Lutheran. Club: Order Eastern Star. Office: PO Box 225 Jenkintown PA 19046

FRIEDELL, JOANN, social service adminstr.; b. Bklyn., Feb. 4, 1951; d. George and Edna F.; B.A. in Psychology, SUNY, Stony Brook, 1974; M.S. in Ednl. Psychology, Coll. St. Rose, 1979. Auditor, N.Y. State Social Services, Albany, 1974-78, supr. computer piloting, 1978-79, supr. computer installation, 1979-81, mgr. computer ops., 1981—; renovator, mgr. income-producing property. Mem. Nat. Assn. Female Execs. Club: Am. Health and Racquet (Albany). Office: 40 N Pearl St Albany NY 12207

FRIEDHEIM, BETTE SWEENEY, editor; b. Bklyn., Mar. 23, 1921; d. Edward and Catherine (Lynch) Sweeney; student N.Y.U., 1946, U. Mexico City, 1947; m. Eric Friedheim, Dec. 31, 1951. Travel editor Am. Life mag., N.Y.C., 1950-51; asso. editor Travel Agt. mag., N.Y.C., 1951—, Hotel Gazette, N.Y.C., 1957-60, Interline Reporter, N.Y.C., 1951—; editor Travel Industry Personnel Directory, N.Y.C., 1951—; sec.-treas. Am. Traveler, Inc., N.Y.C., 1951—, Interline, Inc., N.Y.C., 1951—, Travel Industry, Inc., N.Y.C., 1951—, El Travel Agt. Internat., N.Y.C., 1979—; ins. broker, 1951—. Mem. Soc. Am. Travel Writers (past sec.), Aviation and Space Writers Assn., Overseas Press Club. Republican. Roman Catholic. Home: 860 United Nations Plaza New York NY 10017 Office: 2 W 46th St New York NY 10036

FRIEDLAENDER, L. MARTHA, social work adminstr.; b. N.Y.C., Dec. 15, 1931; d. Georges D. and Rosalind (Kreinik) F.; B.A., Colby Coll., 1953; M.S.S.W., Columbia U., 1956. Supr. of Brownsville, Bklyn. unit United Cerebral Palsy of N.Y.C., 1956-59; asst. dir. group work Fedn. of the Handicapped, N.Y.C., 1960-61; Fulbright scholar social group work U.S. Ednl. Commn. in the U.K., London, 1961-62; supr. cottage life Leake & Watts Children's Home, Yonkers, N.Y., 1962-65; sr. caseworker Windham Children's Service, N.Y.C., 1965-67; program dir. Vacations and Community Services for the Blind, N.Y.C., 1967-70; adminstr. mental health services Health Ins. Plan, N.Y.C., 1970-75; psychotherapist (part-time) Social Service Bd., N.Y. Soc. Ethical Culture, N.Y.C., 1974—; adminstrv. social work supr. L.I. Jewish/Hillside Med. Center, Queens Hosp. Center affiliation, Jamaica, N.Y., 1977-82; asst. dir. dept. social work, also discharge planning coordinator St. Luke's-Roosevelt Med. Center, Roosevelt Div., N.Y.C., 1982—. Mem. nat. council Fellowship of Reconciliation, 1962—, mem. personnel com., 1968—. Cert. social worker, N.Y. Mem. Nat. Assn. Social Workers, Am. Public Health Assn., Am. Orthopsychiat. Assn. Home: 382 Central Park W New York NY 10025 Office: St Luke's Roosevelt Med Center Roosevelt Div 428 W 59th New York NY 10019

FRIEDLAND, BENICE UDELLE, psychologist, educator; b. Akron, Ohio, June 18, 1935; d. Hymen H. and Ida S.; B.Sc., Ohio State U., 1956; M.Ed., Frostburg State Coll., 1969; Ed.D., W.Va. U., 1972; children—by previous marriage—Holli, David Michael. Asso. prof. psychology Coppin State Coll., 1972-80; adj. prof. Bowie State Coll., Loyola Coll.; pvt. practice psychology, Balt., 1976—; psychologist Spring Grove State Hosp., Balt., 1978—; bd. dirs. Blind Industries and Services of Md.; bd. advisors rehab. div. Balt. Goodwill Industries, 1979—; cons., inservice trainer ednl. and vocat. rehab. agys. Mem. Am. Personnel and Guidance Assn., Am. Psychol. Assn., Nat. Rehab. Assn., N.Am. Soc. Adlerian Psychology. Author: (with W. McKelvie) Career Goal Counseling, 1978; editor Individual Psychologist, 1976—; mem. editorial bd. Jour. Rehab., 1979—; contbr. articles to profl. publs. Home: 6819 Cherokee Dr Baltimore MD 21209 Office: 2 E Read St Baltimore MD 21202

FRIEDLAND, LILLI, psychologist; b. Bad Gastein, Austria, Feb. 24, 1947; came to U.S., 1950, naturalized, 1956; d. Joseph and Marie (Bjerkenhejm) Rebhun; B.A., U. Oreg., 1966; Ph.D., U. So. Calif. 1975; m. David Lee Friedland, Feb. 22, 1969; 1 son, Jered. Research asst. Research Service Bur., Los Angeles, 1968-70; cons. to Council of Jewish Fedn., N.Y.C., 1969-70; research analyst Los Angeles Mental Health Dept., 1970-73; chief planning div. Office of Alcohol Abuse and Alcoholism, Los Angeles County, 1973-74, chief program and system evaluation, 1973-74; chief drug abuse planning Los Angeles County Dept. Health Services, 1973-76; dir. family devel. program Suicide Prevention Center, Los Angeles, 1975-77; pres. Friedland Psychol. Assos., Inc., Beverly Hills, Calif., 1975—; cons. to pvt. secondary schs., Calif., 1973—; condr. workshops. Chairperson Devel. Disabilities Area Bd., Calif., 1977-79, Program Planning and Evaluation Com. Area Bd., 1975-77; mem. exec. com., community service com., leadership devel. com., mem. program planning and budgeting com. Jewish Fedn. Council, 1981—. Recipient certs. of appreciation Bd. Suprs. Los Angeles County, 1980, Los Angeles County Narcotics and Dangerous Drugs Commn., 1975. Mem. Am. Psychol. Assn., Calif. Psychol. Assn., Los Angeles Psychol. Assn. (profl. conduct com. 1979—, editor Newsletter 1979-81, treas. 1982), Los Angeles County Psychol. Assn. (dir. 1980—), Los Angeles County Clin. Psychol. Assn. (dir. 1980—), Women in Bus., Women's Referral Service, Hadassah. Republican. Jewish. Home: 1216 Daniels Dr Los Angeles CA 90035 Office: 2080 Century Park E Suite 204 Los Angeles CA 90067

FRIEDLAND, RUTH VOLID, art gallery owner; b. Chgo.; d. Ben and Ida (Saykowitch) Volid; ed. Art Inst. Chgo., U. Chgo., Chouinard Art Sch., Otis Art Inst., Am. Acad. Art; 2 daus. Art tchr., Chgo., 1950-52; owner, designer Fashion Hat Bus., 1945-47; interior designer, graphic designer, copy chief Meyer Both Co., 1939-45; owner, designer Dude Ranch, 1947-50; creative dir. King Kor Stamp Co., Chgo., 1962-70; public relations staff Merchandising Group, N.Y.C., 1970-72; owner Ruth Volid Gallery, Ltd., Chgo., 1970—. Mem. U.S. affiliated bd. Mus. Contemporary Art, 1976; mem. woman's bd. Sinfonia Musicale. Mem. Archives Am. Art, Am., Soc. Interior Designers Industry Found., Nat. Home Fashion League, Soc. Archtl. Historians, North Shore Art League, Arts Club Chgo. Club: President's. Office: 225 W Illinois St Chicago IL 60610

FRIEDLANDER, ANNA FAY, economist, writer; b. Newark, July 23, 1935; d. Haney Fay and Mary Lillian Rodgers; B.S. in Journalism cum laude, U. Minn., 1957; M.A. in Broadcast Film Arts, So. Meth. U., 1968, M.A. econs., 1975; children—Paul C., Mark T. Editor, Richardson (Tex.) News, 1960; asst. editor Sun News, Sun Oil, Dallas, 1960-69; field research dir. Corp. for Public Broadcasting, Dallas-Ft. Worth, 1972-75; pres. Multi-Media, Inc., Dallas, 1968-70; instr. econs. So. Meth. U., Dallas, 1973-74, Richland Coll., Dallas, 1975-78, Northlake Coll., Irving, Tex., 1978-80; exec. and founding editor Solar Engring. Mag., Dallas, 1975-81; pub. First Person Singular, 1981-82; staff economist Keplinger Cos., energy cons., Houston, 1982—. Mem. Internat. Solar Energy Soc. (gen. chmn. ann. meeting Am. sect.), ASHRAE, Tex. Solar Energy Soc. (founder, dir. 1978-80), Center for Renewable Resources (dir., officer 1978-80). Author: The Shared Time Strategy, 1966; Dallas Food Finds, 1974. Home: 361 N Post Oak Ln Apt 342 Houston TX 77024 Office: 3200 Entex Bldg Houston TX 77002

FRIEDMAN, ARLENE, editor; b. Newark; d. Isador and Dorothy Friedman; grad. Katharine Gibbs Sch., N.Y.C.; m. Harold Shepherd, Nov. 7, 1971. With William Morris Agy., 1966; with Fawcett Publs., N.Y.C., 1966—, mng. editor, then editor, 1972-73, editor-in-chief Crest and Gold Medal Books, 1973-79; editor-in-chief Fawcett Books Group unit CBS Publs., 1979-81, v.p., 1981—. Address: 30 E 9th St Apt 6CC New York City NY 10003

FRIEDMAN, BARBARA ALLYN BERNSTEIN, pub. co. exec.; b. N.Y.C., June 6, 1946; d. Allan Charles and Frances Ester (Orange) Bernstein; B.A. in Polit. Sci., N.Y. U., 1968; student Rutgers U., 1968-69, U. So. Calif., 1973; m. Arthur Daniel Friedman, Mar. 31, 1968; children—Michael Kenneth, Steven David. With Children's Book Council, N.Y.C., 1964; programmer Prudential Life Ins. Co., Newark, 1968; pres., founder Computer Sci. Press., Inc., Rockville, Md., 1974—. Mem. Washington Pubs. Assn., Assn. Computing Machinery, IEEE, Am. Math Soc., Assn. for Ednl. Data Services, Pi Sigma Alpha. Republican. Jewish. Home: 9301 Sprinklewood Ln Potomac MD 20854 Office: 11 Taft Ct Rockville MD 20850

FRIEDMAN, BARBARA SIEGEL, acct.; b. N.Y.C., Jan. 19, 1953; d. Philip and Laura (Gitlen) Siegel; B.S., Fairleigh Dickinson U., 1973, postgrad., 1974—; m. Bennett Friedman, June 1, 1975; children—Erica Brooke, Brett Ross (twins). Sr. auditor Benjamin Nadel & Co., N.Y.C., 1973-76; acctg. mgr. N.Y. Zool. Soc., Bronx, 1976-79; controller Vera Inst. Justice, N.Y.C., 1979-80; sr. acctg. coordinator Salomon Bros., N.Y.C., 1980-81; controller N.Y. Bot. Garden, 1981—. Tech. asst. N.Y. State Council on Arts; asst. dist. leader 9th Ward Democratic Club, 1970-71. Mem. Nat. Assn. Female Execs. Democrat. Jewish. Club: Racquetplaza Racquetball. Home: 58 Underhill Rd Scarsdale NY 10583

FRIEDMAN, CAROLYN, fragrance mfg. co. exec.; b. N.Y.C., Dec. 5, 1950; d. Ben and Pauline (Bergman) F.; student Hunter Coll., 1970-71. Sec. to dir. sales Revlon Inc., N.Y.C., 1968-70, asst. to various product mgrs., 1970-71, asst. to mktg. mgr. Salon div., 1971-72; corporate mktg. mgr. Faberge Inc., N.Y.C., 1972—. Mem. Fashion Group, Cosmetic Career Women, Fragrance Found. Office: 1345 Ave of Americas New York NY 10105

FRIEDMAN, COLLETTE SWEET, kitchen designer, interior designer; b. Los Angeles, Feb. 25, 1933; d. Maurice Paul and Ilona M. (Feld) Albert; student Los Angeles Valley Coll., 1961-63; student Calif. State U., Northridge, 1964, Pierce Coll., 1965-67, UCLA, 1968-70; m. Robert A. Friedman, Sept. 16, 1951; children—Scott D., Brian C., Victoria A., Valaree L., Collette. Interior designer, North Hollywood, Calif., 1962-76; owner/designer Better Homes and Kitchens, Westlake Village, Calif., 1976—. Recipient award Bank of America, 1951. Mem. Am. Inst. Kitchen Dealers (sec. So. Calif. chpt. 1979-82), Conejo Assn. Profl. Interior Designers, Westlake Village C. of C., Conejo Valley C. of C. Office: 31121 Via Colinas 1004 Westlake Village CA 91362

FRIEDMAN, DOTTIE JUDITH, retail clothing store exec.; b. N.Y.C., June 5, 1938; d. Max and Hannah (Levy) Shlafer; student Salt Lake City public schs.; divorced; children—Elisabeth, Tracy. Engaged in retail clothing, 1963—; v.p., chief exec. officer Contempo Casuals (sold to Carter, Hawley Hale, 1979), Los Angeles, 1979—. Named Woman of Yr., Cedars Sinai Hosp., 1980. Mem. Fashion Group. Address: 1104 Sunset Vale Los Angeles CA 90069

FRIEDMAN, FRANCES ALMAND, social worker; b. Hazelhurst, Ga., Feb. 3, 1948; d. Edward Felton and Rosemary (Anderson) Almand; B.S., Fla. State U., 1970; M.S.W., U. Md., 1975; postgrad. Nat. Cath. Sch. Social Services, Cath. U., 1975; m. Robert M. Friedman, Mar. 20, 1970; children—Katherine, David. Behavioral asso. Sunland Hosp. for Mentally Retarded, Tallahassee, 1969-70; mem. hotline staff Youth and Family Counseling Agy., Oyster Bay, N.Y., 1971; social work asst. St. Mary's County Dept. Social Services, Leonardtown, Md., 1972-73; med. social worker, med. social work dept. Arnne Arundel County Health Dept., Annapolis, Md., 1973-74; sch. social worker Tri-Agy. Sch. program Crownsville (Md.) Hosp. Center, 1974-75; research asso. Burt Assos., Inc., Inst. for Human Resources Research, Bethesda, Md., 1975; adj. instr. U. South Fla., Tampa, 1977; clin. social worker alcoholism services Hillsborough Community Mental Health Center, Tampa, 1977-78, clin. social worker, children's services, 1978-79; coordinator friend-to-friend program Community Council on Child Abuse and Neglect, Tampa, 1979-80; vis. lectr. dept. social work U. South Fla., Tampa, 1980-81; sch. social worker Hillsborough County Bd. Edn., Tampa, 1981—. Mem. Nat. Assn. Social Workers, Acad. Cert. Social Workers, Fla. Assn. Health and Social Services. Democrat. Home: 14042 Cascade Ln Tampa FL 33618 Office: 411 E Henderson Ave Tampa FL 33602

FRIEDMAN, LESLIE J., scriptwriter, businesswoman, author; b. N.Y.C., Oct. 12, 1948; d. Henry and Bernice A. Friedman; B.A., U. Cin., 1970; M.S., U. Ky., 1972. Children's librarian, then br. librarian trainee Public Library Cin. and Hamilton County, 1970-73; art librarian U. Ga., 1974-77; freelance lectr. women's media image, 1975—; producer: Mr. Whipple Groupies—Looking at Women's Advt. Image; Womanhood: A Pornographic Vision; author: Sex Role Stereotyping in the Mass Media, An Annotated Bibliography, 1977; partner Clarity Corp. Scripts. Mem. advisory bd. Atlanta Vocat. Counseling Center, Atlanta Council Battered Women. Mem. Women's Inst. Freedom Press, Women in Film, Art Libraries Soc. N.Am. (past regional pres.). Home and Office: 136 Terrace Dr NE Atlanta GA 30305

FRIEDMAN, LORRAINE (MRS. NORMAN B. FRIEDMAN), educator; b. Chgo., Sept. 24; d. Leon and Adele Weisman; A.B., U. Ill., 1944; M.A., Sch. Social Service Adminstrn., U. Chgo., 1947; children—Victor, Adele. Social caseworker State of Ill., Chgo., 1944-49; tchr. pub. schs., Chgo., 1960-66, sch. social worker, 1966-79; instr. field work Sch. Social Service Adminstrn., U. Chgo., 1971-79, cons. Ford Tchr. Tng. Program, staff mem. Grad. Sch. Edn., 1971-72, clin. asso. Sch. Social Service Adminstrn., 1974-79, coordinator bd. edn., 1979-80, acting coordinator, 1980-81; tchr. 1st course given on staff, human relations and social work Chgo. Bd. Edn., 1971-72. U.S. Children's Bur. fellow, 1945-47. Registered cert. social worker, Ill.; certified tchr.-social worker Chgo. Bd. Edn. Mem. Nat. Assn. Social Workers (workshop 5th Symposium 1977), Acad. Certified Social Workers. Contbr. articles to profl. jours. Address: 1236 E 57th St Chicago IL 60637

FRIEDMAN, MIRIAM, fin. exec.; b. Poland, Apr. 8, 1919; d. Nathan and Rose (Nelkin) Brook; grad. high sch.; m. Frank Friedman, Dec. 14, 1941; 1 dau., Jacalyn Friedman Walzer. With Midtown Motors, N.Y.C., 1944—, bookkeeper and comptroller, 1955—; controller Etna Products Inc., N.Y.C., 1955—. Mem. Jewish Community Center, Spring Valley, N.Y. Democrat. Club: B'nai B'rith. Office: Etna Products Inc 53 W 23d St New York NY 10010

FRIEDMAN, PAULA ROBBINS, social worker; b. N.Y.C., July 7, 1928; d. Larry and Hazel (Solomon) Robbins; B.A., Syracuse U., 1950; M.S.W., Adelphi U., 1973; m. Rubin Robert Friedman, Jan. 17, 1954; children—Stuart Lee, Andrew Bruce. Public relations office mgr., 1964-66; travel agt., 1966-67; abstractor, 1967-70; caseworker St. Christopher's Sch., Dobbs Ferry, N.Y., 1973-76; counselor Women-in-Self Help-Westchester, 1977-79; caseworker Nat. Nephrology Found., 1979-80; family service worker Swiss Benevolent Soc., N.Y.C., 1980; psychiat. social worker Westchester County Med. Center, Valhalla, N.Y., 1980—. Mem. Nat. Assn. Social Workers, Council of Nephrology Social Workers. Home: 125 Edgemont Rd Scarsdale NY 10583 Office: Vosburgh Pavilion Westchester County Med Center Valhalla NY 10595

FRIEDMAN, PHOEBE LOPATIN, photographer, writer, civil liberties activist; b. N.Y.C., Mar. 25, 1925; d. Israel and Sophie (Friedman) Lopatin; B.A., Hunter Coll., 1947; m. Ralph Friedman, Jan. 11, 1949; 1 dau., Amy. Free lance writer, photographer, 1950—; contbr. articles, photographs to the Nation, N.Y. Times, Los Angeles Times, numerous regional publs., trade jours.; photographs appearing in 7 books on Oregon; instr. Portland Community Coll., 1972—; commentator Sta. KBOO, Portland, 1972—, pres. bd. dirs., 1975-77; sr. paralegal Legal Aid of Multnomah County, 1980—. Mem. Multnomah County Democratic Central Com., 1970—, Oreg. State Dem. Central Com., 1976—; co-founder Portland Women Strike for Peace. Recipient Wayne Morse Tiger award Dem. Party of Oreg., 1981. Jewish. Address: 2845 NE 56th Ave Portland OR 97213

FRIEDMAN, PHYLLIS ARLENE, health service co. exec.; b. Bklyn., June 13, 1935; d. Louis and Mary (Asch) Weingast; student pub. schs., Bklyn.; m. Leonard Green, Mar. 1981; children—Brett, Mark. Mgr., Rochester (N.Y.) area br. Diet Workshop of Boston, 1967-68; pres. Rochester Diet, Inc. (doing bus. as Diet Workshop), 1968—; cons., field rep., mem. advisory bd. Internat. Diet Workshop; v.p. dir. Progress Inc., Balt. Capt. Community TV Fund Raising Auction, Rochester, 1977; pres. Rochester chpt. at large Women's Am. Orgn. Rehab. Tng., 1967-69. Named Diet Workshop Area Dir. of Year Internat. Diet Workshop, 1972. Mem. Rochester C. of C., Am. Mgmt. Assn., ORT, Hadassah, B'nai B'rith Women. Compiler and editor 4 point lifetime weight control plan of Internat. Diet Workshop. Home: 240 Hibiscus Dr Rochester NY 14618 Office: 4 Tobey Village Office Park Pittsford NY 14534

FRIEDMAN, SANDRA MASKALIK, speech pathologist; b. Bklyn., Apr. 26, 1941; d. Sam and Mollie Maskalik; A.A., Nassau Community Coll., 1973; B.A. magna cum laude, Hofstra U., 1975, M.A. (Univ. fellow), 1976; m. Eric Friedman, Dec. 15, 1960; children—Lisa, Adam. Speech cons. Pfizer, Inc., N.Y.C., 1976-77; speech pathologist William Floyd Public Sch., Mastic Beach, N.Y., 1977-78, Gt. Neck (N.Y.) Public Schs., 1978-79, 81—, Herricks Public Sch., Albertson, N.Y., 1979-80, Summit Sch., Forest Hills, N.Y., 1980-81; adj. speech instr. Baruch Coll., CUNY, 1981—. Lic. pvt. practitioner in speech pathology, N.Y. State. Mem. Am. Speech and Hearing Assn. (cert.), N.Y. State Speech ano Hearing Assn., L.I. Speech and Hearing Assn., Internat. Assn. Logopedics and Phoniatrics, Phi Beta Kappa. Office: Great Neck Public Schs Great Neck NY 11020

FRIEDMAN, SARAH LANDAU, psychologist; b. Tel-Aviv, Israel, Nov. 18, 1943; d. Faivel and Esther (Vloska) Landau; B.A., Hebrew U., Jerusalem, 1968; M.A. in Ednl. Psychology, Cornell U., 1971; Ph.D. in Developmental and Exptl. Psychology, George Washington U., 1975; m. Moshe Friedman, June 11, 1967; 1 dau., Daphen-Ruth. Research asst. Cornell Testing and Guidance Center, 1969-70; teaching asst. Cornell U., 1970-71, George Washington U., 1971-74; research fellow NIMH, 1974-76, research psychologist, 1976-79; neonatal research psychologist, dept. perinatal/neonatal pediatrics Washington Hosp. Center, Washington, 1977-79; research asst. prof. psychiatry and behavioral sci. George Washington U. Sch. Medicine, Washington, 1979-80; research asso. Children's Hosps. Nat. Med. Center, Washington, 1979-80; asso. Nat. Inst. Edn., Washington, 1980—. George Washington U. tuition awardee, 1972-73; Sigma Xi grant in aid awardee, 1973-74. Mem. AAAS, Am. Edn. Research Assn., Am. Psychol. Assn., D.C. Psychol. Assn., N.Y. Acad. of Scis., Soc. for Research in Child Devel., Sigma Xi, Psi Chi (co-recipient nat. research award 1974), Phi Kappa Phi, Phi Lambda Theta. Contbr. sci. articles to profl. jours. and books; editor: (with M. Sigman) Preterm Birth and Psychological Development, 1980; research in infant behavior and devel., cognitive devel., picture perception and individual differences. Home: 4511 Yuma St Washington DC 20016 Office: 1200 19th St Washington DC 20208

FRIEDMAN, SONYA ELAINE KIEL, psychologist; b. Bklyn., Mar. 27, 1936; d. Joseph and Frieda (Goldman) Kiel; B.A., Bklyn. Coll., 1956; M.Ed., Wayne State U., 1963, Ph.D., 1967; m. Aug. 5, 1956; children—Sharon, Scott. Speech and hearing therapist Des Moines Public Schs., 1956-59, Pontiac (Mich.) Public Schs., 1959-62; sch. psychologist Rochester (Mich.) Public Schs., 1963-73; newspaper columnist, 1970-74; resident psychologist AM-America and ABC stas., corr. Network News, N.Y.C., Detroit, Cleve. and Chgo., 1974-78; talk show host Radio Crisis Intervention, Sta. WXYZ, Detroit, 1978—, Sonya, Sta. WDIV; pvt. practice psychology, Birmingham, Mich., 1967—; tchr. Oakland U., Oakland Community Coll. Mem. Am. Psychol. Assn., Am. Assn. Sex Educators, Counselors and Therapists, Am. Orthopsychiat. Assn., Am. Assn. Marriage Counselors, Mich. Psychol. Assn., Mich. Interprofl. Assn., Mich. Assn. Marriage Counselors. Author: I've Had It, You've Had It, 1974.

FRIEDMANN, HARRIET SPIEGEL, social worker; b. Chgo., Oct. 5, 1949; d. Joseph and Rita (Weisdorf) Spiegel; B.A., U. Ill., Urbana, 1970; M.S.W., Loyola U., Chgo., 1977; children—Heather Leah, Brett Terrance. Psychiat. social worker Infant Welfare Soc., Chgo., 1977-79; mem. adv. bd. Re-entry Center, Wilmette, Ill., 1979—, vol. clinician, 1980—; maternity social worker St. Francis Hosp., Evanston, Ill., 1981—; mem. adv. bd. Family Focus, Evanston; pvt. practice therapy for children and adults, Wilmette, Ill., 1979—. U. Ill. Bronze Tablet scholar, 1970, James scholar, 1966-70, Levie scholar, 1976-77. Mem. Nat. Assn. Social Workers, Acad. Cert. Social Workers, Phi Beta Kappa, Phi Kappa Phi, Alpha Lambda Delta. Office: 1017 Central St Wilmette IL 60091

FRIEDRICH, LINDA ALISON BERGER, nurse, transp. co. exec.; b. N.Y.C., May 17, 1934; d. Harry Morley Berger and Ethel Agnes (Barnum) Monce; A.A., Chaffey Jr. Coll., 1954; diploma in nursing Good Samaritan Hosp., 1957; B.S. in Nursing, Calif. State U., Los Angeles, 1958, M.S. in Nursing (Shirley Titus fellow, HEW grantee), 1977; children—John, Theresa, William. Critical care nurse, cons. Bur. Critical Care Nursing, Los Angeles, 1978-80; lectr. Med.-Mgmt. Acad., Marina Del Rey, Calif., 1978—; nurse Hosp. of Good Samaritan Med. Center, Los Angeles, 1967-71; prof. nursing Los Angeles City Coll., 1971—; pres. A&A Air Patient Transport Service, Los Angeles, 1980—. Patron, Los Angeles County Mus. Art, 1977—. Mem. Calif. Nursing Assn., Am. Fedn. Tchrs., Nat. Critical Care Inst., U. So. Calif. Alumni Assn., Nat. Assn. Female Execs. Republican. Roman Catholic. Contbr. articles in field to profl. publs. Home: 8622 Vine Valley Dr Sun Valley CA 91352 Office: Los Angeles City Coll 855 N Vermont St Los Angeles CA 90029

FRIEND, EDITH OVERTON, home economist; b. Twin Branch, W.Va., June 5, 1928; d. George Hiram and Carrie Elizabeth Overton; B.A., Asbury Coll., 1950; M.A., W.Va. U., 1961; postgrad. U. Md., 1966, Va. Poly. Inst. and State U., 1970; diploma profl. custom millinery Acad. of Millinery Design, N.J., 1978; m. Warren Glenn Friend, Nov. 21, 1951; children—Kathryn Louise, Mary Elizabeth (dec.), Samuel Warren (dec.). Home economist AE Power Co., Logan, W.Va., 1950-51, Madison, W.Va., 1951-54; home demonstration agt. Perston County, Kingwood, W.Va., 1954-61; instr. home econs. dept. Concord Coll., Athens, W.Va., 1966-68; extension home economist Nelson County, Lovingston, Va., 1968-79, SW dist. chmn., 1980—; substitute tchr. Preston County Bd. Edn., 1961-65; elem. tchr. Preston County Bd. Edn., 1965; home econs. tchr. Mercer County Bd. Edn., 1966. Recording Steward Methodist Ch., Cranesville, W.Va., 1962-65; pres. Women's Soc. of Christian Service, 1969-71, treas. Moorefield dist., 1963-64, sec. missionary edn., 1965-66, mem., 1961-72. Clubs: W.Va. Federated

Women's Cranesville Homemakers Group (pres. 1962-63), Terra Alta Homemakers' Group, Order of Eastern Star (worth matron Nelson County chpt. 1973-74, 1978-79). Author: The Basic Four Weight Control Plan, 1977. Office: 310 W Valley St Abingdon VA 24210

FRIEND, MIRIAM RUTH, temporary personnel co. exec.; b. Scranton, Pa., May 19, 1925; d. Benjamin and Etta (Weiss) Loewy; B.A., Syracuse (N.Y.) U., 1947; cert. Inst. public Welfare Tng., Cornell U., 1950; m. Sidney Friend, Aug. 27, 1950. Social worker child placing div. N.Y. State Dept. Welfare, 1948-52; v.p. Office Help Temporaries, Yonker, N.Y., 1954—; chmn. planning com. Pvt. Industry Council, 1979-80, pres., 1981-82. Bd. dirs. Yonkers Salvation Army, 1977—, Yonkers Gen. Hosp., 1978—; pres. Big Bros.-Big Sisters Yonkers, 1978-80. Recipient Yonkers Safari award for community service, 1978. Mem. Yonkers C. of C. (chmn. breakfast club 1978), Sales and Mktg. Execs. Internat., Adminstrv. Mgmt. Soc., Bus. and Profl. Women, Syracuse U. Alumni Assn., Psi Chi. Clubs: Soroptimists (pres. 1970-72), Racquet (Yonkers). Home: 11 Abbey Pl Yonkers NY 10701 Office: 20 S Broadway Yonkers NY 10701

FRIES, HELEN SERGEANT HAYNES (MRS. STUART G. FRIES), civic leader; b. Atlanta; d. Harwood Syme and Alice (Hobson) Haynes; student Coll. William and Mary, 1935-38; m. Stuart G. Fries, May 5, 1938. Bd. dirs. Community Ballet Assn., Huntsville, Ala., 1968—; mem. nat. nurses aid com. ARC, 1958-59; dir. ARC Aero Club, Eng., 1943-44; supr. ARC Clubmobile, Europe, 1944-46; mem. women's com. Nat. Symphony Orch., Washington, 1959—; vol. docent, sponsor Huntsville Mus. Art; vol. docent Weeden House of Twickenham Hist. Preservation Dist. Assn., Huntsville; bd. dirs. Madison County Republican Club, 1969-70; mem. nat. council Women's Nat. Rep. Club N.Y., 1963—, chmn. hospitality com., 1963-65; bd. dirs. League Rep. Women, 1952-61. Mem. Nat. Soc. Colonial Dames Am., DAR, Nat. Trust Hist. Preservation, D.C., Valley Forge (Pa.), Eastern Shore of Va. hist. socs., Assn. Preservation Va. Antiquities, Greensboro Soc. Preservation, Tenn. Valley Geneal. Soc., Huntsville Hist. Soc., English Speaking Union, Alliance Francaise. Clubs: Washington, Capitol Hill, Army-Navy Country (Washington); Garden (Redstone Arsenal), Redstone (Ala.) Yacht; Army-Navy (D.C.). Home: 409 Zandale Dr Huntsville AL 35801

FRIIS, HELENE ELIZABETH, architect, sculptress; b. Stuttgart, W.Ger., 1948; came to U.S., 1950, naturalized, 1967; d. Kasimerz and Anastasia Rogalski; B.F.A., Ft. Wright Coll. Holy Names, 1967; B.A. in Edn., Wash. State U., 1970, B. Archtl. Studies, 1971, B.Arch., 1972; m. Terry E. Friis, June 13, 1973; 1 dau., Angela Dominique. One-woman shows: Ft. Wright Coll. Holy Names, 1967, Boston U., 1968, Wash. State U., 1970; represented in permanent collections: HEF Design, Architects and Planners, 3D Devel., Inc., Rogalski Collection; instr. fine arts Spokane Sch. Dist., 1969; assoc. architect, designer, planner GFG & Assocs., Spokane, 1972-74; founder, owner, prin. HEF Design Architects & Planners, Spokane, 1975-82, dir. mktg., 1975—; founder, v.p. 3D Devel., Inc., Spokane, 1982—, artist in residence Boston U., 1967-68. Mem. AIA, Council Ednl. Facilities Planners, Urban Land Inst., Nat. Trust Historic Preservation. Roman Catholic. Club: Spokane Bus. Office: W 1520 3d Ave Suite 301 Spokane WA 99204

FRINK, BETTYE JEAN, state ofcl.; b. Crossville, Ala., Feb. 19, 1933; d. Lester Love and Edna Leora (McMillian) Haynes; student bus. coll.; m. William David Frink, July 7, 1951; children—Victor Farrell, William David, Bettye Lynn, Leigh Ellen. Proofreader, Dept. Treasury, 1955-57; with IRS, 1957-59; sec. state State of Ala., 1959-63; auditor State of Ala., Montgomery, 1963-67, 75—. Del., Democratic Nat. Conv., 1960; mem. Ala. Bd. Edn., 1971-75. Mem. Nat. Assn. State Auditors, Comptrollers and Treasurers. Home: 1943 Talbot Terr Montgomery AL 36106 Office: State Capitol Montgomery AL 36130 *

FRISHBERG, TAMARA, psychiatrist; b. Kiev, U.S.S.R., Mar. 5, 1938; came to U.S., 1975, naturalized, 1981; Evsey Israilevich and Cherna (Feldman) Bekker; M.D., Pirogov Med. Sch., Vinnitza, Russia, 1961; m. Anatoly Frishberg, Mar. 15, 1961; 1 son, Alexander. Resident in psychiatry Inst. for Physicians, U. Kiev, 1961-62; psychiatrist Kiev Regional Mental Health Hosp., 1962-74; resident psychiatry Wash. U. Sch. Medicine, 1977-80; supervising psychiatrist Bliss Mental Health Center, St. Louis, 1980—; instr. psychiatry Washington U. Sch. Medicine, St. Louis, 1980—. Mem. Eastern Mo. Psychiat. Assn., Am. Psychiat. Assn. Office: 1420 Gratton St Saint Louis MO 63104

FRISTOE, MACALYNE (WATKINS), speech pathologist, educator; b. Nashville, Tenn., Mar. 14, 1931; d. George Miller and Brownie Mitchell (Appleton) Watkins; B.A., Vanderbilt U., 1953, M.S., 1960, Ph.D., 1972; children by previous marriage—James Houston Fristoe, Andrew McLean Fristoe. Instr. speech pathology Vanderbilt U., 1964-67, instr. psychology, 1971-72, asst. prof. psychology, 1972-74; asst. prof. U. Ala., Birmingham, 1974-76, dir. lang. intervention study project, 1974-76; asso. prof. audiology and speech scis. Purdue U., W. Lafayette, Ind., 1976—, dir. Speech Clinic, 1976-79; cons. to various schs. and health orgns., 1976—. Cert. speech pathologist, Ind.; NDEA fellow, 1969. Mem. Am. Psychol. Assn., Am. Speech and Hearing Assn. (chairperson conv. subcom. lang. devel., lang. disorders 1977-78), Tenn. Speech and Hearing Assn. (editor jours. 1960-61), Ind. Speech and Hearing Assn., Council for Exceptional Children (pres. div. children with communication disorders 1978-79, asso. editor Jour. Childhood Communication Disorders 1975-79), Am. Assn. on Mental Deficiency, Assn. for Women in Psychology, Phi Beta Kappa, Sigma Xi. Unitarian. Co-author: Goldman-Fristoe Test of Articulation, 1969; Goldman-Fristoe-Woodcock Test of Auditory Discrimination, 1970; Goldman-Fristoe-Woodcock Auditory Skills Test Battery, 1975; author articles on speech disorders, mental deficiency and audiology, chpts. on communication disorders and mental retardation. Home: 2113 S 7th St Lafayette IN 47905 Office: Dept Audiology and Speech Scis Purdue Univ W Lafayette IN 47907

FRITTER, GENEVIEVE DAVISSON, violinist, composer; b. Clarksburg, W.Va., Dec. 13, 1915; d. Dorsey Achilles and I. Maude (Wilcox) Davisson; B.Mus., Judson Coll., 1937; postgrad. Juilliard Summer Sch., 1937-38, Birmingham Conservatory of Music, 1939-40, Cin. Conservatory of Music, 1941-43; m. C. Eldon Fritter, Aug. 30, 1940 (dec. 1975); children—Jean Louise, Thelma Priscolla. Supr. music Lafayette (Ala.) Pub. Schs., 1937-39, Fairfield, Ala., 1939-40; violinist Birmingham Symphony, 1939-40; tchr violin and theory Quinn Sch. Music, Lakewood, Ohio, 1944-49; freelance violinist, Washington, 1959—; concertmaster Nat. Ballet Orch., 1965-70; music dir., resident composer Montgomery Ballet Co., 1960-80; violinist Kennedy Center Opera House Orch., Washington, also Filene Center Orch., Wolf Trap Farm Park, Vienna, Va., 1971—; lectr. on composition; compositions include: Sinfonietta No. 1, 1978; Poem for Flute and Orch., 1981; Theme and Variations for String Orch., 1976. Recipient 1st prize song div. Nat. Fedn. Music Clubs, 1940, Outstanding Alumna award Judson Coll., 1966. Mem. Am. Music Center, ASCAP, Am. Fedn. Musicians, Am. Women Composers, Inc., Friday Morning Music of Washington, Mu Phi Epsilon. Congregationalist.

FRITTS, LILLIAN ELIZABETH, nurse; b. N.Y.C., July 19, 1923; d. William Franklin and Elzora Jane (Hodge) Bowen; A.D.N., R.N., Central Piedmont Community Coll., 1969; m. Thurman Luther Fritts, Aug. 5, 1944; children—William Luther, Franklin Lee, George Allen. Emergency room nurse Lexington (N.C.) Mem. Hosp., 1953-58; office nurse James T. Welborn, M.D., Lexington, 1958-60; staff nurse Haven Nursing Center, Lexington, 1960-61; pvt. duty nurse, 1961-63; owner, partner Buena Vista Nursing Center, Lexington, 1964—; adult extension tchr. Davidson County Community Coll., 1978, adv. bd. nursing program, 1969-79. Mem. Am. Nurses Assn., N.C. Nurses Assn., Lic. Practical Nurse Orgn. (state sec. 1958-60), N.C. Lic. Practical Nurse Assn., Dist. 9 Nurse Assn. N.C., N.C. Health Care Facilities Services Assn. Baptist. Home: Everhart Rd PO Box 419 Lexington NC 27292

FRITTS-WILLIAMS, MARY LOUISE MONICA, anatomist; b. Detroit, Apr. 16, 1940; d. Myron Matthias (Kolodziejski) Fritts; B.S., U. Detroit, 1962, M.S., 1964; Ph.D. (NIH fellow), Wayne State U., Detroit, 1971; m. Milton James Williams; 1 dau., Anne Mara. Grad. research asst. U. Detroit, 1962-64, adj. asst. prof., 1968-69; research asst. Johns Hopkins U., 19 ; instr., then asst. prof. Mercy Coll., Detroit, 1964-68; research asst. Wayne State U. Med. Sch., 1970-71, asst. prof. devel. biology, 1971—; vol. tchr. Rochester (Mich.) Pub. Schs. Fellow Mich. Cancer Edn. Found., 1965; grantee Inst. Sci. and Tech., U. Mich., 1963-64, Sigma Xi, 1973. Mem. AAAS, Genetics Soc. Am., Am. Soc. Microbiology, Soc. Devel. Biology, N.Y. Acad. Scis., Mich. Citizens Lobby. Office: 627 W Alexandrine St Detroit MI 48202

FRITZ, ETHEL MAE HENDRICKSON, writer; b. Gibbon, Nebr., Feb. 4, 1925; d. Walter Earl and Alice Hazel (Mickish) Hendrickson; B.S., Iowa State U., 1949; m. C. Wayne Fritz, Feb. 25, 1950; children—Linda Sue, Krista Jane. Dist. home economist Internat. Harvester Co., Des Moines, 1949-50; writer Wallace's Farmer mag., Des Moines, 1960-64; free-lance writer, 1960—. Accredited master flower show judge. Mem. Women in Communications (pres. Phoenix profl. chpt.; nat. task force com. 1980—), Am. Soc. Profl. and Exec. Women, Am. Home Econs. Assn., PEO, Phi Upsilon Omicron, Kappa Delta.

FRITZ, JEAN GUTTERY, author; b. Hankow, China, Nov. 16, 1915; d. Arthur Minton and Myrtle (Chaney) Guttery; B.A., Wheaton Coll., 1937; LL.D. (hon.), Washington and Jefferson Coll., 1982; m. Michael Fritz, Nov. 1, 1941; children—David, Andrea. Research asst. Silver Burdett Co., N.Y.C., 1937-41; book reviewer San Francisco Chronicle, 1941-43; children's librarian, Dobbs Ferry, N.Y., 1952-55; tchr. writer's workshop, Katonah, N.Y., Bd. Coop. Ednl. Services, Yorktown, N.Y., 1961-69; mem. faculty Appalachian State U., Boone, N.C., summer, 1980-82; writer, lectr., 1960—. Recipient nonfiction award Children's Book Guild, 1978; named Author of Yr., Pa. Sch. Librarians, 1979. Mem. Authors Guild. Author: Fish Head, 1954; The Cabin Faced West, 1958; The Animals of Dr. Schweitzer, 1958; How To Read a Rabbit, 1959; Brady, 1960; San Francisco, 1962; I, Adam, 1963; Magic To Burn, 1964; Early Thunder, 1967; George Washington's Breakfast, 1969; (adult biography) Cast for a Revolution, 1972; And Then What Happened, Paul Revere?, 1973; Why Don't You Get a Horse, Sam Adams?, 1974; Where Was Patrick Henry on the 29th of May?, 1975; Who's That Stepping on Plymouth Rock?, 1975; Will You Sign Here John Hancock?, 1976; What's the Big Idea, Ben Franklin?, 1976; Can't You Make Them Behave, King George?, 1977; Brendan the Navigator, 1979; Stonewall, 1979; Where Do You Think You're Going, Christopher Columbus, 1980; The Man Who Loved Books, 1981; Traitor, 1981; Homesick: My Own Story, 1982. Contbr. articles to numerous mags. Home: 50 Bellewood St Dobbs Ferry NY 10522

FRITZ, MADELEINE ALBERTO, geologist, educator; b. St. John, N.B., Can., Nov. 3, 1896; d. Edwin John and Jessie Marie (Osborne) F.; B.A., McGill U., 1919; M.A., U. Toronto, 1923, Ph.D., 1927. Successively asst. prof. geology U. Toronto (Ont.), asso. prof., prof., 1952-67, prof. emeritus, 1967—; research asso. Royal Ont. Mus., Toronto, 1967—. Fellow Royal Soc. Can., Geol. Soc. Am., Paleontol. Soc. Am., Geol. Assn. Can. Recipient Centennial medal, 1967. Anglican. Clubs: Faculty (hon. life); Royal Ont. Mus. (hon. life). Contbr. articles to sci. jours. Home: 70 Delisle Ave Toronto ON M4V 1S7 Canada Office: 100 Queens Park Toronto ON M5S 2C6 Canada

FRITZELL, STELLA HOUGE, state govt. ofcl.; b. Bucyrus, N.D., Oct. 3, 1909; d. Gunder and Carrie (Engen) Houge; B.S. cum laude, U. Minn., 1931; m. Kenneth E. Fritzell, June 24, 1933 (dec. Feb. 1957); children—Peter, Sara, Erik, Anne. Research technician Univ. Hosp., U. Minn., 1932-34; nutritionist Mpls. Dept. Welfare, 1934-40; stockbroker Piper, Jaffray, Hopwood, Grand Forks, N.D., 1959-71; mem. N.D. Senate from 43d Dist., 1972—, mem. appropriations com. Mem. Grand Forks Park Bd., 1960-74, pres., 1972-74; mem. Grand Forks Planning and Zoning Commn., 1971-76; state hon. chmn. Wildlife Week, 1977, 78. Recipient Pub. Service award U. Students for Environ. Def., 1971; named Most Outstanding Women in Legislature by newspaper poll, 1975, Legis. Conservationist of Year, Wildlife Fedn., 1975. Mem. Nat. (dir.), N.D. wildlife fedns., League Women Voters, Bus. and Profl. Women. Republican. Clubs: Grand Forks Country, Grand Forks Gun (dir. 1961-71; state trapshooting champion 1969). Address: 112 Cottonwood St Grand Forks ND 58201

FROEHLICH, ADELE, newspaper editor; b. Chgo., July 8, 1918; d. A. I. and Frances Elizabeth (Welch) F.; Vocal instr., McHenry (Ill.) High Sch., 1944-68; writer McHenry Plaindealer, 1941-47, editor, 1947—. Co-dir., McHenry County Vocal Festival, 1972. Republican. Roman Catholic. Clubs: McHenry Choral. Recipient 1st place editorial award Ill. Agrl. Assn., 1954; 1st place editorial award Ill. Press Assn., 1973, 3d place individual column award, 1977, 2d place individual column award, 1981; Woman of Yr. award McHenry Bus. and Profl. Women's Club, 1976. Home: 3621 W John St McHenry IL 60050 Office: 3812 W Elm St McHenry IL 60050

FROLICHSTEIN, SUSAN HEYMAN, social worker; b. Chgo., May 12, 1941; d. Herbert Hugh and Goldyne Reta (Hoffman) Heyman; B.A., U. Mich., 1962; M.A., U. Chgo., 1964; m. Seymour Rees Frolichstein, June 28, 1964; children—Rita Diane, Michael Wolff. Social caseworker No. Dist., Jewish Family and Community Service, Chgo., 1964-65, United Charities Legal Aid Bur., 1965-66; intake worker vocat. adjustment center Jewish Vocat. Service, Chgo., 1967-68; social worker Chgo. Met. chpt. Epilepsy Found. Am., 1974-76; social service coordinator Chgo. chpt. Nat. Multiple Sclerosis Soc., 1976-81; alcoholism counselor, trainee Luth. Center for Substance Abuse, 1981; employee assistance counselor J.W. Crawford Assos., Chgo., 1981—; social work vol. O.A.T.E.S., St. Francis Hosp., Evanston, Ill., 1981—; pvt. practice social work, 1982—. Bd. dirs. LWV, Evanston, 1970-72, PTA, Evanston schs., 1971-79. Mem. Nat. Assn. Social Workers (bd. dirs. North Suburban chpt. 1979—), Evanston Mental Health Assn. Jewish. Home: 916 Lee St Evanston IL 60202 Office: 53 W Jackson St Chicago IL 60604

FROMM, ERIKA (MRS. PAUL FROMM), clin. psychologist; b. Frankfurt, Germany, Dec. 23, 1910; d. Siegfried and Clementine (Stern) Oppenheimer; came to U.S., 1938, naturalized, 1944; Ph.D. magna cum laude, U. Frankfurt, 1933; postgrad. child care program, Chgo. Inst. for Psychoanalysis, 1949-51; m. Paul Fromm, July 20, 1938; 1 dau., Joan (Mrs. Greenstone). Chief psychologist Apeldoorn State Hosp. (Holland), 1935-38, Francis W. Parker Sch., 1944-51; supervising psychologist Inst. for Juvenile Research, 1951-53; asst. prof. to asso. prof. Northwestern U. Med. Sch., 1954-61; prof. U. Chgo., 1961-76, prof. emeritus, 1976—. Diplomate Am. Bd. Examiners in Profl. Psychology, Am. Bd. Examiners Clin. Hypnosis. Fellow Am. Psychol. Assn. (pres. div. 30, 1972-73), Am. Orthopsychiat. Assn. (dir. 1961-63), AAAS, Soc. Clin. Exptl. Hypnosis (sec. 1965-67, pres. 1975-77); mem. Am. Bd. Psychol. Hypnosis (pres. 1971-74), Ill. Psychol. Assn. (council 1951-53, 55-57, bd. examiners 1959-62, v.p. bd. examiners 1960-61), Soc. Projective Techniques, Sigma Xi. Author: (with L.D. Hartman) Intelligence-A Dynamic Approach; (with Thomas M. French) Dream Interpretation, A New Approach, 1964; (with Ronald E. Shor) Hypnosis: Developments in Research and New Perspectives, 1972, 2d edit., 1979; also numerous articles in profl. jours. Mem. editorial bd. Jour. Clin. and Exptl. Psychopathology, 1951-59; clin. editor Internat. Jour. Clin. and Exptl. Hypnosis, 1968—; mem. adv. bd. Jour. Imagination, Cognition and Personality, 1981—; assoc. editor Brit. Jour. Hypnosis, 1982—. Home: 5715 S Kenwood Ave Chicago IL 60637 Office: Dept Behavioral Sciences U Chicago Chicago IL 60637

FROMMER, JEANETTE, ins. agy. exec.; b. Sebree, Ky., Feb. 27, 1943; d. Robert L. and Lola B. (Myers) Sauls; student Phoenix Coll., 1977, also various ins. seminars; m. Donald R. Frommer, Nov. 22, 1963 (dec. 1969); children—James D., Brian K., Michele L. With Holland-Benson Agy., Inc. (name changed to Holland-Frommer Agy., Inc. 1978), Phoenix, 1969—, officer mgr., 1970-78, pres., owner, 1978—. Recipient Very Important Parent award Orangewood Elem. Sch., 1981. Mem. Profl. Ins. Agts. Ariz. (sec. 1978-81, dir. 1981—, Officer of Yr. 1981), Ind. Ins. Agts. Am., Ariz. Ind. Ins. Agts., Maricopa County Ind. Ins. Agts., Profl. Ins. Agts. Republican. Methodist. Home: 1802 W Claremont Phoenix AZ 85015 Office: 5800 N 19th Ave Suite 101 Phoenix AZ 85015

FROMSON, ANTOINETTE DUVAL, civic worker; b. Chgo., May 22, 1925; d. Ralph A. and Yvonne (Duval) Brown; Barnard Coll., 1947; m. Howard A. Fromson, Oct. 12, 1946; children—Michele Yvonne, Michael Erik, Timothy Arthur, Brett Duval. Plaintiff, Women vs. Conn., legal action about the right of women to control their bodies, 1969; convenor, 1st chmn. Conn. Women's Polit. Caucus, 1970; organizer Westport-Weston (Conn.) chpt. NOW, 1972, organizer, convenor, pres. Southwestern Conn. chpt., 1974-78; del. Conn. Democratic Conv., 1974; mem. Weston Town Dem. Com., 1972-74. Mem. Unitarian-Universalists Women's Fedn., Barnard Alumni Assn. Democrat. Unitarian. Clubs: Cedar Point Yacht, Aspetuck Valley Country, Fairfield Organic Gardening. Home: 15 Rogues Ridge Rd Weston CT 06883

FRONAPFEL, LINDA LOUISE PHILLIPS, public relations co. exec.; b. Peoria, Ill., Apr. 11, 1940; d. John Charles Phillips and Mary Louise (Boyd) Shepherd; B.A., U. Wyo., 1976; postgrad. N.Y. U., 1978—; m. Richard William Fronapfel, Oct. 8, 1960; children—Paige Allyn, Richard William. Asso. publicity dir. Simon & Schuster, N.Y.C., 1969-70; publicity dir. Drake Pubs., N.Y.C., 1972; dir. publicity, promotion Chatham Press, Greenwich, Conn., 1973-74; founder, pres. Phillips Publicity Services, Darien, Conn., 1976—; guest lectr. public relations New Sch. for Social Research, N.Y.C., 1977-78, So. Conn. State Coll., 1977—. Mem. Democratic Town Com., 1976-81, vice chmn., 1976-77; bd. dirs. Darien YWCA, 1976-78. Mem. Conn. Press Women, Nat. League Am. Penwomen, Actors Equity Assn., Pubs. Publicity Assn. N.Y., Alumnae Assn. Kappa Kappa Gamma. Democrat. Club: Tokeneke (Darien). Miss Wyo., Miss Am. pageant, 1959; named 1st Miss U.S. Air Force Acad., 1959. Home: 33 Old Farm Rd Darien CT 06820

FROOKS, DOROTHY, lawyer, author; b. Saugerties, N.Y.; d. Reginald and Rosita (Siberez) F.; LL.B., Hamilton Coll., 1918, LL.M., 1919; spl. courses Harvard U., N.Y. U., St. Lawrence U., U. N.C. Law Sch., Tulane U., Duquesne U.; Ps.D., Nat. Inst. Psychology, 1946; student Indsl. Coll. Armed Forces, 1953. Admitted to N.Y. State bar, 1920, U.S. Customs Ct., 1932, U.S. Supreme Ct., 1934, Fed. bar P.R., 1925, Alaska bar, 1935, Calif. bar, 1926, La. bar, 1929, U.S. Ct. Claims, 1950, U.S. Ct. Mil. Appeals, 1954, Hawaii bar, 1958, C.Z. bar, 1959; atty. Salvation Army, N.Y.C., 1920-21; organizer Poor Man's Ct., 1921; atty. for com. U.S. Coast Guard, 1939-40; counsel N.Y. State Bd. Edn., 1940-41; owner, editor Public Service Record, N.Y.C., 1920-21; pub. Murray Hill News, Oyster Bay News, 1916-19; columnist N.Y. Evening World, 1929-32; del. 1st Inter-Am. Bar Conf., Havana, 1921, Internat. Law Conf., Oxford, Eng., 1932, Atty. Gen.'s Crime Congress, Washington, 1934, Gov.'s Crime Conf., Albany, 1935; candidate for Congress-at-large State N.Y., 1934; nat. judge adv. Vets. of World War I, Inc., 1969; arbitrator Small Claims Ct., 1970—. Served as chief yeoman U.S. Navy in charge woman enrollments and recruiting, World War I; served in Judge Adv. Office, U.S. Army, World War II. Recipient medal for patriotic service by Woodrow Wilson, 1918. Mem. Nat. Assn. Woman Lawyers (organizer, chmn. mil. and naval law com. 1946), Nat. Aero. Assn., Am. Judicature Assn., Wis. Archaeol. Soc., Am. Bar Assn., N.Y. State Bar Assn., Westchester County Bar Assn., Inter-Am. Bar, Women of Greater N.Y. (pres.), Murray Hill Assn. (pres.), Iota Tau Tau, Epsilon Eta Phi. Presbyterian. Clubs: Westchester Jr. League, Eastern Star, Peekskill Country (dir.). Author: The American Heart, 1919; Civilization, 1922; Criminal Obscenity, 1923; Chronology of the Catholic Church; Loves Law, 1927; Wills and Estates, 1929; All in Love, 1932; Over the Heads of Congress, 1935; Portia on Horseback, 1943; The Olympic Torch, 1946; Girls Get Their Men, 1947; How to Use the Small Claims Court, 1979; Wills, 1981; Lady Lawyer, 1975. Office: Lake Mohegan Peekskill NY 10547 also 237 and 261 Madison Ave New York NY 10016

FROSCH, HELEN NELL MORRIS, psychoanalytic psychotherapist; b. Bklyn., Feb. 3, 1943; d. Stanley Jerome and Sophye Morris; B.A., N.Y. U., 1965; M.S.W., Adelphi U., 1973; cert. Inst. for Study of Psychotherapy, 1978; m. Allan Frosch, June 30, 1974; 1 dau., Samantha Cassidy. Child psychotherapist, dept. child psychiatry Brookdale Hosp., Bklyn., 1973-75; chief psychiat. social worker Yonkers (N.Y.) Youth Services Agy., 1975-78; staff therapist Bklyn. Center for Psychotherapy, 1978-79; patient services coordinator Nat. Huntington's Disease Assn., N.Y.C., 1978-79, nat. patient services coordinator, 1979—; pvt. practice individual, family, group psychotherapy, and treatment of individuals and families experiencing psychol. stress of illness, N.Y.C., 1977—; cons. to Huntington's disease orgns., social work supr. Mem. Nat. Assn. Social Workers, Acad. Cert. Social Workers, Soc. for Advancement of Psychoanalytic Devel. Psychology (pres. N.Y.C.). Author: Huntington's Disease: Differential Clinical Care, 1982; sr. author (pamphlet) Support Groups for Huntington's Disease Families, 1982. Office: 100 Riverside Dr New York NY 10024

FROST, ALBERTA CAROLYN, govt. ofcl.; b. Fargo, N.D., May 14, 1944; d. J. A. and Mildred A. (Sanders) F.; B.A. with honors, U. Colo., 1966, tchrs. cert., 1967. With Dept. Agr., 1967—, dir. nat. food stamp program, 1979-81, dir. civil rights and EEO div. Food and Nutrition Service, 1982—. Recipient Superior Performance award Dept. Agr., 1971, 78. Mem. Am. Public Welfare Assn., Phi Beta Kappa. Office: Park Office Center Bldg 3101 Park Center Dr Alexandria VA 22302

FROST, ARETA LUE, savs. and loan assn. exec.; b. Seattle, June 10, 1938; d. Jesse Raymond and Carolyn Lee (Green) Hurley; B.A. magna cum laude in Speech and Hearing Pathology, U. Wash., 1960; also various profl. courses and seminars; m. June 11, 1960 (div. 1971); children—John, Jeff, Chris. Speech and hearing pathologist, Seattle, Spokane (Wash.), Everett (Wash.), and N.J., 1960-71; communications-public relations dir. Mayor's Office, City of Everett, 1971-73; mktg. cons., tng. instr. Gen. Telephone Co., Everett, 1973-75; account exec. Investor's Diversified Services, Seattle, 1975; exec. recruiter, mgr. Seattle office Acme Personnel, Inc., Seattle, 1976-78; mktg. mgr. Home Savs. & Loan Assn., Burien, Wash., 1978—, asst. v.p., 1979-80; asst. v.p., mktg. mgr. Umpqua Savs. & Loan Assn., Roseburg, Oreg., 1980—; weekly radio show on bus. Chmn., U. Wash. 10-Yr. Reunion, 1970; pres. Greeters, Roseburg C. of C.; bd. dirs. Downtown Mchts. Assn.; 1st v.p.

United Way 1982, pres., 1983, also bd. dirs., mem. budget allocations com. Mem. U.S. League Savs. and Loans, Wash. Savs. League, Mortar Bd., Phi Beta Kappa. Contbr. articles to profl. publs. Home: 1818 NE Todd Roseburg OR 97470 Office: Umpqua Savs & Loan Assn 445 SE Main St Roseburg OR 97470

FROST, CAROL SHIRLEY, mfg. co. exec.; b. Boston, Oct. 1, 1929; d. Charles J. and Agnes R. (Carroll) Popp; student Boston schs.; m. Donald Frost, Oct. 15, 1949 (dec.); children—Donald, Lorraine, Charles, Linda. Pres., owner Klarmann Rulings, Inc., Waltham, Mass., 1960-76, Manchester and Litchfield, N.H., 1976—. Mem. Soc. Photog. Scientists and Engrs. Office: Bancroft Hwy Route 3A Litchfield NH 03108

FROST, DIANNE BAILEY, psychologist; b. West Point, Ga., Sept. 6, 1949; d. Odie Lee and Frances Georgia (Hester) Bailey; B.S. magna cum laude, U. Ga., 1972, M.Ed., 1974, Ph.D., 1976; postgrad. Masters and Johnson Inst., 1980; m. Kenneth Bradley Frost, Aug. 16, 1975. Community psychologist, co-dir. marital sexual co-therapy service U.S. Govt., W. Ger., 1976-79; psychologist Ogeechee Psycho-Ednl. Center, Midville, Ga., 1979; part-time instr. U. Alaska, Cordova, 1980-81; co-dir. Mental Health and Alcohol Clinic, Cordova, 1980-81; co-founder, co-dir. Frost Found., sex therapy clinic, Augusta, Ga., 1981—. Mem. Am. Assn. Sex Educators, Counselors, and Therapists (cert. sex therapist), Am. Psychol. Assn., Sex Info. and Edn. Council of U.S., NOW, Phi Kappa Phi, Phi Delta Kappa, Kappa Delta Pi. Home: 1554 Walton Way Augusta GA 30904 Office: PO Box 3699 Augusta GA 30904

FROST, MARY KATHERINE, clin. exec.; b. Windsor, Ont., Can., Nov. 13, 1928; came to U.S., 1951, naturalized, 1967; d. Philip Francis and Elizabeth Eppert; cert. in acctg. Windsor Bus. Coll., 1946; student Toronto Conservatory Music, 1946-47, Am. Inst. Banking, 1954-57; A.S., Wayne State U., 1967; m. William Max Frost, July 17, 1948; Teller, bookkeeper, asst. acct. Toronto Dominion Bank, Windsor, 1947-51; with Nat. Bank Detroit, 1951-54; mgr., customer relations officer City Nat. Bank Detroit, 1954-62; psychobiology research supr., adminstrv. asst. dept. mental health Lafayette Clinic, Detroit, 1964—; co-founder, coordinator, polysomnographer Lafayetter Clinic Sleep Center, 1975—. Mem. citizens adv. council Lafayette Clinic, chmn. membership, 1979-82, vice chmn., 1982—; bd. dirs. Travelers Aid Soc., 1973—, Casa Maria, 1974-81, Casgrain Hall, 1974—; trustee League Catholic Women, 1974—, mem. adv. bd., 1982—; co-founder Windsor Light Opera Co., 1948. Named Disting. Employee of 1981, Lafayette Clinic, 1982. Mem. Mich. State Employees Assn. (pres. mental health dept. Lafayette Clinic chpt. 1975-81), Assn. Polysomnography Technologists, Nat. Assn. Female Execs., Mich. Assn. Govt. Employees, Econ. Club Detroit. Republican. Clubs: Five o'Clock Forum, U. Detroit, U.S. Senatorial. Contbr. articles to profl. jours. Home: 1 Lafayette Plaisance Suite 1617 Detroit MI 48207 Office: Dept Psychobiology Lafayette Clinic 951 E Lafayette St Detroit MI 48207

FROST, OLIVIA PLEASANTS, research cons.; b. Asbury Park, N.J.; d. William Henry and Theresa (Mitchell) Pleasants; B.A., Hunter Coll.; M.A. in Sociology, Columbia U., 1951; Ph.D., N.Y.U., 1972; children—Carolyn Olivia, James William, Charles S. Research asso. N.Y.C. Youth Bd., 1956-59; research asso. HARYOU, Youth in the Ghetto, 1963-70; research dir. N.Y. Urban League, 1965-66; dir. research and program evaluation Bedford Stuyvesant Youth in Action, 1966-68; program devel. adminstr. City U. N.Y., 1972-75; asso. prof. dept. acad. affairs Medgar Evers Coll., City U. N.Y., 1976-77; research cons. Columbia U. Sch. Library Sci., Malcolm King Coll. Harlem Extension, 1975—; pres. OFRA. Warburg fellow, 1968; Dept. Labor grantee. Mem. Nat. Assn. Social Workers, Assn. Black Social Workers, N.Y. Urban League, NAACP, Assn. Black Women in Higher Edn. Contbr. articles to profl. jours. Address: 1550 York Ave New York NY 10028

FROST-WELMERS, NAN ELICE, airline flight attendant; b. Albion, Mich., Sept. 8, 1947; d. Robert J. and Norma L. (Adams) Frost; student Grand Valley State Coll., 1965-68; m. Anthony J. Welmers, Sept. 12, 1970. Flight attendant North Central Airlines, 1968—. Mem. Mich. Women's Commn., 1978—, chmn., 1979—. Mem. Assn. Flight Attendants (rep. Detroit), Coalition Labor Union Women, Stewardesses for Women's Rights (nat. coordinator, pres. 1973-75, chairperson Detroit chpt. 1973—; co-founding mem.), NOW (pres. Mich. state 1977-79, convenor Mid-Western chpt.; pres. 1975-76), Mich. Women's Polit. Caucus, Nat. Women's Polit. Caucus. Democrat. Home: Dearborn MI 48126

FRUHMANN, KAREN ANNE, lab. adminstr.; b. Orange, N.J.; d. Robert Whitin and Anna (Harvey) Mullin; B.A. magna cum laude in Psychology and Biology, William Paterson Coll., 1974; cert. med. tech. St. Mary's Hosp., 1975; M.S. summa cum laude in Med. Tech., Fairleigh Dickinson U., 1977; postgrad. Southeastern U., 1982—. Biochemistry technologist Raritan Valley Hosp., Greenbrook N.J., 1975-76; asst. supr. enzymology, tech. writer quality assurance, diagnostic researcher, chemistry adminstr. Warner Lambert Gen. Diagnostics, Morris Plains, N.J., 1976-78; dir. lab. services Kessler Inst. for Rehab. W. Orange, N.J., 1979—. Mem. Am. Soc. Clin. Pathologists (affiliate mem.), N.Y. Acad. Scis., Am. Soc. Med. Tech., N.J. Soc. Med. Tech., Assn. for Women in Sci., Nat. Certification Agy. (clin. lab. scientist), Alpha Mu Tau. Presbyterian. Contbr. articles on hematology to profl. jours. Office: Kessler Inst 1199 Pleasant Valley Way W Orange NJ 07052

FRUMBERG, GLORIA, pub. co. ofcl.; b. N.Y.C., Mar. 26, 1927; d. Joseph Morris and Ruth Sarah (Berlinger) Grossman; student public schs.; m. Ira Herbert Frumberg, May 15, 1949; children—Lawrence Lee, Charles Iver. Sec. public relations mfg. co., 1946-49; asst. advt. and promotions dir. mfg. corp., 1949-51; dist. mgr. World Book Ency., 1962-70; sr. regional mktg. mgr. Ency. Brit., Atlantic Beach, N.Y., 1970—. Pink Lady vol. Long Beach (N.Y.) Meml. Hosp., 1961-63; former pres. South Shore chpt. Kidney Found. N.Y. Mem. Women's Direct Response Group (pres. N.Y. chpt. 1980-82, nat. pres. 1982-84), Direct Mail Mktg. Assn., Hundred Million Club. Office: PO box 57 Atlantic Beach NY 11509

FRY, BARBARA ANN, govt. ofcl.; b. St. Charles, Ill., Nov. 10, 1937; d. Robert Nicholas and Marianne Eloise (Earhart) Wilford; B.S., U. Ill., 1959; M.B.A., Roosevelt U., 1976; m. Ronnie Darrel Fry, June 15, 1974; children—Kim Buskirk, Gena Buskirk. Budget analyst, then budget officer Navy Electronics Supply Office, Great Lakes, Ill., 1962-73; regional budget officer IRS, Chgo., 1973-75, Atlanta, 1975-76, regional fiscal mgmt. officer, 1976—; former mem. adv. com. EEO. Past treas. Loch Lomond Property Owners Assn., PTA. Served with USAF, 1959-61. Mem. AAUW (past treas.), Federally Employed Women (past co-chmn. Inter-Agy. Council, pres. Atlanta chpt.), Atlanta Assn. Fed. Execs. (treas. 1981-82), A Woman's Place (chairperson membership com.), Am. Soc. Mil. Controllers (past v.p. North Shore chpt.).). Home: 1511 Montevallo Circle Decatur GA 30033 Office: 275 Peachtree St NE Rm 744 Atlanta GA 30043

FRY, JOAN HELEN, author; b. Glen Ridge, N.J., Jan. 26, 1942; d. William Gustav and Helen Martha (Brombach) Mebius; B.A., U. Mich., 1965; postgrad. U. Calif., Santa Barbara, 1967-69; m. John A. Fry, Dec. 31, 1978. Head tchr. Rio Blanco Sch., Belize, 1962-63; manuscript editor ABC-Clio Press, Santa Barbara, Calif., 1971; free lance writer, 1972—; editor Grossmont Press, San Diego, 1976-77, AMAI/BBDO, Chgo., Rancho Santa Fe, Calif., 1977-81. Mem. Calif. Press Women, San Diego Writers/Editors Guild, Calif. Dressage Soc. Club: Nat. Writers. Contbr. articles, short stories to profl. jours. incl. Colorado, 1970-76, Western Horseman, 1973-74, Boston Globe, 1975, Transatlantic Rev., 1977, Westways, 1979, Country Jour., 1979, Horse World, 1980-81, Saddle and Bridle, 1982—; author: (with Kathryn Denby-Wrightson) The Beginning Dressage Book, 1981. Address: 331 Deodar Ln Bradbury CA 91010

FRY, MAURINE ANN, psychologist, educator; b. Akron, Iowa, Aug. 22, 1935; d. Waldon J. and Pearl M. (McKellar) F.; B.S. cum laude, U. S.D., 1957, Ed.M., 1963; Ph.D. in Ednl. Psychology, U. Iowa, 1967. Tchr. pub. schs., Calif. and Wis., 1957-62; grad. asst. ednl. psychology U. S.D., 1962-63; sch. psychologist North Iowa Spl. Edn. Dist., Mason City, 1963-64; spl. research asst. Children's Reading Clinic, U. Iowa, Iowa City, 1964-66, instr. ednl. psychology, 1966-67; asst. prof. ednl. psychology Ariz. State U., Tempe, 1967-71, assoc. prof., 1971-76, prof., 1976—, chmn. dept. ednl. psychology, 1977—. Mem. Am. Psychol. Assn., Western Psychol. Assn., Internat. Reading Assn., Am. Ednl. Research Assn., AAUP (exec. com. 1975-77, 81—), Ariz. State U. Faculty Assn., Sigma Xi. Author: (with I. Swenson) Adolescent Psychology in the Classroom, 1977; contbr. articles on ednl. psychology to profl. jours.

FRY, PATTI L., mktg. exec.; b. Youngstown, Ohio, Feb. 26, 1949; d. James W. and Lucille F. Fry; B.S. with distinction, Stanford U., 1972, M.B.A., 1977. Nurse, Kaiser Found. Hosps., Redwood City, Calif., 1972-74; asst. head nurse Mills Meml. Hosp., San Mateo, Calif., 1974-75; summer intern Chase Manhattan Bank, N.Y.C., 1976; cons. Booz, Allen & Hamilton, Chgo., 1977-80; mktg. exec. IBM, Oakland, Calif., 1980—.64 79 Frederick Bronson Cooley fellow, 1976-77; John C. and Emilie D. Cosgrove fellow, 1975-76. Mem. Assn. Western Hosps., Phi Beta Kappa, Mu Phi Epsilon. Home: 1171 Compass Lane Foster City CA 94404 2901 Peralta Oaks Ct Oakland CA 94404

FRY, ZELLA JEANNE OLIVER (MRS. ALVIN ABRAM FRY), educator; b. Moyie, B.C., Can., Oct. 30, 1909; came to U.S., 1951, naturalized, 1958; d. Walter and Mary (Congdon) Oliver; B.A., U. Alta., 1931, diploma in secondary edn., 1932, Cert. d'Etudes Françaises, 1936; M.A., Columbia U., 1944, postgrad., 1945-51; postgrad. U. B.C., 1940, U. Wash., 1941; m. Alvin Abram Fry, Dec. 29, 1950. Tchr. Alta. pub. schs., 1932-42; asst. prin. High River High Sch., Alta., 1935-38; supervising prin. Lomond Consol. Schs., Alta., to 1935; tchr. Edmonton (Alta., Can.) City Schs. and univ. demonstration tchr., Alta., 1938-42; lectr. Alta. Normal Schs., 1942-45; asst. prof. lang. arts, theatre U. Alta., Edmonton, 1945-50, asso. prof., 1951; grad. asst. Tchrs. Coll., Columbia, N.Y.C., 1951-52; asso. prof. adolescent psychology Glassboro (N.J.) State Coll., 1953; adj. prof. elem. edn. U. Del., Dover extension center, 1955-57; tchr. Selbyville (Del.) Public High Sch., 1955-57; asso. prof. speech, theatre, media studies Kean Coll. N.J. (formerly Newark State Coll.), Union, 1958-77, adjudicator play festivals, 1970—; moderator panel, 1975; dir. workshops; adjudicator state drama festival U. Del., 1978, Chatham, N.J., 1979. Mem. sr. citizens council ARC, Plainfield, N.J., 1981—. Kappa Delta Pi grantee Kent State U., 1971, 72. Recipient awards Kean Coll. N.J., 1976, 77, studio theatre named in her honor. Mem. Am. Community Theatre Assn., Am. Theatre Assn., AAUP, AAUW (chpt. pres. 1954-55, chmn. state com. on ednl. TV 1954, 55), Am. Coll. and Univ. Theatre Assn., Nat., N.J. edn. assns., Speech Assn. N.J. (v.p. 1968-70, pres. 1970-72, mem. exec. bd. 1972-74), Horatio Alger Soc., Speech Assn. Eastern States, Speech-Theatre Assn. N.J. Inc. (chmn. research study com. 1974-76), Children's Theatre Assn. Am., Secondary Sch. Theatre Assn., Canadian Studies Conf. N.J., Somerset County (dir. bus-theatre trip program 1979—), Union County (chmn. com. info. and protective services 1978—) ret. educators assns., Speech Communication Assn., Kappa Delta Pi (Compatriot in Edn. award 1976), Pi Lambda Theta. Episcopalian. Contbr. articles to profl. publs., poems to mags. Co-editor: A Consumer's Guide to the Nursing Homes of Union County, 1980. Home: 6 Edgewood Ct North Plainfield NJ 07060

FRYAR, MARIDELL FISHER, ednl. adminstr.; b. Osage County, Okla., Aug. 18, 1935; d. Fred Lewis and Leah Genevieve (Parrack) Fisher; B.A., Hardin Simmons U., 1957; M.A., Tex. Tech. U., 1972; M.A., U. Tex., Permiam Basin, 1978, adminstrv. cert., 1978; m. Jack D. Fryar, June 3, 1957; children—Fred Eric, Delanna Lynn. Tchr. speech, Lake Worth High Sch., Fort Worth, 1957-60; tchr. English, Vallecito Jr. High Sch., San Rafael, Calif., 1960-62; tchr. speech, debate coach Lee High Sch., Midland, Tex., 1963-67; dir. forensics, 1970-79; dir. forensics Hardin Simmons U., Abilene, Tex., 1967-68, coordinator fine arts and speech Midland Ind. Sch. Dist. (Tex.), 1979—. Named Midland Tchr. of Yr., 1966, Tex. Speech Tchr. of Yr., 1967; recipient Trinity U. Disting. Service award, 1976, Notre Dame Outstanding Coach award, 1975. Mem. Tex. Speech Communication Assn., Tex. Forensic Assn. (pres. 1975-76), So. Speech Communication Assn., So. Forensic Assn., Speech Communication Assn. (pres. 1982-83), Am. Forensic Assn. (sec. 1980-82), Tex. Art Educators Assn., Tex. Music Educators Assn., Nat. Forensic League, NEA, Tex. Tchrs. Assn., Pi Kappa Delta. Republican. Baptist. Edit. bd. Tex. Speech Communication Jour., 1976—, Jour. Am. Forensic Assn., 1979—; author: (with David Thomas) Basic Debate, 1979, Successful Problem Solving, 1979; Successful Business Speaking, 1980; Lincoln-Douglas Debate, 1981; contbr. articles to profl. jours. Home: 2409 Auburn Pl Midland TX 79701 Office: 702 North N St Midland TX 79701

FRYE, DOROTHY MARIE, plumbing and heating contracting co. exec.; b. Ft. Wayne, Ind., Aug. 4, 1929; d. Carl and Velma Ilo (Waldron) Hancher; student Sparland (Ill.) public schs.; m. John B. Frye, Sept. 1, 1973; children by previous marriage—Timothy, David and Danny Gray. Exec. sec. R.G. LeTourneau, Peoria, Ill., 1947-48; sec., bookkeeper Household Fin., 1948-50; co-owner Gray's Trailer Sales, 1965-69; design supr., constrn. mgr. Gray's Constrn., 1969-71; Watts Line advt. specialist Peoria Jour. Star, 1973-74; exec. sec. Illini Plumbing & Heating, Champaign, Ill., 1974-80, v.p., 1980—; co-owner, mgr. Lexington Apts., Urbana, Ill., 1974—. Cub Scout leader, 1960-65. Mem. Nat. Assn. Women in Constrn., Nat. Assn. Plumbing, Heating and Cooling Contractors Aux. Methodist. Clubs: Lincolnshire Fields Country, Women of Moose. Home: 4001 Club House Dr Champaign IL 61820 Office: 2100 S Neil St Champaign IL 61820

FRYE, EVELYN MCCRARY, psychologist; b. Nashville, Tenn.; d. Robert and Lillian (Benson) McCrary; B.S., Middle Tenn. State U., 1963; M.A., Peabody Coll., 1967, Ed.S., 1971, Ph.D., 1976; 1 dau., Ashley Ann. Tchr. psychology Met. Nashville public schs., 1963-77; adj. asst. prof. George Peabody Coll., Nashville, 1975-77; asso. prof. psychology dept. U. Tenn., Nashville, 1977-79; asso. prof. psychology Tenn. State U., Nashville, 1979-81; pvt. practice clin. psychology, Nashville, 1979—; clin. dir. Nashville Pain and Stress Clinic, Inc., 1981—; cons. Nashville Meml. Hosp., 1980—, Rape and Sexual Abuse Center, Nashville, 1980—. Bd. dirs. Crisis Call Center, Nashville, 1978—. Mem. Am. Psychol. Assn., Southeastern Psychol. Assn., Tenn. Psychol. Assn. Episcopalian. Home: 1051 Nesbitt Dr Nashville TN 37207 Office: Doctors Bldg Nashville Meml Hospital Madison TN 37115

FRYE, HELEN JACKSON, fed. judge; b. Klamath Falls, Oreg., Dec. 10, 1930; d. Earl Clifford and Elizabeth Belle (Kirkpatrick) Jackson; children—Eric M., Karen Lynn, Heidi Elizabeth. Public sch. tchr., Eugene, Oreg., 1956-63; admitted to Oreg. bar, 1966; pvt. practice law, Eugene, 1966-71; judge Oreg. Circuit Ct., Eugene, 1971-80; judge U.S. Dist. Ct. Oreg., Portland, 1980—; public speaker. Office: US Courthouse Portland OR 97205

FRYE, JUDITH ELEEN MINOR (MRS. VERNON LESTER FRYE), printing co. exec.; b. Seattle; d. George Edward and Eleen G. (Hartelius) Minor; student U. Calif. at Los Angeles, evenings 1947-48, U. So. Calif., 1948-53; m. Vernon Lester Frye, Apr. 1, 1954. Accountant, office mgr. Colony Wholesale Liquor, Culver City, Calif., 1947-48; credit mgr. Western Dist. Co., Culver City, 1948-53; partner in restaurants, Palm Springs, Los Angeles, 1948, in date ranch, La Quinta, Calif., 1949-53; partner Imperial Printing, Los Angeles, 1955-67, owner, 1969—; editor New Era Laundry and Cleaning Lines, Huntington Beach, Calif., 1962—. Sec., Energy and Pollution Info. Council. Mem. Laundry and Cleaning Allied Trades Assn., Calif. Coin-Op Assn. (exec. dir., service award 1976), Laundry and Dry Cleaning Suppliers Assn., Nat. Automatic Laundry and Cleaning Council (outstanding service award 1971), Women in Laundry and Dry Cleaning (past pres.), Am. Soc. Assn. Execs., So. Calif. Soc. Assn. Execs. Office: 22031 Bushard St Huntington Beach CA 92646

FRYE, LINDA BETH (HISLE), tchr.; b. Ada, Okla., Apr. 15, 1947; d. Roland Earl and Paralee M. (Jones) Hisle; B.A. in Art and Elem. Edn., E. Central State U., Ada, 1970; M.Ed. in Elem. Edn., E. Tex. State U., Commerce, 1975; m. Dennis Franklin Frye; 3 sons, Byron Franklin, Cody Earl, Matthew Cole. Tchr. Sherman (Tex.) Ind. Sch. Dist., 1971—. Mem. Tex. State Tchrs. Assn. (profl. rep. 1974-75), NEA, Classroom Tchrs. Assn. Cert. tchr., Tex.; specialist in lang., learning disabilities in special edn. Home: 413 Hidden Valley Trail Sherman TX 75090 Office: Fairview Sch Woods and Taylor Sherman TX 75090

FRYER, ELSIE BETH, nutritionist, educator; b. Kopperl, Tex., June 25, 1925; d. Robert E. and Erna (Schuhmann) Alsup; B.S., U. N.Mex., 1945; M.S., Ohio State U., 1949; Ph.D., Mich. State U., 1959; m. Holly Claire Fryer, Dec. 27, 1966. Tchr. home econs. pub. schs., Belen and Raton, N.Mex., 1945-48; asst. prof. S.D. State U., Brookings, 1949-56, asso. prof., 1956; asso. prof. foods and nutrition Kans. State U., Manhattan, 1959-75, prof., 1975—. Mem. Am. Home Econs. Assn., Am. Inst. Nutrition, Am. Dietetic Assn., Inst. Food Tech., Soc. Nutrition Edn., Nutrition Today Soc., Am. Assn. Cereal Chemists. Republican. Methodist. Contbr. to profl. jours. Office: Dept Foods and Nutrition Kans State U Manhattan KS 66506

FU, HELENA DA-SHEU SUEN, pharmacist; b. Amoy, Fukien, China, May 7, 1924; came to U.S., 1948, naturalized, 1961; d. Sze-Tsang and Su-Sen (Wu) Suen; B.S. Pharm., Franco-Chinoise U., Shanghai, China, 1945; B.S. in Pharmacy, U. Ill., Chgo., 1949, M.S., 1951; m. Peter W. Fu, Aug. 25, 1951; children—Enoch, Timothy, Daniel. Pharmacist, St. Elizabeth Hosp., Shanghai, China, 1945-48; research biochemist St. Lukes Hosp., Chgo., 1951-59; instr. pharmacy U. Ill., 1959-65; pharmacist Westpoint Pharmacy, Skokie, Ill., 1966-68; research asso. dept. drugs AMA, Chgo., 1968-74; pharmacist Swedish Covenant Hosp., Chgo., 1974-76, Weiss Meml. Hosp., Chgo., 1977; dir. pharmacy The Admiral Retirement Home, Chgo., 1978—. Chinese sec. Chgo. Chinese Baptist Ch. Mem. Am. Pharm. Assn., Ill. Pharm. Assn., Evanston Art Center, Little City Found. for Retarded Children, Sigma Xi, Rho Chi, Lambda Kappa Sigma. Contbr. articles to various publs. Baptist. Home: 5935 N Newark Ave Chicago IL 60631 Office: The Admiral Retirement Home 909 W Foster Ave Chicago IL 60640

FUCCI, LINDA DEAN, banker; b. Roanoke, Ala., July 2, 1947; d. Alton Hershall and Irma Nell (Trimble) Dean; A.S., So. Union State Jr. Coll., Opelika, Ala., 1974; spl. courses Am. Inst. Banking, Am. Inst. Real Estate, Auburn U., Air U. (Lanett, Ala.); m. Bob Fucci, Aug. 1981. With Bank of East Ala., Opelika, 1968-72; adminstrv. asst. charge investments, money mgmt., and corr. banking Auburn Nat. Bank (Ala.), 1972-80, asst. v.p., 1980—; recruiter, pilot Air Trans, Auburn, 1979—. Treas. Lee County Heart Assn., 1979—; crusade chmn. Lee County Cancer Soc., 1980, pres., 1980; mem. Auburn Heritage Soc. Cert. flight instr. Mem. Nat. Assn. Bank Women, Am. Heart Assn., Am. Inst. Banking (pres. East Ala. chpt. 1981), Aircraft Owners and Pilots Assn., Pilots Lobby. Roman Catholic. Home: PO Box 592 Auburn AL 36830 Office: PO Box 711 Auburn AL 36830

FUCCI, MAUREEN ANNE, real estate broker; b. Inglewood, Calif., Apr. 20, 1943; d. Louis Michael and Una Hope (Ball) Fucci; student El Camino Jr. Coll., 1961-63. With Surfside Realty, Manhattan Beach, Calif., 1981—, pres., broker, 1979—. Mem. Nat. Assn. Female Execs., Am. Soc. Profl. and Exec. Women, S. Bay Bd. Realtors (bd. dirs. until 1981). Clubs: Ironwood Country, Manhattan Beach Country. Office: 3627 N Sepulveda St Manhattan Beach CA 90266

FUCHS, JOYCE KAPLAN, magazine publisher; b. New Orleans, Feb. 6, 1947; d. Murrel Herman and Louise May (Goldman) Kaplan; B.A., U. Denver, 1967; M.B.A., Fordham U., 1976; m. Stanley Fuchs, June 20, 1970 (separated Sept. 1980); children—Belinda Louise, Melissa Eleanor. Mgr. women's div. M.N. Nelson & Assos., personnel recruiting, Denver, 1967-68; sales rep. World of Sleep, retail furniture, Denver, 1968-69; sales dir. Tina Michelle div. Alfred Angelo, Inc., bridal accessories, N.Y.C., 1969-70; adminstrv. asst. to v.p. and corp. counsel Raymond Lee Orgn., N.Y.C., 1970; sales cons. Modern Bridge mag., 1971-74; dir. advt. Complete Buyers Guide to Stereo/Hi-Fi Equipment, N.Y.C., 1975-77, publisher, 1977—; dir. advt. Cameo mag., N.Y.C., 1979—; adj. instr. mktg. Fordham U.; propr. Joyce K. Fuchs, mktg. and sales cons. Recipient Top Producer award M.N. Nelson & Assos., 1967, 68. Mem. Am. Mgmt. Assn., Inst. High Fidelity, Advt. Women N.Y. Democrat. Office: 50 Rockefeller Plaza Suite 921 New York NY 10020

FUCHS, LILLIAN, violist, educator, composer; b. N.Y.C.; d. Philip and Kate (Weiss) F.; diploma with honors Inst. Musical Art; m. Ludwig Stein; children—Barbara Stein Mallow and Carol Stein Amado (twins). Co-founder, mem. Perole String Quartet; soloist with Casals Festival, Prades, France; soloist with numerous orchestras, including N.Y. Philharmonic; toured in concert U.S. and Europe; prof. viola Juilliard Sch. Music, Manhattan Sch. Music, N.Y.C.; soloist, tchr. Aspen (Colo.) Music Festival, Banff (Can.) Centre; composer 8 published works for viola, violin and piano, 1947-72; rec. artist Decca, Columbia records. Recipient Artist-Tchr. award Am. String Tchrs. Assn., 1979; scroll 9th Internat. Viola Congress, 1981. Address: 186 Pinehurst Ave New York NY 10033

FUCHS, NANALEE L. HOLVE, chem. engr.; b. Santa Ana, Calif., Dec. 3, 1954; d. Herbert Raymond and Joyce Nanalee (Chapman) Holve; B.S. in Chem. Engring., U. Wash., 1978. Engr., E. I. du Pont de Nemours & Co., Wilmington, Del., 1978—; research engr. Chevron Chem. Co., Richmond, Calif., 1980—. Mem. Am. Inst. Chem. Engrs., Sierra Club. Office: 940 Hensley St Richmond CA 94804

FUCHS, NINA, moving co. exec.; b. N.Y.C., Sept. 8, 1953; d. Harry and Shirley (Hochreich) F.; student Franklin Pierce Coll., 1971-72, Nassau Community Coll., 1972-73. Mem. Kibbutz Adamit, Israel, 1975-76; with Century-Franklin Moving & Warehouse Corp., N.Y.C., 1976-81, sales mgr. in charge comml. storage and household moving sales, 1979-81; sales account exec. Air Couriers Internat., N.Y.C., 1981-82; v.p. sales and mktg., Century-Franklin M & W Corp., N.Y.C., 1982—; dir. ops. and account services Allied Air Freight and Warehouse Sales. Mem. The

Exec. Female, Nat. Assn. Female Execs., NOW, Assn. Record Mgrs. and Adminstrs., Women's Action Alliance N.Y. Office: Century-Franklin Corp 233-35 E 38th St New York NY 10016

FUDALA, JANET BARKER, ednl. adminstr.; b. Ft. Dodge, Iowa, Nov. 20, 1935; d. Lawrence Kendall and Bernice Irene (Geary) O'Neill; B.A., U. Ariz., 1957, M.A., 1959; Ph.D., U. Wash., 1973; m. John Fudala, July 25, 1969; children—Teresa Fudala Simon, Steven John, Theresa Barker Freeman, Marie Barker. Specialist in communication disorders Tucson Public Schs., 1960-61, Seattle Pub. Schs., 1961-73; cons., coordinator learning disabilities research Seattle Public Schs., 1973-75; dir. spl. edn. and spl. programs Port Townsend (Wash.) Sch. Dist., 1978—; adj. faculty Seattle, Seattle Pacific, Western Wash. univs.; speaker to bus. and civic groups. Fellow Am. Speech-Lang.-Hearing Assn. (councilor, 1978-80; recipient grants 1964, 70); mem. Council for Exceptional Children (pres. Wash. council, 1978-79), Council Adminstr. Spl. Edn., Assn. for Gifted, Wash. Assn. Children with Learning Disabilities (v.p. 1975-80, pres. 1980—), Div. Children With Learning Disabilities, Div. Children With Communication Disorders, Wash. Assn. Sch. Adminstrs., C. of C., Zeta Phi Eta (recipient grants 1970). Roman Catholic. Author various tests including Arizona Articulation Proficiency Scale, 1963, Auditory Pointing Test, 1974, Prescriptive Reading Performance Test, 1978; Quickscreen, 1980; asso. editor: Teaching Exceptional Children, Lang. Speech and Hearing Services in Schools; cons. editor Acad. Therapy Publs.; contbr. articles to profl. jours. Home: PO Box 429 Kingston WA 98346 Office: Port Townsend Sch Dist 1610 Blaine St Port Townsend WA 98368

FUENTES, MARTHA AYERS, playwright; b. Ashland, Ala., Dec. 21, 1923; d. William Henry and Elizabeth (Dye) Ayers; B.A. in English (Ione Lester creative writing award), U. South Fla., 1969; m. Manuel Solomon Fuentes, Apr. 11, 1943. Author plays: The Rebel, 1970; Mama Don't Make Me Go To College, My Head Hurts, 1963; Two Characters in Search of An Agreement, 1970; contbr. articles to local, regional and nat. newspapers, feature articles to nat. mags.; author TV plays and feature articles for children and young adults; lectr., condr. workshops on drama, writing for TV. Recipient George Sergel drama award U. Chgo., 1969. Mem. Authors Guild, Authors League Am., Dramatists Guild, Soc. Children's Book Writers, Southeastern Writers Assn., Am. Theatre Assn., Internat. Women's Writing Guild. Roman Catholic. Club: U. South Fla. Alumni. Home and Office: 102 Third St Belleair Beach FL

FUHRER, LINDA LARSEN, social worker; b. Bayonne, N.J., Aug. 29, 1940; d. Joseph Martin and Metha Kirsten (Sorensen) Larsen; student U. Aix-Marseile (France), 1960-61; A.B., Taylor U., 1962, M.S.W. (VA fellow 1963-64, NIMH grantee 1964-65), 1965; m. Larry R. Fuhrer, Dec. 31, 1962; 1 son, Lance. Social worker children's div. Cook County (Ill.) Dept. Public Aid, 1962-63; dir. camp for delinquent girls under auspices Gov. Ind., 1969; social worker Wheaton (Ill.) Public Schs., 1965-68; family counselor La Grange (Ill.) Family Services, 1968; instr. social work Wheaton Coll., 1969-70; social worker spl. project for disadvantaged, elem. schs. Naperville (Ill.) Schs., 1971-72; social worker Regional Program of Hearing Imparied Students, Hinsdale Twp. (Ill.) High Sch., 1975—; dir. Equity Realty Group, 1978—; dir. Presdl. Services Inc., 1978—; pvt. practice social work, 1979—; founding bd. dirs. DuPage Pastoral Counseling Center, Glen Ellyn, Ill., 1975-78. Deacon, 1st Presbyn. Ch., Glen Ellyn, 1973-76; co-chmn. Wheaton Swim Team Parents Group, 1977-80; Class IV swim ofcl. AAU; bd. dirs. scholarship com. Longfellow Sch. PTA, Wheaton, 1976-77. Cert. social worker, Ill. Mem. Nat. Assn. Social Workers, NEA, Acad. Cert. Social Workers, Taylor U. Alumni Assn., Alpha Chi. Home: 125 W Seminary Ave Wheaton IL 60187

FUJII, GERTRUDE SUGIOKA, educator; b. Hollister, Calif., Feb. 10, 1918; d. Seijiro and Kameno (Takeda) Sugioka; B.A., UCLA, 1961, M.A., 1962; Ph.D., U. So. Calif., 1970; m. George S. Fujii, Sept. 9, 1945. Adminstrv. asst. So. Calif. Council Protestant Chs., 1947-52; tchr. English, Los Angeles Unified Dist., 1962-66; asso. prof. Los Angeles Community Coll., 1966-70; prof. English, chmn. dept. Los Angeles Valley Coll., 1970—; vis. lectr. grad. English dept. UCLA, 1980-82. Pres. evening group United Ch. Women Los Angeles, 1958; pres. congregation and bd. adminstrn. Wilshire Christian Ch. (Disciples of Christ); sec. bd. dirs. div. higher edn. Christian Chs. Nat., St. Louis; chmn. English div. Calif. Adv. Com. on Basic Skills; mem. intersegmental com. on writing Calif. Postsecondary Edn. Commn. Mem. Calif. Assn. Tchrs. English, Nat., So. Calif. councils tchrs. English, NEA, Calif. Tchrs. Assn., Los Angeles Coll. Tchrs. Assn., MLA, Am. Studies Assn., English Council Calif. Two Yr. Colls. (pres.), Phi Delta Gamma. Club: Altrusa (past pres. Los Angeles, pres. found.). Editorial adv. bd. Teaching English in the Two-Yr. Coll.; contbg. writer Chronicle of Higher Edn. Office: Los Angeles Valley Coll 5800 Fulton Ave Van Nuys CA 91401

FUKUNAGA, CAROL, state legislator; b. Honolulu, Dec. 12, 1947; B.A., J.D., U. Hawaii. Admitted to Hawaii bar; hearings officer Hawaii Public Employment Relations Bd.; mem. Hawaii Ho. of Reps. Del., Democratic convs., 1976, 78, Constl. Conv., 1978. Mem. Hawaii State Bar Assn., U. Hawaii Law Sch. Alumni Assn., Bus. and Profl. Women's Club. Office: State Capitol Rm 432 Honolulu HI 96813 *

FUKUSHIMA, BARBARA NAOMI, accountant; b. Honolulu, Apr. 5, 1948; d. Harry Kazuo and Misayo (Kawasaki) Murakoshi; B.A., U. Hawaii, 1970; postgrad. Oreg. State U., 1971, 73, U. Oreg., 1972; m. Dennis Hiroshi Fukushima, Mar. 23, 1974; 1 son, Dennis Hiroshi. Intern, Coopers & Lybrand, Honolulu, 1974; auditor Haskins & Sells, Kahului, Hawaii, 1974-77; pres. Book Doors, Inc., Pukalani, 1977—; pres. Barbara N. Fukushima C.P.A., Inc., Wailuku, 1979—; sec. treas. Target Pest Control, Inc., Wailuku, 1979—; internal auditor, acct. Maui Land & Pineapple Co., Inc., Kahului, 1977-80. Recipient Phi Beta Kappa Book award, 1969. Mem. Am. Inst. C.P.A.'s, Hawaii Soc. C.P.A.'s, Nat. Assn. Accts., Am. Womens Soc. C.P.A.'s, Hawaii Assn. Public Accts., Bus. and Profl. Womens Club. Tenrikyo. Address: 1498 Lower Main St Suite F Wailuku HI 96793

FULCHON, CELESTINE MARIA, mgmt. tng. co. exec.; b. Phila., Nov. 9, 1944; d. Thomas Edmond and Celestine Alice (Tyson) Fulchon; A.B., N.Y.U., 1966, postgrad. (Warburg Scholar, 1975-76), 1968—; student U. Ky., 1966-68. Dir. day care center Atlantic Human Resources, 1966; nat. tchr. corps. intern U. Ky., Louisville, 1966-68; asst. dir. community services Ky. Commn. on Human Rights, Louisville, 1968-71; tng. dir. Hunter Found. for Health Care, Inc., Lexington, 1971-73; grad. asst. student affairs div. N.Y.U., 1973-76, sr. clin. supr., 1979-82, human relations and social policy div., 1973-76; v.p. H.B. Reynolds Assos., N.Y.C., 1976—; cons. natural supports program Community Service Soc., N.Y. Mem. bd. clin. examiners Human Relations and Social Policy Program N.Y.U.; bd. sec. Louisville Urban League, 1971; v.p. NAACP Lexington-Fayette County, 1973; mem. community planning com. Louisville Red Cross, 1968-70; mem. Louisville planning com. White House Conf. for Children and Youth, 1969-70; youth conf. planning com. Nat. Council Negro Women, 1974; mem. faculty council Sch. Health, Nursing and Arts Professions N.Y.U., also mem. employee grievance com., v.p. grad. student orgn. Recipient Braithwaite award, 1975. Mem. Nat. Assn. Women Deans, Adminstrs. and Counselors, Am. Coll. Personnel Assn., Am. Personnel and Guidance Assn., Am. Psychol. Assn. Home: 77 W 15th St Apt 1-J New York NY 10011

FULFORD, CHARLOTTE ANN, acct.; b. St. Petersburg, Fla., July 10, 1925; d. Percival Liden and Ruth (Stiles) Roberts; grad. St. Petersburg Public Schs., 1943; m. Fred Vernon Fulford, Jan. 30, 1944; children—Sue Ethel, Margaret Elizabeth, Rebecca Ann, Fred Vernon. With OPA, Pinellas County, Fla., 1946-47; bookkeeper P.L. Roberts Plumbing Co., St. Petersburg, 1952-58; with H.P. Hood & Sons, Dunedin, Fla., 1959-60; sec.-treas., office mgr., acct. So. Roofing Co., Inc., Clearwater, Fla., 1965-80; acct. D.&F. Warehouses Ltd., Pinellas Park, Fla., 1980—. Mem. Nat. Assn. Women in Constrn. (pres. St. Petersburg chpt. 1978-80, nat. dir. region 3 1980-82), Nat. Roofing Contractors Assn., Fla. Roofing, Sheet Metal and Air Conditioning Assn. Mem. Church of Christ. Home: 8638 10th St N Saint Petersburg FL 33702 Office: 4317 62d Ave N Pinellas Park FL 33526

FULKERSON, TAVI, TV personality; b. Detroit, Sept. 21, 1953; d. George J. and Ruth (Black) F.; B.A. with high honors, U. Mich., 1974. Producer, host jazz show Sta. WUOM-FM, U. Mich., Ann Arbor, 1974-76; promotions dir., producer/host daily talk show Sta. WIQB-FM, Ann Arbor, 1976-79; host Tavi show TV-31, Ann Arbor, 1980—; fashion editor Ann Arbor News, 1980—. Bd. dirs. Mich. Theater, Ann Arbor. Mem. Ann Arbor C. of C. (dir. 1982). Unitarian. Club: Nautilus Sports Fitness. Office: 216 S State St Suite 1 Ann Arbor MI 48104

FULLER, ANDREA LORRAINE, writer; b. Cambridge, Mass., Dec. 30, 1938; d. F.W. and E.W. (Danforth) Dorey; B.A. in Creative Writing, San Jose State U., 1978; m. E. Ray Fuller, Sept. 25, 1960; 1 dau., Andrea Rae. Stringer, Valley Jour., Sunnyvale (Calif.) Scribe, 1971; feature writer Cupertino (Calif.) Courier, San Jose (Calif.) Sun, 1972; producer TV cablevision series Gracia's People, 1973; creator, producer TV pilot The Time Tree, 1974; co-editor Met. Adult Edn. Program Anthology, San Jose, 1975, editor, 1976; instr. creative writing, adult edn. Met. Adult Edn. Program, 1974-78, coordinator writing contest, 1976, pres. Senate, 1975-76, editor-in-chief the Cross Town Rag (Internat.), 1979—; creator TV pilot Gentle Invader, 1982; cons. fiction and non-fiction to authors, 1975—; dir. PACE, Inc., Nor-Cal, 1978-82. Recipient achiever award Internat. League Am. Penwomen, 1972. Mem. Calif. Writers Club (panelist, forum, 1976), Am. Penwomen (Santa Clara Br.).

FULLER, ANNE ELIZABETH HAVENS, univ. ofcl., dean, educator; b. Pomona, Calif., Jan. 20, 1932; d. Paul Swain and Lorraine Elizabeth (Hamilton) Havens; A.B., Mt. Holyoke Coll., 1953; B.A. with honours, Oxford U., 1955, M.A. with honours, 1959; Ph.D., Yale U., 1958; m. Martin E. Fuller, June 17, 1961; children—Katharine Hamilton, Peter David Takashi. Instr. English, Mt. Holyoke Coll., 1957-59; instr., asst. prof. English, Pomona Coll., 1959-61; asst. prof. humanities U. Fla., Gainesville, 1961-63; lectr. English, U. Denver, 1964-68, 71-73; assoc. prof. English, chmn. Ctr. for Langs., Prescott Coll., 1968-70; sr. tchr. English, Colo. Rocky Mountain Sch., 1970-71; dean faculty, prof. English, Scripps Coll., 1973-80; spl. asst. to pres. Claremont (Calif.) U. Ctr., 1980-82; v.p. acad. affairs, dean faculty, prof. English, Austin (Tex.) Coll., 1982—. Chmn. adv. bd. Project on Status and Edn. of Women, Washington, 1980—; mem. S.W. Dist. Rhodes Scholar Selection Com., 1975-81. Fulbright grantee, 1953-55, others. Mem. Assn. Am. Colls. (dir. 1977-81, chmn. 1979-80), Am. Council on Edn. (dir. 1979-81, mem. Commn. on Women in Higher Edn. 1981—), Am. Council Acad. Deans (dir. 1977-79), Am. Assn. Higher Edn., MLA, Modern Humanities Research Assn., New Chaucer Soc., Nat. Women's Studies Assn., Phi Beta Kappa. Democrat. Episcopalian. Contbr. articles to profl. jours. Home: 823 N Grand Ave Sherman TX 75090 Office: Dean's Office Austin Coll Sherman TX 75090

FULLER, ETHEL GRAVES, social worker; b. Yanceyville, N.C., July 3, 1939; d. Henry T. and Annie W. (Watlington) Graves; B.A., Bennett Coll., 1960; M.S.W., Howard U., 1966; m. Roy Wilson Fuller, May 20, 1961; children—Adrai Lalita, Frank Brian. Counselor, Bennett Coll., Greensboro, N.C., 1960-61; clk. customer relations Hecht Co., Washington, 1962-63; child welfare worker Charles County Welfare Bd., La Plata, Md., 1963-67; supr. family and children's services, coordinator child abuse team Caswell County Dept. Social Services, Yanceyville, N.C., 1967—. Bd. dirs. Big Bros., Big Sisters; program dir. Caswell County Program Assuring Coll. Edn.; co-chmn. Caswell County Voters League; mem. adv. com. on aging Piedmont Triad Council Govt.; vice pres. Caswell Family Med. Center, Inc.; pres. Young Willing Workers; pres. Area Suprs. Group; Mem. Nat. Assn. Social Workers, N.C. Social Services Assn., NAACP. Baptist. Club: Ind. Order St. Luke (sec. Yanceyville chpt.). Home: Route 1 Box 211 Yanceyville NC 27379 Office: PO Box 187 Yanceyville NC 27379

FULLER, MARY FALVEY, fin. exec.; b. Detroit, Oct. 28, 1941; d. Lawrence C. and Mathilde G. Falvey; B.A. with honors in Econs., Cornell U., 1963; M.B.A., Harvard U., 1967; m. James W. Fuller, Aug. 22, 1981. Systems engr. IBM Corp., N.Y.C., 1963-65, 66; mgmt. cons. McKinsey & Co., Inc., N.Y.C., 1967-75; v.p. Citibank N.A., N.Y.C., 1975-78; sr. v.p., dir., mem. exec. and operating coms., head adminstrn. div. Blyth Eastman Dillon & Co., N.Y.C., 1978-80; pres. M. C. Falvey Assos., Inc., N.Y.C., 1980-81; v.p. fin. Shaklee Corp., San Francisco, 1981-82; ind. mgmt. cons., 1982—; pres., dir. Falvey Autos, Inc., Troy, Mich. Mem. Nat. Commn. Social Security Reform, Human Resources Fin. Council, Cornell U. Council; adminstrn. and legal processes adv. council Mills Coll.; bd. trustees San Francisco Performances; mem. Pres. Reagan's Transition Task Force on Social Security; com. N.Y. Philharmonic, 1975-77. Harvard Bus. Sch. grantee, 1965-67. Republican. Episcopalian. Clubs: Recess, (N.Y.C.); Fin. Officers No. Calif., Fin. Execs. Inst. Home: 2584 Filbert St San Francisco CA 94123 Office: 2584 Filbert St San Francisco CA 94123

FULLER, MARY MARGARET, editor; b. Lincoln, Nebr., Apr. 23, 1914; d. Ewald Ortwin and Marie Daisy (Douglass) Stiehm; B.A., U. Wis., Madison, 1938; m. Curtis G. Fuller, Sept. 24, 1938; children—Nancy Abigail, Michael Curtis. Freelance writer, Wilmette, Ill., 1940-52; sec. Clark Pub. Co., Highland Park, Ill., 1949—; asst. editor Fate mag., Highland Park, 1952-54, exec. editor, 1954-56, editor, 1956—, asso. pub., 1977—; v.p., sec. Woodall Pub. Co., Highland Park, 1965—. Mem. Ill. Soc. Psychic Research (pres. 1966-68), Soc. Psychical Research London, Theta Sigma Phi. Democrat. Universalist-Unitarian. Home: 815 E Deerpath Rd Lake Forest IL 60045 Office: 500 Hyacinth Pl Highland Park IL 60035

FULLER, NANCY FAY, librarian; b. Oxford, Miss., Sept. 23, 1945; d. Joe Bailey and Mattie Burris (Moore) F.; A.A., Wood Jr. Coll., 1965; B.A. in Edn., U. Miss., 1967, M.L.S. (NDEA fellow), 1968. Periodicals librarian George Peabody Coll. for Tchrs., Nashville, 1968-69; asst., asso. prof. and asst. librarian State Tech. Inst., Memphis, 1969-74, prof. and chmn. library dept., 1974-76; pharmacy librarian U. Miss., University, 1976—. Mem. ALA, Am. Assn. Colls. Pharmacy (membership chmn. libraries-ednl. resource sect. 1980-82), Southeastern Library Assn., Miss. Library Assn., U. Miss. Grad. Sch. Library and Info. Sci. Alumni Assn. (pres. 1979-80), U. Miss. Library Staff Assn. (pres. 1979-80), Med. Library Assn., Kappa Delta Pi. Baptist. Club: Pilot (dir. Oxford 1982—). Office: Austin A Dodge Pharmacy Library U Miss University MS 38677

FULLER, NELL BENTON, med. librarian; b. Rock Hill, S.C., Apr. 6, 1917; d. James Newton and Annie Clementine (Bolling) Benton; A.B., U. N.C., Greensboro, 1940; M.S. in L.S., U. N.C., Chapel Hill, 1968; m. Henry Shephard Fuller, Dec. 15, 1962 (dec.). High sch. tchr., Stony Point, N.C., 1940-43; asst. librarian Bowman Gray Med. Sch., Wake Forest U., Winston-Salem, N.C., 1944-45, librarian, 1945-62; mem. faculty and staff Claude Moore Health Scis. Library, U. Va. Med. Center, Charlottesville, 1966—, asst. prof., 1970-75, asso. prof., 1975—, head tech. services, 1970—. Mem. Med. Library Assn. Democrat. Presbyterian. Home: 118 Dorset Ct Charlottesville VA 22901 Office: Box 234 U Va Med Center Charlottesville VA 22901

FULLER, SUE, artist; b. Pitts.; d. Samuel Leslie and Carrie (Cassedy) F.; B.A., Carnegie Inst. Tech., 1936; M.A., Columbia U., 1939. One-woman shows: Bertha Schaefer Gallery, McNay Art Inst., San Antonio, Norfolk Mus. Currier Gallery, Corcoran Gallery, Smithsonian Instn., Plum Gallery, Kensington, Md., others; exhibited in group shows: Aldrich Mus., Corcoran Gallery, Phila., Mus., Whitney Mus., Bklyn. Mus., others; represented in permanent collections: Addison Gallery Am. Art, Larry Aldrich Mus., Chgo. Art Inst., Des Moines Art Center, Ford Found., Met. Mus., Guggenheim Mus., Whitney Mus. Am. Art, Tate Gallery London, Library of Congress, All Souls Unitarian Ch., N.Y.C., others; tchr. Pratt Inst., Bklyn., 1964-65. Recipient Alumni Merit award Carnegie Mellon U., 1974; Louis Comfort Tiffany fellow, 1948; John Simon Guggenheim fellow, 1949; Nat. Inst. Arts and Letters grantee, 1950; Eliot Pratt Found. fellow, 1966-68; Mark Rothko Found. grantee, 1973. Producer movies String Composition, 1970, 74. Patentee embedded string compositions. Home: PO Box 1580 Southampton NY 11968 Office: Chalette Internat 9 E 88th St New York City NY 10028

FULLERTON, DIANE CAROLINE, property mgmt. co. exec.; b. Mpls., Feb. 6, 1943; d. Carl and Mildred (Christensen) Hansen; student U. Minn.; children—Scott Anthony, Kristen Marie. Asst. to pres. Nat. Car Rental, Mpls.; asst. controller Imperial Oil Co., Los Angeles; profl. model and instr., Los Angeles; regional mgr. Alta Property Mgmt., 1978-80; exec. v.p. Mercury Property Mgmt., Irvine, Calif., 1980—; also cons. Mem. Community Assn. Insts., Bldg. Industry Assocs. Republican. Office: 4670 Barranca Pkwy Irvine CA 92714

FULLERTON, GAIL JACKSON, sociologist, univ. pres.; b. Lincoln. Nebr., Apr. 29, 1927; d. Earl Warren and Gladys (Marshall) Jackson; B.A., U. Nebr., 1949, M.A., 1950; Ph.D., U. Oreg., 1954; m. Snell Putney, July 28, 1950 (div. 1966); children—Gregory S., Cindy Gail; m. 2d, Stanley James Fullerton, Mar. 27, 1967. Lectr. sociology Drake U., Des Moines, 1955-57; asst. prof. sociology Fla. State U. at Tallahassee, 1957-60; asst. prof. sociology San Jose (Calif.) State U., 1963-68, asso. prof., 1968-72, prof. sociology, 1972—, dean grad. studies and research 1972-76, exec. v.p., 1977-78, pres., 1978—. Bd. dirs. San Jose Symphony; bd. govs. Santa Clara County region NCCJ. Mem. Am. Sociol. Assn., Internat. Sociol. Assn., San Jose C. of C. (dir.), AAAS, Phi Beta Kappa. Author: (with Snell Putney) Normal Neurosis, 1964, The Adjusted American, 1966; Survival in Marriage, 2d edit., 1977. Home: 226 Wave Crest Ave Santa Cruz CA 95060 Office: Office of Pres San Jose State U. San Jose CA 95192

FULLING, KATHARINE PAINTER, educator, writer; b. Dodge City, Kans., Aug. 6; d. William George and Carrie (Lopp) Painter; B.A., Northwestern U., 1945; M.A., Columbia U., 1947; postgrad. Vassar Coll., 1948, San Marcos U., Lima, Peru, 1948-49, (fellow) Inst. Internat. Edn., U. Madrid, Spain, 1952-53; m. Virgil H. Fulling, Sept. 24, 1948. Asst. dir. Casa Panamericana, Mills Coll., 1944; asst. to dir. Fine Arts Dept., Columbia U., N.Y.C., 1945-47; tchr. public schs. Port Washington, L.I., N.Y., 1953-55; lectr. Global Edn., UN, N.Y.C., 1953-56; public relations dir. Nat. League Am. Pen Women, Washington, 1958-60; Non-Govtl. Orgns. rep. United Women of the Ams., UN, N.Y.C., 1959-62; lectr. Asia and Africa Halls, Smithsonian Inst., Washington, 1965-69; lectr. Folger Shakespeare Library, Washington, 1969-73; art reviewer Wyo., Denver Art Mus., 1974—. Mem. Wyo. Council for Humanities, 1979-80. Mem. Asia Soc., Inter-Am. Center, AAUW, Nat. League Am. Pen Women, LWV (pres. 1967-69), Mark Twain Soc. (hon. mem.), Sigma Alpha Iota. Author: The Cradle of American Art, 1948; Mantillas and Silver Spurs, 1952; contbr., columnist numerous jours. and mags. Address: 715 S Durbin St Casper WY 82601

FULLMER, LOIS MARIE, recreation center exec.; b. Grandview, Iowa, Nov. 28, 1931; d. Charles and Margaret (Coder) Howell; student State U. Iowa, 1955-56, Mason City (Iowa) Jr. Coll., 1956-57; m. Edward E. Fullmer, Feb. 24, 1956; children—Sara, Jay Edward. Mgr. farm, 1956-64; sales rep. Russell Stover Candies, 1966-70; buyer Disneyland, Anaheim, Calif., 1970-79; corporate sr. buyer retail merchandise div. Walt Disney Prodns., Burbank, Calif., 1979—. Served with WAVES, 1951-52; Korea. Home: 244 Canyon Crest Dr Monrovia CA 91016 Office: 500 S Buena Vista Burbank CA 91521

FULLWOOD, KAY FRANCES, nursing service adminstr.; b. Beaufort, S.C., Aug. 28, 1940; d. Oliver and Dorothy (Lee) Green; L.P.N., Helen Fuld Sch. Practical Nursing, 1967; A.D.N. with honors, Fla. Jr. Coll. Sch. Nursing, 1974; B.S. in Nursing, U. North Fla., 1979; div.; 1 dau., Sharon Evon (Mrs. Sidney H. Dees). Staff nurse Hosp. for Joint Disease, N.Y.C., 1967-68; staff nurse Mt. Sinai Hosp., N.Y.C., 1970-71; office nurse, physician's asst., N.Y.C., 1968-71; staff nurse orthopedics Bapt. Med. Center, Jacksonville, Fla., 1971-74, team leader, 1974-76, head nurse, 1976-80, project coordinator nursing service, 1979—, also mem. primary nursing com., 1979—, mem. audit com., procedure com. Mem. Orthopedic Nursing Assn. (pres. Jacksonville chpt. 1976-79), Am. Nurses Assn., Fla. Nurses Assn. (dir. 1981—). Jewish. Office: Baptist Med Center 800 Prudential Dr Jacksonville FL 32207

FULNER, JACQULYN GRIZZARD, social worker; b. Louisville, Mar. 9, 1953; d. John P. and Louise M. Grizzard; B.A. with high distinction, Eastern Ky. U., 1974; M.S.S.W., U. Louisville, 1979; m. John D. Fulner, Jan. 4, 1980. Family service worker Child Devel. Services System, Louisville, 1974-75; social worker Ky. Dept. Human Resources, Louisville, 1976-78; project dir. Louisville Urban League, 1979-80; protective service worker Dept. Human Services, Jefferson County, Ky., 1980—. Recipient Flood Disaster assistance award ARC, 1977. Mem. Nat. Assn. Social Workers. Methodist. Home: 4621 S 2nd St Louisville KY 40214

FULTON, ETHEL MARGARET, coll. pres., educator; b. Birtle, Man., Can., Sept. 8, 1922; d. Ernest Bain and Ethel Mary (Futers) F.; cert. Winnipeg Normal Sch., 1942; diploma, U. Minn., 1946; cert. U. Toronto, 1956, 61; M.A., U. B.C., 1960; Ph.D., U. Toronto, 1968. Pub. and secondary sch. tchr., Ont., 1948-53; head Eng. Coll. Inst., Thunder Bay, Ont., 1960-63; teaching fellow in English, U. Toronto, 1963-66; asst. prof. English, Wilfred Laurier U., 1967-74; dean women U. B.C., 1974-78; pres., prof. English Mt. St. Vincent U., Halifax, N.S., Can., 1978—; dir. Fireman's Fund Ins. Co. of Can. Recipient Ont. Grad. Fellowships; William P. Huffman scholar-in-residence, U. Miami, Oxford, Ohio. Mem. Interam. U. Assn. (dir.), Can. Congress Learning Opportunities for Women, Can. Assn. Univ. Tchrs., Assn. Can. Univ. Tchrs. English, Assn. Univs. and Colls. Can., Assn. Commonwealth Univs., Assn. Atlantic Univs., Assn. Can. and Que. Lit., Can. Council Tchrs. English, Can. Soc. Study Higher Edn., Victorian Studies Assn., Can. Research Inst. Advancement Women, Am. Assn. Higher Edn. Mem. NDP. Mem. United Ch. of Can. Clubs: Voice of Women, Univ. Women's, Zonta. Home: 12A Sherbrooke Dr Halifax NS B3M 1P6 Canada Office: Mount St Vincent University 166 Bedford Hwy Halifax NS B3M 2J6 Canada *

FULTON, JOYCE ROSALIE, banker; b. Ware, Mass., Jan. 21, 1938; d. Joseph E. and Rose A. (Regin) Rabschnuk; student Clark U., U. Mass.; grad. Williams Coll. Sch. of Banking, 1971; m. Harlan W. Fulton, June 15, 1958; children—Catherine Joy, Margaret Beth. With Ware Trust Co. (Mass.), 1960—, v.p., 1973-75, exec. v.p., 1975-77, pres., 1977—, chmn. bd., 1980—. Bd. dirs. Mary Lane Hosp., Gilbertville (Mass.) Library Assn.; trustee New Eng. Sch. Banking at Williams Coll. Mem. Nat. Assn. Bank Women, Mass. Bankers Assn. (dir.), Bank Adminstrn. Inst. (pres. Western Mass. chpt., state dir. 1980-82, dist. dir.). Office: Ware Trust Co 73 Main St Ware MA 01082

FULTON, LEILA, educator; b. Pitts.; d. John Robert and Cordelia (Greiner) F.; B.S., U. Pitts., 1937, M.A., 1954; postgrad. U. Hawaii. Head tchr. Highland Sch., Castle Shannon, Pa., now tchr. Hillsdale Sch., Keystone Oaks Dist., critic for student tchrs. from Duquesne U., U. Pitts., Point Park Coll. and Edinburg Coll. Named Educator of Yr., Pa. Jaycees, 1981. Mem. NEA, Pa., Dormont (pres.) edn. assns., Phi Delta Gamma, Delta Kappa Gamma (pres. 1976-78). Club: Dormont Coll. (pres.) Methodist. Home: 2979 Glenmore Ave Pittsburgh PA 15216

FULTON, SUSAN E.O. BREAKEFIELD (MRS. RICHARD A. FULTON), fin. planner; b. Winthrop, Mass., Dec. 10, 1939; d. Durward Ellsworth and Annabelle (Owens) Breakefield; B.A., Wilson Coll., Chambersburg, Pa., 1961; m. Richard Alsina Fulton, Apr. 13, 1971. Editor, Lititz (Pa.) Record-Express, 1961-62; account exec. Holyoke (Mass.) Transcript-Telegram, 1962-64; account exec. Washington Daily News, 1964-69; account exec. Sta. WASH, Metromedia Radio, Washington, 1969-73, local sales mgr., 1973-75, gen. sales mgr., 1975-77, v.p. and gen. mgr., 1977-81; registered rep. Linsco Corp., Alexandria, Va., 1981-82; fin. planner Manna Corp., Fairfax, Va., 1982—; partner Fulton Broadcasting WRCV, Mercersburg, Pa. Vice chmn. bd. trustees Wilson Coll. Cert. fin. planner Coll. Fin. Planning. Mem. Wilson Coll. Alumnae Assn., Internat. Assn. Fin. Planners, Woman's Network. Republican. Episcopalian. Home: 3813 Garrison St NW Washington DC 20016 Office: Manna Corp 8315 Lee Hwy Fairfax VA 22031

FULTZ, SUE CAROL, advt. agy. exec.; b. Conroe, Tex., July 15, 1946; d. Kelton Benton and Harriett Sue (Woodson) Fultz; B.A., U. Houston, 1967. Vice-pres. Lloyd G. Jakeway Advt. and Public Relations, Houston, 1968-74; dir. press relations First Mktg. Group, Inc., Houston, 1974-77; pres. Suzy Fultz Advt. and Public Relations, Houston, 1974—. Recipient Franklin award U. Houston, 1964-67. Mem. Houston Advt. Fedn. (dir. 1977-78, editor newsletter 1977-80), Am. Women in Radio and TV (past dir.), Houston Assn. Broadcast Execs. in Tex., Delta Zeta. Methodist. Clubs: Art Dir., Press, One Hundred (Houston). Office: 2041 Westcreek Suite 111D Houston TX 77027

FULWEILER, PATRICIA PLATT, civic worker; b. N.Y.C., Mar. 19, 1923; d. Haviland Hull and Marie-Louise (Fearey) Platt; A.B. cum laude, Bryn Mawr Coll., 1945; M.B.A., Columbia U., 1950; m. Spencer Biddle Fulweiler, Oct. 5, 1946; children—Marie-Louise Fulweiler Allen, Pamela Spencer, Hull Platt, Spencer Biddle. Jr. copywriter, asst. account exec. Dorland Internat. Pettingell & Fenton, N.Y.C., 1945-46; statistician, fin. staff treas.'s office Gen. Motors Corp., N.Y.C., 1950-52; asst. account mgr. investment dept. Fiduciary Trust Co., N.Y.C., 1953-61; bd. dirs. Chapin Brearley Exchange, Inc., N.Y.C., 1964-74, treas., 1966-71, pres., 1971-73; bd. dirs. Knickerbocker Greys, 1965—, treas., 1970-75; bd. dirs., treas. City Gardens Club, N.Y.C., 1974-79, chmn. ways and means com., 1974-81; bd. dirs. Nat. Soc. Colonial Dames State N.Y., 1973-82, asst. treas., 1973-82; mem. fin. com. Alumnae Assn. Bryn Mawr Coll., 1970-76; bd. dirs. Daus. of Cin., 1974-81, scholarship adminstr., 1976-81; Pres. Ladies Christian Union, 1982—; rec. sec. Women's Assn. St. James Ch., N.Y.C., 1972-75, co-chmn. Spring Festival, 1974-75, chmn., 1975-76, mem. Altar Guild, 1975—, treas., 1981—; treas. Churchwomen's League for Patriotic Service, 1982—; mem. scholarship com. Youth Found., 1981—. Mem. Soc. Sponsers of U.S. Navy. Republican. Clubs: Colony, Wilson Point Beach Assn. Home: 158 E 83d St New York NY 10028

FUNK, CAROL ANN NORCIA, psychologist; b. Jersey City, Feb. 7, 1947; d. Gerard Thomas and Evelyn Elizabeth (Iaccarino) Norcia; B.A. (scholar), Caldwell Coll., 1968; M.A. (scholar), St. Bonaventure U., 1970; Psy.D. in Psychology, Rutgers U., 1980; m. Ronald Edward Funk, Apr. 4, 1971; 1 son, Matthew. Staff psychologist Passaic (N.J.) Public Schs., 1970-73, project leader Title VI program, 1972-73; staff psychologist Spotswood (N.J.) Public Schs., 1973-76, dir. spl. services, 1975-76; extern psychologist New Brunswick (N.J.) Public Schs., 1976-77, Princeton (N.J.) Public Schs., 1977-78; cons. psychologist Center for Human Relations, East Brunswick, N.J., 1978—. Exec. sec. Puerto Rican Inst. for Devel., 1972-73; mem. citizen's adv. bd. Rutgers Community Mental Health Focus Team, 1974-75; mem. adv. com. Middlesex County Arts Council, 1979; vol. New Brunswick Ret. Srs. Vol. Program, 1978-79. Cert. supr. spl. edn., sch. psychologist; NIMH fellow, 1976-77. Mem. Am. Psychol. Assn., N.J. Psychol. Assn., N.J. Acad. Psychology, N.J. Assn. Sch. Psychologists, Am. Bus. Women's Assn., Phi Delta Kappa. Home: 9 Wellington Pl New Brunswick NJ 08901 Office: B-2 Cornwall Dr East Brunswick NJ 08901

FUNK, ELLA FRANCES, genealogist, author; b. Domino, Ky., Apr. 7, 1921; d. Roy William and Edna Rene (Cummins) Roach; B.Liberal Studies, Mary Washington Coll., Fredericksburg, Va., 1982; m. Eugene Boyd Funk, June 20, 1942; children—Susan Teresa, Eugene Boyd. Exec. sec. Lang. Labs., Inc., Bethesda, Md., 1969-70; office mgr. legal firm Donovan Leisure Newton & Irvine, Washington, 1970-76; genealogist, hist. researcher, writer, 1976—; vol. Assn. Preservation Va. Antiquities. Named Exec. of Week, Sta. WGMS, Washington, June 1975. Life mem. Nat. Geneal. Soc.; mem. Hist. Fredericksburg Found., DAR, Alpha Phi Sigma, Sigma Phi Gamma. Mem. Christian Ch. (Disciples of Christ). Club: Order Eastern Star. Address: Box 557 LOW Locust Grove VA 22508

FUNK, SANDRA GAIL, educator; b. Balt., Dec. 6, 1945; d. Louis Paul and Alice Freddy (Kraemer) F.; B.A., U. Calif., Santa Barbara, 1967; M.A., U. N.C., Chapel Hill, 1972, Ph.D., 1976; Research asst. dept. psychology San Diego State Coll., 1967-72; research and teaching asst. L.L. Thurstone Psychometric lab., 1968-72, statis. and data processing cons., 1972-73; statis. and computer cons. Social Sci. Statis. Lab. U. N.C., 1973-76, instr. Sch. Nursing, 1976-77, asst. prof., 1977-81, assoc. prof., 1981—, coordinator grad. research, 1979—; adj. asst. med. research prof. dept. psychiatry Duke U., 1980—. NDEA fellow 1969. Mem. Am. Psychol. Assn., Psychometric Soc., Gamma Phi Beta. Mem. editorial bd. Jour. Representative Research in Social Psychology, 1969-75, assoc. editor, 1970-71; contbr. in field. Office: School Nursing Carrington Hall 214H University of North Carolina Chapel Hill NC 27514

FUNKHOUSER, SARA ANN, musicologist, educator; b. Santa Rosa, Calif., Apr. 21, 1934; d. Charles William and Maurice (Monroe) Reinking; student Juilliard Sch. Music, 1952-54, Manhattan Sch. Music, 1954-57; B.M., U. Mo., Kansas City, 1974, M.M. (Univ. fellow), 1976, D.M.A., 1981. First oboist Calgary (Alta., Can.) Philharm. Orch., 1958-59, Kansas City (Mo.) Philharm. Orch., 1959-70, Kansas City (Mo.) Lyric Opera, 1963-73; asst. prof. music Kans. State U., 1975—; dir. Kansas City (Mo.) Early Music Consort, 1975—; summer research fellow U. Mo., Kansas City, 1975. Recipient Luther Leavengood Outstanding Tchr. award Kans. State U., 1976. Mem. Coll. Music Soc., Am. Musicological Soc., Am. Fedn. Musicians, Nat. Assn. Tchrs. wind and Percussion Instruments, Pi Kappa Lambda, Phi Kappa Phi. Home: 921 Bertrand Manhattan KS 66502 Office: 223 McCain Auditorium Manhattan KS 66506

FURBUSH, MARY CHAPMAN, clubwoman; b. Danville, Va., Feb. 16, 1913; d. Fred L. and Martha L. (Hubbard) C.; student Goucher Coll., 1929-32; m. Spencer Sanderson Furbush, Aug. 24, 1940. N.H. state chmn. Flag of the U.S. com. DAR, 1959-62, state rec. sec. N.H., 1962-65, chpt. regent, 1960-62, state chmn. sch. com., 1974-77, nat. vice chmn. motion picture com., 1968-71, Constn. Week com., 1977-80; gov. N.H., Gen. Soc. Mayflower Descs., 1965-67, asst. gen., 1969-78, dep. gov. gen., 1978—; v.p. N.H. soc. Nat. Soc. Daus. Colonial Wars, 1968-71, pres. N.H. soc., 1971-74, nat. chaplain, 1974-77, nat. 1st. v.p., 1977-80; mem. Orders of Distinction com. Nat. Soc. Daus. of Barons of Runnymede. Mem. Sch. Bd. Somersworth (N.H.), 1946-49; trustee Trust Funds City of Somersworth, 1954-66, Forest Glade Cemetery, 1946-65. Recipient Valuable Service award Pres. U.S., 1948. Mem. Order of Americans of Armorial Ancestry, Nat. Hist. Soc., N.H. Hist. Soc., Somersworth Hist. Soc., Smithsonian Assos., N.H. Huguenot Soc., Mass. Huguenot Soc., Strawbery, Banke, Nat. Soc. Daus. Am. Colonists, Huguenot Soc. N.H. (v.p.), Piscataqua Pioneers (v.p. 1970-75), Nat. Soc. Dames of Ct. of Honor (N.H. v.p. 1975-79), Jamestowne Soc., Nat. Soc. Colonial Dames XVII Century, Nat. Soc. Daus. Colonial Wars (nat. chmn. awards com. 1982-83). Democrat. Episcopalian. Address: 20 Noble St Somersworth NH 03878

FURGASON, MAIYA KATHRYN, stock brokerage firm account exec.; b. Milw., Sept. 14, 1944; d. Howard and Florence (Mahoney) Herzog; B.A., Rutgers U., 1977; postgrad. N.Y. U., 1977; m. Robert Furgason; children—Maija Kristine, Aaron Robert. Account exec. Merril Lynch, Pierce, Fenner and Smith, N.Y.C., 1977-80; fin. mktg. specialist N.Y. Stock Exchange, 1979; account exec., fin. planning E.F. Hutton Co., N.Y.C., 1980—; vis. faculty mem. Rutgers U. Inst. Mgmt. and Labor Relations, New Brunswick, N.J., 1979—; faculty mem. New Sch. Div. Bus. and Fin., N.Y.C., 1979—. Mem. Women's Econ. Round Table, Am. Econ. Assn., Assn. Alumnae Douglass Coll., N.Y. Stock Brokers Soc., Fin. Women's Assn. N.Y., AAUW, Omicron Delta Epsilon. Clubs: Wings; Metedeconk Yacht. Contbr. various articles on fin. to profl. publs. Home: 5 Dorset Way Edison NJ 08820 Office: E F Hutton Co 605 3d Ave New York NY 10158

FURGESON, BARBARA ANN, mktg. cons.; b. Suffern, N.Y., Nov. 2, 1941; d. James Burr and Marie Josephine (McCormick) F.; B.S., Rutgers U., 1968. Adminstrv. asst. Am. Cyanamid Co., 1959-63; dir. personnel vol. services Passaic (N.J.) Gen. Hosp., 1964-67; dir. personnel Admiral Corp., Rutherford, N.J., 1967-69; dir. personnel store mgmt. Bloomingdales Dept. Store, Bergen County, N.J., 1969-80; v.p. personnel, labor relations and adminstrv. services Gaylords Nat. Corp., Secaucus, N.J., 1973—; pres. Opinions, Inc., Torrance, Calif., 1981—; mem. steering com. Nat. Mass Retailing Inst.; adv. Bergen Community Coll. Home: 17404 Falda Ave Torrance CA 90504

FURGIUELE, MARGERY WOOD, educator; b. Munden, Va., Sept. 28, 1919; d. Thomas Jarvis and Helen Godfrey (Ward) Wood; B.S., Mary Washington Coll., 1941; postgrad U. Ala., 1967-68, Catholic U. Am., 1974, 76, 80; m. Albert William Furgiuele, June 19, 1943; children—Martha Jane Furgiuele MacDonald, Harriet Randolph. Advt. and reservations sec. Hilton's Vacation Hide-A Way, Moodus, Conn., 1940; sec. Tenn. Valley Authority, Knoxville, 1941-43; adminstrv. asst., ct. reporter, Moody AFB, Valdosta, Ga., 1943-44; tchr. bus. Edenton (N.C.) High Sch., 1944-45; tchr. bus., coordinator coop. office edn. Culpeper (Va.) County High Sch., 1958-82; tchr. Piedmont Tech. Edn. Center, 1970-81; co-owner Zinn Wood Antiques & Collectibles Shop, Ruckersville, Va., 1980—. Co-leader Future Bus. Leaders Am., Culpeper, state advisor 1978-79, mem. state bd., 1978-82, exec. bd., 1978-81, Va. Bus. Edn. Assn. Com. chmn., 1978-79. Certified geneal. record Searcher. Mem. Nat., Va. bus. edn. assns., Am., Va. vocat. assns., Smithsonian Assos. Club: Country (Culpeper). Home: 2 Stonybrook Ln Culpeper VA 22701 Office: Country Store Antique Mall Ruckersville VA 22968

FURNESS, BETTY, broadcast journalist, consumer adviser, actress; b. N.Y.C., Jan. 3, 1916; d. George Choate and Florence (Sturtevant) F.; student Brearly Sch., N.Y.C., Bennett Sch., Millbrook, N.Y.; LL.D. (hon.), Iowa Wesleyan Coll., 1968, Pratt Inst., 1978; D.C.L. (hon.), Pace U., 1973, Marymount Manhattan Coll., 1976; m. John Waldo Green, Nov. 27, 1937 (div. Aug. 1943); 1 dau., Barbara Sturtevant; m. 2d, Hugh B. Ernst, Jr., Jan. 3, 1945 (dec. Apr. 1950); m. 3d, Leslie Midgley, Aug. 15, 1967. Movie actress, 1932-37; appeared stage plays Golden Boy, My Sister Eileen, Doughgirls; commls. for Westinghouse Corp., 1949-60; appeared on CBS-radio in Dimension of a Woman's World, Ask Betty Furness, 1961-67; spl. asst. to Pres. U.S. for consumer affairs, 1967-69; chmn. Pres.'s Com. Consumer Interests, 1967-69; exec. sec. Consumer Advt. Council, 1967-69; columnist McCall Mag., 1969-70, 72; chmn., exec. dir. N.Y. State Consumer Protection Bd., 1970-71; commr. N.Y. Dept. Consumer Affairs, 1973; now with NBC News, N.Y.C. Bd. dirs. Consumers Union, 1969—, Common Cause, 1971-75. Office: WNBC-TV 30 Rockefeller Plaza New York NY 10020

FURNISS, SUSAN WEST, polit. scientist, educator; b. Mpls., Aug. 8, 1924; d. David Ripley and Blanche (Sheffield) West; B.A., Smith Coll., 1946; M.A., U. Minn., 1967; M.A., Colo. State U., 1967; Ph.D., U. Colo., 1970; m. J. Leo Cefkin, Dec. 27, 1976; children—David Furniss, Stephenson Furniss, Robert Furniss. Asst. prof. polit. sci. Colo. State U., Ft. Collins, 1967-72, assoc. prof., 1972-80, adj. prof., 1981—, dir. Robert A. Taft Inst. Govt., 1970-74; dir. Colo. office U.S. Sen. Gary Hart, 1975—. Mem. Colo. bd. dirs. LWV, 1958-64, also v.p.; vice chmn., chmn. Larimer County Democratic Com., 1970-74; vice chmn. Colo. Dem. Com., 1974-76; mem. Nat. Dem. Com., 1974-76; chmn. Western States Conf. Dems., 1976-80. Mem. Phi Kappa Phi, Pi Gamma Mu, Pi Sigma Alpha. Democrat. Episcopalian. Home: 1901 Mohawk St Fort Collins CO 80525 Office: Sen Gary Hart 1748 High St Denver CO 80218

FURNIVAL, PATRICIA ANNE, social worker; b. Poughkeepsie, N.Y., Feb. 3, 1938; d. Edwin A. and Esther L. Smith; B.A., Maryville (Tenn.) Coll., 1960; M.A., U. Chgo., 1970; m. George E. Furnival, Feb. 15, 1967. Sr. caseworker Dutchess County Dept. Social Services, Poughkeepsie, 1961-67; rural resources dir. OEO, Freeport, Ill., 1967-68; program coordinator H. Douglas Singer Zone Center, Rockford, Ill., 1968-72; family therapist Bur. Alcohol Rehab., Avon Park, Fla., 1973-74; dir. Tri-County Alcoholism Rehab. Services, Inc., Avon Park, 1974-80; exec. dir. Tri-County Alcoholism Rehab. Services, Inc., Winter Haven, Fla., 1980—; field instr. Fla. State U. Sch. Social Work, 1977—; instr. S.Fla. Jr. Coll., 1979; pvt. practice psychotherapy, 1973—; cons. in field. Mem. Nat. Assn. Social Workers, Acad. Cert. Social Workers, Fla. Alcohol and Drug Abuse Assn., Alcohol and Drug Problems Assn. N. Am. Democrat. Mem. United Ch. Christ. Home: PO Box 1761 Avon Park FL 33825 Office: PO Drawer 9306 Winter Haven FL 33880

FURSE, MARGARET LEWIS, educator; b. Bay City, Tex., Oct. 25, 1928; d. James Claire and Meta (Hawkins) Lewis; B.A. in Philosophy, U. Tex., Austin, 1950; M.A., Columbia U., 1954, Ph.D. in Religion, 1968; m. Austen H. Furse, Feb. 19, 1955; children—Jane, Austen H., III, John L., Mary E. Lectr. religious studies Rice U., Houston, 1970-73; lectr. Am. studies program U. Tex., 1974—, chmn. religious studies com., 1980—. Past mem. Tex. Democratic Exec. Com.; past del. Dem. Nat. Conv. Mem. Am. Acad. Religion, Am. Philos. Assn., Am. Studies Assn. Episcopalian. Author: Mysticism: Window on a World View, 1977; Nothing But The Truth?, 1982; also articles, revs. Home: 1801 Lavaca St Apt 14-D Austin TX 78701 Office: Am Studies U Tex Austin TX 78712

FURST, CARYN MELODY, public relations counselor; b. N.Y.C., Aug. 15, 1949; d. S. Robert and Ann (Bruder) Furst.; B.S., Cornell U., 1971. Asst. editor Madison Ave. mag., N.Y.C., 1971-73; asso. editor Parade mag., 1973-74; features editor Women's Life mag., N.Y.C., 1974; v.p. The Softness Group, Inc., N.Y.C., 1974-78; v.p. Carl Byoir & Assocs., Inc., N.Y.C., 1978—. Recipient Thoth award Washington chpt. Public Relations Soc. Am., 1980; Silver Anvil, Public Relations Soc. Am., 1981, 82. Home: Mill Ln Old Lyme CT 06371 also 36 E 36th St New York NY 10016 Office: 380 Madison Ave New York NY 10017

FURST, NORMA FIELDS, univ. ofcl., educator; b. Bklyn., Feb. 26, 1931; d. Nathan B. and Anne Platzer (Cooper) Fields; B.A., Bklyn. Coll., 1951; M.Ed., Temple U., 1963, Ed.D., 1967; m. M. Lawrence Furst, Sept. 9, 1951; children—Merrick Lawrence, Laura Furst Jacobs. Research librarian N.Y. Pub. Libraries, N.Y.C., 1950-51; registrar Pakistan Mission to UN, N.Y.C., 1951-55; tchr. Bridgeport (Conn.) Pub. Schs., 1959-60; instr. Harcum Jr. Coll., Bryn Mawr, Pa., 1961-62; mem faculty Temple U., Phila., 1963—, prof. psychoednl. processes, 1973—, dean student affairs, 1974—; cons. in field. Trustee Am. Jewish Com., Phila., 1978, Fedn. Jewish Agys., Phila., 1980-82, March of Dimes, Phila., 1979; pres. bd. dirs. Phila. Jewish Campus Activities, 1980-82; sec., v.p. B'nai B'rith Internat. Hillel Commn., Washington, 1976, Jewish Publs. Soc. Am., Phila., 1974; v.p. Jewish Community Relations Council, Phila., 1981. Recipient Lindback award Lindback Found., 1969, Career and Counselling award B'nai B'rith, 1976. Mem. Am. Ednl. Research Assn., Am. Psychol. Assn., Am. Council Edn., Nat. Assn. State and Land Grant Colls. and Univs. (chmn. task force student affairs 1982—, Nat. Assn. Student Personnel Adminstrs. Democrat. Jewish. Contbr. articles in field, chpts. to books. Home: 644 Pine St Philadelphia PA 19106 Office: Temple Univ Philadelphia PA 19122

FURST, RUTH ANN, escrow co. exec.; b. Newark, May 29, 1941; d. Lewis A. and Yetta M. Furst; B.A., U. Calif., San Fernando Valley, 1962. With Heritage Escrow Co., Encino, Calif., 1966—; with Pacific Coast Escrow Co., 1973—. Active Young Democrats; mem. Jewish Nat. Fedn. Mem. Calif. Escrow Assn. Club: Soroptimist. Office: 41-500 Monterey Ave Palm Desert CA 92260 *

FURSTMAN, SHIRLEY ELSIE DADDOW, pub. co. exec.; b. Butler, N.J., Jan. 26, 1930; d. Richard and Eva M. (Kitchell) Daddow; grad. high sch.; m. Russell A. Bailey, Oct. 1, 1950 (div. Oct. 1967); m. 2d, William B. Furstman, Dec. 24, 1977. Asst. corp. sec. Hydrospace Tech., West Caldwell, N.J., 1960-62; sec. to pres. R.J. Dick Co., Totowa, N.J., 1962-63, Microlab, Livingston, N.J., 1963; asst. corp. sec. Astrosystems Internat., West Caldwell, N.J., 1963-65; corp. sec. Internat. Controls Corp., Fairfield, N.J., 1965-73; sec. Global Fin., Nassau, Bahamas, 1974, Internat. Barter Co., Nassau, 1975; corp. sec., sec. to pres. Haas Chem. Corp., Taylor, Pa., 1976-77; asst. to pub. and pres. Am. Home Mag., N.Y.C., 1977-78; adminstrv. coordinator, sec. to sr. v.p. Gilbert, Whitney & Johns, Whippany, N.J., 1979—. Address: 11A Foxwood Dr Morris Plains NJ 07950

FURTADO, DOLORES, microbiologist; b. West Warwick, R.I., July 4, 1938; d. Jesse and Mary Estelle (Moniz) F.; B.S., Cornell U., 1960; M.S. (USPHS fellow, F. G. Novy fellow), U. Mich., 1963, Ph.D., 1966. USPHS fellow Guy's Hosp. Med. Sch., London, 1966-67; postdoctoral research fellow Yale U. Med. Sch., 1976-79; mem. faculty U. Kans. Med. Sch., Kansas City, 1970—, assoc. prof. microbiology, 1976-82, prof., 1982—. Recipient Chancellor's Teaching award U. Kans., 1979. Mem. Am. Soc. Microbiology, N.Y. Acad. Scis., Am. Soc. Nephrology, Soc. Exptl. Biology and Medicine, Infectious Disease Soc. Am., Sigma Xi. Author papers, abstracts in field. Office: Dept Microbiology U Kans Med Center Kansas City KS 66103

FURUMOTO, VIOLA GILBERTINE, librarian; b. Blue Earth, Minn., June 26, 1921; d. William John and Nola Mae (Peacock) Ferris; B.S., U. Minn., 1943; postgrad. Kans. State U., 1946-48; M.L.S., U. Hawaii, 1969; m. Howard H. Furumoto, Jan. 13, 1946; children—William K., Wesley H., Alice Furumoto Dawson, David J., Nancy L., James N., Edward L. Med. technologist U. Minn., 1943-46; instr. zoology Kans. State U., 1946-50; med. technologist, office mgr. Care Animal Hosp., Honolulu, 1954-60; librarian dept. planning and econ. devel. State of Hawaii, 1969-70; head librarian Hastings H. Walker Med. Library, Leahi Hosp., U. Hawaii, 1970-75; ref. librarian, head sci. tech. ref. dept. Hamilton Library, U. Hawaii, Honolulu, 1975—. Mem. ALA, Med. Library Assn., Spl. Library Assn., Assn. Coll. and Research Libraries, Hawaii Library Assn., Med. Library Group Hawaii, John Howard Assn., AVMA Aux., Beta Phi Mu, Gamma Sigma Delta. Methodist. Club: Outdoor Circle. Home: 4433 Aukai Ave Honolulu HI 96816 Office: Hamilton Library University of Hawaii 2550 The Mall Honolulu HI 96822

FURY, KATHLEEN DUNIGAN, writer, editor; b. N.Y.C., June 18, 1941; d. John Raymond and Virginia Elizabeth (Barrows) Dunigan; student Ohio Wesleyan U., 1959-61; B.A., Purdue U., 1964; m. Leonard Wayne Fury, Dec. 26, 1965. Asso. editor Redbook mag., 1964-67; editorial cons. Jasmin mag., Munich, Germany, 1968; sr. writer, articles editor Ladies' Home Jour., 1974-77; founding editor-in-chief Your Place mag., McCall Pub., 1978; free lance writer, 1968-74, 78—; cons. editor Savvy mag., 1979—; articles editor Family Circle mag., 1981—; lectr. diploma in mag. pub. program N.Y. U., 1981—. Mem. Am. Soc. Mag. Editors, N.Y. Women in Communications, Women's Media Group (pres. 1982). Contbr. articles to mags. Office: Family Circle 488 Madison Ave New York NY 10022

FUSCO, LAURIE SMITH, art historian; b. Boston, Oct. 31, 1941; d. Byron Hobart Smith and Geraldine (Peterson) Smith Hershorn; B.A., Wellesley Coll., 1963; M.A., N.Y. U., 1969, Ph.D., 1978; m. Peter Fusco, Apr. 28, 1972. Robert Lehman fellow Inst. Fine Arts, N.Y. U., 1969-72; Fulbright-Hays grantee to Rome, 1972-73; asst. prof. art history U. So. Calif., Los Angeles, 1975-76; head photo archives J. Paul Getty Mus., Malibu, Calif., 1976-78, head acad. affairs, 1978—. Samuel H. Kress grantee, 1974-75; Harvard U. fellow at Villa I Tatti, Florence, 1983. Mem. Coll. Art Assn., Renaissance Soc., Art Historians So. Calif. Home: 1356 N Ogden Dr Los Angeles CA 90046 Office: J Paul Getty Mus 17985 Pacific Coast Hwy Malibu CA 90265

FUSILLO, LISA ANN, educator; b. Washington, Jan. 11, 1951; d. Matthew Henry and Alice Elbert (Zeigler) Fusillo; student Butler U., 1969-72; teaching cert. Royal Ballet Sch., 1975; B.S., George Washington U., 1976; M.A., Tex. Womans U., 1978, Ph.D., 1982; m. Robert Forshay Smith Jr., June 19, 1982. Dancer, Butler Ballet, Indpls., 1969-72; mus. asst. Royal Ballet, London, 1973-75; dancer Liz Lerman Group, Washington, 1975-76; teaching asst. Tex. Womans U., Denton, 1976-77, mem. adj. faculty, 1978, 81; choreographic asst. Leonide Massine, W. Ger., London, Paris, San Francisco, N.Y., 1976-78; instr. Skidmore Coll., Saratoga Springs, N.Y., 1978-80; asst. prof. ballet Tex. Christian U., Fort Worth, 1981—; free lance choreographer, master tchr. in U.S. and Europe. Mem. AAHPER, Imperial Soc. Tchrs. Dancing, Royal Acad. Dancing, AAUP, Sigma Alpha Iota, Alpha Chi, Pi Lambda Theta, Chi Tau Epsilon. Office: Texas Christian Univ Division of Ballet and Modern Dance Box 32889 Fort Worth TX 76129

FUTRELL, KATHLEEN HUNT, educator; b. N.Y.C., Jan. 13, 1926; d. Robert Emmett and Margaret Mary (Fitzgerald) Hunt; B.A., Ladycliff Coll., 1947; M.A. in Edn., Goddard Coll.; diploma Washington Montessori Inst., 1967, 73; m. Alvin F. Futrell, June 5, 1946; children—Jonathan, David, Alison, Daniel. Dir., Aquinas Montessori Sch., Alexandria, Va., 1965—; lectr. Washington Montessori Inst., 1979—; cons. N.Am. Montessori Schs. Mem. N.Am. Montessori Tchrs. Assn., Assn. Montessori Internat. Author: The Normalized Child, 1967. Home: 3007 Cunningham Dr Alexandria VA 22309 Office: 8334 Mount Vernon Hwy Alexandria VA 22309

FUTRELL, MARY FELTNER, educator; b. Cadiz, Ky., Jan. 5, 1924; d. George Edison and Louise (Carr) Feltner; B.S., Austin Peay U., 1944; M.S., U. Wis., 1949, Ph.D., 1952; m. Maurice C. Futrell, Apr. 18, 1947; children—Edison Leon, John Maurice. Asst. prof. home econs. Tex. A&M U., College Station, 1952-56; lectr. Ahmadu Bello U., Nigeria, 1964-66; prof. nutrition and home econs. Miss. State U., 1967—; cons., Panama, India, Haiti, Honduras, Ecuador. Tech. com. Title XII Internat. Sorghum and Millet, 1978—; bd. dirs. Agrl. Missions Found. Fellow Am. Inst. Chemists; mem. Am. Dietetic Assn., Am. Home Econs. Assn., Soc. for Nutrition Edn., Sigma Xi (research award 1972), Gamma Sigma Delta, Omicron Nu. Baptist. Club: Student Agrl. Missions. Contbr. articles to profl. jours. Home: 409 Sycamore St Starkville MS 39759 Office: PO Drawer HE Mississippi State MS 39762

FYFE, MYRNA CATHERINE, mem. Can. provincial legis. assembly; b. Simpson, Sask., Aug. 20, 1941; d. Phillip and Rhyra Parker; B.Ed. in Indian and Metis Edn., U. Sask., Saskatoon, 1966; postgrad. in sociology U. Alta. (Can.), 1975; m. George William Fyfe, Aug. 25, 1965; children—Catherine, Jane. Tchr. public schs., N.W. Terrs., 1960-64; instr. in children's creative devel., 1969-76; consumer services officer, 1977-78; mem. Alta. Legis. Assembly, Edmonton, 1979—. Mem. St. Albert (Alta.) City Council, 1973—. Progressive Conservative. Roman Catholic. Office: Legis Bldg Govt Mems Edmonton AB Canada

FYKE, VIRGINIA TIMM, hosp. adminstr.; b. London, July 17, 1953; d. Bertram R. and Margaret Mary (Gillespie) Harrigan (parents Am. citizens); student Los Angeles Pierce Coll., 1971-74; cert. in Mgmt. and Adminstrn. of Health Care Facilities, UCLA, 1978; m. Robert H. Fyke, Feb. 17, 1979; children—Jennifer, Robert Van. Receptionist, Damon Med. Labs., Van Nuys, Calif., 1971-72; admitting clk. Sherman Oaks Community Hosp., Van Nuys, 1972-73; admitting supr. Encino (Calif.) Hosp., 1973-77; dir. admissions St. John's Hosp. and Health Center, Santa Monica, Calif., 1977—. Mem. Nat. Assn. Hosp. Admitting Mgrs. (accredited admitting mgr.), Calif. Assn. Hosp. Admitting Mgrs., So. Calif. Chpt. of Admitting Officers (dir.). Office: 1328 22d St Santa Monica CA 90404

GAARDER, MARIE, speech pathologist; b. New Britain, Conn., July 19, 1935; d. Nicholas and Clara (Sangeloty) Sarris; B.S., U. Ill., 1957; postgrad. U. Md., 1962-63, Our Lady of Lake U. Grad. Sch. Social Work, San Antonio, 1976-77; m. Kenneth R. Gaarder, Dec. 8, 1962; children—Jason, Galen. Founder speech therapy program Flossmoor (Ill.) Sch. Dist. 161, 1957-59; speech pathologist Prince George's County (Md.) Bd. Edn., 1959-65, Sidwell Friend's Sch., Washington, 1966-67, St. Maurice Sch. for Learning Disabilities, Potomac, Md., 1968-69; pvt. practice speech therapy, Chevy Chase, Md., 1967—; adminstrv. officer Gaarder Med. Corp., Chevy Chase, 1977—. Pres., Prince George's chpt. Council for Exceptional Children, 1963-64; mem. Florence Crittenton Circle, 1966-69, Hospitality and Info. Service for Diplomats, 1967—; chmn. activities com. Jr. Teens, 1979-80; chmn. publicity YWCA Internat. Fair, 1977-79; mem. internat. com. Woman's Nat. Democratic Club; co-chmn. Adv. Com. for Quality Integrated Edn. in Montgomery County, 1977-78; bd. dirs. D.C. br. YWCA, 1981—; chmn. Career Day, Nat. Symphony Ednl. Activities, 1981—. Recipient cert. of appreciation Opera Guild San Antonio, 1977. Mem. Am. Speech, Lang. and Hearing Assn. (advanced cert.), Md. Speech, Lang. and Hearing Assn., Internat. Assn. Logopedics and Phoniatrics, Zeta Phi Eta. Greek Orthodox. Club: Capitol Speakers (Washington). Contbg. author: San Antonio Cookbook II, 1976. Home and office: 4221 Oakridge Ln Chevy Chase MD 20815

GABAY, GALINA VICTOROVNA, speech pathologist; b. Moscow, Feb. 2, 1937; came to U.S., 1974, naturalized, 1980; d. Victor Ivanovich and Zinaida Grigoryevna (Karpova) Samokhin; Masters, Moscow State Pedagogical Inst., 1958-63; 2 children. Speech pathologist and tchr. for deaf, schs. for hearing impaired, Moscow, 1963-73; speech pathologist, tchr. for deaf Protestant Guild for Blind, Watertown, Mass., 1975-77; speech pathologist Fernald State Sch., Waltham, Mass., 1978—; instr. Russian lang., cons. speech pathology Harvard U.; lectr. total communication course Lesley Coll. Grad. Sch. Spl. Edn., Cambridge, Mass., 1980—. Cert. secondary tchr. Russian, cert. speech pathologist and tchr. for deaf, Mass. Mem. Am. Speech Lang. and Hearing Assn. (cert. clin. competence), Mass. Assn. Speech Pathologists and Audiologists. Home: 662 Moody St Waltham MA 02154 Office: Walter E Fernald State Sch 200 Trapelo Rd Waltham MA 02154

GABER, JOANNE GARTEN, clin. psychologist; b. N.Y.C.; d. Stanley and Hannah Rosalind (Frank) Garten; B.S. in Edn., Adelphi Coll., 1949; M.A. in Ednl. Psychology, Tchrs. Coll., Columbia, 1950, profl. diploma, 1969; m. Morton Gaber, Aug. 20, 1950 (div.); 1 dau., Evelyn Jean. Ednl. therapist, 1963-67; psychology intern North Jersey Tng. Sch., Totowa, N.J., 1967-68, clin. psychologist, 1969—; psychology intern Middlesex County Mental Health Clinic, 1968-69; adj. clin. psychologist N.J. Coll. Medicine and Dentistry, Jersey City, 1971—. Ednl. therapist Shield of David Inst., Maimonides Inst. for Exceptional Children, 1963-67. Program dir. Play Schs. Assn., 1959, 60. Mem. Am., N.J. psychol. assns., N.J. Assn. for Brain Injured Children, Assn. for Help Retarded Children, Am. Assn. on Mental Deficiency, Assn. N.J. Instl. Psychologists (sec. 1975—). Home: 28 Highland Cross Rutherford NJ 07070 Office: NJ Tng Sch PO Box 169 Totowa NJ 07511

GABLE, MARTHA ANNE, educator; b. Phila.; d. James F. and Stella (Gingrich) Gable; B.E., Ind. U., 1942; M.Ed., Temple U., 1935. Tchr. Phila. Public Schs., 1926-41, asst. dir. phys. and health edn., Phila., 1942-48, asst. dir. sch. and community relations, 1948-55, dir. radio-TV edn., 1955-66, dir. instrnl. materials, 1966-68; editor Am. Assn. Sch. Adminstrs., 1968-73; cons. ednl. tech., 1973—. Mem. Pa. Gov.'s Adv. Commn. Edn., 1956-58; mem. White House Conf. Edn., 1955; cons. Joint Council Ednl. TV, Washington. Del. Internat. Conf. Ednl. TV, London, 1954; judge Olympic Games, London, 1948, Helsinki, 1952, Melbourne, 1956, Rome, 1960, Tokyo, Japan, 1964; v.p. Women for Greater Phila. Recipient Temple U. Alumni award, 1964; named Disting. Dau. of Pa. Mem. Phila. Public Relations Assn. (sec., Hall of Fame award), Am. Women in Radio and TV, NEA, Public Relations Soc. Am., TV-Radio Advt. Club, AAUW, Am. Assn. Sch. Adminstrs., Am. Newspaper Womens Clubs, Women in Communications. Presbyterian. Clubs: Cosmopolitan; Nat. Press (Washington). Home: 2601 Pkwy Philadelphia PA 19130

GABRIEL, PAT (MRS. GENE F. GABRIEL), club woman; b. Rock Island, Ill., May 2, 1922; d. Max Voyle and Faye (Crist) Wolfe; grad. Canterbury Sch. Fine Arts, 1939; m. Gene Floyd Gabriel, 1980-82), 8, 1941; 1 dau., Patricia Gene. Soc. columnist Coral Gables Times-Guide, now drama critic. Drama chmn. Morgan Park Jr. Woman's Club, Chgo., 1952-54, 3d Dist. Jrs., 1952-54; children's theatre dir. Beverly Hills Jr. Woman's Club, Chgo., 1954; dist. coordinator Mothers March of Dimes Chgo., 1952-55, Coral Gables, Fla., 1956-61; publicity chmn. woman's com., pres. woman's com. Variety Children's Hosp.; 2d v.p. women's com. Project Hope; women's campaign mgr. Senator Doyle Carlton, Jr. for Gov., Coral Gables, 1960; pres. Dade County com. Project Hope, 1973-74; mem. public relations com. Country Club Coral Gables; mem. Coral Gables Beautification Com., 1980-81; permanent chmn. Coral Gables com. Performing and Allied Arts. Recipient Israel 25th anniversary medal Women's div. Greater Miami Jewish Fedn., 1973; named Beautiful Activist, 1974. Mem. DAR (rec. sec. 1962-64), Fla. Fedn. Women's Clubs (drama co-chmn. 1960-62), Theater Arts League (pres.), Women in Communications, Sigma Delta Chi. Methodist. Clubs: Coral Gables Garden (pres. 1980-82 Coral Gables Sr. Women's (1st v.p. 1962-64, pres. 1964-66). Author: The Villager's Book of Outstanding Homes of Miami, 1975. Home: 3915 Monserrate St Coral Gables FL 33134

GABRIELE, SHERRY LEE SOSKIN, accountant; b. Cleve., Jan. 1, 1943; d. Zelman and Molly (Miller) Soskin; B.S., UCLA, 1964; M.Bus. Taxation, U. So. Calif., 1976. Acct. various firms, Calif., 1960-69; acct. Wolf and Co., Los Angeles, 1969-75, mgr., 1969-73, partner in charge tax dept., 1973-75; pvt. practice acctg. specializing in tax planning and compliance, Los Angeles, 1975—; substitute instr. acctg. UCLA, 1965-66. C.P.A., Calif. Mem. Am. Inst. C.P.A.s, Calif. Soc. C.P.A.s, Am. Women's Soc. C.P.A.s, Calif. Scholarship Soc. (seal bearer life mem.). Contbr. articles to profl. publs. Office: 2049 Century Park East Suite 1100 Los Angeles CA 90067

GACHICH, LILLIANA, chemist; b. Belgrade, Yugoslavia, June 11, 1945; d. Dushan and Obrenija (Nesic) G.; B.S., Queens Coll., 1965, M.S., 1967. Lectr. chemistry U. Ill., Chgo., 1968-70; lab. asst. dir. Ill. Racing Bd., 1970-78; lab. mgr. Mobil Oil Corp., Joliet, Ill., 1978—. Mem. Am. Chem. Soc., ASTM. Office: PO Box 874 Joliet IL 60434

GADDIS, IRIS CHARLENE, mil. and hist. reprodns. co. exec.; b. Tyler, Tex., Oct. 22, 1958; d. Charles Fred and Ruth Wanda (Baker) G.; A.A., San Jacinto Coll., 1980; B.A., U. Houston at Clear Lake City, 1981, postgrad., 1982. Pres., founder Ragnarok Enterprises, La Porte, Tex., 1979—. Mem. adv. bd. Northbrook Teen-Age Republicans, 1977—; founder La Porte Young Ams. for Freedom, 1974, chairwoman, 1974—. Second lt. CAP. Baptist. Address: 710 E Main St La Porte TX 77571

GADE, DARLENE KAY, credit exec.; b. Hammond, Ind., Dec. 1, 1935; d. Cecil A. and Virginia M. (Normand) Stonecipher; m. Thor G. Gade, Sept. 28, 1973; children—Laura, Lisa, Russell. With Am. Furniture Stores, Inc., El Paso, Tex., 1965—, credit mgr., 1972-81; nat. panelist Alternatives to Bankruptcy. Mem. Leadership El Paso; chmn. adv. bd. Debit Counseling Service of YWCA. Named Credit Exec. of Yr., State of Tex., 1978-79, Woman of Yr. in Bus. and Fin., El Paso Women's Polit. Caucus, 1981. Cert. consumer credit exec. Mem. Internat. Consumer Credit Assn. (Disting. Service award 1980), Credit Mgmt. Assn., Tex., Credit women Internat., El Paso C. of C., El Paso Credit Women (Outstanding Mem. 1981), El Paso Bar Aux. Office: 105 N Oregon St El Paso TX 79999

GADOLA, NANCY LEE, county ofcl.; b. Flint, Mich., Nov. 9, 1940; d. John Warner and Marion Helen (Lundsten) Brown; student Mott Community Coll., 1962-64, Baker Bus. U., 1964-66; children—Deborah Helen, Diana Lee, Daniel N. With customer relations dept. Mich. Bell Telephone Co., 1966-69; para legal to Paul Godola, atty., Flint, 1969-77; mem. Genessee County (Mich.) Bd. Commrs., 1977—. Del. Republican Nat. Conv., Kansas City, Mo., 1976, del.-at-large, Detroit, 1980. Mem. Nat. Assn. Counties, Mich. Assn. Counties, Am. Conservation Union, Mich. Conservation Union. Home: 6087 W Hill St Swartz Creek MI 48473 Office: 1101 Beach St Flint MI 48502

GAFFNEY, CAROL TARLIN, automated sytems cons.; b. Cambridge, Mass., Sept. 22, 1941; d. Eliot B. and Lola Tarlin; B.A., Brown U., 1962. Tchr. English, Hope High Sch., Providence, 1962-65; test adminstr. Miller Assos., Boston, 1965-69; mgmt. cons. Bio Dynamics, Cambridge, Mass., 1969-73; dir. systems and reporting Nat. Med. Assn. Found., Washington, 1973-74; mgmt. cons. Gorby & Assos., Greenwich, Conn., 1974-76; dir. tng. Center for Health Planning, Phila., 1976-77; dir. ACORN psychol. services to bus., Phila., 1977-82; pres. SynergisTechs, cons. automated systems support, Phila., 1982—. Trustee, treas. Veritas, Phila., 1977-80; trustee Mid-City YWCA, 1981—. Mem. Phila. Womens Network (pres. 1978-80). Office: SynergisTechs 4000 Gypsy Ln Suite 314 Philadelphia PA 19144

GAFFORD, CHARLOTTE KELLY, writer, educator; b. St. Louis; d. Walter Joseph and Charlotte Everett (d'Ailly) Kelly; A.B., Birmingham-So. Coll., M.A., 1962; M.F.A., U. Iowa, 1971; m. Franklin Gafford (dec. 1969); children—Franklin H., Charlotte E., Mary Kelly. Mem. faculty U. Ala., Birmingham, 1968-75, asst. prof. English, 1971-75; vis. writer-in-residence Woodstock Country Sch., South Woodstock, Vt., 1974-75; v.p., story editor Interlock Film Studios, Birmingham, 1967—; assoc. prof. English Norwich U., Northfield, Vt., 1976—. Bd. dirs. Birmingham Art Assn., Birmingham Ballet. Recipient Ellen Gregg Ingalls teaching award U. Ala., Birmingham, 1969; Silver Bowl, Birmingham Festival Arts, 1974; fellow MacDowell Colony, 1975-76. Mem. MLA, Am. Film Inst., Vt. Council on Arts, Touring Arts Register, Vt. Council on Humanities. Jr. League, Kappa Delta. Author: The Moon Peelers: Poems by Four Women, 1973; also articles, revs., poems. Address: Dept English Norwich U Northfield VT 05663

GAGE, DOROTHY JEAN, acctg. technician; b. Howe, Okla., June 13, 1928; d. Seaman and Ruby Euretta (Phillips) Claborn; student pub. schs. Ark. and Calif.; m. Roy C. Gage, May 5, 1949; children—Roy Charles, Seaman Lynn, Christine, Terry Lee. Payroll clk. Saticoy Lemon Assn., Saticoy, Calif., 1946-48; comptometer operator Foremost Dairy, Ventura, Calif., 1948-57, Carnation Co., Ventura, 1957-67; acctg. technician Naval Ship Weapon Systems Engrng. System, Port Hueneme, Calif., 1969—; driver handicapped children, 1957-72. Charter mem. Ventura County Muscular Dystrophy Assn., 1955—, officer or v.p., 1955-81, Ventura county chmn., 1958—; bd. dirs. Ventura County Health Agys., 1968-80. Recipient award for service to Muscular Dystrophy Assn., Calif. Assembly, 1980, others; also named in Congressional Record. Mem. Ventura County Health Agy., Tri-Counties Muscular Dystrophy Assn., Jaycees. Democrat. Clubs: Eagles, Toastmistresses. Office: PO Box 395 Port Heuneme CA 93041

GAGNON, EDITH MORRISON, ballerina, singer, actress; b. Chgo., Apr. 8; grad. Chalif Sch. Dancing, N.Y.C.; student Northwestern U.; voice student Forest Lamont of Chgo. Opera Co.; m. Joseph Agatsten; children—Joyce, Morton; m. 2d, Alfred Gagnon, Feb. 3, 1977. Premiere ballerina Pavley and Oukrainsky Russian Ballet of Chgo., performer with Chgo., Met., Ravinia Opera Cos. and on tour; appeared Birthday of Infanta, Greenwich Follies, The Five O'Clock Girl; founder, dir., instr. Sch. of Dance, St. Louis; singer in concert, Carnegie Hall; commentator radio programs Women on the Home Front, Sta. KSD, St. Louis, and CD program Sta. WEW, St. Louis U.; voice coach, producer, performer benefit performances, St. Louis, San Francisco area. Pres. Pets Unlimited, San Francisco; bd. dirs. Artists Embassy. Mem. Pacific Musical Soc. (pres. San Francisco), Equity Guild. Clubs: Burlingame Country; International, Francisca Hillsborough CA 94010

GAGNON, GABRIELLE VIRGINIA, state legislator; b. Nashua, N.H., Mar. 5; d. Joseph O. and Kathleen (Brousseau) Boliard; student public schs. Nashua; m. Sylvio A. Gagnon, Sept. 18, 1937; children—Sylvia E. Gagnon Kapsack, Beverly V. Gagnon Murray. Insp., Nashua Mfg. Co., 1933-42; checker Textron Co., Nashua, 1943-52; basement mgr. Gordons Ladies Store, 1954-63; insp., tester Sprague Electric Co., Nashua, 1964-77, laser operator, 1977—; mem. N.H. Legislature, 1974—. Pres., Nashua Democratic Womens Club, 1964-65; v.p. Nashua Dem. City Com., 1975-77. Recipient awards for Americanism and publicity Am. Legion Aux., 1964. Mem. Nat. Order Women Legislators, Am. Legion (pres. unit 3), Cath. War Vets. Aux. (chmn. publicity), N.H. Order Women Legislators (corr. sec.). Clubs: Emblem (pres. 1959-60, pres. N.H. 1977-78, Sister of Yr. award 1980), Sr. Citizens Nashua (treas.), Golden Age, Sr. Power. Office: NH House of Reps State House Concord NH 05301 *

GAIA, PAMELA A., state legislator; b. Boston, Feb. 19, 1946; B.A., Memphis State U.; M.A., U. Ala. Mem. Tenn. Voters Council, Shelby County Democratic Voters Council; now mem. Tenn. Ho. of Reps., 88th-91st Gen. Assemblies. Bd. dirs. Mid-South Med. Center Council. Recipient Outstanding Women award Dem. Women's Club, 1974-75. Office: Tenn Ho of Reps State Capitol Nashville TN 37219

GAINER, RUBY JACKSON (MRS. HERBERT P. GAINER), educator, civic leader; b. Buena-Vista, Ga.; d. William B. and Lovie (Jones) Jackson; student Miles Meml. Coll., 1932-35; B.S., Ala. State Tchrs. Coll., 1939; M.A. in English and Social Studies, Atlanta U., 1953; postgrad. Fla. A&M U., 1962-63, Western Wash. State Coll., 1964, U. Conn., 1965, Okla. State U., 1968. H.H.D. (hon.) Selma U., 1968, Daniel Payne Coll., 1971; LL.D. (hon.), Birmingham Bapt. Coll., Faith Coll., Birmingham, 1976; L.H.D. (hon.), Bishop Coll., 1977; m. Herbert P. Gainer, June 2, 1946; children—Ruby Paulette, James H., Cecil F. Tchr. J. B. Turner High Sch., Milton, Fla., 1947-48, public schs., Birmingham, Ala., Washington Jr. High Sch., Pensacola, Fla., 1955-68; guidance counselor Wedgewood Jr.-Sr. High Sch., Pensacola, 1968—; tchr. English, Woodham High School. Brought 2 successful legal cases against Jefferson County (Ala.) Sch. Bd. for equalization of Negro tchr. salaries, 1946-47, re-instatement Negro tchrs. under Tchr. Tenure Act; organized 1st tchrs. union, Birmingham; also organized local high sch. chpt. Future Tchrs. Am., local tchr. aide and teen service groups, local and county assns. edn.; local capt. Heart Fund, Mothers March of Dimes, Cancer Fund; active local PTA, past chmn. Fla. PTA Workshop, 1966; participant Gov. Fla. Conf. Edn., Tallahassee, 1967, Nat. conf. Profl. Rights and Responsibilities, Arlington, Tex., 1968; participant, chmn. numerous profl. ednl. confs. So. U.S.; mem. Escambia County Guidance Council; mem., past officer Fla. Guidance Council. Bd. dirs. United Negro Coll. Fund, Pensacola, Partners for Progress, Pensacola, Escambia County Tb Assn.; mem. Pensacola Democratic Exec. Com., 1981—; area IV dir. Top Teens Am., 1981—. Named Tchr. of Yr., Dist. 1 Fla. State Tchrs. Assn., 1966, also recipient award meritorious service, Disting. Service award, 1966, DuShane Outstanding Service award, 1967; recipient DuShane Outstanding Dir. award Escambia County Tchrs. Assn., 1967, Disting. Service award civil, human, profl. rights, 1965; recipient Outstanding Tchr. and Leader award Fla. Edn. Assn., honor award NEA Fla. State Tchrs. Assn., 1966, awards youth, community orgns.; Disting. Achievement in Edn. award, Outstanding Educator award, Honor award, Recognition Day award, Public Service award, Disting. Community Service award, Parent of Yr. award, Top Educator award (all 1970), human relations award Student Com. of Woodham High Sch., 1972, Polish award as outstanding tchr. of yr. 1981, others; cited Pitts. Courier, NAACP, 1946-47; Ruby J. Gainer Day proclaimed by mayor Pensacola, 1970, 81; Pensacola's Woman of Yr., Pensacola Voice Newspaper, 1974, awards Ala. State U., 1974, 75; Top Lady of Yr. as Disting. Am., 1981; Top Educator of Yr. award, 1981; Disting. Service award Five Flag Toastmasters Club, 1981; Human Relations in Edn. award Fla. Teaching Profession, 1981; Human Relations award S.E. Region Classroom Tchrs., 1981. Mem. Jefferson County (past. sec., past pres.), Escambia County (past sec., past pres,), Fla. (past bd. dirs. dist. 1, past pres. dist. 1, mem. tchr. edn. and profl. standards commn. and evaluation com., bd. advisers dept. classroom tchrs.), Ala. (past. chmn. secondary sch. tchrs.), Am. tchrs. assns., AAUW, Jefferson County Tchrs. Union (past pres.), NEA (v.p. assn. classroom tchrs. 1969-70), Nat. Council English Tchrs., Nat. Council Social Studies Tchrs., Escambia County League Justice, Future Tchrs. Am. Advisers Council, City-Wide Fedn. Women's Clubs (past officer), Internat. Platform Assn., LWV, Gen. Alumni Assn. Ala. State U. (exec. bd.), Top Ladies of Distinction (organizer, pres. Pensacola chpt., Pensacola Top Lady of Yr. 1980, Top Lady of Decade 1980, Area Top Lady of Yr. 1980), Nat. Gen. Alumni Assn. (v.p. 1981—), Alpha Kappa Alpha (Achievement award South Atlantic region 1970). Baptist (mem., pres. bd. ushers). Mem. Order Eastern Star. Clubs: Mary M. Bethune, New Idea Art and Study. (Pensacola). Composer: God Planted You Here, Talking to the Moon, It Is Better Not to Know, In the Quiet of the Day. Contbr. articles, poems publs. Address: 1516 W Gadsden St Pensacola FL 32501

GAINES, EDYTHE JONES, state ofcl.; b. Asheville, N.C., Sept. 6, 1922; A.B., Hunter Coll., 1944; M.A., N.Y.U., 1947; C.A.S., Harvard U., 1966, Ed.D., 1969; LL.D., Montclair (N.J.) State U., 1977; postgrad. Columbia U., CUNY, U. P.R. Tchr., Prospect Jr. High Sch., N.Y.C., 1945-48, Joan of Arc Jr. High Sch., 1948-52; core curriculum coordinator Jr. High Sch. Div., N.Y.C. Public Schs., 1952-55; asst. prin. Joan of Arc Jr. High Sch., N.Y.C. Public Schs., 1955-60, prin., 1960-67; community supt. schs. Community Sch. Dist. 12, N.Y.C. Public Schs., 1967-71, exec. dir. ednl. planning and support, 1973-75; dir. The Learning Coop., N.Y.C., 1971-73; supt. schs., Hartford, Conn., 1975-78; cons. Bd. Govs., Greater Hartford Consortium for Higher Edn., 1978-79; now commr. State Conn. Public Utilities Control Authority, Hartford; lectr. Columbia U., N.Y.U. Trustee Hartford Coll. for Women, Hartford Sem. Found.; bd. dirs. Hartford Stage Co., Conn. Opera Assn., United Way Greater Hartford, Community Council Capital Region, Urban League Greater Hartford; corporator Mt. Sinai Hosp., Hartford, Hartford Hosp.; nat. sponsor Com. for Middle East Studies in Secondary Edn.; mem. Com. for Study Nat. Service; mem. nat. adv. bd. Eric Clearing House on Ednl. Mgmt., U. Oreg.; mem. nat. task force on Desegregation Strategies; mem. Gov. of Conn. Task Force on South African Investment Policy, 1982—. Recipient award Pi Lambda Theta, 1966, award Assn. Bronx Community Orgns., 1973, Mary McCleod Bethune award African Am. Hist. Assn., 1971, Ecumenical award Bronx Council Chs., 1971, Woman of Year award NAACP, Family of Man Medallion award, 1975, award Montclair-North Essex YWCA, 1975, award AAUW, Distinction in Ednl. Service award United Negro Coll. Fund, 1978, citation Conn. Bilingual Edn. Assn., 1978; fellow Nat. Inst. Edn., 1975. Office: Public Utilities Control Authority One Central Park Mall New Britain CT 06051

GAINES, MARION LUCEINE, educator; b. Columbia, S.C., Sept. 21, 1925; d. Marion Little and Eloise (Cave) Gaines; student U. S.C., 1941-43, M.B.A., 1964; B.S., U. N.C. 1945; m. Thomas Clark Fitzgerald, Jr., June 7, 1947; children—Thomas Clark, Gaines Marion, Carolyn Sarah; m. 2d, John Thomas Rice, June 19, 1963 (dec. July 1969). Staff accountant Peat Marwick Mitchell Co., Greensboro, N.C., 1943-47, Darmody Todd & Co., Boston, 1947-48; accountant J.P. Stevens & Co., Greensboro, 1948-51; partner Fitzgerald & Co., C.P.A.s, Columbia, 1951-63; controller Cardinal Chem. Co., Columbia, 1964-66; head acctg. dept. Palmer Coll., Columbia, 1966-70, Midlands Tech. Edn. Center, 1970-74; asst. prof. acctg. Winthrop Coll., Rock Hill, S.C., 1975-81;

asso. prof. Lander Coll., Greenwood, S.C., 1981—. Chmn. fin. com. Girl Scouts Am., Columbia, 1960-63; bd. dirs. Jr. Achievement. Nominated Young Woman of Year, Jr. C. of C., 1960; C.P.A., S.C., N.C. Mem. Nat. Assn. Accountants (sec., dir.), Nat. Assn. Security Dealers, Am. Inst. C.P.A.s, S.C. Assn. C.P.A.s, Inst. Internal Auditors, Phi Beta Kappa, Beta Gamma Sigma. Episcopalian. Club: Zonta (treas. 1965-67, dir. Columbia chpt. 1965-68). Home: 427 Cambridge Ave Greenwood SC 29646

GAINES, MARTHA WREN, equal opportunity officer; b. Jefferson County, Ga., May 20, 1939; d. Paul Mundy and Zada (McTier) Wren; A.B.J., U. Ga., 1961; 1 dau., M. Kelly. Advt. mgr. Smyrna (Ga.) Herald, 1961-62; asst. to dir. info. Ga. Dept. Edn., Atlanta, 1962-64; info. dir. Met. Sch. Devel. Council, Atlanta, 1964-67; freelance writer, Atlanta, 1967-69; asso. sec. for systems design Ga. Manpower Planning Council, Atlanta, 1969-74; cons., lectr., 1974-77; EEO compliance officer Met. Atlanta Rapid Transit Authority, 1977—. Pres. Ga. Abortion Rights Action League, 1979-81; bd. dirs. Ga. ACLU, 1975—, pres., 1981—; mem. nat. bd. dirs. ACLU, 1981—; mem. Carter Mondale Nat. 51.3% Adv. Council, 1976; pres. Atlanta chpt. NOW, 1970-71, Ga. coordinator, 1973-74, nat. bd. dirs., 1971-73, So. region dir., 1976-77, Atlanta Feminist of Yr., 1974; mem. Leadership Atlanta, 1972-73, Atlanta 2000 Edn. Task Force, 1975; bd. dirs. Met. Atlanta YWCA, 1972-78, N.W. Ga. council Girl Scouts U.S.A., 1971-77; exec. com. Dem. Party, 1974-75. Mem. Atlanta Women's Transp. Seminar, Colony Sq. Bus. and Profl. Women (Woman of Yr. award 1981). Home: 2444E Adina Dr NE Atlanta GA 30324

GAINES, ROSSLYN, psychologist, educator; b. Toronto, Ont., Can.; d. Edward A. and Ruth E. (Goldin) Stiegel; B.S. summa cum laude, Northwestern U., 1948; M.A. with honors, U. Chgo., 1961, Ph.D. (NIH fellow), 1963; children—Katherine, John. Counselor and clin. psychologist Chgo. Psychol. Inst., 1951-55; pvt. practice psychotherapy, Chgo., 1959-63; clin. psychologist Resthaven Rehab. Hosp., Chgo., 1960-61; research asst. U. Chgo., 1961-62, instr. dept. psychology, 1963; asst. prof. in residence UCLA, 1963-64, assoc. prof. psychiatry and psychology, 1971-78, prof. in residence psychiatry and psychology, 1978—, dir. hearing impaired infants, children and their families, 1981—; lectr. dept. ednl. psychology U. Calif., Berkeley, 1968-71, assoc. research psychologist Inst. Human Devel., 1966-71; cons. NSF, 1971, Office of Child Devel., Washington, 1974-78, U.S. Office of Edn., 1965-70, Golden Gate Regional Center for Retardation, San Francisco, 1970-71; vis. fellow Oxford (Eng.) U. 1978-79, 80; vis. prof. People's Republic of China, 1981; mem. adv. council Mental Health Clinic for Deaf, St. John's Hosp., 1974-77. Nat. Tng. Labs. fellow, 1966. Mem. Am. Psychol. Assn. (travel award 1969), Soc. for Research in Child Devel., Western Psychol. Assn., Internat. Soc. for Study of Behavioral Devel., Am. Speech and Hearing Assn., Phi Beta Kappa, Sigma Xi. Contbr. articles on child psychology to profl. jours.; mem. editorial bd. Child Devel., 1974-80; cons. editor various psychol. jours.

GAINES, SUSANN FOSTER, retail exec.; b. Gainesville, Ga., Jan. 31, 1947; d. George Almiran and Ann Ella (Foster) Gaines; student Pasadena Coll., 1965-67. Asst. mgr. Gaines Dept. Store, Riverside, Calif., 1967-69; dept. mgr. Broadway Dept. Stores, Montclair Plaza, 1969-70, buyer lingere, Los Angeles, 1970; buyer, office mgr., personnel mgr., part owner Gaines Dept. Store, Corona, Calif., 1970—, also dir.; owner, pres. Astro Bus. Services, Corona, 1979—. Bd. dirs. Marching with Christ, Inc., 1976-80; election officer Riverside County Republican Com., 1980; bd. dirs. Corona Music Theater, 1974. Mem. Nat. Assn. Female Execs., Smithsonian Assos., Nat. Trust Hist. Preservation, Animal Protection Inst. Am., Am. Soc. Profl. and Exec. Women, AFTRA. Mem. Ch. Nazarene. Office: 400 N Main St Corona CA 91720

GAITHER, DOROTHY JAMES, ednl. adminstr.; b. Englewood, N.J.; d. Quinton and Agnes (Belton) James; B.S., William Paterson Coll., 1953; M.S., Mt. St. Mary's Coll., Los Angeles, 1973; m. Frank T. Gaither, Oct. 26, 1962 (dec.); 1 son, Thomas Frank. Tchr. public schs., Bergenfield, N.J., 1953-58; with Los Angeles Unified Sch. Dist., 1958—, reading specialist, 1966-70, cons., 1970-72, dir. STAR program, 1972-75, asst. prin., 1975-77, 82—, prin., 1977-80, asst. dir. ESAA, 1980-82. Mem. Calif. Tchr. Preparation and Licensing Commn. Adv. Bd., 1977-78. Mem. Nat. Assn. Elem. Sch. Prins., Assn. Elem. Sch. Adminstrs., Assn. Calif. Sch. Adminstrs., Nat. Assn. Supervision and Curriculum Devel., Council Black Adminstrs., Links, Inc., Delta Kappa Gamma. Mem. Ch. of Christian Fellowship. Office: 450 N Grand Ave Los Angeles CA 90012

GALANE, IRMA ADELE BERESTON, electronic engr.; b. Balt., Aug. 23, 1921; d. Dr. Arthur and Sarah (Hillman) Bereston; B.A., Goucher Coll., 1940; postgrad. Johns Hopkins, 1940-42, Mass. Inst. Tech., 1943, George Washington U., 1945, 65, 73, 77, 79, U. Md., 1958, Army Mgmt. Sch., 1964; 1 dau., Suzanne Felice Galane Duvall. Physicist, Naval Ordnance Lab., 1942-43; electronic engr. Navy Bur. Ships, 1943-49, Army Office Chief Signal Officer, 1949-51, Navy Bur. Aeros., 1951-56, Air Research and Devel. Command, USAF, 1956-57, FCC, 1957-60, NASA, 1960-62; supervisory electronic engr. USCG Hdqrs., 1962-64; sci. specialist engring. scis. Library of Congress, 1964-65; project engr. Advanced Aerial Fire Support System, Army Materiel Command, 1965-66; engr. Naval Air Systems Command, 1966-71; electronic engr. Spectrum Mgmt. Task Force, FCC, 1971-76, sr. research engr. FCC, 1976—; Judge nat. capitol awards for engrs. and architects, 1975. Registered profl. engr., D.C. Mem. IEEE (sr.), Am. Inst. Aeros. and Astronautics, Nat. Soc. Profl. Engrs. (chmn. publs. com. 1959-60, co-chmn. civil def. com. 1965, spl. asst. to pres. 1965), Soc. Women Engrs. (sr. mem.; nat. membership chmn. 1952, nat. dir. 1953, mem. nat. scholarship com. 1958), Armed Forces Communications and Electronics Assn., Fedn. Profl. Assn., Am. Ordnance Assn., Johns Hopkins Alumni Assn., AAAS, U.S. Naval Inst., Marine Tech. Soc., Internat. Platform Assn., Smithsonian Inst. (asso.). Editor: The Met. Washington Profl. Engr., 1958-60. Home: 4201 Cathedral Ave NW Washington DC 20016

GALANTE, JANE HOHFELD, pianist, music historian; b. San Francisco, Feb. 14, 1924; d. Edward and Lillian (Devendorf) Hohfeld; A.B., Vassar Coll., 1944; M.A., U. Calif., Berkeley, 1949; m. Clement Galante, Dec. 26, 1956; children—Edward Elio, John Clement. Instr., U. Calif., Berkeley, 1948-52, Mills Coll., Oakland, Calif., 1950-52; music editor Berkeley, A. Jour. of Modern Culture, 1944-52; founder, dir. Composer's Forum of San Francisco, 1946-56; concert pianist German tours for USIS, 1952-54; Young Audience Concerts, San Francisco, 1963-70; now mem. Lyra Chamber Music Ensemble; trustee Morrison Chamber Music Center at San Francisco, 1956—. Mem. Am. Fedn. of Musicians, Women Musicians Club of San Francisco, Sierra Club., Nat. Wildlife Fedn., Am. Farmland Trust.

GALBRAITH, BERNICE WOOD, food co. exec.; b. Woods Cross, Utah, Apr. 13, 1923; d. C.C. and Mary A. (Walton) Wood; student Latter Day Saints Bus. Coll., 1942; m. Jay W. Galbraith, Feb. 23, 1944; children—Jerry, Robert, Christy, Lynn. Co-owner Utah Central Airport, Salt Lake City, 1958-63, JayLynn Portrait Studio, Salt Lake City, 1947-72; sec.-treas. Ute Aviation, Salt Lake City, 1959-72, pres., 1972—; pres. Intermountain Freeze Dried Foods, Ogden, Utah, 1974—. Mem. dean's adv. council Coll. Bus., Utah State U. Mem. Rocky Mountain Photographers Assn. (various awards), Airport Owners and Operators, Salt Lake City C. of C., Ogden C. of C. Mormon. Club: Altrusa (pres. Salt Lake 1955-59, treas. dist. 10 1959-61, gov. dist. 10 1963-65). Office: Intermountain Freeze Dried Foods 3025 Washington Blvd Ogden UT 84401

GALBRAITH, LILYAN KING, educator; b. Smithfield, Pa.; d. Jasper Thompson and Iona (Ewing) King; B.S., U. W.Va., 1927, M.S., 1946; Ed.D., Pa. State U., 1953; m. Carl Bennett Galbraith, April 28, 1923 (div. 1939). Tchr. home econs., Rivesville, W.Va. 1927-29, Clarksburg, W.Va., 1942-44; tchr. trainer W.Va. U., Morgantown, 1944-46; supr. home econs. edn. State Coll., Mansfield, Pa., 1946-53; head home econs. dept. Western Mich. U., Kalamazoo, 1953-55; prof., head home econs. edn. dept. S.D. State U., Brookings, 1955-68; prof. Western Ky. U., Bowling Green, 1968-70; prof. home econs. edn. W.Va. U., summers 1971, 72. Recipient citation of merit for meritorious and devoted service to vocat. home econ. edn. program in S.D., 1967; named S.D. Home Economist of Yr., 1968. Mem. Am. Home Econs. Assn., NEA, AAUP, Am. Vocat. Assn., Am. Ednl. Research Assn., AAUW (pres. Brookings br. 1961-63, Uniontown br. 1974-76, named Outstanding Woman of Yr. Uniontown Br. 1982), Bus. and Profl. Women's Club (pres. Brookings 1967-68, historian Uniontown 1974-76, chmn. legis. com. 1980-81, chmn. by-laws com. 1981-82, named Woman of Yr. 1980-81), Future Homemakers Am. (hon.), Fayette County Home Economics Assn. (pres. 1977-79, historian 1979—), Kappa Omicron Phi (chmn. nat. project com. 1954-60), Phi Lambda Theta, Delta Kappa Gamma (pres. chpt. 1964-66, 82-84, corr. sec. 1980-82), Kappa Delta Pi. Republican. Club: Uniontown Coll. (pres. chpt. 1981-82). Methodist (mem. ofcl. bd., trustee 1972-75, adminstrv. bd. 1972-82, chmn. 1978-82, v.p., pres. local unit United Meth. Women, 1971-81, dist. membership chmn. 1979-82). Contbr. articles to profl. publs. Home: 47 Water St Smithfield PA 15478

GALBRAITH, RUTH LEGG, univ. dean; b. Lecompte, La., Nov. 5, 1923; d. Byron S. and Dora Ruth (Lindley) Legg; B.S., Purdue U., 1945, Ph.D., 1950; m. Harry W. Galbraith, June 16, 1950; 1 son, Allan Legg. Chemist, E. I. duPont de Nemours, Waynesboro, Va., 1945-46; textile chemist Gen. Electric Co., Bridgeport, Conn., 1946-47; teaching asst. chemistry Purdue U., 1947-48, research fellow, 1948-50; prof. textiles and clothing U. Tenn., Knoxville, 1950-55; asso. prof. U. Ill., Urbana, 1956-64, prof., 1964-70, chmn. textiles and clothing div., 1962-70; prof., head consumer affairs dept. Auburn (Ala.) U., 1970-73, dean Sch. Home Econs., head home econs. research, 1973—; mem. task force on quality of living Dept. Agr., 1967-68; mem. Carpet and Rug Inst. Consumer Action Panel, 1975; mem. nat. adv. com. Flammable Fabrics Act, 1971-73; mem. home econ. subcom. Agrl. Expt. Sta. Com. on Policy, 1975-79, 81-83, sec., 1977-79; mem. U.S. Dept. Agr. Com. Nine, 1981-83, sec., 1982. Recipient Disting. Alumni award Purdue U., 1970. Fellow Am. Inst. Chemists; mem. Am. Home Econs. Assn. (chmn. research sect. 1978-80), Am. Assn. Textile Chemists and Colorists, Am. Chem. Soc., ASTM (3d v.p. com. D-13 textiles 1975-79, hon. mem. 1980), Assn. Coll. Profs. Textiles and Clothing, Assn. Adminstrs. Home Econs., Nat. Council Adminstrs. Home Econs., AAUW, Ala. Home Econs. Assn. (pres. 1983-84), Sigma Xi, Omicron Nu, Phi Kappa Phi, Delta Kappa Gamma. Mem. editorial bd. Research Jour. Home Econs., 1973-77, chmn. policy bd., 1978-80; contbr. articles in field to profl. jours. Home: 368 Singleton St Auburn AL 36830 Office: Sch Home Econs Auburn U Auburn AL 36849

GALBRAITH, VIRGINIA LEE, educator; b. Boise, Idaho; d. Eugene Robert and Ione (Atkinson) Galbraith; A.B., U. Calif., Berkeley, 1941, Ph.D., 1954. Instr., Vassar Coll., 1945-47, U. Calif., Berkeley, 1949-50; prof. econs. Mt. Holyoke Coll., South Hadley, Mass., 1950—; vis. prof. U. Minn., summers 1959, 61. Mem. Consumer Council Mass., 1958-63; trustee Arthur D. Little Mgmt. Edn. Inst. Mem. Am. Econ. Assn. Democrat. Author: World Trade in Transition, 1965; contbg. author: South of the Sahara, 1973. Contbr. articles to profl. jours. Home: 7 Greenwood Ln South Hadley MA 01075 *

GALE, BARBARA R(ANSEL), mathematician, educator; b. Latrobe, Pa., Aug. 25, 1936; d. James B. and Dorothy A. (Thomas) Ransel; B.S., Indiana (Pa.) U., 1957; M.Ed., 1962; D.Ed., George Washington U., 1974; m. Walter J. Gale, Oct. 25, 1969 (dec.). Math. tchr. Pa. Public Schs., 1957-60; asst. prof. math. Pembroke (N.C.) State U., 1961-63, St. Joseph's Coll., Phila., 1963-69; prof. math. Prince George's Coll., Largo, Md., 1969—, chmn. dept. math. and engring., 1975-77. Mem. Nat. Council Tchrs. of Math., Math. Assn. Am., Md. Assn. Community and Jr. Colls. (treas. 1979—), Md. Council Tchrs. of Math., Am. Math. Assn. Two Yr. Colls., Md. Math. Assn. Two Yr. Colls., Phi Delta Kappa. Roman Catholic. Home: 7812 Lusby's Turn Brandywine MD 20613 Office: 301 Largo Rd Largo MD 20870

GALE, MARLA, clin. social worker; b. Uniontown, Pa., July 20, 1935; d. Saul and Sarah (Lisowitz) Krongold; A.B. magna cum laude, U. Miami, 1971; M.S.W., Barry Coll., 1972; m. Edward Gale, June 12, 1954; children—Jeffrey, Wendy, Lori. Research social worker VA Hosp., Miami, Fla., 1971; caseworker Jewish Family Service Broward County, Hollywood, Fla., 1971-81, supr. profl. staff, 1981—; mem. clin. faculty Barry U., Miami Shores, Fla.; parent effectiveness trainer instr.; real estate salesperson; builder, investor. Mem. Nat. Assn. Social Workers, Acad. Cert. Social Workers, Common Cause, Project Newborn, Met. Mus., Animal Protection Soc., Womens Advocacy Majority Minority. Democrat. Jewish. Office: 1909 Harrison St Hollywood FL 33020

GALE, PATRICIA SUZANNE, tax cons.; b. Detroit, Mar. 17, 1950; d. Charles Jack and Julia Celine (Vidal) Lefler; B.S. in Social Sci. and Edn., Mich. State U., 1972; m. Vern Walter Gale, Sept. 9, 1972; children—Kristopher Walter, Michael Charles. Tchr., Alcona (Mich.) Community Schs., 1972-75, Gerrish-Higgins Sch. Dist. (Mich.), 1975-77, Coor Intermediate Sch. Dist. (Mich.), 1975-77; owner-mgr. H&R Block, Grayling, Mich., 1976—, tchr. Block Basic Tax Sch. Recipient Mich. Higher Edn. award. Republican. Roman Catholic. Clubs: Burning Oak Golf, Dunham Hill Golf and Country, Ye Olde Country, Rebekahs, Ind. Order Foresters. Home: 2125 E Pioneer St Roscommon MI 48653 Office: Grayling MI 49738

GALER, MARY JANE, state legislator, librarian; b. Port Arthur, Tex., June 30, 1924; d. Harry F. and Clara Williams (Graham) Perkins; B.S.L.S., Carnegie Inst. Tech., 1947; B.A. in Edn., U. Pitts., 1945; m. Robert Fulton Galer, Nov. 7, 1951; children—Frank Fulton, Barbara Jean, Robin Robson. Librarian, U.S. Army, Korea, Japan and Calif., 1948-52, Ft. Benning, Ga., 1960-65, Mobile (Ala.) Public Library, 1966; asso. prof. library sci. Columbus (Ga.) Coll., 1967-76; mem. Ga. Ho. of Reps., 1977—. Co-founder, bd. dirs. Contact Teleministries, 1978-82; bd. dirs. Columbus Symphony, 1979-82; mem. Ga. Democratic Com.; del. Dem. Nat. Conv., 1980. Recipient Columbus Public Service award, 1975; Women Helping Women award Soroptimist Internat., 1975; others. Mem. LWV, AAUP, Ga. Library Assn., AAUW (pres. 1975-79), Phi Delta Kappa, Alpha Delta Kappa. Presbyterian. Club: Soroptimist (public affairs chmn. 1977, dir. 1978). Indexer: (with others) microfilm collection Herstory.

GALES, CHARLOTTE LEMMON, retail security ofcl.; b. Ashtabula, Ohio, Dec. 20, 1927; d. Lewis Newton and Opal Marguerite (Fairchild) Lemmon; B.S. in Bus. Adminstrn. magna cum laude, Kent State U., 1967; m. George W. Gales, July 4, 1974; children by previous marriage—Randall Lynn Zelenak, Michelle Marguerite Zelenak Roberts. Sr. auditor Peat, Marwick, Mitchell & Co., Cleve., 1967-71; internal auditor Strouss, Youngstown, Ohio, 1971-72; dir. internal audit, shortage control and systems May Co., Cleve., 1972-74; dir. loss prevention Miller's Inc., Knoxville, 1974—; public speaker on retail shortage and security. Asst. treas. Knox County (Tenn.) Republican Com., 1978—. Mem. Am. Soc. Indsl. Security, Inst. Internal Auditors, Am. Soc. Women Accts., Nat. Acctg. Assn., Beta Gamma Sigma, Beta Alpha Psi. Baptist. Home: 521 W Meadecrest Dr Knoxville TN 37923 Office: 600 Henley St Knoxville TN 37902

GALES, PATRICIA PHILLIPS, educator; b. Pitts., Dec. 15, 1934; d. Michael and Catherine Phillips; A.A., Community Coll. Allegheny County, 1970; B.S. cum laude, U. Pitts., 1971, M.Ed., 1976; m. Donald A. Gales, Dec. 31, 1952; children—Patrice Andrea, Dawn Michelle, Christopher S. Receptionist, St. Joseph Hosp., Pitts., 1950, Liberty Mut. Ins. Co., 1953; tchr. Pitts. pub. schs., 1971-76; elem. tchr. Garrett County Bd. Edn., Oakland, Md., 1977—; owner, operator Mountain Mama's Vacation Resort. Treas., Grad. Council of Edn., 1974-76; musician Ursina Community Band; emergency med. technician Confluence Ambulance Service. Mem. Am. Fedn. Tchrs., Cath. War Vets. Aux., NOW, Farm Vacation Assn. Pa. (sec.-treas.). Home: Box 212 Rural Route 3 Confluence PA 15424 Office: Friendsville Sch Friendsville MD 21531

GALEY, MARGARET ELIZABETH, govt. ofcl.; b. Pitts., Nov. 7, 1939; d. John Taylor and Blanche Georgene (Fishback) Galey; A.B., Vassar Coll., 1961; Ph.D., U. Pa., 1970. Postdoctoral fellow U. Pitts., 1970-71; research asso. UN Inst. Tng. and Research, N.Y.C., 1971-72; asst. prof. polit. sci. Purdue U., West Lafayette, Ind., 1972-77; staff asso. subcom. internat. orgns. Com. Internat. Relations, U.S. Ho. of Reps., 1977-79, staff cons. Com. Fgn. Affairs, 1979—. Mem. exec. bd. Commn. to Study Orgn of Peace, N.Y.C., 1974—; cons. EPA, 1974-75. Mem. Internat. Studies Assn., Am. Soc. Internat. Law. Club: Vassar (N.Y.C.). Home: 3419A S Stafford St Arlington VA 22206 Office: Com Fgn Affairs 2170 Rayburn House Office Bldg Washington DC 20515

GALEY, MARY DUBOIS SCHAUB, architect; b. Washington, May 20, 1948; d. Benton Hall and Rosemary Duvall (Sands) Schaub; B.Arch., Tulane U., 1971; m. Gary Ray Galey, July 15, 1972. Intern architect Fed. Bur. Prisons, 1971-72; staff architect Hallmark Cards, Inc., Kansas City, Mo., 1972-74; with Office Facilities Devel., Fed. Bur. Prisons, Washington, 1974—, project mgr., architect, 1975—; co-owner Design Assos., Crownsville, Md., 1978—. Mem. AIA. Episcopalian. Club: Indian Landing Boat (pres. 1979-80). Home: 1098 Plum Dr Crownsville MD 21032 Office: 320 1st St NW Washington DC 20534 also Box 515 Crownsville MD 21032

GALKIN, FLORENCE, social worker; b. N.Y.C., Dec. 27, 1925; d. Victor and Sadie (Sobel) Greenwald; B.A., Hunter Coll., 1946; M.S.W., U. Pa., 1951; advanced cert. Columbia U., 1961, postgrad., NIMH fellow, 1962-64; m. Bernard Galkin, Dec. 18, 1948; children—Judith, William Seth. Caseworker, Jewish Child Care Assn., N.Y.C., 1951-57; field instr. community orgn. Bird S. Coler Hosp., 1968; cons. ombudsman program Community Council Greater N.Y., 1978—; research asso. Center Policy Research, 1980—; exec. dir. Community Action and Resources for the Elderly, 1976—; trainee leadership in public affairs Coro Found., 1981—. Bd. dirs. Nat. Coalition for Nursing Home Reform, 1978-79; mem. met. coordinating council Am. Jewish Congress; mem. Met. Coordinating Council on Jewish Poverty. Recipient Louise Waterman Wise Humanitarian award Am. Jewish Congress. Mem. Nat. Assn. Social Workers. Jewish. Author: People and Nursing Homes, 1977; (with others) Neighborhood Information Center: A Study and Some Proposals, 1966; (with Hochbaum) The New York State Patient Advocacy Program, Patients and Their Complaints, 1978, Discharge Planning-No Deposit, No Return, 1982. Home: 400 E 56th St New York NY 10022

GALLAGHER, DOLORES ELIZABETH, psychologist; b. N.Y.C., Aug. 7, 1944; d. Joseph and Elizabeth (Goehringer) Ruebeck; B.S., Fordham U., 1965; M.A., Duquesne U., 1967; Ph.D. (NIMH fellow), U. So. Calif., 1979; m. William J. Gallagher, Aug. 27, 1966 (dec. 1979); m. 2d, Larry W. Thompson, Dec. 12, 1981. Rehab. psychologist Fedn. Handicapped, N.Y.C., 1965-72; staff psychologist Altoona (Pa.) Hosp. Community Mental Health Center, 1972-74; clin. psychologist Los Angeles County Occupational Health Services, 1975-77; intern Neuropsychiat. Inst. of UCLA, 1977-78; staff psychologist Adult Counseling Center, Andrus Gerontology Center, U. So. Calif., 1978-79, acting dir., 1980-81; adj. asst. prof. psychology U. So. Calif., 1978-80; co-dir. interdisciplinary team tng. program in geriatrics Palo Alto VA Med. Center, 1981—; lectr. Stanford U.; research cons. aging projects in Los Angeles and San Francisco Bay areas. Bd. trustees Suicide Prevention and Crisis Center San Mateo County, 1981—; cons. Los Angeles County Suicide Prevention Center, 1981—. Recipient grants Nat. Inst. Aging, NIMH; lic. psychologist, Calif.; cert. Nat. Register Health Service Providers in Psychology. Mem. Am. Psychol. Assn., Soc. Psychotherapy Research, Gerontol. Soc. Am., Western Gerontol. Assn., Western Psychol. Assn., Calif. Council Gerontology and Geriatrics. Democrat. Mem. Self-Realization Fellowship. Club: Sierra. Author: (with others) Depression in the Elderly: A Behavioral Treatment Manual, 1981; contbr. articles profl. jours. Home: 355 Los Altos Ave Los Altos CA 94022 Office: Geriatric Research Edn and Clin Center 182B Palo Alto VA Medical Center 3801 Miranda Ave Palo Alto CA 94304

GALLAGHER, HELEN, actress, singer, dancer; b. Bklyn., 1926; student Am. Ballet Sch.; m. Frank Wise, Oct. 14, 1956. Debut in Seven Lively Arts, N.Y.C., 1947; appeared in plays Mr. Strauss Goes to Boston, 1945, Billion Dollar Baby, 1945, Brigadoon, 1947, High Button Shoes, 1947, Tough and Go, 1949, Make a Wish, 1951, Pal Joey, 1952, Hazel Flagg, 1953, Annie Get Your Gun, 1954, Guys and Dolls, 1955, Finian's Rainbow, 1955, Pajama Game, 1954, Brigadoon, 1957, Portofino, 1958, Oklahoma, 1958, Guys and Dolls, 1958, No, No Nanette, 1970-72, Hot House, 1974, Tickles by Tucholsky, 1976, The Gingerbread Lady, 1977, The Misanthrope, 1977; toured with Bus Stop, 1956, The Gershwin Years, 1973; appeared on TV in Shangri-La, Hallmark Hall of Fame, 1960, Colgate Comedy Hour, Ed Sullivan Show, Kraft Television Theatre, Ryan's Hope, The American Woman: Portraits of Courage; performed at nightclubs including Thunderbird, Las Vegas, 1951, Mocambo, Hollywood, Cal., 1951, Persian Room, Plaza Hotel, N.Y.C., 1954, revue Too Good for the Average Man, Camelot, N.Y.C., 1960. Recipient Tony award as best actress in musical for No, No Nannette, 1970. Office: Actors Equity Assn 165 W 46th St New York NY 10036 *

GALLAGHER, JOAN KILLIAN, design firm exec.; b. N.Y.C., Oct. 14, 1949; d. Thomas Francis and Mary O'Shea G.; B.A. in Journalism, Am. U., 1971; m. John Sheppard Warden, June 1, 1974. Founder, pres. Warden-Brooks, Ltd., N.Y.C., 1978—, The Killian Corp., Conn., 1981—. Mem. Am. Mgmt. Assn. Office: 113 E 37th St New York NY 10016

GALLAGHER, MARIAN GOULD, law librarian, educator; b. Everett, Wash., Aug. 29, 1914; d. John H. and Grace (Smith) Gould; student Whitman Coll., 1931-32; A.B., U. Wash., 1937, LL.B., 1937, M.L.S., 1939; m. D. Wayne Gallagher, Oct. 1, 1942 (dec. 1953). Admitted to Wash. bar, 1937; instr. law U. Utah, 1939-44, law librarian, 1939-44; asst. prof. law U. Wash., 1944-49, asso. prof., 1948-53, prof., 1953-81, law librarian, 1944-81; vis. prof. law, disting. law librarian U. Calif.-Hastings, 1982. Fellow Am. Bar Found.; mem. Am. Assn. Law Libraries (pres. 1953-54), Wash. State Bar Assn., Seattle-King County Bar Assn., Am. Bar Assn. (council legal edn. sect.), PEO, Delta Delta Delta, Phi

Alpha Delta. Presbyterian. Home: 1000 8th Ave Seattle WA 98104 Office: U Wash MS Gallagher Law Library Condon Hall 1100 NE Campus Pkwy Seattle WA 98105

GALLAGHER, MARJORIE CURTIS, psychiatrist; b. Columbus, Ohio, Nov. 14, 1948; d. Clarence Mankopf and Mary Curtis (Garvin) G.; A.B., Mount Holyoke Coll., 1970; M.D., Ohio State U., 1973; m. Ralph F. Henn II, Feb. 9, 1974; children—Ralph F. III, Lucas Webster, Katherine Curtis. Intern, Hosp. of Good Samaritan Med. Center, 1973-74; resident in psychiatry Los Angeles County-U. So. Calif. Med. Center, 1974-77; asst. clin. prof. Ohio State U., Columbus, 1978—; practice medicine specializing in psychiatry, Columbus; mem. staff Ohio State U. Hosp.; program dir. in psychiatry, family practice residency Grant Hosp. Trustee, Ronald McDonald House, 1982—. Mem. Am. Psychiatric Assn., Neuropsychiatric Soc. Central Ohio, Ohio Psychiatric Soc., Ohio Med. Assn., Mental Health Assn. Franklin County, Acad. Medicine of Columbus and Franklin County. Office: 300 E Town St Suite 712 Columbus OH 43215

GALLAGHER, MARY CAMPBELL, lawyer, linguist; b. Chgo., May 17, 1938; d. Joseph Raymond and Jane Patricia (O'Hara) G.; student St. John's Coll., 1956-58; A.B. in Philosophy, Barnard Coll., 1960; postgrad. M.I.T., 1968-69; Ph.D. in Linguistics, U. Ill., 1969; J.D., Harvard U., 1974. Asst. prof. linguistics Grad. Center CUNY and Queens Coll., 1969-71; asso. firm Herrick & Smith, Boston 1974-75; adj. asst. prof. New Eng. Sch. Law, 1974; sole practice law, Washington, 1978—. Bd. visitors and govs. St. John's Coll., 1976-81, mem. exec. com., 1978-79, NDEA fellow, 1964-68; Sr. Fulbright lectr. Mem. Ripon Soc. (mem. nat. governing bd. 1980-81), ABA, D.C. Bar Assn., Assn. Trial Lawyers Am., Women's Bar Assn. Washington, Nat. Assn. Women Bus. Owners. Republican. Roman Catholic. Author: (with Thomas J. Brown, Rosemary Turner) Teaching Secondary English: Alternative Approaches 1975; (with others) Curriculum Materials for Gifted Students of English, Grades Seven through Twelve; contbr. numerous articles to profl. jours. Office: Suite 300 1919 Pennsylvania Ave NW Washington DC 20006

GALLAGHER, PATRICIA CECILIA, author; b. Lockhart, Tex.; d. Frank Joseph and Martha Leona (Rhody) Bienek; student Trinity U., 1951; 1 son, James Craig. Novels include: The Sons and the Daughters, 1961, Answer To Heaven, 1964, The Fires of Brimstone, 1966, Shannon, 1967, Shadows of Passion, 1971, Summer of Sighs, 1971, The Thicket, 1974, Castles in the Air, 1976, Mystic Rose, 1977, No Greater Love, 1979, All for Love, 1981, Echoes and Embers, 1983. Mem. Women in Communications, San Antonio Mag. Council. Office: Scott Meredith Literary Agency Inc 845 3d Ave New York NY 10019

GALLAHER, SANDRA LEE, psychologist; b. Portland, Oreg., Jan. 24, 1938; d. David Lenore and Clara (Luck) G.; B.S., Mt. Angel Coll., 1959; M.Ed., Wash. State U., 1964; Ph.D., U. Wash., 1974. Tchr. 5th grade, Quincy, Wash., 1959-61, 3d grade, Camas, Wash., 1961-62; instr. psychology, counselor Yakima Valley Coll., 1963-65; instr. psychology, reading, coordinator, adv. Green River Community Coll., Auburn, Wash., 1965-73, counselor, 1973—; psychologist, Kent, Wash., 1976—; cons. on communications to bus. and agys. Lic. psychologist, Wash. Mem. NEA, Wash. Edn. Assn., Am. Personnel and Guidance Assn., N.W. Family Tng. Inst., Wash. Psychol. Assn., Western Psychol. Assn., Am. Psychol. Assn., Assn. Advancement Psychology. Democrat. Home: 20850 102d Ave SE Kent WA 98031 Office: 12401 SE 320th St Auburn WA 98002

GALLANT, CLAIRE B., social worker; b. New Haven, Mar. 17, 1923; d. Anton F. and Winifred (Kling) Bradoc; B.S., So. Conn. State Coll., 1943, 6th yr. cert. 1972; M.S.W., U. Denver, 1948; m. Edward B. Gallant, Nov. 13, 1945; children—Keith Bradoc, Anne Claire. Head sch. social worker Hamden (Conn.) Bd. Edn., 1964-67; cons., sch. social work services, hearing officer spl. edn. parent appeals, chief mediator spl. edn. parent appeals, Conn. State Dept. Edn., Hartford, 1967-79; prin. trainer personnel preparation program, tng. for mediation skills in 9 states, Dept. Edn. Bur. of Handicapped grant awarded to Nat. Assn. Social Workers, New Haven, 1979— Bd. edn. Wallingford, Conn., 1958-63; bd. dirs. Stony Creek Assn., 1981—. Mem. Nat. Assn. Social Workers (del. 1981 Assembly, exec. bd. Conn. chpt., nat. com. on social work services, recipient first sch. social work award Conn. chpt. 1981, profl. award 1976), Conn. Assn. Sch. Social Workers. Author: Mediation in Special Education Disputes. Editorial bd. Social Work in Education; contbr. articles to publs. in field. Office: 79 Trumbull St New Haven CT 06510

GALLANT, MAUREEN VICTORIA, speech pathologist; b. Exeter, N.H., Nov. 29, 1954; d. Hubert Anselum and Victoria Mildred (Waleryszak) Gallant; B.S. in Communication Disorders, U. N.H., 1976; M.A. in Communication Disorders, Calif. State U., 1980. Aphasia tchr. New Sch. for Child Devel., Van Nuys, Calif., 1980; diagnostician for severely developmentally delayed children, Los Angeles, summer, 1981; lang. and speech specialist Los Angeles County Supt. Schs., 1979-82; speech pathologist Singer & Brown, Inc., Arcadia, Calif., 1982—. Mem. Am. Speech, Lang. and Hearing Assn., Calif. Speech, Lang. and Hearing Assn. Home: 3642 Parrish Ave Los Angeles CA 90065 Office: 650 W Duarte Rd Arcadia CA 91006

GALLANT, MAVIS, author; b. Montreal, Que., Can., Aug. 11, 1922. Author: Green Water, Green Sky, 1959, 60; A Fairly Good Time, 1970; The Other Paris (short stories), 1956, 57; My Heart Is Broken; 8 Stories and a Short Novel (Brit. title An Unmarried Man's Summer), 1964; The Affair of Gabrielle Russier (introductory essay), 1971; The Pegnitz Junction, a Novella and Five Short Stories, 1973; The End of the World and Other Stories, 1974; (short stories) From the Fifteenth District, 1979; contbr. to New Yorker, 1951—. Home: 14 rue Jean Ferrandi Paris VI France *

GALLANT, SANDRA KIRKHAM, psychologist; b. Dallas, July 15, 1933; d. Eugene Raley and Anita Bernice (Brandenburg) Kirkham; A.B., Hollins Coll., 1954; M.S., Va. Commonwealth U., 1956; m. Wade Miller Gallant, Jr., Sept. 15, 1979. Psychologist aide Lynchburg Tng. Sch. and Hosp., 1954-56, Rehab. Center of Rapides Parrish, 1956; clin. psychologist Bowman Gray Sch. Medicine, Wake Forest U., 1956-64, staff psychologist, acting dir. reading, speech and psychology center, 1962-64; staff psychologist Reading Speech and Psychology Center, part-time 1964-74; sch. psychologist Winston-Salem/Forsyth County Schs., part-time, 1974-75; clin. psychologist Child Guidance Clinic, Winston-Salem, N.C., 1975—; cons. to various community orgns. and agys. Bd. dirs. Family Services, 1964-66; bd. dirs. Little Theatre, 1963-66, pres., 1964-65; trustee to exec. com. Arts Council, 1965-68, v.p., 1967-68; bd. dirs. Mental Health Assn. Forsyth County, 1971-77, 79—, pres., 1974-75; bd. dirs. Mental Health Assn. N.C., 1975—, sec., 1977-79, v.p., 1979-81. Named Vol. of Yr., Mental Health Assn. Forsyth County, 1976; co-recipient Forsyth Mental Health Bell award, 1981. Mem. Am. Psychol. Assn., N.C. Psychol. Assn. Episcopalian. Home: 2534 Warwick Rd Winston-Salem NC 27104 Office: Child Guidance Clinic 1200 Glade St Winston-Salem NC 27101

GALLASPY, DIXIE YATES, interior designer; b. Franklinton, La., Dec. 12, 1934; d. Fred Whithurst and Camille (Gardner) Yates; B.A. in Fine Arts, Tex. Woman's U., Denton, 1957; m. John N. Gallaspy, June 14, 1958; children—John Whithurst, Gardner Weeks, Leland Redding. Interior design asst. Muller's Dept. Store, Lake Charles, La., 1957-58; mem. interior design dept. Gabriel & Reams, Architects, Lake Charles, 1958-59; owner, mgr. Dixie's Designs, Bogalusa, La., 1963—; interior design dir. Gulf States Theatres, Inc., New Orleans, 1976—; interior design dir. United Artists Cinemas Corp., Dallas, 1979—; pres. Dixieland Woods Land Co. Membership drive chmn. Washington Parish Community Concerts Assn., 1976-77, bd. dirs., 1976-80; Sunday sch. tchr. sr. high class Methodist Ch., 1977—, mem. adminstrv. bd., 1979-80, sec. bd. trustees, chmn. parsonage com.; bd. dirs. Bogalusa Arts Found., 1981—, Washington Parish Fair Assn., 1982—; mem. exec. com. 1st La. Conf. on Women. Named Woman of Yr., Bogalusa, 1977; named Queen of 1st Mardi Gras of Bogalusa; Queen I, Magic City Carnival Assn., 1981-82. Mem. Am. Soc. Interior Designers, Bus. and Profl. Womens Club. Republican. Methodist. Home and Office: 1737 Gaylord Dr Bogalusa LA 70427

GALLIK, MILDRED DOROTHY, home economist; b. Yonkers, N.Y., Oct. 15, 1926; d. Samuel and Susan (Vitek) G.; B.S., Cornell U., 1948; postgrad. CCNY, 1953. Home econs. adv. Public Service Electric and Gas Co. N.J., 1948-53; asso. equipment editor Today's Woman mag., N.Y.C., 1953-54; food asso. Family Circle mag., N.Y.C., 1954-55; home service dir. Bruno-N.Y., Inc., N.Y.C., 1956-65; dir. consumer affairs The Soap and Detergent Assn., N.Y.C., 1966—. Mem. Am. Home Econs. Assn., Home Economists in Bus., Elec. Women's Roundtable (bd. dirs., nat. v.p. 1972-74), Soc. Consumer Affairs Profls., Nat. Safety Council Women's Conf. (mem.-at-large), Cornell Alumni Assn. of Coll. Human Ecology. Office: Soap and Detergent Assn 475 Park Ave S New York NY 10016

GALLIN, ALICE, assn. adminstr.; b. N.Y.C., Dec. 30, 1921; d. William L.H. and Alice Teresa (Monteith) G.; B.A., Coll. New Rochelle (N.Y.), 1942; M.A., Fordham U., 1944; Ph.D., Cath. U. Am., 1955. Joined Order St. Ursula, Roman Cath. Ch., 1946; prof. history Coll. New Rochelle, 1950-76; asso. exec. dir. Assn. Cath. Coll. and Univs., Washington, 1976-80, exec. dir., 1980—. Mem. Am. Hist. Assn., Am. Cath. Hist. Assn. Author: German Resistance to Hitler, 1955. Office: 1 Dupont Circle Washington DC 20136

GALLITERO, BETTY JO, mfg. co. exec.; b. Yakima, Wash., Sept. 27, 1933; d. Babe Frank and Maudie Lee (Mondier) Payton; B.S., Coll. Notre Dame, Belmont, Calif., 1979, Ryan credential, 1982; m. William Harold Gallitero, Nov. 5, 1960 (dec. Dec. 1981); children—Paul William, David Joseph. Corp. sec. Rainbow Novelties, Inc., amusement machines, San Francisco, 1971-81, pres., owner, 1981—; pres. Future Enterprises Inc., 1982—. Mem. alumni bd. Coll. Notre Dame, 1979—. Regent Merit scholar, 1978, 79. Mem. AAUW, Delta Epsilon Sigma. Republican. Roman Catholic. Home: 12780 Dianne Dr Los Altos Hills CA 94022 Office: 1133 Mariposa St San Francisco CA 94107

GALLIVAN, MELISSA, lawyer; b. Cleve., June 1, 1953; d. William Francis and Donna Dahlen (Kerr) G.; A.B., Brown U., 1975; student London Sch. Econs., 1874; J.D., Vanderbilt U., 1978; m. Paul G. Youngk, Dec. 2, 1978; 1 son, William. Admitted to Tenn. bar, 1978; legis. asst. to U.S. Senator Howard Baker, 1979—. Bd. dirs. Ft. Ellsworth Unit Owners Assn., 1981—. Mem. Tenn. Bar Assn. Club: Jr. League (Washington). Republican. Roman Catholic. Office: 4123 Dirksen Senate Office Bldg Washington DC 20510

GALLMEIER, TERRI MARIE, psychologist; b. Oklahoma City, Oct. 7, 1948; d. Seimund H. and Ruth Pearl (Bunker) G., B.S. with honors, U. Tulsa, 1970, M.A., 1972; Ph.D., U Okla., 1978; m. Alan Cotton Schlessman, Mar. 8, 1980. Psychologist, dept. head Okla. Cerebral Palsy Center, Norman, 1973-75; teaching asst. U. Okla., Norman, 1975-76, teaching asso., research center coordinator, 1977-78; hon. vis. fellow U. Sheffield (Eng.), 1976-77; dir. Child Guidance Center, Okla. Dept. Health, Miami, 1978-80, N.E. Okla. regional coordinator Child Guidance Clinics, dist. supervising psychologist Okla. Dept. Health, Tulsa, 1980—, chmn. peer rev. com., mem. ethics com.; chmn. Okla. adv. com. on child abuse and neglect, 1980—. Mem. Am. Psychol. Assn., Nat. Women's Polit. Caucus, NOW (treas. Tulsa 1979—, Okla. del. nat. conv. 1980), Okla. Public Health Assn. (mental health rep. legis. com. 1980—), Okla. Psychol. Assn., Phi Gamma Kappa. Democrat. Unitarian. Contbr. articles to profl. jours. Home: 9118 S Lakewood Tulsa OK 74136

GALLO, MARIANNE THERESE, social worker; b. Bklyn., Aug. 4, 1953; d. Cono J. and Marie Gallo; B.S.W., Adelphi U., 1975; M.S.W., Columbia U., 1976; M.P.H., U. Calif., Berkeley, 1978. Counselor, tchr. Tr.Y.A. Hostel, Hempstead, N.Y., 1976-77; social worker L.I. Center for Behavior Therapy, Commack, N.Y., 1977; maternal and child health trainee U. Calif., Berkeley, 1977-78; mem. health team Appalachian Corps, Athens, Ohio, 1978; with Shawnee Mental Health Center, Portsmouth (Ohio) Receiving Hosp., 1978-79; sr. social worker Maryhaven Day Treatment Center, Yaphank, N.Y., 1979-80; psychiat. social worker Pilgrim Psychiat. Hosp., 1981—. Mem. Nat. Assn. Social Workers, Am. Public Health Assn. Roman Catholic.

GALLOWAY, ANN MARIE, travel agy. exec.; Perrysburg, Ohio, July 6, 1924; d. Peter and Mary Julia (Letso) Blazier; student Western Res. U., 1944, Toledo U., 1947; m. Robert E. Galloway, Aug. 23, 1947; children—David, Thomas, Kathryn, Susan. Job analyst Willys Motors, Toledo, 1947-55; partner Galloway-Humber-Stone Pub. Relations, 1955-57; patient aid dir. Leukemia Soc., Toledo, 1955-60; v.p., sec. Galloway Travel, Inc., Toledo, 1959—. Chmn. Toledo Symphony; mem. pres.'s council Toledo Mus. of Art; bd. dirs. Village Players, Toledo Opera Assn., Health Clinics Internat., March of Dimes; mem. exec. bd. St. Vincent Hosp. and Med. Found., Com. on Relations with Spain. Mem. Am. Soc. Travel Agts., Women's Advt. Club. Republican, Roman Catholic. Clubs: Zonta, Sylvania Country. Home: 2219 E Grecourt Toledo OH 43615 Office: 4153 Monroe St Toledo OH 43606

GALLOWAY, DIANE LENOIR, found. exec.; b. Phila., Aug. 24, 1941; d. Howard William and Florence Eleanor (Wagner) Galloway; B.A., Am. U., 1963, postgrad. 1963-64. Staff asst. Mfg. Chemists Assn., Washington, 1963-64; research asst. Federazione Italiana dei Consorzi Agrari, Washington, 1964; asst. Office of the Chief of Protocol, N.Y. World's Fair Corp., Flushing Meadow, N.Y., 1964-65; research asst. Population Office, Ford Found., N.Y.C., 1965-66, sr. staff asst. Office of the Pres., 1966-67, adminstrv. asst. Office of the Sec., 1967-68, exec. asst. Office of Sec. and Gen. Counsel, 1968-72, asst. adminstrv. officer 1972-78, asst. to gen. counsel and adminstrv. officer, 1978—. Mem. Women and Found./Corporate Philanthropy, Am. Soc. Profl. and Exec. Women, Nat. Assn. Female Execs., Alpha Chi Omega, Pi Sigma Alpha. Presbyterian. Clubs: Rockaway River Country, U.S. Senatorial. Home: 327 Morris Ave Boonton NJ 07005 Office: 320 E 43 St New York NY 10017

GALLOWAY, EILENE MARIE (MRS. GEORGE BARNES GALLOWAY), cons.; b. Kansas City, Mo., May 4, 1906; d. Joseph Locke and Lottie Rose (Harris) Slack; A.B., Swarthmore Coll., 1928; postgrad. Am. U., 1937-38, 43; m. George Barnes Galloway, Dec. 23, 1924; children—David Barnes, Jonathan Fuller. Tchr. polit. sci. Swarthmore Coll., 1928-30; editor Student Service, Washington, 1931; staff mem., edn. div. Fed. Emergency Relief Adminstrn., 1934-35; asst. chief info. sect., div. spl. info. Library of Congress, 1941-43, editor abstracts Legis. Reference Service, 1943-51, nat. def. analyst, 1951-57; specialist in nat. def., 1957-66; sr. specialist internat. relations (nat. security) Congl. Research Service, 1966-75; cons. internat. space activities, 1975—. staff mem. Senate Fgn. Relations Com., 1947; profl. staff mem. U.S. group Interparliamentary Union, 1958-66; cons. Senate Armed Services Com., 1953-74, Ford Found., 1958; spl. cons. spl. Senate Com. on Space and Astronautics, 1958; spl. cons. to Senate Com. on Aero. and Space Sci., 1958-77; cons. to Senate Com. on Commerce, Sci. and Transp., 1977—; chmn. com. edn. and recreation Washington, 1937-38; forum leader program on adult edn. U.S. Office Edn., 1938; mem. Internat. Inst. Space Law of Internat. Astronautical Fedn., 1958—, U.S. mem. bd. dirs., v.p., 1967-79, hon. dir., 1979—, Fedn. ofcl. observer at sessions UN Com. on Peaceful Uses Outer Space, 1981, 82, mem. com. for relations with internat. orgns., 1979—; mem. Am. Rocket Soc.'s Space Law and Sociology Com., 1959-62; mem. adv. panel Office Gen. Counsel, NASA, 1971; adviser outer space del. U.S. Mission to UN Working Group on Direct Broadcast Satellites, 1973-75, legal subcom., 1976; observer UN Conf. Exploration and Peaceful Uses of Outer Space, Vienna, 1982; lectr. Nat. Acad. Sci., 1973, U.S. CSC, Exec. Seminar Center, Oak Ridge, 1973, 74, 75, 76, 78; ednl. counselor Purdue U., 1974; lectr. Inst. Air and Space Law McGill U., 1975, Inter Am. Def. Coll., 1977, 78; ofcl. observer legal subcom. UN Com. Peaceful Uses of Outer Space, 1977, 78, 79, 80; mem. panel on solar power for satellites and U.S. space policy Office Tech. Assessment, 1979-80. Pres., Theodore Von Karman Meml. Found., 1973—; mem. alumni council Swarthmore Coll., 1976-79. Rockefeller Found. scholar-in-residence, Bellagio, Italy, 1976. Recipient Andrew G. Haley gold medal Internat. Inst. Space Law, 1968; Wilton Park fellow, Eng., 1968. Mem. LWV (chmn. study groups housing, welfare in D.C., 1937-38, mem. tech. com. on law and sociology task force on legal aspects 1979—), AIAA (tech. com. on legal aspects of aeros. and astronautics 1980—), World Peace Through Law Center, Am. Soc. Internat. Law, Am. Astronautical Soc., Lamar Soc. Internat. Law, Internat. Studies Assn., Internat. Acad. Astronautics (trustee 1982-85), Internat. Law Assn., Phi Beta Kappa, Delta Sigma Rho, Kappa Alpha Theta. Episcopalian. Author: Atomic Power: Issues Before Congress, 1946; (with Bernard Brodie) The Atomic Bomb and the Armed Services, 1947; History of United States Military Policy on Reserve Forces, 1775-1957, 1957; Guided Missiles in Foreign Countries, 1957; The Community of Law and Science, 1958; United Nations Ad hoc Committee on Peaceful Uses of Outer Space, 1959; Satellites: A Force for World Peace, World Security and the Peaceful Uses of Outer Space, 1960; International Cooperation and Organization for Outer Space, 1965; Space Treaty Proposals by the United States and U.S.S.R., 1966; Treaty on Principles Governing the Activities of States in the Exploration and Use of Outer Space, Including the Moon and Other Celestial Bodies: Analysis and Background Data, 1967; Remote Sensing of the Earth by Satellites: Legal Problems and Issues, 1973, 75; The Future of Space Law, 1976; Consensus as a Basis for International Space Cooperation, 1977; others; editor: Space Law Symposium, 1958; The Legal Problems of Space Exploration, 1961; United States International Space Programs, 1965; International Cooperation in Outer Space: A Symposium, 1972; The Role of the United Nations in Earth Resources Satellites, 1972; Settlement of Space Law Disputes, 1980; Perspectives of Space Law, 1981; Conditions for Success of International Space Institutions, 1982; Space Manufacturing, 1981; U.S. Space Policy and Programs, 1982; Expanding Article IV of 1967 Space Treaty, 1982; History and Development of Space Law, 1982; asso. editor Advances in Earth Oriented Applications of Space Tech., 1978—; mem. editorial adv. bd. Jour. Space Law, U. Miss. Law Sch., Space Communication and Broadcasting. Home: 4612 29th Pl NW Washington DC 20008

GALLOWAY, PATRICIA DENESE, civil engr.; b. Lexington, Ky., June 14, 1957; d. John Howard and Lou Maudine (Jones) Frisby; B.S. in civil engring., Purdue U., 1978; postgrad. N.Y. Inst. Tech., 1983—; m. Drew Alan Galloway, May 20, 1978. Project engr., inspector CH2M Hill, Milw., 1978-79, master program scheduler, 1979-81; sr. cons. Nielsen-Wurster Group, N.Y.C., 1981—; lectr. Columbia U. Mem. Soc. Women Engrs., Project Mgmt. Inst., ASCE, Sigma Kappa. Club: Toastmasters. Office: 275 Madison Ave New York NY 10016

GALOSY, JULIA REID, training ofcl.; b. Chgo., Nov. 7, 1948; d. Paul C. and Kathryn (Lambrechts) Reid; B.A., W.Wash. U., 1970; M.Ed., U. N.C., 1974, Ph.D., 1978. Project mgr., U. N.C., 1971-74; pvt. practice cons. field of tng., 1974-78; project mgr. tng. and devel. J.C. Penney Co., N.Y.C., 1978-80; dir. tng. and mgmt. devel. Dun & Bradstreet, N.Y.C., 1980—; adj. prof. N.Y.U.; devel. cons. Mem. Am. Soc. Tng. and Devel., Fgn. Policy Assn. Co-author: Basic Course for Residential Child Care Workers, 1978; contbr. articles to publs. in field. Office: 99 Church St New York NY 10007

GALT, FLORENCE TAYLOR, nurse; b. Little Rock, Ark., Sept. 22, 1918; d. Charles Edward and Lena Coffer Taylor; R.N., Washington U., 1940; m. Charles E. Galt, Jr., July 18, 1942 (div. 1958); children—Elizabeth Anne, Charles E., Mary Louise. Pvt. duty nurse, St. Louis, 1940-41; stewardess Am. Airlines, 1941-45; staff nurse Carlsbad (N.Mex.) Regional Med Center, 1970-77, Guadalupe Med. Center, Carlsbad, 1977-82. Pres. Eddy County Women's Republican Club, 1955, Eddy County Women's Med. Aux., 1957-58; chmn. home nursing ARC, 1958; pres. parents council Roosevelt Sch., 1959; state chmn. Am. Med. Edn., 1959; pres. Carlsbad Women's Club, 1962-63; charter mem. Carlsbad Area Art Assn.; mem. LWV of N.Mex.; active Campfire Girls Am., 1956-61. Republican. Presbyterian. Clubs: Carlsbad Horsemen's Assn. (sec. 1962-63), Chpt. Y, PEO. Home: 601 W Orchard Ln Carlsbad NM 88220

GALVIN, KATHLEEN MALONE, educator; b. N.Y.C., Feb. 9, 1943; d. James Robert and Helen (Sullivan) G.; B.S., Fordham U., 1964; M.A., Northwestern U., 1965, 80, Ph.D., 1968; m. Charles A. Wilkinson, June 19, 1973; children—Matthew, Katherine, Kara. Tchr. speech Evanston (Ill.) Twp. High Sch., 1967-68; mem. faculty Northwestern U., 1968—, prof. communication edn., 1980—, chmn. speech edn. dept., 1971—; workshop leader, cons. in field. Mem. Speech Communication Assn., Nat. Council Family Relations, Assn. Tchr. Edn., Central States Speech Assn. (Outstanding Young Tchr. award 1973). Co-author: Person to Person: An Introduction to Speech Communication, rev. edit., 1978; Growing Together: Classroom Communication, 1976; Family Communication: Cohesion and Change, 1982. Editor workshop series. Contbr. articles to profl. jours. Office: 6 Harris Hall Northwestern U Evanston IL 60201

GALVIN, MARYANNE, psychologist, educator; b. Worcester, Mass., Mar. 6, 1954; d. Stephen F. and Bernadette M. (McGinn) Galvin; B.S., Wheelock Coll., 1976; M.Ed. (Mass. Fedn. of Women's Clubs fellow), U. Mass., Amherst, 1978, Ed.D., 1980. Psychologist, Wellesley (Mass.) Public Sch., 1980-81, U. Mass. Med. Sch., Worcester, 1980-81; asst. prof. U. N.H., Durham, 1981—; pvt. practice psychology, Durham, 1981—. Cert. of commendation UN, 1975. Mem. Personnel and Guidance Assn., Am. Psychol. Assn., Mass. Assn. for the Advancement of Individual Potential, Mass. Psychol. Assn. Roman Catholic. Club: New Eng. Masters Competitive Swim. Contbr. articles on psychology to profl. jours. Office: Morrill Hall U N H Durham NH 03824

GAMAN, RACHEL SIMMI, social worker; b. Chgo., July 14, 1949; d. Garrison George and Aldythe Phyllis (Wood) G.; student Mount San Antonio Coll., 1967-69, Calif. State U., Fullerton, 1969-70; B.S., Calif. Poly. U., 1973; M.S.W., U. So. Calif., 1975; 1 adopted dau., Ronda Renee. Dir. social rehab. Met. Psychiat. Services, Los Angeles, 1975-76; dir. rehab. services Continuity of Care Home Health Agy., Los Angeles, 1976; med. social worker Kern Med. Center, Bakersfield, Calif., 1976-78; coordinator geriatric services Kern View Community Mental Health Center, Bakersfield, 1978-80; dir. social services Greater Bakersfield Meml. Hosp., 1980—; tchr. U. Calif. Santa Barbara Extension Program,

Chapman Coll., Bakersfield Coll., 1978—; cons. Hilltop Convalescent Hosp., Colonial Convalescent Hosp., 1979—, Parkview Julian Convalescent Hosp., Parkview Real Convalescent Hosp., 1980—, Westchester Rehab. Agy., 1981—; pvt. practice psychotherapy, Bakersfield, 1979—. Lic. clin. social worker, Calif. Mem. Nat. Assn. Social Workers, Med. Social Workers Kern County, Coordinating Council Sr. Services, Am. Cancer Soc. (service com., profl. edn. com.), Direct Alcohol Service Com. Democrat. Jewish. Club: Quota (dir.). Home: 1921 Pacific Dr Bakersfield CA 93305 Office: 420 34th St Bakersfield CA 93301

GAMBEE, ELEANOR BROWN, writer, civic worker; b. N.Y.C., Apr. 10, 1904; d. Robert Rankins and Elizabeth (Turner) Brown; A.B., Vassar Coll., 1925; postgrad. Columbia U., 1926; m. A. Sumner Gambee, June 1, 1928; children—Sumner Brown, Craig, Eleanor Fay, Robert Rankin. Publicity chmn. Maternal Health Center Bergen County, Englewood, N.J., 1934-38; v.p., mem. bd. Planned Parenthood Assn. Bergen County, Englewood, 1938-46; publicity chmn. No. Valley chpt. ARC, 1939-43; 1st v.p. Social Service Fedn. Englewood, 1948-52; editorial bd. Vassar Alumnae Mag., 1954-55; trustee Dwight Sch., Englewood, 1957-63; freelance writer, lectr., 1961—; mem. Englewood Hosp. Devel. Com., 1965—; instr. N.Y. Bot. Garden, 1967-74, mem. garden council, 1970—, chmn. chemurgic garden, 1977—; publs. com. Hort. Soc. N.Y., 1972-75; pres. Herb Soc. Am., 1978-80; cons. Readers Digest Guide to Gardening, 1978. Recipient Garden Club Am. Hort. award, 1962, award of Merit, 1979; Disting. Service award N.Y. Bot. Garden, 1980. Contbr. articles to hort. publs. Home: 220 Speer Ave Englewood NJ 07631

GAMBLE, PATRICIA P., savs. and loan exec.; b. Seattle, Nov. 13, 1930; d. Jay Salisbury and Prilla Clementine (Foster) Platt; student Savs. and Loan Inst.; m. Roy Lloyd Gamble, Sept. 15, 1950; children—Ralph Lloyd, Howard M. Payroll clk. S.H. Kress & Co., Seattle, 1948-49; cashier-bookkeeper Am. News Co., Seattle, 1949-51, 52-53; dining room cashier Moana Hotel, Honolulu, 1951-52; teller Ballard Fed. Savs. & Loan Assn., Seattle, 1954-55; teller, acctg. clk., loan service dept. mgr. Fidelity Savs. & Loan, Seattle, 1955-65; with Shoreline Savs. Assn., Seattle, 1965-66; asst. mgr. mortgage loan dept. Queen City Savs. and Loan Assn., Seattle, 1966-74; v.p., corp. sec., mgr. home office Family Savs. & Loan Assn., Seattle, 1966—. Mem. Nat. Assn. Profl. Mortgage Women, Nat. Assn. Am. Bus. Women, Puget Sound Assn. Profl. Mortgage Women, Seattle Assn. Profl. Mortgage Women. Office: 1100 Aurora Village Plaza N Seattle WA 98133

GAMBRELL, SARAH BELK, retail exec.; b. Charlotte, N.C., Apr. 12, 1918; d. William Henry and Mary (Irwin) Belk; B.A., Sweet Briar Coll., 1939; D. Humanities, Erskine Coll., 1970; m. Charles Gambrell; 1 dau., Sarah Belk. Vice pres., dir. Belk Stores, various locations, 1947—, pres. 32 stores. Bd. overseers and bd. dirs. Sweet Briar (Va.) Coll.; trustee Princeton (N.J.) Theol. Sem., Johnson C. Smith U., Charlotte, N.C.; trustee nat. bd. YWCA; bd. dirs. YWCA, N.Y.C. and Charlotte, N.C., Women's Bible Soc. N.Y., Parkinson's Disease Found., N.Y.C.; hon. trustee Cancer Research Inst., N.Y.C. Mem. The Fashion Group, Inc., Jr. League N.Y.C., Nat. Soc. Colonial Dames, D.A.R. Presbyterian. Home: 580 Park Ave New York NY 10018 also 300 Cherokee Rd Charlotte NC 28207 Office: 111 W 40th St New York NY 10018 Also PO Box 2727 Charlotte NC 28234

GAMESTER, SHARON VIRGINIA, med. technologist; b. Winchester, Ind., Feb. 18, 1941; d. John Earl and Lillymae (Matteson) Hardesty; M.T., Ball State Tchrs. Coll., 1962; m. Larry Eugene Gamester, Jan. 1, 1963. Med. technologist, blood bank Ball Meml. Hosp., Muncie, Ind., 1962-67; rotating med. technologist Jay County Hosp., Portland, Ind., 1967-68; rotating med. technologist Reid Meml. Hosp., Richmond, Ind., 1969-71, dept. chemistry, 1971-77; med. technologist Doctor C. Deckard, Lynn, Ind., 1972; sr. med. technologist, float technician Kino Community Hosp., Tucson, 1978—; co-owner, operator Gamester's Abbattoir, 1963-68, Gamester Restaurant, 1965-74, Pine Lane Acres, 1978—, Pine Lane Arabians, 1970—. Mem. Am. Soc. Clin. Pathology (cert. med. technologist), Half Arabian Assn. Ariz. Club: Order Eastern Star. Home: 4510 N Fairview St Tucson AZ 85705

GAMMO, MARY LOU CHANDLER, educator; b. Johnson City, Tenn., Feb. 23, 1934; d. Claud Earl and Annie Eller (Norman) Chandler; B.S., East Tenn. State U., 1956; M.B.A., Auburn U., 1959; m. Frank Joseph Gammo, Feb. 1963 (div. 1970); 1 dau., Melanie Patricia. Instr., Auburn (Ala.) U., 1956-59; systems analyst EDP div. RCA, Cherry Hill, N.J., 1959-63; tchr. math. Mt. Hebron Jr. High Sch., Upper Montclair, N.J., 1963-65; tchr. acctg. Columbia High Sch., South Orange, N.J., 1965-66; prof. acctg. East Tenn. State U., Johnson City, 1966—; cons. computer systems. C.P.A., Tenn. Mem. Am. Inst. C.P.A.s (computer edn. com., EDP auditing curriculum task force). Democrat. Baptist. Home: 815 E Watauga Ave Johnson City TN 37601 Office: PO Box 23800A East Tenn State U Johnson City TN 37601

GANDY, KIM ALLISON, lawyer; b. Shreveport, Jan. 25, 1954; d. Alfred K. and Roma Rae (Young) Gandy; B.S., La. Tech. U., 1973; J.D., Loyola U., New Orleans, 1978. Mgr., statistician div. revenue S.Central Bell Telephone Co., 1973-77; student practitioner Loyola U. Law Clinic, 1977-78; bd. dirs. La. State NOW, 1974-75, treas., 1975-77, pres., 1978-81; treas. E.R.A. United Coalition La., 1977-78; admitted to La. bar, 1978; sr. asst. dist. atty. Orleans Parish, La., 1978-79; practice law, New Orleans, 1979—. Bd. dirs. Women's Lobby Network, 1980—; del. La. State Democratic Conv., 1980, 82, chmn. Orleans Parish del., 1982. Recipient award Loyola U. Law Sch. Alumni Assn., 1976; award Am. Jurisprudence Soc., 1976, 77; Milton Sheen award, 1978. Mem. Am. Bar Assn., Am. Trial Lawyers Assn., La. Trial Lawyers Assn., La. Assn. Women Attys., Assn. Women Law Students (pres. 1977-78), Common Cause, ACLU, Nat. Women's Polit. Caucus, New Orleans Bus. and Profl. Women, Delta Theta Phi (pres. 1977-78; Scholarship key 1977). Mem. bd. Loyola U. Law Rev., 1976-78. Address: 5509 Coliseum St New Orleans LA 70115

GANDY, SHARON GAYLE, home economist; b. Cairo, Ga., Feb. 19, 1953; d. Hugh Irwin and Maxine (Andrews) G.; student Abraham Baldwin Agr. Coll., 1971-72; B.S., U. Ga., 1975, M.Ed., 1976; cert. in mgmt. Women's Program in Mgmt., U. Balt., 1981, postgrad. in bus. adminstrn., 1981—; m. Donald Kimball Tag, Jr., Aug. 1, 1981. Instr. consumer edn. Dalton (Ga.) Vocat. Sch. Health Occupations, 1974-76; home economist, residential energy services customer edn. rep. Ga. Power Co., Gainesville, 1976-79; regional edn. programs specialist, public relations and consumer info. services Montgomery Ward & Co., Balt., 1979-80; freelance cons., 1980-81; dir., community specialist Harford County YWCA, Bel Air, Md., 1981—; dir. GanTag Assos., mgmt. tng. and communication cons., 1981—; resident coordinator Future Women Seminars, 1981—. Recipient N.E. Ga. Outstanding Home Economist in Bus. award, 1979, Outstanding Accomplishment in Customer Edn. award, 1979, Internat. Youth in Achievement award, 1980. Mem. Am. Home Econs. Assn., Md. Home Econs. Assn. (by-laws com. 1979-80, family econs. chmn., time mgmt. seminar chmn. and exec. bd. 1980-82, career seminar 1982-83), Ga. Home Econs. Assn. (pub. relations chmn. 1974-76, vice chmn., newsletter editor 1977-77, chmn.-elect, program chmn. 1977-78, area chmn. 1978-79, exec. bd. 1978-79), Home Economists in Bus. (ways and means chmn. 1980-81), Elec. Women's Round Table, Soc. Consumer Affairs Profls. in Bus., Balt. Met. Area Assn. Home Economists (pres. 1981-83), Balt. Exec. Women's Network, Nat. Assn. Female Execs., Harford Council Community Services, Kappa Delta Pi. Contbr. articles to profl. jours. Home: 641 Burlington Ct Edgewood MD 21040

GANG, MARJORIE PAUL, advt. agy. exec.; b. New Kensington, Pa., May 31, 1935; d. August Gerard and Vera Ione (Mahaffey) Canne; student U. Pa., 1952-53, U. Tex., 1953-55; m. Stuart W. Gang, Aug. 14, 1979; children by previous marriage—Linda Sue Paul, David William Paul. Exec. asst. to bd. dirs. Decathlon Athletic Club, Bloomington, Minn., 1969-71; edit. promotion mgr. Webb Publishing Co., St. Paul, 1971-73; acct. exec. Jensen Printing Co., Mpls., 1973-74; savers club dir. Minn. Fed. Savs. and Loan, St. Paul, 1974-76; v.p. Arrowhead Advt. Agy., St. Paul, 1976-80, Stu Gang & Assos., 1980—. Served with USAF, 1953-55. Mem. Advt. Fedn. Minn., Twin Cities Litho Club. Home: 1355 Colonial Dr Roseville MN 55113 Office: 355 Minnesota St Saint Paul MN 55101

GANN, PAMELA BROOKS, lawyer; b. Monroe, N.C., Nov. 2, 1948; d. Levi James and Virginia Willodene (Brooks) G.; A.B. U. N.C., Chapel Hill, 1970; J.D., Duke U., 1973; m. William W. Van Alstyne, Jan. 15, 1981; stepchildren—Marshall, Allyn, Lisa Van Alstyne. Assoc. firm King & Spalding, Atlanta, 1973, Fleming, Robinson & Bradshaw, N.C., 1973-75; asst. prof. law Duke U., Durham, N.C., 1975-78, assoc. prof., 1978-81, prof., 1981—; mem. vis. faculty U. Mich., 1977, Washington U., St. Louis, 1977, U. Colo., summer 1980. U. Va., fall 1980, U. San Diego, summer 1981; apptd. by U.S. Dist. Ct. for D.C. as ind. dir. for 3 publicly held corps., 1979. Mem. ABA, N.C. Bar Assn., Am. Law Inst., Internat. Fiscal Assn., Order of Coif, Phi Beta Kappa. Author: (with D. Kahn) Corporate Taxation and Taxation of Partnerships and Partners, 1979; contbr. articles to profl. jours. Home: 3712 Darwin Rd Durham NC 27707 Office: Sch Law Duke U Durham NC 27706

GANNON, SISTER, ANN IDA, educator, former coll. pres.; b. Chgo., 1915; d. George and Hanna (Murphy) Gannon; A.B., Clarke Coll., 1941; A.M., Loyola U., Chgo., 1948, LL.D., 1970; Ph.D., St. Louis U., 1952; Litt.D., DePaul U., 1972; L.H.D., Lincoln Coll., 1965, Columbia Coll., 1969, Luther Coll., 1969, Marycrest Coll., 1972, Ursuline Coll., 1972, Spertus Coll. Judaica, 1974, Holy Cross Coll., 1974; hon. degrees Rosary Coll., 1975, St. Ambrose Coll., 1975, St. Leo Coll., 1976, Mt. St. Joseph Coll., 1976, Stritch Coll., 1976, Stonehill Coll., 1976, Elmhurst Coll., 1977, Manchester Coll., 1977, Marymount Coll., 1977, Governor's State U., 1979, Seattle U., 1981. Mem. Sisters of Charity; tchr. English, St. Mary's High Sch., Chgo., 1941-47; residence, study abroad, 1951; chmn. philosophy dept. Mundelein Coll., 1951-57, pres., 1957-75, mem. faculty philosophy dept., 1975—; dir. NICOR, SFN, ICM. Mem. Adv. Bd. Sec. Navy, 1975-80, Chgo. Police Bd., 1979—; bd. dirs. Am. Council on Edn., 1971-75, chmn., 1973—; nat. bd. dirs. Girl Scouts U.S.A. 1966-74, nat. adv. bd., 1976—; trustee St. Louis U., 1974—, Ursuline Coll., St. Michael Coll.; bd. dirs. Newberry Library, 1976—, WTTW Pub. TV, 1976—, Sears Roebuck Found.; mem. Gannon-Proctor Commn. (Ill. gov.'s commn. on equality for women), 1982—. Recipient Laetare medal, 1975; LaSallian award, 1975; Aquinas award, 1976; Chgo. Assn. Commerce and Industry award, 1976. Mem. Am. Cath. Philos. Assn. (exec. council 1953-56), Am. Colls. (dir. 1965—, chmn. 1969-70), Religious Edn. Assn. Am. (pres. 1973, chmn. bd. 1975-78), N. Central Assn. (commn. on colls. and univs. 1971-78, chmn. exec. bd. 1975-77, dir.), Assn. Governing Bds. Colls. and Univs. (dir. 1979—), AAUW, Metaphys. Soc. Contbr. articles philos. jours. Address: 6363 Sheridan Rd Chicago IL 60660

GANNON, ANNE DURNEY, banker; b. Bethlehem, Pa., May 15, 1952; d. Joseph J. and Barbara J. (Graveline) Durney; B.A. in Polit. Sci. and History, Rosemont Coll., 1974; postgrad. in bus. adminstrn. Temple U., 1974-77, Stonier Grad. Sch. Banking, Rutgers U., 1977-80; m. Joseph H. Gannon, Oct. 11, 1980. Mut. fund adminstr. Provident Nat. Bank, Phila., 1974-76, mgr. fed. funds dept., 1976—, head Eurodollar trader Nassau br., 1980—. Mem. Greater Phila. Money Marketeers, Rosemont Coll. Alumnae Assn. (dir. and treas. 1978-80). Republican. Roman Catholic. Club: Cynwyd (Pa.). Home: 919 Old Manoa Rd Penfield Downs PA 19083 Office: 1632 Chestnut St Philadelphia PA 19101

GANNON, LILLIAN J., pub. co. exec.; b. Bridgeport, Conn., Apr. 7, 1921; d. Jack B. and Betty Brown; student Hunter Coll., 1938-42. Bus. mgr. Interior design Mag., N.Y.C., 1948-52; treas. Graham Gannon Advt. Co., Inc., 1953-59; bus. mgr. Contract Mag., N.Y.C., 1960-63; bus. mgr. Am. Sports Pub. Co., Inc., N.Y.C., 1963-64; treas. controller Select Publs., Inc., N.Y.C., 1964-70; asst. to pres. Media Networks, Inc., N.Y.C., 1971-72, dir. adminstrv. services, 1973-79, bus. mgr., 1979-81; controller Columbia Communications Inc., N.Y.C., 1981—. Mem. Am. Soc. Personnel Adminstrn., Internat. Assn. Personnel Women, Adminstrv. Mgmt. Soc. Office: 600 3d Ave New York NY 10016 also 370 Lexington Ave New York NY 10017

GANT, CYNTHIA, educator; b. Shreveport, La., Dec. 27, 1954; B.A. in English and Social Studies cum laude, La. Tech. U., 1976; M.Ed. in Adminstrn. and Supervision, U., 1981; postgrad. La. State U., 1981—. Tchr. English and social studies, Green Oaks High Sch., Caddo Parish Sch. Bd., Shreveport, La., 1976—, softball coach, asst. track coach, dir. Green Oaks Dance Troupe and Highsteppers, 1977-81, Green Oaks Flag Corps, 1977-82. Active PTA, Cooper Rd. Civic Club, Citizen Study Com. City-Parish Govts.; asst. recreation dir. Caddo Community Action Agy., 1979-80; first female police aux. officer Shreveport Civil Def., 1980; youth dir. Willow Chute Baptist Ch., 1980-81, mem. women's council. Recipient civic and profl. awards including Tchr. of Distinction, 1977-78, Educator of Year, Shreveport Times, 1978-79, Outstanding La. Educator, 1981, Dr. Mitchell Williams curriculum award, 1981. Mem. NEA, La. Edn. Assn., Caddo Edn. Assn. (faculty rep., service awards, 1980-82), Caddo Council Tchrs. of English, Sigma Tau Delta, Zeta Phi Beta. Address: 3004 Stafford St Shreveport LA 71107

GANT, CYNTHIA ELEANOR, microbiologist; b. Detroit, Oct. 23, 1948; d. Harold William and Mildred (Phillips) Gant; B.S., Tex. Women's U., 1970, M.S., 1980; M.T., Terrell's Labs. Sch. Med. Tech., 1971. Registered med. technologist All Saints Hosp., Ft. Worth, 1971-74, Baylor Med. Center, Dallas, 1974-75; teaching asst. Tex. Women's U., Denton, 1975-78; med. technologist Med. Plaza Hosp., Ft. Worth, Tex., 1976; asst. microbiologist Abbott Lab., Diagnostic Div., Dallas, 1976-78; quality control technician Miller Brewing Co., Ft. Worth, 1978—. Recipient Award for Outstanding Achievements in the Community, Sickle Cell Anemia Assn. of Tex., 1980. Mem. Soc. Indsl. Microbiology, Am. Soc. Microbiology, Am. Soc. Clin. Pathologists, Zeta Phi Beta. Club: Order Eastern Star. Contbr. articles to profl. jours. Home: PO Box 50335 Fort Worth TX 76105 Office: 6600 Will Rogers Blvd Fort Worth TX 76101

GANTER, GRACE, social worker, educator; b. Pitts., July 21, 1922; d. Frank V. and Agnes (Green) G.; B.S.W., U. Pitts., 1945, M.S.W., 1948; D.S.W., Case-Western Res U., 1961. Social worker, Chgo., 1948-50, Cleve., 1950-53, Cleve. Child Guidance Center, 1953-64; assoc. prof. social work SUNY, Buffalo, 1964-66, Smith Coll. Sch. Social Work, Northampton, Mass., 1966-71; prof. social work Sch. Social Adminstrn., Temple U., Phila., 1971—; regional chmn. Am. Psychiat. Clinics for Children, 1962; cons. Family Ct., Phila. 1972-76. NIMH grantee, 1960-63. Fellow Am. Orthopsychiat. Assn., Nat. Assn. Social Workers, Council on Social Work Edn., Common Cause. Author: Retrieval from Limbo, 2d edit., 1971; Human Behavior and the Social Environment, 1980. Home: 7 Decatur Rd Havertown PA 19083 Office: Sch Social Adminstrn Temple U 13th and Columbia Sts Philadelphia PA 19122

GANTMAN, CAROL ANN, psychologist; b. Phila., Apr. 3, 1949; d. Jack A. and Syliva (Liedman) G.; B.S., B.A., U. Pa., 1970; M.A., Bryn Mawr Coll. (grantee, fellow), 1972, Ph.D. (dept.fellow), 1976. Psychologist, Changing Times Center, Community Mental Health Center, Havertown, Pa., 1972-76; sr. staff psychologist Friends Hosp., Phila., 1976—; clin. asst. prof. Hahnemann Med. Coll., Phila., 1978—; pvt. practice psychology, 1976—; vol. psychologist Human Services Center, Phila., 1976-80, also bd. dirs. Mem. leadership devel. com. Phila. Jewish Fedn., 1974—, chmn. membership, 1978-79, chmn. tng. program, 1979. Recipient Feinstein Young Leadership award, 1979. Mem. Am. Psychol. Assn., Assn. Women in Psychology, Am. Group Psychotherapy Assn., Phila. Soc. Clin. Psychologists, Delaware Valley Group Psychotherapy Assn. Home: 612 Carpenter Ln Philadelphia PA 19119 Office: 65B Bldg Suite 206 1 Belmont Ave Bala Cynwyd PA 19004

GANZHORN, BETTY JANE, psychologist, educator; b. Ann Arbor, Mich., Oct. 16, 1921; d. Edwin Carl and Margaret (Flowers) G.; B.S., U. Mich., 1946, M.A., 1949, Ph.D., 1952. Psychometrist, U. Ill., Chgo., 1949-50; asst. prof. psychology, counselor Ball State Tchrs. Coll., Muncie, Ind., (now Ball State U.), 1952-55, assoc. prof., counselor, 1955-61, prof., 1961—; cons. pub. schs., Muncie, 1952-58. Mem. Delaware County Mental Health Bd., 1957-58. Mem. Am. Psychol. Assn., Midwest Psychol. Assn., Ind. Psychol. Assn., AAUP, AAAS, Am. Personnel and Guidance Assn. Contbr. articles to profl. jours. Home: 4204 W Beechwood Ave Muncie IN 47304

GARBATY, MARIE LOUISE, art collector, patron of arts; b. Berlin, Ger., Mar. 9, 1910; widowed. Patron, Met. Opera, N.Y.C. State Opera; patron, hon. mem. Allentown (Pa.) Art Mus.; mem. N.Y.C. Opera Guild; fellow in perpetuity Met. Mus. Art; life fellow Mus. Fine Arts, Boston; internat. centennial patron Mus. Fine Arts, Boston; benefactor, life mem. Chrysler Mus., Norfolk, Va.; assoc. mem. Solomon Guggenheim Mus., N.Y.C., co-founder Am. Shakespeare Festival Theater, Stratford, Conn.; friend N.Y.C. Library; mem. Am. Fedn. Art, China Inst. Am. Inc., N.Y.C., Asia Soc., N.Y.C., Art Mus., Palm Beach, Fla.; donations numerous museums, libraries, profl. socs., including Met. Mus. Art, N.Y.C., U. Wash., Cooper Union Mus., Boston U. Library, Calif. State Coll. Library, Fullerton, Yale U. Library, Hoover Library, Stanford U., Library of Congress, Art Inst., Chgo., Carnegie Inst. Art, others. Address: 923 5th Ave New York NY 10021

GARBETT, ROSEMARY SCHNEIDER, restauranteur; b. Houston, July 9, 1935; d. Rudolph George and Lorena (Boenker) Schneider; m. Thomas M. Garbett Jr., Jan. 30, 1954 (dec. 1976); children—Susan Garbett Kendrick, Thomas M., Katherine A. Michael S. Owner, mgr. Los Tios Mexican Restaurants, Inc., Houston, 1970—, chief exec. officer, 1976—; dir. Great So. Bank, Houston, 1978—Westchase Corp., Houston, 1980—. Bd. dirs. Greater Houston Conv. and Visitors Council, 1979—, Leukemia Soc., Houston, 1980—, Kidney Found., Houston, 1980-82. Recipient Outstanding Restauranteur award City of Houston, 1980-81. Mem. Houston Restaurant Assn. (pres. 1982-83, dir. 1980-82), Tex. Restaurant Assn. (dir. 1982-83). Clubs: Warwick, Maxim, Univ., Bob Smith Yacht (charter mem.), Houston Livestock and Rodeo Show (life). Home: 7810 High Star St Houston TX 77036 Office: 10550 Westpark Houston TX 77042

GARBO, GRETA, actress; b. Stockholm, Sweden, Sept. 18, 1905; came to U.S., 1925, naturalized, 1951; d. Sven and Louvisa Gustaffson; ed. Royal Dramatic Acad., Stockholm. Won her first film recognition in Goesta Berling, 1924, through work in Royal Acad.; came to U.S. and appeared in The Temptress, 1926, The Torrent, 1926, Love, 1927, Flesh and the Devil, 1927, Anna Christie, 1930, Susan Lenox, 1931, Mata Hari, 1931, Grand Hotel, 1932, As You Desire Me, 1932, Queen Christina, 1933, The Painted Veil, Anna Karenina, 1935, Camille, 1936, Conquest, 1937, Ninotchka, 1939, Two Faced Woman, 1941. Recipient Spl. Acad. award, 1954. *

GARCIA, GAYE LAMAR, theatre dir.; b. Colorado Springs, Colo., Oct. 19, 1951; d. Bernard Johnston and Mary Ellen (Hardy) Lamar; B.A., U. Colo., 1973, M.A., 1978; postgrad. in ednl. adminstrn. U. Denver; m. Rudolph Angelo Garcia, Aug. 26, 1976. Communications, group dynamics instr., Denver area, 1972-73; with Denver Public Sch. System, 1973—, arts mgmt./theatre dir., 1973—. Vol., Colo. Arts and Humanities Council as lectr., workshop coordinator, 1974-75. Cert. bicultural/bilingual instr. Mem. Am. Theatre Assn., Women in Theatre, Nat. Council Tchrs. English, Nat. Assn. Female Execs. Author: Celebration (rock musical), 1979; dir., designer, producer profl. and ednl. theatrical prodns. including Godspell, 1974, Guys and Dolls, 1975, My Fair Lady, 1976, Carousel, 1977, Music Man, 1978, Celebration!, 1979, Annie Get Your Gun, 1980, Jesus Christ Superstar, 1982. Home: 18985 E Kent Circle Aurora CO 80013 Office: PO Box 12013 Denver CO 80212

GARCIA, HENEDINA CRUZ, physician; b. Manila, May 14, 1941; d. Nazario Luis and Remedios Cruz; M.D., Manila Central U., 1964; m. Jose Golez Garcia, May 14, 1967; children—Geraldine, Dinamarie. Physician, med. dir. Peekskill (N.Y.) Area Health Care Center; assoc. attending physician Peekskill Community Hosp. Mem. Women's Med. Assn., Geriatric Med. Assn., Am. Soc. Internal Medicine. Roman Catholic. Office: 1037 Main St Peekskill NY 10566

GARCIA, JOSEFINA MARGARITA, dancer, nurse, educator; b. Mascota, Jalisco, Mex., May 2, 1906; came to U.S., 1923, naturalized, 1944; d. Manuel Garcia Perez and Margarita (Garcia) Flores; diploma Nat. Coll., Kansas City, Mo., 1933; tchrs. cert. State Tchrs. Coll., Queretaro, Mex., 1935; R.N., Bethany Hosp. Sch. Nursing, 1939; diploma in psychiat. nursing Inst. of Living, Hartford, Conn., 1941; B.S., Tchrs. Coll., Columbia U., 1943, M.A. in Health and Phys. Edn., 1945; Ph.D. in Dance and Related Arts, Tex. Woman's U., 1958. Elem. tchr. Meth. Normal Sch., Puebla, Mex., 1934-36; dir. religious edn., nurse, coordinator phys. edn. George O. Robinson Sch., San Juan, P.R., 1939-40; psychiat. nurse Psychiat. div. N.Y. Okla. White Plains, 1941-43; tchr. health Poly. Inst., San German, P.R., 1943-44; charge corrective gymnastics Hosp. for Spl. Surgery, N.Y.C., 1944-45; nurse Bellevue Hosp., N.Y.C., 1945-50; tchr., performer La Meri's Ethnologic Center, N.Y.C., 1945-47; lectr., dancer Pearl Buck's East and West Assn., 1947-49; artist, tchr., nurse Jacob's Pillow U. of Dance, Lee, Mass., summers 1949-55; pvt. duty nurse Harkness Pavillion, N.Y.C., 1952-55; supr. psychiat. div. Parkland Meml. Hosp., Dallas, 1956-58; grad. asst. in dance Tex. Woman's U., Denton, 1956-58; chmn. health, phys. edn. and recreation dept. Okla. Coll. for Women, Chickasha, 1958-63 (on leave), instr., 1934-36, 39-40, prof., 1963-64; vis. prof. edn. Miami U., Coral Gables, Fla., 1963-64; dir. dance in dept. health and phys. edn., prof. phys. edn. Madison Coll., Harrisonburg, Va., 1964-67; tchr. English as secondary lang., bilingual edn. N.Y.C. Bd. Edn.; part-time staff Grady Meml. Hosp. Chickasha, 1962-63; numerous dance recitals and workshops, 1940—; tchr. Mexican and Latin Am. dance Tina Ramirez Dance Studio, N.Y.C.; cons. Sacred Dance Guild; choreographer on Mexican themes Alliance Latin Am. Arts, summers 1973-74; artist-in-residence Spelman Coll., Atlanta, 1978-79; prof. geriatric health and exercises Williams Residence, N.Y.C. Vol., Channel 13 Public TV; founder Center for Internat. Security Studies; mem. Am. Security Council. Fellow AAHPER; mem. Am. Asso., N.Y. State (dir.) nurses assns., Nat. So., Va. assns. phys. edn. coll. women, ANTA, Okla. Okla. Assn., Va. Assn. Health, Phys. Edn. and Recreation (chmn. 1962-63), AAUW, Chickasha Bus. and Profl. Women's Club (past chmn. internat. relations com.), Nat. Dance Tchrs. Guild, Nat. Council Arts in Edn., Mus. Natural History, Dance Notation Bur., Internat. Platform

Assn., Pan Am. Women's Assn. (dir. 1967—, v.p.), Dance Film Library Assn. (dir. 1967—), Film Soc. (dir.), Profl. Dance Tchrs. Assn., Nat. Council Sr. Citizens, Met. Opera Guild, Cooper-Hewitt Mus., Nat. Geog. Soc., N.Y. YWCA, Kappa Delta Pi, Phi Sigma Iota. Contbr. articles on dance to profl. publs., Groliers Ency., Richards Ency. Home: 720 West End Ave Suite 1603 New York NY 10025

GARCIA, KAY WELLING, univ. ofcl.; b. Salina, Kans., Oct. 3, 1946; d. John Hubert and Doris Lucille (Errebo) Welling; student Chadron State Coll., 1964-66; B.S., Mont. State U., 1968; div.; 1 dau., Lani Leigh. Med. tech. intern St. James Community Hosp., Butte, Mont., 1968-69; med. technologist, lab. supr. various hosps., Colo., Mont., 1970-73, 75-76; spl. chemist Anaconda Co. (Mont.), 1974-77; field health officer Mont. Dept. Health, Butte, 1978, dir. clin. lab. tng., cons., Helena, 1978-80; dir. Office of Continuing Edn. for Health Profl., Mont. State U., Bozeman, 1980—. Mem. Am. Soc. Clin. Pathologists, Am. Soc. Med. Technologists (bd. dirs. Mont. chpt. 1975-76, 80-82), Am. Soc. Healthcare Edn. and Manpower (nominating com. 1981, pres. Mont. chpt. 1981-83), Mont. Public Health Assn. (nominating com. 1981-82). Home: 1910 S Black St Bozeman MT 59715 Office: 104B Lewis Hall Mont State Univ Bozeman MT 59717

GARCIA, MARIA E., lawyer; b. N.Y.C., Nov. 8, 1948; d. Marie Camargo and Carmen E. Garcia; B.A., Barnard Coll., 1969; J.D., Columbia U., 1974; children—Carmen Mary O'Shea, Kieran Robert O'Shea. Admitted to N.Y. bar, 1975; with IBM, White Plains, N.Y., 1974—, staff atty. field engring. div., 1977-78, area counsel systems products div., Kingston, N.Y., 1980-82, sr. atty. nat. accounts div., White Plains, 1982—. Bd. dirs. No. Dutchess Hosp., Rhinebeck, N.Y., 1981-82. Mem. N.Y. State Bar Assn., Am. Bar Assn., Ulster County Bar Assn. Republican. Roman Catholic. Home: RD 3 Sunnyridge Rd Katonah NY 10536 Office: IBM 1133 Westchester Ave White Plains NY 10604

GARCIA, NELDA LILIA, retailer, rancher; b. Ben Bolt, Tex., May 26, 1935; d. Alfredo and Olaya (Chapa) G.; B.S., U. Tex., Austin, 1957, M.Ed., 1960; student Sch. Real Estate, Walnut Creek, Calif., 1970. Tchr., girls' athletic coach Premont (Tex.) High Sch., 1957-60; tchr., coach Mt. Diablo Sch. Dist., Concord, Calif., 1960-70; real estate sales rep., Walnut Creek, 1970-73; owner, mgr. restaurant and lounge, Oakland, Calif., 1973-75, Garcia's Country Store, Ben Bolt, 1975—; owner, breeder Nopalera Beefmasters Ranch, Ben Bolt, 1975—; partner Garcia's Land Improvement Co., 1979—; chmn. bd. Garcia's Land, Inc. Vice pres. Jim Wells County Water Dist., 1975—; chairperson Community Council and Policy Bd., Ben Bolt-Palito Blanco Sch. Dist. Tchrs. Corp., 1979—; bd. dirs. Mex.-Am. C. of C., 1979—. Recipient nat. hon. rating in women's basketball officiating. Mem. Nat. Fedn. Ind. Bus., Beefmaster Breeders Universal, S. Tex. Beefmasters Breeders Assn., NOW, Southwestern Cattlemen's Assn., Land Improvement Contractors Am. Home and Office: PO Box 546 Ben Bolt TX 78342

GARCIA, OFELIA, artist; b. Havana, Cuba, Feb. 12, 1941; came to U.S., 1961, naturalized, 1967; m. Ramon and Nieves (Gomez-De-Molina) Garcia-Castro; student Escuela Nacional de Bellas Arts, Havana, 1958-60; B.A., Manhattanville Coll., 1969; M.F.A., Tufts U., 1972; postgrad Duke U., 1975—. One woman shows Galeria Universitaria, San Juan, 1970, Cohen Art Center, Boston, 1972, Duke U. Gallery, 1974; group shows include Biennial Latin Am. Printmakers, 1970, 74, 76, 79, group travelling show, Venezuela and Argentina, 3d Miami Graphics Biennial, 1977, Print Club, 1977, N.J. State Mus., 1978, Newark Mus., 1979, Afro-Am. Mus., 1980, Moravian Coll. Gallery, 1980, Mus. of Civic Center, Phila., 1981, Deshong Mus., Chester, Pa., 1982; represented in permanent collections The Museo Grafico, Inst. Puert. Rican Culture, Latin Am. Print Collection, Phillip Morris, Argentina, The Free Library, Phila., Princeton U., N.J. State U., Barnard Coll., also numerous pvt. collections; asst. prof. printmaking and drawing Newton Coll., Mass., 1969-73, chmn. dept. art, 1970-73, dir. div. humanities and fine arts, 1970-73; asst. prof. Boston Coll., 1975-76, dir. studio art program, 1975-76; dir. The Print Club, Phila., 1978—; bd. dirs. Phila. Area Cultural Consortium; bd. dirs. Citizens for Arts in Pa.; mem. adv. bd. Afro-Am. Hist. and Cultural Mus. Kent fellow, 1975-80. Fellow Soc. Values in Higher Edn.; mem. Coll. Art Assn., Women's Caucus for Art, Am. Acad. Religion, AAUP. Roman Catholic. Office: 1614 Latimer St Philadelphia PA 19103

GARD, BETSY ANN, educator; b. Detroit, May 1, 1951; d. Arthur W. and Nancy (Schiller) Schlesinger; B.A., U. Mich., 1972; Ph.D., Washington U., 1978; m. Steven J. Gard, Aug. 20, 1971. Clin. intern Meml. Hosp., U. N.C., Chapel Hill, 1975-76; cons. Judevine Center for Autistic Children, St. Louis, 1977-78, St. Louis State Hosp. Day Treatment Center, 1977-78; asst. prof. psychiatry Emory U. Sch. Medicine, 1978—; cons. in field. Lic. clin. psychologist, Ga. Mem. Am. Psychol. Assn., Ga. Psychol. Assn., Mortar Bd. Jewish. Contbr. articles to profl. jours. Home: Bryn Mawr Atlanta GA 30027 Office: 5825 Glenridge Dr NW Atlanta GA

GARD, CONNIE RAE, computer service office mgr. b. Glasgow, Mont., Jan. 16, 1936; d. Arthur A. and Margaret (Crest) Oslund; cert. Greene's Bus. Coll., 1966. Exec. night auditor Drug Supply Co., Anchorage, 1962-67; office mgr. Sonoma County Computer Service, 1969—; ops. mgr. Sonoma County Data Processing, 1969—. Served with USN, 1954-57. Cert. computer service instr. Mem. Am. Mgmt. Assn., Data Processing Mgmt. Assn. Democrat. Lutheran. Office: 2615 Paulin Dr Santa Rosa CA 95401

GARDELL, CAROL SAYER WALLINE, builder-developer mgmt. co exec.; b. Naval Sta., Trinidad, B.W.I., Jan. 17, 1951 (parents Am. citizens); d. Charles S. and Shirley A. (Anderson) Walline; student No. Va. Community Coll.; m. Gary T. Gardell, June 5, 1971; 1 dau., Emily C. Head bookkeeping dept. Philipsborn, Inc., 1970; br. mgr. Philipsborn T/A Beydas Petites, 1971-74; mgr. mdsg. and mktg. Frank R. Jelleff, 1975-78; retail mktg. dir. Charles E. Smith Mgmt., Inc., Arlington, Va., 1978-80, dir. mktg., 1980—; sec.-treas., bd. dirs. Crystal Under Ground Mchts. Assn. Sec., bd. dirs. Blakeview Homeowners Assn., 1979; v.p. Mosby Woods Condo Assn., 1977-78; tchr. St. Leo's Catholic Ch., Fairfax, Va., 1979—. Mem. Internat. Council Shopping Centers. Office: 1735 Jefferson Davis Hwy Arlington VA 22202

GARDENIER, EDNA FRANCES, nurse; b. Teaneck, N.J., June 30, 1935; d. Andrew Cairns and Edna Frances (Manney) O'Neil; B.S. in Nursing, Seton Hall U., S. Orange, N.J., 1965; M.Ed., Columbia U., 1970; doctoral candidate in ednl. adminstrn. SUNY, Albany; m. Harvey James Gardenier, Aug. 25, 1961; children—Andrew, William. Staff nurse N.J. hosps., 1955-65; public health nurse, 1965-70; mem. nursing faculty Dutchess Community Coll., Poughkeepsie, N.Y., 1970—, program chmn. nursing, 1971, acting head dept. health technologies, 1979-80; mem. overall faculty com. on external degrees in nursing N.Y. State Regents, 1981—; mem. nurse edn. com. SUNY; mem. Dutchess County chpt. Am. Heart Assn., 1974—; nutrition adv. council Dutchess County Coop. Edn., 1970-79. USPHS trainess, 1968-70. Mem. Am. Assn. Women in Jr. and Community Colls., N.Y. Assn. Degree Nurse Council, N.Y. State Nurses Assn., N.Y. State Two Year Coll. Assn. Home: RD 1 Box 85 Holsapple Rd Dover Plains NY 12522 Office: Dutchess Community Coll Pendell Rd Poughkeepsie NY 12601

GARDINE, JUANITA CONSTANTIA FORBES, sch. adminstr.; b. St. Croix, V.I., Aug. 6, 1912; d. Alphonso Sebastian and Petrina (Actien) Forbes; B.A., Hunter Coll., 1934; M.A., Columbia U., 1940; postgrad. U. Chgo., 1949, N.Y.U., summers 1960-66, Cheyney State Coll., summer 1967 m. Cyprian A. Gardine, Apr. 23, 1942; children—Cyprian A., Vicki Maria Camilla, Letitia Theresa, Richard Whittington. Tchr. elem. schs., 1934-35; tchr. math. high sch., 1935-41, 48-49; acting asst. high sch. prin., 1941; jr. high sch. prin., 1941-47; substitute tchr. math., physics, Montclair, N.J., 1947-48; asst. supt. edn., 1949-55; asso. dean Community Colls., 1955-57; high sch. prin., 1957-58; supr. ednl. stats., 1958-62; social worker Dept. Welfare, 1962-63; prin. Christiansted (St. Croix) Public Grammar Sch., 1963-74; tchr. math. evening session extension classes Cath. U. P.R., 1960-62; part time instr. math. Coll. V.I., 1974-75, 80-81; partner St. Croix Tutorial Sch.; bookkeeper St. John's Ch.; testing supr. Ednl. Testing Service. Past sec. bd. dirs. St. Croix Fed. chpt. ARC; chmn. supervisory com., dir. St. Croix. Fed. Credit Union; past sec. St. Croix Sch. Health Com.; past pres. St. Croix (V.I.) Mental Health Assn. Pres., Tchrs. Assn., 1940, Municipal Employees Assn., 1942. Grammar sch. named in her honor. Mem. Am. Statis. Assn., Nat. Assn. Elem. Sch. Prins., V.I. Fedn. Bus. and Profl. Womens Clubs (past sec.), Episcopal Ch. Women of V.I. (past chmn. world affairs com., past pres. Women of Ch.), Christiansted Bus. and Profl. Women's Club (treas., past pres., Woman of Yr. 1966), Daus. King (sec.). Home: 142 Whim Frederiksted VI 00840 also PO Box 1505 Christiansted St Croix VI 00820

GARDINER, LILLIAN JOHNSON (MRS. LAURENCE B. GARDINER), author, club woman; b. Humboldt, Tenn., Aug. 15, 1910; d. Tyree LeRoy and Lillian Janette (Campbell) Johnson; student Peabody Coll. and Vanderbilt U., 1928-31, Falls Bus. Coll., Nashville, 1931-32; m. Laurence Bridges Gardiner, Dec. 12, 1944. Author: (with Mrs. L. D. Bejach) Williamson County Marriages 1800-50, 1956; (with Mrs. J. B. Cartwright) North Carolina Land Grants in Tennessee 1778-1791, 1958, Hess-Daviess Family Booklet, 1958; editor, originator Ansearchin' News, organ Memphis Geneal. Soc., 1953-59; editor geneal. column in nat. mag. U.D.C. Named Ky. col., 1967. Mem. Tenn. Civil War Centennial Com.; mem. woman's adv. council, speakers bur. Civil Def.; hon. life mem., dir. woman's bd. Mid-South Fair. Fellow Huguenot Soc. London; mem. Nat. League Am. Pen Women (br. pres.; state pres.), Tenn. Woman's Press and Authors Club, Sons and Daus. Pilgrims, Memphis Little Theatre (patron), Nat. Geneal. Soc., Colonial Dames Am. (chpt. parliamentarian, v.p.), D.A.R., Daus. Am. Colonists (hon. Tenn. pres.), Huguenot Soc. (hon. pres. Tenn. 1955—; hon. nat. pres. 1967-69) Descs. Colonial Clergy, Dames Ct. Honor (pres. Tenn. 1961-63, nat. trustee), Decs. Knights Garter, St. George's Chapel Windsor Castle, U.S. Daus. 1812, Assn. Preservation Tenn. Antiquities (chpt. parliamentarian), Order First Families Va., Order of Crown in Am., Jamestowne Soc. (dep. gov. Tenn. 1970-72), U.D.C. (chpt. pres. 1958-62), Tenn. Geneal. Soc. (past pres.), Kings Daus. and Sons (leader), Daus. of Barons of Runnemede, Friends Memphis Pub. Library, Nat. Fedn. Press Women, Ladies Hermitage Assn., Nat. Trust Historic Preservation, Bates Family Assn. Old Va., Wynne Family Assn., Murray (Fleming) Clan Assn., Nat. Gavel Club, Brooks Art Gallery League (life). Presbyn. Home: 1863 Cowden Ave Memphis TN 38104

GARDNER, ANNE LANCASTER, lawyer; b. Corpus Christi, Tex., Aug. 19, 1942; d. Jack Quinn and DeWitte (Benton) Lancaster; B.A., U. Tex., 1964, LL.B., 1966; 1 son, Travis Gregory. Admitted to Tex. bar, 1966; asst. dir. continuing legal edn. State Bar Tex., 1966-67; law clk. to U.S. Dist. Ct. judge, 1967-71; partner firm Brown, Crowley, Simon & Peebles, Ft. Worth, 1971-78, Simon, Peebles, Haskell, Gardner & Betty, Ft. Worth, 1978—. Mem. Am., Ft. Worth-Tarrant County (dir.) bar assns., State Bar Tex. (chmn. dist. 7 admissions com.), U. Tex. Law Sch. Assn. (dir.), Young Lawyers Assn. Ft. Worth, Kappa Beta Pi, Delta Zeta. Editor legal jours. Office: 200 Baker Bldg Fort Worth TX 76102

GARDNER, AVA, motion picture actress; b. Smithfield, N.C., Dec. 24; d. Jonas B. and Mary Elizabeth Gardner; student Atlantic Christian Coll.; m. Mickey Rooney, Jan. 10, 1942; m. 2d, Artie Shaw, 1945; m. 3d, Frank Sinatra, 1951 (div.). Motion picture debut in We Were Dancing, 1942; other motion pictures include Lost Angel, Three Men in White, Maisie Goes to Reno, Whistle Stop, The Hucksters, Singapore, One Touch of Venus, Great Sinner, East Side West Side, My Forbidden Past, Show Boat, Pandora and the Flying Dutchman, Lone Star, Snows of Killmanjaro, Ride Vaquero, Mogambo, Knights of The Roundtable, The Barefoot Contessa, Bhowani Junction, The Little Hut, The Sun Also Rises, Naked Maja, On the Beach, 55 Days to Peking, Night of the Iguana, The Bible, Mayerling, Tam-Lin, Devil's Widow, 1971, Life and Times of Judge Roy Bean, 1972, Earthquake, 1974, The Sentinel, 1976, Permission to Kill, 1976, The Bluebird, 1976, The Cassandra Crossing, 1977, City on Fire, 1978, The Kidnapping of the President, 1979, Priest of Love, 1980, Regina, 1982. Address: care Jess S Morgan & Co Inc 6420 Wilshire Blvd Los Angeles CA 90048

GARDNER, BARBARA ELAINE, programmer analyst; b. Sandia Base, N.Mex., Sept. 5, 1950; d. Orville Kenneth and Gladys (Hancock) Gardner; B.S., U. Colo., M.B.A., 1978. Instr. adult basic edn., Independence, Iowa, 1971; merit grad. asst. U. Colo., Boulder, 1976, 77, 78, grad. adminstr. simulated production game, 1977, grad. teaching asst., 1976-77, research asst. to Bur. Econ. Research, 1977, computer lab. advisor, statis. tutor, 1977-78, instr. prodn. mgmt., 1980-81; devel. programmer IBM, Boulder, 1979—. Organizer, coordinator legal aid program Welfare Rights Orgn.; protective payee and conservator Social Service Dept.; worker Drug Councils, Planned Parenthood, Probation Office, Council on Alcoholism, 1970-72. Mem. Am. Prodn. and Inventory Control Soc., Sigma Iota Epsilon, Beta Gamma Sigma. Home: 209 29th St Boulder CO 80303 Office: IBM 3131 28th St Boulder CO 80303

GARDNER, KATHLEEN THERESE, staff mem. U.S. Congress; b. Billings, Mont., Apr. 1, 1949; d. Richard James and Jeanne Ruth (Doucette) G.; B.A. in French and Art History, U. Mont., 1971; postgrad. Harvard U., 1972-74; M.S. in Criminal Justice, Am. U., 1977; m. David Lawrence Cravedi, Mar. 6, 1982. Mem. Staff Harvard Center Advancement Criminal Justice, Cambridge, Mass., 1972-73; office mgr. Harvard Voluntary Defenders, Cambridge, 1973-74; legis. asst. to U.S. Congressman Claude Pepper, Washington, 1975-76; profl. staff mem. U.S. Ho. Select Com. on Aging, Ho. of Reps., Washington, 1971—; co-dir. Nat. Conf. Mental Health, Washington, 1979; del. White House Conf. on Aging Mini Confs. Mental Health, San Diego, 1980, participant, Washington, 1982. Mem. Kappa Alpha Theta. Roman Catholic. Club: Congressional Staff. Author numerous congressional reports. Office: 811 House Office Bldg Annex I House of Representatives Washington DC 20515

GARDNER, LAURA REID, holding co. exec.; b. Elkart, Ind., Aug. 17, 1915; d. Clarence Edward and Clara Sophie (Gardner) Reid; grad. high sch.; m. Stewart Franklin Gardner, Aug. 8, 1936; children—Ann Gardner Lempke, Stewart Eddy, Susan Gardner Bressler. Tchr., Bristol, Ind., Dallas, 1955-67; sec.-treas. Stewart Coach Industries, Bristol, 1946—; cons. interior decorating. Bd. dirs. March of Dimes, 1950-60, Mental Health, 1963-65, Civic Music, 1955-60, YWCA, 1968. Methodist. Club: Garden (pres. Bristol 1958). Home: 17812 CR 10 Bristol IN 46507 also 3951 Gulfshore Blvd N Naples FL 33940 Office: Stewart Coach Industries Inc Bristol IN 46507

GARDNER, MADELEINE MURPHY, ednl. adminstrn. cons.; b. Mpls., Jan. 1, 1920; d. Francis Eugene and Romelle (Comrie) Murphy; B.S., U. Minn., 1942; cert. bus. adminstrn. Harvard U.-Radcliffe Coll. Program, 1947; M.B.A., N.Y. U., 1962; m. Milton M. Gardner, Feb. 22, 1948; children—Leslie Gardner Pantucci, Deborah, Cecilia, Samuel, Mara. Asst. to dir. personnel Columbia-Presbyterian Hosp., N.Y.C., 1947-49; lectr. in mgmt. Nassau Community Coll., cons. Nassau County (N.Y.) Drug Abuse Commn., 1960's; asst. to dir. Inst. of Arts, Hofstra U., 1969-71; dir. cert. program in mgmt. for women Adelphi U., 1972-78, acting dean Univ. Coll., 1979-80, cons. Sch. Bus., 1980—; dir. N. Am. Philips Corp. Overseer Friends of Fin. Edn., Adelphi U.; trustee Heckscher Museum, Huntington, N.Y. Served to maj. WAC, 1942-46. Named Women of Yr., Bus. and Profl. Women's Clubs Nassau County, 1982; named L.I. Achiever, 110 Center for Bus. and Profl. Women, 1982; recipient Am. Assembly Collegiate Schs. Bus Innovation award, 1980. Mem. L.I. Assn. Commerce and Industry (founder Women's Council 1979). Club: Harvard Bus. of N.Y. Home: 26 Hamilton Pl Garden City NY 11530 Office: Sch Bus Adelphi U Garden City NY 11530

GARDNER, MARIA EVRARD, pharmacist; b. Allentown, Pa., June 20, 1949; d. August E. and Helen Evrard; B.S. in Pharmacy, Phila. Coll. Pharmacy, 1972. Pharm.D., 1974; m. Lee Allan Gardner, July 5, 1975; 1 dau., Anne Christine. Intern, Thomas Jefferson U. Hosp., 1972-73, resident in pharmacy, 1973-74, clin. pharmacist med. service, 1974-76, primary care pharmacist, 1974-76; adj. clin. instr. Phila. Coll. Pharmacy and Sci., 1974-76; outpatient clin. pharmacist Tucson VA Hosp., 1976-78; clin. pharmacist Tucson Gen. Hosp., 1978—; asst. prof. pharmacy practice U. Ariz., Tucson, 1977—. Mem. Am. Soc. Hosp. Pharmacists, So. Ariz. Soc. Hosp. Pharmacists (dir. 1979-80, sec. 1977-78), Ariz. Council Hosp. Pharmacists, Am. Assn. Colls. Pharmacy, Rho Chi. Republican. Roman Catholic. Contbr. articles on pharmacology to profl. publs. Home: 1432 N Sarnoff Dr Tucson AZ 85715 Office: College Pharmacy Univ Arizona Tucson AZ 85721

GARDNER, MARJORIE HYER, chemist, educator; b. Logan, Utah, Apr. 25, 1923; d. Saul Edward and Gladys Ledingham (Christiansen) Hyer; B.S., Utah State U., 1946, Ph.D. (hon.), 1975; M.A., Ohio State U., 1958, Ph.D., 1960; cert. Ednl. Mgmt. Inst., Harvard U., 1975; m. Paul Leon Gardner, June 6, 1947; children—Pamela Jean, Mary Elizabeth. Tchr. sci., journalism and English high schs., Utah, Nev., Ohio, 1947-56; instr. Ohio State U., Columbus, 1957-60; asst. exec. dir. Nat. Sci. Tchrs. Assn., 1961-64; vis. prof. Australia, India, Yugoslavia, 1965; asso. dean, dir. Bur. Ednl. Research and Field Service, College Park, Md., 1975-76; dir. Sci. Teaching Center, U. Md., College Park, 1976-77, prof. chemistry, 1964—; div. dir. NSF, 1979-81; cons. UNESCO, NSF. UNESCO grantee, 1970—; NSF grantee, 1964—. Fellow AAAS (council), Am. Inst. Chemistry; mem. Am. Chem. Soc. (council), Chemistry Assn. Md. (pres.), Internat. Union of Pure and Applied Chemistry (exec. com.), Internat. Orgn. Chemistry in Devel. (edn. panel), Assn. Edn. of Tchrs. of Sci., Nat. Assn. Research in Sci. Teaching, NEA, Nat. Sci. Tchrs. Assn., Am. Assn. Higher Edn., Soc. Coll. Sci. Tchrs., Higher Edn. Group Washington, Fulbright Alumni Assn. (pres., dir.), Phi Delta Kappa, Phi Kappa Phi. Author: Chemistry in the Space Age, 1965; editor: Theory in Action, 1964, Vistas of Sci. Series, 1961-63; Investigating the Earth, 1968, Interdisciplinary Approaches to Chemistry, 1973, 1978-79; Under Roof, Dome and Sky, 1974, Toward Continuous Professional Development: Designs and Directions, 1976; contbr. articles in fields of chemistry, sci. edn. to profl. jours. Office: Dept Chemistry U Md College Park MD 20742

GARDNER, MARY ADELAIDE, educator; b. Kingston, Ohio, July 19, 1920; d. Jennet Porter and G. Wyland (Davis) G.; B.A., Ohio State U., 1942, M.A., 1953; Ph.D., U. Minn., 1960. Bacteriologist, Mead Johnson & Co., Inc., 1942-43; dir. civilian club Land Upper Austria Commn., U.S. Army, 1948-51; program asst. Mpls. Star, also Minn. World Affairs Center, 1957-59; teaching asst. U. Minn., 1959-60, lectr., 1960-61; copy editor Mpls. Star, 1960-61; asst. prof. journalism U. Tex., 1961-66; mem. faculty Mich. State U., East Lansing, 1966—, prof. journalism, 1975—; cons. El Norte, Monterrey, Mex., 1970—. Served with USMCR, 1943-46. Recipient commendation U. Antioquia (Colombia), 1962, Teaching Excellence award U. Tex., 1966, diploma de merito ICCTC, Costa Rica, 1979, Disting. Faculty award Mich. State U., 1982; Mpls. Woman's Club fellow, 1956-57; Buenos Aires fellow to Peru, 1953-54; Tozer Found. award, 1959-60; OAS research fellow, 1959-60. Mem. Inter Am. Press Assn. (spl. citation 1975), Women in Communication (Nat. Headline award 1978), Assn. for Edn. in Journalism (pres. 1978-79), Midwest Assn. Latin Am. Studies, NOW. Author: Inter American Press Association: Its Fight for Freedom of the Press, 1967; Press in Guatemala, 1971; also articles. Office: Sch Journalism Comml Arts Bldg Mich State U East Lansing MI 48824

GARDNER, MARY BERTHA HOEFT CHADWICK, postmaster; b. Vernal, Utah, June 13, 1914; d. Edward and Hazel (Burgess) Hoeft; B.S. in Elem. Edn., Utah State U., 1950; m. Rulon Chadwick, Sept. 3, 1935 (div. July 1949); children—Mary Jo Chadwick Wight, Adriana Chadwick Forsgren; m. Leon D. Gardner, July 14, 1951 (dec. May 1974). Bookkeeper, Model Dairy, 1935-49, Weber Central Dairy, 1949-51, Bishops Storehouse, 1950-51; sch. tchr., Ogden, Utah, 1950-51; clk. Post Office, Honeyville, Utah, 1956-72, postmaster, 1972-81; ret., 1981. Pres., Relief Soc. Ch. Jesus Ch. of Latter-day Saints, mem. stake bd. relief soc., mem. stake bd. Sunday Sch., mem. stake bd. mut. improvement assn. orgn. Mem. Nat. League Postmasters (exec. v.p. state br., editor newsletter), Nat. Assn. Postmasters, AAUW (treas.), Daus. Utah Pioneers, Bus. and Profl. Women's Club (treas. Brigham City). Home: RFD #1 Honeyville UT 84314

GARDNER, RUTH ANN, mining engr.; b. Seward, Nebr., Sept. 8, 1930; d. Russell Francis and Alta Cornelia (Carse) Richmond; B.S. in Mech. Engring., U. Nebr., 1956; M.S. in Mining Engring. (Henry DeWitt Smith Trust Scholar), Mackay Sch. Mines, U. Nev., 1978; m. Kenneth C. Nolte, 1957 (dec.); children—Shannon Kay, Jean Wyndham; m. 2d, John D. Gardner, 1981. Engr., Kennecott Copper Corp., Salt Lake City, 1956-58, EtE Mgmt. Corp., Scottsdale, Ariz., 1969-72, Sudbeck Engring. Co., Scottsdale, 1972-73; mining engr. TVA, Casper, Wyo. 1976-77, Mullen Engring., Casper, 1977-78, Fed. Am. Partners, Gas Hills, Wyo., 1978-79; mng. partner Benchmark Mineral Engrs., Laramie, Wyo., 1979—. Bd. dirs. Family Outdoor Recreation Unltd., 1971-72. Mem. Soc. Mining Engrs. of AIME, Sigma Kappa. Office: Benchmark Mineral Engrs Box 3101 University Station Laramie WY 82071

GARDNER, VIRGINIA D., extension home econs. agt.; B.S., Fla. A. and M., U.; postgrad. Howard U., Prairie View A. and M. Coll., Tuskegee Inst., Cornell U., U. Fla., U. N.C., Greensboro; M.Ed., N.C. State U. Coop. extension work agr. and home econs. State of Fla., home demonstration agt., Jackson County, Marianna, Fla., Columbia County, Lake City, Fla., Pinellas County, Clearwater Fla., asst. home demonstration agt., Largo, Fla., asst. county extension home econs. agt., extension home econs. I, Largo, Fla., extension home econs. agt. II, Largo, extension agt. III home econs., program leader U. Fla., Gainesville, home econs. program leader Pinellas County Coop. Extension Service, Largo. asso. prof. extension home econs. U. Fla. Chmn. Jackson County Health Assn., Marianna, Fla., past sec. Jackson County Tng. Sch. P.T.A., chmn. March of Dimes Drive, Clearwater; mem. Friends of Ridgecrest Assn. Bd. dirs. Upper Pinellas Council on Human Relations, adv. com., nominating com.; treas. Fla. Parent Child Center, Inc.; former pres. Neighborhood Community Orgn. Named Agent of the Year, Fla. State Assn. Negro Home Demonstration Agents, also by Nat. Negro Home Demonstration Agts. Assn.; recipient award 4-H Club, Clearwater Heights, Fla. Mem. Fla. Assn. County and Home Demonstration Agts. (past fin. sec., past chmn. civic com., past chmn. resolution com., past asst. sec., past 2d v.p.), Fla. State Assn. Negro Home Demonstration Agts. (past pres., v.p., mem. conv. com.), Nat. Negro Home Demonstration Agts. Assn., Am., Fla., West Coast home econs. assns., Nat., Fla. (2d v.p., policy com., nominating com., public relations com., disting. service com.) assns. extension home econ. agts., Epsilon Sigma Phi, Zeta Phi Beta. Baptist (treas. ch. jr. women, sec. trustee com., ch. clk., chmn. com. trustees).

GARIN-VARGAS, PURA GEMARINO, physician; b. Guimbal, ILoilo, Philippines; d. Ricardo G. and Purificacion Garin; A.A., U. San Augustin, Philippines, 1952; M.D., U. Santo Tomas, 1958; m. Andres I. Vargas, Mar. 15, 1960; children—Andrew, Albert, Arthur. Intern, Lynn (Mass.) Gen. Hosp., 1958-59, resident in pathology, 1959-60; resident in ob-gyn Balt. City Hosp., 1960-61, Sinai Hosp., Balt., 1961-62; resident in anesthesiology Montefiore Hosp. and Med. Center, Bronx, N.Y., 1962-65; chief resident in anesthesiology, ho. physician internal medicine Suburban Hosp., Cleve., 1969; jr. attending anesthesiologist St. Vincent Charity Hosp., Cleve., 1970; chief anesthesiologist Fisher Titus Meml. Hosp., Norwalk, Ohio, 1971—, asst. med. dir. respiratory therapy and ICU, 1977—, med. chief of staff, 1979—. Treas., bd. dirs. South Shore Lung Assn.; bd. dirs. Huron County chpt. Am. Cancer Soc. Diplomate Am. Bd. Anesthesiology. Fellow Am. Coll. Anesthesiology; mem. AMA, Ohio State Med. Assn., Huron County Med. Assn., Ohio Soc. Anesthesiologists, Am. Soc. Anesthesiologists, Internat. Anesthesia Research Soc., Regional Anesthesia Soc., Am. Women Med. Assn., Norwalk Area Hosp. Assn., Profl. Women's Assn. Norwalk. Roman Catholic. Home: 555 Ridge Rd North Willard OH 44890 Office: 257 Benedict Ave Norwalk OH 44857

GARLAND, GEORGIA DIANE, nurse; b. Kansas City, Mo., Oct. 8, 1942; d. George Warren and Helen Bell (Grindstaff) Byrd; R.N., Deaconess Hosp., St. Louis, 1964; B.S., Lindenwood Coll., 1965; M.B.A., Rockhurst Coll., 1980; divorced; children—Jerrod Lee, Jason Lowell. Supr. operating room U. Kan. Med. Center, Kansas City, 1965; mem. faculty St. Luke's Hosp. Sch. Nursing, Kansas City, Mo., 1965-70; supr. operating room Menorah Med. Center, Kansas City, 1970-71; dir. nursing Lakeside Hosp., Kansas City, 1970-75; dir. nursing Reid Meml. Hosp., Richmond, Ind., 1976-77; asst. adminstr. Bethany Med. Center, Kansas City, Kans., also adminstr. alcohol rehab. unit, 1977-80; sr. v.p. Methodist Hosps. Memphis, 1980-82; v.p. Am. Med. Mgmt., Memphis, 1982—; sr. v.p. Meth. Health Systems, Memphis, 1982—; pres. Meth. OutReach, Inc., 1982—; bd. dirs. Home Health and Hospice Memphis. Del., People to People program People's Republic of China, 1980. Mem. Am. Soc. Nursing Service Adminstrs., Tenn. Soc. Nursing Service Adminstrs. Tenn. Nurses Assn. Office: 1735 Madison St Memphis TN 38104

GARLAND, HAZEL BARBARA, journalist; b. Burnett, Ind., Jan. 28, 1913; d. George and Hazel P. Hill; student U. Pitts., 1952; m. Percy A. Garland, Jan. 26, 1935; 1 dau., Phyllis T. With New Pitts. Courier, 1943—, reporter, 1946-52, feature editor, 1952-60, women's editor, 1960-72, entertainment editor, 1966-72, city editor, 1972-74, editor-in-chief, 1974-77, asst. to pub., 1977—, editorial coordinator, cons., 1977—. Past v.p. Pitts. Communications Found.; bd. dirs. Civic Light Opera, 1970-84; past bd. dirs. McKeesport YWCA, Pitts. Urban League. Named Editor of Yr., Nat. Newspaper Pubs. Assn., 1974; recipient Orgn. Rehab. and Tng. Service award Jewish Women, 1974, Sojourner Truth award Bus. and Profl. Women, 1974, Nat. Headliner award Women in Communications, 1975. Mem. Women in Communications, Inc., Nat. Girl Friends, Inc. (chatterbox editor), Black Women's Polit. Crusade, Black Women's Assn., Allegheny County Women's Polit. Caucus, Iota Phi Lambda (hon.). Baptist. Clubs: Altrusa (McKeesport, Pa.), Semper Fidelis (past pres.) (McKeesport); Girl Friends (past pres.) (Pitts.). Office: New Pitts Courier 315 E Carson St Pittsburgh PA 15219

GARLAND, JOAN BRUDER, social worker; b. Cleve., Sept. 30, 1931; d. Henry Ignatius and Mary (Maher) Bruder; A.B., Mt. Holyoke Coll., 1952; postgrad. Wellesley Coll., 1952-53, U. Sao Paulo (Brazil), 1965-66; M.S., Sarah Lawrence Coll., 1974; M.S. in Social Work, Columbia U., 1977; m. Paul Griffith Garland, Aug. 28, 1954; children—Bonnie (dec.), Patrick, John, Cathryn. Grad. asst. chemistry dept. Wellesley (Mass.) Coll., 1952-53; chemist Polaroid Corp., Cambridge, Mass., 1953-54, 55-56; CAPES research fellow U. Sao Paulo, 1954-55; clin. instr. retardation N.Y. Med. Coll., Valhalla, 1978-80; social worker, psychiat. day treatment program Jewish Child Care Assn., Pleasantville (N.Y.) Cottage Sch., 1980; founder, v.p. Crime Victims Assistance Agy., Inc., 1981—. Treas. council Girl Scouts, Sao Paulo, 1965-67; bd. dirs. PTA, 1972-73; bd. deacons Scarsdale (N.Y.) Congl. Ch., 1975; patient rep. White Plains (N.Y.) Med. Center, 1977; bd. dirs. Hudson Valley chpt. Leukemia Soc., 1981—. Cert. in family therapy, Center for Family Learning, also Family Inst. of Westchester; cert. social worker, N.Y. State. Mem. Nat. Assn. Social Workers, Acad. Cert. Social Workers, Soc. Clin. Social Work Psychotherapists, Am. Orthopsychiat. Assn., AAUP, Am. Soc. Human Genetics, Nat. Soc. Genetic Counselors, N.Y. Acad. Scis. Clubs: Mt. Holyoke, Wellesley (Westchester). Home: 28 Oak Ln Scarsdale NY 10583

GARLAND, SARA G., senatorial legis. asst.; b. New Rockford, N.D., May 1, 1946; d. John A. and Annabelle (Stephenson) G.; B.A., U. N.D., 1968, M.A., 1972; m. Kim E. Uhl, Aug. 10, 1979; children—Stephanie Garland, Joshua Edward, Jonathan Stewart. Reporter, Sta. KXJB-TV, Fargo, N.D., 1968-69; instr. speech, U. N.D., 1969-72; asst. dir. public affairs Corp. Public Broadcasting, 1972-76; legis. asst. to Rep. Margaret Heckler, 1976-77, to Sen. Quentin Burdick, 1977—; asst. Senate Appropriations Com. Mem. Capitol Hill Women's Polit. Caucus. Presbyterian. Home: 137 13th St NE Washington DC 20002 Office: Room 451 Russell Senate Office Bldg Washington DC 20510

GARLICK, NANCY BUCKINGHAM, conductor, musician; b. White Plains, N.Y., Feb. 1, 1946; d. Robert and Betty (Bonnar) Buckingham; B.S., SUNY, Potsdam, 1968; M.M., Manhattan Sch. Music, 1970; postgrad. Ecoles Americaines des Beaux Arts, Fontainebleau, 1973, Tanglewood, 1974; m. D. Stevens Garlick, Aug. 30, 1980. Clarinetist, Am. Wind Symphony, 1969, Opera Orch. of N.Y., 1970, Nat. Orch. Assn., 1970, New Haven Symphony, 1971-75, Waterbury Symphony, 1974, Lakeside Symphony, 1976-81, Shenandoah Valley Music Festival of Am. Symphony Orch. League, 1977-78, Mo. Symphony Soc. Performing Arts Center, 1979; music dir. Wooster (Ohio) Symphony Orch., 1977—; asso. prof. music Coll. Wooster, 1975—; clarinetist Wooster Trio, 1980—; N.Y. debut Wooster Trio, 1981; soloist Boston Pops Orch., in Weber's Concertino, New Haven Coloseum, 1973. Westchester Music Tchrs. Assn. grantee, 1964; Coll. Wooster Faculty grantee, 1977; recipient Nat. Orch. Assn. Accomplishment award, 1970. Mem. Internat. Clarinet Soc., Coll. Music Soc., Am. Fedn. Musicians. Home: 1439 Jones St Wooster OH 44691 Office: Dept Music Coll of Wooster Wooster OH 44691

GARNER, CONNIE MCCANNON, data processing analyst; b. Ila, Ga., Oct. 14, 1924; d. Howard Walter and Margaret Naomi (Butler) McCannon; A.A., U. Ga., 1942; m. Eugene Frederick Garner, Mar. 15, 1944; children—Constance, Cary. Instr. data processing Internat. Inst., Ramsey, N.J., 1969-73; instr. data processing Athens (Ga.) Area Vo-Tech. Inst., 1974-76; mgr. mgmt. info. systems for vocat. edn. State of Ga. Dept. Edn., Athens, 1976—. Mem. Am. Vocat. Assn., Am. Vocat. Info. Assn., Ga. Assn. Educators, Ga. Vocat. Assn., Nat. Assn. Female Execs. Democrat. Baptist. Home: N Main St Ila GA 30647 Office: US Hwy 29 N Athens GA 30601

GARNER, JOY DIANNE, med. social worker; b. Mineral Wells, Tex., July 21, 1945; d. John Calvin and Joy Roebuck (Harris) G.; B.S., U. Ark., 1968; M.S.W., Tulane U., 1970; postgrad. Sch. Social Work, Hunter Coll., 1980—. Dir. activities Youth Home, Inc., Little Rock, 1968; social work supr. Ohio State U. Hosp., Columbus, 1970; social worker adolescent unit Miss. State Hosp., Whitfield, 1971; dir. dept. med. and psychiat. social work St. Vincent Hosp., Little Rock, 1971—; lectr. U. Ark., 1977—; cons. in field; med. adv. com. Ark. Arthritis Found. Bd. dirs. Women's Polit. Caucus Ark., 1979-80. Named Ark. Social Worker of Yr., 1977. Mem. Acad. Cert. Social Workers, Nat. Assn. Social Workers (dir. 1979—, pres. Ark. chpt. 1975-78, mem. exec. com. 1979-80, bd. rep. Midwest 1979—), Am. Hosp. Assn., Soc. Hosp. Social Work Dirs., Council Social Work Edn., Ark. Human Services Assn., Am. Group Psychotherapy Assn., Phi Theta Kappa. Democrat. Methodist. Author articles; mem. editorial bd. Jour. Gerentol. Social Work, 1978—. Home: 3119 Millbrook St Little Rock AR 72207 Office: St Vincent Infirmary Little Rock AR 72201

GARNER, KATE BAUCOM, educator; b. Union County, N.C., Jan. 21, 1930; d. Brice Lee and Dora Alice (Little) Baucom; B.S., Tift Coll., 1951; M.S., U. N.C., 1959; m. Max Garner, June 28, 1952; children—Eric, Kathy. Tchr. social studies Southmont High Sch., 1954-57; tchr. family life edn. Grimsley High Sch., Greensboro, N.C., 1957-59; instr. child devel. and family relations U. N.C., Greensboro, 1959-68; exec. dir. Family Life Council of Greater Greensboro, Inc., 1971-77; instr. psychiatry Bowman Gray Sch. of Medicine Wake Forest U., Winston-Salem, N.C., 1977—; cons. in field. Bd. dirs., Human Betterment League N.C., pres., 1982—; co-chairperson Gov.'s Task Force on N.C. Families, 1979—; mem. steering com. Gov.'s Youth Conf., 1978-79. Mem. Nat. Council Family Relations (pres. 1980—), Southeastern Council Family Relations (past pres.), N.C. Family Life Council (past pres.), Groves Conf. on Marriage and the Family (dir.). Democrat. Baptist. Home and Office: 11 Piccadilly Circle Greensboro NC 27410

GARNER, OLLIE BELLE, contracting co. exec.; b. Waynesburg, Ky., Feb. 6, 1928; d. Rufus D. and Nettie B. (Hubble) Stonecypher; Rogers Bus. Coll., Somerset, Ky., 1947; m. Leo M. Garner, May 26, 1947. Sec., Pulaski County (Ky.) Extension Office, Somerset, 1948-50; bookkeeper W.C. Brass & Assos., Indpls., 1951-62; sec., bookkeeper Acme Constrn. Co., Indpls., 1963-65; sec., v.p., dir., co-owner J & O Contractors, Inc., Indpls., 1965—. Mem. Early Am. Soc., Marion County Art League, Network of Women in Bus., Women in Constrn., Internat. Platform Assn. Home: 7515 W Mooresville Rd Camby IN 46113 Office: 3906 W Washington St Indianapolis IN 46241

GARNER, SHELIA CAROLINE, dietitian; b. Morehead City, N.C., Feb. 8, 1953; d. Roy Thomas and Nellie Cannon Garner; B.S., U. N.C., Greensboro, 1975; Registered Dietitian, N.Y. Hosp.-Cornell Med. Coll., 1976; Therapeutic dietitian Charlotte (N.C.) Meml. Hosp., 1976-77; adminstrv. dietitian Moses Cone Hosp., Greensboro, N.C., 1977-80; food service dir. Carteret Gen. Hosp., Morehead City, N.C., 1980—; cons. Morehead Meml. Hosp., Eden, N.C. Mem. Am. Hosp. Assn., N.C. Dietetic Assn., Am. Dietetic Assn. (pub. bus. mgr., treas.), Am. Diabetes Assn. Democrat. Baptist. Home: PO Box 868 Newport NC 28570 Office: 3500 Arendell St Morehead City NC 285575

GARNES, MARLENE CAROL, auditor; b. Portland, Oreg., Oct. 21, 1944; d. Johnie and Florence (Alwell) Garnes; student Ga. State U., 1976-78, Grove St. Coll., Oakland, Calif., 1971; 1 dau., Marlo. Mgmt. analyst City of Atlanta, 1974-78; mgmt. cons. Parametrics, Inc., Washington, 1978; analyst/programmer Security Nat. Bank, Concord, Calif., 1978-80; EDP auditor Crocker Nat. Bank, San Francisco, 1980-82; systems analyst Wells Fargo Bank N.A., San Francisco, 1982—; data processing petty officer Naval Supply Center Reservists, Oakland, 1979—. Served with USNR, 1979. Mem. Black Assn. Data Processing Profls. (dir.). Office: 425 Market St San Francisco CA 94163

GARNET, SHELLEY, social worker; b. N.Y.C., Oct. 18, 1951; d. Daniel David and Ruth (Rothstein) G.; B.A. cum laude, City U.N.Y., 1972; M.S.W., Hunter Coll., 1974. Dir. youth services 92d St. YM-YWHA, N.Y.C., 1974-77; psychotherapist, child abuse program, psychotherapist United Hosps. of Newark Family Life Edn. Center, 1977-78; dir. social services Abused Womens Aid in Crisis, N.Y.C., 1978-82, exec. dir., 1982—. Mem. Acad. Cert. Social Workers, Nat. Assn. Social Workers. Jewish. Office: GPO Box 1699 New York NY 10001

GARNETT, LYNNE, counseling psychologist; b. Balt., Sept. 4, 1942; d. William L. and Kate V. Wolfe; M.P.H., UCLA, 1971; Ph.D. in Ednl. Psychology, U. So. Calif., 1974. Cons. Placement and Career Center UCLA, 1973, counseling psychologist UCLA Psychol. and Counseling Services, 1973-78, cons. campus and community orgns., 1973-78; faculty YMCA Jr. Coll., Nagoya, Japan, 1978-79; dir. counseling Chaminade U., Honolulu, 1980-82; prof. psychology West Oalue Coll., Pearl City, Hawaii, 1982—. NIH fellow, 1970-71. Mem. Hawaii Psychol. Assn., Am. Personnel and Guidance Assn., Hawaii Personnel and Guidance Assn., AAUW, Western Psychol. Assn., Nat. Assn. Women Deans, Adminstrs. and Counselors, Assn. Univ. and Coll. Counseling Center Dirs., Soc. Internat. Edn. Tng. and Research, Nat. Assn. Fgn. Student Affairs. Contbr. writings to publs. in field. Office: 1400 Kapiolani Blvd Suite B26 Honolulu HI 96814

GAROUTTE, BIRDIE BELLE STEPHENS, banker; b. Jasper County, Mo., Oct. 6, 1929; d. Willis Warren and Josephine Belle (Jones) Stephens; grad. Nat. Trust Sch., Northwestern U., 1974; m. Glenn I. Garoutte, May 14, 1950 (dec.); 1 dau., Glenna L. Garoutte Peck. Sec., bookkeeper Hornaday's, Joplin, Mo., 1946-49; legal sec. Scott & Scott, Joplin, 1949-52; civil service employee, Ft. Monmouth, N.J., 1952, White Sands Proving Ground, N.Mex., 1952-53; legal sec. Cowgill Blair, Jr., Joplin, 1956; with First Nat. Bank and Trust Co. of Joplin, 1957—, asst. trust officer, 1969-73, trust officer, 1973—; dir. W.J. Nelson Electric Co., Ozark Investment Co. Sec. adv. bd. Salvation Army; sec. adv. bd. Joplin Humane Soc. Mem. Nat. Assn. Bank Women (chmn. Ozark group), Am. Inst. Banking, Joplin Hist. Soc., P.E.O. Mem. Christian Ch. (Disciples of Christ). Clubs: Pilot (dir.), Woman's (Joplin); Briarbook Golf and Country (sec., dir.). Home: Route 6 Box 218 Joplin MO 64801 Office: First Nat Bank and Trust Co 4th and Main Sts Joplin MO 64801

GARRARD, JEANNE, editor, educator, writer; b. Birmingham, Ala., Apr. 9, 1923; d. Oscar and Jeanne (Holoman) Garrard; student Stetson U., 1940-42; postgrad. Lindsey Hopkins Hotel Sch., 1959; m. Huber S. Ebersole, Oct. 1, 1957 (div. Nov. 1960). Radio dir., writer, commentator Sta. WDBO, WLOF, Orlando, Fla., 1942-43; columnist Sentinel-Star, Orlando, 1943; radio commentator, writer for Burdine's, Palm Beach, Fla., 1943, Miami, Fla., 1943-44, Sta. WKAT, Miami Beach, Fla., 1944-45; commentator Sta. WIOD, Miami, 1944, commentator, writer Sta. WGBS, 1945; program dir. Melody, Inc., Miami Beach, 1945-48; writer Grant Advt., Inc., 1946; columnist Miami Beach Sun Star, 1946; writer Sta. WVCG, Coral Gables, Fla., 1949-50; columnist, Miami Beach, 1950, Riviera-Times, Coral Gables, 1950, Miami Daily News, 1950-51; writer Sta. WIOD, Miami, 1951; feature editor Miami Visitor Pub. Co., Miami Beach, 1952-55, mng. editor, 1955-56, editor, 1956-58; now cons. exec. editor Visitor Pub. Co.; free-lance writer, photographer in various publs. including Am. Home mag., Stag mag., newspapers; scout asst. Better Homes & Gardens, Des Moines, 1959—; asst. mgr., housekeeper Anson Hotel, Surfside, Fla., 1959; asst. to editor, photographer Meredith Pub. Co., Des Moines, 1961—; editor, writer Beach & Town mag., 1981-82; instr. writing adult edn. North Miami (Fla.) High Sch., 1956—; editorial asst. Ortho Garden Guide, Calif. Chem. Co., San Francisco, 1964; bus. mgr., exec. editor Beach and Town, Visitor Pub. Co., Miami Beach, 1964—; columnist, editor South Fla., Flower and Garden Mag., Kansas City, Mo., 1976-82; also writer and pub. relations counselor; lectr. Bd. dirs. Miami Beach Garden Center and Conservatory. Recipient Nat. Lit. Hort. award Nat. Council Garden Clubs, 1967. Mem. South Fla. Orchid Soc., Met. Miami Flower Show Assn., Gold Coast Unlimited Orchid Soc. (hon. life), Naples Orchid Soc. (hon.), Theta Sigma Phi (chpt. pres. 1966-67), Pi Beta Phi. Club: Miami Beach Garden (pres. 1966-68). Author: Growing Orchids for Pleasure (Nat. Garden Club Hort. award); Potted; Tropical Flowers of Florida, 1970; Flowers of the Caribbean, 1970; Flowers of the Bahamas, 1970; Flowers of Bermuda, 1970; Fairchild Tropical Gardens, 1971, rev. edit., 1981; Tropical Flowers, 1973; contbr. articles to pictorial mags. Home: 5768 Pine Tree Dr Miami Beach FL 33140

GARRARD, MARY MARGARET KERN (MRS. HERBERT L. GARRARD), mag. editor; b. Lafayette, Ind.; d. Charles B. and Flora (Work) Kern; B.S. with distinction, Purdue U., 1927; postgrad. Northwestern U., 1927-28; m. Herbert L. Garrard, Dec. 31, 1932; children—Flora Jane (Mrs. Ronald K. Richard), Bruce Kern, Sara Ann Grepp. Editor Mortar Bd. Quar., 1928-30; woman's editor Purdue Alumnus, 1929-30; asso. editor Union League Club Bull., Chgo., 1930-32; editor Internat. Altrusan, 1932-38, also exec. sec. Altrusa Internat., 1935-38; editor Kappa Alpha Theta Mag. 1958-73; free-lance writer of articles in nat. and religious press, including Parents' mag., Better Homes and Gardens, Today's Health, Guideposts, 1946—; tchr. creative writing Ind. U.-Purdue U., Indpls., 1976-79. Chmn. steering com. City Mgr. Plan, Homewood, Ill., 1952. Recipient Flora Roberts medal Purdue U., 1927. Mem. Woman's Press Club Ind., D.A.R., Nat. Fedn. Press Women (nat. award feature story 1965, 78, interview 1977, spl. edit. mag. 1970), Nat. Panhellenic Editors Conf. (chmn. Operation Brass Tacks 1969-71), Women in Communications, Mortar Board, Alpha Lambda Delta, Kappa Delta Pi, Kappa Alpha Theta (trustee found. 1974-76). Presbyterian. Author: The Family of Conrad Kern, 1968; Be A Better Parent, 1979. Home: 19740 Heather Ln Craig Highlands Noblesville IN 46060

GARRETT, DONNA GARRICK, jewelry co. fin. exec.; b. Tintic, Utah, Dec. 12, 1927; d. Morrison H. and Zelma Ora (Baldwin) Garrick; B.S., Brigham Young U., 1949; postgrad. in fin. planning U. So. Calif., 1963; m. Ernest T. Garrett, Dec. 20, 1947. Budget adminstr. Indsl. div. Airesearch, Los Angeles, 1953-67; mgr. fin. planning EG & G Inc., Las Vegas, Nev., 1967-74; dir. corp. acctg. Southwestern Portland Cement, Los Angeles, 1974-77; acctg. mgr. NBC, Los Angeles, 1977-78; bus. mgr. ABC, Los Angeles, 1978-79; controller Admiral Glass Co., Los Angeles, 1979-82, Schaffer & Sons, Canoga Park, Calif., 1982—. Mem. Nat. Assn. Accts., Am. Soc. Women Accts., Nat. Assn. Female Execs. Democrat. Mormon. Club: Spring Valley Lake. Designed and implemented co. budgetary systems, 1963, 69. Home: 444 Piedmont Ave Apt 301 Glendale CA 91206 Office: 6925 Canoga Ave Canoga Park CA 91303

GARRETT, HELEN MARIE, former state senator; b. Paducah, Ky.; d. J. Frank and Helen Eunice (Bean) Rickman; m. Tom Garrett, Aug. 17, 1952 (dec.); children—Tom, Carol. Mem. Ky. Senate, 1962-79, majority party whip. Mem. Ky. Democratic Central Exec. Com.

GARRETT, JENNIE, florist; b. Los Angeles, Dec. 8, 1925; d. Corneles and Hendrika (Van den Bosch) Bout; student Pasadena City Coll., 1940-42; m. Thomas Garrett, Dec. 8, 1945; children—Candyce, Denise, Susan, Thomas, Edward. Owner, mgr. Monrovia (Calif.) Floral, 1958—. Commr., City of Monrovia, 1972-79. Mem. Monrovia C. of C., Foothill Devel. Delayed Children (dir.). Club: Quota of Monrovia. Home: 373 Norumbega St Monrovia CA 91016 Office: 432 W Foothill Monrovia CA 91016

GARRETT, LILA, producer, dir., writer; b. N.Y.C.; d. Joseph and Hilda Glass; B.A., Wis. U., 1948; postgrad. Yale U. Drama Sch., 1952-53, Columbia U., 1953-54; children—Eliza, April. Writer, dir., producer 7 TV comedy pilots and various TV series including: All In The Family, Maude; producer, dir., writer Terraces, NBC-TV movie, 1977; creator, exec. producer, writer Baby, I'm Back, CBS-TV series, 1977-78; dir. Archie Bunker's Place, 1979; The Trouble with Celia (TV pilot), 1980; The Cook, 1980, Barney's Law Suit, 1980; dir. off-Broadway shows, including: Begger's Opera; owner, pres. Lila Garrett Prodns., Beverly Hills, Calif. Candidate Calif. State Senate, 1968. Recipient 3 Emmy awards for writing, producing, Mother of the Bride, 1973, Emmy award, for Girl Who Couldn't Lose, 1975, Emmy nomination for Julie Andrew's Show, 1972. Mem. Writers Guild Am. (dir.), Dirs. Guild Am., Acad. TV Arts and Sci., Caucus Producers and Writers, Women for Women in Films. Office: 228 Lasky Dr Beverly Hills CA 90212 *

GARRICK, BARBARA LAUFER, hosp. adminstr.; b. Syracuse, N.Y., Aug. 10, 1926; d. Emil Joseph and Gertrude Mara Laufer; B.S. in Biology, Ohio Dominican Coll., Columbus, 1948; m. Charles Peter Garrick, Nov. 3, 1951; children—Peter Laufer, Trudi Garrick Kasparek. Staff med. technologist St. Vincent's Med. Center, Bridgeport, Conn., 1949-50, 59-62, supr. hematology, 1950-51, coordinator edn. Sch. Med. Tech., 1962-80, program dir. Sch. Med. Tech., 1980—, lab. mgr. dept. lab. service, 1976—; adj. asst. prof. med. tech. U. Bridgeport. Bd. dirs. S.E. Fairfield County chpt. ARC. Mem. Conn. Assn. Med. Lab. Educators, Clin. Lab. Mgmt. Assn., Am. Soc. Clin. Pathologists, Conn. Assn. Lab. Mgrs., Nat. Council Catholic Women, Kappa Gamma Pi. Roman Catholic. Contbg. author: Dolan's Comprehensive Review for Medical Technologists, 1968; editor: Pre-Test Hematology for Medical Technologists, 1979. Home: 70 Bassick Rd Trumbull CT 06611 Office: 2800 Main St Bridgeport CT 06606

GARRISON, DOLLY DAWSON, utility co. mktg. exec.; b. Waxahachie, Tex., Apr. 3, 1939; d. John Franklin and Rosa Mae (Pool) Dawson; student U. Ark., 1975-76, Upper Iowa U., 1981-82; m. Charles W. Garrison, July 20, 1957; children—Todd Lincoln, Lance Dayton. Bookkeeper, Elliott Oil Co., Pine Bluff, Ark., 1955-64, Pine Bluff Motel-Plantation Embers Restaurant, 1964-67; service rep. Southwestern Bell Telephone Co., Pine Bluff, 1967-71, mktg. rep., 1971-73, communications cons., 1973-77, customer service supr.-adminstr., 1977—. Mem. edn. com. Pine Bluff C. of C., 1980, mem. community improvement com., 1981; active Ark. Assn. for Children with Learning Disabilities, 1972-82, pres., 1977-80, chairperson state conv., 1975-78. Recipient cert. appreciation Ark. Assn. Learning Disabilities, 1980; named Outstanding Community Relations Mem., Southwestern Bell Telephone Co., 1980, Boss of Yr., Pine Bluff Bus. and Profl. Women, 1982. Mem. Southwestern Bell Telephone Community Relations, Fedn. Bus. and Profl. Women, Pine Bluff Bus. and Profl. Women (pres.-elect). Home: 138 W Lake Dr Pine Bluff AR 71603 Office: 7 SW Plaza Pine Bluff AR 71603

GARRISON, JOAN MARIE, educator; b. Chgo., Feb. 27, 1919; d. Frank Spirkle and Elsie Johanna (Dreiske) Wichman; A.B., Oberlin (Ohio) Coll., 1941; M.S., Ind. U., 1950; m. William A. Garrison, Dec. 1, 1950 (dec. Nov. 1979); 1 son, Kenneth William (dec.). Instr. phys. edn. Geneva Coll., Beaver Falls, Pa., 1941-45; asst. prof. phys. edn. Ind. U., Bloomington, 1945-55, Westminster Coll., Salt Lake City, 1955-64; asso. prof. phys. edn. Washington U., St. Louis, 1964—; phys. edn. dir. Central Inst. Deaf, St. Louis, 1972—; bd. ofcls. Gov. Utah Council Phys. Fitness; instr. ARC Inst. Swimming Handicapped. Harpist, Westminster

Community Symphony, 1955-64, David Thornton Chorale and Ch. Choir, St. Louis, 1966-78. Recipient Helen Manley award, 1981. Mem. AAHPER, AAUP, Mo. Assn. Health, Phys. Edn. and Recreation, Nat. Archery Assn., Central Assn. Health, Phys. Edn. and Recreation, St. Louis Folk and Sq. Dance Fedn. Congregationalist. Club: Ind. U. Alumni St. Louis (dir.). Home: 9049 McNulty Dr Saint Louis MO 63114 Office: Box 1188 Washington U Saint Louis MO 63130

GARRISON, KAREN GAIL, hosp. adminstr.; b. Los Angeles, Jan. 21, 1944; d. Albert B. and Gertrude R. (Pew) Doran; student Santa Monica Coll., 1961-64, UCLA, 1963-64, Immaculate Heart Coll., 1964-66; B.S., Calif. State U., 1973; M.S., Loma Linda U., 1978; m. James Patrick Garrison, Oct. 20, 1978. Tchr. elem. grades public and parochial schs., Los Angeles, 1966-71; instr. critical care Glendale Adventist Med. Center, Glendale, Calif., 1974-76; critical care nurse Loma Linda U. Med. Center, 1976, nursing supr., 1977, dir. human resources devel., 1977-80; asst. adminstr. patient care services Feather River Hosp., Paradise, Calif., 1980-82; asst. adminstr. Mt. Diablo Hosp. and Med. Center, Concord, Calif., 1982—; cons. mgmt. and edn., 1978-82. Mem. Am. Hosp. Assn., Nat. League Nursing, Am. Nursing Assn., Am. Assn. Critical Care Nursing, Nat. Critical Care Inst., AAUW, Calif. Soc. Nursing Service Adminstrs., Calif. Soc. Risk Mgmt., Sigma Theta Tau. Home: 22 Valley View Orinda CA 94563 Office: 2540 East St Concord CA 94520

GARRISON, MARY LEE KATHARINE, economist; b. Phoenixville, Pa., July 29, 1951; d. James Lee and Helen Mary (Krystopik) G.; B.S. Fgn. Service, Georgetown U., 1973. With Dept. State, 1973—, consular officer, Saigon, 1974-75, spl. asst. to Asst. Sec. State African Affairs, 1975-76, fin. economist, Kinshasa, Zaire, 1977-79, Zaire desk officer, Washington, 1979-81, dep. dir. econ. policy staff Bur. African Affairs, 1981—; mem. U.S. del. 35th UN Gen. Assembly, 1980; vis. lectr. Boston Coll., 1981. Recipient Meritorious Honor award Dept. State, 1976. Mem. Smithsonian Assos. Roman Catholic. Office: Econ Policy Staff African Affairs Room 5242A Dept State 2201 C St NW Washington DC 20520

GARRISON, PATRICIA MEDLEY, speech pathologist; b. Phila., Oct. 5, 1944; d. Thomas St. Clair and Cassie Rhea (Robinson) M.; B.A., Howard U., 1966; postgrad. Temple U., summer 1967; M.S., Rutgers U., 1978; m. George C. Garrison, June 24, 1967; children—Renetta, George III, D'Vell. Counselor, D.C. Family and Child Services, 1964, YWCA, Washington, 1966; comprehensive English tchr., Public Schs. Phila., 1966-67; student speech clinician Douglass Coll. Rehab., 1977, Muhlenberg Hosp., Plainfield, N.J., 1978, Middlesex Gen. Hosp., New Brunswick, N.J., 1978; speech correctionist New Brunswick (N.J.) Bd. Edn., 1978—; adj. instr. Douglass Coll./Rutgers U., 1980—, vis. lectr. Sch. Health Scis. and Profl. Studies, 1981, cons., 1982—; cons. and lectr. on man, communication/sign lang. Vice pres. Evergreen PTA, Plainfield, 1974-75; program planner YWCA Plainfield, 1975; den mother Cub Scouts, Watchung council Boy Scouts Am.; tchr. English to non-English speakers N.J. Bell Labs., 1975; mem. gospel choir Calvary Bapt. Ch., Plainfield. Recipient Scholarship award Assn. Bus. and Profl. Women, 1962, Nat. Office Mgmt. Assn. award, 1962, Dickerson Estate award, 1962, PTA Service award, 1974-77, Service award Howard U., 1966; Urban League scholar, 1962 cert. of clin. competence in speech and lang. pathology; Mem. Plainfield Hearing Soc., Christian Workshops, Inc., Am. Speech, Lang. and Hearing Assn., Nat. Black Assn. Speech, Lang. and Hearing, Alexander Graham Bell Assn., Orton Soc., Am. Biog. Inst. (asso.), Library of Spl. Edn., Am. Audiology Soc., NAACP, NEA, N.J. Edn. Assn., Middlesex County Edn. Assn., New Brunswick Edn. Assn., Howard U. Alumni Assn., LWV, Delta Sigma Theta (chpt. chaplain 1975, chpt. historian 1979, chpt. sec. 1980). Democrat. Mem. George Garrison Singers. Home: 920 Carnegie Ave Plainfield NJ 07060 Office: 24 Bayard St New Brunswick NJ 08903

GARRISS, LOIS RANDOLPH, real estate broker; b. McDowell Flack, County, N.C., Nov. 16, 1930; d. Sam Lidge and Ruth (Huffman) Randolph; children—Michael Paul, Lois Elaine Flack, Patrick Randolph Flack, Elizabeth Ann Flack. Dental asst., 1976-77; asst. sales dir. Bluff's Town Houses, Morehead City, N.C., 1979, also pres. Garriss Investment Corp., 1978-79; real estate broker, owner Lois R. Garriss Realty, Atlantic Beach, N.C., 1980—. Sec. East Marion (N.C.) Elem. Sch. PTA, 1958, pres., 1959; mem. Art Soc. Jr. Woman's Club, Roanoke Rapids, N.C., 1962; v.p. Women's Soc. Christian Service, commn. steward East Marion Methodist Ch., 1960; mem. Valley Arts Council, Roanoke Rapids, N.C., 1981—. Mem. N.C. Art Soc., Atlantic Beach C. of C. Democrat. Methodist. Home: 915 W 2d St Roanoke Rapids NC 27870 Office: 224 Pond Dr PO Drawer G Atlantic Beach NC 28512

GARROTT, IDAMAE, state legislator; b. Washington, Dec. 24, 1916; A.B., Western Md. Coll., 1936; married; 2 children. Mem. Md. Ho. of Dels., 1979—, mem. ways and means com., joint com. on energy. Mem. Montgomery County Council, 1966-74, chmn. planning com., 1970-74, pres., 1971; bd. dirs. Washington Met. Area Transit Authority, 1972-74; bd. dirs. Washington Suburban Transit Commn., 1971-74, chmn., 1972; bd. dirs. Met. Washington Council Govts., pres., 1974, chmn. land use com., 1969-74; bd. dirs. Solid Waste Mgmt. Agy. Met. Washington, 1969-74; pres. Montgomery County LWV, 1963-66, Montgomery County Humane Soc., 1976-77; bd. dirs. Am. Soc. Planning Ofcls., 1970-73, v.p., 1972-73; sec.-treas. Md. Assn. Counties, 1973-74; mem. nat. panel Nat. Acad. Public Adminstrn., 1975-77; del. Montgomery County Civic Fedn. Democrat. Author: Paying Our Way, Maryland State Taxes and You, 1958. Office: 221 Lowe Bldg Annapolis MD 21401 *

GARTLEY, MELLODY BRUMMETT, utility co. sales exec.; b. Great Bend, Kans., Nov. 23, 1948; d. William Collett and Beverly (Phillips) Brummett; B.A., U. Ill., 1971; postgrad. Pepperdine U., 1982—; m. Edward Preston Gartley, Jr., Dec. 4, 1971; 1 dau., Rachel Colleen. Service rep. Ill. Bell Telephone Co., Waukegan, Ill., 1974-77, communications cons., Chgo., 1977-78; mktg. adminstr. AT&T Long Lines, Los Angeles, 1978-81, account exec., 1981—. Active LaHabra Leisure and Cultural Soc., LaHabra Children's Mus. Mem. Am. Mgmt. Assn. Home: 651 W LaPresa Dr LaHabra CA 90631 Office: 615 S Flower St Los Angeles CA 90017

GARVER, LOUISE, editor; b. North Tarrytown, N.Y., Aug. 15, 1950; d. Orazio and Carmela (Spataro) Cicero; B.S., Va. Commonwealth U., 1972; M.A., Marshall U., 1974. Mng. editor Yorba Linda (Calif.) Star, 1977-79; freelance writer, photographer, Anaheim, Calif., 1979-80; editor Carl Karcher Enterprises, Anaheim, 1980—. Mem. Women in Communications, Orange County Press Club, Public Relations Soc. Am., Internat. Assn. Bus. Communicators (awards 1980, 81). Office: PO Box 4349 Anaheim CA 92803

GARVIN, GERALDINE MCKINLEY, educator; b. Boyne City, Mich., Jan. 3, 1922; d. Donald A. and Isabel (Phillips) McKinleu; student U. Mich., 1939-41; A.B. (Durant scholar), Wellesley Coll., 1943; postgrad. Vassar Coll., 1955; M.Ed., U. Del., 1963; m. James Hinkley Garvin, Mar. 4, 1944; children—James Hinkley, Nancy Garvin Shor. Adminstr., Del. Presch. Assn., 1949-76; lectr. U. Del., 1965-66; asst. prof. Brandywine Coll., 1966-79; asso. prof. psychology Widener U., Chester, Pa., 1979—, also child devel. field experience coordinator. Mem. Del. Foster Care Rev. Bd., 1980—; mem. jr. bd. Wilmington Med. Center, 1954—; bd. mgrs. Wilmington Flower Market, 1972. Honored by U. Del., 1981. Mem. Am. Psychol. Assn., Del. Psychol. Assn., Eastern Community Coll. Social Sci. Assn., Phi Beta Kappa, Alpha Lambda Chi. Presbyterian. Clubs: Greenville Country; Del. Wellesley. Editor: The World of Learning in Delaware Women Remembered, 1977; contbr. articles to profl. jours. Home: 2302 Delaware Ave Wilmington DE 19806 Office: Concord Pike Wilmington DE 19803

GARVIN, JOAN LAVONNE, educator; b. St. Peter, Minn., Mar. 6, 1936; d. Harold John and Pearl Verna (Wendelschafer) G.; B.S., Mankato (Minn.) State U., 1958, M.S., 1968. Tchr. public schs. in Calif. and Minn., 1958—; project dir. staff devel. project, then project dir. health edn. liaison project, Bloomington, Minn., 1972-77; instructional generalist Bloomington elem. schs., 1976—; cons. in health edn., 1972—. Rep., Minn. Lung Assn., 1975—. Recipient numerous golf championship titles in Minn., 1966—; Joan Garvin Golf Classic founded, 1977. Mem. AHPER (health edn. chmn. central dist. 1976), Minn. Assn. Health, Phys. Edn. and Recreation (pres. 1978-79, Paul Schmidt award 1978), Minn. Assn. Supervision and Curriculum Devel. (dir. 1977-79), Trans-Nat. Golf Assn. (state rep. 1976—), NEA, Minn. Edn. Assn., Assn. Supervision and Curriculum Devel., Minn. Women's Golf Assn., Assn. Non-Smokers Rights, Phi Delta Kappa, Delta Kappa Gamma. Club: Mpls. Golf. Home: 8569 Dunkirk Ln Maple Grove MN 55369 Office: 8900 Portland Ave S Bloomington MN 55420

GARWOOD, BARBARA ANN, psychologist, educator; b. Cleve., Jan. 7, 1936; d. Bradford Earl and Hazel Elizabeth (Obrock) Garwood; B.S. John Carroll U., 1963; M.A., Case-Western Res. U., 1968; Ph.D., Kent State U., 1973. Tchr., sr. high sch. English, Euclid (Ohio) Pub. Schs., 1966-68; cons. sch. psychologist Mayfield (Ohio) City Schs., 1973-76; sch. psychologist Cleve. City Schs., 1968-72; pvt. practice psychology, Mentor, Ohio; prof. psychology Lakeland Community Coll., Mentor; mem. Ohio Bd. Psychology, 1976-81, pres., 1980-81. Mem. Lakeland Faculty Assn. (pres. 1980-81), Cleve. Psychol. Assn. (v.p. 1974-75), Ohio Sch. Psychologists Assn. (pres. 1976-77). Club: Pavilion Skating. Contbr. articles to profl. jours. Home: 6361 Candlewood Ct Mentor OH 44060 Office: 9953 Johnnycake Ridge Rd Mentor OH 44060

GARY, BEVERLY A., govt. ofcl.; b. Uniontown, Pa., Oct. 6, 1942; d. Dorothy J. Wilson; student Southeastern U., 1961, U.S. Dept. Agr. Sch., 1967-68, Bowie State Coll., 1981, U. Mass., 1982; m. James A. Gary, Feb. 24, 1962; 1 son, James A. With Bur. Public Rds., Dept. Commerce, 1960-65; with Equal Opportunity Commn., Washington, 1965—, dir. personnel, 1974—. Pres., Randolph Village Elem. Sch. PTA, 1969-70. Mem. Internat. Personnel Mgmt. Assn., Nat. Assn. Female Execs., Washington Urban League, Sr. Exec. Assn., NAACP. Baptist. Club: Helping Hand. Home: 11506 Accolade Terr Clinton MD 20735 Office: 2401 E St NW Room 3214 Washington DC 20506

GARY, JULIA THOMAS, chemist, educator, coll. dean; b. Henderson, N.C., May 31, 1929; d. Richard Collins and Julia (Thomas) G.; B.A., Randolph-Macon Woman's Coll., Lynchburg, Va., 1951; M.A., Mt. Holyoke Coll., 1953; Ph.D., Emory U., 1958. Instr. chemistry Mt. Holyoke Coll., 1953-54, Randolph-Macon Woman's Coll., 1954-55; mem. faculty Agnes Scott Coll., Decatur, Ga., 1958—, prof. chemistry, 1971—, dean coll., 1969—; trustee Randolph-Macon Woman's Coll., 1976—. Chmn. fin. com. Decatur 1st United Methodist Ch., 1981, chmn. elect adminstrv. bd., 1982. Mem. Am. Chem. Soc., AAUW, Am. Conf. Acad. Deans, Phi Beta Kappa, Sigma Xi. Clubs: Druid Hills Golf, Atlanta Zonta (pres. 1980-81). Author articles in field. Home: 117 Bruton St Decatur GA 30030 Office: Agnes Scott Coll Decatur GA 30030

GARY, SHARON DELIGHT, psychol. examiner; b. Decatur, Tex., June 14, 1951; d. Dorthea (Sommerville) Gary; B.S. with honors in Psychology, State Coll. Ark. (name changed to U. Central Ark.), 1973; M.S. in Clin. Psychology, Memphis State U., 1975. Liaison worker Foster Home and Group Home programs N.E. Community Mental Health Center, Memphis, 1975-76; psychol. examiner, asst. dir. Hutt Psychol. Group, Memphis, 1976-79; cons. psychol. examiner Sequoyah Center, Tenn. Psychiat. Hosp. and Inst., Memphis, 1976-77; coordinator, instr. foster care program Center for Govt. Tng., U. Tenn., Memphis, 1978—; owner, psychol. examiner Psychol. Services of Memphis, 1979—; active workshops, seminars on learning disabilities and foster children's devel.; mem. Women's Resource Center, 1977—, Multidisciplinary Child Abuse Rev. Team, 1979—, active NOW march for ERA; participant in lobbying for Ark. Assn. Children with Learning Disabilities. Recipient Ark. Traveler cert., 1978, cert. of appreciation Tenn. Foster Care Assn., 1979. Mem. Am. Psychol. Assn., Tenn. Psychol. Assn., Memphis Psychol. Assn., Nat. Rehab. Assn., Council on Adoptable Children, Assn. for Children with Learning Disabilities, Psi Chi. Mem. Unity Ch. Christianity. Club: Zonta. Home: 3163 Highmeadow Dr Memphis TN 38128 Office: PO Box 28317 Memphis TN 38128 also 1835 Union Ave Suite 203 Memphis TN 38104

GARZARELLI, ELAINE MARIE, economist; b. Phila., Oct. 13, 1950; d. Ralph J. and Ida M. (Pierantozzi) G.; B.S., Drexel U., 1969, M.B.A., 1977; A.B.D., N.Y.U., 1980. With Drexel Burnham, Phila., 1969-71; with A.G. Becker, N.Y.C., 1971—, v.p., economist, 1975—; lectr. in field; Recipient award for bus. achievement YWCA, 1976. Mem. Nat. Assn. Bus. Economists, Women's Fin. Assn., Am. Statis. Assn., Women's Bond Assn. Author: Financial Techniques, 1976; contbr. articles to profl. jours. Developer Sector Analysis, econometric model for predicting industry profits and stock price movements. Home: 280 Butler Rd Springfield PA 19064 Office: 55 Water St New York NY 10041

GASPER, JO ANN, govt. ofcl.; b. Providence, Sept. 25, 1946; d. Joseph and Jeanne (VanMatre) Shoaf; B.S., U. Dallas, 1967, M.B.A., 1969; m. Louis Clement Gasper, Sept. 21, 1974; children—Stephen Gregory, Monica Elizabeth, Jeanne Marie. Adminstrv. asst. U. Dallas, 1964-68; dir., asst. adminstr. Britain Convalescent Center, Irving, Tex., 1964-68; pres. Medicare Centers, Inc., Dallas, 1968-69; bus. mgr., treas. U. Plano (Tex.), 1969-72; ins. agt., 1972-73; systems analyst Tex. Instruments, Inc., 1973-75; acctg. and bus. cons., 1976-81; editor, pub. The Right Woman—Congl. News for Women and the Family, also Register Report, 1980-81; dep. asst. sec. social services policy Office Asst. Sec. Planning and Evaluation, Dept. Health and Human Services, 1981—; bd. dirs., treas. Council Inter-Am. Security, 1978-80; instr. George Mason U., Fairfax, Va., 1976. Mem. nat. family policy adv. bd. Reagan/Bush Campaign, 1980; del. White House Conf. Families, 1979-80; mem. Franklin Area Citizens Neighborhood Watch, McLean, Va., 1980-81, Fairfax County Citizens Coalition for Quality Child Care, 1980-82; co-chmn. St. John's Refugee Resettlement Com., 1975-77. Recipient award Eagle Forum, 1979, Wanderer Found., 1980. Mem. AAUW. Republican. Roman Catholic. Author articles in field, also columnist. Office: 200 Independence Ave Room 433F Washington DC 20201

GASPERONI, ELLEN JEAN LIAS (MRS. EMIL GASPERONI), auto wash exec.; b. Rural Valley, Pa.; d. Dale S. and Ruth (Harris) Lias; student Youngstown U., 1952-54, John Carrol U., 1953-54, Westminster Coll., 1951-52; grad. Am. Inst. Banking; m. Emil Gasperoni, May 28, 1955; children—Sam, Emil, Jean Ellen. Bd. dirs. Fill-Up Up Auto Wash Co., Inc., Ft. Lauderdale, Fla., 1968—, sec., 1968—. Mem. Jr. Bus. Women's Club (dir. 1962-64). Presbyterian. Clubs: Coral Ridge Country, Le Club International (Fort Lauderdale). Home: 4201 NE 25th St Fort Lauderdale FL 33308

GASSETT, KATHRYN MARIE, banker; b. Rhinebeck, N.Y., Apr. 24, 1937; d. John Edward and Helen Marie (Apgar) Wisbauer; student Dutchess Community Coll.; m. Ronald Lee Gassett, June 25, 1977 (dec.). Bookkeeper, Colonial Bank & Trust Co., N.Y.C., 1955-57; bookkeeper First Nat. Bank of Rhinebeck (N.Y.), 1958-78, cashier, 1978—; mem. Milan (N.Y.) Town Council. Mem. No. Dutchess Bus. and Profl. Women Assn. Republican. Methodist. Office: 20 Mill St Rhinebeck NY 12572

GASSMANN, ANNE MARIE, nurse; b. Detroit, Feb. 11, 1949; d. Albert G. and Mary B. G.; B.S. in Nursing, Coll. Mt. St. Joseph, 1971; M.S., U. Ariz., 1976. Staff nurse, asst. head nurse, head nurse Good Samaritan Hosp., Cin., 1971-74; cardiology clin. nurse specialist VA Hosp., Tucson, 1975-77; instr., asst. prof. U. Ariz. Coll. Nursing, Tucson, 1977-82; cardiovascular clin. nurse specialist St. Mary's Hosp., San Francisco, 1982—. USPHS trainee, 1974-75. Mem. Am. Heart Assn. (CPR instr., trainer 1977—, so. Ariz. nursing edn. com. 1977-82, vice chairperson 1978-79, chairperson 1979-80, adv. LPN edn. com. 1979-80, state nurses task force 1979-82, so. Ariz. program com. 1979-82, Ariz. affiliate program com. 1979-82, dir., sec. 1981), Am. Nurses Assn., Am. Assn. Critical Care Nurses, Sigma Theta Tau. Contbr. articles to profl. jours. Home: 3 Commonwealth Ave #2 San Francisco CA 94118 Office: Saint Mary's Hosp 450 Stanyan St San Francisco CA 94117

GASSNER, BEVERLY JEAN, lawyer; b. Homestead, Pa., June 20, 1931; d. Jack Lewis and Mildred (Fogel) Kaplan; B.S., Carnegie Inst. Tech., 1953; M.A., Claremont Grad. Sch., 1968, postgrad. 1970; J.D., U. La Verne, 1977; m. Lawrence M. Gassner, Nov. 26, 1953; children—Michael Joseph, David Benjamin, Stephen Isaac. Social group worker YWCA, Pitts., 1953-54, YM & WHA, Pitts., 1954-55; instr. Am. history San Antonio Community Coll., Walnut, Calif., 1968-71, Chaffey Coll., Rancho Cucamonga, Calif., 1971-73; admitted to Calif. bar, 1977; individual practice law, Ontario, Calif., 1977—. Mem. Western San Bernardino Bar Assn. (trustee), ACLU (exec. com. 1979-80), NOW, Calif. State Bar (standing com. on custody and visitation family law sect.), San Bernardino County Bar Assn. (chmn. resolutions com.), Inland Counties Women in Law, Am. Bar Assn., Calif. Attys. for Criminal Justice, Calif. Women Lawyers, Calif. Bar Assn., Democrat. Jewish. Editor-in-chief U. LaVerne Coll. Law Jour. Juvenile Law, 1977. Office: 367 N 2d Ave Upland CA 91786

GATENBEE, ELIZABETH ROBBINS (MRS. ROBERT JAMES GATENBEE), bearings co. exec.; b. Louisville, Feb. 24, 1916; d. Orlando Douglass and Elizabeth (Holtzhauer) Robbins; spl. student Tarkio Coll., 1955-56; m. Robert James Gatenbee, Sept. 11, 1934; children—Robert James, John Douglass. Sec., Ky. Bearings Service, Inc., Louisville, 1934-48, 57-60, exec. v.p., sec., 1973-80, chmn. bd dirs., 1980—, also dir.; exec. sec., dir. So. Bearings Service, Inc., Knoxville, Tenn., 1976—. Home: PO Box 336 Pewee Valley KY 40056 Office: 1524 Algonquin Pkwy Louisville KY 40210

GATES, ANITA, writer; b. Childersburg, Ala., Jan. 12, 1948; d. J.C. and Ethel M. (Dison) G.; B.A. in Journalism, U. Ala., 1969. Staff supr. public relations South Central Bell, Birmingham, Ala., 1969; supervisory asst. environ. affairs AT&T, N.Y.C., 1969-71; writer Clairol Inc., N.Y.C., 1971-72, editor, 1972-74, publs. mgr., 1974-78; freelance writer, N.Y.C., 1978—; author: The 90 Most Promising Careers for the '80s, 1982; contbr. articles to various mags. including Mademoiselle, Harper's Bazaar, Weight Watchers mag., Am. Baby, Young Miss; contbg. editor Frequent Flyer mag. Mem. Authors Guild, Mensa, St. Bartholomew Community Club. Home and Office: 200 E 72d St New York NY 10021

GATES, BETTY RUSSELL, artist, sculptor; b. Davenport, Okla., Aug. 10, 1927; d. Robert R. and Lela M. Brannon Russell (Creekmore); student Ark. A&M, 1946, Ft. Worth Art Center, various workshops; m. David Winston Gates, July 1, 1945; children—Jerry (dec.), David, Ann, Julie, Alexander. Comml. artist Liberty Glass, Sapulpa, Okla., 1945; tchr. local classes, 1965-70; exhibited works in 15 one-man shows; exhibited works at Williamsons Gallery, Dallas, Gallery Americana, Santa Fe, Blue Door, Taos, others; asst. tchr. gifted children Trinity Art Found., 1979-80. Mem. North Shore Arts Assn., Allied Artists Am., Nat. League Am. Pen Women (Maharishi award 1979), Trinity Art Guild (organizer, pres. 1962-63), Dallas Artists and Craftsmen, Catherine Lorillard Wolfe Art Club, others. Home: 4900 Wondol Hurst TX 76053

GATES, DOROTHY LOUISE, educator; b. National City, Calif., Feb. 21, 1926; d. Harold Roger and Bertha Marjorie (Lippold) Gates; B.A., U. Calif., Santa Barbara, 1949; M.A., U. Hawaii, 1963, Ph.D., 1975; postdoctoral student U. Uppsala (Sweden), 1976, Bedford Coll., London, 1978, Cuban Ministry of Justice, 1979. Dept. probation officer, Riverside County, Calif., 1950-54, 55-61; dir. La Morada, probation facility, Santa Barbara County, 1963-65; asso. prof. sociology San Bernardino (Calif.) Valley Coll., 1965—; part-time tchr. criminology U. Redlands (Calif.), 1975—; chmn. Riverside County Juvenile Justice and Delinquency Prevention Commn., 1971—. Pres. Women's Equity Action League, Hawaii, 1972; mem. adv. group Riverside County Justice System, 1982. Nat. Endowment for Humanities fellow U. Va., 1977. Mem. Western Gerontology Assn., Am. Soc. Criminology, Calif. Probation, Parole and Correctional Assn. (award 1969), LWV. Address: 4665 Braemar Pl Riverside CA 92501

GATES, JANE KROHN, speech pathologist; b. N.Y.C., Jan. 13, 1940; d. Martin L. and Ellen I. (Polson) Krohn; B.A., U. Mass., 1961; M.A., U. Conn., 1965; m. John Milton Gates, Jan. 30, 1965; children—Jonathan, Sander. Lang. pathologist Mt. Diablo Unified Sch. Dist., Concord, Calif., 1965-70; coordinator communications services grant Dept. Edn. R.I., Providence, 1971-73; asst. prof. speech pathology U. R.I., Kingston, 1971-73; prof. edn. Mt. St. Joseph Coll., Wakefield, R.I., 1973-75; speech/lang. pathologist S. Kingston (R.I.) Public Schs., 1976—; pvt. practice speech/lang. pathology, Kingston, 1976—; affiliate med. staff So. County Hosp., Wakefield, 1978—; speech/lang. cons. Washington County Public Nursing Assn., Inc., Wakefield, 1977—. Mem. spl. edn. adv. com. S. Kingston, R.I., 1979-80; mem. Historic Dist. Commn., S. Kingston, 1978—. Mem. R.I. Speech and Hearing Assn., Am. Speech and Hearing Assn. (cert.). Address: Thistledown Ln Kingston RI 02881

GATES, MARGARET JANE, lawyer; b. Annapolis, Md., Oct. 21, 1936; d. Charles Philip and Helen Elizabeth (Stull) Gates; B.A., U. Md., 1958; M.A., Inst. Tech., Monterrey, Mex., 1967; J.D., Georgetown U., 1971; 1 dau., Elizabeth Sophia. Co-dir. Center for Women Policy Studies, Washington, 1972-79; dep. insp. gen. U.S. Dept. Agr., Washington, 1979-81; research fellow Kennedy Sch. Govt., Harvard U., 1981—. Sec.-treas. Center for Women Policy Studies 1972—. Mem. ABA, D.C. Bar Assn., Women's Legal Defense Fund. Home: 1504 44th St Washington DC 20007

GATES, NINA MICHAEL, mining co. exec.; b. Veregin, Sask., Can., June 25, 1935; came to U.S., 1960; d. Michael M. and Annie T. (Chernoff) Evdokimo; m. Oliver Perry Gates, Aug. 25, 1973 (dec.). Engaged in exploration and devel. of mineral lands, 1964—; pres. Atacami Corp., 1970—; mem. U.S. Senatorial Bus. Adv. Bd., Washington. Home: 812 Country Club Dr Ojai CA 93023 Office: PO Box 1143 Ojai CA 93023

GATHERS, BARBARA BROWN, pest control co. exec.; b. Bklyn., Jan. 24, 1952; d. Azel and Sudie Cleo (Robbins) Brown; B.S. in Edn. cum laude, L.I. U., Bklyn. Center, 1978; m. Victor Gathers, Mar. 6, 1976; 1 son, Sekuleo. With A. Brown Pest Control & Exterminating Supplies Co., Bklyn., 1964—, v.p. in charge adminstrn., 1978—; tchr. Day Care Center, Bklyn., 1974-75. Recipient L.I. U. award for service to community and sch., 1978. Founder, Barbara & Co., 1978—. Mem. Nat. Pest Control Assn., Profl. Pest Control Assn., Empire Pest Control Assn. Office: A Brown Pest Control & Exterminating Supplies Co 173 Utica Ave Brooklyn NY 11213

GATLIFF, JANE WANDA, librarian; b. Chillicothe, Ohio; d. Earl Maurice and Duanna (Thomas) G.; B.S. in Bus. Edn., Wilberforce (Ohio) U., 1939; M.S. in L.S., Atlanta U., 1953. Various secretarial and clerical positions, 1941-52; reference librarian Ohio State U. Libraries, Columbus, 1953-59, head interlibrary loan, 1959—. Carnegie Library scholar, 1953. Mem. ALA, Acad. Libraries Assn. Ohio, Northeasterners, Delta Sigma Theta. Episcopalian. Home: 5165 B Stone Ridge Rd S Columbus OH 43213 Office: Ohio State U Libraries 1858 Neil Ave Columbus OH 43210

GATTON, DEBORAH JAN, bank examiner; b. Statesville, N.C., Aug. 26, 1953; d. Frank Delano and Nancy Joanne (Wilson) G.; B.A., N.C. State U., 1975. Asst. mgr. S.S. Kresge Co., Raleigh, N.C., 1975; asst. nat. bank examiner Comptroller of Currency, U.S. Dept. Treasury, Charlotte, N.C., 1975-76, Winston-Salem, N.C., 1976-80, Charleston, W.Va., 1980-81, nat. bank examiner, 1981—. Mem. Nat. Assn. Female Execs. (network dir.), Am. Mgmt. Assns., Charleston Women's Forum, Smithsonian Assos., N.C. State U. Alumni Assn. Democrat. Methodist. Club: Wolfpack. Address: PO Box 308 Charleston WV 25321

GAUDIO, MATHILDA CAROLINE, hosp. exec.; b. Bklyn., Apr. 17, 1916; d. Frederick Andrew and Carrie (Cook) Moretti; student public schs., Bklyn; m. Eugene Gaudio, June 16, 1940; children—Lois Gaudio Woodhull, June Gaudio Croon. Head stock Bonwit Teller Co., N.Y.C., 1933-41; sec. Intra Am. Co., Ltd., N.Y.C., 1960-62; exec. sec. Mazahua Albert Schweitzer Hosp., 1962-78, N.Y.C.; exec. dir. Am. Womens Hosps. Services, N.Y.C., 1978—. Bd. dirs. Mazahua Albert Schweitzer Hosp., Binder Schweitzer PanAm. Indian Found. Office: 225 W 34th St New York NY 10001

GAUNTT, EUGENIA HELEN, physician; b. Deport, Tex., Apr. 6, 1913; d. Robert Alexander and Jessie Elizabeth (Westbreck) Tate; student U. Tex., Austin, 1939-43; M.D., U. Tex., Galveston, 1945; m. William C. Gauntt, June 30, 1944 (div. 1952); children—Charles T., Glenn Gary. State field rep. of health Nat. Youth Adminstrn., Austin, Tex., 1940-41; intern Charity Hosp., New Orleans, 1945-46; gen. practice medicine, Kountze, Tex., 1947—. Mem. Kountze Ind. Sch. Bd. Dirs., 1960-62; bd. dirs. Hardin Meml. Hosp., 1971-81. Fellow Am. Acad. Family Practice (charter); mem. ABA, Tex. Med. Assn., So. Med. Assn., U. Tex. Ex-Students Assn., U. Tex. Med. Br. Alumni Assn. (Galveston), Alpha Omega Alpha. Baptist. Club: Kountze Woman's. Home: Vaughn Dr Kountze TX 77625 Office: Redwood Kountze TX 77625

GAUNTT, WANDALEEN, accountant; b. Vernon, Tex., Apr. 24, 1927; d. Luther Lawton and Ada Faye (Patterson) Gauntt; B.S., Tex. Woman's U., 1948. With Joske's Houston div. Allied Stores, Houston, 1948—, office mgr., 1948-66, internal auditor, 1966-71, asst. controller, 1971-81, asst. to controller-treas., 1981—; asst. sec., Allied Stores of Tex., Houston, 1966—; sec. Post Oaks Corp.; dir. Indo-Asia Corp.; instr. Retailing Inst., U. Houston, 1972-74. Mem. Bus. and Profl. Women's Club (past pres. San Jacinto chpt.), Epsilon Sigma Alpha. Democrat. Mem. Ch. of Christ. Club: Alice Freeman Palmer Literary. Home: 5442 Apple Creek Houston TX 77017 Office: Joske's Houston 4925 Westheimer Houston TX 77032

GAUSMAN, EDITH MARIE, found. exec.; b. N.Y.C., Jan. 17, 1919; s. George and Eliza (Heuermann) G. Fiduciary acct. Sage Gray Todd & Sims, N.Y.C., 1950-64; asst. v.p. Scudder, Stevens & Clark, N.Y.C., 1964-72; asst. treas. Commonwealth Fund, N.Y.C., 1972-75, treas., 1975—. Vice pres. bd. trustees Riverside Ch., N.Y.C., 1976-78; bd. dirs. Westside Ecumenical Ministry to the Elderly, Inc., 1979—. Mem. Bus. and Profl. Women's Club. Home: 11 Riverside Dr New York NY 10023 Office: 1 E 75th St New York NY 10021 *

GAUSS, PAMELA JO, ins. agy. exec.; b. Indpls., Mar. 14, 1946; d. William and JoAnne E. (Caldwell) McCarty; m. David L. Gauss, Nov. 26, 1966; children—Robert L., Christopher D., Tracy Ann. With Leo P. Gauss Ins. Agy., Indpls., 1979—, owner, 1982—. Mem. Profl. Ins. Assn. Roman Catholic. Club: PEO. Office: Suite 200 King Cole Bldg 7 N Meridian St Indianapolis IN 46204

GAUTT, SANDRA WHAYNE, educator; b. Chgo., Nov. 12, 1943; d. Thaddeus Alonzo and Alyce Louise Whayne; B.Ed. cum laude, U. Mo., Columbia, 1964, M.Ed., 1966, Ph.D., 1975; m. Prentice Gautt, June 5, 1971. Tchr., Woodhaven Learning Center, Columbia, 1966-68; supr. Hosp. Sch., U. Mo., Columbia, 1968-69; tchr. supr. Spl. Sch. Dist., St. Louis County, Mo., 1969-71; instr. dept. spl. edn. U. Mo., 1971-76, asst. prof., 1977-81, asso. prof., 1981—; cons., field reader spl. edn. program Div. Innovation and Devel. and Div. Personnel Preparation, U.S. Dept. Edn., U.S. Dept. Edn. grantee, 1978-81, 81-82. Mem. Council for Exceptional Children, Pi Lambda Theta, Phi Delta Kappa, Kappa Delta Pi, Alpha Kappa Alpha. Office: Dept Spl Edn U MO 515 S 6th St Columbia MO 65211

GAVETT, KATHARINE JEANNE, state legislator; b. Bangor, Maine, Dec. 12, 1952; B.A., U. Maine, 1975, B.S., 1977, M.B.A., 1982. Mem. Maine Ho. of Reps., 1979—. Home: 67 Mill St Orono ME 04473

GAY, CAROL VIRGINIA LOVEJOY, cell biologist; b. Belfast, Maine, Apr. 8, 1940; d. Delmar Boynton and Charlotte Mariam (Stuart) Lovejoy; B.A., U. Maine, 1962; M.S., Pa. State U., 1967, Ph.D., 1972; m. Fred Dana Gay, Mar. 6, 1964; 1 son, Zachary Lewis. With biophysics dept. Pa. State U., University Park, 1972-75, research assoc. in biophysics, dept. biochemistry, microbiology, molecular and cell biology, 1975-81, sr. project assoc., 1981—. NIH fellow, 1973-75; recipient NIH Research Career Devel. award, 1979—. Mem. AAAS, Am. Physiol. Soc., Am. Soc. for Cell Biology. Contbr. articles in field to sci. jours. Office: Dept Biochemistry Microbiology Molecular and Cell Biology 508 Mueller Lab Pa State U University Park PA 16801

GAY, CLAUDINE MOSS, physician; b. Alma, Ga., Nov. 30, 1915; d. Fred and Rosa Mae (Mercer) Moss; B.S., Coll. William and Mary, 1935; M.D., U. Va., 1939; m. Lendall C. Gay, June 29, 1940 (dec.); children—Gordon B., Spencer B.; m. J. Marion Bryant, 1974. Intern, Gallinger Mcpl. Hosp., Washington; practice medicine specializing in family practice, Washington, 1940—; mem. staff, exec. bd. Sibley Meml. and Capitol Hill Hosp., Washington; mem. Pres.'s Council on Malpractice, 1965; mem. health adv. commn. HEW, 1971-78; U.S. del. Med. Women's Internat. Congress, 5 times; del. Pres.'s Workshop on Non-Govtl. Orgn. Trustee Moss Charity Trust Fund, 1966—; adv. bd. Med. Coll. Pa., 1977. Fellow Am. Acad. Family Practice (del. 1971—; alt. del. to ho. dels. 1964-71); mem. Assn. Med. Women Internat. (del. 1967-72, councillor 1978), Royal Acad. Medicine, Pan Am. Med. Soc., D.C. Acad. Gen. Practice (pres.), Am. Med. Women's Assn. (councilor orgn. and mgmt. 1972-73, v.p. 1974, nat. pres. 1977), D.C. Med. Women's Assn. (pres.), AMA, D.C. Med. Soc. (dir., exec. bd., past v.p., mem. nominating com. 1970, 81, relative value study com. 1970-72, house and bldg. com. 1971-72, sec. family practice sect. 1966, 69, 78). Clubs: Women's Roundtable for Health Issues, Washington Forum, Zonta (dir.). Home: 5030 Loughboro Rd NW Washington DC 20016 Office: 403 E Capitol St SE Washington DC 20003

GAY, DAWN VIRGINIA, exec. recruiter, med. cons.; b. N.Y.C., Sept. 1, 1951; d. John and Grazina Lillian (Vizbara) G.; student St. Xavier Coll., 1969-71, Morraine Valley Community Coll., 1972-73, Rush U., 1974-75, DePaul U., 1975-77; grad. Way Internat. Ministry, Knoxville, Ohio, 1980; grad. fellows program in community and organizational systems Johns Hopkins U., 1981; 1 son, Christopher Alan. EKG technician, med. transcriber Christ Hosp., Oak Lawn, Ill., 1972-73; nursing asst. Rush Presbyn. St. Lukes Hosp., Chgo., 1974-75; adminstrv. asst. to Jean C. Alexandre, M.D., Broadview, Ill., 1975-78; clinic mgr. Chgo. Osteo. Hosp., 1978; cons. Med. Bus. Cons. & Assos., LaGrange Park, Ill., 1979; pres. bd. dirs. CHIPS, Council for Health, Info. and Public Service, Inc., Maywood, Ill., 1979-80; pres., corp. officer Med. Practice Mgmt., Inc., Maywood, 1979-80; clinic mgr. Alma Comprehensive Med. Center, Ltd., Maywood, 1978-81; health care specialist Mgmt. Recruiters Internat., Frederick, Md., 1980-81; med. cons. and partner Profl. Med. Services, Bensenville, Ill., 1982—; exec. recruiter Health Profls. Internat., Winnetka, Ill., 1982—. Mem. Am. Soc. Profl. and Exec. Women, Ill. Group Mgmt. Assn., Med. Group Mgmt. Assn., Am. Assn. Med. Assts. (cert.). Office: PO Box 195 Bensenville IL 60106

GAY, ELIZABETH DERSHUCK, artist; b. Phila., Nov. 27, 1927; d. John Raymond and Marguerite Sloane (Bright) Dershuck; B.A., Sweet Briar Coll., 1949; postgrad. Nat. Acad. Fine Arts, N.Y.C., 1957-58; m. Frank Lipscomb Gay, Jan. 8, 1955; children—Frank, Jack, Rutherford. One-woman shows include: Little Gallery, Katonah, N.Y., 1975, Mamaroneck Artists Guild, 1977, Hazleton (Pa.) Art League, Cassandra Gallery, White Plains, 1980; group shows include: Beaux Arts Finale, 1975, Westlake Gallery, White Plains, 1976, Lever House, 1977, Union Carbide, 1977, Knickerbocker Artists, 1976, 77, 79, 80-81, Nat. Arts Club, 1977, 79, New Eng. Exhbn. at Silvermine, 1977, Hudson Valley Arts Assn., 1975, 77, 79, Salmagundi Club, 1978, 81, NAD, 1980, traveling exhbns. Nat. Assn. Women Artists, 1980-82; instr. Watercolor North Castle Adult Edn., 1974-77, Pelham Art Center, 1979—; represented by Left Bank Gallery, Wellfleet, Mass., Images, Briarcliff Manor, N.Y. Mem. Artists Equity Assn. N.Y., Knickerbocker Artists N.Y., Mamaroneck Artists Guild, Nat. Assn. Women Artists, Catherine Lorillard Wolfe Art Club N.Y. Republican. Clubs: Whippoorwill, Green Acres Garden. Home: 37 Round Hill Rd Armonk NY 10504

GAY, GRETCHEN M., nurse, hosp. adminstr.; b. Burlington, Kans., May 7, 1930; d. Donald Melvin and Millie Jane (Mattox) Remer; A.A. in Nursing, Johnson County Community Coll., 1973; student parapsychology under Joaquin Cunanan, Manila, 1978. Student, then grad. nurse Olathe (Kans.) Community Hosp., 1972-73; night supr. VA Hosp., Leavenworth, Kans., 1973-77; asst. dir. nursing Mid Continent Psychiat. Hosp., Olathe, 1978—; dir. nursing Troost Nursing Home, 1980—; owner cons. firm Endless Horizons; co-writer grant and co-founder 1st Level Six Treatment Center of Kans. for Wayward Children, Olathe, 1979; an organizer Nurse Adv. Tng. Program, Chgo., 1977. Lic. nursing home adminstr.; R.N. Mem. Metasci. Found., Soc. for Improvement Human Functioning, Am. Nurses Assn., Martin Psychiat. Research Found., Brain Mind. Mem. Unity Ch. Home: 811 Layton Dr Olathe KS 66061 Office: 122 N Cooper Olathe KS 66061

GAY, JORDANA (ROBYN), internat. corp. negotiator; b. Los Angeles; d. H. Bruce Humberstone and Gay Robinson; student (scholar) UCLA, 1970-72; student seminars Interpol, Paris, Scotland Yard, London, 1973-74. Mem. internal affairs staff IWTG, European holding co., Los Angeles, 1974-77; asst. dir. corp. and indsl. counter-espionage unit Teltec Investigations, Inc., Beverly Hills, Calif., 1977-80; partner, dir. Elective Info. Cons.'s, West Los Angeles, 1980—; condr. seminars for legal bus., consumer affairs groups. Co-chairwoman Women's Def. League Los Angeles, 1978-79; vol. legal aid investigations Los Angeles County, 1980—; founder, dir. Paralegal Hotline, 1980—. Fellow Internat. Acad. Criminology; mem. Nat. Crime Prevention Assn., Am. Fedn. Investigators, Beverly Hills C. of C. (mem. crime council), Nat. Assn. Chiefs of Police. Office: 1414 Greenfield Ave Suite 306 West Los Angeles CA 90025

GAY, PATRICIA EILEEN, behavioral pharmacologist; b. Cleve., Oct. 13, 1941; d. William A. and Marjorie (Elliott) Gay; A.B., Middlebury Coll., 1963; M.A., U. Wis., Madison, 1965; Ph.D., Rutgers U., 1973; m. Jack A. Madsen, Jan. 17, 1980; 1 dau., Jonelle Carroll. Statistician, Smith, Kline & French Labs., Phila., 1966-70; mem. faculty Rutgers U., Camden, N.J., 1970-80, assoc. prof. psychology 1978-82; research assoc. prof. neurology U. Utah Coll. Medicine, Salt Lake City, 1978—; assoc. dir. Mark K. Allen Epilepsy Center, Utah State Tng. Sch., American Fork, 1980-82; cons. Epilepsy Assn. Utah, 1980-82. NSF grantee, 1962-63; NIH grantee, 1972-77; Busch Found. grantee, 1980-81. Mem. AAAS, Eastern Psychol. Assn., Am. Psychol. Assn., N.Y. Acad. Scis. Contbr. articles to profl. publs. Office: Dept Neurology Univ Utah Coll Medicine 50 N Medical Dr Salt Lake City UT 84132

GAYLE, CRYSTAL, singer, rec. artist; b. Paintsville, Ky.; d. Melvin Ted and Clara Marie (Ramey) Webb; student public schs., Wabash, Ind.; m. Vassilios Gatzimos, June 3, 1971. Recorded for MCA Records, 1970-72; recorded for United Artists Records, 1973—, latest album We Must Believe in Magic (Gold record); country hits include Beyond You, 1975, Wrong Road Again, 1974, This My Year for Mexico, 1975, Somebody Loves You, 1975, One More Time, 1976, Do It All Over Again, 1977, Never Miss a Real Good Thing, 1976, I'll Get Over You, 1976, Don't It Make My Brown Eyes Blue (Gold record), 1977; albums include Crystal Gayle, 1975, Somebody Loves You, 1975, Crystal, 1976, We Believe in Magic, 1977. Recipient Outstanding Female Vocalist awards Acad. Country Music, 1976, Country Music Assn., 1977. Address: Gayle Entertainments 51 Music Sq E Nashville TN 37203* *

GAYLORD, NELLIE WOLFE, sch. adminstr.; b. Luthersville, Ga., Aug. 20, 1922; d. John Thomas and Madie (Jones) Wolfe; B.A. (scholar), Clark Coll., 1943; M.S. (scholar), Atlanta U., 1950; postgrad. Temple U., U. Pa.; m. Clyde Felton Gaylord, Jr., Aug. 2, 1953; 1 son, Clyde Felton III. Tchr., Atlanta pub. schs., 1944-46; tchr. Sch. Dist. of Phila., 1946-69, tchr. on spl. assignment, 1969-70, adminstrv. asst. to dist. supt., 1970-72, vice prin., 1972-75, prin. secondary sch., 1975—; guest lectr. West Chester State Coll., Pa. State U. Vice chmn. Moorestown (N.J.) Zoning Bd. of Adjustment, 1981, chmn., 1982; vice Moorestown Shadetree Adv. Com., 1976, chmn., 1977; merit badge counselor Boy Scouts Am., 1974—; mem. Citizens Adv. Com. on Drug Abuse, 1970; bd. dirs. West End Community Center, Moorestown, N.J., pres. 1973; membership solicitor YMCA; vestryman Episcopal Ch. Recipient Meritorious Service award United Negro Coll. Fund, 1958; service award Cancer Crusade, 1969; NSF grantee, 1963-66. Mem. Phila. Assn. Sch. Adminstrs., Black Women Ednl. Alliance, Assn. for Supervision and Curriculum Devel., Phila. Clark Coll. Alumni, Alpha Kappa Alpha (N. Atlanta regional dir., past chpt. pres.). Republican. Clubs: Links; The Ems (Moorestown). Home: 405 Glen Ave Moorestown NJ 08057 Office: Sulzberger 48th and Fairmount Ave Philadelphia PA 19139

GAYNOR, ELIZABETH ANNE, editor; b. Balt., Feb. 21, 1946; d. Emanuel A. and Anne K. G.; B.A. cum laude, Conn. Coll., 1967; m. John William Meakin, Apr. 14, 1979. Fashion coordinator Boussac of France, N.Y.C., 1968-71; at home editor Glamour mag., N.Y.C., 1971-76; home furnishings editor Family Circle mag., N.Y.C., 1976-79; decorating editor Ladies Home Jour., N.Y.C., 1979-80; asso. editor House and Garden, N.Y.C., 1980—. Mem. Am. Soc. Interior Decorators, Nat. Home Fashion League, Women in Communications, Am. Soc. Mag. Editors. Office: 350 Madison Ave New York NY 10017

GAYNOR, LEAH, publicist; b. Irvington, N.J.; d. Jack and Sophia Kamish; A.A., Miami Dade Community Coll., 1970; B.A., Fla. Internat. U., 1975, postgrad., 1975—; m. Robert Merrill, Mar. 27, 1954; children—Michael David, Lisa Heidi, Tracy Lynn. Owner, operator Lee Gaynor Assos., pub. relations, Miami, Fla., 1970-72; exec. dir. Ft. Lauderdale (Fla.) Jaycees, 1970-71; host interview program Sta. WGMA, Hollywood, Fla., 1971-73, Stas. WWOK and WIGL-FM, Fla., 1973-79; occupational specialist Lindsey Hopkins Edn. Center, Dade County Pub. Schs., with publicity-pub. relations dept., Miami, 1971—. Mem. N.E. Citizens Adv. Com. Career and Vocat. Edn., 1973-79; mem. adv. com. North Miami Beach High Sch., 1977-79; mem. communications com. Council Continuing Edn. Women Miami, 1972—. Mem. Women in Communications, Am. Women in Radio and TV (dir. publicity Goldcoast chpt. 1974-76), Public Relations Soc. Am., Internat. Assn. Bus. Communicators (treas. chpt. 1983). Democrat. Home: 1255 NE 171 Terr North Miami Beach FL 33162 Office: 1410 NE 2d Ave Miami FL 33132

GAYNOR, MITZI (FRANCESCA MITZI VON GERBER), actress; b. Chgo., 1930; m. Jack Bean. Dancer with Los Angeles Light Opera Co.; acting roles include; Fortune Teller, Song of Norway, Louisiana Purchase, Naughty Marietta The Great Waltz, South Pacific; motion pictures include My Blue Heaven, Anything Goes, The Joker, Les Girls, South Pacific, Happy Anniversary, Surprise Package, Anniversary Waltz, Birds and the Bees, There's No Business Like Show Business, Bloodhounds of Broadway, Take Care of My Little Girl, Golden Girl, The I Don't Care Girl, We're Not Married, For Love or Money; concert tour U.S., 1972-73; made TV comedy-variety appearance. *

GAYTON, BARBARA JEANNE, food co. mgr.; b. Somerville, Mass., Oct. 8, 1948; d. Harold Russel and Sophia Eva Theresa (Minkiel) G.; A.A., Fairleigh Dickinson U., 1968, B.S., 1974, postgrad. With Thomas J. Lipton, Inc., Englewood Cliffs, N.J., 1968—, sales coordinator, 1973-75, asst. sales promotion mgr., 1975-79, asst. mgr. mktg. info., 1979—. Republican. Roman Catholic. Office: Thomas J Lipton Inc 800 Sylvan Ave Englewood Cliffs NJ 07632

GDOWSKI, SANDRA, software engring. co. exec.; b. Utica, N.Y., Nov. 3, 1953; d. Michael and Frances (Carzo) G.; B.A., U. Calif., San Diego, 1975; postgrad. in elec. engring. U. So. Calif., 1978-81. Programmer analyst Tech. Service Corp., Santa Monica, Calif., 1975-79; software design engr. TRW, Def. and Space Systems Group, Redondo Beach, Calif., 1979-80; mgr. advanced tech. The BDM Corp., Hawthorne, Calif., 1980—. Mem. Nat. Assn. Female Execs., Am. Soc. Profl. and Exec. Women. Office: 5155 Rosecrans Ave Hawthorne CA 90250

GEACINTOV, TAMARA, business exec.; b. Disna, Poland, Dec. 5, 1931; came to U.S., 1952, naturalized, 1954; d. William and Erna Olga (Kentler) Bosianok; B.A., Rutgers U., 1968; m. Cyril Geacintov, Oct. 18, 1953 (div. 1979); children—Elizabeth, Alexis. Research asst. Bell Labs., Piscataway, N.J., 1969-75; founder DRG Internat. Inc. Trading Co., Westfield, N.J., 1971-81, v.p., gen. mgr., 1975-81; founder, pres. Amlab, Inc., Mountainside, N.J., 1980—; lectr. on trade. Contbr. articles to profl. jours. Home and Office: 149 Knightsbridge Rd Mountainside NJ 07092

GEAKE, CAROL LYNNE, veterinarian; b. Grand Rapids, Mich., Feb. 19, 1941; d. John Edward and Alice Geraldine (Bussler) Rens; B.S. in Zoology, U. Mich., 1961, M.S. in Parasitology, 1963; D.V.M., Mich. State U., 1968; m. Raymond Robert Geake, June 9, 1962; children—Roger Rens, Tamara Lynne, William Rens. Research asst. Mus. Zoology, U. Mich., Ann Arbor, 1960-63, research asso. dept. indsl. toxicology, 1963-66; asso. veterinarian Plymouth (Mich.) Vet. Hosp., 1969-70; pvt. practice Vet. medicine, Northville, Mich., 1971—; field investigator Parke-Davis & Co., Ann Arbor, Mich., 1975—; cons. in field. Leader Wayne County (Mich.) 4-H Vet. Sci. Project, 1968-72; trustee St. Mary Hosp., Livonia, Mich., 1980—. Mem. Am., Mich., Southeastern Mich., Women's vet. med. assns., Am. Assn. Equine Practitioners, Northville Bus. and Profl. Women's Club, Phi Sigma, Phi Zeta. Home and office: 48525 W Eight Mile Rd Northville MI 48167

GEARON, CATHLEEN, airline exec.; b. Bay Shore, N.Y., Jan. 28, 1931; d. Joseph Michael and Oonagh Frances (Keown) Gearon; student SUNY, 1948-51; student Calif. State U., 1978—. Operator, N.J. Bell Telephone, Mount Holly, N.J., 1951-52; with Brit. Airways, 1955—, supr. interline sales, N.Y.C., 1960-63, supr. reservations sales, Century City, Calif., 1969-72, computer troubleshooter and coordinator services, 1969—, supr. tng., Los Angeles, 1972—; faculty Los Angeles Trade-Tech. Coll., 1973-75, pvt. travel schs., 1979-80. Served with USAF, 1952-55. Mem. Am. Legion (post comdr. 1980-81, dist. vice comdr. 1981-82, dist. 2d vice comdr. 1982—), Nat. Assn. Female Execs., Air Force Sgts. Assn. Republican. Roman Catholic. Clubs: Past Comdrs., 20 and 4 Honor Soc. Women Legionaires. Home: 6153 Manton Ave Woodland Hills CA 91367 Office: 1901 Ave of the Stars Suite 1000 Los Angeles CA 90067

GEBHARDT, CAROL ANN, neuropsychologist; b. Phila., Oct. 24, 1952; d. Edwin James and Mildred Victoria (Holt) G.; B.A. with honors in Psychology (Nat. Merit scholar 1970-74, Phila. Bd. Edn. Merit scholar 1970-74), Allegheny Coll., 1974; A.M. (teaching fellow 1974-75, grad. scholar 1975-76, advanced teaching fellow 1976-77), Boston U., 1977, Ph.D. (advanced teaching fellow 1977, grad. scholar 1977-78), 1981; m. Abe Shliferstein, Feb. 9, 1980. Animal neuropsychology research asst. Boston VA Hosp., 1975-76; histology research technician Beth Israel Hosp., neurology unit Harvard U. Med. Sch., Boston, 1976; research asst in human neuropsychology Boston U. Sch. Medicine at Boston VA Med. Center, 1977-78; research asst , computerized tomography scan Boston VA Med. Center, 1978-79; Nat. Research Service Award trainee Boston U. Sch. Medicine, 1980-81; cons. neuropsychology, Leonardo, N.J., 1981—. Nat. Research Service awardee NIH, 1980-81. Mem. Internat. Neuropsychol. Soc., Am. Psychol. Assn. Research, publs. in field. Home: 19 Kelvin Ave Leonardo NJ 07737

GEBRE-HIWET, JOCELYN DORSEY, broadcasting co. exec.; b. Boston, Oct. 30, 1950; d. Robert Sherwood and Helena Fredericka (Harris) Dorsey; grad. in journalism, Ohio State U., 1968-72; postgrad. Ga. State U., 1975-76; m. Makonnen Gebre-Hiwet, Aug. 2, 1976; children—Tewodros Makonnen, Robert Fassil Makonnen. Co-moderator Lets Talk About It, Sta. WOSU-TV, 1971; with Sta. WKRC-TV, Cin., 1972; anchorwoman Sta. WSB-TV, Atlanta, 1973—. Mem. Nat. Assn. Media Women, Atlanta Assn. Black Journalists. Episcopalian. Office: Station WSB-TV 1601 W Peachtree St NE Atlanta GA 30309

GEDDES, ANN, talent agy. dir.; b. Evanston, Ill., Nov. 25, 1943; d. Robert Allen and Sara Elizabeth (Bonham) Geddes; student St. Petersburg (Fla.) Pub. Schs.; 1 son, Peter Allen. Profl. model, Chgo., 1963-67; owner, dir. Geddes Agy., Chgo., 1968—; cons. Am. Nat. Bank, 1969, 76, 77, Walter Heller Corp., 1977, Worldbook Child Craft Internat., 1978; dir. Chgo. Unltd., Inc. Mem. Chgo. Assn. Radio and TV Agents. Office: 875 N Michigan Ave Chicago IL 60611

GEDDES, LANELLE EVELYN, nurse-physiologist; b. Houston, Sept. 15, 1935; d. Carl Otto and Evelyn Bertha (Frank) Nerger; B.S.N., U. Houston, 1957, Ph.D. (fellow), 1970; m. Leslie Alexander Geddes, Aug. 3, 1962. Staff nurse Houston Ind. Sch. Dist., 1957-62; instr. to asst. prof. physiology Baylor U. Coll. Medicine, 1972-75; asst. prof. nursing Tex. Women's U., 1972-75; prof., head Sch. Nursing, Purdue U., 1975—. Recipient teaching awards. Mem. Am. Nurses Assn., Nat. League Nursing, Am. Assn. Critical-Care Nurses, AAAS, N.Y. Acad. Scis., Phi Kappa Phi, Sigma Theta Tau, Iota Sigma Pi. Lutheran. Contbr. articles sci. jours., chpts. in books. Office: Sch Nursing Purdue University West Lafayette IN 47907

GEDIMAN, HELEN KORNFELD, clin. psychologist, psychoanalyst; b. N.Y.C., Mar. 23, 1931; d. Louis B. and Minnie (Mabel) Kornfeld; A.B., Radcliffe Coll.-Harvard U., 1952; A.M., Boston U., 1953; Ed.M., Harvard U., 1954; Ph.D. in Clin. Psychology, N.Y.U., 1959, cert. in psychoanalysis and psychotherapy, 1968; 1 son, Paul Henry. Pvt. practice psychoanalysis, N.Y.C., 1961—; asst. clin. prof. psychiatry Albert Einstein Coll. Medicine, 1973—; adj. assoc. prof. psychology N.Y.U., 1972—. Mem. Am. Psychol. Assn., N.Y. Freudian Soc., Inst. for Psychoanalytic Tng. and Research. Contbr. articles to profl. jours. Home: 50 E 89th St New York NY 10028 Office: 40 E 89th St New York NY 10028

GEDMAN, NANCY JOYCE, pub. co. exec.; b. Chgo., Aug. 25, 1951; d. Donald Kent and Elaine Joyce (Newman) G.; B.A. in Journalism, U. Minn., 1973, J.D., 1977; m. Robert D. Hunter, May 8, 1976. Asst. dir. U. Minn. Alumni Assn., St. Paul, 1973-74; admitted to Minn. bar, 1977; partner firm Margoles & Gedman, St. Paul, 1978-80; mgr. acquisitions and mktg. Mason Pub. Co., St. Paul, 1980-81; pres. Butterworth Legal Pubs. div. Butterworth (London-established 1818)-Reed Internat. P.L.C., Newton Upper Falls, Mass., 1981—. Mem. Mass. Bar Assn. Office: Butterworth Legal Pubs 381 Elliot St Newton Upper Falls MA 02164

GEERS, ROSE MAE, real estate exec.; b. Berlin, Md., Jan. 25, 1922; d. Daniel Alexander and Rose Effie (Bassett) Scott; student public schs.; m. Norman Francis Geers, June 14, 1960; children—Bonnie Lee Geers Waldhaus. Propr. Rose Geers, Realtor, Quincy, Ill., 1949—. Mem. Quincy Bd. Realtors (pres. 1973-74; Realtor of Yr. award 1978). Republican. Roman Catholic. Clubs: Spring Lake Country, Elks Ladies Aux. Office: 1012 Maine St Quincy IL 62301

GEETEH, HOLLY SNYDER, calligraphy designer; b. Dallas, Mar. 26, 1920; d. Frederick Albert and Lucie (Holbrook) Snyder; student So. Meth. U., 1950-53; pvt. art lessons DeForest Judd, 1952-53, Jerry Bywaters, 1950-53; m. Samuel Selig Geeteh, Sept. 15, 1940; children—David Harris, John Leslie. Mgr., J.C. Penney Co., North Park, Dallas, 1970-74, Nieman-Marcus, Dallas, 1974-77; owner/designer Holly Specialized Service, Dallas, 1977—. Mem. DAR. Democrat. Mem. Ch. of Christ. Address: 6027 McCommas Blvd Dallas TX 75206

GEFFEN, AMY JILL, coll. adminstr.; b. Bklyn., Apr. 24, 1949; d. Julius Dan and Rose (Kardonsky) G.; B.A., Bklyn. Coll., 1970; M.A. (scholar), Harvard U., 1971; Ph.D., N.Y.U., 1980; postgrad. Institut d'Etudes Françaises - Bryn Mawr summer, 1968; m. George L. Shapiro, June 22, 1980. Tchr., N.Y.C. Bd. Edn., 1972-79, bilingual coordinator Dist. 18, 1978-80; adj. lectr. N.Y. Tech. Coll., 1980; adj. assoc. prof. N.Y.U., 1982—; dir. spl. programs, dir. corp. programs L.I.U. Inst. Continuing Edn., Bklyn., 1980—; pres., founder Resumes for a Change, N.Y.C., 1981—. N.Y. State Regents scholar, 1966-70, Regents fellow, 1970-71; recipient A. U. N. Camera award, 1970. Mem. Am. Council Edn., Nat. Identity Program for Women, Nat. Assn. Women Deans, Adminstrs. and Counselors, Am. Council Higher Edn., MLA, Phi Beta Kappa, Pi Delta Phi. Home: 210 E 15 St New York NY 10003 Office: LIU Inst Continuing Edn University Plaza Brooklyn NY 11201

GEFFEN, BETTY ADA, theatrical personal mgr.; b. Lachine, Que., Can., May 12, 1911; came to U.S., 1942, naturalized, 1945; d. Joseph and Minnie (Illievitz) Gottheil; student public schs., Montreal, Que.; m. Jacob N. Geffen, Dec. 23, 1944; 1 dau., JoAnn Merle. Sec., Saul Cohen/Trustee in Bankruptcy, Montreal, 1926-28, Maxwell Cummings Real Estate, 1928-30, Monroe Abbey, Atty., 1930-31; with Tic-Toc, Stanley Grill and Chez Maurice, Montreal, 1931-41; sec. H.L. Green, N.Y.C., 1941-44; pvt. personal mgr., casting cons., N.Y.C., 1950—; cons. Consab Assos. Corp., N.Y.C., 1966—. Trustee Israel Cancer Research Fund; vol. Floating Hosp. Mem. N.Y. Acad. TV Arts and Scis., Motion Picture Pioneers. Democrat. Clubs: Variety Women (v.p. 1977-81, pres. 1982), Brandeis U., Pioneer Women. Address: 17 W 71st St New York NY 10023

GEFFNER, DONNA SUE, speech pathologist, audiologist, educator; b. N.Y.C., June 24, 1946; d. Louis and Sally (Weiner) G.; B.A. magna cum laude, Bklyn. Coll., 1967; M.A., N.Y.U., 1968, Ph.D. (NDEA fellow), 1970, postgrad. student Advanced Inst. Analytic Psychotherapy, 1973-75. Asst. prof. Lehman Coll., 1971—; prof. dept. speech St. John's U., 1976—, dir. Speech and Hearing Center, 1976—; cons. corp. communications; TV producer and hostess NBC, 1977-78, CBS, 1978-79. Emmy nominee for Outstanding Instrnl. Program, 1978; recipient award Pres.'s Com. on Employment of Handicapped; N.Y. State Edn. Dept. grantee, 1976-78; City U. N.Y. Research Found. grantee, 1972. Fellow Am. Speech, Lang. and Hearing Assn. (legis. councillor 1978—); mem. N.Y. State Speech and Hearing Assn. (pres. 1978-80), Audiology Study Group N.Y., Aphasia Study Group N.Y. Contbr. articles to profl. jours. and textbooks; issue editor Jour. Topics in Lang. Disorders, 1980. Office: St John's Univ Speech and Hearing Center Grand Central Pkwy Jamaica NY 11439

GEHR, PAULA JOY, bank exec.; b. Syracuse, N.Y., June 18, 1946; d. Arthur Cleveland and Helen Joy (Suiter) G.; student Lake Forest Coll. 1964; A.B., Mt. Holyoke Coll., 1968; M.B.A., U. Pa. 1970. With dept. computer applications Merrill Lynch, N.Y.C., 1970-77; with Bradford Trust Co., N.Y.C., 1977; sr. cons. Investment Supervision Consulting Group, Peart Marwick Mitchell & Co., N.Y.C., 1977-80; v.p. Bankers Trust, N.Y.C. 1980—; vice chmn. Trust Universe Comparison Service, 1981, chmn., 1982. Office: 280 Park Ave New York NY 10017

GEHRAND, DENISE MASON, publisher; b. Red Bank, N.J., Aug. 5, 1952; d. William F. and June E. McGourley; A.A., Burlington Community Coll., 1973; student Monmouth Coll., 1974, Stockton State Coll., 1975. Prodn. mgr. Neighbor Newspaper, Tampa, Fla., 1976-77; advt. dir. Pinch-A-Penny, Inc. Clearwater, Fla., 1977-79; mng. editor Baylife Mag., Clearwater, 1979-80; editor Condo Jour., 1980; owner, operator Continental Pub., Inc., Via Newsletters, Clearwater, 1980—; pres. Wakecrest Advt., Inc., 1981—. Mem. Ad Club 2 (editor 2's News 1979-80). Home: 358 State Route 580 Clearwater FL 33519 Office: 5300 Ulmerton Rd Clearwater FL 33520

GEIGER, RUTH, pianist; b. Vienna, Austria, Jan. 30, 1923; came to U.S., 1938, naturalized, 1944; d. Bernhard and Olga (Schreier) Geiger; grad. with honors Juilliard Grad. Sch., 1944. N.Y. debut recital as winner of Naumburg award, 1944; appearances as soloist in recitals and on radio, and with orchs. in U.S.; 1st European concert tour, 1957; ann. tours to Britain, Holland, Belgium, Switzerland, Sweden; concerto soloist with English Chamber Orch., Orch. de Suisse Romande, London Philharmonia; extensive appearances on BBC, Eng., Scotland; pvt. tchr. N.Y.C.; participant summer music sch. U. Sussex, 1971; annual participant as featured pianist in Chamber Music Summer Festival, N.C., Warren Wilson Coll., Asheville, 1972—. Finalist Leventritt contest, 1946, Rachmaninoff contest, 1948. Mem. Sigma Alpha Iota. Recs. include Ruth Geiger Plays Schubert, 1978. Address: 160 W 73 St New York NY 10023

GEIGERMAN, CLARICE FURCHGOTT, pub. relations and ins. co. exec.; b. Charleston, S.C., Sept. 24, 1916; d. Melvin and Doreta (Brown) Furchgott; student Draughon Sch. Commerce, 1934-35, U. Ga., 1935, 36, Am. Inst. Banking, 1936-41, Ga. Inst. Real Estate, 1972; m. Henry David Geigerman, July 4, 1941 (dec. 1967); children—Henry David, Robert M. Sec. to v.p. investment dept. Citizens and So. Nat. Bank, Atlanta, 1935-41; personnel dir. Atlanta Ordnance Dept., 1941-43; pub. relations counselor in pvt. practice, Atlanta, 1944—; agt. Nat. Life Ins. Co., Atlanta, 1968—; real estate agt. First Atlanta Equity, 1972-77, Haunson Realty, 1978—. Bd. dirs. So. Regional Opera, 1968-75, pres., 1968-69; dir. Active Voters, 1965—; pres. Atlanta Playhouse Theatre, 1973—; pres. Atlanta Civic Ballet, 1962-64, bd. dirs., 1962-67; mem. Atlanta Ballet Assos., 1962—; mem. adv. bd. Muscular Dystrophy Assn., 1968—; mem. bd. sponsors Atlanta Symphony Guild, 1969—, v.p. women's bd., 1966-68, mem. policy bd., 1966—; bd. dirs. Atlanta Youth Symphony, 1974—, Atlanta Funds Rev. Bd., 1973-75, Atlanta Music Club, 1972—, Shoestring Opera Co., 1978—; trustee Atlanta Press Club, 1974—, Pro Mozart Soc. Named H. Col. Ga. Gov.'s Staff. Mem. Pub. Relations Soc. Am., Victorian Soc. Am., Nat. Council Jewish Women, Marquis Library Soc., Nat. Acad. TV Arts and Scis., Am. Women in Radio and TV, Women's C. of C., English Speaking Union, Epicurean Soc. Am.; Italian Cultural Soc., Atlanta Hist. Soc., World Assn. Women Journalists. Jewish. Clubs: W. Paces Ferry Raquet, Atlanta Music (dir. 1973—), Oaks, Standard, Ga. Writers. Contbr. articles on arts and music to mags.; co-editor Atlanta Music Club Newsletter and Atlanta Music Club Mag., 1973—; contbg. editor Arts Mag., 1962-63, TV Digest, 1961-62; contbr. articles So. Israelite Newspaper. Home: 620 Peachtree St NE Atlanta GA 30308 Office: 151 Ellis St Atlanta GA 30308

GEISLER, ROSEMARY, computer dealer/lessor co. exec.; b. Chgo., Apr. 5, 1947; d. James Vincent and Raffaella Mary (DeSeno) Pastorello; student Triton Coll., 1970-72; B.A., DePaul U., 1981; m. Ervin R. Geisler, Aug. 17, 1968. Asst. market analyst Evans Products Co., Rolling Meadows, Ill., 1970-76; office services mgr., asst. market analyst Comdisco, Inc., Rosemont, Ill., 1976-78, asst. mktg. product mgr., 1978-80, dir. dealer relations, 1980-81, mktg. product mgr., market maker, 1981—. Mem. Des Plaines (Ill.) Youth Commn. Mem. Computer Dealers/Lessors Assn., DePaul U. Alumni Assn. Home: 85 Brinker Rd Barrington Hills IL 60010 Office: Comdisco Inc 6400 Shafer Ct Rosemont IL 60018

GELBER, LOUISE CARP, lawyer; b. Detroit, Oct. 24, 1921; d. Jacob and Gusta (Schneider) Carp; student Los Angeles City Coll., 1940, U. Mich., 1941; B.A., UCLA, 1942; LL.B., U. Calif., Berkeley, 1943; m. Milton Gelber, July 10, 1943; children—Jack, Bruce, Julie. Admitted to Calif. bar, 1944; research asst. to Judge Roger Traynor, Calif. Sup. Ct., San Francisco, 1944-45; ptnr. Gelber & Gelber, El Monte and Arcadia, Calif., 1945—; judge protem Mcpl. Ct., El Monte Jud. Dist., County Los Angeles, 1962. Asst. treas. Los Angeles County Democratic Congl. Dist., Calif. Dem. State Central Com., 1968. Recipient award of honor El Monte C. of C., 1968. Mem. Arcadia C. of C., Tournament of Roses Assn., LWV, Foothill Bar Assn., Eastern Bar Assn. Home: 1225 Rancho Rd Arcadia CA 91006 Office: 1225 Rancho Rd Arcadia CA 91006

GELFAND, JANICE ROHRS, chem. co. mktg. exec.; b. Balt., Dec. 6, 1951; d. Frederick Vernon and Hazel Regina (Reid) Rohrs; B.S. in Chemistry with honors, U. Del., 1973; postgrad. in bus. adminstrn. Temple U., 1978—; m. Jeffrey Marc Gelfand, Oct. 21, 1979; 1 son, Joshua Elliott. With Rohm and Haas Corp., 1973—, tech. sales rep., Bristol, Pa., 1974-79, asst. sales mgr. specialty chems., Phila., 1979-80, product mgr.-mktg., splty. chems., 1980—. Mem. Chem. Club Phila., Cooling Tower Inst., Chem. Spltys. Mfrs. Assn., Am. Mgmt. Assn. Home: 2 Jonathan Rd Cherry Hill NJ 08003 Office: Rohm and Haas Corp Indsl Chems N Am Independence Mall W Philadelphia PA 19105

GELLER, ETHELL ANN, clin. psychologist; b. Linz, Austria, Sept. 26, 1946; came to U.S., naturalized, 1948; d. Morris and Golda (Braun) Schwartz; B.A. summa cum laude with honors in Psychology, Hunter Coll., 1973; M.A., CUNY, 1975, Ph.D., 1977; m. Ronald D. Geller, June 21, 1964. Tng. fellow Inst. for Advanced Study in Rational Psychotherapy, N.Y.C., 1975-77; grad. teaching fellow Hunter Coll., N.Y.C., 1976-77, adj. asst. prof., 1977; mem. faculty Inst. for Behavioral Therapy, N.Y.C., 1977-78; staff psychologist, supr. Inst. for Rational Psychotherapy, N.Y.C., 1978—; pvt. practice clin. psychology, N.Y.C., 1978—; condr. workshops for Nat. Council on Alcoholism, Am. Humanist Soc., others, 1975—. Mem. Am. Psychol. Assn., Assn. for Advancement Behavior Therapy, Soc. Behavioral Medicine, N.Y. Acad. Scis., Phi Beta Kappa, Psi Chi. Office: 952 Fifth Ave New York NY 10021

GELLER, SHIRLEY FLORENCE, occupational therapist; b. Tarnapol, Poland, Jan. 17, 1921; came to U.S., 1923, naturalized, 1945; d. Isak and Rose (Marder) Scherker; cert. fine arts Cooper Union U., 1944, B.F.A., 1976; cert. occupational therapy Va. Commonwealth U., 1945; m. Murray Geller, Aug. 10, 1946; children—William, Judith. Color engr. Internat. Printing Ink, N.Y.C., 1942-44; chief textile designer Herman Studio, N.Y.C., 1948; occupational therapist Aspinwall (Pa.) VA Hosp., 1949; chief psychiat. day treatment hosp., dir. art therapy Creedmoor Hosp., Queens Village, N.Y., 1963-70; chief occupational therapy Silver Spring (Md.) Day Treatment Center, 1972-74; supr. psychiat. occupational therapy VA Hosp., Washington, 1974-78; dir. adjunctive therapies Community Hosp. of North Hollywood, Los Angeles, 1978-80; chief occupational therapist VA Out-patient Clinic, Los Angeles, 1980—. Dir. dramatic prodn. Bklyn. Coll. Hillel Found., 1946-49; arts and crafts and dancing instr. Lighthouse for the Blind, N.Y.C., 1948; cons. Inst. Holistic Personality Research, N.Y.C., 1950-52, Assn. for Feeling Truth and Living It, N.Y.C., 1964-77; adult edn. painting instr. N.Y.C. Bd. Edn., 1954-57; set designer, actress Great Neck (N.Y.) Community Theater, 1957-70; cons. Nat. Paraplegia Found., 1962-76; human relations group leader Walt Whitman High Sch., Bethesda, Md., 1970-72, Ethical Culture Soc., Washington, 1972-73. Exhibited paintings in group shows: Mus. Modern Art, N.Y.C., 1938, N.Y. World's Fair, 1939, Bklyn. Mus., 1943, Met. Mus. Art, N.Y.C., 1945, Mus. Modern Art, N.Y.C., 1950, Hofstra Coll., 1950-58, L.I. Art Show, Levittown (2d prize), 1952, Contemporary Arts Gallery, N.Y.C., 1958, L.I. Art Show, Manhasset (1st prize 1960). Registered occupational therapist. Mem. Am. Occupational Therapy Assn., World Fedn. Occupational Therapy, D.C. Occupational Therapy Assn., L.I. Occupational Therapy Assn., Calif. Occupational Therapy Assn. Office: 425 S Hill St Los Angeles CA 90013

GELLER, SUSAN CAROL, mathematician, educator; b. Newark, Oct. 27, 1948; d. Albert Seleg and Bernice Ruth (Friedman) G.; B.S., Case Inst. Tech., 1970; M.S., Cornell U., 1972, Ph.D., 1975. Computer programmer Chem. Abstracts Services, Columbus, Ohio, 1970; asst. prof. Purdue U., West Lafayette, Ind., 1975-81; faculty fellow Mary Ingraham Bunting Inst., Radcliffe Coll., Harvard U., Cambridge, Mass., 1980-82; assoc. prof. math. Tex. A&M U., College Station, 1981—. Mem. Community Singers Bryant, Tex., 1981—. NSF fellow, 1970-72; Purdue U. grantee, 1976, 77; NSF grantee, 1977-79, 82—. Mem. Math. Assn. Am., Am. Math. Soc., Am. Women in Math. Contbr. articles to profl. jours. Office: Dept Math Tex A&M Univ College Station TX 77843

GELORMINO, JOAN ANN, educator; b. Torrington, Conn., Jan. 3, 1939; d. Erminio and Jennie Rose Gelormino; B.S., Western Conn. State Coll., Danbury, 1960; M.S., U. Hartford, 1966; Ed.D., Nova U., Ft. Lauderdale, Fla., 1975. Tchr., Torrington Bd. Edn., 1960-62; tchr. Hartford (Conn.) Bd. Edn., 1962-68, tchr., dir., resource tchr. Early Childhood Learning Center, adj. faculty U. Hartford, 1969-71; dir. Lower Sch., Univ. Sch., Nova U., 1971—, asso. dir. Sch. Center, 1973—; cons. Early Childhood Program, Waterbury, West Hartford, Farmington, Conn., 1970-72, Long Beach, N.Y., Half Hollow, N.Y., Merrick, N.Y., Learning Inst. N.C.; cons. migrant edn., Fla., 1973-75, Seminole Pre-Sch. Programs, Fla., Broward County, Fla.; bd. dirs., v.p. United Way Child Care Centers, Broward County, 1975—, pres., 1976-78. Mem. Broward County Environ. Control Bd., 1979-80. Mem. Nat. Assn. for Edn. Young Children, Assn. for Childhood Edn. Internat., Soc. for Research Child Devel., Am. Montessori Assn., AAUW, Fla. Assn. for Children Under Six (conf. chmn. Hollywood 1980). Author: Pre-Number and Mathematic Skill Sequence With Activities, 1969; Constructing Games for Early Childhood Classrooms, 1974; Transactional Analysis For Parents and Teachers of Young Children, 1975. Home: 3630 Citrus Trace Apt 4 Fort Lauderdale FL 33328 Office: 7500 SW 36th St Fort Lauderdale FL 33314

GELWICK, BEVERLY PROSSER, psychologist, educator; b. Lewiston, Maine, Sept. 6, 1932; d. Edward Everett and Beulah Marie (Morrison) Prosser; B.S., Temple U., 1955; M.Ed., U. Mo., Columbia, 1971, Ph.D., 1975; m. Richard Lee Gelwick, May 14, 1955; children—Jennifer Lee Gelwick Luecke, Allen Morrison. Counseling intern, teaching fellow Counseling Service, U. Mo., Columbia, 1971-73, counseling psychologist Coll. Edn., 1974-75; dir. counseling service Univ. Without Walls, Stephens Coll., Columbia, 1975-76, counseling psychologist, counseling service, 1976-78, dir. counseling service, 1978—; adj. asso. prof. Tchrs. Coll., Columbia U., N.Y.C., 1982; vis. lectr. grad. guidance and counseling dept. U. Reading (Eng.), 1973-74. Lic. psychologist, Mo. Fellow Soc. Values in Higher Edn.; mem. Am. Psychol. Assn., Am. Coll. Personnel Assn., Mo. Psychol. Assn., Nat. Register Health Service Providers in Psychology. Mem. United Ch. Christ. Author: Up the Ladder: Women, Professional and Clients in College Student Personnel, 1979. Contbr. articles to profl. jours. and books. Office: Box 2025 Stephens Coll Columbia MO 65215

GEMMELL, SUZANNE, univ. dean; b. Pomona, Calif., June 6, 1938; d. Phil B. and Frances (Holbrook) G.; B.S., U. Oreg., 1960; M.A., U. N.Mex., 1968; Ed.D., Ind. U., 1974. Elem. sch. tchr., Calif., 1960-66; asst. dean women Miami U., Oxford, Ohio, 1967-71; assoc. instr. founds. of edn. Ind. U., Bloomington, 1971-74; assoc. dean students, then dean admissions and records Calif. State U. Dominguez Hills, Carson, 1974-77, dean Univ. Coll., 1977—; cons. in field. Named Outstanding Woman in Edn., Torrance (Calif.) YWCA, 1978. Mem. AAUW, Am. Assn. Higher Edn., Am. Personnel and Guidance Assn., Nat. Assn. Student Personnel Adminstrs., Student Personnel Assn. Calif. Democrat. Episcopalian. Address: Univ Coll Calif State Coll Dominguez Hills Carson CA 90747

GEMMILL, ELIZABETH H., lawyer, banker; b. Phila., Dec. 7, 1945; d. Kenneth W. and Helen H. Gemmill; A.B., Bryn Mawr Coll., 1967; J.D., Boston U., 1970; m. Douglas B. Richardson, July 15, 1977. Admitted to Mass. bar, 1970, Pa. bar, 1973; assoc. firm vom Baur, Coburn, Simmons & Turtle, Boston, 1970-71; staff atty. Cape Cod Legal Services, Inc., Hyannis, Mass., 1971-73; asst. dist. atty. City of Phila., 1973-74; atty., asst. sec. Girard Bank, Phila., 1974-75, sec., treas., counsel, 1975-76, v.p. customer services, 1976-78, v.p., gen. auditor, 1979-81, sr. v.p. personnel dept., 1981—. Active Children's Country Week Assn., Com. of 70, United Way, Contact Phila.; treas. Butera for Gov. Com. Mem. ABA, Pa., Phila. bar assns., Am. Soc. Corp. Secs. (pres. Middle Atlantic group), Nat. Investors Relations Inst., Forum for Exec. Women, Phila. Coll. Textiles and Sci., Greater Phila. Fedn. Settlements, Third Dist. Automated Clearing House, Nat. Found. Women's Health. Home: 3817 The Oak Road Philadelphia PA 19101 Office: Girard Bank Girard Plaza Philadelphia PA 19101 *

GENETTI, MARIANNE ELIZABETH, real estate broker; b. Hazleton, Pa., Dec. 9, 1937; d. August H. and Della Elizabeth (Fox) Genetti; B.S., Pa. State U., 1959; postgrad. Am. U., 1967-68, Rollins Coll., 1971-72. Contract adminstr. Dept. Def. Personnel Support Agy., Phila., 1960-63; asst. mgr. Gus Genetti Hotels, Wilkes-Barre and Hazleton, Pa., 1963-65; project specialist Econ. Devel. Adminstrn., Dept. Commerce, Washington, 1965-69; comptroller Gus Genetti Hotel, Hazleton, 1969-71; contracts specialist Sprint missile Martin-Marietta Corp., Orlando, Fla., 1971-73; broker-salesman Borgon Realty Corp., Orlando, Fla., 1973—; dir. Best Western Genetti, Hazleton; instr. Valencia Community Coll. Open Campus, Orlando, 1982. Grad. Realtors Inst.; recipient Superior Performance award Dept. Commerce, 1969. Mem. Orlando Winter Park Bd. Realtors, Fla. Assn. Realtors, Central Fla. Investors, Mensa. Home: 1401 E Church St Orlando FL 32801 Office: Borgon Realty 110 Wisteria Ave Orlando FL 32806

GENOVESE, LOUISE MARIE, food mgmt. exec.; b. Cleve., Nov. 17, 1937; d. Lorenzo and Louise H. (Salanetro) Genovese; B.S.H., Ohio U., 1959; postgrad. Mills Coll., 1959-60. With Stouffer Restaurant div. Stouffer Foods Corp., Cleve., 1960-68; dir. foods dept. Stouffer Food Service div., 1968-75; dir. food services Fono's Unltd., San Francisco, 1975-77; div. dietitian Servomation Corp., San Francisco, 1977-78; mgr. ops. purchasing Magic Pan, Inc., San Francisco, 1978-81; cons. on food service State of Calif. VA Home, Yountville, Calif., 1977-78, 80; coordinator quality assurance Greyhound Food Mgmt. Inc., div. Greyhound Corp., Phoenix, 1981—. Mem. women's bd. YWCA of San Mateo County, 1980-82. Mem. Am. Dietetic Assn., Ariz. Dietetic Assn., Bus. and Profl. Women's Assn., Cath. Alumnae Assn., Mills Coll. Alumnae Assn. Republican. Roman Catholic. Club: Soroptimist (v.p. 1974-82). Contbr. articles to profl. jours. Office: Greyhound Towers Bldg 2 Sta 3113 Phoenix AZ 85012

GENSEL, PATRICIA GABBEY, paleobotanist; b. Buffalo, Mar. 18, 1944; d. Scott Seburn and Elinor (Dikeman) Gabbey; B.A., Hope Coll., Holland, Mich., 1966; M.S. (NDEA fellow 1967-69), U. Conn., 1969, Ph.D., 1972; m. William H. Gensel, June 1, 1968. Research asst. King's Coll., London, 1966-67; research assoc. U. Conn., 1972-75; mem. faculty U. N.C., Chapel Hill, 1975—, assoc. prof. botany, 1980—. NSF fellow, 1969-72, grantee, 1974-75, 77-79, 80-83. Mem. Bot. Soc. Am. (rep. editorial bd. 1976-82), Am. Fern Soc., Am. Assn. Stratigraphic Palynologists, Palaeontol. Assn., Congress Internat. Microflores Palaeozoique, Internat. Commn. Palynology, Internat. Orgn. Paleobotanists, Sigma Xi, Mortar Bd. Author papers in field. Office: 405 Coker Hall U NC Chapel Hill NC 27514

GENTLEMAN, JULIA B., state senator; b. Des Moines, Aug. 24, 1931; d. John and Marguerite Brooks; B.S., Northwestern U., 1953; m. Gregor Gentleman, 1954; 5 children. Formerly mem. Iowa Ho. of Reps., 1975-78; mem Iowa Senate, 1979—. Office: Iowa State House Des Moines IA 50319

GENTRY, WANDA MARKHAM, utility exec.; b. Franklin, Ky., Oct. 7, 1939; d. Thomas Harris and Edith Nell (Dinwiddie) Markham;

student Bowling Green Bus. U., 1957-58; m. William Henry Gentry, Dec. 30, 1961; children—Jonathan Markham, Laura Leigh. Sec. to gen. mgr. N.H. Granite State Ins. Co., Jacksonville, Fla., 1958-60; sec. Ky. State Hwy. Dept., 1960-63; sec. to dir. of nurses East Ridge Community Hosp., Chattanooga, 1974, adminstrv. asst., 1974-76; adminstrv. asst. to pres. and chmn. bd. Tenn. Natural Gas Lines, Inc., and Nashville Gas Co., 1976—. Mem. Exec. Women Internat. (dir. Nashville chpt. 1978—, sec. 1980). Republican. Baptist. Home: 104 Trout Valley Dr Hendersonville TN 37075 Office: 2000 Parkway Towers Nashville TN 37219

GENUNG, MARJORIE EVELYNN TOWER-TOOKER (MRS. LOUIS T. GENUNG), educator, media specialist, librarian; b. Atkinson, Nebr., Mar. 12, 1925; d. Albert Ralph and Vera Marie (Rickover) Tower-Tooker; student U. Nebr., 1951, Wayne State Coll., 1942-47; B.A., Colo. State Coll., 1966, U. No. Colo., 1970; postgrad. Doane Coll., 1967-68, U. Utah, 1973-74, Ph.D. (hon.), 1973; m. Louis T. Genung, Feb. 2, 1944 (dec. Jan. 1982); 1 son, Louis Thompson. Elem. tchr. Atkinson Public Schs., 1958-69; dir. libraries and audiovisual communications Clay County Dist. I-C, Fairfield, Nebr., 1972-81; media specialist Albion (Nebr.) City Schs., 1981—; mem. Neb. Gov.'s White House Conf. on Libraries. Mem. NEA (life), Nebr., Colo. edn. assns., Assn. Childhood Edn. Internat., ALA, Nebr., Mountain Plains library assns., Nat. Council Tchrs. English, AAUW, Nebr. Ednl. Media Assn., Assn. Supervision and Curriculum Devel., Assn. Ednl. Communications and Tech., Internat. Visual Literacy Assn., Nat. Council Exceptional Children, Alumni Assn. U. No. Colo. (life charter), Women Educators Nebr., Am. Legion Aux., Nebr. Lay Citizens Edn. Assn. (exec.), Am. Nat. Cowbelles, Nebr. Cowbelles, DAR (regent 1971, dist. treas. 1968-71), Internat. Platform Assn., LWV, Women's Soc. Christian Service, Ak-Sar-Ben. Methodist. Mem. Order Eastern Star. Home: 902 E 7th St Hastings NE 68901 also Atkinson NE 68713

GEO-KARIS, ADELINE JAY, state senator; b. Tegeas, Greece; student Northwestern U., Mt. Holyoke Coll.; LL.B., DePaul U. Admitted to Ill. bar; prin. Adeline J. Geo-Karis & Assocs., Zion, Ill.; mcpl. and legis. atty., Mundelein, Vernon Hills, Libertyville Twp., Long Grove Sch. Dist.; formerly justice of peace; former asst. state's atty.; former mem. Ill. Ho. Reps.; now mem. Ill. State Senate, minority spokesman labor and commerce com., environment, energy and natural resources com., chmn. alt. energy com.; chmn. Ill. Energy Resources Commn.; mem. Nuclear Safety Com., AEC, Consumer's Coordinating Council, numerous other coms.; sponsor Nuclear Safety Preparedness bill, 1979. Office: Ill Senate 1 State Capitol Springfield IL 62706

GEORGE, DOROTHY BELLE GIBBS, former social worker, civic worker; b. New Bern, N.C., Oct. 2, 1928; d. Edward and Lillian (Boone) Gibbs; student Hampton Inst., 1947-48; B.A. in English, Morgan State U., 1951; postgrad. U. Md., 1967; m. Liston Alvor George, Sept. 17, 1950; children—Brenda Claryce, Liston Alvor, LaVerne Yvette. Social welfare caseworker, St. Thomas, V.I., 1951-52; caseworker Balt. Dept. Social Services, 1954-67, supr., 1967-68; dir. neighborhood center Urban Services Agy., Balt., 1967-72, dir. youth devel. program, 1972-77; cons. on resolution of day care center audits to Md. sec. human resources, 1977-80, ret., 1980. Bd. dirs. Md. Credit Union Ins. Corp., 1975—; cons. on consumer edn., credit union and youth devel. programs to civic, religious and govt. groups, 1968—; past mem. Balt. Mayor's Citizens Coordinating Council; mem. Balt. City Women Job Corps Com; organizer low-income credit union, Balt., 1968, also organizer, consumer coordinator 4 ltd. credit unions, 1968-69. Cert. econ. developer Nat. Council for Equal Bus. Opportunity, cert. organizer, operator, counselor Nat. Credit Union Adminstrn. Mem. Balt. Bridge Congress, NAACP. Democrat. Episcopalian. Clubs: Holidays, Gems Social. Home: 201 Suter Rd Baltimore MD 21228

GEORGE, DOROTHY EVELYN, educator; b. Stewart, Miss., Dec. 26, 1922; d. James Thomas and Linda Sharron G.; Asso. in Religious Edn., Southwestern Bapt. Theol. Sem., 1952; B.S. in Elem. Edn., Miss. Coll., 1955. Secretarial position United Gas Pipe Line Co., Jackson, Miss., 1943-49; elem. dir. Highland Baptist Ch., Dallas, 1952-53; dir. Bapt. Student Union, Lakeland, Fla., 1954-55; elem. dir. First Bapt. Ch., Jackson, 1956-59; cons. presch. and children's work, ch. tng. dept. Miss. Bapt. Conv., Jackson, 1959—; cons. in work with mentally retarded in chs. in Miss. Mem. So. Bapt. Religious Edn. Assn., Assn. for Childhood Edn. Internat., Miss. Bapt. Religious Edn. Assn., So. Assn. for Children Under Six, Miss. Assn. for Children Under Six. Home: 237 Lorenz St Jackson MS 39216 Office: Miss Bapt Conv Box 530 Jackson MS 39205

GEORGE, ELIZABETH HARRIS, TV sta. ofcl.; b. Washington, Dec. 19, 1953; d. William L. and Janie Sybil (Beach) Harris; bus. adminstrn. degree, King's Coll. Bus., 1976; grad. Southeastern Coll. Beauty, 1980; m. May 29, 1982. With Susie Casuals, Charlotte, N.C., 1970-78; sales cons. Belk's, Charlotte, 1979; buyer, sales rep. The Fruit Basket Inc., Charlotte, 1979-81; adminstrv. asst. PM Mag., Sta. WBTV-TV Charlotte, 1981—; make-up cons. Lic. cosmotologist. Mem. Nat. Assn. Female Execs., Nat. Audubon Soc., Smithsonian Instn.

GEORGE, ETHEL TODD, artist, author; b. Montgomery, Ohio, Oct. 9, 1906; d. Clifford and Mary-Jane (Perin) Todd; B.S., U. Cin., 1928; M.A., Western Res. U., 1962; m. Harold Andrew Manderson, Jan. 18, 1930 (dec. Aug. 1950); children—Martha Perin Manderson Phillips, Sarah Evans Manderson Luebbe; m. 2d, Alonzo Milton George, July 11, 1970. Sports broadcaster Sta. WLW, Cin., 1927-30; instr. art, public schs. Cleve., 1959-60; art supr. public schs., Kenston, Ohio, 1960-63; art supr., master tchr. Aurora (Ohio) High Sch., 1964-70; exhibited over 30 one-woman shows including: St. Francis Parish House, Stamford Conn., 1971, Stamford Yacht Club, 1973, Easter Seal Rehab. Center, Stamford, 1974-76, Eagle Towers, Stamford, 1976, Perrot Meml. Library, Old Greenwich, Conn., 1978, Town Club, Cin., 1979, 1st Presbyn. Ch., Stamford, 1979, Whitney Shop, New Canaan, Conn., 1980, Court Galleries, Cin., 1981, Garden Center Greater Cleve., 1981, Stone Studio, Stamford, 1981, Boca Grande Gallery, Gasparilla Island, Fla., 1982; exhibited over 100 group shows including: Conn. Women Artists, Norwich, 1973-74, Hudson Valley Art Assn., White Plains, N.Y., 1974-76, Conn. Classics, Trumbull, 1975-78, Catharine Lorillard Wolfe Art Club, N.Y.C., 1975-78, Nat. Arts Club, N.Y.C., 1975, Salmagundi Club, N.Y.C., 1976-78, Pen and Brush, N.Y.C., 1976-78, Conn. Watercolor Soc., Hartford, 1976, Bergen Guild travelling shows, 1977-78; artist, instr., owner Hidden Acre Studio, Stamford, Leader, Girl Scouts U.S.A., 1928-48; condr. demonstrations and workshops; art show judge; instr. ARC. Recipient Bronze plaque Conn. Exhbn. Nat. League Am. Pen women, 1973; Anna Hyatt Huntington Bronze medal Nat. Arts Club N.Y.C., 1975; Grumbacher award Pen and Brush Exhbn. N.Y.C., 1976 Dorothy L. Ferris award, 1981; spl. award Conn. state Pen Women exhibit, 1981; Grumbacher bronze medallion Catharine Lorillard Wolfe Art Club, 1981. Mem. Nat. League Am. Pen Women (pres. Pioneer chpt. 1980-82), Salmagundi Club N.Y.C., Pen and Brush Club N.Y.C., Catherine Lorillard Wolfe Art Club N.Y.C., Am. Watercolor Soc. (asso.), Whiskey Painters Am., Am. Crafts Council, Stamford, Old Greenwich art socs., Kappa Delta, Phi Delta Pi. Republican. Episcopalian. Author: Painting Flowers with Watercolor, 1980. Home: 200 Hunting Ridge Rd Stamford CT 06903

GEORGE, GAYLE MARSH, med. technologist; b. Charlotte, N.C., Feb. 18, 1944; d. David Pardue George and Elizabeth (Marsh) Quackenbush; student N.Y.U., 1980—. Med. technologist Dr. T.H. Byrns Lab., Charlotte, 1964-67; med. technologist Mercy Hosp., Charlotte, 1967-70, Med. U. S.C., Charleston, 1970-72; asst. supr. med. technologists VA Med. Center, Charleston, 1972-77, supr. med. technologists, Salem, Va., 1977—. Asst. chmn. EEO, Salem, 1980-82. Recipient spl. recognition award Combined Fed. Campaign of United Way, 1976. Mem. Am. Assn. Med. Technologists, Nat. Assn. Female Execs., Am. Soc. for Clin. Pathologists, Nat. Accredited Agy. for Med. Lab. Scientists, DAR, UDC. Republican. Episcopalian. Home: PO Box 683 Salem VA 24153 Office: 1970 Blvd Salem VA 24153

GEORGE, MARY SHANNON, state senator; b. Seattle, May 27, 1916; d. William Day and Agnes (Lovejoy) Shannon; B.A. cum laude, U. Wash., 1937; postgrad. U. Mich., 1937, Columbia U., 1938; m. Flave Joseph George; children—Flave Joseph, Karen George Van Hook, Christy, Shannon George Lowrey. Prodn. asst., asst. news editor Pathe News, N.Y.C., 1938-42; mem. fgn. editions staff Readers Digest, Pleasantville, N.Y., 1942-46; columnist Caracas (Venezuela) Daily Jour., 1953-60; councilwoman City and County of Honolulu, 1969-74; senator State of Hawaii, 1974—, asst. minority leader, 1978-80, chmn. transp. com., 1981-82; mem. Nat. Air Quality Adv. Bd., 1974-75. Vice chmn. 1st Hawaii Ethics Commn., 1968; mem. budget com. Aloha United Fund, 1970; co-founder Citizens Com. on Constl. Conv., 1968; vice-chmn. platform com. Republican Nat. Conv., 1976, co-chmn., 1980; bd. dirs. Hawaii Planned Parenthood, 1970-72, 79—, Hawaii Med. Services Assn., 1973—. Recipient Jewish Men's Club Brotherhood award, 1974; named Woman of Yr., Honolulu Press Club, 1969, Hawaii Fedn. Bus. and Profl. Women, 1970; Citizen of Yr., Hawaii Fed. Exec. Bd., 1973, 76. Mem. LWV (pres. Honolulu 1966-68), Mensa, Phi Beta Kappa, Kappa Alpha Theta. Episcopalian. Author: A Is for Abrazo, 1961. Home: 782-G N Kalaheo Ave Kailua HI 96734 Office: Hawaii State Capitol Honolulu HI 96813

GEORGE, META WADE, librarian, educator; b. Sumter, S.C., Sept. 19, 1923; d. M.L. and Meta (Long) Wade; B.A. in English, Morris Coll., 1944; certificate Bank Street Coll. of Edn., 1976; postgrad. N.Y. U., N.Y. State U., 1973; cert. in supervision and adminstrn. Fordham U., 1980; m. Albert L. George; children—Beverly June George Ruhe, Margaret A. Elec. inspector Western Electric Co., N.Y.C., 1946-50; tchr. Mid-Westchester Sch., Eastchester, N.Y., 1959-60; reading specialist Mt. Vernon (N.Y.) Bd. Edn., 1963—, media librarian, 1975—, tchr., 1963-78. Pres., Aspire Girls' Club, 1973-76; organizer Langdon-Oneida Block Assn., 1966—; coordinator adult Bible class 1st Presbyn. Ch., Mt. Vernon, N.Y., 1970-76, ruling elder, 1970-74, chmn. bd. Christian edn., 1970-76; bd. dirs. Post Rd. council Girl Scouts U.S., 1960-78. Recipient Jenkins award for outstanding service to young people, 1980. Mem. Am. Assn. for Study of African-Am. Life and History (v.p. Westchester chpt. 1963-78), League of Women Voters. Home: 825 Gramatan Ave Mount Vernon NY 10552 Office: Board of Education Mount Vernon NY 10553

GEORGE, PHYLLIS, sports broadcaster; b. Denton, Tex.; student N. Tex. State U., Tex. Christian U.; m. Robert Evans, Apr. 14, 1977 (div. 1978); m. 2d, John Y. Brown, Jr., Mar. 17, 1979; 1 son, Lincoln Tyler George. Joined staff CBS Sports, 1975, co-host NFL Today Show, CBS Control; co-host Miss America Pageant, 1972-78, also Candid Camera; other TV appearances include: Tonight Show, Kraft Music Hall, Muppets Show, Charlie Brown's 30th Birthday; host TV series People, 1978; co-host Tournament of Roses Parade and Macy's Thanksgiving Day Parade; lectr. Named Miss America, 1971. Office: care Governors Office State Capitol Frankfort KY 40601

GEORGE, VIRGINIA MAXWELL, nurse; b. Birmingham, Ala.; d. William Robert and Kittye Lee (Bradford) Maxwell; B.S. in Nursing, Vanderbilt U., 1947; M.S., U. Ala., 1963; M.A., George Peabody Coll., Nashville, 1972; m. Ralph Thaddeus George, Nov. 15, 1944; children—Kittye Lynn, Lee Anne. Instr. nursing N.E. La. State U., Monroe, 1963-64; mem. faculty Vanderbilt U. Sch. Nursing, Nashville, 1964—, assoc. prof. nursing, 1972—, dir. family nurse clinician program, 1975—; nurse practitioner grant application reviewer, div. nursing HEW; bd. dirs. United Neighborhood Health Services, 1978-81, sec., 1978-80, treas., 1980-81; bd. dirs. Ctr. Health Services, 1974—. Recipient Shirley Titus award Vanderbilt U. Sch. Nursing, 1970; HEW grantee, 1978-83. Mem. Am. Nurses Assn., Sigma Theta Tau. Home: 3716 Belmont Blvd Nashville TN 37215 Office: Vanderbilt U Sch Nursing Nashville TN 37240

GEORGES, LINDA SWINSON, anesthesiologist; b. Orangeburg, S.C., Feb. 26, 1948; d. Rodney Southerland and Marian Edwards Swinson; B.S., Emory U., 1970; M.D., Med. Coll. Ga., 1976; m. Gregory L. Georges, Aug. 21, 1982. Intern in surgery Med. Coll. Ga., Augusta, 1976-77, resident in anesthesiology, 1977-79; fellow in anesthesiology U. Utah, Salt Lake City, 1979-80, instr. anesthesiology, 1979-82, asst. prof., 1982—, asst. to med. dir. pediatric intensive care unit, 1982—; asst. chief anesthesiology Shriners' Hosp. for Crippled Children, Salt Lake City, 1979—. Med. lic. S.C., Ga., Utah. Diplomate Am. Bd. Anesthesiology, Nat. Bd. Med. Examiners. Mem. AMA, Utah State Med. Assn., Salt Lake County Med. Assn., Am. Soc. Anesthesiologists, Internat. Anesthesiology Research Soc., Am. Med. Women's Assn., Soc. Critical Care Medicine, Alpha Omega Alpha. Presbyterian. Home: 1665 Sherman Ave Salt Lake City UT 84105 Office: U Utah Med Center 50 N Medical Dr Salt Lake City UT 84132

GEORGESON, KATHLEEN MIELE, social worker; b. N.J., June 27, 1945; d. John F. and Kathryn (McDonough) Foulkrod; B.A., Chestnut Hill Coll., 1967; M.S.W., Fordham U., 1971; postgrad. Nathan Ackerman Family Inst., 1974-77; m. Carl L. Georgeson, June 4, 1977. Social worker Spence Chapin Adoption Service, N.Y.C., 1967-70; psychiat. social worker St. Vincents Hosp. and Med. Center, N.Y.C., 1971-79; clin. social worker Fair Oaks Hosp., Summit, N.J., 1980—; pvt. practice clin. social work, Summit, 1977—. Mem. steering com. Womens Network St. Bartholomew Community Club, 1978-79. NIMH grantee, 1970-71. Fellow Soc. Clin. Social Work Psychotherapists; mem. Nat. Acad. Cert. Social Wrokers, Am. Assn. Marriage and Family Therapists (clin. mem.). Home: 90 West End Ave Summit NJ 07901 Office: 19 Prospect St Summit NJ 07901

GEORGETTE, FRANCES, mgmt. cons. co. exec.; b. Los Angeles; B.A. magna cum laude, U. So. Calif., 1956, Ph.D., 1977; 1 dau., Jane L. Watson. Cons. Reiss-Davis Child Study Inst., Los Angeles, 1959-63, Los Angeles Psychiat. Service, 1963-66, Los Angeles City Sch. Child Guidance Centers, 1963-66; teaching asst. grad. dept. clin. psychology U. So. Calif., 1964-65; cons. Washington Sch. Psychiatry, 1966-70; pres. Frances Georgette Watson Assos., Washington, 1969-72, Planning & Human Systems, Inc., Washington, 1972—; mem. vol. staff Small Bus. Guidance and Devel. Center, Howard U., 1968-72. Trustee, Women's Equity Action League, Washington, 1978; active NOW. Recipient Service award U. So. Calif. Alumni Assn., 1977. Mem. Am. Psychol. Assn., D.C. Psychol. Assn., Soc. Internat. Devel., Mensa, Phi Beta Kappa. Club: U. So. Calif. Alumni (pres. club 1970-76) (Washington). Contbr. articles to profl. jours. Office: 3201 New Mexico Ave NW Washington DC 20016

GEORGINA, CYNTHIA CUTTER, radio sta. exec.; b. Peterborough, N.H., May 25, 1936; d. Howard Clifton and Frances M. (King) Cutter; student Keene State Coll., 1975 Franklin Pierce Coll., 1982; m. Malcolm L. Georgina, Apr. 16, 1954; children—William L., Daniel H., Susan G., Diane B. With Keene (N.H.) Sentinel, 1963-72; with Sta. WKNE, Keene, 1972—, hostess daily talk show, 1976—, supr. ops., 1978-81, sta. mgr., 1981—. Active civic groups. Democrat. Methodist. Home: 41 Bent Ct Keene NH 03431 Office: Box 466 Stanhope Ave Keene NH 03431

GERARD, BARBARA, educator, visual artist; b. N.Y.C., Apr. 21, 1943; d. Arthur and Edith (Perrone) De Bernarda; B.S., N.Y.U., 1963, M.A., 1966, postgrad., 1972; profl. diploma, City Coll. of CUNY, 1975; postgrad. Columbia U., 1977-79; m. Marvin Hartenstein, Sept. 18, 1976; 1 son by previous marriage—David Gerard. Graphic designer C. A. Parshall Advt. Agy., N.Y.C., 1962; art tchr. Herman Ridder Jr. High Sch., N.Y.C., 1963-65; free lance designer Sam Muggeo Advt. Inc., N.Y.C., 1965-67; art chmn. Herman Ridder Jr. High Sch., 1967-70; program counselor recruitment and tng. of Spanish-speaking tchrs., N.Y.C. Bd. Edn., 1970-72, program coordinator bilingual pupil services Center for Bilingual Edn., 1972-75, dir. bilingual tchr.-intern program, 1975-79, dir. Center for Dissemination, 1979-81; owner, v.p. George Gerard Assocs., Inc., Port Washington, N.Y., 1981—; cons. Yeshiva U., Pace U., 1973, Aspiria of N.Y., 1974, Children's TV Workshop - Sesame St., 1975; adj. lectr. CCNY, 1973-74, N.Y.U., 1974-75, Coll. New Rochelle, 1974-75; cons., participant WNBC-TV, 1970, 75, 79; one woman shows: Lincoln Inst. Gallery, N.Y., 1968, Henry Hicks Gallery, Bklyn., 1976, Second Story Spring St. Gallery, N.Y., 1976, Viridian Gallery, N.Y., 1977, 79; exhibited in group shows Loeb Student Center Gallery, N.Y.C., 1962, 63, Riverdale Community Gallery, N.Y., 1965, Environment Gallery, N.Y.C., 1969, Metamorphosis, N.Y., 1970, Concepts II, N.Y.C., 1971, Union Carbide, N.Y., 1972, Lever House, 1973, Westchester Arts Soc., White Plains, N.Y., 1973, Gillary Gallery, Jericho, L.I., 1974, Manhattan Savs. Bank, 1976, Bklyn. Acad. Music, 1976, Pvt. Viewings/The Erlichs, The Colins, 1976, Gallery 91, Bklyn., 1976, Henry Hicks Gallery, Bklyn., 1975, 76, 77, Lincoln Center, Avery Fisher Hall N.Y., 1976, Second Story Spring St. Gallery, 1976, Bergdorf Goodman, White Plains, 1976, First Women's Bank, 1976, 80, Viridian Gallery, 1976, 77, 80, Womanart Gallery, 1976, Norman Kramer Gallery, Danbury, Conn., 1976, Mfrs. Hanover Bank, N.Y., 1977, Guild Hall Mus., East Hampton, N.Y., 1977, 80, Union of Maine Artists, Portland, 1977, Northeastern U., Boston, 1978, Vered Internat. Gallery, East Hampton, 1978, Women in the Arts Gallery, 1979, Rensselaer Inst., Troy, 1979, Marie Dellicone Gallery, 1981; represented in permanent collections Mus. Contemporary Crafts, N.Y.C., BBD&O Advt., Inc., N.Y.C.; also pvt. collections. Chmn., Pres.' Task Force on Bilingual Edn., 1972; v.p. Viridian Gallery, 1976-77; bd. dirs. Nat. Assn. Italian-Am. Dirs., 1982; v.p. Italian Bilingual Bicultural Educators Assn., 1982. HEW/Fed. Govt. ESEA Title VII grantee, 1975-79; recipient Nat. Scene Award for Achievement in Arts and Culture, 1979. Mem. NEA, Nat. Assn. Bilingual Edn., N.Y. State Assn. Bilingual Edn., Council Supervisory Adminstrs., NOW, Am. Council for Arts, Coalition of Women Artists Orgn., Assn. of Artist-Run Galleries, Women in the Arts, Advt. Women N.Y., Women Bus. Owners of N.Y. Contbr. articles to profl. jours. Home: 3 Briarcliff Dr Port Washington NY 11050 Office: 270 Main St Port Washington NY 11050

GERARD, JEAN BROWARD SHEVLIN, UNESCO ofcl., civic worker; b. Portland, Oreg., Mar. 9, 1938; d. Edwin Leonard and Ella (Broward) Shevlin; B.A., Vassar Coll., 1959; J.D., Fordham U., 1977; m. James Watson Gerard, II, June 20, 1959; children—James Watson, Harriet Coster. Area dir. Europe Res. Officers Ladies, 1960-61; sec. aux. Sheltering Arms Children's Service, 1967-68, 69-70; co-chmn. Viennese Opera Ball, N.Y.C., 1967-82; bd. govs. Women's Nat. Republican Club, 1967-73, 74-80, rec. sec., 1968-70, pres., 1971-73, treas., 1974, chmn. 53d ann. luncheon, 1974; bd. dirs. Knickerbocker Greys, 1968-74; sec. Com. to Unite Am., 1970—; bd. dirs. Youth Found., 1973—, sec., 1973-77, U.S. Flag Found., 1974—; trustee Hancock County Trustees of Pub. Reservations, 1977—; alt. del. Rep. Nat. Conv., 1980; ambassador, permanent del. of U.S. to UNESCO, Paris, 1981—, exec. bd., 1982—. Recipient medal of appreciation SAR, 1970; medal of honor VFW, 1982. Mem. N.Y. County Lawyers Assn., ABA, D.C., Fla., N.Y. State bar assns., Women's Econ. Round Table, Colonial Dames Am., DAR, Nat. Soc. New Eng. Women, Nat. Soc. Magna Carta Dames, France-Am. Soc., Order of Lafayette, Phi Alpha Delta. Presbyterian. Clubs: Colony, Republic, City Midday; Capitol Hill; Racing de France. Home: 201 E 79th St New York NY 10021 Office: 1 Rue Miollis Paris 75015 France

GERBI, SUSAN ALEXANDRA, biology educator; b. N.Y.C.; Mar. 13, 1944; d. Claudio and Jeanette Lena (Klein) Gerbi; B.A. (N.Y. State Regents scholar), Barnard Coll., 1965; M.Phil., Yale, 1968, Ph.D. (NIH fellow), 1970; m. James Terrell McIlwain, April 10, 1976. NATO and Jane Coffin Childs Fund fellow Max-Planck Institut fur Biologie, Tubingen, W. Ger., 1970-72; asst. prof. biology Brown U., Providence, 1972-77, assoc. prof., 1977-82, prof., 1982—; vis. assoc. prof. Duke U., Durham, N.C., 1981-82; mem. genetics research grants rev. panel NSF, 1979-81; mem. genetic basis of disease com. NIH, 1981—. Dist. commr. Palmer River Pony Club, 1973-75. NIH research grantee, 1974—, research career devel. awardee, 1975-80. Mem. Am. Soc. for Cell Biology, Soc. for Devel. Biology, Genetics Soc., Sigma Xi. Contbr. articles to profl. jours. Office: Biomedical Div Brown U Providence RI 02912

GERBIG, LINDA MARY, med. found. adminstr.; b. Winchester, Va., Sept. 29, 1948; d. Emery Noel and Charlotte Florence (Williams) G.; student Murray State U., 1966-70, Trevecca Nazarene Coll., 1970-71, Tulane U., 1980—. Staff nurse pediatric surgery, Vanderbilt U. Hosp., Nashville, 1970-71; emergency room head nurse, Bapt. Hosp., Nashville, 1971-77; regional coordinator Tenn. Found. for Med. Care, Nashville, 1977-79; hosp. rev. mgr. S.E. La. Med. Quality Rev. Found., 1978-80, dir. program ops., 1980—; instr. Tulane U. Sch. Community Medicine, 1981—. Mem. Women's Aux. Christian Counseling Services. Mem. Am. Coll. Utilization Rev. Physicians. Republican. Nazarene. Home: 801C Wilshire Blvd Metairie LA 70005 Office: 3000 Magazine St Suite 200 New Orleans LA 70115

GEREAU, MARY C., legis. asst.; b. Winterset, Iowa, Oct. 10, 1916; d. David Joseph and Sarah Rose (Stack) Condon; B.A., U. Iowa, 1939, M.A., 1941; student Mt. Mercy Jr. Coll., 1935-37; m. Gerald Robert Gereau, Jan. 14, 1961. Program dir. ARC, India, 1943-45; dean of students Eastern Mont. Coll., 1946-48; supt. pub. instrn. state of Mont., 1948-56; sr. legis. cons. NEA, 1957-73; dir. legislation Nat. Treasury Employees Union, 1973-76; legis. asst. to Sen. Melcher, Mont., 1976—. Mem. Council Chief State Sch. Officers (dir. 1953-56, pres. 1956), Rural Edn. Assn. (exec. bd. 1953-56), Nat. Women's Party (sec.), Equal Rights Ratification Council (nat. chmn.), NEA. Named Conservationist of Yr., Mont. Conservation Council, 1952; recipient Disting. Service award VFW, 1951; Disting. Service award, Chief State Sch. Officers, 1956. Contbr. articles on state govt., edn. to profl. jours. Office: Rm 1123 Dirksen Senate Office Bldg Washington DC 20510

GERHARDT, DORIS VIRGINIA, real estate co. exec.; b. Atlanta, Aug. 19, 1932; d. Oscar Claude and Dora Lee (Tolbert) Wilson; student Pasadena City Coll., Mission Coll.; m. James Walter Wade, Jan. 1948 (div. 1950); 1 dau., Debra Darlene; m. 2d, Herman Frederick Gerhardt, Mar. 5, 1959. Dental asst. Dr. A.J. Helfenbein, Montrose, Calif., 1957-61; bookkeeper Max Factor, Hollywood, Calif., 1961-66, Gianera Pontiac, LaCrescenta, Calif., 1966-70; sales mgr. Pro Realty, Calif., 1974-81; with D. Pro Realty, Paradise, 1981—. Mem. Nat. Bd. Realtors, Calif. Bd. Realtors, Los Angeles Bd. Realtors, Sunland-Tujunga C. of C. Republican. Home: 4901 Clark Rd Paradise CA 95969

GERKE, ROBERTA, free lance writer; b. State Center, Iowa, Mar. 2, 1903; d. William H. and Mary (Oehlsen) Gerke; A.B., Mills Coll., 1940. Sec. Calif. Gov. James Rolph, Jr., 1931-33; sec. Louis B. Mayer, Metro-Goldwyn-Mayer Studios, Hollywood, 1933-34; wrote and presented radio program Todays Career Women, 1940-46; pub. relations dir. The Robert Dollar Co., 1946-59; travel dir. Nob Hill Travel Service, 1960—, Jet Travel, Inc., Manila, Philippines, 1963—; Open Doors columnist, State Center (Iowa) Enterprise, 1962-68, Radio Post, Fredericksburg, Tex., 1962-63, Oakland (Calif.) Tribune, 1964-65, Calif. Sr. Citizen News, 1969—. Am. corr. London, covered wedding of Princess Elizabeth, 1947, and coronation, 1953. Recipient Woman of Distinction award City-County Record, San Francisco, 1954; Janice Wilkin Gavel award, Armed Forces Service League, 1963; awards Calif. Press Women, 1970, 72; award Pacific Northwest Writers Conf., 1971. Mem. Calif. Hist. Soc., English-Speaking Union, San Francisco Women's C. of C., Women in Communication. Clubs: Mills (San Francisco); Washington Press. Am. Newspaper Women's (Washington); Calif. Writers; Calif. Press Women; Nat. Fedn. Press Women. Author: Highlights-Dollar Line Case, 1951; Open Doors in Europe, 1953; European Adventure, 1958; also mag. articles. Home: 1233 California St San Francisco CA 94109

GERKE, SUSAN AUFDERHAAR, info. mgmt. co. ofcl.; b. Celina, Ohio, Feb. 14, 1951; d. Norman Robert and Eleanor Belle (Shook) Aufderhaar; B.G.S., U. Nebr., Omaha, 1978; cert. M.I.T., 1980; m. David Joseph Gerke, Dec. 17, 1973; 1 dau., Laura Michelle. Programmer/systems analyst Dept. Def., U.S. Air Force, 1969-75; sr. programmer, analyst, mgr. quality assurance Majers Market Research, 1978-79; staff mgr. bus. systems Northwestern Bell Telephone Co., Omaha, 1979-82, staff mgr. area tech. support Am. Bell Telephone Co., Omaha, 1982—. Active scouting program for inner-city youth, YWCA, Joslyn Mus., Fontennelle Forest, Voices of Omaha; past worthy advisor Rainbow for Girls; active United Way campaign, Emmy Gifford Children's Theater. Served with USAF, 1969-75; Vietnam. Decorated Air Force Commendation medal. Mem. Assn. Computing Machinery (past sec.), Data Processing Mgrs. Assn. (exec. bd., sec.), Nat. Assn. Female Execs., Am. Mgmt. Assn., Smithsonian Instn., Applewood Heights Home Owners, Nat. Honor Soc. Republican. Mem. United Ch. of Christ. Club: Eastern Star. Office: Northwestern Bell Telephone Co 100 S 19th St Omaha NE 68102

GERLING, INGRID HELGA, nurse; b. Cottleus, Germany, Feb. 24, 1934; came to U.S., 1952, naturalized, 1958; d. Adolf and Herta (Lehmann) G.; B.S. in Nursing, U. Utah, 1964, M.S.W., 1967; R.N., Midstate Bapt. Hosp., Nashville, 1957; children—Christian A., Michael K. Generic social worker Bur. Indian Affairs, Fairbanks, Alaska, 1967-69; sch. social worker Pocatello Sch. Dist., 1969-76; nursing supr. Woodland Park Mental Health Center, Portland, Oreg., 1976-79; dist. nurse Estacada (Oreg.) Sch. Dist., 1979—. Chmn. social com. Met. Youth Symphony, 1979-81. Recipient award for outstanding services Bur. Indian Affairs, 1967. Mem. Nat. Assn. Social Workers (Fairbanks Area rep. 1968-69, treas. East Idaho br. 1971-74), Acad. Cert. Social Workers. Home: 7525 Springhill Dr Gladstone OR 97027 Office: PO Box 108 Estacada OR 97023

GERMAIN, ANNE CROFT, newspaper editor, publisher; b. Helena, Mont., Feb. 14; d. George Noel and Mary Alice (Blaisdell) Middlemas; student U. Mont., 1947-51, U. Calif., 1954-56; m. Richard L. Croft, 1949; children—Laren V. Croft Brill, Wendy A.; m. 2d, Richard K. Germain, 1957. Editor, photographer, writer Los Gatos (Calif.) Times-Observer, 1958-61, Sta. KSBW-AM-TV, Salinas, Calif., 1962-64; editor, feature writer San Jose (Calif.) Mercury, 1961-62; asst. to pub., book editor Monterey (Calif.) Peninsula Herald, 1965-70, editor, columnist, 1970—; founding pres. Town and Country Press, Monterey, 1975—. Mem. Newspaper Guild, ACLU (dir.). Author: Pebble Beach: The Way It Was, 1976. Office: Box 271 Monterey CA 93940

GERMAN, JOAN ALICE WOLFE, author; b. Phila., Feb. 9, 1933; d. Merrill Pierce Wolfe and Jeanette (Anderson) Evans; student Temple U., 1951-54; m. Donald Robert German, Sept. 4, 1954; 1 son, Donald Robert. Various secretarial positions, 1954-57; adminstrv. asst. dept. public relations Vertol Aircraft Corp., Morton, Pa., 1958; freelance writer, 1964—; books: (with D.R. German) The Bank Teller's Handbook, 1970, rev. edit., 1981, Successful Job Hunting for Executives, 1974, Bank Employee's Marketing Handbook, 1975, Tested Techniques in Bank Marketing, vol. 1, 1977, vol. 2, 1979, Make Your Own Convenience Foods, 1979, How to Find a Job When Jobs are Hard to Find, 1981, The Money Book, 1981, The Bank Employee's Security Handbook, 1982, The Only Money Book for the Middle Class, 1982; contbr. to Bankers Mag., Brides, Compass, Consumers Digest, poetry jours.; editor Warren, Gorham & Lamont, Inc., N.Y.C., 1968—. Founder, bd. dirs. Community Craft Center, Hopkinton, Mass., 1968-69; bd. dirs. Berkshire Mental Health Assn., Pittsfield, Mass., 1981-82. Mem. Nat. League Am. Pen Women (br. pres. 1974-76, state pres. Mass. 1976-78), Am. Soc. Journalists and Authors, Inc. (dir-at-large 1979-81), Authors Guild, Boston Authors Club, Berkshire Poets Workshop (founder), Phi Gamma Nu (pres. Temple U. chpt. 1954). Unitarian. Address: West Mountain Rd Cheshire MA 01225

GERMI, KATHERINE NAVARRE, transformer mfg. co. exec.; b. Lansing, Mich., Oct. 31, 1947; d. Frederick Earl and Mary Jane (Navarre) Tripp; B.A. in Bus. Adminstrn., Mich. State U., 1969; m. August Germi, Apr. 1, 1978. Asso. mgr. Mid-Am. Club, Chgo., 1973-77; corp. sec. Quality Transformers, Inc., Chgo., 1977-78, v.p., 1978-80, pres., chief exec. officer, 1980—, also dir. Mem. U.S. C. of C., Am. Nat. Standards Inst., Nat. Assn. Catering Execs., Nat. Assn. Female Execs., Nat. Assn. Women Bus. Owners, Power Conversion Products Council Inc. Club: Lake Point Tower (Chgo.). Office: 3110 North Sheffield Ave Chicago IL 60657

GERNON, HELEN RUTH, educator; b. Portchester, N.Y., Nov. 6, 1946; d. Frank Ellis and Mary (White) G.; student U. N.C., Greensboro, 1964-66; B.B.A. in Acctg. with honors, U. Ga., 1968; M.B.A. in Acctg., Fla. Atlantic U., 1972; Ph.D. in Acctg. (Am. Assembly Collegiate Schs. Bus. fellow; grad. teaching fellow), Pa. State U., 1978. Auditor, Ernst and Whinney, Atlanta, 1968-69; instr. Fla. Atlantic U., 1972-73; asst. prof. U. Oreg., 1978—; cons. to corps.; coordinator U. Oreg. C.P.A. Rev. Course. Recipient Harry A. Jacobs, Jr. Profl. Service award U. Oreg., 1982; C.P.A., Oreg. Mem. Am. Inst. C.P.A.s, Oreg. State Soc. C.P.A.s (dir.), Nat. Assn. Accts., Am. Acctg. Assn., Acad. Internat. Bus., Beta Alpha Psi, Phi Kappa Phi, Beta Gamma Sigma, Zeta Tau Alpha. Club: Toastmasters. Author: The International Accounting and Tax Researchers' Publication Guide, 1982; Financial Statement Translation and Multinational Enterprise Performance Evaluation, 1981; contbr. articles to profl. jours. Home: 3440 Onyx St Eugene OR 97405 Office: Dept Acctg Coll Bus U Oreg Eugene OR 97403

GERONEMUS, DIANN FOX, social work cons.; b. Chgo., July 4, 1947; d. Herbert J. and Edith (Robbins) Fox; B.A. with high honors, Mich. State U., 1969; M.S.W., U. Ill., 1971; m. Robert Geronemus, Aug. 24, 1969; 1 dau., Heather Eileen. Social worker neurology, neurosurgery and medicine Hosp. of Albert Einstein Coll. Medicine, 1971-74; prin. social worker ob-gyn and newborn infant service Rush-Presbyn.-St. Luke's Med. Center, Chgo., 1974-75; social worker neurology, adminstr. Multiple Sclerosis Treatment Center, St. Barnabas Hosp., Bronx, N.Y., 1975-77, socio-med. researcher (Nat. Multiple Sclerosis Soc. grantee), dept. neurology and psychiatry, 1977-79, dir. social service, 1979-80; field work instr. Fordham U. Grad. Sch. Social Service, 1979-80; mem. edn. com., med. adv. bd., program cons. Nat. Multiple Sclerosis Soc., 1980—; pvt. practice med. social work and consultation, 1980—. Mem. Acad. Cert. Social Workers, Nat. Assn. Social Workers, Soc. Hosp. Social Work Dirs., Am. Orthopsychiat. Assn., Adult Edn. Assn., Council Nephrology Social Workers, Am. Assn. Sex Educators, Counselors and Therapists. Jewish. Contbr. articles to profl. jours. Home and office: 833 NW 81st Way Plantation FL 33324

GERRICK, EDNA W., business exec.; b. Phila., Aug. 8, 1950; d. Robert W. and Sally S. (Robins) G.; B.S., U. Pa., 1972, M.B.A., 1975. Clk., Colonial Ins. Co., Phila., 1972-74; adminstrv. asst. Acme Stores, Inc., Phila., 1974-75, office mgr., 1975-78; asst. to pres. Johnstone Mfg. Co., Phila., 1978-80, adminstrv. v.p., 1980—. Mem. Am. Soc. for Tng. and Devel., Am. Mgmt. Assn., Phi Mu. Club: Toastmistress (Phila.). Office: Werik Bldg Lower Level Suite 100 9600 Roosevelt Blvd Philadelphia PA 19115

GERRINGER-BUSENBARK, ELIZABETH JACQUELINE, systems analyst; b. Edmund, Wis., Jan. 7, 1934; d. Clyde Elroy and Matilda Evangeline Knapp; student San Francisco State Coll., 1953-54, Los Angeles City Coll., 1960-62, Santa Monica (Calif.) Jr. Coll., 1963; Ph.D., 1979; m. Roe Devon Gerringer-Busenbark, Sept. 30, 1968 (dec. Dec. 1972); stepchildren—David, Yvonne. Actress, Actors Workshop San Francisco, 1959, 65, Theatre of Arts Beverly Hills (Calif.), 1963, also radio; cons. and systems analyst for banks and pub. accounting agys.; artist, singer. Pres., Environ. Improvement, Originals by Elizabeth, San Francisco, 1973—; ordained minister, 1978. Author: The Virgin Twenty, 1967; Happening—Impact-Mald, 1971; Seven Day Rainbow, 1972; Zachary's Adversaries, 1974; Fifteen from Iowa, 1977; Bart's White Elephant, 1978; Skid Row Minister, 1978; Points in Time, 1979; Special Appointment, 1979. Address: PO Box 1640 7th and Mission Station San Francisco CA 94101

GERRISH, JAYNE ANN, banker; b. Denver, Jan. 7, 1953; d. Frederick Matthew and Marie (Stinson) Calender; mgmt. cert. Nat. Assn. Bank Women, 1981; diploma Am. Inst. Banking, 1981; grad. Nat. Consumer Compliance Sch., 1979; 1 son, Ian Matthew. Real estate servicing clk., new accounts, sec. First Interstate Bank, Portland, Oreg., 1973-75; sec. loan servicing, new accounts Estes Park Bank (Colo.), 1975-78, compliance officer, loan officer, 1978-82; comml. loan aide IntraWest Bank of Southglenn, N.A., Littleton, Colo., 1982—. Named Young Career Woman local chpt. Bus. and Profl. Women, 1978. Mem. Nat. Assn. Bank Women, Nat. Assn. Female Execs. Club: Rainbow for Girls (majority mem.). Office: 2350 E Arapahoe Rd Littleton CO 80122 also Box 2559 Littleton CO 80161

GERSHENFELD, MATTI KIBRICK, psychologist; b. Phila., Mar. 26, 1926; d. Hyman and Esther Kibrick; A.B., U. Pa., 1946, M.A., 1951; Ed.D., Temple U., 1967; student U. Pa. Med. Sch., 1971-72; m. Marvin Aaron Gershenfeld, Mar. 23, 1947; children—Robert, Howard, Richard, Kenneth. City planner Phila. City Planning Commn., 1946-51; exec. dir. Fedn. Community Councils of Phila., 1951-53; producer U. of Air TV Program, Citizen in Action, 1952-54; adj. prof. Temple U. Grad. Sch., 1966—, Pa. State U., Ogontz; creator, dir., cons. Inst. Awareness, Sch. for Women, Phila., 1968-75; cofounder, pres. Couples Learning Center, Jenkintown, Pa., 1976—; pres. Matti Gershenfeld Assos., P.C., Jenkintown, 1974—; pvt. practice psychology, Jenkintown, 1974—; project dir. Transition Stages for Women, Network; pres., Pa. Council on Family Relations, 1980—. Internat. co-chmn. Internat. Disciplinary Congress on Women, Israel, 1981-82; bd. dirs. Am. Jewish Com., Jewish Campus Activities Bd.,; chmn. midlife task force Fedn. Jewish Agys.; chmn. president's council Gwynedd Mercy Coll. Lic. psychologist, Pa., Fellow Pa. Psychol. Assn.; mem. Am. Assn. Marriage and Family Therapists, Internat. Transactional Analysis Assn. (clin. mem.), Am. Psychol. Assn. (exec. bd. div. 35), Nat. Council Family Relations, Pa. Council Family Relations. Jewish. Author: Groups: Theory and Experience, 1973; Instructors Handbook, 1973, 2d edit., 1981; Impact of Changing Roles of Women on Women, 1975; Marriage: Public or Private Responsibility, 1980; Couples Handbook, 1981. Home: Pepper and Winter Rds Rydal PA 19046 Office: Benson East Suite A-13 Jenkintown PA 19046

GERSHON, ANNE ANGEN, pediatrician; b. Pa., Aug. 30, 1938; d. Willard F. and Elda (Yarborough) Angen; A.B., Smith Coll., 1960; M.D., Cornell U., 1964; m. Michael D. Gershon, June 10, 1961; children—Perry, Timothy, Dana. Pediatric Intern N.Y. Hosp., N.Y.C., 1964-65, resident in pediatrics, 1966-68; fellow in infectious diseases Oxford U., 1965-66, N.Y.U., 1968-70; mem. faculty N.Y.U. Med. Center, N.Y.C., 1970—, prof. pediatrics and virology, 1980—. NIH grantee. Mem. Am. Acad. Pediatrics, Soc. Pediatric Research (council 1975-79), Am. Soc. Microbiology, Phi Beta Kappa, Sigma Xi. Jewish. Author papers in field. Office: 550 1st Ave New York NY 10016

GERSHOWITZ, SONYA ZIPORKIN, nursing home adminstr.; b. Bronx, N.Y., July 30, 1940; d. David and Rose (Falkin) Ziporkin; R.N., Sinai Hosp., Balt., 1960; B.S. in Nursing, U. Md., 1973, M.S. in Nursing Adminstrn., 1978; children—Benjamin, Sharon. Staff nurse Sinai Hosp., 1960-63; evening supr. Happy Hills Convalescent Home, Balt., 1963-64; dir. nurses Ashburton Home, Balt., 1963-64, Mt. Sinai Nursing Home, Balt., 1968-71, 73-74, Multi-Med. Convalescent and Nursing Center, Towson, Md., 1974-75; owner, Fed. Hill Nursing Center, Inc., Greater Pa. Ave. Nursing Center, Inc., Balt., Lafayette Sq. Nursing Inc., Balt.; adminstr. Fed. Hill Nursing, Inc., Balt., 1980—; adminstrv. dir. Chai Mgmt. Co., Inc.; lectr. and cons. in field, summer camp nurse; mem. White House Conf. Aging, 1971, Md. Task Force Nosocomial Infections, 1974—; chmn. subcom. innovation survey procedures Md. Dept. Health and Mental Hygiene, 1977; mem. labor market adv. com. Mayor Balt. Office Manpower Resources, 1978; mem. Md. Gov.'s Conf. on Aging, 1980, Senator Humphrey's Washington Legal Found., 1980-81; bd dirs., mem. sr. high sch. scholarship com. Randallstown Sr. High Sch., Balt., 1974-76. Fellow Am. Coll. Nursing Home Adminstrs. (chmn. edn. com. 1977, pres. elect com. 1978), Am., Md. nurses assns., U. Md., Sinai Hosp. Nurses alumni assns., Health Facilities Assn. Md., Am. Health Care Assn., Md. Assn. Quality Assurance Profls., Stoneybrook Improvement Assn., (pres. 1974), Mt. Royal Improvement Assn., Md. League Horsemen (past dir.), South Balt. Businessmen Assn., Orchard Bittle Assn. Jewish. Office: 1400 John St Baltimore MD 21217

GERSONI-EDELMAN, DIANE CLAIRE, author, editor; b. Bklyn., Apr. 16, 1947; d. James Arthur and Edna Bernice (Krinski) Gersoni; B.A. cum laude, Vassar Coll., 1967; m. James Neil Edelman, Oct. 5, 1975; children— Michael Lawrence, Sara Anne. Asst. editor, then asso. editor Sch. Library Jour. Book Rev., 1968-72; free lance writer, 1972-74, 77—; writer, editor Scholastic Mags., Inc., N.Y.C., 1974-77; author: Sexism and Youth, 1974; Work-Wise: Learning About the World of Work from Books, 1980; cons., speaker in field. Jewish religion. Club: Vassar (N.Y.C.). Contbr. articles, book revs. to anthologies, newspapers, mags. Home: care Edelman 301 E 78th St New York NY 10021

GERSOVITZ, SARAH VALERIE, painter, printmaker; b. Montreal, Que., Can., Sept. 5, 1920; d. Solomon and Eva (Gampel) Gamer; student MacDonald Coll., Montreal Mus. Fine Arts, Ecole des Arts Appliques; diploma comml. arts, diploma communication arts, M.A., Concordia U.; m. Benjamin Gersovitz, June 22, 1944; children—Mark, Julia, Jeremy. Tchr. painting and drawing Bronfman Centre, Montreal, 1972—; one-woman shows include Montreal Mus. Fine Arts, 1962, 65, Art Gallery Greater Victoria, 1966, U. Alta., 1968, Burnaby Art Gallery, 1969, Art Gallery Hamilton, 1969, Mt. St. Vincent U., 1971, Coll. St. Louis, 1972, Inst. Cultural Peruano, Lima, 1973, Confedn. Art Gallery, 1976, St. Mary's U., 1976, Confedn. Art Gallery, 1976, U. Sherbrooke, 1979, Peter Whyte Gallery, 1982, London Regional Art Gallery, 1982, Holland Coll., others; represented in permanent collections Library of Congress, N.Y. Pub. Library, Nat. Gallery South Australia, Inst. Cultural Peruano, Lima, Am. Embassy, Ottawa, numerous Can. mus., univs. and embassies including Nat. Gallery Can., Montreal Mus. Fine Arts, Le Musée du Québec, Le Musée d'Art Contemporain; group exhbns. include 3d Internat. Play Group Exhbn., N.Y.C., 1973, Internat. Triennial, Grenchen, Switzerland, 1961, VI and V Internat. Biennial, Ibiza, Spain, 1972, 74, 82, II Internat. Biennial, Norway, 1974, 76, III and IV Internat. Biennial, Frechen, Germany, 1974, 76, 1st Internat. Bienal, Segovia, Spain, 1974, III Biennial Graphic, Cali, Colombia, 1976, 11th Biennale, Lljubljana, Yugoslavia, 1975, 13th, 1979, ann. exhbn. NAD, N.Y.C., 1975, 11th Bienale Internat. d'Art de Menton, France, 1976, contemporary miniature Exhbn., U. Mich., 1977, XVIII Premio Internat. de Dibujo, Barcelona, 1979, XV Internat. Bienal de São Paulo (Brazil), 1979, Bienal des Grabado, Maracaibo, Venezuela, 1977, Premio Internat. per l'Incisione, Biella, Italy, 1980, Internat. Biennale des Arts Grafiques, Brno, Czechoslovakia, 1980, 1st Internat. Miniature Print Exhbn., Seoul, 1980, Wesleyan Internat. Exhbn. Prints and Drawings, Macon, Ga., 1980, Salón Nacional de Grabado, Lima, Peru, 1981, Exhbn. Que. Graphics, Hong Kong, 1982, numerous others U.S. and abroad. Recipient 1st prize Seagram Fine Arts Expn., 1968; Graphic Art prize Winnipeg Art Gallery Bienial, 1962, Anaconda award Can. Soc. Painters-Etchers, 1963, 67; 1st prize Concours Graphique, U. Sherbrooke, 1977, Canadian Playwriting Competition, 1982; purchase award Mus. de Que., 1966, Nat. Gallery South Australia, 1967, Dawson Coll., 1974, Thomas More Inst., 1977, Law Faculty U. Sherbrooke, 1979; hon. mention Miniature Painters, Sculptors, and Engravers, Washington, 1976. Mem. Royal Can. Acad. Arts (council 1981-82), Societe des Graveurs du Que. Address: 5173 Mayfair Ave Montreal PQ H4V 2E8 Canada

GERSTEIN, DIDRI ARNEL PICOULT, speech pathologist; b. Ellenville, N.Y., Aug. 19, 1949; d. Ben and Barbara J. (Morris) Picoult; A.A.S., Dutchess Community Coll., 1969; B.S., SUNY, Oneonta, 1972; M.S., Adelphi U., 1973; m. Jeffrey Gerstein, Nov. 26, 1976; 1 dau., Robyn Beth. Trainee, Rehabilitative Services Adminstrn., 1972; speech pathologist Ulster County Health Dept., Kingston, N.Y., 1973-78, Head Start Program, Ellenville, 1979, Middletown, 1980; pvt. practice. Cert. tchr., lic. speech pathologist, N.Y. State. Mem. Am. Speech and Hearing Assn., N.Y. State Speech and Hearing Assn. Home: 5 R Dean Pl Middletown NY 10940

GERSTEIN, LOIS APRIL KINGSDORF, social worker; b. Bronx, N.Y., Sept. 7, 1953; d. Julius and Leah Kingsdorf; B.A. cum laude in Sociology, Queens Coll., 1975; M.S.W., N.Y. U., 1977; m. Ralph Gerstein, Aug. 18, 1974. Social worker White Plains Nursing Home, Bronx, 1977, Holy Family Home, Bklyn., 1977-79; med. social worker VA, Northport, N.Y., 1979—. Cert. social worker, N.Y. Mem. Nat. Assn. Social Workers (council of aging), Acad. Cert. Social Workers, Queens Coll. Alumni Assn., N.Y. U. Alumni Assn. Home: 512 Unqua Rd Massapequa NY 11758 Office: VA Hospital Middleville Rd Northport NY 11768

GERSTER, JUDY ELLEN, retail chain exec.; b. Nevada, Mo., June 1, 1946; d. Jewell Richard and Mary Ellen (Hutchison) G.; student public schs.; Various positions Dunbrooke Shirt Factory, El Dorado Springs, Mo., 1964-66; sec., bookkeeper Taylor's Acctg. Co., Nevada, Mo., 1966-72; sec., bookkeeper, receptionist Davison Enterprises, Nevada, 1972—, sec. of corp. for subs., exec. sec., 1976—. Mem. Citizens' Com. for Updating Comprehensive Plan for City of Nevada, 1975; pre-sch. Sunday sch. dir., children's ch. dir., com. mem. First Baptist Ch., Nevada, Mo. Named to Outstanding Young Women in Am., 1976. Mem. Nat. Secs. Assn., Nat. Assn. Female Execs. Club: Soroptimist Internat. (pres. chpt. 1979-80) (Nevada). Home: 210 N Elm St PO Box 179 Nevada MO 64772 Office: 122 1/2 N Cedar PO Box 285 Nevada MO 64772

GESAMAN, ROSE MARIE, nurse; b. Marion, Ind., Sept. 16, 1944; d. George Paul and Joan Marceille (Cary) Wiegand; R.N., St. Joseph's Sch. Nursing, 1965; m. Steven Ray Gesaman, Dec. 6, 1969; children—Stephanie Louise, Dustan Ray. Staff nurse Whitley County Hosp., Columbia City, Ind., 1965; head nurse orthopedic unit Darnall Army Hosp., Ft. Hood, Tex., 1967; staff nurse Murphey Med. Center, Warsaw, Ind., 1968, ho. mgr., 1968-69, operating room supr., 1969-70; staff nurse Whitley County Hosp., Columbia City, Ind., 1974, ho. mgr., 1975-77; dir. nursing Miller's Merry Manor, Warsaw, Ind., 1977-81; ho. mgr. Whitley County Meml. Hosp., Columbia City, Ind., 1981—. Served to 1st lt., Nurse Corps, U.S. Army, 1966-67. Recipient Kosciusko County Med. Aux. Scholarship award, 1965—; Scottish Rite Scholarship award, 1965—; Outstanding Cath. Youth Kosciusko County award, 1965. Mem. Whitley County Meml. Hosp. Nurses Assn., Am. Legion, Beta Sigma Phi. Democrat. Roman Catholic. Home: Box 191 North Webster IN 46555 Office: Box 409 353 N Oak St Columbia City IN 46725

GESELL, INEZ PATRICIA, concrete co. exec.; b. Fosston, Minn., Feb. 25, 1917; d. Elmer Olof and Esther Marie (Peterson) Solberg; student public schs.; m. William John Gesell, Dec. 31, 1938 (dec. 1975); children—William Lester, Gary John, Mary Ann. With Gesell Concrete Products Inc., Bagley, Minn., 1945—, pres., 1975—. Treas. ladies aux. St. Ann Roman Catholic Ch., Bagley. Home: Route 3 Box W43 Bagley MN 56621 Office: Gesell Concrete Products Inc Route 2 Bagley MN 56621

GESNER, CAROL, educator; b. Colon, Panama, July 7, 1922 (parents Am. citizens); d. Ralph L. and Elsie W. Gesner; B.S., N.J. State Coll., 1944; M.A., U. N.H., 1949; Ph.D. in English, La. State U., 1956. Mem. faculty Berea (Ky.) Coll., 1954—, prof. English, 1967—. Bd. dirs. Ky. Humanities Council. Mem. MLA, AAUP. Episcopalian. Author: Shakespeare and The Greek Romance, 1970; Plymouth, 1978; also poems, articles; mem. editorial bd. U. Ky. Press. Address: 863 Berea Coll Berea KY 40404

GETLAN, PHYLLIS JANE, social worker; b. N.Y.C., June 23, 1928; d. Harry Aaren and Sadye (Leshnower) Kolbrener; B.A., L.I. U., 1950; M.S. in Social Work, Columbia U., 1957; m. Norman Getlan, Nov. 4, 1954; children—Robert, Nancy. With Bur. Public Assistance, Children's Placement Services, Foster Home Care div. N.Y.C. Dept. Social Services, 1951-56; with Muscular Dystrophy Assn., N.Y.C., 1957-59; mem. staff home care dept., outpatient dept., hemodyalysis program Elmhurst (N.Y.) Hosp., 1964-69, sr. social worker, hemodialysis program, 1969-81; asst. dir. social service dept. New Rochelle (N.Y.) Hosp., 1981—. Mem. Council Nephrology Social Work (chmn. nat. legislation), Acad. Cert. Social Workers, Nat. Assn. Social Workers, Nat. Kidney Found., others. Home: 198 Hickory Grove Dr E Larchmont NY 10538

GETTLE, KARAN STEWART, occupational therapist; b. Indpls., Aug. 10, 1949; d. Lester Franklin and Ruth Irene (Wainwright) Stewart; B.S. (HEW scholar), Ind. U., 1972, postgrad., 1975—; m. Stewart Gettle, Jan. 18, 1980; 1 son by previous marriage, Brant Harmon. Occupational therapist Marion County Gen. Hosp., Indps., 1972-74, Meth. Hosp., Indpls., 1974-76; occupational therapist Hand Rehab. Center of Ind., Indpls., 1976-78, dir., 1978—; practicum instr. clinic Ind. U. Med. Center, Indpls., 1973—. vol. St. Vincent Hosp. Mem. Am., Ind. (membership com. 1972-73, treas. 1973-75) occupational therapy assns., Am. Soc. Hand Therapists (founding mem. 1978—, nominating and research coms.), Alpha Omicron Pi. Alumni. Mem. Christian Ch. (Disciples of Christ). Club: Job's Daus. Author: Hand Principles and

Methods, 1980; contbr. articles to profl. jours. Home: 4273 Centennial Ct Carmel IN 46032

GETTY, KATHLEEN ANN, engr.; b. Schenectady, Dec. 28, 1955; d. Robert William and Clara Gene Getty; A.A.S. in Journalism, SUNY, Morrisville, 1976; B.A. in English, SUNY, Oswego, 1978. Procedure and specification writer Stone & Webster Engring. Corp., 1978-80, constrn. specialist, River Bend Nuclear Station, St. Francisville, La., 1980-81, field engr., 1981—. Mem. ASME. Home: 1957 General Cleburne Ave Baton Rouge LA 70810 Office: Stone & Webster Engring Corp N Access Rd Saint Francisville LA 70775

GETTYS, VESTA SKEES, indsl. psychologist; b. Princeton, Ky., Oct. 21, 1935; d. Hugh Shelby and Merle Owen Skees; B.A., U. Calif., Berkeley, 1960; M.A., U. Louisville, 1963; Ph.D., Ohio State U., 1970; m. Charles F. M. Gettys, Mar. 28, 1964; children—Vesta, Ann. Research asso. U. Louisville, 1965-66; teaching asst. Ohio State U., 1967-68; adj. asst. prof. U. Okla., 1972-82; vis. asst. prof. San Diego State U., 1975-76; dir. Law Enforcement Psychol. Services, Inc., Norman, Okla., 1979—; dir. Exec. Stress Mgmt. Inc., Norman, 1980—; cons. indsl. psychology. Mem. AAAS, So. Soc. Philosophy and Psychology, Am. Psychol. Assn., Okla. Psychol. Assn., LWV. Democrat. Baptist. Home: 703 Jona Kay Terrace Norman OK 73069 Office: 2221 W Lindsey St Suite 200E West Oaks Office Park Norman OK 73069

GETZ, VIRGINIA ANN, heating and air conditioning co. ofcl.; b. Memphis; d. Fred William and Marion Agnes (Brennan) G.; B.S., Memphis State U., 1970. Fin. counselor St. Joseph Hosp., 1969-78; office mgr. St. Francis Hosp., 1978-79; ops. mgr. Bryant Air Conditioning Co. div. Carrier Corp., Memphis, 1979—. Mem. Memphis Assn. Credit Execs., Nat. Assn. Female Execs., Memphis Assn. Credit Women. Home: 4283 Chickasaw Rd Memphis TN 38117 Office: 3727 Air Park Memphis TN 38118

GETZENDANNER, SUSAN, judge; b. Chgo., July 24, 1939; d. William B. and Carole (Muehling) O'Meara; B.B.A., Loyola U., Chgo., 1966, J.D., 1966; children—Alexandra, Paul. Admitted to Ill. bar, law clk. U.S. Dist. Ct., 1966-68; assoc. firm Mayer, Brown & Platt, Chgo., 1968-80; judge U.S. Dist. Ct., Chgo., 1980—. Office: 219 S Dearborn St Chicago IL 60604

GETZOFF, CAROLE IRIS, broadcaster; b. N.Y.C., Dec. 29, 1943; d. Alexander and Frances Evelyn (Kramer) G.; B.A., Hunter Coll., 1965; Editorial asst. Pageant Mag., N.Y.C., 1965, asso. editor, 1966, photoeditor, 1967; mem. dance and drama workshop La Mama ETC., N.Y.C., 1967-70; host A Woman's Pl. and New Morning, Sta. WPLJ, ABC, N.Y.C., 1975-80, reporter, anchorman, 1980—; asso. producer 20/20, ABC-TV, N.Y.C., 1979-80; tchr. women in media course New Sch. for Social Research, 1977-80. Recipient Grace Schulberg Essay prize Hunter Coll., 1965. Mem. AFTRA, Actors Equity, Screen Actors Guild, Am. Women in Radio and TV. Democrat. Jewish. Author: The Natural Cook's First Book, 1973; contbr. articles to mags., 1970-80, including Ms., Village Voice, Harper's, Cosmopolitan. Home: 39 Plaza St Brooklyn NY 11217 Office: ABC 1330 Ave of Americas New York NY 10019

GEWELBER, RHONA WEINBERG, dairy feed co. exec.; b. Lynwood, Calif., Apr. 23, 1953; d. Bob and Marcha (Wallin) Weinberg; student Oxford U. (Eng.), 1973-74; grad. Stephens Coll., 1975; m. Ytzhak Gewelber, Mar. 27, 1977; 1 dau., Hali Morrisa. Mgr., buyer Golden Boutique, Honolulu, 1975-76; exec. sec. Zellerbach Paper Co., Los Angeles, 1976-78; adminstrv. asst. Coast Grain Co., Norwalk, Calif., 1978-80, v.p., 1981—. Vice-pres. Ida Mayer Cummings Aux. of Jewish Homes for Aging. Named Vol. of Yr., Jewish Homes for Aging, 1982. Republican. Home: 15510 Olive Branch Dr La Mirada CA 90638 Office: 12948 S Pioneer Blvd Norwalk CA 90650

GEWIRTH, MARCELLA TILTON, editor, environ. planner; b. Blue Island, Ill., May 21, 1928; d. Herbert Fleming and Rose Imogene (Moore) Tilton; M.S., U. Chgo., 1954; m. Alan Gewirth, Mar. 18, 1956; children—Andrew Alan, Daniel Tilton, Letitia Rose. Instr. U. Chgo., 1955-57, research asst. in medicine med. sch., 1958-59; editor The Audubon Compass, WNIB Radio, Chgo., 1972-75; environ. editor Hyde Park Herald, Chgo., 1975-80; environ. planner Gt. Lakes nat. program office EPA, Chgo., 1980—. Pres. Joint PTA Music Commn., 1967-72; dir. Hyde Park Kenwood Community Conf., 1976. Ford Found. fellow, 1954-55. Recipient Environ. Quality award Region V, EPA, 1974. Mem. LWV Chgo., Cook County LWV (dir. Met. Study 1963-66), Chgo. Audubon Soc. (dir. 1971-75; Protector of Environ. award 1978), AAAS, Nat. Audubon Soc., Nat. Wildlife Fedn., Friends of the Earth, Ill. Wildlife Soc., Lake Mich. Fedn., Environ. Action. Episcopalian. Home: 1365 E Park Chicago IL 60637 Office: 536 S Clark St Chicago IL 60604

GEWIRTZ, GERRY, editor, publisher; b. N.Y.C., Dec. 22, 1920; d. Max and Minnie (Weiss) G.; B.A., Vassar Coll., 1941; m. Eugene W. Friedman, Nov. 11, 1945; children—John Henry, Robert James. Editor, Package Store Mgmt., 1942-44, Jewelry mag., 1945-53; freelance editor promotion dept. McCall's mag., Esquire, 1953-56; free-lance fashion and gifts editor Jewelers Circular Keystone, N.Y.C., 1955-71; editor, pub. The Fashionables, 1971-74, The Forecast, 1974—, Nat. Jeweler, Ann. Fashion Guide, 1976—, asso. pub., editor-in-chief Exec. Jeweler, 1980—. Mem. exec. com. Cardinal Cooke's Inner City Council; trustee Marymount Coll., Tarrytown, N.Y.; bd. dirs. Israel Cancer Research Fund; exec. com. med. div. Greater N.Y. Campaign State of Israel Bonds; trustee Central Synagogue; mem. Am. Jewish Com., Nat. Interreligious Commn. Recipient Jewelry Industry Div. award Am. Jewish Com., 1978, (with husband) Tower of Hope award, 1981. Mem. N.Y. Fashion Group, Nat. Home Fashions League, Nat. Assn. TV Arts and Scis. Clubs: N.Y. Vassar; Overseas Press. Home: 55 E 86th St New York NY 10028 Office: 420 Madison Ave New York NY 10017

GEYER, GEORGIE ANNE, columnist, author, speaker, educator; b. Chgo., Apr. 2, 1935; d. Robert George and Georgie Hazel (Gervens) G.; B.S., Northwestern U., 1956; postgrad. (Fulbright scholar) U. Vienna (Austria), 1956-57; Litt.D. (hon.), Lake Forest Coll., 1980. Reporter, Southtown Economist, Chgo., 1958; soc. reporter Chgo. Daily News, 1959-60, gen. assignment reporter, 1960-64, Latin Am. corr., 1964-67, roving world corr., 1967-75; syndicated columnist Los Angeles Times Syndicate, 1975-80, Universal Press Syndicate, 1980—; Spencer prof. journalism Syracuse U., 1976; John J. Fitzpatrick lectr. U. Utah, 1977; mem. bd. courses by newspaper project U. Calif., San Diego; speaker on trips to Africa, Asia and Iceland for Internat. Communication Agy., 1979, 81, 82; mem. steering com. Latin Am. governance project Aspen. Inst. Active Orgn. for S.W. Community Chgo., 1960—; trustee Am. U., Washington. Recipient 1st prize Am. Newspaper Guild, 1962; 2d prize Ill. Press Editors Assn., 1962; award for best reporting in Latin Am., Overseas Press Club, 1967; Alumni Merit award Northwestern U., 1968, Alumnae award, 1981; Maria Moors Cabot award Columbia U., 1971; Hannah Solomon award Nat. Council Jewish Women, 1973. Mem. Chgo. Council Fgn. Relations (dir.), Internat. Inst. Strategic Studies (London), Mortar Bd., Theta Sigma Chi. Author: The New Latins, 1970; The New 100 Years War, 1972; The Young Russians, 1975; Buying the Night Flight, 1983; contbr. articles to Atlantic Mag., Sat. Rev. Lit., Nat. Observer, New Republic, others. Address: 800 25th St NW Washington DC 20037

GHAFFARI, AVIDEH BEHROUZ, service co. exec.; b. Tehran, Iran, Apr. 17, 1943; came to U.S., 1975, naturalized, 1982; s. Zabih and Homa Behrouz; B.A., Art and Design Sch. Scotland, 1966; m. Abbas Ghaffari, Feb. 2, 1976; children—Narsi Azima, Borzou Azima. Founder, pres. Polydecor Co., Tehran and Paris, France, 1962-68; pres. Pakab Co. Ltd., Tehran, 1963-75; pres. Avidecor Co., Inc., N.Y.C., 1979—; sec.-treas., dir. Metavi Inc., N.Y.C., 19 —. Recipient Award of Merit, Imperial Govt. Iran, 1969. Mem. Nat. Assn. Female Execs., Iran Inst. Interior Design. Home: 425 E 58th St New York NY 10022 Office: 790 Madison Ave New York NY 10021

GHALY, MARY S.D., physician; b. Cairo, Egypt, Jan. 27, 1938; d. Shafik Daoud and Saddika Loza (Sikka) Ghaly; M.D. with honors, Cairo U. Med. Sch., 1960; postgrad., 1962-63; M.B.B. Ch., diplomas in internal medicine and anesthesiology. Clin. researcher Shoubra Gen. Hosp., Cairo, Egypt, 1960-61; intern Cairo U. Hosp., 1962-65; staff anesthesiologist chest surgery dept. Chest Disease Hosp.-Abassia, Cairo, Egypt, 1965-69; attending staff R.I. Med. Center, Howard, 1969-70; clin. anesthesiology resident anesthesiology dept. U. Iowa, Iowa City, 1970-73; fellow intensive care units Ind. U., Indpls., 1972-73; asso. dir. clin. research Pfizer, Inc., Groton, Conn., 1973—; Recipient Laila Darwish prize Egyptian Ministry Edn., 1954, 55. Mem. Nat. Assn. Female Execs., Am. Soc. Anesthesiologists, Conn. Soc. Anesthesiologists, Internat. Assn. Asthma. Home: Churchwood Condominiums Apt 5B Niantic CT 06357 Office: Clin Research Dept Pfizer Inc Groton CT 06340

GHIRALDINI, JOAN, telecommunications co. exec.; b. Bklyn., Mar. 31, 1951; d. Robert and Anne (Centineo) G.; B.A., Smith Coll., 1972; M.B.A., U. Pa., 1975. Econ. specialist Western Electric Corp., N.Y.C., 1975-76; sr. fin. analyst Internat. Paper Co., N.Y.C., 1976-78, mgr. strategic planning, 1978-81; dir. fin. planning Executone, Inc., Jericho, N.Y., 1981-82, dir. strategic planning, 1982—. Mem. Fin. Womens Assn. N.Y., Am. Fin. Assn., Wharton Bus. Sch. Club N.Y., Smith Coll. Club N.Y. Home: 155 E 38th St Apt 3G New York NY 10016

GHOLSTON, BETTY JEAN, ednl. specialist; b. Wagram, N.C., Feb. 1, 1942; d. Lacy and Sarah M. (McLean) Blue; B.S., N.C. Central U., 1963; postgrad. U. N.C., 1979; M.S., N.C. A and T. U., 1979; m. Willie Gunter Gholston, Aug. 17, 1963; children—Lisa Regina, Betty Cornelia, Saranarda, Willie Gunter. Librarian, Shaw High Sch., Laurinburg, N.C., 1966-67, Rohannen High Sch., Rockingham, N.C., 1968; tchr.-librarian Cameron Morrison Sch., Hoffman, N.C., 1968-77; ednl. specialist Cameron Morrison Youth Center, Hoffman, 1977—. Mem. Wagram Bd. Commrs., 1974—, mayor protem, 1976, 77, 80—; organizer Newtown Community Orgn., 1973; founder Scotland County br. Wagram Library, 1976. Named Tchr. of Yr., N.C. Dept. Youth Services, 1977. Mem. NEA, N.C. Assn. Educators, N.C. Assn. Classroom Tchrs., Polit. Assn. for Concerned Educators, Assn. Coll. Women. Democrat. Baptist. Home: Rt 1 Box 283 Wagram NC 28396 Office: PO Box 169 Hoffman NC 28347

GHOLSTON, HELEN ALBERTA, educator; b. Lawrence, Mass., May 13, 1923; d. Albert Clinton and Helen Gertrude (Mitchell) McIlwain; B.A. in English with distinction, San Diego State U., 1976, M.A. in Edn., 1980; m. Andrew J. Gholston, Apr. 25, 1944; children—Andrea, Juanita, Corale, Wendy, Michael, Andrew J. Microfilm operator San Diego City Civil Service, 1957-58; engaged in real estate, 1961-70; tutor EEO program San Diego Community Colls., 1971-75; tchr. San Diego city schs., 1977—, tchr. English, Abraham Lincoln Sr. High Sch., 1979—, chmn. dept., 1980—, mem. textbook com. San Diego city schs. Mem. Nat. Council Tchrs. English, Assn. Supervision and Curriculum Devel., Nat. Council Negro Women, Am. Bus. Women's Assn. Baptist. Author articles, Curriculum materials. Home: 5322 Hilltop Dr San Diego CA 92114 Office: Lincoln High Sch 150 S 49th St San Diego CA 92113

GHORMLEY-GOIRAN, MARY VIRGINIA, sales exec.; b. Oklahoma City, July 22, 1953; d. Luthur Wayne Ghormley and Jessica Ellen Van Vleck Stone; B.A., Stephens Coll., Columbia, Mo., 1974; m. Philip De La Hogue Goiran, Feb. 6, 1982. Salesperson, Gabrielle's, Denver, 1978; territory mgr. Wallace Berrie & Co., Van Nuys, Calif., 1978-79; dist. sales mgr. Wallace Berrie & Co., Van Nuys, 1979-81, regional sales mgr., 1981—. Named Rookie Salesperson of Year, Wallace Berrie & Co., 1978. Mem. Nat. Assn. Female Execs., NOW, League Women Voters, Am. Mgmt. Assn. Democrat. Roman Catholic. Home: 5200 Montview Blvd Denver CO 80207

GIADROSICH, SHIRLEY ERLAND, nurse; b. N.Y.C., Sept. 24, 1947; d. Endre and Sigrid (Hoiland) Erland; diploma Meth. Hosp. Sch. Nursing, 1968; B.S., Adelphia U., 1981. Surg. nurse Meth. Hosp., Bklyn., 1968-70; staff nurse J. B. Thomas Hosp., Peabody, Mass., 1971-73; staff nurse Mercy Hosp., Rockville Centre, N.Y., 1973-75, critical care nurse, 1975-78, staff nurse CCU, 1978—. Mem. Am. Assn. Critical Care Nurses, Am. Heart Assn., N.Y. State Nurses Assn., Sierra Club. Club: Sons of Norway. Home: 2120 Wantagh Ave Wantagh NY 11793 Office: 1000 N Village Ave Rockville Centre NY 11579

GIANNINI, MARGARET JOAN, physician, govt. ofcl.; b. Camden, N.J., May 27, 1921; d. Francis and Rose Ann (Giordano) G.; ed. Boston U., 1929-40, Temple U., 1940-42; M.D., Hahnemann Med. Coll., Phila., 1945; H.H.D. (hon.), Mercy Coll., 1972; m. Louis J. Salerno, Feb. 1, 1948; 4 sons. Intern, N.Y. Med. Coll., 1945-46, resident in pathology, 1946-47, in pediatrics, 1947-48; prof. pediatrics Met. Hosp. Med. Center, N.Y.C.; clin. assoc. prof. Smith Coll., Mass., 1974-79; founder, dir. Mental Retardation Inst., N.Y. Med. Coll.; dir. Nat. Inst. Handicapped Research, U.S. Dept. Edn., Washington, from 1979; dir. rehab. research and devel. VA, Washington; interregional adv. mental retardation, dept. world tech. cooperation UN, 1978—; spl. cons. mental retardation constrn. unit NIH; cons. Pres.'s Com. Mental Retardation; mem. sci. adv. bd. Kennedy Child Study Center, N.Y.C.; mem. adv. council system of advocacy N.Y. State Assn. Retarded Children; mem. N.Y. State Council Developmental Disabilities, also chmn. planning com.; mem. hon. com. N.Y. State Spl. Olympics; chmn. mental retardation task force statewide planning for vocat. rehab. services N.Y. State Dept. Edn.; mem. adv. com. Retarded Infant Service; past mem. children's com. N.Y. State Dept. Mental Hygiene; mem. nat. adv. bd. Rehab. Internat., USA; numerous lectures and presentations. Bd. dirs. Internat. Inst. Developmental Disabilities, Children's Brain Research Fund; trustee Capital Children's Mus., Washington, Museo Italo-Americano, San Francisco. Diplomate Am. Bd. Pediatrics, Nat. Bd. Med. Examiners; lic. physician, N.Y. State, D.C. Recipient award Assn. Pediatric Research, 1956; Achievement award Am. Med. Women's Assn., 1960; Achievement award AMITA, 1960, 75; Wyeth Med. Sci. Achievement award, 1966; named Woman Doer by Lady Bird Johnson, 1968; recipient Enrico Fermi edn. award, 1971; Woman of Yr. award, Westchester Fedn. Women, 1972; Dr. Giannini Day declared in her honor Variety Club Women, 1972; recipient key to City of Bologna (Italy), 1974; plaque City of San Francisco, 1980; Leadership award Children's Holistic Inst. for Life Devel., 1979; citation Gov. of N.Y., 1980; Mary Switzer award World Rehab. Fund, 1980; seal Inner London Edn. Authority, 1970; numerous others. Fellow Am. Acad. Pediatrics (nat. com. children with handicaps; Bronze medal), Am. Assn. Mental Deficiency (past pres.; founder prevention com.; past chmn. nominations and elections com.; v.p. for medicine; ad hoc com. on tng.); mem. Inst. Medicine of Nat. Acad. Scis., Am. Assn. Univ.-Affiliated Programs (past pres.), Am. Woman's Med. Assn., AMA, Am. Acad. Cerebral Palsy, AAUP, Pan Am. Med. Assn. (hon.), N.Y. State Med. Assn., D.C. Med. Soc., Israel Med. Soc. (dir.), Internat. Health Soc. (dir. developmental disabilities). Contbr. articles to med. jours. Office: VA 810 Vermont Ave NW Washington DC 20420

GIANNONE, TONI LYNNE, speech pathologist; b. Bridgeport, Conn., Nov. 3, 1950; d. Peter Anthony and Eleanor Bridget (Scinto) G.; B.A., U. Conn., Storrs, 1972; M.A. with honors, Western Mich. U., Kalamazoo, 1973; m. Kenneth M. Nowak, Aug. 9, 1975. Speech pathologist Found. Sch., Orange, Conn., 1973-74; clin. coordinator Southeastern Conn. Hearing & Speech Center, Norwich, 1974-77; dir. speech pathology Lawrence and Meml. Hosp., New London, Conn., 1975-77; dir. primary unit Found. Sch., Orange, 1977—; prof. U. R.I., Kingston, 1976—; speech pathologist Am. Cancer Soc., 1974-78. Recipient DAR Good Citizen award, 1968. Mem. Am. Speech and Hearing Assn., Conn. Speech and Hearing Assn., Beta Phi Beta. Roman Catholic. Home: 470 Lawlor Terr Stratford CT 06497 Office: 719 Derby Milford Rd Orange CT 06477

GIANTURCO, ADRIANA, state govt. ofcl.; b. Berkeley, Calif., June 5, 1939; d. Elio and Valentine Trant (McGillicuddy) G.; B.A. magna cum laude, Smith Coll., 1960; postgrad. in econs., U. Calif., Berkeley, 1962; m. John L. Saltonstall, Jr., Jan. 8, 1976. Researcher, Time Mag., Paris, 1962-64; economist Planning Services Group, Cambridge, Mass., 1966-68; dir. planning and evaluation Action for Boston Community Devel., Inc., Boston, 1968-73; dir. planning Office of State Planning and Mgmt., Boston, 1973-75; asst. sec. Bus. and Transp. Agy., Sacramento, 1975-76; dir. Calif. Dept. Transp., Sacramento, 1976—. Mem. Transp. Research Bd. (exec. com.), Phi Beta Kappa. Office: 1120 N St Sacramento CA 95814

GIANUTSOS, ROSAMOND ROCKWELL, psychologist, educator; d. Samuel Forbes Rockwell and Ursula Ingalls Hazen; B.A., Barnard Coll., 1966; Ph.D., N.Y.U., 1970; m. John Gerasimos Gianutsos, Sept. 11, 1965; children—Gerasimos John, Matthew Nicholas. Asst. prof. Adelphi U., Garden City, N.Y., 1970-74, assoc. prof., 1974—; sr. psychologist, adj. assoc. prof. N.Y.U. Med. Center, 1978—. Fellow N.Y. Acad. Scis.; mem. Am. Psychol. Assn., Psychonomic Soc., Eastern Psychol. Assn., Am. Congress Rehab. Medicine, Internat. Neuropsychol. Soc., AAUP. Author: Computer Programs for Cognitive Rehabilitation, 1981; Contbr. numerous articles to profl. jours. Office: Dept Psychology Adelphi U Garden City NY 11530

GIARDIELLO, MADELINE SAYOC, cosmetic co. exec.; b. Bkyn., May 26, 1942; d. Salvatore and Viola Altieri; ed. Vivian Woodard Acad., 1968; m. John Giardiello, June 10, 1975; children—Cesar, Sabrina, Christina. Owner chain beauty salons, Fla., 1968-78; nat. sales mgr. M.A.F. Enterprises, Hollywood, Fla., 1975; distbr. Vivian Woodard Cosmetics, 1968-72, Gaubaud of Paris Cosmetics, 1972-74; distbr., pres. Evermond Cosmetics Inc., 1975-79; pres. Fabriella Cosmetici, Inc., North Miami Beach, Fla., 1979—. Mem. Fla. Cosmetic and Fragrance Assn. (pres.), Foragers Am., Miami Shores Bus. and Profl. Women's Assn. Home: 1170 NE 170 St North Miami Beach FL 33162 Office: 2120 NE 162 St North Miami Beach FL 33162

GIBB, ELIZABETH GLENADINE, mathematician; b. Biggsville, Ill., June 8, 1919; B.Ed., Western Ill. State U., 1941; M.A., George Peabody Coll., 1944; Ph.D. in Math. Edn., U. Wis., 1953. Tchr. math. and sci. Mendon Twp. High Sch., 1941-45; tchr. math. Geneseo Twp. High Sch., 1945-46; prof. math. edn. U. No. Iowa, 1946-65; prof. math. edn. U. Tex., Austin, 1965—. Mem. Am. Ednl. Research Assn., AAAS. Office: Dept of Mathematics University of Texas Austin TX 78712 *

GIBBONS, DELORES JACKSON, educator; b. Halltown, W.Va., Jan. 24, 1938; d. Daniel David and Mary Frances (Taylor) Jackson; B.A., Shepherd Coll., 1960; M.A., Jersey City State Coll., 1974; postgrad. Mid-Atlantic Assn. Tng. and Cons., 1979-81; 1 son, Mark Darnell. Tchr., Page-Jackson High Sch., Charles Town, W.Va., 1959-60; tchr. Dickinson High Sch., Jersey City, 1960-73, coordinator work-study programs, 1971-73, guidance counselor, 1973-75, coordinator guidance dept., 1975-82, acting vice prin., 1982—; condr. workshops No. N.J. Sch. Systems, 1981—; mem. vis. com. Middle States Assn. Commn. Secondary Schs. Mem. community adv. bd. Upward Bound program, 1975—. Mem. N.J. Edn. Assn., Hudson County Edn. Assn., Jersey City Edn. Assn., N.J. Personnel and Guidance Assn., Hudson County Personnel and Guidance Assn., Jersey City Personnel and Guidance Assn., Coll. Women (pres. 1981—), N.J. Black Educators, NAACP. Mem. Christian Ch. Co-author manual: Integrating the Classroom with the World of Work, 1980. Address: 71 Ellington St East Orange NJ 07017

GIBBONS, MRS., JOHN SHELDON (CELIA VICTORIA TOWNSEND), editor, publisher; b. Fargo, N.D.; d. Harry Alton and Helen (Haag) Townsend; student U. Minn., 1930-33; m. John Sheldon Gibbons, May 1, 1935; children—Mary Vee, John Townsend. Advt. mgr. Hotel Nicollet, Mpls., 1933-37; contbg. editor children's mags., 1935—; partner Youth Assos. Co., Mpls., 1942-65; pub., art dir. Mines and Escholier mags., 1954-65; founder Bull. Bd. Pictures, Inc., Mpls., 1954, pres., 1954—; founder Periodical Litho Art Co., Mpls., 1962-65, pres., 1962-65. Active St. Paul Internat. House, Friends of Inst., St. Paul Arts and Sci. Center. Republican chairwoman Golden Valley, Minn., 1950; alternate del. Hennepin County Rep. Conv., 1962. Mem. Mpls. Inst. Arts, Ft. Lauderdale Mus. Arts, Art Guild Boca Raton. Delta Zeta. Clubs: Woman's Minikahda; Woman's of Minneapolis; Woman's (Deerfield Beach, Fla.). Home: 1416 Alpine Pass Tyrol Hills Minneapolis MN 55416 Office: 1057 A1A Hillsboro Beach FL 33062

GIBBONS, VIRGINIA LEE, lawyer; b. Martinsburg, W.Va., Oct. 11, 1946; d. Pierce Gladstone and Goldie Garland (Hinkle) G.; B.S. in Polit. Sci., Shepherd Coll., Shepherdstown, W.Va., 1968; J.D., George Washington U., 1976. Personnel mgmt. specialist U.S. Navy, Washington, Phila., 1969-71, 72-73, Dept. Transp., Washington, 1971-72; law clk. Fed. Energy Adminstrn., Washington, 1975; law clk. EPA, Washington, 1975-76, staff atty., 1976-81, sr. atty.-adv. and dep. dir. Office of Legislation, 1981—; admitted to Va. bar, 1976. Mem. Am. Bar Assn., Va. Bar Assn., Va. Women's Bar Assn. Office: 401 M St SW Washington DC 20460

GIBBS, ANN, chemist; b. Corpus Christi, Tex., May 19, 1941; d. Frank James and Elizabeth Ann (Setzer) G.; student Tulane U., 1958-59; B.A., U. Tex., Austin, 1961; M.S., U. Ark., 1964. Research asst. Inst. Marine Sci., U. Tex., 1960-62; chemist DuPont Co., Savannah River plant, Aiken, S.C., 1966—; mem. ad hoc com. NDA instrumentation U.S. Dept. Energy, 1980-82. AEC fellow, 1962-65. Mem. Am. Chem. Soc. (chmn. Savannah River sect. 1980), Am. Phys. Soc., AAAS, Am. Nuclear Soc., ASTM, Inst. Nuclear Materials Mgmt. Presbyterian. Research in nuclear spectroscopy and nondestructive instrumentation. Home: PO Box 6624 North Augusta SC 29841 Office: Bldg 779A Savannah River Lab Aiken SC 29808

GIBBS, CAROLE ANN, accountant; b. Sioux City, Iowa, Apr. 2, 1937; d. Paul S. and Linnea D. Ferner; B.B.A., U. Hawaii, 1964; m. Douglas Gibbs, Oct. 1, 1956; children—Karen Sue, Kathleen. Mem. staff Coopers & Lybrand, C.P.A.s, Honolulu, 1964-75, tax mgr., 1975—; v.p. Hawaiian Trust Co. Ltd., 1981—; mem. nat. adv. council SBA, 1977-78. Vice chmn. Honolulu City and County Com. Status Women, 1978—. Mem. Nat. Assn. Accts. (dir. 1978-80), Am. Soc. Women Accts. (pres. 1967-68), Hawaii Soc. C.P.A.s (pres.-elect), Hawaii Acctg. Edn. Found.

(pres. 1979-80), PEO, Delta Zeta. Home: 1935 Makiki St Honolulu HI 96822 Office: PO Box 3170 Honolulu HI 96802

GIBBS, EFFIE LAJANE, accountant; b. Winnfield, La., Feb. 4, 1944; d. Finis James and Vivian (Dean) G.; student La. State U., Alexandria, 1976—, La. State U., Shreveport, 1970-74. Sec., acct. receptionist Herman Gorham, gen. contractor, Winnfield, La., 1967-69; acct. Virginia Dickerson, acctg. and tax service, Winnfield, 1970-74; owner, operator LaJane's Acctg. & Tax Service, Winnfield, 1974—. Mem. Nat. Assn. Female Execs., Am. Mgmt. Assn., Early Am. Soc., Nat. Hist. Soc., Am. Security Council, Nat. Trust for Historic Preservation, Am. Soc. Profl. and Exec. Women, U.S. Senatorial Club, Smithsonian Assos. Mem. Assemblies of God. Home and Office: 1004 San Pedro St Winnfield LA 71483

GIBBS, ELIZABETH LENORE, mining engr.; b. Washington, Sept. 13, 1943; d. Harold Ray and Bessie Margaret (Johnson) G.; student Va. Poly. Inst., 1960-64; E.M. (AIME Women's Aux. scholar), Colo. Sch. Mines, 1969, M.S., 1972; m. Donald Eldhart, July 6, 1979; children—Cora A., Teresa E.; children by previous marriage—Tanya P., Ian H. Mining engr. Consol. Coal Co., Pitts., 1969-71, Continental Oil Co., Denver, 1971-72; teaching asst. Colo. Sch. Mines, 1971-72; sr. mining engr. Climax Molybdenum Co. (Colo.), 1973-76, Gulf Mineral Resources Co., Denver, 1976-81; asst. prof. Colo. Sch. Mines, Golden, 1981—. Pres., bd. dirs. Mitchell Sch., Inc., Leadville, Colo., 1974-82. Mem. Soc. Computer Simulation, AIME (2d Pl. Student Paper award 1969), Colo. Mining Assn. Editor: Mining Software Rev., 1981—. Home: Salina Star Route Boulder CO 80302 Office: Basic Engring Dept Colo Sch Mines Golden CO 80401

GIBBS, GLADYS WADE, bank exec.; b. Smith County, Tenn., Feb. 14, 1922; d. Bemon and Ruth (White) Wade; grad. Sch. Banking of South, La. State U.; cert. mgmt. Nat. Assn. Bank Women; m. Emmett C. Gibbs, July 18, 1953; 1 dau., Mary Friss Wilburn. Bookkeeper, Smith County Bank, Carthage, Tenn., 1946-47, sec. to cashier, 1947-59, asst. cashier, 1959-64, v.p., 1964-78, sr. v.p., 1978—, also dir., mem. exec. com. Mem. Carthage Bus. and Profl. Women's Club (pres. 1963), Smith County C. of C., Nat. Assn. Bank Women (chmn. Middle Tenn. Group 1965-66), Baptist. Clubs: Green Hills Golf and Country, Eastern Star (worthy matron 1960-61), Carthage Past Matrons. Home: Route 1 Brush Creek TN 38547 Office: 101 Main St Carthage TN 37030

GIBBS, JEWELLE TAYLOR, psychologist, educator; b. Stratford, Conn., Nov. 4, 1933; d. Julian Augustus and Margaret Pauline (Morris) Taylor; A.B. cum laude, Radcliffe Coll., 1955; postgrad. Harvard-Radcliffe Program in Bus. Adminstrn., 1959; M.S.W., U. Calif., Berkeley, 1970, Ph.D., 1980; m. James Lowell Gibbs, Jr., Aug. 25, 1956; children—Geoffrey Taylor, Lowell Dabney. Jr. mgmt. asst. U.S. Dept. Labor, Washington, 1955-56; market research coordinator Pillsbury Co., Mpls., 1959-61; clin. social worker Stanford (Calif.) U. Student Health Service, 1970-74, 78-79, research asso. dept. psychiatry, 1971-73; asst. prof. Sch. Social Welfare U. Calif., Berkeley, 1979—. Bd. regents U. Santa Clara (Calif.), 1980-84; mem. Minn. State Commn. on Status of Women, 1963-65; co-chairperson Minn. Women's Com. for Civil Rights, 1963-65. NIMH fellow, 1979; Soroptimist Internat. grantee, 1978-79. Fellow Am. Orthopsychiat. Assn.; mem. Am. Psychol. Assn., Nat. Assn. Social Workers, Western Psychol. Assn. Democrat. Mem. editorial bd. Am. Jour. Orthopsychiatry, 1980—; bd. publs. Nat. Assn. Social Workers, 1980-82; contbr. chpts. to books, articles to profl. jours. Office: Haviland Hall Sch Social Welfare U Calif Berkeley CA 94720

GIBBS, JUNE NESBITT, Republican nat. committeewoman; b. Newton, Mass., June 13, 1922; d. Samuel Frederick and Lulu (Glazier) Nesbitt; B.A. in Math., Wellesley Coll., 1943; M.A. in Math., Boston U., 1947; m. Donald T. Gibbs, Dec. 8, 1945; 1 dau., Elizabeth. Republican nat. committeewoman, R.I., 1969-80; sec. Rep. Nat. Com., 1977-80; mem. def. adv. com. Women in Services, 1970-72, vice chmn., 1972; mem. Middletown Town Council, 1974-80, pres., 1978-80. Served to lt. (j.g.) USNR, 1942-46. Home: 163 Riverview Ave Middletown RI 02840

GIBSON, ALTHEA, tennis player, golfer, state ofcl.; b. Silver, S.C., Aug. 25, 1927; d. Daniel and Annie B. (Washington) Gibson; B.S., Fla. A. and M. Coll., 1953; m. William A. Darben, Oct. 17, 1965. Amateur tennis player in U.S., Europe and S.Am., 1941-58; asst. instr. dept. health and phys. edn. Lincoln U., Jefferson City, Mo., 1953-55; appeared in movie in The Horse Soldiers, 1958; made profl. tennis tour with Harlem Globetrotters, 1959; community relations rep. Ward Baking Co., 1959; won world profl. tennis championship, 1960; joined Ladies Profl. Golf Assn. as profl. golfer, 1963; apptd. to N.Y. State Recreation Council, 1964; staff mem. Essex County Park Commn., Newark, 1970, recreation supr., 1970-71; dir. tennis programs, profl. Valley View Racquet Club, Northvale, N.J., 1972; tennis pro Morven, 1973—; athletic commr. State of N.J., 1975—; recreation mgr. City of East Orange (N.J.), 1980. Named Woman Athlete of Year, AP Poll, 1957-58; named to Lawn Tennis Hall of Fame and Tennis Mus., 1971. Mem. Alpha Kappa Alpha. Author: I Always Wanted to Be Somebody, 1958. Home: PO Box 768 East Orange NJ 07019

GIBSON, BARBARA B., former state legislator; b. Burlington, Vt., July 4, 1935; grad. pub. schs.; m. David A. Gibson, Jan. 2, 1982; children from previous marriage—Donna, Robert, Mary, David. Mem. Ward II Democratic Com., 1970-81, chmn., 1972-77; mem. Burlington City Dem. Com., 1973-80; mem. Chittenden County Dem. Com., 1977-80; mem. Vt. Ho. of Reps., 1979-82. Pres., Friends of Speech and Hearing, 1970-71; mem. Burlington Sch. Bd., 1973-77; mem. Burlington Bd. Aldermen, 1977-79. Mem. Chittenden Dem. Women, Grand Isle County Dem. Women, Vt. Dem. Women, Brandon Tng. Sch. Assn. (trustee). Roman Catholic.

GIBSON, CATHERINE WILLIAMS, educator, ednl. adminstr.; B.S., W.Va. State Coll., 1947; M.S., Western Res. U., 1954; postgrad. (scholar) U. Boston, summer 1961-62; Ph.D. in Edn. (teaching asst.), U. Akron, 1977. Tchr., Cleve. Public Schs., 1947-65, 67-70; dir. edn. AID for NEA, Washington, Nairobi, Kenya, 1965-67; research asso. U. Ariz., Tucson, 1970-73; prin. Clarkston Elem. Sch., Lorain, Ohio, 1976-79, on-site inservice coordinator tchr. corps project, 1979—; asso. prof. Coll. Edn., Margai Tchr. Tng. Coll., Freetown, Sierra Leone, summer 1964; instr. curriculum and supervision, Kenya, summer 1968. Active St. Andrews Episcopal Ch., NAACP, Urban League, Nat. Council Negro Women; bd. dirs. Lorain County Drug and Alcohol Abuse Council, Erie Shores council Girl Scouts U.S.A; vol. ARC; sponsor Reading Club; counselor Girl Guides; mem. Community Center Service, Women's Civic League Cleve., Cleve. Council Human Rights. Recipient PTA Tchr. award, 1962. Mem. NEA, Ohio Adminstrs. Assn., Assn. Supervision and Curriculum Devel., Internat. Reading Assn., Ohio Reading Assn., Ohio Edn. Assn., Am. Assn. Sch. Adminstrs., Nat. Assn. Female Execs., Kappa Delta Pi, Delta Sigma Theta. Club: Quota. Office: 1020 7th St Lorain OH

GIBSON, CHARLOTTE, utility co. exec.; b. Glancy, Miss., Nov. 12, 1927; d. John William and Louise (Hall) Gibson; B.S. in Home Econs., Miss. U. for Women, 1949. Homemaking tchr., Moss Point, Miss., 1949-50, McComb, Miss., 1951-53; regional home economist Crosley Major Appliance Co., Cin., 1954-56; home service adviser Dallas Power & Light Co., 1956-70, appliance coordinator, 1971-77, energy conservation rep., 1978—; cons. to project bus. div. Jr. Achievement, Inc.; chmn. Dallas consumer exchange com. FDA, 1979, 80. Recipient citation for meritorious service to consumers Maj. Appliance Consumer Action Panel, 1979; certificate of appreciation Dallas Ind. Sch. Dist., 1979. Mem. Am. Home Econs. Assn., Nat. Home Improvement Council, Nuclear Energy Women, Home Economists in Bus. (treas. N. Tex. chpt.), Elec. Women's Round Table (nat. dir., nat. energy affairs chmn. 1980—). Methodist. Home: 5818 E University Blvd Apt 229 Dallas TX 75206 Office: Dallas Power & Light Co 1506 Commerce St Dallas TX 75201

GIBSON, DIANE LUCIENNE, commodities trading commn. ofcl.; b. Chgo., Feb. 4, 1942; d. Edgar Arthur and Denise Louise (Waymel) Theriault; A.A., Chgo. City Colls. Loop Br., 1972; children—Scott A., Heidi, Matthew, Peter. Statement and file clk. N.W. Nat. Bank, Chgo., 1961-62; public relations Candlewick Lake, Elmhurst, Ill., 1973; employment counsellor Ivy Personnel, Chgo., 1973-74, Dunhill Personnel, Chgo., 1974-75; agt. New Eng. Life Ins., Chgo., 1975-80; asso. Commodity Futures Trading Commn., 1981—. Planning com. Lincoln Park Conservation Assn.; parish group leader Fourth Presbyn. Ch.; active Chgo. Heart Assn. Mem. Chgo. Assn. Life Underwriters (bd. dirs.). Contbr. article to jour. in field. Office: 180 N LaSalle St Suite 3200 Chicago IL 60601

GIBSON, ELEANOR BEATRICE, artist, library cons.; b. London, Eng., Mar. 8, 1905; d. Harry Hepburn and Anne Elizabeth (White) Gibson; brought to U.S., 1905, derivative citizenship, 1914; student Loomis-Chaffee Sch., 1923; A.B., Cornell U., 1928; student St. Joseph Coll., West Hartford, 1937-38; M.S. in Library Sci., Syracuse U., 1957. With Aetna Life & Casualty Co., Hartford, Conn., 1928-42, librarian research div., 1933-42; librarian Logan Lewis Library, Carrier Corp. Research Center, Syracuse, N.Y., 1947-67, spl. adviser, 1967-70; tech. supr. computerized union catalogue project Conn. State Library, Hartford, 1968-71; now artist, library cons. Served from 1st lt. (WAAC) WAC, AUS, 1942-46; capt., 1950-51. Recipient Honors award, Spl. Libraries Assn., 1968, named to Hall of Fame. Mem. Spl. Libraries Assn. (pres. Western N.Y. 1959-60; nat. chmn. metals materials div. 1961-62), Conn. Acad. Fine Arts (sustaining mem.), West Hartford Art League (hon. life), Alumni Assn. Syracuse U. Sch. Library Sci. and Info. (pres. 1967-68, Am. Legion, Pi Lambda Sigma (pres. 1958-59), Beta Phi Mu (local pres. 1959-60). Episcopalian. Editor: Guide to Metallurgical Information, 1965. Contbr. articles to profl. jours. Home: White Studio Leighton Hill Rd Newbury VT 05051 also 23 Fernridge Rd West Hartford CT 06107

GIBSON, ELEANOR JACK (MRS. JAMES J. GIBSON), psychologist, educator; b. Peoria, Ill., Dec. 7, 1910; d. William A. and Isabel (Grier) Jack; B.A., Smith Coll., 1931, M.A., 1933, D.Sc. (hon.), 1972; Ph.D., Yale U., 1938; D.Sc. (hon.), Rutgers U., 1973, Trinity Coll., 1982; m. James J. Gibson, Sept. 17, 1932; children—James J., Jean Grier. Asst., instr., asst. prof. Smith Coll., 1931-49; research asso. in psychology Cornell U., Ithaca, N.Y., 1949-66, prof., 1972—, Susan Linn Sage prof. psychology, 1972—; fellow Inst. for Advanced Study, Princeton U., 1959-60, Inst. for Advanced Study in Behavioral Scis., Stanford, Calif., 1963-64; vis. prof. M.I.T., 1973, U. Calif., Davis, 1978, U. Minn., 1980; vis. scientist Salk Inst., 1979. Recipient Wilbur Cross medal Yale U., 1973. Guggenheim fellow, 1972-73. Fellow Am. Psychol. Assn. (disting. sci. contbn. award 1970, pres. div. 3 1977, G. Stanley Hall medal div. 7) AAAS (chmn. 1982); mem. Nat. Acad. Edn., Psychonomic Soc., Eastern Psychol. Assn. (pres. 1968), Brit. Psychol. Soc. (hon.), Soc. Exptl. Psychologists (Howard Crosby Warren medal 1977), Soc. Research in Child Devel. (governing council 1980—, disting. contbn. award 1981), Nat. Acad. Sci., Am. Acad. Arts and Scis., Phi Beta Kappa, Sigma Xi. Author: Principles of Perceptual Learning and Development (Century award), 1969; (with H. Levin) The Psychology of Reading, 1975.

GIBSON, ELISABETH JANE, educator; b. Salina, Kans., Apr. 28, 1937; d. Cloyce Wesley and Margaret Mae (Yost) Kasson; A.B., Colo. State Coll., 1957; M.A., San Francisco State Coll., 1968; Ed.D., U. No. Colo., 1978; m. Harry B. Gibson, July 1, 1970. Tchr. various public schs., 1957-67; tchr. Central Kans. Diagnostic and Remedial Edn. Center, Salina, 1968-70; instr. Loretto Heights Coll., Denver, 1970-72, Regis Coll., Denver, spring 1973; instr. Met. State Coll., Denver, summer 1972, asst. prof., spring 1979; co-owner, v.p. Ednl. Cons. Enterprises, Inc., Greeley, Colo., 1974-77; exec. dir. Colo. Fedn. Council Exceptional Children, Denver, 1976-77; resource coordinator Mile High Consortium, Denver, 1976-77; cons. Mont. Dept. Public Instrn., Helena, 1978-79; spl. edn. dir. N.E. Colo. Bd. Cooperative Ednl. Services, Haxtun, 1979—. Mem. Colo. Comprehensive Personnel Planning Com., 1977-81; mem. bd. dirs. MacIntosh Acad. for Gifted Children, Denver, 1977-79; mem. adv. council Denver Public Schs. Spl. Edn. Com., 1978-79, Colo. Title IV Council, 1980-82; acting co-chmn. Colo. Coalition for Edn. Handicapped Persons, Denver, 1978-79; pres. bd. dirs. Found. Exceptional Children, Reston, Va., 1980-81, bd. dirs., 1976-82; pres. bd. dirs. N.E. Colo. Services for Handicapped, Inc., Sterling, 1981-82; mem. Denver City and County Commn. Disabled, 1978-79. Recipient Ann. Service award Colo. Fedn. Council Exceptional Children, 1981; Office of Edn. fellow San Francisco State Coll., 1967-68, grad. research fellow U. No. Colo., 1972-74. Mem. Colo. Assn. Sch. Execs., Council Adminstrs. Spl. Edn. Colo., Rural Edn. Assn., Am. Assn. Mental Deficiency, Colo. Assn. Gifted and Talented. Republican. Methodist. Club: Order of Eastern Star. Contbr. articles and ednl. minicourses in field to profl. publs. Home: 2443 S Colorado Blvd Apt 227 Denver CO 80222 Office: NE Colo Board Cooperative Ednl Services Haxtun CO 80731

GIBSON, JACQUELYN JORDAN, electrologist; b. Phila., Aug. 2, 1924; d. Ira Andrew and Emma Ercyal (Brickley) Jordan; grad. Kree Electrologist Sch., 1946; m. Morgan Stone Gibson, Mar. 9, 1946; children—Bruce Morgan, Ronald Wayne, Jeffrey Jordan. Prin., Jacquelyn Jordan Gibson, electrologist, Balt., 1946-61, Salisbury, Md., 1961-81, Jupiter, Fla., 1982—. Numerous ch. activities including adminstrv. bd., sec. Council on Ministries, Altar Guild and Missionary Circle; vol. worker Bd. Elections. Mem. Md. Electrolysis Assn. (charter), C. of C. Republican. Methodist. Clubs: Elks Aux., Soroptimists (past chpt. pres., past chpt. treas.), Women of Moose. Home: 102 E Beverly Rd Jupiter FL 33458 Office: 390 Tequesta Dr Tequesta FL

GIBSON, MARY ELIZABETH (PSEUDONYM MARALEE G. DAVIS), writer, novelist; b. Springfield, Mass., Jan. 9, 1924; d. Francis Clarence and Beatrice Grace (Tait) Gagnier; student, Bay Path Jr. Coll., 1941-42; m. Francis Charles Davis, July 18, 1942 (div. Aug. 1964); children—Beverley Tait Davis Clarke, Susan Olds Davis English, Maralee Ruth Dana Davis Chris; m. 2d, David Joel Thibault, Nov. 9, 1964 (div. Oct. 1967); m. 3d, William Carter Gibson, Jan. 21, 1970. Co-owner dairy farm, Amherst, Mass., 1951-60; with Amherst Jour., 1952-54; with Sta. WHMP, Northampton, Mass., intermittently 1955-73; owner Maralee G. Davis, real estate, Amherst, 1956-58; with Sta. WHYN Radio-TV, Springfield, Mass., intermittently, 1958-60; breeder Gt. Pyrenees dogs, 1959-62; with Greenfield (Mass.) Recorder, 1958-62, WTTT, Amherst, 1963-64; free-lance advt. and writing, 1963—; asst. editor Sportsman's News, Northampton, 1963-64; founder, co-owner, pres., treas. Amherst Employment Service, 1968-69; asso. Heiser Real Estate, Northampton, 1973-74. Guest poet Sta. WMUL-TV series on poets for ednl. TV, 1971; guest poet and speaker Vt. Writers Seminar, U. Vt., 1970, Morris Harvey Coll., 1970-71. Treas. Hillcrest Cemetery Marker Service, Springfield, 1972—; bd. dirs. Franklin/Hampshire (Mass.) Community Mental Health Center, 1975-76; coordinator Sunrise art seminars, 1977. Recipient awards for poems Nat. Fedn. Poetry Socs., 1970; citation World Poetry Soc., 1970; citation Shenandoah Valley Acad. Lit., 1978, 79. Mem. N.H., Ariz., W. Va. poetry socs., Martin County (Fla.) Writers Group, Poetry Soc. Am. Author: (under pseudonym Maralee G. Davis) Soliloquy's Virgin (poetry), 1964; The Valley of Self (poetry), 1969. Contbr. poems to various anthologies. Home: PO Box 337 Jensen Beach FL 33457 also PO Box 301 North Amherst MA 01059

GIBSON, RENEE DYER, draftsperson; b. Wenatchee, Wash., Oct. 6, 1944; d. William Russell and Shirley Marguerite (Spencer) Dyer; cert. RCA Insts. Sch. Drafting, 1970; student Modesto Jr. Coll., 1973—, Calif. State Coll., Stanislaus, 1974, N.Y. Inst. Photography, 1979-80; m. Clyde Pierce Gibson, Dec. 24, 1974; children—Lisa Eleana Zabroski, Stefani Yvonne Zabroski, Nicolette Elizabeth Gibson. Detailer/draftsperson Varco-Pruden, Turlock, Calif., 1971-73, 76-77; electronics draftsperson Auto-Weigh, Inc., Modesto, Calif., 1977; detailer/draftsperson Cuckler Steel Bldgs., Turlock, 1978-79, Andersen Steel Bldgs., Lockeford, Calif., 1979-82; electronics drafting cons. ESS, Inc., Sacramento, 1979. Mem. Asso. Photographers Internat.

GIBSON, ROSE CAMPBELL, social scientist; b. Detroit, May 30, 1925; d. John Henry and Lela Gertrude (Long) Campbell; M.A., U. Mich., 1968, Ph.D., 1977; m. Ralph Milton Gibson, Dec. 31, 1947; children—Ralph Milton, John S. Lectr., cons. U. Mich., Ann Arbor, 1977-78, research asso., 1978-79, research scientist, 1982—; cons. Nat. Inst. Edn., 1979—. Mem. Ann Arbor Bd. Health, 1965-66; mem. exec. bd. Ann Arbor Democratic Women's Club, 1957; mem. Ann Arbor Mayor's Com. on Urban Renewal, 1957. USPHS fellow, 1979; Adminstrn. on Aging grantee, 1979. Mem. Am. Psychol. Assn., Biofeedback Soc. Am., AAAS, AAUP, Links, Delta Sigma Theta. Office: 520 E Liberty St Ann Arbor MI 48109

GIBSON, ROXIE ELIZABETH, author; b. Spring City, Tenn., Jan. 24, 1934; d. James Mac and Ethel Cawood; student public schs.; m. James Clyde Gibson, May 29, 1952; 1 son, James Clyde. Sec., Christian edn. dept. First Presbyn. Ch., Nashville, 1970-76, Oak Hill Sch., Nashville, 1976—; author: Hey, God, Listen, 1971, Hey God, Where Are You?, 1972, Hey, God, What Is Christmas?, 1974; Hey, God, Hurry, 1976, Just Me, Lord, 1978, Two Little Fishes and Five Loaves of Bread, 1975; (musicals) Hey, God, Listen, 1972, Hey God, What is Christmas?, 1974, Hey, God, Hurry, 1976, Hey, God, What is America?, 1981. Mem. Nat. League Am. Pen Women, ASCAP, Nat. Acad. Rec. Arts and Scis., Nashville Woman's Press and Author's Club. Presbyterian. Home: 898 Van Leer Dr Nashville TN 37220 Office: 4815 Franklin Rd Nashville TN 37220

GIBSON, SAMANTHA LYNN, preventive maintenance analyst; b. Mesa, Ariz., Dec. 9, 1941; d. Burr and Gwendolyn (Porter) Webb; student No. Ariz. U., Flagstaff, 1961, Coll. San Mateo, Calif., 1969, U. Ariz., Tucson, 1977; m. David Kent Gibson, June 2, 1981; children by previous marriage—Laurence, Donald and Danielle Livingston. Public relations ofcl. Sahara Tahoe Hotel, Stateline, Nev., 1969-71; with South Lake Tahoe C. of C., 1972-75; mgr. Winslow (Ariz.) C. of C., 1975-76; preventive maintenance analyst S.W. Forest Industries, Snowflake, Ariz., 1976—; cons. troubleshooting mech. problems through vibration analysis. Mem. Snowflake Planning and Zoning Commn., 1977-78. Mem. Paper Industry Mgmt. Assn., Ariz. Assn. Indsl. Devel. (dir. 1975-76), Indsl. Devel. Endeavor Assn. (dir. 1975-76), Snowflake-Taylor C. of C. Republican. Research on trending in vibration analysis, analyzing mech. problems in rotating equipment. Home: PO Box 997 Snowflake AZ 85937 Office: PO Box 128 Snowflake AZ 85937

GIBSON, SANDRA DELL, television exec.; b. Hammond, Ind., May 29, 1941; d. John Roy and Helen Louise (Ostovich) Strickland; student Hollywood Profl. Sch., 1958-59, Woodbury Bus. U., 1959-61. Adminstrv. asst. Voi-Shan Mfg., Culver City, Calif., 1961-66; asso. Larson/Walker & Assos., Los Angeles, 1966-73; sta. mgr. KMEX-TV, Los Angeles, 1973—; producer, dir. Navidad en el Barrio Telethon, 1975—. Mem. Los Angeles County Com. for White House Conf. on Families. Recipient Nosotros Public Service award; cert. Navidad en el Barrio. Mem. Nat. Assn. Female Execs., So. Calif. Broadcasters Assn. Republican. Home: 1200 N Flores St Los Angeles CA 90069 Office: 5420 Melrose St Hollywood CA 90038

GIBSON, SUSAN PAMELA, health systems analyst; b. Washington, July 15, 1945; d. Albert Carlisle and Anna Irene (Tafuri) Gibson; B.S., Valparaiso U., 1968; postgrad. Cambridge U., 1968, LaSalle Extension U., 1968-69, U. Md., 1980-81. Sr. asst. mgr. Household Fin. Corp., Bladensburg, Md., 1974-75; tng./ upward mobility officer Bur. Med. Services, Hyattsville, Md., 1975-78, asst. asso. dir. for ops., 1978-81; health systems cons. Wyman Park Health System, Inc., Balt., 1981-82; systems analyst, planning mgr. Group Health Assos., Inc., Washington, 1982—; exec. dir. WAE, Inc., 1976-80; v.p. corp. affairs, GO Enterprises, Inc., 1978—. Active Am. Cancer Soc., Pinecrest Civic Assn.; pres. Parkside Civic Assn., 1972-74; bd. dirs. Constellation House Condominium Assn., 1981-83. Recipient Public Health Service Case award, 1980, Bur. of Med. Services Dirs. award for sustained performance, 1981. Mem. Nat. Assn. Female Execs., Group Health Assn. Am., LWV, Valparaiso U. Alumni Assn., Am. Public Health Assn. Democrat. Roman Catholic. Club: Toastmistress. Home: 10504 Lorain Ave Silver Spring MD 20901 Office: 2021 L St NW Washington DC 20036

GIDDENS, ZELMA KIRK, broadcasting co. exec.; b. Lafayette, Ala.; d. James William and Eunice (Rice) Kirk; grad. So. Union Jr. Coll., 1932; student Auburn U., 1934-35; m. Kenneth R. Giddens, May 19, 1934; children—Ansley Giddens Green, Therese Giddens Greer, Sara Kay. With Sta. WKRG-AM, 1947-55; with Sta. WKRG-AM-FM-TV, Mobile, Ala., 1955—, pres., 1969—. Mem. English Speaking Union (v.p. 1964-76), Smithsonian Assos., Mobile Art Assn., Mobile C. of C.s Lion Aux., Nat. Press Club, Am. Newspaper Women's Assn. Home: 2555 N Delwood Dr Mobile AL 36606 Office: 555 Broadcast Dr Mobile AL 36616

GIDDINGS, LUCILLE CASSELL, nurse; b. Port Chester, N.Y., Jan. 30, 1947; d. Curtis Emmitt and Rose (Lucente) Cassell; R.N., St. Clare's Hosp., N.Y.C., 1969; B.A., Coll. Mt. St. Vincent, Bronx, N.Y., 1979; M.P.A., N.Y.U., 1982; m. William Alfred Giddings, Apr. 2, 1977. Staff nurse hosps. in N.Y. State, 1969-71; elementary sch. nurse Port Chester-Rye Town Bd. Edn., 1971-82; dir. interdepartmental services Misericordia Hosp. Med. Center, Bronx, N.Y., 1982—; chmn. Port Chester br. ARC, 1978. Recipient Rev. Mother Jean Marie award, 1969. Mem. Am. Hosp. Assn., Am. Soc. Public Adminstrn., Nat. Assn. Female Execs., Am. Coll. Hosp. Adminstrs., N.Y.U. Alumni Assn., Coll. Mt. St. Vincent Alumni Assn. Home: 139 S Regent St Port Chester NY 10573 Office: 600 E 233d St Bronx NY 10466

GIDDINGS, MANYA KOSHKO, aircraft service co. exec.; b. Kansas City, Kans., Sept. 21, 1922; d. Stefan and Mehelena (Zybko) Koshko; A.A., Cerritos Coll., 1967; B.A., Calif. State U., Fullerton, 1970; m. Edwin Wight Giddings, July 12, 1948 (dec. Apr. 1970); 1 son, David Wight. Sec., aircraft mfg. co., airlines, 1941-48; co founder, owner, pres. Elsinore Aerospace Services, Inc., Downey, Calif., 1971—, pres., chmn. bd., dir. subs. On Line Computer Center. Mem. adv. bd. Downey Community Hosp. Mem. Nat. Bus. Aircraft Assn., Air Transp. Assn., Assistance League. Republican. Roman Catholic. Club: Aero.

GIELE, MILDRED LEWIS (MILDRED LEWIS KERR), author; b. Middleport, Ohio, July 21, 1897; d. Thomas Franklin and Laura Estelle (Wells) Lewis; student Ohio U., 1915-17, Emerson Coll., Boston, 1919-20; B.S., Ohio State U., 1936; m. James William Kerr, Oct. 14, 1921 (dec. 1953); children—Dorothy Jean, Marjorie Ann; m. 2d, Lester C. Giele, June 28, 1958 (dec. 1968). Dir. music dept. Rio Grande Coll. (Ohio), 1918-19; concert pianist, reader Affiliated Lyceum Bureaus, 1920-21; kindergarten tchr. Oakwood Elementary Schs., 1932-40, supr. music, 1940-47, 54-58; literary editor Lorenz Pub. Co., Dayton, Ohio, 1947-54. Head fine arts dept. Am. Youth Found. Camps, Mich., summers 1937-47; sec. Theater Guild, 1930; pres. Woman's Soc., First Bapt. Ch., Dayton, 1966, 71; v.p. Shafor Blvd. PTA, 1931-33; mem. bd. edn., exec. bd. and music com. First Bapt. Ch., Dayton, 1929-72. Mem. Ohioana Library Assn., Nat. Ret. Tchrs. Assn., Pi Beta Phi. Clubs: Woman's Literary (pres. 1962-64), Dayton Woman's (mem. bd., v.p. 1962-65), Kiwanis Women, French Study Group, Drama Reading Group (Dayton). Author: First Fairy Tales, 1946; A Rainbow in My Hand, 1973; operettas: Steamboat A'Comin, 1948; Johnny Appleseed, 1947; D. Boone Killed a Bear, 1952; Let There Be Light, 1965; lyricist numerous solos including Wedding Prayer, 1950, choruses including Night-Rise, 1948, Proclaim Liberty, 1976.

GIERHART, MILDRED LOUISE, banker; b. Wheeler, Tex., Feb. 11, 1928; d. James W. and Nora E. (Osborne) Henderson; student W. Tex. State U., Canyon, 1945-46; m. Milton L. Gierhart, Sept. 26, 1947; 1 son, Milton L., Jr. Stenographer, U.S. Dept. Welfare, 1956-58; with First Bank & Trust Co., and predecessor, Shamrock, Tex., 1958—, asst. v.p., 1970-74, cashier, 1974—, v.p., 1980—. Bd. dirs., cons. nat. bus. leaders Shamrock High Sch.; bd. dirs. Pioneer West Museum, Shamrock; bd. dirs., treas. Shamrock Community Concert Assn. Mem. Shamrock C. of C. (dir.). Democrat. Baptist. Clubs: Thursday Fine Arts (pres. Shamrock 1980), Order Eastern Star. Home: 209 W 8th St Shamrock TX 79079 Office: 305 N Main St Shamrock TX 79079

GIESSLER, EMILY SWEARINGEN, cosmetics sales ofcl.; b. Fort Wayne, Ind., Oct. 19, 1940; d. Milton Park and Sarah Lucile (Engle) Swearingen; B.A., Tex. Christian U., 1962; M.A., St. Francis Coll., 1966; children by previous marriage—James Hugh Engle, Melinda Sue Engle. Dir. edn. Am. Cancer Soc., Fort Worth, 1963; tchr. North Adams Community Sch., Decatur, Ind., 1963-79; sr. sales dir. Mary Kay Cosmetics Co., Decatur, Ind., 1978—. Treas. 1st United Meth. Ch., Decatur. Mem. Nat. Assn. Female Execs., Internat. Platform Assn., Tri Kappa. Republican. Address: 422 N 3d St Decatur IN 46733

GIEZENTANNER, DORIS PATTON, county ofcl., civic ofcl., civic worker; b. Alexander, N.C., Aug. 7, 1927; d. Oscar Jerome and Elizabeth Jane (Hunter) Patton; exec. sec. degree Blanton Bus. Coll., 1946; student U. Tenn., 1947-49; m. John Henry Giezentanner, Jan. 20, 1948; children—Debra Ann, John Henry. Sec., Interagy. Narcotic Squad, 1973-76; mem. Woodfin (N.C.) Bd. Aldermen, 1971-76; commr. Buncombe County, Ashville, N.C., 1976—, vice chmn., 1976—. Vice chmn. Blue Ridge Mental Health Bd.; bd. dirs. U. N.C. at Asheville Found., Western N.C. Health Systems Agy., Caring for Children, N.C. Gov.'s Working Group on Energy; mem. Asheville Community Sch. Bd.; co-chmn. Yr. 2000 Historic Commn. Recipient spl. award Blue Ridge Mental Health Bd.; named one of Buncombe County's Outstanding Women, 1981. Mem. N.C. Assn. County Commrs. (dir.), Asheville Bus. and Profl. Womens Club, VFW Aux. Democrat. Baptist. Club: Asheville City. Address: Box 8462 Asheville NC 28804

GIFFIN, MARGARET ETHEL (PEGGY), mgmt. cons.; b. Cleve., Aug. 27, 1949; d. Arch Kenneth and Jeanne (Eggleton) G.; B.A. in Psychology, U. Pacific, Stockton, Calif., 1971; M.A. in Psychology, Calif. State U., Long Beach, 1973. Psychometrist, Auto Club So. Calif., Los Angeles, 1973-74; dir. Equal Employment Opportunity Compliance Services div. Psychol. Services, Inc., Los Angeles, 1975—; mem. tech. adv. com. on testing Calif. Fair Employment and Housing Commn., 1974—, mem. steering com., 1978—. Mem. Internat. Personnel Mgmt. Assn. Assessment Council, Am. Psychol. Assn., Western Psychol. Assn., Personnel Testing Council So. Calif. (pres. 1980, chmn. bd. dirs. 1982). Club: Athletic (Los Angeles). Home: 330 S Westmoreland Ave Los Angeles CA 90020 Office: 3450 Wilshire Blvd Suite 1200 Los Angeles CA 90010

GIFFIN, PATRICIA KELLY, accountant; b. Milan, Ind., Jan. 14, 1940; d. George Arthur and Doris Pearl (Koehler) Kelly; B.S. in Acctg., U. Ala., Birmingham, 1974; M.B.A., U. Cin., 1978, M.S. in Taxation, 1982; m. Terry Giffin, June 21, 1958; children—Madeline, Michael. Asst. controller Johnson Rast & Hays, Birmingham, 1971-74; staff acct. Mowery Burke & Co., Cin., 1974-76; acctg. mgr. Levi Accessories, Cin., 1976-78; cost acctg. supr. Schenley Distillers, Cin., 1978-79; instr. U. Cin., 1980—; ind. cons. practice in acctg. and taxes, West Chester, Ohio, 1980—. C.P.A., Ohio. Mem. Am. Inst. C.P.A.s, Am. Women's Soc. C.P.A.s, Am. Soc. Women Accts. (dir. Cin. chpt. 1980-82), Ohio Soc. C.P.A.s (editorial adv. bd.), Cin. Women's Soc. C.P.A.s (an organizer). Address: 9145 Sunderland Way West Chester OH 45069

GIFFUNI, FLORA BALDINI, artist, ednl. adminstr., interior design co. exec.; b. Naples, Italy; B.F.A., N.Y. U., 1942, M.F.A., Columbia, 1945; postgrad. U. Madrid (Spain), 1959, U. Pisa (Italy), 1960, Institute d'Allende Mex., 1966, N.Y. Sch. Interior Design, 1959, also Art Students League; m. Joseph Giffuni, June 22, 1941; children—JoAnn, Vincent, Catherine. Exhibited in 7 one-person shows; exhibited in group shows including Lever House, Am. Artists Profl. League, N.Y.C., Nat. Acad., N.Y.C., Hudson Valley Art Assn., Nat. Arts Club, N.Y.C., Nat. Art League, Douglaston, N.Y., Copley Soc., Boston, Salmagundi Club, N.Y.C.; dir. Giffuni Art Studio, Bronx, N.Y., 1942-50 ; instr. art Immaculate Conception Sch., Jamaica Estates, N.Y., 1955-65; pres. F.B.G. Interiors, Jamaica Estates, 1959—; pres. Flora B. Giffuni Art Sch., Jamaica Estates, 1960—; past dir. Catan Rose Sch. Art, Jamaica, 1962-74; past editor Catharine Lorillard Wolfe Art Club, N.Y.C., 1973-76. Recipient Amita award Interior Design, Am. Italian Awards for Women Achievement, 1959, pastel awards Lever House, Am. Artists Profl. League, 1966; spl. award Nat. Acad., 1970; Talens award, 1970; Bocur award, 1971; Josephson award, 1973; 1st prize Pastel, Grand Central Gallery, N.Y.C., 1977; elected to Pastel Hall of Fame. Mem. Nat. Arts Club (gov., award 1972), Nat. Art League (award 1971, 73, 75, 77, 78, 80), Catharine Lorillarde Wolfe Art Club (Awards 1976, 77), Am. Artists Profl. League, Art Students League, Nat. Soc. Interior Designers, Pastel Soc. Am. (founder, pres. 1975—), Smithsonian Inst., Accademia d'Arte (Parma, Italy), Salmagundi Club (hon.). Works included in How to Paint Figures in Pastel, Palette Talk, Today's Art. Address: 180-16 Dalny Rd Jamaica Estates New York NY 11432

GIFT, HELEN CHOATE, sociologist; b. Kingsport, Tenn., Jan. 20, 1943; d. Wesley Edgar and Clara Barton (Choate) G.; B.A., Emory U., 1965, M.A., 1969, Ph.D., 1971. Instr. high sch. biology DeKalb County, Ga., 1965-66; dir. research and manpower planning Comprehensive Health Planning, Chgo., 1970-73; chief behavioral scis. ADA, Chgo., 1973-75, dir. econ. research, 1975-81; asst. prof. Northwestern U., 1974-81; asso. research dir. D'Arcy-MacManus & Masius, Inc., Chgo., 1981—; mem. periodontal adv. com. NIH, 1978-80, mem. adv. com. Nat. Inst. on Aging, 1980—; Vol., Five-Hosp. Homebound Elderly Program. NIMH fellow, 1966-69; Emory U. grad. fellow, 1969-70. Mem. Am. Sociol. Assn., Internat. Assn. Dental Research, Behavioral Scientists in Dental Research, Phi Beta Kappa. Clubs: University Circle, Found. for Ill. Archeology. Contbr. articles to profl. jours.

GIGNAC, JUDITH ANN, county supr.; b. Detroit, Mar. 21, 1939; d. Durward Arthur and Gertrude Marian (Maneck) DuPont; student Broward Bus. Coll., 1957-58, U. Colo., 1967-69, Cochise Coll., 1975-76; m. Paul Ross Gignac, Sept. 12, 1964; children—Beth Andrea, Christopher Ross. Data processor Kettelle & Assos., Colorado Springs, Colo., 1968-69; computer programmer RCA Ballistic Missile Early Warning Systems, Colorado Springs, 1962-68; mem. Cochise County Bd. Suprs., Bisbee, Ariz., 1977—, chmn., 1978-79; dir. Huachuca Fed. Credit Union, 1979-80; participant profl. confs., 1979—; dir. Bank of Cochise; founder Women as Leaders seminar series, 1981; mem. task force Ariz. Wastewater Treatment Facilities Mem. council Govt. affairs Ariz. Hosp. Assn.; v.p. Sierra Vista (Ariz.) Indsl. Devel. Authority, 1976-78; bd. dirs. Safford Dist. Public Land Adv. Council; pres. Thunder Mountain Republican Women, 1972-74; treas. Ariz. Rep. State Com., 1976-77; chmn. Cochise County Rep. Com., 1972-75; sub-com. chmn. Nat. Rep. Platform Com., 1980. Named Lady of Yr., Sierra Vista chpt. Beta Sigma Phi, 1978, Woman in Action, AAUW, 1975. Mem. Am. Soc. Public Adminstrn., Ariz. Assn. Ind. Developers, Ariz. Acad., U.S. Border Cities, Counties and States (dir.), Southeastern Ariz. Govt. Orgn. (dir.), Ariz. Assn. Counties (exec. com. 1981), Assn. U.S. Army (dir. 1980-82), Federally Employed Women, Thunder Mountain Republican Women, Sierra Vista C. of C., Bisbee C. of C. Club: Bus. and Profl. Women (Woman of Yr., Huachuca chpt. 1974-75). Home: 565 Raymond Dr Sierra Vista AZ 85635 Office: PO Box 225 Bisbee AZ 85603

GIGUIERE, MICHELE LOUISE, lawyer; b. Spokane, Feb. 11, 1944; d. Karl Earl and Mildred Elaine (Phillips) G.; B.A., U. Pacific, 1965; M.S., U. So. Calif., 1969; J.D., Lincoln Law Sch., 1980. Exec. trainee J.W. Robinson Co., Los Angeles, 1965-66; tchr. Novato (Calif.) Unified Sch. Dist., 1967-78; asst. dept. mgr. Emporium, San Rafael, Calif., 1970-74; admitted to Calif. bar, 1980, since practiced in Citrus Heights and Fair Oaks, Calif. Mem. Am. Bar Assn., State Bar Calif., Sacramento County Bar Assn., Calif. Women Lawyers, Women Lawyers Sacramento, LWV. Democrat. Presbyterian. Clubs: Network. Home: 4824 Minnesota Ave Fair Oaks CA 95628 Office: 4777 Sunrise Ave Fair Oaks CA 95628

GILBERT, ALMA MAGGIORE, broadcasting exec.; b. Canton, Ohio; d. Vincent Dominick and Florence Antoinette (Manack) Maggiore; student pvt. sch., Canton, Ohio; m. Richard B. Gilbert, July 17, 1953; 1 son, Gary Richard. Dir., sec. Ariz. Aircasters, Inc., Scottsdale Broadcasting Co., 1955-58; program dir. Sta. KOPK, Scottsdale, Ariz., 1956-58; dir., sec. No. Ariz. Aircasters, Inc., 1957-59; program dir. Sta. KZOK, Prescott, Ariz., 1957-59; dir., v.p., sec. KYND Radio Corp., program dir. Sta. KYND, Tempe, Ariz., 1960-66; dir., v.p., sec. Aircasters, Inc., Scottsdale, Ariz., 1966-82; dir., v.p., sec. Ariz. Communications Corp., program dir. Sta. KXTC, Glendale/Phoenix, 1968-78; pres. Sta. KQST, Sedona, Ariz., 1982—; pres. Am. Aircasting Corp., Scottsdale, 1979—. Home and Office: Box 182 Scottsdale AZ 85252

GILBERT, CAROLYN DIANE, mfg. co. exec.; b. Birmingham, Ala., Aug. 14, 1945; d. Jim Hardy Gilbert and Alberta (Berry) Gilbert Halsell; student Seattle Pacific U., 1977-78, Seattle Community Coll., 1963-64, 77; 1 son, Theodore Steven Harris. Sec., Pacific Northwest Bell Co., Seattle, 1965-69; claims adjuster Farwest Assurance Co., Seattle, 1969-71, 74-75; claims adjuster Airborne Freight Corp., Seattle, 1971-73; asst. credit mgr. Foss Launch & Tug Co., Seattle, 1975-80; with Marco Seattle, 1981—. Mem. Nat. Assn. Female Execs., Nat. Assn. Credit Mgmt. (chairperson marine trade group), NAACP Nat. Assn. Credit Women. Democrat. Home: 1300 Puget Dr #403 Renton WA 98055 Office: 2300 W Commodore Way Seattle WA 98199

GILBERT, EDWINA SMITH, airlines exec.; b. 1932; attended U. Miami; married. With Eastern Air Lines, Inc., Miami, Fla., 1956—, beginning as flight attendant, successively instr. flight attendant tng., mgr. flight attendant tng., acctg. dir. in-flight services, div. v.p. in-flight services, 1956-73, v.p. inflight services, 1973—. Office: Eastern Air Lines Inc Miami International Airport Miami FL 33148 *

GILBERT, ELIZABETH MALIN, speech pathologist; b. N.Y.C., Dec. 21, 1952; d. Lewis S. and Jeannette L. (Wolin) Hollins; B.S. magna cum laude, N.Y.U., 1974; M.S., Adelphi U., 1975; m. Bruce R. Gilbert, June 30, 1974. Clin. speech pathologist, undergrad. instr. Adelphi Speech and Hearing Center, Garden City, N.Y., 1974-75; clin. speech pathologist, vocat. counselor N.Y.C. Bd. Edn., 1975-78; dir. tng. and devel./ employee relations BBDO, Inc., N.Y.C., 1978-80; dir. tng. and human resources Young & Rubicam, Inc., N.Y.C., 1980—; cons. in oral communications. Recipient Acad. Merit award, grad. clin. fellowship Adelphi U., 1974; Career Guidance award Assn. Bus., Labor and Edn., 1978; Partner in Edn. award, N.Y.C. Bd. Edn., 1978, others. Mem. Advt. Agy. Personnel Assn. (pres. 1980—), Am. Speech and Hearing Assn., L.I. Speech and Hearing Assn., Am. Soc. for Personnel Adminstrs., Am. Soc. for Tng. and Devel., Am. Mgmt. Assn., Assn. for M.B.A.s. Office: 285 Madison Ave New York NY 10017

GILBERT, FRANCES BIRSCH, human services info. system adminstr.; b. Blackstone, Va., Dec. 12, 1917; d. William L. and Frances Ann (Turner) Birsch; B.A., Old Dominion U., 1971, M.Urban Studies, 1975; postgrad. U. Va., 1979; m. Robert O. McLean, Apr. 4, 1937 (dec. 1951); 1 dau., Frances; m. 2d, Foster Ingram Gilbert, Dec. 11, 1954; children—Charles Francis, Foster Ingram. Asst. adminstr. Health Info. Center, Norfolk, Va., 1965-68, adminstr., 1968-71; dir. Info. Center of Hampton Roads, The Planning Council, Norfolk, 1971—; mem. faculty Eastern Va. Med. Sch., Norfolk, 1976—; cons. United Way of Am., VA, Washington, Mgmt. and Community Studies Inst., and others; chmn. Virginia Beach Community Mental Health and Mental Retardation Services Bd., 1970-72; mem. exec. com. Va. Mental Health Study Commn., 1963-65. Mem. Va. Task Force on Mental Health Manpower, 1974-76; sec. United Drug Abuse Council, Inc., 1970-72; bd. dirs. Tidewater Health Found., 1962-67, Va. Mental Health Fund, 1971-76. Bd. dirs. Virginia Beach Democratic Women's Club; del. Va. Dem. Conv. Registered social worker, Va. Mem. Am. Soc. Public Adminstrs., Alliance of Info. and Referral Services, Va. Assn. for Mental Health (dir. 1963-71), Va. Council on Social Welfare, AMA (com. services for children 1962-72), Va. Fedn. Women's Clubs (pres. Tidewater dist. 1962-64, chmn. mental health div. 1970-73). Episcopalian. Author: Information and Referral-How to Do It, vol. 1, part 1, 1976, part 2, 1976, part 3, 1976, part 4, 1976; contbr. articles to profl. jours. Home: 7605 Atlantic Ave Virginia Beach VA 23451 Office: 101 St Paul's Blvd Norfolk VA 23510

GILBERT, HEATHER CAMPBELL, bus. services co. exec.; b. Mt. Vernon, N.Y., Nov. 20, 1944; d. Ronald Ogston and Mary Lodivia (Campbell) G.; B.S. in Math. (Nat. Merit scholar), Stanford U., 1967; M.S. in Computer Sci. (NSF fellow), U. Wis., 1969. With Burroughs Corp., 1969-82, sr. mgmt. systems analyst, Detroit, 1975-77, mgr. mgmt. systems activity, Pasadena, Calif., 1977-82; mgr. software product mgmt. Lolean Data Mgmt. Inc., Covina, Calif., 1982—. Mem. Assn. Computing Machinery, Am. Product and Inventory Control Soc., Stanford U. Alumni Assn. (life), Stanford Profl. Women Los Angeles County (pres. 1982-83), Nat. Assn. Female Execs., Town Hall. Home: 2020 Dacian Dr Walnut CA 91789 Office: 529 S 2d Ave Covina CA 91723

GILBERT, HELEN LOUISE, nurse practitioner, family planning adminstr.; b. Grand Rapids, Sept. 21, 1927; d. Reginald George and Jessie Louise (Hilton) Read; diploma U. Mich. Sch. Nursing, 1949; asso. degree Marshalltown Community Coll., 1972; cert. Family Planning Specialist, U. Nebr., 1973; m. Kenneth Robert Gilbert, Feb. 1, 1947; children—Kristin Louise Gilbert Strittmatter, Mark Alan, William Walter. Sch. office hosp. nurse ARC, 1950-58; staff nurse, in service coordinator Community Hosp. Marshalltown, Iowa, 1969-71; family planning nurse Mid-Iowa Community Action, Ames, 1971-73; founder, nurse, exec. dir. Central Iowa Family Planning Inc., Marshalltown, 1973—. Pres. bd. dirs. Marshalltown Community Sch. Nursing Found. Recipient Woman of Achievement award, 1982. Mem. Iowa Nurses Assn., Nurses Assn. of Am. Coll. Obstetricians and Gynecologists (cert. excellence in practice in maternal, gynecol., neonatal nursing 1976-77), Nat. Family Planning and Reproductive Health Assn. (dir. 1973—, internat. family planning com.). Home: Union Grove Lake Garwin IA 50632 Office: PO Box 375 704 May St Marshalltown IA 50158

GILBERT, JEANNE GIFFORD (KOCH), psychologist; b. Haddonfield, N.J.; d. Henry Andrew and Eva Florence Gifford; B.A., Cornell U., 1925; B.A., U. Pa., 1926; Ph.D., Columbia U., 1936; m. George Walton Koch, Aug. 1, 1951; stepchildren—Barbara Carol Koch, Walton Boston. Chief psychologist St. Charles Guidance Clinic, Bklyn., 1935-60, dir. psychology, 1960-66; dir. research Mt. Carmel Guild, Newark, 1966-73; mem. adj. faculty St. Johns U., St. Joseph Coll., N.Y.U., L.I. U., Fairleigh Dickinson U., Passaic County Coll., Fordham U., N.Y.C., 1937—; pvt. practice psychology, Newark, 1958—. Diplomate Am. Bd. Profl. Psychology; lic. psychologist, N.J.; cert. psychologist, N.Y. State. Mem. Am. Psychol. Assn., Eastern Psychol. Assn., N.J. Psychol. Assn., N.Y. Acad. Scis., Gerontol Assn., N.J. Gerontol Assn. Contbr. articles to profl. jours. Home: 19 Oak Hill Rd Short Hills NJ 07078 Office: 352 Mt Prospect Ave Newark NJ 07104

GILBERT, JUDITH ARLENE, lawyer; b. Los Angeles, Jan. 9, 1946; d. Beril B. and Dorothy Marilyn (Stern) Gilbert; student U. Calif., Berkeley, 1963-64; B.A., UCLA, 1967; J.D., Harvard U., 1970; m. Joel Philip Schiff; 1 dau., Lauren Michelle Schiff. Admitted to Calif. bar, 1971; practiced in Los Angeles; asso. firm Rosenfeld, Meyer & Susman, 1970-72, Quittner, Stutman, Treister & Glatt, Los Angeles, 1972-73, Abeles & Markowitz, and predecessor, Beverly Hills, Calif., 1974-76; sr. counsel Bank of Am., 1977—; judge protem Beverly Hills Small Claims Ct., also Los Angeles County Mcpl. Ct., Los Angeles Superior Ct.; mem. arbitration panel Calif. Superior Ct.; atty. client disputes mediator, mem. arbitration com. Los Angeles Superior Ct. Mem. Los Angeles County Com. Human Resources; active Girl Scouts U.S.A., Cystic Fibrosis, City of Hope. Mem. Beverly Hills Bar Assn. (sec. 1982-83), Women Lawyers Assn. Los Angeles, Calif. Women Lawyers, Los Angeles County, Bar Assn., Calif. State Bar (conv. del. 1975-82), Thespians, Collegian Singers, Brick Muller Soc., Internat. Law Club (social co-chmn. 1970), UCLA Alumni Assn. (adv. com., scholarship com.), Tower and Flame, Phi Beta Kappa, Gamma Delta Epsilon, Pi Gamma Mu, Omega Delta Epsilon, Phi Chi Theta, Delta Phi Epsilon. Clubs: Merchants, Sutherland (sec.-treas. 1968-69). Office: Bank of America Dept 4017 555 S Flower St Los Angeles CA 90071

GILBERT, KATHIE SIMON, educator; b. Akron, Ohio, Feb. 28, 1943; d. John Nicholas and Bernadine Mary (Ilg) S.; B.A., U. Ala., 1964; M.A., La. State U., 1966, Ph.D., 1972; m. John Randalph Gilbert, Jr., Jan. 28, 1964; children—Mark Ivan, Adam Stacy. Asso. prof. econs. Miss. State U., Mississippi State, 1968-78, prof. econs., 1978-81, prof. econs. and polit. sci., 1981—. Mem. Oktibbeha County Democratic Exec. Com., 1976-80; vice chmn. Miss. Internat. Women's Yr. Com., 1977. Am. Council on Edn. fellow, 1979-80; Miss Econ. Council fellow; Miss. Com. for Humanities grantee, 1975—. Mem. Am. Econ. Assn., So. Econ. Assn., Southeastern Econs. Assn., Southwestern Social Scis. Assn., Nat. Women's Studies Assn., Southeastern Women's Studies Assn. (pres.), Am. Women in Sci., AAAS, AAUW (pres. Starkville br. 1977-79, 1st v.p. Miss. div. 1980-82, pres. 1982—), Starkville LWV (treas.), Phi Kappa Phi, Omicron Delta Epsilon, Pi Alpha Alpha. Democrat. Roman Catholic. Club: Miss. State U. Faculty Women's. Contbr. articles to profl. jours. Office: Drawer JE Mississippi State MS 39762

GILBERT, LYNN TENDLER, exec. search co. exec.; b. Bklyn., Apr. 26, 1938; d. William and Henrietta (Glicksman) Tendler; B.S. in Math., U. Fla., 1959; children—Jay Gilbert, Allison Gilbert. Asso., Personnel Assos., Miami, 1960-63; dir. tech. recruiting Dunhill Personnel, N.Y.C., 1963-68; pres., co-founder Gilbert Tweed Assos., Inc., N.Y.C., 1972—. Treas., Riverdale Community Assn., 1976—; mem. adv. bd., fin. com. Spuyten Duyvil Infantry Sch., 1975—, chmn., 1973-75, trustee, 1982. Mem. Internat. Assn. Personnel Women, Nat. Assn. Corp. and Profl. Recruiters. Home: 11 Sigma Pl Riverdale NY 10471 Office: 630 3d Ave New York NY 10017

GILBERT, MYRNA JEAN, anthropologist; b. Boulder, Colo., Aug. 11, 1935; d. Albert L. and Elizabeth (Goggin) Hall; B.A., Ariz. State U., 1957, M.A. in English, 1964; M.A. in Anthropology, U. Calif., Santa Barbara, 1974, Ph.D., 1980; m. Richard Leon Gilbert, Mar. 24, 1956 (dec. 1979); 1 dau., Lisa Anne. Instr. English secondary schs., Md., 1957-59, Ariz., 1960-61; research asso. Social Process Research Inst., U. Calif., Santa Barbara, 1974-76, Spanish Speaking Mental Health Research Inst., UCLA, 1976-78; research project dir. Centro Familiar de Santa Barbara, 1978-81; program officer founds. and corp. relations Direct Relief Internat., Santa Barbara, 1981-82; research cons. Calif. Office Alcohol and Drug Programs, Sacramento, 1976-77, Calif. Commn. on Alcoholism for Spanish Speaking, Sacramento, 1978; researcher kinship networks in Mex., 1973-74. Bd. dirs. Santa Barbara Family Care Center, 1972-75, Community TV of Santa Barbara, 1972, Santa Barbara Mus. Art, 1970-72. NIMH grantee, 1978-81, 82-84; Office Child Devel. grantee, 1976-78. Mem. Am. Anthrop. Assn., Soc. Applied Anthropology, Santa Barbara Mus. Art (pres. docent council 1970-72). Contbr. articles on research in Hispanic communities and families to profl. jours. Home: 5254 Calle Morelia Santa Barbara CA 93111 Office: Dept Anthropology U Calif Santa Barbara CA 93106

GILBERT, RACHEL SHAW, state legislator, real estate broker; b. Ottawa, Kans.; d. Herbert M. and L.C. Ferris (Pile) Shaw; B.A., U. Nebr., 1956; M.A., Coll. of Idaho, 1969; children—Cheryl Allison Glibert Brady, Kimberly Lynn. Sch. tchr., Nebr., 1952-57; broker Walker & Co. Real Estate, Boise, Idaho, 1969-71; broker-owner Gilbert & Assocs. Realtors, Boise, 1972-82; mem. Idaho Ho. of Reps., 1980—. Bd. dirs. United Way, Boise, 1963-68, Boise Philharm. Orch., 1966-68; chmn. Idaho Legis. Dist. 15, 1980. Mem. Nat. Assn. Realtors (dir.), Idaho Assn. Realtors (dir. 1978-80), Idaho Assn. Commerce and Industry (dir.), Boise C. of C. (v.p. 1979). Republican. Home: 1111 Marshall St Boise ID 83706 Office: 1475 N Cole St Boise ID 83704

GILBERT, ROSE BENNETT, communications co. exec.; b. High Point, N.C., July 11, 1938; d. Ellis Howard and Sadie B. (Vernon) Bennett; B.A., Mary Washington Coll., 1960; postgrad. George Washington U., 1964-65; children—Scott Randolph, Bennett J. Reporter, Richmond (Va.) News-Leader, 1960-64; editor 1,001 Decorating Ideas Mag., N.Y.C., 1973-75; columnist Chgo. Tribune-Daily News Syndicate, 1975-77; v.p., partner Sweet & Co., N.Y.C., 1978-80; pres. Gilbert/ Green Communications, N.Y.C., 1980—; asso. editor Country Decorating Mag., N.Y.C. Adult Sch. Maplewood/South Orange (N.J.) Adult Sch., 1975—. Mem. Mary Washington Coll. Alumni Assn. (v.p. 1966-67), Nat. Home Fashion League, Fashion Group. Episcopalian. Author: You-Do-It Book of Early American Decorating, 1978; Decorating Country-Style, 1980. Home: 73 Jefferson Ave Maplewood NJ 07040 Office: 141 E 33 St New York NY 10016

GILBERT, RUTH LOUISE, tax mgr.; b. Hammond, Ind., Dec. 27, 1933; d. Alonzo Boyer and Eva Ella (Mills) Luyster; B.S. summa cum laude, in Acctg., U. Mo., 1972; m. Milton Caleb Gilbert, Jr., Mar. 10, 1951 (div.); children—David Donald, Steven Craig. Staff acct. Touche Ross & Co., St. Louis, 1973-75; sr. tax acct. Rubin, Brown, Gornstein & Co., St. Louis, 1975-77; mgr. tax research and planning Mallinckrodt, Inc., St. Louis, 1977—. C.P.A., Mo. Mem. Am. Inst. C.P.A.s, Nat. Assn. Accts. (dir.), Mo. Soc. C.P.A.s (sec. state taxation com. 1982-83), Beta Gamma Sigma (v.p. 1972-73), Beta Alpha Psi. Republican. Lutheran. Home: 503 Gatehall Ln Ballwin MO 63011 Office: 675 McDonnell Blvd PO Box 5840 Saint Louis MO 63134

GILBERT, VIRGINIA LEE, poet, educator; b. Elgin, Ill., Dec. 19, 1946; d. Blair Edward and Florence Amelia (Swailes) G.; B.A. (Harlan fellow), Iowa Wesleyan Coll., 1969; M.F.A., U. Iowa, 1971. Contbr. numerous poems to jours., newspaper and anthologies, including New Poets—Women, I Hear My Sisters Saying, Lyrical Iowa, Back Door, Cameos, New Small Press Women Poets, Crazy Horse, Beloit Poetry Jour., New Voices in Am. Poetry: An Anthology, I Love You All Day, It Is That Simple, The Seneca Rev., Prairie Schooner, Sumac, N.Y. Quarterly, N. Am. Rev., So. Poetry Rev., 80 for the 80's; tchrs. aide Head Start Program, Iowa City, Iowa, 1969-70; Peace Corps vol. Korean middle sch., 1973-74; teaching fellow in creative writing U. Utah, Salt Lake City, 1974-75; instr. English to Iranian Naval Forces, Rasht, Iran, 1976-77; instr. English, Iranian Army Aviation Forces, Isfahan, Iran, 1977-79; asst. prof. English, Ala. A & M U., Normal, 1980—. Creative writing fellow Nat. Endowment for Arts, 1976-77. Mem. AAUP, Poets and Writers, Inc., Poetry Soc. Am., Associated Writing Programs, Internat. Platform Assn., Royal Asiatic Soc., Sigma Tau Delta. Methodist. Office: Alabama A&M University Normal AL 35762

GILBERTSON, MILDRED GEIGER, author; b. Galena, Ill., June 9, 1908; d. Henry George and Mildred Ann (Palmer) Geiger; B.B.A., U. Tex., 1933; m. Philip R. Gilbertson, Sept. 6, 1935; children—Bruce, Gay. Author 34 juvenile books, 1945—, over 500 short stories; co-author U. Oreg. Rhetoric Textbooks, 1969—. Mem. Author's Guild, Author's League. Democrat. Author: Champions Don't Cry, 1959; The Unchosen, 1962; A Dog for Joey, 1967; See Yourself in Print, 1967; The Strange New World Across the Street, 1976. Home: 950 Park Ave Eugene OR 97404

GILCHRIST, DELORES LENORE, govt. employment cons.; b. Payette, Idaho, Aug. 9, 1936; d. John Daniel and Evelyn Doris (Edwards) Harriman; student public schs., Hillsboro, Oreg., Myrtle Point, Oreg.; children—Randy Terrell Kellems, Jamie Ray Kellems, Danny Jay Kellems. Communications specialist Nat. Security Agy., Washington, 1955-56, Army Security Agy., Frankfurt, Germany, 1956-57, Oakland County (Mich.) Sheriff Dept., 1965-69; communications/office services supr. BP Alaska Inc. (now Sohio Petroleum Co.), Anchorage, 1969-77, EEO coordinator, 1977-79; cons. EEO employment. Houston, 1979—. Pres. bd. dirs. BP Alaska Employees' Club, 1977-78; adv. Jr. Achievement, Anchorage, 1976-78. Served with WAC, U.S. Army, 1954-57. Recipient Recognition award March of Dimes, 1977, Jr. Achievement, 1978. Mem. Nat. Assn. Female Execs., Internat. Assn. Desk and Derrick (dir. Anchorage chpt. 1977-78). Republican. Editor: Sohio/BP Co. Newsletter, 1975-79. Home and Office: Ryde Inc Route 2 Box 159 Hemphill TX 75948

GILCHRIST, JANE GILMARTIN, mag. exec.; b. Montauk, Point, N.Y., Aug. 1, 1931; d. Richard Timothy and Winifred (O'Brien) Gilmartin; B.A. (tuition scholar), Cornell U., 1952. Market research staff Procter & Gamble Co., 1952-54; with Time Inc., 1955—, publicity dir. Sports Illus. mag., 1979—; bd. dirs. Women's Sport Found. Contbr. articles to mags., newspapers. Office: Room 1972 1271 Ave of the Americas New York NY 10020

GIL DEL REAL, MARÍA TERESA, health found. researcher; b. Cúcuta, Colombia, Jan. 5, 1941; came to U.S., 1962, naturalized, 1969; d. Antonio E. and Rosa (Calvo) Gil del R.; Asso., Bogotá Bus. Coll., 1961; B.A. in Anthropology, Rutgers U., 1979; m. John R. Romano, Oct. 10, 1964; children—Christina M., John Alexander. Freelance translator, simultaneous interpreter, 1977-79; bilingual editor Princeton Internat. Translations, Princeton Junction, N.J., 1979-80; research asst. Robert Wood Johnson Found., Princeton, 1980—; cons. epidemiology, internat. public health. Mem. Alpha Sigma Lambda. Home: 76 Princeton Ave Rocky Hill NJ 08553 Office: Robert Wood Johnson Found PO Box 2316 Princeton NJ 08540

GILDSTON, PHYLLIS SYLVIA, educator; b. N.Y.C.; d. David and Nettie (Drexel) Gurfein; A.B., Cornell U., 1951; M.S. Queens Coll., 1959; Ph.D., Columbia U., 1964; m. Harold Gildston, Sept. 2, 1951; children—Eva, Jessica. Speech pathologist and audiologist, research coordinator Mill Neck Manor Lutheran Sch. for Deaf, 1958-59; organizer, adminstr. system-wide program for rehab. speech and hearing handicapped Garden City Pub. Schs., 1959-62; audiologist N.Y. League for Hard of Hearing, 1959-62; prof. speech pathology and audiology, coordinator diagnostics tng. and services dept. speech Bklyn. Coll., CUNY, 1962—; adj. prof. C.W. Post Coll., L.I. U. and Hunter Coll., CUNY; cons. in audiology Rockville Gen. Hearing and Speech Center, 1962—, Indsl. Home for Blind, 1966-70, Gt. Neck Speech and Hearing Center, N.Y. State Sch. Indsl. and Labor Relations, Cornell U. Chairperson noise pollution subcom., bd. dirs. N.Y. Scientists Com. for Pub. Info. Fellow Scientists Inst. for Pub. Info.; mem. Am., N.Y. State (sec.) speech and hearing assns., N.Y. Acad. Scis., AAAS, Acoustical Soc. Am., Phi Beta Kappa, Sigma Xi. Author: Diagnostic Laboratories in Speech Pathology, 1974, rev. edit., 1975. Contbr. articles to profl. jours. Home: 2 Hilltop Dr Great Neck NY 11021 Office: Dept Speech Bklyn Coll City U NY Ave H and Bedford Ave Brooklyn NY 11210 *

GILE, JANICE ANN, educator; b. Richland, Wash., Jan. 16, 1948; d. John Alexander and Sarah Helen (Grant) Gile; A.A., Columbia Basin Coll., 1968; B.A. in Edn., Eastern Wash. U., 1970, M.Ed., 1979. Tchr. kindergarten Keene-Riverview Elem. Sch., Prosser, Wash., 1970-75, Summer Migrant Sch., Prosser, 1971, 80, Title I math remediation, Prosser, 1973; tchr. Title VII bilingual kindergarten program Keene-Riverview Elem. Sch., 1975-81; tchr. 1st grade, Prosser, 1981—, bldg. rep. Prosser Edn. Assn., 1971-72, sec., 1972-74, negotiator, 1977-78; NSF participant math workshop Eastern Wash. U., summer 1974; Bilingual-Bicultural Inst. participant Wash. State U., summer 1977. Co-leader Bluebird Group, Prosser, 1972-73; mem. choir Luth. Ch., Prosser, 1970—. Mem. Prosser Edn. Assn., Wash. Edn. Assn., NEA, Assn. for Supervision and Curriculum Devel., Wash. Assn. Supervision and Curriculum Devel., Phi Delta Kappa, Alpha Delta Kappa. Lutheran. Home: 1026 Hemlock St Prosser WA 99350 Office: 832 Park Ave Prosser WA 99350

GILE, RUTH MARY, social worker; b. Manchester, N.H., June 5, 1948; d. Hugh Edward and Doris H. (Luippold) Gile; B.A., U. Mass., 1970; M.S.W., Boston Coll., 1977. Hosp. social worker Walter Reed Gen. Hosp., ARC, 1970-71, Clark AFB Hosp., Philippine Islands, 1971-72, Roger Williams Gen. Hosp., Providence, 1973, New Eng. Meml. Hosp., Stoneham, Mass., 1973-76, Beth Israel Hosp., Brookline, Mass., 1977-79; clin. social worker Family Service Orgn. of Worcester (Mass.), Inc., 1979—; field instr. Boston Coll. Grad. Sch. Social Work, 1979-80, Boston U. Grad. Sch. Social Work, 1980-82. Mass. alt. del. White House Conf. on Families, 1980; adv. com. on status of women City Mgr.'s Office, Worcester, 1980—; chmn. Task Force on Day Care, Worcester; bd. dirs. Regional Environ. Council, Worcester, 1980—; profl. edn. com. Am. Cancer Soc., Worcester, 1979—. Mem. Nat. Assn. Social Workers (chpt. dir. 1980—), Acad. Cert. Social Workers, Social Work Oncology Group, Sidney Farber Inst. Office: 31 Harvard St Worcester MA 01608

GILEADI, AVIVA EVA, nuclear engr.; b. Budapest, Hungary, Nov. 26, 1917; came to U.S., 1959, naturalized, 1973; d. Samuel and Gisela (Kupferstein) Fischmann; Ph.D. in Physics, Peter Pazmany U., Budapest, 1941; M.Sc. in Nuclear Engring., U. Mich., Ann Arbor, 1960; m. Michael Gileadi, May 2, 1946; children—Amos Noah, Ruth Hannah. Tchr., Israel, 1948-58; lectr., dir. lab. Technion-Israel Inst. Tech., Haifa, 1958-63; reactor physicist BONUS Nuclear Power Plant, P.R., 1963-65; dir. nuclear engring. dept. U. P.R., also dir. div. nuclear engring. P.R. Nuclear Center, 1970-71, prof. nuclear engring., chief scientist center, 1965-75; prin. scientist KMS Fusion, Inc., Ann Arbor, 1976-79; prin. engr. nuclear engring. div., generation engring. dept. Detroit Edison Co., 1979—; vis. scientist Brookhaven Nat. Lab., 1968. Named Woman Scientist of Yr., Am. Technion Soc., 1967. Mem. Am. Nuclear Soc., Health Physics Soc. Jewish. Co-author: Applied Nuclear Power Engineering for Practicing Engineers, 1972; contbr. articles profl. jours. Home: 2711 Somerset Blvd Troy MI 48084 Office: 3331 W Big Beaver Rd Troy MI 48084

GILES, ANNE DIENER, flutist; b. Rochester, N.Y., Oct. 13, 1948; d. Frederick William and Alma Mary (Bastian) Diener; B.M., Juilliard Sch., 1970, M.S., 1971; m. Allen L. Giles, Sept. 26, 1970; 1 dau., Katherine Anne. Prin. flutist Los Angeles Philharmonic, 1971—; rec. artist Deutsche Grammaphon, London, Crystal Records, 1972-82. Recipient Walter and Elsie Naumberg award Juilliard Sch., 1970, Bronze medal Internat. Concours de Geneve, 1973. Mem. Nat. Flute Assn., Music Tchrs. Nat. Assn., NOW, Mu Phi Epsilon. Home: 4150 Chestnut Ave Long Beach CA 90807 Office: Los Angeles Philharmonic Orch 135 N Grand Ave Los Angeles CA 90012

GILES, BERNICE RIGGS, educator; b. Tuscaloosa, Ala., July 2, 1927; d. Ezekiel and Bessie Elizabeth (Willett) Riggs; student Stillman Coll., 1944-46; A.B., Daniel Payne Coll., 1948; B.S., Ala. State U., 1951, M.Ed., 1967; postgrad. U. Ala., U. Tenn., Miss. State U., So. U., Shelton Community Coll.; m. James Giles, Aug. 21, 1975; children by previous marriage—Donald Jerome, Janice Romelia, James Albert, Jacqueline Elizabeth, Lucretia Ann. Tchr. elem. sch., Five Points, Ala., 1948-50; tchr. Carver High Sch., Eutaw, Ala., 1950-54, Coahoma (Miss.) Jr. High Sch., 1955-56; tchr., supr. reading program, asst. prin. Parkview and Poplar Springs elem. schs., Meridian, Miss., 1962-74; tchr. Gen. Edn. Devel. program Tuscaloosa County Bd. Edn., 1979; supr. I, Family and Child Care Center, Birmingham, Ala., 1979; tchr./counselor, supervisor I, Gen. Edn. Devel. and coll. prep. classes U. Ala., Tuscaloosa, 1976—. Trio Program fellow, 1980, Mem. NEA, SCLC, NAACP, Miss. Edn. Assn. Democrat. Methodist. Clubs: Excelsior, Order of Eastern Star. Home: 2834 19th St Tuscaloosa AL 35401

GILES-HOLMES, GWEN BURDETTE, city assessor; b. Atlanta; d. Dennis Wood and Irene (Griffin) Burdette; ed. St. Louis U.; m. John W. Holmes, Jr., Mar. 1, 1980; children—Carla Giles, Karl Stephon. Exec. sec. St. Louis Council Human Relations; dir. community affairs KMOX-TV; dir. civil rights City of St. Louis; mem. Mo. State Senate, 1977-81; assessor City of St. Louis, 1981—. Active United Way of Greater U. St. Louis, 1981—; del. Democratic Nat. Conv., 1980; mem. Archdiocesan Commn. Human Rights, St. Louis Conf. Religion and Race, Panel Am. Women, St. Louis Council Black People; campaign mgr. Congressman William L. Clay, 1968; mem. Pres. Carter's 51.3% Adv. Com. on Women; mem. Dem. State Com. Named Citizen of Yr., Omega Psi Phi, 1977; recipient award Daus. of Elks; named Outstanding Negro Woman of 1977, Internat. Daus. of Isis, 1978, Woman of Yr., Omega Psi Phi, 1978; recipient achievement award Nat. Urban Affairs Council, 1979, Mary Rhodes award Sisters of Loretto, 1981; cited Mo. chpt. Am.s. Dem. Action, 1981. Mem. Mo. Black Leadership Assn., St. Louis Roundtable of Congl. Black Caucus. Roman Catholic. Home: 6048 W Cabanne Pl Saint Louis MO 63112 Office: City Hall Saint Louis MO 63103

GILES-VANCE, IDA RUTH, mfg. co. exec.; b. Collins, Miss., Oct. 2, 1943; d. Buren and Ruth Cooper; diploma Detroit Inst. Commerce, 1970; children—Jerome, Tyrone, Michael. With Honeywell, Inc., 1965—, regional adminstrv. aide, then asso. br. adminstr., 1970-76, br. adminstr., Southfield, Mich., 1976—. Bd. dirs. Crary St. Mary's Community Council, 1980—. Named Alumni of Year, Detroit Inst. Commerce, 1970. Mem. Women's Conf. of Concerns. Office: 17515 W 9 Mile Rd Southfield MI 48075

GILGER, MARGARET LOUISE, ch. music dir.; b. Kiowa, Kans., May 5, 1927; d. Arthur Briggs and Lottie Mabelle (Eary) Dungan; B.A., Southwestern Coll., 1949; postgrad. Colo. State Coll., 1942, 54, 55; m. Robert W. Gilger, May 29, 1949; children—Roberta, Nancy. Asst. dir. adult choir, organist Grace Methodist Ch., Winfield, Kans., 1946-48; secondary public sch. music tchr. Montezuma, Kans., 1948-50; dir. children's choirs United Meth. Ch., Pratt, Kans., 1950-52; dir. adult choir and ch. organist Ulysses, Kans., 1952-63; dir. adult choir Garden City (Kans.) United Meth. Ch., 1965—, coordinator, dir. music, 1976—; cons. for music program, dir. Assn. for Migrant Workers in Western Kans., 1965-68. Bd. dirs. Kans. Arts Commn., 1974-75; mem. City of Garden City Humanities Commn., 1975-78; mem. Meth. Conf. Diaconal bd., 1980—; bd. dirs. Community Choral & Symphony Assn., Garden City, 1972-78. Mem. Piano Tchrs. League (pres. 1974-76), Choristers Guild, Assn. of Community Arts Council of Kans., Kans. Music Educators Assn., Fellowship of United Meth. Musicians. Home: 714 Ridgeway Pratt KS 67124 Office: Main at Kansas St Garden City KS 67846

GILKES, CHERYL LOUISE TOWNSEND, sociologist, minister; b. Boston, Nov. 2, 1947; d. Murray Luke, Jr., and Evelyn Annette (Reid) Townsend; B.A., Northeastern U., M.A., Ph.D. Lectr. Univ. Coll. Northeastern U., 1973-78, also instr. sociology Boston State Coll., 1974-78; asst. prof. sociology Boston U., 1978—; assoc. minister Union Baptist Ch., Cambridge, Mass.; vis. lectr. Tufts U., 1974; instr. sociology U. Mass., 1976; research assoc., vis. lectr. sociology of religion Harvard U. Div. Sch., 1981-82; vis. lectr. Afro-Am. studies Simmons Coll.; faculty fellow Bunting Inst., Radcliffe Coll., 1982-84. Sec. Cambridge Civic Unity Com., 1978—; pres. Cambridge Black Cultural and Hist. Assn., 1978—. Spivak Dissertation fellow Am. Sociol. Assn., 1977-78; Nat. Fellowships Fund dissertation fellow, 1977-78; Socialization Tng. fellow Northeastern U., 1970-73. Mem. Am. Sociol. Assn., Eastern Sociol. Soc., Mass. Sociol. Assn., Soc. Study of Social Problems, Assn. Humanist Sociology, Soc. Study of Symbolic Interaction, Assn. Black Sociologists, Sociologists Women in Soc., Soc. Sci. Study of Religion, Phi Kappa Phi. Contbr. articles and revs. to profl. jours., chpts. in books. Office: 96 100 Cummington St Boston MA 02215

GILL, ABIGAIL STANTON, mfg. co. exec.; b. Boston, Sept. 11, 1945; d. Robert J. and Gertrude E. (Clukay) Stanton; student Skidmore Coll., 1963-65; B.S. in Acctg. magna cum laude, N.H. Coll., 1977; m. Paul H. Gill, Jr., Mar. 29, 1975; 1 dau., Katherine Donovan. Comptroller, Austin-Gordon Design, Inc., Nashua, N.H., 1975—; treas. Gill Security Service, Inc., Hollis, N.H., 1979—, also dir. Mem. Nat. Fedn. Ind. Bus., So. N.H. Assn. Commerce and Industry. Home: PO Box 455 Hollis NH 03049 Office: Pine St Extension Nashua NH 03060

GILL, EVALYN PIERPOINT, editor, publisher; b. Boulder, Colo.; d. Walter Lawrence and Lou Octavia Pierpoint; student Lindenwood Coll., B.A., U. Colo.; postgrad. U. Nebr., U. Alaska, M.A., Central Mich. U., 1968; m. John Glanville Gill, Nov. 10, 1943; children—Susan Pierpoint, Mary Louise Glanville. Lectr. humanities Saginaw Valley State Coll., University Center, Mich., 1968-72; mem. English faculty U. N.C., Greensboro, 1973-74; editor Internat. Poetry Rev., Greensboro, 1975—; pres. TransVerse Press, Greensboro, 1981—. Bd. dirs. Eastern Music Festival, Greensboro, 1981—; bd. dirs. Greensboro Symphony, 1982—, Greensboro Opera Co., 1982—. Mem. Am. Lit. Translators Assn., MLA, N.C. Poetry Soc., Phi Beta Kappa. Author: Poetry By French Women 1930-1980, 1980; contbr. poetry to numerous mags. Home: 1501 Kirkpatrick St Greensboro NC 27408 Office: PO Box 2047 Greensboro NC 27402

GILL, JANE ROBERTS, clin. social worker; b. Boston, Dec. 6, 1923; d. Penfield Hitchcock and Cecilia (Washburn) Roberts; student Wellesley Coll., 1941-43; B.A., Boston U., 1954, M.S.W., 1956; m. Peter Lawrence Gill, Dec. 24, 1943 (div. 1973); children—Jonathan Penfield, Dorcas Pearson, Nicholas Brinton, Timothy Roberts. Social worker Beth Isreal Hosp., Boston, 1956-57, South End Family Program, Boston, 1957-58, Margaret Gifford Sch., Cambridge, Mass., 1963-65; Adams House Psychiat. Clinic, Boston, 1967—; coordinator outpatient clinic and cardiac rehab. program Falkner Hosp., Boston, 1975—, sr. clin. social work supr., 1976—; staff Headache Research Found., 1976—; pvt. practice social work, Brookline, 1970—; clin. instr. Simmons Coll. Sch. of Social Work, 1971-79. Mem. social service com. Am. Heart Assn., 1979—; program chmn. Mass. Mental Health Center, 1969-71; mem. Democratic Town Com., Newton-Wellesley, 1959-64. Lic. ind. clin. social worker, Mass. Mem. Acad. Cert. Social Workers, Register Clin. Social Workers, Mass. Acad. Psychiat. Social Workers, Acad. Psychosomatic Medicine, Peacham Hist. Assn., Putney Sch. Alumni Assn. Contbr. papers to profl. meetings. Office: 318 Allandale Rd Chestnut Hill MA 02167 and Faulkner Hosp Center St at Allandale Rd Boston MA 02130

GILL, JOAN EPSTEIN (JOAN BLANK), journalist, illustrator; b. Buffalo, Apr. 3, 1928; d. Ralph C. and Miriam A. Epstein; A.A., Stephens Coll., 1947; A.B., Sarah Lawrence Coll., 1949; m. Harvey Blank, Sept. 14, 1975; children—Robin, Susan, Prudence; editor, art dir. Investment Sales Monthly, Coral Gables, Fla., 1964-68; editor, art dir. Fla. Commentary, Hollywood, 1973-75; editor, art dir. Communique, Miami, Fla., 1974-75; editor, designer Born of The Sun, 1975-76; freelance writer, 1950—; cons. in field, 1963—; pres. Grapetree Productions, Inc., 1981—. Mem. Nat. Press Club (Washington), Phi Theta Kappa, Chi Delta Phi. Democrat. Author: Laugh Lines, 1982 (Joan Blank illustrator); (Joan Blank) Give Your Whole Self, 1981. Contbr. articles, photo-features to mags. Address: 600 Grapetree Dr Apt 10CN Key Biscayne FL 33149

GILL, MABEL CHARLENE, cartographer, feminist; b. Alton, Ill., July 3, 1924; d. Charles Baker and Katherine Freda (Dehne) Meisenheimer; B.A., Tarkio Coll., 1976; m. Fred L. Gill, Feb. 3, 1946; children—Charles Winfield, Frederic Kent. Cartographic aide Aero. Chart Plant, St. Louis, 1948-53; cartographer Aero. Chart & Info. Center, St. Louis, 1953-62, supervisory cartographer, 1962-70; program mgr. Def. Mapping Agy. Aerospace Center, St. Louis, 1970-81. Chmn. for Mid-Continent Region, ERA, 1980-82; founder Alton (Ill.) Mus. History and Art, 1971, bd. dirs., 1971—; sec. Landmarks Preservation Council of Ill./SW, 1980-81; regional mgr. Federally Employed Women, 1978-79, charter pres. Arsenal '76 chpt., 1976; dir. dist. VII, Nat. Women's Conf. Com., 1982—; Mo. chmn. Homemaker's Equal Rights Assn., 1981—. Recipient 1st pl. award for community service Fed. Women's Program Council, 1976; Equal Opportunity award Def. Mapping Agy., 1978; named Woman of Yr., Aero. Chart & Info. Center, 1966. Mem. Am. Soc. Photogrammetry (award 1977, pres. 1977-78), Am. Congress of Surveying and Mapping (dir. 1969-70), AAUW, LWV, Mo. Coalition for ERA (treas. 1980-82), NOW, Women's Register of Mo., Methodist. Clubs: Zonta (chpt. v.p. 1980-81, pres. 1981-82, historian 1982—), Toastmasters (adminstrv. v.p. 1979-80, edn. v.p. 1981-82). Editor Newsletter of Photogrammetric Engring. & Remote Sensing, 1974-79, Apocalypse, 1972-75. Home: 4244 Lasata Dr Saint Louis MO 63123

GILL, MARGARET MARY, family therapist; b. Yonkers, N.Y., May 7, 1946; d. Patrick Joseph and Margaret (Reynolds) G.; B.A., Coll. Mt. St. Vincent, 1967; M.A., DePaul U., 1972; cert. family therapist Northwestern U., 1978; postgrad. Inst. Psychoanalysis, 1973-75, Ill. Inst. Tech., 1975-76, Jane Adams Coll. Social Work, U. Ill., 1981—; m. Gary K. Benz, July 5, 1980. Therapist in-patients Chgo. Alcoholic Treatment Center, 1969; caseworker Chgo. Foundlings Home, 1969-71; adoption counselor Luth. Child and Family Services, River Forest, Ill., 1971-78, family therapist, 1976—, supr. spl. needs adoption program, 1978-80; pvt. practice family therapy, 1979—; sec. open door soc. com. Adoption Info. Service, 1971-72. Mem. Nat. Assn. Social Workers, Nat. Council Illegitimacy (sec. 1972-73 Chgo.), Coalition Adoptive Parents and Agys. (practice com. adoption info. service 1979-80), Ranch Triangle Assn., Lincoln Park Conservation Assn., Am. Psychol. Assn., Child Care Assn. Ill., Family Inst. Chgo. (alumni bd. 1981—), Pi Gamma Mu. Contbr. articles to profl. jours. Office: 125 N Manor Oak Park IL 60301 also 2121 N Dayton Chicago IL 60614

GILLEECE, MARY ANN, lawyer, mem. congressional staff; b. Effingham, Ill., Sept. 3, 1940; d. Howard Edward and Margaret Mary (Harris) Weinrich; B.S., U. Conn., 1962; J.D., Suffolk U., 1972; LL.M. George Washington U., 1982; 1 dau., Tricia Marie. Tchr. structural linguistics and English lit., Conn., 1962-65; expediter Cole Hersee Co., Boston, 1966, 67; mem. investigative staff Mass. Atty. Gen., 1970-72, asst. atty. gen., 1972-75; asso. firm Gargiulo and Holian, Cambridge, Mass., 1972-77; counsel U.S. Ho. of Reps. Com. Armed Services, Washington, 1977—; admitted to Mass. bar, 1972; U.S. Supreme Ct. bar, 1978; lectr. Suffolk U. Law Sch., 1972. Recipient Spl. Leadership award Bd. Trustees Suffolk U., 1978, Outstanding Alumni award, 1979. Mem. ABA, Fed. Bar Assn. (v.p. nat. circuit). Office: Room 2120 Rayburn House Office Bldg Washington DC 20515

GILLENWATER, ANNE RIDINGS, maintenance planner; b. Detroit, Apr. 23, 1936; d. James Clarence and Mary Sue (Hughes) Ridings; B.S. in Bus. Adminstrn., U. Tenn., Knoxville, 1971, also postgrad. With Aluminum Co. Am., Alcoa, Tenn., 1962—, various secretarial positions, 1962-71, adminstrv. analyst, 1971-73, indsl. engr., 1973-75, systems analyst, 1975-76, systems design engr., 1976-80, maintenance planner, 1980—. Adviser Alcoa Jr. Achievement; chmn. plant savs. bond campaign, 1972; mem. Tenn. Commn. on Women, 1974-81, chmn., 1975, 80, 81; bd. dirs. Laurel Lake Youth Camp, treas., 1977—; co-sponsor White House Conf. on Domestic and Econ. Affairs, 1975; bd. dirs. Blount County Girls Club, 1980—. F.T. Bonham scholar, 1953-54. Cert. profl. sec. Mem. Am. Inst. Indsl. Engrs., Soc. Women Engrs. (sec., 1976, SE student activities coordinator, 1977-79, pres. Knoxville, 1979, nat. chmn. new student sects., 1979-80, dir., 1981), Am. Soc. Tng. and Devel. (pres. 1981), Tenn. Valley Personnel Assn. (TIPC chmn., 1981, treas. 1982), Nat. Secs. Assn. (pres. 1972-74), AAUW. Republican. Baptist. Clubs: Knoxville Club LeConte, Delta Zeta. Speaker workshops, seminars, confs.; instr. human relations and adminstrn. Home: Route 5 Box 200 24 Fairoaks Dr Maryville TN 37801 Office: PO Box 9158 Alcoa TN 37701

GILLESPIE, JACQUELYN RANDALL, psychotherapist, ednl. psychologist; b. Paris, Oct. 10, 1927; d. John Roberts and Hazel Marine (Hammel) Hunter (parents Am. citizens); B.A., Calif. State U., Long Beach, 1960; M.S., Calif. State U., Fullerton, 1965; Ph.D., Calif. Grad. Inst., 1977; m. Thomas Gilbert Gillespie, Apr. 27, 1947; children—Thomas Randall, Catherine Claire Gillespie Laroche. Psychologist, Fullerton (Calif.) Union High Sch. Dist., 1969-82; dir. CGI Counseling

Center, Orange, Calif., 1982—; pvt. practice ednl. psychology and psychotherapy Learning Assos., Fullerton, Calif., 1975—; instr. Calif. Grad. Inst., 1978-80, asst. prof., 1980—. Bd. dirs. North Orange County Child Guidance Center, 1973-78, Pacific Acad., Fullerton, 1980—; project dir. Career Edn. Incentive Act Grant, 1979-80. Recipient Research award, Calif. Assn. Sch. Psychologists, 1972. Mem. Calif. Assn. Lic. Ednl. Psychologists (sec. 1979-80, pres. elect 1981), Am. Psychol. Assn., Calif. State Psychol. Assn., Calif. Tchrs. Assn., Calif. Assn. Sch. Psychologists. Author: Diagnostic Analysis of Reading Errors, 1980. Home: 1037 Avocado Crest Rd La Habra CA 90631 Office: Learning Assos 2720 N Harbor Blvd Suite 120 Fullerton CA 92635

GILLESPIE, JUDITH ANNE, ednl. adminstr.; b. Appleton, Wis., June 28, 1939; d. Clarence Joseph and Cora Jane (Beilke) Boyle; diploma Prospect Hall Secretarial Sch. Girls, Milw., 1959; m. William Gillespie, Sept. 9, 1961; 1 dau., Suzanne Elizabeth. Office mgr. Thomas M. Loescher, M.D., Appleton, 1962-77, Appleton Allergists, Ltd., 1977—; tchr. on-line-real time computer terminals, 1968—; exec. coordinator Vols. of Appleton Sch. Dist., 1982—. Pres., ch. counselor Lutheran Girl Pioneers, Mt. Olive Evang. Luth. Ch., Appleton, 1980-81, v.p. dist. 10, 1980-81; sec., bd. dirs. Outagamie County Humane Soc., 1980-81. Mem. Women in Mgmt. (historian, bd. dirs. Fox Cities chpt. 1980-81). Home: 5316 N Ballard Rd Appleton WI 54911 Office: 436 E Longview Dr Appleton WI 54911

GILLESPIE, MINTIE (DENA), archtl. drafting co. exec.; b. Vallejo, Calif., Dec. 14, 1945; d. John Junior and Mintie Jeanne Da Vee (Parker) Windsor; B.A., San Diego State U., 1967, postgrad., 1968; m. William John Gillespie, Aug. 29, 1965; children—Robert Windsor, Brock Bill, Taila Mintie. Tchr. English and modern dance Monte Vista High Sch., La Mesa, Calif., 1967-72, dean student activities, 1973-75; archtl. draftswoman Design Assos., El Cajon, Calif., 1976; owner, designer Gillespie Resdl. Drafting, El Cajon, 1976—. Active PTA, 1975-82; bd. dirs. El Cajon Girls' Club, 1977-78. Mem. Am. Inst. Bldg. Designers (home design award 1981), Calif. Tchrs. Assn., AAUW, Aztec Alumni Assn., El Cajon C. of C. (mem. ambassador com. 1975-76). Office: 1283 E Main St Suite 102 El Cajon CA 92021

GILLETT, MARGARET, educator, writer; b. Wingham, Australia, Feb. 1, 1930; d. Leslie Frank and Janet Alene (Vickers) Gillett; B.A., U. Sydney, 1950, diploma in edn., 1951; M.A., Russell Sage, 1957; Ed.D., Columbia U., 1961. Tchr., Australia, 1951-53, Eng., 1953-54; edn. officer Govt. of Australia, Sydney, 1954-57; asst. prof. edn. Dalhousie U., Halifax, N.S., Can., 1961-62; registrar Haile Sellassie I U., Ethiopia, 1962-64; assoc. prof. edn. McGill U., Montreal, Que., Can., 1964-67, prof., 1967-82, MacDonald prof. edn., 1982—; mem. Can. Nat. Commn. for UNESCO Sub.-Commn. on Status Women; mem. exec. bd. Women's Info. and Referral Centre, Montreal, 1981-84. Can. Council grantee, 1976; Social Sci. and Humanities Council grantee, 1977, 78, 79; Social Sci. Fedn. Can. grantee, 1980; McGill Faculty Grad. Studies grantee, 1976, 78. Mem. Am. Ednl. Studies Assn. (founder 1969), Comparative and Internat. Edn. Soc. Can. (pres. 1977-79), Comparative and Internat. Edn. Soc. U.S., World Council Comparative Edn. Socs. (exec. council), Can. Research Inst. for Advancement of Women, Can. Soc. for Study of Edn. (exec. 1977-79), James McGill Soc. (exec. council McGill U. 1978—). Clubs: Ste. Adele Tennis, McGill U. Faculty. Author: A History of Education: Thought and Practice, 1966; (with Momika Kehoe) The Laurel and the Poppy, 1967; Readings in the History of Education, 1969; (with John Laska) Foundation Studies in Education, 1973; Educational Technology, 1973; We Walked Very Warily: A History of Women at McGill, 1981; founding editor McGill Jour. Edn., 1966-77. Home: 4800 de Maisonneuve W Apt 610 Montreal PQ H3Z 1M4 Canada Office: 3700 McTavish McGill U Faculty Edn Montreal PQ H3A 1Y2 Canada

GILLETTE, ETHEL MORROW, columnist; b. Oelwein, Iowa, Nov. 27, 1921; d. Charles Henry and Myrne Sarah (Law) Morrow; student Coe Coll., 1939-41; B.A., Upper Iowa U., 1959; M.A., Western State Coll., 1969; m. Roman A. Gillette, May 6, 1944; children—Melody Ann, Richard Alan, William Robert. Stenographer, Penick & Ford, Cedar Rapids, Iowa, 1941-43, FBI, Washington, 1943-44; tchr. Fayette (Iowa) High Sch., 1959-60, Jordan Jr. High Sch., Mpls., 1960-64, Montrose (Colo.) High Sch., 1964-68; family living, religion editor The News-Record, Gillette, Wyo., 1977-79, columnist Distaff Side, 1979—. Mem. Wyo. Writers Assn., Western Writers Am. (asso.). Contbr. articles to various mags. Home: 1804 E Locust St Montrose CO 81401

GILLETTE, JOYCE LYNNE, nurse; b. Youngstown, Ohio, Oct. 8, 1948; d. Frederick Thomas and Eleanor Elsie (Kulow) G.; R.N., Mt. Sinai Hosp., Cleve., 1969; B.S. in Nursing, U. Rochester (N.Y.), 1973; M.A. in Health Edn. Kent (Ohio) State U., 1980. Nursing supr. Shaker Med. Center, Cleve., 1973-74; public health nurse Cuyahoga County Bd. Health, Cleve., 1974-77; nurse Ob-Gyn clinic Cleve. Met. Gen. Hosp., 1977-79; grad. teaching asst. Kent State U., 1979-80; inservice instr. St. Francis Med. Center, Lynwood, Calif., 1980-81, asst. coordinator med. and profl. edn., 1981—. Mem. Am. Coll. Health Assn., Am. Public Health Assn., Am. Soc. Health Manpower Edn. and Tng. (local and nat.), Inservice and Health Edn. Council Los Angeles, Diabetes Teaching Nurses of So. Calif., Eta Sigma Gamma, Sigma Theta Tau. Lutheran. Author articles in field. Office: 3630 E Imperial Hwy Lynwood CA 92042

GILLEY, BARBARA JOAN, civic worker; b. Birmingham, Nov. 13, 1941; d. Colon Taft and Vivian Loraine (Adams) Dunn; student Alvin Jr. Coll., 1971-72; m. Glen E. Gilley, Aug. 6, 1960; children—Glenn Gregory, Steven Scott, Shaun Michael. Convenor, Miss. Gulf Coast NOW, 1974; dir. public relations Walter Anderson Players, Ocean Springs, Miss., 1975—; mem. Jackson County Democratic Exec. Com., 1975—; mem. Gulf Islands Nat. Seashore Adv. Commn., 1978—. Episcopalian. Home: 6129 Gruich St Ocean Springs MS 39564

GILLIAM, GWYNN HENRIETTA, govt. ofcl.; b. Omaha, June 7, 1945; d. David and Margaret Lucille (Moore) Eleby; B.A., U. Nebr., Omaha, 1967. Community organizer Greater Omaha Community Action, 1967; guidance counselor Neighborhood Youth Corps, Omaha, 1967-70; from field rep. to sr. field rep. Nebr. Equal Opportunity Commn., Omaha, 1970-74; with Women's Bur., Dept. Labor, Kansas City, Mo., 1976-78, 78—, regional adminstr., 1980—; pvt. cons. Eleby Gilliam & Assos., Kansas City, Mo., 1978—; partner UJAMA Enterprises, 1982—. Bd. overseers St. Georges' Half-Way House, 1976-77; mem. exec. steering com. Blue Hills Neighborhood Coalition, 1976-77; adv. bd. Greater Kansas City Urban League, 1980—; pres. elect Central Kansas City Bus. and Profl. Women, 1976-77; exec. bd. Union Apprenticeship Readiness Tng. Systems, 1979—; adv. council Survival Skills Urban Women, 1979-81, Met. United Citizens Prison Reform, 1976-81; sec. bd. dirs., exec. bd. LWV Omaha, 1972-75; bd. dirs. Greater Kansas City YWCA, 1981—. Fellow Dundee Women's League, 1964-67; Osborne scholar, 1963-67. Mem. Mo. Black Leadership Assn. Office: 911 Walnut St Room 2511 Kansas City MO 64106

GILLIAM, JULIANNE KEMPER, video tape producer; b. Kansas City, Mo., May 11, 1927; d. James Madison and Gladys Woods (Grissom) Kemper; student Bennington Coll., 1945-48; m. William Sutherland Beckett, 1948; 1 dau., Deirdre Beckett; m. 2d Digby Gallas, 1958 (dec. 1965); children—Marina Gallas, Evan Gallas; m. 3d Gardner Burnett Gilliam, Oct. 18, 1975. Founder, owner, operator Helicon Video and Visuals, Pacific Palisades, Calif., 1978—. Mem. Assos. Barnsdall Mcpl. Art Gallery. Producer video tape biographies of artists and art collectors. Home: 501 Latimer Rd Santa Monica CA 90402 Office: PO Box 614 Pacific Palisades CA 90272

GILLIAM, MARTHA ANN, microbiologist; b. Dallas, Nov. 15, 1940; d. Hugh Edgar, Jr. and Mary Lola (Davis) G.; B.A., U. Tex., 1963; M.S. with honors, U. Wyo., 1966; Ph.D. (Dept. Agr. grantee), U. Ariz., 1973. Research asst. U. Tex., 1963-64, U. Ariz., 1966-69; radiochemist Wadley Research Inst., Dallas, 1964-65; research microbiologist Dept. Agr., Tucson, 1969—, research leader, acting ctr. dir., 1981—; research assoc. in microbiology U. Ariz., 1973—. Recipient research award Apiary Insps. Am., 1979. Mem. Soc. Invertebrate Pathology, AAAS, Ariz.-Nev. Acad. Sci., Sigma Xi, Gamma Sigma Delta. Author papers in field. Home: 9720 E Lorain Pl Tucson AZ 85710 Office: 2000 E Allen Rd Tucson AZ 85719

GILLIAM, PAULETTE MARIE, communications cons.; b. Houston, July 21, 1947; d. Bert James and Marie Hester (Hardcastle) Gilliam; B.S. in Radio-TV-Film, U. Tex., 1969; M.A. in Communications, Ariz. State U., 1977. TV producer KLTV-TV, Tyler, Tex., 1969, KLRN-TV, Austin, Tex., 1970, WQED,-TV, Pitts., 1970-72; devel. dir., TV producer KAET-TV, Phoenix, 1973-76; lectr. Ariz. State U., 1974-75; adminstr. Ariz. Cactus-Pine council Girl Scouts U.S., 1977-78; owner PMG Enterprises, Phoenix, 1978—; chief info. div. Ariz. Game and Fish Dept., 1982—; cons. various orgns. including Fed. Emergency Mgmt. Agy.; cons. Consortium for Learning through Mediated Instruction Ariz. (C.L.A.I.M.), 1978—. Mem. Govs. Adv. Council Emergency Edn. and Tng., 1980—. Recipient awards including Nat. Gold Medal award, Nat. Assn. Ednl. Broadcasters, 1973; TV Promotion award, Corp. Public Broadcasting, 1973-74; Fed. Cert. of Superior Service, 1980; HEW grantee 1979. Mem. Nat. Assn. Govt. Communicators, Nat. Orgn. Female Execs., Internat. E.S.T. Network. Contbg. editor The Family Game, 1972.

GILLIARD-PAYNE, BARBARA, govt. ofcl.; b. Washington, July 15, 1941; d. William Frank Gilliard and Ruth (Lee) Gilliard Thomas; student Howard U., 1959-60; student U. Md., 1971-74; M.P.A., Am. U., 1979; m. Richard T. Payne, May 10, 1958 (dec.); children—Teresa, Regina, Monica. Personnel mgmt. specialist Bur Outdoor Recreation, Dept. Interior, Washington, 1967-72; equal opportunity and tng. officer Fish and Wildlife Service, Washington, 1972-74, chief OEO, 1974-78, asst. to dir. for civil rights, 1978-80, asst. dir. OEO, 1980—; mem. adv. com. for fish, game and wildlife U. D.C., 1974-76. Chairperson, Fin. Disclosure Rev. Commn. of Howard County (Md.), 1976-78. Named Mgr. of Month, Fed. Exec. Bd., 1976. Mem. Am. Soc. Public Adminstrn., Conf. Minority Public Adminstrs., Com. for Women in Public Adminstrn., NAACP, Am. Soc. Profl. and Exec. Women, Nat. Assn. Female Execs., Sr. Execs. Assn., Internat. Platform Assn., Fed. Exec. Inst. Alumni Assn. Roman Catholic. Club: Toastmasters (adminstrv. v.p. Interior club 1974). Office: 18th and C Sts NW Washington DC 20240

GILLIATT, ANNE FOLEY, exec. recruiter; b. Rio de Janeiro, Brazil, Sept. 18, 1947; d. Arthur D. and Anne N. (Nichols) Foley; B.A., Manhattanville Coll., 1969. Internat. underwriter First Boston Corp., N.Y.C., 1969-71; internat. economist Morgan Guaranty Trust Co., N.Y.C., 1971-78; v.p. Tully and Hobart, Inc., Chgo., 1978—. Mem. Assn. Exec. Recruiting Cons., Inc., Spl. Libraries Assn. Democrat. Home: 850 N State St Chicago IL 60610 Office: 333 N Michigan St Chicago IL 60601

GILLIATT, PENELOPE ANN DOUGLASS, author; b. London; d. Cyril and Mary (Douglass) Conner; student Queen's Coll., London, Bennington Coll., Vt.; m. R.W. Gilliatt (div.); m. 2d, John Osborne (div.); 1 dau., Nolan. Film critic Observer (London), 1961-67, theatre critic, 1965; guest film critic New Yorker, 1967, regular film critic, 1968—; writer feature film scripts and plays filmed for BBC-TV; novelist; double play-bill at Am. Pl. Theatre, N.Y.C.: Property and Nobody's Business, 1980. Recipient award for creative work in lit. Am. Acad.-Nat. Inst. Arts and Letters, 1972. Fellow Royal Soc. Lit. Mem. Brit. Labour Party. Author: One by One, 1965; A State of Change, 1968; The Cutting Edge, 1979; (short stories) Come Back If It Doesn't Get Better, 1970, Nobody's Business, 1972; Splendid Lives, 1979; Sunday, Bloody Sunday (original film script) (Oscar nomination 1971; awards for 1971 best original screenplay Writers Guild Am., Writers Guild Eng., Nat. Soc. Film Critics, N.Y. Film Critics), 1971; Penguin Modern Stories, 1971; (film and theatre essays) Unholy Fools, 1973; Jean Renoir: Essays, Conversations, Review, 1975; Jacques Tati, 1976; (short stories) Splendid Lives, 1977; Three-Quarter Face, 1979; (play) But when all's said and done, 1981. Office: New Yorker Mag 25 W 43d St New York NY 10036 *

GILLICE, SONDRA JUPIN, fuels co. personnel exec.; b. Champaign, Ill.; d. Earl Cranston and Laura Lorraine (Rose) Jupin; B.S., Lindenwood Coll., 1958; M.B.A., Loyola Coll., Balt., 1982; m. Gardner Russell Brown, Jan. 12, 1980; 1 son by previous marriage, Thomas Alan Gillice. Div. tng. supr. Liberty Mut. Ins. Co., N.Y.C., 1958-68; personnel officer Citibank, N.Y.C., 1968-70, First Nat. Bank Chgo., 1970-73; mgr. human resources Potomac Electric Power Co., Washington, 1973-81; dir. personnel U.S. Synthetic Fuels Corp., Washington, 1981—; chmn. tng. and mgmt. devel. com. Edison Electric Inst., 1979-80, chmn. exec. and mgmt. program, 1980-81; mem. adv. com. Pa. State U., Behrend Coll. Mem. Am. Soc. Personnel Adminstrn., Am. Soc. Tng. and Devel., Washington Personnel Assn. (sec. 1975-76), Internat. Platform Assn., DAR, Soc. Magna Charta Dames, AAUW (pres. br. 1976-78). Episcopalian. Clubs: Army Navy Country, Edgartown (Mass.) Yacht; Soroptomists (pres. Washington club 1979-80, Golden Gravel award 1980). Home: 309 N Maple Ave Falls Church VA 22046 Office: 2121 K St NW Washington DC 20586

GILLIG, BARBARA JEAN, ins. co. ofcl.; b. Victoria, Tex., Apr. 18, 1943; d. Lucian Goldie M. (Barber) Walleck; student Bank Adminstrn. Inst., Victoria, 1976-81, Victoria Coll., 1976—; m. Walter C. Gillig, Jr., Oct. 21, 1972; children—Christopher, Gianna Marie; children by previous marriage—Kristie Lynn Timme, Elaine Deniece Timme, Jeanne Annette Timme. Asst. sec. Coastal Loans, Inc., 1964; office mgr. Statewide Leasing and Ins., 1964; comml. loan sec. First Victoria Nat. Bank, 1964-74; asst. cashier Bank of Victoria, 1975-76, asst. v.p., 1976-79, v.p., 1979-81; solicitor Joe N. Pratt Ins., Victoria, 1981—. Bd. dirs., past sec. Victoria County Sr. Citizens Assn., Inc. Named Woman of Achievement, Victoria Regional Mus. Assn., 1981; cert. consumer credit exec. Internat. Consumer Credit Assn., 1981. Mem. Credit Mgmt. Assn. Tex. (dir. region IV, Credit Mgmt. Assn. Victoria (past sec., v.p., pres.), Victoria C. of C. (chmn. arts and culture com. 1980), Nat. Assn. Bank Women, Am. Bus. Women's Assn. (past sec. DeLeon chpt., past pres., named Women of Yr.), Nat. Secs. Assn. (past sec. DeLeon chpt., past v.p., past pres., Sec. of Yr.). Roman Catholic. Clubs: Golden Agers, Inc., Jaycee-Ettes (Victoria chpt. past sec., pres. 1976, 78; Tex. past area v.p.). Home: Route 2 Box 64-P Victoria TX 77901 Office: 2955 1706-A N Navarro St Victoria TX 77902

GILLILAND, JEANETTE WINN, educator; b. Stanford, Ky., Sept. 15, 1948; d. Robert Clifton and Susan Elizabeth (Taylor) Winn; student (acad. scholar), Ky. So. Coll., 1966; A.B. in Speech and Theatre, Western Ky. U., 1971, M.A. in Counselor Edn., 1975; postgrad. in Adult Edn., Alaska Pacific U., 1978; postgrad. in Ednl. Evaluation, U. Alaska, Fairbanks, 1978-79; postgrad. in Adult Edn., S.W. Tex. State U., 1980; m. Victor Pence Gilliland, Feb. 8, 1971; 1 son, Eric Clifton Conner Gilliland. Adminstrv. asst. Diversified Edn. and Research Corp., N.Y.C., 1967-68; actress profl. theatre, Atlanta Town and Country Dinner Theatre, Ky. Belle Dinner Theatre, Bowling Green, Mammoth Dave Nat. Park Outdoor Theatre, Cave City, Ky., 1967-70; substitute tchr. Ky. and Tenn. public schs., 1972-73; instr. Austin Peay State U. Prep. Program, Ft. Campbell, Ky., 1974, Enterprise (Ala.) State Jr. Coll., 1976-77; acad. diagnostician Regional Adult Learning Center, Fairbanks, Alaska, 1977-78, dir. urban programs, 1978-79; coordinator credit programs and tng., U. Tex., San Antonio, 1979—; cons. in field. Choral dir., church musician, Stanford, Ky., Bowling Green, Ky., Clarksville, Tenn., Ft. Wainwright, Alaska, San Antonio. Recipient Danforth Leadership award, 1966, acting award Western Players Theatre Group, 1970, program award Alaska Adult Edn. Assn., 1979. Mem. Nat. Univ. Continuing Edn. Assn., Nat. Assn. Women Deans, Adminstrs. and Counselors, Adult Edn. Assn. U.S., Am. Soc. Tng. and Devel., Alpha Psi Omega, Zeta Phi Eta. Contbr. writings to profl. publs. in field. Home: 6503 Greentop San Antonio TX 78233 Office: 6900 Loop 1604 W San Antonio TX 78285

GILLILLAND, CORA LEE CRITCHFIELD, art historian; b. Falls City, Nebr., Apr. 12, 1932; d. Edward J. and Hazel M. (Ratekin) Critchfield; A.B. with high honors in Art, Lindenwood Coll. for Women, 1954; A.M., U. Chgo., 1960; postgrad. State U. Iowa; m. Thomas Gillilland, Aug. 23, 1956; children—Shaun, Ruth, Ginger. Edn. specialist Dept. Edn., Trust Ter. Pacific Islands, 1957-58, 62-65; prin. Truk High Sch., Caroline Islands, 1962-63; lectr. art history Dept. Agr. Grad. Sch., 1960-61; mus. specialist div. numismatics Smithsonian Inst., Washington, 1965-71, collaborator, 1971—; lectr. art history Montgomery Coll., Takoma Park, Md., 1975—. Chmn. Arlington County (Va.) Art Advisory Com., 1972-74; mem. Arlington County Humanities Com., 1975—. Mem. Am. Numismatic Soc., Am. Numismatic Assn., Assn. for Social Anthropology in Oceana, P.E.O. Republican. Congregationalist. Author: The Stone Money of Yap—A Numismatic Survey, 1975. Contbr. articles in field to profl. jours. Home: 3713 N Glebe Rd Arlington VA 22207 Office: Bureau of the Mint Dept of Treasury Washington DC 20220

GILLIS, CHRISTINE DIEST-LORGION, fin. planner, stockbroker; b. San Francisco; d. Evert Jan and Christine Helen (Radcliffe) Diest-Lorgion; B.S., U. Calif., Berkeley; M.S., U. So. Calif.; children—Barbara Gillis Pieper, Suzanne Gillis Seymour (twins). Account exec. Winslow, Cohu & Stetson, N.Y.C., 1962-63, Paine Webber, N.Y.C., 1964-65; sr. investment exec. Shearson Hammill, Beverly Hills, Calif., 1966-72; fin. planner E.F. Hutton & Co., Glendale, Calif., 1972—. Cert. fin. planner. Mem. Inst. Cert. Fin. Planners, Town Hall of Calif. (life, treas. 1974-75, dir., gov. 1976-80), Women Stockbrokers Assn. (founding pres. 1963), Women of Wall Street West (pres. 1979-83), Navy League (life; dir.), Assistance League Pasadena, AAUW (life; trustee Ednl. Found.), Bus. and Profl. Women, Phi Chi Theta (life). Democrat. Episcopalian. Club: U. So. Calif. Town and Gown (life). Home: 1495 Pegfair Estates Dr Pasadena CA 91103 Office: 225 W Broadway Glendale CA 91204

GILLIS, EILEEN FLEMING, educator; b. Boston, Dec. 9, 1930 d. James Joseph and Anna Theresa (Brosnahan) Fleming; A.B., Emmanuel Coll., 1946; M.Ed., Boston U., 1972; m. Joseph L. Gillis, June 17, 1948; children—Kathleen G. Pope, Joseph Leo, Julie Anne G. Dutcher, Daniel Edward, Michael Kerby, F. Brian. Math. researcher M.I.T., Cambridge, 1946-49; reading specialist Milton (Mass.) public schs., 1972-79, core evaluation chmn., 1979-82, resource tchr., 1982—, dir. inservice tng. program for secondary tchrs. in reading, 1978-79. Mem. Milton Town Meeting, 1975—; trustee Milton Library, 1976—, rec. sec., 1981—, chmn. computer study com., 1982—; dir. Coll. Entrance Exam. Bd., Milton High Sch., 1980; chmn. Ann. Charity Ball, 1980; bd. dirs. Jr. Guild of Cath. Charities, Boston, 1979-82; asst. med. and patient edn. project, Center for Nutritional Research, M.I.T., summer 1977; cons. in field. Mem. Internat. Reading Assn., New Eng. Reading Assn., Mass. Reading Assn., S. Shore Reading Assn., Nat. Tchrs. Assn., Mass. Tchrs. Assn., Mass. Assn. Children with Learning Disabilities, Friends of Milton Library, Milton Hist. Soc., Mus. Fine Arts Boston, China Trade Mus., LWV, AAUW (pres. Milton area br. 1982—). Clubs: Jr. Guild Cath. Charities, Milton Hoosic, others. Home: 1278 Canton Ave Milton MA 02186 Office: Milton Public Schs Milton MA 02186

GILLIS, PHYLLIS LESLIE, author; b. Cleve., July 3, 1945; d. Sidney and Joan (Greenis) Helper; B.A., Mich. State U., 1967; M.S.J., Northwestern U., 1968; m. David Gillis, Nov. 25, 1971; 1 son, Jordon Clayton. Staff writer Urban Am., Inc., Washington, 1967; reporter Nat. Jour., Washington, 1968-70; staff asso. Office of Urban Affairs, CUNY, N.Y.C., 1970-72; exec. dir. Gallup Internat. Research Inst., Princeton, N.J., 1972-76; v.p. Louis Harris & Assocs., N.Y.C., 1976-78; mng. partner Carversville Inn, Inc. (Pa.), 1979—; columnist Parents Mag., 1980—; dir. Solebury Equip. Corp. (Pa.), 1981—. Mem. LWV, Am. Soc. Journalists and Authors, Authors Guild, Bucks County Writers Guild, Women in Communications. Author: The New Pregnancy, 1979; contbr. articles to profl. jours. Address: RD 1 PO Box A309 New Hope PA 18938

GILLISPIE, BETH JACOBS, human resource devel. cons.; b. Lansing, Mich., June 4, 1950; d. Durand Frank and Lenore May (Sobel) Jacobs; B.A., Mich. State U., 1972; postgrad. in public adminstrn. Washington Public Affairs Center, U. So. California, 1974-76; m. C. Stephenson Gillispie, June 27, 1976; 1 stepdau., Sasha Rebecca; 1 son, Sean Wallace. Trainer, course developer Abt Assos./Nat. Drug Abuse Tng. Center, Washington, 1972-74; cons. human resources devel., Washington, 1974-76; course devel. mgr. HCS, Inc./Nat. Drug Abuse Center, Gaithersburg, Md., 1976-79; prin. Tudor House, Richmond, Va., 1979—; mem. faculty Duke U. Summer Alcoholism Inst., 1980, 81; keynote speaker Va. Women's Task Force; nat. conf. presentations; mem. Va. Tng. and Edn. Sub-com for Credentialing Drug Counselors, 1979-80. Mem. Am. Soc. Tng. and Devel., Nat. Assn. Female Execs., Ginter Park Residents Assn. Author books, most recent being: (with others) Adolescence: Intervention Strategies, 1977; sr. author: Women in Treatment, 1979. Home and office: 1605 Confederate Ave Richmond VA 23227

GILLROY-POSCHEL, MARY MARGARET, writer; b. Stamford, Conn., Mar. 25, 1942; d. John Henry and Mildred Bridget (Daly) Gillroy; B.S.L.S., Tex. Woman's U., 1964; student Univ. Coll., Dublin, 1962-63; m. Jerome R. Poschel, Dec. 20, 1969. Children's librarian Perrot Meml. Library, Old Greenwich, Conn., 1965-66; supplemental recreational activities specialist ARC, S. Vietnam, 1966-67; young adult librarian Arlington County (Va.) Library, Arlington, 1968-69; free-lance writer, 1972—; ARC caseworker, public relations chmn. MacDill AFB, Tampa, Fla., 1980—; public speaker, 1967—; author/editor: Women Helping Women, 1979; also articles. Bd. dirs. local ARC, 1972-74; pres. women's assn. Quinnipiac Coll., 1973, 74, dir., 1975. Recipient Civilian Service in Vietnam medal; Culpepper Found. scholar, 1960-64. Mem. ALA, NOW (dir.), Nat. Cat Protection Soc., Pet and Wildlife Preservation. Overseas Service League, Tex. Woman's U. Alumnae Assn., Alpha Beta Alpha. Home: 572 Marmora Ave Tampa FL 33606

GILMAN, CAROL ANN, retail co. fin. ofcl.; b. Plattsburgh, N.Y., Nov. 13, 1947; d. A. W. and Patricia (Vidock) G.; grad. Am. Inst. Banking, Atlanta, 1972; B.B.A., Ga. State U., Atlanta, 1978. Research analyst Fed. Res. Bank Atlanta, 1968-76; internal audit mgr. Haverty Furniture Companies, Inc., Atlanta, 1978-82; systems auditor J.C. Penney Co., 1982—; speaker on auditing. Fin. v.p., co-founder Nat. Action Archery Assn., 1978; mem. DeKalb County Militia Dists. Commn. Recipient public service certificates, Ga. Wheelchair Athletic Program. Mem. Inst. Internal Auditors EDP Auditors Assn., Ga. State U. Alumni Soc., Ga. Women's Polit. Caucus. Democrat. Roman Catholic. Clubs: Order of

Robin Hood (archery champion), ERA (Ga.). Home: 3663 Salem Dr Lithonia GA 30058 Office: 715 Peachtree St NW Atlanta GA 30308

GILMAN, CYDNI KAYE, lawyer; b. Manhattan, Kans., June 18, 1953; d. Kenneth A. and Carole R. (Branch) G.; B.A., U. Kans., 1975; J.D., Washburn Law Sch., 1978. Admitted to U.S. Dist. Ct. bar, 1978; Kans. bar, 1978; intern to Public Defender of 18th Jud. Dist. Kans., 1977, to judge of 28th Jud. Dist., Salina, Kans., 1976; atty. Legal Aid Soc. Wichita (Kans.), 1978—; asst. adj. prof. Wichita State U., 1981—; also adviser legal asst. program; vol. mediator Victim-Offender Mediation Program; speaker on role of women in law to community groups. Vol., Kans. Spl. Olympics State Meet. Mem. Am. Bar Assn. (Kans. del. to Young Lawyers div. 1981 Conv.), Kans. Bar Assn. (mem. citizenship com. 1982-83). Wichita Bar Assn., Wichita Young Lawyers Assn. (v.p. 1980-81, pres. 1982-83), Kans. Legal services Staff Assn. (v.p. 1980-81, pres. 1981-82), NOW, Delta Delta Delta. Democrat. Methodist. Office: 502 Century Plaza Bldg 111 W Douglas Wichita KS 67202

GILMAN, ETHEL ZENA, social worker, assn. exec.; b. Reading, Pa., Sept. 15, 1945; d. George and Beatrice (Korn) G.; B.A., Pa. State U., 1967; M.A., N.Y. U., 1974. Youth guidance technician N.Y.C. Youth Bd., 1967-68; caseworker N.Y.C. Dept. Social Services, 1969-70; youth services specialist, asst. supr. youth services N.Y.C. Youth Services Agy., 1970-74; single intake youth counselor II, Fla. Dept. Health & Rehab. Service, Miami, 1974-77; project supr. juvenile projects Miami (Fla.) Police Dept., 1977-80; exec. dir. Fla. chpt. Nat. Assn. Social Workers, Tallahassee, 1980—. Mem. Am. Psychol. Assn., Am. Personnel and Guidance Assn., Nat. Assn. Social Workers, Fla. Soc. Assn. Execs. Home: 1616 Kay Ave Tallahassee FL 32301 Office: NASW Fla Chpt 222 W Pensacola St Tallahassee FL 32301

GILMORE, BARBARA LEE, filmmaking, media co. exec.; b. Los Angeles, Apr. 3, 1938; d. Arthur Lee and Ruth Eleanor (Ryan) Cahill; B.S. in Secondary Edn., Ind. U., 1961; Calif. Teaching Credential, Calif. State U., 1966; m. James Gilmore, Oct. 28, 1961; children—Kasey Lee, Michael William. Tech. writer Aerojet-Gen. Corp., Sacramento, 1961-65; substitute tchr. Conejo Valley Unified Sch. Dist., Thousand Oaks, Calif., 1966-72; film producer Atlantis Prodns., Inc., Thousand Oaks, 1972-79; participant CORO Founds. Public Affairs Program for Women, Los Angeles, 1979; program mgr. Calif. Assn. Realtors, Los Angeles, 1979-80; pres. Forecast, Inc., Thousand Oaks, Calif., 1980—; dir. Multicultural Media Assos., Thousand Oaks, 1979-82, Atlantis Prodns., Inc., Thousand Oaks, 1976-82; cons., lectr. time mgmt., Thousand Oaks, 1981—. Chmn. community devel. com. Ventura County Grand Jury, 1977-78; chmn. Conejo Future Founds. Sch. Unification Task Force, 1973. AAUW fellowship grantee, 1974, research grantee, 1981-82, 82-83. Mem. AAUW (pres. 1972-73; mem. bd. 1968-79), CORO Found. Assos., Women in Public Affairs, Nat. Assn. Female Execs. Club: Community Leaders. Home: 2909 Raleigh Pl Thousand Oaks CA 91360 Office: 31220 La Baya Suite 110 Westlake Village CA 91362

GILMORE, MARJORIE HAVENS, lawyer, club woman; b. N.Y.C., Aug. 16, 1918; d. William Westerfield and Elsie (Medl) Havens; A.B., Hunter Coll., 1938; J.D., Columbia, 1941; m. Hugh Redland Gilmore, May 8, 1942; children—Douglas Hugh, Anne Charlotte Gilmore Decker, Joan Louise. Admitted to N.Y. State bar, 1941, Va. bar, 1968; research asst. N.Y. Law Revision Commn., 1941-42; asso. firm Spence, Windels, Walser, Hotchkiss & Angell, N.Y.C., 1942, Chadbourne, Wallace, Parke & Whiteside, N.Y.C., 1942-43; atty. U.S. Army, Washington, 1948-53. Sec., Thomas Jefferson Jr. High Sch. PTA, 1956-58; parliamentarian Wakefield High Sch. PTA, 1959-60, chmn. citizenship com., 1960-61; publicity chmn. Patrick Henry Sch. PTA, sec., 1964-65; parliamentarian Nottingham PTA, 1966-69; mem. extra-curricular activities com. Arlington County Sch. Bd.; area chmn. fund drive Cancer Soc., 1955-56; active Girl Scouts U.S.A., 1963-70; mem. '41 com. Columbia Law Sch. Fund. Recipient Constl. Law award Hunter Coll., 1938. Mem. Arlington Fedn. Women's Clubs (rec. sec. 1979-80), Columbia Law Sch. Alumni Assn., Alpha Sigma Rho. Presbyn. Club: Williamsburg Woman's of Arlington (corr. sec. 1970-72, 1st v.p. 1972-74, pres. 1974-76, chmn. communications 1981—). Home: 3020 N Nottingham St Arlington VA 22207

GILMORE, SUZANNE ELLEN, nursing adminstr.; b. Worcester, Mass., Oct. 8, 1945; d. Richard Fay and Ruth Myrtle (Rogers) Gilmore; B.S. in Nursing, St. Olaf Coll., 1967; M.B.A., Boston U., 1977. Staff nurse Columbia-Presbyn. Hosp., N.Y.C., 1967-68; asst. head nurse Univ. Hosp., N.Y.U. Med. Center, N.Y.C., 1968-69; successively staff nurse, sr. staff nurse, head nurse, supr., neurology clin. leader Mass. Gen. Hosp., Boston, 1970-76; br. mgr. Medox, Inc. div. Drake Internat., Boston, 1977-78; dir. nursing Goddard Meml. Hosp., Stoughton, Mass., 1979—; lectr. various hosps., N.H. Heart Assn., Mass. Office Emergency Med. Services. Mem. ednl. adv. bd. Massasoit Community Coll.; mem. nat. council Community Hosp Task Force. Mem. Am. Assn. Nursing Service Adminstrs., Save Children Fedn., Mass. Soc. Nursing Service Adminstrs., Am. Soc. Profl. and Exec. Women, Am. Hosp. Assn., Quincy Hist. Soc., Mass. Cultural Alliance, St. Olaf Coll. Alumni Assn., Boston U. Alumni Assn., New Eng. AAU. Home: 1047 S Artery Apt 609 Quincy MA 02169 Office: Goddard Meml Hosp 909 Sumner St Stoughton MA 02072

GILPIN, MARGARET, social worker, family therapist; b. N.Y.C., Dec. 19, 1942; d. Edward and Reba G. (Canzano) G.; B.A., C.W. Post Coll., 1964; M.S.W., Adelphi U., 1966. Coordinator div. psychosomatic medicine N.Y. Med. Coll., N.Y.C., 1971-72, mem. faculty div. group and family process, 1972-74; cons. Pan Am. Health Orgn., UN, N.Y.C., 1978, 79; dir. psychosocial edn. residency program in social medicine Montefiore Hosp., Bronx, N.Y., 1976—; asst. prof. dept. community health Albert Einstein Coll. Medicine, N.Y.C., 1976—; pvt. practice family therapy, 1970—. NIMH fellow, 1963-64; Lester Martin Found. scholar, 1965-66; VA fellow, 1965-66. Fellow Am. Orthopsychiat. Assn.; mem. Nat. Assn. Social Workers, Acad. Cert. Social Workers, Am. Family Therapy Assn. Contbr. articles to profl. jours. Home: 545 West End Ave New York NY 10024 Office: 3412 Bainbridge Ave Bronx NY 10467

GILSON, CHRISTINE MOTE, librarian; b. Denver, Sept. 8, 1946; d. Edwin J. and Esther E. (Heckman) Westermann; B.A., Grinnell Coll., 1968; M.S., U. Ill., 1970; m. Preston A. Gilson, Dec. 27, 1969; 1 dau., Genevieve Rose. Interlibrary loan librarian U. Okla., Norman, 1970-72; adminstrv. librarian Lincoln (Ill.) Public Library, 1972—. Mem. adv. bd. Salvation Army; bd. dirs. Logan County Heritage Found. Named Woman of Month, Lincoln Courier, 1976. Mem. LWV, Ill. Library Assn. (pres. public library sect. 1983), Right to Read Adv. Council, Lincoln C. of C. Episcopalian. Home: 803 N Logan Lincoln IL 62656 Office: 725 Pekin Lincoln IL 62656

GILSON, JAMIE MARIE, writer; b. Beardstown, Ill., July 4, 1933; d. James Noyce and Sallie Anna (Wilkinson) Chisam; B.S. with honors in Speech, Northwestern U., 1955; m. Jerome Gilson, June 19, 1955; children—Tom, Matthew, Anne. Tchr., Thacker Jr. High Sch., Des Plaines, Ill., 1955-56; writer for ednl. radio, TV and film, producer div. radio and TV, Chgo. Public Schs., 1956-59; continuity dir. Sta. WFMT, Chgo., 1959-63; writer column and articles Chgo. Mag., 1977—; author children's books, including: Harvey, the Beer Can King (Merit award Friends Am. Writers 1979), 1978; Dial Leroi Rupert, D.J., 1979; Do Bananas Chew Gum (Carl Sandburg award Friends Chgo. Public Library 1981), 1980; Can't Catch Me, I'm the Gingerbread Man, 1981; Thirteen Ways to Sink a Sub, 1982; tchr. creative writing 6th grade students, 1974—; lectr. on writing. Mem. Soc. Midland Authors, Children's Reading Round Table, Soc. Children's Book Writers.

GILSON, JO ELAINE, county ofcl.; b. Purcell, Okla., Jan. 10, 1947; d. Charley C. and Wanda Jo Johnston; children—Marta Lynn, Neal I. Supr., Oklahoma County Treas. Office, Oklahoma City, 1967-80, sr. supr., 1980-81, chief dep. county treas., 1981—. Mem. State and County Treas. Assn., State Officers and Deps. Assn., Exec. Women's Club. Democrat. Baptist. Home: 8208 NW 38th St Bethany OK 73008 Office: County Treasurer's Office 360 Oklahoma County Office Bldg Oklahoma City OK 73102

GILTNER, DELORIS MARGARET, nurse; b. Princeton, Ill., Nov. 1, 1922; d. Hugh Verner and Margaret Elizabeth (Hess) G.; B.S. with spl. honors, U. Colo., Boulder, 1959; M.S., U. Calif., San Francisco, 1963; Ph.D., U. Denver, 1979. Supr., instr. Colo. State Hosp., Pueblo, 1949-56; clin. instr., nursing coordinator psychiat. unit St. Mary Corwin Hosp., Pueblo, 1959-64; asst. prof., acting dir. nursing So. Colo. State Coll., Pueblo, 1964-69; asso. prof., acting dir. nursing Met. State Coll., Denver, 1969-74; acting head dept. nursing Carroll Coll., Helena, Mont., 1975; dir. patient care, asst. adminstr. clin. services Boulder (Colo.) Psychiat. Inst., 1976-81; asso. dean student affairs/asso. prof. U. Colo. Sch. Nursing, Denver, 1981—; health oriented counselor Nativity Parish, Broomfield, Colo., 1981. Mem. Am. Nurses Assn. (mem. psychiat. mental health rev. team of nat. rev. com. for accreditation of nurse practitioner programs 1975-76), Nat. League Nursing (mem. forum for adminstrs. nursing 1977-81), Mile Hi Continuing Edn. Network for Nursing (sec.), Creative Ednl. Found., Am. Assn. Higher Edn., Western Soc. Research Nursing, Colo. Nurses Assn. (pres. 1973-74, 80-81, Nurse of Year 1974, Past Pres. award 1981), Colo. League Nursing, Colo. Soc. Health Care Nursing Service Adminstrs. Roman Catholic. Home: 36 Irene Ct Broomfield CO 80020 Office: 4200 E 9th Ave Box C288 Denver CO 80262

GIMOVSKY, ARLENE JOAN, biomed. engr.; b. Jamaica, N.Y., May 18, 1953; d. Gerald W. and Ethel (Friedman) Glaser; B.S. in Chem. Engring., Columbia U., 1973; M.S. in Bio Engring., N.Y.U., 1976; m. Martin L. Gimovsky, June 10, 1973. With med. products div. Union Carbide Corp., Tarrytown, N.Y., 1973-80, project mgr. immunoassay systems, 1973-80; project mgr. urol. products Pharmaseal div. Am. Hosp. Supply Corp., Glendale, Calif., 1980-82, dir. spl. markets research and devel., 1982—. Recipient Creelman prize math. Williston Northampton Acad., 1969; grantee NSF summers 1968, 69. Registered profl. engr., Calif. Mem. Am. Inst. Chem. Engrs., Am. Assn. Clin. Chemistry, Nat. Soc. Profl. Engrs., Health Industry Mfrs. Assn. (com. on aids for ostomy and incontinence), Soc. Women Engrs. Author, patentee in field. Office: 1015 Grandview Ave Glendale CA 91201

GINALSKI, JUNE JOYCE IRENE HOUGLUND, mgmt. systems co. exec.; b. Kimberley, B.C., Can., May 6, 1938; came to U.S., 1961, naturalized, 1972; d. Charles A. and Elsie Joyce (Hartley) Houglund; A.S., Victoria Coll., 1958; B.S., U. B.C., 1959; Ph.D., Oreg. State U., 1963; postgrad. Harvard U., 1976; m. William Ginalski, Nov. 28, 1969; 1 stepson, Mark. Dir. computing lab. Oreg. State U., 1961-66; cons. Gen. Electric Co., 1966-71; mgr. research and devel. Ramada Inns, Inc., Phoenix, 1972-73; asst. v.p. First Nat. Bank-Western Bancorp. Corp., Phoenix, 1973-78; v.p. planning Gt. Western Bank & Trust Co., Phoenix, 1978-80; asso. Continental Mgmt. Systems, 1980—. Mem. Nat. Assn. Bank Women (past dir.), Assn. for Research and Enlightenment, Futurist Soc. Democrat. Club: Harvard. Home: 5501 E Calle Tuberia Phoenix AZ 85018 Office: Continental Mgmt Systems 2701 E Indian Sch Rd Phoenix AZ 85016

GINES, MERRY CAYFORD, money mgmt. co. exec.; b. Emmett, Idaho, Apr. 23, 1949; d. Weston Lloyd and Meredith June (Cone) Cayford; B.S. summa cum laude, Calif. State U., 1975; m. Feb. 4, 1967 (div.); 1 son, Christopher. Mktg. mgr. Itel Corp., San Francisco, 1973-76; div. mgr. Newmedia Mktg., Inc., N.Y.C., 1976-77; account supr. John Blair & Co., N.Y.C., 1977-78; pres. Merry Gines Mgmt. Corp., registered SEC investment advisers, N.Y.C., 1978—; lectr., fin. cons. Mem. N.Y. State Republican Com.; mem. presdl. task force com.; mem. George Bush for Pres. Com.; active Mus. Modern Art; Guggenheim Mus. Registered rep. N.Y. Stock Exchange. Mem. Econ. Roundtable, Fin. Women's Assn. Home: 342 Apt 87th St New York NY 10028 Office: 1185 Ave of Americas Suite 3665 New York NY 10036

GINGOLD, HERMIONE FERDINANDA, actress; b. London; d. Jame and Kate (Walter) Gingold; student pvt. schs., London, governesses in Paris; m. Michael Josef; children—Leslie, Stephen. Actress, Old Vic, Shakespeare at Stratford on Avon, also Paris; film appearances include Gigi, Naked Edge, Music Man, Gay Paree, Harvey Middleman-Fireman, I'd Rather Be Rich, Promise Her Anything, Rocket to the Moon, A Little Night Music; mem. cast Almanac, 1st Impressions, The Sleeping Prince, Fallen Angels, From A to Z, Milk and Honey, Oh Dad, Poor Dad, A Little Night Music, Side by Side by Sondheim, N.Y.C.; made TV appearances on Ed Sullivan Show, Omnibus, Matinee Theatre, The Importance of Being Ernest, Jack Paar, Alfred Hitchcock Presents, This is Your Life, Hallmark Hall of Fame, Merv Griffin Show, Girl Talk, Mike Douglas Show, The Girl from U.N.C.L.E. Recipient Donaldson award; dame Knights of Malta. Author: The World is Square: My Own Unaided Work; Sirens Should be Seen and Not Heard, 1963. Recordings: La Gingold, Life of the Party, Facade, Lysistrata, A Little Night Music, Peter and the Wolf (Grammy award), Carnival of Animals, Chitty Chitty Bang Bang. Home: 405 E 54th St New York NY 10022 *

GINN, DONNA LYNETTE, mgmt. cons.; b. Middletown, Ohio, Sept. 1, 1948; d. Donald Jerome and Audrey Elaine (Scroggins) G.; student Miami U., Oxford, Ohio, 1966-71, U. Cin., 1976; postgrad. Nat. Tng. Labs., 1977-79; B.A. in Psychology. Lab technician Middletown (Ohio) Hosp., 1965-67, Kettering (Ohio) Meml. Hosp., 1967-68; research technician Ind. U.-Wright Patterson AFB, Ohio, 1968, Miami U., 1968-71, St. Louis U. Med. Sch., 1971-73; research technician Procter & Gamble, Miami Valley Labs., Cin., 1973-77, mgr. orgnl. devel. cons., 1977—. Vol. counselor Butler County Mental Health Assn., 1977—; founder, pres. Daus. of Sophia, 1976—; dir., moderator Black Student Action Assn. radio and TV program, 1968-71; mem. youth motivation task force Nat. Alliance Bus., 1979—, Black Exec. Exchange Program, 1979—; active Big Sisters, Cin., 1968-71. Am. Assn. Clin. Pathology-Middletown Hosp. acad. scholar, 1966; Martin Luther King fellow, 1970; recipient Letters of Appreciation, Minority Counselor, Middletown High Sch., 1976, Dept. Air Force, 1969; named Outstanding Young Woman Am., 1979. Mem. Am. Soc. Tng. and Devel., Orgnl. Devel. Network, Am. Mgmt. Assn., AAAS. Baptist. Club: Girls Assembly Order Eastern Star (sec. 1960-64). Office: 6210 Center Hill Rd Cincinnati OH 45224

GINNETTI, CYNTHIA JULE, psychologist; b. Atlantic City, Jan. 22, 1942; d. John and Frances Inez (Mosca) G.; B.A., Rosemont Coll., 1963; M.A., U. Ariz., 1974, Ph.D., 1977; m. June 9, 1979; 1 dau., Heather Marie King. Women's editor, drama critic, journalist Miami (Fla.) Herald, 1967-69; psychology extern Palo Verde Hosp., 1973-74; psychology intern Ariz. Med. Center, 1974, 77; psychologist Comprehensive Care Center, Lexington, Ky., 1976-77; asso. in clin. tng. U. Ariz., Tucson, 1978—; dir. Pima County Court Clinic, Tucson, 1978—; adj. faculty U. Ariz., 1978—. Mem. So. Ariz. Psychologists Assn. (pres.), Ariz. Psychologists Assn., Am. Psychol. Assn. Home: 6015 Paseo Ventoso Tucson AZ 85715 Office: 45 W Pennington St Tucson AZ 85701

GINSBURG, RUTH BADER, judge; b. Bklyn., Mar. 15, 1933; d. Nathan and Celia (Amster) Bader; B.A., Cornell U., 1954; postgrad. Harvard Law Sch., 1956-58; J.D. (Kent scholar), Columbia U., 1959; LL.D., Lund (Sweden) U., 1969, Am. U., 1981; m. Martin David Ginsburg, June 23, 1954; children—Jane Carol, James Steven. Admitted to N.Y. bar, 1959, D.C. bar, U.S. Supreme Ct. bar; law clk. to dist. judge So. Dist. N.Y., 1959-61; research asso. Columbia Law Sch. Project on Internat. Procedure, 1961-62, asso. dir., 1962-63; asst. prof. law Rutgers U., Newark, 1963-66, asso. prof., 1966-69, prof., 1969-72; prof. law Columbia, N.Y.C., 1972-80; U.S. circuit judge U.S. Ct. of Appeals for D.C. Circuit, Washington, 1980—; gen. counsel ACLU, 1973-80, bd. dirs, 1974-80. Mem. Am. Bar Assn. (bd. editors jour. 1972-78, council sect. individual rights and responsibilities 1975-81), Bar Assn. N.Y.C. (exec. com. 1974-80), Am. Law Inst. (council 1979—), Am. Bar Found. (dir. 1979—, exec. com. 1980—), Am. Acad. Arts and Scis., Council Fgn. Relations, Phi Beta Kappa (vis. scholar 1973-74), Phi Kappa Phi. Author: (with Anders Bruzelius) Civil Procedure in Sweden, 1965, The Swedish Code of Judicial Procedure, 1968; A Selective Survey of English Language Studies on Scandinavian Law, 1970; Constitutional Aspects of Sex-Based Discrimination, 1974; (with others) Sex-Based Discrimination, Text, Cases and Materials, 1974, supplement, 1978. Bd. editors Am. Jour. Comparative Law, 1966-72. Contbr. articles to legal jours. Home: 700 New Hampshire Ave NW Washington DC 20037 Office: US Ct of Appeals US Courthouse Washington DC 20001

GINTHER, CYNTHIA SUSAN, mktg. exec.; b. Laramie, Wyo., Dec. 31, 1953; d. Howard Glen and Marie H. (Hansen) Ginther; A.A., Northwest Coll., Seattle, 1974; B.A., U. Wyo., 1976; M.B.A., Colo. State U., 1980. Advt., promotions, publicity mgr. McDonald Corp., Ft. Collins, Colo., 1976-78; dir. public relations dir. music Colo. State U., Ft. Collins, 1978-80; corporate mktg. mgr. Tele-Communications, Inc., Denver, 1980—; public relations, mktg. and customer services cons.; tchr. courses in public relations, fund raising, gen. mktg.; TV co-host for telethons; free lance photographer, writer. Mem. Nat. Assn. Female Execs., Rocky Mountain Cable Assn., Denver Advt. Found., Women in Cable, Cable TV Adminstrn. and Mktg. Assn., Nat. Wildlife Fedn., Audubon Soc., Sierra Club. Clubs: Denver Cable. Home: 4982 S Ulster St Pkwy 613 Denver CO 80237 Office: Call Box 22595 Wellshire Station Denver CO 80222

GIOE, CHARLOTTE, cons. co. exec.; b. Bklyn., Nov. 15, 1942; d. Joseph and Lena (DiGiovanna) Marrone; B.A. cum laude, CUNY, 1964, M.S., 1969; m. Louis Gioe, Sept. 1963; children—Leah, Dana. Early childhood educator Lindenhurst (N.Y.) public schs., 1964-81, early childhood coordinator, 1977-78; exec. dir. Joy Acad. Center, Lindenhurst, 1975—; pres. Forum Internat. Exchange, Inc., Babylon, N.Y., 1981—; cons. Rose Motors Internat., Inc., 1980-81, Mountaindale Spa, 1982. Team capt. Am. Cancer Soc., 1981; sponsor Children to Children Project, UNICEF, 1981. Recipient Jenkins Meml. award PTA and Community Service, 1976, 81. Mem. Nat. Assn. Female Execs. (nat. adv. council), Am. Entrepreneurs Assn., AAUW, N.Y. State Early Childhood Edn. Council, N.Y. State Teaching Assn., Kappa Delta Pi. Roman Catholic. Club: L.I. Network Council, 110 Center for Bus. and Profl. Women. Author: Individualized Instruction Activities, 1978; contbr. articles to profl. jours. Address: 104 Beverly Rd Babylon NY 11704

GIOIA, KATHLEEN ROURKE, microbiologist; b. Waterbury, Conn., Jan. 7, 1933; d. James Michael and Kathleen Anetta (Classey) Rourke; B.A. in Microbiology, U. Conn., 1956; postgrad. Nova U. Grad. Sch., 1976-79; m. Anthony A. Gioia, Sept. 25, 1954 (div. 1966); children—Patrick, Kathleen, Michael. Intern Riverside (Calif.) Community Hosp., 1958-59, med. technologist, 1959-61; microbiologist, serologist Univ. Mo. Med. Center and Hosps., Columbia, 1961-64; supr. dept. microbiology St. Francis Hosp., Miami Beach, Fla., 1967-69; asst. to dir. research and quality control Gray Industries, Ft. Lauderdale, Fla., 1971-73; supr. dept. microbiology Fla. Med. Center, Ft. Lauderdale, 1973-75; microbiologist spl. testing North Ridge Gen. Hosp., Ft. Lauderdale, 1975—. Treas. Coral Springs Women's Club, 1975-77. Mem. Am. Soc. Microbiology, Am. Acad. Microbiology. Club: Coral Springs Women's. Office: 5757 North Dixie Hwy Fort Lauderdale FL 33334

GIOMI, THELMA ANNE, psychologist; b. Albuquerque, Feb. 26, 1947; d. James E. and Esma Anne (Snyder) Giomi; B.A. cum laude, U. N.Mex., 1969, M.A., 1972, Ph.D. (Univ. fellow), 1974. Psychometrician, Albuquerque Pub. Schs., 1969; teaching asst. introductory psychology U. N.Mex., 1970, instr. child psychology, 1973, teaching asst. exptl. child psychology, 1974, clin. staff psychologist, asst. prof. psychiatry Programs for Children, 1976-81; pvt. practice psychology, Albuquerque, 1981—; clin. psychology intern Pitts. Child Guidance Center, 1974-75; cons. Child Abuse Program, Albuquerque, 1976-80; mem. sci. staff Bernalillo County Med. Center. Active, N.Mex. Youth Work Alliance. NSF grantee, 1968. Mem. Am. Psychol. Assn. (assoc.), Nat. Registry Health Care Providers, AAAS, Rio Grande Writers Assn., Phi Beta Kappa, Phi Kappa Phi. Home: 713 Manzano St NE Albuquerque NM 87110 Office: 406 San Mateo Blvd NE Suite 8-B Albuquerque NM 87106

GIORDANO, JUDITH LUCIA, publishing exec.; b. Bronx, N.Y., Feb. 11, 1954; d. Joseph Francesco and Elida Felicia (Buccino) G.; B.A. in Archaeology and Anthropology, Friends World Coll., 1976. Student archaeologist, Kyoto (Japan) Govt., 1973-74; free lance archaeologist, Rome, Italy, 1974-77; circulation clk. Natural History Mag., Am. Mus. Natural History, N.Y.C., 1978-79, fulfillment mgr., 1979-80; asst. circulation mgr. Bill Communications, N.Y.C., 1980, circulation mgr., 1981, dir. circulation plastics/chem. div., 1981—; free lance cons. direct mail and circulation fulfillment. Recipient public service award Asahi Shimbun, Japan, 1974. Mem. Nat. Assn. Female Execs., Am. Bus. Press, Women in Communications, Fulfillment Mgr. Assn., Nat. Bus. Circulation Assn. Office: Bill Communications 633 3d Ave New York NY 10017

GIRION, BARBARA MICHELLE, author; b. N.Y.C., Nov. 20, 1937; d. Samuel and Blanche Belle (Taub) Warren; B.A., Montclair (N.J.) State Coll., 1958; m. Heywood Jay Girion, Nov. 27, 1957; children—Jeffrey, Eric, Laurie. Jr. high sch. tchr., Hillside, N.J., 1959-63; free-lance writer, journalist; contbr. to children's mags.; author children's books: The Boy with the Special Face, 1978, Joshua, The Czar and the Chicken Bone Wish, 1978, A Tangle of Roots (a Best Book of 1979 ALA; Kenneth B. Smilen/Present Tense Lit. award), 1979, Misty and Me, 1979, Like Everybody Else, 1980, A Handful of Stars, 1981; lectr. Hofstra U., summers 1976, 78, 79, U. R.I., summer 1980, 81. Trustee YM-YWHA Met. N.J., 1973-78, The Jewish News, 1976—, Jewish Edn. Assn., 1973-76; v.p. edn. women's div. Jewish Community Fedn., 1974-78; mem. Council Jewish Fedns. and Welfare Funds, 1973-78. Recipient Nat. Young Leadership award Council Jewish Fedns. and Welfare Funds, 1973. Mem. Soc. Children's Book Writers. Home: 25 Wildwood Dr Short Hills NJ 07078

GIRLING, BETTIE JOYCE MOORE, home health exec.; b. Midlothian, Tex., Feb. 10, 1930; d. Robert and Florence Irene (Shaw) Moore; B.S. in Edn., Daniel Baker Coll., 1952; M.S.S.W., U. Tex., Austin, 1956; m. Robert George William Girling, III, Sept. 2, 1960; children—Robert George William V, Maria Julia Anastasia, Samuel Marcus Shaw, Katherine Susan Jane. Tchr., Clairemont (Tex.) Ind. Sch. Dist., 1952-53;

caseworker Tex. Dept. Public Welfare, 1953-57, licensing supr., Dallas, 1960; caseworker Austin State Sch. for Mentally Retarded, 1957-60; with adoption intake Edna Gladney Home, Ft. Worth, 1961-65; researcher Child Welfare League Am., N.Y.C., 1966; organizer, exec. dir. Girling Home Care, Austin, 1967-69; asst. dir. agy. programs Girling & Assos. Home Health Services, Inc., Austin and Central Tex., 1969—, also dir.; owner, operator child care facility, 1973-75; organizer, condr. profl. workshops; dir. Girling Hospices of Austin, San Antonio, Brownwood, Abilene, Ft. Worth, Houston and Corpus Christi. Mem. Nat. Assn. Social Workers, Tex. Hosp. Assn., Tex. Home Health Assn., Nat. Hospice Orgn., Nat. Assn. Home Health Agys. Democrat. Baptist. Home: 2608 Pembrook Trail Austin TX 78731 Office: 4902 Grover Ave Austin TX 78756

GIROD, JUDY, interior design firm exec.; b. Alexandria, La., Aug. 24, 1948; d. John James and Lily (McKnight) Capdevielle; B.F.A. in Interior Design, La. State U., 1971; m. Jerold S. Girod, Aug. 22, 1970. Interior designer Dowles Inc., 1970-72; interior designer, mgr. dept. Clyde W. Smith Co., 1972-75; interior designer Blitch Architects, 1975-79; owner, pres. Judy Girod Interior Design Inc. (now Judy Girod Design Group), New Orleans and Lafayette, La., 1979—. Bd. dirs. Coliseum Sq. Assn., 1980—, St. Charles Ave. Bus. Assn., 1982. Mem. La. State U. Alumni Assn. (dir. Greater New Orleans Met. chpt. 1979-80), Am. Soc. Interior Designers (pres. La. dist. chpt. 1982), Inst. Bus. Designers, Delta Zeta. Republican. Roman Catholic. Clubs: Spring Fiesta Assn., La. Landmarks. Contbr. series on interior design to Gambit Mag. Home: 1402 Magazine St New Orleans LA 70130 Office: 1070 Saint Charles Ave New Orleans LA 70130

GIRONE, JOAN CHRISTINE CRUSE, county ofcl.; b. Kingston, Ont., Can., Aug. 30, 1927; naturalized U.S. citizen; d. Arthur William and Helen Wilson Cruse; m. Joseph Michael Girone, June 26, 1954; children—Susan, Richard, William. Buyer, Franklin Simon, Inc., N.Y.C., 1946-54; supr. Midlothian dist. Chesterfield County (Va.) Bd. Suprs., 1976—, vice chmn., 1982—; Founding mem. Capitol Area Agy. on Aging, 1973—; commr., sec. Richmond (Va.) Regional Planning Dist. Commn., 1976—; chmn. community edn. adv. com. Va. Bd. of Edn., 1972-79; mem. Va. Gov.'s Adv. Bd. on Aging, 1980—; chmn. Richmond Met. Transp. Planning Orgn., 1981—; bd. visitors Va. State U.; chmn. Chesterfield County Com. to elect John Warner Republican Senator, 1979; Chesterfield chmn. Marshall Coleman for Gov., 1981—. Club: Huguenot Republican Woman's. Home: 2609 Dovershire Rd Bon Air VA 23235

GIRONELLA, OLIVA CARINO, psychologist; b. Manila, Philippines, Aug. 1, 1934; d. Francisco Alambat and Clara Madamba (Palafox) Carino; B.A. cum laude (coll. scholar), U. Philippines, 1955; M.A., U. Nebr., 1956, Ph.D. (tuition fellow), 1959; m. Hilarion Gironella, June 4, 1960; children—Ninette Aileen, Claire Ann, Stephen Karl, Bryan Clive. Clin. intern, psychometrist U. Counseling Service, U. Nebr., 1958-59; staff counselor U. Student Counseling, U. Wis., 1959-61, instr. U. Extension Div., 1960-61; pvt. practice psychology Western Psychol. Services, Madison, Wis., 1960-61; child psychologist Central Wis. Colony and Tng. Sch., Madison, 1960-61; staff psychologist unit for emotionally disturbed children U. Hosp., Edmonton, Alta., Can., 1961-62; dir. psychol. services Alta. Alcoholism and Drug Abuse Commn., Edmonton, 1962-71; cons. for psychol. services Alta. Sch. for Deaf, Edmonton, 1971-81; prof. dept. psychology U. Alta., Edmonton, 1969—; pvt. practice psychology Oliva Carino Psychol. Services, Ltd., Edmonton, 1976—; conf. coordinator 1st Can. Symposium on Mental Health and Hearing Impairment, 1980—. Mem. Am. Psychol. Assn., Psychologists Assn. Alta. (chmn. standards and qualifications com. 1980—), Phi Kappa Phi, Pi Gamma Mu, Psi Chi, Pi Lambda Theta, Sigma Delta Epsilon. Club: Faculty of Univ. Alta. Home: 15103 Rio Terrace Dr Edmonton AB T5R 5M6 Canada Office: Psychology Dept Biol Scis Bldg U Alta Edmonton AB T6G 2E1 Canada

GIRTH, MARJORIE LOUISA, lawyer, educator; b. Trenton, N.J., Apr. 21, 1939; d. Harold Brookman and Marjorie Mathilda (Simonson) Girth; A.B., Mt. Holyoke Coll., 1959; LL.B., Harvard U., 1962. Admitted to N.J. bar, 1963, N.Y. bar, 1976, U.S. Supreme Ct. bar, 1969; pvt. practice, Trenton, 1963-65; research asso. Brookings Instn., 1965-70; asso. prof. law SUNY Law Sch., Buffalo, 1971-79, prof., 1979—; vis. prof. U. Va. Law Sch., 1979-80. Bd. dirs. Buffalo and Erie County YWCA, 1972-76, Buffalo Unitarian Universalist Ch., 1981—; mem. commn. peace, justice and human rights Internat. Assn. Religious Freedom, 1976-79. Mem. Am. (chmn. bankruptcy law com. 1980-82, exec. com. banking, corp., bus. sect. 1981—), N.Y. (mem. bus. law com. 1977—), Erie County bar assns., Law and Soc. Assn. (trustee 1976-77), Mt. Holyoke Alumnae Assn. (Centennial award 1972). Author: Poor People's Lawyers, 1976; Bankruptcy Options for the Consumer Debtor, 1981; co-author: Bankruptcy: Problem, Process, Reform, 1971. Office: O'Brian Hall SUNY North Campus Buffalo NY 14260

GIRTON, LYDA GENE, psychologist; b. Lafayette, Ind., July 28, 1946; d. Charles Harold Girton and Virginia Irene (Sheek) Girton Schneider; B.S., Ind. U., 1968, M.S., 1971, Ed.D. (fellow), 1973; postgrad. UCLA, U. Calif., Irvine; m. H. Marshall Goldsmith, July 20, 1974; children—Kelly Ann, Bryan Christopher. Tchr. English, Frankfort (Ind.) Sr. High Sch., 1968-70; tchr., research asst. Ind. U., 1970-73; psychol. counselor Loyola Marymount U. Counseling Center, Los Angeles, 1973-75, asst. dir. counseling services, 1975-77, dir. counseling services, 1977-81; sr. partner Human Systems Devel., Inc., 1979—; pvt. practice marriage, family and child counseling, 1976—, as psychologist, 1980—; lectr., cons. Recipient Outstanding Service award Loyola Marymount U. Student Body, 1975. Mem. Am. Personnel and Guidance Assn., Am. Psychol. Assn., Am. Coll. Personnel Assn., Nat. Assn. Student Personnel Adminstrs., Calif. Assn. Marriage, Family and Child Therapists, Calif. Women in Higher Edn., Western Psychol. Assn., Ind. U. Alumni Assn. (life), Pi Lambda Theta, Zeta Tau Alpha. Contbr. articles to profl. jours. Home: 5505 Soledad Rd La Jolla CA 92037 Office: 1298 Prospect St La Jolla CA 92037

GISH, LILLIAN, actress; b. Springfield, Ohio; d. James Lee and Mary (Robinson) Gishi; A.F.D., Rollins Coll.; H.H.D., Mt. Holyoke Coll.; D.F.A. (hon.), Bowling Green State U., 1976, Middlebury Coll. Debut on stage at 5; appeared in motion pictures, 1913—, including Birth of a Nation, Hearts of the World, Borken Blossoms, Way Down East, Orphans of the Storm, Scarlet Letter, Annie Laurie, The Wind, The Enemy, Night of the Hunter, The Cobweb, Miss Susie Slagle's, Duel in the Sun, Portrait of Jennie, Orders to Kill, The Unforgiven, 1960, Follow Me Boys, 1966, The Comedians, 1967, La Boheme, A Wedding, 1978, (TV) Thin Ice, 1980; movies made in Italy: The White Sister, Romola; appeared in the theatre, 1930—, plays include Uncle Vanya, Camille, 9 Pine Street, Within the Gates, Ophelia in Hamlet, Star Wagon, Life with Father, The Marquise, Legend of Leonara, Crime and Punishment, 1948, title role in Miss Mabel, 1950, The Curious Savage, 1950, The Trip to Bountiful, Portrait of a Madonna, The Wreck of the 5:25, The Family Reunion, (Pulitzer Prize play) All the Way Home, 1960-61, nurse in Romeo and Juliet, 1965, Anya, 1966, I Never Sang for My Father, 1967, 68, Too True To Be Good, 1963, A Passage to India, 1963, Uncle Vanya, 1973, A Musical Jubilee, 1975; also many TV plays including Twin Detectives, 1976, Sparrow, 1977. Toured Europe, Russia as lectr. on art films, 1969, 71-72, U.S.A., 1969-73; Royal Command appearance Queen Elizabeth the Queen Mothers, 1980. Recipient hon. Acad. Award, 1971; Handel medallion, City of N.Y., 1973. Author: The Movies, Mr. Griffith and Me, 1969; Dorothy and Lillian Gish, 1973. Address: 430 E 57th St New York NY 10022 *

GITT-EDWARDS, PATRICIA E., communications co. exec.; b. N.Y.C., Mar. 8, 1941; d. Michael A. and Cornelia K. (Cunn) Gitt; B.S. in Home Econs., U. Vt., 1962; M.B.A. in Mktg., Fordham U., 1980; m. Lee A. Edwards, Nov. 1, 1981. Acct. exec. The Rowland Co., Inc., 1968-71; account exec. Hill & Knowlton, Inc., N.Y.C., 1973-75; mgr. communications Life Savers, Inc., N.Y.C., 1976-80; owner, mgr. Patricia Gitt Co., N.Y.C., 1980—. Mem. Am. Women in Radio and TV (tres. N.Y.C. chpt. 1981-83). Office: 305 E 24th St New York NY 10010

GITTELL, MARILYN, polit. scientist, educator; b. N.Y.C., Apr. 3, 1931; d. Julius and Rose (Meyerson) Jacobs; B.A., Bklyn. Coll., 1952; M.P.A., N.Y. U., 1953, Ph.D., 1960; m. Irwin Gittell, Aug. 20, 1950; children—Amy, Ross. Instr. polit. sci. Queens Coll., CUNY, 1960-62, asst. prof., 1962-65, asso. prof., 1965-67, prof., 1967-71, prof. urban studies, 1971-73, dir. Inst. Community Studies, 1967-73, chmn. dept. urban studies, 1971-73; prof. polit. sci. Bklyn. Coll., CUNY, 1973-78, asst. v.p. and asso. provost, 1973-78; prof. polit. sci. Grad. Center, CUNY, 1978—; cons. N.J. Dept. Higher Edn., Ford Found., Nat. Inst. Edn., UN. Mem. adv. bd. P.R. Research Center, Washington, 1971-75; mem. Queens Lay Advocate Service, 1972—; mem. community com. Met. Mus. Art, 1971—; mem. planning com. White House Conf. Children and Youth, 1970; mem. asso. task force on manpower U.S. Dept. Labor, 1970-74; mem. Nat. Study Commn. Undergrad. Edn. and Tchr. Edn., N.Y. State Regent Com. on Exams.; trustee Interface; mem. N.Y. State adv. com. Resource Center for Women; mem. Middle States evaluation teams Lafayette Coll., Inter-Am. U., U. P.R. Tax Found. fellow. Mem. Phi Beta Kappa. Author: Local Control in Education, 1972; (with Fantini) Decentralization: Achieving Reform, 1973; School Boards and School Policy, 1973; (with Cook and Mack) City Life: A Documentary History of the American City, 1973; What Was It Like: When Your Grandparents Were Your Age, 1976; Limits to Participation: The Decline of Community Organizations, 1980. Office: 33 W 42d St New York NY 10036

GITTLER, CAROL SPEAR, real estate broker; b. Chgo., Aug. 13, 1940; d. Louis L. and Esther (Katz) Spear; B.A., Roosevelt U., Chgo., 1978; m. Marvin Gittler, July 9, 1960; children—Michelle, Caryn, Susan, Mandy, Debra. Engaged in real estate, 1975—; real estate researcher U. Chgo., 1976-77; sec. Forus Investment Corp., Chgo., 1978—; pres. C.A.T.S. Realty, Chgo., 1980—. Mem. 5th Ward Citizens Com., Chgo., 1975—; bd. dirs. Hyde Park Community Conf., Chgo., 1981; cons. to Rep. Carol Braun, 1978—. Mem. Nat. Assn. Realtors, Hyde Park Hist. Soc., Franklin Honor Soc. Jewish. Home: 5458 Hyde Park Blvd Chicago IL 60615 also 10332 Ward Ave Union Pier MI 49129 Office: 120 W Madison St Chicago IL 60602

GIUFFRE, MARY MARGARET, educator; b. Burlington, Vt., July 11, 1945; d. Joseph J. and Courana (Le Clerc) Bishop; B.S., Trinity Coll., 1967; M.Ed., U. Vt., 1976; postgrad. U. Vt., 1980-82; m. Martin J. Giuffre, July 29, 1968; children—James, Rebecca. Faculty, Champlain Valley Union High Sch., Hinesburg, Vt., 1967-69; instr. to asst. prof. Trinity Coll., Burlington, Vt., 1970-78, chmn. Dept. Bus., 1976-78; asst. prof. dept. bus. and econs. St. Michael's Coll., Winooski, Vt., 1978—; cons. curriculum Vt. State Colls., 1981—, mem. standing com. exptl. learning, 1978-81. Mem. citizens adv. com. South Burlington Sch. System, 1975-76; mem. Vt. Diocesan Ecumenical Commn., 1974-77. Kappa Gamma Pi scholar, 1966. Home: 34 Sunset Ave South Burlington VT 05401 Office: 118 Sullivan Hall Saint Michaels Coll Winooski VT 05404

GIUFFRE, VIRGINIA M., banker; b. N.Y.C., Mar. 28, 1945; d. John M. and Mary J. (McLoughlin) McGovern; B.A., Coll. White Plains of Pace U., 1966; m. Joel G. Giuffre, Dec. 10, 1972. Mgmt. trainee Citicorp. Fin. Div., N.Y.C., 1970-73, data processing projects Services Mgmt. Group, 1975-77, asst. v.p. Personnel Group, 1977-78, v.p., dir. subs. Thrift Resources, Inc., 1978-82, dir. mktg. devel. and strategic planning Citicorp. Remittance Service, 1982—. Mem. Fin. Woman's Assn., NOW. Office: 425 Park Ave York NY 10043

GIVAN, DOROTHY MAE, educator; b. St. Louis; d. John William and Stella Marie (Pietsch) G.; B.S., Central Mo. State Coll., 1950, B.S. in Edn., 1951; M.Ed., St. Louis U., 1963, postgrad. summer 1964. Recreation supr. St. Louis State Tng. Sch., summers 1950-54; tchr. Spl. Sch. Dist. St. Louis, 1961-63; recreation supr. Dept. Army Spl. Services, Europe, 1954-61; tchr. mentally retarded, Oakland, Calif., 1961-64; tchr. orthopedically, multiple handicapped, Oakland, 1964—; house mother, facilities supr. Family Living Project - Cerebral Palsied, summer 1968, asst. dir. Family Living Project-Cerebral Palsied, 1969. Mem. Council Exceptional Children, NEA, Calif. Tchrs. Assn., Oakland Tchrs. Assn., East Bay Dachshund Club (treas. 1978-79), No. Calif. Dachshund Club, Alpha Delta Kappa. Home: 3368 Victoria Ave Lafayette CA 94549 Office: 3031 E 18th St Oakland CA 94601

GIVEN, MARIAN ZORK, guidance center exec.; b. El Paso, Tex., Oct. 1, 1923; d. Luis and Ruth (Schwartz) Zork; B.A., Mills Coll., 1945; M.A., Columbia U. Tchrs. Coll., 1946; M.Ed., U. Tex., El Paso, 1973; m. Robert H. Given, Oct. 26, 1946; children—Barbara, Tom. Psychol. asso. El Paso Guidance Center, 1973—, exec. dir., 1981—, pres., 1963. Pres., El Paso Family Services, 1967-69, El Paso council Nat. Council Jewish Women, 1955-56, White Sch. PTA, 1962, Morehead PTA, 1965; v.p. El Paso Sun Carnival, 1961; chmn. bd. trustees El Paso Mental Health-Mental Retardation Center, 1968-71; bd. dirs. El Paso Housing Authority, 1975-78; trustee Bridges Sch., 1980—; co-chmn. United Fund Planning, 1962-64. Mem. Am. Psychol. Assn., Tex. Psychol. Assn., Delta Kappa Gamma. Jewish. Home: 4935 Meadowlark El Paso TX 79922 Office: 1501 N Mesa St El Paso TX 79902

GIVNISH, MEG, psychodramatist; b. Phila., 1939; B.A. in Speech and Drama, Chestnut Hill Coll., Phila., 1961; postgrad. U. Del., 1962-64; cert. psychodrama, Moreno Inst., Beacon, N.Y., 1971; M.A. in Humanities, Beaver Coll., Glenside, Pa., 1981. Clin. dir. psychodrama dept. Horsham Clinic, Ambler, Pa., 1974—; exec. dir. Acad. Psychodrama and Sociometry, Ambler, 1977—; dir., founder Problem Solving Theatre, Ambler, 1980—; pres. Moreno Inst./Acad. Psychodrama, 1982—; editor Beacon House, Inc., Pubs., 1981—; cons. in field, 1969—. Fellow Am. Soc. Group Psychotherapy and Psychodrama (exec. coucil 1980—); mem. Fedn. Trainers and Tng. Programs in Psychodrama (membership chmn. 1978-79), Phi Sigma Tau, Kappa Delta Pi. Author papers in field. Address: Acad Psychodrama and Sociometry Welsh Rd and Butler Pike Ambler PA 19002

GLAD, BEVERLY JOYCE, librarian; b. Washington, Pa., Apr. 7, 1941; d. John Robinson and Rose Alma (Smith) Smithson; A.B., Lycoming (Pa.) Coll., 1963; M.L.S., Emory U., 1965; divorced. Cyrillic serials librarian Columbia U., 1966-69; librarian Stone & Webster Securities Corp., N.Y.C., 1969-74; dir. research Boyden Assos., N.Y.C., 1974-75; head librarian Salomon Bros., Inc., N.Y.C., 1975-78, v.p., library mgr., 1978—; cons., lectr. in field. Fellow Slavic and E. European Inst., Ind. U., 1963-64; grantee U. Colo.-Kans. U., 1963, Ind. U., 1964. Mem. Spl. Libraries Assn., ALA, Assoc. Info. Mgrs., Am. Soc. Info. Sci., Citizens Exchange Council. Editor: Fin. News Checklist, 1976—, New Bus. Publns., 1976—, Investment Banking Subject Headings, 1975—, Library News, 1982—. Home: 160 Columbia Heights Brooklyn Heights NY 11201 Office: 1 New York Plaza New York NY 10004

GLADSTEIN, BARBARA ABRAMS, psychologist; b. Chgo., July 30, 1930; d. Benjamin and Rose Leona (Mostow) Abrams; B.Ed., Nat. Coll., 1951; M.Ed., U. Rochester, 1972, Ed.D., 1979; m. Gerald Allen Gladstein, Aug. 16, 1951; children—Richard, Deborah, Rose, Laura. Tchr., Avon, Conn., 1951-54; psychologist Webster (N.Y.) Schs., 1973-75; lectr. U. Rochester (N.Y.), 1975-77; research coordinator Holcomb Learning Center, SUNY, Geneseo, 1977-79; psychologist Monroe Devel. Center, Rochester, 1979-81, Bloomfield Schs., East Bloomfield, N.Y., 1981—; pvt. practice psycho-ednl. counseling, Rochester, 1979—; people-to-people psychology del. to Peoples Republic of China, 1982. Mem. Am. Psychol. Assn., Assn. Advancement of Behavior Therapy, Genesee Valley Psychol. Assn., Tri-county Counselors Assn. Jewish. Home: 204 Oakdale St Rochester NY 14618

GLANSTEIN, PHYLLIS JOY, fin. planning cons.; b. Jersey City, May 22, 1945; d. Harry and Katherine G.; B.A., U. Rochester, 1967; M.S., So. Ill. U., 1970; Ph.D., U. Conn., 1975. Employment counselor Mich. Employment Security Commn., 1967-68; counselor So. Ill. U., Carbondale, 1968-70; dir. student personnel U. Conn., Storrs, 1970-72; cons. Aetna Life Ins. Co., Hartford, 1973; mgr. human resources Conn. Mut. Life Ins. Co., Hartford, 1973-79, agt., supr., Orange, Calif., 1979-80; pres. Planning Concepts, fin. planning cons. firm., 1980—. Mem. adj. faculty U. Hartford, 1975-77. Recipient Leadership award Hartford YWCA, 1978. Mem. Orange County Life Underwriters Assn., Am. Psychol. Assn., Assn. Profl. Cons., NOW. Office: 500 City Pkwy W Suite 100 Orange CA 92668

GLASER, BARBARA LOIS, social worker; b. Boston, Mar. 19, 1929; d. Richard and Miriam LeVine; student Bates Coll., 1946-48; B.A., Syracuse U., 1950; M.S.S., Bryn Mawr Coll., 1969; postgrad. Case Western Res. U., 1974, U. Chgo., 1977, 78; m. Anthony J. Glaser, June 18, 1950; 1 dau., Terry Glaser Bieri. Program dir. YWCA, Syracuse, N.Y., 1960-63; dir. Helpmate Vol. Bur. for Elderly, Phila., 1964-66; asst. dir. Foster Grandparents, Phila., 1966, acting dir., 1967; social worker Public Child Welfare, Media and Washington, Pa., 1969-71; dist. supr. Children's Home Soc. Va., Arlington, 1971-73; chief Bur. Child, Family, Adult Service, Arlington, 1973-76; dir. social service div. Dept. Human Resources, County of Arlington, 1976—; mem. Gov.'s Conf. on Aging, 1979; adv. bd. HEW Study of Domestic Violence, 1980. Mem. Acad. Cert. Social Workers, Nat. Assn. Social Workers, Am. Public Welfare Assn., Va. League Social Service Execs., Va. Conf. Social Welfare, Nat. Council Refugee Resettlement, Va. Refugee Council. Contbr. to The Field of Social Work. Home: 9512 Kingsley Ave Bethesda MD 20814 Office: PO Box 7266 Arlington VA 22207

GLASER, CAROL GROVEMAN, therapist; b. Bronx, N.Y., June 30, 1949; d. M. Arnold and Margaret (Moskowitz) Groveman; B.A., City U. N.Y., 1971; M.A., Calif. Sch. Profl. Psychology, 1977, Ph.D., 1979; m. Donald Howard Glaser, Aug. 5, 1979. Tchr. public schs., Bronx, N.Y., 1971-73; ednl. coordinator, tchr. Southwood Mental Health Center, Chula Vista, Calif., 1973-75; pvt. practice psychotherapy, San Diego, 1978—. Mem. Am. Psychol. Assn., Calif. Psychol. Assn., Acad. San Diego Psychologists (asso.). Office: 2423 Camino Del Rio S Suite 111 San Diego CA 92108

GLASGOW, MARIAN KATZEN, educator; b. Pa., July 27, 1941; d. Harry and Margaret Cecelia (Gordon) Katzen; B.S., Brandeis U., 1963; postgrad. U. Chgo. Sch. Social Service Adminstrn., 1963-64; M.S.W., Columbia U., 1965; m. Arthur H. Glasgow, June 21, 1964; children—Adam, Jason, Sarah. Psychotherapist, Residential Treatment Ctr., Rochester, N.Y., 1965-67; counselor, supr. Community Sex Info., Brookline, Mass., 1972-73; asst. prof. human sexuality Med. Sch., Boston U., 1974—, dir. human sexuality teaching program, 1979—; cons. schs., social agys. Mem. Am. Assn. Sex Educators, Counselors and Therapists, Soc. Sci. Study Sex, Child Study Assn. Mass., Am. Pub. Health Assn. Jewish. Contbr. articles to profl. jours. Office: Med Sch Boston U 80 E Concord St Boston MA 02118

GLASGOW, NORMA FOREMAN, state ednl. ofcl.; b. Hollis, Okla., Nov. 3, 1927; d. Edd Terell and Ruby (Battles) Holly; B.S. in Edn., Southwestern Okla. State Coll., 1947; M.S. in Edn., U. So. Calif., 1951; Ph.D. in Communication (Emmett Walters grad. fellow 1968-70, Ida N. Scharff scholar 1970-71), U. Tex., Austin, 1971; m. Maurice J. Foreman, Feb. 13, 1953 (dec. 1958); children—Kim Alan, Kerry Joan Foreman Bellomy; m. 2d, Keith W. Glasgow, Aug. 9, 1980. Project adminstr. Ednl. Testing Service, Los Angeles, 1947-50; asst. to prodn. mgr. Pacific Press, Inc., Los Angeles, 1950-52; partner farming and cattle operation, Kalamazoo, 1952-58; instr. journalism public schs. in Mich., Okla. and Tex., 1958-64, West Tex. State U., Canyon, 1964-67; communications specialist S.W. Ednl. Devel. Lab., Austin, Tex., 1967-70; asst. to commr. higher edn., coordinating bd. Tex. Coll. and Univ. System, Austin, 1971-77, head sr. coll. and univs. div., 1977-80, asst. commr. for sr. coll. and univ., 1980-81; commr. higher edn. State of Conn., 1981—; mem. ednl. adv. com. Gov. Tex. Commn. Status Women, 1977-78; chmn. Tex. Adv. Com. Faculty Workloads, 1977-78; chmn. planning com., nat. leadership seminar State Chief Acad. Program Officers, 1980; chmn. Tex. Bilingual Edn. Adminstrs. Conf., 1978; mem. Tex. planning com., nat. identification program women higher edn. adminstrn. Am. Council Edn., 1979-81; bd. dirs. Conn. Student Loan Assn., 1981—; adv. bd. Conn. Edn. Policy Seminar, 1981—; mem. Conn. State Council on Edn. for Employment, 1981—, Conn. State Occupational Info. Coordinating Com., 1981—; cons. in field. Newspaper Fund fellow, summer 1964. State Higher Edn. Exec. Officers Assn., Edn. Commn. of States, Kappa Tau Alpha, Phi Kappa Phi. Democrat. Editor reports in field. Office: 61 Woodland St Hartford CT 06105

GLASIER, JOAN LARSON, audiologist, educator; b. Salem, Mass., Feb. 10, 1949; d. Lawrence Nicholas and Mary Jane (DeCoulos) L.; B.A., Salem State Coll., 1971; M.Ed., Smith Coll., 1972; postgrad. Northeastern U., 1973-77; m. James Crocker Glasier, 1975 (div. 1978). Tchr. Beverly (Mass.) Sch. for the Deaf, 1972-75; clinic dir. Hearing and Speech Center Beverly Hosp., 1973-75; speech lang. and hearing cons. Developmental Sch. for N. Shore, Inc., United Cerebral Palsy Assn. N. Shore, Peabody, Mass., 1977; audiologist Gracewood (Ga.) State Sch. and Hosp., 1977-78; audiologist, tchr. Neuroassessment Center, Napa State Hosp., Imola, Calif., 1979—; tchr. Napa Valley (Calif.) Coll., 1980—; cons. in field. Lic. in audiology, Calif. Mem. Am. Speech Lang. and Hearing Assn. (cert. clin. competency), Calif. Speech Lang. and Hearing Assn., Council Exceptional Children, Computer Users in Edn., Am. Acoustical Soc., Alexander Graham Bell Assn., Conv. Am. Instrs. for Deaf. Author: Introduction to Neuropsychology for the Clinician, 1981. Home: PO Box 7217 Napa CA 94558 Office: Neuroassessment Center Napa State Hospital Box A Imola CA 94558

GLASS, ELIZABETH MAYLON, edn. cons.; b. Hartford, Conn., Aug. 24, 1922; d. Robert Anderson and Marion Gibson (Low) G.; student Hartford Coll. for Women, 1940-41; B.S., U. Conn., 1944, M.S., 1951. Tchr. math. and sci. Newington (Conn.) Jr./Sr. High Sch., 1945-50, Litchfield (Conn.) Jr./Sr. High Sch., 1951-52; asso. prof. math. edn. SUNY, Albany, 1952-62; edn. cons. Conn. Dept. Edn., 1965—; part-time faculty St. Rose Coll., Albany, Central Conn. State Coll., Eastern Conn. State Coll. Mem. Westbrook (Conn.) Zoning Commn. NSF fellow. Mem. Nat. Council Tchrs. of Math., Assn. State Suprs. of Math., Conn. Assn. Sch. Supts., U. Conn. Alumni Assn., Phi Delta Kappa. Republican. Author 5 math. textbooks, numerous articles. Home: 369 Linnmoore Hartford CT 06106 Office: PO Box 2219 Hartford CT 06115

GLASS, JODI LYNN, audiologist, feminist activist; b. Bklyn., May 13, 1953; d. Joseph Hillard and Corinne (Bernstein) G.; B.A. in Audiology, SUNY, Buffalo, 1975; M.A. in Audiology, Hofstra U., 1976. Ednl. audiologist Learning Center for Deaf Children, Framingham, Mass., 1976-78, Wrentham (Mass.) State Sch., 1976-78, Meeting Street Sch., East Providence, 1978—; ednl. cons., equal edn. opportunity R.I. Dept. Edn.; ednl. cons., fed. programs Providence Dept. Edn.; mem. edn. subcom. R.I. Adv. Commn. on Women. Coordinator, R.I. Women Against Violence Against Women; founder Feminist Resources Unltd. Mem. Am. Speech-Lang. and Hearing Assn. (cert.; com. equality of sexes), Alexander Graham Bell Assn. (R.I. coordinator children's rights group), Women's Liberation Union (program dir.), NOW (program dir.), LWV, Women's Polit. Caucus, R.I. Citizens for Equality in Lang. (founder). Home: 264 Doyle Ave Providence RI 02906 Office: Meeting Street Sch 667 Waterman Ave East Providence RI 02914

GLASS, MARGARET SMYLLIE, lawyer; b. Hartford, Conn., Dec. 20, 1946; d. Robert Henderson and Dorothy Lee (Jones) Smellie; B.A., Mount Holyoke Coll., 1971; J.D., Hastings Coll. Law, U. Calif., San Francisco, 1975; M.B.A., Duke U., 1980; m. J. Carter Glass, Apr. 9, 1976. Admitted to Calif. bar, 1975, N.C. bar, 1976; v.p. asst. counsel Cameron-Brown Co. subs. First Union Corp., Raleigh, N.C., 1976-79; v.p., counsel Davidson & Jones Corp., Raleigh, 1979-82; asso. gen. counsel Carolina Power & Light Co., Raleigh, 1982—; seminar speaker Mortgage Bankers Assn. Am., 1977; mgmt. game bd. dirs. Fuqua Sch. Bus., Duke U., Durham, N.C., 1981-82. Mem. Am. Bar Assn., N.C. Bar Assn. (mem. corporate counsel com.), Wake County Bar Assn. Democrat. Presbyterian. Home: 3004 Upland Circle Raleigh NC 27607 Office: PO Box 1551 411 Fayetteville St Raleigh NC 27602

GLASS, WENDY DAVIS, art dealer; b. N.Y.C., Aug. 28, 1925; d. Aaron Wise and Helen Miller (Obstler) Davis; B.A., Bard Coll., 1948; children—Robin, Tim. Group worker with children Greenwich House, 1948, Mus. Modern Art, N.Y.C., 1958; owner, dir. Glass Gallery, N.Y.C., 1960—. Campaign worker Democratic candidates. Mem. Antiques Appraisers Assn. (registered), N.Y. Am. Women's Bus. Assn., Ukiyo-e Soc., Japan. Soc. Jewish. Address: 315 Central Park W Apt 8W New York NY 10025

GLASSCOCK, LOIS ANN, coal co. exec.; b. Vansant, Va., Mar. 15, 1945; d. Joe W. and Frankie M. Street; ed. Grundy (Va.) public schs., McClains Bus. Sch.; 1 son, Frank D., Jr. Acct., Orvis Kemp, C.P.A., 1966-67, Dent K. Burke Assos., C.P.A.s, 1968-71; successively acct., asst. controller, controller, v.p. fin., sr. v.p. fin. United Coal Co., Bristol, Va., 1971—; dir. Bank of Va., Bristol. Bd. dirs. Theatre Bristol, Bristol Meml. Hosp. Baptist. Office: PO Box 1280 Bristol VA 24203

GLASSE, LOU, state agency ofcl.; b. Marlow, Okla., Apr. 18, 1927; d. John Andrew and Elsie Vivien (Ward) Howard; B.A. in Social Work, U. Okla., 1949; M.S.W. in Social Casework, U. Conn., 1959; m. John Howell Glasse, June 16, 1950; children—Jeffrey Howell, Paulding Howard. Family counselor Dutchess County (N.Y.) Family Counseling Service, 1965-69, family adv. coordinator, 1970-73; dir. Dutchess County Office for Aging, 1973-76; now dir. N.Y. State Office for Aging, Albany, 1976—; chmn. N.Y. del., dep. dir. for policy White House Conf. on Aging, 1981; mem. N.Y. State Health Planning Commn.; mem. N.Y. State Crime Control Planning Bd.; mem. N.Y. State Gov.'s Council on Handicapped and Domestic Violence Task Force; past pres. Nat. Assn. State Units on Aging; mem. study commn. on alcoholism and aging Nat. Council on Alcoholism; adv. bd. Gerontol. Research Inst. Chmn. human relations com. Dutchess County Council Chs., 1962-64; mem. Dutchess County council State Commn. Human Rights, 1963-69; chmn. Dutchess Democratic Party Issues Com., 1970-73; adv. council Policy Center on Income Maintenance, Heller Sch., Brandeis U. Recipient Margaret Elden Rich Meml. award Nat. Family Service Assn., 1973. Mem. Nat. Council Aging, Nat. Assn. Social Workers (Social Worker of Yr. 1976), Acad. Cert. Social Workers (Social Worker of Yr. N.Y. State chpt. 1982). Presbyterian. Office: Agency Bldg 2 Empire State Plaza Albany NY 12223

GLASSER, KAY ELBAUM, civic worker; b. Lawrence, Mass., July 24, 1918; d. Samuel and Anna Karass; B.A. magna cum laude, Radcliffe Coll., 1940; M.S.W., Simmons Coll., 1956; Ph.D., Brandeis U., 1967; m. Joshua B. Glasser, Nov. 22, 1972. Mental health educator Mass. Dept. Mental Health, 1956-62; asso. prof. social work U. Denver, 1967-73; mem. Sarasota County (Fla.) Sch. Bd., 1978—, now vice chmn.; past mentor Eckerd Coll. Program Experienced Learners; citizens adv. bd. St. Armand's Banking Center, S.E. 1st Nat. Bank of Sarasota. Chmn. planning council United Way of Sarasota; trustee, sec. New Coll. Found.; bd. dirs. Taxpayers Assn. Saratota County, Sarasota County Civic League, 1977-78, United Way Found., 1980—; formerly active Mass. Republican Party; former mem. Newton (Mass.) Bd. Public Welfare; former vice chmn. Newton Rep. City Com.; mem. LWV, former v.p. Newton; bd. dirs. Community Coalition for Families, Sarasota County Informed Parents, L.I.F.E., Asolo Theatre Festival Assn.; mem. Property Adjustment Appraisal Bd.; mem. Fla. Adv. Council on Global Edn.; mem. task force on global edn. Nat. Sch. Bds. Assn. Mem. Acad. Cert. Social Workers, Nat. Assn. Social Workers, Council on Social Work Edn., AAUW, AAUP, Phi Beta Kappa. Clubs: Bird Key Yacht, Sarasota Women's Rep., Sarasota Bay Women's Rep. Home: 603 Longboat Club Rd Longboat Key FL 33548 Office: 2418 Hatton St Sarasota FL 33577

GLASSICK, MADALINE ZEIGLER, elementary sch. tchr.; b. York County, Pa., Sept. 6, 1928; d. John Donald and Pauline Clara (March) Zeigler; B.S., Shippensburg (Pa.) State Coll., 1949; M.Edn. with honors, Pa. State U., York, 1981; m. Robert Carl Glassick, July 14, 1950; 1 son, Robert Carl. Tchr. public schs. in Pa., 1946—; tchr. 4th grade Jackson Sch., York, 1949—; mem. York City Vertical Sci. Com., 1966—; master tchr. student tchrs., 1952—. Tchr. Bible sch. St. Mark's Luth. Ch., Emigsville, Pa., 1958-80, chmn. Christian edn., 1958-80, mem. ch. council, 1972-80. Mem. NEA, Pa. State Edn. Assn., York City Edn. Assn., Jackson Sch. PTA. Home: 3165 N George St Emigsville PA 17318 Office: 177 E Jackson St York PA 17404

GLASSMAN, JUSTINE HELENA, nurse, educator; b. N.Y.C., Feb. 3, 1928; d. George A. and Bessie (Laskin) Rizinsky; B.A., Bklyn. Coll., 1948; M. Nursing, Yale U., 1951; m. Jerome M. Glassman, June 15, 1952; children—Lorna Rae, Martin Jorge, Gary. Public health staff nurse Community Service Soc., 1951-52; public health coordinator Albert Einstein Med. Center, No. Div., Phila., 1952-57; public health instr. Fitzgerald-Mercy Hosp. Sch. Nursing, 1958-59, cons. nursing edn., 1959-62; asst. prof. community health nursing Pace U. Lienhard Sch. Nursing grad. div., Briarcliff Manor, N.Y., 1972—. Chmn. nurses edn. com. Phila. div. Am. Cancer Soc., 1957-60; v.p. United Way of Westchester County, 1981. Recipient meritorious service award, 1956; Disting. Service award Jaycees, 1980-81. Mem. Bucks-Phila. Dist. Nurses Assn. (chmn. public health nurses sect. 1953-55, chmn. mental health workshop planning program, 1956, chmn. joint sect. conf. com. 1955-56, dir. 1953-55), Am. Nurses Assn., Pa. Nurses Assn. (mem. at large public health sect. 1954-55, chmn. public health coordinators workshop planning com. public health sect. 1955-57), Yale Sch. Nursing Regional Alumni Assn. (chmn. 1953-55, 1959-62), Bus. and Profl. Women's Club (health and safety com. 1959-61), Am. Public Health Assn., Pa. Public Health Assn., Nat. League of Nursing, Pa. League of Nursing, Pres. PTA (local), 1966-68; bd. dirs. LWV (local), 1969-75; neighborhood troop organizer Girl Scouts U.S.A., 1968-70; chmn. United Way Office: Pleasantville/Briarcliff Campus Briarcliff Manor NY 10510

GLASSMAN, LANE, clin. psychologist, psychoanalyst; b. Roanoke, Va., Sept. 10, 1942; d. Burnet Samuel and Adeline (Friedman) Kaufer; B.A., N.Y. U., 1963; Ph.D., CCNY, 1972; m. Daniel F. Jones, Feb. 2, 1979; 1 dau., Sarah. Diagnostic testing Jewish Bd. Guardians, N.Y.C., 1968-69; clin. teaching asst. City Coll., CUNY, N.Y.C., 1971; sr. clin. psychologist Bronx (N.Y.) State Hosp., 1969-74; clin. instr. in psychiatry Albert Einstein Coll. of Medicine, Bronx, 1975; pvt. practice psychoanalysis and psychotherapy, N.Y.C., 1973—. Cert. psychologist, N.Y. Mem. Am. Psychol. Assn., N.Y. State Psychol. Assn. Contbr. writings to profl. publ.; asso. editor Jour. Bronx State Hosp., 1973-75. Home: 302 W 12th St New York NY 10014 Office: 51 Fifth Ave New York NY 10003

GLASSON, MURIEL ADA, educator; b. Almena, Kans., Dec. 16, 1900; d. Fred John and May (Williams) G.; B.S., U. Nebr., 1934; postgrad. Kans. State Coll., Columbia, Colo. State Coll., (Internat. Sch. Art Study award 1945) Quadalajara (Mexico) U., U. Calif. at Berkeley, (ARC Study award 1951) Whitworth Coll., Cornell U. Tchr. home econs., Spivey, Kans., 1934-36, Cedar Point, Kans., 1936-38, Sylvan Grove, Kans., 1938-42, Highland, Kans., 1942-43, Waterville, Wash., 1943-45, Lindsay, Calif., 1946, Port Angeles, Wash., 1946-52, 53-56, 57—. Del. Internat. Congress Home Econs., Edinburgh, Scotland, 1953; Balt., 1958; chmn. com. internat. students U. Wash., Seattle, 1959. Fulbright scholar, Netherlands, 1952-53, Burma, 1956-57; Asia Found. grantee, 1957, Sears, Roebuck & Co. Found. award, 1960. Mem. Tchrs. Credit Union (v.p. 1950-53, 58-60), Am. Home Econs. Assn. (internat. chmn. Wash. 1953-54), Wash. Olympic Peninsula Home Economists (area chmn.), Olympic Home Economists (pres. 1953-56), AAUW (legis. chmn. So. Kans. 1934-36), Bus. and Profl. Women's Club (v.p. Lindsay 1946), Wash. Orthopedic Aux. (pres.), DAR (chpt. treas., regent 1964-65, dir. Ranier chpt.), Internat. Platform Assn., Soc. Colonial Dames. Conglist. (past bd. mem.). Rebekah (past noble grand); mem. Order Eastern Star. Contbr. articles to profl. publs. Home: 308 E Republican St Apt 188 Seattle WA 98102 also 1120 B 84th Ave N Saint Petersburg FL 33702

GLAZER, JUDITH S., ednl. adminstr.; b. N.Y.C.; d. Max and Pauline V. Lager; B.A., Smith Coll., 1953; M.A., N.Y.U., 1973, Ph.D., 1981; children—Helen Marcy, George Douglas. Coordinator community services, coordinator spl. projects SUNY Coll., Purchase, 1970-72, asst. to v.p., 1972-73; asst. dean of community services Westchester (N.Y.) Community Coll., 1973-75; research asso. N.Y. State Temporary Commn. on Future of Postsecondary Edn., 1976-77; instr. higher edn. N.Y.U., N.Y.C., 1978-79; assoc. dir. Inter-Univ. Doctoral Consortia Project, N.Y.C., 1978-80; cons. ednl. and pub. affairs, 1975—; dir. N.Y. Alliance for Pub. Schs., N.Y.U., 1980—. Trustee, pres. Blind Brook-Rye Town Bd. Edn., 1963-72; assoc. campaign chmn. Rye Town-Pt. Chester United Way, 1977-79; bd. dirs. Westchester Nat. Council on Crime and Delinquency, 1978-80, Vol. Service Bur., 1974-79; bd. dirs. County Environ. Mgmt., 1973-80. Recipient NACO New County U.S.A. achievement award, 1975. Mem. Am. Assn. for Higher Edn., Assn. for Study Higher Edn., Nat. Assn. Women Deans and Adminstrs., Am. Ednl. Research Assn., Kappa Delta Pi. Contbr. articles to publs. Home: 201 W 70th St New York NY 10023 Office: NY University 32 Washington Pl New York NY 10003

GLAZER, MARJORIE JILL, speech pathologist; b. Boston, July 1, 1947; d. Lewis Joseph and Barbara G.; student Adelphi U., 1964-66; B.S., Boston U., 1968; M.A., Columbia U., 1969. Speech and lang. pathologist Sharon (Mass.) Public Schs., 1969—; pvt. speech pathology practice, Brookline, 1969—; mem. exec. bd. Sharon Tchrs. Assn. Mem. Brookline (Mass.) Town Meeting, Brookline Democratic Town Com., precinct chmn. presdl. and congl. elections, congl. campaign coordinator. Mem. Am. Speech, Lang. and Hearing Assn., Mass. Tchrs. Assn., Sharon Tchrs. Assn., Council Exceptional Children, Assn. Children with Learning Disabilities, NEA, Mass. Speech and Hearing Assn. Home: 45 Green St Apt 6 Brookline MA 02146 Office: 1 School St Sharon MA 02067

GLAZERMAN, ELLEN JOAN COOPERMAN, retail co. exec.; b. Phila., May 4, 1948; d. Jack Joseph and Florence (Cream) Cooperman; B.A., Temple U., 1969; div. Investment research analyst Phila. Investment Co.; systems analyst Fed. Res. Bank of Phila., 1972-75; sr. cons. Touche Ross & Co., Newark, 1975-78; v.p. fin., controller Mark Cross, Inc., N.Y.C., 1978—; cons. ops. and data processing. Del., White House Conf. on Small Bus., 1980. Home: 39 Walnut St Livingston NJ 07039 Office: 16 E 52d St New York NY 10022

GLAZER-WALDMAN, HILDA RUTH, ednl. psychologist, educator; b. Balt., Aug. 14, 1947; d. Maurice and Louise (Merfeld) Glazer; B.A., Beaver Coll., 1969; Ed.M., Rutgers U., 1972, Ed.D., 1976; m. David Joel Waldman, May 30, 1976. Staff specialist for curriculum assessment Balt. City Public Schs., 1974-76; adj. asst. prof. edn. U. Mo., St. Louis, 1977-79; asso. Evaluative Research Assos., St. Louis, 1977-78; asst. prof. psychology Fontbonne Coll., St. Louis, 1978-79; research asst. prof. dept. allied health edn. Sch. Allied Health Scis., U. Tex. Health Sci. Center, Dallas, 1980-82, asst. prof. allied health edn., 1982—. Mem. educator's taskforce Mo. region Anti-Defamation League, B'nai B'rith, 1978-79. Mem. Am. Psychol. Assn., Eastern Psychol. Assn., Am. Ednl. Research Assn., Southwestern Ednl. Research Assn. Co-editor book on gerontology. Contbr. articles to profl. publs., research reports. Office: Dept Allied Health Edn Sch Allied Health Scis U Tex Health Sci Center at Dallas 5323 Harry Hines Blvd Dallas TX 75235

GLEASON, JANICE MONICA, nurse, lawyer; b. N.Y.C., Aug. 14, 1932; d. John Patrick and Sarah Agnes Casey; R.N., Mercy Coll. Nursing, San Diego, 1953; M.A. in Human Behavior, U.S. Internat. U., San Diego, 1973; B.S. in Law, Western State U., San Diego, 1978, J.D., 1978; m. Matthew Campbell Gleason, Dec. 10, 1953; children—Mark Manning, Sheila Agnes, Sharon Mercedes. Mem. nursing staff Balboa Hosp., San Diego, 1953-55, Cook County Hosp., Chgo., 1956, St. Luke's Hosp., Chgo., 1956, Plastic Surgery Med. Clinic, San Diego, 1958-68; nurse Vietnam Orphan Airlift, 1975; cons. continuing edn. Calif. Parapsychology Found., San Diego, 1972—; v.p. Progressive Social Services Tech., sr. citizens legal services; spokesperson Martha Movement, San Diego County; lectr. in field. Mem. NOW, 1971—, nat. bd. dirs., 1976-77, chmn. speakers bur., San Diego, 1977—, chmn. San Diego chpt., 1971—, chmn. child care Calif chpt., 1972; del. Internat. Women's Conf., Mexico City, 1975, Houston, 1977; pres. Catholics for a Free Choice, 1975-77; founding mem. 1st Internat. Abortion Rights Assn., 1975; bd. dirs. Sr. Citizens Legal Services. Named Mother of Year, San Diego chpt. NOW, 1975, recipient Susan B. Anthony award, 1977; Corpus Juris Secundum award ARC, 1975; Am. Jurisprudence award, 1976. Mem. Christian Legal Soc., Am. Assn. Plastic and Reconstructive Surg. Nurses, Nat. Women's Polit. Caucus. Democrat. Address: 6333 Castejon Dr La Jolla CA 92037

GLEASON, JEAN BERKO, psycholinguist; b. Cleve., Dec. 19, 1931; d. Arthur E. and Alice (Gelberger) Berko; A.B., Radcliffe Coll., 1953, A.M., 1955; Ph.D., Harvard U., 1958; m. Andrew Mattei Gleason, Jan. 26, 1959; children—Katherine, Pamela, Cynthia. Research assoc. Harvard U. Grad. Sch. Edn., 1969-70; prin. research assoc., dept. psychiatry Harvard U. Med. Sch., 1970-72; vis. asst. to assoc. prof. psychology Boston U., 1972-75; vis. schlar com. on linguistics Stanford U., spring 1974; prof. psychology Boston U., 1976—, research assoc. Aphasia Research Ctr., Med. Sch., 1961—; research scholar in residence Hungarian Acad. Scis., Budapest, spring 1981; mem. mental retardation research com. Nat. Inst. Child Health and Human Devel., 1981—. NSF grantee, 1977-80; Internat. Research and Exchanges Bd. travel grantee, 1981. Fellow Am. Psychol. Assn., AAAS; mem. Linguistic Soc. Am. (chmn. program com. 1980-81), Acad. Aphasia, Internat. Neuropsychol. Soc., Soc. Research in Child Devel., Radcliffe Grad. Soc., New Eng. Psychol. Assn., New Eng. Child Lang. Assn., Phi Beta Kappa. Contbr. articles to profl. jours. Home: 110 Larchwood Dr Cambridge MA 02138 Office: 64 Cummington St Boston MA 02215

GLEASON, JEAN WILBUR, lawyer; b. St. Louis, Oct. 31, 1943; d. Ray Lyman and Martha (Bugbee) Wilbur; B.A., Wellesley Coll., 1965; LL.B. cum laude, Harvard U., 1968; m. Gerald Kermit Gleason, Aug. 28, 1966; children—Charles Blake, Peter Wilbur. Admitted to Calif. bar, 1969, D.C. bar, 1978; law clk. U.S. Ct. Appeals, 9th Circuit, 1968-69; asso. firm Brobeck, Phleger & Harrison, San Francisco, 1969-72; spl. counsel to dir. div. corp. fin. SEC, 1973-76, asso. dir. div. investment mgmt., 1976-78; mem. firm Fulbright and Jaworski, Washington, 1978—. Mem. Am. Bar Assn. (fed. regulation of securities com.), D.C. Bar (steering com. corp. sect.), Phi Beta Kappa. Home: 3320 Highland Pl NW Washington DC 20008 Office: Fulbright and Jaworski 1150 Connecticut Ave NW Washington DC 20036

GLEICH, CAROL SUE, edn. specialist; b. Kewanee, Ill., Jan. 18, 1935; d. Carl and Edna (Krause) Gleich; A.B., U. Iowa, 1958, M.S., 1967, Ph.D., 1972. Program dir. med. tech. program, asst. prof. dept. pathology U. Iowa, Iowa City, 1972-77; health manpower edn. specialist, div. asso. health professions Bur. Health Professions, Health Resources Adminstrn., HHS, Hyattsville, Md., from 1977, now allied health cons. to Egypt; adj. asso. prof. U. Md. Sch. Medicine; mem. Iowa Health Manpower Com., 1976—; cons. U. Wis. System Acad. Affairs, 1976; panelist and participant workshops. Cert. clin. chemistry technologist, Nat. Registry Clin. Chemistry. Mem. Am. Soc. Allied Health Professions, Am. Soc. Clin. Pathologists (asso.; cert. med. technologist; sec. Bd. Registry, 1975-77), Am. Soc. Med. Tech., Iowa Soc. Med. Tech. (Outstanding Med. Technologist of Yr. 1975), Beta Beta Beta. Asso. editor Am. Jour. Med. Tech., 1974—, Jour. Allied Health, 1982—; contbr. articles to profl. publs., papers to confs. Home: 5125 Norbeck Rd Rockville MD 20853 Office: Center Bldg Room 541 3700 East-West Highway Hyattsville MD 20782

GLEIT, CAROL JOYCE, nurse; b. Madison, Wis., Jan. 6, 1934; d. Roy Sophus and Lillian Ruby Marie (Kroncke) Hansen; B.S.N., Boston U., 1957; M. Nursing Edn., U. Pitts., 1960; Ed.D., N.C. State U., Raleigh, 1976; children from previous marriage—Ruthe, Natalie, Robert, Nathan. Head dept. fundamentals of nursing Contra Costa Coll., San Pablo, Calif., 1961-64; acting dir., course coordinator Rex Hosp. Sch. Nursing, Raleigh, N.C., 1964-74; asst. prof. nursing U. N.C., Chapel Hill, 1974-77; asso. prof. nursing U. Va., Charlottesville, 1977—. Bd. dirs. Contra Costa County Heart Assn., 1963-64; trustee Triange chpt. Multiple Sclerosis Soc., 1973-74; bd. dirs. N.C. United for ERA, 1974-77; community resource coordinator Chapel Hill Carboro Rape Crisis Center, 1976-77. Mem. Am. Nurses Assn., Adult Edn. Assn., Sigma Theta Tau, Phi Kappa Phi. Democrat. Home: 2 Tennis Dr Charlottesville VA 22901 Office: McLeod Hall U Va Charlottesville VA 22903

GLENN, CAROLYN LOVE, high sch. choral dir.; b. Raleigh, N.C., June 30, 1933; d. Lawson Hilman and Geneva McGee (Foster) G.; B.M.E., cert. in voice, Fla. State U., 1956. Elem. music tchr., 1956-59; jr. high sch. choral dir., 1959-71; tchr., choral dir. Amos P. Godby High Sch., Tallahassee, 1971—; pvt. voice and piano tchr.; singer; debut Carnegie Recital Hall, N.Y.C., 1965; performed in concerts in Fla., Ga., W.Va., N.J. and N.Y., concert tour Europe, 1970; soprano solo, asst. choir dir. St. Paul's Methodist Ch., also children's choir dir. Vol. emergency room Tallahassee Meml. Regional Med. Center. Rockefeller Found. grantee to Oberlin Conservatory of Music, 1963. Mem. Am. Choral Dirs. Assn., Fla. Vocal Assn., Music Educators Nat. Conf., Nat. Assn. Tchrs. Singing, Delta Kappa Gamma, Delta Zeta. Democrat. Home: 2310 Don Andres St Tallahassee FL 32304 Office: 1717 W Tharpe St Tallahassee FL 32303

GLENN, CLETA MAE, lawyer; b. Clinton, Ill., Sept. 24, 1921; d. John and Mattie Sylvester (Anderson) Glenn; B.S., U. Ill., 1947; J.D., DePaul U. Coll. Law, 1976; m. Rex Eugene Loggans, Sept. 3, 1948 (div.); 1 dau., Susan. Real estate builder, developer, 1959-69; communications dir. Transp. Research Center, Northwestern U., Evanston, Ill., 1969-72; admitted to Ill. bar, 1977; practice law, Chgo., 1977—; lectr. Assn. Trial Lawyers Am., John Marshall Law Sch. Served with U.S. Navy, 1943-59. Recipient Real Estate Humanitarian award Kislak Co., Miami, Fla., 1962. Mem. Am. Bar Assn. (sect. chmn. 1980—), Ill. Bar Assn. (assembly rep., standing com.), Chgo. Bar Assn., Assn, Trial Lawyers Am., Ill. Trial Lawyers Assn., Lex Leggio, Phi Alpha Delta. Editor: Collective Bargaining and Technological Change in American Transportation, 1979; contbr. articles to profl. publs. Home: 880 N Lake Shore Dr Chicago IL 60611 Office: 69 W Washington St Chicago IL 60602

GLENN, CONSTANCE W., univ. art mus. dir.; b. Topeka, Oct. 4, 1933; d. Henry A. and Madeline S. (Stewart) White; B.F.A., U. Kans., 1955; postgrad., U. Mo., 1964-69; M.A. in Art History, Calif. State U., Long Beach, 1974; m. Jack W. Glenn, June 19, 1955; children—Laurie Frances, Caroline Elizabeth, John Christopher. Prin. Constance W. Glenn Interiors, 1958-68; co-owner Jack Glenn Gallery, Corona del Mar, Calif., 1970-75; lectr., asst. prof., asso. prof. art, Calif. State U., Long Beach, 1973—, dir. Univ. Art Mus., 1973—, dir. Mus. Studies Cert. Program; dir. Center for So. Calif. Studies in Visual Arts. Mem. Am. Assn. Mus., Coll. Art Assn., Art Mus. Assn., Archives of Am. Art (chmn. So. Calif. adv. bd.), Friends of Photography (bd. trustees), Los Angeles Center Photog. Studies (bd. trustees), Kappa Alpha Theta. Art cons. Architectural Digest; author books, catalogues, articles on contemporary art. Office: Calif State Univ Long Beach Art Mus 1250 Bellflower Blvd Long Beach CA 90840

GLENN, DONNA BRILEY, journalist; b. Shenandoah, Iowa, June 21, 1941; d. Harold Vinton and Lela Catherine (Winkler) Briley; B.A., Grinnell Coll., 1963; M.A., Stanford U., 1964; M.A. in Journalism, Am. U., 1977; student U. Guadalajara (Mex.), summer 1962; m. Michel Keith Glenn, Oct. 3, 1964; children—Rory Harold James, Jason Briley Glenn. Speech therapist Bd. Coop. Ednl. Services, Westchester County, N.Y., 1965-66; speech dir., dir. video studio Chase Manhattan Bank, N. Am., N.Y.C., 1966-69; cons. in oral communications, N.Y.C., 1969-72; reporter Sta. WAMU-FM, Washington, part time 1976—; acting dir. editorials Sta. WMAL, 1978; freelance writer and photographer, 1976—; asso. producer Kaleidoscope, WAMU-FM, Am. U., Washington, 1979-80. Bd. dirs. Rec. for the Blind, Inc., Washington, 1978-79, Fgn. Student Service Council, 1978-81; mem. Women's Nat. Democratic Club. Mem. Am. Speech and Hearing Assn., Am. Women in Radio and TV, Women in Film, Capital Press Women, PEO (state officer). Methodist. Club: Jr. League (dir. 1978-79; vice chmn. vols. at battered women's shelter 1979-80). Home: 5220 Watson St NW Washington DC 20016 Office: Am U Washington DC 20016

GLENN, JUDY CAROLE, nurse, naval officer; b. Birmingham, Ala., July 2, 1946; d. Talmadge William and Maude Elizabeth (Steading) G.; diploma in nursing Univ. Hosp., Birmingham, 1967; B.S.N., Samford U., 1975; M.S.N. in Cardiovascular Nursing, U. Ala., Birmingham, 1978;

Staff nurse Univ. Hosp., 1967-68; charge nurse CCU, Lloyd Noland Found., Fairfield, Ala., 1968-70; charge nurse Bessemer (Ala.) Carraway Med. Center, 1970-75, unit coordinator, 1975-76, cardiovascular clin. specialist, 1978-80; commd. lt. U.S. Naval Res., 1979; asst. charge nurse intermediate intensive care Naval Regional Med. Center, San Diego, 1981—; instr. CPR, corpsman cardiology course; mem. regional area CPR com. Ala. Heart Assn., 1979-80, CPR regional course coordinator, 1977-78. Camp nurse Assembly of God Ch., Montgomery, Ala., 1968, 77, 78. Recipient citation Ala. Heart Fund, 1975; USPHS Title II trainee, 1977-78. Mem. Am. Nurses Assn., Am. Heart Assn. (council on cardiovascular nursing), Am. Assn. Critical Care Nursing (tech. assistance panel 1978-79). Republican. Office: Naval Regional Med Center San Diego CA 92134

GLENN, JUNE CAMP, ins. co. exec.; b. Phila., Dec. 11, 1932; d. Raymond Sterling and Lilly (Becker) Camp; B.S., Stockton State Coll., 1980; m. Alan L. Glenn, Oct. 20, 1951. Claim adjuster Crawford & Co., Atlantic City, 1960-67; supr. Oliver & Co., Atlantic City, 1967-73; claim supr. Prudential Property & Casualty Co., Linwood, N.J., 1973, claim unit mgr., 1975, regional ops. cons., 1975-76, mgr. South Jersey field service office, 1976-79, sr. claim cons., Holmdel, N.J., 1979—. Mem. Ins. Advisory Com., Atlantic Community Coll., 1973-76; chairperson Atlantic-Cape May County Traffic Safety Com., N.J. Safety Council, 1976-79. Recipient Insurors Press Edn. award, 1970; chartered property and casualty underwriter; cert. profl. ins. woman; designated asso. in claims Ins. Inst. Am. Mem. Atlantic County Claim Assn. (pres. 1974-76), Ins. Women Atlantic County (pres. 1964-66), Nat. Assn. Ins. Women (Nat. Claims Woman of Yr. 1975), Soc. Chartered Property and Casualty Underwriters. Home: 53 River Dr Marlboro NJ 07746 Office: PO Box 419 Holmdel NJ 07733

GLENN, KATHLEEN GLORIA, motivational sales tng. specialist; b. Monterey, Calif., Aug. 20, 1943; d. Antonino Jack and Josephine (Spataro) Costanza; B.A., San Jose State U., 1965; div.; 1 son, Bradley Stewart. Owner, pres. Fashions Unltd., B. Stewart Glenn Co., Fancy That, Monterey, Calif., 1965-74; Western regional mgr. Mary Quant Co., 1974-77; exec. account dir. Princess Marcella Borghese, No. Calif., 1977-80; dir. tng., pres. Sales Plus Co., San Jose, Calif., 1980—. Office: 137 Manton Dr San Jose CA 95123

GLICK, BETTY JANE, accountant; b. Carlisle, Pa., Sept. 15, 1935; d. Benjamin Burns and Margaret Irene (Brinkerhoff) Bailey; student pub. schs., Carlisle; m. Carl Samuel Glick, Jr., Sept. 4, 1953; children—Elizabeth Rose, Carl Samuel III (dec.), John Robert, William Joseph. Sec., Bedford Shoe Co. div. G.R. Kinney Co., Carlisle, 1953-54, bookkeeper, 1956-57, lacer pre-fit room, 1959; acct. M.G. Riley, C.P.A., Kenai, Alaska, 1966-82. Program chmn. Kenai PTA, 1968-69, pres., 1969-70; mem. Kenai Planning & Zoning Adv. Com., 1974-76, chmn., 1976; mem. Kenai City Council, 1976-82, vice mayor, 1979-82; mem. Kenai Peninsula Borough Assembly, 1982—; parliamentarian Kenai Peninsula Borough Planning and Zoning Com., 1976-77, vice chmn., 1977-81, chmn., 1981-82; treas. Jr. Achievement, Kenai, 1978-81, chmn., 1981-82; bd. dirs. Jr. Achievement Alaska, 1982-83. Named Citizen of Month, Kenai C. of C., 1977. Mem. Alaska Mcpl. League (dir. 1980-81, 2d v.p. 1981-82, 1st v.p. 1982-83), Billiken Bus. and Profl. Women's Club (named Woman of Yr. 1978). Club: Peninsula Petroleum Wives. Home: PO Box 528 Highbush and E Aliak St Kenai AK 99611

GLICK, HARRIET BRIER, theatre sch. dir.; b. Phila., Aug. 29, 1922; d. Ben and Gertrude (Lerner) Brier; grad. Phila. Sch. Drama Art, 1940; student U. Pa., 1940-42, St. Joseph Coll., 1965, Barnes Found., 1969-76; postgrad. theater arts Villanova U., 1975; m. Bernard Fine, May 23, 1942 (div. Mar. 1971); children—Diane Davids, Kenneth; m. 2d Milton Glick, Mar. 19, 1971. Practice tchr. creative dramatics Phila. Sch. System, 1962; dir. children's theater New Hope, Bucks County, 1963; dir. high sch. theater Cornelia Otis Skinner Playhouse, Lower Merion Sch. System, 1967; instr. improvisational theater Harcum Jr. Coll., 1967, Main Line Sch., 1971; tchr. Lower Merion Sch. Dist., 1971-74; dir. children Bala Cynwyd Library, Narberth, Pa., 1964-74; instr. creative dramatics Merion Elem. Sch., 1971; dir. Belmont Hills Sch., Narberth, Pa., 1972—; instr. guides Bicentennial hist. tours Walnut St. Theater, Phila., 1975-76; instr. creative drama for children Main Line Center Arts, Haverford, Pa., 1975-79; dir. ednl. activities Walnut St. Theater, Phila., 1979; mem. staff Mainline Center Arts, Haverford, 1975-79; dir. theater workshop, dir. children's theater Royal Palm Theater, Boca Raton, Fla., 1979—. Mem. Am. Ednl. Theater Assn. Author: What Makes An Actor and Artist and Not Just a Performer, 1969. Home: 605 Conshohocken State Rd Penn Valley Narberth PA 19072 also 3400 Ocean Blvd Palm Beach FL 33480

GLICK, JOYCE DEBRA, retail exec.; b. Chgo., Mar. 26, 1951; d. Sam and Bernice G.; B.S.J., Northwestern U., 1972. Asst. editor Odyssey mag., Chgo., 1972-75; dir. communications Apparel Center, Chgo., 1975-78; account exec. Janet Diederichs & Assos., Public Relations, Chgo., 1978; dir. mktg. Albany Bank & Trust Co., Chgo., 1979; dir. mktg. Handmoor Women's Stores, Chgo., 1980—. Mem. women's telethon com. United Cerebral Palsy, 1981, fund raising com. Chgo. Internat. Film Festival, 1981. Mem. Am. Israeli C. of C. and Industry (dir., 1978-80). Jewish. Office: Handmoor Women's Stores 300 N Michigan Ave Chicago IL 60601

GLICK-COLQUITT, KAREN LYNNE, coll. adminstr.; b. Bucyrus, Ohio, Sept. 2, 1945; d. Phillip Dole and Bernice Grace (Shasteen) Glick; B.S.J., Bowling Green State U., 1967, M.A., 1979; m. Michael Colquitt, Apr. 6, 1968; children—M. Todd, K. Christine. Editor, Bowling Green (Ohio) State U., 1972-74; account exec. Howard E. Mitchell, Jr., Advt., Findlay, Ohio, 1974-77; asst. to dir. Student Devel. Program, Bowling Green State U., 1977-79; dir. public info. Bluffton (Ohio) Coll., 1980—. Public relations officer Findlay chpt. NAACP, 1982—. Mem. Women in Communications, Public Relations Soc. Am., Coll. Sports Info. Dirs. Am., Council Advancement and Support of Edn., Nat. Assn. Intercollegiate Athletics, Sports Info. Dirs. Assn. Episcopalian. Office: Riley Ct Bluffton Coll Bluffton OH 45817

GLICKENHAUS, SARAH BRODY, speech therapist; b. Mpls., Mar. 8, 1919; d. Morris and Ethel (Silin) Brody; B.S., U. Minn., 1940, M.S., 1945; m. Seth Morton Glickenhaus, Oct. 23, 1944; children—James Morris, Nancy Pier. Speech therapist, Davison Sch. Speech Correction, Atlanta, 1940-42; speech pathologist U. Minn., Mpls., 1945-46; speech therapist Queens Coll., N.Y.C., 1946-48; speech therapist VA, N.Y.C., 1949-50; pvt. practice, New Rochelle, N.Y., 1950-71; speech therapist Abbott Sch. United Free Sch. Dist. 13, Irvinton, N.Y., 1971—; tutor learning disabled children New Rochelle Public Schs., 1968-71. Mem. Am. Speech Hearing And Lang. Assn., N.Y. State Speech and Hearing Assn., Westchester Speech and Hearing Assn., AAAS. Club: Harvard (N.Y.C.). Jewish. Home and office: 100 Dorchester Rd Scarsdale NY 10583

GLICKMAN, LAURA LEE, lawyer; b. Bklyn., Apr. 26, 1946; d. Daniel Bernard and Miriam K. (Friedman) Glickman; A.B. with honors, UCLA, 1967, J.D., 1970; m. James D. Leewong, Feb. 18, 1979; Admitted to Calif. bar, U.S. Supreme Ct. bar, U.S. Ct. Appeals bar, U.S. Dist. Ct. bar; practiced in Pacoima, Calif., 1971-72, Los Angeles, 1972—; staff atty. San Fernando Valley Neighborhood Legal Services, Inc., Pacoima, 1971-72, directing atty., 1972; clin. supervising atty. Legal Aid Found. Los Angeles, 1972-74; adj. clin. prof. Loyola U. Sch. Law, Los Angeles, 1972-74. Mem. lawyers com. ACLU, 1972-74; chmn. young profl. leadership group Jewish Fedn. Council Greater Los Angeles, 1977-78, also mem. community relations com., 1978, leadership devel. com., 1978; referee bd. retirement Los Angeles County Employees Retirement Assn., 1975—. Recipient Bancroft-Whitney award, 1968, Appellate Advocacy award UCLA Law Sch., 1970. Mem. State Bar Calif., Beverly Hills Bar Assn., Los Angeles County Bar Assn., Women Lawyers Assn. Los Angeles, Japanese-Am. Bar Assn., So. Calif. Chinese Lawyers Assn., UCLA Law Alumni Assn. (dean's counsel), Calif. Women Lawyers Assn. Office: 3325 Wilshire Blvd Suite 700 Los Angeles CA 90010

GLICKMAN, SYLVIA, social worker, columnist, freelance writer; b. Maynard, Mass., Apr. 1, 1920; d. Joel and Fannie (Marcus) Glickman; B.A., U. Mich., 1943; postgrad. U. Chgo., 1944-45; M.S. in Social Service, Boston U., 1950. Psychiat. research asst. Mich. Child Guidance Clinic, 1943—44, Ill. Neuropsychiat. Inst., Chgo., 1944—45; home service worker Boston Red Cross, 1945-48; family service worker Jewish Family Service, Boston, 1950-56, Worcester, Mass., 1956—61, Providence, 1964-66; social work cons. St. Joseph's Hosp., Providence, 1966-69; supr. social workers Mass. Rehab. Commn., 1971-73; columnist Forum for the Handicapped, Worcester Sunday Telegram, 1973—; social worker div. spl. edn. Worcester Public Schs., 1975-78, vocat. edn. counselor, 1978-80, affirmative action com., 1978-80; mem. Worcester Area Com. on Employment of Handicapped, 1973—, Inter-Campus Com. on Handicapped Students, Boston, 1976-78; del. Mass. council Orgns. of Handicapped, 1974-78; asso. mem. Mass. Gov.'s Com. on Employment of Handicapped, 1972-78; organizer, mem. steering com. Coalition for Handicapped Citizens, Worcester, 1976—; chmn. Mass. State Task Force Attitudinal Barriers, 1977 White House Conf. Handicapped Individuals; mem. Mass. Coalition of Citizens with Disabilities, 1979—, award, 1981; mem. minority adv. bd. Channel 27, Worcester, 1978—; producer segment on handicapped: Inside Worcester, 1979—; scriptwriter, exec. producer All Ordinary People, 1981. Mem. planning com. This Is Worcester, 1979-80; organizer, chmn. Media Council on Handicapped Issues, 1980—. Recipient News award Epilepsy Soc. of Mass., 1974; Service Above Self award Mass. Assn. Paraplegics, 1976; Carla Harling Cody Meml. award Worcester Area Employ the Handicapped Com., 1976; Communications award Nat. Easter Seal Soc., 1979. Registered clin. social worker, Mass. Mem. Nat. Assn. Social Workers (chairwoman task force on handicapped Greater Mass. chpt. 1973—), Mass. Assn. of Paraplegics (dir. 1973-76, legis. chmn. 1975-76), Acad. Certified Social Workers. Jewish. Clubs: Business and Profl. Women, B'nai B'rith. Contbr. articles to profl. jours. Home: 45 Harley Dr Apt 4 Worcester MA 01606

GLIEWE, UNADA GRACE, author, illustrator; b. Rochester, N.Y., July 10, 1927; d. Edwin Herman and Unada Belle (Hinckley) G.; B.F.A. in Painting and Illustration magna cum laude, Syracuse (N.Y.) U., 1949. Staff artist advt. agys., Rochester, 1949-54, Lutheran Bd. Parish Edn., Phila., 1955-67; freelance author, illustrator, 1967—, instr. illustration Hussian Sch. Art; illustrator numerous books, 1967—, latest being The Old Witch and the Dragon, 1979, The Trouble With Leslie, 1979, The Steps to My Best Friends House, 1980, Rosalie at Eleven, 1980; also ednl. material; author, illustrator: Ricky's Boots, 1970, Andrew's Amazing Boxes, 1971; author: The Marvelous Monster of Mulligan Heights, 1981. N.Y. State Acad. scholar, 1945-49; Art scholar Syracuse U., 1945-49. Mem. Phila. Children's Reading Round Table, Plays and Players. Democrat. Lutheran. Address: 2300 Pine St Apt 6 Philadelphia PA 19103

GLOBERMAN, NORMA P., devel. economist; b. N.Y.C., Jan. 19, 1932 d. Herbert and Rebecca (Mitler) Globerman; B.A. summa cum laude, Hunter Coll. with UN, 1953—, devel. program info. officer, N.Y.C., 1953-59, spl. asst. civil ops. in Congo, 1960-61, spl. asst. Office Sec. Gen., 1961, project officer, 1962-73, chief div. for SE Asia, 1973-78, chief div. South and West Asia, 1979—; cons. Marymont Coll. Mem. Council Fgn. Relations. Painting represented in N.Y., Mass., Pa. Home: 300 E 56th St New York NY 10022 Office: One UN Plaza New York NY 10017

GLODE, KATHLEEN KAISER, retail hardware store exec.; b. Volga, S.D., July 1, 1949; d. Robert Albert and Joan (Janda) Kaiser; B.S. in Math., Creighton U., 1971; m. Michael S. Glode, Nov. 28, 1970; children—Mary Jane, Johanna, Michael Shively. Secondary math. tchr. Omaha Public Schs., 1970-71; part-owner, dept. mgr. Shively Hardware Co., Saratoga, Wyo., 1973—; v.p. T & G Enterprises, 1981—. Mem. evaluation team Saratoga Schs., 1976, 80; mayor Town of Saratoga, 1977-79; sec. Carbon County Council Govts., 1977-78; vice-chmn., treas. 1977-79; sec. Carbon County Impact Joint Powers Bd., 1977-80; precinct committeewoman, 1978—; chmn. Sr. Citizens Housing Task Force, 1980; mem. Carbon County Library br. building com., 1982—. Mem. Saratoga Hist. and Cultural Assn., Council Cath. Women, LWV, Wyo. Archeol. Soc., C. of C. (retail bus. com. 1979), Alpha Sigma Nu. Democrat. Roman Catholic. Address: PO Box 605 Saratoga WY 82331

GLOGAU, LILLIAN FLATOW FLEISCHER, ednl. adminstr.; b. N.Y.C., Feb. 15, 1924; d. Henry and Diana (Heller) Flatow; B.A. cum laude, Bklyn. Coll., 1946; M.A., Columbia U., 1949; Ed.D., N.Y. U., 1969; m. F.E. Fleischer, 1948 (dec. 1957); children—Jordan, Laurence, Alexander; m. 2d, Jerome N. Glogau, Nov. 20, 1963. Tchr. public schs., N.Y.C., 1946-49; tchr. Plainview (N.Y.) schs., 1959-61, adminstr., 1961-66; prin. Spring Valley (N.Y.) Schs., 1966—; pres. Pragmatix, edn. corp., South Orange, N.J.; exec. dir. Applied Learning Center Found., N.Y.C.; mem. adj. faculty Fairleigh Dickinson U., Madison, N.J., Caldwell (N.J.) Coll.; lectr., cons. to sch. dists. Recipient Founders Day award N.Y. U., 1970. Mem. Am. Assn. Sch. Adminstrs., Assn. for Supervision and Curriculum Devel., Sch. Adminstrs. Assn. N.Y. State, Nat. Assn. Elem. Sch. Prins., Kappa Delta Pi, Pi Lambda Theta. Author: Nongraded Primary, 1967; You and N.Y. City, 1970; Let's See, 1971; The Elementary School Media Center, 1972; contbr. articles to profl. jours. Office: East Ramapo Central Sch Dist Spring Valley NY 10977

GLOISTEN, KATHLEEN MARY, media specialist; b. Flushing, N.Y., Feb. 19, 1950; d. Bernard Joseph and Mary Beatrice (Langer) Gloisten; B.A., U. Denver, 1972; M.A., U. No. Coll., 1977; cert. U. Paris, 1982. Tchrs. aide elem. sch., Aurora, Colo., 1972-73; tchr. elem. sch., Belleview, Colo., 1973-76, Independence Elem. Sch., 1976-82; media resource center specialist Sch. Dist.; coordinator Computertown U.S.A. Aurora Public Library. Chmn. precinct Democratic Party, 1976-77. Mem. Alliance Française, Kappa Delta Pi. Author: French Pronunciation Lang. Guide to the Young Learner, 1982. Home: 10001 E Evans 41C Denver CO 80231 Office: 4700 S Memphis Aurora CO 80014

GLOS, MARGARET BEACH, assn. exec., mgmt. cons.; b. N.Y.C.; d. Stewart Taft and Josephine (Cushman) Beach; B.A. summa cum laude, Smith Coll., 1958; postgrad. Columbia U., 1959-61, M.I.T., 1978; m. Stanley Glos, June 1, 1961; children—Alexander Beach, Maya Cushman, Andrew Bishop. Editor Nucleonics Mag., McGraw Hill Co., 1959-66; asst. mng. editor Sci. Research Mag., 1966-67; exec. dir. Soc. Nuclear Medicine, N.Y.C., 1967-79; exec. sec. Edn. and Research Found., 1975-79; adminstr. Am. Bd. Nuclear Medicine, 1975-80; pres. G & T Mgmt., Inc., N.Y.C., 1979—; exec. dir. Am. Assn. Clin. Histocompatiblity Testing, 1980—, Internat. Assn. Personnel Women, 1981—, Soc. Radiol. Engring., 1982—, Am. Assn. Music Therapy, 1982—; exec. v.p. Soc. Gastrointestinal Assts., 1980—; exec. dir. Internat. Assn. Personnel Women, Am. Assn. Music Therapy. Mem. Soc. Nuclear Medicine, Am. Soc. Assn. Execs., Profl. Conv. Mgmt. Assn., Phi Beta Kappa, Sigma Xi. Contbr. articles to profl. jours; author children's books. Office: 211 E 43d St New York NY 10017

GLOSSBRENNER, ERNESTINE VIOLA, state legislator; b. Troup, Tex., Nov. 1, 1932; d. Ellwood Leslie and Ica Louise (Perry) G.; A.A., Kilgore Jr. Coll., 1952; B.A. in Chemistry, U. Tex., 1954; M.A. in Math., Tex. A&I U., 1971. Tchr. sci. and math. secondary schs. Alice (Tex.) Ind. Sch. Dist., 1954-76, chmn. math. dept. Alice High Sch., 1962-76; mem. Tex. Ho. of Reps., 1977—. Chmn. stewardship com., chmn. worship com., deaconess First Christian Ch.; urban renewal commr., Alice, 1973-76; del. county and state Dem. convs., 1974, 76, 78, 80, 82; mem. Tex. Sunset Commn., 1981. Recipient Common Cause award, 1980. NSF fellow, 1960-61; profl. teaching cert. in math. and supervision, Tex. Mem. Orgn. Women Legislators, Bus. and Profl. Women's Club, Tex. Assn. Elected Women, Nat. Woman's Polit. Caucus, Tex. Woman's Polit. Caucus (Woman of Yr. 1974), Tex. Tchrs. Assn., AAUW, Delta Kappa Gamma, Phi Delta Kappa. Office: 101 N Wright St Alice TX 78332

GLOSSER, BEVERLY JUNE, nurse, civic worker; b. Canton, Ohio, June 2, 1942; d. Alfred Earl and Grace LaVerne (Huth) Ransom; student Bethany (W.Va.) Coll., 1960-62; B.S. in Nursing, Case Western Res. U., Cleve., 1965; m. Jack Glosser, June 19, 1965; children—Kristen Elizabeth, Eric Ryan, Erin Leigh. Staff nurse Univ. Hosps., Cleve., 1965-66, Warren (Ohio) Gen. Hosp., 1967-68, Trumbull Meml. Hosp., Warren, 1970-71; pvt. duty nurse, Warren, 1979—; tchr.'s asst. Christ Episcopal Presch., 1978—; clinic aide North Road Sch., 1976-79; substitute sch. nurse Howland Twp. Schs. Pres. Women's Panhellenic Assn. Trumbull County, 1977-78, 1st v.p., 1976-77, 2d v.p., 1975-76. campaign worker charitable drives; rec. sec. PTA, 1978-79; chmn. bd. Christ Episc. Coop. Presch., 1975-77, Warren Civic Music Assn., 1968-69; active YWCA, Girl Scouts U.S.A., Cub Scouts; bd. deaconesses, mem. pulpit com., Sunday Sch. tchr. Central Christian Ch., mem. bd. Christian edn., 1981-82; treas. Parent Tchr. Orgn., 1981-82; bd. dirs. March of Dimes. Republican. Clubs: Weeds to Roses Garden (past pres.), Job's Daus. Home: 3775 Bellwood St SE Warren OH 44484

GLOSSER, ELIZABETH BARBARA, bus. cons.; b. Plymouth, Pa., June 25, 1939; d. Charles B. and Elizabeth (Ruddy) G.; B.A., Coll. Misericorida, Dallas, Pa., 1961; M.Ed. (NDEA fellow), Rutgers U., 1965; M.B.A., Fairleigh Dickinson U., 1978. Tchr., Neptune (N.J.) High Sch., 1961-64; counselor, Westwood, N.J., 1965-69; tchr., River Dell, N.J., 1969-71; mgr. sales adminstrn. Xerox Corp., 1972-73, cons., 1971-72, product mgr., 1972, sales mgr., 1973-79; asst. prof. bus. and econs. Marymount Coll., Tarrytown, N.Y., also pres. Women at Work, 1979-81; mng. dir. The Exec. Exchange, Englewood Cliffs, N.J., 1981—. Fund raiser Multiple Sclerosis Soc., Am. Cancer Soc. Mem. Nat. Assn. Female Execs. (network dir.), Am. Mgmt. Assn., AAUP, Assn. Children with Spl. Needs. Roman Catholic. Author: Moments Matter, 1977. Home: 115 Main St Avon By The Sea NJ 07717 Office: 210 Sylvan Ave Englewood Cliffs NJ

GLOVER, KATHLEEN DEBORAH BROWN, retail exec.; b. New Orleans, Nov. 7, 1952; d. Willie Leo and Kathleen Norris (Wilson) Brown; B.A.J., La. State U., 1974; m. John Armand Glover, Jr., July 26, 1974. Advt. mgr. Daily Reveille, La. State U., 1973-74; asst. buyer Halsey, Stakelum & Brown, Inc., New Orleans, 1975; asst. buyer Media Investment Service/McCann-Erickson Inc., Metairie, La., 1975-76, media buyer media investment service, 1976-80; now owner, mgr. Kat's Meow, New Orleans. Mem. jr. opera com. New Orleans Opera Assn., 1974—; com. mem. New Orleans Area council Boy Scouts Am., 1977-78. State Dept. grantee World Congress Women Journalists and Writers, Israel, 1973. Mem. Women in Communications (treas. New Orleans profl. chpt. 1975-76, pres. La. State U. chpt. 1973-74), Metairie Art Guild, Vieux Carre Art Guild, Ladies of the Madonna, Board Soc. (v.p), U.D.C. (pres. chpt. 1981-82). Roman Catholic. Club: Candlelighters. Home: 1521 Haring Rd Metairie LA 70001 Office: 817 Decatur St New Orleans LA 70116

GLOVER, LAURICE WHITE, psychoanalyst, musician; b. Los Angeles, Oct. 15, 1930; d. Lawrence Francis and Alice Violet (King) White; B.A., Occidental Coll., 1951; M.S. in Social Work, Columbia, 1956; cert. in psychoanalysis and psychotherapy Postgrad. Center Mental Health, N.Y.C., 1971, cert. in supervision of psychoanalysis, 1975; student pipe organ Norman Wright, Robert Owen, Virgil Fox; m. Norman James Glover, Aug. 18, 1956 (div. 1963). Pvt. practice psychoanalysis, N.Y.C., 1968—; faculty and sr. supr. psychoanalysis Postgrad. Center Mental Health, N.Y.C., 1976—; asst. clin. prof. psychiatry Albert Einstein Coll. Medicine, Yeshiva, U., N.Y.C., 1975—; adj. asst. prof. psychology Bronx Community Coll., 1974; tng. analyst Nat. Psychol. Assn. for Psychoanalysis, 1974-76; psychoanalysis faculty Nat. Inst. Psychotherapies, 1978—; faculty, sr. supr. psychoanalysis, tng. analyst Tng. Inst. Mental Health Practitioners, 1979—. Organist, choir dir. Throggs' Neck Lutheran Ch., Bronx, N.Y., 1964-67; jazz organist Hotel Barbizon for Women, 1965-66; organist, choir dir. 4th Ave. Meth. Ch., Bklyn., 1967—74. Mem. Soc. Clin. Social Workers, Nat. Assn. Social Workers, Am. Group Psychotherapy Assn., Am. Guild Organists, Am. Theatre Organists Soc., Am. Fedn. Musicians. Contbr. articles to profl. publs. Office: 271 Central Park W New York NY 10024

GLOWA, MARJORIE JANE, consumer credit reporting co. exec.; b. Long Beach, N.Y., Oct. 12, 1941; d. Bernard and Dorothy (Schulman) Deutsch; B.A., Syracuse U., 1963; m. Theodore A. Glowa, Sept. 28, 1974; children—Pamela Reid Bressen, Laura Ashley Bressen. Vice pres., gen. mgr. Central Credit Bur., Schenectady, 1973—; mem. faculty consumer credit SUNY, Albany, SUNY, Cobleskill; speaker on consumer edn., local high schs., colls., Am. Inst. Banking, 1978-81; bd. dirs. Capital region Consumer Credit Counseling Services. Chmn., Clifton Park Halfmoon Ednl. TV fundraising, Saratoga County, N.Y., 1969-71; coordinator Saratoga (N.Y.) Cancer Soc., 1969, Saratoga County ARC, 1970; leader Saratoga County 4H, 1971; chmn. Shenendehowa Community Festival, Saratoga, 1970; mem. secretarial and sci. adv. com. Cobleskill Coll. Recipient ERA award TRW, 1981. Mem. Internat. Consumer Credit Assn., N.Y. State Consumer Fin. Assn., Soc. Consumer Credit Execs., Adminstrv. Mgmt. Soc., Credit Mgmt. Eastern N.Y., N.Y. State Council Retail Credit, Asso. Credit Burs., C. of C. Home: Box 1001 Schenectady NY 12301 Office: 243 State St Schenectady NY 12305

GLOWACKI, LINDA R., ins. co. ofcl.; b. Phila., Dec. 25, 1950; d. Roland E. and Dolores T. (Wilkie) Yocum; m. Thaddeus G. Glowacki, Sept. 19, 1970. With Colonial Penn Group, Inc., Phila., office mgr. law dept., 1975-76, mgr. office services, 1976-77, mgr. purchasing adminstrn., 1977-79, group mgr. purchasing, 1979-80, mgr. adminstrn. for data processing div., 1981—; instr. mgmt. and data processing; freelance writer on mgmt. topics. Mem. Internat. Word Processing Assn., Adminstrv. Mgmt. Soc., Nat. Assn. Purchasing Mgrs. (cert. purchasing mgr.), Nat. Assn. Female Execs. Office: 21st Floor Five Penn Center Philadelphia PA 19103

GLUCK, LOUISE ELISABETH, poet; b. N.Y.C., Apr. 22, 1943; d. Daniel and Beatrice (Grosby) Gluck; student Sarah Lawrence Coll., 1962, Columbia, 1963-65; m. Charles Hertz (div.); 1 son, Noah Benjamin Gluck; m. 2d, John Dranow, 1977. Vis. poet Goddard Coll., U. N.C., U. Va.; vis. poet U. Iowa; Elliston prof. U. Cin., 1978; vis. faculty Columbia U., 1979; faculty M.F.A. program Goddard Coll., 1976-80, Warren Wilson Coll., Swannanoa, N.C., 1981—; Holloway lectr. U. Calif., Berkeley, 1982. Recipient award for creative work Am. Acad. and

Inst. Arts and Letters, 1981; Rockefeller Found. grantee; NEA grantee, 1979-80; Guggenheim Found. grantee. Author: Firstborn, 1968; The House On Marshland, 1975; Descending Figure, 1980. Address: Creamery Rd Plainfield VT 05667

GNADT, JOAN THERESE HARNEY, cardiologist; b. Milw., July 20, 1949; d. Thomas Holland and Rose Caroline (Kriege) Harney; student Marquette U., 1967-68; B.S. in Zoology, U. Wis., Milw., 1971; M.D., Med. Coll. Wis., 1976; m. Gregory James Gnadt, June 25, 1971; 1 son, Geoffrey James. Intern, Martinez (Calif.) VA Med. Center, 1977-78, resident in internal medicine, 1978-80, fellow in cardiology, 1980-82, staff in cardiology, 1982, acting asst. chief cardiology, 1982—; asst. clin. prof. medicine U. Calif., Davis, 1982—. Mem. ACP (asso.), Am. Coll. Cardiology (affiliate in tng.), Am. Med. Women's Assn. Roman Catholic. Home: 5745 Colton Blvd Oakland CA 94611 Office: 150 Muir Rd Martinez CA 94553

GOANS, JUDY SUSANNA WINEGAR, lawyer; b. Knoxville, Tenn., Sept. 27, 1949; d. Robert Henry and Lula Mae (Myers) Winegar; student Sam Houston State U., 1967-68; B.S. in Engring. Physics, U. Tenn., 1971, postgrad., 1971-74, J.D., 1978; m. Ronald E. Goans, June 18, 1971. Teaching asst. dept. physics U. Tenn., Knoxville, 1971-74; instr. legal rights Women's Opportunities and Referrals of Knoxville, 1977-78; patent analyst nuclear div. Union Carbide Corp., Oak Ridge, 1978-79; atty. Office of Asst. Gen. Counsel for Patents, U.S. Dept. Energy, Washington, 1979-82; atty. Office Legislation and Internat. Affairs, U.S. Patent and Trademark Office, Washington, 1982—. Mem. Knoxville Women's Center, 1977—; del. Nat. Women's Conf., Internat. Women's Year; mem. legal bd. Knoxville Rape Crisis Center, 1979; mem. Knox County Republican Exec. Com., 1978-79. Mem. ABA, Tenn. Bar Assn., NOW (dir. 1977-79), Govt. Patent Lawyers Assn. (sec. 1981-83), Am. Patent Law Assn., Sigma Pi Sigma, Tau Beta Pi. Methodist. Home: 2233 Pinefield Rd Waldorf MD 20601

GOBELI, VIRGINIA CLAIRE, home economist; b. Providence, July 14, 1942; d. Albert and Claire Estelle (Plante) Ouellette; B.A. in Foods and Nutrition, Salve Regina Coll., 1964; postgrad., U. R.I., 1972; m. Garrett Frederick Gobeli, Aug. 17, 1974; children—Gayla Elizabeth, Gregory Alfred. Student dietitian Newport (R.I.) Hosp., 1961-64; adminstrv. dietitian N.Y. Hosp.-Cornell Med. Center, N.Y.C., 1965-67; county extension home economist U. R.I., Providence, 1967-69; dairy food publicist N.E. region Am. Dairy Assn., Chgo., 1969-72; state 4-H leader home econs. U. Mass., Amherst, 1972-73; state 4-H specialist Coop. Extension Service, U. Nev., Reno, 1973—; bd. dirs. Redwood Recreation Leadership Lab. Active No. Nev. Childcare Assn.; com. for Community Christmas Carnival; mem. Miss Nev. Hostess Guild, Arts Festival Bd. U. Nev. Mem. Nat. Recreation and Park Soc., Nat. Home Econs. Assn., Nev. Home Econs. Assn., Nat. 4-H Agts. Assn. (service award 1978), Nev. 4-H Agts. Assn., Am. Camping Assn., Epsilon Sigma Phi. Democrat. Roman Catholic. Club: Soroptimists Internat. (Reno-South). Author various 4-H manuals. Home: Box 608 Chepachet RI 02814 Office: State 4-H Office FA236 University of Nevada Reno NV 89557

GOBER, PEGGY GRACE, real estate ofcl.; b. Odessa, Tex., Aug. 12, 1934; d. Matthew Emmit and Vera Belle (Green) Nelson; diploma real estate cum laude Odessa Coll., 1978; student Seminar for Suprs.; m. Walter David Gober, Jr., May 21, 1955; children—Jana Wylene Gober Zimmerman, Dana Francene Gober Sandison, Rhonda Gale. Various office positions, 1949-57, 67-69; bookkeeper, office mgr. W. Tex. White Trucks, Inc., Odessa, 1970-74; office mgr. Bob's Casing Crews, Inc., also Emco Machine Works Co., Odessa, 1974-80; real estate broker Zant & Assos., Odessa, 1979-81; office mgr., sec.-treas. Royal Mud, Inc., Abilene, Tex., 1980—; sales agt. Rayburn Leon Brazzel Real Estate, Abilene, 1981—. Active local Cystic Fibrosis campaign, 1968; precinct rep. Ector County Democratic Conv., 1976; coach Wormettes, Internat. Oil Field Rodeo, Abilene. Mem. Nat. Assn. Female Execs. Baptist. Club: Bob's Casing Crews Wives. Home: 2510 Stonecrest Dr Abilene TX 79606 Office: 4818 Kirkman Abilene TX 79605

GOCHNEAUR, PATRICIA ANN, ins. agt.; b. McMechen, W.Va., July 14, 1934; d. James Wallace and Mabel (Anderson) Pastorius; B.A., Wellesley Coll., 1955; m. Vernon G. Gochneaur, Dec. 16, 1972; children from previous marriage—Deborah Dru Faul, Terri Lisa Faul. Tchr. math. Moravian Sem. for Girls, Bethlehem, Pa., 1955-56; tchr. math Anthony Wayne Schs., Maumee, Ohio, 1963-64; cons., mgr. Fashion Two Twenty Cosmetics, Toledo, 1964, dir., studio owner, Columbus, Ohio, 1965-72; owner, mgr. Credit Card Alert, Simsbury, Conn., 1977-78; pres. Credit Card Alert, Inc., Aurora, Ohio, 1978-79; agt. Northwestern Mut. Life Ins. Co., Bloomfield, Conn., 1979—; owner, breeder standardbred race horses, 1975—. Mem. Nat. Assn. Life Underwriters, Akron Assn. Life Underwriters, U.S. Trotting Assn.

GODBEY, KAROLYN LUSSON, nurse, educator; b. San Diego, Aug. 11, 1937; d. Victor William and Velma Alice (Caskey) Lusson; diploma St. Luke's Hosp. Sch. Nursing, Jacksonville, Fla., 1958; B.S. in Nursing, U. Fla., 1974, M.S. in Nursing, 1975; postgrad. Fla. State U., 1982—; children—Michael Lawrence, Kevin Scott. Pvt. duty nurse Shands Teaching Hosp., Gainesville, Fla., 1959, staff nurse, 1959-62; gynecology nurse practitioner U. Fla. Student Infirmary, 1972-73; pvt. practice psychotherapy, Gainesville, 1972—; instr. nursing U. Fla., 1975-77, asst. prof., 1977—. Pres., Soccer Booster Club Gainesville High Sch., 1977-78, treas., 1977-78; sec. Citizens Adv. Council, 1980-81; block capt. Forest Ridge/Henderson Heights Neighborhood Crime Watch Assn., Gainesville, 1981—. Mem. Sigma Theta Tau, Phi Kappa Phi. Democrat. Roman Catholic. Contbr. in field. Home: 1615 NW 21st St Gainesville FL 32605 Office: Box J-187 JHMHC Gainesville FL 32610

GODDARD, FRANCES BYRD, clin. social worker; b. Greensboro, N.C., Aug. 11, 1939; d. Henry Davis and Blanche Newton (Leavell) Blake; B.A. with honors, Converse Coll., 1961; M.S.W., U. N.C., 1963; m. Anthony Edward Goddard, Oct. 10, 1964; 1 dau., Caroline Stuart. Sr. social worker Children's Home Soc. Va., Richmond, 1963-71; supr. services Culpeper County Dept. Social Services, Culpeper, Va., 1971-74; dir. Culpeper Mental Health Clinic, 1974-76; dir. Culpeper Family Counseling Service, 1976—; mem. Va. Bd. Social Workers, 1978—; cons. Va. State Dept. Welfare on Child Abuse. Pres., Culpeper County Mental Health Assn., 1973. Fellow Am. Orthopsychiat. Assn.; mem. Nat. Assn. Social Workers (pres. Va. chpt. 1978), Otto Rank Assn., Va. Council on Social Welfare, Acad. Cert. Social Workers, Va. Soc. Clin. Social Workers, Am. Assn. State Bds. of Social Work (pres. 1982—), Va. Bd. Social Workers (chmn. 1979-82), Mental Health Assn. of Culpeper (pres. 1980). Episcopalian. Author: A Social Profile of a Southern Community, 1961; Difference Without Distance: Identification with Function in the Helping Process, 1963. Home: Quaint Acres Boston VA 22713 Office: 102 N Main St Culpeper VA 22701

GODDARD, PAULETTE, actress; b. Whitestone, N.Y., June 3, 1915; ed. at pub. schs.; m. Edgar James; m. 2d, Charles Chaplin; m. 3d, Burgess Meredith, June 21, 1944 (div.); m. 4th, Erich Maria Remarque, Feb. 25, 1958 (dec. 1971). Began on New York stage; went to Hollywood for small part in Kid from Spain; played in Modern Times, 1936, Duffy's Tavern, 1945, Kitty, 1945, Standing Room Only, 1944 Diary of a Chambermaid, 1946, Proudly We Hail, 1943, Unconquered, 1947, An Ideal Husband, 1947, Hazard, 1948, On Our Merry Way, 1948, Anna Lucasta, 1949, Woman of Vengeance, 1948, The Torch, 1949, Time of Indifference, 1966; TV movies include the Snoop Sisters, 1972. *

GODFREY, AGNES MULVEY, educator; b. N.Y.C., July 24, 1915; d. Charles Watt and Mary Elizabeth Mulvey; B.A. in Elem. Edn., Columbia U., 1937, M.A. in Child Devel., 1938; m. Raymond V. Godfrey; children—James Terrance, Raymond Michael, Lynn Ellen, Susan Marie. Teaching fellow Columbia U., 1936-37; research asst. Erpi Ednl. Films and Sci. Sch. of Air, 1937-38; tchr. Cranford, N.J., Rye, N.Y., 1938-41; staff div. cultural relations U.S. Dept. State, 1942; staff Nat. Cathedral Sch., Washington, 1943-44, Burroughs Sch., China Lake, Calif., 1947-50; curriculum coordinator Univ. Park Elem. Sch., Melbourne, Fla., 1961-68; dir. curriculum and materials center Brevard County (Fla.) Schs., Melbourne, 1968-69, dir. instrn., 1969-70, area reading clinician, 1971-77; curriculum coordinator, 1977—. Bd. dirs. Friends of Melbourne Library, 1968-70. Named Tchr. of Yr., 1961; recipient citation of merit Nat. Multiple Sclerosis Soc., 1976. Mem. Assn. Childhood Edn., AAUW, Am. Assn. Supervision and Curriculum Devel., Internat., Brevard County (dir.) reading assns., Ringling Art Mus., Delta Kappa Gamma. Author sch. publs.

GODFREY, JUDY JERRELL, assn. exec.; b. Richmond, Va., Aug. 7, 1947; d. William Dandridge and Brantley Hartson (Williams) Jerrell; B.S. in Home Econs. Edn., Longwood Coll., 1969; m. Kent Garff Godfrey, Oct. 7, 1978; 1 son, Christopher Wesley Dandridge. Tchr. home econs. Parker Gray Middle Sch., Alexandria, Va., 1969-71; home economist Dairy Council of Upper Chesapeake Bay Inc., Balt., 1971-72, program dir., 1972-76, exec. dir., 1976—; mem. nutrition edn. adv. coms. Essex Community Coll., Balt. Public Schs., Md. State Health Dept., Morgan State U.; com. mem. nat. nutrition curriculum devel. Nat. Dairy Council; v.p. Md. Agr. Week, Inc., bd. dirs., 1981-82; chmn. Md. Agrl. Dinner Com.; mem. Nat. Food and Nutrition Info. Center Users' Group. Mem. Am. Home Econs. Assn., Md. Home Econs. Assn., Soc. Nutrition Edn., Md. Soc. Assn. Execs., Md. Press Women (charter/founder mem.), Cousteau Soc. Republican. Methodist. Office: 8600 LaSalle Rd 202 Carroll Bldg Towson MD 21204

GODFREY, LORETTA SACHS, advt. exec.; b. Bloomfield, Ind., Dec. 19, 1946; d. Dennis Maurice and Betty Jean (Huber) Sachs; student Ind. U., 1964-69; B.A., Fordham U., 1983. Distbn. supr. Ednl. TV Stas. Program Service, Bloomington, Ind., 1967-69; mgr. traffic dept. Nat. Ednl. TV, N.Y.C., 1969-71; traffic mgr. Benton & Bowles Advt., N.Y.C., 1971; account exec. BBDO Advt., N.Y.C., 1973-76; supr. broadcast ops. and bus. affairs The Lever Media Group div. Lever Bros. Co., N.Y.C., 1976-82; advt. mgr. Publs. Clearing House, Port Washington, N.Y., 1982—. Chmn. communications com. Country Club Estates Civic Assn., Hempstead, N.Y., 1980-81. Mem. NOW. Club: Order Eastern Star. Office: 382 Channel Dr Port Washington NY 11050

GODLES, EILEEN SUSAN, communications co. exec.; b. Kew Gardens, N.Y., Dec. 21, 1948; d. Harry and Rosalind Pauls; B.A., Queens Coll., 1966-71; postgrad. Seton Hall U., 1980. Layout engr. N.Y. Telephone Co., 1972-74; sales coordinator Texfi Industries, N.Y.C., 1974-75; adminstrv. specialist Mobil Oil Co., N.Y.C., 1975-76; service order control supr. ITT, N.Y.C., 1976-77, tng. and documentation specialist, 1977-79; communications systems rep. AT&T, N.Y.C., 1979-81, tech. cons., 1981—. Mem. Nat. Assn. Female Execs. Home: 209 Raymond Av Nutley NJ 07110 Office: 32 Ave of Americas New York NY 10013

GODWIN, GAIL KATHLEEN, author; b. Birmingham, Ala., June 18, 1937; s. Mose Winston and Kathleen (Krahenbuhl) G.; student Peace Jr. Coll., Raleigh, N.C., 1955-57; B.A. in Journalism, U. N.C., 1959; M.A. in English, U. Iowa, 1968, Ph.D., 1971. News reporter, Miami Herald, 1959-60; rep., cons. U.S. Travel Service, London, 1961-65; editorial asst. Saturday Evening Post, 1966; lectr. Iowa Writers Workshop, 1972-73; lectr. Vassar Coll., 1977, Columbia U. Writing Program, 1978, 81; author novels including: The Perfectionists, 1970, Glass People, 1972, The Odd Woman, 1974, Violet Clay, 1978; A Mother and Two Daughters, 1982; short stories: Dream Children, 1976; author librettos (with Robert Starer) The Last Lover, 1975, Apollonia, 1979, Anna Margarita's Will, 1981; fellow Center for Advanced Study, U. Ill., Urbana, 1971-72; Am. specialist USIS, 1976. Nat. Endowment Arts grantee, 1974-75; Guggenheim fellow, 1975-76; recipient award in lit. Am. Acad. and Inst. of Arts and Letters, 1981. Mem. PEN, Authors Guild, Authors League, Nat. Book Critics Circle, ASCAP. Address: care John W Hawkins The Paul Reynolds Agy 12 E 41st St New York NY 10017 *

GODWIN, JOELLA BUSTER, artist; b. Lewisville, Tex.; d. John E. and Emma (Mayfield) Buster; student So. Meth. U., 1930-32, La. State U., 1943, Dallas Mus. Fine Arts Sch., 1962-66, Kathryn Hail Travis Art Sch., Ruidoso, N.Mex., 1966; pvt. study piano with Harold von Mickwitz, 1933-35; m. David George Godwin, Apr. 18, 1936. Piano tchr., Dallas, 1933-37; exhibited art Tex. Fine Arts Regional exhibits Highland Park Town Hall, Dallas, 1965, North Park, Dallas, 1966, Walnut Hills Pub. Library, Dallas, 1966; Region 2 Citation Exhbn. Tex. Fine Arts Assn., 1965-67. Mem. Fine Arts Previewers of So. Meth. U. Mem. Tex. Fine Arts Assn. (v.p. v.p. 1966-67), Dallas Fedn. Music Clubs, DAR, United Meth. Women, Ch. Women United, Dallas Art Assn., Dallas Art Mus. League, Hist. Preservation League, Delta Delta Delta. Methodist. Clubs: Dallas Woman's, Mickwitz (pres. Dallas 1955-57, treas. 1969-70), Mary K. Craig Class, Lyceum.

GOEI, SIOE TIEN, chem. engr.; b. Semarang, Indonesia, Jan. 4, 1940; came to U.S., 1969, naturalized, 1976; d. Henry Kiauw-Bok and Molly Kiam-Nio (Lie) Liem; B.Sc. in Chem. Engring., Bandung Inst. Tech., 1961, M.Sc. in Chem. Engring, 1964; m. Bert T. Goei, May 26, 1966; children—Kimberley Hendrika, Gregory Fitzgerald. Chief lab technician Pomona Wine and Syrup Industries, Bandung, Indonesia, 1965-67; lab. technician serology dept., Alpha Therapeutic Corp., Los Angeles, 1970-72, sr. lab technician biochemistry dept., 1973-74, research scientist research and devel. dept., 1975-77, mgr. process and product devel., 1978-80, dir. process and product devel., 1981—; pres., treas. United Gruno U.S.A. Corp., 1980—. Recipient Corp. Pres.'s award, Alpha Therapeutic Corp., 1979. Mem. Am. Inst. Chem. Engrs., Permai Indonesian Am. Soc. Home: 154 Ladera St Monterey Park CA 91754 Office: 5555 Valley Blvd Los Angeles CA 90032

GOELL, ABBY JANE, painter, appraiser; b. N.Y.C.; d. Stanley Mendel and Anne (Bellin) Wershof; B.A., Syracuse U., 1949; cert. N.Y. Sch. Interior Design, 1958; M.F.A., Columbia U., 1965; postgrad. Attingham Park, Shropshire, Eng., summer 1963, Pratt Graphic Art Center, 1966; 1 son, Mark Jordan. One-woman show: Automation House, N.Y.C., 1973; group shows include: Lumley-Cazalet, London, 1976; AAAL, 1977, Childe Hassam Purchase Exhbn., N.Y.C., 1977, U.S. Dept. State, Havana, Cuba, 1979, Sculpture Center, N.Y.C., 1981, Silvermine Ann., 1981, 82; represented in permanent collections: Chase Manhattan Bank, Mus. Modern Art, N.Y.C., Atlantic Richfield Oil Co., Yale U., Sloane-Kettering Meml. Center, N.Y.C., Grafisches Kabinet, Munich, W.Ger.; co-pub. Arcadia Press, N.Y.C., 1980—; tchr. Hunter Coll., 1967, Lab. Inst. Merchandising, 1967-70. Yaddo fellow, 1968; Va. Center for Creative Arts fellow, 1981. Mem. Am. Soc. Appraisers (sr.), Women's Caucus for Art, Victorian Soc. in Am., Nat. Trust for Historic Preservation. Democrat. Editor: English Silver 1675-1825, 1980. Home and office: 37 Washington Square W New York NY 10011

GOEN, CYNTHIA DOLORES, nurse; b. Houston, Apr. 22, 1948; d. Simon and Consuelo Barbara (De La Garza) Elizondo; B.S. in Nursing, Dominican Coll., 1971; m. Herbert Don Goen, June 8, 1969; children—Anne Marie, Kelly Colleen, Philip Jeffery. Staff nurse med.-surg. unit St. Joseph Hosp., Houston, 1971-74; office nurse Michael K. O'Heeron, M.D., urologist, Houston, 1974; staff nurse CCU, Meml. Hosp. System-S.E. Unit, Houston, 1975-76, asst. head nurse med. unit, relief charge nurse duty emergency room, intensive care unit and CCU, 1976-79; cardiovascular nurse specialist Cardiology Lab., Kelsey-Seybold Clinic, Houston, 1979—. Mem. Am. Assn. Critical-Care Nurses, Am. Cardiology Technologists Assn. Home: 8315 Glenalta St Houston TX 77061

GOERNER, LINDA C., real estate broker, editor; b. Pocahontas, Iowa, Jan. 12, 1948; d. Reynold Russell and Darlene Lucille (Hoffert) G.; student Creighton U., Omaha, U. Iowa. Sales asso. Urban Investment and Devel. Co., real estate, Chgo., 1974-76; sales mgr. Village West Sales Co., Hazel Crest, Ill., 1976-78, B & B Investment Co., 1978-79; broker/sales mgr. Chgo. Service Realty, 1979-81; broker Four Sales Sales Co., 1981—; creator, editor Condo. minium mag., Chgo., 1981—. Mem. Million Dollar Sales Club, 1977, 78. Mem. Nat. Assn. Realtors. Lutheran. Home: 2332 Wehrli Rd Naperville IL 60565 Office: 5541 East Lake Dr Lisle IL 60532

GOETZ, FAITH HENDERSON, advt. research firm exec.; b. Chgo., June 12, 1918; d. James Robertson and Mary (Cook) Henderson; student Stephens Coll. for Women, 1935-37, Moser Bus. Coll., 1937-38; m. John W. Goetz, Jr., Oct. 29, 1949. Adminstrv. asst. Clark Subs. Agy., Chgo., 1938-50; asst. to exec. placement mgr. Carson Pirie Scott & Co., Chgo., 1967-70; v.p., personnel dir. Gallup & Robinson, Inc., Princeton, N.J., 1970—, dir., 1977—. Mem. Princeton Personnel Assn. Presbyterian. Office: 575 Ewing St PO Box 525 Princeton NJ 08540

GOETZ, THERESE ELIZABETH, orgnl. cons.; b. Orange, N.J., Nov. 23, 1950; d. Henry G. and Mathilde (Cornely) Goetz; B.A., Douglass Coll., Rutgers U., 1972; M.A., U. Ill., Champaign-Urbana, 1975, Ph.D., 1978; m. Ronald J. Lipinski, July 30, 1977; 1 dau., Valerie Anne. Teaching asst. U. Ill., 1972-77; asst. prof. psychology U. N.Mex., 1977-81, part-time, 1981—; orgnl. cons. Therese Goetz and Assos., Albuquerque, 1981—. U. N.Mex. research allocation grantee, 1977-80; NSF undergrad. research grantee, summer 1971. Mem. Profl. Orgn. for Women (exec. task force 1980-81, dir. 1981-82), Am. Mgmt. Assn., Am. Psychol. Assn., Am. Soc. Tng. and Devel., N.Mex. Network for Women in Sci. and Engring., Sigma Xi, Psi Chi. Roman Catholic. Office: 4800 Southern Ave SE Albuquerque NM 87108

GOFF, GIGI E., advt. agy. mgr.; b. Los Angeles, July 28, 1937; d. William Allen and Florence Roberta (Roberts) Glynn; student Central Oreg. Community Coll., 1954-55; divorced; children—Darrell, Dale, Nancy, Lynda, David. Partner, office mgr. Waco Auction House (Tex.), 1960-63; partner Goff & Assos., ins., 1963-75; mgr. Walter W. Cribbins Co., splty. advt., Beaverton, Oreg., 1976—. Recipient Creativity in Advt. awards (5), 1979-81. Mem. Sales and Mktg. Execs. Internat. (v.p.), Inst. Mangerial Women, Nat. Assn. Female Execs., Portland Advt. Fedn., Greater Portland Conv. and Visitors Assn., Portland C. of C., Beaverton C. of C. Home: 13175 SW Oakwood St Beaverton OR 97005 Office: 4175 SW Cedar Hills Blvd Beaverton OR 97005

GOFF, JACQUELINE ANN, bus. exec.; b. Kittery, Maine, May 25, 1943; d. Jacob Benjamin Millard and Leila Ann (Camp) G.; B.M., La. State U., 1967. Sec., Dow Chem. Co., 1968-69; with Hydrocarbon Constrn. Co., Houston, 1970-74, asst. expediter, 1972-74; material expediter Pullman-Kellogg, Houston, 1974, sr. expediter, 1974, material coordinator, expediting supr., 1975—. Mem. Assn. Profl. Expediters. Republican. Presbyterian. Home: 2155 Winrock Apt 2 Houston TX 77057

GOFF, PATRICIA JOAN, sales exec.; b. Balt.; d. John R. and Catherine M. (Miller) Moore; m. Joseph Goff, Aug. 9, 1975; children by previous marriage—Kathleen, Jimmy, Danny and Maureen Quinn. Mgr., sales rep. Tupperware Home Parties, Wayne, N.J., 1962-67; sales rep. Airbrook Limousines, Saddle Brook, N.J., 1974-76; sales rep. Photo Corp. of Am., Edison, N.J., 1976-78; sales mgr., sales rep. Natpac, Inc., Union, N.J., 1978-82; sales exec. Vacation Concepts Inc., McAfee, N.J., 1982—. Recipient several awards Natpac, including Salesperson of Yr., 1979. Home: 18 Beaver Brook Dr RD 5 Sussex NJ 07461 Office: PO Box 638 McAfee NJ 07428

GOFF, REGINA MARY, educator; b. St. Louis; d. Ward Wellington and Annabelle (Young) Goff; B.A. in Edn., Northwestern U., 1934; M.A., Columbia, 1940, Ph.D., 1948; m. Josiah F. Henry, Jr., Sept. 23, 1960. Dir. nursery sch., St. Louis, 1935; tchr. kindergarten, Kansas City, Kans., 1936-39; instr. Lincoln U., Jefferson City, Mo., 1940-46; dir. student teaching Stowe Tchrs. Coll., St. Louis, 1947-48; prof. child devel. Fla. A. and M. Coll., Tallahassee, also supr. Fla. Dept. Edn., 1949-50; mem. faculty Morgan State Coll., Balt., 1950-65, chmn. dept. edn., 1963-65; asst. commr., office of programs for disadvantaged U.S. Office Edn., Washington, 1965-71; prof. U. Md., 1971—; Union Grad. Sch., Union Exptl. Colls. and Univs., 1976—; cons. Ministry Edn. Iran, 1955-56. Mem. child welfare com. Md. Conf. and Welfare, 1960-62; pres. Urban League Md., 1961-63, bd. dirs., 1959-64; bd. dirs. UN of Md., Children's Guild Md., UNICEF of Md. Recipient Pub. Service in Edn. awards Urban League Balt., 1963, St. Louis Assn. Negro Women's Clubs, 1965, Nat. and Profl. Bus. Women's Clubs, 1966, Alpha Kappa Alpha, 1966; Rockefeller Found. fellow, 1945-46. Mem. Am. Psychol. Assn., Md. Assn. Tchr. Edn. (pres.), NEA, Pi Lambda Theta, Kappa Delta Pi, Psi Chi, Phi Delta Kappa, Alpha Kappa Alpha. Democrat. Roman Catholic. Contbr. articles on ednl. studies, cultural influence on personality devel. to ednl. jours. Home: 2306 Montebello Terr Baltimore MD 21214

GOFFEN, RONA, art historian; b. N.Y.C., June 7, 1944; d. William and Stella G.; A.B. cum laude, Mt. Holyoke Coll., 1966; M.A., Columbia U., 1968, Ph.D. with distinction, 1974. Lectr, Ind. U., Bloomington, 1971-73; lectr. Princeton (N.J.) U., 1973-74, asst. prof. art and archeology, 1974-78; asst. prof. art Duke U., Durham, N.C., 1978-80, assoc. prof., 1980—; vis. prof. Barnard Coll., 1980. Com. to Rescue Italian Art/Ford Found. fellow, Venice, 1970-71; vis. scholar Am. Acad. Rome, 1976; Am. Council Learned Socs. fellow, 1976-77; Villa I Tatti fellow, 1976-77; G.K. Delmas Found. grantee, 1980; Am. Philos. Soc. grantee, 1982. Mem. Coll. Art Assn. Am., Renaissance Soc. Am. Contbr. articles to profl. jours. Office: Dept Art Duke U Durham NC 27708

GOFMAN, FEYGA, chemist; b. Kishinev, USSR, June 18, 1938; d. Khaim and Lea (Shtienberg) Rawitsky; student Kishinev State U., 1955-60; m. Semyon Gofman, Feb. 28, 1965; children—Yefim, Margarita. Chem. engr., Shoe factory, Zorile, Kishinev, USSR, 1960-63, mgr. chem. dept., 1963-79; chief chemist Davis Mfg. Co., Inc., San Antonio, 1979—. Jewish. Home: 518 Red Cliff San Antonio TX 78216 Office: 1023 Morales San Antonio TX 78285

GOGATE, SHASHI ANAND, physician; b. Indore, India, July 9, 1938; d. Kashinath M. and Manorama R.; M.B.B.S., M.G.M. Med. Coll., 1962; M.S., Ohio State U., 1969; m. Anand B. Gogate, June 20, 1962; children—Sangita, Soniya, Sanjay. Instr., research asso. Ohio State U., 1970-73, asst. prof. pathology, 1973-75, asst. clin. prof., 1975—; dir. lab. Columbus Pathology Lab., 1975-79, chief pathology, 1976—; pres. S.A. Gogate M.D., Inc., 1978—. Mem. adv. bd. Internat. Mediation Soc., Columbus. Fellow Coll. Am. Pathologists, Am. Soc. Clin. Pathologists;

mem. AMA, Ohio Med. Assn., Franklin County Med. Soc., Fairfield County Med. Soc., Internat. Acad. Pathology, Republican. Hindu. Contbr. articles to profl. jours. Home: 6112 Sedgwick Rd Worthington OH 43085 Office: Lancaster Farifield Community Hosp 401 N Ewing St Lancaster OH 43130

GOGGINS, PHYLLIS MORGAN ASHFORD, health care adminstr.; b. New Haven, Aug. 5, 1926; d. Daniel D. and Mildred R. (Hobbs) Morgan; B.S. in Nursing, Fla. Internat. U., 1974; M.S. in Nursing, U. Conn., 1979; m. William J. Goggins, May 8, 1971; children—Karen, Andrea, Christopher, Eric. Public health nurse, Fairfax County, Va., 1948-50; vol. clinic nurse, New Delhi, India, 1952-54, Asuncion, Paraguay, 1957-59, San Pedro Sula, Honduras, 1961-64; staff nurse Univ. Community Hosp., Tampa, Fla., 1969-71; evening charge nurse pediatrics Naples (Fla.) Community Hosp., 1971-73; public health nurse Collier County Health Dept., Naples, 1973-75; supr. Northwest Community Nursing and Health Service, Harmony, R.I., 1975-77, asst. dir., 1977-79, exec. dir., 1979—; clin. instr. community health nursing R.I. Coll., Providence, 1981-82. Mem. R.I. Gov.'s Commn. Home Health Care Needs, 1981-82, Gov.'s Adv. Council on Zambarano Hosp., 1980-81. Mem. Am. Public Health Assn., Nat. League Nursing, New Eng. Public Health Assn., Am. Nurses Assn., R.I. Assn. Home Health Agys. (chmn. council dirs. 1980-82), Glocester Bus. Assn., N. Providence Bus. and Profl. Women's Assn., Alumni Assn. Mass. Gen. Hosp. Home: 33 Hillcrest Ave Greenville RI 02828 Office: PO Box 234 Harmony RI 02829

GOGICK, KATHY CHRISTINE, mag. editor; b. Passaic, N.J., Aug. 3, 1945; d. Joseph John and Emeline (Radwin) Wadowski; student Emmanuel Coll., 1963-64; B.S., Fairleigh Dickinson U., 1967; m. Robert Joseph Gogick, Feb. 24, 1968; 1 son, Jonathan. Asst. beauty editor Cosmopolitan Mag., N.Y.C., 1967-68; merchandising mgr. Co-ed Mag., 1968-69, editor-in-chief, 1976—; creative mgr. Estee Lauder, Inc., N.Y.C., 1969-72; asso. editor Town & Country Mag., 1972-76. Trustee, Fairleigh Dickinson U., 1980—. Mem. Am. Soc. Mag. Editors, Women in Communications, Fashion Group. Office: Co-ed Magazine 50 W 44th St New York NY 10036

GOHDE, SANDRA ESHRICH, speech and lang. pathologist; b. Hackensack, N.J., June 7, 1950; d. Charles Henry and Gilda Rita (Volpe) Eshrich; B.A. magna cum laude, Montclair State Coll., 1972, M.A., 1978; m. Robert P. Gohde, May 5, 1974. Adult edn. lipreading instr. Montclair (N.J.) Bd. Edn., 1974-75; speech and lang. pathologist Parsippany-Troy Hills Bd. Edn., Parsippany, N.J., 1972—. Mem. Am. Speech, Lang. and Hearing Assn., N.J. Speech and Hearing Assn., Morris County Speech and Hearing Assn. Roman Catholic. Home: 16 Adler Ct Rockaway Boro NJ 07866 Office: Parsippany-Troy Hills Bd of Education PO Box 52 Parsippany NJ 07054

GOINES, BEVERLY TERRELL, writer, bank ofcl.; b. Knoxville, Dec. 10, 1953; d. William French and Catherine Terrell; B.S. in Communications (Am. Newspaper Pubs. Assn. scholar), U. Tenn., 1975; M.A. in Communications (Kiplinger fellow), Ohio State U., 1976; m. James Edward Goines, Aug. 8, 1981. Intern-reporter Knoxville News-Sentinel, 1972, gen. assignment reporter, 1972-75, religion editor, gen. assignment reporter, 1976-81; public relations rep. First Tenn. Bank N.A., Memphis, 1981—. writer U. Tenn. Public Relations Office, Knoxville, 1975; teaching asso. Ohio State U. Journalism Sch., 1975-76. Named Outstanding Sr. Woman U. Tenn., 1975. Mem. Women in Communications, Inc., Knoxville Newspaper Guild, Diet Workshop (life), Sigma Delta Chi, Delta Sigma Theta. Democrat. Baptist. Home: 516 Whitestone Memphis TN 38109 Office: 165 Madison Ave Memphis TN 38103

GOKBORA, MARY JANE MCKEE, social worker; b. Mankato, Minn.; d. John Cecil and Claire (Nieberle) McKee; B.A., U. Iowa, 1946, M.S.W., 1958; m. Ahmet Gokbora, Jan. 11, 1946 (div. June 1956); children—Gail M., Erol K. Pub. assistance worker Iowa Dept. Social Welfare, Linn County, 1951-56; child welfare worker, Marshall and Tama Counties, 1958-59; psychiat. social worker, mental health team Div. Mental Health, Iowa Bd. Control State Instns., 1959-60; dir. social services Iowa State Tng. Sch. for Boys, Eldora, 1960-62; supt. Mo. State Tng. Sch. for Girls, Chillicothe, 1962-71; social work cons. to Mo. Law Enforcement Assistance Council, Jefferson City, Mo., Women in Community Service, Lincoln, Nebr., St. Francis Homes, Albany, N.Y., 1971-75; clin. asst. prof. Sch. Social Welfare, State U. N.Y., Albany, 1975-78; psychiatric social worker div. Devel. Disabilities, State of N.Y., 1978—. Certified social worker, N.Y. Mem. Nat. Fedn. Bus. and Profl. Womens Clubs, AAUW, U. Iowa Alumni Assn., Nat. Assn. Social Workers (chpt. v.p. 1965-66, sec. 1974—), Nat. Council Crime and Delinquency, Joint Commn. Correctional Manpower and Tng., Nat. Assn. Tng. Schs. and Juvenile Agys. (v.p. 1963-69), Nat. Conf. Supts. of Correctional Instns. for Girls and Women (pres. 1965-66), Acad. Certified Social Workers, Register Clin. Social Workers. Episcopalian. Address: 22 Tulip Terr Clifton Park NY 12065

GOLAN, MARGO ELIZABETH, business exec.; b. Lafayette, Ind., Aug. 23, 1916; d. Charles Fenton and Sarah Elizabeth (Fisher) May; grad. high sch.; m. Samuel L. Golan, Dec. 2, 1944 (dec. Dec. 1969); 1 dau., Kim (Mrs. Marvin Chancellor Norton, Jr.); stepchildren—Leonard Walter, Frederick Joseph. With Kauffman & Wulf Dept. Store, Hammond, Ind., 1935-36; dept. head Goldblatt Bros., Inc., Hammond, 1936-42; with Holiday Inn, Key West, Fla., 1960—, innkeeper, 1962—; dir. Key West & Lower Kays Devel. Corp., Key West Redevel. Agy., 1979-80. Chmn., Monroe County Advt. Commn., 1969-76; mem. Monroe County Master-Plan Adv. Council; bd. dirs. Monroe County Public Library; commr. governing bd. Lower Fla. Keys Hosp. Dist. Recipient Community Service award Lions Club, 1975; Outstanding Community Service award NAACP, 1975; Outstanding Service to Community award Fla. Keys Community Coll., 1976; Community Service award Key West Navy League, 1977; Outstanding Community Service award Fla. State Grand Lodge Masons, 1977; Outstanding Generosity and Service to Community award City of Key West, 1978; Jaycee award, 1980; Appreciation award Boy Scouts Am., 1982; award Key West C. of C. Hall of Fame, 1982. Mem. Key West C. of C. (dir., recipient Community Service award 1971), Internat. Assn. Holiday Inns (advt. com. 1971, reservation com. 1972). Club: Key West Women's (dir., recipient Outstanding Mem. award 1972). Home: 2 Go-Ln Key West FL 33040 Office: 1111 N Roosevelt Blvd Key West FL 33040

GOLD, BARBARA ROSE, actuary; b. Bklyn., Mar. 7, 1948; d. Harry and Esther (Leibowitz) Comisar; B.A. magna cum laude with honors in Math., Bklyn. Coll., 1968; m. Jeffery Gold, Sept. 1, 1968; 1 dau., Erica Rachael. With Met. Life Ins. Co., N.Y.C., 1968-77; asso. actuary Guardian Life Ins. Co., N.Y.C., 1977-81, actuary, 1980-81; v.p. and asst. actuary Prudential Life Ins. Co., N.J., 1981—. Fellow Soc. Actuaries (examination com. 1976-78, com. on life and health corp. affairs 1980—); mem. Am. Acad. Actuaries, Phi Beta Kappa. Home: 29 Foxburn St New City NY 10956 Office: Prudential Plaza Newark NJ 07101

GOLD, CAROL SAPIN, mgmt. cons., lectr., writer; b. N.Y.C., June 28; d. Cerf S. and Muriel L. (Fudin) Rosenberg; B.A., U. Calif., Berkeley, 1955; m. Joseph B. Weinstein, Dec. 26, 1976; children—Kevin Bart, Craig Paul, Courtney Byrens. Pub. relations cons. Braun & Co., Los Angeles, 1964-67; corp. dir. personnel tng. Great Western Fin. Corp., Los Angeles, 1968-70; pres. Carol Sapin Gold & Assos., Los Angeles, 1971—, mgmt. cons., 1968—; lectr. various univs. including U. Calif. at Los Angeles, 1971, 75, Calif. Inst. Tech., 1974; guest speaker radio and TV programs, 1972—; cons. to fed. govt. agys., Fortune 500 Co., also comml. orgns., 1971—; radio-TV guest, 1976-78. Mem. Am. Soc. for Tng. and Devel., Nat. Speakers Assn., Am. Mgmt. Assn. (mem. staff 1971-74), Sales and Marketing Execs., Am. Mgmt. Research Internat. (mem. staff 1972—). Author: If You Don't Say Green, You Can't Grow, 1975; Success Secrets; Leadership in Customer Relations, 1980; contbr. numerous articles on mgmt. and communication to profl. jours.; featured in films on interpersonal communication, latest being Instant Replay, 1978. Address: 4121 Redwood Ave Los Angeles CA 90066

GOLD, DORIS (BAUMAN), publicist; writer, publisher; b. N.Y.C., Nov. 21, 1919; d. Saul and Gertrude (Reiss) Bauman; B.A., Bklyn. Coll., 1946; M.A., Washington U., St. Louis, 1955; m. Bernard G. Gold, Oct. 18, 1953; children—Albert, Michael. Instr. in English, U. Kans., 1946-48, SUNY, Farmingdale, 1957-59; editor Young Judaean Mag., 1963-72; astronomy educator Hall of Sci., N.Y.C., 1969-73; writer Fedn. Jewish Philanthropies, N.Y.C., 1972-74; exec. dir. Pete McGuinness Sr. Center, Bklyn., 1974-77; public relations Assoc. YM-YWHAs of N.Y., 1978—; pub. Biblio Press, Fresh Meadows, N.Y., 1979—; Eastern region coordinator task force women and volunteering NOW, 1973-76; mem. adv. bd. Lilith, Jewish women's mag., 1977—; author: Stories for Jewish Juniors, 1967; (poetry) Honey In The Lion, 1979; essay in Woman In Sexist Society, 1971, Opposition To Volunteerism Bibliography, 1979; freelance writer, researcher, 1948—. Founder, Mid-Island YM-YWHA, Wantagh, N.Y., 1957.

GOLD, SHERRY SHIFRA, social worker; b. Lithuania, Aug. 13, 1928; d. Philip and Nechama Gerber; B.A. cum laude, Ohio U., 1949; M.A., Bank Street Sch., 1960; M.S.W., Yeshiva U., 1975; m. Melvin L. Gold, Jan. 29, 1950; children—Charles, Neil, Ronald, Nina. Dir., Coop. Nursery Sch., Paterson, N.J., 1950-52; tchr. schs., Israel, 1954-56; prin. Sholem Alecheim Folk Sch., Verona, N.J., 1957-60; social worker Jewish Counseling and Service Agy., Millburn, N.J., 1975-77; caseworker Jewish Family Service of N. Jersey, Wayne, 1977—; bd. dirs. Center for Family Studies; cons. Quality Care, Inc. Bd. dirs. Am. Jewish Congress; mem. exec. bd. LWV; mem. bd. edn. Temple B'nai Abraham. Mem. Nat. Assn. Social Workers, Assn. for Mental Health Affiliation with Israel. Home: 29 Lakeview Dr West Orange NJ 07052 Office: 1 Pike Dr Wayne NJ 07470

GOLD, SHIRLEY JEANNE, state legislator, labor relations specialist; b. N.Y.C., Oct. 2, 1925; d. Louis and Gussie (Lefkowitz) Diamondstein; B.A. in Music, Hunter Coll., 1945; M.A. in Behavioral Sci. (Crown-Zellerbach Corp. scholar), Reed Coll., 1962; m. David E. Gold, June 22, 1947; children—Andrew, Dana. Tchr., Portland (Oreg.) Public Schs., 1954-68; pres. Portland Fedn. Tchrs., Am. Fedn. Tchrs./AFL-CIO, 1965-72, pres. Oreg. Fedn. Tchrs., 1972-77; cons. labor relations to univs., coll., Portland, 1977-80; mem. Oreg. Ho. of Reps., Salem, 1980—; mem. Oreg. Tchr. Tenure Rev. Bd., 1965-72; mem. Nat. Multi-State Consortium, 1974; mem. Speak Out Oreg. com. to White House and Congress, 1978; mem. Oreg. Task Force on Tax Reform; AFL-CIO scholar George Meany Inst., 3 times, 1976-77. Chairperson precinct com., conv. del. Oreg. Democratic Party, 1960-80, dist. leader, chairperson edn. com., 1978-80; charter mem., mem. exec. bd., v.p. Oreg. Council for Cts., 1977-80. Mem. Hunter Coll. Alumni Assn., Reed Coll. Alumni Assn., Pacific N.W. Labor History Assn., Portland Fedn. Tchrs., Oreg. Fedn. Tchrs., Oreg. Fedn. Dem. Women, Oreg. Coalition for Nat. Health Security, Oreg. Women's Polit. Caucus, ACLU, Coalition Labor Union Women. Jewish. Contbr. articles on labor relations to Willamette Week newspaper, 1977-80; editor Oreg. Tchr. newspaper, 1970-72. Office: H493 State Capitol Bldg Salem OR 97301

GOLDAMMER, JANN HUNT, retail exec.; b. Council Bluffs, Iowa, Nov. 24, 1946; d. Jerome K. and Helena O. Miller; student Gemological Inst. Am., 1973-74, Ill. Central Coll., 1981-82; m. James H. Goldammer, Aug. 29, 1980; children—Randy Lee Hunt, Nancy Lynn Hunt. Jewelry buyer C. B. Brown, Omaha, 1966-67; admissions U. Nebr., Omaha, 1968; service rep. Northwestern Bell Telephone Co., Omaha, 1965-66; area mgr. Brandeis Dept. Stores subs. Selco, Inc., Omaha, 1969-75; v.p., gen. mgr. Finlay Fine Jewelry, Peoria, Ill., 1975-82; corp. sales mgr. Rich's Dept. Store, Atlanta, 1982—. Mem. stewardship com., bd. dirs. Our Savior Lutheran Ch., Pekin, Ill.; active Pekin Am. Bus. Club Ann. Charity Auction. Office: 45 Broad St SW Atlanta GA 30303

GOLDBERG, BARBARA BERNICE, librarian; b. Phila., June 20, 1951; d. Nathan Freda (Sokolic) G.; B.A., Temple U., 1972; M.S. in L.S. (NIH grantee), Case Western Res. U., 1973; postgrad. Baruch Coll., 1977-79. Librarian dept. pediatrics Rainbow Baby and Children's Hosp., Cleve., 1972-73; dir. med. libraries Doctors Hosp., Columbus, Ohio, 1973-76; asst. librarian Beth Israel Med. Center, N.Y.C., 1976-77, asso. librarian, 1977-78; med. librarian VA Hosp., Bklyn., 1978-79; chief library services VA Med. Center, Bklyn. Extended Care Center, St. Albans, OPC Ryerson St., 1979—; guest lectr. Ohio U. Sch. Library Tech., 1975, 76; chmn. VA Dist. 3 Library Council, 1981-82; chmn. steering com. Consumer Health Info. Group, 1981-83; mem. Med. Library Center Planning Subcom., 1981-83; speaker NLM Medline Update, 1980. Nat. Library of Medicine trainee Aug. 1977, Apr. 1978. Mem. Med. Library Assn. (cert., N.Y. regional group 1976—, chmn. small health scis. libraries group 1979-80), AAUW, Spl. Library Assn., Franklin County Assn. Health Sci. Librarians (vice chmn. 1975-76), Bklyn. Queens S.I. Health Services Libraries. Jewish. Home: 155 E 23d St Apt 509 New York NY 10010

GOLDBERG, GERALDINE ELIZABETH, clin. psychologist; b. Neptune, N.J., Mar. 22, 1939; d. Albert V. and Katherine Irene (Mulholland) McCormick; B.S. cum laude, East Stroudsburg (Pa.) State Coll., 1967; M.A. in Psychology, Fairleigh Dickinson U., 1971; m. Arthur Goldberg, July 1, 1961. Staff clin. psychologist Youth Devel. Clinic, Newark, 1971-75; psychotherapist in clin. psychology Mental Health Consultation Center, N.Y.C., 1975—; human resources specialist Age Corp., Livingston, N.J., 1979—, v.p., 1980—, sec. bd. dirs., 1977—. Mem. Am. Psychol. Assn. (asso.), N.J. Assn. Profl. Psychologists (v.p. 1978-81, pres. 1982), N.J. Psychol. Assn. (asso.).

GOLDBERG, JANE ELLEN, banker; b. N.Y.C., Nov. 25, 1947; d. Albert H. and Frances (Wolf) G.; A.B., Barnard Coll., 1968. Credit analyst Morgan Guaranty Trust Co. N.Y., 1968-70, fin. analyst, 1970-73, loan work-out officer, 1973-76, comml. banking officer, 1976-78, real estate fin. officer, 1978—, v.p., 1980—. Bd. dirs., trustee Joyce Theatre Found., Inc.; chmn. 310 Lexington Tenants Orgn., 1980-82. Mem. Nat. Assn. Corp. Real Estate Execs. (past v.p., treas. N.Y.C. chpt.), Fin. Women's Assn. Home: 310 Lexington Ave New York NY 10016 Office: 23 Wall St New York NY 10015

GOLDBERG, JO-ANNE KATHLEEN RZEPKA, social work cons.; b. Elizabeth, N.J., Apr. 4, 1952; d. Joseph Valentine and Mildred Helen (Barron) Rzepka; B.A., B.S.W., Syracuse U., 1974, M.S.W., 1975; m. Robert M. Goldberg, Mar. 6, 1977. Social worker, supr. VA Hosp., Syracuse, N.Y., field instr. Coll. Human Devel., Syracuse U., 1975-76; social work specialist in cardiac care Muhlenberg Hosp., Planifield, N.J., field instr. Sch. Social Work, Livingston Coll., 1976-77; social worker U. Pa. Hosp., Phila., field supr. Sch. Social Work, U. Pa., Pa. State U., West Chester State Coll., 1977-80; social work cons. for pvt. facilities specializing in long-term care; dir. in-service tng. programs for allied health care profls., Phila., 1980—; mem. long-term care adv. com. Health Systems Agy. Southeastern Pa., 1979—. Sloan Kettering Cancer Center fellow Meml. Hosp., N.Y.C., 1978. Mem. Alumni Presdl. Classroom for Young Ams., Nat. Assn. Social Workers, Acad. Polit. and Social Scis., Acad. Cert. Social Workers, Phi Beta Kappa, Phi Kappa Phi, Eta Pi Upsilon. Democrat. Jewish. Home: Bldg #U5 Sea Aire Chapman Blvd Somers Point NJ 08244

GOLDBERG, JUDITH MARION, resort ranch exec.; b. N.Y.C., Apr. 15, 1945; d. David and Frances (Chachanowsky) Katz; B.S., Empire State Coll., 1981; postgrad. Pace U. Grad. Sch. Bus., 1981—; m. Norman Goldberg, Feb. 23, 1973. Adminstrv. asst., staff coordinator, staff dir. local and statewide polit. campaigns, 1965-72; office mgr. firm O'Dwyer & Bernstien, N.Y.C., 1972-74; co-owner, mktg. dir. Sunnycroft Ranch Resort, Wallkill, N.Y., 1974—; v.p., bd. dirs. Orange County Tourism and Promotion Corp.; lectr. Mem. Am. Soc. Profl. and Exec. Women, Nat. Assn. Female Execs. Office: RD 1 Brunswick Rd Wallkill NY 12589

GOLDBERG, KAREN JOY, high fashion optical co. exec.; b. Evergreen Park, Ill., Apr. 2, 1942; d. A.F. and E.R. (Davison) Knauf; student U. Chgo., U. Ill., Lawrence Inst. Tech.; m. H.D. Goldberg, Nov. 22, 1970; children—Marc Steven, Cydney Anne. Asst. traffic dir. MPD, Mitsubishi Internat. Corp., Chgo., 1961-63; asst. Barton Distilling Co., Chgo., 1963; asst. to pres., clinic coordinator, asst. registrar Chgo. Coll. Osteo. Medicine, Chgo., 1964-70; pres. Multi Corp Ops., Hamtramck, Mich., 1977—; dir. Automated Eyecare Corp., Infomatrix Corp. Mem. Nat. Assn. Female Execs., Am. Optometric Assn., Opticians Assn. Mich., Hamtramck C. of C. (dir.), Mich. Profl. Women's Network (dir.). Clubs: Hadassah, B'nai B'rith. Office: Campau Optical Div MCO 9727 Joseph Campau Hamtramck MI 48212

GOLDBERG, LEE WINICKI, furniture co. exec.; b. Laredo, Tex., Nov. 20, 1932; d. Frank and Goldie (Ostrowiak) Winicki; student San Diego State U., 1951-52; m. Frank M. Goldberg, Aug. 17, 1952; children—Susan Arlene, Edward Lewis, Anne Carri. With United Furniture Co., Inc., San Diego, 1953—, corporate sec., dir., 1963—, dir. environ. interiors, 1970—; founder Drexel-Heritage store Edwards Interiors, subs. United Furniture, 1975; founding partner, v.p. FLJB Corp., constrn., 1976. Den mother Boy Scouts Am., San Diego, 1965; vol. Am. Cancer Soc., San Diego, 1964-69; chmn. jr. matrons United Jewish Fedn., San Diego, 1958; del. So. Pacific Coast region Hadassah Conv., 1960, pres. Galilee group San Diego chpt., 1960-61; supporter Marc Chagall Nat. Mus., Nice, France, Smithsonian Instn., Los Angeles County Mus., La Jolla (Calif.) Mus. Contemporary Art. Recipient Hadassah Service award San Diego chpt., 1958-59. Mem. Nat. Home Furnishings Inst. Democrat. Jewish religion.

GOLDBERG, LOUISE BERNSTEIN, educator; b. N.Y.C., June 3, 1931; d. Joseph and Anna (Wainrober) Bernstein; B.A., Bklyn. Coll., 1965; M.S., Queens Coll., City U. N.Y., 1968; m. Marvin Goldberg, May 2, 1953; children—Steven, Gary. Various secretarial positions, 1951-54; piano instr., 1961-62; tchr. 3d grade May Moore Sch., Deer Park, N.Y., 1965—. Mem. NEA, PTA, Deer Park Tchrs. Assn., Am. Numismatic Soc. Republican. Jewish. Home: 8 Belmont Pl Hicksville NY 11801 Office: 239 Central Ave Deer Park NY 11729

GOLDBERG, MARCY REINITZ, insurance exec.; b. Detroit, Aug. 23, 1945; d. George Joseph and Terry (Epps) Reinitz; B.S., Northwestern U., 1967; postgrad. Purdue U., 1973; C.L.U., DePaul U., Chgo., 1975, postgrad. in taxation, 1975—; m. Joseph Michael Goldberg, Oct. 20, 1968; 1 dau., Rachel Ann. Life underwriter Guardian Life Ins. Co., Chgo., 1971-73; life underwriter, corp. fringe benefit analyst Coordinated Fin. Programming, Chgo., 1973-75; founder, pres. Creative Compensation Plans, Chgo., 1975—; guest lectr. Ill. Bar Assn., Grad. Sch. Accountancy, DePaul U.; cons. Ill. C.P.A. Found.; faculty S.W. La. U. Sch. Life Ins., 1977. Active, Art Inst. Chgo., 1968—, Lyric Opera Guild, 1972—, Chgo. Symphony Soc., 1973—; bd. dirs. Young Leadership div. Chgo. Jewish Fedn., 1974—, pres., 1979-80; bd. dirs. Bd. Jewish Edn. Met. Chgo., 1982—, Israel Scholarship Found., 1982—; mem. Chgo. com. Simon Wiesenthal Center for Holocaust Studies. Recipient Nat. Quality award, 1973; mem. Million Dollar Roundtable, 1973—; 1st and only female mem. Five Million Dollar Forum, 1977—. Mem. Am. Soc. C.L.U.s, Nat. Assn. Life Underwriters, Chgo. Estate Planning Council. Columnist, Round the Table mag., 1976—. Office: 180 N LaSalle St Suite 1701 Chicago IL 60601

GOLDBERG, MICHELE WYMAN, communication tng. specialist, career cons.; b. Phila., Aug. 27, 1954; d. Joseph and Florence (Edelsman) Wyman; B.A. in Writing, Pa. State U., 1976; m. Alan Goldberg, Apr. 2, 1978; 1 son, Jesse Wyman. Copywriter, public relations asst. Tract Advt. and Public Relations, Inc., Bala Cynwyd, Pa., 1976-77; student services dir., instr. Phila. Sch. Office Tng., 1978-81; partner Progressive Tng. Assos., Phila., 1981-82; pres. Goldberg ETC, Phila., 1982—; cons. careers, Phila., 1981—; guest lectr., cons. for various community and profl. groups. Mem. N.E. Profl. Adv. Com., dir. Lifeline Telephone Hotline, Plymouth Meeting, 1971. Mem. Internat. Transactional Analysis Assn., Am. Personnel and Guidance Assn., Nat. Vocat. Guidance Assn., Pa. Personnel and Guidance Assn., Pa. Vocat. Guidance Assn., Nat. Assn. Female Execs., Am. Soc. Tng. and Devel., Am. Entrepreneurs' Assn. Pen and Pencil Club. Columnist Times Publs., 1982—; also articles. Home: 2813 Tremont St Philadelphia PA 19136

GOLDBERG, RYLLA MAY ROCKEY, business exec.; b. Muleshoe, Tex., May 1, 1934; d. Richard Matthew and Ruth Hester (Bearden) Rockey; B.M., U. Puget Sound, 1957; grad. N.W. Intermediate Banking Sch., Lewis and Clark Coll., 1977; children—Shana Dian. Sec. to v.p. and cashier Bank of Tacoma, 1968-70; tech. writer Seattle-1st Nat. Bank, 1970-73, ops. publs. officer, 1973-74, mgr. check mgmt., 1974-76, asst. v.p., mgr. prodn. control in corp. purchasing, 1976-78, asst. v.p., mgr. furnishings in corp. purchasing, 1978-79, v.p., mgr. adminstrv. services, 1979-80; asst. to pres. Pioneer Bus. Forms, Tacoma, 1980-81; pres. The Goldberg Co., Tacoma, 1981—; tchr., cons. magnetic ink printing, banks and printers. Mem. Sigma Alpha Iota. Author: Magnetic Ink Printing and Evaluation Guide, 1976; contbr. book revs. to Seattle Post-Intelligencer. Composer: Theme and Variations for Cello and Piano, 1959. Office: PO Box 98299 Tacoma WA 98499

GOLDBERGER, NORMA MILLER, clinic adminstr.; b. Toronto, Ont., Can., Dec. 25, 1945; d. Alec and Faye (Shapiro) Miller; B.A., U. Toronto, 1966, M.A., 1967; postgrad Boston Coll., 1969-70; m. Apr. 28, 1968; children—David Benjamin, Joshua Elliott, Jessica Renee. Instr., Pine Manor Jr. Coll., Boston, 1970-71; dir. Problem Pregnancy Counseling Service, Open Door Clinic, Columbus, Ohio, 1972-73; counselor N.W. Womens Clinic, Columbus, 1973-74, dir., 1974-76; pres., dir. Akron Womens Clinic, Inc. (Ohio), 1976—. Mem. NOW, Nat. Abortion Rights Action League, ACLU. Jewish. Clubs: Rubber Capital Harmonica, Newcomers. Office: 513 W Market St Akron OH 44303

GOLDBLATT, JAN H., educator; b. Chgo., Nov. 26, 1949; d. Joel Goldblatt and Lynne Walker Durocher; student U. Mich., 1970; B.A., Ariz. State U., 1971; M.A., 1976. Tchr., Tempe (Ariz.) Schs., 1972—, gifted program, 1976-79; tchr. Fees Sch., 1979—. Mem. Nat. Assn. for Gifted, Ariz. Assn. for Gifted and Talented. Republican. Jewish. Office: Sam Fees Intermediate Sch 1600 E Watson St Tempe AZ 85283

GOLDEN, JESSIE GRAY, ret. librarian, genealogist; b. Seagoville, Tex., Oct. 23, 1903; d. William Tapley and Eula Lavina (Herring) Gray; B.A., W. Tex. U., 1929; postgrad. N. Tex. U., 1948; m. Joe Bob Golden, July 29, 1928; children—Jeanelle Zellane (Mrs. Lawrence Henry

Warburton, Jr.), Joe Bob. Librarian, prin. Kaufman County, Tex., 1924-27; tchr. Wichita County, Tex., 1927-44; tchr., dir. Camp Fire Girls, Bonham, Tex., 1946-49; docent Tex. State Library, Austin, 1953-65, genealogy librarian, 1965—; free lance researcher Tex. history, 1972-75. Chmn., Daus. Republic Mus. Com., 1969—; dist. officer PTA, 1942-49; mem. Woman's Forum Bd., Wichita Falls, Tex., 1940-44; election judge, 1968-71. Mem. Austin Geneal. Soc. (dir. 1969-72), AAUW, Daus. Republic Tex. (chmn. mus. com. 1969—), Tex. State Geneal. Soc. (pres. 1982-83), Tex. Woman's Forum (pres. Vernon Tex. 1952-53), Santa Rosa Hort. Soc. (treas. 1951-53), Alpha Story League (pres. 1941-43). Baptist (Sunday sch. tchr.). Clubs: Bonham Garden (pres. 1947-49); Austin Woman's. Home: 2100 Hartford Rd Austin TX 78703

GOLDEN, KATHLEEN CLARE, systems analyst; b. Alamagordo, N.Mex., Nov. 9, 1956; d. Charles C. and Clare Eileen (Fites) Golden; student DeAnza Jr. Coll., Cupertino, Calif., 1974-75, Foothill Coll., Mountain View, Calif., 1980—. Dental asst., San Jose, Calif., 1974-75, 76-77, Berkeley, Calif., 1975-76; disk-to-tape operator CIS div. Intel Corp., San Jose, 1978-79; data entry systems analyst Sperry Univac, San Francisco, 1979—; cons. installation and tech. support of equipment. Recipient Rookie Systems Analyst of Yr. award Sperry Univac, 1980. Roman Catholic. Office: Three Embarcadero Center Suite 1100 San Francisco CA 94111

GOLDEN, LAURA LORETTA, educator; b. Lexington, Ky., June 11, 1940; d. Hubert Anthony and Caroline Garrard (Holt) G.; B.S., Fla. State U., 1964; M.Ed., Ga. Coll., 1971. Instr., Fla. State U., Tallahassee, 1964-70, Middle Ga. Coll., Cochran, 1971-73; asst. prof. Ga. Coll., Milledgeville, 1973-75; asst. prof., co-dir. athletics head coach women's basketball Colo. Coll., Colorado Springs, 1975-81; asst. prof. phys. edn., head coach womens basketball Central Mich. U., Mount Pleasant, 1981—. Mem. Mich. Basketball Coaches Assn., Womens Nat. Basketball Coaches Assn. Office: Central Michigan University Rose Arena Mount Pleasant MI 48859

GOLDEN, TERESA VITAGLIANO, mktg. rep.; b. Mt. Vernon, N.Y., June 5, 1955; d. Vincent Jack and Audrey Mildred (Fabini) Vitagliano; B.A. in Econs., Coll. Mt. St. Vincent, 1975; M.B.A. in Corp. Fin., Pace U., 1979; m. George Patrick Golden, Jan. 3, 1976; 1 dau., Helen Marie. Accounts receivable mgr. ITEL Corp., White Plains, N.Y., 1975-78; fin. systems cons. Sci. Timesharing Corp., White Plains, 1978-79; systems analyst IBM, Poughkeepsie, N.Y., 1979-80, graphics mktg. rep., 1980—. Republican. Roman Catholic. Home: 14 Sarah Ln Hopewell Junction NY 12533 Office: IBM South Rd Poughkeepsie NY 12602

GOLDENBERG, IRENE TOBY, clin. psychologist, educator; b. Memphis, Apr. 18, 1934; d. Morris and Isobel (Erenberg) Feinstein; B.A., U. Calif., Berkeley, 1956; M.A., Calif. State U., Los Angeles, 1960; Ed.D., UCLA, 1969; m. Herbert Goldenberg, Feb. 17, 1963; children—Philip, Erica, Karen. Tchr. elem. sch. Los Angeles City Unified Sch. Dist., 1957-61; sch. psychometrist Pasadena (Calif.) City Coll., 1861-62, sch. psychologist, 1962-64; psychol. cons. ednl. handicapped program Alamitos (Calif.) Sch. Dist., 1964-66, Monrovia (Calif.) Unified Sch. Dist., 1965-68; dir. psychol. services Operation Head Start, Pasadena, 1965; psychol. cons. mental retardation services Bur. Maternal Health, Los Angeles County Health Dept., 1966-67; sr. mental health cons. (Head Start) Los Angeles Fedn. of Settlements and Ctrs., 1966-67; sch. psychologist spl. presch. program Dubnoff Sch. for Ednl. Therapy, North Hollywood, Calif., 1967-69; asst. prof. psychology Calif. State U., Los Angeles, 1969; asst. prof. in residence Neuropsychiat. Inst., UCLA, 1969-84, acting supr. outpatient psychology div., 1971-75, adj. asst. prof., 1975-77, adj. assoc. prof., 1977—, dir. psychol. services mental supr. psychology assessment lab., 1969-75, inpatient child psychology div., 1972-75. Recipient Book of Yr. award Am. Jour. Nursing, 1980. Diplomate Am. Examiners in Profl. Psychology; lic. marriage, family and child counselor, psychologist, Calif.; cert. elem., jr. coll., orthopedically handicapped tchr., sch. psychologist, Calif. Mem. Nat. Register of Health Service Providers in Psychology, Am. Bd. Profl. Psychology (trustee), (trustee 1981—), Psychol. Assn., Calif. Psychol. Assn., Am. Orthopsychiat. Assn., Los Angeles County Psychol. Assn., Am. Personnel and Guidance Assn., Am. Family Therapy Assn. Democrat. Jewish. Co-author: Family Therapy: An Overview, 1980. Office: UCLA-NPI 760 Westwood Plaza Los Angeles CA 90024

GOLDEN STEWART, ARLENE JEAN, designer, stylist; b. Chgo., Nov. 26, 1943; d. Alex Emerald and Nettie (Rosen) Golden; B.F.A. (Ill. State scholar), Sch. Art Inst. Chgo., 1966; m. Randall Edward Stewart, Nov. 6, 1970; 1 dau., Alexis Anne. Designer, stylist Formica Corp., Cin., 1966-68; pattern designer Armstrong World Industries, Lancaster Pa., 1968-73, interior furnishing analyst, design and color forecasting, 1974-76, internat. staff project stylist, 1976-78, sr. stylist Corlon flooring, 1979-80, sr. exptl. project stylist, 1980—. Exhibited textiles: Art Inst. Chgo., 1966, Ox-Bow Gallery, Saugatuck, Mich., 1966. Home: 141 E Marion St Lancaster PA 17602 Office: Armstrong Tech Center Product Design 2500 Columbia Ave Lancaster PA 17604

GOLDENTHAL, JOLENE BLEICH, playwright, art critic; b. Boston; d. Abraham H. and Lillian (Hochberg) Bleich; A.B., Smith Coll.; M.A., Trinity Coll., Hartford, Conn.; m. Carol Goldenthal; children—Peter, Lance. Art critic West Hartford (Conn.) News, 1966-70, Hartford Courant, 1970-80; plays include: Mequasset by the Sea, Album, Birthday, Island, The Station, Five P.M., A Stranger in a Strange Land, I Thought I Saw a Snowman, Rachel, Charne, Remembering Mrs. Crowley. Recipient 2d place award Galaxy Competition, 1977, 1st prize Readers and Playwrights Theatre, 1979, Cedar Rapids Theatre Playwrighting Competition, 1979, also hon. mentions Mem. Hartford Playwrights (founder, artistic dir.), Dramatists Guild. Women in Communications, Smith Coll. Alumnae Assn., Hartford Smith Coll. Club, Am. Jewish Congress. Office: 132 Jefferson St Hartford CT 06103

GOLDFARB, ANITA JUNE, career counselor; b. Chgo., June 24, 1928; d. Herman and Ida (Kaufman) Stern; B.A., Calif. State U., Northridge, 1968; M. Liberal Arts, U. So. Calif., 1972; certificate social service U. Calif., Los Angeles, 1969, adult counseling specialist, 1973; m. A. Eddy Goldfarb, Oct. 18, 1947; children—Lyn, Fran, Martin. Tchr. history Simi (Calif.) United Sch. Dist., 1968-69; counselor Suicide Prevention Center, Los Angeles, 1969-71; edn./vocation and career adviser Extension Info. Advisory Service, U. Calif., Los Angeles, 1971-75; co-dir., trainer Center for New Directions, Van Nuys, 1972-74; pvt. practice career and edn. counseling, Northridge, Calif., 1974—; instr. U. So. Calif., 1974, Calif. State U., Northridge, 1975; educator, trainer adults in non-traditional settings. Mem. Mayor's Bicentennial Com. to Honor Volunteers; mem. advisory com. on minority affairs Ventura County (Calif.) Coll. Dist., 1977-78. Mem. Am. Personnel and Guidance Assn., Nat. Council Family Relations, Internt. Assn. Counseling Services, Calif. Psychol. Assn., Catalyst/Assn. for Tng. and Devel. Author, editor newsletter Transitional Woman, 1974-76. Home: 4614 Monarca Dr Tarzana CA 91356 Office: 19434 Londelius St Northridge CA 91324

GOLDHABER, GERTRUDE SCHARFF, physicist; b. Mannheim, Germany, July 14, 1911; d. Otto and Nelly (Steinharter) Scharff; student univs. of Freiburg, Zurich, Berlin; Ph.D., U. Munich, 1935; m. Maurice Goldhaber, May 24, 1939; children—Alfred Scharff, Michael Henry. Came to U.S., 1939, naturalized, 1944. Research asso. Imperial Coll., London, 1935-39; research physicist U. Ill., Champaign, 1939-48; asst. prof., 1948-50; asso. physicist Brookhaven Nat. Lab., Upton, N.Y., 1950-58, physicist, 1958-62, sr. physicist, 1962-79; adj. prof. Cornell U., 1980—; cons. Brookhaven Nat. Lab., 1980—. Cons. to nuclear data group NRC, 1966, AEC Labs., 1946—; mem. research adv. com. NSF, 1973-74; mem. Com. on Problems of Women in Physics, 1971; mem. physics vis. com. Harvard U., 1973-79; chmn. ad hoc panel on nuclear data compilations, NRC-Nat. Acad. Sci. Com. on Nuclear Sci., 1969-71; sci. cons. ACDA, 1974-78; mem. nominating com. Presdl. Medal of Sci., 1977-79. Trustee Nat. Accelerator Lab. Univ. Research Assn., Batavia, Ill., 1972-77. Recipient L.I. Achievers award in sci. Fellow Am. Phys. Soc. (program com. nuclear physics div. 1973-74, councillor-at-large 1978-81), AAAS; mem. Nat. Acad. Scis. (report rev. com. 1973-81, forum com. 1974-81, com. for edn. women in sci. and engring. 1978—), Sigma Xi. Editorial com. Ann. Revs. Nuclear Sci., 1972-78; bd. editors Jour. Physics Eng. (Europhysics Jour.), 1978-79. Home: 91 S Gillette Ave Bayport NY 11705 Office: Brookhaven Nat Lab Upton NY 11973

GOLDHAMMER, FLORIE BRETTLER, lawyer; b. Plainfield, N.J., May 5, 1933; d. Sol and Hilda (Ettlinger) Brettler; student U. Chgo., 1949-53, New Sch. Social Research, 1954-55; B.A. summa cum laude, U. Pitts., 1972, J.D., 1975; m. Robert Goldhammer, Dec. 26,1954 (dec.); children—Anne Middleton, Elizabeth Percy. Admitted to Pa. bar, 1975; assoc. firm Johnson and Johnson, Pitts., 1975-77, Greenwald and Greenwald, Pitts. and Monroeville, Pa., 1979-81; bar examiner Commonwealth of Pa., 1981—. individual practice law, Pitts., 1977-79. Mem. Allegheny County Bar Assn. (chairperson com. juvenile law 1979-81), Pa. Bar Assn., Am. Bar Assn., Pa. Trial Lawyers Assn., Am. Trial Lawyers Assn. Office: 824 Frick Bldg 437 Grant St Pittsburgh PA 15219

GOLDIN, AUGUSTA, educator, columnist, author; b. N.Y.C., Oct. 28, 1906; d. Jacob and Fanny (Harris) Reider; B.A., Hunter Coll., 1927; M.S., CCNY, 1929; Ed.D., Columbia U., 1946; m. Oscar Goldin, Oct. 25, 1933; children—Kenneth, Valerie. Tchr. elem. sch., 1927-42; prin. elem. sch., N.Y.C., 1944-72; asst. prof. edn. St. John's U., 1972-75; edn. columnist S.I. (N.Y.) Advance, 1968—; author 14 books including: Let's Read and Find Out Science Books, 7 vols., 1963-69; How To Release the Learning Power in Children, 1970; Grass: The Everything, Everywhere Plant, 1977; Oceans of Energy, 1980; Geothermal Energy, 1981. Named to Hunter Coll. Hall of Fame, 1982; recipient Outstanding Educator award Am. Legion, 1982. Mem. Nat. Audubon Soc., Nat. Council Adminstrv. Women in Edn., Authors Guild, Phi Delta Kappa. Office: The Staten Island Advance Fingerboard Rd Staten Island NY 10305

GOLDINGER, SHIRLEY BOTANE, county agy. ofcl.; b. Newark, June 27, 1925; B.S., N.Y. U., 1946; M.S. in Home Econ. Edn., UCLA, 1951. Home economist Gen. Electric Co., Los Angeles, 1948; dir. Los Angeles County Dept. Consumer Affairs, 1975—. Mem adv. com. Bur. Automotive Repair; chmn. Democratic State Party, 1973-75. Recipient commendations Calif. State Assembly, Los Angeles City Council for Consumerism, 1971; Achievement award Women in Public Affairs, 1978; E. Dykstra award Am. Soc. Public Adminstrs., 1979. Mem. Comsumer Fedn. Am. (dir.), Nat. Assn. Consumer Agy. Adminstrs. (dir. 1977-79), Calif. Consumer Affairs Assn. Democrat. Office: 500 W Temple St Los Angeles CA 90012

GOLDIZEN, CAROLYN SNYDER, nurse; b. Lahmansville, W.Va., Mar. 17, 1936; d. Lloyd Neil and Eva Lucretia (Parker) Snyder; R.N., Winchester (Va.) Meml. Hosp., 1956; postgrad. Potomac State Coll., Keyser, W.Va., Parkersburg (W.Va.) Community Coll., St. Joseph Coll., North Winham, Maine; m. Lee Allen Goldizen, June 6, 1956; children—Lucretia Ann, Lee Allen (dec.), Cristina Leigh. Pediatric staff nurse Winchester Meml. Hosp., 1957; with Grant Meml. Hosp., Petersburg, W.Va., 1957—, beginning as head nurse med. surg. wing, successively staff operating room nurse, nurse cons. diet kitchen, med. and surg. supr., 1958-77, instr. area coal miners' emergency med. technician tng. program, 1977, emergency room supr., 1977—; dir. Grant County Ambulance Service, 1977—; mem. W.Va. Emergency Med. Service Testing Team; vocat. edn. instr. for emergency med. technicians Grant County Schs.; mem., sec. Northeastern W.Va. Regional Emergency Med. Services Council; mem. W.Va. Paramedic Curriculum Com.; cardiopulmonary affiliate faculty Am. Heart Assn.; advanced life support instr. Mem. Am. W.Va. Nurses Assn. (past pres. subdist. 6) Emergency Dept. Nurses, Nat. League Nursing. Methodist. Clubs: Home Demonstration, Hosp. Aux., Ladies Aide Soc., Eastern Star (worthy matron). Home: Knollview Star Route 1 Box 4 Lahmansville WV 26731

GOLDMAN, ARLENE LESLIE, apparel co. exec.; b. Paterson, N.J., July 7, 1956; d. Jacob and Bertha (Deck) G.; student Am. U., 1974. Asst. store mgr., asst. buyer Latt's Country Store, Washington, 1976-77; ops. mgr. Complement, Washington, 1977-78; with Bidermann Industries, 1978—, prodn. mgr. Jean-Paul Germain, div., N.Y.C., 1979-80, dir. ops., 1980-81, v.p., 1981—. Mem. Whitney Mus., Nat. Assn. Female Execs., ORT. Home: 120 E 34th St Apt 3N New York NY 10016 Office: 1 E 57th St New York NY 10022

GOLDMAN, BARBARA LINDA, clin. psychologist; b. Boston, July 31, 1950; d. Philip Charles Goldman and Selma L. (Goldblatt) Goldman Cohen; B.A. magna cum laude, Brandeis U., 1972; M.S., U. Miami, 1974, Ph.D. in Clin. Psychology, 1977; m. Philip C. Boswell, Sept. 9, 1979. Lectr. psychology U. Miami, Coral Gables, Fla., 1976, now adj. asst. prof. psychology dept.; psychologist United Family and Children's Services, Miami, Fla., 1976-78; clin. dir. Teenage Living Community, Miami, 1977-79; pvt. practice clin. psychology, Coral Gables, 1978—; cons. Miami Mental Health Center. NIMH fellow, 1972-75. Mem. Am. Psychol. Assn., Dade County Psychol. Assn. Home: 533 Giralda Ave Coral Gables FL 33134 Office: Catalonia Bldg Suite 401 250 Catalonia Ave Coral Gables FL 33134

GOLDMAN, DIANE CYDNEY, personnel agency exec.; b. Paterson, N.J., Oct. 6, 1949; d. Jacob and Bertha (Deck) G.; B.A. in Bus. Adminstrn., Boston U., 1971. Employment counselor Career Center, Inc., Hackensack, N.J., 1974; asst. mgr. Hallmark of Lyndhurst (N.J.) Inc., 1975-76, pres., 1977—, pres. Hallmark of Union (N.J.) Inc., 1977—, pres. Hallmark of Parsippany (N.J.), 1979—, Hallmark at Paramus Plaza I (N.J.), 1982—. Mem. Nat. Assn. Personnel Cons.'s, N.J. Assn. Personnel Cons. Home: 160 Overlook Ave Apt 26B Hackensack NJ 07601 Office: 140 Route 17 N Paramus NJ 07652 also 2401 Morris Ave Union NJ 07083 also 1099 Wall St W Lyndhurst NJ 07071 also 333 Littleton Rd Parsippany NJ 07054

GOLDMAN, LISA, social worker; b. Phila., Feb. 11, 1951; d. Gerald and Elaine (Freeman) S.; B.A. in Theatre Arts cum laude, Adelphi U., 1972; M.S.W. magna cum laude, N.Y. U., 1974. Case aide Creedmoor Mental Hosp., 1970-72; counselor Hawthorne Cedar Knolls Residential Treatment Center, 1972; group worker Rhinelander Center, Children's Aid Soc., 1973-74; supr. rapid intervention project Queens (N.Y.) Family Ct., 1974-75; asst. project dir., cons. Assn. Jr. Leagues of Am. Inc., N.Y.C., 1976; program cons. Nat. Council of Jewish Women, Inc., N.Y.C., 1976—, developer programs and publs. in juvenile justice and child abuse; field instr. Columbia U. Grad. Sch. Social Work; account exec., pub. relations/promotion dir. film premiere The Chosen, Rapid Am. Corp., 1981. Active Tenants and Block Assn., 1972—; mem. Nat. Assembly Juvenile Justice Program Collaboration Task Force, 1976—. Mem. Am. Mgmt. Assn., Nat. Assn. Social Workers, NOW, Acad. Polit. Sci., Women's Equity Action League. Home: 35 Clark St Apt 1A Brooklyn Heights NY 11201

GOLDMAN, PATRICIA ANN, govt. ofcl.; b. Newton, N.J., Mar. 22, 1942; d. Jacob Joseph and Miriam Louise (Cassiday) G.; B.A. in Econs., Goucher Coll., 1964; m. Charles A. Goodell, July 1, 1978. Research asst. Joint Econ. Com. of Congress, 1964-65; legis. asst. ad hoc subcom. on war on poverty, edn. and labor com. U.S. Ho. of Reps., 1965-66; research cons. U.S. C. of C., 1966, dir. manpower and poverty programs, 1967-71; legis. counsel Nat. League Cities, also U.S. Conf. of Mayors, 1971-72; exec. dir. The House Wednesday Group, U.S. Ho. of Reps., 1972-79; mem. Nat. Transp. Safety Bd., Washington, 1979—, vice chmn., 1982—; vis. prof. Woodrow Wilson Nat. Fellowship Program; lectr. Brookings Instn. Program for Sr. Govt. Execs. Trustee, Goucher Coll.; former treas. Nat. Women's Edn. Fund; former mem. adv. bd. Nat. Women's Polit. Caucus, also past chmn. Republican Women's Task Force; former chair governing bd. Ripon Soc. Fellow Kennedy Inst. Politics, Harvard U., 1978. Named Woman of Yr., Women's Transp. Seminar, 1982. Office: 800 Independence Ave SW Washington DC 20594

GOLDMAN-RAKIC, PATRICIA SHOER, neuroscientist, educator; b. Salem, Mass., Apr. 22, 1937; d. Irving and Jennie (Pearl) Shoer; A.B., Vassar Coll., 1959; Ph.D., UCLA, 1963; m. Pasko Rakic, Feb. 18, 1979. USPHS postdoctoral fellow dept. psychiatry Brain Research Inst., UCLA, 1963-64; research assoc. dept. animal behavior Am. Mus. Natural History, N.Y.C., 1964-65; staff fellow sect. neuropsychology Lab. Psychology, NIMH, Bethesda, Md., 1965-68, research physiologist, 1968-78, chief sect. on devel. neurobiology, 1978-79; prof. neurosci. sect. neuroanatomy Yale U. Sch. Medicine, New Haven, 1979—; vis. scientist M.I.T., Cambridge, 1974—; mem. nat. adv. research task force NIMH, 1972-74, grantee, 1980—; mem. neurobiology study sect. NIH, 1981—; Herbert Birch meml. lectr. Internat. Neuropsychology Soc., 1981. Recipient Sr. Scientist award, 1980—; Aldon Spencer award Columbia U., 1982. Fellow AAAS, Am. Psychol. Assn.; mem. Soc. for Neurosci., Internat. Soc. for Devel. Psychobiology, Am. Anat. Assn., NEI-NIMH-NINCDS Assembly of Scientists (pres. 1974-75). Contbr. numerous articles to profl. jours. Office: Sect Neuroanatomy Yale U Sch Medicine 333 Cedar St New Haven CT 06510

GOLDRICK, JANET MARIE, lawyer, ednl. adminstr.; b. Newton, Mass., Sept. 23, 1939; d. Charles Drummy and Mabel Esther (Kivlehan) Goldrick; B.A., Regis Coll., 1961; M.Edn., Boston U., 1962; J.D., Suffolk U. Law Sch., 1976. Admitted to Mass. bar, 1977, U.S. Supreme Ct. bar, 1980; tchr., prin. Newton (Mass.) Public Schs., 1962—, Bogota, Colombia, S.Am., 1969-70; pvt. practice law, Newton, Mass., 1977—. Recipient Lawyers Co-operative Pub. Co. Am. Jurisprudence award for Family Law, 1976. Mem. Newton Tchrs. Assn. (pres. 1981—), Mass. Edn. Assn., NEA, Mass. Bar Assn., Boston Bar Assn., Nat. Orgn. Legal Problems Edn. Roman Catholic. Office: Charles C Burr Sch 171 Pine St Auburndale MA 02166

GOLDSCHMIDT, FAITH KNABE, public health analyst; b. Springfield, Mass., Sept. 25, 1940; d. Henry Walter and Ruth Irene (Dupree) Knabe; B.A., Clark U., 1962; M.A., Smith Coll., 1963; postgrad. Rutgers U., 1965-67; M.P.H., Columbia U., 1978; m. Paul Goldschmidt, June, 1963 (div. 1973); 1 son, Jeffrey Scott. Research asst. Waksman Inst., Rutgers U., Piscataway, N.J., 1964-65; research microbiologist Johnson & Johnson Research, North Brunswick, N.J., 1967-78; analyst DRG project, health econ. services N.J. Dept. Health, Trenton, 1978-81, health econs. research specialist DRG project, 1981—. Mem. Am. Soc. Microbiology, N.Y. Acad. Sci., Am. Burn Assn., Am. Public Health Assn., N.J. Public Health Assn., Sigma Xi. Home: 61 Herbert Dr East Brunswick NJ 08816 Office: PO Box 1540 NJ State Dept Health Trenton NJ 08625

GOLDSMITH, BARBARA JANE, environ. cons.; b. Providence, Dec. 4, 1949; d. James and Marion (Jagolinzer) G.; B.A., George Washington U., 1971; M.CityPlanning, Harvard U., 1974. Asst. to dir. Met. Washington Coalition Clean Air, 1971-72; con. to environ. directorate OECD, Paris, 1974-75; mgr. program devel. Regulatory Info. Services, Environ. Research and Tech., Inc., Concord, Mass. and Washington, 1973—. Mem. council Harvard Grad. Sch. Design Assn., 1980-83. EPA spl. fellow, 1972-74; fellow Dept. Transp., 1972. Mem. Air Pollution Control Assn. Club: Harvard (Washington). Author articles in field. Home: 282 Mt Auburn St Watertown MA 02172 Office: 696 Virginia Rd Concord MA 01742

GOLD-SMITH, DIANA, systems exec.; b. N.Y.C., Oct. 3, 1944; d. Hugo and Herta (Rosenthal) Goldsmith; B.A., Hunter Coll., CUNY, 1966. With Duca di Roma, Rome and Florence, Italy, 1967-68; div. leader Lloyd H. Hall Co., Inc., N.Y.C., 1968-72; corp. dir. research Lebhar-Friedman Publs., N.Y.C., 1972-78; v.p. ASI, Inc., Los Angeles, 1978-81; corp. staff-systems Smith Cline Beckman, Fullerton, Calif., 1981—; mgmt. cons. Mem. Am. Mktg. Assn. Office: 2500 Harbor Blvd Fullerton CA 92634

GOLDSMITH, ELIZABETH BEARD, educator; b. Buffalo, Nov. 24, 1949; d. Irving William and Betty Amelia Beard; B.A., Fla. State U., 1971; M.A., Mich. State U., 1972, Ph.D., 1977; m. Ronald Earl Goldsmith, July 31, 1971; 1 son, David Scott. Asst. prof. dept. home econs. N.Mex. State U., Las Cruces, 1976-78; asst. prof. Sch. Home Econs., U. Ala., Tuscaloosa, 1978-81; asso. prof. dept. home and family life Coll. Home Econs., Fla. State U., Tallahassee, 1981—. Inst. Higher Edn. Research and Services postdoctoral scholar, 1980, U. Ala. grantee and fellow, 1977-80. Mem. Am. Assn. Housing Educators (state chmn.), Am. Home Econs. Assn., Am. Council Consumer Interests, AAAS, Sigma Xi, Omicron Nu. Christian Scientist. Manuscript reviewer Prentice Hall, John Wiley, Allyn and Bacon, 1977—. Office: 215 Sandels Bldg Fla State U Tallahassee FL 32306

GOLDSMITH, GERTRUDE, wholesale co. exec.; b. Bremen, Ger., Nov. 10, 1909; came to U.S., 1939, naturalized, 1944; d. Emil and Selma (Mendel) Meyer; ed. in Ger., also Pittmann's Coll., London; m. Henry R. Goldsmith, Sept. 18, 1938 (dec); children—Susan Lillian, Richard Michael. Founder (with husband) Compact Novelites, N.Y.C., 1945, now pres. Mem. C. of C. of U.S., Gifts and Decorative Accessories Assn. Jewish. Home: 85-15 Main St Jamaica NY 11435 Office: 303 Fifth Ave New York NY 10016

GOLDSMITH, ISABELLE GAN, dietitian; b. Chgo., Apr. 25, 1925; d. Louis and Anna (Tay) Gan; B.S., U. Ill., 1947; student (coll. scholar), Ill. Inst. Tech., 1943-44; cert., UCLA, 1972, U. Calif., Berkeley, 1964; m. Paul Goldsmith, Aug. 9, 1947; children—Larry, Susan, Carol. Nutritionist Chgo. Health Dept., 1947-50, Pasadena (Calif.) Health Dept., 1962-64; nutrition parent interviewer Child Health Study, U. Calif., Berkeley, 1965; nutrition cons. Villa Esperanza, Pasadena, 1968, Pasadena Vis. Nurses Assn., 1969-70, Pasadena City Schs. Head Start program, 1965-66; nutrition supr. Community Planning Council Head Start Program, Pasadena, 1965-70; dir. Personal Achievement Asso., Pasadena, 1972-78; cons. nutritionist U. So. Calif. Sch. Medicine, 1979—; cons. in pvt. practice, Los Angeles County, 1978—. Cons. to planning com. Am. Heart Assn., 1979—, Los Angeles Day Care and Devel. Council, 1979—; mem. task force on foods and nutrition, Com. on Aging, Pasadena Community Council, 1965-70; mem. task force on hunger, State of Calif., 1965-70; edn. dir. San Gabriel Valley Dial-A-Dietitian project, 1961-66. Named Chgo.'s Outstanding Student, also recipient Mayor's medal, 1943. Registered dietitian; cert. adult counseling specialist. Mem. Am. Dietetics Assn., Am. Public Health Assn., Am. Home Econ. Assn., Greater Los Angeles Nutrition Council (treas. 1973-76), Soc. Nutrition Edn., Group Psychotherapy Assn. So. Calif.,

Internat. Transactional Analysis Assn., AAUW, NOW. Club: Happy Hearts. Home: 28408 Ridgehaven Ct Rancho Palos Verdes CA 90274 Office: Skylark Profl Bldg 23560 Madison St Suite 106 Torrance CA 90505

GOLDSMITH, MARGIE, film dir., writer, producer; b. San Francisco, Jan. 3, 1944; d. Eugene M. and Nancy Goldsmith; student Boston U., 1961-64; B.S., Columbia U., 1965. State mgr., summer stock and N.Y. Shakespeare Festival, 1962-65; asst. dir. off-Broadway and Broadway theatrical prodns. including Les Blancs, Boesman & Lena, People Are Living There, The Crucible, Othello, 1966-72; asso. producer, writer, dir. narration IS IS Christ, TV spl., 1972; sr. v.p. Planned Communication Services, film prodn., N.Y.C., 1973—; author novel: Screw-Up, 1972. Recipient Gold, Silver, Bronze awards Internat. Film and TV Festival N.Y., 1978, 79, 80, 81, Andy award for excellence Advt. Club N.Y., 1978, Cine Golden Eagle award, 1975, also others. Songwriter; playwright SOS, 1973. Office: 12 E 46th St New York NY 10017

GOLDSMITH, RUTH STAFFORD, state legislator; b. Bluefield, W.Va., Jan. 17, 1924; student W.Va. U.; m. William F. Goldsmith; children—Karen Goldsmith Johnston, William F. Mem. W.Va. Ho. of Dels., 1980—, mem. govt. orgn., industry, and labor coms. City committeewoman, South Charleston, W.Va.; mem. South Charleston City Council; pres. W.Va. Fedn. Republican Women; bd. dirs. Nat. Fedn. Rep. Women; mem. Kanawha Arts Alliance, YMCA, YWCA, South Charleston Commn. for Visual Arts and Beautification, Kanawha County Rep. Women, Sunrise Found., Kanawha Bicentennial Commn. Mem. AAUW. Methodist. Club: South Charleston Women's. Office: Va Ho of Dels Charleston WV 25305 *

GOLDSMITH, SILVIANNA, filmmaker, educator; b. N.Y.C.; d. Roy and Anna Lewis (Lefkowitz) Goldsmith; B.A., Bklyn. Coll., 1963; M.A., N.Y.U. 1966. Films include: Orpheus Underground, 1975, Lil, Lil Picard, Art Is a Party, 1974, Mexico, 1975, Nightclub, Memories of Havana in Queens, 1975; one-woman shows Millenium, 1975, Goethe House, 1976, Irvington and Westchester, N.Y., 1978, S.I. Mus., 1978; film shows include: Calif. Inst. Arts, 1973, Graz Mus., Austria, 1974, Mus. Modern Art, Vienna, 1974, Modern Mus., Basle, Switzerland, 1975, Paris Mus. Modern Art, 1974, S.I. Mus., 1978, N.Y.U. 1975, Ashawagh Hall, East Hampton, N.Y., 1975, 2d Internat. Festival Women's Films, Berlin, 1976, Soho Festival Arts, 1976, Exptl./Personal Film Festival, Women's Interart Center, 1977, Anthology Film Archives, 1977, 78, 81, Mus. Modern Art, Innsbruck, Austria, 1977, Bklyn. Mus., 1977, Berlin Arsenal, 1977, Ford Found., 1979; tchr., film coordinator Women's Interart Center, N.Y.C., 1972—. Grantee N.Y. State Council Arts, Nat. Endowment Arts, 1974-77. Mem. Women/Artist/Filmmakers, Inc. (past sec., project dir., pres. 1980), Millenium Film Workshop, Women's Salon. Home: 411 E 10th St New York NY 10009 Studio: 151 W 18th St New York NY 10011

GOLDSTEIN, AILEEN, investment co. exec.; b. Rosenberg, Tex., June 26, 1914; d. Cecil and Raye (Levine) Robinowitz; B.B.A., U. Tex., 1934; postgrad. in econs. Trinity U., San Antonio, 1959-61; m. Eli Goldstein, Jan. 27, 1935; 1 son, Gerald H. Cotton buyer R.B. Stores, Ft. Bend and Wharton Counties, Tex., 1934; legal sec., 1935-38; sec. Spl. Services, U.S. Air Force, Santa Maria, Calif., 1943; account exec. Dempsey-Tegler, San Antonio, 1961-66, E.F. Hutton, San Antonio, 1966-78; investment exec. Shearson/Am. Express, San Antonio, 1978—; lectr., condr. seminars. Mem. investment com. Temple Beth El, 1979—; pres. San Antonio sect. Nat. Council Jewish Women, 1940-42; 1st pres. San Antonio chpt. Brandeis U. Women's Com., 1949-50, nat. bd. dirs., 1950-51; an organizer Vis. Nurse Service San Antonio, 1952, Sr. Citizens Center, 1958-62; mem. San Antonio Parks and Recreation Bd., 1960-64; charter mem. for San Antonio and Bexar County, Alamo Area Council Govts., 1968. Mem. Friends of McNay Art Inst., Friends of San Antonio Library, San Antonio Mus. Assn., Smithsonian Assos., S.W. Research Found. Forum, Women's Aux. San Antonio Bar Assn. (charter), ACLU, Jewish Community Center, Am. Jewish Com. Democrat. Clubs: San Antonio, Giraud. Home: 6803-B West Ave San Antonio TX 78213 Office: 110 E Crockett St San Antonio TX 78298

GOLDSTEIN, CHARLOTTE LEAH TAYLOR, writer, pub. co. exec.; b. Phila., Feb. 7/8, 1923; d. Harry and Fannie (Goldberg) Taylor; m. S. Edward Goldstein, Feb. 28, 1942; children—Jeffrey-Allan, Sharon-Leigh, Charles-Terry, James-Stephan. Owner, Postal Instant Press, Los Angeles, 1971—, Printing Plant, Los Angeles, 1972—; owner, v.p. S/C Enterprises, Inc., Culver City, Calif., 1972—; developer Drug Control Hotline, Hot Meals on Wheels, Free Clinic Program; designer group therapy programs Los Angeles Hosps. Mem. exec. com. Calif. J.F. Kennedy for Pres., 1960; co-organizer, Temple Beth Ami, Reseda, Calif., 1950, Hadassah, Encino, 1954, B'nai Brith, West Los Angeles, 1964; chmn. Hollywood USO, 1954-60; adult tng. dir. Boy Scouts Am., recipient Silver Bruin award, 1965. Mem. Printing Industry Am. Republican. Clubs: B'nai B'rith, Elks, Emblem. Author: The American Flag, American Presidents, The Stars Cry, Sea and Sand, Time and Tide, Call An Ambulance, Tomorrow is for the Living, others; co-author, dir. nat. pioneer Stay Well program for sr. citizens, 1967-71. Home: 2136 Benedict Canyon Dr Beverly Hills CA 92010 Office: 9900 Washington Blvd Culver City CA 90230

GOLDSTEIN, DIANE RUDNER, banker; b. Memphis, Mar. 17, 1950; d. William B. and Jocelyn Rudner; B.A., U. Md., 1972; m. Edward J. Goldstein, Aug. 19, 1972. Asst. dir. psychol. services Asso. Professionals Inc., Memphis, 1972-74; asst. dir. mktg. research and planning Mfrs. Hanover Trust Bank, N.Y.C., 1974—, asst. v.p., 1977-80, v.p., 1980—; instr. Am. Inst. Banking. Mem. Bank Mktg. Assn., Fin. Womens Assn., Phi Beta Kappa. Home: 200 E 74th St New York NY 10021 Office: 350 Park Ave 10th Floor New York NY 10022 *

GOLDSTEIN, HANNAH, import co. exec.; b. N.Y.C., Apr. 6, 1934; d. William and Cecil (Rock) Rosenblatt; A.A., U. Fla., 1953; B.S. in Bus. Adminstrn., N.Y. U., 1955; children—Joyce Dara, Mitchell Bruce, Stephen Elliott, Russell Jay. Self-employed, N.Y.C., 1954-65; with Equitable Life Assurance Soc., N.Y.C., 1962-65; with Creative Programs and Paul Breiff Assocs., N.Y.C., 1965-70; mem. N.Y. Mercantile Exchange and Nat. Stock Exchange, 1967-70; pres. J. Pierre Internat., N.Y.C., 1968-73, Discovery Internat. Ltd., Scottsdale, Ariz., 1972—, Goldwest Internat. Ltd., Scottsdale, 1980—. Bd. dirs. Friends of Channel 8, Tempe, 1977—; mem. econ. devel. com. Scottsdale Town Enrichment Program, 1981-82; Democratic Precinct committeewoman, 1980—; State Dem. Committeewoman, 1981—; mem. econ. devel. com. Animal Welfare League, others. Mem. English Speaking Union, Ariz. World Trade Assn., Nat. Assn. Cable TV, Nat. Assn. TV Programming Execs., Am. Statis. Assn., Am. Mgmt. Assn., Nat. Acad. TV Arts and Scis., Alumni Assn. N.Y.U. Sch. Commerce, Beta Gamma Sigma. Clubs: University. Home: 8132 E Valley View Rd Scottsdale AZ 85253 Office: 10810 N Scottsdale Rd Scottsdale AZ 85254

GOLDSTEIN, JOAN, sociologist; b. Bklyn., Feb. 15, 1932; d. Harry and Ethel (Goldstein) Goldstein; B.A., U. Iowa, 1954; M.S., Bank St. Coll., 1967; Ph.D., Grad. Center, CUNY, 1978. High sch. tchr., N.Y.C., 1955-65; counsellor Practical Nurse Tng. Program, Manpower Devel. Tng. Act, N.Y., 1965-68; state health manpower planner Comprehensive Health Planning Agy., N.J. Health Dept., Trenton, 1968-72; asso. dir. Community Health Inst., N.Y., 1972-74; prof. sociology Bklyn. Coll. and Pace U., 1974—; research sociologist Grad. Center, City U. N.Y., 1975—; asst. prof. Rutgers U.; cons. Policy Research Corp.; mem. adv. com. Center for Women in Medicine, Med. Coll. Pa.; research Gateway Planning, Nat. Park Service. Mem. N.J. Gov.'s Pinelands Rev. Com., 1977, N.J. Public Health Council; mem. tech. adv. com. on off-shore oil leasing Dept. Interior. Fellow, Resources for Future Found., Inc., Washington, 1976—. Mem. NOW (nat. coordinator Women and Health Task Force, 1972-74, state coordinator Women and Aging Task Force 1973-74), Assn. Women in Sci. Author: Environmental Decision Making in Rural Locales: Pine Barrens, 1981; The Politics of Offshore Oil, 1982. Home and Office: B-15 Lakeview Terr Princeton NJ 08540

GOLDSTEIN, KAREN JAFFE, speech pathologist; b. New Haven, May 20, 1948; d. Samuel Abraham and Frances Diane (Molstein) J.; B.S., Emerson Coll., 1969; M.Ed., Northeastern U., 1971; D.Sc., Boston U., 1977; married; children—David, Michael. Clin. supr. Boston U., 1973; clin. dir. speech pathology U. Mass. Med. Center, 1978; pvt. practice speech, voice and lang. pathology, Concord, Mass., 1978-82, Portland, Oreg., 1982—; cons. in field. Mem. Am. Speech and Hearing Assn. (cert.), Mass. Speech and Hearing Assn., Am. Cleft Palate Assn. Editor: Annual Abstracts of Speech, Voice, Language and Hearing, 1979. Home: 10360 SW Hawthorne Ln Portland OR 97225

GOLDSTEIN, SANDRA, inflatable toys importing co. exec.; b. Chgo., Dec. 7; d. Jack Julius and Esther Judith (Glickman) Gilbert; student U. Wis., U. Ill., Champaign-Urbana; m. Seymour Leo Goldstein, Aug. 12, 1951; 1 dau., Jennie S. Co-founder, sr. v.p., sales mgr. Jennie G. Sales Co., Inc., Lincolnwood, Ill., 1961—. Mem. Nat. Assn. Convenience Stores, Nat. Oil Jobbers Assn., Ill. Petroleum Assn., Iowa Oil Jobbers Assn. Clubs: Carleton (Chgo.); Turnberry Yacht (Miami, Fla.). Office: 3770 W Pratt Ave Lincolnwood IL 60645

GOLDSTEIN, SHIRLEY MARIE, mgmt. cons. co. exec.; b. Bklyn., Dec. 1, 1927; d. William and Rita (Mohsberg) Lavine; grad. high sch.; m. Manfred Goldstein, Aug. 27, 1950; children—Ciny Marie, Lynn Alyse. Dental technician, Bklyn., 1946-48; teller First Nat. City Bank, Bklyn., 1948-56, bookkeeper, 1956-57, safe deposit mgr., 1957-59; sec., treas. Positive Cons., Inc., Bellmore, N.Y. 1964—, also dir. Mem. Long Island Aviation Council (sec. 1970-72), L.I. Assn. Commerce and Industry. Republican. Home and office: 2255 Arby Ct Bellmore NY 11710

GOLDSTEIN-SAULTER, RITA, psycho therapist; b. N.Y.C., Jan. 4, 1929; d. Joel Herbert and Pauline Birns; A.A., Santa Monica Coll., 1966; B.A., Calif. State U., Northridge, 1970, M.A., 1974; postgrad., Profl. Sch. Humanistic Studies, 1980—; m. Leon Saulter, May 7, 1982; children—Michael Alan Goldstein, Robert Steven Goldstein. Group facilitator Hamilton High Sch., Los Angeles, 1969; dir. new counselor program, supr. So. Calif. Counseling Center, Los Angeles, 1971-76; pvt. practice marital and family therapy, Beverly Hills and Van Nuys, Calif., 1974—; supr. Anando Marga Family Unity Center, Los Angeles, 1977; oral commr. Bd. Behavioral Scis., Sacramento, Calif. Lic. marriage, family and child counselor. Mem. Am. Psychol. Assn., Am. Assn. Marriage and Family Therapists, Calif. Assn. Marriage and Family Therapists (recipient Service award, 1980), Group Psychotherapy Assn. So. Calif. (recipient Service award 1980), Nat. Council Family Relations, Assn. Humanistic Psychology. Home: 13854 Vanowen St Van Nuys CA 91405 Office: 321 S Beverly Dr Suite F Beverly Hills CA 90212

GOLDSTON, LINDA LEEBOV (MRS. EDWARD M. GOLDSTON), lawyer; b. Pitts., Aug. 17, 1942; d. Mike and Florence (Labovitz) Leebov; A.B., U. Pitts., 1964; student U. Seven Seas, fall 1963; J.D., U. Pitts., 1967; m. Edward M. Goldston, Apr. 12, 1969; children—Joseph Leebov, Samuel Morris. Admitted to Pa. bar, 1968; shareholder Baskin and Sears, P.C., Pitts., 1968—. Vice-pres., Temple Sinai. Mem. Am., Pa., Allegheny County bar assns., Nat. Assn. Women Lawyers, Nat. Council Jewish Women, Women's Am. O.R.T., Ladies Hosp. Aid Soc., Ladies Aux. Jewish Home for Aged, B'nai B'rith. Home: 1309 Beechwood Blvd Pittsburgh PA 15217 Office: Frick Bldg Pittsburgh PA 15219

GOLDSZER, BATH-SHEBA, artist, export co. exec.; b. Warsaw, Poland, Jan. 26, 1932; came to U.S., 1953, naturalized, 1958; d. Zygmund and Ada (Patt) Danziger-Milbow; B.A. in Edn., Hertzelia Tchrs. Sem., 1953-56; studied with Gustav Rehberger, Art Students League; pvt. studies with Joe Hing Lowe, Ludmila Morosova; m. Joel Goldszer, June 2, 1956; children—Ronald I., Lita F. Two-person show Fellowship Gallery, Hollis, N.Y., 1972; group shows include: Lever House Gallery, N.Y.C., Twin Towers Custom House Gallery, N.Y.C., Union Carbide Gallery, N.Y.C., MHT Gallery, N.Y.C., Hudson Valley Art Assn., Westchester County Center Gallery, White Plains, N.Y., 1973-82, Catharine Lorillard Wolf Art Club, 1973-82, Nat. Art League Gallery, Douglaston, N.Y., 1974-82, Art League Nassau County, 1974-82, St. John U. Chung Cheng Art Gallery, 1979, 80; represented in numerous pvt. collections in U.S.A., Israel, Poland and Argentina; bookkeeper, office mgr. Louis Hornick & Co., N.Y.C., 1956-59, 69-75; controller, investment, cons. Freedco Products, Long Island City, N.Y., 1975—. Served to sgt. Israeli Army, 1950-52. Recipient numerous art awards; nominated gold medal Academie Italia Delle Arti de del Lavoro, 1980. Mem. Am. Artists Profl. League N.Y.C. (life fellow), Hudson Valley Art Assn., Catharine Lorillard Wolfe Art Club, Nat. Art League, Art League Nassau County, Big Six Art League (chmn., treas. 1970-82). Club: Hadassah. Home: 46-10 61st St Woodside NY 11377

GOLDWATER, MARILYN, state legislator; b. Boston, Jan. 29, 1927; d. Frederick and Rebecca (Geller) Rubin; R.N., Mt. Sinai Hosp. Sch. Nursing, 1948; m. William H. Goldwater, Aug. 8, 1948; children—Charles A., Diane L. Gen. duty, pvt. duty, emergency room, camp nurse, 1948-62; mem. Md. Ho. of Dels., Annapolis, 1974—. Bd. mem. Woman's Suburban Democratic Club, Bethesda, Md., 1966, pres., 1971-73; bd. mem. Woman's Nat. Dem. Club, 1966-67; vice chmn. 16th Legis. Dist., Precinct 7-23, Montgomery County, Md., 1965-66, chmn., 1966-68; exec. v.p. Western Suburban Dem. Club, Bethesda, Md., 1967-68; mem. adv. bds. women public ofcls. internship program Goucher Coll., 1979—; mem. Md. State Soc. Autistic Children, 1978—. Recipient Ann London Scott award for legis. excellence Md. div. NOW, 1979, Nurse of Yr. award Md. Nurses Assn., 1977, citations VFW, 1976, March of Dimes, 1965, ARC, 1979; Recognition award Am. Nurses Assn., 1980. Mem. Nat. Order Women Legislators (legis. chmn. 1978), Am. Nurses Assn., Nurses Coalition for Action, Nat. Assn. Jewish Legislators, LWV, Concerned Citizens for Juvenile Justice, Women Legislators Md. (chmn. 1979-81), Mt. Sinai Hosp. Sch. Nursing Alumni Assn., Sigma Theta Tau. Democrat. Jewish.

GOLDWYN, JUDITH S., typographer; b. N.Y.C., Apr. 1, 1940; d. Raymond B. and Rosetta (Van Gelder) Schlessel; B.A., N.Y.U., 1962; M.A., L.I.U., 1973; m. Ronald M. Goldwyn, Aug. 20, 1961; children—Ira D., Laura-Jill. Tchr., Gt. Neck, N.Y., 1972-77; owner The Word Factory, Gt. Neck, 1977—. Mem. Gt. Neck Village Bus. Assn. (sec.), Gt. Neck C. of C. (dir.), Typographers Assn. N.Y. Office: 621 Middle Neck Rd Great Neck NY 11023

GOLEMBESKI, KAREN ANN, jewelry corp. exec.; b. Providence, May 23, 1947; d. Joseph John and Marion Elizabeth (Isaacson) G.; B.S., U. R.I., 1968; postgrad. in bus. Providence Coll., 1970-72. Purchasing dir. Hedison Mfg. Co., Providence, 1968-71; account exec. Vanguard Metals Co., North Attleboro, Mass., 1971-75; pres. Am. Pewter Co., Inc., N.Y.C., 1982—; owner, sales rep. Elite Assos., Providence, 1982—. Active Big Sisters program; mem. Republican Nat. Com. Mem. Jewelers and Silversmiths of Am., Nat. Council Salesmen's Orgns., Nat. Assn. Female Execs. Club: Playoff Racquetball. Office: 2 Jacksonwalk Way Providence RI 02903

GOLICZ, PEGGY LOUISE, real estate appraiser; b. Washington, May 21, 1946; d. Ernest P. and Alicia A. (Peter) Erickson; student Wash. State U., Pullman, 1968; m. Lawrence J. Golicz, Aug. 3, 1968; children—Eric John, Karl Peter, Mark Joseph. Various secretarial and adminstrv. asst. positions, 1968-74; engaged in real estate, 1974—; broker, v.p. property mgmt., dir. Total Realty, Inc., Madison, 1978—; v.p. Am. Appraisal & Feasibility Corp., Madison, 1978—, also dir.; cons. in field. Mem. Nat. Center Housing Mgmt., Inst. Real Estate Mgmt., Soc. Real Estate Appraisers (asso.), Nat. Assn. Realtors, Greater Madison Bd. Realtors, Nat. Assn. Female Execs., Westmoreland Youth Hockey Assn., Alpha Phi, Alpha Sigma Epsilon. Clubs: Order Eastern Star, Order Forresters. Author papers in field. Home: 1619 Elderwood Circle Middleton WI 53562 Office: 6510 Schroder Rd Madison WI 53711

GOLIGHTLY, ANNIE LUCILLE, home economist; b. Gadsden, Ala., Dec. 26, 1920; d. Renfroe Selman and Zenobia (Morris) G.; student Ala. Coll. for Women, 1939-41; B.S. in Home Econs., Ala. Poly. Inst. (now Auburn U.), 1946, postgrad., summer 1947; M.S. in Textiles, Clothing and Related Art, U. Tenn., Knoxville, 1955; postgrad. in clothing and textiles Iowa State U., summer 1964, Colo. State U., summer 1970; Ph.D., Utah State U., 1974. Tchr. home econs., secondary sch., Chatom, Ala., 1944-45, Biloxi (Miss.) High Sch., 1946-52; sewing tchr. Singer Co., Anniston, Ala., 1945; tchr. Pensacola (Fla.) High Sch., 1952-57, acting dean girls, 1957-58; asst. prof. clothing and textiles Ga. So. Coll., 1958-70, acting chmn. div. home econs., 1961-63; instr. Va. Poly. Inst. and State U., 1972-73; asso. prof. Memphis State U., 1973—. Mem. Assn. Coll. Profs. Textiles and Clothing, Am. Home Econs. Assn., Tenn. Home Econs. Assn., West Tenn. Home Econs. Assn., AAUW, Alpha Delta Kappa, Kappa Omicron Phi. Baptist. Home: 4749 Audubon View Circle Apt 2 Memphis TN 38117 Office: Manning Hall Memphis State U Memphis TN 38152

GOLIN, ANNE KEEFE, psychologist, educator; b. Tulsa, May 17, 1932; d. James L. and Frances M. (Harrison) Keefe; B.A., Newcomb Coll., Tulane U., 1954; Ph.D., U. Iowa, 1960; div.; children—Carol, Eric, Sarah. Instr., U. Wis., Milw., 1960-65, field assessment officer tng. program Peach Corps, 1964-65; mem. faculty U. Pitts., 1966—, prof. edn., 1972—, dir. rehab. counseling program, 1980—. Mem. Am. Psychol. Assn., Am. Soc. Allied Health Professions, Council Exceptional Children. Co-author: The Interdisciplinary Health Care Team: A Handbook, 1979; The Interdisciplinary Team: A Handbook for the Education of Exceptional Children, 1981. Office: 5K32 Forbes Quad U Pitts Pittsburgh PA 15260

GOLOMB, CLAIRE, psychologist; b. Frankfurt, Germany, Jan. 30, 1928; d. Chaskel and Fanny (Monderer) Schimmel; B.A., Hebrew U., Jerusalem, 1954; M.A., New Sch. for Social Research, N.Y., 1959; Ph.D., Brandeis U., 1968; m. Dan Golomb, Feb. 23, 1954; children—Mayana, Anath. Instr., Wellesley (Mass.) Coll., 1968-69; asst. prof. Brandeis U., Waltham, Mass., 1971-74; assoc. prof. psychology U. Mass., Boston, 1974-82, prof., 1982—. Mem. Am. Psychol. Assn., Soc. Research in Child Devel. Author: Young Children's Sculpture and Drawing: A Study in Representational Development, 1974. Home: 61 Plainfield St Newton MA 02168 Office: U Mass Harbor Campus Boston MA 02125

GOLOMB, LYNNE ROOTH, ednl. psychologist; b. Chgo., Sept. 2, 1945; d. Eli and Florence (Goodman) Rooth; B.A., U. Pitts., 1966, M.S., 1968; Ed.D., Loyola U., 1980; m. Harvey Golomb, Dec. 28, 1965; children—Adam Simon, Sara Rooth. Grad. asst. Arsenal Family Childrens Center, Pitts., 1967-68; tchr., therapist League Sch., Boston, 1968-69; tchr., developer infant day care program Dept. Labor Nat. Capitol Area Day Care, Washington, 1969-71; cons. Programs for Handicapped, Chgo., 1974-78; pvt. practice ednl. psychology, Chgo., 1978—; lectr. Loyola U., Chgo., 1981—. NIMH fellow, 1966. Mem. Am. Psychol. Assn., Nat. Assn. Edn. Young Children, Council Exceptional Children, Ill. Sch. Psychologists Assn. Home and office: 5412 S Blackstone Ave Chicago IL 60615

GOLUB, SHARON BRAMSON, psychologist; b. N.Y.C., Mar. 25, 1937; R.N., Mt. Sinai Hosp. Sch. Nursing, 1957; B.S., Columbia U., 1959, M.A., 1966; Ph.D., Fordham U., 1974; m. Leon M. Golub, June 1, 1958; children—Lawrence E., David B. Head nurse Mt. Sinai Hosp., N.Y.C., 1957-59; contbg. editor RN Mag., Oradell, N.J., 1967-74; asst. prof. psychology Coll. of New Rochelle (N.Y.), 1974-79, dir. women's studies, 1978-79, assoc. prof., chairperson, 1979—; adj. assoc. prof. psychiatry N.Y. Med. Coll., Valhalla, 1980—; pvt. practice individual and group psychotherapy; cons. Mental Health Assn. of Westchester, 1970-78. NIH fellow, 1971-74; cert. psychologist, N.Y. State. Mem. Am. Psychol. Assn., Eastern Psychol. Assn., Assn. for Women in Psychology, AAUP, N.Y. Acad. Scis., Am. Assn. of Sex Educators, Counselors and Therapists, Soc. for Menstrual Cycle Research (pres. 1981-83), Phi Beta Kappa, Sigma Xi, Psi Chi. Contbr. articles to profl. jours. Home: 32 Runyon Pl Scarsdale NY 10583 Office: Coll of New Rochelle New Rochelle NY 10801

GOMBERG, EDITH LISANSKY, psychologist; b. N.Y.C., Jan. 14, 1920; d. Barnet and Dorothy (Resnick) Silverglied; M.A., Columbia U., 1940; Ph.D., Yale U., 1949; m. Henry Jacob Gomberg, June 24, 1967; children—Stephen, Judith, Eugene, Richard, Robert. Lectr., research asst., research asso. Center Alcohol Studies, Yale U., 1949-67; asso. prof. dept. psychology U. P.R., 1968-71; prof. Sch. Social Work, U. Mich., Ann Arbor, 1974—. Mem. Town Meeting, Hamden, Conn., 1964-65; mem. Nat. Council on Alcoholism Blue Ribbon Study Commn. on Alcoholism and Aging, 1979—; chmn. panel on prevention, mem. steering com. study to assess sci. opportunities of alcohol related research Inst. Medicine, Nat. Acad. Sci. Mary E. Ives fellow, 1944; AAUW Elizabeth Avery Colten fellow, 1955. Mem. Am. Psychol. Assn., Psychonomic Soc., Council Social Work Edn., Sociedad Interamericana de Psicologia, Gerontol. Soc., Sigma Xi. Jewish. Author: Gender and Disordered Behavior, 1979; Alcohol, Science and Society Revisited, 1982; contbr. chpts. to books, articles to profl. jours. Office: 1065 Frieze Bldg U Mich Ann Arbor MI 48109

GOMEZ, ANA LYDIA MAS, ret. govt. ofcl., educator; ofcl.; b. San Juan, P.R., Sept. 30, 1913; d. Jose and Concepcion (Marti) Mas Nadal; B.A., U. P.R., 1937; M.A., Columbia, 1948; m. Edmundo Gomez, Dec. 24, 1934. Jr. econ. analyst U.S. Dept. State, 1945-48, agrl. econ. asst., econ. officer, 1948-52, asst. agrl. attache, 1952-54, econ. officer, attache, 1965-73; asst. agrl. attache U.S. Dept. Agr., 1954-65; lectr. econs. U. Ams., Mexico City, 1975—. Recipient Superior Service award U.S. Dept. Agr., 1956. Mem. Am. Econ. Assn. Home: Explanada 1210 Lomas de Chapultepec Mexico 10 DF Mexico

GOMEZ, GAYNELL REGINA, banker; b. St. Louis, Apr. 6, 1947; d. Gerald D. and Joyce R. Lenoir; B.B.A., U. Wis., 1968; M.B.A. (Edward W. Carter Fellow), UCLA, 1976; m. Frank C. Gomez, Oct. 18, 1968; 1 son, Frank C. Corporate banking officer Beverly Hills office United Calif. Bank, 1972-74, asst. v.p. internat. div., Los Angeles, 1977-78, v.p. Spl. Industries div., 1978-80; v.p. strategic planning First Interstate Bancorp, 1980—. Mem. Beta Gamma Sigma. Democrat. Roman Catholic. Home: 1152 Point View St Los Angeles CA 90035 Office: 707 Wilshire Blvd Los Angeles CA 90017

GOMEZ D'CASTRO, NILDA MARIA, med. technologist; b. San German, P.R., July 14, 1933; d. Modesto and Enriqueta (D'Castro Gutierrez) Gomez L.; B.S., Cath. U. P.R., 1955; med. technologist, Jackson Meml. Hosp., U. Miami, 1957; m. German Fragoso, Mar. 25, 1969. Chief med. technologist Dept. Health, Aguadilla Dist. Hosp., 1969-75; adminstrv. technologist Dept. Health, Mayaguez Med. Center, 1971-76; regional supr. Western Health Region, Mayaguez, 1967-76; adminstr., owner Western Lab. Service P.R., 1981—; pres. Multi-Media Corp. Mem. Am. Soc. Med. Tech., Am. Soc. Clin. Pathology, Am. Bd. Bioanalysis, Am. Soc. Blood Banks, Coll. Med. Tech. P.R. Office: PO Box 81 San German PR 00753

GOMPERS, GAYE JOANNE, psychologist; b. N.Y.C., Jan. 9, 1945; d. Joseph Placid and Annette (Schneiderman) Sacca; adopted d. Seymour Stich; B.A. with honors and spl. distinction in psychology, Fla. Internat. U., 1974, M.S., 1977; postgrad. U. Miami, 1977, Nova U. Sch. Profl. Psychology, 1978—; m. Richard William Gompers, Mar. 31, 1961; children—Teri Jo, Cori Ann, Robert, Dani Lynn. Child care dir., 1971-73; instr. Sunrise Sch. for Exceptional Children, 1973-74; instr. Beth Am Schs., 1974-75; sr. counselor Community Center, 1975; therapist with disturbed children Grant Center Hosp., Miami, Fla., 1975-76; clin. dir. drug-rehab. program Operation ReEntry, Miami Beach, Fla., 1976-79; mem. tng. faculty Humanistic Inst. Fla., Miami, 1978; co-founder, program developer Growth Inst., North Miami, Fla., 1979; clin. caseworker, psychotherapist with emotionally disturbed adolescents and families, Bertha Abess Children's Center, Miami, 1979-81; supr. Children's Home Soc., 1981-82. Cert. of tng. in Gestalt therapy; tchr.'s cert., Fla. Mem. Nat. Assn. Sch. Psychologists, Am. Psychol. Assn. Democrat. Jewish. Home: 11309 SW 167th Terr Miami FL 33157

GONCHAR, SUSAN ADAMS, govt. ofcl.; b. Milw., Mar. 21, 1936; d. George Matthew, Jr. and Jo Ellen (Maxson) Adams; m. Donald James Gonchar, Dec. 4, 1954; children—Laura Ann, Nancy Maxson. Personnel staff asst. Def. Mapping Agy. Topographic Center, Washington, 1976-79, writer-editor DMA Office Distbn. Services, 1979-81, public affairs specialist, 1981—; mem. edn. com. Def. Mapping Fed. Credit Union, 1980—. Recipient Outstanding Performance award Def. Mapping Agy., 1977, 79, 80, 81, 82, beneficial suggestion award, 1979, 80, Outstanding Employee of Yr. award, 1981; George Washington medal Freedoms Found. Valley Forge, 1981, Combined Fed. Campaign Merit award, 1980. Mem. Nat. Press Club, Nat. Assn. Govt. Communicators, DAR (chpt. regent 1967-69, adv. bd. sch. 1971-74, nat. chmn. jr. membership 1971-74, nat. chmn. mag. 1980—, chaplain Outstanding Jr. Club 1981-83; named Va. Outstanding Jr. Mem. 1966), Magna Charta Dames, Daus. Colonial Wars. Republican. Episcopalian. Home: 9514 Miranda Ct Fairfax VA 22031

GONG, MERY LEE, data processor; b. Cleve., June 14, 1931; d. Wing and Shee (Woo) Gong; B.S., Ohio State U., 1954. Computer operator Instrn. and Research Computer Center, Ohio State U., Columbus, 1954-56, programmer, cons., 1956-61, ops. supr., 1961-65, adminstrv. asst., 1965-72, asst. dir., 1972-81, asso. dir., 1981—; computer cons. Cole-Layer-Trumble Co.; instr. Ohio State U. continuing edn. Children's Hosp., Columbus, 1969. Mem. Ohio Commn. on Status of Women. Mem. Am. Mgmt. Assn., Assn. Computing Machinery, Data Processing Mgmt. Assn., Air Force Assn., Assn. for Systems Mgmt., Ohio State U. Alumni Assn., N.W. Area Council for Human Relations, LWV, Upper Arlington Civic Assn., Columbus Area Civil Rights Council. Club: Quota (Columbus). Home: 1776 Ridgecliff Rd Columbus OH 43221 Office: 1971 Neil Ave Columbus OH 43210

GONYA, PATRICE YEAGER, ins. co. ofcl.; b. Bremen, Ga., Aug. 17, 1951; d. Forest William and Madge Moore (Cain) Yeager; B.S., U. Mo., Columbia, 1972, M.B.A., 1978; m. David E. Gonya. Devel. trainee State Farm Ins. Co., Columbia, 1972-73, jr. acct., 1973-74, acct., 1974-77, asst. acctg. mgr., Springfield, Pa., 1977-79, acctg. supt., 1979—. Vol. drives Heart Fund, 1975, 76; office co-chmn. United Way, 1979, chmn., 1980, mem. campaign effectiveness council, 1982. C.P.C.U. Mem. Nat. Assn. Accts., Nat. Assn. Female Execs.

GONZALES, LUCILLE CONTRERAS, ednl. adminstr.; b. Colton, Calif., Nov. 30, 1937; d. Antonio Colunga and Ramona (Arroyo) Contreras; A.A., San Bernardino Valley Coll., 1958; B.A., U. Calif., Santa Barbara, 1960; M.A., Claremont Grad. Sch., 1969; m. Enrique Gonzales, Aug. 27, 1960; children—Leticia Maria, Cecilia Maria. With Chino (Calif.) Public Schs., 1960—, bilingual classroom tchr., 1970-74, bilingual coordinator, 1974-76, coordinator consol. application-intergroup relations, 1976-78, supr. spl. projects, 1978, adminstr. spl. projects, 1978-82, dir. spl. projects, 1982—. Mem. Migrant Regional Exec. Bd.; mem. Bilingual Dirs. Task Force. Mem. Nat. Assn. Female Execs., San Bernardino County Assn. Compensatory Edn. Dirs. (pres., v.p.), P.E.O., Assn. Secondary Spl. Projects, Assn. Calif. Sch. Adminstrs., Pi Lambda Theta, Delta Kappa Gamma. Office: 5130 Riverside Dr Chino CA 91710

GONZALEZ, CRISTINA, lang. profl., educator; b. Gijón, Spain, Apr. 9, 1951; came to U.S., 1976; d. Cesar González and Maruja Sánchez; M.A., U. Oviedo, Spain, 1976; M.A., Ind. U., Bloomington, 1978, Ph.D., 1981; m. Richard A. Cohen, Aug. 8, 1979. Tchr. Spanish, Academia Clarín, Oviedo, Spain, 1976; asso. instr. Spanish, Ind. U., Bloomington, 1976-79; lectr. Spanish, Tufts U., 1980; asst. prof. Spanish, Purdue U., West Lafayette, Ind., 1981—. Ind. U. grantee, summer 1977. Mem. Société Internationale Arthurienne, Medieval Acad. Am., Semiotic Soc. Am., Am. Assn. Tchrs. Spanish and Portuguese, MLA, Centro Español de Documentación y Estudios. Author: Aproximación al Libro del Cavallero Zifar, 1983, also articles; mem. editorial bds. Dieciocho, Third Woman. Home: 3332 Peppermill Dr West Lafayette IN 47906 Office: Dept Fgn Langs Purdue U West Lafayette IN 47907

GONZALEZ, DIANE KATHRYN, social worker; b. Cin., Aug. 20, 1947; d. Joseph Curtis and Kathryn Mary (Diskin) Gonzalez; B.A. in Social Work, U. Dayton, 1969; A.M. in Social Work, U. Chgo., 1973; m. Thomas Connolley Leibig, July 5, 1974; 1 dau., Abigail. Social worker Hamilton County Welfare Dept., Cin., 1969-71; social worker obstetrics dept. and prenatal clinic social service dept. St. Francis Hosp., Evanston, Ill., 1973-78; rap group leader Teen Scene, Planned Parenthood Assn., Chgo., part-time, 1979-80; social worker Chgo. Comprehensive Care Center, part-time, 1980—; chmn. adv. com. Evanston Continuing Edn. Center, 1978-80. Cert. social worker, Ill. Mem. Nat. Assn. Social Workers, Acad. Cert. Social Workers. Roman Catholic. Home: 218 W Menomonee St Chicago IL 60614 Office: Chicago Comprehensive Care Center 3639 S Michigan Ave Chicago IL 60653

GONZALEZ, LINDA ANTONIA, univ. ofcl.; b. Los Angeles, July 13, 1955; d. Domingo and Otilia (Ponce) G.; B.B.A. (Data Processing Mgmt. Assn. scholar 1973), U. Tex., El Paso, 1977. Mem. adminstrv. staff U. Tex., El Paso, 1973—, student devel. specialist Office Student Fin. Aid, 1977-81, asst. dir. office, 1981—. Mem Nat. Assn. Student Fin. Aid Adminstrs. Democrat. Roman Catholic. Home: 305 Pecos St El Paso TX 79905 Office: 202 W Union Bldg U Tex El Paso TX 79968

GONZALEZ, LITA DEBORAH, county ofcl.; b. Manhattan, N.Y., Jan. 25, 1949; d. Thomas Anthony and Nieves Maria (Gutierrez) G.; B.A., SUNY, New Paltz, 1969, M.S., 1973, M.P.A., Brockport, 1980. Sr. instn. tchr. N.Y. State Div. Youth, Highland, 1970-74, asst. cottage coordinator, 1974-76, asst. foster care coordinator, Rochester, 1976-78, foster care coordinator met. team, 1978-79; coordinator Monroe County Human Relations Commn., Rochester, 1979—. Bd. dirs. Rochester Camp Fire Girls, 1978-79, 82—, spl. projects coordinator, 1979; mem. allocation com. sect. F, Rochester Community Chest, 1979—; mem. Finger Lakes Health Systems No. Subarea Council, 1979-81. Recipient cert. of appreciation Henrietta Kiwanis Club, 1977, Rochester Camp Fire Girls, 79. Mem. Woman's Career Network. Home: 759 Woodbine Ave Rochester NY 14619 Office: 80 W Main St Rochester NY 14614

GONZALEZ-SANABRIA, OLGA DORIS, chem. engr.; b. Patillas, P.R., Apr. 6, 1956; d. Meliton and Ana Matilde (Rivera) Gonzalez; B.S. in Chem. Engring. cum laude, U. P.R., 1979; postgrad. U. Mich. Continuing Edn., summer 1979, U. Toledo, 1980—; m. Rafael Sanabria, Nov. 22, 1979; 1 dau., Naomi. Ops. engr. chem. engring. practice Yabucoa Sun Oil Co. (P.R.), 1978; chem. engr. NASA Lewis Research Center, Cleve., 1979—. Recipient Incentive award NASA, 1981. Mem. Electrochem. Soc., Chem. Engring. Soc., Tau Beta Pi. Patentee in field. Office: NASA Lewis Research Center 21000 Brookpark Rd Cleveland OH 44135

GONZLIK, PAMELA JOAN, cable TV performer b. N.Y.C., Apr. 20, 1948; d. John Martin and Regina (Cohen) G.; secretarial diploma, A.O.S. acctg. degree, Taylor Bus. Inst., 1975; student in acctg Pace U., 1975. Stock records clk. G. A. Saxton & Co., N.Y.C., 1970-71; sec., bookkeeper Acme Quilting Co., Inc., N.Y.C., 1971-73; acct., sec., office mgr. Alwyn Partners, N.Y.C., 1975-77; treas. Independence Plaza Tenants Orgn. and Rent Strike Com., 1977-78; sec. Atalanta Corp., N.Y.C., 1978-80; legal sec. City of N.Y. Law Dept., 1980—; cable TV vol., producer, host, performer Musical Interludes cable TV show Exptl. TV Coop., Inc., N.Y.C., 1978-82; vol., adminstrv. asst. ETC Studios, 1978-82; developer cable TV game shows. Mem. Phi Chi Theta (rec. sec. Gamma Xi chpt. 1976-77). Home: 40 Harrison St Apt 38E New York NY 10013

GOOD, ANNE LEEPER (MRS. JOHN CARTER GOOD), civic worker; b. Jackson, Tenn., Nov. 10, 1923; d. Robert Allen and Ola (Crittenden) Leeper; A.B., B.S. cum laude, Lambuth Coll., 1944; m. John Carter Good, Oct. 28, 1945; children—John Robert, Carter Crittenden, William Allen. Co-chmn. Introduction to Washington com. The Hospitality and Info. Service, 1968-71, treas., 1971-75, v.p., 1975-77, pres., 1977-79; membership chmn. Spanish Portuguese Study Group, 1968-69, v.p., 1969-70, pres., 1970-71; mem. ladies' bd. House of Mercy, 1970—, treas., 1972-74. Bd. dirs. D.C. br. Nat. Capitol Area YWCA, 1971-78, 79—, rec. sec., 1974, treas., 1974-76, 81—; com. Hannah Harrison Career Sch., 1971-78, 79—, chmn., 1976-77; bd. dirs. Nat. Capital Area YWCA, 1973-79, fin. com., 1978—; bd. dirs. Rosemount Infant Day Care Ctr., 1972-82, v.p., 1974-76; bd. dirs. Washington chpt. Achievement Rewards for Coll. Scientists, 1971-72, Alliance Francaise, Club d'Amitie Franco-Internationale. Clubs: St. Albans School Mothers (pres. Washington 1964-65), Air Force Officers Wives (mem. bd. Washington 1959-61).

GOOD, JOSEPHINE LOUISE, govt. ofcl.; b. Denver, Mar. 10, 1918; d. George Washington and Lena Pearl (Wooley) G.; student Parks Sch. Bus., Denver, 1935. Sec., several congl. offices, Washington, 1946-53; confidential adminstrv. aide to postmaster gen., Washington, 1953-56; conv. dir. Republican Nat. Com., Washington, 1956-82; dir. Exec. Secretariat, GSA, Washington, 1982—, Served with USCGR, 1943-45. Mem. Def. Adv. Com. on Women In Service. Roman Catholic. Home: 1800 Old Meadow Rd Apt 1217 McLean VA 22102 Office: Exec Secretariat GSA 18th and F Sts NW Washington DC 25045

GOOD, LINDA LOU, educator; b. Zanesville, Ohio, May 30, 1941; d. John Robert and Alice Laura (Fulkerson) Moore; B.S. in Elem. Edn., Ohio U., 1964; m. Larry Alvin Good, Jan. 11, 1964; children—Jason (dec.), Alicia and Tricia (twins), Amy Jo. Tchr., West Muskingum Sch. Dist., 1962-64; first grade tchr., Bellevue, Ohio, 1964-68, 2d grade tchr., Zanesville Sch. System, 1970—. Co-chmn. Zane Trace Commemoration. Mem. NEA, Ohio Edn. Assn., Zanesville Edn. Assn., Eastern Ohio Tchrs. Assn. Methodist.

GOOD, MARY JANE, temporary employment co. exec.; b. Indpls., Sept. 15, 1934; d. Street W. and Helen Blanche (Sarchet) Butler; student Public Relations Sch., Cleve., 1968, Real Estate Sch., Calumet Coll., Gary, Ind., 1976; m. Howard Ray, Dec. 5, 1952; children—Rae Jane Araujo, Eric Howard. Marketing mgr. Suburbs Ahead, Bolingbrook, Ill., 1972-73; dir. field services Am. Heart Assn., Cin., 1974-76; mgr. Norrell Services, Chgo., 1976-79, dist. mgr. Ohio-W.Va., Atlanta, 1979—, mem. Norrell Pres. Club, 1978, 81, Leaders Panel, 1981. Ward com. chmn. Republican party, Strongsville, Ohio, 1967-69; chmn. Well Baby Clinic, Bolingbrook, 1972-73; com. mem. Strongsville Recreational Com. Library Com., 1968-69; chmn. Crown Point (Ind.) chpt. Am. Heart Assn., 1977-78, public relations chmn. Ind., 1978. Recipient Outstanding Citizen award Bolingbrook Women's Club, 1973; named hon. Ky. Col. Mem. Epsilon Sigma Alpha. Home: 1577 Pinehurst Dr Pittsburgh PA 15241 Office: 3092 Piedmont Rd NE Atlanta GA 30305

GOOD, SUSAN PAULINE, banker; b. Sanger, Calif., Aug. 17, 1953; d. Alfred Anton and Elsbeth (Grimm) Good; A.A., Reedley Coll., 1973; B.A. summa cum laude, Calif. State U., Fresno, 1975; m. David Lehman, May 22, 1976. Advt. asst. Bell Public Relations Agy., Fresno, Calif., 1976-77; account exec. Meeker Advt., Fresno, Calif., 1977-78; dir. advt. First Savs. and Loan, Fresno, Calif., 1978-81 (merger with Central Fed. Savs. and Loan 1981), asst. v.p., br. promotions mgr., br. mgr., 1981—. Mem. mktg. com. U.S. League Savs. Assn., 1980-81; chmn. Fresno City-County Commn. on Status Women, 1979; sec. Fresno County Democratic Central Com., 1981-82; pres. Calif. State U. Fresno Alumni Assn., 1981; sec., bd. dirs. Fresno Rape Counseling Service, 1981. Recipient cert. of achievement Inst. Fin. Edn., 1982. Mem. Fresno Advt. Fedn. (pres. 1982—), Nat. Assn. Female Execs., Inst. Fin. Edn., Calif. Press Women, Nat. Women's Polit. Caucus. Roman Catholic. Club: Arthur Murray Dance. Office: 600 W Main St Visalia CA 93291

GOODALE, HOPE KAUFMANN, educator; b. N.Y.C., Apr. 23, 1926; d. Charles Barnard and Nettie (Cramer) Kaufmann; A.B. with honors in Spanish, Bryn Mawr Coll., 1948, M.A., 1950, Ph.D., 1965; m. Robert Lincoln Goodale, Aug. 2, 1951. Music librarian Free Library of Phila., 1949-51; instr. dept. Spanish, Bryn Mawr Coll., 1952-59; asst. prof. modern langs. Widener Coll., Chester, Pa., 1964-67, assos. prof., 1967-71, prof., 1972—; corp. Internat. Inst. of Spain, Madrid. Fulbright fellow, Madrid, 1960-61. Mem. MLA, Phila. Vicinity MLA, Pa. MLA, Am. Assn. Tchrs. Spanish and Portuguese. Democrat. Contbr. articles to profl. jours. Home: 411 S Providence Rd Wallingford PA 19086 Office: LC 137A Widener Univ Chester PA 19013

GOODALE, RONDA ANDELMAN, educator; b. Boston, June 16, 1949; d. Louis and Rose (Post) Andelman; B.S., Boston State Coll., 1967; Ed.M. in Spl. Edn., Northeastern U., 1968; Ph.D. in Ednl. Psychology, Boston Coll., 1982; children—Chandler Michael, Lara Faith. Spl. educator Boston public schs., 1968—, core evaluation team leader, 1976-77, support tchr., 1977-78, compliance specialist dept. spl. services, 1979—; spl. educator Mass. Mental Health Center, 1969-72; ednl. dir. Boston-Brookline Collaborative Center, 1972-75; supr. student tchrs. Boston Coll., 1975-76; lectr. dept. psychology, U. Mass., Boston, 1968—, spl. edn. adv.; 1977—, lectr. spl. edn. Regis Coll., Weston, Mass., 1977-81; lectr. Tchr. Corps., 1979—. Mem. Council for Exceptional Children. Home: 42 Alton Pl Brookline MA 02146 Office: 26 Court St Boston MA 02108

GOODALE, TONI KRISSEL, devel. cons.; b. N.Y.C., May 26, 1941; d. Walter DuPont and Ricka Krissel; A.B. cum laude, Smith Coll., 1963; student U. Geneva, 1962-63; postgrad. Hunter Coll., 1964-65; m. James Campbell Goodale, May 3, 1964; children—Timothy Fuller, Ashley Krissel. Congl. intern Senator Keating, U.S. Senate, Washington, 1963; broadcast analyst FCC, Washington, 1963-64; adminstrv. asst., dir. grant research dept. Ford Found., N.Y.C., 1964-67, cons. public edn. dept., 1968-69; N.Y. rep. Smith Coll., N.Y.C., 1975-78, asst. dir. devel., 1978-79; pres. TKG Assocs., N.Y.C., 1979—; mem. bd. advs. First Women's Bank. Mem. alumnae fund com. Smith Coll.; trustee, alumnae fund chmn., mem. alumnae council Brearley Sch.; mem. exec. com. Parents Assn., St. Bernard's Sch.; trustee, bd. govs. Churchill Sch.; trustee N.Y. Inst. Child Devel.; mem. women's div. Legal Aid Soc.; mem. N.Y. com. Joffrey Ballet; mem. benefit com. Grosvenor House; vice chmn. N.Y.C. Opera Benefit; mem. N.Y. com. Sch. of Am. Ballet, Superskates. Mem. Nat. Soc. Fund Raising Execs., Brearley Sch. Alumnae Assn., Smith Coll. Alumnae Assn. Clubs: Cosmopolitan, Doubles Internat., Smith Coll., Washington Tennis. Author preface Effective Corporate Fund Raising. Office: 3 W 51st St New York NY 10019

GOODEN, OPAL, editor, writer; b. Ft. Worth, Oct. 13, 1911; d. Juewell and Winnifred (Eastus) Gooden; A.B., Tex. Christian U., 1931; student U. Chgo., 1931-33, Chgo. Theol. Sem., 1931-33. Writer, Paterson (N.J.) Call, 1937-38, Youth Employment Project, WPA, Duluth, Minn., 1938; mem. program staff YWCA, Summit, N.J., 1939-42; writer, internat. specialist U.S. Dept. Labor, Washington, 1942-47; free lance writer, 1947-49; info. officer U.S. War Claims Commn., Washington, 1949-51; writer, editor Internat. Press Service, USIS, Washington, 1951-53; careers cons., editor Am. Assn. Med. Social Workers, Nat. Assn. Social Workers, Washington, 1954-56; personnel asst., editor Miners Meml. Hosp. Assn., Washington, 1957-64; editor, adminstrv. asst. United Mine Works of Am. Welfare and Retirement Fund, Washington, 1964-74; editorial cons. Health and Med. Care, 1974—. Mem. Citizens Assn. Georgetown; v.p. Friends Non-Profit Housing, Inc., 1965-71; bd. dirs. Ionia R. Whipper Home, 1969-72; patron Heard Mus. and Wild Life Sanctuary, McKinney, Tex., 1976—. Fellow Am. Pub. Health Assn.; mem. Physicians Forum, Am. Med. Writers Assn. (chpt. sec. 1967-68), Am. Newspaper Womens Club (2d v.p. 1963-64), Smithsonian Assos., Friends of Nat. Zoo, Sierra Club. Democrat. Mem. Soc. of Friends. Club: Washington Press (Washington). Home and office: 3320 Dent Pl NW Washington DC 20007

GOODHUE, MARY BRIER, lawyer, state senator; b. London, July 24, 1921; d. Ernest and Marion H. (Hawks) Brier; came to U.S., 1923, naturalized, 1942; B.A., Vassar Coll., 1942; LL.B., U. Mich., 1944; m. Francis A. Goodhue, Jr., May 15, 1948; 1 son, Francis A., III. Admitted to N.Y. State bar, 1945; asso. firm Root, Clark, Buckner & Ballantine, N.Y.C., 1945-48; asst. counsel N.Y. State Crime Commn., 1951-53, N.Y. State Moreland Commn., 1953-54; mem. firm Goodhue Lange Banks & Arons, and predecessors, Mt. Kisco, 1955—; mem. N.Y. State Assembly from 93d Dist., 1975-78, N.Y. State Senate, 1979—. Trustee, No. Westchester Hosp., Presbyn. Hosp., N.Y.C.; N.Y. del. Nat. Women's Conf., Houston, 1977. Decorated Order St. John. Mem. Am. Bar Assn., No. Westchester Bar Assn., Westchester Bar Assn. Office: 126 Barker St Mount Kisco NY 10549

GOODKIN, HELEN FAIRBANK, rehab. specialist; b. Chgo., Mar. 6, 1945; d. John Young and Laverne L. (Dulfer) Fairbank; A.B., Bryn Mawr Coll., 1967; postgrad. Grad. Sch. Bus., U. Chgo., 1969; m. Michael Goodkin, Oct. 1, 1971; children—Graham Laird, Nathalie Fairbank. Securities analyst Continental Ill. Nat. Bank, 1968-72; membership coordinator Better Govt. Assn., 1972-73; dir. Access Chgo., Rehab. Inst. Chgo., 1973-74; prin. Helen F. Goodkin & Assos., 1975—; mem. Ill. Gov.'s Com. Employment of Handicapped, 1974-75; cons. White House Conf. on Handicapped Individuals, 1976-77; mem. transp. com. Mayor's Office for Senior Citizens and Handicapped, Chgo., 1978; mem. arts and edn. com. Chgo. Planning Council on Aging and Rehab., 1978. Bd. dirs. Chgo. Area Project, 1969-71, asst. treas., 1971; bd. dirs. Rec. for the Blind, 1980—, Access Living, 1981—; mem. aux. bd. Art Inst. Chgo., 1973-75, co-chmn. Sculpture in the Park, 1974, mem. libraries com., 1977; mem. steering com. Library Soc., Regenstein Library Soc., U. Chgo., 1977; mem. resources com. Bryn Mawr Coll., 1977. Mem. Chgo. Soc. Composers (trustee 1978). Episcopalian. Clubs: Friday, Racquet, Casino. Author: A Guide to Community Action for the Handicapped, 1976; co-author: Environmental Aspects of Rehabilitation, 1979; editor: Access Chicago: A Guide to the City, 1973; Architect's and Designer's Handbook of Banier-Free Design, 1974. Office: 537 W Arlington Pl Chicago IL 60614

GOODMAN, ARDEN PATRICIA, med. optical co. exec.; b. N.Y.C., Aug. 16, 1949; d. Sheldon Stuart and Elizabeth Lillian (Weiss) Goodman; B.S. in Chemistry and Life Scis., U. Ill., 1971; m. Joseph Theodore Gacsi, Dec. 26, 1976; children—Ted, Vickie. Chemist, Ferro Corp., Huntington Beach, Calif., 1971-72, Beckman Instruments, Fullerton, Calif., 1972-73; research chemist Edwards Labs. div. AHSC, Irvine, Calif., 1974-80; mgr. quality assurance Am. Med. Optics div. AHSC, Irvine, 1980-81, mgr. quality assurance engring. 1981—. Mem. Am. Soc. Quality Control, Am. Chem. Soc., Am. Horse Show Assn., Internat. Arabian Horse Assn. Contbr. articles on chemistry and med. device research to profl. jours. Office: 1402 E Alton Ave Irvine CA 92714

GOODMAN, ARLENE FRANCES BROWN, real estate broker; b. Lewiston, Maine, Sept. 2, 1937; d. Ethan Wood and Methyl Vernice (Cox) Brown; m. Jeffery Robert Goodman, Nov. 22, 1969; children—Pamela Dobson Arsneault, Wanda Dobson McLocklin, Jeffrey Scott Dobson, Timothy Michael Dobson, Michael Anthony Goodman. Waitress, Edwards, Lewiston, Maine, 1964-67; data sorter Pioneer Plastics Co., Auburn, Maine, 1967; with Gen. Devel. Co., Port St. Lucie, Fla., 1967; with Gen. Devel. Corp., Port St. Lucie, Fla., 1967—, saleswoman, 1969-81, broker, 1981—. Mem. Nat. Assn. Female Execs. Democrat. Baptist. Home: 4901 Oleander Ave Fort Pierce FL 33450 Office: 11111 S Federal Hwy Port Saint Lucie FL 33452

GOODMAN, BERNICE EVELYN, psychotherapist; b. Hot Springs, Ark., June 27, 1927; d. Bernard and Dorothy (Neumann) G.; B.S., U. Wis., 1948; M.S., Columbia U., 1952. Dir. program city and country brs. Children's Aid Soc., N.Y.C., 1963-71; pvt. practice psychotherapy, N.Y.C., 1969—; cons. youth service systems Region II, HEW, 1971-72; co-founder, chairperson 1st bd. dirs. Inst. Human Identity, 1972-76; co-chairperson Nat. Task Force Lesbian/Gay Issues. Mem. Nat. Assn. Social Workers (co-chmn. task force gay issues 1979—), Acad. Cert. Social Workers. Author book and articles in field. Address: 32 E 3d St New York NY 10003

GOODMAN, CARENE GOODWIN, nurse; b. Mebane, N.C., Feb. 10, 1930; d. James Garland and Esther Pauline (Wellington) Goodwin; R.N. diploma with honors (N.D. Bitting award) Watts Hosp. Sch. Nursing, Durham, N.C., 1950; m. Elstun Flournoy Goodman, Feb. 1, 1957; children—Susan, Timothy, Bentley, Elstun Flournoy. Staff nurse Watts Hosp., 1950-51, head nurse, 1955-56; operating room nurse U. N.C. Meml. Hosp., Chapel Hill, 1952-55; head nurse St. Luke's Hosp., Houston, 1957; indsl. nurse Foley's Dept. Store, Houston, 1958; supr. Bellaire Gen. Hosp., Houston, 1966-67, asst. dir. nursing, 1968-76, dir.

nursing service, 1977-78, asso. dir. nursing service, 1980-81, dir. nursing service, 1981-82; Active ARC, Am. Cancer Soc., Am. Heart Assn. also sponsor health occupations career for high sch. students; in-service edn. instr. Rosewood Gen. Hosp., Houston, 1978—. Asso. pres. Windsor Village PTA, Houston, 1968; coach girls softball team Windsor Village Youth Assn., Houston, 1968-70. Mem. Tex. Hosp. Soc. Nursing Service Adminstrs., Am., Tex. hosp. assns., Soc. Nursing Service Adminstrs. Methodist. Clubs: Order Eastern Star, Lakeway Tennis. Home: 11710 Hornbrook Dr Houston TX 77099 Office: 5314 Dashwood Houston TX 77081

GOODMAN, CHRISTINE, psychoanalyst, clin. psychologist; b. New Brighton, Pa., Aug. 12, 1939; d. Charles Christian and Jean (Graham) Blattner; B.A., Oberlin Coll., 1961; M.A., Ind. U., 1963; Ph.D., Fordham U., 1975; cert. in psychoanalysis and psychotherapy Adelphi U., 1980. Psychologist, Indsl. Home for Blind, N.Y.C., 1963-66, Bur. Child Guidance, N.Y.C., 1967-80; mem. com. on handicapped N.Y.C. Bd. Edn., 1980—; pvt. practice psychoanalysis, N.Y.C., 1976—. Mem. Am. Psychol. Assn. Home and office: 204 W 14th St New York NY 10011

GOODMAN, DODY (DOLORES), actress, comedienne; b. Columbus, Ohio, Oct. 28; d. Dexter and Leona G.; student Sch. Am. Ballet, Met. Opera Ballet Sch., N.Y.C. Stage debut as dancer with corps de ballet Radio City Music Hall, N.Y.C., 1940; Broadway debut as dancer High Button Shoes, 1947; in chorus Miss Liberty, 1949; appeared stage shows: Call Me Madam, 1950, Wonderful Town, 1953, Shoestring '57, 1956, Parade, 1960, Fiorello!, 1962, A Rainy Day in Newark, 1963, A Thurber Carnival, 1965, Ben Bagley's Cole Porter Revue, 1965, My Daughter, Your Son, 1969, The Front Page, 1969, The Matchmaker, 1971-72, Lorelei, 1974, George Washington Slept Here, Kindling, Side by Side by Sondheim; toured in Once Upon a Mattress, 1960-61; author play Mourning in a Funny Hat; author film script Women, Women, Women!; regular on TV series Mary Hartman, Mary Hartman, 1976-77, Fernwood Forever, 1977, The Mary Tyler Moore Hour, 1979; other TV appearances include: Caesar's Hour, The Martha Raye Show, You'll Never Get Rich, The Ray Bolger Show, The Jack Paar Show, The Merv Griffin Show, Girl Talk, The Tonight Show, Love Boat; appeared in film Bedtime Story, 1964, Grease, 1978, Valentine Day on Love Island. Mem. AFTRA. Office: care Hussong Agy 8271 Melrose Ave Suite 108 Los Angeles CA 90046 also Ruth Webb Enterprises 9229 Sunset Blvd Suite 509 Los Angeles CA 90069 *

GOODMAN, ELLEN HOLTZ, author, columnist; b. Newton, Mass., Apr. 11, 1941; d. Jackson Jacob and Edith (Weinstein) Holtz; B.A. cum laude, Radcliffe Coll., 1963; 1 dau., Katherine Anne. Researcher, reporter Newsweek Mag., 1963-65; feature writer Detroit Free Press, 1965-67; feature writer columnist Boston Globe, 1967—; syndicated columnist Washington Post Writers Group, 1976—; radio commentator Spectrum, CBS, 1978-79. Named New Eng. Newspaper Woman of Year, New Eng. Press Assn., 1968; recipient Catherine O'Brien award Stanley Home Products, 1971; Media award Mass. Commn. Status Women, 1974; Columnist of Year award New Eng. Women's Press Assn., 1975; Pulitzer prize, 1980; prize for commentary Am. Soc. Newspaper Editors, 1980; Nieman fellow, Harvard U., 1974. Author: Turning Books, 1979; Close to Home, 1979; At Large, 1981. Office: care Press Relations Simon & Schuster Inc 1230 Ave of Americas New York NY 10020

GOODMAN, JUDITH G., communications co. ofcl.; b. N.Y.C., Oct. 5, 1952; d. Jerome D. and Florence B. (Rosen) Greenberg; B.A., Stephens Coll., 1972; M.B.A., Nova U., 1982; Publicist, Harry N. Abrams, Inc., art book pubs., N.Y.C., 1972-73; media dir. CAPR Corp., advt. agency, Palm Beach, Fla., 1973-76; prodn. mgr. WPEC-Channel 12, ABC-TV, West Palm Beach, Fla., 1976-78; corp. relations mgr. Photoelectronics Corp./WPEC-TV, 1978—. Organizer, chmn. Palm Beach County Council of Arts, 1981-82; bd. dirs. United Way Palm Beach County, S. Fla. Fair, Big Bros./Big Sisters. Mem. Advt. Club Palm Beaches, Nat. Assn. Realtors, Royal Palm Festival. Home: 350 Seabreeze Ave Palm Beach FL 33480 Office: WPEC-Channel 12 Fairfield Dr West Palm Beach FL 33407

GOODMAN, JUDITH ROSS, psychotherapist; b. St. Louis, June 12, 1950; d. Bernard Alan and Elizabeth (Schnitzer) Ross; B.A. in Psychology, Newcomb Coll., Tulane U., New Orleans, 1972; M.S.W., Brown Sch., Washington U., St. Louis, 1974; advanced tng. St. Louis Psychoanalytic Inst., 1981—; m. Mark Goodman, June 23, 1979; children—Lauren, William Scott. Community health educator St. Louis County Health Dept., 1972-73; after-sch. program coordinator St. Louis County Juvenile Ct., 1973-74; med. social worker Ob-Gyn/family planning services St. Louis County Dept. Community Health and Med. Care, 1974-80; pvt. practice psychotherapy, founder Women's Care Group, St. Louis, 1980—; adj. prof. Brown Sch. Social Work, 1975-77; Am. rep. English social work exchange program Council Internat. Programs, 1977; cons. and lectr. in field. Mem. Acad. Cert. Social Workers, Nat. Assn. Social Workers, Am. Public Health Assn., Psi Chi. Author article in field. Home: 364 Mission Ct Saint Louis MO 61330 Office: 7396 Pershing Saint Louis MO 63130

GOODMAN, LILLIAN RACHEL, nurse educator; b. Hanover, N.H., May 20, 1923; d. Benjamin and Anna (Tapper) G.; R.N., Peter Bent Brigham Hosp. Sch. Nursing, 1947; B.S., Boston U. Sch. Nursing, 1950, M.S., 1954, Ed.D., Sch. Edn., 1969. Dir. nurses Boston State Hosp., 1955-63; asst. chief supr. psychiat. nursing Mass. Dept. Mental Health, Boston, 1963-69; prof., acting dean U. Mass. Sch. Nursing, Amherst, 1970-73; prof., chmn. Worcester State Coll. Dept. Nursing, 1973—; asso. clin. prof. Boston U. Sch. Nursing, 1957-69; cons. VA Hosp., Brockton, Mass., 1960-67. Pres. Worcester Vis. Nursing Assn., 1982—, co-chmn. program ops. com., 1980—. Am. Jour. of Nursing fellow, 1967-68; recipient Mass. Nurses Assn. Leadership award, 1979. Mem. New Eng. Council on Higher Edn. for Nursing (mem. exec. com. 1974-76), Am. Nurses Assn., Mass. Nurses Assn., Nat. League Nursing, Sigma Theta Tau. Club: Quota of Worcester. Mem. editorial bd. Perspectives in Psychiatric Care, 1961-75; co-author The Schizophrenic's Mother, 1963; co-moderator videotape: Living with Dying, 1976. Home: 68 Topsfield Circle Shrewsbury MA 01545 Office: 486 Chandler St Worcester MA 01602

GOODMAN, LINDA BERSHAD, speech pathologist; b. N.Y.C., Oct. 8, 1940; d. Michael and Florence (Eisenberg) Bershad; B.A. magna cum laude, Adelphi Coll., 1960, M.S., 1963; m. Carl R. Goodman, Aug. 27, 1960; children—Dawn, Jordan. Tchr. speech and hearing handicapped Mineola (N.Y.) Vocat. Edn. and Extension Bd., 1962-63; speech pathologist St. Mary's Hosp. for Children, Bayside, N.Y., 1963-64; speech cons. U.S. Naval Hosp., St. Albans, N.Y., 1967-69; speech and reading therapist Maria Montessori Sch., New Rochelle, N.Y., 1969-73; speech pathologist Montgomery Hosp., Norristown, Pa., 1973—. Mem. Am. Speech and Hearing Assn. (cert.), Phi Beta Kappa, Psi Chi, Sigma Alpha Eta. Home: 12 Mimosa Circle Lafayette Hill PA 19444 Office: Montgomery Hosp Norristown PA 19401

GOODMAN, LINDA GOLD, banker; b. Wallingford, Pa., Mar. 29, 1951; d. George and Rya Gold; B.A. in Econs., Goucher Coll., 1972. Research asso., project dir., bur. econ. research, disability and health div. Rutgers U., New Brunswick, N.J., 1972-73; corporate lending officer U.S. banking dept. Bankers Trust Co., N.Y.C., 1974-76, asst. treas. utilities div., 1976-77, asst. v.p. petroleum div., 1977-79, v.p., 1979—, head petroleum unit, 1981, sect. head coal, 1982—. N.Y. admission rep. Goucher Coll., Towson, Md., 1975, 76, career devel. rep., 1979—; vol. worker, therapeutic activities div. Mt. Sinai Hosp., N.Y.C., 1977; mem. campaign com. N.Y. Young Republican Club, 1979—; mem. energy group Am. Jewish Com. Mem. N.Y. Real Estate Group (founder, pres. 1979—). Jewish. Home: 315 W 70 St Apt #15D New York NY 10023 Office: 280 Park Ave New York NY 10017

GOODMAN, LISL MARBURG, psychologist; b. Vienna, Austria, Dec. 26, 1921; came to U.S., 1948, naturalized, 1950; d. Emil and Hermine Marburg; B.A., Monmouth (N.J.) Coll., 1964; M.A., New Sch. Social Research, 1966, Ph.D., 1969; m. Samuel Goodman, Aug. 28, 1946; children—Ronald E., Jeffrey Marburg. Research asst. New Sch. Social Research, 1966-68; mem. faculty Jersey City State Coll., 1969—, asso. prof. psychology, 1975—; staff psychologist Psychiat. Services Center, White Plains, N.Y., 1970—, sr. clin. psychologist, 1976—. Recipient Outstanding Profl. in Human Services award Am. Acad. Human Services, 1974. Mem. Assn. Former Intelligence Officers, Am. Psychol. Assn., Assn. Advancement Psychology, Found. Thanatology, AAUP, Eastern Psychol. Assn., N.Y. Acad. Sci. Author: Death and the Creative Life, 1981; contbr. articles to profl. jours. Home: 175 Palmer Ln Thornwood NY 10594 Office: Psychology Dept Jersey City State Coll Jersey City NJ 07305

GOODMAN, MADELEINE JOYCE, human geneticist; b. N.Y.C., Sept. 11, 1945; d. Joseph and Pauline (Applebaum) Schwarzbach; A.B., Barnard Coll., 1967; diploma in human biology Oxford U., 1968; Ph.D., U. Hawaii, 1973; m. Lenn E. Goodman, Aug. 29, 1965; children—Allegra, Paula. Asso. prof. gen. sci. and women's studies U. Hawaii, Honolulu, 1975—; pres. Pacific Health Research Inst.; dir. Women's Studies Program, U. Hawaii. NSF grantee, 1976-77, 81-83; NIH trainee, 1972-73; NDEA fellow, 1970-72; Straub Trust grantee, 1977-78; A.C.S. grantee, 1982-83. Mem. AAAS (pres.), Hawaii Assn. for Women in Sci., Soc. Social Biology, Am. Soc. Human Genetics. Condr. research on menopause, breast cancer and age related changes in women; contbr. articles to profl. sci. jours. Office: 721K Porteus Hall Univ Hawaii Honolulu HI 96822

GOODMAN, MARGARET NORMA, broadcaster; b. Regina, Sask., Can., Sept. 14, 1930; came to U.S., 1952, naturalized, 1959; d. Douglas Hector and Mary Lillian (Baxter) Campbell; student public schs., Vernon, B.C., Can.; m. John Stuart Goodman, Oct. 4, 1952; children—Fraser, Leslie, Kelly, Stuart. Copywriter, Sta. KBYR, Anchorage, 1952-53; with Sta. KTVA, Anchorage, 1954—, anchor morning news, 1977-78, mid-day news, 1977-78, co-anchor Eyewitness News, nightly, exec. adminstrv. asst., 1978-81, asst. v.p., 1981—. Bd. dirs. YMCA, Anchorage; mem. Def. Adv. Com. on Women in the Service, 1963-66; bd. dirs. Salvation Army, Anchorage, 1978—, Am. Cancer Soc., 1967—; mem. Sudden Infant Death Syndrome task force, 1978—; bd. dirs. Multiple Sclerosis Soc., 1979—. Recipient Americanism medal DAR, 1974; March of Dimes Service award, 1972; N.G. Bur. Guardsman award, 1977; Army and Air N.G. Meritorious Service award, 1972; Muscular Dystrophy Assn. citation of merit, 1974, 79; Anchorage Republican Women's Club Press and Media award, 1976, 78; U.S. Navy Recruiting Cert. of Appreciation, 1972; named Outstanding Citizen, Mayor George Sullivan, 1974; Alaska Children's Services service award, 1979; The Ninety-Nines, Inc. Interest in Aviation award, 1977; McCalls Gold Mike award, 1961; Heart Assn. Merit award; Alaska Paramed. Assn. Outstanding Service award, 1978, others. Mem. Assn. U.S. Army, Beta Sigma Phi. Republican. Episcopalian. Club: Anchorage Woman's. Home: 4015 Merrill Dr Anchorage AK 99503 Office: 1007 W 32d Ave Anchorage AK 99503

GOODMAN, NATALIE COHAN, psychologist, educator; b. Cleve., July 1, 1928; d. Benjamin G. and Bessie E. Cohan; B.A., Ohio State U., 1950, M.A., 1950; Ed.D, Harvard U., 1969; m. Philip Goodman, Sept. 23, 1950; children—Marcia, Kenneth, Miriam. Head State psychologist Cambridge (Mass.) Guidance Center, 1969-70; dir. research Concord (Mass.) Mental Health Center, 1970-74; research assoc. Radcliffe Ins., Cambridge, 1974-75; psychologist Lesley Coll., Cambridge, 1975-79; co-founder, dir. Affiliates for Adult Devel., Bedford, Mass., 1976—; pvt. practice clin. psychology, Bethesda, Md., 1978—; psychologist Easter Seal Treatment Center, Rockville, Md., 1979—, Kingsbury Center, Washington, 1979—. Mem. Am. Psychol. Assn., Md. Psychol. Assn., D.C. Psychol. Assn. Contbr. articles to profl. jours. Home and office: 5219 Wapakoneta Rd Bethesda MD 20816 Office: Kingsbury Center 2138 Bancroft St NW Washington DC 20008

GOODMAN, PATRICIA, social worker; b. N.Y.C., Mar. 17, 1940; d. Alexander and May (Frank) Morton; B.A., Hofstra Coll., 1961; M.S.W. (NIMH scholar 1962-63, JBG-JWYWHA scholar 1967-68), Hunter Coll., 1968; postgrad. N.Y. U., 1977—; m. Kenneth D. Goodman, Dec. 23, 1970; children—Roslyn B. Levitt, Anne K. Goodman, Heather Goodman. Case aide Bklyn. Home for Children, 1961-62; dir. teen programs YM-YWHA, Little Neck, N.Y., 1963-70; asst. dir. social services Creedmoor Psychiat. Center, Queens, N.Y., 1970-72, dir. edn. and tng., 1972-73; dir. clin. services Pope Pius XII Sch., Chester, N.Y., 1973-74; dir. social service Manhattan Psychiat. Center, 1974-77; unit chief Bronx Psychiat. Center, 1977-79; dir. social work services Univ. Hosp., Stony Brook, N.Y., 1979—; adj. prof. C.W. Post Grad. Sch. Counselling, 1972-73; field faculty Hunter Sch. Social Work, 1975-79, Adelphi Sch. Social Work, 1971-77; asso. clin. prof. SUNY Sch. Social Welfare, Stony Brook, 1980—; cons. in field; lectr. in field; adv. bd. mem. NIMH grant on tng. clin. mental health workers Hunter Sch. Social Work. Mem. Assn. to Advance Adminstrn. Curriculum for Social Workers (dir.). Contbr. articles to profl. jours. Office: Univ Hosp State Univ of NY Stony Brook NY 11794

GOODMAN, PHYLLIS LOUISE, public relations exec.; b. N.Y.C., Sept. 7, 1946; d. Bernard Jacob and Claire (Rosenberg) Goodman; B.S., Cornell U., 1967. Extension home economist Nassau County Extension Service, Mineola, N.Y., 1967-68; asst. editor Funk & Wagnalls, N.Y.C., 1968-69; sr. v.p. Glick & Lorwin, Inc., N.Y.C., 1969-80; sr. v.p. sci. and medicine div. Medicus Intercon Internat., Inc., 1981-82; account supr. Hill and Knowlton, Inc., N.Y.C., 1983—. Mem. public relations com. Cornell U., mem. land-grant affairs legis. support group, 1979. Mem. Am. Home Econs. Assn., Home Economists in Bus. (chmn. N.Y.C. chpt. 1979-80, program chmn. nat. conv. 1981), Public Relations Soc. Am., Pharm. Advt. Council, AAHPER and Dance, AAUW, Pi Lambda Theta. Home: 205 West End Ave New York NY 10023 Office: 420 Lexington Ave New York NY 10017

GOODMAN, YETTA M., educator; b. Cleve., Mar. 10, 1931; d. William and Dora (Shapiro) Trachtman; B.A. in History, Los Angeles State Coll., 1952, M.A. in Elem. Edn., 1956; Ed.D. in Curriculum Devel., Wayne State U., 1967; m. Kenneth S. Goodman, 1952; children—Debra, Karen Goodman Castro, Wendy Hood. Elem. and secondary tchr., public schs., Los Angeles, 1952-63; supr. pre-service teaching experiences Wayne State U., 1963-67; asst. to asso. prof. U. Mich., Dearborn, 1967-75; prof. edn., co-dir. program in lang. and literacy U. Ariz., 1975—; cons. in field. Active in orgns. concerned with children's rights. Recipient Faculty Recognition award Tucson Trade Bur., 1978. Mem. Nat. Council Tchrs. English (nat. dir. 1976—, pres. 1978-79), Center Expansion of Lang. and Thinking (dir. 1972—, pres. 1976-79), Internat. Reading Assn. (chairperson and active mem. various coms. 1962—), Assn. Supervision and Curriculum Devel., Am. Ednl. Research Assn., Assn. Childhood Edn. Internat. Jewish. Author books, including: (with C. L. Burke) Reading Miscue Inventory: A Procedure for Diagnosis and Evaluation, 1972; (with C. Burke and B. Sherman) Reading Strategies: Focus on Comprehension, 1981; contbr. numerous articles, chpts. to profl. publs.; also audio tapes scripts video, films. Home: 5649 E 10th St Tucson AZ 85711 Office: Program in Lang and Literacy Coll Edn Room 402 U Ariz Tucson AZ 85721

GOODNER, JO ANN, educator; b. Idabel, Okla., Sept. 15, 1934; d. Dudley and Jewell (Stout) Goolsby; student Okla. State U., 1952-55, U. Tex., El Paso, summers, 1959-69, Utah State U., 1961; B.S., Tex. Women's U., 1973; postgrad. N.Tex. State U., 1973, Richland Community Coll., 1974-78, Northeastern Okla. State U., 1979-80, Okla. U., 1981; m. George David Goodner, Aug. 29, 1954; children—Darla Jo Ann Goodner Ures, Victoria Louise. Tchr., Ysleta (Tex.) Ind. Sch. Dist., 1959-69, Plano (Tex.) Ind. Schs., 1972-77; real estate asso. residential div. Henry S. Miller, Dallas, 1974-78; elem. tchr. Muskogee (Okla.) Public Schs., 1980—; mem. Muskogee County Literacy Council, 1979. Founding bd. dirs., chmn. fin. Prespectives, Muskogee Women's Resource Center, 1979-80; bd. dirs. Muskogee County Hist. Soc., 1979; vol. Leukemia Assn., El Paso, 1965-69, Dallas, 1972-79, Muskogee, 1980-82; v.p. LWV, Muskogee, 1979-82, chmn. water com., 1981, bd. dirs., 1979—; bd. dirs. Muskogee Educators Polit. Action Com., 1981. Recipient Ysleta Classroom Tchrs. award, 1958. Mem. Okla. Edn. Assn., NEA, Eastern Okla. Reading Council (local rep.), Okla. State Assn. Gifted and Talented, PTA, Choctaw Hist. Soc., Muskogee County Coalition ERA, Omega Rho Alpha, Delta Kappa Gamma, Kappa Delta (chpt. advisor U. Tex at El Paso chpt. 1963). Baptist. Home: 200 Foltz Ln Muskogee OK 74401 Office: Franklin Elem Sch Muskogee OK 74401

GOODPASTER, MARY JOSEPHINE, accountant; b. Liberal, Kans., July 17, 1946; d. Aurelio and Luz Maria (Renteria) Andrade; B.A., Wichita State U., 1975; m. John Goodpaster, June 10, 1967; children—Nina, John, Michele. With fluid power div. Cessna Aircraft Co., Hutchinson, Kans., 1968—, clk. cost acctg., 1968-70, payroll clk., 1971-73, cost acct. jr., 1973, acct., 1974, cost acct. sr., 1975-79, budget supr., 1979-80, cost acctg. supr., 1980—; treas. bldg. com. Cessna Employees Club, 1977-79. Mem. Hutchinson Acctg. Assn., Beta Gamma Sigma, Phi Kappa Phi, Beta Sigma Phi. Roman Catholic. Club: Toastmasters. Home: 7300 Pony Acres Hutchinson KS 67501 Office: RFD 4 Hutchinson KS 67501

GOODRICH, DOROTHEA ROSEMARY, stock exchange exec.; b. Indpls., June 14, 1927; d. Homer I. and Dorothy Ellen (Allen) Cutsinger; student Miami U., 1945-47; m. Russell E. Goodrich, Dec. 17, 1954; 1 son, William Allyn. With Cin. Stock Exchange, 1952—, exec. sec., 1973—. Mem. Pilot Club Internat., Pilot Club Cin. (pres.). Office: 205 Dixie Terminal Bldg Cincinnati OH 45202

GOODRICH, GAIL LEE, personnel adminstr.; b. Nashville, June 17, 1947; d. Jack B. and Mildred A. (Redmon) G.; B.S., U. Tenn., 1969; M.B.A., U. Chgo., 1979. Tchr., Knox County Schs., Knoxville, Tenn., 1969-70; flight attendant United Airlines, Chgo., 1970-71, instr., 1971-73, field supr., 1973-76, tng. supr., 1976-77, indsl. relations rep., 1977-80, affirmative action mgr., 1980-81, mgr. human resources, 1981, personnel adminstr., 1982—; mem. Ill. Gov.'s Grievance Panel, 1982—. Bd. dirs. No. Cook County div. Jr. Achievement, 1981—. Mem. Am. Soc. Personnel Adminstrn., U. Chgo. Women's Bus. Group, U. Tenn. Alumni Assn., U. Chgo. Alumni Assn. Republican. Methodist. Clubs: Women's Golf League, Management, Women's Bus. Group. Home: 2020 Lincoln Park W Chicago IL 60614 Office: PO Box 66100 Chicago IL 60666

GOODRICH, GRACE MARIE, sculptor, educator; b. Sioux Falls, S.D., Sept. 22, 1913; d. Edward Benjamin and Julia Margaret (Roache) G.; student U. Chgo., 1963-64; M.A. in Art Edn., Art Inst. Chgo., 1964; postgrad. Temple U., summer 1967; M.S. in Visual Design, Ill. Inst. Tech., 1968; M.F.A., Inst. Allende, San Miguel de Allende, Mexico, 1974; m. Edward W. Enthof, Aug. 31, 1940; 1 dau. Art educator, artist, 1932—; art dir. Lake Forest (Ill.) Public Schs., 1951-68; lectr. art edn. Lake Forest Coll., 1952-68; asso. prof. art Dakota Wesleyan U., Mitchell, S.D., 1968-74; prof. history of art Inst. Allende, San Miguel de Allende, Guanajuato, Mexico, 1974—; exhibited drawings, paintings, printmaking and all media of sculpture, throughout U.S. and Mexico; one-woman shows include U. Calif., Berkeley, 1978, Galeria La Princesa San Miguel de Allende, 1978, Marin County Civic Center, San Rafael, Calif., 1981; represented by Karanar Gallery, Tiburon, Calif.; commd. six limestone panels at entrance for Deer Path Jr. High Sch., Lake Forest. Mem. Coll. Art Assn. Am., Civic Fine Arts Assn. Sioux Falls, Nat. Art Edn. Assn., Mus. Modern Art N.Y.C., Art Inst. Chgo., San Francisco Mus. Art, Ill. Inst. Tech. Alumni Assn., Phi Kappa Phi. Episcopalian. Club: Order Eastern Star. Author: The Ideal Art Center, 1968. Home: 387 S Morning Sun Ave Mill Valley CA 94941

GOODRICH, PATRICIA ANN, state legislator; b. Jefferson City, Mo., Jan. 13, 1933; d. Eli Oscar and Eleanor Elizabeth (Hunt) Axon; student Jefferson City Jr. Coll., 1951-52, Park Coll., Parkville, Mo., 1952-54; m. Philo W. Goodrich, Oct. 3, 1954; children—Phillip, James, John. Title I tchr.'s aide, 1968-69; mem. Wis. Ho. of Reps. from 72d Dist., 1975—. Active local PTA, Boy Scouts Am., 1958-75. Republican. Mem. Federated Ch. Club: Athena. Office: Room 309N State Capitol Madison WI 53702

GOODSON, JOANNE, nurse adminstr., cons., publisher; b. Atlanta, Nov. 20, 1930; d. C. Herbert and Corinne (Johnson) G.; grad. Crawford W. Long Hosp. Sch. Nursing, 1952; B.S.N.E., Med. Coll. Ga., 1960; M.Nursing, Emory U., 1965; student Woodrow Wilson Coll. Law, 1980. Mem. faculty Crawford W. Long Hosp. Sch. Nursing, Atlanta, 1952-56; mem. staff, supr. VA Hosps., Dublin, Ga. and Houston, 1956-59; dir. dept. nursing services Med. Coll. Ga. Hosp., Augusta, 1960-64; dir. nursing service and health services Wesley Woods Health Center, Atlanta and asso. prof. nursing Emory U. Sch. Nursing, 1965-70; cons. in field, Atlanta, 1971-74, Tucker, Ga., 1979—; dir. Emory Community Nursing Service, Sch. Nursing Emory U., Atlanta, 1975-77, dir. internat. nursing center, 1975-79; pub., 1979—. Mem. Am. Public Health Assn., Ga. Health Care Assn., Internat. Nursing Services Assn. Home: 4419 Cowan Rd Suite 306 Tucker GA 30084

GOODWILLIE, JANET MCCOLLOUGH, social worker, county social services adminstr.; b. Pasadena, Calif., Feb. 8, 1925; d. Charles Nathan and Gladys Eva (Stewart) McCollough; B.A. magna cum laude, U. Redlands, 1946; postgrad. Boston U., 1948-49; M.S.W., Columbia U., 1952; m. Byron Douglas Goodwillie, Nov. 7, 1953 (dec. Mar. 1980); children—Heather McCollough, Bruce Douglas. Social worker, San Diego Dept. Welfare, 1946-48, 73-79; child welfare worker, 1949-50, 51-53, social work supr., 1953-56; sr. social work supr. San Diego Dept. Social Services, 1979—; bd. dirs. Indochinese Community Health and Edn. Project, 1979-80; mem. Indochinese Coalition, 1979-80. Leader, recruiter, cons., mem. nominating com. San Diego-Imperial council Girl Scouts U.S., 1965-69; treas., pres., bd. dirs. Turning Point Alcoholic Recovery Home for Women, San Diego, 1979—; bd. dirs. Big Sisters League, San Diego, 1980—. Mem. Nat. Assn. Social Workers, Acad. Cert. Social Workers. Clubs: Trafalgar, Sierra. Office: 311 S Tremont St Oceanside CA 92054

GOODWIN, DOROTHY CHENEY, legislator, ret. educator; b. Hartford, Conn., Sept. 2, 1914; d. Charles Archibald and Ruth (Cheney) G.; A.B., Smith Coll., 1937; Ph.D., U. Conn., 1957. With various agys. Fed. Govt., 1937-45; librarian FAO, UN, Washington, 1945-46; agrl.

economist Allied Powers in Japan, 1947-52; mem. faculty U. Conn., Storrs, 1957-74, asso. prof. econs., asst. provost, dir. instl. research, now emeritus; dir. Conn. Natural Gas Corp., from 1972; mem. Conn. Gen. Assembly from 54th Dist., 1974—, chmn. edn. com., 1979—. Chmn. Joshua's Tract Conservation and Historic Trust, Windham Planning Region, Conn., 1968-74; mem. Mansfield (Conn.) Bd. Tax Rev., 1959-61, 65-71, Mansfield Town Council, 1971-75; mem. Dem. Town Com., Storrs, 1965—; trustee Hartford Coll. for Women, 1960—, co-chmn., 1975-76; bd. regents U. Hartford, 1971-77; bd. dirs. U. Conn. Found., 1966—, N.E. Conn. Community Devel. Corp., 1972—; trustee Conn. chpt. Nature Conservancy, 1970-77, Mansfield Tng. Sch. Found., 1976—; former trustee Conn. Prison Assn.; former exec. bd. Indian Trails council Eastern Conn. Boy Scouts Am.; corporator Windham Community Meml. Hosp., 1971—, Hartford Hosp., 1972—. Mem. LWV. Democrat. Episcopalian.

GOODWIN, ELEANOR, govt. ofcl.; b. Fayetteville, N.C., Apr. 12, 1941; d. Vernon F. and Edna Pauline (Rountree) Goodwin; B.A., U. N.C., 1963; M.Ed., Ga. State U., 1978; student Meredith Coll., 1959-61. With C & S Bank, Atlanta, 1963-64, Am. Oil Co., Atlanta, 1964-66; mgmt. intern U.S. Civil Service Commn., Atlanta, 1966; with U.S. Office Personnel Mgmt., Atlanta, 1966—, asst. regional dir. S.E. Region, 1980—; asso. cons. Deely, Fenton & Assos., 1982—; adv. bd. Atlanta Federally Employed Women. Mem. Am. Soc. Tng. and Devel., Atlanta O.D. Network, Internat. Personnel Mgmt. Assn., Atlanta Women's Network, Am. Soc. Pub. Adminstrn. Unitarian. Clubs: Sierra, Atlanta Sporting. Contbr. articles to profl. jours. Home: 942 Canterbury Rd Atlanta GA 30324 Office: 75 Spring St Atlanta GA 30303

GOODWIN, KATIE MAXINE-AGIN, rehab. co. exec.; b. Cleve., Feb. 26, 1952; d. Jerome and Cecile Sarah (Gray) Agin; B.S., Ohio State U., 1975. Occupational therapist Ga. Retardation Center, Atlanta, 1975-76; rehab. specialist Internat. Rehab. Assocs., Atlanta, 1976-78, account rep., 1978-79, Midwest regional mktg. mgr., Chgo., 1979-80, dist. sales mgr., Detroit, 1980-82, sales tng. tchr., 1979—; mem. rehab. counseling adv. com. Mich. State U., 1982-85. Mem. Ga. Self-Insured Assn. (com. rep. 1978-79), So. Assn. Workers Compensation Adminstrn., Mich. Assn. Rehab. Profls. (membership chmn. 1981-82), Mich. Rehab. Assn. (chmn.), Am. Occupational Therapy Assn., Nat. Rehab. Assn., Detroit Adjusters Assn., Nat. Assn. Profl. Saleswomen (Mich. publicity com.), NOW. Home: 32013 W Twelve Mile Rd Apt 210 Farmington Hills MI 48018 Office: R&P Assocs Inc 3250 W Big Beaver Suite 127 Troy MI 48084

GOODWIN, LINDA GRACE, performing arts adminstr.; b. Abington, Pa., Oct. 22, 1951; d. Robert Peter and Betty Grace Goodwin; B.Mus. in Music Edn., Peabody Inst. Music, Balt., 1976; postgrad. Johns Hopkins U. Ensemble mgr. Peabody Conservatory, Balt., 1975-78; asso. dir. ensemble activities Peabody Inst., Johns Hopkins U., 1978—. Recipient award ASCAP, 1980. Mem. Am. Symphony Orch. League, Internat. Soc. Performing Arts Adminstrs., Musicians Union. Office: 1 E Mt Vernon Pl Baltimore MD 21202

GOODWIN, MARIA ANGELA, travel agy. exec.; b. Norwood, Mass., Jan. 15, 1952; d. Pelligreno and Elvira Jean (Depari) C.; student Hartford Conservatory Music, 1970-72. Dancer, Hartford Ballet Co., 1970-73; travel cons. Bernardini Travel, Wrentham, Mass., 1976-78; pres., chmn. bd., coordinator group tours Walpole Travel (Mass.), 1978—; lectr. to various women's groups. Mem. Am. Soc. Travel Agts., Nat. Assn. Female Execs., Cruise Lines Internat. Assn., Boston Women in Travel, Internat. Fedn. Womens Travel Orgns., Inst. Cert. Travel Agts., Boston Bon Vivants, Mass. Businessmen's Assn., C. of C., Downtown Mchts. Assn. (sec. 1978-80, v.p. 1980—), Common Cause. Office: Walpole Travel 942 Main St Walpole MA 02081

GOODWIN, NORMA JEAN, physician; b. Norfolk, Va., May 14, 1937; d. Stephen C. and Helen (Jefferson) Goodwin; B.S., Va. State Coll., 1956; M.D., Med. Coll. Va., 1961. Intern, resident, chief resident in internal medicine Kings County Hosp. Center, Bklyn., 1961-65, clin. asst. in medicine, 1965-67, asst. vis. physician in medicine, 1967—; clin. asst. instr. medicine SUNY Downstate Med. Center, Bklyn., 1964-65, asst. instr. medicine, 1965-67, instr. medicine, 1967-70, asst. prof. medicine, 1970-72, clin. asst. prof. family practice, 1972—, clin. dir. hemodialysis unit, 1967-69, dir. unit, 1969-71; v.p. for community health and ambulatory care services N.Y.C. Health and Hosps. Corp., 1971-74, sr. v.p., 1974-75; mgmt. cons. health care planning, evaluation and adminstrn., 1975—; lectr. in field; founder, pres. AMRON Mgmt. Cons., 1976—. Past pres., treas. Provident Clin. Soc. Bklyn. Inc., 1967-69, pres., 1969-72; past mem. health task force N.Y. Urban Coalition; cons., mem. health services research study sect. Nat. Center Health Services Research HEW; past mem. regional adv. group N.Y. Met. Regional Med. Program; advisor to com. on community medicine Comitia Minora; mem. N.Y. State Gov.'s Health Adv. Council, 1981—; past 1st vice chmn. Bedford Stuyvesant Comprehensive Health Planning Council; past mem. health sci. career adv. com. La Guardia City U. N.Y. Past chmn. bd. dirs. McDonough St. Community Center; past mem. bd. dirs. N.Y. Assn. Ambulatory Care, N.Y. Coll. Podiatric Medicine, ARC Greater N.Y., N.Y. Heart Assn.; trustee Atlanta U. Center. Fellow nephrology NIH, 1965-67. Mem. Nat. Med. Assn. (trustee, past speaker, vice speaker and sec. ho. dels., past 2d v.p., chmn. publs. com. 1980—, mem. exec. com. bd. trustees 1979-82, chmn. task force on concerns women physicians 1982, mem. exec. com. region I, 1978—), Am. Public Health Assn. (governing council 1978-82, mem. com. on affiliates 1978—, chmn. 1979-80), Empire State Med. Assn. (exec. com. 1972—), Public Health Assn. N.Y.C. (dir., treas., mem. com. on pub. policy and legislation, past sec., affiliate rep. to Am. Pub. Health Assn. governing council), Nat. Assn. Health Services Execs. (past pres. N.E. regional chpt.), Sigma Xi, Alpha Kappa Mu, Beta Kappa Chi. Contbr. numerous articles to jours., chpt. to book. Office: 747 E 37th St Brooklyn NY 11210

GOODWIN, P(AMELA) JANETTE (JAN), editor; b. London, Feb. 10, 1944; came to U.S., 1974; d. Charles Henry and Lilian G.; Diplome, Ecole des Langues, Geneva, 1965. News corr., Israel, 1970, Greece, 1971, radio reporter BBC-Radio, London, 1970; news editor Fleet St. News Agy., London, 1969-72; diary editor Woman's Realm mag., London, 1972-74; gen. editor Nat. Enquirer, Lantana, Fla., 1974-77; exec. editor Us mag., publ. N.Y. Times Co., N.Y.C., 1977; sr. editor Ladies' Home Jour., N.Y.C., 1978—. Mem. Cambodian Crisis Com., White House, 1978-80. Mem. Am. Soc. Mag. Editors, N.Y. Press Club, Nat. Press Club. Office: 641 Lexington Ave New York NY 10022

GOOLISHIAN, HELEN WADE, educator; b. Holyoke, Mass., July 23, 1935; d. Melvin and Elaine Ellen (Pickup) Wade; A.A., Cape Cod Community Coll., 1969; A.B., Mount Holyoke Coll., 1971; M.Ed., U. Mass., 1972, Ed.D., 1981; m. Gregory A. Goolishian, Dec. 29, 1955; children—Wade Thomas, Gregory A. Exec., Arthur Murray Dance Studios, Waco, Tex., 1953-58, Boston, 1958; sch. psychologist Greenfield (Mass.) public schs., 1972-74; dir. community services and continuing edn. Cape Cod Community Coll., West Barnstable, Mass., 1974-75, prof. psychology, 1975—. Mem. Nat. Assn. Women Deans, Counselors and Adminstrs., AAUW, Jean Piaget Soc., Delta Kappa Gamma. Home: 1216 Main St East Dennis MA 02641 Office: Cape Cod Community Coll Route 132 West Barnstable MA 02668

GOOLSBY, JANETTE DORTCH, newspaper editor; b. Sheridan, Ark., Nov. 10, 1947; d. Home. Edward and Flora Agnes (Brown) Dortch; scholar, Little Rock U., 1965-67; m. Alan Eugene Goolsby, Jan. 21, 1967; children—Gloria Amanda, Shaw Edward, Drake Hershel. Toy mgr. J.C. Penney Co., Maryville, Tenn., 1967-69; editor, co-owner South Ark. Accent, Hampton, 1973—. Active, Cancer Soc., Band Boosters, Jaycettes, Physicians Recruitment Com.; officer PTA, 1976. Mem. Ark. Press Assn., Ark. Press Women, United Meth. Women (trustee). Democrat. Home and Office: PO Box 455 Hampton AR 71744

GOPPERS, VELTA MANEKS, chemist; b. Gostini, Latvia, Feb. 28, 1915; d. Karlis and Milda (Udris) Maneks; came to U.S., 1949, naturalized, 1954; B.S., U. Riga, 1942, M.S., 1944; m. Sergejs Goppers, 1941 (div. 1947); 1 dau., Ilze Goppers Oredson. Asst., U. Riga, 1940-44; analytical chemist Farben Industries, Germany, 1944-45; instr. Tech. Sch., Stuttgart, Germany, 1945-47; mgr. Pharmacy and Chem. Preparation Lab., Esslingen, Germany, 1947-49; analytical chemist Twin City Testing & Engring. Lab., St. Paul, 1949-52; technologist sci. dept. U. Minn., 1952-53, jr. scientist dept. physiology, 1953-59, sr. scientist environ. health, 1959-68, sr. scientist Space Sci. Center, 1968-70, Environ. Health and Research Center, 1970—, tchr. microchemistry and chromatography dept. environ. health Grad. Sch. Recipient Recognition award planetary quarantine dept. NASA, 1974. Fellow Am. Inst. Chemists, AAAS; mem. Am. Chem. Soc., Am. Indsl. Hygiene Assn. (treas. 1966-68), Sigma Xi, Iota Sigma Pi (pres. Mercury chpt. 1973-74, research award in chemistry 1976), Sigma Delta Epsilon (treas. 1966-69). Lutheran. Contbr. research articles to profl. publs. Home: 5164 Abercrombie Dr Minneapolis MN 55435 Office: Dept Environ Health U Minn Minneapolis MN 55455

GORCHYNSKI, SYLVIA ANNE, psychologist; b. Yorkton, Sask., Can.; came to U.S., 1960; d. Stanley Walter and Stephanie Alice (Fedoruk) G.; B.Sc., R.N., U. Sask., 1959; cert. public health nursing (NIMH scholar), U. Calif., San Francisco, 1963, M.Sc. in Psychiat. Nursing (NIMH scholar), 1964, cert. nursing service adminstrn. (NIMH scholar), 1965; Ph.D. in Personality and Social Psychology (USPHS scholar) Boston U., 1973. Nurse hosps. in Santa Barbara, Calif., 1960-62; instr. continuing edn. U. Calif., San Francisco, 1964-65; vis. lectr. Calif. State U., San Francisco, 1964-65; resident nursing service adminstrn. St. Mary's Hosp., San Francisco, 1964-65; clin. psychology intern Kaiser Hosp., San Francisco, 1970; Jungian pre-tng. analysis, 1973; clin. psychologist San Francisco Community Mental Health Services, research coordinator Center Spl. Problems, 1974-80; pvt. practice psychotherapy and consultation, San Francisco, 1975—, Edmonton (Alta., Can.), 1981—; ind. cons. Arthur D. Little, Cambridge, Mass., 1973-76; cons. Research Triangle Inst., 1977—; mem. adv. com. San Francisco Vol. Bur., 1978-80. Mem. Am. Psychol. Assn., Assn. Women in Sci., Sigma Theta Tau. Club: Order Eastern Star. Author papers in field. Address: 2305 Van Ness Ave San Francisco CA 94109 also 43S-10830 Jasper Ave Edmonton AB T5J 2B3 Canada

GORDON, BERTHA COMER, ret. ednl. adminstr.; b. Louisville, Ga., Feb. 24, 1916; d. Willie and Viola (Hill) Comer; B.S., N.Y. U., 1945; M.A., Hunter Coll., 1955, profl. cert. 1965; m. Carlton Gordon, Nov. 6, 1942. Registered nurse N.Y.C. Dept. Hosps., from 1937; tchr. Manhattan Schs., N.Y.C., 1950-52, counselor, 1952-62; dept. head Eli Whitney Vocat. High Sch., Bklyn., 1962-69; high sch. prin., Bronx, N.Y., 1969-72, asst. supt., 1972-74, supt., from 1974; adj. prof. grad. div. CUNY, 1970-75; cons. N.Y.C. Bd. Edn., 1980—. Mem. Friends of Westchester Community Coll.; mem. supt.'s adv. com. White Plains Public Schs.; bd. dirs. Am. Lung Assn., White Plains (N.Y.) Child Devel. Ctr.; nurse ARC. Treas., Friends of Westchester Community Coll., 1982—. Mem. N.Y.C. Adminstrv. Women in Edn. (past pres.), NAACP (life), Nat. Assn. Secondary Sch. Prins., N.Y.C. Supts. Assn., Am. Assn. Sch. Adminstrs., Am., N.Y. State, N.Y.C. Dist. 14 nurses assns., Doctorate Assn., N.Y.C. Acad. Public Edn. (exec. bd.), Hunter Coll. (Hall of Fame), N.Y. U. alumni assns., Westchester Hist. Soc., Kappa Delta Pi (past pres. Greater, N.Y. chpt.). Clubs: N.Y.U. (house com.), Women's City of N.Y. Mem. editorial bd. N.Y.U. Quar., 1971-73. Home: 1002 Hall Ave White Plains NY 10604

GORDON, CAROLYN ROSE, interior designer; b. Kansas City, Kans., Apr. 9, 1939; d. Peter M. and Louise M. Bizal; B.S. in Art Edn., Pittsburg (Kans.) State U., 1961; postgrad. U. Wash., 1961-62; m. Robert L. Gordon, June 24, 1961; children—Michelle, Peter. Tchr. art, public schs., Burien. Wash., 1961-63, head dept. art Redwood Wash. Sr. High Sch., 1966-67; tchr. art Purahou Sch., Honolulu, 1967-68; instr. interior design Harper Coll., 1973-74; founder, owner, pres. Design Workshop Ltd., Northbrook, Ill., 1980—; tchr. interior decorating for adult edn. Pres., Panhellenic of Hawaii, 1972-73; troop leader Moraines council Girl Scouts U.S.A., 1973-74. Named Miss Pittsburg, Pittsburg Jaycees, 1959. Mem. Am. Soc. Interior Design, Women in Mgmt., Nat. Assn. for Self-Employed, Nat. Assn. for Future Women, Theater in the Rough, Alpha Gamma Delta (chairwoman installation). Episcopalian. Home: 1601 Wilmot Ln Deerfield IL 60015 Office: 1020 Waukegan Rd Northbrook IL 60062

GORDON, DOROTHY MARILYN, maintenance service exec.; b. Nyack, N.Y., Mar. 19, 1939; d. David Edward and Louise Marie (Miller) G.; student New Sch. for Social Research, 1961-63, Printing Industries of Met. N.Y., 1968; 1 dau., Victoria Ferman. Prodn. mgr. T.A.B. Litho, N.Y.C., 1963-65, Select Mag.'s, N.Y.C., 1965-67, ASARCO, N.Y.C., 1968-71; dir. purchasing New Century Edn., Piscataway, N.J., 1977-79; pres. Multi-Service Co-op, Highlands, N.J., 1979; founder, pres. The House Doctor, Inc., home cleaning and improvement service, Highlands, 1980—. Legis. aide N.J. Assembly, 1978-79; mem. N.J. Dept. Community Affairs Div. on Women, Displaced Homemakers task force, 1978-80; adv. bd. Women's Resource & Survival Center, 1978—. Recipient award Women's Resource & Survival Center, 1979. Mem. Highlands C. of C., NOW (state del. 1976-78, chpt. v.p. 1978), N.J. Orgn. Women's Plan of Action. Creator programs: Women's Affairs, 1979; Sunlite and Moonbeams, 1980; Sr. Citizens Speak Out, 1980. Address: G-12 Twin Lights Highlands NJ 07732

GORDON, DRUSILLA DELECE, educator; b. Geary, Okla., Aug. 13, 1927; d. Bryan Jack and Vanda Johnnie (Browning) Griffin; student UCLA, 1945, U. Tex., 1945-48; B.S., U. Okla., 1949, Ed.M., 1951; postgrad. Tex. Christian U., 1956-57, U. Ark., 1965-66; Ed.D., U. Miss., 1974; m. Richard Allen Gordon, Jr., Aug. 16, 1952; 1 son, Richard Allen, III. Tchr., Corpus Christi (Tex.) Ind. Sch. Dist., 1951-52, St. Ann's Sch., Midland, Tex., 1963-65; mem. faculty Westark Community Coll., Ft. Smith Ark., 1966—, chmn. dept. psychology and edn., 1979-80. NSF grantee, 1967. Mem. AAUP (pres. 1975-77), Ark. Two-Yr. Coll. Tchrs. Assn., NEA, Ark. Edn. Assn., Phi Delta Kappa, Phi Kappa Phi, Alpha Gamma Delta. Office: Westark Community Coll PO Box 3649 Fort Smith AR 72913

GORDON, ELAINE TRAVIS, counselor, therapist; b. Chgo., Aug. 11, 1932; d. James and Doris (Gittelsohn) Travis; B.S. in Health Sci., Columbia U. and U. Ill., 1955; M.A. in Edn., N.Y.U., 1957; postgrad. U. Calif., Berkeley, 1957-59; Ph.D. in Counseling Psychology, Union Grad. Sch., San Francisco, 1977; m. Milton Gordon, Jan. 1, 1955; children—David Bryan, Karen Rose, Nancy Lynn, Peter Wallace. Occupational therapist Hosp. for Joint Diseases, 1955-57; instr. family life edn. Seattle Pub. Schs., 1959-67; founder, pvt. practice Self-Discovery Service, Seattle, 1978—; tchr. social psychology and communication skills U. Wash. Exptl. Coll.; mem. allied health profl. staff Fairfax Psychiat. Hosp., Kirkland, Wash.; v.p. Allied Health Professions; sexual dysfunction therapist U. Wash., 1978-80; project dir. drama therapy North Seattle Mental Health, 1976-77; counselor clin. psychology Seattle Mental Health Rehab.; bd. dirs. N.W. Neurol. Rehab., 1981—. King County Arts Commn. grantee, 1976-77. Mem. Am. Occupational Therapy Assn. (cert.), Internat. Transactional Analysis Assn. (cert.), Am. Assn. Marriage and Family Therapists (cert.), King County Health Planning Council, Am. Psychol. Assn., Am. Personnel and Guidance Assn., Lake City C. of C., Women's Bus. Exchange, Fedn. Bus. and Profl. Women. Author: Personalized Guidelines, 1979; contbr. articles to psychotherapy and rehab. jours. Home: 8255 45th Ave NE Seattle WA 98115 Office: 11000 Lake City Way NE Suite 314 Seattle WA 98125

GORDON, ELAINE YVETTE, state legislator; b. N.Y.C., Sept. 8, 1931; d. Henry and Freda Weitzman; student CCNY, 1950, Fla. Internat. U., 1980; children—Pamela Beth, Brian, Seth. Salesperson, Duke Industries, Hialeah, Fla., 1978—; lectr.; mem. Fla. Ho. of Reps., 1972—, chmn. house adminstrn. com. Bd. dirs. and officer Fla. Center for Children and Youth; mem. adv. bd. Crime Prevention Commn. Recipient spl. recognition and award Inst. for Women, Fla. Internat. U., 1978; Good Govt. award North Miami Beach Jaycees, 1974; Woman of Yr. award Dade Bus. and Profl. Women's Club, 1973. Mem. Nat. Conf. State Legislatures, Nat. Women's Polit. Caucus (organizer), Dade County Bus. and Profl. Women. Jewish. Office: 11866 W Dixie Hwy Miami FL 33161 *

GORDON, GUANETTA STEWART, writer, poet; b. Kansas City, Mo.; d. Samuel Lewis and Minnie Anna (Brown) Stewart; ed. Baker U., U. Kan.; m. Lynell F. Gordon; children—Stewart Lynell, Krista Sharon (Mrs. Morris). Radio dramatist sta. KMBC, Kansas City, Mo.; radio script writer, dramatist, lectr., book reviewer; free lance writer; author: Songs of the Wind, 1953; Under the Rainbow Arch, 1965; Petals From the Moon, 1971; Shadow Within the Flame, 1973; Above Rubies, 1976, Red Are the Embers, 1980; The Aurora Tree, 1982, also poetry various mags. Recipient feature writing awards Nat. League Am. Pen Women, 1954, spl. award for quantity of good articles submitted to 1956 contest; named Kans. Poet of Year, Midwest Fedn. Chaparrals, 1966, J. Donald Cuffin Book award Kans. Authors Club, 1981, award of personal achievement in writing, 1982; Della Crowder Miller Meml. award for Petrarchan sonnet, 1982; numerous other nat. and internat. awards in prose and poetry. Mem. Nat. League Am. Pen Women (pres. Alexander br. 1956-58, nat. 1st v.p. 1970-72), Am. Poetry League, D.A.R., Poetry Soc. Va., World Poetry Soc. (distinguished service citation 1970), Ariz., Phoenix (pres. 1973) poetry socs., Phoenix Writers Club, Poetry Soc. Am., Fedn. Chaparral Poets, Delta Delta Delta. Address: 11847 Hacienda Dr Sun City AZ 85351

GORDON, JAN IRENE STRAIGHT, ins., estate and fin. co. exec.; b. Portland, Oreg., May 28, 1951; d. Lyle Henry and Juanita Jean Vandercook; student Ga. So. Coll., 1971-72; B.S. in Adminstrn. of Justice/Sociology, Portland State U., 1975; m. Stephen R. Gordon, Dec. 28, 1980; 1 dau., Jennifer Spring. Saleswoman, Lincoln Nat. Life Ins. Co., San Mateo, Calif., 1975-81; owner, mgr. Jan Straight & Assocs., San Mateo, 1981—; dir. Material Handling Corp., Oreg. Handling Equipment Co., Inc., speaker in field; local chairwoman Life Underwriters Polit. Action Com. C.L.U. Mem. Nat. Assn. Life Underwriters, Peninsula Assn. Life Underwriters (v.p., editor bull.), Calif. Assn. Life Underwriters (mem. State Consumer Edn. Task Force), Nat. Speakers Team (charter). Christian Scientist. Club: Friends of the Winemakers (club photographer) (Santa Clara). Office: 400 S El Camino Real Suite 900 San Mateo CA 94402

GORDON, JO ANN CUSHMAN, journalist; b. Green Cove Springs, Fla., Oct. 9, 1946; d. Joseph Henry and Delma Faye (Wilson) Cushman; student Indian River Community Coll., Ft. Pierce, Fla., 1974-76; 1 son, Frederick Brian Lee. Reporter, Today Newspaper, Cocoa, Fla., Vero Beach News Bur., 1970-73, Sta. WTTB, Vero Beach, Fla., 1973-74, comml. writer, 1974-76; reporter Pensacola (Fla.) News Jour., Milton (Fla.) News Bur., 1976-77, bur. chief, 1977-78, edn. writer, 1978-80, Pensacola city govt. reporter, 1980—. Recipient Friend of Edn. award Santa Rosa Profl. Educators, 1978; Outstanding News Media Covering Edn. award Phi Delta Kappa, 1981, Newsmaker award Fla. Teaching Profession, NEA, 1980; Charles Stewart Mott award Edn. Writers Assn., 1980. Mem. Santa Rosa Press Club (former officer). Democrat. Home: 1315 E La Rua St Pensacola FL 32501 Office: One News Journal Plaza Pensacola FL 32574

GORDON, LENORE DORIS, educator; b. Shenandoah, Pa., Nov. 23, 1931; d. Daniel and Betty (Mainker) G.; B.S. cum laude, Fairleigh Dickinson U., 1955; M.A. in Edn., Health Care, Central Mich. U., 1977. Microbiologist, Babies Hosp., Columbia U., N.Y.C., 1955-59, Belinson Hosp., Petah Tikva, Israel, 1960-72; head microbiology sect. Barnert Meml. Hosp., Paterson, N.J., 1972-75; instr. infection control U. Medicine and Dentistry N.J., Newark, 1977—. Mem. Am. Soc. Microbiology, Assn. Practitioners in Infection Comtrol, Am. Soc. Med. Tech., Central Mich. U. Alumni Assn. Home: 215 Passaic Ave Passaic NJ 07055

GORDON, LYNNE L., jewelry co. exec.; b. N.Y.C., Jan. 18, 1923; d. Curtis and Lillian (Berman) Lewin; lic. tchr. Ethical Culture Tchr. Tng. Sch., 1943; student N.Y.U. Sch. of Engring., 1943-44, Boston Mechanics Sch., 1943; m. Alfred Gordon, Dec. 25, 1947; children—Ronni Anne, Diane Beth. Kindergarten tchr., 1943; civilian insp., ordance dept. U.S. Army, 1944-46; owner, operator Lynne's Boutique, N.Y.C., 1946-68; partner MYLU Design Co. div. Coro Jewelry Co., 1968-71; designer, exec. v.p., partner Tancer and Two Inc., N.Y.C., 1971—. Mem. Fashion Group. Office: Tancer and Two Inc 366 Fifth Ave New York NY 10001

GORDON, MALVINA, social worker, psychotherapist, educator; b. N.Y.C., June 27, 1922; d. Henry and Ethel (Brinker) Marcus; B.A., Hunter Coll., 1943; M.A., N.Y. U., 1951; M.S.W., Adelphi U., 1961; m. Michael Gordon, Nov. 25, 1954; 1 dau., Amy. Ednl. dir. Eisman Day Nursery, 1950-52; dir. Greenwich House Child Care Center, 1952-59; supr., sr. caseworker Family Service Assn. Five Towns, 1961-69; pvt. practice psychotherapy, N.Y.C., 1965—; asso. prof. Sch. Social Work, Adelphi U., Garden City, N.Y., 1969—. Cert. social worker, N.Y. Mem. Nat. Assn. Social Workers, AAUP, Council Social Work Edn. (accreditation commn.), NOW. Contbr. articles, book revs. to profl. publs. Home: 171-13 Mayfield Rd Jamaica Estates NY 11432 Office: Adelphi Univ School Social Work Garden City NY 11530

GORDON, MARILYN LU, health care co. exec.; b. Los Angeles, July 11, 1954; d. Frank Ephraim and Seemah Kitty (Masliah) G.; B.A. in Health Services Adminstrn., Antioch U., 1977. Med. equipment and supply buyer Am. Med. Internat., Beverly Hills, Calif., 1972-73, computer coordinator, 1973-77, asst. to v.p. purchasing, 1977-80, dir. materials systems, 1980-82; pres. Medi-Genics, Inc., Sherman Oaks, Calif., 1982—; cons. in field. Mem. Am. Inst. Hosp. Cons., Internat. Materials Mgmt. Soc., Calif. Assn. Hosp. Purchasing Agents. Office: 15445 Ventura Blvd Suite 10-309 Sherman Oaks CA 91413

GORDON, MILDRED HARRIET GROSS (MRS. IVAN H. GORDON), hosp. exec.; b. Phila., Mar. 13, 1934; d. Nathan and Kate (Segal) Gross; student U. Pa., 1952-56; B.S., Kutztown (Pa.) State Coll., 1960; M.S. (Falk Found. fellow), Med. Coll. Pa., 1970, Ph.D. in Psychiatry (fellow), 1972; m. Ivan H. Gordon, June 13, 1954; 1 dau., Radene Lara. Tchr. sci. public schs., 1961-66; with Family Guidance Center, 1966-70; dir. dept. psychiatry Mental Health Treatment Center, Reading Hosp.,

West Reading, 1972—; clin. instr. dept. psychiatry Med. Coll. Pa., Phila., 1972-78; clin. asst. prof. dept. psychiatry Temple U. Med. Sch.; pvt. practice DGR Assos., Wyomissing, Pa.; mem. Pa. Gov.'s Council on Drug and Alcohol Abuse, 1972-78. Bd. dirs. Confront, 1971-73, Council on Chem. Abuse, 1971-73. Mem. Am. Psychol. Assn. Home: 1850 Oak Ln Reading PA 19604 Office: Reading Hospital K Bldg Reading PA 19603 also 845 Park Rd N Wyomissing PA 19610

GORDON, PAMELA ANN, pharm. co. rep., cytotechnologist; b. Bklyn., Feb. 17, 1953; d. Norman Anthony and Louise Regina (Cooper) G.; student Barry Coll., 1971-74; Cytotechnologist, U. Miami, 1975; B.B.A., Fla. Atlantic U., 1980. Staff cytotechnologist, instr. U. Miami (Fla.) Med. Sch., 1975-77; chief cytotechnologist Diagnostic Lab., North Palm Beach, Fla., 1977-78; pharm. rep. Glaxo Inc., Ft. Lauderdale, Fla., 1981—; didactic and microscopic instr. U. Miami Sch. Cytotechnology, 1975-77. Mem. Am. Soc. Cytology, Am. Soc. Clin. Pathologists, Fla. Soc. Cytology, So. Assn. Cytotechnologists, Delta Sigma Pi. Home: 104 Oriole Ct Royal Palm Beach FL 33411 Office: 1900 W Commercial Blvd Fort Lauderdale FL 33309

GORDON, PAMELA MARTIN, psychologist; b. San Jose, Calif., Aug. 19, 1948; d. Cuyler North and Florence (Incerpi) Martin; B.A., U. Calif., Berkeley, 1971; M.S., Rutgers U., 1975; Ph.D., SUNY, Binghamton, 1979; m. William C. Gordon, Sept. 29, 1973; children—Jason Cuyler and William Scott (twins). Staff psychologist Binghamton (N.Y.) Psychiat. Center, 1976-77, Albuquerque Child Guidance Center, 1978-80, VA Hosp., Albuquerque, 1980—; clin. asst. prof. dept. psychiatry U. N.Mex., 1980, adj. asst. prof. dept. psychology, 1981. Mem. Am. Psychol. Assn., N.Mex. Psychol. Assn. (treas. 1980-82). Office: VA Hosp 2100 Ridgecrest Rd SE Albuquerque NM 87108

GORDON, RUTH, actress; b. Quincy, Mass., Oct. 30, 1896; d. Clinton Annie Tapley (Ziegler) Jones; student Quincy Public Schs.; m. Gregory Kelly, 1918; 1 son, Jones Harris; m. 2d, Garson Kanin, Dec. 4, 1942. First appearance as actress Empire Theatre, N.Y.C., 1915, as Nibs in Peter Pan, with Maude Adams; other appearances include: Seventeen, 1917-19, Saturday's Children, 1928, Serena Blandish, 1929, Hotel Universe, 1930, the Church Mouse, 1930-31, Ethan Frome, 1935, The Count Wife, 1936-37, Nora in a Doll's House, 1938, Natasha in The Three Sisters, 1942-43, Over Twenty-One, 1943-45, The Leading Lady, 1948, The Smile of the World, 1949, The Matchmaker (London and Berlin), 1954, N.Y.C., 1955, The Good Soup, 1960, A Time to Laugh (London), 1962, Mother, My Father and Me, 1963, The Loves of Cass McQuire, 1966, Dreyf in Rehearsal, 1974, Mrs.-Warren's Profession, 1976; (films) Mary Todd Abe Lincoln in Illinois, 1939, Mrs. Ehrlich in Dr. Ehrlich's Magic Bullet, 1939, Two Faced Woman, Action in the North Atlantic, Edge of Darkness, Inside Daisy Clover, 1965, Lord Love a Duck, 1966, Rosemary's Baby (acad. award Best Supporting Actress), 1968, Whatever Happened to Aunt Alice?, 1969, Where's Poppa?, 1970, Harold and Maude, 1971, Every Which Way But Loose, 1978, Brighton Beach, 1979; Any Which Way you Can, 1980; (TV films) Isn't It Shocking, 1973, Prince of Central Park, 1975, Rosemary Baby II, 1976, The Great Houdini, 1976, Perfect Gentlemen, 1978, Scavenger Hunt, 1979; guest appearance TV shows Kojak, 1975, Rhoda, Medical Story, 1975; playwright Star A Very Rich Woman, 1965, Ho! Ho! Ho!, 1976; (TV) Mommy in the American Dream, 1963, Madame Arcati Elithe Spirit. Recipient Emmy award for Taxi, 1979, Oscar for Rosemary's Baby. Author plays: Over Twenty One, Years Ago, The Leading Lady; screenplays (with Garson Kanin) A Double Life, Adam's Rib, The Marrying Kind, Pat and Mike; author: Myself Among Others, 1971, My Side, 1976, An Open Book, 1980, Shady Lady, 1982; contbr. articles in field to profl. jours. Office: 200 W 57th St New York NY 10019

GORDON, RUTH, brokerage firm exec.; b. Plain City, Ohio, June 30, 1941; d. Calvin M. and Cleetus M. (Loveless) Tumlin; student U. South Fla., 1974; m. Anthony Glenn Arango, June 27, 1981; 1 dau. by previous marriage, Alyssa Susan Elkinton. Account exec. E.H. Russell & Co., Chgo., 1962-66; freelance writer, actress, N.Y.C., 1966-68; advt. mgr. Playboy Enterprises, Chgo., 1968-70; pres. The Gordon Agy., Tampa, Fla., 1971-73; v.p. corp. communications Medfield Corp., St. Petersburg, Fla., 1973-79; chmn. bd., pres. Securities Discount Corp., Clearwater, Fla., 1981-82; securities prin., investment officer Jerry Williams, Inc., 1982—. Republican. Home: 4402 Beach Park Dr Tampa FL 33609

GORDON, SUSAN AMBER, venture capital co. exec.; b. N.Y.C., Sept. 9, 1954; d. George S. and Jeanne Gordon Goldman; B.A. summa cum laude with honors in Psychology, Barnard Coll., Columbia U., 1976. Mng. editor TUBE Mag., Doubleday & Co., N.Y.C., 1977-78; with Boardroom Reports, N.Y.C., 1978-80, book mktg. dir., 1980; v.p. Weinrich-Zitzmann-Whitehead, 1980-81; v.p. Biotech Capital Corp., 1981—. Mem. Phi Beta Kappa. Office: 11 Hanover Sq New York NY 10005

GORE, BARBARA LINDHOLM, research adminstr., educator; b. N.Y.C., Feb. 11, 1937; d. Lauri E. and Anna M. (Johnson) Lindholm; B.A. cum laude, Mercy Coll., 1974; postgrad. Cornell U., 1977-78, L.I. U., 1978-80; children by previous marriage—Andrew Spano, David R. Spano, Christine L. Spano, Karen Spano. Claims examiner N.Y. State Dept. Labor, 1975-78; personnel dir. Rockland Research Inst., N.Y. State Office of Mental Health, Orangeburg, 1978—; instr. health adminstrn. dept. psychiatry, N.Y.U. Coll. Medicine, 1979—; oral examiner N.Y. State Dept. Civil Service, 1980. Del., Dem. Nat. Conf., 1972; town chmn. Yorktown Dem. Com., 1977-78; mem. Westchester County Dem. Com., 1968-78. Mem. Soc. Research Adminstrs., Assn. Mental Health Adminstrs. Office: Rockland Research Inst Orangeburg NY 10962

GORE, CATHERINE ANN, social worker; b. Mullens, W.Va., Feb. 2, 1937; d. Bernard Joseph and Agnes Cecilia (Spradling) G.; B.A., Thomas More Coll., 1968; M.S.W., Ohio State U., 1971, now postgrad. Caseworker, Cath. Charities, Cin., 1967-69, 71-72; psychiat. social worker Mcpl. Ct. Psychiat. Clinic, Cin., 1973; mem. faculty Ct. Psychiat. Center, U. Cin., 1974-80, asst. prof. psychiat. social work, coordinator consultation services, 1979-80; cons. Hamilton County Welfare Dept.; instr. No. Ky. U.; grad. research assoc. Ohio State U., 1981-82. Mem. Nat. Assn. Social Workers, Acad. Cert. Social Workers. Democrat. Roman Catholic. Home: 2599 Scioto View Ln Columbus OH 43221

GORE, SAUNDRA SUE, nurse; b. Terre Haute, Ind., July 23, 1942; d. Robert Warren and Reba Louise (Burkholder) Guyer; diploma in nursing, Barnes Hosp., St. Louis, 1963; m. Neil Robert Gore, Mar. 4, 1967; 1 son, Vance Robert. Staff and head nurse coronary care Barnes Hosp., 1963-67, 70-71; mem. staff San Pedro (Calif.) Peninsula Hosp., 1968-70, 74—, dir. cardiology, 1979—; instr. Calif. State U., Long Beach; CPR instr. R.N.; cert. in critical care. Mem. Am. Heart Assn., Am. Assn. Critical Care Nurses, Nat. Mgmt. Assn. Home: 3534 Newridge Dr Rancho Palos Verdes CA 90274 Office: 1300 W 7th St San Pedro CA 90732

GORE, SUSAN ANNE, psychologist; b. San Diego, Nov. 5, 1949; d. Leonard F., Jr. and Helene W. Gore; B.A., Fla. State U., 1971; M.A. (USPHS fellow), Vanderbilt U., 1973, Ph.D., 1975. Asst. prof. psychology Memphis State U., 1975-76, Tex. Christian U., Ft. Worth, 1976-81; dir. Nat. Women's Studies Assn., U. Md., College Park, 1981—; ednl. services coordinator Family and Individual Services Assn., Ft. Worth, 1980; lectr. European div. U. Md., 1980-81; cons. in field. Vice pres., bd. dirs. Ft. Worth Women's Center, 1976-78. Russell Sage summer intern, 1973. Mem. Nat. Women's Studies Assn. (a founder; coordinating council 1979-80), Am. Psychol. Assn., Assn. Women in Psychology, NOW, S. Central Women's Studies Assn. (a founder 1978, steering com. 1978-80), Gamma Phi Beta. Club: Zonta. Home: 1309 Lawrence St NE Washington DC 20017

GORECKI, DANUTA MARIA, librarian; b. Lwow, Poland, June 29, 1922; came to U.S., 1969, naturalized, 1974; d. Stanislaw and Teodora (Okoll) Wojnar; M.S., Jagiellonian U., Cracow, Poland, 1952, Ph.D., 1966; M.S., U. Ill., Urbana, 1973; m. Jan Gorecki, Dec. 25, 1954; children—Piotr Stanislaw, Marie Joanna. Corp. lawyer several state-owned enterprises, Cracow, 1952-68; librarian spl. langs. dept. U. Ill. Library, Urbana-Champaign, 1971-74, law cataloguer, 1974-81, rare book room cataloguer, 1982—, asso. prof. library adminstrn., 1980—. Served as 2d lt., mem. Polish Underground Anti-Nazi Home Army, 1939-45; mem WIN, Cracow, 1945-46; polit. prisoner, 1946-50. Mem. Am. Assn. Law Libraries, ALA, Mediaeval Acad. Am. Home: 510 W Washington St Urbana IL 61801 Office: 1408 W Gregory Ave Urbana IL 61801

GORENA, MINERVA, educator; b. Edinburg, Tex., Mar. 30, 1943; d. Humberto and Eva (Benavides) Gorena; B.A., Pan Am. Coll., 1963; M.Ed., U. Tex., Austin, 1975. Tchr., Hidalgo County Common Sch. Dist., Runn, Tex., 1963-64, Mission (Tex.) Ind. Sch. Dist., 1964-67, Pharr-San Juan-Alamo Ind. Sch. Dist., Pharr, Tex., 1967-69; counselor Out-of-Sch. Neighborhood Youth Corps, asso. City County Econ. Devel. Corp., Edinburg, Tex., 1969-70; materials specialist Title VII Bilingual Edn. Program, Region XIII Edn. Service Center, Austin, Tex., 1970-74; cons. div. bilingual edn. Tex. Edn. Agy., Austin, 1974-77; mgr. user services Nat. Clearinghouse for Bilingual Edn./Inter-Am. Research Assos., Inc., Rosslyn, Va., 1978-81, asso. dir., 1981—, exec. asso. 1978—. NDEA fellow, 1967. Mem. Austin Area Assn. for Bilingual Edn. (sec. 1975-76), Nat. Assn. for Bilingual Edn. (del. 1979), Tex. State Tchrs. Assn. (Region XIII chpt. pres. 1973-74), Nat. Assn. Female Execs., Va. Assn. Bilingual Edn., Va. Assn. Hispanic Am. Democrats, Nat. Assn. Latino Elected Ofcls., YMCA, Phi Delta Kappa. Roman Catholic. Editor: Information and Materials to Teach the Cultural Heritage of the Mexican American, 1972, Resources in Bilingual Education: A Preliminary Guide to Government Agency Programs of Interest to Minority Language Groups, 1979; Sources of Materials for Minority Languages: A Preliminary List, 1979. Home: 2805 S Columbus St Arlington VA 22206 Office: 1555 Wilson Blvd Suite 600 Rosslyn VA 22209

GORKE, KAREN MARIE, truck terminal exec.; b. Long Beach, Calif., Aug. 23, 1955; d. Rudolph Eric and Marlene Shirley (Elitzer) G.; student Orange Coast Coll., 1976-77, U. Calif., 1977-78, 81—. Dietary supr. Anaheim Meml. Hosp., 1971-75; bookkeeper Iverpac Corp., Fountain Valley, Calif., 1975-76; asst. controller For Better Living, Inc., Laguna Niguel, Calif., 1976-79; div. controller Tower Industries, Inc., Fonatana, Calif., 1979-81; gen. mgr. Bandini Truck Terminal, Los Angeles, 1981—. Mem. Credit Mgrs. Assn. So. Calif., Nat. Soc. Public Accountants. Assembly of God. Office: 3152 Bandini Blvd Los Angeles CA 90023

GORMAN, AUDREY JANE, ednl. media and materials cons.; b. Albany, N.Y., Oct. 26, 1946; d. Frank Joseph and Audrey Margaret (Mulligan) G.; B.A. in English cum laude, Coll. St. Rose, 1968; M.L.S., SUNY, Albany, 1970. Youth and children's librarian East Orange (N.J.) Public Library, 1970-78; instructional media specialist Ednl. Improvement Center, N.E., West Orange, N.J., 1978-81; ednl. media and materials cons., 1981—. Mem. N.J. State Library Task Force on Computer Applications in Libraries, 1980; juror Am. Film Festival, 1980-81. Mem. Spl. Libraries Assn., N.J. Library Assn., N.J. Ednl. Media Assn. Home and office: 29 S Munn Ave 3A East Orange NJ 07018

GORMAN, ELAINE LABOUR, journalist; b. Wilmington, Del., Oct. 12, 1935; d. Harry E. and Edythe Mae (Young) LaBour; B.A., U. Del., 1957; m. Cecil Francis Gorman, June 6, 1981. Actress profl. theatre, N.Y.C., 1957-64; various newspaper staff positions, Wilmington, Del., Tokyo, Wheaton, Ill., Coatesville, Pa., 1968-73; reporter, drama critic, sect. asst. editor Suburban Life Newspapers, LaGrange Park, Ill., 1973-76; editor-in-chief SCOPE, Sperry Univac Customer Engring. Employee Publ., Blue Bell, Pa., 1976—. Mem. Internat. Assn. Bus. Communicators, Internat. Women's Press Assn., Women in Communications, LWV. Democrat. Methodist. Clubs: Ikebana Internat.; Gilbert and Sullivan Players (Phila.). Office: PO Box 500 Blue Bell PA 19424

GORMAN, JUDY A., life ins. co. exec.; b. Dayton, Ohio, Feb. 9, 1939; d. Mark and Bernice Adele Goldman; B.F.A., Boston U., 1961. TV actress appearing on The Nurses, The Defenders, The Patty Duke Show, 1961-65; account exec. Staff Builders, Inc., 1961-66; sr. account exec. Uniforce, Inc., 1966-68; consumer affairs officer Chase Manhattan Bank, N.Y.C., 1968-74; dir. consumer and community services Am. Council Life Ins. Co., N.Y.C., 1974-76; 2d v.p. Office Corp. Responsibility, N.Y. Life Ins. Co., N.Y.C., 1976-78, v.p., 1978-82, v.p. mktg., 1982—. Mem. Soc. Consumer Affairs Profls. in Bus. (dir. 1975-79, pres. 1977-78), Council Better Bus. Burs. (dir. 1978—). Office: NY Life Ins Co 51 Madison Ave New York NY 10010

GORMAN, LILLIAN R., bank personnel exec., indsl. psychologist; b. N.Y.C., July 4, 1953; d. Helmuth H. and Ida A. (Malitsch) Degen; B.A. in Psychology, Lehman Coll., City U. N.Y., 1975; M.A., Case Western Res. U., 1978, Ph.D. in Indsl. Psychology, 1979; m. Mark R. Gorman, Oct. 23, 1976. Econ. benefits asst. Girl Scouts U.S.A., N.Y.C., 1971-75; staff cons. Personnel Research & Devel. Corp., Cleve., 1977-78; research asst. Case Western Res. U., 1975-79; v.p. personnel research and planning First Interstate Bank Los Angeles, 1979—; cons. psychology. Mem. Am. Psychol. Assn., Personnel Testing Council So. Calif., Phi Beta Kappa. Lutheran. Home: 2305 Overland Ave Los Angeles CA 90064 Office: 600 S Spring St Los Angeles CA 90014

GORMAN, LINDA KORN, psychologist; b. Phila., June 1, 1953; d. Samuel and Muriel (Grass) Korn; B.A., Dickinson Coll., 1975; M.A., Temple U., 1978, Ph.D., 1980; m. Thomas Joseph Gorman, Jan. 7, 1979. Clinic asst. Psychol. Services Center, Temple U., 1976-77, clinic supr., teaching asst., 1978-80; clin. psychology intern Norristown (Pa.) State Hosp., 1977-78; psychologist Program of Aux. Services for Students, non-pub. schs., Bala-Cynwyd, Pa., 1980—; psychologist St. Gabriel's Hall, Phoenixville, Pa., 1981. Cert. sch. psychologist, Pa. Mem. Am. Psychol. Assn., Eastern Psychol. Assn., Pa. Psychol. Assn., Phila. Soc. Clin. Psychologists, Assn. Advancement Psychology, AAUW, Mensa, Dickinson Coll. Alumnae, Phi Beta Kappa Alumnae, Pi Beta Phi Alumnae. Home: 1000 Conestoga Rd Apt B332 Rosemont PA 19010 Office: 725 Conshohocken State Rd Bala-Cynwyd PA 19004

GORMAN, MARCIE SOTHERN, franchise exec.; b. N.Y.C., Feb. 25, 1949; d. Jerry R. and Carole Edith (Frendel) Sothern; B.S., Memphis State U., 1970; m. N. Scott Gorman, June 14, 1969 (div.); children—Michael Stephen, Mark Jason. Tchr., Memphis City Sch. System, 1970-73; tng. dir. Weight Watchers of Palm Beach County and Weight Watchers So. Ala., Inc., West Palm Beach, Fla., 1973—, area dir., then pres., 1977—; pres. Markel Ads, Inc. Hon. lt. col. a.d.c. Ala. Militia. Mem. Women' Am. ORT (program chmn. 1975), Optometric Soc. (sec. 1973), Weight Watchers Franchise Assn., Am. Bus. Women's Assn., Nat. Assn. Female Execs. Home: 3253 Hoy Lake Rd Lake Worth FL 33463 Office: 6801 Lake Worth Rd Suite 119 Lake Worth FL 33463

GORMAN, S(ARAH) JOANNE, psychotherapist; b. Asheboro, N.C., Sept. 3, 1937; d. Shuford Tobias and Madie Hester (Sasser) Plott; B.A., U. N.C., Greensboro, 1959; M.S. in Social Work (Univ. fellow 1960-62), Columbia U., 1962; m. Edward G. Gorman, Dec. 15, 1962; children—Monica, David, Nicole. Caseworker, Lutheran Child Welfare Assn., N.Y.C., 1962-63, Allegany County (N.Y.) Dept. Adoptions, Angelica, 1964-66, Los Angeles County Dept. Adoptions, Long Beach, Calif., 1966-67, 69-72; cons. Psychiat. Clinic for Children, San Pedro, 1974-76; pvt. practice psychotherapy, Redondo Beach, Calif., 1974—. Mem. Nat. Assn. Social Workers, South Bay Assn. Licensed Clin. Social Workers. Democrat. Home: 2607 Pinale Ln Palos Verdes Estates CA 90274 Office: 1801 S Catalina Ave Suite 307 Redondo Beach CA 90277

GORMAN, THEOPHILE, writer, newspaper reporter; b. Richland Center, Wis., June 24, 1921; d. Elmer and Ada (Flamme) Smith; B.A. magna cum laude, Carroll Coll., 1943; postgrad. U. Wis., 1962; m. William P. Gorman, June 28, 1941; children—Kathleen, Carole. Editor women's page, news reporter Waukesha (Wis.) Freeman; instr. Spanish Waukesha County Tech. Inst., 1954-67; reporter, feature writer Waukesha (Wis.) Freeman, 1970-76; reporter Post Publs., 1977-81; free lance writer, 1981—. An organizer Waukesha Jaycettes, Waukesha Symphony Aux.; chmn. publicity numerous clubs and orgns. Recipient journalism awards for news stories, features and interviews. Mem. Nat. Fedn. Press Women (bd. dirs. 1975), Wis. Press Women (v.p. 1974-76, sec. 1976-80). Episcopalian. Home: 114 E Wabash Ave Waukesha WI 53186

GORME, EYDIE, singer; b. N.Y.C., Aug. 16; m. Steve Lawrence, Dec. 29, 1957; children—David, Michael. Various night club engagements; mem. Steve Allen's TV troupe Tonight Show, 1954; Broadway debut (with husband) in Golden Rainbow, 1967; numerous theater appearances throughout U.S. Emmy award winning TV spls. include Steve and Eydie honoring Gershwin, Porter and Berlin. Chairwoman entertainment com. Cerebral Palsy. Recipient Grammy award as best female vocalist of yr. for If He Walked into My Life, 1967. Office: care Lee Solters 9255 Sunset Blvd Los Angeles CA 90069

GOROCHOW, MONICA SCHAEFFER, psychologist; b. Linden, N.J., Jan. 28, 1952; d. Hans A. and Lilo (Jacobsohn) Schaeffer; B.S. summa cum laude, U. Md., 1973, M.A. in Behavioral Psychology, 1979; m. Mitchell E. Gorochow, Aug. 3, 1975. Behavioral scientist Westinghouse Behavioral Safety Center, Columbia, Md., 1973-76; mgr. tng. and edn. programs occupational safety and health div. JRB Assos., Inc., McLean, Va., 1976-79; asst. dir. tng. and info. div. safety NIH, Bethesda, Md., 1979—; workshop leader; cons. in field. Mem. Am. Psychol. Assn., Am. Soc. Tng. and Devel., Phi Beta Kappa, Psi Chi, Phi Kappa Phi. Author papers in field. Home: 26 Bannister Ct Gaithersburg MD 20879 Office: 9000 Rockville Pike Bldg 13 Room 2E43 Bethesda MD 20205

GOROVE, MARGARET JOAN, educator; b. N.Y.C., Aug. 30, 1935; d. James Joseph and Katherine Sarah (Boles) Beasley; B.A., Manhattanville Coll., 1957; M.F.A., U. Miss., 1968; m. Stephen Gorove, July 31, 1958; children—Katherine Marie, Stephen James, Margaret Colleen, Michael Alexander. Free-Lance research editor Grolier Corp., N.Y.C., 1957-63; instr., asst. prof., assoc. prof., chmn. dept. art U. Miss., University, 1969—, chmn., 1978—; NEH grantee, 1979, 81, 82. Mem. Coll. Arts Assn., Nat. Assn. Schs. Art and Design, Nat. Council Arts Adminstrs., Humanities and Tech. Assns., Miss. Assn. Women in Higher Edn., Miss. Art Assn., S.E. Coll. Art Conf. (pres. 1981), Internat. Astronautical Fedns. (Am. coordinator humanities sessions meetings 1978—), Miss. Inst. Arts and Letters (dir.). Contbr. articles to profl. jours. Home: 320 Country Club Rd Oxford MS 38655 Office: Dept Art Univ Miss University MS 38677

GORSUCH, ANNE MCGILL, lawyer, govt. ofcl.; b. Casper, Wyo., Apr. 21, 1942; d. Joseph John and Dorothy Jean (O'Grady) McGill; student Nat. U. Mexico, summers 1955, 56, 58, Regis Coll., Denver, summer 1959; B.A., U. Colo., 1961, LL.B., 1964; m. David Gorsuch, June 4, 1964; children—Neil, Stephanie, J.J. Admitted to Colo. bar, 1964; Fulbright scholar, Jaipur, India, 1964-65; asst. trust adminstr. First Nat. Bank of Denver, 1966-67; instr. Metro State Coll., 1966-67; asst. dist. atty. Jefferson County, 1968-71; dep. dist. atty., Denver, 1971-73; hearing officer Real Estate Commn., State Bds. Cosmetology, Optometric Examiners, Profl. Nursing and Vet. Medicine, 1974-75; corporate counsel Mountain Bell Telephone Co., Denver, 1975-81; mem. Colo. Ho. of Reps., 1977-81, chmn. state affairs com., 1979—, chmn. legal services com., 1980—; del. Nat. Conf. State Legislators; mem. Nat. Conf. Commrs. on Uniform State Law, 1979—; loaned exec. mgmt. and efficiency task force Colo. Dept. Regulatory Agys., 1976; adminstr. EPA, Washington, 1981—. Active Christ the King Parish and Sch. PTA, Jewish Community Center; bd. dirs. YMCA. Mem. Am., Colo., Denver bar assns., Mortar Bd., Phi Alpha Delta, Delta Delta Delta. Republican. Roman Catholic. Office: Environ Protection Agy 401 M St SW Washington DC 20460 *

GORSUCH, CAROL DOTY, communications/public relations exec.; b. Plainfield, N.J., July 3, 1943; d. Wilbur Aaron and Ellen Anna (Strom) Doty; B.A. in Journalism, Colo. State U., 1965; m. Keith Edward Gorsuch, Aug. 13, 1966; children—Kim Lynn, Mark David. Reporter, photographer Brighton (Colo.) Blade, 1965-66; asst. to dir. publs. Tacoma Public Schs., 1966-69; owner Gorsuch Communications-Public Relations/Publs., Tacoma, 1969—; public info. officer City of Tacoma Human Relations Dept., 1977-81; instr. Ft. Steilacoom Community Coll., 1978, Tacoma Community Coll., 1981; mgmt. tng. instr. City of Tacoma Tng. and Devel. Dept.-Media Relations, 1981. Vol. instr. United Way of Pierce County/Mgmt. Assitance Program-Public Relations for Vol. Agys., 1981; bd. dirs. Sharing, 1976-82; bd. dirs. South Sound Women's Network, 1980-82, v.p. membership, 1980-81; chmn. City of Tacoma Beautification Com., 1977-78; co-chmn. public relations com. Jr. League Tacoma, 1978, asst. evening active chmn., 1979-80; chmn. City of Tacoma Human Relations Dept., United Way Campaign, 1978; co-chmn. City of Tacoma U.S. Savs. Bond Campaign, 1978; mem. City of Tacoma Legis. Analysis Com., 1980-81; press sec., mktg. dir. Doug Sutherland for Mayor Campaign, 1981. Recipient Disting. Servica citation Keep America Beautiful, 1977. Mem. Women in Communications (chpt. v.p. 1975-77), Internat. Assn. Bus. Communicators, Tacoma-Pierce County C. of C. (communications council 1981), Colo. State U. Alumni Assn., Kappa Delta. Episcopalian. Home and Office: 7203 N 27th St Tacoma WA 98407

GORTNER, SUSAN REICHERT, univ. dean; b. San Francisco, Dec. 23, 1932; d. Frederick Leet and Frida L. (Leuschner) Reichert; A.B., Stanford U., 1953; M.Nursing, Western Res. U., 1957; Ph.D., U. Calif., Berkeley, 1964; m. Willis Alway Gortner, Aug. 25, 1960; children—Catherine Willis, Frederick Aiken. Surg. staff nurse, instr.-supr. Johns Hopkins Hosp. Sch. Nursing, 1957-58; instr., then asst. prof. U. Hawaii, 1958-64; staff scientist, research adminstr. USPHS, 1968-78; prof. family health care U. Calif., San Francisco, 1978—, assoc. dean research, 1978—, acting chmn. dept. family health care nursing, 1982—, also mem. affiliated faculty Inst. Health Policy Studies and Aging Health Policy Center; cons. in field. Fellow Am. Acad. Nursing (governing council 1979-81); mem. Am. Nurses Assn. (chmn. exec. com. council nurse researchers 1978-80), Nat. League Nursing, Am. Ednl. Research Assn., Am. Assn. Higher Edn., Western Soc. Research Nursing, Sigma Theta Tau, Pi Lambda Theta. Author articles, abstracts, monographs in field; assoc. editor: Nursing Practice in the 80's, 1982. Home: 470 Cervantes Rd Portola Valley CA 94025 Office: Sch Nursing U Calif San Francisco CA 94143

GORTON, ARLENE ELIZABETH, educator; b. Providence, Mar. 16, 1931; d. Kingdon D. and Eveline (Wright) G.; A.B., Brown U., 1952; M.Ed., U. N.C., Greensboro, 1954. Asst. prof. phys. edn. Conn. Coll., New London, 1954-60; asso. prof. phys. edn. Brown U., Providence, 1960-71, prof., 1971—, asso. dir. athletics, 1973—; dir. phys. edn. Pembroke Coll., Providence, 1954-60; cons. Providence Sch. Dept., Curriculum Guide in Phys. Edn., 1964-66; chmn. ethics and eligibility com. Assn. Intercollegiate Athletics for Women, 1981-82. Recipient Outstanding Woman of Yr. award YWCA, 1978. Mem. AAHPER (Presdl. medallion). Nat. Assn. Phys. Edn. Coll. Women, ACLU, R.I. Assn. Health, Phys. Edn. and Recreation (honor award 1971), Brown Alumni Assn. Club: Rotary. Office: Dept Athletics and Phys Edn Brown U Providence RI 02912

GORTON, LAURIE ANN, editor; b. Buffalo, Nov. 26, 1949; d. James Wallace and Doris Ida (Torke) G.; B.A. in Journalism cum laude, U. Wis., Madison, 1971. Asso. editor Cooking for Profit, Madison, 1971-74; editor, pub. dir. Baking Industry, Putman Pub. Co., Chgo., 1974—. Mem. Old Town Players (Chgo.). Mem. Inst. Food Technologists, Am. Assn. Cereal Chemists, Am. Soc. Bakery Engrs., Bakers Courtesy Club (dir.), Phi Beta Kappa. Christian Scientist. Office: 301 E Erie St Chicago IL 60611

GOSS, JANELL JONES, duplicating and info. processing equipment co. mgr.; b. Arcadia, La., May 29, 1936; d. Grady Edward and Ethel Jane (Peevy) Jones; B.S. magna cum laude, La. State U., 1973; children—Frederick Stuart, Sherilyn Goss Short, Sharla Goss Bates. Regional equipment order entry supr. Xerox Corp., Dallas, 1973-75, mgmt. info. system analyst, 1975-76, nat. systems devel. analyst, Rochester, N.Y., 1976-78, regional mgr. equipment order entry/commn. acctg., Dallas, 1978-81, nat. mgr. equipment planning/control, Office Products Div., Dallas, 1981—. Recipient plaques for outstanding service Xerox Corp., 1978, 79, 80. Mem. Xerox Mgmt. Assn. (dir. 1975-76), AAUW, LWV, Phi Kappa Phi, Phi Lambda Pi (pres. 1972-73). Democrat. Baptist. Club: Order Eastern Star. Home: 2501 Winterstone Dr Plano TX 75023

GOSS, PATRICIA BELLAMY, missiles and space co. ofcl.; b. Montreal, Que., Can., May 21, 1944; d. Clifford J. and May Glenn (Black) Bellamy; naturalized, 1966; A.B., UCLA, 1966, M.A., 1967; Ph.D., N.Y. U., 1978; m. David J. Goss, Aug. 1, 1973; children—Jennifer Suzanne, Geoffrey Bellamy. Lectr., dir. forensics UCLA, 1967-73; asst. prof. dept. speech and theatre Herbert Lehman Coll., City U. N.Y., 1973-79; human resources specialist Lockheed Missiles and Space Co., Sunnyvale, Calif., 1980—. Named Debate Coach of Yr., Georgetown U., 1971; recipient H.A. Wichelns award for outstanding article in Free Speech Yearbook, Speech Communication Assn., 1975. Mem. Speech Communication Assn. (freedom of speech commn. 1977-79), Am. Soc. Tng. and Devel., Internat. Communication Assn. Democrat. Editor: Media Ecology Rev. 1975-76; contbr. articles to jours. Home: 2481 Alpine Rd Menlo Park CA 94025 Office: 1111 Lockheed Way Sunnyvale CA 94086

GOSS, SUSAN LEIGH, writer, editor; b. Hornell, N.Y., Feb. 14, 1951; d. Leigh Buckner and Janet Ann (Johnson) Egbert; B.A. in English, Alfred U., 1973; postgrad. (Gannett Newspaper scholar) Mich. State U. Sch. Journalism, 1976-77; m. Edward Alexander Clay, Sept. 9, 1978; 1 dau., Rachel Scott. Tech. writer/editor Nat. Elevator Industry Ednl. Program, Rochester, N.Y., 1979—. Mem. Kappa Tau Alpha. Episcopalian. Writer, editor Elevator Constructor jour., 1979—; editor: NEIEP Elevator Terms, An Illustrated Glossary, 1980. Home: 66C Windsorshire Dr Rochester NY 14624 Office: 1664 N Clinton Ave Rochester NY 14621

GOSSETT, DORIS ELLIS, govt. EDP ofcl.; b. Wilmington, Ohio, Dec. 27, 1939; d. John Leonard and Rachel Jeanette (Wilson) Ellis; B.A. in Math., Miami U., 1961; cert. in tech. of mgmt. Am. U., 1977. Programmer/mathematician Research Computation Div., Naval Research Lab., Washington, 1961-66, supervisory mathematician, 1967, tech. cons., 1968-74, dep. head, 1974—. Mem. NOW, Pi Mu Epsilon. Democrat. Office: Code 2801 Naval Research Lab Washington DC 20375

GOSSMAN, JOYCE MAVIS MILLER, dietitian; b. Oconto Falls, Wis., Sept. 28, 1923; d. Reinhold Edward and Florence Ann (Miller) Miller; B.S., U. Wis., Stout, 1945; M.S., Mankato State U., 1980; m. John J. Cahill, June 7, 1947 (dec.); 1 son, Edward Jefferson; m. 2d, Karl William Gossman, Apr. 25, 1952 (dec.); children—Karl William, David Paul. Pediatric dietitian Anchor Hosp., St. Paul, 1950-51; dietitian Riverview Hosp., St. Paul, 1952; clin. dietitian Rochester (Minn.) Meth. Hosp., 1956-60, head dietitian, 1960-66, head adminstrv. dietitian, 1966-76, dir. dietary edn., 1976—. Served with AC, U.S. Army, 1946-47. Recipient Alumni Distinguished Service award U. Wis., Stout, 1976. Mem. Am., Minn. (past state pres.) dietetic assns., Am. Home Econs. Assn., Soc. for Nutrition Edn., AAUW, Am. Legion Aux. (past pres.), Phi Upsilon Omicron, Phi Kappa Phi. Republican. Lutheran. Home: 2062 26th Ave NW Rochester MN 55901 Office: Rochester Meth Hosp Rochester MN 55901

GOSS-MOFFITT, NINA BESS, psychiatrist; b. Brookhaven, Miss., Aug. 13, 1926; d. Isaac Alanson and Aubrey Reid (Corban) Goss; B.S., Millsaps Coll., 1946; M.D., Tulane U., 1950; m. Ellis M. Moffitt, June 12, 1954; children—John Ellis, Virginia Ellen. Intern, St. Elizabeth's Hosp., Washington, 1950-52; staff physician Miss. State Hosp., Whitfield, 1952-53, 54-61; practice medicine specializing in family medicine, Natchez, Miss., 1953-55, Jackson, Miss., 1955-61; staff physician Western State Hosp., Staunton, Va., 1961-62; resident in psychiatry U. Louisville, 1962-64, U. Miss., 1965-66; cons. psychiatry Bur. Mental Health Services, Miss. State Bd. Health, Jackson, 1965-69, dir. bur., 1970-75; practice medicine specializing in psychiatry, Jackson, 1975—; mem. staff U. Miss. Med. Center, Doctors Hosp.; asst. clin. prof. U. Miss. Med. Center; bd. dirs. Miss. Found. for Med. Care; cons. alcohol and drug unit Doctors Hosp. Pres. PTA, Lester Sch., Jackson, 1968-70. Mem. Central Med. Soc., Miss. State Med. Assn., So. Med. Assn., Miss. Psychiat. Assn. (newsletter editor 1973-81, treas. 1981-82), Am. Psychiat. Assn. Babtist. Office: 940 N State St Jackson MS 39201

GOTHAM, DONNA SORENSON, devel. group exec.; b. Valley City, N.D., Sept. 21, 1944; d. Frank H. and Ellen Lindner Sorenson; B.S., N.D. State U., 1967; M.B.A., Keller Grad. Sch. Bus., 1977; m. Robert M. Gotham, May 26, 1973; children— Brooks Miller, Hunter Matthew. Consumer specialist Hotpoint-GE, Chgo., public relations 1967-72; Nat. Portion Control, Chgo., 1972-72; research home economist Central Soya, Chgo., 1973-76; owner, mgr. Gotham Interiors and Apts., Chgo., 1976—. Mem. Claridon Park Owners Assn. Presbyterian. Club: Ski. Home: 3721 N Greenview Chicago IL 60613 Office: 921 Belle Plaine Chicago IL 60613

GOTHARD, DONITA, psychologist, educator, rancher; b. Minden, La., June 9, 1932; d. Donald Elmer and Nita (Brunt) Gothard; B.A., Northwestern State U. La., 1954, M.Ed., 1961; Ph.D., U. Ala., 1970. Tchr., Bossier (La.) Parish Schs., 1954-61, counselor, 1961-67; instr. Northwestern State U. of La., 1967-68; dir. human relations Caddo (La.) Parish Schs., 1970-71, sch. psychologist, 1971-73; asst. prof. psychology La. State U., Shreveport, 1973-76, asso. prof., 1976-81, prof., 1981—, also coordinator specialist degree of sch. psychology; founder, pres. West Park Psychol. Services, Inc. Mem. adv. bd. N.W. La. Childbirth Edn. Assn. Mem. Am., La., N.W. La. (past pres.) psychol. assns., La. Acad. Scis., Am. Miniature Schnauzer Assn. Home: Route 1 Box 166 Keatchie LA 71046

GOTHARD, HEATHER MCCLOUD, educator; b. Birmingham, Eng., Feb. 4, 1947; came to U.S., 1947; d. Frank James and Barbara (Bax) McCloud; B.S., U. Tenn., Chattanooga, 1972, M.Ed., 1974; m. Terry Joseph Gothard, Aug. 31, 1967. Tchr. Daisy Child Devel. Center, Chattanooga, 1968-72; lead tchr. Summit Child Devel. Center, Chattanooga, 1972-73, Bakewell Child Devel. Center, Chattanooga, 1973-75; ednl. coordinator, career devel. coordinator Hamilton County Child Devel. Program, Chattanooga, 1975—; extension tchr. Western Ky. U., Chattanooga State Tech. Community Coll.; adv. com. Child Care Center, Chattanooga State Tech. Community Coll.; mem. craft com. child care program Sequoyah Vocat. Sch.; leader workshops, speaker, lectr. in field. Mem. planning com. Chattanooga Nature Center, 1978, chmn. pre-sch. sect., 1978. Cert. child devel. asso. Mem. Nat. Assn. Edn. Young Children, So. Assn. Edn. Young Children, Tenn. Assn. Young Children (exhibits chmn. 1979), Chattanooga Assn. Young Children (workshop chmn. 1980), Am. Contract Bridge League, Ranger Rick Nature Club, Smithsonian Instn. Democrat. Methodist. Home: 5 Shingle Rd Chattanooga TN 37409 Office: 201 Broad St Chattanooga TN 37402

GOTT, HELEN J., social services agy. adminstr.; b. Gainesville, Mo., June 30, 1934; d. Lonza Daniel and Helen Margaret (Ebrite) Blisard; B.S., Drury Coll., 1971; student Nat. Judicial Coll., Reno, 1979-81; m. Charles L. Gott, June 8, 1954 (div.); children—Joseph L., Lynette, With Ozark County Times, Gainesville, 1953-54; with Modern Telephone Co., Gainesville, 1955-57; caseworker div. family services Mo. Dept. Social Services, Mountain Grove, 1958-71, county dir., 1971-73, asst. dist. supr., 1973-75, fair hearing officer, 1975-79, hearings unit supr. and adminstrv. asst. to gen. counsel gen. counsel div., Jefferson City, 1979—. Mem. Nat. Assn. Adminstrv. Law Judges, Am. Public Welfare Assn. Mem. Order Eastern Star (past matron). Home: Shepherd Hills Manor Apt 306 Jefferson City MO 65101 Office: Gen Counsel Div Dept Social Services Broadway State Office Bldg Jefferson City MO 65101

GOTTESMAN, ELEANOR BELL, psychologist; b. Cleve.; d. George and Jeanette (Klein) Gluckman; B.A. in Psychology, George Washington U., 1947, M.A. in Clin. Psychology, 1963; postgrad. Ackerman Family Inst., 1974-75; m. Callman Gottesman, Aug. 2, 1964; children—Erika Bell, Barbara Bell Sudbury, Carol Gottesman Siegel. Psychologist, D.C. Gen. Hosp., 1961-64, Bethesda (Md.) Community Psychiat. Clinic, 1961-64, Nassau (N.Y.) County Schs., Rockville Center, East Rockaway, N.Y., Hempstead, N.Y., Elmont, N.Y., 1965-70, Richardson-Bellows Henry Mgmt. Cons., N.Y.C., Washington, 1970-71, Jewish Child Care Assn., N.Y.C., Pleasantville, N.Y., 1973—; pvt. practice psychology, N.Y.C., 1974—; chmn. social service com. Stephenwise Free Synagogue; mem. exec. com., 1981—. Agnes and Eugene Meyer grantee; lic. clin. psychologist, sch. psychologist, N.Y. State; Nat. Register Health Service Providers in Psychology. Mem. Am. Psychol. Assn., Council for Nat. Register Health Service Providers in Psychology, Psi Chi. Originator body image identification test; contbr. articles to profl. jours. Home and Office: 1 W 72nd St New York NY 10023 also Pleasantville Cottage Sch Pleasantville NY 10570

GOTTFRIED, MARTHA ANN, real estate broker; b. Evansville, Ind., Apr. 21, 1937; d. Francis J. and Mildred E. (Schatz) Heines; student U. Evansville, 1958, Palm Beach Jr. Coll., 1971; m. Robert W. Gottfried, Nov. 13, 1970. Sec. production control Mead Johnson & Co., Evansville, 1956-61, sec., v.p. internat. div., 1961-63, sec., pres. internat. div., 1963-67, adminstrv. asst., chmn. bd., 1967-70; corp. sec.-treas., dir. Robert W. Gottfried, Inc., Palm Beach, Fla., 1970—; pres. Martha A. Gottfried, Inc., Real Estate, Palm Beach, 1977—; owner Gwen Fearing Real Estate, Palm Beach, 1979—; mem. adv. bd. First Am. Bank, Palm Beach, 1978—. Mem. Internat. Fedn. Real Estate Fedn., Nat. Womens Council Realtors, Palm Beach Bd. Realtors (dir.), Palm Beach Civic Assn. Roman Catholic. Club: Poinciana (Palm Beach). Home: 301 Polmer Park Palm Beach FL 33480 Office: 241 Worth Ave Palm Beach FL 33480

GOTTLER, THELMA ELIZABETH, home economist; b. Pensacola, Fla., Aug. 19, 1950; d. John Peter and Thelma Shepard G.; B.S., U. Montevallo, 1972, M.A.T., 1974. Tchr. home econs. Geneva County High Sch., Hartford, Ala., 1972-73; with 4-H home econs. program Morgan County Extension Service, Hartselle, Ala., 1974—, asso. county agt. 4-H, 1978—; adv. Morgan County Cowbelles, 1977—. Historian, Holy Family Catholic Ch., Hartselle, 1978—. Recipient Home Econs. scholarship Baldwin County Homemakers Council, 1968. Mem. Nat. Assn. Extension 4-H Agts., Nat. Assn. Extension Home Economists, Nat. Home Econs. Assn., Ala. Assn. Extension 4-H Agts. (sec., v.p., then pres.), Ala. Assn. Extension Home Economists, Ala. Home Econs. Assn. Roman Catholic. Club: Ladies (Hartselle). Office: PO Box 98 Hartselle AL 35640

GOTTLIEB, LUCILLE MONTROSE FOX, ret. state ofcl.; b. Hartford, Conn., May 30, 1929; d. Louis Paul and Rose Tomasina (Vignone) Montrose; student Cambridge Sch. Bus. Sci., 1948, Hillyer Jr. Coll., 1950; m. Francis R. Fox, Jr., June 26, 1954; m. 2d, Ralph Gottlieb, Sept. 28, 1979. Adminstrv. fiscal mgmt. officer Conn. Hwy. Dept., Hartford, 1950-61, asst. pub. relations dir., 1961-65, personnel asst., 1965-70; liaison officer Conn. Dept. Transp., 1970—; sec., treas. Shoreline Communications Inc., 1976—. Chmn. Rocky Hill Park Com., 1968, Pool and Teen Center Com., 1976-77, Park and Recreation Adv. Bd., 1969; mem. Govs. Environ. Policy Com., 1972-74; chmn. Park and Recreation Adv. Bd., 1970; v.p. Gov's. Environ. Policy Panel on Travel and Transp.; trustee Bicentennial Council 13 Original States, 1978. Mem. NCCJ, Antiquarian Landmarks Soc. Conn., Fedn. Bus. and Profl. Women (chmn. pub. relations com.), Pub. Personnel Assn. Greater Hartford (v.p.), Conn. Employees Assn., Nat. Resources Council Conn., Great Meadow Conservation Trust, Conn. Pub. Health Assn., Women in Communications (v.p. Conn. chpt. 1978), Conn. Hist. Com., Conn. Italian-Am. Cultural Assn. (pres. 1978), Met. Opera Guild. Democrat. Roman Catholic. Clubs: Lady Hilton VIP, Cosmopolitan Hartford, Officers of Conn. (gov.). Creator Gertie Glitter anti litter symbol. Home: 150 Crestview Rd Manchester NH 03104 also 3500 Galt Ocean Dr Fort Lauderdale FL 33308

GOTTLIEB, MARISE SUSS, epidemiologist; b. N.Y.C., July 16, 1938; d. Lester J. and Fannie (Freeman) Suss; A.B., Barnard Coll., 1958; M.D., N.Y.U., 1962; M.P.H. in Epidemiology, Harvard U., 1966; m. A. Arthur Gottlieb, June 8, 1958; children—Mindy C., Joanne M. Intern in medicine Mass. Meml. Hosp., Boston, 1962-63; med. officer NIH, Bethesda, Md., 1963-65; resident in epidemiology Harvard U. Med. Sch., 1965-68, from research fellow to instr. medicine, 1966-70; dir. chronic disease services and public health N.J. Dept. Health, 1970-72; asst. prof. dept. community medicine Coll. Medicine and Dentistry N.J., Rutgers U. Med. Sch., Piscataway, N.J., 1972-75; assoc. prof. medicine Sch. Medicine, Tulane U., 1975—, assoc. prof. epidemiology, Sch. Pub. Health, 1975-80; chief chronic disease control program Office Health Services and Environ. Quality, La. Dept. Health and Human Resources, 1975—. Mem. health effects rev. panel EPA, 1981—; sec.-treas. S.E. La. Med. Quality Rev. Fedn., 1979—; spl. research fellow Nat. Inst. Arthritis and Metabolic Diseases, 1966-68. Mem. Am. Fedn. Clin. Research, Soc. Epidemiol. Research, Am. Diabetes Assn., Am. Public Health Assn., Am. Heart Assn. (epidemiology council). Author papers in field. Office: 1430 Tulane Ave New Orleans LA 70112

GOUDY, JOSEPHINE GRAY, social worker; b. Des Moines, Nov. 30, 1925; d. Gerald William and Myrtle Maria (Brooks) Gray; B.A., State U. Iowa, 1953, M.S.W., 1966; m. John Winston Goudy, June 5, 1948; children—Tracy Jean, Paula Rae. Child welfare supr. Iowa Dept. Social Services, 1960-68; psychiat. social worker Community Mental Health Center Scott County (Iowa), 1966-71; social work instr. Palmer Jr. Coll., Davenport, Iowa, 1967-70; psychiat. social worker, chief social services Jacksonville (Ill.) State Mental Hosp., 1971-74; coordinator community mental health outpatient services McFarland Mental Health Center, Springfield, Ill., 1974; exec. dir. Macoupin County Mental Health Center, Carlinville, Ill., 1974—; chmn. Human Services Edn. Council, Springfield, 1979-81; past exec. Davenport Community Welfare Council. Mem. Nat. Assn. Social Workers, Acad. Cert. Social Workers, Am. Personnel and Guidance Assn., AAUW (br. pres. 1964-66, mem. state bar 1966-68, br. grantee 1975), Internat. Fedn. U. Women, U. Iowa Alumni Assn., Bus. and Profl. Women, Delta Kappa Gamma. Republican. Methodist. Club: Carlinville Women's (pres. 1975-77). Home: 364 W Tremont St Waverly IL 62692 Office: 100 N Side Sq Carlinville IL 62626

GOUGÉ, SUSAN CORNELIA JONES (MRS. JOHN OSCAR GOUGÉ), microbiologist; b. Chgo., Apr. 18, 1924; d. Harry LeRoy and Gladys (Moon) Jones; student Am. U., Washington, 1942-43, La. Coll., 1944-45; B.S., George Washington U., 1948; postgrad. Georgetown U., 1956-58, 66-69, Goddard grad. program Vt. Coll., Norwich U., 1981—; m. John Oscar Gougé, Aug. 7, 1943; children—John Ronald, Richard Michael, Claudia Renée Gougé Carr. Med. technician Children's Hosp. Research Lab., Washington, 1948-49; bacteriologist George Washington U. Research Lab., D.C. Gen. Hosp., 1950-53; med. microbiologist Walter Reed Army Inst. Research, Washington, 1953-61; research asst. Dental Research, Walter Reed Army Med. Center, 1961-62; microbiologist antibiotics div. FDA, 1962-63; supr. quality control John D. Copanos Co., Pharms., Balt., 1963-64; research tng. asst., infectious diseases and tropical medicine Howard U. Med. Sch., 1964-65; research asso. Georgetown U. Lab. Infectious Diseases, D.C. Gen. Hosp., 1966-69; mycologist Georgetown U. Hosp. Lab., 1969-70; microbiologist The Research Found. of The Washington Hosp. Center, 1971-73; dir. quality control Bio-Medium Corp., Silver Spring, Md., 1973-76; microbiologist Alcolac, Balt., 1976-77; microbiologist div. of labs. Dept. Human Resources, Community Health and Hosps. Adminstrn., Washington, 1978-79; microbiologist div. ophthalmic ENT and dental devices Office Med. Devices, Nat. Center Devices and Radiol. Health, FDA, 1979—. Sec. to exec. bd. Bethesda Project Awareness, 1970-71; cons. lead poisoning detection testing project D.C. Office Vols. for Internat. Tech. Assistance, 1970-71, recipient medal for community service; vol. Zacchaeus Free Med. Clinic, Washington, 1979—; mem. Parish Social Concerns Com. Mem. Nat. Capital Harp Ensemble, 1941-65. Mem. Women's Suburban Democratic Club. Registered microbiologist Nat. Registry Microbiologists; specialist microbiologist, Am. Acad. Microbiology. Mem. AAAS, Am. Soc. for Microbiology, Am. Assn. Clin. Chemists, Am. Chem. Soc., Am. Inst. Biol. Scis., N.Y. Acad. Scis., Am. Public Health Assn., Albertus Magnus Guild, Capital Bus. and Profl. Women's Club (rec. sec. 1973-74, 1st v.p. 1974-75, pres. 1975-76), Pi Kappa Delta. Roman Catholic. Club: Toastmasters (sec. 1979-80). Home: 4101 Maryland Ave Bethesda MD 20816 Office: Bur Med Devices FDA 8757 Georgia Ave Silver Spring MD 20910

GOUGH, JESSIE POST (MRS. HERBERT FREDERICK GOUGH), ret. educator; b. Nakon Sri Tamaraj, Thailand, Jan. 26, 1907 (parents Am. citizens); d. Richard Walter and Mame (Stebbins) Post; B.A., Maryville Coll., 1927; M.A. in English, U. Chgo., 1928; Ed.D., U. Ga., 1965; m. Herbert Frederick Gough, June 30, 1934; children—Joan Acland (Mrs. Alexander Reed), Herbert Frederick. Tchr. English, Linden Hall, Lititz, Pa., 1930-32; tchr. Fairyland Sch., Lookout Mountain, Tenn., 1955-64; research asst. English curriculum studies center U. Ga., 1964-65; asso. prof. elem. edn. LaGrange (Ga.) Coll., 1965-73, prof., 1973-75; prof. N.W. Ga. area tchr. edn. services, 1969-71. Mem. Walker County (Ga.) Curriculum Council, 1959-61, Walker County Ednl. Planning Bd., 1958-60. Mem. Am. Ednl. Research Assn., Internat. Reading Assn., East Tenn. Hist. Soc., Nat., Ga. edn. assns., Delta Kappa Gamma. Home: 8111 Savannah Hills Dr Ooltewah TN 37363

GOUGH, MARGARET ELLEN, newspaper pub., editor; b. Boise, Idaho, Jan. 6, 1926; d. Everett Bancroft and Mabel Jean (Kennington) Knipe; student Coll. of Idaho, Caldwell, 1944-46; m. Theron McParlin Gough, Aug. 23, 1946 (dec. 1979); children—Teresa Ellen, Theron Thayne Timothy McParlin, Thomas Everett. Pub., editor Parma (Idaho) Rev., 1979—. Tchr. ch. sch., del. nat. women's conv., elder, youth leader United United Presbyterian Ch.; past pres. local PTA; organizer, past pres. West Canyon County Republican Women, Treasure Valley Toastmistress Club; bd. dirs. Caldwell Community Found., 1980—; adv. bd. Canyon County Soil Conservation Dist. 208; former Cub Scout leader; registrar of elections, head election judge, 1955-79. Recipient Jaycee Disting. Service award Parma Jaycees, 1955. Mem. Idaho Press Assn., Nat. Press Assn., Coll. of Idaho Alumni Assn., Parma C. of C. (dir.). Home: 4th and Tucker Sts Parma ID 83660 Office: Parma Review 2d St Parma ID 83660

GOUGH, PAULINE BJERKE, magazine editor; b. Wadena, Minn., Jan. 7, 1935; d. Luther C. and Zita Pauline (Halbmaier) Bjerke; B.A., U. Minn., Mpls., 1957; B.S., Moorhead (Minn.) State Coll., 1970; M.S., Ind. U., Bloomington, 1972, Ed.D., 1977; children—Mary Pauline, Sarah Elizabeth, Philip Clayton. Reporter women's page San Jose (Calif.) Mercury-News, 1957-58; with research dept. Campbell-Mithun Advt., Mpls., 1958-60; tchr. Univ. Elem. Sch., Bloomington, 1970-79; freelance writer Agy. Instructional TV, Bloomington, 1974-80; mem. adj. faculty Ind. U.-Purdue U., Indpls., summers 1976, 77; asst. editor Phi Delta Kappan, Bloomington, 1980-81, mng. editor, 1981—; mem. profl. staff Phi Delta Kappa, 1981—, also leader insts. on writing for publ. Recipient Disting. Alumna award Moorhead State U., 1982. Mem. Women in Communications, Phi Beta Kappa, Phi Delta Kappa, Pi Lambda Theta. Author articles in field. Home: 113 N Concord Rd Bloomington IN 47401 Office: Phi Delta Kappa PO Box 789 Bloomington IN 47402

GOULARD, SARAH REED, banker; b. Washington, Aug. 31, 1945; d. Everett Maurice and Marion Reed (Ganzenmuller) G.; grad. Smith Coll., 1967; m. Hiram I. Moudy, Jr., May 24, 1980. With Morgan Quaranty Trust Co., N.Y.C., 1967—, portfolio mgr. investment dept., until 1978, v.p. banking group, 1979—. Corporator Dana Hall Sch., Wellesley, Mass. Home: 14 E 90th St New York NY 10028 Office: 23 Wall St New York NY 10015

GOULD, JANE S., coll. adminstr.; b. Pleasantville, N.Y., Mar. 25, 1918; d. Irvin and Helen (Hays) Auerbach; B.A., Barnard Coll., 1940; M.A., Tchrs. Coll., Columbia U., 1970; m. Bernard M. Schwartz, Aug. 4, 1942 (dec. Jan. 1967); children—Nancy, David; m. 2d, Jay M. Gould, Oct. 17, 1969. Asst. dir. Alumnae Adv. Center, N.Y.C., 1954-65; dir. placement and career planning Barnard Coll., N.Y.C., 1965-73, dir. Women's Center, 1972—; bd. dirs. Seven Coll. Vocat. Workshops, 1962-66, supr. Community Service Workshops, 1966-68; bd. dirs. Women's Counseling Project, 1976—. Mem. Nat. Assn. Women Deans and Counselors. Author: Part-Time Employment: Employer Attitudes on Opportunities for the College Trained Woman, 1964. Contbr. articles to ednl. jours. Home: 302 W 86th St New York NY 10024 Office: Women's Center Barnard Coll 606 W 120th St New York NY 10027

GOULD, JANICE SANDRA, stockbroker; b. St. Louis, Dec. 20, 1942; d. Gilbrt Raymond and Frances Elizabeth (Ellingsworth) Caldwell; B.A., U. Iowa, 1967; student Simpson Coll., 1961-62, Drake U., summer 1974; children—Troy Bryan, Jonna Ryon. Med. sec., 1965-67; legal sec., 1967-68; real estate salesperson Las Vegas, 1973-75; stockbroker Dain Bosworth Inc., Des Moines, 1974-82, Edward D. Jones & Co., Ankeny, Iowa, 1982—; substitute tchr. high sch., Las Vegas, 1973; condr. investment/market seminars. Mem. citizens ad hoc com. Law Sch. U. Nev. Las Vegas, pres., sec., organizer, lobbyist; mem. adv. bd. Bd. Regents Law Sch., also adv. bd. historian; bd. dirs. Clark County Central Republican Com., 1969-82, state conv. del., election bd. chm., state credential com.; mem. Warren County Rep. Central Com., 1979—, county conv. del., 1980, 82; pres. Tri T.A.G. parents gifted children; tchr. secondary level Sunday Sch. Mem. PEO (charter chpt. pres., state conv. del.), AAUW (state legis. chmn., del. nat. conv. 1975), U. Iowa Alumni Assn., Alpha Xi Delta. Clubs: Zonta (fin. com., advt. com. for projects, seminar speaker 1982), La. Sertoma. Home: 1307 E Detroit St Indianola IA 50125 Office: 106 SW Linden St Suite 1E Ankeny IA 50021

GOULD, JUDITH CAPLAN, legal guardian, former mental health agy. ofcl.; b. Phila., June 6, 1933; d. Albert Joseph and Sylvia (Bayuk) Caplan; A.B. in Polit. Sci., Goucher Coll., 1955; M.P.A., U. South Fla., 1980; children—Julia Bayuk, Gwendolyn Elspeth. Asst. to mng. editor Phila. Legal Intelligencer, 1955-61; commr. City of Dunedin (Fla.), 1972-76, mayor, 1976-78; adminstrv. asst. Pinellas-Pasco Dist. Mental Health Bd. V, Largo, Fla., 1980-81; legal guardian, 1981—; mediator Citizens Dispute Settlement Program; instr. St. Petersburg (Fla.) Jr. Coll., Clearwater, Fla., 1979. Chmn., Pinellas Planning Council, 1976-77; sec. Met. Planning Orgn., 1977-78; pres. LWV of Clearwater Area, 1969-71; active Sci. Center Pinellas County, Common Cause; pres. Dunedin Friends of Library, 1982; bd. govs. Dunedin Civic Assn. Recipient Women Honoring Women award Soroptimist Internat. Upper Pinellas County, 1977, Voice of Democracy cert. VFW, 1977, citation for service DAV, 1977. Mem. Am. Soc. Public Adminstrn., Dunedin C. of C., Dunedin Hist. Soc., Jr. Service League Dunedin. Republican. Jewish. Clubs: Hadassah, Zonta of Upper Pinellas County. Home: 2346 Demaret Dr Dunedin FL 33528

GOULD, JULIETTE L., pub. co. exec.; b. N.Y.C., Nov. 11, 1935; d. Jack and Nettie K. Lobsenz; B.A., Syracuse U., 1955; M.A., N.Y. U., 1957; M.A., Tchrs. Coll., Columbia U., 1968; m. Gene G. Gould, June 27, 1959; children—Jason Harris, Evan Lewis. Asst. to fashion dir. Doyle Dane Bernbach, N.Y.C., 1957-59, Town & Country Shoes, N.Y.C., 1959-61; promotion coordinator Simplicity Patterns, N.Y.C., 1961-64; v.p. corp. ratings Standard & Poor's Corp., N.Y.C., 1967—. Mem. Women's Econ. Round Table. Independent Democrat. Office: Standard & Poor's Corp 25 Broadway New York NY 10004 *

GOULD, MAXINE LUBOW, oil and gas co. exec.; b. Bridgeton, N.J., Feb. 28, 1942; d. Louis A. and Bernice L. (Goldberg) Lubow; B.S., Temple U., 1962, J.D., 1968; m. Sam C. Gould, June 17, 1962; children—Jack, Herman, David. Head resident dept. student personnel Temple U., 1962-66; dir., treas. Hilltop Interest Program, Inc., Los Angeles, 1973-74; law clk. law firms, Los Angeles, 1975-77; with Buffalo Resources Corp., Los Angeles, 1978-82, corp. sec., 1979-82; corp. sec., securities prin. Buffalo Securities Corp., Los Angeles, 1979-82; corp. sec. LaMaur Devel. Corp., Los Angeles, 1979-82; contracts analyst, land dept. Texaco Inc., Los Angeles, 1982—. Mem. Roscomare Valley Assn. Edn. Com., Bel Air, Calif., 1975-76; subcom. chmn. Roscomare Rd. Sch. Citizens Adv. Council, Bel Air; active various community drives. Recipient Joseph B. Wagner Oratory award B'nai B'rith, 1959, Voice of Democracy award, 1958-59, award Commentator Club, 1959. Mem. Nat. Assn. Female Execs. (network dir.), Calif. Women Lawyers, Women in Bus., Am. Assn. Petroleum Landmen, Los Angeles Assn. Petroleum Landmen, Phi Alpha Theta, Alpha Lambda Delta. Jewish. Home: 2501 Roscomare Rd Bel Air CA 90077

GOULSON, JO PINNELL, biomed. research adminstr., sculptor, musician; b. Birmingham, Ala., July 31, 1926; d. John W. and Frances (Moores) Pinnell; B.S., U. Ala., 1947; postgrad. Yale U. Div. Sch., 1947-48, Woman's Med. Coll. Pa., 1948-50, U. Mich. Med. Sch., 1950, Tulane U. Med. Sch., 1951; M.S. in Public Health, U. N.C., 1954; m. Hilton Thomas Goulson, Aug. 21, 1954; children—Daniel Thomas, Amy Frances. Adminstrv. asst. Wyeth Inst. Applied Biology, Phila., 1951-53; research asst. U. N.C. Sch. Medicine, Chapel Hill, 1954-61, research asso. Center for Research in Pharmacology and Toxicology, 1965-67, research asso. U. N.C. Dental Research Center, 1968-82, head office of communication/edn., 1976-82, research asso., tchr. sci. writing seminar dept. parasitology Sch. Public Health, 1977—; free lance editor and grants cons., 1961—; vol. editorial cons. Schs. Dentistry and Medicine, 1968—; wood sculpture tchr. Durham (N.C.) Arts Council, 1974-76; percussion tchr.; percussionist with U. N.C. Symphony Orch., 1954-68, U. N.C. Playmakers Theater, 1955-64, U. N.C. Opera Theater, 1953-55, Village Band, Chapel Hill, 1974—, Durham Symphony, 1978; percussionist Community Youth Theater, Chapel Hill, 1977—, v.p. band parents assn., 1981-82; vol. sculpture lectr. Chapel Hill public schs., 1969. Mem. subcom. on research and innovation Gov.'s Commn. on Public Sch. Edn. in N.C., 1968-69; vol. United Fund; ch. sch. supt. United Ch. of Christ, 1958-60, chmn. bd. deacons, 1973-74, chmn. pastoral relations com., 1979—; pres. Chapel Hill Ch. Women United, 1972; sec. Inter-Ch. Council for Social Services, 1968-70; bd. dirs. Orange County Mental Health Assn., 1974-75. Mem. Am. Crafts Council, Carolina Designer Craftsmen (sec. 1970-73, 78-80, pres. 1982—), Nat. Woodcarvers Assn., S.E. Sculptors Assn., N.C. Crafts Assn., N.Y. Acad. Scis., Durham Art Guild, N.C. Fedn. Women's Clubs (historian dist. 8 1971-72, pres. 1969-70), U. N.C. Public Health Alumni Assn. (sec. 1979-80), Am. Assn. Med. Writers, Soc. Tech. Communicators, AAAS, Sigma Xi, Alpha Epsilon Delta. Club: Chapel Hill Woman's (pres. 1963-66, trustee 1967-70, chmn. fin. com. 1977—). Home: 52 Oakwood Dr Chapel Hill NC 27514 Office: Dept Parasitology Sch Public Health U NC Chapel Hill NC 27514

GOUNARIS, ANNE DEMETRA, biochemist, educator; b. Boston, Oct. 27, 1924; d. Demetrios Themistocles and Kaliope (Gouvalaris) G.; diploma Mass. Gen. Hosp. Sch. Nursing, 1946; A.B., Boston U., 1955; Ph.D., Harvard U., 1960; M.A. (Ann Horton research fellow), Newnham Coll., Cambridge U., 1980. Research asso., NIH fellow, Brookhaven Nat. Lab., 1960-62; research asso. Carlsberg Lab., Copenhagen, 1962-64, Rockefeller U., N.Y.C., 1964-66; prof. chemistry Vassar Coll., Poughkeepsie, N.Y., 1966—; vis. fellow in medicine Mass. Gen. Hosp., 1978—. Rask-Osted fellow, Denmark, 1963-64; NIH research grantee, 1968-71, 72-75; named to Collegium of Disting. Alumni, Boston U., 1974. Mem. Am. Soc. Biol. Chemists, Am. Chem. Soc., AAAS, N.Y. Acad. Scis., AAUP, Phi Beta Kappa, Sigma Xi. Contbr. articles to biochemistry jours. Office: Vassar College PO Box 349 Poughkeepsie NY 12601

GOURDINE, VANESSA WRYDER, writer, publisher, psychologist; b. Orange, N.J., Nov. 13, 1953; d. William and Beatrice Celeste (Comito) G.; B.A., Rutgers U., 1975, D.Clin. Psychology; M.A., Montclair State Coll., 1978. Pres., owner Tng. Tech. for Bus., Montclair, N.J., 1978—; editor, owner Human Resource Mgmt. Newsletter, 1980—; writer EDP Tng. News, 1979-81; editor Lowe Investment and Fin. Letter, Lowe Stock Adv., 1978-80; writer, researcher AT&T, 1980-81; psychologist St. Mary's Hosp., Passaic, N.J., 1981—; adj. instr. Middlesex County Coll., Edison, N.J., 1981—; cons. Midatlantic Nat. Bank, Wessex Assos.; columnist N.J. Voice, 1978—. Mem. Am. Soc. Tng. and Devel., Writers' Guild. also PO Box 394 Montclair NJ 07042 Office: Social Scis Dept Middlesex County College Edison NJ 08817

GOURLEY, ANN BOOSE, univ. mgmt. services officer; b. Somerset, Pa., Aug. 9, 1947; d. George Park and Nancy (Boose) G.; student U. Pitts., 1965-67; A.B. magna cum laude in Psychology (NSF undergrad. research fellow), Clark U., Worcester, Mass., 1970; Mgmt. fellow U. Calif., San Francisco, 1980. Asst. to dir. summer sch. Clark U., 1970-72; asst. to pres. Innerspace Environs., Inc., San Francisco, 1972-75; mgmt. services officer U. Calif., San Francisco, 1975—. Mem. Nat. Assn. Adminstrv. Coordinators, Gen. Clin. Research Centers, NIH, Soc. Research Adminstrs., Clark U. Alumni Council, Phi Beta Kappa, Psi Chi. Home: 330 Parnassus Ave #105 San Francisco CA 94117 Office: 1202 Moffitt Hospital U Calif San Francisco CA 94143

GOVINDJEE, RAJNI VARMA, biophysicist; b. Meerut, India, May 31, 1936; came to U.S., 1957, naturalized, 1972; d. Avadh and Nand (Rani) Narain; B.Sc. in Biology and Chemistry, U. Allahabad, 1953, M.Sc. in Botany (Srivilas scholar 1953-54, Univ. scholar 1953-55), 1955; Ph.D. in Botany, U. Ill., Champaign-Urbana, 1961; m. Govindjee, Oct. 24, 1957; children—Anita, Sanjay. Govt. of India sr. research scholar U. Allahabad, 1955-57; grad. fellow botany U. Ill., 1957-59, research asst., then USPHS postdoctoral fellow, 1959-63, research assoc. botany, 1963-68, sr. research assoc. in biophysics, 1968—; vis. scientist CNRS, France, 1967, U. Leiden (Netherlands), 1976. Mem. Am. Soc. Photobiology, Sigma Xi. Author articles in field. Home: 2401 S Boudreau Dr Urbana IL 61801

GOVONI, JEAN OFFUTT, advt. agy. exec.; b. Washington, Sept. 24, 1951; d. William Ernest, Jr. and Jean (Riggles) Offutt; B.F.A. cum laude, Syracuse (N.Y.) U., 1973. Art dir. Rozicer Trotter Advt., Washington, 1973; graphic designer Fannell Studio, Boston, 1973; with Dancer Fitzgerald Sample, Inc., N.Y.C., 1974—, art dir., 1975—, producer, 1978—, v.p., 1980—; mem. faculty Sch. Visual Arts, N.Y.C., 1980—. Recipient award N.Y. Art Dirs. Club, 1981, U.S. TV Comml. Festival, 1980, One Club, 1981, C/10 award, 1981. Office: 405 Lexington Ave New York NY 10017

GOVONI, VIRGINIA DELISO, aluminum foundry exec.; b. Bklyn., Mar. 24, 1934; d. Joseph John and Jennie Adeline (Ambrosino) D.; B.A., Coll. New Rochelle, 1955; student Springfield Coll., 1970; m. Veni Govoni, Jan. 21, 1967. Cost analyst Toolkraft Corp., Springfield, Mass., 1959-62; mgr. personnel, adminstrv. asst. Hampden Brass & Aluminum Co., Springfield, 1962—, vice-pres. HBA Cast Products Co., 1976—; dir. Pioneer Valley Refrigerated Warehouse, Chicopee, Mass., Stevens-Walden Corp., Worcester, Mass.; trustee Springfield Instn. for Savs., 1978—. Bd. dirs. Springfield Civic Center-Symphony Hall, Am. Heart Assn., YMCA; trustee, treas. Springfield Library and Mus. Assn.; corporator Mercy Hosp., Springfield. Mem. Greater Springfield C. of C. (dir. 1976—, pres. 1976-77, named Woman of Yr. 1982), Nat. Assn. Female Execs., Soc. Die Cast Engrs., Bus. and Profl. Women Assn. Club: Zonta Internat. (sec. 1980—pres. elect 1982-83). Office: 262 Liberty St Springfield MA 01104

GOWENS, VERNEETA VIOLA, journalist; b. South Holland, Ill., Mar. 19, 1913; d. William and Mary Cawthorne (Fowler) Gibson; ed. public schs., Bryant and Stratton Bus. Coll.; m. Albert Gowens, July 17, 1936; children—Victoria Ann Gowens Utke, Mary Ann Gowens Weiss. Clk., public relations worker Chgo. and Riverdale Lumber Co., Chgo., 1934-45; feature writer, women's editor Tribune Publs., Harvey, Ill., 1960-62; feature writer, women's editor Star-Tribune, Williams Press, Chicago Heights, Ill., 1963-78; freelance writer; script writer variety shows Ship Ahoy, 1963, Fair 'n' Square, 1964; contbr. to Internat. Altrusan, 1974, Church Herald, 1977. Sunday sch. tchr., youth leader 1st Ref. Ch., South Holland; mem. editorial council Ch. Herald, Reformed Ch. in Am., 1976—; pres. Dist. 150 P.T.A., 1965-66; adv. com. program in ltd. occupation tng. Thornton High Sch., 1963-69; mem. South Holland Indsl. Commn., 1965-68; bd. dirs. Family Service and Mental Health Center of South Cook County, Ill., 1974-77; mem. South Holland unit Salvation Army, 1958—; judge Internat. Teen Pageant, 1969; mem. South Holland Community Chest, 1978—; adv. bd. Thornton Community Coll. nursing program, 1976—; active South Holland Diamond Jubilee, 1969. Recipient award South Holland C. of C., 1970, Genoa council K.C., 1974, Village of South Holland, 1969, 1st pl. in contest No. Ill. U., 1974, 75, award Suburban Press Found., 1969, 1st pl. award Ill. Press Assn., 1973, 50 other awards in writing. Mem. Ill. Women's Press Assn. (Woman of Yr. 1974, award 1978), Nat. Fedn. Press Women (1st pl. Sweepstakes award 1976). Home: 16830 S Park Ave South Holland IL 60473

GOWER, ALICE MARIE, ednl. adminstr.; b. Windsor, Mo., Aug. 28, 1922; d. Warren Leslie and Gladys Pearl (Whitesell) Beck; B.S. in Social Studies, Central Mo. State U., 1943, M.S. in Edn. and Library Sci., 1961, Ed.S., 1971; m. Henry D. Gower, Jan. 6, 1945; children—Henry D., Kolyn Nancy Gower Cochran, Phillip B. Tchr., various elem. schs., U.S.A., W.Ger., 1955-62; librarian Central Mo. State U. Residence Center, Independence, 1962-67, dean women, 1967-81, Warrensburg, dir. spl. student services, 1981—. Mem. Nat. Women in Higher Edn. Adminstrn., Nat. Assn. Women Deans, Adminstrs., and Counselors, Nat. Assn. Student Personnel Adminstrs., Mo. Student Personnel Assn., AAUW, Assn. for Women Students, Alpha Xi Delta. Presbyterian. Club: Order of Eastern Star. Home: PO Box 456 Warrensburg MO 64093 Office: Union G-8 Warrensburg MO 64093

GOWETZ, MARGARET REID, food service exec.; b. Advocate, N.S., Can.; came to U.S., 1939, naturalized, 1945; d. Herman Layton and Edith Lenore (Spicer) Reid; B.S., Acadia U., Wolfville, N.S., 1939; postgrad. Mass. Gen. Hosp., 1939-40; m. Ralph Hemenway Gowetz, Oct. 8, 1944. Adminstrv. dietitian Meml. Hosp., Worcester, Mass., 1940-41; mgr. Central Kitchen, Worcester, 1942-44; instr. nutrition and diet therapy Worcester City Hosp., Meml. Hosp., Worcester, 1945-48; adminstrv. dietitian Belmont Hosp., Worcester, 1946-47; instr. Fanning Trade High Sch., Worcester, 1945-47; dietitian, dir. food services Paul Revere Life Ins. Co., Worcester, 1948—; mem. evaluating team for Hennessy trophy program USAF, 1980. Mem. budget panel United Way, Worcester, 1958-62; bd. dirs. Friendly House, Inc., 1962-60, v.p., 1971-77, chmn., 1971-73; bd. dirs. ARC, 1975-80, YWCA, 1960-64, 70-72; trustee Andover Newton Theol. Sch., Newton Centre, Mass., 1980—. Recipient Golden Laurel award Food Service mag., 1971; Nat. award for outstanding kitchen design Girl Scouts U.S.A., 1973, hon. cert. for support, 1973; registered dietitian. Mem. Mass. Restaurant Assn. (dir. 1964-72), Nat. Indsl. Cafeteria Mgrs. Assn. (dir. 1973-77), Soc. Foodservice Mgrs. (sec. 1977, treas. 1978, v.p. 1979, exec. bd. 1979—), AAUW, Nat. Restaurant Assn., Am. Dietetic Assn., AAUW. Republican. Baptist. Contbr. articles to profl. jours. Home: 24 Valley Hill Dr Worcester MA 01609 Office: 18 Chestnut St Worcester MA 01608

GOWIN, MARILYN J., fin. and tax cons.; b. Morrisonville, Ill., May 20, 1939; d. Robert Edgar and Marjorie Lucille (Cloyd) G.; B.S., U. Ill., Urbana, 1961. With Price Waterhouse, N.Y.C., 1961-65, Arthur Andersen & Co., Tampa, Fla., and N.Y.C., 1965-72, Coopers & Lybrand, N.Y.C., 1972-78; fin. and tax cons., N.Y.C., 1978—. Vol. Community Tax Aid; mem. Ocean Beach Assn. C.P.A. Mem. Am. Inst. C.P.A.s, N.Y. State Soc. C.P.A.s, Am. Soc. Women Accts. (past dir. N.Y.C.), Am. Woman's Soc. C.P.A.s, Nat. Assn. Accts. (past dir. N.Y.C.), Mensa. Club: U. Ill. Alumni (past dir.) (N.Y.C.). Office: 240 Central Park S New York NY 10019

GOYDEN, DENISE D., chem. research technician; b. Trenton, June 16, 1955; d. Edward Bernard and Helen (Capik) Ducko; cert. lab. asst. St. Francis Hosp., 1974; student Mercer County Community Coll., 1979-81, Trenton State Coll., 1981—; m. Anthony Joan Goyden, Oct. 15, 1977. With lab. tech.-microbiology dept. St. Francis Med. Center, Trenton, 1974-76; quality control technician Wampole Lab. div. Carter Wallace, Princeton, N.J., 1976; microbiologist Yardley Lab., Woodhaven, Pa., 1976-79; chem. research technician FMC Corp., Princeton, N.J., 1979—. Mem. Am. Soc. Clin. Pathologists (assoc.). 106 Abernethy Dr Trenton NJ 08618 Office: FMC Corp PO Box 8 Princeton NJ 08540

GOYNE, JANET (HOBBS) MARTINDALE, editor trade publ.; b. Gary, Ind., Apr. 3, 1944; d. Wirth C. and Bernice A. (Hutchens) Hobbs; B.A., Purdue U., 1966; m. Jeffery L. Goyne; 3 stepchildren. Advt. mgr. J.C. Penney Co., Indpls., 1966-70; pub. relations asst. Ind. Farmers/ Town & Country Mut. Ins. Cos., Indpls., 1970-73; asst. dir. sales promotion Indpls. Life Ins. Co., 1973-74; editorial asst. Nat. Assn. Mut. Ins. Cos., also editor monthly publ., permanent sec./treas. Profl. Ins. Communicators Am., Indpls., 1974—. Mem. Nat. Assn. Ins. Women (pres. chpt. 1980-81), Internat. Assn. Bus. Communicators (accredited), Indpls. Assn. Ins. Women, Ind. Bus. Communicators (dir. 1980), Women in Communication (1st. v.p. 1972-73). Democrat. Presbyterian. Mem. bd. advisors Insights for the Insurance Woman mag., 1981. Office: PO Box 68700 Indianapolis IN 46268

GRABER, HELEN ELAINE, bus. exec.; b. Fergus Falls, Minn., Nov. 19, 1930; d. Thomas William and Agnes (Bertram) Lee; A.S., St. Luke's Hosp. Sch. Nursing, Fergus Falls, Minn., 1948, 49; student U. Minn., 1952; m. Gordon C. Graber, Jan. 31, 1953; children—Kristina Ann, Leesa Beth, Stacia Ruth, Gordon Carl, Maria Grace. Nurse Abbott Hosp., Garvue Nurses Registry, Mpls., Good Samaritan Hosp., Spokane, Wash., 1949-79; pres., founder, dir. Alegra Products, Inc., Long Lake, Minn., 1979—. Mem. Nat. Assn. Female Execs. Lutheran. Patentee in med. field. Home: Route 1 Box 14 Montrose MN 55363 Office: Alegra Products Inc 524 Brimhall Ave Long Lake MN 55356

GRACE, DIXIE LEE, clin. psychologist; b. Mpls., Dec. 30, 1948; d. Harry A. and Emma C. (Ashauer) Super; B.A. summa cum laude, U. Minn., 1971; M.A., SUNY, Buffalo, Ph.D., 1976; m. Thomas A. Grace, July 14, 1973. Psychologist, Center for Behavior Therapy, Mpls., 1976-77, Inst. for Psychol. Therapies, Mpls., 1977—. Lic. cons. psychologist, Minn. Mem. Am. Psychol. Assn., Minn. Psychol. Assn., Minn. Women Psychologists (treas. 1979-80), Am. Soc. Psychologists in Pvt. Practice, Minn. Psychologists in Pvt. Practice (sec. 1979-80), Nat. Register Health Service Providers in Psychology, Phi Beta Kappa. Home: 2536 Millwood St Roseville MN 55113 Office: 204 W Franklin Ave Minneapolis MN 55404

GRACE, HELEN KENNEDY, ednl. adminstr.; b. Beresford, S.D., Mar. 30, 1935; d. Walter James and Ethel Elvira (Soderstrom) Kennedy; B.S. in Nursing, Loyola U., Chgo., 1963; M.S. in Nursing, U. Ill., Chgo., 1965; Ph.D. in Sociology, Northwestern U., 1969; m. Elliott A. Grace, Nov. 20, 1961; 1 dau., Elizabeth Ann. Nursing adminstr. Ill. Dept. Mental Health, 1963-67; faculty Coll. of Nursing, U. Ill., Chgo., 1967—, instr., 1967-69, asst. prof., 1969-71, asso. prof., 1971-73, prof., asso. dean for grad. study, 1973-77, dean coll. of Nursing 1977—. Recipient Disting. Alumnus award Loyola U., Coll. of Nursing U. Ill. Mem. Am. Nurses Assn., AAAS, Nat. League for Nursing (governing bd. 1978—), Am. Acad. of Nursing (governing council 1976-80), Am. Sociol. Assn. Author: Mental Health Nursing: A Psychosocial Approach, 1977, 2d edit., 1981; Families Across the Life Cycle: Family Studies for Nursing, 1977; The Development of a Child Psychiatric Treatment Program, 1971; Current Issues in Nursing, 1981. Office: 845 S Damen Ave Chicago IL 60612

GRACE, JULIANNE ALICE THOMPSON, mfg. co. exec.; b. Riverdale, N.Y.; d. Arthur Edward and Julia (McCarthy) Thompson; B.A., Marymount Manhattan Coll., 1959; M.A., Fordham U., 1960; m. Daniel V. Grace, July 2, 1960; children—Daniel V., III, Deirdre Elizabeth. Economist, Research Birthdate, N.Y.C., 1963-67; asst. dir. admissions Marymount Manhattan Coll., N.Y.C., 1967-68, dir. admissions, 1968-72; project adminstr. Perkin—Elmer Corp., Wilton, Conn., 1972—74, mgr. indsl. relations, 1974-79, dir. indsl. relations, 1979-82, asst. to v.p. semiconductor equipment group, 1982—. Voting rep. Coll. Entrance Exam. Bd., 1968—72. Rep., Nat. Scholarship Service for Negro Students, 1968-72; mem. Conf. Bd. Mgmt. and Personnel Seminar, 1977. Observer Hudson Inst. Sem., 1975; bd. dirs. Greater Norwalk Community Council, 1976-81, Norwalk-Wilton chpt. ARC, 1976—. Woodrow Wilson Found. fellow, 1959-60. Mem. Am. Council Admissions Counselors, Assn. Coll. Admissions Counselors, N.Y. Personnel and Guidance Assn., Am. Soc. Personnel Adminstrs., Internat. Assn. Personnel Women, AAU (distance running div.). Home: 104 Conrad Rd New Canaan CT 06840 Office: 50 Danbury Rd Wilton CT 06856

GRACE-MCCOY, MARY ELLEN, interior design corp. exec.; b. Cleve., Apr. 19, 1952; d. Raymond Wesley and Mary Elizabeth (Foley) Grace; Assoc. Interior Design, Art Acad. Chgo., 1973; m. Thomas W. McCoy, II, Oct. 15, 1977. Asst. mgr. Bruno Furniture Co., Chgo., 1973-74; project coordinator Contract Interiors, Chgo., 1974-75; sr. designer Gilcor Inc., Cleve., 1975-76; sr. designer, partner Creative Designer Concepts, Cleve., 1976-78; pres. GDA Inc. (Grey Design Assos.), Cleve., 1978—; participant local coll. work-experience programs, 1978—; career counselor for high sch. students, 1979—. Vol. phone counselor, public rep. Reach-Out, 1975-78; active Greater Cleve. Growth Assn., 1979—; organizer Ronald McDonald House, 1979. Mem. Inst. Bus. Designers (assoc.). Clubs: Cleve. Athletic, Univ. of Cleve. Office: GDA Inc 3 Commerce Park Sq 23200 Chagrin Blvd Cleveland OH 44122

GRADISON, HEATHER JANE, govt. ofcl.; b. Houston, Sept. 6, 1952; d. David Lowe Stirton and Dorothy Johanne Flatt Cox; B.A., Radford Coll., 1975; postgrad. George Washington U., 1976, 78; m. Willis D. Gradison, Jr., Nov. 29, 1980; 1 dau., Maile Jo. Summer intern So. Rwy. System, Washington, 1974, mgmt. trainee, 1975-76, market research asst., 1976-77, asst. rate officer, 1978-80, rate officer, 1978-82; commr. Interstate Commerce Commn., Washington, 1982—; mem. Transp. Research Forum, 1978-80, Women's Transp. Seminar, 1978-81. Republican. Office: 12th and Constitution Ave NW Room 4136 Washington DC 20423

GRADY, ARVETA CHARLENE, social worker; b. Memphis, Jan. 16, 1951; d. Arthur L. and C. Mary (Taylor) G.; B.S., Eastern Mich. U., 1972; M.S.W., Wayne State U., 1976. Welfare service worker foster care dept. Wayne County Dept. Social Service, Detroit, 1976; clin. social worker outpatient dept. Dept. Mental Health, Lafayette Clinic, Detroit, 1976—. Mem. Nat. Assn. Social Workers, Nat. Assn. Black Social Workers, Cert. Clin. Social Workers Mich., Delta Sigma Theta. Democrat. Methodist. Office: 951 E Lafayette St Detroit MI 48207

GRADY, SHERRY ANN, engr.; b. Alexandria, Va., May 2, 1953; d. John David and Dorothy (Howard) Grady, Jr.; B.S. in Engring., N.C. State U., 1977. Engr. in charge chem. lab. Contractors Engrs. Services Inc., Goldsboro, N.C., 1976—, engr. in charge engring. ops., 1978—, corp. sec., 1978—, design engr., 1979—, also dir.; mem. adv. panel Chem. Week Mgmt., 1981-82. Mem. N.C. Soc. Profl. Engrs., Soc. Am. Mil. Engrs. (nominating com. Goldsboro post), Soc. Women Engrs. (charter mem. N.C. State U. sect.). Republican. Methodist. Club: N.C. State U. Women Engrs. (1st v.p.). Home: 203 N Slocumb St Goldsboro NC 27530 Office: PO Box 762 1304 N William St Goldsboro NC 27530

GRAEB, THELMA SAVARD, ins. agt.; b. Rochester, N.Y., July 16, 1934; d. Basil Eugene and Thelma Lucile (Daus) Savard; B.S., Syracuse U., 1956, Ph.D., 1974; M.A., Northwestern U., 1958; m. Harold Sigfreid Graeb, Jr., July 19, 1958; children—Bruce, Jacqueline, Sharon, T. Randall. Supr., Hearing and Speech Center, Yale Sch. Medicine, New Haven, 1956-57; pvt. practice speech pathology, Newport, R.I., 1959-62; supr. hearing and speech Suffolk Rehab. Center for the Physically Handicapped, Inc., Commack, N.Y., 1963-66; asst. prof. spl. edn. N.J. State Coll., Jersey City, 1966-67; cons. speech and hearing dept. Mountainside Hosp., Montclair, N.J., 1967-69; dir., div. audiology Hearing & Speech Center of Rochester (N.Y.), Inc., 1969-71; U.S. Office Edn. fellow Syracuse U., 1971-73, dir. BOCES, 1973-75; ednl. cons. Organizational Change & Staff Devel., Manlius, N.Y., 1976; prin. Rockwell Elem. Sch., Nedrow, N.Y., from 1976; now agt. Donohue Agy., Equitable Life Assurance Soc. Mem. Am. Assn. Sch. Adminstrs., Nat. Council for Exceptional Children, Am. Speech and Hearing Assn., Assn. Profl. Women in Mgmt., Greater Syracuse C. of C. (pres.' cabinet), Phi Delta Kappa, Pi Lambda Theta, Zeta Phi Eta, Kappa Alpha Theta. Contbr. articles to profl. jours. Home: 7619 Glencliffe Rd Manlius NY 13104 Office: Donohue Agy Equitable Life Assurance Soc 1200 Carrier Tower Syracuse NY 13202

GRAESCH, ALICE IRENE, banker; b. Maynard, Iowa, Mar. 8, 1930; d. George Edward and Irene Esther Trower; student public schs., Maynard; m. Walter R. Graesch, Mar. 11, 1951; children—Allan Lee, Marcia Ann. Graesch Hughson. With Oelwein State Bank (Iowa), 1947-50, 53—, asst. cashier, 1971-79, asst. v.p., 1979—; with Security State Bank, San Diego, 1951-52. Republican. Lutheran. Home: Rural Route 1 Box 66 Maynard IA 50655 Office: Oelwein State Bank Oelwein IA 50662

GRAF, JENNY HINES, real estate exec.; b. Somerset, Ky., July 7, 1933; d. Walter Bolen and Elta (Lester) Hines; student U. Miami, 1957-58, Broward Community Coll., Ft. Lauderdale, Fla., 1966-69; m. Jay J. Hammond, May 29, 1958 (div. Mar. 1966); children—Vivian, James, Robert, Heidi; m. 2d, Robert J. Graf, Aug. 30, 1969 (div. May 1974). Project mgr. W. Plantation Devel. Corp., Ft. Lauderdale, 1964-69; asst. to pres. Investment Co. Fla., Ft. Lauderdale, 1970-72; pres., dir. Wellington Realty Fla., also asst. sec., dir. Breakwater Housing Corp. and v.p. Bahamas Mortgage Co. (all Ft. Lauderdale), 1973-76; gen. partner Ideaction Inst., also Specific Markets Assos. (both N.Y.C.), 1976-77; v.p. Palm Beach Assos. div. Gould Inc., also broker/salesman Gould Realty Fla. and owner Specific Market, Inc. (all West Palm Beach, Fla.), 1977—; tchr. career counseling seminar Success Patterning, 1976—; mem. mgmt. bd. First Am. Bank Palm Beach County, 1978—. Mem. Fla. com. Libertarian Party, 1976-80; mem. citizens adv. bd. Palm Beach Legis. Del., 1978-80; bd. dirs. Assn. Spl. Dists., 1979—. Hon. mem. Inst. Residential Mktg.; mem. Am. Mktg. Assn., Nat. Assn. Home Builders (sales and mktg. council). Club: Zonta. Office: 12230 Forest Hill Blvd Wellington West Palm Beach FL 33411

GRAFFLIN, CECILIA, real estate exec.; b. Manchester, Eng., Feb. 3, 1929; came to U.S., 1961, naturalized, 1977; d. James and Mary (Gallagher) Cavanagh; m. Douglas G. Grafflin, Jr., July 20, 1962; children—Jill Elizabeth, Victoria Wendelin. Employee, contbg. columnist British European Airways, 1952-57; community relations officer British Air Ministry, 1957-61; advt. mgr. Officers Wives Club, mag. Shaw AFB, Sumter, S.C., 1964-65; real estate asso. Howe and Sibley, then Randolph Properties, Chappaqua, N.Y., 1973—; founder, owner Grafflin Assos. Campaign worker New Castle Democratic party, 1974-76, del. Westchester Caucus, 1979; mem. adv. bd. New Castle Community Centre, 1978; sec. North Bedford Rd. Civic Assn.; active United Way No. Westchester, 1974-79, dist. chmn. Chappaqua, 1980; mem. planning com. Upper Harlem Commuter Council. Mem. Nat. Assn. Female Execs., Westchester County Bd. Realtors. Club: Town (bd. govs. 1980-81, membership chmn., treas.) (New Castle). Home: 162 N Bedford Rd Chappaqua NY 10514 Office: 31 S Greeley Ave Chappaqua NY 10514

GRAFTON, CHARLINE DUBAIL, educator; b. Derby, Conn., Sept. 10, 1944; d. Charles A. and Edna (Reiss) DuBail; B.A. in Psychology, Am. Int. Coll., Springfield, Mass., 1966; M.A. in Edn., W. Conn. Coll., Danbury, 1974; m. Theodore C. Grafton. Med. tech. U.S. Govt., West Haven, Conn., 1966-68; tchr. of learning disabilities Danbury (Conn.) Bd. Edn., 1968—; counselor Monroe Youth Group, 1965—; presenter and chmn. Writing Short Term Objectives for Ind. Edn. Plans Workshop; mem. Human Relations Program for Danbury Schs. Named outstanding elementary tchr. nominee, Monroe, Conn., 1968. Mem. NEA, Danbury (rep.) edn. assns., Conn. Assn. Children with Learning Disabilities, Acad. Social and Polit. Sci., Assn. Religious Concerns, Council of Religious Assns. (pres. 1963-64), Sigma Lambda Kappa. Home: 92 Highland Ave Danbury CT 06810 Office: Gen Delivery Pembroke Sch Danbury CT 06810

GRAFTON, MARY ANNA, accountant; b. Hattiesburg, Miss., Sept. 1, 1947; d. Joseph Eugene and Iris May (Neville) Pratt; B.A., Minot State Coll., 1975; children from previous marriage—Jill Kathleen, Sean Anthony Eugene, Andrew Raymond. Bookkeeper, Household Fin. Co., San Diego, 1969, Sears Roebuck Co., Minot, N.D., 1973-75; supr. gen. acctg. No. States Power Co., Minot, 1975—. Pres., PTA, 1979-80; leader Girl Scouts, Minot, 1973-75; active Foster Parent Program, Minot, 1978-82. Served with USN, 1966-68. Republican. Episcopalian. Club: Toastmistress (v.p. 1978-79). Home: 2043 NW 8th St Minot ND 58701

GRAGG, LINDA JO, ins. broker; b. Houston, Apr. 7, 1945; d. Richard Lee and Mary Francis (Grimes) Gavin; B.S., N. Harris County Coll., 1978; m. Jerry Gragg, Apr. 20, 1975; children—Wade Kendall, John Wesley. Sec., Cravens, Dargan, Houston, 1963-68; with Adams & Porter, marine ins. brokers, Houston, 1968—, supr., 1976-79, asst. corp. sec., 1979—. Mem. Republican Nat. Com. Mem. Nat. Assn. Female Execs., Ins. Women Houston, Ind. Ins. Agts. Houston. Lutheran. Office: 1819 St James Houston TX 77056

GRAHAM, ANNE, govt. ofcl.; b. Annapolis, Md., Dec. 28, 1949; grad. Bradford Coll.; postgrad. Columbia U. Spl. asst. to dep. dir. for communications Republican Nat. Com., from 1971; with White House News Summary Office, 1973; mem. staff Sec. Simon, Dept. Treasury, 1974-75; press sec. to Senator Harrison Schmitt of N.Mex., 1976-79; asst. press sec. Reagan-Bush 1980 Presdl. campaign; dep. spl. asst. to Pres. for communications, Washington, 1980-81; asst. sec. for legis. and public affairs U.S. Dept. Edn., Washington, 1981—. Office: Dept Edn 400 Maryland Ave SW Washington DC 20202 *

GRAHAM, CATHEY ANNE, psychotherapist, clin. social worker; b. Seattle, May 24, 1949; d. Wesley Franklin and M. Louise (Cathey) G.; A.A., Citrus Community Coll., Azusa, Calif., 1970; B.A. with honors in Behavioral Scis., B.S. with honors in Social Services, Calif. State U., Pomona, 1973; cert. in social services UCLA, 1974; M.S.W. (Delta Theta Tau scholar, Kappa Kappa Gamma scholar, March of Dimes scholar, Calif. State scholar), U. So. Calif., 1976. Grad. student asst. day treatment center Met. State Hosp., Norwalk, Calif., 1973-74, cons. in youth and aging, 1974-76, psychiat. social worker, program trainer, 1976-77, cons. in stress mgmt., 1979; group leader encore program YWCA, Pasadena, Calif., 1979; clin. social worker Huntington Meml. Hosp., Pasadena, 1977-79, coordinator social work services in cardiac rehab., 1979-81; guest lectr. continuing edn. for nurses, 1979; pvt. practice psychotherapy, biofeedback and stress mgmt., 1979—; dir. Therapeutic Alliance Inc., Long Beach, Calif.; cons. in stress mgmt. to various community agys. and orgns., 1978—. Lic. clin. social worker, Calif.; cert. community coll. counselor, community coll. student personnel worker, community coll. instr., Calif. Mem. Biofeedback Soc. Am., Biofeedback Soc. Calif. (cert), Am. Youth Hostels (life, nat. trips leader). Presbyterian. Office: 2401 San Pasqual Suite L Pasadena CA 91107

GRAHAM, EFFIE IRENE ANDERSON, nurse, psychologist; b. Colbert, Wash., Sept. 6, 1924; d. Andrew Bror and Anna Helena (Brattlund) Anderson; B.S. in Nursing, U. Wash., 1949; M.S., U. Colo., 1959; Ph.D., Boston U., 1972; m. Donald W. Graham, Apr. 7, 1972. With Deaconess Sch. Nursing, Spokane, Wash., 1949-56, acting dir., 1955-56; asst. dir. Lic. Practical Nurse program USPHS, Mt. Edgecumbe, Alaska, 1956-58; exec. officer Alaska Bd. Nursing, 1959-61; coordinator Lic. Practical Nurse program Anchorage Community Coll., 1961-66; dean Coll. Nursing, Alaska Meth. U., Anchorage, 1971-75; asso. prof., acting dept. head (med.-surg.) Coll. Nursing, U. Ill., Chgo., 1976-78; asst. dean Coll. Nursing, U. Ill., Rockford, 1978-82; prof. Sch. of Nursing, U. Alaska, Anchorage. Mem. adv. com. Center for Study of Alcoholism, U. Alaska, Anchorage, 1973-75; bd. dirs. Ill. Heart Assn. Served with Nurse Corps, U.S. Army, 1945-46. Am. Nurses Found. research grantee, 1971-73. Mem. Am. Nurses Assn., Nat. League Nursing, Am. Psychol. Assn., Soc. Menstrual Cycle Research (founder mem., treas.), Phi Beta Kappa, Sigma Xi. Editor: (with A. Dan and C. Beecher) The Menstrual Cycle: A Synthesis of Interdisciplinary Research, 1980. Home: Box 321 Sutton AK 99674 Office: Sch Nursing U Alaska Anchorage AK

GRAHAM, JORY, author, columnist; b. Chgo., Feb. 7, 1925; d. Ralpha A. and Rose-Frances (Kramer) Reis. Columnist, Jory Graham's City, Chgo. Sun-Times, 1969-74; syndicated columnist A Time for Living, Universal Press Syndicate, 1977—, The Patient's View, Your Patient and Cancer, 1982—; author: I'm Driving My Analyst Crazy, 1959, Brit. edit., 1960; Children on a Farm, 1962; Katie's Zoo, 1962; Chicago: An Extraordinary Guide, 1968; Instant Chicago—How to Cope, 1973; In the Company of Others: Understanding the Human Needs of Cancer Patients, 1982, Brit. edit., 1983; creator, editorial dir. Something's Got to Taste Good: The Cancer Patient's Cookbook, 1981; author booklets including An Alternative to Mastectomy, 1981, also contbr. articles to jours. and mags.; vis. prof. So. Ill. U., 1981. Founder, v.p. One/Fourth, The Alliance for Cancer Patients and Their Families; adviser to adv. bd. Full Circle Counseling, Inc., Staunton, Va.; mem. adv. bd. Horizon Hospice, Chgo. Designated Chgo. ambassador Mayor Daley and Chgo. Conv. and Tourism Bur., 1974; recipient 1st Jory Graham award Friends of the Parks, Chgo., 1977; citation for contbn. to architecture Ill. council AIA, 1977; Community Recognition award Nat. Assn. Negro Bus. and Profl. Women's Clubs, 1980; Alamo award Daus. Republic Tex., 1980; Outstanding Individual Achievement award in communications YWCA Met. Chgo., 1981; Testimonial for devotion One/Fourth, The Alliance for Cancer Patients and Their Families, 1982. Mem. Am. Soc. Journalists and Authors, Soc. Profl. Journalists/Sigma Delta Chi, Soc. Midland Authors. Club: Arts (Chgo.). Address: 1560 N Sandburg Terr Chicago IL 60610

GRAHAM, KATHARINE, newspaper co. exec.; b. N.Y.C., June 16, 1917; d. Eugene and Agnes (Ernst) Meyer; student Vassar Coll., 1934-36; A.B., U. Chgo., 1938; m. Philip L. Graham, June 5, 1940 (dec. 1963); children—Elizabeth Morris Graham Weymouth, Donald Edward, William Welsh, Stephen Meyer. Reporter San Francisco News, 1938-39; pres. Washington Post Co., 1963-73, chmn. bd., chief exec. officer, 1973—; dir. Newspaper Advt. Bur., Inc., AP, Bowaters Mersey Paper Co. Ltd., Newsweek, Inc. Trustee Urban Inst., George Washington U., U. Chgo., Fed. City Council, Conf. Bd.; adv. com. Inst. Politics, John F. Kennedy Sch. Govt., Harvard U. Mem. Am. Soc. Newspaper Editors (adv. com.), Am. Newspaper Pubs. Assn. (chmn., pres. 1980—), Ind. Commn. on Internat. Devel. Issues, Sigma Delta Chi. Clubs: Washington Press, 1925 F St., Nat. Press (Washington); Cosmopolitan (N.Y.C.). Office: 1150 15th St NW Washington DC 20071 *

GRAHAM, LAURA MARGARET (LAURA GRAHAM FORBES), artist; b. Washington, Ind.; d. Ray Austin and Eugenia Bruce (Winston) Graham; student Sacred Heart Convents (Grosse Pointe, Mich., Noroton, Conn., N.Y.C.) Westover and Nightingale Schs.; studied art Art Students League, with Bridgman and Frank du Mond; Grand Central Art Sch.; Traphagen Art Sch.; pvt. study with Mead Schaeffer, Henry Rittenberg, N.A. and Edward Dufner, N.A.; grad. Sch. Adult Edn., N.Y. U., 1965; m. Clifford Lee Forbes, May 4, 1940 (div.); 1 son. Exhibited paintings John Herron Art Mus., Indpls., N.Y. Water Color Club, Am. Water Color Soc., N.A.D. (youngest artist exhibiting Nov. 1932), Pa. Acad. Boston Art Club, Montclair Art Mus., World's Fair 1940, Contemporary Art Bldg., Conn. Acad. Fine Arts Exhibit, Allied Arts of Am., Ogunquit (Maine) Art Center, 50th Anniversary Celebration Westover Sch., Newport Art Assn., Nat. Arts Club. A sponsor N.Y. U. Chamber Music Concert, 1954—, concerts in Washington Sq. Park, 1954-55. Recipient Alexander Wall prize, 1943, Allied Artists Am. exhbn., N.Y. Nat. Arts Club, 1st prize for painting, 1939; 2d prize, 1940, 41, hon. mention, 1947, 48, 72; hon. mention Allied Artists, 1948, Art Assn. Ogunquit, Maine, 1947, 49; hon. mention and war bond, Terry Art Exhbn., Miami, Fla., 1952. Mem. Nat. Assn. Women Artists, Allied Artists of Am., Conn. Acad. Fine Arts (artist mem.), N.Y. U. Alumni Assn., N.Y. Hist. Soc., Museum City N.Y., Nat. Trust Historic Preservation, Victorian Soc. Am., English Speaking Union, Friends of the Philharmonic, Am. Artists Profl. League, Art Students League (life). Clubs: Nat. Arts, Pen and Brush, Women's Nat. Republican (N.Y.C.). Address: 10 Washington Sq N New York NY 10003

GRAHAM, LINDA, computer co. exec.; b. N.Y.C., Sept. 6, 1948; d. Frank P. and Mary R. (Ficaro) Bommicino; student Katharine Gibbs Sch., 1967. With IBM, 1967—, word processing systems adminstr., 1975-76, systems mktg. support rep., 1976-81, tech. support analyst, 1981—. Recipient various IBM awards, including Achievement in Mktg. Support Conf. award, 1977, 78, 79, 80. Mem. Internat. Word Processing Assn. (v.p. membership, newsletter editor Music City chpt.), Democrat. Roman Catholic. Club: YWCA Cable. Home: 3025 Westforest Dr Dallas TX 75229 Office: 2100 One Main Pl Dallas TX 75250

GRAHAM, LOLA AMANDA (BEALL) (MRS. JOHN JACKSON GRAHAM), photographer, author; b. nr. Bremen, Ga., Nov. 12, 1896; d. John Gainer and Nancy Caroline Idella (Reid) Beall; student Florence Normal Sch., 1914; m. John Jackson Graham, Aug. 3, 1916; children—Billy Duane, John Thomas, Helen (Mrs. D. Hall), Donald, Beverly (Mrs. Bob Forson). Tchr. elem. public sch., Centerdale, Ala., 1914, Eva, Ala., 1915; free lance photographer and writer, 1950—; editor poetry column Mobile Home News, 1968-69; designer jacket cover for Reader's Digest book Our Amazing World of Nature. Recipient numerous nat. prizes, 1950—; Crossroads of Tex. grand nat. in poetry for For Every Monkey Child, 1980; executed prize-winning Sioux Indian and heirloom photog. quilts. Mem. Ina Coolbrith Poetry Soc., Chapparal Poets. Author: (booklet) How to Recycle Ancestors and Grandcestors. Contbr. photographs to Ency. Brit., also numerous mags. and books. Address: 225-93 Mount Hermon Rd Scotts Valley CA 95066

GRAHAM, LORRAINE HUNT, state legislator; b. Burlington, Vt., July 20, 1925; m. Foster J. Graham; 5 sons, 2 daus. Mem. Vt. Ho. of Reps., 1966—. Mem. St. Joseph's Home and Sch. Assn., Gov.'s Commn. on Children with Learning Disabilities, 1967, Burlington Sch. Bd.; trustee Fletcher Free Library, 1974-79; mem. adv. com. for spl. edn., 1978—; mem. Ad Hoc Com. for Child Abuse, 1978; bd. dirs. Burlington Boys' Club, Vt. Dental Care Program. Mem. N.G. Officers' Wives, Order Women Legislators (program chmn. 1967-70, pres. 1973-74). Roman Catholic. Office: Vt Ho Reps State Ho Montpelier VT 05602 *

GRAHAM, MARGARET EDNA (MRS. WILLIAM B. GRAHAM), club woman; b. Weedsport, N.Y.; d. James Leo and Grace (Van Duzer) Kanaley; grad. St. Xavier Coll., 1932; m. William Burden Graham, June 15, 1940; children—William J., Elizabeth Ann (Mrs. Dennis Muckermann), Margaret Edna (Mrs. Benson Caswell), Robert Byron. Past pres. Am. Assn. Maternal and Infant Health; past sec. Chgo. Chamber Music Soc.; governing mem. Chgo. Orchestral Assn.; mem. woman's bd. Mercy Hosp., Ill. Children's Home and Aid Soc., Children's Meml. Hosp., Chgo. Rehab. Inst., Loyola U., De Paul U., English Speaking Union, U. Chgo., U. Chgo. Cancer Research Found., Alliance Francaise; exec. bd. women's assn. Chgo. Symphony; mem. U.S.O.; vice chmn. women's bd., trustee Ravinia Festival; bd. govs. Ill. Club Cath. Women; mem. bd. Kenilworth Home and Garden Club. Clubs: Women's Athletic, Casino (Chgo.); Westmoreland, Mid Am., Kenilworth, Indian Hill, Eldorado Country; Lost Tree (Fla.). Home: 40 Devonshire Ln Kenilworth IL 60043

GRAHAM, MARTHA, dance, choreographer; b. Pitts., May 11, 1894; studied with Ruth St. Denis; LL.D., Mills Coll., Brandels U., Smith Coll., Harvard, 1966, also numerous others. Soloist, Denishawn Co., 1920, Greenwich Village Follies, 1923; faculty Eastman Sch., 1925; debut as choreographer-dancer 48th St. Theatre, N.Y.C., 1926; founder, artistic dir. Martha Graham Dance Co., Martha Graham Sch. Contemporary Dance; Guggenheim, Fellow, 1932; choreographer 150 works including Appalachian Spring, Letter to the World, Clytemnestra Tragic Patterns, Frontier, Phaedra, Cortege of Eagles, Myth of a Voyage, Scarlet Letter, Point of Crossing, Owl and the Pussycat, Flute of Pan, with music composed by Aaron Copland, Paul Hindemith, Carlos Chavez, Samuel Barber, Gian-Carlo Menotti, William Schuman, Edgar Varese, others: guest soloist leading U.S. orchs. in solos Judith, Triumph of St. Joan; Guggenheim fellow, fgn. tours with Martha Graham Dance Co., 1950, 54, 55-56, 60, 62-63, 67, 68, some under auspices U.S. Dept. State; U.S. tours, 1966, 70, sponsored by Nat. Endowment for Arts. Recipient Aspen award, 1965; Creative Arts award Brandeis U., 1968; Distinguished Service to Arts award Nat. Inst. Arts and Letters, 1970; Handel medallion City of N.Y., 1970; Presdl. medal of freedom, 1976; Capezio Dance award, 1960, others. Author: Notebooks of Martha Graham, 1973. Address: 316 E 63rd St New York NY 10021 *

GRAHAM, PAMELA SMITH, distbg. co. exec.; b. Winona, Miss., Jan. 18, 1944; d. Douglas LaRue and Dorothy Jean (Hefty) Smith; student U. Colo., 1962-65, U. Cin., 1974-76; m. Thomas P. Harley, Dec. 4, 1976; children—Jennifer, Eric, Janice, Tom. Profl. artist, craft tchr., art exhibitor, Colo., N.J. and Ohio, 1968-73; acct., word processor Borden Chem. Co., Cin., 1974-78, also real estate, property mgmt. and investor, Cin., 1972-77; owner, pres. Hargram Enterprises, Cin., 1977-81; owner, pres. Graham & Harley Enterprises, Denver area, 1981—; cons. leadership tng. County committeewoman, Bergen County, N.J., 1972; clk. of session Glendale Presbyterian Ch., 1975-79; cadet sgt. CAP, 1960; treas. United Sales Leaders, 1979-80; campaign chmn. United Appeal, Borden Chem. Co., 1977. Recipient awards for art, leadership and bus. achievements. Mem. Nat. Assn. Female Execs., Mus. Modern Art, Kappa Kappa Gamma. Republican. Club: Queen City Racquet. Home and Office: 4303 S Taft St Morrison CO 80465

GRAHAM, PATRICIA ALBJERG, educator; b. Lafayette, Ind., Feb. 9, 1935; d. Victor L. and Marguerite (Hall) Albjerg; B.S., Purdue U., 1955, M.S., 1957, D.H.L. (hon.), 1980; Ph.D., Columbia U., 1964; D.H.L. (hon.), Manhattanville Coll., 1976, Beloit Coll., 1977, Clark U., 1978, Suffolk U., 1978, Ind. U., 1980, St. Norbert Coll., 1980; m. Loren R. Graham, Sept. 6, 1955; 1 dau., Marguerite Elizabeth. Tchr. high sch., Norfolk, Va., 1955-56, 57-58, N.Y.C., 1958-60; lectr., asst. prof. Ind. U., 1964-66; asst. prof. Barnard Coll. and Columbia Tchrs. Coll., N.Y.C., 1965-68, asso. prof., 1968-72, prof., 1972-74; dean, v.p. Radcliffe Coll., Cambridge, Mass., 1974-77; prof. Harvard U., Cambridge, 1974-79, Charles Warren prof. history of edn., 1979—, dean Grad. Sch. Edn., 1982—; dir. Nat. Inst. Edn., HEW, Washington, 1977-79; dir. Northwestern Mut. Life Ins. Co., SRA. Bd. dirs. Dalton Sch., 1973-76, Beloit Coll., 1976-77, 79-82, Josiah Macy Jr. Found., 1976-77, 79—. Am. Council on Edn. fellow Princeton U., 1969-70; Guggenheim fellow, 1972-73; Radcliffe Inst. fellow, 1972-73; Woodrow Wilson Center fellow, 1981-82. Mem. History Edn. Soc. (pres. 1972-73), Am. Hist. Assn., Phi Beta Kappa. Episcopalian. Author: Progressive Education: From Arcady to Academe, 1967; Community and Class in American Education: 1865-1918, 1974; (with W. Todd Furniss) Women in Higher Education, 1974. Home: 7 Francis Ave Cambridge MA 02138

GRAHAM, PATRICIA ANN, fund raiser; b. Winnsboro, La., Jan. 25, 1932; d. Emory Tanner and Dema Clotele (Newsom) Phillips; diploma Draughons Bus. Coll., Shreveport, La., 1960; student spl. fund rasing courses; m. J.T. Cook, Jr., Oct. 16, 1949; children—Louanne, Barbara, Jeanette; m. 2d, Charles J. Graham, June 10, 1962; 1 dau., Kama. With Vivian Woodard Corp., Van Nuys, Calif., 1963-69, Air Control Products Co., Shreveport, 1969-70; mem. devel. staff Nat. Jewish Hosp./Nat. Asthma Center, Denver, 1970—, dir. S.W. region, 1974—. Recipient cert. of disting. service Nat. Jewish Hosp./Nat. Asthma Center. Mem. Nat. Soc. Fund Raising Execs. (pres. Dallas chpt. 1982). Republican. Baptist. Club: Chandlers Landing Yacht. Author manual in field. Home: 322 Columbia Dr Rockwall TX 75087 Office: 2900 Turtle Creek Plaza Suite 430 Dallas TX 75219

GRAHAM, POLLY LAGAIL, heavy constrn. co. exec.; b. Troy, Ala., Oct. 25, 1943; d. Max Leslie and Clara Mae (Austin) Griffin; student U. Montevallo (Ala.), 1961-62; m. Simmie Rayvon Graham, Apr. 14, 1962; children—Brandan Josh, Shadron Austin. Bookkeeper, Brundidge Milling Co. (Ala.), 1963; with S.A. Graham Co., Inc., Brundidge, 1963—, sec.-treas., 1964—; sec.-treas. Ray Chevrolet, Inc., Brundidge, 1977-81; pres. Dalco Constrn. Co., Brundidge, 1980—. Methodist. Home: Route 2 Box 34 Brundidge AL 36010 Office: PO Box 546 MBE Corp Brundidge AL 36010

GRAHAM, RUTH CORNELIA, nurse; b. Asheville, N.C., Sept. 8, 1925; d. Clyde Stevenson and Allie Missouri (Vaughn) Long; R.N., Grady Meml. Hosp., Atlanta, 1949; m. James Rowley Graham, Nov. 24, 1954; 1 son, James Rawley. Staff nurse, then supr. Aston Park Hosp., Asheville, 1946-54; asst. dir. nurses, Wilkes Gen. Hosp., North Wilkesboro, N.C., 1955—. Bd. dirs. Wilkes County Cancer Soc., New River Mental Health Assn., Wilkes Home Health Bd., Wilkes Hospice. Mem. Am. Nurses Assn., N.C. Nurses Assn. (dist. pres. 1975-81). Democrat. Baptist. Home: Route 3 Box 15 Wilkesboro NC 28697 Office: Wilkes Gen Hosp North Wilkesboro NC 28659

GRAHAM, SAUNDRA M., state legislator; b. Cambridge, Mass., Sept. 5, 1941; d. Charles B. and Roberta (Betts) Postell; student U. Mass., 1971-73; children—Carl, Rhonda, Tina, Darryl, David. Mem. Cambridge City Council, 1971—; mem. Mass. Ho. of Reps., Boston, 1977—. Bd. dirs. Cambridge Community Center. Recipient Disting. Citizen award Mass. Assn. Afro-Am. Policement, 1974, award for community service Boston Masons, 1974, Sojourner Truth award Nat. Assn. Negro and Profl. Women's Clubs, 1976, citations Gov. Michael Dukakis and Sec. of State Paul Guzzi, 1976. Mem. Mass. Legis. Assn. Office: Room 20 State House Boston MA 02133 *

GRAHAM, THEODORA RAPP, educator; b. Kearny, N.J., Feb. 5, 1938; d. Stanley W. and Mary B. Rapp; A.B., Rutgers U., 1959; M.A., Columbia U., 1964; Ph.D., U. Pa., 1974; m. Robert J. Graham; 1 son, Devin. Secondary sch. tchr. English and French, N.J., 1960-63; instr. English, Moravian Coll., Bethlehem, Pa., 1963-65; mem. faculty Pa. State U., 1965—, assoc. prof. humanities and English, Capitol campus, Middletown, 1977—, coordinator grad. program humanities, 1975-82. Mem. MLA, Phi Beta Kappa. Author articles in field, chpts. in books. Editor: William Carlos Williams Rev., 1975—. Office: Humanities Div Pa State U Capitol Campus Middletown PA 17057

GRAHAM, VIRGINIA, radio, television and theatrical performer, lectr.; b. Chgo., July 4; d. David Stanley and Bessie (Feiges) Komiss; B.A., U. Chgo.; M.A., Northwestern U.; m. Harry G. Guttenberg, May 2, 1935; 1 dau., Lynn Guttenberg Bohrer. Radio writer, 1936-38; emcee Internat. Beauty Show, 1947-51; performer TV shows including Dave Garroway Show, Where Was I, 1950, Food for Thought, 1951-57, This Is Your Life, 1956; co-hostess radio program Week Day, NBC, 1956; goodwill ambassador Clairol Co., 1961; emcee TV program Girl Talk, 1962-69, rerun of Girl Talk, 1980; emcee The Virginia Graham Show, Hollywood, 1970-74; various performances, Las Vegas. Active Am. Cancer Soc., March of Dimes, Kidney Found., ARC, mental health and cerebral palsy orgns., others; appeared on numerous fundraising telethons. Named Woman of Yr., K.P., 1957; Am. Cancer Soc., 1961, Internat. Woman of Yr., Women's Clubs Am., 1959; recipient numerous citations for civic activities. Author: There Goes What's Her Name, 1965; Don't Blame the Mirror, 1967; Tonight or Never Cook Book, 1968; If I Made It, So Can You, 1979. *

GRAHAME, PAULA PATTON (MRS. ORVILLE FRANCIS GRAHAME), artist, writer; b. Clearfield, Iowa; d. Harry T. and Betsey J. (Jacobs) Patton; B.A., U. Iowa, 1926; m. Orville F. Grahame, Nov. 3, 1923; 1 dau., Sarah Grahame Cairns. Artist and sculptor exhibited at Ind. Artists, N.Y.C., Worcester Art Mus., Rockport Art Assn. Dir. Protective Ins. Assn. of Can., 1962-70; corporator Worcester Girls' Club; corporator, dir. Edward Street Day Nursery, 1954-60, Children's Friend Soc., 1963-67; pres. Unitarian Women's Alliance, 1966-68, dir. Youth Guidance Center, 1963-67; founder art scholarship fund U. Iowa, Distinguished Service award U. Iowa, 1969. Mem. Nat. Soc. Lit. and Arts, Worcester Hist. Soc., Western Sci. Center, D.A.R., State Hist. Soc. Iowa, Nat. Hist. Soc., Smithsonian Assos., Asso. Nat. Archives, Worcester Art Museum, Music Festival Assn., Rockport Art Assn., AAUW (pres. Worcester br. 1959-61). Unitarian. Author poems, short stories, Palimpsest hist. stories; editor Memorial Hospital News, 1951-54. Home: 6 Bancroft Tower Rd Worcester MA 01609

GRAHAM-LIPPITT, JANICE ELIZABETH, psychologist; b. Wyandotte, Mich., Oct. 31, 1948; d. Robert Lewis and Wanda Elizabeth (Janice) Rutt; B.A., Eastern Mich. U., 1971, M.S., 1973; Ph.D., Kent State U., 1977; m. Lawrence Lee Lippitt, Jan. 1, 1980; stepchildren—Stephanie, Karman. Coordinator staging psychologists ACTION, Peace Corps, Washington, 1973-74; grad. asst., teaching fellow Kent (Ohio) State U., 1974-77; counselor Akron (Ohio) U., 1977-79; med. psychologist Akron Gen. Med. Center, 1979-80; pvt. practice, 1980—; rehab. psychologist Boulder (Colo.) Meml. Hosp., 1981—; co-founder, coordinator Oncology Support Group. Mem. Am. Psychol. Assn., Am. Personnel and Guidance Assn., Assn. Humanistic Psychology, Forum Death Edn. and Counseling, Phi Delta Kappa, Omicron Delta Kappa. Home: 535 S 44th St Boulder CO 80303

GRAINGER, HELEN ELAINE, sch. bus driver; b. White Cloud, Mich., Aug. 29, 1927; d. Myron Eugene and Bernice Ethel (Tanquary) Clary; student public schs., Baldwin, Mich.; m. Eugene Orton Grainger, Aug. 23, 1946; children—Larry E., Barbara L., Sue E., Daniel B. Real estate salesperson Obrecht Realty, Lansing, Mich., 1964-65; bus driver, field trip driver Lansing Sch. Dist., 1965—; driver examiner State Mich., 1974—. Supt. nursery Mason First Bapt. Ch., 1966—. Recipient Mich. Minute Man Gov's. award, 1976, award Mason C. of C., 1976; Mich. Bicentennial award, 1976. Mem. Pioneer Hist. Soc., Marble Collectors Soc. Am., Mich. Hist. Soc., Greater Lansing Hist. Soc. (pres. 1977-78, award 1976), Mason Area Hist. Soc. (award 1976), Downtown Bus. Council. Author: Pictorial Lansing Great City of the Grand, 1976. Home: 3905 Circle Dr Mason MI 48854 Office: 2817 Chamberlain Dr Lansing MI 48912

GRAN, VIOLA MARGARET, real estate broker; b. LaCrosse, Wis.; d. Bernard George and Margaret Caroline (Cain) Kramer; student Wis. Sch. Real Estate, 1967; grad. Realtors Inst., Mpls., 1974; student U. Wis. Bus. and Mgmt. Extension, 1966, 73; m. James K. Gran, Sept. 16, 1937 (dec. Aug. 1977); 1 son, James B. Real estate broker, La Crosse, 1967—, owner, mgr. V. M. Gran Realty, La Crosse, 1967—, La Crescent, Minn., 1969—; owner, mgr. VMG Rentals and Advt., La Crosse, 1965—; instr. Wis. Sch. Real Estate, Milw., 1968—. Mem. Nat. Assn. Realtors, Wis., Minn. (legis. com. 1981-82) realtors assns., Greater LaCrosse, Southeastern Minn. bds. realtors, Realtors Nat. Mktg. Inst., LaCrosse, LaCrescent chambers commerce, Mississippi Valley Exchange (pres.), VFW Ladies Aux., Women of Moose (chmn. 1981-82). Methodist. Office: Jackson Plaza 1013 East Ave S LaCrosse WI 54601

GRANDE, CAROL SENZEK, ins. co. rep.; b. Bismarck, N.D., May 25, 1944; d. Virgil Dorothea (Josephson) Senzek; B.A., Gustavus Adolphus Coll., 1966; M.Ed. (Jesse Noyes Found. scholar), U. Houston, 1974; m. Owen A. Grande, Oct. 5, 1968. Med. technologist-educator, Mpls. and Houston, 1966-73; coordinator edn. Am. Soc. Med. Tech., Houston, 1974-75, dir. membership, 1975-77; sales asso. Acacia Mut. Life, Houston, 1978—; instr. displaced homemaker program U. Houston, 1978-79; tchr. fin. seminars. Bd. dirs. Houston Credit Coalition, 1977-78; co-chairperson membership subcom. Houston Area Women's Center. Recipient Climbers award Gen. Agts. and Mgrs. Assn., 1980. Mem. Houston Assn. Life Underwriters, Nat. Assn. Life Underwriters, Profl. Women Execs., Nat. Assn. Women Bus. Owners (div. sec. 1980—), AAUW (pres. Greater Houston area interbr. council 1980—, Tex. dir. 1981-83). Office: 11 Greenway Plaza Suite 608 Houston TX 77046

GRANDE, SARINA ROSARIA, designer, civic worker; b. N.Y.C., June 22, 1910; d. Francis and Maria D'Amato; pvt. tutors; numerous coll. courses; m. Frank Grande, Dec. 7, 1962. In various design and mfg. positions, garment industry, 1929-35; prin. design studio, clothing designs, N.Y.C., 1935-65; cons. to garment trade; cons. interior design; participant, coordinator Pageant of Lace for Ziegfield Club, 1941; cons. on synthetic fabrics I.E. DuPont de Nemours & Co., 1942-50; feature writer Italian Am. Rev. Active fund raiser for arts, charitable orgns., 1974—; mem. exec. bd., treas. Stanley Richter Assn. for Arts, Danbury, Conn., New Cannan (Conn.) Soc. for Arts, Rowayton (Conn.) Arts Center, Ridgefield (Conn.) Community Center, Adrich Mus., Ridgefield, Danbury Music Center, Scott Fanton Mus., Danbury, Hist. Soc. Danbury, Met. Opera Guild, N.Y.C., Am. Mus. Natural History, N.Y.C.; chmn. bd. Italian Am. Democratic Orgns. N.Y. N.Y.C., 1960-65; bd. dirs., mgr. Songcrafters Opera Workshop, Lake Mayopac, 1973-77; mem. Danbury Cultural Commn., 1982—; active Delphi Mini Opera, N.Y., Boys' Towns Italy, Girls' Towns Italy. Recipient George B. DeLuca award Fedn. Italian Am. Dem. Orgns., 1959, Humanitarian award United Jewish Appeal and Friendship Internat., 1959; named Lady of Month, Italian Am. mag., 1962; cert. of recognition Vol. Bur. Greater Danbury, 1982. Mem. Ams. Italian Descent Inc. (chmn. bd. 1971-79), Am.-Italy Soc., French Alliance, Les Grands Vivants (founder and pres. 1974). Roman Catholic. Clubs: Princeton (N.Y.); Danbury Dem. Designer for films: Three Men on a Horse, 1938; Black Magic, 1945; Power Unlimited, 1945; designer spl. garments for series This is America, 1945; patentee garment constrn., U.S., Can.; author Social Scene and Opera Scene columns Il Popolo weekly nat. newspaper, 1962-64. Home and office: Villa Grande Candlewood Lake Reynolds Rd Danbury CT 06810

GRANDINETTI, MICHELLE ANN, nurse; b. Chicago Heights, Ill., Sept. 4, 1950; d. Nicholas and Anne Caroline Quigley; A.A.S. (coll. scholar 1968-70), Prairie State Coll., Chicago Heights, 1970; B.S. in Nursing, Governors State U., Park Forest South, Ill., 1982; m. James Robert Grandinetti, Jan. 2, 1971. Staff and charge nurse nurse hosps. in Ill., 1970-78; night supr. Nat. Orthopedic and Rehab. Hosp., Arlington, Va., 1978-79; asst. dir. nursing Palos Community Hosp., Palos Heights, Ill., 1981—. Roman Catholic. Home: 18558 May St Homewood IL 60430

GRANFIELD, ELIZABETH JANE, psychiat. social worker; b. Hollywood, Calif., Aug. 31, 1928; d. Estill Brown and Bernice (Cornell) Hicks; B.A. in Psychology, UCLA, 1949; M.S.W., N.Y. U., 1970; postgrad. Center for Family Learning, New Rochelle, N.Y., 1975-76, Nathan Ackerman Inst. Family Therapy, N.Y.C., 1976-79; m. William M. Granfield, Apr. 26, 1952; children—Jeffrey, Anne, Mary. Psychiat. aide Waikiki Med. Group, Honolulu, 1951-55; electroencephalographic technician Stanford U. Hosp., San Francisco, 1955-59; psychiat. social worker Mid-Fairfield Child Guidance Clinic, Norwalk, Conn., 1970-71; sr. psychiat. social worker Child Guidance Clinic Greater Stamford (Conn.), 1971—; pvt. practice psychotherapy, marriage counseling, Stamford, 1975—. Mem. Nat. Assn. Social Workers, Acad. Cert. Social Workers, Am. Assn. Marriage and Family Counselors, Conn. Soc. Clin. Social Workers, Nat. Registry Health Care Providers, Am. Orthopsychiat. Assn., Pi Beta Phi. Democrat. Presbyterian. Home: 33 Fairty Dr New Canaan CT 06840 Office: 103 W Broad St Stamford CT 06902

GRANGER, NOELLE AUDREY, devel. biologist; b. Bristol, Conn., Aug. 25, 1944; d. John Martin and Audrey Frances (LaCourse) Parsons; A.B., Mt. Holyoke Coll., 1965; Ph.D., Western Res. U., 1970; m. R. Eugene Granger, Aug. 19, 1967. Lectr. biol. scis. U. Calif., Irvine, 1971-77; research asso. dept. biol. scis. Northwestern U., Evanston, Ill., 1977-81; asst. prof. anatomy Med. Sch., U. N.C., Chapel Hill, 1981—. Nat. Acad. Scis. exchange fellow Czechoslovak Nat. Acad. Scis., 1975-76; NSF grantee, 1976-81; Whitehall Found. grantee, 1976-81; NIH grantee, 1978—. Mem. Am. Women in Sci., Entomol. Soc. Am., European Soc. Comparative Endocrinologists, AAAS, Am. Soc. Zoologists. Democrat. Roman Catholic. Contbr. articles to profl. jours. Home: 1415 Gray Bluff Trail Chapel Hill NC 27514 Office: Dept Anatomy U NC Chapel Hill NC 27514

GRANGER, THERESE, pay TV mktg. ofcl.; b. Rutland, Vt., Aug. 2, 1953; d. O. Henry and Beatrice Florence (Mario) G.; B.S. in Acctg., U. Vt., 1975; M.B.A., Harvard U., 1980. Sr. auditor Arthur Andersen & Co., Boston, 1975-78; fin. analyst Time Life Films, N.Y.C., 1980-81; nat. mktg. mgr. Home Box Office, N.Y.C., 1981—. C.P.A. Mem. Am. Inst. C.P.A.s. Home: 250 W 85th St New York NY 10024 Office: 1271 Ave of the Americas New York NY 10020

GRANNES, A(PPLONIE) JANICE, mayor, partner hardware store; b. Montivedeo, Minn., Apr. 27, 1937; d. Fred and Applonie E.A. (Hartleben) Reber; B.S., Concordia Coll., 1961; m. Douglas L. Grannes, Aug. 4, 1962; children—Dean J., Dana J. With Farmers & Mchts. State Bank, Breckenridge, Minn., 1955-60; tchr. Canby (Minn.) Elem. Sch., 1961-63, Park Knoll, St. Louis Park, Minn., 1963-64, Centennial Elem. Sch., Circle Pines, Minn., 1964-65, Spring Lake Park Sch., 1966-68, Robbinsdale Schs., Minn., 1968-75; partner Carlton Hardware (Minn.), 1975—; mayor City of Carlton, 1977—. Mem. Brooklyn Center (Minn.) Park and Recreation Commn., 1972-75; active United Way campaign, 1979—; active No. Carlton County Coop Vocat. Center, 1979—; mem. Arrowhead Regional Bd. of Corrections, Carlton County adv. com., 1979—; Republican precinct vice chmn., 1972—, city vice chmn., 1974-75. Lutheran. (Stonecroft Bible leader 1977—). Club: Carlton Study. Office: 213 Walnut St Carlton MN 55718

GRANT, ALTHEA MILDRED, social work adminstr.; b. Detroit, Dec. 25, 1947; d. Wycliffe and Annie Pearl (Rivers) G.; B.A., Wayne State U., 1973, M.S.W., 1975. Dir. social services Highland Park (Mich.) Gen. Hosp., 1975-76; social worker Rape Counseling Center, Detroit Police Dept., 1976-77, dir., 1977—; v.p. community adv. bd. Mich. Osteo. Medicine Center, Inc., 1979—; adj. prof., field instr. Wayne State U., U. Detroit, U. Windsor (Ont., Can.), 1977-82. Nat. co-chmn. violence against women com. NOW, 1980—; bd. dirs. Women's Center, Inc., Southeastern Mich. Anti-Rape Network, 1976—; chmn. grants com. Detroit Police Commr.'s Task Force. Mem. Womens Econ. Club Detroit, Detroit Mcpl. Profl. Women (pres.), Acad. Cert. Social Workers, Nat. Assn. Social Workers, Nat. Assn. Black Social Workers (chmn. continuing edn.). Democrat. Office: 4201 Saint Antoine St Detroit MI 48201

GRANT, DORIS JEAN, sch. prin.; b. Hattiesburg, Miss., Sept. 1, 1932; d. George C. and Annie Mae (Brown) Kelly; B.S., Alcorn State U., 1954; M.A., Calif. State U., Long Beach, 1975; m. John C. Grant, Feb. 26, 1956; children—Rita Renee, Cynthia Delise, Gregory Darryl, Joyce Yvonne. Tchr., Compton (Calif.) Sr. High Sch., 1967-73, adminstrv. asst., 1973-75; adminstrv. asst. Harriet Tubman Sr. High Sch., Compton, 1976, asst. prin., 1976-77; prin. Roosevelt Jr. High Sch., Compton, 1978—; instr. Compton Community Coll., nights 1970-75. Recipient Disting. Tchr. award, 1973. Mem. Calif. Tchrs. Assn., Assn. Compton Unified Sch. Adminstrs (treas.), Assn. Calif. Sch. Adminstrs. Democrat. Mem. A.M.E. Ch. Club: Order Eastern Star. Home: 1332 Kramer Dr Carson CA 90746 Office: 1200 E Alondra Blvd Compton CA 90221

GRANT, GERALDINE HUGHES, govt. ofcl.; b. Warren, Ark., June 27, 1923; d. Willie and Daisy (Hunter) Hughes; student Ark. Bapt. Coll., 1940-41, 44-46, Los Angeles Jr. Coll. Bus., 1957, Los Angeles City Coll., 1958-60; M.Sci. of Adminstrn., Calif. State U., 1979; m. Joseph Grant, Jan. 12, 1962; 1 son, William Thomas. Tchr. elem. public schs., Ark., 1944-47; posting machine operator, Kansas City, Mo., 1952-53; file clk. Immigration and Naturalization Service, Dept. Justice, Los Angeles, 1954-56, info. clk., 1956-62, supervisory contact rep., 1962-70, immigration insp., 1970-75, immigration examiner, 1975-78, acting immigration examiner supr., 1978, supervisory immigration examiner, 1978—. Minister of music children's dept. Sunday sch. Victory Bapt. Ch., 1955-61, adult Sunday sch. tchr., 1962—, mem. Voices of Victory Choir, 1953—. Recipient Cert. of Appreciation, Shelley Sch. Child Devel. Center, Raleigh, N.C., 1979. Mem. Nat. Council Negro Women (life), Am. Inst. Parliamentarians (pres. local chpt. 1977-78, 80-81), Eta Phi Beta (pres. local chpt. 1973-74, 80-82, rec. sec. 1965-66, western regional dir. 1969-73, grand dir. edn. 1974-78), Black Women's Forum. Democrat. Club: Toastmistress (council del. 1979-80). Home: 3010 S Bronson Ave Los Angeles CA 90018 Office: 300 N Los Angeles St Los Angeles CA 90012

GRANT, HELEN KAY, occupational therapist; b. Lima, Ohio, Nov. 6, 1937; d. Nye and Martha (Sherman) G.; B.S., Ohio State U., 1959, M.S., 1968; doctoral candidate, 1982. Occupational therapist Highland View Hosp., Cleve., 1959-62; chief occupational therapist Children's Hosp., Columbus, Ohio, 1962-64; mem. faculty Ohio State U., 1964-68, asst. dir. occupational therapy services, 1968-70, dir. occupational therapy ednl. program, 1970—; mem. adv. com. Ohio Dept. Health Arthritis Care, 1978-81; vice chmn. com. allied health edn. and accreditation AMA, 1982. Fellow Am. Occupational Therapy Assn.; mem. Ohio Occupational Therapy Assn. (award of merit 1981). Office: 1583 Perry St Columbus OH 43210

GRANT, HELEN LILLIAN, health spa chain exec.; b. Joliet, Ill., Jan. 2, 1925; d. Carmen and Lucia L. (Pistilli) Palleschi; student Met. Bus. Coll., 1943-44; student Budde Flying Sch., 1947-49, U. Houston, 1967-68; m. Michael D. Grant, June 20, 1958; children—Laura Grant Chamblin, Mary Helen, Michael Daniel, Troy. Bookkeeper, acct., comptroller, v.p., cost clk. Am. Can. Co., Joliet, Ill., 1943-45; bookkeeper Aylin Advt. Agy. and Naman Hotel Supply, Houston, 1951-55; acct. Houston Bus. Service, 1955-65; comptroller Slenderbolic Health Spa, Houston, 1965-72, Dynamics Health Equipment Co., Houston, 1972-77; comptroller Figure World, Inc., San Antonio, 1972-79, v.p., 1980—. Active Blue Bird Aux., S.W. Tex. Meth. Hosp., San Antonio, 1980—. Served with WAVES, 1945-47. Roman Catholic. Club: Tex. A&M Mother's. Home: 200 Prinz St San Antonio TX 78213 Office: 508 W Rhapsody St San Antonio TX 78216

GRANT, JULIET, coll. ofcl.; b. Newark, Jan. 27, 1933; d. Katherine Pearsall; A.S., Essex County Coll., 1973; B.A., Shaw U., 1976; m. Frank Grant, Aug. 27, 1950; 1 son, Eric Frank. Community organizer Urban League Essex County (N.J.), Newark, 1969-73; dir. welfare rights tng. project, sec. Welfare Rights Orgn., Newark, 1973; community coordinator Coll. Medicine and Dentistry N.J., Newark, 1973—. Democratic committeewoman West Ward, 18th Dist.; del. Nat. Dem. Conv., 1980, Midterm Dem. Conf., 1978; candidate for councilwoman at large Newark, 1982; mem. Essex County Dem. Women, N.J. Hypertension Study Group. Recipient award Newark Emergency Services for Families, 1979; Community Achievement award P.A.G. Prodns., 1982; cert. of achievement Mayor's Policy Bd. Newark, 1980; Acad. Distinction award Shaw U., 1976; cert. of recognition, citizens adv. bd. Coll. Medicine and Dentistry Community Mental Health Center, 1979. Mem. Coalition of 100 Black Women, LWV, Nat. Displaced Homemakers. Home: 410 S 16th St Newark NJ 07103

GRANT, LINDA KAY, journalist; b. Peoria, Ill., May 24, 1940; d. Virgil V. and Esther (Lundberg) G.; B.S. in Journalism, Northwestern U., 1962; m. Charles Ruby, Nov. 27, 1979. Copy editor Saturday Evening Post, N.Y.C., 1962-64; researcher Newsweek mag., N.Y.C., 1965-66; freelance journalist, Vietnam and Hong Kong, 1966-70; asso. editor Fortune mag., Time, Inc., N.Y.C., 1971-77; staff writer bus. sect. Los Angeles Times, 1978-79, asst. fin. editor, 1980, N.Y. fin. bur. chief, 1980—; asso. dir. Women of Wall Street West. Recipient Best Reporting from Abroad award Overseas Press Club, 1967; Gerald Loeb award for disting. bus. and fin. journalism, 1981. Author: The Face of Hong Kong, 1970. Home: 32 Water's Edge Rye NY 10580 Office: 220 E 42 St New York NY 10017

GRANT, MARGARET ELLEN, psychiatrist; b. Clinton, Okla., July 5, 1948; d. Gilbert Richard and Bernice (Bledsoe) G.; B.A. in Biology, Rice U., 1970; M.D., U. Ark., 1975. Research asst. U. Ark. Sch. Medicine, Little Rock, 1970-72, intern, 1975-76; resident in psychiatry U. Colo., Denver, 1976-80; career resident Colo. State Hosp., Pueblo, 1978-79; practice medicine specializing in psychiatry, Denver, 1980—; psychiat. cons. Jefferson County Mental Health Center, Lakewood, Colo., 1980—; vol. U. Colo. Med. Center, 1980—; mem. staff Bethesda, Mt. Airy, St. Joseph hosps. Diplomate Am. Bd. Psychiatry. Mem. Am. Psychiat. Assn., Colo. Psychiat. Soc., Colo. Women's Med. Assn. Democrat. Office: 105 Fillmore St Suite 230 Denver CO 80206

GRANT, MARY CHRISTINE, psychologist; b. Rochester, N.Y., Feb. 24, 1941; d. Francis Kirk and Kathryn (Blind) Vassaw; B.A. in English, Nazareth Coll. of Rochester, 1963; M.A. in Psychology, Fordham U., 1965, Ph.D. in Clin. Psychology, 1977; m. Thomas Nicholas Grant, July 2, 1966; 1 dau., Christine Ann. VA psychology trainee, N.Y.C., 1964-65; sch. psychologist Monroe County Dist. No. 1, Penfield, N.Y., 1965-66; psychology intern Kennedy Child Study Center, N.Y.C., 1966-67; psychologist Mental Retardation Clinic, Flower and Fifth Ave. Hosps., N.Y.C., 1967-68; staff psychologist Bellevue Psychiat. Hosp., clin. instr. psychiatry Postgrad. Med. Sch., N.Y.U., N.Y.C., 1968-75; psychotherapist Bleuler Psychotherapy Clinic, N.Y.C., 1976-77; cons. Lavelle Sch. for Blind, N.Y.C., 1977-80; pvt. practice psychotherapy, N.Y.C., 1975-80; cons. psychologist Rochester (N.Y.) Sch. for Deaf, 1980-81. Mem. Am. Psychol. Assn.

GRANT, MARY KATHRYN, educator, health assn. exec.; b. Bklyn., July 24, 1941; d. John Thomas and Mary Linus (Guerin) Grant; B.A., Mercy Coll., 1964; M.A., U. Notre Dame, 1969; Ph.D., Ind. U., 1974. Tchr. secondary English and journalism, Mich. and Iowa, 1964-68; asst. prof., asst. to dean Mercy Coll., Detroit, 1969-77; exec. dir. Detroit Area Consortium of Cath. Colls., 1976-77; assoc. acad. dean, dir. continuing edn. Mt. St. Mary's Coll., Los Angeles, 1977-80; adj. asst. prof. English, UCLA, 1980; exec. dir. Mercy Health Conf., Farmington Hills, Mich., 1980—; mgmt., editorial cons. Mem. Mayor's Commn., Detroit, 1976, Women and the Bicentennial. NSF grantee, 1979-80. Mem. Mich. Cath. Health Assn. (chairperson quality worklife spl. com.). Contbr. articles to profl. jours. Home: 5846 Staghorn Dr Ypsilanti MI 48197

GRANT, MIMI (MARICELESTE KELLEY), mktg. communications co. exec.; b. Long Beach, Calif., June 29, 1948; d. Christopher and Beatrice Edwina (Hebert) Mathewson; B.A., Loyola-Marymount U., 1970; postgrad. Harvard U. Grad. Sch. Bus.; m. Robert P. Kelley, 1976; children—Robert P. Kelley III, Laura Suzanne Grant, Elizabeth Rachel Kelley. Prodn. asst. BBD&O Advt., Los Angeles, 1970-72; asst. public affairs Mazda Motors Am., Compton, Calif., 1972-74, head public affairs, 1974-75; publicity and entertainment programming mgr. Knott's Berry Farm, Buena Park, Calif., 1975-76; pres. Five Star Mktg. Services, Inc., Santa Ana, Calif., 1976—; hostess TV show Women at the Top. Founder, pres. weCan Women's Network, Santa Ana. Recipient PROTOS award of excellence Public Relations Soc. Am., 1976, 77, Best Continuing Publicity Program award Publicity Club Los Angeles, 1977, award Los Angeles Ad Women, 1981. Mem. Women in Bus., Nat. Speakers Assn., Publicity Club Los Angeles, Am. Soc. Tng. and Devel., Kappa Gamma Phi. Republican. Mem. Christian Ch. (Disciples of Christ). Author: weCan Seminar Handbook, 1978; Success Secrest, 1979; contbr. articles to newspapers. Home: 13992 Malena Dr Tustin CA 92680 Office: 555 Parkcenter Dr Santa Ana CA 92705

GRASSMANN, MARGARET OTTILIE, social worker; b. N.Y.C., June 22, 1928; d. Max Richard and Frieda Lucy (Schwenn) Grassmann; student City CCNY, 1958-62; B.A., U. Denver, 1967, M.S.W., 1973. Clk.-typist Met. Life Ins. Co., N.Y.C., 1946-47, sec. Health and Welfare div., 1947-60; sec. Nat. Life Ins. Co., N.Y.C., 1960; adminstrv. asst.

Beech-Nut Lifesavers Co., N.Y.C., 1960-62; sec. family services div. Denver Dept. Social Services, 1962-69, caseworker, 1969-72, social worker, 1972-76, prin. social worker specializing in protective services for adults, 1976-82, adult protective services social caseworker, Capitol Hill Dist., 1982—. Vol. dir. Tb ward Bellevue Hosp., N.Y.C., 1950-52; vol. N.Y. Foundling Hosp., 1953; bd. dirs. Am. Lung Assn., Denver, 1975-79. Mem. Acad. Cert. Social Workers, Nat. Assn. Social Workers, Pi Gamma Mu, Alpha Kappa Delta. Democrat. Roman Catholic. Home: 130 Pearl St Apt 403 Denver CO 80203 Office: Denver Dept Social Services 320 W 8th Ave Denver CO 80204

GRASSO, DORIS TENEYCK (MRS. DOMINIC LAWRENCE GRASSO), artist; b. Sullivan County, N.Y., May 3, 1914; d. Eugene Oscar and Elsie (TenEyck) Teschner; student Ednl. Alliance, N.Y.C., 1957-57; student art centers and pvt. art tng.; m. Dominic Lawrence Grasso, Nov. 29, 1933; children—Robert Eugene, Virginia Ann. Art dir., instr. Doris Grasso Sch. Fine Arts, Bayonne, N.J., 1952-61; exhibited in numerous group shows, including Thomson Gallery, N.Y.C., Pen and Brush Club, N.Y.C., Terry Art Inst., Miami, Fla., Newark Art Mus., Montclair (N.J.) Art Mus., Lever House, N.Y.C., Nat. Arts Club, N.Y.C.; one man shows Burr Gallery, N.Y.C., Bennett Coll., Bayonne Pub. Library, others; represented in Paul Whitener Meml. Collection, Hickory (N.C.) Mus. Art, George B. Burr Permanent Collection, N.Y.C., Bambergers Collection Famous People N.J., Jersey City Art Mus. Trustee, Jersey City Mus. Art, 1955-57. Recipient Pauline Wick award, 1961, Windsor Newton awards, 1958, 61, Jersey City Mus. award, 1958; gold medallion Jersey Jour. award, gold medal Woman's Club, 1963; award for nat. achievement in art Amita, Inc., 1966; 1st award for sculpture Fedn. Women's Clubs, Ridgewood, N.J., 1971; 1st sculpture award Womens Club, Atlantic City, N.J., 1971; others. Fellow Am. Artists Profl. League, Internat. Arts and Letters (Switzerland); mem. Burr Artists, Hudson Artists (pres. 1960-62), Jersey City Mus. Assn., N.J. Painters and Sculptors Soc. (dir., rec. sec.), Trailside Art Mus. (permanent mem.), Essex Watercolor Soc. Bayonne Mus. Arts, Whistler Art Soc., Burr Galleries, Village Art Center Galleries, Sarasota Mus. Art Assn., Hunterdon Art Center Assn., Newark Art Center, Hudson Artists (dir.), Gotham Painters Rutherford, Plainfield art assns., Rockport Artists Assn. (asso.), Elks Aux. (pres. 1950-52), Ch. Guild (pres. 1950-52). Club: Bayonne Women's (art chmn.). Address: Doris TenEyck Grasso Gallery 15 Langsford St Lanesville Cape Ann Gloucester MA 01930

GRATZ, PAULINE, educator; b. N.Y.C., Mar. 30, 1924; d. John and Rose (Berman) Gratz; B.A., Hunter Coll., 1945; M.A., Columbia, 1948, Ed.D., 1961; m. Sidney Aaronson, July 25, 1969. Jr. bacteriologist Queens (N.Y.) Gen. Hosp., 1945-47; research technician Jewish Hosp. Bklyn., 1947-48; instr. biol. and phys. scis. Bayonne (N.J.) Hosp. Sch. Nursing, 1948-51; sci. coordinator phys. and biol. scis. N.Y. Med. Coll. Sch. Nursing, 1951-56, New Rochelle (N.Y.) Hosp. Sch. Nursing, 1956-61; instr. nursing edn. Columbia U. Tchrs. Coll., 1961-62, asst. prof. natural scis. and nursing edn., 1963-65, asst. prof. natural scis., 1965-67, asso. prof., 1967-69; prof. human ecology Duke U. Sch. Nursing, 1969—; vis. prof. physiology N.C. Health Manpower Project, summer 1973; cons. Kingsborough Community Coll., Bklyn., 1967-68, Medi-Visuals, Inc., N.Y.C., 1968-72; bd. dirs. N.C. League Nursing, New Hope Audubon Soc. NSF fellow, 1965; Shell merit fellow, 1969. Fellow AAAS; mem. Am. Assn. Higher Edn., AAUP, Am. Pub. Health Assn., Audubon Soc., Nat. Sci. Tchrs. Assn., Nat. Geographic Soc., Nat. Assn. Research in Sci. Teaching, Nat. League Nursing, Nat. Wildlife Fedn., Durham Mental Health Assn., Fedn. Associated Scis. and Bioologists, Center for Personalized Learning, Kappa Delta Pi, Pi Lambda Theta, Iota Sigma Pi, Sigma Theta Tau (hon.). Author: Integrated Science: An Interdisciplinary Approach, 1966; (with Morrison, Cornett and Tether) Human Physiology, 1981; Experiments in Physiology, 1981; Teachers Guide in Human Physiology, 1981; contbr. chpts. to books in field. Office: 132 Hanes House Duke U Sch Nursing Durham NC 27710

GRAU, SHIRLEY ANN (MRS. JAMES KERN FEIBLEMAN), writer; b. New Orleans, July 8, 1929; d. Adolph and Katherine (Onions) Grau; B.A., Tulane U., 1950; m. James Kern Feibleman, Aug. 4, 1955; children—Ian, James, Nora Miranda, William, Katherine. Writer for Holiday, New Yorker, New World Writing, Mademoiselle, Sat. Eve. Post, Atlantic, The Reporter, 1954—. Author: The Black Prince and Other Stories, 1955; The Hard Blue Sky, 1958; The House on Coliseum Street, 1961; The Keepers of the House (Pulitzer prize for fiction 1965), 1964; The Condor Passes, 1971; The Wind Shifting West and Other Stories, 1973; Evidence of Love, 1977. Mem. Phi Beta Kappa. Office: care Brandt and Brandt 1501 Broadway New York NY 10036

GRAVES, BETH ARNOLD, clin. social worker; b. Batesville, Ark., Apr. 12, 1954; d. William Joshua and Bobbye McAlister (Reed) Arnold; student Southwestern at Memphis, 1972-73, Hendrix Coll., 1973-74; B.A., U. Ark., 1976, M.S.W., 1977; m. Daniel Graves, Dec. 1976; 1 dau., Blair Danielle. Staff mem. Senator John L. McClellan, Washington, summers 1972-73, Mid South Center on Alcohol Problems, Little Rock, summers 1976-77; clin. social worker S.W. Ark. Counseling and Mental Health Center, Nashville, 1977-81; cons. to various nursing homes, 1977—. Mem. Nat. Assn. Social Workers, Acad. Cert. Social Workers, DAR. Democrat. Methodist. Home: 3719 W Markham St Little Rock AR 72205 Office: PO Box 1867 Conway AR 72032

GRAVES, ELIZABETH STEPHENS, interior designer; b. Mich., Oct. 1, 1930; d. Arthur W. and Isabella (Balhoff) Stephens; student Mich. State U., 1948-51, Layton Sch. Art. 1960, 61, Louisville Art Center, 1968, 69; m. Lee Kimball Graves, July 7, 1950; children—Wendy Leary, Joy, Barbara Clum. Dir., WHAS Gallery, Louisville, 1968, 69; designer P.L. Mahan Interiors, Inc., Birmingham, Mich., 1971-74; designer, owner Pine Tree Interiors, Birmingham, 1975—. Mem. women's com. directorship Cranbrook Art Acad./Mus.; chmn. Louisville Salutes the Arts, 1969; chmn. rental and sales gallery Milw. Art Center, 1962-66, Speed Mus., Louisville, 1967, 68. Republican. Presbyterian.

GRAVES, HELEN ALVERA MATAYA, educator; b. Pittsburg, Ill., Feb. 21, 1925; d. Lawrence and Pauline (Starcevich) Mataya; B.S., So. Ill. U., 1946; M.A., U. Minn., 1949; Ph.D., Wayne State U., 1975; m. James H. Graves, June 26, 1949; children—Christina, James W., Nicholas. Ueland fellow U. Minn., Mpls., 1947, grad. research asst., 1946-48, research asst., lab. social relations, 1948-49; mem. faculty U. Mich., Dearborn, assoc. prof. polit. sci., 1981—, dir. polit. internship seminar, 1973—, founding mem., chmn. women's commn., 1974-77, organizer 1st women's studies minor; organizer 1st polit. internship program Ont. Provincial Legislature, 1977-81. Mem. bd. canvassers Grosse Pointe (Mich.) Bd. Edn., 1964—; Democratic precinct del., 1964—; exec. bd. 14th Congressional Dist. Dem. Party Orgn., 1964-76, v.p., 1970-74; alt. del. Nat. Dem. Conv., Miami, Fla., 1972. Recipient Disting. Faculty award U. Mich., 1975, Internat. Women's Yr. award, 1976; named Disting. Faculty, Mich. Assn. Governing Bd., 1982; U. Mich. Rackham grantee, 1977, 78, U. Mich. at Dearborn Campus grantee, 1976; Can. Faculty Enrichment grantee, 1981. Mem. Am., Midwest polit. sci. assns., LWV, ACLU, NAACP, Mich. Conf. Polit. Scientists (pres. 1978-79), NOW. Unitarian. Clubs: Econ. of Detroit. Home: 1304 Buckingham St Grosse Pointe Park MI 48230 Office: U Mich 4901 Evergreen Rd Dearborn MI 48128

GRAVES, NANCY STEVENSON, artist; b. Pittsfield, Mass., Dec. 23; B.A., Vassar Coll., 1961; B.F.A., Yale U., 1961, M.F.A., 1964. Numerous one-man shows, including: Whitney Mus. Am. Art, N.Y.C., 1969, Nat. Gallery Can., Ottawa, 1971, Neue Galerie der Stadt Aachen (Ger.), 1971, Mus. Modern Art, N.Y.C., 1971, Inst. Contemporary Art, U. Pa., Phila., 1972, La Jolla (Calif.) Mus. Art, 1973, Art Mus. South Tex., Corpus Christi, 1973, André Emmerich Gallery, Inc., N.Y.C., 1974, 77, Janie E. Lee Gallery, Houston, 1977, 78, M. Knoedler & Co., 1979, 80, 81; retrospective show travelled to Albright Knox Gallery, Buffalo, Akron (Ohio) Art Inst., Contemporary Arts Mus., Houston, 1980, Brooks Art Gallery, Memphis, Neuberger Mus., Purchase, N.Y., Des Moines Art Center, Walker Art Center, Mpls., 1981; numerous group shows, including: Whitney Mus. Am. Art, N.Y.C., 1970, 76, Corcoran Gallery Art, Washington, 1971, 76, Parc Floral, Paris, 1971, Neue Galerie, Kassel, Ger., 1972, Serpentine Gallery, London, 1973, Project 74, Cologne, Ger., 1974, Berlin Nat. Galerie, 1976, Vancouver (B.C.) Art Gallery; represented in permanent collections: Mus. Modern Art, N.Y.C., Whitney Mus. Am. Art, N.Y.C., Ludwig Mus., Cologne, Nat. Gallery Can., Ottawa, Des Moines Art Center, La Jolla Mus. Contemporary Art, Art Mus. South Tex., Berkeley (Calif.) Mus. Art, Albright-Knox Art Gallery, Buffalo, N.Y., Art Inst. Chgo. Vassar Coll. fellow, 1971-72; Fulbright-Hayes grantee, 1965-66, Paris Biennale grantee, 1971; Nat. Endowment for Arts grantee, 1972-73; Creative Artist Pub. Service grantee, 1974-75. Subject of numerous profl. publs., films. Office: care Knoedler Gallery 19 E 70th St New York NY 10021 *

GRAVES, PIRKKO MAIJA-LEENA, clin. psychologist; b. Tampere, Finland, Jan. 20, 1930; came to U.S., 1957; d. Frans Vilho and Bertta Katariina (Katajisto) Lahtinen; Mag.Phil. (Finnish State scholar 1949-52), 1954; French Govt. scholar, U. Paris, 1954-55; Ph.D. (Fulbright scholar 1957-58, Lucy E. Elliott scholar 1958-59), U. Mich., 1964; postgrad. Washington Psychoanalytic Inst.; m. Irving Lawrence Graves, Dec. 31, 1969. Psychologist, U. Mich. Psychol. Clinic, 1960-63, asst. study dir. Survey Research Center, 1961-63, instr. psychology, 1964-70; asst. prof. Johns Hopkins U., 1970-76, lectr., sr. research psychologist precursors study Med. Sch., 1979—; dir. research Mental Health Study Center, NIMH, 1976-79; cons. in field. Fellow Md. Psychol. Assn.; mem. Am. Psychol. Assn. Author articles in field, chpts. in books. Home: 2235 Kentucky Ave Baltimore MD 21213 Office: 550 N Broadway Baltimore MD 21205

GRAVETT, ETHEL M. F., realtor asso.; b. Ashland, Ky., Dec. 29, 1934; d. Kenneth V. and Virginia W. (Little) Fannin; student Palm Beach Jr. Coll.; m. Gerwood Bruce Gravett, Feb. 10, 1957; children—Anthony, Jeffrey, Phillip. Realtor asso. Wilcox Gallery of Homes, Inc., Tequesta, Fla. Commr., Gulf Stream council Boy Scouts Am., 1975—, recipient unit commr. award; pres. Loxahatchee Hist. Soc., 1973-78. Mem. Jupiter, Tequesta and Hobe Sound Bd. Realtors. Republican. Baptist. Club: River Edge, Jr. Woman's of Jupiter-Tequesta (pres. 1969, v.p. 1968), Woman's of Jupiter-Tequesta (dir. 1971-78), Phi Beta Lambda. Home: 200 River Dr Tequesta FL 33458 Office: 361 Tequesta Dr Tequesta FL 33458

GRAY, ANN MAYNARD, broadcasting co. exec.; b. Boston, Aug. 22, 1945; B.A., U. Mich., 1967; M.B.A., N.Y.U., 1971; m. Richard R. Gray, Jr. With Chase Manhattan Bank, N.Y.C., 1967-68; with Chem. Bank, 1968-73, asst. sec., 1971-73; asst. to treas. ABC, Inc., N.Y.C., 1973, asst. treas., 1974-76, treas., 1976-81, v.p. corp. planning, 1979—. Office: 1330 Ave of Americas New York NY 10019

GRAY, BERNICE MARIE, nursing home adminstr.; b. Hudson, Wis., Aug. 29, 1913; d. Albert Oliver and Frances Elizabeth (Vlieland) Fillbach; grad. R.N., Meth. Hosp., Madison, Wis., 1935; m. Eldon Gray, Jan. 18, 1937; children—Pamela, Dennis (dec.). Charge nurse Hazel Green (Wis.) Hosp., 1935-40, dir. nursing, 1958-64; night supr. St. Luke's Hosp., Milw., 1940; owner, adminstr. Gray's Nursing Home, Platteville, Wis., 1965—; dir. nurses Parkview Terrace, Platteville, 1969-71; v.p. bd. dirs. Parkview Terrace Commn. on Aging. Mem. S.W. Wis. Vocat.-Tech. Adv. Com. Mem. Am. Nurses Assn. (past pres. dist. 19), Wis. Nurses Assn. (sec. gerontol. div.), Am. Coll. Nursing Home Adminstrs., Nat. Geriatric Soc., Am. Health Care Assn., C. of C. Lutheran. Club: Quota. Home: 35 Preston Dr Platteville WI 53818 Office: Gray's Nursing Home 555 N Chestnut St Platteville WI 53818

GRAY, CATHERINE GARRISON, personnel exec.; b. Allen, Tex., Dec. 30, 1926; d. Larkin Guy and Ella Ruth (Keyworth) Garrison; m. Hoyle Mack Gray, June 6, 1945; 1 son, Jim Mack. Office clk. Tex. Bond Reporter, Dallas, 1944-45; acctg. clk. Dallas Title & Guaranty Co., 1946-48, sec., bookkeeper, 1949-70; personnel coordinator USLIFE Title Ins. Co., Dallas, 1971-75, v.p. personnel adminstrn., 1975—. Cert. graphoanalyst. Mem. Internat. Graphoanalysis Soc., Tex. Graphoanalysts, Dallas Personnel Assn. Mem. Ch. of Christ. Home: 208 Whisenant Dr Allen TX 75002 Office: 1301 Main St Dallas TX 75202

GRAY, CATHLEEN ANN, social worker; b. N.J., June 9, 1943; d. Hugh Edward and Elinore (O'Donnell) Wisely; B.A., U. Dayton, 1965; M.S.W., Boston U., 1968; postgrad. U. Md.; m. James J. Gray, July 13, 1968; children—Liam, Justin. Clin. social worker Hahnemann Hosp., Phila., 1968-70; clin. social worker Dept. Human Resources, Washington, 1970-72, Potomac Found. for Mental Health, Rockville, Md., 1972-74; pvt. practice, Chevy Chase, Md., 1974—; mem. faculty Nat. Cathedral Sch. Social Services Cath. U., Washington, 1975—. NIMH grantee, 1966-68. Mem. Nat. Assn. Social Workers, Acad. Cert. Social Workers, Nat. Assn. Clin. Social Workers, AAUP. Democrat. Roman Catholic. Home: 7312 Maple Ave Chevy Chase MD 20015 Office: Nat Cathedral Sch Social Service Catholic U Washington DC 20064

GRAY, DORA EVELYN, accountant; b. Smith County, Tex., Mar. 26, 1924; d. H. Esten and Mattie E. (Payne) Clyburn; grad. Fed. Inst., 1944; m. Harvie A. Gray, Dec. 22, 1945 (dec.); children—Dennis H., Ladell L. Gray Green. Treas., asst. mgr. Wagner Office Equipment, 1948-61; asst. treas. Pool. Co., San Angelo, Tex., 1962-72; loan officer, acting mgr. Concho Educators Fed. Credit Union, San Angelo, 1972-75; warehouse accountant M System Food Stores, Inc., San Angelo, 1976—. Precinct del. county convs., 1976—; active various community drives; active in legislation regarding ERA, 1959—. Mem. Bus. and Profl. Women's Club (local pres., dist. chmn. for personal devel., legislative chmn., past state bd. dirs.). Democrat. Mem. Ch. of Christ. Home: 915 N Adams St San Angelo TX 76901

GRAY, DOROTHY HELEN, writer, lawyer, legis. cons.; b. Chgo., June 3, 1936; d. Milton R. and Grace (Daley) Kamer; B.A., U. Calif., Berkeley, 1957; postgrad. Loyola U., Los Angeles, 1963-65; J.D. cum laude, U. Santa Clara, 1979; children—Michele, Daniel, Jeremy, Timothy, Matthew, Teddy. Press sec. re-election campaign Calif. state senator, 1974; cons. to sec. of resources State of Calif., Sacramento, 1975-76; cons. to dir. State of Calif. Dept. Parks and Recreation, Sacramento, 1975-77, Nat. Inst. for Law and Econs., Santa Clara, Calif., 1978-79; cons. State of Calif. Native Am. Heritage Commn., Sacramento, 1978—; dep. city atty. City of San Jose (Calif.), 1981—. law, Los Altos, Calif. Instr. law U. Santa Clara, 1980-81. Chmn. Save the Murphy Bldg. Com., 1973-76; vice chmn. Santa Clara Hist. Heritage Commn., 1973-76; del. Calif. Democratic State Central Com., 1968, 70; sec. Santa Clara County chpt. Calif. Dem. Com., 1970-71; Santa Clara county co-chmn. Citizens for Kennedy, 1979-80; del. Dem. Nat. Conv., 1980. Mem. Californians for Preservation Action, Calif. State Bar Assn. Roman Catholic. Club: Commonwealth of Calif. Author: Everywoman's Guide to Political Awareness, 1975; Women of the West, 1976; Protecting Native American Cultural Resources, 1979. Staff U. Santa Clara Law Rev., 1978-79. Home: 762 Edgewood Ln Los Altos CA 94022

GRAY, ELVA MAE, mfg. co. ofcl.; b. Wichita Falls, Tex., Aug. 15, 1926; d. Joseph and Ella Maude (Drinkard) Matthews; student Delta Jr. Coll., Stockton, Calif., 1962, 70, 75, Humphrey Bus. Coll., 1973-74, Calif. State U., Hayward, 1978; m. Odies Gray, Aug. 15, 1948; children—Donna Sue Gray Jackson, Randolph. Clk.-typist Sharpe Depot, U.S. Army, 1944, Stockton, traffic clk., 1956-62; beautician Cameo Beauty Salon and Elva's Beauty Salon, 1945-54; owner-operator G.I. Cleaners, Stockton, 1962-68; payroll clk. Johns-Manville Co., Stockton, 1968-73, purchasing agt., 1973—, asst. regional purchasing agt., San Mateo, 1979—. Pres. Young Women's Christian Council; pres., dir. choir, youth leader New Hope Ch. of God in Christ, Stockton, 1965-76. Recipient Superior Performance award Sharpe Depot, U.S. Army, 1961. Mem. Nat. Assn. Purchasing Mgrs. Home: 2155 Eric Ct Apt 3 Union City CA 94587 Office: 2600 Campus Dr San Mateo CA 94403

GRAY, ENID MAURINE, librarian; b. Galveston, Tex., Sept. 2, 1943; d. Willis James and Enid (Childress) G.; B.A., N.E. La. State U., Monroe, 1966; M.L.S., N. Tex. State U., Denton, 1969. Jr. high sch. librarian Caddo Parish Sch. Bd., Shreveport, La., 1966; library dir. City of Beaumont (Tex.), 1966—; prof. Sch. Library Sci., Sam Houston State U., Huntsville, Tex., 1976; chmn. Tex. Library Systems Act Bd., 1976-79; mem. Tex. Library Systems and Constrn. Act Adv. Bd., 1971-73. Recipient Disting. Alumnus award N. Tex. State U. Sch. Library and Info. Scis., 1980. Mem. ALA, Southwestern Library Assn., Tex. Library Assn. (pres. 1973-74, legis. chmn. 1978-81), Tex. Mcpl. Librarians Assn. (pres. 1971-72), Jefferson County Library Assn. (pres. 1971-72), Beta Phi Mu, Delta Kappa Gamma. Methodist. Clubs: Altrusa (v.p. 1980-81, pres. 1981-83), Jr. League (Beaumont). Author: History of Medicine in Beaumont, Tex., 1969; Beaumont Libraries - Then and Now, 1976. Home: 485 Longmeadow Dr Beaumont TX 77707 Office: PO Box 3827 Beaumont TX 77704

GRAY, ETHEL MCCULLOUGH, farmer, ch. ofcl.; b. Hastings, Fla., July 29, 1912; d. Charles Henry and Cuba (Doak) McCullough; grad. high sch.; D.H.L. (hon.), Fla. So. Coll., 1975; m. Bruce Gray, Jan. 30, 1929 (dec. Aug. 1962); children—Donna (Mrs. Donald L. Myhre), Jennie (Mrs. James J. Boyer), David Bruce, Dale Marie, Alan Neil. Owner-operator Gray Farms, Putnam County, Fla., 1962—; coop. weather observer U.S. Weather Bur., 1962—. Mem. World Methodist Council, 1966-71; del. Gen. Conf. Meth. Ch., 1968, 76, del. Jurisdictional Conf., 1968, 72, 76, pres. Womans Soc. Fla. Conf., 1966-70, del. Spl. Session of Gen. Conf. United Meth. Ch., 1970; del. World Meth. Council, 1971, 76; del. gen. conf. United Meth. Ch., 1972, 80, S.E. Jurisdictional Conf., 1980; lay leader DeLand dist. United Meth. Ch., 1975-79, Fla. Conf., 1980—, mem. Council Fin. and Adminstrn., 1980—; pres. Fla. Council of Chs., 1972-74. Mem. women's adv. bd. Bethune Cookman Coll., Daytona Beach, Fla.; mem. pres.'s council Fla. So. Coll., trustee, 1980—. Mem. Putnam-St. Johns County Farm Bur., (past dir.), Fla. Planter, Fla. Fruit and Vegetable Assn. Home: PO Box 36 Hastings FL 32045 Office: Route 2 Box 183 East Palatka FL 32031

GRAY, FRANCINE DU PLESSIX, author; b. Warsaw, Poland, Sept. 25, 1930; came to U.S., 1931, naturalized, 1952; d. Bertrand and Tatiana (Jacovleff) du Plessix; B.A., Barnard Coll., 1952; LL.D., CUNY, 1981; m. Cleve Gray, Apr. 23, 1957; children—Thaddeus Ives, Luke Alexander. Free-lance writer essay, fiction, lit. criticism; works included New Yorker mag., N.Y. Times, N.Y. Times Book Rev., N.Y. Rev. Books, New Republic, others; author books: Divine Disobedience, 1970; Hawaii: The Sugar-Coated Fortress, 1972; Lovers and Tyrants, 1976; World Without End, 1981; Disting. vis. prof. CUNY, 1975; vis. prof. Yale U., 1981; writer-in-residence Am. Acad. in Rome, 1980. Recipient Nat. Cath. Book award, 1970, Newswomen's Club N.Y. Front Page award, 1972. Mem. Am. P.E.N., Authors' Guild, Nat. Book Critics Circle (dir.). Democrat. Roman Catholic. Address: Cornwall Bridge CT 06754 Address: Cornwall Bridge CT 06754

GRAY, HANNA HOLBORN, univ. pres.; b. Heidelberg, Germany, Oct. 25, 1930; d. Hajo and Annemarie (Bettman) Holborn; came to U.S., 1934; naturalized, 1940; A.B., Bryn Mawr Coll., 1950; Ph.D., Harvard U., 1957; M.A. (hon.), Yale U., 1971; LL.D., (hon.), Dartmouth Coll., 1978 Brown U., 1979, Wittenberg U., 1979 U. Rochester, U. Notre Dame, 1980, U. So. Calif., 1980; D.Litt. (hon.), Oxford U., 1979, numerous others; m. Charles Montgomery Gray, June 19, 1954. Instr., Bryn Mawr (Pa.) Coll., 1953-54; instr. Harvard U., 1957-59, asst. prof., 1959-60; asst. prof. U. Chgo., 1961-64, asso. prof., 1964-72, pres., prof., 1978—, also trustee; prof. Northwestern U., Evanston, Ill., dean Coll. Arts and Scis., 1972-74; provost, prof. Yale U., New Haven, 1974-78, successor trustee, 1971-74, acting pres., 1977-78; Phi Beta Kappa vis. scholar, 1971-72; dir. Cummins Engine Co., Morgan Guaranty Trust Co., J.P. Morgan Co., Atlantic Richfield Co. Mem. Pulitzer Prize Com.; trustee Center for Advanced Study in Behavioral Scis., Bryn Mawr Coll., Mus. of Sci. and Industry, Mayo Found., Brookings Instn.; bd. dirs. Chgo. Council on Fgn. Relations, Council on Fin. Aid to Edn., Andrew W. Mellon Found. Newberry Library fellow, 1960-61; Center for Advanced Study in Behavioral Scis. fellow, 1966-67; hon. fellow St. Anne's Coll., Oxford. Fellow Am. Acad. Arts and Scis.; mem. Am. Philos. Soc., Am. Hist. Assn., Renaissance Soc. Am., Phi Beta Kappa (senate). Editor: (with Charles Gray) Jour. Modern History, 1965-70; contbr. articles to profl. jours. Office: Office of Pres U Chgo 5801 S Ellis Ave Chicago IL 60637

GRAY, INA FERN PARKER, civic worker; b. McKinney, Tex., Dec. 20, 1922; d. Louis A. and Oma E. Parker; B.S., Hardin Simmons U., 1948; M.A., Eastern N.Mex. U., 1955; m. W. Connie Gray, Apr. 27, 1940 (dec.); children—Christine Gray Polvado, Bill Gray, Glorietta Gray Yancy, Carolyn Gray McClung. Tchr., Benjamin, Tex., 1944-48; tchr. music edn. and migrant edn., Morton, Tex., 1948-76; ret., 1976. Pres. Cochran County Tchrs. Assn., 1964, Cochran County Tchrs., 1965; active heart, cancer, tuberculosis and mental health drives; pres. Town and Country Study Club; mem. Gov.'s Council Arts and Humanities, 1966-76; del. workshop Office on Aging, Austin, Tex. Named Tchr. of Year, Area Federated Study Clubs, 1963. Mem. Am. Assn. Ret. Persons, Tex. Tchrs. Assn. (bd. dirs. workshops on needs of ret. people), Classroom Tchrs. Assn., Music Educators, NEA, Delta Kappa Gamma. Democrat. Baptist. Clubs: Cochran County Federated, Eastern Star. Pianist. Home: Apt 109-A SW 5th St Morton TX 79346

GRAY, JANE, biologist, educator; b. Omaha, Apr. 19, 1931; d. Ernest Benjamin and Muriel Ethel (Barrett) G.; B.A., Radcliffe Coll., 1951; Ph.D., U. Calif., Berkeley, 1958. Instr. dept. geology U. Tex., Austin, 1956-58; research asso. geochronology labs. U. Ariz., Tucson, 1958-62; research asso. Mus. Natural History, U. Oreg., Eugene, 1962-63, curator paleobotany, 1963-77, asst. prof. biology, 1963-66, asso. prof., 1966-72, prof., 1972—. NSF fellow, 1952-53; Genevieve McErney fellow, 1953-55. Mem. Paleontol. Soc. Am., Bot. Soc. Am., AAAS, Internat. Union Geol. Scis. (subcom. silurian stratigraphy), Internat. Geol. Correlation Programme (New World sec.), Sigma Xi, Phi Beta Kappa. Editorial bd. Evolutionary Monographs, N.W. Geology. Author articles in field. Office: Dept Biology U Oreg Eugene OR 97403

GRAY, MARGARET EDNA, nursing educator; b. Norfolk Va., June 11, 1931; d. William E. and Margaret E. (Smith) G.; diploma Norfolk Gen. Hosp. Sch. Nursing, 1952; B.S. in Nursing, Columbia U., 1956;

M.S., U. Md., 1966; Ed.D., Va. Poly. Inst. and State U., 1980. Staff nurse Norfolk Gen. Hosp., 1952-55, asst. night supr., 1953-54, instr. med.-surg. nursing, 1956-58; instr. med.-surg. nursing Riverside Hosp. Sch. Nursing, Newport, Va., 1958-64; ednl. dir. Va. Bd. Nursing, Richmond, 1965-69; coordinator health technology Va. Dept. Community Colls., Richmond, 1969-72; asso. prof. nursing, dir. nursing program, Va. Appalachian Tricoll., Abingdon, 1972-78; grad. research asst. Va. Poly. Inst. and State U., Blacksburg, 1979; asst. prof. nursing grad. program U. Va. Sch. Nursing, Charlottesville 1980-82, mem. adj. faculty outreach grad. program, 1977-79; chmn. dept. nursing Va. State U., Petersburg, 1982—; cons. nursing programs various community colls. in Va., 1969—; mem. adv. com. ARC Health Systems Agy., Va. and Tenn. 1977-78. Mem. Nat. League Nursing, Va. League Nursing (fin. com. 1981—, dir. 1982), Am. Nurses Assn., Va. Nurses Assn. (sec. 1976-79, com. mem. 1980—). Presbyterian. Club: Women's (Abingdon). Contbr. articles on health care edn. to profl. publs. Office: Meml Hosp Va State U Dept Nursing Petersburg VA 23803

GRAY, MARY TAYLOR, bowling center exec.; b. Waxahachie, Tex., Jan. 12, 1928; d. Frank Camillus and Christine Elizabeth (Rader) Taylor; B.B.A., So. Methodist U., 1950; m. John Preston Gray, June 30, 1950; children—Sharon Elizabeth, Carol Ann, Mary Jo. Various secretarial positions, 1950-52; corp. sec.-treas., bookkeeper Gray's Lanes, Texas City, Tex., 1955—; sec.-treas. S.W. Bowling Proprietor's Conv., 1971-76. Republican. Baptist. Home: 1921 15th Ave N Texas City TX 77590 Office: 2404 Palmer Hwy PO Box 2007 Texas City TX 77590

GRAY, MIRIAM MARY, educator; b. Nevada, Mo., Nov. 29, 1905; d. Chester H. and Pearl (Welch) Gray; A.A., Cottey Coll., 1925; B.S., U. Mo., 1927; M.A., Columbia U., 1932, Ed.D., 1943. Tchr. phys. edn. high sch. and jr. coll., Moberly, Mo., 1927-30, jr. and sr. high sch., Chickasha, Okla., 1930-31, elem. and jr. high sch., Tulsa, 1934-41; phys. edn. dir. Knox Sch. for Girls, Cooperstown, N.Y., 1932-33; instr. phys. and health edn. U. Tex., 1943-46; asso. prof. health and phys. edn. Ill. State U., 1946-57, prof., 1957-72, emerita, 1972—, dance coordinator, 1946-69; dir. advanced study insts. in dance edn. U.S. Office Edn., summers 1968, 69; dir. Wayside Farm Inc., 1970—, pres., 1980—. Dir., mem. adv. bd. Vernon County unit Ret. Senior Vol. Program, 1975-78, chmn. bd., 1977-78. Hon. fellow AAHPER and Dance (chmn. midwest dance sect. 1954-55, chmn. nat. sect. on dance 1958-60, editor dance div. 1966-70, program chmn. conf. on dance as a discipline 1965; v.p., chmn. dance div. 1970-73, dir. 1971-72, nat. dance assn. parliamentarian 1974-75, Heritage honoree 1975, NDA scholar 1978-79); mem. Nat., Ill. edn. assns., Ill. (hon. life), Mo. (hon. life) assns. health phys. edn. and recreation, Nat. (nat. editorial com. 1955-60, editor biennial publ. 1957-59), Midwest assns. for phys. edn. of coll. women, Internat. Assn. Phys. Edn. and Sports for Girls and Women, Nat. Found. for Health, Phys. Edn. and Recreation, Internat. Council Health, Phys. Edn. and Recreation, Am. Dance Guild, Sacred Dance Guild, Congress on Research in Dance (dir. 1969-73, parliamentarian 1973-74), Nat. Conf. Grad. Edn. (editorial com. 1967), Dance Notation Bur., Am. Dance Therapy Assn., Ill. Square Dance Callers Assn. (roving dir. 1955-57, central dir. 1960-62), Ill. Fedn. Square Dance Clubs (devel. chmn., editor newsletter 1955-57), Vernon County Hist. Soc. (dir. 1973—, corr. sec. 1974-76), AAUP (chpt. pres. 1953-54, Ill. conf. pres. 1955), Nat., Mo., Vernon County (sec.-treas. 1973-74, pres. 1974-76) ret. tchrs. assns., Am. Assn. Ret. Persons, Ill. State U. Annuitants Assn., Bus. and Profl. Women's Club, AAUW (program topic chmn. 1975-77, dir. 1975-78), Am. Cancer Soc. (v.p. Vernon County unit 1977, dir. 1977—), Delta Kappa Gamma (chpt. 2d v.p. 1964-66, pres. 1978-80), Phi Theta Kappa (pres. 1924-25), Kappa Delta Pi, Pi Lambda Theta. Clubs: Idlers (pres. 1963-64), Nevada Camera (pres. 1976-78). Author: The Physical Education Demonstration, 1946; A Century of Growth, 1951; editor: Purposeful Action, Workshop Report of NAPECW, 1956; Focus on Dance V, Composition, 1969; co-editor; Designs for Dance, 1968; contbr. to profl., ednl. and lay publs. Dance dir. centennial pageants: The Past Is Prologue, Ill. Edn. Assn., 1955; With Faith in the Future, Ill. State U., 1957. Address: The Wayside Route 1 Nevada MO 64772

GRAY, MYRTLE EDWARDS, ednl. adminstr.; b. Tuscaloosa, Ala., Nov. 20, 1914; d. Burton and Alabama Bryant Edwards; B.S., Ala. State U., M.Ed., 1950; Ed.S., U. Ala., 1971; m. Samuel Alfred Gray, Mar. 13, 1938; children—Myrtle Imogene, Samuel A. Elem. sch. tchr., Tuscaloosa County, 1935-36, Tuscaloosa, Ala., 1936-54, prin. elem. schs., 1954-63, supervising prin., 1963—. Bd. dirs. YMCA, 1975-80, Salvation Army, 1975-80; chmn. Westside Cancer Drive, 1979; v.p. Ala. Bapt. State Women's Conv., pres. Northwest Dist., 1981—. Mem. Ala. Edn. Assn., Elem. Prins. Assn., Ala. Reading Assn. (1st v.p. 1970-74), U. Ala. Alumni Assn., Ala. Assn. Women and Girls Clubs (pres. 1968-72), Nat. Assn. Colored Women's Clubs, Inc. (2d v.p. 1980—), Nat. Bapt. U.S.A. Women's Aux. Democrat. Clubs: Nightingale, Cosmos Study, Tuscaloosa City Fed. (past pres.). Home: 49 Washington Sq Tuscaloosa AL 35401

GRAY, NAOMI THOMAS, bus. and govt. cons., co. exec.; b. Hattiesburg, Miss., May 18, 1922; d. Simon S. and Rosa (Henry) Thomas; B.S., Hampton Inst., 1945; M.A., Ind. U., 1948. Field dir. Planned Parenthood Fedn. Am., N.Y.C., 1952-68, v.p. field services, 1968-70; pres. Naomi Gray Assos., N.Y.C., 1970-72, San Francisco, 1972—; vice chmn. Pyramid Savs. & Loan, San Francisco, 1979—. Treas., Black Leadership Forum, 1976-79; mem. hosp. aux. bd. U. Calif. Med. Center, San Francisco, 1977—; bd. dirs. Fort Mason Found., 1977—. Mem. Nat. Assn. Social Workers, Am. Public Health Assn., Assn. Black Psychologists, Nat. Assn. Negro Bus. and Profl. Women's Clubs. Contbr. articles to profl. jours. Office: 1724 Fillmore St San Francisco CA 94115

GRAY, NICOLIN JANE PLANK, botanist, educator; b. Yakima, Wash., Apr. 24, 1921; d. Laurence Lubin and Clara Nicoline (Larsen) Plank; B.S., U. Wash., 1942, M.S. (Alpha Chi Omega scholar), 1945; m. Alfred Orren Gray, Sept. 5, 1947; children—Robin, Richard. Instr. biology Yakima Valley (Wash.) Jr. Coll., 1942-44; instr. Whitworth Coll., Spokane, Wash., 1944-46, asst. prof., 1946-48, 1956-72, asso. prof., 1972-78, prof. biology, 1978-80, prof. emeritus, 1980—, chmn. natural sci. div., 1977-79; bot. cons. Inland Empire Poison Center, Spokane, 1963—; herbarium curator Whitworth Coll., 1963—; cons. Ragged Ridge Outdoor Ednl. Opportunities Center, Spokane, 1973-80; cons. mycologist to various groups, 1975—. Whitworth faculty research grantee, 1960, 64, 69; NSF grantee, 1962, 65, 71-72; NIH grantee, 1960-61. Mem. Bot. Soc. Am., N.W. Sci. Assn., AAAS, Washington Native Plant Soc., Eastern Wash. State Hist. Soc. (trustee 1979—), Phi Beta Kappa (sec.-treas. Inland Empire assn. 1951-52, 66-67, 70-71), Sigma Xi, Pi Lambda Theta. Democrat. Presbyterian. Author: A Manual of Common Fungi of the Inland Northwest, 1982. Contbr. articles to profl. jours.

GRAY, PENNY ULBRICHT, nursing adminstr.; b. San Antonio, Feb. 27, 1940; d. Hilmar August and Mary Elizabeth (Moore) Ulbricht; R.N., Seton Sch. Nursing, Austin, 1961; B.S. in Nursing, Incarnate Word Coll., 1963; M.S. in Nursing, U. Tex., Austin, 1973; m. Arnold Louis Gray, Nov. 22, 1969; 1 dau., Nicole Michelle. Float nurse Santa Rosa Hosp., San Antonio, 1962; staff nurse Guadalupe Valley Hosp., Seguin, 1963; asst. head nurse labor and delivery Nix Meml. Hosp., San Antonio, 1964-65; instr. L.V.N. Sch., Gary Job Corps, 1965-67; prof. San Jacinto Coll., 1967-77; dir. nursing support services St. Joseph Hosp., Houston, 1977—. Spl. lectr., Tex. Woman's U., Houston; cons. hosp. computers; adv. bd. Houston chpt. ARC. Mem. Nat. Assn. Nurse Recruiters, Nat. League Nursing, Tex. Nurses Assn., Tex. Assn. Nurse Recruiters, Houston Assn. Nurse Recruiters. United Methodist (chmn. council on ministries 1981). Home: 1701 Norwood St Deer Park TX 77536 Office: St Joseph Hosp 1919 LaBranch St Houston TX 77002

GRAY, RACHEL GILLEAN, state senator; b. N.C., Sept. 26, 1930; d. Jesse Frank and Janet (Miller) Gillean; student Catawba Coll., 1948-50, High Point Coll. Evening Sch.; m. William Bruce Gray, June 26, 1950; children—William Bruce, James Frank, Thomas Edward. Mem. N.C. Senate, 1977—; mayor protem City of High Point, 1973, 75; mem. N.C. Council on Status of Women, N.C. Adv. Council on Tchr. Edn.; bd. dirs. Uwharrie council Boy Scouts Am.; mem. Mayor's Com. on Status of Women High Point; pres. Ferndale Jr. High Sch. PTA. Recipient Catawba Coll. Disting. Alumni award. Mem. High Point Garden Council, Women's Soc. Christian Service (past pres.), Mental Health Assn. (past pres.), Women's Profl. Forum, Women's Forum N.C., High Point Hist. Soc., LWV. Clubs: Sheraton Hills Swim (organizer, 1st v.p.), Newcomers (past city hostess, organizer). Methodist. Office: NC Senate State Capitol Raleigh NC 27602 *

GRAY, REGINA BERICE, social worker; b. San Diego, Feb. 10, 1944; d. Harry and Helen (Raphael) G.; B.A., U. Calif., 1965; M.S.W. (Tommi Frank award), U. Denver, 1977; m. Bernard Simon Mayer, Oct. 1, 1978; 1 son by previous marriage Ethan Marshal Greene. Tchr., Pinole Jr. High Sch., 1965-67, Georgetown Day Sch., 1968-69; social worker Boulder County (Colo.) Community Corrections, 1977-78; family therapist Boulder County Mental Health Center, Boulder, Colo., 1973-76, 78-81; faculty Naropa Inst., 1980—, U. Denver Grad. Sch. Social Work; lectr., cons. in field; mem. Boulder County Child Abuse Review Team, 1979. Mem. community devel. bd. City of Boulder. Mem. Nat. Assn. Social Workers, Alumni Assn. of U. Denver Grad. Sch. Social Work (treas.), Am. Orthopsychiat. Assn. Home: 1028 Juniper St Boulder CO 80302 Office: 1333 Iris St Boulder CO 80302

GRAY, SHEILA HAFTER, psychiatrist, psychoanalyst; b. N.Y.C., Oct. 19, 1930; M.D., Harvard U., 1958; cert. Washington Psychoanalytic Inst., 1969; m. Oscar Shalom Gray, Apr. 8, 1967. Intern, St. Elizabeths Hosp., Washington, 1958-59; resident McLean Hosp., Belmont, Mass., 1959-61; clin. and research fellow Mass. Gen. Hosp., Boston, 1961-62; staff psychiatrist Chestnut Lodge, Inc., Rockville, Md., 1962-64; practice medicine, specializing in psychiatry and psychoanalysis, Washington, 1964—; clin. asst. prof. psychiatry U. Md. Sch. Medicine, Balt., 1968-75, clin. assoc. prof., 1975—; instr. Washington Psychoanalytic Inst., 1971-75, teaching analyst, 1975—; mem. staff U. Md. Hosp., Balt.; physician mem. Commn. on Mental Health, Superior Ct. of D.C., 1972—; bd. govs. Nat. Capital Reciprocal Ins. Co., 1981—. Fellow Am. Psychiat. Assn.; mem. Am. Psychoanalytic Assn. (diplomate Bd. of Profl. Standards), Washington Psychiat. Soc. (councillor 1981—) Med. Soc. D.C. (exec. bd. 1982—). Office: PO Box 40612 Palisades Station Washington DC 20016

GRAYBEAL, BARBARA, writer, editor; b. Mountain City, Tenn., Sept. 21, 1935; d. Claude Harold and Ruby Lucille (Hodge) Graybeal; B.A. magna cum laude, Marietta Coll., 1957; m. Lewis N. Kremer, June 7, 1958 (div.). With New Yorker mag., N.Y.C., 1957-58; asso. editor Sat. Eve. Post, Phila., 1958-62, Episcopalian mag., Phila., 1962-69; asst. editor Luth. Mag., Phila., 1971-72; instr. journalism Temple U., Phila., 1972—; editor CGA World mag., account exec. Mktg. Communications Mgmt., Inc., Phila. Mem. com. on interpretation and promotion, dept. overseas missions Nat. Council Chs., 1966-68. Mem. Phila. Dem. Com., 1968. Bd. dirs., sec. Friends of Free Library Phila. Mem. Women in Communications (v.p. Phila. chpt.), Marietta Coll. Alumni Assn., AAUW, Sigma Delta Chi-Soc. Profl. Journalists, Phi Beta Kappa, Alpha Xi Delta. Episcopalian (lay reader). Editorial cons. Good Ideas for Decorating. contbr. articles, photography, poetry and book revs. to various publs. Home: Street Rd Pocopson PA 19366 Office: 1420 Walnut St Philadelphia PA 19102

GRAYDON, HELEN MARIE, utilities co. exec.; b. N.Y.C., Apr. 8, 1918; d. Albert W. and Helen C. (Bartos) G. With Gen. Pub. Utilities Corp., Parsippany, N.J. 1937—, formerly asst. comptroller, now corp. sec. Mem. Am. Soc. Corp. Secs. Republican. Office: 100 Interpace Pkwy Parsippany NJ 07054

GRAYER, MERYL ROMAINE, ins. co. exec.; b. N.Y.C., Mar. 7, 1933; d. Harry and Betty (Hurwick) Grayer; B.S., N.Y. U., 1948, M.A., 1949, Ph.D., 1980; C.L.U., Am. Coll. Life Underwriters; postgrad. N.Y. Sch. Bus., 1958, Sobelsohn Sch., 1958-59; children—Melody Anderson, Morgan Meredyth Held. Exec. asst. Federated Brokerage Group, N.Y.C., 1958; asst. v.p. Standard Security Life Ins. Co. N.Y., N.Y.C., 1959-69; corp. asst. sec. Madison Life Ins. Co., N.Y.C., 1969-71, also corp. sec. Asso. Madison Cos., Inc., N.Y.C., 1969-71; industry liaison cons. Met. Life Ins. Co., N.Y.C., 1972—; adj. asst. prof. Coll. Ins., N.Y.C., 1973—; lectr. in field. Mem. fund-raising com. Alumni Fedn. N.Y. U., commr. N.Y.C. Commn. on Status of Women, 1982—. Named Outstanding Bus. Woman, Bus. and Profl. Women's Clubs of N.Y. State, 1978; recipient Outstanding Achievement award and Explorers award Boy Scouts Am., 1977, 78; Outstanding Achievement award Myopia Research Found., 1977; Women Leaders Round Table, 1974, 77; Humanitarian award Doctorate Assn. N.Y. Educators, 1982. Mem. Am. Soc. C.L.U.s (sec. and dir. N.Y. chpt. 1974-75, dir. 1972-75, program chmn. 1976-78, 82—, public relations chmn. 1978-82), N.Y. League Bus. and Profl. Women (pres. 1975-76, dir. 1973-76, Woman of Yr. 1981), Golden Key Soc., Nat. Assn. Life Underwriters, N.Y. Press Women (v.p. 1975-76, 78-82), Women in Communications (job chmn. 1977-79), AAUW, N.Y. Chamber Commerce and Industry, Doctorate Assn. N.Y. Educators (Laurel Wrealth award 1982), Nat. Orgns. Adv. Council for Children (bd. dirs. 1982—), Accts. for Public Interest (nat. bd. dirs. 1980—), Nat. Fedn. Bus. and Profl. Women's Clubs (legis. platform com. 1976-77, nat. bd. dirs. 1981-82, mem. nat. legislation com. 1982—), Nat. Council Women of U.S., Bus. and Profl. Women's Clubs N.Y. State (1st v.p. 1979-80, 2d v.p. 1978-79, rec. sec. 1977-78, legis. chmn. 1976-77, pres. 1981-82, chair state PAC 1982—), Am. Mgmt. Assn., Assos. Lincoln Center, Friends City Center. Clubs: Women's City, N.Y. U., N.Y. U. Alumnae (dir. 1976-80, corr. sec. 1980-82, v.p. 1982—), N.Y. Fin., Zonta (dir. 1975-82, rec. sec. 1976-77, v.p. 1977-78, pres. 1978-80), Touchdown of Am. (dir. 1980—), N.Y. Alumni Fedn. (dir. 1982—). Editor: Life Underwriters Bull., 1973—. Contbr. articles to profl. jours. Home: 130 E 18th St New York NY 10003 Office: 1 Madison Ave New York NY 10010

GRAY-LITTLE, BERNADETTE, psychologist; b. Washington, N.C., Oct. 21, 1944; d. James and Rosalie Lanier Gray; A.B., Marywood Coll., 1966; M.S., St. Louis U., 1968, Ph.D., 1970; m. Shade Keys Little, Nov. 21, 1970; children—Maura, Mark. Psychology intern Malcolm Bliss Mental Health Center, St. Louis, 1968-69; Fulbright fellow Copenhagen U., 1970-71; asst. prof. psychology U. N.C., Chapel Hill, 1971-76, asso. prof., 1976-82, prof., 1983—. NIMH fellow, 1967-68; grantee Social Sci. Research Council, Spencer Found., Carolina Population Center; NRC fellow, 1982-83. Mem. Am. Psychol. Assn., Phi Beta Kappa. Contbr. articles to profl. jours. Office: Dept Psychology U NC Chapel Hill NC 27514

GRAYSON, JIMI PAYNE, guidance counselor; b. Letohatchie, Ala., Nov. 21, 1934; d. James Dixon and Ella Mae (Wilson) Payne; B.S., S.C. State Coll., Orangeburg, 1956, M.Ed., 1967; divorced; children—Stephanie Claire, Siobhan Benita. Sec. to dean of women S.C. State Coll., Orangeburg, 1958-66; tchr. Bur. Land Mgmt., Dept. Interior, Mountain Home, Idaho, 1966-69; dean of women Tenn. State U., Nashville, 1969-73; guidance counselor Bryant Intermediate Sch., Alexandria, Va., 1974—, dir. career edn., 1978—; dir. career edn. Herndon (Va.) Internat. Sch., 1975. Dir. summer activities Episcopal Youth Group, Orangeburg, 1963-65. Mem. Va. Assn. Guidance and Counseling, Fairfax County Tchrs. Edn. Assn. Address: 1111 R St NW Washington DC 20009

GRAYSON, KATHRYN, singer; b. Winston-Salem, N.C., Feb. 9, 1929; student Minnaletha White, M.-G.-M. Studio Schoolhouse. Stage appearances in musicals include The Merry Widow, 1961, Naughty Marietta, 1961, Rosalina, 1962, Camelot, 1962-64, also S.Am. tour in Show Boat; motion picture appearances include Andy Hardy's Private Secretary, Anchors Aweigh, Two Sisters from Boston, It Happened in Brooklyn, Till the Clouds Roll By, That Midnight Kiss, Grounds for Marriage, The Toast of New Orleans, Show Boat, Lovely to Look At, So This Is Love, Kiss Me Kate, The Vagabond King, The Amazing World Psychic Phenomena, Now I Lay Me Down to Sleep; TV appearances Die Fledermaus, 1966; numerous appearances on concert stage, TV and radio; recs. include Time After Time, Love Is Where You Find It, Make Believe, Smoke Gets In Your Eyes, Romance, Serenade, (All of a Sudden) My Heart Sings, Jealousy, Un Bel Di, Sempre Libera, So in Love. Address: care Impersario 12214 Viewcrest Rd Radio City CA 91604 *

GRAZIANO, FLORENCE VERONICA MERCOLINO (MRS. NATALE GRAZIANO), artist; b. Plainfield, N.J.; d. Michael and Florence (Sheriff) Mercolino; student R.I. Sch. Design, Columbus Coll. Art and Design, 1963—, Art Students League, 1968-70; m. Natale Graziano, Dec. 11, 1954. Exhibited in one-man shows Chase Gallery, N.Y.C., Bullock's-Wilshire Gallery, Los Angeles, Washington County Mus. Fine Arts, Hagerstown, Md., G. & G. Gallery, Plainfield, N.J.; exhibited in group shows throughout N.J., Crespi Gallary, N.Y.C., Mansfield Art Gallery, Columbus, Ohio, Marion, Ohio; represented in permanent collections: Columbus Coll. Art and Design, Rutgers U., Eureka Coll., U. Maine, Wittenberg U., Coll. City N.Y., Payne Whitney Clinic, Washington County Mus. Fine Arts, Hagerstown, Sheldon Swope Art Gallery, Terre Haute, Ind., others; owner, dir. G & G Gallery, Plainfield, The Workshop Gallery, Flemington, N.J.; dir., instr. Graziano Sch. Fine Arts, N.J., Graziano Summer Art Workshop, Flemington. Mem. Art Students League N.Y. (life), Am. Artists Profl. League (past pres. N.J. chpt.), Pen and Brush N.Y., Painters and Sculptors Soc. N.J. Clubs: Salmagundi, Nat. Arts, Catherine Lorillard Wolfe Art (N.Y.C.). Address: RD 3 Box 672 River Rd and Railroad Ave Flemington NJ 08822

GRAZIANO, MARY E, banker; b. Flushing, N.Y., June 23, 1929; d. Salvatore and Nina (Greco) Sisinni; m. Joseph John Graziano, May 30, 1948 (dec.); children—Joseph, John, Steven. Vice-pres. Hillside Contracting Co., New Hyde Park, N.Y., 1958-69; asst. v.p. Chem. Bank, Lake Success, N.Y., 1969—. Mem. Assn. Records Mgrs. and Adminstrs. (past pres.), Nat. Assn. Bank Women, Nat. Microfilm Assn. Roman Catholic. Club: Garden City Country. Address: Chemical Bank 2 Ohio Dr Lake Success NY 10040

GREACEN, NAN, artist; b. Giverny, France, Mar. 6; d. Edmund and Ethol (Booth) G.; student Grand Central Sch. Art, 1926-30; m. Rene Bard Faure, Dec. 7, 1936; children—Nancy Faure Waesche, Renee. Tchr., Grand Central Sch. Art, 1931-43; portrait painter, still life and landscapes; watercolor painter; tchr. pvt. art classes; works rep. Gateway Art Gallery (Palm Beach, Fla.), Kobra Gallery (Jacksonville Beach, Fla.), Grand Central Art Galleries, N.Y.C., Beeches Gallery (Carmel, Calif.), Brush and Palette Gallery, St. Augustine, Fla. Recipient numerous awards for art, 1931-79, including: 1st prize Manhattan Savs. Bank exhibit Westchester Artists, 1963, Best in Show award Nat. Arts Club, 1964, purchase award and medal Montclair Mus., 1966, Landscape prize Nat. Arts Club, 1967, Kathleen Grumbacher medal 1969, Best in Show award St. Augustine Art Assn., 1972, Benedictine competition award, 1976, 1st watercolor prize St. Augustine Honor Show, 1977, 1st prize for oil, St. Augustine Mems., 1978, 1st prize for watercolor, St. Augustine Honor Show, 1979. Mem. NAD, Fla. Watercolor Soc. (awards 1973, 74), Hudson Valley Art Assn. (Medal of Honor 1976, Gumbacher award 1968, John Newington award 1970), Allied Artists Am., Audubon Artists, St. Augustine Art Assn., Scarsdale Art Assn. Presbyterian. Clubs: Ponte Vedra, Sawgrass. Author: The Magic of Flower Painting, 1965; Still Life is Exciting, 1970. Studio: 184 San Juan Dr Ponte Vedra Beach FL 32082

GREASER, CONSTANCE UDEAN, research orgn. exec.; b. San Diego, Jan. 18, 1938; d. Lloyd Edward and Udean (Rohr) G.; B.A., San Diego State Coll., 1959; postgrad. U. Copenhagen Grad. Sch. Fgn. Students, 1963, Georgetown U. Sch. Fgn. Service, 1967; M.A., U. So. Calif., 1968; Exec. M.B.A., UCLA, 1981. Advt., publicity mgr. Crofton Co., San Diego, 1959-62; supr. Mercury Publs., Fullerton, Calif., 1962-64; supr. engrng. support services div. Arcata Data Mgmt., Hawthorne, Calif., 1964-67; mgr. computerized typesetting dept. Continental Graphics, Los Angeles, 1967-70; v.p., editorial dir. Sage Publs., Inc., Beverly Hills, Calif., 1970-74; head publs. Rand Corp., Santa Monica, Calif., 1974—. Publicity dir. National City March of Dimes Parade, 1961-62. Mem. Women in Bus. (pres. 1977-78), Soc. for Scholarly Pubs. (nat. bd. dirs.), Orgn. Women Execs., So. Calif. Bookbuilders Assn., Women in Communication, UCLA Exec. Program Assn. Editor: Urban Research News, 1970-74; mng. editor Comparative Polit. Studies, 1971-74; contbr. articles to various jours. Home: 4735C La Villa Marina Marina Del Rey CA 90291 Office: 1700 Main St Santa Monica CA 90406

GREATHOUSE, LILLIAN ROSALEA, educator; b. St. Louis, Nov. 13, 1943; d. Ambrose and Rosalea Greathouse; B.A., Ouachita Baptist U., Arkadelphia, Ark., 1966; M.S., So. Ill. U., Carbondale, 1970, Ph.D., 1981. Tchr. bus. Acorn Consol. Schs., Mena, Ark., 1966-68; mem. faculty So. Ill. U., 1968—, asso. prof. tech. careers, 1982—, asst. dean Sch. Tech. Careers, 1979-82; co-owner Career Assos., Carbondale, 1979—; cons. in field. Mem. Assn. Records Mgrs. and Adminstrs., Am. Vocat. Edn. Assn., Nat. Bus. Edn. Assn., Nat. Assn. Women Deans, Adminstrs. and Counselors, Office Systems Research Assn., Midwestern Research Assn., Bus. and Profl. Women's Club, Delta Pi Epsilon, Iota Lambda Sigma, Phi Delta Kappa. Author: Records Management, 1975; Time Management, 1979; also articles. Home: 513 N Springer St Carbondale IL 62901 Office: Sch Tech Careers So Ill U Carbondale IL 62901

GREAVES, BETTINA BIEN (MRS. PERCY L. GREAVES, JR.), economist; b. Washington, July 21, 1917; d. Van Tuyl Hart and Bertha (Conn) Bien; B.A. Wheaton Coll., 1938; postgrad. Strayer Sch. Bus., 1939, N.Y. U., 1951-52; M.L.S., Columbia, 1967; m. Percy L. Greaves, June 26, 1971. Various secretarial positions, 1939-42; adminstrv. asst. Fgn. Econ. Adminstrn., La Paz, Bolivia, Vienna, Austria, 1943-46, sec. export dept. Smith, Kline & French, Phila., 1946-47; asst. to exec. dir. Found. for Freedom, Washington, 1947-48; office mgr. Thomas L. Phillips, realtor, Washington, 1948-51; sr. staff mem., dir. debate materials program, contbg. editor The Freeman, Found. for Econ. Edn., Inc., Irvington-on-Hudson, N.Y., 1951—. Mem. Am. Econ. Assn., Am. Hist. Assn. Author: Free Market Economics, 2 vols., 1975. Compiler: The Works of Ludwig von Mises, 1970; translator 3 monographs by Ludwig von Mises in On the Manipulation of Money and Credit, 1978; contbr. Toward Liberty, Mises Festschrift, 1971, also to profl. jours.

Home: 19 Pine Lane Irvington-on-Hudson NY 10533 Office: 30 S Broadway Irvington-on-Hudson NY 10533

GRECO, ANN FRANCES BREEN, legis. aide; b. N.Y.C., Sept. 1, 1941; d. Joseph and Margaret (Purcell) Breen; B.A., Governors State U., Park Forest, Ill., 1979; postgrad. polit. sci., U. Ill.; student Kent Coll. Law, Ill. Inst. Tech., Chgo., 1982—; m. Frank Greco, Feb. 16, 1973; 1 dau., Colleen Lucia. Market research asst. Market Research Corp. Am., N.Y.C., 1964-67; field supr., market research asst. Cole Bender Assos., N.Y.C., 1967-69; clinic coordinator U. Chgo. Hosps., 1976-77; adminstrv. asst. Sta. WMAQ, Chgo., 1978; survey researcher U. Ill., 1979; legis. aide Congressman Gus Savage (Ill.), Washington, 1980-82; workshop leader, 1980—. Mem. Women's Polit. Caucus (legis. chmn. Capitol Hill chpt. 1981), Chgo. Bar Assn., Ill. Women's Bar Assn. (student div.). Club: St. Bride's Women's (v.p. 1976). Home: 8453 S Colfax St Chicago IL 60617 Office: 1743 E 87th St Chicago IL 60617

GRECO, GLORIA THERESA, librarian; b. N.Y.C., May 25, 1930; d. Alfonso F. and Rosa (Mardi) G.; A.B., Coll. of New Rochelle (N.Y.), 1952; M.L.S., Columbia U., 1954. Library asst., then reference librarian Coll. New Rochelle, 1952-72, library dir., 1972—; trustee Met. Reference and Research Library Agy., 1973—. Mem. Met. Catholic Coll. Librarians (pres. 1962-63), N.Y. Library Assn. (pres. coll. and univ. sect. 1975-76), ALA, Westchester Library Assn., N.Y. Library Club, Archons of Colophon. Roman Catholic. Home: 669 Pelham Rd New Rochelle NY 10805 Office: Gill Library Coll of New Rochelle New Rochelle NY 10805

GREEN, ALICE, librarian; b. nr. Burlington, Kans., Sept. 20, 1916; d. Roy J. and Eliza (Carleton) Green; student Amarillo Coll., 1933-35, W. Tex. State Coll., 1935-37; B.S. in L.S., U. Okla., 1938. Librarian, Tex. Mil. Coll., Terrell, 1938-39; gen. asst. Tex. State Library, Austin, 1939-41; asst. librarian Amarillo Pub. Library, 1941-47, librarian, 1947-82. Mem. Am., Southwestern, Tex. (Librarian of Yr. 1977) library assn. Home: 3704 Clearwell St Amarillo TX 79109

GREEN, ALMA JAMES, city ofcl.; b. Jefferson County, Ala., Apr. 19, 1932; d. Will and Ophelia (Chelley) James; Asso. Sci., Lawson State Jr. Coll., 1972; m. Ben Green, Aug. 18, 1950; children—Tommy Lois, Elaine, Bennie, Chandra, Benja. With Berthon's Dry Cleaners, 1964-67; family worker Jefferson County Com. for Econ. Opportunity, Ensley, Ala., 1967-70, counselor, 1970-72, dir. neighborhood service center, 1973—; chmn. Ensley Neighborhood Fed. Credit Union. Pres. PTA Mulga Jr. High Sch., 1964-67; 2d v.p. Minor High Sch. PTA; mem. Mulga (Ala.) City Council, 1976—; sec. Mulga Civic League, 1975—; dir. youth dept., ch.clk., Sunday sch. tchr. Peace Baptist Ch. Recipient Mother of Yr. award Mulga Jr. High Sch., 1967; Outstanding Service award Zeta Phi Lambda, 1973. Mem. Ala. League of Municipalities, Westfield Alumni Assn. Club: Order Eastern Star. Home: 219 1st St Mulga AL 35118 Office: 210 19th St Ensley AL 35218

GREEN, ANGELA VERA, sorority exec.; b. Washington, Aug. 25, 1950; d. Chester Longworth and Ella (Jones) G.; B.S. in Bus. Adminstrn., N.C. A&T State U., 1972; M.S. in Fin., Benjamin Franklin U., Washington, 1981. Asst. dept. mgr. Woodward & Lothrop, Washington, 1972-74; asst. comptroller Delta Sigma Theta, Inc., Washington, 1974—. Mem. Nat. Assn. Female Execs., Surburban Md. chpt. N.C. A&T State U. Alumni Assn., Delta Sigma Theta. Home: 2115 A Fort Davis St SE Washington DC 20020 Office: 1707 New Hampshire Ave Washington DC 20009

GREEN, ANN A., clothing mfg. co. exec.; b. N.Y.C., May 6, 1925; d. Harry and Pauline (Melzack) Weinstein; B.A., Bklyn. Coll., 1947; postgrad New Sch. Social Research, 1949; m. Milton Green, Nov. 27, 1949 (dec. 1974); children—Denise Lyn, Michael Harris. Pres., sec., Originals by Denise, Inc., N.Y.C., 1974—. Mem. Suit and Coat Assn. Jewish. Clubs: Tennis Port, Fleetwood Tennis. Office: 500 7th Ave New York NY 10018

GREEN, BELVA JEAN, health assn. exec.; b. Eaton County, Mich., Aug. 16, 1927; d. Phillip Clem and Gladys M. Green; student Mich. State Coll., 1945-47, Ind. U., 1959, Purdue U. Ins. Mktg. Inst., 1967. Sec. to pres. Rea Magnet Wire Co., Ft. Wayne, Ind., 1958-63; sec. to corp. purchasing v.p. Magnovox Co., Ft. Wayne, 1963-67; nat. exec. dir. United Cancer Council, Ft. Wayne and Indpls., 1967-71; exec. dir. Allen County Cancer Soc., Ft. Wayne, 1971—; guest lectr. Ind. U., St. Francis Coll., IV-Tech. Coll., nursing, med. assts., LPN, 1971. Co-founder local unit Make Today Count, 1976, regional coordinator nat. group, 1980; nat. pres. United Cancer Council Staff Assn., 1982-83; vol. United Way of Allen County Bd., 1974-76, Speakers Bur., 1975—, mem. public relations com., 1975-76; v.p. adv. bd. Salvation Army, 1976; charter mem. Friends and Families of Nursing Home Residents, 1978-81; vol. Mental Health Assn., 1978; mem. med. assts. adv. bd. Ind. Vocat. Tech. Coll., 1980-81; mem. No. Ind. Health Systems Agy. Hospice Panel, 1979; co-founder, bd. dirs. Hospice of Fort Wayne, Inc. Recipient Woman of Influence awards Toastmistress Clubs, Fort Wayne Club and Council #6, 1971, united Way Leadership awards, 1974, 76, Community Service award Seventh-day Adventist Ch., 1979. Mem. Public Relations Soc. Am., Internat. Assn. Bus. Communicators, Women in Communication, Internat. Platform Assn., Allen County Social Service Agy. Adminstrs. Presbyterian. Clubs: Fort Wayne Press, Foster Park Lioness (charter mem., dir. 1980), World Wide Travel, Fort Wayne Toastmistress Internat., Order Eastern Star. Contbr. articles to various publs. Office: Allen County Cancer Soc 2925 E State Blvd Fort Wayne IN 46805

GREEN, CAROL B., diet orgn. exec., banker; b. N.Y.C., Nov. 13, 1938; d. Paul N. and Ruth Forst; B.A., Loretto Heights Coll., 1978; student Queens Coll., Hunter Coll., U. Del.; married; children—Deborah, James David, Daniel J. Vice pres. Weight Watchers of Rocky Mountain Region, Inc., Littleton, Colo., 1968-73, pres., 1974—; partner Truffles Investment Co., Denver, 1979—; founder, dir. Women's Bank N.A., Denver, 1978—; pres. Contemporary Images, Inc.; chmn. bd. Cache Creek Nat. Bank. Mem. exec. bd. Boy Scouts Am., 1969—; chmn., keynote speaker, women and bus. conf. GSA, 1979. Mem. Colo. Small Bus. Council (exec. bd.), Presidents Round Table, World Weight Watchers Franchisee Assn., Denver C. of C. (dir.), Centennial C. of C. (dir.), Nat. Platform Assn. Club: Zonta (pres.). Office: 1449 W Littleton Blvd Littleton CO 80120

GREEN, CAROL H., lawyer, journalist; b. Seattle, Feb. 18, 1944; B.A. summa cum laude in History and Journalism, La. Tech. U., 1965; M.Law (Ford Found. fellow), Yale U., 1977; J.D., U. Denver, 1979. Intern, Shreveport (La.) Times, 1964, reporter, 1965-66; reporter Guam Daily News, 1966-67; city editor Pacific Jour., Agana, Guam, 1967-68; reporter, editorial writer, Denver Post, 1968-75, legal affairs reporter, 1977-79, asst. editor editorial page, 1979-81, house counsel, 1980—, labor relations mgr., 1981—; guest lectr. U. Colo. Journalism Sch.; seminar co-leader ct. news Idaho State U.; cons. San Mateo County (Calif.) Criminal Justice Council; mem. corrections task force Colo. Criminal Justice Standards and Goals, 1974-75. Recipient McWilliams award for ct. reform news, Denver, 1971, award for interpretive reporting Denver Newspaper Guild, 1979. Mem. Soc. Profl. Journalists, Am. (forum on communications law), Colo., Denver bar assns., Am. Judicature Soc. Clubs: Denver Press, Denver Athletic. Episcopalian. Office: Box 1709 Denver CO 80201

GREEN, CAROLYN LOUISE, urban planning cons.; b. Waterloo, Iowa, Apr. 9, 1950; d. Tommie Lee and Madelean (Tanner) G.; B.A., U. Iowa, 1973. Urban planner Calif. Air Resources Bd., Sacramento, 1974-76, Oakland, 1976-77; policy planner air, water, transp. Jack G. Raub Co., Costa Mesa, Calif., 1977-78; mgr. policy planning Jack G. Raub Co., Costa Mesa, 1978—; mem. clean air/clean water task force Calif. Bldg. Industry Assn., 1977—; mem. air quality com. Calif. Council Environ. and Econ. Balance, 1978—; vice-chmn. South Coast Air Quality Mgmt. Dist. Adv. Council; mem. regional issues adv. com., vice chmn. regional issues tech. com. Bldg. Industry Assn. So. Calif., 1979—; mem. Orange County Air Quality Subregional Tech. Com., 1978—; mem. steering com. regional citizens council So. Calif. Assn. Govts., 1981—. vice pres. Am. Lung Assn. Orange County, 1980—; mem. assembly dels. Orange County Health Planning Council, 1977—; chmn. Health Promotion Implementation Task Force; mem. Health Leadership Council, 1980—; founding mem./vice-chmn. steering com. Orange County Wellness Promotion Network; mem. long range planning com., bd. dirs. United Way Orange County North/South., 1980—; sec. bd. dirs. Orange County Urban League, 1982—. HUD urban studies fellow, 1972-73. Cert. urban planner Am. Inst. Cert. Planners. Mem. Am. Planning Assn., World Future Soc., Nat. Assn. Female Execs., Am. Demographics Assn., Nat. Council Negro Women, LWV. Home: 715 Poppy Ave Corona del Mar CA 92625 Office: 125 Baker St Costa Mesa CA 92626

GREEN, CLEOPATRA (PATSY) CAROLEE, communications exec.; b. Electric Mills, Miss., Nov. 6, 1938; d. Ralph and Marg (Eagerton) Green; B.A., U. S.C., 1960; postgrad., N.Y.U., 1981. Asst. dir. info. Savs. Bank Assn., N.Y.C.; lectr. in field. Author: History of Savings Bank Women 1930-1980. Home: 126 W 75th St New York NY 10023 Office: 200 Park Ave New York NY 10166

GREEN, DOROTHY BURKETT (MRS. LONSDALE B. GREEN), bus. exec., club woman; b. Raleigh, N.C., Oct. 28, 1902; d. Charles William and Laura (Weisman) Burkett; B.A., Vassar Coll., 1924; m. Lonsdale Bruce Green, Jan. 8, 1938. Riding tchr. Barnard Camp for Girls, Vt., 1920-24; interior decorator, N.Y.C. and Miami Beach, Fla., 1928—; real estate broker, 1943—; partner Hotel Devon, Miami Beach, 1950-59; partner House Closing & Maintenance Co., 1938-50. Pres., Vassar Club Dade County, 1950-60; pres. John Foster Dulles chpt. Woman's Cancer Assn. U. Miami, 1960-62, 80-81; registrar Biscayne chpt. D.A.R., 1958-60, vice regent, 1960-62, regent, 1962-64, now hon. regent, treas., 1966-68, state insignia chmn., 1958-60, state chmn. D.A.R. mag. advt., 1960-62, recipient nat. award for Insignia, 1960, nat. award mag. advt., 1962-64, rec. sec. Fla. soc., 1964-66, state chmn. Am. heritage com., 1963-64, nat. vice chmn. D.A.R. mag. advt. com., 1965-68, state chmn. membership commn., 1967-68, U.S.A. bicentennial com., 1968-72, pres. Fla. Officers Club, 1969-70, registrar Biscayne chpt., 1970-72, 81-83, treas. chpt., 1972-74, regent chpt., 1974-78, Fla. chmn. protocol, 1974-76, Fla. chmn. Seimes Microfilm Center, 1976-78, regent Biscayne chpt., 1978-80, pres. regent's council Greater Miami; state chmn. colonial courier Daus. Am. Colonists, 1961-64, chpt. regent, 1964-67, rec. sec. Fla. soc., 1967-68, registrar Gov. John West chpt., 1970-73, state chmn. bicentennial com., 1968-76; Fla. chmn. U.S.A. bicentennial com. U.S. Daus. of 1812, 1973-76; trustee Third Century, U.S.A., Miami, 1972-76. Recipient nat. award Am. Heritage, 1964. Club: La Gorce Country (chmn. womans golf assn. 1952-53; chmn. bridge com. 1971-73). Author: Horseback Riding, 1922; Canary Birds, 1931. Home: Oliver House 5333 Collins Ave Apt 11B Miami Beach FL 33140

GREEN, DOROTHY EUNICE, research psychologist; b. Montgomery, Ala., Dec. 18, 1917; d. Cliff and Wilsie J. (May) G.; B.S., Auburn U., 1937; M.A., Peabody Coll., 1941; Ph.D., U. Chgo., 1950. Research psychologist U.S. Air Force, Washington, 1951-54, U.S. CSC, Washington, 1954-67, USPHS, Washington, 1967-77, Chilton Research Services, Radnor, Pa., 1977-82; Audits & Surveys, Inc., 1982—. Mem. Am. Psychol. Assn., Eastern Psychol. Assn., D.C. Psychol. Assn. Presbyterian. Contbr. articles to profl. publs. Home: 3509 N Dickerson St Arlington VA 22207 Office: Audits & Surveys Inc Princeton NJ

GREEN, EDITH STARRETT, former Congresswoman; b. Trent, S.D., Jan. 19, 1910; d. James Vaughn and Julia (Hunt) Starrett; student Willamette U., Oreg., 1927-29; B.S., U. Oreg., 1939; LL.D. (hon.), Linfield (Oreg.) Coll., 1964, Yale U., 1965, Georgetown U., 1966, Reed (Oreg.) Coll., 1966, Oberlin (Ohio) Coll., 1966, Tex. Christian U., 1970, Beloit (Wis.) Coll., 1971; H.H.D. (hon.), U. Portland (Oreg.), 1969; D.Public Adminstrn. (hon.), Willamette U., 1970; children—James S., Richard Allan. Tchr., Salem (Oreg.) Schs., 1931-42; mem. U.S. Congresses from 3d Oreg. Dist., 1955-75, congressional del. Parliamentary Conf., Switzerland, 1958, NATO Conf., London, 1958, UNESCO Gen. Conf., Paris, 1964, 66, WHO Orgn., Switzerland, 1973, World Population Conf., Bucharest, 1974; dir. Pacific Northwest Bell Telephone, Seattle, Benjamin Franklin Savs. and Loan, Portland, Oreg. Physicians Service; mem. Oreg. Bd. Higher Edn. Trustee, Linfield Coll.; mem. adv. bd. U. Oreg. Health Scis. Center; chmn. Oreg. del. Democratic Nat. Conv., 1960, 68; Oreg. chmn. John F. Kennedy Presdl. campaign, 1960, Robert F. Kennedy presdl. primary campaign, 1968, Henry M. Jackson presdl. primary campaign, 1972. Recipient Eleanor Roosevelt Mary McLeod-Bethune World Citizenship award Nat. Council Negro Women, 1965; EE.B. McNaughton award ACLU, 1966; Pres. award Nat. Rehab. Assn., 1967; Disting. Service award NEA, 1968; citation World Conv. Chs. of Christ, 1970; Disting. Service award Nat. Assn. Trade and Tech. Schs., 1971; Outstanding Service award Nat. Assn. Student Personnel Adminstrs., 1972; AAUW Ann. Achievement award, 1974; Oreg. Broadcasters Assn. award, 1978; Portland's First Citizen award, 1978. Mem. Delta Kappa Gamma, Alpha Delta Kappa, Delta Sigma Theta. Home: 8031 Sacajaurea Way Wilsonville OR 97070

GREEN, ERNA JANE (MRS. LEONARD GREEN), exec. recruiting cons.; b. Norwalk, Conn., May 14, 1936; d. Allen A. and Bess R. Feldman; B.B.A., U. Miami, 1958; M.A., U. Bridgeport, 1972; m. Leonard Green, May 14, 1961. With A. G. Becker & Co., Inc., N.Y.C., 1958-61; tchr. sec. schs., Fairfield County, Conn., 1961-68; teaching asst. U. Bridgeport (Conn.), 1968-69; asso. Charles Irish Co., Inc., N.Y.C., 1978-80, sr. asso., 1980—. Mem. Town Council, New Canaan, Conn., 1975-79. Mem. Phi Alpha Theta. Home: 210 Main St New Canaan CT 06840 Office: 420 Lexington Ave New York NY 10017

GREEN, GERALDINE DOROTHY, state ofcl.; b. N.Y.C., July 14, 1938; d. Edward and Lula M. (Albro) Chisholm; student CCNY, 1961-64; J.D., St. John's U., 1968. Tax acct. Coopers & Lybrand, N.Y.C., 1966-68; admitted to N.Y. bar, 1968, Calif. bar, 1972; staff atty. IBM Corp., Gaithersberg, Md., 1969-71, Los Angeles, 1971-72; sr. atty., asst. corporate sec. Atlantic Richfield Co., Los Angeles, 1972-80; commr. Calif. Dept. Corps., Los Angeles, 1980—. Bd. dirs. Los Angeles area USO, 1978—. Mem. NAACP, Nat. Bar Assn., Am. Bar Assn., Nat. Legal Aid and Defender Assn., Calif. Assn. Black Lawyers, Calif. Women Lawyers Assn., Black Women Lawyers Calif., Los Angeles World Affairs Council, Women Lawyers Assn. Los Angeles, U.S. Olympic Soc. Office: California Dept of Corporations 600 S Commonwealth Ave 16th Floor Los Angeles CA 90005

GREEN, GLENDA, artist, educator; b. Weatherford, Tex., Feb. 4, 1945; d. Allen and Alma Green; B.F.A. magna cum laude, Tex. Christian U., 1967; M.A. (Kress fellow), Tulane U., 1970. One-woman shows: Central State U., Edmond, Okla., 1973, N. Tex. State U., 1974, U. Okla., 1975, 1977, Mus. Southwest, Midland, Tex., 1975, Okla. Mus. Art, Oklahoma City, 1976, Philbrook Art Center, Tulsa, 1978, Okla. Hist. Soc., Oklahoma City, 1979; group shows include: U. Tex., Arlington, 1975, Santa Fe Mus. Fine Arts, 1976, Okla. Art Center, Oklahoma City, 1977, 80, S. Tex. Artmobile, 1979-80; represented in permanent collections: Nat. Mus. History and Tech. Smithsonian Inst., Washington, Mus. City N.Y., Williams Coll. Mus. Art, N.Y.C., Tex. Christian U., Ft. Worth, U.S. Senator Allen J. Ellender Meml., Houma, La., Bizzell Meml. Library and Health Scis. Center, U. Okla.; research asst. to dir. Kimbell Art Mus., Ft. Worth, 1968, 69; curator collections Newcomb Art Sch., Tulane U., 1968-72, instr. art history, 1969-72; instr. U. Okla., 1973-75, guest artist on faculty, 1972-75; trustee Okla. Mus. Art; judge numerous exhbns. Adv. trustee George Lynn Cross Acad., Norman, Okla., 1978—. Mem. Coll. Art Assn. Am. Address: 8904-A Trone Circle Austin TX 78758

GREEN, HELEN, educator, cons.; b. Bklyn., Sept. 6, 1929; d. Morris and Rose (Brodsky) Green; B.A., Bklyn Coll., 1958; M.A., N.Y.U., 1968, Ph.D., 1975; m. Michael H. Lee, Nov. 23, 1957; 1 dau., Michele Carla. Counseling supr. Mt. Sinia Hosp., 1970-79; asst. prof. N.Y.U. 1973-81; cons. Standard Security Life Ins. Co., 1975-79, Mktg. Innovations, 1980—; Asso. prof. CUNY, 1981—; Family Ct. Project of ARC, 1960-66. Recipient Pres.s award Met. Rehab. Assn., 1979; Grad. Students award, 1979. Mem. APA, APGA, RCA. Co-author Drug Misuse/Human Abuse, 1975. Editorial bd. Jour. Addictions, 1978-82; contbr. articles to profl. jours. Home: 76 Oxford Dr Tenafly NJ 07670

GREEN, JOAN SHAPIRO, banker; b. Hampton, Va., Nov. 7, 1944; d. Isaac and Doris (Mintz) Shapiro; A.B. in Math. with honors, Mt. Holyoke Coll., 1966; m. Franklin Lewis Green, June 26, 1966; children—Jeffrey, Julia. Statis. analyst instrumentation lab. M.I.T., Cambridge, 1966-68; from calculator applications specialist to dir. mktg. services copiers SCM Corp., N.Y.C., 1968-81; v.p. mktg. Bankers Trust, N.Y.C., 1981—; speaker in field. Bd. dirs. Henderson House Coop. Apt., N.Y.C., 1980—, v.p., 1981—; friend Commn. Status of Women, N.Y.C., 1980—. Mem. Seven Colls. Careers Com. (a founder 1974, pres. 1975-81), Bus. and Profl. Women (chpt. dir. 1980-81). Club: Mt. Holyoke (dir.) (N.Y.C.). Home: 535 E 86th St New York NY 10028 Office: Bankers Trust 280 Park Ave New York NY 10017

GREEN, JOYCE, book pub. co. exec.; b. Taylorville, Ill., Oct. 22, 1928; d. Lynn and Vivian Coke (Richardson) Reinerd; A.A., Christian Coll., 1946; B.S., MacMurray Coll., 1948; m. Warren H. Green, Oct. 8, 1960. Asso. editor Warren H. Green, Inc., St. Louis, 1966-78, dir., 1978—; v.p. Visioneering Advt. Agy., 1972—; exec. sec. Affirmative Action Assn. Am., 1977—; pres. InterContinental Industries, Inc., 1980—; asst. to pres. Southeastern U., New Orleans, 1982—. Mem. Am. Soc. Profl. and Exec. Women, Direct Mktg. Club St. Louis, C. of C. Democrat. Methodist. Clubs: Jr. League, Clayton Women's. Home: 12120 Hibler Dr Creve Coeur MO 63141 Office: 8356 Olive Blvd Saint Louis MO 63132

GREEN, JOYCE BROWN, nurse; b. Sanford, Fla., Feb. 3, 1941; d. Coley and Beatrice Dean (Christian) Brown; B.S.N., Meharry Med. Coll., 1961; M.A., Pepperdine U., 1981; m. 1961; children—Darryl, Luci. Asst. head nurse Rancho Los Amigos Hosp., Downey, Calif., 1962-65; sch. nurse Los Angeles City Schs., 1968-74; asst. nursing dir. Martin Luther King Jr. Hosp., Los Angeles, 1974—. Mem. Pentacostal Ch. Club: United Foursquare Women's Orgn.

GREEN, JOYCE HENS, U.S. dist. judge; b. N.Y.C., Nov. 13, 1928; d. James Stanley and Hedy Emma (Bucher) Hens; B.A., U. Md., 1949; J.D., George Washington U., 1951; m. Samuel Green, Sept. 25, 1965; children—Michael Timothy, June Heather, James Harry. Admitted to D.C. bar, 1951, Va. bar, 1956; individual practice law, Washington, 1951-66; partner firm Green & Green, Washington, 1966-68; asso. judge D.C. Superior Ct. of D.C., 1968-79; U.S. dist. judge for D.C., 1979—. Chmn., Exec. Women in Govt., 1977; trustee D.C. div. Am. Cancer Soc., 1963-72. Recipient award Women's Legal Def. Fund, 1976, Alumni Achievement award George Washington U., 1975; Profl. Achievement award George Washington U. Law Alumni, 1978. Mem. Am. Bar Assn., D.C. Bar, Bar Assn. D.C., Women's Bar Assn. D.C. (Woman Lawyer of Yr. award 1979), Va. State Bar, Arlington County (Va.) Bar Assn., Phi Delta Phi, Kappa Beta Pi. Office: US Dist Ct Washington DC 20001

GREEN, JUNE LAZENBY, fed. judge; b. Arnold, Md., Jan. 23, 1914; d. Eugene H. and Jessie T. (Briggs) Lazenby; J.D., Am. U., 1941; m. John Cawley Green, Sept. 5, 1936. Admitted to Md. bar, D.C. bar, U.S. Supreme Ct. bars; claims adjuster Lumberman's Mut. Casualty Co., 1942-43, claims atty., 1943-47; pvt. practice law, Washington, 1947-68, Annapolis, Md., 1950-68; judge U.S. Dist. Ct. D.C., Washington, 1968—; bar examiner, Washington, 1963-68. Fellow Am. Acad. Matrimonial Lawyers; mem. Bar Assn. D.C. (dir. 1966-68), Women's Bar Assn. D.C. (Woman Lawyer of Year 1965, pres. 1955-57), Inter-Am., Am., Md. bar assns., Zonta, Kappa Beta Pi. Club: Nat. Lawyers (Washington). Home: 464 Joyce Ln Arnold MD 21012 also 550 N St SW Washington DC 20024 Office: US Courthouse 3d and Constitution NW Washington DC 20001

GREEN, LOLA ROSE, personal growth cons.; b. N.Y.C., Jan. 25, 1940; d. Irving and Esther Cohen; B.S., Cornell U., 1961; postgrad. Tulane U., 1961-63, New Sch. for Social Research, 1968-75; m. Walter A. Green, June 30, 1963; children—Jason and Jonathan (twins). Tchr., supr. emotionally disturbed children Judge Baker Guidance Center, Boston, 1961-63; fashion model, 1963-67; free-lance writer, 1967-73; founder, pres. Program Innovators, Glen Cove, N.Y., 1973—. Founder Nutrition Edn. Center of L.I.; nat. chmn. Family Renewal Conf. of Young Pres.'s Orgn. Mem. Nat. Speakers Assn., Meeting Planners Internat., Am. Soc. Tng. and Devel. Author: Great Places by the Sea, 1973; co-author: Success Secrets, 1979; Build A Better You...Starting Now, 1979. Office: Program Innovators Lattingtown Rd Glen Cove NY 11542

GREEN, MARY LOIS, ednl. adminstr., counselor; b. Eufaula, Okla., Feb. 3, 1935; d. Samuel P. and Agnes Burris; B.A., Langston U., 1967; postgrad. Oklahoma City U., 1973-74; M.A., Okla. State U., 1975, postgrad., 1976-78; m. Theodis G. Green, Oct. 23, 1969; 1 son, Theodis G. Tchr. spl. edn. public schs., Okla., 1968-72; supr.-counselor dept. early childhood devel. Langston U., from 1973, now interim dir. Young Hall. Active Langston Beautiful Club. Recipient Outstanding Tchr. award Oklahoma City Public Schs., 1968, named Art Tchr. of Yr., 1969. Mem. Okla. Edn. Assn., NEA, Zeta Phi Beta. Democrat. Baptist. Club: Okla. Federated (princess). Office: Langston U Langston OK 73050

GREEN, MARY VIRGINIA, pediatrician; b. Rockville Centre, N.Y., July 5, 1948; d. Arthur Francis and Rosemary Helen (Gill) Smity; B.A., Coll. of New Rochelle, 1970; M.D., SUNY, Syracuse, 1974; m. Tim D. Green, July 7, 1973; children—Jennifer, Daniel, Julia, David. Resident in pediatrics Bellevue Hosp-N.Y.U. Med. Center, N.Y.C., 1974-76, Upstate Med. Center, Syracuse, 1979-81; practice medicine specializing in pediatrics, Baldwinsville, N.Y., 1981—; clin. asst. prof. pediatrics SUNY Upstate Med. Center, Syracuse; mem. pediatric attending staff St. Joseph's Hosp., Crouse Irving Meml. Hosp., Syracuse. Served to capt., M.C., U.S. Army, 1976-79. Mem. Am. Acad. Pediatrics, Onandaga Pediatric Soc. Roman Catholic. Office: 8280 Willett Pkwy Baldwinsville NY 13027

GREEN, MI MI, actress; b. Waco, Tex., Oct. 3, 1947; s. Jeffrey Davis and Ruthie Lee G.; student Prairie View A. and M. Coll., 1967-69, Al Fann Theatrical Ensemble, 1973-82. Drama instr., dir. public relations, v.p. Al Fann Theatrical Ensemble, Inc., Hollywood, Calif., 1973—; actress in comml.s., films, record albums including Stevie Wonder's Songs in the Key of Life. Mem. The Media Forum, Nat. Assn. Female Execs., Home Ministries Am., Ministries for Higher Mind Devel., Screen Actors Guild, Am. Fedn. TV and Radio Arts Concerned Black Artists for Action. Club: N.Y. Health and Racquet. Office: 6043 Hollywood Blvd Suite 207 Hollywood CA 90028

GREEN, NANCY LOUGHRIDGE, coll. adminstr.; b. Lexington, Ky., Jan. 19, 1942; d. William S. and Nancy O. (Green) Loughridge; B.A. in Journalism, U. Ky., 1964; M.A. in Journalism, Ball State U., 1971; postgrad. U. Ky., 1968, U. Minn., 1968; m. Orrin Edward Young, Dec. 16, 1978. Tchr. English and publs. adv. Clark County (Ky.) High Sch., Winchester, Ky., 1965-66, Pleasure Ridge Park High Sch., Louisville, 1966-67, Clarksville (Ind.) High Sch., 1967-68, Charleston W.Va.) 1968-69; asst. publs. and public info. specialist W.Va. Dept. Edn., Charleston, 1969-70; tchr. journalism and publs. dir. Elmhurst High Sch., Ft. Wayne, Ind., 1970-71; student publs. adv. U. Ky., Lexington, 1971-82; gen. mgr. student publs. U. Tex., Austin, 1982—; pres. Media Cons., Inc., Lexington, 1980; dir. urban journalism workshop program Louisville and Lexington newspaper pubs., 1976; sec. Kernel Press, Inc., 1971-82. Bd. dirs. Jr. League, Lexington, 1980-82, Manchester 1978-82, pres., 1979-82. Recipient Ball State U. Journalism Alumnus award, 1975. Mem. Associated Collegiate Press, Journalism Edn. Assn. (W.Va. state dir. 1968-69), Nat. Council Coll. Publs. Advs. (pres. 1979—; Disting. Newspaper Adv. 1976). AP Mng. Editors, Ky. Intercollegiate Press Assn., Columbia Scholastic Press Assn., So. Interscholastic Press Assn., Internat. Newspaper Advt. and Mktg. Execs., Sigma Delta Chi. Contbr. articles on journalism edn. to profl. publs. Home: 1501 W 6th St Austin TX 78703 Office: Tex Student Publs PO Box D Austin TX 78712

GREEN, ROSE BASILE (MRS. RAYMOND S. GREEN), educator, poet, author; b. New Rochelle, N.Y., Dec. 19, 1914; d. Salvatore and Caroline (Galgano) Basile; B.A., Coll. New Rochelle, 1935; M.A., Columbia U., 1941; Ph.D., U. Pa., 1962; L.H.D. (hon.), Gwynedd-Mercy Coll., 1979, Cabrini Coll., 1982; m. Raymond S. Green, June 20, 1942; children—Carol-Rae (Mrs. Alfred Robert Hoffmann), Raymond Ferguson St. John. Tchr., Torrington (Conn.) High Sch., 1936-42; writer, researcher Fed. Writers Project, 1935-36; free-lance script writer Cavalcade of Am., NBC, 1940-42; assoc. prof. English, univ. registrar Tampa (Fla.) U., 1942-43; spl. instr. English, Temple U., Phila., 1953-57; prof. dept. English, Cabrini Coll., Radnor, Pa., 1957-70, chmn. dept., 1957-70. Exec. dir. Am. Inst. Italian Studies; dir. lit. com. Phila. Art Alliance; bd. dirs. Phila. Opera Co.; bd. dirs., trustee Free Library of Phila.; v.p., dir. Nat. Italian-Am. Found.; chair Nat. Adv. Council Ethnic Heritage Studies; adv. bd. Women for Greater Phila.; dir. Balch Inst. Phila. Decorated cavalier Republic of Italy; named Woman of Yr. Pa. Sons of Italy, 1975, Disting. Dau. of Pa., 1978; recipient Nat. Amita award for lit., 1976, Nat. Bicentennial award for poetry DAR, 1976, other awards for contbns. to lit. and edn. Mem. Am. Acad. Polit. and Social Sci., Acad. Am. Poets, Acad. Polit. Sci., Am. Studies Assn., Ethnic Studies Assn., AAUW (dir.-at-large), Nat. Council Tchrs. English, Am.-Italy Soc. (dir. 1952—), Eastern Pa. Coll. New Rochelle Alumnae (pres. 1951-54), Kappa Gamma Pi. Club: Cosmopolitan (Phila.). Author: Cabrinian Philosophy of Education, 1967; (poetry) To Reason Why, 1971, Primo Vino, 1974, 76 for Philadelphia, 1975, Century Four, 1981, Songs of Ourselves, 1982; (criticism) The Italian-American Novel, 1974; Woman, The Second Coming, 1977; Lauding the American Dream 1980; The Life of St. Francis Cabrini, 1982; Songs of Ourselves, 1982; editor faculty jour. A-Zimuth, 1963-70. Home: 308 Manor Rd Philadelphia PA 19128

GREEN, RUTH NELDA (CUMMINGS), educator; b. Greenway, Ark., Aug. 25, 1928; d. William Harrison and Opal Lee (Davis) G.; B.S. in Edn., U. Omaha (now U. Nebr., Omaha), 1966, postgrad.; m. Robert C. Green, Jr., Apr. 22, 1951 (dec.); children—Dana Lynn Green Schrad, Lisa Jane Green Noon. Tchr., Public Schs. Greenway, 1948-51, Hancock County (Miss.), 1951-53, Bellevue (Nebr.), 1961—. Bd. govs. edn. com. Fontenelle Forest Nature Center. NSF scholar, 1968-73. Mem. NEA, Nebr. Wildlife Assn., Nat. Audubon Soc. (Edn. award 1975), Omaha Audubon Soc., Bellevue Edn. Assn., Nebr. Edn. Assn., Inland Bird Banding Assn., Am. Birding Assn., Nebr. Ornithologists Union (state pres. 1982, dir.), Alpha Delta Kappa. Mem. Ch. of Christ. Columnist for Audubon Soc. Omaha Newsletter, Nebr. Ornithologists Union Newsletter. Home: 506 W 31st Ave Bellevue NE 68005 Office: 700 Galvin Rd Bellevue NE 68005

GREEN, SHIA TOBY RINER, therapist; b. N.Y.C., July 1, 1937; d. Murray A. and Frances Riner; student CCNY, 1954-57; B.A., Antioch Coll., 1974, M.A., 1976; m. Gary S. Green, Sept. 4, 1957; children—Margot Laura, Vanessa Daryl, Garson Todd. Press. and legis. sec. U.S. Ho. of Reps., Washington, 1960-71; cons. Rehab. Services Adminstrn., Social and Rehab. Services, HEW, 1972-73; asst. dir. State of Md. Foster Care Impact Dmonstration Project, 1977-78; therapist Alexandria (Va.) Narcotics Treatment Program, 1979—; mem. treatment com. Alexandria Case Mgmt. and Treatment of Child Sexual Abuse. Mem. exec. bd. Children's Adoption Resource Exchange, Washington; vol. worker Girl Scouts U.S.A., also Boy Scouts Am., 1970-74. Mem. Am. Psychol. Assn., Md. Psychol. Assn., Am. Assn. Marriage and Family Therapy. Co-author: Permanent Planning in Maryland—A Manual for the Foster Care Worker. Home: 7609 Hackamore Dr Potomac MD 20854 Office: Alexandria Narcotics Treatment Program 517 N St Asaph St Alexandria VA 22314

GREENAWALT, MARTHA SLOAN (MRS. KENNETH WILLIAM GREENAWALT), civic worker; b. Clarksburg, W.Va., Sept. 8, 1906; d. Herbert Elias and Louella (Dye) Sloan; A.B., Wilson Coll., 1928; M.A., Columbia, 1929; m. Kenneth William Greenawalt, Sept. 3, 1929; children—William Sloan, Robert Kent, Ann Cornell (Mrs. William Beaven Abernethy), Kim Chandler. Tchr., Berkeley Inst., Bklyn., 1929-33; pres. Westchester council Women's Coll. Clubs, 1952-53; mem. housing research com., mem. bd. Westchester Council Social Agys.; chmn. Greenburgh Urban Renewal Commn., 1961-75; mem. bd. Westchester citizens com. Nat. Council on Crime and Delinquency, 1975-82; mem. com. for constl. reform, 2d regional plan com., mem. bd. dirs. Regional Plan Assn., Westchester Alliance Juvenile and Criminal Justice; mem. Nat. Adv. Com. on Comprehensive Health Planning, 1972-74; mem. adv. bd. Greenburgh Neighborhood Health Center, 1974—; bd. dirs. Westchester County Urban League, 1957-62; v.p. United Way of Westchester, 1979-81; mem. exec. com. Women of Westchester; chmn. Westchester Women's Council, 1981—; mem. citizens adv. panel Tri-State Regional Planning Commn.; adv. council Women's Center; mem. Social Services Community Adv. Council, 1979-81; vice chmn. Legal Awareness for Women, 1981—. Mem. LWV (pres. Greenburgh 1953-56, pres. Westchester County 1957-59, pres. N.Y. 1963-67, mem. nat. bd. 1968-74, trustee Overseas Edn. Fund, pres. tri-state met. area 1981—), Scarsdale-Hartsdale UN Assn., NOW (dir. Central Westchester chpt. 1973-78), Wilson Coll. Alumnae Assn. (dir. 1979-82). Address: 65 Highridge Rd Hartsdale NY 10530

GREENBAUM, SHEILA, lawyer; b. Phila., Mar. 31, 1949; d. Albert and Libbie Greenbaum; B.A. Case Western Res. U., 1971; postgrad. Cleve. Marshall Coll. Law, 1971-73; J.D., U. Mo., Kansas City, 1974; m. Gary M. Wasserman. Admitted to Mo. bar, 1974; counselor ACLU Western Mo., 1974-75; asso. mem. firm Arthur A. Benson II, Kansas City, Mo., 1974-76; chief regional civil rights atty. HEW-Region VII, Kansas City, 1976-80, Dept. Edn., 1980-82; presiding ofcl. Merit Systems Protection Bd., St. Louis, 1982—. Mem. Regional Task Force on Reduction of Adolescent Pregnancy, Mayors Adv. Commn. on Human Relations. Bd. dirs. Jewish Community Relations Bur. (vice chmn.), ACLU (1st v.p.), Western Mo. Mem. Fed., Kansas City, Am. bar assns., Womens Polit. Caucus, Assn. Women Lawyers, Friends of Art, Com. for Free Choice. Home: 1539 Woodroyal W Dr Saint Louis MO 63017 Office: 1520 Market St Saint Louis MO 63103

GREENBERG, JEANNE LECRANN, corp. exec.; b. N.Y.C., Dec. 23, 1935; d. Vincent and Anne LeCrann; student Fairleigh Dickenson U., 1959-60, Rider Coll., 1974-78, Princeton U.; m. Herbert M. Greenberg, July 30, 1969; children—Scott, Phillip, Holly. Dir. field ops. Market Psychology, Inc., N.Y.C., 1958-61; dir. field ops., then v.p., dir. govt. services Mktg. Survey and Research Corp., Princeton, N.J., 1961-70, pres., 1975—; dir. placement and counseling OEO, New Opportunities Program, San Juan, P.R., 1965-66; dir. placement and counseling Social Research Corp., 1968-70; pres., gen. mgr. Progressive Communications, Inc., Sta. WIMG, Trenton, N.J., 1973—; exec. v.p. Personality Dynamics, Inc., Princeton, 1970—; founder, 1977, since pres. N.J. Radio Network; workshop leader, speaker in field. Trustee Del. Valley United Way, 1978—, chmn. publicity com., 1979—. Grantee OEO, 1965-66, Dept. Labor, 1968-69. Mem. Assn. Women in Radio and TV, Nat. Assn. Broadcasters, Nat. Radio Broadcasters Assn., N.J. Assn. Broadcasters, N.J. Press Club, Women's Equity Action League, Princeton C. of C., Mercer County C. of C. Democrat. Author articles in field. Home: 99 Ridgeview Circle Princeton NJ 08540 Office: PO Box 2050 Princeton NJ 08540

GREENBERG, JUDITH ANN, advt. exec.; b. Pitts., July 8, 1951; d. Jack Z. and Mary A. (Chayet) G.; B.B.A. in Mktg., SUNY, Binghamton, 1972. Asst. account exec. Wells Rich Greene, Inc., N.Y.C., 1973-75; account exec. Weltin Advt., Atlanta, 1975-76, Grey Advt., Toronto, 1976, N.Y.C., 1976-77; v.p., account supr. N.W. Ayer Internat., N.Y.C., 1977—. Home: 300 Fillow St West Norwalk CT 06850 Office: NW Ayer Internat 1345 Ave of Americas New York NY 10105

GREENBERG, JUDITH LYNN, social worker; b. N.Y.C., Feb. 9, 1947; d. Sam Paul and Celia (Lidofsky) G.; B.A. with distinction (Adelia Cheever scholar 1966), U. Mich., 1967; M.A., U. Chgo., 1970; postgrad. (univ. grantee) Adelphi U., 1979—. Elem. sch. tchr. Willow Run (Mich.) public schs., 1967-68; urban planner Chgo. Dept. Devel. and Planning, 1970-71; social worker Inst. Juvenile Research, Chgo., 1971; med. social worker St. Luke's Hosp., N.Y.C., 1972-73; social worker immigration and absorption dept. Jewish Agy., Jerusalem, 1973-74; social worker, student supr. Jewish Bd. Family and Children's Services, N.Y.C., 1974-82; dir. Queen's Preventive Services, Jewish Bd. Family and Children's Services, 1982—; instr. St. Joseph's Coll., Bklyn., 1979—; participant TV programs, family life edn. workshops. HEW fellow, 1968-70. Mem. Nat. Assn. Social Work, Assn. Sex Educators, Counselors and Therapists, Acad. Cert. Social Workers, Soc. for Sex Therapy and Research, Am. Soc. Tng. and Devel. Jewish. Home: 210 W 89th St Apt 1C New York NY 10024 Office: Queen's Preventive Services 89-14 Parsons Blvd Jamaica NY 11432

GREENBERG, LAURY REINER, camp dir.; b. N.Y.C., July 11, 1927; d. Louis Leon and Minnie (Berkowitz) Reiner; B.A., Queens Coll., 1948; postgrad. Hunter Coll., 1949-50; m. Jerry Greenberg, Sept. 12, 1948; children—Mara Sue, Mark Daniel, Lida Beth. Statistician, Boy Scouts Am., N.Y.C., 1948-49, Paramount Movies, N.Y.C., 1949-50; camp dir., owner Camp Birchwood, West Goshen, Conn., 1947—. Mem. Am., Conn. camping assns., Assn. Ind. Camps, Conn. Camp Dirs. Assn. Home: 140 Ash Dr Roslyn NY 11576

GREENBERG, LEAH, psychologist; b. Jan. 2; d. Laib and Hannah (Denman) G.; B.S., Johns Hopkins U.; B.H.L., Balt. Hebrew Coll.; M.A., Johns Hopkins U. Psychologist, Boys Village, Cheltenham, Md., 1963—. Mem. Am. Psychol. Assn., Eastern Psychol. Assn., Md. Psychol. Assn., Johns Hopkins Alumni Assn., Phi Delta Kappa, Phi Delta Gamma. Contbr. articles to profl. jours. Home: 3812 Glengyle Ave Baltimore MD 21215 Office: Boys Village Cheltenham MD 20623

GREENBERG, ROSALIE, child psychiatrist; b. Bklyn., Dec. 21, 1950; d. Sam and Molly G.; B.A., N.Y.U., 1972; student Upstate Med. Center, Syracuse, 1972-73; M.D., Columbia U., 1976; m. Soly Baredes, Aug. 25, 1973. Intern, Overlook Hosp., Summit, N.J., 1976-77; resident in gen. psychiatry Columbia Presbyn. Med. Center, N.Y. State Psychiatric Inst., N.Y.C., 1977-80, fellow in child and adolescent psychiatry, 1979-81, dep. dir. pediatric psychiatry outpatient clinic, 1981-82; dir. child and adolescent outpatient services Fair Oaks Hosp., Summit, N.J., 1982—; instr. Columbia U., 1981—. Mem. Am. Psychiat. Assn., Am. Acad. Child Psychiatry, N.Y. Acad. Scis., AMA. Office: Fair Oaks Hospital 19 Prospect St Summit NJ 07901

GREENBERGER, ELLEN, educator; b. N.Y.C., Nov. 19, 1935; d. Edward Michael and Vera (Brisk) Silver; B.A., Vassar Coll., 1956; M.A., Harvard U., 1959, Ph.D., 1961; m. Michael Burton, Aug. 26, 1979; children by previous Marriage—Kari Greenberger, David Greenberger. Instr., Wellesley (Mass.) Coll., 1961-63, asst. prof., 1963-67; sr. research scientist Johns Hopkins U., Balt., 1967-75; prof. social ecology U. Calif., Irvine, 1975—, dir. program in social ecology, 1975-80. USPHS fellow, 1956-59; Margaret Floy Washburn fellow, 1956-58; Ford Found. grantee, 1979-81; Spencer Found. grantee, 1979-81. Mem. Am. Psychol. Assn., Western Psychol. Assn., Am. Anthrop. Assn. Contbr. articles to profl. jours. Office: Program in Social Ecology U Calif Irvine CA 92717

GREENDORFER, SUSAN LOUISE, educator; b. San Francisco, Aug. 30, 1940; d. William Benjamin and Justine Louise (Nascimento) G.; A.B. cum laude, U. Calif., 1962, M.A., 1965; Ph.D., U. Wis., 1974. Tchr., San Francisco Unified Sch. Dist., 1963-69; asst. prof. sociology of sport, U. N.Mex., 1974-75; asst. prof. sociology of sport U. Ill., Champaign, 1975-80, assoc. prof., 1980—. NCAA grantee, 1982—. Fellow Assn. Anthrop. Study of Play; mem. AAHPER and Dance, Internat. Sociol. Assn., Internat. Com. Sport Sociology, N.Am. Soc. Psychology of Sport and Phys. Activity, Midwest Sociol. Soc., N.Am. Soc. for Sociology of Sport (co-founder, treas.). Editor: Sociology of Sport; Diverse Perspectives, 1981; contbr. in field. Home: 2204 Briar Hill Champaign IL 61820 Office: 3 ICBD 51 Gerty Dr Champaign IL 61820

GREENDORFER, TERESE RICH, fashion editor; b. Newark, Apr. 4, 1924; d. Robert D. and Rose Hannah (Rich) Grosman; student Centenary Jr. Coll., N.J., 1943, Tobe-Coburn Sch. Fashion Careers, N.Y.C., 1944; m. Sidney Greendorfer, Nov. 15, 1972; children—Richard Rogel, Todd Rogel, Rory Rogel. Mgr., lingerie buyer Junure House, N.J., 1945-47; feature writer Newark Star Ledger, 1965-66, fashion and beauty editor, 1966—. Recipient Frany, Fashion Reporting of N.Y. award, 1974; Israel Fashion medal, 1975; Fur Council Nat. Retail Merchants Assn. awards; Emba Mink Breeders awards. Mem. Nat. Fedn. Press Women, Inc., Newswomen's Club N.Y., Inc. Republican. Jewish. Home: Claridge House #2 Verona NJ 07044 Office: The Star Ledger Newark NJ 07101

GREEN-DORSEY, JEAN AUDREY, info. systems exec.; b. Cleve., Oct. 27, 1940; d. Sydney Howard and Bennie Irene (Blake) Green; B.A., L.I. U., 1962; m. William R. Dorsey, Nov. 1, 1980. With IBM, N.Y.C., 1966-72; mktg. mgr. office automation Olivetti, N.Y.C., 1972-80; dep. dir. N.Y.C. Mgmt. Info. Systems, 1981—; sr. cons. Inst. Mgmt. Devel., 1980—; adv. editor Hearst Pubs., 1981—, others; lectr. in field. Bd. dirs. Fair Harbor Community Assn., 1981—. Recipient cert. Fresh Air Fund, 1980. Mem. Internat. Word and Info. Processing Assn., Am. Mgmt. Assn. Clubs: Sales Execs. of N.Y., The Club at N.Y. World Trade Center. Contbr. articles to profl. jours. Office: 44 Beaver St New York City NY 10004

GREENE, BEVERLY ANN, psychologist; b. Orange, N.J., Aug. 14, 1950; B.A., N.Y.U., 1973; M.A., Inst. Advanced Psychol. Studies, 1977, Ph.D., 1983; postgrad. Marquette U., 1973-74. Psychologist div. child/adolescent psychiatry Downstate Med. Center, also clin. instr. King County Hosp., 1973-74; psychology fellow Mental Retardation Inst., N.Y. Med. Coll., Valhalla, N.Y., 1974-76; cons. psychologist Williamsberg Child Devel. Center, Bklyn., 1976-78; research asst. N.J. Coll. Medicine and Dentistry, also VA Med. Center, 1979-80; psychology trainee Brookdale Hosp. and Med. Center, 1980; sch. psychologist N.Y.C. Public Schs., 1980—. Mem. Internat. Neuropsychol. Soc., Am. Psychol. Assn., N.Y. Assn. Black Pyschologists, N.Y. Neuropschology Group.

GREENE, DANA KATHERINE, historian; b. Orange, N.J., May 20, 1942; d. Charles Dresser and Dorothea (Benson) G.; B.A., Coll. New Rochelle, 1963; M.A., No. Ill. U., 1967; Ph.D., Emory U., 1971; m. Richard Roesel, Dec. 21, 1968; children—Kristin, Justin, Lauren, Ryan. Vol., Peace Corps, Costa Rica, 1963-65; asst. prof. history St. Mary's Coll. Md., St. Mary's City, 1971-75, assoc. prof., 1975—; ednl. policy fellow Office Edn., Div. Internat. Edn., 1975-76, cons., 1977—. Mem. D.C. com. on observance Internat. Woman's Year; commn. mem. Fairfax County History Commn. Nat. Endowment for Humanities summer seminar grantee, 1974, 78; Am. Philos. Soc. grantee, 1979; AAUW grantee, 1979, Radcliffe Coll. grantee, 1981; African study/travel grantee Am. Hist. Assn., 1982. Mem. AAUW (dir. Ednl. Found., mem. bd. D.C. br.), Am. Hist. Assn. (coordinating com. women in hist. professions), NOW, Fellowship Reconciliation, Council Adoptable Children, Women's Internat. League for Peace and Freedom. Democrat. Roman Catholic. Editor: Lucretia Mott: Complete Sermons and Speeches, 1981. Office: Calvert Hall St Mary's Coll Md Saint Mary's City MD 20686

GREENE, ELIZABETH BOWEN, state ofcl.; b. Ashville, N.C.; d. Robert Alexander and Lillian Elizabeth (Collins) Bowen; B.A., Meredith Coll., 1951; M.S., Hunter Coll., 1978; children—Anne, Robert, Laura. Actress, The Lost Colony Co., Manteo, N.C., 1951; staff The Barter Theatre, Abingdon, Va., 1953; commentator WWNC Radio, WLOS-TV, Ashville, 1955-56; employment counselor Youth Opportunity Center, Jamaica, N.Y., 1965-69; sr. counselor Sheridan Rehab. Center, N.Y.C., 1969-71; asso. counselor Queensboro Rehab. Center, L.I., 1971-76, program dir., 1975-76; supr. div. substance abuse Manhatton Outreach, 1976-79; supr. specialized treatment services N.Y. State Div. Substance Abuse Services, N.Y.C., 1979—. Legis. chmn. Forest Hills Neighbors Assn., 1973, v.p., 1974; mem. Queensboro Pres.'s Council on Drug Addiction, 1973-76; mem. Dist. Adv. Council on Human Services, 1974-79; mem. county com. Queens Liberal Party, N.Y., 1972-76, vice chmn., 1972-74; bd. mgrs. St. Clement's Episcopal Ch. Cert. rehab. counselor. Mem. Nat. Rehab. Assn., Nat. Rehab. Counselors Assn., Nat. Fedn. Bus. and Profl. Women's Clubs, Nat. Assn. Female Execs. Democrat. Author: Demographic Characteristics of Successful Clients in Drug Abuse Rehabilitation, 1977. Home: 85-44 67 Dr Rego Park NY 11374 Office: 80 Centre St Room 332 New York NY 10013

GREENE, GERALDINE MARIE, clin. social worker; b. N.Y.C., Aug. 5, 1944; d. Daniel Joseph and Helen Mary Callahan; B.A., Mercy Coll., 1966; M.S.W., Fordham U., 1968; postgrad. Hunter Coll., 1978—; m. Sept. 3, 1966; 1 son, Sean. Group homes supr. St. Germaine's Home, Peekskill, N.Y., 1969-75; asso. exec. dir., dir. group homes St. Mary's-in-the-field, Valhalla, N.Y., 1975-77; dir. family services Family and Community Services, Roman Catholic Archidiocese of Paterson, N.J., 1977-79; exec. dir. Scarsdale Family Counseling Service (N.Y.), 1979—; instr. Fordham U. Sch. Social Work, 1973-75. NIMH fellow, 1966-68. Mem. Nat. Assn. Social Workers, Acad. Cert. Social Workers. Home: Dogwood Ct Goldens Bridge NY 10526 Office: 403 Harwood Ct Scarsdale NY 10583

GREENE, HELEN FINCH, psychologist, educator; b. Schenectady, Oct. 3, 1920; d. Raymond J. and May (Tandy) Finch; B.A., Elmira Coll., 1942; M.A., Columbia U., 1943; Ph.D., Fla. State U., 1954; m. Philip S. Greene, Mar. 26, 1955; children—John, Margaret. Instr. child devel. E. Carolina Tchrs. Coll., Greenville, N.C., 1943-44; instr., asst. prof. child devel., dir. nursery sch. Winthrop Coll., 1944-46; asst. prof. child devel. Auburn U., 1946-52; grad. teaching asst. Fla. State U., 1952-54, asso. prof. child devel. and family relations, 1954-57; sch. psychologist Coventry (R.I.) Sch. Dept., 1958-71; asst. prof. child devel. and family relations U. R.I., 1971-73, asso. prof., dir. Child Devel. Center, 1973—; psychologist Aptitude Testing Service, Providence, 1958-59; cons. psychologist Smithfield (R.I.) Sch. Dept., 1965-68, Green Acres Country Day Sch., Providence, 1964-67. Mem. Gov.'s Commn. for Internat. Yr. of the Child, 1979. Mem. Am., R.I. (v.p. 1976) home econs. assns., Internat. Fedn. Home Econs., New Eng. Measurement and Evaluation in Guidance. Club: North Kingstown (R.I.) Women's. Office: Quinn Hall U RI Kingston RI 02881

GREENE, JOANNE ROSENZWEIG, radio sta. exec.; b. Boston, Feb. 14, 1954; d. Max Israel and Irene (Mittleman) Rosenzweig; student Northwestern U., 1971-73; B.S., Emerson Coll., 1975; m. Fred S. Greene, June 21, 1980. Public affairs dir. Sta. KRE, Berkeley, Calif., 1975-78; news dir. Sta. KSAN, San Francisco, 1978-80; public affairs dir. Sta. KFRC, San Francisco, 1981—; consumer reporter Evening Mag., Sta. KPIX-TV, San Francisco, 1981-82; freelance producer radio series. Bd. dirs. Youth News, Oakland, Calif., Vietnam Veterans Project, San Francisco. Recipient Armstrong award, 1977, Gabriel award, 1981, San Francisco State Broadcast award, 1982. Mem. Am. Women in Radio and TV, Radio and TV News Dirs. Assn. Democrat. Jewish. Office: 415 Bush St San Francisco CA 94108

GREENE, JUDITH ANN, nurse, educator; b. Cleve., June 11, 1946; d. J. Wesley and Maryle (Tallente) G.; nursing diploma Baroness Erlanger Hosp. Sch. Nursing, Chattanooga, 1967; B.S.N. cum laude, So. Missionary Coll., 1974; M.S.N. in Psychiat. Mental Health Nursing, Vanderbilt U., 1975; postgrad. (NIH trainee) U. Ala., Birmingham, 1977-78; Ph.D. in Higher Edn. Adminstrn., George Peabody Coll. for Tchrs., Vanderbilt U., 1980. Clin. nurse Moccasin Bend Psychiat. Inst., Chattanooga, 1967-68, nurse mgr. acute care facility, 1969-73, nurse mgr. longterm care facility, 1974; cons. nursing Medicare div. Blue Cross/Blue Shield, Chattanooga, 1968-69; clin. nurse T. C. Thompson Children's Hosp., Chattanooga, 1973; clin. specialist Westcott Psychiat. Pavillion, Dalton, Ga., 1977-78; instr. Columbia (Tenn.) Community State Coll., summer 1975; instr. U. Tenn., Chattanooga, 1975-76, asst. prof., 1976-77; asst. prof., coordinator psychiat. mental health nursing, dir. nurse practitioner unit Meharry Med. Coll., 1978-80; asst. prof. nursing U. Tenn., Knoxville, 1980-82, assoc. prof., 1982—, also coordinator psychosocial nursing; workshop, conf. presentations; blood pressure screening Am. Heart Assn., Knoxville, 1981; test rev. cons. R. N. Licensure Exam Revs., Es-Di-En-Ci, Inc., Lexington, Ky. Vol. counselor Crisis Call Center, Nashville, 1978-80. Mem. Am. Nurses'

Assn., Tenn. Nurses' Assn., Nat. League Nurses, Am. Nurses' Found. (charter), Sigma Theta Tau. Contbr. articles to profl. jours. Office: 1200 Volunteer Blvd Knoxville TN 37916

GREENE, LOUISE ROBERTS, coll. adminstr.; b. Bedford, Va., Sept. 7, 1929; d. James Rush and Ethel (Wright) Skinnell; B.S. in Secondary Edn., U. Tenn., 1970, M.S. in Ednl. Adminstrn. and Supervision, 1974, Ed.D. in Ednl. Adminstrn. and Supervision, 1981; m. Sterling Roberts, Mar. 31, 1950 (dec. 1967); children—Lucinda Roberts Baird, Elizabeth Roberts Heaton; m. 2d, Raymond A. Greene, Jr., Nov. 23, 1972; stepchildren—Susan Greene Dickson, Elizabeth Greene Cooley, Karen Lee. Personnel asst. Carbide Nuclear Co., 1946-53; tchr. Oak Ridge High Sch., 1970-71; dir. admissions and records Roane State Community Coll., Harriman, Tenn., 1971-78, dir. ednl. services, 1978—. Mem. Tenn. Assn. Collegiate Registrars and Admissions Officers, So. Assn. Collegiate Registrars and Admissions Officers, Am. Assn. Collegiate Registrars and Admissions Officers, Phi Kappa Phi, Alpha Lambda Delta, Pi Lambda Theta. Republican. Presbyterian. Research on relationships between managerial style and effectiveness. Home: PO Box 4 Kingston TN 37763 Office: Roane State Community College Harriman TN 37748

GREENE, MARY NOLIN, clin. social worker; b. Auburn, N.Y., July 1, 1927; d. Charles Joseph and Myrna Josepha (Tallman) Nolin; B.A., Marymount Coll., 1949; M.S.W., Syracuse U., 1976; m. James Greene, Aug. 27, 1949; children—Charles, Michael, James, Mary. Sch. social worker Cayuga-Onondaga B.O.C.E.S., Auburn, 1976-77; psychiat. social worker Cayuga County Community Mental Health Center, Auburn, 1977—; geratric/phobic control cons.; individual, group and family therapist. Pres., Auburn Service League, 1957-58; pres. Cayuga County Homemakers, Inc., 1965-66. Mem. Nat. Assn. Social Workers, LWV. Republican. Roman Catholic. Home: 16 Teller Ave Auburn NY 13021 Office: 146 North St Auburn NY 13021

GREENE, NANCY ELLEN, clin. psychologist, speech pathologist; b. Miami, Fla., July 4, 1948; d. Morris Edward and Leona Betty (Hoffman) G.; A.A., Colby Jr. Coll., 1968; B.S., Boston U., 1970, M.Ed., 1971; M.A., Calif. Sch. Profl. Psychology, 1975, Ph.D., 1977. Staff speech pathologist Lemuel Shattuck Rehab. Hosp., Boston, 1971-72, supr. speech and hearing dept., 1972-73; psychol. intern Catholic Family Services, San Diego, 1975-76; County Mental Health Services, San Diego, 1976-77; pvt. practice speech pathology, San Diego, 1974—; clin. psychologist San Diego Group, 1976—, speech pathologist, 1979—; cons. to numerous hosps., agys. Mem. Am. Speech and Hearing Assn., Am. Psychol. Assn., Calif. Psychol. Assn. Office: 7670 Opportunity Rd Suite 165 San Diego CA 92111

GREENE, SHARON ELIZABETH, chem. co. sec.; b. White Plains, N.Y., Aug. 24, 1946; d. Conway Elwood and Georgette Julia (Dailey) G.; exec. secretarial diploma Berkeley Secretarial Sch., 1970, word processing diploma, 1982; A. Applied Secretarial Scis., Berkeley-Claremont Sch., 1975; student in bus. adminstrn. and mktg. Pace U., 1975—. Sec., Mut. N.Y., N.Y.C., 1970-71, U.S. div. mfg. dept. Mobil Oil Corp., N.Y.C., 1971-72; sec. dept. central distbn. Mobil Chem. Europe, N.Y.C., 1972—; mem. career mktg. bd. Mademoiselle mag., 1979—; working women's panel Glamour mag., 1980—; nat. adv. bd. Today's Sec. mag., 1980—. Internat. chairperson Nat. Council Negro Women, Bronx, N.Y., 1977-80, rec. sec., 1977-79, del. nat. conv., 1979, 81, 2d v.p., 1979-81, 1st v.p., 1981-82; hon. mem. nat. adv. bd. Am. Biog. Inst. Recipient Mary McLeod Bethune Achievement award Nat. Council Negro Women, 1977. Mem. Profl. Secs. Internat. (corr. sec. N.Y.C. chpt. 1980-81, chpt. v.p. 1981-82), Am. Mktg. Assn., Nat. Assn. Female Execs., Nat. Assn. Negro Bus. and Profl. Women's Clubs (asst. rec. sec. chpt. 1976-78), N.Y. League Bus. and Profl. Women's Clubs, Internat. Platform Assn., N.Y.C. Jr. C. of C., LWV. Club: Toastmistress (sec. 1981-82; council nominating com.). Home: 54 Lytton Ave Hartsdale NY 10530 Office: 150 E 42d St New York NY 10017

GREENFIELD, HELEN MEYERS, former insp. and test service exec.; b. Albany, N.Y., Aug. 4, 1908; d. Stephen and Catherine (Bronkov) Meyers; grad. Baker's Bus. Sch., 1924; m. Frank L. Greenfield, Apr. 1, 1929; children—Stuart Franklin, Val Shea. Accounts supr. George G. McCaskey Co., N.Y.C., 1924-29; spl. assignments purchasing dept. McCall's Pub. Co., 1929, Fgn. Affairs Publs., Inc., 1929-31; with purchasing dept. Glidden-Buick Corp., 1931-32; interviewer Civil Works Adminstrn., supr. filing and payroll systems Houston St. Project Center, 1933-36; with dept. accounting Reuben H. Donnelley Co., 1936-37; supr. layouts, makeup prins. of semi-monthly publs. Tide Publs., Inc., 1939-41; asst. to purchasing agt., supr. maintenance perpetual inventory Hopeman Bros., 1941-43; with money order div., corr. dept. U.S. Govt., P.O. Dept., N.Y.C., 1943-44; v.p. Frank L. Greenfield Co., Inc., N.Y.C., 1945-59; v.p. All Purpose Chair Corp., 1950-55; pres. Val Equipment, Inc., 1950-62; v.p. Am. TestingLabs., Inc., 1950-63; supr. personnel, purchases Irving Lampert Co., 1951-52; account assignment coordinator, advt. contracts dept. Newsweek, N.Y.C., 1970-78, ret., 1978; owner, operator Princess Helen Antiques, Helen M. Greenfield Realty Corp., New York Bd. Elections, 1936; active New York Heart Assn.; producer hostess ann. banquet Mt. Laurel Chapel, 1960—. Named Hon. princess Cherokee Tribe by Chief Rising Sun of Richmond, Va. Club: Order Eastern Star (past matron).

GREENFIELD, LOIS BRODER, educator; b. Chgo., Feb. 5, 1924; d. Samuel and Rose (Michel) Broder; B.S., U. Chgo., 1945, M.S., 1946; Ph.D., U. Calif., Berkeley, 1953; 1 dau., Ellen Beth. Faculty, U. Wis., Madison, 1956—, prof. engring., 1958—. Mem. Am. Soc. Engring. Edn., Am. Psychol. Assn., Am. Ednl. Research Assn., Soc. Women Engrs. Contbr. articles to profl. jours. Office: General Engineering Bldg U Wis Madison WI 53706

GREENFIELD, MEG, journalist; b. Seattle, Dec. 27, 1930; d. Lewis James and Lorraine (Nathan) Greenfield; B.A. summa cum laude, Smith Coll., 1952, L.H.D. (hon.), 1978; L.H.D., Georgetown U., 1979; Fulbright scholar Newnham Coll., Cambridge (Eng.) U., 1952-53. With Reporter mag., 1957-68, Washington editor, 1965-68; editorial writer Washington Post, 1968-70, dep. editorial page editor, 1970-79, editorial page editor, 1979—; columnist Newsweek mag., 1974—. Recipient Pulitzer prize for editorial writing, 1978. Mem. Am. Soc. Newspaper Editors, Phi Beta Kappa. Club: Federal City (Washington). Home: 3318 R St NW Washington DC 20007 Office: 1150 15th St NW Washington DC 20005

GREENFIELD, SUSAN COHEN, mktg. specialist; b. Houston, June 27, 1943; d. Aaron J. and Felice W. Cohen; student U. Tex., 1963; B.S. in Psychology, U. Houston, 1965; systems engring. cert. IBM, 1967; children—Elizabeth Ann, Alysha Lynn. Br. mgr., fin. cons. FLC Fin. Services, Sherman Oaks, Calif., 1973-75; salesperson, ter. mgr. C.R. Bard Inc., Murray Hill, N.J., 1975-77; OEM mktg. specialist high tech. sales Honeywell, Inc., Los Angeles, 1977—. Bd. dirs. Orange County Easter Seal Soc., Rehab. Inst. Orange County, del. Calif. state conv., 1982; mem. Orange County Music Center. Named to Honeywell Pres.'s Club, 1980. Mem. Mensa, Psi Chi. Photographs pub. in book of poetry, 1970. Home: 432 Roni Ln Anaheim CA 92807 Office: 6620 Telegraph Rd Los Angeles CA 90040

GREENFIELD, THELMA NELSON, educator; b. Portland, Sept. 11, 1922; d. Ivar Emanuel and Lulu Ruth (Maxwell) Nelson; B.A., U. Oreg., 1944, M.A., 1947; Ph.D., U. Wis., 1952; m. Stanley B. Greenfield, Jan. 22, 1951; children—Tamma L., Sayre N. Instr., Queens (N.Y.) Coll. Sch. Gen. Studies, 1955-56; mem. faculty U. Oreg., Eugene, 1963—, prof. English, 1972—; vis. prof. U. Regensburg, 1974-75; guest lectr. Oreg. State Penitentiary. Mem. MLA, Shakespeare Assn. Am., Renaissance Soc. Am., Philol. Assn. Pacific Coast. Club: Shakespeare (Eugene). Author: The Intduction in Elizabethan Drama, 1969; The Eye of Judgment, 1982; contbr. articles in field to profl. jours. Office: Department of English University of Oregon Eugene OR 97403

GREENHOUSE, SALLY ELLEN, govt. ofcl.; b. Washington, Jan. 2, 1949; d. Ferd D. and Angelina (Manthos) O'Donnell; student No. Va. Extension, U. Va., 1968, 70; B.S., Radford State Tchrs. Coll., 1971; m. Waymon G. Hefner; 1 dau., Angelina. With Dept. Air Force, full and part-time, 1966-74, personnel specialist, to 1974; personnel specialist Fed. Energy Office, 1974; supervisory personnel specialist Dept. Treasury, Washington, 1974-78; with D.C. Govt., 1978-80, dep. asso. dir. for staffing services, to 1980; mgr. staffing and classification Bur. Govt. Fin. Ops., Dept. Treasury, 1980, mgr. policy and evaluation, 1980—. Recipient various outstanding performance ratings. Home: Route 1 Box 910 Washington VA 22747 Office: Treasury Annex Madison Pl and Pennsylvania Ave NW Washington DC 20226

GREENLEAF, KATHERINE MAXIM, lawyer, ins. co. exec.; b. N.Y.C., Oct. 28, 1948; d. George Lionel and Mildred Norris (Jameson) Maxim; B.A. with honors, Conn. Coll., 1970; J.D., Boston U., 1973; m. Peter Greenleaf, July 1, 1972; children—Julia Tyler, Robert Morgan. Admitted to Maine bar, 1973, Mass. bar, 1973; atty. Union Mutual Life Ins. Co., Portland, Maine, 1973-78, asso. counsel, 2d v.p. litigation, 1978-79, 2d v.p. benefits div., 1979-80, v.p. adminstrn., 1980—; trustee Portland Savs. Bank. Mem. Internat. Claim Assn., Maine Bar Assn., Maine Trial Lawyers Assn.

GREENLEE, JANET STELLE, social worker; b. Washington, Jan. 22, 1946; d. Bernard Keith and Lillian (Kirtzman) Johnpoll; B.S., Ohio State U., 1967; M.S.W., W.Va. U., 1973; M.B.A. in Acctg. and Fin., UCLA, 1978; m. James K. Greenlee, Sept. 1, 1967; 1 son, David Karl. Dir. homemaker team Family Service Agy., Fairmont, W.Va., 1973-74; adminstrv. dir., controller Portals House, Inc., Los Angeles, 1977-78; analyst Arthur Andersen & Co., Los Angeles, 1978-79; dir. Russian resettlement Jewish Family and Children's Service, Denver, 1979-80; mgmt. cons. for nonprofit orgns., 1979—; mem. adj. faculty U. Denver Grad. Sch. Social Work, 1980-81. Mem. Nat. Assn. Social Workers. Home: 6642 E Peakview Pl Englewood CO 80111 Office: U Denver Grad Sch Social Work 2148 S High St Denver CO 80208

GREENMAN, JILL DANFORTH, public relations exec.; b. Lafayette, Ind., Oct. 9, 1947; d. Frederick Snow and Eugenie (Doran) G.; B.A., DePauw U., 1969; M.S.J., Northwestern U., 1976. Pub. relations specialist Harris Trust & Savs. Bank, Chgo., 1976-78; account supr. Burson-Marsteller, Chgo., 1978-81; account group supr. Golin/Harris Communications, Inc., Chgo., 1982—; pub. relations cons.; press relations mgr. for Ill. State Rep., 1978. Recipient award Internat. Assn. Bus. Communicators, 1978. Mem. Pub. Relations Soc. Am., Northwestern U. Alumni Assn., Alpha Phi. Republican. Roman Catholic. Home: 70 W Burton Pl Chicago IL 60610 Office: 500 N Michigan Ave Chicago IL 60611

GREENSLADE, GERTRUDE SCHROEDER, economist, educator; b. Albuquerque, Feb. 20, 1920; d. Thomas B. and Elsa E. (Koch) Guyton; B.S., Colo. State Coll., 1936; M.A., Johns Hopkins U., 1948, Ph.D., 1953. Economist various fed. agys., 1941-69; prof. econs. U. Va., 1969—. Mem. Am. Econ. Assn., Assn. Comparative Econ. Studies, AAAS. Author: Growth of Major Steel Companies in the United States, 1900-1950, 1954; contbr. in field. Home: 1800 Jefferson Park Ave Charlottesville VA 22903 Office: Rouss 114 University of Virginia Charlottesville VA 22901

GREENSTEIN, RUTH LOUISE, lawyer; b. N.Y.C., Mar. 28, 1946; d. Milton and Beatrice (Zutty) Greenstein; B.A., Harvard U., 1966; M.A., Yale U., 1968; J.D., George Washington U., 1980; m. David Seidman, May 19, 1972. Fgn. service info. officer USIA, Washington and Tehran, Iran, 1968-70; adminstrv. asst. Export-Import Bank of the U.S., Washington, 1971-72; asst. dean Woodrow Wilson Sch. Public and Internat. Affairs, Princeton U., 1972-75; budget examiner U.S. Office Mgmt. and Budget, Washington, 1975-79; budget coordinator U.S. Internat. Devel. Coop. Agy., 1979-81; admitted to D.C. bar, 1980; asso. gen. counsel NSF, 1981—. Mem. Am. Bar Assn., D.C. Bar Assn. Office: National Science Foundation 1800 G St NW Washington DC 20550

GREENWALD, CAROLINE MEYER, artist; b. Madison, Wis., Jan. 30, 1936; d. Frank Gustave and Lina Doris (Logemann) Meyer; B.S., U. Wis., 1957, M.A. in Art, 1975, M.F.A. in Art, 1977; U. Notre Dame Dept. Art Workshop, 1976; children—Elaine Kathryn, Geraldine Lynn. One-woman shows: U. Wis. Humanities Gallery, 1975, Source Gallery, San Francisco, 1977, U. Wis. Union Gallery, Madison, 1977, Cin. Acad. Art, 1977, Galleria Kin, Mexico City, 1979, Loyola U., Chgo., 1979, Getler/Paul Gallery, N.Y.C., 1980, Evanston (Ill.) Art Center, 1980, Fendrick Gallery, Washington, 1981, Carleton Coll., Northfield, Minn., 1982, Getter/Paul Gallery, N.Y.C., 1982; group shows include: Nat. Collection Fine Arts, Washington, 1977, Detroit Inst. Arts, 1979, Suibu Mus. Art, Tokyo, 1979, Smithsonian Instn. Traveling Exhbn., 1978-80, Pratt Graphics Center, N.Y.C., 1978, Traveling Exhbn. of Ind. Curators, 1978-80, 10th Internat. Biennial of Tapestry, Lausanne, Switzerland, 1981, Internat. Touring Exhbn. World Print Council, 1981-83, Mus. Applied Art, Belgrade, Yugoslavia, 1981, Am. Craft Mus., N.Y.C., 1982, Arts Council Gt. Britain, 1982, Australian Nat. Gallery, 1982, Fine Arts Mus. L.I., 1982; represented in permanent collections: Mus. Modern Art, N.Y.C., Phila. Mus. Art, Davidson Art Center Wesleyan U., Middletown, Conn., Art Inst. Chgo., Elvehjem Art Center and Madison Art Center, U. Wis., Amoco, Internat. Piper Co, Wis. Union Art Collection U. Wis., Container Corp. Am., EPA, San Francisco, Mpls. Inst. Arts, Owens Corning Fiberglas, Toledo, Owens Ill., Ohio, others; affiliated with Getler/Pall Gallery, N.Y.C., Alice Simsar Gallery, Ann Arbor, Peter M. David Gallery, Mpls., and Fendrick, Washington; vis. artist, lectr., including Unique Print Symposium of Washington Print Club and Nat. Collection Fine Arts, Smithsonian Instn., Washington, 1978, Internat. Hand Papermakers Confs., 1975—, Loyola U., 1979, U. Wis., Stevens Point, 1979, Printmaking Council N.J., 1982, Carleton Coll., 1982. Subject of articles in profl. and popular publs. Address: 3400 Cross St Madison WI 53711

GREENWALD, DOROTHY I., educator; b. Harrison, Ark., Sept. 22, 1920; d. George W. and Caroline (Brown) Neal; student Sch. of Cosmetology, Miami, Okla., 1938-39, Craft Students League, N.Y.C., 1958-62; m. Harry Greenwald, Apr. 17, 1949. Owner, operator beauty salon and ladies ready to wear stores, 1940-58; instr. ceramic dept. Craft Student League, N.Y.C., 1962-80, Queens Museum Sch. of Art, Flushing, N.Y., 1980—; chmn. Craft Students League of YWCA of N.Y.; treas. Greenwald Electro-Mech. Cons., Inc., Whitestone, N.Y. Recipient awards Rockland Center for Art, 1972, L.I. Guild of Craftsmen, 1972, Artist-Craftsmen N.Y., 1975. Mem. World Craft Council, Am. Craft Council, Artist-Craftsmen N.Y. (pres. 1972-75), L.I. Guild of Craftsmen, Queens Alliance for Artists. Republican. Home: 149-47 Powells Cove Blvd Whitestone NY 11357 Office: Craft Student League 610 Lexington Ave New York NY 10022

GREENWALD, LISA, nurse, educator; b. Vienna, Austria, Nov. 13, 1937; came to U.S., 1939, naturalized, 1944; d. Alfred and Grete (Pollack) Hauser; R.N., Mt. Sinai Sch. Nursing, 1958; B.S. in Public Adminstrn., U. New Haven, 1976, M.A. in Indsl. and Organizational Psychology, 1979; m. Harry Greenwald, Aug. 31, 1958; children—Linda, Michael, Thomas. Staff nurse, asst. head nurse, head nurse Mt. Sinai Hosp., N.Y.C., 1958-59; head nurse Hosp. for Joint Diseases, N.Y.C., 1961-63; staff and relief supr. Brookdale Med. Center, Bklyn., 1963-74; adminstrv. supr. St. Vincent's Med. Center, Bridgeport, Conn., 1974—; adj. instr. U. New Haven, 1979—. Chmn., Remedial Reading Program, Bklyn. Public Schs., 1972-74; com. mem. Quinipiac council Boy Scouts Am., 1977-80. Recipient Mt. Sinai Hosp. for Under-grad. Students Scholarship, 1975, also grad. scholarship. Mem. Mt. Sinai Hosp. Sch. Nursing Alumni Assn. Democrat. Jewish. Home: 120 Depot Rd Milford CT 06460 Office: 2800 Main St Bridgeport CT 06606

GREENWALD, SHERI, soprano, opera singer; Debut with Netherlands Opera in The Marriage of Figaro, appeared in The Rake's Progress, 1981-82; singer La Boheme and The Rake's Progress for Washington Opera, 1981-82; soloist in Haydn's Creation, San Francisco Symphony, 1982, The Marriage of Figaro, Santa Fe Opera and George Rochberg's The Confidence Man, 1982, Cendrillon with San Francisco Opera, Arabella with Netherlands Opera and Rigoletto with Ky. Opera, 1982-83; has appeared with Santa Fe Opera, Houston Grand Opera, San Francisco Opera, Opera Theatre St. Louis, Pitts. Opera; orchestral appearances include Boston Symphony, San Francisco Symphony, St. Louis Symphony, Phila. Orch., Rotterdam Philharm., Indpls. Symphony, N.J. Symphony, Pro Arte Chorale. Office: Care Columbia Artists Management Inc 165 W 57th St New York NY 10019 *

GREENWELL, SUSAN OURSELER, mfg. co. exec.; b. Salisbury, Md., Dec. 3, 1946; d. Ira Augustus and Virginia Ruth (Harrington) O.; student Towson State Coll., 1964-66, Chesapeake Coll., 1969; m. Philip Steele Greenwell, Jr., June 18, 1966. Tchr., Head Start, Dorchester County Bd. Edn., Cambridge, Md., 1966-67; with Xerox Corp., various locations, 1967—, region tech. program launch support mgr., Arlington, Va., 1979-80, tech. program mgr. Eastern ops., Rochester, N.Y., 1980—; cons. Interface Group Ltd., Wor-Wic Tech. Community Coll. Mem. Mcpl. Utilities Commn., Cambridge, 1978-80; mem. Wicomico County Commn. on Status of Women, 1977-78. Recipient Region Service Ops. award Xerox Corp., 1980. Mem. Nat. Assn. Female Execs., NOW, Fedn. Planned Parenthood. Democrat. Methodist. Clubs: Cambridge Country, Cambridge Yacht, Bay Country Racquet, Salisbury Racquet. Home: 1202 Race St Cambridge MD 21613 Office: 1616 N Ft Myer Dr Arlington VA 22209

GREENWOOD, JUDITH AYOTTE, interior design co. exec.; b. Lewiston, Maine, July 16, 1943; d. Lawrence C. and Helen Esther (Verrill) Ayotte; student Jacksonville U., 1961-62, Auburn U., 1970-71; B.S., U. Md., 1974; 1 dau., Erin Elizabeth. Chief designer Trend Systems, Inc., Washington, 1974; staff designer Gloria Weissberg Asso., Washington, 1974; founder, pres. Judith Greenwood Designs, Chevy Chase, Md., 1975—. Mem. Am. Soc. Interior Designers, Omicron Nu. Democrat. Lutheran. Club: Washington Ski. Office: Judith Greenwood Designs 1755 18th St NW Washington DC 20009

GREENWOOD, KATY BROWN, educator; b. Wheeler, Tex., Jan. 24, 1935; d. Ray D. and Lena (Baker) Brown; B.S., W.Tex. State U., 1954; M.Ed., 1958; Ph.D., U. Minn., 1978; m. Jim D. Greenwood, July 11, 1954; children—Lisa Kay, Jim L., Joe Kelly, Lesley Ann. Dir. guidance Spearman (Tex.) Ind. Sch. Dist., 1968-71; vocat. cons. for handicapped Regional Ednl. Service Center, Amarillo, Tex., 1972; research asso. U. Minn., 1973-77; asst. prof., coordinator grad. vocat. edn. Tex. A&M U., College Station, 1981—, project dir. tech. assistance in vocat. edn. to Dominican Republic, 1981-82; cons. in policy devel., analysis, evaluation tng. in developing countries. Mem. Brazos Valley Devel. Council. Recipient Outstanding 1st Yr. Counselor award Tex. Edn. Agy., 1969; Leadership Devel. grantee U.S. Office of Edn., 1973-76. Mem. Tex. Vocat. Tchr. Educators Assn. (dir. 1979-81), Am. Vocat. Assn. (chmn. awards com. 1981-82), Phi Delta Kappa. Home: 2812 Camelot Dr Bryan TX 77801 Office: Coll Edn Tex A & M U College Station TX 77843

GREER, BONNIE BETH, educator; b. Toledo, Sept. 13, 1946; d. Therron Otto and Betty Mae Kleckner; A.B., Ind. U., 1968; M.Ed., Okla. U., 1969, Ph.D., 1971; m. John Garland Greer, July 9, 1977; children—Christopher John, Tiffany Maye. Instl. tchr. No. Ind. Children's Hosp., South Bend, 1968; tchr. 6th grade Blanchard (Okla.) public schs., 1968-69; successively grad. asst., spl. instr., lectr. Okla. U., 1969-72; program dir. Stone Belt Center Retarded, Bloomington, Ind., 1972-73; asst. prof. Bridgewater (Mass.) State Coll., 1973-74; mem. faculty Memphis State U., 1974—, asso. prof. spl. edn. and rehab., 1976—; lectr. edn. Ind. U., part-time, 1972-73. Mem. Council Exceptional Children, Am. Assn. Mental Deficiency, Delta Kappa Gamma. Author articles in field, chpts. in books; co-editor: Practical Strategies in Working with the Trainable Mentally Retarded, 1975. Office: Dept Spl Edn and Rehab Memphis TN 38152

GREER, DOROTHY LUCILLE LEECH (MRS. THOMAS KEISTER GREER), bus. exec.; b. Fort Morgan, Colo., Nov. 5, 1921; d. Laurance Blakely and Lucille Otis (Gill) Leech; student Mills Coll., 1939-40; B.A., San Diego State Coll., 1943; m. Thomas Keister Greer, Jan. 9, 1943; children—Nancy Tallaferro (Mrs. William Nelson Alexander II), Giles Carter, Celeste Claiborne. Tchr., Franklin County Schs., Rocky Mount, Va., 1944-45, 48-49, Roanoke (Va.) City Schs., 1949-51; dir., sec.-treas. Franklin County Times, Inc., Rocky Mount, 1968—; v.p. Greer Investment Corp., 1977-79. Mem. central com. Assistance League So. Calif., Los Angeles, 1952-54; mem. patrons com. Internat. Debutante Ball, 1969-71. Mem. D.A.R., Internat. Platform Assn. Christian Scientist. Clubs: Willow Creek Country (sec.-dir. Rocky Mount 1962-64); Roanoke Country; San Diego Yacht. Home: The Grove Rocky Mount VA 24151

GREER, ELMA MAY, editor; b. Hayward, Calif., June 19, 1926; d. Robert and Catherine Margaretta (Dax) G.; student public schs., Berkeley, Calif.; divorced; children—Kathleen Kuhn Anstey, Bill Kuhn. Asst. producer to Al Jarvis and His Make Believe Ballroom, Los Angeles, 1947-49; mem. prodn. staff Bob McLaughlin, 1949-55; exec. sec. Clubtime, 1949-55; with KEY Records, Los Angeles, 1955-57, Eric Distbrs., San Francisco, 1957-58; producer Del Courtney's TV show on KPIX, 1958-60; promotion dir. Chatton Distbrs., 1958-60; music dir. Radio Sta. KSFO, San Francisco, 1960-76, asst. program dir., 1976-78; asso. editor Gavin Report, San Francisco, 1978—; cons. radio programmers; music cons. to students San Francisco State Coll. Recipient Bill Gavin awards for music dir. of year Middle of the Road, 1965, 67, 70. Mem. Country Music Assn. Home: 1915 Green St 105 San Francisco CA 94123 Office: One Embarcadero Center #1816 San Francisco CA 94111

GREER, GERMAINE, author, feminist; b. nr. Melbourne, Australia, Jan. 29, 1939; d. Eric Reginald and Margaret May Mary (Lafrank) Greer; B.A. with honors in English and French Lit., U. Melbourne, 1959; M.A. with honors in English, U. Sydney (Australia), 1961; Ph.D. (Commonwealth scholar), Newnham Coll. of Cambridge U. (Eng.), 1964; m. May 1968 (div.). Lectr. English, U. Warwick (Eng.), 1967-72; now with grad. faculty modern letters U. Tulsa. Author: The Female Eunuch, 1970; The Obstacle Race, 1979. Office: Tulsa Center for Study of Women's Lit U Tulsa 600 S College Ave Tulsa OK 74104

GREER, JOANNE MARIE G., health care researcher, govt. ofcl.; b. New Orleans, Aug. 24, 1937; d. Carl Matthewson and Sydney Marie (Comeaux) Greer; B.S. cum laude, St. Mary's Dominican Coll., 1961; M.Ed., La. State U., 1969; Ph.D., U. Md., 1974; research affiliate Washington Psychoanalytic Inst., 1979—; m. Thomas Vernon Greer, Apr. 23, 1966; children—Marc Bernley, Carl Mathieu Cashen. Tchr., adminstr. Sisters of St. Joseph of Medaille, 1959-65; mem. faculty La. State U., 1966, U. Md., 1969-75; ops. research analyst VA, Washington, 1975, Health Care Financing Adminstrn., 1976, Health Services Adminstrn., Rockville, Md., 1977-80, acting chief spl. studies Office Planning, Evaluation and Legislation, 1978-80; programs specialist NIMH, Rockville, dep. chief Nat. Center for Prevention and Control of Rape, 1980-81; math. statistician advanced techniques staff of insp. gen. HHS, Washington, 1982—; guest worker NIH Clin. Center, 1981-82; cons. psychologist, Washington, 1979—. NSF fellow, 1965; NDEA fellow, 1969-72; recipient Outstanding Performance award USPHS, 1978. Fellow Md. Psychol. Assn.; mem. Am. Psychol. Assn., Psychometric Soc., Am. Statis. Assn., Am. Assn. Sex Educators, Counselors and Therapists. The Co-author: Sexual Aggressor: Current Perspectives on Treatment; Victims of Sexual Aggression: Treatment of Children, Women, and Men; contbr. numerous articles to profl. jours and govt. publs. Home: 12420 Kuhl Rd Silver Spring MD 20902 Office: 330 Independence Ave SW Room 5739 Washington DC 20201

GREER, JUDITH ANN, editor, writer; b. N.Y.C., May 9, 1946; d. Mortimer and Ruth (Neslie) Greer; B.A., Hunter Coll., 1968. Editorial and prodn. mgr. Greene & Labiner, Inc., pubs. reps., N.Y.C., 1967-69; asso. editor Travel Agt. Mag., Am. Traveler, Inc., N.Y.C., 1969-70; editor Westchester (N.Y.) Sports News, 1970-71; mng. editor Ski Mag., Ski Bus. Mag., Times Mirror Mags., Inc., N.Y.C., 1971-76; sr. editor Cue mag., N. Am. Pub., N.Y.C., 1976-77; editor Ski Bus. newspaper, 1980-81; pub. U.S. Sports Letter, N.Y.C., 1981—; U.S. bur. chief Fall Line mag., South Melbourne, Australia, 1981—; free lance writer N.Y. Mag., Cue Mag., House and Garden, Ingenue, Budget Decorating, Argosy, So. Living, Home Garden mags. Mem. U.S., Eastern ski writers assns. Home: 44 E 63d St New York NY 10021 Office: 44 E 63d St New York NY 10021

GREER, LAVERNE GRITTON, musician, ret. educator; b. Penfield, Ill., June 12, 1916; d. Shelby Lylburn and Maudie Ann (Fetters) Gritton; B.A., U. Ill., 1937; student MacPhail Coll. Music, Mpls., 1951-53; m. E. Edward Greer, Mar. 25, 1937; 1 son, Lylburn. Tchr. music Woodbine (Kans.) pub. schs., 1944-45, schs. in Ill. and Minn., 1948-54, Rantoul (Ill.) pub. schs., 1954-76; pvt. music tchr., 1945—. Mem. Nat. Guild Piano Tchrs., Music Educators Nat. Conf., Ill. Music Educators Assn., Internat. Soc. Music Educators, Am. Choral Dirs. Assn. (life), Nat. Assn. Organ Tchrs., Internat. Platform Assn., AAUW (br. pres.). Mem. Christian Ch. Home: 513 Eden Park Rantoul IL 61866

GREER, MARION PLATNER, speech and lang. pathologist; b. Schenectady, Oct. 18, 1931; d. Harold B. and Margaret (Koch) Platner; B.A., Syracuse U., 1953; M.S., Coll. St. Rose, 1968; student hotel tech. Schenectady Community Coll.; m. Wilbur Greer, Nov. 1, 1953; children—Barbara, David, Laura. Speech therapist Hartford (Conn.) Schs., 1953-54; lang. therapist League of Hard of Hearing, Hartford, 1954; speech therapist South Colonie Sch. Dist., Albany, N.Y., 1964; speech and lang. therapist Scotia Sch. Dist., 1966-69; speech and lang. pathologist Ballston Spa (N.Y.) Sch. Dist., 1969—; cons. Skidmore Coll. New Family Life Project; mem. task force Coll. St. Rose. Mem. Capitol Area Speech, Lang. and Hearing Assn. (sec.), Am. Speech, Lang. and Hearing Assn., N.Y. State Speech and Hearing Assn., Internat. Platform Soc. Republican. Home: 619 Glen Ave Scotia NY 12302 Office: 70 Malta Ave Ballston Spa NY 12020

GREER, SALLY ANN, psychologist; b. Boston, Jan. 16, 1942; d. James H. and Gertrude C. (Helfer) G.; B.A. summa cum laude, U. San Diego, 1976, M.A., 1977; Ph.D., Calif. Sch. Profl. Psychology, 1980; children—Leah Anne, Andrew Arthur, Christopher Paul. Interviewer, Am. Field Service, El Cajon, Calif., 1972-74; parent adv. battering parent's program San Diego County, 1973-75; mental health worker, pre-doctoral intern Mercy Hosp., San Diego, 1976-77; pre-doctoral intern Catholic Family Services, San Diego, 1978; research plastic surgery dept. U. Calif. Med. Center, San Diego, 1979, asst. clin. prof., 1981—; sr. staff mem. counseling and psychol. services U. Calif., La Jolla, 1980—. Grantee Plastic Surgery Research Found., 1978. Mem. Am. Psychol. Assn., Soc. Behavioral Medicine, San Diego Soc. Clin. Hypnosis, Alpha Gamma Sigma, Psi Chi (charter pres. 1976). Office: George Washington U 1229 25th St NW Washington DC 20037

GREGG, DOROTHY ELIZABETH, chem. co. exec.; b. Tempe, Ariz.; d. Alfred Tennyson and Mamie Elizabeth (Walker) G.; B.A., U. Tex., 1944, M.A. (grad. fellow), 1945; Ph.D. (all-univ. grad. fellow), Columbia U., 1951, L.H.D. (hon.), 1967; m. Paul Hughling Scott, 1952; children—Kimerly, Gregg. Lectr., Columbia U., 1946-52, asst. prof. econs., 1952-54; asst. dir. public relations U.S. Steel Corp., N.Y.C., 1956-74; dir. corp. communications Celanese Corp., N.Y.C., 1974-75, corp. v.p. communications, 1975-81, corp. v.p. external affairs, 1981—; dir. Ednl. Testing Service of Princeton U. Mem. adv. bd. edn. and tng. Sec. of Navy; mem. civilian public relations adv. com. U.S. Mil. Acad. Mem. Found. Public Relations Research and Edn. (pres.), Women in Communications (pres. N.Y. chpt., Nat. Headliner award 1980), Nat. Com. U.S.-China Relations, Phi Beta Kappa, Pi Sigma Alpha. Clubs: Princeton, Zonta (N.Y.C.). Contbr. articles profl. mags., P.F. Collier & Son Ency. Home: 425 E 58th St New York NY 10022 Office: 1211 Ave of Americas New York NY 10036

GREGG, ROSALIE MANN, social service agy. ofcl.; b. Hayden, N.Mex., Sept. 17, 1920; d. John Patterson and Lona Estella (Butler) Mann; grad. Decatur Bapt. Jr. Coll., 1942; m. Robert Nolen Gregg, Dec. 16, 1945; children—Sherry Lynn Gregg Harris, Marsha Jill Gregg Eder, Robbie Zane Gregg Weaver, Dana Rene. Sec., Govt. of Wise County, 1957-65; ins. clk. Allied Ins. Agy., Decatur, Tex., 1965-68; sec. Decatur C. of C., 1968-75; adminstrv. asst. Wise County Council on Alcoholism, Decatur, 1976—. Chmn., Wise County Hist. Commn., 1964—; exec. dir. Wise County Hist. Soc., 1970—; treas. SHARE; sec.-treas. Pleasant Grove Cemetery No. 1. Mem. Tex. Assn. Mus., Tex. Hist. Found., Tex. Assn. Alcoholism Counselors, Tex. Assn. Traffic Safety, Wise County Archaeol. Assn., Dallas County Hist. Assn., Tarrant County Geneal. Soc., Am. Legion Aux. (sec.-treas.). Democrat. Methodist. Club: Decatur Woman's (past pres.). Editor: Do You Know About...Wise County, 1965; History of Wise County...A Link with the Past, 1975; also monthly hist. newsletter. Home: 1602 S College Decatur TX 76234 Office: 105 S Church Decatur TX 76234

GREGGS, ELIZABETH MAY BUSHELL (MRS. RAYMOND JOHN GREGGS), librarian; b. Delta, Colo., Nov. 7, 1925; d. Joseph Perkins and Ruby May (Stanford) Bushell; student Colo. Coll., 1943-44; B.A., U. Denver, 1948; m. Raymond John Greggs, Aug. 16, 1952; children—David M., Geoffrey B., Timothy C., Daniel R. Children's librarian Grand Junction (Colo.) Pub. Library, 1944-46, Chelan County Library, 1948, Wenatchee Pub. Library, 1948-52, Seattle Pub. Library, 1952-53; children's librarian Renton Pub. Library, 1957-61, dir., 1962, br. supr. and children's services, 1963-67; area children's supr. King County Library, Seattle, 1968-79, asst. coordinator children's services, 1979—; cons., organizer Tutor Center Library, Seattle South Community Coll., 1969-72; mem. Puget Sound Council for Reviewing Children's Media, chmn., 1974—; adj. prof. Seattle Pacific U., 1980—; cons. to children's TV programs. Chmn. dist. advancement com. Kloshee dist. Boy Scouts Am., 1975-78; mem. Bond Issue Citizens Group to build a new Renton Library, 1958, 59. Recipient Hon. Service to Youth award Cedar River dist. Boy Scouts Am., 1971, award of merit Kloshee dist., 1977. Mem., ALA (mem. Boy Scout com. children's services div. 1973-78, chmn. 1976-78, mem. Newbery com. 1978—, membership com. 1978-80, exec. bd. 1979-81, editorial adv. bd. Top of News), Pacific N.W. (vice chmn. children's div. 1981-83), Wash. (exec. bd. children's and young adult services div. 1970-78) library assns., King County Right to Read Council (co-chmn. 1973-77), Pierce-King County Reading Council, Assn. Library Services to Children, Wash. State Literacy Council (exec. bd. 1971-77), Wash. Library Media Assn., Puget Sound Orton Soc. Methodist. Editor: Cayas Newsletter, 1971-74; cons. to Children's Catalog, Children's Index to Poetry. Home: 800 Lynnwood Ave NE Renton WA 98056 Office: 300 8th Ave N Seattle WA 98109

GREGOIRE, MARY BUSCH, educator; b. Crosby, N.D., Dec. 12, 1952; d. Henry M. and Eileen F. (Goven) Busch; B.S., N.D. State U., 1974, M.S., 1975; postgrad. Kans. State U., 19 —; m. Wayne Thomas Gregoire, June 7, 1975; 1 dau., Theresa Marie. Adminstrv. dietitian St. Luke's Hosp., Fargo, N.D., 1975-76; dir. dietetics Jasper County Hosp., Rensselaer, Ind., 1976-78; asst. dir. food services Lake County Convalescent Home, Crown Point, Ind., 1978-81; instr. dietetics and instl. mgmt. Kans. State U., Manhattan, 1981—. Sysco Corp. scholar, 1982. Mem. Am. Dietetic Assn., Kaw Valley Dietetic Assn., Kans. Dietetic Assn. Roman Catholic. Home: K-4 Jardine Terrace Manhattan KS 66502 Office: Kansas State University Manhattan KS 66502

GREGONIS, JUNE ELLEN, med. technologist, microbiologist; b. Roanoke, Va., July 29, 1941; d. Ellis Aaron and June L. (Doyle) Musselman; B.S. in Med. Tech., Roanoke Coll., 1963; cert. med. tech. Beckley Meml. Sch. Med. Tech., 1962; postgrad. Duke U., 1979-82, Central Mich. U., 1981—; m. William J. Gregonis, May 8, 1965 (div. 1975); 1 son, Theodore John. Research med. technologist Duke U. Med. Center, Durham, N.C., 1964-65, anaerobic microbiologist, 1974-77, parasitologist, 1978-80, quality control, continuing edn. coordinator hosp. labs., 1980—; chief med. technologist Med. Clinic, Newport News, Va., 1965-66, med. technologist Newport News Shipbuilding and Dry Dock Co., 1966-67; sr. research technologist Va. Poly. and State U., Blacksburg, 1967-68; sr. research technologist Queens U. and Kingston Gen. Hosp., Kingston, Ont., Can., 1968-70; chief technologist Ongwanada Hosp., Kingston, 1970-72; med. technologist Roanoke Meml. Hosp., 1962-64, Geisinger Med. Center, Danville, Pa., 1972-74. Mem. Am. Soc. for Microbiology, N.C. Soc. Med. Tech., Am. Soc. Clin. Pathologists (affiliate mem., cert. med. technologist), Nat. Certification Agy. for Med. Lab. Personnel (cert.), Am. Soc. Med. Tech. (cert.). Clubs: Chapel Hill Ski, Durham Savoyards (tech. crew). Contbr. articles on microbiology to profl. jours. Home: 2836 Chapel Hill Rd Apt 18C Durham NC 27709 Office: Box 2929 Duke U Med Center Durham NC 27710

GREGORIUS, BEVERLY JUNE, obstetrician and gynecologist; b. Ottawa, Ill., June 21, 1915; d. Henry Godfrey and Arline (Barry) Pruette; B.S., Madison (Tenn.) Coll., 1935; M.D., Loma Linda (Calif.) U., 1946, M.S., 1953; m. Hans Harvey Gregorius, Aor. 6, 1939 (dec.); 1 dau., Joan Gregorius Jones. Intern, Los Angeles County Gen. Hosp., 1946-47; resident in ob-gyn, White Meml. Hosp., Los Angeles, 1949-52; practice medicine specializing in ob-gyn, Burbank, Calif., 1953-77; assoc. clin. prof. Loma Linda U. Med. Sch., also U. So. Calif. Med. Sch., 1956—; program dir. ob-gyn residency program Glendale (Calif.) Adventist Med. Center, 1977-81, chmn. dept. ob-gyn, 1981—. Diplomate Am. Bd. Ob-Gyn. Fellow Am. Coll. Ob-Gyn, ACS, Internat. Coll. Surgeons; mem. Los Angeles Ob-Gyn Soc. (council 1979—sec.-treas. 1982-83). Adventist. Home: 10635 Lansdale St North Hollywood CA 91602 Office: 1509 Wilson Terr Glendale CA 91206

GREGORY, ANN YOUNG, editor, publisher; b. Lexington, Ky., Apr. 28, 1935; d. David Marion and Pauline (Adams) Young; B.A. with high distinction (Ky. Broadcasters Assn. scholar), U. Ky., 1956; m. Allen Gregory, Jan. 29, 1957; children—David Young, Mary Peyton. Sec., Ky. edit. TV Guide, Louisville, summer 1956; traffic mgr. Sta. WVLK, Lexington, 1956-61; part time tchr. adult basic edn. Wise County (Va.) Sch. Bd., St. Paul, 1966-72; adminstrv. asst. Appalachian Field Services, Children's TV Workshop, St. Paul, 1971-74; editor, co-pub. Clinch Valley Times, pres. Clinch Valley Pub. Co., Inc., St. Paul, 1974—. Vice pres. St. Paul PTA, 1970-73; trustee Lonesome Pine Regional Library Bd., 1972-80, chmn., 1978-80; chmn. com. to establish br. library in St. Paul, opened 1975; mem. adv. bd. Pro-Art (Wise County chpt. Va. Mus. Fine Arts), 1979—; co-leader Brownie troop Girl Scouts U.S.A., 1971-76; mem. adv. bd. Wise County (Va.) YMCA, 1977—; mem. Wise County Bd. Edn., 1975—, vice chmn., 1981—; mem. Va. Edn. Block Grants Adv. Com., 1981—; pres. Wise County Humane Soc., Inc.; bd. dirs. Va. Sch. Bds. Assn., 1979—. Named Outstanding Clubwoman of Year, St. Paul Jr. Women's Club, 1964, 66; Outstanding Citizen, S.W. Va. dist. Va. Fedn. Women's Clubs, 1968. Mem. Va. Press Assn. (1st place award for editorial writing 1976), Nat. Press Women, Va. Press Women, Nat. Newspaper Assn., Women in Communications, Mortar Bd., Phi Beta Kappa, Alpha Delta Pi. Democrat. Methodist. Clubs: Lake Bonaventure Country, Saintly Squares. Editor, text writer The Flood of '77 in the St. Paul Area, 1977. Home: PO Box 303 Longview Dr Saint Paul VA 24283 Office: PO Box 817 Russell St Saint Paul VA 24283

GREGORY, ANNE ELIZABETH, editor; b. Leamington, Ont., Can., Nov. 2, 1936; d. Herbert Thorp and Helen Elizabeth (Ewald) G.; B.A. in Psychology with honors, Hollins (Va.) Coll., 1958. With Merrill Lynch, Pierce, Fenner & Smith, N.Y.C., 1958—, exec. editor Investor's Reader, Bus. News Mag., 1972-74, publs. mgr. individual investment div., 1974, asst. v.p., 1975-77, v.p., 1977, editor-in-chief Merrill Lynch Market Letter, 1976—. Mem. Financial Women's Assn., Pi Epsilon Mu. Republican. Episcopalian. Club: Meadow (Southampton, N.Y.). Office: Merrill Lynch 165 Broadway New York NY 10006

GREGORY, ARYEAR, travel agy. exec.; b. Cleve., July 28, 1918; d. Aristos Harry and Anne (Leka) John; student Cleve. Coll., 1945-47, Baldwin Wallace Coll., 1956; cert. Inst. Cert. Travel Agts., 1972; m. John V. Gregory (dec.); 1 son, Jim Aristos. Dressmaker, 1945-53; jr. acct. Greyhound Rent-a-Car, 1958-59; various positions travel agys., 1960-72; owner, mgr. Greg-Lil Travel Center, Inc., 1972-75; pres., mgr. Cleve. Travel Center, Inc., 1979—; owner, dir., instr. Travel Agts. Tng. Sch., Parma, Ohio, 1972—; cons. in field. Great Books Discussion group leader, 1948-56. Mem. Inst. Cert. Travel Agts. Greek Orthodox. Author: The Travel Agent-Dealer in Dreams, 1975. Home: 5356 Pearl Rd Rear Parma OH 44129

GREGORY, CLAIRE DISTELHORST, TV producer; b. Chgo., Mar. 6, 1926; d. Robert Henry and Genevieve (McCall) Distelhorst; student Cornell Coll., 1943-46; A.B., Ind. U., 1947, M.S., 1954, postgrad., 1959; children—Charles, Martha. Tchr. public schs., Bismarck and Rossville, Ill., 1947-50, Helmsburg, Ind., 1950-51; grad. asst. Audio Visual Center of Ind. U., 1953-55, lectr., dir. women's, children's and social service programs radio and TV, 1956-59; exec. dir. Community Service Council, Inc., Bloomington, Ind., 1971-75; asst. supr. instructional TV program devel. Ind. U. Radio and TV Service, 1975-81, dir. spl. projects, 1982—; chmn. Bloomington Telecommunications Council, 1975-80; writer, producer: Russian Revolution and Arts, Parts I and II, 1976; Teleconference on Mass Transportation, 1976; Transportation Briefing, 1977; videotapes on profl. devel. Internat. Devel. Inst., 1975-80; 16 videotapes on computer instrn., 1978-80; Getting There, 1980; Living Africa, 1979-82; Programming for Microcomputers, 1982; TV advisor Mostly Moliere Troupe, 1981—. Mem. United Way of Monroe County, 1982; treas. Blue Ridge Assn., 1978-81. Mem. Psi Iota Xi. Club: Univ. Office: 212 Radio and TV Bldg Indiana University Bloomington IN 47405

GREGORY, CYNTHIA KATHLEEN, (MRS. TERRENCE S. ORR), ballerina; b. Los Angeles, July 8, 1946; d. Konstantin and Marcelle (Tremblay) Gregory; grad. high sch.; m. Terrence S. Orr, May 14, 1966. Ford Found. scholar San Francisco Ballet, 1961, soloist, 1962-65; with Am. Ballet Theatre, N.Y.C., 1965—; soloist, 1966, prin. dancer, 1967—; appeared on TV with San Francisco Opera, 1963-64, in film Girl Most Likley, 1955; TV appearance on The Edge of Night, 1981. Recipient Silver Bowl, Dance Mag., 1955. Address: 310 W 94th St New York NY 10025 *

GREGORY, DELLA ARLENE ARLEDGE, educator; b. Martinsville, Ohio, Oct. 6, 1938; d. George and Lucille Irene (Shiverdecker) Arledge; B.A., Ohio State U., 1959, M.A., 1977, doctoral candidate, U., 1979—; student Ohio Wesleyan U., summers 1969, 70, 72, 74, 75, 77, 78; m. James Andrew Gregory, Dec. 20, 1959; children—James Andrew, Julie Ann, Janis Arlene. Tchr., Delaware (Ohio) City Schs., 1960—; part-time communications instr. Marion Tech. Coll.; also ednl. cons. Mem. adv. bd. Help Anonymous, 1974—; adv. 4-H Club, 1969—; adv. Am. Field Service, 1973-79, host mother, 1974-75; mem. edn. com. local Methodist ch., 1977—; publicity coordinator Delaware Arts Festival, 1977-79; vol. family outreach program Juvenile Ct. Annie Webb Blanton scholar Delta Kappa Gamma, 1979—, Louise and Marguerite Morse scholar, 1981. Mem. United Teaching Profession, Ohio Council Tchrs. of English Lang. Arts (sec. 1973-76), Nat. Council Tchrs. of English (com. on poets in schs. 1974-76, judge writing awards 1975-79), Delaware City Tchrs. Assn. (pres. 1979-81), AAUW (charter pres. Delaware br. 1965-67), Delta Kappa Gamma (pres. Iota chpt.), Pi Lambda Theta. Contbr. articles to profl. jours. Home: 240 Homestead Ln Delaware OH 43015 Office: 289 Euclid Ave Delaware OH 43015

GREGORY, ELEANOR ANNE, artist, educator; b. Seattle, Jan. 20, 1939; d. John Noel and Eleanor Anne G.; B.A., Reed Coll., 1963; M.F.A., U. Wash., 1966; M.Ed., Columbia U., 1978, Ed.D., 1978. Art tchr. Seattle Public Schs., 1970-75; instr. N.Y.C. Community Coll., 1977, Manhattan Community Coll., N.Y.C., 1978; asst. prof. N.Mex. State U., Las Crucas, 1978-79; asst. prof. art Purdue U., West Lafayette, Ind., 1979—; one woman shows: Columbia U. Tchrs. Coll., 1976, Watson's Crick Gallery, West Lafayette, 1980, 81, Gallery I, Purdue U., 1980; group shows include: El Paso (Tex.) Art Mus., 1979, Ind. State Mus., Indpls., 1980, Lafayette (Ind.) Art Mus., 1982; represented in permanent collections: Portland (Oreg.) Art Mus. mgr. Watson's Crick Gallery, West Lafayette, 1982—. Mem. Nat. Art Edn. Assn., Chgo. Calligraphy Collective, Internat. Soc. Edn. Through Art. Episcopalian. Home: 6347 Sand Point Way NE Seattle WA 98115 Office: Dept Art West Tex State U Box 207 WT Station Canyon TX 79016

GREGORY, HARRIET STELLA, physician; b. St. Paul, Oct. 1, 1915; d. Charles George and Minnie Henrietta (Anderson) G.; A.B., Macalester Coll., 1937; M.D., U. Minn., 1941; m. Ernest A. Bragg, Jr., Aug. 14, 1943; children—Edith Gail, Margaret Anne, Carol Mather, Alice Gregory, Russell Bartlett. Intern, Bethesda Hosp., St. Paul, Mn. 1940-41; resident Mass. Meml. Hosp., Boston, 1942-43; cytopathologist Sturdy Meml. Hosp., Attleboro, Mass., 1963—. Mem. Attleboro Sch. Com., 1968-74. Named Woman of Yr., Mass. Fedn. Bus. and Profl. Women, 1978; honor roll Mass. div. AAUW. Mem. AMA, Mass. Med. Soc., Bristol North Med. Soc., Attleboro Drs. Club (past pres.), AAUW (pres. Mass. div. since 1982—). Unitarian. Club: Attleboro Area Bus. and Prof. Women. (past pres.). Office: 211 Park St Attleboro MA 02703

GREGORY, JEWELL KIRCHNER, personal services co. exec.; b. Carthage, Mo., Jan. 14, 1934; d. Carl Otto and Ruth Mildred (Jones) Kirchner; B.A., U. Pa., 1955; M.A., U. Ill., 1969; m. Edward Haig Gregory, May 31, 1953; children—Susan Faith, Jane Hope. Freelance newspaper columnist, club speaker, 1969-74; relocation specialist Equitable Relocation Service, Equitable Life Assurance Soc., N.Y.C., 1975-79, nat. mgr. home search services, N.Y.C., 1980—. Pres., Maine Twp. (Ill.) High Sch. Scholarship Fund, 1972-73. Mem. Assn. Alumnae U. Pa. (dir. 1961-64), Internat. Soc. Preretirement Planners. Democrat. Episcopalian. Contbr. articles to profl. jours. Home: 36 Elmwood Pl Short Hills NJ 07078 Office: 1700 Broadway New York NY 10019

GREGORY, JUSTINA WINSTON, educator; b. Brattleboro, Vt., Sept. 24, 1946; d. Richard and Clara (Brussel) Winston; A.B., Smith Coll., 1967; M.A., Harvard U., 1972, Ph.D., 1974; m. Patrick Bolton Gregory, Aug. 2, 1969; children—Tobias, Nora. Asst. prof. classics Yale U., New Haven, 1974-75; asst. prof. classics Smith Coll., Northampton-Mass., 1975-80, asso. prof., 1980—. Fulbright fellow, 1967-68; Woodrow Wilson fellow, 1968-69; Am. Council Learned Socs. fellow, 1977. Mem. Classical Assn. New Eng., Am. Philol. Assn., Phi Beta Kappa. Translator: (with Patrick Gregory) Aesop's Fables, 1975; contbr. articles to scholarly jours. Office: Smith College Northampton MA 01063

GREGORY, LINDA BRANDENBURG, editor; b. Frederick, Md., May 7, 1949; d. Austin Toms and Grace Eleanor (Rohrer) Brandenburg; B.A. in Polit. Sci., Hood Coll., 1972; m. Fred Watkins Gregory; 1 dau., Melissa Kay. Mem. staff Frederick News-Post, 1972—, family editor, 1973—, editor children's page, 1975—. Mem. Nat. Fedn. Press Women (Communications award 1979, 80), Md. Press Women (awards), Frederick Arts Council. Republican. Lutheran. Club: Frederick Jr. Women's (hon.), Zonta. Contbg. writer Hood Mag. Home: 615 Wyngate Dr Frederick MD 21701 Office: 200 E Patrick St Frederick MD 21701

GREGORY, LYDIA MAY JENCKS, librarian, club woman; b. Cumberland, R.I., Nov. 6, 1903; d. Gerard Dallas and Florence May (Perkins) Jencks; B.S., U. R.I., 1926; A.M., Brown U., 1929; postgrad. in library sci. SUNY, Geneseo, 1932; m. William Gregory, Dec. 21, 1935. Tchr., librarian Central Sch., Franklin, N.Y., 1929-30; asst. librarian, registrar, librarian, instr. library sci. State Tchrs. Coll., Geneseo 1930-32; librarian, instr. library sci. State Tchrs. Coll., Gorham, Maine, 1932-35; past lectr. Cumberland (R.I.) Grange. Trustee, Attleboro (Mass.) Pub. Library, 1941—; state librarian Mass. DAR, 1950-53; state librarian Daus. Am. Colonists, 1958—, Mass. regent, 1961-64, nat. chaplain, 1964-67 nat. chmn. nat. awards com.; clk. Bethany Congl. Ch.; mem. Attleboro Republican City Com. Mem. Children Am. Revolution (sr. state pres., 1953-57), Mass. Library Trustees Assn., Attleboro Mus. Art and History, Daus. of Founders and Patriots, Woman Descs. Ancient and Honorable Arty. Co., Nat. Trust Hist. Preservation, New Eng. Hist. Geneal. Soc., Friends of Lincoln Circle of Blind, People of the Attleboros. Author: Course of Study in Use of Library, 1935; contbr. articles to profl. jours. Home: 39 Angeline St S PO Box 155 Attleboro MA 02703

GREGORY, PHYLLIS ABIGAIL, stained glass artist; b. Detroit, Sept. 7, 1947; d. Joseph Edgar and Leverta Audrey (Johnson) Wisby; B.S., Colo. Women's Coll., Women's Coll., 1970; M.B.A., Pepperdine U., 1981; m. William E. Gregory May 24, 1969; children—Allison Francis, Ryan Matthew. Med. technologist Sacred Heart Hosp., Pensacola, Fla., 1969-70, White-Wilson Clinic, Ft. Walton Beach, Fla., 1970-71; asso. Path. Labs., Las Vegas, 1972-73, supr. hematology lab., instr. Hermann Hosp., U. Tex. Sch. Allied Health Scis., Houston, 1975-77; lab. dir. Alief Gen. Hosp., Houston, 1977-78, med. technologist, 1980-81; med.

technologist Mt. Vernon Hosp., Alexandria, Va., technirep. Skonie Mktg.; free lance stained glass artist, 1981—; tech. mktg. rep. Hycel, Inc., Houston, 1978-79; sales rep. Curtin-Matheson Sci., Houston, 1979-80. Republican. Episcopalian. Home: 8349 Orange Ct Alexandria VA 22309

GREGORY, WANDA JEAN, ct. reporter, singer, musician; b. Little Rock, Sept. 7, 1925; d. John Albert and Angie (Thompson) Deming; student pub. schs. Little Rock; m. G. C. Gregory, Jan. 15, 1945 (div.); 1 son, Rex Carleton. Ofcl. ct. reporter, Nueces County, Tex., 1959-76, 36th Jud. Dist. Ct., San Patricio, Live Oak, McMullen, Aransas and Bee Counties, Tex., 1979-82; freelance court reporter, Corpus Christi, Tex., 1976-78, 82—, Honolulu, 1979. Vocalist with dance bands and jazz combos; pvt. tchr. jazz and pop singing; appeared in Tex. Jazz Festival, 1961-82; soloist Jazz Mass, 1976-82, Corpus Christi Interdenominational Choir. Mem. Tex. Shorthand Reporters Assn. (cert.), Tex. Jazz Festival Soc. (founder 1969, past pres., now bd. dirs.), Am. Fedn. Musicians, LWV, Bus. and Profl. Women's Club. Democrat. Methodist. Home and Office: 3926 Panama St Apt 133 Corpus Christi TX 78415

GREIF, BONNIE E., corp. controller; b. Washington, Mar. 14, 1953; d. Paul E. and Marjorie A. (Cook) Lipp; B.S., Calif. State U., Los Angeles, 1978; m. Terrence M. Greif, Jan. 1, 1982. Staff acct., acctg. supr. Owens-Ill., Vernon, Calif., 1976-78; cost acct., asst. controller Kaiser Aluminum, Vernon, 1978-79; plant controller Tower Industries, Sante Fe Springs, Calif., 1979-81; corp. controller NOA Airscrew Howden, Inc., Anaheim, Calif., 1981—. Mem. Anaheim C. of C. Republican. Mem. Moravain Ch. Office: PO Box 6317 1380 N McCan Anaheim CA 92806

GREIMAN, LIELA RUMBAUGH, univ. ofcl.; b. Oak Park, Ill., Apr. 22, 1939; d. Jack and Lydia (Keller) Berman; B.A., So. Ill. U., 1962; M.A., Northwestern U., 1964, Ph.D., 1969; m. William H. Greiman, Apr. 19, 1980. Instr., U. Ill., Chgo., 1964-65; teaching fellow Northwestern U., 1965-68; asst. prof., then assoc. prof. English North Central Coll., Naperville, Ill., 1968-78, chmn. dept., 1973-78, acting dean div. lang. and lit., spring-summer 1975; acting dean Sch. Gen. Studies, John F. Kennedy U., Orinda, Calif., 1979-80, acad. v.p., prof. lit. and aesthetics, 1978—. Recipient Elsie O. and Philip D. Sang Disting. Teaching award, 1975; Nat. Endowment for Humanities grantee, 1977. Mem. AAUP, Calif. Concerns. Author articles, reports in field. Home: 1522 Madera Ct El Cerrito CA 94530 Office: 12 Altarinda Rd Orinda CA 94563

GREJCZYK, CAMILLE LOUISE, acctg. co. mgr.; b. Chgo., June 7, 1947; d. Jerome N. and Louise M. (Aniolowski) Ptaszynski; B.A., DePaul U., 1982; m. Gary Grejczyk, June 13, 1970. Various positions Montgomery Ward & Co., Chgo., 1965-80, mgmt. support mgr., 1975-80; mgr. office systems practice area Arthur Young & Co., Chgo., 1980—. Recipient Word Processing Achievement award Word Processing/Info. Systems mag., 1980. Mem. Word Processing Mgmt. Assn. Chgo. (pres. 1979 program chmn. 1978). Home: 401 Webster St Chicago IL 60614 Office: Arthur Young & Co 1 IBM Plaza Chicago IL 60611

GREM, JUNE OLSON, publishing co. exec.; b. Chgo., Sept. 14, 1920; d. David G. and Ebba (Sandberg) Olson; B.A., Stanford U., 1940; m. Frank M. Grem, Apr. 3, 1943; children—Ann Grem Bregent, Marsha Grem Lopez, Philip C., Joan Grem Porschakin (dec.), Jean. Underwriting trainee then researcher Coronet-Esquire Mag.; pres. Enterprise Publs., Inc., Oak Park, Ill., 1971—. Active Girl Scouts U.S.A., 1956-60. Recipient Congress of Freedom award, 1974. Mem. AAUW. Mem. Libertarian Party. Author: The Money Manipulators, 1971; Karl Marx, Capitalist, 1972; The Liberty Amendment Money Trap, 1979; Guide to New Money System, 1981. Home: 155 Maplewood Dr Laflin Wilkes-Barre PA 18702 Office: PO Box 1658 Wilkes Barre PA 18701

GRENNAN, CYNTHIA FRANCES, sch. supt.; b. Sterling, Ill., Jan. 4, 1938; d. Francis John and Elza M. (Pippert) G.; B.S., Ill. State U., 1958; M.A., Ariz. State U., 1964. Tchr., Palatine, Ill., 1959-61, Chandler, Ariz., 1961-64; tchr. Anaheim (Calif.) Union High Sch. Dist., 1964-67, head counselor, 1967-72, psychologist, spl. edn. coordinator, 1972-76, asst. prin., 1976-77, prin., 1977-78, asst. supt. curriculum, 1978-79, supt., 1979—. Recipient hon. service award PTA. Mem. Am. Assn. Sch. Adminstrs., Assn. Supervision and Curriculum Devel., Assn. Calif. Sch. Adminstrs., Anaheim C. of C., Phi Delta Kappa. Episcopalian. Clubs: Altrusa (v.p. 1978—); Ebell (named outstanding educator) (Anaheim). Office: PO Box 3520 Anaheim CA 92803

GRENZEBACH, ELIZABETH STEWART, med. technologist; b. Richlands, Va., July 12, 1939; d. Frederick Fitzgerald and Margaret (Bronson) Stewart; student Mary Washington Coll., 1957-60; B.S., Med. Coll. Va., 1961; m. James Austin Grenzebach, May 12, 1973. With dept. pathology, Med. Coll. Va., Richmond, 1961-63, chief technologist Kidney Transplant Lab., 1963-66; research technologist Med. Coll. Wis., Milw., 1966-70, research asso. dept. environ. medicine, 1970-72; lab. dept. head Silver Hill Found., New Canaan, Conn., 1973—. Mem. Am. Soc. Clin. Pathologists. Republican. Episcopalian. Club: Country of New Canaan. Home: 106 Elm Pl New Canaan CT 06840 Office: PO Box 1177 Valley Rd New Canaan CT 06840

GRESHAM, JESSIE LEE, spl. edn. adminstr.; b. Cin., Apr. 27, 1924; d. Early and Elsie (Moore) Brown; B.Ed., Chgo. Tchrs. Coll., 1955; M.Ed., 1961; m. William A. Gresham, July 6, 1959 (dec.); children—Marian, Bonnie, Colleen. Microphotographer, U.S. Treasury Dept., Chgo., 1948-52; tchr. Chgo. Bd. Edn., 1955-67, adminstr. Bur. Socially Maladjusted Children, Chgo., 1969—. Supervising team leader Nat. Tchr. Corps, 1967-69. Mem. Council Exceptional Children, Council Adminstrs. Spl. Edn., Council Children with Behavior Disorders, Chgo. Tchrs. Union, Phi Delta Kappa. Democrat. Baptist. Home: 5201 Cornell Ave Chicago IL 60615 Office: 228 N LaSalle St Chicago IL 60601

GRESS, GARNETTA MARGARET, equal employment opportunity specialist; b. Balt., May 10, 1943; d. Harold James and Garnetta Margaret (Ramsay) Potee; student East Carolina U., 1967-71, Pitt Community Coll., 1969-70, Coastal Carolina Community Coll., 1973-74, Pepperdine U., 1975, Syracuse U., 1977—; EEO law cert. Antioch Sch. Law, 1982; m. James A. Gress, Mar. 11, 1978; children—William Potee Klages, Jenifer Raye Klages. Fed. Women's program mgr. U.S. Marine Corps, Camp Lejeune, N.C., 1979—. Mem. Onslow County Council on Status of Women, 1979—, vice-chmn. 1980-81; mem. USO Council for Jacksonville, 1975—; bd. dirs. Balt. Regional chpt. ARC, 1960-61. Mem. N.C. Assn. EEO Personnel, Am. Soc. Mil. Comptrollers, Am. Bus. Women's Assn. (Chpt. Woman of Yr. 1974), Federally Employed Women, Inc., NOW, Beta Sigma Phi (Chpt. Woman of Yr. 1975-76). Home: PO Box 1347 Swansboro NC 28584

GREWELL, MARY, oil and gas co. exec.; b. Dover, Ohio, Jan. 27, 1936; d. Paul and Maria E. Sica; student Inst. for Energy Devel., 1979-81; m. Floyd M. Grewell, Sept. 19, 1953; children—Brenda J., Gail E., Tammy K. Clk. bookkeeping dept. Reeves Steel & Mfg. Co., Dover, 1953-54; adminstrv. asst. prodn. and land dept. Resource Exploration, Inc., Dennison, Ohio, 1974-77, Canton, Ohio, 1977-79; land adminstr. Berea Oil & Gas Corp., New Philadelphia, Ohio, 1979-80, v.p. land, 1980—. Dist. chmn. Del. dist. Girl Scouts U.S.A., 1971-74. Recipient Thanks badge Girl Scouts U.S.A., 1970. Mem. Am. Assn. Petroleum Landmen, Am. Right of Way Assn., Ohio Oil and Gas Assn., Ind. Oil and Gas Assn. W.Va. Mem. Moravian Ch. Club: Tuscarawas Valley Desk and Derrick, Internat. Mgmt. Council. Office: Progress St Dover OH 44622

GREY, CONSTANCE KOHLER, real estate broker; b. Buffalo, Nov. 18, 1922; d. William David and Elizabeth Velma (Barnes) Kohler; student Buffalo State Coll. Tchrs. (now SUNY, Buffalo), 1944-48; m. Roger P. Grey, June 12, 1947; children—Roger Harland, Richard David, Cheryl Lynn. Salesperson, Dorothy Derby Realty, Frewsburg, N.Y., 1959-60; salesperson, then asso. realtor Marshall Dunn Realty Co., Jamestown, N.Y., 1960-69; owner Connie Grey Realty, Lakewood, N.Y., 1969—; mem. bd. assessment rev. Town of Ellicott (N.Y.), 1976; tchr. career edn. Frewsburg Central Sch.; sponsor weekly radio show. Bd. dirs. Chautauqua County (N.Y.) Women's Republican Club; trustee Village of Coloron (N.Y.), 1976. Mem. Nat. Assn. Realtors, Jamestown Bd. Realtors (chmn. multiple service), N.Y. Assn. Appraisers, Jamestown Area C. of C., Chautauqua County C. of C. (dir.), Chautauqua County Vacationlands Assn. (dir.), Nat. Council Women Realtors, Bus. Profl. Women's Club, Lakewood C. of C. (dir.), Nat. Fedn. Bus. and Profl. Women. Unitarian. Clubs: Zonta (publicity com., dir. 1982-83), Lakewood Woman's. Address: 2095 Southwestern Dr Lakewood NY 14750

GREY, JEAN SCHWARTZ, accountant, plastics co. exec.; b. N.Y.C., June 14, 1925; d. Isidore and Edithe (Sarette) Schwartz; B.B.A., CCNY, 1950; m. Charles Grey, Nov. 22, 1945; children—Scott, Shari. Pub. acct. Kipnis & Karchmer, C.P.A.s, N.Y.C., 1942-44; pub. acct., then asst. head tax dept. Clarence Rainess Co., C.P.A.s, N.Y.C., 1944-54; ind. tax specialist, estate acct., Syosset, N.Y., 1950—; organizer, 1952, since treas., dir. Cee-Jay Extruders, Inc., plastics co.; lectr., cons. in field. C.P.A., N.Y. Mem. Am. Soc. Women Accts., Am. Women's Soc. C.P.A.s, N.Y. State Soc. C.P.A.s, Acctg. Inst. C.W. Post Coll. Art League, Bus. and Profl. Women's Club, U.S. Coast Guard Aux., Société des Vignerons. Clubs: Tappan Beach Yacht, Sagamore Yacht. Home: 9 Spruce Ln Syosset NY 11791 Office: 5 Sidney Ct Lindenhurst NY 11757

GRICE, JULIA HAUGHEY, author; b. Battle Creek, Mich., May 28, 1940; d. Wilfrid H. and Jean F. (Ayers) Haughey; B.A., Albion Coll., 1962; m. Lee Butcher, Feb. 12, 1980; children by previous marriage—Michael Grice, Andrew J. Grice. Books include: Lovefire, 1977, Emerald Fire, 1978, Daughters of the Flame, 1979, Wild Roses, 1980, The Passion Star, 1980; contrb. articles and fiction to various mags.; speaker various civic and profl. orgns. Mem. Detroit Women Writers (pres. 1975-77).

GRIDER, SYLVIA ANN, coll. dean; b. Pampa, Tex., Oct 21, 1940; d. R.C. and Huba Mildred (Holt) G.; B.A. in Latin, U. Tex., 1963, M.A. in History, 1967; Ph.D. in Folklore, Ind. U., 1976. Tchr., Tex. high schs., 1963-70; mem. faculty Tex. A&M U., 1976—, asso. prof. English, 1979—, asst. dean Grad. Coll., 1981—. Mem. Internat. Soc. Folk Narrative Research, Am. Folklore Soc., Children's Lit. Assn., South Central MLA, Western Lit. Assn., Tex. Folklore Soc. (pres. elect 1981), Tex. Council Tchrs. English, Delta Kappa Gamma, Phi Kappa Phi. Office: Grad Coll Tex A&M U College Station TX 88843

GRIDLEY, DAILA SEFERS, microbiologist; b. Riga, Latvia, Jan. 16, 1944; came to U.S., 1949, naturalized, 1954; d. Videvuds and Marta (Snikers) Sefers; B.S., U. Oreg., 1966, M.S., 1971; Ph.D., Loma Linda U., 1978; m. Larry Brown Gridley, Mar. 9, 1968; children—Laila and Laura (twins), Lisa. Med. technologist U. Oreg., 1966-69; sr. med. technologist Loma Linda (Calif.) Med. Center, 1971-74; researcher asso. Loma Linda U., 1978-81, asst. prof., 1981—; lectr. in field; faculty Calif. Poly. U., 1982—. Recipient Pres.'s award, Loma Linda U., 1978; Clinton Reed Brower scholar, 1978; Oreg. State scholar, 1962; Elsa U. Pardee Found. grantee, 1979-81, Nat. Dairy Council grantee, 1979-81. Mem. Am. Soc. Clin. Pathology, Am. Soc. Microbiology, Nat. Registry Microbiologists, AAAS, Sigma Xi, Delta Gamma. Republican. Lutheran. Club: Mothers of Twins, Casa Colina. Contbr. articles to profl. jours. Home: 784 Hillcrest Dr Pomona CA 91768 Office: Barton and Anderson Rds Loma Linda CA 92350

GRIER, BARBARA G. (GENE DAMON), author, editor, pub.; b. Cin., Nov. 4, 1933; d. Philip Strang and Dorothy Vernon (Black) G.; student public schs. Kansas City, Kans. Fiction, poetry editor The Ladder, Reno, 1966-67, editor, 1968-72; pub., 1970-72; dir. promotion NAIAD Press, Reno, 1973—, treas. NAIAD Press, Inc., 1976—, v.p., 1981—, also dir. Recipient President's award Gay Acad. Union, 1982. Author: (with Lee Stuart) The Lesbian in Literature, 1967, 3d edit., enlarged, 1981; chpt. in Sisterhood is Powerful, 1970; editor: (with Coletta Reid) Lesbian Lives: Biographies of Women from the Ladder, 1976; The Lesbian's Home Journal, 1976; The Lavender Herring, 1976; Lesbiana, 1976; Neither Profit Nor Salvation in the Lavender Culture, 1978; The Garden Variety Lesbian in The Lesbian Path, 1979, in The Coming Out Stories, 1980. Democrat. Address: PO Box 10543 Tallahasse FL 32302

GRIER, LINELLE NOLAN, home economist; b. Okmulgee, Okla., Sept. 15, 1917; d. Chester Author and Alberta (Bennett) Evans; B.S., Langston U., 1937; M.S., U. Wis., 1949; M.S., Alcorn State U., 1978; Ph.D. (hon.), Colo. State Christian Coll., 1973; m. Harold Edwin Grier, Jan. 24, 1964; 1 son by former marriage—Prentis Clamore Nolan. Tchr. vocat. home econs. Okla., 1937-58; dir. home mgmt., So. U., Baton Rouge, La., 1958-61; dormitory asst., profl. study U. Wis., Madison, 1961-62; asso. prof. home econs., Alcorn State U., Lormen, Miss., 1962—; cons. in field. Grantee HEW, 1968-69, U.S. Dept. Agr., 1968-71. Mem. Am. Home Econs. Assn., Miss. Home Econs. Assn., Am. Vocat. Assn., Miss. Consumer Assn. (dir.), AAUW, Kappa Omicron Phi. Baptist. Clubs: Ainwell Federated Women's (asst. sec. 1973-75), Parmi Nous Bridge (sec. 1978—), Claiborne County Bus. and Profl. Women's Club (corr. sec.). Home: PO Box 724 Alcorn State U Lorman MS 39096 Office: PO Box 763 Alcorn State U Lorman MS 39096

GRIEST, DOROTHY, coll. adminstr., mktg. cons.; b. Iota, La., Sept. 30, 1924; d. Henry R. and Dicie (Stakes) Hebert; B.S., U. Colo., 1945, M.B.A., 1951; Ph.D., La. State U., 1966; m. John M. Griest, July 18, 1972; children—Gibson H. Sandham, Jennifer S. Guillory. Prof., Northeast La. U., 1973-76; prof. Coll. Bus. Adminstrn., U. Colo., Boulder, 1956-77, chmn. bus. environment and policy, 1978-81; head dept. mgmt. and adminstrv. studies U. Southwestern La., 1981—. Dir., Monroe Civic Center, 1973-76. Mem. Acad. Mgmt., Southwest Fedn. Adminstrv. Disciplines, Beta Gamma Sigma, Phi Kappa Phi, Pi Sigma Epsilon, Beta Sigma. Democrat. Presbyterian. Home: 601 Camellia Blvd Lafayette LA 70503 Office: Univ Southwestern LA PO Box 40598 Lafayette LA 70504

GRIEST, GUINEVERE LINDLEY, govt. ofcl.; b. Chgo., Jan. 14, 1924; d. Euclid Eugene and Marianna (Lindley) Griest; A.B., Cornell U., 1944; A.M., U. Chgo., 1947, Ph.D., 1961; postgrad. (Fulbright fellow) Cambridge (Eng.) U., 1953-55. Instr., U. Ill., Chgo., 1947-61, asst. prof., 1961-66, asso. prof. English, 1966-72; program officer div. of fellowships Nat. Endowment for Humanities, Washington, 1969-73, dep. dir. div. of fellowships, 1973—. Mem. MLA, Phi Beta Kappa, Phi Kappa Phi. Episcopalian. Author: Mudie's Circulating Library and the Victorian Novel, 1971; contbr. articles to profl. jours. Office: Div of Fellowships Nat Endowment for Humanities 806 15th St NW Washington DC 20506

GRIEVE, JOSEPHINE HENDERSON, psychologist; b. Sturgis, Mich., Nov. 30, 1928; d. Homer H. and Josephine M. (Byrne) Henderson; B.M., U. Mich., 1950, Ph.D., 1978; M.A., Western Mich. U., 1970; m. L. Dale Grieve, Mar. 5, 1971; children—Mary, Patricia. Tchr. elem. schs., Chelsea, Mich., 1950-53, Muskegon, Mich., 1964-68; counselor public schs., Muskegon, 1968-71; clin. psychologist West Shore Mental Health Clinic, Muskegon, 1967-77; pvt. practice clin. psychology, Muskegon, 1977—; lectr., cons. to profl. assns. and ednl. agys., 1975—. Named Profl. and Bus. Woman of Yr., Quadrangles Club Mich., 1979; lic. psychologist, Mich. Mem. Am. Psychol. Assn., Mich. Psychol. Assn., Am. Soc. Clin. Hypnosis, Internat. Transactional Analysis Assn. (clin. mem.). Home and office: 1627 Jefferson St Muskegon MI 49441

GRIFFEE, CAROL MADGE, journalist; b. Washington, Dec. 30, 1937; d. John Franklin and Leda Mae (Woodruff) G.; B.A. with honors, U. Tulsa, 1959, M.A., 1966. Reporter. Ft. Smith (Ark.) Times-Record, 1955, Tulsa Daily World, 1958-60; news editor Annandale (Va.) Free Press, 1961-62; staff writer Washington Eve. Star, 1963-66; city editor No. Va. Sun, Arlington, Va., 1967-69, exec. editor, 1969-72; capitol reporter Walter E. Hussman Co., Camden, Ark., 1973; reporter Ark. Gazette, Little Rock, 1973—. Past pres. George Mason Republican Women's Club; past dir. research Fairfax County Rep. Com.; past bd. dirs. Arlington chpt. ARC; past bd. visitors George Mason U., Fairfax, Va. Recipient Very Spl. Lady award Advt. Club Met. Washington, 1967, Spl. award Ark. Sanitarians Assn., 1977, also awards Nat. Fedn. Press Women, Ark. Press Women. Mem. Nat. Fedn. Press Women (dir. 1977-78, legislations-resolutions dir. 1979-80), Ark. Press Women (pres. 1977-78), Mortar Bd., Sigma Delta Chi (chpt. v.p. 1979-80), Phi Delta Epsilon, Phi Gamma Kappa, Phi Delta Theta, Pi Gamma Mu, Phi Mu, Sigma Delta Chi. Project dir. Horizons: 100 Arkansas Women of Achievement, 1980. Home: 2610 N Taylor St Little Rock AR 72207 Office: PO Box 1821 Little Rock AR 72203

GRIFFEE, NOREEN JOANNE KILEY, home economist; b. Newhall, Calif., Nov. 14, 1938; d. Clifford James and Mary Elizabeth (Kanaly) Kiley; student U. So. Calif., 1955-57; B.S. in Home Econs., U. Mont., 1961; children—Glenn, Daniel. Food research asst. Schilling div. McCormick & Co., San Francisco, 1961-62, ednl. rep., 1962-63; asso. home economist McCall Pattern Co., N.Y.C., 1969-70; dir. home econs. and consumer services Calif. Raisin Adv. Bd., Fresno, 1974-81; dir. consumer services Sun-Diamond Growers Calif., San Ramon, 1981—; community resource guest lectr. Calif. State U., Fresno; mem. consumer edn. com. Fresno City Coll.; oral bd. mem. Fresno County CSC. Mem. Am. Home Econs. Assn., Home Economists in Bus., Soc. Nutrition Edn., Inst. Food Technologists, Soc. Consumer Affairs Profls., Kappa Kappa Gamma Alumnae Assn. Office: c/o Sun-Diamond Growers of Calif 1320 El Capitan Dr San Ramon CA 94583

GRIFFES, DONNA BERSE, TV comml. rep.; b. Woodbridge, N.J., June 15; d. H. Benjamin and Mazie (Traiman) Berse; R.N., Mt. Sinai Hosp. Sch. Nursing, 1950; m. Arthur Raynes Griffes, Jr., Dec. 20, 1952; children—Benjamin William, Susan Barbara, Peter Lynch. Head nurse pediatric div. Mt. Sinai Hosp., N.Y.C., 1950-52; free-lance fashion model Darcy Sheehan Agy., Ft. Lauderdale, Fla., 1971-75; asst. to pres. Internat. Yacht Brokerage, Ft. Lauderdale, 1975-79; asst. to pres. Berton Group, Culver City, Calif., 1979-80; exec. asst. Lonnie Dunn Co., Los Angeles, 1980-81; staff nurse St. John's Hosp., Santa Monica, Calif., 1981-82. Mem. Mayor's Prayer Breakfast Com., Ft. Lauderdale, 1974-76; participant Presdl. Prayer Breakfast, Washington, 1976; campaign worker J.F. Kennedy, Broward City, 1962, Jack Eckerd for Gov., Broward County, 1976; vol. reader for the blind, 1968-70; bd. dirs. Community Concert Assn., 1970-78; mem. Ft. Lauderdale Symphony Soc., Ft. Lauderdale Mus. of Art. Recipient Total Family Recognition award 1st Presbyn. Ch., Ft. Lauderdale, 1963-64. Mem. Nat. Assn. Female Execs. Republican. Address: 3700 S Sepulveda Blvd Apt 314 Los Angeles CA 90034 Office: care William Jeffreys Agy Los Angeles CA

GRIFFIN, ALBERTA LOGAN, librarian; b. Rutherfordton, N.C., Apr. 28, 1928; d. Rogers Harrison and Hattie Rogenus (Whiteside) Logan; B.S., Albany State Coll., 1964; M.Ed., Columbus Coll., 1976, Asso. Library Media Specialist, 1976; m. John R. Griffin, May 6, 1945; children—Ange Lene, Linda Jean, Barbara, Elaine, Mary Louise, Delmarie, Vanessa. Substitute tchr. public schs. Columbus, Ga., 1955-59; asst. librarian 4th Ave Public Library, Columbus, 1960-73; dir. Baker Village br. Chattahoochee Valley Regional Library, Muscogee County Sch. Dist., Columbus, 1973—. Mem. exec. bd. LWV, 1979; pres. AME Ministers Wives Alliance Columbus and Phenix City, 1977—, AME South West Ga. Wives Alliance, 1979. Mem. Ga. Library Assn., Southeastern Library Assn., AAUW (sec. Columbus 1978), Columbus Coll. Alumni Assn. (dir. 1979), Nat. Council Negro Women, Urban League, Phoenix Arts and Culture Center (dir. Columbus chpt.), Alpha Kappa Alpha. Club: Continental Socs. Inc. Home: 3031 8th St Columbus GA 31906 Office: 124 Benning Dr Columbus GA 31903

GRIFFIN, BARBARA BIONDO, social worker; b. Detroit, June 19, 1950; d. Sam John and Irene Theresa (Przygoda) Dimaria; M.S.W., U. Mich., 1975, planning specialist in gerontology cert., 1975; m. Dec. 17, 1977; 1 son, Stephen Bennett. Founder, owner, operator day care center, 1971; cons. to nursing homes, 1972—; geriatric social planner, 1976-77; cons., asst. dept. head St. Joseph Hosp., Bellingham, Wash., 1977—; cons. social worker Mt. Baker Kidney Center, 1980—. Bd. dirs. Rape Relief; active local Democratic campaigns, Ohio, 1968-69. NIMH scholar, 1975. Mem. Nat. Assn. Social Workers, Gerontol. Soc., Nat. Assn. Gerontology, NOW (chmn. bd. 1971-77), Women of Western. Home: 1016 Key St Bellingham WA 98225 Office: care St Joseph Hosp 3201 Ellis St Bellingham WA 98225

GRIFFIN, BETTY RUTH, educator; b. Miami, Fla., Nov. 13, 1940; d. Willie Frank and Lealer (Marshall) Garrison; B.A., U. Miami, 1981; children—Elaine, Samuel. Sec., Liberty City Ch. of Christ, Miami, 1973—; editor, pub. Christian Women at Work mag., Miami, 1981—; tchr. journalism and English, Dade County (Fla.) Public Schs., 1981—. Mem. Sigma Delta Chi. Mem. Churches of Christ. Author booklets. Home: 1425 NW 56th St Miami FL 33142

GRIFFIN, DIANE CAROLYN, physician; b. N.Y.C., Nov. 29, 1933; d. William and Nancy Lorraine (Trattler) Griffin; R.N., Luth. Med. Center, 1955; B.A. in Biology and Chemistry, Luther Coll., 1960; postgrad. Columbia U., 1960-63, L.I.U., 1963-64; M.D., U. Rome, Italy, 1974. Nurse Luther Coll., Decorah, Iowa, 1957-59; med. surg. instr. Luth. Med. Center, Bklyn., 1960-63; pvt. duty nurse Maimonides Med. Center, Bklyn., 1964-75; resident N.Y. U., 1975-77, resident physician, 1977-81; trainee in rehab. medicine Bellevue Hosp., VA Hosp., Goldwater Meml. Hosp., N.Y.C., 1978-81; staff physician Geriatric Medicine Nursing Home, Bklyn., 1981-82; practice medicine specializing in rehab. medicine, Bklyn., 1982—; health cons. Dept. Health, Rome, Italy, 1969-71. Fellow in rehab. medicine Goldwater Meml. Hosp., 1980. Mem., AMA, Am. Profl. Assn., Christian Med. Assn. Democrat. Lutheran. Clubs: American-Italian (Rome, Italy); Health. Home: 2660 E 19 St Brooklyn NY 11235

GRIFFIN, ELIZABETH LOOMIS, club woman; b. Chgo., Apr. 18, 1922; d. Eustis Holcomb and Elsie Violet (Cole) Loomis; student public schs., Bothell, Wash.; m. Samuel Walker Griffin, Apr. 18, 1967; children—James Loomis Ferguson, Thomas Eustis Wells. Bookkeeper, Bekins Moving Co., 1940-42, Keener's Meat Market, 1957-67. Mem. Northshore Bicentennial Com., Bothell, 1974-76; pres. Colonial Dames XVII Century, 1974-76; dist. pres. Vets. World War I Aux., 1977-78; state regent DAR, Wash., 1978-80. Recipient Americanism award VFW, 1978; medal of appreciation SAR, 1978. Mem. New Eng. Women, Am.

Legion Aux., Daus. Brit. Empire, Bothell Hist. Soc., Wash. Gens., Freedom Found., Daus. Am. Colonists. Republican. Baptist. Clubs: Navy Mother's, Rebekahs. Home: 23816 2d Ave SE Bothell WA 98011

GRIFFIN, ESTHER REITOR, interior designer; b. N.Y.C., Jan. 29, 1947; d. Alejandro and Dora Reitor; student Jersey City State Coll., 1965-66; A.S., Miami Dade Community Coll., 1978. Designer, showroom mgr. D'Art, Miami, 1976-80; designer Esther R. Griffin, Miami, 1980—; product and source researcher Ferendino Grafton Spillis Candela, Coral Gabels, Fla., 1981—. Mem. Inst. Bus. Designers, Am. Soc. Interior Designers Fla. Renaissance Guild. Home: 860 NE 78th St Apt 505 Miami FL 33138 Office: 800 Douglas Entrance Coral Gables FL 33134

GRIFFIN, HARRIET ELIZABETH, educator; b. Parker County, Tex.; d. Minter Crozier and Lillian (Sumner) Griffin; B.A., Tex. Christian U., 1932, M.A., 1935; postgrad. U. Tex., Colo. State U., UCLA, U. So. Calif. English tchr. Milsap public schs., 1933-35; tchr. Ft. Worth public schs., 1935-47, dean Tech. High Sch., also supr. Adult Evening Sch., 1947-63, coordinator guidance testing and vs. tchrs., 1963-67, dir. profl. relations, 1967-76; part time human relations instr. Tarrant County Jr. Coll. Del. World Confederation Orgn. of Teaching Professions, Korea, 1966, Ireland, 1968, London, 1972; bd. dirs. NCCJ, Sickle Cell Anemia Found.; mem. lay mem. com. on unauthorized practice of law State Bar Tex.; cons. Edna Gladney Home; mem. Adv. Bd. for Sr. Vols.; mem. edn. com. Ft. Worth Human Relations Agy.; mem. Camp Fire Bd.; del. Nat. White House Conf. on Aging, 1981. tchr. Aldersgate group 1st Meth. Ch. Named Exec. Woman of Yr., Zonta Internat., 1976; recipient award of distinction Nat. Council Adminstrv. Women in Edn., 1976; City of Ft. Worth Human Relations award, 1976; named Sr. Citizen of Yr., 1979; Harriet Griffin Human Relations award Ft. Worth Schs. named in her honor. Mem. Bus. and Profl. Women's Club, Tex. Tchrs. Assn. (pres. 1966, Adminstr. of Yr. 1976), Council Adminstrv. Women (past pres.), C. of C., Nat. Ret. Tchrs. Assn. (asso. v.p.), Ft. Worth Ret. Tchrs. Assn. (pres.), U.S.-China Peoples Friendship Assn., Friends of Library (dir.), Kappa Kappa Iota (hon.), Delta Kappa Gamma, Kappa Delta Pi. Methodist. Clubs: Altrusa (past pres.), Woman's, Shakespeare. Former author ednl. column One Small Voice, Ft. Forth Press (Sch. Bell award 8 yrs.). Contbr. articles to profl. publs. Home: 2555 Greene Ave Fort Worth TX 76109

GRIFFIN, JANE FLANIGEN, research scientist; b. Buffalo, Mar. 26, 1933; d. Charles Francis and Edith Mae (O'Connor) Flanigen; B.A. in Chemistry (N.Y. State Regents scholar), D'Youville Coll., Buffalo, 1954; Ph.D. in Chemistry (Danforth predoctoral fellow), SUNY, Buffalo, 1974; m. Richard F. Griffin, Dec. 27, 1954; children—Richard F., Thomas More, Mary T., Anne Elizabeth, Charles (dec.). Indsl. lab. technician Linde Corp., summers 1952-53; jr. research scientist Lind Corp. Research Lab., 1954-55; teaching asst. SUNY, Buffalo, 1971-73; postdoctoral research fellow molecular biophysics Med. Found. of Buffalo, Inc., 1974-77, research scientist, 1977—; chmn. various profl. congresses; lectr. Gordon Conf., 1976. Recipient Brotherhood award NCCJ, 1967; Danforth grad. fellow for women, 1967-72. Mem. AAAS, Am. Chem. Soc., Am. Crystallographic Assn., Am. Andrology Soc., Royal Soc. Chemistry, Am. Women in Sci., Kappa Gamma Pi. Republican. Roman Catholic. Editor: Molecular Structure and Biological Activity, 1982; contbr. articles profl. jours., chpts. in books. Office: 73 High St Buffalo NY 14203

GRIFFIN, MARGARET ANN, nurse; b. Hastings, Minn., June 3, 1925; d. Ray H. and Bertha M. (Thomas) Knotz; diploma in nursing St. Marys Hosp., Mpls., 1946, student Sch. Anesthesia, 1952; m. John H. Griffin Sept. 19, 1959 (dec. Oct. 1979); 1 dau., Linda Marie. Staff nurse Mpls. Gen. Hosp., 1946-48, Mercy Hosp., Sacramento, 1948-50; anesthetist St. Marys Hosp., Mpls., 1952-57; anesthetist Carbon County Meml. Hosp., Rawlins, Wyo., 1957-67, nurse, 1969—, now day house supr.; head nurse Park Manor Nursing Home, Rawlins, 1968-69. Mem. Am. Nurses Assn., Am. Assn. Nurse Anesthetists. Roman Catholic.

GRIFFIN, MARY ELIZABETH WILSON (MRS. DONALD F. GRIFFIN), metals mfg. co. exec., educator, city ofcl.; b. Yuba City, Calif., May 24, 1932; d. Zacharias Walters and Mary (Nickerson) Wilson; A.A., Yuba Coll., 1952; A.B. cum laude (Calif. Congress PTA scholar), Chico State Coll., 1954; postgrad. Sacramento State Coll., 1956, San Francisco State Coll., 1957-58; m. Donald F. Griffin, Sept. 6, 1958; children—John Malcolm, Mimi Elizabeth, Zachary Paul. Tchr. pub. elem. schs., Santa Rosa, Calif., 1954-57; asso. prof. edn. San Francisco State Coll., 1957-59, temporary tchr. Campus Elem. Sch., 1960-67; v.p. Griffin Metal Products, San Francisco, 1960-63, sec.-treas., 1963—; tchr. South San Francisco Unified Sch. Dist., 1973—. Treas. library trust fund French-Am. Bi-Lingual Sch., San Francisco, 1965-67; active PTA, 1967—, dir. county parent edn. program, 1972—; mem. Millbrae (Calif.) Beautification Com., 1971-78; bd. dirs. San Francisco Boys Chorus, until 1981; mem. Millbrae City Council, 1976—, mayor, 1980-81; chmn. North San Mateo County Council of Cities, 1978-79; bd. dirs. San Mateo County Easter Seal Soc., 1977—, 1st v.p., 1981-82; chmn. legis. com. San Mateo County Council of Mayors; 1st v.p. Peninsula div. League Calif. Cities, 1981-82. Recipient appreciation cert. Cub Scouts Am., 1969, 70, 71, Hon. Service award Calif. Congress PTA, 1973; named Woman of Yr., Calif. Fedn. Women's Clubs, 1980. Mem. Millbrae C. of C. Democrat. Presbyterian. Club: Millbrae Woman's. Home: 67 Aura Vista Millbrae CA 94030 Office: 1320 Underwood Ave San Francisco CA 94124

GRIFFIN, MARY FRANCES, library cons.; b. Cross Hill, Laurens County, S.C., Aug. 24, 1925; d. James and Rosa Lee (Carter) G.; A.B., Benedict Coll., 1947; M.S.L.S., Ind. U., 1957; student S.C. State Coll., summers 1948-51, Atlanta U., 1953, Va. State Coll., 1961. Tchr.-librarian Johnston (S.C.) Tng. Sch., Edgefield County Sch. Dist., 1947-51; librarian Lee County Sch. Dist., Dennis High, Bishopville, S.C., 1951-52, Greenville County (S.C.) Sch. Dist., 1952-66; library cons. S.C. Dept. Edn., Columbia, 1966—; vis. tchr. U. S.C., 1977. Recipient Cert. of Living the Legacy award Nat. Council Negro Women, 1980. Mem. ALA, Assn. Ednl. Communications and Tech. S.C., Assn. Curriculum Devel., AAUW (pres. Columbia br. 1978-80), Southeastern Library Assn. (sec. 1978-80), S.C. Library Assn. (sec. 1979), S.C. Assn. Sch. Librarians. Baptist. Home: PO Box 1652 Columbia SC 29202 also 1100 Skyland Dr Columbia SC 29210

GRIFFIN, PRISCILLA LORING (MRS. JOHN J. GRIFFIN), wax mfg. co. exec.; b. Winchester, Mass., Apr. 1, 1930; d. John Alden and Madeleine (Libby) Loring; student Pembroke Coll., Brown U., 1947-49, Katherine Gibbs Coll., 1949-50; m. John J. Griffin, Jan. 27, 1951; children—Patricia, Michael, Peter. Sec. to project Mass. Inst. Tech. (now Draper Labs.), 1950-52; adminstrv. asst., asst. treas. Roger A. Reed, Inc., Reading, Mass., 1971-72, pres., treas., 1972—; mem. corp. Reading Savs. Bank, 1977—, trustee, 1980—. Chmn., Camp Fire Girls of Reading, 1964-66, mem. state bd., 1966-68; mem. Reading Town Meeting, 1957-68; chmn. League Women Voters, Ipswich, 1969-70; trustee Roger A. Reed, Inc. Profit Sharing and Trust, 1968. Mem. New Eng. Women Bus. Owners (treas.), Asso. Industries Mass., Small Bus. Assn. New Eng. Unitarian. Clubs: Ipswich Bay Yacht, E. Lake Woodlands. Home: 1 Riverside Dr Ipswich MA 01938 Office: 167 Pleasant St Reading MA 01867

GRIFFIN, SHIRLEY ANN, freelance writer; b. Chgo., Dec. 2, 1949; d. L.F. and Thelma G.; B.S., Mundelein Coll., 1970; M.A., Atlanta U., 1972; postgrad. in mgmt. Northwestern U. Acad. services coordinator, student counseling service U. Ill. Med. Center, Chgo., 1974-77; mgr. spl. projects Coll. Dentistry, U. Ill., Chgo., 1977-80; adminstrv. mgr. Central YMCA Coll., Chgo., 1980-81; bus., ednl. tng. cons., Chgo., 1981-82. Active, Multicultural TV Council, Chgo. Mem. Women in Mgmt., Nat. Assn. Female Execs., League Black Women. Address: 5415 N Sheridan Rd Chicago IL 60640

GRIFFIN, SUZANNE REBER, publishing co. exec.; b. Rockville Centre, N.Y., Oct. 15, 1947; d. John Walter and Louise August (Duvelius) Reber; B.S., Boston U., 1969; M.A., Catholic U., 1975, Ph.D., 1978; postgrad. U. Calif., Berkeley; m. June 17, 1975. Editor, Nat. Assn. Counties, Washington, 1969; asst. press sec. to Senator Hugh Scott from Pa., 1970; research editor Am. Psychol. Assn., Washington, 1970-71; asst. editor Anthrop. Quar., Washington, 1972-75; reporter Dubuque (Iowa) Telegraph Herald, 1975-76; editorial dir. Aldine Pub. Co., Chgo., 1977-78; mgr. communications services McKinsey and Co., Chgo., 1978-80; research cons. McKinsey & Co., San Francisco, 1980-81. Contbr. to Ency. of Anthropology, 1977. Home: 270 32d Ave San Francisco CA 94121

GRIFFIN, SYLVIA F., home economist; b. Bklyn., Mar. 14, 1926; d. Alfred L. and Florence (Markel) Futterman; B.S. in Home Econs., Pratt Inst., 1947; M.Ed. in Adult Edn., Rutgers U., 1967, postgrad., 1976—; m. Russell E. Griffin, Apr. 4, 1971; children—Lance Meehan, Kevin Meehan, Barret Meehan. Decorating cons. John Wannamaker Dept. Store, N.Y.C., 1947; dietitian Schrafft's Resraurants, N.Y.C., 1948-49; free lance mag. writer, 1955-56; extension home economist Rutgers U., New Brunswick, N.J., 1961—, parliamentarian Extension Forum, sec. personnel com. home econs. dept. Cook Coll., Rutgers U. Women's Center adv. bd. Brookdale Community Coll., 1975—. Mem. Am. Home Econs. Assn., N.J. Home Econs. Assn., Nat. Assn. Extension Home Economists (disting. service award for N.J. 1972, Florence Hall award 1971), N.J. Assn. Extension Home Economists. Author monthly newsletter HOME ECogram, 1976—; contbr. to USDA publ. Office: 20 Court St Freehold NJ 07728

GRIFFITH, BARBARA LEE, ins. co. exec.; b. Evanston, Ill., May 25, 1938; d. Gordon and Doris Griffith; B.S., cert. phys. therapy, U. Wis., 1960; M.H.A., Ind. U., 1975. Staff therapist Mary Free Bed Hosp., Grand Rapids, Mich., 1960-61; asst. chief phys. therapist Curative Workshop, Milw., 1961-64; staff therapist Australian Multiple Sclerosis Soc., also Royal South Sydney Rehab. Hosp., Sydney, 1964-65; chief phys. therapist Curative Workshop Milw., 1966-73; mgr. health service research and evaluation Blue Cross-Blue Shield Ind., 1975-81, mgr. market research and planning, 1981—. Recipient Guy Spring award Ind. Hosp. Assn., 1974. Mem. Am. Phys. Therapy Assn., Am. Hosp. Assn., Am. Assn. Female Execs., U. Wis. Alumni Assn., Ind. U. Alumni Assn., Audubon Soc., Nature Conservancy. Methodist. Home: 6755 Washington Blvd Indianapolis IN 46220 Office: 120 W Market St Indianapolis IN 46204

GRIFFITH, DOROTHY AUBINOE, interior designer; b. Washington, Feb. 19, 1927; d. Alvin Love and Dorothy (Barron) Aubinoe; A.B., Rollins Coll., 1948; grad. teaching cert. U. Md., 1949; diploma Internat. Inst. Interior Design, 1958; children—June, Paul, Tod, Holly. Owner, interior designer Griffith Assos., Inc., Bethesda, Md., 1958-78; owner, dir. Griffith Gallery, Miami, Fla., 1978—. Mem. Am. Soc. Interior Designers. Home: 932 Tendilla Ave Coral Gables FL 33134

GRIFFITH, GENEVA ELLERBEE, photojournalist; b. Orange, Tex., May 17, 1922; d. Odie Leslie and Lottie Layne (Cherry) Ellerbee; student public schs., Port Arthur, Tex.; m. D.W. Griffith, Apr. 29, 1944 (dec. Apr. 1973); children—Leslie D., Cherie Kay. Photojournalist, Cameron (La.) Pilot, 1957—, Lake Charles (La.) Am. Press, 1967—; sec. Office of Cameron Parish Dist. Atty., 1973—. Bd. dirs., v.p. La. Fur and Wildlife Festival; mem. La. Bicentennial del. to France, 1976; bd. dirs. Cameron Parish chpt. Am. Heart Assn., Am. Cancer Soc. Recipient award for stories and photos La. Press Women's Assn., La. Press Assn. Mem. Nat. Fedn. Press Women, Council for Devel. of French in La., Am. Legion Aux., La. Press Women's Assn. Baptist. Home and office: PO Drawer I Cameron LA 70631

GRIFFITH, JANE ELIZABETH, museum ofcl.; b. Edgefield, S.C., Sept. 19, 1939; d. William Arthur and Elizabeth (Pritchard) Byrd; B.A., Winthrop Coll., 1961; M.A.T., U. N.C., 1965; postgrad. Duke U., 1962, Tex. A.&M. U., 1970-80; m. George Wayne Griffith, 1966 (dec. 1972). Tchr., Columbia (S.C.) Public Sch. System, 1961-63; biologist Nat. Marine Fisheries Lab., Oxford, Md., 1963-64; tchr. Texas City (Tex.) Ind. Sch. Dist., 1965-67, Galveston (Tex.) Coll., 1967-71; research asst. U. Tex. Med. Br., Galveston, 1972-73; spl. projects analyst Amoco Chem. Co., Alvin, Tex., 1974-82; pres. Griffith Enterprises, Hitchcock, Tex., 1981—; dir. edn. BTA Mus., 1982—. George W. Griffith Scholarship Program dir., 1972—; bd. dirs. Hitchcock Library, 1973-74; mem. City of Galveston Anti-litter Com., 1971-72. Mem. AAUW (state bd. 1972-74). Home: PO Box 812 Rye TX 77369

GRIFFITH, JANET EILEEN, investment broker; b. Indpls., Jan. 8, 1949; d. George Willis and Margaret Olive (Finnicum) Corney; student Goethe-Institut, Passau, W. Ger., 1969; B.A. magna cum laude, Augustana Coll., 1971; m. Alan Lee Griffith, July 24, 1976. Tchr., Woodland Community Unit Dist., Streator, Ill., 1971-74; pub.'s rep. Macmillan Pub. Co., N.Y.C., 1974-76; tchr. Iowa City Community Schs., 1976-77; sec. Peoples Bank & Trust Co., Cedar Rapids, Iowa, 1978-79; registered rep. Dain Bosworth Inc., Cedar Rapids, 1979—; instr. Kirkwood Community Coll. Mem. Women's Profl. Network, AAUW (exec. bd. Iowa div., chmn. div. topic 1981-83), Phi Beta Kappa. Home: 318 Nassau St SE Cedar Rapids IA 52403 Office: 105 IE Tower Cedar Rapids IA 52401

GRIFFITH, JESSIE HORNE, educator; b. Rocky Mountain, N.C., Jan. 17, 1935; d. Jesse and Mary (Battle) Horne; B.S., Winston Salem (N.C.) State U., 1957; M.Ed., Suffolk U., Boston, 1980; m. Albert E. Griffith, Dec. 21, 1957 (div. 1961); 1 son, Vincent Earl. Elem. sch. tchr., Boston, 1957, Saugus. Mass., 1964—; fin. cons. Oliver Fin. Service, Providence, 1981; propr. Mgmt. Cons. Service, Saugus, 1979—. Bd. dirs. Camp Rotorary-Lynn WMCA, Lynn, Mass., 1980—. Mem. Nat. Assn. Industry-Edn. Coop., Nat. Assn. Exec. Females, Nat. Assn. Elem. Sch. Prins., Assn. Supervision and Curriculum Devel., Mass. Assn. Supervision and Curriculum Devel., Am. Assn. Ind. Investors. Democrat. Home: 2 Staaf Rd Saugus MA 01906 Office: VW Evans Sch E Denver St Saugus MA 01906

GRIFFITH, MARY LOUISE KILPATRICK (MRS. EMLYN I. GRIFFITH), civic worker; b. Gadsden, Ala., Mar. 22, 1926; d. Lewis A. and Willie (Reid) Kilpatrick; A.B., Huntingdon Coll., 1947; m. Emlyn I. Griffith, Aug. 13, 1946; children—William L., James R. Pres. Evergreen Twig, hosp. charity group, Rome, 1966-67; bd. dirs. Rome Art and Community Center, 1967-72; mem. Bd. Edn. Rome City Sch. Dist., 1967-77; bd. dirs. Rome chpt. Am. Field Service, 1969-77; trustee Utica Coll. Found., 1974—, George Jr. Republic, 1974—, Pub. Broadcasting Council Central N.Y., 1977—, 1st Presbyn. Ch., Rome, 1979—; pres. Rome Home, 1973-75; permanent adviser Rome Newcomers Club. Recipient Rose for Living award Rotary Club, 1973; Civic award for conspicuous service Colgate U., 1978. Presbyn. Mem. PEO (pres. 1965-66), AAUW, Nat. Soc. Lit. and Arts. Club: Wednesday Morning (pres. Rome 1968-70). Home: Golf Course Rd Rome NY 13440

GRIFFITH, RHETA, banker; b. Memphis, June 3, 1947; d. Edward M. and Mary Elizabeth (Bateman) G.; student Stephens Coll., 1965; B.A., U. Ark., 1970. Corp. sec., dir. Merchants and Planters Bank, Clarendon, Ark., 1976—. Dist. dir. Monroe County Soil Conservation Dist., 1976-79. Episcopalian. Home: 221 N 3d St Clarendon AR 72029

GRIFFITHS, KAREN LYNN, lawyer, legislator; b. Junction City, Kans., Jan. 19, 1953; d. John Joseph and Elsie Pearl (Paden) Beavers; B.A., Washburn U., 1975, J.D., 1978; m. Douglas Craig Griffiths, Aug. 12, 1978. Admitted to Kans. bar, 1978; atty., prosecutor City of Wichita, Kans., 1978-79; asso. Morgan & Reid, Newton, Kans., 1979—; mem. Kans. Ho. of Reps., 1979-82. Bd. dirs. Hospice, Inc., 1971—, Family Health Plan, 1981—. Mem. Nat. Assn. State Legislators, Am. Bar Assn., Kans. Bar Assn., Harvey County Bar Assn., P.E.O., Newton C. of C., Bus. and Profl. Womens Club. Republican. Methodist. Office: 127 E 7th St Newton KS 67114

GRIGGS, MARGARET DUNHAM, artist; b. Atlanta, May 30, 1922; d. Cornelius Thomas and Margaret Couper (Traylor) Dunham; grad. Finch Coll., 1942; student Art Students League, N.Y.C.; m. Eugene A. McCain, 1946; children—Margaret Dunham, Thomas Ward, Eugene Augustus; m. 2d, Maitland Lee Griggs, Aug. 25, 1962. Part owner, mgr. Gallery in the Barn, Westchester, N.Y., 1952-55; artist, 1955—; v.p., then pres. Watershed, Inc., Newcastle, Maine, 1975-80, also dir.; critic and instr. of painting; one-woman exhbns. include Hudson River Mus., Yonkers, N.Y., Maine Art Gallery, Wiscasset; group exhbns. include Art Inst., Albany, N.Y., Wadsworth Atheneum, Hartford, Conn., Katonah (N.Y.) Gallery, Frost-Gully Gallery, Portland, Maine, Finch Mus., N.Y.C., Saranac (N.Y.) Gallery. Bd. dirs. Group Home, Bristol, Maine, 1980—. Mem. Westchester Art Soc., Maine Art Gallery, Katonah Art Gallery. Democrat. Clubs: Ausable, St. Hubert's (N.Y.). Address: Ardsley Ave W Ardsley-on-Hudson NY 10503

GRIGGS, PHYLLIS KAY, fast food chain exec.; b. Grand Island, Nebr., Aug. 26, 1937; d. Fritz and Kathryn Rieger; grad. Nat. Sch. Bus., 1957; m. Norman E. Griggs, Dec. 31, 1956 (div., 1971); 1 dau., Tracy Kay. With Corner Constrn. Co., Rapid City, S.D., 1957-71; owner, mgr. Mister Donut Franchise, McAllen, Edinburg and Brownsville, Tex., 1972—; pres., chief exec. officer Ahora Que, Inc., McAllen, 1972—; adv. council chmn. Mister Donut of Am.; v.p. Poquito Mas, Inc., 1982—. Mem. adv. council SBA. Bd. dirs., 2d v.p. McAllen Boy's Club. Home: 1700 Fern St McAllen TX 78501 Office: 4309 N 22d St McAllen TX 78501

GRIGORY, MILDRED ANNE, data processing co. exec.; b. Leesburg, Va., Jan. 31, 1948; d. Alexander Perrow and Ruby (Conner) McGhee; B.A. in Bus. Mgmt. magna cum laude, Coll. William and Mary, 1968; hon. doctorate in humanities and sci. Harvard U., 1979; cert. in data processing, 1977; m. Larry David Grigory, Apr. 19, 1974. Dir. data processing Best Products Co., Richmond, Va., 1968-71, Parish Murrell & Co., C.P.A.s; dir. data processing, prin. Judd Thomas Beasley & Smith, C.P.A.s, Dallas, 1974-77; pres. Cert. Resources Corp., Dallas, 1979— mem. President's Adv. Council for Small Bus. Reform, 1978, 79, 81. Named Woman of Yr., Data Processing Mgmt. Assn., 1973, 76, 78. Mem. Assn. for Systems Mgmt., Internat. Platform Assn. (Public Speaker of Yr. 1979), Internat. Entrepreneurs Assn., Fellowship of Christian Athletes (nat. lectr.), Data Processing Mgmt. Assn., Bus and Profl. Women, EDP Auditors Assn., Nat. Hist. Soc., C. of C. of U.S., Nat. Trust for Historic Preservation, Smithsonian Assos., Alpha Beta Chi. Home: 318 Swan Ridge Pl Duncanville TX 75137 Office: Cert Resources Corp 8730 King George Dr Suite 115 Dallas TX 75235

GRILL, JOYCE BABLER, musician, educator; b. Monroe, Wis.; d. Harry W. and Emma (Yossi) Babler; Mus.B., U. Wis., 1958, Mus.M., 1977; postgrad. Sch. Fine Arts, Fontainbleau, France, 1959; m. Karl P. Grill, Aug. 12, 1962; children—Karen Anne, Karl Erik Kristian. Mus. accompanist CBS-TV, N.Y.C., 1958-61; music tchr. Madison (Wis.) Public Schs., 1961-67; pvt. music tchr., Chgo., 1967-70; piano instr. St. Mary's Coll., Winona, Minn., 1972-73, U. Wis., LaCrosse, 1974—. Mem. Music Educators Nat. Conf., Music Tchrs. Nat. Assn., Wis. Music Tchrs. Assn., LaCrosse Area Music Tchrs. Assn., Wis. Music Educators Conf., AAUW, Sigma Alpha Iota, Phi Kappa Phi. Club: Town and Country Garden. Office: University of Wisconsin Fine Arts Bldg LaCrosse WI 54601

GRILL, NANNETTE LOUISE, writer, producer, composer, educator; b. Los Angeles, Mar. 26, 1935; d. Raymond James and Ethel Mae (Rogers) G.; student Stanford U., 1952-55; B.A. summa cum laude, Immaculate Heart Coll., 1965; M.A., U. Calif., Los Angeles, 1969. Teaching sister Los Angeles Area Catholic Parochial schs., 1956-68; coordinator juvenile program Culver City (Calif.) High Sch., 1968-69; assoc. prof. English, Pasadena (Calif.) City Coll., 1969—; freelance writer, 1970-74; partner Scarecrow Publs., Los Angeles, 1971-73; co-founder So. Calif. chpt. Reading is Fundamental, 1972; cons. in field. Nat. Endowment for Humanities fellow, 1973-74; NDEA grantee, 1966. Mem. ASCAP, TV Acad. Arts and Scis., Los Angeles Womens C. of C., U. Calif. Alumni Assn., Stanford U. Alumni Assn. Author: (with Charonne Wali) Mister Abracadabra, 1971; Clothe the Naked, 1980; also papers. Interview guest on TV shows including Dinah's Place, Tom Snyder's Sunday Show. Designed and produced children's public service shows, 1972-73; producer, writer TV spl. Dear Bear's Christmas, 1980. Christmas (Emmy nominee), Home: Marina Del Rey CA Office: Pasadena City College Department of English 1560 E Colorado Blvd Pasadena CA 91106

GRILLO, JEANNE MAEROSE, mfg. co. exec.; b. Chgo., Sept. 15, 1952; d. Ernest S. and Genevieve M. (Bartelak) G.; B.A. with honors and high distinction in English (Tchr. Edn. scholar), U. Ill., 1973, M.A., 1974. From customer service rep. to quality control supr. Wilton Enterprises/Pillsbury Co., Chgo., 1975-78; buyer Eagle Sheet Metal Co., Niles, Ill. 1978-79; prodn. planner Wittek div. Microdot Co., 1979; mfg. liaison Sun Chem. Co., 1979-80; direct materials buyer Papermate div. Gillette Co., LaGrange Park, Ill., 1980—. Mem. Nat. Assn. Female Execs., Lambda Iota Tau. Roman Catholic. Home: 437 Bayview Ave Naperville IL 60565 Office: 825 26th St LaGrange Park IL 60525

GRIMES, (ALICE) BEVERLY, med. technologist; b. Mobile, Dec. 7, 1925; d. Hopie Smith and Alice May (Parsons) Tatum; B.S., Springhill Coll., 1981; m. John Andrew Grimes, Jr., June 3, 1950; children—John Andrew, III, Alan Tatum. Operator retail drug store, 1940-63; with Tatum's Pharmacy, Mobile, 1963-81; lab. technologist, parasitologist Mobile Infirmary, 1963—; tchr. Sch. Med. Technologists; Sales group leader Avon Products, 1982—. Mem. Am. Soc. Clin. Pathologists, Am. Assn. Med. Assts. (pres. chpt. 1982-83). Republican. Episcopalian. Home: 2781 S Sherwood Dr Mobile AL 36606

GRIMES, CAROLYN LEE, acct.; b. Winchester, Va., Sept. 9, 1951; d. Albert Julian and Nannie Rose G.; A.A., Smithdeal Massey Bus. Coll., 1971; student Ohio State U. Coll. Continuing Edn.; 1 son, Philip Isaiah. Bookkeeper, Shockey Bros., Inc., Winchester, 1971-73; exec. sec., payroll clk. Gen. Electric Co., Winchester, 1973-75; acct., personnel mgr. Supreme Council of House Jacob, Coshocton, Ohio, 1975—. Mem. Nat. Assn. Female Execs. Republican. Home: Route 1 Box 143 Coshocton OH 43812 Office: PO Box 300 Coshocton OH 43812

GRIMES, DARCEL CLARNISE, TV anchor, reporter; b. washington, July 6, 1954; d. John Henry and Hattie Lee (White) G.; B.A. in Communications and Sociology, Am. U., 1977. Writer, Morningline News Program, Sta. WAMU-FM, Washington, 1974; intern Sta. WMAL, Washington, 1975; editorial clk. Dept. Interior, Washington, 1974-76; intern NBC Network Radio and TV, Washington, 1975-76, desk asst., 1976; reporter, writer, anchor Sta. WRBC, Jackson, Miss., 1976-77; anchor, producer, reporter Sta. WTVA-TV, Tupelo, Miss., 1977-81; anchor, reporter Sta. WLDS-TV, Asheville, N.C., 1981—. Mem. Women in Communications. Democrat. Baptist. Club: Capital Press. Home: 40E Foxfire Dr Ashville NC 28803 Office: PO Box 2150 Asheville NC 28802

GRIMES, FRANCES SELLS, former bus. cons. co. exec.; b. Johnson City, Tenn., Feb. 8, 1930; d. Samuel Hayward and Helen (Milligan) Sells; student Agnes Scott Coll., 1948-50; B.S., East Tenn. State U., 1952; m. Alton Barger Grimes, Mar. 24, 1979; children—Helen Doss Chapaitis, Dorothy Doss Dance, Robert McB. Doss. Vice pres. Farnsworth Cannon, Inc., McLean, Va., 1970-77; dir. Chalet de la Paix, Arlington, Va., 1975-78, King's Inc., Johnson City, 1968—, Gen. Shale Products Corp., Johnson City, 1977—. Bd. dirs. Sells Found., 1973—. Mem. Daus. Am. Colonists, DAR, Colonial Dames XVII Century, Nat. Soc. So. Dames Am. Republican. Presbyn. (elder). Home: 6613 McLean Ct McLean VA 22101

GRIMES, JUDITH ELIZABETH, educator; b. Indpls., July 3, 1945; d. William T. and Edith Florence (Roberts) Gill; B.M., Butler U., 1967, M.S., 1973; m. Tom Davisson, July 4, 1976; children—Gina, Brandon. Dir. instrumental music Danville Community Schs., Danville, Ind., 1968-72; head instrumental music Univ. Sch., Ind. State U., Terre Haute, 1972—, also assoc. prof. music; state chmn. nat. Music In Our Schs. Week movement, 1979-81; guest clinician, conductor; dir. Terre Haute All City High Sch. Concert and Jazz Bands. Recipient Caleb Mills Teaching Award, Ind. State U., 1979; named One of 10 Outstanding Music Educators, Sch. Musician and Tchr., 1982. Mem. Women Band Dirs. Nat. Assn. (charter mem., nat. ednl. chmn. 1982—, Silver Baton award 1981), Developer instrumental music program high sch. level, Montego Bay, Jamaica. Home: 228 S 21st St Terre Haute IN 47803 Office: Univ Sch Ind State U Terre Haute IN 47809

GRIMES, JUDY THIELEN, real estate exec.; b. Oakland, Calif., Feb. 7, 1955; d. Jack and Lyla (Knudson) Thielen; ed. Cabrillo Coll.; m. Jerry Summers Grimes, Jan. 16, 1982. With Tree & Sea Realty, Aptos, Calif., 1975-78, Coast Counties Realty, Santa Cruz, Calif., 1978-78, Steward Realtors, Santa Cruz, Calif., 1979-81; broker, woner Cypress Realty, Santa Cruz, 1981—. Mem. Santa Cruz Bd. Realtors, Nat. Assn. Realtors, Calif. Assn. Realtors. Lutheran. Home: 322 Los Altos Dr Aptos CA 95003 Office: 2-2596 E Cliff Dr Santa Cruz CA 95062

GRIMES, MARIETTA MARIE, real estate sales exec.; b. Maryville, Mo., May 25, 1946; d. Homer Leon and Neva Marie Council; B.S. in Vocat. Home Econs., N.W. Mo. State U., Maryville, 1968, M.S. in Counseling, 1974; m. William H. Grimes, Jr., Aug. 29, 1975. Tchr., Harrison County RIV Schs., Gilman City, Mo., 1969-72; counselor Jefferson Schs., Conception Jct., Mo., 1974-75; sales asso. Estill & Greenlee Realtors, Charleston, W.Va., 1976-78; exec. dir. Sexual Assault Center, Charleston, 1977-78; sales mgr. Levy, Malone & Co., Des Moines, 1978-80; sales rep. Lew Clarkson Real Estate, Des Moines, 1980—; exec. mgr. Beeline Fashions, 1981—; adj. prof. counseling W.Va. Coll. of Grad. Studies; del., workshop leader Internat. Women's Yr. Conf. W.Va., 1977. Grantee U. Mo., 1975. Home: 422 NW Greenwood Ankeny IA 50021 Office: 6000 Douglas St Des Moines IA 50312

GRIMES, MARJORIE GOLDSCHMIDT, elec. mfg. co. exec.; b. Elizabethtown, Ky., Feb. 8, 1929; d. John Arthur and Elsie Marie (Long) Goldschmidt; B.A. in Psychology, U. Cin., 1951; m. Joseph K. Grimes, July 2, 1972; 1 son, Jay Van Arsdall. With Gen. Electric Co., 1954—, mgr. personnel practices, mgr. relations systems and tng., Phila., 1968-72, mgr. managerial skills devel. course, Crotonville, N.Y., 1972-74, mgr. employee and community relations, Waynesboro, Va., 1974—; adj. instr. U. Cin. Med. Sch., 1960-68. Founding mem., pres. Waynesboro, East Augusta County Jr. Achievement, Inc., 1977-80; bd. dirs. Waynesboro Heart Assn., 1978-80, pres., 1979; mem. Gov.'s Com. for Arts, 1979-80, Gov.'s Com. on Handicapped, 1979; chmn. Waynesboro ARC, 1982; bd. dirs. Nat. Soc. for Prevention of Blindness, 1981-82. Recipient Leadership award Nat. Bus. Leadership Conf., 1979. Mem. Shenandoah Valley Personnel Assn. (pres. 1976), Waynesboro C. of C. (dir. 1978-80, pres. 1980). Author: All About Personnel Testing, 1959; The Law and Personnel Testing, 1972. Home: 211 Pelham Dr Waynesboro VA 22980 Office: Gen Elec Dr Waynesboro VA 22980

GRIMES, TAMMY, actress, singer, comedienne; b. Lynn, Mass., Jan. 30, 1936; d. Luther Nichols and Eola Willard (Niles) Grimes; grad. Beaver Country Day Sch., 1951; grad. with honors Stephens Jr. Coll., 1953; m. Christopher Plummer, Aug. 16, 1956 (div. 1960); 1 dau., Amanda Michael. Mem. staff Westport Playhouse, Conn., 1954; N.Y. debut in Neighborhood Playhouse, 1955; singer, actress Littlest Review, Off Broadway Phoenix Theatre, 1956; appeared Stratford (Ont.) Shakespeare Festival, 1958; performed Cambridge (Mass.) Drama Festival, in Shakespeare's Twelfth Night, summer 1959; role of Moll in Marc Blitzstein's opera, The Cradle Will Rock, N.Y.C. Center, 1960; role in Unsinkable Molly Brown, on Broadway, 1961-62, later on tour; appeared in musical 42nd Street; theatrical appearances in Father's Day, 1979, A Month in the Country, 1979-80; TV performer NBC-TV on Omnibus, 1959, Hollywood Sings, 1960, series Hour of Great Mysteries, 1960; in Four Poster, CBS-TV, 1962; Horror at 35,000 Feet (Movie of the Week) CBS-TV, 1973; The Borrowers, Hallmark Hall of Fame, 1974; appeared in Broadway prodn. Rattle of A Simple Man, 1964, High Spirits, 1965-66, Jubilee, 1973; starred in Mollie, 1978, Tartuffe, 1977, California Suite, 1976-77; appeared in films Three Bites of the Apple, 1966, Play It As It Lays, 1972, Somebody Killed Her Husband, 1977, The Runner Stumbles, 1979, Can't Stop the Music, 1980. Recipient Comoedia Matinee Club award, 1961; Antoinette Perry award, 1960; Variety Drama Critics award, 1961, Tony award for Private Lives, 1970. Republican. Address: care William Morris Agy Inc 151 El Camino Beverly Hills CA 90212 *

GRIMMELL, KAREN ETHEL, psychiatrist; b. Bklyn., Mar. 20, 1937; d. Charles H. and Ethel H. (Haggren) G.; B.S., Wagner Coll., 1957; M.D., N.Y. Med. Coll., 1961; m. George W. O'Rourke, July 27, 1962; children—Robert, Stephen, Erin. Intern, Mountainside Hosp., Montclair, N.J., 1961-62; resident Western State Hosp., Ft. Steilacoom, Wash., Greystone Park (N.J.) Hosp.; unit chief Hall Brooke Hosp., Westport, Conn., 1972-75; clin. dir. Stamford (Conn.) Methadone Maintenance Program and Woman Center, Stamford, 1975-79; dir. day treatment Greater Bridgeport (Conn.) Mental Health Center, 1979-81, dir. outpatient dept., 1981—; practice medicine specializing in psychiatry, 1972—; mem. staff St. Vincent's Hosp., Bridgeport, Park City Hosp., Bridgeport. Diplomate Am Bd. of Psychiatry 1978. Mem. Am. Psychiat. Assn., Am. Med. Women's Assn., Conn. Psychiat. Assn. Home: 17 Old Barn Rd Trumbull CT 06611 Office: 1635 Central Ave Bridgeport CT 06610

GRIMMER, MARGOT, dancer, choreographer, dir.; b. Chgo., Apr. 5, 1944; d. Vernon and Ann (Radville) Grimmer; student Lake Forest Coll., 1963, Northwestern U., 1964-68. Dancer, N.Y.C. Ballet prodn. of Nutcracker Chgo., 1956-57, Kansas City Starlight Theatre, 1958, St. Louis Mcpl. Theatre, 1959, Chgo. TentHouse-Music Theater, 1960-61, Lyric Opera Ballet, Chgo., 1961, 63-66, 68, Ballet Russe de Monte Carlo, N.Y.C., 1962, Ruth Page Internat. Ballet, Chgo., 1965-70; dancer-choreographer Am. Dance Co., Chgo., 1972-82, artistic dir., 1972-82; dancer, choreographer Bob Hope Show, Milw., 1975, Washington D.C. Bicentennial Performance, Kennedy Center, 1976, Woody Guthrie Benefit Concerts, 1976-77, Assyrian Cultural Found., Chgo., 1977-78, Iranian Consulate Performance, Chgo., 1978, Israeli Consulate Concert, Chgo., 1980 Chgo. Council Fine Arts Programs, 1978-82, U.S. Boating Indsl. Show, 1981-82; dir.-tchr. Am. Dance Sch., 1971-82; appeared in TV commls. and indsl. films for Libbys Foods, Sears, Gen. Motors, others, 1963-81; soloist in ballet Repertory Workshop, CBS-TV, 1964, dance film Statics (Internat. Film award), 1967; soloist in concert Ravinia, 1973. Ill. Arts Council grantee, 1972-74, 78, Nat. Endowment for Arts grantee, 1973-74. Mem. Actors Equity Assn., Screen Actors Guild, Am. Guild Mus. Artists. Important works include ballets In-A-Gadda-Da-Vida, 1972, The Waste Land, 1973, Rachmaninoff: Theme and Variations, 1973, Le Baiser de la Fee and Sonata, 1974, Four Quartets, 1974, Am. Export, 1975, Earth, Wind and Fire, 1976, Blood, Sand and Empire, 1977, Disco Fever, 1978, Pax Romana, Xanadu, 1979, Ishmael, 1980, Vertigo, 1982, others. Home: 970 Vernon Ave Glencoe IL 60022 Office: 442 Central Ave Highland Park IL 60035

GRIMSLEY, LYNN GRIFFIN, assn. exec.; b. Fort Oglethorpe, Ga., Sept. 15, 1943; d. Homer Howard and Alice Cecelia (Hoopes) Griffin; student U. Tenn., Chattanooga, 1979—; m. David Slater Grimsley, Aug. 25, 1962; children—Mary Lynn, Stephen Michael. Sec., Vol. State Life Ins. Co., 1961-62; sec. Pioneer Bank, 1962-63; legal sec. firm Strang, Fletcher, Carriger, Walker, Hodge & Smith, Chattanooga, 1967-71; exec. sec. Office Mayor Chattanooga, 1971-72, adminstrv. aide to mayor, 1972, adminstrv. asst., 1973-75; exec. dir. Allied Arts Fund Greater Chattanooga, and Chattanooga Arts Council, 1976—; mem. community devel. adv. panel Tenn. Arts Commn. Bd. dirs. Goodwill Industries, 1975—; vice chmn. residential div. United Fund, 1979; mem. met. ministry com. Episcopal Commn. S.E. Tenn., 1979—. Mem. Chattanooga C. of C. (central city council), Am. Council for Arts, Am. Coll., Univ. and Community Arts Adminstrs., Nat. Assembly Community Arts Councils. Office: 16 Patten Pky Chattanooga TN 37402

GRISEUK, GAIL GENTRY, fin. cons.; b. Providence, Jan. 24, 1948; d. Marvin Houghton and Gertrude Emma (Feather) Gentry; student (Fla Power Corp. scholar), Fla. State U., 1966-70; m. Steven Paul Griseuk, Oct. 20, 1979; 1 dau., Christina Deborah. Asst. div. controller Mobile Home Industries, Tallahassee, 1968-70; owner, mgr. BDI Services, Tallahassee and Lake Charles, La., 1970-78; fin. cons. Aylesworth Fin., Inc., Clearwater, Fla., 1978—; instr., dir. vet. outreach Angelina Coll., Lufkin, Tex., 1975-76. Vol., Sunland Tng. Center, 1970-72, George Criswell House, 1969-73. Mem. Am Kennel Club. Methodist. Contbr. short stories to Redbook, McCall's, Christian Home. Home: 1024 Woodcrest Ave Clearwater FL 33516 Office: 1321 US Hwy 18 S Suite 102 Clearwater FL 33516

GRISWOLD, MADELEINE MASSEY, nursing adminstr.; b. Raleigh County, W.Va., Mar. 18, 1921; d. James G. and Alice Gay (Toler) Massey; R.N., Charleston Gen. Hosp. Sch. Nursing, 1942; student Morris Harvey Coll., 1939-42, U. Ala., 1965, Wake Forest U., 1980; m. Frederick C. Griswold, Dec. 12, 1944; children—Sandra Griswold Wise, Frederick C., James Mark. Head nurse surg. unit Rex Hosp., Raleigh, N.C., 1947-48; staff nurse Kiowah Indian Hosp., Lawton, Okla., 1958-61; asso. head nurse pediatrics U.S. Army Hosp., Fort Riley, Kans., 1961-64; head nurse pediatrics Huntsville (Ala.) Hosp., 1965-66; asso. head nurse surgery and pediatrics Redstone Army Hosp., Redstone Arsenal, Ala., 1967-68; supr. first aid clinic PPG Industries, Huntsville, Ala., 1968-71; adminstrv. supr. Raleigh Gen. Hosp., Beckley, W.Va., 1971-77; dir. nursing service Plateau Med. Center, Ltd., Oak Hill, W.Va., 1977—; mem. adv. com. W.Va. Inst. Tech., Montgomery, 1978-82, Vocat. Tech. Sch., Oak Hill, 1979-82. Served with U.S. Army, 1942-46. Mem. Am. Nurses Assn., W.Va. Nurses Assn. (council health planning and legis.). Home: Box 146 Glen Daniel WV 25844 Office: 430 Main St Oak Hill WV 25901

GRITZ, JANET MERLE WEISBLUT, speech-lang. pathologist; b. Washington, Jan. 3, 1944; d. Harold and Jessie (Glassman) Weisblut; B.A., George Washington U., 1965, M.A., 1966; postgrad. U. Md., 1970-80; m. Richard Gritz, Mar. 14, 1965; children—Larry, Bonnie. Supr. speech and hearing services D.C. Soc. Crippled Children and Adults, 1966-68; pvt. practice speech-lang. pathology, Silver Spring, Md., 1968—; dir., pres. Janet M. Gritz, P.A., Silver Spring, 1975—; instr. U. Md., 1974; mem. profl. edn. com. Am. Cancer Soc.; mem. Montgomery County Stroke Club Com. Sec., PTA, 1979-80; vol. Am. Cancer Soc., 1979-80, Am. Heart Assn., 1979-80. Mem. D.C. Speech-Lang.-Hearing Assn. (chmn. com. aging and nursing homes 1978-81), Md. Speech-Lang.-Hearing Assn. (liaison to Md. Coalition of Long Term Health Care Providers 1979—), Speech and Hearing Discussion Group Met. Washington Area (past pres.), Am. Speech-Lang.-Hearing Assn. (cert. clin. competence in speech pathology), Am. Acad. Pvt. Practitioners in Speech Pathology and Audiology, Met. Area Dirs. of Clinics and Pvt. Practices. Democrat. Jewish. Home and Office: 200 Kimblewick Dr Silver Spring MD 20904

GRIVNA, MARY ALLENE, adminstrv. asst.; b. Dexter, Minn., Sept. 30, 1942; d. Kenneth Ray and Lois Lorene (Schiefelbein) Coleman; student Des Moines Area Community Coll., 1975-78; m. Donald Lee Grivna, Aug. 5, 1961; children—Mark Allen, Ellen Kay. Sec. dept. vet. physiology and pharmacology Iowa State U., Ames, 1972-77, adminstrv. asst. dept. biochemistry and biophysics, 1977-81; adminstrv. asst. dean's office Sch. Law, U. Calif., Davis, 1982—. Mem. Am. Bus. Women's Assn. Democrat. Lutheran. Home: 8277 Moss Oak Ave Citrus Heights CA 95610 Office: 1011 King Hall U Calif Davis CA 95616

GRIZZELL, JUNE LAVERNE, data processing exec; b. Knoxville, Tenn., July 7, 1937; d. Richard and Reva O. (Sharp) Grizzell; student U. Tenn., 1955-62, Lincoln Meml. U., 1959-61; B.S., Manfield State Coll., 1964. Med. research technician U. Tenn. Hosp., Knoxville, 1960-62; programming aide computer dept. Gen. Electric Co., Huntsville, Ala., 1965-66; programmer Computer Scis. Corps., Huntsville, 1966-69; computer specialist U.S. Army Corps of Engrs., Huntsville, Ala., 1969—. Chmn., Fed. Women's Program for Huntsville div. U.S. Army C.E., 1979—; active Am. Diabetes Assn. Mem. Assn. of Computing Machinery, AAUW, Zeta Tau Alpha. Clubs: Huntsville Alumnae, Order Eastern Star. Home: 8009 Navios St Huntsville AL 35802

GRIZZLE, MARY R. (MRS. BEN F. GRIZZLE), state senator; b. Lawrence County, Ohio, Aug. 19, 1921; ed. Portsmouth Interstate Bus. Coll.; m. Ben F. Grizzle; children—Henry, Polley, Lorena, Mary Alice, Betty, Jeanne. Mem. Fla. Ho. of Reps., 1963-78; mem. Fla. Senate, 1978—, mem. econ. community and consumer affairs, health and rehab. services, natural resources and conservation coms. Past chmn. Fla. Commn. on Status of Women; govt. rep. Nat. Conf. Women Community Leaders for Hwy. Safety; active P.T.A.; mem. Pinellas County (Fla.) Civil Service Com., Pinellas County Planning Com. Former town commr.; past pres. Women's Rep. Com. Named One of Ten Outstanding Women, St. Petersburg Times, 1966; recipient Achievement award Fla. Rehab. Assn., 1979; hon. life mem. Pinellas County Sch. Food Services, 1979; Largo Jr. Women's Club Woman of Year, 1980. Mem. League Women Voters, Largo Bus. and Profl. Womens Club, Altrusa, Woman's Club, Nat. Soc. Arts and Letters, Delta Kappa Gamma (hon. Alpha Phi chpt.). Episcopalian. Author: (with others) Thimbleful of History. Office: 2601 Jewel Rd Suite C Belleair Bluffs FL 33540 *

GROAH, LINDA KAY, nursing adminstr. and educator; b. Cedar Rapids, Iowa, Oct. 5, 1942; d. Joseph David and Irma Josephine (Zitek) Rozek; diploma St. Luke's Sch. Nursing, Cedar Rapids, 1963; student San Francisco City Coll., 1976-77; B.A., St. Mary's Coll., Moraga, Calif., 1978; m. Patrick Andrew Groah, Mar. 20, 1975; 1 dau., Kimberly; stepchildren—Nadine, Maureen, Patrick, Marcus. Staff nurse to head nurse U. Iowa, 1963-67; clin. supr., dir. operating and recovery room Michael Reese Hosp., Chgo., 1967-73; dir. operating rooms Med. Center Central Ga., Macon, 1973-74; dir. operating and recovery rooms U. Calif. Hosps. and Clinics, San Francisco, 1974-82, asst. dir. hosps. and clinics, 1982—; clin. instr. U. Calif. Sch. Nursing, San Francisco, 1975—; cons. to operating room suprs., to div. ednl. resources and programs Assn. Am. Med. Colls., 1976—; condr. seminars. Mem. Nat. League for Nurses, Am. Nurses Assn. (vice chmn. operating room conf. group 1974-76), Assn. Operating Room Nurses (com. on nominations 1979-82), Center for Study Dem. Instns. Author: Perioperative Nursing Practice, 1983; contbr. articles on operating room techniques to profl. jours. and textbooks; author, producer audio-visual presentations. Home: 5 Mateo Dr Tiburon CA 94920 Office: M423B 3d and Parnasus Sts San Francisco CA 94143

GROEBEL, LILLIAN S., educator; b. Yonkers, N.Y., Oct. 29, 1918; d. Max and Marie (Andritzke) Hollander; B.A. with high distinction, Ariz. State U., M.A., 1961; m. Oscar Groebel, Dec. 28, 1940; 1 son, Richard Lee. Elem. sch. tchr., Phoenix, 1958-69; seminar leader, demonstration tchr. U. Hawaii, 1966-68; lectr. U. Haifa (Israel), 1969—, head dept. fgn. langs., supr. pre-acad. Mem. NEA, Ariz. Edn. Assn., U. Tchrs. English in Israel, Hadassah, Kappa Delta Pi. Jewish. Author: The Reading of English, 1972, A Reading Program for Students of English, 1975; also articles. Office: Univ Haifa Mt Carmel Haifa Israel

GROH, CAROL ANN, grahic designer; b. Grand Rapids, Mich., Dec. 28, 1943; d. Robert and June (Bogdanik) Stoll.; B.A., N.Y.U., 1964; postgrad. Pratt Inst., 1964; m. Donald Smith, July 17, 1976; children—Justin Daniel, Christopher Charles. Sr. designer Skidmore, Owings & Merrill, N.Y.C., 1968-73, participating asso., 1973-79; founding partner GN Design Assos., Inc., N.Y.C., 1979—, now exec. v.p. Mem. Allegiance Women in Architecture (sr.). Office: 595 Fifth Ave New York NY 10022

GROMFIN, ANNETTE MAY, educator; b. Chgo., May 1, 1927; d. Harry and Esther Gromfin; B.A., U. Ill., 1952; postgrad. Law Sch. DePaul U., 1955-58. Asso. researcher Sch. Public Adminstrn. U. So. Calif., Los Angeles, 1962-66, dir. Tchr. Corps tng. Sch. Edn., 1966-76, adj. faculty, dept. ednl. adminstrn., 1980—; nat. dir. tech. assistance/tng. program Tchr. Corps, U.S. Dept. Edn./U. So. Calif., 1976-80; bd. dirs., cons. Western Interstate Commn. on Higher Edn. Bd. dirs. Womens Legal Services, 1982-83. Recipient Merit cert. HEW, 1980, Appreciation cert. and Achievement award U.S. Office Edn., 1977; Coro Found. assoc., 1981-82. Mem. Sociology Edn. Assn. (pres. 1980-81), Am. Ednl. Research Assn., Women in Cable. Home: 6137 W Alcott St Los Angeles CA 90035 Office: Sch Edn Univ So Calif University Park Los Angeles 70012

GRONDIN, FRANCES GRACE (MRS. J.W. GEORGES GRONDIN), solicitor broadcaster, real estate agt.; b. Worcester, Mass., July 25, 1932; d. Joseph Anthony and Rose Ester (Belculfine) Franchi; R.N., Meml. Hosp. Sch. Nursing, 1953; student Jackson Coll. Women, 1953-54; B.A., U. Moncton, 1976, LL.B., 1982. m. J.W. Georges Grondin, Jan. 29, 1955; children—Georges, Jean-Paul, Joseph, Rosanne. Supr., Rochester (N.Y.) Gen. Hosp., 1956-58, Hotel Dieu Hosp., Moncton, N.B., Can., 1958-59; free-lance broadcaster CBC radio, Moncton, 1974—; researcher, reporter documentaries CKEW-ATV, Moncton, 1976-77; also real estate agt. Pres., Meals on Wheels, 1972-73, mem. adv. bd., 1973-74; chmn. profl. collections United Way, 1975. Mem. adv. bd. YMCA, 1971-72, East End Boys Club, 1972-74; bd. dirs. Moncton Flying Sch., 1966-68. Mem. Can. Assn. for Children with Learning Disabilities (treas. 1971-3), Moncton Council Women (chmn. recreation 1973-74, mem. exec. bd. 1973-74), Moncton Drug Aid Assn. (exec. sec. 1971-72), Atlantic Symphony Assn. (chmn. variety show 1972), Can. Bar Assn., Barristers Soc. N.B., N.B. Assn. Registered Nurses, Can. Owners and Pilots Assn. Roman Catholic. Clubs: Moncton Golf and Country, Moncton Flying (Moncton). Home: 294 Westmount Blvd Moncton NB Canada

GROSE, EDITH (KATE) MARGARETHE, newspaper editor, printer; b. Scotia, N.Y., Mar. 7, 1917; d. Nelsen and Beatrice Edith (Yates) Geertsen; A.A., Schenectady Jr. Coll., 1937; m. Harold J. Hogan, June 17, 1938; children—David H., Charles J.; m. 2d, C.H. Grose, June 25, 1971; stepchildren—Lawrence C., Peter S., Susan K. Sec., Internat. Gen. Electric Co., 1937-41, 44-46; editor Scotia-Glenville Jour., 1960-80, Ballston Jour., Ballston Spa, N.Y., 1971—; chmn. bd. Ballston Printing Co., Inc.; sec. Jour. Newspapers, Inc. Mem. N.Y. State Ednl. Conf. Bd., 1954-55; chair Schenectady County Ednl. Conf. Bd., 1956-57; mem. Scotia-Glenville Bd. Edn., 1957-63, v.p., 1958-60; mem. Schenectady County Child Guidance Bd., 1961-62; bd. dirs. N.Y. State congress Parents and Tchrs., 1950-53, legis. chmn., 1954-55, life mem. Fellow Internat. Conf. Newspaper Editors; mem. Printing Industries Am., N.Y. State Press Assn., Saratoga County His. Soc. Presbyterian. Clubs: Pinehurst Country, Ballston Spa Country. Home: 72 W High St Ballston Spa NY 12020

GROSKOPF, DORIS MARIE, trucking co. exec.; b. Thief River Falls, Minn., Jan. 8, 1924; d. Ernest Norman and Minnie (Tommerdahl) Rude; student public schs., Crookston, Minn.; m. Charles Joseph Groskopf, Feb. 20, 1944; children—Ronald Stewart, Charlene Ann, Barbara Ann. Sec., U.S. Air Force Washington, 1942-43; teller Bank of Am., Sonoma, Calif., 1943-44; with Groskopf-Weider Trucking Co., Inc. and G-W Tank Lines, Inc., Sonoma, 1944—, sec.-treas., dir., 1956—, chief exec. officer, 1960—; partner Groskopf-Weider Leasing Co., 1946—; expert witness for public utilities commn. State of Calif. rate hearings, 1979-80. Mem. Am. Field Service. Republican. Lutheran. Clubs: Sonoma Valley Bus. and Profl. Women's (pres. 1953-54), Soroptimist, Sonoma Nat. Women's Golf. Address: 1761 Denmark St Sonoma CA 95476

GROSS, BEATRICE SCHAAP, educator, author, cons.; b. N.Y.C., Jan. 23, 1935; B.A. in Am. Studies, Syracuse (N.Y.) U., 1956; M.S. in Edn., Bank Street Coll., Edn., N.Y.C., 1958; married, 2 children. Adj. instr. Sch. Continuing Edn., N.Y. U., N.Y.C., 1968-80; asso. prof. humanities SUNY, Old Westbury, 1972-76; author teaching materials McGraw Hill, Sci. Research Assos.; mem. adv. bd. The Feminist Press; syndicated columnist The Family Viewpoint. Mem. World Edn. Recipient Disting. Achievement award Ednl. Press Assn. Am., 1974; Faculty Exchange Scholar's award SUNY, 1975. Cert. pre-sch. and elem. edn. Author: Radical School Reform, 1970; Will It Grow In a Classroom?, 1974; The Childrens Rights Movement, 1977; The New Old, 1978; Teaching Under Pressure, 1979; Towards Improved Compensatory Education; editor: Future Needs and Goals for Adult Learning 1980-2000; Improving Compensatory Education in the Primary Schools, 1982; contbr. articles to profl. jours., newspapers, mags. Home: 17 Myrtle Dr Great Neck NY 11021

GROSS, CAROLE DOLPH, publishing co. exec.; b. Camden, N.J., May 13, 1942; d. Earl Walter and Ruth (Sinclair) Dunham; B.A. in Polit. Sci., Bucknell U., Lewisburg, Pa., 1964; m. Stephen Henry Gross, Aug. 1, 1977; 1 dau., Wendy Sinclair. Advt. copywriter BBDO, 1966-67; sales promotion mgr. Macmillan Pub. Co., 1967-71; with Doubleday Pub. Co., N.Y.C., 1972-80, mktg. mgr., promotion dir., 1976-80, advt. mgr., sales and promotion, chmn. mktg. com., to 1980; v.p., mktg. and editorial dir. Davis Publs., N.Y.C., 1980—; mktg. dir. Denver Pub. Inst., summers 1975-78; lectr. Columbia U. Bus. Sch., also Sch. Journalism. Fellow Florence (Italy) Renaissance Art Program, 1963; White House intern, summer 1962. Mem. Assn. Am. Pubs. (chmn. mktg. com.), Book Critics Circle, Pubs. Publicity Assn., Pubs. Advt. Club. Democrat. Presbyterian. Club: Princeton (N.Y.C.). Contbr.: The Business of Publishing, 1980; contbg. editor: Pushcart Prize, 1977. Office: 380 Lexington Ave New York NY

GROSS, CAROLINE LORD (MRS. MARTIN L. GROSS), state legislator; b. Laconia, N.H., May 5, 1940; d. William Shepard and Marion (Manns) Lord; A.B., Radcliffe Coll., 1963; M.A.T., Harvard U., 1964; postgrad. Franklin Pierce Coll., 1981—; m. Martin L. Gross, Nov. 5, 1960. Research asst. Supr. Schs., Concord, N.H., 1965-66, N.H. Legis. com. ann. sessions, Concord, 1966, N.H. Fiscal com. 1967-68; adminstrv. asst. N.H. gov., Concord, 1969-70; coordinator N.H. fed. funds, Concord, 1971-72; supr. checklist, Concord, 1969—; mem. N.H. Ho. of Reps., 1973—. Mem. N.H. Commn. Status Women, 1972-75; del. N.H. Republican Conv., 1968, 70, 74, 76, 78, 80, 82; legis. policy asst. N.H. Ho. of Reps., 1974-81; trustee Concord Library, 1974-77, Granite State Public Radio, 1979-82; Rep. candidate for N.H. State Senate, 1980. Mem. LWV, N.H. Council Better Schs. Home: 15 Rumford St Concord NH 03301 Office: NH Ho of Reps Concord NH 03301

GROSS, CYNTHIA DOROTHY LAVERNE, civic worker; b. Green Bay, Wis., Sept. 28, 1944; d. Walter George and Loretta Wilhemina Ida (Brandt) Boettcher; B.S., U. Wis., 1966, postgrad., 1973, 78; m. Lawrence Henry Gross, June 17, 1967; children—Aaron, Rebecca. Playgroud dir. Oshkosh (Wis.) Public Schs., 1965-66; tchr. public schs., Valders, Wis., 1966-67, Pierce Sch., Milw., 1967-68, Hawthorne Sch., Milw., 1968-70, St. John's Sch., Portage, Wis., 1975-76; head Med. Foster and Emergency Receiving Home, 1978—; dir. Family Day Center, 1981—; pres. Lincoln-Brener PTA, 1981—; mem. Headstart Policy Com. and Seven County Council, 1979—. Mem. Wis. Edn. Assn., Wis. Fedn. Foster Parents, Shawano Jaycettes (state dir. 1972—), U.S. Jaycettes, Wis. Jaycettes. Lutheran. Author: (with Lawrence Gross and Jerry Sterneigle) Pen and the Prof, 1964. Contbr. short articles to newsletters and newspapers. Home: 224 S Andrews St Shawano WI 54166

GROSS, EVELYN RHODA, sch. psychologist; b. N.Y.C., Aug. 30, 1922; d. Sam and Esther (Rauch) November; A.A., Norwalk Community Coll., 1969; B.A. magna cum laude, U. Bridgeport, 1973, M.S., 1975, profl. diploma advanced study, 1977; m. Herbert Gross, May 9, 1948; children—Jonathan, David, Lewis, Deborah. Acting sch. psychologist Burr Farms Sch., Westport, Conn., 1978; cons. Trumbull (Conn.) Schs., 1979; pvt. practice counseling, Norwalk, Conn., 1980; psychologist Mid Atlantic and Caribbean Regional Center for Services to Deaf-Blind Children, N.Y.C., 1980—; cons. in field. Rec. sec. Guild for Visually Handicapped Children; vol. dance tchr. Temple Shalom and Temple Israel. Mem. Am. Psychol. Assn., Conn. Assn. Sch. Psychologists, Am. Personnel and Guidance Assn., Nat. Assn. Deaf Blind, Assn. Edn. of Visually Handicapped, Council Exceptional Children, Psi Chi. Club: Swinging Eights Square Dance (pres. 1972-73). Founder, editor Group Discussion Newsletter. Home: 32 Deerwood Manor Norwalk CT 06851 Office: 999 Pelham Pkwy New York NY 10469

GROSS, EVELYN ROSENBERG, real estate co. exec., educator; b. Greenwood, S.C., Sept. 30, 1926; d. Ernest Royal and Alyce (Kahn) Rosenberg; B.A., Sophie Newcomb Coll., 1947; grad. Realtors Inst., Orlando, Fla., 1976; m. Leonard Gross, Aug. 31, 1950 (div. 1977); children—Gayle, Sally, Ernest. Caseworker Mt. Sinai Hosp., N.Y.C., 1947-49; partner, tchr. modeling sch., Oklahoma City, 1956-57; pvt. practice as Realtor, Ft. Lauderdale, Fla., 1969—; v.p. GlobeSpan Real Estate Co., Ft. Lauderdale, 1973—; adminstr., instr. Real Estate Edn. Center, Ft. Lauderdale, 1975-81; exec. dir. MCK Real Estate Edn. Centers, Ft. Lauderdale, 1977-81; owner Real Estate Salesmanship Centers, Ft. Lauderdale, 1974-77; sales tng. cons. Sun Banks of Fla., 1982—. Trustee Ft. Lauderdale U., 1971-75, vice chmn., 1975. Mem. Nat., Fla. assns. Realtors, Ft. Lauderdale Bd. Realtors, Women's Council Realtors. Jewish. Author: (with L. Gross) Real Estate for the New Practitioner, 1976. Office: 2691 E Oakland Park Fort Lauderdale FL 33306

GROSS, HARRIET P. MARCUS, public info. specialist; b. Pitts., July 15, 1934; d. Joseph William and Rose (Roth) Pincus; A.B. magna cum laude, U. Pitts., 1954, postgrad., 1954-55; cert. Religious Teaching, Spertus Coll. of Judaica, Chgo., 1962; postgrad. U. Chgo., 1972-73; children—Sol Benjamin, Devra Lynn. Asso. editor Jewish Criterion of Pitts., 1955-56; publs. writer B'nai B'rith Vocat. Service, 1956-57; leader recreation program for handicapped adults United Cerebral Palsy of Greater Chgo., 1957-58; group leader Jewish Community Centers of Met. Chgo., 1958-63; columnist Star Publs., Chicago Heights, Ill., 1964-80; public info. specialist Operation ABLE, Chgo., 1980-81; free-lance public info. specialist, Dallas, 1981—; tchr. creative writing Homewood-Flossmoor (Il.) Park Dist.; adv. com. journalism program Prairie State Coll., Chicago Heights, 1978—; adv. bd. The Creative Woman quar. publ. Governors State U., Park Forest South, Ill. Bd. dirs., sec. Family Service and Mental Health Center of South Cook County, Ill., 1965-71; mem. Park Forest (Ill.) Commn. on Human Relations, 1969-80, chmn., 1974-76; bd. dirs. Ill. Theatre Center, 1977-80, Park Forest Bus. and Profl. Assn., 1979-80, Greater Dallas sect. Nat. Council Jewish Women, 1981—, Jewish Family Service of Dallas, 1982—. Recipient Fellowship for Action Humanitarian Achievements award, 1974; Anti-Defamation League of B'nai B'rith Honor award, 1978; Dr. Charles E. Gavin Found. Community Service award, 1978. Mem. Nat. Fedn. Press Women, Ill. Woman's Press Assn. (named Woman of Yr. 1978), Intertel (v.p. Gateway Forum of Dallas 1981—), Mensa, Sigma Delta Chi, Phi Sigma Sigma. Jewish. Developed 1st community newspaper action line column, 1966. Address: 7320 La Cosa Dr Dallas TX 75248

GROSS, NANCY LYNN, mfg. co. exec.; b. St. Joseph, Mo., Nov. 2, 1952; d. Claude C. and Helen Fay (Oliver) Boner; B.S. in Acctg., U. Ky., 1975; M.B.A., U. Cin., 1980; m. Gary Lloyd Gross, May 29, 1976. With Armco Steel Corp., Kansas City, Mo. and Middletown, Ohio, 1974-80, credit rep., Middletown, 1975-80; acct. Armco, Inc., Middletown, 1980-81, sr. acct., 1981—; lectr. Miami U., Middletown, part-time 1980—. Mem. Beta Alpha Psi, Beta Gamma Sigma. Baptist. Home: 607 S Highview Rd Middletown OH 45042 Office: 703 Curtis St Middletown OH 45042

GROSS, SHIRLEY MARIE, farm mgr., artist; b. Beardstown, Ill., Apr. 4, 1917; d. Robert Lee and Marie Elizabeth (Ellrich) Northcutt; A.A., Stephens Coll., 1936; B.A., Ill. Coll., 1938; m. Carl David Gross, Oct. 4, 1941; children—David Lee, Susan Jean Gross Conner. Med. technologist St. John's Hosp., Springfield, Ill., 1938-41, Schmidt Meml. Hosp., Beardstown, 1957-64; librarian Beardstown Public Library, 1970-76; pvt. practice farm mgmt., Beardstown, 1958—; exhibitor various art shows, Ill., 1969—. Bd. dirs. Beardstown Hosp., Head Start. Winner art awards various shows. Mem. Am. Soc. Clin. Pathologists (med. technologist), Jacksonville Area Artist League. Democrat. Congregationalist. Clubs: Beardstown Woman's, Cass County Council for the Arts, Beardstown Bus. and Profl. Women's (pres., 1968-70). Home: 1116 Jefferson Beardstown IL 62618

GROSSHANS, MAXINE ZBIKOWSKI, law librarian; b. Pitts., Sept. 16, 1941; d. Frank J. and Stella (Kolodziejski) Zbikowski; A.B., U. Pitts., 1963; M.A., U. Chgo., 1969; m. Frank David Grosshans, June 3, 1967; 1 dau., Laura Schoe. Asst. librarian Continental Nat. Am. Group, Chgo., 1964-68; asst. cataloger Biddle Law Library, U. Pa., Phila., 1969-70; librarian Venable, Baetjer & Howard, Balt., 1970-74; reference librarian, head reference services U. Md. Law Sch. Library, Balt., 1974-81, sr. reference librarian Thurgood Marshall Law Library, 1981—. Mem. Law Library Assn. Md., Md. Library Assn., Pvt. Library Assn., Law Librarians Soc. D.C., Am. Assn. Law Libraries. Home: 307 Woodbourne Ave Baltimore MD 21212 Office: 20 N Paca St Baltimore MD 21201

GROSSHEIDER, REBECCA KAY, constrn. and land devel. co. exec.; b. Marshfield, Wis., Apr. 24, 1951; d. Ceylon Lester and Patricia Mae (Meyer) Greunke; B.A., Concordia Coll., 1973; student Ill. Benedictine Coll., 1978-79, DuPage Sch. Real Estate, 1979; m. Nelson Lloyd Grossheider, June 10, 1972. Comml. loan asst. Oak Park Trust & Savs. Bank (Ill.), 1970-73; tchr. St. John Luth. Sch., Lombard, Ill., 1973-74; acctg. supr. GTE Fed. Credit Union, Northlake, Ill., 1974-78; dir. data processing and acctg. D.F. Hedg Inc., Naperville, Ill., 1978—, sec., also dir., 1979—. Mem. bd. edn. St. Mark's Lutheran Ch. Mem. Nat. Assn. Women in Constrn., Nat. Assn. Female Execs., Nat. Assn. Home Builders (bus. mgmt. com.), AAUW. Republican. Home: 1700 Windjammer Ln Hanover Park IL 60103 Office: 782 Gartner Rd Naperville IL 60540

GROSSI, EDITH A., chiropractor; b. Chgo., Apr. 25, 1955; d. Arthur A. and Frances R. Grossi; D.C., Palmer Coll. Chiropractic, 1979. Asst. chiropractor, 1971-76; practice chiropractic medicine, Chgo., 1980—. Mem. Am. Chiropractic Assn., Ill. Chiropractic Assn., Council Roentgenology, Council Nutrition. Office: 700 W North Ave Chicago IL 60635

GROSSINGER, TANIA SEIFER, writer, pub. relations cons.; b. Evanston, Ill., Feb. 17, 1937; d. Max and Karla (Seifer) Grossinger; B.A., Brandeis U., 1956. Pres. Grossinger Assocs., N.Y.C., 1959—; dir. broadcast promotion Playboy Mag., 1963-69, Roger & Cowan Pub. Relations, 1969-70; dir. pub. relations Stein & Day Pubs., N.Y.C., 1970-72; free-lance writer, 1972—; moderator, panelist Am. Soc. Journalists and Authors writers confs., 1977-82. Active Christopher Street Block Assn., 1976—. Mem. Am. Soc. Journalists and Authors. Author: Growing Up at Grossingers, 1975; The Book of Gadets, 1974; (with Andrew Neiderman) Weekend, 1981; The Great Gadget Catalogue, 1978; contbr. articles to various mags. Home and Office: 1 Christopher St New York NY 10014

GROSSKOPF-MARKLEY, DIANNE, pub. co. exec.; b. Los Angeles, Sept. 20, 1953; d. Walter Henry and Anne Mary (Pisano) Grosskopf; A.A. summa cum laude, Los Angeles Valley Coll., 1973; B.S. summa cum laude, Calif. State U., Northridge, 1975; m. Theodore E. Markley, III, July 17, 1976. Writer, UPI, Los Angeles, 1975; writer, then editor Men's Apparel News, Los Angeles, 1975-76; exec. editor Men's Apparel News and Calif. Apparel News, 1976-79; exec. editor Playgirl mag., 1979-81; v.p., exec. editor Ritter/Geller Communications, Santa Monica, Calif., 1981—; lectr. Named Outstanding Alumna, Calif. State U., 1981. Mem. Women in Communications, NOW. Office: 3420 Ocean Park Blvd Suite 3000 Santa Monica CA 90405

GROSSMAN, EDITH K., psychologist; b. Waltershausen, Ger., Feb. 6, 1931; came to U.S., 1939, naturalized, 1944; d. Morris and Selma (Goldner) Hammerschlag; B.A., Hunter Coll., 1952; M.A., CCNY, 1955; cert. Queens Coll., 1964; Ph.D., N.Y.U., 1970, cert. in psychoanalysis, 1975; m. Alfred E. Grossman, Feb. 18, 1951; children—Gene Michael, Maura Robin. Tchr., N.Y.C. Schs., 1952-55, Plainview (N.Y.) Schs., 1960-64; psychologist Levittown (N.Y.) Schs., 1964-66; teaching fellow N.Y.U., 1966-68; lectr. Queens Coll., 1968-70, asst. prof. psychology, 1970—, coordinator grad. program in sch. psychology, 1981—. Mem. Am. Psychol. Assn., Eastern Psychol. Assn., N.Y. Psychol. Assn., N.Y. Soc. Clin. Psychologists, Sch. Psychology Educators Council N.Y. Contbr. articles to profl. jours.

GROSSMAN, ELIZABETH KORN, nursing adminstr., coll. dean; b. S.I., N.Y., May 15, 1923; d. George and Ethel (Elliot) Korn; B.A., Hunter Coll., 1944; M.N., Western Res. U., 1947; M.S. in Nursing Edn., Ind. U., 1960, Ed.D., 1972; m. Thomas Grossman, Feb. 23, 1952; 1 son, Thomas. Researcher, Columbia Carbon Corp., Bklyn., 1944; staff nurse, asst. head nurse, head nurse, supr. Univ. Hosp., Cleve., 1947-52; Instr. Mt. Sinai Hosp. Sch. Nursing, Cleve., 1952-53; supr. maternity nursing Meth. Hosp., Indpls., 1953-57; instr. maternity nursing, 1957-59; instr. DePauw U., Indpls., 1959-62; asst. prof., asso. prof., grad. maternity Ind. U., Indpls., 1959-66, chairperson grad.-undergrad. maternity nursing, 1966-73, dean Sch. Nursing, 1973—. Fellow Am. Acad. Nursing; mem. Am. Nurses Assn., Nat. League Nursing, Am. Assn. Colls. Nursing (treas.), Nurses Assn. of Am. Coll. Ob-Gyn (chmn. edn. com.), Midwest Alliance Nursing (treas. 1979-81), Sigma Theta Tau (Disting. Service award 1977), Am. Assn. Maternal Child Health, Delta Kappa Gamma, Alpha Xi Delta. Republican. Roman Catholic. Contbr. articles to profl. jours. Home: 11201 Westfield Blvd Carmel IN 46032 Office: 1100 W Michigan St Indianapolis IN 46223

GROSSMAN, JUDY BELMONT, computer design co. ofcl.; b. San Francisco, Nov. 20, 1947; d. Morrison Harry and Joy (Kaufman) Belmont; B.S. in Bus. Adminstrn., U. Colo., Boulder, 1969; m. Gary F. Grossman, Aug. 19, 1979. Flight attendant Trans Internat. Airlines, Oakland, Calif., 1972-76; mgr. contract adminstrn. Itel Corp., San Francisco, 1976-78, mgr. vendor leasing, 1978-79; dir. new product devel. Friends Amis Inc., San Francisco, 1979—. Bd. dirs. San Francisco Jewish Community Center, 1981—, chmn. youth com., 1981—; mem. steering com. profl. women's div. Jewish Welfare Fedn., San Francisco, 1981—. Clubs: San Francisco Bay, Mt. Tam Racquet. Home: 79 W Clay Park San Francisco CA 94121

GROSSMAN, MAURINE NETCHIN, speech pathologist; b. Chgo., Mar. 26, 1947; d. Jack F. and Fay Netchin; B.S. in Speech and Hearing Handicapped, N.Y. U., 1969, M.A. in Speech Pathology and Audiology, 1970. Itinerant speech therapist N.Y.C. Bd. Edn., 1969-70, 70-71, speech therapist, 1972—; speech therapist Chgo. Bd. Edn., 1971-72; pvt. practice speech pathology, N.Y.C., 1972—; research asst. N.Y. Law Sch., 1982—; salesperson L & S Real Estate, N.Y.C., summers 1978-80. Office Edn. fellow, 1970, City U. N.Y. grantee, 1979; cert. tchr. speech and hearing handicapped, cert. speech pathologist, N.Y. State. Mem. Am. Speech, Lang. and Hearing Assn. (cert. clin. competence), N.Y. State Speech, Lang. and Hearing Assn., N.Y. U. Alumni Assn., United Fedn. Tchrs. Home: 63 E 9th St New York NY 10003 Office: 400 1st Ave New York NY 10010

GROSSO, CAMILLE MARIE, nurse; b. Geneva, N.Y., Sept. 28, 1938; d. Frank Leo and Gaetana Nicolina (Luongo) Balistreri; diploma Willard State Hosp. Sch. Nursing, 1959; B.S. in Nursing, George Mason U., 1976; M.S. in Nursing, Cath. U., 1978; m. Gerard M. Grosso, Apr. 8, 1961; children—Gerard M., Gina M. Staff nurse Univ. Hosp., Syracuse, N.Y., 1959-61; head nurse, care coordinator Project Hope, Saigon, S. Vietnam, 1961-62; vol. Am. Red Cross, Colorado Springs, Colo. and No. Va., 1963-71; staff nurse and head nurse The Fairfax Hosp., Falls Ch., Va., 1973-76; cons. mental health and alcoholism nursing, Va., 1976—; mental health nursing clin. specialist Arlington (Va.) Hosp., 1978-79, dir. nursing, 1979-82; dir. forensic psychiat.-mental health program Cath. U. Am., Washington, 1982—, adj. asst. prof. nursing, now asst. prof.; adj. faculty mem. U. Va. Continuing Edn. Center, Falls Church. Chairperson advisory council Fairfax Community Action Alcoholism Program; bd. dirs. Fairfax Community Action Program, 1976-78. NIMH traineeship, 1976-78; named Dist. 8 Outstanding Nurse, Va. Nurses Assn., 1975; recipient Service award, George Mason U., 1976. Mem. Am., Va. (bd. dirs. Dist. 8) nurses assns., Nat. Council on Alcoholism, Council on Alcoholism for Fairfax County, Nat. Nurses Soc. on Alcoholism, Alumni Assn. Cath. U., Alumni Assn. George Mason U., Va. Nurses Coalition for Action in Politics (chairperson 1978 annual meeting), Sigma Theta Tau, Alpha Chi. Club: Italian Cultural Soc. of Washington. Home: 7853 Danby Dr Annandale VA 22003 Office: Sch Nursing Cath U Am Washington DC 20064

GROSVENOR, CAROL ANN, computer cons; b. Lansing, Mich., July 19, 1949; d. Robert C. and Barbara J. (Brown) G.; B.S. in Computer Sci. and Music, Central Mich. U., 1972; M.S. in Computer Sci., West Coast U., 1978. Programmer-analyst Am. Bank & Trust, Lansing, Mich., 1973-75; systems analyst GTE Data Services, Los Angeles, 1975-78; mem. tech. staff Transaction Tech. Inc., Los Angeles, 1978-79; nat. software support mgr. Computer Communications, Inc., Los Angeles, 1979-80; cons., prin. Chocolate Chip Computer Co., Inglewood, Calif., 1980—; founder, edn. cons. Los Angeles Women's Computer Center. Mem. Assn. Women in Computing (pres. Los Angeles chpt. 1981-83. Outstanding Achiever award 1981), Nat. Assn. Women Bus. Owners (dir. 1982—, Service award 1982), Inglewood C. of C., Bus. and Profl. Assn., IEEE, Assn. Computing Machinery. Mem. Metropolitan Community Ch. Office: PO Box 4637 Inglewood CA 90309

GROTE, E. ENID (MRS. JOHN HENRY GROTE, JR.), artist, librarian, editor; b. N.Y.C., Sept. 26, 1909; d. Lewis and Mary Katherine (Engle) Granath; student (Louise Graham Hinsdale scholar) Columbia U., 1928-31, Sch. Library Sci. and Sch. Journalism, 1933-35; m. John H. Grote, Jr., Dec. 28, 1935. With Free Public Library, East Orange, N.J., 1932-37; mem. editorial staff fgn. and Washington news AP, N.Y.C., 1937-43; chief librarian, organizer news reference library Pan Am. World Airways, N.Y.C., 1943-44; organizer U.S. Info. Libraries, Office War Info., U.S. State Dept., N.Y.C. and Washington, 1944-45; chief librarian Hort. Soc. N.Y., N.Y.C., 1947-61; free-lance cons. editor to N.Y.C. pubs.; hort. manuscript evaluator, 1950-61; editor, contbr. book revs. and articles The Bulletin; group shows include: Woodstock (N.Y.) Artists Assn., Catskill Art Soc., Hurleyville, N.Y., also other art assn. shows, pvt. galleries; represented in pvt. collections. Mem. Spl. Libraries Assn., Woodstock Artists Assn., Catskill Art Soc., Internat. Soc. Artists, LWV, Internat. Platform Assn., Smithsonian Assocs. Republican. Presbyterian. Club: Woodstock Country. Home and studio: Windmill Point 341 Tulip Blvd Port Saint Lucie FL 33452

GROTH, BETTY, conservationist, author, photographer; b. Oak Park, Ill.; d. Herman A. and Bertha L. (Luepke) G.; grad. Vassar Coll., 1932. Sec., Oak Park YMCA, 1935-42; sec. Ill. Commn. for Handicapped Children, 1943-46; pvt. sec. Chgo. Assn. of Commerce and Industry, 1947-53, Chgo. Heart Assn., 1953-75. Mem. Save-The-Dunes Council, North Central Audubon Council; sec., dir. Natural Resources Council of Ill., 1967-71, v.p., 1969-71; v.p., dir. Du Page County Clean Streams, 1967-69; founder, chmn. Northern Conservation Cabinet, 1971-75; landscape gardener Audubon Sanctuary, Wayne, Ill., 1977-79; color film nature lectr. Mem. Nat. Audubon Soc., Ill. Audubon Soc. (v.p. conservation, dir. 1962-73, sec. bd. dirs. 1973-74), Big Bluestem Audubon Soc. (dir., sec.), Du Page Audubon Soc., Nat. Wildlife Fedn., Conservation Explorers Club (pres. 1975-76), Morton Arboretum, Sarasota Jungle Gardens, Am. Bald Eagle Club. Baptist. Club: Wis. Vassar. Author: Open Spaces in Illinois, 1962; Surprise in the North Woods, 1966; Wildlife by John Burroughs Cabin, 1967; King's Ransom to Save a Prairie, 1968; Ivory Bills Found Alive in Texas Big Thicket, 1969; Great Swamp Wildlife Refuge Versus Jetport, 1970; The Fate of Thorn Creek Woods, 1971; Man's Dominion of the Green Earth, 1972; Country Estate, 1973; King of Sky, Land and Water, 1974; North Woods Shoreline, 1975; Vanished Illinois Prairie Returns, 1976; contbr. articles to profl. jours. Home: Gull Shores Gills Rock Ellison Bay WI 54210

GROTS, INTA AELITA, physician; b. Riga, Latvia, Oct. 23, 1927; d. Fridrichs A. and Silvija (Palcers) Gusmanis; came to U.S., 1951, naturalized, 1956; B.S., Simmons Coll., 1953; M.D., Boston U., 1957; m. Andrejs Grots, June 6, 1953; children—Martin P., Andris C. Intern, Beth Israel Hosp., Boston, 1957-58; resident in dermatology Boston U. Hosps., 1958-61; assoc. clin. prof. dermatology Boston U. Med. Sch., 1978—; mem. staff Univ. Hosp., Boston. Diplomate Am. Bd. Dermatology. Mem. Am. Acad. Dermatology, Soc. Investigative Dermatology, Am. Soc. Dermatopathology, Daugaviete. Republican. Lutheran. Contbr. articles to profl. jours. Office: 80 E Concord St Boston MA 02118

GROTTA, SANDRA BROWN, interior designer; b. Detroit, June 7, 1934; d. John Leonard and Ada Victor Brown; student U. Mich., 1952-55, N.Y. Sch. Interior Design, 1964; m. Louis William Grotta, Sept. 8, 1955; children—Thomas Howard, Tracy Ann. Sr. partner HSG Interiors, South Orange, N.J., 1964—. Mem. Am. Soc. Interior Designers. Home: Maplewood NJ

GROTZINGER, LAUREL ANN, educator, univ. dean, b. Truman, Minn., Apr. 15, 1935; d. Edward F. and Marian Gertrude (Greeley) G.; B.A., Carleton Coll., 1957; M.S., U. Ill., 1958, Ph.D., 1964. Instr., asst. librarian Ill. State U., 1958-62; asst. prof. Western Mich. U., Kalamazoo, 1964-66, asso. prof., 1966-68, prof., 1968—, asst. dir. Sch. Librarianship, 1965-72, dean, chief research officer Grad. Coll., 1979—. Mem. ALA (sec.-treas. Library History Roundtable 1973-74), Assn. Am. Library Schs., Acad. Mgmt., Mich. Acad. Sci., Arts and Letters (v.p. 1980-81, pres.-elect 1981—), Am. Assn. for Higher Edn., Council Grad. Schs., Nat. Council Univ. Research Adminstrs., AAUP (sec. W.M. chpt. 1968-70), Phi Beta Kappa (pres. S.W. Mich. 1977-78), Beta Phi Mu (v.p., pres. Kappa chpt.), Pi Delta Epsilon, Alpha Beta Alpha. Author: The Power and the Dignity, Scarecrow, 1966; mem. editorial bd. Jour. Edn. for Librarianship, 1973-77; contbr. articles to profl. publs. Home: 2729 Mockingbird Dr Kalamazoo MI 49008

GROVATT, PATRICIA ARLENE, nurse; b. Joliet, Ill., Aug. 4, 1940; d. Arthur Hilding and Leona Gladys (Woodman) Sandbloom; R.N., Swedish Covenant Hosp. Sch. Nursing, 1961; B.S. in Nursing, Wheaton Coll., 1964; m. Benjamin Charles Grovatt, Nov. 4, 1967; 1 dau., Amy Lee. Nursing instr. Swedish Covenant Hosp., Chgo., 1964-67; staff Burlington County Meml. Hosp., Mt. Holly, N.J., 1968—, head nurse nursery, 1968-69, asst. dir. nursing, dir. inservice edn., 1969-74, asso. dir. nursing, 1974-79, dir. nursing edn. and evaluation, 1979-82; pres. S. Jersey Inservice Exchange, 1973-74. Accreditation surveyor N.J. Dept. Higher Edn., 1977; bd. dirs. Pub. Health Nursing Assn. of Burlington County, 1975—; mem. Broad St. Bapt. Ch., 1968—, organist, 1969—, choir dir., 1975—; lectr. Contact Telephone Counselling Ministry, 1972-74. Mem. Am. Soc. for Health Care Edn. and Training, Nursing

Service Adminstrs., Nat. League Nursing, Sigma Theta Tau. Republican. Office: 175 Madison Ave Mount Holly NJ 08060

GROVE, VIVIAN LORRAINE, social service agy. adminstr.; b. Trenton, N.J., June 21, 1923; d. Charles E. and Edythe (Inman) G.; B.S., N.J. State Coll., 1945; M.Ed., Springfield Coll., 1953; M.S.S., Bryn Mawr Coll., 1962. Tchr., Chatham (N.J.) Public Schs., 1946-47; dir. programs YWCA, Trenton, 1947-51, Springfield, Mass., 1953-56; exec., Mid-City br. YWCA, Phila., 1956-59, asso. met. exec. dir. Phila., 1959-60, field cons., later teenage cons. nat. bd., 1962-66, exec. dir. Seattle, 1966-70, dir. services to urban assns., nat. bd., N.Y.C., 1971-76, exec., personnel and tng. services unit, nat. bd., N.Y.C., 1976—. YWCA scholar, 1951-53, 60-61. Mem. Nat. Assn. Social Workers, Acad. Cert. Social Workers, Nat. Social Welfare Assembly, Nat. Adult Edn. Assn., Council Social Work Edn., Am. Mgmt. Assn. Author YWCA pamphlets, adminstrv. handbooks. Home: 229A Convent Rd Cranbury NJ 08512

GROVER, EVE RUTH, banker; b. Germany, Mar. 9, 1929; d. George and Gisa Hubseh (Deutsch) Bergmann; came to U.S., 1946, naturalized, 1951; grad. degree in bank mgmt., U. Va., 1974; grad. Am. Inst. Banking, 1973; m. Sept. 19, 1948; children—Ronald George, Jeffrey Louis. With First Nat. City Bank, N.Y.C., 1946-51, Citizens Bank of Takoma Park, Md., 1956-60, Am. Security & Trust Co., Washington, 1960-64; asst. br. mgr. Pub. Nat. Bank, Washington, 1964-69; asst. treas., br. mgr. Union Trust Co. of Md., Balt., 1969-71; v.p. State Nat. Bank, Bethesda, Md., 1971-78, dir. womens hdqrs., 1975-78; pres., chief exec. officer First Women's Bank Md., 1978—. Former mem. Women's Commn. Montgomery County (Md.); bd. dirs. Montgomery County Community Child Care Council, 1976-77; adv. bd. Mt. Vernon Coll. Sch. Bus. Adminstrn.; vice-chmn. Small Bus. Devel. Financing Authority; bd. govs. Hugh O'Brien Youth Found. Recipient award Montgomery County Public Schs. and Commn. for Women, 1980; Mother of Year, I. Magnin, 1980; Susan B. Anthony award Fedn. Orgns. Profl. Women, 1978; resolution of recognition Md. State Senate, 1977; others. Mem. Am. Inst. Banking, Nat. Council Career Women (dir. 1976-80), Nat. Assn. Bank Women, Md. Bankers Assn. (mgmt.-ops. com.), Nat. Assn. Women Bus. Owners, Federally Employed Women (hon.), Rockville C. of C. (dir.), Bus. and Profl. Women. Democrat. Jewish. Coordinator, speaker at seminars related to women and finance. Home: 4306 Emden Ave Wheaton MD 20906 Office: PO Box 2022 Rockville MD 20852

GROVES, MARTHA ODESSA, nurse; b. Winston, Mo., July 25, 1925; d. Clem Seward and Nora Beatrice (Harris) Gould; B.S.N., U. Mo., 1948; A.B. in Edn., W.Va. Wesleyan U., 1965; M.Nursing, U. Fla., 1971; postgrad. W.Va. U., 1977-78; m. Jay Voelker Groves, May 24, 1948; children—Lester Martin, Sarah Jayne, Catherine Jeanette. Staff nurse Boone County Hosp., Columbia, Mo., 1947-48; operating room nurse Lynch Clinic, Fairbury, Nebr., 1948-49; staff nurse Hord Meml. Hosp., Central City, Nebr., summer, 1952, U. Mich. Hosp., Ann Arbor, 1952-54, summer, 1955; relief nurse Potomac Valley Hosp., Keyser, W.Va., 1956-57; supr. nurse Holbrook Rest Home, Buckhannon, W.Va., 1959-60; staff nurse U. Minn. Hosp., Mpls., summer 1962; staff nurse Med. Center. W.Va. U., Morgantown, summer, 1965; teaching asst. W.Va. Wesleyan Coll., 1965-68; grad. asst., 1969-71, instr., 1971-72; instr. Alderson Broaddus Coll., 1972-74, asst. prof., 1974-76; adminstr. Holbrook Nursing Home, Inc., Buckhannon, 1976-80; staff nurse Eye & Ear Clinic of Charleston (W.Va.), 1981—; lectr. in field. Mem. Am. Nurses Assn., W.Va. Nurses Assn., Dist. 4 Nurses Assn., Nat. League for Nursing, W.Va. League for Nursing, W.Va. Profl. Nursing Home Adminstrs., W.Va. Health Care Adminstrs., AAUW. Democrat. Baptist. Contbr. articles to profl. jours. Home: 1637 Franklin Ave Charleston WV 25311 Office: 1306 Kanawha Blvd East Charleston WV 25301

GROWE, JOAN ANDERSON, sec. state Minn.; b. Mpls., Sept. 28, 1935; d. Arthur F. and Lucille M. (Brown) Anderson; B.S., St. Cloud State U., 1956; cert. in spl. edn. U. Minn., 1964; children—Michael, Colleen, David, Patrick. Tchr. elem. pub. schs., Bloomington, Minn., 1956-58; tchr. for exceptional children elem. pub. schs., St. Paul, 1964-65; spl. edn. tchr. St. Anthony (Minn.) Pub. Schs., 1965-66; mem. Minn. Ho. of Reps., 1973-75; sec. of state State of Minn., St. Paul, 1974—; mem. adv. com. Fed. Elections Commn.; participant exec. mgmt. program for state and local govt. Harvard U., 1979; mem. Minn. Bd. Investment, Jud. Planning Com. Recipient Minn. Sch. Bell award, 1977, Outstanding Achievement award YWCA, 1978. Mem. Nat. Assn. Secs. of State (pres. 1979-80), Bus. and Profl. Women's Club, Women's Polit. Caucus, Minn. LWV, Common Cause, Nat. Order Women Legislators, NOW, AAUW, Infact, Minn. Women's Network, Ams. for Democratic Action, Citizen's League, Democratic Statewide Elected Ofcls., Minn. Assn. for Retarded Citizens, Minn. Shares for Hunger, Urban Concerns. Mem. Democratic Farm Labor Party. Roman Catholic. Club: Zonta. Office: 180 State Office Bldg Saint Paul MN 55155

GROY, GEORGIA ANN, med. technologist; b. Reno, Nev., June 20, 1937; d. George Elwood and June Rose (Spear) Markell; student N.C. State U., 1972-73; B.S., U. Nev., 1976, postgrad., 1980—; m. Richard Vernon Groy, June 1, 1956; children—Rae Jeanine, Denise Ann, Dina Louise, Michelle. Med. asst. Dr. M. H. Duxbury, Reno, Nev., 1958-62; lab. technician Dr. Howard Smith, Roswell, N.Mex., after 1962; now med. technologist, bacteriology supr. W. 6th St. Lab., Reno. Served with USAF, 1955-56. Mem. Am. Soc. Med. Technologists, Nev. Soc. Med. Technologists, Phi Kappa Phi. Democrat. Roman Catholic. Clubs: University, Women of Moose, Non-Commd. Officers Wives (sec. 1970). Home: 330 Richards Way Sparks NV 89431 Office: 129 W 6th St Reno NV 89503

GRUBBE, DEBORAH LYNN, chem. corp. exec.; b. Chgo., Apr. 10, 1955; d. Jerome Walter and Domenica Veronica (Salce) G.; B.S. in Chem. Engring. with highest distinction, Purdue U., 1977; cert. (Winston Churchill fellow) U. Cambridge (Eng.), 1978. Chem. engr. E.I. duPont de Nemours & Co., Inc., East Chicago, Ind., 1978, services engr., Edge Moor, Del., 1978-80, area engr. constrn. div., Deepwater, N.J., 1980-81, div. engr., Wilmington, Del., 1981—. Mem. Am. Inst. Chem. Engrs. (chmn. nat. program subcom. 1980-82), Wilmington Women in Bus. (subchmn. program com. 1982—), Zeta Tau Alpha (pres. Wilmington alumnae chpt. 19 , province pres. Eastern Pa. region 1981-83), Tau Beta Pi, Phi Kappa Phi. Roman Catholic. Home: 22 Spectrum Dr Newark DE 19713 Office: Constrn Div E I duPont de Nemours & Co Inc Exptl Sta Wilmington DE 19898

GRUBBS, DEBRA ANN, pub. co. exec.; b. Washington, Aug. 13, 1953; d. Jack Lewis and Marilyn Miller (McElroy) G.; student Old Dominion U., 1971. Real estate sales mgr. Long & Foster Real Estate, Inc., McLean, Va., 1976-79, real estate broker, 1979—; pres. New Start Publs., Inc., Sterling, Va., 1981—. Mem. N.Am. Vegetarian Soc. Home: 750 Ridge Dr McLean VA 22101 Office: 100 Glenn Dr Sterling VA 22170

GRUBBS, PEGGY JOYCE BALLARD, liquefied petroleum gas co. exec.; b. Salisbury, N.C., Jan. 26, 1936; d. Carl Monroe and Eva Mae (Plyler) Ballard; student public schs.; m. Marvin Lester Grubbs, Jan. 5, 1956. With Queen Gas Co. Inc., Barnwell, S.C., 1953—, office and credit mgr., 1960-72, gen. mgr., v.p., 1972—. Mem. Barnwell C. of C. Republican. Baptist. Club: Sweetwater Country. Home: PO Box 372 Route 3 Snelling Barnwell SC 29812 Office: 2314 Marlboro Ave PO Box 386 Barnwell SC 29812

GRUBBS, SUSAN GALE LIKINS, nurse adminstr., cons.; b. Salt Lake City, July 8, 1948; d. Corwin Hale and Virginia Louise (Snyder) Likins; B.S. cum laude in Nursing, U. Utah, 1971, M.S. in Nursing, 1981; m. Samuel Galen Grubbs, Sept. 12, 1969 (div.). Staff nurse Sisters of the Holy Cross Hosp., Salt Lake City, 1971-73, Sisters of Mercy Hosp., Buffalo, 1973, St. Joseph's Hosp., Syracuse, N.Y., 1973-74; staff nurse Holy Cross Hosp., Salt Lake City, 1974-75, supr., 1974-81, critical care nurse clinician, 1981-82, clin. dir. critical care services, 1982—; mem. clin. faculty Weber State Coll., U. Utah; instr., trainer Utah Heart Assn.; teaching cons. Hewlett Packard, Sorenson Research Co., Salt Lake Fire Dept.; lectr. in field. Mem. nursing edn. com. Utah Heart Assn. Mem. Am. Assn. for Critical Care Nurses (Utah chpt.), Sigma Theta Tau (Gamma Rho chpt.), Alpha Lambda Delta. Republican. Congregationalist. Home: 7655 S 2700 E Salt Lake City UT 84121 Office: 1045 E 1st S Salt Lake City UT 84102

GRUBER, KATHRYN CLINE (MRS. OWEN MARSHALL GRUBER), pianist, educator; b. Belton, Tex., Sept. 22; d. William Edwin and Permilla (Mitchell) Cline; B.A. in Latin, B. Music in Piano, U. Mary Hardin-Baylor, 1931; postgrad. U. Tex., Austin, 1938, 41, UCLA, 1957; pvt. studies in piano; pupil of Walter Gilewicz; m. Owen Marshall Gruber, Sept. 16, 1946. Tchr. Latin, Belton High Sch., 1931-46; concert and studio pianist, Los Angeles, 1946-55; accompanist for husband, concert baritone, 1946—; tchr. piano, Santa Monica, Calif., 1948-51, also San Fernando Valley; pianist various chs., Tex. and Calif. Recipient B. R. Stocking medal, 1931; Outstanding Alumna award Mary Hardin-Baylor U., 1977. Mem. Nat. Piano Guild, Music Tchrs. Assn. Calif., Music Tchrs. Assn. San Fernando Valley W., Palisades Fine Arts Soc. (v.p. 1950-54, pres. 1956-58), Opera Guild So. Calif., San Fernando Valley Symphony Assn., San Fernando Valley Community Concert Assn. (dir., v.p. publicity), Mary Hardin-Baylor U. Alumni So. Calif. (pres. 1960-64), DAR, Pi Gamma Mu, Alpha Chi, Sigma Alpha Iota. Composer musical settings for poetry of Horace. Home: 6450 Quakertown Ave Woodland Hills CA 91367

GRUCCIO, LILLIAN JOAN (MRS. WILLIAM TAYLOR HARRINGTON THORMAN), lawyer; b. Camden, N.J.; d. Joseph and Millie (Fornataro) Gruccio; grad. Steelman Bus. Sch., Camden, 1945; A.A., Rutgers U., 1947, LL.B., 1951, LL.D., 1968. Admitted to N.J. bar, 1952, U.S. Dist. Ct., N.J. dist., 1952, U.S. Supreme Ct. bar, 1960; partner firm Frank C. Propert, Camden, 1952-55; asso. firm Lewis and Hutchinson, and successors, Camden, 1956-61; with legal dept. Campbell Soup Co., Camden, 1955; practiced in Pennsauken, N.J., 1961-73, Medford, N.J., 1973—. Mem. Camden City Juvenile Conf. Com., 1957-62; bd. dirs. Camden County Health and Welfare Council, 1957-61. Bd. dirs. Camden and Vicinity YWCA, 1959-67, chmn. adult program com., 1957-67, fashion show com., 1967; budget com. United Fund of Camden County, 1968. Mem. Am., N.J., Burlington County, Camden County bar assns., Rutgers U. Law Sch. Alumni Assn. (chancellor South Jersey div. 1962, bd. mgrs. 1952-64), S. Jersey Pub. Relations Assn., Pennsauken (charter, 1st v.p. 1967-73, mem. legislative com. 1967-72, corr. sec. 1972, chmn. personality devel. com. 1972-73) Burlington County (scholarship com. 1974, legislative com. 1973-74) bus. and profl. women's clubs, LeisureTowne Civic League (rec. sec. 1974-75; by-laws com. 1975). Clubs: Aux. United Republican (chmn. legislative com. 1971-72). Home: 63 Sheffield Pl Vincentown NJ 08088 Office: Cedarbrook Bldg Taunton Blvd Medford NJ 08055

GRUEBEL, BARBARA JANE, internist; b. Honolulu, May 12, 1950; d. Robert William and Elenor Jane (Perry) G.; B.S., Stephen F. Austin State U., 1971; M.D. (Robert Wood Johnson Found. scholar, Coll. Women's Club scholar), Baylor U., 1974. Intern in internal medicine U. Rochester, 1974-75, resident in internal medicine, 1974-77; pulmonary fellow U. Mich., 1977-79; mem. med. staff Anthony L. Jordan Health Center, Rochester, N.Y., 1976-77, Univ. Health Service, Ann Arbor, Mich., 1978-79; med. dir. progressive respiratory care unit Meth. Hosp. of Dallas, 1979-80; asst. prof. medicine U. Tex. Health Sci. Center, Dallas, 1979-80; cons. in pulmonary disease, Dallas, 1980—; med. dir. pulmonary services Southeastern Meth. Hosp.; clin. asst. prof. medicine U. Tex. Health Sci. Center; nat. affiliate faculty Am. Heart Assn. Active TEXPAC. Recipient award for gen. excellence in pediatrics, 1974, Stanley W. Olson award for acad. excellence, 1974, John Richard Fox award, 1974, Stuart A. Wallace award in pathology, 1974; Welch Found. grantee, 1970; Am. Lung Assn. tng. fellow, 1977-79. Diplomate Nat. Bd. Med. Examiners. Fellow ACP, Am. Coll. Chest Physicians (named Young Pulmonary Physicians of Future 1979); mem. Am. Med. Women's Assn. (scholastic excellence award 1974), Am. Thoracic Soc., Am. Lung Assn., AMA, Dallas County Med. Soc., Tex. Med. Soc., Soc. Critical Care Medicine, Nat. Assn. Female Execs., Nat. Assn. Med. Dirs. Respiratory Care, Dallas Acad. Internal Medicine, Am. Cancer Soc. (dir. Oak Cliff area), Women Meeting Women, Dallas Acad. Medicine, Dallas C. of C., Oak Cliff C. of C., Alpha Omega Alpha, Beta Beta Beta. Office: 221 W Colorado St Suite 470 Dallas TX 75208

GRUEN, SHIRLEY JEAN, psychologist; b. San Antonio, Jan. 22, 1945; d. Clarence Edward and Frieda Helen (Schafer) Neugebauer; B.S. in Edn., S.W. Tex. State U., 1965; M.A., U. Houston, 1971; Ph.D., Tex. A&M U., 1978; m. Frank Xavier Gruen, Sept. 18, 1965; children—Sheryl Robin, Scott Xavier. Speech therapist Houston Ind. Sch. Dist., 1966-68, asso. sch. psychologist, 1971-73; psychol. asso. Region IV Edn. Service Center, Houston, 1973-78; pvt. practice psychology, Sugar Land, Tex., 1980—. NIMH grantee, 1969-71. Mem. Am. Psychol. Assn., Tex. Psychol. Assn., Houston Psychol. Assn., Houston Behavior Therapy Assn., Am. Soc. Clin. Hypnosis, Houston Group Psychotherapy Soc., Am. Assn. Marriage and Family Therapists. Republican. Club: Sugar Creek Country. Home: 1629 Country Club Dr Sugar Land TX 77478 Office: 4915 S Main St Sugar Land TX 77477

GRUGER, AUDREY LINDGREN, county ofcl.; b. Minot, N.D., May 17, 1930; d. Swan Magnus and Mabel Johnson Lindgren; B.A., U. Wash., 1952; postgrad. U. Calif., Davis, 1966-67; m. Edward Hart Gruger, Jr., June 27, 1952; children—Sherri, Lawrence, Linda. Mem., Wash. State Ho. of Reps., 1977-82; mem. King County (Wash.) Council, 1981—. Mem. LWV, AAUW, Womens Polit. Caucus, Nat. Order Women Legislators. Democrat. Mem. United Ch. of Christ. Home: 3727 NE 193d St Seattle WA 98155

GRUMBACHER, MIRIAM LOUISE, engr., oil co. exec.; b. Toulouse, France, June 6, 1948; came to U.S., 1970, naturalized, 1980; d. Louis F. and Arlette C. (Dubourg) Pelissier; B.S. in Engring., Ecole Polytechnique Feminine, 1970; M.Elec. Engring., CCNY, 1972; children—Rebecca, Gabrielle. Elec. pipeline engr. Bechtel Corp., Houston, 1974-77; staff engr. Continental Oil Co., Houston, 1977-80; pres. Petro-World Inc., Houston, 1980—, Tex-oil Investments Inc., Houston, 1980—; v.p. Malou Steel Inc.; dir. Houston Steel & Pipe. Named Outstanding Woman of Yr., Conoco Inc., 1980; registered profl. engr., Tex. Mem. Tex. Soc. Profl. Engrs. Office: 5850 San Felipe Suite 120 Houston TX 77057

GRUNER, VIRGINIA SHAW (MRS. GEORGE JOHN GRUNER), club woman; b. Chgo., Feb. 19, 1912; d. Neil John and Rose (Tenwick) Shaw; grad. Chgo. Tchrs. Coll., 1931; B.S., Northwestern U., 1932; Ph.D. (hon.), Colo. Christian Coll., 1973; m. George John Gruner, Nov. 6, 1935; children—Valerie Dale, Diane Rae. Tchr., Parker Practice Sch. of Chgo., Chgo. Tchrs. Coll., 1935-40. Active Girl Scouts Am., 1949-53; v.p. Factotums, Scarsdale (N.Y.) Woman's Club, 1953; mem. member's guild High Mus. Art, Atlanta. Recipient Civic Achievement award City of Chgo. Mem. Internat. Platform Assn., Pi Lambda Theta, Cui Bono, Alpha Omicron Pi. Republican. Presbyn. Clubs: Scarsdale Golf (chmn. women's golf assn. 1954-56); American Yacht (Rye, N.Y.); Druid Hills Golf (Atlanta). Home: 2609 174th Ave NE Redmond WA 98052

GRYCZ, ANNE ELIZABETH, mental health services co. exec.; b. San Francisco, Apr. 7, 1944; d. Albert Winters and Elizabeth Gertrude (Bogle) Cunningham; B.A., U. San Francisco, 1965; m. June 25, 1966 (div.); children—Michael Joseph, Anastasia Christina. Tchr. Spanish, history Santa Clara (Calif.) Unified Sch. Dist., 1966-67; tchr. theology, in charge parish edn. programs and tchr. tng. Roman Cath. Archdiocese of San Francisco, 1970-76; sec. Behaviordyne, Inc., Palo Alto, Calif., 1976-78, asst. to pres., 1978-80, v.p. consumer services, 1980—; condr. workshops in field; cons. handicapped children. Bd. dirs. Palo Alto Adolescent Services Corp. Mem. AAUW, Nat. Assn. Female Execs., Am. Bus. Women's Assn., Peninsula Women's Exec. Group, Alpha Sigma Nu. Democrat. Roman Catholic. Author: The Guide Pak, 1978; contbr. articles to Migrant Echo, 1974-76. Home: 1142 Guinda St Palo Alto CA 94301 Office: 599 College Ave Palo Alto CA 94306

GUARINO, NANCY L., civic worker; b. Rolling Rock, Pa., Nov. 14, 1930; d. Samuel Porch and Margretta Marie (Reep) Roadman; student Seton Hill Coll., 1955-57; m. Ralph Guarino, Dec. 17, 1949; children—Randy Ralph, Sharon Lynn, Gavin Gary. Vice pres. Jr. Women's Club, 1977; Maple Princess judge Somerset County, Pa., 1978; litter control chmn. Garden Club Fedn. Pa., 1977, bd. dirs., 1976-80; founder Indian Lake Ski Club, 1969; leader Brownie Troop, 1960; owner, operator Ski Shop, 1968, beauty salons, Latrobe, Pa., 1960-64, Indian Lake Lodge, Pa., 1970; pres. Somerset Garden Club, 1978-79; judge of elections Indian Lake Boro, 1977-79; chair Heart Fund, 1964; mem. Roadside Council Pa.; oil painter, works exhibited public showings. Recipient ski and golf awards. Mem. Ski Industries of Am. Republican. Methodist. Club: Indian Lake Golf. Home: RD 1 Indian Lake Central City PA 15926

GUDMUNDSEN, ANNE MYERS, nurse, educator; b. Waukegan, Ill., Apr. 18, 1940; d. Glen Isenhour and Grace Alberta (Maier) Myers; B.S. (Harding-Ky Kendall scholar 1958-60), Tex. Woman's U., 1962; M.S., U. Colo., 1967; Ph.D., U. Denver, 1975; m. John Woolford McFarland, Jan. 31, 1981; children—Richard Andrew, Kathryn Lynne. Instr., Tex. Woman's U., Denton, 1965-66, asso. prof., 1976-77, coordinator doctoral program, 1977-78, asso. dean for grad. studies Coll. Nursing, 1977-78, dean Coll. Nursing, 1978—, provost Inst. Health Scis., 1979—; asst. prof. U. Colo., 1967-73; cons. Colo. Dept. Health, 1975-76; grant reviewer predoctoral fellowships Div. Nursing, Dept. Health and Human Resources. Block chmn. March of Dimes, 1967-70; active Another Mother for Peace, 1967—, ARC. Served as lt. (j.g.) Nurse Corps, USN, 1962-65. Recipient award Tex. Legislature, 1982. Mem. Am., Tex. nurses assns., Am. Heart Assn., Sigma Theta Tau, Phi Kappa Delta, Kappa Delta Pi, Pi Lambda Theta, Alpha Kappa Gamma, Phi Kappa Psi. Author: (with Peggy L. Chinn) Child Health Maintenance, 1978; contbg. author Medical-Surgical Nursing of the Ill or Injured Adult. also articles, book revs., audiovisual prodns. Office: Texas Woman's U Denton TX 76204

GUENTERT, MARGARET, educator; b. Cin., Feb. 28, 1941; d. Fred and Helen (Kramer) G.; B.S. in Edn., Ohio U., 1962; M.S. (univ. fellow), Ind. U., 1964. Tchr., Princeton High Sch., Cin., 1962-66; tchr., chmn. English dept. Norwood (Ohio) High Sch., 1966-76, asst. prin., 1976-78; tchr. Walnut Hills High Sch., 1978—, chmn. English dept., 1982—; research cons. Cin. Public Schs., 1981—; camp dir. Camp Towaki, 1964, Camp William Butterworth, 1965, Camp Ross Trails, 1966-68, Camp Natarswi, 1969-72. Mem. Nat. Council Tchrs. English (dir. 1968-69, 71, 81), English Council Greater Cin. (pres. 1969-70), Mortar Bd., Kappa Delta Pi. Author: (poetry) Running Free, 1975; editor: A Bicentennial Remembrance, 1976.

GUENTZEL, EVELYN CAROL NELSON, educator; b. Mpls., July 2, 1939; d. Victor John and Alice M. (Thompson) Nelson; B.S., St. Cloud State U., 1961; M.S., Mankato State U., 1977; m. Richard Dale Guentzel, Aug. 7, 1965; children—Melanie, Heather. Tchr. English, Pine City, Minn., 1961-63, Mound, Minn., 1963-65, Lincoln, Nebr., 1966-67, Austin, Minn., 1968-70; tchr. reading Austin public schs., 1973—. Mem. NEA, Minn. Edn. Assn., Austin Edn. Assn., Internat. Reading Assn., LWV, Southeastern Minn. Reading Council, Minn. Reading Assn., AAUW. Mem. Democratic Farm Labor Party. Lutheran. Home: 1104 6th Ave Austin MN 55912

GUERNETTE, JOANNE GERDES, psychologist; b. Sacramento, Calif., Mar. 22, 1931; d. Fred Paul and Pauline Clements (Haines) Gerdes; B.A., Sacramento State U., 1954, M.A., 1966; Ph.D., Tex. A&M U., 1974; m. Gene Sutphen; children—Eric, Keslie. Speech pathologist, therapist Sacramento County Supt. of Schs. Office, 1957-60; sch. psychologist Sacramento County Office of Edn., 1960-66; staff psychologist St. Joseph Community Mental Health Center, Houston, 1967; clin. psychologist Hauser Neuropsychiat. Clinic, Houston, 1967-70; cons. Brazos County Mental Health Center also Milam County Mental Health Center, 1972-74; sr. psychologist, clin. dir. Devereux Found., Victoria, Tex., 1974—; pvt. part-time practice neuropsychology, Victoria, Tex., 1979—; vol. cons. Brazos County Mental Health Center; Child Study Clinic, Victoria. Mem. Sacramento Area Sch. Psychologists Assn. (pres.-elect 1966), Calif. Assn. Sch. Psychologists and Psychometrists (dir. 1965), Am. Psychol. Assn., Tex. Psychol. Assn., Southwestern Psychol. Assn., Council for Exceptional Children. Home: 403 W Stayton Ave Victoria TX 77901 Office: PO Box 2666 Victoria TX 77902

GUERNSEY, MARY LINDA, nurse; b. Wilmington, N.C., Mar. 13, 1945; d. Hugh Johnston, Jr. and Dorothy Margaret (Watson) Sloan; R.N., Miami Valley Hosp., Dayton, Ohio, 1966; postgrad. Wright State U., Dayton, Sinclair Community Coll., Dayton, Coll. Mt. St. Joseph, 1981-82; m. Donald Alan Guernsey, July 22, 1967; children—Michael Hugh, Kristina Nicole. Mem. nursing staff Miami Valley Hosp., 1966—, charge nurse self care hemodialysis piloted program Regional Artificial Kidney Center, 1980—. Sunday sch. tchr. Aldersgate United Methodist Ch., Huber Heights, Ohio, 1980—. Mem. Am. Assn. Nephrology Nurses and Technicians. Republican. Clubs: Order Eastern Star, Order Rainbow Girls (Grand Cross of Color 1963). Author manuals in field; contbr. articles to profl. jours. Home: 5201 Beechview Dr Huber Heights OH 45424 Office: 1 Wyoming St Dayton OH 45409

GUERRA, MIRTHA, accountant; b. Havana, Cuba, Mar. 11, 1946; came to U.S., 1961, naturalized, 1970; d. Jose R. and Mirtha (Regalado) Guerra; B.B.A., U. Miami, 1972. Acct., Ernst & Whinney (formerly Ernst & Ernst), Miami, Fla., 1972-82 also mgr. in charge tax dept.; acct. Alexander Grant & Co., Miami, 1982—. Active United Way Dade County, Latin Orange Festival Council; bd. dirs. Greater Miami United, Spanish Am. League against Discrimination, The Forum. C.P.A., Fla. Mem. Am. Soc. Women Accts. (past pres. Miami chpt.), Am. Inst. C.P.A.s, Fla. Inst. C.P.A.s, Am. Women Soc. C.P.A.s, Cuban Soc. Accts., Cuban Am. C.P.A.s (sec.), Interam. Soc. Latin Businessmen, Latin C. of C., Latin Bus. and Profl. Women's Club (pres.), Internat. Center. Clubs: Cuban Women's, Coconut Grove Sailing, Tiger Bay, Banker's, Vizcayans. Office: 1000 Brickell Ave Suite 500 Miami FL 33131

GUERRIERI, MARILYN WEALE, electronics co. exec.; b. Buffalo, July 5, 1943; d. Marion Barnard and Helen (Brennan) Weale; B.A.,

Elmira Coll., 1965; M.B.A., SUNY, Buffalo, 1975; children by previous marriage—Edith, Peter. Cost acct. Fairchild Camera & Instrument Corp., Semi Condr. Group, Mountain View, Calif., 1975-76, fin. analyst, 1976, mgr. fin. analysis and reporting, 1976-77, product line controller, 1977-78; fin. mgr. Intel Corp., Santa Clara, Calif., 1978—. Mem. Phi Beta Kappa, Beta Gamma Sigma. Unitarian. Office: 1350 N Mathilda Ave Sunnyvale CA 94086

GUERTIN, JUDITH LANSKY, career planning cons.; b. Boston, July 19, 1946; d. Merton Warren and Ida (Waitzkin) Lansky; B.A., Barnard Coll., 1968; M.A. (tuition scholar), U. Rochester, 1969; M.B.A. with distinction, DePaul U., 1979; m. Mario A. Guertin, Nov. 3, 1973. Coordinator acad. programs Reid Hall, Paris, 1969-70; grants adminstr. Inst. Internat. Edn., Chgo., 1974-76; dir. student employment services Columbia Coll., Chgo., 1976-78; mktg. adminstr. W.B. Dolphin & Assos., Chgo., 1978-79; mktg. cons. Technomic Consultants, Chgo., 1980-81; adminstr. pediatric nursing Rush-Presbyn.-St. Luke's Med. Center, Chgo., 1981-82. Bd. dirs. Flexible Careers, Chgo., 1975-78, Chgo. Coalition on Women's Employment, 1976-78; steering com. mem. Ill. Women's Agenda, 1976-77. Mem. Women in Mgmt., Chgo. Health Execs. Forum, Women's Health Execs. Network. Editor: The Job Hunter's Notebook, 1975. Home: 100 E Walton Pl Chicago IL 60611

GUEST, BARBARA, writer; b. Wilmington, N.D., Sept. 6, 1920; d. James H. and Ann (Hetzel) Pinson; B.A., U. Calif., Berkeley, 1943; m. Stephen Haden-Guest, Aug. 1948 (div. 1954); 1 dau., Hadley; m. 2d, Trumbull Higgins, Aug. 1954; 1 son, Jonathan Van Lennep. Editorial assoc. Art News, N.Y.C., 1951-55. Recipient Longview award Longview Found., 1960; Yaddo fellow, 1958; Nat. Endowment for Arts grantee, 1980; Mem. PEN, Poetry Soc. Am. Author: (plays) The Ladies Choice, 1953; The Office, 1961; Port, 1965; (poems) The Location of Things, 1960; Poems, 1963; The Blue Stairs, 1968; Moscow Mansions, 1973; The Countess from Minneapolis, 1976, The Turler Losses, 1980; Bibliography, 1981; Quilts, 1981; (novel) Seeking Air, 1978; (with B.H. Friedman) Robert Goodnough, Artist, 1962; (with Sheila Isham) I Ching: Poems and Lithographs, 1969; (biography) Images of H.D.: The Poet and Her World. Home: 116 Meeting House Ln Southampton NY 11968

GUEST, BERNETTE PARKER, oil and gas co. exec.; b. Salt Lake City, May 18, 1952; d. Robert Farnsworth and Ilona Leiola (Wiebke) Parker; B.S. in Fin., Colo. State U., 1973; m. Russel Paul Guest, Sept. 15, 1973; children—Forrest Farnsworth, Robert Russel. Transfer agt., corp. sec.-treas. Am. Stock Transfer, Inc., Denver, 1969-70, v.p., dir., 1971-74; corp. sec., controller Golden Oil Co., Denver, 1974-78, treas., 1977—, v.p., 1978—, dir., 1976—; cons., sec.-treas., dir. G & S Service Co., Inc., Tulsa, 1977-79. Mem. Am. Soc. Profl. and Exec. Women, Ind. Petroleum Assn. Mountain States, Inst. Energy Devel. Office: 530 Denver Club Bldg Denver CO 80202

GUEST, DEBRA DIANE, state ofcl.; b. Honolulu, June 19, 1951; d. Frederick Howard and Josephine Ann (Lech) G.; student Auburn (Ala.) U., 1969-70; M.S., U. South Fla., Tampa, 1972; Ed.D., Nova U., Ft. Lauderdale, Fla., 1980. Mem. staff MacDonald Tng. Center for Mentally Retarded, Tampa, 1972-74, acad. cons. Civitan pre-sch. program, 1973-74; with Fla. Dept. Health and Rehab. Services, 1974—, dir. dist. VI Diagnosis and Evaluation Center, Tampa, 1980—; mem. adj. faculty U. Tampa, 1973-75, Hillsborough Community Coll., 1976—. Chmn. promotion and entertainment com. dist. 8, Fla. Spl. Olympics, 1981—. HEW grantee, 1980-82. Mem. Am. Speech and Hearing Assn., Am. Assn. Mental Deficiency, Am. Soc. Profl. and Exec. Women, Nat. Assn. Female Execs., Fla. Speech and Hearing Assn., Network Exec. Women. Author papers in field. Office: 4000 W Buffalo Ave Tampa FL 33614

GUEST, JEAN HADEN, TV exec.; b. N.Y.C.; d. Albert G. and Freda (Muldavin) Hindes; student N.Y. U.; m. Peter Haden Guest, Dec. 29, 1945; children—Christopher, Nicholas, Elissa. Dir., Am. Nat. Theatre and Acad., N.Y.C., 1954-67; v.p. Wender & Assos., N.Y.C., 1968-74; dir. Theatre Communications Group, N.Y.C., 1974-75; v.p. talent and casting CBS-TV, Los Angeles, 1975—. Mem. Acad. TV Arts and Scis. Office: 7800 Beverly Blvd Los Angeles CA 90036 also 198 Old Stone Hwy Easthampton LI NY

GUEST, LOUISE BLAKE, nurse, educator; b. N.Y.C., Feb. 17, 1929; d. Charles H. and Helen (Kissel) Blake; diploma in nursing Mt. Sinai Hosp. Sch. Nursing, 1951; B.S. in Nursing, Johns Hopkins U., 1958; M.A. in Edn., Bradley U., 1969, bus. cert., 1974; m. Marion I. Guest, Aug. 5, 1961; children—Matthew Blake, Laura Louise. Staff nurse Mt. Sinai Hosp., N.Y.C., 1951; head nurse operating room Presbyn. Hosp., N.Y.C., 1951-53; staff nurse Fresno County (Calif.) Gen. Hosp., 1953; head nurse Ill. Research and Edn. Hosp., Chgo., 1954; head nurse operating room Johns Hopkins Hosp., Balt., 1954-58; pvt. instrumenteer for physician, N.Y.C., 1959-60; head nurse Presbyn. Hosp., N.Y.C., 1960-61; nurse cons. Takau Med. Coll. Hosp., Republic of China, 1961-62; asso. dir. Sch. Nursing, Meth. Hosp., Peoria, Ill., 1968-69, dir., 1969—; mem. com. nursing examiners Ill. Dept. Registration and Edn., 1974-75. Mem. Nat. League Nursing (council of diploma programs exec. com. 1977-81), Ill. League Nursing, Peoria Area Council Dirs. Nursing Edn. (chmn. 1975—), Midwestern Assn. Student Fin. Aid Adminstrs., Am. Assn. Higher Edn., AAUW, Bradley U. Alumni Assn., Johns Hopkins Alumni Assn., Mt. Sinai Hosp. Sch. of Nursing Alumni Assn. Presbyterian. Home: 1410 W Covington Ct Apt 5 Peoria IL 61614 Office: 221 NE Glen Oak Ave Peoria IL 61636

GUEST, MARTHA LOU, psychologist, govt. agy. ofcl.; b. Fayetteville, Tenn., July 26, 1950; d. George Paschal and Thelma B. (Wallace) Moyers; B.S. in Psychology, U. Tenn., 1973, M.S. in Indsl. and Organizational Psychology, 1975; m. Joe Warlick Guest, Jr., June 9, 1972. Residence hall adminstr. U. Tenn., Knoxville, 1970-75; account exec. Techni-Search, Inc., Milw., 1976; investigator security clearances CSC, Paducah, Ky., 1977-78; employee devel. specialist U.S. Office Personnel Mgmt., Louisville, 1978-80, labor relations specialist, Atlanta, 1980—. Mem. Am. Psychol. Assn., Soc. Fed. Labor Relations Profls., Internat. Personnel Mgmt. Assn., Mortar Bd., Phi Beta Kappa, Phi Kappa Phi, Alpha Delta Pi. Mem. Church of Christ. Home: 1501 Clairmont Rd Apt 227 Decatur GA 30033 Office: 940 Russell Fed Bldg 75 Spring St SW Atlanta GA 30303

GUIA, ROMANA NORMA ILAGAN, physician; b. Mabini, Batangas, Philippines, Nov. 18, 1930; d. Nicomedes Alcayde and Cresilda Amboy (Ilagan) G.; A.A., Manila Central U., 1952, M.D., 1957. Resident physician Batangas Provincial Hosp., Philippines, 1957-60, staff physician, ob-gyn, 1960-68; staff physician Western Mental Health Inst., Bolivar, Tenn., 1968-76; resident in psychiatry U. Tenn., Memphis, 1976-79; staff physician VA Med. Center, North Little Rock, Ark., 1979—. Lic. Ednl. Council for Fgn. Med. Grads., Philippines, State of Fla., S.C., Okla. Mem. Am. Psychiat. Assn., Nat. Assn. VA Physicians, Ark. Psychiat. Soc., Philippines Women's Med. Assn., Philippines Med. Assn., Batangas Med. Soc. Roman Catholic. Home: 24 E Fort Roots St North Little Rock AR 72114 Office: Bldg 89 Fort Roots Mental Health Center North Little Rock AR 72114

GUIDO, SALLY ANN, cons. co. exec.; b. N.Y.C., Nov. 16, 1937; d. Vincent James and Rose Marie (Caruso) Guido; B.S., N.Y.U., 1962; M.B.A. summa cum laude, Baruch Coll. CCNY, 1965. Sr. analyst and planner Batten, Barton, Durstine & Osborn, N.Y.C., 1964-68; sr. planner ITT Rayonier, N.Y.C., 1968-70; prin. S. Guido & Assos., N.Y.C., 1970-72; sr. asso. Booz, Allen & Hamilton, N.Y.C., 1972-75; practice dir. mktg. and bus. planning cons. Peat, Marwick, Mitchell, N.Y.C., 1975-79; sr. v.p., prin. Johnson, Smith, Knisely, Inc., N.Y.C., 1980—; sr. adv. Vol. Urban Cons. Group; lectr. mktg. and planning; mem. exec. panel Pa. State U. Coll. Bus. Adminstrn., M.B.A. communications panel, M.B.A. program, 1978, 80; bd dirs. N.Y.U. Coll. Bus. and Public Adminstrn., 1978-81, v.p., 1982. Mem. N.Y.U. Alumni Fedn. (dir. 1978-82, chmn. student relations com. 1980, seminar leader Dean's Day activities 1978-82) recipient Founder's Day Award), Am. Mktg. Assn., Baruch Coll. Alumni Assn., Fin. Women's Assn. (asso.), Beta Gamma Sigma. Contbr. articles in field to profl. jours. Home: 40 Park Ave New York NY 10016 Office: 275 Madison Ave New York NY 10016

GUIDROZ-GREEN, FAY THRASHER, psychologist; b. Wyhne, Ark., Dec. 17, 1935; d. Andrew Justin and Joy Maud (Charles) Thrasher; B.S., Miss. State U., 1958; M.Ed., McNeese State U., 1963; M.A., La. State U., 1968, Ph.D., 1970; m. Richard E. Green, Feb. 1978; children—Jeffrey Kane, Sidney Joseph. Chief psychologist Lake Charles (La.) Mental Health Center, 1970-73; clin. psychologist VA Hosp., Salisbury, N.C., 1973-76; chief psychology service VA Outpatient Clinic, San Antonio, 1976-77; chief psychology service, coordinator research and devel. VA Hosp., Murfreesboro, Tenn., 1977—; regional trainer Tng. in Ind. and Group Effectiveness, 1974-76. Lic. psychologist. Mem. Am. Psychol. Assn., Menninger Found., Nat. Register Health Care Providers, Smithsonian Assn., Maze Found., Oaklands Found., AMA Aux., Assn. Advancement Psychologists, Assn. VA Chief Psychologists. Home: 1027 E Main St Murfreesboro TN 37130 Office: VA Med Center Lebanon Rd Murfreesboro TN 37130

GUILD, CAROL ELIZABETH (MRS. WILLIAM H. GUILD), telecaster, producer; b. Minnet, Wash.; d. David Pringle and Grace (McFadden) Williams; student U. Nev., 1937-40, Pasadena Community Playhouse, 1940-41, Keystone Jr. Coll., Pa., 1966, Pa. State U., 1972; m. William H. Guild; children—Diane, Nita, William H., Ruth. Broadcaster, telecaster, producer KOH, Reno, KOLOTV, Reno, 1951-59, KPIX, San Francisco, 1958-59, WAFM, Miami, Fla., 1959-60, Monitor, NBC, N.Y.C., 1958-61, WDAU-WNEP-TV, Scranton, Pa., 1960-63, daily shows Carol and Friends, Time With Carol, Magic Window, A Visit with Carol, Party Line, PBS-WVIA-TV, Scranton, 1966—, weekly show Carol's Phone 44, PBS cablevision; owner, pres. Guild Video Features, N.Y.C. Mem. Nev. Gov.'s Welfare Com., 1958-59. Vice chmn. Lyon County (Nev.) Republicans, 1956-58. Bd. dirs. Crippled Children's Soc. Scranton. Recipient Nat. awards Am. Women in Radio and TV, Nat. Assn. Ednl. Broadcasters. Mem. Internat. Platform Assn., Delta Delta Delta, Beta Sigma Phi. Mem. Order Eastern Star. Home: Route 1 Box 69 New Milford PA 18834 Office: WVIA-TV Old Boston Rd Pittston PA 18640

GUILLEMETTE, GLORIA VIVIAN, dressmaker, designer; b. North Attleboro, Mass., June 27, 1929; d. Wilfred Anthony Roy and Sylviana (Bonnoyer) King; student Nat. Sch. Dress Design, 1976; m. Thomas William Guillemette, Mar. 24, 1963; children—Sylvia Marie, Katherine Anne, John Thomas. Machine operator dress mfg. cos., 1945-60; asst. to dressmaker and designer, Windsor, Conn., 1960-63; owner Mrs. G's Studio, Enfield, Conn., 1963—; dir. Fashion Show, 1973, 76. Cub Scout commr. Boy Scouts Am., 1980-82; mem. Enfield Fair Rent Commn., 1979-83; justice of peace Conn., 1979—; mem. Republican Town Com., 1978-79; sec. United Meth. Women, 1977-82. Club: Republican Women's.

GUILLERMO, LINDA SUE, social worker; b. Chgo., July 4, 1951; d. Triponio Pascua and Helen Elizabeth (Moskal) G.; B.A., U. Ill., Chgo., 1973, M.S.W., 1975, postgrad., 1980; postgrad. Jane Addams Coll. Social Work, 1980-82. Mktg. research interviewer Rabin Research Co., Chgo., 1970-73; mktg. research interviewer, coder Marcor Mktg. Research, Inc., Chgo., 1973-75; social work intern Child and Family Services, Chgo., 1973-74, Chgo. Bd. Edn., 1974-75; social worker, therapist child abuse and neglect, case investigator, case planning cons., social service program planner Ill. Dept. Children and Family Services, Chgo., 1975-78, social service program planner, contract negotiator, monitoring agt. Central Resources Contracts and Grants, 1978-79; sales person Sentry Realty, Chgo., 1978-80; social worker, therapist, program coordinator, casework supr. of child abuse assessment and intervention program, proposal writer Casa Central, Chgo., 1979-82, casework cons. of child abuse assessment and intervention program, proposal writer, program dir. and casework supr. of early intervention program, 1979—; tng. specialist City Coll. of Chgo., 1980; adj. asso. researcher Asher Feren Law Office, Chgo., 1980-81. Treas. Greenleaf Condominium Assn., Chgo., 1980-81. Lic. real estate salesperson, Ill. Mem. Nat. Assn. Social Workers, Acad. Cert. Social Workers, Ill. Cert. Social Workers, North Side Real Estate Bd. Home: 1510 W Greenleaf St Chicago IL 60626

GUIN, GRACE HUGHES, physician; b. Birmingham, Ala., July 23, 1912; d. Ernest Smith and Grace Allen (Hawkins) Hughes; B.S., Birmingham-So. Coll., 1938; M.D., Vanderbilt U., 1943; 1 dau., Grace Guin Schiff. Intern, Albany (N.Y.) Hosp., 1945-46; resident pathology Garfield Hosp., Washington, 1950-52, Children's Nat. Med. Center, Washington, 1952-53; fellow pathology Meml. Hosp., N.Y.C., 1953-54; assoc. dir. lab. Children's Nat. Med. Center, Washington, 1954-60, dir. lab., 1960-64; staff pathologist Arlington (Va.) Hosp., 1964-67; staff pathologist VA Med. Center, Washington, 1967-80, asst. to dir. pathology service VA Central Office, Washington, 1967—; clin. prof. pathology George Washington U. Med. Center, Washington, 1960—. Nat. Cancer Inst. postdoctoral fellow, 1952. Diplomate Am. Bd. Pathology (AP and CP). Mem. Internat. Acad. Pathology, Coll. Am. Pathologists, Washington Soc. Pathology, Med. Soc. D.C. Republican. Contbr. articles in field to med. jours. Home: 3600 N Abingdon St Arlington VA 22207 Office: VA Central Office 810 Vermont Ave NW Washington DC 20420

GULLAHORN, JEANNE ERARD, psychologist, educator; b. Springfield, Mass., Mar. 11, 1932; d. Hector Langevin and Malvina Elmire (Lanctot) Erard; B.A., Radcliffe Coll., 1954; postgrad. U. Paris, 1955; M.A., U. Kans., 1958; Ph.D., Mich. State U., 1964; m. John T. Gullahorn, May 7, 1955; children—Gregory M., Lorriane L., Leslie J. Asst. prof. psychology Mich. State U. East Lansing, 1965-69, assoc. prof., 1969-74, prof., 1974—, chmn. social-personality program, 1970-72, 77-79, assoc. dean Grad. Sch., 1982—; vis. scientist System Devel. Corp., Santa Monica, Calif., 1965-66; vis. prof. Univ. Coll., Cardiff, Wales, 1972-73; health scientist adminstr. on Intergovtl. personnel act exchange NIMH, Rockville, Md., 1979-81. NIMH grantee, 1968-72; NSF grantee, 1965-69, 77-79. Mem. Am. Psychol. Assn. (chmn. planning bd. 1981), North Central Assn. Commn. Instns. Higher Edn. Soc. Psychol. Study Social Issues, Assn. Women in Psychology. Author: Women: A Psychological Perspective, 1977; Psychology and Women: In Transition, 1979; contbr. articles to profl. jours. Home: 313 E Brookfield East Lansing MI 48823 Office: Grad Sch 246 Adminstrn Bldg Michigan State Univ East Lansing MI 48824

GULLION, SALLIE ROGERS, med. adminstr.; b. Houston, Sept. 29, 1935; d. Murray Maurice and Mary Henrietta (Parkins) Rogers; B.S. in Biology, Rice U., 1957; m. Jerry Campbell Gullion, Dec. 22, 1955; children—Guy Rogers, Laura Michelle, Gregg Campbell (dec.). Intern in med. tech. Parkland Meml. Hosp., Dallas, 1957-58; chief technologist spl. hemotology Wadley Research Center, Dallas, 1958-59; clin. lab. technologist Garland (Tex.) Meml. Hosp., 1959, 60; pathology lab. technologist Drs. Grossman and Smith, Dallas, 1960-63, nuclear medicine technologist Dr. M.H. Mitchell and Assos., Lubbock, Tex., 1965-66; clinic adminstr. Marshall (Tex.) Internal Medicine Assos., 1968—; pres. J&S Rentals, Inc., Marshall, Pres. LWV Marshall/Harrison County, 1978-79; mem. Meml. Hosp. Aux., Harrison County Med. Soc., Aux.; sec.-treas. E. Tex. Pastoral Counseling Center; mem. City of Marshall Citizen Adv. Com.; chmn. bldg. com. Marshall Public Library; mem. Marshall Planning and Zoning Commn. Cert. med. technologist Am. Assn. Clin. Pathologists; cert. med. asst. Mem. Med. Group Mgmt. Assn., Marshall C. of C. (chmn. med. com. 1969-82, mem. water ways com.). Home: 2800 Waubun Dr Marshall TX 75670 Office: 1900 S Washington St Marshall TX 75670

GULLIVER, ADELAIDE CROMWELL, sociologist, educator; b. Washington, Nov. 27, 1919; d. John Wesley, Jr. and Yetta Elizabeth (Mavritte) Cromwell; A.B., Smith Coll., 1940; M.A., U. Pa., 1941; cert. in social work, Bryn Mawr Coll., 1943; Ph.D., Radcliffe Coll., 1952; L.H.D., U. Southwestern Mass., 1972; m. Philip H. Gulliver, May 12, 1973; 1 son by previous marriage, Anthony C. Hill. Mem. faculty Hunter Coll., 1942-44, Smith Coll., 1945-46; mem. faculty Boston U., 1951—, now prof. sociology. Mem. adv. com. vol. aid AID; mem. Nat. Council Humanities, 1968-70; adv. com. corrections Commonwealth Mass., 1955-68, mem. commn. instns. higher edn., 1973-74; adv. com. to dir. IRS, 1970-71, to dir. census, 1972-75. Mem. bd. Wheelock Coll., 1971-72, Nat. Center Afro-Am. Artists, 1970—, African Am. Scholars Council, 1971—, Nat. Fellowship Fund, 1974-75. Mem. African Studies Assn. (dir. 1966-68), Am. Acad. Arts and Scis., Am. Sociol. Assn., Council on Fgn. Affairs, Phi Beta Kappa. Home: 51 Addington Rd Brookline MA 02146 Office: 138 Mountfort St Brookline MA 02146 *

GUMPEL, LISELOTTE, educator; b. Berlin; d. Karl and Grete Gumpel; came to U.S., 1954, naturalized, 1961; B.A. summa cum laude (Honors Merit award 1963, Honors award 1964), Calif. State U., San Francisco, 1964; M.A., Stanford U., 1966, Ph.D. (Stanford-Wilson dissertation fellow), 1971. Radiologic technologist, tchr. Mt. Zion and St. Mary's med. centers, San Francisco, 1956-64; mem. faculty U. Minn., Morris, 1968—, asso. prof. German, 1973—; Helen Cam vis. fellow Girton Coll., Cambridge (Eng.) U., 1977-78. Nat. Endowment for Humanities fellow, 1972. Mem. AAUP, MLA, Nat. Soc. Lit. and Arts. Democrat. Author: 'Concrete' Poetry From East and West Germany: The Language of Exemplarism and Experimentalism, 1976; Metaphor Reexamined in Terms of Non-Aristotelian Semantics, 1983; contbr. articles to profl. jours. Address: PO Box 650 Univ Minn Morris MN 56267

GUMUCIO, SUSAN HARRISON, advt. and graphic artist; b. Kansas City, Mo., June 3, 1950; d. William Henry and Marjorie Ellen (Stark) Harrison; B.F.A. in Advt. and Editorial Art with distinction, U. Kans., 1972; m. René V. Gumucio, Sept. 14, 1974; stepchildren—Michael, Lisa, Kathleen, Gregory, Debby. Staff artist Praco Advt. Co., Colorado Springs, Colo., 1972-74; advt. dir. Kaufman's Dept. Store, Colorado Springs, 1974-77; owner, artist Susan H. Gumucio Advt., Littleton, Colo., 1977—; v.p. Gubilico, Inc., Littleton, 1979—. Recipient awards Pikes Peak Advt. Fedn., 1st pl. award Am. Advt. Fedn. Dist. XII, 1976, MAME award Denver Home Bldg. Assn., 1979. Mem. Am. Inst. Graphic Arts. Republican. Office: 5575 S Sycamore St Suite 126 Littleton CO 80120

GUNASON, SEBA ANNE, educator; b. Terre Haute, Ind., July 19, 1935; d. Harold W. and Seba Collings; B.A., Butler U., 1964; postgrad. Ind. State U., 1965-66; children from previous marriage—Robert, Joseph, Kenneth, Jennifer. Psychiat. social worker Midtown Mental Health Center, Indpls., 1969-74; asst. prof. Center for Youth Devel. and Research, U. Minn., St. Paul, 1975-77; dir. adolescent services, asst. prof. Ind. State U., Indpls., 1978—; mem. Ind. Juvenile Justice Task Force, 1978-79. Mem. adv. bd. Mayor Indpls., 1980—, adv. com. Indpls. Community Services Council, 1979; mem. affirmative action com. Hoosier Capital Girl Scouts, 1979. Lilly Endowment grantee, 1978-79, 80-81. Mem. Nat. Assn. Social Workers, AAUW. Home: 5758 Big Oak Dr Indianapolis IN 46254 Office: 143 N Meredian St Suite 309 Indianapolis IN 46204

GUNDERSEN, ALICE MARSHALL, ins. co. adminstr.; b. Groveton, N.H., Nov. 19, 1934; d. Daniel Weeks and Eleanor Marshall; student Fisher Jr. Coll., Boston, 1952-53, Boston U., 1956, Northeastern U., 1957-59, Madonna Coll., 1966; B.M., U. Mich., 1970; m. Carl A. Gundersen, Apr. 11, 1959; children—Daniel Carl, M. Scott. Exec. sec. with New Eng. Colls. Fund, Boston, 1956-58, with John Hancock Mut. Life Ins. Co., Boston, 1958-59; office supr. dept. human genetics U. Mich., Ann Arbor, 1964-67; adminstrv. coordinator and mgr. brokerage adminstrn. Alexander Hamilton Life Ins. Co., Farmington, Mich., 1973-75; supr. data services Delta Dental Plan of Mich., Southfield, 1976—; pres. Data-Word Services, Southfield, Mich.; cons. Nat. Med. Mgmt. Systems, Flint, Mich.; music dir. St. Timothy Presbyterian Ch., Livonia, Mich., 1964-72, Trinity Episcopal Ch., Farmington, 1975-77; CESA cons. Presbytery of Detroit, 1975-77, mem. task force on women, 1978—; mem. Livonia City Council, 1980—; cons. women re-entering work force; systems cons. Adv. com. Livonia Sch. Bd., 1967-68; campaign coordinator City Council Candidate, 1970; active Livonia Com. for Better Human Relations, 1965-74. Mem. Assn. Systems Mgmt. (publicity chmn. 1978, membership chmn. 1979-80, officer 1980-81, v.p., 1981-82), Women's Econ. Club Detroit (membership com., 1976, program com., 1977), Mich. Women's Polit. Caucus (polit. action chmn. 1979—, state chmn. 1981—), Nat. Women's Polit. Caucus (adminstrv. com. 1981—). Home: 15715 Southampton St Livonia MI 48154 Office: 21700 Northwestern Hwy Southfield MI 48037

GUNDERSEN, JOAN REZNER, educator; b. Chgo., Nov. 9, 1946; d. Charles Louis and Lois Gladys (Baskin) Rezner; B.A., Monmouth Coll., Ill., 1968; M.A., Coll. William and Mary, 1969; Ph.D., U. Notre Dame, 1972; m. Robert P. Gundersen, Sept. 13, 1969; 1 dau., Kristina. Mem. assoc. faculty Ind. U., South Bend, 1971-74; vis. asst. prof. history Vanderbilt U., Nashville, 1974-75; asst. prof. history St. Olaf Coll., Northfield, Minn., 1975-82, assoc. prof., 1982—. Choir dir. All Saints Episcopal Ch., Northfield, 1975-81, mem. vestry, 1978-81, clk., 1981—. Colonial Williamsburg research grantee, 1971, Newberry Library fellow in family history, 1973. Mem. Am. Hist. Assn., Orgn. Am. Historians, So. Hist. Assn., Women Historians Midwest, Minn. Hist. Soc., Northfield Hist. Soc., Nat. Hist. Soc., Phi Alpha Theta. Republican. Author: (with others) American History at a Glance, 3d edit., 1975, 4 edit., 1979, America: Changing Times, 1st edit., 1979, 2 edit., 1981; bd. editors Hist. Mag. of Episcopal Ch., 1977—; contbr. articles in field to profl. jours. Home: 315 Cherry St Northfield MN 55057 Office: Dept History St Olaf Coll Northfield MN 55057

GUNDERSON, JUDITH KEEFER, golf assn. exec.; b. Charleroi, Pa., May 25, 1939; d. John R. and Irene G. (Gaskill) Keefer; student public schs., Uniontown, Pa.; m. Jerry L. Gunderson, Mar. 19, 1971; children—Jamie L., Jeff S.; stepchildren—Todd G., Marc W., Lisa J. Bookkeeper, Fayette Nat. Bank, 1957-59, gen. ledger bookkeeper, 1960-63; head bookkeeper First Nat. Bank Broward, 1963-64; bookkeeper Ruthenberg Homes, Inc., 1966-69; bookkeeper, asst. sec./treas. Pennisular Properties, Inc. subs. Investors Diversified Services Properties, Mpls., 1969-72; comptroller, sec.-treas. Am. Golf Fla., Inc., Deerfield Beach, 1972—, also dir. County committeewoman, Broward County, Fla., 1965-66. Mem. Nat. Golf Found., C. of C., Beta Sigma Phi.

GUNDLACH, VIRGINIA PEARL EVERSOLE, public accountant; b. Mishawaka, Ind., Feb. 8, 1924; d. Amos N. and Gladys E. (Seals) Eversole; student Pan Am. Coll., Fla., 1946, South Bend (Ind.) Coll. Commerce, 1949-50; m. William Gundlach, Sept. 30, 1966; 1 dau., Gladys Dian. Factory worker U.S. Rubber Co., 1942-44; secretarial positions Patnaude Ins. Agy., Lakeville, Ind., 1949-60; prin. Virginia Gundlach Pub. Acct., LaPaz, Ind., 1960—. Served with USAAF, 1944-46. Office: PO Box 253 LaPaz IN 46537

GUNDRUM, LAETTA JUNE, petrochem. co. exec.; b. East St. Louis, Ill., June 13, 1927; d. Norman Henry and Fern L. (Seibel) Gundrum; student Rockford Coll., 1943-44; B.S. in Chemistry, U. Chgo., 1947. Tech. editor U.S. Dept. Agriculture, Peoria, Ill., 1950-51; tech. writer E. I. DuPont deNemours & Co., Wilmington, Del., 1951-58; advt. mgr. Amoco Chems. Corp., Chgo., 1965—. Named Person of Yr., Soc. Plastics Industry, 1977. Mem. Assn. Nat. Advertisers, Bus. and Profl. Advertisers Assn., Soc. Tech. Communicators, Women's Advt. Club Chgo., Am. Chem. Soc. Office: 200 E Randolph St Chicago IL 60601

GUNN, DEBRA CLARK, physician; b. Mound Bayou, Miss., Sept. 11, 1950; d. Clarence Benderson and Gladys (Garrett) Clark; grad. Fisk U.; M.D., Washington U., St. Louis; 1 dau., Gabrielle. Practice medicine specializing in ob-gyn, Houston. Mem. AMA, Tex. Med. Assn., Harris County Med. Soc., Houston Women's Ob-Gyn Assn. (corp. mem.). Home: 8523 Hearth Dr Apt 34 Houston TX 77054 Office: 7000 Fannin Rd Suite 1111 Houston TX 77030

GUNTER, ANNIE LAURIE, state ofcl.; b. Hollow Twp., N.C., June 23, 1919; d. Samuel Franklin and Daisy (Callahan) Cain; grad. Lake Wales (Fla.) High Sch., 1937; m. William Adams Gunter, Oct. 14, 1946; 1 son, William Adams. Sec., Lake Wales Public Schs., Lake Wales State Bank, 1942-45; apptd. coordinator Ala. Office of Hwy. and Traffic Safety, Montgomery, 1971-72, apptd. dir. Office of Consumer Protection, 1972-78; apptd. treas. State of Ala., 1978, elected treas., 1978—. Mem. Nat. Democratic Platform Com., 1972, 76; elected to Ala. Dem. Exec. Com. from Dist. 81, 1974-78; mem. career devel. adv. bd. U. Ala.; mem. adv. bd. Sch. Home Econs., Auburn U.; mem. president's adv. council Marion (Ala.) Inst. Mem. Soc. Consumer Affairs Profls., Am. Council Consumer Interests, Nat. Assn. Consumer Agy. Adminstrs., D.A.R., Daus. of Am. Colonists, Women in Communications. Presbyterian. Club: Soroptimist. Office: State Capital Bldg Room 111 Montgomery AL 36130

GUNTER, GRETCHEN, beverage co. lobbyist; b. Ft. Worth, Tex., Apr. 13, 1942; d. William Clinton and Frances Virginia (Spinks) Weeden; student Gulf Park Coll., 1960; B.A., Tex. Christian U., 1963; M.A., U. Denver, 1979; m. Edward C. Gunter, Dec. 29, 1964; children—Garrett Edward, Holli Gretchen. Tchr., Ft. Worth (Tex.) public schs., 1963-64, Denver public schs., 1965-69; pub. relations dir. Classic Chorale, Denver, 1974-75; asso. producer Noonday-KOA-TV, Denver, 1978; with Mountain Bell, Denver, 1979; dir. Vols. Callaway for Senate, 1980; orgnl. dir. Bradford for Congress, 1980; producer Pub. Access, United Cable TV, 1980; local govt. lobbyist Adolph Coors Co., Denver, 1980—. Mem. Women in Communications (pres-elect 1980-81). Republican. Episcopalian. Clubs: Mile High Republican Women's Forum (charter pres. 1982—), Colo. Fedn. Rep. Women, Nat. Fedn. Rep. Women, Aurora Rep. Women's. Home: 1839 S Nile Ct Aurora CO 80012 Office: 1535 Grant St Suite 300 Denver CO 80203

GUNTER, LITRA O'LINA, govt. ofcl.; b. Bessemer, Ala., Oct. 3, 1952; d. Ailue O'Dell and Louise L. Gunter; B.A., Spelman Coll., 1974; postgrad. Atlanta U., 1974-78, Substitute tchr. Atlanta Bd. Edn., 1977; with IRS, 1977; collection agt. HEW, Atlanta, 1977-78, mgmt. analyst, Washington, 1978-80; mgmt. analyst Dept. Edn., Washington, 1980, asst. on-site monitor ADP contract, 1980—; dir. Diversified Investments Inc. Mem. Nat. Assn. Female Execs. (network dir.), Ga. Assn. of Historians, Assn. Records Mgrs. and Adminstrs., Am. Forum for Internat. Study (bd. dirs.), Am. Soc. Profl. and Exec. Women. Home: 200 Randolph Rd Silver Spring MD 20904 Office: 7th and D Streets SW Washington DC 20202

GUNTER, MARY ANN, univ. adminstr.; b. Ardmore, Okla., May 19, 1949; d. Deward Earl and Verna Mae (Toups) Bannister; student Oscar Rose Jr. Coll., 1978, U. Okla., 1981—; children—Brandon Joseph, Rebecca Ann. Bookkeeper, Webbs Office Supply, Ardmore, 1968; asst. mgr. Beneficial Fin. Co., Dallas, 1969-73; apt. reservationist U. Okla. Housing Programs, 1977-80, mgr., 1980—. Chairperson, Norman (Okla.) Fair Housing Resource Bd., 1981-82. Mem. Assn. Coll. and Univ. Housing Officers, Southwest Assn. Coll. and Univ. Housing Officers (state dir.), U. Okla. Managerial Staff Assn. (sec. 1982-83). Roman Catholic. Clubs: Trosper Archery, Okla. State Archery Assn. (sec. 1980-81), Fellowship of Robin Hood. Office: 1406 Asp St Norman OK 73019

GUNTER-HUNT, GAIL, social worker; b. South Bend, Ind., Aug. 17, 1950; d. William E. Gunter and Lois Fisher Hardy; B.A. with honors, Ark. State U., 1972; M.S.W., U. Ark., 1977; cert. specialist in aging U. Mich., 1978; m. Michael Edward Hunt, May 21, 1977. Nursing home rep. Ark. Social Services, Little Rock, 1972-75; field instr. social work U. Mich., Ann Arbor, 1978-82; clin. social worker U. Mich. Med. Center, 1978-80, sr. social worker, 1980-82; field supr. social work U. Wis., 1982—; social worker Wm. S. Middleton Meml. VA Hosp., Madison, 1982—. Bd. dirs. Juvenile Diabetes Found., Greater Huron Valley chpt., Ann Arbor, 1980-81. Cert. social worker, Mich. Mem. Acad. Cert. Social Workers; Nat. Assn. Social Workers, Am. Assn. Diabetes Educators, Am. Diabetes Assn., Am. Public Health Assn., Arthritis Found. Home: 7 Hiawatha Circle Madison WI 53711 Office: 2500 Overlook Terr Geriatrics Program Bldg 6 Madison WI 53705

GURFEIN, HADASSAH NEIMAN, clin. psychologist; b. Bklyn.; d. Morris and Dorothy (Wagner) Neiman; B.A., Barnard Coll., 1960; M.A., CCNY, 1962; Ph.D., Fordham U., 1977; postgrad. in psychoanalysis and psychotherapy N.Y.U., 1977, in hypnosis Inst. of Pa. Hosp., 1982; m. Elisha Gurfein, July 31, 1966; children—Joshua Noah, Jonathan Daniel, David Michael. Clin. psychologist Hadassah Hosp., Israel, 1962-63; psychologist, clin. fellow Bklyn. Coll., 1963-64; cons. psychologist L.I. Consultation Center, 1963-64; psychologist Lynbrook and Fairfield Public Schs., 1964-67; adj., dept. psychology Fairleigh Dickinson U., Teaneck, N.J., 1977-78; psychologist, chmn. child study team Dumont (N.J.) Pub. Schs., 1977—; cons. psychologist Tourette and Tic Lab., Mt. Sinai Hosp., N.Y.C., 1981—; pvt. practice clin. psychologist, N.Y.C., 1977—; mem. Fedn. of Jewish Philanthropies Task Force on Mental Health. Mem. Am. Psychol. Assn., N.Y. State Psychol. Assn., N.J. Psychol. Assn., N.Y. Assn. Clin. Psychologists, N.J. Assn. Sco. Psychologists, Soc. for Clin. and Exptl. Hypnosis, Psi Chi, Phi Delta Kappa (Ph.D. dissertation award, 1976). Jewish. Home: 156 Sherwood Pl Englewood NJ 07631 Office: 40 E 89th St New York NY 10028

GURKE, SHARON MCCUE, naval officer; b. Bklyn., Apr. 4, 1949; d. James Ambrose and Marion Denise (Coombs) McCue; B.A., Molloy Cath. Coll., 1970; M.S. in Systems Mgmt., U. So. Calif., 1977; m. Lee Samuel Gurke, Apr. 16, 1977; children—Marion Dawn, Leigh Elizabeth. Commd. ensign U.S. Navy, 1970; advanced through grades to lt. comdr., 1979; aircraft maintenance duty officer Orgn.-Intermediate Maintenance Officer, Comdr. Naval Air Force U.S. Pacific Fleet, Naval Air Sta., North Island, San Diego, 1974-77; head quality assurance div. Intermediate Maintenance Dept. Supporting Aircraft, Naval Air Sta., Miramar, San Diego, 1977-78, avionics div. officer, 1978-80; officer in charge Naval Aviation Engring. Service Unit Pacific Naval Air Sta., North Island, 1980-82; aircraft intermediate maintenance officer Naval Air Sta., Alameda, Calif., 1982—. Lic. pilot; first female naval officer selected for aero. engring. tng.; recipient Capt. Winifred Q. Collins award USN, 1980. Mem. Ninety Nines, San Diego Naval Women Officers Network (chmn.). Home: 3324 Fir Ave Alameda CA 94501

GURNE, PATRICIA DOROTHY, lawyer; b. Phila., May 25, 1941; d. George Albert and Dorothy (Hammett) G.; B.A., MacMurray Coll., 1965; J.D., George Washington U., 1969; grad. Nat. Inst. Trial Advocacy, 1974. Admitted to Colo. bar, 1969, D.C. bar, 1971; law clk. to Judge Joyce H. Green, Superior Ct. D.C., Washington, 1969-71; asso. firm Jackson, Campbell & Parkinson, and predecessors, Washington, 1971-75, partner, 1975—; mem. D.C. Ct. Appeals Jud. Conf., 1977—, D.C. Circuit Jud. Conf., 1979—. Trustee, George Washington U., 1981—; bd. dirs. D.C. Women's Com. for Crime Prevention, 1978-79. Mem. ABA, Bar Assn. D.C. (exec. council young lawyers sect. 1974-77, vice chmn. young lawyers sect. 1976-77, Young Lawyer of Yr. award 1979), Women's Bar Assn. (pres. 1978-79, dir. 1980—), Women's Bar Found. (dir. 1981—), D.C. Bar sec., dir. 1978-79, ethics com. 1979-82), George Washington U. Law Alumnae Assn. (dir.). Office: 1120 20th St NW Washington DC 20036

GURNSEY, KATHLEEN W., state legislator; b. Donnelly, Idaho, June 23, 1927; d. Robert Gilmore and Thelma (Halferty) Wallace; B.S.B.A., Boise State U., 1974; m. Vern L. Gurnsey, May 7, 1950; children—Kristina, Steven, Scott. Mem. Idaho Ho. of Reps., 1974—, chmn. ho. appropriations com. Mem. def. adv. com. Women in Service. Mem. AAUW. Presbyterian (elder).

GURSKA, PATRICIA, hosp. exec.; b. Rye, N.Y., Jan. 9, 1950; d. Richard Gurska and Patricia (Hatley) Kreiser; B.S., Pa. State U., 1974. Early childhood specialist Farrell (Pa.) Day Care Center, 1974-75; dir. Day Care Center-Eduplay, Mpls., 1975-76; dir. public relations Children's Home Soc. Day Care Programs, St. Paul, 1976-79, St. Mary's Hosp. and Rehab. Center, Mpls., 1979—. Bd. dirs. Children's Lobby, 1978-79; coordinator, Upper Midwest chpt. Jews-by-Choice, 1982—. Recipient MacEachern award Acad. Hosp. Public Relations, 1980. Mem. Minn. Council for Hosp. Public Relations (v.p. 1980-81, pres. 1981-82), Women in Communications (dir. 1980-81, Clarion award 1981), Minn. Assn. for Edn. Young Children (dir. 1981-82), Greater Mpls. Day Care Assn. (dir. 1977-78), Minn. Jaycees (coordinator several fund raising activities 1978-79). Home: 5036 France Ave S Minneapolis MN 55410 Office: St. Mary's Hosp and Rehab Center 2414 S 7th St Minneapolis MN 55454

GURTIN, LEATRICE KAGAN, ednl. adminstr.; b. Bklyn., May 6, 1936; d. David and Gertrude (Goldstein) Kagan; student Russell Sage Coll., 1953-55; B.A. in English, Brown U., 1967; M.A. in English, Carnegie-Mellon U., 1975; m. Morton Edward Gurtin, June 12, 1955 (div. 1981); children—Amy Lynn, William Robert. With customer service dept. So. Calif. Gas Co., Los Angeles, 1955-56; creative drama instr. YMCA and YMHA, Barrington and Providence, R.I., 1961-63; English and drama tchr. Winchester Thurston Sch., Pitts., 1967-74; dir. admissions and placement Sch. Urban and Public Affairs, Carnegie-Mellon U., Pitts., 1975-78; dir. placement and career planning Grad. Sch. Bus., U. Pitts., 1978—, also mem. faculty; lectr. to corps.; actress local radio and TV commls. Sta. WPRO, Providence, 1963. Mem. personnel adv. bd. Alleghany County Health Dept., 1976—; mem. fund raising com. Am. Sch. of Florence, 1974, Brown U., 1975-78; tchr. Favela children Ambulatorio da Praia do Pinto, Rio de Janeiro, 1970, recipient Spl. Service award, 1970. Recipient Spl. Service award Liberty Sch., Pitts., 1973. Mem. Pitts. Personnel Assn., Middle Atlantic Placement Assn., Coll. Placement Council, Midwest Placement Assn., Exec. Women's Council Pitts. Clubs: Brown (Pitts.). Contbr. articles to profl. jours. Home: 732 College Ave Pittsburgh PA 15232 Office: U Pitts Pittsburgh PA 15260

GUSSEN, RUTH, physician; b. N.Y.C., May 6, 1925; d. Joseph and Charlotte (Herman) Marcus; B.A., Cornell U., 1946, M.D., 1950; m. John Gussen, Dec. 25, 1949; 1 son, James. Intern, then resident in pathology Bellevue Hosp., N.Y.C., 1950-54; asst. pathologist VA Hosp., Oklahoma City, 1955-58; mem. faculty UCLA Med. Sch., 1966—, prof. pathology, 1979—, dir. Temporal Bone Lab., 1966—. NIH grantee, 1966—. Mem. Am. Acad. Otolaryngology, Am. Otol. Soc., Assn. Research Otolaryngology. Author articles in field, chpts. in books. Address: 31-24 Rehab Center UCLA Med Sch Los Angeles CA 90024

GUSTAFSON, ROSE ELAINE, city ofcl.; b. Alta., Can., July 11, 1927; came to U.S., 1927; d. Albert Allen and Ronghild (Olsenberg) Olson; student Seattle Pacific U., 1964-65, Am. Inst. Banking, 1966-70, Inst. Fin. Edn., 1972-76; m. David E. Gustafson, Dec. 26, 1946; children—Gail Lynne, Shirley Jean, Jeffery David. With Rainier Bank, Seattle, 1957-70; v.p. br. ops. Queen City Savs. & Loan, Seattle, 1970-78; exec. v.p. Sound Savs. & Loan, Seattle, 1978-81; asst. city treas. Seattle, 1981—; regional mem. Pres.'s Commn. on White House Fellowships, 1979. Trustee Alki Found.; v.p. Small Bus. Council, Seattle C. of C., 1981—, trustee, 1979—; trustee Visitors & Conv. Bur., 1980-81; bd. dirs. Cardiopulmonary Research Inst., 1982—; mem. Virginia Mason Assos., 1982—. Mem. U.S., Wash., Seattle savs. leagues. Republican. Clubs: Zonta (pres. 1978-79), Women & Bus. (pres. 1980-81, trustee 1978-81). Office: 103 Municipal Bldg Seattle WA 98104

GUSTIN, ANN WINIFRED, psychologist; b. Winchester, Mass., Oct. 21, 1941; d. Bertram Pettingill and Ruth Lillian (Weller) G.; B.A. with honors in Psychology, U. Mass., 1963; M.S. (USPHS fellow), Syracuse U., 1966, Ph.D., 1969; m. Carl George Beal, Sept. 17, 1966. Research asst., psychology trainee U. Mass., Tufts U., Harvard U., Syracuse U., 1961-66; psychology intern VA, Canandaigua, N.Y., 1967-68; asst. prof. psychology U. Regina (Sask., Can.), 1969-74, asso. prof. psychology, dir. counseling services, head clin. tng., 1974-78; pvt. practice psychology, Carrollton, Ga., 1978—; staff tng. cons. Frobisher Bay Dept. Social Services, N.W. Territories, Can., 1979-80; cons. staff Tanner Hosp. Membership chmn. Carroll County Mental Health Assn., 1979-81. Registered psychologist, Sask.; lic. psychologist, Ga. Mem. Am. Psychol. Assn., Can. Psychol. Assn., Ga. Psychol. Assn., Sask. Psychol. Assn. (mem. exec. council 1971-72, registrar 1972-73). Office: 401 Bradley St Carrollton GA 30117

GUSTUS, DAWN CHISHOLM, advt. mgr.; b. Chgo., Nov. 26, 1951; d. James Lawrence and Florence Louella (Engebretson) Chisholm; student Miami U., Oxford, Ohio, 1970-72; B.A., U. Ill., Champaign-Urbana, 1974; m. Leon Truman Gustus, Aug. 4, 1973. Communications designer Abana Press, Inc., Urbana, 1974-77; owner Solo Flite, Champaign, 1977-79; public info. officer City of Clearwater (Fla.), 1979-81; advt. mgr. Dessein & Co., Ltd., Clearwater, 1981—. Mem. Nat. Assn. Female Execs., Bank Mktg. Assn., Internat. Assn. Bus. Communicators, C-U Advt. Club (dir.), Clearwater Advt. Fedn. (dir., editor newsletter), Internat. Ombudsman Inst., Gamma Phi Beta. Club: Champaign-Urbana Symphony Guild (chmn. decorations for benefit 1978). Office: 301 S Jupiter Ave Clearwater FL 33515

GUTEKUNST, BERYL SNYDER, coll. adminstr.; b. Scranton, Pa., July 11, 1939; d. Percy Guy and Louise Emily (Lewis) Snyder; A.B., Gettysburg Coll., 1961; M.S., U. Pa., 1965; m. Donald P. Gutekunst, June 23, 1962; children—David Paul, Peter John. Tchr., Upper Moreland Sch. Dist., Willow Grove, Pa., 1968-72, Wissahickon Sch. Dist., Spring House, Pa., 1968-74, Lower Moreland Sch. Dist., Huntingdon Valley, Pa., 1974-76; personnel cons. TLC Assos., Huntingdon Valley, 1977-78; sales rep. G&G Talmage Assos., Willow Grove, 1979-80; dir. communications program and women in mgmt. program Chestnut Hill Coll., Phila., 1980—. Trustee, Upper Dublin Library Bd., 1980—; mem. Pa. Gov.'s Planning Council for Library Services, 1982—. Mem. AAUW (pres. br. 1977-79, state v.p. 1981-83), Am. Personnel and Guidance Assn., Am. Coll. Personnel Assn., Am. Assn. Higher Edn. Club: Old York Rd. Country (Spring House). Contbg. editor: Domestic Tour Manual, 1980. Home: 1825 Howe Ln Maple Glen PA 19002 Office: Chestnut Hill College Philadelphia PA 19118

GUTH, CARYL JOY (MRS. JOHN FALSTAD), anesthesiologist; b. Peoria, Ill., Sept. 17, 1935; d. Walter Christian and Helen Josephine (Whitaker) G.; A.A., Mars Hill Jr. Coll., 1955; B.S. cum laude, Wake Forest U., 1957; postgrad. N.C. Baptist Hosp. Sch. Cytology, 1957-58; M.D., Bowman Gray Sch. Medicine, 1962; m. John Falstad, Aug. 24, 1968. Intern, U. Kans. Med. Center, Kansas City, 1962-63; resident in anesthesiology U. Pa. Hosp., Phila., 1963-65; instr. anesthesia Bowman Gray Sch. of Medicine, Winston-Salem, N.C., 1965; anesthesiology fellow Queen Victoria Hosp., E. Grinsted, Sussex, Eng., 1966; vis. instr. anesthesia U. Nijmegan, Netherlands, 1966; chief anesthesia Kaiser Med. Center, Santa Clara, Calif., 1967; anesthesiologist Mills Meml. Hosp., San Mateo, Calif., 1967—, asst. chief anesthesiologist, 1969-71, chief anesthesiologist, 1976-80. Mem. bldg. com. Mills Meml. Hosp., 1971-79, mem. acute care, surgery rev. coms., 1972-80, governing exec. com., 1974—. Diplomate Am. Bd. Anesthesiology. Mem. Am. Soc. Anesthesiology (ho. of dels. 1980—, communications com. 1980—), Calif. Soc. Anesthesiology (dir. 1977—, editor bull. 1977-80, asst. treas. 1977-81, pres. 1982-83), AMA, Calif. Med. Assn., San Mateo County Med. Assn. (community relations com. 1981—), Am. Med. Tennis Assn., Beta Beta Beta, Alpha Epsilon Delta, Kappa Mu Epsilon. Patentee gen. anesthesia mask and chin holder. Home: 145 Rizal Dr Hillsborough CA 94010 Office: 100 S Ellsworth St Suite 802 San Mateo CA 94401

GUTHRIE, ANN GERTRUDE, health adminstr., phys. therapist, cons.; b. Boulder, Colo., Aug. 4, 1943; d. John T. and Ruth I. Guthrie; B.S. in Phys. Therapy, 1966; M.S., U. Notre Dame, 1977. Phys. therapist Mass. Gen. Hosp., Boston, 1965-67, Univ. Hosp., Denver, 1967-70; dir. phys. therapy Mercy Med. Center, Denver, 1970-72, dir. allied services, 1972-76, patient rep., 1976—, adminstrv. dir., 1979—; instr. U. Colo., 1967-70; cons. HEW, 1973-79, grant reviewer, Rockville, Md., 1979; acting dir., adminstr. McNamara Hosp. and Nursing Home, Fairplay, Colo., 1975; mem. State Bd. Phys. Therapy, 1973-76. Lic. phys. therapist, Colo. Mem. Nat. Soc. Patient Reps., Colo. Soc. Patient Reps. Democrat. Baptist. Contbr. articles on phys. therapy to profl. jours. Office: 1619 Milwaukee Denver CO 80206

GUTHRIE, BETTY JUNE, clin. social worker; b. Clinton, Okla., June 4, 1926; d. David G. and Laura (Simpson) G.; student Christian Coll., Columbia, Mo., 1944-45; B.A., U. Okla., 1948; M.S.W., Tulane U., 1956. Child welfare worker Okla. Child Welfare Div., Oklahoma City, 1949-56; dist. child welfare supr. Okla. Child Welfare Div., Ponca City, 1957-67; clin. social worker Bi-State Mental Health Found., Ponca City, 1967-74, chief clin. social worker, 1974—; pvt. practice psychotherapy Fair Clinic, Inc., Ponca City, 1968—; asso. prof. Okla. U.; regional vice chmn. White House Confs. Children and Youth, 1960, regional sec., 1970; pres. Kay Council Community Services, 1964-67; exec. bd. Kay County Youth Shelter, 1972-77; mem. Kay County Child Welfare Adv. Bd., 1967—. Mem. Mayor's Com. on Drug Abuse, chmn., 1976-77. Lic. clin. social worker, Okla. Mem. Acad. Cert. Social Workers, Registered Social Workers in Okla., Nat. Registry Health Care Providers in Clin. Social Work, Nat. Assn. Social Workers, Okla. Health and Welfare Assn., Delta Delta Delta. Methodist. Office: Doctor's Park 404 Fairview Ponca City OK 74601

GUTHRIE, HELEN ANDREWS, educator; b. Sarnia, Can., Sept. 1925; came to U.S., 1946, naturalized, 1957; d. David and Helen Parker (Sweet) Andrews; B.S., U. Western Ont., 1946; M.S., Mich. State U., 1948; Ph.D., U. Hawaii, 1968; D.Sc., U. Western Ont., 1982; m. George M. Guthrie, June 4, 1949; children—Barbara, Jane, James. Asst. prof. nutrition Pa. State U., 1948-69, asso. prof., 1969-72, prof., 1972—, head dept. nutrition, Coll. Human Devel., 1979—; dir., Nabisco Brands Inc. Chmn., State College (Pa.) Bd. Health, 1978-82. Mem. Am. Inst. Nutrition, Soc. Nutrition Edn., Am. Dietetic Assn. Home: 1316 S Garner St State College PA 16801 Office: 106 Human Development University Park PA 16802

GUTHRIE, JANET, racing driver; b. Iowa City, Iowa, Mar. 7, 1938; d. William Lain and Jean Ruth (Midkiff) Guthrie; B.S. in Physics, U. Mich., 1960. Comml. pilot and flight instr., 1958-61; research and devel. engr. Republic Aviation Corp., Farmingdale, N.Y., 1960-67; publs. engr. Sperry Systems, Sperry Corp., Great Neck, N.Y., 1968-73; racing driver Sports Car Club Am. and Internat. Motor Sports Assn., 1963—; profl. racing driver U.S. Auto Club and Nat. Assn. for Stock Car Racing, 1975—. Recipient Curtis Turner award Nat. Assn. for Stock Car Racing-Charlotte World 600, 1976; First in Class, Sebring 12-hour, 1970; N.Atlantic Road Racing champion, 1973. Mem. Madison Ave. Sports Car Driving and Chowder Soc. First woman to qualify for and race in Indpls. 500, 1977, finished 9th, 1978.

GUTHRIE, JOYCE WOODSON, communications co. mktg. exec.; b. Washington, Oct. 9, 1945; d. Frank Edward and Vernice Valaria (Meadows) Woodson; B.A. cum laude, Howard U., 1967; M.B.A., Harvard U., 1971; 1 dau., Vernice Irene. Asst. buyer Filene's, Boston, 1971-72, dept. mgr., 1972-73; sr. cons. asso. Mark Battle Assos., Washington, 1973-74; asst. mgr. market mgmt. AT&T, Morristown, N.J., 1974-78, div. mgr., residence strategic market analysis, Parsippany, N.J., 1981—; div. staff mgr., residence mktg. Bell Telephone Pa., Phila., 1978-81. Mem. fin. com. Phila. council Girl Scouts U.S.A. Mem. Alliance Black Mgrs., Nat. Black M.B.A. Assn., Council Concerned Black Execs., Forum Exec. Women. Episcopalian. Office: 5 Wood Hollow Rd Parsippany NJ 07054

GUTHRIE, MARILYN EDITH, assn. exec.; b. Auburn, N.Y., Oct. 5, 1946; d. George Nelson and Marjorie Estelle (Field) G.; A.A.S., SUNY, Morrisville, 1966. Various secretarial positions, 1966-75; exec. asst. Northeastern Retail Lumbermens Assn., Rochester, N.Y., 1975-79, sr. v.p., Wellesley, Mass. and Rochester, 1979—. Mem. Meeting Planners Internat., Hotel Sales and Mgmt. Assn., Nat. Assn. Exhibit Mgrs. Republican. Club: Oakley Country (Watertown, Mass.). Office: 180 Linden St Wellesley MA 02181

GUTMAN, JUDITH MARA, writer, producer, lectr.; b. N.Y.C., May 22, 1928; d. Victor and Anna (Zimmerman) Markowitz; B.A., Queens Coll., 1949; M.S., Bank Street Coll. Edn., 1957; postgrad. N.Y.U., 1958; m. Herbert Gutman, June 18, 1950; children—Marta Ruth, Nell Lisa. Lectr., cons. U. Wis., Madison, 1953-54; dir. Montefiore Nursery Sch., N.Y.C., 1954-57; lectr. Hunter Coll., N.Y.C., 1957-58; writer, prodr. film strips including Immigration, Migration and Urbanization, 6 strips, 1977, Labor in America: Its Growth and Development, 4 strips, 1978; lectr. art, photography and culture throughout world, 1977—; guest curator Internat. Center Photography, N.Y.C., 1980; mem. bd. Centre for Photography, Bombay, 1982—. Am. Inst. for Indian Studies sr. faculty research fellow, 1978, 79; Ford Found. research and travel grantee, 1978; Smithsonian Instn. grantee, 1978, 79, 80; Social Sci. Research Council postdoctoral faculty fellow, 1979. Mem. Soc. Photog. Edn., Authors Guild. Author: The Colonial Venture, 1966; Lewis W. Hine and the American Social Conscience, 1967; (with Edwin Rozwenc) The Making of American Society, 1972, 73; Lewis Hine: Two Perspectives, 1974; Is America Used Up?, 1973; Buying, 1975; Through Indian Eyes, 1982; contbr. articles and reviews to various periodicals including N.Y. Times, Washington Post, Dictionary of American Biography, Popular Photography. Home: 976th Ave Nyack NY 10960 Office: The Internat Center of Photography 1130 Fifth Ave New York NY 10028

GUY, MARLENE, social worker; b. N.Y.C., Jan. 15, 1946; d. Renee Givens; B.A. in Psychology, City U.N.Y., 1969; M.S.W., Columbia U., 1972. Asst. psychiat. social worker N.Y. State Dept. Mental Hygiene, N.Y.C., 1969-72; psychiat. social worker Harlem Interfaith Counseling Service, N.Y.C., 1972-74, Met. Hosp. Community Mental Health Center, N.Y.C., 1974-78; asst. regional dir. Planned Parenthood Fedn. Am., Inc., N.Y.C., 1979—. Vol., Haryou Action Community Corp., 1963—; research interviewer Northside Center for Child Devel., 1964—; co-chmn. vols. United Negro Coll. Fund, 1977—. Cert. social worker, N.Y. State. Mem. Acad. Cert. Social Workers, Nat. Assn. Social Workers, Nat. Assn. Black Social Workers, Coalition 100 Black Women, Am. Public Health Assn., Am. Mgmt. Assn.

GUY, MILDRED DOROTHY, educator; b. Brunswick, Ga.; d. John and Mamie Paul (Smith) Floyd; B.S. in Social Sci., Savannah State Coll., 1949; M.A. in Am. History, Atlanta U., 1952; postgrad. U. So. Calif., U. Colo.; m. Charles H. Guy, Aug. 18, 1956 (div. 1979); 1 dau., Rhonda Lynn. Tchr. social studies L.S. Ingraham High Sch., Sparta, Ga.; tchr. English and social studies North Jr. High Sch., Colorado Springs, 1958—; cooperating tchr. Tchr. Edn. Program, Col. Coll., 1968-72. Fund raiser for Citizens for Theatre Auditorium, Colorado Springs, 1979; bd. dirs. Urban League, 1971-75; del. to County and State Democratic Conv., 1972, 76, 80; mem. Pike's Peak Community Coll. Council, 1976—. Recipient Viking award North Jr. High Sch., 1973; Outstanding Black Woman of Colorado Springs award, 1975; named Pacesetter, Atlanta U., 1980-81, Outstanding Black Educator of Yr., Black Educators of Dist. II, Colorado Springs, 1981. Mem. NEA, Colo. Edn. Assn., Colorado Springs Tchrs. Assn., Fedn. of Bus. and Profl. Women, AAUW, Colo. Council of Social Studies, Assn. for Study of Afro-Am. Life and History, Colo. LWV, NAACP, Alpha Delta Kappa, Alpha Kappa Alpha. Baptist. Club: Elks. Home: 3132 Constitution Ave Colorado Springs CO 80909 Office: 612 E Yampa St Colorado Springs CO 80903

GUY, ROXANNE JOSEPHINE, physician; b. Galesburg. Ill., Aug. 15, 1952; d. Robert Edward and Gertrude Josephine (Hoegg) Bowman; B.S., Ill. State U., 1974; postgrad. Salzburg Coll., 1973; M.D., So. Ill. U., 1977; m. Curtis Eguene Guy, May 17, 1980. Resident So. Ill. U. Sch. Medicine Affiliated Hosps., Springfield, 1977-81, chief resident gen. surgery, 1981-82, resident in plastic surgery, 1982—. Diplomate Nat. Bd. Med. Examiners. Mem. AMA, Am. Med. Women's Assn., Ill. State Med. Soc., Sangamon County Med. Soc., Sol. Ill. U. Sch. Medicine Alumni Soc. Methodist. Contbr. articles to profl. jours. Home: 2052 S Lincoln Ave Springfield IL 62704 Office: PO Box 3926 Room D334 Springfield IL 62708

GUYRE, JUDITH PITZO, indsl. drive co. exec.; b. Phila., Nov. 27, 1945; d. Frank Joseph and Carolyn Marie (Miller) Pitzo; student parochial schs., spl. courses; m. Ronald T. Guyre, Aug. 19, 1978; 1 son, Garrett M. Sec. to pres. Alpha Lithograph, Camden, N.J., 1964-67; adminstrv. asst. Transam. Ins. Co., Phila., 1967-70; office mgr. Power Quip/C.J. Kitching Assos., Pennsauken, N.J., 1972-78; v.p. Brisbane Indsl. Drive Co., Jim Thorpe, Pa., 1978—; seminar leader. Asst. to dir. Voorhees Community, Edn. and Recreation Program. Mem. Nat. Assn. Female Execs., Power Transmission Reps. Assn. Republican. Roman Catholic. Home: Star Rt 2 Box 16A Blakeslee PA 18610 Office: Box 12 2d Star Rt Jim Thorpe PA 18229

GUZIEC, JOAN ANN, lawyer; b. Holyoke, Mass., Aug. 23, 1943; d. Joseph John and Ann Victoria (Zagrocka) Wdowiak; B.S., Am. Internat. Coll., 1967; M.Ed., Springfield Coll., 1969; J.D., Western New Eng. Sch. Law, 1976; m. Walter Paul Guziec, Jr., July 28, 1961 (div.); 1 dau., Joy A. Tchr., Minnechaug Regional High Sch., Wilbraham, Mass., 1967—; admitted to Mass. bar, 1977, U.S. Dist. Ct. bar, 1977; individual practice law, Springfield, Mass., 1977—. Mem. Am. Bar Assn., Mass. Bar Assn., Hampden County Bar Assn. Democrat. Roman Catholic. Home: 1715 Carew St Springfield MA 01104 Office: 31 Elm St Suite 651 Springfield MA 01103

GUZMAN, LOURDES A. LACAP, physician; b. Masantol, Pampanga Philippines, Sept. 22, 1930; came to U.S., 1969, naturalized, 1974; d. Roman Yabut and Victoria Lugtu (Alfonzo) Lacap; A.A., U. Santo Tomas, 1950; M.D., U. Manila, 1955; m. Jose G. Guzman, Dec. 8, 1962; children—Don Christopher, Madonna Therese, Joseph Paul, Suzanne Victoria. Rotating intern, med. resident Newark Beth Israel Hosp., 1955-56, Sacred Heart Hosp., Allentown, Pa., 1956-58, Princeton (N.J.) Hosp., 1958-59, Lawrence Meml. Hosp., New London, Conn., 1959-60; practice medicine specializing in internal medicine, Masantol, Pampanga, 1961-66; mcpl. health officer, Masantol, Rhu, 1966-69; house physician Suburban Community Hosp., Cleve., 1969-70, Broadview Center, Brecksville, Ohio, 1970-71; med./psychiat. staff Allentown State Hosp., 1972—. Active, Notre Dame Sch. Assn., Bethlehem, Pa., Becahi Sch. Assn., Bethlehem, St. Luke's Ladies Aide Soc. Mem. Philippine Med. Women's Assn. (life), Pa. Assn. State Mental Hosp. Physicians, Lehigh Valley Med. Women's Assn., Allentown Med. Staff Assn. (sec.-treas.). Home: 1203 Dalehurst Dr Bethlehem PA 18018 Office: 1600 Hanover Ave Allentown PA 18103

GWALTNEY, MILDRED, librarian; b. Richmond, Va., June 1, 1946; d. Milton N. and Helen (Davis) G.; B.A., Longwood Coll., 1967; M.L.S., George Peabody Coll., 1970; postgrad. U. Ky., 1974-76. Tchr. English, Henrico High Sch., Richmond, 1967-69, librarian, 1970-71; instr. dept. library sci. and instructional media Western Ky. U., Bowling Green, 1971-76, asst. prof., 1976—. Mem. Southeastern, Ky. library assns., Ky. Sch. Media Assn., 3d Dist. Librarians Assn., Children's Lit. Assn., Mortar Bd., Beta Phi Mu, Alpha Psi Omega, Zeta Tau Alpha. Home: 621 Cabell Dr Apt 4 Bowling Green KY 42101 Office: Dept Library Sci and Instructional Media Western Ky U Bowling Green KY 42101

GWALTNEY, VIRGINIA VIOLA, social services ofcl.; b. Nashville, Nov. 6, 1942; d. Raymond Pasco and Kathryn June G.; B.A., U. Fla., 1964; 1 son, Grayson Brook. Tng. cons. Clairol, Inc., Faberge, Inc., Eve of Roma, Atlanta, 1965-71; mktg. mgr. Field Creations, Inc., Atlanta, 1972-76; owner, mgr. Global Publs., Ft. Myers, Fla., 1976—; dir. Lee County Medicare Program, Ft. Myers, 1978—. Bd. dirs. United Way, Community Coordinating Council. Recipient cert. of merit Health Care Financing Adminstrn., 1981. Mem. Am. Mensa Soc. Democrat. Home: 311 Whittier Ave North Fort Myers FL 33903 Office: 3830 Evans Ave Fort Myers FL 33901

GWIN, DAWN SIMMONS, graphic designer; b. Marshall, Tex., Aug. 23, 1951; d. Aura L. and Janette Fason (Ryan) Simmons; B.A., Trinity U., 1973; postgrad. U. Tex., San Antonio, 1978—. Communications mgr. Frost Nat. Bank, San Antonio, 1976-80; editor San Antonio Mag., 1980-81; dir. mktg. 1776, Inc., San Antonio, 1981; owner The Drawing Room, San Antonio, 1981—. Mem. Internat. Assn. Bus. Communicators (awards of merit 1980, award of excellence 1978, dir. 1982), Women in Communications (award of excellence 1981), Am. Mktg. Assn. (dir.), San Antonio Press Club (1st v.p.), Chi Beta Epsilon, Kappa Delta Pi. Republican. Roman Catholic. Home: 14806 Gallant Fox San Antonio TX 78248

GWINN, RUTH HEITMAN, nurse; b. Kirkwood, Mo., Jan. 20, 1922; d. John Frank and Florence Louise (Tiesler) Wagner; L.P.N., O'Fallon Tech. Sch., St. Louis, 1974; R.N., Maryville Coll., St. Louis, 1978; m. Robert E. Gwinn, Aug. 30, 1980; children—John, Robert, Catherine, Jim, Michael, Cynthia. Supr., Chastians Retirement Center, Des Peres, Mo., 1960-78; dir. nursing Chastians of Clinton (Mo.), 1978-80; asst. dir. nursing, in-service dir. St. Sophia Geriatric Center, Florrisant, Mo., 1980—. Recipient Vol. award Am. Nursing Home Assn., 1969. Mem. Bus. Women's Assn. Roman Catholic. Home: 2675 Dougherty Ferry Des Peres MO 63122 Office: 936 Charbonier St Florrisant MO 63130

GYOR, HARRIET SUE, therapist, author; b. Holbrook, Nebr., Dec. 25, 1942; d. William A. and Helen Joyce (Davis) Gardner; student Compton Jr. Coll., 1960-61, U. Calif., Berkeley, 1961-62; m. Jon Wesley Gyor, July 6, 1962 (div. 1979); children—Julie Ann, William Jon. Teaching asst. sign lang. elem. sch., Santa Fe Springs, Calif., 1971-74; dir. TERRAP, Orange County, Calif., 1976—; owner PGI Pub. Co., Westminster, Calif., 1980—. Vol., Norwalk State Hosp., 1965-67; asst. coordinator seminars for nurses, on phobias Golden West Coll., 1979, 81. Cert. leader TERRAP programs. Mem. Phobia Soc. Am., Am. Booksellers Assn. Mem. Ch. of Religious Sci. Author: Living in Hell: An Agoraphobic Experience, 1980. Office: 14140 Beach Blvd Suite 204 Westminster CA 92683

HAAG, CAROL ANN GUNDERSON, consumer products co. exec.; b. Mpls.; d. Glenn Alvin and Genevieve Esther (Knudson) Gunderson; B.J., U. Mo., 1969; postgrad. Roosevelt U., Chgo., 1975—; m. Lawrence S. Haag, Aug. 30, 1969. Reporter, Waukegan (Ill.) News Sun, summers 1966-69; pub. relations writer, advt. copywriter Am. Hosp. Supply Corp., Evanston, 1969-70, also free-lance editor Lake County (Ill.) Circle weekly newspaper; asst. dir. pub. relations Rush-Presbyn.-St. Luke's Med. Center, Chgo., 1970-71; asst. mgr. pub. and employee communications Quaker Oats Co., Chgo., 1971-72, mgr. editorial communications, 1972-74, mgr. employee communications programs, 1974-77, also mem. corp. office planning com., 1972-77; dir. public relations Shaklee Corp., San Francisco, 1978—. Bd. dirs. Calif. League for Handicapped; adv. bd. San Francisco Spl. Olympics; mem. public relations com. San Francisco Recreation and Parks Dept., San Francisco Vol. Bur. Recipient 1st Place Cert. award Printing Industry Am., 1972, 74, 1st Place Spl. Communication award Internat. Assn. Bus. Communicators, 1974, First Place Citation for Outstanding Editorial Achievement award Chg. Assn. Bus. Communicators, 1974. Mem. Nat. Acad. TV Arts and Scis. (Chgo. and San Francisco chpts.), Indsl. Communication Council, Public Relations Soc. Am., San Francisco C. of C. (public relations com.), San Francisco Press Club. Presbyn. Home: 133 Fernwood Dr Moraga CA 94556 Office: Shaklee Corp 444 Market St San Francisco CA 94111

HAAG, MAUREEN ELIZABETH, graphic designer; b. Ft. Wayne, Ind., Feb. 2, 1943; d. Robert Gerald and Beulah Elizabeth (Fetter) McDougall; B.A., Purdue U., 1965; 1 dau., Jennifer Liann; m. Melvin William Haag; 1 son, Eric Melvin. Mktg. cons. Ind. Lumbermens Mutual Ins. Co., Indpls., 1966; advt. asst. The Singer Co., N.Y.C., 1966-67; customer service rep. Wash. Natural Gas Co., Bellevue, 1968-69; communications cons. Gen. Telephone Co. Ind., 1976-79; owner, cons., graphic designer M. Haag & Co., Ft. Wayne, 1979—. Mem. Purdue Alumni Assn. Lutheran. Club: Kappa Alpha Theta. Home: 6625 Quail Ridge Ln Fort Wayne IN 46804 Office: 6625 Quail Ridge Ln Fort Wayne IN 46804

HAAS, CAROLYN BUHAI, author, ednl. cons.; b. Chgo., Jan. 1, 1926; d. Michael and Tillie (Weiss) Buhai; B.Ed., Smith Coll., 1947; postgrad. Nat. Coll. Edn., 1956-58; m. Robert Green Haas, June 29, 1947; children—Andrew, Mari, Thomas, Betsy, Karen. Tchr., Francis W. Parker Sch., Chgo., 1947-49; art tchr. Glencoe (Ill.) Pub. Schs., 1969-70; co-founder and partner Parents As Resources Leadership Tng. Found., Northfield, Ill., 1970-81; pres. cbh Pub. Inc., Glencoe, Ill., 1979—; co-author children's books including: I Saw a Purple Cow, 1972, A Pumpkin in a Pear Tree, 1976, Children are Children are Children, 1978; author: The Big Book of Recipes for Fun, 1980; Recipes for Fun and Learning, 1982; Purple Cow to the Rescue, 1982; co-author: Backyard Vacation, 1980; Magic Magnets: How to Lure Your Child to Reading, 1981; co-author syndicated comic strip Recipes for Fun; cons. Look at Me! PBS series for parents; contbr. articles to mags. and jours. Chmn., West Sch. PTA, 1962-64; bd. mem. Chgo. chpt. Am. Jewish Com., Ill. Commn. on Child Abuse, Family Counseling Service of Glencoe; bd. dirs. Friends of Glencoe Pub. Library, pres. 1981—; bd. dirs. LWV of Glencoe, Glencoe Human Relations Com.; pres., bd. dirs. Scholarship and Guidance Assn.; co-founder Glencoe Art Fair. Mem. Soc. Children's Book Writers, Nat. Assn. Edn. of Young Children, Assn. Childhood Edn. Internat., Children's Reading Roundtable, Council for Exceptional Children, Internat. Reading Assn. Clubs: Chgo. League of Smith Coll. (pres. 1972-74). Home: 280 Sylvan Rd Glencoe IL 60022 Office: Box 236 Glencoe IL 60022

HAAS, CHRISTINA LEONE, nurse; b. Dayton, Ohio, Sept. 19, 1940; d. Harold Houser and Leone (Moore) H.; R.N., Miami Valley Hosp. Sch. Nursing, 1961; B.S. cum laude in Nursing, Ohio State U., 1963; M.A., N.Y.U., 1970. Staff nurse critical care Ohio State U. Hosp., Columbus, 1961-64; staff The N.Y. Hosp., N.Y.C., 1964—, sr. staff nurse, 1965-66, CCU head nurse, 1966-68, cardiac clin. nurse specialist, 1970-76, clin. nursing dept. head Burn/Emergency Nursing Dept., 1976—, asst. dir. nursing service, 1976—; lectr. in field; cons. in field. Bd. dirs. Hosp. Chaplaincy, 1981—; bd. dirs. N.Y. Heart Assn., 1974-76, mem. dirs.' council, 1976—. Mem. Am. Nurses Assn., Am. Burn Assn., Am. Assn. Critical Care Nurses, Emergency Dept. Nurses Assn., N.Y. Heart Assn., Am. Heart Assn. Contbr. articles to profl. jours. Office: 525 E 68th St New York NY 10021

HAAS, DEBRA KAYE, nurse; b. Parkersburg, W.Va., Mar. 28, 1952; d. John Martin and Donna Jean (Grubb) Pugh; A.Nursing, Parkersburg Community Coll., 1977; m. Thomas Lee Haas, Aug. 21, 1975. Dir. nursing Christian Anchorage Nursing Home, Marietta, Ohio, 1977-80; rev. coordinator Area VIII Peer Rev., Zanesville, Ohio, 1980-81; dir. nursing Hickory Creek Nursing Center, The Plains, Ohio, 1981-82, Marietta Convalescent Center, 1982—. Mem. Ohio Nurses Assn., Am. Nurses Assn. Mem. Decatur Chapel Ch. Home: Rt 1 Newport OH 45768 Office: 117 Bartlett St Marietta OH

HAAS, DOROTHY FRANCES, editor; b. Racine, Wis., June 17; d. Allen Leo and Elizabeth Grace (Sweetman) H.; B.S., Marquette U., 1955. Editor, Whitman Pub. Co., Racine, 1955-68; sr. editor Field Enterprises Ednl. Corp., Chgo., 1968-70; mng. editor children's books Rand McNally & Co., Skokie, Ill., 1970—; lectr. in field. Mem. Women in Mgmt. (dir. 1978-79), Soc. Midland Authors (treas. 1978-79, dir., 1979—), Children's Reading Round Table (dir. 1981-82), Women in Communications, ALA, Authors Guild, Chgo. Book Clinic, Soc. Childrens Book Writers, Internat. Bd. on Books for Young People. Club: Arts (Chgo.). Author: Men of Science, 1958; The Bears Upstairs, 1978, Poppy and the Outdoors Cat, 1981. Home: 336 W Wellington Ave Chicago IL 60657 Office: PO Box 7600 Chicago IL 60680

HAAS, ELEANOR (MRS. PETER RALPH HAAS), mktg. and communications cons.; b. Jersey City, Mar. 12, 1932; d. Nicholas Mark and Eleanor (Cochran) Alter de Csanytalek; B.A., Smith Coll., 1953; cert. N.Y. Sch. Interior Design, 1960; m. Peter Ralph Haas, Oct. 22, 1966. Exec. sec. MCA Artists, Ltd., N.Y.C., 1954-56, Young & Rubicam, Inc., N.Y.C., 1956-58, J. Walter Thompson Co., N.Y.C., 1958-59, Stanford Research Inst., N.Y.C., 1959, Deafness Research Found., N.Y.C., 1960, Earl Newsom & Co., N.Y.C., 1961-65; account exec. Ruder & Finn, Inc., N.Y.C., 1965-68; founder, pres. The Haas Group, Inc., N.Y.C., 1968—; co-founder, pres. DeNigris, Haas & England, Inc., 1978-79; adj. instr. dept. journalism N.Y.U., 1980, adj. asst. prof. Sch. Continuing Edn., 1980—. Mem. N.Y. Women in Communications, Fin. Communications Soc., Internat. Radio and TV Soc., Nat. Acad. TV Arts and Scis., Public Relations Soc. Am., Indsl. Communication Council, Women Execs. in Public Relations, Advt. Women N.Y., Hajji Baba Club. Home: 171 W 79th St New York NY 10024 Office: 59 E 54th St New York NY 10022

HAAS, MARY KATHRYN, actress; b. Milan, Ind., May 4, 1931; d. Harold W. and Ada M. (Meyer) Barkhau B.A. in Theatre, Hanover (Ind.) Coll., 1952; postgrad. No. Ky. U., 1973; m. Donald Joseph Haas, Oct. 4, 1952; children—Eric Alan, Faye Ellen. Stage appearances in Mame, Funny Girl, Promises, Company, Little Me, Picnic, Joe Egg, Skin of Our Teeth, Under Milkwood, Dark of the Moon, Don't Drink the Water, The Women, Solid Gold Cadillac, Strange Bedfellows, Gazebo, Pillow Talk, His and Hers, Lo and Behold, Sabrina Fair, Ohio and Ky., Gypsy, Starting Here, Starting Now, The Pleasure of his Company; on tour in What's a Nice Country Like Us Doing in a State Like This?, 1977; appearances on local and nat. radio and TV, also local cafe appearances; dir. St. Johns United Ch. of Christ Choristers, Newport, Ky., 1966—; asst. to artistic dir. Cin. Sch. for Creative and Performing Arts. Bd. dirs., past sec. Cin. Assn. Community Theatres; Southwestern rep. Ohio Community Theatre Assn.; bd. dirs., past pres. No. Ky. Arts Council; mem. alumni bd. Hanover Coll. bd. dirs. Footlighters, Cin., Ft. Thomas Village Players. Mem. woman's com. St. Luke's Hosp., Ft. Thomas; bd. dirs. Holly Hill Children's Home, Campbell County. Recipient Corbett award Cin. Post-Times Star, 1977. Mem. A.C.T. Cin. (Art Rouse award 1978, past sec. and dir., 1st v.p.), Ohio Community Theatre Assn. (S.W. rep.), No. Ky. Arts Council (past pres. and dir.). Address: 262 Scenic View Dr Fort Thomas KY 41075

HAAS, MILDRED REIFEISS, singer, educator; b. St. Louis, July 5, 1911; d. Walter Fred and Bertha Johanna (Bopp) Reifeiss; student Interlocken Music Camp, 1946, Coenraad V. Bos, 1950-54, Rosa Raisa and Nellie Gardinia, Chgo., 1952-57; m. Edwin W. Haas, July 14, 1937; m. 2d, Eugene J. Binkley, Feb. 16, 1980. Soloist churches, St. Louis, 1935—; performances in civic opera, light opera; recitals given for various instns., to 1966; pvt. instr. voice, St. Louis, 1940—. Mem. Nat. Assn. Tchrs. Singing, Music Tchrs. Nat. Assn., Mo. Music Tchrs., Nat. Fedn. Music, Mus. Research Club, Morning Etude, Jr. Fedn. Music Clubs. Mem. Divine Sci. Fedn. Internat. Studio: 7341 Forest Haven Estates Saint Louis MO 63123

HAASE EWIN, JEANNETTE VALAIRE, univ. adminstr.; b. Ely, Nev., Feb. 5, 1937; d. H. O. Thompson and Ruby V. Thompson Holzapfel; B.A. with honors, Goucher Coll., 1959; Ph.D., U. Md. Sch. Medicine, 1963; m. Richard A. Ewin, Mar. 30, 1982; children—Leslie Ann, Sharon Lee. Research fellow Harvard Sch. Public Health, Boston, 1965-66, research assoc. dept. nutrition, 1966-68; planning and evaluation coordinator No. New Eng. Regional Med. Programs, Burlington, Vt., 1968-69; project adminstr. Tri-State Regional Med. Program, Boston, 1968-71; dir. tech. ops. Health Planning Council Greater Boston, Newton, Mass., 1972-73; dir. programs in health care Radcliffe Coll., Cambridge, Mass., 1973-76; dir. Center African and Middle Eastern Health Programs, Boston U., 1979—, assoc. acad. v.p., 1977-81, assoc. v.p. European ops., 1981—; vis. lectr. Harvard U. Sch. Public Health, 1976-77; asst. prof. Simmons Coll., Boston, 1968; cons. in field. NIH fellow, 1961-63. Fellow Royal Soc. Medicine; mem. Am., Mass. public health assns. Contbr. articles to profl. jours. Office: 147 Bay State Rd Boston MA 02215 also 152 Shakespeare Tower Beech St Barbican London EC2 England

HABADA, PATRICIA ADELAIDE BREEDLOVE, textbook editor; b. Flint, Mich., Mar. 17, 1929; d. Robert Wiley and Lillie Savannah (Bowden) Breedlove; B.S., Kutztown (Pa.) State Coll., 1968; M.Ed., U. Pitts., 1976, Ph.D., 1982; m. Joseph Paul Habada, June 5, 1949; children—Shirley Dawn Habada Harvey, Beverly Kay, Paula Jo. Service rep. Heath Co., Benton Harbor, Mich., 1952-55; classroom tchr., Ohio and Pa., 1958-70; prin., Pa., 1970-73; research asst. U. Pitts., 1973-75; assoc. supt. schs. Pa. Conf. Seventh-day Adventists, Reading, Pa., 1975-79; sr. editor elem. reading textbooks Gen. Conf. Seventh-day Adventists, Washington, 1979—; leader family life seminars and workshops; cons. to sch. dists., colls., univs. Vice pres. Seventh-day Adventists Gen. Conf. Women's Aux.; v.p. edn., lay adv. bd. Pa. Conf. Seventh-day Adventists. Cert. in elem. teaching, adminstrn., supervision of instrn., Ohio, Pa., Seventh-Day Adventists. Mem. Internat. Reading Assn., Assn. Supervision and Curriculum Devel., N.Am. Div. Curriculum Com., Assn. Adventist Women. Writer family life curriculum materials, tchrs. guides to Pa. resources; contbr. articles to various jours. Office: General Conference of Seventh-day Adventists 6840 Eastern Ave NW Washington DC 20012

HABER, AUDREY RUTH, psychologist, author; b. N.Y.C., Feb. 4, 1940; d. Eugene Jerome Friedman and Sally (Reit) Brenner; B.A., Adelphi U., 1960, Ph.D. (USPHS fellow), 1963; m. Jerome Jassenoff, Dec. 19, 1969; children—Laurie Beth, David Scott. Asso. prof. psychology C.W. Post Coll., Greenvale, N.Y., 1964-70; research psychologist UCLA, 1971-78; author, 1967—; books include: Business Statistics, 1982; Fundamentals of Behavioral Statistics, 4th ed., 1980; Fundamentals of Psychology, 3d ed., 1983; General Statistics, 3d ed., 1977; Psychology of Adjustment, 1983; contbr. articles profl. jours. Recipient Acad. of Distinction award Adelphi U., 1977. Mem. Western Psychol. Assn. Am. Psychol. Assn., Psi Chi. Home and Office: 2349 Vermont Ave Toms River NJ 08753

HABERLAND, SUSAN ROBERTA, agrl. products co. mgr.; b. Cleve., Oct. 29, 1946; d. Frederick Christian and Mildred Elizabeth (Schlater) H.; B.S. in Chem. Engring., Carnegie-Mellon U., 1968; M.B.A. (Rockefeller fellow), Harvard U., 1973. Chem. engr. Polaroid Corp., Waltham, Mass., 1968-71; mktg. cons. Pechiney-Ugine Kuhlamann, Paris, summer 1972; exec. trainee, asst. buyer Bloomingdale's, N.Y.C., 1973-74; cons., devel. mgr. Squibb S.A., Tehran, Iran, 1974-75; prin. cons. Khadamat Modiryat Sanaye, Tehran, 1976-78; mgr. bus. planning Union Carbide Agrl. Products Co., N.Y.C., 1978—. Mem. Delta Gamma. Clubs: Sierra, Harvard of N.Y., Eastern Star. Home: The Lausanne 333 E 45th St New York NY 10017 Office: 20th Floor 270 Park Ave New York NY 10017

HACH, LISA PETERS, pub. co. fin. exec.; b. N.Y.C., Dec. 31, 1943; d. Gilbert S. and Constance S. (Carpp) P.; student Hunter Coll.; m. William Hach, Oct. 19, 1979. Bookkeeper, Hans Eichler Motor Cars, N.Y.C., 1967-70, Cars of France, Inc., N.Y.C., 1970-78; asst. controller Diversion Publs. Inc., N.Y.C., 1978—; prin. Sheridan Bookkeeping Service, N.Y.C. Office: 60 E 42d St New York NY 10165

HACHE, MARLENE DOLORES, educator; b. Winslow, Maine, Apr. 4, 1942; d. William Edward and Georgianna (Roberge) H.; B.A., Mich. State U., 1963; M.S. in Edn., So. Ill. U., 1966, Ph.D., 1973; children—

Troy Nader Moslemi, Michelle Farah Moslemi. Tchr. English, Mason (Mich.) High Sch., 1964-65, Fowlerville (Mich.) High Sch., 1965-66; grad. research asst. So. Ill.U., 1967-68, teaching asst., 1969-70; lectr. Pahlavi U., Shiraz, Iran, 1970-71, asst. prof. lit. and English as fgn. lang., 1970-71; dir. English, Internat. Sch., Shiraz, 1971-72; prof. English, Wash. State U., 1975—; mem. All Univ. Council on Tchr. Edn. Gen. chmn., fund-raising chmn. Corelli Ensemble, youth string chamber music group, Moscow, Idaho. Mem. NEA, Nat. Council Tchrs. English, Mich. Edn. Assn., AAUW, Nat. Assn. Fgn. Student Affairs, NOW. Contbr. articles, research on coll. freshmen writing ability. Home: 1435 Chinook St Moscow ID 84843 Office: Dept English 391 Avery Hall Wash State U Pullman WA 99164

HACKER, HELENA, movie studio exec.; b. San Antonio, Feb. 28, 1948; d. Harold Arthur and Pauline F. Shapiro; Am. Field Service exchange student, Sacre Coeur des Chartres, Lyons, France, 1965-66; B.A. cum laude, Stanford U., 1970. Editorial asst. New Yorker Mag., N.Y.C., 1970-72; copy editor Random House Pub. Co., N.Y.C., 1972-74; copychief The Village Voice, N.Y.C., 1974-75, assoc. editor, 1976, sr. editor, 1977; v.p. for prodn. Universal Pictures, Universal Studios, Universal City, Calif., 1978—. Mem. Women in Film. Office: 100 Universal City Plaza Universal City CA 91608

HACKER, KERRY VARINA, lawyer; b. Abilene, Tex., Feb. 27, 1944; d. Leslie Earl and Katherine Emily (Senior) Foreman; B.A., UCLA, 1967; J.D., Western States Coll. of Law, 1978; m. Wesley D. Hacker, Dec. 29, 1966; children—Dean, Stephanie, Valerie, Douglas. Controller, Sea Foamed Lightweight Concrete, Inc., Pico Rivera, Calif., 1967-70, treas., 1970-76; admitted to Calif. bar, 1978, since practiced in Whittier; dir. Sea Foamed Lightweight Concrete, Inc., Western Gypsum Floors. Mem. Whittier com. Spastic Children's League, 1980-82, 2d v.p., 1981-82; treas. PTA, 1976-77; legal counsel Friendly Hills Homeowners Assn., 1979-82. Recipient Am. Jurisprudence award, 1976. Mem. Am. Bar Assn., Los Angles County Bar Assn., Orange County Bar Assn., Whittier Bar Assn. Episcopalian. Club: Los Angeles Athletic. Contbr. articles to profl. jours. Office: 7915 S Painter Ave Whittier CA 90602

HACKETT, ANNE M., fgn. service officer; b. Mass., Aug. 13, 1946; d. Edward F. and Mary (Fenton) Hackett; B.A., Coll. New Rochelle, 1968; M.A., N.Y.U., 1970. Program coordinator Am. Field Service, N.Y.C. and Los Angeles, 1970-74; vice consul Am. Consulate, Istanbul, Turkey, 1976-78, Am. Embassy, Singapore, 1978-80; 1st sec., consul Am. Embassy, Djibouti, 1981—. Mem. Am. Fgn. Service Assn. Address: Villa Plateau du Serpent Blvd Marechal Joffre BP 185 Djibouti

HACKETT, CAROL ANN HEDDEN, physician; b. Valdese, N.C., Dec. 18, 1939; d. Thomas Barnett and Zada Loray (Pope) Hedden; B.A., Duke, 1961; M.D., U. N.C., 1966; m. John Peter Hackett, July 27, 1968; children—John Hedden, Elizabeth Bentley, Susanne Rochet. Intern. Georgetown U. Hosp., Washington, 1966-67, resident, 1967-69; clinic physician DePaul Hosp., Norfolk, Va., 1969-71; chief spl. health services Arlington County Dept. Human Resources, Arlington, Va., 1971-72; gen. med. officer USPHS Hosp., Balt., 1974-75; pvt. practice family medicine, Seattle, 1975—; mem. staff Overlake Meml. Hosp. Mem. bd. Mercer Island (Wash.) Preschool Assn., 1977-78; coordinator 13th Ann. Inter-profl. Women's Dinner, 1978. Mem. Nat. Assn. Residents and Interns, Wash., King County (chmn. com. TV violence) med. socs., NW Women Physicians (v.p. 1978), Seattle Symphony League, Sigma Kappa. Episcopalian. Club: Wash. Athletic. Home: 4304 E Mercer Way Mercer Island WA 98040 Office: 1128 112th Ave NE Bellevue WA 98004

HACKETT, EDWINA ROGERS, clin. social worker; b. Memphis, Mar. 15, 1943; d. H. G. and Roseanne (Brown) Rogers; B.S., Memphis State U., 1969; M.S.W., U. Tenn., 1974; children—Stephen A., John E. Psychiat. social worker City of Memphis Hosp., 1969-76; clin. social worker U. Tenn. Mental Health Center, Memphis, 1976-80; clin. social worker Midtown Mental Health Center, Memphis, 1980—, geriatric coordinator, 1981—; instr. psychiatry U. Tenn. Med. Sch.; field instr. U. Tenn. Sch. Social Work, 1980—. Pres., Memphis and Shelby County Council on Aging, 1981, 82. Mem. Nat. Assn. Social Workers, Tenn. Soc. Clin. Social Workers, Psi Chi. Contbr. article to jour. Hypnosis, 1979. Home: 1218 Faxon Memphis TN 38104 Office: 969 Madison St Memphis TN 38104

HACKETT, JOAN, actress; b. N.Y.C., Mar. 1; d. John and Mary (Esposito) Hackett; scholarship from Uta Hagen and Mary Welch; studied with Lee Strasberg, 1956; m. Richard Mulligan, Jan. 3, 1966 (dissolved 1973). Broadway debut in A Clearing in the Woods, 1959; stage appearances include The Play's the Thing, Call Me by My Rightful Name, Two Queens of Love and Beauty, Journey to the Day, Peterpat, Park, Night Watch; TV appearances include Ellery Queen, Alcoa Premiere, Alfred Hitchcock Theatre, Bob Hope Chrysler Theatre, Bonanza, Mission: Impossible; The American Woman; Portraits of Courage, series Another Day; TV movies include How Awful About Allan, The Other Man, Five Desperate Women, Reflections of Murder, The Young Country, Dead of Night, Possessed, Stonestreet, Long Days of Summer, Paper Dolls; appeared in TV series Young Doctor Malone, 1959-60, The Defenders, 1961-62; films include Will Penny, 1968, Support Your Local Sheriff, 1969, Assignment to Kill, 1969, The Rivals, 1972, The Last of Sheila, 1973, The Terminal Man, 1974, Mackintosh and T.J., 1976, Treasure of Matecumbe, 1976, Mondo Video, 1979, One Trick Pony, 1980, Mourning Becomes Electra (PBS), Only When I Laugh (Golden Globe award, Oscar nominee), 1981; also nightclub appearances. Recipient Obie award Village Voice, 1961, Vernon Rice award, 1961, Theatre World award, 1961; Emmy nomination for Ben Casey. Mem. AFTRA, Screen Actors Guild, Actors Equity Assn. Office: care Kimble/Parseghian Inc 250 W 57th St New York NY 10019

HACKETT, MARY CATHERINE, state agy. adminstr.; b. Newport, R.I., Feb. 6, 1925; d. James Edward and Katherine Cecilia (Murphy) H.; B.A., Seton Hill Coll., 1947. With State of R.I., Providence, 1947—; statistician Dept. Labor, 1947-54; chief div. standards and planning Dept. Employment Security, Providence, 1959-69, dir., 1969—; dir. R.I. Blue Cross, Providence; corporator Citizens Bank, Providence. Bd. dirs. Newport County Girls and Boys Clubs; mem. Providence Dist. Adv. Council, U.S. SBA; adv. com. John E. Fogarty Center; mem. Statewide Planning Council; mem. Gov's. Adv. Commn. on Women; mem. State Manpower Services Council; mem. State Adv. Council Vocat. Edn.; mem. steering Com., Leadership Greater Providence; mem. regional bd. advs. New Eng. Congressional Inst.; mem. adv. com. U. R.I. Women in Polit. and Govtl. Careers. Mem. Internat. Assn. Personnel in Employment Security, AAUW, Am. Soc. Public Adminstrn., Interstate Conf. Employment Security Agys. Club: Turks Head.

HADAWAY, EVELYN N., med. social worker; b. Sioux City, Iowa, Apr. 12, 1921; d. Willis D. and Elsa (Alwes) Noakes; B.S. in Nursing, U. Nebr., 1943; M.S.W., U. Wash., 1953; div.; children—Margaret, David, Bruce. Nursing instr. U. Nebr., Omaha, 1943; head nurse Cottage Hosp., Santa Barbara, Calif., 1946-48; med. social worker U. Wash. Hosp., 1966-72; with Virginia Mason Research Center, Seattle, 1972—, project coordinator, research asso. Breast Cancer Research Project, 1973—. Served with U.S. Army Nurse Corps, 1944-46. Mem.Nat. Assn. Social Workers, Acad. Cert. Social Workers. Office: Breast Cancer Research Project Virginia Mason Med Center 1000 Seneca St Seattle WA 98101

HADDON, ELEANOR DYGERT, journalist; b. Pitts., Nov. 23, 1915; d. Warren Benson and Gertrude Brown Dygert; B.S., U. R.I., 1937; postgrad. Newark State Coll., 1961-63; m. William Pyner Haddon, Oct. 19, 1937; children—Warren D., Trudie Haddon Wanchow, Sharon Haddon Dorner. With F.J. Low Co., N.Y.C., 1937-40; tchr. public schs., Mountain Lakes, N.J., 1962-64; with E.B. Vreeland Travel Agy., Boonton, N.J., 1964-65, Bay Head Travel Agy., 1981—; columnist Citizen, Denville, N.J., 1958-75, Ocean County Rev., Seaside Heights, N.J., 1976—. Leader Boy Scouts Am., Girl Scouts U.S.A., 1950-60; sec. Ladies Aux. of Dover, Brick Beach First Aid, 1981—; trustee, fin. sec. Union Ch. of Lavallette (N.J.), 1981—Mem. Nat. Panhellenic Conf., Boonton Bus. and Profl. Women's Club (pres. 1956-58, state officer 1959-60), Am. Assn. Ret. Persons (rec. sec. Breton Woods chpt.), DAR (chpt. regent 1968-74, treas. 1981—), Ocean Beach Sr. Citizens (sec.), Deborah (sec. Seaside chpt.), Sigma Kappa (province officer 1956-68, nat. 2d v.p. 1968-74, nat. pres. 1974-76, sec.-treas. 1978-80, found. trustee 1980—). Republican. Clubs: Order of Eastern Star (grand officer 1966-67), White Shrine of Jerusalem (past worthy high piestess), Ocean Beach and Bay (trustee, sec. 1976—). Home: 33 E Dolphin Way Ocean Beach III Lavallette NJ 08735 Office: 1717 W 86th St Suite 600 Indianapolis IN 46260

HADEN, DONNA JOHNSON, med. technician; b. Salem, N.J., Mar. 26, 1943; d. Donald V. and Evelyn Rose (Johnson) Johnson; student Rutgers U., 1961-63, Glassboro State U., 1971-72, Salem County Community Coll., 1965-66; M.T., Salem County Meml. Hosp., 1965; m. James duVal, Jan. 16, 1971; children—Sue Elizabeth. Med. technician Salem County Meml. Hosp., Salem, N.J., 1965-69, Wilmington (Del.) Med. Center, 1969-71; asst. dir. Army Edn. Center, Pedricktown, N.J., 1971-72; tchrs. asst. Pedricktown Elementary Sch., 1972-73; adminstrv. asst. Brookside Park Condominiums, Oxon Hill, Md., 1982—. Health/safety chmn. PTA, 1982; active Girl Scouts U.S.A. N.J. State scholar, 1961-63. Mem. Am. Soc. Clin. Pathologists. Democrat. Club: NCO Wives.

HADLEY, DONITA GRACE, newspaper writer and editor; b. Jasonville, Ind., Feb. 4, 1951; d. Guy E. and Bessie F. (Burlingame) H.; B.S. cum laude, Ind. State U., 1973, M.S. cum laude in Communications, 1975. Entertainment editor, feature writer, theatre, film, and music critic Terre Haute (Ind.) Tribune, 1976—. Mem. Wabash Valley Press Club. Office: 721 Wabash Ave Terre Haute IN 47808

HADLEY, ELEANOR MARTHA, economist; b. Seattle, July 17, 1916; d. Homer More and Margaret Sarah (Floyd) H.; B.A., Mills Coll., 1938; M.A., Radcliffe Coll.-Harvard U., 1941-43, Ph.D., 1949. With OSS, 1943-44, Dept. State, 1944-46; mem. Gen. MacArthur's Staff, Tokyo, 1946-47, President Truman's Commn. Migratory Labor, 1950-51, Nat. Assn. Social Workers, 1953-56; mem. faculty Smith Coll., 1956-65; economist U.S. Tariff Commn., 1967-74, GAO, 1974-81; mem. faculty George Washington U., 1972—, adj. prof. econs., 1981—. Fellow AAUW, 1946-47, Japanese Econ. Found., 1982; Fulbright research scholar, 1962-63. Mem. Am. Econ. Assn., Assn. Asian Studies, Inter-univ. Seminar Japan, Nat. Economists Club, Soc. Woman Geographers, Mills Coll. Alumnae Assn., Radcliffe Coll. Alumnae Assn., Phi Beta Kappa. Author: Antitrust in Japan, 1970; Japan's Export Competitiveness in Third World Countries, 1981. Home: 5040 Klingle St Washington DC 20016 Office: Econs Dept George Washington U Washington DC 20052

HADLEY, JANE BYINGTON, psychotherapist; b. N.Y.C., Apr. 24, 1929; d. David and Ruth (Johnson) Millar; B.A., U. V., 1951; M.A., Columbia U., 1967; m. Arthur Twining Hadley, Feb. 24, 1979; children—Elisabeth Danish, Caroline Danish. Intern Queens Coll., 1969; pvt. practice psychotherapy, N.Y.C., 1971—; mem. Staff Met. Center for Mental Health, N.Y.C., 1976-79. Mem. Am. Psychol. Assn. Democrat. Episcopalian. Clubs: Cosmopolitan, Doubles, Edgarton Yacht.

HADLEY, KAREN MARIE, landscape contractor; b. Pasadena, Calif., May 1, 1945; d. Donald Russel and Virginia Frances (Jones) H.; student Los Angeles City Coll., 1967, Orange Coast Coll., 1973—. Mail carrier U.S. Post Office, 1963-64; musician, singer, songwriter, 1964—; owner, operator Hadley Gallery, Newport Beach, Calif., 1968-72, Hadley Landscape Co., Costa Mesa, Calif., 1972—. Mem. Am. Fedn. Musicians, Costa Mesa C. of C. Democrat. Club: Jaks and Jils of Orange County. Home and Office: 358 Hamilton St Costa Mesa CA 92627

HADLEY, LEILA ELIOTT BURTON, author; b. N.Y.C., Sept. 22, 1925; d. Frank V. and Beatrice (Boswell-Eliott) Burton; ed. Green Vale Sch., L.I., St. Timothy Sch., Md.; student U. Witwatersrand, Johannesburg, S. Africa, 1954-55, also postgrad.; children by previous marriages —Arthur T. Hadley III, Victoria Smitter Barlow, Matthew Smitter, Caroline Smitter. Books: Give Me the World, 1958; How to Travel with Children in Europe, 1963; Manners for Children, 1967; Fielding's Guide to Traveling with Children in Europe, 1972, rev. edit. 1974; Traveling with Children in the U.S.A., 1977; Tibet, Twenty Years after the Chinese Takeover, 1979; contbr. articles to newspapers and mags. including Saturday Evening Post, Diplomat, McCall's, Harpers Bazaar, Newsday, Ladies' Home Jour., N.Y. Times; asso. editor Saturday Evening Post, N.Y.C., 1965-67; asso. editor Diplomat Mag., N.Y.C., 1964-65; book reviewer Palm Beach (Fla.) Life, 1967-72. Mem. Royal Soc. Asian Affairs (London), Asia Soc., Women's Nat. Book Assn., Soc. Woman Geographers. Presbyterian. Club: Nat. Press. Home: 300 E 75th St New York NY 10021

HAEFER, ELAINE JUNE, bus. exec.; b. Reedsburg, Wis., July 9, 1946; d. Maynard Leslie and Phyllis June (Prouty) Colvin; student Madison Area Tech. Coll., 1964-65; m. LaMoine Vern Haefer, Sept. 4, 1965; children—Jenine Ellen, Denise Kay. Legal sec., 1964-65; stenographer State of Wis., 1965-66; exec. sec. Mass. Mut. Life Ins. Co., Madison, Wis., 1971-72; bookkeeper Amp Electric Co., Monona, Wis., 1972—, v.p., 1978—; bookkeeper Action Heating and Air Conditioning, Monona, 1977—, asst. sec.-treas., 1979—. Vol., ARC; leader 4-H Club. Lutheran. Home: 6223 Winnequah Rd Monona WI 53716 Office: 103 Owen Rd Monona WI 53716

HAEGEN, FLORENCE VIRGINIA, former polit. party ofcl.; b. Lincoln, Nebr., May 6, 1925; d. Branson Washburn and Claudia Birdie (Chaplin) Stewart; student Colo. Coll., 1943-45; B.A., Coll. of Great Falls, 1971; m. Leo Francis Haegen, Jan. 31, 1946; children—Noel (Mrs. A.J. Hauser), Stewart, Leslie Ruth, Prentice, Allison Priscilla. Tchr., Fergus County High Sch., Lewistown, Mont., 1966-72; precinct committeewoman, 1952-80; county chmn. Fergus County, 1971-73; vice chmn. Mont. Republican Party, 1973-75, chmn., 1975-79; mem. exec. com. Rep. Nat. Com., until 1979. Vice chmn. Western States Chmns. Assn., 1975-79; candidate for Rep. nomination for gov. Mont., 1980; active Mont. Fedn. Rep. Women. Mem. LWV, Internat. Platform Assn., Mont. Cowbelles, Fergus County Cowbelles. Club: Order Eastern Star. Home: Three Smokes Ranch Buffalo MT 59418

HAEGER, PHYLLIS M., assn. mgmt. co. exec.; b. Chgo., May 20, 1928; d. Milton O. and Ethel M.; B.A., Lawrence U., 1950; M.A., Northwestern U., 1952. Midwest editor Tide Mag., Chgo., 1952-55; exec. v.p. Smith, Bucklin & Assos., Inc., Chgo., 1955-78; pres. P. M. Haeger & Assos., Inc., Chgo., 1978—. Mem. Nat. Assn. Women Bus. Owners, Am. Soc. Assn. Execs., Chgo. Soc. Assn. Execs., Inst. Assn. Mgmt. Cos., Chgo. Fin. Exchange, Chgo. Network. Club: Chgo. Execs. Office: P M Haeger & Assos Inc 500 N Michigan Ave Chicago IL 60611

HAFER, MARILYN DURHAM, psychologist; b. Guthrie, Okla., Feb. 10, 1924; d. Walker Philip and Elizabeth (Gooch) Durham; student U. Okla., 1941-42; B.A., Tex. Woman's U., 1966; Ph.D., Tex. Tech. U., 1971. Bank teller First State Bank, Guthrie, Okla. and Odessa, Tex., 1944-57; asst. prof. dept. psychology Ill. Inst. Tech., Chgo., 1971-77; asst. prof. mgmt. rehab. services Adminstrn. Studies Center, DePaul U., Chgo., 1977-78; psychologist U.S. CSC, Chgo., 1977-79; asso. prof. Rehab. Inst., So. Ill. U., Carbondale, 1979—. NSF fellow, 1966-70; Southwestern Psychol. Assn. and Psi Chi cert., 1977; registered psychologist, Ill. Mem. Nat. Rehab. Adminstrs. Assn. (chmn. legis. com. 1979-80), Am. Psychol. Assn., Nat. Rehab. Assn., Nat. Rehab. Adminstrn. Assn., Ill. Rehab. Assn. Democrat. Contbr. articles to profl. jours.; cons. editor Jour. Rehab. Adminstrs., 1978, 81—, Research and the Retarded, 1978-79, Vocat. Evaluation and Work Adj. Bull., 1980—. Home: 2021 A Woodriver Dr Carbondale IL 62901 Office: Rehab Inst So Ill Univ Carbondale IL 62901

HAFFORD, SAUNDRA BURRIS, banker; b. Pontiac, Mich., July 9, 1950; d. Thomas and Frances Kay (Bessent) Burris; diploma Taylor Bus. Inst., N.Y.C., 1970, N.H. Coll., Manchester, 1974. Various secretarial positions, 1968-70, 72-73; substitute tchr. Milford (N.H.) Area Sr. High Sch., 1973-74; with Bankeast, Bedford, N.H., 1974—, br. teller supr., 1977-78, br. mgr., 1978—. Dir. Miss Bedford Pagent, 1980, 81; asst. producer Miss N.H. Pageant, 1980, 81. Mem. Nat. Assn. Bank Women, Bedford Mall Mchts. Assn. (pres. 1980). Address: 473 Hevey St Manchester NH 03102

HAGAN, SHIRLEY SMITH, med. technologist; b. Sherman, Tex., Apr. 20, 1936; d. J.B. and Frances Winnifred (Groce) Smith; diploma med. tech., Parkland Meml. Hosp., Dallas, 1961; B.S., Southeastern Okla. State U., 1977; M.S., Tex. Woman's U., 1981; m. George Phillip Hagan, Apr. 16, 1954; children—Philip Ray, Stephen Russell. Med. technologist hosps. in Tex., 1956-75; instr. med. lab. tech. Grayson County Coll., Denison, Tex., 1974—. Mem. Am. Soc. Clin. Pathologists (affiliate), Am. Soc. Med. Technologists, Tex. Soc. Med. Technologists, Tex. Jr. Coll. Tchrs. Assn. Baptist. Home: PO Box 684 Sherman TX 75090 Office: 6101 Grayson Dr Denison TX 75020

HAGARTY, LOIS SHERMAN, state legislator, lawyer; b. Phila., Sept. 28, 1948; d. Daniel and Evelyn (Wolpert) Sherman; B.S. cum laude in Edn., Temple U., 1970, M.S. in Edn., 1973; J.D., Temple U., 1976; m. John Joseph Hagarty, June 9, 1974; 1 son, Mathew Sherman. Elem. tchr. Upper Merion Area (Pa.) Public Schs., 1970-73; admitted to Pa. bar, 1976; trial atty. Montgomery County Dist. Atty.'s Office, 1976-79, 1st asst. dist. atty., 1979-80; rep. Pa. Legislature, 1980—. Mem. Montgomery County Bar Assn., Pa. Bar Assn. Republican. Jewish. Office: House of Representatives Box 175 Main Capitol Bldg Harrisburg PA 17120

HAGEN, EILEEN LOUISE, psychologist; b. Cleve., Aug. 23, 1947; d. Robert Charles and Margaret Rose (Zachar) H.; B.A., Case Western Res. U., 1971; M.A., Ohio State U., 1972, Ph.D., 1975. With Exxon Co., 1975-81, indsl. organizational psychologist, Linden, N.J., 1978-81; with AT&T Long Lines, Bedminster, N.J., 1981—; adj. staff mem. Profl. Counseling Center, Westfield, N.J., 1982—; cons. in field. Lic. psychologist, N.Y. Mem. Am. Psychol. Assn. Office: PO Box 23 Linden NJ 07036

HAGEN, UTA, actress; b. Gottingen, Germany, June 12, 1919; d. Oskar F. L. and Thyra A. (Leisner) H.; D.F.A. (hon.), Smith Coll., 1978, Wooster Coll., 1982; L.H.D. (hon.), De Paul U., 1981; m. Herbert Berghof, Jan. 24, 1951; 1 dau., Leticia. Played Ophelia, Dennis, Mass., 1937, Nina in Sea Gull, N.Y.C., 1938, Key Largo, 1939, Vicki, 1942, Othello, 1943-45; appeared in (plays) Whole World Over, Faust, Masterbuilder, 1947, Angel Street, 1948, Street Car Named Desire, 1948, 50, Country Girl, 1950, G.B. Shaw's Saint Joan, 1951-52, Tovarich, City Center, 1952, In Any Language, 1952, The Deep Blue Sea, 1953, The Magic and the Loss, 1954, The Island of Goats, 1955, A Month in the Country, 1956, Good Woman of Setzuan, 1957, Who's Afraid of Virginia Wolff, 1962-64, The Cherry Orchard, 1968, Charlotte, 1980 (also univ. tour 1981-82), (films) The Other, 1972, The Boys from Brazil, 1978; TV appearances include A Month in the Country, 1956, Out of Dusk, 1959; tchr. acting Herbert Berghof Studio, N.Y.C., 1947—. Recipient Antoinette Perry award, 1951, 63; N.Y. Drama Critics award, 1951, 63; Donaldson award best actress, 1951; London Critics award for best actress 1963-64 season; Outer Circle award; named to Theatre Hall of Fame, 1981. Author: Respect for Acting, 1973; Love for Cooking, 1976; Sources, 1982. Address: Herbert Berghof Studio 120 Bank St New York NY 10014

HAGENS, LOYCE MCGEHEARTY, psychologist; b. Henderson, Tex., May 31, 1920; d. Edwin Hannaford and Ada Izetta (Hollingworth) Dawson; B.S., U. Tex., Austin, 1941, M.Ed., 1950, Ph.D., 1965; m. Robert Charles Hagens, July 24, 1971; children by previous marriage—Michael Jerome McGehearty, Patrick McGehearty. Lectr. U. Tex., Austin, 1960-63, field coordinator, 1963-66; asst. prof. S.W. Tex. State U., San Marcos, 1964-66; dir. guidance services, prof. psychology U. Corpus Christi (Tex.), 1966-73; prof. psychology Corpus Christi State U., 1975—; pvt. practice psychotherapy, Corpus Christi, 1972—; cons. in field to drug abuse councils, adult treatment centers, Head Start programs, 1972—; mem. adv. bd. Pastoral Counseling Center, 1973—; mem. bd. Assn. Family Counseling Service, 1970-72, Inst. for Child Devel., 1972-73, Parents without Partners, 1969-71, Women's Shelter, 1977-78 (all Corpus Christi); vice chmn. com. on children, youth and families Coastal Bend Council Govts., 1978-79 NDEA grantee, 1967-68. Mem. S.W. Psychol. Assn., Tex. Sch. Psychologist Assn., Am. Personnel and Guidance Assn., Am. Sch. Counselors Assn., Assn. Counselor Educators and Suprs., Assn. Measurement and Evaluation in Guidance, Nat. Vocat. Guidance Assn., Tex. Personnel and Guidance Assn., Tex. Assn. Counselor Educators and Suprs., Tex. Soc. Coll. Tchrs. in Edn. Democrat. Methodist. Column editor: Elem. Counseling, 1969-74; contbr. articles to profl. publs. Home: 5448 Stonegate Way Corpus Christi TX 78411 Office: 4330 S Alameda St Corpus Christi TX 78412

HAGENSON, MARY JANE SKOGEN, biomed. engr.; b. Blue Earth, Minn., Dec. 16, 1951; d. Norman Stanley and Virjean Loy (Thorland) Skogen; B.S. in Physics and Math., Iowa State U., 1974, M.S. in Biomed. Engring. (Coulter Electronics fellow), 1976, Ph.D. (N.W. Coll. and Univ. Assn. for Sci. fellow), 1980; m. Randy Lee Hagenson, Mar. 5, 1971; children—Leigh Christine, Lara Catherine. Grad. research asso. Los Alamos Sci. Lab., 1975-79; dir. flow cytometry facility U. Iowa, Iowa City, 1979-80; research asso. Iowa State U., Ames, 1980—. Mem. AAAS, Iowa Acad. Sci., Sigma Xi. Patentee (with Gary C. Salzman) parabolic cell analyzer. Home: 215 Cypress Dr Huxley IA 50124 Office: 10 Curtiss Hall Dept Genetics Iowa State U Ames IA 50011

HAGER, THRESSA MAY, nursing supr.; b. Centre County Center Hall, Pa., Apr. 14, 1914; d. Charles Edgar and Blanch Esther (Reiber) Fye; R.N., Conemaugh Valley Meml. Hosp., 1935; m. Arlie Clyde Hager, July 4, 1954. Staff nurse Centre County Hosp., Bellefonte, Pa., 1935-39, head nurse operating room, 1939-47; head nurse operating room DePaul Hosp., Norfolk, Va., 1948-49; clin. nurse USPHS Hosp., Norfolk, 1949-54, head nurse out-patient dept., 1954-72, asst. dir. nursing, 1972—, supervisory clin. nurse, 1980—. Recipient Superior Performance award USPHS Hosp., 1955, Quality Performance award,

1974. Mem. Am. Nurses Assn., Va. Nurses Assn., Nat. Assn. Parliamentarians. Methodist. Clubs: Eastern Star, Ladies Oriental Shrine N. Am., Daus. Nile, Royal Order Jesterrettes, Toastmistress. Home: 8840 Granby St Norfolk VA 23503 Office: 6500 Hampton Blvd Norfolk VA 23508

HAGERMAN, RAE LAVONNE, med. technologist; b. St. Helen's, Oreg., Mar. 28, 1932; d. Raymond Fredrick and Ruth Eliza (Rubens) Stroud; student Multonomah Jr. Coll., 1950-52, Lewis and Clark Coll., 1953-54, B.S., 1954; M.T., Good Samaritan Med. Tech., 1955; m. David Harvey Hagerman, May 29, 1951; children—Frederick, Barbara, Susan. Med. technologist Good Samaritan Hosp., Portland, Oreg., 1955-57; gen. med. technologist Holladay Park Hosp., Milwaukie, Oreg., 1958—, lab. mgr., 1962—. Pres. bd. Dwyer Holladay Fed. Credit Union, 1975-82, supervisory chmn., 1982—. Mem. Am. Soc. Med. Technologists, Am. Soc. Clin. Pathologists, Coll. Am. Pathologists. Club: Happy Rock's Sq. Dance. Address: 13121 SE Briggs St Milwaukie OR 97222

HAGERTY, MARGARET SOMERS FREY (MRS. FRANCIS W. HAGERTY), broadcasting exec.; b. Moline, Ill.; d. Harry and Helen (Somers) Frey; student Christian Coll., 1937-38, Parsons Coll., 1938-39; B.A., Grinnell Coll., 1941; m. Francis W. Hagerty, Apr. 30, 1960. Acting city editor Fairfield (Ia.) Daily Ledger, 1943-44; office mgr., prodn. mgr., media dir., sec.-bookkeeper R. L. Sines & Assos. Advt., San Francisco, 1946-47; tchr. pub. schs., Newburg, Ia., 1948; promotion asst. radio sta. KOMO, 1948-50, promotion mgr., 1950-53; advt. and promotion mgr. KOMO-TV, Seattle, 1953-72, mgr. press relations, 1972—. Mem. Nat. Acad. Television Arts and Scis., P.E.O., Broadcast Promotion Assn. Methodist. Home: 6543 46th St NE Seattle WA 98115 Office: 100 4th Ave N Seattle WA 98109

HAGGART, VERONICA A., govt. ofcl., lawyer; b. Lincoln, Nebr., Sept. 6, 1949; B.A., U. Nebr., 1971; J.D., Georgetown U., 1976. Admitted to D.C. bar; spl. asst. to asst. sec. U.S. Dept. Agr., 1973-75; law clk. criminal div. U.S. Dept. Justice, Washington, 1975; law clk. firm Cole Corette & Bradfield, 1976; asso. firm Pope Ballard & Loos, 1978-81; partner firm Heron, Haggart, Ford, Burchette & Ruckert, Washington, 1981; mem. U.S. Internat. Trade Commn., Washington, 1982—. Office: US Internat Trade Commn 701 E St NW Washington DC 20436 *

HAGGER, ZAREF BARBARA, restauranteur; b. Duluth, Minn., June 13, 1915; d. Charles Mitri and Mary (Batach) Saloum: student Duluth Bus. Coll., 1934-36; m. George Frederick Hagger, May 24, 1937; 1 son, Charles Joseph. Mgr. Gophershoe Rebuilder Shop, 1936-38; head dept. time and statistics Chance Vought Aircraft Co., Stratford, Conn., also Dallas, 1943-51; mgr. Venture Inn, Corry, Pa., 1969-72; co-owner, mgr. Colonial Squire Restaurant, Ripley, N.Y., 1972—. Pres., Corry YMCA Aux., Corry Meml. Hosp. Aux.; chmn. Corry Centennial Ball; pres. Lillian Guild, Emmanuel Episcopal Ch.; bd. dirs. Erie County March of Dimes, 1968-73. Named Woman of Year by Corry Citizens, 1968. Served to lt. ARC Motor Corps, 1942-45. Mem. Corry C. of C. (tourist promotion com. chmn. 1970-71). Republican. Clubs: Corry Country, Lakdeview Country, Order Eastern Star. Home: RD 3 W Columbus Ave Corry PA 16407 Office: RD 3 Box 460 Turnpike Rd Corry PA 16407

HAGGERTY, CHARLOTTE FRANCES, recreation co. exec.; b. Cleve., May 16, 1930; d. George Walter and Anna Marie (Kapitan) Mueller; m. Ambrose G. Haggerty, Sept. 16, 1950; children—Thomas Patrick, Patricia Ann. Mgr., Putt-Putt Golf Course, Middleburgh Heights, Ohio, 1968, Fairlawn, Ohio, 1969; mgr., owner Putt-Putt Golf Course, Willoughby, Ohio, 1970—; owner, pres. Marvanco Enterprises, Inc. DBA Putt-Putt Golf Course, Maple Heights, Ohio, 1975—, Tom-Pat Enterprises, Inc. DBA Putt-Putt Golf Course of Milw., 1978—; partner, Chattanooga, Tenn., 1981—; owner Up to Par Ltd., Inc., Willoughby, Ohio, 1980—, North Olmstead, Ohio, 1981—, Cleve. Area Advt. Co., Willoughby. Named Mrs. Putt-Putt in U.S., 1972. Mem. Profl. Putters Assn. (dir. 1979-80), Willoughby C. of C. (trustee 1979-81). Office: 36212 Euclid Ave Willoughby OH 44094

HAGLUND, ELAINE JEAN, educator; b. Los Angeles, Apr. 1, 1937; d. Vernon U. and Lucile Bernadine Haglund; B.A., UCLA, 1958; Ph.D., Mich. State U., 1972. Tchr. pub. schs., Berkeley, Calif., W.Ger., Japan, 1958-69; asst. prof. Calif. State U., Long Beach, 1972-75, dir. Ednl. Psychology Clinic, 1975-78; prof. ednl. psychology and human devel., acad. supr. Internat. Edn. Ctr., 1978-82; prof. English, Hangchow (China) U., 1982-83; marriage, family and child counselor, Long Beach, 1975—. Fulbright-Hays grantee, 1978-80; NDEA grantee, summer 1968; EPDA grantee, summer 1969. Mem. Am. Psychol. Assn., Soc. for Intercultural Edn., Tng. and Research, Internat. Council of Psychologists, Am. Personnel and Guidance Assn., World Council for Curriculum and Instrn., Council for Ednl. Anthropology, Council for Exceptional Children, Internat. Comparative Edn. Soc., Am. Anthropology Assn., Fulbright-Hays Alumni Assn., Amnesty Internat., Am. Field Service, Am. Humanist Assn. Author: On This Day, 1980; A Resource Guide for Mainsteaming, 1982; contbr. articles to profl. jours. Home: 1111 S Coast Dr J-101 Costa Mesa CA 92626 Office: 1250 Bellflower Blvd Long Beach CA 90840

HAGY, LOIS EULALA, paralegal asst.; b. Bristol, Va., Oct. 22, 1950; d. William Kent and Shirley W. (Downs) Hagy; student U. Md., 1969-74, 76-78, Towson State Coll., 1974-76. Legal sec. O'Conor & Sweeney, Balt., 1968-72; asst. dir. mortgage fin. apts. and office parks div. Monumental Properties, Inc., Balt., 1972-75, project coordinator constrn. regional shopping mall div., 1975-76; with Wolpe Enterprises, Inc., Real Estate Developer and Comml. Leasing, Washington, 1976; office mgr. Stemmy & Tidler, C.P.A.s, College Park, Md., 1977; v.p., sec., treas. Metro Builders, Inc., Washington, 1977-80, also dir. residential and comml. renovation, constrn. mgmt., project mgr. condominium conversions; real estate broker David Bandy Real Estate, Washington, 1980-81; paralegal asst. firm Goodell, Landfield, Becker and Green, Washington, 1981—; dir. Capital Devel. Corp., Stemmy & Tidler, Metro Builders, Inc. Notary public. Mem. Washington Bd. Realtors. Home: 1508 17th St NW Washington DC 20036 Office: 1220 19th St NW Washington DC 20036

HAHN, BERNICE ELIZABETH, nurse; b. Askam, Wilkes-Barre, Pa., Nov. 22, 1920; d. Fran and Sophia (Blaszczak) Tanski; R.N., Allentow (Pa.) Hosp., 1943; postgrad. Cook County Sch. Nursing, Chgo., 1944; m. Carl Leonard Hahn, Jan. 4, 1947; children—Carl Leonard, Susan Marguerite. Head nurse emergency room clinics Allentown Hosp., 1944-48, staff nurse emergency room clinics, 1966-74; pvt. duty nurse, 1949-66; charge nurse Lehigh Structural Steel Co., Allentown, 1974—. Recipient Meritorious Service award USPHS, 1945. Mem. Nat. Fedn. Occupational Health Nurses, Am. Nurses Assn., Am. Assn. Bus. and Profl. Women, Pa. Nurses Assn., Berks County Assn. Indsl. Nurses, Allentown Hosp. Alumni Assn. (life), Lehigh County Hist. Soc., St. Catherine's Woman's Alliance. Republican. Roman Catholic. Home: 331 N Franklin St Allentown PA 18102 Office: 1 Allen St Allentown PA 18105

HAHN, EMILY, author; b. St. Louis, Mo., Jan. 14, 1905; d. Isaac Newton and Hannah (Schoen) Hahn; B.S., U. Wis., 1926; postgrad. Columbia U., 1928-29, Oxford U., 1934-35; m. Charles R. Boxer, Nov. 28, 1945; children—Carola, Amanda. Mining engr. Deko Oil Co., St. Louis, 1926; courier, Santa Fe, 1927-28; instr. geology Hunter Coll., N.Y.C., 1929-30; with Red Cross in Belgian Congo, 1930-31; writer of stories and scenarios, N.Y.C. and Hollywood, also travels and newspaper work in Eng., Continent and North Africa, 1931-32; instr. English and writing Customs Coll., Shanghai, China, 1935-38, Chungking, China, 1940; instr. Customs U., Hong Kong. 1941. Author books including Hongkong Holiday, 1946; China A to Z, 1946; Picture Story of China, 1946; Raffles of Singapore, 1946; Miss Jill, 1947; England to Me, 1949; Purple Passage, 1950; Love Conquers Nothing, 1952; Chiang Kai-Shek, 1955; Diamond, 1956; The Tiger House Party, 1959; China Only Yesterday, 1963; China to Me, 1963; Indo, 1964; Africa to Me, 1964; Animal Gardens, 1967; Times and Places, 1970; On the Side of the Apes, 1971; Once Upon a Pedestal, 1974; Mabel, 1977; Look Who's Talking, 1978; Love of Gold, 1981. Interned by Japanese govt. Dec. 1941; returned to U.S. on Gripsholm Dec. 1943. Address: care Brandt & Brandt 1501 Broadway New York NY 10036 *

HAHN, LORENA GRACE, nurse; b. Kalvesta, Kans., Apr. 16, 1914; d. Albert H. and Myrtle (Bingham) Barnes; student Los Angeles County, U. So. Calif. Sch. Nursing, 1944-47, also numerous profl. courses; m. Robert Elwyn Hahn, May 2, 1935. Tchr. tng. Kans. State Normal Sch., 1934-35; Wesleyan ministerial tng. course, including counseling youth career tng., pub. speaking, 1935-44; staff nurse Los Angeles County Sch. Nursing, 1947-50; head nurse Los Angeles County-U. So. Calif Med. Center, 1950—; staff nurse White Meml. Med. Center, 1967—. Recipient 37 yr. perfect attendance cert. Los Angeles County-U. So. Calif. Nurses Alumni Assn., County of Los Angeles Health Dept., 39 Yr. Service award Los Angeles County-U. So. Calif. Med. Center, 1974, Outstanding Employee Recognition award, 1977, 16 Yr. Service award White Med. Center, 1977, Faculty Achievement award, 1982; named Nurse of Yr., C.A.R.E.S. 1981; cert. critical nurse. Mem. Am., Calif., Region 6 nurses assns., Am. Assn. Critical Care Nurses, Nat. Critical Care Inst. Edn., Los Angeles County U.-So. Calif. Nurses Alumni Assn., Nat. Honor Soc. (hon. life). Republican. Home: 2431 Sichel St Apt 207 Los Angeles CA 90031

HAIGHT, DONNA MARIE, chem. mfg. co. sales exec.; b. Prineville, Oreg., Sept. 30, 1950; d. Don Forrester and Leone Minerva (Graham) H.; student Eastern Oreg. Coll., 1968-70; B.S., Oreg. State U., 1972. Vol., Peace Corps, Nepal, 1972-74; tech. sales rep. Am. Cyanamid Co., 1975—, asst. to mktg. mgr., Wayne, N.J., 1979, dist. sales mgr., Charlotte, N.C., 1979-81, sales specialist, Ocala, Fla., 1981—. Recipient Extra Effort award Am. Cyanamid Co., 1978. Mem. Water Pollution Control Fedn., Bus. and Profl. Women (named Young Career Woman, Cardinal club Charlotte and Dist. VII, N.C. 1980), Hunger Project. Home: 300 NE 52d Ct Ocala FL 32670 Office: PO Box 32787 Charlotte NC 28232

HAIL, BARBARA ANDREWS (MRS. EDWARD G. HAIL), museum curator; b. Phila., Nov. 2, 1930; d. James Wickersham and Elizabeth Alice (Woolridge) Kirk; student (Elisha Benjamin Andrews scholar) Brown U., 1948-50; A.B., Cornell U., 1952, A.M., 1953; postgrad. (Danforth Grad. fellow) Columbia U., 1965-67; m. Peter B. Andrews, Dec. 23, 1950 (dec. 1964); children—Clinton J., Elizabeth D., Cynthia K.; m. 2d, Edward G. Hail, May 29, 1969; stepchildren—Ted, Andrew, Peter, Elinor. Tchr. history high sch., Ithaca, N.Y., 1953-54; edn. coordinator Haffenreffer Mus. Anthropology, Brown U., Bristol, R.I., 1968-72, asst. curator, 1972-77, asso. curator, 1977-82, chief curator, 1982—. Mem. R.I. Women's Intergroup Com., 1971-72; mem. R.I. New Democratic Coalition, 1971-72; bd. dirs. Luethi-Peterson Internat. Camps, George Hail Free Library, 1978—. Nat. Endowment Arts fellow, 1975. Mem. Am. Assn. Museums, Phi Beta Kappa. Club: Lake Placid (N.Y.). Author: Hau, Kola! A Catalogue of the Plains Indian Collection of the Haffenreffer Museum of Anthropology. Home: 220 Rumstick Point Rd Barrington RI 02806 Office: Haffenreffer Museum Mount Hope Grant Bristol RI 02809

HAILEY, EVELYN MOMSEN, state senator; b. St. Paul, Apr. 12, 1921; d. Charles Bowers and Anne Lyles (Offutt) Momsen; student George Washington U., 1939-40, U. Hawaii, 1940-41; m. Robert Hailey, Mar. 26, 1943; children—Anne Momsen, Robert Harwell, Christopher Thomas. Mem. Va. Ho. of Dels., 1974-82, Va. Senate, 1982—. Mem. Va. Mental Health Adv. Council, 1978—. Bd. dirs. Chesapeake Bay Found., Va. Mental Health Assn.; past local pres. PTA, LWV. Recipient Lamp Lighter award Norfolk (Va.) Edn. Assn., 1975; life mem. Va. PTA. Democrat. Methodist.

HAIMOWITZ, NATALIE READER, psychologist; b. N.Y.C., May 27, 1923; d. Philip and Esther (Fetner) Reader; B.A., Bklyn. Coll., 1944; M.A. in Clin. Psychology, Ohio State U., 1945; Ph.D. in Human Devel., U. Chgo., 1948; m. Morris L. Haimowitz, Dec. 31, 1948; children—Carla, Myrna, Louise. Research asst. com. on human devel. U. Chgo., 1945-46; lectr. Bklyn. Coll., 1947-48; instr. U. Chgo., 1953-58; pvt. practice psychology, Evanston, Ill. and Kenosha, Wis., 1955—; chief psychologist Women's and Children's Hosp., Chgo., 1955-59; psychologist Milw. Psychiat. Services, 1960-64; co-dir. Haimowoods Inst., 1972—. Mem. Am. Psychol. Assn., Internat. Transactional Analysis Assn., Assn. Advancement of Psychotherapy. Author: (with Morris Haimowitz) Human Development, 1960, Suffering is Optional, 1976. Home and office: 1101 Forest Ave Evanston IL 60202

HAINES, DOROTHEA MARY, acctg. co. exec.; b. Chgo., Oct. 20, 1948; d. Daniel Stanley and Dorothea Mary Hejna; grad. Calif. State U., Fullerton, 1982; m. James Hewson Haines, Apr. 27, 1979; children—Michelle, Christine. Co-founder, acct., chief exec. officer Profls. Tax & Fin. Services, Costa Mesa, Calif., 1979—. Mem. Nat. Assn. Public Accts., Inland Soc. Tax Cons., Nat. Assn. Female Execs., Roman Catholic. Office: 1503 S Coast Dr Suite 315 Costa Mesa CA 92626

HAINES, GAIL KAY, author; b. Mt. Vernon, Ill., Mar. 15, 1943; d. Samuel Glenn and Audrey Claire (Goin) Beekman; A.B. in Chemistry, Washington U., St. Louis, 1965; m. Michael Philip Haines, May 8, 1964; children—David Michael, Cindy Lynn. Analytical chemist Mallinckrodt Chem. Works, St. Louis, 1965-70, freelance writer, 1970—; author: The Elements, 1972; Fire, 1975; Explosives, 1976; Supercold/Superhot, 1976; What Makes a Lemon Sour?, 1977; Natural and Synthetic Poisons, 1978; Brainpower, 1979; Cancer, 1980; Cooking on a Can, Baking in a Box, 1981; Test Tube Mysteries, 1982. Mem. Am. Chem. Soc., Authors Guild. Address: 4145 Lorna Ct SE Olympia WA 98503

HAINES, J. PAGE, newspaper ofcl.; b. Falfurrias, Tex., July 26, 1948; d. Marion Siegal and Janis Marie (Newman) Calhoun; B.A. in Journalism, Tex. Tech U., 1970; M.B.A., U. Houston, 1982; m. C.L. Haines, May 16, 1970. Asst. spl. events mgr. Houston Post, 1971-72, spl. events mgr., 1973-74, circulation promotion mgr., 1974-78; creative mgr. promotion Houston Chronicle, 1978-80, spl. projects mgr. sales and mktg., 1981—; del. White House Conf. on Small Bus., 1980; vice chmn. nat. adv. council SBA, 1980-81. Bd. dirs. Houston March of Dimes, 1979-81. Mem. Houston Advt. Fedn. (various awards), Internat. Newspaper Promotion Assn., Internat. Circulation Mgrs. Assn., Presbyterian. Club: River Oaks Women's Breakfast. Home: 534 Foxbriar Ln Sugarland TX 77478 Office: 801 Texas Ave Houston TX 77002

HAINESWORTH, MARILYN BRYANT, accountant; b. Warren, Ohio, Feb. 27, 1947; d. William and Rovenia (Brogdon) Bryant; B.A. in Acctg., Hiram (Ohio) Coll., 1981; postgrad. Baldwin Wallace Coll.; m. Wayne Hainesworth, Mar. 28, 1964; children—Melani Lynn, Mario Dwayne. Acct., Packard Electric Co., Warren, 1965—; acct., mgr. Williams Electric Co., Warren, 1975—. Exec. adv. Warren Jr. Achievement. Mem. Nat. Assn. Female Execs., Distributive Edn. Clubs Am., Kent State U. Alumni Assn., Assn. M.B.A. Execs., Hiram Coll. Alumni Assn. Office: E&R Bldg N River Rd Warren OH 44483 also 2855 Peerless St Warren OH 44485

HAINSKI, MARTHA BARRIONUEVO, biochemist; b. Buenos Aires, Argentina, Feb. 18, 1932; d. Ricardo and Balbina (Bargados) Barrionuevo; M.B.A., Pepperdine U., 1980; Ph.D. in Biochemistry, U. Buenos Aires, 1957; m. Steven Hainski, Sept. 22, 1962; 1 dau., Alexandra. Research asso. physiol. chemistry Sch. Medicine, Wayne State U., Detroit, 1957-58; research asso. biochemistry Phila. Gen. Hosp., 1958-63, NIH fellow, 1963-65; asso. biochemist Clin. Lab. Med. Group, Los Angeles, 1965-66; dir. protein chem. research Hyland div. Travenol Labs., Los Angeles, 1966-70; mgr. protein chem., research and devel. Abbott Sci. Products Div., Los Angeles, 1970-76, dir. research and devel., 1977-78; v.p. research and devel. Alpha Therapeutic Corp., Los Angeles, 1978—. Bd. dirs. Purple Circle Hoover High Sch., Glendale, Calif., 1980-81. Recipient Presdl. awards Abbott Labs., 1975, 76, 77. Fellow Am. Inst. Chemists; mem. Am. Chem. Soc., AAAS, Am. Mgmt. Assn. Republican. Roman Catholic. Club: Los Angeles Athletic. Contbr. articles to various publs. Patentee in field. Office: 5555 Valley Blvd Los Angeles CA 90032

HAKES, PATRICIA PALMER, clin. social worker; b. St. Paul, Mar. 18, 1936; d. Theodore Hoover and Harriette (Linzee) Palmer; student U. Colo., 1954-55; B.A. cum laude, U. Minn., 1958; M.S. S.W., U. Tex., 1964; M.S. H.P., S.W. Tex. State U., 1981; 1 dau., Caroline Linzee Hakes. Social worker Child and Family Service, Austin, Tex., 1963-64, Austin Child Guidance Center, 1963-66; supr. Harris County Child Welfare Dept., Houston, 1969-70; dir. social work services Shoal Creek Hosp., Austin, 1971-81; pvt. practice psychotherapy and hosp. consultation, Austin, 1971—; cons. Children's Hosp. Med. Center, Boston, 1967-68, Huth Meml. Hosp., Yoakum, Tex., 1981—; individual care cons. State of Ill. Dept. Mental Health and Developmentally Disabled, 1976—. Apptd. by Austin City Council to bd. advisors Brackenridge Hosp., 1975-78, by Austin Area Conf. Chs. to Chaplaincy Commn. bd. advisors, 1978-80. Clin. social worker, psychotherapist, Tex. Mem. Nat. Assn. Social Workers, Acad. Cert. Social Workers, Tex. Soc. Hosp. Social Work Dirs. (pres., 1981-82), Am. Hosp. Assn. Soc. of Hosp. Social Work Dirs., Am. Orthopsychiat. Assn., Am. Cancer Soc. (med. social work com.), Alpha Phi. Clubs: U. Tex. Alumni Assn., Bus. and Profl. Women's Assn. Office: 720 W 34th St Austin TX 78705

HALASI-KUN, ELISABETH CHRISTINA SZORAD, educator; b. Vrsac, Yugoslavia; came to U.S., 1958, naturalized, 1963; d. Nicholas and Mary Juliana (Honig) Szorad; B.S., Columbia U., 1966, M.A., 1968; M.Ed., U. Munich, 1967; Ph.D., N.Y.U., 1972; m. George J. Halasi-Kun, Mar. 10, 1945; children—Beatrice P., Georgie E. Asst. to librarian Barnard Coll., N.Y.C., 1961-66; instr. German, head div. German, Marymount Manhattan Coll., N.Y.C., 1965-69; assoc. Columbia U., 1971—; asst. prof. Mercer County Coll., 1981—. Mem. AAUP, MLA, Internat. Lenau Soc., Am. Folklore Assn. Author: Oral Epic Poetry of the South-Slavs, 1968; Historical, Cultural and Social Influences in the Epics of Nicholaus Lenau, 1973. Home: 31 Knowles Ave Pennington NJ 08534

HALBERT, JANET ROSE, controller; b. Los Angeles, Apr. 6, 1955; d. Samuel and Edith Lucille (Schwartz) H.; B.S., Calif. State U., Northridge, 1977. Sr. tax acct. Arthur Andersen & Co., Los Angeles, 1977-80; tax staff, Tanner & Mainstain, Los Angeles, 1981; pvt. practice acctg., Los Angeles, 1981—; controller Ind. Outdoor Advt., Inc., 1982—. Bd. dirs. Camp JCA; mem. fiscal mgmt. com. Jewish Family Service; leadership devel. com. Jewish Fedn. Council. C.P.A., Calif. Mem. Am. Inst. C.P.A.s, Calif. Soc. C.P.A.s. Democrat. Jewish. Address: 1910 Malcolm Ave Apt 2 Los Angeles CA 90025

HALBERT, SUSAN WHITMAN, extension assn. adminstr.; b. Columbus, Ga., Jan. 23, 1948; d. Stanley James and Helen Winifred (Meade) Whitman; B.A. cum laude, SUNY, Albany, 1970; M.S., U. Rochester, 1979; m. Dana Lee Halbert, Sept. 6, 1975. Adminstr., U.S. Army Service Club, Vietnam, 1970-73; dir. 4-H edn. programs Coop. Extension Assn. of Monroe County (N.Y.), 1973-80; dir. Anchorage Dist. 4-H Program, mem. faculty U. Alaska, 1980—; cons., trainer in field; pres. Rochester Youth Dir.'s Council; chairperson bd. N.W. Youth Center; mem. program bd. Hillside Children's Center Vis. Friends Program. Com. mem., real estate service vol. 19th Ward Community Assn., Rochester. Decorated Vietnam Civilian Service medal. Mem. N.Y. State Assn. Coop. Extension 4-H Agts. (Spl. Service award 1976), Alaska Assn. Vol. Adminstrs., Nat. Assn. Coop. Extension 4-H Agts. (chairperson urban 4-H com. 1975-77, rep. to nat. paraprofl. staff devel. com. 1978-79), Children's Alliance. Author teaching materials in consumer edn., job preparedness, expanding 4-H ednl. opportunities, other subjects for youth. Office: 2651 Providence Dr Anchorage AK 99508

HALE, JANET B., extension agt.; b. Dickson, Tenn., May 16, 1952; d. Alfred Dalton and Sarah Laverne (Thomas) B.; B.S. in Home Econs., U. Tenn., 1974, postgrad. in Agrl. Extension Edn., 1977-80; m. Darrell E. Hale. Asst. extension agt. agrl. extension service DeKalb County, Tenn., Smithville, from 1974, now asso. extension agt. Bd. dirs. County Softball Assn., 1977, pres., 1978; chmn. Smithville Jamboree Com., 1976-80. Mem. Nat. Assn. Extension 4-H Agts., Tenn. Assn. Extension 4-H Agts. (young agts. award 1979, Disting. Service award 1981, v.p. 1981, pres.-elect 1982), Murfreesboro Area Home Economists, Nat. Assn. Extension Home Economists. Methodist. Home: PO Box 426 Smithville TN 37166

HALE, JANET FRASER, nurse, educator; b. Oak Ridge, Nov. 16, 1946; d. Harvey Reed and Jean Adele (Mueller) Fraser; B.S. (Kellas scholar), Russell Sage Coll., 1968, B.S.N. (U.S. Army Student Nurse fellow), 1968; M.A., Central Mich. U., 1978; m. David R.E. Hale, Dec. 17, 1967; children—Heather Jean, David Fraser. Instr. dept. nursing U. Ky. Community Coll., Hopkinsville, 1978-80; asst. prof. Sch. Nursing, U. Alaska, Anchorage, 1980—. Served with Nurse Corps, U.S. Army, 1967-70. Decorated Army Commendation medal; registered nurse, Calif., Ga., Kans., Ky., N.Y., S.D., Alaska; registered nurse educator. Mem. Am. Assn. Critical Care Nurses, Res. Officers Assn. Office: Sch Nursing Suite 106 U Alaska Fairbanks AK 99701

HALE, JEANNIE GIBBS, assn. exec.; b. Lexington, S.C., Apr. 26, 1938; d. William Edward and Mattie Lee (Ivey) Gibbs; student U. S.C., 1971, Austin Peay State U., 1965-66, also Sacramento City Coll., Balboa Jr. Coll., grad. U.S. Chamber Inst., 1982; m. Nov. 23, 1979; children—Eddie Robert (dec.), Michael Richard (dec.), A. Scott, Scarlett Autumn, Tara (dec.). With A.S. Beck, Columbia, S.C., part-time 1953-56; guidance counselor Escola Americana, Rio De Janeiro, Brazil, 1961-62; with various law firms, 1955-70; sec. S.C. Gov.'s Manpower Office, Columbia, 1970; adminstrv. asst. to v.p. Graves Constrn. Co., Hilton Head Island, S.C., 1971-72, to pres., 1972-73, coordinator, interior decorator, 1972-74; v.p., exec. mgr. sales promotions Carmichael C. of C., 1974-78; exec. v.p. Rosemead C. of C., 1978; v.p. Ft. Worth C. of C., 1978—, also mem. area councils A founder, dir. preservation Charles Jensen Bot. Gardens, Carmichael, 1975; sect. chmn. United Way, 1982. Recipient Outstanding Community Service award, Rosemead, 1978, Carmichael, 1975, 76, 77, 78. Mem. Ft. Worth Bus. and Profl. Women, Am. Mgmt. Assn., Nat. Assn. Female Execs., Am. Soc. Profl. and Exec. Women, U.S. C. of C., Am. C. of C. Execs. Republican. Baptist. Clubs: Ft. Worth, Petroleum, Colonial Country, Woodhaven, Cowtown Carnegians, (a founder, sec.), Sundialers, VIP, HERS. Home: 5501 Chimney

Rock Rd Fort Worth TX 76112 Office: 700 Throckmorton St Fort Worth TX 76120

HALE, JUDY ENGLANT, chemist; b. Canton, Ohio, Mar. 12, 1940; d. John Ramsey and Marie (Scott) Englant; B.S. in Chemistry, Kent (Ohio) State U., 1962; m. Arthur A. Hale, Feb. 2, 1974. Analytical chemist Harshaw Chem. Co., Cleve., 1963-65; chemist Spindle Top Research Co., Lexington, Ky., 1965-66; with Goodyear Tire & Rubber Co., Akron, Ohio, 1966—, mgr. info. services, 1979—. Mem. Am. Chem. Soc., Nat. Assn. Female Execs., Tech. and Bus. Women Goodyear, LWV. Author papers in field. Office: 1144 E Market St Akron OH 44316

HALE, LINDA DIANA, mgmt. cons.; b. E. St. Louis, Ill., Feb. 5, 1942; d. Joseph and Cecelia (Murian) Soffranko; B.A., So. Ill. U., 1972, M.A., 1973. Tchr. piano and organ, 1962-70; research asst. U. Kans., Lawrence, 1972-73; instr. E. Carolina U., Cherry Point, N.C., 1973-74; prin. Hays Assos., mgmt. cons., Washington, 1974-77; dir. social systems research dept. Gen. Research Corp., McLean, Va., 1977-80; sr. cons. Hay Assos., Washington, 1980—; asso. dir. Pres.'s Commn. Mil. Compensation, Dept. Def., 1977-78. Tchr. CPR, 1979-80; counselor Fairfax County Offender Aid and Restoration Program, 1979-80; mem. fin. com. United Methodist Ch., Fairfax, Va., 1980—, vice chmn. adminstrv. bd., 1982—. Mem. Am. Sociol. Assn., So. Sociol. Soc., Am. Compensation Assn., Compensation and Classification Soc., Pi Mu Epsilon. Author, spealer in field. Home: 9804 Ward Ct Fairfax VA 22032 Office: 1110 Vermont Ave NW Washington DC 20005

HALE, MARY HELEN PARKER, univ. adminstr.; b. Merryville, La., May 25, 1920; d. James Carroll and Mollie (Dear) Parker; B.A. in English (scholar), La. Coll., 1940, B.A. in Music, 1940; M.A. in English (fellow), La. State U., 1942; Ph.D. in Fine Arts (hon.), U. Alaska, 1965; m. George Erwin Hale, June 12, 1942; children—John Parker, James Milton, Nancy Anne. Instr., dir choral music, Boston 1944-45, Albany, N.Y., 1945, Washington, 1946-49, Anchorage, 1949-50; dir. Anchorage Community Chorus, 1951-59; founder, dir. Alaska Festival of Music, 1956-62; vice chmn. N.Am. Assembly Arts Agys., 1968-70; coordinator arts and community affiliates offices Anchorage Community Coll. and U. Alaska, Anchorage, 1970-76; dir. public services Anchorage Community Coll., 1977-81, asst. to pres., 1979-81. Founder Alaska Southcentral High Sch. Music Festival, 1950; mem. Alaska Centennial Commn., 1963-65; charter mem. Alaska State Council on Arts, 1966, chmn., 1967-71; founder, mem., sec. Alaska Humanities Forum, 1974-79; mem. adv. bd. No. TV, Inc., 1979—; mem. various coms. Anchorage Multi-Purpose Sr. Center; vice-chmn. citizens adv. council Anchorage Community Coll., 1981—, chmn. scholarship com. Recipient Mayor's Disting. Service award, Anchorage, 1965; 49'er award, elected to Hall of Fame, Alaska Press Club, 1970, 72; Outstanding Vol. award U. Alaska, Anchorage, 1976; Outstanding Alumni award La. Coll., 1979; President's citation Anchorage C. of C., 1979. Mem. Anchorage Arts Council (charter mem.), U. Alaska Anchorage Alumni Assos., Internat. Platform Assn., LWV, AAUW, Nat. Assn. Women Deans, Adminstrs. and Counselors, Mu Phi Epsilon, Beta Sigma Phi (hon.). Presbyterian. Clubs: Anchorage Woman's, Soroptimists (hon. mem., pres. 1956) (Anchorage). Home: Star Route A Box 1635 Anchorage AK 99507

HALEVY, HILDA MARIA, anesthesiologist; b. Havana, Cuba; d. Juan and Raimunda (Valdes) Cheng; B.S., Instituto de Segunda Ensenanza de la Nabana, Havana, 1949; M.D., U. Havana, 1957; m. Simon Halevy, 1968; 1 son, Daniel A. Sr. house physician and surgeon Mother Cabrini Meml. Hosp., N.Y.C., 1957-58; resident in anesthesiology Met. Hosp., N.Y.C., 1958-60; fellow in anesthesiology, various hosps., N.Y.C., 1960-67; attending anesthesiologist Astoria (N.Y.) Gen. Hosp., 1967—; vis. scholar to Mexico, Holand, Israel. Mem. AMA (Physician's Recognition award), Am. Soc. Anesthesiologists, Med. Soc. State N.Y., N.Y. State Soc. Anesthesiologists, Med. Soc. County Queens. Democrat. Jewish. Office: 25-10 30th Ave Astoria NY 11102

HALEY, DEBRA ANN, educator; b. Wichita, Kans., June 14, 1953; d. Robert Gail and Anna Ellen H.; B.S. in Bus. Adminstrn. (acad. scholar), Kans. Newman Coll., 1975; M.B.A., Emporia State U., 1979; postgrad. Okla. State U., 1981—. News reporter KFH-Radio, Wichita, summer 1974; acct. Koch Oil Co., Wichita, 1975-78; instr. mktg., mgmt. Wichita State U., 1979-81, faculty adv. bus. and univ. students, 1980-81; instr. mktg. Okla. State U., Stillwater, 1981—. Mem. Am. Mktg. Assn. Roman Catholic. Home: Apt 211 222 N Duck St Stillwater OK 74074 Office: Coll Bus-Mktg Okla State U Stillwater OK 74074

HALEY, ERTTA REILIO, editor/writer; b. Kuusankoski, Finland, Dec. 18; came to U.S., 1922, naturalized, 1941; d. Andrew and Miina (Rasi) Reilio; B.A., Lake Forest Coll., 1939; M.S. in Journalism, Northwestern U., 1941; postgrad. Ill. Inst. Tech., 1950; children—Bonnie Margaret, Christine Ann, Ronald Guy. Food/women's editor Western Newspaper Union, Community Press Service, Chgo., 1941-67; food editor Nat. Livestock and Meat Bd., Chgo., 1964-69, Cooking Can Be Fun, Sta. WGN-TV, Chgo., 1949-50; mng. editor Chart mag. Ill. Nurses Assn., Chgo., 1970-72; food editor/writer United Dairy (now Am. Dairy Assn.), Des Plaines, Ill., 1973—. Public relations dir. Bethel Nursery Sch., Chgo., 1953-55; active PTA, Darwin Sch. Mem. Women in Communications, Sigma Tau Delta. Office: 6300 N River Rd Rosemont IL 60018

HALEY, JOHNETTA RANDOLPH, educator; b. Alton, Ill., Mar. 19, 1923; d. John Alexander and Willye Ethel (Smith) Randolph; B.S. in Music Edn., Lincoln U., 1945; postgrad. U. Ill., 1947, Washington U., St. Louis, 1958; Mus.M., So. Ill. U., 1972; m. David Haley, Apr. 7, 1947; children—Karen Louise, Michael David. Tchr. piano, voice, choral dir. Lincoln High Sch., East St. Louis, Ill., 1945-48; tchr. music Turner Elem. Sch., Kirkwood, Mo., 1950-55, Turner Jr. High Sch., 1950-55, Niplier Jr. High Sch., 1955-72; assoc. prof. music So. Ill. U., Edwardsville, 1972—, acting dir. East St. Louis campus. Active St. Louis Met. YWCA; chmn. fund raising St. Louis council Girl Scouts Am.; dinner chmn. United Negro Coll. Fund, Inc., 1975-77; nat. chmn. Job Corp Com., Cleve. Job Corps for Girls, 1974-78; treas. Council of Lutheran Chs., 1975—; pres. bd. of curators Lincoln U., 1974—; bd. dirs. Luth. Mission Assn. Recipient Disting. Citizen award St. Louis Argus Newspaper, 1970, Vol. Service award YWCA, 1968, Community Service award Alpha Kappa Alpha, Duchess of Paducah award Paducah, Ky. 1973, Key to City, Gary, Ind., Signal award St. Louis Sentinel Newspaper, 1974; Outstanding Service award Drifters, Inc.; Outstanding Community Service award So. Christian Leadership Conf.; Outstanding Leadership award YMCA, others; named Woman of Year, Greyhound Bus Corp., 1969. Mem. Coll. Mus. Soc., Nat. Choral Dirs. Assn., Artist Presentation Soc., AAUP, Ill. Music Edn. Assn., Assn. Governing Bds. Colls. and Univs. (dir. 1980), Nat. Assn. of Negro Musicians, NAACP, Mid-West Kodaly Music Educators, Urban League, Mu Phi Epsilon, Pi Kappa Lambda, Alpha Kappa Alpha. Lutheran. Clubs: Las Amigas Social, Jack and Jill, Top Ladies of Distinction. Home: 30 Plaza Sq Saint Louis MO 63103 Office: Dept Music Southern Illinois U Edwardsville IL 62026

HALF, MAXINE ELAINE, personnel agy. exec.; b. N.Y.C., Apr. 7, 1924; d. Alfred and Martha (Ernstthal) Levison; student N.Y.U., 1941-44; m. Robert Half, June 17, 1945; children—Nancy Half Asch, Peggy Half Silbert. Office mgr. Ry. Express Agy., N.Y.C., 1941-45; asst. export mgr. 20th Century Fox, N.Y.C., 1945-47; v.p. Robert Half of N.Y., Inc., N.Y.C., 1948; v.p. Robert Half Internat., Inc., franchisor of Robert Half and Accountemps offices in U.S., Can., and Gt. Brit., 1964—. Mem. Assn. Personnel Cons. N.Y., Nat. Assn. Personnel Cons., Nat. Assn. Female Execs. Office: 522 Fifth Ave New York NY 10036

HALFERTY, DIANE HARRIET, land devel. co. exec.; b. Tacoma, Feb. 22, 1937; d. Benjamin and Lavina Eleanor (Simmons) Rosen; student U. Miami (Fla.), 1954-56; B.S., Willamette U., Salem, Oreg., 1958; Tech. Asso. of Law, A.A.S., Edmonds Community Coll. and U. Wash., 1976; m. Guy P. Halferty, III, Apr. 5, 1959; children—Geoffrey David, Denise Diane, Keary Douglas, Courney Caryn. Pres., Creativity Unltd., Inc., Edmonds, Wash., 1966-73; pres. Great Pacific Devel. Co., Inc., Federal Way, Wash., 1975—. Mem. King County Housing Task Force, 1978—, King County Ordinance Adv. Com., 1979—; mem. Land Use Research Council; mem. council Shoreline Sch. Dist. Parent-Tchrs.-Student Assn., 1973, exec. bds. Lake Forest Park Sch., Kellogg Jr. High Sch., 1966-78; chmn. Lake Forest Park Safety Com., 1972; judge AAU, 1978—; mem. King County Juvenile Ct. Guardian ad Litem Program, 1981-82; mem. long-range planning com., action com. Univ. Prep. Acad., 1982-83; co-chmn. Consumers Against Gen. Motors. Mem. LWV, NOW, Assn. Mobile Home Park Owners (v.p. 1980, pres. 1981, bd. dirs. 1982—, chmn. polit. action com.), Wash. State Hunter-Jumper Assn., Wash. State Horse Show Assn., Nat. Assn. Female Execs. Unitarian. Club: Wash. Athletic (asso. mem., community affairs com.). Home: 18036 49th Pl NE Seattle WA 98155

HALICZER, BONNIE DIKMAN, reporter, editor; b. N.Y.C., Sept. 9, 1942; d. George Henry and Ruth (Hymes) Dikman; B.A. in English Edn., U. South Fla., 1968; m. Jonah Henry, Aug. 11, 1963; children—Shera Lyn, Scott Harris. Feature and fashion writer St. Petersburg (Fla.) Times, 1956-64; writer Congl. Quar., Washington, 1961-62; fashion writer Tampa (Fla.) Tribune, 1977—; instr. journalism U. Tampa, 1979. Pres. Tampa Hadassah Group, 1974-76; founder Hillel Sch., Jewish Day Sch., Tampa. Recipient Men's Fashion Assn. Am. award 1980, 81, award J.C. Penney, Mo., 1980. Mem. The Fashion Group, Sigma Delta Chi. Club: Palma Ceia Jr. Women's Westcoast editor Fla. Designer's Quar. mag., 1980—. Contbr. articles to profl. jours. Home: 4804 Culbreath Isles Rd Tampa FL 33609 Office: PO Box 191 Tampa Fl 33601

HALINA, MME. (HALINA JOZEFA LUTOMSKI, MRS. FLOYD MARTIN LUTOMSKI), dance educator, choreographer; b. Lwow, Poland, Feb. 4, 1930; came to U.S., 1947, naturalized, 1950; d. Adam and Katarzyna (Jezierska) Dziekan; student Warsaw Opera Ballet Sch., 1936-38, Wielke Theatre, Lwow, 1939-41; grad. Politechnik, Lwow, 1944; m. Floyd Martin Lutomski, Oct. 31, 1946; children—Norbert Michael, Ilona Maria, Kevin. Dancer, Warsaw Opera Ballet, 1938-39, World's Olympiade, Kiev, Russia, 1939, USO, Germany, 1945-46; producer Dance Capades, 1948—; owner, dir., resident choreographer Sch. of Dance Arts, Elmira and Corning, N.Y. tchr. Nat. Dance Tchrs. Orgns., U.S., P.R., 1950; choreographer children's and classical ballets Kimbo Dance Records, 1954—; founder, artistic dir., choreographer Elmira-Corning Ballet, Inc., 1955—, artistic dir. Nutcracker Suite, 1980 coordinator, also dir. ednl. programs; lectr.; producer, choreographer Four Seasons, 1950, Fairy Doll, 1951, Sleeping Beauty, 1953, 59, 65-67, Nutcracker, 1954, 78-82, Hansel and Gretel, 1955, Cinderella, 1957, 81-82, Les Ballet de Elements, 1958, Schlagobers. 1959, Gaite Parisienne, 1960-61, La Boutique Fantasque, 1961, adaptation of Les Sylphides, 1962, Swan Lake, 1952-64, Masquerade, 1962-63, Snow Maiden, 1964, Copelia, 1965, 68, 70, 77-78, Karnival Kontrasts, 1966, La Bayadere, 1966, Nutcracker, 1969, Aurora's Wedding, 1971, Wooden Prince, 1971, Americana, 1972, La Fille Mal Gardee, 1972, Vignette's Classique-Comedia, 1973, Sylvia, 1974, Cirque, 1975, Am. Alphabet Ballet, 1976, Magic Forest, 1978, Stars and Stripes, 1979, Stardust Trail, 1980, The Americas, 1981; dir., choreographer ballet Nutcracker for Elmira-Corning Ballet, 1965-66, also Red-White and Blue, Comedia del Arte, Masque; dir. Les Petits Riens, 1967; dir. Bicentennial ballet: Witching, Am. Gayeties, Peter and the Wolf, 1976, 80-83, Carnival, Snow White, 1977, Snow Maiden, 1980, Cinderella (Pro Kofiev); staged Once upon a Piper, Interplay, Openspace, 1979; originated Pre Ballet album for presch. age Roper Records, 1977, now chmn. performing arts dept.; lectr. Steuben, Chenung, No. Pa. counties; supr. ballet records Roper label; rep. ballet dept. for Dance Educators Am. to Nat. Council Dance Tchrs' Orgns.; dir. Sch. Dance Arts, Elmira, N.Y., Corning, N.Y.; lectr. Elmira-Corning Sch. Dists., 1969-72, Schulyer County Schs., 1968-71. Recipient Steuben Crystal and Gold award Corning community. Mem. Dance Educators Am. (chmn. ballet exam., com. 1966-67, exec. bd. 1967-69, exec. dir. 1969-71). Roman Catholic. Recs. 36 ballet albums Roper Label, 41 ednl. records. Home: 933 Fassett Rd Elmira NY 14905 Office: 410-14 W Gray St Elmira NY 14905 also 258 Dennison Pkwy E Corning NY 14830

HALL, ADRIENNE A., advt. exec.; b. Los Angeles; d. Arthur E. and Adelina Patty Kosches; B.A., UCLA; m. Maurice Arthur Hall; children—Adam, Todd, Stefanie, Victoria. Co-founder Hall & Levine Advt., Inc., 1960; now vice chmn. Eisaman, Johns & Laws Advt., Inc., Los Angeles; dir. Calif. Life Corp. Exec. com., trustee UCLA; regent, exec. com. Loyola-Marymount U.; mem. pres.'s circle Los Angeles County Mus. of Art; mem. Mex.-Am. Legal Def. and Edn. Fund, Overseas Edn. Fund; Western chmn., mem. exec. com. Com. of 200. Recipient Women in Communications nat. headliner award, 1972; Women of Achievement award, 1981; UCLA Alumni Profl. Achievement award, 1979; Silver Medal of Distinction, Am. Advt. Fedn., 1978, named Woman of Yr., 1973; named Mktg. and Media Decisions Adperson of West, 1982. Mem. Am. Assn. Advt. (chmn. bd. govs.), Western States Advt. Agys. Assn. (pres., leadership in West award 1975), Los Angeles Advt. Club (pres.). Club: Calif. Yacht. Office: 6255 Sunset Blvd Los Angeles CA 90028

HALL, ALIX-MARIE, pub. co. exec.; b. Newburgh, N.Y., July 30, 1941; d. William C. and Alix M. (de Saint Phalle) H.; B.A., Hunter Coll., 1965, M.A., 1972; postgrad. N.Y.U. Math. project editor Am. Book Co., N.Y.C., 1966-69; programming writer, analyst IBM, N.Y.C., 1969-72; sr. editor, sponsoring editor Gregg div. McGraw-Hill Book Co., N.Y.C., 1972-73, coordinator staff projects, exec. dept., 1973-74, editor-in-chief acctg., computing and data processing Gregg div., 1974-77; dir. adminstrn. McGraw-Hill Info. Systems Co., N.Y.C., 1977-78, v.p. adminstrn., 1978—, coordinator guidelines for equal treatment of the sexes, 1974; conf. and seminar leader. Cert. in basic programming and system programming, IBM. Mem. Assn. Computing Machinery. Club: Knickerbocker Toastmasters (ednl. v.p. 1978-79, pres. 1979—). Author: (with others) Introduction to Data Processing, 1977, 83, Data Processing Work Kit, 1977, 83. Home: 333 E 69th St 8K New York NY 10021 Office: 1221 Ave of Americas New York NY 10020

HALL, ANN LOUISE, journalist, author; b. Hartford, Conn., June 17, 1946; d. Frank and Katharine (Birner) Eichinger; B.A., Syracuse U., 1968; m. Daniel Waldron Hall, Jan. 17, 1970; children—Christopher Wagner, Jonathan Lyman. Summer intern Hartford Courant, 1967, religion editor, 1968-71, edn. reporter, 1969-71, mem. State Capitol Bur., 1971-73, book reviewer, 1974—; free-lance writer, 1978—. Recipient Faculty award for service to Sch. Journalism, Syracuse U., 1968. Mem. Women in Communications (pres. Syracuse U. chpt. 1967-68, pres. Conn. chpt. 1972-73, exec. bd., job bank dir. Conn. chpt. 1973—, v.p. for membership Conn. chpt. 1979-81), Sigma Delta Chi, (exec. bd. Conn. chpt. 1972-73). Contbr. to Ency. Year Book, 1969. Home: 40 Croydon Ct Wallingford CT 06492

HALL, ANNE CAROL, engring. co. exec.; b. Medford, Oreg., Mar. 28, 1941; d. Orville W. and Arcola I. (Moore) Taber; student correspondence courses various univs.; student U. Ala., Birmingham, 1980—; m. Richard A. Hall, Oct. 14, 1958; children—Stewart, Teresa, Stanley, Christopher. Cost engr. Bechtel Power Corp., Centralia, Wash. 1971-74; material control estimator Wright-Schuchart-Harbor, Ranier, Oreg., 1974-75; cost. engr. Burns & Roe, Richland, Va., 1975-76; project engr. Temple Industries Contractors, Langview, Va., 1976-77; cost engr. Jelco, Huntington, Utah, 1977-78; estimator Daniel Internat., New Strawn, Kans., 1978-79; project control engr. Rust Engring., Birmingham, Ala., 1979—. Pres. PTA, White Pass Sch. Dist., Randle, Wash., 1965. convenor NOW Lewis County (Wash.), 1972. Mem. Am. Assn. Cost Engrs., Am. Mgmt. Assn., Nat. Assn. Female Execs., Bus. and Profl. Women Am. Club: Toastmasters. Office: PO Box 101 Birmingham AL 35221

HALL, BETTY JEAN, lawyer; b. Richmond, Ky., July 12, 1946; d. James Russell and Lillian Guy Hall; B.A., Berea Coll., 1968; J.D., Antioch Sch. Law, 1976; m. Thomas Michael Burke, Oct. 6, 1979; children—Timothy Michael and Tiffany Michelle (twins). Legal sec. firm Arent, Fox, Kintner, Plotkin & Kahn, Washington, 1968-70; asst. dir. youth program Appalachian Regional Commn., Washington, 1970-73; admitted to D.C. bar, 1977, Va. bar, 1977, Tenn. bar, 1979; asso. firm James W. Lawson, Washington, 1976-77; dir. Coal Employment Project, Oak Ridge, Tenn., 1977-79, gen. counsel, 1979-80, exec. dir., 1980—. Bd. dirs. Highlander Research & Edn. Center, 1978—; mem. steering com. Appalachian Alliance, 1979-82; chmn. Appalachian Research and Edn. Assos., 1979—. Recipient Rockefeller Public Service award, 1981. Mem. Am. Bar Assn. Address: 16221 Sunny Knoll Ct Dumfries VA 22026

HALL, CAROL VIDACOVICH, sales rep.; b. New Orleans, Nov. 26, 1941; d. Vernon Jerome and Anne (Geraci) Vidacovich; B.S., Loyola U., New Orleans, 1963; m. John W. Hall, Jan. 27, 1968. Supervisory technologist to asst. chief technologist pathology dept. Touro Infirmary Hosp., New Orleans, 1963-77; sales rep. Regional Med. Labs., Inc., Pensacola, Fla., 1977-82; regional sales mgr. Biomed. Reference Labs., Inc., Metairie, La., 1982—; quality control cons. Active Goodwill Industries; supporter Gallier House Mus. Mem. New Orleans C. of C., Am. Soc. Clin. Pathologists, Am. Soc. Med. Tech., La. Soc. Med. Tech., New Orleans Soc. Med. Tech. Home: 6508 Ithaca St Metairie LA 70003 Office: 4300 Houma Blvd Suite 201 Metairie LA 70002

HALL, DEANA DAVIS, masonry contractor; b. Seneca, S.C., Sept. 26, 1933; d. Reuben M. and Junie (Richey) Davis; grad. North Greenville Coll.; student DeKalb Coll., 1975; m. William. P. Hall, Dec. 26, 1952; children—Krista, Bill, Alice. With So. Bell Telephone Co., Atlanta, from 1952; office coordinator, sec. H & S Masonry, Inc., Duluth, Ga., 1970, pres., 1975—. Mem. Masonry Assn. Ga., Joan Clancy Hosp. Vol. Service, Gwinnett Christian Women's Assn. of Atlanta. Republican. Methodist. Clubs: Hapeville Garden, Order Eastern Star. Address: 2212 Eagle Ter Duluth GA 30136

HALL, DOROTHY GAY NELL, homebuilder; b. Hatch, N.Mex., July 28, 1941; d. Samuel B. and Estelle R. (Lack) Lusk; student Houston schs.; m. Donald A. Hall, July 30, 1958; children—Donna, Dean, David, Diana. Sec., dir. Superior Homes, Inc., Houston, 1962—; pres., dir. United Thermal Insulators Co., 1980—; founder, dir. Superior Homes Ednl. Found. Active local Pee-Wee and Little League football and baseball, Future Farmers Am., March of Dimes, Leukemia Soc., Lung Assn. Recipient Spl. Ann. Appreciation award Nat. Assn. Women in Constrn., 1976, 77. Mem. Nat. Assn. Home Builders, Am. Builders Assn., Assn. Bldg. Contractors, Sales and Mktg. Council, Tex. Assn. Home Builders, Greater Houston Builders Assn. Democrat. Methodist. Home: 23802 Kuykendahl Tomball TX 77375 Office: PO Box 38290 Houston TX 77088

HALL, ELIZABETH BLODGETT, ret. coll. adminstr.; b. N.Y.C., Nov. 16, 1909; d. Thomas Harper and Margaret Carroll (Kendrick) Blodgett; A.B. magna cum laude, Radcliffe Coll., 1946; Hum.D., (hon.) Am. Internat. Coll., 1965, U. Mass., 1967; m. Livingston Hall, Sept. 13, 1930; children—Thomas Livingston, Margaret Rumsey, Elizabeth Crosby, John Kendrick. Head dept. history Concord (Mass.) Acad., 1948-49, head acad., 1949-63; founder Simon's Rock Coll., Great Barrington, Mass., 1964, pres., 1964-72. Trustee Cambridge Sch., 1946-48, Hall Sch., 1950-67, Mass. Bd. Community Colls., 1968, Simon's Rock Coll., 1964-75, 1979—, Berkshire Sch., 1977-80, Bard Coll., 1979—. Recipient Radcliffe Alumnae Recognition award, 1978; Bard Coll. award, 1982. Mem. New Eng. Assn. Colls. and Secondary Schs., Headmistresses Assn. of the East, (pres. 1956-58), LWV (dir. Mass. 1938-40), Phi Beta Kappa, Pi Beta Phi. Republican. Episcopalian. Author: Through Crowded Ways, 1959; Ladies: 1962, 1962; contbr. articles to profl. jours. Home: Simon's Rock Coll Great Barrington MA 01230

HALL, ELLA TAYLOR, clin. community psychologist; b. Macon, Miss., Nov. 30, 1948; d. Essex and Mamie (Roland) Taylor; B.A., Fisk U., 1971, M.A., 1973; Ph.D., George Peabody Coll., 1978; m. Alan Hall, Oct. 1, 1977; children—Banyikaai Monique, Motiqua Shante. Mental health specialist behavioral sci. div. Meharry Med. Coll., Nashville, 1976-77; asso. psychologist Bronx (N.Y.) Psychiat. Center, 1979; clin. psychologist Wiltwyck Residential Treatment Center, Ossining, N.Y., 1979-81; clin. cons. Abbott House, Irvington, N.Y., 1981—. NIMH trainee; Crusade fellow; Kendall grantee. Mem. Am. Psychol. Assn., Delta Sigma Theta. Episcopalian. Research in field (lit.).

HALL, ELVAJEAN, librarian, author; b. Hamilton, Ill.; d. Henry Nelson and Nellie (Hyer) Hall; A.B., Oberlin Coll., 1930; certificate U. Wis. Library Sch., 1932; M.L.S., Columbia, 1941. Asst. librarian Milw.-Downer Coll., 1932-33; librarian high sch., Elgin, Ill., 1934-37, Milw. U. Sch., 1937-42, Stephens Coll., Columbia, Mo., 1944-46; supr. sch. libraries, Jackson, Mich., 1942-44, Newton, Mass., 1946-75. Instr. Mass. Dept. Edn., 1948; cons. Sch. Library Jour., 1958-63, Grolier Soc., 1959; cons., sch. library expert Library Services br. U.S. Office Edn., Washington, spring 1960; cons. library program Chung Chi Coll., Hong Kong, 1962-63; lectr. Univ. Coll., Dublin, summers 1967-69; lectr. schs. Mem. ALA, Nat. League Am. Pen Women (pres. Boston 1970-72), Am. Assn. Sch. Librarians (nat. recruitment chmn. 1956), NEA. Assn. for Supervision and Curriculum Devel., Women's Nat. Book Assn. (pres. Boston chpt. 1957-59; nat. dir. 1957-62, nat. sec. 1960-62), Authors Guild Am., Am. Assn. U. Women, Kappa Delta, Delta Kappa Gamma. Republican. Author: Books To Build On, 1955; Land and People of Argentina, 1960, 72; Pilgrim Stories, 1962; Argentina Pueblo y Costumbres, 1962; Land and People of Norway, 1963, 72; Pilgrim Neighbors, 1964; The Volga: Lifeline of Russia, 1965; Land and People of Czechoslovakia, 1966; Hong Kong, 1967; The Psalms, 1968; Picture Map Geography of Eastern Europe, 1968; The Proverbs, 1970; (with R.J. Houlehen) Battle for Sales, 1973; Careers in Marketing and Distribution, 1974; Today in Old Boston, 1975; Today in Old New York, 1975; Today in Old Philadelphia, 1976. Contbr. articles and cartoons to ednl. and library jours. Address: 4010 Camelot Dr Apt C-2 Raleigh NC 27609

HALL, ESTHER SUSAN, ednl. adminstr.; b. Bethesda, Md., May 1, 1952; d. Arthur Ryker and Martha Harper Hall; B.A. in Sociology, Guilford Coll., 1974; m. R. Bradley Miller, Dec. 19, 1981. Vol. services coordinator City of Raleigh (N.C.), 1976-78; program cons. Office of Vol. Services, N.C. Dept. Human Resources, Raleigh, 1978-81; dir. tng. and devel. N.C. Friendship Force, U. N.C., Chapel Hill, 1981—. Third vice chmn. Wake County (N.C.) Democratic Party, Raleigh, 1981-83, 3d v.p., 1980-81, editor Phoenix, 1979-80; treas. Young Dems. of N.C., 1980-81. Recipient (N.C.) Gov.'s award, 1980. Mem. Wake Assn. Vol. Adminstrs., N.C. Assn. Vol. Adminstrs. (pres. 1980-81), Assn. Vol. Adminstrs. Episcopalian. Home: 1811 Sunset Dr Raleigh NC 27608 Office: PO Box 12559 Research Triangle Park NC 27709

HALL, EVELYN GAY, educator; b. Roanoke, Va., July 1, 1947; d. William Omer and Hattie Lillie H.; B.S., Coll. William and Mary, 1970; M.S., James Madison U., 1974; Ed.D., U. Va., 1977. Asso. prof. psychol. aspects of sport Sch. Health, Phys. Edn., Recreation and Dance, La. State U., Baton Rouge, 1977—; cons. in sports psychology Nat. Strength Inst., various coll. athletic teams. Auburn U. Young scholar award So. Assn. Phys. Edn. Coll. Women, 1981. Mem. Internat. Soc. Sport Psychology, N. Am. Soc. Psychology of Sport and Phys. Activity, AAHPERD, So. Assn. Phys. Edn. of Coll. Women. Contbr. articles to profl. jours. Home: 1625 Southland Ct Baton Rouge LA 70810 Office: Sch Health Phys Ed Recreation and Dance La State U Baton Rouge LA 70803

HALL, GIMONE TIMOTHEA, author; b. Highland Park, Ill., Apr. 30, 1940; d. Tim L. and Gladys (Gimon) McNamara; B.A., U. Tex., 1962; m. Lawrence C. Hall, July 31, 1963; children—Shannon, Colin. Author: (novels) Blue Taper, 1970; Witch's Sucking, 1970; The Juliet Room, 1973; Devil's Walk, 1971; The Silver Strand, 1972; Hide My Savage Heart, 1976; Rapture's Mistress, 1978; Fury's Sun, Passion's Moon, 1979; Ecstasy's Empire, 1980; The Jasmine Veil, 1982. Mem. Author's Guild. Address: Million Wishes Farm Box 212 Route 1 Ottsville PA 18942

HALL, HARRIET LOUISE, mental health center adminstr.; b. Los Angeles, Oct. 9, 1947; d. Donald Moore and Ethyl Louise (Hartsough) Hall; B.A., Coll. Wooster, 1969; M.A., U. Wis., Madison, 1971, Ph.D., 1973; m. Randy C. Stith, Nov. 26, 1977; children—Carolyn Annaliese Hall-Stith, Daniel Dag Hall-Stith, Timothy Vernon Hall-Stith. Psychologist, dir. inservice tng. Weld Mental Health Center, Greeley, Colo., 1974-78; child advocacy team mgr. Adams County Mental Health Center, Commerce City, Colo., 1978-80; dep. dir. clin. programs, 1980-81; asso. dir. programs Jefferson County Mental Health Center, Wheat Ridge, Colo., 1981—. Mem., Adams County Placement Alternative Commn., 1980-81, Adams County Child Protection Team, 1979-80; mem. handicapped child subcom. Colo. Gov.'s Commn. for Children and Families, 1979-80; bd. dirs. Centennial Area Health Edn. Center, 1978, Partners Inc., Greeley, Colo., 1978. Cert. psychologist, Colo. Mem. Colo. Psychol. Assn., Colo. Women Psychologists, NOW, Colo. Com. for Status of Women in Mental Health (treas. 1981—). Democrat. Home: 11205 E Vassar Dr Aurora CO 80014 Office: 6195 W 38th Ave Wheat Ridge CO 80033

HALL, JANE SUSAN, psychotherapist, psychoanalyst; b. N.Y.C., Aug. 9, 1935; d. Jules and Ethel (Yuckman) H.; B.A., N.Y. U., 1968; M.S.W., Hunter Coll., 1972; grad. N.Y. Freudian Soc., 1981; m. James S. Hall, Sept. 9, 1965; 1 dau., Debra Jean. Sr. supr., therapist Greenwich House Counseling Center, N.Y.C., 1970-76, cons., 1976—; mem. faculty Psychoanalytic Inst. for Clin. Social Workers, 1978-80; founding mem. faculty, exec. v.p. N.Y. Sch. for Psychoanalytic Psychotherapy, 1978—; pvt. practice psychotherapy, N.Y.C., 1978—. Fellow Soc. for Clin. Social Work Psychotherapists; mem. Nat. Assn. Social Workers, Soc. Clin. Soc. Work Psychotherapists, Soc. Advancement of Psychoanalytic Devel. Psychology, N.Y. Freudian Soc. Address: 49 W 12th St New York NY 10011

HALL, JANE W., diversified co. exec.; b. Seattle, May 14, 1942; d. Arthur T. and Joyce Waddell; B.A., U. Wash., 1963; J.D., U. Calif., Berkeley, 1975; m. Samuel F. Hall, June 21, 1968. Various editorial staff positions Seattle Mag., 1964-67; copy editor, advt. mgr. Holden-Day, Inc., San Francisco, 1967-68; employee communications mgr. Transamerica Corp., San Francisco, 1968-72, v.p. corp. relations, 1978—; admitted to Calif. bar, 1975; asso. firm Orrick, Herrington, Rowley & Sutcliffe, San Francisco, 1975-77. Bd. dirs. San Francisco Spring Opera Theater, Legal Aid Soc.; mem. adv. council Mills Coll., 1979—. Mem. Internat. Assn. Bus. Communicators, State Bar Calif., Order of Coif. Office: Transamerica Corp 600 Montgomery St San Francisco CA 94111

HALL, JUDITH IRENE, metall. engr.; b. Phila., Dec. 22, 1952; d. Paul Frank and Irene (Rost) Ellmer; B.S., U. Pa., 1974; M.S. in Engring. Mgmt., U. Pitts., 1978; m. William Roy Hall, Apr. 18, 1974. Research metallurgist Jones & Laughlin Steel Corp., Pitts., 1975-77; tech. services metallurgist Allegheny-Ludlum Steel Corp., Leechburg, Pa., 1977-80; research metall. engr. II, Colt Industries, Pitts., 1980—; instr. Community Coll. of Allegheny County, West Mifflin, Pa., 1976—. Mem. Am. Soc. Metals, Metall. Soc. of AIME, Am. Phys. Soc., Am. Soc. for Engring. Mgmt., Inst. Mgmt. Sci., Am. Solar Energy Soc., Omega Rho, Tau Beta Pi. Home: 113 Kilbuck Dr Monroeville PA 15146 Office: PO Box 88 Pittsburgh PA 15230

HALL, KATHLEEN ANN SHADE, legal asst.; b. Guys Mills, Pa., Sept. 10, 1940; d. Glenn C. and Agnes R. (Maxwell) Shade; student Edinboro State Coll., 1958-59, U. West Los Angeles, 1976; m. Robert E. Hall, Aug. 3, 1968 (div.). Exec. sec. Talon, Inc., Meadville, Pa., 1959-62, McDonnell Douglas, Santa Monica, Calif., 1962-64; legal sec. Leon Leonian, atty., Beverly Hills, Calif., 1965-77; prin. Kathleen A. Hall, legal asst., Van Nuys, Calif., 1977—. Mem. Nat. Notary Assn., State Bar Calif. (probate law sect.), Los Angeles Paralegal Assn. Club: Braemar Country. Home: 3915 Benedict Canyon Sherman Oaks CA 91423

HALL, KATHRYN EVANGELINE, author, lectr.; b. Biltmore, N.C.; d. Hugh Canada and Evangeline Haddon (Jenkins) Hall; B.A., U. N.C., M.A.; diploma Adams Sch. Music, Montreat, N.C.; postgrad. Yale, U. London, Fla. Atlantic U. Author: The Papal Tiara, History of the Episcopal Church of Bethesda-By-The-Sea, 1964, The Architecture and Times of Robert Adam, 1969, The Pictorial History of the Episcopal Church of Bethesda-By-The-Sea, 1970-71, Joseph Wright of Derby, A Painter of Science, Industry, and Romanticism, 1974, A History of English Architecture, 1976-82; Sir John Vanbrugh's Palaces and the Drama of Baroque Architecture, 1982-83; lectr. history, art and architecture, U.S., Eng. and Scotland, 1961—. Vice pres. The Jr. Patronesses, Palm Beach, Fla., 1964. Mem. Nat. League Am. Pen Women (Owl award 1972, 76, 77, pres. Palm Beach chpt. 1975-80), Palm Beach Quills (historian), Palm Beach County Hist. Soc. (gov.), Internat. Platform Assn., Soc. Four Arts, Cum Laude Soc., Palm Beach Civic Assn. Episcopalian. Clubs: Everglades (Palm Beach); English Speaking Union (Palm Beach and London). Home: Acadie PO Box 648 Palm Beach FL 33480

HALL, KATIE BEATRICE GREENE, state legislator; b. Miss., Apr. 3, 1938; d. Jeff Louis and Bessie Mae (Hooper) Greene; B.S., Miss. Valley State U., 1960; M.S., Ind. U., 1968, postgrad., 1972; m. John H. Hall, Aug. 12, 1957; children—Jacqueline, Junifer. Mem. Ind. Ho. of Reps. from 5th Dist., 1974-76; mem. Ind. Senate, 1976-82, chmn. edn. com., from 1977; mem. of 98th Congress of U.S. Ho. of Reps. from Ind. 1st dist., 1983—. Recipient numerous civic awards. Mem. AAUW, Nat. Council Negro Women, Nat. Council Social Studies, Nar. Council Black Legislators, Phi Delta Kappa. Democrat. Address: care US House of Reps Washington DC 20515 *

HALL, KAYE, bus. exec., developer; b. Warnock, Ky., Oct. 29, 1944; d. Ermon Heinard and Ethel Aldean (Boggs) Bradley; 1 son, Keenan Lee Hall. Exec. sec. C&O/B&O Ry. Co., Russell, Ky., 1963-69; exec. Bus. Investment, Ltd., Honolulu, 1969-71, v.p., 1971—, corp. sec., 1975—, also dir.; v.p., corp. sec. West Coast Bus. Investment, Ltd., Portland, Oreg., 1971-77, also dir.; v.p. Calif. Bus. Investment, Ltd., Los Angeles, 1972-78, corp. sec., 1973-78, also dir.; pres. Gen. Mgmt. Corp., Honolulu, 1975—, also dir.; pres. Condominium Mgmt., Inc., Portland, 1972—, also dir.; sec., dir. Econ. Devel. & Cons. Engrs., Inc., Honolulu, 1975—. sec. Russell div. Ry. and S.S. Clks. Union, 1968-69. Bd. dirs. Mental Health/Mental Retardation Greenup County (Ky.), 1966-67, United Fund, Greenup County, 1966-67; chmn. USO Spl. Projects, Greenup County, 1967; adv. dir. Valley Christian Schs., Inc., Beaverton, Oreg., 1975-76. Appt. Ky. Col., 1969. Mem. Oreg. Homebuilders Assn. (multifamily housing council), Nat. Community Assns. Inst. Club: West Hills Racquet. Office: 278 SW Arthur St Portland OR 97201

HALL, LEE, ednl. adminstr., painter; b. Lexington, N.C., Dec. 15, 1934; d. Robert L. and Florence (Fitzgerald) H.; B.F.A., U. N.C., 1955, D.F.A., (hon.), 1976; M.A., N.Y. U., 1959, Ph.D., 1965. Chmn. art dept. Drew U., Montclair, N.J., 1965-74; dean visual arts SUNY, Purchase, 1974-75; pres. R.I. Sch. Design, Providence, 1975—; dir. Old Stone Corp., Quinter, Inc.; paintings exhibited Betty Parsons Gallery, Montclair Mus. Bd. cons. Nat. Endowment Humanities, 1968—. Recipient Scholar's award N.Y. U., 1965, Childe Hassam award Am. Acad. Arts and Scis.; Am. Philos. Soc. fellow U. London, Oxford, 1965, 68. Clubs: Cosmopolitan (N.Y.C.); R.I. Sch. Design (N.Y.). Contbr. writings to profl. jours. Office: 62 Prospect Providence RI 02906 *

HALL, LISA LYNN, state ofcl.; b. Aurora, Ill., Oct. 13, 1948; d. Kenneth F. and Veva R. Hall; B.A. cum laude (Ill. State scholar, Sigma Lambda Sigma scholar, Helen R. Messenger, univ. grantee, High Ridge Sch. PTA scholar, Ill. PTA scholar), No. Ill. U., 1970; M.B.A. magna cum laude, Sangamon State U., Springfield, Ill., 1980; m. H. Huckaby, Oct. 12, 1980. Pres., owner Hall Real Estate Enterprises, Springfield, 1972—; mgr. internal audit Ill. Dept. Adminstrv. Services, 1977-79; mgr. audit and investigation Ill. Dept. Commerce, 1979-80, chief audits and investigations, 1980—. Del., Ill. Republican Conv., 1980. Cert. info. systems and data processing auditor. Mem. Inst. Internal Auditors (internat. com. 1979—, charter pres. Springfield chpt. 1978; seminar instr. 1979—), No. Ill. U. Alumni Assn. (gov. 1979—), Nat. Assn. Female Execs., Ill. Audit Mgrs. Assn., Assn. M.B.A. Execs., Internat. EDP Auditors Assn., Springfield Urban League, Am. Bus. Women's Assn., Cwens. Contbr. articles to profl. jours.

HALL, LOIS RIGGS, state senator; b. Beeville, Tex., May 22, 1930; d. Ira Franklin and Pearl Ophelia (McCoy) Riggs; student Tex. Woman's U., 1947-49, U. Tex., 1949-50; m. Walter William Hall, Jr., Dec. 28, 1950 (dec.); children—Robert Macfarlane, Elaine Denise, Judith Lea. Exec. sec. N.Mex. Symphony Orch., Albuquerque, 1975—; mem. N.Mex. Senate, 1980—. Republican. Office: PO Box 769 Albuquerque NM 87103

HALL, LUCILLE JONES GREY, city ofcl., civic worker; b. Cuyahoga Falls, Ohio, Apr. 15, 1922; d. Mark Barber and Nellie (James) Jones; student U. Miami, 1939-41, Rollins Coll., 1941, U. Fla., summer 1942, Cornell U., 1942-43; m. Hugh Morton Grey, Jr., Sept. 27, 1943 (div. Apr. 8, 1977); children—Leslie Grey Harper, Hugh Morton Grey III, Roderic Marcus Upson, Helen Valerie; m. Daniel Luce Hall, II, Jan. 5, 1982. Mem. Venice (Fla.) City Council, 1980—. Organizing pres. Beaux Arts of Lowe Gallery, Coral Gables, Fla., 1952, Town and Country Garden Club, Concord, N.C., 1956; chmn. vol. guides Mus. Sci. and Natural History, Miami, 1952-54; guide Children's Mus., Charlotte, N.C., 1955-56; leader Girl Scouts U.S.A., Concord, Venice, 1954-68, Cub Scouts, Concord, 1956-57, 64-65, pres. Coll. Club of Venice Area, 1960-61, Band Parents Club, Venice, 1960-61; jr. chmn. Venice Garden Club, 1960-62; bd. dirs. PTA, Merrick Demonstration Sch., 1951-52, Miami Music Club, 1951-53; mem. womens planning com. Venice Yacht Club, 1961-62; sustaining chmn. Sarasota Jr. Welfare League, 1967-68; bd. dirs. Family Service Assn. Sarasota, 1968-70; bd. dirs., rec. sec. Women's Library Assn. of New Coll., Sarasota, 1967-69; mem. adminstrv. bd. Grace United Meth. Ch. Mem. Jr. League Sarasota, DAR (regent Myakka chpt. 1973-75), Colonial Dames XVII Century (sec. William Bassett chpt. 1977-78), Daus. Am. Colonists (regent Venice on Gulf chpt. 1979—), Fine Arts Soc. Sarasota (charter), Upson Family Assn. Am., LWV, Bus. and Profl. Women, Friendly Sons and Daus. St. Patrick, Am. Assn. Ret. Persons, Sarasota Panhellenic, Fla. League of Cities, Venice Taxpayers League, Am. Bus. Women Assn., Paperweight Collectors Assn., Kappa Kappa Gamma (organizing pres. Sarasota County chpt. 1962). Republican. Home: 604 Narvaezi St Venice FL 33595 also 1036 Bird Bay Way Venice FL 33595

HALL, MARNIE L., recording corp. exec.; b. Clay Center, Kans., June 5, 1942; d. Joseph A., Jr. and Edith M. (McIntosh) H.; B.Mus. with honors, U. Kans., 1966; M.Mus., Manhattan Sch. Music, 1968. Violinist, Kansas City Philharmonic Orchestra, 1962-66; freelance violinist, N.Y.C., 1966—; founder Gemini Hall Records, N.Y.C., 1975; founder, pres., producer Leonarda Prodns., Inc., N.Y.C., 1977—. Mem. Internat. League Women Composers (affiliate), Am. Symphony Orchestra. Democrat. Home: 808 West End Ave #508 New York NY 10025 Office: PO Box 124 Radio City Station New York NY 10101

HALL, MARY CAROLYN, state ofcl.; b. Moniteau County, Mo., Aug. 28, 1942; d. Floyd Layton and Delta June (Hume) Allee; student S.W. Mo. State U., 1968, Lincoln U., Jefferson City, Mo., 1976-77; m. Stanley E. Hall, Aug. 30, 1964; children—Lance Edward, Paige Elizabeth. Sec., Mo. Ho. Reps., 1971-73; with Mo. Div. Ins., 1973—, supr. lic. sect., 1975-81, dept. dir. div., 1981—. Pres. Jefferson City Jaycees Wives, 1972, 74. Mem. Nat. Assn. Ins. Women (legis. chmn. Mo. 1981-82), Jefferson City Bus. and Profl. Women (v.p. 1980). Home: 808 Belair St Jefferson City MO 65101 Office: 515 E High St Jefferson City MO 65101

HALL, MIMI, mktg. exec.; b. Memphis, Dec. 6, 1949; d. Anthony Houston and Mary Ellen (Kinsella) Hall; B.A., Memphis State U., 1971; m. Robert A. Osborne, Sept. 1, 1978. Editor, Little Publs., Memphis, 1970-72; communications specialist Shelby County Govt., 1973-75; ombudsman, product devel. specialist Nat. Bank of Commerce, Memphis, 1975-79; v.p. corp. communications, mgr. product devel. Union Planters Nat. Bank, Memphis, 1979-81; mktg. dir. J.C. Bradford & Co., Nashville, 1981—. Mem. profl. adv. com., Memphis State U., 1979-81; mem. adv. com. Plough Devel. Area, 1975-79; charter mem. Provida-Profl. Women's Sponsor group for Girls Clubs, 1976-81; budget subcom. mem. United Way Greater Memphis, 1979-81; host family participant Vanderbilt U., Memphis, 1981—; mem. Downtown Hist. Task Force, Memphis, 1974-76. Mem. Women in Communications, Am. Inst. Banking, Am. Mktg. Assn., Public Relations Soc. Am., Roman Catholic. Contbr. articles to profl. jours. Home: 813 Del Rio Pike Apt G6 Franklin TN 37064 Office: 170 4th Ave N Nashville TN 37219

HALL, PATRICIA DELAY, accountant; b. Texarkana, Tex., Dec. 24, 1930; d. Byron N. and Esther J. DeLay; B.B.A., Lamar U., Beaumont, Tex., 1981; m. Miles A. Hall, Apr. 16, 1969; children—Kathryn, Andrew. Bookkeeper, Am. Bridge div. U.S. Steel Corp., Orange, Tex., 1954-59; with du Pont Co., Orange, 1959—, accountant, 1976-79, acctg. specialist, 1979—. Mem. Am. Soc. Exec. and Profl. Women, Nat. Assn. Female Execs., Phi Kappa Phi. Beta Gamma Sigma. Home: 309 Sandy Dr Bridge City TX 77611 Office: PO Box 1089 Orange TX 77630

HALL, WILHELMINA DYE, ednl. adminstr.; b. Elberton, Ga., Feb. 27; d. William Thomas and Louvenia Vivian (Wilson) Dye; B.A., Hampton Inst., 1948; M.Ed., Valdosta State Coll., 1975; m. Jack Finley Hall, June 29, 1950; 1 dau., Denise Hall Winkfield. Tchr. bus. skills Doughtery County Sch. System, Albany, Ga., 1957-67, coordinator office edn., 1967-79, dir. personnel, 1979—. Trustee, Doughtery County Library, 1976—; bd. dirs., council Girl Scouts Am., 1975—, United Way, 1977—; mem. Area Hist. Commn., 1979—; bd. dirs. Albany Ballet Theater. Named Star Tchr., Monroe High Sch., 1971. Mem. Albany C. of C., Ga. Vocat. Assn. (Educator of Yr. bus. and office edn. 1979), Ga. Bus. Edn. Assn. (pres.), Am. Vocat. Assn., Ga. Vocat. Assn., Nat. Bus. Edn. Assn., Ga. Assn. Personnel Adminstrs., Ga. Assn. Educators, Alpha Kappa Alpha, Phi Delta Kappa. Democrat. Roman Catholic. Home: 512 Mercer Ave Albany GA 31701 Office: PO Box 1470 Albany GA 31703

HALLADAY, LAURIE KOHLER, public relations exec.; b. Monroe, Mich., Aug. 18, 1945; d. Alvin John and Florence Julia (Lowrey) Kohler; B.J., U. Mo., 1967; m. Fredric R. Halladay, May 24, 1980. Staff writer, reporter South Bay Daily Breeze, Torrance, Calif., 1967-69; account exec. to v.p. Furman Assocs., Los Angeles, 1969-74; v.p. Bob Thomas & Assocs., Los Angeles, 1974-78; v.p., sr. ptnr. Fleishman-Hillard, Inc., St. Louis, 1978—. Recipient Prism award Los Angeles Pub. Relations Soc., 1978. Mem. Women in Communications (corr. sec. St. Louis chpt.), Soc. Am. Travel Writers, St. Louis Press Club, Pub. Relations Soc. Am. Home: 50 Waterman Pl Saint Louis MO 63112 Office: One Memorial Dr Saint Louis MO 63102

HALLAS, SUSAN SEYMOUR, civic worker, mgmt./devel. cons.; b. Louisville, July 10, 1942; d. George McClure and Florence Hooker (Leaning) Seymour; B.A. in Philosophy, Wellesley Coll., 1964; M.S. in Urban Edn., Central Conn. Coll., 1972; m. Henry Caryl Hallas, Aug. 29, 1964; children—Katherine Seymour, Elizabeth McClure. Tchr., Hartford (Conn.) Bd. Edn., 1964-68; dir. city/suburb project U. Hartford, 1979-81; now self-employed mgmt./devel. cons. Second v.p. Jr. League of Hartford, 1973-75, pres., 1977-79; mem. area council Assn. of Jr. Leagues, N.Y.C, 1975-76, bd. dirs., 1980-82; chmn. Conn. Council of Jr. Leagues, 1978-79; bd. dirs. Hartford Hosp. Aux., 1971-74; mem. vestry Old St. Andrew's Episcopal Ch., 1975-78; bd. dirs. Wintonbury PTA, 1975-78, pres., 1976-77; bd. dirs. Conn. Valley council Girl Scouts U.S.A., 1979-82, Bushnell Park Found., 1982—; pres. Loomis Chaffee Alumni Assn., 1981—. Home: 635 Bloomfield Ave Bloomfield CT 06002

HALLAS-GOTTLIEB, LISA GAIL, film director; b. Rahway, N.J., Feb. 22, 1950; d. Taras and Mary (Lapchinski) H.; B.A. in Broadcasting, Film and English with distinction, Stanford U., 1972. Second asst. dir. films: Opening Night, 1977, World's Greatest Lover, 1977, The Driver, 1977, Old Boyfriends, 1978, Just You and Me, Kid, 1978, A Small Circle of Friends, 1979; 2d asst. dir. TV show M*A*S*H, 1976; 1st asst. dir. TV shows Nobody's Perfect, 1979, Shirley, 1979, Hellinger's Law, 1980, Dynasty; 1980-81. Home: 1414 N Topanga Canyon Blvd Topanga CA 90290

HALLBAUER, ROSALIE CARLOTTA, educator; b. Chgo., Dec. 8, 1939; d. Ernest Ludwig and Kathryn Marquerite (Ramm) Hallbauer; B.S., Rollins Coll., 1961; M.B.A., U. Chgo., 1963; Ph.D., U. Fla., 1973. Asso. prof. bus. Fla. Internat. U., Miami, 1972—. C.P.A., Ill.; certified mgmt. accountant. Mem. Am. Inst. C.P.A.'s, Am. Accounting Assn., Nat. Assn. Accountants, Am. Woman's Soc. C.P.A.'s, Ill. Soc. C.P.A.'s, Inst. Mgmt. Accounting, Beta Alpha Psi, Pi Gamma Mu. Office: Florida Internat Univ Tamiami Trail Miami FL 33199

HALLECK, CONSTANCE JOYCE, advt. splty. co. exec.; b. Dayton, Ohio, May 23, 1944; d. Curtis Woodrow and Ruth Marjorie (Gray) Harvey; A.S., St. Petersburg Jr. Coll., 1964; B.S., U. Fla., 1965; 1 son, John Robert. Sec.-treas., v.p. Trans Global Corp., Atlanta, 1973-75; sales mgr. NFC Mktg. Assn., Dallas, 1975-76; sales rep. Ran Spltys., Houston, 1976-77; pres., chmn. bd. CHAS, Atlanta, Denver, Washington, Pensacola, Fla., Houston and Berlin, Ger., 1977—. Mem. Splty. Advt. Assn. Internat. (mem. speakers bur., grad. Distbr. Mgmt. Inst. 1979, mgmt. devel. seminar 1980, cert. advt. specialist), Splty. Advt. Assn. Atlanta (treas.), Nat. Assn. Female Execs., Am. Bus. Women's Assn. (chpt. v.p. 1978-79), Atlanta Women Bus. Owners Assn. (hospitality chmn., dir., v.p.), Ga. Small Bus. Council (dir., pres.), Women's Forum, (nat. dir.), Nat. Assn. Profl. Saleswomen (dir. Atlanta chpt.), Atlanta Network, Sales and Mktg. Execs. Office: 4741 Pine Acres Ct Dunwoody GA 30338

HALLEEN, SHIRLEY LOUISE KELLS, state legislator; b. Russell, Iowa, May 17, 1935; d. Ray Lester and Ruth Mae (Lewis) Kells; B.S., Wheaton Coll., 1957; m. Owen Halleen, June 8, 1957; children—Terri, Lynne, David. Tchr. secondary sch., Wurzburg, Ger., 1958-59; secondary and coll. tchr., St. Paul, 1963-68; mem. staff YWCA, Sheridan, Wyo., 1969-71; exercise cons. Sioux Valley Hosp., Sioux Falls, S.D., 1976; mem. S.D. Ho. of Reps., 1980—. Bd. dirs. United Way, Family Service, McCrossan Boys' Ranch, Girls Club, S.D. Symphony. Recipient YMCA Service to Youth award, 1970, Sioux Falls Leadership Luncheon award, 1978; named Outstanding Woman in Sports, 1978. Mem. AAUW, LWV, PTA, YWCA, Sioux Falls Coll. Faculty Folk. Democrat. Baptist. Club: P.E.O. Home: 1013 S Lyndale Sioux Falls SD 57105 Office: Ho of Reps State Capitol Pierre SD 57501

HALLEN, DOROTHY W., librarian, environmentalist; b. Worcester, Mass.; d. Herbert Robert and Hilda (Thayer-Carlson) H.; student pub. schs. Worcester and Holden, Mass.; grad. Worcester Sch. Bus.; student Clark U., Boston U. Past research cataloger Worcester Hist. Soc.; clk. Norton Co., Worcester, 1953-57, asst. librarian, 1957-71, head librarian, 1971-78; library cons. chs., small mus.; freelance writer. Mem. Spl. Library Assn., Worcester Hist. Mus., Art Mus., Cousteau Soc., Mustang Soc., Appalachian Mountain Club, Greenpeace Soc., Am. Nuclear Soc., African Wildlife Leadership Found., Nat. Geog. Soc., World Wildlife Fund, Am. Nuclear Soc. (library mem.). Contbr. poems, short stories to anthologies, mags., newspapers. Home: 100 Parker Ave Holden MA 01520

HALLENBECK, PHYLLIS NEWTON, psychologist; b. N.Y.C., Nov. 15, 1921; d. Philip and Thora (Few) Newton; B.S., Kent State U., 1944; M.A., Western Res. U., 1955, Ph.D., 1964; m. Charles Hallenbeck, Jr., Aug. 18, 1955 (div. June 1963); children—Arthur David, Ann. Research asst. Highland View Hosp., Cleve., 1960-62; research asso. Vocat. Guidance and Rehab. Service, Cleve., 1964-66; clin. psychologist Lake County Mental Health Clinic, Mentor, Ohio, 1966-69; instr. psychology Lakeland Community Coll., Painesville, Ohio, 1967-69, Kent State U., 1978-79, Lake Erie Coll., 1978; dir. psychology Sagamore Hills Children's Psychiat. Hosp., Northfield, Ohio, 1969-75. Founder, dir. Flowerledge Sch. for Retarded Children, Geneva, Ohio, 1946-79; dir. Hallenbeck Psycho-Edn. Center, Willoughby, Ohio, 1972—. Mem. Am., Ohio, Cleve. psychol. assns., Am. Assn. Mental Deficiency, Cleve. Acad. Cons. Psychologists. Contbr. articles to profl. jours. Home: 4805 Wood St Willoughby OH 44094 Office: 4805 Wood St Willoughby OH 44094

HALLETT, CAROL BOYD, state legislator; b. Oakland, Calif., Oct. 16, 1937; d. Thomas Hal and Ruth I. Boyd; student U. Oreg., 1955-57, San Francisco State U., 1957-58; m. James T. Hallett, Jan. 26, 1958. Sec. to asst. supt. schs., Cupertino, Calif., 1959-61; office mgr. O'Dell-McConnell, nat. ednl. cons., Palo Alto, Calif., 1961-63; legal sec.,

1963-66; adminstrv. asst., field rep. Assemblyman/Congressman Bill Ketchum and State Senator Don Grunsky, 1967-75; mem. Calif. Assembly, 1976—, minority leader, 1979-82; now candidate for lt. gov. Calif. Mem. Calif. Women in Agr. (named Monterey County Farm of Yr., Monterey chpt. 1978), San Luis Obispo County Ninety-Nines, San Luis Obispo C. of C., Salinas C. of C., DAR, Delta Delta Delta. Republican. Office: State Capitol Rm 2128 Sacramento CA 95868

HALLIBURTON, JEAN ELIZABETH, journalist; b. Dallas, Nov. 3; d. Orville Garrett and Lydie Jeanne (Houghton) Halliburton; B.A. in Journalism, Stanford U.; m. G. Arnold Stevens, dec.; children—Arnold Jr., Carole Stevens Jackson, Harti Stevens Tucker. Womens editor W. Los Angeles (Calif.) Ind.; asst. fashion editor Los Angeles Herald Examiner; contbg. editor Los Angeles Mag., mem. founding staff, 1960-63; owner JHPR Public Relations Co., Newport Beach, Calif., 1964-77; Lifestyle editor Sutton News Group, Newport Ensign, Costa Mesa News, Irvine Today, Corona del Mar, Calif., 1978-81; v.p. Color Me Beautiful, Inc., 1982—. Mem. Women In Communications, Public Relations Soc. Am., Soc. Profl. Journalists-Sigma Delta Chi. Clubs: Washington Press, Capitol Hill. Home: 154 Lexington Ln Costa Mesa CA 92626 Office: 6817 Tennyson Dr McLean VA 22101

HALLIDAY, HARRIET HUDNUT (HOLLY), editor; b. Springfield, Ill., Dec. 7, 1941; d. William Herbert and Elizabeth Allen (Kilborne) Hudnut; B.A., Coll. Wooster, 1963; postgrad. McCormick Theol. Sem.; 1 son, Tyler Hudnut Colman. Exec. sec. women's bd. Presbyterian Med. Center, San Francisco, 1965-68; editor Am. Bar Found., Chgo., 1968-70, asst. dir. publs., 1970-75, mng. editor Am. Bar Found. Research Jour., 1975-80; research asst. dept. philosophy Australian Nat. U., Canberra, 1980-82. Mem. exec. com. jr. governing bd. Chgo. Symphony Orch., 1969-70, 75-76; officer adv. bd. Unitarian Presch. Center, Chgo., 1974-77; mem. Assos. Rush-Presbyn.-St. Luke's Med. Center, 1974-79; mem. alumni bd. Coll. Wooster, 1978-80, also chmn. public relations com., mem. nominating com., by-laws revision com. Mem. Jr. League Chgo. (vice chmn. profl. women's group 1975-76, chmn. criminal justice interest group 1977-78). Republican. Presbyterian. Home: 422 Rosewood Winnetka IL 60093

HALLIDAY, PHYLLIS BAKER, employment agy. exec.; b. Cleve., Dec. 31, 1923; d. Stanley Joseph and Mary Ellen (Taylor) Ryan; B.A., Ohio Wesleyan U., 1946; m. 2d, William Halliday, May 15, 1966; 1 son, Stanley Ryan Baker. Dir. research Lee County Mental Health Facility, Ft. Myers, Fla., 1978—; founder, 1952, since pres. Baker Employment, Inc., Cleve. Mem. Early Settlers Assn., Western Res. Hist. Assn. Republican. Methodist. Club: Woman's City (Cleve.). Office: Richmond Mall Richmond Heights Cleveland OH 44143

HALLOCK, VIRGINIA LEE, communications cons., author, lectr.; b. Kirksville, Mo., Feb. 3; d. Lee Kelsey and Carrie (Ashlock) Cramb; B.A., U. Oreg., 1959, postgrad., 1959-60; diploma Graphonanalysis Soc., Chgo., 1966; m. Earle D. Hallock (dec.); children—William Lee, David B. Tchr., Oreg. public schs., then Merritt Davis Bus. Coll., Salem, Oreg., 1958-74; office mgr. Mann Constrn. Co., Redmond, Oreg., 1951-56; feature story writer Oreg. Jour., Portland, also Bend (Oreg.) Bull., 1948-57; cons. human relations and communications, Salem, Oreg.; speaker, condr. seminars and workshops in field. Mem. Oreg. Consumers Adv. Council, N.E. Salem Community Area Bd.; Protestant mem. Sacred Heart Sch. Bd., Salem, 1977-79. Mem. Nat. Fedn. Press Women, Oreg. Press Women, Graphoanalysis Soc. (Oreg. graphoanalyst of Yr. 1972), Salem Area C. of C. (chmn. social/econ. council 1979, chmn. speakers bur. 1979-80), Conv. Bur. Salem, P.E.O. Republican. Club: Salem Toastmasters (adminstrv. v.p. 1976 named Outstanding Toastmaster 1975). Author: Business Communication, 1972; Charm and Charisma, 1974. Address: 840 Ree Del Ct NE Salem OR 97301

HALLQUIST, JOANN MILDRED, govt. economist; b. Amery, Wis., Nov. 11, 1933; d. Harry T. and Mildred A. H.; B.A. (Knapp scholar), U. Wis., Madison, 1955; postgrad. Columbia U., 1964-65. Commd. fgn. service officer Dept. State, 1957; embassy econ. officer U.S. embassy, Saigon, Vietnam, 1961-63, Brussels, 1970-71; internat. economist Fgn. Agrl. Service, U.S. Dept. Agr., Washington, 1971—. Home: 3008 R St NW Washington DC 20007 Office: 5530 S Dept Agr Washington DC 20007

HALLSTROM, MARY JEANNE (DOLLY), state legislator; b. East Orange, N.J., Dec. 26, 1924; B.S., Loyola U.; R.N., St. Francis Hosp., Evanston. Communication specialist Regional Service Agy.; exec. sec. Ill. Spl. Events Commn.; now mem. Ill. Ho. of Reps., mem. elem. and secondary and higher edn. coms. Founder, Fund for Perceptually Handicapped Children; incorporator, treas. Nat. Assn. Children with Learning Disabilities; chmn. state study com. on edn. White Ho. Conf. on Children and Youth; mem. Evanston Youth Commn., Ill. Commn. on Children, Commn. on Mental Health and Developmental Disabilities; chmn. Ill. State Adv. Council Edn. of Handicapped Children. Mem. Delta Kappa Gamma. Office: Ill Ho of Reps State Capitol Springfield IL 62706 *

HALPENNY, FRANCESS GEORGINA, editor, professor, b. Ottawa, Ont., Can., May 27, 1919; d. James Leroy and Villa Gertrude (Westman) H.; B.A., U. Toronto, 1940, M.A., 1941; LL.D., U. Guelph, 1968, Dalhousie U., 1978. With editorial dept. U. Toronto Press, from 1941—, editor, 1957-65, mng. editor, 1965-69, asso. acad. dir., 1979—, gen. editor Dictionary of Canadian Biography, 1969—; prof. library sci. U. Toronto, 1972—, dean faculty library sci., 1972-78, chmn. research com., 1979—; chmn. Com. on Bibliog. Service Can., 1977-79; mem. com. on library info Can. Book and Periodical Devel. Council, 1974—, chmn., 1979—; mem. Nat. Library Adv. Bd., 1976—, chmn., 1979—. Served with Women's Div. RCAF, 1942-45. Decorated officer Order of Can., 1979. Fellow Royal Soc. Can.; mem. Can. Library Assn. (chmn. com. on editorial and publs. policy 1973-75), Can. Hist. Assn. (council 1968-70). Editorial bd. Scholarly Pub., editorial com. Collected Works John Stuart Mill; contbr. articles to profl. jours. Clubs: Univeristy Women's Heliconian (pres.). Office: Univ Toronto Press Toronto ON M5S 1A6 Canada *

HALPERIN, CORRINE SANDRA, coll. adminstr.; exec.; b. Providence, Feb. 8, 1936; d. Barney and Rose Ruth (Bilsky) Gordon; student Behrend Coll., Wayne State U., U. Mich.; B.A., Mercyhurst Coll., 1980; children—Karen Lynne Halperin Shor, Michel Jay, Amy Marleene. Freelance market researcher, 1968-72; exec. dir. Council Vols. Erie County, 1971-78; exec. dir. YWCA, Erie, 1978-81; unit dir. Am. Cancer Soc., Erie, 1982; adj. faculty Mercyhurst Hosp., dir. Office Community Edn., 1982—; adj. faculty Behrend Coll.; adviser Hospitality House for Women, 1975—. Sec., Erie Art Festival, 1973-74; chmn. Erie County Commn. Drug and Alcohol Abuse, 1978-80. Recipient Community Service award, 1977. Mem. Am. Soc. Tng. and Devel., AAUW, Nat. Council Jewish Women. Contbg. editor: Vol. Adminstrn., 1973—. Home: 1001 Andover Ln Erie PA 16509 Office: Mercyhurst Coll Glenwood Hills Erie PA 16546

HALPERN, MIMI, neuroscientist; b. Antwerp, Belguim, June 19, 1938; came to U.S., 1948; d. Marcel and Clara (Strulovici) Halpern; A.B., Oberlin Coll., 1960; Ph.D., Adelphi U., 1964; m. Ariel Halpern, June 11, 1961; children—Joann, Jeffrey. Research assoc. dept. anatomy Downstate Med. Center, Bklyn., 1964-67, instr., 1967-69, asst. prof., 1969-74, assoc. prof. dept. anatomy and cell biology and program in biol. psychology, 1974-79, prof., 1979—, asst. dean Sch. Grad. Studies, 1975—, dir. program biol. psychology, 1976—. Mem. Am. Anat. Assn., Am. Psychol. Assn., Soc. for Neurosci., Am. Soc. Zoologists, Animal Behavior Soc., AAAS. Contbr. articles to profl. jours. Home: 262 Central Park W New York NY 10024 Office: 450 Clarkson Ave Brooklyn NY 11203

HALPERN, PATRICIA, sales promotion and premiums co. exec.; b. San Francisco, Jan. 13, 1934; d. William and Alice (Dewey) O'Shaughnessy; student U. Ill., m. Harold Halpern, Apr. 1, 1951; children—Rebecca, Jay. Account exec. React Enterprises, N.Y.C., 1974—. Mem. Ad Specialty Assn., NOW. Home: 132 E 35th St New York NY 10016 Office: 9 E 41st St New York NY 10017

HALPERT, RUTH LEVIN, educator; b. N.Y.C., Dec. 31, 1922; d. Jacob and Celia (Shapiro) Levin; B.A., UCLA, 1943, Ed.D., 1966; m. Saul Halpert, Nov. 4, 1943; children—James, Robert. Tchr., Los Angeles City Schs., 1948-56, Beverly Hills (Calif.) City Schs., 1956-60; counselor UCLA, 1960-66; mem. faculty Calif. State U., Northridge, 1966—, prof. ednl. psychology, 1976—. Named Outstanding Tchr., UCLA, 1981. Mem. Am. Psychol. Assn., Am. Personnel and Guidance Assn., Doctoral Alumni Assn. Sch. Edn. UCLA. Home: 13123 Margate St Van Nuys CA 91401 Office: Dept Ednl Psychology Calif State U Northridge CA 91330

HALPIN, GLENNELLE MCCOLLUM, ednl. psychologist; b. Lineville, Ala., Nov. 12, 1939; d. Henry Ferrel and Ruby (Phillips) McCollum; B.S., Jacksonville State U., 1964; M.A., U. Ga., 1969, Ph.D., 1972; m. Gerald Halpin, June 18, 1960; children—Mike, Mark. Vis. prof. U. Ga., Athens, 1972; lectr. U. Mont., Missoula, 1973-74, vis. prof., 1980; asst. prof. Auburn (Ala.) U., 1974-79, assoc. prof. ednl. psychology, grad. faculty, 1979. NDEA fellow, 1968-71). Mem. Am. Psychol. Assn., Southeastern Psychol. Assn., Am. Ednl. Research Assn., Eastern Ednl. Research Assn., Mid-South Ednl. Research Assn., Nat. Council on Measurement in Edn., Phi Beta Kappa, Phi Kappa Phi, Phi Delta Kappa. Methodist. Contbr. revs., articles to profl. nat., internat. jours. Home: 112 Norwood Ave Auburn AL 36830 Office: Dept Founds Edn 4054 Haley Center Auburn U Auburn AL 36849

HALSBAND, FRANCES, architect; b. N.Y.C., Oct. 30, 1943; d. Samuel and Ruth H.; B.A., Swarthmore Coll., 1965; M.Arch., Columbia U., 1968; m. Robert Michael Kliment, May 1, 1971; 1 son, Alexander H. Architect with Mitchell/Giurgola Architects, N.Y.C., 1968-72; partner R.M. Kliment & Frances Halsband Architects, N.Y.C., 1972—; vis. critic archtl. design Columbia U., 1975-78, N.C. State U., 1978, Rice U., 1979, U. Va., 1980. Harvard U., 1981, U. Pa., 1981. Mem. Archtl. League N.Y. (exec. bd. 1975-81, v.p. arch. N.Y., 1981—), AIA (exec. bd. N.Y.C. 1979), Alliance Women in Architecture, Am. Assn. for State and Local History, Am. Assn. Museums, Catskill Center for Conservation and Devel., Gallery Assn. N.Y. State. Office: 1013 Carnegie Hall New York NY 10019

HALSEY, WANDA PHILPOTT, utilities exec.; b. Winding Gulf, W.Va., Apr. 26, 1932; d. Larkin Shelton and Julia Edith (Spasiuk) Philpott; student Sullins Coll., 1949-50, W.Va. U., 1950-51; A.B. cum laude in Journalism, U. N.C., 1953; m. Stephen Simmons Halsey, Feb. 11, 1956 (div. 1966); children—Alexandra Simmons, Nicholas Van Rensselaer. Buyer, Bloomingdale's, N.Y.C., 1953-54; asst. dir. public relations, fashion coordination Julius Garfinckel & Co., Washington, 1954-56; dir. editorial and spl. services Burson-Marsteller, N.Y.C., 1971-73; account exec. The Continental Group, Inc., N.Y.C., 1973-75, mgr. bus. press. relations, 1975-76, dir. media relations, 1976-78; mgr. communications programs Union Pacific Corp., 1978-79; exec. v.p. The Public Policy Group, 1979-80; dir. corp. communications Orange and Rockland Utilities, Inc., Pearl River, N.Y., 1980—. Bd. dirs. Children's Convalescent Hosp., 1962-65, Rockland County Girl Scouts. Mem. Fgn. Press Assn., Women's Econ. Forum, Publicity Club N.Y., Internat. Assn. Bus. Communicators, Public Utility Communicators Assn., Women's Elec. Roundtable, Nat. Assn. Female Execs. Home: 101 Gedney St Nyack NY 10960 Office: One Blue Hill Plaza Pearl River NY 10965

HALSTEAD, LINDA GLYNN, univ. ofcl.; b. Paso Robles, Calif., May 30, 1944; d. Bruce Walter and Joy Arloa (Mallory) H.; B.A., Loma Linda U., 1966; M.A., U. Calif., Riverside, 1979; children—Linda Gaie Baldwin, Eric Ryan Baldwin. Editor, chief bibliographer World Life Research Inst., Colton, Calif., 1966-70; med. writer depts. pathology and clin. lab. scis. Loma Linda (Calif.) U., 1970-74, coordinator grants resources service, 1975—, instr. dept. biostatistics and epidemiology, 1981—. Bd. dirs. World Life Research Inst. Mem. Nat. Council Univ. Research Adminstrs., Soc. Research Adminstrs. Adventist. Contbr. articles to profl. jours. Home: 22818 Grand Terrace Rd Colton CA 92324 Office: Grants Resources Service Loma Linda U Loma Linda CA 92350

HALVORSON, RUDELLA (MICKEY), travel agt.; b. Coulee, N.D., July 14, 1922; d. Martin J. and Selma C. (Olson) Mikelson; m. Halvor M. Halvorson, Feb. 22, 1941; children—Heidi Halvorson Stejer, Judi Halvorson Rowand, Gail Halvorson DeSmet, Mikel, Ronald Paul. Owner, gen. mgr. Red Carpet Travel, Spokane, Wash., 1970—; owner, sec. H. Halvorson, Inc., Spokane, 1945—. Trustee Wampum. Mem. Eastern Wash. Hist. Soc., Spokane C. of C., Assn. Wash. Bus., Am. Soc. Travel Agts., Assn. Retail Travel Agts., N. Am. Travel Assn., Pacific Cruise Conf. Republican. Clubs: Spokane Country, Spokane, Hayden Lake (Idaho) Country. Home: E 1809 Rockwood Pl Spokane WA 99203 Office: Red Carpet Travel S 3009 Grand Blvd Spokane WA 99203

HAM, JANE F., state legislator; b. Cleve., Dec. 1, 1919; B.A. in Fine Arts, Ohio State U.; postgrad. in Aero. Engring., U. Minn.; postgrad. in Data Processing, Dana McKay Bus Sch., Las Vegas; m. Charles W. Ham (dec.); children—Peter, Susan, Marjorie Ham Parker. Dir. Red Cross Club, Japan, U.S. Army Spl. Services Club, Germany; mem. Nev. Assembly, 1981—. Sec.-treas., regional dir. Nev. Fedn. Republican Women; public relations chmn. Nat. Fedn. Rep. Women; del. Rep. Nat. Conv., 1976; sec., 2d vice chmn. Clark County Rep. Central Com.; mem. St. Rose de Lima Hosp. Aux.; pres. Rep. Women of Las Vegas; mem. Women's Polit. Caucus, NAACP, Conservative Caucus, Pro-Family Coalition, Nat. Taxpayers Union, Nev. Taxpayers Assn., Mem. Ohio State U. Alumni Assn. Anglican-Catholic. Club: Zonta. Office: Legislative Bldg 401 S Carson St Carson City NV 89710 *

HAMAN, SHIRLEY ANN, retail exec.; b. Detroit, Sept. 11, 1921; d. William Harold and Grace Elizabeth (Hall) Tucker; student Wayne U., 1940-43; m. Edward A. Haman, Sept. 1, 1943 (dec.); children—Edward A., Ann Elizabeth. Account and bus. mgr., Mitchell Buick Sales, Mt. Clemens, Mich., 1945-53, sec.-treas., bus. mgr., 1973—. Mem. City Planning Commn., Mt. Clemens, Base Community Council. Roman Catholic. Home: 1212 Burlington Dr Mount Clemens MI 48043 Office: 165 N Gratiot Ave Mount Clemens MI 48043

HAMBERG, MARIE ANTIONETTE, govt. adminstr.; b. Pendleton, S.C., Jan. 18, 1948; d. William Hovey and Goldie Marie (Hill) H.; B.S., S.C. State Coll., 1969; M.S.W., U. Md., 1973; postgrad. George Washington U., 1970; cert. W. E. UpJohn Inst., 1975. Program analyst Social Rehab. Service, HEW, Washington, 1969-74, on spl. assignment, Chgo., 1970; social welfare specialist D.C. Dept. Human Resources, 1974-76, then contract adminstr.; lectr. Sch. Social Welfare, SUNY, Albany, 1976-79; exec. dir. Trinity Instn., Inc., Albany, 1979-80; social sci. program specialist, tech. assistance div. Office Human Devel., Adminstrn. for Children, Youth and Families, Children's Bur., HEW, Washington, 1980—. Mem. S.C. State Coll. Alumni Assn., Nat. Assn. Social Workers, Nat. Assn. Black Social Workers, NAACP, Delta Sigma Theta. Mem. A.M.E. Ch. Home: 2480 16th St NW Washington DC 20009

HAMBLETON, BERNIECE CAMPBELL, nurse; b. Emerson, Ark., Feb. 9, 1926; d. Clarence Henry and Nellie Marie (Moore) Campbell; diploma, R.N., Warner Brown Sch. Nursing, El Dorado, Ark., 1948; m. Clarence Earl Hambleton, Jr., Dec. 23, 1947; children—Julianna Marie, Clarence Earl III. Nurse, Warner Brown Hosp., El Dorado, 1948-51, Alvin (Tex.) Meml. Hosp., 1963-65, St. Luke Episcopal Hosp., Houston, 1967-67, Alvin Gulfcoast Hosp., 1967-68; operating room supr. Caribou Meml. Hosp., Soda Springs, Idaho, 1969—. County chmn. Heart Fund, 1971. Mem. Am., Idaho nurses assns., Assn. Operating Room Nurses, Idaho Soc. for Nursing Service Adminstrs. (chmn. by-laws com.). Republican. Baptist. Home: 360 N 2d E Soda Springs ID 83276

HAMBLEY, SHARON L.R., nurse, govt. health agy. ofcl.; b. Mpls., Aug. 1, 1941; d. Walter Fred Rubinson and Blanche Loretta (Martindale) Clement; B.A., U. Minn., 1963, B.S., 1966; USPHS trainee, Columbia U., 1968-69; M.P.A., Am. U. Coll. Public and Internat. Affairs, Georgetown U. Sch. Medicine, 1982; cert. mental health adminstrn. (fellow) Washington Sch. Psychiatry, 1977; m. William A. Hambley, Jr., Sept. 10, 1965 (div. 1975). Sch. health nurse Arlington County (Va.) Schs., 1966-70; public health nurse Fairfax County (Va.) Health Dept., 1970-71; charge nurse splty. clinics Children's Hosp. Nat. Med. Center, Washington, 1971-72; primary nurse intensive care psychiatry Washington Hosp. Center, 1972-74; asst. to chief supervisory nurse forensic psychiatry Alcohol Drug Abuse and Mental Health Adminstrn., NIMH, Washington, 1974-80; program analyst Office Policy Devel. and Research, White House Conf. Aging, 1981; coordinator pre-trial forensic psychiatry Alcohol and Drug Abuse Adminstrn. NIMH, Washington, 1982—; health care planner Reston (Va.) Community Assn., 1970-73; chairperson D.C. Nurses Assn. Profl. Standards Review Orgn., 1976. Fellow Soc. Advanced Med. Systems; mem. Am. Nurses Assn. (cert. excellence in practice in psychiatry 1977), Nat. Forensic Nurses Assn., Nat. League Nursing, Am. Public Health Assn., Nat. Capital Area Public Adminstrs., Am. Soc. Public Adminstrn. (com. on women in public adminstrn.), Am. Oceanic Soc. Am. Acad. Polit. Sci., Am. Coll. Hosp. Adminstrs. Clubs: Ski, Sailing (Washington). Office: DHHS PHS ADAMHA NIMH CCS DFP Washington DC 20032

HAMBY, JEANNETTE K., state legislator; b. Virginia, Minn., Mar. 15, 1933; d. John W. and Lydia (Soderholm) Johnson; B.S., U. Minn., 1956; M.S., U. Oreg., 1968; Ph.D., Oreg. State U., 1976; m. Eugene Hamby, 1957; children—Taryn Rene, Tenya Ramine. Vice-chairperson Hillsboro High Sch. Dist. Bd., 1973-81; mem. Washington County Juvenile Services Commn., 1980—; mem. Suggested Legis. Commn., Council State Govts., 1981—; mem. Oreg. Ho. of Reps., 1981—, mem. trade and econ. devel., aging and minority affairs, intergovtl. affairs coms., 1981—. Mem. Oreg. Mental Health Assn. (sec., v.p.), Am. Nurses Assn., Oreg. Nurses Assn., Am. Vocat. Assn., Oreg. Vocat. Assn., Oreg. Vocat. Career Adminstrn. Lutheran. Office: Oreg Ho Reps State Capitol Salem OR 97310 *

HAMEISTER, LAVON LOUETTA, social worker; b. Blairstown, Iowa, Nov. 27, 1922; d. George Frederick and Bertha (Anderson) Hameister; B.A., U. Ia., 1944; postgrad. N.Y. Sch. Social Work, Columbia, 1945-46, U. Minn. Sch. Social Work, summer 1952; M.A., U. Chgo., 1959. Child welfare practitioner Fayette County Dept. Social Welfare, West Union, Iowa, 1946-56; dist. cons. services in child welfare and pub. assistance Ia. Dept. Social Services, Des Moines, 1956-58, dist. field rep., 1959-64, regional supr., 1964-65, supr., specialist supervision, adminstrn, Bur. Staff Devel., 1965-66, chief Bur. Staff Devel., 1966-68, chief div. staff devel. and tng., 1968-73, asst. dir. Office Staff Devel. and Tng., 1973-78, continuing edn. mgr., 1978—. Active in drive to remodel, enlarge Oelwein (Iowa) Mercy Hosp., 1952. Mem. Bus. and Profl. Women's Club (chpt. sec. 1950-52), Am. Assn. U. Women, Nat. Assn. Social Workers (chpt. sec.-elect 1958-59), Am. Pub. Welfare Assn., Ia. Welfare Assn. Home: 1800 Grand Ave West Des Moines IA 50265 Office: Hoover State Office Bldg Des Moines IA 50309

HAMEL, IRIT ZELTZER, psychologist; b. Vilna, Russia, Mar. 6, 1946; came to U.S., 1972; d. Mendel and Gitel (Mesinger) Zelcer; B.A. cum laude, Tel-Aviv U., 1968, M.A. cum laude, 1972; Ph.D., Vanderbilt U., 1975; m. Baruch Hamel, Sept. 5, 1967; children—Keren, Eschel A. Teaching asst. Tel-Aviv U., 1969-72; research asso. Vanderbilt U., 1975-77; instr. U. Tenn., 1976-79; psychol. intern Dede Wallace Center, Nashville, 1978-79; clin. psychologist dept. corrections State of Tenn., Nashville, 1979-80; clin. psychologist sex offenders program South Fla. State Hosp., Pembroke Pines, 1980—. Vice pres. for edn. Temple Shir Ami. Lic. clin. psychologist, Tenn. Mem. Am. Psychol. Assn., Am. Assn. Correctional Psychologists, N.Y. Acad. Sci. Office: Sex Offenders Program South Fla State Hosp 1000 SW 84th Ave Pembroke Pines FL 33025

HAMEL, JUDITH ANNE, social worker; b. Boston, Sept. 10, 1954; d. Harvey Harding and Myrtle Elaine (Goldberg) H.; B.Social Work, N. Tex. State U., Denton, 1977; m. Jeffrey A. Kaufman, Sept. 5, 1982. From psychiat. counseling asst. to intensive psychiat. counselor Brookhaven Med. Center, Dallas, 1977-79; social worker, then dir. rehab. services Avodah Work Center, Dallas, 1979—. Mem. Nat. Assn. Social Workers, Assn. Jewish Vocat. Service Profls., Sigma Alpha Mu. Jewish. Club: B'nai B'rith (life). Home: 4153 Hawthorne Dallas TX 75219 Office: 2947 Blystone Dallas TX 75220

HAMER, BERNICE BEATRICE, communications exec., cons.; b. Worcester, Mass., July 24, 1924; d. Frank S. and Anastasia (Richmond) Zagunis; student Perkins Sch. Blind; 1 son, Alan Lee. Owner, mgr. Bus. Men's Exchange, Lawrence, Mass., 1949—, Radio Exchange, Inc., 1969—, Exchange for Merrimack Valley, Inc., 1976—. Mem. Telephone Assn. New Eng., Am. Assn. Telephone Exchanges, Nat. C. of C., Better Bus. Bur., Internat. Platform Assn., Nat. Fedn. of Blind. Home: 31 Dartmouth St Lawrence MA 01841 Office: 245 Stevens St Lowell MA 01851

HAMER, JEANNE HUNTINGTON, soprano, educator; b. Lovell, Wyo., Mar. 1, 1933; d. Edward Olney and Francine M. (Clavier) Huntington; Mus.B. with honors, U. Wyo., 1955, postgrad., 1976-82; postgrad. U. Denver, 1976; m. Roger F. Hamer, Aug. 19, 1955; children—Michael Edward, Kathryn Louise. Grad. teaching asst. U. Wyo., 1955-56; pvt. vocal tchr., Billings, Mont., 1957-58, Miles City, Mont., 1958-59, Grand Rapids, Minn., 1959-61, Torrington, Wyo., 1962—; instr. music Eastern Wyo. Coll., 1968—, chmn. dept. music, 1978—; lead roles in operas, including: The Medium, The Telephone, Cavalleria Rusticana, I Pagliacci, Baby Doe; soloist with Billings (Mont.) Symphony, Casper (Wyo.) Symphony, Scottsbluff (Nebr.) Symphony, Nebr. Panhandle Symphony, U. Wyo. Symphony; soprano Barta Trio, 1972—; adjudicator for music festivals, Wyo., Mont., Nebr.; organist, choir dir. All Saints Episcopal Ch., Torrington, 1974-82; dir. Torrington Community Chorus, 1975—. Mem. Nat. Assn. Tchrs. Singing (gov. Wyo.), Am. Choral Dirs. Assn., Music Educators Nat. Conf. Episcopalian. Clubs: PEO, Order Eastern Star. Home: 515 E 23 Ave Torrington WY 82240 Office: 3200 W C St Torrington WY 82240

HAMID, LOUISE KATHERINE, club woman; b. Manchester, Conn., Jan. 18, 1951; d. Michael Alexander and Loretta Ruth (White) Kasevich; student U. Conn., 1969-71; m. Rashid Hamid, Aug. 14, 1971; children—Sophia Ann, Nadia Rashid. Bookkeeper, Naek Constrn. Co., Inc., Vernon, Conn., 1978—; mem. Greater Vernon Jaycee Wives, 1975-79, archivist, 1976-77, pres., 1977-79, chmn. bd. dirs., 1979—; mem. Tolland County Spl. Olympics Track and Field Com., 1979—; leader Conn.

Valley council Girl Scouts U.S.A., 1974, 80—; mem. Hockanum Valley Dept. Aging, 1978-79; pres. Maple Street Sch. PTO, 1980-82; mem. by-law com. Helping Hands Program of Vernon, 1981; sec. PTO Council, Vernon, 1982—. Democrat. Home: 113 Regan Rd Vernon CT 06066

HAMILL, DOROTHY BLACK, journalist; b. Barbourville, Ky., Sept. 14, 1905; d. Henry C. and Ethel (Fellows) Black; B.A., Ohio Wesleyan U., 1926; postgrad. in journalism Northwestern U., 1927; m. Stuart Hamill, Mar. 27, 1936 (div. 1942); 1 dau., Ellen Douglas Hamill Foster. With Friendship Press, N.Y.C., 1937-42; feature writer Johnson City (Tenn.) Press-Chronicle, 1952—. Recipient cert. Jaycees, 1964. Clubs: Monday, Merry Wives. Home: 720 W Locust St Johnson City TN 27601 Office: 204 W Main St Johnson City TN 37601

HAMILL, DOROTHY STUART, profl. ice skater; b. Chgo., d. Chalmers C. and Carolyn C. (Clough) H.; student Colo. Acad.; hon. degree, Greenwich High Sch. Olympic Gold medalist, 1976; world figure skating champion, 1976; profl. skater Ice Capades, 1977—. Office: care Ice Capades 6121 Santa Monica Blvd Hollywood CA 90038 *

HAMILTON, ALICE OBEE, columnist; b. Whitehouse, Ohio, Feb. 26, 1906; d. Christopher and Electa Rose (Miller) Obee; B.S., Eastern Mont. Coll., 1951; m. Robert L. Hamilton, Feb. 27, 1926; children—Robert Lail, Romedla Joy Hamilton Mueller, Richard Dale. Tchr. public schs., Billings, Mont; gardening columnist Billings Gazette, 1958—; host monthly gardening program Sta. KEMC, Billings, 1981—; instr. artistic design Flower Show Schs., 1958—; design and hort. workshops, 1957—; hostess monthly radio program on gardening Sta. KEMC, 1981—. Pres., Mont. Fedn. Garden Clubs, 1954-56, editor state mag., 1954-56, named Gardener of Yr., 1979. Recipient TV Radio award Nat. Council State Garden Clubs, 1958. Mem. Nat. Press Women, Mont. Edn. Assn., NEA. Presbyterian. Contbr. articles to mags.

HAMILTON, BETH ALLEMAN, librarian; b. Stewartstown, W.Va., Apr. 3, 1927; d. Hubert Charles and Gay Elizabeth (Zearley) Alleman; B.S., W.Va. U., 1948; M.A., Rosary Coll., 1969; C.A.S., U. Chgo., 1977; m. Rex Hamilton, Apr. 17, 1949; children—Shelley Hamilton Hutter, Meredith L., Eric R., Kimberly E., John Z. Chemist, Standard Pharmacal, Chgo., 1948-49; tech. librarian Am. Meat Inst. Found., Chgo., 1949-51; research librarian Glidden Co., Chgo., 1952-53; owner, partner Hamilton Truck Leasing, Elk Grove Village, Ill., 1957-63; editor, bus. analyst Internat. Minerals & Chem. Corp., Skokie, Ill., 1964-69; sci. librarian, asso. prof. U. Ill., Chgo., 1969-72, adj. asso. prof., 1972-79; exec. dir. Ill. Regional Library Council, Chgo., 1972-79; sr. info. scientist Triodyne, Inc., Cons. Engrs., Skokie, Ill., 1979—; vis. lectr. Rosary Coll., 1970-71; vis. asst. prof. U. Ill. Grad. Sch. Library Sci., Urbana, 1977—. Mem. Dist. 25 Bd. Edn., Arlington Heights, Ill., 1966-70; mem. Burr Ridge (Ill.) Bicentennial Commn., 1975-76; exec. v.p. Republican. Women's Club of Lyons Twp., 1975-76; librarian, tchr. First Presbyterian Ch. of Arlington Heights, 1960-69. Mem. Am. Chem. Soc., Spl. Libraries Assn., ALA, Ill. Library Assn., Am. Soc. Info. Sci., Beta Phi Mu. Editor: Libraries and Information Centers in the Chicago Metropolitan Area, 1973; Union List of Serial Holdings in Illinois Special Libraries, 1976, 77; Multitype Library Cooperation, 1977; As Much to Learn as to Teach, 1979; contbr. articles in field to profl. jours. Home: 2420 Fir St Glenview IL 60025 Office: 7855 Gross Point Rd Skokie IL 60077

HAMILTON, CHRISTINA DEE, music educator; b. Bloomfield, Ind.; d. Stanley and Mildred Hamilton; B.S., Miami U., Oxford, Ohio; M.S., Ind. U., Bloomington. Tchr. music Monroe County Community Schs., Bloomington, 1957—; owner pvt. music studio for piano, organ, violin and flute; producer, dir. children's operettas for local TV stas. Mem. Internat. Platform Assn., NEA, Ind. Tchrs. Assn., Monroe County Educators Assn., Music Educators Nat. Conf., Ind. Music Educators Assn., Orff-Shulwerk Assn. Republican. Methodist. Home: 516 N Fess St Bloomington IN 47401 Office: 627 W 8th St Bloomington IN 47401

HAMILTON, DAGMAR STRANDBERG, lawyer, educator; b. Phila., Jan. 10, 1932; d. Eric Wilhelm and Anna Elizabeth (Sjöström) Strandberg; A.B., Swarthmore Coll., 1953; J.D., U. Chgo. Law Sch., 1956; J.D., Am. U., 1961; m. Robert W. Hamilton, June 26, 1953; children—Eric Clark, Robert Andrew Hale, Meredith Hope. Admitted to Tex. bar, 1972; atty., civil rights div. U.S. Dept. Justice, Washington, 1965-66; asst. instr. govt. U. Tex., Austin, 1966-71; lectr. Law Sch. U. Ariz., Tucson, 1971-72; editor, researcher Asso. Justice William O. Douglas, U.S. Supreme Ct., 1962-73, 75-76; editor, research Douglas autobiography Random House Co., 1972-73; counsel Judiciary Com., U.S. Ho. of Reps., 1973-74; asst. prof. L.B. Johnson Sch. Pub. Affairs, U. Tex., Austin, 1974-77, asso. prof., 1977—; vis. prof. Washington U. Law Sch., St. Louis, Spring 1982. Mem. steering com. Westlake Neighborhood Assn.; bd. dirs. ACLU. Mem. So., Am. polit. sci. assns., Tex. Bar Assn., Kappa Beta Phi (hon.), Phi Kappa Phi (hon.). Democrat. Quaker. Contbr. to various publs. Home: 403 Allegro Ln Austin TX 78746 Office: LBJ Sch Public Affairs U Tex Austin TX 78712

HAMILTON, ELEANOR LEIGH, sex therapist; b. Portland, Oreg., Oct. 6, 1909; d. Kenneth and Clara-Belle (Cunningham) Poorman; A.B., U. Oreg., 1930; Ph.D., Columbia U., 1955; m. A.E. Hamilton, Aug. 11, 1932; children—Heather, Mark, Wendy, April. Head girl res. program YWCA, San Jose, Calif., 1930-32; founder, dir. Hamilton Sch., Inc., adult edn. and therapy center, profl. sex counselor tng. center, N.Y.C., 1934-48, Sheffield, Mass., 1948—; lectr. in field; appearances on various nat. TV shows, including Phil Donahue Show, Merv Griffin Show, Today, Tomorrow, Woman '78, Alan Hammel, Jo Davidson, Nat. Edn. TV. Recipient Achievement Award of Yr., Soc. for Sci. Study Sex, 1978; lic. psychologist, Mass., N.Y. State. Mem. Am. Assn. Marital and Family Therapists, Am. Psychol. Assn., Am. Assn. Sex Educators, Counselors and Therapists, Am. Coll. Sexologists, Am. Soc. Clin. Hypnosis, Am. Soc. Journalists and Authors. Republican. Author: Sex Before Marriage, 1969; Your Engagement, 1970; Sex With Love (ALA award), 1978; Partners In Love, 1980; contbr. numerous articles to Modern Bride mag., Science Digest, others. Home and Office: Hamilton Sch Inc Silver St Sheffield MA 01257

HAMILTON, GRACE TOWNS (MRS. HENRY COOKE HAMILTON), state legislator; b. Atlanta, Feb. 10, 1907; d. George Alexander and Nellie (McNair) Towns; A.B., Atlanta U., 1927; M.A., Ohio State U., 1929; m. Henry Cooke Hamilton, June 7, 1930; 1 dau., Eleanor Hamilton Payne. Girls work sec. YWCA, Columbus, Ohio, 1927-28, nat. program staff coll. and community divs., N.Y.C., 1936-43, cons. community relations, 1960-62; instr. Atlanta Sch. Social Work, 1928-29; instr. psychology Clark Coll., Atlanta, 1929-30, LeMoyne Coll., Memphis, 1930-34; dir. Survey White Collar and Skilled Negro Workers, Memphis, 1935-36; asso. dir. So. Regional Council, Atlanta, 1954-55; exec. dir. Atlanta Urban League, 1943-60; community relations cons. Hamilton Assos., Atlanta, 1961-67; dir. Atlanta Youth Council, 1966; mem. Ga. Ho. of Reps., 1965—. Vice chmn. Atlanta Charter Commn., 1971-73. Past mem. exec. com. Citizens Adv. Com. for Urban Renewal, Atlanta; mem. Ga. Gov.'s Commn. on Status Women; mem. Nat. Citizens Adv. Commn. Recreation and Natural Beauty, 1966; mem. exec. com. So. Regional Council; mem. Ga. Gov.'s Spl. Council on Family Planning, Fulton-DeKalb Hosp. Authority, 1971; mem. exec. bd. Ga. div. NCCJ. Mem. Fulton County Democratic Exec. Com., 1970—, Ga. Dem. Exec. Com., 1971—. Bd. dirs. Gate City Day Nursery Assn.; trustee Meharry Med. Coll., Atlanta U. Rosenwald fellow, 1947-48. Recipient numerous awards, 1965—, including Distinguished Achievement award Atlanta U. Alumnae Assn., 1965, certificate of appreciation Atlanta Urban League, 1970, citation for pub. service Sta. WSB-TV, 1972, Nonpartisan Community Service award Fulton County Republican Women, 1971, Good Neighbor award NCCJ, 1973, Law Day-Liberty Bell award Atlanta Bar Assn., 1974; named Alumnus of Year, Atlanta U., 1969. Mem. Nat. Order Women Legislators, Internat. Conf. Social Work, Nat. Conf. Social Welfare. Conglist.

HAMILTON, JEANNE BARRETT, govt. adminstr., small bus. exec.; b. Richmond, Va., Aug. 2, 1944; d. Charles Gilbert and Regina (Maroney) Barrett; student Wheeling Coll., 1962-64, 65-66, Loyola U., Rome br., 1964-65; B.A., Cath. U., 1972; m. L. Clark Hamilton, Dec. 26, 1976. Research positions Library of Congress, Washington, 1966—, tech. info. specialist Congressional Reference div. Congressional Research Service, 1966-72, asst. sect. head gen. reference, 1972-74, asst. coordinator research office of dir., 1974-76, head spl. services, 1976-79, adminstr. Congressional Research Adminstrn. for Interdisciplinary Research, 1979—; pres. Designs for Daisy, 1979—; owner Creative Caterers, 1980-81. Library of Congress spl. recruit program trainee 1970; recipient Community Service award, 1979. Mem. Nat. Council Career Women, Nat. Assn. Female Execs., Washington Women's Network, Library of Congress Profl. Assn. Roman Catholic. Home: 502 Malcolm Pl Alexandria VA 22302 Office: Office of Research Analysis and Rev Congressional Research Service Library of Congress Washington DC 20540

HAMILTON, KATY, newspaper mng. editor; b. Kremerbruch, Germany, May 15, 1937; came to U.S., 1959, naturalized, 1964; d. Otto and Helene (Gaul) Limberg; student bus. coll. Braunschweig, Germany; children—Barbara Hamilton Brown, Brenda. In airline communications, Frankfurt, Germany, 1956-58; TTS operator Chambersburg (Pa.) Public Opinion, 1960-69, gen. assignment reporter, 1969-74, area city editor, 1974-77, mng. editor, 1977—. Bd. dirs. Franklin County chpt. ARC. Mem. Pa. AP Mng. Editors Assn. (dir., pres.). Lutheran. Office: 77 N 3d St Chambersburg PA 17201

HAMILTON, LAURA ANN, social worker; b. Cordele, Ga., Nov. 16, 1939; d. Herbert Williams and Janie LaVerne (Lumpkin) Hamilton; student Valdosta State Coll., 1957-58; B.S., Fla. State U., 1961, M.S.W., 1965; postgrad. U. Ga., 1961-62, U. Chgo., summer 1967, W. Ga. Coll., 1969, Ga. State U., 1970. Vis. tchr. Crisp County Schs., Cordele, 1961-63; social service worker Social Service Dept., Milledgeville (Ga.) State Hosp., 1963; med. social worker Crippled Children's Service, Birmingham, Ala., 1964; psychiat. social worker Fla. State Hosp., Chattahoochee, 1965, Milledgeville State Hosp., 1965-66; cons. for social work projects ESEA Title I, Ga. Dept. Edn., Atlanta, 1966-68, ESEA Title III, 1968-71; cons. program evaluations and audits Robert Davis Assos., Inc., Atlanta, 1971-72; chief Div. Planning, Evaluation, Monitoring and Analysis, S.C. Dept. Social Services, Columbia, 1973-76; regional dir. social services Regions 01 and 02, Tex. Dept. Public Welfare, Lubbock, 1976-77; partner Kaye Fleming Boutique and Bridal Corner, Ft. Worth, 1978—; pvt. practice social work, Ft. Worth, Tex., 1978—; field supr. Kirschner Assos., Inc., Albuquerque, 1972, 73; evaluator for edn. professions devel. act project Waycross (Ga.) City Schs., 1972, W. Ga. Ednl. Service Center, Carrollton, 1972; program auditor Clarke County Schs., Atlanta, 1972; instr. Human Resource Center, U. Tex., Arlington, 1977—; lectr. in field. Mem. Acad. Cert. Social Workers, Am. Public Welfare Assn., Am. Soc. Public Adminstrn., Nat. Assn. Social Workers. Address: 1611 Trailridge Dr Arlington TX 76012

HAMILTON, LINDA KAY, publishing co. exec.; b. Waukegan, Ill., May 13, 1945; d. Lloyd Henry and Vida May (Harms) Fruth; B.A., Mich. State U., 1966; A.M. in Library Sci., U. Mich., 1968; M.B.A., Mich. State U., 1972; m. William Digby Hamilton, Nov. 5, 1966; 1 dau., Arwen Elizabeth. Sect. head Mich. State U. Libraries, 1969-73; head catalog dept. Wayne State U. Libraries, Detroit, 1973-75, network coordinator, 1975-76, asst. dir. Mich. Library Consortium, 1976-77; mgr. bibliographic services Univ. Microfilms Internat., Ann Arbor, 1977-79, mgr. collections ops., 1979-82; v.p. acad. micropublishing Research Publs. Inc., Woodbridge, Conn., 1982—. Mem. ALA, Mich. Library Assn., Nat. Assn. Female Execs. Editor: MLA Intellectual Freedom Newsletter, 1974-75, Cort Cat News, 1974-77. Office: 12 Lunar Dr Woodbridge Ct 06525

HAMILTON, MADRID TURNER, assn. exec.; b. Green County, Ga.; d. Paul and Mary (Hubert) Turner; A.B., Spelman Coll.; M.S.W., Atlanta U.; Ph.D., Union Grad. Sch. West, San Francisco, 1979; m. Norman Woodrow Hamilton, June 9, 1948; 1 son, Alexander Turner. Chmn. tng. task force Nat. YWCA of U.S.A., 1970-73, nat. bd. com. of concern for Angela Davis, 1971-73, vice chmn. Urban Services Com., 1973-76; mem. Research and Program Resources Core Group, and local assn. Fin. Devel. Com., 1973-76, treas., fin. chmn. Redlands (Calif.) 1975-77, v.p., chmn. program com. San Francisco, 1971-74, treas., 1980, mem. nat. bd., 1970—, urban affairs, public relations, public affairs coms., editorial adv. com. for YWCA Interchange, Assn. reviewer, regional v.p. nat. bd. Western States, 1979—; pres. Hamilton Enterprises, Inc., San Francisco, 1972—; asst. prof. sociology Morehouse Coll.; asso. prof. Grad. Sch. Social Welfare, San Francisco State Coll. and U. Redlands; cons. public health social work N.Y.C. Dept. Health. Bd. dirs. Redlands United Way, 1975-77, White Plains (N.Y.) Community Chest, Carver Community Center, San Francisco; developing program dir. Columbia Area YWCA, Phila.; activities dir. YWCA City of N.Y.; regional dir. Planned Parenthood World Population; regional rep. Family Service Assn. Am.; active United Negro Coll. Fund, Urban League, N.Y.C. and San Francisco; mem. Calif. Gov.'s Population Study Commn. Recipient Human Resources award Am. Heritage Found., 1976. Mem. Calif. Assn. Realtors (realtor asso.), Spelman Coll. Alumnae Assn. (Far West Region coordinator), Zeta Phi Beta. Club: Altrusa (San Francisco). Newspaper columnist, author. Home: 136 Geneva Ave San Francisco CA 94112

HAMILTON, MARY ELIZABETH CASEY, civic worker, former educator; b. Moorhead, Miss., Sept. 14, 1910; d. John Lucas and Anna Cordelia (Frank) Casey; B.A., Miss. State Coll. for Women, 1932; m. Charles G. Hamilton, May 23, 1939. Tchr. math. and history schs. in Miss., Tenn. and Fla., 1932-75; mem. staff spectator, Columbus, Miss., 1931-32, Tupelo (Miss.) Jour., 1947-48; editor Jour. Monroe County History, Aberdeen, Miss., 1975—. Chmn., Aberdeen City Beautification Commn., 1976—, Monroe County Bicentennial Horizons, 1975-76; mem. Aberdeen Bicentennial Commn., 1975-76, Keep Miss. Beautiful Com., 1979—, Aberdeen City Hall Preservation Com., 1982—. Named Aberdeen Woman of Yr., Jr. Aux., 1976. Mem. Monroe County Hist. Soc. (pres. 1974—), Aberdeen Woman's Club (pres. 1976—), DAR, Aberdeen Pilgrimage Assn., Am. Legion Aux. Democrat. Episcopalian. Address: 410 S Meridian St Aberdeen MS 39730

HAMILTON, REBECCA, state legislator; b. Jan. 8, 1948; B.S., U. Okla. Mem. Okla. Ho. of Reps., 1981—. Office: Okla Ho Reps State Capitol Oklahoma City OK 73105 *

HAMILTON, RHODA LILLIAN ROSEN, educator; b. Chgo., May 8, 1915; d. Reinhold August and Olga (Peterson) Rosen; grad. Moser Coll., Chgo., 1932-33; B.S. in Edn., U. Wis., 1953, postgrad., 1976; M.A.T., Rollins Coll., 1967; postgrad. Ohio State U., 1959-60; postgrad. in clin. psychology Mich. State U., 1971, 76; postgrad. Yale U., 1972, Loma Linda U., 1972; postgrad. in computer mgmt. systems U. Okla., 1976; postgrad. in edn. U. Calif., Berkeley, 1980; m. Douglas Edward Hamilton, Jan. 23, 1936 (div. Feb. 1952); children—Perry Douglas, John Richard. Exec. sec. to pres. Ansul Chem. Co., Marinette, Wis., 1934-36; personnel counselor Burneice Larson's Med. Bur., Chgo., 1954-56 adminstrv. asst. to Ernst C. Schmidt, Lake Geneva, Wis., 1956-58; asso. prof. fin. aid Ohio State U., 1958-60; tchr. English to speakers of other langs., Istanbul, Turkey, 1960-65; counselor Groveland (Fla.) High Sch., 1965-68; guidance counselor and psychol. cons. early childhood edn. Dept. Def. Overseas Dependents Sch., Okinawa, 1968—; co-owner plumbing, heating bus., Marinette, 1943-49; journalist Rockford (Ill.) Morning Star, 1956-58, Istanbul AP, 1960. Vol. instr. U.S. citizenship classes, Okinawa, 1971-72. Mem. NEA, Okinawa Educators, Overseas Edn. Assn., Am. Personnel and Guidance Assn., Nat. Vocat. Guidance Assn., Assn. Measurement and Evaluation in Guidance, Am. Fedn. Govt. Employees (sec. Okinawa local 1678), Nat. Council Measurement in Edn., Am. Sch. Counselor Assn., Phi Delta Gamma. Clubs: Order Eastern Star (organist Shuri chpt. 1); Ikebana Internat. Author poetry on Middle East, 1959-64; Career Awareness, 1978. Home: 255 E Waldo St Groveland FL 32736 Office: Dept Defense Overseas Dependents Sch Bobe Hope Primary Sch PO Box 3280 APO San Francisco CA 96248

HAMILTON, SYLVIA WALINOW (MRS. RAY A. HAMILTON), pub. relations exec.; b. Kansas City, Kans., Nov. 24, 1919; d. Joseph and Eva (Lasik) Walinow; student Kansas City (Kans.) Jr. Coll., 1936-38; m. Ray A. Hamilton, Nov. 20, 1948. Dir. pub. service Radio Sta. KCKN, Kansas City, Kans., 1945-48; dir. pub. relations 5-County Heart Am. United Campaign, Kansas City, Mo., 1948-58, assoc. dir. in charge pub. relations, 1958-73; nat. pub. relations dir. VFW Aux., Kansas City, 1973—. Pub. relations cons. to study of Bay Area United Crusade, San Francisco, 1965. Recipient Silver Anvil award for best program in philanthropic field Am. Pub. Relations Assn., 1958; George Washington gold medal Freedoms Found., 1974, 75, 76, 78. Mem. Kansas City Pub. Relations Soc. (pres. 1960, dir. 1965—), Kansas City Indsl. Editors Assn. (pres. 1960-61), Women's C. of C., Advt. and Sales Club, United Community Funds and Councils Am. (nat. pub. relations com. 1956—, chmn. midwest regional conf. 1962), Theta Sigma Phi. Home: 2138 Normandy Ln Kansas City KS 64116 Office: 406 W 34th St Kansas City MO 64111

HAMILTON, THERESA MARIE, sales exec.; b. Woburn, Mass., July 10, 1950; d. John Francis and Gertrude Marion (Stoney) H.; R.N., Tewksbury Hosp., 1969; student Emmanuel Coll., 1981. Oncology nurse Lahey Clinic Found., Boston, 1970-76; supr. Care at Home Nursing Services, Newton, Mass., 1976-77; field sales rep. Marsha Brenner Assos., 1977-78; dir. sales and mktg. CW Communications Conf. Mgmt. Group, Framingham, Mass., 1978-82; nat. sales mgr. Mitch Hall Assos., Norwood, Mass., 1982—. Author: (with Richard Oberfield) Hepatic Artery Infusion, 1976. Office: 83 Nahatan St Norwood MA 02062

HAMILTON, VIRGINIA, advt. exec.; b. Phila., Mar. 15, 1945; d. Stanley Malcolm and Anna B. (Woolfendon) Cameron; B.A. in History of Art, U. Pa., 1966; postgrad. Pa. Acad. Fine Arts, 1966-67. Freelance photographer, 1967-77; nat. account cons. Dun & Bradstreet Inc., 1977-78; advt. account exec. Mktg. Showcase, N.Y.C., 1978-79; account exec. l'officiel mag., also Seventeen mag., N.Y.C., 1979-80, Actmedia, Inc., N.Y.C., 1980-81, Mktg. Showcase, 1981—; lectr. Careers for Women, N.Y.C., 1977-78. Home: 265 E 66th St New York NY 10021 Office: 621 Ave of Americas New York NY 10011

HAMILTON, VIRGINIA (MRS. ARNOLD ADOFF), author; b. Yellow Springs, Ohio, Mar. 12, 1936; d. Kenneth James and Etta Belle (Perry) Hamilton; student Antioch Coll., 1952-55, Ohio State U., 1957-58, New Sch. for Social Research; m. Arnold Adoff, Mar. 19, 1960; children—Leigh Hamilton, Jaime Levi. Recipient Ohioana Lit. award, 1969. Author: (children's novels) Zeely (Nancy Block Meml. award Downtown Community Sch. Awards Com.), 1967; The House of Dies Drear (Edgar Allan Poe award for best juvenile mystery, 1969), 1968; The Time-Ago Tales of Jadhu, 1969; Planet of Junior Brown, 1971; W.E.B. Dubois: A Biography, 1972; Time-Ago Lost: More Tales of Jahdu, 1973; M.C. Higgins the Great (John Newbery medal 1974, Nat. Book award 1975), 1974; Paul Robeson: The Life and Times of a Free Black Man, 1974; Arilla Sun Down, 1976, Justice and Her Brothers, 1978, Dustland, 1980, The Gathering, 1980. Editor: Writings of W.E.B. Dubois, 1975. Office: care Greenwillow Books div William Morrow Co 105 Madison Ave New York NY 10016 *

HAMILTON, VIRGINIA VAN DER VEER, historian; b. Kansas City, Mo., Sept. 7, 1921; d. McClellan and Dorothy (Rainold) Van der Veer; A.B., Birmingham (Ala.)-So. Coll., 1941, M.A. (Ford Found. Fund for Adult Edn. fellow), 1961; Ph.D., U. Ala., Tuscaloosa, 1968; m. Lowell S. Hamilton, Aug. 4, 1946; children—Carol, David. Staff writer AP, Washington, 1942-46, Birmingham News, 1948-50; asst. prof. history U. Montevallo (Ala.), 1951-55; asst. prof., asst. to pres. for pub. relations Birmingham-So. Coll., 1955-65; lectr. in history U. Ala., Birmingham, 1965-68, asst. prof., 1968-71, asso. prof., 1971-75, prof., 1975—. U. Ala. at Tuscaloosa faculty research grantee, 1969; U. Ala. at Birmingham faculty research grantee, 1973-74, 74-75. Mem. So., Am. hist. assns., Orgn. Am. Historians, Soc. Am. Historians, Am. Assn. State, local History, Ala. Assn. Historians, Ala. Hist. Soc., Oral History Assn. Author: Hugo Black: The Alabama Years, 1972; Alabama: A History, 1977; The Story of Alabama, 1980; Your Alabama, 1980; Seeing Historic Alabama, 1982; editor: Hugo Black and the Bill of Rights, 1978. Home: 3246 Overbrook Rd Birmingham AL 35213 Office: Dept History U Ala Birmingham AL 35294

HAMILTON-TUCKER, MARY CAROLYN, psychologist; b. Anson Country, N.C., Jan. 4, 1942; d. Lee Jay and Rosa Lee (Hamilton) White; B.A., U. D.C., 1976; M.Ed., Howard U., 1978, postgrad., 1978—; m. Samuel Monroe Tucker, Apr. 20, 1962; children—Yvette Carol, Darryl Monroe. Sec., U.S. Treasury Dept., Washington, 1963-64, personnel clk., 1964-65; legal asst. SBA, Washington, 1967-70, adminstrv. sec., 1970-71; adminstrv. asst. U.S. Action Agy., Washington, 1971-72; research asst. U.S. Dept. Transp., Washington, 1972-75; adminstrv. clk. D.C. Public Schs., Washington, 1979; adminstrv. aide D.C. Bd. Edn., Washington, 1979-80; manpower devel. specialist D.C. Dept. Employment Services, Washington, 1980-81; vol. psychol. counselor St. Elizabeth's Hosp., Washington, 1975-76; teaching asst. Howard U., Washington, 1976-78; spl. edn. tchr. Dept. Human Resources, Therapeutic Nursery Sch., Washington, 1978; research fellow sociology-anthropology dept., Howard U., Washington, 1978-79; vol. research asst. D.C. Sch. Bd., Washington, 1978-79; youth counselor Nat. Council Negro Women, Washington, 1975-76. Adv. Neighborhood Council commr., ward IV, Washington, 1981—, chmn.; rec. sec. D.C. Young Republicans, 1981; del. Nat. Young Rep. Fedn. Conv., 1981; rec. sec. Renaissance Club, D.C. Rep. party, 1981; rec. sec. AFRICARE, Washington, 1981-82; pres. Roosevelt High Sch. PTA, Washington, 1981-82; mem. women's programs, public affairs and program com. Md. Black Republic Council, Prince Georges County, Md., 1981-82; mem. exec. bd. Brightwood United Meth. Ch., Washington. Mem. Assn. Black Psychologists, Council Exceptional Children, Nat. Assn. Profl. Pharmacists Wives, Nat. Assn. Retail Druggists, Am. Psychol. Assn., Nat. Womens Polit. Caucus, Phi Delta Kappa. Clubs: United Meth. Women, Profl. Pharmacists Wives. Home: 5921 2d Pl NW Washington DC 20011

HAMLAR, PORTIA YVONNE TRENHOLM, lawyer, educator; b. Montgomery, Ala., Apr. 30, 1932; d. Harper Council and Portia Lee (Evans) Trenholm; B.A., Ala. State U., 1951; M.A., Mich. State U., 1953; J.D., U. Detroit, 1972; postgrad. U. Mich., Wayne State U.; 1 son, Eric L. Hamlar. Vocal music instr. Detroit public schs., 1953-57, 58-63,

65-66, 68-71; acad. counselor U. Mich., 1957-58; vocal music instr. Pontiac (Mich.) High Sch., 1963-65; legal sec. firm Hyman, Gurwin, Nachman & Friedman, Detroit, 1966-68; legal researcher Mich. Appellate Defender, Detroit, 1971-73; adminstrv. asst. Am. Bar Assn. Lawyers for Housing Program, Los Angeles, 1973; legal counsel Greater Watts Model Cities Housing Corp., Los Angeles, 1973; atty. Chrysler Corp., Detroit, 1973-80; adj. prof. law U. Detroit, 1975-79; prof. law Del. Law Sch., Wilmington, 1980—. Mem. Am. (com on occupational safety and health), Del. Bar Assn., Motor Vehicle Mfrs. Assn. (legis. and draft com.), Washington Orgn. Resources Counselors Occupational Safety and Health Lawyers Group, Alph Kappa Mu, Mu Phi Epsilon. Democrat. Episcopalian. Author, pub. Defending the Employer in Occupational Safety and Health Administration Contests; bd. editors: Hazardous Materials Mgmt. Jour.; also articles on housing law; mem. U. Detroit Law Rev., 1970-72. Office: Del Law Sch PO Box 7474 Concord Pike Wilmington DE 19703

HAMLETT, IONA CUYLER, psychologist; b. Austin, Tex., Dec. 12, 1901; d. Robert Henry and Sarah Iona (McBryde) Cuyler; A.B., U. Tex., 1922, A.M., 1923; Ph.D., U. Ind., 1934; m. G. W. Deluz Hamlett, Aug. 29, 1923 (div. 1934); children—Iona Helen (Mrs. James Richard Mensch), Sarah Suzanne (Mrs. Gordon M. Haggard). Ednl., clin. psychologist Ft. Wayne (Ind.) State Hosp. and Tng. Center, 1934-72, dir. dept. psychol. services, 1966-72; pvt. practice psychology, Ft. Wayne, 1972—. Fellow Am. Assn. on Mental Deficiency (chmn. Gt. Lakes region 1963), Am. Psychol. Assn., Internat. Council Psychologists; mem. Ind. Psychol. Assn. (diplomate clin. psychology), Allen County Assn. Mental Health. Presbyterian. Home: Box 5131 Hazelwood Sta Fort Wayne IN 46895

HAMLIN, BETTY LOU, accountant; b. San Antonio, Aug. 5, 1939; d. Walter Roland and Audrey Jane (Keeling) Hamlin; grad. high sch.; m. Stephen Ronald Stone, Apr. 3, 1965; 1 dau., Nikki René. Operator, Southwestern Bell Tel. Co., Dallas, 1957-60; sec. Chas. Pfizer & Co., Dallas, 1960-61; acctg. clk. Goodyear Tire & Rubber Co., Dallas, 1961-67; sec., bookkeeper B.E. Parker, C.P.A., Carrollton, Tex., 1967-68; chief bookkeeper Computer Industries Inc. div. Univ. Computing Co., Dallas, 1968-70; gen acct. I.C. Deal div. Gt. sec. Chas. Pfizer & Co., Dallas, 1960-61; Corp., Dallas, 1970; gen. ledger staff acct. Harris Communication Systems, Inc., Dallas, 1971-73; project acct. Leadership Housing Systems, Inc., Dallas, 1973-74; acct. LDB Corp. div. Giffen Industries, Inc., Dallas, 1974—. Mem. Nat. Assn. Female Execs., Exec. Program. Democrat. Baptist. Home: 13565 Red Fern Ln Dallas TX 75240 Office: PO Box 47586 Dallas TX 75247

HAMLIN, HELEN RUTH, social worker; b. N.Y.C., Sept. 13, 1922; d. Murray L. and Lee M. (Freiwald) Rosenstein; B.A., Hunter Coll., N.Y.C., 1942; M.S.W., Columbia U., 1945; m. Isadore Hamlin, Sept. 23, 1943; children—Abby, Matthew, Emily. Caseworker, supr. Travellers Aid Soc., Washington, 1946-49; caseworker Jewish Family Service N.Y.C., 1950-51; intake/home service supr. N.Y. chpt. ARC, 1951-54; casework cons. Community Service Soc. N.Y.C., 1963-72; dir. social services Jamaica (N.Y.) Service Program Older Adults, 1972-80, Met. Jewish Geriatric Center, Bklyn., 1981—; adj. lectr. York Coll., City U. N.Y. Mem. Gerontol. Soc., Internat. Gerontol. Soc., Nat. Assn. Social Workers, Acad. Cert. Social Workers. Home: 333 E 66th St New York NY 10021 Office: 4915 10th Ave Brooklyn NY 11219

HAMLIN, MADGE TEMPERANCE SILLS (MRS. PAUL MAHLON HAMLIN), former educator; b. Newport News, Va., Sept. 27, 1897; d. James Everett and Fannie Montgomery (Smith) Sills; B.S., Greensboro Coll., 1920; M.A. in History, Columbia U., 1928; m. Paul Mahlon Hamlin, Feb. 18, 1927 (dec. Aug. 1968); 1 dau., Elizabeth Sills Hamlin Hill. Tchr. of English, Kobe, Japan and McIyeire Sch., Shanghai, China, 1921-22; lectr. Nat. Bd. YWCA, various U.S. colls., 1923-25; tchr. gifted children, Garden City, N.Y., 1928-30, Horace Mann Sch. Girls, N.Y.C., 1930-33; founder, benefactor, dir. Hamlin Country Day Sch. for Brilliant Children, Fair Lawn, N.J., 1933-66; organizer, dir. Orchard Sch. for Slow Learning Students, Fair Lawn, 1943-59. Mem. AAUW, DAR, Jamestown Soc., Nat. Soc. Colonial Dames in State N.J. Republican. Congregationalist. Clubs: Montclair Women's; Garden (Montclair and Rossmoor); Women's Nat. Rep. (N.Y.C.). Contbr. articles on travel and edn. to mags. and newspapers in N.J. and N.C.; lectr. on influence of Western civilization on Oriental culture, changing role of women. Address: 259 Old Nassau Rd Rossmoor PO Jamesburg NJ 08831

HAMM, BONNIE MOFFAT, assn. exec.; b. Bellefonte, Pa., Jan. 8, 1944; d. Reginald Lawton and Marian Eugenia (McElroy) Moffat; B.A. in Polit. Sci., Stetson U., 1966, M.A. (prospective teaching fellow 1969), 1971, M.A. in Polit. Sci., M.A. in Edn., 1971. Mgmt. trainee So. Bell Telephone Co., 1967-69; staff analyst Fla. Local Govt. Study Commn., 1971-73; criminal justice planner Office of Mayor, Jacksonville, Fla., 1973-74; grant mgr. Cathedral Found., 1974-75; pvt. cons. to mental health agencies, 1975-76; exec. dir. Consortium to Aid Neglected and Abused Children, 1976-77; mgr. govt. affairs Jacksonville Area C. of C., 1978-81; dir. Nat. Fedn. Ind. Bus., Tallahassee, 1981—; bd. dirs. Urban Jacksonville, 1973-75; mem. adv. bd. CETA, 1978—; mem. Jacksonville Community Council, 1980—, Leadership Jacksonville, 1981. Bd. dirs. Parent Resource Center, Jacksonville, 1977-79. Recipient Service award Jacksonville Safety Council, 1975. Mem. Am. Polit. Sci. Assn., Fla. Women's Polit. Caucus, Duval Women's Polit. Caucus, Jacksonville Women's Network (founding mem.). Democrat. Episcopalian. Home: 2829 Diamondhead E Tallahassee FL 32301 Office: 201 S Monroe St Suite 203 Tallahassee FL 32301

HAMM, PHYLLIS SCAGLIONE, univ. adminstr.; b. Bklyn., June 19, 1936; d. Orlando and Corinne (Alfonso) Scaglione; B.A. with distinction, U. South Fla., 1979; 1 dau., Karen Hamm Walter. Secretarial position Tamiami Trail Tours, Tampa, 1958-64, Reynolds Metals Co., Tampa, 1964-67; staff asst., dean's office Coll. Basic Studies, U. South Fla., Tampa, 1967-72, equal opportunity specialist, 1972-75, mgr. univ. employee benefits, 1975—; pres. U. South Fla. Career Service Senate, 1979. Del., Fla. Dem. Conv., 1979; bd. dirs. The Spring, 1979—; bd. dirs. Nathan B. Stubblefield Found. (WMNF-FM Radio), 1975—, chmn., pres., 1980—. Recipient Athena award Women in Communications, 1977; Outstanding Supervisory Career Service award U. South Fla., 1979; Women Helping Women award Soroptimist Internat. of Tampa 1980. Mem. NOW (pres. Tampa 1974), Women's Equity Action League (pres. Fla. div. 1973-75), ACLU, Coll. and Univ. Personnel Assn., Career Service Employees Fedn. (pres. local 1976). Home: 201 Deer Park Ave Temple Terrace FL 33617 Office: 4202 Fowler Ave Tampa FL 33620

HAMMAR, CHERYL ANN DERNOVICH, stockbroker, fin. planner; b. Rock Springs, Wyo., Apr. 10, 1950; d. George John and Josephine Louise (Sergio) Dernovich; B.A., U. Colo., 1972. Adminstrv. asst. U. Colo. Coll. Bus., Boulder, 1972; adminstrv. asst. G.D. Meyer & Assos., Mgmt. Cons., Boulder, 1973-74; owner, mgr. United Lumber, Inc., Glenwood Springs, Colo., 1974-76; stockbroker Moseley, Hallgarten, Estabrook, Burlington, Vt., 1976-77; stockbroker E. F. Hutton, Burlington, 1977, resident mgr. E.F. Hutton Fin. Services, Glenwood Springs, 1978-79; satellite mgr. Boettcher & Co., Glenwood Springs, 1979-81; pres. CDH Fin. Corp.; v.p. Aspen Securities and Investments; sec. Rocky Mountain Fin. Planning, Inc.; dir. Mountain Valley Devel. Services. Bd. dirs. Women's Resource Center. Mem. Internat. Assn. Fin. Planners, Glenwood Springs Bus. and Profl. Women (pres.), Glenwood Springs C. of C. (dir.), Young Career Woman of Colo., Nat. Assn. Female Execs., Vail Bus. and Profl. Women, Aspen Women's Forum. Republican. Roman Catholic. Address: 201 Centennial St Glenwood Springs CO 81602

HAMMER, BARBARA UDELL, clin. psychologist; b. Chgo., Aug. 25, 1937; d. Jack Edward and Gertrude (Kucheck) Udell; B.A., Grinnell Coll., 1957; M.S., Purdue U., 1959; Ph.D., U. Md., 1964; m. Charles H. Hammer, Oct. 19, 1958; children—Leslie, Ross, Eric. Staff psychologist Adult Mental Health Clinic, Washington, 1964; lectr. child devel. and psychology Mt. Vernon Coll., Washington, 1966-69; staff psychologist Child Guidance Clinic, Washington, 1968-70; cons., supr. U. Md. Counseling Center, College Park, 1967-70; supr. grad. tng. program clin. psychology George Washington U., Washington, 1970-71; pvt. practice clin. psychology, Washington, 1969—; cons., supr. Pastoral Counseling and Consultation Centers of Washington, 1977—. USPHS fellow, 1962-63; recipient AAUW award, 1962-63. Fellow Md. Psychol. Assn.; mem. Am. Psychol. Assn., D.C. Psychol. Assn. (pres.), Am. Acad. Psychotherapists. Home: Route 2 Box 281 Sterling VA 22170 Office: Suite 230 2939 Van Ness St NW Washington DC 20008

HAMMER, GEORGIANA RUTH, civic worker; b. Ozark, Mich., Mar. 8, 1926; d. George Isaac and Anna (Mahl) Rapson; student Modern Bus. Coll., Kennewick, Wash., 1964; m. Louis Elmer Hammer, May 29, 1948; children—John Austin, Linda Lou. Various positions A.C. Spark Plug Co., Flint, Mich., 1944-45, Munson Decker Hosp., 1947, Modern Bus. Coll., 1964-65, Thompson-Lampson Real Estate, Kennewick, 1972, Cooper Heat Co., 1978-79. Former leader, adv. Cub Scouts, Girl Scouts U.S.A., Rainbow Girls, 4-H. Recipient VA Vol. Service 1500 Hr. award Walla Walla Med. Center, 1980; cert. Tri-Cities Conv. Center, 1978; Grand Cross of Color, Internat. Order Rainbow, 1976. Mem. DAV Aux. (Outstanding Mem. award, 1st sr. vice-comdr. dept. Wash.). Club: Order Eastern Star (past dep. Inst. for Grand chpt. Wash., past matron Roza chpt.) (Benton City, Wash.). Home: 1926 George Washington Way Apt A-1 PO Box 744 Richland WA 99352

HAMMER, JANE NICKELSON, educator; b. Marlin, Tex., July 11, 1946; d. Lad and Rebecca (Rodgers) Nickelson; student Sam Houston State Coll., 1964-66; B.B.A., N. Tex. State U., 1968, M.B.A., 1971; Ed.D., Ind. U., 1981; m. Lawrence H. Hammer, Aug. 6, 1966. Tchr., Sunset High Sch., Dallas, 1968-70, Skyline Career Devel. Center, Dallas, 1970-74; asso. instr. Ind. U., Bloomington, 1974-77; teaching asso. Okla. State U., Stillwater, 1977-82, asst. prof. bus., 1982—. Mem. Nat. Bus. Edn. Assn., Phi Delta Kappa, Delta Pi Epsilon, Beta Gamma Sigma. Office: Okla State U Coll of Bus Stillwater OK 74078

HAMMOND, BARBARA JEAN, retail co. exec.; b. Sacramento, Dec. 19, 1930; d. Richard Alonzo and Jacqueline Faye (Davis) Winnie; m. Howard Lee Hammond, July 3, 1948; children—Nanci Lynne, Richard Arthur. With Home Interiors & Gifts, Inc., Dallas, 1960—, area mgr., 1970-75, asst. nat. sales mgr., 1975—, v.p. sales, 1978—, also dir. Bd. dirs., mem. exec. com. Direct Selling Assn. Ednl. Found. Mem. Direct Selling Assn. (dir. 1979—). Office: 4550 Spring Valley Rd Dallas TX 75234

HAMMOND, BEVERLY BLACK, clin. social worker; b. Wolfeboro, N.H., Jan. 12, 1944; d. Richard James and Ethel May (Elliott) Black; B.S. cum laude, U. N.H., 1966; M.S.W., Simmons Coll., 1969; m. Stanley Frank Hammond, July 12, 1969; children—J. Todd, E. Joshua. Social worker N.H. Div. Welfare, Laconia, 1966-67; social worker Div. Child Guardianship, Lawrence, Mass., 1967-68, James Jackson Putnam Children's Center, Roxbury, Mass., 1969-72; psychiat. social worker Caroll County Mental Health Service, Wolfeboro, North Conway, N.H., 1970-71, acting dir., 1969-80; sch. social worker Kingswood Regional Jr. High Sch., Wolfeboro, N.H., 1980—; social work cons. Meml. Hosp., North Conway, 1978-80; social worker North Conway Children and Youth Project Clinic, 1978-80; mem. N.H. Task Force Child Abuse and Neglect, 1976-78; mem. Carroll County (N.H.) Child Protective Com., 1975. Mem. Nat. Assn. Social Workers, Register Clin. Social Workers, Acad. Certified Social Workers. Home: Maple Rd Chocorua NH 03817 Office: Kingswood Regional Jr High Sch Main St Wolfboro NH 03894

HAMMOND, CAROL ANNE, mgmt. cons.; b. Gainesville, Tex., Jan. 4, 1940; d. Charles Harvey and Alma Gladys (Proffer) Woolfolk; student North Tex. State U., 1957-58; mgmt. cert. Tarrant County Jr. Coll., 1981; children—Vanessa, Jaime, Christopher. Asst. to gen. supr. purchasing dept. Bell Helicopter/Textron, 1964-67; exec. sec. Paul R. Ray & Co., Inc., Ft. Worth, 1968-70, mgr. records and research, 1970-77, asst. corp. v.p., 1977; v.p. Gray & Assos., Inc., Dallas, 1977-78; sr. v.p., corp. sec., chief adminstrv. officer SE Assos. Corp., Dallas, 1978—. Loaned exec. United Way of Met. Tarrant County (Tex.); sr. troop leader Circle T council Girl Scouts U.S.A., 1973-76. Mem. Am. Bus. Women's Assn. (chpt. Woman of Yr. award 1980; pres. 1981), Nat. Assn. Female Execs., Am. Mktg. Assn. Club: Lancers. Home: 112 Stonegate Ct Bedford TX 76021 Office: PO Box 61429 Dallas TX 75261

HAMMOND, DEANNA LINDBERG, linguist; b. Calgary, Alta., Can., May 31, 1942; d. Albin William and Emma Lou (Thompson) Lindberg; B.A., Wash. State U., 1964; M.A., Ohio U., 1968; Ph.D., Georgetown U., 1977; postgrad. Summer Sch., U. Ariz., Guadalajara, Portland State U. With Peace Corps, Colombia, 1964-66; prof. English, Universidad Industrial, Bucaramanga, Colombia, 1966-67; tchr. English, Spanish, Pullman (Wash.) High Sch., 1969-74; lectr. Georgetown U., Washington, 1974-77, dir. summer sch. program Quito, Ecuador, 1977; head lang. services Congressional Research Service, Library of Congress, Washington, 1977—; lectr. English as fgn. lang. No. Va. Community Coll., part-time, 1975—. Coordinator Combined Fed. Campaign, Congressional Research Service, 1978; coordinator Washington Area Foster Parents Support Group. Recipient Community Service Award Sec. Califano, 1978. Mem. Am. Translators Assn. (sec./exec. bd. Nat. Capital Area chpt., dir., editorial bd., rep. Council Communication Socs., chmn. domestic liason com., accreditation com.), Council Communication Socs. (pres.-elect 1982-84, exec., govt. relations, publs. coms.), N.E. Conf. Teaching Fgn. Langs., Assn. Tchrs. Spanish and Portuguese, Teaching English to Speakers Other Langs., Greater Washington Area Tchrs. Fgn. Langs., Library of Congress Profl. Assn., Nat. Assn. Female Execs. (charter), Inter-Am. Translators Assn., TESOL, Nat. Council Returned Peace Corps Vols, World Affairs Council, Phi Beta Kappa, Phi Kappa Phi. Democrat. Editorial bd. Modern Lang. Jour. Home: 3713 S George Mason Dr #701 W Falls Church VA 22041 Office: Congressional Research Service Lang Services Library of Congress Washington DC 20540

HAMMOND, DOROTHY LEE, author, publisher, columnist; b. Fairfax, Mo., Sept. 24, 1924; d. Lee O. and Ella E. (Brunk) Martin; B.S., Maryville (Mo.) State Tchrs. Coll., 1949; m. Robert Byron, Sept. 1, 1944; children—Robert K., Kristy R., Byron K. Syndicated columnist Antiques and Collectibles, Columbia Features, Inc., N.Y.C., 1967—; assoc. editor Colonial Homes mag., 1980—; pres. Hammond Publs., Inc., pubs. The Country Calendar, Western Calendar, Wildlife Calendar, 1978—; author 11 books in field including: Confusing Collectibles, I-III; Mustache Cups; Collectible Advertising; Price Guide to Country Collectibles; The Pictorial Price Guide, Vol. I-VI; cons. Smithsonian Instn. Methodist. Office: PO Box 8212 Munger Sta Wichita KS 67208

HAMMOND, HANNAH, nurse; b. Skibbereen, Ireland, Jan. 26, 1932; came to U.S., 1972, naturalized, 1980; d. Daniel William and Bridget Ellen O'Driscoll; R.N., midwife, Crumpsall Hosp. Sch. Nursing, Manchester, Eng., 1958; B.S. in Health Care Adminstrn., Iona Coll., New Rochelle, N.Y., 1982; m. Joseph Hammond, Apr. 27, 1974; stepchildren—Jodi, Barbara. Mem. Franciscan Missionaries of St. Joseph, Roman Catholic Ch., 1949-69; served in Kenya, 1958-71; charge nurse, instr., matron Kaplong Hosp., Kisii, Kenya, 1962-67; charge nurse, midwife Victoria Hosp., Kisumu, 1967-69; charge nurse, emergency nurse, night supr. hosp. Nairobi Hosp., 1969-71; charge nurse, pvt. duty nurse New Rochelle (N.Y.) Hosp., 1972-79; dir. nursing Bapt. Home for Aged, Bronx, N.Y., 1979—. Mem. N.Y. State Nurses Assn., Grad. Nurses of Westchester, Cath. Nurses Assn.

HAMMOND, JANE LAURA, librarian, lawyer; b. nr. Nashua, Iowa; d. Frank D. and Pauline (Flint) Hammond; B.A., U. Dubuque, 1950; M.S., Columbia U., 1952; J.D., Villanova U., 1965. Cataloguer, Harvard U. Law Library, 1952-54; asst. librarian Sch. Law, Villanova (Pa.) U., 1954-62, librarian, 1962-76, prof. law, 1965-76; law librarian, prof. law Cornell U., Ithaca, N.Y., 1976—; admitted to Pa. bar, 1965; adj. prof. Drexel U., 1971-74; mem. depository library council to pub. printer U.S. Govt. Printing Office, 1975-78. Mem. Am. Assn. Law Libraries (sec. 1965-70, pres. 1975-76), Council Nat. Library Assns. (sec.-treas. 1971-72, chmn. 1979-80), Spl. Libraries Assn., ALA, P.E.O. Episcopalian. Office: Cornell Law Library Myron Taylor Hall Ithaca NY 14853 *

HAMMOND, KARLA MARIE, writer and editor; b. Middletown, Conn., Apr. 24, 1949; d. Lester Arthur and Angelina (Lillian) Lorraine (Fusillo) H.; B.A., Goucher Coll., 1971; M.A., Trinity Coll., 1973. Freelance writer and editor, 1973—; research cons. Futures Group, Glastonbury, Conn., 1981; personnel cons. Barbara Chazan Assos., Hartford, Conn., 1981; exec. staff adminstr. CT Student Loan Found., Hartford, 1982—; free-lance book reviewer Sachem Pubg. Assos., Guilford, Conn., 1981-82. Recipient several prizes local colls. Democrat. Contbr. articles, poems, revs. to over 170 publs. in U.S.A., Eng., Can., Japan, Australia, Greece, Sweden and Italy. Home and office: Rural Route 4 12 West Dr East Hampton CT 06424

HAMPARES, KATHERINE JAMES, educator; b. Grand Rapids, Mich., May 24, 1932; A.A., Grand Rapids Jr. Coll., 1953; B.A. with distinction, U. Mich., 1955, M.A. with distinction, 1956, postgrad (NDEA grantee, 1959); postgrad U. Mexico, 1955; Fulbright scholar U. Valladolid (Spain), 1963; postgrad. U. San Marcos, Lima Peru, 1965, U. P.R., 1968; Ph.D., Columbia U., 1968; cert. English as a second lang., N.Y. U., 1972. Freshman counselor U. Mich., 1955-56 instr. Spanish, French Ottawa Hills High Sch., 1957-60; asst. prof., chmn. Spanish, French, Jersey City State Coll., 1961-66, asso. prof., 1966-67; instr. Spanish Hunter Coll., 1963-66; asst. prof. N.Y. U., 1967-69; asso. prof. Spanish, Finch Coll., 1969-72, also chmn. dept. modern langs.; asst. prof Baruch Coll., City U. N.Y., N.Y.C., 1972-76, asso. prof., 1976—, chmn. dept. Romance langs., 1975-77; cons., proof-reader Harper & Row Pubs. N.Y. rep. Bd. dirs. Spanish Am. Dance Theater, N.Y.C. Mem. MLA, Am. Assn. Tchrs. Spanish and Portuguese, Am. Council Teaching of Fgn. Langs., Council Inter-Am. Relations, (N.Y. rep.) La Liga Def. del Idioma Español, Casa hispánica, Amigos de España, Spanish Inst., N.Y.C. Assn. Fgn. Lang. Tchrs., N.Y. State Assn. Fgn. Lang. Tchrs., AAUP, AAUW, Pi Lambda Theta, Kappa Delta Pi, Sigma Delta Pi. Author: Spanish 2400, 1971, 80; Spanish: A Modular Approach, 1976, 82; Paso a Paso, 1978; contbr. articles to profl. jours. Office: Baruch Coll City U NY 17 Lexington St New York NY 10010

HAMPERS, LAVONNE JOYCE OHL (MRS. CONSTANTINE L. HAMPERS), lawyer; b. Mt. Vernon, Ind.; d. Arthur Joseph and Ruby Fern (Lopp) Ohl; student Ind. U., 1956-59, Northwestern U., 1959-61; LL.M., Boston U., 1969; LL.B., Boston Coll., 1967, J.D., 1969; m. Constantine L. Hampers, May 16, 1964; children—Louis, Mark, Douglas. Gen. mgr. Staff Research Asso. and Indsl. Systems, Inc., Chgo., 1959-64; admitted to Mass. bar, 1967; atty. Wilson, Curran, Malkasian & Winward, Boston, 1968-74; individual practice law, Weston, Mass., 1974-75; asso. commr. Mass. Dept. Corps. and Taxation, mem. Mass. Tax Commn., 1975-78; partner firm Blake & Hampers, Boston, 1978-79; commr. Mass. Dept. Revenue, 1979—. Mem. adv. council Mass. Continuing Legal Edn., Bentley Coll.; trustee Meadowbrook Sch. of Weston. Mem. LWV (mem. com. 1973), Am., Mass. (estate and gift tax com.), Boston bar assns., Northeastern States Tax Ofcls. Assn. (pres.). Club: Weston Golf. Office: 100 Cambridge St Boston MA 02204

HAMPSHIRE, SUSAN, actress; b. London, 1942; m. Pierre Granier-Deferre (dissolved 1974); 1 child; m. Eddie Kulukundis, 1981. Actress, stage appearances in Expresso Bongo, Follow That Girl, Ginger Man, Fairy Tales of N.Y., She Stoops to Conquer, On Approval, The Sleeping Prince, A Doll's House, The Taming of the Shrew, Romeo and Jeannette, Peter Pan, As You Like It, Man and Superman, Miss Julie, The Circle, Arms and the Man, Tribades, An Audience Called Edward, A Cruifer of Blood-Sherlock Holmes Mystery, Night and Day, The Revolt, House Guest; rôles in TV serials, Andromeda, The Forsyte Saga, Vanity Fair, The First Churchills, The Pallisers, Dick Turpin, Barchester Chronicles; films include During One Night, The Three Lives of Thomasina, Night Must Fall, Wonderful Life, Paris in August, The Fighting Prince of Donegal, Monte Carlo or Bust, Rogan, David Copperfield, Living Free, A Time for Loving, Malpertius, Neither the Sea Nor the Sand, Roses and Green Peppers, Bang. Winner Emmy award Best Actress in drama series, 1970, 71, 73. Address: care Midland Bank Ltd 92 Kensington High St London W8 England

HAMPSON, CAROLYN JACOBS, educator; b. Morgantown, W.Va., Feb. 18, 1945; d. David Wood and Kathleen M. (Hennen) Jacobs; B.A., W.Va. U., 1966, M.A., 1967. Instr. in English, W.Va. U., Morgantown, 1968-74, asst. prof., 1976—; sponsor English Club and lit. mag. Active Humane Soc., People for the Am. Way. Named Outstanding Tchr., Coll. Arts and Scis., 1981. Mem. LWV, NOW, Mortar Bd., Thomas Wolfe Soc., Inst. Sport and Social Analysis, Phi Beta Kappa. Democrat. Home: 224 Lebanon Ave Morgantown VA 26505 Office: WVa U Morgantown WV 26505

HAMPTON, KATHLEEN J., office mgr.; b. Dallas, Nov. 22, 1942; d. Irwin Lamar and Velma Jane (Adair) Jones; grad. bus. program U. Okla., 1962; divorced; children—Kerri Jean, Kelly James. Sec. land dept. Hunt Oil Co., 1962; sec. legal office Roy J. True, 1963-78; office mgr. True and McLain, P.C., attys., Dallas, 1979—; scheduling sec. to Mickey Mantle, 1969—. Mem. Lake Highlands High Sch. PTA. Mem. Am. Mgmt. Assn., Alpha Delta Pi Alumni Assn. Methodist. Clubs: Inwood Racquet, Chandlers Landing Yacht. Home: 9635 Crestedge Dallas TX 75238 Office: 1515 Dallas Fed Savs Tower Dallas TX 75225

HAMPTON, THELMA LAVERNE, r.r. ofcl.; b. Jayton, Tex., Mar. 5, 1923; d. Jefferson Ervin and Lavenia (Jones) Billingsley; cert. Lipperts Bus. Coll., Plainview, Tex., 1941; student Amarillo Jr. Coll., 1975-77; m. Joe E. Hampton, Mar. 17, 1945 (dec.); children—Robert, John, JoAnn. Sec., Cactus Ordinance Works, Dumas, Tex., 1942-45; cost acct. Marsh Elec. Supply, Amarillo, Tex., 1945-51; with Santa Fe Ry., Amarillo, 1951-77, Chgo., 1977—, schedule supr., labor relations, 1961-77, mgr. labor relations, 1977—; carrier rep. for public law bds. in labor disputes. Baptist. Home: PO Box 647 Glen Ellyn IL 60137 Office: Ry Exchange Bldg 80 E Jackson Blvd Room 600 Chicago IL 60604

HAMPTON-KAUFFMAN, MARGARET FRANCES, banker; b. Gainesville, Fla., May 12, 1947; d. William Wade and Carol Dorothy (Maples) Hampton; B.A. summa cum laude with honors in French, Fla. State U., 1969; postgrad. U. Nice (France), summer 1969; M.B.A. in Fin. (Alcoa Found. fellow), Columbia U., 1974; m. Kenneth L. Kauffman, May 12, 1973. Fin. analyst, economist Bd. of Govs. of Fed. Res. System, Washington, 1974-75; asst. v.p., banking industry specialist, corp. fin. dept. Mfrs. Hanover Trust Co., N.Y.C., 1975-76; v.p., dir. corp. planning and research Nat. Bank of Ga., Atlanta, 1976-81; sr. v.p. corp. planning and product devel. Bank South Corp., Atlanta, 1981—; dir. Accent Enterprises, Inc., Atlanta, TOMAK, Inc., Atlanta. Past comptroller, past liaison officer Angel Flight; dir. Atlanta Profl. Women's Directory, 1981-83; trustee Ga. chpt. Leukemia Soc., 1980—, treas., 1981-82, 1st v.p., 1982-83. Recipient Outstanding Angel Merit award Angel Flight, 1968. Mem. Planning Execs. Inst., Inst. of Mgmt. Scis., Am. Inst. Banking, Inst. of Fin. Edn., Am. Fin. Assn., Downtown Atlanta C. of C., (govt. affairs subcom. 1976-77; high tech. task force 1982-83), Women's Forum, Ga. Exec. Women's Network (sec. 1982-83, dir. 1982—), Mortar Bd., Alliance Française, Little Sisters (pres., treas.), Phi Beta Kappa, Beta Gamma Sigma, Phi Kappa Phi, Alpha Lambda Delta, Pi Delta Phi, Alpha Delta Pi, Kappa Sigma. Episcopalian. Club: Women's Commerce (charter). Office: Bank South Corp 55 Marietta St Atlanta GA 30302

HAMRICK, JOYCE MCCLESKEY, educator; b. Norfolk, Va., Feb. 11, 1945; d. Benjamin C. and Mary Jane (Ferrell) McCleskey; B.A. in Psychology, W. Fla. U., 1969; M.S. in Reading, S. Miss. U., 1970, Ph.D. in Edn., 1973; m. Robert Augustus Hamrick. Grad. asst. S. Miss. U., 1970-71, grad. fellow, 1971-72; asst. prof. reading Troy State U., Dothan, Ala., 1972-78. Vol. tchr. Children's Resource Center of N.W. Fla. Recipient MS Patient Achievement award, 1978. Mem. Internat. Reading Assn., Ala. Reading Assn., NRC, Ala. Multiple Sclerosis Soc., Kappa Delta Pi, Phi Delta Kappa. Co-author: Reading Diagnostic Handbook. Specialist in diagnosis, remediation of disabled readers, writer handbook for teachers to motivate and remediate disabled readers; research oral lang. inventory for remedial readers, grades 1-5. Home: 825 Bayshore Dr Apt 1002 Pensacola FL 32507

HANAU, LAIA, educator; b. Boston, June 4, 1916; d. Samuel B. and Lucy A. (Greenwood) Pearlmutter; A.B., Smith Coll., 1937; M.A., U. Rochester, 1960; postgrad. U. Mich., 1942-45, U. Ky., 1951-53, U. Ariz., 1973-74; m. Richard Hanau, Jan. 2, 1941; 1 dau., Loren Michael. Copy editor Am. Horseman, Lexington, Ky., 1947-49; asst. editor pubs. Dept. Pub. Info., U. Ky., Lexington, 1949-50, editorial asst. dept. animal pathology, 1950-52; editorial cons. Optical Soc. Am., Rochester, N.Y., 1959; tchr. English, Lexington pub. schs. and Sayre Sch., 1960-66; instr. study methods U. Ky. Coll. Medicine, Lexington, 1967-69, asst. prof., 1970-73; cons. in field; tchr. Sayre Sch., 1974-76; contbr. Breadloaf Writers Conf., 1953; editorial cons. U. Ky. Coll. Medicine, 1963-66; tchr., cons. Hanau Method of Study and Writing Techniques. Recipient Avery and Jule Hopwood Award in nonfiction, 1942. Mem. Authors Guild. Author: The Study Game, How to Play and Win With —Statement Pie—, 1972, 73, 74; The Study Game Workbook: A Guide to Writing and Note Taking, 1976; The Study Game: How to Play and Win, 1979. Address: Route 2 Box 46 Stage Coach Rd Patterson NY 12563

HANAWALT, BARBARA ANN, historian, educator; b. New Brunswick, N.J., Mar. 4, 1941; d. Nelson G. and Pearl (Basset) H.; B.A., Rutgers U., 1963; M.A., U. Mich., 1964, Ph.D. (fellow), 1970; m. Ronald N. Giere, Mar. 20, 1981. Teaching asst. U. Mich., Ann Arbor, 1964-66; instr. San Fernando Valley State Coll., Calif., 1970-72; mem. faculty continuing edn. program UCLA, 1971-72, 74; vis. asst. prof. history U. Oreg., 1972-73; asst. prof. dept. history Ind. U., Bloomington, 1974-78, assoc. prof., 1978—; Nat. Endowment for Humanities sr. research assoc. Newberry Library, 1979-80; mem. Inst. for Advanced Study, Princeton, N.J., 1982-83. Am. Council Learned Socs. fellow, 1979; Can. Council grantee, 1975; Am. Philos. Soc. grantee, 1976, 78, Ind. U. faculty grantee, 1979. Mem. Medieval Acad. Am., Social History Soc., Past and Present Soc., Social Sci. History Assn., Royal Hist. Soc. Author: Crime and Conflict in English Communities, 1300-1348, 1979; Crime in East Anglia in the Fourteenth Century, 1976; contbr. articles on English social history to scholarly jours.; contbr. book revs. to hist. jours. Home: 512 E 8th St Bloomington IN 47401 Office: Dept History Indiana Univ Bloomington IN 47405

HANBACK, HAZEL MARIE SMALLWOOD, mgmt. cons.; b. Washington, Sept. 19, 1918; d. Archibald Carlisle and Mary Louise (Mayhugh) Smallwood; A.B., George Washington U., 1940; M.P.A., Am. U., 1968; m. William B. Hanback, Sept. 26, 1942; 1 son, Christopher Brecht. Archivist, U.S. Office Housing Expediter, 1948-50; mgmt. engr. U.S. Archives, 1950-51; spl. asst.-indsl. specialist Sec. Def., 1951-53; dir. documentation div. Naval Facilities Engring., Alexandria, Va., 1953-81; mgmt. cons., 1981—. Pres., West End Citizens Assn., Washington, 1956-58; trustee George Washington U., 1979—. Nominee Rockefeller Public Service award, 1969, Fed. Woman's award, 1969; recipient cert. of merit Dep. Def., 1965. Mem. Mortar Bd., Phi Delta Gamma, Sigma Kappa. Democrat. Episcopalian. Clubs: George Washington U. (chmn. bd. 1971-75), Columbian Women (pres. George Washington U. 1967-69), Order Eastern Star. Author: Military Color Book, 1960; Status of Women in a Cybernetically Oriented Society, 1968. Home: 2152 F St NW Washington DC 20037 Office: 2154 F St NW Washington DC 20037

HANCE, MARGARET T., mayor of Phoenix; b. Spirit Lake, Iowa, July 2, 1923; student U. Ariz., 1942-44; B.A., Scripps Coll., Claremont, Calif., 1945; widow 1970; children—Richard, Galen, Ted. Mem. Phoenix Parks and Recreation Bd., 6 yrs.; producer pub. affairs documentaries for TV, 1967-69; writer, producer Holiday World Travel Show for radio, 1971-75; former mem. Phoenix City Council and vice mayor; mayor City of Phoenix, 1976—; dir. Valley Nat. Bank; conf. del. OECD, 1979. Mem. Adv. Commn. Intergovtl. Relations, Presdl. Federalism Adv. Com; mem. Ariz. Justice Planning Supervisory Bd; mem. community adv. bd. Salt-Gila Flood Control Study; bd. visitors St. Luke's Hosp.; mem. Jr. League Phoenix; advisor Women's Aux. Ariz. Kidney Found. Named Women of Yr., Phoenix Advt. Club, 1978; recipient Don Bolles Meml. award Ariz. KC, 1978, Alumni Achievement award U. Ariz., 1979, Centennial award Salvation Army, 1978. Mem. U.S. Conf. Mayors (trustee), Nat. League Cities (dir.), Nat. Conf. Republican. Mayors and Elected Mcpl. Ofcls. (pres.), League Ariz. Cities and Towns (treas.). Office: Office of the Mayor 251 W Washington St Phoenix AZ 85003 *

HANCOCK, GINGER LEA, map co. exec.; b. Miami Beach, Fla., Feb. 4, 1953; d. Gerald Lewis and Florence (Searson) McPeek; A.A., Palomar Jr. Coll., 1972; m. Norman Edward Hancock, Nov. 13, 1976; stepchildren—Kristi, Dana, Pam. Clk.-typist Camp Pendleton, Calif., 1972, surveying technician, 1972-76; owner, pres. A.R.T. Maps, Inc., San Marcos, Calif., 1977—. Sec., San Diego County (Calif.) Archaeology Soc., 1977, hist. research chairperson, 1980. Home and Office: 33424 Newberry Rd Newberry Springs CA 92365

HANCOCK, LESLEE DIANE, nurse; b. Roanoke, Va., Jan. 17, 1951; d. John Carlton and Jeanne Helen (Dolinger) H.; B.S. in Nursing, Barry Coll., Miami Shores, Fla., 1973; M.Nursing, Emory U., 1977. Staff nurse Cedars of Lebanon Health Care Center, Miami, Fla., 1973-74; staff nurse ICU, St. Francis Hosp., Miami Beach, Fla., 1974; staff nurse CCU, Dekalb Gen. Hosp., Decatur, Ga., 1974-76; clin. nurse specialist Ga. Baptist Med. Center, Atlanta, 1977-78; instr. nursing Piedmont Hosp. Sch. Nursing, Atlanta, 1978-81; asst. prof. nursing Fla. State U., Tallahassee, 1981—. Mem. Am. Nurses Assn., Am. Assn. Critical Care Nurses, Sigma Theta Tau. Office: 451 SCN Fla State U Tallahassee FL 32306

HAND, DORIS ELIZABETH, librarian; b. Camden, N.J., Feb. 11, 1918; d. Edmund Merritt and Florence Louise (Duncan) Pike; grad. Phila. Bus. Coll., 1936; student Glassboro State Coll., 1969-71, Rutgers State U., Camden, N.J., 19—; m. Lawrence Holmes Hand, Nov. 9, 1940; children—Edmund Lawrence, Joan Elizabeth Newton. Billing clk. Jefferson Hosp., 1936; sec. inland marine dept. Camden Fire Ins. Co., 1937-42; with USO, Battle Creek, Mich., 1942-43; sec., office mgr. Republican Party of Camden County, Haddonfield, N.J., 1961-66; library clk. Collingswood (N.J.) Public Library, 1968-75, library supr., 1975—, coordinator children's services, 1978—. Mem. N.J. Library Assn., Camden County Librarians Assn., Children's Librarians Unltd., Am. Legion Aux. (pres. Tatem Shields unit 17, 1952-53, 69-70, 77-78, pres. Camden County 1966-67), Collingswood-Newton Colony Hist. Soc. (pres. 1977-79), Camden County Hist. Soc. Republican. Methodist. Club: Amaranth. Editor: Collingswood Friends of Library Newsletter, 1977-80. Home: 104 Dayton Ave Collingswood NJ 08108 Office: Collingswood Pub Library Haddon and Frazer Aves Collingswood NJ 08108

HANDCOCK, JULIA COLE, social worker; b. Dunedin, N.Z., Aug. 14, 1935; came to U.S., 1964, naturalized, 1968; d. Thomas Gordan and Clare (Fraser) Cole; M.S.W., SUNY, Albany, 1975; children—Adrienne Clare, James Fraser, Deirdre Julia. Instr. home econs. U. Otago (N.Z.), 1956-58; tchr. home econs. Montreal (Que., Can.) High Sch. for Girls, 1958-59; fieldworker Pawling Center for Children, 1973-76, Berkshire Family & Children's Center, Pittsfield, Mass., 1974-80; pvt. practice social work, Albany, 1975—; instr. dept. human services Hudson Valley Community Coll., Troy, N.Y., 1976-81, asst. prof., 1981—; counselor family therapy Schenectady Cath. Family & Community Services, 1981—; cons. Empire State Coll., N.Y., 1982—. Cert. social worker, N.Y. Mem. Nat. Assn. Social Workers (past div. pres.), Acad. Cert. Social Workers, Nat. Assn. Human Service Educators, State Assn. Gerentol. Educators. Home: 32 Lacy Ln Loudonville NY 12211 Office: Hudson Valley Community College Vandenburg Ave Troy NY 12180

HANDLER, EVELYN E., univ. pres.; d. Dezso and Ilona (Roth) Sass; B.A. in Physiology and Chemistry cum laude, Hunter Coll., 1954; M.S. in Biology, N.Y. U., 1962, Ph.D. (NIH fellow 1961-63), 1963; m. Nov. 24, 1965; children—Jeffrey David, Bradley Philip. Research asso. Sloan Kettering Inst., 19S8-60, Merck Inst. Therapeutic Research, 1958-60; vis. scientist Karolinska Inst., Stockholm, 1971-72; mem. faculty Hunter Coll., 1962-80, prof. biol. scis., 1975-80, dean div. scis. and math., 1977-80; mem. doctoral faculty City U. N.Y., 1975-80; pres. U. N.H., Durham, 1980—; chmn., mem. accreditation rev. coms. Middle States Assn. Colls. and Secondary Schs.; mem. Council Inst. Gen. Med. Scis. NIH, 1980—; rep. Council Pharm. Edn., 1978—; cons., reviewer, evaluator, panelist in field. Grantee NSF, NIH. Fellow N.Y. Acad. Scis. (gov. 1978-79); mem. Tissue Culture Assn., Harvey Soc., AAAS, Am. Soc. Hematology, Internat. Soc. Hematology, Nat. Assn. State Univs. and Land-Grant Colls. (exec. com. 1982—), Phi Beta Kappa, Sigma Xi, Phi Sigma. Author numerous papers in field. Office: 210 Thompson Hall Durham NH 03824 *

HANDLER-PENNINGTON, MARGARET ANGELA, fin. cons., art cons.; b. Birmingham, Ala., Sept. 20, 1942; d. George Frederick and Regina Angela (Moreno) Kirchoff; B.A., U. Tenn., 1963; M.S.W., Smith Coll., 1965; m. Gerald Lee Pennington. Faculty dept. psychiatry Emory U., Atlanta, 1966-69; asso. dir. St. Jude's House, Atlanta, 1969-72; asso. dir. public affairs Mental Health Assn., Atlanta, 1972-73; alcoholism cons. Ga. Dept. Human Resources, Atlanta, 1974-75; fine art cons. Rentar Industries, N.Y.C., 1975—; pres. Marpal, Inc., Nokomis, Fla., 1980—; dir. Penn-Products, Venice, Fla., 1982—. Bd. dirs. New Coll. Music Festival, Sarasota, Fla., 1982-84. Recipient awards, grants: Vocat. Rehab. Adminstrn., Nat. Found., Gen. Tire and Rubber Co., Wallace Silver Co., SCV. Mem. Nat. Assn. Social Workers, Acad. Cert. Social Workers, Am. Assn. Mus., Am. Craft Council, Archives Am. Art, Nat. Assn. Female Execs., Smith Coll. Alumnae Assn., DAR, Colonial Dames XVII Century, Pi Beta Phi. Jewish. Club: Hadassah. Home and Office: 2209 Casey Key Rd Nokomis FL 33555

HANDLEY, HELEN MULLINS, acctg. exec.; b. Trafford, Ala., Nov. 18, 1921; d. James Oliver and Carrie Frances (Abel) Mullins; m. Thomas Harley Handley, Feb. 7, 1941; children—Patricia, Thomas Harley, Cathy. Owner, mgr. Anderson County Adjustment Co., Inc., Oak Ridge, 1961—; editor, pub. TCA Bulletin, 1968—. Pres., Arthritis Clinic for Anderson and Roane Counties, 1963-76; mem. Tenn. State Republican Exec. Com., 1974—; co-chmn. Anderson County Republican. Com., 1970-77, 78—, chmn., 1977-78; bd. dirs. Better Bus. Bur. of Knoxville. Mem. Tenn. Coll. Assn. (pres. 1968-69), Am. Bus. Women's Assn. (pres. 1979—), Associated Credit Burs., Tenn. Collectors Assn. (pres. 1982-83), Am. Collectors Assn., Oak Ridge Bus. and Profl. Women, Exec. Women of Knoxville. Baptist. Clubs: Lions, Oak Ridge Women's. Home: 103 Delaware Ave Oak Ridge TN 37830 Office: 210 Town Hall Oak Ridge TN 37830

HANDLEY, JEAN MARY, telephone co. exec.; b. Manchester, Conn., Aug. 28, 1926; d. Francis P. and Margaret (Ivers) H.; B.A., Conn. Coll., 1948; M.A., Northwestern U., 1949. Public relations asst. So. New Eng. Telephone Co., New Haven, 1960, various positions in advt. and employee info., 1960-66, dist. mgr. employee info., 1966-72, gen. info. mgr., 1973-75, gen. advt. mgr., 1975, v.p. public relations, 1978—; div. mgr. public relations dept., planning and press relations AT&T, N.Y.C., 1972-73, press relations dir., 1976-78; dir. Sci. Park Devel. Corp., New Haven. Bd. dirs. Bus. Council Women, N.Y.C., 1978-80, Hospice Inst., New Haven, 1978-80, Newington (Conn.) Children's Hosp.; v.p. New Haven Symphony Orch. 1981—; mem. pres.'s adv. council Quinnipiac Coll., 1979-80; trustee Conn. Coll., New London. Mem. Public Relations Am., Public Relations Soc. N.Y., Women in Communications, Am. Women in Radio and TV, Greater New Haven C. of C. (women's steering com.). Clubs: Quinnipiack, New Haven Lawn. Office: So New Eng Telephone Co 227 Church St New Haven CT 06506

HANDY, MARY NIXEON CIVILLE, poet; b. Ocean Park, Calif., Mar. 5, 1909; d. Leroy Harvey and Lorena Frances (Casey) Civille; student Pomona Jr. Coll., 1927; B.E., U. Calif., Los Angeles, 1930; M.E., Central Wash. State Coll., 1958; postgrad. U. Wash., 1963, 72, Claremont Sch. Theology, summers 1969, 71; m. Lawrence A. Handy, Feb. 14, 1932; children—William Leroy, Lorena Catherine Handy Pollock, David Lawrence (dec.), Nixon Jay. Tchr. elem. schs., Placentia, Calif., 1931, Wenatchee, Wash., 1954-55; instr. English and journalism Wenatchee Valley Coll., 1956-63, dean of women, 1961-66, dir. Poetry Workshop, 1961-66; dir. Released Time Edn., Visalia, Calif., 1945, YMCA, Lake Wenatchee, 1953-59; dir. girls' and women's program YMCA, Wenatchee, 1954-55; dir. adult edn. United Meth. Ch., Sandpoint, Seattle, 1967-69; supt. Ruth Sch. for Girls, Burien, Wash., 1970; dir. religious edn., Des Moines, Seattle, 1970-71; poetry staff Pacific NW Writers Conf., 1975-81. King County Arts Commn. grantee, 1979. Mem. Nat. Ret. Tchrs. Assn., Nat. League Am. Pen Women, Poetry Soc. Am., Am. Acad. Poets, Wash. Poets Assn. (exec. bd. 1975—), P.E.O. (rec. sec. 1975), Delta Kappa Gamma (pres. chpt. 1973-74, state editor Alpha Sigma News 1969-70, Alpha Sigma (Poets grantee 1972). Presbyterian. Author: (poems) Do Not Disturb the Dance: Enter It, 1973; Earth House, 1978; Grandma Casey, 1982. 1982; contbg. editor Fellowship in Prayer, 1978-83. Home and Studio: 19240 10th Ave NE Seattle WA 98155

HANDY, SUZETTA CATHERINE MILLS, family life specialist; b. Chgo., Sept. 10, 1952; d. Alfred Manly and Fern Evelyn (Clevenger) Mills; A.A., Santa Rose Jr. Coll., 1972; B.A., San Francisco State U., 1974; M.A.T., Mills Coll., 1975; m. Darrell Wayne Handy, June 21, 1975; children—Jonathan, Gabriel. Tchrs., Mills Coll. Children's Sch., Oakland, Calif., 1974-75; pre-sch. dir. Christian Life Sch., Concord, Calif., 1975-77; children's services coordinator Family Stress Center, Concord, 1979-82; instr. family life dept. Diablo Valley Coll., Pleasant Hill, Calif., 1982—. Community coll. tchr. credential. Mem. Contra Costa County Child Abuse Prevention Council, Contra Costa County Child Mental Health Services Task Force. Democrat. Mem. Concord Christian Center. Office: Diablo Valley Coll Pleasant Hill CA 94523 *

HANEY, JACQUELINE TAYLOR, civic worker; b. Gilbertown, Ala., Feb. 10, 1940; d. Robert Long and Billie (Smith) Taylor; B.S., U. So. Miss., 1961; m. Harry Lee Haney, Jr., June 16, 1962; 1 dau., Jacqueline Lee. Tchr. sci. and phys. edn. T.R. Miller Sch., Brewton, Ala., 1961-62; tchr. sci. Freeport (Fla.) High Sch., 1966-67. Co-chmn., Am. Heart Assn., Clarke County, Miss., 1963, Young Reps., Clarke County, 1964; pres. Forestry Wives of Yale U., 1968-69, Yale Dames, 1969-70, Yale Women's Coordinating Council, 1970-71; participant Yale Polit. Union, 1969-74; mem. PTA bd. Ridge Rd. Elem. Sch., North Haven, Conn., 1973-74; vol. Harding Ave. Elem. Sch., Blacksburg, 1974-76, v.p. PTA, 1975-76; co-chmn. publicity Blacksburg Middle Sch. PTA, 1976-77, co-pres., 1977-78, pres., 1978-79; mem. LWV, Blacksburg, Va., 1975-76; parent rep. Roanoke Youth Symphony, 1976-79; mem. Roanoke (Va.) Symphony Aux., 1977-79; chmn. bd. dirs. Little Bros./Little Sisters, 1977-79; pres. adv. council for arts in Montgomery County Schs., 1979—; dist. chmn. cultural arts New River Valley PTA, 1979—; bd. dirs. Voluntary Action Center, 1979—. Recipient Vol. Service awards Harding Ave. Elem. Sch., 1975-76, Little Bros./Little Sisters, 1978, 79; Life Membership award, Va. Congress of PTA's, 1979. Democrat. Presbyterian. Address: 305 Franklin Dr Blacksburg VA 24060

HANEY, MARY BELL, civil engr.; b. Miami, Fla., Nov. 10, 1946; d. James Bell and Suzanna (Allen) Trout; B.S.C.E., Clemson U., 1967, M.S. in Environ. Systems Engring. (USPHS trainee), 1968, postgrad. in mgmt., 1968-76; postgrad. in chemistry U. Tex., San Antonio, 1980-81; m. Donald Lee Haney, Aug. 15, 1967; children—James Reuben, Donald Louis. Vis. lectr. and adj. prof. U. N.Mex., 1970-72; v.p. engring. Ruben Rodriguez Land Devel. Inc., Alburquerque, 1970-74; asst. project mgr. Pape-Dawson Cons. Engrs., Inc., San Antonio, 1976-78, project engr., 1978—. Mem. properties com. Girl Scouts U.S.A., San Antonio. Registered profl. engr., Tex. Mem. Nat. Soc. Profl. Engrs., Tex. Soc. Profl. Engrs. (dir. 1980, treas. 1981, sec. 1982, mem. Speakers Bur. 1979—, Outstanding Young Engr. of Yr. award Bexar chpt. 1982), Soc. Women Engrs., Assn. Women in Sci., Nat. Assn. Female Execs., Am. Statis. Assn., Water Pollution Control Fedn., Planetary Soc., ASCE, San Antonio Council Engring. Edn., NOW, YWCA, Tau Beta Pi (Women's Badge 1965), Phi Kappa Phi, Sigma Tau Epsilon. Methodist. Club: Protestant Women of Chapel (pres. club 1975-76). Contbr. articles to profl. publs. Home: 318 Amistad Blvd Universal City TX 78148 Office: 9310 Broadway San Antonio TX 78217

HANIFORD, JO KATHRYN, city councilwoman; b. Monon, Ind., Mar. 6, 1922; d. Raymond Stephen and Laura Gladys (Minch) Bundy; B.M., DePauw U., 1944; m. D'Maris Gerrard Haniford, Sept. 16, 1945; 1 dau., Kathy Jo Haniford Clouse. Tchr., Anderson (Ind.) Public Schs., 1944-45; music dir. Sta. WBAA, Purdue U., Lafayette, Ind., 1945-49; tchr. North Newton Sch. Corp., Morocco, Ind., 1968-75; mem. Rensselaer (Ind.) City Council, 1976—, pres., 1976—, mayor pro tem, 1976—; tchr. elem. music Purdue U. Sch. of the Air. Sec. bd. trustees Rensselaer Central Sch., 1967-71. Mem. DAR (regent 1965-66), Kappa Kappa Kappa, Mu Phi Epsilon. Republican. Methodist. Home: 304 S Sparling Ave Rensselaer IN 47978

HANKE, BEVERLY JEAN, food co. exec.; b. Jackson, Ohio, Aug. 14, 1944; d. John M. and Alva (Cochran) Albert; grad. Columbus (Ohio) Bus. U.; student Ohio State U.; m. Karl J. Hanke, Feb. 25, 1973; 1 dau., Seanne Nicole. With Farm House Foods Corp., Milw., 1971—, controller, 1972—, v.p., prin. fin. officer, 1976—. Mem. fin. com. Calvary United Methodist Ch., West Allis, Wis. Mem. Nat. Assn. Accts., Nat. Assn. Female Execs., Fin. Execs. Inst., Tempo. Office: 777E Wisconsin St Suite 3450 Milwaukee WI 53202

HANKEL, MARILYN LOPICCOLO, librarian; b. New Orleans, Mar. 19, 1950; d. Anthony and Louise (Distefano) Lopiccolo; B.S. in Mgmt., U. New Orleans, 1972; M.L.S., La. State U., 1980; m. Charles C. Hankel, Oct. 28, 1972. Library asst. govt. documents dept. Earl K. Long Library, U. New Orleans, 1972-81, bus. reference librarian, 1981—. Mem. adv. bd. Friends of U. New Orleans Library, 1980—, chmn. publicity com., 1981—. Recipient Nat. Observer Student Achievement award Dow Jones & Co., Inc., 1972. Mem. La. Library Assn., Beta Gamma Sigma, Beta Phi Mu. Home: 2707 Dauphine St New Orleans LA 70117 Office: U New Orleans Library Lakefront New Orleans LA 70148

HANKIN, CAROLE G., educator; b. N.Y.C., June 7, 1942; d. Ephraim and Rose (Weiner) Sperman; B.A., Sarah Lawrence Coll., 1973; M.A., Columbia U., 1974, M.Ed., 1975, Ed.D., 1978; m. Joseph N. Hankin, Aug. 20, 1960; children—Marc, Laura, Brian. Instr. dept. spl. ednl. services Bronx Community Coll., 1975-77; specialist learning disabilities, reading and study skills Edgemont High Sch., Scarsdale, N.Y., 1976-80, coordinator pupil personnel services, 1980—. Bd. dirs. Purchase Community House, 1973—. Mem. Internat. Reading Assn., N.Y. State Assn. Jr. Colls., N.Y. State Reading Council, Westchester Assn. Children with Learning Disabilities, Harford Opera Theater Assn. Home: 4 Merion Dr Purchase NY 10577

HANKIN, LOIS DUREITZ, mgmt. cons.; b. Cleve., Aug. 6, 1945; d. Arthur Frank and Ruth Gertrude (Renner) DuReitz; student (grantee) Mt. Union Coll., 1963-64, Ohio State U., 1964-65; B.S., Case Western Res. U., 1970; m. Norman Hankin, Oct. 31, 1976. Bookkeeper, Chem. Rubber Co., Cleve., 1965-70; office mgr. Importa Ltd., Washington, 1970-71; controller Nat. Coordinating Council on Drug Edn., Washington, 1971-72; v.p. fin. Am. Footwear Industries Assn., Arlington, Va., 1972-76; legal adminstr., controller Lane and Edson, P.C., Washington, 1977-81; pvt. practice mgmt. cons., 1976-77, 81—. Treas., Sierra Villas Homeowners Assn., 1975; active Young Democrats, 1966-69, Stokes for Mayor campaign, 1968; nat. judge Distbv. Edn. Clubs Am., 1978. Recipient Service award Howard County Handicapped, 1977; resolution of appreciation for service, fin. mgmt. com. of Am. Footwear Industries Assn., 1976. Mem. Nat. Assn. Female Execs., Assn. Legal Adminstrs. (nat. and capital chpt.), Two/Ten Assn. Jewish. Home: 7165 Deer Valley Rd Highland MD 20777

HANKINS, SHIRLEY WILLIAMS, state legislator; b. Colby, Kans., Nov. 9, 1931; d. Mack O. and Florence (Wheaton) Williams; student Columbia Basin Jr. Coll., 1972; m. Myron McFadden Hankins, 1950; children—Myron M., Shelley Don Hankins, Sherrey Ann. Precinct committeewoman Wash. Republican Com., 1962—; rep. 4th Dist. Rep. Com. Wash.; del. Rep. State Conv., 1968-76, mem. rules and order com.,

1972, 76, hostess, 1974; chmn. Benton County Rep. Central Com., 1972-74; alt. del. Rep. Nat. Conv., 1976; now mem. Wash. Ho. of Reps.; dosimetry specialist United Nuclear Industries Inc., 1968—. Mem. Richland Rep. Women's Club, Wash. State Fedn. Women's Clubs, Am. Nuclear Soc., Thomas County Hist. Soc., Florance Merrick Women's Council. Methodist. Office: Wash State Ho Reps State Capitol Olympia WA 98504 *

HANKO, DEBORAH ANN, accountant; b. Benton Harbor, Mich., May 17, 1954; d. Roy Raymond and Lorena Marie (Feller) Litke; B.A. in Acctg. (State of Mich. scholar, Mich. State U. scholar, Mich. State U., 1976; honor grad. Acctg. Specialist Sch., Shephard AFB, Tex., 1977; M.B.A., N.Mex. Highlands U., 1981; m. Leonard Hanko, Mar. 17, 1973; 1 son, Raymond Charles. Bookkeeper, J.C. Penney Co., Benton Harbor, 1972; comptroller Strong-Thorne Mortuary Inc., Albuquerque, 1977—; tutor in acctg. and quantative methods. Served with USAF, 1976-77. Mem. Nat. Assn. Accts. (communications dir. 1981-82, sec. 1982—, del. Rocky Mountain Council 1981—), Roman Catholic. Home: 1655 Estrellita Rio Rancho NM 87124 Office: 1100 Coal SE Albuquerque NM 87106

HANKS, BEVERLY JOAN, accountant, town ofcl.; b. Middlebury, Vt., Mar. 7, 1934; d. Hugh Lewis and Dorothy Emeline (Crossman) Atwood; A.S., Becker Jr. Coll., 1954; B.S. magna cum laude in Bus. Adminstrn., Nathaniel Hawthorne Coll., 1980; m. John King Hanks, Dec. 26, 1954; children—John Hugh, Donna Lynn, Cynthia Jean, Bruce Barton. Bookkeeper to controller Semikron Internat., Hudson, N.H., 1977-79; controller Commonwealth Chem. Corp., Tewksbury, Mass., 1979-80, cons., 1981; town acct. Town of Hudson (N.H.), 1981—. Town chmn. Reagan for Pres., 1976; treas. Town of Hudson, 1975-77, mem. budget com., 1976-77. Mem. Hudson C. of C., Mcpl. Fin. Officers Assn., Nat. Assn. Exec. Females. Home: 39 Hazelwood Rd Hudson NH 03051 Office: 12 School St Hudson NH 03051

HANLEY, MARGARET LUCILLE, real estate agt.; b. Terre Haute, Ind., Feb. 21, 1931; d. Hubert Eli and Dorothy Lucille (Hunter) Dietz; grad. public schs.; m. Alpha Robert Hanley, Apr. 2, 1966. Acct., Reuben H. Donnelley Corp., Terre Haute, 1950-60, F. W. Means Co., Terre Haute, 1960-64, J. C. Penney Co., Orlando, Fla., 1965-66; mem. acctg. dept. J. B. Pfister Co., Inc., Terre Haute, 1966-72, Underhill Real Estate, Terre Haute, 1972-75; mem. acctg. dept. Larry D. Helman "Has the Key," Inc., Terre Haute, 1975-76, corp. sec. Key Mortgage Co., 1975-76; mem. acctg. dept. C. W. Combs Constrn., Terre Haute, 1976-79; mgr. Fagg Oliver Sales, Inc., Brazil, Ind., 1979-81, Hamilton Center Inc., Terre Haute, 1981—; real estate sales Gary Combs Real Estate & Devel., 1978—. Mem. Terre Haute Bd. Realtors (exec. officer 1976-80). Mem. Assembly of God Ch. Home: 1196 Lockport Rd Terre Haute IN 47802 Office: 620 8th Ave Terre Haute IN 47804

HANLON, CAMILLE CAROL, psychologist, educator; b. New Orleans, Dec. 25, 1937; d. Philip Samuel and Mary Sue (Berthelot) H.; student La. State U., 1954-56; B.A., U. Tex., 1958; M.A., 1959; Ph.D., Stanford U., 1964. Asst. prof. psychology U. Iowa, 1964-67; lectr. social relations Harvard U., Cambridge, 1967-68; asst. prof. psychology and child devel. Conn. Coll., New London, 1968-73, asso. prof., 1973—, chmn. dept. child devel., 1979-81. NIH fellow, 1967-68. Mem. New England Child Lang. Assn., Am. Psychol. Assn., Soc. Research in Child Devel., Contbr. articles in field to profl. jours. Office: Conn College PO Box 1488 New London CT 06320

HANNA, INGA HAUGAARD, fin. planner; b. Portland, Maine, Jan. 6, 1930; d. Ejnar Nielsen and Helene Martine (Buje) Haugaard; B.S., Simmons Coll., Boston, 1954; M.B.A., U. Mo., Columbia, 1973; m. John G. Hanna, July 2, 1949; children—Erik H., Charlotte H. Stock broker Putnam, Coffin & Burr, Portland, 1964-67; investment research officer Canal Nat. Bank, Portland, 1967-70; exec. dir. Treemont of Dallas, 1973-75, Portland YWCA, 1976-80; ind. fin. planner, Portland, 1980—; corporator Maine Savs. Bank. Mem. bd. World Affairs Council Maine, 1980-82. Recipient Thomas P. Weill award U. Mo., 1973; Danforth asso., 1981. Mem. Inst. Fin. Planners (cert.), Internat. Assn. Fin. Planners, Am. Soc. Profl. Cons., Maine Econ. Soc.

HANNA, KAROLYN RAE, nurse; b. Mankato, Minn., Jan. 14, 1942; d. William Charles and Irene Isabelle (Johnson) Klammer; B.S. in Nursing, Mankato State Coll., 1964; postgrad. med. surg. nursing, U. Wash., Seattle, 1966-67; M.S. in Guidance, Creighton U., Omaha, 1970; m. Hugh E. Hanna, Jr., Mar. 25, 1967; children—Kirsten R., Mark A. Staff nurse St. Luke's Hosp., St. Paul, 1964; instr. nursing Barnes Hosp. Sch. Nursing, St. Louis, 1964-66; staff nurse, instr. operating room nursing Riverside (Calif.) Community Hosp., 1967-68; instr., then asst. to dean Creighton U. Coll. Nursing, 1968-74; asst. dir. nursing Mercy San Juan Hosp., Carmichael, Calif., 1974-77; instr. Imperial Valley Coll., El Centro, Calif., 1977-78; coordinator inservice edn. dept. Santa Barbara (Calif.) Cottage Hosp., 1978-80; instr. nursing Santa Barbara City Coll., 1980—; cons. in field; past chmn. coms. Nebr. Nurses Assn. Recipient Blue Earth County (Minn.) 4-H Alumni award, 1969, dist. II award Nebr. Nurses Assn., 1973. Mem. Am. Nurses Assn., Nat. League Nursing, Am. Cancer Soc., Am. Heart Assn. Author papers in field. Home: 5235 Toluca Ct Santa Barbara CA 93111 Office: Santa Barbara City Coll 721 Cliff Dr Santa Barbara CA 93109

HANNA, MARILYN CONCHA, educator; b. Chaffee, Mo., Sept. 20, 1922; d. Arthur Clarkson and Mary Thurza (Waters) H.; Asso. Fine Arts, William Woods Coll., 1941; student Cin. Conservatory Music, 1941-42; diploma Juilliard Sch. Music, 1945; Mus.B., U. Mo., 1951, M.A., 1954. Tchr. music, piano and piano lit. Stephens Coll., Columbia, Mo., 1946—. Organist, choir dir. 1st Bapt. Ch., Fulton, Mo.; choir dir. 1st Presbyn. Ch., Columbia. Mem. Phi Beta. Democrat. Presbyterian. Home: 4216 Mexico Gravel Rd Columbia MO 65201 Office: Dept Music Stephens Coll Columbia MO 65201

HANNA, MARY LORETTA, registered nurse; b. Pittsburg, Kans., Jan. 10, 1922; d. John Albert and Willa May (Veale) Chester; R.N., Kans. State Tchrs. Coll., 1942; B.S.N., Drury Coll., 1979; m. Chester Allen Hanna, June 3, 1943; children—Cody Allen, Loretta Ellen. Supr. nursery and delivery room, obstetrics dept. Mt. Carmel Hosp., 1942-43; pvt. duty nurse, 1943-48; acting adminstr. Dallas County Health Dept., Buffalo, Mo., 1954-59; line nurse Nat. Gypsum Co., Parsons, Kans., 1952; supervisory nurse Wallace Hosp., Lebanon, Mo., 1961; staff nurse U.S. Army Hosp., Fort Leonard Wood, Mo., 1962; office nurse Dr. Paul Jenkins, Lebanon, Mo., 1963-64; relief supervisory nurse Mo. State Chest Hosp., Mt. Vernon, 1966; orthopedic, acute med. and surg. head nurse U. Mo. Hosp., Columbia, 1967; supervisory clin. nurse U.S. Med. Center for Fed. Prisoners, Springfield, Mo., 1967-80; psychiat. nurse Lexington (Ky.) Fed. Correctional Inst., 1980—. Named Sweetheart of Med. Center Jaycees, 1974, Miss Florence Nightingale by inmates U.S. Med. Center for Fed. Prisoners, 1976; Law Enforcement Ednl. Program grantee, 1968-79. Mem. Am. Nurses Assn., Mo. Nurses Assn., Kans. Nurses Assn. Mem. Christian Ch. Home: 112 Londonderry Apt #3 Lexington KY 40504

HANNAGAN, ANGELA MARIE, educator; b. St. Louis, Dec. 21, 1917; d. Edward Michael and Helen A. (Piechowski) H.; B.A., Fontbonne Coll., 1940; postgrad. Northwestern U., 1942-43, Ind. U. N.W., summers 1969, 70, 71. Dir. public relations Fontbonne Coll., 1940-41; with Famour-Barr Co., 1941-42, Employers Mut. Ins. Co., 1942; tchr. English, East Lansing (Mich.) High Sch., 1943-44; tchr. English, Lew Wallace High Sch., Gary, Ind., 1944—, chmn. English dept., 1965—. Recipient Viola Briley award local 4 Am. Fedn. Tchrs., 1974. Mem. Nat. Council Tchrs. English (dir.), Ind. Council Tchrs. English (exec. bd. 1967—; E. H. Kemper McComb award 1981), Gary English Council (pres. 1960-61), Am. Fedn. Tchrs. (exec. bd. local 4, 1963—), Internat. Platform Assn., Fontbonne Coll. Alumnae Assn. (sec. 1940-42). Roman Catholic. Home: 430 S Grand Blvd Apt 415 Gary IN 46403 Office: Lew Wallace High Sch 415 W 45th Ave Gary IN 46408

HANNAH, MARY ELIZABETH, psychologist, educator; b. Bklyn., Sept. 8, 1940; d. Richards Wesley and Marie (Eitelbach) H.; B.A., Sweet Briar Coll., 1962; M.A., Alfred U., 1970; Ph.D., George Peabody Coll., Vanderbilt U., 1974. Sch. psychologist Rockford (Ill.) Public Schs., 1973-76; asst. prof. psychology dept. U. Detroit, 1977—. NIMH trainee, 1971-72; faculty research grantee, U. Detroit, 1977. Mem. Am. Psychol. Assn., Nat. Assn. Sch. Psychologists (sec. 1979-81, presdl. service award 1981), Mich. Assn. Sch. Psychologists (regional dir. 1978-80), Psi Chi. Episcopalian. Editor: Challenge, 1976; Horizons, 1977; Tomorrow's Children, 1979; Celebrating Children, 1980; profl. conf. procs.; contbr. articles to research publs. in field. Office: Psychology Dept U Detroit Detroit MI 48221

HANNAMAN, ROSE FAILLA, artist; b. Los Angeles, Mar. 30, 1919; d. Tony and Concetta (Faso) Failla; B.A. in Bus. Adminstrn., Fresno (Calif.) State Coll., 1941; m. John Hannaman, Sept. 7, 1956. U.S. Govt. employee in civilian personnel mgmt., 1941-66, program analyst, 1964-66; exhibited in one woman show at Adminstrn. Bldg., Balboa Heights, C.Z., 1977, USIS, Panama, 1978. Recipient numerous prizes Panama's Internat. Fishing Tournaments, 1971-76, Hon. Mention diploma for abstract oil painting in Xerox Pictorial Art Contest, 1972. Abstract oil painting Esmeralda selected by nat. jury to hang in Nat. League Am. Pen Women Biennial Show at Kennedy Center, Washington. Mem. Nat. League Am. Pen Women (nat. art bd. 1976-78, pres. C.Z. and Panama br. 1976-78, state pres. C.Z. and Panama area 1978-80, art editor Pen Woman mag. 1978-81, Disting. Pen Woman award 1982), Altar-Bible Rosary Soc. of Sacred Heart Chapel. Clubs: Inter-Am. Womens of Panama (pres. 1975-76); Isthmian Coll.; Quarry Heights and Ft. Amador Officers Wives (C.Z.). Editor: The Southern Cross (First Place award), 1971-75. Home: PSC Box 938 APO Miami FL 34002

HANNAN, COLETTE, retail drug chain exec.; b. DeKalb, Ill., Feb. 9, 1943; d. Thomas Henry and Winifred Helen (Hart) H.; B.A. cum laude, Rosary Coll., 1965; M.B.A., Northwestern U., 1972. Tchr. high sch. math., Geneva, Ill., 1965-67; retail analyst Walgreen Co., Deerfield, Ill., 1967-70, fin. analyst, 1970-73, asst. treas., 1973-76, dir. fin., 1976—. Office: 200 Wilmot Rd Deerfield IL 60015

HANNEGAN, MARTHA MARIE, fraternity exec.; b. Kansas City, Mo., Nov. 8, 1932; d. Joseph F. and Mayme A. (Overbay) Carolan; student Baker U., 1950-53; B.A., U. Wichita, 1959; m. Robert Eugene Hannegan, Aug. 30, 1958; children—Lawrence David, Thomas Joseph, John Patrick. Elem. tchr. public schs., Wichita, Kans., 1954-58; vol. officer, alumna pres. Alpha Chi Omega, Lincoln, Nebr., 1963-65, province pres., Nebr. and Iowa, 1969-73, asst. collegiate v.p., Phoenix and Houston, 1973-76, nat. collegiate v.p., Houston, 1976-80, nat. pres., 1980—. Democrat. Mem. United Ch. of Christ. Home: 6519 Spring Valley Rd Dallas TX 75240

HANNIGAN, VERA SIMMONS, bus. exec., former White House ofcl.; b. Bklyn., Aug. 20, 1932; d. John Albert and Sadie Marion (Ziegler) Rogel; student U. Md., 1965-71; m. John J. Hannigan, June 15, 1974; children by previous marriage—Stephen F. Simmons, Vera Marifay Simmons Staup, Susan G. Simmons Bolle. Mem. staff Sen. William B. Saxbe of Ohio, 1972-74; confidential asst. Asst. Atty. Gen. for Legis. Affairs W. Vincent Rakestraw, Dept. Justice, 1974-75; with Office of Legis. Affairs, The White House, Washington, 1975-77; Washington rep. land devel. Union Pacific Corp., Washington, 1977—. Active local Va. politics, Republican Party. Home: 11220 Wedge Dr Reston VA 22090 Office: 1120 20th St NW Suite 6005 Washington DC 20036

HANNON, ELIZABETH HALL, info. service co. exec.; b. Washington, Oct. 16, 1941; d. John Richard and Elizabeth Mae (Garber) H.; B.A., U. Md., 1963; m. Kevin Hayes Hannon, Sept. 12, 1964; children—Patrick Michael, Kathleen Anne, Megan Theresa. Reporter, Sci. Service, Washington, 1963-64; sci. reporter Syracuse (N.Y.) Post Standard, 1964-72; tech. editor Pacific Gas & Electric Co., San Francisco, 1973-74; mgr. Inforum, Atomic Indsl. Forum, Washington, 1974-80; exec. dir. Utility Data Inst., Washington, 1980—. Office: 2011 I St NW Suite 700 Washington DC 20006

HANNON, LUCILE CATHERINE, acct., tax cons.; b. Bellefontaine, Miss., Aug. 3, 1909; d. Robert Louis and Hattie Mae (Redding) H.; B.A. in Journalism and Philosophy, Memphis State Coll., 1933; B.S. in Bus. Adminstrn. and Econs., B.A. in Dramatic Playwriting, Marquette U., Milw., 1937. Self-employed acct., tax cons., Pruitt, Ark., 1938—; recorder, acting mayor Town of Pruitt, 1969-72, mayor, 1973-78. Author: Nature's Rich Soil (play), 1937; patentee electric hair rolling device. Home and Office: Star Rt 1 Pruitt AR 72671

HANNON, MARIAN EDWARDS, travel agency exec.; b. St. Louis, Dec. 16, 1912; d. LeRoy Murray and Cornelia (Erskine) Edwards; B.A., U. Wash., 1936; M.S., Danbury State Coll., 1965; m. Stuart Hannon, Oct. 1, 1936 (div. 1963); children—Brian, Denis, Neill, Maureen. Tchr. pub. schs., Danbury, Conn., 1962, Belmont, Calif., 1967-68; tchr.-counselor pub. schs., Templeton, Calif., 1969-70; founder, owner, pres. Atherton Travel (Calif.), 1973—. Exec. pres. Parents Without Partners, chpt. 48, 1976-77. Mem. AAUW (dir. Atherton chpt.). Home and Office: 52 Wilburn Ave Atherton CA 94025

HANNON, MURIEL FRANCES, personnel cons.; b. Bklyn., July 15; d. Martin John and Catherine Monica (Flannery) H. Assignment mgr. Coopers & Lybrand, C.P.A.s, N.Y.C., 1951-66; dir. personnel Laventhol & Horwath, N.Y.C., 1967-73; pres. Muriel F. Hannon Placement Bur., N.Y.C., 1973—. Served with CIC, AUS, 1948-51. Cert. personnel cons. Mem. N.Y. Personnel Mgmt. Assn. (dir.), Internat. Assn. Personnel Women. Home: 7 Grandview Ln Thornwood NY 10594 Office: 366 Madison Ave New York NY 10017

HANNON, PATRICIA MARIE, cons.; b. Boston, May 26, 1952; d. Frederick Francis and Catherine Louise (Bubinski) H.; B.A. in Psychology, U. Mass., 1974; M.Ed., Lesley Coll., 1977. Salesperson, Lauriat's, Boston, 1970-74; child care worker Boston Center for Blind Children, 1974-75; tchr. spl. edn. Boston Public Schs., 1977-82; cons. Gemini Communications, Boston, 1982—. Student mem. Grad. Sch. Council, U. Mass., Boston, 1974. Clubs: Waltham Racquet, Wigs and Whiskers Theatre Group, Wellesley Players Theatre Group. Home and Office: 299 N Harvard St Boston MA 02134

HANRAHAN, LINDA ANN, social service adminstr.; b. Albany, N.Y., Aug. 26, 1951; d. Edward Vincent and Evelyn Clare (White) H.; A.A.S., Broome Community Coll., 1971; B.S., State U. N.Y., Cortland, 1974; M.S., Cornell U., 1978. Dental hygienist, Cortland, 1971-73, Albany, 1974; human ecology tchr., Niskayuna, N.Y., 1974-75; teaching asst. Cornell U., 1976-77; coordinator Aid to Women Victims of Violence, Cortland, 1977—; sec. N.Y. State Coalition Against Domestic Violence, 1980—; vol. coordinator Ithaca (N.Y.) Rape Crisis Service; mem. Task Force on Battered Women; counselor suicide prevention, 1975-77. Tompkins County del. N.Y. State Women's Meeting, 1977. Mem. Sigma Phi Alpha. Office: care YWCA 14 Clayton Ave Cortland NY 13045

HANRAHAN, NANCY M., ednl. adminstr.; b. Pelham, N.Y., Oct. 2, 1954; d. G. Michael and Florence Mary (Quinn) Hanrahan; B.S. in Urban Studies summa cum laude, Worcester State Coll., 1978; M.A. in Mgmt., Brandeis U., 1979. Asst. dir. Worcester (Mass.) Area Drug Coalition, 1975-78; sr. planner Worcester Community Mental Health Center, 1978-79; asso. dir. exec. programs and master's program Brandeis U., Waltham, Mass., 1979—; research asso. White House Task Force on Youth Employment, 1979-80; faculty mgmt. Clark U., 1979—; Worcester State Coll., 1981—; cons. in field. Mem. Newton Community Sch. Bd., 1979; bd. dirs. Chandler St. Center, 1979; mem. adv. com. Plymouth Women's Shelter, Boston, 1979; bd. dirs. Crisis Center, Worcester, 1978; mem. adv. bd. Health Systems, Worcester, 1977-79. Office of Edn. Public Service fellow, 1978-79. Mem. Assn. M.B.A. Execs., New Eng. Human Service Providers. Home: 20 Ledyard St Wellesley MA 02181 Office: Florence Heller Sch Brandeis Univ Waltham MA 02254

HANS, VALERIE PATRICIA, psychologist; b. South Bend, Ind., Jan. 24, 1951; d. John Julius and Mary Frances (Roberts) H.; B.A. with highest honors (U. Calif. Regents scholar), U. Calif., San Diego, 1973; M.A. in Social Psychology (Mary Beatty fellow, U. Toronto Open scholar, Ont. Grad. scholar), U. Toronto (Ont., Can.), 1974, Ph.D., 1978. Lectr., U. Toronto, 1976-78; vis. asst. prof. Ariz. State U., 1978-79, Simon Fraser U., Burnaby, B.C., 1979-80; asst. prof. criminal justice and psychology U. Del., Newark, 1980—; mem. jury adv. bd. Law Reform Commn. Can., 1977-78; cons. in field. Grantee, Law Reform Commn. Can., Simon Fraser U., B.C. Ministry Justice. Mem. Am. Psychol. Assn., Am. Psychology-Law Soc., Law and Society Assn., Soc. Personality and Social Psychology. Author papers in field. Office: Criminal Justice U Del Newark DE 19711

HANSBURG, SUSAN RITA, psychologist; b. N.Y.C., Nov. 11, 1941; d. Sam and Florence (Hans) Fremer; B.A., Adelphi U., 1962; M.A. (Ford Found. scholar), N.Y. U., 1963, Ph.D., 1977. Tchr. public schs., N.Y.C., 1963-65; sch. psychologist public schs., Bayshore, N.Y., 1970-73, Port Washington, N.Y., 1973-77, Herricks, N.Y., 1977-79; pvt. practice clin. psychology, Roslyn, N.Y., N.Y.C., 1978—. adj. asso. prof. C.W. Post Coll., L.I. U., Greenvale, N.Y., 1977—. Chmn. budget adv. com. Roslyn Bd. Edn., 1972-74, mem. adv. com. on kindergarten and primary edn., 1973; trustee Roslyn Nursery Sch., 1969-72. Mem. Am. Psychol. Assn., Nassau County Psychol. Assn., Nat. Assn. Sch. Psychologists, Assn. for Children with Learning Disabilities, Nassau County Mental Health Assn. Home: 93 Revere Rd East Hills NY 11577 Office: 80 Fifth Ave Suite 902 New York NY

HANSEN, CHARLOTTE HELGESON, publishing co. exec.; b. Jamestown, N.D., June 1, 1922; d. Louise S. and Ida (Clough) Helgeson; student Jamestown Coll., 1940-41; B.S., U. Minn., 1944; m. Gordon H. Hansen, Oct. 31, 1945; 1 dau., Jo-Ida C. Hematologist, Hanford Engring., Richland, Wash., 1944-45; serologist Tex. Dept. Health, Wichita Falls, 1945-46; instr. microbiology Jamestown Coll., 1951-61; food editor Jamestown Sun, 1949—; v.p., sec.-treas. Hansen Bros., Inc., Jamestown, 1972—; dir. First Bank Jamestown, First Bank System, Mpls., Hansen Bros., Inc. Bd. dirs. Jamestown Indsl. Devel. Corp., James River Sr. Citizens, Inc., Camp Rokiwan; trustee Jamestown Coll.; mem. N.D. Gov.'s Human Resources Council, 1982. Recipient Thanks badge Girl Scouts U.S.A., 1969; Outstanding Citizen in Community Service award State of N.D., 1974; Outstanding Citizen award City of Jamestown, 1978. Mem. Jamestown C. of C. (dir.), Nat. Assn. Bank Women, Nat. League Am. Pen Women, N.D. Press Women, AAUW, Nat. Fedn. Press Women, Nat. Food Editors and Writers Assn., PEO, Am. Legion Aux., Delta Kappa Gamma, Sigma Delta Chi. Republican. Clubs: Zonta, Order Eastern Star. Author: Kitchen Magic, 1964; Favorites of My Family, 1972; Let's Entertain, 1980. Editors and Writers Assn., PEO, Am. Legion Aux., Delta Kappa Gamma, Sigma Delta Chi. Republican. Clubs: Zonta, Order Eastern Star. Author: Kitchen Magic, 1964; Favorites of My Family, 1972; Let's Entertain, 1980. Home: 309 11th Ave NE Jamestown ND 58401 Office: 122 2d St NW Jamestown ND 58401

HANSEN, DIANA WILLIAMS, home economist; b. Rushville, Ind., Feb. 26, 1937; d. John Thomas and Dorothy June (Jackson) Williams; B.S., Purdue U., 1959; M.B.A., Bellarmine Coll., 1982; m. Gunnar Oscar Hansen, Sept. 1, 1968; children—Christina Diana, Gunnar Thomas. Editorial home economist Gen. Mills, Inc., 1959-62; public relations home economist J. Walter Thompson Advt., 1962-65; range dept. specialist home economist Gen. Electric Co., 1965-70; freelance home economist, 1970-74; mgr. home econs. range dept. Gen. Electric Co., Louisville, 1974-80, mgr. cooking performance devel., 1980—. Mem. Louisville Home Econs. Assn. (pres. 1970-71), Home Economists in Bus., Am. Home Econs. Assn., Internat. Microwave Power Inst. (chmn. membership, chmn. public relations cooking appliance sect. 1976-80, bd. govs. 1982-83). Author: The Microwave Guide and Cookbook, 1977, 78, 79, 80, rev., 1982; The Combination Range Guide and Cookbook, 1980; The Grill-Griddle-Range Guide and Cookbook, 1981; also articles. Home: 91 Valley Rd Louisville KY 40204 Office: Bldg 2 Room 219 Appliance Park Louisville KY 40225

HANSEN, ELLENMAE CURTIS, nurse; b. Akron, Ohio, June 12, 1920; d. James Oliver and Bertha Belle (Christensen) Curtis; R.N., Akron City Hosp. Sch. Nursing, 1942; B.S., Ariz. State U., 1970, M.A., 1972; m. Peter Christian Hansen, Feb. 19, 1944; children—Judith Ellen. Faculty, Eastern Ariz. Coll., Thatcher, 1974-75, Mesa (Ariz.) Community Coll., 1975-76; staff nurse Villa View Community Hosp., San Diego, 1977-78; asst. dir. Psychiat. Technician Program, Hillcrest Coll., San Diego, 1978; dir. Vocat. Nurse Program, Palo Vista Coll. Nursing, Vista, Calif., 1978—; adv. com. Vocat. Nurse Program, Mira Costa Coll., Oceanside, Calif., 1981—. Pres. bd. dirs. Palo Vista Coll. Nursing, 1980—; substitute precinct judge, 1977. Served as ensign, Nurse Corps, USNR, 1943-44; ATO. Mem. Calif. Vocat. Nurse Educators, Navy League of U.S., Calif. Assn. Health Career Educators, Alumni Assn. Akron City Hosp., Calif. Assn. Post-Secondary Schs., Nat. Assn. Health Career Schs., Nat. League Nursing, So. Calif. Dirs. Vocat. Nursing Programs, Alumni Assn. Ariz. State U., Pi Lambda Theta. Republican. Episcopalian. Home: 10564 Avenida Magnifica San Diego CA 92131 Office: 1593 E Vista Way Vista CA 92083

HANSEN, FLORENCE MARIE CONGIOLOSI (MRS. JAMES S. HANSEN), social worker; b. Middletown, N.Y., Jan. 7, 1934; d. Joseph James and Florence (Harrigan) Congiolosi; B.A., Coll. New Rochelle, 1955; M.S.W., Fla. State U., 1960; m. James S. Hansen, June 16, 1959; 1 dau., Florence M. Caseworker, Orange County Dept. Pub. Welfare, N.Y., 1955-57, Catholic Welfare Bur., Miami, Fla., 1957-58; supr. Catholic Family Service, Spokane, Wash., 1960, Cuban Children's Program, Spokane, 1962-66; founder, dir. social service dept., adminstr. supr. Spokane and Inland Empire artificial kidney center Sacred Heart Med. Center, Spokane, 1967—. Asst. in program devel. St. Margaret's Hall, Spokane, 1961-62; mem. budget and planning div. United Way, 1964-77, chmn. projects com., 1972-73; mem. Spokane Quality of Life Commn., 1974-79; mem. kidney disease adv. com. Wash.-Alaska Regional Med. Program, 1972-75. Mem. Nat. Assn. Social Workers (pres. Inland Empire chpt. 1972-74, sec., mem. exec. bd. Wash. chpt. 1975-78), Acad. Certified Social Workers (charter), Am. Soc. Hosp. Social Work Dirs., Nat. Kidney Found. Council Nephrology Social

Workers. Roman Catholic. Home: 5609 Northwest Blvd Spokane WA 99205 Office: Sacred Heart Med Center W 101 8th St Spokane WA 99204

HANSEN, FLORENCE PARSONS, home economist, educator; b. Auburn, Maine, Mar. 27, 1929; d. George Francis and Luella Louise (Small) Parsons; B.S., Nasson Coll., Springvale, Maine, 1950; M.S., Columbia U., 1954; postgrad. Mich. State U., 1978—; m. Walter Jacob Hansen, Aug. 27, 1957; children—Walter Jacob, Christian Frederick. Therapeutic dietitian N.Y. Hosp., White Plains, N.Y., 1953-55; asst. prof. home econs. Nasson Coll., Springvale, 1955-65; adminstrv. dietitian Goodall Hosp., Sanford, Maine, 1965-75; instr. home econs. U. N.H., Durham, 1975-81; asst. prof. home econs. SUNY Coll. Arts and Sci., Plattsburgh, 1981—; cons. in field. Mem. Am. Dietetic Assn., Am. Public Health Assn., Am. Home Econs. Assn., AAAS, Sanford-Alfred Hist. Soc. Kappa Delta Pi. Republican. Mem. United Ch. Christ. Club: Sanford-Springvale Coll. Home: 116 Main St Springvale ME 04083

HANSEN, GLADYS OLGA, word processing systems cons.; b. Chgo., Nov. 19, 1920; d. Charles and Olga (Kubis) Vlas; grad. Bryant and Stratton Bus. Coll., 1938; student Wright Jr. Coll., 1941-42, Coll. of Lake County, 1978; m. Robert Roy Hansen, Mar. 2, 1947 (div. Dec. 1963); children—Gail Melody, James Drew, Lynn Diane (dec.), Diane Kathleen, Karen Lynn. Exec. sec. to pres. Universal Equip. Co., Chgo., 1964-68; sec. to chmn. bd., pres. No. Electric Co., Chgo., 1968-69; word processing mgr. Baxter Travenol Labs., Inc., Deerfield, Ill., 1969-79; word processing cons., Deerfield, 1979—; pub. Kamely Press, Deerfield, 1980. Mem. adv. com. Oakton Community Coll., Morton Grove, 1976-82, Loop Coll., Chgo., 1977-78; sec.-treas. Union Drainage Dist. 1 of W. Deerfield Twp., 1973-78; pub. chmn. PTA, Aurora, Ill., 1956; active Boys Scouts Am., Girl Scouts U.S.A. Mem. Word Processing Mgmt. Assn. Chgo. (sec. 1978-79), Internat. Word Processing Assn., Nat. Assn. Women Bus. Owners, Am. Mgmt. Soc., Women in Mgmt., Am. Soc. Profl. Cons. (div. v.p. 1982), Waukegan/Lake County C. of C., Deerfield C. of C. Republican. Presbyterian. Clubs: Questers (v.p. 1979-80), Order Eastern Star. Author: Word Processing Systems Procedures Manual for Originators, 1976, rev., 1980; Word Processing Systems Procedures Manual for Support Staff, 1976, rev., 1980, 2d rev. edit., 1982. Home: 825 Waterview Circle Vernon Hills IL 60061 Office: 701 W Deerfield Rd Deerfield IL 60015

HANSEN, INA, nursery co. exec.; b. Schiedam, Netherlands, Jan. 2 1937; d. Johan and Johanna (Bezemer) van den Berge; A.A., El Camino Coll., 1978; B.S. summa cum laude in Bus. Adminstrn., Calif. State U., Dominquez Hills, 1981; 1 dau., Valentina Kacani. Freelance med. sec., Rancho Palos Verdes, Calif., 1972-75; tchr. med. assisting Harbor Coll., Los Angeles, 1975, 76, So. Regional Occupational Center, Torrance, Calif., 1976-77, Cerritos (Calif.) Coll., 1977-78; owner, operator Marina Orchids, Marina Del Rey, Calif., 1978—. Dir., treas. Netherlands Social Service Orgn. (under auspices Consul Gen. of Netherlands in Los Angeles), 1981. Cert. Adminstrv. med. asst. Mem. Am. Orchids Soc., Bromeliad Soc., Apt. Owners Assn. (So. Los Angeles County). Republican. Office: 800 Washington St Marina Del Rey CA 90291

HANSEN, JOAN MARIA MALIN, pharm. co. adminstr.; b. Chgo., Jan. 26, 1944; d. Charles Joseph and Leona Joan (Bednarek) Malin; A.B. with high honors, DePaul U., 1968; M.S. in Edn. (Ill. Tchr. Spl. Edn. scholar), No. Ill. U., 1975; 1 son, Eric William. Tchr. disadvantaged children Dist. 26, Mt. Prospect, Ill., 1968; tchr. Sacred Heart Sch., Chgo., 1968-69; tchr. Dist. 21, Wheeling, Ill., 1969, 70; tchr., coordinator Ray Graham Assn. for Handicapped, Elmhurst, Ill., 1973-75, dir. children's and adolescent's services, 1976-77, asso. dir., 1977-79; tng. mgr. Baxter Travenol Labs., Inc., Round Lake, Ill., 1979—; lectr. on community opportunities for handicapped to various local civic groups; developer Babysitters for Handicapped program; developer in-service tng. for parents, program staff, and adminstrs. of social services programs; internal cons. mgmt. devel. Mem. Am. Mgmt. Assn., Soc. Advancement of Mgmt., Am. Soc. for Tng. and Devel., Women in Mgmt. Home: 2005 Oxford Ct Schaumburg IL 60194 Office: PO Box 490 Round Lake IL 60073

HANSEN, KATE PEGGY, editor; b. Washington, Sept. 11, 1948; d. Lester and Louise (Blanton) Leopold; M.A., Bob Jones U., 1970; M.A., San Diego State U., 1979. Instr., Christian Heritage Coll., San Diego, 1970-76; asso. prof. speech San Diego City Coll., 1976-80; editor Where Mag., San Diego, 1980—; communications cons. U.S. Marine Corps, 1979-82. Mem. Western Speech Communications Assn., Communication Arts Group. Republican. Home: 5046 Ducos Pl San Diego CA 92124 Office: 2165 San Diego Ave San Diego CA 92110

HANSEN, KATHRYN GERTRUDE, former state ofcl., assn. editor; b. Gardner, Ill., May 24, 1912; d. Harry J. and Marguerite (Gaston) Hansen; B.S. with honors, U. Ill., 1934, M.S., 1936. Personnel asst. U. Ill., Urbana, 1945-46, supr. tng. and activities, 1946-47, personnel officer, instr. psychology, 1947-52, exec. sec. U. Civil Service System Ill., also sec. for merit bd., 1952-61, adminstrv. officer, sec. merit bd., 1961-68, dir. system, 1968-72; lay asst. firm Webber, Balbach, Theis and Follmer, P.C., Urbana, Ill., 1972-74. Bd. dirs. Univ. YWCA, 1952-55, chmn., 1954-55; bd. dirs. Champaign-Urbana Symphony, 1978-81. Mem. Coll. and Univ. Personnel Assn. (hon., life mem., editor Jour. 1955-73, Newsletter, Internat. pres. 1967-68), Annuitants Assn. State Univs. Retirement System Ill. (state sec.-treas. 1974-75), Pres.'s Council U. Ill. (life), U. Ill. Alumni Assn. (life), U. Ill. Found., Campus Round Table U. Ill., Nat. League Am. Pen Women, AAUW (state 1st v.p. 1958-60), Bus. and Profl. Women's Club, Champaign-Urbana Symphony Guild, Secretariat U. Ill. (life), Fortnightly Club Urbana, Delta Kappa Gamma (state pres. 1961-63), Phi Mu (life), Kappa Delta Pi, Kappa Tau Alpha. Clubs: Medra, Order Eastern Star. Author: (with others) A Plan of Position Classification for Colleges and Universities; A Classification Plan for Staff Positions at Colleges and Universities, 1968; Grundy Corners, 1982. Editor: The Illini Worker, 1946-52; Campus Pathways, 1952-61; This is Your Civil Service Handbook, 1960-67. Author, lectr., cons., editor publs. on personnel practices. Home: 1004 E Harding Dr Apt 307 Urbana IL 61801

HANSEN, MARIE SABATA, former gas co. exec., civic worker; b. nr. Bruno, Nebr.; d. Alois and Marie (Egr) Sabata; grad. Am. Bus. Coll., Omaha, 1929; student U. Nebr., Omaha; m. Gilbert P. Hansen, Nov. 16, 1945 (dec. Mar. 1956). With No. Natural Gas Co. (now InterNorth Co.), Omaha, 1931-72, dir. investor research and relations, 1969-72. Charter mem. Omaha Mayor's Commn. on Status of Women, 1969; bd. dirs., treas., chmn. fin. com. and policy and procedures coms. Uta Halee Girls Village, Omaha, 1982—; bd. dirs., parliamentarian Vols. Intervening for Equity, sr. citizens advocacy, Omaha, 1981—. Mem. Nat. Assn. Parliamentarians (registered), Nebr. Assn. Parliamentarians (treas. 1982), Cath. Daus. Am. (ct. parliamentarian 1981-82), Omaha C. of C. (past pres. women's div.). Clubs: Omaha Press (charter), Omaha Altrusa (pres. 1968-69, dist. treas. 1972-74, parliamentarian 1980-82).

HANSEN, MATILDA ANNE, state legislator; b. nr. Paullina, Iowa, Sept. 4, 1929; d. Arthur J. and Sada G. (Thompson) Henderson; B.A., U. Colo., 1963; M.A., U. Wyo., 1971; m. Robert Michener, 1950; children—Eric, Douglas; m. 2d, Hugh G. Hansen, Aug. 8, 1965. Tchr. Am. history Englewood (Colo.) Sr. High Sch., 1963-65; dir. adult edn. Albany County Sch. Dist., Laramie, Wyo., 1966-78; mem. Wyo. Ho. of Reps. from Albany County, 1975—, ranking minority mem. judiciary com., 1981—, mem. rules and procedures com., 1981—; mgr. Laramie Plains Civic Center; mem. human resources com., state/fed. relations assembly Nat. Conf. State Govts. Gen. Electric Co. fellow, 1965. Mem. Laramie C. of C., LWV (bd. Wyo. chpt. 1969-74). Democrat. Quaker. Club: Univ. Women's. Address: 1306 Kearney St Laramie WY 82070

HANSEN, PENELOPE MILLER, govt. ofcl.; b. Washington, July 4, 1938; d. David S. and Majorie (Taylor) Miller; student Skidmore Coll., 1956-58; B.S. cum laude, Johns Hopkins U., 1972; m. R. Brock Hansen, Nov. 18, 1972; children—Layne, David, Jared. Recycling coordinator, bd. dirs. Ecology Action, Balt., 1970-72; environ. protection specialist EPA, Washington, 1972-75, mgr. materials recovery program resource recovery div., 1975-78, mgr. Office Solid Waste, 1978-79, mgr. minerals and energy program, 1979-81, mgr. analysis and assessment program indsl. waste div., 1981—. Recipient Bronze medal award EPA, 1975, Outstanding Service award, 1981. Mem. Am. Public Works Assn., Am. Polit. Sci. Assn. Author: Residential Paper Recovery, 1975; Decision-Makers Guide in Solid Waste Management, 1976; editor: National Recycling Directory, 1974; contbr. articles on hazardous waste treatment and waste recycling to profl. mags.; Home: 5158 Phantom Ct Columbia MD 21044 Office: EPA 401 M St SW Washington DC 20460

HANSENS, EUNICE DODD, civic worker; b. Vancouver, Wash., Nov. 11, 1919; d. William Wylie and Ada Eugenia (Wernette) Dodd; student Whitman Coll., 1937-39; m. Curtis Glenn Hansens, Feb. 6, 1948; children—Linda Yvonne, Glenn Elton, John Eric, Helen Aline. Exec. sec. United Way, Walla Walla, Wash., 1976-79; sec. Einan's Funeral Home, Richland, Wash., 1979-81; office mgr. Richland Bell Furniture, 1981—; mem. economic devel. com. Walla Walla C. of C., 1977-78; pres. Republican Women of Walla Walla County, 1978-79; mem. Walla Walla Community Service Council, 1976—; mem. exec. com. Walla Walla Bicentennial Com., 1975-76; pres. Women's Guild of Walla Walla Symphony Soc., 1963, 73; mem. citizens study and adv. group, Walla Walla Regional Planning Com., 1974-81; mem. Walla Walla County Rep. Govtl. Conf., 1976-81. Mem. D.A.R. Republican. Lutheran. Mem. Order Eastern Star, P.E.O. (pres. Wash. chpt. 1971-72). Home: 507 Comstock St Richland WA 99352 Office: 714 Parkway Richland WA 99352

HANSFORD, SUSAN WRIGHT, gallery dir., artist; b. Howell, Mich., May 31, 1952; d. William R. and Martha Jane (Massoll) Myers; B.A., Grand Valley State Coll., 1973. Sr. staff artist Sta. WGVC-TV, Grand Rapids, Mich., 1971-74; art and photo dir. Sta WXXI TV, Rochester, N.Y., 1974-75; pres., creative dir. Wright Angle Graphics, Rochester, 1974-79; mng. partner Wright-Angle-Young, Rochester, 1979-81; owner, dir. Gallery 696, 1982—. Trustee, Grand Rapids Art Mus., 1973-74; active fund raising Pres. Ford reelection, 1976; bd. dirs., chmn. public relations Rochester Gen. Hosp. Found., 1980. Mem. Nat. Assn. Ednl. Broadcasters (Gold award 1974), Women in Communication, Bus. Profls. Advt. Assn., Mktg. Execs. Communication, Inc. Office: 696 Park Ave Rochester NY 14607

HANSON, ANN H., state legislator; b. St. Albans, Vt., May 10, 1935; student U. Vt., 1956; m. Daniel J. Hanson. Mem. R.I. Ho. of Reps., 1980—; v.p. Barrington (R.I.) Town Council, 1976-78, pres., 1978-80, mem., 1975-80; pres. Barrington LWV. Republican. Office: RI State House Providence RI 02903 *

HANSON, ANNE COFFIN, art historian; b. Kinston, N.C., Dec. 12, 1921; d. Francis Joseph Howells and Annie Roulhac (Coffin) Coffin; B.F.A., U. So. Calif., 1943; M.A. in Creative Arts, U. N.C., 1951; Ph.D., Bryn Mawr Coll., 1962; m. Bernard Alan Hanson, June 27, 1961; children by previous marriage—James Warfield Garson, Robert Coffin Garson, Ann Blaine Garson. Instr., Albright Art Sch., U. Buffalo, 1955-58; vis. asso. prof. art Cornell U., 1963; asst. prof. Swarthmore Coll., 1963-64, Bryn Mawr Coll., 1964-68; dir. Internat. Study Center, Mus. Modern Art, N.Y.C., 1968-69; adj. asso. prof. N.Y. U., 1969-70; prof. history art Yale U., New Haven, 1970—, chmn. dept., 1974-78; resident Am. Acad. Rome, spring, 1974. Nat. Endowment for Humanities fellow, 1967-68; Am. Council Learned Socs. grantee, summer 1963. Mem. Coll. Art Assn. Am. (pres. 1972-74), Comité Internationale de l'histoire de l'Art (nat. mem.). Author: Jacopo della Quercia's Fonte Gaia, 1965; Edouard Manet, 1966; Manet and the Modern Tradition, 1977; contbr. articles to profl. jours; editorial bd. The Art Bull., 1971—; editor monograph series Coll. Art Assn., 1968-70; governing bd. Yale U. Press, 1977—; editorial com. Art Jour., 1979—. Home: 28 Lincoln St New Haven CT 06511 Office: Dept History Art 56 High St Yale U New Haven CT 06520 *

HANSON, CAROL COOPER, escrow service co. exec.; b. Sacramento, Apr. 2, 1939; d. Charles James and Helen Margaret (Malaspina) Cooper; student San Jose State U., 1956-58; B.A., U. Hawaii, 1973; m. Joe A. Hanson, Feb. 14, 1969; children—Christopher James, Jeffrey Charles, Mark Phillips. With Nat. Escrow Co., Honolulu, 1973-77, Pali Kai Realtors, Kailua, Hawaii, 1977-78, Transam. Title Ins. Co., Pasadena, Calif., from 1978; now v.p. SP Escrow Services, Inc. subs. Security Pacific Corp., Pasadena. Mem. Calif. Escrow Assn. (dir.), Escrow Assocs. San Gabriel Valley (pres.). Contbg. author: Open Sea Mariculture, 1974. Home: 1100 Madre Vista Rd Altadena CA 91001 Office: 45 S Hudson St 8th Floor Pasadena CA 91101

HANSON, DARLENE OLGA, business exec.; b. Park Rapids, Minn., Aug. 14, 1931; d. Robert Livingston and Olga Marie (Olson) Marshall; student St. Olaf U., 1949-50; m. K. N. Hanson, Nov. 23, 1950; children—Bruce K., Marshall Brad. Owner, operator 2 gift shops, Park Rapids and Nevis, Minn., 1955-58; saleswoman Holmes Realty Co., Fargo, N.D., 1959-61; owner, mgr. Perkins Pancake Houses Fla., St. Petersburg and Clearwater, 1961-66; investment advisor Fin. Programs Inc., St. Petersburg, 1966-67; personnel advisor Clairmont Personnel, Clairmont and La Jolla, Calif., 1967-68; office mgr. Eleo Med. Corp., Sorento Valley, Calif., 1968-69; owner, operator Candy Casa, San Diego, 1969-79, Candy Casa II, St. Petersburg Beach and Madeira Beach, Fla., 1972-73, Vanilla Villa, 1981—; mgr. Squibob Sq. Shopping Center, Old Town, San Diego, 1969-79; mem. planning com. Old Town, San Diego, 1973-78; dir. Perkins Pancake Houses Fla., 4 Seasons. Bd. dirs., v.p. C. of C. Pinellas County (Fla.), 1961-66. Recipient 7 service awards Kiwanis Club, St. Petersburg, 1961-66; named to Top 10 for real estate sales Fargo Bd. Realtors, 1961. Office: 3759 Avocado Blvd La Mesa CA 92041

HANSON, KAREN LINNEA, med. technologist; b. Moline, Ill., Sept. 8, 1936; d. Earl Henning and Rose Linnea (Anderson) Hanson; B.A., Augustana Coll., 1958; cert. med. tech. Rockford Meml. Hosp. Sch. Med. Tech., 1962. Med. technologist chemistry dept. Rockford (Ill.) Meml. Hosp., 1958-60, 1962-71, lab. Quad Cities Pathologist Group, Moline Luth. Hosp., 1971—. Aux. mem. Tri-City Symphony Orch., city chmn., 1978—, chmn., Moline City, 1977-78, vice chmn., 1976-77; mem. ch. council St. John's Luth. Ch., Rock Island, Ill., 1978-81, mem. worship and music com., 1978-81, chairperson program div., 1980-81, mem. altar guild, 1973—, tchr. Sunday sch., 1978-79. Mem. Am. Soc. Med. Technologists, Am. Soc. Clin. Pathologists (affiliate mem., cert med. technologist), P.E.O. Home: 3243 9 Ave Rock Island IL 61201 Office: Lutheran Hosp 501 10 Ave Moline IL 61265

HANSON, MARLYS CUDWORTH, research lab. exec., consultant; b. New Rockford, N.D., July 5, 1939; d. Clair Franklin and Leone Laura (Williams) Cudworth; B.S. in Bus. summa cum laude, Moorhead (Minn.) State Coll., 1962; M.S. in Career Counseling, Calif. State U., Hayward, 1978; m. Merle E. Hanson, Dec. 4, 1958; children—Lori Claire, Brent Leigh. Ct. stenographer Cass County Ct., Fargo, N.D., 1958-60; jr. and sr. high sch. tchr. Los Angeles public schs., 1962-64; counselor, project mgr. career edn. program Socorro (N.M.) unified schs., 1969-73; mgr. mgmt. devel. and tng. Lawrence Livermore (Calif.) Lab., 1974-79, mgr. employment and devel. elec. engring. dept., 1979—; prin. Hanson & Assocs., cons. firm; leader seminars, cons. in field. Mem. Am. Soc. Tng. and Devel. (dir. career devel. div.), Am. Soc. Engring. Edn. Club: Delta Boating. Author articles in field. Office: L-151 Livermore CA 94550

HANSON, MARY LOUISE, banker, polit. worker; b. Bremerton, Wash., Apr. 24, 1944; d. Lawrence Grant and Ruth Louise (Johnson) Dix; student U. Wash., 1962-64, U. Colo., 1973-77; m. Donald G. Hanson, Dec. 19, 1964 (div. June 1973). Adminstrv. asst. U. Pa., Phila., 1965-70, Provident Mgmt. Corp., Providence, 1970-72; with First Nat. Bank of Denver, 1972-80; asst. v.p. mgr. loan analysis dept. United Bank of Denver, 1980—; lectr.; chmn. adv. council Aton Found.; various state bd. positions Colo. Libertarian Party, 1976—; nat. vice chmn. Libertarian Party, 1977-81, mem.-at-large nat. com., 1981—, regional rep. on nat. com., 1977, nat. fin. chmn., 1980; Libertarian candidate for treas. of Colo., 1978. Bd. trustees AMC Cancer Research Inst., 1982—. Mem. Nat. Fedn. Bus. and Profl. Women, Colo. Fedn. Bus. and Profl. Women (1st v.p.), Downtown Denver Bus. and Profl. Women (pres. 1978-80, state legis. chmn. 1980-81), Robert Morris Assos. Office: United Bank 1700 Broadway Denver CO 80217 also Libertarian Party 2300 Wisconsin Ave NW Washington DC 20007

HANSON, PATRICIA ANN, pvt. investigator; b. Chgo., Aug. 17, 1942; d. Walter A. and Bertha (Topp) Troy; student U. Wis., Parkside, 1979—; m. Jan. 22, 1966 (husband dec.); children—Jodi Ann, Heather Leigh; m. 2d, Jeffrey G. Hanson, Dec. 5, 1981. Clk., E.J. Brach & Sons, Chgo., 1960-65; mgr. Lake-of-the-Woods Lodge, Nestor Falls, Ont., Can., 1966-67; tech. coordinator Joliet (Ill.) Wrought Washer, 1971-72; office mgr. dental office, Elkhorn, Wis., 1972-73; communications officer Lake Geneva (Wis.) Police Dept., 1973-81; pvt. investigator Braden & Olson Law Firm, 1981—. Founding, past pres. Assn. Prevention of Family Violence, 1978-79. Recipient Walworth County Mental Health award, 1979. Mem. Lake Geneva Profl. Policemen's Protective Assn. (past pres., chmn. contract negotiations team 1974—), Lake Geneva Bus. and Profl. Women's Club (legis. chmn., 1st v.p.), Lake Como Beach Property Owners Assn. (treas. 1981-82). Republican. Roman Catholic. Home: Route 2 Box 402 Lake Geneva WI 53147 Office: PO Box 512 Lake Geneva WI 53147

HANSON-SEESE, KAREN GRACE, nurse; b. Walla Walla, Wash., Feb. 2, 1948; d. Franklin Bertram and Ruth Elizabeth (Silven) Hanson; B.A. in Social Work, Eastern Wash. U., 1969; B.S. in Nursing, Wash. State U., 1971; M.Ed., Walla Walla Coll., 1981; m. Daniel E. Seese, Oct. 5, 1974; children—Rob, Elizabeth. Staff nurse CCU and med. unit Deaconess Hosp., Spokane, 1971-72; charge nurse VA Hosp., Walla Walla, 1972-73, U.S. Army Med. Center, Camp Kue, Okinawa, 1973; nurse Walla Walla Gen. Hosp., 1973-76; coordinator health continuing edn., clin. instr. nursing program Walla Walla Community Coll., 1982—. Bd. dirs., v.p. Walla Walla Symphony Soc., 1978-80. Mem. Am. Heart Assn. Wash. (Silver award 1978, pres. Eastern Wash. sub area council 1979, gov. 1978-79), Am. Nurses Assn., Emergency Dept. Nurses Assn., Am. Assn. Critical Care Nurses, AAUW, Am. Assn. Higher Edn., Phi Delta Kappa, Sigma Theta Tau. Episcopalian. Home: 50 Brookside Dr Walla Walla WA 99362 Office: 500 Tausick Way Walla Walla WA 99362

HANTOUT, MARY ANN, nurse; b. Oelwein, Iowa, Oct. 10, 1938; d. Donald D. and Mary Mildred (McKibben) Palmer; diploma Evang. Sch. Nursing, 1959; student Marshalltown Jr. Coll., 1956-58, U. San Francisco, 1961-62, Hunter Coll., 1964-66, U. Calif., San Diego, 1972, U. Nev., Las Vegas, 1972; m. Mustapha Hantout, Nov. 5, 1967; 1 dau., Lydia Donann. Nurse, Iowa Methodist Hosp., Des Moines, 1959-61, Los Angeles County Gen. Hosp., 1961-62, Doctors Hosp., N.Y.C., 1962-64, Bellevue Hosp., N.Y.C., 1964-65; evening supr. Gracie Square Hosp., N.Y.C., 1965-68; evening charge nurse pediatrics, asst. charge ICU, Sunrise Hosp., Las Vegas, 1968-71; dir. nursing, interim adminstr. Cedarbrook Hosp., Las Vegas, 1971-74; supr. care unit North Las Vegas Hosp., 1975-77; head nurse, clin. dir. Met. Police Dept., Las Vegas, 1980-81; sr. correctional nurse Dept. Prisons, State of Nev., Jean, 1982—. Bd. dirs. Las Vegas Women's Crisis Shelter. Mem. Am. Nurses Assn., Nev. Alcohol Assn., Nat. League for Nursing, Nev. Nurses Assn., So. Nev. Council on Alcoholism, Interagy. Council on Alcoholism, Beta Sigma Phi. Republican. Methodist. Clubs: Order Eastern Star, Las Vegas Jr. Women's (pres.), Nev. Federated Women's (corr. sec.). Home: 293 Hensley St Las Vegas NV 89109

HAPP, ALTA ELIZABETH, artist, educator; b. Kennewick, Wash., Feb. 19, 1921; d. Henry Lewis and Annie Elizabeth (Yates) Leckliter; student Bakersfield Jr. Coll., 1939-40; m. Richard Clarence Smith (div. 1961); children—Robin (Mrs. Bernard Charles Danylchuk), Alan Montgomery, Shelley (Mrs. Thomas William Stoye); m. 2d., William Morris Happ, Jan. 19, 1967. Instr. oil painting, adult edn. Palomar Coll., San Marcos, Calif., 1958-62; pvt. tchr., lectr. in field, 1962—; one-woman shows The Atheneaum, La Jolla, Calif., 1959, Jeane's Gallery, La Jolla, 1961, Palomar Coll., 1959-61, The Little Galleries, Escondido, Calif., 1964, La Pina Ltd., La Jolla, 1965, 66, 67, Gray's Gallery, Escondido, 1973, Carlsbad Oceanside Art League Gallery, 1973; exhibited in group shows San Diego Mus. Art, San Diego Art Inst., Riverside Mus. Art, San Bernardino Mus. Art, So. Calif. Expn., Del Mar, also various galleries represented in permanent collections; lectr. on psychology and symbology of color in music and art. Active Palomar Hosp. aux., 1957-59; pres. Showcase of Arts, Escondido, 1961-62; rep. to San Diego Council of Visual Arts, 1966-67; mem. Escondido Cultural Arts Com., 1972-73; chmn. Mission Valley (Calif.) Expn. Art, 1967; bd. dirs. Philos. Religious Free Library, 1970-74, Pala Mission Indian Sch., 1965-72. Huntington Hartford Found. fellow, Pacific Palisades, Calif., 1964. Recipient numerous other awards. Mem. San Diego Art Inst., San Diego Art Guild of Fine Arts Soc., San Diego Watercolor Soc., Nat. League of Am. Pen Women (pres. 1974-76), Watercolor West. Home: 2355 Royal Crest Escondido CA 92025

HAQUE, MALIKA HAKIM, pediatrician; b. Madras, India; came to U.S., 1967; d. S. Abdul and Rahimunisa (Hussain) Hakim; M.B.B.S., Madras Med. Coll., 1967; m. C. Azeez ul Haque, Feb. 5, 1967; children—Kifizeba, Masarath Nashr, Asim Zayd. Rotating intern Miriam Hosp., Brown U., Providence, 1967-68; resident in pediatrics Children's Hosp., N.J. Coll. Medicine, 1968-70; fellow in devel. disabilities Ohio State U., 1970-71; acting chief pediatrics Nisonger Center, 1973-74; staff pediatrician Children and Youth Project, Children's Hosp., Columbus, Ohio, also clin. asst. prof. pediatrics Ohio State U., 1974-80; clin. asso. prof. pediatrics Ohio State U., 1981—; staff pediatrician Columbus Children's Hosp.; cons. Central Ohio Head Start Program, 1974-79. Mem. Republican Presdl. Task Force, 1982—. Recipient Physician Recognition award AMA, 1971-83, Gold medals in surgery, radiology, pediatrics and ob/gyn; Presdl. medal of Merit, 1982; diplomate Am. Bd. Pediatrics. Fellow Am. Acad. Pediatrics; mem. Ambulatory Pediatric Assn., Central Ohio Pediatric Soc. Islam. Research on enuresis. Office: 700 Children's Dr Columbus OH 43205

HARBAUGH, VIRGINIA WAYNE, govt. adminstr.; b. Savannah, Ga., Dec. 15, 1930; d. Adrian Bancker and Jeannette Butler (Strong) Talbot; B.A., Smith Coll., 1952; M. Planning and Urban Design, U. Va.,

1971; m. William Henry Harbaugh, Aug. 15, 1953; children—Lyn Hartridge, William Talbot, Henry Richmond. Sr. planner Thomas Jefferson Planning Dist. Commn., Charlottesville, Va., 1973-79, exec. dir., 1979—. Pres. League of Women Voters, Mansfield, Conn., 1957-59, Lewisburg, Pa., 1964-66; pres. Va. Citizens Planning Commn., 1976-78. Mem. Am. Inst. Cert. Planners, Am. Planning Assn. Democrat. Unitarian. Home: 1930 Thomson Rd Charlottesville VA 22903 Office: 401-403 8th St NE Charlottesville VA 22901

HARBIN, DENISE DELL, advt. agy. exec.; b. Akron, Ohio, Nov. 18, 1950; d. Dell Howard and Nester Lillian (Nelson) Harbin; B.A., Miami U., Oxford, Ohio, 1972; postgrad. Parsons Sch. Design. Art dir. Warwick, Welsh & Miller Advt., Inc., N.Y.C., 1972-76; sr. art dir. J. Patrick Moore Advt., Inc., Mpls., 1976-77; exec. v.p., creative dir. Bednar, Harbin & Wright Advt., Inc., Westport, Conn., 1978-80; sr. v.p., creative dir. Internat. Mktg. Group, Inc., Westport, 1978-80; pres. Harbin Communications Group, Inc., N.Y.C., 1980—. Mem. Am. Advt. Fedn. (past v.p. Twin cities chpt.), Art Dirs. Club N.Y., Advt. Club N.Y., Advt. Women N.Y. Republican. Presbyterian. Office: 501 Fifth Ave New York NY 10017

HARBISON, MARGARET WARLICK, educator; b. Cleveland County, N.C., Dec. 19, 1935; d. Walter Theodore and Lessie Lawrence (Downs) Warlick; B.S., Appalachian State U., Boone, N.C., 1957, M.A., 1963; Ed.D., U. Miss., 1974; m. Clyde Hilton Waters, May 31, 1964 (div.); 1 son, Jack Hilton; m. 2d, Paul Dean Harbison, May 16, 1981. Instr. phys. edn. jr. high schs., N.C., 1957-61, Fla., 1961-62; asst. prof. health, phys. edn. and recreation U. Miss., 1963-67; asst. prof. phys. edn. Kennesaw Coll., Marietta, Ga., 1967-70; asst. prof. health, phys. edn. and recreation Delta State U., Cleveland, Miss., 1970-74; prof., coordinator phys. edn. and athletics for women E. Tex. State U., Commerce, 1974—; asst. recreation dir.; supr. summer playgrounds. Bd. dirs. United Way, 1977-80, treas., 1978-80. Recipient Presdl. citation AAHPER, 1974; Disting. Community Service award, 1981. Mem. Am. Alliance for Health, Phys. Edn., Recreation and Dance, Tex. Assn. Health, Phys. Edn. and Recreation, Tex. Assn. Coll. Tchrs., So. Assn. Phys. Edn. for Coll. Women, Nat. Assn. Phys. Edn. in Higher Edn., C. of C. (dir., 1978-81), Delta Kappa Gamma, Kappa Delta Pi. Democrat. Baptist. Club: Psychology (pres., 1978-80). Home: 2824 McCarley Dr Commerce TX 75428 Office: Dept Health and Phys Edn E Tex State U Commerce TX 75428

HARBOUR, JEANNE DULAS, child psychiatrist; b. Labatut, France, Feb. 9, 1921; d. Pierre and Dorothy (Stafas) Dulas; came to U.S., 1958, naturalized, 1967; M.D., Sch. Medicine, Paris, 1947; M.D., Wis. U., 1968; m. Howard Harbour, June 15, 1962. Sch. public health med. insp., France, 1948-58; intern Presbyn.-St. Luke's Hosp., Chgo., 1958-59, resident, 1959-61; clin. asst. psychiatry Ill. U., 1959-61; fellow psychiatry McGill U., 1962, Toronto U., 1963; fellow child psychiatry Chapel Hill Meml. Hosp., U. N.C., 1964-65; cons. child psychiatry North Shore Hosp., Winnetka, Ill., 1966-67, Mendota State Hosp., Madison, Wis., 1968-71; clin. instr. U. Wis., Madison, 1968-71; attending child psychiatrist Children's Meml. Hosp., Chgo., Northwestern U., Chgo., 1973-80, Rush-Presbyterian-St. Luke's Med. Center, Chgo., 1976—; asst. prof. dept. psychiatry Rush Med. Coll. Diplomate in child psychiatry Am. Bd. Psychiatry and Neurology. Fellow Am. Orthopsychiat. Assn.; mem. AMA, Am. Psychiat. Assn., Ill., Chgo. med. soc., Ill. Psychiat. Soc., Am. Med. Womens Assn., Chgo. Council Child Psychiatry. Research on color blindness of sch. children. Home: 535 N Michigan Ave Chicago IL 60611 Office: 2335 W 103d St Chicago IL 60643

HARDAGE, JEANNETTE, nutritionist; b. Vernon, Tex., July 30, 1933; d. Augustus and Pearl (Hobson) H.; B.A., Tex. Christian U., 1969; B.S., Tex. Woman's U., 1953, M.S., 1971, Ph.D., 1973; m. Olan S. Johnson, May 31, 1953 (div. May 1981); children—Layne Jeanette, Dean Olan; m. 2d, Edward Whitaker, Jan. 3, 1982. Tech. writer, mech. design draftsman Gen. Dynamics, Fort Worth, 1953-70; asso. prof. nutrition and food So. U., Baton Rouge, 1973-78; asso. prof. home econs., dir. food sci. and nutrition program Norfolk (Va.) State U., 1978-82; dir. dietetic programs Tidewater Community Coll., Virginia Beach, Va., 1983—; dietitian Manning Convalescent Home, Portsmouth, Va., 1979—. Mem. Women in Communications (pres., 1960, 77), Am. Dietetic Assn. (regional pres. 1980), Am. Home Econs. Assn., Internat. Food Service Execs. Assn., Va. Restaurant Assn., Va. Public Health Assn. Methodist. Home: 937 Leckie St Portsmouth VA 23704 Office: 1700 College Crescent Virginia Beach VA 23456

HARDAWAY, EVELYN RENEE, data processing exec.; b. Columbus, Muscogee, Ga., Dec. 19, 1948; d. Roscoe and Vesta Mae (Mitchell) H.; student Johnson C. Smith U., Charlotte, N.C., 1967-68, Am. Inst. Banking, Columbus, Ga., 1969-70. Auditing clk. First Nat. Bank, Columbus, Ga., 1969-72; office mgr. Cagle, Inc., Omaha, 1972-74; account exec. Flair Personnel Service, Atlanta, 1974-76; tech. adv. Am. Mgmt. Services, Denver, 1976-80; data processing coordinator Lifemark Corp., Houston, 1981—. Recipient Operations Excellence award Am. Mgmt. Services, 1979. Mem. Nat. Assn. Female Execs. Home: 9475 Roark Rd Apt 101 Houston TX 77099 Office: PO Box 656 Katy TX 77449

HARDEN, ANITA JOYCE, nurse; b. Jackson, Tenn., May 17, 1947; d. Percy Lawrence and Marjorie (Robison) H.; B.S. in Nursing, Ind. U., 1968; M.S. in Nursing, Ind. U.-Purdue U., Indpls., 1973; 1 son, Brian Robison Weir. Staff nurse Indpls. hosps., 1968-71; instr. Ind. U. Sch. Nursing, 1973-75; dir. continuing care Gallahue Mental Health Center, Indpls., 1975-80; mgr. psychiatry Community Hosp., Indpls., 1980—; clin. asst. prof. Ind. U., 1977-82, clin. asso. prof., 1982—; clin. asso., trainer Suicide Prevention Service, Indpls., 1974-77; chmn. adv. bd. de-institutionalization project Central State Hosp., Indpls., 1978-79; mem. Ind. Council Community Mental Health Center, 1979-80. Recipient Outstanding Achievement in Professions award Center Leadership Devel., 1981. Mem. Ind. U. Alumni Assn., Christian Women's Fellowship, 500 Festival Assos., Sigma Theta Tau, Chi Eta Phi. Democrat. Mem. Christian Ch. (Disciples of Christ). Author articles in field. Home: 4057 Clarendon Rd Indianapolis IN 46208 Office: 1500 N Riter St Indianapolis IN 46219

HARDER, SARAH SNELL, univ. adminstr.; b. Chgo., Sept. 9, 1937; d. Frank Wen and Margaret Louise (Bryne) Snell; student U. Iowa, 1955-58; B.A., B.S. cum laude, U. Wis., LaCrosse, 1963; M.A., Bowling Green State U., 1966; m. Harry R. Harder, Feb. 7, 1964; children—Richard, Bentley, Jennifer, Aaron. Mem. faculty in English, Bowling Green State U., 1967-68; mem. faculty English, U. Wis., Eau Claire, 1968, adv. to older students, 1975-77, asst. to chancellor for affirmative action, 1975-78, asst. to chancellor for affirmative action and ednl. opportunity, 1978—; mem. U. Wis. regents' task forces on basic skills, status of women, minority/disadvantaged students; cons. women's employment and equity, non-traditional programs in higher edn. Co-chmn. Nat. Women's Conf. Com., 1979—; trustee Eau Claire Public Library, 1980—; founding bd. dirs. Wis. Women's Network. Named one of 80 Leaders for the Eighties, Milw. Jour., 1979; Dept. Edn. grantee, 1978—. Mem. AAUW (nat. dir., award), LWV, Nat. Women's Polit. Caucus (award Wis. br.), Women's Equity Action League, NOW, Delta Kappa Gamma, Alpha Lambda Delta. Democrat. Co-designer Beyond ERA—an Action Plan, 1982; contbr. articles to Redbook, Grad. Woman, Stateswoman. Home: 463 Summit Ave Eau Claire WI 54701 Office: Schofield 225 U Wis Eau Claire WI 54701

HARDESTY, ELSIE NASH, writer; b. West Point, Miss., Jan. 25, 1926; d. Elzie Byron and Gladys (Hilburn) Nash; B.A. cum laude, Miss. U. for Women, 1947; m. Daniel Clark Hardesty, May 23, 1948; children—Daniel Clark, Franklin Nash, Carl Edwards. Women's writer State-Times, Baton Rouge, 1947, 67-71, 78-79; asst. mgr. Sta. WJQS, Jackson, Miss., 1948; organist First Meth. Ch., Baton Rouge, 1949-51; asst. organist Trinity Episcopal Ch., Baton Rouge, 1953-76; music tchr. Trinity Episcopal Sch., 1954-59, kindergarten tchr., 1964-65; organist First Ch. of Christ Scientist, Baton Rouge, 1955-57; women's writer Morning Advocate, Baton Rouge, 1971-78; free-lance writer, Baton Rouge, 1979—. Active, Altar Guild, Trinity Episcopal Ch., pres., 1958-59; lic. lay reader Episc. Diocese of La., 1976-82; bd. dirs. YWCO, 1980-81; vol. Books for the Blind, La. State Library, 1980-82. Recipient writing awards UPI, 1977, Gen. Foods, 1978. Mem. La. Presswomen (awards, 1974, 76, 77), Miss. U. for Women Alumnae Assn. (chpt. pres. 1960, 73), DAR, Mortar Bd., Am. Guild Organists (chpt. dean 1953-54), Zeta Tau Alpha (house corp. memls. chmn. 1965-71), Sigma Alpha Iota, Alpha Psi Omega, Pi Delta Epsilon. Democrat. Clubs: Baton Rouge Music (performing mem.). Home: 1907 Cloverdale Ave Baton Rouge LA 70808

HARDESTY, SARAH JANE, violinist; b. Kansas City, Mo., Sept. 14, 1946; d. Egbert M. and Margaret E. H.; B.Mus. Drake U., 1967; postgrad. Ind. U., 1967-68. Mem. 1st violin sect. Dallas Symphony Orch. 1968—; lectr. in field. Mem. Greater North Tex. Orchid Soc. (past sec.). Office: PO Box 26207 Dallas TX 75226

HARDIN, ANITA MILES, ednl. adminstr.; b. De Funiak Springs, Fla., Dec. 4, 1943; d. Ausphera Schubert and Daisy Belle (LeCroy) Miles; A.A., Chipola Jr. Coll., 1963; B.A., U. South Fla., 1965; cert. Bur. Studies in Adult Edn., Ind. U., 1977, 78, Behavioral Systems Inc., Atlanta, 1977, Personal Dynamics Inst., Adventures in Attitudes, Mpls., 1978, So. Personal and Profl. Devel. Co. Psychology of Winning Seminar, Auburn, Ala., 1981; M.Ed., Auburn U., Montgomery, Ala., 1978; postgrad. in edn. Auburn U., 1978—; 1 son, John William II. Tchr., Hillsborough County (Fla.) Bd. Edn., 1965-68, Escambia County (Fla.) Bd. Edn., 1968-73, Bullock Meml. Found., Union Springs, Ala., 1973-74; adminstr. Bullock County (Ala.) Bd. Edn., 1975-78; ESEA Title IV-C project dir. Auburn City Bd. Edn., 1978—, dir. ednl. services, 1978—; cons. Bullock County Bd. Edn., 1975. Recipient cert. of appreciation Auburn Lions Club, 1979, Ala. Reading Assn., 1980, Assn. Children with Learning Disabilities, 1981. Mem. Am. Assn. Sch. Adminstrs., Ala. Council Sch. Adminstrs. and Suprs., Nat. Assn. Female Execs., Phi Delta Kappa. Democrat. Methodist. Author grant proposals. Home: 1021 Eagle Circle Auburn AL 36830 Office: 855 E Samford Ave Auburn AL 36830

HARDIN, FRANCES LANNING, educator; b. Canton, Ga., Dec. 10, 1925; d. Noah Richard and Mattie Lou (Hulsey) Lanning; student Reinhardt Coll., 1943-44; B.S. in Bus. Adminstrn., Ga. State Coll. for Women, 1948; postgrad. Ga. State U., 1967-68, Queen's Coll., Oxford, Eng., 1979; J.D., Atlanta Law Sch., 1978, LL.M., 1979. Tchr., Fulton County Schs., Atlanta, 1955—; guest naturalist Audubon Colony, Cedar Mountain, N.C., summer 1977. Recipient WSB Radio Willing Service Banner award, 1978; cited in Congl. Record, 1977. Mem. Roswell Bus. and Profl. Women's Club (Woman of Achievement), Ga. Fedn. Bus. and Profl. Women's Clubs (chmn. world affairs 1970, vice chmn. world affairs 1971), Delta Kappa Gamma. Baptist. Writer ednl. programs using travel slides, 1970-71. Home: 336 Mt Vernon Hwy NW Atlanta GA 30328 Office: Northwestern Sch Route 4 Birmingham Hwy Alpharetta GA 30201

HARDIN, LUCILE (MRS. SIDNEY LANIER HARDIN), book reviewer; b. Fate, Tex., Sept. 26, 1899; d. Thomas Preston and Ina Pearl (Davidson) McGraw; student So. Meth. U., 1919-20, 36, 50, U. Dallas, 1959-60; m. J. B. Hill, Sept. 26, 1920 (dec. 1949) children—Peggy Lucille (Mrs. John C. Taylor), J.B., Joy Hill (Mrs. Charles Flach), Martha (Mrs. Tommy Prince), Thomas, David; m. 2d, Sidney Lanier Hardin, Aug. 31, 1957. Profl. reviewer books for book clubs, civic clubs and publs., 1949—. Mem. Delphians, Dallas Story League, Internat. Platform Assn., Bus. and Profl. Women's Club. Baptist. Rebekah, Maccabees; mem. Order Eastern Star. Home: 121 Austin Blvd Edinburg TX 78539 Office: 6362 Malcolm St Dallas TX 75214

HARDIN, M. ELLEN, pub. co. ofcl.; b. Guadalajara, Jalisco, Mex., Mar. 5, 1930; came to U.S., 1932, naturalized, 1958; d. Ernest Edgar and Myrtle (Arkebauer) von Pohle; student Pacific Union Coll., 1947-51, U. Calif., Berkeley, Extension Sch., 1978-79; B.A. in Bus. Mgmt., U. Redlands, 1982; m. James Richard Hardin, Sept. 5, 1949; children—Dorothy Ellen Hardin Valcarcel, Sheryl Elaine Hardin Johnson. Music tchr. piano and children's choir, Oxnard and Glendale, Calif., 1960-67; asst. to office mgr. Verdugo Hills Med. Group, Glendale, 1968-71; med. ins. specialist Tempe (Ariz.) Med. Center, 1971-72, mgr., 1973-75; acct. Pacific Union Conf., Glendale and Westlake, Calif., 1975-78; mgr. Hosanna House Pubs., mktg., mfg., mail order, Newbury Park, Calif., 1978—. Lectr., condr. workshops on religious curriculum and teaching methods for ch. youth groups; prin. organist, minister of music Oxnard Seventh-day Adventist Ch. Mem. Nat. Assn. Female Execs., Direct Mail Mktg. Assn. Author series of four sets of Bible stories for worldwide children's Bible clubs, 1970, series of nature object lesson stories with felt visuals, 1970.

HARDIN, MARTHA LOVE WOOD, civic leader; b. Muncie, Ind., Aug. 13, 1918; d. Lawrence Anselm and Bonny Blossom (Williams) Wood; B.S. with distinction and high honors, Purdue U., 1939; m. Clifford Morris Hardin, June 28, 1939; children—Susan Hardin Wood, Clifford Wood, Cynthia Hardin Milligan, Nancy Hardin Rogers, James Alvin. Librarian, U. Chgo., 1939-40. Chmn. Nebr. Heart Fund, 1967; vol. worker Lincoln Gen. Hosp., 1965, Clarkson Hosp., 1966; hon. chmn. Symphony Ball, Washington, 1970; mem. met. bd. YWCA, Washington, 1969-71. St. Louis, 1973—; mem. Women's Com. of Pres.'s Com. on Employment of Handicapped, 1970—, permanent mem. bd., 1970—; bd. dirs. St. Louis Speech and Hearing Clinic, St. Louis Met. YWCA; co-chmn. nat. fund-raising campaign U. Nebr. Found., 1977-80. Mem. St. Louis Geneal. Soc., DAR, PEO, Mortar Bd., Phi Beta Kappa, Pi Beta Phi. Clubs: Congressional (Washington); Old Warson Country, St. Louis (St. Louis). Contbr. articles to geneal. publs. Home: 10 Roan Ln Saint Louis MO 63124

HARDING, FRANCES KELLER, physician; b. College Place, Wash., June 3, 1906; d. Peter Martin and Florence (Armstrong) Keller; B.S., Walla Walla Coll., 1925; M.D., Loma Linda U., 1929; H.H.D. (hon.), Otterbein Coll., 1975; m. Warren G. Harding 2d, Dec. 23, 1926 (dec.); children—Florence Harding Hiscock, Carolyn Harding Motzel, Peter M. Studied in Edinburgh, Scotland; resident Sydney (Australia) Sanitarium and Hosp., 1933-38; practice medicine specializing in obstetrics and gynecology, Sydney, 8 years; specializing in med. gynecology, Columbus, Ohio, 1949—; asst. prof. student health service Ohio State U., 1948, also lectr. dept. medicine and adj. lectr. health edn.; adj. lectr. health edn. Denison U., Ohio Wesleyan U., Oberlin Coll., Capital U., Otterbein U. Pres., Met. Health Council, Columbus 1950-52; mem. Community Chest Finance Com. and bd., 1953-58; bd. dirs., pres., mem. med. adv. bd. Planned Parenthood Columbus; bd. dirs. Planned Parenthood World Population; mem. bd. Florence Crittenden Home, 1963; mem. Columbus Council Social Agys.; chmn. Ohio Health Edn. Com.; bd. dirs. Columbus Pub. Health Nurses Assn.; trustee Ohio Hist. Soc., 1980—. Recipient Women of Year award Am. Med. Women's Assn., 1959, Elizabeth Blackwell award Hobart and Smith Coll., 1974; Alumna of Year, Walla Walla Coll., 1978, Loma Linda U. Med. Coll., 1979. Mem. AMA, Brit., Ohio, Columbus and Franklin County med. assns., Am. Public Health Assn., Royal Coll. Physicians and Surgeons (Edinburgh, Scotland), Royal Soc. for Promotion Health (Eng.), Am. Sch. Health Assn., Planned Parenthood Physicians U.S.A., Am. Med. Women's Assn. (dir., lectr., v.p., pres. 1972, com. chmn.), Zonta (pres. Columbus br.), Mortar Bd. (hon.). Contbr. articles to med. jours. Home: 1296 La Rochelle Dr Columbus OH 43221

HARDING, JEANNE CROWLEY, indsl. distbg. co. exec.; b. Kingsport, Tenn., Mar. 5, 1937; d. Thomas Henry and Juanita Ruth (Willis) Crowley; student Steed Coll., 1953-54, E. Tenn. State U., 1955-57; A.S., U. Tenn., 1966; m. Harry Harding, July 2, 1969; children—Katherine Jeanne, Michael Kent; stepchildren—Harry Steven, James Elliott, Patricia Patton, Jeffrey Scott. Bus. mgr. Swingle Hosp., 1953-59, Bowman Pediatric Clinic Bus. Office, Johnson City, Tenn., 1960-62; substitute tchr., pub. schs., Knoxville, 1965; sec.-treas., dir. Indsl. Distbrs., Inc., Roanoke Rapids and Canton, N.C., Savannah, Ga., Columbus, Miss. and Prattville, Ala., 1969—. Pres., PTA, Johnson City, 1962; leader brownies Girl Scouts U.S.A., Jonesboro, 1963, leader girl scouts, 1961, den mother, 1964-65; pres. Hosp. Guild, Johnson City, 1956; treas. St. Mark's Episcopal Ch. active Save the Children Program, 1981-82, other charitable orgns. Mem. Roanoke Rapids and Canton C. of C., Pulp and Paper Storekeeper Assn., Paper Industry Mgmt. Assn., Am. Hosp. Assn. Republican. Clubs: Chockoyotte Country, Sea Pines Country, Jr. Woman's (v.p. 1961). Home: 1 River Rd Roanoke Rapids NC 27870 also 17 Old Military Rd Hilton Head Island SC 29928 Office: 801 Weldon Hwy Roanoke Rapids NC 27870

HARDING, LOIS CAROL, interior designer; b. Portland, Oreg., Dec. 25, 1927; d. Claude Albert and Ferne Hildegar (Connelly) Harding. Interior decorator, 1963—; part-owner Harding/Post, Inc. Mem. Am. Soc. Interior Designers, Internat. Soc. Interior Designers. Republican. Office: 316 S Tustin Ave Orange CA 92666

HARDING, MARDI (MAUREEN) WELLS, real estate devel. co. exec.; b. Denver, Nov. 24, 1946; d. Jackson H. and Bernice M. Wells; B.A., U. Denver 1968; m. Frederick H. Harding, June 8, 1968; 1 son, Todd C. Property mgr. Bedford Properties, Inc., Lafayette, Calif. 1976-79, project mgr. 1979-82, v.p. property mgmt., 1982—. Lic. real estate broker, Calif.; cert. property mgr. Mem. Inst. Real Estate Mgmt., Internat. Council Shopping Centers. Office: PO Box 1267 Lafayette CA 94549

HARDISTY, BETTIE CHRISTENE, educator; b. Dora, N.Mex., May 1, 1934; d. Benjamin Temple and Zella Maye (White) Long; B.S., Eastern N.Mex. U., 1974, M.Ed., 1976; m. Dan Preuit Hardisty, Aug. 17, 1952; children—Kathryn Christene, Dennis Dan. Bookkeeper, Hinkle's Dept. Store, Clovis, N.Mex., 1952-53, Clovis Cattle Commn. Co., 1954-56; cashier Southwestern Investment Co., Clovis, 1956; telephone operator Mt. Bell Tel. & Tel. Co., Clovis, 1956-58; home economist Coop. Extension Service, N.Mex. State U., Clovis, 1975—. Pres., James Bickley Parent Tchr. Orgn., Clovis, 1969-70; sec.-treas. Curry County Affiliate of Am. Diabetic Assn., 1975-79; bd. dirs. Meals on Wheels, Clovis, 1975-77. Named Curry County Cowbelle of the Yr., 1969; N.Mex. Assn. Extension Home Economist Communications award for weekly newspaper column, 1978. Mem. Am. Home Econ. Assn., N.Mex. Extension Home Econ. Assn., Nat. Extension Home Econ. Assn., Phi Kappa Phi. Democrat. Baptist. Club: Pilot Internat.

HARDRICK, ELINOR JANICE, nurse; b. Hartford, Conn., Aug. 16, 1943; d. Claude R. and Marion W. (Whaley) H.; R.N., Helene Fuld Sch. Nursing, Provident Hosp., 1973. Psychiat. nurse Provident Hosp., Balt., 1973-74, St. Elizabeth Hosp., Dept. Human Services, Washington, 1974—, supr., 1982—; pres. Hardrick Enterprises Forestville, Md., 1981—. Recipient Outstanding Service award Drake Food Service, Inc., 1981. Mem. Smithsonian Assos. Baptist. Office: 3700 10th St NW Washington DC 20010

HARDS, KATHRYN ELISA, indsl. psychologist; b. Chgo.; b. Arthur O. and D. Caroline (Redcliffe) Olsen; B.A., San Jose State U., 1972, M.S., 1976; m. William C. Hards; 1 son, Eric A. Indsl. psychologist Four-Phase Systems, Cupertino, Calif., 1976-78; pvt. practice as cons. indsl. psychologist, Cupertino, Calif., 1979—; cons. C&H Sugar Co., San Francisco, Real Estate World, Campbell, Calif., Stanford U. Med. Center, Tech. Adv. Service for Attys., Pa., others; adj. prof. psychology San Jose State U., 1978—. Mem. Am. Psychol. Assn., Nat. Assn. Indsl. and Orgnl. Psychologists, Western Psychol. Assn., Société Canadienne de Psychologie, Psi Chi (life).

HARDY, CAMILLE COMBS, univ. ofcl.; b. Mt. Airy, N.C., Oct. 14, 1944; d. James B. and Mary (DePalma) Combs; B.A., Duke U., 1965; M.A., U. N.C., 1968; Ph.D., U. Mich., 1971; m. Michael C. Hardy, Mar. 29, 1965; 1 dau., Miranda C. Asst. prof. dance East Carolina U., Greenville, N.C., 1971-73, Nat. Acad. Arts, Champaign, Ill., 1973-78, U. Tex., Austin, 1978-79; asst. prof. dance U. Ill., Urbana, 1975-78, asst. to dean Coll. Fine and Applied Arts, 1979—; guest dance scholar Cornell U., spring 1982; mem. dance adv. panel, multi arts adv. panel Ill. Arts Council; dance program cons. Nat. Endowment Arts. Recipient Outstanding Achievement in Theatre award U. Mich., 1969, 70, 71; NEA performance arts grantee, 1973; U. Tex. grantee, 1979. Mem. Dance Critics Assn. (chmn. 1980 conf., exec. bd. dirs.), Tex. Inst. Dance Criticism, Congress on Research in Dance, Dance History Scholars (exec. bd. 1982-85). Contbr. articles to Dance Mag., Dance Chronicle, Dance Research Jour., Ballet Rev., Am. Arts Mag. Home: 813 W University Ave Champaign IL 61820 Office: Coll Fine and Applied Arts U Ill Champaign IL 61820

HARDY, CAROLE MORGAN (HASTY), educator, entrepreneur; b. Detroit, July 26, 1946; d. John Clifford and Sophia (Pociask) Hasty; B.A., Wayne State U., 1969; M.A., Met. Collegiate Inst., London, 1973; postgrad. Oxford U. (Eng.), 1977; m. Joseph Carl Hardy, Apr. 18, 1980. Dir. edn. Women's Prison-Detroit House of Correction, Plymouth, Mich., 1969-72; cons. Wayne County Sherriff's Dept., Detroit, 1971-72, adminstrv. asst. to Councilwoman Erma Henderson of Detroit, 1973-74; cons. Western Interstate Commn. Higher Edn., Boulder, Colo., 1977-78; dir. Rape Crisis Center, Pueblo, Colo., 1974-77; project dir. Tng. Assos., Inc., Boulder, 1979-81; dir. Justice Mgmt. Enterprises, Carmel, Calif., 1980—; pres. Dynamax, Inc., Carmel, 1980—; instr. Golden Gate U., San Francisco, 1981-83, Detroit Inst. Tech., 1974, Canada Coll., 1980-81. cons. in field. NIMH-LEAA grantee, 1979-81. Mem. Nat. Assn. Female Execs., Am. Soc. Public Adminstrn., NOW, Am. Correctional Assn., Am. Correction Health Services, Alliance for Am. Innovation, San Jose C. of C., Nat. Women's Polit. Caucus. Contbr. articles to profl. publs. Office: PO Box 222037 560 Carmel Rancho Blvd Suite 6 Carmel CA 93922

HARDY, DEBORAH WELLES, historian; b. Milw., Nov. 2, 1927; d. Frank M. and Doris (Berger) Hursley; B.A., Stanford U., 1949; M.A., U. Calif., Berkeley, 1950; Ph.D., U. Wash., Seattle, 1968; widow; children—Scott, Jonathan, Bridget. TV writer, 1964-72; mem. faculty U. Wyo., Laramie, 1966—, prof. history, 1978—, head dept., 1980—; mem. Wyo. Council Humanities, 1972-76. Grantee Social Sci. Research Council, summer 1971, Am. Philos. Soc., 1976. Mem. Am. Hist. Assn., Am. Assn. Advancement Slavic Studies, AAUP, NEA, Western Social Sci. Assn., Western Slavic Assn., Phi Beta Kappa. Author: Petr Tkachev:

The Critic as Jacobin, 1977; also articles. Home: 2450 Park Ave Laramie WY 82070 Office: History Dept U Wyo Laramie WY 82071

HARDY, JANE ELIZABETH, educator; b. Fenelon Falls, Ont., Can., Mar. 27, 1930; came to U.S., 1956, naturalized, 1976; d. Charles Edward and Augusta Miriam (Lang) Little; B.S. with distinction, Cornell U., 1953; m. Ernest E. Hardy, Sept. 3, 1955; children—Edward Harold, Robert Ernest. Garden editor and writer Can. Homes Mag., Maclean-Hunter Pub. Co., Ltd., Toronto, Ont., 1954-55, 56-62; contbg. editor Can. Homes, Southam Pub. Co., Toronto, 1962-66; instr. Cornell U., 1966-73, sr. lectr. in communication arts, 1979—; mem. Cornell U. Provost's Adv. Com. on Status of Women, 1977-81; lectr., condr. workshops on writing. Pres. ch. council First Congregational Ch., Ithaca, N.Y., 1978-79. Mem. Women in Communications, Inc. (faculty adv. Cornell chpt. 1977—), Garden Writers Assn. Am., Royal Hort. Soc., Pi Alpha Xi, Phi Kappa Phi, Alpha Omicron Pi. Clubs: Toronto Garden, Ithaca Garden, Ithaca Women's. Contbr. numerous articles to mags.; author numerous other publs., including brochures, slide set scripts; editor pro tem Cornell Plantations Quar., 1981-82. Home: 215 Enfield Falls Rd Ithaca NY 14850 Office: 304 Roberts Hall Dept Communication Arts Cornell U Ithaca NY 14853

HARDY, JUNE DORFLINGER, portrait painter and photographer; b. N.Y.C., Feb. 2, 1929; d. William Francis Dorflinger, Jr. and Katheryn (Hait) Dorflinger Manchee; grad. Briarcliff Jr. Coll., 1949; student Parsons Sch. Design, 1949-50, N.Y. Sch. Interior Design, 1953-54, Nat. Acad. Art-Art Students League, 1966-82, Columbia U., 1963; m. John Alexander Hardy, Jr., May 26, 1956. Asst. tchr. Peck Sch., Morristown, N.J., 1950-51; with personnel dept. McGraw Hill, Inc., 1951-52; editorial asst., then asst. editor Better Homes and Gardens mag., 1952-57; editorial asst., then asst. editor Successful Farming mag., 1952-57; freelance portrait painter and photographer, 1969—; tchr. drawing and pastel painting Onteora Club, N.Y., summer 1977. Nat. Home Fashions League scholar, 1953; recipient 1st prize portrait in oil Twilight Park Art Show, 1976, 79, 1st prize portrait photography, 1977, 2d prize pastel landscape, 1979, 2d prize for flower photography, 1982; 1st prize for flower photography Onteona Garden Club Show, 1982. Life mem. Art Students League. Republican. Episcopalian. Clubs: Colony (chmn. entertainment), Wednesday (past pres.), Badminton, Onteora. Address: 14 Sutton Pl S New York NY 10022

HARDY, MARGARETE N., telephone co. exec.; b. Worcester, Mass., June 29, 1948; d. Erving Douglas and Janette (McCreery) Hardy; B.A., Whittier Coll., 1970; M.A., Occidental Coll., 1979; children—Douglas, Sarah. Adminstrv. asst. state senator and then lt. gov. Mervyn Dymally, Los Angeles, 1971-75; sr. asso. Cerrell Assos., Los Angeles, 1975-77; asst. dir. public affairs Calif. State Mus., Los Angeles, 1977-79; public affairs rep. Gen. Telephone Co., Santa Monica, Calif., 1979—. Bd. dirs. Nat. Council Social Services, 1969—, Calif. Spl. Olympics, 1969—; mem. Calif. State Bd. Cosmetology, 1976—, pres., 1980-81; mem. Calif. State Congress of Bds. and Burs., 1978—; mem. Dem. Women's Task Force, 1975—. Recipient Am. Friends of Public Service award, 1978; named Outstanding Woman in Politics, Los Angeles mag., 1975; Urban Affairs fellow, 1973-74. Mem. NOW, Los Angeles Women's Polit. Caucus, LWV, Los Angeles Social Service Soc., Los Angeles Women's Coalition, ACLU, AAUW, Public Relations Soc. Am., Women in Communications, Public Interest in Radio and TV Soc., Radio and TV News Assn., Pi Sigma Alpha. Democrat. Clubs: Chmn.'s Circle, Greater Los Angeles Press. Home: 1843 Midvale Ave Los Angeles CA 90025 Office: 100 Wilshire Blvd Santa Monica CA 90406

HARE, JANICE LUCILE, explosive metal bonding co. exec.; b. Oak Park, Ill., Oct. 12, 1930; d. Robert Anthony and Lucile Veronica (Emerson) Pacl; student Morton Jr. Coll., 1948-50; m. Alan W. Hare, June 24, 1950; children—Cathleen, William, Michael, Desiree, Gregory, Pamela, Teresa. With Ohio Youth Commn., Delaware, 1967-70; treas., office mgr. N.W. Tech. Industries, Sequim, Wash., 1970—. Mem. Port Angeles Sch. Bd., 1971-75, v.p., 1973-75, legis. rep., 1971-75, mem. community action adv. bd., 1975, mem. gifted children adv. bd., 1979-80; mem. platform com. Clallam County Republican Com., 1976. Mem. North Olympic Child Study Group, Arts in Action. Club: Town and Gown Dance. Home: 90 Lindberg Rd Port Angeles WA 98362 Office: 547 Diamond Point Rd Sequim WA 98382

HAREL, MIRIAM, plastic surgeon; b. Tel Aviv, July 1, 1942; came to U.S., 1972, naturalized, 1977; d. Max and Leoni (Silver) Kaiser; M.D., Hebrew U., Jerusalem, 1970; m. Asher Harel, Aug. 12, 1970; children—Noam, Tamar. Tng. in plastic surgery, Jerusalem, 1970-72; resident in gen. surgery, N.Y.C., 1972-75; resident in plastic surgery Albert Einstein Coll. Medicine, Yeshiva U., N.Y.C., 1975-78; practice medicine specializing in plastic surgery, Framingham, Mass., 1979—; speaker on plastic surgery to women's groups. Served with Israeli Air Force, 1960-62. Mem. Am. Soc. Plastic and Reconstructive Surgeons, New Eng. Soc. Plastic and Reconstructive Surgeons, Mass. Soc. Plastic and Reconstructive Surgeons, Am. Med. Womens Assn., Old Girls Network Boston. Home: 24 Jane Rd Newton MA 02159 Office: 350 Union Ave Framingham MA 01701

HARGADINE, MARTHA PARROTT YOUNG, dancer, educator; b. East Grand Rapids, Mich., Dec. 15, 1937; d. Walter Carpenter and Mary Minor (Parrott) Young; B.A., U. Calif., Santa Barbara, 1950; M.A. in Dance Edn., U. Utah, 1965; Ph.D. in Dance and Counseling Edn., U. So. Calif., 1973; divorced; 1 son, Mark Toscan. Tchr. phys. edn. and dance San Francisco Bay area high schs., 1960-63; grad. asst. phys. edn. and dance U. Utah, 1963-65; instr. dance Central Wash. State Coll., Ellensburg, 1965-67; caseworker Wash. State Dept. Pub. Assistance, 1968-70; jr. supr. phys. edn. and dance U. So. Calif., 1971-73; asst. prof. dance and dance therapy Tex. Women's U., Denton, 1973-75; asst. prof. dance N.E. La. U., Monroe, 1975-77; facility instr. La. Dept. Vocat. Rehab.; dir. phys. edn. Hartford House Sch. for Learning Disabled, 1977; counselor, mgr. Diet Center Monroe, 1978; owner, operator Diet Centers, Monroe and Ruston, La., 1978—; mem. nat. profl. adv. bd. Diet Center, Inc.; nursing home dance therapist, Denton, 1973-74. Recipient Hon. Merit award Wash. State Dept. Pub. Assistance, 1970; grantee Tex. Women's U., 1973-74; holder black belt in Tae Kwon Do, Shotokon, brown belt in Shotokan; registered therapeutic recreation specialist. Mem. Am., La. assns. health, phys. edn. and recreation, Com. Research for Dance, Dance Notation Bur., Am. Dance Therapy Assn., Am. Dance Guild, All South Karate Assn., House of Greek (Havanas). Episcopalian. Contbr. articles to profl. jours. Address: PO Box 5066 Monroe LA 71203

HARGRAVE, CECILLE TERRY, interior designer; b. Paris, Tex., July 23, 1917; d. Carl C. and Una Lila (Sealy) Terry; B.A., East Tex. State U., 1938; postgrad. So. Meth. U. Downtown Coll., 1952-53, Little Sch. of Fine Arts, 1953; m. Glenn M. Hargrave, Oct. 9, 1937. Interior designer; specifiers-interior cons. Garland (Tex.) City Hall; guest editor Tex. Contractor, 1954, Furniture Age, 1956. Recipient Instns. Mag.'s award for Sam Rayburn Meml. Student Center, 1964; named Distinguished Alumna, East Tex. State U., 1975. Mem. K.T. Ednl. Found. (hon.), East Tex. State U. Alumni Assn. (pres. Dallas county chpt.), Women in Architecture, Dallas Council World Affairs, Southwest Homefurnishing Assn. Alpha Alpha Gamma, Chi Omega. Episcopalian. Clubs: Park Cities Toastmistress (founder, past pres.) (Dallas). Projects include Sam Rayburn Meml. Student Center, East Tex. State U., Commerce, Tex., Midway Park Elementary Sch., Euless, Tex., 1st Nat. Bank, Garland, 1st Security Nat. Bank Dallas, 1st Security Fin. Systems, Inc., Dallas, Parkdale State Bank, Corpus Christi, Tex. Home: 6938 Winchester St Dallas TX 75231

HARGRAVES, EMILY RAINBOLT, artist; b. Bedford, Ind.; d. Lee Ellis and Katherine (Duncan) Rainbolt; student Chgo. Art Inst., 1932-33, Art Student's League, 1955; B.A., Ariz. State U., 1950, M.F.A., 1963; m. Howard Hargraves, 1935 (dec. May 1943); 1 dau., Martha Ellen. Tchr., painter Studio-Workshop & Gallery, Mesa, Ariz., 1957-67; exhibited Sally Robbins Gallery, East Orange, N.J., from 1959, Am. Gallery, Copehagen; tchr. life and anatomy Phoenix Mus. Sch., 1957—; one-man shows Phoenix Art Mus.; asst. prof. art Stephen F. Austin State U., Nacogdoches, Tex., 1967—. Hartford Found. fellow, 1955-56; Yaddo fellow, Saratoga Springs, N.Y., 1957-58; named Artist of Yr., City of Mesa and State of Ariz. Mem. Nat. Assn. Women Artists, Artists Equity, Ariz. Artists Guild (pres. 1957-58). Address: 911 Mocking Bird Ln Nacogdoches TX 75961

HARGROVE, LINDA ANN, child care co. exec.; b. Quincy, Fla., Feb. 3, 1955; s. John Gus and Geraldine (Collier) Washington; B.S. in acctg. Fla. A & M U. 1978; m. Don Lamarr Hargrove, May 24, 1980; 1 son, Don Lamarr. Receptionist, Fla. State U. 1973-78, clk. 1978-79; controller, acct. Fernandina Beach News Leader, Inc., Fernandina Beach, Fla. 1979-82, fiscal officer, Big Bend 4-Council Inc. 1982—. Democrat. Baptist. Home: Rt 6 Box 523 Quincy FL 32351

HARING, GENE FRANCES, psychiatrist; b. San Francisco, Apr. 7, 1940; d. Arnold Walter and Esther Katherine (Huisman) H.; B.S., Jamestown Coll., 1961; M.D., Med. Coll. Pa., 1965. Intern, Med. Coll. Pa., Phila., 1965-66; resident Eastern Pa. Psychiatric Inst., Phila., 1966-69; staff psychiatrist, coordinator structured services, med. dir. Luzerne-Wyoming County Mental Health Center, Wilkes-Barre, Pa., 1976-79; practice medicine specializing in psychiatry, Kingston, Pa., 1979—; mem. staffs Wilkes-Barre Gen. Hosp., New Med. Center; clin. asso. prof. Hahnemann Med. Sch., 1974—. Bd. dirs. Mental Health Assn. of Luzerne County, 1969—, Domestic Violence Center, 1981-82. Mem. Am. Psychiatric Assn., Internat. Assn. Social Psychiatry, Am. Assn. Social Psychiatry, Am. Med. Womens Assn., Am. Group Psychotherapy Assn., Pa. Psychiatric Assn. Office: 841 Wyoming Ave Kingston PA 18704

HARING, PATRICIA ANN, legal asst.; b. L.I., N.Y., Mar. 31, 1944; d. Michael S. and Anna (Balchunas) Zwer; B.S., Hunter Coll., 1976; postgrad. New Sch. Social Research; grad. Paralegal Inst., Phila., 1972; 1 dau., Jill St. Jude. Legal sec. firm Davis Polk & Wardwell, 1966-69; adminstrv. asst. to press sec. and campaign mgr. N.Y. Mayoralty Campaign, 1969-70; system controller firm Skadden Aprs Slate Meagher & Flom, 1970-71; confidential asst. to pres. Webcor Electronics Corp., L.I., N.Y., 1972-73; office mgr. Frank L. Miller, N.Y.C., 1973-74; legal asst. environ. law Union Oil Co. Calif., 1976-77; asst. to treas. Mission Hills Property Corp., Palm Springs, Calif., 1977; pres. Palm Springs Resume Service & Career Counseling, 1977-78; office mgr. Freeman, Meade, Wasserman & Schneider, N.Y.C., 1978-80; freelance writer, 1980; legal asst. to gen. counsel Diamond Dealers Club of N.Y., Inc., 1981, to corp. partner Pryor, Cashman, Sherman & Flynn, N.Y.C., 1981-82; legal asst. Weil, Gotshal & Manges, N.Y.C., 1982—. Vice pres. public relations Roosevelt Island (N.Y.) Residents Assn., 1980. Cert. scuba diver. Mem. Ind. Press Assn., Am. Soc. Profl. and Exec. Women, Am. Mus. Natural History (asso.), Smithsonian Instn. (asso.), Internat. Platform Assn., Nat. Assn. Female Execs., HALT, City News Agy., Bus. and Profl. Women's Club, Am. Mus. Natural History, Smithsonian Inst., Nat. Assn. Female Execs. Roman Catholic. Clubs: Am. Legion Ladies Aux. Contbr. articles to profl. jours. Home: 540-1900 Main St Roosevelt Island NY 10044 Office: 767 Fifth Ave New York NY 10153

HARITUN, ROSALIE ANN, clarinetist, music educator; b. Johnson City, N.Y., May 30, 1938; d. George and Helen (Ternosky) H.; B.Music Edn., Baldwin-Wallace Conservatory of Music, Ohio, 1960; M.S. in Music Edn., U. Ill., 1961; profl. diploma Tchrs. Coll., Columbia U., 1965, Ed.D., 1968, postdoctoral, 1971-72. Tchr. instrumental music elem. schs., Patchogue, L.I., N.Y., 1961-63, jr. high schs., 1963-65; instr. music edn. Sch. Music, Temple U., Phila., 1968-71; instr. instrumental music N.Y.C. Bd. Edn., 1971-72; asst. prof. music edn. Sch. Music, East Carolina U., Greenville, N.C., 1972—, del. to faculty assembly, Raleigh, N.C., 1981—; clarinetist/saxophonist Greenville Summer-in-the Park Orch., 1975-79; clarinetist Albemarle Players prodn. South Pacific, Elizabeth City, N.C.; cons. curriculum devel., 1976-82; adjudicator choral/instrumental festivals, solo/ensemble contests, 1975-82. Mem. Coll. Music Soc. (council mem. music edn. div. Mid-Atlantic chpt. 1982), Delta Kappa Gamma (chpt. exec. bd. 1980-82) Sigma Alpha Iota (chpt. pres. 1966-68), Pi Kappa Lambda (chpt. pres. 1977—). Democrat. Baptist. Contbr. articles on music edn. to prof. publs. Home: 206 N Oak St Greenville NC 27834 Office: Sch Music East Carolina U 10th St Greenville NC 27834

HARKER, CHARLOTTE STUART, nutritionist; b. Dubuque, Iowa, Apr. 23, 1923; d. Bert Everett and Charlotte Ann (Atkinson) Stuart; B.S., Iowa State U., 1945; M.S., Purdue U., 1963, Ph.D., 1966; m. Robert James Harker, Apr. 14, 1945; children—Robert Jeffrey, Craig Stuart. Mem. faucity Ind. State U., Terre Haute, 1960—, assoc. prof. nutrition, 1968-74, prof., 1975—; cons. Internat. Minerals and Chems. Co., Fla. Internat. U., Am. Home Econs. Assn. Gen. Foods fellow, 1964-65; Mortar Bd. scholar, 1965-66; recipient grants Ind. State U., USPHS. Mem. Am. Dietitic Assn., Ind. Dietitic Assn., Am. Home Econs. Assn., Ind. Home Econs. Assn., Ind. Nutrition Council, Nutrition Today Soc., Soc. Nutrition Edn., Mortar Bd., Iota Sigma Phi, Sigma Delta Epsilon, Pi Beta Phi, Phi Upsilon Omicron. Author: Questions and Problems on Nutrition, 1974.

HARKER, LUCY KATHLEEN, banker; b. Janesville, Wis., July 18, 1944; d. Donald James and Lucy Jean (Gray) H.; B.A., U. Wis., 1966; M.B.A., U. Chgo., 1969. Jr. investment advisor, trust investment div. Continental Ill. Nat. Bank & Trust Co., Chgo., 1966-67, fin. economist, 2d v.p. econ. research div., 1967-75, v.p., market mgr. multinat. banking services, 1975—. Chairperson, bd. mgrs. Home for Destitute Crippled Children, Wyler Children's Hosp. Mem. Nat. Assn. Bank Women. Office: 231 S LaSalle St Chicago IL 60693

HARKER, VIRGINIA RAE, phys. therapist; b. Ellensburg, Wash., Mar. 21, 1937; d. Ray Hans and Margaret Lilian (McBride) Mordhorst; student U. Puget Sound, 1955-57; B.S., U. So. Calif., 1959; div.; 1 dau., Karen Lynne Harker. Phys. therapist Rancho Los Amigos Hosp., Downey, Calif., 1960-71; dir. phys. therapy Long Beach (Calif.) Gen. Hosp., 1971-77; owner, mgr. Home Health Phys. Therapy, Ellensburg, 1977—; cons. Haven House, Gold Leaf Nursing Homes, Ellensburg. Mem. Am. Phys. Therapy Assn. Republican. Methodist (supt. ch. sch., trustee, council ministries). Home: 1920 Judge Ronald Rd Ellensburg WA 98926

HARKEY, JOYCE ANNETTE, ednl. psychologist; b. Crystal City, Tex., Oct. 7, 1930; d. David Crockett and Ruth Brown Carr; B.S., S.W. Tex. State U., 1968, M.Ed., 1972; m. Harold Leslie Harkey, Jr., June 30, 1949; children—Joyce Elizabeth Harkey Winn, Hal Leslie III, Ronald Martin, Wayne King. Homemaking tchr. Crystal City (Tex.) Ind. Sch. Dist., 1966-71, Carrizo Springs (Tex.) Ind. Sch. Dist., 1971-73; ednl. diagnostician Cluster V Spl. Edn. Coop., Carrizo Springs, 1973-77, asso. sch. psychologist, 1977—, mem. Cluster V Spl. Edn. Coop. Adv. Council. Cert. psychol. asso., asso. sch. psychologist, Tex. Mem. Am. Psychol. Assn., NEA, Tex. Psychol. Assn., Tex. State Tchrs. Assn., Alamo Area Ednl. Diagnosticians Assn., Women's Soc. Christian Service (life), PTA, Delta Kappa Gamma (pres. Theta Upsilon chpt. 1978-80), Alpha Chi. Democrat. Methodist. Clubs: Athena Study (pres. 1956-57); Carrizo Springs Athletic Booster. Home: 520 N 12th Ave Crystal City TX 78839 Office: 102 N 5th St Carrizo Springs TX 78834

HARKEY, VERNA RAE, pianist, educator; b. Ft. Worth, Nov. 20, 1928; d. Verne and Rachel Isabelle (Beam) Morrill; B.A., George Pepperdine Coll., 1950; m. Kenneth L. Harkey, Sept. 21, 1951; children—Karl M., Kevin L. Tchr. piano, Long Beach, Calif., 1950—. Mem. Nat. Guild Piano Tchrs., Nat. Music Tchrs. Assn., Music Tchrs. Assn. Calif., Southwestern Youth Music Festival, Epsilon Eta, Mu Phi Epsilon (founder Long Beach alumae chpt.) Republican. Mem. Ch. of Christ. Clubs: Ebell of Long Beach, Musical Arts (Long Beach). Home and Studio: 2243 Canehill Ave Long Beach CA 90815

HARLAN, KATHLEEN T., bus. cons., lectr.; b. Bremerton, Wash., June 9, 1934; d. Floyd Kenneth and Rosemary (Parkhurst) Troy; grad. Sanford-Brown Bus. Coll., St. Louis, 1955; m. John L. Harlan, Feb. 16, 1952; children—Pamela Kay, Kenneth Lynwood, Lianna Sue; m. 2d, Merlin Habig, June 30, 1979. Owner, distbr. Safeguard N.W. Systems, Tacoma, 1969-79; pres. Greenapple Graphics, Inc., Tacoma; developer, mgr. Poulsbo Profl. Bldg., 1969-79; owner, mgr. Iskrem Hus Restaurant, Poulsbo, Wash., 1972-75; pres. Bus. Seminars Tacoma, 1977—; pres. New Image Confs., 1979-81; mem. Organizational Renewal, Inc., Tacoma, 1978-81; asso. mem. Effectiveness Resource Group, Inc., Tacoma, 1979-81; owner, mgr. Safeguard Acctg. and Data Systems, Bremerton, Wash., 1982—; speaker on mgmt. in small bus. Mem. Wash. State Bd. Boundary Rev., Kitsap County, 1970-76; mem. local bd. Selective Service, 1971-76. mem. Selective Service Bd. 19, 1971-76. Mem. Nat. Speakers Assn., Nat. Assn. Female Execs., Nat. Assn. Accts. Contbr. chpt. to Here Is Genius, 1980; author various bus. manuals. Home: 434 Buena Vista Fircrest WA 98466 Office: 1702 6th St Bremerton WA 98310

HARLAN, MARY JANE, consumer products co. exec.; b. Knoxville, Tenn., Nov. 22, 1948; d. Robert Beardslee and Gladys Lura (Waller) Spence; student Elmira Coll., 1966-67; B.S. in Zoology, U. Tenn., 1970; m. Richard Sorrells Ticknor, July 9, 1972; 1 dau., Katherine Luray. Sales rep. L'eggs, Knoxville, 1973-74, Lever Bros., Knoxville, 1974-76; resource developer Knoxville Women's Center, 1976-78, bd. dirs., 1979—, pres. bd. dirs., 1982—; ter. mgr. E. Tenn., Beecham Products, Knoxville, 1978—. Mem. NOW (nat. employment com. 1979—, pres. Knoxville 1976, chmn. state employment com. 1975-77). Mem. council Appalachian Women, Inc., 1978-80; mem. adv. bd. Knoxville Head Start, 1977-78. Club: Carnegians. Contbr. articles on employment to profl. jours. Home: 2222 Island Home Blvd Knoxville TN 37920 Office: 1745 Old Springhouse Ln Suite 417 Atlanta GA 30338

HARLAN, NANCY MARGARET, lawyer; b. Santa Monica, Calif., Sept. 10, 1946; d. William Galland and Betty M. (Miles) Plett; B.S. magna cum laude, Calif. State U., Hayward, 1972; J.D., U. Calif., Berkeley, 1975; m. John Hammack, Dec. 1, 1979; children—Laryssa Maria Rebello, Leea Elyce Harlan. Admitted to Calif. bar, 1975, Fed. bar, U.S. Dist. Ct. for Central Dist., 9th Circuit, 1976; asso. firm Poindexter & Doutré, Los Angeles, 1975-80; residential counsel Coldwell Banker Residential Brokerage Co., Fountain Valley, Calif., 1980-81; counsel for real estate subs. law dept. Pacific Lighting Corp., Santa Ana, Calif., 1981—; tchr., designer courses in real estate ethics, professionalism and law. Exec. v.p. student body U. Calif., Berkeley, 1974-75. Lic. real estate broker, Calif. Mem. State Bar Calif., Am. Bar Assn., Los Angeles County Bar Assn., Orange County Bar Assn. (dir. corp. counsel sect. 1982—), Calif. Women Lawyers Assn., Orange County Women Lawyers Assn., Los Angeles Women Lawyers Assn., Nat. Assn. Female Execs. Office: 18 Brookhollow Dr Santa Ana CA 92705

HARLAN, ROMA CHRISTINE, portrait painter; b. Warsaw, Ind.; d. Charles William and Fern (McCormick) Harlan; student Purdue U., Art Inst. Chgo.; pvt. study with Ralph Clarkson, Chgo., Francis Chapin, Chgo., Weyman Adams, N.Y.C., Marie Goth, Indpls. One-man shows Lake Shore Club Chgo., Little Gallery of Esquire Theater, Chgo., Purdue U. Gallery, West Lafayette, Ind., George Washington U. Gallery, Washington, Hoosier Salon, Indpls., All.-Ill. Soc. Fine Arts, Kaufmann's Gallery, Chgo., Lafayette (Ind.) Art Assn., Arts Club Washington; exhibited numerous group shows; represented in permanent collections at U.S. Supreme Ct., U.S. Capitol Bldg., SEC, D.C. Fed. Ct. House, Nat. Guard Bldg., Washington, Nat. Fedn. Bus. and Profl. Women's Clubs, Washington, Lake Shore Club, Chgo., Purdue U., West Lafayette, Ind., Nat. Presbyn. Ch., Washington, St. Stevens Sch., Alexandria, Va., Walter Reed Army Med. Center. Art chmn. D.C. Fedn. Women's Clubs. Daus. of Ind. scholar. Mem. Ind. State Art Assn. Presbyterian. Club: Arts, Washington Forum, Zonta, D.C. Fed. Women's Clubs (Washington). Address: 1600 S Joyce St Apt A-1607 Arlington VA 22202

HARLAN, ROSA JANE (SMITH), ins. agt.; b. Okatie, S.C., Apr. 24, 1924; d. George Franklin and Anna Maud (Pricher) Smith; student public schs., also various ins. courses; diploma in fin. Armstrong Coll., Savannah, Ga., 1943; m. Richard Houston Harlan, Jr., June 29, 1945; children—Richard Houston, III, Donald Franklin, Hollace Joanna. Meteorologist, U.S. Weather Bur., 1943-44; airline stewardess, 1944-47; model, also freelance spl. events dir. and fashion dir., 1955-70; fashion dir. May Cohens Co., Jacksonville, Fla., 1961-62, Jordan Marsh Co., Boston, 1963-64; buyer Furchgotts Stores, Jacksonville, 1973-75; spl. agt. John Hancock Mut. Life Ins. Co., Jacksonville, 1975—; founder, 1978, since pres. Internat. Fin. Cons., fin. counseling, Jacksonville; real estate agt. ERA, 1981—, real estate broker, 1982—. Pres., Duval Med. Center Aux., 1958-59; mem. Duval County Welfare and Hosp. Bd., 1960-61; lead in Little Theatre plays; star local movie Story of Fashion. Recipient numerous appreciation awards for civic work; winner various beauty pageants. Mem. Nat. Assn. Life Underwriters, Fla. Assn. Life Underwriters, Jacksonville Assn. Life Underwriters, Life Underwriters Tng. Council, Am. Soc. Profl. and Exec. Women (internat. platform com.), Nat. Assn. Female Execs. (network dir.). Republican. Episcopalian. Clubs: Quota, Inonsphere. Home: 4237 Verona Ave Jacksonville FL 32210 Office: 4539 Beach Blvd Jacksonville FL 32207

HARLEY, BARBARA WEST, psychologist; b. Columbia, S.C., May 28, 1948; d. Ralph Thomas and Euleita Frances (Black) West; A.B., Dickinson Coll., 1970; Ph.D., U. Pa., 1980; m. John Barker Harley, Aug. 8, 1972; children— Andrew West Harley, Issac Thomas West Harley. Intern, Horizon House, Phila., 1974-75; dir. psychol. services Cath. Home for Girls, Phila., 1975-76; coordinator Crisis Program for Runaway Adolescents and Families, Cath. Social Services, Ansonia, Conn., 1978-79; counseling psychologist Day Care Cons. Program, The Child Center, Rockville, Md., 1979-80; pvt. practice, Rockville; lectr. U. Pa., 1975-76, teaching asst., 1972. Mem. counseling and guidance adv. com. Montgomery County (Md.) Bd. Edn.; mem. communications com. Plymouth Woods, Rockville. EPDA fellow, 1971-73; Lightner Witmer fellow U. Pa. Mem. Am. Psychol. Assn., Assn. Advancement of Psychology, Soc. Psychol. Study of Social Issues.

HARLEY, ROSE MADELINE, tng. sch. exec.; b. Paris, Ark.; d. Charles V.B. and Ella O. (McVay) H.; B.A. cum laude, Columbia U., M.A. in Adult Edn., 1976. Area mgr. N.Y.-L.I., Dale Carnegie orgn., 1960-63, instr. trainer internat. hdqrs., 1963-67, regional mgr. internat.

hdqrs., 1967-76, mgr. Dale Carnegie Inst. of N.Y.C., 1976-79; pres. Harley Inst., Inc., presenting Dale Carnegie courses in No. N.J., Hackensack, 1979—. Bd. dirs. Council for Noncoll. Continuing Edn., now v.p. Mem. Mensa, Columbia U. Alumni Assn., Sales Execs. Club N.Y.C. Club: Princeton. Home: 280 Prospect Ave Hackensack NJ 07601 Office: 25 E Salem St Hackensack NJ 07601

HARLIN, VIVIAN KRAUSE, physician; b. Seattle, Dec. 26, 1924; d. Louis Joseph and Julia (Rommel) Krause; B.S. in Zoology, U. Wash., 1946, M.S. in Preventive Medicine, 1970; M.D., U. Oreg., 1950; m. Allan J. Harlin, June 26, 1948; children—Sandra Jeanne Heim, Julie Ann Harlin Baldwin, Andrew Edward. Intern, Swedish Hosp., Seattle, 1950-51, resident, 1951-52; practice medicine, Seattle, 1952-53; clinic physician Snohomish County (Wash.) Health Dept., 1953; examiner physician Seattle Public Schs., 1953-57, dir. health services, 1957-79; sr. fellow dept. preventive medicine U. Wash., 1968-69, clin. instr. Sch. Public Health and Community Medicine, 1969—; dir. health services Office of Supt. of Public Instrn., Tumwater, Wash., 1979—; cons. HEW. Mem. ch. council Luth. Ch. Recipient Sch. Bell award Physicians and Schs. Conf., 1969; Golden Acorn award Wash. Congress Parent-Tchr.-Student Assn., 1973; Disting. Alumni award Sch. Pub. Health and Community Medicine, U. Wash., 1982. Mem. Am. Med. Women's Assn. (past pres. br. 37, pres. 1981), Am. Sch. Health Assn. (pres. 1974, mem. governing council 1978-80, mem. editorial bd. 1978-79; Howe award 1979), AMA (Physician Recognition award 1970, 80), Wash. Med. Assn., King County Med. Soc., Wash. Public Health Assn. (life), Wash. Tb and Respiratory Disease Assn. (dir. 1972-73), Seattle-King County Tb and Respiratory Disease Assn. (dir. 1970-73), Wash. Lung Assn. (dir., mem. King County regional council 1973-74), Wash. Soc. for Prevention of Blindness, Eta Sigma Gamma (honor award 1975), Delta Kappa Gamma. Contbr. articles to profl. jours.

HARLOW, BARBARA ANN, mgmt. cons.; b. Kansas City, Kans.; d. James Vernon and Jennie Alice (Flint) Bigler; B.A., U. Nebr., 1970; children—Ronald Eric Harlow, Gregory Brent Harlow. Exec. dir. March of Dimes, Omaha, 1970-71, regional cons., Kansas City, Mo., 1971-73, nat. cons., 1973-74; public relations dir. Crown Center Hotel, Kansas City, 1974-78; corp. dir. tng. and devel. Woolf Bros., Kansas City, 1978-80; pres. Mgmt. Assos., Inc., cons. human resource devel., 1980—; cons. women in mgmt. Active public relations Clark Welfare Council, Clark AFB, Philippines; counselor Neighborhood Youth Corps, Kansas City; mem. women's div. Kansas City Philharm. Orch. Mem. Public Relations Soc. Am., Am. Soc. Tng. and Devel., Kansas City C. of C. Club: Kansas City Ski. Home: 7615 E Gregory Blvd Kansas City MO 64133

HARLOW, ROSE MARY, telephone equipment co. exec.; b. Coblence, Germany, July 2, 1917; d. Jacob and Charlotte (Burgauer) Meyer; ed. Pitman Sch., London; m. Ronney L. Harlow, May 4, 1938; children—Jacqui, Judi. Ops. mgr. Glovemakers, Inc., Chgo., 1942-46; with Pritec, Chgo., 1946—, comptroller, pres., 1979—; graphoanalyst. Past pres. Temple Emanuel Sisterhood, bd. dirs. Emanuel Congregation. Mem. Telephone Interconnect Assn. Club: Exec. (Chgo.). Home: 2900 W Greenleaf Ave Chicago IL 60645 Office: 5800 N Lincoln Ave Chicago IL 60659

HARMAN, MARYANN WHITTEMORE, artist, educator; b. Roanoke, Va., Sept. 13, 1935; d. John Weed and Clifford Kelly Whittemore; B.A., Mary Washington Coll., 1955; M.A., Va. Poly. Inst., 1974; m. R. Phillip Harman, July 26, 1955; children—Mary Kelly, John Whittemore, Phillip Mears. Faculty, Va. Poly. Inst., Blacksburg, 1963—, prof. art 1981—; one-woman shows: Andre Emmerich Gallery, N.Y.C., 1976, 78, Rubiner Gallery, Detroit, 1977, 78, Meredith Long Gallery, N.Y.C., 1980, Haber Theodore Gallery, N.Y.C., 1981-82, Osuna Gallery, Washington, 1982; group shows include: Va. Mus. Art, Richmond, 1973, 74, 75, 80, 81, Southeastern Center for Contemporary Art, Winston Salem, N.C., 1963, 65, 67, 71, 76, Boston Mus., 1981, Roanoke (Va.) Mus., 1963-79, Butler Inst. Contemporary Art, Youngstown, Ohio, 1969, 72; represented in permanent collections: Boston Mus., General Motors, Detroit, Hunter Mus., Chattanooga, Roanoke Mus., Phillip Morris Corp., Richmond and N.Y.C., Mfrs. Hanover Trust, N.Y.C., Am. Can Corp., N.Y.C., Shawnert Bank of Boston, others. Mem. Coll. Art Assn., Nat. Hon. Art and Architecture Soc., Tau Sigma Delta. Episcopalian. Home: 602 Landsdowne Dr Blacksburg VA 24060 Office: Va Poly Inst Blacksburg VA 24061

HARMON, ARTICE WARD, occupational therapist; b. Hughes, Ark., Oct. 2, 1940; d. William Oscar and Alice Williams (Turner) Ward; B.S., Ind. U., 1973; M.P.H., U. Ill., 1975; m. Luther Harmon, Dec. 5, 1959. Occupational therapy intern St. Elizabeth's Hosp., Washington, 1973, Helen Hayes Rehab. Hosp., W. Haverstraw, N.Y., 1973; staff occupational therapist Mercy Hosp. and Med. Center, Chgo., 1973-76; dir. occupational therapy program Westside Parents Center, of Retarded Children United, Chgo., 1976-77; head occupational therapy dept. Americana Health Care Center, Champaign, Ill., 1977-81; dir. occupational therapy program Chgo. State U., 1981— guest lectr. allied health curriculum U. Ill., Urbana-Champaign, fall 1975, grad. teaching asso. occupational therapy curriculum Coll. Asso. Health Professions, 1978-80, instr., 1980-81; chmn. steering com. Ill. Council Occupational Therapy Edn.; cons. in field. Mem. Am., Ill. occupational therapy assns., Am. Pub. Health Assn., Am., Ill. vocat. assns., People United to Save Humanity, Phi Delta Kappa, Kappa Delta Pi. Roman Catholic. Home: 748 E 104th St Chicago IL 60628 Office: Coll Allied Health Chgo State U 95th St at King Dr Chicago IL 60628

HARMON, BARBARA SAYRE, artist; b. Yerington, Nev., Aug. 8, 1927; d. Ruth (Barker) and Fred Grayson Sayre; student Bisttram Sch. Fine Art, 1947-49, Black Mountain Coll., 1950; m. Cliff Franklin Harmon, July 7, 1949; 1 son, Jonathan Henry. Founder, mgr. Children's Gallery, Taos, 1963—, Children's Gallery Press, 1967—; paintings, graphics shown in pvt. galleries; author, illustrator: Tabbigail's Garden, 1967; Little People's Counting Book, 1968; This Little Pixie, 1969; Monday's Mouse, 1970; The Tumpfee Wood Acorn Book, 1977; Thimbly Hill, 1980; cover designer, illus. N.Mex. mag. Christmas story, 1981. Home: Box 202 Taos NM 87571

HARMON, DOROTHY ANN, univ. adminstr.; b. El Paso, Tex., Aug. 1, 1924; d. Willis Wayne and Katie Irene (Jarrell) Ransom; B.A., Wichita State U., 1946; m. Francis E. Harmon, Aug. 23, 1948; children—Karen Lynn, Wayne Eugene. Field house mgr., Wichita (Kans.) State U., 1967-74, acad. coordinator athletic dept., 1968-74, asst. athletic dir., 1971-72, asso. dir. Marcus Center Continuing Edn., 1974—. Bd. dirs. Sr. Services, Inc., 1982; mem. planning div. United Way, 1977—. Named to Shocker Hall of Fame, 1981. Mem. Nat. Assn. Edn. Secs. (state chmn. 1974-75), Kans. Assn. Edn. Secs. (fall workshop chmn. 1977), Wichita Assn. Edn. Secs. (mem. bd.), Wichita State U. Alumni Assn., Alpha Chi Omega. Democrat. Methodist. Clubs: Wichita State U. Dames (2d v.p. 1982-83), Air Capital Track (bd. dirs.), Downtown Lioness (past pres.). Home: 2418 N Belmont St Wichita KS 67220 Office: Marcus Center Wichita State U Wichita KS 67208

HARMON, KATHLEEN MARY, state program adminstr.; b. Elizabeth, N.J., Mar. 11, 1934; d. Bernard Florian and Mary Catherine (Jarvais) Grall; cert. S.W. Computer Coll., 1970; BUS, U. N.Mex., 1973, M.A., 1979; m. Clinton Harmon, Jan. 9, 1953 (div.); children—Sandra, Victoria, Mary, Walter, William. Computer programmer N.Mex. Employment Security Dept., Albuquerque, 1971-78, coordinator handicapped programs, 1978—; vice chairperson bd. dirs. Career Services for Handicapped; chairwoman N.Mex. Com. on Concerns of Handicapped, 1976—; mem. Pres.'s Com. for Employment Handicapped; mem. UN Planning Council 1981 Yr. of Disabled. Mem. Internat. Assn. Personnel in Employment Security, Nat. Rehab. Assn. (consumer bd.), N.Mex. Rehab. Assn. (dir., pres.-elect job placement div.), Mensa, Am. Bus. Women's Assn. (Tramway chpt Woman of Yr. 1978), Nat. Women's Polit. Caucus, Bernalillo County Woman's Polit. Caucus. Roman Catholic. Club: Toastmasters. Home: 83 Calle Vadito NW Albuquerque NM 87120 Office: 401 Broadway NE PO Box 1928 Albuquerque NM 87103

HARMON, LILY, artist; b. New Haven, Nov. 19, 1912; d. Benjamin and Bessie (Horowitz) Perelmutter; student Yale U. Sch. Art, 1929-31, Academie Colarossi Paris, 1931-32, Art Students League, 1932-33; m. Joseph H. Hirshhorn, 1945 (div. 1956); children—Amy, JoAnn; m. Milton Schachter, Oct. 1972. One-man shows Asso. Am. Artists Galleries, N.Y.C., 1944, 50, 53, 56, 57, Silvermine Art Assn., 1954, Westchester County Arts & Crafts, 1950, Ann Ross Gallery, N.Y.C., 1959, Selected Artists Gallery, N.Y.C., 1960, HCE Gallery, Provincetown, Mass., 1961, Yamada Gallery, Kyoto, Japan, 1963, Scargo Lake Gallery, Dennis, Mass., 1964, Tirca Karlis Gallery, Provincetown, Krasner Gallery, N.Y.C., 1966, Provincetown Group Gallery, 1966, Internat. Salon Palace of Fine Arts, Mexico City, 1973, U. Richmond, Marsh Gallery, George M. Modlin Fine Arts Center 1973, Krasner Gallery, N.Y.C., 1977, 81, others; 50-yr. retrospective exhbn. Wichita (Kans.), 1982-83; drawing show Summit Gallery, 1982-83; represented in permanent collections Butler Art Inst., Youngstown, Ohio, Whitney Mus. Am. Art, N.Y.C., Newark Mus., Ein Harod and Tel Aviv (Israel) mus., U. Mass. at Amherst, Kalamazoo (Mich.) Art Inst., Smithsonian Art Inst., Washington, St. Lawrence U. Mem. Provincetown Art Assn., Artists Equity Assn., Nat. Acad. Design, Provincetown Art Assn. Illustrator: Pride and Prejudice (Jane Austen), 1950; Sounds of a Distant Drum (Bill Martin, Jr.), 1967; (Japanese books) Buddenbrooks (Thomas Mann), 1965, Symphonie Pastorale (Andrié Gide), 1965, The Counterfeiters (André Gide), 1965, Dirty Hands (Jean Paul Sartre), 1965, The Castle (Franz Kafka), 1965, Metamorphosis (Franz Kafka), 1965, Lafcadio's Adventures (André Gide), 1972; Therese (Francois Mauriac), 1972; House of Mirth (Edith Wharton), 1975; Short Stories of Guy de Maupassant, 1976; author: (autobiography) Freehand, 1981. Home: 151 Central Park West New York NY 10023 also 629 Commercial St Provincetown MA 02657

HARMS, KATHLEEN MONTECILLO, pathologist; b. Cebu, Philippines, Sept. 27, 1946; d. Jesus A. and Guadalupe (Abellana) Montecillo; B.S., U. San Carlos, 1965; M.D., Cebu Inst. Medicine, Philippines, 1970; m. Larry Duane Harms, June 13, 1971; children—Brigitte M., Keith L. Rotating intern McLaren Gen. Hosp., Flint, Mich., 1972-73; resident in pathology Hurley Med. Center, Flint, 1973-77; practice medicine specializing in pathology, Lapeer, Mich., 1977-79; dir. pathology South La. Med. Center, Houma, 1979—; asso. clin. prof. Tulane U. Sch. Medicine; cons. pathologist Lapeer County Gen. Hosp., Wheelock Hosp., Community Hosp. Diplomate Am. Bd. Pathology. Mem. Am. Soc. Clin. Pathologists, Coll. Am. Pathologists, Mich. Soc. Pathologists, AMA. Republican. Roman Catholic.

HARMSEN, MARYANNE JOAN, ins. account exec.; b. Bklyn., Dec. 22, 1945; d. Francis P. and Anne M. (Mannelli) Romano; student St. Peter's Coll., 1963, N.J. State Tchrs. Coll., 1964, Coll. Ins., 1977-78, Bergen Community Coll., 1979; m. Arnold B. Harmsen, Aug. 4, 1979; children by previous marriage—Andrea Francesca and Jennifer Patricia Lamendola. Agt., Met. Life Ins. Co., Newark, 1974-76, Western World Ins. Co., Ramsey, N.J., 1977-80; account exec. Foxcroft Agy., Inc., Milford, Pa., 1980—; risk mgmt. cons. N.Y. health care facilities. Bd. advisors Acad. St. Aloysius, 1973-74; charter mem., officer, dir. nat. chpt. Ladies of Unico, 1969-70. Recipient Leaders award Met. Life Ins. Co. Leaders Conf., 1975. Mem. Am. Hosp. Assn., Assn. Profl. Ins. Women, Risk and Ins. Mgmt. Soc. (asso.), Nat. Assn. Female Execs., N.J. Democratic Assn. Roman Catholic. Club: Franklin Lakes Newcomers (past pres.). Home: 22 Myrtle Ave Ramsey NJ 07446 Office: 403 Broad St Milford PA 18337

HARNSBERGER, THERESE COSCARELLI (MRS. FREDERICK OWEN HARNSBERGER), librarian; b. Muskegon, Mich.; d. Charles and Julia (Borrell) Coscarelli; B.A. cum laude, Marymount Coll., 1952; M.L.S., U. So. Calif., 1953; postgrad. Rosary Coll., River Forest, Ill., 1955-56, UCLA Extension, 1960-61; m. Frederick Owen Harnsberger, Dec. 24, 1962; 1 son, Lindsey Carleton. Free-lance writer, 1950—; librarian San Marino (Calif.) High Sch., 1953-56; cataloger, cons. San Marino Hall, South Pasadena, Calif., 1956-61; librarian Los Angeles State Coll., 1956-59; librarian dist. library Covina-Valley Unified Sch. Dist., Covina, Calif., 1959-67; librarian Los Angeles Trade Tech. Coll., part-time 1972—, Pasadena City Coll. Library, 1973—; librarian, evening instr. East Los Angeles Coll., 1970—; tumor registrar, med. librarian Alhambra Community Hosp., 1975-79; med. library cons., 1978—; pres. Research Unltd., 1980—; freelance reporter L.A.'s Best Bargains Newsletter, 1981—. Chmn. spiritual values com. Covina Cordinating Council, 1964-66; telephone chmn. Fremont Sch. PTA, Alhambra. Mem. Calif. Assn. Sch. Librarians (chmn. legis. com.), Covina Tchrs. Assn., Book Publicists of So. Calif., AAUW (historian 1972-73), U. So. Calif. Grad. Sch. Library Sci. (life), Nat. Tumor Registrars Assn., So. Calif. Med. Library Group (jobs com. 1977—), LWV, Am. Nutrition Soc. (chpt. Newsletter chmn.), Calif. State Poetry Soc., Pi Lambda Theta. Author poetry. Office: 2809 W Hellman Ave Alhambra CA 91803

HARPER, DONNA T., mortgage broker, comml. real estate broker; b. Chgo., Nov. 2, 1943; d. Vito J. and Eileen L. (Kennelly) Tassone; children—Jeanne Marie, Melissa Leigh. Sec., Pullman-Standard; adminstrv. aide Ill. Supt. Public Instrn., 1964-66; pres. Venture Property Services, Inc., 1980—; broker, owner Valley Income Properties, Phoenix, 1979—. Office: 1611 E Camelback Rd Suite 6 Phoenix AZ 85016

HARPER, GLADYS COFFEY (MRS. THOMAS A. HARPER), health services agy. adv.; b. Pitts.; d. Clarence William and India Anna (James) Jackson; B.A., U. Pitts., 1970, M.P.A., 1972, M.S.H., 1973; m. Thomas A. Harper, Jan. 21, 1968. With Allegheny County (Pa.) Health Dept., 1958—, chief office tng. and edn. adminstr., 1975-76, adv. curriculum devel. and health adminstrn., 1976—; health technician specialist office health affairs OEO, Washington, 1965; vis. lectr. Grad. Sch. Public and Internat. Affairs, U. Pitts., 1970—; panelist Sta. WQED-TV White House Conf. Food, Nutrition and Health; trustee Mayview State Hosp., 1975—, v.p. bd. trustees, 1978, trustee clin. pastoral edn. program, 1979-80. Program chmn. Law Day, Allegheny County Assn. Lawyers' Wives, 1975, v.p., 1978, pres., 1980; program chmn. Pa. Bar Assn. Wives Program, 1978; trustee Louis Little Meml. Fund, Allegheny County Bar Assn., 1979. Named Woman of Yr., Greyhound Corp., 1967, 1 of 25 Outstanding Pittsburghers, Wayfarer Mag., Chrysler Corp., 1967, Health Services award Pitts, Club United, 1970, Harold B. Gardner award-Md. Citizen Health award, Allegheny County Med. Soc., 1973, Drug Edn. recognition Pitts. Press, 1971, citation for environ. health curriculum devel. and supervision Chatham Coll., 1976. Mem. Am. Public Health Assn., Royal Soc. Health, Am. Soc. Public Adminstrn., Conf. Minority Public Adminstrs., Legis. Council Western Pa. (dir., v.p. elect 1982), Western Pa. Genealogy Soc. (pres. elect 1982), League Community Health Workers, AAUW, NAACP (Isabel Strickland Youth Advisor award 1967, Daisy E. Lampkin Human Rights award 1969), Program to Aid Citizen Enterprises. Co-producer documentary: What's Buggin' The Blacks?, Sta. KDKA-TV, 1968. Home: 5260 Center Ave Coronada Apts 502 Pittsburgh PA 15232

HARPER, JANE CAMPBELL (CHAMBERLAIN), journalist; b. Albert Lea, Minn., Dec. 18, 1925; d. George Vernon and Edith Jean (Christie) Chamberlain; student U. Colo., 1943-44; B.A., U. Minn., 1947; m. Michael Hoye, Sept. 15, 1947; m. 2d. Ralph Harper, Sept. 3, 1955; children—Jennifer, Douglas, Megan. Editorial asst. Radio Showmanship mag., 1945-47, Modern Medicine, 1947-48; editor World-Ind., Walsenburg, Colo., 1951-55; news editor Sta. KATE, Albert Lea, 1956-58; editor Colo. Trumpet, Denver, 1960-66, 69-73; asst. dir. govt. and polit. edn. Colo. Edn. Assn., Denver, 1968-70; free-lance writer govt. politics, 1973-78; press aide to speaker Colo. Ho. of Reps., 1979-80; adminstrv. asst. Colo. Press Assn., 1979—. Presdl. elector, 1972; precinct committeewoman, 1975—. Mem. Nat. Fedn. Press Women, Colo. Press Women (pres., 1961-62), N.Eng. Hist. and Geneal. Soc., Colo. Genealogy Soc., Conn. Genealogy Soc., Soc. Mayflower Descendants, Theta Sigma Phi. Republican. Episcopalian. Author publicity manuals, 1957, 63, 70, series polit. and govtl. guides, 1969; co-author polit. handbook, 1970, legis. directory, 1979, 81, Colo. newspaper yearbook, 1980. Home: 1365 Iola St Aurora CO 80010 Office: 1336 Glenarm Pl Denver CO 80204

HARPER, JEAN ELIZABETH PAYNE, photojournalist; b. Richmond, Va., June 7, 1929; d. Martin Sly and Emma Louise (Brock) Payne; student Va. Commonwealth U., 1969-76; m. James William Harper, Oct. 23, 1944; children—Charlotte, Sandra, Billy, Pat, John, Betsy, Jane, Brendan. Reporter, photographer Northumberland Echo, Heathsville, Va., 1967—; asst. editor, 1980-82; owner, Jean Harper Photos, Heathsville, 1969—; editor, pub. Rap-po-peake Illustrated Press, 1982—; press aide Congl. campaign for Dr. Kenneth Wells, 1st dist. Va., 1972; campaign photographer for mem. Ho. of Dels., 1975-77; lectr. in field. Va. Young Homemakers scholar, 1970; named Young Homemaker of Yr., 1973-74; Va. Press Assn. awards, 1968, 69, 70, 72, 73, 74, 75, 76, 77, 78, 79; Va. Press Women awards, 1973, 74, 80. Mem. Va. Press Photographers, Va. Press Women, Young Homemakers of Va. (pres. 1965-66). Republican. Roman Catholic. Home: PO Box 106 Lodge Rd Callao VA 22435 Office: Callao VA

HARPER, M. JEANNETTE PUGH, cosmetic and beauty salon exec.; b. Lead, S.D., Jan. 16, 1926; d. Louis A. and Madeleine I. (DeKelso) Wiman; m. Ralph Allen Harper, Mar. 6, 1977. Sales and prodn. mgr. White Pine Lumber Co., Oreg., Calif. and Nev., 1945-52; secretarial positions, Sacramento, 1952-59; chief acct. Sierra Mt. Mills., Celestial Valley, Calif., 1959-61; co-owner Sierra Nevada Pine Lumber Co., Grass Valley, Calif., 1961-70; owner, mgr. Merle Norman Cosmetic Studio & Beauty Salon, Grass Valley, 1970—, Great Looks Hair Designs, Nevada City, Calif., 1970—. Recipient service awards local Lions, Jaycees, others; lic. cosmetologist, Calif. Mem. Grass Valley Bus. and Profl. Women's Club (pres. 1975-76), Capital Dist. Bus. and Profl. Women's Club (pres. 1979-80), Calif. Fedn. Bus. and Profl. Women's Clubs (dir. 1979-82), Grass Valley Area C. of C. (pres. 1975, Earl Covey award), Grass Valley Central Bus. Dist., Gold Country Cosmetologists Assn. (sec. 1981-82) Nat. Hairdressers and Cosmetologists Assn., Calif. Cosmetology Assn., Nat. Assn. Female Execs., Internat. Entrepreneurs Assn. Office: 120 Mill St Grass Valley CA 95945

HARPER, NANCY LEA, educator; b. Hays, Kans., Feb. 27, 1947; d. Joe O. and Willa L. (Webster) Brown; B.A., Emporia State U., 1969; M.A., U. No. Iowa, 1970; Ph.D., U. Iowa, 1973. Instr. English, U. No. Iowa, Cedar Falls, 1970-71; asst. prof. communication Rutgers U., New Brunswick, N.J., 1973-76; asst. prof. communication U. Iowa, Iowa City, 1976-78, assoc. prof., 1979—, asst. dean liberal arts, 1978-82, assoc. dean, 1982—, asst. prof. communication and journalism, 1978-79; mem. adv. com. edn. U.S. Dept. Edn., 1980-81; guest lectr. communication various colls. and profl. groups, 1976—. Dept. Edn. grantee, 1981, N.W. Area Found. grantee, 1979, 80-82. Mem. Assn. for Communication Adminstrn., Speech Communication Assn., Internat. Communication Assn., Central States Speech Communication Assn., Midwest Cooperative Edn. Assn., AAUP. Author: Human Communication Theory, 1979; The History of a Paradigm and The Clusters Source Book: Balancing Liberal Learning and Career Preparation, 1980; contbr. articles on communication to profl. jours.; editor: Human Communication: Core Readings, 1974. Home: 10 Glendale Ct Iowa City IA 52240

HARPER, OLLYE HOBGOOD, educator; b. Newellton, La., Jan. 11, 1916; d. Walter David and Nellie Catherine (Triche) Hobgood; B.S., Delta State U., 1937; Ed.M., Miss. Coll., 1960; Ph.D., U. So. Miss., 1970; m. Matthew Harper, Jr., Aug. 27, 1939; 1 dau., Judith Katherine. Tchr., McComb (Miss.) public schs., 1937-39, Silver City (Miss.) public schs., 1942-43, Laurel (Miss.) public schs., 1944-45, 48-50; ofcl. hostess Gov.'s Mansion, State of Miss., 1956; tchr. Jackson (Miss.) public schs., 1957-62, Laurel (Miss.) public schs., 1962-81; adj. prof. U. South Fla., Tampa, Summer 1967 U. Miss. at Jackson, U. So. Miss., 1973, Hattiesburg, 1969-75, William Carey Coll., Hattiesburg, Miss., 1973—. Pres. Jr. Aux., 1948-49; chmn., March of Dimes, Jones County (Miss.), 1950-51; del. Nat. Democratic Conv., 1956; mem. Nat. Platform Com., 1956; sec. treas. Jones County Democratic Com., 1969-73; pres. Laurel Little Theatre, 1949-50; trustee Miss. Hosp. Sch. for Cerebral Palsy, 1957-63. Named Woman of Yr., Bus. and Profl. Women's Club, 1970. Mem. Internat. Reading Assn., Delta Kappa Gamma (chpt. pres. 1976-78). Democrat. Presbyterian. Home: 549 N 6th Ave Laurel MS 39440

HARPER, ROSALINDE MARIE, cable TV producer; b. Kansas City, Mo., June 19, 1954; d. Connie Esther Harper; B.S. in Communications (Univ. Equal Opportunity grantee), Ga. State U., 1976. Producer, announcer Sta. WRAS, Atlanta, 1973-76; producer, announcer, salesperson, Sta. WIIN, Atlanta, 1974-75; writer Atlanta Jour. newspaper, 1975-76; news reporter/anchor Sta. WRNG, Atlanta, 1976-77, Sta. WSAV-TV, Savannah, Ga., 1977-79, Eastside corr., bur. chief Sta. KSD, St. Louis, from 1979; now editor, producer Cable News Network, Atlanta; stringer CBS Radio N.Y., Nat. Pub. Radio, Washington, 1976-78. Recipient Sr. award Ga. State U., 1976; Black Achievement award So. Christian Leadership Conf., 1981, lic. radio operator FCC. Mem. Nat. Assn. TV Arts and Scis., Atlanta Communications Club, Women in Communication, Ga. Assn. Ednl. Broadcasters, Assn. Black Journalists, Sigma Delta Chi. Contbr. articles to newspapers. Home: 1150 Collier Rd Apt A6 Atlanta GA 30318 Office: Cable New Network 1050 Torchwood Dr Atlanta GA

HARPER, RUTH B., state legislator; b. Savannah, Ga., Dec. 24, 1927; d. Thomas and Sallie (Bryant) Deloach; grad. Berean Inst. Sch. Cosmetology and Bus., Phila., Flamingo Modeling and Charm Sch., Phila., Phila. Miniversity, m. James Harper, Sept. 24, 1950. Mem. Pa. Ho. of Reps., chmn. minority subcom. basic edn. com. Founder, past pres. North Central Phila. Women's Polit. Caucus; ward leader 13th Ward Phila. Democratic Com.; mem., past treas. Pa. Legis. Black Caucus; nat. Dem. committeewoman; founder, dir. Ruth Harper's Modeling and Charm Sch., Phila.; producer Miss Ebony Pa. Scholarship Pageant; bd. mem. YMCA Columbia br.; past mem. bd. dirs. N.W. Phila. br. ARC; bd. mem. Women Greater Phila. Recipient award Phila. Women's Polit. Caucus, Service award Bright Hope Baptist Ch., Service award Third World 76 Inc. Black Expo, Pyramid award Elks, Outstanding Service award Order Eastern Star. Mem. NAACP (life), Nat. Council

Negro Women, Bus. and Profl. Women Phila. Baptist. Home: 1427 W Erie Ave Philadelphia PA 19140

HARPER, SARA JUANITA, ret. judge; b. Cleve., Aug. 10, 1926; d. James Weldon and Leila (Smith) Harper; B.B.S., Western Res. U., 1948; LL.B., 1952; m. George W. Trumbo; 5 children. Admitted to Ohio bar, 1952; individual practice law, 1952-66; atty. Legal Aid Soc., 1966-67; prosecutor City of Cleve., 1967-69, asso. dir. law, 1969-70; judge Cleve. Mcpl. Ct., 1970-82, ret., 1982; splty. instr. on evidence; hostess radio program The Adminstrn. of Justice and Preventive Law. Presiding officer Ohio Nat. Women's Internat. Year, 1977; ednl. adv. counselor Case Western Res. U., 1975—; co-chmn. Freedom Fund Dinner, NAACP, 1971, chmn. membership drive, 1978; trustee Goodwill Industries Greater Cleve., sec. bd. trustees; trustee Cleve. Animal Protective League, Salvation Army; Republican candidate for chief justice Ohio Sup. Ct., 1980. Served to maj., USMCR, 1973-78, lt. col. Res. Cert. mil. judge; recipient Superior Jud. Service award Ohio Supreme Ct., 1978, Law and Order with Justice and Humanity award, 1971, commendation VA, 1978, Tribute to Greatness award, 1971, Vol. Service award, 1976, Woman of Year award, 1972. Mem. Nat. Bar Assn. (pres. jud. council 1975-76), Ohio Jud. Council, John Harlan Law Club, Cleve. Women Lawyers Assn., Nat. Council Negro Women, Alpha Kappa Alpha, Gamma Phi Delta, Eta Phi Beta. Republican. Baptist (chmn. bd. religious edn.). Clubs: Daus. of Elks, Eastern Star. Appeared in Career Vignette Series of Real People at Work, Edn. Research Council Am., 1974, in movie on minorities in positions of influence in Am., USIS, 1975. Office: 1475 Davenport St Cleveland OH 44114

HARPER, SHIRLEY FOLKESTAD, librarian; b. Sauk Centre, Minn., Dec. 11, 1926; d. Otto and Pauline (Hansen) Folkestad; student U. Minn., 1944-47; M.A., U. Chgo., 1952; m. James R. Harper, Jr., 1947 (div. 1978); 1 son, James R. III. Librarian, A. G. Bush Library, Indsl. Relations Center, U. Chgo., 1949-75; librarian N.Y. State Sch. Indsl. and Labor Relations and dir. Martin P. Catherwood Library, Cornell U., Ithaca, N.Y., 1975—. Mem. Spl. Libraries Assn. (coms.; Profl. award 1967), Am. Soc. Info. Sci. (coms.), Com. Indsl. Relations Libraries, ALA, Indsl. Relations Research Assn., World Future Soc. Author: (with Thomas L. Whisler) Performance Appraisal: Research and Practice, 1962; (with com.) Special Libraries: A Guide for Management, 1966, rev. edit., 1974; ILR Thesaurus, 1977, rev. edit., 1981. Home: 16 D Strawberry Hill Rd Ithaca NY 14850 Office: Cornell U Ithaca NY 14853

HARPHAM, VIRGINIA RUTH, violinist; b. Huntington, Ind., Dec. 10, 1917; d. Pyrl John and Nellie Grace (Whitaker) Harpham; A.B., Morehead State U., 1939; m. Dale Lamar Harpham, Dec. 25, 1938; children—Evelyn, George. Violinist, Nat. Symphony Orch., Washington, 1956—, prin. of second violin sect., 1964—; mem. Lywen String Quartet, 1960-69. Nat. Symphony String Quartet, 1973—. Episcopalian. Home: 3816 Military Rd NW Washington DC 20015 *

HARPP, JACQUELINE, auditor; b. Stewart County, Ga., Dec. 23, 1952; d. James and Elsie Lou (Thomas) Harp; B.S. in Bus. Adminstrn., Morris Brown Coll., 1974; postgrad. Ga. State U., 1978. Mgmt. auditor-evaluator GAO, Atlanta, 1974—. Mem. Am. Soc. for Public Adminstrn., Nat. Assn. for Female Execs. Democrat. Mem. African Methodist Episcopalian Ch. Home: 3008 Rolling Meadows Ct Lithonia GA 30058 Office: 221 Courtland St NE Atlanta GA 30043

HARRELL, CAROLYN HARDISON, nursing home adminstr.; b. Washington, N.C., Feb. 25, 1942; d. Dewey Jasper and Emma Blanche (Lilley) Hardison; R.N., Petersburg (Va.) Gen. Hosp., 1963; B. Nursing, Pacific Western U., 1981, D. Sc. in Health Care Adminstrn., 1982; m. Jerry W. Harrell, Apr. 18, 1979; children by previous marriage—Natalie Dawn and John Michael Cameron. Staff nurse Petersburg Gen. Hosp., 1963-66; staff nurse, supr., inservice dir. Central State Hosp., Petersburg, 1963-73; owner, operator Cameron's Day Care Center, Colonial Heights, Va., 1973-74; dir. nurses Guarian Corp., Petersburg, 1974-76; adminstr. Am. Health Care Corp., Richmond, Va., 1976-77, Beverly Enterprises, Greenville, N.C., 1977—. Vocat. adv. com. Martin Community Coll., 1979. Recipient Citizenship award, 1960; named Employee of Month, Guardian Corp., 1974. Mem. Am. Coll. Nursing Home Adminstrs., Va. Health Care Facilities Assn., N.C. Health Care Facilities Assn. Republican. Club: Bus. and Profl. Women. Home: 1403 Red Banks Rd Greenville NC 27834 Office: PO Box 5046 Greenville NC 27834

HARRELL, MABEL JANET, med. technologist; b. Selma, N.C., Oct. 15, 1927; d. Joseph McNeil and Bessie Mabel (Greene) Butts; student Richmond Profl. Inst. of Coll. of William and Mary, 1945-47, 59-60, 60-61; M.T., Stuart Circle Hosp., 1948; m. Stewart Havens Harrell, June 3, 1967; children—Joseph Stewart, Diantha Rhea. Med. technologist Maria Parham Hosp., Henderson, N.C., 1950-58, Moses Cone Hosp., Greensboro, N.C., 1958-59, Richmond (Va.) Meml. Hosp., 1959-60; chief technologist Warren Gen. Hosp., Warrenton, N.C., 1960-62, 64; blood bank supr. Wake Meml. Hosp., Raleigh, N.C., 1962-63, 65-68; chief technologist Roanoke Rapids Hosp., Roanoke Rapids, N.C., 1969-72; med. technologist Halifax Meml. Hosp., Roanoke Rapids, 1980—. Treas., Quankie Bapt. Ch., 1966-73, Sunday sch. tchr., 1967-81, dir. Women's Missionary Union, 1979-82, Vacation Bible Sch. dir., 1976-82, chmn. history com., 1976-82; dir. Women's Missionary Union and Vacation Bible Sch., S. Rosemary Bapt. Ch., 1982—. Mem. Am. Soc. Clin. Pathologists, Am. Soc. Med. Technologists, N.C. Soc. Med. Technologists. Address: Route 2 Box 409A Roanoke Rapids NC 27870

HARRELL, RUTH FLINN, psychologist; b. Americus, Ga., Apr. 19, 1900; d. Dan and Neva (Poley) Flinn; B.S., Wesleyan Coll., Macon, Ga., 1920; M.A., Columbia U., 1924, Ph.D., 1942; m. William Lee Harrell, Nov. 24, 1928; 1 dau., Ruth Harrell Capp. Psychologist, Norfolk (Va.) Schs., 1926-37; rehab. psychologist neuro-surgery Johns Hopkins Hosp., Balt., 1936-47; prof. psychology Old Dominion U., Norfolk, 1965-70, research prof., 1976—. Found. nutritional Advancement grantee, 1976. Mem. Am. Psychol. Assn., N.Y. Acad. Sci., Va. Psychol. Assn., NEA. Presbyterian. Author: Effect of Mothers Diets on the Intelligence of Offspring; Effect of Added Thiamin on Hearing, 1943, Further Effects of Added Thiamin on Learning and Other Processes, 1947; co-author: Can Nutritional Supplements Help Mentally Retarded Children?: An Exploratory Study, 1981. Home and Office: 6411 Powhatan Ave Norfolk VA 23508

HARRELSON, TERESA LYNN, pharmacist; b. Mt. Airy, N.C., Oct. 25, 1950; d. James Earle and Wilma Martin H.; A.S., Paducah Community Coll., 1970; B.S., U. Ky., 1973. Pharmacist, Drug World Pharmacy, Louisville, 1973-76; dir. pharm. services Health Care of Louisville, 1976-78; dir. pharmacy Christian Ch. Home, Louisville, 1978—. Mem. Jefferson County Acad. Pharmacy (pres. 1980, bd. govs. 1973-79), Ky. Pharmacist Assn. (sec., bd. govs. 1978-80), Am. Pharm. Assn., Nat. Assn. Retail Druggists, Am. Soc. Cons. Pharmacists, Council Women Pres. (pres. 1982), Derby City Bus. and Profl. Women's Assn. Republican. Baptist. Home: 1008 Lake Way Louisville KY 40222 Office: 942 S 4th St Louisville KY 40203

HARRIMAN, PAMELA DIGBY CHURCHILL, polit. action com. adminstr.; b. Farnborough, Eng., Mar. 20, 1920; came to U.S., 1959, naturalized, 1971; d. Edward Kenelm and Constance Pamela Alice (Bruce) Digby; B. Domectic Sci.-Economy, Downham (Eng.) Coll., 1937; postgrad. Sorbonne, Paris, 1937-38; m. Randolph Churchill, 1939; 1 son, Winston Spencer; m. 2d, Leland Hayward, May 4, 1960; m. 3d, W. Averell Harriman, Sept. 27, 1971. With Ministry of Supply, London, 1942-43; with Churchill Club for Am. Servicemen, 1943-46; journalist Beaverbrook Press, Europe, 1946-49; mem. nat. fin. council Democratic Nat. Com.; mem. Democratic House and Senate Council; co-chmn. Democratic Congressional Dinner 1979; founder Democrats for the 80's, 1980—. Named Democratic Women of Yr., Women's Nat. Democratic Club 1980. Roman Catholic.

HARRINGER, HELEN EHRAT, social worker; b. Chgo., June 20, 1936; d. Charles William and Dorothy (Glanz) Ehrat; B.A., U. Mich., 1958; M.S.W., U. Conn., 1962; m. Olaf Harringer, Dec. 20, 1975; children—H. L., Karen Hedges. Program supr. Hartford (Conn.) Neighborhood Centers, 1959-62; program dir. Evanston (Ill.) Children's Home, 1963-64; dir. student activities Evanston Twp. High Sch., 1975-76; social worker Wheaton (Ill.) Public Schs., 1977-79, Libertyville (Ill.) Public Schs., 1979-81; dir. Gehring Hall, St. Joseph Hosp., 1981—; leader Liberal Youth on North Shore, 1969-71; counseling cons. People Against Pornography, 1980-81. Mem. bd. Juvenile Protective Assn., 1963-68, Glenview United Fund, 1969-76, Family Service Wilmette, Glenview, Northbrook and Kenilworth, 1970-76, Grove Heritage Assn., 1979-81. Grantee Hartford Community Chest, 1960-62. Mem. Nat. Assn. Social Workers. Unitarian. Home: 530 Hunter Rd Glenview IL 60025 Office: 2130 N Kenmore St Chicago IL 60614

HARRINGTON, ELIZABETH DALLAS, food mfg. co. exec.; b. Jackson, Miss., Nov. 9, 1942; d. William Lee and Louise Landis (Crowder) Dallas; B.A., Cornell U., 1965; m. Robert William Harrington, Aug. 21, 1965; children—Elizabeth Brooke, Kristin (dec.). Fashion coordinator, commentator Marshall Field & Co., Chgo., 1965; asst. brand mgr. Procter and Gamble Co., Cin., 1966-68; account exec. J. Walter Thompson Co., Chgo., 1968-72, account supr., 1972-76, v.p., 1973-76, v.p. mgmt. supr., 1976-79; v.p. advt., pres. Ad Com subs. Quaker Oats Co., Chgo., 1979—; lectr. advt. Barat Coll. Adv. to bd. dirs. Grove Sch. for Handicapped Children, Lake Forest, Ill. Recipient Family Circle Nutrition award, 1973; YWCA Leadership award, 1977; named Outstanding Young Bus. Woman of Yr., Glamour mag., 1977; Advt. Woman of Yr., 1980; Outstanding Corp. Advt. Exec., Gallagher Report, 1981. Mem. Chgo. Advt. Club, Women's Advt. Club of Chgo., Am. Advt. Fedn. (dir. 1979—), Nat. Assn. Better Bus. Burs. (dir. children's advt. rev. unit 1979—), Chgo. Network. Office: Quaker Oats Co Merchandise Mart Plaza Chicago IL 60654

HARRINGTON, SISTER, MARIA MAURICE, coll. ofcl.; b. Holyoke, Mass., July 3, 1921; d. Maurice John and Mary T. (Courtney) Harrington; B.S., Coll. of Our Lady of Elms, 1944; M.S. in Chemistry, Fordham U., 1960. Joined Sisters of St. Joseph, Roman Catholic Ch., 1939; tchr. Sister Joseph's High Sch., Pittsfield, Mass., 1944-50; instr. chemistry Coll. Our Lady of Elms, 1950-65, asst. prof., 1965-77, asso. prof., 1977—, acad. dean, 1973-79, v.p., 1979—; mem. Sisters Senate, 1971-78, pres., 1972-74. NSF grantee Oak Ridge Summer Inst., 1968, Renssalaer Poly. Inst., 1970. Recipient Disting. Alumna award Coll. Our Lady of Elms, 1977. Mem. AAUP, AAUW, Am. Chem. Soc. Home and Office: 291 Springfield St Chicopee MA 01013

HARRINGTON, MARY KENNEY, nursing adminstr.; b. Boston; B.S. in Nursing, Boston Coll. Sch. Nursing, 1969; m. John F. Harrington, June 14, 1970; children—Jennifer, Eric. Asst. dir. nurses Plymouth County Hosp., Hanson, Mass., 1980—. Mem. Mass. Soc. Nursing Service Adminstrs., South Shore Nurse Assn.

HARRINGTON, SANDRA MAY, ednl. adminstr.; b. Geneva, N.Y., Sept. 21, 1948; d. James Jerome and Julia Mary (Deeb) H.; A.A., Niagara County Community Coll., 1968; B.S. in Secondary Edn., SUNY, Buffalo, 1970; M.S., Nova U., 1979. Tchr. trainable mentally handicapped Okeechobee (Fla.) Public Schs., 1971-79, tchr. educable mentally handicapped, 1979-81, dean of students Okeechobee High Sch., 1981-82, Okeechobee Jr. High Sch., 1982—. Recipient Entricy Herald Achievement award Niagara County Community Coll., 1968; Cert. of Appreciation, Okeechobee Cub Scouts, 1977; winner Fla. Learning Resources System/Alpha contest, 1979; Fla. Dept. Edn. grantee, 1976. Mem. Fla. Assn. Sch. Adminstrs., Assn. Supervision and Curriculum Devel., Council Exceptional Children, PTA. Democrat. Home: PO Box 1331 1605 W Virginia Blvd Okeechobee FL 33472

HARRIS, ADRIENNE WYNN, ednl. adminstr.; b. Milw., Feb. 3, 1947; d. Sherburn and Marjorie Deen (Tarrant) Wynn; student Nat. Coll. Edn., 1965-66, Marquette U., 1966-68; m. Harold L. Harris, June 16, 1968; children—Ralph, Geoffrey. Houston br. adminstr. Stanley H. Kaplan Ednl. Center, 1975—. Vice pres. Willow Meadows Civic Assn., 1976. Mem. Houston C. of C. (edn. com.). Address: 7011 Southwest Freeway Suite 520 Houston TX 77074

HARRIS, AMANDA KENYON, pharm. co. exec.; b. Wilmington, Del., Nov. 11, 1943; d. James M. and Bessie (Symonds) Kenyon; m. Roger E. Harris, Nov. 30, 1963; children—Eric, Aaron. Reporter, Herald Jour./Am., Syracuse, N.Y., 1961-63; reporter Democrat & Chronicle, Rochester, N.Y., 1963-65, feature news reporter, 1971-73; co-owner, pub. Dundee (N.Y.) Observer, 1967-71; editor employee publs. Xerox Corp., Rochester, 1973-76, mgr. communication projects, 1976-77, mgr. affirmative action, 1977-78; mgr. communications Merck & Co., Inc., Rahway, N.J., 1978-81, dir. communications and research, 1981—. Mem. steering com. for regional conf. on Women's Issues and Concerns; spl. liaison N.Y. State Office of Lt. Gov. and N.Y. State dels. to First Nat. Women's Conf., Houston; mem. steering com. for regional conf. Women and Money Mgmt.; mem. adv. com. Monroe Community Coll.; chmn. regional conf. Women and Employment; mem. steering com. nat. conf. on the changing employee population; mem. nat. action com. Women and Employment Discrimination; career counselor Rochester Women's Career Center and Women in Communication, Inc. Recipient awards including Excellence in Design and Publ. Internat. Assn. Bus. Communicators, 1977; Spl. Merit award Xerox Corp., 1977; named Young Woman of Achievement, Nat. Council Women, 1978, Outstanding Young Women Am., 1979. Mem. Internat. Assn. Bus. Communicators, Women in Communication, Internat. Communication Council, Internat. Communications Assn., Sigma Delta Chi. Democrat. Episcopalian. Office: PO Box 2000 Rahway NJ 07065

HARRIS, ANNE M. F., furniture, graphics and interior designer; b. Duluth, Minn., July 23, 1921; d. Fred David and Florence Amelia (Wickstrom) Harris; student U. Minn., 1939-42, 75-78; grad. Hans Krieks Masterclass, 1978; m. Howard Liss, July 5, 1952 (div. Nov., 1974); children—Jodi Robin, Dana Jennifer. Art dir. Calif. Mags., Los Angeles, 1946-49; art editor, cover designer Pines Publs., N.Y.C., 1952-55; art editor Street and Smith, N.Y.C., 1955-57; designer, art dir. Stravon Pub. Co., N.Y.C., 1954-65; designer, illustrator C.B.S. Publs., N.Y.C., 1970—; cons. design Highlights for Children, Honesdale, Pa., 1976-79; store and window design, sales Castro Convertible, N.Y.C., 1979-81; with Harris & Kaye Interior Designs, N.Y.C., 1981-82; owner, mgr. Anne Harris, Designs, N.Y.C., 1979—. Fund raiser UN Internat. Sch., 1962-71, editor parent's newsletter; mem. N.Y. Mayor's Adv. Council for Interior Furnishing and Design Industry, 1981—; adv. Dept. Cultural Affairs of N.Y.C., 1981—. Recipient 1st prize for publ. design Western Trade Editors, 1948. Mem. Am. Soc. Interior Designers, Internat. Soc. Artists, Am. Craft Council. Office: 40 W 72d St New York NY 10023

HARRIS, BARBARA, actress; b. Evanston, Ill., 1935; d. Oscar and Natalie (Densmoor) Harris; m. Paul Sills (div.). Appeared with Second City Co., Chgo., 1960-61, with Second City Co. in From the Second City, N.Y.C., 1961-62, Oh Dad, Poor Dad, Mama's Hung You in the Closet and I'm Feelin' So Sad, N.Y.C., 1962, Mother Courage and Her Children, N.Y.C., 1963, Dynamite Tonight (off-Broadway), On a Clear Day You Can See Forever, 1965, The Diary of Adam and Eve, The Lady or the Tiger?, Passionella, The Apple Tree, 1966, The Rise and Fall of the City of Mahagonny, 1970; appeared in films Oh Dad, Poor Dad, A Thousand Clowns, Who is Harry Kellerman and Why Is He Saying Those Terrible Things About Me?, 1971, Plaza Suite, 1971, The War Between the Men and the Women, 1972, Mixed Company, 1974, Nashville, 1975, Freaky Friday, 1977, Movie, Movie, 1978, The North Ave. Irregulars, 1979, The Seduction of Joe Tynan, 1979, Second-Hand Hearts, 1980; also TV appearances. Recipient N.Y. Drama Critics award for most promising new actress, Variety Poll, 1961, 62; Off-Broadway award Village Voice, 1962. Address: care Robinson & Assos Inc 132 S Rodeo Dr Beverly Hills CA 90212 *

HARRIS, BARBARA HULL (MRS. F. CHANDLER HARRIS), social agy. adminstr.; b. Los Angeles, Nov. 1, 1921; d. Hamilton and Marion (Eimers) Baird; student UCLA, 1939-41, 45-47; m. F. Chandler Harris, Aug. 10, 1946; children—Victoria, Randolph Boyd. Pres., Victoria Originals, 1955-62; partner J.B. Assos., cons., 1971-73; statewide dir. vols. Children's Home Soc. Calif., 1971-75. Pres., Silver Spoons vol. group Calif. Pediatric Center, 1958; Los Angeles County Heart Sunday chmn. Los Angeles County Heart Assn. (recipient Outstanding Service award 1965), 1965, bd. dirs., 1966-69; mem. exec. com. Hollywood Bowl Vols., 1966—, chmn. vols., 1971, 75; chmn. Coll. Alumni of Assistance League, 1962; mem. exec. com. Assistance League So. Calif., 1964-71, 72-80, pres., 1976-80; bd. dirs. Nat. Charity League, Los Angeles, 1965-69, 75, sec., 1967, 3d v.p., 1968; ways and means chmn., dir. Los Angeles Am. Horse Show, 1969; dir. Coronet Debutante Ball, 1968, ball bd. chmn., 1969-70, 75, mem. ball bd., 1969—; pres. Hollywood Bowl Patroness com., 1976; v.p. Irving Walker aux. Travelers Aid, 1976, 79; pres. So. Calif. alumni council Alpha Phi, 1961, fin. adviser to chpts. U. So. Calif., 1961-72, U. Calif. at Los Angeles, 1965-72; benefit chmn. Gold Shield, 1969, 1st v.p., 1970-72; chmn. Golden Thimble III Needlework Exhbn., Hosp. of Good Samaritan, 1975; bd. dirs. U. Calif. at Los Angeles Affiliates, 1976-78; pres. Jr. Philharmonic Com., 1981-82. Recipient Ivy award as outstanding Alpha Phi alumna So. Calif., 1969; outstanding alumni award for community service UCLA, 1978; Mannequin's Eve award, 1980. Home: 7774 Skyhill Dr Hollywood CA 90068

HARRIS, BARBARA IVEY, accountant; b. Dothan, Ala., Oct. 19, 1951; d. Willie and Hattie Bell (Barnes) Ivey; B.S., Fla. A&M U., 1973. Internal revenue agt. IRS, Fort Lauderdale, Fla., 1974; adminstrv. asst. Internat. Paper Co., Panama City, Fla., 1974-77; sr. adminstr. fin. services, 1977-78, cost analyst, 1978-79; staff acct. S.W. Forest Industries, Panama City, 1979—. Treas., Employees Mut. Benefit Assn., 1978—; active United Way, recipient Outstanding Service award, 1975. Ethel Vereen Meml. scholar, 1969, Union Carbide grantee, 1969. Mem. Nat. Assn. Female Execs., Nat. Notary Assn., Zeta Phi Beta. Democrat. Lutheran. Club: Order Eastern Star.

HARRIS, BERNICE STONE, home economist; b. Nashville, N.C., Jan. 7, 1928; d. Bernice Daniel and Mary Ruby (Mercer) Stone; B.S., E. Carolina U., 1949; student Atlantic Christian Coll., 1964, N.C. State U., 1965-66; m. Baxter Harris, Dec. 23, 1950 (dec.); children—Myra Harris Wright, Daniel Robert. Vocat. home econs. tchr., Wilson County, N.C., 1949-53; asst. case worker Dept. Public Welfare, Nash County, N.C., 1960-64; ext. home economist N.C. Agrl. Ext. Service, Louisburg, N.C., 1964—. Mem. N.C. Home Econs. Assn., Nat. Assn. Extension Home Economists (Disting. Service Assn. 1977), N.C. Assn. Extension Home Economists, Am. Home Econs. Assn. Southern Baptist. Home: Route 2 Box 153 Spring Hope NC 27882 Office: 307 E Nash St Louisburg NC 27549

HARRIS, BETH, journalist; b. Balt., Aug. 27; d. John J. and Pauline (Seligman) Mendes; m. Maurice Harris, Mar. 30, 1959. Writer, producer radio and TV, San Francisco and Los Angeles; advt. account exec., San Francisco; book reviewer Desert Sun, Palm Springs, Calif., 1977—. Program chmn. Friends of Library, Coll. of Desert. Mem. Nat. League Am. Pen Women, Palm Springs Women's Press Club (charter). Jewish. Address: PO Box 2569 Palm Springs CA 92263

HARRIS, BETTY CHAFFMAN, educator; b. Balt., May 2, 1928; d. David Henry and Ida Irene (Roberts) Chaffman; R.N., Columbia Union Coll., 1950; B.S. in Nursing, Incarnate Word Coll., 1969; M.S., U. Tex., 1971; postgrad. Ohio State U., 1974—; m. E. Vernon Harris, Sept. 24, 1950; children—Ellen, Dale, Carol, Sharon. Nursing supr. Harding Hosp., Worthington Ohio, 1960-66; instr. nursing Tex. Woman's U., Denton, 1971-73; instr. Ohio State U., Columbus, 1973—. Mem. adv. com. Marion Tech. Coll., Ohio, 1980—. Mem. Am. Nurses Assn., Ohio Nurses Assn., Assn. Seventh-day Adventist Nurses, Sigma Theta Tau, Phi Kappa Phi. Office: Ohio State U 1585 Neil Ave Columbus OH 43210

HARRIS, BETTY COX, counselor; b. Los Angeles, Nov. 15, 1910; d. Joseph Harris and Mary Belle (Holt) Cox; student Occidental Coll., 1928-29; B.A., U. So. Calif., 1932; m. Gibson Olver Harris, Aug. 3, 1940; 1 dau., Wendy Lynne Harris Replogle. Women's editor, gen. assignment reporter, ch. editor The Daily Report, Ontario, Calif., 1933-41; advt. columnist Pasadena Star News, 1955-59; ct. reporter, with woman's pages West Covina (Calif.) Daily Tribune, 1959-61; salesperson Calif. Dept. Real Estate, 1972—; instr. real estate Mira Costa Coll., Oceanside, Calif., 1979; peer counselor Oceanside Sr. Citizens, 1981—. Mem. Women in Communications (dir. 1954-69), Nat. Assn. Realtors (women's council 1974-76), Alpha Gamma Delta, Republican. Presbyterian. Author: With Courage Adequate, with Dignity Intact, 1971. Address: 6711 Camino del Prado Carlsbad CA 92008

HARRIS, BILENDA, public relations exec.; b. Louisville, Sept. 12, 1949; d. William James and Glenda (McMullin) H.; A.B. in Journalism, U. So. Calif., 1975; postgrad. Calif. State U., Los Angeles, 1981; 1 son, Brendan Bruce Werner. Parish vestry fellow, Sch. Theology, Claremont Colls., 1977; assoc. dir. research Republican Assocs. Research Library, Glendale, Calif., 1975-76; soc. reporter Santa Anita Park Race Track, Arcadia, Calif., 1978-80; communicator Clayton Mfg. Co., El Monte, Calif., 1979-81; asst. advt. mgr. Stoody Co., Industry Calif., 1981-82; press aide, field rep. to Calif. State Assemblyman from 41st Dist., 1982—; research assoc. Inst. Polit. Economy, Calif. State U., Los Angeles, 1980-82. Exec. adv. chpt. Jr. Achievement; bd. dirs. Arcadia (Calif.) chpt. ARC, Verdugo Hills High Sch. Cable TV Co., Tujunga, Calif., 1982—. Mem. Soc. Automotive Engrs. (affiliate), U. So. Calif. Alumni Assn. (life), Arcadia Republican Women, So. Calif. Iris Soc., Calif. Arboretum Found., Arcadia Tournament of Roses Assn., Sigma Delta Chi. Episcopalian. Office: 143 S Glendale Ave Suite 208 Glendale CA 91205

HARRIS, BRENDA (GLORIA) COZART, learning cons.; b. Phila., Aug. 24, 1941; d. Arlington Ronald and Inez E. (Jackson) Cozart; B.A., Howard U., 1963; M.A., Cath. U. Am., 1966; Ed.S., Trenton (N.J.) State Coll., 1979; m. John Wesley Harris, II, Aug. 10, 1974; children—John Cozart, Shawn Wesley, Brendan Aaron. Speech therapist D.C. Bd. Edn., 1965-66; speech pathologist and audiologist Hunterdon Med. Center, Flemington, N.J., 1966-67; tchr. deaf and aphasic children Montgomery County sch., Lansdale, Pa., 1967-71; learning cons. child study team

Camden (N.J.) Bd. Edn., 1971—; founder, dir. House of Mirrors and Faces, charm and awareness sch. for girls, Phila., 1967—, Inn of Beautiful Children, awareness program for toddlers, Phila., 1967—; founder More Opportunities for Mothers to Interact and Exchange Strategies, 1979. Organizer, dir. 1st Miss Black Am. Beauty Pageant, 1967. Mem. Am. Speech and Hearing Assn., N.J. Ednl. Assn., Camden Ednl. Assn., Howard U. Alumni Assn. Methodist. Office: Camden Bd Edn 3d and Walnut Sts Camden NJ 08103

HARRIS, CHERYL MONTGOMERY, air force officer; b. Phoenixville, Pa., Oct. 8, 1949; d. William Howard and Carol (Hecht) Montgomery; student Philipps U., Marburg, W.Ger., 1970-71; B.A., Muhlenberg Coll., 1972; M.S. in Organizational Behavior, SUNY, Binghamton, 1980; M.S. in Systems Mgmt., U. So. Calif., 1981; m. William T. Harris, Dec. 21, 1974. Commd. 2d lt. U.S. Air Force, 1972, advanced through grades to capt., 1976—, chief processing, Hancock Field, N.Y., 1973-74, chief quality force, 1974-76, chief personnel No. Communications Area, Griffiss AFB, N.Y., 1976-78, chief pub. affairs, 1978-79, chief, officer selection br. Directorate of Attaché Affairs, Ft. Belvior, Va., 1979-82; internat. polit.-mil. affairs officer, dep. chief of staff/plans Pacific Air Forces hdqrs., Hickam AFB, Hawaii, 1982—. Decorated Air Force Commendation medal, Meritorious Service medal with oak leaf cluster. Mem. Air Force Assn., Met. Opera Guild, Wolf Trap Assos., Smithsonian Assos., Mensa, Friends of Kennedy Center. Home: 1080 Kaumoku St Honolulu HI 96825 Office: HQ PACAF/XPND Hickam AFB HI 96853

HARRIS, CONNIE DENISE, data processing ofcl.; b. Birmingham, Ala., July 26, 1953; d. Johnnie Mack and Vivian (Redmond) H.; B.B.A. with honors in Acctg., Mich. State U., East Lansing, 1975; postgrad. in biology Roosevelt U., 1976—. Various acctg. intern positions, 1973-74; systems analyst, auditor Arthur Andersen & Co., Chgo., 1975-77; tech. rep. Boeing Computer Services Co., Chgo., 1977-78; systems analyst Tektronix Co., Chgo., 1979-80; VM/CMS coordinator Banker's Life & Casualty Co., Chgo., 1980-82; sr. programmer/analyst/project Leader Velsicol Chem. Co. div. N.W. Industries, Chgo., 1982—; founder, mgr. C&W Bldg. & Maintenance Co., 1978—; tchr. computer classes. Mem. Data Processing Mgmt. Assn., Am. Mgmt. Assn., Mich. State U. Alumni Assn., Mortar Board, Phi Gamma Nu, Beta Alpha Psi. Baptist. Author: Poetry by Me, 1975; inventor consumer durable good. Office: 341 E Ohio Chicago IL 60611

HARRIS, CONSTANCE MALMAR, chemist; b. Flushing, N.Y., Dec. 12, 1937; d. Howard Burgess and Mary Calvin (McKnight) Malmar; B.S., Duke U., 1958, Ph.D., 1965; m. Thomas M. Harris, June 7, 1958; children—Mary Elizabeth, Jennifer Lynn. Research assoc. Vanderbilt U., Nashville, 1965-79, research asst. prof. chemistry, 1979—. Mem. Phi Beta Kappa, Sigma Xi. Contbr. articles to profl. jours. Home: 1706 Graybar Ln Nashville TN 37215 Office: Dept Chemistry Vanderbilt U Nashville TN 37235

HARRIS, DENISE KETORIA, chem. engr.; b. Cleve., Nov. 6, 1951; d. Edward N. and Cora (Parker) H.; B.A. in Biology (Swift scholar), U. Chgo., 1974; cert. mgmt., Case-Western Res. U., 1976. Jr. lab. technician, then lab. technician TRW, Inc., Cleve., 1974-82, chem. engr., 1982—. Treas. choir Greater Abyssinia Baptist Ch., Cleve., 1980-82. Mem. Nat. Assn. Female Execs. Democrat. Clubs: Toastmasters, Toastmistress. Home: 10321 North Blvd Cleveland OH 44108

HARRIS, DIANA KOFFMAN, sociologist; b. Memphis, Aug. 11, 1929; d. David Nathan and Helen Ethel (Rotter) Koffman; student U. Miami, 1947-48; B.S., U. Wis., 1951; postgrad. Tulane U., New Orleans, 1951-52; M.A., U. Tenn., 1967; postgrad. U. Oxford (Eng.), 1968-69; m. Lawrence A. Harris, June 24, 1951; children—Marla, Jennifer. Advt. and sales promotion mgr. Wallace Johnston Distbg. Co., Memphis, 1952-54; welfare worker Tenn. Dept. Public Welfare, Knoxville, 1954-56; instr. sociology Maryville (Tenn.) Coll., 1972-75; instr. sociology Fort Sanders Sch. Nursing, Knoxville, 1971-78; instr. sociology U. Tenn., Knoxville, 1967—. Chmn. U. Tenn. Council on Aging, 1979—; organizer Knoxville chpt. Gray Panthers, 1978; mem. Gov's. Task Force on Preretirement Programs for State Employers, 1973; mem. White House Conf. on Aging, 1981; bd. mem. Knoxville-Knox County Council on Aging, 1976, Sr. Citizens Info. and Referral, 1979, Sr. Citizens Home-Aide Service, 1977; del. E. Tenn. Council on Aging, 1977. Recipient Meritorious award Nat. U. Continuing Edn. Assn., 1982. Mem. Am. Sociol. Assn., AAAS, Gerontol. Soc. Am., Popular Culture Assn., So. Sociol. Soc., So. Gerontol. Soc., N. Central Sociol. Assn. Clubs: London Competitor's; Nat. Contest Assn.; Knoxville Kontestars. Author: Readings in Social Gerontology, 1975; (with Cole) The Elderly in America, 1977, The Sociology of Aging, 1980; contbr. articles in field to profl. jours. Home: 4505 Landon Dr Knoxville TN 37921 Office: Dept Sociology U Tenn Knoxville TN 37916

HARRIS, DIANE CAROL, optical mfg. co. exec.; b. Rockville Centre, N.Y., Dec. 25, 1942; d. Daniel Christopher and Laura Louise (Schmitt) Quigley; B.A. cum laude, Cath. U. Am., 1964; M.S., Rensselaer Poly. Inst., Troy, N.Y., 1967; m. Wayne Manley Harris, Sept. 30, 1978. Analytical chemist Nat. Heart Inst., NIH, Bethesda, Md., 1964-65; with Bausch & Lomb, Inc., Rochester, N.Y., 1967—, line mgr. analytical products, 1976-77, v.p. planning and bus. devel. Soflens div., 1977-80, corp. dir. planning, 1980-81, v.p. corp. devel., 1981—. Pres., Rochester Against Intoxicated Driving, 1979—; bd. dirs. Nat. Council on Alcoholism, Rochester Area. Recipient Disting. Citizens award Monroe County, 1979; Nat. Merit scholar, 1960; N.Y. State Regents scholar, 1960; NSF grantee, 1963. Mem. Am. Chem. Soc., Am. Mgmt. Assn., Planning Execs. Inst., Newcomen Soc. N.Am., I-Cube Investment Club, Phi Beta Kappa, Sigma Xi, Delta Epsilon Sigma, Kappa Beta Gamma. Author articles, papers in field. Home: 123 Blue Ridge Rd Penfield NY 14526 Office: Bausch & Lomb Inc 1 Lincoln First Sq Rochester NY 14601

HARRIS, DOLORES MARGARET, ednl. adminstr.; b. Camden, N.J., Aug. 5, 1930; d. Roland H. and Frances Anna (Gatewood) Ellis; B.S., Glassboro State Coll., 1959, M.A., 1966; postgrad. Rutgers State U., 1973—; children—Morris, Sheila, Gregory. Tchr. adminstr. Glassboro Bd. Edn., N.J., 1959-70; Head Start dir. Glassboro Scope Center, summer 1969, 70; asso. dir. Nat. Tng. Inst., Jersey City State Coll., summer 1971; dir. continuing edn. Glassboro State Coll., 1974—; adult edn. evaluator Millville (N.J.) Public Schs., 1977—; nat. cons. reading and adult edn., 1968—; civil service examiner N.Y. State, 1976—; lectr. and organizer workshops in adult basic edn., 1968—. N.J. del. to Houston Conf., Internat. Women's Year, 1977; mem. N.J. Task Force on Thorough and Efficient Edn., 1977-78; vice chairperson N.J. Coalition of Univ. and Coll. Women, 1978-79; bd. dirs. Glassboro Borough Glass Mus., 1979—, Gloucester County United Way, 1977—; trustee Glassboro Child Devel. Center, 1974-77. Recipient Glassboro State Coll. Disting. Alumnus award, 1971; award Girl Scouts U.S., 1979, others. Mem. Assn. for Continuing Higher Edn., Assn. Adult Edn. U.S. (dir. 1973-76, N.J. del. 1970-79), Assn. Adult Edn. N.J. (pres. 1973-74), Nat. Higher Edn. Assn., Assn. N.J. Coll. and Univ. Profs., N.J. Assn. Community Edn., Gerontol. Assn. N.J., AAUW, Assn. N.J. State Coll. Faculty, N.J. State Fedn. Colored Women's Clubs (pres. 1974-79, trustee 1979—, Outstanding Service award 1973), Nat. Assn. Colored Women's Clubs, Phi Delta Kappa, Delta Kappa Gamma. Baptist. Editor For Adults Only newsletter, 1970-74. Office: Adult Continuing Edn Glassboro State College Glassboro NJ 08028

HARRIS, DONA LINDQUIST, educator; b. Blackfoot, Idaho, Jan. 27, 1945; d. Elvin Alexander and Irene (Ball) Lindquist; B.A. cum laude in Polit. Sci., U. Utah, 1967, M.A. in Ednl. Psychology, 1973, Ph.D. in Ednl. Psychology, 1975; m. E. Kent Harris, Aug. 24, 1968; children—Ashley Dawn, Ryan Kent. Congressional intern. U.S. Ho. of Reps., summers 1965, 66, 67; asso. for evaluation, sect. evaluation and methods devel. Intermountain Regional Med. Program, Salt Lake City, 1969-72, dir. sect., 1972-73; project dir. primary care preceptorship program dept. family and community medicine U. Utah, 1973-75, asst. prof. family and community medicine, project dir. student programs in family medicine Sch. Medicine, 1975—, women's faculty liaison officer to Am. Assn. Med. Colls., 1982—. Mem. Soc. Tchrs. Family Medicine, Assn. Am. Med. Colls., Assn. Behavioral Scis. and Med. Edn. Research in evaluation edn., personality types of med. students, residents and faculty, determinants of career selections; editor edn. column. Family Medicine, 1981—. Home: 2200 S 18th E Salt Lake City UT 84106 Office: IC 303 Med Center 50 N Medical Dr Salt Lake City UT 84132

HARRIS, DORIS OTT, nurse; b. Clarksburg, W.Va., July 1, 1944; d. Nelson Tate and June (Balogh) Ott; R.N., Mather Sch. Nursing, 1965; B.S.N. with honors, Northwestern State U., 1969; M.S. in Nursing, U. Ala., 1970; m. Eugene B. Harris, Jan. 6, 1973; children—Kathleen Leigh, Lesley Jeanne. Instr., Mather Sch. Nursing, New Orleans, 1968-69; asso. prof. nursing William Carey Coll., Hattiesburg, Miss., 1970-74; dir. inservice edn. Charity Hosp., New Orleans, 1974-75; asst. prof. nursing Tex. Women's U., Houston, 1975-80; instr. nursing North Harris County Jr. Coll., Houston, 1981—; dir. nurse recruitment Meml. City Gen. Hosp., Houston, 1981—. Active Girl Scouts U.S.A., 1979-80; vol. Drug Abuse Clinic, New Orleans, 1970-71. Served to capt. Miss. Air N.G., 1969-74. Nurse Tng. act grantee, 1967-68, 69-70. Mem. Am. Nurses Assn., Tex. Nurses Assn., Nat. Nurse Recruiters Assn., Tex. Assn. Nurse Recruiters, Houston Area Nurse Recruiters Assn., Sigma Theta Tau, Phi Kappa Phi. Republican. Baptist. Club: Houston Yacht. Contbr. articles to prof. jours. Home: 13811 Taylorcrest St Houston TX 77079 Office: 920 Frostwood St Houston TX 77024

HARRIS, DOROTHY LIPP, educator; b. Phila., Mar. 15, 1922; d. Samuel Larue and Pamela (Clarke) Lipp; B.S. in Social Scis./Edn., U. Pa., M.S., 1945; Ph.D. in Psychology, Northwestern U., 1952; m. Philip R. Harris, July 3, 1965. Communications specialist pub. relations, dir. Main Chance Camp, Elizabeth Arden Corp., Chgo., 1947-48; instr. Northwestern U., Evanston, Ill., 1951, U. Utah, Salt Lake City, 1945-47; dean women, assoc. prof. psychology Wis. State U., River Falls, 1952-54, U. N.D., Grand Forks, 1954-59; dean women, spl. asst. v.p. Pa. State U., State College, 1959-70; prof., assoc. dean U.S. Internat. U., San Diego, 1971—; mgmt. cons., v.p. Harris Internat., Ltd., La Jolla, Calif., 1971—. UNESCO del. Geneva, 1964, Israel, 1961, Paris, 1963. Northwestern U. Carnegie fellow in behavioral scis. Mem. Acad. Mgmt., Am. Personnel and Guidance Assn., AAUW, Alpha Lambda Delta, Mortar Bd., Pi Lambda Theta. Republican. Club: LaJolla Beach and Tennis. Author: (with P. R. Harris) Improving Management Communication Skills, 1978, Leadership Effectiveness with People, 1978; A Day to Day Key to Successful Employee Negotiations, 1978. Home: 2702 Costebelle Dr LaJolla CA 92037 Office: Sch of Business and Mgmt United States International Univ 10455 Pomerado Rd San Diego CA 92131

HARRIS, ELEANOR, educator; b. Ill., July 7; A.B., U. Chgo., also A.M.; M.Div., Chgo. Cluster Theol. Schs., 1975; D.Min., 1978; Ph.D. in Religion, N.Y. U., 1980. Mem. faculty U. Ill., Chgo., asst. prof. English, 1970—; part-time instr. Ind. U. N.W.; part-time asst. prof. Chgo. City Coll. Named Swedish Lucia for Chgo., 1970; recipient Scripture Reading award Am. Bible Soc., 1975. Mem. Am. Acad. Religion, Soc. Bibl. Lit., Chgo. Soc. Bibl. Research, Religious Edn. Assn., Internat. Assn. Women Ministers, MLA, Midwest MLA, Conf. Christianity and Lit., Am. Scandinavian Found., Mensa. Contbr. articles and poetry to profl. jours. Office: Dept English Box 4348 Univ Ill Chgo Chicago IL 60680

HARRIS, EMMYLOU, singer, rec. artist; b. Birmingham, Ala., 1949. Country music performer, singer; assisted Gram Parsons on albums GP and Grievous Angels, toured with him and Fallen Angel Band; performed across Europe and U.S.; rec. artist Reprise Records; appeared in rock documentary The Last Waltz, 1978; albums include: Pieces of the Sky, 1975, Elite Hotel, 1976, Luxury Liner, 1977, Quarter Moon in a Ten-Cent Town. Winner Grammy award, 1976, 77. Office: care C&R Warren 420 N Orange Dr Los Angeles CA 90036 *

HARRIS, FLORENCE CATHERINE, social worker; b. Phila., Dec. 28, 1941; d. Wilber Fiske and Melda Elizabeth (Beitzel) H.; B.S., High Point (N.C.) Coll., 1963; M.S.W., U. Md., 1972. Social work asst. Calvert County (Md.) Dept. Social Services, Prince Frederick, 1964-69; social work asst. Prince George's County (Md.) Dept. Social Service, Hyattsville, 1969-71; social worker Md. Children's Aid and Family Service, Towson, Md., 1972-80, Crownsville (Md.) Hosp. Center, 1980—. Cons., Contact Balt., 1974—; counselor Family Life Center, Columbia, Md., 1974—; mem. citizens adv. council N.W. Mental Health Balt. County, 1977-78; sec. bd. dirs. Christian Counseling Assos., Burtonsville, Md., 1978—; mem. Faith at Work Team, Columbia, 1973-75, Calvert County Commn. on Aging, 1967-68, Evang. Women's Caucas, Washington, 1976—, N.W. Coalition Social Agys., Balt. County, 1978; cons. Nursing Home Ministry Evang. Presbyn. Ch., Annapolis, Md., 1978. Lic. cert. social worker, Md. Mem. Nat. Assn. Social Workers, Register Clin. Social Workers, Assn. Certified Social Workers, Md. Conf. Social Concern. Democrat. Presbyterian. Home: 8870H Spiral Cut Columbia MD 21045 Office: Meyer Bldg Crownsville Hosp Center Crownsville MD 21032

HARRIS, FRANCES ALVORD (MRS. HUGH W. HARRIS), cons., ret. radio-TV broadcaster; b. Detroit, Apr. 19, 1909; d. William Roy and Edith (Vosburgh) Alvord; A.B., Grinnell Coll., 1929; L.H.D. (hon.), Ferris State Coll., 1980; m. Hugh William Harris, Sept. 24, 1932; children—Patricia Anne (Mrs. Floyd A. Metz), Hugh William, Robert Alvord. With advt. dept. Himelhoch Bros. & Co., Detroit, 1929-31; broadcaster as Julia Hayes, Robert P. Gust Co., 1931-34; tng. and personnel dept. Ernst Kern Co., 1935-36; broadcaster as Nancy Dixon, Young & Rubicam, Inc., 1939-42; women's editor Sta. WWJ, Detroit, 1943-64, Sta. WWJ-TV, 1947-64, spl. features coordinator Sta. WWJ-TV-AM-FM, 1964-74; prin. Fran Harris & Assocs., cons. to social agys., instns., orgns., Detroit, 1974—; pres., chief exec. officer I.C. Harris & Co., Detroit. Mem. exec. bd. Wayne County chpt. Mich. Soc. for Mental Health, 1953-63; chmn. Mental Health Week, 1958-59; mem. Wayne County Commn. on Aging, 1975—, chmn., 1976-77; publicity com. YWCA, 1945, 2d v.p., 1963; mem. publicity com. Tri-County League for Nursing, 1956-61; publicity chmn. Met. Detroit YWCA Bd. Dirs., 1961-66, exec. com., 1962-67; campaign dist. chmn. United Found., 1959, unit chmn., 1960-61, chmn. speakers bur., 1974; exec. bd. United Found. Women's Orgn., 1962-64; governing bd. United Community Services Women's Com., 1961-66; bd. dirs. United Community Services, 1964-67; bd. dirs. Homemaker Service Met. Detroit, pres., 1969-70; bd. dirs. Vis. Nurse Assn., pres., 1974-76; bd. dirs. Camp Fire Girls of Detroit, mem. nat. council, 1967-72, mem. nat. bd., exec. com., 1970-72, pres., 1978-80; bd. dirs. Well Being Service Aging, 1969-74, Sr. Center, 1971-76, Friends Detroit Pub. library, 1972-77, Friends Children's Mus., 1972-74; trustee Detroit Com. Alcoholism, 1961-64; mem. Mayor's Com. for Freedom Festival, 1959, chmn. women's activities, 1965; mem. Mayor's Com. for UN Week, 1959; mem. Gov.'s Commn. Status of Women, 1962-69, Mich. State Women's Commn., 1969-77; mem. nat. council Homemaker Service, 1970-73; mem. adv. com. to trustees Grinnell Coll.; mem. bd. control Ferris State Coll., 1968-78; mem. def. adv. com. Women in the Services, 1970-73, chmn., 1973; program chmn. Met. Detroit YMCA, 1973-75; sec.-treas. Mich. Assn. Governing Bds. State Colls. and Univs., 1975, v.p., 1976-77, pres., 1977-78. Recipient Grinnell Coll. Alumni award, 1959, Mental Health Soc. Mich. award, 1958, Theta Sigma Phi Headliner award for Mich., 1951, nat., 1952; Women's Advt. Club of Detroit Civic award, 1957; named Advt. Woman of Yr., Detroit, 1958, 73, Soroptimist Woman of Yr., 1965; Fran Harris Day in her honor, Detroit, 1960; Vol. State of Mich., 1975; Heart of Gold award, 1976. Mem. Am. Women in Radio and TV (pres. Detroit chpt. 1957-58, gen. chmn. nat. conv. 1966, Outstanding Community Service award 1972), Women's Advt. Club of Detroit (pres. 1959-60, mem. bd. 1974-77), UN Assn. U.S.A. (dir. Detroit chpt. 1962-65, Mich. div. bd. 1963-65), Advt. Fedn. (nat. v.p. women's activities 1964-67), Nat. Fedn. Press Women (hon.), Women in Communications (pres. Detroit 1950-51; del. to Asian-Am. Women in Broadcasting Conf. 1966, nat. 1st v.p. 1968-71, nat. pres. 1971-73, chmn. Communications Conf. Ams., 1968, del. III World Congress Women Journalists 1973), Pi Epsilon Delta. Episcopalian (communications com. local congregation and Diocese of Mich. 1965-66). Club: Women's Econ. (charter mem.; dir. 1975—, membership chmn. 1975, program chmn. 1976, public relations co-chmn. 1977, treas. 1978, sec. 1979, 1st v.p. 1980, pres. 1981-82; charter) (Detroit). Author, editor: Focus: Michigan Women, 1977. Home: 8120 E Jefferson Detroit MI 48214 Office: 1237-1245 First National Bldg Detroit MI 48226

HARRIS, GEORGIA, antiques dealer; b. Edna, Tex., Feb. 8, 1920; d. Lee Thomas and Lillie delilah (Walker) Jacobs; m. Volum Lawrence Harris, Mar. 16, 1938 (dec.); children—Patricia, Martha, Janice, Kathryn. Owner, operator antiques bus., Schulenburg, Tex., 1945-50, Weathervane Antiques, Columbus, Tex., 1950—; mgr. dir. Meml. City Antiques Show, Houston, 1972, Sharpstown Antiques, Houston, 1970-78, Magnolia Antiques Show, Columbus, 1964-68, LaGrange (Tex.) Fair Show, 1969-73; mgr. coordinator Columbus Antiques Show, benefit Am. Legion, 1975-80, Brenham (Tex.) Antiques Show, benefit Heritage Soc., 1979-82, Houston Antiques Show, benefit UN, 1981-82. Baptist. Home and Office: Hwy 90 W Box 187 Columbus TX 78934

HARRIS, GLORIA G., psychologist; b. Chgo., Dec. 10, 1938; d. Theodore G. and Claire (Sirmay) Greenfield; M.S.W., Simmons Sch. Social Work, Boston, 1962; Ph.D., U. Wash., 1972; m. Jay Howard Harris, Aug. 4, 1963; children—Cameron, Merrill. Clin. instr. U. Wash. Med. Sch., 1973-74; adj. prof. Am. U., 1974-76; part-time pvt. practice psychology, 1976—; dir. Behavioral Designs, Washington, 1976—. Mem. Am. Psychol. Assn., Am. Assn. Advancement of Behavior Therapy, Phi Beta Kappa. Co-author (with S. Osborn): Assertive Training for Women, 1975. Editor: The Group Treatment of Human Problems, 1977. Home: 6257 Madra Ave San Diego CA 92120

HARRIS, HELEN CARROLL, univ. ofcl.; b. Weleetka, Okla., July 15, 1938; d. Ambrose and Deborah (Newson) Carroll; student Creighton U., 1957-58, U. Nebr., 1969-76; m. Henry L. Harris, May 19, 1956; children—Alex Maurice, Shaun Rene. Personnel specialist Father Flanagans Boys Home, Boys Town, Nebr., 1976; personnel supr. Quaker Oats Co., Omaha, 1976-77; employment coordinator/nurse recruiter South Bay Hosp., Redondo Beach, Calif., 1977-80; personnel coordinator admissions and fin. aid U. So. Calif., Los Angeles, 1980—. Mem. Am. Soc. for Personnel Adminstrn., Women In Mgmt., Zeta Phi Beta. Home: 6406 Victoria Ave Los Angeles CA 90043 Office: U So Calif 666 Childsway Los Angeles CA 90007

HARRIS, ILENE BARMASH, educator; b. Chgo., Jan. 21, 1945; d. Charles and Shirley (Garfinkel) Barmash; B.A., U. Chgo., 1965, M.A. (Univ. fellow, Ford Found. fellow), 1972, Ph.D., 1979; m. Morton Edward Harris, July 9, 1967. Tchr. social studies Chgo. Public Schs., 1966-68; social studies test materials writer Sci. Research Assos., Chgo., 1969-73; instr. Rutgers U., New Brunswick, N.J., 1971, U. Chgo., 1973; research fellow U. Minn. Med. Sch., Mpls., 1973-78, research asso., 1978—; evaluation cons. Bush Found., St. Paul; ednl. cons. Nat. Endowment for Humanities faculty devel. cons. VA North Central Regional Med. Edn. Center; continuing med. edn. cons. Minn. Med. Assn.; curriculum cons. Southwestern Coop. Ednl. Lab. mem. Am. Ednl. Research Assn., Am. Assn. Med. Colls., Nat. Soc. Study Edn., Assn. Supervision and Curriculum Devel., Evaluation Research Soc. Mem. editorial bd. Sch. Rev. 1969-71; contbr. articles to profl. jours. Home: 4375 Coolidge Ave S Minneapolis MN 55424 Office: 420 Deleware St SE Minneapolis MN 55455

HARRIS, IMOGENE HAIRRELL, lawyer; b. Dunbar, Okla., Jan. 9, 1930; d. J.C. and Janie (Watkins) Hairrell; LL.B., J.D., U. Tulsa, 1959; 1 son, John Jason Hairrell-Harris. Admitted to Okla. bar, 1959; partner firm Howard, Larkin & Harris, 1960-66; atty. Sun Oil Co., 1966-70; asst. prof. law U. Tulsa, 1970-73; asst. city atty. City of Tulsa, 1973—; judge alt. City of Broken Arrow (Okla.). Sec. Met. Tulsa Transit Authority; bd. dirs. Leadership Tulsa; v.p. Citizens for Mass Transit Coalition. Mem. Am., Okla., Tulsa County bar assns., Am. Public Transit Assn. (legal com.), Bus. and Profl. Women, Okla. Mcpl. Lawyers. Democrat. Unitarian. Clubs: Tulsa Ski, Photography. Editor The Tulsa Lawyer, 1969-72. Contbr. articles to Transit Law Review. Home: 3324 E 76th St Tulsa OK 74135 Office: City Hall 200 Civic Center Room 1012 Tulsa OK 74103

HARRIS, IMOGENE MCDANIEL, publisher, editor; b. Gary, Ind., Nov. 20, 1931; d. Lohney L. and Geneva (Scott) McDaniel; B.S., Ind. U., 1959; postgrad. Ind. U., 1960, Purdue U., 1963, Valparaiso U., 1970; m. James T. Harris, Sept. 1, 1950; children—Temple-Jene Harris Fleming, Gaylyn. With Harris Printing Co., Gary, 1950-80, co-owner, 1956-80; sec.-treas. INFO, Inc., Gary, 1963-80, pres., 1980—; tchr., elem. grades Gary Public Schs., 1959-65, librarian, 1965-71; exec. editor Gary INFO Newspaper, 1971; dir. Gary Communications Group, Gt. Lakes Broadcasting. Bd. dirs. Urban League N.W. Ind.; chmn. Gary Commn. for Women, 1981—. Recipient Outstanding Woman award NAACP, 1981, Media award Gary NAACP, 1978. Mem. Nat. Newspaper Publishers Assn., Black Media Inc (regional coordinator), Lake County Assn. Black Communicators (pres. 1979—), NAACP (life), Delta Sigma Theta. Methodist. Home: 1178 Hovey St Gary IN 46406 Office: 1953 Broadway Gary IN 46407

HARRIS, JEAN LOUISE, physician; b. Richmond, Va., Nov. 24, 1931; d. Vernon Joseph and Jean Louise (Pace) Harris; B.S., Va. Union U., 1951; M.D., Med. Coll., Va., 1955; D.Sc. (hon.), U. Richmond, 1981; m. Leslie John Ellis, Sept. 24, 1955; children—Karin Denise, Pamela Diane, Cynthia Suzanne. Exec. dir. Nat. Med. Assocs. Found., Washington, 1969-72; prof. family practice and dir. Center for Community Health Med. Coll. Va., Richmond, 1973-78; sec. human resources Commonwealth of Va., Richmond, 1978-82; v.p. state mktg. programs Control Data Corp., Mpls., 1982—; mem. President's Pvt. Sector Initiatives Task Force; mem. recombinant DNA com. NIH/HEW; mem. adv. bd. Women's Bank, Richmond; chmn. sickle cell adv. bd. NIH/HEW, 1978-79. Named Woman of Yr., Richmond YMCA, 1980; recipient Disting. Service award Nat. Govts. Assn., 1981. Mem. Am. Soc. Pub. Adminstrs., Richmond Med. Soc., Richmond Acad. Medicine, So. Inst. Human Resources (pres. 1980-81), Am. Pub. Health Assn. (chmn. social policy bd. 1976-77), Continental Socs., Delta Sigma Theta. Episcopalian. Clubs: Links Inc., Jack'n Jill. Home: 3318 Chatham St Richmond VA 23227 Office: 8100 34th Ave S Minneapolis MN 55440

HARRIS, JEAN NOTON, music educator; b. Monroe, Wis., Feb. 21, 1934; d. Albert Henry and Eunice Elizabeth (Edgerton) Noton; B.A., Monmouth (Ill.) Coll., 1955; M.S., U. Ill., 1975, adminstrv. cert., 1980; m. Laurence G. Landers, June 7, 1955; children—Theodore Scott, Thomas Warren, Philip John; m. Edward R. Harris, Nov. 27, 1981. Tchr. music schs. in Ill. and Fla., 1955-76; tchr. music Dist. 54, Schaumburg, Ill., from 1976; now tchr. Anne Fox Sch., Hanover Park IL 60103 Named Outstanding Young Woman of Yr., Jaycee Wives, St. Charles, Mo., 1968. Mem. Music Educators Nat. Conf., Ill. Music Educators Assn., NEA (life), Am. Choral Dirs. Assn., U. Ill. Alumni Assn. (life), Mortar Bd., Monsa. Mem. United Ch. Christ. Home: 914 Roxbury Ln Schaumburg IL 60194

HARRIS, JESSIE G. (MRS. HUBERT LAMAR HARRIS), former ednl. adminstr.; b. Athens, Ga., May 12, 1909; d. Wiley Jackson and Dora (Hilley) Ginn; B.B.A., U. Ga., 1956; A.B., Ga. State U., 1960; m. Hubert Lamar Harris, Nov. 25, 1930; children—Mary Ann (Mrs. William Holley), Hubert Lamar, Dorothy (Mrs. Ronald Zazworksy), Martha Susan (Mrs. R. R. McCue, Jr.). Various secretarial positions, ins. and law offices, 1923-30; sec. div. gen. extension U. Ga., 1930-35, asst. dir. div. gen. extension, 1935-47; assisted with compilation survey Univ. System Ga., Atlanta, 1949-50, adminstrv. asst. to regents, 1951-63, asst. exec. sec., 1963-67, asso. exec. sec., 1967-72, asst. vice chancellor personnel, 1972-74, emeritus, 1974—. Asst. exec. dir. Ga. Scholarship Commn., 1965-66; asso. exec. sec. Ga. Med. Edn. Bd., 1952-72. Mem. AAUW (chmn. study group 1964-66, treas. 1972, 73), Atlanta Hist. Assn., So. Hist. Soc., Sandy Springs Arts and Heritage Soc., Crimson Key Honor Soc., Mortar Bd., Phi Chi Theta, Delta Mu Delta, Psi Chi. Club: Atlanta Writers. Home: 765 Douglas Rd NE Atlanta GA 30342

HARRIS, JULIE, actress; b. Grosse Pointe Park, Mich., Dec. 2, 1925; d. William Pickett and Elsie (Smith) H.; student Perry Mansfield Theatre Work Shop, 1941-43, Yale Drama Sch., 1945; m. Jay I. Julien, Aug. 12, 1946; m. 2d, Manning Gurian, Oct. 21, 1954; 1 son, Peter; m. 3d, Erwin Carroll. Appeared in plays Sundown Beach, 1948; The Young and Fair, 1948-49; Magnolia Alley, 1949; Montserrat, 1949; The Member of the Wedding, 1950-51; I Am a Camera, 1951-52, film, 1956; The Lark, 1956; Little Moon of Alban, 1960; A Shot in the Dark, 1961; Marathon 33, 1964; Ready When You Are, C.B., 1964; Break a Leg, 1979; tour, Broadway, The Warm Peninsula; appeared in Skyscraper, 1965, Harper, 1966, And Miss Reardon Drinks A Little, 1971, Voices, 1972, The Last of Mrs. Lincoln, 1973, In Praise of Love, 1974, The Belle of Amherst, 1976; motion pictures Poacher's Daughter, 1960, The Haunting, The Moving Target, Voyage of the Damned, 1976, The Bell Jar, 1979; TV movie The Gift, 1979. Recipient Antoinette Perry award for East of Eden, 1956, best actress in Forty Carats, 1969, for The Last of Mrs. Lincoln, 1973; Grammy award for The Belle of Amherst, 1977. Address: care William Morris Agy 1350 Ave of Americas New York NY 10019 *

HARRIS, JUNE STARKEY, electronics co. exec.; b. Wheeling, W.Va., Nov. 22, 1932; d. Bernard Theodore and Ruth Elizabeth (Bonene) Starkey; student Coll. Commerce, Wheeling, 1950-52; m. Jack William Harris, Nov. 7, 1953; 1 son, Thomas Crown. Various secretarial and sales positions, 1950-59; v.p. sales and mktg. Savoy Electronics, Inc., Ft. Lauderdale, Fla., 1959—. Mem. Radio Club Am., Homeowners Assn., Kennelworth. Democrat. Roman Catholic. Clubs: Zonta, Flying Orchids. Home: 1455 NW 92d Way PO Box 9108 Coral Springs FL 33065 Office: 1175 NW 24th St Fort Lauderdale FL 33305

HARRIS, KAREN KOSTOCK, corp. exec.; b. Chgo., Sept. 11, 1942; d. Kenneth P. and Elsie A. (Raffl) K.; student Mundelein Coll., Chgo., 1979—; m. Roy Lawrence Harris, Feb. 14, 1981. Clk. loan dept. Evanston Fed. Savs. and Loan (Ill.), 1960-63, mgr. collection dept., 1963-65; credit adminstr. Packaging Corp. Am., Evanston, 1965-72, adminstrv. asst. to v.p., 1972-74; credit mgr. trainee Am. Hosp. Supply Corp., 1974-75; cash mgr., asst. to treas. Pullman Standard, Chgo., 1975-76; nat. credit adminstr. Gen. Binding Corp., Northbrook, Ill., 1976-77; treas. C.H. Hanson Co., Chgo., 1977-79, sec.-treas., dir., 1980—; owner Stock Enterprises, Highland Park, Ill., 1980—; partner Harris Enterprises, 1981—; pres. Sirrah Enterprises, Inc., 1982—. Mem. adv. bd. alcoholism program Grant Hosp., Chgo., 1980; founder Weekend Coll. Scholarship Fund, Mundelein Coll., 1981, charter mem. Mundelein Coll. Women's Network. Recipient Cert. of Merit, Chgo. Assn. Commerce and Industry and Industry Youth Motivation Program, 1981. Republican. Club: Swedish (sec., dir. 1981—) (Chgo.). Office: 303 W Erie St Chicago IL 60610

HARRIS, KATHERINE ANNE, advt. exec.; b. Denison, Tex., Aug. 22, 1949; d. J. W. and Mary Jane (Adams) H.; B.A. with honors, Austin Coll., Sherman, Tex., 1969; postgrad. philosophy So. Ill. U., Edwardsville, 1969-70; 1 son by former marriage, Kevin Jeffrey McCarty. Freelance writer Dallas, 1970-73; writer public relations dept. Southland Corp., Dallas, 1974; dir. pub. relations, copywriter, account exec. Arrington Art & Advt., Albuquerque, 1975-77; owner, creative dir. Katherine Harris Communications, Albuquerque, 1977—; co-founder, corp. v.p., treas. Target Mktg., Inc., 1980—; corp. sec., dir. Spectra Med, Inc., 1980—. Bd. dirs. Classics Theatre Co., 1975-76; active Albuquerque Civic Beautification Com., Am. Cancer Soc., Meals on Wheels. Nat. Merit scholar, 1966-69; Firestone scholar, 1966-69. Mem. N.Mex. Advt. Fedn. (copywriting awards 1975-80, dir. 1980—), Albuquerque Press Club. Home: 9609-D El Corte Cajon NE Albuquerque NM 87111 Office: PO Box 26645 Albuquerque NM 87125

HARRIS, LALINE OWENS, sch. prin.; b. Atlanta, Mar. 15, 1924; d. Henry Preston and Leona Vermelle (Miles) Owens; B.S., Miner Tchrs. Coll., 1945; M.A., N.Y. U., 1949, Ed.D., 1956; m. De Long Harris, Dec. 22, 1956. Tchr. mathematics, bus. Shaw Jr. High Sch., Washington, 1947-63; counselor Garnet-Patterson Jr. High Sch., Washington, 1963-64; counselor C. Melvin Sharpe Health Sch., Washington, 1964-68; asst. prin. Woodson Jr. High Sch., Washington, 1968-75, prin., 1975—; organizer, supr. Parent-Aide Program, Summer Inst. for Children with Learning Disabilities, 1967. Recipient Founders Day award, N.Y. U., 1957; NCCJ fellow, 1958; Gen. Electric fellow, 1966; Agnes Myer fellow, 1968. Mem. Nat. Assn. Sec. Sch. Prins., Council of Sch. Officers, Am. Personnel and Guidance Assn., Am. Soc. African Culture, Kappa Delta Pi, Alpha Kappa Alpha. Democrat. Methodist. Clubs: Met. Women's Dem. (pres. 1968-70), Nat. Women's Dem., Order Eastern Star, Daus. of Isis, Order of Golden Circle, Club 20 (chmn. 1960-62), Nat. Barristers' Wives, D.C. Barristers Wives (pres. 1963-65). Home: 1206 Rhode Island Ave NE Washington DC 20018 Office: 4101 Minnesota Ave NE Washington DC 20019

HARRIS, LOUISE, author; b. Warwick, R.I., Sept. 28, 1903; d. Samuel P. and Faustine M. (Borden) Harris; A.B., Brown U., 1926; pvt. study organ with T. Tertius Noble, N.Y., 1938-42. Sec., Samuel P. Harris, Inc., 1928-42; tchr. piano and organ, ch. organist, recitalist, Providence, 1928-46. Mem. corp. R.I. Hosp. Fellow Internat. Biog. Assn. (life patron); mem. Nat. Archives (asso.), Am. Biog. Inst. (life patron), Am. Guild Organists, Hymn Soc. Am., Audubon Soc., Brown Alumnae Assn., Nat. Trust Historic Preservation, Nat., R.I., Western R.I., East Providence hist. socs. Am. Heritage Soc., Library of Human Resource of Am. Bicentennial Research Inst., Library of Human Resource of Am. Heritage Research Assn., Am. Mus. Natural History, Smithsonian Assos. Author: A Comprehensive Bibliography of C.A. Stephens, 1965; None But the Best, 1966; A Chuckle and A Laugh, 1967; The Star of the Youth's Companion, 1969; The Flag Over the Schoolhouse, 1971, sequal Old Glory-Long May She Wave!, 1981; Our Great American Story-Teller, 1978; compiler: Under the Sea in the Salvador (C.A. Stephens), 1969; C.A. Stephens Looks at Norway, 1970; Charles Adams Tales (C.A. Stephens), 1973; Little Big Heart and Other Stories, 1974. Home: 15 Jay St Rumford RI 02916 Office: Box 1926 Brown U Providence RI 02912

HARRIS, LUCY B., systems specialist; b. Fort Smith, Ark., Feb. 25, 1924; d. Joseph Real and Lucy (McDonough) Brown; B.A., U. Ark., 1970; postgrad. U. Tex., Dallas, 1976—; children—Clyde III, Bradford, Sara Randall Maloney, Lucy Randall Nelson, Mark; m. 2d, Mack C. Harris, III, 1981. Owner, mgr. The Other Place, Inc., retail store, Fort Smith, 1965-71; controller Rebmar Inc., Dallas, 1971-75; acctg. mgr. Republic Nat. Factors Corp., Dallas, 1975-76; pvt. practice systems service, Fort Worth, 1976—. Bd. dirs. Hillvale Rehab. Center, Dallas; sustainer Jr. League of Dallas. Republican. Episcopalian. Home: PO Box 25266 Dallas TX 75225 Office: care John Johnson CPA 7001 Grapevine Hwy Suite 430 Fort Worth TX 76118

HARRIS, MARIAN SABRINA, social worker; b. Tallahassee, Mar. 4, 1944; d. Leo and Ida Mae Hoskin; B.A., Fla. A&M U., 1964; M.S.W., Fla. State U., 1977; 1 dau., Trina Shaunaldrea. Social worker Fla. State Div. Social and Econ. Services, Miami, 1965-67; claims clk. Fla. State Dept. Commerce, Tallahassee, 1971-73; statis. aide Fla. State Dept. Edn., Tallahassee, 1973-75; sr. caseworker Children's Home Soc. Fla., Tallahassee, 1977-78; psycho-social rehab. program dir. Archbold Community Mental Health Center, Thomasville, Ga., 1979-81; dir. treatment Broward County div. Mental Health, Ft. Lauderdale, Fla., 1981—; adj. prof. Fla. State U., Barry Coll.; cons. social work Stork's Nest, Quincy, Fla., 1977-78. Active Tallahassee Urban League, Girl Scout Council Apalachee Bend, So. Christian Leadership Conf. Children's Home Soc. Fla. grantee, 1976-77. Mem. LWV, NAACP, Nat. Assn. Social Workers, Internat. Assn. Psycho-Social Rehab. Services, Child Welfare League Am., Fla. Council Community Mental Health, Leon County Mental Health Assn., Thomas County Mental Health Assn., Fla. State U. Alumni Assn., Alpha Kappa Alpha. Democrat. Roman Catholic. Home: 4300 Rock Island Rd Apt 221 Fort Lauderdale FL 33319 also 858 W Dover St Tallahassee FL 32304 Office: 1000 SW 84th Ave Hollywood FL 33025

HARRIS, NATHOLYN DALTON, nutritionist, educator; b. Calvary, Ga., Feb. 26, 1939; d. Martin Luther and Elvie Nathalie (Clinard) Dalton; B.S. with honors, Berry Coll., 1961; M.S., Ohio State U., 1962; Ph.D. (Helena Chamberlain fellow), U. Wis., 1967; m. Ronald Harris, July 15, 1967; children—Rhonda Lynn, Scott Eaton. Instr. food and nutrition Berry Coll., 1962-63; research asst. U. Wis., Madison, 1963-66, lectr., 1966-71; asso. prof. food and nutrition, head dept. food and nutrition Fla. State U., Tallahassee, 1979-81. Named an Outstanding Young Woman Am., U.S. Jaycees, 1965. Mem. Inst. Food Technologists, Am. Home Econs. Assn., Am. Chem. Soc., So. Assn. Agrl. Scientists, Nutrition Today Soc., Am. Oil Chemists Soc., Sigma Xi. Democrat. Baptist. Research, publs. in field. Home: 2019 Lee Ave Tallahassee FL 32312 Office: 413 Sandels Bldg FS4 Tallahassee FL 32306

HARRIS, PATRICIA ANN, museum adminstr.; b. Michigan City, Ind., Oct. 8, 1934; d. Norman G. and Lillian M. (Noveroske) Gruse; student Purdue U., 1952-53, South Bend Coll. Commerce, 1954; m. William H. Harris, June 18, 1955; children—Susan M. Harris Vail, Keith A., Anita C. Harris Young, Kathleen R. Curator, dir. Old Lighthouse Museum, Michigan City Hist. Soc., Inc., 1973—. Leader No. Ind. council Girl Scouts U.S.A., 1963-73; mem. steering com. Michigan City Sesquicentennial, 1833-1983, also project selection chmn. Recipient Cert. of Appreciation, No. Ind. council Girl Scouts U.S.A., 1970, Cert. of Council Recognition, 1971. Mem. Am. Assn. State and Local History, Ind. Hist. Soc., Michigan City Hist. Soc. (trustee 1966—, sec. 1966-74), NW Ind. Geneal. Soc. (trustee 1975-81, v.p. 1977-78), Western Mich. Geneal. Soc., Pi Epsilon Kappa (grand pres. 1973-77). Author: History of St. Mary's of the Immaculate Conception Church, 1967; research in local history. Home: 504 Greenwood Ave Michigan City IN 46360 Office: PO Box 512 Michigan City IN 46360

HARRIS, PATRICIA ANNE, physician; b. Lawrence, Kans., June 10, 1929; d. Earl Julian and Frata Frances (Holiday) Harris; A.B., U. Kans., 1951, M.D., 1954. Intern, St. Francis Hosp., Wichita, Kans. 1954-55; resident, 1955-56; practice medicine specializing in internal medicine, Wichita, 1956-60; postgrad. U. Pa. Grad. Sch. Medicine, 1960-61; mem. staff internal medicine dept. A.T. & S.F. Hosp., Topeka, 1961-67; asst. med. dir. Security Benefit Life Ins. Co., Topeka, 1968-70, asso. med. dir., 1970-77. Mem. Am. Med. Women's Assn., Kans. Thoracic Soc., AMA, Kans., Shawnee County med. soc., Kans. Heart Assn., Pan Am. Med. Women's Alliance, N.Y. Acad. Scis., Royal Soc. Medicine (affiliate mem.), P.E.O., Alpha Omega Alpha. Home: 1617 W 26th Topeka KS 66611

HARRIS, PATRICIA ANNE, govt. systems mgr.; b. Cleve., July 27, 1950; d. George Byron and Lillian Anne (Kippert) Srofe; A.A. cum laude, Anchorage Community Coll., 1979; children—Robert Alan Koski, Mark Andrew Koski. File clk. typist Alcan Aluminum, Warren, Ohio, 1968-69; sec. Manpower, Inc., St. Louis, 1969-70; sec. USAF, Anchorage, 1970-73, adminstrv. systems mgr., 1977-79, chief systems mgmt. div., 1979—; sec. IRS, Anchorage, 1973-75; supervisory clerical asst. Alaska Outer Continental Shelf Office, Anchorage, 1975-77. Recipient USAF Outstanding Adminstrv. officer award, 1979; named Anchorage Fed. Employee of Yr., 1977. Mem. Nat. Assn. Female Execs. Home: PO Box 822 Elmendorf AFB AK 99506 Office: HQ AAC/DAY Elmendorf AFB AK 99506

HARRIS, PATRICIA ROBERTS, sec. HEW, lawyer, educator; b. Mattoon, Ill., May 31, 1924; d. Bert Fitzgerald and Hildren Brodie (Johnson) Roberts; A.B., Howard U., 1945, summa cum laude; J.D., George Washington U., 1960; postgrad. U. Chgo., 1945-47, Am. U., 1949-50; LL.D., Lindenwood Coll., Morgan State Coll., 1967, Russell Sage Coll., Dartmouth Coll., Tufts U., 1970, Johns Hopkins U., MacMurray Coll., U. Md., Williams Coll., 1971, Ripon Coll., Brown U., 1972, Wilberforce U., 1973, Aquinas Coll., 1973, Colby Coll., 1973, Brandeis U., 1973, No. Mich. U., Marquette, 1973, U. Mich., 1973, Smith Coll., Northampton, Mass., 1974, Wittenberg U., Springfield, Ohio, 1974, U. Mass., Amherst, 1975, U. Portland (Oreg.), 1975, Am. U., 1978; D.C.L., Beaver Coll., 1968; D.H.L., Miami U., 1967, Newton Coll. of Sacred Heart, 1972; D.P.Sc., Rollins Coll., 1974; m. William Beasley Harris, Sept. 1, 1955. Program dir. YWCA, Chgo., 1946-49; asst. dir. Am. Council Human Rights, 1949-53; exec. dir. Delta Sigma Theta, 1953-59; admitted to D.C. bar, 1960, U.S. Supreme Ct. bar, 1963; trial atty. Dept. Justice, 1960-61; asso. dean students, lectr. law Howard U., 1961-63, asso. prof. law, 1963-65, prof. law, 1967-69, dean Sch. Law, 1969; partner firm Fried, Frank, Harris, Shriver & Kampelman, Washington, 1970-77; sec. HUD, Washington, 1977-79; sec. HEW, Washington, 1979-80; mem. U.S.-P.R. Commn. Status P.R., 1964-66; U.S. ambassador to Luxembourg, 1965-67; dir. 20th Century Fund, U.S. 1971—; alt. U.S. del. to 21st-22d Gen. Assemblies of UN, 1966-67; U.S. alt. del. 20th plenary meeting Econ. Commn. Europe, 1967; mem. Nat. Adv. Com. Reform Fed. Criminal Laws, 1967-70; mem. Nat. Commn. Causes and Prevention of Violence, 1968-69; mem. Carnegie Commn. on Future Higher Edn., 1969-73; mem. adv. bd. Marshall Scholarship Program; mem. Adminstrv. Conf. U.S., 1967-71. Co-chmn. Nat. Women's Com. Civil Rights, 1963-64; vice chmn. Nat. Capitol Area Civil Liberties Union, 1962-65; exec. bd. D.C. chpt. NAACP, 1958-60, bd. dirs. Legal Def. Fund, 1967-77, UN Assn., 1967-71; bd. dirs. Georgetown U., 1970-76; chmn. welfare com. Urban League D.C., 1961-65; mem. Com. on Admissions and Grievances, U.S. Dist. Ct., D.C., 1970-77; mem. council Rockefeller U., 1972-77; trustee Practicing Law Inst., 1974-77, Am. Bar Found., 1974—; bd. govs. Atlantic Inst., 1967-77; del. Democratic Nat. Conv., 1964, chmn. credentials com., 1972; chmn. D.C. Law Revision Commn., 1975-77; presdl. elector D.C., 1964; mem.-at-large Dem. Nat. Com., 1973-76. Decorated Order of Oaken Crown (Luxembourg); recipient Centennial citation Wilson Coll., 1969; Emma V. Kelly award Dau. Elks, 1968; Distinguished Achievement award Women's Com. of Yeshiva U., 1968; Woman of Year award Women's Aus. Jewish War Vets., 1968; Distinguished Alumni award Howard U., 1966; Alumni Achievement award George Washington U., 1965; Distinguished Service award Washington Alumnae chpt. Delta Sigma Theta, 1963; Aquinas award Aquinas Coll., 1972; One Nation award Phila. Action br. NAACP, 1972; Woman of Year in Bus. and the Professions award Ladies Home Jour., 1974; Black Enterprise Achievement award, 1976; Catalyst award in honor of women dirs. of corps., 1976. Mem. Am. (spl. commn. study legal edn. 1973-77), Fed., D.C. bar assns., Order of Coif, Council Fgn. Relations, Phi Beta Kappa, Delta Sigma Theta, Kappa Beta Pi. Club: Cosmopolitan (N.Y.C.). Office: 200 Independence Ave SW Washington DC 20201 *

HARRIS, ROBERTA ELIZABETH BRUMMAGE, nurse; b. Keyser, W.Va., Oct. 9, 1947; d. Robert Leslie and Elizabeth Jane (Rotruck) Brummage; asso. degree in nursing Fairmont State Coll., 1967; B.S. cum laude in Nursing, W.Va. U., 1978, M.S. in Nursing, cum laude, 1982; m. Howard Lee Harris, July 2, 1966; children—Troy Wayne, Todd Shawn. Staff nurse, intensive care unit W.Va. U. Med. Center, Morgantown, 1967-68; staff nurse, coronary care unit Fairmont (W.Va.) Gen. Hosp., 1969-71; surg. nurse practitioners, evening emergency room supr. Fairmont Clinic, 1971-77; paramedic instr., coordinator regions 6 and 7, Emergency Med. Services, Fairmont, 1977-80; cardiac rehab. nurse United Hosp. Center, Clarksburg, W.Va., 1980-81; asso. inservice edn. coordinator Fairmont (W.Va.) Gen. Hosp., 1981—; pvt. practice nurse clinician, Fairmont, 1980—; mem. curriculum and tng. com. W.Va. Office of Emergency Med. Services, 1977-80; practical tester Nat. Registry Emergency Med. Technicians, 1979; speaker in field. Treas., United Methodist Women's Group, 1981—. R.N., W.Va. Mem. Am., W.Va. (chmn. dist. gen. and economic welfare com., mem. com. 1978-81) nurses assns., Nurses Coalition for Action in Politics, Bus. and Profl. Women's Orgn., Am. Heart Assn. (basic cardiac support instr. 1978—, advanced cardiac life support instr. 1978—, faculty W.Va. affiliate 1979—, nursing com. W.Va. affiliate 1981—). Republican. Club: Y-Sqs. Sq. Dance (pres. 1981—). Contbg. author revision: Employment Standards for Registered Professional Nurses, 1981. Home: Route 3 Box 383 M Fairmont WV 26554 Office: Fairmont Gen Hosp Locust Ave Fairmont WV 26554

HARRIS, ROBERTA LUCAS, social worker; b. St. Louis, Nov. 13, 1916; d. Robert Joseph and Clara Louise (Mellor) Lucas; A.B., St. Louis U., 1955, M.S.W. (NIMH grantee), 1964; m. William F. Sprengnether, Jr., Aug. 21, 1937 (dec. Aug. 30, 1951); children—Robert Lucas, Madelon Sprengnether Gohlke, Ronald John; m. 2d, Victor B. Harris, Sept. 13, 1955 (dec. June 14, 1960). Field instr. Sch. Social Work St. Louis U., 1967-70; chief of domestic relations City of St. Louis, 1966—. Dir., Citizens' Housing Council, 1956-60; del. to Community Family Life Clinic, 1957; dir. Landmarks Assn., 1957-63; pres. Compton Heights Improvement Assn., 1973. Mem. Nat., Mo. assns. social workers, Nat. Council Crime and Delinquency, Assn. Family Conciliation Cts. (dir. 1968—), Greater St. Louis Probation and Parole Assn. (sec. 1976), St. Louis U. Sch. Social Service Alumni Assn. (sec. 1973), LWV (dir. 1956-61). Methodist. Club: Wednesday. Home: 3137 Longfellow St St Louis MO 63104

HARRIS, SANDRA JOAN, educator; b. Marion, Ohio, May 12, 1941; d. John Brooks and Loraine Virginia (Drake) Soulier; B.A. in History and Edn., Calif. State U., 1973, M.S. in Reading, 1980; m. Richard Lewis Harris, June 3, 1961; children—Cynthia Ann, Jeffrey Richard. Tchr., Los Molinos Sch., Hacienda Heights, Calif., 1973-75, Faber Sch., Dunellen, N.J., 1977-78, 80—, Whittier Sch., Dunellen, 1979-80; tchr. Early Childhood Edn. Task Force, 1974-75. Mem. com. Women in 7th Dist., Bernards Twp., N.J., 1978-82. Recipient Dorothy Feddersohn Scholarship award PTA, 1976; Interning for Learning Grant, Dunellen Bd. Edn., 1979. Mem. Internat. Reading Assn., N.J. Edn. Assn., Dunellen Edn. Assn. Republican. Methodist. Club: Welcome Wagon Bridge. Home: 79 Dyckman Pl Basking Ridge NJ 07920 Office: Faber Sch Dunellen NJ 08812

HARRIS, SANDRA LEE, clin. psychologist, educator; b. Seattle, Apr. 15, 1942; d. William W. and Felice (Deitchman) Harris; B.A., U. Md., 1964; Ph.D. in Clin. Psychology, SUNY, Buffalo, 1969. Asst. prof. Douglass Coll., Rutgers U., New Brunswick, N.J., 1969-73, assoc. prof., 1973-79, Grad. Sch. of Applied and Profl. Psychology, Rutgers U., Piscataway, N.J., 1974-79, prof. psychology, 1979—, dir. Douglass Devel. Disabilities Center, 1972—. Fellow Am. Psychol. Assn.; mem. AAUP, Assn. for Advancement of Behavior Therapy, Eastern Psychol. Assn., Nat. Soc. for Autistic Children, Soc. for Pediatric Psychology. Democrat. Jewish. Contbr. articles to profl. jours.; editor The Clin. Psychologist, 1978-81. Home: 23 Ross Hall Blvd S Piscataway NJ 08854 Office: PO Box 819 Rutgers U Piscataway NJ 08854

HARRIS, SARA RICHMAN, gerontol. research center exec., author; b. Cleve., Mar. 17, 1921; d. Aaron L. and Rivella Lillian (Shapiro) Richman; B.A., U. Chgo., 1941; m. Raymond Harris, Dec. 1, 1946; children—Anita, Laura, Jonathan, Alan. Asst. prof. dept. bus. Hudson Valley Community Coll., Troy, N.Y., 1967-69, exec. dir. Ctr. for Study of Aging, Inc., 1957—; adj. prof. SUNY, Albany, 1976-77; lectr. Albany Med. Coll., Union U., 1977—; coordinator, panelist bi-weekly talk program Sta. WQBK, 1979—; organizer, coordinator, presenter program on geriatrics and gerontology N.Y. State Occupational Therapy Assn., 1979; past dir. pvt. children's camps, N.H., tchr. adult edn. art courses. Chmn. Citizens Com. for new Public Library, Albany; mem. Mayor's Adv. Com. on Minority Housing, Albany; upstate chmn. Shapp for Pres., 1975-76; mem. nat. alumni cabinet U. Chgo., 1970—. Recipient Service award Albany Interracial Council, Inc., 1970; Disting. Alumna award Girls Latin Sch./Boston Latin Acad. Assn., 1979; honored as woman leader Albany br. AAUW and Coll. of St. Rose, 1976. Mem. Internat. Gerontol. Soc., Am. Gerontol. Soc., Albany Artists Group, Inc., Schenectady Art Soc., Art Students League N.Y., Health, Edn., and Welfare Club (pres.). Club: U. Chgo. of Capital Dist. (pres. 1981—). Asso. editor: Guide to Fitness After Fifty, 1977. Office: 706 Madison Ave Albany NY 12208

HARRIS, VANESSA LEE, public affairs specialist; b. Columbus, Ohio, Jan. 8, 1948; d. Homer P. and Helen M. (Saunders) Lee; student Wilberforce Central State U., 1968; B.S. in Family and Consumer Resources, Wayne State U., 1976; organizing cert. Nat. Tng. and Info. Center, 1977; children—Kevin Maurice, David Vincent. Tchr. consumer edn. City Sch. Detroit, 1977; consumer edn. specialist Mich. Senator Jack Faxon, 1977-79; sales mgr. Bowers Realty, Detroit, 1979; public affairs specialist Project on Equal Edn. Rights, NOW Legal Def. and Edn. Fund, Milford, Mich., 1979—; pres. Consumer Info. and Research Service; owner Seminar Planners; arbitrator Detroit Better Bus. Bur.; cons. consumer issues and workshops. Mem. New Detroit Anti-Racism Com.; mem. Wayne County Consumer Adv. Bd., Vol. Action Bur.; mem.

adv. bd. WXYZ Talk Radio; active Project Redirection, Urban League; bd. dirs. Brightmoor Community Center, Detroit, Women of Wayne Child Care Center, Detroit; mem. citizen rev. com. Detroit City Planning Commn. Recipient Scholastic Achievement award Wilberforce Central State U., 1970; recognition for community work NOW; Project Headstart award Detroit Pub. Schs. Mem. Awareness Inc., Consumer Credit Assn. Greater Detroit, Consumer Educators Mich., Nat. Coalition Black Women Bus. Owners and Operators, Wayne State U. Alumni Assn., Women of Wayne, Consumer Adv. Research Council, NOW, Nat. Assn. Female Execs. Democrat. Methodist. Home: 8801 Kingswood Apt 105 Detroit MI 48221 Office: City Nat Bank Bldg Suite 880 Detroit MI 48226

HARRIS, VELVA JOY, nursing adminstr.; b. Naylor, Mo., Jan. 16, 1936; d. Jack Seamans and Melba Priscilla (Lassiter) Cunningham; R.N., Mo. Bapt. Hosp. Sch. Nursing, 1956; B.S., Washington U., 1962; postgrad. in psychology U. Tex., 1969; m. Fred L. Harris, Apr. 20, 1956 (div.); 1 dau., Kimberly Jo. Psychiat. nurse Mo. Bapt. Hosp., St. Louis, Mo., 1956-61, clin. instr. psychiat. nursing, 1961-63; asst. dir. nurses Northwest Tex. Hosp., Amarillo, Tex., 1967-69; asst. dir. nurses W. I. Cook Meml. Children's Hosp., Ft. Worth, 1970-73; adminstrv. head nurse II, Santa Barbara (Calif.) Gen. Hosp., 1973-78; dir. nurses Santa Barbara County Health Care Services, 1978—; instr. med. aidman course Tex. Army Nat. Guard, Amarillo, Tex., 1968. Mem., Ventura-Santa Barbara Health Systems Agency, 1976—; pres. Western Addiction Services Program, Inc., 1979-80; mem. adv. com. Health Techs. div. Santa Barbara Community Coll., 1979—. Served as capt. Nurses Corps, USAF, 1963-67. USPHS ednl. trainee, 1961-62. Mem. Calif. Soc. Nursing Service Adminstrs., Advocates for Public Health, Nat. Assn. Public Health, Santa Barbara County Employees Assn. (dir. 1975-78), Washington U. Alumni Assn. Episcopalian. Club: Zonta Internat. Home: 257 Brandon Dr Goleta CA 93017 Office: 300 N San Antonio Rd Santa Barbara CA 93110

HARRIS, VERA EVELYN (CUSIMANO), real estate sales co. exec.; b. Watson, Sask., Can., Jan. 11, 1932; came to U.S., 1957; d. Timothy and Margaret (Popoff) H.; student U. B.C. (Can.), Vancouver; children—Colin Clifford Graham, Barbara Cusimano Page. Office mgr. Keglers, Inc., Morgan City, La., 1964-67; office mgr., acct. John L. Hopper & Assos., New Orleans, 1967-71; office mgr. Elite Homes, Inc., Metairie, La., 1971-73; comptroller Le Pavillon Hotel, New Orleans, 1973-74; controller Waguespack-Pratt, Inc., New Orleans, 1974-76; adminstrv. controller Sizzler Family Steak Houses of So. La., Inc., Metairie, 1976-79; dir. adminstrn. Sunbelt, Inc., New Orleans, 1979-82, sec., dir., 1980—; exec. v.p. Corp. Cons., Inc., 1980—; exec. dir. Nat. Sizzler Franchise Assn., 1976-79; mem. Jefferson Bd. Realtors. Mem. Am. Bus. Women's Assn., Nat. Assn. Female Execs., Metairie Art Guild, New Orleans Art Assn., Le Petit Art Guild. Home: 2202 Caswell Ln Metairie LA 70001 Office: 419 Carondelet 4th Floor New Orleans LA 70130

HARRIS, WANDA GOFORTH, market research co. exec.; b. Gerald, Mo., Mar. 10, 1939; d. Clyde and Artie I. (Clark) Goforth; m. Craig Harris, Apr. 23, 1960; children—Leslie, Wendy, Shannon. Pres., Harris Interviewing, Inc., Concord, Calif., 1975—, Redding, Calif., 1979—. Mem. Concord Cultural Commn., 1974-76; mem. Concord Housing Com., 1973. Recipient Joint Calif. Senate Assembly resolution, 1982. Mem. Am. Mktg. Assn., Mktg. Research Assn., Todos Santos Bus. and Profl. Women (founder, charter pres.), NOW, Nat. Women's Polit. Caucus, Nat. Alliance Homebased Bus. Women. Democrat. Home and Office: 5289 Pine Hollow Rd Concord CA 94521

HARRIS-CROSS, ROSE, social worker; b. Canton, Miss., Mar. 17, 1945; d. R.B. and Estella (Clayton) Harris; B.A., Jackson (Miss.) State U., 1967; M.S.W., Mich. State U., 1973; children—Una-Kariim A., Kha-Lihah. Field coordinator Headstart, 1967-68; med. social worker St. Lawrence Hosp., Lansing, Mich., 1968-71; affective listening skills, substance abuse trainer, Lansing, 1976-78; sch. social worker, Lansing, 1973—; field supr. Mich. State U.; field coordinator Lansing Community Coll., 1974-76. Troop leader Brownies, 1979-80. Mem. Nat. Assn. Social Workers (chpt. chmn. 1978-79, program chmn. 1977-78), Mich. Sch. Social Workers Assn., Lansing Sch. Edn. Assn. (rep. assembly 1974-75, negotiating com. 1976-79), Minority Edn. Assn., NAACP, Urban League, Delta Sigma Theta (past sec.). Home: 6435 Norburn Way Lansing MI 48910 Office: 406 E Holmes Rd Lansing MI 48910

HARRIS-NOEL, ANN GRAETSCH, educator, cons. geologist; b. Cleve., Sept. 6, 1934; d. Albert Walter and Hattie Margaret (Curtis) Graetsch; B.S., Kent State U., 1956; M.S., Miami U., 1958; postgrad. Argonne Nat. Labs., 1967-80, Ohio State U., 1968, U. N.Mex., 1967, Va. Poly. Inst., 1963; m. Charles Dale Noel, Dec. 27, 1980; children—Laurie Ann, Kelli Beth. Research engr. Ferro Corp., Cleve., 1958-59; geologist U.S. Geol. Survey, various locations, 1959-61; mem. faculty Youngstown (Ohio) State U. 1961—, asso. prof. geology, 1977—; cons. geologist pvt. industry, 1977—. Mem. Environ. Rev. Com., City of Youngstown, 1974—. Recipient Jefferson award for pub. service Am. Inst. Pub. Service, 1981; named Woman of Year YWCA, 1978. Fellow Ohio Acad. Sci.; mem. N. Am. Thermal Analysis Soc., Assn. Profl. Geologists, Nat. Assn. Geology Tchrs., No. Ohio Geol. Soc., Geol. Soc. Am., Sigma Xi. Methodist. Author: Geology of National Parks, 1975, 3d edit., 1982. Home: 535 E Judson Ave Youngstown OH 44502 Office: Dept of Geology Youngstown State Univ 410 Wick St Youngstown OH 44555

HARRISON, ANN TUKEY, educator; b. Geneva, N.Y., Apr. 19, 1938; d. Harold B. and Ruth (Schweigert) Tukey; B.A., Mich. State U., 1957; M.A., U. Mich., 1958, Ph.D., 1962; m. Michael J. Harrison, Sept. 1, 1970. From instr. to asst. prof. U. Wis., Madison, 1961-65; from asst. prof. to prof. French, Mich. State U., East Lansing, 1965—. Woodrow Wilson fellow, 1957-58; recipient Disting. Alumni award Mich. State U., 1970; Ruth Dean Ann. lectr. Mt. Holyoke Coll., 1976; Am-Council Learned Socs. grantee, 1981. Mem. MLA, Am. Assn. Tchrs. of French, Am. Council Teaching of Fgn. Langs., Medieval Acad., Mich. Fgn. Langs. Assn. (pres. 1978-80). Author: Charles of Orleans and the Allegorical Mode, 1975; co-editor: Lectures de France et d'Outre Mer, 1967; Si Nous Commencons a Lire, 1968; contbg. linguist: A-L-M French, Level 4, rev., 1972; Nos Amis, 1979; contbg. editor: Pensee et Litterature Francaises, 1971. Home: 277 Maplewood Dr East Lansing MI 48823 Office: Mich State U East Lansing MI 48824

HARRISON, CAROLYN CASSELL, counselor; b. Waterbury, Conn., June 19, 1925; d. Kenneth Parker and Elizabeth Rachel (Emery) Wight; R.N., Mass. Gen. Hosp. Sch. Nursing, 1946; B.S. in Nursing Edn., Catholic U., 1953; M.Ed. in Counseling, U. Md., 1969; m. Thomas Richard Harrison, June 16, 1973; children—Donna Cassell, Stafford Cassell, Jack Carlton Cassell. Nursing supr. Monadnock Community Hosp., Peterboro, N.H., 1947-49; staff nurse Doctors Hosp., VA Hosp., Washington, 1949-52; asst. dir. health services Am. U., Washington, 1949-50; dir. admissions Sch. Nursing, Washington Hosp. Center, 1957-67; dir. records office Coll. Edn., U. Md., College Park, 1968-70; counselor Prince George's Community Coll., Largo, Md., 1970-81; dir. career devel. Isothermal Community Coll., Spindale, N.C., 1981—. Trustee, chairperson edn. com. Gould Acad., Bethel, Maine, 1971—; adminstr. employee assistance program Isothermal Community Coll., bd. dirs. Task Force on Domestic Violence, Rutherford County, N.C., 1982—; mem. adv. com. Statewide Assessment of Career Aspiration and Job Attainment Among Women Returning to Coll. in Md., 1978-80. Mem. NOW, Am. Personnel and Guidance Assn., N.C. Personnel and Guidance Assn., Nat. Assn. Women Deans, Adminstrs. and Counselors, Nat. Council Student Devel., NEA, Counseling and Personnel Assn.-U. Md. Methodist. Clubs: Faculty Women's (Am. U.), Pilot Internat. (dir. 1982—). Home: 617 Brookwood Dr Spindale NC 28160 Office: Isothermal Community Coll PO Box 804 Spindale NC 28160

HARRISON, DEMERICE, systems cons.; b. LaGrange, Ga., Aug. 8, 1940; d. Otis David and Ruby Mae (Wilson) Pike; student Wayne State U., 1962-64, U. Tenn., 1974-76; children—Kenneth Dale, Jeffrey Alan, Melinda Anne. Copywriter, Robinson Furniture, J.L. Hudson Co., Detroit, 1960-66; advt. mgr. Wright Kay Jewelers, Detroit, 1967-69; personnel mgr. Atlantic Envelope Co., Nashville, 1970-72; sales rep. Standard Register Co., Nashville, 1972—. Recipient 5 sales awards. Mem. Hosp. Fin. Mgrs. Assn., Data Processing Mgmt. Assn., Davidson County Bus. and Profl. Women, Davidson County Women's Polit. Caucus. Home: 621 Vivian Dr Nashville TN 37211 Office: PO Box 17443 Nashville TN 37217

HARRISON, EDYTHE COLTON, state legislator; b. Detroit, Sept. 17, 1934; student Finch Coll., Wayne State U.; m. Stanley Leigh Harrison; children—Tim C., Jody L., Julie L. Mem. Va. 2d Dist. Democratic Com.; mem. Va. Ho. of Reps., 1980—. Founding pres. Va. Opera Assn.; mem. pres.'s adv. council Old Dominion U.; bd. dirs. Greater Norfolk Corp.; mem. Norfolk Commn. on Arts and Humanities; bd. dirs. Regional Hospice Council of Tidewater. Mem. Va. Alliance for Arts Edn., Va. State C. of C. (edn. com.). Office: Va Ho Dels State Capitol Richmond VA 23219 *

HARRISON, (ELEANOR) JACQUELINE CROSTON, fin. exec.; b. Morgantown, W.Va., Sept. 17, 1934; d. Guy Alexander and Helen Margaret (McGee) Croston; B.Mus.Ed. (Bd. Govs. scholar), W.Va. U., 1955, Mus.M. (Bd. Govs. scholar), 1956; now postgrad. in history W.Va. U.; m., Oct. 21, m., Oct. 21, 1955; children—Jeannine Louise, David Summers, Laura Suzanne. Instr. music theory, grad. assistance program, W.Va. U. Sch. Music, Morgantown, 1955-56; tchr. music, public jr. high sch., Richmond, Va., 1956-58; choir dir., organist, various chapels, U.S. Army, 1962-69; organist Drummond Chapel United Meth. Ch., Morgantown, 1974—; office asst. W.Va. U. Sch. Nursing, 1974-76; fin. sec. Spruce St. United Meth. Ch., Morgantown, 1976-79; asso. treas. Monongalia Pediatric and Youth Assos., Inc., Morgantown, 1979—. Republican. Methodist. Clubs: Monongalia County Med. Soc. Aux., Order Eastern Star. Home: 1449 Dogwood Ave Morgantown WV 26505 Office: Monongalia Pediatric & Youth Assos Inc 404 Inglewood Blvd Morgantown WV 26505

HARRISON, HATTIE N., state legislator; b. Lancaster, S.C.; grad. Antioch Coll. Former tchr.; mem. Md. Ho. of Dels., 1973—, chmn. rules and exec. nominations com.; cons. Mott Found., Flint, Mich., Internat. Community Edn. Assn., Melbourne, Australia; apptd. to Nat. Community Edn. Adv. Council. Active Eastside Democratic Orgn., Md. Assn. Mental Health, Citizens for Fair Housing, LWV, NAACP, YWCA, East Baltimore Women's League, Nat. Lab. for Advancement of Edn.; mem. Balt. City Dem. State Central Com., Commn. on Women. Recipient various service awards. Mem. Md. Assn. for Community Edn. (pres.). First black woman to chair legis. com. Md. Ho. of Dels.

HARRISON, JEANNE D., lawyer; b. Augusta, Ga., Dec. 22, 1944; d. Frederick L. and Aurelia O.F. (Sancken) H.; B.A., U. Ga., 1966; J.D., Mercer U., 1970. Admitted to Ga. bar, 1971; mem. firm Allgood & Childs, Augusta, 1971-75; individual practice law, Augusta, 1975—. Mem. Am. Bar Assn., Ga. Bar Assn., Augusta Bar Assn., Young Lawyers Club. Episcopalian. Home: 654 Center Court Dr Augusta GA 30909 Office: 563 Greene St PO Box 1565 Augusta GA 30903

HARRISON, JOYCE VIRGINIA, advt. co. exec.; b. Flin Flon, Man., Can., May 3, 1939; d. Peter V. and Amelia (Ohryn) H.; student U. Man., 1957-58, Laurentian U., 1968-69; children—Kim, Marley, Lindsay. Women's editor, program dir. Cambrian Broadcasting, Sudbury, Ont., Can., 1959-70; ops. mgr. Broadcast Services, Evanston, Ill., 1970-72; asso. creative dir. Arthur Meyerhoff & Assos. (now BBDO), Chgo., 1972-79; creative dir., sr. v.p. Draper Daniels (now Bozell & Jacobs), Chgo., 1979—; pres. Rambull Inc., 1973-79; dir. Wax & Assos., Chgo., 1980-81. Mem. Nat. Acad. Rec. Arts & Scis., ASCAP. Democrat. Roman Catholic. Composer songs. Home: 2200 Forestview Rd Evanston IL 60201 Office: 360 N Michigan Ave Chicago IL 60601

HARRISON, (LENORE) RANDY, orgn. exec.; b. N.Y.C., Sept. 19, 1942; d. Randolph George and Eleanor Virginia (Discenza) H.; B.S. in Art Edn., Pratt Inst., Bklyn., 1964; m. Walter S. Walter; children—George Randolph, Clifford Harrison. Tchr. fine arts and ceramics East Brunswick (N.J.) High Sch., 1964-66; pvt. art instr., Heidelberg, W.Ger., 1966-73; art instr. Tidewater Community Coll., Chesapeake, Va., 1976-78; show promoter Broadway summer series Chrysler Hall, Norfolk, Va., 1977, 78; exec. dir. Downtown Norfolk Assn., also asso. dir. Downtown Norfolk Devel. Corp., 1978—. Bd. dirs., theatre liaison chmn. Va. Theatre Guild; bd. dirs. Met. Arts Congress, Friends of Zoo, Norfolk. Mem. Nat. Assn. Female Execs. (network dir.), Internat. Downtown Execs. Assn., Tidewater Artists Assn. (pres.). Office: 201 Granby Mall Suite 101 Norfolk VA 23510

HARRISON, LOIS COWLES, civic worker; b. Des Moines, Iowa, June 23, 1934; d. Gardner and Lois (Thornburg) Cowles; B.A., Wellesley Coll., 1956; m. John Raymond Harrison, June 24, 1955; children—Mark, Pat, Lois; m. 2d, Homer E. Hooks, Nov. 27, 1982. Dir., Cowles Media Co. (formerly Mpls. Star and Tribune Co.). Commr. Gov.'s Commn. on Status of Women, 1973-77, Fla. Ethics Commn., 1974-78; mem. Commn. on Fla. Constl. Revision, 1977-78; mem. Fla. Women's Polit. Caucus, 1973-75; v.p. LWV Fla., 1973-77, pres., 1977—, bd. dirs., 1982-83, dir. edn. fund, 1973-77, dir. LWV U.S. ERA chair, 1980-82; bd. dirs. ERAmerica, 1980-82; pres. Planned Parenthood Central Fla., 1982—; dir. Fla. Fine Arts Council, 1972—; mem. Mayor's Creative and Performing Arts Council, Lakeland, Fla., 1972-75; mem. Am. Bar Commn. on Evaluation of Profl. Standards, 1978—. Episcopalian. Home: 2311 Nevada Rd Lakeland FL 33803

HARRISON, MARGARET BAXTER, tire co. exec.; b. Petersburg, Va., June 18, 1925; d. Morrice Linwood and Verna Margaret (Williams) Baxter; student Va. Commonwealth U., 1944-47; student Pan Am. Bus. Sch., 1955; m. Clyde Warren Harrison, Feb. 4, 1950 (dec. Aug. 1974); children—Holly Preston, Jan Baxter. Dress model Janay Modes, N.Y.C., 1948-50; freelance dress model, 1950—; apprentice optician Baxter Optical Co., Petersburg, Va., 1950-53; optician Morrice Linwood Baxter, Petersburg, 1954; office mgr. Harrison Tire Service, Inc., Hopewell, Va., 1956-74, pres., 1974—; nat. spokesperson Tire Retread Info. Bur., 1975-76. Mem. Nat. Tire Dealers and Retreaders Assn., Am. Retreaders Assn. Methodist. Clubs: Jordon Point Country (Hopewell, Va.); Downtown (Richmond, Va.). Home: 3419 Norton St Hopewell VA 23860 Office: Harrison Tire Service Inc 202 E City Point Rd Hopewell VA 23860

HARRISON, MARY ANNE, lawyer; b. Syracuse, Apr. 15, 1944; d. James Robertson and Ruth (O'Connor) Urquhart; B.A., U. So. Calif., 1966; J.D., U. Calif., Berkeley, 1969; m. Douglas L. Thorpe, Oct. 2, 1977. Admitted to Calif. bar; dep. atty. gen. Calif., 1970-73; sr. atty. Pacific Lighting Corp., 1973-76; v.p., sec., gen. counsel Buena Vista Distbg. Co., Inc., Burbank, Calif., 1976—. Bd. dirs., City of Los Angeles Ofcl. Salaries Authority, 1979-80. Mem. Los Angeles County Bar Assn. (trustee 1979—), Calif. Women Lawyers, Women Lawyers Assn. Los Angeles, Am. Bar Assn., State Bar Calif. (del. 1974—, chmn. conv., 1979). Office: 350 S Buena Vista St Burbank CA 91521 *

HARRISON, NEDRA JOYCE, surgeon; b. Buffalo, Apr. 16, 1951; d. Herman Lloyde and Gertrude (Newsom) H.; B.S., Rosary Hill Coll., 1973; M.D., SUNY, Buffalo, 1977. Resident in surgery Millard Fillmore Hosps., Buffalo, 1977-82, mem. provisional attending staff in gen. surgery, 1982—; practice medicine specializing in gen. surgery, Buffalo, 1982—; mem. faculty SUNY at Buffalo Sch. Medicine. Chmn. United Thank Offering, Episcopal Ch., Buffalo, 1982. Recipient Best Research Paper in Gen. Surgery award Millard Fillmore Hosps., 1978, 81. Mem. AMA, Am. Med. Women's Assn., Christian Med. Soc., Delta Epsilon Sigma. Episcopalian. Office: 405 Linwood Ave Buffalo NY 14209

HARRISON, SHEILA JEAN WHITE, accountant; b. Lufkin, Tex., Mar. 18, 1942; d. Royce Howard and Marguerite (Henry) White; B.B.A., U. Houston, 1970; m. Finis Bennett Harrison, Jr., Oct. 6, 1962; 1 dau., Connie Lynn. Asst. credit mgr., asst. purchasing agt. Eastman Whipstock, Inc., Houston, 1964-67; controller, treas. Toro Petroleum Corp., Houston, 1970-75; project cons. Hooker Chem. Corp., 1975-77; mgr. acctg. Houston Oil and Minerals Corp., 1977-79; owner, cons. Harrison Enterprises, Houston, 1978—; cons., mktg. rep. T.S.R., Inc., Houston, 1979-81; cons. STSC, Inc., 1981—. Auction vol. Assn. Community TV, 1975—. Recognized as top salesperson of yr. T.S.R., Inc., 1979, 80, 81. C.P.A., Tex. Mem. Nat. Assn. Credit Mgmt., Am. Inst. C.P.A.s, Tex. Soc. C.P.A.s, Am. Soc. Women C.P.A.s, Petroleum Accts. Soc., Fin. Planning Execs., U. Houston Coll. Bus. Alumni Assn. (pres., dir.). Republican. Home: 11603 Highgrove St Houston TX 77077 Office: 11 Greenway Plaza Suite 1700 Houston TX 77046

HARROD, EMMA KRALL (MRS. DAVID BIDWELL HARROD), physician; b. Eaton, Ohio, Feb. 25, 1930; d. Bert L. and Mildred I. (Wolverton) Krall; B.A. cum laude, Miami U., 1952; M.D., Harvard U., 1957; m. David Bidwell Harrod, June 15, 1954; children—David A., Eric B., Mary Ellen, Richard. Intern, U. Minn. Hosps., 1957-58; fellow genetics Roswell Park Meml. Inst., Buffalo, N.Y., 1963-66; resident pediatrics Buffalo Children's Hosp., 1966-67; resident in phys. medicine and rehab. Meyer Meml. Hosp., Buffalo, 1977-78; dir. Birth Defects Center, 1968-70; dir. maternal and child health services Erie County Health Dept., 1970-72, dep. commr., 1972-77; med. dir. United Cerebral Palsy Assn., 1978-80; attending dept. rehab. medicine Erie County Med. Center, 1978—; pediatrician Health Care Plan, Inc., 1980—; asso. clin. prof. pediatrics State U. N.Y. Pres., YWCA, 1976-79; bd. dirs. Nat. Found. March of Dimes, 1973-77. Mem. Am. Acad. Pediatrics, Am. Acad. Cerebral Palsy and Developmental Medicine, Teratology Assn., Am. Public Health Assn., AAAS. Club: Zonta. Home: 174 Morris Ave Buffalo NY 14214 Office: 100 Leroy Ave Buffalo NY 14214

HARROLD, LOU ANN, home economist, farmer, educator, businesswoman; b. Findlay, Ohio, Dec. 9, 1935; d. Donald Layman and Carolyn Genevra (Mathews) Putnam; B.S. summa cum laude, Ohio State U., 1956; M.S., Independence U., 1976; M.S. in Ednl. Adminstrn., U. Dayton, 1979; m. Clyde Ellis Harrold, June 10, 1977; children—Robert E. Spangler, Jr., Stacia Lee Spangler. Tchr., Alger High Sch., 1957-59; tchr., dept. head Kenton (Ohio) Jr. High Sch., 1964-79; tchr. home econs., dept. head Kenton St. High Sch., 1979—; farmer, dairy and hog, later grain, Ada, Ohio, 1957—; engaged in housing restoration and rental, 1977—; cons. Ohio Dept. Edn., 1974, 76, 82; dir. sch.-age parent project, 1981—. State adv. bd. Ohio Coop. Extension Service, 1980—, Nutrition Edn. Tng. Program, 1981—; sec. Cessna Twp. Bd. Zoning Appeals, 1974—. Named Ohio Tchr. of Yr. in Home Econs., 1982; recipient service award Coll. Agr. and Home Econs. Ohio State U., 1982. Mem. Am. Home Econs. Assn., Ohio Home Econs. Assn. (state pres. 1980-81, Dist. A pres. 1978-79), Ohio Assn. for Supervision and Curriculum Devel., Internat. Fedn. Home Econs., Nat. Assn. Vocat. Home Econs. Tchrs., Nat. Assn. Female Execs., AAUW, Home Econs. Edn. Assn., Am. Vocat. Assn., Greater Toledo Dairy and Nutrition Council, Home Economists in Bus., Delta Kappa Gamma, Phi Delta Kappa. Republican. Methodist. Club: University II (pres.). Supr. devel. Kenton Middle Sch. Home Econs. Curriculum, distributed nationally, 1981. Home: 8187 TR 90 Ada OH 45810 Office: 200 Harding Ave Kenton OH 43326

HARROUN, ANN PATRICIA BIRON, state legislator; b. Gorham, N.H., May 20, 1935; d. Oscar and Evelyn (Page) Biron; student U. N.Mex., Albuquerque, 1959-62, Moorpark (Calif.) Coll., 1968-70; B.A., Trinity Coll., Burlington, Vt., 1980; m. Thomas V. Harroun, Mar. 24, 1956; children—Leslie, Peter. Clk. Union Mut. Life Ins. Co., Portland, Maine, 1953-55; sec. Stanford (Calif.) U., 1955-56; asst. auditor IBM Employees' Fed. Credit Union, Essex Junction, Vt., 1979; mem. Vt. Ho. of Reps., 1981—. Selectman Town of Essex, 1976—, mem. planning commn., 1972-76; village clk. Village of Essex Center, 1971-72. Mem. LWV, Vt. Natural Resources Council, Nature Conservancy, Orgn. Women Legislators. Democrat. Unitarian. Club: Sierra. Home: 14 Wildwood Dr Essex Junction VT 05452 Office: State House Montpelier VT 05602

HARROUN, DOROTHY SUMMER, painter, educator; b. El Paso, Tex., Nov. 29, 1935; d. Daniel Stuart and Eleanor (Flowers) H.; B.F.A., U. N.Mex., 1957; postgrad. (Fulbright scholar) U. Paris, Sorbonne, 1957-58; M.F.A., U. Colo., 1960. One woman shows: The Gondolier Gallery, Boulder, Colo., 1961, 62, Sta. KAFE-FM Gallery, San Francisco, 1963, 64; Lovelace-Bataan Hosp., Albuquerque, 1976, 79; Eastern N.Mex. U., 1981, Rathaus, Kelkheim, W.Ger., N.Mex. State U. group shows include: Whitte Mus., San Antonio, 1960, shows in Hyannis, Mass., Waterbury, Conn., Newport, R.I., 1964-65, Mus. N.Mex., Santa Fe, 1966, Ogunguit (Maine) Art Ctr., 1977, Am. Watercolor Soc. 112th Ann., N.Y.C., 1979, Coos Art Mus., Coos Bay, Oreg., 1980, Western Slope Show, Montrose, Colo., 1981, 82; represented in permanent collections U. N.Mex., U. Colo., pvt. collections in U.S., France, Italy, W.Ger.; art dir. Wood-Reich Advt. Agy., Boulder, 1960-61; lectr. U. Colo., Boulder, 1961-62; tchr. art Langley-Porter Neuropsychiat. Inst. U. Calif., 1963; lectr. San Francisco State Coll., 1964-65; tchr. Art Center Sch., Albuquerque, 1975-79; tchr. watercolor, drawing U. N.Mex., 1980-81. Mem. Artist Equity Assn. (pres. Albuquerque chpt. 1977-79), AAUW (state cultural dir.), Nat. League Am. Pen Women (pres. Albuquerque br. 1982—). Author and illustrator: Take Time to Play and Listen, 1963, Phun-y Physics, 1975. Address: Star Route Box 982 Corrales NM 87048

HARSHMAN, LAURIAN SEAVERSON, savs. and loan exec.; b. Rawlins, Wyo., May 6, 1935; d. Lester Grant and Estelle Arlee (Slade) Seaverson; B.A. in Internat. Relations, U. Wyo., 1957; J.D., U. Ariz., 1967; trust adminstrn. grad. Pacific Coast Sch. of Banking, 1976; m. John Samual Harshman, Oct. 12, 1974; 1 stepdau., Pamela Harshman Kirk; children by previous marriage—Katherine Arlee Handley, David Landon Handley. Real estate loan processor Ariz. Bank, Phoenix, 1962-64; asst. v.p., trust officer Wells Fargo Bank, San Francisco, 1967-78; v.p., mgr. trust dept. 1st Nationwide Savs., San Francisco, 1978—. Mem. Calif. Savs. and Loan League, P.E.O., Kappa Delta. Republican. Episcopalian. Office: First Nationwide Savs 700 Market St San Francisco CA 94102

HART, CAROL JANE, educator; b. Bklyn., Apr. 7, 1945; d. Charles Edward and Anna (Johnson) Ferguson; student public schs.; m. William John Hart, May 24, 1964; children—Kip Leonard, Kenneth Charles, Karole Jane. Cheerleader, 1959-63; coach elem. and high schs., 1963-65,

69-70; cheer coach St. Jude Catholic Youth Orgn., Hopatcong, N.J., 1970-82; leader workshops, clinics, cheer competitions, 1971—. Recipient various cheer leading prizes; named to Dynamic Cheerleaders Assn. Hall of Fame, 1979; cert. cheerleading competition judge. Mem. Nat. Cheerleaders Coaches Assn., Internat. Cheerleaders Found., U.S. Cheerleaders Assn., Dynamic Cheerleaders Assn., Golden Eagle Cheerleaders Assn., Upper Morris Vicarate Cath. Youth Orgn. Cheerleaders League (sec. 1976-79), Pa. PTA, Sports Acrobatics Fedn., Assn. Intercollegiate Athletics for Women, St. Jude Rosary Altar Soc. Republican. Author research papers, articles in field. Address: PO Box 182 Center Rd Reeders PA 18352

HART, CONSTANCE GRAY, former assn. exec.; b. Bklyn., Feb. 28, 1896; d. Percy R. and Emma (King) Gray; grad. Bklyn. Heights Sem., 1914; student Child Edn. Found., Montessori Normal, 1916-18; m. Jes Jessen Dall, Jr., Nov. 24, 1917 (dec. June 1942); children—Jes Jessen III, Joan (Mrs. Edward C. Patton); m. 2d, Merwin K. Hart, Dec. 9, 1961 (dec. Nov. 1962). Asst. tchr. Montessori dept. Bklyn. Heights Sem., 1915; prodn. control Sperry Gyroscope Co., 1943-44, buyer, 1944-46; with Nat. Econ. Council, Inc., 1946-68, v.p., dir., 1951-58, exec. v.p., 1958-68, dir., 1968-73. Bd. dirs., v.p. Ithaca (N.Y.) Community Chest, Girl Scouts Am., other civic groups, 1927-42. Republican. Episcopalian. Clubs: Women's National Republican (past v.p. bd. govs.); Quantuck Beach; Westhampton Beach. Home: 200 E 66th St New York NY 10021

HART, ELEANORE HAYS, Realtor; b. Pitts., June 4, 1931; d. William James and Jessie E. (Watkinson) Hays; student U. Pa., 1963-65, Duquesne U., 1969-71; grad. Realtors Inst.; m. John M. Hart, Sept. 25, 1953; children—Lynne J., J. David. Sec. H.J. Heinz Co., 1949-53; office mgr. William J. Hays, Realtor, Pitts., 1965-71; owner, broker Hays Real Estate, Pitts., 1971-81; pres. Hart Assocs., Inc., 1982—; owner Allegheny Real Estate Acad.; mem. Electronic Realty Assos.; instr. real estate Duquesne U.; teaching staff Polley Inst. Mem. Greater Pitts. Bd. Realtors (dir.), North Fellowship, Symphony North, Greater Pitts. C. of C. (dir.), Hall Inst. of Real Estate. Club: Wildwood Golf. Home: 319 Hallsborough Dr Pittsburgh PA 15238 Office: Pittsburgh PA 15238

HART, ELIZABETH ANN, psychologist; b. Chgo., Sept. 7, 1924; d. Edwin Philip and Marion Howell (Robinson) H.; B.S. in Psychology, Purdue U., 1946, M.S., 1949. Supervising vocat. appraiser Inst. Psychol. Services, Ill. Inst. Tech., 1949-51; personnel asst. Bell & Howell Co., Chgo., 1951-52; counselor Office Vocat. Guidance and Placement, U. Chgo., 1952-55; psychologist seizure unit Children's Med. Center, Boston, 1955-56; coordinator guidance and testing Lincolnwood (Ill.) Sch., also Fairview Sch., Skokie, Ill., 1956-57; sr. psychologist mcpl. dept. Psychiat. Inst., Circuit Ct. Cook County, 1957-66; clin. asst. psychiatry Northwestern U. Med. Sch., 1968-71; psychologist Barclay Hosp., Chgo., 1973. Mem. Am. Psychol. Assn., Am. Personnel and Guidance Assn., Ill. Psychol. Assn., Chgo. Guidance and Personnel Assn., Chgo. Psychol. Assn. Address: 5415 Sheridan Rd Chicago IL 60640

HART, JOANNE MARIE, food service co. exec.; b. Boston, Jan. 9, 1931; d. Patrick Joseph and Josephine Hanna (Casey) Sullivan; student public schs.; m. Maurice Edmund Hart, Sept. 10, 1955; children—Charleen, Michael, Mary, Joseph, Brenda, Kathleen, Paul. Treas., mgr. Hart Bros. Caterers, Randolph, Mass., 1955—, Lantana Co., Randolph, 1971—; dir. Quincy (Mass.) Savs. Bank. Bd. dirs. Braintree Family Counseling and Guidance Center, South Shore Bus. and Indsl. Polit. Action Com., South Shore Polit. Action; bd. trustees South Shore Hosp., South Weymouth, Mass. Mem. Mass. Restaurant Assn., South Shore C. of C. (dir.), Wedgewood Soc. Roman Catholic. Club: Old Colony Tennis (Hingham, Mass.). Home: 99 Atlantic Ave Cohasset MA 02025 Office: 43 Scanlon Dr Randolph MA 02368

HART, JUDITH ELAINE, banker; b. Danville, Ill., Oct. 24, 1942; d. Raymond Luther and Olive Elaine (Pichon) Van Buskirk; grad. in fin. U. Ill., 1981—, m. Jerry L. Hart, Nov. 15, 1975; children from previous marriage—Bruce Allan Juran, Mark Ian Juran. Loan Officer Busey 1st Nat. Bank, Urbana, Ill., 1973-79; fin. specialist City of Urbana, 1979-82; loan officer Liberty Bank, Honolulu, 1982—. Trustee Fithian (Ill.) Village Bd. Mem. Nat. Assn. Female Execs., Nat. Community Devel. Assn. Am. Inst. Banking, Am. Bank Women Assn., NOW, Ill. Council Women in Real Estate (affiliate), Women's Clubs Am. Author Urbana Rehab. Incentive Loan Program Man., 1981. Home: Kapiolani Blvd Apt 2408 Honolulu HI 96826 Office: Liberty Bank-Ala Moana Branch 1450 Ala Moana Blvd Honolulu HI 96826

HART, KITTY CARLISLE, arts adminstr.; b. New Orleans, Sept. 3, 1917; d. Joseph and Hortence (Holtzman) Conn; ed. London Sch. Econs., Royal Acad. Dramatic Arts; D.F.A. (hon.), Coll. New Rochelle; D.H.L. (hon.), Hartwick Coll., Manhattan Coll.; m. Moss Hart, Aug. 10, 1946; children—Christopher, Cathy. Chmn. N.Y. State Council on Arts; panelist TV Show To Tell the Truth; actress on stage and in films, singer Met. Opera; TV moderator and interviewer. Assoc. fellow Timothy Dwight Coll. of Yale U.; bd. dirs. Empire State Coll.; formerly spl. cons. to N.Y. Gov. on women's opportunities; mem. vis. com., bd. overseers Harvard U. Music Sch.; mem. vis. com. for the arts M.I.T. Contbr. book revs. to jours. Office: 80 Centre St New York NY 10013*

HART, MARIE MOONEY, real estate broker; b. Montgomery, Ala., Jan. 20, 1913; d. Charles France and Marie (Kidd) Mooney; B.S. in Bus., Ind. U., 1939; student U. Wis., summer 1938; m. Arthur Leland Hart, Nov. 20, 1941; children—Jeffrey Mooney, John Scot, Anne Leslie. High sch. tchr. bus., St. Paul, Ind., 1939-41; with USAAF, Army Ordnance and IRS, 1941-50; cofounder Hart Realty Co., Evansville, Ind., 1964-74; owner, mgr. rental housing. Exec. bd. Dexter Sch., 1964. Mem. VFW Aux. Republican. Presbyterian. Clubs: Tri-State Racquet, Central Turners (Evansville). Home: 2919 Washington Ave Evansville IN 47714

HART, MARY TOLEN, motion picture co. exec.; b. Arlington, N.J., June 22, 1915; d. Samuel Thornton and Estella Ware (Pepper) Tolen; student Fla. Jr. Coll., 1973-74; m. John Edward Hart, Sept. 9, 1933; children—John Edward, Marilyn Hart Burke (dec.), Patricia Hart Brock. With ABC Fla. State Theaters, Inc., Jacksonville, 1955—, asst. to dir. advt., 1977—. Named Bus. Woman of Yr., Sta. WMBR, Jacksonville, 1969. Mem. Women Motion Picture Industry Jacksonville (pres. 1959, 67, 68), Women of Motion Pictures Internat. (internat. v.p. 1960-61), internat. pres. 1969-70), Jacksonville Bus. and Profl. Women's Club (pres. 1973). Republican. Presbyterian. Clubs: German American (pres. 1978—), Ortega Forest Garden (pres. 1955, 78-80). Home: 4852 Princess Anne Ln Jacksonville FL 32210 Office: 1 Regency Pl Suite 301 9570 Regence Sq Blvd Jacksonville FL 32211

HART-DANIEL, IVY, paralegal specialist; b. N.Y.C., Sept. 28, 1947; d. Sylvanus Henry and Ruby (Adams) Hart; grad. cum laude Paralegal Inst., 1980-81; m. Victor C. Daniel, Jr., May 28, 1964; children—Eve, Beverly, Victor, Brett. Sec. to exec. asst./office mgr. Washington and Nat. Urban League, 1969-71; sec., acting program analyst Dept. Energy, Washington, 1979-80; program coordinator Gilford, Deringer & Co., Washington, 1980-81; sec./paralegal U.S. Atty.'s Office for D.C., Washington, 1981—; pres. Ivy Hart Assos., Washington, 1980—. Active ann. membership drive Washington Urban League, 1969-71; vol. worker polls, local city council and sch. bd. elections, 1971-72; others. Recipient cert. of achievement Paralegal Inst., 1981; cert. of appreciation U.S. Atty's Office-Grand Jury, 1981. Mem. Nat. Assn. Female Execs., Nat. Capitol Area Paralegal Assn., Nat. Secs. Assn. (sec. 1978-79), Smithsonian Inst. Democrat. Roman Catholic. Club: Nat. Secs. Home: 6619 2nd St NW Washington DC 20012 Office: U S Attys Office US Superior Ct 500 Indiana Ave NW Washington DC 20001

HARTE, SANDRA SUSAN, retail apparel co. exec., designer; b. Atlanta, Aug. 7, 1939; d. John Joseph and Sarah Pauline (Kivette) H.; student Sweet Briar Coll., 1957-58; B.A., Emory U., 1965, M.A.T. (fellow), 1967; M.A. in Journalism, U. Ga., 1975; 1 son, R. Davis Ison IV. Occupational therapist dept. psychiatry Emory U. Med. Sch., 1962-64; curriculum writer, tchr. Atlanta Public Sch. System, 1967-73; owner, mgr. Paragraphics, freelance writing, public relations, Atlanta, 1975-78; dir. public relations Atlanta Market Center, 1979-81; pres. Preferred Buyers Group/The Clothesline Couturier, Atlanta, 1981—. Nat. Endowment fellow, 1978. Episcopalian. Office: 3167 Peachtree Rd NE Atlanta GA 30305

HARTENSTEIN, ROSLYN DAWSON, communications cons., writer; b. Corpus Christi, Tex., Sept. 30, 1952; d. Joseph Turner and Melba Louise (Bruno) Dawson; B.A. in English, Journalism, Baylor U., 1973; M.A. in English Lit., Vanderbilt U., 1974; m. Darrel W. Hartenstein, Sept. 6, 1980. News dir. Sta. KEFC-FM, Waco, Tex., 1972-73; news dir., announcer Nashville Public Radio, 1973-74; news dir., chief copywriter Sta. KEFC-FM, 1974-75; chief copywriter, producer WACO-AM, Waco, 1975; asst. mgr. Sta. KKIK-AM, 1976-77; instr. dept. English McLennan Community Coll., Waco, 1975-77; instr. dept. communications Baylor U., 1976-77; freelance writer and editor, Ft. Worth, 1978; dir. communications publs. Dallas C. of C., 1979-82; ind. communications cons., writer, 1982—; lectr. So. Meth. U., 1980. Chmn. publicity com. Dallas water utilities centennial; chmn. publicity com. Martin Luther King, Jr. birthday celebration, 1980-81. Mem. Am. C. of C. Execs., Public Relations Soc. Am., Internat. Assn. Bus. Communicators, Women in Communications, Inc., Dallas Ad League, Press Club of Dallas, Am. Mgmt. Assn., Jr. League of Dallas. Club: Lancers. Publisher: Dallas mag., 1980-82. Home and Office: PO Box 190453 Dallas TX 75219

HARTIGAN, GRACE, artist; b. Newark, Mar. 28, 1922; d. Matthew A. and Grace (Orvis) Hartigan; student pvt. art classes; m. Robert L. Jachens, May 1941 (dec. 1948); 1 son, Jeffrey A.; m. 2d, Robert Keene, Dec. 14, 1959 (div. 1960); m. 3d, Winston H. Price, Dec. 24, 1960 (dec. 1981). Artist-in-residence Md. Inst. Grad. Sch. Painting, 1965—. One man shows Tibor de Nagy Gallery, N.Y.C., 1951-55, 57-59, Vassar Coll. Art Gallery, 1954, Martha Jackson Gallery, N.Y.C., 1962, 64, 67, 70, U. Chgo., 1967, Gertrude Kasle Gallery, Detroit, 1968, 70, 72, 74, Robert Keene Gallery, Southampton, N.Y., 1957-59, Gres Gallery, Washington, 1960, U. Minn., 1963, William Zierler Gallery, N.Y.C., 1975—, Hamilton Gallery, N.Y.C., 1981; exhibited in numerous group shows including Modern Art in U.S., 1955-56, 3d Internat. Contemporary Art Exhbn., 1957, 4th Internat. Art Exhbn., Japan, 1957, IV Biennial, Sao Paulo, 1957, New Am. Painting Show, Europe, 1958-59, World's Fair, Brussels, 1958, The Figure Since Picasso, Mus. Ghent (Belgium); collections Mus. Modern Art, N.Y.C., Walker Art Center, Whitney Mus. Am. Art, Art Inst. Chgo., Met. Mus., Raleigh Mus., Providence Mus., Bklyn. Mus., Mpls. Mus., Albright-Knox Gallery, Buffalo, numerous others. Recipient Merit award for art Mademoiselle Mag., 1957; Nat. Inst. Arts and Letters purchase award, 1974. Address: 1701 1/2 Eastern Ave Baltimore MD 21231 *

HART-JAMES, FRANCES MIRIAM, business ofcl.; b. Muskegon, Mich., Aug. 9, 1935; d. Frank Halroyed and Miriam Frances (Burghoorn) Hart; student (journalism scholar) Tyler Jr. Coll., 1953-55, (scholar) U. Tex., 1958, U. Va., 1979-81, Old Dominion U., 1981, Tidewater Community Coll., 1978; m. William Luther James, Sept. 6, 1977; children by previous marriage—Frank Paul and Miriam Kirk Fisher. Account exec. Reynolds-Elkin Advt. Agy., Tyler, Tex., 1953-55; agy. mgr. East Tex. Life Ins. Co., Tyler, 1958-66; editor in chief LaGrange (Tex.) Jour., 1966-67; purchasing agt. Invader Boat Co., 1967-69; prodn. mgr. Imperial Am. Co., Owentown, Tex., 1969-71; partner Perkins Assos., Henderson, Tex., 1972-74; mgr. govt. dept., govt. contract mgr., quality mgr. C.E. Thurston & Sons, Inc., Norfolk, Va., 1974—; cons. James & Beane Assos., 1981—. Active East Tex. Symphony Orch., 1951-55, Tyler Civic Theater, 1954-56; Sunday sch. supt. Christ Episcopal Ch., Tyler, 1956-57, All Saints Episcopal Ch., 1957-58; mem. Republican Nat. Com. Mem. Nat. Contract Mgmt. Assn. (past sec.-treas.). Nat. Assn. Female Execs. Contbg. editor to Cert. Ins. Agts. Profl. Jour., Am. Dental Assts. Profl. Jour; writer feature articles Dallas Morning News, 1953-57. Home: 5548 Brookville Rd Norfolk VA 23502 Office: 850 Tidewater Dr Norfolk VA 23504

HARTLEY, MARY DEE, county ofcl.; b. Hagerstown, Md., Mar. 13, 1932; d. George Thomas and Agnes Ogden (Cassidy) Danforth; B.S. in Bus. Adminstrn. cum laude, Wesley Coll., Dover, Del., 1982; children—Robert, Mary, Thomas, Elizabeth, Ann. Program coordinator Kent County (Del.) Public Employment Program, 1971-73; dir. operation mainstream and public employment programs Kent County, 1973-75, dir. comprehensive employment and tng. programs, 1975—. Named Outstanding Woman, Dover Century Club, 1969. Mem. Nat. Assn. Manpower Ofcls., Mid-Atlantic Manpower Planners Assn. Democrat. Roman Catholic. Home: 355 Fidder's Green Dover DE 19901 Office: 417 S State St Dover DE 19901

HARTLEY, RUTH EDITH, psychologist, educator; b. N.Y.C., May 26, 1910; d. Israel and Bertha (Cohen) Shuchowsky; B.A., Cornell U., 1930; M.A., Columbia U., 1932, Ph.D., 1944; m. Eugene Hartley, May 24, 1935; children—Sue Ann, Wendy Ellen. Instr., Bklyn. Coll., N.Y.C., 1945-46, CCNY, 1944, 46-47; psychologist Free Synagogue Child Adoption Com., N.Y.C., 1947-49; asso. prof. L.I. U., N.Y.C., 1961-63; research prof. U. Hawaii, Honolulu, 1967-68; chmn. dept. growth and devel. U. Wis., Green Bay, 1968-76; vis. professorial fellow Murdock U., Perth, Western Australia, 1975; adj. prof. Ariz. State U., Tempe, 1978-80; prin. investigator mental health and children's play Caroline Zachry Inst., N.Y.C., 1947-50; cons. CBS, 1963-64; lectr. Kindergarten Tng. Coll., Christchurch, N.Z., 1967, U. B.C., Can., 1968; evaluator NDEA Tchr. Tng. Project, N.Y.C., 1966-67. Office of Naval Research grantee, 1955-58; lic. psychologist, Wis., N.Y. Fellow Am. Psychol. Assn., Soc. for Research in Child Devel.; mem. Heard Mus. Guild, Nat. Ret. Tchrs. Assn., Phi Beta Kappa, Pi Lambda Theta, Kappa Delta Pi. Author: Sociality in Preadolescent Boys. 1946; (with others) Fundamentals of Social Psychology, 1952, transl. into German, 1955, with E.L. Hartley) Understanding Children's Play, 1952, transl. Dutch, 1958, Hebrew, 1960; Growing Through Play, 1952; (with L.K. Frank and R. Goldenson) New Play Experiences for Children, 1952; Complete Book of Children's Play, 1957, 2nd. edit., 1963; contbr. articles to psychology jours.; co-editor: Outside Readings in Psychology, 1950, 2nd. edit., 1957, 3rd, edit., 1965.

HARTLEY, VIRGINIA HAWGOOD GJEMSO, Realtor; b. Everett, Wash., Aug. 14, 1916; d. Einar S. and Josie Elma (West) Gjemso; B.S., U. Wash., 1940; m. Arthur Phillip Hawgood, Feb. 22, 1944; children—Katherine Hawgood Baker, Christine Hawgood Durvee, Arthur Phillip; m. 2d, Fred Hartley, May 16, 1973. Salesman, Wynn Norton Co., La Canada, Calif., 1955-59; mgr. Jonnie L. Ross Co., La Canada, 1959-62; pres., owner La Canada Valley Realty, 1962-78, Hawgood Assos., La Canada, Palm Desert, Calif., 1972-78. Served with Spl. Services, World War Two. Mem. La Canada Multiple Listing Assn. (pres. 1970-71), La Canada (pres. 1972, dir.), Palm Desert bds. realtors, Calif. Real Estate Assn., Nat. Assn. Realtors (pres. La Canada chpt. women's council 1969-70, dir. 13th dist. 1968-72) U. Wash. Alumni Assn., Mu Sigma, Alpha Gamma Delta. Clubs: Indian Wells Country (Calif.), Everett Golf and Country, Everett Yacht. Address: UC Bank Bldg 650 Foothill La Canada CA 91011

HARTMAN, ANN RUTLEDGE, interior designer; b. Ft. Dodge, Iowa, Sept. 29, 1922; d. Reyburn Lorenzo and Mabel (Mears) Rutledge; student Ft. Dodge Jr. Coll., 1940-41, Iowa State U., 1941-43, Chgo. Art Inst., 1943-44; m. Otto John Hartman, Sept. 14, 1952; children—Leslie, Elizabeth, Martin. With Interior Displays, Sears & Roebuck, Chgo., 1945-47; interior designer Mandel Bros., Chgo., 1947-53, freelance, Terre Haute, Ind., 1953-65, Kansas City, Mo., 1965-68, Chgo., 1968-71, Terre Haute, 1972-80; now pres. Interior Arts, Inc. and Gallery House, Terre Haute. Prize winner, Chgo. Tribune Better Rms. competition, 1948, 49; Cert. of Achievement, Sch. Bus., Ind. State U., 1975; Outstanding Craftsmanship award Mansion House Fabrics, 1978. Clubs: Young Matrons League, PEO, Kappa Kappa Kappa. Home: 114 Southglen Rd Apt 31 Terre Haute IN 47802 Office: 4812 S 7th St Terre Haute IN 47802

HARTMAN, BARBARA JOSEPHINE, librarian; b. Appalachia, Va., Oct. 15, 1936; d. George Luther and Esther Maude (Lowe) Cress; B.S., Emory and Henry Coll., 1958; M.S. in L.S. (Del. State Library Commn. fellow), Drexel U., 1968; m. Robert Douglas Athey Jr., Jan. 10, 1958 (div. 1980); children—Ashley Elizabeth, Carol Scott, Jane Kelsey; m. 2d, John Edward Hartman, Aug. 23, 1980. Mem. staff Enoch Pratt Free Library, Balt., 1961-63; library trainee Dover (Del.) Public Library, 1965-67; librarian St. Francis Hosp. Sch. Nusing, Wilmington, Del., 1968-71, St. Francis Hosp., Wilmington, 1971-73; head reference dept. Taylor Meml. Public Library, Cuyahoga Falls, Ohio, 1976-77; dir. med. library services St. Margaret Meml. Hosp., Pitts., 1978—; pres. Pitts. East Hosp. Library Coop., 1981—. Mem. Med. Library Assn. (sec. Pitts. 1979-81). Home: 1815 Wightman St Pittsburgh PA 15217

HARTMAN, CATHERINE RUDISILL, educator; b. Biscoe, N.C., Mar. 24, 1916; d. Jacob Andrew and Annie (Dietz) Rudisill; B.S., Appalachian State Tchrs. Coll., 1944; M.A., Columbia, 1950, profl. diploma Tchrs. Coll., 1959; student U. London, Heidelberg U., summer 1953, N.Y.U., summer 1954, U. Calif. at Los Angeles, summer 1956; m. Harold R. Hartman, Dec. 26, 1962. Primary tchr. Park Grace Sch., Kings Mountain, N.C., 1936-39; elementary, music tchr. Oakhurst Sch., Charlotte, N.C., 1939-44, Gary Sch., Tampa, Fla., 1945-47; elementary supr. schs. Gaston County Schs., Gastonia, N.C., 1947-55, dir. instrn., 1955-61, asst. supt. in charge instrn., 1961-63; asso. prof. edn. William Paterson Coll. of N.J., Wayne, 1964—, chmn. gen. elementary program com. for curriculum revision, 1967-68, chmn. dept. secondary edn., 1972-78, chmn. dept. adminstrv., adult and secondary programs, 1979—. Mem. Assn. Supervision and Curriculum Devel. of N.E.A. (nat. dir. 1958-61), Nat. Conf. Christians and Jews (Carolinas regional dir. 1952-62), AAUW (dir. Charlotte 1953-55), Assn. Childhood Edn. (life, treas. N.C. 1955-57, adviser Gaston County br. 1955-63), William Paterson Fedn. Coll. Tchrs., Am. Assn. Sch. Adminstrs. (life), Kappa Delta Pi, Pi Lambda Theta. Presbyn. Home: 26 S Middletown Rd Georgian Ct Pearl River NY 10965 Office: Raubinger Hall 426 William Paterson Coll of NJ Wayne NJ 07470

HARTMAN, JOAN FRANCES, ins. agy. exec.; b. St. Louis, July 23, 1931; d. Charles Joseph and Mary Margaret (McDonnell) Brennan; student Loretto Heights Coll., 1949-50; m. Alvin Hartman, Oct. 24, 1950; children—Michael Lee, Michelle Lynn. With creative art dept. Hallmark Greeting Cards, Kansas City, Mo., 1950; with T.F. Daly Ins. Agy., Denver, 1950-53, Mac's Supply Co., Denver, 1955-63, Top Value Enterprises, Denver, 1963-69; mgr. acctg., investments and lic. ins. agts. Ind. Ins. Agts. of Colo., Inc., also Ind. Ins. Agts. of Denver, Inc., 1969-82; prin. Joan Hartman Ins. Agy., 1982—; sec.-treas. Braden Co., Inc., 1982—; co-owner, v.p. H & N Rentals, Denver, 1976—; sales rep. Chrislove of Denver, Inc., 1978-80; dir. Chateau D'Art. Recipient award USO, 1956; Blue Vase award, 1982, Ace, Double Ace, Triple Ace and Super Ace awards, 1982, Knights of Sky award (all Farmers Ins. Group). Mem. Coalition of Bus. Women (co-founder). Democrat. Roman Catholic. Office: 9030 Yukon St Suite 1260 Silo Bus Park Silo Bldg I Westminster CO 80020

HARTMAN, JOANNE ALIFELD, painter; b. Bklyn., Nov. 15, 1931; d. Arthur Alifeld and Anna (Streep) Alifeld Grappel; B.A. in Psychology, Bklyn. Coll., 1952; postgrad. in art Nassau Community Coll., 1970-73; M.F.A., Queens Coll., 1975; m. Robert Hartman, Oct. 5, 1952; children—Ronni, Marjorie, Ellen. In various advt. positions, 1948-54, 62-63; tchr. N.Y.C. Bd. Edn., 1955-56; teaching asst. Queens Coll., 1975; asst. prof. art Suffolk County Community Coll., 1975—; one-man shows: Queens Coll., Flushing, N.Y., 1975, Hofstra U., Hempstead, N.Y., 1980, Ingber Gallery, N.Y.C., 1981; group shows: Heckscher Museum, Huntington, N.Y., 1976, Queens Coll. 1974, Nassau Community Coll., 1971, Firehouse Gallery, Garden City, N.Y., 1972, Nassau County Cultural Arts Competition, 1972, Oyster Bay Twp. (N.Y.) Competition, 1977, Suffolk County Community Coll., 1976, 77, 79, Women's Internat. Arts Festival, N.Y.C., 1975, N.Y. U. Loeb Student Center, 1976, 112 Greene St., N.Y.C., 1978, Landmark Gallery, N.Y.C., 1978, Paul Klapper Library, Queens Coll., 1979, U. Mass., 1980, First Women's Bank, N.Y.C., 1980, N.Y. Kidney Found., 1981, Ingber Gallery, 1981, A.I.R. Gallery, N.Y.C., 1981. Leader, 4-H Club, Jericho, N.Y. Mem. Coll. Art Assn. Home: 42 Flower Ln Jericho NY 11753 Studio: 89 W 3d St New York NY 10012

HARTMAN, NANCY LEE, physician; b. Philipsburg, Pa., July 29, 1951; d. Richard Lee and Ann Hartman; grad. Barbizon Sch. Modeling, 1970; A.A., Harcum Jr. Coll., 1969-71; B.A., Lycoming Coll., 1974; M.S., L.I. U., 1977; M.D., Am. U. of Caribbean in Plymouth, Montserrat, W.I., 1981. Med. technologist Lock Haven (Pa.) Hosp., 1971-72, Williamsport (Pa.) Hosp., 1972-73, Renovo (Pa.) Hosp., 1974; microbiologist Jersey Shore (Pa.) Hosp., 1974, N.Y. Hosp. and Cornell Med. Center, N.Y.C., 1974-75, Drekter and Heisler Labs., N.Y.C., 1975, North Shore Labs., Inc., Syosset, N.Y., 1976-78. Allied Health Professions trainee, 1975-83. Mem. Am. Soc. Clin. Pathologists (registered med. technologist), Am. Soc. Microbiology. Home: PO Box 98 Roslyn NY 11576

HARTMAN, PATRICIA O., state legislator; b. Harrison County, W.Va., Aug. 18, 1925; d. Carroll R. and Mae (Yoho) Ogden; B.A., Marshall U.; m. George W. Hartman, Oct. 4, 1946; children—Georgeann Hartman Ruby, Richard O., Edwin R. Mem. W.Va. Ho. of Dels., 1976—, mem. coms. banking and ins., edn. (vice chmn.), health and welfare. Active Commn. on Aging, LWV, Nat. Order Women Legislators; bd. dirs. Barnett Child Care Center; mem. Region II Community Mental Health Center, Cabell County Bd. Edn. Mem. AAUW, Alpha Xi Delta. Democrat. Lutheran. Club: Pea Ridge Women's (Gen. Fedn. Women's Clubs). Office: West Virginia House of Dels Charleston WV 25305 *

HARTMAN, SUE ANNETTE, ednl. adminstr.; b. Findlay, Ohio, July 10; d. H. Lee and Edythe Eveline H.; B.S. in Edn., Bowling Green State U., 1957, masters, 1961, postgrad., 1974-79; postgrad. U. Toledo, 1977-79, (scholar) Ohio State U., 1969, UCLA, 1972, (Ruth Grimes scholar), Miami U., Oxford, Ohio, 1971, Rider Coll., 1974. Bus. edn. tchr. Whitmer High Sch., Washington Local Schs., Toledo, 1957-68, vocat. intensive office edn. tchr., 1968-74; coop. office edn. coordinator

Whitmer Vocat. Center, Washington Local Schs., Toledo, 1974-76, trade and industry supr., 1976—; cons. Ohio Dept. Vocat. Edn. Delta Kappa Gamma scholar, 1970-71; Ohio Savs. and Loan Fin. scholar, 1969; Ohio Ins. Inst. scholar, 1976. Mem. NEA, Ohio Edn. Assn., Ohio Trade and Indsl. Edn. Suprs. Assn., Am. Vocat. Assn., Ohio Vocat. Assn., N.W. Ohio Edn. Assn., Tchrs. Assn. Washington Local Schs. (Outstanding Educator award 1979-80), Delta Pi Epsilon (corr. sec. 1973, pres.-elect 1979, pres. 1980), Delta Kappa Gamma (rec. sec. 1977, corr. sec. 1980). Methodist. Home: 5679 Monroe St Apt 606 Sylvania OH 43560 Office: Whitmer Vocat Center 5719 Clegg Dr Toledo OH 43613

HARTMAN-GOLDSMITH, JOAN, art historian; b. Malden, Mass., June 3, 1933; d. Hyman and Ruth (Hadler) Lederman; m. Alan Hartman, Jan. 10, 1952 (div.); 1 dau., Hedy Hartman; m. 2d, Robert Goldsmith, Aug. 12, 1976. Instr., coordinator, initiator art history program, China Inst. in Am., N.Y.C., 1967-77; lectr. sch. continuing edn. N.Y.U., N.Y.C., 1976-77; exec. officer, dir. public info. Jewish Mus., N.Y.C., 1977-80; dir. Inst. for Asian Studies, Inc., N.Y.C., 1981—; lectr. Cooper-Hewitt Mus. of Design (Smithsonian Instn.), 1976; lectr. mus. Los Angeles, St. Louis, Pitts., Indpls., Buffalo, Rochester, N.Y., Toronto, Can., Denver Art Mus., Seattle Art Mus., Asian Art Mus. San Francisco; spl. lecture tour for Archaeol. Inst. Am., 1977; condr. seminars on Chinese jade, Met. Mus. Art, N.Y.C., 1977; fellow in perpetuity, mem. vis. com. slide and photograph library Met. Mus. Art; trustee Indpls. Mus. Art; mem. art com. China House Gallery, N.Y.C.; program chmn. ann. conf. MAR/Assn. Asian Studies, Bucknel U., 1974. Nat. Endowment grantee, vis. specialist Buffalo Mus. Sci., 1972, Indpls. Mus. Art, 1971; reviewer Nat. Endowment for Humanities, div. public programs, 1978—. Mem. Am. Oriental Soc., Assn. for Asian Studies (founding mem. Mid-Atlantic Region, 1972, sec./treas., 1973, adv. council, 1974-75), Oriental Club of N.Y. Treas., Upper Eastside Jewish Community Council, N.Y.C. Am. corr. Oriental Art mag., London, 1963—; contbr. feature articles to pubs. in field; guest curator, author catalogue: Ancient Chinese Jades from the Buffalo Museum of Science, China Inst. Am., 1975, Three Dynasties of Jade, Indpls. Mus. Art, 1971, Chinese Jade through the Centuries, China Inst. Am.. 1968-69, Chinese Jade of Five Centuries, 1969; author slide survey: Introduction to Chinese Art, 1973; contbr. articles and book revs. to learned jours. and pubs. Office: Inst for Asian Studies 619 Lexington Ave New York Ny 10022

HARTMANN, PEGGY O'SULLIVAN, retail credit exec.; b. N.Y.C., May 14, 1923; d. John Mortimer and Mary (Roach) O'Sullivan; student Regis Coll., 1941-42, Trinity Coll., 1943-44; B.S., George Peabody Tchrs. Coll., 1973; M.A.T. (fellow), Vanderbilt U., 1975; m. Robert C. Hartmann, Mar. 16, 1946 (div. Aug. 1975); children—Kathleen, Robert C., David, Richard, Margaret M., Ellen. Lab. technician Pa. Hosp., Phila., 1945-46; tchr. Pace Acad., Atlanta, 1975-76; mgr. service desk Neiman-Marcus Atlanta, 1976-77, credit mgr., 1977—. Pres. Vanderbilt Med. Aux., 1959-61, St. Cecilia Parents Club, Nashville, 1962-63, Father Ryan High Sch. Aux., Nashville, 1964-65; pres. Religious Heritage Am., 1969, named Ch. Woman of Yr., 1969; sect. chmn. comml. unit United Way of Met. Atlanta, 1980-81. Recipient St. Thomas More award Nat. Council Cath. Men, 1971; asso. credit exec. Soc. Cert. Consumer Credit Execs. Mem. Atlanta Credit Women Internat. (chmn. bd. 1981), Dixie Council Credit Women Internat., Atlanta Consumer Credit Assn. (dir. 1979-83), Atlanta Women's C. of C., Nat. Assn. Female Execs., Internat. Consumer Credit Assn. (bd. dirs. Dist. III 1983—), Atlanta Vanderbilt Alumni. Roman Catholic. Home: 1443 Hampton Glen Ct Decatur GA 30033 Office: 3393 Peachtree Rd NE Atlanta GA 30326

HARTRANFT, JUDY KAREN EVELAND, cosmetic co. exec.; b. Laurelville, Ohio, Oct. 13, 1944; d. Lloyd Franklin Eveland and Virgie Leota (Bainter) Eveland Cox; student public schs., Laurelville, 1950-62; m. Orman N. Hartranft, Mar. 24, 1962; children—Cheryl Lee, Mindy Sue. Rep., Avon Products, Inc., Cin., 1965-75, dist. mgr., 1975-81, field trainer Springdale br., 1980—, mgmt. asso. trainer, 1981—, nat. panel mem., 1979-80. Pres., Laurelville Little League, 1975-76, girls' softball coach, 1975-78. Avon Circle of Excellence awardee, 1976, 77, 78. Home: 2930 Larchwood Ct Maineville OH 45039 Office: Avon Products Inc 175 Progress Pl Cincinnati OH 45246

HARTSHORN-FLYNN, EDWINA, psychologist; Weymouth, Mass., Mar. 10, 1947; d. George F. and Doris H. (Barnes) Hartshorn; A.B. (Elisha Benjamin Andrews scholar), Brown U., 1969; M.Ed. (Fellow 1969-70), U. N.C., 1971, Ph.D., 1974; m. James F. Flynn, Aug. 13, 1977. Psychologist, program coordinator West Seneca (N.Y.) Developmental Center, 1973—. Bd. dirs. Health Care Plan of Western N.Y., 1979. Mem. Am. Psychol. Assn., Am. Assn. Mental Deficiency, Phi Beta Kappa. Home: 39 Wanakah Heights Hamburg NY 14075 Office: 1200 East and West Rd West Seneca NY 14224

HARTSOOK, ELMA W., civic worker; b. Mt. Gilead, Ohio; d. Isaac W. and Maria (Ulrey) Wheeler; grad. public schs.; m. F.M. Hartsook, June 26, 1919 (dec. Jan. 1951). Treas., Morrow County's Med. Aux., 1958—, Morrow County Mental Health, 1956—; del. Rep. Nat. Conv., 1956; mem. finance commn. Methodist Ch. Mem. 40 and 8, Am. Legion Aux. Clubs: Ladies Oriental Shrine, Order White Shrine of Jerusalem, Order Eastern Star (past matron, past pres. dist.). Home: 133 E Main St Cardington OH 43315

HARTT, SUSAN KAY, lawyer; b. Ypsilanti, Mich., Mar. 21, 1948; d. Harold and Helen Louise (Collins) Hartt; B.A., Coll. of Wooster, 1970; M.A. in Econs., J.D., U. Mich., 1974. Admitted to Ill. bar, 1974, Mich. bar, 1978; asst. atty. gen. State of Ill., 1974-76; asso. firm McDermott, Will & Emery, Chgo., 1976-78; staff atty. Kellogg Co., Battle Creek Mich., 1978-79, food and drug counsel, 1979-80, asst. gen. counsel, 1980—. Mem. Am. Bar Assn., Women Lawyers Assn. of Mich., Mich. State Bar, Ill. State Bar. Office: Kellogg Co 235 Porter St Battle Creek MI 49016

HARTUNG, NOVELLA POLINORI, civic worker; b. Alliance, Ohio, July 9, 1938; d. Hugo George and Jennie (Aquilio) Polinori; student Central Tech. Inst., Los Angeles, 1957, Mt. Union Coll., Alliance, 1959; m. David Lewis Hartung, Dec. 9, 1961; children—David Lewis, Elizabeth Hilty. With Western Airlines, San Francisco, 1957-58, First Nat. Bank, Alliance, Ohio, 1959-61. Mem. exec. bd. Jr. League of Canton, Inc., 1968, 70, 75-77, Woman of the Yr. chmn., 1969, rec. sec., 1970, chmn. pub. relations, 1977-78; mem. exec. bd., cotillian chmn. Children's Aid. Soc., 1967; mem. exec. bd., co-chmn. symphony ball Canton Symphony League, 1971-72, mem. adv. bd., caberet co-chmn. Canton Cultural Center, 1973; v.p. Aultman Hosp. Women's Bd., 1976-78, pres., 1978-79, angel auction chmn., 1975, also mem. hosp. assn. bd.; mem. Mus. Guild bd. of Canton Art Inst., 1977—, publicity chmn., 1979—, mem. exec. bd., 1979—; fashion show coordinator Football Hall of Fame, 1978-79, vice chmn. luncheon, 1980; Grey Lady, ARC, 1969-71; tchr. arts and crafts, pediatrics unit Aultman Hosp.; mem. women's com. Blossom Music Center; co-chmn. Canton Symphony Pop Concert; vol. worker Aultman Hosp. Gift Shop; active worker fund drives Heart Fund, Art Inst., Civic Ballet, United Way, United Arts; mem. ball com. Jewish Center; chmn. fund-raising dr. Jackson High Sch. Marching Band, 1981. Recipient appreciation award Profl. Football Hall of Fame, 1969, 79; dividend of merit cert. Cultural Center for the Arts, 1977; Community Service award Jackson Jaycees, 1981. Republican. Mem. United Church of Christ. Home: 5282 St Andrews Canton OH 44708

HARTY, MARY ANN, librarian; b. Holden, Mass., Oct. 28, 1949; d. Martin Christopher and Arlene Frances (Joyal) H.; student Salzburg (Austria) U., 1972-73; B.A. cum laude, U. N.H., 1974; postgrad. Johns Hopkins U., 1975-76; M.S., Simmons Coll., 1979; m. John Anthony Domini, Dec. 17, 1976. Cataloging asst. Widener Library, Harvard U., 1976-77, intern Baker Library, 1977-79; head tech. services Learning Resource Center No. Essex Community Coll., 1979-80; library project adminstr. Sylvania Systems Group Strategic Systems div. GTE Products Corp., Westboro, Mass., 1980-82. Mem. Spl. Libraries Assn. (co-editor Boston chpt. News Bull. 1981-82), Am. Soc. Info. Sci., Beta Phi Mu (pres. Beta Beta chpt. 1981-82). Home: Brooktree Apts 2790 NW 29th St Corvallis OR 97330

HARTZ, LUETTA BERTHA, ins. co. exec.; b. Stevens Point, Wis., Sept. 29, 1947; d. Alfred Bernard Carl and Bertha Martha (Stauffer) Janz; student Madison (Wis.) Bus. Coll., 1965-66; m. James Patrick Hartz, Dec. 31, 1975. With Employers Ins. of Wausau (Wis.), 1966-68; casualty rater Sentry Ins. Co., Stevens Point, Wis., 1968-70, casualty supr., 1970-71, casualty trainor, 1971-72, customer service corr., 1972-74, bur. technician, 1974-75, customer service and acctg. mgr., Concord, Mass., 1975-79, personal lines property processing mgr., 1979-81, personal lines casualty processing mgr., 1981—. Campaign treas. Republican Party county clk. candidate, Portage County, Wis., 1972. Mem. U.S. Golf Assn. (asso.). Lutheran. Club: Emblem (1st asst. marshal 1980-81, treas. 1981-83) (Concord, Mass.). Home: 40 Drummer Rd Acton MA 01720 Office: Sentry Ins Co Old Road to Nine Acre Corner Concord MA 01742

HARTZ, LYNN RICHARDSON, counselor; b. Charleston, W.Va., Jan. 27; d. Nelson McClure and Mary Grace (Stone) Richardson; A.B., Marshall U., Huntington, W.Va., 1963; M.S. in Child Devel. and Family Relations, U. Ariz., 1973; M.A. in Counseling and Guidance, W.Va. Coll. Grad. Studies, 1976; Ph.D. in Psychotherapy, Union Grad. Sch., Cin., 1978; m. William Leonard Hartz, Oct. 12, 1968 (dec.); children—Nell Marie, Hope Keturah, Mark Thomas Perrin (dec.), Grace Lynn Hartz Thomas. Exec. dir. Tucson Area council Camp Fire Girls, 1968-70; counselor Family Services Kanawha Valley, Charleston, 1972-73; dir. children's mental health services W.Va. Dept. Mental Health, Charleston, 1976-77; exec. dir. Appalachian Women's Cons. Services, also dir. Women's Counseling Center W.Va., Charleston, 1977—; convenor 1st ann. Conf. Rural Am. Women, 1977. Mem. Mental Health Counselors Assn., Am. Personnel and Guidance Assn., Psychology of Birth Assn., Appalachian Women's Network, Council Appalachian Women, Am. Assn. Sex Educators, Counselor and Therapists. Author poems, articles in field. Home: 1325 Summit Dr Charleston WV 25302 Office: 1021 Quarrier St Suite 214 Charlestown WV 25301

HARTZMAN, MELONEE JEAN, chemist, air force officer; b. Shreveport, La., Apr. 1, 1949; d. George Calvin and Norma Jean Raines; B.S., William Carey Coll.; student La. State U. Sch. Med. Technology, 1970-71. Chem. supr. Champlain Physicians Hosp., Plattsburgh, N.Y., 1971-73; sr. staff technologist Willis Knighton Hosp., Shreveport, 1973-74, supr. blood bank, 1978-80; research asso. Albany Med. Coll. br., Alamogordo, N.Mex., 1974-75; lab. night supr. Gerald Champion Hosp., Alamogordo, 1975-78; commd. capt. U.S. Air Force, 1980; officer in charge chemistry David Grant Med. Center, Travis AFB, Calif., 1980-82; chief clin. pathology USAF Hosp., Bitburg, W. Ger., 1982—. Mem. Soc. Clin. Pathology, Am. Assn. Mil. Surgeons, Soc. Armed Forces Med. Lab. Scientists, Nat. Orgn. Exec. Females, NOW. Republican. Roman Catholic. Office: Dept Clin Pathology USAF Hosp Bitburg Box 6212 APO New York NY 09132

HARVELL, ELAINE JOHNSON, home economist, assn. ofcl.; b. Spartanburg, S.C., Feb. 18, 1946; d. Alderman Boreham and Carolyn W. (Mills) Johnson; B.A., Meredith Coll., Raleigh, N.C., 1968; diploma Culinary Arts Inst., Chgo., 1974; m. Charles Lewis Harvell, Apr. 11, 1970. Asst. home extension agt. N.C. State U., Yadkinville, 1968-69; promotion specialist N.C. Dept. Agr., Raleigh, 1969-72; A.M. hostess Sta. WBT-TV, Charlotte, N.C., 1972-73; supr. home econs. S.C. Dept. Agr., Columbia, 1973; account exec. Newman, Saylor & Gregory, advt., Columbia, 1973-78; product publicist, freelance cons., Raleigh, 1978-79; mktg. specialist N.C. Dept. Agr., 1979-80; dir. consumer affairs N.C. Pork Producers Assn., Raleigh, 1980—. Recipient Superior Service award N.C. Dept. Agr., 1970; Coastal Plains Regional Commn. research grantee, 1979. Mem. Am. Home Econs. Assn., Home Economists in Bus., Am. Woman in Radio and TV, N.C./S.C. Home Econs. Assn., Raleigh Public Relations Soc., Columbia Media Club. Office: NC Pork Producers Assn PO Box 25727 Raleigh NC 26711

HARVELL, JUDY ERNEST, food editor; b. Norfolk, Va., Sept. 22, 1939; d. John Walter and Miriam Earle (Turner) Ernest; student Mary Washington Coll., 1957-58, Stuart Circle Sch. Nursing, 1958-59; m. James Wayman Harvell, Jr., Apr. 4, 1959; children—Mark, Miriam, Heather, John. Loan teller Central Nat. Bank, Richmond, Va., 1961-64; bookkeeper J. G. Colby Co., Richmond, 1964-65; food editor Daily Press, Newport News, Va., 1972—. Mem. Nat. Fedn. Press Women, Va. Press Women. Methodist. Home: 42 W Governor Dr Newport News VA 23602 Office: 7505 Warwick Blvd Newport News VA 23607

HARVEY, ALICE SAVINA WILSON, ret. tchr., civic worker; b. Rome, N.Y., Oct. 27, 1915; d. Lester Henry and Laura Alice (Crowell) Wilson; B.A., Wellesley Coll., 1937; postgrad. (scholar) U. Heidelberg (Germany), 1937, U. Catholique d'Angers, France, 1937-38, Middlebury Coll., 1940, 42, U. Lisbon (Portugal), 1971, U. Pisa (Italy), 1979; m. John Edward Harvey, Aug. 30, 1939; children—Diane Harvey Clarke, James Edward and Janet Alice Harvey Graddick (twins). Tchr. French, Mary C. Wheeler Sch., Providence, 1938-39; tchr. French and English, Gambier (Ohio) High Sch., 1952-53; tchr. French, Mt. Vernon (Ohio) High Sch., 1958-66, tchr. advanced French, 1968-69; tchr. French, Kenyon Coll., Gambier, 1970. Sec. bd. county visitors Knox County (Ohio), 1955-57; judge precinct elections, 1976; vol. ARC, Mercy Hosp., Mt. Vernon, 1975-80. Inst. Internat. Edn. fellow, 1937-38; NDEA grantee, 1960; John Hay fellow Colo. Coll., 1963. Mem. LWV (pres. 1977-79), Nat. Ret. Tchrs. Assn., Ohio Ret. Tchrs. Assn., Knox County Ret. Tchrs. (legis. chmn. 1981—). Democrat. Clubs: Town and Country Garden (v.p. 1981—). Home: 201 Woodside Dr PO Box 123 Gambier OH 43022

HARVEY, BARBARA LEE WHITE (MRS. DAVID L. HARVEY), educator; b. Jackson, Tenn., May 2, 1937; d. Berlie Thomas and Grace Lucille (Tapley) White; B.A. (C.M. Gooch scholar), Blue Mountain (Miss.) Coll., 1959; M.A. in Edn., U. LaVerne (Calif.), 1981; m. David Lee Harvey, Sept. 3, 1960; children—Stephen Lee, Victoria Leann. Dir. master tchr. Valley View Christian Preschool, 1973-74; prof., dir. master tchr., chmn. dept. early childhood edn. Early Childhood Devel. Center, Pacific Christian Coll., Fullerton, Calif., 1974—; owner, dir. Christian Pacific Edn. Centers, Fullerton. Mem. adv. bd. Sick Child Observation Clinic, Yorba Linda; Calif.; chmn. S.W. dist. Evangel. Free Ch. of Am., 1968-74. Mem. Nat., So. Calif., Orange County (chmn. career guidance 1974-75, ways and means 1975—, v.p. charge edn. 1976—) assns. for edn. young children, Church Related Nursery Sch. Fellowship, Calif. Assn. Young Children, Assn. Christian Schs. Internat., Nat. Assn. Christian Sch. Adminstrs., Concerned Women of Am. Evangelical Christian. Club: Women's Enrichment (Fullerton). Office: Christian Pacific Edn Centers 1231 E Chapman Ave Fullerton CA 92631

HARVEY, DOROTHY MAY, newspaper editor; b. Bartlesville, Okla., Apr. 3, 1922; d. Paul and Vila May (Ray) H.; B.S. in Commerce, Okla. A&M Coll., 1950. Tech. asst. research dept. Phillips Petroleum Co., 1942-48; program dir., pub. relations dir. Topeka YWCA, 1950-55; asso. editor Capper's Weekly, Topeka, 1955-73, editor, 1974—. Mem. Women in Communications. Republican. Methodist. Home: 2311 Hazelton Ct Topeka KS 66606 Office: 616 Jefferson St Topeka KS 66607

HARVEY, DOROTHY MCDONALD, ret. home economist; b. Junction City, Ark., May 5, 1917; d. Robert John and Annie (Nolley) McDonald; B.S., La. Tech. Coll., 1939; postgrad. La. State U., 1953, 69; M.S., Iowa State U., 1951; Ph.D., Tex. Women's U., 1957; m. J.P. Harvey, June 6, 1946. Tchr., Junction City High Sch., 1937-38; tchr. home econs. Rocky Mount (La.) High Sch., 1939-43; asst. home demonstration agt. Rapids Parish, Alexandria, La., 1943; asso. home demonstration agt. Caddo Parish, Shreveport, La., 1944-46; home demonstration agt. Jackson Parish, Jonesboro, La., 1946-55; asst. prof. clothing and textiles Tex. Woman's U., Denton, Tex., 1957-60; asso. prof. Wis. State U., Stevens Point, 1968-69, Ga. So. Coll., Statesboro, 1969-70; prof. Miss. U. for Women, Columbus, 1970-80. Tex. Woman's U. fellow, 1955-57. Mem. AAUW, La. Home Demonstration Agts. Assn. (sec. 1954), AAUP, Am. Home Econs. Assn., ASTM, Miss. Home Econs. Assn., Central Region Coll. Profs. Clothing and Textiles, Delta Phi Delta, Phi Upsilon Omicron, Epsilon Sigma Phi. Methodist. Democrat. Club: Jonesboro Hodge Garden. Home: 820 Polk Ave S Jonesboro LA 71251

HARVEY, GILLIAN MARY (JILL), legal asst. and sec.; b. Mineola, N.Y., July 10, 1936; d. Rexford Leslie and Olga Anne (Lambert) Thompson; B.S. in Bus., Russell Sage Coll., 1957; cert. litigation specialist, legal asst. U. West Los Angeles, 1974; m. Fene Arthur Henry, Jr., Sept. 20, 1958 (div. 1972); children—Deborah Marie, Bruce Rexford; m. 2d. H. Darwin Harvey, Nov. 9, 1974. Legal asst., legal sec. Coleman & O'Connell, Los Angeles, 1972-74, DJB Corp., Los Angeles, 1974-75; pvt. practice legal asst., Los Angeles, 1975-79; legal asst., legal sec. Ball, Hunt, Hart, Brown & Baerwitz, Beverly Hills, Calif., 1979—. Pres., bd. dirs. Bonner Sch. Parent Group; mem. Santa Monica Homeowners Assn. Mem. Los Angeles Paralegal Assn. Democrat. Episcopalian. Office: Ball Hunt Hart Brown and Baerwitz 450 N Roxbury Dr Suite 500 Beverly Hills CA 90212

HARVEY, HELENE ELNA, social worker; b. Duxbury, Vt., Aug. 22, 1934; d. Harry Francis and Mabel Elna (Johns) H.; B.A., Lebanon Valley Coll., 1967; M.S.W., Our Lady of the Lake U., San Antonio, 1970. Community worker Croagh Patrick Youth Center, Cambridge, Mass., 1957-58, St. Teresa's Social Service Center, Bklyn., 1958-60; area supr. Cath. Social Services, Harrisburg, Pa., 1950-57; caseworker Cath. Charities, Alexandria, La., 1967-68; supr. foster home devel. div., 1970-72, program dir. intake div. and foster home devel. div., 1972-73; with Harris County Child Welfare, Houston, 1970-73; dir. continuing edn., instr. Grad. Sch. Social Work, U. Houston, 1973-79, 80-81, adj. prof., 1979-80; field instr. Harris County Child Welfare; cons. Christian Child Help Found., Permanency Planning Project. Recipient Apt Recognition award U. Tex. Med. Sch., Houston, Herman Hosp., 1975. Mem. Acad. Cert. Social Workers, Nat. Assn. Social Workers, Internat. Assn. Schs. Social Work, Tex. Soc. Adlerian Psychology. Author: (with Barbara Glass) Guides for Foster Parents, 1972. Office: 4200 Scotland St #72 Houston TX 77007

HARVEY, KAREN MARIE, county ofcl.; b. Sioux Falls, S.D., Feb. 20, 1938; d. Harold William and Fern Nelson Pool; B.A. in History, State U. S.D., 1960; m. Richard L. Harvey, Aug. 18, 1960; children—Aaron, Anna. Tchr. history and govt. Hickman High Sch., Columbia, Mo., 1960-62; coordinator non-credit program continuing edn. Ohio U., Athens, 1975-76; county commr., Athens County, Ohio, 1977—. Mem. legis. com. County Commrs. Assn. Ohio, 1978-82; pres. Athens County Bd. Commrs., 1981; pres. Athens County Data Processing Bd., 1977-79; del. Ohio White House Conf. on Libraries and Info. Services, 1978; Ohio del. White House Conf. on Libraries and Info. Services, 1979; pres. Athens County Council on Aging, 1978-79, Friends of the Library of Ohio U., 1979-82; trustee Tri-County Community Action Agy., 1977-82; mem. Athens County Regional Planning Commn., 1977-82; mem. Council Govts Athens City-County Planning, 1977-82; trustee Buckeye Hills-Hocking Valley Regional Planning Dist., 1977-82; mem. Athens County Community Improvement Corp., 1977-82; mem. adv. council Tri-County Joint Vocat. High Sch., 1978-80; trustee Area 6 Health Planning Agy., 1979-81; bd. dirs. Nelsonville Public Square, Inc., 1979-82; mem. research com. Athens Econ. Devel., 1980; trustee Dairy Barn, 1979-80; adv. com. Ohio State Library Bd., 1982—; mem. Ohio State Community Edn. Adv. Com., 1982—. Democrat. Club: Pi Beta Phi Alumnae (treas. 1979-82) (Athens). Office: Athens County Courthouse Athens OH 45701

HARVEY, KATHERINE ABLER, civic worker; b. Chgo., May 17, 1946; d. Julius and Elizabeth (Engelman) Abler; student La Sorbonne, Paris, 1965-66; A.A.S., Bennett Coll, 1968; m. Julian Whitcomb Harvey, Sept. 7, 1974. Asst. librarian McDermott, Will & Emery, Chgo., 1969-70; librarian Chapman & Cutler, Chgo., 1970-73, Coudert Freres, Paris, 1973-74; adviser, organizer library Lincoln Park Zool. Soc. and Zoo., Chgo., 1977-79, mem. soc.'s women's bd., 1976—, chmn. library com., 1977-79, mem. exec. com., 1977—, sec., 1979-81; mem. jr. bd. Alliance Francaise de Chgo., 1970-76, treas., mem. exec. com., 1971-73, 75-76, mem. women's bd., 1977-80; mem. Fred Harvey Fine Arts Found., 1976—; hon. life mem. Chgo. Symphony Soc., 1975—; mem. Phillips Acad. Alumni Council, Andover, Mass., 1977-81; mem. acad.'s bicentennial celebration com, class celebration leader, 1978, co-chmn. for Chgo. acad.'s bicentennial campaign, 1977-79; mem. women's bd. Northwestern Meml. Hosp., 1979—, treas., chmn. fin. com., 1981—; mem. women's bd. Lyric Opera Chgo., 1979—, exec. com. 1980—; mem. Guild Chgo. Hist. Soc., 1978—, Women's Assn. Chgo. Symphony Orch., 1979—; mem. aux. bd. Art Inst. Chgo., 1978—; bd. dirs. Found Art Scholarships, 1982—; mem. Know Your Chgo. com. U. Chgo., 1981—. Clubs: Arts, (Chgo.), Friday (corr. sec. 1981—), Casino (gov. 1982—). Home: 1209 N Astor St Chicago IL 60610

HARVEY, LYNNE COOPER (MRS. PAUL HARVEY), broadcasting exec., civic worker; b. St. Louis County, Mo.; d. William A. and Margaret (Kehr) Cooper; A.B., Washington U., St. Louis, 1939, M.A., 1940; m. Paul Harvey, June 4, 1940; 1 son, Paul (Harvey) Aurandt. Broadcaster ednl. program Sta. KXOX, St. Louis, 1940; broadcaster-writer women's news and WAC Variety Show, Fort Custer, Mich., 1941-43; gen. mgr. Paul Harvey News, ABC, 1944—; pres. Paulynne Prodns., Ltd., Chgo., 1968—, exec. producer Paul Harvey Comments, 1968—. Pres. woman's bd. Mental Health Assn. Greater Chgo., 1967-71, v.p. bd. dirs., 1966-71; pres. woman's aux. Infant Welfare Soc. Chgo., 1969-72 bd. dirs., 1969—; nominating chmn. Salvation Army Woman's Adv. Bd., 1967-69; reception chmn. Community Lectures. Bd., Oak Park-River Forest, Ill., 1963-69; pres. Mothers Council, River Forest, 1961-62; charter bd. mem. Gottlieb Meml. Hosp., Melrose Park, Ill.; mem. adv. bd. Nat. Christian Heritage Found., 1964—recipient Religious Heritage of Am. award, 1974; trustee John Brown U., 1980—. Mem. McGraw's Wildlife Found., Phi Beta Kappa, Kappa Delta Pi, Phi Sigma Iota, Eta Sigma Phi. Clubs: Chicago Golf, Woman's Athletic, Press (Chgo.); Nineteenth Century Woman's, Oak Park Country. Editor, compiler: The Rest of the Story. Office: PO Box 77 River Forest IL 60305

HARVIE, MARION ELINORE, counselor; b. Bklyn., May 15, 1926; d. Harry Richmond and Alice Marion (Morgan) H.; A.A., Green Mountain Coll., 1946; B.S., SUNY, 1977; Adelphi U., 1980—, Rutgers U., 1979. Exec. sec. various corps., N.Y.C., 1947-71; sec. Freeport (N.Y.) Human Rights Commn., 1971-78; dir. Freeport Alcohol and Substance Abuse Center, 1971—, Freeport Employee Assistance Program, 1971—. Employee mem. Stblzn. and Affirmative Housing Task Force Com., 1979—; mem. N.Y. State Alliance on Women, Alcohol Abuse and Alcoholism, 1978—; exec. bd. L.I. region Assn. Labor-Mgmt. Adminstrs. and Cons. on Alcoholism, 1980-82; adv. bd. Freeport Youth Outreach Project, 1974—, Hi-Hello Child Day Care Center, 1979—; mem. Atlantic S.W. Civic Assn., 1963—; adv. bd. Freeport Hosp. for Alcoholism, 1979—. Recipient Woman of Yr. award N.Y. State Alliance on Women, Alcohol Abuse and Alcoholism, 1981; citation N.Y. State, 1981. Mem. Nat. Assn. Alcoholism Counselors, L.I. Alcoholism Counselors Assn., N.Y. Fedn. Alcoholism Counselors, Nassau County Mental Health Assn., Am. Personnel and Guidance Assn. Mem. Christian Ch. Columnist —The Choice is Yours,— The Leader, 1974—. Home: 689 S Bayview Ave Freeport NY 11520 Office: 46 N Ocean Ave Freeport NY 11520

HARWELL, LINDA KAY, assn. exec.; b. Forney, Tex., Oct. 18, 1943; d. Marvin and Ola Modelle (Criswell) Feagin; student Eastfield Coll., 1978-80, Henderson County Jr. Coll., 1980, Comml. Coll. Bus., 1978-79; m. Gary Stephen Harwell, May 8, 1964; children—Gary Stephen, Jason Lloyd. Bookkeeper, Terrell State Bank (Tex.), 1964, Colonial Hosp., Terrell, 1973-76; real estate broker Sedgwick & Assos., Inc., Forney, 1978-82; reporter Forney Heritage Soc., 1981—. Treas. Cub Scouts Am., Forney, 1974-80; mem. Kaufman County Hist. Commn. Mem. Dallas County East Genealogy (dir.). Baptist. Home: Route 2 Box 119 Forney TX 75126

HARWOOD, ELEANOR CASH, librarian; b. Buckfield, Me., May 29, 1921; d. Leon Eugene and Ruth (Chick) Cash; B.A., Am. Internat. Coll., 1943; B.S., New Haven State Tchrs. Coll., 1955; m. Burton H. Harwood, Jr., June 21, 1944 (div. 1953); children—Ruth (Mrs. William R. Cline), Eleanor, James Burton. Librarian, Rathbun Meml. Library, East Haddam, Conn., 1955-56; asst. librarian Kent (Conn.) Sch., 1956-63; cons. to Chester (Conn.) Pub. Library, 1965-71. Served from ensign to lt. (j.g.) USNR, 1944-46. Mem. Am., Conn. library assns., Chester Hist. Soc. (trustee 1970-72), D.A.V., Am. Legion Aux., Soc. Mayflower Descs. Mem. United Ch. Author: (with John G. Park) The Independent School Library and the Gifted Child, 1956; The Age of Samuel Johnson, LL.D., 1959. sec., Home: Maple St Chester CT 06412

HARWOOD, LYNN CATHARINE, ins. co. exec.; b. New Orleans, Mar. 19, 1941; d. John Michael and Marguerite Marie (Ferry) H.; B.A., La. State U., 1962. With Met. Life Ins. Co., New Orleans, 1968-78; mgr. Can. Life, Dallas, 1978—; owner, partner Ins. Service Center, Dallas, 1980—; v.p. Bohs-Harwood Co., Dallas, 1981—; pres. Invideo Prodns., Inc., Dallas, 1981—; partner B&H Investments; leader-trainer counselor selling, exec. mktg. skills. Recipient nat. quality award La. Life Leaders; C.L.U. Mem. Nat. Assn. C.L.U.s, Nat. Assn. Life Underwriters. Home: 3701 Turtle Creek Blvd Dallas TX 75219 Office: 137 World Trade Center PO Box 581365 Dallas TX 75258

HARWOOD, MADELINE B., state senator; b. Newbury, Vt., July 7, 1914; R.N., Mary Fletcher Hosp. Sch. Nursing, Burlington, Vt., 1936; m. Clifford Harwood; 3 sons, 1 dau. Pres., Vt. Fedn. Republican Women, 1965-67; mem. Vt. State Senate, 1969—; del. Rep. Nat. Conv., 1964, 68, 72; nat. committeewoman Rep. Nat. Com., 1973—. Trustee, Champain Coll., 1969-75, U. Vt., Montpelier, 1971-77. Mem. VFW Aux., Am. Legion Aux., DAR, Manchester Bus. and Profl. Women, Aux. Vt. State Med. Soc. (pres.). Office: Vt Ho Reps State Ho Montpelier VT 05602 *

HASBROUCK-MARTIN, PATRICIA MARIE, videotape producer and dir.; b. Dallas, Apr. 26, 1953; d. Theodore and Beverly Hasbrouck; B.F.A. magna cum laude, So. Meth. U., 1976. TV news Sta. WFAA, Dallas, 1972-77; producer/dir. video Dallas Area Hosp. TV System, 1977-80; producer/dir. video tng. tapes Southwestern Life Ins. Co., Dallas, 1980-81; dir. instructional TV Archbishop Sheen Center for Communication, 1981—; video cons. Nat. Arthritis Found., Navarro County Jr. Coll. Mem. Internat. TV Assn., Press Club Dallas, Women in Communications (Matrix award), Poetry Soc. Tex., So. Meth. U. Alumni Assn., Sigma Delta Chi. Home: 4229 Pleasant Run Irving TX 75062 Office: 3915 Lemmon Ave Dallas TX 75219

HASCHEMEYER, AUDREY ELIZABETH VEAZIE, molecular biologist; b. Chgo., Oct. 31, 1936; d. Waldemar and Elizabeth (Gibson) Veazie; B.S. in Chemistry (Bronze tablet 1957), U. Ill., 1957; Ph.D. (NSF fellow 1957-59, Procter & Gamble Co. fellow 1959-60), U. Calif., Berkeley, 1961. Research assoc. M.I.T., 1961-64, Harvard U. Med. Sch., 1965-67; assoc. in biol. chemistry Mass. Gen. Hosp., Boston, 1967-69; mem. faculty Hunter Coll., CUNY, 1969—, prof. biology and biochemistry, 1974—, chmn. dept. biol. scis., 1980—; chief scientist R/V Alpha Helix, 1978, USCG Polar Star, 1981; project leader McMurdo Sta., Antarctica, summers 1978-80; sta. sci. leader Palmer Sta., Antarctica, summer 1982. Fellow USPHS, 1962-64, Helen Hay Whitney Found., 1964-67; research scholar Am. Cancer Soc., 1976; grantee NIH, NSF, Am. Cancer Soc., CUNY, NATO; named Outstanding Woman Scientist, N.Y. chpt. Am. Women in Sci., 1981. Fellow AAAS; mem. Am. Soc. Biol. Chemists, Am. Physiol. Soc., Biophys. Soc. (council 1976-79, exec. com. 1978-79), Am. Soc. Zoologists, Soc. de Chimie Biologique, Am. Inst. Biol. Scis., Marine Biol. Lab., Sigma Xi. Author numerous papers in field. Office: 695 Park Ave New York NY 10021

HASELDEN, ELIZABETH LEE (MRS. KYLE HASELDEN), civic and religious worker; b. Charleston, S.C., Sept. 13, 1913; d. Thomas Oswald and Mary E. (Pettigrew) Lee; Mus.B., Meredith Coll., 1935; student Columbia U., summer 1935, Colgate-Rochester Div. Sch., 1936-37; m. Kyle E. Haselden, Sept. 8, 1936; children—Kyle Haselden II, Alice, Thomas Lee. Tchr. English, music high sch., Florence, S.C., 1935-36; tchr. piano prep. dept. Morris Harvey Coll., Charleston, W.Va., 1959-60. Vice pres. United Ch. Women, Mpls., 1947-49, infer-faith chmn., Charleston, 1958-60, mem. nat. Christian social relations adv. com. of triennium, 1961-64; nat. chmn. Christian social relations Ch. Women United, 1964-67, nat. v.p., 1967-71; nat. dir. urban ministries Ch. Women United, 1971-80; mem. Bapt. Joint Com. Public Affairs, 1962-63; mem. div. Christian social concern Am. Bapt. Conv., 1963-69; mem. commn. on Christian unity, mem. gen. bd. Am. Bapt. Chs. U.S.A., 1970—, v.p., 1980-82, mem. urban policy panel Center Theology and Public Policy, 1978—; coordinator Evanston (Ill.) Ecumenical Action Council, 1980—. Mem. Citizen's Council for Better Schs., Charleston, 1958-60; mem. Mayor's Council on Human Relations, Mpls., 1947-50; pres. Women's Conf. on Human Relations, Mpls., 1946-50, Council on Human Relations, Rochester, N.Y., 1952-54, Charleston, W.Va., 1959-60; mem. Mayor's Community Relations Commn. Evanston. Mem. women's planning com. Japan Internat. Christian U., 1959—. Recipient Luke Mowbray Ecumenical award Am. Bapt. Chs. U.S.A., 1979; Disting. Alumnae award Meredith Coll., 1981. Author study guide, articles. Home: 1507 Lincoln St Evanston IL 60201

HASENSTAB, MARY SUZANNE, audiologist, sch. psychologist educator; b. Cleve., Sept. 1, 1941; d. Jack A. and Helen M. (Williams) Rodda; B.S., Kent State U., 1963, M.Ed., 1968, Ph.D., 1975; postgrad. U. Cin., 1979-80, U. Va., 1980-81; children—Michael, Sally. Tchr. elem. schs., Streetsboro, Ohio, 1963-64, Strongsville, Ohio, 1964-65, Los Angeles Pub. Schs., 1965-66, St. Andrew Sch., 1966-67; reading tutor Kent (Ohio) City Schs., 1967-68, tchr. of hearing impaired, 1968-71; instr. dept. spl. edn. Kent State U., 1971-73, asst. prof., 1975-76; asst. prof. dept. speech pathology and audiology U. Va., Charlottesville, 1976-81, asso. prof., 1981—, dir. services for the hearing impaired, 1976—; cons. to pub. sch. systems, civic groups and pub. agys., 1971—; reviewer for Prentice Hall Pub. Co., 1971-72, Follett Publs., 1976-77. Mem. Speech and Hearing Assn. of Va., Am. Speech and Hearing Assn., Assn. Childhood Edn. Internat., Assn. Coll. Edn. in Hearing Impairment, Internat. Reading Assn., Nat. Council for Exceptional Children, Alexander Graham Bell Assn. for the Deaf, Internat. Council on Edn. in Univs., Phi Kappa Delta, Kappa Delta Pi. Author: (with J.S. Horner) Comprehensive Intervention with Hearing Impaired Infants and Preschool Children, 1982; contbr. articles on audiology to profl. jours. Office: 109 Cabell Hall U Va Charlottesville VA 22903

HASKELL, CHERYL MONA, planning engr.; b. Cheyenne, Wyo., Apr. 23, 1946; d. Bernard William and Ferne Adele (Hofer) Payne; B.S., U. Wyo., 1967, B.S. in Math Edn., 1977; div.; children—Brian Dean, Brad Allen, Monica Lyn. Research asst. Wyo. Game and Fish Commn., Laramie. 1966-67; adminstrv. acct. vocat. rehab. dept. State of Wyo., Cheyenne, 1966-72, dir. stats. and fiscal dept., 1972-73, substitute tchr., 1978; statistician Wyo. Commn. for Women, Cheyenne, 1978; outside plant planning engr. and feeder adminstr. Mountain Bell, Cheyenne, 1978—. Treas., Buffalo Ridge Sch. PTO, 1975-76, v.p., 1974-75; treas. All Christian Fellowship, 1977-78. Mem. Nat. Council Tchrs. Math., Bus. and Profl. Women, Gamma Phi Beta (treas. 1967). Home: 5021 Pineridge Cheyenne WY 82001 Office: 6101 Yellowstone St Room 219 Cheyenne WY 82001

HASKELL, LORI SUSAN, photojournalist; b. Seattle, Sept. 26, 1954; d. Gordon C. and Dorothy M. (Kelly) H.; B.A. in Communications and Polit. Sci. magna cum laude (Mortar Bd. scholar 1975-76, Univ. scholar 1975-76), U. Wash., 1976. Asst. dir. pub. affairs Sta.-KREM-TV, Spokane, Wash., 1975; dir. continuity Sta.-KGW, Portland, Oreg., 1976-77, news photographer Sta.-KGW-TV, 1977; news photographer Sta.-KOMO-TV, Seattle, 1977—. Sea Scout leader Portland council Girl Scouts U.S.A., 1977-78. Mem. Women in Communications, Mortar Bd. (v.p. in charge selections local chpt. 1977, del. nat. conv. 1975), Internat. Alliance Theatrical Stage Employees, Nat. Press Photographers Assn., Alpha Phi. Home: 1516 E Republican St Apt 15 Seattle WA 98112 Office: Sta-KOMO-TV 4th and Denny Sts Seattle WA 98109

HASKINS, LINDA E., lawyer; b. Ft. Worth, Mar. 15, 1950; d. Marshall Earl and Virgie Lee (Lancaster) H.; B.A., U. Tex., Austin, 1974; J.D., U. Houston, 1978; student U. Tex., Arlington, 1968-72. Admitted to Tex. bar, 1978; atty., coordinator legis. affairs dept. United Gas Pipe Line Co., 1978—; lectr. Coll. Bus. and Tech., U. Houston, 1978—. Albert DeLange Meml. scholar, 1977-78; recipient Outstanding Woman award United Gas Pipe Line Co. and Houston YWCA, 1980. Mem. Tex. Young Lawyers Assn. (bd. dirs.), Houston C. of C. (govtl. affairs com. 1980—), LWV, Am. Bar Assn., Fed. Energy Bar Assn., Tex. State Bar, Houston Bar Assn., Women's Law Assn., Am. Soc. Profl. Women (So. regional steering com.), NAM, Tex. Assn. Bus. Address: PO Box 1478 Houston TX 77001

HASLAM, COLLEEN, nurse; b. Clovis, N.M., Apr. 19, 1952; d. David Jeremy and Norma Jean (Deaton) Haslam; B.S. in Nursing cum laude, U. Utah, 1974; M.Orgnl. Behavior, Brigham Young U., 1981. Staff nurse Latter Day Saints Hosp., Salt Lake City, 1974-75, head nurse, 1977-78; mgmt. intern IBM, White Plains, N.Y., 1980; asst. dir. nursing Idaho Falls (Idaho) Consol. Hosp., 1981-82; with nursing mgmt. Cottonwood Hosp., Murray, Utah, 1982—; health coordinator over more than 100 missionaries Taiwan, 1976-77. Mem. Am. Soc. Personnel Adminstrn. Office: 900 Memorial Dr Idaho Falls ID 84302

HASLANGER, MARTHA LOUISE, filmmaker; b. Dearborn, Mich., Sept. 16, 1947; d. John Frederick and June (Loftsgordon) Anderson; A.B. with honors in Germanic Lit., Denison U.; M.F.A., Eastern Mich. U. Fellow in film, Radcliffe Inst., Cambridge, Mass.; film shows include: Whitney Mus. of Am. Art, N.Y.C., 1976, Berlin's (Germany) Arsenal, 5th Internat. Film Competition at Knokke-Heist, Belgium, London (Eng.) Filmmakers' Co-op, the Millenium, N.Y.C., The Collective, N.Y.C., Chgo. Filmgroup, and Munich (Germany) Stadtmuseum, Whitney Biennial, 1979, 81, 83, 3d Internat. Avant-Garde Film Festival, London, Festival Internat. du Jeune Cinema, Hyeres, France, Film as Art, Arts Council Gt. Britain, Internationale Filmfestspiele, Berlin; video shows include: Sao Paulo (Brazil) Biennial, Whitney Mus. of Art, Inst. of Contemporary Art, Phila.; judge numerous film festivals, panels. Recipient grant for video work, Nat. Endowment for the Arts, film grant Royal Film Archives of Belgium and the AGFA-GEVAERT Corp., grant Radcliffe Inst. and Harvard Corp., artist grant CAPS, N.Y. State; Jerome Found. grantee. Author: Memory Book, 1977; Goldy Dances 1978; contbr. works to numerous profl. mags. and jours. Films in collection of Am. Fedn. Arts, Royal Film Archives Belgium, Arts Council Gt. Britain, Internat. Forum of Young Cinema of Berlin.

HASLER, WILLEEN HASTINGS, office mgmt. and employee relations trainer, cons.; b. Bolivar, Mo., Apr. 30, 1929; d. William T. and M. Evah (Barnes) Hastings; student Ventura Coll., 1966-72, U. Calif., Irvine, 1975-76; m. Harry Linn Hasler, Apr. 14, 1973; children by previous marriage—Farrel D. Johnson, Marleen Johnson Clolinger. Adminstrv. sec. Santa Paula (Calif.) High Sch., 1952-66; adminstrv. asst. to pres. Ventura Coll., 1966-73; prin. trainer, cons. employee relations and office mgmt. Willeen Hasler & Assos., Oceanside, Calif., 1974—; cons., trainer U. Calif., Santa Barbara; community colls.; profl. assns., cities, counties. state and fed. employees. Mem. Am. Soc. Tng. and Devel., Nat. Speakers Assn., Nat. Assn. Female Execs., Nat. Assn. Women Bus. Owners. Nat. Assn. Ednl. Office Personnel, Calif. Sch. Employees Assn., Calif. Assn. Ednl. Office Personnel. Author, pub.; ABC's For Office Employees: An Office Bible, 1976; Career Growth for Women, 1978. Home: 276-25 N El Camino Real Oceanside CA 92054

HASSELL, JEAN HAYS, dietitian, educator; b. Rochester, Pa., Mar. 16, 1929; d. Edson M. and Dorothy G. (Treverton) Hays; student Ohio U., 1947-49; B.S. cum laude, Syracuse U., 1951; M.S. in Foods and Nutrition, Kent State U., 1974; postgrad. Ohio State U., 1980; m. Gordon Elmer Hassell, Sept. 8, 1951; children—Karen Lynne, Megan Ann. Therapeutic dietitian Rochester (Pa.) Gen. Hosp., 1951-52; home economist H. J. Heinz Co., Pitts., 1952-54; therapeutic and teaching dietitian St. Vincent DePaul Hosp., Norfolk, Va., 1955-56; therapeutic dietitian Trumbull Meml. Hosp., Warren, Ohio, 1970-75; lectr. Pa. State U., Shenango Valley Campus, Sharon, Pa., 1975-78; instr. Youngstown (Ohio) State U., 1975-79, 80—, coordinator nutrition edn. and tng. program, 1979-80; cons. dietitian Gastroenterology Clinic, Warren, Ohio, 1975—; teaching dietitian Trumbull Meml. Hosp. Sch. Nursing, Warren, 1962—. Pres. Women's Panhellenic Assn. Trumbull County, 1967; bd. dirs. Am. Cancer Soc., Trumbull County unit. Kellogg med. dietetics grantee, 1980. Mem. Am. Dietetic Assn., Soc. Nutrition Edn., Ohio Dietetic Assn., Ohio Nutrition Council, Mahoning Valley Dietetic Assn., Ohio Dietetic Educators of Practitioners (chmn. 1981-82), Omicron Nu, Chi Omega. Republican. Presbyterian. Home: 7401 Mines Rd SE Warren OH 44484 Office: Youngstown State U 410 Wick Ave Youngstown OH 44555

HASSELMEYER, EILEEN GRACE, child health and human devel. agy. adminstr.; b. Bklyn., May 23, 1924; d. Edwin Allen and Margaret Grace (Cody) Hasselmeyer; R.N., Bellevue Sch. Nursing, 1946; B.S., N.Y.U., 1956, M.A., 1956, Ph.D., 1963. Staff nurse, head nurse, supr., study coordinator Pediatric Metabolic and Nutritional Research Service N.Y.U. Children's Med. Service (various assignments in N.Y.C., U. Tex., Mexico City, S.I.); nurse cons. div. nursing resources Bur. Med. Services USPHS, Washington, commd. officer, 1956—; sr. nurse cons., 1963, asst. Surgeon Gen. Dept. Health and Human Services, 1979—, chairperson interagy. panel on Sudden Infant Death Syndrome. Spl. asst. for prematurity Office of Dir. Nat. Inst. Child Health and Human Devel., Bethesda, Md., 1963-66, acting dir. perinatal biology and infant mortality program, extramural programs, 1967-68, dir., 1969-74, asst. to dir. for perinatology, 1974, chief, pregnancy and infancy br. Center for Research for Mothers and Children, 1974-79, acting chief clin. nutrition and early devel. br. Center for Research for Mothers and Children, 1979-80, asso. dir. for Scil. Rev. Office of Dir., 1979—, project officer NICHD Coop. Epidemiologic Study of Sudden Infant Death Syndrome Risk Factors, 1979—; prin. investigator Handling and Premature Infant Behavior Research Project, N.Y.U., 1961-63; Annie W. Goodrich Vis. Prof. Yale U. Sch. Nursing, New Haven, 1968-69; NIH fellow, 1962-63; Am. Nurses Found.'s 1st Devel. grantee, 1962-63; Sigma Theta Tau grantee, 1969; Nat. League for Nursing Commonwealth fellow, 1959-62; Named Bellevue Sch. of Nursing Disting. Alumnae, 1976; recipient HEW, PHS Commendation Medal, 1975; NICHD Recognition of Outstanding Performance, 1973; N.Y.U. Creative Leadership award, 1980. Mem. Am. Nurses Assn., Nat. League for Nursing, Am. Public Health Assn., Perinatal Research Soc., Am. Pediatric Soc., USPHS Commd. Officers Assn., Bellevue Alumnae Assn. Contbr. numerous articles on maternal and infant nursing and sudden infant death syndrome to profl. jours. Office: 7910 Woodmont Ave Bethesda MD 20205

HASSETT, CAROL ALICE, psychologist; b. Bklyn., Apr. 19, 1947; d. Joseph and Anna (Portanova) Lusardi; B.S., St. John's U., 1968; M.Ed., Hofstra U., 1974, Ph.D. in Psychology (teaching asst.), 1981; m. John J. Hassett, June 29, 1968; 1 son, John J. Tchr. Day Elem. Sch., Bklyn., 1968-69; psychologist, alcoholism counselor Nassau County Dept. Drug and Alcohol also Mental Health Assn. Nassau County, East Meadow, N.Y., 1981—; adj. asst. prof. Hofstra U., 1980, 81. Bd. dirs. Malverne Vol. Ambulance Corps, 1976—; bd. govs. Kings County Cadet Corps, 1966-72. Cert. advanced emergency med. technician, pre-hosp. critical care technician; permanently cert. tchr., N.Y. Mem. Am. Psychol. Assn. Republican. Roman Catholic. Contbr. articles profl. jours. Home: 105 Franklin Ave Malverne NY 11565

HASSETT, SISTER, JANE, coll. pres., educator; b. St. Louis, Jan. 3, 1928; A.B., Maryville (Mo.) Coll., 1949; A.M., St. Louis U., 1960, Ph.D. in Modern European History, 1967. Tchr. elem. and secondary schs., St. Louis, Tex. and Mich., 1954-63; lectr. history Fontbonne Coll., St. Louis, 1963-65; instr. to asst. prof., 1965-72, chmn. dept. history, 1965-66, assoc. prof. history, pres., 1972—. Mem. exec. com. Ind. Coll. and Univs. Mem. bd. advisors Women's Adv. Group Mo.; mem. Citizens Com. Mo. ERA, Interreligious Task Force Soviet Jewry. Office of Edn. fellow, 1971-72. Mem. Orgn. Am. Historians, Am. Cath. Hist. Soc., Am. Assn. Higher Edn. Office: Fontbonne College 6800 Wydown Blvd Saint Louis MO 63105 *

HASSLER, SANDRA LEE, controller; b. Allentown, Pa., Jan. 3, 1949; d. Harold Elmer and Ruth Eleanor (Dahlof) H.; A.A. in Bus. Adminstrn., Northampton County Community Coll., 1969; B.S. in Bus. Mgmt., Indiana (Pa.) U., 1971. Engaged in retail fin., 1971-77; corp. controller, asst. to chmn. bd. Apparel Affiliates, Inc., Quakertown, Pa., 1977-81; ind. fin. and retail cons. computer programming and internal auditing, Phila., 1981-82; div. controller Honeybee, women's retail apparel chain, Huntington Valley Pa., 1982—. Mem. Am. Mgmt. Assn., Nat. Assn. Female Execs. Mem. Moravian Ch. Author ops. and retail manuals/booklets for design of data collection devices. Home: 1100 Newportville Rd Apt 830 Croydon PA 19020 Office: 2745 Philmont Ave Huntington Valley PA 19006

HASTE, BETTY GAYLE, sec.; b. Bedford, Ind., Nov. 15, 1957; d. Troy Nelson and June LaVonne (White) H. Perforator operator The Daily Reporter, Greenfield, Ind., 1977-80; sec. III, Purdue U., West Lafayette, Ind., 1980—. Methodist. Home: 2612 South St Lafayette IN 47904 Office: 688 Krannert Purdue U West Lafayette IN 47907

HASTINGS, AGNES MARY, civic worker; b. Buffalo, Oct. 11, 1922; d. Joseph and Sophie (Meyers) Smith; B.A., Golden Gate U., 1974; postgrad San Francisco State U., 1974-76, San Jose State U., 1977; paralegal student St. Mary's Coll., Moraga, Calif., 1981-82; m. Donald Hastings, June 17, 1948; children—Donna, Donald. Copygirl, AP, Syracuse, Washington, 1945-48; sec., stenographer Calif. State Govt., 1963-80, sec., stenographer Calif. Dept. Transp., 1972-76, library clk., 1976-80; census enumerator U.S. Govt., 1980; home care employee Meyer Nursing Services, 1981—. Mem. Alcoholism Adv. Bd. San Mateo County (Calif.), 1977-78; vol. worker Adult Benevolent Assn., 1978—, San Francisco Suicide Prevention; vol. jail aide Service League San Mateo County, 1978; vol. travelers aid San Francisco Internat. Airport, 1978-79, Disaster Unit Palo Alto ARC Unit, 1982—; admissions clk. Sequoia Hosp., 1979; judge, insp. election polls San Mateo County, 1976—; campaign vol. U.S. Rep. Bill Royer, 1980. Named Employee of Month, Meyer Nursing Services, Dec. 1981. Mem. Golden Gate U. Alumni Assn. (sec. Peninsula Group 1982), San Francisco Legal Assts. Assn. Roman Catholic. Home: 613 Bainbridge St Foster City CA 94404

HASTINGS, JOAN, state legislator; b. Drumright, Okla., Oct. 7, 1932; d. Frank R. and Etta Margaret (Newport) Phillips; student Tulsa U., 1949-52, 59-61; children—Michael Joe King, George Patrick King. Owner, operator Joan Hastings Aqua Tots, Tulsa; substitute tchr. in spl. edn. Tulsa Public Schs.; mem. Okla. Ho. of Reps., 1974—. Vice chmn. Tulsa County Republican Party; mem.Young Rep. Nat. Com.; chmn. nat. speakers bur. Young Rep. Nat. Exec. Com.; bd. dirs. Tulsa YMCA, Tulsa Opera Guild, Tulsa Philharm., Tulsa Boys' Home, Tulsa Goodwill Aux., Tulsa Arts Council, Tulsa Soc. Prevention Cruelty to Animals; mem. exec. bd. Tulsa Civic Ballet. Recipient Humanities award Nat. ARC; recognition for spl. edn. Kennedy Found.; State Wildlife Conservation award; award for meritorious service Okla. Firefighters Assn. Mem. Ducks Unltd., Young Republicans (life hon.). Presbyterian. Office: State Capitol Room 546 Oklahoma City OK 74105 *

HASTINGS, MELBA E., state legislator; b. Snyder, Tex., Oct. 25, 1926; student Northeastern Jr. Coll.; m. Vernon Hastings. Acct.; mem. Colo. Ho. of Reps., mem. agr., livestock and natural resources com., local govt. com., state affairs com. Mem. DAR, CowBelles, Hist. Soc. Democrat. Methodist. Club: Jane Jefferson. Office: Colorado House of Reps State Capitol Denver CO 80203 *

HASTINGS, SYBIL BUTLER (MRS. MILO HASTINGS), former business exec.; b. Farmington, Kans.; d. Charles Pardee and Mary (Wright) Butler; student pub. schs., Effingham, Kans.; m. Milo Hastings, Dec. 9, 1916 (dec. Feb. 1957); children—Edith (Mrs. John Charles Callahan Jr.), Warren. Sec., Dept. Labor, Washington, 1918; asst. to editor True Story Mag., 1919; sec. to prodn. mgr., reader, editor Dodd, Mead & Co., 1919-33; book cloth salesman, color cons., advt. mgr. Holliston Mills, N.Y.C., 1934-54; art dir., author, designer Color Notes, Columbia Mills, Inc., N.Y.C., 1954-77. Mem. Am. Inst. Graphic

Arts, Women's Nat. Book Assn. Editor: Women in the World of Words; asst. editor: Americana, As Taught to the Tune of a Hickory Stick. Contbr. articles to profl. publs. Pioneer offset and silk screen book covers. Home: 621 White Plains Rd Tarrytown NY 10591

HASTY, LOU NELLE MOORE, acctg. technician, civic worker; b. Turner County, Ga., Dec. 17, 1922; d. Joseph Ben and Nannie Lucile (Clower) Moore; grad. Albany Freeman Bus. Coll., 1941; m. Parham Jackson Hasty, Nov. 14, 1947. Acctg. technician Colquitt County Dept. Family and Children's Services, Ga. Dept. Human Resources, Moultrie, 1941—. Pres. Am. Legion Aux., Doerun, Ga., 1953-54, Moultrie, 1966-69, 71-72, 76-80; jr. v.p. Ladies Aux. VFW, 1977-78, pres., 1978-79, 81-82. Recipient service awards Gov. of Ga., 1960, 66, 71, 71, 76. Mem. Ga. County Welfare Assn. Methodist. Clubs: Magnolia Garden, Sr. Citizens, Northside Vol. Fire Div. Ladies Aux. Home: Route 3 Indian Lake Moultrie GA 31768 Office: PO Box 906 Moultrie GA 31768

HATCH, ALLENE GATY (MRS. ALDEN R. HATCH), artist, author; b. Morristown, N.J.; d. Theodore Emmett and Jean (Gardner) Gaty; student Bard Coll., 1941-42, Fashion Acad., 1944-45, Columbia U., 1945, Art Student's League, 1963-64; m. Alden R. Hatch, Sept. 9, 1950. Asst. art dir. Allied Display Corp., 1945-47; artist N.Y. Daily News, 1947, Edwin Freed Advt. Agy., 1948-50; illustrator books Henry Holt & Co., Prentice Hall, Inc., Am. Heritage mag., Doubleday & Co., Inc., Crown Pubs., Inc., 1950—; asst. to pres. Scenic Hudson Preservation Conf., 1978—; articles and cartoons for Barrytown Explorer; public relations cons. Travel Dynamics, Aris Gloves; painter portraits in U.S., Europe. Com. mem. Windham Children's Service. Mem. Colonial Dames Am. Republican. Episcopalian. Author, illustrator: Menopause Can Be Fun, 1972; author: Marjorie Merriwether Post, 1977. Home: Quartermile Germantown NY 12526

HATCH, LOIS EDWINA, designer, home bldg. co. exec.; b. Framingham, Mass., June 28, 1926; d. Edwin R. and Doris M. (Roberts) Dayton; student Mass. Sch. Art, 1943-45, Cape Cod Community Coll., 1962-64; children—Maurine L. Prokop, Marcia L. Desmond. Bookkeeper, Cochituate (Mass.) Motors, 1943-45, automotive accountant, 1945-57, mgr. auto parts, 1958; office mgr. Dennisport (Mass.) Motors, 1958; accountant, gen. mgr. Cranberry Motors, Orleans, Mass., 1959-62; real estate broker Emil Hanslin Assos., New Seabury, Mass., 1962-64; residential designer, pres. Handcrafted Homes, Stuart, Fla., 1970—; ind. real estate broker, Fla., 1965—. Recipient Chrysler Motors Accounting award, 1958; lic. pilot, 1968; registered real estate broker, Mass., Fla.; lic. residential contractor, Fla. Mem. Nat. Assn. Registered Real Estate Brokers, Nat. Assn. Home Builders. Treasure Coast Builders Assn., Aircraft Owners and Pilots Assn. Republican. Office: 3411 SE Dixie Hwy Stuart FL 33494

HATCH, MARY GIES, educator; b. Omaha, Feb. 17, 1913; d. Charles George and Jane Elizabeth (Sturman) Gies; A.B., Vassar Coll., 1935; postgrad. (Vassar fellow) U. Heidelberg, 1935; M.A., U. Mich., 1937; Ph.D. (univ. scholar), Syracuse U., 1952; m. David Lincoln Hatch, Aug. 24, 1940; children—Charles Winthrop, Mary Abby (Mrs. Joel Cleland), Faith (Mrs. William Mann), Elizabeth Ann. Tchr., Detroit pub. schs., 1937-38, Montclair (N.J.) High Sch., 1938-40, Dana Hall, Wellesley, Mass., 1940-42; prof. German, Columbia (S.C.) Coll., 1960—, chmn. German dept., 1963—. Columbia Coll. Research grantee, 1964; So. Assn. Research grantee, 1968. Mem. MLA, Am. Assn. Tchrs. German, Am. Sociol. Assn., Phi Beta Kappa. Contbr. articles to profl. jours. Editor S.C. Conf. on Fgn. Lang. Teaching Newsletter. Home: 2420 Terrace Way Columbia SC 29205

HATCHER, BETTY FRANCIS, med. technologist; b. Bryan, Tex., Aug. 9, 1932; d. Bon Nugent and Ruby Mae (Locke) Francis; student U. Houston, 1948-50, St. Joseph Hosp. Sch. Med. Technology, 1950-51; m. David Ellison Hatcher, Oct. 9, 1964; 1 dau., Diane Elizabeth. Chief blood bank technologist St. Josephs Hosp., Houston, 1952-64; founder, dir., supr. cons. and spl. projects Spectra Biols., Inc., East Brunswick, N.J., 1964-69; corp. sec., dir. spl. projects Gamma Biols. Inc., Houston, 1970—; dir. Record Archives, Inc. Mem. Am. Assn. Blood Banks (Ivor Dunsford award 1981), South Central Assn. Blood Banks (Jean Stubbins award 1977), Houston Antibody Club, Internat. Soc. Blood Transfusion. Baptist. Contbr. articles to profl. jours. Home: 9404 Memorial Dr Houston TX 77024 Office: 3700 Mangum St Houston TX 77092

HATCHER, ESTER LEE, home economist; b. College Grove, Tenn., Jan. 2, 1933; d. Marvin P. and Sadie (Kinnard) H.; B.S., Tenn. State U., 1954; M.S., U. Tenn., Knoxville, 1970. Asst. agt. Agr. Extension Services, Eastern Tenn. counties, 1954-65; asst. agt. Madison County, Jackson, Tenn., 1965-69; asst. prof. expanded food and nutrition U. Tenn., Knoxville, 1970-75, asso. prof., 1975—, leader, 1978—; counselor EEO, 1973—. Mem. Soc. Nutrition Edn., Greater Knoxville Nutrition Council, Am. Home Econs. Assn., Tenn. Home Econs. Assn., Knox Area Home Econs. Assn. Baptist. Club: Les Modernettes Social. Home: 5809 Holston Dr Knoxville TN 37914 Office: PO Box 1071 Knoxville TN 37901

HATCHER, MARTHA OLIVIA TAYLOR (MRS. FRANK PRIDGEN HATCHER, SR.), biologist, educator; b. Birmingham, Ala., Feb. 17, 1920; d. Sanford Allia and Mary (McCullough) Taylor; B.S., Howard Coll., 1936-40; M.Ed. in Sci. Edn., U. Ga., 1966, Ed.D., 1973; tchrs. cert. Breanu Coll., 1964; m. Frank Pridgen Hatcher, Sr., Nov. 7, 1941; children—Frank Pridgen, Martha Elizabeth, Nancy Louise. Chief bacteriologist veterinary div. Ga. Dept. Agr., Atlanta, 1943-45; supr. surg. pathology lab. Jefferson Hillman Hosp., Med. Coll. Ala., Birmingham, 1945-46, research asst. in pathology, 1945-46; mgr. offices Fran Mar Farms, Inc., Gainesville, Ga., 1957-66; instr. biology Gainesville Jr. Coll., 1966-67, asst. prof. biology, 1967-74, asso. prof., 1974-77, prof., 1977—, acting chmn. div. natural scis. and maths., 1968-74, chmn., 1974—; accompanist music dept. Brenau Coll., Gainesville, 1959-61. Chmn. Gray Ladies Vol. Services, Gainesville chpt. ARC, 1957-62; sec. Yohah council Girl Scouts U.S.A., 1959-61; bd. dirs. Community Concert Assn. Gainesville, 1968-70. NSF sci. faculty fellow in microbiology, 1970-71. Mem. AAUP, AAAS, Am. Guild Organists, Am. Inst. Biol. Scis., Nat. Assn. Biology Tchrs., Assn. S.E. Biologists, Nat. Assn. Research Sci. Teaching, Ga. Acad. Sci., Nat. Sci. Tchrs. Assn., Am. Legion Aux. (pres. 1948-50), Am. Soc. Zoologists, Southeastern Assn. Educators of Tchrs. Sci. (sec.-treas., editor Newsletter), UDC (chpt. pres. 1949-51), Am. Soc. Microbiology, AAUW, Kappa Delta Pi, Alpha Epsilon Delta, Delta Kappa Gamma, Phi Delta Kappa, Phi Theta Kappa, Delta Zeta. Clubs: Music (pres. 1950-52), Federated Music (sec. 1957-58) Phoenix Soc., Pilot Internat., (Gainesville). Home: 840 Memorial Dr NE Gainesville GA 30501 Office: PO Box 1358 Gainesville Jr Coll Gainesville GA 30501

HATCHETT, SHARON DENISE, lawyer; b. Mayfield, Ky., Nov. 12, 1954; d. William and Helen (Schofield) Hatchett; B.A., Ill. State U., 1976; J.D., DePaul U., 1979. Admitted to Ill. bar, 1979, Mich. bar, 1982; atty. NLRB, Washington, 1979-80, Office U.S. Trustee, U.S. Dept. Justice, Chgo., 1980-81, Office Gen. Counsel, Gen. Motors Corp., Detroit, 1981—. Mem. Ill. Bar Assn., Nat. Bar Assn., Am. Bar Assn., Mich. Bar Assn., Delta Sigma Theta. Methodist. Contbr. articles to profl. jours. Office: Office Gen Counsel Gen Motors Corp 3044 W Grand Blvd Detroit MI 48202

HATELEY, ENID ELLEN, real estate broker; b. Guayaquil, Ecuador, Mar. 22, 1925; came to U.S., 1944, naturalized, 1948; d. Harry Hawkes and Silia (Blanco) Shephard; B.S., Colegio Guayaquil, 1942; B.A., U. So. Calif., 1946; m. James Charles Hateley, II, Aug. 24, 1946; children—James Charles, Robert, Donald. Asst. credit mgr. Bank of Calif., 1946-49; with IBEC, 1950-51, E.H. Imports, 1952-60; trust adminstr. Bank of Am., 1973-75; broker Coldwell Banker, Los Altos, Calif., 1976—. Named Miss Dominican Republic, 1946; named to Coldwell Banker Million Dollar Club, 1976, 77, 78; recipient Silver Circle award Coldwell Banker, 1979-81. Mem. Nat. Assn. Realtors, Calif. Assn. Realtors, Los Altos Bd. Realtors (life mem. Million Dollar Club). Republican. Roman Catholic. Club: Los Angeles Athletic. Home: 2175 Chuleta Ct Los Altos CA 94022 Office: 301 S San Antonio Rd Los Altos CA 94022

HATFIELD, ELAINE CATHERINE, psychologist; b. Detroit, Oct. 22, 1937; d. Charles Ewald and Eileen Catherine (Kalahar) H.; B.A., U. Mich., 1959; Ph.D., Standford U., 1963. Asst., then asst. and assoc. prof. psychology U. Minn., 1963-66; assoc. prof. psychology U. Rochester (N.Y.), 1966-68; assoc. prof. and prof. psychology U. Wis., 1968-81; prof. psychology U. Hawaii, Manoa, 1981—, chmn. dept., 1981—; guest research prof. Sonderforschungsberich 24, Mannheim, W.Ger., 1972; adminstr. various govt. grants, 1965—; mem. small grants com. NIMH, 1977-80; social scis. rev. com. NSF, 1971-74; com. aging Nat. Acad. Scis., 1978-81; research assoc. Wis. Family Studies Inst., 1980-81. Co-recipient Nat. media award Am. Psychol. Assn., 1979. Fellow Soc. Psychol. Study Social Issues, Am. Psychol. Assn. (council reps. 1969-74); mem. Assn. Women Psychologists, Hawaii Psychol. Assn., Soc. Exptl. Social Psychology (exec. com. 1970-73), Am. Assn. Sex Educators and Counselors, Soc. Personality and Social Psychology. Author: A New Look at Love, 1978; Equity: Theory and Research, 1978; Interpersonal Attraction, 1978. Home: 2444 Hihiwai St Apt 2205 Honolulu HI 96822 Office: 2430 Camous Rd Honolulu HI 96822

HATHAWAY, JOYCE ANNE, former banker; b. Osborn, Mo., May 20, 1923; d. Gordon Waldo and Mattie Musette (Squires) Moore; student Platt Gard Bus. U., 1940-41, Pacific Coast Grad. Sch. Banking, 1974-76; standard and grad. certs. Am. Inst. Banking; m. John E. Hathaway, Nov. 16, 1942; children—John G., Janice L., James A. With 1st State Bank, King City, Mo., 1941-42, Capital Nat. Bank, Sacramento, 1942-44, U.S. Dept. Fin., Ft. Lewis, Wash., 1944-45; with Crocker Nat. Bank, Sacramento, 1951-81, asst. mgr., 1964-72, asst. v.p. ops., 1972-75, v.p., mgr., 1977-80, ret., 1980; mem. Nat. Credit Womens Exec. Com., 1968-72, chmn., 1973-74; former speaker on banking history, credit, also related subjects to local and nat. orgns.; instr. effective speaking, credit and collections, 1975-76. Vol., Meth. Hosp. Mem. Nat. Assn. Bank Women (charter, past pres. No. Calif.), Credit Women Sacramento (past pres.), Am. Inst. Banking (past pres. Sacramento chpt.), Nat. Assn. Credit Mgmt. (exec. com.), Assn. Ret. People (area coordinator Act for Ind. Maturity 1980—), Banker Speech Club. Republican. Presbyterian. Club: Soroptimist (treas. South Sacramento 1980). Home: 1014 Johnfer St Sacramento CA 95831

HATHAWAY, NANCY NEEDHAM, banker; b. Boston, Apr. 7, 1948; d. Daniel and Harriet G. (Leatherbee) Needham; B.A., Smith Coll., 1970; m. David R. Hathaway, June 9, 1973; 1 son, David Bradley. Trader fgn. exchange trading Bankers Trust Co., N.Y.C., 1970-73, asst. treas. corporate planning, 1973-76, asst. v.p. investment dept., 1976-78, v.p. internat. investment mgmt. group, 1978—. Mem. Fin. Women's Assn. Republican. Club: Smith Coll. (pres.) (N.Y.C.). Office: 280 Park Ave New York NY 10017

HATHAWAY, SUSAN, educator; b. Columbus, Ind., Jan. 15, 1946; d. John Kimsey and Beryl Frances (McLean) H.; B.A., Purdue U., 1967; M.A., Ind. U., 1969. Research asst. Irwin Mgmt. Co., Columbus, 1969-71; tchr. English and journalism Wheeling (Ill.) High Sch., 1971—; also speaker, instr. coll. workshops. First v.p. bd. dir. Groves of Hidden Creek Condominium II, 1977-78; sec. bd. dirs. Groves of Hidden Creek Community Assn., 1977-78, pres. bd. dirs., 1978-79. Recipient Outstanding Educator award Wheeling Jaycees, 1981; Spl. Recognition Newspaper Adv. award Newspaper Fund, 1981. Mem. Journalism Edn. Assn. (editor newsletter 1978—, medal of merit 1980), Kettle Moraine Press Assn. (dir. 1978-80), No. Ill. High Sch. Press Assn. (dir. 1980—), Nat. Council Tchrs. of English. Presbyterian. Office: 900 S Elmhurst Rd Wheeling IL 60090

HATHCOCK, YVONNE SHIRLEY, state dept. correction adminstr.; b. Elkhorn, Wis., Mar. 21, 1935; d. Edward and Tena (Huisman) Vanden Berg; B.A., U. Ark., Pine Bluff, 1976; M.A., Ark. State U., 1982; m. George Calvin Hathcock, Oct. 4, 1951 (dec); children—Ronald Charles, Patricia Jan, Thomas Edward, Russell Calvin. Printer, Arkadelphia Siftings Herald, 1955-57, Pine Bluff Comml., 1957-61, with Ark. Democrat, 1961-63, Ark. Gazette, 1963-65; asst. dir. public relations U. Ark., Pine Bluff, 1977-79; supr. composing room Ark. Dept. Correction, Pine Bluff, Ark., 1979—. Mem. Ark. Assn. Univ. Women, Nat. Assn. Female Execs., Career Guild, VFW Aux., Lambda Iota Tau. Democrat. Presbyterian. Home: 5711 W Jones St Pine Bluff AR 71602 Office: 8000 W 7th Ave Pine Bluff AR 71603

HATTAN, SUSAN K., legislative asst.; b. Lincoln, Nebr., Jan. 11, 1951; d. Hubert Curtis and Margaret Marie H.; B.A. summa cum laude, Washburn U., 1973; M.A. with distinction, Am. U., 1977. Legis. aide to Sen. Bob Dole, Kans., 1973-77; policy analyst, spl. asst. to adminstr. Food Safety and Quality Service, Dept. Agr., 1977-78; legis. asst. to Sen. Nancy Kassebaum, Kans., 1978—. Mem. Phi Kappa Phi, Zeta Tau Alpha. Office: Room 304 Russell Senate Office Bldg Washington DC 20510 *

HATTON, CAROLYN S., dentist; b. El Campo, Tex., Nov. 26, 1946; d. Rene LaFayette and Gladys Vera (Trojcak) Mood; B.S. in Dental Hygiene, Baylor U., 1969, D.D.S., 1978; 1 son, Jeffrey Carter. Practice gen. dentistry and gnathology, asso. Dr. William L. Comcowich, Aspen, Colo., 1978—. Mem. ADA, Colo. Dental Assn., Western Colo. Dental Assn., Colo. Prosthodontic Assn., Aspen Dental Soc. (sec.), Soc. Occlusal Studies, Am. Equilibration Soc. Office: 420 W Main St Aspen CO 81611

HATVANY, NINA GABRIELE, mgmt. cons.; b. Eng, Oct. 8, 1953; came to U.S., 1974; d. Paul Bernard and Ingeborg (Kirchtag) H.; B.Sc. with 1st class honors, Bristol (Eng.) U., 1974; M.A. in Psychology (Univ. fellow), Stanford U., 1976, Ph.D. in Psychology, 1978. Asst. prof. bus. Grad. Sch. Bus., Columbia U., 1978-81; pres. Hatvany Assocs. Inc., gen. mgmt. cons., San Francisco, 1981—. Mem. Am. Mgmt. Assn., Acad. Mgmt., Am. Psychol. Assn. Editor: (with D. Nadler and M. Tushman) Managerial Behavior, Concepts and Cases, 1982.

HAUCK, MARGUERITE HALL, broadcasting co. mktg. and research exec.; b. Bayside, N.Y., June 30, 1948; d. Carlyle Washington and Anzonette Marguerite (Asmussen) Hall; student Syracuse U., 1966-67; B.A. summa cum laude, Queens Coll., U. City N.Y., 1974. Asso. producer Animatic Prodns., Ltd., N.Y.C., 1968-72; mktg. analyst BBDO, Inc., N.Y.C., 1974-75; mktg. analyst CBS, Inc., N.Y.C., 1975-76, mgr. mktg. and research FM nat. sales, Radio div. CBS, 1976—. Bd. dirs. Queens Coll. Student Services Corp., 1973-74. Recipient Queens Coll. Disting. Service award, 1974. Mem. Nat. Assn. Female Execs. Author: The $321 Billion Dollar Market, 1981; columnist TV/Radio Age mag., 1982. Home: 20 Continental Ave Forest Hills NY 11375 Office: CBS 51 W 52d St New York NY 10019

HAUG, LOUISE CATO SMITH, publisher; b. LaGrange, Ga., June 27, 1929; d. Clifford Levi and Nora (Tidwell) Cato. Sales person, United Educators Co., Chgo., 1949-56, Boone Publs., Lubbock, Tex., 1956-57; owner, operator Smith Pub. Co., Lubbock, 1957—; co-owner, pres. Lubbock Execs. Inc. Mem. Nat. Assn. Female Execs. Office: 1715 Ave K Lubbock TX 79401 also PO Box 5584 Lubbock TX 79401

HAUGAN, GERTRUDE MARION, clin. psychologist; b. New Richland, Minn.; d. Henry Albert and Ella Pauline (Gardson) Haugan; student Rochester Jr. Coll., 1938-40, U. Minn., 1947-48; B.A., George Washington U., 1952, M.A., 1956; Ph.D., U. Md., 1970. Asst. to chief staff D.C. Gen. Hosp., Washington, D.C., 1949-59; research psychologist New Eng. Center Hosp., Boston, 1959-62; pvt. practice clin. psychology, Washington, 1962-66; grad. teaching asst. U. Md., College Park, 1966-67; intern in psychology Hall Psychiat. Inst., Columbia, S.C., 1968-69; postdoctoral fellow in pediatrics Kennedy Inst., John Hopkins Med. Sch., 1970-71; clin. psychologist Developmental Services Center, Washington, 1971-72, chief Children's Program, 1972—; cons. Eastern Shore State Hosp., 1970-71; clin. instr. George Washington U., Washington, 1975—. Mem. Am. Psychol. Assn., Am. Assn. Mental Deficiency, Assn. Advancement Behavior Therapy, Phi Beta Kappa. Home: 4720 S Chelsea Ln Bethesda MD 20814 Office: Developmental Services Center Washington DC 20011

HAUGH, J(OYCE) EILEEN GALLAGHER, psychologist, educator; b. Ironton, Ohio, Sept. 3, 1937; d. Lawrence J. and Frances I. (Wilson) Gallagher; B.S., Coll. of St. Teresa, 1967; Ed.M., Ohio U., 1969; Ph.D., Loyola U., Chgo., 1975; m. Charles Richard Haugh, July 29, 1978; children—Kevin Charles, Maria Frances, Kateri Lynn. Tchr. elem. parochial schs., Chgo., 1958-59, Portsmouth, Ohio, 1959-63, Owatonna, Minn., 1963-64; tchr. secondary schs., Lake City, Minn., 1964-67, Springfield, Minn., 1967-68; instr. psychology Coll. of St. Teresa, Winona, Minn., 1969-72, v.p. student affairs, 1975-76; assoc. prof. psychology St. Mary's Coll., Winona, 1976—, asst. dean acad. advising, 1977-78, dir. grad. program in counseling and psychol. services, 1980—. NDEA fellow, 1968-69. Mem. Am. Personnel and Guidance Assn., Am. Coll. Personnel Assn., Minn. Personnel and Guidance Assn., Am. Psychol. Assn., Nat. Assn. of Women Deans, Adminstrs. and Counselors, Psi Chi, Phi Delta Kappa. Roman Catholic. Home: 74 Hillsdale Ct Winona MN 55987 Office: Saint Mary's College Winona MN 55987

HAUGHTON, JACQUELINE BABETTE, trade show prodn. exec.; b. Memphis, Nov. 11, 1929; d. Charles Henderson and Della Irene (Trumble) Miller; B.S., U. Wis., 1951; postgrad. U. Colo., 1952-53; m. Richard A. Haughton, Feb. 11, 1956 (dec. June 1977); children—Jeffrey Charles, Douglas Alan, Linda Sue. Tchr., Bethesda, Md., 1954-55, Arlington, Va., 1955-56, Denver, 1956-57; founder, dir. Arvada Presbyn. Mothers Day Out Pre-Sch., Arvada, Colo., 1965-76; v.p. Indsl. Expns., Inc., Denver, 1975-77, pres. 1977—; dir. Lakeside Nat. Bank, Denver Colo.; pres. Denver Trade Show Council, 1977—. Vice chmn., Colo. Bd. Edn., Wheat Ridge Festival; chmn. bd. dirs. Colo.. PTA-Parent Teacher Student Assoc. Recipient Spark Plug award U. No. Colo., 1980, Silver Spoon award AAUW, 1979, State Ednl. Leadership award PTA-Parent Teacher Student Assoc., 1980. Mem. Women's Forum, Home and Garden Show Execs. (internat. dir.), Internat. Sport Show Producers Assn. (dir.), Conv. and Visitors Bur., Denver C. of C., Wheat Ridge C. of C., Delta Kappa Gamma. Republican. Presbyterian. Club: P.E.O. Home: 10 Hillside Dr Lakewood CO 80215 Office: 10 Lakeside Ln Denver CO 80212 also PO Box 12297 Denver CO 80212

HAUGLAND, BRYNHILD, state legislator, farmer; b. Ward County, N.D., July 28, 1905; d. Nels and Sigurda (Ringoen) Haugland; B.A., Minot State Coll., 1956. Mem. N.D. Ho. of Reps., 40/50 Dist., 1939—, chmn. social welfare com. Mem. Def. Adv. Com. Women in Services, 1955-58. Vice chmn. N.D. Gov.'s State Health Planning Com., 1944-75; mem. Ward County Zoning Commn., Minot City Planning Commn., N.D. Bicentennial Commn. Bd. dirs. Internat. Peace Garden, 1953—. Named N.D.'s Outstanding Woman in Law, 1973; Outstanding Legislator, Nat. Assembly Govt. Employees, 1979. Mem. Bus. and Profl. Women's Club (named Woman of Yr. 1956, 71), Farmers' Union and Farm Bur., Delta Kappa Gamma. Lutheran. Club: Quota. Address: Box 1684 Minot ND 58701

HAULSEE, ANNE LOUISE, career effectiveness cons.; b. Richmond, Va., Dec. 21, 1946; d. Russell Boykin and Mary Louise (Smith) H.; B.A. in Sociology, Roanoke Coll., 1968; M.A. in Sociology, W.Va. U., 1971; m. Russell Thomas Boyle, Jr., July 21, 1979. Grad. asst. W.Va. U., 1968-69; program asst. Nat. Sch. Public Relations Assn., Washington, 1969-74; mgr. Washington office Western Temporary Services, 1974; cons. women's program div. Transcentury Corp., Washington, 1975-76; co-founder, adminstrv. dir., corp. sec. Martha Movement, nat. assn. devoted to recognition of homemakers, Washington, 1976-77; career effectiveness cons., condr. career planning and mgmt. devel. programs, Washington, 1977—; condr. career tng.; mem. staff Dept. Agr. Grad. Sch. Spl. Programs Div.; mem. Georgetown U. Speakers Bur., Johnson-Butler Agy. Mem. Am. Soc. Profl. and Exec. Women, Nat. Assn. Women Bus. Owners (pres. Capital Area chpt.), Nat. Assn. Female Execs., Federally Employed Women, Nat. Council Career Women, Washington Women's Network, No. Va. Alumnae Panhellenic Assn. (pres. 1982—), Delta Gamma (pres. Alumnae chpt. 1973-75). Presbyterian. Home and Office: 205 Yoakum Pkwy #1511 Alexandria VA 22304

HAUN, FRANCES CONWAY MALONEY, ret. educator, club woman, writer; b. Warrensburg, Tenn., Jan. 2, 1910; d. Hugh Conway and Lena (McCorkle) Maloney; B.S., East Tenn. U., 1933; M.S., U. Tenn., 1956; certificate in journalism Newspaper Inst. Am., 1969; postgrad. U. Tenn., 1970-71, Middle Tenn. State U., summer 1971; diplomat Inst. of Children's Lit., 1973; m. Fred Burwin Haun, Jan. 24, 1936; children—Hugh Leslie, Frances Lavinia Haun Zimmermann, Philip Maloney. Tchr. English and home econs. Warrensburg High Sch., 1930-33, Whitesburg High Sch., Hamblen County, Tenn., 1946-49; hot lunch supr. Hamblen County Schs., 1941-42; Red Cross swimming instr., Morristown, 1946-48, tchr. Sherwood Elementary Sch., Morristown, Tenn., 1956-75. Historian, Morristown-Hamblen, 1970—; mem. Democratic Exec. Com. of Hamblen County, 1966—; v.p. Dem. Women's Club of Hamblen County, 1972-73, Springvale Home Dem. Club, chmn. nominating com., 1973-75; tchr. children's classes Bible Sch. and Sunday Sch. United Methodist Ch., Morristown, 1940-50, mem. adult choir, 1938-42, dir. jr. choir, 1948-54, pres. women's guild, 1967-69, 71-72, 78-80; life mem. United Meth. Guilds #11, 1968; bd. dirs. Hamblen County Farm Bur.; mem. Morristown-Hamblen Bicentennial Commn., Morristown-Hamblen Rose Center Bd.; dir., hostess David Crockett Tavern & Mus., Morristown; bd. dirs. Hamblen Library, Morristown Emergency Youth; Recipient Writers prize City of Morristown, 1955; Morristown Jaycees Speakers award, 1967; award Morristown Edn. Assn., 1969; Red Cross award, 1971; named Outstanding Alumna, E. Tenn. U., 1974. Mem. UDC (Ladies' Reading Circle), D.A.R. (chpt. regent 1979—), Hamblen Humane Soc. (charter), NEA, Tenn. Edn. Assn., East Tenn. (chmn. 1969-70, leadership award 1969), Morristown-Hamblen (chmn. 1968-70) heart assns., Hamblen County Assn. for Preservation of Tenn. Antiquities (dir. 1975-76), Upland Terrace Garden Club (pres. 1949-50), Morristown-Hamblen Hist. Soc. (charter), E. Tenn. U. Alumni Assn. (pres. Hamblen chpt. 1970-72), Morristown-Hamblen Ret. Tchrs. Assn., Morristown Humane Soc. (charter) Hamblen County Farm Bureau (chrmn. ladies' divn. 1981). Author: Beyond the Classroom, 1966; Faraway Places. Contbr. poems to lit. publs. and articles to newspapers. Address: Green Hills Box 51 Route 2 Russellville TN 37860

HAUPTFUHRER, BARBARA BARNES, corp. dir.; b. Greensboro, N.C., Oct. 11, 1928; d. J. Foster and Myrtle (Preyer) Barnes; B.A. cum laude, Wellesley Coll, 1949; m. George J. Hauptfuhrer, Jr., Sept. 9, 1950; children—George J. III, W. Barnes. Dir., Vanguard Group Investment Cos., Valley Forge, Pa., 1972—, Great Atlantic and Pacific Tea Co., Inc., Montvale, N.J., 1975—, Gen. Public Utilities Corp., Parsippany, N.J., 1976-79, Phila. Saving Fund Soc., 1976—, J. Walter Thompson Co., Inc., N.Y.C., 1977—, Knight-Ridder Newspapers, Inc., Miami, Fla., 1979—, Mass. Mut. Life Ins. Co., Springfield, 1979—, JWT Group, Inc., N.Y.C., 1980—, Owens-Ill., Inc., Toledo, 1981—; public mem. regional adv. com. on banking policies and practices 3d Nat. Bank Region, 1976-77. Trustee, Wellesley (Mass.) Coll., 1970—, Com. for Econ. Devel., 1979—; bd. dirs. John and Mary R. Markle Found., 1976—, Greater Phila. Partnership, 1975—; bd. dirs. World Affairs Council Phila., 1977—, vice chmn., 1978-80; bd. dirs. Phila. United Fund, 1960-65, United Way Southeastern Pa., 1979—; trustee Salem Acad. and Coll., 1967-70; mem. Harvard Vis. com. for Harvard and Radcliffe, 1972-78; mem. Presser Found., 1970—; pres. Jr. League Phila., 1958-60, Meadowbrook Sch., 1962-63; mem. Phila. Orch. Council, 1979—; mem. Mayor's Commn. for Women, Phila., 1981—. Mem. Wellesley Coll. Alumnae Assn. (pres. 1970-73). Lutheran. Home: 1700 Old Welsh Rd Huntingdon Valley PA 19006

HAURE, HILDA HELEN, assn. exec.; b. Rayne, La., Oct. 15, 1929; d. Joseph Daniel and Helen Ann (Meyers) Theunissen; grad. parochial schs.; m. J. Curney Haure, Oct. 12, 1952; children—Kim James, Vanessa Ann, Terri Judith, Pierre. Dental asst., Rayne, 1950-53; sec. Haure Machine Shop, Rayne, 1966-72; clk. Rayne Br. Hosp., 1972-74; exec. sec. Rayne C. of C., 1974—. Vice-pres., PTO, 1966; capt. Mothers March of Dimes, 1956-62; chmn. Mental Health Drive, 1974, St. Jude's Children's Hosp., 1972; gen. chmn. Rayne Frog Festival, 1974-79. Mem. Rayne Br. Hosp. Aux., Family Life Ministry. Recipient Bldg. Our Am. Communities award, 1978. Democrat. Roman Catholic (St. Leo's Altar Soc.). Home: 920 Hilda St Rayne LA 70578 Office: 103 N Parkerson Rayne LA 70578

HAUSAFUS, CHERYL OLMSTEAD, home economist educator; b. Cin., Sept. 27, 1946; d. Ralph Maurice and Adelaide Louise (Schweninger) Olmstead; B.S., Fla. State U., 1968; M.S., Pa. State U., 1971; Ph.D., Iowa State U., 1973; m. John Earl Hausafus, May 26, 1973; children—Michael Todd, Tara Ann. Tchr. home econs. Taylor County High Sch., Perry, Fla., 1968-69; food service tchr. Gibbs Comprehensive High Sch., St. Petersburg, Fla., 1970; asst. prof. home econs. edn. E. Carolina U., Greenville, N.C., 1972-75; asst. prof. home econs. edn. Iowa State U., Ames, 1978—; mem. state adv. bd. Future Homemakers Am., 1980—; mem. adv. council Des Moines Home Econs. Adv. Council, 1981—. Grantee, Apple Edn. Found., 1980. Mem. Am. Home Econs. Assn., Am. Vocat. Assn., Council Vocat. Edn., Am. Ednl. Research Assn., Iowa Vocat. Assn. (dir.), Omicron Nu, Phi Delta Kappa. Democrat. Episcopalian. Home: 3700 Rollins Ave Des Moines IA 50312 Office: Dept Home Econs Edn Iowa State U Ames IA 50011

HAUSER, GEORGIA ANN, educator; b. Cleve., Feb. 7, 1947; d. George Eugene and Mary Beshara; B.S., Ohio State U., 1971, M.A., 1978; m. Thomas Hauser, June 27, 1970; 1 son, Thomas. Tchr., coordinator distributive edn. Brookhaven High Sch., Columbus (Ohio) City Schs., 1971—. Treas., Twigs No. 17 Childrens Hosp., 1981—; mem. sustaining bd. Buckeye Boys Ranch, 1978—; vol. Cancer Crusade, 1980—, Barrington Parent-Tchr. Orgn., 1976—. Mem. NEA, Ohio Edn. Assn., Columbus Edn. Assn., Ohio State U. Alumni Assn., Upper Arlington Civic Assn. Office: 4077 Karl Rd Columbus OH 43224

HAUSER, JOYCE ROBERTA, pub. relations and mktg. specialist; b. N.Y.C.; d. Abraham and Helen (Lesser) Frankel; B.A., SUNY, 1976; children—Mitchell, Mark, Ellen. Editor, Art in Flowers, 1955-58; pres. Joyce Advt., 1958-65; partner Hauser & Assocs., Pub. Relations, 1966-75; dir. broadcasting Bildersee Pub. Relations, 1973-75; pres. Hauser & Assocs., Inc., Pub. Relations, 1975-78, Hauser-Roberts, Inc., Pub. Relations/Mktg., N.Y.C., 1978—; moderator show Perceptions, Sta. WEVD, 1975-77, Speaking of Health, WNBC, 1977-80, 97 Health Line, Sta. WYNY, 1980—, Conversations with Joyce Hauser, Sta. WNBC, 1975—; instr. Baruch Coll., CCNY, 1980—. Mem. Citywide Health Adv. Council on Sch. Health, 1970—, treas., 1980—. Named one of 10 Top Successful Women, Cancer Soc., 1976; recipient Professionalism award Sta. WNBC, 1980. Mem. AFTRA, Am. Women in Radio and TV (corr. sec. 1973, chmn. coll. women in broadcasting 1974). Contbg. editor Alive, 1976-77. Home: 115 E 82d St New York NY 10028 Office: 20 E 53d St New York NY 10022

HAUSER, LYNN ELIZABETH, eye surgeon; b. Cleve., Apr. 11, 1951; d. Cavour Herman and Ruth Natalie (Lageman) H.; B.S. in Medicine, Northwestern U., 1974, M.D., 1976; m. Neil L. Ross, June 20, 1975; 1 son, Michael Hauser Ross. Resident in ophthalmology Northwestern U., 1976-80; practice medicine specializing in ophthal. surgery, Dekalb, Ill., 1980—; clin. asst. prof. ophthalmology U. Ill., Chgo.; lectr. in ophthalmology Northwestern U.; project ophthalmologist Nat. Eye Inst. Early Treatment Diabetic Reinopathy Study, 1982. Diplomate Am. Bd. Ophthalmology. Mem. Am. Acad. Ophthalmology, AMA, Dekalb County Med. Soc., Ill. Assn. Ophthalmology, Ill. State Med. Soc., LWV. Office: 8 Health Services Dr Suite 2 Dekalb IL 60115

HAUSER, MARGARET JEAN GOODMON, educator; b. Danville, Ill., Oct. 31, 1939; d. Marvin and Ida Helen (Glynn) Goodmon; B.S. in Journalism and Communications, U. Ill., 1961; M.S. in Instructional Design/Tech., No. Ill. U., 1975, Ed.D., 1980; m. Richard L. Hauser, Sept. 8, 1962; children—Elizabeth Jean, Katherine Lynn. Advt. copywriter Sears, Roebuck and Co., 1961, 64; newspaper reporter Champaign (Ill.)-Urbana Courier, 1962; classroom tchr., Peru, Ill., 1967-69; media specialist, dir. Project Creation, Ill. Dept. Edn., 1974-80; acad. dean Ravenscroft Sch., Raleigh, N.C., 1981-82; pres. Knowledge Group, Inc., Raleigh, 1981—. Past bd. dirs. LaSalle-Peru chpt. LWV, Illinois Valley United Fund, Am. Field Service. Recipient Disting. Service award LaSalle-Peru Jaycees, 1975. Mem. Am. Soc. Curriculum and Devel., AAUW, Adult Edn. Assn. U.S., Am. Soc. Tng. and Devel. Episcopalian. Address: 7320 Grist Mill Rd Raleigh NC 27609

HAUSER, RITA E., lawyer; b. N.Y.C., July 12, 1934; d. Nathan and Frieda Abrams; A.B., Hunter Coll., 1954; Doctorate with highest honors, U. Strasbourg, France, 1955; LL.B., U. Paris, 1958; LL.B., Harvard U., 1959; m. Gustave M. Hauser, June 10, 1956; children—Glen, Patricia. Admitted to D.C. bar, 1960, N.Y. bar, 1961; sr. partner Stroock, Stroock & Lavan, N.Y.C., 1972—; dir. ARA Services, Inc., Wickes Cos. Inc. Trustee, Harvard U. Law Sch. Assn. of N.Y.C., Center for Inter-Am. Relations, Inst. for Internat. Edn., Freedom House; bd. dirs. Friends of the Hague Acad. Internat. Law, N.Y. Philharmonic-Symphony Soc.; mem. bd. govs., v.p. Am. Jewish Com. Fellow Am. Bar Found.; mem. Am. Bar Assn., Am. Fgn. Law Assn. (dir., v.p.), Assn. of Bar of City of N.Y. Office: Stroock Stroock Lavan 61 Broadway New York NY 10006

HAUSMAN-SMITH, KATHRYN ELLEN, designer; b. Cleve., Oct. 9, 1949; d. Morris Hersh and Ruth Adele (Sablowitz) Hausman; student U. Wis., Madison, 1967-69; B.S., Fashion Inst. Tech., N.Y. U., 1971; m. David Smith, July 25, 1975; children—Trevor Leslie, Graham Morrison. Advt. dir. Sheffield Watch Corp., N.Y.C., 1971-72; owner, pres. designer Medusa's Heirlooms, N.Y.C., 1972—. Home: 154 E 89th St New York NY 10028 Office: 385 5th Ave Suite 501 New York NY 10016

HAUT, CLAIRE JOAN, artist, craftsman; b. Moline, Ill., Sept. 26, 1918; d. John Louis and Florence Norton (Cameron) Overholt; student Augustana Coll., 1936-37, Am. Acad. of Art, 1937-38, Sch. of Design (now. Inst. of Design, Ill. Inst. Tech.), 1940-44, 50; m. Edward Joseph Haut, Jr., Jan. 21, 1950; 1 dau., Susan Haut Hedley. Designer, exptl. design unit Ill. Art Project, 1939-42; art editor advt. layout Fairbanks-Morse, 1942-43; art editor layout and design Cudahy Packing Co., 1944-45; freelance advt. artist, Chgo., 1945-52; illustrator, designer Sandia Labs., Albuquerque, 1958-74; pvt. practice painter, craftsman, graphic artist, Albuquerque, 1974—. Works include paintings, constrns., drawings, sculpture; recent one-man shows: Johnson Gallery, U. N.Mex., Albuquerque, 1979, Artichoke Gallery, Albuquerque, 1980, Balloon People Go-Shoppe, Albuquerque, 1980, 81; two-man show: Simms Fine Art Center, Albuquerque Acad., 1982; participant travelling shows including State Dept. tour 8 European countries, 1960, Mus. N.Mex. SW Biennial and Travelling Show, 1968-69; exhibitor shows including 14th Nat. Exhibit, Fall River, Mass., 1970, Washington and Jefferson Coll., Pa., 1971, Greater New Orleans Nat. Shows, 1972, 71, Nat. League Am. Penwomen Biennial and travelling show, 1972-73, Lawton (Okla.) Internationals, 1970, 71, 72, 74, 20th Nat. Sun Carnival Exhibit, El Paso (Tex.) Mus., 1978-79, All Media Art Competition, Houston, 1979, 18th Ann. Artists Salon, Okla. Mus. Art, 1979; participant invitational shows, N.Mex., Tex., N.J.; work represented Ill. Arts Project travelling exhbn. Chgo. Art Inst., Mus. Modern Art, Corcoran Galleries, Carnegie Inst., San Francisco Mus., City Mus. St. Louis, Toledo Mus. Active, One Percent for Art campaign, Albuquerque, 1978-79. Recipient various prizes. Mem. Artists Equity (pres. Albuquerque chpt., 1976-77, exhbns. chmn., 1974-75), Nat. League Am. Penwomen (chpt. pres. Manzanita br., 1970-72, state exhbn. chmn. 1974-76), Albuquerque Designer-Craftsmen. Presbyterian. Home and Office: 9836 McKnight NE Albuquerque NM 87112

HAUTZIG, ESTHER RUDOMIN, author; b. Vilna, Poland, Oct. 18, 1930; came to U.S., 1947, naturalized, 1951; d. Samuel and Chaja (Cunzer) Rudomin; student Hunter Coll., N.Y.C.; m. Walter Hautzig, Sept. 10, 1950; children—Deborah Margolee, David Rudomin. Publicity asst. Children's Book Council, 1952-54; dir. children's book promotion T.Y. Crowell, 1954-59; freelance cons. children's book promotion, 1960—; tchr. classes children's book witing, 1960—; author: Let's Cook Without Cooking, 1955; Let's Make Presents, 1970; Redecorating Your Room for Practically Nothing, 1967; The Endless Steppe (Jane Addams Prize book 1969, Lewis Carroll Shelf book 1970, Boston Globe/Horn Book Honor Book 1968, Chgo. Tribune/Washington Post Spring Children's Books Festival Honor Book 1968, Shirley Kravitz award Assn. Jewish Libraries 1968), 1968; In The Park, 1968; At Home: A Visit in Four Languages, 1968; In School: Learning in Four Languages, 1969; Let's Makes More Presents, 1973; Cook Cooking, 1973; The Case Against the Wind, 1975; Life With Working Parents: Practical Hints for Everyday Situations, 1976; A Gift for Mama, 1981. Pres. Calhoun (N.Y.) PTA, 1964. Mem. Author's Guild. Jewish. Address: 505 West End Ave New York NY 10024

HAVAS, JUDY, exec. search cons.; b. Budapest, Hungary, Feb. 5, 1950; d. Fred and Martha (Friedlander) H.; came to U.S., 1956, naturalized, 1961; B.A. in Psychology, U. Calif., Los Angeles, 1972, M.B.A., 1976. Adminstrv. asst. Towers, Perrin, Forester & Crosby, Los Angeles, 1973; med. sales rep. Pennwalt Corp., Los Angeles, 1973-74; cons. Korn-Ferry Internat., Los Angeles, 1976-81; partner Fell & Co., 1981—. Mem. U. Calif. Los Angeles Mgmt. Alumni Assn. (dir. 1978—). Address: 1901 Ave of the Stars Suite 1611 Los Angeles CA 90067

HAVELOCK, CHRISTINE MITCHELL, educator; b. Cochrane, Ont., Can., June 2, 1924; d. William Waterson and Annie Margaret (Graham) Mitchell; B.A., U. Toronto, 1946; M.A., Harvard U., 1950, Ph.D., 1958; m. Eric A. Havelock, Nov. 21, 1962. Mem. faculty Vassar Coll., 1953—, prof. art history, 1967-78, Sarah Gibson Blanding chair, 1978—, chmn. art dept., 1968-71, asst. to pres., 1972-73, dir. women's studies, 1978-80, curator class. collection. Recipient Charles Eliot Norton Fellowship award, 1950-51. Mem. Coll. Art Assn., Archaeol. Inst. Am., Democrat. Author: Hellenistic Art, 2d edit., 1981. Office: Vassar Coll Poughkeepsie NY 12601

HAVENS, ISABELLE, microbiologist; b. McGill, Nev.; d. George Walter and Helen (Campbell) H.; A.B., Western Coll., Oxford, Ohio, 1935; M.S., U. Chgo., 1956. Asso. dir. clin. microbiology labs. Minn. State Sanatorium, Ah-gwah-ching, 1937, Litchfield County Hosp., Winsted, Conn., 1938-41, Station Hosp., Baer Field, Ft. Wayne, Ind., 1941-42, Charleroi-Monessen Hosp., Charleroi, Pa., 1942-44; with dept. microbiology U. Chgo., 1944-48, research asst. dept. medicine, 1948-58, research asso., asso. dir. clin. microbiology labs., 1958-69; microbiologist St. Joseph Mercy Hosp., Pontiac, Mich., 1969—; clin. instr. med. tech. Coll. Human Medicine Mich. State U.; vis. instr. St. Mary's Coll., Orchard Lake, Mich. Recipient Hillkowitz Meml. award Am. Soc. Med. Technologists, 1957; gold award Ill. State Med. Soc., 1956; named Employee of Yr., U. Chgo. Clinics, 1961, Ill. Med. Technologist of Yr., 1963; Corning award Am. Soc. Med. Technologists, 1964. Fellow Royal Soc. Health; mem. A.A.A.S., Mich. Pub. Health Assn., Am., Mich. soc. microbiology, Am. Mich. (treas.), Oakland socs. med. technologists, Ill. Acad. Sci., Ill. Med. Technologists Assn. (past pres.), Med. Mycol. Soc. of Ams., Sigma Xi, Sigma Delta Epsilon. Research on immunity to cholera, Endamoeba histolytica, surg. infections, and respiratory flora. Home: 323 N Eton St Birmingham MI 48008 Office: 900 Woodward Ave Pontiac MI 48053

HAVERFIELD, MABEL ANNABELLE, cons., author; b. Conway, Iowa, Jan. 16, 1895; d. George Washington and Lillie Day (Coppock) Leach; student Springfield (Mo.) State Tchrs. Coll., 1914-15, summers 1915, 17, Peru (Nebr.) Tchrs. Coll., 1916-17, Washington U., St. Louis, 1958-59, Mo. U., 1963; m. Walter Wildey Haverfield, Sept. 23, 1917; children—Robert Walter, Ruth Maybelle. Tchr. pub. schs., Granby, Mo., 1915-16, Falls City, Nebr., 1916-18; gen. supt. Maplewood Christian Ch. Sunday Sch., 1931-33, 35-37; pres. Maplewood-Richmond Heights League Women Voters, 1933-35; mem. Maplewood-Richmond Heights Sch. Dist. Bd. Edn., 1935-41; pres. Womens Council, Maplewood Christian Ch., 1936-38; prin. weekday Schs. of Religion, 1941-52; dist. chmn. children's work Disciples of Christ, 1952-54, 63-65, state chmn. childrens work, 1954-56, dist. pres. Christian Womens Fellowship, 1956-58; mem. exec. bd. Disciples Council Greater St. Louis, 1956-58; dist. del. Christian Womens Fellowship to Quadrennial Assembly, Purdue U., 1957; mem. United Ch. Women Bd., 1956-58; mem. state bd. Christian Women's Fellowship, 1956-60, state treas., 1958-60, state parliamentarian, 1958-60; del. World Conv. Christian Chs., Edinburgh, Scotland, 1960; tchr. St. Louis Assn. for Retarded Children, 1959-73; tchr. Kanasa City Council Chs., Kansas City Christian Ch. Commn., State Lab. Schs. of Kans., Iowa and numerous Lab. and Observation Schs. in Mo.; dir. ann. 2-week St. Louis Lab. Sch. for teaching-tng., 1953-54, 64; tchr. young retarded adults in ecumenical Sunday A.M. program, 1963-82. Mabel A. Haverfield Scholarship established for needy retarded children by parents and staff of St. Louis Assn. for Retarded Children, 1973. Mem. Nat. Assn. Retarded Citizens, Mo., St. Louis assns. retarded children, Friends of Retarded. Club: Order Eastern Star. Author: Bug Off, 1976. Home: 5329 Jamieson Ave Saint Louis MO 63109

HAVEY, MARGUERITE, organist, composer; b. N.Y.C., Dec. 16, 1910; d. Marshall Lawrence and Edna Hill (Brady) H.; diploma N.Y. Collegiate Inst., 1927, Juilliard Sch. Music, 1933; student Am. Conservatory Music, Chgo., 1948-49, Sch. Sacred Music Union Sem., 1931. Organist, founder, dir., profl. mixed choir Ch. of Epiphany, N.Y.C., 1939-57; condr. Hastings Singers, Hastings on Hudson, N.Y., 1950-68; guest condr. Greenwich (Conn.) Choral Soc., 1967; freelance organist, dir., 1976—; compositions include: O Spirit, Who from Jesus Came, Carol of the Adoration, Noel, In Praise of Mary's Son; mem. music faculty Brearley Sch., N.Y.C., 1957-76, choral dir., 1970-76, chmn. music dept., 1973-76. Trustee, Kinhaven Music Sch., Weston, Vt., 1979-82. Mem. Nat. League Am. Pen Women (pres. So. Vt. chpt. 1978-80; recipient choral arrangement prize 1976), Am. Guild Organists (past nat. council, asso. cert.). Protestant Episcopalian.

HAVILAND, CAMILLA KLEIN, lawyer; b. Dodge City, Kans., Sept. 13, 1926; d. Robert Godfrey and Lelah (Luther) Klein; A.A., Monticello Coll., 1946; B.A., Radcliffe Coll., 1948; LL.B., Kans. U. Sch. Law, 1955, J.D., 1968; m. John Bodman Haviland, Sept. 7, 1957. Admitted to Kans. bar, 1955, Fed. bar, 1955; pvt. practice law, Wichita, Kans., 1955-56, Dodge City, 1956-57, 77—; judge Probate County and Juvenile Cts., Ford County, Kans., 1957-77. Mem. Kans. Atty. Gen.'s Youth Com., 1962-66; mem. probate law study com. Kans. Jud. Council, 1973, mem. probate forms com., 1975-79, mem. juvenile code com., 1979-82. Nat. committeewoman Young Democrats of Kans., 1948-54; v.p. Young Dem. Clubs Am., 1953-55. Mem. president's council St. Mary of Plains Coll., 1961-67; bd. dirs. Cascade (Colo.) Property Owners Assn., 1964-70, mem. adv. bd. Salvation Army, Dodge City, 1956—; mem. adv. council Kans. U. Sch. Religion, 1970—, Kans. U. Sch. Social Welfare, 1972—. Recipient Nathan Burkan Meml. award in copyright law A.S.C.A.P., 1955; cert. of recognition Nat. Council Juvenile Ct. Judges, 1966. Mem. ABA (mem. probate and real estate com. 1955—), Kans., Southwest Kans. (sec., treas. 1957-70, 1971-73; pres. 1970-71, Ford-Gray County (pres. 1979-80) bar assns., Kans. Probate Judges Assn. (pres. 1963-64), P.E.O., DAR, Am. Legion. Club: Soroptimists (Dodge City). Author: Poems by Camilla, 1948; also articles in Kans. Law Rev. Office: 203 W Spruce Dodge City KS 67801

HAVILAND, LEONA, librarian; b. Stamford, Conn., Nov. 10, 1916; d. Howard Brush and Ada Grace (Jewell) Haviland; B.S., U. Ala., 1940; M.S., U. Ill., 1951; postgrad. Columbia, 1943, 56-60; m. Warren John Burke, Sept. 10, 1973. Jr. asst. Ferguson Library, Stamford, 1936-37, summers 1938-39, sr. asst., 1940-44; student asst. U. Ala., 1937-40; asst. to cataloguer U.S. Nat. Mus. Library, Washington, 1944-48; librarian Arts and Industries Mus., Smithsonian Instn., Washington, 1948-50; reference librarian U.S. Mcht. Marine Acad., Kings Point, N.Y., 1952-77. Mem. council YWCA, Washington, 1945-47. Mem. A.L.A., Spl. Libraries Assn. (past group membership chmn.), L.I. Hist. Soc., N.Y. Geneal. and Biog. Soc., Smithsonian Assos., South Street Seaport Mus., Alpha Beta Alpha, Alpha Lambda Delta. Home: 809 Pennsylvania Ave Saint Cloud FL 32769

HAVLIN, NORMA JEAN, psychologist; b. Beardstown, Ill.; d. Rolla and Grace (Reische) DeWitt; B.S., So. Ill. U., Edwardsville, 1964, M.S., 1965, Ph.D., Carbondale, 1969; children—Robert H., James W. Tchr. 1st grade East St. Louis Sch. Dist. #189, 1964-66; psychologist Gardenville project St. Louis Public Schs., 1969-70; psychologist Alton Community Unit Sch. Dist. #11, (Ill.), 1970—; lectr. So. Ill. U., Edwardsville, 1969—; psychologist Madison County Head Start; lectr. St. Louis Tchrs. Learning Center, 1978—; pvt. practice, Godfrey, Ill., 1974—; hearing officer Ill. Bd. Edn.; instr. Parent Effectiveness Tng. Mem. Ill. Psychol. Assn., So. Ill. Psychol. Assn. (pres.), Am. Psychol. Assn., Nat. Assn. Sch. Psychologists, Ill. Sch. Psychologists Assn. Methodist. Home: 5013 Cavalier Ct Godfrey IL 62035 Office: 2512 Amelia St Alton IL 62002

HAVOSTAL, MARJORIE PAINE, investment mgmt. co. exec., writer; b. Mpls., Apr. 29, 1930; d. Franklin and Helen Paine; student U. Calif., Berkeley, 1948, George Washington U., 1960, U. Ariz., 1962-63; m. John J. Havostal, May 6, 1954; children—Ronald, Bruce, Wayne, Gloria. With Nat. Geog. Soc., Washington, 1950-52; personnel sec. U.S. Army, Ft. Myer, Va., 1952-55; exec. sec. Consol. Mut. Trust, Woodbridge, Va., 1980-82, exec. v.p., 1982—; cons. in animal rights. Contbr. articles to health mags.

HAWES, GRACE MAXCY, univ. adminstr., author; b. Cumberland, Wis., Feb. 4, 1926; d. Clarence David and Mabel Hannah (Erickson) Maxcy; student U. Wis., 1944-46; B.A., San Jose State U., 1963, M.A., 1971; m. John G. Hawes, Aug. 28, 1948; children—Elizabeth, John D., Mark, Amy. Library asst. NASA, Langley, Va., 1948-49; archivist Hoover Archives Stanford U., 1976-80; adminstr. Office of Devel., Stanford U., 1980—. Mem. Soc. Am. Archivists, Inst. Hist. Study, Women in Hist. Research, Calif. Archivists Assn. Author: The Marshall Plan for China: Economic Cooperation Administration, 1948-1949, 1977. Home: 410 Sheridan Ave Apt 220 Palo Alto CA 94306 Office: 301 Encina Hall Stanford University Stanford CA 94304

HAWK, NANCY JO, educator; b. Billings, Mont., Mar. 13, 1925; d. Harry Hamilton and Montana Edith (Grady) Skaggs; B.B.A. in Bus. Mgmt., Nat. U., San Diego, 1978; M.B.A., 1979; postgrad. Point Loma Coll.; m. Frank H. Hawk, Aug. 17, 1945; children—Lenore Hawk Dale, Patricia, Steven, Anthony. Owner, operator state beach concession, 1960-64; prin.'s sec., gen. office mgr. San Diego City Schs., 1964-79; tchr. bus. courses San Diego colls., 1976—; mem. Faculty Senate, Miramar Coll., Southwestern Coll.; condr. workshops in field of office edn. Pres., Wegeforth Sch. PTA, 1964-65; chmn. fundraising Tierrasant Little League, 1979; chmn. fund drive Am. Heart Assn. Mem. Nat. Assn. Female Execs., Am. Women in Community and Jr. Colls. (co-chmn. conf.); chmn. fund drive Am. Heart Assn., Alumni Assn. Nat. U., Bus. and Profl. Women's Club. Democrat. Home: 2453 Caminito Ocean Cove Cardiff CA 92007 Office: Miramar Coll San Diego CA 92126 also Southwestern Colls Bonita CA 92010

HAWKINS, CAROLYN SIVLEY, business exec.; b. Ft. Smith, Ark., Feb. 8, 1952; d. Robert Edward and Edith Emily (Sivley) H.; B.S., U. Ark., Little Rock, 1974; Med. Technologist, VA Sch. Med. Tech., 1974; student (Ark. Jr. Miss. scholar), Ouachita Bapt. U., 1970-72. Med. technologist Bapt. Med. Center, Little Rock, 1974-75; tech. dir. United Blood Services, Ft. Smith, 1975-79; sales engr. Hawkins Co., Inc., Ft. Smith, 1980-81, ter. mgr., 1982—. Mem. Gov.'s Youth Council, 1970. Mem. Am. Soc. Clin. Pathologists (registered med. technologist), Am. Assn. Blood Banks, S. Central Assn. Blood Banks (publs. com. 1976-77), Am. Soc. Med. Tech., Ark. Soc. Med. Tech. (dir. 1977-79, chmn. public relations com. 1978-79, nominations com. 1979-80), Jr. League (dir., chmn. Niteliners), Pi Beta Phi Alumnae. Methodist. Home: 3401 Londonderry Fort Smith AR 72903 Office: 222 Towson Ave Fort Smith AR 72901

HAWKINS, DEBORAH HADLOCK, veterinarian; b. Portland, Maine, Sept. 23, 1951; d. Edson Barry and Barbara (Whalen) Hadlock; student Purdue U., 1969-71; B.S., U. Ill., 1975; V.M.D., U. Pa., 1980. Asso. veterinarian Gramercy Park Animal Clinic, N.Y.C., 1981—; surg. cons. Massapequa Animal Hosp. Mem. AVMA, N.Y. State Vet. Med.

Assn., N.Y.C. Vet. Med. Assn., Phi Zeta. Office: 37 E 19th St New York NY 10019 *

HAWKINS, ELINOR DIXON, librarian; b. Masontown, W.Va., Sept. 25, 1927; d. Thomas Fitchie and Susan (Reed) Dixon; A.B., Fairmont State Coll., 1949; B.S., U. N.C., 1950; m. Carroll Woodard Hawkins, June 24, 1951; 1 son, John Carroll. Children's librarian Enoch Pratt Free Library, Balt., 1950-51; head circulation dept. Greensboro (N.C.) Public Library, 1951-56; librarian Craven-Pamlico Library Service, New Bern, N.C., 1958-62; dir. Craven-Pamlico-Carteret Regional Library, New Bern, 1962—; storyteller children's TV program Tele-Story Time, Greensboro, New Bern, 1952-58, 63—. Mem. Tryon Palace Commn., 1974—; mem. New Bern-Craven County Bicentennial Commn., 1973-76; mem. adv. bd. Salvation Army. Mem. N.C. Assn. Retarded Children, N.C. Library Assn., Friends of Library. Baptist. Club: Pilot Internat. (pres. Greensboro 1957-58). Home: PO Box 57 Cove City NC 28523 Office: 400 Johnson St New Bern NC 28560

HAWKINS, GENEVA MCCARTER, ednl. adminstr.; b. Birmingham, Ala., Nov. 16, 1926; d. Will and Georgia Ann (Beard) McCarter; A.B., Fisk U., 1949; M.A., U. Louisville, 1955, Ed.S., 1968; m. John Lewis Hawkins, Feb. 8, 1951 (dec.); children—Deborah H. Sprott, Johnetta Louisa, Vivian Shontee, Donald Vincent. Tchr., Birmingham, Ala., 1949-50; checker Kroger Co., Louisville, 1958-61; tchr. Russell Jr. High Sch., Louisville, 1961-71; counselor Parkland Jr. High Sch., Louisville, 1971-75, asst. prin., 1975-78; prin. Woerner Middle Sch., Louisville, 1978-80; prin. Western Middle Sch., Louisville, 1980—; cons. Focus-Impact, 1970-71; mem. nat. consumer adv. council Kroger Co., 1980. Mem. Emergency Sch. Aid Act Adv. Bd., Solvent Abuse Program Adv. Bd., Community Research Bd., Portland area; dist. pres. Woman's Home and Overseas Missionary Soc., 1982, supt. ch. sch., 1982, sec. quarterly conf., 1982. Recipient Award of Merit, Jefferson County Bd. Edn., 1979, Cert. of Appreciation, Ky. Elem. Schs., 1978, Outstanding Leadership-Ch. Citation, Gov. J. Carroll, 1978. Mem. NAACP (1st v.p. 1979, outstanding leadership award 1980), Women in Sch. Adminstrn., Ky. Assn. Sch. Adminstrs., Jefferson County Assn. Sch. Adminstrs. (bd. dirs.), Phi Delta Kappa. Democrat. Methodist. Clubs: Drifters, Inc. (pres. 1977), Kentuckian Golf (pres. 1976), Order Eastern Star (Louisville); Kentuckiana Ch. Bowling League (pres.); United Golf Assn. (treas.). Home: 401 S 39th St Louisville KY 40212 Office: 2201 W Main St Louisville KY 40212

HAWKINS, IDA FAYE, educator; b. Ft. Worth, Dec. 28, 1928; d. Christopher Columbus and Nannie Idella (Hughes) Hall; student Midwestern U., 1946-48; B.S., N. Tex. State U., 1951; student Lamar U., 1968-70; M.S., McNeese State U., 1973; m. Gene Hamilton Hawkins, Dec. 22, 1952; children—Gene Agner, Jane Hall. Tchr., DeQueen Elem. Sch., Port Arthur, Tex., 1950-54; tchr. Tyrrell Elem. Sch., Port Arthur, 1955-56; tchr. Roy Hatton Elem. Sch., Bridge City, Tex., 1967-68; tchr. Oak Forest Elem. Sch., Vidor, Tex., 1968—. Second vice-pres. Travis Elem. PTA, 1965-66, 1st v.p., 1966-67; corr. sec. Port Arthur City council PTA, 1966-67. Mem. NEA, Tex. State Tchrs. Assn., Classroom Tchrs. Assn., Am. Psychol. Assn., McNeese State U. Alumni Assn. Presbyterian (Sunday sch. tchr. 1951-53, 60-66). Home: 4075 Laurel Apt 73 Beaumont TX 77707 Office: Oak Forest Elem Sch 2400 Hwy 12 Vidor TX 77662

HAWKINS, JULIA MAE YOUNG, social worker, state ofcl.; b. St. Augustine, Fla.; d. Abraham L. and Ida (Pappy) Young; A.B., Talladega Coll., 1931; grad. (Urban League fellow 1931-33) N.Y. Sch. Social Work, 1933; m. Charles Clinton Hawkins, May 31, 1932; children—Charles Clinton, Homer C. Caseworker, St. Louis, 1933-35; sr. med. social worker N.Y. State Dept. Welfare, N.Y.C., 1938; med. social work supr. N.Y.C. Dept. Welfare, 1935-46; dist. case supr. W.Va. Dept. Welfare, 1954-57, dist. casework supr. I, 1957-59, tng. supr., 1959-63, asst. dir. staff devel., Charleston, 1963-66; dir. foster grandparents program W.Va. Dept. Mental Health, Charleston, 1966—. Active civic and community affairs. Mem. Nat. Assn. Social Workers, Acad. Certified Social Workers, Am. Pub. Welfare Assn. (com. on social work edn. and personnel 1963-65), Columbia U. Sch. Social Work Alumni (dir. 1964-66), Delta Sigma Theta. Roman Catholic. Club: Nat. Links (charter mem., 1st pres. 1952-54, certificate of appreciation 1976) (Charleston). Home: 219 Brookhaven Dr Nitro WV 25143 Office: WVa Dept Health State Capitol Bldg Charleston WV 25305

HAWKINS, KAREN FRANCES, banker; b. Portchester, N.Y., Nov. 30, 1947; d. George Lockwood, II and Helen Athena (Raftes) H.; B.A. in Math. and Spanish, Wells Coll., Aurora, N.Y., 1969; grad. Inst. Coop. Leadership, 1978. Asso. in corp. fin. Morgan Stanley & Co., N.Y.C., 1969-71; fin. analyst pvt. placements Travelers Ins. Co., Hartford, Conn., 1971-72; analyst corp. fin. and research Culverwell & Co., Inc., Springfield, Mass., 1972-74; asst. v.p., comml. loan officer Springfield Bank for Coops., 1974-80, Citizens & So. Nat. Bank, Atlanta, 1980-81, mgr. comml. br., 1982—; tchr. classes in field. Mem. Am. Inst. Banking. Republican. Episcopalian. Club: Cross Creek Ladies Twilight Golf League (chmn. 1981-82), Cross Creek Golf Assn. (treas. com. 1982—). Office: 3885 Old Gordon Rd Atlanta GA 30336

HAWKINS, KAREN LEE, lawyer; b. Central Falls, R.I., Oct. 17, 1945; d. Everett Yale and Kathryn Mary (Zagar) H.; B.A., U. Mass., Amherst, 1967; M.Ed., U. Calif., Davis, 1976; J.D., Golden Gate U., 1979, M.B.A. in Taxation, 1981. Asst. dean student affairs U. Calif., Davis, 1973-76; admitted to Calif. bar, 1979; tax cons. Touche Ross & Co., San Francisco, 1979—. Pres. Women's Rep. Assembly, Davis, 1974-75. Rockefeller Found. fellow, 1962-63; Mandarin Chinese grantee, 1976. Mem. Am. Bar Assn., Calif. Bar Assn., Bar Assn. San Francisco, Am. Trial Lawyers Assn., NOW, ACLU. Club: Sierra. Office: 1 Kaiser Plaza 10th Floor Oakland CA 94612

HAWKINS, MARY ELLEN HIGGINS, state legislator; b. Birmingham, Ala.; student U. Ala., Tuscaloosa, 1945-47; m. James H. Hawkins (div., 1971); children—Andrew Higgins, Elizabeth and Peter Hixon. Congl. aide to several mems. U.S. Ho. Reps., 1945-59; chmn. Sumter County (Ga.) Republican Com., 1970-72; vice-chmn. 3d Dist. Republican Com., 1970-72; community adv. council Sm. Bus. Adminstrn., Atlanta, 1970-72; mem. Fla. Ho. Reps., 1974—. Mem. Fla. Adv. Council, U.S. Commn. Civil Rights, 1977-81; art instr. Sumter County Schs., Americus, Ga., 1971-72; staff writer Naples Daily News, Fla., 1972—. Roman Catholic. Club: Zonta. Office: Fla Ho Reps State Capitol Tallahassee FL 32301

HAWKINS, MICHELLE WOODHOUSE, psychiat. found. exec.; b. San Mateo, Calif., May 17, 1934; d. Charles Douglas and Muriel Margaret (Jeffery) Woodhouse; B.A., Mt. Holyoke Coll., 1956; m. Richard Thurber Hawkins, June 30, 1956; children—Charles Sherman, Jeffery Lee, Elizabeth Jackson. Instr. adult edn. U.S. Army, Alaska Command, 1956-58; pres. Citizens for Citizens, Inc., Fall River, Mass., 1966-68; mem. Bd. Prison Insps., Montgomery County, Pa., 1971-74; chief exec. officer Horsham Psychiat., Found., Ambler, Pa., 1978—; dir. Horsham Psychiat. Clinic, 1977—, chaplain, 1982—; postulate for holy orders Episcopal Ch. Mem. Gov.'s Commn. on Youth, 1967-68; bd. dirs. YMCA, Fall River, Mass., 1966-68, Roxborough, Pa., 1968-70; mem. Montgomery County Day Care Assn., 1968-72, Nat. Council on Crime and Delinquency, 1971-74; mem. Episcopal Ch. Commn. on Health and Human Affairs, 1973—, co-chmn., 1979-82. Recipient Public Service award, Fall River Mass., 1968. Mem. Nat. Assn. Pvt. Psychiat. Hosps., Soc. of Companions of Holy Cross; affiliate Coll. Chaplains of Am. Protestant Hosp. Assn. Author: Crisis in Faith, The Challenge of Poverty, 1968; Juvenile Justice, 1973. Home: 826 Pine Tree Rd Lafayette Hill PA 19444 Office: Welsh Rd and Butler Pike Ambler PA 19002

HAWKINS, PAULA, U.S. Senator; b. Salt Lake City, Jan. 24, 1927; ed. U. Utah, L.H.D. (hon.), 1982; m. Walter Eugene Hawkins, 1947; children—Genean, Kevin, Kelley. Mem. U.S. Senate from Utah; vice-chmn. Republican Nat. Com. Mem. Fla. Fedn. Rep. Women; Nat. Fedn. Rep. Women. Recipient numerous awards including Guardian Small Bus., Nat. Fedn. Ind. Bus., 1982. Mem. Ch. Jesus Christ of Latter-day Saints. Office: 1327 Dirksen Senate Office Bldg Washington DC 20510 *

HAWKINS, PAULA, U.S. senator; b. Salt Lake City; student Utah State U.; m. Walter Eugene Hawkins, Sept. 5, 1947; children—Genean, Kevin Brent, Kelley Ann. Public service commr. State of Fla., Tallahassee, 1972-79; v.p. Air Fla., Miami, 1979-80; U.S. senator from Fla., 1980—; Republican precinct committeewoman, Orange County, Fla., 1965-70; speakers chmn. Fla. Rep. Exec. Com., 1967-69; mem. Fla. Rep. Nat. Conv., 1968, 72, 76, 80, Nat. Fedn. Rep. Women, 1965—; bd. dirs. Fla. Fedn. Rep. Women, 1968—; mem. Rep. Nat. Com. for Fla., 1968—; mem. adv. council Nat. Young Rep. Fedn., 1971—; chmn. host com., mem. rules com. Rep. Nat. Conv., 1972; vice-chmn. Rep. Nat. Com., 1972—; presdl. elector, 1972-80. Mem. Maitland Civic Center, 1965-70; charter mem. bd. dirs. Fla. Ams. Constl. Action Com. of 100, 1966-68; mem. Central Fla. Mus. Speakers Bur., 1967-68, Rural Telephone Bank Bd., 1972-78, Gov. Fla. Commn. Status Women, 1968-71; chmn. legis. com. Orange County Drug Abuse Council, 1970; co-chmn. Orange County March of Dimes, 1970. Recipient citation for service Fla. Rep. Party, 1966-67; Above and Beyond award as outstanding woman in Fla. politics, 1968; nominated Orange County Woman of Yr., Maitland Woman's Club, 1969. Mem. White House Fellows, Maitland C. of C. (Good Govt. award). Mem. Ch. Jesus Christ of Latter-day Saints (pres. Relief Soc., Orlando Stake 1963-64, Sunday sch. tchr. 1964—). Office: 1327 Dirksen Senate Office Bldg Washington DC 20510

HAWLEY, LINDA DONOVAN, advt. co. exec.; b. Bryn Mawr, Pa., Nov. 1, 1946; d. John Donovan and Ann (Durnall) H.; diploma in advt. Charles Morris Price Sch. Advt., Phila., 1965. Sr. writer The Bulletin Co., Phila., 1968-72, The Advt. People, Inc., Bala Cynwyd, Pa., 1973-75, Elkman Advt. Co., Inc., Bala Cynwyd, 1975-77; sr. copywriter Mel Richman Inc., Bala Cynwyd, 1977-80; v.p. Hawley & Matthews Inc., Valley Forge, Pa., 1980—; lectr. Charles Morris Price Sch., Pa. State U. Recipient various advt. awards including Neographics award. 1970, Addy award, 1976, Addy awards 2d Dist., 1980, Phila., 1981; Charles Morris Price Sch. Disting. Alumni Award, 1977. Mem. Phila. Club Advt. Women (pres. 1978-80), Phila. Women's Network, Am. Advt. Fedn. (Pa. lt. gov. 1979-81, 2d dist. sec. 1981—), TV and Radio Advt. Club. Roman Catholic. Office: Hawley & Matthews Inc PO Box 927 Davis Rd and Oakwood Ln Valley Forge PA 19481

HAWMAN, DORIS FRISCH, speech clinician; b. Phoenix, Md., Apr. 3, 1933; d. John Christian and Martha (Simms) Frisch; B.S. in Speech Therapy, Towson State U., 1974, M.S., 1977; m. Kenneth J. Hawman, Nov. 24, 1951; children—Scott, Keith, Martha. Speech clinician Mahalia Jackson Elem. Sch., Balt., 1974-77, Martin Luther King Elem. Sch., Balt., 1977-79, Langston Hughes Elem. Sch., Balt., 1979-80, Bear Creek Elem. Sch., Balt., 1980-81, Battle Grove Elem. Sch., Balt., 1981—; speech tutor to learning disabled children and adults, Balt., 1974—. Election registrar 10th Dist. Md., 1958—; active Rep. Club Balt. County, 1958—; pres. couples club Luth. Ch.; judge oratorical contest Optimist Club. Mem. Am. Speech, Lang. and Hearing Assn. (cert.). Club: Order Eastern Star (officer 1976-78). Innovator teaching methods mentally handicapped adults and learning-disabled children. Home: 15013 LaVale Rd Monkton MD 21111 Office: Battle Grove Elem Sch 7828 Saint Patricia Ln Baltimore MD 21222

HAWN, GOLDIE, actress; b. Washington, Nov. 21, 1945; d. Edward Rutledge and Laura (Steinhoff) Hawn; student Am. U.; m. Gus Trinkonis, May 16, 1969 (div.); m. 2d Bill Hudson; children—Oliver, Kate Garry. Profl. dancer, 1965; 1st profl. acting in Good Morning, World, 1967-68; mem. company Laugh-In 1968-70; appeared in TV spl. Pure Goldie, 1971, Goldie and Kids—Listen to Us, 1982; appeared in films Cactus Flower (Acad. award best supporting actress), 1969, There's A Girl In My Soup, 1970, Dollars, 1971, Butterflies Are Free, 1971, The Sugarland Express, 1974, The Girl from Petrovka, 1974, Shampoo, 1975, The Duchess and the Dirtwater Fox, 1976, Foul Play, 1978, Seems Like Old Times, 1980; exec. producer and star Private Benjamin, 1980. Office: care William Morris Agy 151 El Camino Dr Beverly Hills CA 90212 *

HAWORTH, VALARIE ANN, bus. exec., mastectomy cons.; b. Oakland, Calif., May 1, 1935; d. Rex Lowell and Antoinette Marie (Olivier) Wimer; student San Francisco State U., 1953-54; grad. Am. Acad. Husband-Coached Childbirth, 1974; grad. diploma, surg. appliance technician; various profl. seminars Am. Acad. Orthotics and Prosthetics; m. William James Haworth, Aug. 10, 1958 (div.); children—Rene Nicole, Brett Michael. Profl. dancer Contemporary Dance Co., 1954-55; childbirth educator, 1973—; prin. exec. Occasions, San Francisco, 1976—; mastectomy cons. Grigorieff Orthopedic Labs., Inc., Novato, Calif.; guest lectr. U. Calif. Med. Center, San Francisco State U., Coll. of Marin. Mem. Internat. Childbirth Edn. Assn., Edn. for Childbirth Assn. Marin (past pres.). Home: PO Box 13 Dillon Beach CA 94929 Office: Grigorieff Orthopedic Labs Inc 15 Pamaron Way Suite L Novato CA 94947

HAWRYSH, ZENIA JEAN, food scientist; b. Edmonton, Alta., Can., Nov. 4, 1938; d. Onif and Pauline (Keaschuk) Lukianchuk; B.Sc. in Home Econs., U. Alta., Edmonton, 1959; M.Sc. in Foods, Mich. State U., 1960, Ph.D. in Food Sci., 1970. Lectr. foods, dept. home econs. U. Alta., 1960, asst. prof., 1962; grad. asst. dept. food sci. Mich. State U., 1969-70; asso. prof. foods, dept. home econs. U. Alta., 1976-80, prof., chmn. dept. foods and nutrition, 1980—. Gen. Foods Fund fellow, 1966-67; Thelma Porter fellow, 1967-68. Mem. Inst. Food Technologists, Can. Inst. Food Sci. and Tech., Am. Meat Sci. Assn., Am. Dairy Sci. Assn., AAAS, Am. Dietetic Assn., Can. Dietetic Assn., Can. Univ. Tchrs. Home Econs., Am. Home Econs. Assn., Central and East European Studies Assn. Can., Sigma Xi. Ukrainian Greek Orthodox. Club: Ukrainian Profl. and Bus. Office: 308C Home Economics Bldg University of Alberta Edmonton AB T6G 2M8 Canada

HAWTHORNE, BETTY EILEEN, educator, univ. dean; b. Seattle, Nov. 22, 1920; d. Harry Albert and Marcia (Thompson) Hawthorne; B.S., U. Wash., 1941, M.S., 1944. Ph.D., Mich. State U., 1954. Field nutritionist Pacific area ARC, Wash., 1943-44; instr., asst. prof. Oreg. State U., Corvallis, 1946-55, assoc. prof. foods and nutrition, 1955-62, prof., 1962—, dean Sch. Home Econs., 1965—; dir. Curtice-Burns, Inc., Rochester, N.Y.; chmn. home economics subcom., expt. sta. com. on orgn. and policy Nat. Assn. State Univs. and Land Grant Colls., 1977-80; dir. Pacific Power & Light Co., Portland. Bd. dirs. Good Samaritan Hosp., Corvallis, 1970-78. Served with ensign to lt. (j.g.). Supply Corps. USNR, 1944-46. Mem. Am., Oreg. (past pres.) dietetic assns., Am. Pub. Health Assn., Am. Inst. Nutrition, Am. Home Econs. Assn. (past sect. chmn.), Assn. Adminstrs. Home Econs. in Land Grant Colls. and State Univs. (pres. 1976-77), AAUW, AAAS, Soc. Nutrition Edn., Nat. Council Family Relations, Western Gerontol. Soc., Am. Council Consumer Interests, Altrusa Internat. Phi Beta Kappa, Sigma Xi, Phi Kappa Phi, Omicron Nu, Iota Sigma Pi. Home: 144 NW 29th St Corvallis OR 97330 *

HAWTHORNE, LUCIA SHELIA, educator; b. Balt., May 6; d. Edward Wilkin and Daisy (Goins) H.; B.S., Morgan State U., 1964; M.A.T., Wash. State U., Pullman, 1965; Ph.D., Pa. State U., 1971; m. Ward S. Parham, Aug. 18, 1979. Teaching asst. Wash. State U., 1964-65; instr. Morgan State Coll., 1965-67; teaching asst. Pa. State U., 1967-69; asst. prof. Morgan State U., 1969-72, assoc. prof., chmn. dept. speech communication and theatre arts, 1972-75, prof., 1976—, assoc. dean humanities, 1974-75; cons. in field. Am. Council Edn. Acad. Adminstrn. fellow, 1974-75. Mem. Speech Communication Assn., Western Speech Assn., Md. Communications Assn., Assn. Communication Adminstrs. Baptist. Contbr. in field. Office: Morgan State University Baltimore MD 21239

HAWTHORNE, MARTHA ELLEN, educator; b. Monroe, La., Sept. 24, 1938; d. Frank W. and Ellen Mae (Collins) Hawthorne; B.A., La. State U., 1960, B.S., 1961, M.S., 1964. Tchr., Glen Oaks Jr. High Sch., Baton Rouge, 1961-62; grad. asst. La. State U., 1963-64; instr., dir. women's intramurals U. Houston, 1964-70, 71-75; asst. prof., coach women's varsity tennis NE La. U., Monroe, 1976-79; coordinator women's athletics Rice U., Houston, 1979-81, asst. athletic dir., 1981—; mem. Houston Ind. Sch. Task Force Com. Expansion Girls Athletics, 1973-74. Mem. Council of Collegiate Women Athletic Adminstrs., U.S. Tennis Assn., SW Assn. Intercollegiate Athletics for Women (pres. 1977-78), Tex. Assn. Intercollegiate Athletics for Women (pres. 1981-82), La. Assn. Intercollegiate Athletics for Women (v.p. athletics 1976-78), Assn. Intercollegiate Athletics for Women (mem. com. men's athletics 1977-78), Chi Omega. Home: 8513 Merlin Dr Houston TX 77055 Office: Rice U Athletic Dept Houston TX 77001

HAY, ELIZABETH KERR, nurse, educator; b. N.Y.C., Apr. 11, 1943; d. Alexander Wilson and Elizabeth Ransom (Kerr) H.; A.B., Randolph-Macon Woman's Coll., 1965; B.S., Columbia U., 1967; R.N., Columbia-Presbyn. Med. Center, 1967; M.S.N., Vanderbilt U., 1976. Orthopedic staff nurse Presbyn. Hosp., N.Y.C., 1967-69; nursing supr., instr. Firestone Hosp., Harbel, Liberia, 1969; head nurse, supr. Rogosin Kidney Disease Treatment Center, N.Y. Hosp., Cornell Med. Center, 1970-74; staff nurse hemodialysis Nashville VA Hosp., 1974-75; clin. specialist adult neurosurgery/orthopedics, instr. med.-surg. nursing Vanderbilt U., Nashville, 1976-79, asst. prof. med.-surg. nursing, 1979—; cons. profl. adv. bd., quality assurance reviewer Upjohn Health Care Services, 1979—; neurol. cons. critical care program U. Tenn., 1981—. Recipient Shirley Titus award Sch. Nursing, Vanderbilt U., 1981, excellence in clin. instrn. award; Ellen Gregg Ingalls award Vanderbilt U., 1982. Mem. Am. Nurses Assn. (com. to develop standards of orthopedic nursing practice 1982-83), Nat. Assn. Orthopedic Nurses, Tenn. Nurses Assn., Sigma Theta Tau. Office: Vanderbilt U Godchaux Hall 21st Ave S Nashville TN 37240

HAYDEN, MARGARET BLEDSOE, state legislator; b. Ashe County, N.C., Mar. 5, 1939; d. Boss George and Eula (Luther) Bledsoe; B.S., Appalahian State U., Boone, N.C., 1961, M.A. in Spl. Edn., 1972; m. Herman N. Hayden, Jr.; children—Jackson Lane and Steven Zane (twins). Tchr. exceptional children Sparta (N.C.) Elem. Sch.; cons. div. exceptional children N.C. Dept. Public Instrn., 1978—; pres. Future Heirlooms Ltd., handmade quilt exporting, Sparta; mayor of Sparta, 1977-81; mem. N.C. Ho. of Reps. from 28th Dist., 1981—. Elder, past chmn. Presbyn. Ch., Sparta; 1st v.p. Democratic Party. Office: State Legis Bldg Raleigh NC 28611

HAYDEN, MARJORIE SIEWERT, banker; b. Mpls., Dec. 21, 1930; d. Henry Alex and Marjorie Minkler Siewert; B.A., Carleton Coll., 1953; postgrad. U. Minn., 1957-58; children—Joseph, Grace. With First Nat. Bank, Little Falls, Minn., 1949—, pres., 1971—. Past pres. Carnegie Library Bd., Lindbergh Sch. PTA; vestry Episcopal Ch.; past vice chmn. Morrison County Democratic-Farmer-Labor Party. Mem. Nat. Assn. Bank Women, Ind. Bankers Assn., Little Falls C. of C. (dir.), Minn. Civil Liberties Union (past dir.). Office: First Nat Bank Little Falls MN 56345

HAYDEN, RUTH WHEELER, dietitian, educator; b. Seattle, Apr. 19, 1923; d. Noble Curtis and Emma Pearl (Cummings) Remington; B.S., U. Wash., 1964, dietetic intern, 1965, M.S., 1966; postgrad. Oreg. State U., 1978-79; m. Richard Charles Wheeler, Aug. 27, 1944 (dec. 1965); children—Richard Charles, Robert Edward, Deborah Elaine, John Scott; m. 2d, Ralph Horace Hayden, Sept. 13, 1968. Asst. prof. foods and nutrition Utah State U., 1966-69; instr. foods and nutrition, dir. dietetic asst. and dietetic technician programs Portland (Oreg.) Community Coll., 1969—. Chmn. nutrition com. Oreg. Heart Assn., 1979-80, bd. dirs., 1980—. Mem. Am. Dietetic Assn., Oreg. Dietetic Assn., Oreg. Nutrition Council, Am. Soc. for Hosp. Food Service Adminstrs., Coll. and Univ. Tchrs. Foods and Nutrition (chmn. 1980 conf.). Republican. Episcopalian. Home: 26001 NE Butteville Rd Aurora OR 97002 Office: 12000 SW 49th St Portland OR 97219

HAYDEN, VIRGINIA EVA, pharm. co. ofcl.; b. Midland, Mich., May 20, 1927; d. Robert James and Altheda Mae (Wood) H.; B.A. in Acctg. and Econs., Mich. State U., 1949; m. Donald Conrad, Feb. 15, 1952 (div.). Stock inventory clk. Dow Chem. Co., 1949-50; budget clk., analyst, specialist, coordinator Upjohn Co., Kalamazoo, 1950-72, mgr. corp. budgeting, 1972-78, exec. devel. cons., 1978—, also co-founder, advisor Greater Opportunities for Women (GROW); speaker mgmt. classes; speaker on career planning and women in mgmt. to profl. orgns.; tchr. women in mgmt. Kalamazoo Coll. Advisor Center Women's Services of Western Mich. U.; bd. dirs. Kalamazoo Alcohol and Drug Abuse Council. Recipient W.E. Upjohn award, 1970. Mem. Kalamazoo Network (dir., co-founder), Am. Soc. Tng. and Devel., Kalamazoo Personnel Assn., Nat. Wildlife Assn., Kalamazoo Nature Center, Audubon Soc., YWCA. Club: Kalamazoo Altrusa (pres.). Home: 8207 Bruning St Kalamazoo MI 49002 Office: Upjohn Co 7000 Portage Rd Kalamazoo MI 49001

HAYEK, MARY ANNIE, psychologist; b. Paterson, N.J., Feb. 13, 1925; d. Anthony T. and Mary N. (Sara) Haddad; B.A. with distinction in Psychology, Fla. Internat. U., 1975, M.S. in Counselor Edn., 1978; Ph.D. in Clin. Psychology, Heed U., Hollywood, Fla., 1980; m. James Paul Hayek, Aug. 12, 1945; children—George Anthony, James Paul, Joanne Christine. Alcohol counselor, therapist South Miami Hosp., Miami, Fla., 1977-78; cons. psychologist, psychotherapist Victims Advocates for Sexually Abused Children, Miami, 1980-81; psychotherapist Counseling and Stress Control Center, Coral Gables, Fla., 1978-80, pvt. practice with Center, 1980—. Master and Johnson fellow, 1979-82. Mem. Am. Mental Health Counselors Assn., Am. Personnel and Guidance Assn., Am. Psychol. Assn., Fla. Assn. Practicing Psychologists, Fla. Assn. Profl. Hypnosis, Fla. Mental Health Counselors Assn., Nat. Rehab. Assn., Mental Health Assn. Dade County, Phi Theta Kappa, Phi Lambda Pi, Psi Chi. Author: Recovered Alcoholic Women With and Without Incest Experience, 1981. Home: 1801 SW 84th Ct Miami FL 33155 Office: 115 Madeira Ave Coral Gables FL 33134

HAYES, ALBERTA PHYLLIS WILDRICK, ret. health service exec.; b. Blakeslee, Pa., May 31, 1918; d. William and Maude (Robbins) Wildrick; diploma Wilkes Barre Gen. Hosp. Sch. Nursing, 1938-41; student Wilkes Coll., 1953-54, Pa. State U., 1969—; m. Glenmore Burton Hayes, Oct. 9, 1942; children—Glenmore Rolland, William

Bruce. Nurse, Monroe County Gen. Hosp., East Stroudsburg, Pa., 1941-44; pvt. duty nurse, 1944-56; with White Haven (Pa.) Center, 1956-82, dir. residential services, 1966-82, ret., 1982. Pres. Tobyhanna Twp. Sch. PTA, 1948-49, Top-o-Pocono Women of Rotary, 1975-76; nurse ARC, 1955; adv. council Luzerne County Foster Grandparent Program, 1977—, Health Services Keystone Job Corps, Drums, Pa., 1977—. Mem. Am. Assn. Mental Deficiency, Am. Legion Aux. (unit pres. 1946-47). Club: Pocono Mountains Women's (Blakeslee). Home: PO Box 11 Blakeslee PA 18610

HAYES, ALICE BOURKE, biologist, educator; b. Chgo., Dec. 31, 1937; d. William Joseph and Mary Alice (Cawley) Bourke; B.S., Mundelein Coll., Chgo., 1959; M.S., U. Ill., 1960; Ph.D., Northwestern U., 1972; m. John J. Hayes, Sept. 2, 1961. Researcher, Mcpl. Tb Sanitarium, Chgo., 1960-62; mem. faculty Loyola U., Chgo., 1962—, chmn. dept. natural sci., 1968-77, dean natural scis. div., 1977-80, asso. prof., 1974-79, prof., 1979—, asso. acad. v.p., 1980—. Fellow in botany U. Ill., 1959-60, NSF, 1969-71; grantee Am. Orchid Soc., 1967, HEW, 1969, NSF, 1975, NASA, 1980—. Mem. Am. Soc. Plant Physiology, Bot. Soc. Am., Soc. Ill. Microbiologists, Am. Soc. Microbiology, Internat. Soc. Human and Animal Mycology, AAAS, Am. Inst. Biol. Scis., Assn. Midwest Coll. Biology Tchrs. Roman Cath. Contbr. profl. publs. Home: 6190 N Indian Rd Chicago IL 60646 Office: 820 N Michigan Ave Chicago IL 60611

HAYES, BETTINE J., investment mgr.; b. Boston, Sept. 6, 1928; d. Reginald W. P. and Ethel (Thomas) Brown; B.A., Wellesley Coll., 1950; m. M. Vinson Hayes, June 10, 1961; children—M. Vinson III, Juliet Dorothy. Security analyst Merrill Lynch, Pierce, Fenner & Smith, Inc., N.Y.C., 1950-60, 76—, portfolio analyst, 1960-73, Canadian research coordinator, 1967-69; mgr. N.Y. Wellesley Club, 1973-74; researcher Nat. Info. Bur., 1974-76. Mem. D.A.R. (chpt. treas. 1958-59, historian 1961-62, rec. sec. Colonielles, 1961-71, 74-77, treas. Colonielles 1971-73), N.Y. Soc. Security Analysts. Home: 39 Gramercy Park New York City NY 10010 also 11 Spring Close Ln East Hampton NY 11937 Office: 1 Liberty Plaza 165 Broadway New York NY 10080

HAYES, GLORIA LOUISE PAYNE, credit mgr.; b. Dover, N.J., Aug. 4, 1930; d. Theodore Eaton and Irene Payne Stubblebine; grad. Reading Bus. Inst.; student Valencia Coll., 1978-79; m. James Allen Hayes, Sept. 12, 1981; children—Christine, Diane, Sharon, Cindy, Alan. Office clk. Weiner's Clothing Co., Reading, Pa., 1948-52; adminstrv. asst. Pottsgrove Schs., Pottstown, Pa., 1959-69; billing supr. Baker Equipment Co., 1969-74; accounts receivable mgr. Green Thumb Co. div. Stratford of Tex., Orlando, Fla., 1974-77; terminal acctg. mgr. Green Thumb Co. div. Ralston Purina Co., Orlando, 1977-79, credit mgr. Deco Plants Co. div., St. Louis, 1979—; bus. cons. Spring Garden Products, Apopka, Fla., 1979. Pres., PTA, West Pottsgrove, 1960-66; softball coach, Fenton, Mo.; v.p. Bowling League, Orlando. Named Woman of Yr., Pottstown Mercury newspaper, 1967; awarded life membership Pa. PTA. Mem. Nat. Assn. Female Execs., Am. Mgmt. Assn. Baptist. Clubs: Nat. Travel, Ionosphere. Composer. Home: 9571 Fredricksburg Ct Saint Louis MO 63126 Office: Checkerboard Sq Saint Louis MO 63188

HAYES, HELEN, actress; b. Washington, Oct. 10, 1900; d. Francis Van Arnum and Catherine Estell (Hayes) Brown; grad. Sacred Heart Acad., Washington, 1917; L.H.D., Hamilton Coll., Clinton, N.Y., 1939, Smith Coll., 1940; L.H.D., Elmira (N.Y.) Coll.; Litt.D., Columbia U., 1949 U. Denver, 1952; D.F.A., Princeton U., St. Mary's Coll.; m. Charles MacArthur, Aug. 17, 1928 (dec. Apr. 1956); 1 son, James. First appeared on stage at age of 6; mem. Columbia Players, Washington, 4 seasons; later toured with Lew Fields and John Drew; played in Old Dutch, Prodigal Husband, Pollyanna, Penrod; appeared with William Gillette in Dear Brutus; appeared in Clarence, Bab, To the Ladies, We Moderns, Dancing Mothers, Caesar and Cleopatra, What Every Woman Knows, Croquette, Mr. Gilhooley, Mary of Scotland, 1934, Victoria Regina, 1937-38, Ladies and Gentlemen, 1939-40, Twelfth Night, 1940-41, Candle in the Wind, 1941-42, Harriet, 1943-45, Happy Birthday, The Glass Menagerie, London, 1948, Farewell to Arms, Vanessa, The Wisteria Trees, 1950, Mrs. McThing, 1952, Mainstreet to Broadway, 1953, Skin of Our Teeth, Europe and U.S., 1955, Harvey, Long Days' Journey Into Night, 1971, others; appeared in motion pictures The Sin of Madelon Claudet, Arrowsmith, My Son John, 1951, Anastasia, 1956, Airport (Acad. award as best supporting actress 1971, 1970, Herbie Rides Again, 1974, Helen Hayes: Portrait of an American Actress, 1974, One of Our Dinosaurs is Missing, 1975, Candleshoe, 1978; numerous TV appearances including series The Snoop Sisters, 1972-74; others; Mrs. Derth in TV revival of Barrie's Dear Brutus, 1956; mem. A.P.A. Phoenix Repertory Co., 1966—. Recipient best actress award Motion Picture Acad. Arts and Sciences, 1932, in The Sin of Madelon Claudet; Emmy award, 1954; Antoinette Perry award for best actress in Time Remembered, 1958; Medal of City N.Y.; Medal of Arts, Finland; Am. Exemplar medal Freedoms Found., 1978; Laetare medal U. Notre Dame, 1979. Hon. pres. Am. Theatre Wing; pres. Am. Nat. Theatre and Acad.; 2d v.p. Actors Fund, 1975—. Chmn. Women's activities Nat. Found. for Infantile Paralysis. Republican. Roman Catholic. Author: A Gift of Joy, 1965; On Reflection, 1968; (with Anita Loos) Twice Over Lightly, 1971; Star on Her Forehead, 1949. *

HAYES, ISABELLA MALLORY, civic worker; b. Kewanee, Ill., Mar. 27, 1908; d. George Adelbert and Ella Bowie (Swayze) Mallory; B.A., Knox Coll., 1930, B.L.S., U. Wis., 1931; postgrad. U. Md., 1953; m. Walter Harold Hayes, Nov. 9, 1935; 1 dau., Anne Hayes Hume. With Kewanee Public Library, 1926-30; head reference dept., public library, Roanoke, Va., 1931-43; instr., asst. reference librarian U. Md. Library, College Park, 1949-58, head Md. and rare book room, also in charge displays and public relations, 1958-69, editor Library News, 1952-69. Exec. dir. Nat. Library Week in Md., 1962; chmn. First Citizens Conf. on Libraries in Md., 1965. Mem. State Adv. Com. on Day Care to Md. Dept. Social Services, 1962-72; chmn. Health and Welfare Council Prince Georges County, 1965-68. Bd. dirs. Health and Welfare Council Nat. Capital Area, Washington, 1964-68, Md. Com. for Day Care of Children, Balt., 1964-69, Prince George's County Retarded Day Care Center, 1962-69, St. John's County (Fla.) ARC, 1975-78; mem. St. Johns County (Fla.) Welfare Bd., 1976-77. Recipient Community Service award Health and Welfare Council Nat. Capital Area, Washington, 1968. Mem. LWV (county pres. 1957-58, mem. state bd. 1958-62), AAUW (2d v.p. br. 1972-77, dir. 1978—, legis. chmn. St. Augustine br. 1981—), Mothers Club Kappa Alpha Theta, Alpha Delta Pi (patroness). Author: Ethics of Advertising: a Selected Bibliography, 1931; Financing Presidential Campaigns, A Selected Bibliography, 1953. Home: 70 Willow Dr Saint Augustine FL 32084

HAYES, JANET GRAY, mayor San Jose (Calif.); b. Rushville, Ind., July 12, 1926; d. John Paul and Lucile (Gray) Frazee; A.B., Ind. U., 1948; M.A. magna cum laude, U. Chgo., 1950; m. Kenneth Hayes, Mar. 20, 1950; children—Lindy, John, Katherine, Megan. Psychiat. caseworker Jewish Family Service Agy., Chgo., 1950-52; vol. Denver Crippled Children's Service, 1954-55; vol. Adult and Child Guidance Clinic, San Jose, 1958-59; mem. San Jose City Council, 1971—, vice-mayor, 1973-74, mayor, 1975—; trustee U.S. Conf. Mayors, 1977—, mem. sci. and tech. task force, 1976—; bd. dirs. League Calif. Cities, 1976—, mem. property tax reform task force, 1976—; chmn. State of Calif. Urban Devel. Adv. Com., 1976-77; mem. Calif. Commn. Fair Jud. Practices, 1976—; mem. Democratic nat. campaign com., 1976; mem. Calif. Dem. Commn. Nat. Platform and Policy, 1976; del. Dem. Nat. Conv., 1980; bd. dirs. South San Francisco Bay Dischargers Authority; chmn. Santa Clara County Sanitation Dist.; mem. San Jose/Santa Clara Treatment Plant Adv. Bd.; chmn. Santa Clara Valley Employment and Tng. Bd. (CETA); past mem. EPA Aircraft/Airport Noise Task Group; bd. dirs. Calif. Center Research and Edn. in Govt.; bd. dirs., chmn. adv. council Public Tech. Inc. AAUW Edn. Found. grantee. Mem. Assn. Bay Area Govts. (exec. com. 1971-74, regional housing subcom. 1973-74, regional housing subcom. 1973-74), LWV (pres. San Francisco Bay Area chpt. 1968-70, pres. local 1966-67), Phi Beta Kappa. Democrat. Club: Century. Office: City Hall 801 N 1st St San Jose CA 95110

HAYES, JUNE DOLORES, psychologist, behavioral cons.; b. Phila., Dec. 26, 1946; d. Charles Alfred and June Delores (Beckman) Hayes; B.S., Coll. Misericordia, 1968; M.Ed., Kutztown State Coll., 1972; Ph.D., Calif. Grad. Inst., 1978. Tchr., Birdsboro (Pa.) Sch. Dist., 1968-69, Eastern Lebanon County Schs., Myerstown, Pa., 1969-70; houseparent Talbot Hall, Jonestown, Pa., 1969-72; psychol. asso. Wernersville (Pa.) State Hosp., 1972-74; psychiat. aide Santa Ana (Calif.) Psychiat. Hosp., 1974-76; intern Inst. Family and Group Therapy, Riverside, Calif., 1975-77; psychol. intern Psychiat. Clinic for Children, Meml. Hosp., Long Beach, Calif., 1975-76; pvt. practice marriage, family and child counseling, Riverside, Calif., 1977-80, Glen Avon, Calif., 1980—; behavioral and ednl. cons., supr. Lakeview Develop. Disabilities Center, Pedley, Calif., 1977-81; mental health clinician Central Valley Comprehensive Community Mental Health Project, San Bernardino County, Calif., 1977—, chmn. peer rev. com., 1978-79; clinic mgr. New Day Mental Health Clinic, Rialto, Calif., 1980—; part-time instr. Chapman Coll., Residential Edn. Center, 1979-80. Mem. Am. Assn. Sex Educators, Counselors and Therapists, Calif. Psychol. Assn. Episcopalian. Home: 4006 Campbell St Glen Avon CA 92509 Office: New Day Mental Health Clinic 301 N Riverside Rialto CA

HAYES, KAREN WOOD, state legislator; b. Cedar City, Utah, Oct. 16, 1935; d. Lalif and Roma (Pollock) Wood; B.S., Brigham Young U.; widow; children—Garry, Leslie, Lisa, Kristen, Bryan, Heidi. With traffic dept. Las Vegas (Nev.) Police Dept., 1954-55; exec. sec. Harlingen AFB, Tex., 1955-57; legal sec., 1976; mem. Nev. Ho. of Reps., 1975—, chmn. judiciary com., 1979-80, chmn. study com. mobile homes, 1979-80, chmn. transp. com., 1977-79, speaker pro tem, 1981. Named Mother of Year, City of Hope, 1976. Mem. Nat. Order Women Legislators, Nat. Conf. State Legislators Bus. and Profl. Women, Citizens for Responsible Govt. Mormon.

HAYES, MARNELL LAROE, educator; b. Eustis, Fla., July 24, 1939; d. Clarence Crooks LaRoe and Edna (Rogers) LaRoe Matousek; B.A., U. Fla., 1961, M.Ed., 1965, Ed.D., 1971; 1 dau., Valerie Pierce Howell. Regional rep. Fla. Div. Retardation, Gainesville, 1969-70; asst. prof. spl. edn. U. So. Miss., Hattiesburg, 1970-71; asst. prof. spl. edn. U. Toledo, 1971-73; prof. spl. edn. Tex. Woman's U., Denton, 1973—; ednl. cons.; speaker gifted students and learning-disabled students. Bd. dirs. Theatre Onstage, Dallas. Postdoctoral fellow Project FLAME, 1977-78. Mem. Council for Exceptional Children, Am. Orthopsychiat. Assn., Mensa (pres. N. Tex. chpt. 1977), Pi Lambda Theta, Phi Delta Kappa, Alpha Omicron Pi. Mem. editorial adv. bd. Acad. Therapy, 1978—. Office: Dept Spl Edn Tex Woman's Univ Denton TX 76204

HAYES, MARTHA LEE, educator; b. Oklahoma City, July 14, 1936; d. Clyde Eugene and Aita (Zornes) Kirkhan; B.A., Central State U., Edmond, Okla., 1962; M.A.T., Oklahoma City U., 1970; Ed.D., U. Okla., 1982; m. June 13, 1968 (div.); 1 son, Brian Lee. Tchr. public schs., Oklahoma City, 1962-68; team leader Tchr. Corps, Oklahoma City Public Schs., 1969-71, curriculum cons., 1971-74, dir. state and federal projects, 1974-76, prin. Moon Middle Sch., 1976-78, also dir. right to read; dir. tchr. corps Central State U., 1978—; adj. prof. U. Okla., 1976-78. Mem. Nat. Womens Polit. Caucus, ACLU, Coop. Council Okla. Adminstrs., Women in Ednl. Adminstrn., Okla. Assn. Secondary Schs. Prins. (pres.), Okla. Assn. Tchr. Educators, Phi Delta Kappa. Democrat. Unitarian. Club: Fellowship Internat. Home: 7610 NW 36th St Bethany OK 73008 Office: 100 University St ON 302 Edmond OK 73034

HAYES, MARY ESHBAUGH, newspaper editor; b. Rochester, N.Y., Sept. 27, 1928; d. William Paul and Eleanor Maude (Seivert) Eshbaugh; B.A. in English and Journalism, Syracuse (N.Y.) U., 1950; m. James Leon Hayes, Apr. 18, 1953; children—Pauli, Eli, Lauri Le June, Clayton, Merri Jess. With Livingston County Republican, Geneseo, N.Y., summers, 1947-50, mng. editor, 1949-50; reporter Aurora (Colo.) Advocate, 1950-52; reporter-photographer Aspen (Colo.) Times, 1952-53, columnist, 1956—, reporter, 1972-77, asso. editor, 1977—; tchr. Colo. Mountain Coll., 1979. Mem. Nat. Fedn. Press Women (1st prizes in writing and editing 1976-80), Colo. Press Women's Assn. (writing award 1974, 75, 78-80, sweepstakes award for writing 1976, 77, 78, 2d pl. in state 1982). Mem. Aspen Community Ch. Photographer, editor: Aspen Potpourri, 1968. Home: PO Box 497 Aspen CO 81611 Office: Box E Aspen CO 81611

HAYES, PATRICIA ANNE, govt. ofcl.; b. Chgo., Jan. 26, 1921; d. Frank Ambrose and Annabel (Fanning) Hayes; A.B., Coll. St. Teresa, 1942; B.S., U. Md., 1956; M.Ed., Coll. William and Mary, 1961; M.A., George Washington U., 1961; certificate in meteorology U. Chgo., 1945. Tchr. pub. schs., Chgo., 1942-44; meteorologist U.S. Weather Bur., Washington, 1945-49, climatologist U.S. Dept. Army, 1949-52; commd. 1st lt. U.S. Air Force, 1951, advanced through grades to maj., 1966; meteorologist A.F. Cambridge Research Center, Boston, 1952-54; base weather officer, Molesworth, Eng., 1954-57; team chief Forecast Center, Langley AFB, Va., 1957-58, asst. chief climatology div. hdqrs. 2d weather group, 1958-64; weather officer European Theater Forecast Center, 1964-67, aerospace scis. officer 8th Weather Squadron, Westover AFB, Mass., 1967-70, S.E. Asia Weather Center, 1970-71; wing climatologist 4th Weather Wing Ent AFB, Colo., 1971-72; claims rep. HEW, 1973—. Mem. Am. Meteorol. Soc., AAUW, Ret. Officers Assn., Kappa Gamma Pi. Home: 8145 N Harding St Skokie IL 60076

HAYMAN, CAROL BESSENT, poet, author: b. Southport, N.C., June 9, 1927; d. George Howard and Minnie May (Guthrie) Bessent; A.A., Louisburg (N.C.) Jr. Coll., 1945; student East Carolina U., 1945, 65; m. Louis De Maro Hayman, Aug. 30, 1945; children—Richard Louis, Susan Carol Hayman Lynch. Columnist, Onslow Herald, Jacksonville, 1974-76; works include: Keepsake, 1962, These Lovely Days, 1971-72, 76, Collection of Writings Published in North Carolina Christian Advocate, 1972, What is Christmas?, Tidings, 1974, reprinted, 1975-78; contbr. articles and poems to numerous mags. including Vista, Listen, Marriage and Family Living, The Upper Room Pathways to God and Ideals, Hallmark, Inc.; guest instr. Coastal Carolina Community Coll. lectr., poetry contest judge. Trustee Louisburg Coll., 1965-72, recipient Distinguished Alumnus award, 1978. Recipient numerous awards poetry confs. N.C., Ga., Fla. Named Goodwill Ambassador by Mayor, City of Jacksonville, 1973. Mem. Nat. League Am. Pen Women (Southeastern regional editor Pen Woman 1972-74, mem. exec. bd. 1974-75), Southeastern Writers' Assn, (charter), World Poetry Soc., Acad. Am. Poets, Authors Guild, N.C. Poetry Soc., Internat. Platform Assn., D.A.R., Onslow County Arts Council, N.C. Symphony. Methodist. Club: N.C. Congl. Home and office: 220 Club Point Dr Cape Carteret Swansboro NC 28584

HAYMOND, PAULA JO, hosp. adminstr.; b. Warsaw, Ind., Sept. 29, 1949; d. George Milton and Phyllis Anita (Freeman) H.; B.A. in Psychology, Butler U., Indpls., 1971, M.S. in Edn., 1973; Ed.D. in Counseling and Counselor Edn., Ind. U., 1982. Behavioral clinician Ind. Boys Sch., Plainfield, 1973-77, behavioral clinician, affirmative action expeditor juvenile diagnostic unit, 1977-78; behavioral clinician juvenile diagnostic unit Ind. Girls Sch., Indpls., 1978-80; head div. human systems devel. Lund Cons., Inc., Mohegan Lake, N.Y, 1981-82; asst. dir. residential services Faith Home, children's psychiat. hosp., Houston, 1982—; instr., guest lectr. Ind. U.; past sec. Ind. State Employees Assn. Fed. Credit Union. Mem. Delta Delta Delta, Kappa Kappa Kappa. Author studies in field. Office: 100 Sandman St Houston TX 77007

HAYNES, DOROTHY MARIE, special edn. tchr.; b. Henryetta, Okla., Apr. 16, 1943; d. William Madison and Claire (Pistorius) Haynes; B.S. in Edn., Our Lady of Lake U., San Antonio, 1964; M.Ed. in Reading, Loyola U., New Orleans, 1975, Reading Specialist, 1975; Certificate U. New Orleans, 1971. Tchr. San Antonio Ind. Sch. Dist., 1964-66, Orleans Parish Sch. Bd., 1966-67, Jefferson Parish Sch. Bd., Gretna, La., 1967-70, tchr. learning disabilities, 1970—; tchr. behavior disorder/emotionally disturbed Children's Med. Center Developmental Center, Tulsa, 1982—; mem. learning disabilities com. office Edn. Archdiocese New Orleans. Mem. Council Exceptional Children, Assn. Children with Learning Disabilities, La. Tchrs. Assn. Research in problems exceptional children. Cert. tchr. mentally retarded, learning disabilities, reading specialist, emotionally disturbed. Address: care Dr W M Haynes 306 Warren Rd Henryetta OK 74437

HAYNES, JANET-LINDA, med. biologist; b. Bklyn., Nov. 26, 1947; d. Fred Howard and Juliette Lillian (Dreifuss) H.; diploma in med. tech. (hosp. scholar) Beekman-Downtown Hosp. Sch. Med. Tech., N.Y.C., 1969; B.S. (N.Y. State Regents scholar, Empire State Assn. Med. Technologists scholar, N.Y. State Soc. Pathologists scholar), L.I.U., 1969, M.S., 1972; M.Phil., N.Y.U., 1982, postgrad., 1982—. Teaching fellow in scis. L.I.U., Bklyn., 1969-72, mem. faculty, 1973—, adj. asst. prof. biology, 1975-80, adj. asso. prof. biology, 1980—, adj. mem. grad. faculty med. biology C.W. Post Coll., L.I.U., 1979—; research technologist Jewish Hosp. and Med. Center of Bklyn., 1972-77; faculty mem. Physician Asst. Program, Bklyn.-Cumberland Med. Center, 1976—; adj. asst. prof. biology Pace U., N.Y.C., 1977-78; asst. prof., clin. coordinator dept. med. tech. Health Scis. Center, Sch. Allied Health Professions, SUNY, Stony Brook, 1981—; adj. lectr. City U. N.Y., 1973-81; teaching fellow biology N.Y.U., 1979—. Active, Operation Baby Track, ARC, N.Y.C., 1981, Am. Cancer Soc., 1982—; mem. ad hoc. com. on status of women SUNY, Stony Brook, 1982. Recipient Charlotte Pann Meml. award N.Y.U., 1981; Phi Sigma grad. research awardee, 1972; Conn. State fellow, 1974-75; NIH trainee, 1974-75; N.Y.U. grantee in biology, 1980—; Sigma Xi grantee, 1981-82. Mem. Am. Soc. Clin. Pathologists (cert. med. technologist), Am. Soc. Med. Tech., Assn. for Women in Sci., AAUW, N.Y. Acad. Scis., Women's Health Alliance of L.I., Sigma Xi, Alpha Epsilon Delta, Phi Sigma. Contbr. articles to profl. jours. Office: Dept Med Tech Sch Allied Health Professions Health Scis Center SUNY Stony Brook NY 11794

HAYNES, MARIAN AQUILLA, mgmt. cons.; b. St. Louis, Sept. 8, 1948; d. Neal Jefferson and Ollie Mae (Hart) H.; B.S. in Fashion Mdsg., U. Mo., Columbia, 1970. Asst. dept. mgr. Saks Fifth Ave., St. Louis, 1970-71; fashion copywriter Wohl Shoe Co., St. Louis, 1971-74; resource mgr. APC Skills Co., Palm Beach, Fla., 1974—; v.p. Creative Ins. Services, Inc., Atlanta, 1981—. Recipient Flair award Advt. Women St. Louis, 1973. Mem. Nat. Council Negro Women (adv. bd.), Alpha Kappa Alpha. Baptist. Office: 3485 N Desert Dr Suite 134 East Point GA 30344

HAYNES, MARTHA PATRICIA, astronomer; b. Boston, Apr. 24, 1951; d. William Veech and Louise Mary (Healy) Haynes; B.A., Wellesley Coll., 1973; M.A., Ind. U., 1978, Ph.D., 1978. Assoc. instr. Ind. U., 1974-76; jr. research assoc. Nat. Radio Astronomy Obs., Charlottesville, Va., 1976-78, asst. dir. Green Bank (W.Va.) Ops., 1981—; instr. Piedmont Va. Community Coll., 1978; postdoctoral fellow Nat. Astronomy and Ionosphere Center, Arecibo Obs., P.R., 1978-80. Mem. Am. Astron. Soc., AAAS, Sigma Xi. Address: PO Box 2 Green Bank VA 24944

HAYNICZ, LACY ANN, hosp. exec.; b. Riverside, N.J., Sept. 12, 1950; d. Joseph Charles and Minnie May (Jones) Hale; student La. State U., 1968-70, Rider Coll., 1971-74, Stephens Coll., 1979—; m. Michael S. Haynicz, Dec. 21, 1974. Salesperson accessories dept. Pomeroy's, Willingboro, N.J., 1970; with Strawbridge & Clother, Cherry Hill, N.J., 1971-72; clk. typist R. M. Hollingshead Co., Camden, N.J., 1972-74; exec. sec. to corporate controller The Hibbert Co., Trenton, N.J., 1974-75; dir. med. records Cumberland Regional Health Plan, Vineland, N.J., 1975-78; asst. dir. med. records Phila. Coll. Ostopathic Medicine, 1978; dir. med. records in care pavilion and Mt. Laurel Convalescent Centers, Geriatric and Med. Centers, Phila., 1979-80; dir. med. records, Vineland (N.J.) State Sch. Hosp., 1980—. Coach Little League cheerleading squad, 1972-73. Recipient Records Technician cert. Am. Med. Record Assn., 1977. Mem. N.J. Med. Record Assn., Hort. Soc., Alpha Chi Omega (pres.). Home: 267 Dogwood Ln Clarksboro NJ 08020 Office: 1676 E Landis Ave Vineland NJ 08360

HAYNIE, MARY ELIZABETH, vol. services adminstr.; b. Atlantic City, N.J., Dec. 14, 1923; d. Edwin N. and Mary Rose (Dolan) Donaldson; ed. Atlantic City Bus. Coll., 1944-46, U. Del., 1982; m. John Francis Haynie, Oct. 29, 1944; children—Paul Stephen, Mark Christopher. Long distance operator, supr. N.J. Bell Telephone Co., Atlantic City, 1942-65; dir. vol. services Children's Seashore House, Atlantic City, 1965—. Democratic state committeewoman, 1969-81; chmn. bd. trustees Woodbine State Sch., 1969—; bd. dirs. Atlantic County chpt. ARC, 1973; vice chmn. gen. adv. com. Atlantic County Vocat. Sch.; chmn. Atlantic-Cape May County Traffic Safety Commn. mem. Atlantic County Council, So. N.J. Health Systems Agy., 1977—; mem. Atlantic County Bd. Chosen Freeholders, 1971-75. Mem. Am. Soc. Dirs. Vol. Services, N.J. Soc. Dirs. Vol. Services, Council for Exceptional Children, Atlantic City Bus. and Profl. Women's Club, Common Cause (charter), N.J. Fed. Bus. and Profl. Women's Clubs (v.p.). Roman Catholic. Home: 211 N Washington Ave Ventnor NJ 08406 Office: Children's Seashore House 4100 Atlantic Ave Atlantic City NJ 08401

HAYS, MARY KATHERINE JACKSON (MRS. DONALD OSBORNE HAYS), civic worker; b. Flora, Miss.; d. Rufus Lafayette and Ada (Collum) Jackson; student U. Miss., 1925-26, Millsaps Coll., 1926-27, 43-44; grad. Clark Bus. Sch., 1934; student Columbia U., 1935, Strayer Bus. Coll., 1951; m. Halbert Puffer Oliver, Aug. 9, 1927 (dec. 1934); m. 2d, Donald Osborne Hays, Aug. 30, 1937. Sec. to pres. McCullough Box and Crate Co., Pharr, Tex., 1934-36; sec. to field supr. Miss. Unemployment Compensation, 1936-37; rep. Homes of Tomorrow, 1940 N.Y. World's Fair; sec. to head interior design Lord & Taylor, N.Y.C., 1940; sales dept. Knabe Piano Co., N.Y.C., 1941-43. Active, Little Theatre, Wilkes Barre, Pa., 1937-39; charter mem. and incorporator Conf. State Socs., Washington, 1952; vol. worker Am. Cancer Soc., Washington, 1956—; mem. Center City Residents Assn., Phila., 1956; mem. women's com. Nat. Symphony Assn., vol. worker USO, 1945-48, symphony sustaining com. drives, 1957-66; mem. women's com. Corcoran Gallery Art, Washington, 1957-62; mem. Pierce-Warwick Adoption Assn. of Washington Home for Foundlings; vol. Washington Heart Assn., 1959-66; mem. Nat. Capital Area chpt. United Ch. Women, 1957—; mem. D.C. Episcopal Home for Children, 1961—, D.C. Salvation Army Aux., 1962—. Mem. Miss. State Soc. D.C. (sec. 1950-53), Nat. Trust for Historic Preservation, Miss. Women's Club D.C., DAR (vice regent chpt. 1970-72, regent chpt. 1972-74, vice chmn.

D.C. com. celebration Washington's birthday 1972-76, state librarian 1974-76), UDC, Johnstone Clan Am. (exec. council 1976-81). Episcopalian. Club: The Washington. Home: 4000 Massachusetts Ave NW Washington DC 20016

HAYS, MIRIAM PEGGY WALL, counselor; b. Little Rock, Sept. 12, 1937; d. Harry Boykin and Verna Estelle (Bates) Wall; student Randolph Macon Woman's Coll., 1955-56; B.A., U. Ark., Fayetteville, 1956-59; M.S.W., U. Ark., Little Rock, 1976; m. Marion Steele Hays; children—Leonard Lee Thompson, Harry Boykin Thompson, Miriam Lyde Thompson. Counselor, Counseling Assos., Little Rock, 1976-79, Little Rock Counseling Clinic, 1979—; speaker civic and ch. groups. Former mem. vestry St. Mark's Episcopal Ch., now lay reader. Mem. Acad. Cert. Social Workers, Nat. Assn. Social Workers, Ark. Bd. Social Workers, Internat. Transactional Analysis Assn., Jr. League Little Rock (treas., com. chmn.). Home: 5113 Crestwood Little Rock AR 72207 Office: 1405 N Pierce Suite 209 Little Rock AR 72207

HAYS, WILMA RUBY, health agy. exec.; b. Pleasant Hill, Mo., Apr. 25, 1923; d. Floyd George and Ruby Margaret (Overton) Shurtleff; student Okla. State U. Tech., 1978-80; m. Thomas Richard McCullagh, Dec. 29, 1943; children—Patricia Ann McCullagh, Claudia Kay McCullagh; m. Thomas Marshall Hays, Oct. 29, 1954; children—Mary Margaret, Cecilia Marie. Exec. sec. Armed Forces Induction Sta., Tulsa, 1941-43; sec. Guaranty Abstract Co., Tulsa, 1943-49, Earlougher Engrng. Co., Tulsa, 1949-51, Bethlehem Supply Co., Tulsa, 1951-54; exec. dir. Kidney Found. of Okla., Oklahoma City, 1969—; treas. Nat. Health Agys., Okla., state chmn., 1981-83. Mem. Profl. Staff Assn. of Nat. Kidney Found., Okla. Soc. Assn. Execs., Am. Mgmt. Assn., LaPetite Seur Book Rev. Club, LWV. Republican. Roman Catholic. Clubs: Bus. and Profl. Women's (rec. sec. 1978, pres. 1980) (Oklahoma City); Christian Women's of Okla. Home: 4040 NW 61st St Oklahoma City OK 73112 Office: 3313 NW Classen Oklahoma City OK 73118

HAYWARD, LUCILLE BAINBRIDGE, army officer; b. St. Petersburg, Fla., Aug. 27, 1939; d. Bainbridge and Gertrude (Caswell) H.; A.A., St. Petersburg Jr. Coll.; B.S., U. S. Fla., 1966; M.S., Jacksonville State U., 1977; Med. technologist Mound Park Hosp. Lab., St. Petersburg, 1960-68; commd. lt. U.S. Army, 1968, advanced through grades to maj., 1977; Mil. Police co. cmdr., Fort Gordon, Ga., 1974-75, bn. exec. officer, Ft. McClellan, Ala., 1975-76, personnel officer, 1976-77; organizational effectiveness staff officer, hdqrs. Tng. and Doctrine Command, Ft. Monroe, Va., 1977—. Mem. Am. Soc. Clin. Pathologists, Assn. Med. Technologists, Assn. U.S. Army. Office: HQ TRADOC DCST Fort Monroe VA 23651

HAYWARD, SAMMANTHA LYNNE MARIE, customer service ofcl.; b. Pasadena, Calif., Nov. 18, 1949; d. Louis George and Ethelyn Georgia (Hale) Nichols; A.S., San Diego Mesa Coll., 1976; B.B.A., Nat. U., 1980, postgrad.; m. James Donald Hayward, Feb. 7, 1970 (separated); 1 dau., Nicole Charise. Customer info. rep. San Diego Gas and Electric, 1970-72, 1974-80, customer info. analyst, 1980-81, customer service supr. Beach Cities Dist. Office, 1981—. Seminar leader, trainer Energy Speakers Corp., 1980—. Mem. citizens adv. com. Sandburg Elem. Sch., San Diego, 1974-75, v.p., 1974, pres., 1975; area coordinator San Diego Sch. Bond Election, 1974. Recipient Sch. Citizens Adv. Com. Service award San Diego City Schs., 1975. Mem. Career Womens Assn., Am. Mgmt. Dimensions Assn. Democrat. Mem. editorial bd. Women's Basic Tng. Manual, 1981-82. Home: 17159 W Bernardo Dr Apt 102 San Diego CA 92127 Office: 4901 Morena Blvd Suite 210 San Diego CA 92117

HAYWOOD, ANNE MOWBRAY, physician, educator; b. Balt., Feb. 5, 1935; d. Richard M. and Margaret (Mowbray) H.; B.A. in Chemistry, Bryn Mawr Coll., 1955; M.D. (Harriet Judd Sartain scholar) Harvard U., 1959. Intern in pediatrics U. Calif. Med. Ctr., San Francisco, 1959-60; fellow in biochemistry Columbia U., 1961-62; fellow div. biology Calif. Inst. Tech., 1960-61, 62-64; resident in pediatrics U. Wash., Seattle, 1974-75, fellow in pediatric infectious deseases, 1975-76; pediatric infectious disease fellow Vanderbilt U., Nashville, 1976-77; asst. prof. microbiology Northwestern U. Med. Sch., Chgo., 1964-66, Yale U. Med. Sch., New Haven, 1966-73; vis. asst. prof. Rockefeller U., 1971-72; vis. scientist biophysics unit Agrl. Research Council, Inst. Animal Physiology, Cambridge, Eng., 1972-74; sr. assoc. pediatrician Strong Meml. Hosp., Rochester, N.Y., 1977—. Assoc. prof. pediatrics and microbiology U. Rochester, 1977—. NIH fellow, 1971-73; European Molecular Biology Orgn. fellow, 1973; diplomate Am. Bd. Pediatrics. Mem. Am. Soc. Microbiology, Am. Soc. Biol. Chemists. Democrat. Contbr. articles on biochemistry and virology to profl. jours. Office: Dept Pediatrics Univ Rochester 601 Elmwood Ave Rochester NY 14642

HAYWOOD, LUCILLE ANNE GARITY BLOSE, retail mcht.; b. Balt., Aug. 18, 1926; d. Charles Henry and Grace Elizabeth (Rogers) Garity; student Knoxville Bus. Coll., 1944-45, 74, U. Tenn., 1978-79; 1 son, Thomas R. Blose. With Sta. WROL, Knoxville, Tenn., 1944-45; library asst. TVA, Knoxville, 1945-48; traffic mgr., continuity writer Sta. WBIR, Knoxville, 1953-63; promotion mgr. WBIR-TV, Knoxville, 1963-66; co-owner, officer, bookkeeper Haywood House, Inc., Gatlinburg, Tenn., 1969-78; owner, mgr., pres. House of Clocks & Gifts, Inc., Gatlinburg, 1978—. Ruling elder, treas. Gatlinburg Presbyn. Ch. Mem. Exec. Women's Assn. Office: House of Clocks and Gifts Inc Craft Center Hwy 73 E Gatlinburg TN 37738

HAZALEUS, MARGARET BENNINGTON, univ. dean; b. Center, Colo., Mar. 8, 1919; d. Frank and Jessie Lynnanne (Scarff) Bennington; B.S. in Food Sci. and Nutrition, Colo. State U., 1941, M.S. in Sociology, 1960; m. Melvin Harp Hazaleus, Jan. 2, 1943; children—John Melvin, Susan Lynn. Dietitian sch. lunch program, LaJunta, Colo., 1941-42; tchr. chemistry and biology Del Norte High Sch., 1942-43; elem. tchr. Center Consol. Schs., 1945-46; asst. to dean Coll. Home Econs., Colo. State U., 1961-67, coordinator student programs, 1967-71, asst. dean Coll. Human Resource Scis., 1971—; conf. presenter. Mem. Poudre R-1 Citizens Com., Gov.'s Commn. Status of Women; vol. Reach to Recovery unit Am. Cancer Soc., 1974—; leader Cub Scouts, Brownie Scouts; mem. 4-H Devel. Com., Larimer County 4-H Scholarship Com. Named Outstanding Faculty Mem., Colo. State U. Coll. Home Econs., 1969; Outstanding Woman Adminstr., Colo. State U., 1973, Very Important Prof., 1980, recipient Disting. Service award in undergrad. advising, 1980. Mem. Am. Home Econs. Assn., Colo. Home Econs. Assn., Assn. Acad. Affairs Adminstrs., Nat. Council Family Relations, Coll. Home Econs. Alumni Assn., Colo. State U. Alumni Assn. (honor alumna 1977), Coll. Home Econs. Alumni Council, Mortar Bd. Alumni Group, Gamma Sigma Delta, Delta Kappa Gamma, Phi Kappa Phi, Omicron Nu, Alpha Delta Kappa, Delta Delta Delta. Republican. Presbyterian. Club: PEO. Student patio on Gifford Bldg., Colo. State U. dedicated to biographee, 1982. Home: 1213 Green St Fort Collins CO 80524 Office: Gifford 100A Coll of Human Resource Scis Colo State U Fort Collins CO 80523

HAZARD, HELEN HUTCHINSON, realty exec.; b. Balt., Aug. 13, 1916; d. David William and Fannie S. (Swanson) Hutchinson; B.S., Johns Hopkins U., 1938; m. Claude Jack Hazard, Sept. 29, 1947; children—Linda Delaney, Claudia Hazard Hughes. Tchr. secondary edn. Balt. City Sch. System; instr. English dept. Morgan State Coll., Balt.; pres. Helen Hazard Realtors, Inc., Stamford, Conn., 1957—. Mem. Stamford Bd. Realtors, bd. dirs., 1966-67. Mem. Nat., Conn. assns. real estate bds., AAUW, Women's Council Realtors, Johns Hopkins Alumni Assn. Clubs: Stamford Duplicate Bridge, Midday (pres. 1975-76). Home: 82 Boxwood Dr Stamford CT 06906 Office: 500 Newfield Ave Stamford CT 06905

HAZELBAKER, EILEEN GENEVA, med. technologist; b. Decatur County, Kans., Nov. 2, 1928; d. Clint Leonard and Edith Helen (Vermilion) Huff; degree in gen. sci. Ft. Hays (Kans.) State Coll., 1953; m. Fred R. Hazelbaker, Oct. 5, 1974; 1 son by previous marriage, Wayne Leroy Wohler. Intern, Stormont-Vail Hosp., Topeka, 1953; med. technologist hosps. in Kans. and Wash., 1954-67; med. technologist Syringa Gen. Hosp., Grangeville, Idaho, 1967—. Mem. Am. Soc. Clin. Pathologists. Mem. Christian Ch. (Disciples of Christ). Clubs: Extension, Rebekahs. Home: Route 1 Box 64 Grangeville ID 93530 Office: Syringa Gen Hosp Grangeville ID 83530

HAZELIP, EDWINA KAY, registered nurse; b. Louisville, Jan. 25, 1952; d. Edwin O'Neil and Lorraine Esta (Nicols) H.; grad. High Point (N.C.) Hosp. Sch. Nursing, 1975. Nurses aide Wilkes Gen. Hosp., North Wilkesboro, N.C., 1971-72; day care center worker Child's Kingdom, Wilkesboro, N.C., 1971-72; head nurse coronary and intensive care unit Wilkes Gen. Hosp., North Wilkesboro, 1972—, pres. nurses' staff, 1976, 78, v.p., 1977, 81, sec., 1980, sec. coronary care staff, 1977-78, 79, chmn., 1980-82; instr. cardiac defibrillation. Bd. dirs. Wilkes County unit Am. Heart Assn. Cert. instr. CPR. Mem. Am. Nurses Assn., N.C. Nurses Assn. Home: 1120 Myers Park North Wilkesboro NC 28659

HAZELTON, LUCY REED, advt. writer, artist; b. St. Louis, Sept. 9, 1929; d. Ferdinand Maximillian and Elizabeth Emily (Benson) Schaeffer; student Washington U., St. Louis, 1947-48, St. Louis U., 1954-56; writers workshops, U. Colo., summer 1968, U. Houston, summer 1971; m. Burton W. Hazelton, Feb. 15, 1958 (dec.); children—Terence G. Reed (dec.), Deborah Lucy Reed, Ellen Frisch. Writer, artist for ednl. programming Webster Pub. Co., 1962-63; with Scharr Printers, 1966-67; advt. writer, artist Christian Bd. Publs., 1967-69; mgr. advt., public relations A.G. Edwards & Sons, Inc., brokerage, St. Louis, 1969-82; freelance writer/public relations, 1982—; monthly columnist Arts mag., Poetry Center Speaking. Bd. dirs. St. Louis Poetry Center, v.p., 1976-77, pres. bd. chancellors, 1980-81; bd. dirs. Big River Assn. Recipient 1st place E. Oscar Thalinger award for verse play, The Still Point, 1965, 2d pl. for verse play, The River Laughs, 1966; Merit awards Financial World mag., 1973-75, 76, 77, 78, 79; Bicentennial award St. Louis Poetry Center, 1975, Marianne Moore award, 1977. Mem. St. Louis Writers Guild (treas. 1975), Advt. Prodn. Club St. Louis, Acad. Am. Poets, ACLU, Women in Communications, Advt. Fedn. St. Louis. Author: Three Circles and the Princess, 1976; editor Poetry Center Speaking, 1973—; contbr. poetry to mags., revs. Home and Office: 668 Kirkshire Dr Kirkwood MO 63122

HAZELTON, PENNY ANN, law librarian; b. Yakima, Wash., Sept. 24, 1947; d. Fred Robert and Margaret (McLeod) Pease; B.A. cum laude, Linfield Coll., 1969; J.D., Lewis and Clark Law Sch., 1975; LL.M., U. Wash., 1976; m. Norris J. Hazelton, Sept. 12, 1971; 1 dau., Victoria MacLeod. Admissions counselor Linfield Coll., 1969-71; serials librarian Linfield Coll. Law Library, 1972-75; admitted to Wash. bar, 1976; assoc. law librarian, assoc. prof. U. Maine, 1976-78, law librarian, assoc. prof., 1978-81; asst. librarian for research services U.S. Supreme Ct., Washington, 1981—; tchr. legal research, legal research for paralegals, Indian law, law and medicine; cons. Maine Adv. Com. on County Law Libraries. Mem. Law Librarians New Eng. (pres. 1979-81), Am. Assn. Law Libraries (cert.), Law Librarians' Soc. Washington, Am. Bar Assn., Fed. Bar Assn. Republican. Contbr. articles to Environ. Law. Office: 1 1st St NE Washington DC 20543

HAZENFIELD, SUSAN LONG, speech pathologist; b. Akron, Ohio, Jan. 17, 1955; d. Ralph Patrick and Margaret Katherine (Thompson) Long; B.A., Ohio State U., 1977; M.A., Case-Western Res. U., 1979; m. John Erwin Hazenfield, Dec. 2, 1978. Speech pathologist Wicomico County Bd. Edn., Salisbury, Md., 1979-80, Roanoke-Chowan Hosp., Ahoskie, N.C., 1980, Summit County Bd. Mental Retardation and Developmental Disabilities, 1980—. Standard profl. teaching cert., Md.; lic. speech pathologist, N.C., Md. Mem. Am. Speech, Lang. and Hearing Assn. (cert. clin. competence in speech pathology), N.C. Speech, Lang. and Hearing Assn., Md. Speech, Lang. and Hearing Assn., Ohio State U. Alumni Assn., Ohio Speech, Lang. and Hearing Assn., Weaver Tchrs. Assn., NEA, Md. Tchrs. Assn., Wicomico County Edn. Assn. Home: 2384 Silver Spring Dr Stow OH 44224 Office: Weaver Sch 89 E Howe Rd Tallmadge OH 44278

HAZI, HELEN MARIE, educator; b. Pitts., Dec. 20, 1951; d. Julius and Helen (Rostosky) Hazi; B.A. cum laude, U. Pitts., 1972, M.Ed., 1975, Ph.D., 1980. Tchr., Ringgold Sch. Dist., Monongahela, Pa., 1972-74; research asst. U. Pitts., 1974-76; research asst. Learning Research and Devel. Center, Pitts., 1976-77; supr. curriculum and instrn. Quaker Valley Sch. Dist., Sewickley, Pa., 1978-80; asst. prof. ednl. adminstrn. West Va. U., Morgantown, 1981—. Mem. Assn. Supervision and Curriculum Devel., W.Va. Assn. Sch. Adminstrs., Council Profs. of Instructional Supervision, Phi Delta Kappa. Democrat. Byzantine Catholic. Home: 3601 Collins Ferry Rd H14 Morgantown WV 26505 Office: WVa U 1130 Ag-Sci Bldg Morgantown WV 26506

HAZZARD, GENEVIEVE CATHERINE, educator; b. Mpls.; d. Francis Joseph and Margaret (Ryan) Hazzard; student St. Joseph's Acad., St. Teresa's Coll. Asst. mgr. Century Advt. Co., Detroit, 1948-49; account exec. Chevrolet Women's Program, from 1950; v.p. Campbell-Ewald, Detroit, 1958-71; mem. faculty Chevrolet Sch. Mgmt. and Merchandising, Detroit, 1957-68, counselor Chevrolet div. Gen. Motors, 1960-68; instr. speech in industry, Detroit, 1948-70. Active, Civic Searchlight Commn. Named Nat. Advt. Woman of Yr., 1959; recipient Golden Plate award Acad. of Achievement, 1960. Mem. Fashion Group, Inc., Theta Sigma Phi. Roman Catholic. Clubs: Questers, Women's Ad. Died Sept. 3, 1982.

HAZZARD, SHIRLEY, author; b. Sydney, Australia, Jan. 30, 1931; d. Reginald and Catherine (Stein) H.; ed. Queenwood Sch., Sydney, to 1946; m. Francis Steegmuller, Dec. 22, 1963. With Combined Services Intelligence, Hong Kong, 1947-48, U.K. High Commr.'s Office Wellington, N.Z., 1949-51, UN (Gen. Service Category), N.Y.C., 1952-62; Christian Gauss lectr. Princeton U., 1982. Trustee N.Y. Soc. Library. Recipient 1st prize O. Henry Short Story Awards, 1976; grantee in lit. Nat. Inst. Arts and Letters, 1966; Guggenheim fellow, 1974; Nat. Book Critics Circle award for Fiction, 1981. Mem. Nat. Inst. Arts and Letters. Author: Cliffs of Fall and Other Stories, 1963; (novel) The Evening of the Holiday, 1966; (fiction) People in Glass Houses, 1967; (novel) The Bay of Noon, 1970; (social history) Defeat of an Ideal: A Study of Self-Destruction of the United Nations, 1973; (novel) The Transit of Venus, 1980; contbr. short stories to New Yorker mag. Address: 200 E 66th St New York NY 10021

HEAD, LAURA DEAN, educator; b. Los Angeles, Nov. 3, 1948; d. Marvin Laurence and Helaine (Springer) H.; student Coll. of the Holy Names, Oakland, Calif., 1966-68; B.A., San Francisco State U., 1970; M.A. in Sociology, U. Mich., Ann Arbor, 1974, Ph.D. in Devel. Psychology, 1977. Teaching asst., asst. project dir. U. Mich., 1970-73; instr. U. Calif., Riverside, 1973-76; project dir., research scientist Urban Inst. Human Services, 1978-80; project dir., sr. research analyst Far West Lab. for Ednl. Research and Devel., San Francisco, 1980-81; instr. dept. black studies San Francisco State U., 1981—. Am. Psychol. Assn. fellow, 1976-77. Mem. Soc. Research in Child Devel. (reviewer nat. conf. 1981), Am. Psychol. Assn., Assn. Black Psychologists, Black Women's Forum, Nat. Black Child Devel. Inst., Children's Def. League. Club: Commonwealth of San Francisco. Interviewed on local TV and radio shows. Home: 26 Burgess Ct Marin City CA 94965 Office: Black Studies Dept San Francisco State U 1600 Holloway Ave San Francisco CA 94132

HEAD, MARY JOHNSTON, corp. dir.; b. Shawnee, Okla., Feb. 28, 1930; d. Paul Xenophon and Helen Elizabeth (Alford) Johnston; student Wellesley Coll., 1947-48, U. Okla., 1949; m. Benjamin Thomas Head, June 17, 1949; children—Marcia Lee, Paul Johnston, Eric Talbott. Mem. Citizens Adv. Com. on Transp. Quality, Washington, 1968-73, Urban Transp. Adv. Council, Washington, 1973; dir. Amtrak, 1974-80, vice chmn., 1975-79; dir. Household Internat., Butler Mfg. Co., CertainTeed Corp., The Sun Co., Am. Hosp. Supply Corp., Delta Air Lines. Pres., Jr. League Oklahoma City, 1968-69; treas., dir. Youth Services for Okla. County, 1973-75; exec. com. Oklahoma City Beautiful Com., 1970-73; trustee Nat. Council Crime and Delinquency, 1971-75; mem. com. for probation officer tng. Fed. Jud. Center, Washington, 1971-72. Trustee Presbyn. Med. Center, Oklahoma City, 1969-75, Mary Baldwin Coll., 1976—; bd. dirs. St. Anthony Hosp., Oklahoma City, 1973-75; bd. visitors U. Pitts. Grad. Sch. Bus., 1978—. Recipient Law Day award-Liberty Bell award Oklahoma Bar Assn., 1971; named to Okla. Hall of Fame, 1978; Disting. Service citation U. Okla. Mem. Conference Board, Pi Beta Phi. Presbyterian (elder). Address: 3232 Tarryhollow Austin TX 78703

HEAD, MARY KALEEL, educator; b. Wilmington, Del., Dec. 13, 1934; d. Charles Samuel and Mary Rose (Rist) Kaleel; B.S., U. Del., 1956; M.S., U. Wis., 1958; Ph.D., Purdue U., 1963; m. William J. Head, June 16, 1962; children—A. Kevin, Sarah N. Dietetic intern Ohio State U., 1956-57; instr., asst. prof. foods and nutrition Purdue U., West Lafayette, Ind., 1958-60, 66-69; dietitian St. Elizabeth Hosp., Lafayette, Ind., 1963-66; extension asst. prof., extension assoc., prof. food sci. N.C. State U., Raleigh, 1969-76; vis. lectr. Sch. Nursing. W.Va. U., Morgantown, 1977-79, assoc. prof. family resources, 1979—; cons. W.Va. Dept. Edn., research orgns. Gen. Foods fellow, 1960-62; recipient Disting. Service award Instn. Nutrition N.C., 1977. Mem. N.C. Dietetic Assn. (Mem. of Yr. 1976), Am. Dietetic Assn., Nutrition Today Soc., Roman Catholic. Contbr. articles to profl. jours. Office: Dept Family Resources WVa U Morgantown WV 26506

HEAD, TONI GODDARD, editor, pub.; b. Valparaiso, Ind., Sept. 27, 1917; d. Glen Joseph and Mildred Mae (Mock) Goddard; student U. Ill, 1936-37, Syracuse U., 1937-39, U. Pa., 1946; m. Richard W. Couch, June 21, 1941 (div.); children—Richard W., Deborah. Asst. editor Pulp & Paper, Evanston, Ill., 1956-58; med. copywriter Lee Ramsdaell Agy., Phila., 1958-60; advt. dir. Head Ski Co., Balt., 1960-65; founder Femsignal publ., Satellite Beach, Fla., 1976, editor, 1976-78, editor emeritus, 1978—; founder Mother Ch., feminist religion, 1978, matriarch, 1978—, editor, pub. Mother Ch. Bull., Tallahassee, 1977—; pres. Women Together, Inc.; bd. dirs. Aware Woman Clinic. Founder Brevard County (Fla.) chpt. NOW, 1972, pres., 1977-78; by-laws coordinator Fla. NOW; mem. Fla. council Fla. Women's Polit. Caucus. Home: 2105 Cheeke Nene Tallahassee FL 32301

HEADLEY, LEE ADELE, psychotherapist; b. Eureka, Calif., July 8, 1925; d. Edward and Ida Joanna (Johnson) Fleming; B.A., U. Calif., Berkeley, M.S.W., 1948; Ph.D. in Psychology, Am. Acad. Asian Studies, 1970. Social worker VA Hosp., San Francisco, 1948-52; supr. Agnew State Hosp., 1952-56; pvt. practice psychotherapy, Palo Alto, Calif., 1956-70; with Family and Child Psychiat. Med. Clinic, Campbell, Calif., 1970-77; practice psychotherapy, Los Altos, Calif., 1977—; cons. Children's Health Council, Stanford U., 1956-67, Mental Health Clinics, Santa Clara County, Calif., 1964-68; instr. family therapy Palo Alto Mental Research Inst., 1965-67. Mem. Am. Assn. Suicidology, Internat. Assn. Suicide Prevention, World Fedn. Mental Health, Am. Group Therapy Assn. Democrat. Author: (with others) Suicide in Different Cultures, 1975; Adults and Their Parents in Family Therapy, 1977; People Around You Can Make You Fat, 1979; contbr. articles to profl. jours. Home and Office: 12210 Brookmill Rd Los Altos CA 94022

HEALD, EMILY EASTHAM, civic worker; b. Lawrence, Mass., July 14, 1917; d. Ernest Eugene and Elsie (Eastham) H.; grad. Katharine Gibbs Sch., Boston, 1935. With Mass. Electric Co., 1935-81; ret., 1981; trustee First Essex Savs. Bank, Lawrence, 1977—. Mem. Girl Scout Council Greater Lawrence, Inc., 1935-63, pres. leaders assn., 1938-42, adviser sr. Girl Scouts planning bd., 1949-51, dir., 1951-63, sec. bd. dirs., 1952-53, v.p., 1957-61, pres., 1961-63, nat. council mem. 1949-51, 63-69, dir., pres. Merrimack River Girl Scout Council, Inc., 1963-70; dir. Methuen chpt. ARC, 1952-54, chmn., 1953-54, dir. Greater Lawrence chpt., 1954-81, sec., 1957-60, 1st vice chmn., 1961-63, chmn., 1963-65; sec. dist. 1 Mass. regional blood program, 1960-63, exec. com., 1963-66; chmn. Methuen div. Community Chest Drive, 1951; mem. budget com. United Fund, Lawrence, 1954-56, chmn. spl. gifts, Methuen, 1960; chmn. social action com. Greater Lawrence Council of Chs., 1959-61; sec. bd. dirs. Greater Lawrence Guidance Center; trustee Methuen Meml. Music Hall, Inc., 1949-81, sec., 1949-53, 55-56, 60-63, clk., 1951-55, 60-66, v.p., 1966-69, pres., 1969-73. Episcopalian (dir. choir mothers 1956-67, pres. Eureka club 1957-59, vestryman 1972-75, sr. warden 1976-78). Clubs: Quota (Lawrence); Appalachian Mountain (Boston). Home: 54 Striper Lane E Falmouth MA 02536

HEALEY, E. CLAIRE, educator; b. Providence, Mar. 9, 1924; d. Frank J. and Josephine A. (Powers) Voyer; B.A. magna cum laude, Boston U., 1950; M.A., Columbia U., 1954, Ph.D., 1968; m. Raymond F. Healey, Dec. 20, 1947; children—Ray, Todd, Glenn, Leah, Grant. Instr. English, Hunter Coll., N.Y.C., 1965-68; mem. faculty Montclair (N.J.) State Coll., 1968—, prof. English and Am. lit., 1979—, grad. coordinator English, 1973-76, chmn. dept., 1976-82. Mem. Gov. N.J. Vets. Facilities Council, 1980—; mem. president's com. intercollegiate Athletics Am. Council Edn., 1980—. Govt. fellow Am. Council Edn., 1979-80. Mem. MLA, Coll. English Assn., Am. Assn. Higher Edn., Nat. Assn. Women Deans, Adminstrs. and Counselors. Author articles in field, chpts. in books. Office: Montclair State Coll Upper Montclair NJ 07043

HEALY, ALICE FENVESSY, psychologist, educator; b. Chgo., June 26, 1946; d. Stanley J. and Doris (Goodman) Fenvessy; A.B. summa cum laude, Vassar Coll., 1968; Ph.D., Rockefeller U., 1973; m. James Bruce Healy, May 9, 1970. Asst. prof. psychology Yale U., New Haven, 1973-78, asso. prof., 1978-81, jr. faculty fellow, 1977-78, sr. faculty fellow, 1980-81; research asso. Haskins Labs., New Haven, 1976-81; asso. prof. psychology U. Colo., 1981—; mem. basic behavioral processes research rev. com. NIMH, 1979-81. USPHS grantee, 1975-77; NSF grantee, 1977-82; Spencer Found. grantee, 1978-80. Mem. Psychonomic Soc., Am. Psychol. Assn. (div. exptl. psychology), Rocky Mountain Psychol. Assn., Cognitive Sci. Soc., Eastern Psychol. Assn., Soc. Math. Psychology, Phi Beta Kappa, Sigma Xi. Mem. editorial bd. Memory and Cognition, 1976—, acting asso. editor, 1978-79; mem. editorial bd. Jour. Exptl. Psychology: Human Learning and Memory, 1980-81, Learning, Memory and Cognition, 1981—; contbr. articles to profl. jours. Home: 840 Cypress Dr Boulder CO 80303 Office: Dept Physchology U of Colo Muenzinger Psychology Bldg Boulder CO 80309

HEALY, JOAN J., sales exec.; b. Los Angeles, Aug. 30, 1945; d. John Donald and Maude Lenore (Doudna) H.; B.A. in Psychology with high honors, Northeastern Ill. U., 1975; postgrad. in bus. adminstrn. De Paul

U., 1978—; 1 dau., Kimberly Healy Maurer. Pharm. research asst. Abbott Labs., North Chicago, Ill., 1966-79; biomed. sales engr. Nicolet Instrument Corp., Madison, Wis., 1979—. Mem. Nat. Assn. Female Execs., Nat. Network Women in Sales. Home: 435 Swallow Ln Deerfield IL 60015 Office: 1345 Wiley Rd Suite 121 Schaumburg IL 60195

HEALY, THERESA ANN, ambassador; b. Bklyn., July 14, 1932; d. Anthony James and Mary Catherine (Kennedy) H.; B.A., St. John's U., 1954. Tchr. elem. and secondary schs., N.Y.C., 1951-55; with U.S. Fgn. Service, 1955—; ambassador to Sierra Leone, 1980—. Mem. Am. Fgn. Service Assn. Roman Catholic. Office: Dept of State 2201 C St NW Washington DC 20520

HEAP, SYLVIA STUBER, civic worker; b. Clifton Springs, N.Y., Sept. 25, 1929; d. Stanley Irving and Helen (Hill) Stuber; B.A. cum laude, Bates Coll., 1950; postgrad. U. Conn. Sch. Social Work, 1952-54, Boston U. Sch. Social Work, 1953-54, SUNY, Brockport, 1979, SUNY, Potsdam, 1980, Syracuse U., 1980-81; m. Walker Ratcliffe Heap, June 9, 1951; children—Heidi Anne, Cynthia Joan, Walker Ratcliffe III. Dir. Y-Teens, YWCA, Holyoke, Mass., 1950-51; social group worker West Haven (Conn.) Community House, 1951-54; program dir. YWCA, Ann Arbor, 1954-55, part-time, 1955-59; mem. adv. bd. div. continuing edn. Jefferson Community Coll., 1965—, chmn. adv. bd., 1968—; pres. Jefferson County Med. Soc. Aux., 1971-72; bd. dirs. St. Lawrence Valley Ednl. TV, 1973—, sec., 1976-80, treas., 1980—, bd. dirs. Watertown Lyric Theatre, 1973—; bd. dirs. N.Y. State Med. Soc. Aux., 1974—, 2d v.p. bd., 1979-80; fitness instr. Jefferson Community Coll., Watertown, 1977—; chmn. health projects N.Y. State Med. Soc. Aux., 1981—. Named Citizen of Yr. Greater Watertown C. of C., 1975. Mem. Friends of Public TV, AAUW, Coll. Women's Club Jefferson County, Phi Beta Kappa. Unitarian Universalist.

HEAP, VIRGINIA SKINKLE, interior designer; b. Chgo., July 29, 1907; d. George Elliot and Blanche (Randolph) Skinkle; student Sorbonne, Paris, France, 1925-27; m. Sydney Heyworth Heap, Nov. 12, 1932; 1 son, Randolph Heyworth. Owner Virginia Heap Interiors, Los Angeles, 1940—. Precinct capt. Rep. Club, Los Angeles, 1945—; bd. dirs. Los Angeles unit Pro Am., v.p. edn., 1977-78; mem. Freedoms Found., Valley Forge, 1979—. Mem. Am. Assn. Interior Designers, Jr. League Los Angeles, English Speaking Union, Park LaBrae Republicans, Nat. Fedn. Republican Women, Bel Air Republicans. Author column In One Ear, 1933-35, Urban Phenomena, monthly mag. page, 1930-32. Address: 435 S Curson Ave Los Angeles CA 90036

HEARD, MARY ALICE, editor; b. Gallup, N.Mex., Nov. 8, 1931; d. Henry Herbert and Lucy Georgia (Blain) H.; student U. Wyo., 1949-50, Kans. State U., 1950-52. Mem. staff Clay Center (Kans.) Dispatch, 1952—, society editor-reporter, 1952—. Sec. Clay Center chpt. ARC, 1956-80; publicity dir., sec. Clay Center chpt. Am. Cancer Soc., 1956—; ch. sch. tchr. St. Paul's Episcopal Ch., Clay Center, 1954-79, also mem. Altar Guild, 1979-82; active Clay Center Assn. Retarded Citizens. Mem. Nat. Fedn. Press Women, Kans. Press Women, Clay Center Bus. and Profl. Women (publicity dir. 1954—). Republican. Clubs: Helianthus (publicity chmn. 1969—), Sisters of Martha (pres. 1978-81), Order Eastern Star (25 yr. mem.). Office: 805 5th St Clay Center KS 67432

HEARNES, BETTY COOPER, state legislator; b. Brinkley, Ark., July 24, 1927; B.S. in Public Sch. Music, U. Mo., 1952; H.H.D. (hon.), Lindenwood Coll., 1971; m. Warren E. Hearnes, July 2, 1948; 3 daus. Mem. Mo. Ho. of Reps., 1979—. Recipient Disting. Woman of Am. award Columbia Coll., 1971; Alumni award U. Mo., 1974; Hon. Alumnus, William Woods Coll., 1972. Mem. Mississippi County Hist. Soc., Bus. and Profl. Women's Club, Acad. Mo. Squires, PEO. Baptist. Clubs: Jr. Study, Kathryn Boone Music. Democrat. Office: Mo State Ho of Reps Jefferson City MO 65101

HEARST, AUSTINE MCDONNELL, former columnist, feature writer, radio commentator; b. Boston, Nov. 22, 1928; d. Austin and Mary (Belt) McDonnell; grad. Notre Dame of Md., King-Smith Jr. Coll.; m. William Randolph Hearst, Jr., July 29, 1948; children—William Randolph III, John Augustine Chilton. Reporter, columnist Washington Times Herald, 1944-54; syndicated columnist King Features Syndicate, 1949-54; radio commentator CBS Mut. network. Active, North Salem Hist. Soc. Mem. Daus. Soc. Cincinnati, Nat. Soc. Barons of Runnemede, Soc. Descs. King William I the Conqueror and His Companions at Arm., Colonial Dames Am. Clubs: Nat. Press, Sulgrave (Washington); American Fox Hound; Colony, Cosmopolitan (N.Y.C.).

HEARST, BELLA RACHAEL, physician, artist; b. Pitts.; d. Aba and Bertha (Aipern) Hearst; B.M., Chgo. Med. Sch., 1949, M.D., 1950; postgrad. Johns Hopkins U., 1952-53, Art Inst. Chgo., 1958-68. Rotating intern Norwegian Am. Hosp., Chgo., 1949-50; jr. asst. pathologist Cook County Hosp., Chgo., 1950-52; fellow med. legal pathology U. Md., 1953-54; sr. pathology resident Charity Hosp., New Orleans, 1955-56; spl. cardiac research Armed Forces Inst. Pathology, Washington, 1956-57; dir., coordinator pathology dept. Hosp. O'Horan Menda Yucatan, Mex., 1957-58; founder Bertha Hearts Found., Inc., 1958, exec. dir., 1958-63; founder Diabetic Inst. Am., Inc., Chgo., 1959, exec. dir., 1959-63; founder Internat. Diabetic Inst., Inc., Chgo., 1963, exec. dir., 1963—; dist. med. dir. compensation U.S. Dept. Labor, Chgo., 1968—; with Chgo. Dept. Health, 1977—, Uptown Neighborhood Health Center, 1977-78, Copernicus Multipurpose Center, 1978-79, Lakeview Neighborhood Health Center, Chgo., 1979—; research dir. Fed. Safety and Fire Council, Chgo.; research assn. microbiology Stritch Sch. Medicine, Loyola U., Chgo.; staff physician Western Ill. U., 1971-72; asso. prof., 1971-72. Art exhibit Shuster Art Gallery, N.Y., 1966, Internat. Dermatology Congress, Munich, 1967. Recipient 3d prize AMA Conv., Chgo., 1962; testimonial plaque for work sr. citizens Chelsea House, Chgo. Fellow Am. Coll. Angiology, Internat. Coll. Angiology, Am. Geriatric Soc., Royal Soc. Pub. Health; mem. Internat. Acad. Pathology, Am. Women's Med. Assn., Am. Soc. Microbiology, Am. Assn. for Study Neoplastic Diseases, Reticuloendothelial Soc. Author: Diabetes and Juvenile Delinquency, 1964; Diabetes and Fitness, 1964; Diabetic Statistical Research Survey, 1961-65; Diabetes and Blood Groups, 1965; Diabetes and Agin, 1965; Diabetes and Newborns; contbr. articles to various publs. Office: 8 S Michigan Blvd Chicago IL 60603

HEARST, CATHERINE CAMPBELL (MRS. RANDOLPH A. HEARST), civic worker; m. Randolph Apperson Hearst, Jan. 12, 1938 (div.); children—Catherine, Virginia, Patricia, Anne, Victoria. Mem. bd. regents U. Calif. Address: care Hearst Corp 959 8th Ave New York NY 10019 *

HEARST, GLADYS WHITLEY HENDERSON, writer; b. Wolfe City, Tex.; d. William Henry and Helen (Butler) Whitley; student Trinity U., 1924-26; B.A., U. Tex., 1928, M. Journalism, 1928, postgrad., 1938-40; m. Robert David Henderson, May 17, 1933 (dec. 1941); m. 2d, Charles Joseph Hearst, Oct. 30, 1943 (dec. Nov. 1980). Editor, Future Farmer News, Austin, Tex., 1930-33; dir. Service Bur., Tex. Congress Parents and Tchrs., Austin, 1933-36; dir. Student Union, U. Tex., 1939-42; free lance writer, 1945—; instr. U. No. Iowa, 1946-47. Instr. writing Waterloo YWCA, 1966-69. Vice chmn. Black Hawk County Democratic party, 1945-57; mem. County Extension Program Planning Com., 1965-68; past deaconess United Ch. of Christ, chmn. long-range planning com., 1975-79. Served to lt. WAVES, USN, 1942-45. Mem. AAUW (life, Iowa chmn. Status of Women 1954-56, past pres. Cedar Falls br.), Women in Communications (nat. pres., Disting. Service award 1962, 73, nat. chmn. by laws 1969-74, nat. citation 1969, Task Force Long Range Planning Com. 1973-74; charter mem., v.p. NE Iowa chpt. 1978), PEO, Zeta Tau Alpha, Kappa Tau Delta, Sigma Delta Chi (scholarship award). Club: Capital Gains Investment (past pres., treas. 1970-73) (Cedar Falls). A writer Cedar Falls Centennial Pageant, 1952; writer, editor hist. book Cedar Falls Naval Station 1942-45, Anthology Family Histories Northeast Iowa (Iowa Arts Council grant), 1978; editor pictorial directory United Church of Christ, 1982. Address: 4100 Jackson St Apt 230 A Austin TX 78731

HEATH, KAREN S., mem. staff Congress; b. Washington, Jan. 10, 1943; d. Dominic and Holly Perrucci; student Westhampton Coll.; B.A., George Washington U.; M.A., Johns Hopkins U.; m. Edgar Andrew Heath. Tchr., Baltimore County, Md.; legis. asst. Rep. Bob Wilson of Calif., then adminstrv. asst.; profl. staff mem. Ho. Com. on Armed Services, Washington. Mem. Phi Beta Kappa, Zeta Tau Alpha. Office: Room 2120 Rayburn Ho Office Bldg Washington DC 20515 *

HEATH, MARIWYN DWYER, polit. cons.; b. Chgo., May 1, 1935; d. Thomas Leo and Winifred (Brennan) Dwyer; B.J., U. Mo., 1956; m. Eugene R. Heath, Sept. 3, 1956; children—Philip Clayton, Jeffrey Thomas. Mng. editor Chemung Valley Reporter, Horseheads, N.Y., 1956-57; self-employed freelance writer, speech writer, editor Tech. Transls., Dayton, Ohio, 1966—; cons. Internat. Women's Commn., 1975-76; ERA coordinator Nat. Fedn. Bus. and Profl. Women's Clubs, 1974—; mem. polit. and mgmt. cons. ERAmerica, 1976—; mem. Gov. Ohio Task Force Credit for Women, 1973; mem. Midwest regional adv. com. SBA, 1976—; chmn. Ohio Coalition ERA Implementation, 1974-75. Bd. dirs. Dayton YWCA, 1968-74. Recipient various service awards. Mem. AAUW (dir. Dayton 1965-72; Woman of Year award Dayton 1974), Nat. Fedn. Bus. and Profl. Women's Clubs (pres. Dayton 1967-69, Ohio 1976-77; Woman of Year award Dayton 1974, Ohio 1974), Ohio Women. Republican. Roman Catholic. Address: 10 Wisteria Dr Dayton OH 45419

HEATHERLEY, ELINOR ELIZABETH, nurse; b. Trenton, N.J., Aug. 10, 1949; d. Eli John and Thelma Virginia (Dansbury) Parent; Asso. Nursing Tarrant County Jr. Coll., 1973; m. James Heatherley, June 14, 1968 (div. Mar. 1975); 1 dau., Charlotte Kelly. Nurse's aide Arlington (Tex.) Community Hosp., 1969-72; registered nurse Ft. Worth Osteo. Hosp., 1974—, head nurse, 1975-78, clin. nurse leader, 1978—. Active ARC, Girl Scouts U.S.A.; asst. coach Green Gator Soccer Team, Arlington. Democrat. Presbyterian. Home: 1003 Waverly Dr Arlington TX 76015 Office: 1000 Montgomery St Fort Worth TX 76107

HEATON, ELOISE KLOTZ, educator, composer; b. Baldwinsville, N.Y., June 1, 1909; d. John Adam and Lena (Parry) Klotz; B.Mus., Syracuse U., 1933, M.A., 1960; postgrad. New Eng. Conservatory Music, summers 1945, 46, 48, Boston U., summer 1952, Eastman Sch. Music, U. Rochester, summer 1969, 72, 74; certificate in choir tng. Royal Conservatory Music, U. Toronto, summer 1950; m. Charles Toll Heaton, Aug. 29, 1934. Pvt. piano tchr., Syracuse, N.Y., 1933—; instr. music Peterboro (N.Y.) Union Sch., 1936-38; instr. piano, voice, chorus Itawamba Jr. Coll., Fulton, Miss., 1950-51; substitute tchr. Syracuse Pub. Schs., 1952-54, 55-60; instr. N.W. Miss. Jr. Coll., Senatobia, 1954-55; Mem. Music Tchrs. Nat. Assn., Am. Musicol. Soc., Music Educators Nat. Conf., N.Y. State Sch. Music Assn., Composers and Authors Assn. Am., Poetry Soc. Va., AAUP, AAUW, Am. Soc. for Aesthetics, Am. Guild Organists, Internat. Musicol. Soc. Republican. Episcopalian. Composer sacred songs The Lord is Merciful, 1937, One Prayer, 1946, My Soul is Athirst for God, 1948, Hear Me When I Call, O Lord, 1965, 91st Psalm, 1962; sacred cantatas Christ in Gethsemane, 1944, Law of the Harvest, 1946; secular songs Lady at the Harpsichord, 1945, The Springtime Is My Mother, 1930; children's study pieces Play-time Music for Kindergarten, 1953; First Piano Duets, 1961; violin solo, Invocation, 1956; operetta The Queen's Garden, 1938. Author: Around the Sun, 1948. Contbr. to anthology American Lyricists, 1954. Home and studio: 135 Kensington Pl Syracuse NY 13210

HEATON, JANE, religious ofcl.; b. Centralia, Ill., Nov. 23, 1931; d. Wilbur Estle and Nina (Huddleston) Heaton; B.Music Edn., DePauw U., 1953; M.Religious Edn., Christian Theol. Sem., 1968. Sec., Div. Overseas Ministries, Christian Ch., Indpls., 1953-58, deptl. asso., 1958-61, dir. curriculum and edn. dept. ch. women Div. Homeland Ministries, 1961-72, dir. leadership devel., dept. ch. women, 1972-74; course adminstr. Pan-African Leadership Course for Women, Mindolo Ecumenical Centre, Kitwe, Zambia, 1975-78; asst. in curriculum and program sales Christian Bd. Publ., St. Louis, 1978-79, dir. curriculum and program sales, 1979-80, v.p. curriculum and program sales, 1980—; missionary in Zaire, 1959-60; ordained to ministry Christian Ch., 1970; tchr. Mindolo Ecumenical Centre, Kitwe, Zambia, 1973. Sec.-tres. Irvington Community Council, Indpls., 1972-75. Mem. Indpls. Radio Club, Theta Phi. Club: Zonta. Author: And What of Ourselves, Bible study guide on Hebrews, 1968; Journey of Struggle, Journey in Hope, 1983. Home: 4400 Lindell Apt 8-O Saint Louis MO 63108 Office: 2721 Pine St Box 179 Saint Louis MO 63166

HEATON, MARY JONES, lumber co. exec.; b. Milan, Ga., Dec. 31, 1934; d. Monroe Collen and Ruby Lee (Evans) Jones; student LaSalle Extension U., 1965, S. Ga. Coll., 1978; children—Marilyn, William M. Heaton, Jr. Loan clk. Bank of Eastman (Ga.), 1966-69; bookkeeper Jones Lumber Co., 1953-65; asst. sec.-treas. M.C. Jones Lumber Co., Inc., Milan, Ga., 1969—. Former pres. P.T.A., Parents Without Partners. Baptist. Club: Eastern Star (past treas.). Address: PO Box 205 Milan GA 31060

HEATWOLE, THELMA MARGARET, reporter; b. Hastings, Nebr., Nov. 17, 1912; d. Harry Lattimore and Pearl Margaret (Robertson) Renick; m. Don Franklin Heatwole, June 3, 1933; children—Bruce Earl, David Allan. News reporter, asso. editor Glendale (Ariz.) Herald, 1946-62; staff writer Arizona Republic, Phoenix, 1962-77, feature writer, 1977—; speaker in field schs. and clubs. Pres. Ariz. State Firemen's Aux., 1956; mem. Ariz. Hist. Soc., Glendale Hist. Soc., Glendale Sister City Assn.; bd. dirs. Glendale Salvation Army, 1972; chmn. bd. Ch. of the Brethren, 1978-79. Recipient City of Tolleson, Ariz., award, 1978, Glendale C. of C. community service awards, 1960, 61, 77, award Glendale Union High Sch. Bd. Edn., 1977. Mem. Ariz. Press Women (charter, various contest awards, pres. 1967-68), Nat. Fedn. Press Women (various awards), Ariz. Press Club (various awards). Author: Ghost Towns and Historical Haunts in Arizona, 1981. Thelma Heatwole awards given by Ariz. Press Women for stories about teenage accomplishments, 1968-78. Home: 5741 W Morten Ave Glendale AZ 85301

HEAVEY, IRENE ELIZABETH, personnel exec.; b. Exeter, R.I., Dec. 10, 1932; d. Achilles Joseph and Eugenia Marie (Duguay) Carrier; student Boston U., 1952-54, Northeastern U., 1955-57, Am. U., 1978-80; m. Thomas Francis Heavey, Oct. 23, 1958; 1 dau., Joan Marie. Advt. copywriter Parke Snow, Inc., Waltham, Mass., 1950-52; asst. buyer Star Market Co., Newton, Mass., 1952-59; adminstr. logistics Project Hope, Washington, 1960-61; adminstrv. mgr. Electronic Teaching Labs., Washington, 1961-63; exec. asst. to pres. Security Credit Corp., Silver Spring, Md., 1964-72, corp. sec., 1964-72; with Sperry Univac, McLean, Va., 1972—, now mgr. employee benefits/services personnel dept. Election ofcl. Montgomery County, Md., 1970-74; treas. PTA, 1976; sec. Civic Assn., Silver Spring, 1974-78. Recipient award United Way, 1979, 80, 81, ARC, 1980, service award Sperry Univac, 1977-79. Mem. Nat. Employee Services and Recreation Assn. (dir. 1980—), Washington Area Recreation and Employee Services Council (pres. 1980, v.p. 1981-82), Am. Soc. Personnel Adminstrs., Am. Soc. Bus. and Profl. Women, Nat. Assn. Female Execs., Am. Assn. Fitness Dirs. in Bus. and Industry. Republican. Roman Catholic. Office: 8008 Westpark Dr McLean VA 22102

HEBERT, KATHLEEN JOYCE, computer co. exec.; b. Huntingdon, Pa., Sept. 28, 1950; d. Raymond Francis and Marjorie May (Walters) H.; student public schs., Schenectady, 1967-68. Various secretarial positions, 1968-74; with Estimation, Inc., Linthicum Heights, Md., 1974-81, mgr. programming dept., 1976-81, corp. treas., 1979-81; programming mgr. Eastern region Diversified Electronics, Mountain View, Calif., 1981—. Office: 1700 Stierlin Rd Mountain View CA 94043

HEBERT, MARY OLIVIA, librarian; b. St. Louis, Nov. 11, 1921; d. Arthur Frederick and Clara Marie (Golden) Meyer; certificate librarianship, Washington U., St. Louis, 1972; m. N. Hal Hebert, Sept. 9, 1943 (dec. Mar. 1969); children—Olivia, Stephen, Christina, Deborah, Beth, John, James. Secretarial positions in advt., 1942-43; v.p. Hebert Advt. Co., 1955-66; adminstrv. asst. communications Blue Cross, St. Louis, 1966-69, librarian, 1969—. Mem. Spl. Libraries Assn. (pres. elect. St. Louis Metro chpt.), St. Louis Med. Librarians. Roman Catholic. Office: 4444 Forest Park Blvd St Louis MO 63108

HECHT, DIANE MELESKI, interior designer; b. Kingston, N.Y., Oct. 17, 1945; d. Vincent J. and Rose S. (Fasce) Meleski; B.F.A., Boston U., 1967; m. Stephen S. Hecht, Aug. 17, 1968. Interior designer M. Brown & Co., Boston, 1966-67, Hans Krieks Assos., Boston, 1967-68, F.A. Stahl & Assos., Boston, 1968-69, Interspace, Inc., Phila., 1969-70, William Sklaroff Design Assos., Ardmore Pa., N.Y.C., 1970-81; partner Hecht & Marler (HMI), N.Y.C., 1981—. Recipient Outstanding Achievement in field of design award Women in Design Internat., 1981. Mem. Archtl. League, Environ. Design and Research Assn., Women in Design Internat., Preservation League N.Y. State, Westchester Preservation League (trustee, v.p., dir. county wide archtl. survey), Com. for Preservation of Archtl. Records, Mcpl. Art Soc., Nat. Trust Historic Preservation, Classical Am. Democrat. Home: 30 Emerson Rd Larchmont NY 10538 Office: Hecht & Marler 225 Park Ave S 19th Floor New York NY 10003

HECHT, MARIE BERGENFELD, educator, author; b. N.Y.C., Oct. 21, 1918; d. Frank Falle and Marie (Trommer) Bergenfeld; B.A., Goucher Coll., 1939; M.A., New Sch. for Social Research, 1971; m. Morton Hecht, Jr., Dec. 17, 1937 (div.); children—Ann (Mrs. David Bloomfield), Margaret, Laurence, Andrew. Tchr. Am. history Mineola High Sch., Garden City Park, N.Y., 1960-80. Mem. Am. Hist. Assn., Orgn. Am. Historians. Author (with Herbert S. Parmet): Aaron Burr: Portrait of an Ambitious Man, 1967; Never Again: A President Runs for a Third Term, 1968; John Quincy Adams: A Personal History of An Independent Man, 1972; The Women, Yes, 1973; Beyond the Presidency: The Residues of Power, 1976; Odd Destiny: The Life of Alexander Hamilton, 1982. Address: 5 Hewlett Pl Great Neck NY 11024

HECKART, EILEEN, actress; b. Columbus, Ohio, Mar. 29, 1919; d. Leo Herbert and Esther (Stark) Purcell; B.A., Ohio State U., 1942, L.H.D. (hon.), 1981; student Am. Theatre Wing, 1944-48; LL.D., Sacred Heart U., Bridgeport, Conn., 1973; D.F.A. (hon.), Niagara U., 1981; m. John Harrison Yankee, Jr., June 26, 1943; children—Mark Kelly, Philip Craig, Luke Brian. Actress Broadway plays, Voice of the Turtle, 1944, Brighten the Corner, 1946, They Knew What They Wanted, 1948, Stars Weep, 1949, The Traitor, 1950, Hilda Crane, 1951, In Any Language, 1953, Picnic, 1953, Bad Seed, 1955, A View From the Bridge, 1956, Dark at the Top of the Stairs, 1958, Invitation to a March, 1960, Everybody Loves Opal, 1961, Family Affair, 1962, Too True To Be Good, 1963, And Things That Go Bump in the Night, 1965, Barefoot in the Park, 1965-66, You Know I Can't Hear You When the Water's Running, 1967, The Mother Lover, 1968, Butterflies Are Free, 1969, Veronica's Room, 1973, The Effect of Gamma Rays on Man-in-the-Moon Marigolds, 1971, Remember Me, 1975, Mother Courage and Her Children, 1975, Mrs. Gibbs in Our Town, 1976, (one-woman show) Eleanor, 1976, Ladies at the Alamo, 1977; movies: Miracle in the Rain, Bad Seed, Somebody Up There Likes Me, Bus Stop, Hot Spell, Heller in Pink Tights, My Six Loves, 1962, Up the Down Staircase, 1966, No Way To Treat A Lady, 1968, Butterflies Are Free, 1972, Zandy's Bride, 1974, The Hiding Place, 1975, Burnt Offerings, 1975, Wedding Band, 1975; TV actress, 1947—. Recipient Outer Circle award, 1953, Daniel Blum award, 1953, Sylvania TV award, 1954, Donaldson award, 1955, Oscar nomination, 1956, Hollywood Fgn. Press award, 1956, Film Daily citation, 1956, Variety Poll of N.Y. Drama Critics award, 1958; N.Y. Emmy for Save Me A Place at Forest Lawn, 1967; March Dimes award, 1970; Aegis award, 1970; Ohio State U. Centennial award, 1970; Acad. award for Butterflies Are Free, 1973; Straw Hat award, 1973, 75, 77; Gov.'s award of Ohio, 1977; Ohiana Library award, 1978. Mem. Pi Beta Phi. Home: 135 Comstock Hill Rd New Canaan CT 06840 Office: care STE Representation 888 7th Ave New York NY 10019 *

HECKER, SUSAN JUNE, pre-engineered bldg. mfg. co. exec.; b. Bethlehem, Pa., Oct. 23, 1945; d. George Lee and Thelma Mae Billheimer; student Northampton County Community Coll. Accounts receivable dept. staff Bethlehem (Pa.) Steel Corp., 1964-70; regional sec. Butler Mfg. Co., Phila., 1970-75, adminstrv. asst., 1975-76, area mgr. Eastern Pa., 1976—. Republican. Methodist. Clubs: Quota, Soaring Soc. Am. Home: RD 1 William Church Ln Hellertown PA 18055

HECKLER, MARGARET M. O'SHAUGHNESSY, congresswoman; b. Flushing, N.Y., June 21, 1931; d. John and Bridget (McKeown) O'Shaughnessy; B.A. (scholar), Albertus Magnus Coll., 1953, LL.D., 1972; LL.B. (scholar), Boston Coll., 1956; postgrad. U. Leiden (Netherlands), 1953; L.H.D., Northeastern U., 1970, Emanuel Coll., 1969; D. Law and Letters, Stonehill Coll., 1969; LL.D. honoris causa, Regis Coll., St. Bonaventure U., 1975; m. John M. Heckler, Aug. 29, 1953; children—Belinda West, Alison Anne, John M. Admitted to Mass. bar, 1956; mem. Mass. Gov.'s Council, 1962-66; mem. 90th to 97th congresses from 10th Dist. Mass., mem. Agrl. Com., Joint Econ. Com., Vets. Affairs Com., Select Com. on Ethics, Sci. and Tech. Com.; founder, co-chair Congressional Caucus on Women's Issues; keynote speaker Nat. Women's Republican Conv., 1967. Mem. pres.'s adv. com. Wheaton Coll.; mem. corp. Madeira Sch.; mem. nat. adv. com. Hampshire Coll.; bd. dirs. March Dimes; hon. bd. dirs. Epilepsy Found. Am.; trustee Heart Research Found.; hon. trustee Newton Wellesley Hosp.; mem. U.S. Commn. on Observance of Internat. Women's Year. Recipient numerous civic and profl. awards. Mem. Am. Bar Assn. (com. on govt., legis. and public interest of food, drug and cosmetic law div.), Boston Bar Assn., Mass. Trial Lawyers, Mass. Women Lawyers, Catholic Women's Coll. Alumnae Assn. (past pres.). Club: Ninetieth (v.p.) (Washington). Office: 2312 Rayburn House Office Bldg Washington DC 20515

HEDAHL, BEULAH MINERVA, psychologist, educator; b. Bismarck, N.D., Sept. 12, 1920; d. Edwin N. and Clara (Berge) H.; A.A., Bismarck Jr. Coll., 1941; B.A., Concordia Coll., Moorhead, Minn., 1946; M.A., Wash. State U., 1948; M.A., U. Minn., 1954, Ph.D., 1958. Asst. prof. English, Pacific Lutheran U., 1948-51, dean women, 1948-51; teaching asst., instr. U. Minn., 1952-56; instr. Mich. State U., 1956-58, asst. prof., 1958-63, assoc. prof., 1963-64, counselor, 1956-64; dir. Counseling Ctr., U. N.D., 1964-79, sr. staff counseling psychologist, 1979—, assoc. prof., 1964-75, prof., 1975—, chmn. psychology dept.,

1979-81. Mem. Am. Psychol. assn., Am. Personnel and Guidance Assn., Am. Assn. Higher Edn., N.D. Psychol. Assn., N.D. Personnel and Guidance Assn. AAUW, Pi Lambda Theta. Lutheran. Cons. editor: Jour. Counseling Psychology, 1975-81. Home: 2825 Knight Dr Grand Forks ND 58201 Office: University of North Dakota Counseling Center Grand Forks ND 58202

HEDITSIAN, CORINNE ADRIENNE, govt. info. agy. ofcl.; b. Providence, Nov. 22, 1939; d. Tateos and Mantoohe (Serjenian) H.; B.A. magna cum laude in Govt., Jackson Coll., Tufts U., 1961; M. Internat. Affairs, Columbia U., 1963; spl. acad. year in Cinema Studies (USIA grantee, 1978-79), Sch. of Arts, N.Y.U., 1978. Jr. officer in tng. USIA, Washington, 1963; asst. info. officer Am. Consulate, Bombay, India, 1964-69; program officer Near East Area Office, Washington, 1969-71; cultural attache Am. Embassy, Beirut, Lebanon, 1971-75; dir. speakers and artists bur. for Africa and Middle East, Am. Embassy, Paris, 1975-78; press officer Fgn. Press Center, U.S. Internat. Communication Agy. (formerly USIA), N.Y.C., 1979—. Active NOW. Recipient meritorious honor award USIA; Nat. Endowment for Humanities fellow, summer 1981. Mem. Am. Fgn. Service Assn., Women's Action Orgn. (founding), various fgn. service agys., Nat. Assn. Women Execs. Armenian Apostolic. Contbr. various catalogs on art, film, film festival programs. Office: Foreign Press Center 18 E 50th St New York NY 10022

HEDLEY, MARTHA KAY, educator; b. Terre Haute, Ind., Sept. 20, 1940; d. Harry Wildon and Helen Marie (Baker) H.; B.B.A. summa cum laude, Memphis State U., 1962; M.S., U. Tenn., 1963; Ph.D., Ind. State U., Terre Haute, 1971. Instr. bus. edn. Tenn. Wesleyan Coll., Athens, 1963-65, Memphis State U., 1965-66, Ind. State U., 1966-71; prof. bus. edn., chmn. dept. Ala. State U., Montgomery, 1971-73; prof. bus. edn. U. Ala., Birmingham, 1973—; chmn. Birmingham City Sch. Vocat. Adv. Council, 1975—; cons. in field. Mem. Nat. Bus. Edn. Assn., Am. Vocat. Assn., Nat. Assn. Bus. Tchr. Educators, Ala. Bus. Edn. Assn., Alpha Xi Delta (past chpt. adv.), Phi Delta Kappa, Delta Pi Epsilon. Author, editor in field. Home: 936 Ryecroft Rd Pelham AL 35124 Office: 136 Ullman Hall U Ala Birmingham AL 35294

HEDLUND, EMMA, fabric warehouse co. exec.; b. St. George, Utah, May 14, 1923; d. Gordon and Blanche (Beckstrom) Sullivan; student Phoenix Coll., 1970-72; m. Carl B. Hedlund, June 25, 1960; children—Melinda Marlene Hedlund Millsap, Terry Gordon, Carlene Laurie. With, Hedlund Fabric Supply Co., Phoenix, 1968—, v.p., dir., 1970—. Mem. citizens adv. council Phoenix Union High Sch. Dist., 1977—. Mem. Nat. Assn. Decorative Fabric Distbrs., Automotive Service Industry Assn., Phoenix Met. C. of C. Republican. Mormon. Office: Hedlund Fabrics Supply Co 1710 E Washington St Phoenix AZ 85034

HEDLUND, NANCY LEE, psychologist; b. Chgo., Dec. 3, 1940; d. Sexten W. Hedlund and Lorraine (DeRoche) Hedlund Hamilton; B.S., U. Okla., 1964, M.S. in Human Ecology, 1970; Ed.M. in Nursing, Columbia U., 1972, Ph.D. in Social Psychology, 1977; m. Finis Breckenridge Jeffery, Nov. 2, 1979. Instr. nursing U. Okla., 1965-67; dir. nursing Central Okla. Community Mental Health Center, Norman, 1967-69; instr. psychiat. nursing Sch. Nursing, Cornell U., N.Y.C., 1969-71; clin. specialist mental health nursing N.Y. Hosp., Cornell U., N.Y.C., 1971-74; pvt. practice psychotherapy, N.Y.C., 1974—; asso. prof. Yale U. Sch. Nursing, New Haven, 1976—, chmn. program in nursing research, 1977—; cons. research Baystate Med. Center, Springfield, Mass., 1980—, Hosp. of St. Raphael, New Haven, 1981-82. Mem. Am. Nurses Assn., Am. Psychol. Assn., Am. Assn. Social Psychiatry, Am. Orthopsychiat. Assn., Sigma Theta Tau. Episcopalian. Contbr. articles on nursing research and social psychology to profl. publs. Home: 380 Riverside Dr 7L New York NY 10025 Office: 57 Dawson Ave Apt 3 West Haven CT 06516

HEDTKE, DELPHINE L., educator, designer; b. Wayzata, Minn., Mar. 25, 1932; d. Herbert and Wyona Hedtke; B.S., Gustavus Adolphus Coll., 1953; M.S., U. Minn., 1968; postgrad. UCLA, 1961-62, Fashion Inst. Tech., N.Y.C., 1976; Ph.D., U. Mo., 1978. Tchr. fine arts, home econs. Minn. Public Schs., 1953-56; tchr. fine arts, adminstr. home econs. Calif. Public Schs., 1956-60; fashion apparel workshop coordinator, haute couture and theatre costume designer Coll. Edn., Home Econs. Edn., U. Minn., 1974—; dist. cons. home econs., asst. vocat. program dir. Roseville Area Schs., St. Paul, 1963—; dir. Creative Design Ltd., Calif.; lectr., cons. in field. Mem. AAUW, Am. Home Econs. Assn., Am. Vocat. Assn., Home Econs. Edn. Assn., Minn. Assn. Vocat. Adminstrs., Minn. Edn. Assn., Minn. Home Econs. Assn., Minn. Met. Council Adminstrv. Women in Edn., Minn. Assn. Vocat. Educators, Minn. Vocat. Assn., Nat. Assn. Female Execs., Nat. Council Local Adminstrs., NEA, Nat. Suprs. Home Econs., Mpls. Soc. Fine Arts, Friends of the Goldstein Gallery, Walker Art Center. Lutheran. Author: Apparel Fashion Dimensions: A Multidisciplinary Approach, 1978; illustrator: Tiny Tunes for Tiny Tots, 1976; contbr. articles to profl. jours., newspapers. Home: 1661 Western Ave N Saint Paul MN 55117 Office: Kellogg Sch 15 E County Rd B2 Saint Paul MN 55117

HEDWALL, JEANETTE NICKEL, keyboard co. sales exec.; b. Madison, Wis., Mar. 21, 1937; d. George and Sophie Marie (Lorenzen) Nickel; student extension classes; m. Edward A. Hedwall, June 30, 1979; children—Tammy, Tom; stepchildren—Julie, Jeff. Real estate broker Jeanette Klevgaard Realty, Gehrke Realty, Kemps Realty; sales rep. Forbes Meagher Music, Madison, Wis., 1970-77; saleswoman Sherman Clay, Seattle, 1977—, sales trainer, 1977—; speaker in field. Home: 14510 SE 47th Pl Bellevue WA 98006 Office: 1624 4th Ave Seattle WA 98101

HEENEY, MARY ELLEN, newspaper editor; b. Portland, Kans., Oct. 17, 1903; d. John Joseph and Fannie Alberta (Aker) Burger; student Phillips U., 1926-27, Colo. U., summer 1924, Emporia Tchrs. Coll., summers 1928, 30; m. David Geeslin Heeney, Sept. 2, 1931; children—Mary Lou Heeney Boettcher, John David, Patricia Ann Reich. Tchr., rural schs., Kans., 1923-25, 28-31; writer Wellington Daily News, 1939-45; local editor South Haven (Kans.) New Era, 1947—, Pianist, Christian Ch. Mem. Fedn. Womens Clubs (state bd.), Kans. Authors Club, Kans. Press Assn., Sumner County Hist. Soc. Chistorian 1961—). Republican. Club: Order Eastern Star. Office: Box 98 South Haven KS 67140

HEERDT, NATALIE RENEE, fin. exec.; b. Johannesburg, South Africa, Aug. 29, 1950; came to U.S., 1981; d. Fritz Adolf and Golda (Ross) Sonntag; B.S., U. Witwatersrand, 1970; I.M.P., London Bus. Sch., 1980, Stanford U., 1981. Ground stewardess South African Airways, Johannesburg, 1970-71; computer systems design, installation and liaison officer Computer Package Systems, Johannesburg, 1971-72; systems design Johannesburg Stock Exchange, 1973-77; partner, portfolio mgr. Mathison & Hollidge, Johannesburg, 1977-80; dir. fixed income services Century Capital Assos., N.Y.C., 1981—. Mem. Money Marketeers. Jewish. Clubs: Soroptimist, Barclays Exec. Bus. Women's. Office: 767 3d Ave New York NY 10017 *

HEFFELFINGER, GLORIA MAE, nurse; b. Mpls., July 27, 1928; d. Charles King and Josephine (Lowe) H.; B.S. in Nursing, Coll. St. Catherine, 1957; M.S. in Nursing (USPHS scholar), U. Minn., 1968, postgrad., 1977. Operating room supr., clin. instr. St. Michael's Hosp., Grand Forks, N.D., 1957-62; operating room and emergency room supr. St. Joseph's Hosp., St. Paul, 1962-64; asst. dir. nursing St. Luke's Hosp., St. Paul, 1964-68; asso. dir. nursing St. Joseph's Hosp., St. Paul, 1968—. Mem. Am. Nurses Assn., Minn. Nurses Assn. Republican. Roman Catholic. Office: 69 W Exchange St Saint Paul MN 55102

HEFFERNAN, PATRICIA CONNER, law sch. ofcl.; b. N.Y.C., Oct. 11, 1946; d. Arthur S. and Catherine (Center) Conner; B.A., U. Va., 1968; M.B.A., Suffolk U., 1980; m. John Joseph Heffernan, Sept. 13, 1969. Office restaurant mgr. Wobbly Barn, Killington, Vt., 1968-72; bus. mgr. Woodstock Country Sch., Vt., 1972-74; bus. mgr. Vt. Law Sch., Royalton, Vt., 1974-79, asso. dean for bus. affairs, 1979-81, asso. dean, treas., 1981—. Trustee, Killington Mountain Sch., 1978, pres., 1980—; mem. Killington Planning Commn., 1975, vice chmn., 1976, chmn., 1977-79; mem. Killington Zoning Bd., 1979—; mem. Vt. Epilepsy Assn., 1977—; mem. Vt. steering com. for ACE Nat. Indentification Prgm. for Women in Higher Edn., 1978—. Mem. Inst. Mgmt. Accts., Nat. Assn. Coll. and Univ. Bus. Officers, Am. Assn. Univ. Adminstrs. Home: PO Box 34 W Park Rd Killington VT 05751 Office: Vermont Law Sch South Royalton VT 05068

HEFFINGTON, KATHLYN ALLENE, educator, real estate broker; b. Lawrenceburg, Tenn., May 19, 1920; d. Dendon Selar and Reba Allene (Hughes) Grisham; B.A. cum laude, Athens Coll., 1968; M.A., Middle Tenn. State U., 1971, Ed.S., 1978; m. Charles Alexander Heffington, July 26, 1938; children—Charles Alexander, Jack Grisham, Margaret Rebecca Heffington Scroggins, Kathryn Leah Heffington Fitzpatrick. Rural letter carrier U.S. Postal Dept., Lawrence County, Tenn., 1945-61; tchr. Lawrence County Dept. Edn., Lawrenceburg, 1965—; real estate broker Heffington Real Estate Co., Lawrenceburg, 1975—; sec.-treas. Middle Tenn. Mortgage Co.; dir. Key Life Ins. Co. Mem. NEA, Tenn. Edn. Assn., Lawrence County Edn. Assn., Tenn. Real Estate Assn., Lawrenceburg Community Theatre, Tenn. Performing Arts, Epsilon Sigma Alpha (Lawrenceburg chpt. organizer, 1st pres.). Mem. Ch. of Christ. Club: Thursday (pres. 1978). Home: Route 7 Box 70 Lawrenceburg TN 38464 Office: Heffington Real Estate Co 320 E Gaines St Lawrenceburg TN 38464

HEFFLEFINGER., CLARICE MAE, real estate broker; b. Oregon, Ill., Oct. 5, 1937; d. Ralph Wayne and Wyota Anita (Nashold) Thorpe; A.A., Coll. Sequoias, Visalia, Calif.. 1967; m. Jack Kenneth Hefflefinger. Jan. 24, 1970; children—Kenneth, Jack, Deborah, Kevin. Various positions in banking and ins., 1956-76; real estate asso. Scotsman Realty, Tulare, Calif.. 1977—; substitute tchr. Tulare City Schs., 1979—. Mem. Tulare County SSS Draft Bd. Mem. Nat. Assn. Realtors, Calif. Assn. Realtors (dir.), Tulare Bd. Realtors (dir., pres. 1982), Amvets Aux. (pres. post 1982). Republican. Club: Quota. Home and Office: 1351 Williams St PO Box 1213 Tulare CA 93274

HEFFNER, PHOEBE J., real estate co. exec.; b. Chgo., June 2, 1929; d. Frank Leventhal and Anne Stanley; B.S. in Commerce, DePaul U., 1977; 1 son, Michael. Closing sec. Baird & Warner, Inc., Chgo., 1963-68, personnel mgr., 1968-75. asst. v.p., 1975-80, dir. of personnel, 1977—, v.p., 1980—, asst. sec., 1981—. Active Lakeview Citizens Council, Ind. Voters of Ill., Metro-Help, Inc. Mem. Soc. of Personnel Adminstrs. (membership com. 1979-80), Am. Soc. for Personnel Adminstrs. (affiliate), Am. Bus. Women's Assn. (scholarship chmn. 1976-79). Home: 2800 N Lake Shore Dr Chicago IL 60657 Office: Baird & Warner Inc 115 S LaSalle Chicago IL 60603

HEFFRON, ANNE ABEL, social agy. exec.; b. Dallas, Nov. 3, 1933; d. Henry Odell and Ruby E. (Powell) Abel; B.A., Hendrix Coll., 1954; m. Robert N. Heffron, Sept. 13, 1957; children—Robert Michael, Richard Douglas, Laura Michelle, Kelly Anne. Tchr., Calhoun County, Tex., 1954-55; field dir. CampFire, Inc., Corpus Christi, Tex., 1955-56, dist. dir., Long Beach, Calif., 1956-57, exec. dir. Cooke County council, Gainesville, Tex., 1977—, mem. faculty core tng. for exec. dirs., 1980; tchr., San Luis Obispo, Calif., 1957-58; employment security officer State of Calif., 1960-62, 64-66. Pres., Gainesville (Tex.) Newcomers Club, 1976; mem. Texoma Regional Criminal Justice Adv. Com., 1979-80, Gainesville City Council, 1980—; mem. adv. com. 4-H, 1977-78; dir. Texoma Regional Planning Commn., 1981-82. Republican. Presbyterian. Home: 506 Line Dr Gainesville TX 76240 Office: 400 S Weaver St Gainesville TX 76240

HEFKO, RUTH MARILYN, country club mgr., floral designer; b. Marshfield, Wis., June 25, 1926; d. Theodore Dmyterko and Mabel Crystal (Hood) H.; student U. Wis., Marshfield Extension, 1946; m. Freeman J. Powell, Nov. 22, 1957 (dec.); m. 2d, Joseph P. McGuire, Dec. 12, 1964 (dec.). Sec., inventory control Appleton (Wis.) Renault Sales, Wis. Auto Wrecking Co., cost acct. Auto Body Works, Inc., until 1952; floral designer Geraldine Hale, Florist, Burton's Orchids & Flowers, mgr. Baylor Flower Shop, Dallas, 1952-62; floral designer Mangel's Florist, Drake Hotel, front desk receptionist and cashier Millionaires' Club, Broadway, Chgo., 1962-71; mgr. Lincoln Hills Country Club (formerly Westview Country Club), Marshfield, 1972—. Presbyterian. Home: 409 B W 5th St Marshfield WI 54449

HEFNER, CHRISTIE ANN, publishing/entertainment co. exec.; b. Chgo., Nov. 8, 1952; d. Hugh Marston and Mildred Marie (Williams) H.; B.A. summa cum laude in English Lit., Brandeis U., 1974. Free lance journalist, Boston, 1974-75; spl. asst. to chmn. Playboy Enterprises, Inc., Chgo., 1975- 77, v.p., 1977-82, pres., 1982—; bd. dirs. Playboy Found.-Playboy Enterprises, Inc. Active Nat. Assn. Repeal Abortion Laws, ACLU (mem. Pres.'s com.), Brandeis Nat. Women's Com. (life); mem. Com. of 200; mem. nat. adv. bd. Nat. Women's Polit. Caucus. Mem. NOW, Phi Beta Kappa. Democrat. Club: Economic. Office: 919 N Michigan Ave Chicago IL

HEGARTY, MARION MIKE, speech pathologist; b. Youngstown, Ohio, May 10, 1948; d. Michael Ablen and Marion Charlotte (Saba) Mike; B.S., Ohio U., 1969; M.S., Kent State U., m. Christopher J. Hegarty, Nov. 25, 1982; children—Christine, Mahren, Cahill, Melissa, Michael, Monika (foster child). Speech pathologist Youngstown Hearing and Speech Center, 1970-72, Reading (Pa.) Spl. Edn. Center 1972-76, Manoning County Sch. Dist., Youngstown, after 1976; cons. in field. Bd. dirs. Hearing Impaired for Burks County (Ohio), 1973. Mem. Nat. League Am. Pen Women (writer award 1981), Broadcast Music Inc., Nat. Forensic League, Sigma Alpha Eta. Composer, writer lyrics I Like Me and What's So Bad About Different; creator, producer Kids Are Talking for Cable TV. Office: PO Box 1152 Novato CA 94948

HEGEDUS, ARLEEN HAZEL, nurse, educator; b. Wyandotte, Mich., Aug. 9, 1939; d. Joseph and Helen I. Hegedus; diploma Harper Hosp. Sch. Nursing, 1960; B.S. in Nursing, Ind. U., 1966, M.S., 1967; postgrad. U. Mich., 1973-75. Staff nurse Harper Hosp., Detroit, 1960-61, Meml. Hosp., Long Beach, Calif., 1961; office nurse, Lakewood, Calif., 1961-62; staff nurse Belleville (Ill.) Nursing Home, 1964; camp nurse Camp Linden, Huron Valley council Girl Scouts U.S.A., Mich., summer 1970; ofcl. nurse of U.S. Auto Club, Indpls. 500 race, 1967-75; asst. prof. nursing U. Mich. Sch. Nursing, Ann Arbor, 1969-74, asso. prof., 1974—; tchr. med.-surg. nursing and nursing mgmt., also forensic nursing Univ. Hosp., Ann Arbor, Mich., 1979—; cons. to profl. nursing groups, 1981—. Served to 1st. lt. Nurse Corps, USAF, 1962-64. Recipient Lucy D. Germain award Harper Sch. Nursing, 1959. Mem. Am. Nurses Assn., Nat. League Nursing, Am. Heart Assn., Nat. Forensic Center, AAUP, Nutritional Acad., Sigma Theta Tau, Pi Lambda Theta. Contbr. articles to profl. jours. Home: 2323 Faye St Ann Arbor MI 48103 Office: U Mich Sch Nursing 1355 Catherine Ann Arbor MI 48109

HEGG, DOLORA MARIA, civic worker; b. Boyd, Minn., Feb. 26, 1924; d. Henry Edward and Marie Louise (Kelm) Kammeyer; student schs. Palouse, Wash.; m. Walter George Hegg, Dec. 27, 1946; children—Yvonne, Yvette, Sharon, Shirley, Ronald. Organized first local Milwaukie (Oreg.) Loaves and Fishes program, 1973, vol. dir., chmn. steering com., 1973—, vol. driver, Fish; vol. office worker Luth. Family Services; vol. driver Meals-on-Wheels; Sunday Sch. treas. and tchr. Luth. Ch., 1946-69; pres. Jr. High Sch. PTA, 1956-57; elem. sch. PTA pres., 1962-63; 4-H leader, 1958-65; organizer, dir. Sr. Citizens program in Milwaukie Center, 1980. Recipient vol. of year award, Kiwanis, 1975, Community Service award Milwaukie Grange, 1979. Home: 13838 SE Matilda Dr Milwaukie OR 97222 Office: 5440 SE Kellogg Creek Dr Milwaukie OR 97222

HEGGINS, MARTHA JEAN ADAMS, educator; b. Florence, S.C., May 9, 1942; d. Thomas Lee and Mable L. Adams; B.S., S.C. State Coll., 1960; M.S., Bank Street Coll. Edn., 1969; Ed.D., Rutgers U., 1975; 1 son, Willie J., III. Tchr. nursery and elem. schs., S.C., 1964-71, N.J., 1971-75; dir. Demonstration Day Care Learning Center, New Brunswick, N.J., 1972-73; teaching asst. urban edn. dept. Keen Coll., Montclair State Coll., Livingston Coll. (all N.J.), 1973-75; mem. adj. faculty dept. home econs. Montclair State Coll.. Upper Montclair, 1974-75; instr. edn. S.C. State Coll., Orangeburg, 1969-70, asst. dir. student teaching, 1970-71, asst. prof., 1975-78. asso. prof. early childhood edn., 1978—, dir. day care tng. program, 1978—. Chmn. work area on edn. Trinity United Meth. Ch., 1977-78. Named Tchr. of Yr., Sch. Home Econs., S.C. State U., 1977; Leadership Devel. grantee Ford Found., 1967-68; Martin Luther King, Jr. fellow, 1971-74. Mem. S.C. Home Econs. Assn., NEA, Nat. Assn. Edn. of Young Children, S.C. Assn. Edn. of Young Children, S.C. State Employees Assn., Day Care and Child Devel. Council Am., Assn. Childhood Edn. Internat., Am. Home Econs. Assn., Parent Fedn. Am., Kappa Omicron Phi, Phi Delta Kappa, Delta Sigma Theta. Home: PO Box 1706 South Carolina State Coll Orangeburg SC 29117 Office: 205 Staley Bldg South Carolina State Coll Orangeburg SC

HEGHINIAN, ELIZABETH ALBAN TRUMBOWER, artist, educator; b. N.Y.C., Jan. 11, 1917; d. Eli Cadwallader and Maria Lucas (Coyle) Trumbower; certificate dept. indsl. design Pratt Inst., 1938; B.S. magna cum laude, N.Y. U., 1950, M.A., 1952, Ph.D., 1957; postgrad. Bklyn. Inst. Arts and Scis., 1963-66, Bklyn. Mus. Art Sch., L.I. U., 1963-66, Fairleigh Dickinson U., 1970; studied under Richard Mayhew, Georgiana Brown Harbeson, Edith Fetterolf, Katheryn I. Young, Howard W. Arnold, I.-Ching Ku; m. Aram Lincoln Heghinian, Aug. 24, 1957; children—Elizabeth Alban, Marie Hunazant. Indsl. designer Belle Kogan Assos., 1938-40; art dir. Norcross Pubs., 1940-42; buyer for battle damaged U.S. naval vessels and equipment Arma Corp., 1942-45; dir. arts and crafts YWCA Camp Program, 1946; designer Cosmopolitan Crafts, Camp Fire Outfitting Co., 1946-47; faculty N.Y. U., 1947-61, asst. prof. edn., 1957-61; specialist consultation services nat. arts and crafts com. Boys' Clubs Am., 1949-65; research and practicum in remedial reading techniques N.Y.C. Pub. Sch., Bklyn., 1966-68; exhibited in group shows Pratt Inst., 1936-38, N.Y. U., 1948-52; represented in permanent collection Bklyn. Mus. Art Sch., pvt. collections. Mem. nat. adv. com. on recreation programs and activities arts and crafts sect. Nat. Recreation Assn., 1958-62; pres. Camp Jefferson, Inc., N.Y.C., dir. Camp Jefferson, Palisades Interstate Park, N.Y., 1945—; active town wide camping and sch. year program Girl Scouts U.S.A., 1969-73; mem. N.Y. Assn. for Brain Injured Children, 1963—. Recipient Founders Day certificate N.Y. U., 1950. Mem. Am. Watercolor Soc. (asso.), AAUW, Nat. Congress Parents and Tchrs., Tenafly Nature Center Assn., Palisades Interstate Park Camp Dirs.' Assn., Pi Lambda Theta, Kappa Delta Pi, Epsilon Pi Tau. Author: The Contribution of Craft Activities to the Philosophy and Objectives of Boys Clubs of America, 1957; (monograph) Crafts in Boys' Clubs, 1958. Address: 52 Howard Park Dr Tenafly NJ 07670

HEID, BEVERLY ANN, investment broker; b. Indpls., July 4, 1938; d. Raymond E. and Anna Lucile Carmichael; B.A. in Econs., Ind. U., 1960; M.B.A. in Fin., Ind. U., 1964; m. Robert L. Heid, Oct. 28, 1961; children—Beth Ann, Sara Diane. Fin. analyst Eli Lilly & Co., Indpls., 1960-63; mgr. market research Ind. Nat. Bank, Indpls., 1964-68; founder, pres. Heid Research, Indpl., 1968-75; pres. Heid Econ. Research subs. Mchts. Nat. Corp., Indpls., 1975-81; v.p. Mchts. Nat. Corp., Indpls., 1979-81; investment broker J.J.B. Hilliard-W.L. Lyons, Inc., Indpls., 1981—. Bd. dirs. Jr. Achievement Central Ind. Mem. Am. Mktg. Assn. (past pres. Ind. chpt.), Ind. Econ. Forum (past pres.), Ind. U. Alumni Assn. (exec. council), Bank Mktg. Ind. U. Sch. Bus. Alumni Assn. (past pres.), Beta Gamma Sigma. Presbyterian. Club: Indpls. Athletic. Office: Hilliard-Lyons Inc 1414 E Merchants Plaza Indianapolis IN 46204

HEIDELBERGER, KATHLEEN PATRICIA, physician; b. Bklyn., Apr. 13, 1939; d. William Cyprian and Margaret Bernadette (Hughes) H.; B.S. cum laude, Coll. Misericordia, 1961; M.D. cum laude, Womans Med. Coll. Pa., 1965; m. Charles William Davenport, Oct. 8, 1977. Intern, Mary Hitchcock Hosp., Hanover, N.H., 1965-66; resident in pathology, 1966-70; mem. faculty U. Mich., Ann Arbor, 1970—, assoc. prof. pathology, 1976-79, prof., 1979—. Mem. Am. Soc. Clin. Pathologists, Internat. Acad. Pathology, Pediatric Pathology Club, Coll. Am. Pathologists. Office: Dept Pathology Box 045 U Mich Ann Arbor MI 48109

HEIDEN, ANTONIETTE LOUISE (TONI), real estate broker; b. Santa Monica, Calif., Feb. 3, 1948; d. Donald Maurice and Marguerite Louise (Rosenberger) Mandrillo Torres; student Pierce Jr. Coll., 1967, San Fernando Valley State Coll., 1968, Mesa Coll., 1973-74, Colo. U., 1978-80; children—Chad Wesley, Trent Ashly. Owner, Clubhouse Crafts, Grand Junction, Colo., 1976-78; real estate broker Target Realtors, 1978-80, Home Owners Realty, 1980-81, Bray & Co., div. Better Homes & Gardens, 1981—. Mem. Nat. Assn. Realtors, Women's Council Realtors (ednl. chairperson), Grand Junction Bd. Realtors. Roman Catholic. Home: 2658 Bahamas Way Grand Junction CO 81501 Office: Bray & Co 1015 N 7th St Grand Junction CO 81501

HEIDKE, FLORITA LAUGHLIN (MRS. ROY ALBERT HEIDKE), educator, civic worker, artist; b. Chgo., Mar. 22, 1927; d. John Thomas and Florence (Hilb) Laughlin; B.E., Chgo. Tchrs. Coll., 1948; M.A., Northwestern U., 1952; student Chgo. Acad. Fine Arts, 1950; grad. work Chgo. Art Inst. and Chgo. Acad. Comml. Arts, U. Ill., 1976-80, Ariz. State U., 1980; m. Roy Albert Heidke, June 23, 1951 (div. Mar. 1982); children—Michel Marie Heidke Shane, Patricia Ann Heidke Diaz, William Geoffrey II, Amanda Jon. Tchr. public schs., Chgo., 1948-52; profl. muralist, 1955—; treas. Look & Heidke, Inc., Oak Lawn, Ill., 1958; featured columnist Southtown Economist Newspaper, 1959-63; supr. art Blue Island (Ill.) schs.; head ceramics sch. adult edn. Blue Island; tchr. art Community High Sch. Dist. 218, 1970—. Founder, Oak Lawn Youth Commn., 1955, sec., 1955-57, v.p., 1957-59; founder Ranch Manor Homeowners Assn. and Aux., 1954, v.p., 1955-58, pres., 1965-67; pres. Lawn Manor PTA, chmn. gov.'s commn. on Day Care Centers, 1970—; bd. dirs. March of Dimes Nat. Found., 1960—, Ill. Animal Welfare; v.p., social chmn. Christ Community Hosp. Women's Aux., 1971-73. Mem. Northwestern U. Alumni Assn., Chgo. Tchrs. Coll. Alumni Assn., Chgo. Tchrs. Union (social sec. to pres. 1951-62), AAUW, Am. Bicentennial Research Inst., ARC Assn., Nat. Soc. Lit. and Arts, Nat. Indian Arts Council. Home: 11024 S Keeler Ave Oak Lawn IL 60453 also 4800 N 68th St Scottsdale AZ 85251 Office: 5210 W 95th St Oak Lawn IL 60453

HEIDLER, NICOLE ROUSSEAU, ins. co. ofcl.; b. Suresnes, France, Apr. 9, 1915; d. Rene Jules and Genevieve (Abadie) Rousseau; came to U.S., 1947, naturalized, 1955; Baccalaureat Es Lettres, Lycee de Sevres (France), 1935; exchange student Ohio U., 1935-36; License es Lettres, U. Paris Sorbonne, 1943; certificate in Gen. Ins. Ins. Inst. Am., 1970; m. Harrison Hodgson, Nov. 26, 1948. Co-owner Maison Itard, home for exceptional children, Suresnes, 1942-47; asst. in French, Elmira Coll., 1947-48; Case Western Res. U., summer 1947; asst. prof. French and psychology Middle Ga. Coll., 1947-51; sec. to asst. purchasing agt. Turner-Supply Co., Mobile, Ala., 1951-54; sec. Thomas McElveen & Son, ins. adjusters, Miami, Fla., 1955-57; claims supr. casualty claims Ins. Servicing & Adjusting Co., Miami, 1957-80; instr. Fla. Internat. U., 1980. Mem. Fla. Ad Hoc Com. Ins. Reform Study, 1977-78; mem. adv. Council Ins. Inst., U. Miami, 1981—. Named Ins. Woman of Yr., Ins. Women Miami, 1970; lic. ins. adjuster, Fla.; cert. profl. ins. woman. Mem. Nat. Assn. Ins. Women (Region III Claims Woman of Yr. 1976, dir. Region III 1977-78, mem. exec. bd. 1977-78), Ins. Women South Dade (County, Fla.) (founding pres. 1973), South Fla. Claims Assn., Early Am. Soc. Democrat. Episcopalian. Editor: South Dade Pioneer, South Florida Claimsman. Home: PO Box 570758 Perrine Miami FL 33157

HEIFETZ, SONIA, ret. pharmacist; b. Rowne, Poland; d. Zise and Toiba (Ehrlich) Heifetz; came to U.S., 1929, naturalized, 1934; Ph.G., Temple U., 1933. Asst. chief pharmacist Grad. Hosp. U. Pa., Phila., 1937-49, dir. pharmacy services, 1949-77; formerly pharmacist-mgr. Rite-Aide Corp., now ret. Cert. tchr. of Russian, Phila. Bd. of Edn. div. sch. extension. Mem. Am. Soc. Hosp. Pharmacists, Del. Soc. Hosp. Pharmacists (hon.), Phila. Guild Hosp. Pharmacists (v.p. 1966, treas. 1967-77), AAUW. Home: 2665 Willits Rd Apt 32H Philadelphia PA 19114

HEIGHT, DOROTHY I., social worker; b. Richmond, Va., Mar. 24, 1912; M.A., N.Y. U.; postgrad. N.Y. Sch. Social Work. Mem. adv. com. on women in service Dept. Def., 1952-55; vis. prof. Delhi Sch. Social Work, New Delhi, India, 1952; now pres. Nat. Council of Negro Women, Inc., Washington. Mem. nat. bd. YWCA, dir. YMCA Center for Racial Justice; mem. N.Y. State Bd. Social Welfare, 1958-74; mem. Pres.'s Com. of Employment of Handicapped; mem. ad. hoc com. pub. welfare HEW; cons. for African affairs to sec. State, mem. women's com. Office Emergency Planning, Pres.'s Commn. on Status of Women, Pres.'s Commn. for Equal Employment Opportunity. Bd. dirs. CARE, Community Relations Service; bd. govs. A.R.C. Address: Nat Assn Negro Women 1819 H St NW Suite 900 Washington DC 20006 *

HEIKEN, BARBARA ELLEN, mgmt. cons.; b. Hartford, Conn., Apr. 25, 1949; d. Robert M. and Shirley (Mandell) Rayburn; A.B. (Univ. fellow) N.Y.U., 1971. Asst. to v.p. mktg. Am. Express Lang. Centers, N.Y.C., 1971-73; sr. tng. specialist Citibank, Long Island City, N.Y., 1973-75; orgn. devel. cons. internat. div., then adminstrv. mgr. personnel planning Chem. Bank, N.Y.C., 1975-78; v.p. human resources Kenmore, Inc., N.Y.C., 1979-81; pres. Randell-Heiken, Inc., N.Y.C., 1981—; instr. English as 2d lang. Mem. Am. Soc. Tng. and Devel., Human Resource Planning Soc., OD Network, Nat. Assn. Female Execs., Women Bus. Owners N.Y. Home: PO Box 307 Scarborough NY 10510 Office: 77 Bleecker Ct New York NY 10012

HEILMAN, LEONA (LEE) MARIE, educator; b. Denver, Sept. 21, 1929; d. Richard James and Marie Elizabeth (Smith) Lawrence; B.S., Colo. State U., 1951, M.S., No. Ill. U., 1974; m. Donald E. Heilman, Aug. 19, 1951; 1 son, Alan Edward. Owner, Easter Creations by Lee 1954-72; vocat. foods instr. DeKalb (Ill.) Sch. Dist. 428, 1966-77; asst. prof. dietitics, nutrition and food sci. No. Ill. U. 1977—; cons. in field. Mem. Am. Home Econs. Assn., Am. Vocat. Assn., Nat. Inst. Food Service Industries (recipient award for disting. service 1978), PEO, Delta Delta Delta. Congregationalist. Author: Eating Your Way Thru College Makes Good Sense 1979; Principles and Procedures of Basic Food Cookery 1980; Chicken-A Collection of Easy, Economical, Diet Delicious Chicken Recipes 1981. Home: 828 Dorken Ln DeKalb IL 60115 Office: 304 Wirtz Hall Northern Illinois University DeKalb IL 60115

HEILOMS, MAY, artist; b. Russia; d. Mark A. and Eugenie (Mogilensky) Levinson; naturalized, 1932; student Hunter Coll., 1929; student Art Students League; m. Samuel Heiloms, June 12, 1938. One man shows include: Silvermine Guild, Conn., Barry Coll., Miami, Fla., Jeannette Nessler Gallery, N.Y.C., Tex. Western Coll., El Paso, E. Central State Mus., Ada, Okla., S. Western State Coll., Weatherford, Okla., U. Wyo., Laramie, Oconee County Library, Walhalla, S.C., Cortland Art Center, N.Y., Paducah Art Guild, Ky., Okla. Baptist U., Shawnee, Warder Pub. Library, Springfield, Ohio, La Salle Coll., Phila., U. Maine, Utica (N.Y.) Pub. Library, Lafayette (Ind.) Art Assn., Hudson Guild Gallery, N.Y.C., Madison Sq. Garden Sports Gallery, N.Y.C., Madison Sq. Mus. of Sports, numerous others; group shows include: Pa. Acad. Fine Arts, Jersey City Mus., Butler Inst. Am. Art, Bklyn. Mus., Denver Mus., NAD, Am. Acad. Arts and Letters, also in Argentina, Mex., numerous others; traveling exhbns. include: Cleve. Mus. Art, Allbright Art Gallery, Buffalo, Dallas Mus., Corcoran Gallery, Washington, Rochester Meml. Art Gallery, others, also in Portugal, Greece, Italy, Belgium; represented in permanent collections: Phila. Mus. Art, Norfolk (Va.) Mus. Art, Samuel S. Fleisher Meml. Art Found., Bat Yam Mus. and Safad Mus. (Israel), Kenny Internat. Found., Smithsonian Instn., others; mem. faculty Fashion Inst. Tech.; adviser Ford Found. Program in Humanities, 1958, 59. Recipient numerous prizes and awards, including: Jersey City Mus., 1956; M. Grumbacher prize for watercolor, 1963; prize for oil Nat. Arts Soc., 1975. Fellow Royal Acad. Art (London); mem. Painters and Sculptors N.J. (hon. life pres. 1st prize 1952-55, prize for oil 1974, 75), Audubon Soc. Artists (past v.p.), Am. Painters and Sculptors (dir.), Nat. Soc. Painters Casein (dir., prize for casein 1973, 75), Am. Soc. Contemporary Artists (prizes for oil 1966, 68, 71, 72, 80), Allied Artists, N.Y. Soc. Women Artists (corr. sec.), Artists Equity, Nat. Assn. Women Artists (Atwood Klinger prize 1954), Bklyn. Soc. Artists, Knickerbocker Artists, Manhattan Gallery Group, Silvermine Guild, Conn. Women Artists. Studio: 340 W 28th St New York NY 10001

HEIMAN, JULIA RUE, clin. psychologist; b. Phoenix, Oct. 27, 1948; d. Edward and Ruth H.; B.A., Ariz. State U., 1970; Ph.D., SUNY, Stony Brook, 1975. Sr. research scientist and research instr. L.I. Research Inst. and SUNY, Stony Brook, 1975-77, research scientist V and research asst. prof., 1979-81; asso. dir. research services Sex Therapy Center at Stony Brook, 1978-81, chief Lab. Marital and Interpersonal Problems, 1978-81; asst. prof. psychiatry and behavioral scis. U. Wash., Seattle, 1981—; research coordinator Harborview Community Mental Health Center, Seattle; cons., workshop leader Am. Assn. Sex Educators, Counselors and Therapists; lectr. community orgns. NIMH grantee, 1976-79, 79—; NIH grantee, 1976-81. Mem. Am. Psychol. Assn., Soc. Psychotherapy Research, Internat. Acad. Sex Research, N.Y. Council Research Scientists, Soc. Sci. Study of Sex, Phi Kappa Phi. Editorial rev. bd. Jour. Applied Behavior Analysis, 1976-79, Archives Sexual Behavior, 1979—, Jour. Sex Research, 1978—; author: Becoming Orgasmic: A Sexual Growth Program for Woman (with L. and J. LoPiccolo), 1976; co-author films for therapeutic use. Home: 4006 Greenwood Av N Seattle WA 98103 Office: U Wash Z-A-31 Seattle WA 98195

HEIMANN, JUDITH BARTMANN, state ofcl.; b. Frankfurt/Main, Germany, Aug. 23, 1920; came to U.S., 1947, naturalized, 1949; d. Peter and Margarethe Helene (Hahn) Bartmann; B.A. in Bacteriology, U. Ariz., 1950; m. Ernest Heimann, Aug. 23, 1947; children—Stephen Bartmann, Marga Linotte. Interpreter, Am. Mil. Govt., 1945-47; researcher in biochemistry U. Ariz., 1950-52; partner Greystone Assos., 1977—; commr. Md. Nat. Capital Park and Planning Commn., 1979—. Trustee, LWV Edn. Fund, 1974-78, LWV Overseas Edn. Fund, 1974-80; mem. Commn. for Women Montgomery County, 1972-73; mem. Bicentennial Commn. Montgomery County; vice chmn. Ethics Commn., Montgomery County, 1976-79. Recipient citation Montgomery County Council, 1976; Md. Gov.'s citation, 1979. Mem. Am. Planning Assn., Am. Acad. Polit. and Social Sci., LWV (pres. Montgomery County 1969-73, v.p. Md., 1973-74, nat. dir. 1974-78), Phi Beta Kappa, Phi Kappa Phi. Democrat. Office: 8787 Georgia Ave Silver Spring MD 20907

HEIMANN, SANDRA W., ins. co. exec.; b. Cin., Feb. 16, 1943; d. William Franklin and Margot Lestor (Warner) Woeste; student U. Cin.; m. Robert Alvin, Dec. 7, 1968; children—Robert Alvin, Paige Ann. Vice pres. Am. Fin. Corp., 1969—, also v.p., sec. various subs; v.p. Great Am. Ins. Co., 1973—. Mem. Cin. Downtown Council; dir. Hospice; trustee Hyde Park Community Methodist Ch. Republican. Home: 7315 Sanderson St Cincinnati OH 45243 Office: 1 E 4th St Cincinnati OH 45202

HEIN, LUCILLE ELEANOR, author; b. Chgo., June 11, 1915; d. Ernest and Sena Elena (Midthun) H.; B.A., U. Wis., 1937, M.A., 1938. Grad. fellow, teaching aide U. Wis., 1938-40; instr. English, Wagner Coll., S.I., 1940-44; occasional tchr. N.Y.C. area, 1944—; freelance writer, 1950—; author: Enjoy Your Children, 1959; One Small Circle, 1962; Enjoying the Outdoors with Children, 1966; We Talk With God, 1968; Thinking of You, 1969; I Can Make My Own Prayers, 1971; Entertaining Your Child, 1971; Prayer Gifts for Christmas, 1972; Walking in God's World, 1972; A Tree I Can Call My Own, 1974; My Very Special Friend, 1974; From Sea to Shining Sea, 1975; That Wonderful Summer, 1978; Thank You God, 1981. Editor: The Complete Book of Campfire Programs, 1958; She Maners: The Teen Girl's Book of Etiquette, 1959; Leadership in Voluntary Enterprises, 1961; The Book of Outdoor Winter Activities, 1962; Rainy Day Fun for Kids, 1962. Lutheran. Address: 33 Central Ave Staten Island NY 10301

HEINEMANN, KATHERINE (KAKI), poet; b. St. Louis, Aug. 13, 1918; d. Herbert N. and Elsa S. (Straus) Arnstein; B.S., Washington U., St. Louis, 1950, M.A. (Arts and Scis. Faculty award 1950), 1956; m. Morton D. May, 1937; children—David A., Philip F.; m. 2d, Sol Heinemann, July 8, 1950; 1 dau., Kate Heinemann Tauscher. Freelance writer, poet, 1960—; tchr. English composition and lit. U. Tex., El Paso, 1968-74; condr. poetry readings, workshops, 1968—; mem. El Paso Art Resources Dept. Bd., 1980-81; author: Brandings, 1968; reading for Poetry Archives of Library of Congress, 1982. Mem. PEN, Nat. Soc. Arts and Letters. Clubs: Coronado Country, El Paso Tennis, Sunset Heights Garden, First Wednesday History. Home: 4252 Ridge Crest Dr El Paso TX 79902

HEINRICH, LAURA JEAN, corp. communications specialist; b. Saginaw, Mich., Sept. 21, 1938; d. William and Edna Margaret (Stiehl) H.; A.B., Kalamazoo Coll., 1959; M.A. in Library Sci., U. Mich., 1968, M.A., 1970, Ph.D., 1972; m. W.A. Haselhorst, May 29, 1976; 1 son, William. Public sch. tchr., 1959-70; mem. faculty Kans. State U., 1971-73; mgmt. cons., 1970-74; dir. EEO, Macomb County Community Coll., 1974-75; asst. prin. Van Hoosen Jr. High, Rochester, Mich., 1975-76; asst. dir. Ala. Info. and Devel. Systems, 1976-77; mem. faculty U. Ala., Birmingham, 1977-78, U. Cin., 1978-79; ombudsperson, coordinator mgmt. tng., mgr. socio-tech. programs aircraft engine group Gen. Electric Co., 1979-82; dir. corp. communications and orgnl. devel. Pneumo Corp., 1982—. Trustee, Sch. Found. Greater Cin. Mem. Am. Soc. Tng. and Devel., NOW, Nat. Women's Polit. Caucus, Organizational Devel. Network. Office: 3781 E 77th St Cleveland OH 44105

HEINS, ETHEL LEAH, magazine editor, critic; b. N.Y.C., Apr. 9, 1918; d. H.H. and Rose Yaskin; A.B., Douglass Coll., Rutgers U., 1938; postgrad. Columbia U., Harvard U.; m. Paul Heins, June 27, 1943; children—Peter S., Margery E. Children's librarian N.Y. Public Library, 1938-43, Louisville Free Public Library, 1943-44, Boston Public Library, 1956-62; instructional media specialist Lexington (Mass.) Public Schs., 1962-74; editor Horn Book mag., Boston, 1974—; mem. faculty Center Study Children's Lit., Simmons Coll., Boston; lectr., cons., author, reviewer, judge children's book awards. Recipient citation Rutgers U., 1979, named to Douglass Soc., 1981. Mem. ALA, Nat. Council Tchrs. English, Children's Lit. Assn., Internat. Research Soc. Children's Lit., New Eng. Library Assn., New Eng. Roundtable Children's Librarians, Mass. Library Assn., Mass. Tchrs. Assn. Office: Horn Book Park Sq Bldg Boston MA 02116

HEINTZ, BONNIE LEE, educator; b. Junction City, Kans., June 28, 1924; d. Ralph and Dorritt Margaret (Wilgocki) H.; student Midland Coll., Pacific Lutheran U.; B.A., U. Puget Sound, 1949; M.A., U. Wash., 1961, later postgrad. With Tacoma Times; editor U. Puget Sound Alumnus; staff U. Wash., 1949-50, Skagit Valley Jr. Coll., 1950-52; dist. dir. GSA, 1952-59; prof. English, humanities div. Seattle Pacific U., 1960—; editor Lambda Iota Tau newspaper; Ogham adviser, dept. geophysics U. Tex. Mem. Gov.'s Com. for Year 2000, 1965-73, mem. steering com., 1972-73; active Friends of Library, 1969—; bibliographer Pondicherry Lodge, Baker St. Irregulars, 1961-75, Dorothy L. Sayers Soc., 1976—. Named Outstanding Educator, 1972, 73. HEW grantee, 1971. Mem. Nat. Council Tchrs. English, Royal Irish Acad. (corr.), Am. Camping Assn., World Wildlife Soc., Nat. Hist. Archaeologists Soc., Internat. Underwater Archeology, Nat. Hist. Soc. Methodist. Clubs: Egotist, L.I.T. Author: Spindrift, 1949; Tomorrow and Tomorrow and Tomorrow, 1973; Ternion, 1978; The Stones of the Field, 1978-79; From Under the Horns of the Unicorns, 1981. Office: Dept Humanities Seattle Pacific U Seattle WA 98119

HEINTZ, JANICE ROWENA STRUM, editor; b. Rock Island, Ill., Jan. 21, 1936; d. Morris and Rebecca (Baron) Strum; B.A., Art Inst. Chgo., 1957; M.A., U. Chgo., 1958; m. Larry Deane Heintz, Mar. 6, 1965; 1 son, Baron Strum. Advt. illustrator M.L. Parker Co., Davenport, Iowa, 1958-59; reporter, artist, feature editor Quad-City Times, Davenport, 1959-62; advt. copywriter Disney Studios, Chgo., 1962-63; copywriter, creative promotional writer and designer Better Homes and Gardens mag., Des Moines, 1963-65; freelance illustrator and writer, 1965-76; lifestyle editor Daily Dispatch, Moline, Ill., 1976—. Bd. dirs. Davenport Mcpl. Art Gallery, 1979—. Mem. Nat. Fedn. Press Women, Ill. Press Women, Mississippi Valley Press Club (founder), Fashion Group, Midwest Women in Art, Nu Kappa Kappa. One-woman art exhbns. advt. design, portraits and comml. designs, Chgo., 1957. Office: 1720 5th Ave Moline IL 61265

HEINTZELMAN, CAROL ANN, social worker; b. Allentown, Pa., Sept. 24, 1942; d. Allen George and Emma Amanda (Strauss) H.; B.A., diploma social work (Luth. Ch. Am. fellow), Muhlenberg Coll., Pa., 1965; M.S.W. (Luth. Ch. Am. fellow), Howard U., 1970 D.S.W., Cath. U. Am., 1980. Instr. social welfare and sociology Shepherd Coll., Shepherdstown, W.Va., 1971-75; teaching asst. Cath. U. Am., 1975-76; asst. prof. social work Elizabethtown (Pa.) Coll., 1976-77, Millersville (Pa.) State Coll., 1978—; pres., bd. dirs. Eastern region Luth. Social Services, Elizabethtown Child Care Center. Mem. Nat. Assn. Social Workers, AAUW, Council Social Work Edn., Acad. Cert. Social Workers, Delta Kappa Gamma. Democrat. Home: 409 N Market St Elizabethtown PA 17022 Office: 225 McComsey Hall Millersville PA 17552

HEINZ, ELISE BROOKFIELD, lawyer; b. Plainfield, N.J., Jan. 14, 1935; d. Winfield Bernard and Rachel Edwards (Clarke) H.; B.A., Wellesley Coll., 1955; LL.B. cum laude, Harvard U., 1961; m. James Edwin Clayton, 1961; children—Jonathan Brown Clayton, David Lake Clayton. Admitted to D.C. bar, 1961, Va. bar, 1969, U.S. Supreme Ct., 1969; asso. firm Fowler, Leva, Hawes & Symington, Washington, 1961-64; individual practice law, Washington, 1964-69, Arlington, Va., 1969—; mem. Va. Ho. of Dels., 1978-82; adj. prof. Georgetown U. Law Center. Mem. Chesapeake and Ohio Canal Nat. Hist. Park Commn., 1982—. Mem. ABA, Va. State Bar, Arlington County Bar Assn., D.C. Bar, Va. Women Lawyers Assn., Am. Law Inst., Nat. Women's Polit. Caucus, LWV, AAUW, Women's Equity Action League, Nat. Parks Assn., Izaak Walton League, Appalachian Tr. Conf. Democrat. Office: 2728 N Fillmore St Arlington Va 22207

HEINZE, RUTH-INGE, profl. assn. exec.; b. Berlin, Nov. 4, 1919; came to U.S., 1955, naturalized, 1962; d. Franz Albert and Louise Auguste Marie (Preschel) Heinze; diploma, Interpreter Coll., Berlin, 1952; B.A., U. Calif., Berkeley, 1969, Ph.D., 1974. Lectr., course designer adult edn., San Francisco, 1956-72; editor Follett Pub. Co., Chgo., 1955-56; lectr., course designer adult edn. Berlin, 1963-68; producer, writer monthly ednl. radio program, Berlin, 1963-73; research fellow Nat. Mus., Bangkok, Thailand, 1972; lectr. U. Chiangmai, 1972, Mills Coll., Oakland, Calif., 1974; staff research asst. U. Calif., San Francisco, 1975; Fulbright Hays research fellow Inst. S.E. Asian Studies, Singapore, 1978-79; research assoc. Center for S. & S.E. Asia Studies, U. Calif., Berkeley, 1974—; dir., editor Asian Folklore Studies Group, 1977—; nat. dir. Ind. Scholars of Asia, 1981—; lectr. in field. Am. Inst. Indian Studies grantee, 1975, 78; named Outstanding German-Am. Citizen of East Bay, Internat. Inst., 1980. Mem. Assn. for Asian Studies, Internat. Assn. Study of Traditional Asian Medicine, Ind. Scholars of Asia, Asian Folklore Studies Group, U. Calif. Alumni Assn., Langley Porter Psychiatric Inst. Alumni Faculty Assn., Fulbright Alumni Assn. Club: Friends of Ethnic Art. Contbr. numerous articles to profl. jours.; author: The Biography of Ajhan Man, 1977; Tham Khwan-How to Contain the Essence of Life, a Socio-Psychological Comparison of a Thai Custom, 1982; The Role of the Sangha in Modern Thailand, 1977, others. Home: 2321 Russell Apt 3A Berkeley CA 94705 Office: 260 Stephens Hall Univ Calif Berkeley CA 94720

HEISER, LORAINE MARY, state legislator; b. Chgo., Apr. 20, 1928; d. Michael S. and Helen Rams; B.S., No. Ill. U., 1949; m. Richard S. Heiser, Aug. 21, 1952; children—James Stevens, Claire Ann. Nutritionist, Cook County Hosp., Chgo., 1949; home economist Commonwealth Edison Co., 1950-52; tchr. Chgo. Public Schs., 1950-53; mem. Pa. Ho. of Reps., 1980—. Bd. dirs. Women's Center and Shelter Greater Pitts.; alt. del. Republican Conv., 1976; chmn. Ross Twp. Rep. Com.; pres. Women's Center North Hills; mem. Allegheny County Rep. Com. Rules; chmn. Leadership Tng. Com. Recipient Good Govt. award Jr. C. of C., 1978. Mem. Am. Legis. Exchange Council, AAUW (Outstanding Woman 1978), Bus. and Profl. Women (Woman of Yr., North Hills 1981). Club: Zonta. Office: PO Box 179 Main Capitol Bldg Harrisburg PA 17120

HEISLER, NORMA BOODMAN, psychotherapist; b. N.Y.C., Nov. 11, 1933; d. David Louis and Belle (Hochstein) Boodman; cert. Pratt Inst., 1956; B.A. in Psychology, Bklyn. Coll., 1972; M.S.W., N.Y. U., 1977; postgrad. N.Y. Sch. for Study of Psychoanalytic Psychotherapy, 1979-82; m. Arthur Heisler, Aug. 9, 1952; children—Miriam, Daniel. Personnel asst. A. H. Miller, N.Y.C., 1952-56; free lance comml. artist Wolf Studios and Lowenstein Studios, 1957-69; art therapist, N.Y., 1970-71; tchr. Yeshivak Ohel Moshe, N.Y.C., 1971-72; family counselor, art therapist Lillian Sklar Filler Day Care Center, N.Y.C., 1973-76; therapy intern L.I. Coll. Hosp., N.Y.C., 1976-77; tchr. adult edn. Kingsborough Community Coll., N.Y.C., 1978-79; psychotherapist N.Y. Psychotherapy and Counseling Center, 1978—, also pvt. practice; one-woman shows of paintings include: Jewish Community House, N.Y.C., 1960; 2-person show: Ahda Artzt Gallery, 1969; group shows include: Caravan Art Gallery, 1953, 54, 55, Bklyn. Mus. (award), 1956, 57, Duncan Gallery, 1958, Art U.S.A., 1958, Kottler Mus., 1958, Directions Gallery, 1959, Boston Art Festival, 1960, Pa. Acad. Fine Arts, Phila., 1961, St. Louis U., 1962, Ruth Sherman Gallery, 1965, N.Y. World's Fair, Ahda Artz Group, 1970, 71. Recipient Latham award for brotherhood, 1954, 55, 56, 57, 59; Grumbacher award of merit, 1960; other art awards. Mem. Nat. Assn. Social Workers, Soc. Advancement of Psychoanalytic Developmental Psychology. Jewish. Home: 2373 E 7th St Brooklyn NY 11223 Office: 796H Drew St Brooklyn NY 11208

HEISTAD, MURIEL HUBBARD, ret. speech pathologist; b. Weatersfield, Vt., Apr. 25, 1908; d. Fred B. and Josephine (Flint) Hubbard; B.S., Arnold Coll., 1929; M.A., U. Mass., 1973; m. Erling Heistad, Apr. 1, 1933; children—Mary Frederica, Erling Harlan, Donna Lou. Instr. phys. edn., coach, referee Lebanon (N.H.) High Sch., 1929-30, Claremont (N.H.) Public Schs., 1930-33; child welfare worker Grafton County (N.H.) Welfare Dept., Woodsville, 1956-62; speech pathologist Pittsfield (Mass.) Schs., 1969-72, Brandon (Vt.) Schs., 1972-78, Poultney (Vt.) Schs., 1978-79, Fair Haven (Vt.) Schs., 1979-80. Mem. Am. Speech and Hearing Assn. (cert. clinician in speech pathology). Author: Stuttering and Respiration, 1977. Address: 12 Riverdale Pkwy Lebanon NH 03766

HEITMAN, BETTY GREEN, polit. party ofcl.; b. Malvern, Ark., Nov. 27, 1929; d. George Anderson and Inell (Cooper) Green; B.S., Tex. Women's U., 1949; m. Henry Schrader Heitman, Apr. 3, 1951; children—Donna Inell, Thomas Haile, Perry Schrader, Paul Anderson. Adminstrv. dietician Hotel Dieu Hosp., New Orleans, 1950-51, Clarkson Meml. Hosp., Omaha, 1951-52; pediatric dietician Charity Hosp., New Orleans, 1952-53; pres. Nat. Fedn. Republican Women, Washington, 1978-80; mem. Republican Nat. Com., Washington, 1974-77, co-chmn., 1980—, del. convs., 1968, 76. Co-chmn. La. 6th Congressional Dist. Rep. Action Council, 1964-66; membership chmn. La. Fedn. Rep. Women, 1964-66, pres., 1967-71; mem. La. State Rep. Central Com., 1972-79. Recipient Disting. Alumna award Tex. Women's U., 1980; named Hon. Citizen Tex., 1980. Episcopalian. Office: 310 1st St SE Washington DC 20003

HEITSCHMIDT, DONNETTA LYNN, educator; b. Manhattan, Kans., Apr. 20, 1952; d. Bobby Charles and Lavel Ann (Russell) H.; B.S., Kans. State U., 1973; M.A. in Journalism and Communications, U. Fla., 1974; Ph.D. (Coll. Student Personnel Adminstrn. scholar, 1978-79), U. No. Colo., 1979. Instr. English and journalism, student publs. adviser Daytona Beach (Fla.) Community Coll., 1974-77, 82—; resident advisor U. No. Colo., Greeley, 1977-78, fin. aid counselor, grad. asst., 1978-79; dir. student activities Odessa (Tex.) Coll., 1979-80; ednl. services coordinator Nat. Assn. for Campus Activities, Columbia, S.C., 1980-82; part time English instr. Midlands Tech. Coll., Columbia; leader human potential seminars. Mem. local com. to review ecumenical statement of Luth. Ch. Am. synod; charter mem. Profl. Bus. Women of Odessa. Mem. Women in Communication, Nat. Council Coll. Publ. Advisers, Nat. Assn. Student Personnel Adminstrs., Kans. State U. Alumni Assn., Chimes, Kappa Delta Pi. Compiler Programmers' Handbook, 1981; editor, contbr. article to publ. in field. Home: 500 Shadow Lakes Blvd Apt 135 Ormond Beach FL 32074 Office: Daytona Beach Community College PO Box 1111 Daytona Beach FL 32015

HELD, BARBARA SUSAN, psychologist; b. N.Y.C., Mar. 5, 1950; d. Milton H. and Harriette (Kornblum) H.; B.A. in Psychology, Douglass Coll., Rutgers U., 1972; Ph.D. in Psychology (NIMH tng. fellow), U. Nebr., Lincoln, 1979; m. David C. Bellows, Aug. 18, 1974. Intern in psychology Tex. Research Inst. Mental Scis., Tex. Med. Center, Houston, 1978-79; psychol. cons. Bath-Brunswick Area Mental Health Center, Brunswick, Maine, 1979-81; asst. prof. psychology Bowdoin Coll., Brunswick, 1979—, Mellon Fund new course devel. grantee, 1980; pvt. practice clin. psychology, Brunswick, 1981—; supr., cons. specializing in family therapy for Maine mental health profls. Lic. psychologist, Maine. Mem. Am. Psychol. Assn., Phi Beta Kappa. Contbr. articles to profl. publs. Office: Psychology Dept Bowdoin Coll Brunswick ME 04011

HELD, NANCY JEAN GRAFFAM, educator; b. Winnipeg, Can., Oct. 27, 1932; d. Harry Earl and Gladys (Fie) Graffam; student Iowa State U., 1950; B.S., Drake U., 1954, M.S., 1955; m. Charles Holborn Held, Mar. 25, 1967; children—Heidi Alice, Kirstin Lucretia. Dir. Visual edn. tchr. sch. Northbrook (Ill.) pub. schs., 1954-55; tchr. pub. schs., Deerfield, Ill., 1956; asso. prof. edn. and psychology, head dept. elementary edn. Iowa Wesleyan Coll., Mt. Pleasant, 1957-60; prof. edn. Albion (Mich.) Coll., 1960—; vis. prof. edn. Mich. State U., 1965. Mem. AAUW, Phi Beta Kappa, Phi Kappa Phi, Kappa Delta Pi. Presbyterian. Home: 1155 River's Bend Albion MI 49224 Office: Albion Coll Albion MI 49224

HELD, SHIRLEY ELAINE, educator, weaver; b. Hinton, Iowa, Aug. 21, 1923; d. Albert Herbert and Neva Lucille (Royer) H.; B.S., Iowa State U., 1945, M.S., 1952. Tchr. home econs., Lake City (Iowa) Public Schs., 1945-46, LeMars (Iowa) Public Schs., 1946-47, Humboldt (Iowa) Public Schs., 1947-51; asst. prof. clothing, textiles Utah State U., Logan, 1952-53; prof. art and design Iowa State U., Ames, 1953—. Mem. Iowa Fedn. Handweavers and Spinners, Midwest Weavers Assn., Handweavers Guild Am., Am. Crafts Council, World Crafts Council. United Methodist. Author: Weaving: A Handbook of the Fiber Arts, 2d edit., 1978. Office: Design Coll Iowa State U Ames IA 50011

HELD, VIRGINIA, philosopher; b. Mendham, N.J., Oct. 28, 1929; d. John Howard Nott and Margaretta (Wood) Potter; A.B., Barnard Coll., 1950; Ph.D., Columbia U., 1968; divorced; children—Julia, Philip. Mem. staff Reporter mag., 1954-65; lectr. philosophy Barnard Coll., 1964-66; mem. faculty Hunter Coll., CUNY, 1965—, prof. philosophy Grad. Sch., 1977—; vis. lectr. Yale U., 1972; dir. Nat. Endowment Humanities Summer Seminar, Stanford U. Law Sch., 1981; vis. scholar Harvard U. Law Sch., 1981-82. Fulbright fellow, 1950; fellow Rockefeller Found., 1975-76. Mem. Am. Philos. Assn. (exec. com. Eastern div. 1979-81), Columbia U. Seminars (assoc.), Conf. Methods (exec. com. 1971—), Internat. Assn. Philosophy Law and Social Philosophy (pres. Am. sect. 1981-83), Soc. Philosophy and Public Affairs (chmn. 1972), Soc. Women in Philosophy. Democrat. Author: The Public Interest and Individual Interests, 1970; also articles. Editor: The Property, Profits and Economic Justice, 1980; co-editor: Philosophy and Political Action, 1972; Philosophy, Morality and International Affairs, 1974. Office: Dept Philosophy City U NY Grad Sch 33 W 42d St New York NY 10036

HELFERT, KAREN ELIZE, nurse; b. Mpls., May 18, 1941; d. Donald Arthur and Ardeth Eileen (Olson) Sander; B.A., U. Md., 1963; R.N. (Outstanding Nursing Grad. 1976), Montgomery Coll., Takoma Park, Md., 1976; M.S. in Nursing, Catholic U. Am., 1979; widow; children—Kathrine, Samantha, Lisa. Instr. nursing Georgetown U., 1979—, cons. adolescent intervention team, 1979. Vice pres., chmn. coms. Commn. Women Montgomery County (Md.), 1970-75; adv. council Suburban Hosp., Bethesda, Md., 1979; vice chmn. Code 3, citizens criminal justice orgn.; Democratic precinct chmn., Montgomery County; newsletter editor parish council Holy Cross Ch., Garrett Park, Md.; area coordinator Yellow Ribbons for the Hostages, 1980-81. Mem. Am. Nurses Assn., Md. Nurses Assn., Montgomery County Gifted/Talented Assn., Club des Admirateurs de Gaëtan Duchesne (pres. 1981—), Sigma Theta Tau, Gamma Phi Beta. Author papers in field. Home: 11429 Ashley Dr Rockville MD 20852 Office: St Mary's Georgetown Univ Washington DC 20057

HELGANZ, BEVERLY BUZHARDT, telephone co. exec.; b. Tampa, Fla., June 7, 1941; d. M. Owain and Virginia Myers (Crabb) Buzhardt; A.A., Jacksonville U., 1962, B.A., 1974; m. Charles F. Helganz, Jr., June 26, 1964 (dec.). With So. Bell Tel. and Tel. Co., Jacksonville, Fla., 1959—, bus. office supr., tng. supr., 1966-76, employee relations supr., 1977-78, staff supr. equal employment opportunity, 1978-79, asst. mgr. bldg. ops., 1979-80, asso. mgr. real estate, staff mgr. personnel 1980—. Mem. Am. Bus. Women's Assn. (past pres.), Jacksonville Alumnae Panhellenic Assn. (formerly rec. sec., v.p., pres. 1981-82), Jacksonville Mus. Arts and Scis., Jacksonville U. Alumni Assn., Zeta Tau Alpha (past pres., dist. pres. 1979-81), Beta Sigma Phi (past pres.). Methodist. Clubs: Pilot Internat., University. Home: PO Box 1825 Jacksonville FL 32201

HELGESON-GONYA, NANCY LEE, educator; b. Emmetsburg, Iowa, July 20, 1952; d. Clarence Tilbert and Doris Jean (Clark) Helgeson; B.S., Iowa State U., 1974; postgrad. UCLA, 1979—. With Calif. Dept. Corrections, Parole Services, Santa Barbara, 1975-76; trainer/counselor Los Angeles Innovative Counselor Training and Placement Program, 1976-77; placement dir. Los Angeles Job Corps, 1977-79; program dir. TWA Univance Career Center, Los Angeles, 1979; personnel officer/career devel. coordinator Union Bank, Los Angeles, 1980-82; instr. dept. human devel. UCLA Extension, 1981-82; cons. in career planning and mgmt. Mem. Los Angeles Jr. C. of C. (chmn. 1980), Personnel and Indsl. Relations Assn., Am. Soc. Tng. and Devel., Women in Bus., Internat. Assn. for Personnel Women, Nat. Women's Polit. Caucus, Am. Personnel and Guidance Assn.

HELIOFF, ANNE GRAILE, painter; b. Liverpool, Eng.; d. Max and Frances Elizabeth (Beilenson) H.; student Columbia U., Art Students League, N.Y.C.; m. Benjamin Michael Hirschberg. One-woman exhbns. include: Capricorn Gallery, N.Y.C., 1966-69, Phoenix Gallery, N.Y.C., 1972, 74, 76, 82; group exhbns. include Milch Gallery, N.Y.C., 1940, Nat. Gallery Art, Pa. Acad. Ann., Art U.S.A., also 6 Americans in France, traveling show, 1976, museums in Florence and Naples, Italy; mem. U.S. del. 5th Congress Internat. Assn. Art, Tokyo, 1966; mem. Phoenix Gallery, N.Y.C., Ann Leonard Gallery, Woodstock, N.Y.; dir. exhbns. Recipient Silver medal Albany (N.Y.) Mus. Art and Sci., 1957; Homer Boss scholar, 1939; Y. Kuniyoshi scholar, 1940-45. Mem. Woodstock Artists Assn. (life, past dir.), Art Students League (past dir.), Am. Soc. Contemporary Artists (past dir.; award in oil, watercolor and acrylic), Nat. Assn. Women Artists, N.Y. Soc. Women Artists (past dir.). Home: 14 Neher St Woodstock NY 12498 Office: 340 W 28th St New York NY 10001

HELLER, JANET EGGLESTON, credit union mgr.; b. Middletown, N.Y., Sept. 16, 1934; d. John Francis and Alwilda Zella (DeGraw) Eggleston; B.A.S., Hartwick Coll., 1956; m. Owen E. Heller, July 5, 1956; children—Erich E., Gretchen E. With Nuri Mirro Co., Egg Harbor City, N.J., 1957-58, Navy Exchange, Quonset, R.I., 1958-60, Credit Union, Long Beach Naval Sta., Calif., 1967-68; with Lakehurst (N.J.) Naval Fed. Credit Union, 1969—, gen. mgr., 1976—. Vice pres. PTA, Long Beach Elem. Sch., 1966-68; pres. PTA, Lakehurst Elem. Sch., 1970-72; treas. Lakehurst Little League, 1970-75; mem. Lakehurst Bd. Edn., 1973-76; sec. cub pack Boy Scouts Am., Lakehurst, 1973-76, sec. troop 10, 1974-76; leader Girl Scouts U.S.A., Lakehurst, 1976-78. Mem. Credit Union Exec. Soc. (program dir. N.J. council 1979—), N.J. Credit Union League (edn. dir. chpt. 1969—, sec. chpt. 1980—), Hartwick Coll. Alumni Assn., Alpha Omicron Pi. Republican. Lutheran. Clubs: Eagles Aux., Women of Moose. Home: 413 Union Ave Lakehurst NJ 08733 Office: Lakehurst Naval Fed Credit Union NAEC Lakehurst NJ 08733

HELLER, JOAN CAROL, social worker; b. Detroit, Dec. 1, 1948; d. Raymond K. and Elise (Cohen) Rubiner; B.A., U. Iowa, 1970; M.S.W., U. Ill., 1973; postgrad. Northwestern U. Inst. Psychiatry, 1975-77; m. Richard H. Heller, Aug. 31, 1969. Cons. Northbrook Police Dept., Family Service Center of Wilmette, Glenview, Northbrook and Kenilworth, Wilmette, Ill., 1973-76, dir. Crisis Intervention Unit, Northbrook (Ill.) Police Dept., 1976—; pvt. practice social work, Glencoe, Ill., 1976—; cons. Mem. Evanston Community Com., 1970-73. Mem. Nat. Assn. Social Workers, Assn. Police Social Workers. Home: 430 Oakland Dr Highland Park IL 60035

HELLER, JOYCE COFFEY, speech pathologist, audiologist; b. Newark, Sept. 29, 1930; d. Meyer William and Helen (Nass) Coffey; B.S., Syracuse U., 1952; M.A., City U. N.Y., 1954; Ph.D., N.Y. U., 1968; m. Joseph Heller, July 1, 1954; children—Scott, Patricia. Faculty, Kean Coll. of N.J., Union, 1964—, prof. speech pathology, dept. spl. edn. 1975—; research asso. in speech pathology, div. plastic surgery, Center for Craniofacial Disorders, Montefiore Hosp., Bronx, N.Y., 1969—; cons. speech pathology N.J. Dept. Spl. Edn., Trenton, 1970—; asst. prof. orthodontics Fairleigh Dickinson U. Dental Sch., Teaneck, N.J., 1973—. Mem. Internat. Assn. Logopedics and Phoniatrics, Am. Speech and Hearing Assn., N.J. Speech and Hearing Assn. (pres. 1975-76), Am. Cleft Palate Assn., Am. Cleft Palate Ednl. Found. (pres. 1979—), Pi Lambda Theta. Contbr. articles in field to profl. jours. Office: Kean Coll of NJ Dept Speech Pathology/Audiology Morris Ave Union NJ 07083

HELLER, LOIS JANE, physiologist; b. Detroit, Jan. 4, 1942; d. John and Lona Elizabeth (Stockmeyer) Skagerberg; B.A., Albion (Mich.) Coll., 1964; M.S., U. Mich., 1966; Ph.D., U. Ill., Chgo., 1970; m. Robert E. Heller, May 21, 1966; children—John Robert, Euzanne Elizabeth. Instr., then asst. prof. physiology U. Ill. Med. Center, Chgo., 1970-72; mem. faculty U. Minn. Med. Sch., Duluth, 1972—, assoc. prof. physiology, 1977—, asst. dean student affairs, 1973-76; mem. research com. Minn. chpt. and Gt. Plains region Am. Heart Assn., 1978-82, chmn. bd. Minn. chpt., 1982-83. Recipient Outstanding Alumnus award Albion Coll., 1982. Mem. Am. Physiol. Soc., Sigma Xi. Co-author: Cardiovascular Physiology, 1981. Contbr. articles to profl. jours. Home: 311 Halsey St Duluth MN 55803 Office: Dept Physiology U Minn Med Sch Duluth MN 55812

HELLER-MAIBOR, DEBRA KAY, speech and lang. pathologist; b. Wilkes Barre, Pa., Nov. 17, 1951; d. Ralph Reuben and Jean Arlene (Sullum) H.; B.S. summa cum laude, Ohio U., Athens, 1973; M.S., U. Mich., 1974. Speech and lang. pathologist Beverly (Mass.) Public Schs., 1975-78, Perkins Sch. for Blind, Watertown, Mass., 1978—; field supr. student clinicians Boston U., Northeastern U. Mem. United Cerebral Palsy Assn., Nat. Head Injury Found. Mem. Am. Speech and Hearing Assn., Mass. Speech and Hearing Assn., Phi Kappa Phi. Club: B'nai B'rith Women (charter mem. Greater Boston single unit). Home: 32 Whites Ave 114 Watertown MA 02172 Office: 175 N Beacon St Watertown MA 02172

HELLMAN, LILLIAN, playwright; b. New Orleans, June 20, 1907; d. Max B. and Julia (Newhouse) H.; ed. N.Y.U., Columbia U.; M.A., Tufts Coll., 1940; Litt. D. (hon.), Wheaton Coll., 1961, Rutgers U., 1963, Brandeis U., 1965, Smith Coll., 1974, N.Y.U., 1974, Yale U., 1974, Franklin and Marshall Coll., 1975; Columbia U., 1976; m. Arthur Kober (div.). With Horace Liveright, Inc., N.Y.C., 1924-25; theatrical play-reader, 1927-30; book reviewer for Herald Tribune, 1925-28; writer, 1926—, scenario writer, 1935—. Recipient Gold medal for drama Nat. Inst. and Acad. Arts and Letters 1964. Fellow Am. Acad. Arts and Scis.; mem. AAAL, Dramatists Guild. Author: The Children's Hour, 1934; Days to Come, 1936; The Little Foxes, 1939; Watch on the Rhine, 1941; The Searching Wind, 1944; Another Part of the Forest, 1946; Adapted Roble's Montserrat, 1949; The Autumn Garden, 1951. Dramatized for movies: The Dark Angel, 1935; These Three, 1935-36; Dead End, 1937; The Little Foxes, 1940; The North Star, 1943; The Searching Wind, 1945; An Unfinished Woman (a memoir), 1969; Pentimento: A Book of Portraits, 1973; Scoundrel Time, 1976; Maybe, 1980. Editor: The Letters of Anton Chekhov, 1955; musical version of Voltaire's Candide, 1955; Adaptation of Anouilh's play. The Lark, 1955; Toys in the Attic, 1960; Adaptation My Mother, My Father and Me, from Burt Blechman's How Much, 1963. Author motion picture: The Chase. Editor: The Big Knockover (Dashiell Hammett), 1966; The Collected Plays, 1972. Contbr. articles and stories to mags. Home: 630 Park Ave New York NY 10021

HELLMAN, SANDRA ANN, hosp. adminstr.; b. Mpls., Oct. 17, 1937; d. Wallace McKinley and Alice Mae (Lee) Wadtke; B.A., U. Minn.; M.P.H. (USPHS fellow), U. Calif., Berkeley, 1962, D.P.H. (USPHS fellow), 1971; M.B.A., St. Mary's Coll., 1982; m. Stanley Hellman, July 23, 1964; children—Dara, Carrie. Dir. edn. and services Am. Cancer Soc., Hennepin County, Minn., 1959-60; cancer control and accident prevention cons. Minn. Dept. Public Health, 1960-61; project coordinator Action Research Project Dept. Public Health, San Francisco, 1962-64; ednl. cons., field staff supr. Calif. Nurses Assn., San Francisco, 1964-68; asst. adminstr. Pacific Med. Center, San Francisco, 1972-74, dir. div. edn., 1974-76, cons. div. edn., 1972-74; pres. Merritt Hosp. Found., Oakland, Calif., 1979—. Active San Francisco Symphony Assn., Neighborhood Home Owners Bds. Recipient Nat. Am. Cancer Soc. Awards for Pub. Health Edn. Programs, 1961. Mem. Am. Coll. Hosp. Adminstrs., Nat. Assn. for Hosp. Devel., Calif. Publ. Health Assn., Soc. Pub. Health Educators, Am. Hosp. Med. Educators. Republican. Contbr. articles to profl. jours. Home: 16 Tweed Terr San Rafael CA 94901 Office: Hawthorne Ave and Webster St Oakland CA 94609

HELLMANN, NORMA JANELLE, cytotechnologist; b. Honolulu, Jan. 21, 1949; d. Norman Louis and Margaret Janelle (Baker) Hellmann; B.A., Carthage Coll., 1971; cert. Johns Hopkins Hosp. Sch. Cytotech. 1972. Asso. cytotechnologist Johns Hopkins Hosp., Balt., 1972-74; supr. cytology lab. Clin. Labs. of Nashville, 1974; ednl. coordinator Sch. Cytotech. Vanderbilt U., Nashville, 1974-76; supr. cytology lab. Clin. Labs. of Black Hills, Rapid City, S.D., 1976—; program coordinator CDC Workshops on Cytology, Rapid City, 1978. Mem., comdr. Rushmore Composite Squadron CAP, 1982—, dir. blood flight program of S.D., 1976—; exec. sec. Wonderland Homes Water and Service Co., 1979-80. Mem. Am. Soc. Cytology, Am. Soc. Clin. Pathologists (affiliate mem., cert. cytotechnologist), Am. Soc. for Cytotech., AAUW (recipient woman of worth award 1982), Aircraft Owners and Pilots Assn., Soaring Soc. of Am., Beta Beta Beta, Alpha Mu Gamma. Republican. Lutheran. Home: Rt 9 Box 170 D Rapid City SD 57701 Office: PO Box 238 Rapid City SD 57709

HELM, MARIE THERESE HYNES, fin. analyst; b. N.Y.C., July 25, 1950; d. Edward Gibson and Dorothy Gertrude (Heide) Hynes; B.A., George Washington U., 1972; m. John P. Helm, Mar. 24, 1979. With Capital Analysts, San Francisco, 1972-79; sr. fin. advisor, sales rep. Capital Concepts Investment Corp., San Francisco, 1979—. Mem. Nat. Assn. Life Underwriters, San Francisco C. of C. (women's council), Embarcadero Center Forum. Republican. Roman Catholic. Clubs: Fin. Women's (past pres.), Commonwealth of Calif. Home: 1948 Green St San Francisco CA 94123 Office: 425 California Suite 2600 San Francisco CA 94104

HELMLINGER, TRUDY BENITA, social worker; b. Seattle, Jan. 2, 1942; d. Benjamin V. and Birdie L. (Pettigrove) H.; B.A. in Psychology, Calif. State U., Sacramento, 1967, M.S.W. (Nat. Assn. Social Workers scholar), 1969. Psychiat. social worker Children's Protective Services, Sacramento, 1969-70, Placerville, Calif., 1970-71; pvt. practice clin. social work, Sacramento, 1971—; tchr. American River Coll., Sacramento, U. Calif., Davis, U. Calif., Irvine. Lic. clin. social worker, Calif.; lic. marriage, family and child counselor, Calif. Mem. Nat. Assn. Social Workers, World Fedn. Mental Health, Am. Soc. Journalists and Authors, Sacramento Mental Health Assn. Democrat. Methodist. Author: After You've Said Goodbye, 1977. Office: 2740 Fulton Ave Suite 113 Sacramento CA 95821

HELMS, MARY ANN, nurse; b. Compton, Calif., Jan. 7, 1935; d. Raymond Whitfield and Amanda Zelpha (Hancock) Spencer; A.A. in Nursing, El Camino Coll., 1971; B.S. in Nursing, Calif. State U., Los Angeles, 1976; M.A. in Mgmt., St. Mary's Coll., 1978; postgrad. Ariz. State U., 1981—; m. Willard Ford Helms, Mar. 15, 1958; children—Michael Steven, Steven Allen. Med. sec., bookkeeper Palm Springs (Calif.) Med. Clinic, 1956-61; office mgr. William R. Stevens Ins. Agy., Santa Ana, Calif., 1961-63, I.J. Weinrot & Son Ins. Agy., Los Angeles, 1963-67; staff nurse Kaiser Found. Hosp., Harbor City, Calif., 1971-76; supr., coordinator pediatrics Maricopa County Gen. Hosp., Phoenix, 1976-80; critical care nurse Phoenix Baptist Hosp., 1980-81, critical care mgr., 1981—. Mem. Am. Nurses Assn., Am. Soc. Women Accts., Natural History Mus., Met. Mus. Art, Smithsonian Instn., Phoenix Zoo, Phoenix Art Mus., Cousteau Soc., Calif. State U. Alumni Assn., KAET Public Broadcasting System, Am. Assn. Critical Care Nurses, Ariz. Nurses Assn. (treas., co-editor Update, Dist. 1), Nat. League Nursing, Phi Kappa Phi, Alpha Gamma Sigma. Republican. Mormon. Research on noise pollution on phys. and mental health of citizenry, phenylketonuria testing in Los Angeles, measurement of attitudes toward children in pediatric nurses. Home: 1007 E Michelle Dr Phoenix AZ 85022 Office: 6025 N 20th Ave Phoenix AZ 85015

HELPERN, BEATRICE LIEBOVITZ NIGHTINGALE, civic worker; b. N.Y.C., July 23, 1907; d. Abraham L. and Hannah (Weinberg) Liebovitz; B.A. summa cum laude, N.J. Coll. for Women, 1928; m. 2d, Lester M. Nightingale, Dec. 1, 1935 (dec. 1951); children—William L., Stuart L.; m. 3d, Milton Helpern, Jan. 1, 1955 (dec. 1977); stepchildren—Nancy H. (Mrs. Edward Moldover), Susan H. (Mrs. Paul Nettler), Alice (Mrs. Elliot M. Gross). Vol. sec. to chief med. examiner City of N.Y., 1960-74, now vol. med.-legal archivist; sec. to Dr. Helpern, 1974-77; vol. sec. Milton Helpern Library of Legal Medicine, N.Y.C., 1962—, trustee, 1977—, asst. treas., 1978—; vol. sec. Inst. Forensic Medicine, N.Y. U. and City N.Y., 1968-74, dept. forensic medicine N.Y. U., 1960-72, vol. med.-legal archivist, 1974—. Mem. ladies organizing com. Internat. Meetings Forensic Medicine, N.Y.C., 1960, London, 1963; hon. chmn. women's com. 1st World Meeting Med. Law, Belgium, 1967; chmn. 2d World Meeting, Washington, 1970; hospitality com. Internat. Assn. Accident and Traffic Medicine, chmn., 1967-69; chmn. hospitality com. Symposia on Forensic Medicine, N.Y.C., 1962-74. Bd. dirs. N.Y. chpt. Am. Jewish Com., 1950—, League for Emotionally Disturbed Children, Hemophilia Found., 1961-63; bd. dirs. Womens Aux. Med. Soc. County of N.Y., 1973—, 2d v.p., 1979-80, pres. 1980, 81, chmn. symposium, 1976, 79, 81, 82. Recipient Silver Medal Alliance Francaise, 1928. Mem. Mystery Writers Am. (hon.), Phi Beta Kappa. Home: 303 E 57th St New York NY 10022

HELPERN, JOAN MARSHALL GRUEN, designer, mfg. co. exec.; b. N.Y.C., Oct. 10, 1926; d. Edward S. and Ethel (Tilzer) Marshall; B.A., Hunter Coll., 1947; M.A., Columbia U., 1948; postgrad. Harvard U., 1960; m. David M. Helpern, Aug. 14, 1960; children—David M., Elizabeth Joan. Psychologist, Hunter Coll., 1946-48; lectr., cons., coordinator child devel. program N.Y.C. Bd. Edn., 1948-60; psychologist, counselor, tchr., coordinator guidance services, 1948-60; dir. pupil personnel services Lexington (Mass.) Bd. Edn., 1960-67; designer, S.R.O. Shoes, Boston, 1964-65; fashion cons. Melville Shoe Co. Boston, 1967-69; designer, pres. Joan & David Helpern, Inc., N.Y.C., 1969—; lectr. child guidance Hunter Coll., Yeshiva U., Harvard U., Lesley Coll.; exec. v.p., dir. Suburban Shoe, Inc., 1969—. Mem. Com. of 200, 1982—. Columbia U. scholar, 1947; recipient Coty Fashion award, 1978. Mem. Am. Sch. Counseling Assn. (gov. 1966-68). Club: Harvard (Boston). Author: Guidance of Children in Elementary Schools, 1957; mem. editorial bd. Am. Sch. Counselors Assn. Jour., 1964-67. Home: 1010 Memorial Dr Cambridge MA 02138 Office: 4 W 58th St New York NY 10019

HELSEL, E. KATHRYN, city ofcl.; b. Blackwell, Okla., Dec. 10, 1943; d. Harold F. and Goldia M. (DeShazer) Crow; B.S., Okla. State U., 1965; m. Allan J. Helsel, Feb. 20, 1965. Tchr. home econs. South High Sch., Wichita, Kans., 1965-66, Flour Constrn. Co., Seoul, Korea, 1966; head start dir. Six Sandoval Indian Pueblos, Inc., Bernalillo, N.Mex., 1968-69, exec. dir., 1969—; partner Hunnewell Elevator, South Haven, Kans., 1975—; dir. Aging Projects, Inc., Hutchinson, Kans., 1976—; cons. Native Am. Tech. Asst., Am. Coalition for Indian Programs; v.p. Tewan, Inc., 1975—. Coordinator Kans. Coalition on Aging, 1979—; spokeswoman for Concerned Farm Wives, 1976; pres. N.Mex. Indian Community Action Program dirs., 1974; active various nat. legis. on Indian issues. Mem. Nat. Assn. Nutrition and Aging Services Programs (v.p. 1979-80, pres. 1981-82), Nat. Assn. Nutrition Dirs. (spokeswoman 1978), Am. Agri-Woman, Kans. Assn. Nutrition and Aging Services Programs (pres. 1979-82), Kans. Livestock Assn., Nat. Wheat Growers Assn. Democrat. Methodist. Club: Order Eastern Star. Home: Route 1 South Haven KS 67140 Office: Reno County Courthouse Hutchinson KS 67501

HELTON, MARY VIRGINIA, civil engr.; b. Collin County, Tex., Feb. 4, 1919; d. Walter Ennis and Laurine Lavinia (Neighbors) Williams; B.A. in Math., McMurry Coll., Abilene, Tex., 1940; m. Beryl Thomas Helton, Dec. 22, 1945 (div.); 1 dau., Virginia Beryl. Tchr. math. Stamford Jr. High Sch., 1940-43; head math. dept. Ranger Jr. Coll., 1943-45; with Tex. State Dept. Hwys. and Public Transp., Dallas, 1945—, sr. design engr. dist. 18, 1973—. Dir., Mesquite (Tex.) Social Services, 1971-73; mem. Mesquite Coordination Council, 1976-79; ruling elder Emmanuel Presbyn. Ch., Mesquite, 1970-73, clk. session, 1970-73; ruling elder St. Mark Presbyn. Ch., Dallas, 1974-77, del. to Presbytery, 1970-77. Mem. Am. Soc. Profl. and Exec. Women, Tex. Public Employees Assn., Tex. State Employees Assn. (dir. 1977-79). Democrat. Presbyterian. Clubs: Bus. and Profl. Women's, Altrusa (pres. 1977-79) (Mesquite). Home: 3526 Bonito Vista Circle Mesquite TX 75150 Office: Box 3067 Dallas TX 75225

HELTON, WENDY (WINIFRED WENDOLYN HARRISON), state ofcl.; b. Lexington, Ky., Sept. 6, 1941; d. Damon Wilson and Helen Evelyn (Tuttle) Harrison; B.S., Western Ky. U., 1963; M.A., Ind. U., 1970. Tchr., Huntingberg (Ind.) High Schs., 1963-65, New Albany-Floyd County Consol. Schs., Floyd Knobs and Georgetown, Ind., 1965-68, Ellettsville (Ind.) High Sch., 1968-69, Ripley (W.Va.) High Sch., 1970, Ravenswood (W.Va.) High Sch., 1970-73; state FHA/HERO advisor Ind. Dept. Pub. Instrn., Div. Vocat. Edn., Indpls., 1973-75, state cons. Home Econs. Edn., 1975-80; state coordinator civil rights guidelines Ind. State Bd. Vocat. Tech. Edn., Indpls., 1980-81, state coordinator for reduction of sex bias, 1981—. Membership on adv. com. on sex discrimination Ind. Civil Rights Commn., 1981—; mem. N. Central Evaluation teams, 1975—; active Big Sis. Greater Indpls., 1980—; dist. advisor Future Homemakers of Am., Ind., 1968-70. Recipient Ind. Hon. Membership FHA award, Ind. Assn. Future Homemakers of Am., 1975; Ind. U./Purdue U. fellow, 1975; Purdue U. grantee, 1978. Mem. Ind. U. Home Econs. Alumni Assn. (treas.-sec. 1974, treas. 1981-82), Am. Vocat. Assn., Ind. Vocat. Assn., Ind. Council Vocat. Adminstrs., Vocat. Edn. Equity Council, Nat. Assn. Female Execs., Ind. Vocat. Home Econs. Assn. Presbyterian. Home: 6267 N Washington Blvd Indianapolis IN 46220 Office: 17 W Market St Room 401 Indianapolis IN 46204

HELVERN, JANE ALVIES, public relations cons.; b. Hollywood, Calif., Aug. 5, 1913; d. Robert Lincoln and Edna May (McKay) Alvies; A.B. (gold medal), U. So. Calif., 1935; postgrad. Yale U. Law Sch., other law schs.; m. A. Wallace Helvern, Mar. 29, 1952 (dec. 1957). Asso. editor Fed. Rules Service, Washington, 1938-40; feature writer Palo Alto (Calif.) Times, 1940; dir. with OWI, 1942-45; writer-producer public service programs Sta. KFOX, Long Beach, Calif., 1945-46; dir. public relations Youth Films, Inc., Hollywood, 1947-48; exec. sec. pro tem So. Calif. Broadcasters Assn., 1948; editorial asst. Calif. Agr. mag., 1949-50; chmn. exec. council Delta Alpha chpt. Alpha Gamma Delta, 1961-62, activities adv., 1962-63, chmn. Calif. grand council study com., 1967-69, public relations chmn. internat. conv., Phoenix, 1972; dir.-organizer Inter-Greek Soc., U. So. Calif., 1976-80, sec., 1978-79, v.p., 1979-80, life membership chmn., 1980-81; cons. in field, chmn. numerous fund raising campaigns. Recipient numerous cert. of appreciation awards of merit. Mem. U. So. Calif. Gen. Alumni Assn., Trojan League Los Angeles (publs. chmn., dir. 1980-81), Inter-Greek Soc., Three Arch Bay Assn. (past pres. property owners legal com. 1960-63), Nat. Aero. Assn., Los Angeles World Affairs Council, Phi Beta Kappa, Phi Kappa Phi, Zeta Phi Eta (past chpt. pres.), Phi Alpha Delta. Christian Scientist. Clubs: Yale, Town and Gown, Woman's of Hollywood, Dionysians. Author articles, plays, songs and lyrics. Address: 1965 Canyon Dr Hollywood CA 90068

HELZEL, REBEKAH SPIEKHOUT, banker; b. Chgo., Jan. 7, 1951; d. John Andrew and Genevieve (Van Hattem) Spiekhout; B.A., Hope Coll., 1973; m. Lawrence Helzel, May 15, 1977. Internat. asst. Toronto Dominion Bank of Calif., San Francisco, 1974-76; fgn. exchange trader Bank of Am., San Francisco, 1976-78, fgn. exchange adv., 1978-79; v.p. Fgn. Exchange Exposure Mgmt. Workshop, San Francisco, 1979-80, Internat. Treasury Services, San Francisco, 1980—. Mem. Fgn. Exchange Assn. N.Am. Clubs: Commonwealth, San Francisco Bay, San Francisco Tennis. Contbr. articles to profl. publs. Office: 555 California St Suite 4850 San Francisco CA 94104

HEMENWAY, RUTH ORA, real estate exec.; b. Cottage Grove, Oreg., Aug. 9, 1945; d. James William and Julia May H.; student Puget Sound Bible Coll., 1963-65. Salesperson, Hemenway Realtors, Cottage Grove, 1966-67, office mgr., 1967-69, broker, 1969—, property mgr., 1972—. Named Realtor of Yr., Cottage Grove, 1976. Mem. Bd. Realtors (sec. 1974, v.p. 1975, pres. 1976). Mem. Ch. of Christ. Club: Cottage Grove Soroptimists. Home: 610 Wood Ave Cottage Grove OR 97424 Office: 1807 E Main St PO Box 647 Cottage Grove OR 97424

HEMINGWAY, BETH ROWLETT, author, columnist, lectr.; b. Richmond, Va., May 6, 1913; d. Robert Archer and Evelyn Lucille (Doggett) Rowlett; B.Mus., Hollins Coll., 1934; m. Harold Hemingway, Apr. 2, 1938; children—Ruth Hartley, Martha Scott. Writer, Richmond-Lifestyle mag.; columnist Artistry in Bloom, Richmond Times-Dispatch; author: A Second Treasury of Christmas Decorations, 1961; Flower Arrangement with Antiques, 1965; Christmas Decorations Say Welcome, 1972; Antiques Accented by Flowers, 1975; Beth Hemingway's No Kin to Ernest, 1980; lectr. numerous states, also Australia, 1966, Eng., 1977. Vol., Hermitage Meth. Home, 1977-79. Mem. Nat. League Am. Pen Women, Va. Writers Club, Richmond Hort. Assn., Va. Fedn. Garden Clubs (book rev. chmn.), Richmond Council Garden Clubs (flower arrangement chmn.), Clay Spring Garden Club (pres. 1953-55), Barton Garden Club (pres. 1959-61, 74). Republican. Methodist. Home: 1604 Derek Ln Richmond VA 23229

HEMLOW, JOYCE, educator, author; b. Liscomb, N.S., Can., July 30, 1906; d. William and Rosalinda (Redmond) Hemlow; B.A., Queen's Coll., Kingston, Can., 1941, M.A., 1942; A.M., Radcliffe Coll., 1944, Ph.D., 1948; LL.D. (hon.), Queen's, 1967, Dalhousie U., 1972. Mem. faculty McGill U. 1945—, Greenshields prof. English lit. and lang., 1965—, prof. emerita, 1975—. Guggenheim fellow, 1951-52, 66-67; recipient James Tait Black Meml. book prize for best biography in U.K., The History of Fanny Burney, 1958, also Gov. Gen. Can. medal for academic non-fiction, 1958, Rose Mary Crawshay prize Brit. Acad., 1960; Distinguished Achievement medal Radcliffe Coll., 1969. Fellow Royal Soc. Can.; mem. Johnsonians, Phi Beta Kappa. Editor: Journals and Letters Fanny Burney (Madame d'Arblay). Home: 3555 Atwater Ave Montreal PQ H3H 1Y3 Canada also Liscomb NS Canada

HEMMENS, JEAN ANN, retail exec.; b. Chgo., Jan. 29, 1936; d. Raymond T. and Thelma F. (Brown) Doherty; A.B. in English, U. Ill., Urbana, 1957; postgrad. U. N.C. Sch. Library Sci., 1965-69; divorced; children—Craig, Eric, Ann. Pres. The Bentwood Ltd., retail home furnishings, Chapel Hill and Raleigh, N.C., 1970—. Mem. Chapel Hill C. of C. Democrat. Home: 512 E Rosemary St Chapel Hill NC 27514 Office: The Bentwood Ltd University Mall Chapel Hill NC 27515

HEMMERLE, PATRICIA ANNE, med. technologist, adminstr.; b. Lebanon, Ind., Feb. 17, 1953; d. Charles Richard and Shirley Dorothy (Driscoll) Hemmerle; A.B. in Chemistry, Ind. U., 1975, M.S., 1978; cert. med. tech. St. Joseph Hosp. Sch. Med. Tech., 1976. Med. technologist Community Hosp. of Indpls., 1976-79, program dir. Sch. Med. Tech., 1981—; clin. instr. clin. chemistry, adj. prof. U. S. Ala. Med. Center, Mobile, 1979-81; mem. examination council for Nat. Certification Agy. for Med. Lab. Personnel. Mem. Am. Soc. Med. Tech. (cert. med tech., specialist in clin. chemistry), Am. Soc. Clin. Pathology (affiliate mem.), Consortium of Ind. Med. Lab. Educators, Am. Assn. Clin. Chemists. Home: 4761 Alsuda Dr Indianapolis IN 46205 Office: 1500 N Ritter Indianapolis IN 46219

HEMPEL, KATHERINE ANNE, govt. ofcl.; b. Buffalo, July 12, 1954; d. Edwin Arthur and Marie Katherine (Niles) Hempel; B.A. magna cum laude, Syracuse U., 1976. Asst. dir. govt. affairs Menswear Retailers of Am., Washington, 1977-80; adminstrv. asst. Resources for the Future, Inc., Washington, 1980-81; congl. staff asst. U.S. House of Reps., Washington, 1981—. Mem. AAUW, Nat. Assn. Female Execs., Phi Beta Kappa. Episcopalian. Home: 1301 S Scott St Apt 717 Arlington VA 22204

HEMPFLING, LINDA LEE, nurse; b. Indpls., July 28, 1947; d. Paul Roy and Myrtle Pearl (Ward) Hempfling; diploma Meth. Hosp. Ind. Sch. Nursing, 1968. Charge nurse Meth. Hosp., Indpl., 1968; staff nurse operating room Silver Cross Hosp., Joliet, Ill., 1969; charge nurse operating room Huntington (N.Y.) Hosp., 1969-73; night supr. operating room Hermann Hosp., Houston, 1973-76; unit. mgr. operating rooms, 1976—. Future Nurses Am. scholar, 1965. Mem. Nat. League Nursing, Am. Nurses Assn., Houston Soc. Central Service Personnel, Assn. Operating Room Nurses. Office: 1203 Ross Sterling Ave Houston TX 77030

HEMPHILL, BERNICE MONAHAN, blood bank exec.; b. San Francisco; d. Thomas E. and Anne J. (McGinerty) Monahan; ed. U. Calif.; m. Charles D. Hemphill, June 30, 1939. Supervising technologist Honolulu Blood Plasma Bank, 1941-43; exec. dir., sec. Irwin Meml. Blood Bank, San Francisco Med. Soc., 1944—. Treas. Am. Assn. Blood Banks, 1949-74, chmn. nat. com. on clearinghouse program, 1953—, pres., 1976, com. on govt. liaison; mem. com., exec. com., fin. com. Am. Blood Commn., 1978—; founder, sec. Calif. Blood Bank System, 1951-57; mem. state adv. com. on blood and blood derivatives Calif. Dept. Pub. Health, 1964—; mem. consumer adv. council San Francisco Med. Soc. Health Plan, cons. on blood banking projects; mem. nat. adv. communicable disease council HEW, 1969-72. Active United Way San Francisco; mem. Mayor's Citizens Com. for Centennial Golden Gate Park, 1969; bd. dirs. Catholic Social Service San Francisco, 1957-62; pres. Am. Women for Internat. Understanding, 1973—; mem. Women for Nixon-Agnew Com., 1968; co-chmn. Com. to Re-elect Pres., 1972; mem. nat. adv. com. Women for Pres. Ford, 1976; mem. adv. com. fiscal affairs Republican Nat. Com., 1977-80; mem. nat. steering com. George Bush for Pres., 1980; mem. adv. bd. U. Santa Barbara Sch. Bus.; bd. dirs. Nat. Center Vol. Action, 1976-79; bd. dirs., public info. com. San Francisco unit Am. Cancer Soc., 1977—; mem. coordinating com. Calif.-Internat. Women's Year, 1977 chmn. sponsoring com. Nat. Conf. Social Welfare, 1975; mem. steering com. LIVE (Learn through Internat. Vol. Effort), 1975-76. Recipient John Elliott award Am. Assn. Blood Banks, 1960, commendation Ft. Miley VA Hosp., San Francisco, 1961, award of merit Catholic Charities San Francisco, 1962, Lane Bryant citation, 1965, 66, 67, 68, Key of Guild award Medico-Dental Study Guild Calif., 1973; lectr. award So. Central Assn. Blood Banks, 1975; Thomas Owen Meml. award Calif. Blood Bank System, 1978; named Disting. Woman, San Francisco Examiner, 1960, U.S. Lady-of-Month, U.S. Lady publ., 1963; 1st Disting. Adminstr. award Am. Assn. Blood Banks, 1981; Woman of Achievement award Bus. and Profl. Women's Club San Francisco, 1981. Mem. Women's Forum West, U. Calif. Hosp. Aux., U. Calif. Doctor's Wives Club, St. Francis Hosp. Aux., Laguna Honda Home Aux., San Francisco Assn. Mental Health, Little Children's Aid Aux., World Affairs Council No. Calif., Internat. Soc. Blood Transfusion, Women's Aux. San Francisco Dental Soc., Pan Am. Fedn. Vol. Blood Donations (hon.), San Francisco C. of C. (dir.); exec. com. 1980-82, founder women's council), Women's Forum West (v.p., program chmn. 1980-81), UN Assn. U.S.A. (steering com. internat. women's com. 1975; nat. com. on U.S.-China relations). Conceived and created 1st blood bank clearinghouse, 1951. Clubs: Franciso, Commonwealth (San Francisco); Capitol Hill (Washington). Home: 1070 Green St Apt 1301 San Francisco CA 94133 Office: 270 Masonic Ave San Francisco CA 94118

HEMPHILL, LINDA TAXIS, assn. exec.; b. Richmond, Va., Jan. 16, 1945; d. John Otto and Doris Rebecca (Chew) Taxis; B.A., Am. U., 1966; 1 dau., Lindsay Rebecca. Asst. to the pres. Sci. Communication, Inc., Washington, 1966-67; mng. editor, advt. dir. Am. Indsl. Arts Assn., Washington, 1967-71; dir. publs. Nat. Soc. Public Accountants, Washington, 1971-78; conf. coordinator Soc. Nat. Assn. Publs., 1978; dir. publs. and communications Internat. and Am. Assns. Dental Research, 1978—. Block capt. Brookville/Seminary Valley Civic Assn., 1977—; asst. music dir. Alexandria Community Singers, 1977—; founder, asst. music dir., sec., treas. Ad Hoc Singers, Ltd., 1977-80; organist, choirmaster Church of the Covenant, Arlington, Va., 1975—. Mem. Am. Soc. Bus. Press Editors, Soc. Nat. Assn. Publs. (bd. dirs. 1981—), D.C. Fedn. Bus. and Profl. Women's Clubs, Cosmopolitan Bus. and Profl. Women's Club, AAUW, Gamma Sigma Sigma. Republican. Episcopalian. Home: 5006 Regency Place Alexandria VA 22304 Office: International and American Associations for Dental Research 734 15th St NW Suite 809 Washington DC 20005

HENDERSON, ALICE ELIZABETH, broadcasting exec.; b. Freeport, N.Y., Dec. 12, 1947; d. Harry G.A. and Alice L. (Modin) McManus; student Wood Secretarial Sch., N.Y.C., 1966; m. Robert B. Henderson, Jan. 3, 1973 (div.). Editor program practices CBS, Inc., N.Y.C., 1966-71, dir. program practices, 1975-77, v.p., 1977—; asst. to v.p. Bloomingdale's, N.Y.C., 1972. Trustee, AWRT Edn. Found., 1979-80. Mem. Am. Film Inst., Acad. TV Arts and Scis., Hollywood Radio and TV Soc., Am. Advt. Fedn., Am. Women in Radio & TV. Office: 51 W 52d St New York NY 10019

HENDERSON, ANNE FORTUNE, educator, cattle farmer; b. Arrington, Va., July 25, 1928; d. Harry Pierce and Cecil Dorothy (Fortune) Henderson; diploma Va. Intermont Coll., 1948; B.S., Va. Commonwealth U., 1950; M.Ed., U. Va., 1958. Tchr., R.E. Lee Jr. High Sch., Lynchburg, Va., 1950-52, E.C. Glass High Sch., Lynchburg, 1952-62; asst. prof. health, phys. edn. and recreation Mary Washington Coll., Fredericksburg, Va., 1962-69; asst. prof. health, phys. edn. and recreation Lynchburg Coll., 1969-81, asso. prof., 1981—; owner, mgr. cattle farm, Nelson County, Va., 1969—. Mem. AAHPER, Va., So. assns. health, phys. edn. and recreation, Va. Angus Assn., Va. Beef Cattle Assn., Nelson County Farm Bur., Amateur Fencers League Am. Republican. Episcopalian. Club: Winton Country (Clifford, Va.). Home: Cherry Hill Arrington VA 22922 Office: Lynchburg College Lynchburg VA 24504

HENDERSON, CAROLYN EVANGELINE WHITE, hosp. adminstr.; b. Washington, Oct. 30, 1946; d. William Bryant Henderson and Pinkey Moore (foster mother); R.N. diploma Lincoln Hosp. Sch. Nursing, Durham, N.C., 1971; B.S. in Bus. Adminstrn., N.C. Central U., 1978; postgrad. in nursing U. N.C., Greensboro, 1980—. Operating room technician Lenoir Meml. Hosp., Kinston, N.C., 1965-68; operating room nurse Lincoln Hosp., 1971-75; operating room ednl. coordinator Lincoln Hosp. and Watts Hosp., Durham, 1975-76; program coordinator Durham County Gen. Hosp., Durham, 1976—, ednl. coordinator, 1980—; workshop coordinator/cons.; tchr. in field; chmn. operating room adv. com. Durham Tech. Inst., 1977-78; vice chmn. grad. nursing staff Lincoln Hosp., 1974-75. Recipient Operating Room Achievement award Lincoln Hosp., 1971; Public Speaking award N.C. Central U., 1972, Choral Music award, 1976, J.C. Scarborough Community Service award, 1977, Hosp. Service pin Durham County Gen. Hosp., 1978. Mem. Am. Nurses Assn., N.C. Nurses Assn. (chmn. operating room conf. group 1973-74), Assn. Operating Room Nurses (chmn. continuing edn. com. Tar Heels East chpt. 1978-79), Lincoln Nursing Alumni Assn. (pres. 1973-78), N.C. Central U. Alumni Assn. (dir. 1979-80), Nat. Assn. Female Execs., Santa Filomena Nursing Honor Soc., Am. Nurses' Found. Democrat. Mem. African Methodist Episcopal Ch. Home: 3311 Shannon Rd Apt 26C Durham NC 27707 Office: 3643 N Roxboro St Durham NC 27704

HENDERSON, EDITH NELL GUNN, mail order co. exec.; b. Amarillo, Tex., Apr. 20, 1927; d. William Baugh and Edith (Ratliff) Gunn; student Christian Coll., Columbia, Mo., 1945-47; A.A., U. Okla., 1950; m. Walter Andrew Henderson, Jr., Apr. 15, 1949; children—Hilda, Julie, Jenny. Gift buyer Gunn Bros., Amarillo, 1956-70, sec.-treas., 1970-75; v.p. Gunn Bros. and Serendipity, mail order catalog, Amarillo, 1975—. Chmn., Suicide Prevention-Crises Intervention, 1968-70, 71-72, vice chmn., 1970-71; chmn. Ad Hoc Com. on Drug Abuse; trustee Mental Health Retardation Regional Bd., 1972-74; mem. Amarillo Rehab. Com., 1967; sec. Family Service Bd., 1969; mem. Central Youth Adv. Council, 1969-72; mem. solicitation com. United Way. Recipient Woman of Yr. award Beta Sigma Phi, 1972; Appreciation award Amarillo Mental Health Mental Retardation Regional Bd. Trustees, 1974, Suicide Prevention-Crises Intervention - Operation Drug Abuse, 1976. Mem. Direct Mail Mktg. Assn., Kappa Kappa Gamma. Mem. Ch. of Christ. Club: Amarillo Jr. League (pres. 1965-66). Office: Gunn Bros and Serendipity 616 Harrison St Amarillo TX 79101

HENDERSON, EILEEN JOYCE, educator; b. Elton, Wis., Jan. 9, 1928; d. Sherman Hobert and Vesta Millie (Tate) Roe; certificate Langlade County Coll., 1957; B.Edn., Pestalozzi Frobel, Chgo., 1969; reading specialist certificate Nat. Coll. Edn., 1975; m. Charles Henderson, May 14, 1969; children—James, Robert. Tchr. pub. schs., Pickeral, Wis., 1957-58, Wilson Grade Sch., White Lake, Wis., 1958-62, White Lake Pub. Schs., 1962-65; tchr. Birnamwood (Wis.) Elementary Sch., 1965-66; tchr. pub. schs. Zion, Ill., 1966—. Mem. NEA, Ill., Zion edn. assns. Mem. Assembly of God Ch. Home: 12300 39th Ave Kenosha WI 53142 Office: Elmwood Sch 31st and Ezra Ave Zion IL 60099

HENDERSON, ELAINE JOYCE, restaurant exec.; b. Salt Lake City, July 29, 1932; d. Russell Adams and Pearl Kathleen Davies; grad. high sch.; children—Gregory, Julie, Christopher. Dist. mgr. Guckenheimer Enterprises, Redwood City, Calif., 1971-77; owner Lane's Foods, Sunnyvale, Calif., Sugar Loaf Restaurant, Penn Valley, Calif., Esté Catering Co., Sunnyvale, 1977—. Mem. Am. Restaurant Assn., C. of C. Grass Valley. Republican. Home: 18979 Chaparral Dr Penn Valley CA 95946 Office: PO Box 564 Cupertino CA 95015

HENDERSON, ELIZABETH BAKER, craftswoman; b. East Lansing, Mich., June 18, 1912; d. James Frederick and Bessie Irene (Buskirk) Baker; B.A., Mich. State U., 1933; A.M., U. Chgo., 1942; m. Dorland John Henderson, Dec. 28, 1955. Dir. social service and camp Abraham Lincoln Centre, Chgo., 1933-42; child care cons. Children's Bur., Va. Dept. Public Welfare, 1942-44; exec. sec. Neighborhood Center and Council, Montclair, N.J., 1944-48; sch. social worker East Orange (N.J.) Bd. Edn., 1948-59; handweaver, potter, 1960—; restorer (with husband) Sydenham House, Newark, 1955—. Mem. Nat. Assn. Social Workers, Am. Crafts Council, So. Calif. Handweavers Guild, N.J. Hist. Soc., Nat. Trust Historic Preservation, Newark Mus., English Speaking Union. Democrat. Club: Williams (N.Y.C.). Author: The Integration of Case Work and Group Work at Abraham Lincoln Centre, 1942. Address: Old Rd to Bloomfield Newark NJ 07104

HENDERSON, GWENDOLYN WITHERSPOON, educator; b. Charleston, S.C., Sept. 11, 1931; d. James William and Myrtle Louise (Ruff) Witherspoon; A.B., Fisk U., Nashville, 1951; M.S., Oreg. State U., 1974, Ph.D., 1976; divorced; children—Valton D., Alan C. Researcher, Sloan-Kettering Inst., N.Y.C., 1951-53; tchr. sci., chmn. dept. W.A. Perry Jr. High Sch., Columbia, S.C., 1956-62; tchr. math. and chemistry, div. chmn. Tolleston High Sch., Gary, Ind., 1962-68; tchr. phys. scis., chemistry, chmn. sci. dept. Lower Richland High Sch., Columbia, 1968-73; instr. sci. edn. Oreg. State U., 1973-76, EOP dir., acad. coordinator 1974-79; asso. dir. govt. contract leadership/mgmt. tng. Atlanta U., 1979-80; asso. prof., coordinator math. and sci. dept. edn. U. N.C., Asheville, 1980—; past pres. Richland County Edn. Assn. Exec. bd., exec. com., chmn. budget com. United Way Benton County (Oreg.), 1974-79; exec. bd., exec. com. Consumer Credit Counseling Service, Asheville, 1980—; pres. Corvallis NAACP, 1976-79; mem. exec. bd. LWV, Columbia, 1968-73; mem. Oreg. Gov.'s Commn., 1976-78; exec. bd. YWCA, Asheville, 1982—. Recipient award S.C. Edn. Assn.; grantee Carnegie Corp., 1954-55, NSF, 1957, 59-60, 71-73, Oreg. State U. Found., 1973, 75, 77; N.C. State Dept. Public Instrn. grantee. Mem. Nat. Sci. Tchrs. Assn., Nat. Assn. Women Deans, Adminstrs. and Counselors, N.C. Sci. Tchrs. Assn., N.C. Assn. Colls. Tchrs. Edn., Urban League (exec. bd. Columbia 1970-73), Phi Delta Kappa, Delta Sigma Theta (chpt. community relations com. chmn. 1949, service cert. 1981). Methodist. Club: Altrusa (v.p., chmn. internat. relations com. Corvallis, Oreg. 1977-79, Asheville, 1980—). Author articles in field. Home: 24 Pinecroft Ln Fletcher NC 28732 Office: PO Box 8467 University Heights Asheville NC 28814

HENDERSON, JILL, pub. relations and personnel exec.; b. Cambridge, Mass., June 15, 1938; d. George Maës and Daphne (Foster) Henderson; M.Ed., Antioch Coll., Yellow Springs, Ohio. Adminstrv. asst. Apollo project, instrumentation lab. M.I.T., 1959-68; asst. tech. dir. Boston's SUMMERTHING, 1968-70; asst. to dir. Shady Hill Sch., Cambridge, 1970-74; dir. personnel Charles River Assos., Inc., Boston, 1974—, dir. public relations, 1982—; adv. council, mem. adj. faculty Bentley Coll. Trustee White Mountain Sch., Littleton, N.H. Mem. Internat. Assn. Personnel Women (chpt. dir., chmn. publicity and public relations com.), Profl. Mgmt. Assn. (dir.), Am. Soc. Personnel Adminstrs., Am. Soc. Tng. and Devel., Employment Mgmt. Assn., Coll. Placement Council, Boston Women's Luncheon Group, Antioch Inst. Open Edn. Alumni Assn. (pres. 1980-82), White Mountain Sch. Alumnae Assn. (pres. 1981—). Episcopalian. Club: Women's Athletic (Boston). Author articles in field. Office: 200 Clarendon St Boston MA 02116

HENDERSON, JOYCE R., mktg. and mgmt. cons.; b. Berkeley, Calif., Apr. 14, 1944; d. Sylvester T. and Elizabeth Marie Hardiman; B.S. in Nursing, San Francisco State Coll., 1966, postgrad. 1966-68; postgrad. Calif. State U., Los Angeles, 1968-69; m. William Edward Merritt, III. Public health nurse Alameda County Health Dept., Oakland, Calif., 1966-68; clinic nurse Planned Parenthood, Inc., Oakland, 1968, Planned Parenthood World Population, Los Angeles, 1968-69; supervising obstet. nurse Park Avenue Hosp., Pomona, Calif., 1969-71; asso. dir. program ops. Los Angeles Regional Family Planning Council, 1969-71, exec. dir., 1971-77; dir. enrollment and group relations Kaiser-Permanente Med. Care Program, So. Calif. regional office, Los Angeles, 1977-81; cons. mgmt. and mktg., Culver City, Calif., 1981—; mem. faculty (part-time) Occidental Coll., 1976; cons. Westinghouse Learning Corp., Los Angeles, 1972; dir. Lomod Corp., 1975—. Mem. adv. bd. United Negro Coll. Fund, 1978-79; chairperson Citywide Task Force on Health Edn., Los Angeles Unified Sch. Dist., 1977-78; bd. dirs. People's Coordinated Services, 1977—, Goodwill Industries of So. Calif., 1980—. Recipient citation of merit Los Angeles Bd. Public Works, 1976, resolution of appreciation City Council Los Angeles, 1976. Mem. Am. Public Health Assn., Am. Mgmt. Assn., Soc. Advancement Mgmt., Sales and Mktg. Execs. Assn., Delta Sigma Theta, NAACP. Club: Soroptimist (dir. 1978-79).

HENDERSON, KATHERINE LOUISE, librarian; b. Carmel, Calif., Jan. 26, 1935; d. Frederick Peter and Harriet Ruth (Severance) H.; B.A., U. Calif., Berkeley, 1957; J.D., U. Santa Clara (Calif.), 1972; M.L.L., U. Denver, 1979; children—John Jeffrey Nelson, David Alexander Nelson, Diane Charmian Slocum. High sch. and elem. sch. tchr. in Calif., 1964-70; legal research asst., 1970-72; dir. Clark County Law Library, Las Vegas, Nev., 1972-82; asst. law librarian McGeorge Sch. Law, Sacramento, 1982—; mem. Nev. Adv. Council Libraries. Bd. dirs. Las Vegas Art Mus., 1976. Mem. Am. Assn. Law Libraries, So. Calif. Assn. Law Libraries, Nev. Library Assn., So. Nev. Assn. Women Attys., AAUW (rec. sec. Nev. 1974-76), LWV (treas. Nev. 1975-77), Artists Coop. Las Vegas, Alpha Phi. Republican. Episcopalian. Author monographs in field. Office: Mc George Sch Law Library 3200 5th Ave Sacramento CA 95817

HENDERSON, KATHRYN SILVERTHORNE, profl. soc. exec.; b. Buffalo, 1916; d. Frederick William and Florence (Krause) Silverthorne;

student Northwestern U. Sch. Journalism, 1934-35, Irvine Studio of Drama, N.Y.C., 1938, Feagin Sch. Acting, N.Y.C., 1939; m. Edward Henderson, 1944 (dec.); children—Edward Bell, Susan Lee. Sec. to advt. mgr. Esquire mag., Chgo.; sec. to pub. Radio Guide mag., Chgo. and N.Y.C., Miami (Fla.) Tribune; actress Mae Desmond Players, radio and summer stock; staff commentator Sta. WBAB, Atlantic City; traveling fashion show commentator Lever Bros. Co.; publicity dir., account exec. Posner Advt. Agy., N.Y.C.; nat. advt. time salesperson N. Central Broadcasting System, N.Y.C.; asst. to exec. dir. Am. Geriatrics Soc., N.Y.C., 1962-73, exec. dir., 1973—; editor monthly newsletter, 1979—. Mem. Gerontol. Soc. Am. Presbyterian. Home: 220 Central Park S New York NY 10019 Office: 10 Columbus Circle New York NY 10019

HENDERSON, LORRIE (LEORA FOSTER), psychiat. social worker, adminstr., educator b. Cedar Rapids, Iowa, July 30, 1924; d. Floyd Percy and Rosetta Mae (Bair) Foster; student Cornell (Iowa) Coll., 1942-44; B.A. in Psychology, U. Tex., Austin, 1964, M.S.W., 1967; m. Charles Perry Henderson, Sept. 15, 1945; children—Charles Timothy, Jane Ann Henderson Herrin. Psychiat. social worker Austin State Hosp., 1964-65; foster home finder, licensing worker Austin-Travis County Child Welfare, 1967-68; successively psychiat. social worker, program dir. Title IVA, sr. therapist social worker Austin Guild Guidance Center, 1968-76; dir. social services children's psychiat. unit Austin State Hosp., 1976—; asso. prof. practicum Worden Sch. Social Work, 1975—; field instr. U. Tex. Grad. Sch. Social Work, Austin, 1980—, St. Edwards U. Social Welfare Dept., 1980—; cons. in field. Bd. dirs. Austin Christmas Bur., 1973-75, v.p., 1974-75; patron Austin Mental Health Assn., 1978-80; mem. Regional Network for Children, 1979—. Served with WAVES, 1945. Alfred Noyes scholar, 1943-44, 63-64, 65-67; recipient Franklin Lindsay student loan 1963-64, 65-67; NIMH grantee, 1965-66, TDPW Student stipent, 1966-67. Mem. Acad. Cert. Social Workers, Nat. Assn. Social Workers, Am. Assn. Marriage and Family Therapy (approved supr.), Tex. Exes (life, newsletter editor grad. sch. social work 1972-73, mem.-at-large exec. com. 1976-80). Office: 4110 Guadelupe St Austin TX 78751

HENDERSON, MARGUERITE PETTITT, accountant; b. Dallas, May 22, 1925; d. James Dolphus and Sarah Elizabeth (Maupin) Pettitt; student acctg. So. Meth. U., 1968. Operator, Girl Friday Bookeeping and Income Tax Service, Dallas, 1968—; asst. controller Brookhaven Med. Center, Farmers Branch, Tex., 1981—; treas. Farmers Branch Hosp. Authority, Brookhaven Med. Center Credit Union. Mem. Nat. Assn. Accts. Home: 1865 Greendale St Dallas TX 75217 Office: 12100 Webb Chapel Farmers Branch TX 75234

HENDERSON, MARTHA MAE SAUNDERS, museum dir.; b. Spartanburg, S.C., Dec. 18, 1924; d. Alex Pinkney and Mildred Ruth (Clemons) Saunders; A.A., A.S., Burlington County Coll.; B.S. with honors, So. Ill. U., M.B.A., Central Mich. U.; m. Mark Henderson, Jr., Nov. 23, 1941; children—Sondra, Woodrena, Markette, Mark, III, Alexis. Girl Scout coordinator, Far East, 1966; founder Mus. Edn. and Research in Am. Black Art, Sci. and History, Camden, N.J., 1968, mem. staff, 1971—, pres., 1977—, dir., 1972—; mem. Cultural Commn. Burlington County, 1974; trustee N.J. State Mus. Friends; cons. in field. Recipient various recognition awards, certs. appreciation. Mem. Nat. Fedn. Press Women, Female Execs., Am. Assn. Mus., Nat. Conf. Artists, Afro Am. Mus. Assn. Democrat. Episcopalian. Author mus. materials. Office: Merabash Museum Rutgers Univ Camden NJ 08102

HENDERSON, MARY RUTH, educator; b. Sweetwater, Tenn., Oct. 25, 1951; d. Bill Hooper and Edna Lee (Largen) H.; B.S. in Home Econs., U. Tenn., 1973, M.S. in Agr., 1975. Asst. extension agt. U. Tenn. Agrl. Extension Service, Sequatchie County, Tenn., 1975-77; asst. prof. 4-H, state 4H specialist U. Tenn. Agrl. Extension Service, Knoxville, 1977—. Mem. Vol. Knoxville, Tenn. 4-H Alumni, Inc., Knoxville Area Home Econs. Assn., U. Tenn. Century Club. Mem. Nat. Assn. Extension 4-H Agts., Tenn. Assn. Extension 4-H Agts., Tenn. Assn. Agrl. Agts. and Specialists, Profl. Adminstrs. Vol. Services, Epsilon Sigma Phi, Gamma Sigma Delta. Baptist. Editor The 4-H Leader, 1977—; author 4-H publs., handbooks, visuals, newsletters. Office: PO Box 1071 209 Morgan Hall Knoxville TN 37901

HENDERSON, MAXINE LEE, nursing adminstr.; b. Halstad, Minn., Apr. 23, 1946; d. Albert Victor and Idelle Bernice (Norum) Johnson; R.N., St. Luke's Hosp. Sch. Nursing, Fargo, N.D., 1967; student Baylor U. Med. Center, 1969-70, N.D. State U., Fargo, 1970-76; m. Mark E. Henderson, May 4, 1974; children—Megan, Kristen. Staff nurse St. Barnabas Hosp., Mpls., 1967-68; instr. operating room St. Luke's Hosp. Sch. Nursing, Fargo, 1968-70, head nurse operating room, 1970-76; dir. nursing Halstad Lutheran Meml. Home, 1977—; mem. adv. council medication program Moorhead Area Vocat. Tech. Inst.; CPR instr. Mem. Assn. Operating Room Nurses, Geriatric Nursing Conf., Gen. Fedn. Womens Clubs. Republican. Lutheran (mem. ch. council, meml. sec.). Clubs: Happy Homemakers, Halstad Woman's (treas.), Red River Racquet. Home: Route 2 Halstad MN 56548 Office: 133 4th Ave E Halstad MN 56548

HENDERSON, MAXINE OLIVE BOOK (MRS. WILLIAM HENDERSON III), ednl. cons., assn. exec.; b. Rush, Colo., Apr. 22, 1924; d. Jesse Frank and Olive (Booth) Book; B.A., U. Colo., 1945; m. William Henderson III, Apr. 10, 1948; children—William IV, Meredith. Personnel adminstr. Gen. Electric Co., Schenectady and N.Y.C., 1945-54; asst. dir. placement Katherine Gibbs Sch., N.Y.C., 1967-70; v.p., dir. William Henderson Cons., Inc., N.Y.C., 1969—; dir. recruitment Girl Scouts U.S.A., N.Y.C., 1973-78, dir. human resources, 1978-82, dir. career devel., 1982—. Pres., Goddard-Riverside-Trinity Sch. Thrift Shop, N.Y.C., 1964-65, Trinity Sch. Mothers' Orgn., N.Y.C., 1965-66; treas. Brearley Sch. Parents Assn., N.Y.C., 1966-67. Episcopalian. Clubs: North Suffolk Garden, Nissequogue Beach, Nissequogue Platform Tennis Assn. (St. James, L.I., N.Y.). Home: 606 W 116th St New York NY 10027 also Nissequogue River Rd Saint James NY 11780 Office: 830 3d Ave New York NY 10022

HENDERSON, MYRTICE WINSLETT, educator; b. Wilkinson County, Ga., Dec. 21, 1928; d. William Thomas and Bertha Lucile (Butler) Winslett; B.S. in Edn., Georgia Coll., 1950, M.Ed., 1973; D. Arts candidate, Carnegie-Mellon U.; m. Howard James Henderson, July 31, 1950; children—Howard James, William Winslett. English tchr., choral music dir. Manor (Ga.) High Sch., 1950-57, Twiggs County (Ga.) High Sch. 1957-64, Cochran (Ga.) High Sch., 1964-73; voice instr. Middle Ga. Coll., 1965-70, asst. prof. English, music, 1973—; music dir. 1st Methodist Church Cochran, 1970—; organizer, dir. Cochran Jr. Women's Club Vocal Ensumble; soprano soloist, choral dir. coll. theater prodns. Recipient Spl. Music award Ga. C. of C., 1975; Service award Ga. 4-H Club, 1976; Fred Waring Choral Music Workshop grantee, 1975. Mem. NEA, Ga. Assn. Edn., D.A.R., Internat. Platform Assn., Southeastern Conf. Teaching of English in Two-Year Coll., Delta Kappa Gamma (Ga. state scholar 1978). Clubs: Cochran Woman's (co-chmn. fine arts com.), Ga. Federated Women's, Cochran Pilot (charter). Office: Middle Ga Coll Cochran GA 31014 *

HENDERSON, NAOMI HAIRSTON, market research co. exec.; b. Alexandria, La., Jan. 2, 1944; d. Joseph Henry and Anna Lee (Allen) Hairston; B.A. in Elem. Edn., Am. U., 1964, M.Ed. in Spl. Edn., 1968; m. Licius Samuel Henderson, III, Aug. 8, 1964. Sr. analyst Verve Research Corp., Rockville, Md., 1976-78; pres. Prism Corp., market research, Washington, 1978-81; dir. market research Goldberg/Marchesano & Assos., Inc., Washington, 1981-82; partner Riva market research div. R.J. Sobus & Partners, Washington, 1982—; est seminar leader; focus group moderator; cons. in field; lectr. market research. Mem. Market Research Assn., Leadership Forum Washington (vice chmn. 1981-82). Address: 4417 Brandywine St NW Washington DC 20016

HENDERSON, ROSEMARY GNAEDINGER, govt. ofcl.; b. Chgo., Nov. 30, 1921; d. Robert Joseph and Mary Edna (Metz) Gnaedinger; B.A., Mills Coll., 1943; m. Ralph Allen Henderson, Dec. 8, 1945; children—Judith Ellen, Scott Allen, Bruce Evan, Keith Richard, Craig Philip. Publicist various local and nat. polit. campaigns; public participation coordinator region 6 EPA, Dallas, 1976—. Mem. steering com. Dallas County Jr. Coll., 1963-65; mem. Dallas City Plan Commn., 1973-77; mem. Dallas County Grand Jury, 1970; mem. budget com. Dallas County United Fund, 1979; mem. Hist. Designation Task Force, Dallas; bd. dirs. Bethlehem Center of Dallas. Mem. Nat. Assn. Support of Public Schs., Tex. Com. for Public Edn., Nat. Urban League, LWV, Phi Beta Kappa. Democrat. Roman Catholic. Home: 5830 Desco Dr Dallas TX 75225 Office: 1201 Elm St Dallas TX 75270

HENDERSON, SARAH COTHRAN, civic worker, former educator; b. Greenwood, S.C., Feb. 2, 1915; d. Thomas White and Willie Maude (Boswell) Cothran; A.B., Lander Coll., 1937; M.Ed., Furman U., 1963; postgrad. Clemson U., 1971-73, LaVerne Coll., 1971, Furman U., 1976; m. William Edward Henderson, Dec. 30, 1936 (dec. Jan. 1980); 1 son, William Edward. Tchr., Greenville (S.C.) County Schs., 1950-78. Regent, Nathaneal Greene chpt. DAR, 1974-76, state chmn. public relations S.C. soc., 1976-79, state conf. chmn., 1982, dist. 1 dir., 1979-82, historian Palmetto State Officers Club, S.C. Mem. Greenville Art Assn., Greenville Geneal. Soc. (charter, archivist), Nat. Soc. Magna Carta Dames, Plantagenet Soc., S.C. Geneal. Soc., Greenville Hist. Soc., Ligon Family Assn., Huguenot Soc. S.C., DAR, Lander Coll. Alumni Assn., Furman U. Alumni Assn., Nat. Trust Hist. Preservation, Nat. Archives, Friends of Greenville Library. Club: Greenville Woman's. Presbyterian. Home: 114 Woodruff Rd Route 6 Greenville SC 29607

HENDREN, MERLYN CHURCHILL, furniture co. exec.; b. Gooding, Idaho, Oct. 16, 1926; d. Herbert Winston and Annie Averett Churchill; student U. Idaho, 1944-47; m. Robert Lee Hendren, June 14, 1947; children—Robert Lee, Anne Aleen. With Hendren's Furniture Co., Boise, 1947-69; co-owner, v.p. Hendren's Inc., Boise, 1969—. Bd. dirs. Idaho Law Found., 1978—; chmn. Coll. of Idaho Symposium, 1977-78, mem. adv. bd., 1981—; pres. Boise Council on Aging, 1959-60; mem. Gov.'s Commn. on Aging, 1960, Idaho del. to White House Conf. Aging, 1961; trustee St. Luke's Regional Hosp., 1981—; mem. adv. bd. dirs. Boise Philharm. Assn., Inc., 1981—. Mem. Boise C. of C. Republican. Episcopalian. Home: 3504 Hillcrest Dr Boise ID 83705 Office: 516 S 9th St Boise ID 83706

HENDRICK, EUNICE MAY, club woman; b. Pocasset, Okla., June 17, 1933; d. Alfred Floyd and Ruby Gladys (Key) Barton; student public schs.; m. Jerald Dean Hendrick, July 20, 1950; children—Valerie Ann, Vicky Lee, Jerry Randall. Various secretarial positions, 1958, 67-70, 76—; co-owner Hendrick-Reding Ins. Agy., Mustang, Okla., 1973-76; treas. S.W. Toastmasters Club, 1977-78; pres. Eagle Forum Mustang, 1979-80; organizer Okla. Crime Seminar, Mustang, 1975. Republican. Home: 115 S Lakepark Dr Mustang OK 73064 Office: 130-A E Hwy 152 Mustang OK 73064

HENDRICK, ZELWANDA, educator; b. Rusk, Tex., Nov. 28, 1925; d. Lloyd Irvin and Viola Alice (McGuire) Hendrick; A.A., Lon Morris Coll., 1945; B.S., N. Tex. U., 1947; M.A., So. Meth. U., 1958. Tchr. theatre arts Overton (Tex.) High Sch., 1947-49, Nacogdoches (Tex.) High Sch., 1949-50, Boude Storey Sch., Dallas, 1950-53, Kimball High Sch., Dallas, 1953-62; tchr. theatre arts H. Grady Spruce High Sch., Dallas, 1962-78, chmn. fine arts dept., 1963-77, ret., 1978; drama and psychology tchr. Alexander Sch., 1978—; substitute tchr. Highland Park High Sch., Dallas, 1980—; part-time tchr. John Robert Powers Finishing Sch., 1951—; teaching fellow N. Tex. U., 1964-65. Active, Tyler (Tex.) Civic Symphony, 1949-50, Tyler Civic Theatre, 1949-50, Dallas Theatre Center, 1960-61; mem. adv. com. Smithsonian Instn., 1975; co-sponsor U.S. Inst. Tech. Theatre; del. Democratic Dist. Conv., 1980; candidate Tex. State Legislature, 1980; chmn. Dallas County Transp. Bd., 1982—. Mem. Internat. Thespians (state dir.), Tex. Speech Assn. (sec. 1973—), Am. Assn. Ednl. Theatre, Dallas Ednl. Drama Assn. (governing bd.), Tex. Tchrs. Assn., Nat. Forensic League, AAUW, Classroom Tchrs. Dallas, Internat. Platform Assn., Ednl. Arts Assn., Tex. Congress Parent Tchr. Assn. (hon. life), DAR, Daus. Republic of Tex., N. Texas Collie Club, Nat. Assn. Royalty Owners, Tex. Ind. Producers and Royalty Owners Assn., Delta Kappa Gamma. Club: Order Eastern Star. Contbr. to A Guide to Student Teaching in Music, 1968-70. Home: 3016 Westminster St Dallas TX 75205

HENDRICKS, DOROTHY KAPROTH (KAPPY HENDRICKS), art gallery exec.; b. Foley, Minn., June 28, 1935; d. Casper and Stella (Gapinski) Kaproth; student Coll. St. Scholastica, Duluth, Minn., 1952-54; B.S., U. Colo., 1956, postgrad., 1957-61; postgrad. U. Md., 1961-63, Naganuma (Tokyo Sch. Japanese Lang.), 1965-70; M.S. in Applied Linguistics, Japanese Lang., Georgetown U., 1973; m. Marshall L. Hendricks, Apr. 2, 1956; children—Jeffrey, Lisle. Food economist Safeway Stores, Denver, 1956-58; tchr. Denver Public Schs., 1958-61, Prince George's County Public Schs., 1961-63; prof. Jissen Joshi Daigaku, Tokyo, 1966-70; pres. The Hendricks Art Collection Ltd., Bethesda, Md., N.Y.C. and Tokyo, 1965—; lectr. in field. Mem. Am. Soc. Appraisers. Republican. Author: Tadashi Nakayama: His Life and Work, 1983; contbr. articles in field. Home and Office: 6502 Hillmead Rd Bethesda MD 20817

HENDRICKS, HELEN MARIE, banker; b. Holdrege, Nebr., July 7, 1923; d. Samuel Truman and Helen Marie (Sauer) Schrock; B.A., U. Nebr., 1949; m. Harlan Hendricks, June 18, 1949; children—Jacqueline Jo, Kristy Marie, Wayne G. Various clerical and secretarial positions, 1942-46, 58-62, 65-66; asst. cashier, 1970-80, asst. v.p. First Nat. Bank, David City, Nebr., 1980— Trustee, St. Luke's United Methodist Ch., David City, mem. David City Planning Commn., 1971-82, sec.-treas., 1979. Trustee, chmn. St. Luke's United Meth. Ch. David City (Fin. com.), 1982—. Mem. Nat. Assn. Bank Women, David City C. of C., PEO, Am. Legion Aux., Northside Extension Club. Democrat. Club: Couples Bridge.

HENDRICKS, MARY JO, elec. engr.; b. Steubenville, Ohio, Apr. 26, 1956; d. James Albert and Mary Joan (Dougherty) Deist; B.S. in Elec. Engring., W.Va. Inst. Tech., 1978; m. Michael K. Hendricks, June 3, 1978. Elec. design engr. Union Carbide Corp., Charleston, W.Va., 1978-82, lead elec. engr. energy systems Institute plant (W.Va.), 1982—. Mem. IEEE (chmn. W.Va. sect. 1981-82; rep. Kanawha Valley Joint Tech. Council 1982-83), Eta Kappa Nu. Republican. Presbyterian. Home: 102 Green Dr Hurricane WV 25526 Office: Union Carbide Corp Box 2831 BL-271 Charleston WV 25330

HENDRICKS-RAUCH, MAUREEN CALISTA, marriage/family/feminist therapist; b. Bklyn., Dec. 23, 1934; d. Edwin Vincent and Mary Frances (Taaffe) Hendricks; B.S.N., Seton Hall U., 1969; M.S., U. Colo., 1971; Ed.D., U. No. Colo., 1979; m. Thomas McQuie Rauch, Aug. 13, 1972. Staff nurse, various hosps., 1957-69; community health nurse City of Denver, 1970; teaching asso. community health nursing U. Colo., Boulder, 1971-72; sr. instr. Community Health Nursing, U. Colo., 1972-75; family nurse practitioner 895 S. Logan Med. Clinic, Denver, 1973-76; pvt. practice marriage, family, and feminist therapy, Denver, 1979—; coordinator marriage team St. Elizabeth Roman Cath. Ch., Denver, 1979—. Mem. preventive and maint. care subcom. Denver Area Wide Comprehensive Health Planning Council, 1973-76; cons. to community health nurses, S.D., 1975, Wyo., 1977. Cert. family nurse practitioner Am. Nurses Assn., 1977, 82; USPHS nurse traineeship, 1969, 70-71; grad. nurse scholarship award N.J. League Nursing, 1968; fellow in marital and family therapy Internat. Council Sex Edn. and Parenthood, Am. U. Mem. Am. Assn. Marriage and Family Therapy, Nat. Council Family Relations, Colo. Assn. Holistic Health, Nat. Writers Club, Am. Nurses Assn., Council Primary Care, Colo. Nurses Assn., Am. Psychol. Assn., Sigma Theta Tau, Kappa Delta Pi, Delta Epsilon Sigma, Psi Chi. Roman Catholic. Club: Women's Ordination Conf. Contbr. articles to profl. jours. Office: 3710 E 5th Ave Denver CO 80206

HENDRIE, ELAINE, public relations exec.; b. Bklyn., d. David and Pearl (Saltzhauer) Kostell; m. Joseph Mallam Hendrie, July 9, 1949; children—Susan, Barbara. Asst. account exec. Benjamin Sonnenberg Public Relations firm, N.Y.C., 1953-57; public relations cons., writer, editor, 1957-72; dir. public relations and media Religious Heritage of Am., Washington, 1973-75; producer, interviewer Woman to Woman radio program, WRIV and WALK AM and FM, L.I., N.J., Westchester County, N.Y., Conn., 1974-77; exec. dir. Women in New Directions, Inc., Suffolk County, N.Y., 1974-77, cons. 1978—; nat. media coordinator NOW, Washington, 1978; media dir. Am. Speech-Lang.-Hearing Assn., Washington, 1979-80; public info. officer, head media and mktg. Dept. Navy, Washington, 1980-81; pres. Triangle Enterprises, 1982, Hendrie & Pendzick, 1982—; resource person for media Nat. Commn. on Observance of Internat. Women's Yr., 1977—; cons. Multi-Media Prodns. Inc., N.Y.C., 1978—, Women in New Directions, Inc., 1981—. Club: Bellport Bay Yacht. Home: 50 Bellport Ln Bellport NY 11713

HENDRIX, BEVERLY VIOLA, nurse, educator; b. Martin, S.D., Aug. 17, 1935; d. John William and Elva (Searby) Allard; B.S. in Nursing, Augustana Coll., Sioux Falls, S.D., 1957; M.S., Marquette U., Milw., 1970; m. Val E. Hendrix, June 3, 1956; children—Evelyn, Steven. Instr. nursing Hendricks Meml. Hosp., Abilene, Tex., 1958-60, U. Wis., Milw., 1970-76; hosp. and sch. nurse, Rapid City, S.D., 1961-63; dir. hosp. edn. St. Michael's Hosp., Milw., 1976-78; coordinator staff devel. Family Hosp., Milw., 1978-81; asst. prof. George Mason U. Sch. Nursing, Fairfax, Va., 1981—. Mem. Am. Nurses Assn., Nat. League Nursing. Presbyterian. Address: 6593 Braddock Rd Alexandria VA 22312

HENDRIX, KATHRYN ANN, trade assn. exec.; b. Olean, N.Y., July 6, 1934; d. George Tobias Whipp and Kathryn Elizabeth (Green) H.; B.S., Carnegie Mellon U., 1955. Sec., NASA, 1955-57; with Forging Industry Assn., Cleve., 1957—, corp. sec., 1977—, asst. v.p. adminstrn., 1980—. Mem. Greater Cleve. Soc. Assn. Execs. (dir., sec.-treas.), Cleve. Area Meeting Planners, Club: Women's City of Cleve. Home: 4400 Clarkwood Pky #615 Warrensville Heights OH 44128 Office: 55 Public Sq Rm 1121 Cleveland OH 44113

HENDSEY, SUSANNE B., librarian; b. Providence, R.I., Mar. 19, 1936; d. Laurence J. and Harriet (Delaplane) Brennan; B.A., U. Conn., 1960; M.L.S., U. Mich., 1967. Head, MBA Library, U. Conn., Hartford, 1964-66; sr. asst. librarian Grad. Sch. Bus., Public Adminstrn., Cornell U., 1967-72; chief readers' services FTC, Washington, 1972-79, library dir., 1979—. Mem. Law Librarians Soc. (dir. 1980-81), Spl. Libraries Assn. (chairperson social sci. group Washington chpt. 1982), D.C. Library Assn., Am. Assn. Law Libraries, Law Librarians Soc. D.C., Beta Phi Mu. Office: FTC 6th and Pennsylvania Aves NW Washington DC 20580

HENKALINE, SHARON TERUE, real estate broker; b. Greenville, Ohio, Dec. 5, 1946; d. Ronald Leroy and Francis Pauline (Daniel) Brown; MTI Bus. Sch., 1965; cert. in bus. adminstrn., U. Dayton, 1975; student Ohio State U., 1977; m. Jack Blaine Henkaline, Aug. 12, 1966; 1 son, Christopher Blaine. With aero. systems div. Wright Patterson AFB, Dayton, Ohio, 1965-66; with office adj. gen. U.S. Army, Fort Belvoir, Va., 1966-67; with purchasing and inventory control dept. Greenville (Ohio) Mfg., 1971-74; sales asso. Paul Clark Realty, Van Wert, Ohio, 1974-76, office mgr., 1976-78; partner Newert Co., Van Wert, 1976-78; owner, broker King & Co. Realty, Van Wert, 1979-80; pres., broker Shannon Realty Assos. Inc., Van Wert, 1980—. Mem. Nat. Assn. Realtors, Am. Bus. Women's Assn., Ohio Assn. Realtors, Van Wert Bus. and Profl. Womens Club, Van Wert County Bd. Realtors (v.p. 1978—), C. of C. Republican. Club: Elks. Home: UPP Rd Route 4 Van Wert OH 45891 Office: Shannon Realty Assos Inc 1043 S Shannon St Van Wert OH 45891

HENKE, M(ARY) BETH, public health specialist; b. Richmond, Va., June 16, 1947; d. William W. and Wanda J. Beckner; B.A. in Biology, Sweet Briar Coll., 1969; cert. med. tech. U. N.C., 1974, M.P.H. (USPHS grantee), 1981. High sch. tchr. biology, health scis. and English, Malawi, 1969-71; condr. public health survey, Zaire, 1971-72; med. lab. technologist U. N.C. Student Health Service, Chapel Hill, 1974-77, tng. asso. Program for Internat. Tng. in Health, 1981-82, acting dir. Program for Internat. Tng. in Health, 1982—; tchr. bacteriology, med. tech. program U. Nairobi Med. Tng. Center, Kenya, 1977-79. Mem. Am. Soc. Clin. Pathologists (cert. med. technologist), Am. Soc. Tng. and Devel., Nat. Council Internat. Health, Delta Omega. Office: 208 N Columbia St Chapel Hill NC 27514

HENKELS, NANCY LEE BULLOCK, former social service supr.; b. Bryn Mawr, Pa., July 26; d. George Reginald and Dorothy Lindsay (Black) Bullock; student Linden Hall Jr. Coll., 1944-46, U. Pa., 1947, Adelphia Bus. Sch., 1975; Cert. Main Line Bd. Realtors, 1975; children—Lindsay, Scott, David, Susanne. Vol. dir. arts and crafts Cathcart Home, Devon, Pa., 1967-69; child care supr. Devereux Found., Devon, 1974-75; supr. Evans Sch. for Retarded, Exton, Pa., 1975; companion-aid R.N. Health Services, 1975; housemother, supr. Charles E. Ellis Sch. for Girls, Newtown Square, Pa., 1976; houseparent, counselor Overbrook Sch. for the Blind, Phila., 1976-80; teaching asst. Delaware County Intermediate Unit, Presbyn. Children's Village, Rosemont, Pa., 1981. Local chmn. Pitts. Symphony Orch., 1963; vol. Melmark Home for Exceptional Children, Valley Forge Army Hosp.; sec. local PTA Bd. Recipient cert. Nat. Police Officers Assn., 1973. Mem. Assn. for Edn. (cert.), Am. Soc. Profl. and Exec. Women, Valley Forge Hist. Soc. Home: Devon Park Apts PO Box 143 Devon PA 19333

HENKIND, JANICE VERONICA, editor, adminstr.; b. N.Y.C., Feb. 3, 1951; d. William I. and Veronica A. Benjamin; B.A., Mercy Coll., 1972; M.Sc., U. Bridgeport, 1977; m. Paul Henkind, May 22, 1977; 1 son, Aaron Samuel. Electron microscopist Boyce Thompson Inst. for Plant Research, 1972-74, dept. ophthalmology Montefiore Hosp. and Med. Center, 1974-76; exec. adminstr. Assn. for Research in Vision and Ophthalmology, New Rochelle, N.Y., 1977—; mng. editor Ophthalmology, Jour. Am. Acad. Ophthalmology, 1979—, Acta, 24th Internat. Congress Ophthalmology, 1982-83; v.p. Med. Dialogues, Inc. Mem. Assn. Women in Sci., Nat. Assn. Female Execs., Electron Microscopist Soc. Am. Address: 276 Overlook Rd New Rochelle NY 10804

HENLE, GERTRUDE, virologist; b. Manheim, Germany, Apr. 3, 1912; d. Theophil and Eleneore (Baumgart) Szpingler; came to U.S., 1937, naturalized, 1943; M.D., U. Heidelberg (Germany), 1936; D.M.S. (hon.), Med. Coll. Pa., 1975; m. Werner Henle, Mar. 13, 1937. Intern, Inst. Hygiene, U. Heidelberg, 1936-37; mem. faculty U. Pa., 1937—, instr. to prof. bacteriology Sch. Medicine, 1940—, asst. to prof. virology in pediatrics, 1940—, mem. research staff Children's Hosp. of Phila., 1940—. Recipient Mead-Johnson award Am. Acad. Pediatrics, 1950. Variety of Heart award City of Phila., 1970, Smith, Kline and French award for excellence in research, 1971, Robert-Koch medaille and Robert-Koch preis Robert-Koch-Stiftung, 1971; Robert de Villiers award Leukemia Soc. Am., Inc., 1975, Virus Cancer Program award Nat. Cancer Inst., 1975, Sci. award Phila. chpt. Am. Cancer Soc., 1977, Disting. Achievement in Cancer Research award Bristol Myers Co., 1979. Mem. Am. Acad. Microbiology, Nat. Acad. Scis., Tissue Culture Assn. Contbr. numerous articles on influenza, mumps, hepatitis, infectious mononucleosis and tumor viruses to sci. jour. Home: 533 Ott Rd Bala-Cynwyd PA 19004 Office: 34th St and Civic Center Blvd Philadelphia PA 19104 *

HENLEY, HELEN MCTAGGART (MRS. W. BALLENTINE HENLEY), rancher; b. Pawnee, Ill., Mar. 20, 1910; d. Albert Thomas and Edith L. (Fallenstein) McTaggart; student Washington U., St. Louis, 1935-38; m. William Ballentine Henley, Dec. 15, 1942. Co-owner, mgr. Delmar Farm, Momence, Ill., 1943-58, Creston Circle Ranch, Paso Robles, Calif., 1958—; income property owner devel. and mgmt., 1955—. Mem. Am. Saddle Horse Assn., Am. Aberdeen-Angus Assn., Calif. Saddle Horse Breeder's Futurity (dir. 1945-48, 58-71). Home: 1224 Geneva St Glendale CA 91207 Office: Creston Circle Ranch Creston Star Route Paso Robles CA 93446

HENLEY, LILA JO SELMAN, social worker; b. Winter Haven, Fla., Feb. 9, 1936; d. Harold James and Hazel Louise (Collier) Selman; B.A., Tenn. Temple U., Chattanooga, 1961; prof. cert. Fla. State U., Tallahassee, 1963; M.S.W., Ind. U., 1967; m. James Wilson Henley, Jr., Feb. 2, 1968; 1 dau., Joy Selman. Child welfare worker Douglas County (Ga.) Dept. Family Service, 1961-62, Cobb County (Ga.) Dept. Family and Children's Service, 1963-66; dir. Cobb County Mental Health Bd., 1967-68; sch. social worker Atlanta Bd. Edn., 1968—; cons. in field. Adult mem. Girl Scouts Am. Mem. Nat. Assn. Social Workers, Acad. Cert. Social Workers, NEA, Ga. Assn. Educators, Atlanta Assn. Educators, Ga. Vis. Tchrs. Assn., Ga. Mental Health Assn., Phi Psi Sigma. Republican. Baptist. Club: Douglas County Pilot. Home: 3177 Hwy 166 Douglasville GA 30135

HENLEY, SALLIE HAMLET, artist, deaf interpreter; b. Norfolk, Va., Sept. 29, 1933; d. Charles McDowell and Sarah Speight (White) Hamlet; student pub. schs., Norfolk; m. William Franklin Henley, Jr., July 21, 1951; children—William Franklin III, Robert Matthew. Pub. speaker, Milw., 1968-71, Houston, 1971—; book dramatist, Milw., 1969-71, Houston, 1971-72; interpreter for deaf, Milw., 1969-71, Houston, 1971—; free-lance artist, Atlanta, 1963-65, Houston, 1975—; exhibited Sportsmans Gallery, The Galleria, Houston. Interpreter to deaf Elmbrook Ch., Brookfield, Wis., 1969-70; vol. tchr. deaf retardate Fairview North Elementary Sch., Brookfield, 1970; narrator, interpreter Deaf Olympics, 1969; sec. Quail Valley Civic Assn., 1974-75; bd. dirs. Ephphatha, Inc., Milw., 1969-70. Mem. Registry Interpreters for Deaf. Republican. Home: 2806 E Pebble Beach Dr Missouri City TX 77459

HENLINE, FLORENCE, pianist; b. Ft. Wayne, Ind.; d. Samuel and Caroline Dorothy (Mollet) Henline; B.M., Chgo. Mus. Coll., 1928; m. Milson Jezek, Sept. 2, 1936. Made first concert appearance at age of 13; appeared with Ill. Symphony and Grant Park Orch., Chgo., Women's Symphony (ofcl. pianist); accompanist; staff pianist NBC network, 1930-32; pianist, soloist Chgo. Symphony String Ensemble, 1946-56, Chgo. Pops Symphonette; soloist Indpls. Symphony String Ensemble Symphonette, 1970; solo concert engagements throughout U.S.; faculty mem. Chgo. Conservatory, 1959. Judge auditions piano solo contest 35th ann. Chicagoland Music Festival, 1964, ann. competition soloists Young Judea Symphony Orch. Chgo., 1965, 67. Fellow Internat. Inst. Arts and Letters (life); mem. Lake View Mus. Soc., Musicians' Club Women, Alliance Francaise (Chgo.), Ill. Opera Guild, Chgo. Artists Assn., Mu Phi Epsilon (soloist at internat. conv. 1972). Club: Cordon. Home: 9715 S Vanderpoel Chicago IL 60643

HENN, CAROL DEAN, ednl. adminstr.; b. Bethlehem, Pa., Jan. 30, 1947; d. Dean Richard and Irene Caroline (Kuzma) H.; B.A. with honors in Polit. Sci., Moravian Coll., 1968, postgrad., Moravian Theol. Sem., 1981—. Asso. dir. devel. Moravian Coll., Bethlehem, 1970-72, dir. ann. fund, 1972-74, dir. publs., 1974-77, dir. instl. relations, 1977—. Analyst, John D. Rockefeller campaign for W.Va. Ho. of Dels., 1966. Recipient Gold award United Way, 1977. Mem. Council for Advancement Support Edn. (Am. Alumni Council award 1971), Northampton County Tourism Council (dir.), Bethlehem Fine Arts Commn., Bermuda Nat. Trust, Underwater Explorers Soc. Democrat. Moravian Lutheran. Drawings represented in permanent collection Royal Danish Theatre Mus., Copenhagen; contbr. articles to ch. mags. Home: 2119 Cloverdale Rd Bethlehem PA 18018 Office: Moravian Coll Bethlehem PA 18018

HENN, SHIRLEY EMILY, librarian; b. Cleve., May 26, 1919; d. Albert Edwin and Florence Ely (Miller) Henn; A.B., Hollins Coll., 1941; M.S., U. N.C., 1966; m. John Van Bruggen, July 14, 1944 (div. May 1947); 1 son, Peter Albert (dec.). Library asst. Hollins (Va.) Coll., 1943-44, 61-64, reference librarian, 1965—; advt. mgr. R.M. Kellogg Co., Three Rivers, Mich., 1946-47; exec. sec. Hollins Coll. Alumnae Assn., 1947-55; real estate salesman Fowlkes & Kefauver, Roanoke, Va., 1955-61. Pres. Soc. for Prevention Cruelty to Animals, 1959-61, 69-72, bd. dirs., 1972-81. Mem. Am. Alumni Council (dir. 1952-54, dir. women's activities 1952-54), ALA, Va. Library Assn., Pub. Documents Forum Va., Nat. DAR (librarian Nancy Christian Fleming chpt. Roanoke 1977—), Collie Club Am., Roanoke Bird Club, Roanoke Kennel Club. Club: Quota (chpt. pres. 1958-60) (Roanoke). Author and illustrator: Adventures of Hooty Owl and His Friends, 1953; editor: Hollins Alumnae Bull., 1947-56. Home: 6915 Tinkerdale Hollins VA 24019 Office: Fishburn Library Hollins College VA 24020

HENNER, MARILU, actress; b. Chgo.; student U. Chgo. Films include: Between The Lines, Blood Brothers; TV appearances: The Paper Chase, Off-Campus, Seventh Avenue, Leonard, Like Father Like Daughter, Taxi; theatre appearances: Grease, Over Here, Pal Joey. Office: care Susan Smith and Assos 850 7th Ave New York NY 10019 *

HENNESSEE, ELIZABETH LEE, stockbroker; b. Raleigh, N.C., Sept. 1, 1953; d. William Edward and Mary Frances H.; B.A. in Edn. and Psychology, Randolph Macon Women's Coll., 1974. Tchr., So. Christian Acad., Raleigh, 1975; asst. dir. Raleigh Guidance Center, 1976; stockbroker Thomson McKinnon Securities, Inc., N.Y.C., 1976—, NOW asst. v.p. Active, Girl Scouts Greater N.Y.; mem. Jr. Com., Guggenheim Mus., 1979-82. Mem. Investment Assn. N.Y.C., Careers for Women (speaker). Methodist. Club: Jr. League (N.Y.C.). Office: 1 State St Plaza New York NY 10004

HENNESSEY, HELEN BURT, rare book dealer; b. Hydeville, Vt., Apr. 18, 1910; d. Sherrie Howard and Ethel Maude (Clark) Burt; grad. Bishop Hopkins Hall, Burlington, Vt., 1927; m. Joseph P. Hennessey, May 15, 1943; 1 dau., Sherri Burt. Machine operator Pratt & Whitney Aircraft Co., World War II; vol. radiographic technician Bellevue Hosp., N.Y.C., 1952-54; with Canterbury Book Shop, N.Y.C., 1954-62; propr. Hennesseys Old and Rare Books, Saratoga, N.Y., 1962—. Collector sch. taxes, Low Hampton, N.Y., 1947-50; Gray Lady, nurses aide VA Hosp., Albany, N.Y., 1960-62. Mem. Antiquarian Book Seller Assn. Am. Democrat. Address: The Hennesseys 4th and Woodlawn Ave Saratoga NY 12866

HENNESSY, BARBARA MCDONNELL, psychotherapist; b. N.Y.C., Apr. 18, 1931; d. James F. and Anna (Murray) McDonnell; B.A., Manhattanville Coll., 1953; M.S.W., N.Y. U., 1975; children—John F. III, Kathleen, James M., Kevin, Peter, David. Founder, research asst. Vitam Center, Inc., 1972; asst. to pres. Thorson Investment Co., Greenwich, Conn., 1973; asst. prof. U. Bridgeport (Conn.), 1976; founder, dir. Anuk, Inc., Stamford, Conn., 1977, therapist, dir. field placements, 1978—, co-dir. character disorder program, 1980—; dir. New Canaan Center for Devel. Whole Person, 1978—; field supr. Fordham U., N.Y.C., 1979—. Sec. bd. trustees SUCASA, Conn. Psychotherapy Center, 1976—. Mem. Internat. Transactional Analysis Assn., Acad. Cert. Social Workers, Nat. Assn. Social Workers. Clubs: Country, Winter (New Canaan, Conn.). Home and Office: Duck Pond Rd East Norwalk CT 06855

HENNIGE, MARIANNE AMALIE, accountant; b. Stuttgart, Germany, Apr. 18, 1926; came to U.S., 1952, naturalized, 1956; d. Eugen Albert and Julie Pauline (Groezinger) H.; B.B.A. magna cum laude, Northwood Inst., Midland, Mich., 1981; children—Shirley I., Sharon C. Office mgr. Dept. Army, Europe, 1946-52; supr. acctg. dept. Mich. Farm Bur. Ins., 1953-58; sec. to prin. Peck (Mich.) Community Schs., 1958-61; asst. treas., mgr. acctg. dept. Proctor Homer Warren, Inc., 1961-77; chief acct., mgr. data processing dept. Mich. Products., Inc., distbrs. ednl. materials, Lansing, 1977—; officer, dir. Sanilac County Bd. Edn. Credit Union, Sandusky, Mich. Mem. Peck Library Bd.; chmn. com. for fgn. student exchange Greater Detroit Area YMCA. Mem. Nat. Assn. Female Execs., Am. Mgmt. Assn., Lansing Accts. Assn., AAUW, Phi Theta Kappa, Beta Sigma Phi (life; chpt. pres. 1962, 64, 69-70). Office: 1200 Keystone Ave Lansing MI 48910

HENNING, FAY MARIE, mfg. co. exec.; b. Eau Claire, Wis., June 25, 1942; d. Bernard T. and Mildred (Strobel) H.; B.A., Luther Coll., 1964; postgrad. Tex. Tech. U., 1967-71, Ind. Purdue U., 1971-79; M.A., U. Iowa, 1969. Tchr. Spanish, Public Schs. Davenport (Iowa), 1965-69, Slaton, Tex., 1969-71; counselor, social worker Met. Sch. Dist. Washington Twp.-Indpls., 1971-73; dir. edn. and tng. Community Addiction Services Agy., Inc., Indpls., 1973-77; purchasing agt., personnel mgr. Paper Art Co., Indpls., 1978-79; personnel and adminstrn. mgr. E-A-R div. Cabot Corp., Indpls., 1979—; v.p. The Woman's Touch, Inc., 1977. Mem. community adv. com. Fairbanks Hosp., Inc., Indpls., 1978—, co-chmn. women's issues task force, 1979-80; co-chmn. Ind. Task Force to Certify Substance Abuse Counselors, 1975-77; mem. adv. com. Pike High Sch., 1979—; bd. dirs. Julian Center, 1981—, Indpls. YWCA, 1982—; bd. dirs. Cabot Corp. Polit. Action Com., 1981—. Mem. Women's Polit. Caucus, Network Women in Bus. (sec. 1979, v.p. 1981—), Am. Soc. Personnel Adminstrn. Home: 4015 N New Jersey St Indianapolis IN 46205 Office: 7911 Zionsville Rd Indianapolis IN 46268

HENNING, GERTRUDE WERFELMANN, publishing co. exec.; b. Froid, Mont., Oct. 26, 1913; d. Arthur Henry and Beatrice (Duever) Werfelmann; student Luther Inst., 1930, Northwestern U., Elgin Community Coll.; m. Albert W. Henning, Nov. 20, 1940; children—Beatrice Henning Haase, Suzanne Henning Krahn. Mem. investment com. David C. Cook Found., 1972—, sec. bd., 1972—; fin. sec., adminstrv. asst. to pres. David C. Cook Pub. Co., Elgin, Ill., 1965—. Organ accompanist St. John's Luth. Ch., Elgin, 1972—; bd. dels. Luth. Home and Service for the Aged, Arlington Heights, Ill., 1974—. Mem. Elgin Musicians Assn., Elgin Choral Union. Home: 78 S Edison Ave Elgin IL 60120 Office: 850 N Grove Ave Elgin IL 60120

HENNING, LAURA HELENE, info. mgmt. engr.; b. Patuxent River, Md., Apr. 16, 1948; d. Charles William and Julia Marie (Wainscott) H.; B.A., U. Calif., at Berkeley, 1970; M.L.S. (scholar), U. Oreg., 1971. Reference librarian Calif. State Coll., Stanislaus at Turlock, 1971-73; librarian Contra Costa County Library, Pleasant Hill, Calif., 1973; head librarian Electric Power Research Inst., Palo Alto, Calif., 1973-80; records systems specialist Wash. Public Power Supply System, Richland, 1980-82; project engr. Inst. Nuclear Power Ops., Atlanta, 1982—; mem. nat. environ. studies project adv. bd. Atomic Indsl. Forum, 1975. Mem. Spl. Libraries Assn., World Affairs Council, Assn. Records Mgrs. and Adminstrs., Nuclear Records Mgmt. Assn., Beta Phi Mu. Contbr. articles to profl. jours. Address: 60 Arlene Ln Walnut Creek CA 94595

HENNINGS, DOROTHY GRANT (MRS. GEORGE HENNINGS), educator; b. Paterson, N.J., Mar. 15, 1935; d. William Albert and Ethel Barbara (Moll) Grant; A.B., Barnard Coll., 1956; M.Ed. (NSF Acad. Yr. Inst. grantee), U. Va., 1959; Ed.D. (Field Enterprise grantee), Columbia, 1965; m. George Hennings, June 15, 1968. Tchr., Pierrepont Elementary Sch., Rutherford, N.J., 1956-58, Thomas Jefferson Jr. High Sch., Fair Lawn, N.J., 1959-64; prof. edn. Kean Coll. of N.J., Union, 1965—. Recipient Edn. Press. award, 1974. Mem. Nat. Council Tchrs. English, Nat. Council Social Studies, N.J. Reading Assn., Internat. Reading Assn., Phi Beta Kappa, Phi Delta Kappa, Phi Kappa Phi, Kappa Delta Pi. Author: (with B. Grant) Teacher Moves, 1971; Content and Craft: Written Expression in the Elementary Sch., 1973; Smiles, Nods and Pauses: Activities to Enrich Children's Communication Skills, 1974; Mastering Classroom Communication: What Interaction Analysis Tells the Teacher, 1975; (with G. Hennings) Keep Earth Clean, Blue and Green: Environmental Activities for Young People, 1976; Words, Sounds, and Thoughts: More Activities to Enrich Children's Communication Skills, 1977; Communication in Action: Teaching the Language Arts, 1978, 2d edit., 1982; (with D. Russell) Listening Aids Through the Grades, 1979; (with G. Hennings) Today's Elementary Social Studies, 1980; Written Expression in the Language Arts, 1981. Contbr. articles to Edn., The Record, Lang. Arts, Sci. Tchr., Tchr. to Tchrs., Sci. and Children, Early Years, others. Home: 21 Flintlock Dr Warren NJ 07060 Office: Kean Coll of NJ Morris Ave Union NJ 07083

HENNINGS, JOSEPHINE SILVA (HALPIN), ret. govt. ofcl.; b. St. Louis; d. Francois P. and Mary Josephine (Barrick) Silva; B.A., Washington U., polit. sci. George Washington U.; m. Breen Halpin (dec.); children—Breen, Joan; m. 2d, Thomas C. Hennings, Jr. (dec.). News broadcaster, analyst Sta. KMOX, St. Louis, WINS, N.Y.C., ABC, N.Y.C.; broadcaster, news analyst Sta. KGU, Honolulu; fgn. corr. St. Louis Globe-Democrat, CBS, Caribbean, Pacific; columnist, feature writer Honolulu Advertiser; features editor, columnist St. Louis Star Times; editor Inter-Am. Affairs, USIA, Dept. State; sr. radio officer UN; news analyst, TV panelist ABC; editor U.S. Comptrollers Office, St. Thomas; then fed. govt. liaison officer Dept. of Def., Washington. Named top Am. woman broadcaster in internat. field UN, U.S. Dept. Labor. Clubs: Am. Women in Radio and TV, Washington Press, Nat. Press, Federal Editors (Washington); Overseas Press (N.Y.C.). Home: 2501 Calvert St NW Washington DC 20008

HENNINGTON, JOANN, educator, univ. exec.; b. Hereford, Tex., Apr. 10, 1932; d. Frank Gordon and Myra C. Witherspoon; B.A., Ariz. State U., 1964, M.B.A., 1966, D.B.A., 1972, Ed.D., 1972; m. Robert Leo Hennington, Apr. 10, 1950; 1 dau., Suanne. Exec. sec. Southwestern Pub. Service Co., Hereford, Tex., 1950-55; dept. chmn. bus. edn. Scottsdale (Ariz.) Pub. Schs., 1964-74; faculty mem., asst. dean Coll. Bus. Adminstrn., Ariz. State U., Tempe, 1974—, assoc. prof., 1978—, seminar leader Center for Exec. Devel., 1975—. Bd. dirs. Scottsdale Pub. Schs. Vocat. Adv. Council, 1975—; bd. dirs. Big Sisters of Ariz., 1978-80, mem. exec. bd. Aux., 1975-80. Mem. Nat. Bus. Edn. Assn., Am. Bus. Communication Assn., Western Bus. Edn. Assn., Ariz. Bus. Edn. Assn., Faculty Women's Assn. Ariz. State U., Women in Higher Edn. Ariz., Ariz. State U. Coll. Bus. Adminstrn. Alumni Assn. (bd. dirs. 1977-81), Delta Pi Epsilon (Outstanding Leadership award Alpha Sigma chpt. 1964, nat. pres. elect 1982-83), Beta Gamma Sigma (pres. Beta chpt. of Ariz. 1982-83), Pi Omega Pi, Pi Lambda Theta, Phi Kappa Phi, Kappa Delta Pi. Author: Selfpace English Composition, 1976. Contbr. chpts. to yearbooks, articles to profl. jours. Home: 8254 E Hubbell St Scottsdale AZ 85257 Office: Coll Bus Adminstrn Ariz State U Tempe AZ 85287

HENRION, ROSEMARY, nurse; b. Greenville, Miss., Oct. 2, 1930; d. Vincent and Camille (Portera) Provenza; R.N., St. Mary's Sch. Nursing, Galveston, Tex., 1951; B.S. in Nursing, U. Tex. Med. Br., Galveston, 1963; M.S.N. (NIMH fellow 1971), Vanderbilt U., 1972; M.Secondary Edn., U. So. Miss., 1974; m. Albert Joseph Henrion, Sept. 8, 1956 (dec.); 1 son, Albert Joseph. Staff nurse St. Mary's Hosp., Galveston, 1951-52; office nurse and pvt. duty surg. nurse, Galveston, 1952-53; head nurse Ob and med.-surg. nursing, Greenville (Miss.) Gen. Hosp., 1953-54, supr. obstetrical nursing, 1954-56; nursing instr. Providence Hosp. Sch. Nursing, Waco, Tex., 1957-59; dir. inservice edn. Meml. Hosp., Gulfport, Miss., 1966-67, asst. dir. nursing service, 1966-67, dir. nursing service, 1967-68; psychiat. clin. nurse specialist Biloxi (Miss.) VA Med. Center, 1972—, in-house cons., 1975—; participant research projects So. Region Edn. Bd., 1973-75; asst. clin. prof. psychiat.-mental health nursing Grad. Sch. Nursing, La. State U., New Orleans, 1975-77; mem. Miss. Bd. of Nursing, 1975-79, pres., 1976-78. Mem. Planning com. Family Counseling, St. Thomas Ch., Long Beach, Miss., 1974—, ministry of canonical affairs, 1975-77; mem. Pass Christian Carnival Assn., 1975-78; ednl. council local chpt. Am. Cancer Soc., 1977. Recipient service award Biloxi VA Center, 1970, 79; Menninger Found. fellow, 1978—. Mem. Am. Nurses Assn., Dist. Nurses Assn. (membership com., 1964-66, chmn., 1966-67), Miss. Nurses Assn. (vice chmn., program chmn. spl. interest group 1972-75), Council Advanced Practitioners Psychiat.-Mental Health Nursing, Internat. Transactional Assn., Gulf Coast Mental Health Assn. (planning com. Women's Worry Clinic 1972), U. Tex. Alumni Assn., Vanderbilt U. Alumni Assn., U. So. Miss. Alumni Assn., Am. Bus. Women's Assn., Sigma Theta Tau. Roman Catholic. Club: Officers. Researcher, speaker, panelist profl. confs., contbr. articles in field to publs. Home: 19 Wenmar Ave Pass Christian MS 39571 Office: VA Med Center Biloxi MS 39571

HENRY, JEN ELLEN, psychiat. social worker; b. Ironton, Ohio, May 16, 1945; d. Allen T. and Wilma L. Christy; B.A. in Religion, Coll. Wooster (Ohio), 1967; cert. in ch. and community McCormick Theol. Sem., Chgo., 1971; M.S.W., U. Ill., 1971. Social worker Kirkdale Child Guidance Clinic, London, 1971-74; sr. psychiat. social worker Child and Adolescent Psychiat. Clinic, Inc., Buffalo, 1975—. Mem. Nat. Assn. Social Workers, NOW. Presbyterian. Office: 3350 Main St Buffalo NY 14214

HENRY, KATHERINE SAVAGE, physician; b. Marietta, Ga., Aug. 30, 1944; d. James Ernest and Audrey Louise (Armstrong) Savage; B.A., Birmingham-So. Coll., 1966; M.D., Emory U., 1971. Intern, resident in internal medicine Ga. Bapt. Hosp., Atlanta, 1971-73; emergency room physician Baylor Med. Center, Dallas, 1973-74; family physician The Family Clinic, Garland, Tex., 1974; family practice medicine, Richardson, Tex., 1974—; chmn. dept. family practice Richardson Gen. Hosp., 1975; cons. health care Richardson YWCA; exec. com. Richardson Med. Center, 1975- 78; first physician, designer health service U. Tex., Dallas, 1974-76. Diplomate Am. Bd. Family Practice. Fellow Am. Acad. Family Physicians; mem. AMA (physicians recognition award), Am., Tex. acads. family practice, Dallas County Med. Soc., Tex. Med. Assn., Am. Med. Women's Assn. (charter pres. Dallas chpt. 1980). Home: 16007 Ranchita Dr Dallas TX 75248 Office: 721 W Arapaho Suite 2 Richardson TX 75080

HENRY, KATHLEEN MARIE, mktg. exec.; b. Stillwater, Okla., Sept. 24, 1950; d. Irl Wayne and Hulda Mary (Duncan) Henry; B.S., Central State U. (Okla.), 1972. Community relations dir./account exec. Lowe Runkle Advt., Oklahoma City, 1972-74, account coordinator, 1975; sales promotion cons. McDonald's Corp., Houston, 1974; regional advt. supr. McDonald's Southfield (Mich.), 1975, regional advt. mgr., 1976-78, local store mktg. mgr., Oak Brook, Ill., 1978-80, staff dir., store mktg./sales promotion, 1980-82, home office dir. store mktg./sales promotion, 1982—. Publicity chmn. Keep Okla. Beautiful, 1973-74; publicity chmn. Muscular Dystrophy Assn. Am., 1973-74; bd. dirs. Southfield Arts Council, 1976-78. Recipient Pres.'s award, McDonald's Corp., 1978; Chgo. YWCA Leadership award, 1978; Disting. Former Student award, Central State U., 1979, Outstanding Sr. Woman, 1972, Outstanding Greek Woman, 1972. Mem. Central State U. Alumni Assn. (dir. 1974), Nat. Assn. Female Execs., Women's Advt. Club Chgo., Sigma Kappa. Home: 6386 Kindling Ct Lisle IL 60532 Office: McDonalds Plaza Oak Brook IL 60521

HENRY, MARGARET MARY, assn. exec.; b. Medford, Mass., Feb. 4, 1930; d. James Francis and Etta Mabel (McCobb) Hazel; A.B., Regis Coll., 1952; m. Charles Eric Henry, Nov. 1, 1963. Technician dept. pharmacology Harvard Med. Sch., 1952-54; research asst. dept. pharmacology Yale U. Med. Sch., 1954; research technician Children's Med. Center, Boston, 1955-56; research asst. Mallory Inst. Pathology, Boston City Hosp., Boston U. Med. Sch., 1956-60; tech. writer, advt. dir., exhibits mgr. Grass Instrument Co., Quincy, Mass., 1960-65; pres. Med. Assn. Mgmt. Inc. Willoughby, Ohio, and Midlothian, Va., 1965—; exec. sec. Am. Electroencephalographic Soc., Willoughby, 1970-80; exec. sec. Am. Soc. EEG Technologists, 1974-76; exec. sec. Am. Epilepsy Soc., 1977-80; exec. dir. Am. Soc. Neuroimaging, 1981—; exec. dir. Health Scis. Communications Assn., 1982—, Assn. Med. Investigators, 1982—, Central Va. Epilepsy Soc., 1982—; cons. prodn. Am. Jour. EEG Tech., 1966-69; manuscript editor Archives Phys. Medicine and Rehab., 1968-71; sec. Anticonvulsant Glossary Com. Internat. Bur. Epilepsy, 1968-71; mem. exec. bd. Nat. Com. Research and Communicable Disorders. Charter mem. Kirtland Ednl. Found., 1964-65; chmn. Cleve. Com. on Epilepsy, 1975-76; pres. exec. bd., staff wives com. Cleve. Clinic Found., 1975-76; bd. dirs. Central Va. Epilepsy Assn., 1981—; mem. women's com. Richmond Symphony. Mem. Central Assn. Electroencephalographers, Profl. Conv. Mgmt. Assn., Am. Soc. Assn. Execs., Va. Soc. Assn. Execs., Meeting Planners Internat. (pres. No. Ohio chpt.). Clubs: Herb Soc.; Mrs. Hudson's Lodgers. Contbr. articles to profl. jours. Home: Route 1 Box 311F Midlothian VA 23113

HENRY, MARTHA FRANCES, dietitian; b. Columbia, Mo., Sept. 19, 1920; d. James William and Martha Frances (Robinson) Shock; B.S., U. Mo., 1941; postgrad. Iowa State U., 1940, Tex. A&M U., 1973-74; m. Walter Keith Henry, Feb. 13, 1943; children—Stephen Allen, Dale Lee, Carl Bruce. County supr. Nat. Youth Adminstrn., Jefferson City, Mo., 1941-42; dietitian Mo. State Sanatorium, Mt. Vernon, 1942-43; cafeteria mgr. Scruggs-Vandervoort-Barney, St. Louis, 1943-45; dir. food service McQuay-Norris Mfg. Co., St. Louis, 1945; asst. dir. residence halls U. Mo., Columbia, 1946-47; lab. technician Tex. A&M U., College Station, 1965-71; dietitian Bryan (Tex.) Hosp., 1972-74; cons. dietitian Sherwood Health Care Facility, Bryan, 1974-75, Hennesey Nursing Home, Giddings, Tex., 1982—; adminstrv., clin. dietitian St. Joseph Hosp., Bryan, 1976-78; pvt. cons. nutritionist College Station, 1978—. Flower chmn. A&M Methodist Ch., 1958—; active Brazos County chpt. ARC. Mem. Am. Dietetic Assn., Am. Diabetes Assn., Gerontol. Nutritionists Assn., Tex. Dietetic Assn., Mid-East Tex. Dietetic Assn. (pres.), Brazos Valley Home Econs. Assn., Cons. Nutritionist-Pvt. Practice Group, DAR, Daus. Am. Colonists, U.S. Daus. of 1812, Nat. Geneal. Soc., Brazos Valley Geneal. Assn., Magna Carta Dames. Republican. Club: Order Eastern Star. Home and Office: 1202 Caudill St College Station TX 77840

HENRY, NANCY LOUISE, conf. center-hotel exec., mayor; b. Somerville, N.J., July 18, 1940; d. Robert Lewis and Mary Louise (Skinner) Twyman; student Rutgers U., 1973-75, Trenton State Coll., 1976-77; children—Lionel N., Robert Lewis. With Johnson & Johnson, New Brunswick, N.J., 1959-77, v.p., 1965-77; conv. coordinator Nat. Conf. Center, East Windsor, N.J., 1977-78; sales mgr. Scanticon-Princeton (N.J.) Conf. Center-Hotel, 1982—; dep. mayor City of Somerset (N.J.), 1982—; mayor Franklin Twp. (N.J.), 1982—; spl. asst. to gov. State of N.J., Trenton, 1978-79, dir. resources and community participation Office of Ombudsman for Instnl. Elderly, Trenton, 1979—. Councilwoman Franklin Twp. (N.J.), 1977—; committeewoman 4th Ward, Franklin Twp., 1977-79, ward chmn., 1978-79; mem. adv. council Somerset County Employment and Tng. Agy., 1977-81, chmn. youth adv. council, 1978-80; del. Democratic Nat. Conv., 1980; v.p. N.J. Fedn. Dem. Women. Methodist. Home: 15 DeWald Ave Somerset NJ 08873 Office: Scanticon-Princeton 100 College Rd E Princeton NJ 08540

HENRY, PATRICIA ANN, home economist mgmt. co. ofcl.; b. Fostoria, Ohio, Oct. 4, 1947; d. Joseph I. and Betty Jean (Feasel) Pocs; student St. Francis Sch. of Nursing and St. Mary of Spring Coll., 1965-66, Ohio State Sch. Nursing, 1974; external degree in nursing SUNY, 1976; B.S. in Home Econs., Ohio State U., 1975 postgrad in bus. adminstrn., 1982; realtor, Columbus Tech. Inst., 1978; m. David Strubie Henry, July 2, 1966 (div. Jan. 1971); 1 dau., Jennifer; m. 2d, Barry Wayne Cox, Mar. 7, 1980 (div. July 1981). Office nurse, Fredericktown, Ohio, 1966-67, Mt. Vernon, Ohio, 1969-71; nursing tech. St. Anthony Hosp., Columbus, Ohio, 1971-72; lab. tech. Ohio State U. Hosp., 1972-75; nursing coordinator Med. Evaluation Services, Columbus, 1975-76; sales rep. Ryan Homes, Inc., Columbus, 1976-78, Virginia Homes, Inc., Columbus, 1978-79, Crest Communities, 1979-81; sales mgr. condominiums Kling Beil Mgmt. Group Co., Columbus, 1981—. Mem. Nat. Assn. Realtors, Ohio Bd. Realtors, Home Economists in Bus., Am. Home Econs. Assn., Ohio State U. Alumni Assn. Home: 5384 Fortress Trail Columbus OH 43230 Office: 2890 Chateau Circle N Ave Columbus OH 43221

HENRY, SANDRA JANE, advt. and pub. relations co. exec.; b. Indpls., Dec. 22, 1953; d. Ernest Leroy and Carol Ann (Gipson) Lester; B.F.A. in Journalism, So. Methodist U., 1975; m. Thomas Joseph Henry, July 28, 1979; 1 stepson, James Christopher. Intern in advt. and public relations, Dallas and Tulsa, 1972-75; instr. student workshop Oral Roberts U., Tulsa, 1973; copywriter, media buyer Venus Advt., Indpls., 1975-76; account exec. Joe Newman Advt., Indpls., 1976-77, v.p., 1977-80; owner Sandra J. Henry & Assocs., Indpls., 1980—; condr. motivation seminars; guest, instr. Nat. Crime Prevention Inst. seminars U. Louisville, 1980, 81; guest instr. advt. classes Clark Coll., Indpls., 1980, Wabash (Ind.) Coll., 1978; lectr. relaxation seminar SMCI Programs, Inc.; guest lectr., speaker on sales tng., motivation, advt. and pub. relations to various groups. Vol., March of Dimes, Ind. Competitive Swim Com., Ind. Sports Corp. Recipient award March of Dimes, 1980; Talent Award scholar, 1972-74. Mem. Nat. Assn. Female Execs., Ind. Fedn. Advt. Agys., Indpls. C. of C., Network Women in Bus., Advt. Club Indpls. Republican. Office: 4274 Larkspur Trace Indianapolis IN 46227

HENRY, SARAH TABB, home economist; b. Owensboro, Ky., July 17, 1934; d. William Roy and Lockett (Ford) Tabb; B.S., U. Ky., 1956, M.S., 1959, Ed.S., 1969, Ed.D. (EPDA fellow), 1977; m. William Keith Henry, July 31, 1963; 1 dau., Mary Keith. Tchr. home econs., Georgetown, Ky., 1956-60; area supr. Ky. Dept. Edn., Frankfort, 1960-63, asst. dir. home econs. unit, 1969-74; curriculum writer Curriculum Devel. Center Vocat. Edn., U. Ky., 1964-69; asst. prof. Morehead (Ky.) State U., 1977-78; asst. prof. Sch. Edn., U. Louisville, 1978-80, dir. nutrition edn. project, 1979; asst. dean Coll. Home Econs., U. Ky., Lexington, 1980—; tchr. summer course N.D. State U., 1969; cons. in field. Bd. dirs. Georgetown Day Care Center, 1979-82; mem. Christian edn. com. First Presbyn. Ch., Georgetown, 1980-81. Named Ky. col., 1960. Mem. Am. Vocat. Assn., Am. Home Econs. Assn., Nat. Assn. Tchr. Educators Home Econs., Home Econs. Edn. Assn., Ky. Assn. Future Homemakers Am. (hon.), Ky. Home Econs. Assn. (past pres., treas.), U. Ky. Alumni Assn. (life), U. Ky. Coll. Home Econs. Alumni Assn. (past pres.), Women's Assn. Georgetown Coll., Am. Legion Aux., Phi Delta Kappa, Phi Upsilon Omicron, Iota Lambda Sigma, Alpha Xi Delta. Democrat. Club: Spindletop Hall. Home: Route 2 Gunnell Rd Georgetown KY 40324 Office: U Ky 206 Erikson Hall Lexington KY 40506

HENRY, VIRGINIA DEXTER (MRS. JAY E. HENRY), civic worker; b. Lone Rock, Wis., June 5, 1908; d. Forrester L. and Rosetta (Zimmerman) Dexter; B.A. (Panhellenic Council scholar 1932-33), U. Wis., 1934; m. Jay Everett Henry, Sept. 29, 1934; children—Terry Jay, Steven Dexter. Nat. editor Phi Chi Theta, 1934-48; social worker Wis. Gen. Hosp., Madison, 1930-36. Mem. spl. housing com. City of Wheeling, 1958-59; pres. Wheeling YWCA, 1957-60, dir., 1954-61; nat. rep. nat. support com., nat. bd. YWCA, 1962-64, mem. nat. bd., 1964-73; bd. dirs. Charleston YWCA, 1966-71, pres., 1970-71; pres. Charleston Aux. Profl. Engrs. Soc., 1967-69, 79—; chmn. state council W.Va. Soc. Profl. Engrs., 1970-72; vice-chmn. central region Nat. Soc. Profl. Engrs., 1976-78, editor, 1978-80, chmn.-elect, 1980-81, nat. chmn. Aux., 1981-82; mem. Meals-on-Wheels, Inc.; pres. United Ch. Women of Greater Wheeling Council of Chs., 1955-57, Women's Assn. First Presbyn. Ch., Wheeling, 1951-55, Wheeling Presbyterial, 1959-62; sec. Human Rights Commn. Wheeling; v.p. Synodical W.Va., U.P. Ch. U.S.A., 1968-70; mem. Charleston Meml. Hosp. Aux.; chmn. dept. conservation W.Va. Fedn. Women's Clubs, 1974-76, 80-82, environ. action dept., 1982. Life mem. Phi Chi Theta. Club: Charleston Women's (chmn. public affairs dept. 1970-72, chmn. conservation 1972-74; dir. 1975-77, co-chmn. blood pressure clinics 1973—, treas. 1978—). Home: 116 McGovran Rd South Hills Charleston WV 25314

HENSLER, SUE, educator; b. Greenway, Ark., July 27, 1932; d. Albert Newton and Minnie Elgiva (Overton) Harris; student Southwestern (Tenn.) U., Memphis, 1949-50; B.S. in Kindergarten-Primary Edn., Tex. Woman's U., Denton, 1953; m. William Harry Hensler, Oct. 30, 1954; children—Patricia Ann, Kay Marie, Vern Harris. Tchr., Denver, 1953-55; tchr. Aurora (Colo.) Pub. Schs., 1957—, also resource person, mem. com. profl. growth; cons. art collecting. Mem. speaker's bur. Aurora Pub. Library. Mem. Tex. Woman's U. Nat. Alumnae Assn. (life), Nat. Audubon Soc., Pacific N.W. Indian Center, Southwestern Assn. Indian Affairs, Western Heritage Art Found., Colo. State, Aurora (life, dir.) hist. socs., Aurora Arts and Humanities Council, Denver Mus. Natural History, Denver Art Mus., Denver Zool. Found., Zeta Tau Alpha (life), Pi Lambda Theta, Delta Kappa Gamma. Republican. Protestant. Home: 1081 Jamaica Ct Aurora CO 80010 Office: Aurora Pub Schs 1085 Peoria St Aurora CO 80010

HENSLEY, BONNIE KEATON, nurse; b. Hinton, W.Va., Nov. 19, 1917; d. Hugh and Lucretia Adeline Keaton; diploma in nursing, Johns Hopkins Hosp., 1940; B.S., U. N.C., Chapel Hill, 1964; M.S. (HEW Dept. Nursing trainee 1967), Duke U., 1969; m. Laurence S. Hensley, Aug. 25, 1942; children—Laurence S., R. Stephen. Staff nurse, supr., tchr. Duke U. Med. Center, 1952-67; mem. faculty U. N.C. Sch. Nursing, Chapel Hill, 1968—, asso. prof., 1975—, continuing edn. program dir., 1973-74. Mem. Am. Nurses Assn., AAUP, N.C. Nurses Assn. (chmn. com. continuing edn. planning 1979-81, dist. pres. 1973-74, dist. dir. 1978—) N.C. Adult Edn. Assn., N.C. Group Behavior Soc., U. N.C. Chapel Hill Sch. Nursing Alumni Assn. (dir. 1980-82), Sigma Theta Tau. Author articles, papers, videotapes in nursing mgmt., assertive behavior tng. and interpersonal relations. Home: 3237 Pickett Rd Durham NC 27705 Office: Carrington Hall U NC Chapel Hill NC 27514

HENSLEY, DOROTHY LUCILLE, retail toy exec.; b. DeQueen, Ark., Aug. 24, 1937; d. S.O. and Lucille (Clayton) Clark; A.B. in Spanish, Speech and Edn., Bethany (Okla.) Nazarene Coll., 1959; postgrad. Okla. U., Central State U.; m. Manuel Hensley, Aug. 21, 1960; children—Michael Clarke, John Allison. Tchr. Spanish and speech, Maize, Kans., 1959-60; elem. Spanish tchr. Sta. KETA-TV, Oklahoma City Public Schs., 1960-65; elem. sch. tchr., St. Louis Park, Minn., 1970; owner-mgr. The Toy Store, Enid, Okla., 1977—; pres. Glenwood Elem. Sch. PTA, Enid, 1974-75; pres. Coordinating Council PTA's of Enid, 1974-75. Founder, dir. Enid Boys Choir, 1976-78; exec. bd. Enid-Phillips Symphony Assn., 1974-80, pres. 1976-78. Mem. Enid C. of C. Republican. Mem. Ch. of Nazarene. Devel. curriculum guides Okla. Dept. Edn. Home: 1021 Westwood Rd Enid OK 73701 Office: 1218 B W Willow St Enid OK 73701

HENSLEY, ELIZABETH CATHERINE, nutritionist; b. Mpls., Feb. 27, 1921; d. Erich Christian and Lulu Mabel (Elliott) Selke; B.S. in Edn., 1942; M.S., Cornell U., 1944, postgrad., 1950-51; m. Eugene B. Hensley, June 10, 1954. Instr. food and nutrition U. Del., 1944-47; asst. prof. Okla. A&M U., 1947-50; mem. faculty U. Mo., Columbia, 1951—, prof. food and nutrition, 1954—, chmn. dept. home econs., 1954-55, head dept. food and nutrition, 1955-65, co-chmn. dept. human nutrition, 1973-76. Mem. Am Home Econs. Assn., Nutrition Today Soc., Mo. Home Econs. Assn., PEO, Pi Lambda Theta, Omicron Nu, Phi Upsilon Omicron, Gamma Sigma Delta, Kappa Alpha Theta. Mem. Christian Ch. (Disciples of Christ). Author: Basic Concepts of World Nutrition, 1981. Home: 802 Greenwood Ct Columbia MO 65201 Office: 217 Gwynn Hall U Mo Columbia MO 65211

HENSLEY, KAREN MARIE, hosp. adminstr., nurse; b. Ravenna, Ohio, Apr. 4, 1950; d. John J. and Rose E. (Scalera) Ruschak; diploma U. Akron and Akron City Hosp. Sch. Nursing, 1970; B.S.P.A., St. Joseph's Coll., North Windham, Maine, 1983; m. John R. Hensley, Jan. 19, 1979; 1 son, Michael. Head nurse CCU, Mercy Hosp., Toledo, 1971-75; charge nurse, acute neurology St. Mary Corwin Hosp., Pueblo, Colo., 1975-76; peer rev. coordinator Cuyahoga Falls (Ohio) Gen. Hosp., 1976-79; dir. nursing Hamilton Meml. Hosp., McLeansboro, Ill., 1979-81; nursing service coordinator Franklin Hosp., Benton, Ill., 1981—. Mem. Am. Soc. Nursing Adminstrs., Ill. Soc. Nursing Adminstrs. (pres. Region 5 chpt. and mem. state exec. com. 1981—), Nat. Assn. Quality Assurance Profls. (dir. 1978-80, award 1980), Am. Heart Assn. Home: 6th and Main Dahlgren IL 62828

HENSLEY, ROBIN MARIE, audio-visual co. cons.; b. Atlanta, Apr. 29, 1956; d. James Milton and Murray L. (Loyless) H.; B.S. in Acctg., Ga. State U., 1977. Mem. audit staff Ernst & Whinney, Atlanta, 1977-80, mem. mgmt. cons. staff, 1980-82; pres. Audio Visual Services, Atlanta, 1982—. Pres., Atlanta Ballet Assos., 1981-83; mem. exec. com., bd. dirs. Atlanta Ballet Inc., Rich's Enterprising Woman, Atlanta. Recipient Sr. award Ga. State U., 1977, Catherine Miles recognition award, 1977; C.P.A., Ga. Mem. Nat. Alliance of Exec. and Profl. Women's Networks (nat. sec. 1980-83), Ga. Exec. Women's Network (co-founder 1979, pres. 1979, mem. adv. bd. and dir. 1980-83), Ga. Soc. C.P.A.s, Am. Soc. Personnel Adminstrs. (membership com.), Clubs: Atlanta City (intermediate bd. dirs.), Women's Commerce. Home: 8 Carlisle Way NE Atlanta GA 30308 Office: 2642 Batavia St Atlanta GA 30344

HENSON, HAZEL LAY, clothing co. exec.; b. Winder, Ga., June 12, 1916; d. Marion R. and Mamie E. (Haynie) Lay; student Ga. State Coll. for Women, 1933-35; m. J. Ivory Henson, Apr. 15, 1939 (dec. 1974); children—Richard L., James W. With Henson Garment Co. Inc., Athens, Ga., pres., 1974—. Mem. Nat. Fedn. Ind. Bus., Am. Apparel Mfrs. Assn., Ga. Bus. and Industry Assn. Methodist. Home: 810 E Broad St Winder GA 30680 Office: Henson Garment Co Inc 125 Paradise Blvd Athens GA 30607

HENSON, LINDA LEE, accountant; b. Salem, Ohio, May 4, 1941; d. Wade Arnold and Elizabeth Helen (Melitshka) Caufield; B.S.B.A. with highest honors, Dominguez Hills State U., 1975; m. James Richard Henson, Dec. 24, 1960; children—Lisa Ann, Krista Lynn, Jana Marie. Acct., Atherton Industries, Menlo Park, Calif., 1975-76; acctg. supr. Field Communications, San Francisco, 1976-77; fiscal officer San Francisco Art Inst., 1977-79; cons. acctg., San Francisco, 1979—; controller Am. Electronics Assn., Palo Alto, Calif., 1980—. Mem. Republican. Home: 1519 Spinnaker Ln Half Moon Bay CA 94019 Office: 2680 Hanover St Palo Alto CA 94304

HENSON, LOUISA WEEKS, radio exec.; b. Louisville, Oct. 26, 1948; d. Clarance Edward and Cora (Bradford) H.; B.A., U. Ky., 1970. Gen. mgr. Sta. WLRS Radio-WLRS TV, Louisville, 1971—; exec. v.p. Henson Broadcasting Co., Inc., Louisville, 1971—. Vice-chmn. Third Century-Louisville Central Area Inc., 1981-82; bd. dirs. Louisville chpt. YWCA, 1981—; adv. bd. Louisville Deaf Oral Sch., 1981—; chmn. Ohio Valley chpt. March of Dimes Bd., 1977-79, chmn. March of Dimes Adv. Bd., 1980—. Mem. Nat. Radio Broadcasters Assn. (state dir. 1977-81), Am. Broadcasting Co. Affiliate Bd. (sec. 1978-79), Louisville Area Radio Stas. (pres. 1981-82), Am. Women in Radio and TV, Ky. Broadcasters Assn., Advt. Club Louisville (dir.). Democrat. Baptist. Home: 2322 Carlton Terr Louisville KY 40205 Office: 800 S 4th St Louisville KY 40203

HEPBURN, AUDREY, actress; b. Brussels, May 4, 1929; d. Joseph Anthony and Baroness Ella (van Heemstra) H.; ed. Day Sch., Arnhem, Netherlands, Conservatory of Music, Arnhem; student ballet with Sonia Gaskel, Amsterdam, Marie Rambert, London; m. Melchor Gaston Ferrer, Sept. 25, 1954; 1 son, Sean; m. 2d, Andrea Dotti, 1969; 1 son, Luca. Mem. Corps de Ballet with Sauce Tartare, also Sauce Piquante, West End, London, also Cabaret on TV; small parts in motion pictures Laughter in Paradise, Lavender Hill Mob, Young Wives' Tale, Secret People, Nous irons à Monte Carlo; leading roles in Am. motion pictures Roman Holiday, 1953, Sabrina Fair, 1954, War and Peace, 1955, Funny Face, 1956, Love in the Afternoon, 1956; first legitimate play, Gigi, N.Y.C., 1951; appeared in Ondine, N.Y.C., 1954, Producers Showcase, TV, 1957; films: Green Mansions, 1958, The Nun's Story, 1959, The Unforgiven, Breakfast at Tiffany's, 1960, The Children's Hour, Charade, 1962, My Fair Lady, 1963, Paris When it Sizzles, 1964, How to Steal a Million, 1965, Two for the Road, 1966, Wait Until Dark, 1967, Robin and Marian, 1976, Bloodline, 1979, They All Laughed, 1981. Recipient Acad. Award for Roman Holiday, 1953; Spl. Tony award, 1968. Office: care Kurt Frings 9440 Santa Monica Blvd Beverly Hills CA 90210 *

HEPBURN, KATHARINE, actress; b. Hartford, Conn., 1909; m. Ogden Ludlow (div.). Awarded first honors, 1934, by vote of Acad. of Motion Picture Arts and Scis. for performance in Morning Glory, 1933; appeared in Little Women, Spitfire, The Lake (play), Alice Adams, Sylvia Scarlett, Mary of Scotland, Women Rebels, Quality Street, Stage Door, Bringing Up Baby, Holiday, Break of Hearts, Christopher Strong, The Philadelphia Story (play), others; Women of the Year, 1942; Without Love (play), 1942; Keeper of the Flame, 1943; Dragon Seed, 1944; Undercurrent, 1946; Sea of Glass, 1946; Song of Love, 1947; State of the Union, 1948; Adams's Rib, 1949; As You Like It (play) (Rosalind), 1950; African Queen, 1951; Pat & Mike, 1952; The Millionairess (play Eng. and U.S.A.), 1952; Summertime, 1955 (award Acad. Motion Picture Arts and Scis. 1955); Iron Petticoat, The Rainmaker, The Desk Set, 1957; (plays) Taming of the Shrew, Merchant of Venice, Measure for Measure (Eng. and Australia), 1955; Much Ado About Nothing, 1957 (plays); Suddenly Last Summer, 1959 (film); Long Days Journey into Night (motion picture), 1962; Guess Who's Coming to Dinner (motion picture), 1967 (Acad. award for best performance by actress 1968); Lion in Winter (Acad. award best actress 1969); Mad Woman of Chaillot, 1969; Trojan Women, 1971; appeared on stage in CoCo (musical), N.Y.C., 1970, on tour 1971; A Delicate Balance (movie), 1973; Glass Menagerie (TV movie), 1973; Love Among the Ruins (TV movie), 1975; A Matter of Gravity, N.Y. and tour, 1976-77; The Corn is Green (movie for TV), 1979; On Golden Pond (motion picture), 1981. Recipient gold medal as world's best motion picture actress, Internat. Motion Picture Expn., Venice, Italy, 1934; N.Y. Critic's award for performance in picture The Philadelphia Story, 1940; Annual award Shakespeare Club N.Y.C., 1950; Whistler Soc. award, 1957; Hasty Pudding Club's ann. Woman of Yr. award, 1958.

HEPWORTH, CAROLYNE, soils engring. co. exec.; b. Augusta, Ga., Jan. 3, 1942; d. Samuel and Patricia A. (Timm) Steffen; student U. Denver, 1975, Community Coll. Denver, 1976-78, Columbia Coll., 1979; B.S. in Acctg., 1981; m. Richard C. Hepworth, Apr. 25, 1981; children—Michelle Denise, Michael John, Diana Lynnette. Sec., U.S. Army Records Center, St. Louis, 1960-61, Goodyear Tire & Rubber Co., St. Louis, 1963-67; bookkeeper, office mgr. Hayes C.T.S., Inc., Ironton, Mo., 1971-73; controller Chen & Assos., Inc., Denver, 1974—. Active dist. orgn. Rep. Party, 1978-79. Mem. Women in Constrn., Am. Soc. Women Accountants, Nat. Assn. Accountants, Profl. Services Mgmt. Assn. Roman Catholic. Home: 3333 E Florida #86 Denver CO 80210 Office: 96 S Zuni St Denver CO 80223

HERBERT, CECILIA HEALY, banker; b. Tacoma, Wash., Mar. 22, 1949; d. James Peter and Dorothy (Kiely) Healy; B.A., Stanford U., 1971; M.B.A., Harvard U., 1973; m. James Hall Herbert, II, Dec. 18, 1976; 1 son, James Hall. Internat. fin. mgmt. exec. Morgan Guaranty Trust Co., N.Y.C., 1973-76, v.p. internat. banking, San Francisco, 1979—; nat. div. v.p. Bank of Va., Richmond, 1976-78. Mem. Fin. Women's Assn., Bay Area Profl. Women's Network. Club: Harvard of N.Y. Home: 2368 Broadway San Francisco CA 94115 Office: 400 Montgomery St San Francisco CA 94104

HERBERT, CHARLYNE TOWNSEND, clin. psychologist; b. Denver, June 28, 1907; d. Charles Hooker and Helen Marie (Kelly) Townsend; B.A., UCLA, 1941, Ph.D., 1947; m. Frank Lawrence Herbert, Sept. 10, 1960 (div. 1966). Asst. chief psychology service VA Med. Center, Long Beach, Calif., 1952-77, chief clin. psychologist, 1952-77; research psychologist emeritus, 1977—; asso. clin. prof. psychology UCLA, 1950-77, emeritus, 1977—. Diplomate Am. Bd. Examiners in Profl. Psychology (bd. dirs. Western region), Am. Bd. Profl. Hypnosis; lic. psychologist, Calif. Fellow Am. Psychol. Assn., AAAS; mem. Western Psychol. Assn., Sigma Xi, Pi Gamma Mu, Psi Chi. Republican. Episcopalian. Club: Huntington Harbour Beach and Tennis. Contbr. articles to profl. jours. Office: 5901 E 7 St Long Beach CA 90822

HERBST, CAROL JEAN, air force non-commd. officer; b. Cleve., Dec. 15, 1937; d. William James and Mildred Marie (Schlesinger) H.; grad. Park Coll., Parkville, Mo., 1980; postgrad. in bus. adminstrn. Golden Gate U. Enlisted in U.S. Air Force, 1956; sta. at Clark AB, Philippines, 1969-70, Ramstein AB and Wiesbaden AB, Ger., 1959-62; recruiter in Cleve., 1963-67; non-commd. officer in charge personnel affairs, Shu Lin Kou As, Taiwan, 1971-73, Nat. Security Agency, Ft. Meade, Md., 1973-77; non-commd. officer in charge personnel affairs Luke AFB, Phoenix, 1977—; also base sgt. maj. Republican. Methodist. Home: 9509 W Pierce St Tolleson AZ 85353

HERBST, MARIAN G., mfg. co. exec.; b. N.J., Apr. 5, 1925; d. Charles A. and Bessie M. (Crutts) Moore; B.A., Syracuse (N.Y.) U., 1962; children—Gwen Hamel, Charles Molnar. Pres., mgr. Paramount Ins. Agy., 1950-59; pres., owner Broaster Hut Franchises, 1959-68; mcpl. clk., treas., purchasing agt., Chester, N.J., 1970-74; exec. fin. dir. PTL-TV Network, 1975-79; v.p., gen. mgr. C.G. Mfg., Inc., 1975-81; owner, pres. mfg. co., Lake Wylie, S.C., 1981—. Ordained to ministry Full Gospel Ch. Mem. Nat. Assn. Female Execs. Republican. Address: Box 5067 Lake Wylie SC 29710

HERBSTMAN, BARBARA DUBIN, former educator; b. N.Y.C., Apr. 7, 1938; d. Joshua Hyman and Irene Eleanor Dubin; B.S., Syracuse U., 1959; M.A., Columbia U., 1961; Ph.D., U. Ill., 1973; m. Joe Herbstman, Feb. 16, 1975; children—Joshua Tobias, Deborah Marsha. Tchr. elem. schs., N.Y.C., 1960-64, Tucson, 1964-68; instr. So. Ill. U., 1971-72; asst. prof. edn. Western Ill. U., 1974-75; edn. cons. Ill. Office of Edn., 1973-75. Pres., Tchrs. Council N.Y.; public edn. chmn. Am. Cancer Soc. Mem. Philosophy Edn. Soc., Am. Edn. Study Assn., Midwest Philosophy Edn. Soc., AAUW (v.p.), Dental Soc. Aux. (pres.), Kappa Delta Pi, Pi Lambda Theta, Phi Kappa Phi. Clubs: B'Nai Israel Sisterhood (v.p.), Hadassah (pres. Gainesville chpt.). Columnist, Tucson Edn. Assn. Bull., 1965-68; writer, editor Synagogue Bull., 1975-79. Home: 407 S W 80th Dr Gainesville FL 32607

HERD, CHARMIAN JUNE, educator, singer, actress; b. Waterville, Maine, June 1, 1930; d. Samuel Braid and Jennie (Lang) Herd; B.A., Colby Coll., 1950; M.Ed., U. Maine, 1964; postgrad. Boston U., 1951; ednl. cert. No. Conservatory, Bangor, Maine, 1954; also study voice with Roger A. Nye. Dir. music State Sch. for Girls, Hallowell, Maine, 1950-51; head English, French, dramatics dept. St. George High Sch., Tenants Harbor, Maine, 1951-52; dir. music pub. schs. Albion, Unity, Maine, 1952-54, Troy, Freedom, Maine, 1953-54; dir. music pub. sch. system Belgrade, Maine, Waterville Jr. High Sch., 1954-55; dir. vocal music Waterville Jr. and Sr. high schs., 1954-58; head English and dramatics depts. Besse High Sch., Albion, 1959-62; tchr. French, English and drama Skowhegan High Sch., 1962-69; tchr. French, Adult Edn. Sch., 1963—; dir. dramatic arts program Skowhegan Sch. Adult Edn., 1966-69; instr. French, Lawrence Sr. High Sch., Fairfield, Maine, 1969-71, chmn. dept. drama and speech, 1972-79; dramatics instr. U. Maine at Farmington 1969-70; soloist various chs., Maine, 1951—; soloist numerous club, ch., conv., coll. concerts, oratorios. 1st pres., performing mem. Waterville Theatre Guild, music dir., 1967—; performing mem. Theatre at Monmouth (Maine), Portland Lyric Theatre; chmn. bd. Augusta Players; mem. Camden Civic Theatre; mem. Titipu Choral Soc.; program chmn. Albion PTA; mem. Waterville Community Ballet Theatre, 1975—; bd. dirs. Waterville Opera House, 1975—; trustee Theater at Monmouth, 1970—, sec. bd. trustees, 1977—; 1st v.p. New Eng. Theatre Conf., 1976-77, fall conf. chmn., 1977; theatre chmn. Ann. Maine Festival of Arts, Bowdoin Coll., Brunswick, 1978. Mem. Waterville Friends Music, DAR (music chmn. Winslow (Maine) 1955-57, sec. 1957-59, vice regent 1959-61, regent 1961-62, Maine advt. chmn. 1958-60); Actors' Equity, Ednl. Speech and Theatre Assn. of Maine (state pres. 1972-74), Waterville Bus. and Profl. Women's Club (program chmn. 1957-58, v.p. 1958-59, pres. 1959-61, chmn. drama dept.

1961), Albion-Burnham Tchrs. Club. (sec. 1960-61), Bay State Post Card Club, R.I. Post Card Club, Pine Tree Post Card Club (chmn. Portland Mini-Show 1980-82, exec. bd. 1979-82), Internat. Platform Assn., New Eng. Theatre Council (dir. 1975—), NEA, Maine Tchrs. Assn., Theatre Assn. Maine (exec. bd. 1972-74, 2d v.p. 1973-74, exec. sec. 1975-76, state pres. 1976—), Actors Equity, Portland Lyric Theatre (sec. bd.). Club: Cecilia (Augusta, Me.). Composer sacred music: Babylon, 1959, The Greatest of These is Love, 1961; Pan, 1963; Keep Not Thy Silence, O God; Remember Now Thy Creator; Slow, Slow, Fresh Fount; A Witch's Charm; Hymn to God The Father. Home: The Riverview Main St RFD 5 Scarborough ME 04074

HERDA, ELLEN ANN, anthropologist, educator; b. New Rockford, N.D., June 13, 1940; d. Alvin Louis and Alta Irene (Bestul) H.; B.A., U. Minn., 1963; B.S., Mankato State U., 1967; M.S., Calif. State U., Hayward, 1974; M.A. (research fellow), U. Oreg., 1977, Ph.D., 1978, postgrad., 1981—; m. Paul Jennings Jensen, Oct. 23, 1971 (div. 1982). Tchr., Peace Corps, Monrovia, Liberia, 1963-64; tchr., French, social studies, also bilingual/bicultural edn. Calif. migrant workers, Riverside, 1968-75; ednl. researcher, project mem. Alaskan Rural Edn., Architecture and Curriculum, U. Oreg., 1976-78, asso. dir. Univ. Council for Ednl. Adminstrn., 1978-80; asst. prof. edn. and anthropology U. San Francisco, 1980—; adj. prof. Ohio State U.; cons. U.S. Office Edn. NSF grantee, 1981. Mem. Am. Edn. Research Assn., Am. Anthropol. Assn., Soc. Applied Anthropology, Nat. Soc. Study of Edn., S.W. Anthropol. Assn., Council Exceptional Children. Editor: Univ. Council and Adminstrn., 1978-80; contbr. articles to profl. publs. Office: Univ San Francisco Rossi Wing San Francisco CA 94117

HERICH, JANE MARIE, telephone co. exec.; b. St. Louis, June 7, 1950; d. Joseph Michael and Frances Juanita (Randolph) Herich; student public schs., St. Louis County, Mo. Records clk. Southwestern Bell Telephone Co., St. Louis, 1968, clk. to dist. plant engr., 1969-71, personnel sec., 1971-73, sec. to gen. personnel relations supr., 1973-76, staff supr. payroll procedures, 1976-81, asst. staff supr. functional acctg., 1981—. Roman Catholic. Home: 9 Oakwood Ln Saint Louis MO 63129 Office: Southwestern Bell Telephone Co 1010 Pine St Saint Louis MO 63101

HERITAGE, DORRIS EVELYN (KILLAM), personnel exec.; b. Beverly, Mass., Aug. 2, 1924; d. Raymond and Aleda Maude (Beauregard) Killam; grad. Salem Comml. Sch., 1944; student Boston U., evenings 1948-49, Harvard U., 1949-50, Northeastern U., 1966-70; 1 dau. by previous marriage, Susan. Sec. and tech. asst. Beverly Farms (Mass.), 1950-51; sec. to bus. mgr. food and flavor group, life scis. div. Arthur D. Little, Inc., Cambridge, Mass., 1951-70; adminstrv. asst. firm Goodwin, Procter and Hoar, Boston, 1970-71; founder, pres. Heritage Personnel, Inc., Hampton, N.H., 1972—. Served with WAVES, World War II. Mem. Nat. Assn. Female Execs., Bus. and Profl. Women's Club. Office: 820 Lafayette Rd Hampton NH 03842

HERITEAU, JACQUELINE, author; b. Vendee, France, Oct. 12, 1925; came to U.S., 1955, naturalized, 1971; d. Marcel and Piney (Sutherland) H.; student Montreal (Que., Can.) U., 1942-44, Sorbonne, Paris, 1948-49; children—Krishna Littledale Hunter, David Hunter, Holly Hunter. Author numerous gardening and cooking books, 1969—, including How to Grow and Cook It, 1970, Oriental Cooking The Fast Wok Way, 1972, Potpourris and other Fragrant Delights, 1973, How to Grow and Can It, 1975, Take-It Along Cookbook, 1975, Herbs, 1975, Home Canning and Freezing, 1975, Tomato Growing and Cooking, 1975, Easy Garden Projects, 1975, Small Vegetable and Fruit Gardens, 1975, The Office Gardener, 1977, The Complete Book of Beans, 1978, A Feast of Soups, 1982; gen. editor Good Housekeeping Illustrated Ency. of Gardening, 1972-73; hort. cons. Family Circle mag.; contbr. articles to various mags. Home: 1049 Park Ave New York NY 10028

HERLEHY, DONNA MARIA TICCHI, univ. ofcl.; b. Brockton, Mass., Sept. 11, 1950; d. James Joseph and Frances Katherine Ticchi; B.A. cum laude, Emmanuel Coll., 1972; M.A., Mich. State U., 1973; m. Thomas James Herlehy, Aug. 26, 1972. Adminstrv. asst. Office Research Adminstrn., Kent (Ohio) State U., 1974-75; asst. dir. Grant and Contract Adminstrn., Children's Hosp., Boston, 1975-77; asst. dir. Office Sponsored Programs, M.I.T., Cambridge, 1977-79, adminstrv. officer Lab. Architecture and Planning, 1979—. Docent, mem. docent council Boston By Foot, 1977—, chmn. acad. affairs, 1978—, mem. editorial staff, 1978—. Recipient Disting. Service award Boston By Foot, 1979. Mem. Soc. Research Adminstrs., Nat. Council Univ. Research Adminstrs., Kappa Gamma Pi. Home: 22 Addington Rd Brookline MA 02146 Office: Lab Architecture and Planning MIT 77 Massachusetts Ave Cambridge MA 02139

HERMAN, CARLENE EMILY, tax cons., acct., real estate broker; b. Deep Cove, B.C., Can., Sept. 10, 1912; d. William J. and Emily M. (Miller) Smith; student U. Wash., Seattle, 1930-33; m. Alby O. Gaydon, June 10, 1931 (dec.); children—Allene Gaydon, Kathy King Neelands, Leonard Gaydon (dec.); m. 2d, Richard Herman, 1956 (dec.). Pvt. practice acctg., also real estate broker, Auburn, Calif., 1941—. Vol., Friends of Library, Auburn Faith Hosp. Guild. Mem. Soc. Calif. Accts., Nat. Assn. Tax Consultors, Auburn Bus. and Profl. Women's Club. Republican. Congregationalist. Clubs: Republican Women's, Soroptomist Internat. (Auburn), Order Eastern Star, White Shrine of Jerusalem (Auburn, Calif.). Home: 13070 Lincoln Way Auburn CA 95603 Office: 13118 Lincoln Way Auburn CA 95603

HERMAN, GRETA SUE, psychiatrist; b. Galveston, Tex., June 22, 1949; d. Frank W. and Ann L. (Caplovitz) H.; B.S., Sophie Newcomb Coll., 1970; M.D., Tulane U., 1974. Intern in surgery Tulane U.-Charity Hosp. of La., New Orleans, 1974-75; med. dir. Desire Neighborhood Health Center, New Orleans, La., 1976-77; resident in psychiatry Mt. Sinai Med. Sch., City U. N.Y., 1977-80; unit chief clin. unit Bronx VA Hosp., 1980-82; coordinator residency tng., dept. psychiatry Mt. Sinai Med. Ctr., N.Y.C., 1982—, unit chief, 1982—. Diplomate Am. Bd. Psychiatry and Neurology. Mem. Am. Psychiat. Assn., Am. Assn. Dirs. of Psychiat. Residency Tng., AMA. Democrat. Jewish. Office: Mt Sinai Med Center One Gustave L Levy Pl New York NY 10029

HERMAN, LUCY-JO, mail order exec.; b. Petersburg, Va., Nov. 5, 1935; d. Joseph John Malloy and Lucy (Powell) Malloy Miller; B.A., U. Pa., 1956, M.A., 1972; postgrad. Phila. Sch. Psychoanalysis, 1972-75; m. M. William Herman, Nov. 15, 1975; 1 dau., Emily Anne; children by previous marriage—Stephen Michael, Philip Joseph and Elisabeth-Jo Constantine Stephano. Exec. dir. Arts Found., 1967, C & B Toys, 1968-72; exec. cons., 1972-75; v.p. spl. projects Harriet Carter, Inc., Montgomeryville, Pa., 1975—, charge Lynne's Miniature Treasures div., 1975—. Mem. bd. Republican Women, 1966; publicity dir. County Reps., 1967, personnel dir., 1967-68. Mem. Nat. Assn. Miniature Enthusiasts, Miniature Industry Assn. Am., Delaware Valley Lyric Opera, Mensa (cert. of merit 1972). Contbr. articles to periodicals. Office: Harriet Carter Inc Stump Rd Montgomeryville PA 18936

HERMAN, PHYLLIS G., psychotherapist; b. N.Y.C., July 18, 1930; d. Abraham and Bertha (Burg) Goldapel; B.S., CCNY, 1951, grad. student, 1953; M.S.W., N.Y. U., 1976; m. Harold C. Herman, June 6, 1951; children—Aline, Shelly, Lorette. Tchr., N.Y.C. Schs., 1951-56, Center for Individual Help, Woodmere (N.Y.) Sch. Dist., 1966-73; psychotherapist New Hope Guild, Howard Beach, N.Y., 1973—; pvt. practice psychotherapy, Woodmere, N.Y., 1973—. Mem. Nat. Assn. Social Workers. Jewish. Mem. B'nai B'rith, Nat. Council Jewish Women. Home: 1115 Fordham Ln Woodmere NY 11598

HERMAN, SUSAN JANE, psychologist, health services adminstr.; b. Chgo., May 2, 1939; d. Leonard T. Goodman and Dorothea K. Blumenthal; B.A., U. Md., 1962; M.A., Rollins Coll., 1965; Ph.D. (univ. fellow), U. Fla., 1970; certificate in psychoanalysis N.Y. U., 1979. Tchr., Orange County, Fla., 1963-66, counselor, 1966-67; grad. asst. U. Fla., Gainesville, 1967-68, 69-70; instr. psychology, counseling intern Valencia Jr. Coll., Orlando, Fla., 1968-69; counseling and research asst. U. Fla., pub. relations dir. Community Drug Center, Gainesville, 1969-70; psychologist Mental Health Center, Newark, 1970-72; cons. psychologist Fairleigh Dickinson U., Teaneck, N.J., 1972—; dir. psychol. services Montclair (N.J.) State Coll., 1973—; pvt. practice psychotherapy, Union, N.J., 1972—. Mem. Psychoanalytic Soc. of Postdoctoral Program for Study and Research in Psychology, Am., N.J. psychol. assns., N.Y. Assn. Feminist Psychotherapists. Home: 1296 Oxford Ln Union NJ 07083 Office: Psychol Services Montclair State Coll Upper Montclair NJ 07043

HERMAN, TRUDY ANNE, state ofcl.; b. Munich, Germany, Sept. 25, 1949; d. Frank and Ruth Mary (Sickinger) Gallic; A.A., Potomac State Coll., 1969; B.A., W.Va. U., 1971, M.P.A., 1972; m. Frederick R. Herman, Aug. 18, 1973; 1 son, Nicholas Frederick. Asst. to city mgr. City of Wheeling (W.Va.), 1972-74; project officer Gov.'s Office Fed. State Relations. Charleston, 1974-77; exec. asst. to dir. community devel. Gov.'s Office Econ. and Community Devel., Charleston, 1977-78, dep. dir. indsl. devel., 1978-81; credit analyst W.Va. Econ. Devel. Authority, Charleston, 1981—. Mem. Nat. Assn. Female Execs., Women in Community Devel., Am. Inst. Banking, W.Va. U. Alumni Assn. Home: 111 Shaw Ln Hurricane WV 25526 Office: Bldg 6 Rm 525 State Capitol Charleston WV 25305

HERMANN, HELEN LESLIE, duplicating equipment co. mgr.; b. Phoenix, Aug. 5, 1954; d. William LaMar and Helen Higginbotham H.; B.A. cum laude in Spl. Edn./Elem. Edn., Ariz. State U., 1976. Tchr. spl. edn. Self-contained State Mandated Classroom for Severely Mentally Disturbed Children, Madison Sch. Dist., Phoenix, 1976-78; sales account rep. Xerox Corp., Phoenix, 1978-81, sales planning mgr., 1981—. Recipient Profl. award Xerox Corp., 1979. Home: 7120 E Wilshire Apt 9 Scottsdale AZ 85257 Office: 3030 N Central St Suite 1400 Phoenix AZ 85012

HERMANN, MARY KEVIN HOWARD, nurse, educator; b. St. Lawrence, Ky., Oct. 26, 1934; d. Charles Kevin and Mary M. Howard; R.N., St. Mary's Sch. of Nursing, Evansville, Ind., 1955; B.S. cum laude in Nursing, U. Evansville, 1970, M.A., 1972, M.S. in Nursing, 1974; postgrad. Ind. U., 1979—; m. Robert R. Hermann, Feb. 2, 1957; children—Michael R., Barbara K., Leah M., Daniel J. Staff nurse St. Mary's Med. Center, Evansville, Ind., 1955-56, head nurse, 1956-58, asst. dir. nursing service, 1965-68; instr. nursing U. Evansville, 1970-73, asst. prof., 1973-76, assoc. prof., 1976—, asst. dean baccalaureate program, 1974-80. Mem. adv. com. Am. Heart Assn. Program, Evansville, 1981. Mem. Am. Nurses Assn., Ind. Nurses Assn. (co-chmn. commn. on edn., chmn. task force on competencies, dir., dir. dist. 4 1982-84), Am. Assn. Critical Care Nurses. Home: 8011 Maple Ln Newburgh IN 47630 Office: Box 329 Evansville IN 47702

HERNANDEZ, SHERRY LEE, assn. exec.; b. San Francisco, Oct. 25, 1942; d. Eugene Francis and Beryl Delora (O'Connor) Corrigan; student San Jose City Coll., 1960-61, Foothill Coll., 1965-67, DeAnza Coll., 1976-81; m. Danny Hernandez, Nov. 15, 1969; 1 son, Terrence. Adminstrv. asst. De Anza Coll., Cupertino, Calif., 1967-81; owner, designer Color & Designer Concepts, Boulder Creek, Calif., 1981—; exec. mgr. Plumbing-Heating-Cooling Contractors Assn. Greater Bay Area Inc., Mountain View, Calif., 1981—; interior design cons. Vol., Santa Clara Valley Youth Hockey, 1975-79. Mem. Nat. Assn. Plumbing-Heating-Cooling Contractors, Calif. Exec. Mgrs. Council. Home: 18286 Hwy 9 Boulder Creek CA 95006 Office: 2672 Bayshore Frontage Rd Mountain View CA 94043

HERNDON, LILLIE EDENS, broadcasting exec.; b. Sumter, S.C., Jan. 15, 1916; d. Robert Manning and Lillie A. (Frazier) Edens; student public schs.; L.H.D. (hon.), Columbia (S.C.) Coll., 1979; m. Wayne Woodrow Midiffer, Apr. 7, 1939; children—Sandra Kay, Wayne Woodrow; m. 2d, James Marvin Herndon, 1953 (div. 1968). With Kay's Dept. Store, 1932-51; owner Edens Norge Village, 1964-73; pres. Nat. PTA, 1973-75; mem. S.C. Bd. Edn., 1974-77; bd. dirs. Corp. Public Broadcasting, 1975—, chmn., 1978—; v.p. Nat. Assn. State Bds. Edn., 1975-76; chmn. Nat. Action Com. Foster Children, 1974-75. Named South Carolinian of Year, 1978; hon. fellow Am. Sch. Health Assn. Republican. Baptist. Office: 1111 16th St Washington DC 20036

HERNSTADT, JUDITH FILENBAUM, broadcasting exec., city planning and real eastate cons.; b. N.Y.C., Nov. 18, 1942; d. Alex and Ruth Selena (Silberman) Filenbaum; student Sophie Newcomb Coll., Tulane U., 1960-61; B.A., Washington Sq. Coll., N.Y.U., 1964; M.A. in Urban and Regional Planning and Housing (Carnegie Found. fellow), N.Y.U., 1966; cert. Smaller Co. Mgmt. Program, Harvard U. Bus. Sch., 1977; m. William Henry Hernstadt, Oct. 12, 1973. With N.Y. State Office Planning Coordination, 1966-68; partner Devel. Planning Assos., 1967-68; with engrng. scis. dept. Service Bur. Corp., N.Y.C., 1968-69; with Llewelyn-Davies Assos., planning cons., N.Y.C., 1969-71; planning cons., 1971-73; with Arlen Realty & Devel. Corp., N.Y.C., 1973-74; partner Planning and Devel. Team, N.Y.C., 1974—; v.p. Nev. Ind. Broadcasting Corp. (KVVU-TV 5), Las Vegas, 1974-75, 77-79, pres., 1976-77; pres. Hernstadt Broadcasting Corp. (Sta. WKAT), Las Vegas, 1978—, Miami, Fla., 1979-81; cons. real estate market analysis and feasibility studies throughout country. Del., Fine Arts Fedn. N.Y., 1970—; mem. Pres.'s council Tulane U., U.S. Dept. State Fine Arts Com. Mem. Am. Inst. Planners, Am. Soc. Planning Ofcls., Assn. Women in Radio and TV. Clubs: Las Vegas Country; Sleepy Hollow Country (Tarrytown, N.Y.); Harmonie (N.Y.C.). Contbr. articles to profl. jours. Home: 927 Fifth Ave New York NY 10021 also 3111 Bel Air Dr Apt 25G Las Vegas NV 89109 Office: 1759 Bay Rd Miami Beach FL 33139

HERON, JEAN ELLEN, hosp. assn. ofcl.; b. Worcester, Mass., Nov. 22, 1942; d. Peter F. and Hedwidge T. (Sampson) Heron; B.A., Regis Coll., 1964; M.B.A., Northeastern U., 1970; postgrad. U. Mass., 1976—, U. Pa., 1977. Personnel systems and procedures analyst E.G. & G. Corp., Bedford, Mass., 1964-69; systems analyst Interactive Bus. Data, Boston, 1969-70; mgr. program devel. Mass. Hosp. Assn., Burlington, 1970-74, dir. spl. projects, 1974-77, dir. mktg., 1977-78; mktg. mgr. Shared Med. Systems, King of Prussia, Pa., 1978—; mem. Mass. Gov.'s Mental Health and Mental Retardation Advisory Council, Mass. Statewide Emergency Med. Systems Council. Expt. in Internat. Living scholar, 1962. Mem. Health Care Mgmt. Assn. Mass. (past pres.), Hosp. Fin. Mgmt. Assn., Am. Coll. Hosp. Adminstrs., New Eng. Hosp. Assembly, Catholic Hosp. Assn., Mass. Assn. for Mental Health, Am. Mgmt. Assn., Boston Jr. C. of C., Pi Gamma Mu. Home: 12 Fox Run Rd Lincoln NH 03251 Office: Box 675 King of Prussia PA

HERPST, MARTHA JANE, artist, art educator; b. Titusville, Pa.; d. Henry Howard and Lou (Cupler) Herpst; student Pa. Acad. Fine Arts, Phila., 1931, Grand Central Sch. Art, N.Y.C. (medalist 1932), 1931-33; studied with Guy Pene DuBois, 1941. Began painting in oils at age of 9 yrs; sold first portrait at 12 yrs.; specializes in portraits; exhibited Nat. Arts Club, N.Y.C., 1933—, Butler Art. Inst., Youngstown, O., 1938, Ogunquit (Me.) Art Assn. Summer Show, 1951, 53, Catherine Lorillard Wolfe Art Club, 1954, 57, Am. Artist Profl. League, 1953—; represented in permanent collection Nat. Arts Club. Titusville (Pa.) Masonic Lodge, with portrait of Charles T. Evans, Titusville Woman's Club with portrait of Laura W. Luce, Titusville YWCA with portrait of Mrs. Fred B. Howland, USMC League with portrait of Capt. Robert Lee Green, Titusville Recreation Center with portrait of Mrs. Charles Burgess, Gannon Coll. with portrait of Archbishop John Mark Gannon, St. Benedict's Convent, Erie, Pa. with portraits of Sisters. Tchr. art St. Joseph Acad. High Sch., Titusville, 1955-69; portrait of Martha McKinney Fleming, McKinney Hall U. Pitts. Titusville Campus. Mem. Am. Artists Profl. League, Titusville Bus. and Profl. Women's Club. Clubs: Nat. Arts, Woman's Titusville Country. Republican. Roman Catholic. Home: 118 W Main St Titusville PA 16354

HERR, ARBA REBECCA OWEN, editor; b. Harrisburg, Pa., Nov. 17, 1912; d. Harry Garman and Rebecca Caldwell (Stine) Owen; B.S. cum laude in Edn., Elizabethtown (Pa.) Coll., 1945; M.S. in Edn., Temple U., Phila., 1965; m. Paul Stumpf Herr, May 3, 1940; children—Paula Herr Arwood, Paul Arden, Nora Herr Allen. Tchr., Pa. schs., 1933-50; tchr. weaving Elizabethtown Coll., 1950-51; editor Bd. Publn., Evangelical United Brethren Ch., Dayton, Ohio, 1964-68; editor United Methodist Pub. House, Nashville, 1968—; cons. workshops, ministries with younger children, children's studies; curriculum cons. African Bibl. studies, Monrovia, Liberia, 1979-80; mem. commn. pub. edn. Nat. Council Chs., 1966-68; dir. children work council Eastern Pa. Conf. Bd. Christian Edn., 1963-64. Mem. Common Cause, Nat. Assn. for Edn. Young Children, Tenn. Bot. Gardens and Fine Arts Center. Clubs: Altrusa (corr. sec. 1972-74, chmn. com. internat. relations 1974-76), Eastern Star, Music City Shell (charter). Author: Primary Course Plan: Middle East, 1972; Everbody Needs a Home, 1973. Home: 6832 Highland Park St Nashville TN 37205 Office: 201 S 8th Ave Nashville TN 37202

HERR, VALERIE JEAN, economic geographer, demographer; b. Birmingham, Eng., Oct. 21, 1936; d. John and Ada (Jones) Shaw; came to U.S., 1966; B.Comm., U. Birmingham, 1957; M.A., U. Calif., Berkeley, 1967, Ph.C., 1970, Ph.D., 1977; m. Richard Herr, Aug. 28, 1968; children—Sarah, Jane. Research statistician City of Birmingham, 1957-58; prof. stats. and social scis. U. Birmingham, 1958-62; researcher demography and housing demand, 1962-66; research demographer U. Calif., Berkeley, 1966-67; free lance demographic cons., 1967—; dir. Internat. Inst. in Spain, Madrid, 1979-80; vis. lectr. demographer U. Calif., Santa Cruz, 1981-82. Mem. Council for European Studies. Author: Population in The Countryside, 1969; co-author: Population Growth and Planning Policy, 1968; Colour and Citizenship, 1970. Address: 1541 Hawthorne Terr Berkeley CA 94708

HERRE, SAUNDRA RUVOLDT, broadcasting co. exec.; b. Reynoldsburg, Ohio, Aug. 3, 1936; d. James Oran and Margaret (Devore) Ruvoldt; B.S., Miami U., Oxford, Ohio, 1958; 2 children. Tchr. English pub. schs., Groveport, Ohio, 1958-59, Racine, Wis., 1961; account exec. WFNY Radio, Racine, 1970-75; owner Sandi Herre Pub. Relations and Advt., 1975-76; v.p. Portfolio, Ltd., Racine, 1976—; partner Schoolhouse Shoppes, Racine, 1976—; v.p., dir. El Sol Broadcasting, Inc., Milw., 1980—; instr. U. Wis., Parkside, 1980-82; lectr. in field. Mem. Gov.'s Conf. on Small Bus.-Capital Formation Task Force, Wis., 1981—; testifier U.S. Senate, Small Bus. Com., 1981; del. White House Conf. on Small Bus., 1980, others; mem. Racine Urban Aesthetics Commn., 1973, 82, Racine County Planning Council, 1974-82, Wis. Bus. Devel. Fin. Corp., 1981-82; exec. dir. Racine Literacy Council, 1982. Mem. Wis. Council on Edn. for Women in Bus., Ind. Bus. Assn. Wis. (bd. dirs.), Wis. Women Entrepreneurs (pres.). Address: 4101 Pennington Ln Racine WI 53403

HERREMANS, IRENE MARIE, educator, accountant; b. Ravenna, Mich., Oct. 5, 1948; d. Albert August and Eleanor Dorothy (Link) H.; B.S., Ferris State Coll., 1970; M.B.A., Roosevelt U., 1976, M.S. in Acctg., 1980. Instr. bus. Waukegan (Ill.) East High Sch. 1970-80, girls' track coach, 1980; instr. Coll. Lake County, Grayslake, Ill., 1975—, Roosevelt U., Chgo., 1978—; lectr. bus. mgmt. and acctg. U. Wis.-Parkside, Kenosha, 1980—; market researcher Proficiency Specialists, San Diego, 1978-80; tax and acctg. cons., 1977—. Recipient Outstanding Tchr. award Waukegan East High Sch., 1980; named Adv. of Yr., Women In Bus. Club, U. Wis., Parkside; C.P.A. Mem. Nat. Assn. Female Execs., Am. Bus. Women's Assn. (pres.; woman of yr. 1978, del. nat. conv.), Nat. Assn. Accts., Racine Women's Network (dir. profl. devel.), Phi Gamma Nu, Beta Gamma Sigma, Delta Zeta. Roman Catholic. Clubs: Indoor Tennis Am., Lake Bluff Yacht. Home: 4811 Emstan Hills Rd #103 Racine WI 53406 Office: U Wis-Parkside Kenosha WI 53141

HERRICK, CAROLE LYNN, educator, trumpet player; b. Washington, June 16, 1949; d. Harold Colton and Doris Lorene (Cosper) H.; Mus.B. with high honors, U. Tex., Austin, 1971, Mus.M., 1972; Ph.D. in Music Edn., North Texas State U., 1981. Trumpet player Midland (Tex.)-Odessa Symphony, 1966-67, Austin Symphony, 1967-73, Irving (Tex.) Symphony, 1974-76; Ark. Symphony, 1981—; band dir. Dallas Ind. Sch. Dist., 1973-76; mem. brass faculty, teaching fellow North Tex. State U., Denton, 1976-78; mem. brass faculty Brookhaven Coll., Dallas, 1978-80; asst. prof. music Hendrix Coll., Conway, Ark., 1980—; clinician and adjudicator instrumental music, 1976—. North Tex. State U. research grantee, 1979-80; Hendrix Coll. research grantee, 1982. Mem. Music Educators Nat. Conf., Ark. Music Educators Assn., Ark. State Band and Orch. Assn., Ark. Elem. Music Educators Assn., Ark. Bandmasters Assn., Alpha Lambda Delta, Phi Kappa Phi, Pi Kappa Lambda, Sigma Alpha Iota, Pi Lambda Theta. Presbyterian. Office: Box 135 Hendrix Coll Conway AR 72032

HERRICK, DORIS EILEEN SCHLESINGER, assn. exec.; b. Salina, Kans., Mar. 6, 1928; d. Jefferson Seligman and Jessie Merle (Nothern) Schlesinger; B.A., Ottawa (Kans.) U., 1949; m. William F. Herrick, June 5, 1948 (div. 1973); children—William Robert, David Michael, Susan Carol. Reporter, Arkansas City (Kans.) Daily Traveler, 1947; writer commls. Arkansas City Radio Sta., 1949; office mgr. Charlotte Finn Interior Design, White Plains, N.Y., 1973-78; exec. dir. Eastern Tennis Assn., White Plains, 1978—, Eastern Youth Tennis Found., 1979—; mem. membership com. U.S. Tennis Assn., 1980—. Trustee, First Bapt. Ch. White Plains, 1979—, pres., 1977-79, pres. woman's guild, 1960-64, 73; bd. dirs. Purchase (N.Y.) Community House, 1967-69; pres. Lake St. Sch. PTA, Harrison, N.Y., 1965-67, Purchase Sch. PTA, 1967-69; v.p. Met. Assn. Bapt. Women, 1962-64. Mem. AAUW (last v.p. Westchester br. 1966), N.Y. Soc. Assn. Execs. Democrat. Club: White Plains Woman's (pres. 1970-72). Home: 24 Fairview Ave White Plains NY 10603 Office: 202 Mamaroneck Ave White Plains NY 10601

HERRICK, KATHLEEN MAGARA, social worker; b. Mpls., Oct. 18, 1943; d. William Frank and Mary Genevieve (Gill) Magara; B.A. in Social Work and French, Coll. St. Benedict, St. Joseph, Minn., 1965; M.S.W. (Mildred B. Erickson fellow 1975), Mich. State U., E. Lansing, 1976; m. John Middlemist Herrick, Feb. 5, 1966; children—Elizabeth Jane, Kathryn Mary. Social worker II, Carver County Social Services, Chaska, Minn., 1965-70; therapist St. Lawrence Community Mental Health Center, Lansing, Mich., 1974-75; sch. social worker Ingham Intermediate Sch. Dist., Mason, Mich., 1975-76; home/sch. coordinator Eaton Intermediate Sch. Dist., Charlotte, Mich., 1976-81; caseworker St.

Vincent Home for Children, Lansing, 1979-80; tchr. cons. for severely emotionally impaired, 1981—; bd. dirs. Catholic Social Services, Lansing. Mem. Nat. Assn. Social Workers, Nat. Assn. Retarded Citizens, Am. Orthopsychiat. Assn., Mich. Assn. Sch. Social Workers, Mich. Assn. Emotionally Disturbed Children, Eaton County Assn. Retarded Citizens, Feingold Assn. SE Mich., NOW, Nat. Women's Health Network, Amnesty Internat., Phi Kappa Phi, Phi Alpha. Democrat. Roman Catholic. Home: 2330 Shawnee Trail Okemos MI 48864 Office: 1790 E Packard Hwy Charlotte MI 48813

HERRIGES, ROSEMARY PATI, bus. exec.; b. N.Y.C.; d. Joseph Vincent and Sally G. Pati; student New Eng. Conservatory Music, 1950-52, Wheaton Coll., 1956; m. Raymond C. Herriges, July 1, 1969; (dec. Oct. 1975); 1 son, Gerald Joseph. Engaged in radio and TV, Boston and N.Y.C., 1955-65; mgr. Med. Personnel Pool, Boston, 1965-68; pres. Med. Personnel Pool Palm Beach, Inc. (Fla.), 1969—; cons. Personnel Pool Am. Recipient Small Bus. Woman of Yr. award SBA, 1975; Commendation, Personnel Pool of Am., 1979, 80, 81; Appreciation cert. Republican party, 1981; Mem. Internat. Backgammon Assn. Republican. Roman Catholic. Clubs: Lacoquille, South Seas Plantation, Breakers Beach, Palm Beach Yacht. Home: 1200 S Flagler Dr West Palm Beach FL 33401 Office: Med Personnel Pool Palm Beach Inc 211 Royal Poinciana Way Palm Beach FL 33480

HERRIN, DIAN, alcoholism and drug therapist; b. San Diego, Oct. 16, 1932; d. Maurice Simpson and Lota Mitchell (Chambers) Todd; A.A. in Bus. Adminstrn., Soule Coll., New Orleans, 1952; student Calif. Lutheran Coll., Moorpark; B.S. in Behavioral Sci., UCLA; m. Richard Lee Herrin, May 7, 1955; adopted children—Richard Lee, Dawn Lea. Various secretarial and office positions, 1950-75; dir. Tri Valley Alcohol Info. and Referral Center, Simi Valley, Calif., 1975-76, various temporary positions, 1976—; lead facilitator Driving While Intoxicated Pilot Program, Ventura County, Calif., 1976-77; office mgr. Counselors of Alcohol Addictions and Related Disorders, Van Nuys, Calif., 1977-79; owner, operator Pet Experience, Simi Valley, Rancho Capri Dobermans; asst. project dir. ASSERT, Simi Valley, 1978-80; part-time crisis intervention counselor Interface Community, Newbury Park, Calif., 1978-81; adult edn. tchr., 1976—; chmn. Ventura County Alcoholism Adv. Bd., 1975-76; sec.-treas. Calif. Assn. Alcoholism Adv. Bds., 1976. Mem. Doberman Pinscher Club Am., Counselors on Alcohol Addictions and Related Disorders, Nat. Assn. Alcoholism Counselors, Sierra Club. Republican. Home: 1179 Cadiz Dr Simi Valley CA 93065 Office: 2902-F-1 Cochran Ave Simi Valley CA 93062

HERRING, BILLIE GRACE, librarian, educator; b. Flatonia, Tex., Nov. 16, 1932; d. William and Minnie Louise (Minzenmeyer) Ungerer; B.S. in Elem. Edn., U. Tex., Austin, 1953, M.L.S. (fellow 1967-68), 1968, Ph.D., 1974; m. James Craig Herring, Jan. 11, 1956; children—William Dale, Theodore Craig. Dir. edn. First Luth. Ch., also Westminster Presbyn. Ch., Austin, 1953-57; tchr., librarian Fly Jr. High Sch., Crystal City, Tex., 1961-62; librarian Harris Sch., Austin, 1962-67; asso. prof. library sci. U. Tex., Austin, 1968—; cons. in field, condr. continuing edn. workshops. Ruling elder Trinity Presbyn. Ch., Austin, 1979-81. Mem. AAUW (historian Austin br. 1968-70), Assn. Ednl. Communications and Tech., ALA, Assn. Am. Library Schs., Assn. Supervision and Curriculum Devel., Tex. Ednl. Tech. Assn., Southwestern Library Assn., Tex. Library Assn. Author curriculum materials. Home: 1510 Glencrest Dr Austin TX 78723 Office: Box 7576 Univ Tex Austin TX 78712

HERRING, SUSAN WELLER, anatomist; b. Pitts., Mar. 25, 1947; d. Sol William and Miriam (Damick) Weller; B.S. in Zoology, U. Chgo., 1967, Ph.D. in Anatomy, 1971; NIH postgrad. fellow U. Ill. Med. Center, 1971-72; m. Stephen E. Herring, Nov. 18, 1967. Asst. prof. oral anatomy and anatomy U. Ill. Med. Center, 1972-77, assoc. prof., 1977—; vis. assoc. prof. biol. scis. U. Mich., 1981. Woodrow Wilson hon. fellow, 1967; NSF predoctoral fellow, 1967-71; grantee NIH, Muscular Dystrophy Assn. Mem. Am. Soc. Zoologists (chmn. elect div. vetebrate morphology 1981-82), AAAS, Am. Assn. Anatomists, Am. Soc. Mammalogists, Soc. Vertebrate Paleontologists, Sigma Xi. Author research papers in field. Office: 801 S Paulina Ave Chicago IL 60612

HERRINGTON, DOROTHY EVANGELINE MEANS, educator; b. Moberly, Mo., Jan. 17, 1920; d. Lewis Manning and Evangeline (Boggs) Means; student Central Meth. Coll., 1937-39; B.A. in Polit. Sci., U. Mo., 1941, B.S. in Edn., 1961, M.Ed. in Guidance and Counseling, 1961; postgrad. U. Ind., summer 1964, U. Tex., 1964-65, U. Mo.-Columbia, 1972-73, 77-81; m. Frank Dwight Waddell, Aug. 1, 1942 (dec. July 1943); 1 son, Frank Dwight; m. 2d, William Palmer Oliver, Jr., Jan. 13, 1945 (div. Oct. 1946); 1 son, Thomas Means (dec.); m. 3d, Kenneth Frank Herrington, Jr., Feb. 1, 1950 (div. June 1961); children—Kenneth Frank III, Dorothy Evangeline, Martha Diane, Nancy Katherine (dec.), Lewis Gaylord, Geoffrey Royal. Sec. Mo. Dept. Edn., Jefferson City, 1940, 41; adminstr. asst. to comdg. gen. Mo. State Guard, Jefferson City, 1941-42; fin. clk. VA, St. Louis, 1946-47, jr. adminstrv. asst. to dir. personnel Army Finance Center, 1947-49; tchr. public schs., Fayette, Mo., 1949-50; tchr. U.S. Air Force Acad., Colorado Springs, Colo., 1961-62; guidance counselor Ritenour Sr. High Sch., St. Louis, 1962-64; mgr. children's dining room Mayfair-Lenox Inn, St. Louis, 1963-64; counselor Gary Job Corps Tng. Center, San Marcos, Tex., 1965-66; counselor specialist, sch. psychologist Psychol. Services and Ednl. Research div. Milw. Pub. Schs., 1967-70; substitute tchr., counselor Columbia (Mo.) Pub. Schs., 1973-75; sr. sec. U. Mo., Columbia, 1975-76; nurse asst. Colonial Manor Nursing Home, Glasgow, Mo., 1979-80, Cooper County Hosp., Boonville, Mo., 1980-81. Mem. Am., Mo. personnel and guidance assns., Internat. Assn. Ednl. and Vocat. Counselors Assn., NEA, Nat. Council Social Studies, Am. Psychol. Assn., Am. Sch. Counselor Assn., Assn. Counselor Edn. Supervision, U. Mo. Alumni Assn., Nat. Vocat. Counselors Assn., Pilots Internat. Assn., Ninety-Nines Internat., Aircraft Owners and Pilots Assn., Nat. Student Nurses Assn., UN Assn. U.S.A., Kappa Alpha Theta, Phi Beta Internat., Alpha Phi Zeta. Home: 504 N Linn Ave and 909 W Davis St Fayette MO 65248

HERRON, CAROL OLIVIA, author; b. Washington, July 22, 1947; d. Oscar Smith and Georgia Carol (Johnson) Herron; A.B., Eastern Bapt. Coll., 1969; M.A., Villanova U., 1972; postgrad. U. Pa., 1980—. Asst. instr. English, Villanova (Pa.) U., 1971-72; med. sci. writer Freedmen's Hosp., Washington, 1972-73; editorial asst. Nat. Park Service, Washington, 1974; tech. publs. editor U.S. Bur. Land Mgmt., Albuquerque, 1975-77; sr. tech. writer, editor Stanford Research Inst., 1978-80. Stage mgr. Back Alley Theatre, Washington, 1972-73. Recipient U.S. Spl. Achievement award Bur. Land Mgmt., Dept. Interior, 1976; fellow Folger Shakespeare Library, 1982. Author: Sojourner, 1968; Sea Songs, 1979; Therafter Johnnie, 1979; editor; Pacemaker Maintenance System, 1972; Carcinoma of Esophagus, 1972; Carotid Endartectomy, 1973; Hypertension, 1973; Pediatric Cardiovascular Surgery, 1973; Regional Potash Environmental Analysis Record, 1975; Rio Puerco Grazing Environmental Statement, 1977; Star Lake Bisti Regional Coal Draft Environmental Statement, 1977; Wood Dust Criteria Document, 1979; Anacrusis, 1982. Home: 6514 7th St NW Washington DC 20012 Office: PO Box 5662 Takoma Park MD 20912

HERRON, ELLEN PATRICIA, Judge; b. Auburn, N.Y., July 30, 1927; d. David Martin and Grace Josephine (Berner) H.; A.B., Trinity Coll., 1949; M.A., Cath. U. Am., 1954; J.D., U. Calif., Berkeley, 1964. Asst. dean Cath. U. Am., 1952-54; instr. East High Sch., Auburn, 1955-57; asst. dean Wells Coll., Aurora, N.Y., 1957-58; instr. psychology and history Contra Costa Coll., 1958-60; dir. row Stanford, 1960-61; asso. firm Knox & Kretzmer, Richmond, Calif., 1964-65; admitted to Calif. bar, 1965; partner firm Knox & Herron, 1965-74, Knox, Herron and Masterson, 1974-77 (both Richmond, Calif.); Judge Superior Ct. Calif., 1977—; gen. partner Real Estate Syndicates, Calif., 1967-77. Active numerous civic orgns.; bd. dirs. Rhonoh Sch., Richmond, YWCA, Econ. Devel. Council Richmond; mem. alumni bd., Boalt Hall, U. Calif., 1980—. Mem. Am., Contra Costa (exec. com. 1969-74), Richmond bar assns., State Bar Calif., Nat. Women Judges Assn., Nat. Assn. Women Lawyers, Calif. Women Lawyers, Applicants Attys. Assn., Calif. Judges Assn. (ethics com. 1977-79, criminal procedure com. 1979-80), Queen's Bench, Nat. Women's Polit. Caucus. Democrat. Club: Commonwealth of Calif. Home: 51 Western Dr Point Richmond CA 94801

HERSHENSON, IRIS J., business exec.; b. Bklyn., June 11, 1952; d. Joe and Clara (Sher) Hershenson; B.A., Hunter Coll., 1974; M.B.A., Fordham U., 1982; m. Jaimie M. Blackman, July 31, 1977. Asso. dir. dept. sch. food services Bd. Jewish Edn., N.Y.C., 1974-81; v.p., gen. mgr. Musication, Inc., Bklyn., 1981—; cons. in field; pres. The Hershenson-Blackman Corp., 1981—. Vice pres. Bradley Palisade Tenants Assn., 1980—. Recipient cert. of recognition, Bd. Jewish Edn. Sch. Food Service Assn., 1980. Mem. Assn. M.B.A. Execs., Speech and Communications Assn., Phi Beta Kappa. Jewish. Exec. producer (documentary film) A Kosher Approach to School Lunch, 1980; contbr. articles to profl. jours. Home: 2465 Palisade Ave Riverdale NY 10463 Office: 1206 Bay Ridge Ave Brooklyn NY 11219

HERSHEY, LENORE, (MRS. SOLOMON G. HERSHEY), editor; d. Max and Frances (Grombecker) Oppenheimer; B.A., Hunter Coll., 1938; m. Solomon G. Hershey, Dec. 21, 1942; 1 dau., Jane. Sr. editor McCall's mag., 1952-68; mng. editor Ladies Home Jour., N.Y.C., 1968—, editor-in-chief, 1973-81; v.p. Charter Pub., Inc.; pres. Charter Pub. Devel., Inc., Cable TV, 1981—. Mem. Pres.'s Adv. Council on Econ. Role of Women, 1972—; sec. Com. for Gracie Mansion, 1964-67; mem. Pres.'s Commn. observance Internat. Women's Year, 1975, also mem. media com. Bd. dirs. Nat. Center for Vol. Action, Women's Forum, N.Y.C.; mem. Nat. Commn. Prevention Child Abuse. Recipient Extraordinary Woman of Achievement award NCCJ; named One of 25 Most Influential Women in U.S., NEA and World Alumnae, 1977, 78; Mother of Yr., 1978; named to Hall of Fame, Hunter Coll. Author short stories, articles. Home: 750 Ladd Rd New York NY 10471 Office: 641 Lexington Ave New York NY 10022

HERSKOVITZ, FRIEDA SCHREIBER, psychologist; b. Phila., July 8, 1917; d. Abner and Mary (Lamm) Schreiber; B.A., Bryn Mawr Coll., 1938, M.A., 1961; Ed.D., U. Pa., 1969; postgrad. Georgetown U. Med. Sch., 1975-79; m. Alexander M. Herskovitz, Jan. 1, 1941; children—Richard, Barton, Marshall. Fellow, Univ. Counseling Service, U. Pa., 1961-63, counselor, 1961-69; prof. early childhood edn. Temple U., Phila., 1970-75; pvt. practice family therapy, Bala Cynwyd, Pa., 1975—; cons. to early childhood edn. programs. Mem. commn. on campus affairs Fed. Jewish Agys.; mem. profl. services com. Jewish Employment and Vocat. Service. Mem. Am. Psychol. Assn., Am. Personnel and Guidance Assn., Pa. Psychol. Assn., Pa. Personnel and Guidance Assn., Assn. Humanistic Psychology. Jewish. Home and Office: 103 Rock Hill Rd Bala Cynwyd PA 19004

HERSON, DIANE S., microbiologist; b. N.Y.C., Apr. 23, 1944; d. Morris A. and Esther K. (Goldman) H.; B.S., Cornell U., 1964; M.S., Rutgers U., 1966, Ph.D., 1968; m. Stephen H. Franklin, Oct. 21, 1973; children—Pamela Allison Franklin, Daniel Jonathan. Lab instr. Cornell U., Ithaca, N.Y., 1964; research asst. Rutgers U., New Brunswick, N.J., 1964-66, research asso., 1966-68; asst. prof. biol. scis. U. Del., Newark, 1968-74, asso. prof. 1974—. Recipient research grants U. Del. Research Found., 1969-71, 75-76, Del. Inst. Med. Edn. Research, 1973-74, Water Resources, 1974-76, EPA, 1977-80. Mem. Am. Soc. for Microbiology, AAAS, N.Y. Acad. Sci., Sigma Xi. Contbr. articles to profl. jours. Office: Sch of Life and Health Sci U of Del Newark DE 19711

HERSTEAD, LOU ANN, retail monument co. exec.; b. Scottsbluff, Nebr., Sept. 10, 1952; d. Lewis John and Doris T. (Luther) H.; A.A., Nebr. Western Jr. Coll., 1972; B.S. in Econs. (Rodeo scholar), U. Wyo., 1974, postgrad. in econs. and bus. adminstrn. (Univ. grantee), 1974-75. Stat. research asst., div. stats. Wyo. Dept. Labor, Cheyenne, 1974; grad. asst. M.B.A. program U. Wyo., 1974-75; summer intern First Nat. Bank of Bayard, Nebr., 1975; trainee Herstead Monument Co., Scottsbluff, 1976-80, exec. v.p., 1980—. Named Nat. Collegiate All-around Cowgirl, Girls Rodeo Assn., 1973, World Championship Goattyer, 1976. Mem. Rocky Mountain Monument Builders (trustee 1980—, pres. 1979, 82), Monument Builders N. Am. Republican. Episcopalian. Club: U. Wyo. Rodeo. Writer Wyo. Econ. Indicators mag., fall 1974. Home: Route 1 Mitchell NE 69357 Office: 1319 Ave A Scottsbluff NE 69361

HERTZBERG, HAZEL WHITMAN, educator; b. Bklyn., Sept. 16, 1918; d. Charles Theodore and Grace (Wood) Whitman; student Middlebury Coll., 1935-37; B.A., U. Chgo., 1958; M.A., Columbia U., 1961, Ph.D., 1968; m. Sidney Hertzberg, Aug. 25, 1941; children—Hendrik, Katrina McClintock. Exec. sec. India Famine Emergency Com., 1946, Nat. Sharecroppers Fund., 1947-49; editor India Today, 1944-47; tchr. social studies/English, Ramapo Central Sch. Dist. 1, Suffern, N.Y., 1957-62; instr. Tchrs. Coll., Columbia U., N.Y.C., 1963-68, asst. prof., 1968-69, assoc. prof., 1970-78, prof. history and edn., 1978—; cons. Am. Indian Center Newberry Library, others; panelist Nat. Endowment for Humanities, 1980-82; co-dir. summer seminars in social studies, N.Y. State Hist. Assn., 1965-68; cons. N.Y. Dept. Edn., 1962-67. Nat. Endowment for Humanities fellow, 1974-75; Woodrow Wilson Internat. Center for Scholars fellow, 1975. Mem. Am. Hist. Assn., Orgn. Am. Historians, Social Sci. Edn. Consortium, Nat. Council Social Studies, Ann. Conf. on Iroquois Research. Democrat. Quaker. Author: Social Studies Reform, 1880-1980, 1981; The Great Tree and the Long House, 1966; The Search for An American Indian Identity: Modern Pan-Indian Movements, 1971; contbr. articles to profl. jours. Home: 35 Iroquois Ave Palisades NY 10964 Office: PO Box 222 525 W 120 St New York NY 10027

HERTZBERGER, NANCY ELDER, banker; b. Knoxville, Tenn., Apr. 7, 1938; d. J. Robert and Ethel B. (Bailey) Elder; grad. U. Fla. Sch. Banking; m. Donald G. Hertzberger, May 26, 1979; children—Robert Buren Hall, Lee Anne Hall. With Hamilton Nat. Bank, Knoxville, 1956-60, 1st Bank Clewiston (Fla.), 1962-64, Fla. Nat. Bank, West Palm Beach, 1964-69; with Mall Bank, West Palm Beach, Fla., 1969—, sr. v.p., 1978—. Mem. Nat. Assn. Bank Women, Am. Inst. Banking, DAR. Home: 231 Lake Arbor Dr Palm Springs FL 33461 Office: 1801 Palm Beach Lakes Blvd West Palm Beach FL 33401

HERTZOG, BEVERLY MEYER, nurse; b. Puunene, Maui, Hawaii, Oct. 17, 1941; d. Arthur Edward and Sophie (Tavares) Meyer; R.N., Queen's Sch. Nursing, 1962; 1 son, Edward Everett Meyer Hertzog. Staff nurse Maui Meml. Hosp., Wailuku, 1962-64, 68-70; office nurse Dr. W.G. Pfaeltzer, Kahului, Hawaii, 1965-66, Dr. L.S. Rockett, Wailuku, Maui, 1970-71; supr. Hale Makua, Wailuku, 1971-76, head nurse, 1976; supr. Maui Meml. Hosp., 1978—; cons. in field. Active Commn. on Aging, 1976-77. Cert. geriatrics, nursing adminstrn. Am. Nurses Assn. Mem. Hawaii Govt. Employees Assn. Roman Catholic. Home: 387 S Mokapu St Kahului Maui HI 96732 Office: Maui Meml Hosp 221 Mahalani St Wailuku Maui HI 96793

HERTZOG, KARLA JANE, personnel service exec.; b. Denver, Jan. 3, 1951; d. Theodore Karl and Charlene (Walker) Cobb; student Colo. State U., 1969-71, Metro State Coll., 1972; 1 dau., Kara Ann. With TOPS*, 1971—, area mgr. Calif. offices, San Diego, 1973—; v.p. Placements, Inc. Mem. Calif. Assn. Temporary Services (pres. San Diego chpt., treas., sec. state), Independent Office Service Inst. (sec.), Nat. Assn. Temporary Services. Republican. Presbyterian. Office: 7851 Mission Center Ct Suite 210 San Diego CA 92108

HERVEY, PATRICIA ANN (DALY), structural steel draftsman; b. Houston, Aug. 8, 1953; d. Cornelius Francis and Elizabeth Ann (Caffrey) Daly; A.A.S., San Jacinto Coll., 1973; m. Perry David Hervey, Nov. 15, 1975; children—Sarah Paige, Vanessa Leigh. Civil draftsman Bayshore Surveying, Deer Park, Tex., 1972, Mcpl. Engrng., Houston, 1973; structural draftsman Brown & Root, Inc., Houston, 1974-76; illustrator Norwegian Petroleum Cons., Oslo, 1976-77; structural draftsman, illustrator Matthew Hall Engrng., Houston, 1981-82. Club: Am. Women's Club of Oslo (illustrator 1976-79, membership chmn. 1978-79). Home and office: 312 Downham Ct Walnut Creek CA 94598

HERWIG, BARBARA LYNN, lawyer; b. Los Angeles, Nov. 1, 1944; d. Karl Edmund and Gertrude Dorothy (Ernst) H.; B.A., Stanford U., 1967; J.D., U. Calif., Berkeley, 1970. Admitted to Calif. bar, 1971; with Dept. Justice, Washington, 1970—, atty. civil div., appellate staff, 1972-81, asst. dir. torts br., civil div., 1981—. Mem. Am. Bar Assn., State Bar Calif. Office: Dept Justice Washington DC 20530

HERWIG, JOAN EMILY, educator; b. Chgo., Apr. 7, 1943; d. Roger Miles and Joyce Ivah (Mahlke) H.; student Merrill-Palmer Inst., 1964; B.S., U. Wis., Stout, 1965; M.S., Iowa State U., 1971; Ph.D. (David Ross fellow), Purdue U., 1978. Tchr. jr. high sch., Port Huron, Mich., 1965-69; dir.-tchr. Head Start, Port Huron, summers 1965-69; teaching asst. Iowa State U., 1969-70, asso. prof. child devel., 1971—; research asst. Purdue U., 1976-78; cons. child devel., early childhood edn. Bd. dirs. Ames (Iowa) Presch., 1971-73, Pammel Nursery Sch., Ames, 1975-76; mem. governing bd. Episcopal Parish of Ames, 1982—. Mem. Soc. for Research in Child Devel., Nat. Assn. Edn. Young Children, Midwest Assn. Edn. Young Children, Iowa Assn. Edn. Young Children (sec. 1979-82, v.p. 1982—), Am. Home Econs. Assn., Nat. Assn. Early Childhood Tchrs. Educators, Omicron Nu, Phi Delta Kappa. Contbr. chpts., articles to profl. publs.; research in cognitive devel. young children. Office: 215 Andrews Iowa State U Ames IA 50011

HERZENBERG, CAROLINE LITTLEJOHN, physicist; b. East Orange, N.J., Mar. 25, 1932; d. Charles Frederick and Caroline Dorthea (Schulze) Littlejohn; B.S., M.I.T., 1953; M.S., U. Chgo., 1955, Ph.D., 1958; m. Leonardo Herzenberg, July 29, 1961; children—Karen Ann, Cahterine Stuart. Research assoc. U. Chgo., 1958-59; research assoc. Argonne (Ill.) Nat. Lab., 1959-61; asst. prof. physics Ill. Inst. Tech., Chgo., 1961-67, research physicist, 1967-70, sr. physicist, Research Inst., 1970-71; assoc. prof. physics U. Ill. at Med. Center, Chgo., 1972-74; lectr. physics Calif. State U., Fresno, Calif., 1975-76; physicist Argonne (Ill.) Nat. Lab., 1977—. Mem. LWV, NOW (co-organizer Freeport chpt.), Am. Phys. Soc. (chmn. com.), Assn. Women in Sci. (nat. sec. 1972-74), Fedn. Am. Scientists, AAAS, Sigma Xi. Club: Chicago Physics (bd. dirs.). Contbr. articles to profl. jours. Home: 1814 Valley View Dr Freeport IL 61032 Office: Argonne National Lab Argonne IL 60439

HERZIG, JEAN BURROWS, social worker; b. Indianola, Iowa, May 26, 1925; d. Charles N. and Sadie L. (Bryan) Burrows; student Simpson Coll., 1943-46; B.A., Trinity U., 1947; m. O. Paul Herzig, June 25, 1949; children—Paul A., Karen, Amy, Heidi. Sec., U.S. Dept. State Fgn. Service, La Paz, Bolivia, 1947-49; social worker State Fla. Health and Rehab. Services, Clearwater, 1968-73, social and rehab. services supr., 1973—. Bd. mem., treas. Pinellas Opportunity Council, 1974—; pres. Pinellas Health Coalition, 1977-79; mem. task force Alternate Birthing Center, 1979; active Women's Polit. Caucus, Pinellas Coalition ERA. Recipient Merit award State Fla., 1973. Mem. Am. Public Welfare Assn., Nat. Assn. Social Workers. Republican. Methodist. Office: 1100 Cleveland St Clearwater FL 33515

HERZOG, FAY ANN, social work adminstr.; b. New Orleans, Aug. 22, 1946; d. Anthony George and Aline Helen (Mauer) Herzog; B.A., La. State U., 1968; M.S.W., Tulane U., 1972; m. Marion Robert Neyrey, Aug. 15, 1975. Supr. social work Office Human Devel., New Orleans, 1968-77; clin. social work supr. Child Protection Center, New Orleans, 1977-79; social service adminstr. La. Tng. Inst., New Orleans, 1979—; mem. La. State Bd. Cert. Social Workers, 1974—; owner, operator Fleur de Lis Photography, 1976—. Active River Road Civic Improvement Assn. Mem. Nat. Assn. Social Workers, Acad. Cert. Social Workers, Bougalie Rebels Cat Club (v.p. 1979-81), Greater Baton Rouge Cat Club, Vieux Carre Cat Club. Home: 3782 Herald St New Orleans LA 70114 Office: 3225 River Rd Bridge City LA 70094

HESLIN, CATHLEEN JANE, designer; b. Bklyn., Feb. 24, 1929; d. Charles Jenkins and Katherine (Bauer) Hunter; A.A., Packer Collegiate Inst., Bklyn., 1950; postgrad. Duke U., Pratt Inst.; m. John Thomas Heslin, June 24, 1950. Sr. artist, designer Klopman Mills, Rockleigh, N.J., 1966-72; free-lance designer, 1972-78; propr. Quilters Corner, Tappan, N.Y., 1978—; historian Borough of Rockleigh (N.J.), 1973—, councilwoman, 1974—, chmn. environ. com., 1974, chmn. fin. com., 1977; chmn. Rockleigh Historic Adv. Com., 1978—. Recipient various certs. of appreciation. Mem. Tappantown Hist. Soc. (dir.), Soc. Archtl. Historians, Am. Soc. Planning Ofcls., Bergen County Hist. Soc., Historic Homes Assn. N.J. Republican. Author: History of Rockleigh, N.J., 1648-1973, 1973. Inventor Quilters Quarter, measuring device. Obtained Nat. Historic Dist. status for Borough of Rockleigh, 1976. Home: Piermont Rd Rockleigh NJ 07647 Office: 92 Main St Tappan NY 10983

HESLIN, MARY MAZUREK, state ofcl.; b. Hartford, Conn., Aug. 15, 1929; d. John Thomas and Sophie Anna (Yanda) Mazurek; student Albertus Magnus Coll., 1947-48; B.A., U. Conn., 1951; M.A. in History, Trinity Coll., 1968; m. Thomas Patrick Heslin, Apr. 26, 1952; children—Joanne, Mary Ellen, Thomas, Jr., John. Tchr. Weaver High Sch., Hartford, Conn., 1951-70; city councilwoman, City of Hartford, 1971-72, dep. mayor, 1972-75; commr. Consumer Protection, Hartford, Conn., 1975—. Adv. bd. Consumer Product Safety Commn.; adj. prof. econs. Central Community Coll.; chmn. Gov.'s Metric Coordinating Com. Co-chmn. inter local agreement com. Met. Dist. Commn., 1971-73; co-chmn. Commn. Right to Read, 1970-72; mem. Hartfords Bicentennial Com., 1973-74. Recipient Polonia State Disting. Service award United Polish Socs., 1978; named woman of year Greater Hartford Jr. C. of C., Nat. Fedn. Bus. and Profl. Women, 1977. Mem. Nat. Assn. Consumer Affairs Adminstrs. Officers Assn., Am. Food and Drug Ofcls., Internat. Narcotics Enforcement Officers Assn., New Eng. Food and Drug Ofcls., Bus. and Profl. Women's Orgn., Hartford Women's Network. Democrat. Roman Catholic. Clubs: Hartford Federated Democratic Women's; Polish Democratic; Ellington Ridge Country; Wampanoag Country. Office: 165 Capitol Ave Hartford CT 06115

HESS, ADELINE LAYAOU (MRS. CHARLES FREDERICK HESS, JR.), ret. librarian; b. Dorranceton, Pa., Nov. 6, 1915; d. Francis B. and Jennie (Decker) Layaou; cert. Bloomsburg State Tchrs. Coll., 1934; B.S., Mansfield State Tchrs. Coll., 1952; postgrad. Pa. State U., 1956-58, Clarion State Tchrs. Coll., 1958; M.L.S., Marywood Coll., 1962; m. Charles Frederick Hess, Jr., Dec. 8, 1934; children—Charles Frederick, III, Donald Francis, Jane (Mrs. Curtis H. Bonser). Tchr.,

Kingston Twp., Pa., 1934, Wellsboro, Pa., 1952-58; sch. librarian Central Dauphin Schs., Harrisburg, Pa., 1964-65; asst. prof. library edn. Mansfield State Coll., supr. Campus Tng. Sch. Library, 1965-66, mem. faculty adv. council, 1965-66; sch. library advisor Pa. Dept. Pub. Instrn., Harrisubrg, 1966-75; supr. libraries Indochinese refugee sch. Pa. Dept. Edn., Indiantown Gap, Pa., 1975. Editor radio program Dateline: Edn., WNBT, Wellsboro, 1962-63. Treas., Tioga County Council PTA's 1955-56, chmn. by-laws and legislation, 1956-58, pres., 1958-60; vol. nurse's aide ARC, probation worker for parolees Commonwealth of Pa., 1961-63. Mem. Rep. Women's Club; bd. dirs. Central Dauphin Taxpayers League, 1975-76. Hon. mem. Future Farmers Am., 1952. Mem. Bus. and Profl. Women, Am. Assn. U. Profs., Assn. Pa. State Coll. Faculties, Pa., Am. library assns., Pa. Learning Resources Assn., Pa. Edn. Assn., NEA, Tioga County Assn. Sch. Librarians (a founder, pres. 1962), Internat. Platform Assn., Assn. Ednl. Communications and Tech., Delta Kappa Gamma, Kappa Delta Pi. Methodist (mem. ofcl. bd. ch., cert. lay speaker, tchr. Ch. Sch.). Home: 7645 Jonestown Rd Harrisburg PA 17112

HESS, ANNE LETCHWORTH, psychologist; b. Rocky Mount, N.C., Aug. 25, 1940; d. Samuel and Oma Wilba (Lewis) Letchworth; B.A., Trenton State Coll., 1962; M.S., Ohio U., 1967, Ph.D., 1971; m. Charles Thomas Hess, Sept. 1, 1966; 1 son, Samuel Timothy. Clk., Gallup & Robinson, Princeton, N.J., 1962-64; grad. asst., teaching asst. Ohio U., Athens, 1964-68; psychology intern U. Fla., Gainesville, 1968-69; staff psychologist U. Maine, Orono, 1969-82, cooperating asso. prof. psychology, 1972-82; postdoctoral fellow clin. neuropsychology, Houston, 1979-80; psychologist Eastern Maine Med. Center, 1981—; pvt. practice psychology, 1982—; mem. Maine Bd. Examiners Psychologists, 1977-82, sec., 1977-78, chmn., 1978-81. Active Maine Multiple Sclerosis Soc., Internat. Women's Year. Mem. Am. Psychol. Assn., Maine Psychol. Assn. (mem. exec. com., chmn. ad hoc com. on sexism), Maine Coll. Health Assn. (sec.-treas. 1971-74), Internat. Neuropsychol. Soc., Am. Assn. State Psychology Bds. Author: (with H. L. Bradshaw) Positiveness of Self-Concept and Ideal Self as a Function of Age, 1970. Contbr. articles to profl. publs. Home and Office: 103 Spring St Stillwater ME 04489

HESS, CAROL PRUSAN, speech pathologist; b. Bklyn., Nov. 30, 1946; d. Irving E. and Frieda F. (Mendelson) Prusan; B.A., Hofstra U., 1967, M.A., 1969; m. Alan M. Hess, Sept. 30, 1967; children—Erika Jill, Alex Martin. Chief speech clinician Speech Clinic, Hofstra U., 1967-70; chief pathologist Assn. for Advancement Blind Children, Inc., Jamaica, N.Y., 1967-70; tchr. speech correction Sayreville (N.Y.) Public Schs., 1970-71; co-owner Gift Gallery of Freehold (N.J.), 1972—, Erika Enterprises, Freehold, 1972—; speech pathologist Freehold Area Hosp., 1979—. Consumer affairs local assistance officer Freehold Twp., 1975-77; founding mem. Temple Beth Shalom, Freehold. Cert. speech correctionist, N.J.; permanent cert. N.Y. State Dept. Edn.; cert. in speech-lang. pathology Am. Speech, Lang. and Hearing Assn., 1980. Mem. Am. Speech, Lang. and Hearing Assn., N.J. Speech and Hearing Assn., Monmouth County Speech and Hearing Assn., Hadassah (life, v.p. Freehold 1974-75), Levitt Home Owners Assn., Sigma Pi. Office: Freehold Area Hosp County Route 537 Freehold NJ 07728

HESS, FLORENCE SMITH, ret. psychiat. social worker, adminstr.; b. Pitts., Jan. 1, 1916; d. Grover Cleveland and Alice Mae (Weber) Smith; B.A., Chatham Coll., 1939; M.S.W., Smith Coll., 1941; m. William W. Hess, Jan. 1, 1942; children—J. Bruce, Margaret, Marilyn, Gretchen. Caseworker, Family Service of Phila., 1941-43; social worker Children's Bur. Del., 1943-45; social service supr. Del. State Hosp., 1971-73; social work supr. of worker Terry Children's Psychiat. Center, 1973-76; social work supr. of admissions Del. State Hosp., Wilmington, 1976-81. Vice-pres. Travelers Aid Soc. Del., 1958-61; mem. exec. com. United Fund No. Del., 1965-69; pres. bd. dirs. Florence Crittendon Home, 1956-58; bd. dirs. Family Soc. No. Del., 1965-70; local bd. dirs. Travelers Aid Soc., 1954-67, nat. bd., 1969-71. Mem. Nat. Assn. Social Workers, Assn. Lic. Clin. Social Workers. Republican. Presbyterian. Clubs: Smith Coll. of Del., Torch. Home: 4601 Beechwold Rd Wilmington DE 19803 Office: Delaware State Hosp Newcastle DE 19720

HESS, MARGARET JOHNSTON, religious writer, educator; b. Ames. Iowa, Feb. 22, 1915; d. Howard Wright and Jane Edith (Stevenson) Johnston; B.A., Coe Coll., 1937; m. Bartlett Leonard Hess, July 31, 1937; children—Daniel, Deborah, John, Janet. Bible tchr. Community Bible Classes Ward Presbyn. Ch., Livonia, Mich., 1959—, Christ Ch. Cranbrook (Episcopalian), Bloomfield Hills, Mich., 1980—. Co-author: (with B.L. Hess) How to Have a Giving Church, 1974, The Power of a Loving Church, 1977; author: Love Knows No Barriers, 1979; Esther: Courage in Crisis, 1980; Unconventional Women, 1981; contbr. articles to religious jours. Home: 16845 Riverside Dr Livonia MI 48154

HESS, PAULA KAY, mem. staff Pa. Ho. of Reps.; b. Hershey, Pa., Dec. 4, 1947; d. Paul Warren and Judith Alice (Morrett) H.; B.A., Lebanon Valley Coll., 1969; Ed.D., Pa. State U., 1980. Tchr., Cornwall-Lebanon (Pa.) Sch. Dist., 1969-77; fed. curriculum coordinator Joint Task Force New Arrivals, Ft. Indiantown Gap, Pa., 1975; grad. asst. dept. ednl. adminstrn. Pa. State U., 1977-79; dir. profl. devel. Pa. State Edn. Assn., Harrisburg, 1979-80; dir. govt. relations Pa. Assn. Sch. Adminstrs., Harrisburg, 1980-82; adminstrv. asst. to majority leader for legis. ops. Pa. Ho. of Reps., Harrisburg, 1982—; presenter Edn.-Law Inst., Lehigh U., 1981. Registered Lobbyist, 1980-82. Mem. Nat. Orgn. Legal Problems in Edn., Nat. Assn. Female Execs., Pa. Assn. Sch. Adminstrs., Pi Gamma Mu, Phi Delta Kappa, Pi Lambda Theta. Republican. Home: 4212-E Society Park Ct Harrisburg PA 17109 Office: PO Box 1 House Post Office Main Capitol Harrisburg PA 17120

HESS, SHARYL JANEEN, public relations counsel; b. Travis AFB, Calif., Aug. 15, 1952; d. Lawrence Allen and Dora Louise (Krug) H.; B.S., Purdue U., 1974; M.B.A., N.Y. U., 1979. Extension agt. Purdue U., 1975-76; mem. staff personnel and community relations Monsanto Textiles Co., Decatur, Ala., 1976-78, mem. staff tng. and devel., 1978, public relations exec., N.Y.C., 1978-80; carpet merchandising, Atlanta, 1980-81; public relations dir. Atlanta Market Center (John Portman & Assos.), 1981—. Capt., United Way, Kokomo, Ind. and Decatur, Ala., 1976-78; adv. Jr. Achievement, Decatur, 1977-78. Recipient Jr. Achievement citation of outstanding service, 1978. Mem. Public Relations Soc. Am., N.Y. Publicity Club, Am. Assn. Textile Chemists and Colorists. Clubs: High Mus. Young Careers, Bicycle, Ski (Atlanta). Home: 2100 Palmyra Dr Marietta GA 30067 Office: 240 Peachtree Suite 2200 Atlanta GA 30043

HESS, SUSAN VIRGINIA, chemist; b. Abington, Pa., Apr. 1, 1953; d. Herbert I. and Virginia M. (Kern) H.; B.S., Ursinus Coll., 1975; postgrad. Temple U., 1979—. Chemistry tchr. West Chester (Pa.) Area Sch. Dist., 1975-77; research and devel. chemist Amchem Products, Ambler, Pa., 1977—. Research in devel. non-polluting, non-toxic pretreatments for metal substrates. Office: 300 Brookside Ave Ambler PA 19002

HESS, WANDA JEAN, audiologist; b. Rochester, N.Y., June 30, 1949; d. Edwin and Irene (Miller) H.; B.S., Geneseo State Coll., 1972; M.A. in Speech Pathology, U. Kans., 1974, M.A. in Audiology, 1975; postgrad U. Buffalo, 1978—. Joined Order Sisters of Mercy of Rochester, Roman Catholic Ch., 1973; audiologist U. Kans. Med. Center, Kansas City, 1972-73; instr., master clinician speech pathology Geneseo (N.Y.) State Coll. 1976-77; therapeutic dir., staff coordinator United Cerebral Palsy, Rochester, N.Y., 1977-78; audiologist, asst. prof. Brockport State Coll., SUNY, 1978—, area chmn. univ., 1980—. Nat. Child Health grantee, 1973-74; Disting. Prof. award, 1976-77, Geneseo. Mem. Am. Speech Lang. Hearing Assn., N.Y. State Speech and Hearing Assn., Alexander Graham Bell Assn., Acoustical Soc. Am., Nat. Physics Assn., Volta Assn., Genesee Valley Speech and Hearing Assn. (v.p. 1982-83), Learning Disabilities Assn., Audecibel, Hearing Edn. and Research Found. Home: 55 Martha St Spencerport NY 14559 Office: Audiology Clinic SUNY Brockport NY 14420

HESSELBART, SUSAN CAROL, sociologist; b. Detroit, May 30, 1946; d. Rubin R. and Naomi Lois (Hendelman) Losh; B.A., U. Mich., 1968, M.A., 1971, Ph.D., 1973; m. John C. Hesselbart, July 30, 1966. Asst. prof. sociology Fla. State U., 1973-77, asso. prof., 1978—; dir. Project TAL, opinion survey of Tallahassee, 1974—; survey cons. legal cases State Office Public Defender, Fla. Jud. Ct. Circuit U.S. Navy, Fla. Legislature; cons. State Supreme Ct. Fla.; panel mem. small grants rev. com. NIMH, 1980—. Mem. Am. Sociol. Assn. (nominating com. social psychology sect. 1980), So. Sociol. Assn. (com. status of women 1978-79, exec. com. 1979-82), Sociologists for Women in Soc. (newletter editor So. region 1976-78), Am. Assn. Pub. Opinion Research, Phi Beta Kappa, Alpha Kappa Delta. Head sociology editor Sex Roles: A Jour. of Research, 1977—; asso. editor Social Forces, 1978-82; editorial bd. Social Sci. Quar., 1978—; Teaching Sociology, 1982—; contbr. articles to profl. jours. Home: Greenwood 1124 Alachua Ave Tallahassee FL 32308 Office: Dept Sociology Fla State U Tallahassee FL 32306

HESTON, LILLA ANASTACIA, educator; b. St. Helen, Mich., Oct. 1, 1927; d. Chester L. and Lilla (Charlton) H.; B.S., Northwestern U., 1949, M.A., 1958, Ph.D., 1965. Instr., Vassar Coll., 1958-60; mem. faculty dept. interpretation Sch. Speech, Northwestern U., Evanston, Ill., 1961—, NOW prof., chmn. dept. Mem. Speech Communication Assn., AAUP, Ill. Speech and Theatre Assn., Central States Speech Assn. Editor: Man in the Dramatic Mode, books 1-6; Drama Lives, books 1-3; contbr. articles in field to profl. jours. Office: 1979 Sheridan Rd Northwestern U Evanston IL 60201

HESTON, LYNNE KAREN, ins. co. exec.; b. N.Y.C., Dec. 30, 1951; d. Charles and Joan Heston; B.A., U. Pa., 1973; M.B.A., U. Hartford, 1980; m. Nicholas Paindiris, Oct. 26, 1975. Research analyst The Futures Group, Glastonbury, Conn., 1973-77; mktg. research analyst Barclays Am./Bus. Credit, Inc. (formerly Aetna Bus. Credit, Inc.), East Hartford, Conn., 1977-79, mgr. mktg. research, 1979-81, asst. v.p. mktg. planning and research, 1981; mgr. mktg. research Conn. Gen. Life Ins. Co., Hartford, 1981-82; asst. v.p. mktg. research CIGNA, Hartford, 1982—; cons. in field. Mem. Am. Mktg. Assn. Home: 119 Butler Dr Glastonbury CT 06033 Office: CIGNA Hartford CT 06152

HESTON, MADELINE MARIE, country club corp. exec.; b. Dallas County, Iowa, Aug. 30, 1919; d. Henry Peter and Hazel Lee (Mader) Manders; student Capital City Comml. Coll., Des Moines, 1938; m. Russell Eugene Heston, Oct. 31, 1942; children—Carole Heston Weidaw, Russell Eugene, Margot Heston Mickle, Marlene Heston Howell. Sec. for Iowa State Agrl. Conservation Com., Des Moines, 1938-41; with personnel div. REA, Washington, 1941, sec. to power cons. to adminstr., office of adminstr., Washington, 1941-43, sec. to head of priorities sect., St. Louis, 1943-44; sec.-treas. Country Club Corp. of Grinnell, Iowa, 1960—. Sec.-treas. bd. dirs. Grinnell Girls Camp Assn., 1969—. Republican. Methodist. Clubs: T.T.T. Soc. (chpt. Iowa AU), Sunset. Home and Office: 1023 East St Grinnell IA 50112

HETER, MARTHA LOUISE, pressure vessel mfg. co. adminstr.; b. Hutchinson, Kans., Nov. 3, 1949; d. Waid and Gladys (Richardson) H.; student Southwestern Coll., 1967-68; B.S., Kans. State U., 1971; postgrad. U. Kans., 1980-81. Adminstrv. asst. Gril-lite, Inc., Shawnee Mission, Kans., 1972-73, sales coordinator, 1973-75, mdse. coordinator, 1975-76; contract adminstr. Chgo. Heater Co., Inc. subs. Marley Co., Mission, Kans., 1976-80, purchasing agt., 1980—; pvt. piano instr., 1977-81. Mem. Lenexa (Kans.) Bicentennial Choir, 1976, Johnson County Republican Run, 1980, Mothers March of Dimes, Spl. Olympics, 1982. Mem. AAUW, Am. Home Econs. Assn., Nat. Assn. Purchasing Mgrs., Four Colonies Homes Assn., Kans. State U. Alumni Assn. Republican. Methodist. Clubs: Overland Park Racquet; Kansas City Ski. Home: 12224 W 79th Terr Lenexa KS 66215 Office: Chgo Heater Co Inc subs Marley Co 5800 Foxridge Dr Mission KS 66202

HETHERINGTON, KAY, coll. adminstr.; b. San Pedro, Calif., Aug. 26, 1953; d. Robinson and Elizabeth Marion (Reiland) Hetherinton; B.A. in Psychology and Biblical Lit., Azusa Pacific Coll., 1976, M.A. in Sociology, 1978. Dir. student activities Pacific Christian Coll., Fullerton, Calif., 1976; dir. student activities and vol. services St. Benedict's Coll., St. Joseph, Minn., 1977; asst. dean students, head coach women's basketball Huron (S.D.) Coll., 1980; resident dir. Boise State U., 1981-82; dir. residence life Ill. Benedictine Coll., Lisle, 1982—. Mem. Nat. Assn. Student Personnel Adminstrs. Address: 5700 College Rd Lisle IL 60532

HETRICK, ETHEL WIEST, psychologist, educator; b. Canon City, Colo., Nov. 4, 1943; d. Joseph Emory and Ethel May (Hyatt) Means; B.S., U. Tex., 1965, M.A., 1966; cert. Sch. Counselor, U. Houston, 1971; Ph.D., Tex. Women's U., 1976; m. Robert Hugh Hetrick, Feb. 14, 1970; children—John Emory, Samuel Logan. Tchr., Friendswood (Tex.) Sch., 1966-67, Clear Creek schs., League City, Tex., 1967-71; spl. edn. counselor Iving (Tex.) schs., 1971-73; teaching fellow in psychology Tex. Women's U., 1973-74; intern Fairhill Sch., Dallas, 1975-76; psychologist Northwestern State U., Natchitoches, La., 1976-78, head div. spl. edn., 1978-81; psychologist Tangue Verde Schs., Tucson, 1981—. Bur. Edn. for Handicapped grantee, 1979. Lic. psychologist, La.; cert. psychologist, Ariz. Mem. Council Exceptional Children, Am. Psychol. Assn., Assn. Children with Learning Disabilities, La. Psychol. Assn., Southwestern Ariz. Psychologists, Natchitoches Assn. Children with Learning Disabilities (bd. advisors 1977-80). Contbr. articles to profl. jours. Home: 11261 E Hash Knife Tucson AZ 85715 Office: Tangue Verde Sch Dist 13 Tucson AZ

HETZLER, FLORENCE M., educator; b. Rochester, N.Y., June 6, 1926; B.A. magna cum laude (Gerard scholar), Marymount Coll., 1946; M.A. magna cum laude, L'Universite Laval, Que., Can., 1947, postgrad. summers 1947, 48, 51; Ph.D. in Philosophy, Fordham U., 1959; postgrad. U. Rochester, summer 1959; Fulbright scholar, Sorbonne U., Paris, 1960; postgrad. voyage aboard the Canberra, Fla. Inst. Tech., summer 1973. Tchr. French and Latin, chmn. lang. dept. Royalton Hartland Sch., Middleport, N.Y., 1947-50; tchr. French and Latin, Scarsdale (N.Y.) High Sch., 1950-61, tchr. French and philosophy, 1963—; instr. Canisius Coll., Buffalo, 1961-62; adj. asso. prof. philosophy Fordham U., 1968—, faculty adv. Gen. Studies Student Council, 1972—; philosopher cons., adv. bd. Center for Interdisciplinary Creativity, So. Conn. State Coll., New Haven, 1972—; participant, moderator, chmn. sessions, profl. confs. in field, U.S., Israel, Can., W.Ger., Greece, Eng., Kenya, Mex., Colombia. Active N.Y.C. mus. including Met. Mus. of Art, Whitney Mus. of Art, Bklyn. Mus. of Art, Jewish Mus., Solomon R. Guggenheim Mus.; mem. Met. Opera Guild, Am. Mus. Natural History, N.Y. Bot. Garden, Friends of Neuberger Mus., Friends of Scarsdale Public Library, others. Recipient outstanding tchr. of Yr. award, Fordham U., 1971, profl. devel. grantee, Bd. of Edn., Scarsdale, 1983. Mem. Am. Soc. for Aesthetics, Asia Soc. (N.Y.C.), Am. Philos. Assn., Am. Cath. Philos. Assn. (v.p. Met. Div., 1980—), Metaphys. Soc. Am., Internat. Soc. for Metaphysics, Soc. for Advancement of Am. Philosophy, Nat. Council Tchrs. of English, Am. Romanian Acad. Arts and Scis., Internat. Soc. for Philosophy and Lit., Archaeol. Inst. Am., Brit. Soc. for Aesthetics, Met. Round Table of Philosophy (pres. 1981—), Internat. Brancusi Soc. (pres., chmn., moderator various confs.), Alpha Sigma Lambda. Organizer, chmn. colloquium, editor book: Brancusi: The Complementarity of Art and Philosophy, 1976; author books including: Death and Creativity, 1974, Philosophical Aspects of Thanatology, vols. I and II, 1978, The Courage to Love: Brancusi; invited lectr., panelist profl. confs.; contbr. articles, writings to publs.; radio panelist, interviews. Address: Chateau Rochambeau Scarsdale NY 10583

HEULER-ZALENSKI, MARY ROSE, records mgmt. analyst; b. Glendale, N.Y., Feb. 18, 1934; d. Ignatius George and Margaret Mary (Kelsch) Blinn; A.A.S. in Bus., N.Y.U., 1972; m. Herbert W. Heuler, May 5, 1952 (dec.); m. 2nd, Theodore A. Zalenski, June 25, 1977. With M & T Chem., Inc., N.Y.C., 1958-69, office services supr., 1968-69; records analyst Ebasco Services, Inc., N.Y.C., 1969-72; records mgr. Citizens Utilities Co., Stamford, Conn., 1972-79; v.p., treas. Records Systems Assos. Inc., New Canaan, Conn., 1979-81; records mgmt. analyst TAB Products Co., 1981—. Sec., Milford Entertainment Civic Assn., 1979-81. Named Chpt. Mem. of Yr., Wes-Con chpt. Assn. Records Mgrs. and Adminstrs., 1976. Mem. Assn. Records Mgrs. and Adminstrs. (Region VII v.p. 1976-79), Nat. Assn. Female Execs. Democrat. Roman Catholic. Club: New Haven Community Chorus. Editor: Wes-Con Bull., 1974-81. Address: 1131 Naugatuck Ave Milford CT 06460

HEUN, GISELA MARIA, univ. adminstr.; b. Stuttgart, Ger., Aug. 4, 1944; came to U.S., 1968; d. Wilhelm Otto and Else Klara Jaeger; B.B.A., U. Frankfurt/Main, 1964; student mgmt. seminars U. Mich., 1974; m. Hartmut Heun, Jan. 9, 1969. Exec. asst. export div. VDO Instruments, Frankfurt/Main, 1962-68, asst. to gen. mgr., Detroit, 1968-69; translator/editor Lang. and Lang. Behavior Abstracts Jour., U. Mich., 1971-72, adminstrv. asst. in Germanic langs. and lit., 1972-73, bus. mgr. Coll. Lit., Sci. and Arts Adminstrn., 1973-79, adminstrv. mgr. physiology Med. Sch., 1979—; cons. in fin. and personnel mgmt., grants mgmt.; translator and interpreter German/English, U. Mich. Mem. Am. Assn. Med. Colls. Club: German/Am. Cultural Exchange. Home: 2125 Churchill Dr Ann Arbor MI 48103 Office: 1335 E Catherine St U Mich Ann Arbor MI 48109

HEURING, GRETCHEN SNOOK, computer co. exec.; b. Corvallis, Oreg., Nov. 22, 1941; d. Louis Farra and Eve G. (Niemeyer) Snook; student U. Oreg., 1959-62; B.S., U. Cin., 1972; postgrad. Chase Law Sch., 1973-74; m. Vincent P. Heuring, Apr. 15, 1971; children—James, Karen, Richard, Gail, Katheryn, Maureen, Steven. Dir. grants program Community Chest, Cin., 1972-75; account exec. Merrill Lynch, Cin., 1975-77; v.p. fin. Intelligent Devices Inc., Cin., 1977-81; exec. v.p. Future Now, Inc., Cin., 1981—; lectr. on fin. for women U. Cin.; cons. on various grant devel. projects to govt., non-profit assns.; registered rep. N.Y. Stock Exchange. Bd. dirs. Met. Area Religious Coalition of Cin., 1976-77; mem. C. of C. Leadership, Cin., 1977-78; pres. Citizens Com. for Justice and Corrections, 1976-78. Recipient Community Service award AFL-CIO, 1975, award C. of C. Leadership Cin., 1978. Mem. Nat. Assn. Securities Dealers, Nat. Assn. Grant Developers (charter), Cin. Controllers Assn., Women's Polit. Caucus. Democrat. Episcopalian. Clubs: Banker's, Women's City of Cin. Author: A Manual for Grantsmanship, 1975. Home: 4040 Beechwood St Cincinnati OH 45229 Office: 16 Convention Way Cincinnati OH 45202

HEWELL, GRACE L., ednl. adminstr., govt. ofcl.; b. Atlanta, Dec. 18, 1918; d. John Lee and Josie (Harris) Hewell; A.B., Spelman Coll., 1940; M.S.W., Atlanta U., 1943; M.A., Columbia U., 1952, E.D., 1958, M.S. in Public Health Edn., 1954. Service club dir. U.S. Armed Forces Europe, 1945-50; public health educator Dept. Health, City of N.Y., 1954-60; program coordination officer Office of Asst. Sec. for Legis., HEW, 1961-65; edn. chief Com. on Edn. and Labor U. S. Ho. Reps., Washington, 1965-66; adult edn. program officer Office of Edn., N.Y. region, 1967-78; specialist ednl. telecommunications Dept. Edn., Washington, 1978—; commr. U. S. Nat. Commn. for UNESCO, 1975-80; cons. Job Corps Centers for Women, Pres.'s Task Force on War on Poverty, 1964-65; staff liaison rep. Pres. Kennedy's Commn. on Status of Women, HEW; cons. continuing edn. program Spelman Coll. Served with WAC, 1943-45; founder Acad. on Human Rights and Peace, 1977; Social Action Inst., 1975; U.S.A. del. to UNESCO Internat. Human Rights Congress, 1978. Recipient numerous awards in field of edn. including disting. service award for contributions in health, edn. and welfare, Commn. on Status of Negro Women of Greater N.Y., 1963. Fellow AAAS, Am. Public Health Assn.; mem. AAUW, Adult Edn. Assn. of U.S.A., Nat. Assn. for Public Continuing and Adult Edn. (recipient outstanding service award 1973, 81), Nat. Assn. Social Workers, N.Y. Acad. Scis., Nat. Council Negro Women, Kappa Delta Pi, Pi Lambda Theta, Phi Delta Kappa, Delta Sigma Theta. Baptist. Club: Altrusa, Inc. (chmn. internat. relations com., recipient citation for disting. contributions to human rights, Washington). Home: 240 Central Park S Apt 150 New York NY 10019 Office: Dept Edn 400 Maryland Ave SW Washington DC 20202

HEWITT, BETTY JANE, journalist; b. Akron, Ohio, Aug. 31, 1922; d. Emerson I. and Ethel Mae (Ammon) Hurd; student Warren Bus. Coll., 1941-43, Kent State U., 1971-72, Eastern Coll. St. David, Pa., summers 1977, 78, 79; m. Herbert D. Hewitt, Sept. 12, 1947; children—James Charles, Jane Ann, Kenneth Lee. News corr., feature writer Warren (Ohio) Tribune Chronicle, 1966-67; reporter The Record Courier, Ravenna, Ohio, 1968-73, now news corr. and columnist; county reporter The Youngstown (Ohio) Vindicator, 1978-80, now news reporter and feature writer; sec. Luxaire Cushion Co., Newton Falls, Ohio, 1973-76; tchr. writing Warren G. Harding High Sch., 1978-79; columnist Kinsman (Ohio) Jour., 1979-80; freelance writer and public speaker Newton Falls. Mem. lay life and work com. Eastern Ohio Assn., United Ch. of Christ. Recipient 2d pl. non-fiction award Greater Canton Writer's Conf., Malone Coll., 1976, 77. Mem. Nat. Press Women (nat. award 1971), Nat. Writers Club, St. David's Christian Writers Conf., Ohio Press Women (1st pl. awards 1971, 79), Newton Falls Bus. and Profl. Women's Club. Republican. Contbr. articles to Christian, gen. and women's mags., including Family Devotions. Home and Office: 2731 W River Rd SW Newton Falls OH 44444

HEWITT, NANCY BAUER, conv. planner; b. Lansing, Mich., July 25, 1934; d. Theodore and Maurine (Foote) Bauer; B.S., U. Mich., 1956; m. Howard C. Hewitt, 1955 (separated 1981); children—Gayle, Andrew, Amy. Partner, Conv. and Touring Coordinators, 1975-81; pres. Calif. Conv. Events, 1981—. Bd. dirs. Am. Cancer Soc., 1960-65; pres. Children's Home Soc., 1975; pres. Sharp Hosp. Aux. Com., 1978; mem. San Diego Leadership Devel. Council, 1979; mem. HOST Conv. and Vistors Bur., 1980-83. Mem. Hotel Sales Mgmt. Assn., Meeting Planners Internat., Children's Home Soc., San Diego Symphony. Republican. Episcopalian.

HEWITT, PATRICIA WIMAN (MRS. WILLIAM ALEXANDER HEWITT), agriculturalist; b. Chgo., Jan. 17, 1925; d. Charles Deere and Pattie (Southall) Wiman; student Conn. Coll. for Women, 1942-44, U. Calif. at Santa Barbara, 1944-45, George Washington U., 1946-47; m. William Alexander Hewitt, Jan. 3, 1948; children—Anna Hewitt Wolfe,

Adrienne Deere, Alexander Southall. Asst. to mgr. Midvale Farms Corp., Tucson, 1945-47, dir., sec., 1945-80, half owner, 1963-80; owner, mgr. Friendship Farms, East Moline, Ill., 1955—; owner, joint mgr. Camelot Vineyards, Rutherford, Calif., 1960—; dir. Diagnostic Data Inc., Mountain View, Calif. Operation coach Japanese Self Def. Forces, 1967-68. Mem. Jr. League, San Francisco, 1951—; asst. to field dir. ARC, San Francisco, 1944-45, service cons., 1950-54; bd. dirs. YWCA, San Francisco, 1951-52, Moline Welfare Agy., 1959-69; governing mem. Arabian Horse Club Registry Am., 1963-64; trustee, pres.'s council Marycrest Coll., Davenport, Iowa, 1969-73; v.p. U.S. Modern Pentathlon Assn., 1971-76; mem. U.S. Olympic Games Com., 1970-76; mem. nat. bd. advisers Nat. Assn. for Retarded Children, 1967—; mem. Ill.-Iowa Assn. for Children with Specific Learning Problems, 1970-79; mem. Ill. State Adv. Council Edn. Handicapped Children, 1973-75; mem. exec. com. Nat. Reading Council, 1970-72; trustee Charles Deere Wiman Meml. Trust, Morris Animal Found., Lincoln Acad. of Ill., Rock Island Franciscan Hosp., Knox Coll., Galesburg, Ill., 1975—; chmn. bd. trustees Butterworth Meml. Trust; trustee Arabian Horse Owners Found., 1961-73, mem. adv. bd., 1973—; mem. women's bd. Field Mus. Natural History, Chgo., 1972-81; bd. dirs. Family YMCA, Rock Island, 1975-79; mem. service council United Way Rock Island, Ill. and Scott County, Iowa, 1973-76; bd. trustees Am. Farmland Trust, 1981—; governing life mem. Art Inst. Chgo., 1972—; mem. Nat. Com. on U.S.-China Relations, 1974—, Ill. Racing Bd., 1973-77, Nat. Assn. State Racing Commrs., 1973-77; mem. nat. bd. dirs. U.S. Equestrian Team, 1977—; mem. citizens com. U. Ill., 1974-77, animal sci. adv. com. Coll. Agr., 1974-77; mem. mental health adv. com. Rock Island County Pub. Health Bd., 1974—; mem. adv. bd. Assn. for Retarded Children and Adults Rock Island County, 1972—; mem. corp. vis. com. for dept. psychology M.I.T., 1977—. Mem. Internat. Arabian Horse Assn. (dir. 1964-67), Grayson Found., Arabian Horse Racing Assn., Am. Horse Show Assn. (life, mem. drugs and medications com.). Episcopalian. Clubs: Santa Barbara Yacht; Arts (Chgo.). Home: 3800 Blackhawk Rd Rock Island IL 61201 Office: Friendship Farms Rural Route 2 Box 612 East Moline IL 61244

HEWITT, SANDRA ELAINE STUARD, banker; b. Springfield, Tenn., May 30, 1951; d. Clarence Connell and Madge Delma (White) Stuard; B.S., Austin Peay State U., Clarksville, Tenn., 1973; grad. various banking courses; m. Richard W. Hewitt, Sept. 2, 1972; 1 dau., Lesley Elaine. With Commerce Union Bank, Nashville, 1973-82, asst. v.p., 1981-82, mgr. Madison br., 1980-82; v.p., dir. br. adminstrn. United So. Bank, Nashville, 1982—. Chmn., Robertson County chpt. Am. Heart Assn., 1979-80, memls. chmn. Mid Tenn. chpt., 1980; mem. allocations com. Nashville Area United Way, 1978-79. Mem. Nat. Assn. Bank Women, Am. Inst. Banking (counsel Nashville chpt. 1978), Rivergate Mall Mchts. Assn. (treas. 1979), Springfield Bus. and Profl. Women's Club (v.p., treas. 1979; Young Careerist award 1979, Bus. Woman of Yr. award 1979), Chi Omega. Club: Soroptimist (rec. sec. 1982-83). Home: Route 1 Cedar Hill TN 37032 Office: 200 4th Ave N Nashville TN 37219

HEWLETT, GLADYS FAYE, banker; b. Raceland, Ky., Dec. 24, 1924; d. Joseph and Belva (Mowery) McClanahan; student Am. Inst. Banking, Ashland, Ky., 1957-62; m. Wayne B. Hewlett, May 11, 1946; children—William Wayne, Joetta Dean. Treas., Raceland Bd. Edn., 1943-47; with 1st and Peoples Bank, Russell, Ky., 1957—, asst. cashier, 1975—. Mem. Working Women Cleve. Democrat. Methodist. Club: Eastern Star. Home: 816 Raceland Ave Raceland KY 41169

HEWLETT-KIERSTEAD, NANCY CARRICK, psychologist, educator; b. Schenectady, Feb. 19, 1927; d. Clarence Wilson and Mary Stephens (Carrick) Hewlett; B.F.A., Cornell U., 1949; M.A. (Univ. fellow), U. Mich., 1952; Ph.D. (Univ. fellow), U. Conn., 1972; m. Andrzej T. Romer, June 19, 1952 (div. 1969); children—Jan Edward, Anna Louise, Mary Helena; m. 2d, Henry A. Kierstead, July 26, 1981. Tchr. art Thomaston (Conn.) High Sch., 1960-63; freelance artist, potter, 1962-67; asso. prof. psychology Eastern Conn. State Coll., Willimantic, from 1969; pvt. practice sch. and family counseling IMD, Lombard, Ill. Asst. clk. Storrs (Conn.) monthly meeting Soc. of Friends, 1978-80, clk., 1980. Mem. Am. Psychol. Assn., Ill. Psychol. Assn., Sierra Club, Clearwater. Office: IMD 2200 22d St Lombard IL

HEXNER, LILA M., entrepreneur, educator, cons.; b. Kimberly, Wis., May 14; d. Harold George and Florence Esther (McCabe) Fird; B.S. in Edn., U. Wis.; M.Phil.Ed., Newton Coll. Sacred Heart, 1973; m. Peter E. Hexner, Dec. 28, 1951; children—Michael T., Holly A., Thomas S. Women's adv., mem. adminstrn. Middlesex Community Coll., 1971-78, founder, dir. women's center, 1971-75, founder dir. Widening Opportunity Research Center, 1975-78, founder, dir. div. community services, 1978; founder, mgr. No. Energy Corp., N.E. Regional Solar Energy Center Edn. Dept., Boston, 1978-82; pres. Cons. Exchange, Inc., 1982—; mem. adv. com. Internat. Solar Renewable Energy Conf., 1981; cons. in field. Mem. Mass. Adv. Council on Vocat. Tech. Edn., 1972-79; mem. Mass. Gov.'s Spl. Commn. on Youth Unemployment, 1978—; mem. exec. com. Mass. coordinating com. Internat. Women's Yr., 1978. Recipient Disting. Service award Middlesex Community Coll., 1973; grants include Fund for Improvement Postsecondary Edn., 1976-78. Mem. Women in Solar Energy (nat. adv. bd. 1980-82). Home: 105-1 Trowbridge Cambridge MA 02138

HEYCK, GERTRUDE PAINE DALY (MRS. THEODORE R. HEYCK), club woman; b. Houston, Nov. 30, 1910; d. David and Gertrude (Paine) Daly; student Wellesley Coll., 1929, Pembroke Coll., 1931-34; B.A., Brown U., 1934; m. Theodore R. Heyck, May 1, 1935; children—Jane Peel (Mrs. Donald H. Gaucher), Theodore Daly. Dir., Union Stock Yards, San Antonio, 1961-64. Mem. Jr. League. Clubs: Wellesley, Brown-Pembroke (v.p.). Home: 1907 Bolsover Rd Houston TX 77005

HEYDE, MARTHA BENNETT (MRS. ERNEST R. HEYDE), psychologist; b. New Bern, N.C., Jan. 31, 1920; d. George Spotswood and Katherine (McIntosh) Bennett; A.B., Barnard Coll., 1941; M.A., Columbia, 1949, Ph.D., 1959; m. Ernest R. Heyde, Aug. 17, 1946. Instr. psychol. founds. and services Tchrs. Coll., Columbia U., N.Y.C., 1953-60, research asst., career pattern study Horace Mann-Lincoln Inst., Tchrs. Coll. Columbia U., 1957-59, research asso., 1960-70, cons., 1970-73. Mem. Barnard Coll. Alumnae Council, 1956-61, 69—, pres. class, 1956-61. Trustee, Barnard Coll., 1974-78. Mem. Am. Psychol. Assn., Am. Personnel and Guidance Assn., Sigma Xi, Kappa Delta Pi, Pi Lambda Theta. Contbr. to research monograph The Vocational Maturity of Ninth Grade Boys, 1960, Floundering and Trial After High Sch, 1967; co-author Vocational Maturity during the High School Years, 1979. Home: 140 Cabrini Blvd Apt 109 New York NY 10033

HEYMAN, ELINORE SHRAGER, adminstr.; b. Plainfield, N.J., July 29, 1922; d. Herman Louis and Besse B. (Silverstone) Shrager; student Columbia U., New Sch. Social Research; m. Nathaniel M. Heyman, May 21, 1942; children—Susan Heyman Understein, Gail Heyman Karp, Linda Heyman Horlacher, Richard X. Dir. Founder's Room, fashion show dir. Tepper's, Plainfield, N.J., 1964-69, copywriter, asst. advt. mgr., Plainfield and Short Hills, N.J., 1969-73; office mgr. Timesaver, Inc., Kensington, Md., 1974-76, v.p., 1976-78; asst. to pres. Info. Planning Asso., Inc., Gaithersburg, Md., 1978-80, v.p. fin. and adminstrn., 1980-81. Pres., Sisterhood Temple Sholom, Plainfield, 1962-64, bd. dirs. temple, 1964-65; sec. bd. dirs. Westlake Park A Condominium Assn., Bethesda, 1979-81. Lic. owner thoroughbred race horses, Md., Del., N.J., Pa. Club: Women's Aux. of Hebrew Home Greater Washington. Contbr. articles on racing to Backstretch mag. Home: 7425 Democracy Blvd Bethesda MD 20817

HEYMAN, GERTRUDE, retail store exec.; b. Newark, June 29, 1933; d. Stanley and Anna Pocius; student public schs., Newark; m. Jay Heyman, Mar. 25, 1972; children by previous marriage—Yvonne Janks Kellogg, Anita Janks, Susan Janks Hook, Alan Janks; children—Karen, Bruce. Asst. mgr. Ann's Sewing Center, Livingston, N.J., 1951-62; with Fabric Land, North Plainfield, N.J., 1962—, pres., 1977—. Recipient Internat. Retailers award, 1978. Mem. Nat. Retailers Mdse. Assn., Women's Fashion Fabric Assn., Fashion Group, Am. Mchts. Assn. Office: Fabric Land 855 Route 22 North Plainfield NJ 07060

HEYN, DALMA VICTORIA, magazine editor; b. N.Y.C.; d. Ernest Victor and Ethel Elizabeth (Kenyon) H.; B.A., U. So. Calif., 1967. Asso. editor Travel Age West mag., San Francisco, 1970-72, Redbook mag., N.Y.C., 1972-74; articles editor Lithopinion, Graphics and Public Affairs Jour., N.Y.C., 1974-76; editor Family Health mag., N.Y.C., 1977—. Mem. Am. Soc. Mag. Editors. Author articles for consumer publs., Ency. Brit., travel publs., Sunday supplements. Office: 149 Fifth Ave New York NY 10010 *

HIATT, HELEN, wholesale co. exec.; b. Paxton, Ind., Mar. 18, 1922; d. Lewis and Crystal (Glass) Rogers; student Purdue U., 1970; m. Robert S. Hiatt, Oct. 12, 1941; children—Robert H., Dereatha Ann. Owner, Pin Up Beauty Shop, Indpls., 1941-42; bookkeeper Lafayette Radio Supply (Ind.), 1947-65; head bookkeeper Smith Candy & Tobacco Co., Lafayette, 1965—, treas., 1969—, credit mgr., 1969—; treas. Am. Vending Corp., Wabash Data Products. Lic. realtor, Ind. Mem. Bus. and Profl. Womens Club, Kappa Kappa Sigma. Methodist (trustee 1980-83). Home: 3915 S Orchard Ct Lafayette IN 47905 Office: 2300 S 30th St Lafayette IN 47905

HIATT, JANE CRATER, ednl. cons., state ofcl.; b. Winston-Salem, N.C., May 26, 1944; d. Howard Rondthaler and Irene May (Sides) Crater; student U. N.C., Greensboro, 1962-63; B.A., U. N.C., Chapel Hill, 1966; M.A., Wake Forest U., 1972; postgrad. Hofstra U., summer 1973; m. Wood C. Hiatt, May 12, 1978; 1 son, Jonathan David. Tchr. English, tchr. gifted Winston-Salem/Forsyth County Schs., 1966-70, 72-73; exec. dir. Tenn. Com. for Humanities, Inc., affiliate Nat. Endowment for Humanities, Nashville, 1973-77; project dir. Peoples of the South, 9 state and Nat. Endowment for Humanities project, Nashville, 1976; free-lance project exec., cons., and scholar for various agys., Ocean Springs, Miss., 1977—; mem. Tenn. Gov.'s Com. for Sesquicentennial Celebration, 1977; moderator/panelist in field; reviewer Nat. Endowment for Humanities; reporter on Faces, Miss. Ednl. TV; asst. dir. Miss. Com. for Humanities, Jackson, 1981—. Sec. Gulf Coast Arts Council, Biloxi, Miss., 1979—, Mental Health Assn. in Miss., 1981-82; bd. dirs. Gulf Coast Mental Health Assn., Harrison County, Miss., 1979—, Gulf Coast Symphony, Biloxi, 1979—; mem. adv. bd. Images '79, Women in the South of U. So. Miss.; mem. Tenn. Commn. Internat. Women's Yr., 1977. Mem. AAUW, Nat. Assn. Female Execs., Miss. Soc. Arts and Letters, Phi Beta Kappa. Editor: (with William C. Havard) Peoples of the South: Heritages and Futures, 1976; exec. producer The South, Sta. WDCN-ETV, Nashville, 1976. Home: 4310 Deer Creek Dr Jackson MS 39211 Office: 3825 Ridgewood Rd Jackson MS

HIATT, MARY POTT, educator; b. Wusih, China; d. Walter Hawks and Elizabeth Washington (Fisher) Pott (parents Am. citizens); A.B., Elmira Coll.; M.A., Columbia U., Ph.D., 1971; m. Norman W. Storer, Feb. 1975; 1 son, Andrew. Instr. English, Rutgers U., New Brunswick, N.J., 1969-71; asst. prof. Baruch Coll., CUNY, 1971-75, asso. prof., 1975-79, prof., 1979—, dept. chmn., 1981—. Mem. Nat. Council Tchrs. English, MLA, Phi Beta Kappa. Author: Artful Balance: The Parallel Structures of Style, 1975; The Way Women Write, 1977. Office: Baruch College CUNY English Dept 17 Lexington Ave New York NY 10010

HIATT, MAURINE GARDNER, former hosp. adminstr.; b. Provo, Utah, Aug. 5, 1923; d. Ivin Estelvin and Eunice Stella (Iverson) Gardner; student hosp. adminstrn. Utah Tech. Coll., Provo, 1973-75, UCLA, 1973-75; m. M. Ray Hiatt, June 9, 1942; children—Sylvia, Grant, Lorraine and Lucille (twins), Vernon, Noel. Sec., Utah Public Service Commn., Salt Lake City, 1941, U. Utah, Salt Lake City, 1942; sec., acct. Latter Day Saints No. States Mission, Chgo., 1943-45; sec. U.S. Bur. Reclamation, Spanish Fork, Utah, 1950-51, U.S. Steel Corp., Provo, 1953-57; sec., personnel dir., public relations dir. Payson (Utah) Hosp., 1968-74, adminstrv. asst., public relations dir., 1974-80; adminstrv. asst. Mountain View Hosp., Payson, 1974-80, public relations dir., 1974-80. Sec. Youth Activities Com., 1949-52; pres. jr. high sch. PTA, 1958; bd. Nebo Sch. Dist., 1977-80, pres., 1979; sec. Payson Citizens Polit. Party, 1970—; mem. Utah County Rep. Central Com., 1974-77; active Mormon Ch., pres. Relief Soc., 1966-68, MIA pres., 1954-56, 60-62, jr. Sunday Sch. coordinator, 1947-48, Sunday Sch. organist, 1962-64, adult tchr., 1962-65, chorister, 1980, Stake Sunday Sch. tchr., 1970-72, Relief Soc. tchr., 1978-80. Mem. Nat. Secs. Assn. (Sal-Ute chpt., organizer Timp View chpt., Provo, charter pres. 1954-55). Lyricist Songs for Special Occasions, 1968. Home: 618 S 700 W Payson UT 84651

HIBBS, EUTHYMIA DOUVALETAS, research clin. psychologist; b. Mytilini, Greece, Dec. 13, 1937; came to U.S., 1971, naturalized, 1974; d. George A. and Maria (Palaiologos) Douvaletas; M.S. in Psychology, U. Brussels, 1965; M.Ph., Internat. Sch. Psychology, Brussels, 1971; postgrad. Am. U.; m. Russell Schuler Hibbs, May 15, 1971; 1 dau., Anna Maria. Clin. psychologist Titeca Clinic, Brussels, 1964-67; mem. personnel staff NATO, Brussels, 1967-71; dir. Mental Health Center, Columbia Pt.-Tufts U., Boston, also lectr. psychiatry Tufts U. Med. Sch., 1971-74; sch. psychologist, Tripoli, Lybia, 1974-77; clin. research psychologist NIMH, 1977—. Bd. dirs. Internat. Study Center Children and Families. Mem. Am. Psychol. Assn., Washington Acad. Sci., Internat. Council Psychologists, Phi Delta Gamma. Office: 2340 University Blvd E Adelphi MD 20783

HIBNER, DIXIE LANE, ednl. adminstr.; b. Dawson Springs, Ky., Jan. 16, 1942; d. Euel Matthew and Ester May (Beshears) Johnston; B.S., Eastern Mich. U., 1963, M.A., 1966; postgrad. U. Mich., 1978—; m. Edward Joseph Hibner, Aug. 10, 1963; children—Bradly Alan, Michael Ryan. Tchr., Elmhurst (Ill.) Public Schs., 1963-64; tchr., curriculum cons. Wayne-Westland Community Schs., Wayne, Mich., 1964-77; prin., Title I dir., curriculum adv. com. chmn., profl. staff devel. coordinator Saline (Mich.) Area Schs., 1977—. Active Assn. Retarded Citizens. Mem. Assn. Supervision and Curriculum Devel., Mich. Assn. Supervision and Curriculum Devel. (dir. pres. 1982-83), Mich. Elem. and Middle Sch. Prins. Assn., Nat. Assn. Elem. Sch. Prins., Mich. Council Women in Ednl. Adminstrn. Author: (with Liz Cromwell) Finger Frolics, 1976, Explore and Create, 1979. Office: 203 Risdon Dr Saline MI 48176

HIBNER, JANET LOUISE, state legislator; b. Tippecanoe County, Ind., July 26, 1935; d. Harvey Delbert and Alta Pearle (Lucas) Nelson; A.B., Ind. U., 1957; children—Kevin C., Jill A. Asso. microbiologist Eli Lilly & Co., Indpls., 1957-61; office mgr. Sommer & Barnard, Indpls., 1980; mem. Ind. Ho. of Reps. from 40th Dist., 1976—. Vice chmn. Wayne County Republican Com., 1974-76. Mem. Nat. Conf. State Legislators.

HICKCOX, BONITA ANN, nurse; b. Spring Green, Wis., Dec. 5, 1928; d. Sidney Hood and Mildred Veronica (Snyder) Runyan; R.N., Meth. Hosp. Sch. Nursing, 1950; student U. Wis., 1971, St. Petersburg Jr. Coll., 1976-77; m. Marvin Jackson Hickcox, Oct. 15, 1954; children—Kimberley, Jeffrey, Mark. Staff nurse Meth. Hosp., Madison, 1950-52, Reedsburg (Wis.) Hosp., 1952; supr. Meth. Hosp., Madison, 1952-53, asst. head nurse, 1953-55, emergency room nurse, 1956-58; staff nurse/head nurse Central Wis. Center, Madison, 1969-73; dir. nurses Extended Care Facilities, St. Petersburg, Dunedin and Largo, Fla., 1974-82; health care coordinator Abilities, Inc., Fla. Rehab. Center, 1982—. Home: 1729 Valencia Dr W Largo FL 33540 Office: 2735 Whitney Rd Clearwater FL 33518

HICKEY, DELINA ROSE, state legislator; b. N.Y.C., Mar. 25, 1941; d. Robert Joseph and Marie (Ripa) H.; B.S. in Edn., SUNY, Oneonta, 1963; M.A., Manhattan Coll., 1967; Ed.D. in Counselor Edn. and Psychology, U. Idaho, 1971; m. David Andrews; 1 son by previous marriage, Jon Robert. Elem. sch. tchr., counselor, Westchester, N.Y., 1963-68; part-time instr. psychology St. Thomas Aquinas Coll., Sparkhill, N.Y., 1971-72; asst. prof. edn. Nathaniel Hawthorne Coll., Antrim, N.H., 1972-75; mem. faculty Keene (N.H.) State Coll., 1975—, assoc. prof. edn., 1978—; mem. N.H. Legislature from 13th Dist., 1981—; mem. adv. council Title IV, 1979-82. Trustee, Big Bros./Big Sisters, Keene, 1978-80, Family Planning Services S.W. N.H., 1976—; mem. N.H. Juvenile Conf. Com., 1976-81. Mem. N.H. Order Women Legislators, New Eng. Research Orgn., Am. Vocat. Assn., N.H. Personnel and Guidance Assn. Democrat. Author articles in field. Office: Rhodes Hall Keene NH 03431

HICKEY, HAZEL SEBREN, banker; b. Belmont, La., Aug. 25, 1929; d. Lucien H. and Nettie Hampton (Skinner) Sebren; student public schs., also various specialized banking courses; m. J.J. Hickey, Mar. 14, 1959; children—Kenneth Webb, David Webb, Michael Webb, Rick Webb. Teller, First Nat. Bank, Shreveport, 1953-63, 63-66; savs. and comml. teller Mechanics Nat. Bank Burlington County, Burlington, N.J., 1963; loan teller Longview Nat. Bank (Tex.), 1967; with Longview Bank & Trust Co., 1968—, sr. v.p., dir. mktg. and personnel, 1981—; adv. bd., dir. La. Bankers Sch. Supervisory Tng.; coordinator fin. seminars. Treas., Longview Symphony Guild, 1978-80; bd. dirs. Longview Symphony League, Longview unit Am. Heart Assn.; chmn. Gregg County Heart Fund, 1979, pres. Heart Assn., 1982—; past dir. Longview Civic Chorale; mem. adv. bd. LaTourneau Coll., 1981. Citizenship scholar, 1947. Mem. Sales and Mktg. Execs. (charter, past dir.), Am. Inst. Banking, Nat. Assn. Bank Women, Bank Mktg. Assn., Longview C. of C., Fedn. Women's Clubs (1st v.p.). Baptist. Clubs: Oak Forest Country, Summit (Longview); E. Tex. Knife and Fork (dir., past pres.). Home: NF 40 Lake Cherokee Longview TX 75603 Office: 300 W Whaley St Longview TX 75601

HICKEY, JUDITH MARGARET, mfg. co. exec.; b. Mpls., July 10, 1950; d. Rene Vernon and Margaret Lucille (Byam) Carlson; B.S. in Bus. Adminstrn., U. Mo., 1972; M.B.A., Coll. St. Thomas, 1980; m. Joseph L. Hickey, Jr., May 16, 1973. Credit rep. Mobil Oil Corp., Milw., 1972-73; ter. mgr. Cheseborough-Pond's, Inc., Milw., 1973-75; sales rep. Ortho Pharm., Milw., 1975-76; ter. mgr. Am. Can Co., Mpls., 1976-77; product mktg. mgr. Green Giant Co., Mpls., 1977-81; dir. sales and mktg. Community Electronics Corp., 1981—; gen. partner Kiss & Make Up, Mpls., 1981—; lectr. in field. Mem. Am. Mktg. Assn., Nat. Assn. Female Execs., Am. Soc. Exec. and Profl. Women. Club: Minn. Sidekicks, Inc. (dir. 1977-81, corp. sec. 1979-80). Office: 911 Plymouth Ave Minneapolis MN 55411

HICKEY, MARY LYNNE, fin. exec.; b. Evanston, Ill., Oct. 25, 1951; d. Lawrence and Ada (Fox) H.; B.A., St. Louis U., 1973; M.B.A., Northwestern U., 1976. Sr. auditor Arthur Andersen & Co., Chgo., 1976-80; account exec. E.F. Hutton & Co., Inc., Chgo., 1980—. C.P.A., Ill. Mem. Am. Inst. C.P.A.s, Ill. Soc. C.P.A.s, Chgo. Women's Soc. C.P.A.s, Northwestern U. Mgmt. Alumni Assn. (dir. 1980—), Northwestern U. Profl. Women's Assn. (pres. 1980-81). Office: Chgo Bd Trade Bldg Suite 338 141 W Jackson Blvd Chicago IL 60604

HICKEY, VALERIE CONSTANT, banker, mayor; b. Bklyn., Oct. 7, 1928; d. Frank and Augusta (Hardt) Constant; student bus. adminstrn., CCNY, 1947-49; m. 2d, John M. Patton, June 23, 1979; children—Valerie Hickey Lindstrom, James L. Hickey. Supr., First Nat. Bank, Miami (Fla.), 1949-58; with Mchts. Bank Miami, 1961—, br. mgr., asst. cashier, 1975-82, asst. v.p., 1982—; mem. West Miami City Council, 1974-82, pres., 1978-79 mayor, 1982—, chmn. Fla. Citizens Com. Edn., 1977—; bd. dirs. Dade League Cities; pres. Women in Govt. Service, 1979-80; mem. West Miami Charter Revision Com., 1980. Past pres. women's aux. Flagami Khoury League. Named Woman of Achievement, Sta. WTVJ, 1978. Mem. Am. Inst. Banking, Fla. Fedn. Bus. and Profl. Women's Clubs (past pres. Miami chpt., dist. dir. 1981—). Democrat. Roman Catholic. Home: 5930 SW 10th St Miami FL 33144 Office: 6600 SW 66th Ave Miami FL 33144

HICKINGBOTHAM, BARBARA ANN, assn. exec.; b. Eudora, Ark., Dec. 7, 1937; d. Herren Iveson and Marnette Sophia (Dardelle) Peacock; grad. Center Interior Design, 1964; cert. N.Y. Sch. Interior Design, 1965; cert. achievement Martin McDaniel Sch. Real Estate, 1977; m. Frank D. Hickingbotham, Aug. 21, 1955; children—Herren Curtis, Frank Todd. Interior decorator, Little Rock, 1965-68; with sales dept. Nat. Investor Life Ins. Co., Little Rock, 1968-70; co-organizer A. Q. Restaurants, Little Rock, 1970-72; mgr. restaurants Dogpatch USA, Harrison, Ark., 1972-74; dir. internat. affairs Ark. Sec. State, Little Rock, 1974-77; exec. dir. Nat. Soc. to Prevent Blindness, Little Rock, 1979-82; single parent program devel. Campus Crusade for Christ, 1982—. Fund raiser March of Dimes. Mem. Ark. Health Assn., Ark. Vol. Coordinators Assn. Baptist. Clubs: Pleasant Valley Country, Altrusa (dir.) (Little Rock). Home: 73 Valley Club Circle Little Rock AR 72212 Office: 5905 Forest Pl Suite 100 Little Rock AR 72207

HICKMAN, BONITA DORIS, nurse cons. and psychotherapist; b. Marietta, Ga., Feb. 9, 1944; d. James Coleman and Dora Estella (Quiroz) Watson; B.S., Med. Coll. Ga., 1973, M.S., 1974; m. William Benjamin Hickman, Apr. 29, 1969; children—Jason Willis, Amber Olivia. Psychiat. nurse cons. dept. nephrology Med. Coll. Ga., Augusta, 1974-75, instr., 1975-77; cons. Wash. State Dept. Devel. Disabilities, 1977-79, Continuing Edn. Unltd., Atlanta, 1977-79; outreach coordinator USO, Hanau, W. Ger., 1979-80; instr. Central Tex. Coll. Overseas, Hanau, 1979-80; sch. health nurse Hanau Am. High Sch., 1980—. Served with Army Nurse Corps, 1967-69. Mem. Am. Assn. Marriage and Family Therapists, Am. Nurses Assn., Nat. League Nursing, Overseas Sch. Health Nurses Assn. (co-chmn.), Sigma Theta Tau. Contbr. articles to profl. jours. Home: 222/1 Neu Argonner 6450 Hanau 11 Federal Republic of Germany Office: 92d Med Detachment APO New York NY 09165

HICKMAN, ELIZABETH PODESTA, counselor educator; b. Livingston, Ill., Sept. 30, 1922; d. Louis and Della (Martin) Podesta; B.E. summa cum laude, Eastern Ill. State U.; M.A., George Washington U., 1966; postgrad. U. Chgo., 1945, U. Va., 1964-66, (fellow) Northeastern U., 1967-68; Ed.D. (Exxon Found. grantee, Raskob Found. grantee), George Washington U., 1979; m. Franklin Jay Hickman, Mar. 17, 1944; children—Virginia Hickman Hellstern, Franklin. Tchr. public schs., Ill., Ohio, Va., Naples, Italy, 1944-64; dir. coll. transfer guidance Marymount Coll. of Va., Arlington, 1964-67, dir. Counseling Center, 1974-81, asso. dean counseling and residence life, 1981—; community counselor div. Mass. Employment Security, Newton, 1968-69; tchr. English conversation, Fuchu, Japan, 1969-73; placement dir., career counselor Coll. Great Falls (Mont.), 1973-74; lectr. Far East div. U. Md., Fuchu, 1971-73; spl. adv. Internat. Ranger Camps, Denmark and Switzerland, 1974-81; spl. cons. Internat. Quaker Sch., Wekhoven, Netherlands, 1959-63; mem. steering com. Pres.'s Com. on Employment of Handicapped, 1975—. Vol., ARC, 1967-78, Family Services, 1954-75; mem. youth subcom. Va. Manpower Com. Served with WAVES, 1943-44. Lic. counselor, Va. Mem. Am. Personnel and Guidance Assn., Nat. Assn. Women Deans, Adminstrs. and Counselors (liaison to president's com.), Nat. Vocat. Guidance Assn., Am. Coll. Personnel Assn., No. Va. Counselors Assn., Delta Epsilon Sigma, Pi Lambda Theta. Roman Catholic. Home: 4708 38th Pl N Arlington VA 22207 Office: 2807 N Glebe Rd Arlington VA 22207

HICKMAN, EVALYN PROUTY, artist, educator; b. Elyria, Ohio, Nov. 25, 1918; d. Frank Harrison and Lolita (Snell) Prouty; B.F.A., U. Colo., 1940; postgrad. U. Denver, 1940-41; M.A., U. No. Colo., 1960; m. Charles Parker Hickman, Dec. 26, 1959; children—Tia, Lyn Lolita, John Prouty, Ada Louise. Tchr. art and music Public Schs., Dahlgren, Va., 1950-53, Oakland (Calif.) Public Schs., 1955-56; mem. faculty art dept. Colo. State U., Fort Collins., 1957—, tchr. design, 1957—, asso. prof., 1979—; one-woman shows: 1st Nat. Bank, Ft. Collins, 1978; Lodestone Gallery, Boulder, Colo., 1979, Monroe Indsl. Bank, Ft. Collins, 1979, 80, Colo. State U., 1980, U. No. Colo., 1980, Salina (Kans.) Art Center, 1981, Lincoln Center, Ft. Collins, 1981; group shows include: Gallery East, Loveland, Colo., 1978, 79, 80, Hart Gallery of Western Art, Saratoga, Wyo., 1978, 79, 80, Colo. Women in the Arts, Ft. Collins, 1979, Maxim's High Plains 5 State Annual, 1980-81, Thompson Valley Regional, Loveland, 1981; represented in permanent collections: 1st Nat. Bank, Loveland, 1st Nat. Bank, Ft. Collins, Monroe Indsl. Bank, Ft. Collins, Colo. State U., Univ. Nat. Bank, Ft. Collins, Sun Am. Bank, Greeley, Colo., Cheyenne Indsl. Bank, City and County Bldg., Ft. Collins; represented in pvt. collections, Eng., N.Z., Australia, Hawaii, Can., Mex., others. mem. visual arts com. Fort Collins Lincoln Community Center, 1978-82; mem. arts and furnishings com. St. Luke's Episcopal Ch., 1959—. Recipient award Colo. Women in the Arts, Larimer County Program, 1979. Mem. Nat. Art Edn. Assn., Colo. Art Edn. Assn., Sigma Alpha Iota, Kappa Delta Pi, Delta Phi Delta, Pi Beta Phi. Republican. Episcopalian. Clubs: Reviewers, Culture, Wampum Indian Arts Interest Group, Mortar Board, PEO. Home: 1812 Stover St Fort Collins CO 80525 Office: Art Dept Colo State U Fort Collins CO 80523

HICKMAN, GENEVA KILBURN, marriage and family therapist; b. Percilla, Tex., Nov. 12, 1922; d. Jessie Eugene and Cannie Bell (Adams) Kilburn; cert. Austin Sch. Bus., 1940; B.A. with highest honors, Calif. State U., San Diego, 1964, postgrad., 1964-68; M.A., Chapman Coll., 1974; postgrad. Newport Internat. U., 1978-79; children—Sydnie Gene, Gail Denise, Georgia Ann. Sec. to asst. dist. atty. City of Austin (Tex.), 1939-40; asst. sec. to dir. Tex. State Employment Service, 1940-43; sec. to dean architecture U. Tex., Austin, 1943; asst. acct. Krueger Jewelers, Austin, 1945-48; partner Hickman & Hickman Public Accts., San Diego, 1950-59; tchr. Calif. Public Sch. System, 1964-73; head dept. bus. Lutheran High Sch., Orange, Calif., 1973-74; counselor Chapman Community Clinic, Orange, 1973-75; counselor Garden Grove Christian Counseling Center, 1974-75; psychologist Human Services of Western Ark., Russellville, 1975-78; marriage and family counseling, Russellville, 1978-80; cons. psychologist Mental Health dept. State of Okla., Lawton, 1980; psychologist Jim Taliaferro Mental Health Clinic, Lawton, 1980—; cons. in field. Organizer, leader Mothers March of Dimes, El Cajon, Calif.; active Better Water Com., National City, Calif.; mem. Calif. State PTA Mother Singers; youth dir., Sunday sch. tchr. Methodist Ch., El Cajon; lay reader Episcopal Ch. Recipient Sr. Woman's Honor award Calif. State U., San Diego, 1964. Mem. Bus. Edn. Tchrs. Assn., Nat. Educators Fellowship, Nat. Assn. Social Workers, Am. Assn. Marriage & Family Therapists, Southwest Psychol. Assn., Ark. Psychol. Assn., Mortar Bd., Pi Omega Pi, Kappa Delta Pi, Beta Gamma Sigma. Republican. Author articles in field.

HICKS-BRUUN, MILDRED M., research chemist; b. Evington, Va., Jan. 30, 1900; d. Everdell Altamont and Minnie Hay (Patrick) Hicks; A.B., Randolph-Macon Woman's Coll., 1921; M.S., U. Iowa, 1925, Ph.D., 1930; postgrad. summers Cornell U., 1922, U. Va., 1923, Columbia U., 1929, U. S.C., 1922-23, George Washington U., 1928-29; m. Johannes Hadeln Bruun, May 1, 1930. Instr. chemistry and physics Columbia (S.C.) Coll., 1921-23; head sci. dept. Biwabik (Minn.) High Sch., 1923-24; grad. asst. in chemistry U. Iowa, 1924-25; head analytical dept., research asst. to tech. dir. Am. Aniline Products Co., Lock Haven, Pa., 1925-26; research chemist Nat. Bur. Standards, Washington, 1926-32, cons., 1932-36; asst. dir. research Sun Oil Co., Phila., 1932-42; research chemist Meml. Hosp. for Cancer, N.Y.C., 1943-45; tech. writer, 1946-78; contbr. over 20 research papers to profl. publs. including Jour. Phys. Chemistry, Bur. Standards Jour. Research, Jour. Am. Chem. Soc., Indsl. and Engring. Chemistry, Chem. Ency.; author (hist. narrative) Polly's Journal Vol. 1, 1978, Vol. II, 1980; patentee petroleum field. Past bd. dirs. League Women Voters, Council Social Agencies; chmn. program com. Meml. Hosp. Aux., Niagara Falls, N.Y., 1956-57; publicity com., del. nat. meeting Am. Hosp. Auxiliaries, 1956; publicity com. Vis. Nurse Assn.; pres. Easton Council Republican Women, 1963. Mem. Am. Chem. Soc. (chmn. women chemists nat. meeting 1941, chmn. women's tech. service com. 1943-45), Am. Petroleum Inst., AAUW (past dir., ann. del. UN seminar 1971-79, Outstanding Woman citation Pa. div. 1979), Fgn. Policy Assn., Phi Beta Kappa, Sigma Xi. Presbyterian. Clubs: Skytop (Cresco, Pa.); Women's Nat. Rep. (N.Y.C.). Home: Cathedral Village Apt A409 600 E Cathedral Rd Philadelphia PA 19128

HICKSON, CHARLOTTE ANN, librarian; b. Brownfield, Tex., Jan. 8, 1947; d. Robert Alison and Bernice Viola (Doyle) Martin; B.A., Tex. Woman's U., 1968, M.L.S., 1969; m. Ronnie B. Hickson, Apr. 19, 1965; children—Kurt Leldon, Brandi Katrice. Reference librarian Tex. Tech. U., Lubbock, 1968-70, catalog librarian, 1970-75, acquisitions librarian monograph sect., 1975-79, dept. chmn., acquisitions librarian, 1979—. Bd. dirs. Mae Murfee PTA, Lubbock, 1979-80. Mem. NOW, Tex. Library Assn. Democrat. Methodist. Author articles in field. Home: 3412 74th St Lubbock TX 79423 Office: Texas Tech U Library Acquisitions Dept Lubbock TX 79423

HICKSON, PATRICIA LOUISE, ednl. adminstr.; b. Hanover, N.H., Mar. 15, 1951; d. Jerome B. and Hazel M. (Fitzgerald) H.; B.A., Colby Coll., 1973; M.A., Central Mich. U., 1976; postgrad. George Washington U., 1974-76. Colby Coll. European rep., 1973; asst. registrar Georgetown U. Law Center, Washington, 1974; head evening programs U.S. Dept. Agr. Grad. Sch., Washington, 1974-78; dir. career planning Colby Coll., Waterville, Maine, 1978—; Title III cons. Unity (Maine) Coll. Vol., Natural Resources Council Maine; coll. coordinator Rotary Internat. Grad. Fellowships. Mem. Coll. Placement Council, Eastern Coll. Personnel Officers (profl. devel. com.), Nat. Assn. Advs. Health Professions, N.E. Assn. Pre-Law Advs., Am. Personnel and Guidance Assn., Am. Assn. Univ. Adminstrs., Chi Omega. Home: RFD 1 Box 998 Middle Rd Fairfield ME 04937 Office: Colby College Waterville ME 04901

HICKS-SIEGFRIED, KATHLEEN, savs. and loan exec.; b. Calif., May 2, 1950; d. Paul and Barbara Frances Shultz; student Long Beach (Calif.) City Coll., 1969-70; m. John Meredith Siegfried, Dec. 31, 1980; 1 dau., Kristianne Noel. With Security Pacific Nat. Bank, Lakewood, Calif., 1972-78; from teller to asst. br. mgr. Allstate Savs. and Loan Assn., Long Beach area, 1972-78; br. mgr., asst. v.p. U.S. Life Savs. and Loan Assn., Long Beach, 1978-81; br. mgr., v.p. Imperial Savs. and Loan Assn., Seal Beach, Calif., 1981—. Mem. Spl. Olympics Boosters Com., 1980. Mem. Long Beach C. of C., Bay City Center Bus. Assn. (pres. 1981), Seal Beach Old Town Bus. Assn. (dir. 1980). Office: 610 Pacific Coast Hwy Seal Beach CA 90740

HIEATT, CONSTANCE BARTLETT, educator; b. Boston, Feb. 11, 1928; came to Can., 1968, naturalized, 1975; d. Arthur Charles and Eleonora (Very) Bartlett; student Smith Coll., 1945-47; B.A., Hunter Coll., City U. N.Y., 1953, A.M., 1957; Ph.D. (univ. and Lewis-Farmington fellow), Yale U., 1959; m. Allen Kent Hieatt, Oct. 25, 1958. Lectr. CCNY, 1959-60; asst. prof., asso. prof. Queensborough Community Coll., City U. N.Y., 1960-65; asso. prof., then prof. English, St. John's U., Jamaica, N.Y., 1965-68; prof. English, U. Western Ont., London, Can., 1968—. Recipient fellowships, grants Can. Council and Social Sci. and Humanities Research Council Can. Fellow Royal Soc. Can.; mem. Medieval Acad. Am., MLA, Soc. for Advancement of Scandinavian Studies, Societe Rencesvals, Internat. Arthurian Soc., Anglo-Norman Text Soc., Children's Lit. Assn., Assn. Can. Univ. Tchrs. of English. Anglican. Editorial bd.: English Studies in Canada; adv. bd. Publs. of MLA; author: The Realism of Dream Visions, 1967; Essentials of Old English, 1968; Karlamagnus Saga, vols. I, II, 1975, vol. III, 1981; (with Sharon Butler) Pleyn Delit: Medieval Cookery for Modern Cooks, 1976; eight children's books; translations and editions; contbr. articles to scholarly jours. Home: 2 Grosvenor St London ON N6A 1Y4 Canada Office: Dept English Univ Western Ontario London ON N6A 3K7 Canada

HIEBERT, ELIZABETH BLAKE (MRS. HOMER L. HIEBERT), civic worker; b. Mpls., July 18, 1910; d. Henry Seavey and Grace (Riebeth) Blake; student Washburn U., 1926-30; B.S., U. Tex. 1933; m. Homer L. Hiebert, Aug. 29, 1935; children—Grace Elizabeth (Mrs. John E. Beam), Mary Sue (Mrs. Donald Wester), John Blake, Henry Leonard, David Mark. Sec. Topeka Regional Sci. Fair, 1958-60, bd. dirs., 1964—; bd. dirs. YMCA 1968-74, Topeka (Kans.) Friends of the 300; water safety instr. and swimming tchr. of handicapped; freelance writer. Shawnee County chmn. Arthritis Found. Hon. fellow Harry S. Truman Library. Mem. D.A.R., Daus. Am. Colonists, AAUW (dir. 1944-62, 65—), N.E. Hist. and Geneal. Soc., Tex. U. Alumni, Am. Home Econs. Assn., Shawnee County Med. Aux. (past pres.), Nat. Audubon, Met. Mus. Art, P.E.O. (past local pres. coop. bd.), Topeka Art Guild, Nat. Soc. Ancient and Hon. Arty., Nat. Trust Historic Preservation, Internat. Oceanographic Found., Nat. League Am. Pen Women (pres. Topeka 1970-72), Washburn Alumnae Assn., Am. Assn. State and Local History, Colo. Hist. Assn., Shawnee County Hist. Soc., Mont., Minn., Kans. hist. socs., Smithsonian Assos., Oceanic Soc., Internat. Platform Assn., Topeka Friends of the Library, Cousteau Soc., Am. Assn. Zookeepers, Nat. Assn. for Mature People, Am. Assn. Ret. Persons, K. U. Spencer Mus. Art, Conn. Soc. Genealogists, Nat., New Eng. geneal. socs., Topeka Beautification Assn. (sec.), Can Help, People to People, Archives Assos., Oriental Inst., Delta Kappa Gamma (hon.), Delta Gamma. Club: Topeka Knife and Fork. Editor children's page Household mag., 1934-39. Home: 1517 Randolph Topeka KS 66604

HIEBERT, NANCY BRAMLEY, polit. cons., fundraiser; b. Hutchinson, Kans., Dec. 4, 1941; d. Harold Leslie and Lois Daile (Kitch) Bramley; B.S. in Nursing, U. Kans., 1963, M.S. in Ednl. Psychology and Research, 1977, Ph.D. in Ednl. Psychology and Research, 1982; m. John Blake Hiebert, Aug. 25, 1962; children—Eric Blake, Rebecca Joan. Staff nurse U. Kans. Med. Center, 1962-63, nursing instr., 1963-65, 68; sch. nurse Shawnee Mission (Kans.) High Sch., 1965-67; nursing instr. new parent edn. Research Hosp. and Med. Center, 1970; Montessori presch. tchr. Johnson County Presch. and Kindergarten, 1971-73; teaching asst. dept. ednl. psychology and research U. Kans., 1976, grad. asst. Emily Taylor Women's Resource Center, 1978-80, vis. fellow Research Inst. Women's Public Lives, 1980-81; field coordinator Watkins campaign 3d Congl. Dist. Kans., 1980; dir. Century Club Builders' campaign Kans. Democratic Com., 1982—; project asst. Title IX Equity Workshop Project, Region VI, 1977. Chmn. com. on women Kans. div. AAUW, 1979—; conv. adviser Intercollegiate Assn. Women Students, 1979, 80; co-chmn. steering com. UN Mid-Decade Conf. for Women Region VII, 1980; co-chmn. steering com. Kans. Women's Connection, 1981-82; chmn. Kans. Women's Polit. Caucus, 1981-82; fin. council Kans. Democratic Com.; mem. Victory Club Douglas County Dem. Party. Named Outstanding Woman Staff Mem., U. Kans. Women's Recognition Com., 1979; vis. fellow Research Inst. Women's Public Lives, 1980-81. Mem. Nat. Assn. Women Deans, Adminstrs. and Counselors (exec. bd. 1981-82, Ruth Strang Research award 1981), Nat. Women's Polit. Caucus, Phi Delta Kappa, Pi Lambda Theta, Sigma Theta Tau. Home: 1521 Stratford Rd Lawrence KS 66044 Office: PO Box 1914 Topeka KS 66601

HIERHOLZER, JOAN, artist; b. Grand Rapids, Mich., Sept. 26, 1928; d. Frank R. and Bernice H. (Cooper) H.; B.F.A., Lindenwood Coll. for Women, Tex. U., 1952; M.F.A., Rutgers U., 1969; m. Harlan B. Pratt, May 3, 1980; children by previous marriage—Charles Cooper Bennett, David Pine Bennett. Fashion illustrator, San Antonio, 1947-56; tchr. art Summit (N.J.) Art Center and Public Schs., 1969-73; one-woman shows of paintings include: Exxon Refinery, Linden, N.J., 1975-82, Marion Koogler McNay Art Inst., San Antonio, 1959, Summit Art Center, 1964, 81, Ednl. Testing Service, Princeton, N.J., 1981, Allied Chem. Corp., Morristown, N.J., 1980, AT&T Galleries, Basking Ridge, N.J., 1983; group shows include: Bodley Gallery, N.Y.C., 1957, 58, Dallas Mus. Fine Arts, 1953, 54, 55, Equitable Life Assurance Co., N.Y.C., 1979, 80, Fairleigh Dickinson U., Madison, N.J., 1974, Lever House, N.Y.C., 1973, Montclair (N.J.) Art Mus., Mus. N.Mex., Santa Fe, 1956, NAD, N.Y.C., 1972, N.J. State Mus., Trenton, 1969, 82, Rutgers U. Art Gallery, New Brunswick, N.J., 1969, Witte Mus., San Antonio, 1952-55, N.J. State Mus. Art, Trenton, 1963, 82, Fed. Bldg., N.Y.C., 1981, 82; mem. Phoenix Gallery, N.Y.C.; represented in permanent collections: Exxon Corp., Overlook Hosp., Summit, also pvt. collections. Mem. Nat. Assn. Women Artists, Kappa Kappa Gamma, PEO. Republican. Christian Scientist. Address: RD 1 PO Box 659 Pittstown NJ 08867

HIGBEE, FLORENCE SALICK, librarian; b. Milw.; d. Otto Thomas and Mary (Reiter) Salick; B.A., U. Wis., 1933; M.A. in Library Sci., Cath. U. Am., 1965; 1 dau., Joan Florence. Reference librarian Shirlington br. of Arlington County Public Libraries, Arlington, Va., 1965-67; br. librarian Glencarlyn br. Arlington County Public Libraries, Arlington, 1967, Columbia Pike br., 1967-73; translator, archivist. Mem. nominating com. Literacy Council No. Va., Inc., 1973-74. State of Va. Grad. fellow, 1964-65. Mem. ALA, Am. Malacological Union. Home: 13 N Bedford Arlington VA 22201

HIGGINS, AGNES CHARLOTTE, dietitian, nutrition service adminstr.; b. Finley, N.D., June 18, 1911; d. Edward G. and Sadie H. (Nelson) Quamme; B.S. cum laude, U. Minn., 1933; LL.D. (hon.), Concordia U., 1975; hon. diploma Dawson Coll., Que., Can., 1982; m. Benjamin Howard Higgins, June 1, 1936 (div. 1952); children—Holway, Benjamin, Edward. Home economist Northeast Settlement House, Mpls., 1933-34, Betty Crocker Kitchen, Gen. Mills Inc., Mpls., 1935-36, 37-38; profl. dietitian Montreal (Que.) Diet Dispensary, 1948-58, exec. dir., 1958-81, adminstr. Can. intensive tng. program perinatal nutrition, 1981-82, adminstr. March of Dimes program in perinatal services, 1979-81; pres. Corp. of Dieticians of Que., 1968-69; cons. to Food Prices Rev. Bd., Can. Govt., 1973, Internat. Childbirth Assn., 1982; participant Nat. Conf. on Food Strategy, Can., 1978. Mem. Citizens Com. on Slum Clearance and Low Rental Housing, 1952-54; del. Can. Conf. on Aging, 1966; bd. dirs. Point St. Charles Community Services, 1968-70, Elizabeth House for Unmarried School-age Pregnant Adolescents, 1968-72; mem. Canadian Minister's Consumer Council, 1974-75; trustee United Red Feather Services, 1972-81. Decorated Order of Can., Her Majesty Queen Elizabeth the Second, 1975; recipient Woman of Achievement award YWCA, 1975; Agnes Higgins award established in her honor by March of Dimes Birth Defects Found., 1981, Disting. Vol. Leadership award, 1981. Fellow Royal Soc. of Health (Eng.); mem. Can. Dietetic Assn. (Goodhost award for outstanding achievement 1979), Canadian Home Econs. Assn., Soc. for Nutrition Edn., Nutrition Soc. of Can., Can. Public Health Assn., Internat. Childbirth Edn. Soc., Profl. Corp. of Dietitians of Que., Omicron Nu. Contbr. numerous articles on nutrition to profl. publs. Mem. United Ch. of Can.

HIGGINS, BLANCHE, Realtor; b. Cleve., Sept. 30, 1921; d. Andrew Martin and Marie (Webster) Martin; student Western Res. U., Wayne State U.; m. Edward Weston Higgins, Nov. 27, 1965. Propr., pres. Blanche Fey Sedam, Inc., Ft. Lauderdale, Fla., 1958—; pres. AAA Realty of Ft. Lauderdale, Inc., 1966—; sec.-treas. Lauderdale Sixteen Corp. Mem. Internat. Real Estate Fedn., Lauderdale Area Bd. Realtors, Fla. Assn. Realtors, Realtors Nat. Inst., Nat. Assn. Realtors, Women's Council Realtors. Clubs: Internat., Am. of Costa Del Col (Spain), Internat., Exchangers. Home: Villa Muneca La Montua Marbella Province of Malaga Spain also 1711 SE 7th St Fort Lauderdale FL 33316 Office: 1011 SE 17th St Fort Lauderdale FL 33316

HIGGINS, DOLORES, nursing adminstr.; b. Astoria, L.I., N.Y., Nov. 12, 1924; d. Philip Joseph and Grace Marie (Houseman) H.; R.N., Hackensack (N.J.) Hosp. Sch. Nursing, 1946; B.S. in Nursing, U. Pa., 1951, M.A. in Nursing Edn., 1955; Ed.D., U. Sarasota, 1977; postgrad. Catholic U. Am., 1960-61, U. Va., 1970. Staff nurse Hackensack Hosp., 1946-47; head nurse St. Luke's Hosp., Bethlehem, Pa., 1947-48; adminstrv. asst. in nursing Albert Einstein Med. Center, Phila., 1949-51; instr. U. Pa., Phila., 1951-52; asst. prof., dir. maternal-child health Georgetown U. Sch. Nursing, Washington, 1955-61; asso. prof. adminstrv. nursing program U. Ky., Lexington, 1962-65; dean Center for Nursing, Ursuline Coll., Cleve., 1978—; chmn. nursing program, asso. prof. Radford (Va.) Coll., 1968-72; dir. dep. nursing edn. Gadsden State Jr. Coll., 1972-78. Named Woman of Achievement, Gadsden, Ala. Mem. Am. Nurses Assn., Nat. League for Nursing, AAUP, NEA, Am. Assn. Cardiac Care Nursing, Greater Cleve. Nurses Assn., Citizens Area League Nursing, Nat. Assn. Women Deans, Adminstrs. and Counselors, Am. Heart Assn. (nursing edn. com. N.E. Ohio), AAUW. Roman Catholic. Club: Pilot Internat. of Cleve. (1st v.p. 1981—, 2d v.p. 1980-81, dir. 1980—). Home: 6811 Mayfield Rd 1497 Mayfield Heights OH 44124

HIGGINS, LUCY MILLER, mfg. co. exec; b. Oklahoma City, Mar. 31, 1954; d. Charles Ferdinand and Marijo (Brigham) Miller; B.B.A., U. Okla., 1976; postgrad. So. Meth. U., 1981—; m. Thomas Corlett Higgins, Jan. 28, 1978. Sales rep. Kerr-McGee Chem., Chgo., 1976-78, Western Omega Chem. Co., Los Angeles, 1978-79; sales rep. Celanese Corp., Los Angeles, 1979-80, field devel. engr., 1980; field devel. specialist Gen. Electric Corp., Dallas, 1980—. Mem. Soc. Plastics Engrs., Dallas Hist. Soc., LWV, Nat. Assn. Female Execs. Republican. Episcopalian. Clubs: Brookhaven Country, St. Mary's Guild. Home: 6135 LaCosa Dr Dallas TX 75248 Office: 4141 Blue Lake Circle Suite 108 Dallas TX 75234

HIGGINS, MARGARET MARY, govt. ofcl.; b. Meriden, Conn., Dec. 11, 1944; d. Joseph C. and Katherine T. (Roche) H.; B.A., Albertus Magnus Coll., 1966; postgrad. Northeastern U., 1973. With U.S. Office of Personnel Mgmt., 1966—, mgr. Augusta (Maine) area office, 1970-72, personnel specialist, Boston regional office, 1972-74, mgr. Providence area office, 1974-79, chief adv. services office, Washington, 1979-82, chief recruiting testing and info. br., 1982—. Bd. dirs. Opportunities for Women, Providence, 1977-79. Recipient Office of Personnel Mgmt. Dirs. award for superior accomplishment, 1981. Mem. Internat. Personnel Mgmt. Assn., New Eng. Fed. Personnel Council (chmn. 1978-79), Am. Soc. Public Adminstrn. (chpt. pres. 1977-78).

HIGGINS, MARGE, state legislator; b. Lincoln, Nebr., Aug. 3, 1931; student St. Joseph's Coll., Owensboro, Ky.; m. David Higgins, Mar. 24, 1956. Mem. radio advt. sales staff Wall Street Jour.; advt. mgr. Daily Record; real estate salesman; owner, operator Higgins TV & Appliances; owner, mgr. Howell Ins. Agy., Omaha; mem. Nebr. Legislature, 1980—. Chmn. Douglas County Democratic Party, 1974-76; past chmn. Douglas County Correction Advisors Com.; bd. dirs. YWCA; mem. jud. nominating com. Juvenile Ct. Douglas County. Mem. Am. Legion Aus. Club: Eagles. Office: 6820 J St Omaha NE 68117 *

HIGGINS, SHIRLEY ALICE MILLER, hosp. ofcl.; b. Marshall, Mo., Oct. 7, 1946; d. Shearman Harry and Ursa Edna (Bodwell) Miller; B.S., Missouri Valley Coll., 1968; M.Ed., U. Ill., 1969; M.A., Ball State U., 1980; m. Thomas Joseph Higgins, June 6, 1970; children—Trevor Michael, Tyler Thomas. Asst. head resident, teaching asst. English, Mo. Valley Coll., Marshall, 1967-68; research asst. U. Ill., Urbana, 1969; tchr. English, social studies and speech Brookens Jr. High Sch., Urbana, 1970-71; spl. edn. tchr. Webster Hall and Decatur (Ill.) Community Schs., 1970-72; dir. program evaluation and research New Castle (Ind.) State Hosp., 1975-76, dir. staff devel. and tng., 1976—. Mem. Nat. Assn. Retarded Citizens, Am. Assn. on Mental Deficiency, Am. Soc. Tng. and Devel., Adult Edn. Assn., Bus. and Profl. Women, Alpha Psi Omega, Pi Delta Epsilon, Sigma Tau Delta. Home: 3601 S 10th St New Castle IN 47362 Office: New Castle State Hospital 100 Van Nuys Rd New Castle IN 47362

HIGGINS, SISTER, THERESE, coll. pres.; b. Winthrop, Mass., Sept. 29, 1925; d. James C. and Margaret M. (Lennon) H.; A.B. cum laude, Regis Coll., 1947; M.A., Boston Coll., 1957; Ph.D., U. Wis., Madison, 1963; D.H.L., Emmanuel Coll., 1977. Joined Sisters of St. Joseph, 1947; area councillor Sisters of St. Joseph, 1969-74; asso. prof. English, Regis Coll., 1968—, coll. pres., 1974—; trustee Cardinal Spellman Philatelic Mus., 1976—; adv. bd. pastoral devel. office Archdiocese of Boston, 1981—. Mem. Gov.'s Commn. on Status of Women, 1977-79. Mem. AAUW, Assn. Ind. Colls. and Univs. Mass. (exec. com.), Women's Coll. Coalition (exec. com. 1981-84). Roman Catholic. Office: Regis Coll Weston MA 02193

HIGGS, FLORENCE BESSOM (MRS. GEORGE W. HIGGS), sculptor; b. Marblehead, Mass., Nov. 30, 1905; d. Frank L. and Elise (Loberg) Bessom; grad. sculpture course Mass. Coll. Art, 1927; evening study NAD; m. George W. Higgs, Sept. 15, 1929; children—Virginia, Donald, Gerry. Exhibited sculpture in group shows at Balt. Mus. Art, Richmond Mus. Art, Corcoran Gallery Art, Syracuse Mus. Art, John Herron Art. Mus., Indpls., Smithsonian Instn.; represented in numerous pvt. collections; co-founder The Artists Mart in Georgetown, D.C., 1951-70, also 2-man shows; tchr. art Mrs. Cooks Pvt. Sch., 1943-49; commd. to do bas-relief in post office, Staunton, Va.; sculptures in St. Andrew's Ch., Arlington, Va., Hartford (Conn.) Sem., Woodson High Sch., Fairfax, Va., Holy Cross Monastery, West Park, N.Y., Howard B. Owens Sci. Center, Md., Abbot Public Library, Marblehead, Mass. Recipient ceramic sculpture award Art Alliance Am.; bronze medal for sculpture Soc. Washington Artists, 1940, 57; sculpture award Corcoran

Gallery Art, 1959. Club: Kiln of Washington (pres. 1956, Winthrop award for ceramic sculpture 1st ann., Ferro enamel award for ceramic sculpture 2d ann., 4 ann. awards Ceramic Internat. at Smithsonian). Episcopalian. Home: 4133 N 25th St Arlington VA 22207

HIGHSMITH, WANDA LAW, assn. exec.; b. Cleveland, Mo., Oct. 25, 1928; d. Lloyd B. and Nan (Sisk) Law; student U. Mo., 1954-56; 1 dau., Holly. Legal sec., firms in Mo. and D.C., until 1960; various staff positions Am. Coll. Osteopathic Surgeons, 1960-72, asst. exec. dir., conv. mgr., Coral Gables, Fla., 1974—. Mem. Profl. Convention Mgmt. Assn., Fla. Soc. Assn. Execs., Meeting Planners Internat. Republican. Methodist. Home: 1150 Madruga Ave Apt C-304 Coral Gables FL 33146 Office: 3132 Ponce de Leon Blvd Coral Gables FL 33134

HIGHTSHOE, NANCY, civic worker; b. St. Louis, May 11, 1947; d. Edwin and Mary Ann (LaBarge) Kalbfleish; B.A. magna cum laude in Psychology, U. Mo., St. Louis, 1972; M.A. in Human Relations and Adminstrn. of Justice, Webster Coll., 1978. Commd. female police officer sexual assault investigative unit City of St. Louis, 1972-81; pres. RAPE Seminars, St. Louis, 1982—; conv. speaker on rape cause, effect and prevention. Mem. Nat. Speakers Assn., Women's Crusade Against Crime, Women's Info. Network, Psi Chi. Office: PO Box 31155 Saint Louis MO 63131

HILBERT, IRMALEEN, internat. ins. co. exec.; b. Chgo., Nov. 5, 1931; d. Forest and Lucy Pearl (Howerton) Brame; children—George Edward Hilbert Jr., Janice Lynn Hilbert, John Forest Hilbert, Robert Louis Hilbert. Office mgr. Woodland Hills Ins. (Calif.), 1959-76; personal accounts mgr. Alexander & Alexander, Los Angeles, 1976-77, Wellnigton Agys., Los Angeles, 1977-80; v.p. Bayly, Martin & Fay Inc., Los Angeles, 1980—. Bd. dirs. Valley Hot Line Crises Intervention, Van Nuys, Calif., 1974-76. Mem. Woodland Hills Bus. and Profl. Women (pres. 1970-71, Woman of Yr. award 1974), Woodland Hills Chamber (freedom season sec. 1972), Women in Mgmt. (v.p. 1981, pres. 1982-83), So. Calif. Marine Underwriters, Ins. Women of Los Angeles, Democrat. Home: 4346 Matilija St Apt 12 Sherman Oaks CA 91423 Office: 3200 Wilshire Blvd Los Angeles CA 90010

HILBISH, BARBARA SMITH, singer, actress, voice educator; b. Canton, Ohio, July 27, 1928; d. Ellsworth Price and Mary Ernestine (Strock) Smith; B.M., Westminster Choir Coll., 1950, M.M., 1958; m. Thomas Hilbish, July 2, 1950; children—Catherine Moore, Jennifer Sabina. Dir. choirs Trenton (N.J.) State Home for Girls, 1950-51; voice tchr., Ann Arbor, Mich., 1955—; vis. lectr. voice U. Mich., Ann Arbor, 1966; voice tchr. Nat. Music Camp, Interlochen, Mich., 1966-69, 1974-82; soloist 1st Presbyterian Ch., Ann Arbor, 1969-75; soloist Phila. Orchestra, Detroit Symphony, 1971. Active Jr. League, Canton, 1950. Mem. Nat. Assn. Tchrs. Singing, Ann Arbor Civic Theatre, Saline Area Players, St. Andrew's Players, Sigma Alpha Iota. Republican. Home: 2189 S 7th St Ann Arbor MI 48103

HILDEBRAND, VERNA LEE, educator; b. Kans., Aug. 17, 1924; d. C. E. and Florence (Smyth) Butcher; B.S., Kans. State U., 1945, M.S., 1957; Ph.D., Tex. Woman's U., 1970; m. John R. Hildebrand, June 23, 1946; children—Carol Ann, Steve Allen. Mem. faculty Okla. State U., 1955-56, Kans. State U., 1958, Tex. Tech U., 1962-67; mem. faculty Mich. State U., East Lansing, 1967—, prof. family and child ecology Coll. Human Ecology, 1967—. Mem. Nat. Assn. Early Childhood Tchr. Educators (pres. elect 1982), Nat. Assn. Edn. Young Children, Am. Home Econs. Assn., Latin Am. Studies Assn., Midwest Latin Am. Studies Assn., Mich. Assn. Edn. Young Children (Significant Service award 1981). Author: Introduction to Early Childhood and Workbook, 3d edit., 1981; Guiding Young Children, 2d edit., 1980; Parenting and Teaching Young Children, 1981; China's Families: Experiment in Societal Change, 1981. Home: 308 Michigan St Apt 8 East Lansing MI 48823 Office: HE 203 Michigan State U East Lansing MI 48824

HILDEBRANDT, JEANNE MARIE, shopping center mgr.; b. Detroit, May 12, 1931; d. Jack and Jeanne Katherine (Kaukola) Beaubien; student Detroit public schs.; children—James, Mark, Lori. Comptroller, Maintenance Engring. Co., 1953-62; from comptroller to mgr. Livonia Mall Shopping Center (Mich.) 1963—. Mem. Livonia Indsl. Devel. Commn., 1972—, NCCJ, 1981; steering com., fund raiser Madonna Coll., Livonia, 1979—. Mem. Nat. Assn. Women Execs., Internat. Council Shopping Centers, Livonia C. of C. (dir.). Republican. Lutheran. Office: 29514 Seven Mile Rd Livonia MI 48152

HILDEBRANDT, LIESELOTTE MARGARETE, educator; b. Stettin, Ger., Feb. 22, 1920; d. Richard Albert and Elisabeth Maria (Pechtoldt) Prochnow; came to U.S., 1963, naturalized, 1972; M.A., U. Hamburg (Ger.), 1961; m. Bruno F.O. Hildebrandt, Apr. 7, 1949. Instr. German, U. Colo., Boulder, 1963-65, U. Ill., Chgo., 1965-69; asst. prof. German, U. N.D., Grand Forks, 1969-80, asso. prof., 1980—; instr. German, Stanford U., summers 1961, 62, 64, 65, Ind. U., summer 1967, Middlebury (Vt.) Coll., summers 1968, 69, U. Minn., summer 1977. U. N.D. faculty research grantee, 1974. Mem. AAUP, Modern Lang. Assn. Am., Am. Assn. Tchrs. German, Linguistic Soc. Am., Linguistic Circle Manitoba and N.D., Fgn. Lang. Assn. N.D., Midwest, Rocky Mountain modern lang. assns. Fgn. Lang. Assn. Red River, Delta Phi Alpha (hon.). Author: Drills in German Pronunciation, 1964; Deutsche Phonetik fuer Amerikaner, 1976. Home: 916 29th Ave S Grand Forks ND 58201 Office: U ND Grand Forks ND 58202

HILDERLEY, JERIANN GERTRUDE, data processing exec., arts adminstr.; b. Saginaw, Mich., July 17, 1937; d. Clifton Tabor and Gertrude Anna (Volz) H.; student Smith Coll., 1955-57; B.A. in Art, U. Calif., Berkeley, 1959; M.A. in Art, U. Mich., Ann Arbor, 1961; m. Jerome A. Badanes, July 7, 1965 (div.). Teaching asst. U. Mich., 1960-62; instr. art Henry St. Settlement, N.Y.C., 1963-65; dir. Burning City St. Theater, N.Y.C., 1966-69, Painted Women Ritual Theater, N.Y.C., 1970-73, Sea Wave Music Prodns., N.Y.C., 1974-80, Sea Wave Records, N.Y.C., 1979—; tchr. women's studies, continuing edn. SUNY, Purchase, also Empire Coll., 1977-79; prodn. supr. Books dept. Am. Inst. C.P.A.s, N.Y.C., 1977-81; data conversion coordinator BRS Med., N.Y.C., 1981—; performer, cons. in theater and music Bard, Vassar and Goddard colls., Stanford U., U. Mass., 1973-80; editor CAW Mag.-Polit. Arts Jour., 1965-67; books include: A Feminist's History of Music Notation, 1978; (novel) Mariposa, 1979. Organizer, Angry Arts to Stop Vietnam War, 1968; art adv. Faculty for a Democartic Soc., 1969-71; cons. Human Rights Coalition, Woodstock, N.Y., 1980; adv. bd. Feminist Music and Politics issue Heresies Mag. Collective, 1980; Creative Artists Program grants jurist, 1982. Ann Arbor Arts Council grantee, 1961; N.Y. State Council Arts grantee, 1971-73; recipient grants for women artists, 1978. Mem. Smith Coll. Alumnae Assn., BMI, Wise Women Enterprises, Inc., Producers of Feminist Music. Democrat. Record producer: Jeritree's House of Many Colours, 1980. Contbr. articles to periodicals. Office: BRS Med 380 Madison Ave New York NY 10017

HILEMAN, SALLY JEAN, social worker; b. Ogden, Utah, Sept. 5, 1929; d. John A. and Molly Naomi (Arnovich) Sugar; B.S., Ariz. State U., 1971, M.S.W., 1973; children—Paul William, Jay Aron. Psychiat. social worker Riverside County Mental Health, Indio, Calif., 1973-76; dir. social service dept. Inter-Community Hosp., Covina, Calif., 1976—; cons. police depts.; field instr. U. Calif., Long Beach; pvt. practice, Covina. Pres., Calif. Human Services Orgn., 1975-76; pres. bd. dirs. East Valley Free Clinic, 1978; trustee, sec. Hospice of East San Gabriel Valley, Inc.; bd. dirs. Handicapped Resource Center. Mem. Nat. Assn. Social Workers, Lic. Clin. Social Workers (Calif.), Nat. Assn. Clin. Social Workers. Address: 174 W College St Covina CA 91723

HILFSTEIN, ERNA, historian; b. Kraków, Poland; came to U.S., 1949, naturalized, 1954; d. Leon and Anna (Schornstein) Kluger; B.A., CCNY, 1967, M.A., 1971, Ph.D., City U. N.Y., 1978; m. Max Hilfstein; children—Leon, Simone Juliana. Tchr. secondary schs., N.Y.C., 1968—; vis. prof. Queens Coll., 1973; affiliate Grad. Sch./Univ. Center, CUNY. Mem. History Sci. Soc., Medieval Acad. Am., Polish Inst. Arts and Scis. in Am., United Fedn. of Tchrs. (chpt. chmn. 1978—). Democrat. Jewish. Author: Starowolski's Biographies of Copernicus, 1980; collaborator English transl. Nicholas Copernicus' Complete Works, Vol. I, 1972, Vol. II, 1978, Vol. III, 1983; contbr. articles and revs. to profl. jours. Editor: Science and History, 1978. Address: 1523 Dwight Pl Bronx NY 10465

HILGEMAN, CHARLOTTE ANN, auditor; b. Sarasota, Fla., July 7, 1943; d. Joseph Lawrence Hilgeman and Margaret Eileen (Johnson) Hilgeman Lindsey; student San Francisco City Coll., 1962-63, San Francisco State Coll., 1963, Cumberland County Coll., 1969-71, Rutgers U., 1976. Vol., VISTA, Fla., 1965-66; N.J., 1966; propr. Wishing Well Motel, Vineland, N.J., 1971-77, Mario's Restaurant, Ocean City, Md., 1980—, Harrison Hall, Ocean City, 1980—; real estate salesperson Charles L. Scarani, Vineland, 1974-78; pres. Strawberry Enterprises, Ltd., Ocean City, Md., 1979—; night auditor Fairmont Hotel, New Orleans, 1980—; orientation dir. CETA, Cumberland County, 1974-75; state insp. multiple dwellings State of N.J., 1976-77, state compliance officer, 1977-78; cons. rural housing Farmworkers Corp., Vineland; also freelance writer. Mem. Cumberland County Democratic Exec. Com., 1973-76; v.p. Vineland Dem. Club, 1974-76; team capt. United Way, 1975; vol. worker Vineland Tiny Tim Fund, 1972-75; bd. dirs. Cumberland County Community Concerts, 1976-79. Mem. Cumberland County Bd. Realtors (asso.), Vineland C. of C., N.J. Assn. Notary Publics, NOW. Office: 1800 Esplanade Ave New Orleans LA 70116

HILGER, IRMA, nun, nursing home adminstr.; b. Reno County, Kans., July 12, 1917; d. Peter M. and Katherine (May) H.; R.N., St. Johns Sch. Nursing, Tulsa, 1942; B.S.N., Coll. of St. Teresa, Winona, Minn., 1952; M.S. in Nursing Edn. Adminstrn., St. Louis U., 1961. Joined Sisters of Sorrowful Mother, Roman Catholic Ch., 1935; supr. obstetrics St. Johns Hosp., Tulsa, 1942-49, nursing service dir., 1949-55; supr. obstetrics, St. Francis Hosp., Wichita, Kans., 1955-59; dir. nursing St. Johns Sch. Nursing, 1959-61; missionary, St. Lucia, W.I., organizer Victoria Sch. Nursing, Castries, St. Lucia, 1961-65; rehab. old AF hosp. into St. Jude Hosp., Vieux Fort St. Lucia, 1965-76; nursing home adminstr. Franciscan Villa, Broken Arrow, Okla., 1979—, pres., 1980—. Mem. Kans. Nurses Assn., Okla. Nurses Assn., Okla. Nursing Home Adminstrs. Assn. Club: Villa Garden. Home: 17110 E 51st St S Broken Arrow OK 74012 Office: Franciscan Villa Broken Arrow OK 74012

HILKER, YVONNE KNIGHT, banker; b. Buckeye, Ariz., July 10, 1937; d. Lawrence James and Thelma Pearl (McKinney) Knight; grad. Am. Inst. Banking, 1968; m. Dennis Carl Hilker, Apr. 6, 1957. Messenger, Valley Nat. Bank, Phoenix, 1956-68, mgmt. trainee, 1968-70, corp. officer, asst. br. mgr., 1970-73, br. mgr., 1973-80, v.p., br. mgr., 1980—. Mem. Valbanqueras (past pres.), Nat. Assn. Bank Women (past chmn.), Am. Inst. Banking (past dir.), West Phoenix Maryvale C. of C. (incoming pres.). Republican. Lutheran. Club: Soroptimist Internat. of Kachinas (treas.). Office: PO Box 2947 Phoenix AZ 85062

HILL, ADDIE VIRGINIA, fencing co. exec., real estate broker; b. Florence, S.C., Oct. 31, 1942; d. Vesper and Maebell (Turner) Powell; grad. Carolina Coll. Commerce, 1961; student in bus. adminstrn. Francis Marion Coll., 1976, 82, in real estate Florence Darlington Tech. Coll., 1979—; m. Sam Hill, July 12, 1959; children—Shannon Rae, Alfred. With So. Bell Telephone Co., Florence, 1961-74, dial clk., 1969-70, assignment clk. long distance direct dial office, 1974; exec. sec., co-owner Sam Hill Fencing, Inc., Florence, 1974—; real estate agt., sec.-treas. corp., dir. Florence Realty, 1979—. Pres., Women's Aux., Christian Assembly Ch., Florence, 1978-80. Mem. Nat. Assn. Female Execs., Florence Bd. Realtors. Home: 1015 Howe Springs Rd PO Box 12010 Florence SC 29501

HILL, ANITA CARRAWAY, state legislator; b. Chatfield, Tex., Aug. 13, 1928; d. Archie Clark and Martha (Butler) Carraway; B.A. in Journalism, Tex. Woman's U., 1950; m. Harris Hill, Sept. 20, 1952; children—Stephen Victor, Virginia Evelyn. Reporter Garland (Tex.) Daily News, 1950-51; ednl. dir. First Meth. Ch., Garland, 1951-53; chemist Kraft Foods Co., Garland, 1953-56; legis. aide, Tex. Legislature, 1975-77; mem. Tex. Ho. of Reps., 1977—, mem. mcpl. bond and revenue sharing coms., 1971-74. Awards chmn. City of Garland Environ. Council; mem. City of Garland Park and Recreation Bd., 1971-77, chmn., 1976-77; life mem. PTA. Named Disting. Alumna, Tex. Woman's U., 1981. Mem. Garland C. of C., Rowlett C. of C., Bus. and Profl. Women's Club (Garland Woman of Year, 1980), AAUW, Tex. Assn. Elected Women. Republican. Methodist. Office: 203 Republic Bank Bldg 700 W Ave B Garland TX 75040

HILL, BARBARA MAE, librarian; b. Keene, N.H., Sept. 19, 1924; d. Gale Earl and Gertrude Wiseman (Reed) Hill; B.E., Keene Tchrs. Coll., 1946; M.S., Simmons Coll., 1952. Tchr. sci. and math. Thayer High Sch., Winchester, N.H., 1946-47; children's librarian Keene Public Library, 1947-52; asst. librarian Mass. Coll. Pharmacy and Allied Health Scis., Boston, 1952-58, asso. librarian, 1958-69, librarian, 1969—. Mem. AAUP, Drug Info. Assn., Am. Assn. Colls. Pharmacy (ho. of dels. 1979-80, chmn. libraries-edn. resources sect. 1982—), Med. Library Assn. (chmn. pharmacy group 1965-66), Spl. Libraries Assn. (vice chmn. pharm. div. 1972-73, chmn. 1973-74), Kappa Delta Pi, Rho Chi. Office: Massachusetts College of Pharmacy and Allied Health Scis 179 Longwood Ave Boston MA 02115

HILL, BETTYE JEAN, nurse; b. St. Louis, Aug. 12, 1947; d. James William and Maggie Pearl (DeBose) Hill; B.S. in Nursing, So. Ill. U., 1969, M.S. in Edn., 1982. Staff nurse Barnes Hosp., St. Louis, 1969-71; health educator Metro-East Health Services Council, E. St. Louis, Ill., 1971-72; city-wide health edn. coordinator City of E. St. Louis, 1972-76; inservice coordinator Christian Welfare Hosp., E. St. Louis, 1976-78; instr. nursing St. Louis Mcpl. Sch. Nursing, 1978-81; dir. nursing Community Hosp., E. St. Louis, 1981—. Bd. dirs. St. Louis Met. Sickle Cell Anemia Assn., St. Clair County Alcoholism and Drug Abuse Dependence Council; mem. Region IV Alcoholism Adv. Com., Sch. Dist. 189 Health Adv. Com.; mem. nursing adv. com. State Community Coll.; pres. E. St. Louis Urban League Guild. Recipient Public Service award St. Clair County Urban League, 1978. Mem. Am. Nurses Assn., Mo. Nurses Assn., Ill. Spc. Nurse Adminstrs., Alpha Upsilon Sigma (chpt. pres. 1972-74), Sigma Gamma Rho. Democrat. Baptist. Office: 1509 Dr ML King Dr East St Louis IL 62201

HILL, BETTYE OWENS, cosmetic co. exec.; b. N.Y.C., Feb. 21, 1944; d. Frank Joseph and Isabel (DeMoustes) Owens; B.A., St. Josephs Coll. for Women, 1965; M.S., Adelphi U., 1975; m. Robert John Hill, Nov. 20, 1965; children—Robert, Lara. Speech pathologist Bur. Speech Improvement, N.Y.C. Public Schs., 1965-66, West Hempstead (N.Y.) Public Schs., 1970-78; mem. faculty St. Josephs Coll., Brentwood, N.Y., 1975-78; v.p. Blackhorse, Inc., West Hempstead, 1975-77; mgr. tng. and design Avon Products Inc., N.Y.C., 1978—. Co founder, treas. Voice for Handicapped, 1974-75. Lic. speech pathologist, N.Y. Mem. Am. Speech and Hearing Assn. (cert. clin. competence), Am. Soc. Tng. Dirs. Home: 483 Cold Spring Rd Laurel Hollow NY 11791 Office: 9 W 57th St New York NY 10019

HILL, CAROL AUDREY, business exec.; b. South Gate, Calif., Apr. 19, 1934; d. Verne Thomas and Beatrice Audrey (White) Holman; student Butte Coll., 1974-77; m. James Arthur Pennington, 1981 (div. 1982); stepchildren—Deborah Ann, George James. Display and advt. mgr. J. C. Penney Co., Chico, Calif., 1954-60; owner, operator Chico Pet Shop (name later changed to Carol's Dog.-Cat Care Center), 1961—; owner, operator Designs by Carol, Chico, 1979—; owner, instr. dog obedience sch., 1963—. Recipient various ribbons and trophies for showing dogs, fish and reptiles, various awards for tropical fish articles; cert. adult edn. tchr., Calif. Mem. Nat. Dog Groomers Assn. Am., Nat. Assn. Female Execs., Internat. Platform Assn. Assoc. with Judy Chicago in nat. needlework art project. Home: 282 Camino Norte Chico CA 95926 Office: 973-Q Fairview Center East Ave Chico CA 95926

HILL, CAROLINE KELLER, home economist; b. Birmingham, Ala., Mar. 28, 1941; d. William McMurray and Florence Patterson (Kleybecker) H.; B.S. in Home Econs., Auburn (Ala.) U., 1961, M.S., 1966; m. Donald Oliver Hill, Dec. 26, 1959; children—William Oliver, Jamie Caroline. Supr. home mgmt. house Auburn U., 1962; tchr. high schs. in Ala., 1963-64, 71-73; instr. clothing and textiles U. Ala., 1969-70, asst. dir. continuing edn. in home econs., 1970-71; mem. faculty Miss. State U., 1974—, asst. prof. home econs., 1977—, originator fashion mdsg. program, 1975; cons. in field. Mem. Am. Home Econs. Assn., Assn. Coll. Profs. Textiles and Clothing, Miss. Home Econs. Assn., Midsouth Ednl. Research Assn., Miss. Consumers Assn., Gamma Sigma Delta, Omicron Nu, Phi Delta Kappa, Kappa Delta Pi. Mem. Ch. of Christ. Author papers in field. Home: 105 Clarmont Circle Starkville MS 39759 Office: Drawer HE Miss State Univ Mississippi State MS 39762

HILL, CAROLYN ANN, condr., educator; b. Oklahoma City, May 1, 1938; d. Virgil Fred and Flora (Evans) H.; Mus.B., U. Okla., 1961, Mus.M., 1963; diploma in conducting Mozarteum, Salzburg, Austria, 1968. Tchr., Chapin Sch., N.Y.C., 1964-68; head dept. Columbia Prep. Sch., N.Y.C., 1968-72, UN Internat. Sch., N.Y.C., 1972—; European conducting debut, Salzburg, Austria, 1968; N.Y. conducting debut N.Y. Music Soc. Chamber Orch., Town Hall, 1972; music dir. nat. touring co. of '1776', 1972; music dir., cond. Livingston (N.J.) Symphony Orch., 1973—; lectr. conducting, symphonies; music dir., organist St. Cloud Presbyterian Ch., West Orange, N.J. Mem. Am. Fedn. Musicians. Author workbooks in field of music. Office: 24-50 East River Dr New York NY 10010

HILL, DIANE SELDON, psychologist; b. Mpls., Sept. 17, 1943; d. Earl William and Geraldine (Le Veille) Seldon; B.A., Mt. Holyoke Coll., 1965; M.A., U. Minn., 1968, Ph.D., 1974; m. David Reuben Hill, May 14, 1966; children—Anna, Jason. Instr., counselor Student Counseling Bur., U. Minn., Mpls., 1968-70; instr. dept. psychology Augsberg Coll., Mpls., 1970-71; adv. women's programs U. Minn., 1970-71; counselor, instr. humanities Emma Willard Sch., Troy, N.Y., 1972-75; dir. counseling and reengagement Colo. Women's Coll., Denver, 1976-77; pvt. practice clin. psychology, 1979—; asst. clin. prof. psychology U. Colo. Health Scis. Center, 1979—; mem. Colo. Psychologist Examiners, 1981—. Bd. dirs. Park Hill Elem. Sch. Assn., 1976-78. NDEA fellow, 1967; cert. psychologist, Colo. Mem. Am. Psychol. Assn., Colo. Psychol. Assn. (dir. 1979—), Rocky Mountain Psychol. Assn., Colo. Assn. Women's Studies, Women's Forum Colo., Colo. Assn. Gifted and Talented. Democrat. Episcopalian. Club: Mount Holyoke of Colorado (pres. 1978-80). Home: 2052 Bellaire St Denver CO 80207 Office: 2250 S Albion Denver CO 80222

HILL, DONNA MARIE, editor, librarian, educator, writer; b. Salt Lake City; d. Clarence Henry and Emma Charlotte (Wirthlin) Hill; A.B., George Washington U., 1948; M.S., Columbia U., 1952. Cryptographic technician U.S. Embassy, Paris, 1949-51; librarian N.Y. Pub. Library, 1952-59; asst. to librarian CCNY, 1962-63; lectr. Hunter Coll. Library, N.Y.C., 1964-70, instr. library, 1970-75, asst. prof., 1975-79, head Tchrs. Central Lab., 1974—, assoc. prof., 1980—. Recipient Scholar Incentive award CUNY, 1981-82. Mem. AAUP, Library Assn. of CUNY, Phi Beta Kappa, Pi Gamma Mu, Delta Kappa Gamma (2d v.p. Gamma Alpha chpt. 1982—), Kappa Delta. Mormon. Club: N.Y. Amateur Computer. Author: Catch a Brass Canary, 1965; Third Book of Junior Authors (with Doris de Montreville), 1972; The Picture File: A Manual and Curriculum Related Subject Heading List, 1975; Joseph Smith: The First Mormon, 1977; Ms. Glee Was Waiting, 1978; Mr. Peeknuff's Tiny People, 1981; That Thing and Other Eerie Animal Tales, 1983; author-illustrator Not One More Day, 1957; illustrator: The Sea Cart (by Janet Konkle), 1961. Office: Hunter Coll Library 695 Park Ave New York NY 10021

HILL, EMILY JONAS, electronic controls mfg. co. exec.; b. Chgo., Mar. 2, 1927; d. Emil and Renee (Lovas) Jonas; B.S., Northwestern U., 1949, M.A., 1952; m. Roger Gettys Hill, Dec. 10, 1949; children—Wendy, Roger. Tchr., part-time, Racine, Wis., 1957-72; v.p. public relations Gettys Mfg. Co., Inc., Racine, 1966-78, exec. v.p., 1976—, dir., 1966—; officer Gettys Mfg. GmbH, Germany, 1972—; dir. Gettys Ltd., Eng., 1970—, Gettys Italy, 1977—; Gettys Ireland and Gettys France, 1978—, Marine Trust Co., Milw., 1980—. Mem. steering com. Wis. Theatre Assn., 1972—; bd. dirs. Florentine Opera, Milw., 1978—, Festival Theatre, Milw., 1979—; trustee YWCA, Racine, 1979—. Named Woman for All seasons, Racine Children's Theatre Council, 1970. Mem. Mfrs. and Employers' Assn. (mgmt. council 1972—), Oasis Soc., Hungarian-U.S. Econ. Council, World Trade Assn. Milw., Wis. Dist. Export Council, Wis. Women Entrepreneurs. Methodist. Mem. editorial bd. Wis. Jour. Small Bus., Madison, Wis., 1979—; one-woman photo show Racine Public Library, Children's Div., 1962. Office: 2700 Golf Ave Racine WI 53404

HILL, HELEN LOUISE, county ofcl.; b. Marceline, Mo., May 22, 1938; d. Gordon and Kathleen Mae (Olinger) Courtney; grad. Parks Bus. Coll., 1958; children—Jacob, Jeffrey, John J., Jesse J., Joseph J., Jennifer N. Field worker Schlumberger Well Survey Corp., Cortez, Colo., 1958-59; title clk. supr. Adams County Clk. and Recorder, Commerce City, Colo., 1966-69; mgr. Hill Hauling Service, Eastlake, Colo., 1965-74; public trustee Adams County, Brighton, Colo., 1975-79, treas., 1979—. Mem. Commn. on Women, State of Colo., 1973-79; mem. Colo. State Democratic Central Com., 1972-74, Adams County Dem. Central Com., 1970-79; mem. Adams County Retirement Bd., 1979-82. Recipient Appreciation awards Gov. Colo., 1977, 78; named Outstanding Woman of Yr., Adams County Dem. Women's Caucus, 1978-79. Mem. Met. Treas.' Assn., Colo. Treas.' Assn., Colo. Public Trustees Assn., Bus. and Profl. Women's Assn. (dist. chmn. 1974-75), Adams County Mental Health Assn., Virginia Neal Blue Center, NOW, Adams County Jane Jefferson, Adams County C. of C., Colo. Women's Polit. Caucus. Lutheran. Home: 3225 E 124th Ave Denver CO 80241 Office: 450 S 4th Ave Brighton CO 80601

HILL, HYACINTHE (VIRGINIA KAIN), poet; b. N.Y.C., May 24, 1920; d. Joseph Thomas and Angela Virginia (Bradley-Bruen) Cronin; B.A. cum laude with honors in English, Bklyn. Coll., 1961; M.A. in English and Comparative Lit., Hunter Coll., 1965; postgrad. Fordham U., 1965-69; Ph.D. (hon.), No. Pontifical Acad., Sweden, 1969; D.Arts and Letters (hon.), Gt. China Arts Coll., 1969; D. Hum., Coll. Alfred the Great, Hull, Eng., 1970; L.H.D. (hon.), L'Universite Libre d'Asie,

India, 1974; m. Johan Anderson, July 15, 1940 (dec.); children—John Luke Anderson, Matthew Mark Anderson (dec.); m. 2d, John H. Kain, Dec. 28, 1978. Tchr. English, James Monroe High Sch., Bronx, N.Y., 1969-81; del. World Congress Poets, Manila, 1969, Taiwan, 1973; hon. v.p. Centro Studi e Scambi, Rome, 1974; Author: Shoots of a Vagrant Vine (Avalon Nat. Sonnets prize 1950), 1950; Promethea (Cameo Press book award 1957), 1957; Squaw, No More, 1975; also numerous individual poems; co-editor Diamond Year Anthology, 1970; editor North Atlantic edit. Great Am. World Poets Anthology, 1973; poems included in An Anthology of Women Poets from Deborah and Sappho to the Present. Recipient Poetry Soc. Am. prizes, 1958—; N.Am. Chapbook award, 1966; 1st prize Eleanor Otto award N.Y. Poetry Forum, 1969, 70; 1st prize Internat. Inst., 1970; York (Eng.) poetry prize, 1974; named champion Order United Religions, 1975; Keats Poetry prize London Lit. Edits., 1975; proclamation Mayor of Yonkers, 1975; named Dau. of Mark Twain for contbn. to modern Am. Poetry; numerous other awards. Mem. Acad. Am. Poets, Poetry Soc. Am., League Am. Pen-Women, Cosmosynthesis League (hon. life mem.), Alpha Delta Kappa. Quaker. Home: Merlin's Gleam Bell Hollow Rd Putnam Valley NY 10579

HILL, JACKIE, exec. search co. exec.; b. Los Angeles, Dec. 10, 1934; d. Major and Margaret (Firestone) Donee; grad. high sch.; children—Robert Scott, Kim Denise. With Jackie Hill & Assos., Agy., now pres., chmn. bd. Mem. Bur. Employment Agys. Club: Balboa Ski. Home: 1409 Dolphin Terr Corona Del Mar CA 92625 Office: 2041 Bus Center Dr #201 Irvine CA 92715

HILL, JANE ELEANOR, orgn. and personal devel. cons.; b. Kansas City, Mo., Dec. 29, 1921; d. Wilber Wilkerson and Virginia May (Brandenburg) Rhoads; student U. Mo., 1940-41, Los Angeles Bus. Coll., 1942; m. Ernest Clifton Hill, Nov. 5, 1943; children—Jane Eleanor Hill Elder, Elizabeth Ann Hill Davis. Loan teller Bank of Am., 1944-45; founding mem. Cons./Trainers Southwest, Tulsa, 1968—, mgr. cons. and continuing edn., 1972—; founder, exec. dir. Resonance: Listening and Growth for Women, Inc., Tulsa, 1977—. Ordained deacon Episcopal Ch., 1977—; mem. staff St. Dunstan's Episcopal Ch., Tulsa, 1977—; mem. deacon formation com. Episcopal Diocese Okla., 1981—; bd. dirs. Tulsa Police and Fire Chaplaincy Corp., 1980-82. Mem. Assn. Creative Change, Fellowship of Women in Diaconate, PEO, Alpha Gamma Delta. Republican. Home: 5258 S Joplin Pl Tulsa OK 74135 Office: 2524 E 41st St Tulsa OK 74105

HILL, JULIA SANDRA, electrologist; b. Nashville, Dec. 11, 1942; d. Edgar Thomas Simpson and Edna Simpson Ferguson; student Shelby State Electrolysis Seminar, Memphis, 1974-82, Henderson Sch. of Electrology, Winston-Salem, N.C., 1973; m. Claude Lee Hill, May 7, 1974; children—Kenneth Lee, Tina Marie. Pvt. practice electrology, Nashville. Registered electrologist; lic. under healing arts, 1975. Mem. Tenn. Electrologist Soc. (pres., 1976-78, 80-81). Democrat. Baptist. Office: 109 29th Ave N Suite 8 Nashville TN 37203

HILL, LYDA HUNT, investment co., travel agy. exec., civic worker; b. Dallas, Sept. 17, 1942; d. Albert G. and Margaret (Hunt) H.; student Stanford U., 1960-61; B.S. in Math., Hollins Coll., 1964. With Seven Falls Co., tourist attraction, oil and gas and real estate co., Dallas and Colorado Springs, Colo., 1964—, sec., 1970-74, pres., 1974—; founder, chmn. bd. Hill World Travel, Dallas, 1968—; pres. Hill Decel. Co., oil, gas, real estate investments, Dallas, 1974—. Chmn. Crystal Charity Ball, Dallas, 1975; bd. dirs. Dallas Soc. Crippled Children, Hope Cottage Children's Bur., Dallas; chmn. bd. Am. Heart Assn., Dallas, 1978-80; mem. regional governing council Assn. Jr. Leagues, Dallas, 1975-76, 2d v.p. Jr. League of Dallas, 1975-76, treas., 1979-80, pres., 1982-83, editor Jr. League Mag., 1974; condr. workshops for Hogg Found. for Mental Health, Austin, Tex., 1975. Named an Outstanding Young Women Am., U.S. Jaycees, 1977, 79. Mem. Young Pres. Orgn. Author Jr. League Bylaws Resource, 1976. Home: 3525 Turtle Creek Blvd 15B Dallas TX 75219 Office: 2500 1st Nat Bank Bldg Dallas TX 75202

HILL, MARION PHYLLIS, social worker; b. Lawrenceville, Va., Sept. 21, 1928; d. Vernon Algie and Harriet Ann (Rhodes) Jones; B.A., Hampton (Va.) Inst., 1948; postgrad Atlanta U., 1948-49; M.S.W., U. Mich., 1964, cert. Inst. Gerontology, 1981; m. Walter W. Hill, Dec. 31, 1950; children—Walter W., Patricia Francine. Child welfare worker Bur. of Social Services, Richmond, Va., 1949-50; sr. child placement worker dept. public welfare City of Chgo., 1951-54; nursery sch. dir. Neighborhood House Assn., Buffalo, N.Y., 1960-61; clin. social worker Med. Center U. Mich., Ann Arbor, 1964-75, sr. social worker, 1975—, field instr. social work, 1968—, Social work supr., 1979—. Mem. City of Ann Arbor Recreation Bd., 1964-70, City of Ann Arbor Housing Commn., 1977-82, v.p., 1979-80, mem. exec. com. Community Devel. Block Grants, 1978-82. Mem. NAACP (corresponding sec. 1976—), Nat. Assn. Negro Bus. and Profl. Women (founder, pres. Ann Arbor chpt. 1976-78, chmn. nat. bd. health task force 1980—), Nat. Assn. Social Workers, Acad. Cert. Social Workers, Nat. Conf. of Social Welfare, Am. Burn Assn., Phi Kappa Phi, Alpha Kappa Alpha. Episcopalian. Home: 701 Sunset Rd Ann Arbor MI 48103 Office: University of Michigan Medical Center 1405 E Ann St Ann Arbor MI 48108

HILL, MARTHA ADELE, chemist; b. London, Ont., Can., Apr. 13, 1922; came to U.S., 1949, naturalized, 1956; d. Rowland and Elsie (Wilkins) Hill; B.S., Wheaton (Ill.) Coll., 1943; M.Sc., Rutgers U., 1945; Ph.D., U. Toronto, 1949. Chem. lab. asst. Wheaton Coll., 1942-43; grad. asst. N.J. Coll. for Women, Rutgers U., New Brunswick, N.J., 1943-45; demonstrator in chemistry U. Toronto, Ont., Can., 1945-48; analytical chemist Dow Chem. Co., Sarnia, Ont., summer, 1944; research chemist Eastman Kodak Co., Rochester, N.Y., 1949-56, research asso., 1957-64; faculty Engring. Sci., U. Western Ont., 1973-80; exec. asst. VI Internat. Fermentation Symposium, 1978-80; ind. cons. chemist doing research for U. Tex., El Paso, 1981—, Faculty of Engring. Sci., U. Western Ont., London, 1982—. Mem. Am. Chem. Soc., Sigma Pi Sigma. Club: London Christian Women's. Contbr. articles to profl. jours.; patentee in field. Home: 103 Wychwood Ct London ON N6G 1S6 Canada

HILL, MARY ANN, mktg. exec.; b. Binghamton, N.Y.; d. Charles L. and Mary (Roscoe) H.; B.Mus., Syracuse U., 1968, M.Mus., 1970; postgrad. Syracuse U. at Florence, Italy, 1967-68, at Vevey, Switzerland, 1969. Mktg. rep. IBM, N.Y.C., 1973-75, account mgr., 1975-76, mktg. mgr., 1976-78, program mgr., office v.p. sales, N.Y.C., 1979-81, with mktg. practices div., N.Y.C., 1981—; spl. asst. U.S. Dept. Energy, 1978-79. Mem. Pres. Com. on Exec. Exchange Alumni, 1979. Mem. Syracuse U. Alumni Assn., Friends of Carnegie Hall. Republican. Clubs: St. Bartholomews Community, St. Bartholomews Players, Blue Hill Troupe. Soprano soloist, Binghamton Symphony Orch., 1970-73, Syracuse Opera, 1968-70, Syracuse U. Opera, 1968-70. Home: 310 E 70th St New York NY 10021 Office: IBM One Citicorp Center 153 E 53d St New York NY 10022

HILL, MARY FRANCES, health care profl.; b. Newton, N.J., Oct. 7, 1942; d. Ellsworth Roger and Frances (Carrubba) Hill; A.A., County Coll. of Morris, 1979; student Montclair State Coll., 1979—. Mem. staff Newton (N.J.) Meml. Hosp., 1964-66, St. Clare's Hosp., Denville, N.J., 1966-70, Chilton Meml. Hosp., Pompton Plains, N.J., 1972-79; quality assurance coordinator Profl. Standards Review Orgn., Wayne, N.J., 1979—; chmn. Passaic Valley PSRO med. record adv. com.; mem. med. care evaluation com. N.J. PSRO. Served with USMC, 1961-63. Cert. med. record technician. Mem. Am. Med. Records Assn., Med. Record Assn. N.J., Nat. Assn. Female Execs., Assn. for Health Records, Internat. Platform Assn., Handgun Control Inc., Group Against Smokers Polution, Safe and Nuclear Free Environment, NOW, ACLU, Common Cause. Home: 289 Mount Hope Ave Apt B21 Dover NJ 07801 Office: 573 Valley Rd Wayne NJ 07470

HILL, MARY LUSAN, health care exec.; b. Decatur, Ill., May 21, 1940; d. Carl McCrae and Mary Jayne (Ahrens) Hill; B.S., Webster Coll., 1962; M.T., Northwestern U., 1963. Chief lab. instr. Clin. Pathology Course, Northwestern Med. Sch., Chgo., 1964, sr. research technologist, 1964-75; research asso. dept. pathology, Duke U. Med. Center, Durham, N.C., 1975—. Vol. Ind. Voters of Ill., Ind. Precinct Orgn., 1972. Mem. Am. Soc. Clin. Pathologists. Roman Catholic. Clubs: Durham-Chapel Hill Ski and Sports (sec. 1978-79), Bus. and Profl. Women's (pres. 1977-78, legis. chmn. 1978-80). Contbr. articles to profl. jours. Home: 2800 Croasdaile Dr Durham NC 27705 Office: PO Box 3712 Durham NC 27710

HILL, MARY MARGARET, govt. ofcl.; b. Wilmington, N.C., July 31, 1931; d. Norman Douglas Burns and Geneva (Larkins) Burns Knight; B.A. cum laude, Queen's Coll., 1975, M.A., 1977; M.P.A. in Fin. and Budget, N.Y. U., 1980; children—Ralph Jonathan, Anna Maria, Eric Gerald. With budget and purchasing depts., Queen's Coll., Flushing, N.Y., 1963-78; dep. dir. corp. mgmt. Addiction Research Treatment Corp., Bklyn., 1978-79; grants mgmt. specialist U.S. Dept. Energy, N.Y.C., 1980-81; cons. income tax preparation, 1961-82, resume writing for minority youth and women, 1975-82; budget analyst U.S. Dept. Army, Ft. Dix, N.J., 1982—. Active NAACP. Mem. Nat. Assn. Female Execs. Club: Queen's Coll. Women's (fin. officer, 1972-74). Contbr. articles to Rochdale Village community newspaper. Home: Whitehall Apts Bldg C1-4 Mount Holly NJ 08060

HILL, MILLICENT AMELIA, govt. ofcl.; b. Phila., Nov. 12, 1933; d. Arthur Cornelius and Rose Audrey (Thomas) Somers; cert. Temple U. Community Coll., 1954, cert. Manpower Devel. Tng., 1972; m. Ernest G. Hill, Jr., May 4, 1958. Clk.-typist Bur. Employment Security, Phila., 1952-57, unemployment compensation interviewer, 1957-59, unemployment compensation examiner, 1959-66, employment service interviewer outreach program, 1966-68, job corps gatehouse, 1968-71, employee relations rep., 1971—. Recipient Humanitarian award Chapel of Four Chaplains, 1967. Mem. Pa. Employment Security Employees Assn. (election chmn. 1978-82, shop steward 1978-82, employment service-unemployment compensation rep. 1981-82). Lutheran. Club: Dramatic. Office: 667 N Broad St Philadelphia PA 19123

HILL, PAMELA ABEL, TV documentary producer and exec.; b. Winchester, Ind., Aug. 18, 1938; d. Paul Haynes and Mary Frances (Hollis) Abel; B.A., Bennington Coll., 1960; student U. Glasgow (Scotland), 1958-59, Universidad Autonoma de Mexico, 1960-61; m. Thomas G. Wicker, Mar. 9, 1974; children—Christopher Hill; stepchildren—Grey Wicker, Cameron Wicker, Kayce Freed, Lisa Freed. Foreign affairs analyst under Dr. Henry A. Kissinger, Rockefeller for Pres. campaign, N.Y.C., 1961-65; researcher, asso. producer NBC News, N.Y.C., 1965-73, dir. on NBC White Paper series, 1969-72, producer Edwin Newman's weekly network show, 1972; producer ABC News Closeup programs, NYC, 1973-78, exec. producer documentary unit, 1978-79, v.p. ABC News, 1979—. Recipient Emmy award for best direction, 1974, for best show, 1970, 74, for ABC News Closeup, 1979; George Foster Peabody award, 1974; Alfred DuPont award, 1974; Nat. Press Club award for consumer reporting, 1974; Christopher award, 1975, 79, 80, 81; Gabriel award, 1973; Am. Film Festival award, 1970; Columbia-DuPont award for outstanding documentary series, 1979, 80; top prize Monte Carlo Film Festival, 1979; Edward R. Murrow award Overseas Press Club, 1979. Mem. Dirs. Guild of Am., Writers Guild of Am. East, Am. Women in Radio and TV. Author: U.S. Foreign Policy: 1945-65, 1966; contbr. photos various mags. and books. Home: 169 E 80th St New York NY 10021 Office: ABC News 7 W 66th St New York NY 10023

HILL, PAMELA LOUISE, theatre exec.; b. Columbus, Ohio, Apr. 27, 1953; d. Frederick B. and Betty Lou (Heppel) H.; B.A., Otterbein Coll., 1975; M.A., Bowling Green State U., 1976. Sec., Ohio Theatre, Columbus, 1977; publicist Ind. Repertory Theatre, Indpls., 1977-78; public relations dir. Players Theatre of Columbus, 1978-82; dir. pub. relations and mktg. Kenyon Festival Theatre, Gambier, Ohio, 1982—; dir., actor radio, TV, 1980—. Active Ease-On-Downtown, Columbus Devel. Dept., 1980-81. Recipient Outstanding Achievement award in acting Players Theatre of Columbus, 1977. Mem. Women in Communications, Pub. Relations Soc. Am., Ohio Theatre Assn., Ohio Community Theatre Assn. Office: Kenyon Festival Theatre Kenyon Coll Gambier OH 43022

HILL, PATRICIA ARNOLD, govt. ofcl.; b. Balt., Oct. 29, 1936; d. George Henry and Mildred Mae (Kress) Arnold; student No. Va. Community Coll., part time 1966-76; m. Richard Denzil Hill, Oct. 24, 1970; children—Terry Marlene Fomby, Debra Michelle Hill. Sec. firm McEwan & Walker, Chattanooga, 1955; clk.-typist Bur. Aeros., Washington, 1956-58, security clk., 1958, security asst., 1959-62, security specialist Bur. Aeros. and Naval Weapons Washington, 1962-66; security specialist Bur. Naval Weapons, 1962-66, Naval Ordnance Systems Command, 1966-74; security specialist Naval Sea Systems Command, Washington, 1974-75, head classification mgmt. br., asst. dir. security div., 1975-80, dep. dir., head info. security br. security div., 1980—. Mem. Nat. Assn. Female Execs., Nat. Classification Mgmt. Soc., Ind. Sec. Assn., Va. State Soc., Profl. Bus. Women. Baptist. Home: 1003 Collingwood Rd Alexandria VA 22308 Office: Nat Center Bldg 3 Crystal City Arlington VA 22202

HILL, PATTY MAYNARD, nursing educator; b. Forsyth County, N.C., June 9, 1944; d. Ray and Etta Mae (Holleman) Maynard; diploma N.C. Bapt. Hosp. Sch. Nursing, 1966; B.S.N., U. N.C., 1969, M.Ed., 1973; doctoral candidate N.C. State U., Raleigh, 1982—; m. Gary P. Hill, Aug. 20, 1966; children—Gary P., Christopher, Caroline. Office nurse, 1967-69; instr. pediatric nursing Watts Sch. Nursing, Durham, N.C., 1970-74; instr. U. N.C. Sch. Nursing, Chapel Hill, 1974-77, asst. prof., 1977—; reviewer/cons. Duxbury Press; mem. rev. bd. Appleton Century Croft; condr. workshops. Bd. dirs. Chapel Hill Oasis, 1978-80, Chapel Hill Day Care Center, 1977—, Chapel Hill Service League, 1977—; del. St. Thomas More Sch., 1981-82. Mem. Am. Nurses Assn., N.C. Nurses Assn., AAUP, Nat. Assn. Adult Edn., Nat. Assn. Care of Hospitalized Child, Sigma Theta Tau. Methodist. Co-editor, contbg. author: Development throughout Life: A Nursing Perspective, 1982; co-author: Human Development; contbr. articles in field. Home: 414 Sharon Rd Chapel Hill NC 27514 Office: U NC Sch Nursing Chapel Hill NC 27514

HILL, PENNY, computer cons.; b. Phila., Sept. 2, 1944; d. Edward William and Anne Tanguay (Flick) Garrison; B.A., U. Del., 1966; m. John Edlund, Feb. 28, 1981; 1 son, Christopher Townsend Hill. Programmer, analyst, supr. N.C. State U., Raleigh, 1966-68; programmer, analyst Vitro Labs., Wheaton, Md., 1968-69; instr. Control Data Inst., Arlington, Va., 1969-70; sr. analyst Fairfax (Va.) Hosp., 1970-74; systems engr. Dimension Inc., Reston, Va., 1974-75; sr. systems engr. Cincom Systems, Washington, 1975-78, project coordinator, Cin., 1978-79, cons. Profl. Services div., San Francisco, 1979-80; sr. software engr. MicroPro, San Rafael, Calif., 1980-81; pres., computer cons. Computer Solutions, Inc., 1981—. Mem. Assn. Computing Machinery (spl. interest group microcomputers), IEEE Computer Soc., Nat. Assn. Female Execs., Internat. Solar Energy Soc.,

HILL, PHYLLIS MALIE SITES (MRS. RALPH HILL), librarian; b. Indian Springs, Md., Nov. 30, 1923; d. George A. and Mamie (Funkhouser) Sites; student Frostburg State Tchrs. Coll., 1941-43; B.A. in Secondary Edn., Shepherd Coll., 1963; postgrad. U. Md., 1963; M.A. in English, Shippensburg State Coll., 1971; m. Ralph Hill, Oct. 3, 1943 (dec. 1961); children—Ronald Ancil, Christine Anne, Marshall Clifton, Samuel Alexander. Asst. librarian West Frederick Jr. High Sch., 1963; librarian Boonsboro (Md.) Sr. High Sch., 1963-67, Instrnl. Resource Center Library, Washington County Bd. Edn., Hagerstown, Md., 1967—. Recipient Dr. Christian award for play, 1950. Mem. ALA, Md. Internat. Reading Assn., Delta Kappa Gamma. Methodist. Author play: The Rainbow Trail, 1949. Co-author: Thirteen to One, 1969. Editor The Tchr.'s Library, 1977; compiler: Mother's Favorite Quotes, 1979. Home: Route 2 Boonsboro MD 21713 Office: Washington County Bd Edn Hagerstown MD 21740

HILL, PRISCILLA GRANDIN, fin. analyst; b. Shaker Heights, Ohio, June 10, 1953; d. Robert Martin and Jean Culver (Grandin) H.; B.S., Stetson U., DeLand, Fla., 1975; grad. various banking courses. With Mut. Bank Savs., Newton Centre, Mass., 1975-81, asst. comptroller, 1978-80, comptroller, 1980-81; fin. analyst Boston Fin. Data Services, Inc., 1981-82, asst. mgr., 1982—. Player, coach North River Women's Fastpitch Softball League, 1976-77. Mem. Savs. Bank Women Mass., Savs. Bank Assn. Mass. Officers Club, Duxbury Hist. Soc. Republican. Presbyterian. Home: 119 Buckboard Rd Duxbury MA 02332 Office: 1776 Heritage Dr North Quincy MA 02171

HILL, ROSANNA, lab. adminstr.; b. Macon, Ga., July 1, 1949; d. Henry and Julia (Chambliss) Hill; B.S., Clark Coll., 1971; postgrad. Howard U., 1971-72. Med. technologist Ga. Bapt. Med. Center, Atlanta, 1972-77, lab. mgr., 1977-81; lab. ops. mgr. Acculabs, Inc., Atlanta, 1981—, dir., partner, 1981—. Mem. Am. Public Health Assn., Clin. Lab. Mgmt. Assn., Nat. Assn. Female Execs. Mem. A.M.E. Ch. Home: 3110 Godby Rd Apt 21C College Park GA 30349 Office: 160 Boulevard NE Atlanta GA 30312

HILL, RUTH VOLLMERS, town ofcl.; b. Dunsmuir, Calif., May 5, 1920; d. Shelby Allison and Sarah Ruth (Miller) Vollmers; student Chico (Calif.) State Coll., 1939-40, U. Pa., 1967, Rutgers U., 1973, Fairleigh Dickinson U., 1977; m. Robert Eugene Hill, Jan. 26, 1946 (div. 1963); children—Kathleen Hill Schideleff, James Eugene. With Teller Comml. Co. (Alaska), 1938-39; with civil service and surveillance dept. Ordance Dept., U.S. Army, 1941-43; flight operator, instr. Fairbanks (Alaska) Air Service, 1944-45; camp dir. Washington Rock council Girl Scouts U.S., Westfield, N.J., 1958-59, camp chmn., bd. dirs., 1958-60; sec. Recreation Commn., Mayor's Youth Council Westfield (N.J.), 1965-66, sec., asst. dir. recreation, 1967-68, sec., dir. recreation, 1968—; chmn. aviation edn. com. N.J.-N.Y. sect. Ninety-Nines, 1958-62; dir. Interat. Tri-Orgnl. Encampment, also founder Can. Air Rangers, Wings Scouts of Girl Scouts and Ninety-Nines, 1956-62. Recipient Thanks badge Girl Scouts U.S., 1955, Amelia Aerhart medal Ninety-Nines, 1959. Mem. Nat. Recreation and Park Assn., Nat. Community Edn. Assn., N.J. Recreation and Parks Assn., N.J. Community Edn. Council, Union County Recreation and Parks Soc., Recreation and Parks Adminstrn. Assn. N.J., Soc. Recreation and Parks Educators, World Leisure and Recreation Assn., Internat. Orgn. Active Licensed Women Pilots, Ninety-Nines, CAP (lt., pilot 1956-62, sect. instr. aviation edn. 1958-62), Alaska Geog. Soc. Christian Scientist. Home: 800 Forest Ave Apt 8C Westfield NJ 07090

HILL, SANDRA VERNICE, mgmt. analyst, govt. ofcl.; b. Petersburg, Va.; d. Wellington Alexander and Marie Vernice (Wooden) H.; A.A.S., SUNY, 1971; B.A. (State News scholar), Mich. State U.; M.P.A. (Nat. Assn. Schs. Public Affairs and Adminstrn./Ford Found. fellow), Am. U. Fed. intern Naval Ship Research and Devel. Center; program analyst HUD; now mgmt. analyst U.S. Gen. Acctg. Office, Washington; freelance writer, photographer; former tchr. undergrads. Am. U. Participant Bread for the City Program. Scripps Howard Found. awardee. Mem. Am. Soc. Public Adminstrn., Com. for Women in Pub. Adminstrn., Federally Employed Women, Pi Alpha Alpha, Phi Theta Kappa, Delta Psi Omega, Phi Delta Gamma. Baptist. Clubs: Toastmasters Internat., Bus. and Profl. Women's. Contbr. articles to profl. jours.

HILL, SANDY, broadcast journalist; b. Centralia, Washington; B.A., U. Wash. Formerly adminstrv. asst. Seattle-First Nat. Bank; newswriter, reporter KIRO-TV, Seattle; news anchorwoman KNXT-TV, Los Angeles; reporter KABC-TV, Los Angeles; now co-host, newscaster Good Morning Am., ABC. Address: ABC Good Morning Amer 7 W 66th St New York NY 10023 *

HILL, SARA LYNN, architect; b. Montclair, N.J., May 25, 1951; d. Lawrence and Mary (Allanson) H.; B.Arch. cum laude, Tulane U., 1974; B.F.A. magna cum laude, Newcomb Coll. Art, 1974. Chief designer Mathes, Bergman & Assos., New Orleans, 1974-75; archtl. designer J. Buchanan Blitch & Assos., 1975-76; archtl. cons. F. Monroe Labouisse Jr., 1976-79; staff architect, plans examiner Vieux Carre Commn., 1979-80; owner, partner V.C. Builders Gen. Contractors, 1980—; owner, mgr. Hill Co., 1980—. Mem. AIA, La. Contractors Assn., Soc. Archtl. Historians. Club: So. Yacht. Office: 721 Louisa St New Orleans LA 70117 also 620 Louisa St New Orleans LA 70117

HILL, SHIRLEY YARDE, psychologist; b. Galesburg, Ill., Nov. 2, 1941; d. Clyde and Lorraine Louise (Bryant) Yarde; A.B., Grinnell Coll., 1963; Ph.D. (USPHS fellow), Washington U., St. Louis, 1971; 1 son, John Adrian. Instr. psychiatry Washington U. Med. Sch., St. Louis, 1971-74, asst. prof., 1974-77; research asso. prof. psychiatry Western Psychiat. Inst. and Clinic, U. Pitts. Med. Sch., 1977, asso. prof., 1982—; cons. Nat. Center for Alcohol Edn.; mem. initial rev. group Nat. Inst. Alcoholism and Alcohol Abuse, 1980—; cons. Presidents Commn. on Mental Health. Grantee Nat. Inst. Drug Abuse, Nat. Inst. Alcohol Abuse and Alcoholism. Mem. N.Y. Acad. Sci., Research Soc. in Alcoholism, Am. Psychol. Assn., Sigma Xi. Contbr. numerous articles to profl. jours. Office: 3811 O'Hara St Pittsburgh PA 15261

HILL, TOMMIE ANN, mathematician; b. Clearwater, Fla., Nov. 23, 1948; d. Willie James and Bernice Lee (Walker) H.; B.A. in Math., Emory U., 1969; M.S. in Math., Northwestern U., 1970; Ed.D. in Curriculum and Instrn. (Univ. fellow), U. Houston, 1976. Instr. math. Spelman Coll., 1970-71, W.Va. State Coll., 1971-74; asst. prof. math., freshman studies Prairie View A&M U., 1976—; summer instr. Tufts U., 1972; instr. math. North Harris County Coll. 1975—; summer fellow Hampton Inst.-NASAS Research Program, 1979. Parliamentarian M.E. Rickmeyer Missionary Soc., Wesley Chapel AME Ch., Houston, 1979, 81-82, publicity chmn., 1980. Mem. Math. Assn. Am., Nat. Council Tchrs. Math., S.W. Ednl. Research Assn., Am. Ednl. Research Assn., Phi Beta Kappa, Kappa Delta Epsilon, Kappa Delta Pi, Phi Delta Kappa. Democrat. Mem. African Methodist Episcopal Ch. Author: (with Frank Hawkins) Trigonometry: A Laboratory Manual, 1979. Home: 1106 Carlton St Clearwater FL 33515 Office: PO Box 2845 Prairie View TX 77445

HILLBERRY, SHEILA MARIE STUEHRENBERG, microbiologist; b. Breckenridge, Minn., Apr. 19, 1945; d. Henry Ernest Fredrick and Marian Violet (Sandberg) Stuehrenberg; B.S., Moorhead State U., 1966;

M.S., Purdue U., 1970; m. Joseph Hillberry, June 25, 1967; children—Russell Henry, Joseph Martin. Tchr. jr. high. sci. Wausau (Wis.) Public Schs., 1966-67; tchr. sci. Robert G. Cole High Sch., San Antonio, 1967-68; substitute tchr. Rapid City (S.D.) Schs., 1970-71; supr. clin. microbiology sect. Rapid City Regional Hosp., 1971—; adj. prof. S.D. Sch. Mines and Tech., 1979—. Organist, dir. choir, chmn. bd. edn. Lutheran Ch. Mem. Am. Soc. Clin. Pathology, Am. Soc. Microbiology, Black Hills Soc. Med. Technology. Home: 1938 Fremont St Rapid City SD 57701 Office: Laboratory 353 Fairmont Blvd Rapid City SD 57701

HILLE, RITA KATHRYN, real estate broker; b. Fairfield, Ohio, Oct. 26, 1933; d. Clarence Henry and Delma Lurella (Wetzel) Gordon; A.A. in Social Service, San Jose City Coll., 1972; B.S. in Bus. Mgmt., San Jose State U., 1974; grad. Realtors Inst., 1980; m. Paul K. Bond, Dec. 28, 1953; children—Lani, Sheila; m. 2d, Peter F. Hille, Sept. 4, 1959; children—Julia, Lisa. Sales asso. Bell Realtors, Inc., 1975-77; owner, mgr. RKH Realty, Los Altos, Calif., 1977—; pres. Hille Enterprises, Inc., 1977—; phys. fitness instr., 1970—. Chmn. Los Altos Equal Opportunity Com., 1978-79; bull. editor La Volante, 1974-76. Served with M.C., USN, 1951-53. Lic. pvt. pilot; cert. resdl. broker specialist. Mem. Million Dollar Club Los Altos, Nat. Assn. Realtors, Calif. Assn. Realtors, San Jose Bd. Realtors, Los Altos Bd. Realtors, Palo Alto/Mountain View Bd. Realtors, Menlo Park Bd. Realtors, Sunnyvale Bd. Realtors, LWV. Republican. Episcopalian. Founder Creekside Chronicle, 1969. Home: 1640 Wakefield Terr Los Altos CA 94022 Office: 133 Main St Los Altos CA 94022

HILLEBERT, MINTA CAROL, nurse; b. Charleston, W.Va., Feb. 2, 1949; d. Oliver Wendell and Minta Ruth (Davis) Halstead; A.D.N., Salem (W.Va.) Coll., 1973; student Fla. Atlantic U., 1982—; m. John D. Hillebert, Oct. 25, 1968; children—David Troy, Eric Wendell, Mark Edward. Head nurse Med./Surg. Div., Kettering Med. Center, Dayton, Ohio, 1975; nursing supr. Southeastern Med. Center, North Miami Beach, Fla., 1976-77; adminstrv. asst./nursing supr. Community Hosp. of South Broward, Hollywood, Fla., 1978; quality assurance dir. Drs. Hosp. of Hollywood, 1979-80; quality assurance coordinator Quality Care Rev., U. Miami/James M. Jackson Meml. Med. Center, Miami, 1981; quality assurance dir. U. Miami/Bascom Palmer/Ann Bates Leach Eye Hosp., Miami, 1982—. Recipient Outstanding Employee Performance Recognition for contbns. to quality assurance techniques for hosps., 1980. Registered nurse. Mem. Am. Nurses Assn., Nat. League Nursing, Nat. Assn. Quality Assurance Profls., South Fla. Risk Mgrs. Assn., Adminstrs. Forum, South Fla. Hosp. Assn. Club: Optimrs. Contbr. articles to profl. jours. Home: 7812 Alhambra Blvd Miramar FL 33023 Office: U Miami/Ann Bates/Leach Eye Hosp 900 NW 17th St Quality Assurance Dept Miami FL 33136

HILLER, WENDY, actress; b. Stockport, Eng.; d. Frank and Marie (Stone) Hiller; ed. Winceby Sch.; m. Ronald Gow, Feb. 25, 1937; children—Ann, Anthony. Broadway debut in Love on the Dole, 1936; stage appearances in N.Y. include The Heiress, 1947, Moon for the Misbegotten, 1957, Flowering Cherry, 1959, Aspern Papers, 1961-62; appeared in Crown Matrimonial, London, 1973, Waters of the Moon, London, 1979; motion pictures include Pygmalion, 1939, Major Barbara, 1941, I Know Where I'm Going, 1945, Separate Tables (Acad. award for Best Supporting Actress 1958), 1958, Sons and Lovers, 1960, Toys in the Attic, 1963, A Man for All Seasons, 1966, David Copperfield, 1969, Murder on the Orient Express, 1973, Voyage of the Damned, 1976, Elephant Man, 1980. Decorated Order Brit. Empire, 71, dame Brit. Empire, 1975. Office: care ICM 22 Grafton St London W1 England *

HILLERY, KATHRYN ZAFRAS, real estate broker; b. Cleve., Jan. 3, 1925; d. James and Esther (Malavit) Zafras; student Walsh Inst. of Acctg., Detroit, 1943-44; m. Aug. 18, 1946 (div. Sept. 1966); children—Kathleen P., James F., Marie A., Jane L., Jennifer J., John C. Legal sec., office mgr., acct. various cos., Detroit, 1942-52; asst. buyer, supr. grocery sales dept. Meijer Markets, 1964-65; office mgr., acct. Top Value Enterprises Co., Grand Rapids, Mich., 1965-68; dir. Fla. Home Center, broker R.J. Ide, Inc., Grand Rapids, 1968-74; prin., pres., dir. Red Apple Real Estate, Grand Rapids, 1974-75; owner, broker Solar Real Estate Co. II, Grand Rapids, 1975-77; prin., asso. real estate broker, exec. v.p.-treas., dir. Platinum Exchange Group, Inc., Grand Rapids, 1977-81, pres., 1981—; partner, owner Hilfree Leasing Co., Platinum Equity, Grand Rapids, 1981—; dir. Four Winds Corp., Platinum Capital Corp., others; mem. adv. bd. Resorts Condominium Internat. Active local youth groups, 1956, 58, 59; bd. dirs. Forest Hills PTA, 1961-62. Recipient Award of Excellence, Nat. Land Devel. Assn., 1982. Mem. Mich. Assn. Realtors, Grand Rapids Bd. Realtors. Democrat. Mem. Unity Ch. Home: 6407 Wainscot St SE Grand Rapids MI 49506 Office: Platinum Exchange Group Inc 3637 Clyde Park SW Grand Rapids MI 49509

HILLERY, MARY JANE LARATO, editor; b. Boston, Sept. 15, 1931; d. Donato and Porzia (Avellis) Larato; Asso. Sci. (scholar), Northeastern U., 1950; B.S., U. Mass., 1962; m. Thomas H. Hillery, Feb. 25, 1961; 1 son, Thomas H. Sales agt., linguist Pan Am. Airways, Boston, 1955-61; interpreter Internat. Conf. Fire Chiefs, Boston, 1966; tchr. Spanish, YWCA, Natick, Mass., 1966-67; community relations cons., adv. bd. dirs., lectr. for migrant edn. project div. Mass. Dept. Community Affairs, Boston, 1967-69; editor-in-chief Sudbury (Mass.) Citizen, 1967-76; area editorial adviser Beacon Pub. Co., Acton, Mass., 1970—; editor Beacon Publs., 1977-80; dir. public affairs com. Mass. Dept. Environ. Quality Engring., 1981—. Mem. bus. adv. com. Town of Sudbury, 1972-77; mem. Sudbury Sch. Com., 1976-77; mem. Meml. Day Celebration Com., 1972—, master ceremonies, 1973-82, parade marshal, 1973, 74, 75, 82, chmn., 1974; panelist Internat. Women's Yr. Symposium, 1975; bd. dirs., incorporator Sudbury Nonprofit Housing Corp., 1973-74, chmn. Sudbury Town Report, 1969-72. Served with WAVES, 1950-54; maj. U.S. Army Res., 1975—; liaison officer to U.S. Mil. Acad., 1976—. Named Editor of Yr., Beacon Pub. Co., 1970; recipient cert. of appreciation DeMolay, 1969, Boy Scouts Am., 1974, CD Preparedness Agy., 1975, Mass. Bicentennial Commn., 1976, Woman of Achievement citation Mass. Senate, 1979, 82. Mem. Nat. Editorial Assn., Nat. Newspaper Assn., Internat. Platform Assn., New Eng. Press Assn., Res. Officers Assn. (life mem., sec. 1978-79, Outstanding Service award 1979), Bus. and Profl. Womens Club (1st v.p. 1973-74, pres. 1974-76, parliamentarian 1976-78, mem. state elections com. 1976, state bylaws com. 1977-78, 79-81, chmn. state legis. com. 1979-81, Woman of Yr. 1979, Woman of Achievement award 1982), LWV (dir. 1964-68), Nat. League Am. Pen Women (exec. bd. Boston 1974-76, pres. 1976-78, master ceremonies 50th anniversary Boston br. 1977, parliamentarian 1978—, auditor 1980-82), Omega Sigma. Contbg. editor Beacon, 1979—, Towne Talk, 1975-79, Citizen's Forum, 1975-81. Home: 66 Willow Rd Sudbury MA 01776 Office: 20 Main St Acton MA 01720

HILLIARD, ANNIE PEARL, educator; b. Roxboro, N.C., Dec. 24, 1944; d. Jessie Melvin and Mary Jane (Lawson) Toler; B.S., Elizabeth City State U., 1967; M.A., Trinity Coll., 1971; M.S., Johns Hopkins U., 1978; m. Ronald E. Hilliard, Apr. 25, 1969. Tchr., Washington Sch. System, 1968—, bus. mgr., 1980—. Mem. Nat. Assn. Female Execs., Nat. Geog. Soc., Nat. Bus. Edn. Assn., Eastern Bus. Tchrs. Assn., Zeta Phi Beta (Md. state dir. 1980-81). Club: Johns Hopkins. Home: 5372 Phelps Luck Dr Columbia MD 21045 Office: 24th and Benning Rd NE Washington DC 20002

HILLIARD, DONNA JEAN, nurse; b. Fairfield, Ill., Oct. 18, 1951; d. James F. and Norma Jean (Montgomery) Curry; diploma Burnham Hosp. Sch. Nursing, Champaign, Ill., 1972; m. Carroll Eugene Hilliard, Sept. 9, 1972; 2 daus., Melinda Suzanne, Megan Denise. Staff nurse Burnham City Hosp., Champaign, 1971; dir. nursing Scott County Nursing Center, Winchester, Ill., 1972—; mem. Nursing Continuing Edn. Council Region III, Ill. Instr., ARC; mem. Scott County Ambulance Bd. Republican. Mem. Christian Ch. Club: Bridge. Home: 201 E Cherry St Winchester IL 62694 Office: RR 2 Winchester IL 62694

HILLINGS, JENNIFER ANN, press secretary; b. Washington, D.C., Oct. 7, 1954; d. Patrick Jerome and Phyllis Kaye (Reinbrecht) H.; B.A. in Public Relations, U. So. Calif., 1976. Account exec. Palisades Communications, Los Angeles, 1978-79; press dir. Calif. Senate Republican leader, Sacramento, 1979-81; press sec. Calif. Reagan-Bush campaign, Los Angeles, 1980; mem., press sec. Republican Nat. Com., Washington, 1981—. Mem. Delta Gamma. Home: 2305 Commonwealth Ave Alexandria VA 22301 Office: 310 First St SE Washington DC 20003

HILLIS, MARGARET, musician, choral conductor; b. Kokomo, Ind., Oct. 1, 1921; d. Glen R. and Bernice (Haynes) Hillis; B.A., Ind. U., 1947; postgrad. choral conducting, Juilliard Sch. Music, 1947-49; D.Mus. (hon.), Temple U., 1967, Ind. U., 1972, Carthage Coll., 1979, Wartburg Coll., 1981; D.F.A. (hon.), St. Mary's Coll., 1977, Lake Forest Coll., 1980. Dir. Met. Youth Chorale, Bklyn., 1948-51; asst. condr. Collegiate Choral, N.Y.C., 1952-53; mus. dir., condr. Am. Concert Choir, N.Y.C., 1950—, Am. Concert Orch., 1950—; condr., instr. Union Theol. Sem., 1950-60, Juilliard Sch. Music, 1951-53; dir. choral dept. Third St. Music Sch. Settlement, 1953-54; founder, music dir. Am. Choral Found., Inc., 1954—; choral dir. N.Y.C. Opera Co., 1955-56, Chgo. Mus. Coll. of Roosevelt U., 1961-62; condr., choral dir. Santa Fe Opera Co., 1958-59, Chgo. Symphony Chorus, 1957—; music dir. N.Y. Chamber Soloists, 1956-60; choral condr. Am. Opera Soc., N.Y.C., 1952-68; mus. asst. to music dir. Chgo. Symphony Orch., 1966-68; music dir., condr. Kenosha Symphony Orch., 1961-68; condr., choral dir. Cleve. Orch. Chorus, 1969-71; prof. conducting, dir. choral orgns. Northwestern U. Sch. Music, 1970-77; resident condr. Chgo. Civic Orch., 1967—; music dir. Choral Inst., 1968-70, 75; mus. dir., condr. Elgin (Ill.) Symphony Orch., 1971—; condr. Do-It-Yourself Messiah, 1976—; vis. prof. conducting Ind. U., 1978—. Guest condr. Chgo. Symphony, Cleve. Orch., Minn. Orch., Nat. Symphony Orch., others. Artists' adv. Nat. Fedn. Music Clubs Youth Auditions, 1966-70; mem. vis. com. dept. music U. Chgo., 1971—; chmn. choral panel Nat. Endowment for Arts, 1974-81; hon. mem. Roosevelt U. Council of 100, 1976—; adv. bd. Cathedral Choral Soc. Washington Cathedral, 1976—. Recipient Golden Plate award Am. Acad. Achievement, 1967; Alumnus of Yr. award Ind. U. Sch. Music Alumni, 1969; Steinway award, 1969; Chgo. YWCA Leader Luncheon I award, 1972; Friends of Lit. award, 1973; SAI Found. Circle of 15 award, 1974; Grammy award for best choral performance, 1977, 78, 79; Leadership for Freedom award Women's Scholarship Assn. of Roosevelt U., 1978; award for contbn. to choral art Assn. Profl. Vocal Ensembles, 1980; named Woman of Yr., music category, Ladies Home Jour., 1978. Civilian flight instr., USN CAA, WTS, World War II. Mem. Nat. Fedn. Music Clubs (hon., citation for contbns. to music 1981), Am. Choral Dirs. Assn., Assn. Choral Condrs., Am. Music Center, Assn. Profl. Vocal Ensembles (exec. bd.), Am. Symphony Orch. League, Nat. Soc. Lit. and the Arts, PEO, Sigma Alpha Iota (hon.), Pi Kappa Lambda (hon.), Kappa Kappa Gamma (Alumni Achievement award 1978). Club: Musicians of Women (hon.). Office: Am Choral Found Inc 130 W 56th St New York NY 10019 also 220 S Michigan Ave Chicago IL 60604

HILLIS, MARY O., chemist, educator; b. Beardstown, Ill., Dec. 11, 1919; d. Arthur Burl and Maude B. (Schaefer) Hillis; A.B., MacMurray Coll., 1941; D.Sc. (hon.), 1982; M.S., U. Ill., 1942, Ph.D., 1944. Mem. faculty Vassar Coll., Poughkeepsie, N.Y., 1944—, prof. chemistry, 1962-82, prof. emeritus, 1982—. Mem. Am. Chem. Soc., AAAS, N.Y. Acad. Scis., Sigma Xi, Phi Beta Kappa. Republican. Congregationalist.

HILLMAN, CAROL ELLIS, speech-lang. pathologist, hosp. adminstr.; b. DuBois, Pa., May 5, 1953; d. Ralph Sheldon and Margaret (Girman) Ellis; B.S., Pa. State U., 1974, M.S., 1975; m. Robert Edward Hillman, Nov. 27, 1976; 1 dau., Sarah Ellen. Speech pathologist N.H. Easter Seal Soc., Manchester, 1975, Lawrence (Mass.) Gen. Hosp., 1975-76, Logansport (Ind.) Spl. Services, 1976-77; speech-lang. pathologist Lafayette (Ind.) Home Hosp., 1977-79; pvt. practice speech-lang. pathology, Stoneham, Mass., 1979-80; mgr. speech-lang. pathology dept. Beverly (Mass.) Hosp., 1980-81, dir. diagnostic/support services, 1981—; cons. speech-lang. pathology services Harbor Schs., Newburyport, Mass. Bd. dirs. United Cerebral Palsy, Lafayette, 1978-79. Recipient outstanding speech pathology student award Pa. State U., 1974. Mem. Am. Speech-Lang. and Hearing Assn. (cert. clin. competence), Mass. Speech-Lang. and Hearing Assn. Home: 4 Flint St Wakefield MA 01880 Office: Beverly Hosp Beverly MA 01915

HILLMAN, ELSIE HILLIARD (MRS. HENRY LEA HILLMAN), polit. worker; b. Pitts., Dec. 9, 1925; d. Thomas Jones and Marianna (Talbott) Hilliard; student Westminister Choir Coll., 1944-45; m. Henry Lea Hillman, May, 1945; children—Juliet (Mrs. J. Todd Simonds), Audrey (Mrs. Timothy O. Fisher), Henry Lea, William Talbott. Mem. 14th ward Republican Com., 1956, chmn. 1964-70; mem. Rep. Fin. Com., 1963; mem. Pa. State Adv. Com., 1963—; mem. Rep. State Exec. Com., 1963—; alt. del. Rep. Nat. Conv., 1964, del., 1968, dep. del., 1976, del.-at-large, 1980; chmn. Rep. Exec. Com. Allegheny County, 1967-70; co-chmn. Re-elect Nixon Dinner, 1971; mem. Rep. Nat. Com., 1975—. Trustee, Ellis Sch., Pitts., 1951-66, hon. bd. mem. 1966—; trustee Carlow Coll.; bd. dirs. WQED Pub. TV, Pitts. Oratorio Soc.; bd. dirs., v.p. Pitts. Symphony Soc.; bd. dirs. Squirrel Hill Urban Coalition, 1972, v.p. 1972—. Named Women of Yr., Squirrel Hill Kiwanis, 1965; recipient Humanitarian award Guardians of Greater Pitts., 1973; Nat. Brotherhood award (with husband) NCCJ, 1973; Pa. Disting. Rep. award, 1974; Disting. Dau. of Pa. award, 1975. Mem. Urban League of Pitts. (dir., 1st v.p. 1970). Episcopalian (mem. vestry 1976). Home: Holyrood Rd Morewood Heights Pittsburgh PA 15213

HILLMAN, JANET SUE HARRISON, pension cons.; b. Charleston, W.Va., Apr. 19, 1939; d. William Edward and Dorothy Marie (Jones) Harrison; A.B., Albion Coll., 1966; m. Allan Hillman, June 11, 1972. Contract underwriter Travelers Ins. Co., Hartford, Conn., 1969-72; spl. agt. Prudential Ins. Co., Ft. Lee, N.J., 1972-74; benefits adminstr. J. C. Penney Co., Inc., N.Y.C., 1974-77; employee benefits cons. Johnson & Higgins, N.Y.C., 1977-80; pension cons. Frank B. Hall Cons. Co., N.Y.C., 1980-81, sr. pension cons., 1981—. Mem. Am. Pension Conf., Nat. Assn. Female Execs., NOW, LWV. Congregationalist. Home: 7 Macopin Ave Upper Montclair NJ 07043 Office: Frank B Hall Cons Co 261 Madison Ave New York NY 10016

HILLMAN, LESLIE WIGINGTON, editor; b. Pawhuska, Okla., Sept. 19, 1954; d. John Henry and Virginia Lee (Conger) Wigington; B.A. (H.H. Herbert hon. pub. relations scholar), U. Okla., 1976; m. Stephen Alan Hillman, May 23, 1976; 1 dau., Erica Michelle. News reporter Ada (Okla.) Evening News, 1977-78; editor Southside Times, Tulsa, 1978-79; wire editor Broken Arrow (Okla.) Daily Ledger, 1979-80; mng. editor Tulsalite mag., Tulsa, 1980—; editor Spotlite, Tulsa Performing Arts Center, 1980, 81. Recipient Irene Bowers Sells award, 1976, Service award Cystic Fibrosis Found., 1981. Mem. Women in Communications (2d v.p. Tulsa 1981-83). Office: 5523 E Skelly Dr Tulsa OK 74135

HILLMAN, SANDRA MARY, nursing educator; b. Waterbury, Conn., May 12, 1947; d. Domenic M. and Marguerite R. (Ciarlelli) Rinaldi; B.S. in Nursing, U. Conn., 1969; M.S. in Nursing, Boston U., 1976; Ph.D. in Higher Edn. Boston Coll.; m. Henry M. Hillman, Nov. 22, 1970. Public health nurse Dept. Health, Waterbury, 1969-75; instr. public health nursing Coll. Health Profls., U. Lowell (Mass.), 1976-77; instr. public health nursing Northeastern U. Sch. Nursing, Boston, 1977-78, coordinator contemporary nursing, 1977-78; asst. prof. Boston Coll. Sch. Nursing, Chestnut Hill, 1978—; partner Boston Nursing Network Cons. Bd. dirs. Brockton (Mass.) Vis. Nurses Assn., 1979-82, Lynn (Mass.) Vis. Nurses Assn., 1982; mem. Gov.'s Health Issues Task Force. Mem. Am. Nurses Assn., Mass. Nurses Assn., Am. Public Health Assn., Mass. Public Health Assn., Nat. Assn. Women Deans, Adminstrs. and Counselors, Sigma Theta Tau. Home: 420 Ward St Newton MA 02159 Office: Boston Coll Commonwealth Ave Chestnut Hill MA 02167

HILLMAN, SHEILAH ARCHAMBAULT, writer, pub.; b. Quincy, Mass., May 22, 1935; d. Alcide Joseph and Shirley Veronica (Griswold) Archambault; B.A. magna cum laude, Tufts U., 1957; m. Robert S. Hillman, Aug. 31, 1957; children—Kimberly Ann, Robert Joseph. Reporter, The Patriot Ledger, Quincy, 1954-57; mng. editor Gold Medal Books, Fawcett Pubs., N.Y.C., 1957-61; journalism tchr., public relations cons., 1972—. Mem. Women in Communications, Authors Guild. Author: Public Relations for Private Schools, 1976; (with Dr. Robert S. Hillman) Traveling Healthy: A Complete Guide to Medical Services in 23 Countries, 1980; The Baby Checkup Book, 1982.

HILLMAN-JONES, GLADYS CORNELIA, ednl. adminstr.; b. Albany, N.Y., Jan. 15, 1938; d. Thomas Benjamin and Minnie Geneva (Colclough) Brooks; B.S., SUNY, Oneonta, 1960; M.A., Kean Coll. (formerly Newark State Coll.), 1970; m. Harold Jones, Apr. 19, 1980; 1 son by previous marriage, George I. Hillman III. Tchr. public schs., Albany, N.Y., 1960-64, Newark, 1964-69; vice prin. Chancellor Ave. Sch., Newark, 1969-76; prin. Marcus Garvey Sch., Newark, 1976-78, George Washington Carver Elem. Sch., Newark, 1978-81; dep. exec. supt. Newark Public Schs., 1981—. Mem. NAACP (life), Am. Assn. Sch. Adminstrs., Internat. Reading Assn., Assn. Supervision and Curriculum Devel., United Council Negro Women, N.J. Reading Assn., Essex County Council Sch. Adminstrs., Delta Sigma Theta (chmn. scholarship com. 1973-77). Baptist (chmn. Black coll. com. 1978-81, chmn. bd. Christian edn. 1982—). Office: 2 Cedar St Newark NJ 07102

HILLS, ARGENTINA SCHIFANO, editor, publisher; b. Pola, Italy, Oct. 4, 1921; d. Vincent and Argentina (Tomat) Schifano; student U.N.Y., 1940-42; hon. degree, Interam. U., 1969, Queens Coll., Charlotte, N.C., 1971, U. Miami (Fla.), 1978; m. Lee Hills, Oct. 31, 1963. Exec. Buitoni-Perugina, N.Y.C., 1941-51; editor, pub. El Mundo, San Juan, P.R., 1960—; pres. Telemundo, Inc., 1960, Radio Mundo, Angel Ramos Found. Pres. women's com. Detroit Art Inst., 1972-74; mem. women's com. Detroit Symphony, 1970-75; chmn. Dade County Council Arts and Scis., 1978-80; bd. dirs. ARC, 1961-65, Salvation Army, 1965-68, Americas Soc. N.Y., Miami Downtown Devel. Authority; trustee Barry U., Miami, Fla., U. Detroit. Recipient Maria Moors Cabot gold medal Columbia, 1968; Americas Found. award, 1977. Mem. Inter-Am. Press Assn. (dir., pres. 1977-78), Am. Soc. Newspaper Editors (dir.), Am. Newspaper Pubs. Assn. Clubs: Bath (Miami); Bankers (San Juan); Detroit, Grosse Pointe, Dorado Beach. Home: Banyan Ln Bay Point Miami FL 33137 Office: El Mundo Apartado 2408 San Juan PR 00936

HILLS, BARBARA JEAN, clin. social worker; b. Chgo., Dec. 2, 1938; d. Stanley Clarence and Estelle Marie (Bonk) Piontek; B.S. magna cum laude, Eastern Mich. U., 1973; M.S.W., U. Mich., 1976; m. Michael Hills, Dec. 22, 1956; children—Stanley Stuart, Estelle Ann, Edward Thomas, Cynthia Stevens. Med. social worker South Macomb Hosp., Warren, Mich., 1976; clin. social worker Children's Center, Detroit, 1976-78; clin. social worker, bd. dirs. Family Human Potential Services, Livonia, Mich., 1977-81; clin. social worker Franklin Center for Behavioral Change, 1981—; panelist for workshops, 1976—; field instr. U. Mich. Sch. Social Work, 1977-78; trainer post-grad. level mental health profls., 1976—. Tchr. aide Lafayette Clinic, Detroit, 1971; co-chmn. Concerned Citizens Highland Park, Mich., 1970; pres. Mayflower Co-op. Nursery, Detroit, 1968-69; treas., newsletter editor Livonia Co-op. Nursery, 1964-65. Mem. Nat. Assn. Social Workers, Assn. Cert. Social Workers, Detroit Women's Forum, Women's Justice Center, Mich. Assn. Emotionally Disturbed Children, Women's Exchange, Am. Orthopsychiat. Assn., Phi Theta Kappa, Kappa Delta Pi. Club: Univ. Mich. Alumni of Dearborn. Office: 29260 Franklin Rd Suite 167 Southfield MI 48034

HILLS, CARLA ANDERSON, lawyer; b. Los Angeles, Jan. 3, 1934; d. Carl H. and Edith (Hume) Anderson; A.B. cum laude, Stanford U., 1955; postgrad. St. Hilda's Coll., Oxford (Eng.) U., 1954; LL.B., Yale U., 1958; LL.D. (hon.), Pepperdine U., Los Angeles, 1975, Washington U., St. Louis, 1977, Mills Coll., 1977, Lake Forest (Ill.) Coll., 1978, Williams Coll., 1981; m. Roderick Maltman Hills, Sept. 27, 1958; children—Laura Hume, Roderick Maltman, Megan Elizabeth, Alison Macbeth. Admitted to Calif. bar, 1959, D.C. bar, 1977, U.S. Supreme Ct. bar, 1965; asst. atty. civil div. Dept. Justice, Los Angeles, 1958-61; partner firm Munger, Tolles, Hills & Rickershauser, Los Angeles, 1962-74; adj. prof. UCLA Law Sch., 1972; asst. atty. gen. civil div. Dept. Justice, Washington, 1974-75; sec. HUD, 1975-77; partner firm Latham, Watkins & Hills, Washington, 1978—; vice chmn. President's Commn. Housing, 1981-82; dir. Am. Airlines, Inc., Corning Glass Works, IBM Corp., Signal Companies, Inc., Standard Oil Co. Calif., Fed. Nat. Mortgage Assn. Co-chmn. adv. com. presdl. debates LWV, 1980. Mem. Am. Bar Assn. (chmn. sect. antitrust law 1982-83), Fed. Bar Assn. (pres. Los Angeles chpt. 1963), Women Lawyers Assn. (pres. 1964). Republican. Episcopalian. Co-author: Federal Civil Practice, 1961; co-author, editor: Antitrust Adviser, 1971. Office: 1333 New Hampshire Ave NW Washington DC 20036

HILPERT, BRUNETTE KATHLEEN POWERS (MRS. ELMER ERNEST HILPERT), civic worker; b. Baton Rouge; d. Edward Oliver and Orvilla (Nettles) Powers; A.B., La. State U., 1930, B.S. in L.S., 1933; postgrad. Columbia U., 1937; m. Elmer Ernest Hilpert, Aug. 1, 1938; children—Margaret Ray, Elmer Ernest II. Cataloguer, La. State U. Library, Baton Rouge, 1930-36, La. State U. Law Sch. Library, 1936-38; librarian Washington U. Law Sch. Library, St. Louis, 1940-42; reference librarian Washington U. Library, St. Louis, 1952-54. Drive capt. United Fund, St. Louis, 1956; del. White House Conf. on Edn., St. Louis, 1962; trustee John Burroughs Sch., 1959-63; bd. dirs. Grace Hill Settlement House, 1957-63, v.p., 1960-62; bd. dirs. Internat. Inst., 1964-68; bd. dirs. Neighborhood Health Center, 1964-67, sec., 1964—; dir. Arts and Edn. Council, 1967—; pres., dir. Women's Assn. St. Louis Symphony Soc., 1969-71; exec. com., dir. St. Louis Symphony Soc., 1969—; bd. dirs. Miss. River Festival, 1969-74; dir. women's adv. bd. Continental Bank & Trust Co., 1970-77, 79—; bd. dirs. St. Louis Inst. Music, 1971-75; bd. dirs. St. Louis String Quartet, 1971-77, pres., 1975-77; bd. dirs. Community Music Sch., 1973-75, Little Symphony Concerts Assn., 1975-78, St. Louis Conservatory and Schs. for Arts, 1975—, Dance Concert Soc., 1977—, Women's Aux. Bd. Bethesda Gen. Hosp., 1981—. Recipient Woman of Achievement award St. Louis Globe Democrat, 1967. Mem. Nat. Soc. Arts and Letters (dir. 1964-65, 80-82), Dance Concert Soc., Delta Zeta. Republican. Presbyterian. Clubs: Wednesday (rec. sec. 1963-64), St. Louis Woman's. Home: 630 Francis Pl Apt 1-N Saint Louis MO 63105

HILSENBECK, FLORENCE CAROLYN BURNS, registered nurse; b. Kimberlin Heights, Tenn., Sept. 24, 1917; d. Charles Earl and Florence Elizabeth (Anthony) Burns; student Milligan Coll., 1935-37; B.S. in Nursing, Vanderbilt U., 1940; m. John Robert Hilsenbeck, June 19, 1941; children—Patricia, John, Charles, Richard. Instr., Methodist Hosp. Sch. Nursing, Memphis, 1940-41; obstetrical nurse Henry Ford Hosp., Detroit, 1941; head nurse obstetrics New Grace Hosp., Detroit, 1942; inservice instr. North Shore Med. Center, Miami, Fla., 1970-71, dir. inservice edn., 1971-74, dir. nursing, 1974-82. Mem. PTA Council, Miami Shores, 1954-56; active Girl Scouts U.S., Boys Scouts Am., 1950-62. Mem. Am. Soc. Hosp. Nursing Service Adminstrs., Fla. Soc. Hosp. Nursing Service Adminstrs., Am. Heart Assn. Greater Miami, S. Fla. Soc. Dirs. Nursing (sec. 1976-77), Med. Aux. North Shore (pres. 1955-56), PEO (chpt. pres. 1960-62, chmn. state conv. Fla., 1964), Sigma Theta Tau (Iota chpt.). Republican. Presbyterian. Home: 9350 NE 12th Ave Miami Shores FL 33138 Office: 1100 NW 95th St Miami FL 33150

HILT, NANCY ELAINE, nurse; b. Wrightsville, Pa., Sept. 8, 1943; d. Paul Albert and Harriet Mae (Grove) H.; R.N., Reading (Pa.) Hosp., 1964; B.S. in Nursing, Med. Coll. Ga., 1976, M.S. in Nursing, 1977. Staff nurse Reading Hosp., 1964-65; asst. head nurse Children's Hosp. Med. Center, Boston, 1965-67; staff nurse Newington (Conn.) Crippled Children's Hosp., 1970-71; orthopedic nurse specialist Emory U. Clinic, 1971-73, Henrietta Egleston Hosp. Children, Atlanta, 1971-76; nursing supr., clin. specialist Children's Rehab. Center, U. Va. Med. Center, Charlottesville, 1977—, instr. dept. orthopedics and rehab. Sch. Med. U. Va., 1977—, clin. instr. Sch. Nursing, 1977—; cons. in field, vis. lectr., condr. seminars and workshops. Served to capt. Nurse Corps, U.S. Army, 1967-70. Mem. Am., Va., Orthopedic (dir. 1972-74, editor newsletter 1972-74) nurses assns., Am. Humane Assn., Assn. Child Care Hosps. Co-author: Pediatric Orthopedic Nursing, 1975; Manual of Orthopedics, 1980; contbr. profl. jours., producer audio-visual materials. Office: Children's Rehab Center Unit Va Med Center Charlottesville VA 22901

HILTON, SAMANTHA LYNN, orthopedic surgeon; b. Boulder, Colo., Dec. 1, 1948; d. Weston Tyler and Phoebe Salome (Johnson) Lord; M.D., Ohio State U., 1976. Intern, then resident San Francisco Gen. Hosp., 1976-78; practice medicine specializing in orthopedic surgery, San Francisco, 1978—; instr. sports medicine and orthopedics. Mem. Nat. Com. on Sports Medicine, AMA, San Francisco Med. Soc., Women in Med. Careers, Greenpeace, Sierra Club. Democrat. Contbr. articles to profl. jours. Home: 287 Church St San Francisco CA 94114 Office: 2299 Post San Francisco CA 94102

HILTON-LEONARD, JEANNE, clin. social worker; b. Rockford, Ill., Sept. 1, 1934; d. Harry King and Caroline (Albers) Hilton; B.S. with honors, Ind. U., 1973, M.S.W. (Kappa Alpha Theta scholar), 1975; married; children—Stuart, Julie, Susan. Psychiat. social worker, then social work supr. LaRue D. Carter Meml. Hosp., Indpls., 1975-79; supr. counselors Family and Childrens Services, Ft. Wayne, Ind., 1979—. Cert. alcoholism counselor. Mem. Nat. Assn. Social Workers, Acad. Cert. Social Workers. Home: 3810 Ironwood Ct Fort Wayne IN 46815 Office: 2712 S Calhoun St Fort Wayne IN 46807

HILTZ, STARR ROXANNE, sociologist; b. Little Rock, Sept. 7, 1942; d. John Donald and Mildred V. (Koons) Smyers; A.B., Vassar Coll., 1963; M.A., Columbia U., 1964, Ph.D., 1969; children—Jonathan David, Katherine Amanda. Prof. sociology, chmn. dept. sociology, anthropology and social work Upsala Coll., 1969—; assoc. dir. Computerized Conferencing and Communications Center, N.J. Inst. Tech., 1978—; pres. Computerized Conferencing, Inc., 1978—; cons. social impacts of computer systems. Mem. Am. Sociol. Assn., Assn. Computing Machinery, Internat. Communication Assn., Am. Soc. Info. Sci., World Future Soc. Unitarian. Author: Creating Community Services for Widows, 1976; (with M. Turoff) The Network Nation, 1978; (with E. Korr) Computer-Mediated Communication, 1982; Online Communities, 1982. Home: 1531 Golf St Scotch Plains NJ 07076 Office: Upsala College East Orange NJ 07019

HIMLER, MARSHA SUE, career info. systems cons.; b. Indpls., Mar. 26, 1943; d. John Milton and Ruth Devona (Burks) Himler; B.S., Ind. U., 1964; postgrad. Syracuse U., 1968-72, Cornell U., 1969-72. With N.Y. State Dept. Labor, Albany, 1966—, now career info. systems cons.; owner Himler Data Services, Syracuse, N.Y., 1974-76. Mem. Duryea for Gov. campaign, 1979. Served to lt. comdr., USNR, 1973—. Mem. Internat. Assn. Personnel in Employment Security, Mensa, Welsh Pony Soc. Am., Am. Driving Soc. (recognized judge), Northeastern Welsh Pony Assn. (life mem., dir. 1970—). Republican. Episcopalian. Club: Bus. and Profl. Women. Home: 688 Gorge Rd Middleburgh NY 12122 Office: Bldg 12 State Campus Albany NY 12240

HIMONAS, JILL, bus. exec.; B.A. in Speech and English Lit., Hunter Coll., 1966; m. James Himonas, Jr. Sales rep. Lanvin-Charles of the Ritz, N.Y.C., 1966-68, dir. dept. store promotions, 1969; brand mgr. Prince Matchabelli div. Chesebrough-Ponds, N.Y.C., 1970-71; with Max Factor & Co., Los Angeles, 1972—, mktg. mgr., 1972-74, v.p. mktg., dir., 1975-81, sr. v.p. cosmetics/toiletries, 1981—; mem. faculty Town Hall Exec. Seminar Series; speaker bus. colls., mgmt. seminars. Bd. councillors Coll. Continuing Edn., U. So. Calif., also adv. bd. continuing edn. for women. Club: Flintridge Riding. Office: Max Factor & Co 1655 N McCadden Pl Hollywood CA 90028

HINCHEE, RUTH JOAN, nurse, educator; b. Orlando, Fla., Oct. 28, 1926; d. Andrew Herbert and Ina Hattie (Hart) Tice; R.N. diploma Charity Hosp. Sch. Nursing, New Orleans, 1947; B.S.N., McNeese State U., 1974; M.S.N., U. Tex., 1976; m. Benjamin H. Hinchee, Feb. 4, 1948; children—Richard, Laura, Charles. Staff nurse hosps., Calif., Fla., La., 1947-53; hosp. nursing supr. Lake Charles (La.) Meml. Hosp., 1953-66; public health nurse Calcasieu Parish Health Unit, Lake Charles, 1966-74; instr. in nursing McNeese State U., 1975-77, asst. prof., 1977-82, assoc. prof., 1982—, community health nursing coordinator, 1975—, faculty adv. Student Nurses Assn., 1978—; chmn. nursing/health services Calcasieu-Cameron chpt. ARC, 1979—. Recipient Disting. Service award ARC, 1957, Kiwanis Internat., 1975. Mem. Am. Nurses Assn., Nat. League Nurses, La. State Public Health Assn., Am. Public Health Assn., La. State Nurses Assn., Lake Charles Dist. Nurses Assn. (treas. 1981—), Am. Bus. Women's Assn., Phi Lambda Pi. Republican. Home: 735 Jefferson Lake Charles LA 70605 Office: McNeese State U Dept Nursing Lake Charles LA 70609

HINCKLEY, HELEN CLARK, civic worker; b. Gettysburg, Ohio, Aug. 24, 1922; d. Harley Valentine and Mary (Lohridge) Clark; B.S. in Music Edn., Miami U., Oxford, Ohio, 1944; m. Timothy Dwight Hickley, Sept. 7, 1946; children—Deborah, Timothy, Michael. With IBM, Cin., 1944-46; mem. Cin. City Council, 1974-77; mem. Republican Exec. Com. Hamilton County, Ohio, 1977—; pres. Women's Com., Cin. Symphony Orch., 1969-70, Cin. May Festival, 1967-68, Cin. Opera Assn., 1964-65, Cin. Ballet Co., 1971-73; mem. adv. bd. Salvation Army, 1978—; bd. dirs. Central Psychiat. Clinic, 1977, Sch. for Creative and Performing Arts, 1979—, Cin. Clean Com., 1978-80; bd. dirs. Free Store, 1980; mem. Friends of Cin. Conservatory of Music, 1980. Presbyterian. Clubs: Cin. Country, Town, Jr. League, Zonta.

HINDING, ANDREA, librarian, archivist; b. St. Paul, July 15, 1942; d. Haakon and Isabelle Marie (Supan) H.; student Marquette U., 1960-62; B.A. magna cum laude in History, U. Minn., 1966, M.A. in History, 1973; m. William R. Van Essendelft, Apr. 25, 1970 (div. 1976). Library asst. U. Minn. Libraries, Mpls., 1964-66, research asst., 1966-67, curator of manuscrips, 1967-78, dir. Walter Libraries, asso. prof., 1978—; dir. Women's History Sources Survey, 1975-79, Minn. Welfare Records Survey, 1976-77; mem. Nat. Archives Adv. Council, 1977-80, Joint Com. Historians and Archivists, 1980-82. Fellow Soc. Am. Archivists (mem. exec. council 1975-79); mem. Orgn. Am. Historians(mem. exec. council 1977-80), Am. Hist. Assn., AAUP, ALA. Editor: Women's History Sources: A Guide to Archives and Manuscript Collections in the United States, 2 vols., 1979. Office: 107 Walter Library U Minn Minneapolis MN 55455

HINE, PEGGY ANN DAVIDSON, educator, bus. cons.; b. Muskegon, Mich., Jan. 19, 1933; d. Willard J. Nelson and Gertrude E. (Makurat) Nelson Davidson; B.A. cum laude, Western Mich. U., 1954; M.A., Mich. State U., 1969, Ph.D., 1975; m. Edward W. Hine, Aug. 21, 1954; children—Leslie L., Laurel A., Edward W., Eric N., Ethan J. Tchr. secondary schs., Wayne, Mich., 1954-58; mem. faculty Lansing (Mich.) Community Coll., 1970-71; instr. U. Coll., Mich. State U., East Lansing, 1971-74, instr. grad. edn., 1974-76, acting dir. Adult Resource and Referral Center, 1976, dir. grad. workshop Coll. Edn., 1975-76; bus. mgr. Professional Corp., East Lansing, 1969-82; bus. cons. to bus. firms, govt. and edn., 1978—; asst. prof. grad. bus. mgmt. Aquinas Coll., Grand Rapids, Mich., 1978—. Mem. Am. Mgmt. Assn., Mich. Adult Edn. Assn., Adult Edn. Assn. U.S., Mich. Assn. Tng. and Devel., Associated Women Students (v.p. 1950-51), Arista, Phi Delta Kappa, Tau Alpha Kappa. Home: 1850 Abbott Rd East Lansing MI 48823 Office: Aquinas College Robinson Rd Grand Rapids MI 49506

HINER, MARJORIE LOU, trucking co. exec.; b. Crawfordsville, Ind., June 5, 1944; d. Isaac Edwin and Dortha Eileen (Odell) Hoss; B.S., Ball State U., 1966, M.A., 1970; m. Homer F. Hiner, July 14, 1973; children—Richard, David, Marcy. Tchr., Maconaquah High Sch., Bunker Hill, Ind., 1966-67; substitute tchr. various schs., 1970-73; with Hiner Transport, Inc., Huntington, Ind., 1973—, owner, sec.-treas. bd. dirs., 1973—; treas. Hiner Leasing, Inc., also dir.; bookkeeper, dir. Hiner Mgmt. Services, Inc. Bd. dirs. Huntington County United Way; mem. adv. bd. Salvation Army. Mem. Nat. Assn. Female Execs., Am. Bus. Women's Assn. Mem. Ind. Motor Truck Assn., Huntington C. of C., South Side Bus. Assn., Ft. Wayne Executive Club, Ball State U. Alumni Assn., Psi Iota Xi, Alpha Phi. Republican. Home: 1979N-600W Andrews IN 46702 Office: PO Box 621 Huntington IN 46750

HINERFELD, RUTH JEAN, assn. exec.; b. Milton, Mass., Sept. 18, 1930; d. Morris Joseph and Anna Sally (Shoolman) Gordon; A.B., Vassar Coll., 1951; postgrad. Harvard Radcliffe Program in Bus. Adminstrn., 1952; m. Norman M. Hinerfeld, Dec. 25, 1952; children—Lee Ann, Thomas Benjamin, Joshua Gordon. Pres., LWV of U.S., Washington, 1976—; bd. govs. UN Assn. U.S.A., 1974—; mem. White House Adv. Com. for Trade Negotiations, 1975—; mem. exec. com. Overseas Devel. Council, 1976—, Leadership Conf. on Civil Rights, 1978—; trustee Citizens Research Found., 1978—; mem. Nat. Petroleum Council, 1979—, Commn. for Nat. Agenda for the '80's, 1979-80; mem. U.S. del. UN Mid-Decade Conf. on Women, 1980; Presdl. fellow Aspen Inst., 1981. Recipient disting. citizen award Nat. Mcpl. League, 1978. Office: 1730 M St NW Washington DC 20036

HINES, MARY EMMA, educator; b. Bolton, Miss., July 5, 1934; d. Walter and Emma Mae (Johnson) Harvey; B.S., Jackson State Coll., 1958; B.S., UCLA, 1966; m. Theodore Hines, Dec. 3, 1960; children—Emma Corenia, Herbert Lee, Harold Louis, Joel Lynn, Janee Latricia. Tchr., Hinds County, Miss., 1958-64, Los Angeles City Schs., 1966—; partner H & H Tire Service, South Gate, Calif., 1972—. Pres. Mission True Love Dist. Assn., Los Angeles, 1981—; Sunday Sch. tchr., Bible tchr., youth pres. New Covenant Bapt. Ch. Mem. United Tchrs. Los Angeles, Nat. Edn. Assn., Nat. Council Tchrs. Assn., Gompers Faculty Assn., English Council Los Angeles. Home: 16032 Indian Creek Rd Cerritos CA 90701 Office: 9019 Long Beach St South Gate CA 90280

HINES, PATRICIA, social worker; b. Watertown, N.Y., Nov. 4, 1947; d. Arthur and Bella (O'Neil) H.; B.S., SUNY, Oswego, 1969; M.S.W., SUNY, Buffalo, 1975; M.P.A., Fairleigh Dickinson U., 1982. Supr. social work Ocean County Bd. Social Services, Toms River, N.J., 1973-77, adminstrv. supr. social work, 1977—; social work cons. Medicenter and Rainbow Day Care, Lakewood, N.J., 1975—, Ocean County Vis. Homemaker Service, Inc., Toms River, 1975-80, Community Meml. Hosp., Toms River, 1978-79, Country Manor, Toms River, 1981—; prin. Sr. Care Planning Assocs.; instr. social work Georgian Court Coll., Lakewood, 1975—. Chmn., Ocean County Title XX Coalition, 1977-82; bd. dirs. Ocean County Family Planning Program, Toms River, 1969-73. Cert., Dr. Thomas Gordon Parent Effectiveness Trainer. Mem. Acad. Cert. Social Workers, Nat. Assn. Social Workers. Home: 13 Bay Harbor Blvd Brick NJ 08723 Office: 1027 Hooper Ave Toms River NJ 08753

HINKEL, SANDRA VERNA, psychologist; b. Miami, Fla., Apr. 12, 1951; d. Edmund Angelo and Melba Enola Verna; B.A., Tex. Luthern Coll., 1973; M.S., Trinity U., 1975; postgrad. U. Tex., San Antonio, 1978; m. Bruce Hinkel, May 17, 1975. Asst. dir. Coll. Selection and Planning Found., San Antonio, 1973-75; psychol. asso. Behavioral Sci. Assos., San Antonio, 1974-75, Bexar County Hosp. Dist. Mental Health, San Antonio, 1975-78, C.Lee Lowery, Ph.D., Inc., San Antonio, 1979—. Mem. Am. Psychol. Assn., Tex. Psychol. Assn. Democrat. Lutheran. Home: 3118 Royalton San Antonio TX 78228 Office: 206 Oak Hills Med Bldg 7711 Louis Pasteur Dr San Antonio TX 78229

HINKLE, JANE KATHERINE, chem. co. exec.; b. Chgo., July 10, 1937; d. Matthew J. and Ann (Ray) Kasallis; student Rosary Coll., 1959; children—Karla, Keely, Kurt, Kyle. Quality control technician Dept. Agr., 1956-59; quality control supr. Kraft Foods Co., 1959-61; dir. water analysis Suburban Labs., 1961-69; with Magnaflux Surface Conditioners Inc., Chgo., 1966—, v.p., nat. sales mgr., tech. dir., 1974—. Mem. ASTM, Am. Soc. Metals, Soc. Automotive Engrs. Roman Catholic. Home: 1120 High Ridge Rd Lombard IL 60148 Office: 6935 W 62d St Chicago IL 60638

HINKLE, MURIEL RUTH NELSON, naval warfare analysis co. exec.; b. Bayonne, N.J., Mar. 17, 1929; d. Andrew and Florence Martha Ida (Nuber) Nelson; student Md. Coll. for Women, 1947-49; B.A., U. Md., 1951; m. David Randall Hinkle, June 5, 1954; children—Valerie Nelson, Janet Lee, Sally Ann. Mgr., Wildacres Thoroughbred Horse Farm, Waterford, Conn., 1960-70; illustrator Naval Warfare Predictions/Computer Simulated Naval Engagements, Analysis & Tech., Inc., North Stonington, Conn., 1970-73; pres. Sonalysts, Inc., Waterford, 1973—, also dir.; dir. Alpha Mortgage Corp., Beta Computer Corp., Command Engring. & Tech. Services Co.; cons. anti-submarine warfare cruise missile weapon systems Gen. Electric Co., 1974-76; cons. Def. Nuclear Agy. for Tactical Nuclear Effects in anti-submarine warfare, 1974-75; spl. edn. subsitute tchr. Waterford Pub. Schs., 1968-74. Bd. trustees Thames Sci. Center, 1979-82. Recipient commendation for services to submarine force Comdr. Submarine Squadron Ten, 1973. Mem. Conn. Thoroughbred Owners Assn., Nat. Audubon Soc., Submarine Devel. Group Two Wives Club (pres. 1968), Sigma Kappa. Republican. Baptist. Clubs: Westbrook Hunt, Navy Wives. Co-author: Scope of Acoustic Communications Systems in Naval Tactical Warfare, 1974; Non-Acoustic Anti Submarine Warfare, 1974; Nuclear Weapons Effects in Anti Submarine Warfare, 1974; Measures of Effectiveness, Naval Tactical Communications, 1975; co-author: Destroyer ASW Barrier, 1977. Home: RD 1 Box 168-A Stonington CT 06378 Office: Sonalysts Bldg 215 Parkway North Waterford CT 06385

HINRICHSEN, EVELYN ELIZABETH MERRELL (MRS. WALTER HINRICHSEN), corp. exec.; b. Chgo., Nov. 30, 1910; d. Dwight Livingston and Julia (Dodd) Merrell; B.A., Mus.B., Mills Coll., 1938, M.A., 1940; m. Walter Hinrichsen, Aug. 2, 1946 (dec. July 1969); children—Martha Eleanor, Henry Hans. Asst. sec. to pres. Mills Coll., Oakland, Calif., 1942-44; sec. to chief asst. and librarian Library of Congress, Washington, 1944-46; v.p., sec. C.F. Peters Corp., N.Y.C., 1948-69, v.p., sec., owner, 1969-70, owner, pres., 1970-78, owner, chmn. bd., 1978—. Mem. AAUW, Met. Mus. Art, Mus. Modern Art, N.Y. Philharmonic, Alumnae Assn. Mills Coll., Sigma Alpha Iota. Home: 431 E 20th St New York NY 10010 Office: 373 Park Ave S New York NY 10016

HINSCH, GERTRUDE WILMA, devel. biologist; b. Chgo., Oct. 20, 1932; d. Hans R. and Gertrude (Kalb) H.; B.S., No. Ill. U., 1953; M.S., Iowa State U., 1955, Ph.D., 1957; m. Martin Silvers, Oct. 17, 1981. Mem. faculty Mt. Holyoke Coll., 1957-60, Mt. Union Coll., Alliance, Ohio, 1960-67, U. Miami (Fla.), 1966-74; mem. faculty U. South Fla., Tampa, 1974—, prof. biology, 1980—. Mem. Marine Biol. Lab., Am. Inst. Biol. Scis., AAAS, Soc. Study Reprodn., Am. Soc. Zoologists, Internat. Soc. Devel. Biology, Soc. Study Devel. Biology, Sigma Xi. Home: Route 1 Box 110 Thonotosassa FL 33592 Office: LIF 169 U South Fla Tampa FL 33620

HINSON, PEGGY MILDRED, educator; b. Thomaston, Ga., July 19, 1936; d. Robert LeGrand, Sr. and Mildred Sara (Keever) H.; B.S. in Edn., Auburn U., 1958; B.S. in Med. Adminstrn. and Supervision, Ga. State U., 1978. Head English dept. Faith Sch., Ft. Benning, Ga., 1958-61, Daniel Jr. High Sch., Columbus, Ga., 1961-63; tchr. Rothschild Jr. High Sch., Columbus, 1965-75, head English dept., 1976—; secondary English cons., Columbus, 1975-76; curriculum steering com. Columbus Coll. Named Star Tchr., 1975; recipient commendation Pres. of U.S., 1976, commendation U.S. Congress, 1976. Mem. Nat. Council Tchrs. of English, NEA, Ga. Assn. Educators, Muscogee Assn. Edn., Columbus Exec. Club, AAUW, Ga. Walking Horse Assn., Phi Delta Kappa, Alpha Delta Kappa, Delta Delta Delta. Home: 3312 Gail Dr Columbus GA 31907 Office: 1136 Hunt Ave Columbus GA 31907

HINTON, ANN PEARLMAN, psychotherapist; b. Washington, Dec. 25, 1941; d. Earl Ralph and Eleanor Jane (Goldsmith) Pearlman; B.A., U. Pitts., 1964; M.S., Case Western Reserve U., 1966; m. Alfred Fountaine Hinton, Aug. 5, 1965; children—Adam Uhri, Melina Laurel. Dir. research Citizens Com. on Youth, Cin., 1968-70; clin. social worker Detroit House of Corrections, 1976; clin. social worker Kalamazoo Child Guidance Clinic, 1973-77; pvt. practice psychotherapy, Ann Arbor, Mich., 1977—. Bus. Vocat. Rehab. fellow, 1964-65. Mem. Nat. Assn. Social Workers (chmn. polit. action 1969-70, v.p. social policy Mich. chpt. 1980—). Cert. social worker, marriage and family counselor, Mich. Author: Summer in the City, 1969; Self Appraisal of the Cincinnati Out-of-School, 1969; Getting Free, 1982. Office: 117 N 1st St Ann Arbor MI 48104

HINTON, DONNA MARIE, accountant; b. Chgo., Apr. 8, 1955; d. Joseph H. and Mary F. (Clarke) H.; B.B.A. cum laude in Fin., U. Notre Dame, 1977; M. Mgmt. cum laude, Aquinas Coll., 1980. Acct. I, Amway, Ada, Mich., 1977-79, acct. II, 1980-81, chief acct. inventory, 1982—. Mem. Nat. Assn. Accts. (dir. Grand Rapids chpt. 1981-82, Walter J. Mikulski award 1980-81), Beta Gamma Sigma. Club: Notre Dame of Grand Rapids (treas. 1979-80, dir. 1981-82). Office: 7575 E Fulton Rd Ada MI 49355

HINTON, SHIRLEY ANN, market research analyst; b. Raleigh, N.C., Nov. 11, 1943; d. Sharon and Mary Eliza (Cheek) H.; B.S. in Chemistry, Shaw U., 1966. Systems engr. IBM, N.Y.C., 1966-74, regional edn. mgr., 1974-76, sr. forecaster/market research analyst, White Plains, N.Y., 1976-79, sr. market research analyst-internat., 1979—; coll. bus. cons. Nat. Alliance Bus. Alumni speaker United Negro Coll. Fund. Recipient Service award Shaw U., 1974. Mem. Am. Chem. Soc., Am. Mgmt. Assn., Nat. Assn. Female Execs., Delta Sigma Theta. Baptist. Club: Shaw U. Alumni.

HINTON-BRAATEN, KATHLEEN, violinist, writer; b. Ventura, Calif., Sept. 15, 1941; d. Jack C. and Adelaide (Hilford) McNeil; student Oberlin Coll., 1959-61; Calif. State U., Northridge, 1961-62, Calif. State U., San Francisco, 1962-63, Calif. State U., Fullerton, 1966, U. Md., College Park, 1977; 1 son, Randolph Phillip Hinton. Violinist, San Diego Symphony Orch., San Antonio Symphony, Cin. Symphony, Music in Maine String Quartet; co-founder, asst. personnel mgr., adminstr. 20th Century Consort, Nat. Symphony Orch., Washington, 1975-79; violinist Nat. Symphony Orch., 1969—; recitalist; freelance travel, performing arts, history and profile writer; contbr. to N.Y. Times, Washington Post, Symphony mag., Christian Sci. Monitor, Cin. Enquirer, S.W. Art mag., Quest, Internat. Musician, others. Mem. Washington Ind. Writers, Musicians Union Local, Japan-Am. Soc. Home and Office: 4813 S 28th St Arlington VA 22206

HINTZ, JEANNETTE LEIGH, city ct. ofcl.; b. Akron, Ohio, Aug. 5, 1932; d. Alfred Edward and Margaret Lucille (Lee) Leigh; B.A. in Polit. Sci., U. Akron, 1981; divorced; children—Nancy Hintz Fuchs, Eugene F., Jr., Steven Eric. City clk., council clk., sec. to mayor City of Tallmadge (Ohio), 1952-55; legal sec., 1965-77; bailiff Akron Mcpl. Ct., 1977—. Mem. exec. com. Summit County Republican Party, 1976-78; Rep. precinct committeewoman, Akron, 1966—. Mem. Phi Sigma Alpha, Alpha Sigma Lambda. Home: 1033 Kling St Akron OH 44301 Office: 217 S High St Akron OH 44308

HINZ, DOROTHY ELIZABETH, writer, editor, public relations exec.; b. N.Y.C., Nov. 28, 1926; d. Hans and Anna (Borell) Hinz; A.B., Hunter Coll., 1948; postgrad. Columbia U. Copy editor Collier's Mag., 1948-53; asst. to dir. devel. Columbia U., N.Y.C., 1953-55; mng. editor Grace Log, econs. research-analyst, writer speeches, white papers, com. reports Latin Am. affairs, pub. relations dept. W.R. Grace & Co., N.Y.C., 1955-64; staff writer Oil Progress, fgn. news media, speeches, films, internat. petroleum ops., public relations dept. Caltex Petroleum Corp., N.Y.C., 1964-68; fin. editor Merrill Lynch, Pierce, Fenner & Smith, 1969-74; asst. sec., mgr. speakers bur. research-writer, editor speeches, spl. studies and reports corporate communications dept. Mfrs. Hanover Trust Co., N.Y.C., 1974—. Mem. Inter-Am. Round Table, Soc. Am. Med. Writers. Contbr. articles on multinat. corps., devel. nations, trade and finance to various publs. Home: 600 W 115th St New York NY 10025 Office: 350 Park Ave New York NY 10022

HIPP, CAROLYN CASSIDY, real estate broker; b. Lexington, Ky., Sept. 7, 1921; d. William Henry and Della Mae (Poe) Cassidy; m. Donald Harry Hipp, Mar. 9, 1946; student Spencerian Comml. Sch., 1940; children—Donald Harry, Donna Carol, Barbara Dell, Ruth Anne, Steven Douglas. Sec. div. IBM, Louisville, 1939-40; hostess air shows Miss American Aviation, 1940-41; model John Robert Powers, N.Y.C., 1941; sec. Current Surveys div. Census Bur., Dallas, 1942-43; sec. Reynolds Metals Co., 1943-46; asso. broker Harold J. Lawlor & Co., Realtors, Richmond, Va., 1973—. Grad. Realtors Inst. Mem. Women's Council Realtors (pres. Richmond chpt. 1979, sec. Va. chpt. 1981), Va. Assn. Realtors (dir. 1980), Richmond Bd. Realtors, Nat. Assn. Realtors.

Republican. Mormon. Clubs: Roslyn Hills Garden, Richmond Council Garden. Home: 11213 Birchcrest Rd Richmond VA 23233 Office: Parham Med Center Suite 201 Richmond VA 23229

HIPPS, DONNA MARIE (MRS. ROBERT O. HIPPS), librarian; b. Waterloo, Iowa, May 18, 1925; d. George Fred and Mamie Jean (Livingston) Westlic; B.S., Iowa State U., 1946; M.A., U. Minn., 1963; m. Robert O. Hipps, Aug. 9, 1946; Children—Alan, Margaret (Mrs. Douglas A. Peters), James. Tchr. pub. schs., Iowa, 1946-48; teaching asst. Univ. High Sch., U. Minn., Mpls., 1960-63; librarian Lincoln High Sch., Bloomington, Minn., 1963-70; library specialist Jefferson High Sch., Bloomington, 1970-74, dir. resource center, 1974-75, media dir., 1975—. Mem. Am. Fedn. Tchrs., NEA, LWV (state treas. 1958-59, dir. Edina 1955-58), Am. Field Service, AAUW, Sigma Kappa, Beta Phi Mu. Methodist. Home: 6604 Dakota Trail Edina MN 55435 Office: 4001 W 102d St Bloomington MN 55431

HIPSHIRE, LOUISE JOYNER, legal office adminstr.; b. Hampton, Va., Nov. 23, 1945; d. Odis B. and Nannie Leigh (Vick) Joyner; student Ga. State U.; m. James R. Hipshire, Sept. 12, 1980. With Peoples Bank and Trust Co., Rocky Mount, N.C., 1966-69, Avco Fin. Servies, Rocky Mount, 1969-72, Inventories Co., Garner, N.C., 1972-74; comptroller, officer mgr. Moffett and Henderson, P.C., attys.-at-law, Atlanta, 1974—; sec.-treas. Charter Oak Mortgage Corp.; cons. in acctg. systems. Active local Big Sisters, 1979—. Mem. Nat. Assn. Legal Adminstrs., DeKalb County Bd. Realtors. Republican. Methodist. Office: 1916 Piedmont Rd NE Atlanta GA 30324

HIRASAKI, MARSHA PARRISH, valve mgf. co. sales exec.; b. Sullivan's Island, S.C., Oct. 27, 1945; d. Louis August Rohde and Ruth Ann (Hynes) Nelson; B.S.M.E., Duke U., 1967; M.S.M.E., U. Houston, 1971; m. John Kiyoshi Hirasaki, Dec. 29, 1968; children—Kitt Nelson, Parrish Nelson. Aerospace engr. TRW Systems, Houston, 1967-72; design engr. Nat. Maritime Research Center, Galveston, Tex., 1972-74; sales mgr. Cooper Valve & Fitting, Inc., LaPorte, Tex., 1974-76; pres., gen. mgr. Eurasia Valve Corp., Houston, 1976-79; dist. sales mgr. Masoneilan div. McGraw Edison, Freeport, Tex., 1979—. Mem. Instrument Soc. Am. (pres. chpt. 1982-83), NOW (pres. Houston chpt. 1972-73). Home: 931 Shady Oak Dr Dickinson TX 77539

HIRES, CLARA S., bot. researcher; b. Merion, Pa., Apr. 8, 1897; d. Charles E. and Clara K. (Smith) Hires; student Wellesley Coll., 1916-19, Tchrs. Coll., Columbia, others, 1920-32; B.A., Cornell U., 1928. Tchr. sci. Edgewood Sch., Greenwich, Conn., 1920-25, Buxton Country Day Sch., Short Hills, N.J., 1929-32, Shore Rd. Acad., Bklyn., 1932-34; owner, research dir. Mistaire Labs., Millburn, N.J., 1929—. Mem. mgmt. com. Overlook Hosp., Summit, N.J., 1938-42. Mem. AAAS (life), Internat. Fern Soc. (Los Angeles chpt.), Am. Fern Soc. (life), Brit. Pteridological Soc., N.Y. Acad. Scis., (life), N.J. Acad. Scis., Bot. Soc. Am. (paleobot. sect., pteridology sect.), Torrey Bot. Club, N.Y. Micros. Soc., N.Y. Bot. Garden, Internat. Orgn. Paleobotany, Paleontol. Soc., Am. Hort. Soc., N.Y. Hort. Soc., Internat. Soc. Stereology, AAUW, League Women Voters, Wyo. Assn., Sigma Delta Epsilon (Kappa chpt., past local and nat. offices). Clubs: Maplewood Garden, Summit Nature, Wellesley, Cornell. Author: Spores . Ferns . Microscopic Illusions Analyzed, Vol. I, 1965, Vol. II, 1978. Contbr. articles to profl. jours. Address: 152 Glen Ave Millburn NJ 07041

HIRN, DORIS DREYER, health service adminstr.; b. N.Y.C., Dec. 3, 1933; d. James Howard and Dorothy Van Nostrand (Young) Dreyer; student Colby Jr. Coll., 1950-51, Hofstra U., 1953-56; m. John D. Hirn, Oct. 27, 1956; children—Deborah Lynn, Robert William. Owner, Dutchlands Farm, Albany, N.Y., 1957-62, Hickory Hill Farm, Galena, Ill., 1965-75; adminstr. Home Health Service, Chgo., 1972-74, exec. dir. Suburban Home Health Service, 1974— ; pres. Hickory Hill Mgmt. Corp.; dir. Nat. Health Delivery Systems, Serengeti Prodns., Inc.; v.p. Compulease, Inc. Served with WAVES, 1951-52. Mem. Am. Fedn. Home Health Agys., Ill. Council Home Health Agys., Coffee Clubs Ill. (dir.). Contbr. articles to various periodicals. Home: Chicago IL 60610 Office: 2250 E Devon Ave Des Plaines IL 60018

HIRSCH, BARBARA, educator; b. Orange, N.J., Mar. 27, 1943; d. Lee and Abby I. (Parker) Hirsch; B.S., Fairleigh Dickinson U., 1965, M.A. cum laude, 1971; postgrad. Seton Hall U., 1973, Montclair State Coll., 1974, Fordham U., 1976. Dir. spl. edn., dir. gifted and talented edn. Nutley (N.J.) Public Schs., 1965—; pvt. practice ednl. cons., Nutley, 1975—; adj. prof. edn. Fairleigh Dickinson U., Rutherford, N.J., 1968—; nat. lectr. spl. edn. Mem. N.J. Prins. and Suprs. Assn., Nat. Assn. Secondary Prins., N.J. Assn. Spl. Edn. Adminstrs., AAUW, N.J. Assn. Learning Cons., Phi Delta Kappa. Contbr. articles in field to profl. jours.; author ednl. curricula. Home: 477 Washington Ave Nutley NJ 07110 Office: Bloomfield Ave Nutley NJ 07110 also Home and Office: 6526 Masters Blvd Orlando FL 32811

HIRSCH, ELEANOR GULBIS, author, editor; b. Chgo., Nov. 26, 1923; d. Christian and Alvine Katherine (Bauman) Gulbis; B.A. in English, U. Ill., 1946; m. Fred W. Hirsch, Apr. 6, 1951; children—Leslie Kathleen, Melanie Ann. With Scott, Foresman and Co., Chgo., 1947-66, project editor, 1961-66; directing editor Ency. Brit. Ednl. Corp., Chgo., 1966-67; mng. editor Lyons and Carnahan, Chgo., 1967-73; editorial dir. Rand McNally, Skokie, Ill., 1973-75; exec. editor Holt, Rinehart and Winston, N.Y.C., 1975-77; editorial v.p. Scott, Foreman & Co., Glenview, Ill., 1977-78; v.p., dir. reading Ginn and Co., Lexington, Mass., 1978-80; author, ednl. cons., 1980—; author: The Principal's Resource, A Handbook, 1982; exec. editor monthly newsletter Principal's Principles, 1982—. Mem. devel. com. Chgo. Met. YWCA, 1981—. Honoree, Salute to Women in Bus., YWCA. Mem. Acad. Women Achievers (charter), Internat. Reading Assn., Nat. Assn. Elem. Sch. Prins., Nat. Council Tchrs. English. Unitarian. Address: 649 58th St Hinsdale IL 60521

HIRSCH, ELISABETH FEIST (MRS. FELIX HIRSCH), philosopher, ret. educator; b. Mainz, Germany, Nov. 2, 1904; d. Sigmund and Toni (Rawicz) Feist; student U. Freiburg, 1924, U. Berlin, 1924-29; Ph.D., Marburg U., 1930; m. Felix Hirsch, Nov. 6, 1938; children—Roland, Thomas. Came to U.S., 1938, naturalized, 1944. Asst. prof. philosophy Bard Coll., Annandale-on-Hudson, N.Y., 1949-54; asst. prof. philosophy and modern langs. Trenton State Coll., 1956-64, asso. prof. philosophy, 1964-69, prof. philosophy, 1969-72, prof. emeritus, 1972—, chmn. dept. philosophy and religion, 1969-72. Rockefeller Found. award for studies in France, 1929-30; Sterling research fellow, Yale U., 1937-38; Gulbenkian Found. fellow, Lisbon, Portugal, summer 1960; Guggenheim fellow, 1960-61; prize Portuguese Acad. Internat. Culture, 1968. Mem. Renaissance Soc. Am., Am. Soc. Reformation Research, Heidegger Conf., AAUW (May Treat internat. fellow 1954-55). Author: Weltbild und Staatsidee bei Jean Bodin, 1930; Damião de Gois, The Life and Thought of a Portuguese Humanist (1502-1574), 1967. Editor: De Arte Dubitandi et Confidendi. Ignorandi et Sciendi (Sebastian Castellio), 1937, 2d edit., 1981; contbr. articles on history of ideas and philosophy of Martin Heidegger to books, scholarly and profl. jours. Home: Pennswood Village Apt L113 Newtown PA 18940

HIRSCH, FERN JOYCE, psychologist; b. N.Y.C., Aug. 27, 1953; d. Raymond Morton and Alice Jeannette (Slovak) Singer; B.A., SUNY, Binghamton, 1973; Ed.S., U. Kans., 1976; m. Steven Hirsch, Oct. 21, 1973; children—Jami, David, Kelli. Computer operator U. Kans., Lawrence, 1974-75, statistics and research cons., 1974-76, data analyst, 1975-76; sch. psychologist Nat. Sch. Dist., National City, Calif., 1976-79; cons. psychologist Seekonk (Mass.) Sch. Dist., 1979—, Fuller Meml. Hosp., South Attleboro, Mass., 1979-80; suicide prevention counselor Crisis Call, Binghamton, 1971-73. Two/Ten scholar, 1971-73. Mem. Am. Psychol. Assn., Nat. Assn. Sch. Psychologists, Calif. Assn. Sch. Psychologists and Psychometrists, Phi Beta Kappa. Jewish. Home: 14 Evergreen St Barrington RI 02806

HIRSCH, GLORIA TISHLER, family therapist; b. Chgo., Mar. 18, 1928; d. Abraham and Sarah (Mintz) Tishler; B.S., Roosevelt U., Chgo., 1949; M.A., Calif. State U. at Northridge, 1968; postgrad. U. Calif. at Los Angeles, 1968-70; m. Ira Hirsch, May 21, 1950; children—Susan Dee, Lisa Ellen, Karen Barbara. Adult edn. instr. Beverly Hills (Calif.) High Sch., 1957-60; tchr., dir. early childhood edn. programs, Los Angeles, 1949-60; psychol. cons. Project Head Start, Office Econ. Opportunity, Los Angeles County, 1965-70; clin. dir. Friends of Family, family therapy, family edn. and child abuse prevention and treatment center, Van Nuys, Cal., 1972—. Coordinator, Pacoima Community Parent-Child Program; examiner Calif. Bd. Behavioral Sci. Examiners; participant/presenter profl. convs., seminars. Mem. exec. com. Los Angeles Mayor's Adv. Com. on Status of Women, chairperson Child Care Com. Mem. Calif. Assn. Marriage and Family Therapists (trustee), Am. Assn. Marriage and Family Counselors (clin. mem.), Nat. Council on Family Relations, NOW, ACLU. Contbr. to Marriage Today: Problems, Issues and Alternatives; also articles to profl. jours. Office: 14522 Kittridge Van Nuys CA 91411

HIRSCH, JUDITH, journalist; b. Buffalo, Aug. 17, 1944; d. Samuel Albert and Roseann (McCann) Hirsch; B.A., Bowling Green (Ohio) State U., 1966. News dir. WBGU-TV, Bowling Green State U., 1967-68; reporter Daily Sentinel Tribune, Bowling Green, 1968-75; with WOHO Radio, Toledo, 1975-76, Maumee Valley Pub. Co., 1976-77, Toledo Edison Co., 1977—. Cons. advt., public relations to various polit. campaigns, 1972-73. Sec., Citizens Adv. Council on Alcoholism and Drug Abuse, Wood County, Ohio, 1973-74; coordinator Santa's Toybox, Christmas Toy Collection Campaign; coordinator Basic Police Sch., Bowling Green Dept Police. Recipient certs. of appreciation Ohio State Hwy. Patrol, 1971, Nat. Police Officer Assn., 1975, City of Bowling Green, 1976; YWCA TWIN honoree, 1980; regional chmn. Nuclear Energy Women, 1979-81. Mem. Women in Communications (treas. 1981-82), Wood County Peace Officers Assn. (sec.-treas. 1977—), Delta Zeta. Editor: Alumnae Newsletter, 1972-73; TWIN Management Forum, 1981. Home: 315 W 2d St Perrysburg OH 43551 Office: Toledo Edison Emergency Planning 300 Madison Ave Toledo OH 43652

HIRSCH, JULIA CAROL, mgmt. cons.; b. Freeport, Ill., Mar. 18, 1939; d. Muriel Woessner and Lois (Peterman) Woessner Hirsch; B.A., Stanford U., 1960. Program dir. Stanford (Calif.) Alumni Assn., 1960-68; exec. asst. to pres. Calif. Inst. Arts, Valencia, Calif., 1968-72; v.p. Nat. Center for Vol. Action, Washington, 1972-74; Calif. Gubernatorial campaign mgr. for Herb Haffif, San Francisco, 1974; pres. J. C. Hirsch and Assos., San Francisco, 1974-78; v.p. Boyden Assos., Inc., San Francisco, 1978—. Mem. bd. Stanford Alumni Exec. Bd., 1973-76; trustee York Sch., 1979—. Mem. Women in Communications, No. Calif. Indsl. Relations Council, Econ. Round Table. Clubs: World Trade, St. Francis Yacht. Home: 27 Hinckley Walk San Francisco CA 94111 Office: One Maritime Plaza Suite 1760 San Francisco CA 94111

HIRSCH, LINDA GERALDINE, psychotherapist; b. Detroit, Mar. 27, 1946; d. Leopold and Celia (Klopfer) H.; B.S., SUNY, Cortland, 1968; M.A., Calif. State U., Los Angeles, 1972; Ph.D., U. Miami (Fla.), 1975; m. Norman Jules Silber, June 10, 1979. Counselor, St. Luke's Center Methadone Clinic, Miami, 1973-74, dir. Project Intercept, 1974-76; pvt. practice, Miami, 1976—; dir. behavior therapy Cedars of Lebanon Hosp. back rehab. program, Miami, 1977-78; dir. Douglas Gardens Outpatient Mental Health Center, Miami, 1979-80; instr. Fla. Internat. U., 1981—. Mem. organizing com. Planned Parenthood Dade County. Mem. Am. Psychol. Assn., Fla. Psychol. Assn., Internat. Assn. Study of Pain, Am. Assn. Marriage and Family Therapists, Nat. Council Family Relations, Dade Assn. Marriage and Family Therapy (treas.), South Fla. Behaviorist Soc. Republican. Jewish. Home: 1232 Palermo Ave Coral Gables FL 33134 Office: 151 NE 52d St Miami FL 33125 also 1295 NW 14th St Suite G Miami FL 33125 also 470 Biltmore Way Coral Gables FL 33134

HIRSCH, MICHELLE LINDA, psychiatrist; b. N.Y.C., June 12, 1947; d. Eli and Molly (Kinsler) H.; B.S. cum laude, CCNY, 1968; M.D., Upstate Med. Sch., Syracuse, N.Y., 1973; 2 children. Intern, Westchester div. N.Y. Med. Coll., 1974-75; resident in psychiatry, N.Y. State Psychiat. Inst., N.Y.C., 1975-79; fellow in child psychiatry Columbia-Presbyn. Hosp., 1978-80; asst. clin. prof. psychiatry Columbia U., N.Y.C., 1980—; staff Columbia-Presbyterian Hosp.; researcher, instr. U. Chgo., 1967-68. Diplomate Am. Bd. Psychiatry and Neurology. Mem. AMA, Am. Women's Med. Assn., Am. Psychiat. Assn., Am. Acad. Child Psychiatry, Phi Beta Kappa. Speaker profl. confs. in field. Office: 30 Lincoln Plaza New York NY 10023

HIRSCHFELD, MARIE GIFFORD, home economist; b. Schenectady, Aug. 24, 1937; d. Carl W. and Edna Gray (Pearce) G.; B.S., SUNY, Plattsburgh, 1960; m. Robert Hirschfeld, Apr. 15, 1960; children—Alfred, Robin, Michael. Tchr. home econs. Woodland Jr. High Sch., East Meadow, L.I., 1960-61; tchr. home econs. Robbinsdale Sch. Dist., Mpls., 1968-70; home economist Heublein, Inc., Hartford, Conn., 1972—; cons. Lender's Bagel Bakery; Internat. Silver Co. Mem. Am. Home Econs. Assn., Home Economists in Bus. Episcopalian (altar guild, women's club). Home: 330 Sir Walter Dr Cheshire CT 06410 Office: 430 New Park Hartford CT 06101

HIRSCHFELD, SUE ELLEN, educator; b. Ossining, N.Y., Jan. 12, 1941; d. Ira Bertram and Helen Caroline (Rieser) Hirschfeld; B.S., U. Fla., 1963, M.S. (teaching asst.), 1965; Ph.D., U. Calif., Berkeley, 1971. Preparator, illustrator Fla. State Mus., Gainesville, 1959-61, 62-63; engring. aide computer III, Boeing Aircraft Co., Seattle, 1961; illustrator biol. sci. curriculum study Am. Inst. Biol. Scis., Boulder, summer 1960; faculty Calif. State U., Hayward, 1970—, now prof. geol. scis.; cons. geology, lectr. Calif. State U. grantee, 1975, 78. Mem. Assn. Women Geoscientists (organizer, nat. sec. 1979-80), AAAS, Soc. Vertebrate Paleontologists, Paleontol. Soc., Biosystematists, Geol. Soc. Am., Soc. Econ. Geologists and Paleontologists, Internat. Paleontol. Assn., Sigma Xi. Contbr. articles to profl. jours. Office: Dept Geol Sci Calif State Univ Hayward CA 94542

HIRSH, JOYCE APELIAN, banker; b. Paterson, N.J., Sept. 12, 1943; d. Samuel Apelian and Evelyn (Kordja) Orr; B.A., Vassar Coll., 1965; M.A., Columbia U., 1966; M.B.A., Fordham U., 1974; m. Jerome E. Hirsch, Aug. 7, 1966; children—Paul S., Alison Bick. Investment specialist Citibank NA, N.Y.C., 1966-76, manpower planning officer, 1976-77, v.p. ops., 1978-79, v.p., dept. head pvt. banking and investment div., 1979—. Mem. fin. com. Jr. League of Scarsdale, 1982-83. Chartered fin. analyst. Mem. Nat. Assn. Bank Women (pres. chpt. 1982-83). Inst. Chartered Fin. Analysts, N.Y. Soc. Fin. Analysts, Fin. Analyst Fedn., Am. Mgmt. Assn. Home: 64 Walworth Ave Scarsdale NY 10583 Office: 153 E 53d St New York NY 10043

HIRSON, ESTELLE, educator; b. Bayonne, N.J.,; d. Morris and Bertha (Rubinstein) H.; tchr. credential UCLA; B.E., San Francisco State Coll.; student U. So. Calif., summers. Tchr., High St. Homes Sch., Oakland Calif., 1949-54, Prescott Sch., 1955-60, Ralph Bunche Sch., 1960-66, Lockwood Sch., 1966—; owner Puzzle-Gram Co., Los Angeles, 1946-49; pres. Major Automobile Co. Mem. NEA, Calif., Oakland, Los Angeles tchrs. assns., Sigma Delta Tau, Mt. Sinai-Duarte Nat. Med. Center (life mem.; parliamentarian, dir. 1946-50). Democrat. Mem. Order Easter Star, Masons Women's Assn. (v.p. Los Angeles 1982). Home: 8670 Burton Way Los Angeles CA 90048

HIRST, WILMA ELIZABETH, psychologist; b. Shenandoah, Iowa; d. James H. and Lena (Donahue) Ellis; A.B. in Elementary Edn., Colo. State Coll., 1948, Ed.D. in Ednl. Psychology, 1954; M.A. in Psychology, U. Wyo., 1951; m. Clyde Henry Hirst (dec. 1969); 1 dau., Donna (Mrs. Alan R. Goss). Elementary tchr., Cheyenne, Wyo., 1945-49, remedial reading instr., 1949-54; asso. prof. edn., dir. campus sch. Neb. State Tchrs. Coll., Kearney, 1954-56; sch. psychologist, head dept. spl. edn. Cheyenne (Wyo.) pub. schs., 1956-57, sch. psychologist, guidance coordinator, 1957-66; dir. div. of research, pub. relations, Cheyenne Schs., 1966-71; prin. investigator Coop. Research Study, U.S. Office Edn. project, dir. div. research and spl. projects, 1971-74; dir. research, spl. projects, also pupil personnel Laramie County Sch. Dist. 1, 1974—. Vis. asst. prof. U. So. Calif., summer 1957, Omaha U., summer 1958; vis. lectr. U. Okla., summers 1959, 60, U. Nebr., summer 1961, U. Wyo., 1962, summer, 1964; extension asso. prof., Kabul, Afghanistan, 1970, Goiania, Brazil, 1974. Mem. Wyo. Bd. Psychology Examiners, 1965-74, sec.-treas., 1965-66, vice chmn., 1968-73; mem. adv. council div. exceptional children Wyo. Dept. Edn., 1974—; mem. adv. bd. Cheyenne Transit Devel. Program, 1975-77; participant Russian seminar Internat. Fedn. Press Women, 1973, Kent State Comparative Edn. Seminar, South Africa, 1975. Mem. speakers bur., local mental health orgn.; active Little Theatre, 1936-70, Girl Scout Leaders Assn., 1943-50; mem., past chmn. bd. social devel. Cheyenne Model Cities; mem. S.E. Wyo. Mental Health Bd., 1968-69; v.p., bd. dirs. Wyo. Mental Health Assn.; bd. dirs. Wyo. Children's Home Soc., treas., 1977—; mem. exec. com. Wyo. Partners of Ams., 1973-78; mem. adv. bd. Stride Learning Center, 1975-77; elder 1st Presbyterian Ch., Cheyenne, 1978—; bd. dirs. Goodwill Industries Wyo., 1978—, chmn., 1981-82; mem. Friendship Force to Honduras, summer 1979, Child Protection Team, Laramie, County; co-chmn. Tech. Adv. Group Wyo. Dept. Edn., 1982—. Recipient Woman of Year award Cheyenne Bus. and Profl. Women's Club, 1974. Diplomate Am. Bd. Profl. Psychology. Fellow Internat. Council Psychologists (regional chair 1981—); mem. Am. Assn. State Psychology Bds. (sec.-treas. 1970-74), Nat. Fedn. Press Women (dir. 1979—), Wyo. Press Women, AAUP, Wyo. Psychol. Assn. (state sec.-treas. 1958-60, pres. 1962-63, exec. bd.) Am. Personnel and Guidance Assn., NEA (life mem.; mem. seminar People's Republic China 1978), AAUW, Assn. Supervision and Curriculum Devel., Cheyenne Assn. Prin. and Spl. Personnel (pres. 1964-65), Am. Assn. Sch. Adminstrs., Laramie County Council Social Agys. (sec.-treas. 1962), Nat. Assn. Gifted Children (state membership chmn., pres.), Internat. Platform Assn., Am. Ednl. Research Assn., DAR (chpt. vice regent 1976—), Psi Chi, Kappa Delta Pi, Pi Lambda Theta, Alpha Delta Kappa (pres. 1965-66). Mem. Order Eastern Star, Daus. of Nile. Club: Zonta (pres. Cheyenne 1965-66, dist. treas. 1974—). Author: Know Your School Psychologist, 1963; Effective Psychology for School Administrators, 1980; Contbr. articles to profl. jours. Home: 3458 Green Valley Rd Cheyenne WY 82001 Office: Sch Adminstrn Bldg Cheyenne WY 82001

HIRT, JANET ROSE, educator; b. Meadville, Pa., Mar. 14, 1942; d. Ira George and Gladys Gertrude (McLaren) H.; B.A., Eastern Coll., St. David's Pa., 1964; M.A. in English, Allegheny Coll., Meadville, Pa., 1969; M.A. in Counseling, Villanova (Pa.) U., 1973; M.S. in L.S., Drexel U., Phila., 1977; postgrad. Oxford U., 1970, Sussex U., 1977. Copy editor Am. Bapt. Bd. Publs., Valley Forge, Pa., 1964; tchr. English, Springfield (Pa.) High Sch., 1964-73, 76—, counselor, 1973-75. Cert. in comprehensive English, secondary sch. guidance, library sci., Pa. Mem. ALA, Modern Lang. Assn., Nat. Council Tchrs. of English (life), NEA, Pa. Edn. Assn., Springfield Edn. Assn., AAUW, Buten Mus. Wedgwood (life), English Speaking Union, Wedgwood Collectors Soc. (charter). Home: Aronimink Arms Drexel Hill PA 19026 Office: Springfield High School 49 W Leamy Ave Springfield PA 19064

HIRT-KRAVETSKY, PATRICIA CAROL, fin. exec.; b. Jersey City, Apr. 16, 1948; d. Harold James and Gladys (Nitsch) Hirt; B.A., Upsala Coll., 1969; advanced cert. Am. Inst. Banking, 1973; M.B.A., Fairleigh Dickinson U., 1974. Asst. treas. Bank of N.Y., N.Y.C., 1975-77, asst. v.p., 1977-79, v.p., 1979-80; investment broker Garvin Guybutler, N.Y.C., 1980—. Mem. Fin. Women's Assn. Clubs: Binghamton Racquet, Order Eastern Star. Home: 515 Forest Ct Rivervale NJ 07675 Office: 120 Broadway New York NY 10005

HITCHENS, LINDA SUE, import-export co. exec.; b. Milford, Del., Dec. 20, 1949; d. Norris T. and Grace W. (Jones) H.; B.S., U. Del., 1972; J.D. cum laude Loyola U., Los Angeles, 1982. Flight attendant Delta Air Lines, Atlanta, 1972-78; pres. Hitch Oriental Imports, Los Angeles, 1976—. Mem. Am. Bar Assn. Republican. Miss Del. in Miss Am. Pageant, 1970.

HITE, CATHARINE LEAVEY, orch. mgr.; b. Boston, Oct. 1, 1924; d. Edmond Harrison and Ruth Farrington Leavey; B.A., Coll. William and Mary, 1945; m. Robert Atkinson Hite, Aug. 28, 1948; children—Charles Harrison, Patricia Hite Rogers, Catharine Hite Dunn. Restoration guide Williamsburg Restoration, 1944-45; asst. edn. dept. Honolulu Acad. Arts, 1945-46; sec., tour guide edn. dept. office chief curator Nat. Gallery Art, 1946-48; opera liason/coordinator Honolulu Symphony, 1972-73, asst. to gen. mgr., 1973-75, community devel. dir./opera coordinator, 1975-77, dir. ops./opera prodn. coordinator, 1977-79, orch. mgr., 1979—, mem. exec. com., 1965-69, pres. women's assn., 1965-66; com. chmn., opera assn. chmn. Hawaii Opera Theatre, 1966-69. Mem. W. R. Farrington Scholarship Com., 1977-82; mem. community arts panel State Found. Culture and the Arts, 1982. Phi Beta Kappa. Episcopalian. Office: 1000 Bishop St Honolulu HI 96813

HITE, SHERE D., social scientist, author; b. St. Joseph, Mo., Nov. 2, 1942; B.A. cum laude in History, U. Fla., 1964, M.A., 1966; postgrad. Columbia U., 1967-68. Dir., Hite Research Internat., N.Y.C., 1972—; lectr. field women's rights, intellectual history, sexual instns. Named one of Am.'s 25 most influential women World Almanac, 1978. Mem. NOW, Women's History Assn., Women for Freedom of Press, Met. Opera Guild. Author and researcher: Sexual Honesty, By Women For Women, 1974; The Hite Report: A Nationwide Study of Female Sexuality, 1976; The Hite Report on Male Sexuality, 1981. Office: PO Box 5282 FDR Station New York NY 10022

HITTENBERGER, TINA-LAURA, health aids co. exec.; b. San Francisco, Apr. 16, 1950; d. Herman Carl and Janiece Adele (Turner) H.; B.A. in Art magna cum laude, Colo. Coll., 1971; M.B.A., Golden Gate U., San Francisco, 1980. With Hittenbergers, orthotic and prosthetic service, San Francisco, 1972—, v.p., 1975—; profl. relations, program devel. Los Medicos Voladores, 1976; instr. U. Calif. extension program; illustrator Community Workshop, Projects Team, Growing Older, Inc.; cons., designer, lectr. in field. Ford Found. grantee, 1971. Mem. Am. Acad. Orthotists and Prosthetists, Am. Orthotic and Prosthetic Assn., Nat. Ski Patrol, Phi Beta Kappa, Delta Gamma. Presbyterian. Pub.: Orthotic-Prosthetic Reference Guide, 1976; illustrator Once Upon An Organization, 1980; sculpture rep. atrium of library Colo. Coll.; one-woman exhbn. Colorado Springs Fine Arts Center, 1972. Office: 1117 Market St San Francisco CA 94103

HIVELY, EVELYN THOMAS HELMICK, coll ofcl.; b. McKeesport, Pa., July 20, 1928; s. Samuel Blair and Evelyn (Descaunets) Thomas; B.S. (Buhl Found. scholar 1946-50, Andrew Carnegie scholar 1948-50), Carnegie Mellon U., 1950; M.A., U. Miami, 1964, Ph.D., 1969; m. Robert William Hively, June 19, 1972; children—Jon Sommer Helmick, Jennifer Thomas Helmick, Melinda Blair Helmick. Tchr. French and English, Pub. Schs., New Wilmington, Pa., 1950-52; instr. humanities U. Miami, 1964-69, asst. prof., 1969-73, asso. prof. English, 1973-77, dir. Am. studies, 1975-77; acad. dean Salem Coll., Winston-Salem, N.C., 1977-81; v.p. acad. affairs Western Mont. Coll., Dillon, 1982—. Rockefeller Found. fellow, 1963-64. Mem. MLA, Am. Studies Assn., Fla. Coll. English Assn. Contbr. articles to profl. jours. Home: 620 Arizona St Dillon MT 59725 Office: Western Mont Coll Dillon MT 59725

HIXENBAUGH, PAULA JEANNETTE, psychologist; b. Boston, Aug. 19, 1948; d. Walter Henry and Jeannette (Rockwood) H.; B.S., Bridgewater State Coll., 1970; M.A., Tchrs. Coll., Columbia U., 1974, M.Ed., 1976, M.Phil., 1977, Ph.D., 1977; m. Stuart Robert Carter, May 27, 1979; children— Adam Milroy, Christine. Teaching asst. Tchrs. Coll., Columbia U., N.Y.C., 1975-77, research asst., 1976-77; psychologist Middletown (N.J.) Public Schs., 1977-80; lectr. Roehampton Inst., London, 1980—; speaker various parent groups and ednl. groups. NIMH training grantee, 1974-77. Mem. Am. Psychol. Assn., Nat. Assn. Sch. Psychologists, N.J. Psychol. Assn., N.J. Assn. Sch. Psychologists, Monmouth-Ocean County Psychol. Assn. Office: Digby Stuart College Roehampton Inst London SW15 England

HIXON, CHRISTINE PRITCHARD, counselor; b. Wilcox County, Ala., May 13, 1918; d. Hoy Ellsworth and Rosa M. (Bridges) Pritchard; B.S., U. Ala., 1942; M.S., Samford U., 1967; advanced degree and AA cert. U. Ala., Birmingham, 1976; m. Daniel Alexander Hixon, June 14, 1942; children—Daniel Alexander, Charlotte Lisa Hixon Taylor. Tchr. public high schs. Alabama county systems, 1940-45, Birmingham (Ala.) Edn. Systems, 1962-80; guidance counselor Ramsay High Sch., Birmingham, 1967-72, Homewood (Ala.) High Sch., 1972-80; pvt. practice counseling, Birmingham, 1980—; cons. So. Assn. Accreditation, Birmingham, 1975. Student oratory sponsor VFW, Birmingham, 1970-72; student essay competition sponsor Freedom Found., Valley Forge, Pa., 1977-80; active Hoover Service Club, Birmingham; mem. ch. planning com., personnel com. Green Valley Baptist Ch., Birmingham, 1979—. Recipient cert. VFW, 1970, service recognition Am. Youth, 1981. Mem. Ala. Poetry Soc., Ala. Writers Conclave, Kappa Delta Pi (sec., scholarship chmn.). Contbr. poetry to Sampler. Home: 1827 Paulette Dr Birmingham AL 35226

HIXSON, SHEILA ELLIS, state legislator; b. L'Anse, Mich., Feb. 9, 1933; d. Peter Roy and Ruth Marie (Scully) Ellis; grad. No. State Mich. Tchrs. Coll.; divorced; children—Denise, Lynne, Andrew, Todd. Legal aide Democratic Nat. Com.; cons. Blue Shield, ADA; now mem. Md. Ho. of Dels.; cons., v.p. S & H Assocs. Mem. Md. Dem. Central Com., 1974-76; chmn. Bi-County Legis. Com.; vice chmn. State Hospice Commn.; chmn. subcom Natural Death Act. Mem. Order Women Legislators, Women's Nat. Dem. Club, Women's Health on Wed., Plowmen and Fishmen. Lutheran. Office: 1101 17th St Washington DC 20036

HIZA, BEVERLY DIANE, educator, civic worker; b. Sheridan, Wyo., Nov. 12, 1930; d. David Durward and Margaret Julia (Walters) Masters; B.A., U. Colo., 1952, postgrad., 1953; postgrad. Mary Washington Coll., Fredericksburg, Va., 1953-54; m. Michael J. Hiza, Jr., June 7, 1953; children—Michael David, Margaret Mary Hiza Redsteer. Tchr. elem. schs., Denver, 1952-53, tchr. English as a second lang., Boulder, 1976-80; Registered lobbyist Colo. State Legislature, 1969-74. Bd. dirs. LWV Boulder, 1962-69; bd. dirs. LWV Colo., 1969-75, pres., 1973-75, chmn. employment and tng. com., 1978—; mem. Boulder Citizens Com. for Community Improvement, 1969-71, vice chmn., 1969-70; bd. dirs. Citizens Com. on Colo. Legislature, 1973-74; mem. Colo. Balance of State Adv. Council on Employment and Tng., 1974—, chmn., 1977-79; mem. Colo. State Employment and Tng. Council, 1974—, exec. council, 1976-79, 82—, chmn. program rev. com. 1982—; trustee Boulder County Mental Health Found., 1980—, chmn., 1982—; bd. dirs. Boulder County Mental Health Assn., 1974-78, pres., 1975-76; mem. Mountain Bell Consumer Panel, 1981—; Recipient Colo. Excellence in Govt.-Frank E. Johnson Meml. award, 1975. Mem. Colo. Assn. Continuing Adult Edn., Handweavers Guild Boulder, Kappa Delta. Episcopalian. Home: 375 Auburn St Boulder CO 80303

HIZONA, MINA JOY VERDAN, obstetrician, gynecologist; b. Lucena City, Philippines; came to U.S., 1966; d. Restituto Mac and Regina Ramos (Luna) Verdan; A.A., Philippine Union Coll., 1959; M.D., Far Eastern U., 1965; m. Drad F. Hizona, Nov. 6, 1970; 1 son, James Merrill. Rotating intern Waltham (Mass.) Hosp., 1966-67; resident in ob-gyn Boston Lying-in Hosp. for Women, 1968-69; chief resident ob-gyn Wesson Women's Hosp., 1969-70; house officer dept. ob-gyn Cambridge (Mass.) City Hosp., 1971-73; clinic physician Dorchester Health Center and Charles Circle Clinic, Boston, 1973-75, Mountain Comprehensive Health Center, Whitesburg, Ky., 1975-76; chief dept. ob-gyn Whitesburg Appalachian Regional Hosp., 1975-79; practice medicine specializing in ob-gyn, Whitesburg, 1976-79, Georgetown, Ky., 1979-80, Indpls., 1980—. Baptist. Address: Stonegate Profl Plaza 46 Stonegate Dr Indianapolis IN 46127

HJERMSTAD, DIANE DYKMAN, mktg. exec.; b. White Plains, N.Y., May 28, 1933; d. Harry Trowbridge and Sallie (Dodson) Dykman; B.A., U. Mo., Kansas City, 1955; M.A. in L.S., Rosary Coll., River Forest, Ill., 1972; m. Sigurd Karl Hjermstad, Sept. 15, 1951; children—Ross Edward, Ruth Emily. Engaged in market research, 1965-70; reference librarian adult services Northbrook (Ill.) Public Library, 1972-74; head librarian Ela Area Public Library Dist., Lake Zurich, Ill., 1974-77; dir. info. central Direct Mail Mktg. Assn., N.Y.C., 1978-79, dir. ops., 1979-80; account exec. MICOR, N.Y.C., 1980-82; account exec. Dial Am. Mktg., Teaneck, N.J., 1982—; mem. Northbrook Library Bd., 1969-72. Mem. Northbrook Caucus Com., 1968-69; 2d reader Northbrook Christian Sci. Ch., 1972-75 program chmn. Women's Direct Response Group, 1980—. Mem. ALA Spl. Library Assn., Am. Soc. Assn. Execs., N.Y. Soc. Assn. Execs., Art Inst. Chgo., Direct Mail Mktg. Assn. (membership chmn. telephone mktg. council 1980—). Republican. Club: Hundred Million. Author book revs. Home: 75 Skyline Dr Millington NJ 07946 Office: 32 W 40th St Suite 2J New York NY 10018

HOADLEY, IRENE BRADEN, librarian; b. Hondo, Tex., Sept. 26, 1938; d. Andrew H. and Theresa L. (Leobold) Braden; B.A., U. Tex., 1960; M.A. in L.S., U. Mich., 1961, Ph.D., 1967; M.A., Kans. State U., 1965; m. Edward E. Hoadley, Feb. 21, 1970. Cataloger, Sam Houston State Tchrs. Coll. Library, 1961-62; head circulation dept. Kans. State U. Library, 1962-64; grad. asst. U. Mich., 1964-66; asst. dir. libraries and adminstrv. services Ohio State U. Libraries, 1973-74; dir. libraries Tex. A&M U. Library, 1974—; mem. steering com. Gov. Ohio Conf. Library and Info. Services, 1973-74; exec. bd. AMIGOS Inc., 1975-78; bd. dirs. Houston Area Research Library Consortium, 1978—, pres., 1980—; cons., lectr., adviser in field. Recipient Library Lit. award Scarecrow Press, 1971; named Disting. Alumnus, U. Mich. Sch. Library Sci., 1976. Mem. ALA, Assn. Research Libraries, Tex. Library Assn., U. Mich. Sch. Library Sci. Alumni Assn. Republican. Roman Catholic. Editor: Natural Resources Bibliography, 1970; co-editor: Quantitative Methods in Librarianship: Standards, Research, Management, 1972; editorial bd. Protean: Adminstrn., Systems, Management in Libraries, 1971-72. Home: Route 5 Box 1048 College Station TX 77840 Office: TEX A&M Library College Station TX 77843

HOAG, KATHARINE HARRIS, educator; b. Humacao, P.R., June 2, 1906; d. Van Alen and Edith (Thacher) Harris; m. Gilbert Thomas Hoag, June 25, 1927; children—Katharine Hoag McLean, Margery Hoag Freeman, Elizabeth Hoag Turner. Founder, Little Red Schoolhouse, Amherst (Mass.) Coll., 1933; mem. staff Shellmar Research Lab., Mt. Vernon, Ohio, 1941-44, Consumers Research Co., N.Y.C., 1944-45; instr. remedial reading Temple U., Phila., 1948-51; tchr. remedial reading Haverford (Pa.) Friends' Sch., 1952-68. Haverford Boys Sch., 1952-68; vol. Shanta Bhawan Hosp., Kathmandu, Nepal, 1969-70; lectr. slide shows at schs., colls., orgns., nursing homes, 1956—; tchr. English to Asian refugees Berkeley Adult Sch., 1980—. Author: Exploring Mysterious Kathmandu, 1976. Home: 449 Vassar Ave Berkeley CA 94708

HOAGLAND, PAMELA REDINGTON, ednl. adminstr.; b. Phoenix, June 2, 1937; d. George Appleton and Margaret Tweed (Rae) H.; B.A. with distinction, U. Ariz., 1959, M.Ed., 1965, Ed.D., 1973. Tchr., Tucson Unified Sch. Dist., 1959-73, dir. reading, lang. arts and library services, 1980—; curriculum specialist supr. Pima County Spl. Edn. Coop., Tucson, 1973-76; co-founder, co-dir. Learning Devel. Center, Tucson, 1970-74; pres. Redington Cons. Corp., Tucson, 1980—; lectr. U. Ariz., Tucson, 1965-66, U. Colo., Boulder, 1977, So. Oreg. Coll., Ashland, 1978. Bd. dirs. Behavior Assos., Tucson, 1969—, chmn., 1978-80; mem. adv. bd. Ariz. Right to Read Council, Phoenix, 1976-79, chmn., 1978-80; edn. supr. Grace Episcopal Ch., Tucson, 1965-67; bd. dirs. Tucson Westside Neighborhood Coalition, 1979-81. Recipient Cert. of Recognition, U. Ariz., 1970; Pi Delta Kappa Disting. Lecture Series award Hendrix Coll., Conway, Ark., 1978. Mem. Tucson Edn. Assn. (dir. 1967-73), Nat. Council Tchrs. of English, Internat. Reading Assn., (field cons. 1974—), Assn. Supervision and Curriculum Devel., LWV, Alpha Delta Kappa (chpt. pres. 1965-66), Pi Beta Phi Alumni Assn. Democrat. Episcopalian. Contbr. articles to profl. publs. Office: 2025 E Winsett St Tucson AZ 85719

HOARD, JUNE ELIZABETH (JULIE), eyewear mktg. co. exec.; b. Henderson County, Tex., Mar. 12, 1936; d. C.L. and Gladys Elizabeth (Ruth) Grasham; foster dau. Richard D.A. and Marian (Gray) Russell; student John Robert Powers Finishing Sch., 1957-58, Tex. Christian U., 1965-67, Fla.Internat. U., 1975-76, U. Okla., 1976-77; m. Robert E. Hoard, Oct. 30, 1964; children—Kelly Lynne, Kimberlee, Kevin, Kande. Narrator, audio and fashion modeling NBC-TV, 1954-67; partner June Russell Wigs, Inc., 1962-67; editor Roadrunner mag., Red Ball of Dallas, 1967-70; public relations tng. dir. Diplomat Hotel, Hollywood, Fla., 1970-76, Fairmont Hotel, Dallas, 1969-70; regional sales mgr. Rainbow Optics, N.Y.C., 1980—; hon. community prof. Sch. Hotel, Food and Travel Services, Fla. Internat. U., 1976. Okla. chairperson Ralph Nadar's campaign, 1976; charter mem. bd. dirs. Okla. Med. Research Council, Oklahoma City, 1982—; mem. Republican Presdl. Task Force, 1982—. Named Okla. Mother of Yr., U. Okla., 1977. Mem. Am. Profl. and Bus. Women (pres. chpt. 1967-68), Nat. Assn. Female Execs., Am. Women in Radio and TV, Theta Sigma Chi. Methodist. Club: U. Okla. Faculty. Home: 800 Firewheel Trail Ft Worth TX 76112

HOBAUGH, BEVERLY GAYLE, brokerage co. exec.; b. Long Beach, Calif., Apr. 10, 1941; d. Frank Edward and Thelma Dolorus (Knuppe) H.; B.A. in Sociology, Calif. State U., Fullerton, 1971; postgrad. in bus. Pepperdine U. Probation and group counselor Orange County Juvenile Hall, 1968; credit reporter Dun & Bradstreet, 1971, agy. sales rep., 1971-72; sec., mng. dir., v.p., dir. S&W Engineered Products, Anaheim, Calif., 1972-82; account exec. Merrill Lynch, Pierce, Fenner & Smith, Los Angeles, 1982—; dir. Ronson Equities Calif. Corp. Mem. Exec. Women, NOW. Democrat. Office: 523 W 6th St Los Angeles CA 90017

HOBBS, JOAN MCLEAN, mgmt. cons.; b. Detroit, Oct. 12, 1943; d. William Hector and Ruth Ellen McLean; student Albion Coll., 1961-63; B.A., Mich. State U., 1964. Clearing asst., office of sec. Fed. Res. Bd., Washington, 1965-66, supr. office of sec., 1966-71, adminstrv. asst., office of mng. dir. for ops., 1971-77, exec. asst. to staff dir. for mgmt., 1977-79; pvt. practice mgmt. cons., Houston, 1979—. Recipient spl. achievement award for profl. performance Fed. Res. Bd., 1978. Mem. Nat. Assn. Exec. Women. Methodist. Home and Office: 2929 Buffalo Speedway Houston TX 77098

HOBBS, MARIAN LAURETTA, educator; b. Kansas City, Kans., May 1, 1920; d. Frank Burley and Mary (Olson) H.; A.A., Kansas City (Kans.) Jr. Coll., 1940; diploma acctg., LaSalle Extension U., 1954, law student, 1954-56; B.S., U. Mo., Kansas City, 1960, M.S., 1967. Bacteriology technician Jensen-Salsbury Labs., Kansas City, Mo., 1940-42, bacteriologist, 1964-66; bacteriology technician Peters Serum Co., Kansas City, Mo., 1942; research asst. Dental Sch., U. Mo., Kansas City, 1942-43; pub. acct. Kansas City, Kans., 1954—; food technologist Rutherford Food Corp., Kansas City, Mo., 1960-63; tchr. biology and chemistry Sumner Acad., Kansas City, Kans., 1966—; tchr. indsl. prodn. of enzymes U. Mo., Kansas City, 1980. Mem. Ft. Leavenworth (Kans.) Officer Retiree Council, 1975—; Officer Retiree Adv. Council to Chief Staff U.S. Army, 1979-83. Served as officer WAC, 1943-46. Recipient Letter of Commendation Signal Security Agy., World War II, Master Sci. Tchr. award U. Mo. chpt. Sigma Xi, 1974; scholar Kansas City Bank Clearing House Assn., 1968. Mem. Am. Soc. Microbiology, AAAS, NEA, Nat. Assn. Biology Tchrs., Nat. Sci. Tchrs. Assn., AAUP, AAUW, Am. Soc. Curriculum Devel., Nat. Parks and Conservations Assn., U. Mo. Kans. City Alumni Assn., Ret. Officers Assn. (chpt. treas. 1958-62), Delta Kappa Gamma (rec. sec. 1978-80, membership chmn. chpt. 1980-82; Internat. scholar 1976-77). Republican. Methodist. Clubs: Women's Aux. of Scandinavian of Greater Kansas City, Woman's Kans. Day. Author articles in field. Patentee flavor test smog filter. Office: Sumner Acad 8th and Oakland Sts Kansas City KS 66101

HOBBS, NILA ALENE, mfg. co. exec.; b. Colorado Springs, Colo., Mar. 11, 1949; d. Harold Carl and Wilma Ella (French) H.; B.S. with high distinction, Colo. State U., 1971, M.B.A., 1973. Systems analyst Colo. div. Eastman Kodak Co., Windsor, 1974-80, sect. supr. systems devel., 1980—. Mem. Am. Prodn. and Inventory Control Soc. Republican. Home: 1037 Parkview Dr Fort Collins CO 80525 Office: DP&SD Bldg C 42 Floor 3 Windsor CO 80551

HOBBS, SONIA AKOL BLANCO, nurse; b. Iloilo City, Philippines, Feb. 3, 1945; d. Antonio R. and Francisca de Tomas (Akol) Blanco; came to U.S., 1969, naturalized, 1977; diploma in Nursing, U. Philippines, 1966; B.S. in Nursing, Central Philippine U., 1968; m. George Ira Hobbs, June 6, 1970 (dec. 1974); 1 son, Christopher Alan (dec. 1982). Pvt. duty nurse, Philippines, 1968-69; exchange visitor nurse Vanderbilt U., Nashville, Tenn., 1969-74; head nurse intensive care unit Meharry Hosp., Nashville, 1974-76; charge nurse intensive care unit Parkview Hosp., Nashville, 1976—. Timawa scholar, 1961-62. Mem. Am., Middle Tenn. heart assns., Am. Assn. Critical Care Nurses. Democrat. Roman Catholic. Home: 480 Sunliner Dr Nashville TN 37209 Office: Parkview Hospital 230 25th Ave N Nashville TN 37203

HOBBY, OVETA CULP (MRS. WILLIAM P. HOBBY), former sec HEW, newspaper publisher; b. Killeen, Tex., Jan. 19, 1905; d. I.W. and Emma (Hoover) Culp; student Mary Hardin Baylor College, L.H.D. (hon.), 1956; L.H.D. (hon.), Bard Coll., 1950, Lafayette Coll., 1954; LL.D. (hon.), Baylor U., Sam Houston State Tchrs. Coll., U. Chattanooga, 1943, Bryant Coll., Ohio Wesleyan U., 1953, Columbia, Smith Coll., Middlebury Coll., 1954, U. Pa., Colby Coll., 1955, Farleigh Dickinson, Western Coll.; D.Litt. (hon.), Colo. Women's Coll., 1947, C. W. Post Coll., 1962; m. William P. Hobby, Feb. 23, 1931 (dec. 1964); children—William, Jessica (Mrs. Henry Catto, Jr.). Parliamentarian, Tex. Ho. of Reps., 1926-31, imcomplete terms 1939, 41; joined Houston Post as research editor, 1931, successively lit. editor, asst. editor, v.p., exec. v.p., editor, 1931-53, editor, pub., 1952-53, pres., editor, 1955-65, chmn. bd., editor, 1965—; dir. Sta. KPRC AM-TV, 1945-53, 55-69, chmn. bd., 1970—; chmn. bd., dir. Channel Two TV Co., 1970—; vice chmn. Channel Five TV, Nashville, Channel Eleven, Meridian, Miss.; chief women's interest sect. War Dept. Bur. Public Relations, 1941-42; apptd. dir. WAAC, 1942, commd. col. AUS, dir. WAC, 1943-45; fed. security adminstr., 1953; sec. HEW, 1953-55. Gov., ARC; nat. vice chmn. Am. Cancer Soc. campaign, 1949; mem. Am. design awards com., mem. nat. com. Am. Mus. Immigration, 1956. Mem. nat. adv. com. Citizens for Eisenhower, 1956; sponsor Clark Sch. for Deaf; mem. Coll. Commn. Diocese of Tex., 1956; trustee Eisenhower Birthplace Meml. Park; mem. President's coms. on Employment Physically Handicapped, Civilian Nat. Honors; trustee Am. Assembly, 1957-66, Eisenhower Exchange fellowship; bd. dirs. Houston Symphony Soc.; mem. SW adv. bd. Inst. Internat. Edn.; mem. Com. of 75, U. Tex., 1958—; mem. So. regional com. Marshall Scholarships, 1957—; mem. Rockefeller Bros. Fund Spl. Studies project. Bd. dirs. Com. for Econ. Devel.; mem. nat. bd. devel. Sam Rayburn Found.; mem. Crusade for Freedom, Inc.; nat. council Eleanor Roosevelt Meml. Found.; trustee Rice U., until 1975, Soc. Rehab. Facially Disfigured. Recipient Disting. Service medal, 1944; Philippine Mil. Merit medal, 1947; Pub. of Yr. award, 1960; Living History award, Research Inst. Am., 1960; Honor award National Jewish Hosp., 1962. Mem. So. Newspapers Pubs. Assn. (pres. 1949), Acad. Tex. (charter), Gamma Alpha Chi (hon. vice chmn.). Episcopalian. Clubs: Houston Country, Bayou, Ramada, Junior League (Houston). Author: Mr. Chairman (parliamentary law textbook), also syndicated column same title. Home: Houston TX Office: Houston Post 4747 Southwest Freeway Houston TX 77001

HOBSON, LAURA ZAMETKIN, author; b. N.Y.C.; d. Michael and Adella (Kean) Zametkin; A.B., Cornell U.; m. Thayer Hobson, July 23, 1930 (div. 1935); children—Michael and Christopher (adopted). Advt. writer, until 1934, except for year as reporter N.Y. Eve. Post; promotion writer Time, Life, Fortune mags., 1934-40, becoming copy chief of all Time, Inc. mag. promotion, then dir. promotion for Time mag.; wrote first short story, 1935, continued spare-time writing short stories, 1935-41; devoted full time to writing, including fiction, daily newspaper columns, 1941-56, promotion cons. Time, Fortune, Sports Illustrated mags., 1956-62; cons. editor Saturday Rev., 1960—; full-time novelist, 1963—. Overseer Coll. of V.I. Mem. Authors League Am. (nat. council 1947-75), P.E.N., A.C.L.U. Club: Regency Whist. Author: A Dog of His Own (juvenile), 1941; The Trespassers, 1943; Gentleman's Agreement, 1947 (made into motion picture, winning Acad. Award as best picture of 1947); The Other Father, 1950; The Celebrity, 1951; First Papers (Lit. Guild main selection), 1964; I'm Going to Have a Baby (juvenile), 1967; The Tenth Month (also TV movie), 1971; Consenting Adult (alt. selection Lit. Guild and other book clubs), 1975; Over and Above, 1979; Untold Millions, 1982. Office: care Harper & Row 10 E 53d St New York NY 10022 *

HOBSON, THERESA R. KELLY, med. services co. exec.; b. Utica, N.Y., Feb. 14, 1946; d. Thomas Vincent and Emily (Herubin) Kelly; student Utica Sch. Nursing, 1965; A.S., Monroe Community Coll., 1978; B.S., Rochester Inst. Tech., 1981; m. Robert J. Hobson, Jan. 8, 1966; children—Leahanne, Denise. Personnel coordinator Upjohn Health Care Services, Rochester, N.Y., 1972-77, service dir., 1977-78; mgr. nat. patient aid div. George Heisel Corp., Rochester, 1978-80, asst. gen. mgr., 1980—. Mem. Nat. Assn. Female Execs., Nat. Affiliation Durable Med. Equipment Cos., Rochester Inst. Tech. Alumni, Monroe Community Coll. Alumni. Club: St. Agnes High Sch. Parents. Home: 1291 Crittenden Rd Rochester NY 14623 Office: 177 University Ave Rochester NY 14605

HOBSON, VIRGINIA PRINCE CALVIN, bookstore owner, educator; b. Birmingham, Ala.; d. Earle Pegram and Virginia (Robinson) Calvin; student Sullins Coll., 1941-43, George Peabody Coll., 1946-48, postgrad., 1979—; A.B., Vanderbilt U., 1948, M.S., 1979; postgrad. Memphis State U., 1965, U. North Fla., 1982, Jacksonville U., 1981-82; m. John L. Hobson, Sept. 9, 1950 (div. 1974); children—John Lewis, Ginger. Head gen. cargo for Brit. Ministry, N.Y. Central RR., N.Y.C., 1944; with United Air Lines, N.Y.C., 1945; tchr. Caldwell Sch., Nashville, 1948-50, Venetia Sch., Jacksonville, Fla., 1950-51, Hutchison Sch., Memphis, 1959-65; owner, operator Lee St. Book and Art Shops, Brunswick, Ga., 1970-74, Golden Isles Book Distbr., Brunswick, 1970-74; antiquarian bookman, 1970—; mgr., buyer B. Dalton, Bookseller, Mobile, Ala., 1974-78; dir. studies, head upper sch., English tchr. Bartram Sch., Jacksonville, 1981—. Trustee Sullins Coll., 1965, bd. visitors, 1965-70; exec. bd. dirs. Jr. League Memphis, 1956-60, chmn. publicity, 1959; pres. YWCA Glynn County (Ga.), 1968, Glynn County Med. Aux., 1970; exec. bd. Women's Aux. Med. Soc. Ga., 1968-70, also state v.p. and historian; exec. bd. Women of Ch., St. Paul's Episcopal Ch., Mobile, 1975-76; mem. evaluation com. Jacksonville Episc. High Sch.; head counselor Camp Nakanawa, Crossville, Tenn., 1981. Mem. English Speaking Union, MLA, So. Renaissance Assn., Am. Booksellers Assn., Antiquarian Bookmen, Mid-S. Sullins Alumnae Assn. (pres. 1964), Ala., Tenn. hist. assns., Am. Assn. State and Local History, Nat. Trust Historic Preservation, Ala. Allied Arts Council, Assn. Preservation Tenn. Antiquities, Smithsonian Assos., Stoneridge Assn. (dir.), Christian Booksellers Assn., Daus. Am. Colonists (v.p. Midway, Ga. 1965-75), Jr. League Nashville, Friends Museum City Mobile, Sullins Coll. Alumnae Assn., Cheekwood Assn., Phi Delta Kappa. Clubs: Pilot, Univ. Memphis. Home: 5811 Atlantic Blvd #181 Jacksonville FL 32207

HOCHHEIMER, LAURA, musician; b. Worms, Germany, Apr. 18, 1933; came to U.S., 1938, naturalized, 1947; d. Otto and Trude Hochheimer; student Beaver Coll., 1951-52; B.M., Eastman Sch. Music, 1955; M.F.A., Ohio U., 1957; Ph.D., Ind. U., 1966. Tchr. strings and vocal music, conductor Bainbridge (N.Y.) High Sch., Jr. High Sch. Orchs., Bainbridge Elem. and Bainbridge High Sch., 1957-58; tchr. gen. music Chgo. Public Schs., tchr. mentally retarded and physically handicapped children Spalding Sch. for Handicapped Children, 1958-64; mem. Chgo. Chamber Orch., Northwestern U. Chamber Orch., Roosevelt U. Symphony, 1958-64; grad. asst. in violin Ind. U., Bloomington, tchr. strings and orch. Ind. U. Lab. Sch., 1964-66; tchr. music West Liberty (W.Va.) State Coll., 1968-70; vis. asst. prof. music U. B.C., Vancouver, 1970-71; tchr. music edn. Towson State Coll., 1971-73; asst. prof. music edn. U. Cin., 1973-76; asso. prof. music James Madison U., Harrisonburg, Va., 1976-81; asst. prof. music edn. Cin. Coll. Conservatory Music, mem. grad. faculty U. Cin., 1973-76; asso. prof. music Clemson (S.C.) U., 1981—; violinist solo, chamber music and symphony orchs; cons. music in spl. edn. Orff-Schulwerk and Kodaly approaches in schs. and state convs. throughout U.S. and Can. Recipient George Eastman award Eastman Sch. Music, 1955; Fulbright scholar, Vienna and Salzburg, Austria, 1966-67. Mem. Music Educators Nat. Conf., Am. Orff Schulwerk Assn., Coll. Music Soc., S.C. Music Educators Assn. Author: A Sequential Sourcebook for Elementary School Music, 1980; contbr. articles in field to profl. jours. Office: Strode Tower Box 48 Clemson U Clemson SC 29631

HOCHSTADT, JOY, biochemist, microbiologist; b. N.Y.C., May 6, 1939; d. Julius Louis and Edith (Tabatchnick) Hochstadt; A.B., Barnard Coll., 1960; A.M. in Biol. Scis., Stanford U., 1963; Ph.D. in Microbiology, Georgetown U., 1968; m. Harvey L. Ozer, Feb. 3, 1960; 1 dau., Juliane Natasha Hochstadt-Ozer. Research fellow in devel. biochemistry Stanford U., 1961-62; instr. biology Coll. San Mateo (Calif), 1963; vis. fellow Karolinska Inst., Stockholm, Sweden, 1964-65; research fellow in biol. chemistry Harvard U., 1965-66; teaching asst. in microbiology Georgetown Med. Sch., 1967-68; NIH, USPHS postdoctoral fellow Nat. Heart and Lung Inst., Bethesda, Md., 1968-70; Am. Heart Assn. established investigator, 1970-75; sr. scientist Worcester Found. Exptl. Biology, Shrewsbury, Mass., 1972-76; research prof. N.Y. Med. Coll., Valhalla, 1977-81; dir. div. clin. biochemistry, head cell genetics research lab. Cath. Med. Center, Woodhaven, N.Y., 1981—; USPHS spl. trainee Cold Spring Harbor Lab., 1973; adj. prof. biochemistry Central New Eng. Colls., 1974-75; vis. prof. Weizmann Inst. Sci., Israel, 1976, U. R.I., 1976-77; dir. N.Y. Eldorado, 300 CPN Apts. Corp.; lectr., convener nat. sci. symposia, workshops, confs.; prin. investigator several research grants NIH, NSF; mem. postdoctoral fellowship evaluation panel NSF; mem. cell biology study sect., biomed. scis. rev. com. NIH; chmn. com. to distribute and administer instl. award Am. Cancer Soc., 1973-74. Mem. alumnae council Barnard Coll. Fellow Am. Acad. Microbiology, Am. Inst. Chemists (profl. opportunities com., legis. com.); mem. Am. Heart Assn. (basic sci. council 1970—), Am. Soc. Microbiology (com. on status of women 1970-73, sec. physiology div. 1972-74, nominating com. metabolism and physiology div. 1973—, internat. travel award), Genetics Soc. Am., Am. Soc. Biology Chemists, AAAS, Fedn. Am. Scientists, Am. Assn. Cancer Researchers, Assn. Women in Sci. (affirmative action rep. 1973-75), Profl. Women's Caucus (nat. policy com. 1970-73), N.Y. Acad. Scis., Harvey Soc., Am. Assn. Clin. Scientists, Am. Assn. Clin. Chemists. Contbr. research articles to profl. lit. Mem. editorial bd. Jour. Bacteriology, 1975-80. Discovered that penicillinase is involved in bacterial cell wall metabolism (differentiation to spore-wall in bacillus); elucidated mechanisms of utilization of several purines and pyrimidines in bacteria and animal cells; developed first cell-free vesicle system permitting study of nutrient transport across membranes isolated from mammalian cells in culture; identified that transport changes with growth, quiescence and reactivation involve membrane alterations. Office: Cell Genetics Research Lab CMC St Anthony's Hosp Woodhaven NY

HOCKER, BETTYE ACHOR, nurse, educator; b. Anderson, Ind., May 6, 1922; d. Thomas Riley and Mary Esther (Mills) Achor; R.N., Meth. Hosp., Dallas, 1948; B.S., Ball State U., 1970, M.A., 1976; Ph.D., Columbia Pacific U., 1981; m. Robert James Hocker, Aug. 15, 1971; children—Barbara Cavallo, Tom Pettit. Dir. nurses Shores Retirement Center, Bradenton, Fla., 1979; tchr. Manatee Sch. Bd., Bradenton, 1979-81; prof. health sci. Nova U., Ft. Lauderdale, Fla., 1981; mem. Manatee Opportunity Council, Bradenton, Fla., 1981-82; dir. Sr. Centers of Manatee County, Bradenton, 1981—. Mem. Nat. Council on Aging, 1981-82. Mem. AAUW (hospitality chmn. 1981—), Mem. ARC, Manatee County Sr. League, Am. Fedn. Musicians, NEA, Nat. Council Community Mental Health Centers, Nat. Center Social Gerontology, Eta Sigma Gamma. Republican. Mem. Ch. of God. Address: 4535 Nassau Rd Bradenton FL 33507

HOCKETT, SHERI LYNN, radiologist; b. Cleburne, Tex., Apr. 20, 1953; d. Dale and Rosamond (Prater) Hockett; B.A., So. Meth. U., 1974; M.D., Southwestern Med. Sch., 1978; m. David Alexander Campbell, Apr. 22, 1978. Resident diagnostic radiology St. Paul Hosp., Dallas, 1978-81, chief resident, 1980-81; fellow, 198-82; staff radiologist Meml. Hosp. of Garland (Tex.), and Garland Community Hosp. Diplomate Am. Bd. Radiology. Mem. Am. Assn. Women Radiologists, Am. Coll. Radiology, Radiol. Soc. N.Am., Tex. Radiol. Soc., AMA, Dalls-Ft. Worth Radiol. Soc. Home: 1101 Quail Hollow Garland TX 75043 Office: 2300 Marie Curie Dr Garland TX 75042

HODES, BARBARA, orgn. cons.; b. Chgo., Nov. 30, 1941; d. David and Tybe Zisook; B.S., Northwestern U., 1962; m. Scott Hodes, Dec. 19, 1961 (div. 1977); children—Brian, Valery. Partner Just Causes, cons. not-for-profit orgns., Chgo., 1978—; Chgo. cons. Population Resource Center, 1978-82. Woman's bd. dirs. Mus. Contemporary Art; bd. dirs., vice chmn. Med. Research Inst. Council, Michael Reese Med. Center; bd. dirs., chmn. Midwest Women's Center; trustee Francis W. Parker Sch. Office: Just Causes 1405 N Dearborn Pkwy Chicago IL 60610

HODES, FRANCINE RONNIE, clin. social worker; b. Bklyn., Aug. 31, 1950; d. Leo Louis and Sylvia (Leventhal) Hodes; B.A. magna cum laude in Sociology, SUNY, Buffalo, 1972; M.S.W., U. So. Calif., 1974; M.A., Hebrew Union Coll., 1974; m. Warren B. Churg, Apr. 2, 1978; 1 dau., Jennifer Hodes Churg. Social service cons. Calif. Dept. Health, Los Angeles, 1974-77; dir. social services Hollywood Presbyn. Med. Center, Los Angeles, 1977-78; clin. social worker Pasadena (Calif.) Day Nursery, 1978-80; clin. asso. U. So. Calif. Sch. Social Work, 1979-80, field work instr., 1979-80, clin. social worker Children's Speech and Hearing Center, Van Nuys, Calif., 1979-81; oral commr. Bd. Behavioral Sci. Examiners, Sacramento, 1980—; clin. interviewer Project Step, UCLA Sch. Social Welfare, 1981—. Cert. marriage, family and child counselor, Calif.; lic. clin. social worker, Calif. Mem. Acad. Cert. Social Workers, Nat. Assn. Social Workers, Phi Beta Kappa. Home: 4520 Tyrone Ave Sherman Oaks CA 91423 Office: 900 Hilgard Ave Los Angeles CA 90024

HODES, LINDA STEICHEN, psychotherapist; b. N.Y.C., July 4, 1928; d. William Lon Martin and Mary (Steichen) Martin (Mary S. Calderone); B.A., Vassar Coll., 1948; M.S.W., George Williams Coll., 1976; m. Stuart Taylor Hodes, June 11, 1949 (div. 1974); children—Edward Steichen, Bruce Ira. Dir., host radio talk show Spotlight, Sta. WHOA, San Juan, P.R., 1965-67; exec. dir. Hotline crisis intervention service, Mexico City, 1972-73; pvt. practice psychotherapy, Downers Grove, Ill., 1974—; co-dir. Transactional Analysis Assos., Downers Grove, 1977—; co-dir. New Decision, 1980—; instr. Coll. DuPage, George Williams Coll., 1976-81. Cons., dir. DuPage Women Against Rape, 1975-82. Mem. Nat. Assn. Social Workers, Acad. Cert. Social Workers, Internat. Transactional Analysis Assn. (clin. mem., provisional teaching mem.), Chgo. Transactional Analysis Inst. (pres.), Ill. Soc. Clin. Social Work. Unitarian. Office: 2777 Finley Rd Suite 1 Downers Grove IL 60515

HODGE, ALICE MACNAUGHTON, retail advt. exec.; b. Honolulu, Feb. 11, 1953; d. Malcolm and Winifred (Sperry) MacNaughton; A.B., Stanford U., 1975; postgrad. Foothill Coll., 1975; m. James Blythe Hodge, Jan. 3, 1981; stepchildren—Eric, Terra. With Emporium Capwell Co., San Francisco, 1975—, spl. events, public relations dir., 1979-81, broadcast advt. mgr., 1981—. Mem. public relations com. Vol. Bur., San Francisco, 1980-82; mem. spl. events adv. com. Asso. Merchandising Corp., N.Y.C., 1978-81; mem. public relations com. San Francisco Fine Arts Mus., 1981; area co-chmn. San Francisco chpt. Stanford Ann. Fund, 1975-81; mem. campaign fund adv. com. Sacred Heart Schs., Menlo Park, Calif., 1981-83. Mem. San Francisco Jr. League, San Francisco Women in Advt., Bay Area Exec. Women's Forum, San Francisco Bay Area Publicity Club. Republican. Episcopalian. Club: Commonwealth. Contbr. articles to profl. publs. Home: 3101 Clay St Apt 5 San Francisco CA 94115 Office: 835 Market St San Francisco CA 94103

HODGE, ELAINE KAY, retail exec. b. Denver, Aug. 30, 1950; d. Keith Wallace and Wanda Mary (Yurga) Bland; student U. So. Colo., 1968-70; B.A., Met. State Coll., Denver, 1973; m. Joseph Eugene Hodge, Jan. 22, 1971. With J.C. Penney Co., Denver, 1973—, personnel and office supr., 1980-81, retail mdse. mgr., 1981—. Chmn., United Way Campaign at J.C. Penney, Downtown Denver, 1975-81; vol. dist. probation officer Denver; bd. advs. Distributive Edn. Clubs Am., 1977-78, Outstanding Mcht. award, 1978; asst. instr. self def. for women. Mem. LWV, Nat. Assn. Female Execs., Met. State Coll. Alumni Assn. Home: 1255 Birch St Denver CO 80220 Office: 2580 S Colorado Blvd Denver CO 80222

HODGE, MARY JO (MRS. CHARLES CEDRIC HODGE), health service adminstr.; b. Talladega, Ala., June 15, 1935; d. John Bowling and Martha Allene (Royal) McKinney; B.S., Auburn U., 1956; M.S. (fellow), U. Miss., 1958; D.Pub. Adminstrn., N.Y. U., 1978; m. Charles Cedric Hodge, Aug. 6, 1955; children—Donna, Holly. Psychometrist, Student Guidance Center, Auburn U., 1956-58; psychologist McGuffey Reading Clinic U. Va., Charlottesville, 1962-64, U. Va. Hosp., 1964-65; psychologist St. Lawrence Psychiat. Center, Ogdensburg, N.Y., 1966-73, mental hygiene treatment team leader, 1973-78; dir. Instn. Edn. and Tng., Gowanda Psychiat. Center, Helmuth, N.Y., 1978, dir. treatment services, 1979-81, dir. community services, 1981—. Mem. Am., Eastern psychol. assns., Gerontol. Soc. Am., Northeastern Gerontol. Soc., Acad. Polit. Sci., Assn. Mental Health Adminstrs., N.Y. State Assn. Human Services, Am. Soc. Pub. Adminstrn., Jefferson County Assn. for Mental Health, Assn. for Rural Mental Health, Kappa Delta Pi, Chi Delta Phi, Pi Tau Chi. Home: PO Box 234 Helmuth NY 14079 Office: Gowanda Psychiat Center Helmuth NY 14079

HODGE, TERRY-LINDA, cons. co. exec.; b. N.Y.C., Jan. 20, 1951; d. Charles Whitmore and Rita (Frazier) H.; B.A. in Psychology, U. Conn., 1973, M.S.W. in Med. Social Work (Conn. State fellow), 1976. Dir. Community Sch. Bd. 3, N.Y.C., 1976-77; dir. adminstrv. services Colls. Arts and Scis., U. San Francisco, 1978-81; owner, operator TCL & Assos., San Francisco, 1981—; data supr. Pacific Telephone, Hayward, Calif., 1982—; guest lectr. Bank St. Coll., 1977. Named Outstanding Young Woman Am., U.S. Jaycees, 1980. Mem. Nat. Assn. Black Social Workers, Bay Area Consortium for Quality Health Care, Assn. Univ. Women Adminstrs. Democrat. Methodist.

HODGE, VIRGINIA FRAPS, writer, editor; b. Darby, Pa., Sept. 15, 1940; d. Junius Page and Margaret Adele (Burges) Fraps; student U. Ariz., 1958-62; m. Carle O. Hodge, May 1, 1963 (div. Jan. 1971); 1 dau., Margaret Otis. Reporter, Ariz. Daily Star, Tucson, 1962-65, asst. women's editor, 1965-66, women's editor, 1966-72, asst. mng. editor for features, 1972-76; info. specialist, editor faculty-staff news U. Ariz., Tucson, 1976—. Asst. dir. Western Inst. for Study of Degree-Enhancement Modes. Mem. Ariz. Press Women (1st pl. awards 1965, 67, 70, 71, 78, 81, 82), Nat. Fedn. Press Women, Women in Communications. Democrat. Episcopalian. Home: 1827 E Linden St Tucson AZ 85719 Office: U Ariz Tucson AZ 85721

HODGES, ANN ELIZABETH, mktg. cons.; b. Los Angeles, June 20, 1931; d. Rex Lucien and Bess (Johnson) H.; B.A., Principia Coll., Elsah, Ill., 1951; M.F.A., State U. Iowa, 1955. Sales rep. Eagle Publs., Maywood, Calif., 1974-75; gen. mgr. Systems Engring., Compton, Calif., 1976; sales mgr. Chambers Pub. Service, Santa Fe Springs, Calif., 1978-79; mktg. cons. specializing in motivational recruitment, mktg. plans and mgmt., Long Beach, Calif., 1980—. Mem. Nat. Assn. Female Execs. Office: PO Box 7722 Long Beach CA 90807

HODGES, JUNE VALENTINA, businesswoman; b. Chgo., June 5, 1928; d. Stanley and Rose (Hall) Banez; student Ill. Wesleyan Coll., 1946-47; A.A., Mira Costa Coll.. 1974; m. Earl McGuire, Sept. 18, 1947 (div. 1967); m. H. David Hodges, May 4, 1971; children—Theresa Lynn Stephens, Victoria Lee Biagini, Valerie Jeanne Mellusi. Vice-pres., sec. Electro-Way, Lincoln, Nebr., Omaha, San Diego, 1955-62; regional supr. Parents Inst., San Diego, 1963-65; service rep. Pacific Telephone, San Diego, 1966-67; dist. mgr. Field Enterprises, San Diego, 1968-73; regional dir. Weight Reduction Med. Clinics, San Diego, 1973—; v.p. Pro Ins. Services, San Diego, 1977—; pres. J & J Sales Mgmt., Escondido, Calif., 1979-80. Mem. Am. Mgmt. Assn., Nat. Assn. Female Execs., Asian-Pacific Am. Women's Caucus, Asian Pacific Am. Women of San Diego County (pres. 1979-81), Smithsonian Assos., Zool. Soc. San Diego, Beta Sigma Phi, Democrat. Roman Catholic. Clubs: Fedn. Woman's Clubs; Women's (pres. 1968-69) (Chula Vista, Calif.); Soroptimist Internat. (President's award 1976-77, 81-82, 1st v.p. 1979-81); Toastmasters (club pres. 1980). Office: 4295 Gesner Suite 2A San Diego CA 92117

HODGES, MARGARET MOORE, educator, author; b. Indpls., July 26, 1911; d. Arthur Carlisle and Anna Marie (Mason) Moore; A.B., Vassar Coll., 1932; M.L.S., Carnegie Inst. Tech., 1958; m. Fletcher Hodges, Jr., Sept. 10, 1932; children—Fletcher Hodges, III, Arthur Carlisle, John Andrews. Children's librarian, storyteller Carnegie Library, Pitts., 1953-65; story specialist Pitts. public schs., 1964-68, sta. WQED-TV, Pitts., 1964-68; mem. faculty U. Pitts. Grad. Sch. Library Info. Services, 1964—, prof. library sci., 1975-77, prof. emeritus, 1977—; established Elizabeth Nesbitt Room for children's hist. books U. Pitts. Grad. Sch. Library Info. Services; author numerous juveniles, 1958—, latest being Knight Prisoner, 1976; The High Riders, 1980; The Little Humpbacked Horse, 1980; The Avenger, 1982. Recipient award Pa. Sch. Librarians Assn., 1977; named Disting. Dau. Pa., 1970. Mem ALA, Pa. Library Assn., Beta Phi Mu. Home: 5812 Kentucky Ave Pittsburgh PA 15232 Office: Room 660 LIS Bldg U Pitts Pittsburgh PA 15260

HODGES, V(IVIAN) PAULINE, educator; b. Liberal, Kans., Sept. 20, 1929; d. Paul W. and Dora Dean (Wilson) Arnett; A.B. in English summa cum laude, Okla. Panhandle State U., 1958; M.A. in Secondary Reading and English Edn. summa cum laude, U. Colo., 1973, Ph.D. in Reading summa cum laude, 1977; m. Albert Hodges, Sept. 5, 1947; children—Albert Brent, Mark Eugene. Tchr. English and speech Forgan (Okla.) Public Schs., 1950-66; remedial English tchr. Unified Dist. 480, Liberal, 1966-67; reading tchr. Douglas County High Sch., Castle Rock, Colo., 1970-76; dir. research and devel. Edn. Cons. Assos., Englewood, Colo., 1980-81; asso. prof. Colo. State U., Ft. Collins, 1976—; conf. speaker; curriculum cons.; workshop leader. Mem. Internat. Reading Assn. (dir. Colo. council 1974-77), Colo. Lang. Arts Soc. (pres. 1980-81), Nat. Council Tchrs. of English, Western Writers Am., Am. Fedn. Tchrs. (treas. 1979-80), Phi Delta Kappa (Leadership award). Author: Improving Reading Study Skills, 1979; A Resource Guide to Teaching Reading in the Content Area, 1980; author resource and curriculum guides; editor Jour. Secondary/Adult Reading, 1981; editor: History of Beaver County, Cimarron Territory, 2 vols., 1970; contbr. articles to profl. jours. Office: Dept of Education 200C Colorado State Univ Fort Collins CO 80523

HODGKISS, JUNE ELAINE, businesswoman; b. Scobey, Mont., Apr. 22, 1925; d. Cecil Gerald and Mila Ellen (McKay) Marlenee; grad. Emanuel Hosp. Sch. Nursing, Portland, Oreg., 1946; children—Edwin G., Michael R., Leslie D., Gerald N., Stanley W., Kit W. Staff nurse Silverton (Oreg.) Hosp., 1953-62, supr. maternity dept., 1959-62; intensive care nurse St. Vincent Hosp., Tacoma, 1969, Puyallup (Wash.) Valley Hosp., 1970-73; owner, mgr. Draperies by Delaine, Kailua Kona, Hawaii, 1973—. Chmn., March of Dimes Mothers March, Pierce County, Wash., 1968-72; charter sec. W. Hawaii Youth Council Steering Com. Mem. Kailua Kona C. of C. Club: Soroptimists. Home: 74-5149 Hookolii St Kailua Kona HI 96740 Office: 75-5995 Kuakini Hwy Kailua Kona HI 96740

HODGSON, AURORA SAULO, food scientist; b. Manila, Philippines, Feb. 24, 1950; came to U.S., 1973, naturalized, 1982; d. Serafin Bumanlag and Natividad David (Alfonso) Saulo; B.S. cum laude in Chemistry, Coll. of the Holy Spirit, Philippines, 1971; M.S. in Chemistry, U. Mass., 1977, Ph.D. in Food Sci., 1978. Flavor chemist United Brands Corp. Research and Devel.-Quality Control Labs., Newton, Mass., 1978-81, food processing engr., 1981; food technologist Hunt-Wesson Foods, Inc., Fullerton, Calif., 1981—. Sec., Christian Life Community, Manila, 1968-69, pres., 1969-70. Fulbright Hays grantee, 1973. Mem. Inst. Food Technologists, Am. Chem. Soc. Contbr. in field. Office: 1645 W Valencia Dr Fullerton CA 92634

HODGSON, JACQUELINE LOU, ednl. adminstr.; b. Rocksprings, Wyo., Feb. 3, 1927; d. Louis Ludwig Hodgson and Frances Catherine (Barto) Hodgson Smith; B.S., U. Puget Sound, 1951, M.A., 1952; Ph.D., U. Wis., 1968. Chmn. econs. dept. Universidad de las Americas, Mexico City, 1966-72, chmn. econs. and bus. depts., 1972-73 dean continuing edn. Centro de Estudios Universitarios, adult edn. extension, 1973-81, v.p. instnl. devel. of univ., 1981—, also editor econ. monographs. Fulbright scholar; Earhart Found. scholar. Mem. Northam. Econ. Studies Assn. (v.p.), Am. C. of C. in Mexico (dir.-at-large 1979—), Am. Econ. Assn., Am. Assn. Adult Edn., Assn. Social Econs., Nat. Assn. Continuing Pub. Edn., Alpha Delta Kappa (nat. pres. Mex. 1980-81), Omicron Delta Epsilon (charter mem. Alpha chpt.). Contbr. articles to profl. jours. Home: Carretera San Mateo 13-3 Contadero-Cuajimalpa Mexico DF Mexico Office: Universidad de las Américas AC Hamburgo 250 Mexico DF 06600 Mexico

HODGSON, JANE ELIZABETH, obstetrician and gynecologist; b. Crookston, Minn., Jan. 23, 1915; d. Herbert Heber and Adelaide (Marin) H.; B.S., Carleton Coll., 1934; M.D., U. Minn., 1940, M.S. in Ob-Gyn, 1947; m. Frank W. Quattlebaum, Feb. 22, 1940; children—Gretchen, Nancy. Intern, Jersey City Med. Center, 1939-40, resident internal medicine, 1940-41; fellow ob-gyn Mayo Clinic, 1941-44; practice ob-gyn, St. Paul, 1944-72; med. dir. Preterm Clinic, Washington, 1972-74; mem. staff Charles T. Miller, St. Paul Ramsey hosps.; mem. cons. staff St. Luke's, St. Joseph's, Midway hosps.; asso. prof. ob-gyn U. Minn. Med. Sch.; vis. prof. ob-gyn Al Azhar U. Med. Sch., Cairo, 1979; med. dir. Planned Parenthood Minn., 1980—; tchr. St. Paul Ramsey Hosp. Mem. med. adv. com. Met. Council, 1969-70; chmn. med. adv. bd. St. Paul Planned Parenthood, 1968-72; v.p. No. Assn. Med. Edn., 1960-70; tour of duty on Ship Hope, 1963, 64, 66. Recipient Republican Care award, 1964; WCCO Good Neighbor award 1964; Hope cert. of merit People-to-People Found., 1969; Marshmann S. Wattson award ACLU, 1970; Alumni award Carleton Coll., 1974; Humanitarian award Nat. Abortion Fedn., 1981; named Woman of Year in Professions, YWCA, 1980. Diplomate Am. Bd. Ob-Gyn. Fellow Am. Coll. Ob-Gyn (founding); mem. AMA, So. Minn. Med. Soc. (medal 1952, Bus. and Profl. Woman's award 1958), Minn. (spl. com. to study abortion 1968-69), Ramsey County med. socs., Minn. Soc. Obstetricians and Gynecologists (pres. 1964), Internat. Fertility Assn., St. Paul Surg. Soc. Contbr. articles to med. jours. Home: 1537 N Fisk St Saint Paul MN 55117

HODGSON, MYRA COFER, writer, research analyst; b. Newport News, Va., Oct. 5, 1949; d. Frank M. and Grace (Brelsford) Cofer; student Va. Commonwealth U., 1968-69; B.A., U. Calif., Berkeley, 1972; M.L.S., San Jose State U., 1978; m. Keith O. Hodgson, June 14, 1969. Bookkeeper, corr. Rotary Internat., Zurich, Switzerland, 1972-73; research analyst SRI Internat., Menlo Park, Calif., 1974-78; owner, info. broker Acquire Info., Palo Alto, Calif., 1977-80; research analyst Semiconductor Industry Assn., Cupertino, Calif., 1980—; owner, operator Worden Fraser Pubs., Palo Alto, 1980—. Mem. Spl. Librarians Assn. Author: Cover to Cover: A Guide to San Francisco Bay Area Bookstores, 1980. Office: 605 Cowper St Palo Alto CA 94301

HODNETT, BARBARA MILTON, ednl. counselor; b. Mobile, Ala., Mar. 31, 1942; d. Samuel and Mary Alice (Williams) Milton; student Dillard U., 1960-62; B.A., U. S.Ala., 1974; M.A. (Tchr. Corps fellow), Oakland U., 1976; m. Robert O. Hodnett, Sept. 2, 1967; 1 dau., Maki Danielle. Psychologist asst. Ala. Dept. Mental Health, Searcy Hosp., 1969-72; correctional counselor, Ala. Dept. Corrections, 1974; tchr. Clark County Sch. Dist., Las Vegas, Nev., 1976-78, elem. sch. counselor, 1978-81, 81—, participant spl. edn. conf. on parent involvement, 1981, chmn. ethnic adv. com., 1981—; parole and probation officer State of Nev., 1981; participant profl. confs. Mem. youth affairs com. NAACP. Recipient Clark County Classroom Tchrs. Assn. service award, 1978. Mem. Am. Personnel and Guidance Assn., Nev. Personnel and Guidance Assn., Clark County Sch. Counselors Assn., Delta Sigma Theta. Methodist. Office: 1030 N J St Las Vegas NV 89106

HODSON, JAN CUNNINGHAM, univ. adminstr.; b. Athens, Ohio, Dec. 1, 1951; d. John Kientz and Donna Eileen (King) Cunningham; B. Interior Design, Ohio U., 1973; postgrad. Capital U., 1976-77; m. Thomas Scott Hodson. Paralegal, Lavelle & Yanity Law Firm, Athens, 1977-78, Yanity, DeVeau & Weisenberger, Athens, 1978-79; dir. planned giving Ohio U., 1979—. Mem. exec. com., treas. Athens County Democratic party; bd. dirs. Athens Met. Housing Authority. Mem. Council Advancement and Support of Edn. Office: 201 McGuffey Hall Ohio U Athens OH 45701

HOEBER, AMORETTA MATHEWS, govt. ofcl.; mil. policy analyst; b. Austin, Tex., Nov. 14, 1941; d. J. Chesley and Pearl (Cieri) Mathews; B.A. in Polit. Sci., Stanford U., 1963, postgrad., 1965-69; m. Francis P. Hoeber, Aug. 28, 1965; 1 son, Mark Chesley; stepchildren—Christopher Francis, Richard Halverson (dec.), Anthony Niles. Researcher, Stanford Research Inst., Menlo Park, Calif., 1963-66; mem. tech. staff Analytic Services, Inc., Falls Church, Va., 1966-68, Rand Corp., Santa Monica, Calif., 1968-72; cons. Gen. Research Corp., Santa Monica, 1972-74, dir. dept. mil. policy analysis, 1974-75; asst. dir. policy and strategy analysis div. System Planning Corp., Arlington, Va., 1975-81; prin. dep. asst. sec. for research devel. and acquisition Dept. Army, Washington, 1981—; mem. Center for Study of Democratic Instns., Santa Barbara, 1965—. Mem. Dem. Women's Club Santa Monica, 1971-75, Dem. Women's Forum, Los Angeles, 1971-75; chairperson Nat. Women's Polit. Caucus, Los Angeles, 1973-75; mem. Dem. Nat. Com. Task Force on Fgn. Affairs, 1974-76; chmn. No. Va. Women's Polit. Caucus, 1980, Mem. Republican Women's Forum, 1980—; bd. dirs. Com. on Present Danger. Mem. Am. Acad. Polit. Sci., Am. Polit. Sci. Assn., Air Force Assn., Am. Security Council, U.S. Naval Inst., Ops. Research Soc. Am., U.S. Stragetic Inst., Mil. Ops. Research Soc. (dir. 1977—, v.p. 1980-81, pres. 1981-82), AIAA, Women's Inst. Internat. Relations (treas., dir.), NOW. Co-author: Soviet Strategy for Nuclear War, 1979; Conventional War and Escalation, 1981; author: Chemistry of Defeat, 1982. Home: 5151 Williamsburg Blvd Arlington VA 22207 Office: Room 2E672 The Pentagon Washington DC 20310

HOEFERT, LYNN LUCRETIA, botanist; b. Billings, Mont., July 7, 1935; d. Arthur Carl and Lucretia H.; B.S., Mont. State Coll., 1958, M.S., 1961; Ph.D., U. Calif., Davis, 1965. Postgrad. research botanist U. Calif., Santa Barbara, 1965-66; botanist Agrl. Research Service, Dept. Agr., Logan, Utah, 1966-69, botanist Sci. and Edn. Adminstrn., Salinas, Calif., 1969—. Mem. Bot. Soc. Am., Electron Microscope Soc. Am., Am. Phytopath. Soc., Am. Soc. Sugar Beet Technologists, Sigma Xi.

Mem. editorial adv. bd. Jour. Ultrastructure Research. Home: 405 Lena Ave Gilroy CA 95020 Office: PO Box 5098 Salinas CA 93915

HOEFNER, ELEANOR MORLAND, civic worker; b. Robinson, Ill., Oct. 10, 1920; d. Benton DeFord and Goldye (Fidler) Morland; student Morton Jr. Coll., 1939-40; B.S., U. Ill., 1942; postgrad. Western State Coll., 1954-58; m. Victor C. Hoefner, Jan. 1, 1942; children—Victor C. III, Susan, Kenneth, Elizabeth. Statistician, Continental Casualty Ins. Co., summers 1940-42; substitute tchr. Morton High Sch., 1942-46; partner, crafts tchr. Yarn Cellar, Montrose, Colo., 1964-69; bus. mgr. Victor C. Hoefner, D.O., Grand Junction, Colo., 1969-80; dancer various events. Pres., PTA, Montrose, 1958-59; mem. lay com. Montrose Sch. Bd., 1964-65; active Girl Scouts U.S.A., including pres. Chipeta council, 1976-78; active local ch., ch. sch. tchr., 1950-65, supt., edn. chmn., 1973-74, bldg. chmn., 1975; trustee United Meth. Ch.; vol. coordinator 2 gift shops. Named mem. Methodist Family of Yr., Montrose, 1956; recipient Thanks badge Girl Scouts U.S.A., 1977, Lioness of Yr. award Grand Junction (Colo.) Lioness Club, 1977. Mem. Am. Osteo. Assn. Aux. (hon. life; nat. pres. 1971-72, AAUW (dir. Colo. State div. 1975-80, pres. Colo. State div. 1978-80, public relations chmn.), Women's Soc. Christian Service (hon. life), Federated Women's Club (local pres. 1958-59), Alpha Gamma Delta, PEO (pres. chpt.). Republican. Club: Sojourners (membership chmn.). Contbr. numerous articles to AAUW div. bull., The Record, Aux. to Am. Osteo. Assn. mag.

HOEFT, THEA MARIE, educator, therapist; b. Milw., Feb. 9, 1950; d. Peter Kazin and Renatte Katherine (Kaniewski) Zidonowitz; B.S. in Recreation, U. Wis., LaCrosse, 1972; M.S. in Leisure Studies, U. Utah, 1973; Ed.D., Va. Poly. Inst. and State U., 1979. Playground dir. Watertown (Wis.) Dept. Parks and Recreation, 1969; dir. Bluffview playground LaCrosse Dept. Parks and Recreation, 1970; instr. Ind. State U., Terre Haute, 1973-74; day camp dir. Vigo County Extension Service, Terre Haute, Ind., 1974; instr. Radford (Va.) U., 1974-75; phys. edn. tchr. St. Patrick Cathedral Sch., Harrisburg, Pa., 1975; receptionist crisis worker Holy Spirit Hosp. Community Mental Health Center, Camphill, Pa., 1975; adj. faculty U. So. Miss., Hattiesburg, 1976; master recreational therapist Ellisville (Miss.) State Sch. for Mentally Ill and Retarded, 1976; instr. Radford U., 1976-77; mental retardation profl. Hearthside Rehab. Center, Brown Deer, Wis., 1979; asst. prof., coordinator therapeutic recreation curriculum Ariz. State U., Tempe, 1979—; cons. 4-H, 1976, Crippled Children's Hosp., Va., 1978, others. Mem. Miss. Com. Spl. Olympics, 1976; rep. United Way Ariz., 1979; mem. Mayor's Adv. Drug Com., 1972; bd. dirs. Youth Treatment and Evaluation Center, Phoenix, 1979-82; mem. Phoenix spl. populations adv. council on recreation, 1980-82; vol. Phoenix Panhellenic Council, 1982; mem. Ariz. State U. Centennial Com., 1981-83, chairperson disabled students services adv. bd., 1981-83. Wis. Leadership grantee, 1968; recipient Disting. Service award Montgomery County Cardiac Therapy Center, 1979, United Way, 1980, Recreation Com. U. Wis., LaCrosse, 1971, 72; H. Roe Bartle Recruiting award, 1981. Mem. Am. Camping Assn., Ariz. Parks and Recreation Assn., Va. Parks and Recreation Assn., Nat. Recreation and Park Assn., AAHPER and Dance (editorial bd.), Nat. Leadership Inst., Phi Delta Kappa, Sigma Kappa Sigma, Sigma Lambda Sigma, Gamma Sigma Sigma. Republican. Catholic. Contbr. articles to profl. jours. Home: 3212 N 70th St Apt I Scottsdale AZ 85251 Office: Ariz State U Tempe AZ 85287

HOEHN, MARGARET M., neurologist; b. San Francisco, Nov. 24, 1930; d. Peter Paul and Eve (Till) Maier; B.A., U. Sask., 1950; M.D., U. B.C., 1954; m. Robert J. Hoehn, June 27, 1961; children—Robert Anthony Till, Margaret Eve Maier. Intern, Vancouver (B.C.) Gen. Hosp., 1954-55, resident, 1956-59; resident Shaughnessy Hosp., 1955-56; mem. staff Nat. Hosp. Nervous Disease, London, 1960, 62-63, Boston VA Hosp., 1961-62, Presbyn. Hosp., Denver, St. Joseph's Hosp., Denver, Swedish-Porter Hosps., Denver; asst. prof. neurology Coll. Physicians and Surgeons, Columbia U., 1963-70; asst. prof. U. Colo., Denver, 1970-77, asso. clin. prof., 1977—; mem. med. adv. bd. United Parkinson Found., FDA; bd. dirs. Parkinson Assn. of the Rockies. Fellow Am. Acad. Neurology, ACP, Royal Coll. Physicians (Can.); mem. Am. Neurol. Assn., Assn. Research in Nervous and Mental Diseases, Western EEG Soc., Colo. Soc. Clin. Neurologists, Colo. Med. Soc., Denver Med. Soc., Mensa, Alpha Omega Alpha. Research and publs. in Parkinson's Disease, other diseases of basal ganglia. Home: 3851 S Xanthia St Denver CO 80237 Office: 3535 Cherry Creek North Dr Suite 407A Denver CO 80209

HOENACK, PEG COURSE, music educator; b. Moses Lake, Wash., Mar. 6, 1916; d. Herbert Moore and Mary (Hart) Course; B.A. in Music and Edn., magna cum laude, Wash. State U., 1937; M.Mus., Catholic U. Am., 1972; m. August Hoenack, June 14, 1939; children—Stephen A., Judith Hoenack Schultz, Francis A., August Jeremy. Tchr., cons. music edn. in Washington, Va. and Md., 1940-53; music specialist, Bethesda, Md., 1954-65; group piano instr. Montgomery County (Md.) public schs., 1960-70; lectr. elem. music edn. Am. U., 1972-74, George Mason U., Fairfax, Va., 1976, Trinity Coll., Washington, 1977, Chautauqua (N.Y.) Inst., 1977, Cath. U., Washington, 1979; music cons. and workshop clinician Montessori, parochial and public schs., 1967—; founder, 1967, since dir. Music for Young Children, studios and pub., Bethesda; founder Com. for Music in Public Schs., Montgomery County, 1953; steering com. Cultural Arts in Schs., 1970-75; bd. dirs. Concerned Citizens for Arts in Public Schs., 1972-80. Grantee Rockefeller Found., 1967, EPDA, 1968, Philip Stern Family Fund, 1967-68. Mem. Internat. Soc. Music Edn., Music Educators Nat. Conf., Md. Music Educators, Am. Montessori Soc., Assn. Childhood Edn. Internat., Nat. Assn. Edn. Young Children, Am. Orff Schulwerk Assn., Am. Recorder Soc., N.Y. Koto Club, Washington Koto Club (performing mem.), Washington Friday Morning Music Club (performing mem., violist), Phi Kappa Phi, Pi Lambda Theta, Psi Chi, Mu Phi Epsilon. Presbyterian. Club: Podickory Sailing Assn. Author music textbooks, charts, teaching aids, programmed learning materials; contbr. profl. jours. Home: 8409 Seven Locks Rd Bethesda MD 20817

HOENIG, JUDITH ANNE, nurse; b. Putnam, Conn., Nov. 11, 1943; d. Thomas Francis and Charlotte Zoe (King) Gorey; R.N., Joseph Lawrence Sch. Nursing, 1965; m. Michael J. Hoenig, III, Aug. 6, 1977. Supervising nurse Westview Convalescent Center, Dayville, Conn., 1968-73; asst. dir. nurses Stula Pavilion Nursing Home, Danielson, Conn., 1973-75; dir. nurses Westview Convalescent Center, Dayville, 1975-78, staff nurse, 1981-82; dir. nurses Beechwood Manor Convalescent Hosp., New London, Conn., 1982—; dir. nurses Norcliffe Rest Home, Inc., Brooklyn, Conn., 1979-81. Mem. profl. auditing com. Conn. Community Care, Inc., 1981—. Club: Bus. and Profl. Women's (sec. 1977). Contbr. poem to 1982 Anthology Twentieth Century Greatest Poems. Home: RFD 1 Wauregan Rd Danielson CT 06239 Office: 31 Vauxhall St New London CT 06320

HOFER, INGRID INGEBORG, artist; b. N.Y.C., Aug. 25, 1926; d. William D. and Martha M. (Gaertner) Kassul; B.A., Meisterschule fuer Mode, Hamburg, Germany, 1948; postgrad. U. Hamburg, Traphagen, 1951; m. Peter H. Hofer, Mar. 10, 1951; children—Mark A., Constance R. Sr. instr. adult edn. YWCA, Summit, N.J., 1967-73; instr. Trailside Mus., Mountainside, N.J., 1968-70; instr. watercolors War Meml., Grosse Pointe, Mich., 1974-78, Countryside Art Center, Arlington Heights, Ill., 1981—; one-woman shows include: Studio 4, Roseland, N.J., 1970, Lochmore Country, 1974, Couch House Gallery, 1975, The Covenant Club of Ill., 1979; group shows include: Jersey City Mus., 1968, 70, 73, Nat. Academy Galleries, N.Y.C., 1971, 72, 73, 74, Discovery Art Galleries, 1974, 80, 81, 82, Scarab Club, Detroit, 1974-75, Gallery 9, 1975, Tweed Mus., Duluth, Minn., 1978, Union League Club, Chgo., 1981, Aqueous 81, Ky. Mem. Am. Artist Profl. League, Catharine Lorillard Wolfe Art Club, N.J., Midwest watercolor socs., Internat. Platform Assn. Home: 25561 Blakely Pkwy Barrington IL 60010

HOFER, VIRGINIA EVA HOLLY, educator; b. Beadle County, S.D., July 10, 1928; d. Rufus Holly and Louisa (Huether) Holly Patrick; B.S. in Elem. Edn., Evangel Coll., Springfield, Mo., 1961; M.A. in Curriculum and Instrn., U. Minn., Mpls., 1969; m. Kenneth Eugene Hofer, June 2, 1948 (dec. (Aug. 1951). Tchr., Huron (S.D.) Ind. Sch. Dist., 1953-60, substitute tchr., 1980-82; elem. edn. tchr. St. Paul Ind. Sch. Dist., 1961-70, spl. edn. tchr., 1970-77; curriculum specialist career competency S.D. Vital Info. Edn. and Work, Huron, 1978-79, cons., 1979-80, adminstrv. asst., 1981; substitute tchr. St. Martin Ch. Sch., Huron, 1980-82; cons. S.D. Career Competency and Huron Career Model, 1978-79, S.D. Occupational Coordinating Com., 1979-80, 4-H Club, 1979—; kindergarten tchr. James Valley Christian Sch., Huron, 1982-83; spl. needs coordinator Rural Alternatives Inst., Huron, 1982-83; adj. instr. Huron Coll., 1982. Cert. elem. tchr., S.D. Office: Box 163 Huron SD 57350

HOFFBERG, JUDITH ANN, art pub. co. exec.; b. Hartford, Conn., May 19, 1934; d. George and Miriam (Goldenberg) H.; B.A. cum laude, UCLA, 1956, M.A. in Italian Literature and Lang., 1960, M.L.S., 1964. Cataloger Johns Hopkins U. Bologna (Italy) Center, 1964-65; intern cataloger in prints and photographs Library of Congress, 1965-67; fine arts librarian U. Pa., 1967-69; bibliographer art literature and lang. U. Calif., San Diego, La Jolla, 1969-71; librarian Brand Art Center, Glendale, Calif., 1971-73; exec. sec. Art Libraries Soc. N.Am., 1973-78; freelance archivist, 1978—; dir. Umbrella Assos., Glendale, Calif., 1978—; lectr. in field. Mem. Art Libraries Soc. N. Am. (founder, chmn. 1973-74), Coll. Art Assn. (dir. 1975-79), Soc. Architecture Historians (dir. 1977-82), ALA, Am. Printing History Assn., Internat. Council Mus., Women's Caucus for Art, Internat. Assn. Art Critics, Art Writers of So. Calif. Jewish. Editor: (with S. Hess) Directory of Art Libraries & Visual Resource Collections in North America, 1978; publisher, editor Artists' Publications in Print, 1980, 81, 82; contbr. articles and revs. in field. Home: PO Box 40100 Pasadena CA 91104 Office: PO Box 3692 Glendale CA 91201

HOFFER, DIANE LYNN, psychologist; b. Coral Gables, Fla., Dec. 29, 1953; d. Harold Herman and Charlotte May (Bernstein) H.; B.A. in Sociology, U. Miami, 1974; M.Ed. in Psychology, Counseling and Psychol. Services, Ga. State U., 1975; Dr. Psychology, Nova U., 1981. Practicum student Community Mental Health S. Dade, Dade County, Fla., 1978-79; clin. psychology intern Univ. Health Services U. Mass., Amherst, 1980-81; psychologist in pvt. practice, Coral Gables, 1981—; dance instr.; instr. Parent Effectiveness Tng. Lic. marriage and family therapist, mental health counselor. Mem. Am. Psychol. Assn., AAHPER, Nat. Dance Assn., Internat. Windsurfing Class Assn., Assn. Sex Educators, Counselors and Therapists, Fla. Psychol. Assn. Democrat. Jewish. Contbr. articles to profl. jours.

HOFFMAN, DARLEANE (CHRISTIAN), chemist; b. Terril, Iowa, Nov. 8, 1926; d. Carl Benjamin and Elverna E. (Kuhlman) Christian; B.S. in Chemistry, Iowa State U., 1948, Ph.D. in Phys. Chemistry, 1951; m. Dec. 26, 1951; children—Maureane, Daryl. Chemist, Oak Ridge Nat. Lab., 1952-53; mem. staff radiochemistry group Los Alamos Sci. Lab., 1953-71, asso. group leader, 1971-79, leader chemistry-nuclear div., 1979—. NSF fellow, 1964; Guggenheim fellow, 1978-79. Fellow Am. Inst. Chemists; mem. Am. Chemistry Soc. (mem. exec. com. 1976-78, chmn. div. of nuclear chemistry and tech. 1979), AAAS, Am. Phys. Soc. Methodist. Contbr. numerous articles in field to profl. jours. Office: Los Alamos Sci Lab CNC-DO MS-760 Los Alamos NM 87545

HOFFMAN, DIANA LYNN, architect; b. N.Y.C., Mar. 14, 1947; d. Robert Louis and Lillian Josephine (Macheras) H.; B.Arch., CCNY, 1976. Designer, Design Plus, Saddle River, N.J., 1973-75; exchange student Chiba U., Japan, 1975; grad. asst. CCNY, 1975-76, seminar instr., 1976; designer/planner Perkins & Will Architects, N.Y.C., 1977; chief designer, sr. asso. Robert Larsen Architect, N.Y.C., 1977-78; v.p. James Barclay Assos., N.Y.C., 1978—. Mem. Archtl. Rev. Bd., Dobbs Ferry, N.Y. Registered architect, N.Y. Mem. AIA. Home: 120 Bellair Dr Dobbs Ferry NY 10522 Office: 271 Madison Ave New York NY 10016

HOFFMAN, DORIS JEAN, acct.; b. Rockford, Ill., June 7, 1929; d. Herschel Herbert and Ollie Mae (Sherlock) Wolfe; student LaSalle Extension U., 1950-51, Broward Community Coll., 1969-71; m. Rodney V. Hoffman, Feb. 14, 1949 (dec. 1968); children—Judith Hoffman Olson, Sandra Hoffman Hardy, Kurt Allyn. Operator, Ill. Bell Telephone Co.. Rockford, 1946-49; acct., head tax dept. Fed. & State Tax Record Systems, Rockford, 1949-66, Ft. Lauderdale, Fla., 1966-69; pvt. practice acctg., Ft. Lauderdale, 1969-79; acct., pres. Hoffman & Assos., Inc., Ft. Lauderdale, 1979—; lectr. in field. Mem. bus. edn. adv. com. Fla. Dept. Edn., 1979—; chmn. Fla. del. to White House Conf. on Small Bus., 1979-80; mem. exec. bd., adminstr. adv. council SBA. Named Bus. Woman of Yr., Broward County Women in Communication, 1979; Woman of Yr., Am. Soc. Woman Accts., 1975; Soroptimist Woman of Yr. in Acctg., 1976, 77; Woman of Yr. in Acctg., Zonta, 1978; Bus. Person of Yr., FBLA, 1980. Mem. Fla. Accts. Assn. (pres. 1978-79), Nat. Soc. Public Accts., Internat. Platform Assn. Contbr. articles to profl. jours. Office: 3929 N Andrews Ave Fort Lauderdale FL 33309

HOFFMAN, ELLENDALE MCCOLLAM, psychologist, pastoral counselor; b. Alexandria, La., Apr. 3, 1951; d. William and Hope (Joffrion) McCollam; A.A., Briarcliff Coll., 1971; B.A., Manhattanville Coll., 1973; M.Div., Episcopal Div. Sch., 1976; D.Min., Andover Newton Theol. Sch., 1978; m. Charles L. Hoffman, Nov. 27, 1976. Ordained deacon Episcopal Ch., 1976, ordained priest, 1977; clin. supr. Pastoral Inst. for Tng. in Alcohol Problems, Cambridge, Mass., 1976-78; pvt. practice psychology and pastoral counseling, Falmouth, Mass., 1976—; dir. growth and learning center Marion (Mass.) Center for Human Services, 1978-79; clin. dir. Cape Counseling Center, Hyannis, 1979-82. Chmn., Commn. on Today's Families, Diocese of Mass., 1980-82. Named Woman of Yr., Falmouth Bus. and Profl. Women's Assn., 1982; Roothbert fellow, 1974-76; Episcopal Women's scholar, 1974-76; Robbins fellow, 1976-78; cert. alcoholism counselor, Mass. Fellow Am. Assn. Pastoral Counselors; mem. Am. Psychol. Assn., Am. Assn. Marriage and Family Therapists, Assn. Christian Therapists, LWV. Designer, writer driver's alcohol edn. curriculum, 1977. Home and Office: 78 Main St Falmouth MA 02540

HOFFMAN, KARLA LEIGH, mathematician; b. Paterson, N.J., Feb. 14, 1948; d. Abe and Bertha (Guthaim) Rakoff; B.A., Rutgers, U., 1969; M.B.A., George Washington U., 1971, D.Sc. in Ops. Research, 1975; m. Allan Stuart Hoffman, Dec. 26, 1971; 1 son, Matthew Douglas. Ops. research analyst IRS, Washington, 1970-72; research asst. George Washington U., 1972-75; asso. professorial lectr., 1978—; NSF postdoctoral research fellow Nat. Acad. Sci., Washington, 1975-76; mathematician Nat. Bur. Standards, Washington, 1978—; vis. asso. prof. ops. research U. Md., spring 1982; cons. to govt. agys. Mem. Ops. Research Soc. Am. (sec.-treas. computer sci. tech. sect. 1979-80, vice chmn. sect. 1981, chmn. sect. 1982, vis. professorial lectr. 1980—), Math. Programming Soc. (editor newsletter 1979—, chmn. com. algorithms 1982—). Club: Clifton Horse Soc. Contbr. articles on ops. research to profl. jours. Home: 6921 Clifton Rd Clifton VA 22024 Office: Center Applied Math Nat Bur Standards Washington DC 20234

HOFFMAN, LINDA M., chemist, educator; b. N.Y.C., Dec. 18, 1939; d. Theodore and Esther (Schaeffer) Weiss; B.S., Queens Coll., 1956; M.S., N.Y.U., 1967, Ph.D., 1970; m. Robert G. Hoffman; 1 son, Samuel A. Teaching fellow N.Y.U., 1965-68; postdoctoral fellow Sloan-Kettering Inst. Cancer Research, N.Y.C., 1972-73; research asso. Kingsbrook Jewish Med. Center, N.Y.C., 1973-77; mem. faculty Baruch Coll., CUNY, 1977—, prof. chemistry, 1982—. Recipient Moore award Am. Soc. Neuropathologists, 1980. Mem. AAAS, Am. Chem. Soc., Am. Women in Sci., N.Y. Acad. Sci., Sigma Xi. Contbr. articles to profl. jours. Office: 17 Lexington Ave New York NY 10010

HOFFMAN, LOIS WLADIS, psychologist; b. Elmira, N.Y., Mar. 25, 1929; d. Gustave and Etta Wladis; B.A., SUNY, Buffalo, 1951; M.S., Purdue U., 1953; Ph.D., U. Mich., 1958; m. Martin Hoffman, June 24, 1951; children—Amy G., Jill A.; m. 2d, Herbert Zimiles, Oct. 25, 1981. Research assoc. Inst. Social Research, U. Mich., 1954-60; editor Rev. Child Devel. Research, 1962-67; lectr. psychology U. Mich., 1967-72, assoc. prof., 1972-77, prof., 1977—; research cons. Catalyst. Recipient book award Child Study Assn., 1964, Lewis award Am. Philos. Soc., 1978; research grantee. Mem. Am. Psychol. Assn., Soc. Psychol. Study of Social Issues, Soc. Research in Child Devel. Author: (with M.L. Hoffman) Child Development Research, Vol. 1 and 2, 1964, 66; (with E.I. Nye) The Employed Mother in America, 1963, Working Mothers, 1974; (with M. Mednick and S. Tangri) Women and Achievement, 1975; (with R. Gandelman and R. Shiffman) Parenting—Its Causes and Consequences, 1982. Office: Dept of Psychology University of Michigan Ann Arbor MI 48109

HOFFMAN, MARGARET GROSS, ednl. adminstr.; b. Glassport, Pa., Jan. 14, 1940; d. Albert Frederick and Marguerite Bridget (Murphy) Gross; B.S., Slippery Rock State Coll., 1961; M.Ed., U. Pitts., 1972, Ph.D., 1980. children—Daniel Keith, Diane Lynn. Tchr. health and phys. edn. W. Mifflin Sch. Dist., Pa., 1961-63; tchr. Arroyo High Sch., Los Angeles, 1964-65; asst. prof. Community Coll. of Allegheny County, West Mifflin, Pa., 1970-75, athletic dir., 1975-76, asst. to v.p., exec. dean South Campus, 1976-82, asst. dean learning resources, 1982—. Mem. fin. campaign Pine Run Meth. Ch. Mem. Am. Assn. Higher Edn., Am. Assn. Women in Community and Jr. Colls. (participant in Leaders for 80's Program), Am. Council on Edn. (instl. rep. Nat. Identification Program for Women, Pa., 1981-82), Nat. Sch. Public Relations Assn., AAHPERD, Nat. Council on Community Services and Continuing Edn., Nat. Assn. Female Execs., Mon-Yough C. of C. (chmn. edn.). Editor and writer: Data from the Dean. Home: 471 Dennison Dr West Mifflin PA 15122 Office: 1750 Clairton Rd Rt 885 West Mifflin PA 15122

HOFFMAN, MARGARET MARY, mfg. co. exec.; b. Hammonton, N.J., July 29, 1946; d. Stephen M. and Helen M. (Holland) H.; A.S., Gloucester County Coll., 1981; student Glassboro State Coll., 1981—. Service rep. N.J. Bell Telephone Co., Camden, N.J., 1964-67; systems analyst NCR Corp., Cherry Hill, N.J., 1967-69; data processing mgr. Hussmann Refrigerator Co., Cherry Hill, 1969-77; data processing mgr. flavors div. MacAndrews & Forbes Co., Camden, 1977—; part-time instr. data processing Gloucester County Vocat. Tech. Sch., Sewell, N.J., 1974—. Mem. nat. adv. bd. Am. Security Council, 1979—. Lic. vocat.-tech. tchr., notary public, N.J. Mem. Smithsonian Assos., Nat. Assn. Female Execs., Internat. Mgmt. Council, Citizens Choice. Roman Catholic. Home: 900 Winslow Rd Williamstown NJ 08094 Office: 3rd St and Jefferson Ave Camden NJ 08104

HOFFMAN, MARY ANN, psychologist, educator; d. Paul Gordon and Patricia Ann (Patrick) H.; B.A. magna cum laude, Macalester Coll., 1971; Ph.D. in Psychology, U. Minn., 1975; m. Damon L. Silvers. Instr. psychology U. Minn., 1973-75, intern psychology, 1974-75; asst. prof. Whitworth Coll., Spokane, Wash., 1975-77; asst. prof. grad. program counseling and personnel U. Md., College Park, 1977—; cons. mental health Washington, D.C. Job Corps; pvt. practice psychology. Vol. therapist community mental health centers, Spokane, Minneapolis. Mem. NOW, Am., Eastern, Western psychol. assns., Am. Personnel and Guidance Assn., Phi Beta Kappa (sustaining). Democrat. Presbyterian. Contbr. articles to publs. in field. Home: 3262 Worthington St NW Washington DC 20015 Office: Dept Counseling and Personnel U Md College Park MD 20742

HOFFMAN, MARY CATHERINE, nurse anesthetist; b. Winamac, Ind., July 14, 1923; d. Harmon William Whitney and Dessie Maude (Neely) H.; R.N., Methodist Hosp., Indpls., 1945; cert. obstet. analgesia and anesthesia, Johns Hopkins Hosp., 1949, grad. U. Hosp. of Cleve. Sch. Anesthesia, 1952; Staff nurse Meth. Hosp., 1945-49; research asst., then staff anesthetist Johns Hopkins Hosp., 1949-62; staff anesthetist Meth. Hosp., 1962-64, U. Chgo. Hosps., 1964-66; chief nurse anesthetist Paris (Ill.) Community Hosp., 1966-80; staff anesthetist Hendricks County Hosp., Danville, Ind., Ball Meml. Hosp., Muncie, Ind., 1981—; instr.-trainer CPR, 1975-81; mem. Terr. 08 CPR Coordinating Com., 1975-80. Mem. Am. Assn. Nurse Anesthetists, Am. Heart Assn., Ind. Fedn. Bus. and Profl. Women's Clubs (Ill. dist. chmn. 1977-78, state found. chmn. 1978-79; found. award 1979). Republican. Presbyterian. Home: 1700 N Maddox Dr Muncie IN 47304 Office: Ball Meml Hosp 2401 University Ave Muncie IN 47303

HOFFMAN, MERLE HOLLY, psychologist, polit. activist, health services adminstr.; b. Phila., Mar. 6, 1946; d. Jack Rheins and Ruth (Dubow) H.; B.A. magna cum laude in Psychology, Queens Coll., 1972; postgrad. CUNY, 1972-75; m. Martin Gold, June 30, 1979. Founder, exec. dir. Choices, Forest Hills, N.Y., 1971—; family planning cons. Health Ins. Plan, N.Y.C., 1973—; founder, pres. Center for Comprehensive Breast Services, N.Y.C., 1979—; bd. dirs. Queens div. Health Systems Agy., 1978—; speaker on women's issues. Bd. dirs. Found. for the Creative Community, 1979—. Mem. Nat. Assn. Abortion Facilities (co-founder, pres. 1976-77), Nat. Abortion Fedn. (co-founder, sec. 1977-78), Am. Pub. Health Assn., Nat. Liberty Com. (founder, pres. 1981—), Phi Beta Kappa. Editor, Female Health Topics and Diagnostic Reporter, 1979—; producer TV documentary on abortion; nat. spokeswoman and debater; contbr. articles in field to various publs. Office: Choices 97-77 Queens Blvd Forest Hills NY 11374

HOFFMAN, SUSAN RONNIE, psychologist; b. Bklyn., May 5, 1948; d. Harold Abraham and Connie (Ellman) H.; B.S., Boston U., 1970, Ed.D., 1978. Asst. staff psychologist Judge Stone Child Guidance Center, Brockton, Mass., 1972-74; staff psychologist Dorchester Mental Health Center, Boston, 1974-76, Northeastern U. Counseling Center, Boston, 1976-81; psychologist Hurst Assos., P.C., Boston, 1979-82; pvt. practice psychology, Brookline, Mass., 1981—. Lic. psychologist Mass. Mem. Am. Psychol. Assn., Assn. Women in Psychology. Author articles in field. Office: 1180 Beacon St Suite 4C Brookline MA 02146

HOFFMAN, VIRGINIA MARY, banker; b. Bklyn., Sept. 16, 1936; d. Travis Steven and Margaret Mary (McArdle) H.; student Pace U., 1954-56. With Mfrs. Hanover Trust Co., N.Y.C., 1969—, asst. v.p., 1972-78, v.p. charge mcpl. bond trust dept., 1978—. Mem. Mcpl. Bond Women's Club N.Y.C. Office: 600 Fifth Ave New York NY 10020

HOFFMANN, FRANCES C., educator; b. Dunblane, Sask., Can., July 24, 1921; d. George Percy and Clara (Amerud) Carey; student Nebr.

State Tchrs. Coll., 1943, 51-53; B.S., Iowa State U., 1955, M.S., 1956; m. Albert Theodore Hoffmann, Oct. 21, 1943 (dec. July 1951); children—Gerald Theodore, Thomas Gene. Library asst. Central High Sch., Sioux City, Iowa, 1938-39; dining room asst. St. Joseph's Hosp., 1940-41; underphotographer Elko Photo Co., Sioux City, 1941-42, U.S. Civil Service, 1943-44; grad. research asst. Iowa State U., 1955-56; home econs. instr. Whittier (Calif.) Coll., 1957-66, asst. prof., 1966—, chmn. dept. home econs., 1971-72, 76-81; home econs. dir. Saturday Programs and Summer Day Camps, Found. for the Jr. Blind, Los Angeles, 1964-78, cons. bldg. addition, 1966-68; judge The Greatest Sew on Earth, 1975. Mem. adv. com. Rio Hondo Coll., 1977-82, Rio Hondo Child Devel. Center. Recipient Appreciation award Mchts. Club, 1975. Am. Home Econs. Assn.-Rehab. Svcs. Adminstrn. fellow, 1969-70. Mem. AAUW Am. (mem. rehab. com. 1970-72, com. on coms. 1971), Calif. (adv. coll. chpts. 1968; profl. sect. chmn. coll. chpt. 1968-70 Foothill Dist. council, chmn. colls. and univs. com. 1979) home econs. assns., Internat. Fedn. Home Economists (chmn. 1980-82, chmn. scholarship com. 1982-83), AAUP, Calif. Tchrs. Assn., Am. Textile Chemists and Colorists, Whittier Coll. Assos., Assn. Coll. Profs. Textiles and Clothing, Nat. Assn. Edn. Young Children, Costume Soc. Am., Delta Phi Upsilon, Kappa Omicron Phi (chpt. adv. 1973-82). Methodist. Participant audio-visual documentary Out of Darkness-Light, 1971. Home: 5518 Adele Ave Whittier CA 90601

HOFFMANN, MARY ANN, data processing exec.; b. Yonkers, N.Y., Nov. 19, 1946; d. Robert Augustus and Mary Margaret (Mansfield) Neary; B.A., Coll. Mt. St. Vincent, 1968; M.A., Fordham U., 1971; M.S., Fairleigh Dickinson U., 1978; m. Marvin W. Hoffmann, Mar. 9, 1968; children—Karri, Matthew. Project programmer IBM, Kingston, N.Y., 1977—. NSF fellow, 1968. Mem. IEEE, AAUW, Kappa Gamma Pi. Roman Catholic. Home: RD 1 Box 386E Woodstock NY 12498 Office: IBM Neighborhood Rd Kingston NY 12401

HOFFMANN-BRIGHT, BETTY, state legislator; b. Wanatah, Ind., Dec. 1, 1921; d. Leroy Arthur and Mary J. (Fleming) Black; student Ind. State U., 1940-45; m. Kenneth Bright, Nov. 12, 1981; children—James, Peggy Fermier, Sam Hoffmann. Mem. Iowa Ho. of Reps., 1977—, chmn. transp. appropriations, 1979-80, asst. majority leader, 1980-81. Active Iowa Commn. on Aging, NOW, LWV. Mem. Bus. and Profl. Women. Republican. Methodist. Club: Phoenix Federated. Office: State Capitol Des Moines IA 50319

HOFFNER, MARILYN, univ. ofcl.; b. N.Y.C., Nov. 16, 1927; d. Daniel and Elsie (Schulz) H.; B.F.A., Cooper Union; m. Albert Greenberg, May 29, 1949; children—Doren Roe, Peter Cooper. Art dir. Printers' Ink mag., N.Y.C., 1953-63; art dir. Print mag., N.Y.C., 1960-62; corp. art dir. Vision, Inc., N.Y.C., 1963-75; dir. alumni relations Cooper Union, 1975-82, acting dir. devel., 1982—. Bd. dirs. Art Dirs. Club N.Y., 1973-75, 79—, exec. sec., 1973-75, exec. treas., 1979-82; mem. Citizens Adv. Cultural Arts Com. Dutchess County, 1978-80. Named Alumnus of Yr., Cooper Union, 1968; recipient Gold medal Art Dirs. Club, 1979. Mem. Cooper Union Alumni Assn. (editor-in-chief 1971-74, 1st v.p. 1974-75), Council Advancement and Support of Edn., Type Dirs. Club (numerous awards), Nat. Arts Club (exhbn. com.). Contbg. editor Print mag., 1960-62, Art Direction, 1959-64, Graphics mag., 1959-82; designer mags., children's books. Home: 51 Fifth Ave New York NY 10003 Office: 41 Cooper Sq New York NY 10003

HOFFNUNG, AUDREY SONIA, speech-lang. pathologist, educator; b. N.Y.C., Mar. 15, 1928; d. Nathan and Gussie (Karp) Smith; B.A. cum laude, Bklyn. Coll., 1949; M.A., Columbia U., 1950; Ph.D., City U. N.Y., 1974; m. Joseph Hoffnung, Nov. 26, 1950; children—Bonnie Fern, Tami Lynn. Rehab. therapist Ridgewood Cerebral Palsy Center, 1949-50; dir. speech therapy Kingsbrook Med. Center, Bklyn., 1950-55; therapist and cons. Morris J. Solomon Clinic, Bklyn., 1956-58; therapist Speech and Hearing Center Bklyn. Coll., 1958-62, 63-64; pvt. practice speech therapy Hewlett (N.Y.) Med. Center, 1961-63; pvt. practice speech therapy, Oceanside, N.Y., 1964-71; cons. on staff for aphasic patients Phys. Medicine and Rehab. Center, South Nassau Communities Hosp., 1964-65; part-time lectr. Speech and Hearing Center, Queens (N.Y.) Coll., 1970-72; adj. lectr. dept. speech Bklyn. Coll., 1973-74, asst. prof. speech pathology, 1974-77; asst. prof. dept. speech communication and theatre St. John's U., Jamaica, N.Y., 1977-80, asso. prof., 1980—; guest lectr. N.Y. Orton Soc., 1979, Brookdale Med. Center, 1978; mem. profl. adv. bd. Vis. Home Health Services of Nassau County, 1973—. Cert. and lic. speech pathologist, N.Y. Mem. Am. Speech and Hearing Assn., N.Y.C. Speech, Hearing and Lang. Assn., N.Y. State Speech and Hearing Assn. (chairperson student activities 1978-79), L.I. Speech and Hearing Assn., Aphasia Study Group of N.Y.C., N.Y. Acad. Scis. Contbr. articles on speech pathology to profl. jours. Home: 3282 Woodward St Oceanside NY 11572 Office: Dept of Speech Communication St John's Univ Utopia and Grand Central Pkwys Jamaica NY 11439

HOFFS, EUGENIA SHIMANOVICH, psychiatrist, psychoanalyst; b. Vilna, Poland, Feb. 4, 1925; Mexican citizen, 1940; d. Groim and Aida (Michalowski) Shimanovich; M.A. in Psychology, Nat. U. Mex., 1948, Ph.D. in Philosophy, 1950, M.D., 1960; m. Morris David Hoffs; children—Lorelle, Annabelle. Intern, Psychoanalytic and Psychiat. Insts., Mexico City, 1968; founder Sch. Psychology, Nat. U. Mex., Mexico City, 1948; prof. postgrad. sch. psychology Nat. Med. Sch., Mexico City, 1948-78, mem. Council of Psychiatry, 1976; clin. psychologist Social Security Inst. Mex., 1945-75; practice medicine specializing in psychiatry and psychoanalysis, Mexico City, 1968—; dir. Psychiat. Inst. Mex., 1974-77. Founder, Council for Jewish Women in Mex., Alianza de Mujeres de Mexico; founder, v.p. Inst. for Cultural Relations between Mexico and Israel; active women's rights; mem. Revolutionary Party of Mex., 1943-70; mem. Soc. Friends of Hebrew U., Soc. Weizman Inst. of Rehovot in Mex. Fellow Internat. Council Psychologists; mem. Psychiat. Council Mex., Soc. Psychiatry and Neurology in Mex., Instituto Psiquiatrico de la Cuidad de Mexico (dir. 1974-77). Editor Tribuna Israelita, 1960-72; author: Psychology of Failure, 1958; Application of the Jackson Theory to Psychopalogy, 1953; lectr. various profl. confs. and convs.

HOFFSPIEGEL, JOYCE LASOFSKY, clin. psychologist, educator; b. Paterson, N.J., Feb. 27, 1944; d. Sol and Florence (Goodman) Lasofsky; B.A. (N.J. State scholar), Rutgers U., 1966, Ph.D. (teaching asst.), Inst. Cognitive Studies, 1981; children—Jill Allison, Greg Alan. Clin. intern West Bergen Mental Health Center, Ridgewood, N.J., 1970; dir. spl. services, sch. psychologist No. Highlands Regional High Sch., Allendale, N.J., 1970-80; asst. prof. psychology Mt. Holyoke (Mass.) Coll., 1980-81; dir. grad. program sch. psychology, asst. prof. Rider Coll., Lawrenceville, N.J., 1981—; psychol. cons. Hackensack Hosp. Inst. Child Devel.; pvt. practice clin. psychology. Cert. sch. psychologist, N.J. Mem. Am. Psychol. Assn., Assn. Women in Psychology, N.J. Sch. Psychol. Assn. Contbr. papers to profl. confs. Home: 23 Duryea Rd Upper Montclair NJ 07043 Office: 207 Bellevue Ave Upper Montclair NJ 07043

HOFHEINZ, HARRIET PARKER, social worker; b. Boston, Oct. 8, 1938; s. Haven and Barbara Parker; student Bradford Jr. Coll., 1957-59, U. Geneva, 1959-60; B.A., Harvard U., 1963; M.S.W., Boston U., 1969; m. Roy M. Hofheinz, Jr., June 15, 1963; children—Frederick H., Irene P. Tchr. English, Tokyo, 1963-64; caseworker, div. child guardianship Mass. Dept. Welfare and Childrens Protective Services, 1967-69; pvt. instr. ceramics, Cambridge, Mass., 1969-73; researcher drug rehab. program, Middlesex County, Mass., 1971-72; exec. dir. Cambridge Sch. Volunteers, Inc., 1975—; adminstrv. counselor Tufts U., 1981—; pvt. counselor, 1977—; ceramicist, 1965—. Recipient Nat. Sch. Vol. Inc. award, 1979, citation HEW/ Mass. Commn. Edn., 1979. Mem. Cambridge Mental Health Assn., Cambridge Art Assn., Nat. Sch. Vols., Parents and Childrens Services (exec. bd. 1970-77), Nat. Assn. Social Workers. Democrat. Office: 226 College Ave Medford MA 02115

HOGAN, AMANDA DANIELS, social worker; b. Kenosha, Wis.; d. Peter C. and Alma (Chilingerian) Daniels; B.A., U. Ill., 1934; postgrad. Sch. Social Work, U. Chgo., 1937-39; m. Ivey W. Hogan, Aug. 20, 1946; children—Gary R., Michael W. Supervising social worker Cook County Bur. Pub. Welfare of Ill., 1934-42, 45-46; dir. USO Travelers Aid Service, Galveston, Tex., 1942-43, Waukegan, Ill., 1943-44; tng. officer social workers for Cuban Refugee Assistance Program, HEW, Dade County, Fla., 1962-63; chmn. womens and childrens com. Council Social Agys., Ft. Lauderdale, Fla., 1948-50; mem. organizing com. Broward County (Fla.) Detention Home of Juvenile Ct., 1948-49; mem. Fla. Childrens Comm., 1949-50; mem. coll. admissions com. U. Chgo., 1969. Chmn. philanthropic com. Ft. Lauderdale Womens Civic Club, 1949-52; publicity staff Ft. Lauderdale chpt. Armenian Gen. Benevolent Union, 1974-75; active ARC; mem. organizing com. Broward County chpt. LWV, 1950-52. Recipient spl. recognition for service ARC, 1969. Mem. AAUW (founding pres. Ft. Lauderdale chpt.), Am. Assn. Social Workers. Democrat. Presbyterian. Clubs: Coral Ridge Yacht; Bookfellows. Author: Training Manual for Cuban Refugee Social Workers, 1963. Home: 1840 Coral Ridge Dr Fort Lauderdale FL 33305

HOGAN, ELISABETH W., publisher; b. New Haven, Sept. 11, 1932; d. Charles Lester and Alice (Oviatt) Morris; B.A. in Polit. Sci., Vassar Coll., 1953; married; children—Michele Elisabeth, Pamela Joan. Cons., project dir. Harbridge House, Boston, 1967-71; dir. Betsy Hogan Assos., affirmative action cons., 1972-74; broadcaster Women at Work, radio program, Boston, 1972-74; publisher Equal Employment News, Brookline, Mass., 1971—. Author: Corporate Social Policy, 1975, Women's Yellow Pages, 1978; also articles.

HOGAN, MARY EUPHRASIA, social worker, nun; b. Bremerton, Wash., June 7, 1928; d. Lawrence A. and Inez Marie (White) H.; B.A., Immaculate Heart Coll., 1960; M.S.W., St. Louis U., 1964; cert. in law program for community developers and social workers John Marshall Law Sch., 1981. Joined Sisters of the Good Shepherd, Roman Catholic Ch., 1951; asst. child care exec. dir. Pelletier High Sch., Los Angeles, 1954-64, exec. child care dir. and group coordinator, 1964-72; supervising psychiat. social worker for social service program St. Yves Sch., Las Vegas, 1973-74; cons. psychiat. social worker Half-Way House for Women, New Orleans, 1975; psychiat. social worker, child care worker DeNeuville Heights Sch., Sisters of the Good Shepherd, Memphis, 1975-80; dir. Rose Virginie Residence for Working Women, Chgo., 1980—; field supr., instr. students in B.S.W. program Northeastern Ill. U., 1982. Mem. standards com. State of Tenn., 1977—. Recipient Cert. of Appreciation, Tenn. Dept. of Human Services, 1979; cert. social worker, Calif., Ill. Mem. Nat. Assn. Social Workers, Acad. Cert. Social Workers, Calif. Assn. Health and Welfare, St. Louis U. Alumni Fedn. Address: 1126 W Grace St Chicago IL 60613

HOGAN, MARY SIMRELL, clin. psychologist; b. Evansville, Ind., Feb. 28, 1936; d. Alton Hicks and Edna May (McVey) S.; B.S., Ind. U., 1958; M.S., Butler U., 1964; Ph.D., St. Louis U., 1978; m. Timothy J. Hogan, Dec. 26, 1973; 1 son, Eric. Tchr., Ind., Tex. Schs., 1958-65; counselor Parkway Sch. Dist., St. Louis, 1965-80; family counselor, St. Louis, 1971-81; clin. psychologist, St. Louis, 1980—; lectr. S.E. Mo. U., McPherson U., Mo. Bapt. Coll.; cons. Tufner & Kemp Assos.; cons. Cemrel Inc. Area mem. State of Mo. Advocacy Council for Developmentally Disabled, 1982—; pres. Friends of the Gifted, 1981-82. Licensed Psychologist, Mo.; Certified Psychol. Examiner; Cert. Clin. Hypnotherapist. Mem. Am. Psychol. Assn., Mo. Psychol. Assn., Am. Personnel and Guidance Assn., St. Louis Soc. Psychologists, Womens Commerce Assn., AAUW, Alpha Omicron Pi. Home: 358 S Ballas Rd Kirkwood MO 63122 Office: 3125 LeMay Ferry Rd Saint Louis MO 63125

HOGAN, ROSEMARIE MIHELICH, nurse; b. Cleve., Sept. 19, 1927; d. John Louis and Anna Genevieve (Zwingle) Mihelich; B.S. in Nursing, Case Western Res. U., 1961, M.S., 1971; m. Francis J. Hogan, Aug. 18, 1951; children—Jacqueline, Robert, John, Kathleen, Valerie. Head nurse St. Mary's Hosp., Rochester, Minn., 1949-50; staff nurse Univ. Hosp., Cleve., 1951-52, 1958-65; staff nurse Euclid Gen. Hosp., Cleve., 1953-56; instr. Huron Rd. Hosp. Sch. Nursing, Cleve., 1966-68; asst. prof. nursing Frances Payne Bolton Sch. Nursing, Case Western Res. U., Cleve., 1971-79; asst. prof. nursing Cleve. State U., 1979-80, Kent State U. Sch. Nursing, 1981—; cons. Cleve. Bd. Edn. Named Outstanding Grad. Student St. Mary's Hosp. Sch. Nursing, 1949; recipient Cushing-Robb award Frances Payne Bolton Sch. Nursing, 1961; Cleve. State U. Devel. Found. grantee, 1980. Mem. Am. Nurses Assn., Nat. League for Nursing, Ohio Nurses Assn., Cleve. Area Citizens League for Nursing, Cleve. Oncology Nurses Assn., Alumni Assn. Frances Payne Bolton Sch. Nursing, Sigma Theta Tau. Democrat. Roman Catholic. Home: 17100 Dorchester Dr Cleveland OH 44119 Office: Sch Nursing Kent State U Kent OH 44242

HOGAN, SHIRLEY MAE, fin. corp. exec.; b. St. James, Minn., July 18, 1946; d. Vernon Carl and Helen Rose (Darmer) Stradtman; student Mankato State Coll., Mankato Comml. Coll., U. Minn.; m. David John Hogan, Apr. 3, 1971; 1 son, Jonathan. Sec., Mankato (Minn.) State Coll., 1965-70; with Dain Bosworth Inc., Mpls., 1970—, various positions fixed income div., 1970—, v.p., mgr. govt. securities dept., 1975—. Human rights commr. City of New Brighton, Minn., 1979—. Registered rep. N.Y. Stock Exchange. Mem. Nat. Assn. Securities Dealers, Twin Cities Bond Club, Twin City Investment Women's Club, Govt. Guaranteed Loan Dealers Assn., Mpls. Bus. and Profl. Women. Democrat. Lutheran. Club: Jaycee Women (bd. fin. Minn. 1979—, pres. New Brighton 1977-78, state del. 1976-77). Home: 2003 Pleasant View Dr New Brighton MN 55112 Office: 100 Dain Tower Minneapolis MN 55402

HOGG, HELEN SAWYER, astronomer; b. Lowell, Mass., Aug. 1, 1905; d. Edward Everett and Carrie (Sprague) Sawyer; A.B., Mt. Holyoke Coll., 1926, D.Sc. (hon.), 1958; M.A., Radcliffe Coll., 1928, Ph.D., 1931; D.Sc. (hon.) U. Waterloo, 1962, McMaster U., 1976, U. Toronto, 1977; m. Frank Scott Hogg, Sept. 6, 1930; children—Sarah Longley Hogg MacDonald, David Edward, James Scott. Lectr., Smith Coll., 1927, Mt. Holyoke Coll., 1930-31, asst. prof. astronomy, acting chmn. dept., 1940-41; research asst. Dominion Astrophys. Obs., 1931-35; research asst. U. Toronto, 1936-41, lectr., 1941-50, asst. prof., 1951-55, asso. prof., 1955-57, prof., 1957-76, emeritus, 1976—; program dir. astronomy NSF, Washington, 1955-56; astronomy columnist Toronto Daily Star, 1951—; research asso. David Dunlap Obs., Richmond Hill, Ont., Can., 1941—. Decorated companion Order of Can.; recipient citation Mt. Holyoke Coll., 1952, Rittenhouse Astron. Soc. medal, 1967, Centennial medal, 1967, medal of service, Order of Can., 1968. Fellow Royal Soc. Can. (past pres. sect. 3); mem. Internat. Astron. Union (past pres. sub-com.), Royal Astron. Soc. Can. (hon. pres., service medal 1967), Am. (Annie J. Cannon prize 1950), Canadian (pres. 1971-72) astron. socs., Am. Assn. Variable Star Observers (past pres.), Women's Press Club, Royal Canadian Inst. (pres. 1964-65), Fedn. Ont. Naturalists, Phi Beta Kappa, Sigma Xi. Club: Univ. Womens (Toronto). Contbr. numerous articles to profl. jours. Home: 98 Richmond St Richmond Hill ON L4C 3Y4 Canada Office: David Dunlap Observatory Richmond Hill ON L4C 4Y6 Canada

HOGG, NANCY LAUER, home economist; b. Harrisburg, Pa., Sept. 27, 1927; s. Kurvin William and Eva (Sprenkle) L.; B.S., Carnegie-Mellon U., 1949; M.S., Pa. State U., 1969; divorced; children—Michael D., Stephen J., Allan M. Faculty, Edgewood Park Jr. Coll., Briarcliff Manor, N.Y., 1949-50; instr. consumer edn. adult edn. program State Coll. Pa., 1966; coop. extension home economist Pa. State U., 1968—. Bd. dirs. home-health program Lutheran Social Service, 1970-76, pres., 1975; bd. dirs. Franklin County Meals on Wheels, 1970-79, Head Start Franklin County, 1973—; Pa. del. White House Conf. on Families, Balt., 1980. Mem. Nat. Assn. Extension Home Economists, Am. Home Econs. Assn., Bus. and Profl. Women's Fedn. (chmn. civic partiticaption com. Chambersburg 1972 chmn. personal devel. com. 1977, chmn. fin. com. 1980-81), Pa. Assn. Extension Home Economists (1st pl. award radio contest 1980), Pa. Home Econs. Assn. Home: 123 Colonial Dr Chambersburg PA 17201 Office: 191 Franklin Farms Ln Chambersburg PA 17201

HOGINS, MILDRED HOLDAR, med. technologist; b. Russelville, Ark., Jan. 18, 1939; d. Luther and Frances Eythl (Briscoe) Holdar; cert. in med. tech. Hillcrest Med. Center, Tulsa, 1963; B.S. in Biology, U. Mo., Kansas City, 1969; M.A. in Mgmt. and Supervision, Central City Soc. U., 1976; divorced; 1 son, Mark Holdar. Med. technologist St. Joseph Hosp., Tucson, 1964-66; bacteriologist Providence Hosp., Anchorage, Alaska, 1966-67; med. technologist St. Margaret Hosp., Kansas City, Kans., 1967-68, Providence Hosp., Kansas City, Kans., 1969-71; edn. coordinator Sch. Med. Tech., also asst. chief med. technologist Providence-St. Margaret Health Center, Kansas City, Kans., 1971-76, chief med. technologist, 1976—. Bd. dirs. Mill Creek Run Home Owners Assn., 1979-82, New Sch. Human Devel., Kansas City, Mo., 1982—. Mem. Clin. Lab. Mgrs. Assn., Am. Soc. Microbiology, Nat. Assn. Female Execs., Am. Soc. Clin. Pathologists, Kans. Soc. Med. Tech. (conv. chmn. 1975), Greater Kansas City Soc. Med. Tech. (treas. 1980), U. Mo. Kansas City Alumni Assn., Central Mich. U. Alumni Assn., Tall Clubs Internat., Mensa. Home: 14076 W 88th Terr Lenexa KS 66215 Office: 8929 Parallel Pkwy Kansas City KS 66112

HOHN, AMY-MARIE, social worker; b. Bridgeport, Conn., Feb. 25, 1941; d. William Horner and Amy Adeline (Whiting) Hohn; B.A., Adrian Coll., 1963; M.S.W., N.Y.U., 1971; m. Raymond Stover, July 14, 1973; 1 son, Jeffrey Hohn. Social worker Help Line Telephone Center, N.Y.C., 1971-74, supr., 1974-75, dir., 1975-78, 81—; pvt. practice therapy, N.Y.C., 1979-81; cons. to various groups and orgns., 1979-81; coordinator Personal Dynamics, Mpls., 1979-81; dir. Help Line Telephone Center, N.Y.C., 1981—. Mem. adv. bd. Gramercy Park Inst., N.Y.C., 1979-80; pres. Women of Montclair State Coll., 1979-81. Recipient plaque Help Line Telephone Center, 1979. Mem. Acad. Cert. Social Workers, Nat. Assn. Social Workers, Women's Counseling and Community Service Orgn., Fifth Avenue Forum. Home: 8 Fernwood Pl Upper Montclair NJ 07043

HOHU, MARGARET KUULEI, gerontologist; b. Hilo, Hawaii, Feb. 21, 1924; d. Edmund and Fannie (Werner) Hohu; A.A., U. Houston, 1947; R.N., Jefferson Davis Hosp. Sch. Nursing, Houston, 1947; cert. R.N. anesthetist Baylor U. Med. Center Sch. Nurse Anesthetists, Dallas, 1953; B.S., Colo. Women's Coll., Denver, 1975; M.A., U. No. Colo., 1977, Ed.D., 1979. Shift capt. Women's Air Raid Def., Dept. Army, Hawaii, 1942-44; staff nurse various hosps., Ohio, Colo., 1947-52; staff nurse anesthetist, instr. various hosps., Colo., Hawaii, Utah, 1953-68; pvt. anesthesia practice, Denver, 1967-69; dir. anesthesia services and in-service edn., Deadwood, S.D., 1969-70; staff nurse anesthetist, instr. Fitzsimons Army Med. Center, Denver, 1970-75; nurse anesthetist Anesthesia Assos. of Greeley (Colo.), 1975-78; gerontology cons., Denver, 1979—; adj. prof. gerontology grad. level U. No. Colo., 1979—. Pres., bd. dirs. Greeley Meals on Wheels; mem. steering com., adv. bd. Mt. Evans Hospice, Morrison, Colo. Mem. Colo. Assn. Nurse Anesthetists (trustee 1967), S.D. Assn. Nurse Anesthetists (trustee 1969), Western Gerontol. Soc. (employment com. 1980), Colo. Gerontol. Soc., Internat. Soc. Preretirement Planners, AAUP, Doctoral Vocat. Edn. Assn., Nat. Assn. Female Execs., Nat. Council Aging, Am. Entrepreneurs Assn., Am. Assn. Ret. Persons, Kappa Delta Pi. Author: Pre-retirement and Retirement Education Program: A Leadership Training Manual, 1979; Tomorrow is Mine, 1979. Office: PO Box 159 Evergreen CO 80439

HOIBERG, ANNE LOUISE, research psychologist; b. Elgin, Ill. Mem. staff Naval Health Research Center, San Diego, 1966—, mgr. longitudinal studies program, 1980—; lectr. San Diego State U.; cons. in field. Fellow Inter-Univ. Seminar Armed Forces and Soc. (asso. chmn.); mem. Am. Psychol. Assn., Western Psychol. Assn. Author articles in field. Editor: Women and the World of Work, 1982; asso. editor Psychol. Reports, 1980—; Armed Forces and Soc., 1980—. Address: Naval Health Research Center PO Box 85122 San Diego CA 92138

HOINKES, MARY ELIZABETH, fed. agy. adminstr., lawyer; b. Washington, Aug. 13, 1940; d. Howard Egger and Elizabeth Mae (Lucas) Wahrenbrock; B.A., Randolph-Macon Woman's Coll., 1962; postgrad. Sch. of Law, U. Va., 1962-63; J.D., George Washington U., 1965; m. H. Dieter Hoinkes, July 24, 1965. Admitted to D.C. bar, 1965; asso. firm Clifford & Miller (now Clifford & Warnke), Washington, 1965-68; adminstrv. ofcl. Internat. Labor Office (UN specialized agy.), Geneva, 1969-70, asst. dir. Washington office, 1970-76; atty. adv. U.S. Dept. State, Washington, 1976-77, asst. legal adv., 1977-80; dep. asst. sec. of state, Washington, 1980-81; dep. asst. dir. for multilateral affairs U.S. Arms Control and Disarmament Agy., Washington, 1981—. Office: US Arms Control and Disarmament Agy 320 21st St Washington DC 20451

HOITT, LINDA ANN, elec. mfg. co. mgr.; b. Manchester, N.H., Dec. 11, 1947; d. Proctor and Elizabeth Ann (Tarasuk) H.; grad. Sch. Fashion Design, Boston, 1966-69; student Santa Ana Coll., 1979—. Asst. designer Berkshire Apparel, Malden, Mass., 1969-70; sales corr. AMP Inc., Waltham, Mass., 1970-75; sales engr. ITT Cannon Electric, Wakefield, Mass., 1975-76, product specialist, Santa Ana, Calif., 1976-78, product mktg. mgr., 1978-82 mem. bd. control mgmt. assn., 1981-82; mktg. dir. mil. connector Stanford Applied Engr., Santa Ana, 1982—. Mem. Connector Study Group, Electronic Connector Study Group, Nat. Assn. Female Execs. Home: 1104 N Olive St Santa Ana CA 92703 Office: 2601 S Garnsey St Santa Ana CA 92707

HOKANSON, SHIRLEY ANN, state legislator; b. Morris, Minn., Feb. 8, 1936; d. Clarence Irvin and Gunda Irene (Hagen) Fogle; B.A. in Sociology, U. Minn., 1958; M.S. in Sociology, Mankato State U., 1977; m. Robert Hokanson, Aug. 29, 1959; children—Gregory, Thomas. Social worker: Lacqui Parle County, Madison, Minn., 1958-60, St. Peter (Minn.) State Hosp., 1960-62, Hennepin County Welfare, Mpls., 1963-72; legis. liaison Minn. Social Service Assn., 1973-74; mem. Minn. Ho. of Reps., 1975—, chmn. judiciary subcom. on law reform, vice chmn. house appropriations com., mem. health and welfare, regulated industries coms., elected to house steering com. Democratic Farm Labor Party, past chmn. various interim and standing subcoms. including public safety and gen. transp., human services reorgn., child protection, occupational licensing. Bd. mgmt. Southdale YMCA; bd. dirs. Minn. Safety Council; mem. Hennepin County Task Force on Child Support Enforcement; mem. Joint Religious Legis. Coalition, LWV, Friends of

Augsburg Library, Richfield. Mem. Nat. Conf. State Legislatures (del. assembly). Lutheran. Clubs: Sons of Norway, Am. Legion Aux., VFW Aux. (named Outstanding State Legislator, state VFW Aux., 1978). Office: 248 State Office Bldg Saint Paul MN 55155

HOKE, SHEILA WILDER, librarian; b. Greensboro, N.C., July 15, 1928; d. Herbert Bruce and Virginia Dell (Caylor) Wilder; B.S. in History, U. Kans., Lawrence, 1950, B.S. in Edn., 1951; M.L.S., U. Wis., Madison, 1955; M.S. in Edn., Southwestern Okla. State U., 1977; postgrad. Johns Hopkins U., Montclair State Coll., U. Kans.; m. Robert Edward Hoke, Nov. 21, 1958 (dec.); children—Raymond Fellow II, Philip Wilder. Tchr. history Fredonia (Kans.) High Sch., 1952-54; children's br. librarian Enoch Pratt Free Library, Balt., 1955-58; library dir. service libraries U.S. Army Spl. Services, Bavaria, 1958-59, sch. librarian, 1959-60; cataloger Southwestern Okla. State U. Library, Weatherford, 1963-69, library dir., 1969—; library cons. Concho Sch. Project, 1968-69; spl. projects com. Okla. Dept. Edn., 1974; mem. Okla. State Regents Library Adv. Com., 1975-77; chmn. Adminstrs. Workshop, 1973; TV appearances, 1977, 78. Mem. Okla. Library Assn. (chmn. library edn. div. 1975-76, coll. and univ. div. 1972-73, tech. services div. 1969-70), Southwestern Library Assn., A.L.A., Higher Edn. Alumni Council Okla., AAUW (v.p. Weatherford br.), AAUP, Weatherford C. of C., LWV, Custer County Hist. Soc.), Delta Kappa Gamma. Baptist. Home: 817 N Kansas St Weatherford OK 73096 Office: Al Harris Library Southwestern Oklahoma State University Weatherford OK 73096

HOKR, DOROTHY, state legislator; m. Lee Hokr; children—Thomas, Judith, Paul. Mem. Minn. Ho. of Reps., 1980—, mem. fin. instns. and ins., gen. legis. and vets. affairs, govtl. ops., health and welfare coms. Mem. New Hope City Council. Mem. LWV, N.W. Met. C. of C. Independent Republican. Office: 354 State Office Bldg Saint Paul MN 55155 *

HOLADAY, DEBRA LYNN, communications cons.; b. Mansfield, Ohio, Sept. 4, 1950; d. Nelson and Marcella Frances (Bellew) Jones; student in communications Ariz. State U., 1968-71, U. Calif., Berkeley, 1974, U. Tex., Austin, 1978-79, U. Hawaii, 1981—. Editor, Outreach, United Ch. Directories, Waco, Tex., 1974; dir. sales Grad. Portrait Studies, Waco, 1975-76; v.p. GPS of Tex., Inc., Waco, 1976-77, pres., 1979-81; owner, operator GPS Studios, Austin, 1977-79; asst. editor Trade Pub. Co., Honolulu, 1980; communications cons., 1981—; photography judge Tex. journalism contest Interscholastic League Press Conf., 1977, 78; dir. European Multi-Media Program for Journalists, 1979. Mem. Women in Communications (pres. Honolulu chpt. 1981-82), Internat. Assn. Bus. Communicators. Author: The Gallery of American Presidents, 1978. Home: 2491 Halekoa Dr Honolulu HI 96821

HOLAND, PAMELA KRISIDA, investment/stock broker; b. Dallas, Jan. 22, 1940; d. John Lowery and Mary Elizabeth (Matthews) Vines; student Draughon's Bus. Coll., So. Meth. U., Okla. State U., N.D., State U., U. N.D.; children—David, Deborah, DiAnn, Brian, Michael. Service dir. Upjohn Health Care, Mpls., 1977; mgr. shopping center ops. ThorCo, Inc., Mpls., 1977-79; investment/stock broker Bache, Halsey Stuart Shields, Inc. (formerly Bache, Halsey & Stuart, Inc.), Mpls., 1979-81, Merrill Lynch Pierce Fenner & Smith, Inc., Dallas, 1981—; mem. N.D. Senate from 21st Dist., 1974-76. Chmn., organizer, founding pres. first hosp. aux. in Pawnee, Okla.; gen. chmn. Heart Fund Drive, Am. Cancer Soc. Fund Drive, 1967-69; chmn., organizer com. founding first public library in West Fargo, N.D.; math. tutor Unwed Mother Program Luth. Social Services; area dir. N.D. State Com. for Library Devel.; asst. perceptual motor devel. tng. Opportunity Sch. for Handicapped, Fargo, 1969-72; active LWV, chmn. constl. revision com., 1969-72, bd. dirs. Fargo area, 1972-74; gen. chmn. fund drive, pres. County Am. Cancer Soc., organizer two new chpts.; gen. chmn. com. fundraising com. sta. KFME, ednl. TV, Cass County N.D.; chmn. adv. bd. Fargo Community Day Care Center; bd. dirs. Fargo-Moorhead YWCA, Mpls. YWCA; chmn. legis. com. First Dist. Med. Aux. to Med. Assn.; leader Red River Valley Campfire Girls program; student adv. bd., counseling center N.D. State U. Fargo; adv. com. N.D. State Social Services Bd.; adv. council to N.D. Mental Health Assn., state bd. dirs., sec. N.D. Med. Aux. to N.D. Med. Assn.; bd. dirs. Community Coordinated Child Care Fargo-Moorhead area; state bd. dirs. N.D. Epilepsy Found.; state chmn. bus. adv. com. to Dakota Assn. Native Americans; mem. Tri-Coll. Women's Bur.; campaign mgr. for candidate for Nat. Committeewoman; precinct chmn. polit. dist. 56A; dist. and state del. to polit. convs.; advisory com. to N.D. Social Services Bd.; mem. N.D. Adv. com. U.S. Commn. on Civil Rights; adv. council N.D. Gov.'s Commn. on Comml. Air Transp.; mem. Nat. Mcpl. League, conv. del., 1972-74. Mem. Profl. Women's Group, Nat. Assn. Female Execs. Club: Women's Rotary of Mpls. Home: 9765 Audelia Rd #131 Dallas TX 75238 Office: 2400 RepublicBank-Dallas Tower Dallas TX 75201

HOLBERG, EVA MARIA, civic worker; b. Stralsund, Germany, Apr. 22, 1931; came to U.S., 1957, naturalized, 1962; d. Hans Herbert and Helene Wilhelmine (Engelhardt) Thieshen; student Free U. West Berlin, 1952-55; m. Dieter E. Holberg, May 28, 1955; children—Marion, Astrid. Mgr., Pathways to Music, Mt. St. Mary's Coll., Los Angeles, 1972-74; pres., mgr. Palisades Symphony, Pacific Palisades, Calif., 1974—; pres. Theatre Palisades, 1979-81, 82—, bd. dirs., chmn. ways and means, 1981—; season ticket chmn. Los Angeles Philharm. Affiliated Vols., 1979-81; cultural rep. Palisades Community Council, 1976; bd. dirs. Westside Jr. Philharmonic Com., 1972—, pres., 1975-77, chmn. season ticket sales, 1977—. Named Citizen of Yr. Pacific Palisades, 1981. Mem. Am. Symphony League. Home: 1081 Palisair Pl Pacific Palisades CA 90272 Office: Box 214 Pacific Palisades CA 90272

HOLBERT, DARLENE HATTIE, nurse; b. Warren, Pa., Oct. 24, 1944; d. Swen Victor and Eva Harriet (Ristau) Gustafson; R.N., Capitol City Sch. Nursing, Washington, 1965; m. Burton Louis Holbert, Sept. 7, 1976; children—Darnette Michele, Karl Sven. Staff nurse D.C. Gen. Hosp., 1965-66; staff nurse, asst. head nurse, evening supr. Prince George's Gen. Hosp., Cheverly, Md., 1967-72; nursing supr. Mid Atlantic Nephrology Center, Camp Springs, Md., 1972-73; indsl. nurse Washington Gas Light Co., 1973-74; nursing supr. Police & Fire Clinic, Washington, 1974-77; asst. dir. nursing So. Md. Hosp. Center, Clinton, Md., 1977-79; civilian nurse with U.S. Army, Landstuhl, W.Ger., 1979—. Vol. nurse ARC; CPR instr. Recipient Superior Performance award D.C., 1976, U.S. Army, 1981. Home: 10 Rosenstrasse Hutschenhausen Federal Republic Germany Office: PO Box 5108 APO New York NY 09012

HOLBROOK, PATRICIA ANN, architect; b. Greensboro, N.C., Nov. 28, 1940; d. Bulb Jackson and Pearl Ethylene (Angel) H.; student Coll. William and Mary, 1959-61; B.Arch., N.C. State U., Raleigh, 1967; M.B.A., Loyola Coll., Balt., 1980; m. William Minor May III, Nov. 4, 1961; children—Maria Siena, Jonathan Zwolle, Christopher London, Happy Savannah. Archtl. designer Leviatich & Miller, architects, Ithaca, N.Y., 1968-69, Wells & Koetter, architects, Ithaca, 1969-70; pvt. practice architecture, Balt., 1970-72; prin. architect, partner May & Holbrook, architects, Balt., 1972—; mem. faculty Catonsville Community Coll., 1976-77. Active Montessori Soc. Registered architect, Md.; cert. value engr. Mem. AIA (corp.), Md. Soc. Architects. Office: 901 N Calvert St Baltimore MD 21202

HOLCOMB, MARGUERITE KNOWLES, city ofcl., shorthand reporting co. exec.; b. Dayton Twp., Mich., Apr. 9, 1913; d. Arthur Russell and Catherine (Biermeyer) Knowles; student public schs., Muskegon and Dayton Twp., Mich.; children—Joyce C. Holcomb Filius, John F., June A. Ofcl. circuit ct. reporter 14th Jud. Circuit, Muskegon, 1943-53; pres. Holcomb Reporting Service, Inc., Muskegon, 1953—; commr. City of Muskegon, 1975—, vice-mayor, 1977-79, mayor, 1980—; mem. econ. devel. com. U.S. Conf. Mayors. Mem. adv. council Ferris State Coll., Big Rapids, Mich. Named Businesswoman of Yr., Quadrangle Bus. and Profl. Women's Clubs 1970, State Small Businesswoman of Yr., Mich. Fedn. Bus. and Profl. Women's Clubs, 1973. Mem. Nat. Shorthand Reporters Assn., Mich. Shorthand Reporters Assn., Mich. Ct. Reporters Assn. (pres. 1967-68), Muskegon C. of C. Republican. Clubs: Bus. and Profl. Women's (state pres. 1966-67), Zonta (dir. club), Century. Office: 1891 Lakeshire Dr Muskegon MI 49441

HOLCOMB, MORRIGENE, govt. ofcl.; b. El Paso, Tex., Jan. 22, 1944; d. Morriss Fulton and Mattigene (Palmore) H.; B.S. in Edn., Bucknell U., 1966. Catalogs editor Asso. Book Publs., Ltd., London, 1966-67; asst. to editor Exchange and Commissary News, Washington, 1967; speechwriter Congressional Research Service, Washington, 1967-70, women's rights specialist, 1970-76; women's program officer Library of Congress, Washington, 1976—; employment specialist Pres.'s Civil Rights Reorgn. Task Force and Civil Rights Office of Office of Mgmt. and Budget, Washington, 1979. Recipient meritorious service award Library of Congress, 1974; cert. of appreciation Pres. of U.S., 1979. Mem. Am. Soc. Pub. Adminstrn. (nat. capital area council 1971), ALA, Internat. Personnel Mgmt. Assn., Federally Employed Women, Nat. Women's Polit. Caucus, Washington Women's Network. Mem. editorial adv. bd. Women Today, 1967-80. Office: Library of Congress Washington DC 20540

HOLCOMB, RUTH MARY, warehouse exec.; b. Cleve., Dec. 8, 1920; d. John Albert and Irene Coletta (Hennessey) Klum; student spl. IBM Course, Case Western Res. U., 1960, Am. Mgmt. Assn. course N.Y. U., 1961; Asst. prodn. planning mgr. Hickok Electric, 1940-47; inventory control mgr., asst. purchasing agt. Premier Autoware, 1947-56; asst. warehouse mgr. Curtis Industries, Eastlake, Ohio, 1956-63; warehouse mgr., asst. dir. Cleware Industries, Cleve., 1963-71; v.p., warehouse mgr. H & M Industries, Cleve., 1971—. Democrat. Roman Catholic. Instrumental in award received by Curtis Industries, Am. Material Handling Soc., 1961. Office: H M Automotive Indus 3170 W 106th St Cleveland OH 44111

HOLDEN, FLORENCE ELIZABETH, educator; b. Brattleboro, Vt., Apr. 20, 1923; d. William Henry and Edith Smith (Lane) Cudworth; B.S., U. Vt., 1950; m. Russell Holden (div.); children—Gwen, Russell, Robin, Bruce, Mark, JoAnn, Sandra. Tchr. English, Concord (N.H.) High Sch., 1977—. Bd. dirs. N.H. Community Health Care Assn., pres., 1972-78; sec. bd. Concord Hosp. Assos., 1977—; bd. dirs. YMCA; bd. dirs. Opportunity House, 1979—, Vis. Nurses Assn.; active Girl Scouts U.S., Boy Scouts Am.; trustee U. Vt., 1979—. Served with USNR, 1943-45. Mem. U. Vt. Alumni Assn. (pres. 1976-78), Delta Delta Delta (nat. v.p. 1972-76). Republican. Episcopalian. Club: Concord Country. Home: Birchdale Rd Bow NH 03301 Office: Concord High Sch Warren St Concord NH 03301

HOLDEN, GEORGIE ELIZABETH HOUGH, ret. educator, writer; b. nr. Lucketts, Va.; d. John Wesley and Mary (Barrett) Hough; student Blue Ridge Coll.; B.A., Bridgewater Coll.; postgrad. summer schs. U. Md., Madison Coll.; A.A. with high honors, Prince George's Community Coll., 1973; m. John Hopkins Holden (dec. July 1961); children—Patricia (Mrs. Vincent Squitieri) (dec.), Mary. Tchr. public schs., Montgomery County, Md.; tchr. English, Wicomico High Sch., Wicomico Church, Va.; substitute tchr. Prince George's County Sr. High Sch.; sec. Am. Legion, Washington; clerical asst. higher edn. div. HEW, Washington; sec. Gallaudet Coll., Washington; pub. relations officer; dir. pub. relations, 1960-69, ret.; free-lance writer, 1970—; former asst. Stars and Stripes-The Nat. Tribune. Publicity dir. 5th Internat. Congress Philosophy, Washington, 1957; pub. relations chmn. Workshop Identification Researchable Vocat. Rehab. Problems of Deaf, Washington, 1960, Workshop for Cath. Personnel for Deaf, Washington, 1961, Workshop for Episcopal Workers for Deaf, Washington, 1961; co-chmn. pub. relations Internat. Congress Edn. of Deaf, Washington, 1963; publicity chmn. Workshop for Luths. on Deafness and Rehab., Washington, 1963; mem. nat. adv. bd. Am. Security Council, 1970—; chmn. Generic Drugs Workshop Conf., 1977; co-chmn. Md. Coalition for Generic Equivalants, 1976—; mem. planning com. 1st United Srs. of Md. Day, 1977-78; mem. Tribune sect. Internat. Women's Yr., Mexico City, 1975; pres. Betterment for United Srs., 1977-79, founder, editor Sr. Alert, 1976—, recipient Disting. Achievement award, 1977; charter mem. Republican Presdl. Task Force, 1981. Named hon. citizen Boys Town; recipient award of merit Gallaudet Coll., 1969, Congl. award for vol. assistance, dedicated service and commitment Reps. of 93d Congress, 1973; gifts U.S. div. USSR Fgn. Ministry, 1975; pen used in signing Md. generic drug bill into law, 1977, pen used in signing Md. Pharmacy Assistance-Medicaid bill into law, 1978; Spirited Leadership plaque Betterment for United Srs., 1979; 5 yr. service pin Prince George's County, 1981. hon. fellow Harry S. Truman Library Inst. Mem. Internat. Platform Assn., Nat. Assn. of Deaf, Nat. Trust for Historic Preservation, Am. College Pub. Relations Assn. (hospitality com. nat. conv. 1960, publicity chmn. Mason-Dixon dist. conf. Washington 1961, idea cons. dist. conf. Williamsburg, Va. 1964; dist. sec. 1964-66, planning com. mem. dist. sec. 1964-66, planning com. mem. dist. confs. 1964-66, registrar dist. conf. 1965, nominating com. 1968), Am. News Women's Club, Inc. (publicity com. 1966-67, ad hoc membership com. 1967-68, mem. journalistic tour to China 1980), English-Speaking Union, Am. Assn. Ret. Persons, Smithsonian Assos., Am. Legion Aux., Nat. Symphony Assn., Lancaster-Northumberland Edn. Assn. (chmn. pub. relations com. 1946-48), Puerto Rican Am. Women's League, Nat. Soc. Lit. and Arts, Nat. Religious Publicity Council, Ednl. Press Assn. Am. (steering com. Washington chpt. 1962-63, 66-67, sec.-publicity chmn., editor Edpress Notes 1967-68), Coll. Sports Info. Dirs. Am., Prince George's County Mental Health Soc., Md. Park Improvement Area Assn. (sec. 1963), English-Speaking Union of Commonwealth, Nat. Capital Aux. Vets. World War I (sr. v.p. 1968, group v.p. 1973-74), Delta Zeta (publicity co-chmn. scholarship benefits Gallaudet Coll., 1964-69). Republican. Baptist (pres. adult women's class 1963-66, pres. faith workers class 1963-68). Clubs: U.S. Senatorial (founding); Police and Fire Unit 29; Capitol Heights (Md.) Sr. Citizens (pres. 1978-79, 82—, award for service as pres.). Mem. adv. editorial bd. The Bridgewater Alumnus, 1960-66; editor Gallaudet Record, 1963-69; contbr. articles to profl. publs. Home: 5802 Athena St Maryland Park Capitol Heights MD 20743

HOLDEN, IDA TRAYNER, civic leader; b. La Grande, Oreg., Aug. 8, 1912; d. Jacob Hampton and Lottie (Hill) Trayner; student public schs., Idaho Falls; m. William Sutherland Holden, Nov. 1, 1933; children—William Trayner, Ann Holden Pappas. Exec. sec. Idaho Sch. Trustees Assn., 1956-61. Mem. Bonneville County Bd. Public Assistance, 1945-50; mem. Bonneville County Bd. Edn., 1945-48, Unified Edn. Council, 1953-61; mem. Idaho Falls (Idaho) Sch. Bd., 1947-55, chair, 1954-55; mem. Idaho Dept. Employment, 1960-73; bd. dirs. Eastern Idaho Health and Social Services, 1965-79, Assn. Retarded Children, 1967-71; bd. dirs. Child Devel. Center, 1968-79, chmn., 1968-71; bd. dirs. Devel. Workshop, 1971-78, Idaho Falls Hosp., 1973-82, Idaho Lung Assn., 1968-76, Council Developmental Disabilities, 1971-78; chair Idaho Vocat. Rehab. Bd., 1980-82; bd. dirs. State Health Coordinating Council, 1978-80; mem. Idaho bd. Edn. Commn. of States, 1967-70; bd. dirs. Region 7 Health and Welfare Agy., 1970-82, chair, 1975-80. Recipient service award Am. Humane Assn., 1975, Service to Community award Aden Hyde C. of C., 1977; Woman of Yr., Beta Sigma Phi, 1980. Mem. LWV, PTA (life), Delta Kappa Gamma (hon.). Republican. Club: Toastmistress. Address: 291 S Ridge St Idaho Falls ID 83402

HOLDER, ANGELA RODDEY, lawyer, educator; b. Rock Hill, S.C., Mar. 13, 1938; d. John T. and Angela M. (Fisher) Roddey; student Radcliffe Coll., 1955-56; B.A., Newcomb Coll., 1958; postgrad. Faculty of Laws, King's Coll., London, Eng., 1957-58; J.D., Tulane U., 1960; LL.M., Yale U., 1975; div.; 1 son, John Thomas Roddey Holder. Admitted to La. and S.C. bars, 1960, Conn. bar, 1981; counsel Roddey, Sumwalt & Carpenter, Rock Hill, 1960—; atty. criminal div. New Orleans Legal Aid Bur., 1961-62; counsel York County (S.C.) Family Ct., 1962-64; asst. prof. polit. sci. Winthrop Coll., Rock Hill, 1964-74; research asso. Yale Law Sch., 1975-77, exec. dir. program in law, sci. and medicine, 1976-77; lectr. dept. pediatrics Yale Med. Sch., 1975-77, asst. clin. prof. pediatrics, 1977-79, asso. clin. prof., 1979—; counsel for medicolegal affairs Yale-New Haven Hosp. and Yale Med. Sch., 1977—. Mem. Rock Hill Sch. Bd., 1967-68. Bd. dirs. Family Planning Clinic, chmn., 1970-73. Mem. Am., S.C. (medico-legal com. 1973—), La. bar assns., Am. Soc. Law and Medicine (exec. council). Democrat. Episcopalian. Author: The Meaning of the Constitution, 1968; Medical Malpractice Law, 1975, 2d edit., 1978; Legal Issues in Pediatrics and Adolescent Medicine, 1977. Contbg. editor Prism mag. AMA; also articles. Home: 23 Eld St Apt B New Haven CT 06511 Office: Yale-New Haven Hospital 789 Howard Ave New Haven CT 06504

HOLDER, LILLIAN LYDIA, nursing home adminstr.; b. Sand Draw, Wyo., July 17, 1936; d. Ezra G. and Lillian Lyon; student U. Wyo., 1955, Central Wyo. Coll., 1972-74; A.S. in Nursing, Casper Coll., 1976, student, 1977-79; student St. Joseph's Coll., 1980—; m. William Holder, Aug. 29, 1964; children—Kim Marie (Mrs. Clyde Winckler), Mark Darrell. With Farnsworth Ins. Agy., Riverton, Wyo., 1954-55; bookkeeper Hagstrom Constrn., Riverton, 1955-62; supr. Maddox Well Service, Riverton, 1967-68; nursing asst. Bishop Randall Hosp., Lander, Wyo., 1970-72, Meml. Hosp., Riverton, 1973-74, Natrona County Meml. Hosp., Casper, Wyo., 1974-75; charge nurse, 1976-79; dir. nursing Geriatrics Inc., Greeley, Colo., 1979-80; adminstr. Poplar Living Center, Casper, Wyo., 1980—. Mem. Wyo. Am. Nurses Assn., Wyo. Health Care Assn. Republican. United Methodist. Mem. Order Eastern Star. Home: 338 Columbine St Casper WY 82601 Office: 4305 S Poplar St Casper WY 82601

HOLDSWORTH, CAROLE ADELE, educator; b. Oak Park, Ill., Dec. 3, 1936; d. Merrill Winston and Gladys Ann (Mitchell) Holdsworth; B.A., Elmhurst Coll., 1958; M.A., Northwestern U., 1959, Ph.D., 1965. Instr., Northwestern U., Evanston, Ill., 1962-65; asst. prof. Loyola U. of Chgo., 1965-71, assoc. prof. 1971-80, prof. modern langs., 1980—. Mem. AAUP, MLA, Am. Assn. Tchrs. French, Am. Assn. Tchrs. Spanish and Portuguese, Instituto de Literatura Iberoamericana. Author: Modern Minstrelsy: Miguel Hernandez and Jacques Brel, 1980. Home: 831 S Harvey Ave Oak Park IL 60304 Office: 820 N Michigan Ave Chicago IL 60611

HOLE, VIRGINIA CONNER, cons. co. adminstr.; b. Pasadena, Calif., Mar. 6, 1925; d. Edmund Palmer and Helen Mae Conner; B.S., Pomona Coll., 1947; divorced; children—Theodore W., Victoria E. Hole Boddington, Julie M. Conf. coordinator Los Angeles World Trade Center, 1973-75; dir. membership and promotion Internat. Club Los Angeles, 1975-77; dir. ann. giving Pomona Coll., 1977-80, devel. officer, 1980-81; adminstrv. asst. Richard King Internat., Inc., Los Angeles, 1981—. Bd. dirs. Com. Profl. Women, Los Angeles Philharm. Assn. Mem. Los Angeles World Affairs Council, Calif. Hist. Soc., Pomona Coll. Affiliates, CMC Affiliates, Republican Assocs., English-Speaking Union (dir.), Nat. Art Assn. Episcopalian. Club: Univ. (Los Angeles). Home: 1167 S Orange Grove Blvd Apt 2 Pasadena CA 91105 Office: 811 W Seventh St Suite 206 Los Angeles CA 90017

HOLFORTY, PEARL MARTHA, accountant; b. Detroit, Oct. 31, 1928; s. Johannes and Martha Mary (Francoys) Kramer; student Mich. State U., 1945-47; B.S., Wayne State U., 1970, M.B.A., 1972; m. Clifford W. Holforty, Mar. 27, 1948; children—Kathleen Diane, David Alan, Wendy Lauren, Michael Todd. Controller, Sta. WPON, Pontiac, Mich., 1958-60; bus. mgr. Holforty, Widrig & O'Neill Assos., Inc., Troy, Mich., 1960-69; staff acct. Plante & Moran, C.P.A.s, Southfield, Mich., 1970-77, partner, 1977—; part-time faculty Wayne State U. Recipient Edward G. Erickson award, 1970; Elijah Watts Sells award, 1971; Phi Gamma Mu scholar, 1970. Mem. Am. Inst. C.P.A.s, Mich. Assn. C.P.A.s, Nat. Assn. Accts. (pres. chpt. 1979), Mich. Sch. Bus. Ofcls., Assn. Sch. Bus. Ofcls., Women's Econ. Club, Beta Gamma. Presbyterian. Club: Fairlane. Home: 2783 Hillendale Dr Rochester MI 48063 Office: Plante & Moran PO Box 307 Southfield MI 48037

HOLIAN, GAIL CONCA, educator; b. Jersey City, Sept. 21, 1948; d. Samuel Joseph and Mariejoyee (Contey) Conca; B.A., Georgian Court Coll., 1970; M.A., St. Johns U., 1972; m. John F. Holian, Dec. 26, 1970. Instr. English, Neptune Twp. (N.J.) Bd. Edn., 1971-80; adj. instr. English Ocean County Coll., Toms River, N.J., 1974—; teaching fellow English N.Y.U., N.Y.C., 1978-79; lectr. English Georgian Court Coll., Lakewood, N.J., 1978-80, asst. prof., 1980—. Vol., ARC, 1972—. Georgian Court Coll. grantee, 1968. Mem. Modern Lang. Assn., Nat. Council Tchrs. English, AAUP, Sigma Tau Delta. Club: Soroptomists Internat. (Red Bank Chpt.). Home: 65 Washington St Red Bank NJ 07701 Office: 9th St Lakewood NJ 08701

HOLIDAY, MARTHA JEAN, public relations exec.; b. Charleroi, Pa., Jan. 20, 1926; student Calif. State Tchrs. Coll., 1947-48, N.Y.U., 1948-49. With Slenderlla, N.Y.C., 1952-56; asst. fashion promotion dir. Simplicity Patterns Co., from 1957; producer fashion shows, Biltmore Hotel, N.Y.C., 1957-59, others; freelance fashion show dir.; fashion columnist. Mem. Am. Women in Radio-TV, Women in Allied Alcoholic Beverage Industry. Club: Overseas Press. Address: 119 E 83d St New York NY 10028

HOLLAAR, HESTER M., librarian; b. Hull, N.D., Aug. 7, 1917; d. Aren and Jennie (Groen) Hollaar; B.S., N.D. State Tchrs. Coll., 1959; M.A. in L.S., U. Denver, 1964. Elem. tchr., Hull, 1942-55; tchr., librarian Western Christian High Sch., Hull, Iowa, 1959-64; dir. library Dordt Coll., Sioux Center, Iowa, 1964—. Mem. ALA, Iowa Library Assn., Delta Kappa Gamma. Republican. Mem. Christian Reformed Ch. Home: 829 7th Ave NE Sioux Center IA 51250 Office: Dordt Coll Library Sioux Center IA 51250

HOLLABAUGH WANSERSKI, SUSAN MARIE, greeting card co. exec.; b. St. Louis, July 4, 1954; d. Wilbur Alan and Georgiann Loretta (Molitor) Hollabaugh; B.A. in Psychology magna cum laude, Rockhurst Coll., 1976, postgrad. in bus. adminstrn., 1979-83; m. James Allen Wanserski, Aug. 9, 1975. Editor internal publs. Hallmark Cards, Inc., Kansas City, Mo., 1976-77, process controller I, 1977-78, process controller II, 1978-79, buyer II, 1979-82, sr. bus. analyst, 1982—. Active HALLPAC, Hallmark Polit. Action Com., Bacchus cultural and ednl. found., Prairie Village, Kans., Folly Theater Council, Kansas City; block rep., neighborhood homes assn., Kansas City, 1978. Recipient Indsl. Publs. Award Program Grand Prize of Excellence, United Way Campaign, Kansas City, 1976. Mem. Nat. Assn. Female Execs., Alpha

Sigma Nu. Roman Catholic. Clubs: Brookridge Country, Overland Park. Office: 2501 McGee Kansas City MO 64108

HOLLADAY, WILHELMINA COLE, real estate, printing, and interior design exec.; b. Elmira, N.Y., Oct. 10, 1922; d. Chauncy E. and Claire Elizabeth (Strong) Cole; B.A., Elmira Coll., 1944; postgrad. art history U. Paris, 1953-54, U. Va., 1960-61; m. Wallace Fitzhugh Holladay, Sept. 27, 1946; children—Wallace Fitzhugh, Scott Cole. Exec. sec. Howard Ludington, Rochester, N.Y., 1944-45, Chinese Embassy, Washington, 1945-48; staff Nat. Gallery of Art, Washington, 1957-59; dir. interior design div. Holladay Corp., Washington, 1970—; dir. Holladay-Tyler Printing Corp., 1982—; dir. Woman's Nat. Bank, 1978—, vice chmn., 1978—. Founder archival library of periodicals, books, exhbn. catalogs on women's art for research purposes, 1968—; bd. dirs. Am. Field Service, 1964-80, Internat. Student House, 1973—; mem. council Friends of Folger Mus. Library, 1978—; chmn. com. to establish Nat. Mus. Women's Art, 1980; trustee Corcoran Gallery of Art, 1980—; pres. Holladay Found., 1980—. Mem. Am. Assn. Mus., Am. Fedn. Art, Women's Caucus for Arts, Met. Mus. Art, Mus. Modern Art, Art Libraries of N.Am., Coll. Art Assn., Archives Am. Art, Golden Circle of Kennedy Center, Smithsonian Soc. Episcopalian. Home: 3215 R St NW Washington DC 20007 Office: Holladay Corp 4849 Connecticut Ave NW Washington DC 20008

HOLLAND, DENISE EDGECOMBE, psychiatrist; b. West Palm Beach, Fla., June 13, 1948; d. Erman Wilfred and Mildred Rose (Herndon) Edgecombe; B.S., Howard U., 1970, M.D., 1976; m. Elwood Samuel Holland, June 2, 1973. Adminstrv. asst. NASA, Washington, 1974; extern Alexandria (Va.) Hosp., 1976-78; resident in psychiatry George Washington U. Hosp., Washington, 1976-78, Howard U. Hosp., Washington, 1979-80; physician cons. Dept. Health and Human Services, Balt., 1980-82; physician analyst USPHS, Rockville, Md., 1982—; cons. psychiatrist Bowie (Md.) State Coll., 1979-81, Palmer Park (Md.) Counseling Center, 1981—. Recipient awards Dept. Health and Human Services, 1980, Howard U. Hosp., 1979, D.C. Public Schs., 1981. Mem. AAUW, AMA, Am. Med. Women's Assn., Am. Profl. Practice Assn., Commd. Officers Assn., D.C. Med. Soc., Howard U. Alumni Assn., Howard U. Med. Alumni Assn., Nat. Assn. Residents and Interns, Nat. Med. Assn., Prince George's County Med. Soc., So. Med. Assn., Nat. Med. Assn. Aux. Democrat. Episcopalian. Club: Links (award 1979). Home: 1030 Copperstone Ct Rockville MD 20852 Office: USPHS Room 17-A-55 Parklawn Bldg 5600 Fishers Ln Rockville MD 20857

HOLLAND, DIANNE DAVIS, cytotechnologist; b. Zwolle, La., Dec. 25, 1953; d. Chester Clarence and Eloise Dolores (Ebarb) Davis; student N.E. La. U., 1971-73; B.S., U. S. Ala., 1975, cert. in cytotechnology, 1976. Dental asst. Dr. James R. Cobb, Mobile, Ala., 1974-75; sec. Trail Pontiac, Inc., Mobile, 1976-76; cytotechnologist Physician and Surgeons Hosp., Shreveport, La., 1977—, part-time technologist Willis-Knighton Hosp., Shreveport, 1981—, VA Hosp., Shreveport, 1982—. Registered cytotechnologist. Mem. Am. Soc. Cytology, Am. Soc. Clin. Pathologists, So. Assn. Cytotechnologists, La. Soc. Cytotechnology. Democrat. Roman Catholic. Contbr. articles to profl. jours. Home: 5 Parkway Commons Shreveport LA 71104 Office: 1530 Line Ave Shreveport LA 71101

HOLLAND, GENE GRIGSBY (SCOTTY), artist; b. Hazard, Ky., June 30, 1928; d. Edward and Virginia Lee (Watson) Grigsby; B.A., U. S. Fla., 1968; pupil of Ruth Allison, Talequah, Okla., 1947-48, Ralph Smith, Washington, 1977, Clint Carter, Atlanta, 1977, R. Jordan, Winter Park, Fla., 1979; m. George William Holland, Sept. 22, 1950; 3 children. Various clerical and secretarial positions, 1948-52; news reporter, photographer Bryan (Tex.) Daily News, 1952; clk. Fogarty Bros. Moving and Transfer, Tampa and Miami, Fla., 1954-57; tchr. elem. Schs., Hillsborough County, Fla., 1968-72. One-woman shows of paintings include: Tampa Woman's Clubhouse, 1973, Cor Jesu, Tampa, 1973, bank, Monks Corner, S.C., 1977, Summerville Artists Guild, 1977, 78, Apopka (Fla.) Art and Foliage Festival, 1980, 81, 82, Fla. Fedn. Women's Clubs, 1980, 81, 82; numerous group shows, latest being: Island Gifts, Tampa, 1980-82, Brandon (Fla.) Station, 1980-81, Holland Originals, Orlando, Fla.; represented in permanent collections including Combank, Apopka, also pvt. collections. Vol., ARC, Tampa, 1965-69, United Fund Campaign, 1975-76; pres. Mango (Fla.) Elem. Sch. PTA, 1966-67; sec. Tampa Civic Assn., 1975-76; vol. Easter Seal Fund Campaign, 1962-63. Recipient numerous art awards, 1978-82. Mem. Internat. Soc. of Artists, Council of Arts and Scis. for Central Fla., Fedn. of Women's Clubs (pres. Hillsborough County 1974-75, v.p. Tampa 1974-75), Meth. Women's Soc. (sec. 1976-77), Nat. Trust for Historic Preservation, Nat. Hist. Soc., Central Fla. Geneal. and Hist. Soc., Methodist Soc. Clubs: Musicale (1st v.p. bd. incorporators Tampa 1974-75), Apopka Woman's (pres. 1981-82). Home: 1080 Errol Pkwy Apopka FL 32703 Office: PO Box 700 Plymouth FL 32768

HOLLAND, IRIS DODDS, urban and regional planner; b. DeQueen, Ark., Jan. 27, 1921; d. William Lince and Mary Elvira (Green) Dodds; B.Urban Planning, U. Ill., Champaign-Urbana, 1970, M.Urban Planning, 1972; m. John Clay Holland, Nov. 3, 1948; children—Sara Joyce Holland Sackett, Margaret Lynn Holland Neal. Writer, Quar. Digest Urban Research, Bur. Community Affairs, U. Ill., 1970-71, research asst. dept. urban and regional planning, part-time 1971-72; regional planner Ga. Mountains Area Planning and Devel. Commn., Gainesville, 1972-76, planning dir., 1976-78; researcher, writer, 1979—. Recipient Karl Baptiste Lohmann award U. Ill., 1970. Mem. Am. Planning Assn. (charter), Am. Assn. Ret. Persons (chpt. dir.), Nat. Assn. Ret. Fed. Employees. Democrat. Unitarian. Author: numerous planning documents including Community Development Plan for Clayton, Georgia, 1976; Wildwood Heritage Cookbook, 1979. Address: 1029 Lakemont Dr Gainesville GA 30501

HOLLAND, IRIS KAUFMAN, state legislator; b. Springfield, Mass., Sept. 30, 1920; d. Leo and Sadie Kaufman; grad. Rider Coll., Trenton, N.J.; m. Gilbert S. Holland, Jan. 1, 1941; children—Judy, Richard, Donald. Mem. Mass. Ho. of Reps. from 2d Hampden Dist., 1973—, Republican whip, 1979—; columnist Your State Ombudsman; guest lectr. Mt. Holyoke, Smith, Springfield, Am. Internat., Western New Eng. colls.; Robert A. Taft lectr. Tufts U., U. Mass. Bd. corporators Baystate Med. Center, Goodwill Industries, Springfield, Springfield Day Nursery; adv. bd. Mass. Comm. for Blind; trustee Willis Ross Sch. Deaf; adv. council, exec. com. Bay Path Jr. Coll.; bd. dirs. Pioneer Valley chpt. ARC. Named Woman of Yr., Women's Div., Greater Springfield C. of C., 1980; recipient Woman of Achievement award Mass. Fedn. Bus. and Profl. Women's Clubs. Mem. LWV, Mass. Caucus Women Legislators. Club: Zonta Internat.

HOLLAND, JANET CARLTON, dental hygienist; b. Princeton, N.J., Jan. 4, 1952; d. Ray Deal and Ruth Margaret (Kucher) Carlton; cert. dental hygiene U. N.C., Chapel Hill, 1972, B.S., 1974, M.S. in Dental Aux. Tchr. Edn., 1981; m. James Edward Holland, May 16, 1981. Dental hygienist, Lawrenceville, N.J., 1974-76, Zurich, Switzerland, 1976-79; instr. dental hygiene U. N.C. Sch. Dentistry, Chapel Hill, 1981—. Grantee, Am. Fund Dental Health, 1980. Mem. Am. Dental Hygienists Assn. (Harold Hillenbrand scholar 1980), Am. Assn. Dental Schs., Am. Assn. Public Health Dentists, Assn. Women Faculty, N.C. Dental Hygienists Assn. (chmn. planning com. ho. dels. 1981—), Greater Raleigh Dental Hygiene Study Club (chmn. continuing edn. com. 1981—), U. N.C. Chapel Hill Alumni Assn. Democrat. Author articles in field. Office: U NC Sch Dentistry Chapel Hill NC 27514

HOLLAND, MARJORIE LEE DILDY (MRS. KENNETH A. HOLLAND), educator; b. Hope, Ark.; d. Clell A. and Lucille (King) Dildy; student Lindenwood Coll., 1941; B.S. in Edn., U. Ark., 1945, M.S., 1948, Ed.D., 1963; m. Kenneth A. Holland, July 11, 1948; 1 son, Michael William. Tchr. English, East High Sch., Memphis, 1948-54, 56-59; instr. English, Ark. A. and M. Coll., Monticello, 1959-61; grad. asst. U. Ark., Fayetteville, 1961-63; faculty Northeastern State Coll., Tahlequah, Okla., 1963—, prof. English, 1966—, acting chmn. div. communications, 1971-72, dean Grad. Coll., 1975—. Mem. AAUW (br. v.p. 1967-68), Okla. Edn. Assn. (sec. local unit 1969-70), Nat. Okla. councils tchrs. English, Conf. English Edn., D.A.R., Daus. Am. Colonists, Daus. 1812, Pi Beta Phi, Kappa Delta Pi (chpt. pres. 1962-63), Delta Kappa Gamma (chpt. pres. 1973-76), Phi Delta Kappa. Episcopalian. Clubs: Fortnightly Study (v.p. 1966-68), Muskogee Pi Beta Phi Alumnae. Home: 407 Janet St Tahlequah OK 74464

HOLLAND, SANDRA GUNTER, journalist, editor; b. Mount Airy, N.C., Jan. 12, 1952; d. Joseph Bernard and Rondalene Geralda (Stanley) Gunter; B.S. in Journalism, Va. Commonwealth U., Richmond, 1973; postgrad. N. Tex. State U., Denton, 1975-78, U. Tex., 1974; m. Gasper O. Holland, Feb. 14, 1981. Report writer Va. Dept. Hwys., 1973; newsletter editor Tex. Employment Commn., Austin, 1977-80; free-lance writer, public relations; former tchr. English and journalism. Media contact, advt. rep. Congressional candidate. Served with USAR. Recipient Danforth award, 1973. Mem. Women in Communications, Inc., LWV, Bus. and Profl. Women, Sigma Delta Chi. Republican. Baptist. Home and Office: 529 Oakhaven Rd Pleasanton TX 78064

HOLLAND, SUSAN R., exec. search cons.; b. Chgo., Mar. 24, 1945; d. Edward A. and Christine (Joseph) Rusk; B.A. in Theatre, Knox Coll., 1967; 1 son, Kyle. Tchr. Elgin (Ill.) Public Sch. System, 1967-69; sales and mktg. dir. Bell & Howell Co., Chgo. and Kansas City, Mo., 1971-75; sales dir. Miller/Rossman & Assos. (formerly Women's, Inc.), Hinsdale, Ill., 1975-77; owner, pres. S.R. Holland, Inc., exec. search co., Chgo., 1977—; condr. seminars, speaker. Bd. dirs. B.U.I.L.D., urban devel. league. Mem. Young Execs. Club (membership v.p., now pres.), Chgo. Forum (treas.), Execs. Club of Chgo. Roman Catholic. Office: S R Holland Inc 625 N Michigan Suite 1500 Chicago IL 60611

HOLLANDER, BETTY RUTH, mgmt. cons.; b. Bayonne, N.J., Jan. 13, 1930; d. Irving D. and Gertrude F. Grodberg; B.A., Douglass Coll., 1951; m. Milton B. Hollander, June 8, 1952; children—Eva Lynn, J. Steven, Aaron Joel. Founder, chmn. bd. Omega Group, Stamford, Conn., 1962—; dir. several local cos. Bd. dirs. local community orgns. Jewish. Patentee in field. Office: 1 Omega Dr Stamford CT 06907

HOLLANDER, DORIS A., psychologist, consultant, businesswoman; b. St. Louis, Oct. 13, 1941; d. Samuel and Rose (Heller) H.; B.A., Washington U., 1964; M.A. with distinction, DePaul U., 1972; Ph.D., Loyola U., 1979; m. Jerrold Blumoff, June 9, 1963; children—Sam, Rebecca. Caseworker, Mo. Div. Welfare, St. Louis, 1964-65; research asso. Inst. Juvenile Research, Chgo., 1967-68; instr. ednl. psychology Loyola U., Chgo., 1973-74; psychologist, program developer Women's Achievement Program, Hammond, Ind., 1976-78; pres. Whole Food & Grain Depot, Oak Park, Ill., 1972-78; asst. prof. psychology Webster Coll., St. Louis, 1979—, co-chairperson psychology, sociology and anthropology, dir. adult learner project; pres. Resource Devel. Cons., St. Louis, 1979-81; Exec. v.p., program chmn. Oak Park Mental Health Bd., 1976-79. Mem. Assn. Community Mental Health Authorities Ill. (del.), Am. Psychol. Assn., Midwest Psychol. Assn., Southeastern Psychol. Assn., Mo. Psychol. Assn. (women's issues com.), St. Louis Network Women Psychologists (co-chairperson), Am. Ednl. Research Assn., Am. Personnel and Guidance Assn. Home: 6330 Alexander Dr Saint Louis MO 63105

HOLLEB, DORIS B., urban planner, economist; b. N.Y.C., Oct. 26, 1922; d. Abraham and Rachel Bernstein; B.A., Hunter Coll., 1942; M.A., Harvard U., 1947; postgrad. U. Chgo., 1959-60, 65-66; m. Marshall M. Holleb, Oct. 15, 1944; children—Alan, Gordon, Paul. Economist Fed. Res. Bd., Washington, 1943-44; free lance journalist, cons., 1945-63; econ. cons. Chgo. Dept. City Planning, 1963-64; research asso. Center Urban Studies, U. Chgo., 1966-78, sr. research asso., 1978—, dir. Met. Inst., 1973—; lectr. in field. Bd. dirs. Landmarks Preservation Fund, 1979—; mem. adv. com. Center Study Democratic Instns., 1975-80; mem. adv. council Adlai E. Stevenson Center Internat. Studies, U. Chgo., 1975-79; bd. dirs. Inst. Psychiatry Northwestern Meml. Hosp., 1974-80; mem. vis. com. Oriental Inst. U. Chgo., 1970—; bd. dirs. Bright New City Com., 1968—, Know Your Chfo. Com., 1964—. Mem. Am. Inst. Cert. Planners, Am. Planning Assn., Am. Econ. Assn., NRC, Transp. Research Bd., Lambda Alpha. Clubs: Arts, Tavern Quadrangle, Lincoln Park Tennis, Downtown Ct. (Chgo.); Harvard (N.Y.C.), Bryn Mawr Country. Author: Social and Economic Information for Urban Planning, 1968; The Role of Public Higher Education in Community Service, 1972; contbr. articles to profl. jours. Home: 2650 Lakeview Ave Chicago IL 60614 Office: U Chgo Chicago IL 60637

HOLLEMAN, EDITH A., lawyer; b. Jamestown, Mich., Dec. 31, 1942; d. Hilbert D. K. and Norma B. (Freeman) H.; B.A., Baylor U., 1965; M.S., Columbia U., 1969; J.D., George Washington U., 1976. Admitted to N.Y. bar, 1978; asst. news editor Orange Leader, 1965-68; account exec. Corpcom Services, Inc., 1969-73; researcher Fed. Jud. Center, 1976-77; asst. staff atty. N.Y. State Commn. Jud. Conduct, 1978-79; asst. editor Legal Times, 1979-80; staff counsel govt. ops. com. U.S. Ho. of Reps., Washington, 1980—. Pres., Women's Rights Orgn., George Washington Law Sch., 1975-76; vol. atty. NOW Legal Def. Fund, 1977-78. Mem. Friends of Earth, ACLU, Wilderness Soc., Women's Equity Action League, Women's Legal Def. Fund. Office: Rayburn Office Bldg B371 US House of Representatives Washington DC 20515

HOLLER, MARGARET ANDERSON, publishing co. exec.; b. Denver, Nov. 15, 1943; d. Oscar Arthur and Genevieve J. (Selby) Anderson; A.A., Chaffey Coll., 1963; B.A., U. Calif., Berkeley, 1965; gen. secondary credential Calif. State Coll., San Francisco, 1966. Tchr., Eureka (Calif.) City Schs., 1966-70; with Creative Publs., Inc., Palo Alto, Calif., 1970—, v.p. mktg., 1978-79, v.p. corp. devel., 1980—, asst. corp. sec., 1978—, also dir. Mem. Calif. Math. Council, Nat. Council Tchrs. Math., Calif. Ednl. Exhibitors Assn. (dir. and pres. No. Calif.), Okla. Council Tchrs. Math. (hon. life), Calif. Alumni Assn., Airline Passengers Assn. Author: (with others) Number Sentence Games, 1972. Office: PO Box 10328 Palo Alto CA 94303

HOLLETT, RUTH DUKES, antiques appraiser, lectr.; b. Phila., Dec. 6, 1903; d. George and Laura (Nelson) Dukes; student Pa. Acad. Fine Arts, 1918, Sch. Indsl. Art, Phila., 1920, Baccart Sch., Paris, 1956; m. George Lyon Hollett, Jan. 10, 1936 (dec. 1948). Cons. antiques DAR Mus., Washington, 1942-45; tchr. art Madison Sch., Falls Church, Va., 1942-45; tchr. art therapy St. Elizabeth's Hosp., Anacosta, Md., 1942-45; instr. antiques and Americana, St. Petersburg (Fla.) Jr. Coll., 1962-63; dir. seminars St. Petersburg Hist. Soc. Mus., 1960-63; lectr. various schs. in Fla., 1950-73; condr. seminars Fla. Gulf Coast Art Center, Belleair, 1970-73; lectr. Sci. Center Pinellas County Hist. Soc.; cons. various agys., 1956-75. Mem. Com. 100, Pinellas County; ambassador-at-large, St. Petersburg. Certified expert appraiser antiques and furnishings. Mem. Sun Coast Better Bus. Council, Assn. Fla. Appraisers, Am. Soc. Appraisers (sr.), Nat. Archives and Record Services (asso.), Internat. Platform Assn., Nat. League Am. Pen Women, Co. Mil. Historians, Nat. Hist. Soc., Smithsonian Inst., others. Republican. Mem. Mennonite Ch. Address: 1000 23d Ave N Saint Petersburg FL 33704

HOLLEY, JOAN LOUISE, urban researcher, educator; b. Omaha, June 21, 1931; d. Paul C. and Mae (Straub) Van Valkenburgh; B.S., U. Nebr., 1953, M.Community/Regional Planning, 1976, Ph.D., 1979; m. Jack K. Holley, July 10, 1976; children—Shaun, Erin; stepchildren—Richard, Laura, Michael. Faculty, U. Nebr., Omaha, 1980-82, community service asso. Center for Applied Urban Research, 1980-82. Chmn., 1st Nebr. Neighborhood Workshop/Conf., 1979, asst. chmn. 2d workshop/conf., 1980. Mem. Community Devel. Soc. (pres. Nebr. chpt. 1981-82), Internat. Community Devel. Soc. (urban com., co-editor Vanguard 1980-83), Am. Planning Assn. (chpt. sec.-treas. 1977-78), Neighborhood Orgn. Research Group, Adult and Continuing Edn. Assn., Nat. Adult Edn. Assn., Phi Beta Kappa Regional Assos. (pres. 1981-82). Editor: N.E. Community Devel. Soc. Newsletter, 1980-81; contbr. articles to profl. jours.

HOLLEY, LAUREN ALLANA (MRS. WAYMAN TAYLOR HOLLEY), mental health cons., family therapist; b. Balt., Oct. 9, 1948; d. Winston Willouby and Mary Elizabeth (Hart) Holley; B.S., Morgan State U., 1976; M.A., Antioch U., 1978. Staff Balt. City Schs., 1978—; night communications staff ARC, Balt.; outreach family therapist emergency services Asso. Cath. Charities. Dir., New Life Missionary Bapt. Ch., 1978-80. Recipient Award of Merit, Voter Registration Com., 1980, award outstanding achievement Jobs Project, Morris Goldseker Found., 1979-80. Mem. NAACP (membership com. 1980), Nat. Assn. Female Execs. Office: 4701 N Charles St Baltimore MD 21218 also 320 Cathedral St Baltimore MD 21201

HOLLIDAY, GAY, assn. exec.; b. St. Louis, May 30, 1944; d. Stephen Allen and Imogene (Holder) H.; B.S., Ind. U., 1966, M.S., 1967. Dir. student activities Endicott Jr. Coll., 1967-69; program advisor Meml. Union, Ariz. State U., Tempe, 1969-71, program dir., 1971-74, asst. dir., 1974-79; coordinator ednl. programs and services Assn. Coll. Unions Internat., Bloomington, Ind., 1979—; seminar conductor, coordinator; cons. in field. Volunteer probation officer Maricopa County Juvenile Probation Dept., 1971-72. Mem. Am. Soc. Tng. and Devel., Ind. U. Alumni Assn., AAUW. Club: Zonta. Editor: Regional Newsletter, 1976-79; contbr. articles to profl. jours. Home: 3332 John Hinkle Bloomington IN 47401 Office: 400 E 7th St Bloomington IN 47405

HOLLIDAY, PATRICIA RUTH MCKENZIE, evangelist; b. Jacksonville, Fla., Nov. 17, 1935; d. Robert Irving and Leona Adele (Bell) McKenzie; student Massey Bus. Coll., 1969, Luther Rice Sem., 1976, Southeastern Sem., 1979-80; m. Jan. 20, 1965; children—Connie, Katheryn, Alexander. Sec., Delta Drug Corp., Jacksonville, 1965—; pres. Microfilm Center, Jacksonville, 1974—; pres. Miracle Outreach Ministry, Jacksonville, 1974—. Sec.. Four Found., Inc.; Republican candidate for Fla. Ho. of Reps., 1972; mem. Fla. Republican. Com., 1976-80; lobbyist Fla. Legislature, 1978-80; hostess Pat Holliday TV Show, Jacksonville. Clubs: Minutewomen of Fla. (founder), Univ., Women, Ponte Vedra Women's. Author: Holliday for the King, 1978; Be Free, 1979; Only Believe, 1980; Born Anew, 1981; The Walking Dead, 1982; Anointing Power, 1982; columnist Christian Courier. Home: 9252 San Jose Blvd Apt 2804 Jacksonville FL 32217 Office: Miracle Outreach Ministry PO Box 10126 Jacksonville FL 32207

HOLLIE, ANDRÉA RENEE, public transp. exec.; b. Washington, July 11, 1945; d. Percy Eugene, Jr. and Celestine Marie (Wilson) Ricks; B.S., Portland (Oreg.) State U., 1975; m. Adell Nobu Hollie, III, Aug. 10, 1951. Indsl. coordinator/counselor communications and tech. services div. Philco-Ford Corp., Phila., 1968-70; info. systems supr. Model Cities Program, Portland, 1971-74; coordinator, head research and evaluation dept. Portland Human Resources Bur., 1974-77; dir. conv. activities NAACP, 1977-78; exec. dir. corp. devel. Spiral Works, Inc., Portland, 1978-79; minority bus. enterprise officer Tri-County Met. Transp. Dist., Portland, 1980—. Bd. dirs. Albina Art Center, Portland, 1972-74; mem. Portland Bicentennial Commn., 1976; mem. Portland Cable Communications Regulatory Commn.; mem. Oreg. Museum of Arts, 1974—. Mem. Urban League (dir. Portland 1980—), Schs. for the City (dir. 1980—), Portland Black Women's Network (charter), Delta Sigma Theta (corr. sec. chpt. 1979—). Democrat. Roman Catholic. Club: Portland Met.

HOLLINGER, BETTY JEAN BUSH, educator; b. Selma, Ala.. Mar. 4, 1953; d. Roy Wilson and Betty Jean (Crook) Bush; B.S., U. Montevallo, 1974, M.A.T., 1980; postgrad. U. Ala., 1976, U. Montevallo, 1977, Auburn U., 1978-79; m. Leo Bryant Hollinger, Jr., Nov. 17, 1979 1 son; Leo Bryant III. Asst. head tchr. United Way Day Care, Birmingham, Ala., 1975; clothing tchr. Winston County Area Vocat. Center, Winston County (Ala.) Bd. Edn., 1975-77; asst. county agt. home econs. Auburn U. Extension Services, Camden, Ala., 1977—; lectr. in field. Trustee, mem. adminstrv. bd. Camden United Meth. Ch., 1977—. Mary E. Coleman scholar, 1978. Mem. Ala. Assn. Extension 4-H Agts., Nat. Assn. Extension 4-H Agts., Ala. Home Econs. Assn., Am. Home Econs. Assn., Nat. Assn. Home Extension Agts., Ala. Assn. Home Extension Agts. Methodist. Club: Friday Afternoon, Phi Mu Social. Home: 209 McWilliams Ave Camden AL 36726 Office: First Floor Courthouse Annex Suite 117 Camden AL 36726

HOLLINGER, PAULA COLODNY, state legislator; b. Washington, Dec. 30, 1940; d. Samuel and Ethel (Levy) Colodny; R.N. (Murry Guggenheim award 1961), Mt. Sinai Hosp., N.Y.C., 1961; m. Paul Hollinger, Sept. 16, 1962; children—Ilene, Marcy, David. Mem. Md. Ho. of Dels. from 11th Dist., 1978—. Past sec. Balt. County Commn. Women; past pres. Ind. Democratic Alliance; chmn. Housewives for Humphrey, 1968; del. Dem. Nat. Conv., 1976; mem. U. Md. Chancellor's Commn. on Status of Women, 1979, Md. Health Coordinating Commn., 1979, Md. Gov.'s Commn. on Nursing Issues. Mem. LWV (co-chmn. Pikesville chpt. 1969), Orgn. Rehab. Tng., Nat. Council Jewish Women. Club: B'nai B'rith Women. Office: Room 305C House Office Bldg State Capitol Annapolis MD 21401

HOLLINGSWORTH, HELEN, educator; b. Eldridge, Ala., Jan. 18, 1930; d. Felix Thomas and Julia Arlena (Killingsworth) H.; A.B., U. Ala., 1958, M.A., 1959; Ph.D., U. Tenn., 1971. Instr., U. Ala., 1959-60; personnel officer So. Bell Tel. Co., Mobile, Ala., 1960-61; instr. English, U. N.H., Durham, 1966-71; asst. prof. East Tenn. State U., Johnson City, 1971-76, assoc. prof., 1976—. Served with USAF, 1950-53. Mem. Nat. Council Tchrs. English (state dir. writing achievement awards), AAUP, MLA, Coll. English Assn., Phi Beta Kappa. Editor: The Highlands Bulletin, 1980—. Home: 1109 Southwest Ave Johnson City TN 37601 Office: PO Box 24450 E Tenn State U Johnson City TN 37614

HOLLINGWORTH, BEVERLY ANN, state legislator; b. Haverhill, Mass., Oct. 18, 1935; d. Charles P. and Lillian Evangeline (Brindle) Brindamour; ed. Notre Dame Acad., Tyngsboro, Mass.; m. William Peter Gilligan, Nov. 17, 1978; children by previous marriage—David, Mary Elizabeth, Therese, Kimberly. Patient adv. New Eng. Med. Center, Boston, 1973-75; instr. culinary arts Exeter (N.H.) High Sch., 1977; owner, mgr. Hollingworth Motor Inn and Restaurant, 1958—; mem. N.H. Ho. of Reps., 1981—. Mem. Exeter Hosp. Cancer Clinic, N.H. Consumer Council; adv. bd. vocat.-tech dept. City of Exeter; mem. N.H.

Children and Youth Commn., 1981-82, Hampton Budget Com., 1979-81, Hampton Improvement Land Study Com.; selection team N.H. State Advt. Commn.; chmn. Rockingham County Heart Fund; polit. chmn. for N.H. Seacoast, Gov. King of N.H.; mem. Democratic Policy Com. of N.H., 1982; active Friends of Lane Meml. Library, Exeter Hosp. Vols. Mem. N.H. Order Women Legislators, Nat. Order Women Legislators, Coastal C. of C. (legis. adv. bd., dir.), N.H. Hosp. Assn., Nat. Hosp. Assn. Roman Catholic. Club: Cath. Women's (Hampton); Hampton Democratic. Home: 209 Winnacunnet Rd Hampton NH 03842 Office: A St Hampton Beach NH 03842

HOLLINS, BETTYE, med. researcher; b. Bartow, Ga., Apr. 16, 1946; d. Adolph and Rosa (Brown) Hollins; student Spelman Coll., 1965-67. Lab. technician Med. Coll. Ga., Augusta. 1967-69; research specialist Emory U., Atlanta, 1969-77, lab. supr., 1977—. Mem. Nat. Assn. Female Execs., Inc. Democrat. Baptist. Office: 651 Woodruff Meml Bldg Atlanta GA 30322

HOLLINSHEAD, ARIEL CAHILL, educator; b. Allentown, Pa., Aug. 24, 1929; d. Earl Darnell and Gertrude Loretta (Cahill) H.; student Swarthmore Coll., 1948; A.B., Ohio U., 1951, D.Sc., 1977; M.A., George Washington U., 1955, Ph.D., 1957; m. Montgomery K. Hyun, Sept. 27, 1958; children—William Cahill, Christopher Charles. Asst. prof., fellow in virology Baylor U. Med. Center, Houston, 1958-59; asst. prof. pharmacology George Washington U., Washington, 1959-61, asst. prof. medicine, 1961-64, asso. prof. medicine, head lab. virus and cancer research, 1964-73, prof. medicine, dir. lab., 1974—. Chmn. adv. council Heart to Heart Found. Named Med. Woman of Yr., 1976; decorated Star of Europe medal, 1980. Fellow AAAS, Am. Soc. Microbiology, N.Y. Acad. Sci.; mem. Internat. Assn. Comparative Leukemia Research, Internat. Assn. Study Lung Cancer, Am. Assn. Immunology, Soc. Exptl. Biology Medicine, Am. Soc. Clin. Oncology, Am. Assn. Cancer Research, Washington Acad. Scis., Internat. Agy Research on Cancer, Internat. Union Against Cancer, Grad. Women in Sci., Washington Forum, Sigma Xi, Sigma Delta Epsilon. Clubs: Kenwood Country, Blue Ridge Mountain Country. Contbr. 170 articles to profl. jours.

HOLLIS, BONNIE JEAN, journalist; b. Midland, Mich., Nov. 27, 1939; d. Thomas James and Mildred Lucille (Wells) Smith; B.S., Manchester (Ind.) Coll., 1962; postgrad. edn., Montclair (N.J.) State Coll., 1977; m. James R. Hollis, May 27, 1962; children—Taryn, Timothy. Tchr. English, Millburn (N.J.) Jr. High Sch., 1962-67; reporter Wabash (Ind.) Plain Dealer, 1968-73; gen. assignment reporter, then bus. editor Vineland (N.J.) Times Jour., 1973-78, city reporter, 1978-80; Impressions editor The Press of Atlantic City, 1980—; instr. English lang. English Centre, Zurich, Switzerland, 1977-78; adj. instr. journalism Stockton State Coll., Pomona, N.J., 1979. Recipient award Evening News Assn. Detroit, 1980. Mem. Nat. Fedn. Press Women (2d place award 1980), NOW, N.J. Press Women (treas. 1974-77, 80—; 2 writing awards 1977, 3 writing, editing and layout awards 1978, 4 awards 1980). Home: 2497 Venezia Ave Vineland NJ 08360 Office: Devins Ln Pleasantville NJ 08232

HOLLIS, SHEILA SLOCUM, lawyer; b. Denver, July 15, 1948; d. Theodore Doremus and Emily M. (Caplis) Slocum; B.S. cum laude, U. Colo., 1971; J.D. (Law Sch. scholar), U. Denver, 1973; m. John Hollis; 1 dau., Windsong. Admitted to Colo. bar, 1974, D.C. bar, 1975, U.S. Supreme Ct. bar, 1980; trial atty. FPC, Washington, 1974-75; asso. firm Wilner & Scheiner, Washington, 1975-77; dir. office enforcement Fed. Energy Regulatory Commn., Washington, 1977-79; partner firm Butler, Binion, Rice, Cook & Knapp, Washington, 1980—; profl. lectr. Nat. Law Center, George Washington U., Washington, 1980-82. Mem. Am. Bar Assn. (vice chmn. natural gas com., natural resources sect.), Fed. Energy Bar Assn. (sec., exec. com.), Fed. Bar Assn., Gas Men's Roundtable (exec. com.). Established and developed enforcement program of Fed. Energy Regulatory Commn. Author treatises in field. Office: 1747 Pennsylvania Ave NW Washington DC 20006

HOLLOMAN, JO GASKINS, accountant; b. Charleston, S.C., Apr. 19, 1944; d. Joseph Nathan and Clara Belle (Salter) Gaskins; student Chowan Jr. Coll., 1962, N.C. State U., 1975-78; m. Edward Eugene Holloman, Mar. 8, 1964; children—John Christopher, Jennifer Lynn. Corp. controller, treas. Saieed Constrn. Systems, Inc., Raleigh, N.C., 1973-75; para-profl. to mgr. of mgmt. adv. service Beal & Eilers, Raleigh, 1976-80; owner, acct., fin. planner, mgmt. cons. Jo G. Holloman, C.P.A., Raleigh, 1980—; columnist Garner (N.C.) News, 1981-82. Mem. N.C. C.P.A. Assn. (asso.), Nat. Assn. Female Execs., Nat. Assn. Women Bus. Owners, Garner C. of C. Club: Garner Toastmasters (treas. 1980-81), N. Raleigh Civitan. Editor: Beal & Eilers Newsletter, 1980. Office: PO Box 19105 Raleigh NC 27619

HOLLOWAY, DIANE ELAINE, psychotherapist; b. Tulsa, Oct. 19, 1937; d. Lawrence Lynn and Helen May (Six) Hatcher; B.S., Tex. Woman's U., 1972, M.A., 1974, Ph.D., 1979; m. 1961; children—Brian, Kathleen; m. 2d, Bob Cheney, 1980. Brit. rep. Study Abroad, Inc., London, 1957-59; psychologist Presbyn. Hosp., Dallas, 1970-75, dir. psychol. services and asso. dir. continuing edn. in psychiatry, 1976-78; mental health/mental retardation cons. Drug Rehab. and Law Enforcement Offices, Dallas County, 1975-77; psychotherapist in pvt. practice, Dallas, 1978—; asso. Pain Therapy Assn., Dallas, 1979-81; pres. Security & Mgmt. Systems, Dallas, 1979-81, Mental Health Profl. Group, Dallas, 1980—. Hogg Found. grantee, Southwestern Med. Sch., 1972-73; lic. psychotherapist, Tex. Mem. Am. Med. Writers Assn., Tex. Psychol. Assn., Dallas Psychol. Assn., Am. Psychol. Assn., Tex. Police Assn., Internat. Assn. Chiefs of Police, Archaeol. Inst. Am., Soc. Police and Criminal Psychology. Clubs: Mensa, Paleopathology. Contbr. articles to profl. jours. Home: 11130 Cactus Dallas TX 75238 Office: Suite 619 8210 Walnut Hill Dallas TX 75231

HOLLOWAY, JULIA BOLTON, educator; b. London, Apr. 14, 1937; came to U.S., 1953, naturalized, 1967; d. John Robert Glorney and Sybil Margaret (Rutherford) Bolton; B.A. with great distinction, San Jose State Coll., 1957; M.A., U. Calif., Berkeley, 1967, Ph.D., 1974; m. Halbert H. Holloway, Oct. 10, 1957 (div. June 1967); children—Richard Ben, Colin Lincoln, Jonathan Luke. Teaching asst. U. Calif., Berkeley, 1966-71; asst. prof. English, Quincy (Ill.) Coll., 1971-74, dir. humanities program, 1973-74; asst. prof. English, Princeton U., 1974-81; asst. prof. humanities U. Colo., Boulder, 1981—. Active Princeton Hunger Action, 1974-81; chmn. peace com. Princeton Monthly Meeting, 1975-78; mem. peace com. Phila. Yearly Meeting, 1977-81, clk. policy and legis. subcom., 1980-81; mem. Quaker del. to heads of State, 1980—. Recipient Phelan Lit. award, 1956, 57. Mem. MLA, Medieval Acad., Dante Soc., New Chaucer Soc., James Joyce Found., Bronte Soc. Quaker. Editor, translator: Il Tesoretto (Brunetto Latini), 198; contbr. numerous articles to profl. jours. Office: Center for Interdisciplinary Studies Ketchum 128 U Colo Boulder CO 80309

HOLLOWAY, JULIA FRANCES, air force officer; b. Indianola, Miss., May 3, 1950; d. Harold Francis and Louise Isabelle (Hall) Holloway; B.A., Miss. State U., 1973; postgrad. U. Denver, 1978-80. Commd. capt. USAF, 1974; space surveillance officer Mill Valley AFS, Calif., 1974-77, Clear AFS, Alaska, 1977-78, missile warning officer Cheyenne Mt. Complex, Colo., 1978-79, chief MW Standardization/Evaluation Div., CMC, Colo., 1979-81, dep. dir. MW Ops. Directorate, 1981, MW Software Test/Integration mgr., 1981-82, 1st tech. tng. mgr. Air Force Space Systems Career Field Randolf AFB, Tex., 1982—; cons. in field. Leader Girl Scouts U.S.A., 1975-76; disaster preparedness officer Mill Valley AFS, Calif., 1975-77; disaster preparedness evaluation officer Clear AFS, Alaska, 1977-78; acting chief disaster preparedness evaluation team Hdqrs. N. Am. Aerospace Def. Command, 1979-81. Mem. Air Force Assn., AAUW, Nat. Assn. Female Execs., NOW, Amnesty Internat., Smithsonian Inst. Unitarian. Home: 6935 Ashbrook Dr San Antonio TX 78239 Office: Lowery-Goodfellow Tech Training Div HQ ATC Randolph AFB TX

HOLLOWAY-HENDRIX, RUBY FAYE, educator; d. Frederick Douglass and Ethel Lougenia (Steen) Holloway; B.S., Paul Quinn Coll., Waco, Tex., 1949; M.Ed. with honors, U. Tex., Austin, 1953; m. Allen Hendrix, Apr. 15, 1942. Prin. schs. in Tex., 1941-48; sec., 1948-49; primary tchr. La Marque (Tex.) Ind. Sch. Dist., 1949-51; tchr. exceptional children Galveston (Tex.) Ind. Sch. Dist., 1951—; bd. dirs. Oleander-Sunshine Tng. Center Retarded Children, 1957—; speaker in field. Dir. 10th Episcopal Dist. Sunday Ch. Sch., A.M.E. Ch., 1963-67; co-founder Primm Chapel A.M.E. Ch., LaMarque, 1957. Recipient Vol. Service award U. Tex. Med. Br., Galveston, 1979. Mem. NEA, Assn. Childhood Edn., Tex. Tchrs. Assn. (life), Tex. Classroom Tchrs. Assn., Galveston Edn. Assn. (pres. 1978-79). Democrat. Home: PO Box 243 2629 Lake Park Dr La Marque TX 77568

HOLLY, HELEN ANN, govt. ofcl.; b. Bklyn., Dec. 18, 1922; d. John D. and Ellen Mildred (White) Gough; R.N., Cornell U.-N.Y. Hosp., 1944; B.A. in Psychology, U. Nev., Las Vegas, 1970, M.S. in Counseling, 1980; m. George J. Holly, Jr., Sept. 28, 1944; children—Patricia, George J., III (dec.), John, Michael, Maureen, Rosemary, Charles, Eileen, Kathleen, William. Staff nurse hosps. in Ill. and Va., 1944-50; pvt. duty nurse, Va. and Nev., 1950-65; nurse-jail matron Las Vegas Police Dept., 1965-73; U.S. probation officer, Las Vegas, 1974—; tchr. jail mgmt. Clark County Community Coll., 1977; mem. Gov. Nev. Adv. Bd. Alcoholism, 1971-73. Mem. Gov. Nev. Commn. Status Women, 1968-70. Mem. Fed. Probation Officers Assn., Am. Personnel and Guidance Assn., Nev. Nurses Assn. (pres. 1968), Am. Gold Star Mothers. Democrat. Roman Catholic. Home: 5204 Lytton Ave Las Vegas NV 89102 Office: US Probation 300 Las Vegas Blvd S Room 402 Las Vegas NV 89101

HOLLY, PATRICIA ANN, nursing educator; b. Ft. Wayne, Ind., Mar. 30, 1935; d. Jeremiah J. and Loretta M. (Borchers) H.; B.S. in Nursing, U. Dayton (Ohio), 1964; M.N., U. Pitts., 1970. Joined Franciscan Sisters, Roman Catholic Ch., 1951; supr., instr. pediatric nursing St. Elizabeth Hosp., Dayton, 1960-63, 65-68; med.-surg. nursing supr. St. Elizabeth Hosp., Covington, Ky., 1964; tchr. pediatric nursing Wright State U., Dayton, 1972-74; dir. nursing Franciscan Terr., Cin., 1975-79; asst. prof. nursing edn. U. Cin., 1981—; trustee Our Lady of Bellefont Hosp., Ashland, Ky., 1981-82, Schroder Manor Nursing Home, Hamilton, Ohio, 1975-80; speaker, cons. in field. Mem. Am. Nurses Assn., Nat. League Nursing. Home: 60 Compton Rd Cincinnati OH 45215 Office: 9555 Plainfield Rd Cincinnati OH 45236

HOLLYWOOD, SUSAN ALICE, lawyer; b. Glendale, Calif., Nov. 20, 1953; d. Edwin L. and Merle C. Hollywood; A.B., UCLA, 1974; postgrad. U. Calif., Berkeley, 1974-75; J.D., U. Calif., Hastings, 1978. Admitted to Calif. bar, 1978; legis asst. Congressman Grassley, Washington, 1979-80; legis. asst. to Com. on Fin. U.S. Senate, 1981—. Mem. Calif. Bar Assn. Republican. Episcopalian. Office: Senate Office Bldg Room 232 Washington DC 20510

HOLM, CELESTE, actress; b. N.Y.C.; d. Theodor and Jean (Parke) Holm; ed. Univ. Sch. for Girls (Chgo.), Lycée Victor Durui (Paris), Francis Parker Sch. (Chgo.). Appeared on Broadway in role of Mary L. in the Pulitzer prize play, The Time of Your Life, 1939; opposite George M. Cohan in The Return of the Vagabond, 1940; in Eight O'Clock Tuesday, also My Fair Ladies, 1941; Broadway and on tour in Papa Is All, 1941-42; in The Damask Cheek, 1942-43; first musical comedy role Ado Annie, in Oklahoma, 1943-44; then starred in Bloomer Girl, 1944; made supper club appearance in La Vie Parisienne, 1943, Persian Rm., Plaza Hotel (N.Y.C.), 1944, 45, 53, 54, 55, 57, 59; U.S.O. entertainer, ETO, Aug.-Nov. 1945; appeared in film Three Little Girls in Blue, 1946; starred in films: Gentlemen's Agreement, Snake Pit, Road House, Chicken Every Sunday, Come to the Stable, 1948; Everybody Does It, 1949; Champagne for Caesar, All About Eve, 1950; The Tender Trap, 1955; High Society, 1956; made 21,000 mile tour U.S. Army Air Bases entertaining mil. personnel, 1949; starred on stage in Broadway comedy hit, Affairs of State, Sept. 1950-June 1951; for Dept. State recreated original role in Oklahoma, Berlin Arts Festival (Germany), 1951; starred in revival of Anna Christie (Eugene O'Neill), N.Y.C. Center Theatre, January 1952; appeared on Broadway in The King and I, 1952; Third Best Sport, 1958; Invitation to a March, 1960-61, off Broadway in A Month in the Country, 1963; condr. radio program People at the UN, WNBC radio sta., N.Y.C., 3 yrs.; toured U.S. in program Theatre-in-Concert, 1963, 64, toured 8 Middle Eastern and European countries for State Dept., 1966; appeared as fairy godmother in color TV spl. Cinderella, 1965, 66, 67; starred TV presentations, 1966; star, dir. Affairs of State, Pasadena Playhouse, 1967; starred as Mame in Nat. Co., 1967, 68; appeared in movies Doctor You've Got to be Kidding, 1966, Tom Sawyer, 1972, Secret Files of J. Edgar Hoover, 1976, Bittersweet Love, 1976, on Broadway in Candida, 1970, Habeas Corpus, 1975-76. Mem. governing bd. U.S. Com. for UNICEF; mem. bd. Nat. Assn. Mental Health Bd. Coll. and Career Cons.; v.p. Arts and Bus. Council; mem. Nat. Arts Council, 1982—. Decorated knight Order of St. Olav (Norway); recipient Motion Picture Academy award for best performance by an actress in a supporting role for 1947 for picture, Gentlemen's Agreement; nominated for Acad. Award for work in Come to the Stable, 1950, and again for work in All About Eve; Performer of Year, Variety Clubs Am., 1966; Woman of Yr. award Alliance Francaise; Sarah Siddens award for role in Mame. Address: care Lionel Larner 850 7th Ave New York NY 10019

HOLM, HANYA, choreographer, dir., dancer, dance educator; b. Worms-am-Rhine, Germany; d. Valentin and Marie (Moerschel) Eckert; ed. pvt. schs., Germany; student of music Hoch Conservatory and Dalcroze Inst., Frankfurt-am-Main; grad. Dalcroze Inst., Hellerau; dance diploma Mary Wigman Central Inst., Dresden, Germany; D.F.A. (hon.), Colo. Coll., 1960, Adelphi U., 1969; married and divorced; 1 son, Klaus Holm. Came to U.S., 1931, naturalized, 1939. Chief instr., co-dir. Wigman Inst., Dresden, 10 yrs.; mem. original Wigman Co.; performer, dance dir., choreographer, Europe, until 1931; under auspices Sol Hurok, founder, dir. N.Y. Wigman Sch. Dance, 1931, which later became Hanya Holm Sch. Dance; began Am. concert career, 1936; major prodns.: Trend (N.Y. Times award from John Martin as best dance composition of year), 1937; Metropolitan Daily, 1938; Tragic Exodus (Dance Mag. award for best group choreography in modern dance), 1938; in work with theatre; dir. Eccentricities of Davey Crockett; choreographer: Ballet Ballads, 1948; Kiss Me, Kate (Cole Porter) (best choreographer N.Y. Drama Critics award), 1948, Eng. prodn., 1951; Out of this World (C. Porter), 1950; choreographer, dir. The Golden Apple (Critics Circle citation best musical), 1954; staged dances for re-make of film Vagabond King, 1956; choreography for musical Reuben- Reuben, 1955-56; choreography and mus. numbers My Fair Lady (Tony nominee), 1955-56 (Israeli prodn. 1964), Where's Charley, My Fair Lady (English prodns.), 1958, Christine, and Camelot, 1960-61, Anya, 1965; choreographer television show Pinocchio, 1957, Dinner with the President, 1963, Metropolitan Daily (1st dance prodn. on TV), 1939; dir., choreographer world premiere opera The Ballad of Baby Doe, Central City, Colo. opera house, 1956; dir. dance dept. Mus. Theatre Acad., N.Y.C., 1962—. Pioneer Labanotation for copyright on dance scores musicals Kiss Me, Kate, 1948, My Darlin' Aida, 1952, My Fair Lady, 1956; dir. own sch., N.Y.C., until 1968; dir. summer sessions in dance Colo. Coll., 1941—; mem. staff Alwin Nikolais/Murray Louis Dance Theatre Lab., N.Y.C., 1972—, Juilliard Sch., N.Y.C., 1975—; tchr., lectr. Bretton Coll., Eng., 1979; appeared on Am. Cancer Soc. series, Tactic (NBC), 1959; dir., choreographer opera Orpheus and Euridice (Gluck), Vancouver Internat. Festival, 1959. Recipient Capezio award, 1978; award Fedn. Jewish Philanthropies, 1959; Colo. Centennial award and Gov.'s award, 1973, 74; Heritage Honor award Nat. Dance Assn., 1976; award and medal of distinction in fine arts City of Colorado Springs, 1978. Mem. Am. Arbitration Assn. (nat. panel arbitrators), Soc. Stage Dirs. and Choreographers (v.p.). Address: care Selma Tamber 45 W 54th St New York NY 10019 *

HOLM, SHIRLEY SUE, educator; b. Dayton, Ky., Mar. 29, 1947; d. Joseph W. and Elizabeth D. Hakken; B.A., U. South Fla., 1968; m. Randall L. Holm, June 14, 1969. Tchr., Leto High Sch., Tampa, Fla., 1968-70, Coleman Jr. High Sch., Tampa, 1970-71, Congressional Schs. of Va., Falls Church, 1971-73; tchr. math. Charlotte High Sch., Punta Gorda, Fla., 1974—, also chmn. math. dept., sponsor varsity and jr. varsity football cheerleaders. Named Tchr. of Yr., Charlotte High Sch., 1979, 80, 81. Mem. AAUW, Fla. Council Tchrs. Math., Nat. Council Tchrs. Math., Delta Kappa Gamma. Democrat. Baptist. Home: 880 Silver Springs Port Charlotte FL 33952 Office: 1250 Cooper St Punta Gorda FL 33950

HOLMAN, FELICE, author; b. N.Y.C., Oct. 24, 1919; d. Jac C. and Celia (Hotchner) Holman; B.A., Syracuse U., 1941; m. Herbert Valen, Apr. 13, 1941; 1 dau., Nanine E. Free-lance writer, 1956—. Recipient Lewis Carroll Shelf award Wis. Book Conf., 1974; First Austrian Book prize Austrian Ministry Culture, 1978; Notable Book award ALA, 1975, 79. Mem. Author's Guild. Author: Elisabeth the Birdwatcher, 1962; Elisabeth and the Marsh Mystery, 1964; Silently, The Cat, and Miss Theodosia, 1965; Elisabeth the Treasure Hunter, 1966; Victoria's Castle, 1966; The Witch on the Corner, 1966; The Cricket Winter, 1967; The Blackmail Machine, 1968; A year to Grow, 1968; The Holiday Rat and the Utmost Mouse, 1969; Solomon's Search, 1970; At the Top of My Voice, 1970, 2d edit., 1976; The Future of Hooper Toote, 1972; I Hear You Smiling, 1973; The Escape of the Giant Hogstalk, 1974; Slake's Limbo, 1974; The Drac, 1975; The Murderer, 1978; others. Office: care Charles Scribner's Sons New York NY 10017

HOLMAN, MARTHA BARTRON, civic worker; b. Scranton, Pa., Jan. 23, 1924; d. Jay George and Huldah Tague Bartron; A.S., Scranton Bus. Coll., 1942; student S.W. Tex. State U., 1980; m. William Holman, Jr., Oct. 9, 1948 (dec.); children—Susan, John, William. Sec., Sprague & Henwood, Inc., 1942-43; with Scranton Lackawanna Trust Co., 1943-49; court statement clk. Northeastern Bank Pa., Scranton, 1960—; mem. allocation com. United Way, 1976-78; leader Girls Scouts U.S.A., 1955-73; den mother Boy Scouts Am., 1958-65; council pres. PTA, 1974-76, dist. dir., 1979-81; pres. United Neighborhood Services, 1976-79; bd. dirs. parenting council HSA; chmn. Christian edn. com. Hyde Park Presbyteran Ch., 1970-78, bd. sessions, 1980-82, chmn. building fund 1982—. Mem. Am. Inst. Banking. Republican. Home: 1209 Lafayette St Scranton PA 18504 Office: PO Box 937 Scranton PA 18501

HOLMAN, MARY ALIDA, economist, educator; b. West Point, N.Y., June 26, 1933; d. Jonathan Lane and Anna Alida (Johnson) H.; B.A., George Washington U., 1955, M.A., 1957, Ph.D. (Thomas A. Edison fellow 1962), 1963; m. Theodore Suranyi-Unger, Dec. 15, 1962. Mem. faculty George Washington U., 1963—, prof. econs., 1973—; professorial lectr. Indsl. Coll. Armed Forces, 1965—, Nat. War Coll., 1966-74, Naval Sch. Health Scis., 1979—; cons. NASA, 1966-68, Pres.'s Cost of Living Council, 1971-73. Recipient Watson award Am. Patent Law Assn., 1964. Mem. Am. Econ. Assn. Author: The Political Economy of the Space Program, 1974; co-author: Price Theory and Its Uses, 1978. Office: Dept Econs George Washington U Washington DC 20052

HOLMBERG, LILLIAN, cytotechnologist; b. Bklyn., May 27, 1935; d. Linus Ted and Lillian (Codd) H.; B.A., Bklyn. Coll., 1957; diploma N. Providence (R.I.) Sch. Cytology, 1965. Supr. cytology Boston Lying-In Hosp., 1965-69; cytologist to physician, 1969-71, 1973-74; cytologist St. Anthony's Hosp., St. Petersburg, Fla., 1971-73, Feegel and Howard Lab., Tampa, Fla., 1974-75, Maine Med. Center, Portland, 1978-80, Greenpoint Hosp., Bklyn., 1980-82; cytology supr. Woodhull Med. Center, Bklyn., 1982—. Mem. Am. Soc. Clin. Pathologists, Internat. Acad. Cytology, N.Y. Acad. Cytology, AAUW. Address: Longacre House 317 W 45th St Apt 302 New York NY 10036

HOLME, BARBARA SHAW, state senator; b. Long Beach, Calif., May 24, 1946; d. Harry and Lillian (Walton) Shaw; student UCLA, 1962-63; B.A., Stanford U., 1967; m. Howard Holme, June 16, 1968; 1 son, Timothy Peter. Asst. dir. Met. Denver Urban Coalition, 1969-71; urban cons. Cogen Holt & Assos., New Haven, 1968-69, 1971-72, Denver Housing Adminstrn., 1972-74; mem. Colo. Senate, 1975—, Democratic caucus chmn., 1977-78, Dem. asst. minority leader, 1979-83. Co-pres. Colo. Young Dems., 1973-74; mem. Capitol Hill United Neighborhoods; mem. Colo. Open Space Council; mem. Mayor's Adv. Com. on Youth, Denver, 1969-70; chmn. Colo. Women for Ida Nudel. Recipient award for Outstanding Dem. Senator, Colo. Social Legis. Com., 1979, 80. Jewish. Office: Room 214 State Capitol Bldg Denver CO 80203

HOLMES, BARBARA ANN KRAJKOSKI, real estate asso.; b. Evansville, Ind., Mar. 21, 1946; d. Frank Joseph and Estella Marie (DeWeese) Krajkoski; B.S., Ind. State U., 1968, M.S., 1969, specialist cert., 1976; postgrad. U. Nev., 1976-78; m. David Leo Holmes, Aug. 21, 1971. Acad. counselor Ind. State U., 1968-69, halls dir., 1969-73; dir. residence halls U. Utah, 1973-76; sales asso. Fidelity Realty, Las Vegas, Nev., 1977—; cert. analyst Nev. Dept. Edn., 1981-82; tchr. Clark County Sch. Dist., 1982—. Named Outstanding Sr. Class Women, Ind. State U., 1969; recipient Dir's. award U. Utah Residence Halls, 1973, Outstanding Sales Asso., 1977. Mem. Nev. Assn. Realtors, AAUW, Am. Assn. Women Deans, Adminstrs. and Counselors, Am. Personnel and Guidance Assn., Am. Coll. Personnel Assn., Nevadans for Equal Rights Amendment, Alumnae Chi Omega (treas. Terre Haute chpt. 1971-73, bd. officer Las Vegas 1977—), Clark County Panhellenic Alumnae Assn. (pres. 1978-79). Methodist. Clubs: Job's Daus., Order Eastern Star. Developed personal awareness program U. Utah, 1973-76. Home and Office: 3640 El Toro St Las Vegas NV 89121

HOLMES, BARBARA DEVEAUX, educator; b. Miami, Fla., Nov. 26, 1947; d. Robert Eugene and Lula Mae (Jefferson) DeVeaux; B.A., Stetson U., 1969, M.Ed., 1972; Ph.D., U. Conn., 1974; m. Roosevelt Holmes, Aug. 9, 1971; children—Michael, Courtney. Dir. instl. research and planning Fayetteville (N.C.) State U., 1974-77, asst. to pres., 1977-79; dir. Div. Research and Planning, Mo. Dept. Higher Edn., Jefferson City, 1979-81; v.p. for adminstrv. services and public affairs Hillsborough Community Coll., Tampa, Fla., 1981—; adj. cons. Inst. for Services to Edn., 1979-80. Mem. Bd. of Appeals, City of Fayetteville, 1978-80; bd. dirs. Am. Cancer Soc., Fayetteville, 1979-80. Recipient Outstanding Young Woman award, State of N.C., 1977; named Disting. Grad., U. Conn., 1979. Mem. Assn. Instl. Research, Am. Assn. Higher Edn., Phi Delta Kappa, Pi Lambda Theta. Democrat. Baptist. Author: A Guide for Preparation and Submission of Proposals for Federal and Private Support, 1975; The Black College and Title III, 1979. Home:

5417 Rosemont Ave Tampa FL 33614 Office: 39 Columbia Dr Tampa FL

HOLMES, BARBARA MARIE, pub. co. exec.; b. Petaluma, Calif., Sept. 22, 1950; d. Colin and Dorothy (Gamble) H.; spl. student in art Cuesta Coll., Calif., 1968-71; B.S. in Graphic Design, San Jose State U., 1974. Art cons., buyer, dir. holiday design Lee Wards, San Jose, Calif., 1974-75; tchr. art Peninsula Sch., Palo Alto, Calif., 1975-76; dist. mgr. sales Nat. Fedn. Ind. Bus., San Mateo, Calif., 1976-79; br. mgr. Datapro Research Corp. subs. McGraw Hill Co., Mountain View, Calif., 1979—. Recipient cert. for dedication to underprivilaged children Cuesta Coll., 1969; Sales Achievement award Datapro Research Corp., 1979. Mem. Nat. Saleswomen's Assn., Delta Gamma (Sr. Achievement award 1975, v.p. 1975, rush adv. 1980—). Republican. Episcopalian. Office: 2107 Landings Dr Mountain View CA 94043

HOLMES, DEBORAH LOTT, psychologist, educator; b. Pensacola, Fla., July 13, 1946; d. Roy and Agnes (Medlin) Lott; A.B., Stanford U., 1967; M.S., U. So. Calif., 1968; Ph.D., Harvard U., 1973; m. William C. Holmes, Mar. 27, 1970; children—Dawn Elena, Melissa Lee. Vis. asst. prof. psychology U. Calif., Santa Barbara, 1974-75; assoc. prof. Loyola U., Chgo., 1975—; assoc. in pediatrics Evanston Hosp., 1979—. NSF fellow, 1970-72; March of Dimes grantee, 1979—. Mem. Soc. Research in Child Devel., Am. Psychol. Assn., AAAS, N.Y. Acad. Scis. Author: (with F. J. Morrison) The Child, 1979; contbr. articles to profl. jours. Home: 321 Wesley St Evanston IL 60202 Office: 6525 N Sheridan St Chicago IL 60626

HOLMES, HELEN BEQUAERT, sci., tech. and society researcher; b. Boston, Sept. 6, 1929; d. Joseph Charles and Frances Alice (Brown) B.; A.B. in Chemistry, Oberlin Coll., 1951; M.S. in Zoology, Cornell U., 1953; Ph.D. in Zoology, U. Mass., 1970; m. Francis W. Holmes, June 7, 1953; children—Peter Alan, Sarah Ruth, Joseph Mark. Chmn. sci. dept. Northampton (Mass.) Sch. for Girls, 1965-67; asst. prof. biology Springfield Tech. Community Coll., 1971-73; vis. investigator Amherst Coll., 1973-75; asst. prof. biology Eisenhower Coll., 1975-76; asst. prof. Russell Sage Coll., 1976-78; vis. lectr. in genetics Tufts U., fall 1978, fall 1979; research asso. Fedn. Orgns. for Profl. Women, Washington, 1978-82; vis. scholar in philosophy Spelman Coll., 1982-83; speaker on health care Women of the USSR and the U.S.: Issues of Mut. Concern, LWV, Racine, Wis., 1979; organizer AAAS Symposium, San Francisco, 1980. Trustee, Mt. Toby Friends Meeting, Leverett, Mass., 1960-68, clk., 1979-82. Adelia Field Johnston fellow, 1968-69; NSF grantee, 1978-80, 82-83. Mem. AAAS, Population Biologists New Eng., Inst. Soc. Ethics and Life Sci., Am. Genetic Assn., Assn. Women in Sci., Nat. Women's Studies Assn., Phi Beta Kappa, Sigma Xi, Phi Kappa Phi. Editor-in-chief: Birth Control and Controlling Birth: Women-Centered Perspectives, 1980; The Custom-Made Child? Women-Centered Perspectives, 1981. Home: 24 Berkshire Terr Amherst MA 01002

HOLMES, LAURA GLENN, educator; b. Tampa, Fla., Oct. 21, 1930; d. Glenn Thomas and Beulah S. (Soper) Massey; B.S., U. Tampa, 1951; M.A., U. Colo., 1960; postgrad. U. Chgo., 1965, U. Wis., 1963, U. Fla., 1958, Nova U., 1973, 74, 75; m. G. Harris Holmes, Aug. 21, 1967 (dec. 1979); 1 dau., Jennifer G. Tchr., Broward Elem. Sch., Tampa, Fla., 1951-58; curriculum specialist Hillsborough County Sch. System, Tampa, 1958-59; dean girls Madison Jr. High Sch., Tampa, 1959-61; prin. Robles Sch., Tampa, 1961-62, Ballast Point Sch., Tampa, 1962-67; coordinator instructional services Region 10 Edn. Service Center, Dallas, 1968-73; dir. Lamplighter Sch., Dallas, 1973-75, St. John's Episcopal Sch., Dallas, 1975-81; founder, exec. dir. The Glenwood Sch., Dallas, 1981—; cons. in field. Glenwood Sch. trustee, 1981-83. Mem. Assn. Supervision and Curriculum Devel., Nat. Assn. Elem. Sch. Prins., Delta Kappa Gamma, Alpha Chi Omega. Christian Ch. Home: 6817 Greenwich Ln Dallas TX 75230 Office: 851 S Greenville Richardson TX 75081

HOLMES, LILLIAN OVERTON TODD, banker, Republican nat. committeewoman; b. Toone, Tenn., Sept. 4, 1920; d. Anderson Marsh and Annie Eunice (Black) Overton; B.A., U. Miss., 1973; m. Norman W. Todd, June 15, 1941 (dec. 1972); children—Norman W., Barbara Todd Simard, Alice Todd Perry, Mark O.; m. 2d, C. Ross Holmes, Oct. 6, 1979. With Deposit Guaranty Nat. Bank, Jackson, Miss., 1973—, now bus. devel. cons.; Rep. state vice chmn., 1970-76; Rep. nat. committeewoman for Miss., 1976-80. Episcopalian. Home: 66 Eastbrooke Dr Jackson MS 39216

HOLMES, MARION BERRY WARNER, ednl. adminstr.; b. Abington Twp., Pa., Apr. 13, 1926; d. James Wallace and Hester Hattie (Harrison) Berry; B.S. in Bus. Edn., Temple U., 1948, M.Ed. in Adminstrv. Supervision, 1962; Ed.D. (U.S. Office Edn. fellow), Rutgers U., 1974; m. James Curtis Warner, Aug. 19, 1950; 1 son, James Curtis; m. 2d, Philip H. Holmes, II, July 12, 1975; stepchildren—Philip H., III, Sherrill Holmes Brown. Acct., Walter P. Harris Co., C.P.A., Phila., 1948-55; chm. dept. William Penn Bus. Sch., Phila., 1948-53; tchr. secretarial sci. and acctg. Phila. Public Schs., 1955-65, supr. bus. edn., 1965-75, dir. vocat. edn., 1975—; trustee Rider Coll., Trenton, 1975-79; N.J.; vice chmn. nat. adv. council Nat. Center Research Vocat. Edn., 1978—; cons., lectr. in field. Pres., dir. youth activities First Bapt. Ch. of Crestmont, Willow Grove, Pa., 1970, also trustee; bd. dirs. Bapt. Children's Home, Phila., 1970-80. Recipient Four Chaplains Legion of Honor, 1964, Community Outstanding Service award Brighthope Bapt. Ch., Phila., 1979. Mem. Nat. Bus. Edn. Assn. (exec. bd. 1975-79), Am. Vocat. Edn. Assn., Assn. Supervision and Curriculum Devel., Council for Exceptional Children, Eastern Bus. Edn. Assn. (dir. 1968-79, pres. 1976), Pa. Vocat. Assn., Vocat. Adminstrs. Pa., Phila. Assn. Sch. Adminstrs., Nat. Assn. for Advancement Black Ams. in Vocat. Edn., Black Womens Ednl. Alliance, NAACP (life), Nat. Assn. Large City Dirs. Vocat. Edn. (pres. 1981—), Delta Pi Epsilon, Epsilon Delta Epsilon, Kappa Delta Pi, Phi Delta Kappa, Zeta Phi Beta (Woman of Year award 1974). Co-author: Clerical Typewriting Textbook, 1972. Office: 734 Schuylkill Ave Philadelphia PA 19146

HOLMES, MARTHA HAYDEN KENDALL, social worker; b. Sayre, Okla., Aug. 5, 1945; d. James Milton and Mary Marie (Hayden) Kendall; B.Music, U. Okla., 1970, M.S.W., 1976; m. Fred William Holmes, Sept. 11, 1965 (dec. 1967). Sec., asso. Dist. Atty., Beckham County, Sayre, Okla., 1965-67; social worker Beckham County Welfare Dept., 1970-72; supr. child abuse unit Oklahoma County Child Welfare, Oklahoma City, 1974-75, social worker, 1973-74, 76; social worker neonatal ICU, Okla. Children's Meml. Hosp., Oklahoma City, 1977—. Lic. clin. social worker, Okla. Mem. Acad. Cert. Social Workers, Nat. Assn. Social Workers (program chmn. Oklahoma City unit 1977-78, chmn. profl. standards com. Oklahoma County unit 1981-82), Nat. Assn. Perinatal Social Workers (dir., nat. sec. 1980-83), Oklahoma City Women's Polit. Caucus (membership chmn. 1981-82), AAUW, Okla. Group Process Soc., Forum on Death Edn. and Counseling; Common Cause, Sigma Alpha Iota. Club: Zonta (dir. 1979-81, v.p. 1981-83). Home: 3319 N Youngs Blvd Oklahoma City OK 73112 Office: 940 NE 13th St Oklahoma City OK 73104

HOLMES, PAULINE THOMPSON, nutritionist; b. Mound Bayou, Miss., Feb. 23, 1918; d. Sam and Vanveola (Simmons) Thompson; B.S., Rust Coll., 1939; postgrad. Dillard U., 1959, Marquette U., 1960, Ohio U., 1961-64, Jackson State U., 1967, Delta State U., 1970; m. C. Preston Holmes, July 11, 1943; children—Mercedes, Cornell, Kenneth, Paula, Ralph, Clarence. Biology tchr. Mound Bayou, Miss., 1939-41, 46-51; home econs. instr. Rust Coll., Holly Springs, Miss., 1941-43; war food emergency agt. Fayette, Miss., 1943-46; biology tchr. Eastside High Sch., Cleveland, Miss., 1951-68, chmn. biology dept.; nutritionist Delta Health Center, Mound Bayou, 1968—; pres. Dist. Sci. Fair. Com. Pres., Mound Bayou Civic Club, 1962-77, conf. dir. on youth, 1970-73; active Bethel African Meth. Episcopal Ch. Grantee, Nat. Found., 1959-64; recipient award for Christian service to humanity African Meth. Episcopal Ch., 1977. Mem. NEA, Nat. Biology Tchrs. Assn., Nutrition Soc., Bolivar County Tchrs. Assn. (pres.). Democrat. Clubs: Am. Legion Aux. (pres. State of Miss. 1977-78, chmn. nat. security State of Miss., nat. music chmn. 1978-80, nat. exec. com. State of Miss. 1978, Conf. Debutante-Masters Commr. 1976), Progressive Women's Club, Alpha Kappa Alpha. Condr. research high lysine corn, 1970-71. Home: PO Box 225 Mound Bayou MS 38762 Office: PO Drawer 209 Delta Health Center Mound Bayou MS 38762

HOLMES, PHYLLIS IRENE, educator; b. Crawfordsville, Iowa, Feb. 3, 1940; d. Thomas Julius and Irene Julie (Cassabaum) Holmes; B.S., Greenville (Ill.) Coll., 1961; M.A., U. So. Calif., 1968. Tchr. phys. edn. Winfield (Iowa) Mt. Union High Sch., 1961-64; coach, instr. phys. edn. Biola Coll., La Mirada, Calif., 1964-67; coach, prof. phys. edn. Greenville Coll., 1967—; women's basketball clinician to Sao Paulo, Brazil with Ill. Partners Assn., 1976; asst. coach Midwest women's team Nat. Sports Festival, 1978; asst. coach U.S. women's basketball team to Spartakiade Games, USSR, 1979; commr. Ill. Assn. Intercollegiate Athletics for Women, 1969—, Midwest Assn. Intercollegiate Athletics for Women, 1971-73, 76—. Mem. AAHPER, Nat., Midwest assns. phys. edn. coll. women. Home: 1306 Butternut St Greenville IL 62246 Office: Greenville Coll Greenville IL 62246

HOLMES, RUTH WHITAKER, coll. adminstr.; b. Weaubleau, Mo., May 11, 1933; d. John and Minnie Frost; B.S., Hood Coll., 1955; M.S., U. Mass., 1970; Ph.D., Boston Coll., 1979; m. G. Burtt Holmes, Aug. 16, 1958; children—Richard Holmes, David. Dietetic intern Peter Bent Brigham Hosp., Boston, 1955-56; clin. dietitian Boston Hosp. for Women, 1956-58; instr. U. Mass., Amherst, 1969-71; nutrition coordinator Skilled Nursing Facility Corp., Newton, Mass., 1969-70; mem. faculty Framingham (Mass.) State Coll., 1971-76, dir. coordinated undergrad. program dietetics, 1976—; cons. community health program Framingham Union Hosp. Trustee, Hood Coll., 1975—. Recipient Disting. Service award Mass. State Coll. System, 1980; HEW grantee, 1974-80. Mem. Central Dist. Mass. Dietitians Assn. (chmn.), Am. Dietetics Assn., Mass. Dietetics Assn., Mass. Public Health Assn., Am. Home Econs. Assn., Nutrition Today Soc. Home: 58 Westwood Rd Shrewsbury MA 01545 Office: Framingham State Coll Framingham MA 01701

HOLMES-JOHNSON, ELIZABETH, psychologist; b. Boston, Sept. 2, 1951; d. Charles R. and Evelyn M. (Bedia) Holmes; B.S. in Psychology and Urban/Suburban Studies, U. Bridgeport (Conn.), 1974, M.S. in Sch. Psychology, 1976; Ph.D. in Clin. Psychology, Calif. Sch. Profl. Psychology, 1979; m. Frank C. Johnson, Aug. 2, 1974; children—Erin Kathleen, Adam Michael. Hall dir. U. Bridgeport, 1973-76; counselor Crisis House, San Diego, 1976-77, Tech. Research, Inc., San Diego, 1977-78; psychology intern County Mental Health, San Diego, 1978-79; commd. lt. (j.g.) Med. Service Corps, U.S. Navy, 1979; postdoctoral intern Nat. Naval Med. Center, Bethesda, Md., 1979-80; chmn. dept. behavioral psychology Nat. Naval Dental Center, Bethesda, 1980—, psychol. cons. to dental div. Bur. Medicine and Surgery; trustee Calif. Sch. Profl. Psychology, 1977-79; cons. in field. Mem. Am. Psychol. Assn. Home: 615 Hine St Vienna VA 22180 Office: Nat Naval Dental Center Bethesda MD 20814

HOLMES-ROSS, SHEILA MAUREEN, sales exec.; b. San Jose, Calif., Nov. 1, 1951; d. Douglas F. and Mary A. (Zager) Murphy; B.A., San Jose State U., 1973; m. Lawrence Richard Ross, Dec. 20, 1982. Exec. sec. J.M. Mfg., Santa Clara, Calif., 1972-74; mktg. coordinator Chick, Orthopedic/Hosmer-Dorrance, Campbell, Calif., 1974-75; mgr. mktg. adminstrn. Consol. Video Systems, Sunnyvale, Calif., 1975-77; Regional mgr. Pacific dist. sales mgr. ADDA Corp., Los Gatos, Calif., 1977—. Mem. Nat. Assn. Female Execs., ADDA Corp. Pres. Club. Home and office: 8471 Boothbay Circle Huntington Beach CA 92646

HOLMGREN, PATRICIA KERN, botanist; b. Athens, Ind., Jan. 21, 1940; d. Robert Evan and Ruth Eleanor (Beaudoin) Kern; B.S., Ind. U., 1962; M.S., U. Wash., Seattle, 1964, Ph.D., 1968; m. Noel H. Holmgren, Nov. 25, 1969. Mem. staff N.Y. Bot. Garden, 1968—, head curator herbarium, 1975-81, asst. v.p. sci., dir. herbarium, 1981—; adj. prof. CUNY. Mem. Bot. Soc. Am. (council 1975-84, pres. 1981), Am. Soc. Plant Taxonomists (council 1974-79), Am. Inst. Biol. Scis. (gov. bd. 1981-84), Torrey Bot. Club (council 1982), Internat. Assn. Plant Taxonomy. Editor: Index Herbariorum, 7th edit., 1981; asso. editor Brittonia, 1975—; copy editor Intermountain Flora, 1974—. Office: NY Bot Garden Bronx NY 10458

HOLOWEJ, OKSANA (SANDI), mgmt. tng. and cons. exec.; b. Western Ukraine, Feb. 2, 1944; came to U.S., 1949, naturalized, 1957; d. Dmytro and Maria J. (Hadzaman) H.; B.S., U. Md., 1975. Acct. Edmund J. Bennett Assos., Bethesda, Md., 1964-67, Columbia (Md.) Parks and Recreation, 1967-70; asst. treas. Larsen Products Corp., Rockville, Md., 1970-74; controller Byron Motion Pictures, Washington, 1974-78; controller, fin. mgr. Sterling Inst., Washington, 1978—. Mem. Assn. Women Govt. Contractors, Women in Govt. Relations. Republican. Roman Catholic. Home: 13920 Castle Blvd Apt 311 Silver Spring MD 20904 Office: 1010 Wisconsin Ave NW Suite 700 Washington DC 20007

HOLSER, MARY ANN, human services agy. exec.; b. Detroit, May 21, 1928; d. Ray Ward and Ruth Belle (Ferguson) Harris; B.A., U. Mich., Ann Arbor, 1950; M.S.W., Ohio State U., Columbus, 1954; m. William Thomas Holser, Dec. 23, 1955; children—Thomas Dana, Alec Stuart, Margaret. Young adult dir. YMCA, Amarillo, Tex., 1950-51; recreation leader Columbus (Ohio) Recreation Dept., 1951-53; cottage supr. Juvenile Diagnostic Center, Columbus, 1955; group work specialist Spl. Service for Groups, Los Angeles, 1955-56; psychiat. social worker Met. State Hosp., Norwalk, Calif., 1958-60, League of Latin Am. Citizens, Anaheim, Calif., 1965-67, Crisis Intervention Clinic, U. Calif., Irvine Med. Center, 1967-70; psychiat. social work cons. Los Angeles County Health Dept., 1970; clin. dir. Alcohol Traffic Safety Program, Eugene, Oreg., 1971-76; co-dir. Drinking Decisions, Eugene, 1977-78; dir. Behanna House, Eugene, 1978-79; exec. dir. Lane County Council on Alcoholism, Eugene, 1979—; mental health examiner mental hearings State of Oreg., 1973—; vis. asst. prof. U. Oreg., Eugene, 1973-76; research grantee Max Planck Inst. for Psychiatry, Munich, W. Ger., 1976. Founder, Orange County Free Clinic, 1969; budget chmn. LWV, 1966. Mem. Nat. Assn. Social Workers, Acad. Clin. Social Workers, Oreg. Substance Abuse Assn., Lane County Affirmative Action Com. (chmn.), Oreg. Alcohol Program Mgrs. Assn. (sec.-treas.), Lane County Alcohol Program Mgrs. Assn. (sec.). Democrat. Protestant. Clubs: U. Oreg. Women, Eugene Swim and Tennis. Contbr. articles to profl. jours. Home: 2620 Cresta de Ruta Eugene OR 97403 Office: 795 Willamette Eugene OR 97401

HOLSEY, JOYCE EDLINE (MRS. WILLIAM F. HOLSEY II), lawyer; b. N.Y.C., Jan. 7, 1927; d. Herbert and Emma (Ramsey) Chambers; B.A., Hunter Coll., 1946, M.A., 1951; J.D., U. Ariz., 1971; m. William F. Holsey, II, Dec. 26, 1948; children—Denise, Dorine, William F. III. Elementary sch. tchr., N.Y.C., 1948-53; admitted to Ariz. bar, 1971; staff atty. Pima County Legal Aid Soc., Tucson, 1971-74, supervising atty. Sr. Citizens' Law Project, 1974-77; staff atty. So. Ariz. Legal Aid, Inc., Tucson, 1977—. Precinct committeeman Democratic party, 1970-72. Bd. dirs. Pima County Med. Aux., 1962-63, Tucson br. YWCA, 1971-74, Tucson Girls Club, 1973-76. Mem. Am. Blind Lawyers Assn., Ariz. Women Lawyers Assn., Pima County Bar Assn., NAACP, Delta Sigma Theta (sec. Tucson alumni chpt.). Club: Links (Tucson). Home: 6501 N Camino Arturo Tucson AZ 85718 155 E Alameda St Tucson AZ

HOLSINGER, FAITH WILLIAMS, clubwoman; b. Seymour, Mo., Jan. 7, 1942; d. Wallace Asbury and Gertrude (Moore) Williams; B.A., Drury Coll., 1964; postgrad. U. Mo., 1967-69; m. Kent Corwin Holsinger, Aug. 8, 1970; children—Kristi Lyn, Marcy Elaine. Apprentice ednl. TV sta. KTTS-TV, Springfield, Mo., 1963: fgn. lang. tchr. Hazelwood Sr. High Sch., St. Louis County, 1964-70; substitute tchr., Granite City, Ill., 1970-73. Second v.p. Granite City Republican Women's Club, 1981-82. Mem. NEA, Community Tchrs. Assn., Am. Assn. Tchrs. French, Am. Assn. Tchrs. Spanish and Portuguese, St. Louis Tchrs. Assn., Sigma Delta Pi. Methodist. Clubs: Jr. Service (bd. mem. 1976-82, pres. 1980-81), (Granite City, Ill.); Lesche Literary (pres. 1976-77); PEO (chpt. chaplain 1981-82). Home: 3236 Newell Dr Granite City IL 62040

HOLSTON, SHARON SMITH, govt. ofcl.; b. Cleve., Dec. 15, 1945; d. Charles Coolidge and Eva Mae (Hall) Smith; A.B., Columbia U., 1967; m. Joseph Holston, Jr., Dec. 22, 1973; children—Joseph Ikaweba, Eve Denise. Personnel mgmt. specialist U.S. Commn. Civil Rights, 1967-70, HEW, 1970-72; EEO officer FDA, Rockville, Md., 1972-74, personnel mgmt. specialist, 1975-77, acting exec. officer, 1977-79, spl. asst. to asso. commr. mgmt. and ops., 1979-80, dep. asso. commr. mgmt. and ops., 1980—. Recipient Award of Merit, FDA, 1982. Mem. African Methodist Episcopal Ch. Club: Barnard-in-Washington (dir.). Office: 5600 Fishers Ln Rockville MD 20857

HOLT, ANN BROOKE, veterinarian; b. San Diego, Aug. 10, 1930; d. Walter Coler and Julia Agnes (Douw) H.; B.S., U. Minn., 1953, D.V.M., 1958; P.M.D., Harvard Grad. Sch. Bus. Adminstrn., 1972. Pvt. practice vet. medicine, Minn., 1958-62; Peace Corps vol., Malaysia, 1962-64; vet. med. officer FDA, USPHS, Rockville, Md., 1965—, reviewing officer, 1965-67, br. chief, 1967-72, exec. fellow, 1972-73, dep. dir. div. new animal drugs, 1973-76, dir. div. drugs for ruminant species, 1976-78, assoc. dir. surveillance and compliance, 1978-79, dir. div. of drugs for swine and minor species, 1979-80, assoc. dir. for compliance Bur. Med. Devices, 1980—; officer Dogs-East, Inc. Search and Rescue Unit. Vol. vet. service to Audubon Naturalist Soc. and local Humane Soc. FDA exec. devel. fellow, 1972-73. Mem. AVMA Women's Vet. Med. Assn., D.C. Vet. Med. Assn., Am. Pub. Health Assn. (council vet. sect.). Episcopalian. Home: 4 Orchard Way N Rockville MD 20854

HOLT, BARBARA BERTANY, mgmt. cons.; b. Bridgeport, Conn., Nov. 4, 1940; d. Stephen Edward and Mary G. Bertany; student Regis Coll., 1958-59; B.A. in English, U. Bridgeport, 1962; m. Robert Holt, Dec. 5, 1971; children—Pamela Maren, Laura Kimbel, Mary Brooke. Instr. speech and theatre, U. Bridgeport (Conn.), 1962-69; gen. mgr. BFL Assos., Exec. Recruitment, N.Y.C., 1969-72; founder, pres. Barbara Holt Assos., mgmt. cons., N.Y.C., 1972—; faculty New Sch. for Social Research; mem. N.Y. Fashion Group. Episcopalian. Club: Atrium (N.Y.C.). Developer, producer video career mgmt. series for public TV, 1976. Office: Barbara Holt Assos Box 713 Southport CT 06490

HOLT, BERTHA MERRILL, state legislator; b. Eufaula, Ala., Aug. 16, 1916; d. William Hoadley and Bertha Harden (Moore) Merrill; A.B., Agnes Scott Coll., 1938; LL.B., U. Ala., 1941; m. Winfield Clary Holt, Mar. 14, 1941; children—Harriet Wharton Holt Whitley, William Merrill, Winfield Jefferson. Admitted to Ala. bar, 1941; with Treasury Dept., Washington, 1941-42, Dept. Interior, Washington, 1942-43; mem. N.C. Ho. of Reps. from 22d Dist., 1975—, chmn. legis. ethics com., 1980, chmn. constl. amendments com., 1981, mem. joint commn. govtl. ops., 1982. Pres., Democratic Women of Alamance, 1962, chmn. hdqrs., 1964, 68; mem. N.C. Dem. Exec. Com., 1964-75; pres. Episcopal Ch. Women, 1968; mem. council N.C. Episcopal Diocese, 1972-74, chmn. fin. dept., 1973-75, parish grant com., 1973-80, mem. standing com., 1975-78; chmn. Alamance County Social Services Bd., 1970; mem. N.C. Bd. Sci. and Tech., 1979—; bd. dirs. Hospice N.C., State Council Social Legis. Recipient Outstanding Alumna award Agnes Scott Coll., 1976. Mem. Women's Forum N.C., Law Alumni Assn. U. N.C. Chapel Hill (dir.), N.C. Bar Assn., NOW, English Speaking Union, N.C. Hist. Soc., Les Amis du Vin, Pi Beta Phi. Club: Century Book. Office: PO Box 111 Burlington NC 27215

HOLT, DOROTHY DARLENE, nursing home adminstr.; b. North Henderson, Ill., Feb. 2, 1917; d. Herman Patrick and Martha Estelle (Munson) Devlin; R.N., Galesburg Cottage Hosp. Sch. Nursing, 1940; m. John W. Holt, Mar. 15, 1941; children—John Devlin, Jarrie Allyson. Supr. obstetrics Cottage Hosp., Galesburg, Ill., 1941-43; staff nurse Mayo Gen. Hosp., Galesburg, 1944; staff nurse St. Mary's Hosp., Galesburg, 1972, night floor supr., 1972-73; night supr. Americana Healthcare Center, Galesburg, 1973; owner, adminstr. The Evergreens Retirement Center for Women, Galesburg, 1973—. Mem. Bus. and Profl. Women's Club, Am. Nurses Assn., Galesburg Cottage Hosp. Alumni Assn. Presbyterian. Home: 113 N Arthur Ave Galesburg IL 61401 Office: 1188 W Main St Galesburg IL 61401

HOLT, LINDA ANNE, speech-lang. pathologist; b. Washington, Apr. 15, 1943; d. Walter Henry and Mary Crichton (Jones) H.; B.A., SUNY, Buffalo, 1966, M.A., 1971. Speech pathologist Kenmore-Town of Tonawanda Pub. Sch. System, Kenmore, N.Y., 1966-69, 70-72; grad. asst. U.S. Office of Edn., 1969-70; clin. asst. prof., coordinator clin. services, dept. communicative disorders and scis. SUNY, Buffalo, 1973-76, clin. asst. prof., dir. speech and hearing clinic, dept. communicative disorders and scis., 1977—; pvt. practice speech-lang. pathology; speech-lang. cons. J. Sutton Regan Cleft Palate Clinic Team, Children's Hosp., Buffalo; cons. in field. Lic. speech-lang. pathology, N.Y. State; permanent cert. as tchr. of speech-lang. and hearing handicapped N.Y. State Edn. Dept. Mem. Am. Speech-Lang. and Hearing Assn. (cert. clin. competence), N.Y. State Speech and Hearing Assn., Speech and Hearing Assn. Western N.Y. (past pres.). Blissymbolics Communication Found., Am. Cleft Palate Assn., Council Univ. Suprs. of Practicum in Speech Pathology and Audiology. Republican. Methodist. Clubs: Park Country (Buffalo); Sitzmaker Ski (Colden, N.Y.). Home: 30 Troy-del Way Williamsville NY 14221 Office: SUNY 4226 Ridge Lea Rd Buffalo NY 14226

HOLT, MARJORIE SEWELL, Congresswoman; b. Birmingham, Ala., Sept. 17, 1920; d. Edward Roland and Alice Juanita (Felts) Sewell; B.A., Jacksonville (Fla.) U., 1945; J.D., U. Fla., 1949; m. Duncan McKay Holt, Dec. 26, 1946; children—Rachel Holt Tschantre, Edward, Victoria Holt Stauffer. Admitted to Fla. Bar, 1949, Md. bar, 1962; practice law, Annapolis, Md., 1962; clk. Anne Arundel Circuit Ct., Annapolis, 1966-72; mem. 93d-98th Congresses from 4th Md. Dist., mem. budget com., armed services com. Supr. elections Anne Arundel County, 1963-65; mem. housing com. Anne Arundel County Human Relations Commn., 1964-67; bd. dirs. Office Technol. Assessment, 1976-77, vice chmn., 1977; chmn. Republican Study Com., 1975-76; del. Rep. Nat. Conv., 1968, 76. Recipient Disting. Alumna award U. Fla., 1975. ABA, Md. Bar Assn., Anne Arundel Bar Assn., LWV, Md. Fedn.

Rep. Women, Bus. and Profl. Women's Club, Phi Kappa Phi, Phi Delta Delta. Presbyterian (elder 1959). Mem. staff Fla. Law Rev., 1947-49. Editor, co-author: The Case Against the Reckless Congress, 1976; Can You Afford This House, 1978. Office: 2412 Rayburn House Office Bldg Washington DC 20515

HOLT, MELVA RUTH, health care exec.; b. Lowes, Ky., Apr. 4, 1948; d. Robert Wilson and Mildred Frances (Leath) H.; B.S. in Bus. cum laude, Murray (Ky.) State U., 1973. Various secretarial positions, 1969-72; tchr. bus. Dixie Heights High Sch., Ft. Mitchell, Ky., 1973; exec. sec. to v.p. fin., then coordinator employment Murray State U., 1974-76; dental plan bus. mgr. U. Louisville Dental Sch., 1977, univ. budget analyst, 1978; fin. systems installment engr. HBO & Co., San Mateo, Calif., 1979; coordinator, mgr. fin. data systems Holy Cross Health Systems, S. Bend, Ind., 1980—. Named Ky. Col. Cert. profl. sec. Mem. Nat. Secs. Assn. (membership chmn., pres.-elect), NEA, Nat. Assn. Female Execs., Hosp. Fin. Mgmt. Assn., Alpha Gamma Delta (treas., faculty adv.). Democrat. Baptist. Home: 4115 Coral Dr South Bend IN 46614 Office: 3606 E Jefferson Blvd South Bend IN 46615

HOLT, PHYLLIS MAE, banker; b. Berlin, N.H., Nov. 28, 1933; d. David Donald and Bernadette Evelyn (Gunn) Osborne; student Chamberlain Sch. Retail Mdsg., Boston, 1952; diploma in comml. banking (Norman T. Shepard award), Williams Coll. Sch. Banking, 1975; m. Clyde A. Holt, June 29, 1957. Cashier-sec. Public Service Co. N.H., 1952-59; from teller to mgr. Second New Haven Bank, 1959-74; asst. v.p., br. mgr. Colonial Bank, Milford, Conn., 1974—; instr. Am. Inst. Banking, 1980—; leader seminars and workshops in field. Sec. Milford Progress, Inc., 1977, pres., 1981—; bd. dirs. N. Haven Drug and Alcohol Council, 1972-78, Regional Vis. Nurses Assn., 1972-74, Milford chpt. ARC, 1981—; mem. active corp. execs. SBA, 1981—. Recipient Bus. Advocacy award Conn. Women in Bus., 1982, nat. honor award SBA, 1982. Mem. Nat. Assn. Bank Women (chmn. Conn. 1976, chmn. New Eng. edn. com. 1978-79), Am. Inst. Banking (dir. 1970-80), Milford Fin. Assn. (v.p. 1977-80), Milford C. of C. (dir. 1979), Network Exec. Women Milford (founder, pres. 1979). Roman Catholic. Office: 68 S Broad St Milford CT 06460

HOLT, VICTORIA (PSEUDONYM OF ELEANOR BURFORD HIBBERT), author; b. London, Eng.; d. Joseph and Alice (Tate) Burford; ed. privately; m. G.P. Hibbert. Author: (under pseudonym of Eleanor Burford) House at Cupid's Cross, 1949, Passionate Witness, 1949, Believe the Heart, 1950, Love Child, 1950, Saint or Sinner?, 1951, Dear Delusion, 1952, Bright Tomorrow, 1952, Leave Me My Love, 1953, When We Are Married, 1953, Castles in Spain, 1954, Heart's Afire, 1954, When Other Hearts, 1955, Two Loves in Her Life, 1955, Begin to Live, 1956, Married in Haste, 1956, To Meet A Stranger, 1957, Pride of the Morning, 1958, Dawn Chorus, 1959, Red Sky at Night, 1959, Blaze of Noon, 1960, Night of the Stars, 1960, Now That April's Gone, 1961, Who's Calling?, 1962; (under pseudonym Elbur Ford) Poison in Pimlico, 1950, Flesh and the Devil, 1950, Bed Disturbed, 1952, Such Bitter Business, 1953 (pub. in U.S. as Evil in the House, 1954); (under pseudonym Victoria Holt) Mistress of Mellyn, 1960, Kirkland Revels, 1962, Bride of Pendorric, 1963, The Legend of the Seventh Virgin, 1965, Manfreya in the Morning, 1966, The King of the Castle, 1967, The Queen's Confession, 1968, The Shivering Sands, 1969; The Secret Woman, 1970; The Shadow of the Lynx, 1971; On the Night of the Seventh Moon, 1972; The Curse of the Kings, 1973; The House of 1000 Lanterns, 1974; Lord of the Far Island, 1975; Pride of the Peacock, 1976; The Devil on Horseback, 1977; My Enemy The Queen, 1978; The Spring of the Tiger, 1979; The Mask of the Enchantress, 1980; The Judas Kiss, 1981; The Demon Lover, 1982; (under pseudonym of Jean Plaidy) Beyond the Blue Mountains, 1947, King's Pleasure, 1949 (pub. in Eng. as Murder Most Royal, 1949); Goldsmith's Wife, 1950, Madame Serpent, 1951, Italian Woman, 1952, Queen Jezebel, 1953, Daughter of Satan, 1952, Spanish Bridegroom, 1953, St. Thomas' Eve, 1954, Sixth Wife, 1954, Gay Lord Robert, 1955, Royal Road to Fotheringay, 1955, Wandering Prince, 1956, Health Unto His Majesty, 1956, Flaunting Extravagant Queen, 1957, Here Lies Our Sovereign Lord, 1957, Madonna of the Seven Hills, 1958, Triptych of Poisoners, 1958, Light on Lucrezia, 1958, Louis, The Well-Beloved, 1959, Rise of the Spanish Inquisition, 1959, Road to Compiegne, 1959, Castile for Isabella, 1960, Growth of the Spanish Inquisition, 1960, Spain for the Sovereigns, 1960, The Young Elizabeth, 1961, Meg Roper: Daughter of Sir Thomas More, 1961, The End of the Spanish Inquisition, 1961, Katherine, The Virgin Widow, 1961, The King's Secret Matter, 1962, The Shadow of the Pomegranate, 1962, The Captive Queen of Scots, 1963, The Thistle and the Rose, 1963, The Young Mary Queen of Scots, 1962, Mary, Queen of France, 1964, The Murder in the Tower, 1964, Evergreen Gallant, 1965, The Three Crowns, 1965, The Haunted Sisters, 1966, The Queen's Favourites, 1966, The Spanish Inquisition: Its Rise, Growth and End, 1967, Caroline The Queen, 1968, Katharine of Aragon, 1968, The Prince and the Quakeress, 1968, The Third George, 1969, Catherine de Medici, 1969, Perdita's Prince, 1969, Sweet Lass of Richmond Hill, 1970; Indiscretions of the Queen, 1970; The Regent's Daughter, 1971; Goddess of the Green Room, 1971; Victoria in the Wings, 1972; Captive of Kensington Palace, 1972; The Queen and Lord M, 1973; The Queen's Husband, 1973; The Widow of Windsor, 1974; The Bastard King: the Lion of Justice, 1974; The Passionate Enemies, 1976; The Platagenet Saga, 14 vols., 1976-80; Mary Queen of Scots, 1975; Plantagenet Prelude, 1976; Revolt of the Eaglets, 1977; Heart of the Lion, 1977; Prince of Darkness, 1978; The Battle of the Queens, 1978; The Queen from Provence, 1979; Edward Longshanks, 1979; The Follies of the King, 1980; Uneasy Lies the Head, 1982; (under the pseudonym of Philippa Carr) The Miracle of St. Bruno's, 1976; The Witch from the Sea, 1976; Saraband for Two Sisters, 1977; Lament for a Lost Lover, 1978; The Love Child, 1979; The Song of The Siren, 1980; Will You Love Me in September, 1981; The Adulteress, 1982. Contbr. to newspapers, mags. Office: care Robert Hale Ltd 45/47 Clerkenwell Green London EC1 England

HOLTMAN, LILLIAN C., ednl. adminstr.; b. Phila., Jan. 16, 1934; d. Rudolf Eric and Else Clara (Dietle) Grossmann; diploma Phila. Coll. Bible, 1955; certificate in facilities mgmt. Mass. Inst. Tech., 1974; B.A. magna cum laude in Liberal Arts, U. South Fla., 1977; m. William Albin Holtman, 1980; 1 dau., Lori Rose Yorks. Interpreter, guest and pub. relations cons. Lederle Labs., Pearl River, N.Y., 1955-57; co-ordinator schedules, mgr. space office U. South Fla., Tampa, 1964-73, dir. space utilization and analysis, 1973—; mem. State of Fla. Space Utilization Criteria Com. for Post-Secondary Edn., 1977—; mem. Fla. State Univ. System Capital Outlay Budget Com., 1973—, chmn., 1973-75; lectr. fields space utilization, women in mgmt., women in careers. Active various civic projects, including voter registration, Tampa. Recipient award U.S. Fla., 1980. Mem. Delta Epsilon Chi, Phi Kappa Phi. Home: 10910 61st St Temple Terrace FL 33617 Office: FAO 122 Univ South Florida 4202 Fowler Ave Tampa FL 33620

HOLTON, ANNE LYSBETH, mag. advt. exec.; b. Pitts., June 10, 1950; d. James Leo and Ruth Anna (Homan) H.; B.S. in Psychology, U. Bridgeport, 1972; postgrad. N.Y.U. Legis. aide to Congressman Henry Helstoski of N.J., 1973-74; asst. to advt. dir. New Times Mag., N.Y.C., 1974-75, sales rep., 1975; advt. sales rep. Rolling Stone Mag., N.Y.C., 1975-77; advt. sales rep. Ms. mag., N.Y.C., 1977-78, N.Y. adv. mgr., 1978-79, nat. advt. mgr., 1979, advt. dir., 1979-82; mktg. dir. Gentlemen's Quar. Mag., 1982—. Mem. Mag. Pubs. Assn., Nat. Women's Polit. Party. Republican. Office: 350 Madison Ave New York NY 10017

HOLTON, PRISCILLA BROWNE, sch. adminstr.; b. Hartford, Conn., Dec. 21, 1922; d. Edward Aston and Lucille J. (Ford) Browne; B.S., St. Joseph Coll., 1946; M.Ed., Antioch Coll., 1972; numerous spl. courses; m. John Lyle Holton, Dec. 24, 1944; children—Mary Frances, John Kingsley, Leslie Lucille. Dir., Women's League Day Care Center, Hartford, 1948-49; elementary tchr. Phila. Public Schs., 1954-62; head tchr. Green Tree Sch., Phila., 1963-67, prin., 1969-74; co-therapist parents group Green Tree Sch., 1966-67; dir. North Hill's Day Care Center, Pa., also head start coordinator Eastern Montgomery County, 1967-69; coordinator spl. edn. Antioch Grad. Sch. Edn., Phila., 1974-78, M.Ed. program adminstr., 1978-80, coordinator art exhibits, 1974-80; coordinator Head Start, City of Phila., 1980—; cons.; lectr. chmn. adv. bd. Children's Village; bd. dirs. Mt. Airy Children's House, YWCA, Germantown. Recipient citation Gov. Schaeffer of Pa., 1946, plaque North Hills Day Care Bd., 1968, plaque Green Tree Sch., 1974, plaque V.I.P., 1980, award Chapel of Four Chaplains, 1980; named Outstanding Grad. of Class of 1946, Alumnae of St. Joseph Coll. for Women, 1981. Mem. Pa. Mental Health Assn., LWV, Pa. Tchr. Educators, Assn. Children with Learning Disabilities, Council Exceptional Children, YMCA, Black Women's Ednl. Alliance, Phila. Art Mus., Phila. Hort. Soc., Organisation Mondiale pour l'Education Prescholaire, Nat. Assn. Young Children's Edn., Delta Sigma Theta. Author: (with others) Teacher's Curriculum Guide, 1970; feature writer Hartford Chronicle, 1948. Home: 428 E Montana St Philadelphia PA 19119 Office: 1415 N Broad St Philadelphia PA 19122

HOLTRY, JULIA BERNE, computer mfg. co. exec.; b. Tucson; d. Robert W. Berne and Blossom C. (Chernin) Dorff; B.S., U. Ariz., 1969; M.B.A., Pepperdine U., 1982; m. Frank M. Holtry, Mar. 12, 1972. Flight attendant, dir. customer service, supr. inflight service TWA, N.Y.C. and Los Angeles, 1970-77; mgr. flight attendants Hughes Airwest, San Francisco, 1977-78, sr. dir. inflight services, San Mateo, Calif., 1978-80; staff v.p. Inscan Corp., Petaluma, Calif., 1981—; beauty cons. Mary Kay Cosmetics, Inc., 1979—. Bd. dirs. Big Sisters Am., 1979—. Republican. Jewish. Office: 1364 N McDowell Blvd Petaluma CA 94952

HOLTSBERRY, BARBARA JEAN, mfg. co. exec.; b. Coshocton County, Ohio, Aug. 26, 1938; d. William Raymond and Lena May (Ashcraft) Ramsey; student Ohio State U., 1958-65; B.Sc. in Bus. Adminstrn. summa cum laude, Franklin U., 1972; children—Rosemary, Theresa, Frederick. Sec., Battelle Meml. Inst., Columbus, Ohio, 1966-70; computer programmer Ohio Dept. Edn., Columbus, 1970-71; asst. acctg. supr. Westreco, Marysville, Ohio, 1972-78; supr. adminstrn. and planning engring. dept. Owen's Corning Fiberglas, Newark, Ohio, 1978—. Mem. Nat. Assn. Accts. (pres. Mid-Ohio chpt. 1982—, treas. Ohio council 1982—). Republican. Mem. Ch. of Christ. Clubs: Shalom Christian Singles (treas. 1981), Cambridge (pres. 1981-82). Home: 651 Edgewood Dr Newark OH 43055 Office: Case Ave Newark OH 43055

HOLTZ, VIRGINIA H., librarian; b. Milw., July 6, 1932; d. Lester R. and Helene L. (Crossler) H.; B.A., Wis. State U., 1954; M.S.L.S., U. Wis., 1956. Reference librarian in charge statewide services U. Wis. Med. Library, Madison, asso. librarian W. S. Middleton Med. Library, 1967-71, dir., asso. prof. W. S. Middleton Health Sci. Library, 1971-76, dir. prof. Center Health Sci. Libraries, 1976—; mem. biomed. library review com. Nat. Library Medicine, 1981-84. Mem. Med. Library Assn. (dir. 1976-79, publs. panel 1979-82), Assn. Acad. Health Sci. Library Dirs. (pres. 1981-82, bd. dirs. 1980-83, standards and guidelines com. 1982-85), Am. Library Assn. Office: 1305 Linden Dr Madison WI 53706

HOLTZBERG, BARBARA SUE, public relations exec.; b. Rochester, N.Y., Mar. 26, 1944; d. Milton and Thelma (Baker) Ergas; student U. Buffalo, 1963-64, U. Rochester, 1974-75; children—Lisa Faye, Erin Gayle, Jennifer Anne. Asst. dir. public relations Rochester/Monroe County chpt. ARC, Rochester, 1977-78, dir. public relations nat. capital div., Washington, 1978-80; mgr. press and publicity WRC-TV, NBC, Washington, 1980—. Mem. Women in Communications. Jewish. Office: 4001 Nebraska Ave Washington DC 20016

HOLTZMAN, ELIZABETH, congresswoman; b. Bklyn., Aug. 11, 1941; d. Sidney and Filia (Ravitz) H.; B.A. magna cum laude, Radcliffe Coll., 1962; J.D., Harvard U., 1965. Admitted to N.Y. bar, 1966; asso. firm Wachtell, Lipton, Rosen, Katz and Kern, N.Y.C., 1965-67; asst. to mayor N.Y.C., 1967-70; asso. firm Paul, Weiss, Rifkind, Wharton and Garrison, N.Y.C., 1970-72; mem. 93d-96th congresses from 16th dist. N.Y.; Democratic state committeewoman, dist. leader, Bklyn., 1970; del. Dem. Nat. Conv., 1972; founder Bklyn. Women's Polit. Caucus, 1971. Mem. nat. adv. council Hampshire (Mass.) Coll.; bd. overseers Harvard, 1976; mem. Nat. Commn. on Observance of Internat. Women's Year, 1977. Named 1 of 10 Women of Year, Mademoiselle mag., 1972, Woman of Year, United Hias Service, 1974; Outstanding Woman, Nassau region Hadassah, 1975; Annette Pinsky award ACLU, 1975; Woman of Year, Jewish War Vets., 1975; Spirit of Achievement award Albert Einstein Coll. Medicine, 1977; Distinguished Service award Fairleigh Dickinson U., 1977; recipient Alumnae Recognition award Radcliffe Coll. Alumnae Assn., 1973. Mem. Assn. Bar City N.Y. Democrat. Jewish. Address: 2238 Rayburn House Office Bldg Washington DC 20515

HOLYER, ERNA MARIA, author, educator, artist; b. Weilheim, Bavaria, Germany, Mar. 15, 1925; d. Mathias and Anna Maria (Goldhofer) Schretter; A.A., San Jose Evening Coll., 1964; student San Mateo Coll., 1965-67, San Jose State U., 1968-69, San Jose City Coll., 1980-81; m. Gene Wallace Holyer, Aug. 24, 1957. Free lance writer under pseudonym Ernie Holyer, 1960—; tchr. creative writing San Jose (Calif.) Met. Adult Edn., 1968—; exhibited in group shows Crown Zellerbach Gallery, San Francisco, 1973, 74, 76, 77; I.B.C. Gallery, San Francisco, 1978, Los Angeles 1981. Recipient Woman of Achievement Honor cert. San Jose Mercury-News, 1973, 74, 75; Lefoli award for excellence in adult edn. instrn. Adult Edn. Senate, 1972. Mem. Calif. Writers Club. Author: Rescue at Sunrise, 1965; Steve's Night of Silence, 1966; A Cow for Hansel, 1967; At the Forest's Edge, 1969; Song of Courage, 1970; Lone Brown Gull, 1971; Shoes for Daniel, 1974; The Southern Sea Otter, 1975; Sigi's Fire Helmut, 1975; Reservoir Road Adventure, 1982. Contbr. articles to various mags. and newspapers. Home and Office: 1314 Rimrock Dr San Jose CA 95120

HOLZMAN, ANNE MARIE, retail exec.; b. Binghamton, N.Y.; d. Herman William and Freda Mae (Leonard) H.; student Wagner Coll., Pace Coll., SUNY at Binghamton, Temple U. Steamship broker, 1970-75; with Piercing Pagoda, Inc., chain of jewelry stores, Bethlehem, Pa., 1975—, v.p. charge field ops., 1980—. Mem. Nat. Assn. Female Execs. Home: 394 Thunder Circle Bensalem PA 19020 Office: 65 E Elizabeth Ave Bethlehem PA 18018

HOM, JOAN YEE, mktg. exec.; b. N.Y.C., Oct. 23, 1949; d. Wing Bow and Toy Hong (Gee) Hom; B.A. in Econs. with honors, CCNY, 1971; M.B.A., N.Y.U., 1976. Intern, U.S. Com. for UNICEF, N.Y.C., 1972; research analyst Conf. Bd., Inc., N.Y.C., 1972-75, asso. economist, 1975-77, mktg. research project dir., 1977-80; group mktg. research mgr. AT & T Long Lines, Bedminster, N.J., 1980—. Bd. dirs. N.Y.U., Mgmt. Decision Lab., 1980—, Pan Asian Repertory Theatre, 1981—. Recipient Spl. Commendation, Somerset Hills YMCA, 1981. Mem. Fin. Women's Assn. N.Y. (bd. dirs. 1979—), Am. Mktg. Assn., Nat. Assn. Bus. Economists. Democrat. Club: Columbia Racquet. Contbr. articles to profl. jours. Home: 38 Park St Florham Park NJ 07932 Office: Room 4A220 Bedminster NJ 07921

HOMAN, LETA LADON, educator; b. Salem, Ill., Mar. 5, 1947; d. Donald Walter and Mabel Leta (Rogers) Ball; B.S., So. Ill. U., 1968, M.S., 1973; m. James Lynn Homan, Sept. 4, 1965; children—James Jeffrey, Mark Christopher, Jennifer Lynn. Tchr., Carlyle (Ill.) Grade Sch., 1969, Pinckneyville (Ill.) High Sch., 1969, DuQuoin (Ill.) High Sch., 1970-73, Allendale (Ill.) Grade Sch., 1974-75, Mt. Carmel (Ill.) High Sch., 1975-76; part-time tchr. St. Mary's Catholic Sch., Mt. Carmel, 1976-79; copy writer, producer, hostess Seek and Share, WYER AM-FM, Mt. Carmel, 1976-79; Title I reading specialist Bone Gap (Ill.) Sch., Edwards County Unit, Dist. 1980-81; instr. Wabash Valley Coll., 1981—. Mem. Ill. Edn. Assn., Internat. Reading Assn., Ill. Reading Assn., Wabash Valley Reading Council (past v.p.), Beta Sigma Phi (past pres.). Democrat. Methodist. Clubs: Youth Club of Methodist Ch. (tchr.). Home: 116 Northwood Dr Mount Carmel IL 62863

HOMBS, KAREN KAY, mining co. exec.; b. Denver, Aug. 3, 1942; d. Arthur Clark Eugene and Norma May (Urquhart) Ryman; student U. Denver/Colo. Women's Coll., 1980—; m. Thomas Gibson Hombs, Apr. 12, 1978; 1 son, Timothy John. With Samsonite Corp., Denver, 1960-75, employee relations rep., supr., 1965-71, labor relations rep., 1971-75; labor relations rep. Climax Molybdenum Co. (Colo.) div. AMAX, 1975-78, prin. labor relations adminstr., 1978—. Mem. council Lord of the Mountains Lutheran Ch., Summit County, Colo., 1979-80, founded women's chpt. Luth. Ch. Women, 1976, chpt. chmn., 1976-77, Sunday Sch. supt., 1976-81. Mem. Indsl. Relations Research Assn., Am. Mgmt. Assn. Home: PO Box 805 Dillon CO 80435 Office: Climax Molybdenum Co Labor Relations Dept Climax CO 80429

HOMEIER, KATHRYN MARIE, nurse, educator; b. Akron, Ohio, Nov. 13, 1920; d. Claude William and Anne Helen (Wein) H.; diploma in Nursing St. Thomas Hosp., Akron, 1941; B.S. in Nursing Edn., St. Louis U., 1949; M.S. in Edn., U. Akron, 1963. Mem. nursing staff St. Thomas Hosp., 1941-46, ednl. dir. Sch. Nursing, 1949-62; instr., staff devel. coordinator The Children's Hosp., Akron, 1963-67; asst. prof. nursing U. Akron, 1967-69, assoc. prof., 1969-75, prof., 1975—, coordinator Learning Resource Lab., 1979—. Bd. dirs. St. Edward Home, Akron. Mem. Am. Nurses Assn., St. Thomas Hosp. Alumni Assn., Nat. League for Nursing, U. Akron Alumni Assn. Roman Catholic. Club: Altrusa. Office: College of Nursing The University of Akron Akron OH 44325

HOMRIGHAUSEN, LINDSLEY HARVEY, found. exec.; b. Wilkes-Barre, Pa., Aug. 30, 1945; d. Robert Burgess and Joan Lindsley (Blackman) Harvey; B.A., Lake Erie Coll., Painesville, Ohio, 1967; m. David K. Homrighausen, Apr. 25, 1970; children—Sarah Harvey, Benjamin Burgess. With Mut. of N.Y., N.Y.C., 1967-71, Allied Temp. Service, N.Y.C., 1971-73; adminstr. grants Surdna Found., Inc., N.Y.C., 1973—. Office: 200 Park Ave New York NY 10166

HON, JEANNE ELIZABETH, ednl. adminstr.; b. Lawrence, Mass., Nov. 4, 1931; d. Andrew Paul Sorbo and Marjorie Elizabeth (O'Neill) Nichols; B.A., Calif. State U., Northridge, 1964, M.A. magna cum laude, 1969; Ed.D. with honors, Brigham Young U., 1973; m. Roy Charles Hon. Sr., June 20, 1949; children—Roy Charles, Jr., Kathleen Elizabeth. Sec. to supt. Duarte (Calif.) Unified Sch. Dist., 1959-61; tchr., coordinator, counselor Verdugo Hills Sch., Tujunga, Calif., 1966-75; asst. prin. North Hollywood (Calif.) High Sch., 1975-78; prin. Magnet Sch., Los Angeles Unified Sch. Dist., 1978-82; lectr. grad. studies Calif. Luth. Coll., Thousand Oaks, Calif., 1979—; prin. Sun Valley (Calif.) Jr. High Sch., 1982—. Chmn., United Fund, ARC; mem. coordinating council PTA; sponsor Mexican-Am. Youth Activities Group. Recipient Service award U. So. Calif. chpt. Phi Delta Kappa, 1982, DAV Aux., 1982. Mem. AAUW, Calif. Tchrs. Assn., NEA, Social Studies Assn., Phi Delta Kappa, Theta Sigma Tau. Democrat. Roman Catholic. Home: 6837 Estepa Dr Tujunga CA 91042 Office: 7330 Bakman Ave Sun Valley CA 91352

HONAMAN, JUNE NEWCOMER, state legislator; b. Lancaster, Pa., May 24, 1920; d. Lester W. and Maud (Stauffer) Newcomer; B.F.A., Beaver Coll., Glenside, Pa., 1941; m. Peter K. Honaman, Nov. 20, 1948. Tchr., Lancaster city schs., 1948-54; mem. Pa. Ho. of Reps. from 97th Dist., 1976—, vice chmn. state govt. com., 1979—, chmn. telecommunications subcom., 1979—; gov. bd. Council State Govts., 1980—. Del., mem. platform com. Republican Nat. Conv., 1964, 68, 72; vice chmn. Pa. Rep. State Com., 1964-76. Mem. Bus. and Profl. Women, AAUW, Pa. Farmers Assn., Federated Woman's Club, Lancaster County Conservancy, Nat. Conf. State Legislators. Episcopalian. Club: Lancaster Riding and Tennis. Office: Main Capitol Bldg Harrisburg PA 17120

HONEYWELL, EDITH COLEMAN, educator; b. Andalusia, Ala., July 11, 1932; d. Willie Lee and Gussie (Scover) Coleman; B.S., Bethune-Cookman Coll., 1954; M.Ed., Fla. Atlantic U., 1975; m. Alvin Bush, July 26, 1980; 1 dau., LaVette Edith Huffman. Profl. practices edn. reviewer State of Fla., Tallahassee, 1969-81; communication skills reading specialist Palm Beach County (Fla.) Schs., 1981—; bd. dirs. Tutorial Council. Mem. West Palm Beach (Fla.) Community Action Council, Transcultural Adv. Council, 1975—. Recipient Disting. Service award as outstanding alumni, Behtune-Cookman Coll., 1976. Mem. AAUW (com. on status of women Palm Beach County 1980-82), NAACP, Nat. Urban League, NEA, Equal Rights Amendment State of Fla. Assn., Bethune-Cookman Coll. Alumni Assn., Palm Beach County Tchrs. Assn. (treas. 1980-82), Black Educators Caucus West Palm Beach (pres. 1978—), Lambda Kappa Mu. Democrat. Mem. Pentecostal Ch. Club: Elks (dir. chpt. public relations). Address: 1444 8th St West Palm Beach FL 33401

HONIG, ALICE STERLING, educator, psychologist; b. N.Y.C., Apr. 19, 1929; d. William and Ida (Bender) Sterling; B.A. magna cum laude, Barnard Coll., 1950; M.A. in Exptl. Psychology, Columbia U., 1952; Ph.D. in Developmental Psychology, Syracuse U., 1975; children—Lawrence Sterling, Madeleine, Jonathan David. Program dir. Syracuse (N.Y.) Children's Center and Family Devel. Research Program, 1964-77; assoc. prof. child devel. Syracuse U., 1975-81, prof., 1981—. Mem. Am. Orthopsychiat. Assn., Am. Psychol. Assn., Soc. for Research in Child Devel., Am. Ednl. Research Assn., Nat. Assn. for Edn. of Young Children, Internat. Soc. for Study Behavioral Devel., Jean Piaget Soc., Soc. Pediatric Psychology, Internat. Conf. on Infant Studies, Phi Beta Kappa. Author: Learning Games for Preschoolers, 1982; Infant Caregiving: A Design for Training, 1981; (with J. Lally) Parent Involvement in Early Childhood Education, 1979; contbr. articles to profl. jours. Home: 317 Allen St Syracuse NY 13210 Office: 100 Walnut Pl Syracuse NY 13210

HONIG, NANCY, med. mgmt. cons. co. exec.; b. Oakland, Calif., Jan. 2, 1943; d. Milton and Betty (Street) Marquard; B.A. in Health Service Adminstrn., St. Mary's Coll.; m. Louis Honig, June 2, 1973; children—Michael, Carolyn, Stephen, Jonathan. Mgmt. cons., Oakland, Calif., 1968-75; pres. Nancy Honig & Assos., Inc., San Francisco, 1976—. Mem. Profl. Women's Alliance (founding mem., v.p. 1977-78, pres. 1979-80), Exec. Women's Forum, Com. of 200. Contbr. articles on bus. mgmt. to profl. publs. Office: 1193 Oak St San Francisco CA 94117

HONMYO, MARIE YAMAMOTO, mfg. co. exec.; b. Toppenish, Wash., June 16, 1926; d. Peter K. and Kikuno (Miyamoto) Yamamoto; B.B.A., U. Mich., 1949; m. Masayoshi Honmyo, May 4, 1957; children—Crystal, Cyrus. Acct., City of Seattle, 1950-57, Jack & Heintz Co., Cleve., 1957-59, Republic Electric & Devel. Co., Seattle, 1960-64;

acct., mgr. United Power & Control Systems, Inc., Kirkland, Wash., 1968-77; controller West Coast Machine Tools, Inc., Kent, Wash., 1977—, corp. sec., 1977—. Trustee West Coast Machine Tools Pension and Profit-Sharing Trusts. C.P.A., cert. mgmt. acct. Mem. Nat. Assn. Accts., Am. Women's Soc. C.P.A.s. Mem. Astara. Office: 20826 68th Ave S Kent WA 98031

HONNEN, MARY FRANCES, nun, coll. adminstr.; b. Newport, R.I., Dec. 16, 1921; d. William Henry and Winifred Veronica (Sullivan) H.; B.S., Elms Coll., 1944; M.S., U. Pa., 1959; Ph.D. (Frank Ross Chambers fellow), Columbia U., 1964. Joined Sisters of St. Joseph, 1939; sci. tchr., dept. chmn. Cathedral High Sch., Springfield, Mass., 1946-68, mem. adv. bd., 1968-76; personnel dir. Sisters of St. Joseph, Springfield, 1968-71, mem. exec. bd. congl. govt., 1971-79; acad. dean Elms Coll., Chicopee, Mass., 1979—. Mem. Springfield Diocese Bd. Edn., 1968-70; Chpt. cons. for religious congregations, 1971-79; bd. dirs. Our Lady of Providence Home for Children, Holyoke, Mass., 1968-70; Western Mass. del. United Farm Workers, Calif., 1975, Christian Appalachian Project, 1977. NSF fellow, 1959-60, summer fellow, 1960-62; Kellogg grantee Akron Conf. on Planned Change, 1980. Mem. Nat. Cath. Edn. Assn., Nat. Assn. for Women Religious, Am. Assn. for Higher Edn., Springfield C. of C. Home: 311 Springfield St Chicopee MA 01013 Office: Elms Coll 291 Springfield St Chicopee MA 01013

HOOD, LOUISE B., state legislator; b. Windsor, Vt., Aug. 27, 1916; d. Albert E., Sr., and Gladys H. (Robinson) Buckman; student schs. Windsor; m. Lee B. Hood, Sept. 4, 1938; children—L. Robert, Bonnie Lee, David John. Sec. to attys., payroll clk. Goodyear Tire and Rubber, Windsor, 1947-50; bookkeeper, sec., asst. town clk., justice of peace, notary public, Town of Windsor, 1950-68, treas., 1968-78; mem. Vt. Gen. Assembly, rep. from Town of Windsor, 1979—. Trustee, sec. Windsor Library, Davis Home; sec. Salvation Army, 1975—; treas. Windsor Sr. Center; vice chmn. Rep. Town Com. Methodist. Office: State House Montpelier VT 05602

HOOD, VALERIE LOGAN, seminar adminstr.; b. Kalispell, Mont., Nov. 3, 1937; d. William Regulous and Ione Montana (Swenson) Logan; B.A., Whitman Coll., 1960; M.A., George Washington U., 1963; m. Leroy E. Hood, Dec. 14, 1963; children—Eran William, Marqui Leigh. Tchr., Arcadia (Calif.) Unified Sch. Dist., 1963-67; vis. instr. Pacific Oaks Coll., 1974-78; gen. mgr. Fran W. Meyer Co., Glendale, Calif., 1978-80; dir. mgmt. devel. Indsl. Relations Center, Calif. Inst. Tech., Pasadena, 1981—. Mem. Am. Soc. Tng. and Devel., Personnel and Indsl. Relations Assn. Club: Orgn. for Women-Caltech. Home: 1453 E California Blvd Pasadena CA 91106 Office: 383 S Hill Ave I 90 Calif Inst Tech Pasadena CA 91125

HOOD, VIRGINIA FORD (MRS. FREDERICK REDDING HOOD), civic worker; b. Vinita, Okla., May 1, 1905; d. William Thomas and Demmeria (Byrd) Ford; student Northeastern State Tchrs. Coll., 1920-21, 21-22; A.B., U. Okla., 1924; m. Frederick Redding Hood, Dec. 7, 1924; children—Frederick Redding, William Richard, Virginia Carol (Mrs. Kenneth Lee Pierce). Pres., Ladies Aux. Oklahoma County Med. Soc., 1937, co-chmn. Oklahoma City conv. So. Med. Conv., 1938, chmn. state conv. Okla. Med. Soc., 1950. Dist. chmn. Big One Drive, United Fund, Oklahoma City, 1953; chmn. Okla. Art Center Drive, 1957; capt. spl. gifts div. United Appeal, 1960-69, gen. chmn. Kappa Alpha Theta Found. Drive, 1964-65; chmn. Heritage Hills Hist. Home Tour, 1970-72; pres. Mothers Assn. U. Okla., 1957-58, Okla. Art League, 1960-61, Heritage Hills Aux., 1972-73; mem. Modern Classics, Oklahoma City; dir. YWCA, 1939-41, 66-72, met. bd. dirs., 1969-72, v.p., 1966-69, chmn. personnel com. 1966-68, 70-72, mem. dept. campus Christian life Okla. Assn. Christian Chs., 1964-68; pres. Heritage Hills Women's Com. of Hist. Preservation, 1973—. Mem. Kappa Alpha Theta (Okla. chmn. 1928-31, pres. Oklahoma City alumnae chpt. 1948-51, corp. bd. Alpha Omicron chpt. at U. Okla. 1954-57, 77-83, alumnae dist. pres. 1957-60, grand council 1960-64, v.p. service 1966-70, mem. bd. trustees found. 1966-70). Mem. Christian Ch. (deaconess bd. Oklahoma City 1954-57, 65-68, 72-75, 78-81, past chmn.; pres. Christian Women's fellowship Crow Heights Christian Ch., 1960-61, 61-62, tchr. bus. women's class, sponsor young married class, vice chmn. gen. bd. 1979-80, chmn. gen. bd. 1980-81). Club: Coterie Study (Oklahoma City).

HOOK, PAULA JANE, engring/archtl. co. exec.; b. Fort Leavenworth, Kans., Oct. 1, 1949; d. Paul William and Vida Jane (Brown) Tomlinson; student Foothill Jr. Coll., 1974, West Valley Jr. Coll., 1975; m. Robert Wayne Hook, Apr. 27, 1975; children—Denisie Anne, Leshi Michele, Jerry Paul, Cori Irene. Process and device specialist Fairchild Semicondr., Mountain View, Calif., 1973-75; test specialist, engring. aide Fairchild Research & Devel., Palo Alto, Calif., 1977-79; specifications designer Fairchild Electronics, Mountain View, 1978-79; account adminstr. Advanced Micro Devices, Sunnyvale, Calif., 1980-81; dir. bus. devel. Sullivan & Masson, Sunnyvale, 1981—. Mem. Am. Bus. Women's Assn. (program chmn.), Nat. Assn. Female Execs., Nat. Assn. Profl. Saleswomen, San Jose C. of C. (mem. steering com.), Sunnyvale C. of C. Home: 1804 Wintersong Ct San Jose CA 95131 Office: 1230 Oakmead Pkwy 314 Sunnyvale CA 95131

HOOLEY, DARLENE KAY, state legislator; b. Williston, N.D., Apr. 4, 1939; d. Clarence Alvin and Alyce May (Rogers) Olson; BS., Oreg. State U., also postgrad.; m. John Hooley, June 7, 1964; children—Chad D., Erin B. Choir dir., dean girls, counselor high sch., 1961-69; researcher fed. grant, 1974-79; now mem. Oreg. Ho. of Reps. Mem. West Linn City Council, 1976-80; mem. Park and Recreation Bd., 1974-80; mem. exec. bd. Clackamas County Democratic Com., 1972-75; chmn. Clackamas County Voter Registration Drive, 1972; mem. Clackamas County Mental Health Bd., 1973-75; bd. dirs. Clackamas County Area Agy. Aging, 1981-82. Recipient Solar Advocate of Year award Oreg. State Solar Industries, 1981. Mem. Women's Polit. Caucus, LWV, Tri-A. Democrat. Lutheran. Office: State Capitol Salem OR 97310

HOOPER, ANNE CAROLINE DODGE, physician; b. Groton, Mass., July 16, 1926; d. Carroll William and Bertha Sanford (Wiener) Dodge; A.B., Washington U., St. Louis, 1947, M.D. (Jackson-Johnson research fellow 1949-50), 1952; m. William Dale Hooper, June 17, 1952; children—Elizabeth, Joan, Caroline. Rotating intern Virginia Mason Hosp., Seattle, 1952-53; resident in internal medicine St. Francis Hosp., Hartford, Conn., 1953-54; resident in pathology New Britain (Conn.) Gen. Hosp., 1954-57, Presbyn. Hosp., Phila., 1957-58; forensic pathologist Phila. Med. Examiner's Office, 1958-60; pathologist Coatesville (Pa.) Hosp., 1964, VA Hosp., Coatesville, 1964-66; dir. lab. St. Albans (Vt.) Hosp., 1966-69, Kerbs Hosp., St. Albans, 1966-71, Williamson (W.Va.) Appalachian Regional Hosp., 1971-73, Beckley (W.Va.) Appalachian Regional Hosp., 1974-76; asst. prof. W.Va. Sch. Osteo. Medicine, Lewisburg, 1977-78, assoc. prof. pathology, 1978—. Pres. Fairfield St. Sch. PTA, St. Albans, 1967-68. Recipient Borden Research award, 1952; diplomate Am. Bd. Pathology. Mem. AMA, Am. Soc. Clin. Pathology, Coll. Am. Pathologists, Internat. Acad. Pathology, Am. Acad. Forensic Scis., Nat. Assn. Med. Examiners, Am. Med. Women's Assn., Am. Assn. Blood Banks, W.Va. Med. Soc., W.Va. Pathology Spc., Raleigh County Med. Soc. Home: 104 Elmridge Ct Beckley WV 25801 Office: 400 N Lee St Lewisburg WV 24901

HOOPER, ELSIE SLOTH, travel agt.; b. Orange, N.J., Sept. 11, 1926; d. George Rudolph and Mette (Rasmussen) Sloth; student Silkeborg (Denmark) Sch. Econs., 1947-48; grad. Inst. Cert. Travel Agts., 1977; m. Robert Brundage Hooper, Aug. 26, 1949; children—Robert, William, Barbara, Elizabeth, Bruce. Mem. sales staff Group Air Tours, N.Y.C., 1966-68; owner, mgr. Travel-On Inc., Little Falls, N.J., 1968—. Cert. travel agt. Mem. Am. Soc. Travel Agts. (nat. bd. dirs., nat. edn. chmn.). Republican. Presbyterian. Clubs: Lord's Valley Country. Home: PO Box 1934 Hemlock Farms Hawley PA 18428 Office: 108 Main St Travel On Inc Little Falls NJ 07424

HOOPER, LILLIAN MARGARET, nursing adminstr.; b. Owings Mills, Md., Sept. 13, 1938; d. Lester H. R. and Minnie V. (Talbert) H.; A.A., Balt. Jr. Coll., 1960; diploma in nursing Md. Gen. Hosp., Balt., 1960; student Towson (Md.) State U., 1969-72; cert. Center for Disease Control, Atlanta, 1978. Nurse operating rm. Md. Gen. Hosp., Balt., 1960-64, head nurse operating rm., 1966-69, asst. supr. spl. care unit, 1969-71; gen. duty nurse St. Mary's Hosp., Leonardtown, Md., 1964-66, also supr. operating rm. and recovery rm.; clin. nurse Mt. Wilson (Md.) State Hosp., 1969; supr. med. supply The Good Samaritan Hosp., Balt., 1971-72; nurse clinician Balt. Cancer Research Center, 1972-78; infection control coordinator Levindale Hebrew Geriatric Center and Hosp., Balt., 1978-79, asso. dir. nursing, 1979-81; clin. supr. House in The Pines, Balt., 1981; relief charge nurse Bapt. Home of Md., Inc., Owings Mills, 1981—; asst. dir. nursing Pimlico Manor (formerly House in the Pines), Balt., 1981—. Mem. Assn. of Practioners in Infection Control. Democrat. Episcopalian. Address: 5129 Harney Rd Taneytown MD 21787

HOOPER, SHIRLEY, state ofcl.; b. Meadow, Tex., Nov. 5, 1935; d. Isam Franklin and Lena Cleo (Gregory) Collier; grad. Lovington (N.Mex.) High Sch.; m. Gailen Hooper, May 30, 1953; children—Johnny, Greg. Sec. law firms, N.Mex., 1953-54, 55-63, Elliott & Waldron Abstract Co., Lovington, 1954-55; dep. county clk. Lea County (N.Mex.), 1964; exec. sec. and secretarial supr. N.Mex. Bank & Trust Co. Hobbs, N.Mex., 1964-66; sec. to commr. pub. lands N.Mex. Land Office, Santa Fe, 1969-71; legal sec. to Judges Ray C. Cowan and Lewis R. Sutin, State Ct. Appeals, Santa Fe, 1971-77; sec., jour. clk., asst. chief clk. N.Mex. Ho. of Reps., 1959-73; sec. of state State of N.Mex., Santa Fe, 1979—. Vol. worker for handicapped children, 1967—; chmn. March of Dimes N.Mex. Mothers' March, 1979. Recipient Pioneer award Internat. Assn. Parents of Deaf, 1977, Gold medallion and Mother/Child plaque award March of Dimes, 1976. Mem. N.Mex. Assn. Legal Secs., Nat. Assn. Legal Secs., Beta Sigma Phi. Methodist. Club: Santa Fe County Democratic Women's. Office: Room 400 State Capitol Bldg Santa Fe NM 87503 *

HOOPES, MARGARET HOWARD, psychologist, educator; b. Idaho Falls, Idaho, May 12, 1927; d. James Parley and Elizebeth Joyce (Humphrey) Howard; B.S., Ricks Coll., 1953; M.S., Brigham Young U., 1962; Ph.D., U. Minn., 1969. Tchr. elem. sch., Jerome, Idaho, 1948-50, tchr. jr. high sch., counselor, 1950-52; tchr. high sch., counselor, Ephrata, Wash., 1955-58, Winnetka, Ill., 1958-65, adminstr., 1965-66; instr. U. Minn., Mpls., 1966-69, asst. prof., 1969-70; assoc. prof. marriage and family therapy Brigham Young U., Provo, Utah, 1970-82, prof., 1982—; pvt. practice psychology, Provo; cons. Lic. psychologist, Utah, marriage and family therapist, Utah. Utah Council of Family Relations, Am. Council Family Relations, Am. Assn. Marriage and Family Therapists, Am. Psychol. Assn. Mormon. Contbr. articles to profl. jours. Home: 3532 N Piute Dr Provo UT 84604 Office: 257 CCB Brigham Young U Provo UT 84602

HOOSIN, JANICE LAUTT, social worker; b. Chgo., June 22, 1942; d. Herbert and Ruth Jean (Rubenstein) Lapine; B.A., U. Ill., 1964; M.S.W., Jane Addams Grad. Sch. Social Work, 1966; postgrad. U. Utah, summer, 1977. Psychiat. social worker New Trier Twp. High Sch., East Winnetka, Ill., 1966-70; dir. day hosp. St. Vincent's Hosp., N.Y.C., 1970-73; psychotherapist (part-time) New Trier East High Sch., Winnetka, 1973-74; dir. psychiat. day hosp. dept. psychiatry Evanston (Ill.) Hosp., 1974-78, dir. partial hospitalization, 1978—; clin. assoc., field work supr. U. Chgo. Sch. Social Service Adminstrn., 1974—; cons. Center for Treatment and Rehab., Sheltered Care Facilities, Ill. Div. Vocat. Rehab., 1978—; pvt. practice marital and individual psychotherapy, 1975—; leader human sexuality edn. Northwestern U. Med. Sch., Chgo., 1976—. NIMH fellow, 1964-66; cert. psychiat. social worker, Ill. Mem. Nat. Assn. Social Workers, Internat. Assn. Psychosocial Rehab., Am. Group Psychotherapy Assn. Jewish. Home: 2033 Bissell St Chicago IL 60614 Office: 2530 Ridge Ave Evanston IL 60201

HOOTKIN, PAMELA NAN, pharm. co. exec.; b. N.Y.C., Nov. 14, 1947; d. Louis Arthur and Sally (Perlman) Mash; B.A., SUNY, Binghamton, 1968; M.A. in Econs., Boston U., 1970; m. Stephen Allen, Aug. 2, 1972; 1 dau., Julie Beth Allen. Diversification analyst Champion Internat., N.Y.C., 1971-75; sr. fin. analyst Squibb Corp., N.Y.C., 1975-77, mgr. fin. analyst, 1977-79, dir. fin. planning, 1979—; lectr. econs. U. York, Heslington, Eng., 1970-71. Mem. Fin. Women's Assn. of N.Y. Office: 40 W 57th St New York NY 10019

HOOVER, JANET MADDUX, univ. dean emeritus; b. Plain City, Ohio, Sept. 14, 1916; d. Charles Channing and Elo Fern (Maddux) Thomas; B.A. summa cum laude, Ohio State U., 1937; postgrad. U. N.C., 1943; M.A., Kent (Ohio) State U., 1950; m. William Rotroff Hoover, Dec. 25, 1938 (dec.); 1 son, William Thomas. Social worker YWCA, Canton, Ohio, 1937-39, Cin., 1942-43; asst. dean women U. N.C., 1943-45; med. social worker, Seattle, 1945-46; instr. sociology Kent State U., 1956-68, asst. prof., 1968-76, asso. prof., 1976—, asso. dean Coll. Arts and Scis., 1973-81, emeritus, 1981—; participant Internat. Conf. on Gerontology, Madrid, 1974; bd. dirs. Kentway Retirement Center, Kent. Precinct committeewoman Democratic Party; past mem. bd. dirs. League Women Voters, Campus Ministries. Mem. Am. Sociol. Assn., North Central Sociol. Assn., Am. Studies Assn., Am. Council Adminstrv. Women in Edn., Am. Council Acad. Affairs Adminstrs., Nat. Hist. Communal Socs. Assn. (dir. 1979—), Mortar Bd., Phi Beta Kappa, Alpha Kappa Delta. Mem. United Ch. of Christ. Author: (with Elizabeth Fleming) Manual on The Community, 1967. Home: 5942 Horning Rd Kent OH 44240

HOOVER, JOYCE JANELLE, nurse; b. St. Jo, Tex., Apr. 13, 1927; d. Charley R. and Lela Tisha (Hurd) Hoover; R.N., Harris Hosp., Ft. Worth, 1947; B.S. in Nursing Edn., U. Minn., 1958; M.N., U. Wash., 1965. Commd. ensign U.S. Navy, 1947, advanced through grades to lt. comdr. Nurse Corps; served with naval hosps., flight nursing, ship nursing transports, nurse recruiting; ret., 1968; nursing cons. Tex. Dept. Health, 1968-71; dir. continuing edn. for nurses U. Tex., Austin, 1971—. Mem. Am. Nurses Assn., Tex. Nurses Assn., Nat. League Nursing, Phi Kappa Phi, Sigma Theta Tau. Republican. Home: 3603D Las Colinas Dr Austin TX 78731 Office: U Tex-Austin School of Nursing 1700 Red River St Austin TX 78701

HOOVER, LEE, utility exec.; b. Balt., Oct. 4, 1927; d. Lee Adrian and Ruth Elizabeth (Brown) von Wallenstein; B.A. with honors, Rollins Coll., Winter Park, Fla., 1977; m. Herbert Lowell Hoover, July 21, 1945; children—Michael D., David B., Lee Adrian. Customer service rep. Balt. Gas & Electric Co., 1958-63; substitute tchr., 1964-65; with Fla. Power Corp., 1974—, supr. customer service center Eastern div. office, Winter Park, 1974-81, mgr. customer service, 1981—. Arbitrator, Seminole County Juvenile Arbitration Program; mem. Winter Park City Biracial Com., 1966-76; mem. Seminole Youth Planning Council. Mem. AAUW, LWV, Fla. Council Internat. Visitors, Delta Zeta. Democrat. Quaker (ch. trustee 1982). Home: 1202 Wolverine Trail Winter Springs FL 32708 Office: Box 417 Winter Park FL 32789

HOOVER, SUSAN BETH, advt. agy. exec.; b. Ventnor, N.J., Dec. 14, 1952; d. Clarence Harris, Jr. and Zena (Loukashenok) H.; B.F.A. cum laude, Moore Coll. Art, Phila., 1975; m. Dennis Gererd Connaughton, Feb. 10, 1979. Graphic artist Acad. Natural Scis., Phila., 1975; art dir. Walpert Co., Cherry Hill, N.J., 1975, Group W Advt., Haddonfield, N.J., 1975-77; pres. Graphics One, Cherry Hill, 1975—; v.p., sr. art dir. Brian Advt., Collingswood, N.J., 1977-81; sr. art dir. Detroit office Leo Burnett Advt., Southfield, Mich., 1981—; speaker in field. Recipient NeoGraphic Gold award, 1981; Art Dirs. Club Phila. awards, 1981; Addy award, 1981. Mem. Women's Bus. Profl. Advt. Assn., Art Dirs Club Phila., Phila. Advt. Club. Home: 5 Lafayette Ln Cherry Hill NJ 08003 Office: 26555 Evergreen Rd Southfield MI 48076

HOOVER, THERESSA, religious orgn. exec.; b. Fayetteville, Ark., Sept. 7, 1925; d. James Cortez and Rissie (Vaughn) Hoover; B.A., Philander Smith Coll., 1946; M.A., N.Y. U., 1962. Asso. dir. Little Rock Meth. Council, 1946-48; field worker women's div. Meth. Ch. (now United Meth. Ch.), N.Y. U., 1948-58, Christian social relations worker, 1958-65, head sect. program and edn., 1965-68, exec. sec. womens' div., 1968—. Mem. commn. on chs. participation in devel. World Council Chs. Mem. nat. bd. YWCA, 1963-76; trustee Paine Coll., Augusta, Ga.; mem. exec. bd. Nat. Council Negro Women. Office: 475 Riverside Dr New York NY 10115

HOPE, GLORIA SORRENTINO, nurse, adminstr., educator; b. Rockville Centre, N.Y., Feb. 15, 1924; d. Sylvester and Vera (Milone) Sorrentino; B.S. in Nursing Edn., Tchrs. Coll., Columbia U., 1951; M.A. in Nursing Edn., U. Pitts., 1962; Ph.D. in Ednl. Technology, Cath. U. Am., 1977; m. George Henry Hope, July 3, 1961; 1 son, George Bernard. staff nurse, pvt. duty Mercy Hosp., L.I., 1944-46; head nurse, asst. head nurse N.Y. Hosp., Cornell Med. Center, 1947-49; instr. VA Nursing Service, Sunmount, N.Y., 1951-53; affiliate nurse instr. TB nursing VA Hosp., Sunmount, 1953-58; asst. chief nursing service for edn. VA Med. Center, Butler, Pa., 1958-61, Pitts. U. Drive Hosp., 1961-65; edn. and tng. specialist VA Central Office Nursing Service, Washington, 1965-68, chief edn. and tng. div., 1968-72, dep. dir., 1972-82, ret., 1982; lectr. Continuing Health Edn. Services, Pa. State U., 1961-65; clin. appointment Sch. Nursing, Med. and Surg. Div., U. Pitts., 1961-65; mem. nurse adv. com. U.S. Pharmacopoeia, 1982—. Exec. com. regional adv. group Washington Met. Regional Med. Program, 1974-75; instr. Catholic Christian Doctrine, 1971; lector Mt. Calvary and Our Lady of Good Counsel Cath. Ch., 1971—. Recipient commendations, 1965, 80, 82; adminstr.'s disting. award, 1982. Mem. Am. Nurses Assn., Nat. League for Nursing (rep. White House Conf. on Aging, 1981), D.C. League for Nursing (pres., 1977-79, dir. 1979-82), Inst. of Soc., Ethics and Life Scis., Assn. Mil. Surgeons U.S., Am. Assn. Advancement for Humanities, Am. Soc. Profl. and Exec. Women, Sigma Theta Tau. Republican. Home: Wolftrappe Sq 137 East St NE Vienna VA 22180

HOPE, JOYCE MORTENSEN, nurse, educator; b. Bklyn., Aug. 20, 1936; d. Daniel Theodore and Helen Irene (Maloney) Mortensen; B.S.N., Hunter Coll., 1959, M.S., 1969; postgrad. CUNY, 1978—. Dir. edn. Jersey Shore Med. Center Sch. Nursing, 1963-65; asst. dir. inservice edn. Metro. Hosp., N.Y.C., 1966-68; asst. prof./coordinator Baccalaureate program Hunter Coll., Dept. Nursing, City U. N.Y., 1969-74, chmn. Dept. Nursing, 1974-77, acting dean, Hunter-Bellevue Sch. Nursing, 1977-78, 82—, co-dir. undergrad. program, 1981, assoc. prof., 1979—; faculty Brookdale Ctr. on Aging, N.Y.C., 1978—; advisor Mt. Sinai-Hunter Coll. Long Term Care Gerontology Ctr., 1980—. Adv. com. Community Service Soc. N.Y., 1978—; mem. Nat. Conf. on Aging, 1975—; participant White House Conf. on Aging, 1981. Title II traineeship, USPHS, 1968-69; Fin. awardee, Brookdale Ctr. on Aging, 1978. Mem. Gerontol. Soc. Am., Am. Geriatrics Soc., Aging in Higher Edn., Am. Assn. Ret. Persons, Am. Nurses Assn., Nat. League Nursing, AAAS, N.Y. Acad. Sci., Sigma Theta Tau, Pi Lambda Theta. Club: Vasa Order Am. Office: 425 E 25th St New York NY 10010

HOPE, MARGARET LAUTEN, civic worker; b. N.Y.C., Sept. 11; privately educated; m. Paul C. Debry, Jr., Nov. 9, 1943; m. 2d, Fred H. Hope, Jr., Mar. 30, 1959; 1 son, Frederick H., III. Bd. dirs. Nat. Leukemia Soc., 1974—; co-chmn. giftcom. Heart Ball, Palm Beach, Fla., 1967; mem. ball coms. various charity fund raising events. Episcopalian. Clubs: Everglades, Sailfish (Palm Beach); Women's Nat. Republican (N.Y.C.). Address: PO Box 601 Palm Beach FL 33480-0601

HOPFENSPERGER, DEBORAH LEE, educator, coach; b. New Albany, Ind., Oct. 3, 1955; d. Carl John and Dorothy Lee (Duvall) H.; B.A., U. Evansville, 1978, M.A., 1981. Teacher's aide, volleyball-basketball coach, intramural dir., bldg. supr. women's volleyball, basketball and softball mgr. U. Evansville, 1979-81, intramural dir., bldg. supr., 1981—; volleyball ofcl. Mem. Ind. High Sch. Athletic Assn., Nat. Assn. Intramural and Recreational Sports, Pi Lambda Theta. Democrat. Presbyterian Mem. Internat. Order Job's Daus., Grand Bethel of Ind. Home: 204 Spickert Knobb Rd New Albany IN 47150

HOPKINS, CARTER HUNTER, coll. ofcl.; b. Norfolk, Va., Dec. 8, 1946; d. Henry Blount and Vivian (Smith) Hunter; A.B., Sweet Briar Coll., 1968; M.Ed., Am. U., 1972; m. Edward Meeks Hopkins, July 30, 1977; 1 son, Edward Hunter. Employment counselor Day Personnel, Inc., Washington, 1968; jr. tech. editor TRW Systems Group, Washington, 1969; ins. claims staff Ins. Mgmt., Inc., Washington, 1970; counselor Stone Ridge Country Day Sch., 1972-76; dir. fin. aid and career counseling Sweet Briar (Va.) Coll., 1976-77, dir. career planning, 1977—; cons. in field. IBM Career Planning grantee, project adminstr., 1977-82. Mem. Am. Personnel and Guidance Assn., Am. Coll. Personnel Assn., Middle Atlantic Placement Assn., So. Coll. Placement Assn., Va. Coll. Placement Assn. Episcopalian. Club: Village Garden. Contbr. articles to profl. jours. Home: Ridge Dr Amherst VA 24521 Office: PO Box AT Sweet Briar VA 24595

HOPKINS, CECILIA ANN (MRS. HENRY E. HOPKINS), educator; b. Havre, Mont., Feb. 17, 1922; d. Kost L. and Mary (Manaras) Sofos; B.S., Mont. State Coll., 1944; M.A., San Francisco State Coll., 1958, M.A., 1967; postgrad. Stanford U.; Ph.D., Calif. Western U., 1977; m. Henry E. Hopkins, Sept. 7, 1944. Bus. tchr. Havre (Mont.) High Sch., 1942-44; sec. George P. Gorham, realtor, San Mateo, Calif., 1944-45; escrow sec. Fox & Carskadon, realtors, 1945-50; escrow officer Calif. Pacific Title Ins. Co., 1950-57; bus. tchr. Westmoor High Sch., Daly City, Calif., 1958-59; bus. tchr. Coll. San Mateo, 1959—, chmn. real estate-ins. dept., 1963-76, dir. div. bus., 1976—; cons. to commr. Calif. Div. Real Estate, 1963—, mem. periodic exam. rev. com., 1974—; bd. advisers Glendale Fed./West Coast Fed. Savs. and Loan Assn. Vice chmn. Community Coll. Adv. Com., 1970-71, chmn., 1971-72; mem. adv. com. Chancellor's Community Coll. Endowment, 1975—; mem. Calif. Community Coll. real estate continuing edn. panel, 1979—. Recipient Woman of Achievement award Mateo-Burlingame Soroptimists, 1979. Mem. AAUW, Calif. Assn. Real Estate Tchrs. (state pres. 1964-65, hon. dir. 1962— named Outstanding Real Estate Tchr. 1979), Real Estate Certificate Inst., Calif. Bus. Edn. Assn. (Cert. of Commendation 1978), San Francisco State Coll. Guidance and Counseling Alumni, Theta Alpha Delta, Pi Lambda Theta, Delta Pi Epsilon (nat. dir. interchpt. relations 1962-65, nat. historian 1966-67, nat. sec. 1968-69), Alpha Gamma Delta. Contbr. articles to profl. jours. Home: 504 Colgate Way San Mateo CA 94402

HOPKINS, EDWINA WEISKITTEL, graphic designer; b. Cin., June 7, 1947; d. Edwin and Moody (Bowling) Campbell; student U. Cin.,

1965-66; m. Michael J. Weiskittel, May 1966 (dec. May 1970); 1 son, Todd Michael; m. 2d, Franklin Hopkins, June 1973 (div. June 1977). Asst. to art dir. World Library Publs., Cin., 1965-68; comml. artist Campbell & Assos. Art Studio, Cin., 1969-73; prodn. mgr. William Wilson Advt. Agy., Palos Verdes, Calif., 1973-74; partner Hopkins & Hopkins Design Studio, Redondo Beach, Calif., 1975-76; owner, graphic designer Winnissa Comml. Art Studio, Rolling Hills, Calif., 1976-81; pres. Winnissa, Inc., Redondo Beach, Calif., 1981—. U. Cin. hon. scholar, 1965. Mem. Palos Verdes Peninsula C. of C. Home and office: 718 Ave D Redondo Beach CA 90277

HOPKINS, JEAN SUSANNE, editor; b. Glendale, Calif., Nov. 6, 1947; d. Donald Irwin and Jean Juanita (Ahn) Hopkins; 1 stepson, John J. Kramer; A.A., Ventura Coll., 1967. Reporter, Ventura (Calif.) Star-Free Press, 1970-72; focus editor Redding (Calif.) Record Searchlight, 1972—; guest lectr. Shasta Coll., 1975—; lectr. in field; newspaper critic for amateur and profl. prodns. Mem. adv. com. Shasta Coll. Supportive Services, 1978—; judge Soroptimist Scholarship applicants, 1979, Bus. and Profl. Career Girl Speak-off, 1975, other types competition; co-founder Shasta Dinner Theater, Riverfront Players; performer Little Theater prodns.; mem. council St. James Lutheran Ch., Redding, 1976-78. Named Best actress Simi (Calif.) Horizon Players, 1971, Woman of Achievement, AAUW, 1975; recipient feature story award Nat. Newspaper Contest, 1975, Meritorious Service award 4-H, 1978; pub. service appreciation awards Girl Scouts U.S.A., 1977, 80, Shasta Assn. for Retarded, 1977-78. Office: PO Box 2397 Redding CA 96099

HOPKINS, JEANNE SULICK, accountant; b. FairLawn, N.J., Oct. 14, 1952; d. Peter and Margaret Mary (McLaughlin) Sulick; B.S., Syracuse (N.Y.) U., 1974, M.B.A., 1975; m. Ronald T. Hopkins, Aug. 23, 1975. With Price Waterhouse, C.P.A.s, Syracuse, 1975—, staff acct., 1975-78, sr. acct., 1978-80, audit mgr., 1980—; instr. in field. Mem. fund raising com. Syracuse Symphony Orch.; mem. Nat. Assn. Panhellenics. C.P.A., N.Y. Mem. Am. Inst. C.P.A.s, Planning Execs. Inst., Hosp. Fin. Mgmt. Assn., N.Y. State Soc. C.P.A.s, Syracuse U. Alumni Assn., Delta Delta Delta. Club: Zonta. Office: Price Waterhouse One Mony Plaza Syracuse NY 13202

HOPKINS, LINDA ANN, sch. psychologist; b. Bristol, Va., Aug. 23, 1937; d. James Robert and Trula Mae (Mink) Broce; A.B., King Coll., 1959; M.A., East Tenn. State U., 1977, postgrad., 1977-79; postgrad. Radford U., 1978-79; m. James Edwin Hopkins, Oct. 8, 1960; children—James Edwin, David Lawrence. Social worker Washington County Welfare Dept., Abingdon, Va., 1959-61; social worker Bristol (Va.) Welfare Dept., 1963-65, Washington County Welfare Dept., 1965-68, Bristol Meml. Hosp., 1968-72; psychologist Washington County Public Schs., Abingdon, 1978—; lectr. Va. Highlands Community Coll., Abingdon, 1981—. Mem. Am. Psychol. Assn. (asso.), Nat. Assn. Sch. Psychologists, Va. Psychol. Assn., Va. Assn. Sch. Psychologists, Phi Kappa Phi. Methodist. Club: Dogwood Playhouse. Home: 436 Brookwood Dr Bristol TN 37620 Office: Washington County Public Schs Drawer G Abingdon VA 24210

HOPKINS, LYNETTE LANE, ednl. therapist; b. Los Angeles, Sept. 12, 1934; d. Arthur Henry and LaVaughn Lorene (Beckwith) Lane; B.A., Whittier Coll., 1956; M.S.W., UCLA, 1966; M.S. in Spl. Edn., Mt. St. Mary's Coll., 1978; postgrad. in integrative edn. Internat. Coll., Los Angeles; m. Don J. Hopkins, Nov. 21, 1959; children—Kenneth, Scott, Richard. Elem. sch., jr. high music tchr. Fullerton, Calif., 1956-60; social worker Los Angeles County Dept. Public Social Services, 1960-66, staff devel. specialist, 1966-70; researcher Marianne Frostig Center, Los Angeles, 1974-76; master tchr., ednl. therapist Marianne Frostig Center, Los Angeles, 1976—. Registered social worker, Calif. Mem. Nat. Assn. Social Workers, Acad. Cert. Social Workers, Council for Exceptional Children, Holistic Educators Network. Baha'i. Home: 1144 N Jackson St Glendale CA 91207 Office: 5981 Venice Blvd Los Angeles CA 90034

HOPKINS, MEGAN VICTORIA, med. adminstr.; b. St. Petersburg, Fla., Mar. 24, 1954; d. John Francis and Megan Wanda-Ruth (Morris) Scott; cert. U. History and Tech., Bath, Eng., 1971; student Mary Washington Coll., 1972-74, hosp. adminstrn. Va. Commonwealth U., 1974—; m. David Robert Hopkins, Oct. 5, 1972. Adminstrv. asst. dept. ob-gyn Med. Coll. Va., Richmond, 1975-77; office mgr. Bernard Suher, Gross & Binder, Richmond, 1977; adminstr. Richmond Fertility and Reproductive Medicine Ltd., 1977-80; adminstrv. sec., dept. cardiac surgery Med. Coll. Va., 1981—. Lay therapist Crisis Center Family and Children's Service, Richmond, 1980—. Mem. Nat. Assn. Exec. Females (exec., dir. Va. network), Am. Assn. Med. Assts., Va. Group Med. Mgmt. Assn., Med. Group Mgmt. Assn., Internat. Platform Assn. Democrat. Episcopalian. Contbr. articles to profl. jours. Home: 2421 Park Ave Richmond VA 23220 Office: Box 68 MCV Sta Richmond VA 23220

HOPKINS, THELMA PEGGY, home economist; b. Leverett, Mass., Mar. 12, 1918; d. Maurice Milton and Pluma Effie (Hemenway) Glazier; B.S., U. Mass., 1940; R.D., Western Res. U., Cleve., 1941; attended Kanazawa Real Estate Sch., Honolulu, 1960, U. Hawaii, 1961; m. James Byron Bodensick, Dec. 24, 1975; children by previous marriage—Carole Hopkins Atkinson, David Franklin Hopkins. Staff dietitian Grace New Haven Hosp., 1941-42; home economist Pacific Gas & Elec. Co., Fresno, Calif., 1963-67, PG & E., San Rafael, 1967-69, consumer services rep., 1979—; lectr. community colls. Adv. com. Coll. of Marin, 1971—; mem. Nutritional Edn. Council Sonoma County, 1975—; mem. Easter Seal Soc. Marin County, 1975—, cert. of appreciation, 1974; instr. courses for blind and physically handicapped, 1970—, county heart assns., diabetics socs. Recipient Instr. with Great Merit cert. Pacific Service Employees Assn., 1969, 79, Nat. Home Service award Gas Industry, 1971, cert. of recognition Santa Rosa City Schs., 1975. Mem. Am. Dietetic Assn. (registered), Calif. Dietetic Assn., Bay Area Dietetic Assn., Am. Home Econs. Assn., Calif. Home Econs. Assn., Home Economists in Bus. (chmn. San Francisco group 1978-79, advisor 1979-80). Club: Marin Bus. and Profl. Women. Office: Pacific Gas & Electric Co 3d and Brooks Sts San Rafael CA 94912

HOPKINS, VASHTI JOHNSON, educator; d. Louis Tenner and Matilda (Robinson) Johnson; B.S., Va. Sem. and Coll., 1963; B.S. in Edn., St. Paul's Coll., Lawrenceville. Va., 1967; M.Ed., U. Va., 1969; m. Haywood H. Hopkins, Sr., Oct. 10, 1942; children—Haywood, Yvonne Hopkins Andrews, Sharon Evette. Ret. reading specialist Sandusky Middle Sch., Lynchburg, Va. Mem. NEA, Va. Edn. Assn., Lynchburg Edn. Assn., Va. Reading Assn., Piedmont Reading Assn., NAACP, Episcopal Ch. Women, U. Va. Alumni Assn. (life), St. Paul's Alumni Century Club, Zeta Phi Beta (past basileus Epsilon Kappa Zeta chpt.). Episcopalian. Clubs: Order of Eastern Star (past worthy matron, dep. organizer), Order of Golden Circle (past loyal lady ruler), Daus. of Isis, Amity Social, Bridgette Social. Author poetry.

HOPKINSON, SHIRLEY LOIS, educator; b. Boone, Iowa, Aug. 25, 1924; d. Arthur Perry and Zora (Smith) Hopkinson; student Coe Coll., 1942-43; B.A. cum laude (Phi Beta Kappa scholar 1944), U. Colo., 1945; B.L.S., U. Calif., 1949; M.A. (Honnold Honor scholar 1945-46), Claremont Grad. Sch., 1951; Ed.M., U. Okla., 1952, Ed.D., 1957. Tchr. pub. sch. Stigler, Okla., 1946-47, Palo Verde High Jr. Coll., Blythe, Calif., 1947-48; asst. librarian Modesto (Calif.) Jr. Coll., 1949-51; tchr., librarian Fresno, Calif., 1951-52, La Mesa, Calif., 1953-55; asst. prof. librarianship, instructional materials dir. Chaffey Coll., Ontario, Calif., 1955-58; with Edn. Library San Jose (Calif.) State Coll., 1958-59, asst. prof. librarianship, 1959-64, asso. prof., 1964-69, prof., 1969—, dir. NDEA Inst. for Sch. Library Personnel, 1966. Mem. Am., Calif., library assns., Audio-Visual Assn. Calif., NEA, Sch. Librarians Assn. Calif. (com. mem., treas. No. sect. 1951-52), San Diego County Sch. Librarians Assn. (sec. 1945-55), Calif. Tchrs. Assn., League Women Voters (dir. 1950-51, publs. chmn.), AAUW (social studies chmn., dir. 1957-58), Alpha Beta Bus. and Profl. Women's Club (attendance chmn. 1957-58), Alpha Beta Alpha, Phi Beta Kappa, Alpha Lambda Delta, Delta Kappa Pi, Phi Kappa Phi, Delta Kappa Gamma. Author: Descriptive Cataloging of Library Materials, 1963; Instructional Materials for Teaching the Use of the Library, 1966. Editor: Sch. Librarians Assn. Calif. Bull., 1961-64. Book reviewer Am. Reference Books Ann., Library Jour.; contbr. articles to profl. jours. Office: LN 608 San Jose State U San Jose CA 95112

HOPPE, SUSAN ANDREA, psychologist; b. Racine, Wis., Sept. 16, 1948; d. Clarence Elmer and Beverly Joyce (Anderson) H.; student Wartburg Coll., 1966-69; B.A., Carthage Coll., 1970; M.S., Purdue U., 1974, Ph.D., 1975. Asso. prof. psychology U. S. Ala., Mobile, 1975—. Women's gymnastics judge, 1978—. Mem. Soc. Neurosci., Am. Psychol. Assn., Southeastern Psychol. Assn., Ala. Psychol. Assn., Sigma Xi. Lutheran. Office: Dept Psychology U S Ala Mobile AL 36688

HOPPENFELD, MARILYN PEARL, judge; b. N.Y.C., Dec. 9, 1930; d. Bernard and Anna (Rubin) H.; student Bklyn. Coll., 1948-50; LL.B., Bklyn. Law Sch., 1952; 1 dau., Aphrodite S. Zeitlan. Admitted to U.S. Supreme Ct. bar, 1962; pvt. practice law, specializing in criminal and civil cases, N.Y.C., 1952-78; adminstrv. law judge N.Y. State Dept. Motor Vehicles, N.Y.C., 1978-81, U.S. Dept. Health and Human Services Social Security dept. Office Hearings and Appeals, 1981—; apptd. by ct. to rep. indigent, 1952-78; pre-trial master for Civil Ct. N.Y.; lectr. in field. Bd. dirs. Samaritan Halfway Soc., Jamaica, N.Y., 1963-68; mem. N.Y. State Panel for Indigent, 1965-78. Mem. Queens County Bar Assn., Queens County Criminal Bar Assn., Am. Trial Lawyers Assn., Queens County Women's Bar Assn., Brandeis Assn. Staff writer legal commentary Bklyn. Law Sch. Alumni Bull., 1969-74; contbr. articles to profl. jours.

HOPPER, GRACE BREWSTER MURRAY, mathematician; b. N.Y.C., Dec. 9, 1906; d. Walter Fletcher and Mary Campbell (Van Horne) Murray; B.A., Vassar Coll., 1928; M.A. (Vassar fellow, Sterling scholar), Yale, 1930, Ph.D., 1934; postgrad. (Vassar Faculty fellow) N.Y. U., 1941-42; D.Eng. (hon.), Newark Coll. Engring., 1972; D.Sc. (hon.), C.W. Post Coll. L.I. U., 1973, Pratt Inst., 1976, Linkoping U. (Sweden), 1980, Bucknell U., 1980, Acadia U. (Can.), 1980, So. Ill. U., 1981, Loyola U. Chgo., 1981; LL.D., U. Pa., 1974; D.Public Service, George Washington U., 1981; D.Sc. (hon.), Marquette U., 1982; L.H.D. (hon.), Seton Hall Coll., 1982; m. Vincent Foster Hopper, June 15, 1930 (div. 1945). From instr. to assoc. prof. math. Vassar Coll., 1931-44; asst. prof. math. Barnard Coll., summer 1943; research fellow engring. scis., applied physics Computation Lab., Harvard, 1946-49; sr. mathematician Eckert-Mauchly Computer Corp., Phila., 1949-50, sr. programmer Eckert-Mauchly div. Remington Rand, 1950-59; systems engr., dir. automatic programming devel. UNIVAC div. Sperry Rand Corp., Phila., 1959-64, staff scientist systems programming, 1964-71; ret., 1971; vis. lectr. Moore Sch. Elec. Engring., U. Pa., 1959-63, vis. asso. prof. elec. engring., 1963-74, adj. prof., 1974; professorial lectr. George Washington U., 1971—. Served to comdr. WAVES, 1944-46, 67—, capt. USNR, 1973; presently serving active duty NAVDAC. Decorated Legion of Merit, Meritorious Service award; recipient Naval Ordnance Devel. award, 1946. Connelly Meml. award, 1968, Wilbur L. Cross medal Yale 1972, Sci. Achievement award Am. Mother's Com., 1970, Pioneer award IEEE Computer Soc., 1982, gold medal Armed Forces Communications and Electronics Assn., 1982, others. Disting. fellow Brit. Computer Soc.; fellow Assn. Computer Programmers and Analysts, IEEE (McDowell award 1979), AAAS; mem. Nat. Acad. Engring., Assn. Computing Machinery, Data Processing Mgmt. Assn. (Man of Yr. award 1969), Am. Fedn. Information Processing Socs. (Harry Goode Meml. award 1970), Soc. Women Engrs. (Achievement award 1964), Franklin Inst., U.S. Naval Inst., Internat. Oceanographic Found., DAR, Dames Loyal Legion, Hist. Soc. Pa., Geneal. Soc. Pa., N.H. Hist. Soc., New Eng. Hist.-Geneal. Soc., Valley Forge Hist. Assn., Ret. Officers Assn., Huguenot Soc. Pa., Nat., N.Y. geneal. socs., Pechin Soc., Phi Beta Kappa, Sigma Xi. Contbr. numerous articles to profl. jours. Home: 1400 S Joyce St Arlington VA 22202 Office: Dept of Mgmt Sci George Washington U 2029 G St NW Washington DC 20052

HOPPER, MARY ALICE, consumer credit researcher; b. Balt., Aug. 9, 1942; d. Edward Earl and Anita June (Smith) H.; B.S. in Math., Pa. State U., 1963; M.B.A., U. Chgo., 1981. Data processor Spiegel, Inc., 1964-67, Meiscon div. Control Data Corp., 1967-68; dir. credit research and strategy devel. dir. Montgomery Ward & Co., Chgo., 1968—. Republican. Home: 3940 W Loyola Ave Lincolnwood IL 60645 Office: 1 Montgomery Ward Plaza Chicago IL 60671

HOPPOCK, D. LARUE, educator, antique appraiser; b. San Francisco, Mar. 27, 1933; d. Charles D. and Evelyn (Birdeen) H.; B.A., Western Wash. U., 1958; M.A., Boston U., 1972; postgrad. U. Calif., Berkeley, U. Chgo., U. Md. Prin. high schs. Dept. Def., Paris, Naples, Italy, Istanbul, Turkey and Brunssum, Netherlands, 1963-75; tchr. high sch., Carlsbad, Calif., 1976-79, tchr. elem. sch., 1979—; antique appraiser, 1981—; tchr. evening sch. Mira Costa Coll., 1977—. Named Tchr. of Year, 1963, 65, 68, 69, 81. Mem. Carlsbad Unified Tchrs. Assn. (treas.), Am. Personnel and Guidance Assn., Nat. Educators Fellowship, Delta Kappa Gamma, Assn. Calif. Sch. Adminstrs., Internat. Soc. Appraisers. Contbr. articles in field to profl. jours. Office: 1905 Magnolia St Carlsbad CA 92008

HOPSON, DOLORES ASTRID, data processing exec.; b. Santiago de Cuba, Aug. 7, 1936; came to U.S., 1962, naturalized, 1969; s. Bruno and Rafaela (Cerdeira) Garcia; student Havana U., 1962; B.S., Rutgers U., 1975; children—Edward, Kimberly. Asst. controller Am. Nat. Capitalization Bank, Havana, until 1962; clk. purchasing dept. Hudson Tool & Die Co., Newark, 1962-63; supr. Monroe Data Processing, West Orange, N.J., 1964-71; dir. acctg. applications Automatic Data Processing, Clifton, N.J., 1972—. Mem. Phi Ku Theta. Democrat. Roman Catholic. Home: 55 Bayliss St North Arlington NJ 07032 Office: 405 Route 3 Clifton NJ 07015

HORACEK, CONSTANCE HELLER, graphic designer, educator; b. Campbell, Nebr., Nov. 7; d. Roy B. and Mildred Bernadine (Holt) Heller; B.S. in Edn., Midland Luth. Coll., 1963; M.A. in Ceramic Sculpture, Western Ill. U., 1977, postgrad., 1978—; postgrad. U. Kans., 1974-75, Arrowmont Sch. Arts and Crafts, 1978, 79, 81, 82, Md. Inst. Art, Balt., 1982—; m. Michael Jay Horacek, Aug. 18, 1963; children—Kachina Leigh, Marika Sian. Tchr., Ottawa (Kans.) Jr. High Sch., 1964-68, Bardolph (Ill.) Elem. Sch., 1970; mem. faculty Western Ill. U. Lab. Sch., Macomb, 1970-73, instr. clothing textile design dept. home econs., 1975-80; asst. prof. clothing/textiles Albright Coll., Reading, Pa., 1980—, acting dir. Freedman Gallery, summer 1981; instr. (part-time) extension campus Spoon River Jr. Coll., Macomb, 1980; graphic designer for workshops, seminars and local bus. firms, 1975-80; partner Images Unlimited, Macomb, 1980; cons. visual prodn., 1975—; project dir. Outreach Program, summer 1981; design cons. Tandy Leather Co., Fort Worth. Bd. dirs. Kashasia, Western Ill. U., 1978-80, Downtown Up. Mem. Am. Crafts Council, Am. Home Econs. Assn., Pa. Home Econs. Assn., Surface Design, Kappa Omicron Phi, Kappa Pi, Alpha Psi Omega. Office: Albright Coll Reading PA 19604

HORAI, JOANN, research psychologist, educator; b. N.Y.C., Mar. 9, 1942; B.A. in Psychology and English Lit., U. Miami, 1964, M.S. in Exptl. Psychology and Polit. Sci., 1968, Ph.D. in Social Psychology, 1970. Teaching asst. U. Miami, Fla., 1968-70; asst. prof. psychology Hofstra U., Hempstead, N.Y., 1971-76; adminstrv. officer Office of Programs and Planning, Am. Psychol. Assn., Washington, 1976—, Office Programs and Planning and Office of Nat. Policy Studies, 1978—. Mem. Am. Psychol. Assn., AAAS. Contbr. articles to profl. Jours. Office: 1200 17th St NW Washington DC 20036

HORAN, HOPE DARLENE, psychologist; b. Chgo., Feb. 13, 1954; d. Theodore George and Idelle (Poll) H.; B.S. (Ill. State scholar), U. Ill., Champaign-Urbana, 1976; M.A. (research and teaching asst.), No. Ill. U., 1979. Recreational therapist Evanston (Ill.) Ridgeview Shelter Care Home, summer 1976; psychologist Glenwood (Iowa) State Hosp. Sch., 1979—; cons. Clarinda (Iowa) Mental Health Inst., 1980—. Active Omaha Symphonic Chorus, 1981—; mem. Omaha Public Schs. Citizens Adv. Com., 1980-81; mem. edn. com. Anti-Defamation League, 1980—, chmn. com. anti-Semitism and Jewish youth, 1981—. Mem. Am. Psychol. Assn., Midwest Psychol. Assn., Phi Kappa Phi, Psi Chi. Jewish. Contbr. paper to profl. conf. Office: Glenwood State Hospital-School Glenwood IA 51534

HORELICK, MARY GAIL, phys. therapist; b. Westport, Conn., Apr. 27, 1948; d. Michael and Rita (Hermenze) H.; B.S., Ithaca Coll., 1970. Staff phys. therapist New Rochelle (N.Y.) Hosp. Med. Center, 1971-73, Misericordia Hosp. Med. Center, Bronx, 1974-77, chief phys. therapist/coordinator rehab. services, 1977-80; dir. rehab. services Newington (Conn.) Children's Hosp., 1980—. Vice-Pres. Conn. chpt. Nat. Spinal Cord Injury Found.; mem. phys. therapy adv. council U. Conn. Mem. Am. Phys. Therapy Assn., Am. Coll. Sports Medicine. Home: 24 Conestoga Way Glastonbury CT 06033 Office: 181 E Cedar St Newington CT 06111

HORINE, FREDA LORELEI, twp. ofcl.; b. Bellflower, Ill., Apr. 12, 1901; d. Hugh Monroe and Isabelle (Jordan) McIntyre; student Normal U., 1920; m. Lillard Horine, Sept. 15, 1920; children—Dorothy Marie, Harold Eugene. Grand lectr. Order Eastern Star, Leroy, Ill., 1950-68; mem. Republican Exec. Com. McLean County, Bloomington, Ill., 1970-82; mem. Pres.'s Task Force, Senatorial Com., Arrowsmith, Ill., 1980-82; twp. supr., 1962—. Clubs: Sabina Social, Jr. Maikus, LaRay Woman's, LaRay Country (past pres.), McLean County Woman's (past pres.). Home: Arrowsmith IL 61722

HORKA, LORAYNE ANN, chiropractic physician; b. Hackensack, N.J.; d. Lawrence R. and Cecila Hazel (DuHaime) H.; B.A., Whittier Coll., 1961; M.A., Calif. State U., Los Angeles, 1964; postgrad. McGill U., Montreal, Que., Can., 1965, U. So. Calif., 1966-69; LL.B., Blackstone Coll. Law, 1969, J.D., 1971; D.C., Los Angeles Coll. Chiropractic, 1972. Tchr., El Rancho (Calif.) Unified Sch. Dist., 1961-68; instr. history Calif. State U., Los Angeles, 1967, Pepperdine U., 1969; owner, operator Medico-Legal Services, Glendale, Calif., 1969-72; intern Glendale Chiropractic Clinic, 1971-72, resident in roentgenology, 1972-74; staff physician Morningside Clinic, Los Angeles, 1972-74; instr. roentgenology Los Angeles Coll. Chiropractic, 1973-74; staff physician Manchester-Prairie Group, Inglewood, Calif., 1974-77; partner Western-Jefferson Profl. Group, Los Angeles, 1977-80; pvt. practice, Los Angeles, 1980—. St. Andrew's Research Found. fellow, 1970; Calif. Chiropractic Assn. scholar, 1972. Mem. Am. Chiropractic Council on Roentgenology, Calif. Chiropractic Assn., Am. Chiropractic Assn., Am. Council Women Chiropractors, Sacred Heart of Mary Alumnae Assn., Whittier Coll. Alumni Assn., Pi Lambda Theta, Phi Alpha Theta, Alpha Gamma Sigma. Contbr. roentgenol. articles to profl. jours. Address: 1833 W 8th St Suite 216 Los Angeles CA 90057

HORLOCK, DOROTHY GRAY, rancher, real estate developer; b. Tex., Feb. 8, 1931; d. John Edward and Lee G. Gray; student U. Houston, 1948-49, U. So. Calif., 1956-57; m. Roy M. Norlock, Nov. 22, 1966 (div. Jan. 1976); 1 son, Roy M. Exec. asst. to J. Heflin, Tex. State Rep., 1949-50; v.p. Seaport Realty Co., Inc., Houston, 1950-56; stewardess Trans World Airlines, Los Angeles, 1957-59; owner, operator Sugar Hill Ranch, Hallettsville, Tex., 1960—; property developer; investor; dir. 1100 South Post Oak, Inc., D.G.H. Investments, Inc. Bd. dirs. Houston Grand Opera, 1972-73, chmn. fund dr., 1972; trustee various pvt. trusts; fundraiser Mus. Fine Arts, Houston, Planned Parenthood, Houston. Mem. Tex. Longhorn Assn., Tex. Circle R. Republican. Methodist. Clubs: Houston City, Briar. Home: 11114 Wickway Houston TX 77024 Office: Sugar Hill Ranch Route 2 Box 225 Hallettsville TX 77964

HORMANN, MARILYN SOPHIE, educator; b. Ft. Wayne, Ind., Mar. 12, 1936; d. William August and Clara Marie (Heckmann) Hormann; B.S., Valparaiso U., 1958; M.A., John Carroll U., 1965; postgrad. U. Mich., 1973. Tchr., counselor Cleve. Luth. High Sch. Assn., 1958-62; counselor Cleve. public schs., 1962-72, 73-75, dir. career planning, placement, 1977-80, coordinator organizational devel., 1980-81, coordinator Strategic planning, 1982—; dir. equity career edn. Maple Heights (Ohio) City Schs., 1975-76; pres. Career Life Planning Services, Inc., 1977—; conf. presentor; cons. in field. Gen. Electric Found. guidance fellow, 1967, 82; Mott fellow, 1972-73; Freedoms Found. Valley Forge Tchrs. medal, 1965. Mem. Cleve. Edn. Assn. (pres. 1978—), Am. Personnel and Guidance Assn., NEA, Am. Mgmt. Assn., Assn. for Supervision and Curriculum Devel., Phi Delta Kappa. Episcopalian Contbr. articles to profl. jours. Home: 12550 Lake Ave Suite 1001 Lakewood OH 44107 Office: 1380 E 6th St Cleveland OH 44114

HORN, KAREN NICHOLSON, bank exec.; b. Los Angeles, Sept. 21, 1943; s. Aloys E. and Novella (Hartley) N.; B.A., Pomona Coll., 1965; Ph.D., Johns Hopkins U., 1969; m. John T. Horn, June 5, 1965; 1 son, Hartley John. Economist, bd. govs. Fed. Res. System, Washington 1969-71; v.p., economist First Nat. Bank of Boston 1971-78; pres. Fed. Res. Bank Cleve. 1982—; dir. T. Rowe Price Tax Exempt Money Fund, T. Rowe Price Prime Res. Fund. Trustee, New England Deaconess Hosp., Boston, 1976-78. NSF fellow 1965-68. Office: 1455 E 6th St Cleveland OH 44114

HORN, LAURA TERESA FREY, pharm. co. salesperson; b. Takoma Park, Md., Feb. 24, 1954; d. Robert James and Mary Anne (Bassett) Frey; B.S. in Psychology, Union Coll., Schenectady, 1976; m. James Carl Horn, Sept. 4, 1976. Organizer, dir. Daily Living Skills Program under Golub Coro. grant, Schenectady and Menands, N.Y., 1975-76; tng. supr. Schenectady County Assn. Retarded Children, 1976-77; asso. dir. alumni affairs Union Coll., 1977-78; sr. med. sales rep. G.D. Searle and Co., 1978—; co-producer, co-host TV interview series Conversations, 1977; cons. in field, condr. workshops. Mem. AAUW, Nat. Assn. Female Execs., Am. Mgmt. Assn. Democrat. Club: Union Coll. Alumni (Washington). Home: 11929 Waples Mill Rd Oakton VA 22124 Office: GD Searle & Co PO Box 5110 Chicago IL 60680

HORN, MARCIA T., public relations exec.; b. N.Y.C., Dec. 28, 1947; d. Jacob and Hilda (Savitt) Thomas; B.A., N.Y. U., 1969; A.A., Packer Jr. Coll., 1967; m. Donald Horn, Oct. 10, 1971. Public relations dir. Balmoral Hotel, Nassau, Bahamas, 1969-70; asst. to pres. Casey Assos., N.Y.C., 1970-71; editorial dir. The Design Store, Washington, 1973-75; asso. dir. public info. Investment Co. Inst., Washington, 1975—; contbg. editor The Exec. Female Digest, 1980. Judge, Graphic Arts Awards, 1980, 81; public relations vol. Washington Hebrew Congregation, 1980,

81; judge public relations competition AAUW, 1981. Mem. Women in Communications (pres. chpt. 1982—), Nat. Assn. Female Execs., Kappa Tau Alpha. Contbr. articles to profl. jours. Office: 1775 K St NW Washington DC 20006

HORNAK, LINDA LOUISE, oil corp. exec.; b. Pitts., Nov. 18, 1948; d. John Charles and Isabel S. Demeda; B.A., U. Pitts., 1975; M.A., St. Francis Coll. of Loretto, 1982; m. C.G. Hornak, Aug. 1, 1970. Legal sec. Sheinberg, Raphel & Sheinberg, Pitts., 1966-67; sr. stenographer Bell of Pa., Pitts., 1967-68; with Gulf Oil Corp., Pitts., 1968—, personnel specialist, 1977—. Bd. dirs. Pitts. Alliance for Employment of Handicapped, 1977—. Mem. Pitts. Personnel Assn. Club: Steeltown Corvettes. Office: Gulf Oil Corp PO Box 1166 Pittsburgh PA 15230

HORNBAKER, ALICE JOY, author; b. Cin., Feb. 3, 1927; B.A. cum laude and honors in Journalism, San Jose State U., 1949; children—Christopher Albert, Holly Jo Brocki, Joseph Bernard III. Asst. woman's editor San Jose Mercury-News, 1949-55; owner, mgr. Frisch Big Boy Restaurant Chain, Cin., 1955-68; dir. pub. relations Children's Home Soc. Calif., Santa Clara, 1968-71; asst. dir. pub. relations United Fund Calif., Santa Clara, 1971—; editorial dir. Writers Digest Sch., Cin., 1971-75; columnist, critic, mag. writer, reporter, copy editor People Today sec. Cin. Enquirer, 1975—; tchr. adult edn. Forest Hills Sch. Dist., Thomas More Coll., 1973—; author: Preventive Care: Easy Exercise Against Aging, 1974; byline in People, Modern Maturity, Sr. Advocate, NATR Jour., and others; contbr. fiction to Enquirer mag.; freelance mag. writer. Recipient Bronze award in Am. health journalism, Am. Chiropractic Assn., 1977, 78. Mem. Blue Pencil of Ohio State U. (pres. 1981-82), Women in Communications, Ohio Newspaper Women's Assn. (v.p. 1981-83, 1st place human interest story, 1977, 2d place columnist award 1979, Tops in Ohio award 1982, M.M. McMullen 2d place award 1982, others), Soc. Profl. Journalists (treas. 1981-82). Office: The Cin Enquirer 617 Vine St Cincinnati OH 45201

HORNBECK, EILEEN RUTH, mfg. co. exec.; b. Evansville, Ind., July 10, 1930; d. Adam Jacob and Clara (Rode) Rettig; student public schs., Evansville; children by previous marriage—Michael Slevin, Pat Slevin, Polly Ann Hornbeck. Sec., Cal-Farm Ins. Co., 1951-53, Convair, 1955-56, N. Am. Aviation, 1957-58, Boeing Aircraft Co., 1959-61; salesperson Humming Boyd Sales Co., Tupperware distbr., Los Angeles, 1969—; unit mgr. Tupperware Co., Los Angeles, 1971—. Home: 427 W Gardena Blvd Gardena CA 90247 Office: 9020 Bellanca St Los Angeles CA 90045

HORNBURGER, JANE MELVIN, educator; b. Fayetteville, N.C., Aug. 26, 1928; d. Roy Daniel and Ella (Carter) Melvin; B.S., Fayetteville State U., 1948; M.A., N.Y.U., 1950, Ed.D., 1970; postgrad. UCLA, 1953, 55; m. Thomas Hornburger, Aug. 19, 1950. Tchr., Kinston (N.C.) Public Schs., 1948-54; tchr. Wilmington (Del.) Public Schs., 1954-66, supr. reading, 1966-69, dir. tchr. tng., 1970-72; asst. prof. edn. Boston U., 1972-77, City U. N.Y., 1977—; reading cons.; reviewer comml. publs.; editorial cons. Lang. Arts, 1976-78. Adv. bd. Early Childhood Center, N.Y.C., 1980—; exec. bd. Bronx Reading Council, 1980—. Named Women of Yr., AAUW, Wilmington, Del., 1968; Outstanding Delawarean, Sigma Gamma Rho, Wilmington 1970; N.Y.U. Honors scholar, recipient Founders Day award, 1971; U.S. Office Edn. grantee, 1969. Mem. Nat. Council Tchrs. English (editorial bd.), Internat. Reading Assn. (com. chmn. 1981-83), Mass. Assn. Reading Educators (dir. 1976-77), N.Y.C. Reading Council, N.Y. State English Council, New Eng. Assn. Tchrs. English, AAUP, Phi Delta Kappa, Pi Lambda Theta, Kappa Delta Pi. Episcopalian. Author: So You Have an Aide, 1967; Teaching Multicultural Children, 1977; African Countries and Cultures, 1981; contbr. articles to profl. jours. Home: 1001 Grand Concourse Bronx NY 10452 Office: Bklyn Coll City U NY Bedford Ave and Ave H Brooklyn NY 11210

HORNE, DIANA MARIE, govt. ofcl.; b. Chgo., May 22, 1944; d. Bruno Martin and Anna Mary (Hycz) Sowinski; B.S., Loyola U., Chgo., 1966; Ph.D., Northwestern U., 1973; m. Charles R. Horne, Jan. 2, 1981. Asst. prof. biology Mundelein Coll., Chgo., 1972-74; nat. program mgr. lab. audits EPA, Washington, 1974-80, chief benefits and field studies div., 1980—. Mem. Am. Inst. Biol. Scis., AAAS, Am. Assn. Lab. Animal Scis., Sigma Xi. Home: 7215 Danny Ln Manassas VA 22113 Office: Crystal Mall Bldg 2 Arlington VA 22202

HORNE, JUDITH RAE (DR. RAE ANDERSON), psychologist; b. San Francisco, Feb. 14, 1941; d. Harry Davey and Audrey (Garman) Anderson; A.B., Vassar Coll., 1962; M.A. in Teaching of English, Stanford U., 1965; M.Ed., Boston U., 1972, Ed.D. in Counseling Psychology, 1974; m. Timothy Parmley Horne, Nov. 11, 1965; 1 dau., Tiffany Rae; 1 stepdau., Tara Victoria. Tchr., English, drama, public speaking various schs., 1962-64; resident asst. for dean of women Stanford U., 1964-65; tchr. English Abbot Acad., Andover, Mass., 1966-71, counselor, 1967-71, mem. exec. council, 1969-71; staff psychologist Lawrence Mental Health Center, 1972-73; counselor Salem State Coll., 1973-74, instr. Grad. Sch., 1974-77; pvt. practice, 1974—. Benefit chmn. Boston Pops Benefit for Vassar Scholarships, 1967. Episcopalian. Club: Boston Vassar (area chmn. 1966-68, 69-70, mem. spl. gifts com. 1969), Andover Garden (dir., publicity chmn.). Home: Tiralea 94 Porter Rd Andover MA 01810

HORNE, KATHARYN, ballet dir.; b. Ft. Worth, June 20, 1932; d. William Sullivan and Catherine (Collie) Horn; student Tex. Christian U.; divorced; children—Collie MacCardell, Kirsi Enckell. Soloist, Am. Ballet Theatre, 1950-56; prin. dancer Met. Opera, 1957-65; prin. dancer, dir., tchr. Manhattan Festival Ballet, 1966-69; prin. dancer, tchr. Malmö (Sweden) Stadsteater, 1969-75; co-artistic dir., tchr. Omaha Ballet, 1975-80; artistic dir. Charlotte (N.C.) Ballet and New Reflections Dance Theater, 1981—; Choreographer; stager Classic ballets. mem. guest faculty Adelphi U., Garden City, N.Y., Cornell U., Creighton U., Omaha, No. Ill. U.; cons. to ballets on re-staging of classic ballets. Office: Dance Charlotte 110 E 7th St Charlotte NC 28202

HORNE, MARILYN, mezzo-soprano, soprano; b. Bradford, Pa., Jan. 16, 1934; ed. U. So. Calif.; Mus.D., Rutgers U., 1970, Jersey City State Coll.; D.Litt., St. Peter's Coll. Operatic debut as Hata in The Bartered Bride, Los Angeles Guild Opera, La Scala debut in Oepidus Rex, 1969, Met. Opera debut as Adalgisa in Norma, 1970; other roles include Rosina in Barber of Seville, Neocle in The Siege of Corinth, La Scala, 1969, Isabella in L'Italiana in Algieri, Carmen at Met. Opera, 1972-73, Tancredi, Orlando Furioso, Romeo, Rinaldo; other appearances include Venice Festival (invitation Igor Stravinsky), 1956, San Francisco Opera (Marie in Wozzeck), 1960, Am. Opera Soc., N.Y.C., for several seasons (including roles in Iphigenie en Tauride, Semiramide), Vancouver Opera (Adalgisa in Norma), Philharmonic Hall, N.Y.C., Paris, Dallas, Houston, Covent Garden, London (in Wozzeck); appeared as Italiana, La Scala, 1975, as Rosina, Vienna Opera, 1978; ann. recital at Carnegie Hall; rec. artist for London, Columbia and RCA records; leading exponent florid vocal style. Recipient several Grammy awards. Address: care Columbia Artists Mgmt Inc 165 W 57th St New York NY 10019 *

HORNE, NANCY OALENE, research cons.; b. Norton, Va., Aug. 25, 1931; d. Hoke Irvine and Alice Oalene (Beverly) H.; A.A., Stephens Coll., 1952; B.A., U. N.C., 1954; M.A., Syracuse U., 1956; M.A., Columbia U., 1956, Ph.D., 1969; J.D., U. Richmond, 1980. Adminstrv. asst. Office of Placement, Tchrs. Coll., Columbia U., 1956-57; research asso. Office of Research, Stephens Coll., 1959-60; research asst. Bur. Applied Social Research, Columbia U., 1963-65, project dir. Tchrs. Coll., 1965-67; vis. asst. prof. dept. sociology and rural sociology U. Mo.-Columbia, summer 1971, asst. prof. dept. child and family devel., 1972; program asso. in instnl. research Nat. Lab. for Higher Edn., Durham, N.C., 1972-75; dir. instnl. research State U. Coll., Buffalo, 1975-76; research cons., Richmond, Va., 1976—. Bus. mgr. Home Land and Investment Co., Inc., Norton, Va., 1961-63. Mem. Am. Psychol. Assn., Am. Sociol. Assn., AAAS, N.Y. Acad. Scis., Am. Ednl. Research Assn., Assn. for Instnl. Research, Am. Assn. for Higher Edn., Phi Alpha Delta. Co-author (with others) Institutional Research Handbook, 1974. Asst. editor: The Sociological Quarterly, 1971-73, adv. editor, 1973-75. Address: 10013-B Palace Ct Richmond VA 23233

HORNE, SHARON ROSE, accountant; b. Beaufort, S.C., Feb. 13, 1953; d. Eddie Velmer and Gertrude (Redmond) Horne; B.S. in Bus., U. Md., 1976. Acct., John Hanson Savs. & Loan, Forestville, Md., 1975-76, Group Hospitalization Inc./Med. Service of D.C., Washington, 1976-78, 80—; budget analyst Pepco, Washington, 1978-80. C.P.A., Md. Mem. Am. Inst. C.P.A.s, Nat. Assn. Female Execs., Assn. Women C.P.A.s, Md. Assn. C.P.A.s. Republican. Home: 2600 Brinkley Rd Apt 603 Temple Hills MD 20022 Office: Group Hospitalization Inc 550 12th St SW Washington DC 20024

HORNER, CONSTANCE JOAN, govt. ofcl.; b. Summit, N.J., Feb. 24, 1942; d. David E. and Cecelia M. McNeely; B.A., U. Pa., 1964; M.A., U. Chgo., 1967; m. Charles Horner, May 7, 1965; children—David, Jonathan. Tchr. English lit. and composition East Islip High Sch., Islip Terrace, N.Y., 1964-65; Oak Park (Ill.)-River Forest High Sch., 1965-66; faculty Taiwan Normal U., Taiwan Polit. Sci. U. and U. Md. extension div., Taipei, Taiwan, 1967-69; tchr. Georgetown Day High Sch., Washington, 1972-77; dir. VISTA and service learning programs Action Agy., Washington, 1982—, dep. asst. dir., 1981-82. Office: 806 Connecticut Ave NW Washington DC 20525

HORNER, MATINA SOURETIS (MRS. JOSEPH L. HORNER), coll. pres.; b. Boston, July 28, 1939; d. Demetre John and Christine (Antonopoulos) Souretis; A.B. cum laude, Bryn Mawr Coll., 1961; M.S., U. Mich., 1963, Ph.D., 1968; LL.D., Dickinson Coll., 1973, Mt. Holyoke Coll., 1973, U. Pa., 1975, Smith Coll., 1979, Wheaton Coll., 1979; L.H.D. (hon.), U. Mass., 1973, Tufts U., 1976, U. Hartford, 1980; m. Joseph L. Horner, June 25, 1961; children—Tia Andrea, John, Christopher. Teaching fellow U. Mich., 1962-66; lectr. motivation personality U. Mich. at Ann Arbor, 1968-69; lectr. social relations Harvard U., 1969-70, asst. prof. clin. psychology dept. social relations, 1971-72, assoc. prof. psychology and social relations, 1972—, also cons. univ. health services; pres. Radcliffe Coll., 1972—; dir. Time, Inc. Bd. dirs. Behavioral Edn. Projects; trustee Twentieth Century Fund, bd. scholars Higher Edn. Research Inst.; adv. council NSF, 1977—, chmn., 1980—; mem. President's Commn. for Nat. Agenda for the Eighties, 1979-80, chmn. Task Force on Quality Am. Life in Eighties; bd. dirs. Women's Research and Edn. Inst., 1979—, chmn. research com., 1982—; trustee Groton Sch., 1977—; adv. com. Women's Leadership Conf. on Nat. Security, 1982—. Recipient Roger Baldwin award Mass. Civil Liberties Union Found., 1982; citation of merit NE region NCCJ, 1982. Mem. Nat. Inst. Social Scis., Phi Beta Kappa, Phi Delta Kappa, Phi Kappa Phi. Contbr. psychol. articles on motivation to profl. jours. Address: Office of Pres Radcliffe Coll 10 Garden St Cambridge MA 02138

HORNS, VIRGINIA DRAPER, educator; b. Birmingham, Ala., Apr. 12, 1924; d. John Clifton and Icie (Williams) Draper; B.A., Huntington Coll., Montgomery, Ala., 1945; M.A., U. Ala., 1967, Ph.D., 1969; children—Fred, Lurie, Susan. Tchr., Pinellas County (Fla.) Bd. Edn., 1957-59; tchr., then supr. remedial and developmental reading, Summit, N.J., 1960-66; mem. faculty U. Ala., Birmingham, 1969—, prof. early childhood edn., 1977—, asso. clin. prof. Sch. Nursing, 1974—, dir. Children's Creative Learning Center, 1971-80; pres. Mid-South Ednl. Research Assos., 1976, Jefferson County Child Devel. Council, 1974. Research fellow U. Ala., 1966-69. Mem. Am., Middle South ednl. research assns., Internat. Reading Assn., Kappa Delta Pi, Alpha Psi Omega, Omicron Delta Kappa, Phi Delta Kappa, Delta Kappa Gamma. Methodist. Contbr. articles, revs. to ednl. jours. Home: 2650 Chandalar Ln Pelham AL 35124 Office: Sch Edn Univ Ala in Birmingham University Station Birmingham AL 35294

HORNUNG, GERTRUDE SEYMOUR, art educator; b. Boston; d. Samuel Parker and Rose Anne Seymour; A.B., Wellesley Coll., 1929; M.A., Western Res. U., 1939, Ph.D., 1949; m. Robert M. Hornung, Oct. 31, 1932; 1 dau., Elizabeth Zimri Luce Hornung Smith. Lectr., instr., supr. adult programs Cleve. Mus. Art, 1937-60; lectr. Am. U., Rome, 1974-75; lectr. Tehran, Iran, 1975, Bangkok, Thailand, 1978, Dubin, Ireland, 1970; free lance lectr., Cleve., 1960—. Mem. Nat. Art Educators Assn., Internat. Council Mus., Internat. Com. Mus. Edn., Am. Assn. Mus. Republican. Episcopalian. Home: 2240 Elandon Dr Cleveland OH 44106

HORNUNG, KATHRYNE PFEIFFER, hosp. cons.; b. Hellertown, Pa., Sept. 22, 1935; d. John Frank and Orpha Mae (Diehl) Pfeiffer; R.N., St. Luke's Hosp., 1956; B.S. in Health Care Adminstrn., Lindenwood Coll., 1978; children—Lisa Ann, John Reynold, III. Staff nurse Vis. Nurse Assn., Bethlehem, Pa., 1956-58; staff nurse, San Pedro (Calif.) and Peninsula Hosp., 1969-70, supr. nursing, 1970-72, asst. dir. nursing, 1973-76; dir. nursing Fox Hills Community Hosp., Los Angeles, 1977-80; pres. Kason Co., hosp. cons. Author booklet on staffing alternatives; contbr. articles to health care jours. Address: 2509 Via Anacapa Palos Verdes Estates CA 90274

HORNYACK, MARGARET LOUISE, epidemiologist; b. Rochester, Pa., Mar. 14, 1937; d. Thomas E. and Helen G. (Smith) Sopko; student U. Calif., Irvine, 1977-78; B.S. in Nursing, Calif. State U., Los Angeles, 1971; M.S. in Public Health, U. N.C., Chapel Hill, 1973; doctoral candidate U. Tex. Sch. Public Health, Houston, 1981—; div.; children—James E., Timothy M. Occupational health nurse J & L Steel, Aliquippa, Pa., 1960-61, Hankins Med. Group, Azusa, Calif., 1961-66, Los Angeles Times, 1965-68, TRW Systems Group, Redondo Beach, Calif., 1968-71; cons. San Bernardino County Health Dept., 1971-74; environ. health and safety officer Calif. State Poly. U., Pomona, 1974-77; mem. occupational safety and health study sect. Nat. Insts. Occupational Safety and Health, 1976-79; research asso. Baylor Coll. Medicine, Houston, 1980-81 epidemiologist M.D. Anderson Hosp. Cancer Center, Houston, 1980—; also cons. Vice-pres., treas. Arlington High Sch. Booster Club, 1974-76. Mem. Calif. Assn. Occupational Health Nurses (v.p. 1977-78), Am. Public Health Assn., Am. Indsl. Hygiene Assn., Soc. Occupational and Environ. Health.

HOROSZEWSKI, KATHLEEN MARIA, telecommunications exec.; b. N.Y.C., Mar. 5, 1942; d. George F. and Brigid (Doohan) Hagerty; B.A., Cambridge U., 1968, M.B.A., 1970; m. Roman D. Horoszewski, Aug. 3, 1963; children—Meredith, Roman. Asst. to v.p. fin. Olin Am., Dallas, 1973; staff Arthur Young & Co., Dallas, 1974-77; account exec. Southwestern Bell, 1977, data specialist, 1978, systems mgr., 1979; industry mgr., Am. Tel. and Tel., Basking Ridge, N.J., 1980, staff market mgr., 1981—; cons. in field. Recipient numerous Bell awards for outstanding contbns. to corp. Mem. Am. Mgmt. Assn., NOW, Am. Soc. Profl. and Exec. Women, AIAA. Republican. Home: 2 Overbrook Rd Randolph NJ 07869 Office: 5336 B3 295 N Maple Ave Basking Ridge NJ 07920

HOROWITZ, LAURA RUTH GODOFSKY, editorial service co. exec.; b. Bklyn., Feb. 5, 1943; d. Elias I. and Miriam Esther Newman Godofsky; B.A., U. Chgo., 1964; m. Daniel J. Horowitz, Sept. 5, 1967; children—Ellen Wendy, Natalie Beth. Washington Bur. chief Coll. Press Service, Washington, 1964-65; research asst. Nat. Assn. State Univs. and Land Grant Colls., Washington, 1965-68; public info. specialist. Fed. City Coll., Washington, 1968-69; public info. specialist Mayor's Econ. Devel. Com., Washington, 1969-70; publication cons., Washington, 1969-72; pres. Editorial Experts, Inc., Alexandria, Va., 1972—; tchr. George Washington U., 1976—. Vice pres. Va. Citizens Consumer Council, 1972-80; vice-chmn. Fairfax County Consumer Protection Commn., 1972-78. Mem. Assn. Editorial Bus. (1st pres. 1980-82), Soc. Tech. Communications, Newsletter Assn. Am. EdPress, Washington Ind. Writers. Jewish. Author: Tool Catalog Techniques and Strategies for Successful Action Programs, 1972; contbr. articles in field to profl. jours. Home and office: 5905 Pratt St Alexandria VA 22310

HOROWITZ, NADIA, artist; b. Warsaw, Poland, May 12; came to U.S., 1951; d. Eli and Rose Bartowicz; B.A., Acad. Fine Art, Warsaw; B.A., Ecole Superieure des Arts Graphiques, Brussels, Belgium, 1933; grad. Acad. Fine Art La Grande Chaumiere, Paris, 1934; B.A., Rheiman Schule, Berlin. One-woman shows include: Clasemont Art Center, Haines Falls, N.Y., Gorline Gallery, N.Y.C., 1965, Herzl Gallery, N.Y.C., 1966, Anthroposophical Soc. Am., N.Y.C., 1967, Barsky Med. Center, 1978, Herzl Gallery, 1981; fgn. and U.S. group shows include: Jewish Mus., Gallery of Temple No. Westchester, Groton-on-Hudson, N.Y., 1961-66, Am. Pavilion, World's Fair, N.Y.C., 1964, Hudson Park Library, 1970, Artists Equity Assn., 1970, 78, New Age Gallery, 1978, Internat. Show, Zurich, 1973; works represented pvt. collection of Pablo Casals; pvt. tchr. fine and comml. art. Recipient 1st prize The Gallery, Chgo., hon. mention City Center Group Show, 1st prize Conn. Show, 1978, Gold medal, Academia Italia delle Arti e del Lavoro, Parma, 1980. Mem. Artists Equity N.Y., Nat. Assn. Women Artists. Home and Office: 205 W 89th St New York NY 10024

HOROWITZ, RUTH HYLA LEVY, marriage and family therapist; b. Elizabeth, N.J., Dec. 1, 1910; d. Emanuel and Ethel (Natelson) Levy; B.A., Cornell U., 1931; M.A., Drew U., 1957; cert. advanced marriage counseling U. Pa. Sch. Medicine, 1958; m. Harry Horowitz, June 5, 1935; children—Peter, Elizabeth, Paul. Staff marriage counselor Phila. Marriage Council, div. family studies, dept. psychiatry U. Pa. Sch. Medicine, 1958-59; individual practice, Summit, N.J., 1959—; lectr. Montclair (N.J.) State Tchrs. Coll., 1970-80. Bd. dirs. Child Study Assn. Am., Family Service Assn., Mental Health Assn., Summit, Vis. Nurse Assn. Eastern Union County, Egenolf Day Nursery, Elizabeth. Tchr. first aid ARC Home Service Corps, World War II. Past mem. N.J. Bd. Marriage Counselor Examiners. Mem. Nat. Council Jewish Women, Am. Assn. Marriage and Family Therapy, (clin.), N.J. Assn. Marriage and Family Therapy, Internat. Platform Assn., Summit Med. Soc. (hon.), Am. Jewish Congress (pres. Elizabeth women's div. 1946-47), Hadassah. Jewish (pres. temple sisterhood 1942-43). Club: Madison (N.J.) Golf. Home and Office: 138 Hillcrest Ave Summit NJ 07901

HORRACE, NORMA DELEON, hematologist; b. Jamaica, W.I., Oct. 11, 1938; d. Clinton A. and Louisa Alberta (Crawford) DeLeon; A.A.S., Westchester Community Coll., 1968; B.S., Pace U., 1973; M.S., St. John's U., 1975; m. William Horrace, July 10, 1960; children—William, Brian, Robert. Med. technologist No. Westchester Hosp., Mt. Kisco, N.Y., 1959-73, asst. tech. dir. labs., 1973—, ednl. coordinator Sch. Med. Tech., 1975—; instr. Mercy Coll., Dobbs Ferry, N.Y. Recipient Outstanding Ednl. Coordinator award Am. Soc. Clin. Pathologists, 1976. Mem. Am. Soc. Clin. Pathologists, Am. Assn. Blood Banks. Roman Catholic. Club: Bus. and Profl. Women's. Home: 213 West St Mount Kisco NY 10549 Office: E Main St Mount Kisco NY 10549

HORSLEY, PHYLLIS BLANCHE, mfg. co. ofcl.; b. Boston, June 25, 1940; d. Noah and Blanche P. (Chappelle) Brown; B.S. in B.A., Northeastern U., 1962; grad. Women's Mgmt. Program, Babson Coll., 1978; m. Horace Horsley, Nov. 27, 1978; children—Ralph, Dvora. With Sears, Roebuck & Co., Boston, 1959-67, Plymouth Mfg. Co., Boston, 1962-62; data processing operator Polaroid Corp., Waltham, Mass., 1968-70, computer operator, 1970-72, 74-77, tng. and edn. asso., 1972-74, prodn. supr., SX-70 shutter/sonar, 1978—. VISTA worker, 1970; asst. dir. Christian edn. dept. Grant A.M.E. Ch., 1974-75. Mem. NAACP. Clubs: Black Ski, Sportsman's Bowling League, Martin Luther King Athletic, Cultural and Scholarship Assn. Office: 9 Faxrest Mattapan MA 02126

HORSNELL, MARGARET EILEEN, educator; b. St. Paul, Jan. 3, 1928; d. Kenneth George and Mary Elizabeth (Dowd) H.; B.A., U. Minn., 1961, M.A., 1963, Ph.D., 1967. Instr., U. Minn., Mpls., 1966-68; asst. prof. history Am. Internat. Coll., Springfield, Mass., 1968-76, asso. prof. history, 1976—. Recipient award Tozer Found., 1966; McKnight Found. award, 1968; Am. Internat. Coll. Summer Research grantee, 1970; alt. postdoctoral fellow AAUW, 1974-75. Mem. Inst. Early Am. History and Culture, So. Hist. Assn., Soc. History of Edn., Am. Legal Studies Assn., ACLU, Common Cause, Mass. Audubon Soc., NOW. Home: 15 Atwood Rd South Hadley MA 01075 Office: 24 Lee Hall Am Internat Coll Springfield MA 01109

HORST, JOSEPHINE MONACO, social worker; b. Easton, Pa., May 26, 1930; d. Carmelo and Carmela (Lizza) Monaco; B.A., Pa. State U., 1951; M.S.W., Rutgers U., 1971; m. Samuel L. Horst, Jan. 26, 1951; children—Jory Ann Horst Barone, Jeffrey C., David M. Caseworker, Berks County (Pa.) Bd. of Assistance, 1962-66; social services coordinator Econ. Opportunity Council of Reading and Berks County, 1966-67; social worker Correctional Instn. for Women, Clinton, 1967-69, supr. cottage life, 1969-76; ombudsman N.J. Dept. Corrections, 1976—; instr. Correction Officers Tng. Acad.; cons. Commn. on Accreditation for Corrections. Bd. dirs. Big Bros./Big Sisters of Hunterdon County. Mem. Nat. Assn. Social Workers, Am. Correctional Assn., Acad. Cert. Social Workers. Club: Soroptimist (past pres. Hunterdon County, pres. Hunterdon County 1980-82). Home: Rural Delivery 2 Box 294 Stockton NJ 08559 Office: Whittlesey Rd PO Box 7387 Trenton NJ 08628

HORSTMANN, DOROTHY MILLICENT, physician; b. Spokane, Wash., July 2, 1911; d. Henry J. and Anna (Hunold) H.; A.B., U. Calif., 1936, M.D., 1940; D.Sc. (hon.), Smith Coll., 1961; M.A. (hon.), Yale U., 1961; Dr. Med. Scis. (hon.), Women's Med. Coll. of Pa., 1963. Intern San Francisco City and County Hosp., 1939-40, asst. resident medicine, 1940-41; asst. resident medicine Vanderbilt U. Hosp., 1941-42; Commonwealth Fund fellow, sect. preventive medicine, sch. medicine Yale U., New Haven, Conn., 1942-43, instr. preventive medicine, 1943-44, 45-47, asst. prof., 1948-52, asso. prof., 1952-56, asso. prof. preventive medicine and pediatrics, 1956-61, John Rodman Paul prof. epidemiology and pediatrics, 1961-82, emeritus, 1982—, sr. research scientist, 1982—; instr. medicine U. Calif., 1944-45; NIH fellow Nat. Inst. Med. Research, London, Eng., 1947-48, Master A.C.P.; hon. asso. fellow Am. Acad. Pediatrics; mem. Am. Soc. Clin. Investigation, Am. Epidemiological Soc., Am. Pediatric Soc., Assn. Am. Physicians, Infectious Diseases Soc. Am. (pres. 1974-75), Soc. Epidemiologic Research, Pan Am. Med. Assn., Internat. Epidemiological Assn., Royal Soc. Medicine (hon. mem. sect. epidemiology and preventive medicine), South African Soc. Pathologists (hon. mem.), Nat. Acad. Scis. Home: 11 Autumn St New Haven CT 06511

HORTATSOS, MARY, grocery chain exec.; b. Chgo.; B.A., U. Chgo., 1945. Mem. editorial control dept. Esquire, Inc., Chgo., 1945-46; mem. farm catalog staff Montgomery Ward and Co., Chgo., 1946-47; dept. mgr. Wesley E. Sharer Assos., advt. agy., Chgo., 1947-61; asst. to v.p. research and devel., advt., public relations and long range planning Playskool Inc., Chgo., 1961-73; spl. asst. to pres. Baker & Brichta, Inc., advt. agy., Chgo., 1974; mgr. public relations Convenient Food Mart Inc., Chgo., 1976—. Mem. Publicity Club Chgo., Women in Mgmt. Home: 5757 N Sheridan-13 C Chicago IL 60660 Office: Convenient Food Mart Inc John Hancock Center 875 N Michigan Ave Suite 1401 Chicago IL 60611

HORTON, CARRELL PETERSON, educator; b. Daytona Beach, Fla., Nov. 28, 1928; d. Preston Steward and Mildred Geneva (Adams) Peterson; B.A., Fisk U., 1949; M.A., Cornell U., 1950; Ph.D. (Ford fellow), U. Chgo., 1972; m. Richard G. Horton, Apr. 14, 1954 (div.); 1 son, Richard Preston. Instr., research asso. Fisk U., Nashville, 1950-55; statis. analyst, project adminstr., coordinator pediatric research Meharry Med. Coll., Nashville, 1955-66; instr. to prof., chmn. dept. psychology Fisk U., 1966—, dir. div. social scis.; dir. Rochelle Tng. and Habilitation Center, Nashville, 1968-72, 1975-77, 1977—, vice chmn., 1978-79; mem. child care adv. com. Nashville Wesley Found., 1977—, Nashville area Vocat., 1974-76, vice chmn. Mem. Am. Psychol. Assn., Soc. for Research in Child Devel. Methodist. Office: PO Box 12 Fisk U Nashville TN 37203

HORTON, JANICE FAYE, state senator; b. Barnesville, Ga., Jan. 23, 1945; d. Grover George and Sara Alice (Zellner) Shiver; A.B. in English, Tift Coll., 1967; m. Charles Douglas Horton, Aug. 26, 1967; children—Amy Elaine, Sara Leigh. Tchr. high sch. English, Ga., 1967-72; saleswoman Horton Realty & Investment Co., McDonough, Ga., 1974—; mem. McDonough City Council, 1974-78, Henry County Bd. Commnrs., 1976-80; mem. Ga. Senate, 1978—. Bd. dirs. Am. Cancer Soc. Mem. Bus. and Profl. Women (chpt. v.p.), McDonough C. of C. Democrat. Baptist. Address: 430 Burke Circle McDonough GA 30253

HORTON, KRISTIN EMMA, retail exec.; b. Petoskey, Mich., Oct. 14, 1946; d. Ivar Reuben and Vivian Esther (Carlson) Blomberg; B.Mus., Western Mich. U., 1968; postgrad. Central Mich. U.; m. Victor Charles Horton, Aug. 3, 1968. With accounts receivable dept. Western Mich. U., Kalamazoo, 1965-68; tchr. music Brimley (Mich.) Public Schs., 1968-72, Sault Ste. Marie (Mich.) Public Schs., 1972-80; dist. sales mgr. Knapp Music Co., Grand Rapids, Mich., 1980-81, Marshall Music Co., Lansing, Mich., 1981—; state and dist. adjudicator, mgr. Midwestern Music Conf., 1976-78. Mem. Nat. Assn. Female Execs., NOW, Mich. Sch. Band and Orch. Assn. (sec. 1970-82; State Officer's award 1976-78). Mem. Christian Ch. (Disciples of Christ). Home: 6275 Theisen Rd Elmira MI 49730 Office: 540 Frandor Shopping Center Lansing MI 48912

HORVATH, DOROTHY M., banker; b. Youngstown, Ohio, Nov. 24, 1946; d. Frank Joseph and Mildred Cecelia (Cover) Bogner; student Oberline Coll., 1964-65, Youngstown State U., 1966-73; m. Joseph Dean Horvath, June 10, 1967; 1 son, Joseph Dean. Loan officer, asst. sec. Peoples Bank of Youngstown, 1969-73; asst. cashier BancOhio/Ohio State Bank, Dayton, 1973-74, asst. v.p., 1974-77; v.p., sr. loan officer BancOhio Nat. Bank, Dayton, 1979-82; v.p., nat. accounts corp. banking team mgr. BancOhio Nat. Bank, Columbus, 1982—; mem. adv. bd. on installment credit Am. Bankers Assn., 1974-75; U.S. rep. Tony Hall Small Bus. Adv. Council, 1980—. Trustee Miami Valley Regional Transit Authority, 1981-82, chmn. fin. com., 1981-82. Recipient Golden Coin award Bank Mktg. Assn., 1976, Outstanding Credit Card Mktg. Program award BancSystems Assn., 1975. Mem. Dayton Assn. Credit Mgmt. (dir. 1975-79, pres. 1980-81), Robert Morris Assos. (chmn. Miami Valley group 1981-82, nat. com. on cooperation with Nat. Assn. Credit Mgmt. 1981-82, gov. Ohio Valley chpt. 1980-82, nat. credit council 1982—), Nat. Assn. Bank Women (sec. Greater Cin. chpt. 1979-80, v.p. 1980-81), Dayton Women's Network (treas. 1979-82). Club: Altrusa (treas. 1979-80) (Dayton). Home: 115 Lyndale Dr Westerville OH 43081 Office: 155 E Broad St Columbus OH 43265

HORYCZKO, REBECCA ANN, indsl. sytems specialist; b. Reading, Pa., Nov. 22, 1952; d. Frank Steven and Bernadine (Gaydos) Horyczko; student Rosemont Coll., 1970-71; B.S. in Math., Albright Coll., 1974; postgrad. in bus. adminstrn. St. Jospeh's U. Systems engr. IBM, Wyomissing, Pa., 1974—. Mem. Am. Prodn. and Inventory Control Soc. (v.p. membership). Club: Iris (Wyomissing). Office: 3 Park Plaza Wyomissing PA 19610

HOSKEN, FRANZISKA PORGES, journalist, housing expert, women's rights advocate; b. Vienna, Austria, July 12, 1919; d. Otto and Mary (Low) Porges; came to U.S., 1938, naturalized, 1944; B.A., Smith Coll., 1940; M.Arch., Harvard U., 1944; postgrad. Mass. Inst. Tech., 1963-66; m. 1947 (div. 1961); children—John, Caroline, Andrew. Archtl. designer Skidmore, Owings & Merrill, Chgo., 1946-47; owner, operator Archtl. Color Slides, 1947—; owner, v.p., treas. Hosken, Inc., 1948-53; tchr. interior design Garland Coll., Boston and Cambridge Adult Edn. Center, 1958-61; designer Contract Interiors, Boston, 1958-59; interior designer M. Brown, Boston, 1959-61; writer weekly column Boston Globe, 1964-65; corr.-at-large Archtl. Forum, 1971-74; asso. prof. urban studies U. Without Walls, Boston, 1971-74; pub., editor Womens Internat. Network News, Lexington, Mass., 1975—; internat. coordinator Womens Internat. Network; cons. UN Habitat, 1975, World Bank, 1975; lectr. univs. in U.S., Can., Europe; exhibited paintings in one woman shows at Boston City Hall Gallery, 1973, 74; exhibited in group shows at Mass. Inst. Tech. Hayden Gallery, 1974, Boston Visual Artists Union, 1974. Chairperson subcom. on new towns Nat. Urban League, 1971-72, mem. bd. housing com., 1969-73; bd. dirs. U. Without Walls. Served to ensign USCG Womens Res., 1944-45. Recipient Alpha award for creative imagination, 1940. Mem. AIA (asso. Boston chpt.), Am. Inst. Planners (asso.), Am. Soc. Planning Ofcls., NOW, Womens Equity Action League, Nat. Womens Polit. Caucus, Soc. for Internat. Devel. Author: The Language of Cities, 1968; The Functions of Cities, 1972; The Kathmandu Valley Towns, 1974; International Directory of Women's Development Organizations, 1977; Hosken Report: Genital and Sexual Mutilation of Females, 1979; Female Sexual Mutilations: The Facts and Proposals for Action, 1980. Mem. editorial bd. Smith Coll. Alumnae mag., 1968-69; contbr. articles to newspapers, nat. mags. Home and office: 187 Grant St Lexington MA 02173

HOSKINS, JANINA WANDA EWA KOZLOWSKI, historian, librarian; b. Latvia; came to U.S., 1949, naturalized, 1956; d. Michael K. and Jadwiga (Bialska) Kozlowski; M.A., U. Cracow (Poland), 1946, Ph.D. in History, 1947; postgrad. Catholic U. Am.; m. Francis Wojcicki, Jan. 3, 1931; children—Andrew, Stanley; m. 2d, Halford Lancaster Hoskins, May 9, 1960. Asst. prof. history U. Cracow, 1946-48; researcher in history, Sweden, 1949, Mid-European Study Center, N.Y.C., 1950-54; specialist in Polish affairs Library of Congress, 1951-55, area specialist Poland and East Europe, 1955—; participant internat. congresses; lectr. in field. Mem. Am. Hist. Assn., Medieval Acad., Am. Assn. Advancement Slavic Studies, Kusciuszko Found. Author: Early and Rare Polonica in American Libraries, 1973; Polish Books in English, 1974; Jefferson Views Poland, 1976; also booklets, articles, chpts. in books; compiler: The USSR and Eastern Europe: Periodicals in Western Languages, 1979. Home: 4807 Quebec St NW Washington DC 20016 Office: Library of Congress Washington DC 20540

HOSKINS, SHIRLEY ANN, coll. adminstr.; b. Ft. Worth, July 4, 1947; d. William and Willie (Richards) H.; B.S. in Biol. Scis., U. Calif., 1966, Ph.D. in Higher Edn., 1981; M.S. in Biol. Scis., U. Pacific, 1967. Lab. technician U. Calif., 1967; instr. biol. sci. City Coll. San Francisco, 1967-72, instructional dean, 1972—. Leader Expt. in Internat. Living, 1968-70. Mem. NAACP, Aircraft Owners and Pilots Assn., Council Black Am. Affairs, Am. Soc. Allied Health Professions, Phi Delta Kappa, Alpha Kappa Alpha, Beta Beta Beta. Democrat. Methodist. Clubs: San Francisco Links, All Seasons Ski. Mem. Am. Mt. Everest Expdn. to Tibet, 1981. Office: City College San Francisco Office of Instrn 50 Phelan Ave San Francisco CA 94131

HOSKINS, TERI BLACK, nurse; b. Cin., May 12, 1952; d. Harry Graham and Helen Lorene (Kreisle) Black; A.D.N., Morehead (Ky.) State U., 1973; m. Ralph william Hoskins, Mar. 4, 1978. House supr. Haywood Hosp., Maysville, Ky., 1973-76; team leader med.-surg. ICU, U. Ky. Med. Center, Lexington, 1976-77; staff nurse VA Med. Center, Lexington, 1977-78; house supr. Southeastern Ky. Bapt. Hosp., Corbin, 1978, med./surg. coordinator, infection control nurse, 1979-81, asst. dir. nursing service, 1981—; instr. continuing edn. Army Res. Nurse Corps, 1981; chpt. sec. Am. Heart Assn., 1981—. Bd. dirs. Ephraim McDowell Cumberland Valley Dist., 1981—. Mem. Nat. League Nursing, Assn. Practitioners Infection Control, Ky. Soc. Hosp. Nursing Service Adminstrs., Ky. League Nursing, Bluegrass Oncology Nursing Soc., Res. Officers Assn., Morehead State U. Alumni Assn., U. Ky. Alumni Assn. Club: Order Eastern Star. Home: 61 Winners Circle Trail Corbin KY 40701 Office: 110 Mitchell St Corbin KY 40701

HOSLER, MARY MARGARET, educator; b. Reedsville, Wis., Dec. 8, 1938; d. James Roland and Eleanor Mary (Wojta) O'Connell; B.S., Whitewater State Coll., 1961; M.S., U. Wis., 1963, Ph.D., 1967; m. Russell J. Hosler, Aug. 23, 1968. Bus. edn. tchr. high schs., Orfordville, Madison and Milw., 1961-63; teaching asst. U. Wis., Madison, 1964-66; tchr. Milw. high schs., 1966-67; asst. prof. U. Wis., Whitewater, 1967-69, asso. prof., 1969-76, prof., 1976—, chmn. dept. bus. edn. and office adminstrn., 1976—. Wis. Dept. Public Instrn. grantee, 1978—. Mem. Wis. Assn. Vocat. Adult Educators, Wis. Bus. Edn. Assn. (exec. bd.), Milw. Bus. Edn. Assn., Nat. Bus. Edn. Assn., North Central Bus. Edn. Assn. (adminstrv. bd. 1982—, rep. to nat. exec. com. 1982—), Internat. Soc. Bus. Edn., Am. Bus. Communication Assn., Am. Vocat. Assn., Nat. Assn. Tchr. Educators for Bus. and Office Edn., Nat. Assn. Bus. Tchr. Educators, Pi Lambda Theta, Delta Pi Epsilon. Home: Route 1 Milton WI 53563 Office: Coll Bus and Econs U Wis Whitewater 800 W Main St Whitewater WI 53190

HOSSACK, SHERRYL WILEY, tax cons.; b. Palo Alto, Calif., Mar. 4, 1947; d. Ferrel K. and Betty F. (Joslin) Wiley; B.S., U. Nev., Reno, 1969; M.B.A., Stanford U., 1977; m. Alex B. Hossack, Aug. 25, 1968; 1 son, Aleksandr. With IRS, San Francisco, 1969-74; tax mgr. Coopers & Lybrand, CPAs Palo Alto, 1977-81; controller Holvick deRegt & Koering, Sunnyvale, Calif., 1981—; tchr. adult edn. course Palo Alto schs.; liason to fin. com. Jr. League Palo Alto. Mem. Peninsula Soc. CPAs Peninsula Women's Network, Stanford U. Bus. Sch. Alumnae Assn. Club: Stanford (Palo Alto). Home: 1756 Emerson St Palo Alto CA 94301 Office: 1230 Oakmead Pkwy Sunnyvale CA 94086

HOSTE, HILLAINE ADELINE, med. record technician; b. Monroe, Mich., Mar. 20, 1930; d. George Wilson and Susannah Joanne (Prien) Bondy; student Cleary Coll., Ypsilanti, Mich., 1965-68, Monroe County (Mich.) Community Coll., 1968-72; B.A. in Allied Health Sci., Stephens Coll., 1980; m. Raymond A. Hoste, Mar. 22, 1975; 1 son, Mark Alan. With Gen. Telephone Co. Mich., 1947-60; with VA Med. Center, Ann Arbor, Mich., 1961—, chief med. info. sect., 1976-80, supr. quality assurance unit, 1980—; mem. faculty Joint Commn. Accreditation Hosps.; mem. Bd. Quality Assurance Profls.; cons. in field. Sec. Dundee (Mich.) Community Council, 1954. Recipient Superior Performance award VA, 1974. Mem. Am. Med. Records Assn., Mich. Med. Records Assn., South Eastern Mich. Med. Records Assn., Mich. Assn. Quality Assurance, Profls., Federally Employed Women (sec. Ann Arbor chpt. 1982), Dundee Bus. and Profl. Women (past pres.), NOW. Republican. Presbyterian. Clubs: Metro-Detroit Antique Bottle, Huron Valley Bottle and Insulator, Oddfellows. Home: 366 Main St Dundee MI 48131 Office: 2215 Fuller Rd Ann Arbor MI 48105

HOSTETLER, MARGARET E., legislative asst.; b. Meyersdale, Pa., Mar. 22, 1953; d. James M. and Frances (Bracken) Hostetler; B.S., Pa. State U., 1975; M.B.A., U. Pa., 1980. Fin. analyst U.S. Dept. Def., Washington, now legis. asst. to Rep. Brown of Ohio. Office: Room 1319 Longworth Ho Office Bldg Washington DC 20515 *

HOSTETTER, MARGARET JONES, retirement community ofcl.; b. Louisville, Feb. 4, 1946; d. Harry W. and Doris (Moreland) Jones; B.A., Ind. U., 1978; postgrad. U. Tenn., 1978-80; m. Andrew Stuart Hostetter, Nov. 9, 1973 (dec.); 1 son, Erik Stuart. Nursing personnel hiring ofcl. Americana Healthcare, Indpls., 1976-78; mgr. Harding House Condominium, Nashville, 1978-79; dir. Deer Lake Retirement Community, Nashville, 1979—. Sec. Foster Grandparent Adv. Council, Social Action Group on Aging of Nat. Council Aging. Active ARC, Mental Health, Nat. Alliance Family Life, PTA, Am. Cancer Soc. Cert. nursing home adminstr. Mem. Bellevue Area C. of C., Am. Assn. Ret. Persons, Tenn. Health Care Assn., Nat. Citizens Coalition for Nursing Home Reform, Nat. Assn. Female Execs. Methodist. Home and Office: 368 Deer Lake Dr Nashville TN 37221

HOTCHNER, BEVERLY JUNE, psychologist; b. East St. Louis, Ill., July 13, 1928; d. Benjamin E. and Jennie Louise (Komar) Novack; B.S., U. Ill., 1950; M.A., Washington U., 1963, Ph.D., 1972; m. Selwyn Ross Hotchner, Nov. 22, 1951; children—Kirby, Bradley. Asst. prof. dept. behavioral sci. So. Ill. U. Dental Medicine, Edwardsville, 1973-74, acting chairperson, 1974-75; founder, exec. dir. Center for Human Concern, St. Louis, 1975—; pres. Beverly Hotchner, Inc.; instr. Washington U.; cons. psychologist St. Luke's Hosp., St. Louis, 1978-80. Lic. psychologist, Mo. Mem. Am. Psychol. Assn., Mo. Psychol. Assn., Am. Assn. Marriage and Family Therapists, Am. Assn. Sex Edn. Counselors and Therapists (certification com. 1978-80, regional chairperson plainstates 1976-78), Phi Beta Kappa, Alpha Lambda Delta, Kappa Delta Pi. Home: 7206 Cornell St University City MO 63130 Office: 9378 Olive St St Louis Mo 63132

HOTTENSTEIN, EVELYN KENNY, devel. tng. co. exec.; b. Glasgow, Mont., Mar. 4, 1948; d. Daniel Patrick and Miriam (Phelan) Kenny; B.A., Carroll Coll., 1970; m. Glenn Hottenstein, Dec., 1970; children—Erin, Kimberly. Speech coach, English tchr. Mont. State Sch. for Girls, Helena, 1970-72; exec. dir. Camp Fire council, Helena, 1972-73, mgr. adminstr., exec. orientation program Camp Fire, Inc., Nat. Service Center, Englewood, Colo., 1974-76; owner, mgr. H & G Devel. Co., Cheyenne, Wyo., 1976-78; owner Lifework Assos., Westminster, Colo., 1978—; public speaker; instr. U. Colo., 1982—; cons. Assn. for Vol. Adminstrn. Co-chmn. Mont. Gov.'s Commn. on Status of Women, 1973; mem. Nat. Commn. on Mgmt. Standards, Camp Fire, Inc., 1975-76; mem. adv. bd. Vol. Mgmt. Program, U. Colo., Boulder, 1979, 80; bd. dirs. Unitarian Universalist Service Com. Mem. Am. Soc. Tng. and Devel., Career Devel. Group, Mgmt. Tng. Group, Assn. for Vol. Adminstrn. Unitarian. Home: 3718 Pioneer Ave Cheyenne WY 82009 Office: 4155 E Jewell Suite 405 Denver CO 80222

HOUDE, MARY JEAN, retail co. ofcl.; b. Chgo., Feb. 6, 1927; d. Edmund George and Muriel Alice (Staples) Mailloux; student Eureka Coll., 1945-47, Utah State U., 1971, U. Colo., 1973; m. Thomas R. Houde, Aug. 13, 1949 (dec.); 1 dau., Linda Jean Houde Marquie. Asst. to book editor Ziff-Davis Pub. Co., Chgo., 1947-48; reporter, feature writer, editor Kankakee (Ill) Daily Jour., 1948-71; chief vol. services Ill. Dept. Corrections, 1971-72; nat. dir. women's programs Sears, Roebuck and Co., 1972—, also dir. nat. community improvement program; vice-chmn. Nat. Coalition to Prevent Shoplifting, 1978-80. Advisor, MW CARE; nat. dir. Jr. Women's Clubs, 1964-66. Mem. Women in Communications, Brain Research Found., Ill. Fedn. Women's Clubs (pres. 1970-72), Gen. Fedn. Women's Clubs (dir. 1960—), Community Devel. Soc. (dir. 1973-76), Hands Up (founder; dir. nat. crime reduction program 1974-80). Republican. Roman Catholic. Club: Woman's of Kankakee. Author: The Clubwoman, 1970; co-author: Of the People, 1968. Home: 6371 Kindling Ct Lisle IL 60532 Office: Sears Tower D/703-40/5 Chicago IL 60684

HOUGEN, THERESE YVONNE, mfg. co. exec.; b. Fall River, Mass., Nov. 15, 1922; d. Victor Joseph and Ida Donalda (Riel) Perrault; grad. high sch., 1941; m. Everett Douglas Hougen, July 5, 1941; children—Douglas S., Victor L., Randall B., Bradley R. With Wright Aero., Paterson, N.J., 1943-44, Quackenbushes, Paterson, N.J., 1944-45; with Blair Equipment Co., Flint, Mich., 1953-59, corp. sec., treas., 1959-73, dir., 1977—; with Hougen Mfg. Co., Inc., Flint, 1970—, exec. v.p., 1974—, dir., 1976—. Del., PTO; pres. Hougen Found., 1981—. Mem. U.S. C. of C., Mich. C. of C. Club: East Bay Country (Largo, Fla.). Home: 1184 Normandy Terr Flint MI 48504 Office: G-5072 Corunna Rd Flint MI 48504

HOUGHLAND, SYLVIA M., state ofcl.; b. Saginaw, Mich., Oct. 12, 1938; d. Seymour and Fritzi (Steinber) Seltzer; M. Public Adminstrn., U. So. Calif., 1976; married; children—Kimberley, Kip. Dir., Legal Assistance for Sr. Adults, Shawnee Mission, Kans., 1976-80; sec. Kans. Dept. of Aging, Topeka, 1980—. Mem. Am. Soc. Public Adminstrn., Mid Am. Congress on Aging. Democrat. Office: Dept of Aging 2nd Floor 610 W 10th St Topeka KS 66612

HOULDEN, EDITH IONE, direct selling co. exec.; b. Gratiot County, Mich., Nov. 27, 1919; d. Harold James and Elsie Delilah (Drayer) Anderson; grad. high sch.; m. Lynn Houlden, July 18, 1937; children—Kenlyn Kay, Laurence Lynn. Unit mgr. Sarah Coventry, 1958-61; br. mgr. Judy Lee Jewels, 1961-64; distbr., dir. Viviane Woodard Corp., 1965-75; regional dir. Cameo Coutures, Inc., Ithaca, Mich., 1975—; condr. tng. seminars, 1970-82. Active Ithaca Frontier Festival, Gratiot Agrl. Soc., Ithaca Bicentennial Com.; mem. City Parks and Recreation Commn., 1978—, Community Crime Prevention Com., 1981-82. Recipient Service award Gratiot County, 1976; Spl. Citizen award City of Ithaca, 1977. Mem. Nat. Assn. Female Execs., Gen. Fedn. Women's Clubs, Mich. Fedn. Women's Clubs (resolutions chmn., pres. dist.), Gratiot Hist. Soc. Democrat. Presbyterian. Club: Ithaca Woman's. Address: 229 S Ithaca St Ithaca MI 48847

HOUMANN, CAROLYN ELIZABETH, state legislator; b. Sherwood, N.D., Dec. 23, 1935; d. Carl Johann and Carrie (Aarhus) Knutson; student Minot State U.; m. Alvin C. Houmann, Sept. 22, 1955; children—Shanon Leigh, James Robert, Lisa Jane. Tchr. rural sch.; mem. N.D. Ho. of Reps. Active Girl Scouts U.S.A., Am. Luth. Ch. Women, Hist. Soc. Republican. Clubs: Homemakers, Arts and Humanities. Address: Westhope ND 58793

HOUSE, ANNE W. MCLEMORE, children's clothing mfg. co. exec.; b. Saltillo, Tenn., July 12, 1919; d. Connie D. and Mamie (Craven) Wilkinson; m. James Henry House (dec.); children—Connie McLemore Barker, Samuel T. McLemore. Pres., owner Lil Filly Originals, Inc., Humboldt, Tenn., 1964, also Dallas Showroom, 1981. Activity chmn. Humboldt PTA, 1950-55; activity chmn. West Tenn. Strawberry Festival, 1952-58; troop leader Nischa council Girl Scouts Am., 1951. Democrat. Methodist. Home: Jackson Hwy PO Box 372 Humboldt TN 38343 Office: Milan Hwy PO Box 372 Humboldt TN 38343

HOUSE, OUIDA FRANCINE, wire products co. exec.; b. Converse, La., Nov. 26, 1936; d. Johnny Lee and Opal Lela (Julian) Wright; student Centenary Coll., Shreveport, La., 1966, Morton's Bus. Coll., Shreveport, 1956; m. Jack Edwin House, Sept. 1, 1974 (dec.); 1 dau., Tina Franchelle. Asst. mgr. transit dept. La. Bank & Trust Co., Shreveport, 1958-65; flight attendant, supr. Am. Flyers World Wide Charter Airline, 1968-69; flight attendant, supr. Braniff Internat. Airlines, 1969-76; pres., chmn. bd. AAA Wire Products, Inc., Point, Tex., 1978—; devel. bd. Lakewood Bank, Dallas. Active fund raising telethon Leukemia Soc. Dallas, 1980; vol. air transp. Scottish Rite Hosp., Crippled Children, 1971-73. Recipient Harding Lawrence award in aviation, 1973. Mem. Wire Assn. Internat., Tex. Assn. Bus., Am. Soc. Profl. and Exec. Women, Young Women of Arts of Dallas. Clubs: Dallas Athletic, Chandlers Landing Yacht. Office: PO Box 215 Hwy 69 Point TX 75472

HOUSE, PATRICIA, state ofcl.; b. Nyack, N.Y., Aug. 4, 1947; d. Sumner Joseph and Elaine (Wadlund) H.; B.S.C. in Mgmt., Rider Coll., 1970; M.P.H. in Mgmt. and Adminstrn., U. Minn., Mpls., 1973. Health planner maternal child health program Iowa State Health Dept., Des Moines, 1973-76; mgr. clin. services Planned Parenthood Vt., Montpelier, 1976-78; sr. health planner/analyst Vt. Agy. Human Services, Burlington, 1978—; field supr., lectr. grad. program health edn. and community health U. Vt., Burlington. Mem. adv. bd. Women Helping Battered Women, Burlington; mem. Vt. Right-to-Choose, Green Mountain Film Soc., Burlington; bd. dirs. Learning to Listen, White River Junction, Vt.; charter mem. Vt. Public Radio; co-founder Mpls. Multi-Health Analyst Group, 1972. Co-author: Vermont State Policy for Long Term Care, 1980; editor: State Health Plan for Vermont, 1980; prin. researcher 5-year study IUD utilization among Vt. Women, 1976-81. Home: North Underhill Station Rd Underhill VT 05489 Office: 60 Main St Burlington VT 05401

HOUSE, VICTORIA GAIL, hydrologist; b. Walnut Creek, Calif., Nov. 25, 1956; d. William King and Sylvia (Krieger) House; A.A., Diablo Velly Coll., 1976; M.S., U. Calif., Berkeley, 1979; postgrad. U.S. Dept. Agrl. Grad. Corr. Sch., 1981—. Crew leader Youth Conservation Corps, U.S. Forest Service, Downieville, Calif., 1977, 78; planning intern Tahoe Regional Planning Agy., South Lake Tahoe, Calif., 1979; ski area planning cons. Heavenly Valley Ski Area, South Lake Tahoe, 1979; hydrologic cons. U.S. Forest Service, 1979-81, hydrologist, 1981—; cons. in field. Home: Box 19722 South Lake Tahoe CA 95731 Office: Box 8465 South Lake Tahoe CA 95731

HOUSER, KATHLEEN WELSCH, hosp. public relations ofcl.; b. Pitts., Dec. 26, 1950; d. Robert Francis, Sr., and Bernice Rose (Bruchwalski) Welsch; student U. Pitts.; m. William James Houser, Oct. 7, 1972. Legal sec. Stokes, Lurie & Tracy, Pitts., 1968-72, Kaufman & Harris, Pitts., 1972; legal sec., office mgr. Office of Donnell D. Reed, Pitts., 1973-75; exec. sec. St. Margaret Meml. Hosp., Pitts., 1975-79, community relations asst., 1979-80, asst. dir. community relations, 1980-82, dir. community relations, 1982—. Scouting coordinator Exploring div. Boy Scouts Am. Recipient Superior Achievement awards, Hosp. Assn. Pa., 1979, 80, MacEachern award Acad. Hosp. Public Relations, 1980. Mem. Internat. Assn. Bus. Communications (awards of merit 1980, 81, award of excellence 1978), Public Relations Soc. Health

Care Orgns. Home: 2549 N Lightwood Ave Bethel Park PA 15102 Office: 815 Freeport Rd Pittsburgh PA 15215

HOUSER, LOUISE KELLEY, health care adminstr.; b. Bowman, S.C., Feb. 22, 1919; d. George Quillie and Byrdie Lucile (Stephens) Kelley; B.S., S.C. State Coll., 1941, M.S., 1959; m. John W. Houser, Jr., Sept. 18, 1943; children—John W., George D. Tchr. public schs., Marion County, S.C., 1941-44; tchr. sci. Ga. Sch. for the Deaf, 1959-61; tchr. pub. schs., Rome, Ga., 1961-68; dir. personnel Brentwood (Ga.) Med. Care Home, 1967-71; adminstr. Brentwood Nursing Home, 1972-77; adminstr. Brentwood Park, Three Rivers Health Care Co., Rome, Ga., 1977—. Mem. Rome Council on Human Relations, Ga. Health Care Assn., Am. Health Care Assn., Ga. Soc. Activity Dirs., Ga. Dental Soc. Aux. (past pres.), Am. Cancer Soc. (past pres. Floyd County div.), Aux. Nat. Dental Assn. (past pres., mem. exec. bd.). Home: 121 Jackson St Rome GA 30161 Office: Moran Lake Rd Rome GA 30161

HOUSTON, ALICE VIVIAN, sch. adminstr.; b. Baton Rouge; d. Charles and Sarah Albertha (Scott) H.; B.A., So. U., 1953; M.Ed., La. State U., 1956; Ph.D., U. Tex., 1974. Tchr., Ascension Parish Sch. System, Donaldsonville, La., 1953-57; with East Baton Rouge Parish Sch. System, 1957-77; dir. curriculum Oklahoma City Pub. Schs., 1977-82; asst. supt. for curriculum and instrn. Seattle Pub. Schs., 1982—; cons. SW Ednl. Devel. Lab. Recipient Outstanding Prin. award E. Baton Rouge Parish Edn. Assn., 1975; named Citizen of Yr., Oklahoma City chpt. Omega Phi Psi; NDEA grantee, 1965. Mem. Assn. Supervision and Curriculum Devel. (mem. exec. council 1979-82), Nat. Alliance Black Sch. Educators (mem. exec. bd. 1975-79), NAACP, Urban League, Okla. Reading Council, Kappa Delta Pi, Phi Delta Kappa. Democrat. Methodist. Office: 815 4th Ave N Seattle WA 98109

HOUSTON, SHIRLEY MAE (MRS. THOMAS H. HOUSTON), ct. reporter; b. Jasper, Tex., Oct. 4, 1938; d. Walter Louis and Effie Marie (Hulett) Gordon; student U. Houston, 1957, South Tex. Jr. Coll., Houston, 1958; grad. Robert Krippner Sch. Reporting, 1965; m. Thomas Harold Houston, Aug. 3, 1957. Various secretarial positions, 1956-65; ct. reporter, owner Houston Reporting Service, 1965—; owner H-R-S, 1975—; v.p. Tradewinds Indsl. Park, Inc., 1974—; partner Houston Video Service. Vol. juvenile counselor; advisor Houston Community Coll., 1976-78, Alvin Community Coll., 1980-81. Registered profl. reporter, cert. shorthand reporter, Tex. Mem. Greater Houston Ct. Reporters Assn. (pres. 1975), Nat. Shorthand Reporters Assn. (state chmn. membership com. 1977-78 dir. 1979-80, placement com. 1980-82, co-chmn. word processing com. 1981-82, seminar instr. nat. conv. 1978, 79, 81, 82), Tex. Shorthand Reporters Assn. (advt. chmn. conv. 1967, dir. 1978-80), Nat. Assn. Legal Secs., Tex. Assn. Legal Secs., Houston Assn. Legal Secs. (dir. 1969), DAR, UDC, Harris County Heritage Soc., Theatre Under the Stars. Baptist. Club: Cotillion (Houston). Address: 609 Fannin St Suite 2121 Houston TX 77002

HOUSTON, VIVIAN MCCOY, hotel mgr.; b. Lancaster, Pa., Jan. 30, 1943; d. Charles Lierer and Vivian Elizabeth (Kreider) McCoy; student Park Coll., Parkville, Mo. 1960-63, Temple U., Phila., 1963; m. Mark T. Houston, Aug. 25, 1978. Teller, Fidelity Phila. Trust Co., 1964-67; with Marriott Hotel Corp., 1967—, reservations mgr., New Orleans, 1972-74, gen. mgr. all hotels reservations, Omaha, 1974—. Mem. Am. Bus. Women's Assn. (treas. Omaha chpt. 1978). Home: 9904 Pasadena Ave Omaha NE 68124

HOUX, MARY ANNE, investments; b. Kansas City, Mo., Aug. 16, 1933; d. Rial Richardson and Geraldine Marie (McHale) Oglevie; B.S. in Edn., U. Kans., 1954; postgrad. U. Mo., Calif. State U., Chico; m. Phillip Clark Houx, May 12, 1962 (dec. 1974); 1 son, Clark Oglevie. Tchr. schs. in Mo., 1954-57; asst. to v.p. Woolf Bros., Inc., Kansas City, Mo., 1957-58; Midwest dir. C.A.R.E., Inc., 1960-63; legal sec., 1962-75; co-owner No Bull Custom Meats, Chico, Calif., 1975-79; owner H&P Investments, Chico, Calif., 1979—. Mem. Calif. Republican Central Com., 1972-74; mem. Butte County Rep. Central Com., 1972-76, sec., 1974-76; pres. Chico Rep. Women, 1973; adv. coms. Chico Unified Sch. Dist. Bd., trustee, 1977—, pres., 1979-81; mem. federated council Calif. Interscholastic Fedn., 1980—. Mem. Chico C. of C., Calif. Sch. Bds. Assn. (del. Butte County 1978—), Alpha Phi. Roman Catholic. Clubs: Butte Creek Country, Cosmos, Chico State Assos. (v.p. 1980), Soroptimist, Chico State U. Women, Chico State Faculty Wives (pres. 1969-70). Address: 860 Filbert Ave Chico CA 95926

HOVING, JANE PICKENS, civic worker; b. Macon, Ga.; grad. Curtis Inst. Music, Phila., Juilliard Sch. Music, N.Y.C.; m. 2d, William C. Langley (dec.); 1 dau., Marcella Langley McCormack; m. 3d, Walter Hoving, Sept. 30, 1977. Former singer, actress; appeared on daily Jane Pickens Show, NBC Radio, weekly Jane Pickens Show wint NBC Symphony Orch., weekly Jane Pickens Show for ABC-TV; former mem. Pickens Sisters; starred in musical, Regina, 1949; now civic worker; a founder United Cerebral Palsy Assns., one of chief organizers of ann. telethon; v.p. N.Y. Heart Assn.; pres., chmn. Greater N.Y. adv. bd. Salvation Army; former chmn. all domestic ops., mem. exec. com. ACTION, Washington. Bd. dirs., sec. Cerebral Palsy Research and Ednl. Found.; bd. dirs. Metromedia Inc., Com. for Prevention of Child Abuse, Animal Med Center N.Y., U.S.O., Walter Hoving Home for Seriously Troubled Girls. Recipient Disting. Vol. Service award Mrs. Lyndon B. Johnson, 1968; award Fedn. Jewish Philanthropies N.Y.; achievement award Albert Einstein Coll. Medicine; Humanitarian award United Cerebral Palsy; Meritorious award Govt. of Mex.; USO Woman of Yr. award, 1980; Gold medal Nat. Inst. Social Scis. numerous others. Home: 635 Park Ave New York NY 10021

HOWARD, BARBARA BURROW, cultural affairs cons.; b. Sumiton, Ala., May 17, 1929; d. Eldred Mayo and Alyce Elizabeth (Faught) Burrow; A.A. with honors in Speech, Gulf Park Coll., 1948; B.A., U. Ala., 1950; m. William J. Howard, Jr., Aug. 12, 1952. Feature writer Daily Mountain Eagle, Jasper, Ala., 1945-48; women's editor Tuscaloosa (Ala.) News, 1950-51; legis. asst., press sec. to Congressman Carl Elliott, Washington, 1951-53; press sec., staff writer-editor Congressman Armistead I. Selden, Jr., Washington, 1953-62; mgr. Gerald G. Wagner Assos., pub. relations, Washington, 1962-73; ind. internat. cultural affairs adviser, 1973—; free-lance editor, 1973—; asso. producer ann. UN Concert and Dinner, Washington, 1964-71, editor commemorative publs., 1962-72; writer-editor cultural publs., 1963—. Vol. editorial aide, Presdl. campaigns, 1960, 64. Recipient certificate of Merit, Bus. and Profl. Women's Club, 1950; Distinguished Alumna award U. Ala., 1970. Mem. Nat. Alumni Assn. U. Ala. (pres. Nat. Capital chpt. 1965-67), Smithsonian Nat. Assos., Montgomery County Arts Council, Chi Omega, Theta Sigma Phi. Democrat. Baptist. Club: Pilot. Home and Office: 2305 Sherbrooke Way Rockville MD 20850

HOWARD, CARLOTTA, exec.; b. Phila., May 6, 1920; d. Albert Monroe and Edna (Kraus) Greenfield; B.A., U. Pa., 1942, postgrad. in law; postgrad. Bryn Mawr Coll.; m. Allen R. Howard, Jr.; children—Charles F., Allen R. III, Derek G. Sales tng. dir. Maison Blanche Co., New Orleans; exec. dir. personnel City Stores Co., N.Y.C.; exec. sec. Gov.'s Com. on Aging, Commonwealth of Pa.; pres. ITS Travel, Bryn Mawr, Pa. Sec. Democratic Party, minority insp. elections Lower Merion (Pa.) Twp.; mem. Gov.'s Com. on Jud. Rev., Montgomery County, Pa.; asso. trustee, mem. bd. overseers U. Pa. Sch. Veterinary Medicine; mem. Benjamin Franklin Assos., U. Pa. Served to lt. USNR, World War II. Mem. Montgomery County Kennel Club (dir.). Episcopalian. Author: Gourmet on a Lean Purse, 1979. Home: Rosemont PA 19010

HOWARD, DIANE LEGAN, fountain syrups mfg. co. exec.; b. Macon, Miss., Dec. 7, 1937; d. George Nolan and Nancy (Alexander) Legan; B.A. magna cum laude, Miss. U. for Women, 1969; m. Malcolm B. Howard, Nov. 24, 1956; children—Marion, Diana, Cal, Tommy. Payroll and office mgr. Dr. Pepper Bottling Co., Tuscaloosa, Ala., 1958-65; sales and mktg. Universal Industries Corp., Columbus, Miss., 1968-77, exec. v.p., dir. sales, 1977—. Mem. adv. bd. Miss. State U., Miss. Dept. Social Welfare, Columbus Civic Arts Assn. Mem. Am. Mgmt. Assn. Republican. United Methodist. Clubs: Soroptimist Internat., Milady Garden, Nat. Assn. Jr. Aux. (pres. 1978), Jr. League Tuscaloosa. Home: Route 1 Box 465 Columbus MS 39701 Office: PO Box 192 Hwy 45S Columbus MS 39701

HOWARD, ESTELLE CHARMAINE, personnel cons.; b. Atlantic City, May 22, 1952; d. William James and Geraldine Audrey (Vierra) H.; student public schs.; divorced; children—Devin, Jason. Personnel recruiter Affirmative Action Assos., N.Y.C., 1978-79; officer mgr., personnel cons. Rainbow Cons., N.Y.C., 1979, v.p., 1979—; condr. seminars, cons. in field. Mem. Internat. Assn. Personnel Women, Coalition 100 Black Women, Council Concerned Black Execs., Nat. Assn. Female Execs. Office: 295 Madison Ave New York NY 10017

HOWARD, FRANCES ESTELLA HUMPHREY, govt. ofcl.; b. Wallace, S.D., Feb. 18, 1914; d. Hubert Horatio and Christine (Sannes) Humphrey; B.A. in Sociology, George Washington U., 1937, M.A., 1941; H.H.D. (hon.), Lane Coll., 1967; m. Ray Howard, Dec. 7, 1942 (dec. Jan. 1967); children—William, Anne. With U.S. Office Civilian Def., Washington, 1941-43; liaison officer various vol. agys. for fgn. relief, 1942-60; commd. fgn. service officer Dept. State, 1960, chief liaison officer vol. agys. AID, 1960-67, chief spl. project div., Office of War on Hunger, 1968; liaison officer vol. health orgns. HEW, 1969-70; spl. asst. to asso. dir. for extramural programs Nat. Library of Medicine, NIH, USPHS, Health and Human Services, Bethesda, Md., 1970—; lectr. to various orgns., clubs. Vice pres. U.S. Com. for Refugees, 1975-82; bd. dirs. Universalist-Unitarian Service Com., 1975—, Mus. African Art, Smithsonian Instn., 1962—, Washington Opera, 1977—, Capitol Children's Mus., 1982. Recipient Disting. Service award Grand chpt. Delta Sigma Theta, 1966; Women's Honor award Howard U., 1967; No. Va. service award Altrusa Club, 1967; Emblem of Honor award 6th Ann. Pan Am. Congress Conf. on Social Services, 1968. Fellow Royal Soc. Arts (London); AAUW, Am. Women in Radio and TV, Bus. and Profl. Women's Assn., Am. Sociol. Assn., Pan Am. Conf. Social Work, Soc. Internat. Devel., Internat. Council on Social Welfare, UN Assn. (dir. 1980-82), AAAS. Contbr. articles to nat. periodicals. Office: Nat Library of Medicine NIH 8600 Rockville Pike Bethesda MD 20209

HOWARD, JANA THERESA, lawyer; b. Huntsville, Ala., Apr. 20, 1945; d. Ernest Randall and Mary Regna (Baites) H.; B.S., Auburn U., 1967; M.S., Towson State Coll., 1973; J.D. summa cum laude, U. Balt., 1976. Admitted to Md. bar, 1976; home econs. tchr. Hampton High Sch., Melbourne, Australia, 1967; county ext. home economist U. Ga. Coop. Extension Services, Jefferson, 1967-70; state youth program devel. specialist U. Ga. Coop. Extension Service, Athens, 1970-72; state youth program devel. specialist U. Md. Coop. Extension Service, College Park, 1972-73; asso. law firm Venable, Baetjer & Howard, Balt., 1976—; speaker, cons. EEO Programs, Inc., 1979—, Exec. Enterprises, Inc., 1978—, Profl. Seminar Assos., Inc., 1978-81, Antioch Sch. Law Center for Legal Studies, 1981. Mem. adv. com. Goucher Coll. Women's Mgmt. Devel. Project, 1979—; mem. Greater Balt. Com. Chamber Council, 1980—; pres., bd. dirs. Balt. New Directions for Women, 1980-81, bd. dirs., 1981—. Mem. Am. Judicature Soc., Bar Assn. Balt. City, Fed. Bar Assn., Md. Bar Assn. (spl. com. law and handicapped), Am. Bar Assn. Presbyterian. Club: Loophole Law Balt. Contbr. articles to profl. jours. Office: 1800 Mercantile Bank and Trust Bldg Two Hopkins Plaza Baltimore MD 21201

HOWARD, JANE OSBURN (MRS. ROLLINS STANLEY HOWARD), educator; b. Morris, Ill., Aug. 12, 1926; d. Everett Hooker and Bernice Otilda (Olson) Osburn; B.A., U. Ariz., 1948; M.A., U. N.Mex., 1966, Ph.D., 1969; m. Rollins Stanley Howard, June 5, 1948; children—Ellen Elizabeth, Susan (Mrs. John Karl Nuttall). Instr. U. N.Mex. Sch. Medicine, Albuquerque, 1968-70, mem. staff pediatrics, deaf blind children's program, Albuquerque, 1971-72, asst. dir. N.Mex. programs for deaf blind children, 1972—, instr. psychiatry, instr. pediatrics, coordinator deaf-blind children's program, 1972-76; ednl. cons., 1976—; cons. Mountain-Plains Regional Center for Services to Deaf-Blind Children, Denver, 1971-74, Bur. Indian Affairs, 1974. Active Cystic Fibrosis, Mother's March, Heart Fund, Easter Seal-Crippled Children. Recipient fellowships U. N.Mex., 1965, 66, 66-67, 67-68, U. So. Calif. John Tracy Clinic, 1973. Fellow Royal Soc. Health; mem. Council Exceptional Children, Am. Assn. Mental Deficiency, Nat. Assn. Retarded Children, AAUW, Pi Lambda Theta, Zeta Phi Eta, Alpha Epsilon Rho. Republican. Methodist. Home: 615 Valencia Dr SE Albuquerque NM 87108

HOWARD, KARAL KAY, interior designer, textile designer, educator; b. Houston, Nov. 23, 1943; d. Walker Richard and Hazel Pearl (Hilton) Gray; B.S. in Interior Design, U. Tex., 1965; M.S. in Interior Design, Okla. State U., 1967. Interior designer with Fields & Silverman, Beverly Hills, Calif., 1969-72; prin. Kay Howard Design, Los Angeles, 1972-75, Austin, Tex., 1975—; free-lance textile designer, Los Angeles, 1972-75, Austin, 1975-78; instr. interior design Woodbury Coll., Los Angeles, 1973, Laguna Gloria Art Museum, Austin, 1978, U. Tex., Austin, 1975—; exhibited textile designs 3-woman show, Los Angeles, 1972, nat. show Laguna Beach (Calif.) Mus., 1973; owner Crystal Coyote, retail store, Austin. Guest juror Tex. Designer Craftsmen's Show, 1980. Recipient 1st prize Textile div. Okla. Designer-Craftsmen Statewide Show, 1968. Mem. Am. Soc. Interior Designers (profl. mem., sec. Austin Assn. 1979), Visual Artists Assn., Austin Contemporary Visual Artists Assn. Office: Painter Hall 420 Interior Design Div U Tex Austin TX 78712

HOWARD, LYNN MARSH, newspaper editor; b. Muskogee, Okla., Dec. 26, 1949; d. James B. Marsh and Marguerite H. Ross; student U. Okla., 1967-70; B.Ed. in Journalism, Northeastern State U., 1975; m. James K. Howard; 1 son, Marsh Molloy. Asst. women's editor Muskogee Phoenix, 1972-74; news editor Tahlequah (Okla.) Pictorial Press & Star-Citizen, 1976-80; mng. editor Tahlequah Daily Press, 1980—. Active Tahlequah Arts and Humanities Council, Fedn. Women Democrats; bd. dirs. Help in Crisis, Inc. Recipient H. & R. Block Public Service in Journalism award, 1973; 2d place award for feature Okla. Press Assn., 1981, 1st pl. typography, 1982. Mem. AAUW, Sigma Delta Chi, Delta Delta Delta. Episcopalian. Clubs: Indian Nations Soccer (sec.); Tahlequah Soroptimists (treas. 1980-82). Home: 712 Brentwood Dr Tahlequah OK 74464 Office: PO Box 888 Tahlequah OK 74464

HOWARD, MARGUERITE EVANGELINE BARKER (MRS. JOSEPH D. HOWARD), bus. exec., civic worker; b. Victoria, B.C., Can., July 30, 1921; d. Reuel Harold and Frances Penelope (Garnham) Barker; brought to U.S., 1924, naturalized, 1945; B.A., U. Wash., 1943; m. Joseph D. Howard, June 16, 1952; children—Wendy Doreen Frances, Bradford Reuel. Vice pres., dir. Howard Tours, Inc., Oakland, Calif., 1953—; co-owner, gen. mgr. Howard Travel Service, Oakland, Calif., 1956—, mng. dir. Howard Hall, Berkeley, Calif., 1964-74; co-owner, asst. mgr. Howard Investments, Oakland, 1960—; sec.-treas. Energy Dynamics, Inc. Bd. dirs. Piedmont council Campfire Girls, 1969-79, pres., 1974-79, nat. council, 1972-76, zone chmn., 1974-76, 77-83, nat. bd., 1976-83; bd. dirs. Oakland Symphony Guild, 1969—, pres., 1972-74; bd. dirs. Oakland Symphony Orch., 1972—, mem. exec. bd., 1972-74; bd. dirs. Piedmont Jr. High Sch. Mothers Club, 1968-69. Mem. Oakland Mus. Assn., U. Wash. Alumni, East Bay Bot. and Zool. Soc., Am. Symphony Orch. League, Assn. Calif. Symphony Orchs., Young Audiences, Chi Omega Alumni Seattle, Chi Omega East Bay Alumni, Berkeley. Republican. Clubs: Womens University (Seattle); Womens Athletic (Oakland). Home: 146 Bell Ave Piedmont CA 94611 Office: 526 Grand Ave Oakland CA 94610

HOWARD, MARTHA WALLING, writer; b. Shreveport, La., Jan. 28, 1916; d. Joseph Macon and Moss (Turner) Walling; B.A., Randolph-Macon Woman's Coll., 1937; M.A., George Washington U., 1942; Ph.D., U. Md., 1967; m. George Wilberforce Howard, June 5, 1938; children—George Wilberforce III, James Ewing. Instr. Latin, All Saints Coll., Vicksburg, Miss., 1937-39, Gunstan Hall Jr. Coll., Washington, 1940-42, public schs. Stafford and Fairfax Counties, Va., 1950-66; lectr. Greek and Latin, Am. U., Washington, 1965-66; lectr. humanities U. Ariz., Tucson, 1966-74, asso. prof. humanities, 1974-76; freelance writer, 1976—; books include: All Things to Sea (lyric poetry), 1942; Plutarch in the Major European Literatures of the Eighteenth Century, 1970; Comparative Literature Study (Choice list of outstanding acad. books), 1972. Named to Hall of Fame, U. Ariz., 1975. Mem. Humane Soc. Tucson, Ariz. Hist. Soc., Phi Beta Kappa (Alpha chpt. Ariz.), Mortar Bd. Republican. Episcopalian. Home: 177-C S Paseo Sarta Green Valley AZ 85614

HOWARD, MARY FRANCES, coll. adminstr.; b. Alton, Ill., Mar. 14, 1954; d. John Garfield and Frances Elnora (Banks) H.; B.A., U. Iowa, 1976, M.A., 1977. Research asst. spl. support services U. Iowa, Iowa City, 1976-77; asst. dir. developmental edn. U. Wis., Oshkosh, 1978; dir. spl. services program, asst. dean services Coe Coll., Cedar Rapids, Iowa, 1978—. Commr. Cedar Rapids Civil Rights Commn. Recipient Gwendolyn Brooks award, Alpha award, Penningroth award, J. Reed Delano award, Danforth award. Mem. Nat. Assn. Remedial and Spl. Programs in Postsecondary Edn., NAACP (past exec. bd.), Am. Personnel and Guidance Assn., Mid. Am. Assn. Ednl. Opportunity Program Personnel (pres. Iowa chpt. 1981-82), Am. Coll. Personnel Assn., Nat. Assn. Women Deans, Adminstrs. and Counselors, Assn. Black Women in Higher Edn., Black Women's Civic Orgn. of Cedar Rapids, Delta Sigma Theta. Home: 1716 D Ave NE Apt A3 Cedar Rapids IA 52402 Office: Coe College Box 18 Cedar Rapids IA 52402

HOWARD, NANCY LOUISE, med. technologist; b. Owensboro, Ky., Oct. 23, 1934; d. Augustine and Theresa Pearl (Stallings) Clements; student Brescia Coll., 1952-55; cert. med. tech. St. Joseph Hosp./Marquette U., 1956; children—Jania Kathryn, Norman Francis, Andrea Louise, Renee Ann. Med. technologists Our Lady of Mercy Hosp., Owensboro, 1956-57, Clin. Pathol. Labs., St. Louis, 1957-58, City of St. Louis Koch Hosp., Public Health Labs., 1959-60; lab. supr. Centreville Twp. Hosp., East St. Louis, Ill., 1960-80; lab. mgr., clin. dir. Compton Hill Med. Center, St. Louis, 1980—; instr. Belleville Area Coll. Active Goldwater Presidential campaign. Mem. Am. Soc. Clin. Pathologists (affiliate mem., cert. med. technologist), Am. Soc. Med. Technologists (pres. so. Ill. br. 1978-79), Conf. of Pub. Health Dirs. Republican. Roman Catholic. Club: Columbia Turners Aux. Home: 175 Glendale Dr Columbia IL 62236 Office: 1755 S Grand Blvd Saint Louis MO 63104

HOWARD, PATSY CLIFFENE, educator; b. Gorman, Tex., Nov. 1, 1939; d. James Clifford and Lillian Bell (Daughtery) Howard; student Cisco Jr. Coll., 1958-59; B.S. with honors, Howard Payne U., 1962, postgrad. summer 1964; grad. fellow Calif. State U., 1965-66, U. Md., 1966-67; M.Ed., Tarleton State U., 1979; postgrad. Tex. A&M U., 1980—. Tchr., Fresno (Calif.) Unified Sch. Dist., 1962-63, Spearman (Tex.) High Sch., 1963-65; English instr. Cisco Jr. Coll. and Howard Payne U., 1963; with First So. Bapt. Ch. of Honolulu, 1966; instr. English, Abilene Christian U., 1967-71; editorial asst. Conradiana, McMurry Coll., Abilene 1968-71; editorial dir. Pierian Press, Ann Arbor, Mich., 1971-72; public relations dir. Teheran Am. Sch., 1973-77; exec. dir. Nr. East/S. Asia Council of Overseas Schs., Teheran and Athens, 1974-78; grad. asst. Tex. A.&M. U., College Station, 1980—; mng. editor Thesis Bibl. Series, 1969-71; cons. in field; conf. planner and coordinator. Co-chmn. Bicentennial Celebration Com. for Iran, 1976; mem. housing survey com. Am. Businesses in Iran, 1976-77. Recipient Democracy-in-Action award, 1962; Freedom Found. award, 1962; Dollie Robnett Sr. Woman's award Howard Payne U., 1962; Shell grantee, 1969; U. Tex. computer sci. grantee, 1969-70; Abilene Christian U. faculty research grantee, 1969. Mem. Am. Assn. Sch. Adminstrs., Assn. Advancement Internat. Edn., Ednl. Press Assn., Nat. Sch. Public Relations Assn., Council of Ednl. Facility Planners, Joseph Conrad Soc. (pres. 1973-75), Iran-Am. Soc., Iran-Am. C. of C., AAUW, Mortar Bd., Alpha Chi, Kappa Delta Pi (award 1962), Phi Delta Kappa. Clubs: Am. Women's, Am. Author: Theses in American Literature, 1971; Theses in English Literature, 1971; contbr. articles to profl. jours.; editor The Link, 1973-77, Ye Ole Windbag, 1973-77, Welcome Aboard, 1974-77, The NESA Connection, 1974-78, The Insider, 1975-77, Board-a-Gram, 1976-77, The Pipeline, 1977-78. Home: PO Box 103 Rising Star TX 76471 Office: Tex A & M U Coll Edn Dept Ednl Adminstrn College Station TX 77843

HOWARD, PHYLLIS BERYL, former county commr.; b. Grand Rapids, Mich., Aug. 19, 1928; d. Cornielus George Swart and Helen Marie (Mullennix) Gleason; student public schs., Grand Rapids; m. Harvey W. Kelly, July 8, 1949 (dec.); m. 2d, James A. Yearnd, Mar. 14, 1964 (dec.); m. 3d, Joseph J. Howard, July 8, 1980 (dec. May 1981); children—Mary K. Kelly, Becky D. Kelly, Kimberly J. Yearnd. With Mich. Bell Telephone Co., Fremont, 1946-48, Gerber Products, Fremont, 1948-49; Newaygo County econ. investigator for Probate Ct. and Mich. Crippled Children Conveyor, 1956-58; partner Yearnd Funeral Home, Cadillac, Mich., 1964-79; Wexford County commr., 1975-80, vice chmn., 1977-80; chmn. 4-County Public Health Bd., 1979-80, 4-County Mental Health Bd., 1978-80, 7-County Substance Abuse Adv. Council, 1979-80; vice chmn. region 2, Mich. Assn. Counties, 1979-80; pres. Mich. Asso. Bd. Health, 1978-79; mem. ch. council 1st Congregational Ch., Cadillac. Republican. Clubs: Cadillac Country, Women's Golf Assn.

HOWARD, PHYLLIS RUTH, ceramic mfr., educator; b. Odessa, Tex., Mar. 26, 1947; d. Ganoe J. and Mary J. (Boyd) Howard; Asso. in Nursing, Odessa Coll., 1967; B.S. in Nursing, West, Tex. State U., 1977. Emergency room supr. Med. Center Hosp., Odessa, 1970-75, instr. emergency med. services dept., 1975-80; owner ceramics bus., Odessa, 1980—. Mem. Nat., Tex. emergency med. technicians assns., Nat. Ceramic Mfrs. Assn. Republican. Baptist. Club: Order Eastern Star. Home: 6810 Huber Ave Odessa TX 79762

HOWARD, RUBY MAE, fin. exec.; b. Anderson, S.C., July 23, 1939; d. Tulie and Olga (Robinson) Griffin; diploma Kennedy-King Jr. Coll., 1973; B.S.B.A., Roosevelt U., 1975, M.B.A., 1977; m. Roland Howard, July 1, 1957; children—Rhonda, Renee, Wendy. Payroll clk. and typist Dept. HEW, Chgo., 1957-59; computer clk. and typist Dept. Treasury, Chgo., 1960-61; sec. C.E. U.S. Army, Chgo., 1961-65; sec. to pres. Burr Oak Cemetery, Chgo., 1965-67; asst. editor, bus. mgr. North Central Assn. Colls. and Secondary Schs., Chgo., 1967-70; adminstrv. asst., bus. mgr. Roosevelt U., 1974-77; fin. analyst Chgo. Rock Island R.R., 1977-79; dir. fin., controller Hyde Park Fed. Savs. and Loan Assn., Chgo., 1979—. Mem. Phi Gamma Nu (v.p. Alpha Tau chpt. 1974-76),

Profl. Panhellenic Assn. Home: 50 W 125th Pl Chicago IL 60628 Office: 5250 Lake Park Ave Chicago IL 60615

HOWARD-CLARK, DORIS EDITH, nursing adminstr.; b. Wiltshire, Eng., Mar. 15, 1929; came to U.S., 1969; d. Harold Thomas Daniel and Doris Louise (Avis) Howard; Asso. Sci., Glendale Coll., 1973; student nursing adminstrn. CCNY; m. Kenneth Scofield Clark, Apr. 1, 1950; 1 dau., Heather-Louise Constance; 1 adopted dau., Karen Elizabeth-Janet. Librarian, Woodstock (Ont., Can.) Public Library, 1965-69; staff nurse Meml. Hosp., Phoenix, 1975-76, Bay Area Hosp., Cooj Bay, Oreg., 1976-78; asst. head nurse, dir. nursing service Nursing Home, Everett, Wash., 1979-81; head nurse, mgr. surg.-burn unit United Gen. Hosp., Sedro Wooley, Wash., 1981—. Mem. Audubon Soc., Smithsonian Instn. Mem. Ch. of England.

HOWDER, DELORIS JEAN, costume designer, mfr.; b. Muscotah, Kans., Dec. 28, 1926; d. Ernest Oscer and Lona Ethel (Wiley) Hollenbeck; student Nat. Sch. Dress Design, 1953-54; m. Wilbern B. Obbards; 1 son, Glen Alan; m. 2d, Richard Joseph Howder, Jan. 29, 1968. With Horton Garment Co. (Kans.), 1948-54; with Paramount Studios, Hollywood, Calif., 1955; owner, designer Deloris Square Dance Dresses, Long Beach, Calif., Springfield, Mo., Seligman, Mo. and Horton, 1957—. Mem. Horton C. of C. (mem. arts and crafts show com. 1979), Nat. Costume Assn., Parents Without Partners (editor newsletter 1979-82, N.E. Kans. chpt. 1071 membership dir. 1982—). Office: 847 Central Horton KS 66439

HOWE, JACQUELINE JANE, public info. exec.; b. Springfield, Ohio, June 19, 1955; d. John Norman and Dorothy (Kohl) Ulsh; B.A. cum laude in English, Miami U., 1977; postgrad. Bedford Coll., London, 1978-79; m. James Randall Howe, May 24, 1980. Feature writing intern Cleve. Plain Dealer, 1976; reporter Sumter (S.C.) Daily Item, 1977-78; public relations coordinator Spoleto Arts Festival, Charleston, S.C., summer 1978; coordinator Title VII, Dept. Labor, Springfield, Ohio, 1979-80; editor Advance, monthly mag., U. Tex., Dallas, 1981-82; public info. officer Dallas Fire Dept., 1982—. Public info. officer Am. Cancer Soc., Sumter, 1977-78. Mem. Women in Communications, Miami U. Alumni Assn., Phi Beta Kappa, Omicron Delta Kappa. Club: Baptist Women. Office: City Hall 7AS 1500 Marilla Dallas TX 75201

HOWE, LINDA ARLENE, nurse; b. Pitts., Dec. 12, 1948; d. Alfred Robert and Zella Jane (Lintner) Somerhalder; grad. with honors Columbia Hosp. Sch. Nursing, 1969; grad. with honors Richland Coll., 1981; grad. with honors U. Tex., 1982; postgrad. Tex. Women's U., 1982—; m. John J. Howe, Jr., Dec. 7, 1968; 1 son, Thomas. Nurse intensive care unit, coronary care unit Columbia Hosp., Pitts., 1969-70; nurse Brownsville (Pa.) Hosp., 1970-72; nurse intensive care unit Kennestone Hosp., Marietta, Ga., 1972-74; staff devel. coordinator Autumn Breeze Nursing Home, Marietta, 1974-75; dir. nursing Hideaway Hills Nursing Center, Austell, Ga., 1975-76; geriatric nursing cons. Unicare Services, Inc., Dallas, 1976-79; head nurse Monongalia Gen. Hosp., Morgantown, W.Va., 1979-80; ind. nurse cons., 1980—; critical care supr. Meml. Hosp. Garland (Tex.), 1980—. Leader N.W. Ga. council Girl Scouts U.S.A., Marietta, 1974-76; den leader Pack 168, Circle 10 council Boy Scouts Am., 1977-79. Mem. Am. Nurses Assn., Assn. Rehab. Nurses, Gerontol. Soc., Phi Theta Kappa. Democrat. Roman Catholic. Address: 5001 Roundtable Garland TX 75042

HOWE, MARIE ELIZABETH, state legislator; b. Somerville, Mass., June 13, 1944; d. William Andrew and Amelia Gertrude (McCauley) Howe; J.D., New Eng. Sch. of Law, 1969. Mem. Mass. Ho. of Reps., 1965—, asst. majority leader, 1973—. Mem. Somerville Sch. Com., 1965-68. Mem. Zonta. Home: 19 Pembroke St Somerville MA 02145 Office: State House Boston MA 02133

HOWE, PATRICIA MARY, investment banker; b. Chgo., Sept. 14, 1927; d. Harry Michael and Helen Mary (Maloney) Howe; student Barat Coll., Lake Forest, Ill., 1944-47, Goodman Theatre, Chgo., 1947; m. Ernest O. Ellison, Sept. 23, 1977. Instl. sales asst. Blyth & Co., 1954-55; with L.F. Rothschild & Co., 1957—, mgr. San Francisco br., 1965—, partner, 1968—; dir. Lear Siegler. Trustee U. San Diego, Women's Forum West. Mem. Securities Industry Assn., San Francisco Bond Club, Equestrian Order Holy Sepulchre, Opera Guild, San Francisco Symphony Found. Republican. Roman Catholic. Clubs: World Trade, Metropolitan, Bankers, Villa Taverna, Downtown Assn. (dir.), Bankers (dir.), Bel Air Bay. Office: 4 Embarcadero Center Suite 3300 San Francisco CA 94111

HOWELL, DOROTHY TAYLOR, electronic engr.; b. East Bend, N.C., July 27, 1936; d. Thomas William and Margaret Dorothy (Welch) Taylor; B.A., U. N.C., Greensboro, 1958; postgrad. U. Va., 1958-59, Old Dominion U., 1973, George Washington U., 1974, 75, 81; m. William Edward Howell, June 18, 1960; children—Woodrow Walter, Patricia Ann. Mathematician, NASA, Langley Research Center, Hampton, Va., 1958-68; aerospace technologist data analysis NASA, 1968-80, electronics engr., 1980—. Recipient Apollo Group Achievement award, 1969; Lifting Body Flight Research Team Group Achievement award, 1970; Supersonic Transport NASA Evaluation Team award, 1967. Mem. AIAA, AAUW. Baptist. Club: Federally Employed Women. Contbr. articles to profl. jours. Home: 132 Robanna Dr Seaford VA 23696 Office: NASA Langley Research Center Hampton VA 23665

HOWELL, ELIZABETH FABIAN, psychologist; b. Dallas, June 15, 1946; d. Roy Patton and Emily Fabian (Webster) H.; B.A., Sarah Lawrence Coll., 1968; M.A., N.Y. U., 1974, Ph.D., 1975; postdoctoral fellow Yale U., 1975-77; m. William M. Czander, Jan. 31, 1976; 1 dau., Alicia. Chief psychologist Holyoke Chicopee (Mass.) Area Mental Health Center, 1977-78; pvt. practice, Amherst, Mass., 1977-79, Keene, N.H., 1979-80, N.Y.C., 1981—; adj. faculty Antioch New Eng. U., 1980. Mem. Am. Psychol. Assn. Co-editor: Women and Mental Health, 1981. Address: 325 W 86th St New York NY 10024

HOWELL, JANET DECKER, clin. psychologist; b. Flushing, N.Y., Dec. 12, 1940; d. Benjamin Forbes and Gladys May (Decker) Smith; B.A., Drew U., 1962; M.A., Calif. State U., Northridge, 1972; Ph.D., U. So. Calif., 1975; m. Jerry Dean Howell, Dec. 17, 1978; 1 dau., Jessica May. Tchr. exptl. sch., 1962-63; prin., alternative sch., 1963-65; asst. adminstr. psychiat. facility, 1965-67; adminstr. agy., 1967-70; instr. community coll., 1972-73, 1973—; asst. prof. univ., 1975-78, assoc. prof., 1975-81; pvt. practice in clin. psychology, Woodland Hills, Calif., 1981—. Recipient community service awards for service to youth. Mem. Am. Psychol. Assn., Los Angeles Soc. Psychoanalytic Psychology, Univ. Profs. Calif. Democrat. Unitarian. Office: 4869 Topanga Canyon Blvd Suite 11 Woodland Hills CA 91364

HOWELL, MARGARET CRAWFORD, transp. exec.; b. Huntsville, Ala., Dec. 24, 1941; d. Warren and Ella Lee (Bobo) Crawford; student Howard U., 1966-67, Atlanta U., 1975; B.S. in Bus. Edn., Knoxville Coll., 1963; M.S. in Mgmt. and Supervision Central Mich. U., 1981; 1 child, Leslye E. N. Manpower analyst Huntsville (Ala.)-Madison County Community Action Com., Inc., 1968; tchr. Atlanta public schs., 1969; dir. Community Services Program of Wesley Homes, Inc., Atlanta, 1969-70; contract adminstr. Model Cities Program, City of Atlanta, 1970-71; dir. adminstrv. services Met. Atlanta Rapid Transit Authority, 1972—; vis. prof. Northeastern U., Boston, spring 1979; vis. lectr. Mgmt. Tng. Adv. Council, Morehouse Coll., 1979. Mem. rev. and allocations com. United Way Agy., 1976—, chmn. ad-hoc scholarship com., 1979; bd. dirs. Opportunities Industrialization Center of Atlanta, 1976-81, Black United Fund, 1979; mem. Mid-Atlanta Unit, chmn. individual spl. gifts com. Am. Cancer Soc., 1979. Recipient Sta. WSB Outstanding Name-in-News award, 1969, Superbooster award, 1979; recipient Outstanding Placement award Minority Women's Employment Program, 1975. Lic. Ga. Inst. Real Estate. Mem. Am. Mgmt. Assn., Adminstrv. Mgmt. Soc., Atlanta Women's Network (dir. 1979-81), Am. Bus. Women's Assn., Bldg. Owners and Mgrs. Assn., In-Plant Printing Mgmt. Assn., Atlanta Urban League. Methodist. Home: 4205 Sloop Way Atlanta GA 30349 Office: 2200 Peachtree Summit 401 W Peachtree St NE Atlanta GA 30365

HOWELL, SALLY MAY, univ. center dir.; b. Spokane, Wash., May 19, 1948; d. Raymond D. and Beulah M. (O'Hara) Emley; B.A.Ed., Eastern Wash. U., 1969; m. John Milton Howell, June 20, 1970; 1 dau., Carrie Ann. Bus. tchr. Kiona Benton High Sch., Benton City, Wash., 1969-70; prodn. control staff IBM, Huntsville, Ala., 1970-71; substitute tchr., Las Cruces, N.Mex., 1971-72; dir. univ. center Willamette U., Salem, Oreg., 1976—; artist's rep. for Jim Greeninger, classical guitarist, 1982—. Host, Oreg. Inst. Alcohol Studies, 1981, Young Musicians and Artists Summer Conf., 1976-81, Oreg. Girls State Conv., 1976-81. Cert. in secondary edn. Mem. Assn. Coll. Unions Internat. (host. dir. 1980 regional conf.; women's concerns coordinator 1979-81), Nat. Entertainment and Campus Activities Assn. Home and office: 2161 Eola Dr NW Salem OR 97304

HOWELL, WILMA JEAN, accountant; b. Sharp County, Ark., May 12, 1943; d. Raymond D. and Grace I. (Hughes) Carver; B.A. summa cum laude, Wichita State U., 1980; A.A., Butler County Community Coll., 1978; m. Kenneth Duane Howell, Aug. 26, 1961; children—Kenneth Dale, Kristopher Duane, Korey Dean. Sec., bookkeeper Durling-Richards Ins. Ajudsters, Wichita, Kans., 1961-62; staff acct. Fox and Co., El Dorado, Kans., 1980—; instr. managerial acctg. Butler County Community Coll., 1981-82. C.P.A., Kans. Mem. Kansas Soc. C.P.A.s, Am. Inst. C.P.A.s, Beta Alpha Psi. Mem. Ch. of Christ. Home: Rural Route 1 Leon KS 67074 Office: 228 W Central St El Dorado KS 67042

HOWELLS, MURIEL GURDON SEABURY (MRS. WILLIAM WHITE HOWELLS), civic worker; b. White Plains, N.Y., May 3, 1910; d. William Marston and Katharine Emerson (Hovey) Seabury; student Chapin Sch., 1928; m. William White Howells, June 15, 1929; children—Muriel Gurdon (Mrs. Richard E. Metz), William Dean. Founder Brit. War Relief Soc., Madison, Wis., 1941, pres., 1941-43; apptd. visitor, dept. decorative arts and sculpture Boston Mus. Fine Arts, 1955-72, dept. Am. decorative arts, 1972—; ladies com. Inst. Contemporary Art, Boston, 1955-65, 67-68, asso., 1965-67; bd. dirs. Boston br. English-Speaking Union, 1955-80, v.p., 1973-74; a founder, trustee Strawbery Banke, Inc., Portsmouth, N.H., 1958-75, overseer, 1975-81, hon. overseer, 1981—; a founder, mem. steering com. Guild, 1959—; bd. dirs. Garden Club Am., 1959-62, nat. chmn. medal award com., 1962-65, judge flower arrangements; pres. Piscataqua Garden Club, 1952-54; mem. Harvard Solomon Islands Expdn., Malaita, 1968; chmn. Boston chpt. Venice Com., Internat. Fund for Monuments, 1970-71; vice chmn. Boston chpt. Save Venice Inc., 1971-77, mem. exec. com., 1971—. Recipient King's medal for Service in the Cause of Freedom (Britain), 1946; Historic Preservation award, zone 1 Garden Club Am., 1976. Mem. Nat. Soc. Colonial Dames N.H., Soc. Preservation New Eng. Antiquities (mem. Maine council 1976-78). Clubs: Women's Travel (pres. 1967-69), Vincent, Chilton (Boston); Colony (N.Y.C.). Home: 274 Beacon St Boston MA 02116 also Kittery Point ME 03905

HOWES, BARBARA, poet, anthologist; b. N.Y.C., May 1, 1914; d. Osborne and Mildred (Cox) Howes; B.A., Bennington Coll., 1937; m. William Jay Smith, Oct. 1, 1947; children—David E., Gregory Jay. Author books of poems: The Undersea Farmer, 1948, In the Cold Country, 1954, Light and Dark, 1959, Looking Up at Leaves, 1966, The Blue Garden, 1972, A Private Signal: Poems New/Selected, 1977; editor anthologies: 23 Modern Stories, 1963, From the Green Antilles: writings of the Caribbean, 1966, The Sea-Green Horse (with Gregory Jay Smith), 1970; The Eye of the Heart: Stories from Latin America, 1973; editor lit. quar. Chimera, 1943-47. Guggenheim fellow, 1955; Brandeis U. Creative Arts Poetry grantee, 1958; Award in Lit., Nat. Inst. Arts and Letters, 1971; recipient Golden Rose Award, New Eng. Poetry Club, 1973; recipient Christopher Award, 1974; Bennington Award for Outstanding Contbn. to Poetry, 1980. Mem. Pen Club, Nation Assocs. Home and office: Brook House North Pownal VT 05260

HOWES, PADDY RUDD, writer/editor; b. Coventry, Eng., May 9, 1909; came to U.S., 1925, naturalized, 1941; d. John Alexander and Mary Elizabeth (Doherty) Rudd; student Liverpool Coll., Huyton, Eng., 1920-25; Oxford U., sr. sch. certificate, 1925; student U. Akron, 1934-35, U. Cin., 1941-42, Northwestern U., 1950; m. William R. Howes, Sept. 23, 1946. With Firestone Tire & Rubber Co., Akron, Ohio, 1926-36; sec. Children's Hosp. Research Found., Cin., 1936-42; sr. editor W.B. Saunders Co., Phila., 1942-46; fgn. corre. Country Gentleman Mag., Eng., 1946-48; manuscript editor Jour. Am. Dental Assn., Chgo., 1949-50, news editor, 1950-51; staff writer Survey of Med. Edn., Chgo., 1951-53; free lance writer, editor, publs. cons., Chgo., 1953-56, Phila., 1956-72, Harwich, Mass., 1972—. Bd. dirs. Cape Cod Family and Children's Service and publicity chmn., newsletter editor, mem. accreditation com., 1975-81; corp. mem. bd. dirs. United Way of Cape Cod, 1978—; mem. Cape Cod Community Council, 1975—. Mem. Women in Communications (Chgo. chpt. pres. 1952-53 pres. Phila. chpt. 1962), Phila. Art Alliance, Asso. Country Women of World (life mem.; exec. com. 1946-48, press officer 1946). Writer-Collaborator Medical Schools in the United States at Mid-Century, 1953. Contbr. articles to mags., newspapers and profl. jours. Address: 17 Haromar Heath RFD 3 Harwich MA 02645

HOWES, RUTH HEGE, physicist; b. Montepelier, Vt., Oct. 18, 1944; d. James Landes and Ruth Mavin (Colton) Hege; student Northfield Sch. for Girls, 1960-62; B.A., Mt. Holyoke Coll., 1965; M.A., Columbia U., 1967, Ph.D., 1971; m. Robert Ingersol Howes, June 4, 1966; children—Rachel Tranquility, Prudence Nicole. Adj. instr. Fordham U. at Lincoln Center, 1970-71; vis. asst. prof. physics U. Okla., 1971-72; assoc. instr. Oklahoma City U., 1972-76; asst. prof. Ball State U., Muncie, Ind., 1976-80, assoc. prof. physics and astronomy, 1980—. Nat. Merit scholar, 1962-65; Sarah Williston scholar, 1965-66. Mem. NOW, Am. Phys. Soc., Ind. Acad. Scis., Soc. Archeol. Scis., Sigma Xi, Phi Beta Kappa. Democrat. Research in nuclear physics techniques applied to archeology problems; contbr. articles to profl. jours. Home: 1804 N Reserve St Muncie IN 47303 Office: Dept Physics Ball State U Muncie IN 47306

HOWINGTON, CAROLYN ANN, mfr.'s rep.; b. Wasco, Calif., Aug. 13, 1949; d. Calvin Verble and Pearline (Stutts) Worley; B.S. in Bus., N.E. La. State U., 1971; 1 son, Todd Eugene Howington. With Del-Tex Inc., Claremore, Okla., 1978-79, Oilfield Prodn. Equip., Kans., Okla., 1979-80; owner, pres. R & R Sales, Inc., Tulsa, 1981—. Mem. Nat. Assn. Female Execs., Okla. Minority Purchasing Council, Tulsa Theatre Drive. Republican. Presbyterian. Club: So. Hills Fitness Center. Home: 7446 S Atlanta Ave Tulsa OK 74136 Office: PO Box 7809 Tulsa OK 74105

HOWISON, JUANITA CARMACK, ret. educator, artist; b. nr. Bristol, Va.; d. Alexander Watson and Lillie (Craig) Carmack; student U. Va., summer 1939, George Washington U., 1945-46, summer 1948, Corcoran Sch. Art, 1951; B.S. in Edn., James Madison U., 1959; m. Claude Frederick Howison, May 1, 1948. Tchr., Konnarock (Va.) Sch., 1929-36, Highland View Sch., Washington County, Va., 1936-41, Central Sch., Abington, Va., 1941-42, Herndon (Va.) Elementary Sch., 1942-46, Primary Day Sch., Washington, 1946-50, Fairlington (Va.) Elementary Sch., 1950; private tutor, 1950-56; remedial reading tchr., supr. Ft. Myer Elementary Sch., 1957-59; tchr. Potomac Elementary Sch., McLean, Va., 1960-67, tchr. spl. edn. Markham Sch., Ft. Belvoir, Va., 1967-80; tchr. Haycock Elementary Sch., Falls Church, Va. Exhibited group shows Smithsonian Instn., 1952, 53, 62, Arts Club, D.C., 1966, 67, No. Va. Artists, 1961-68, U. Va., 1966-68, Reston (Va.) Gallery, 1967, others. Mem. Nat. League Am. Pen Women (nat. biennial art exhibit chmn. 1954-56, Va. pres. 1963-64, state art chmn. 1965-66, nat. librarian 1965-66, nat. research chmn. 1966-67, mem. nat. art bd., br. pres. 1978-80), NEA, Internat. Reading Assn., Greater Washington Reading Council, Arlington Council Spl. Edn., Am. Arts League Washington, McLean Art Club (pres. 1978), Art Club Washington, No. Va. Art League, Fine Arts Center Roanoke, Nat. Enamelist Guild, Delta Kappa Gamma. Presbyterian. Clubs: McLean Women's, Order Eastern Star. Home: 1512 Hardwood Ln McLean VA 22101

HOWLAND, ANN, clin. psychologist; b. Cleve., Jan. 7, 1944; d. Richard Moulton and Natalie (Fuller) H.; stepfather—William F. Merrill, III; B.A., Goucher Coll., 1965; M.A., U. Fla., 1971, Ph.D., 1973; children—Andrea Merrill and Joshua Howland Sarver. VA trainee, 1971-72; treatment dir., therapy supr. Clin. Services Community Mental Health Clinic, Nelsonville, Ohio, 1973-75; pres. Athens (Ohio) Psychology Clinic, Inc., 1975-81; pres. Ann Howland, Ph.D. and Assos., Athens, 1981—; chief of staff psychology service O'Bleness Hosp., 1977-80; cons. W.Va. Head Start, 1975-78; instr. case mgmt. for mental health technicians Ohio U., 1975; cons. Athens County Probate Ct., 1975—; mem. Masters and Johnson Inst. Vol. Peace Corps, Colombia, S.A., 1966-68; active Athens Humane Soc., Animal Protection Inst., Save the Whales, Conservation of Endangered Species, NOW. Mem. Am. Psychol. Assn., Ohio Psychol. Assn., Southeastern Ohio Psychol. Assn., Nat. Register Health Service Providers in Psychology. Club: Sawgrass (Fla.). Contbr. chpt. in book. Home and Office: Route 3 Box 163 Athens OH 45701

HOWLAND, JUANITA MAE, fire protection equipment co. ofcl.; b. Kirbyville, Mo., Sept. 7, 1929; d. Thomas Raymond and Ruth Marie (Rowley) Edwards; m. John David Howland, Mar. 24, 1949; children—Juanita Joan Howland Portier, John David, Jerri Ann. Various secretarial and office positions, 1947-72; adminstrv. asst. systems div. Edcor Safety Co., Kansas City, Mo., 1972-77; sales rep. B-H Electronics Co., Kansas City, Mo., 1977-78; pres. Able II Fire Protection Inc., Toledo, 1979—, Tosec, Ltd., Inc., 1982—. Mem. Am. Bus. Women's Assn. (chpt. v.p. 1979-80, pres. 1981-82), Nat. Assn. Women in Constrn. (chpt. v.p. 1979-80), Toledo C. of C., Sylvania C. of C., Nat. Assn. Female Execs. (network dir.). Methodist. Home: 7012 Orvieto Dr Sylvania OH 43560 Office: 709 S Bryne Rd Toledo OH 43609

HOWLETT, PHYLLIS L., athletic conf. adminstr.; b. Indianola, Iowa, Oct. 23, 1932; d. James Clarence and Mabel L. (Fisher) Hickman; B.A., Simpson Coll., 1954; m. Jerry L. Howlett, Jan. 2, 1955 (dec.); children—Timothy A., Jane A.; m. 2d, Ronlin Royer, Dec. 30, 1977. Psychometrist, Drake U., Des Moines, 1956-57, asst. to men's athletic dir., 1974-79; asst. dir. athletics U. Kans., Lawrence, 1979-82; asst. commr. Big Ten Conf., Schaumburg, Ill., 1982—; mem. NCAA Football TV Com. Chair State of Iowa Commn. Status of Women, 1976-79; pres. Vol. Bur. of Greater Des Moines, 1969-70, Arts and Recreation Council of Greater Des Moines, 1975, Iowa Children's and Family Services, 1973; nat. pres. Assn. Vol. Burs., Inc., 1972-73, service award. Recipient certs. of appreciation Des Moines C. of C., State of Iowa, Drake U. Mem. Nat. Assn. Dirs. of Collegiate Athletics, Council Collegiate Women Athletic Adminstrs., Jr. League. Republican. Office: 1111 Plaza Dr Suite 600 Schaumburg IL 60195

HOWORTH, CATHERINE TERESA, high sch. adminstr.; b. South Boston, Mass., Apr. 18, 1928; d. Joseph James and Katherine Frances (White) Sullivan; A.B. in Math., Emmanuel Coll., Boston, 1961; M.A. in Ednl. Adminstrn., Suffolk U., Boston, 1972; m. Gerald Edward Howorth, Feb. 14, 1975. Elem. tchr. St. Mary's Sch., Lawrence, Mass., 1953-54; sec., tchr. prin. St. Mary's High Sch., Lynn, Mass., 1954-65; head dept. math. Hull (Mass.) High Sch., 1965-72, asst. prin., 1972-82; instr. statistics Quincy (Mass.) Jr. Coll., 1978-81; asst. prin. Notre Dame Acad., Hingham, Mass., 1982—; math. cons. Gate of Heaven Sch., South Boston, 1979-80. Mem. Boston province Notre Dame Bd. Edn., Ipswich province Notre Dame Research and Devel. Bd. Mem. Hull Tchrs. Assn. (Tchr. of Yr. 1969), Mass. Tchrs. Assn., NEA, Plymouth County Edn. Assn., Mass. Assn. Secondary Sch. Prins., Nat. Assn. Secondary Sch. Prins., Mass. Assn. Supervision and Curriculum Devel., South Shore Asst. Prins. Assn., Delta Kappa Gamma. Roman Catholic. Home: 16 Surrey Ln Sandwich MA 02563 Office: 1073 Main St Hingham MA 02043

HOWORTH, LUCY (SOMERVILLE), lawyer, internat. trade exec.; b. Greenville, Miss., July 1, 1895; d. Robert and Nellie (Nugent) Somerville; A.B., Randolph-Macon Woman's Coll., 1916; postgrad. Columbia U., 1918; J.D. summa cum laude, U. Miss., 1922; m. Joseph Marion Howorth, Feb. 16, 1928. Asst. in psychology Randolph-Macon Woman's Coll., 1916-17; gauge insp. Allied Bur. Air Prodn., N.Y.C., 1918; indsl. research nat. bd. YWCA, 1919-20; admitted to Miss. bar, 1922; gen. practice Howorth & Howorth, Cleveland, Greenville, Jackson, Miss., 1922-34; U.S. commd. So. Jud. Dist. Miss., 1927-31; assoc. mem. Bd. Vet. Appeals, Washington, 1934-43; legis. atty. VA, 1943-49, v.p., dir. VA Employees Credit Union, 1937-49; assoc. gen. counsel War Claims Commn., 1949-52, dep. gen. counsel, 1952-53, gen. counsel, 1953-54; partner James Somerville & Assocs., overseas trade and devel., 1954-56; pvt. law practice, Cleveland, 1958—; atty. Commn. on Govt. Security, 1956-58; chmn. Miss. State Bd. Law Examiners, 1924-28; treas. com. for econ. survey, 1928-30; mem. Research Commn. Miss., 1930-34; mem. com. on fed. employment policies and practices Pres.'s Commn. on Status of Women, 1962-63; initiator oral history program Delta State U., 1973. Mem. Ho. of Reps., Miss. Legislature, Hinds County, 1932-36, chmn. com. public lands; keynote speaker White House Conf. on Women in Post-war Policy Making, 1944; at conf. on opening 81st Congress; mem. nat. bd. cons. Women's Archives, Radcliffe Coll.; mem. lay adv. com. study profl. nursing Carnegie Corp. N.Y., 1947-48; pres., trustee Monteagle Sunday Sch. Assembly, 1963—; dir. Monteagle Assembly Endowment Fund. Recipient Nellie Nugent Somerville award, 1975; Alumnae Achievement award Randolph Macon Woman's Coll., 1981. Mem. AAUW (nat. bd. dirs.; 2d. v.p., 1951-55, fellowship named in her honor 1973), Fed. Bar Assn., Nat. Assn. Women Lawyers, Am. Soc. Internat. Law (exec. council 1951-54), Am. Bar Assn., DAR, Daus. Am. Colonists, Am. Legion Aux. (past sec. Miss. dept.), Assembly Women's Orgns. for Nat. Security (chmn. 1951-52), Nat. Fedn. Bus. and Profl. Women's (nat. bd. dirs.; rep. Internat. Fedn., Trondheim, Norway, 1939; chmn. internat. conf., N.Y.C., 1946), Miss. Hist. Soc. (dir. 1982-85), Phi Beta Kappa, Pi Gamma Mu, Phi Delta Delta, Alpha Omicron Pi, Delta Kappa Gamma (hon.), Omicron Delta Kappa (hon.). Democrat (del. nat. conv., 1932). Methodist. Clubs: Woman's Nat. Democratic; Soroptimist (Washington). Editor: (with W.M. Cash) Dear Nellie, the Civil War Letters of William L. Nugent, 1977; editor Fed. Bar Assn. News, 1944; assoc. editor Fed. Bar Assn. Jour., 1943-44. Contbr. articles to profl. jours. Address: 515 S Victoria Ave Cleveland MS 38732

HOXIE, SUE ANN, realtor; b. Waterloo, Iowa, Nov. 6, 1947; d. Willard Clair and Opal Marie (Stover) Buzzard; A.A., Sacramento City Coll., 1967; B.S. in Social Sci., Calif. State Poly. U., 1969; postgrad. Sacramento State U., 1969-71; m. Lowell E. Hoxie, May 29, 1976; children— Scott Barrett, Christopher Garrett. Tng. mgr. Arcata Communications, San Francisco, 1971-73; market research analyst Litton BTS, Sunnyvale, Calif., 1973-75; advt. mgr., sales mgr. western region Commex Corp., Sunnyvale, 1975-77; real estate broker, co-owner Buyers' Agt. Saratoga, Calif., 1977-79; corp. sec. Real Estate Advs., Saratoga. Mem. Nat., Calif. assns. realtors, Los Gatos Saratoga Bd. Realtors, San Jose Real Estate Bd. Address: 19502 Via Monte Dr Saratoga CA 95070

HOXSEY, BETTY J., state legislator; ed. public schs.; married; 4 children. Mem. Ill. Ho. of Reps., 1976—, mem. agr., cities and villages and appropriations coms., cost reimbursement public aid com. Mem. Gov.'s Commn. Mandate Programs, Commn. on Orgn. Gen. Assembly, Agrl.-Econ. Fair Commns., Legis. Com. on Ill. Corrections Industries, Agrl. Export Adv. Com., Legis. Adv. Commn., Ill. Law Enforcement Com. Office: Ill Ho of Reps State Capitol Springfield IL 62706 *

HOYLAND, JANET LOUISE, govt. ofcl.; b. Kansas City, Mo., July 21, 1940; d. Robert J. and Dora Louise (Worley) H.; B.A., Carleton Coll., 1962; postgrad. in music (Mu Phi Epsilon scholar 1966), U. Mo. at Kansas City, 1964-67; M.L.A., So. Meth. U., 1979. Policy writer Lynn Ins. Co., Kansas City, 1963-64; music librarian U. Mo. at Kansas City, 1966-68; benefit authorizer Social Security Adminstrn., Kansas City, Mo., 1969-75, tech. specialist, 1976-79, claims authorizer, 1980—; piano tchr. Leta Wallace Piano Studio, Kansas City, 1963, 68; piano accompanist Barn Players, Overland Park, Kans., 1972-75, Off Broadway Dinner Playhouse, Inc., Kansas City, 1973. Co-chmn. Project Equality work area, 1971; work area chmn. on ecumenism Council on Ministries, 1969-70; sec. fair housing action com. Council on Religion and Race, Kansas City, 1968; chmn. adminstrv. bd. Kairos United Meth. Ch., 1982; active ward and precinct work Democratic Com. for County Progress, 1968. Mem. Women's Div. Kansas City Philharmonic, Friends of Art Kansas City, Fellowship House Assn. Kansas City, Internat. Platform Assn., Kansas City Mus. Club (chmn. composition dept. 1967-68), Mu Phi Epsilon (v.p. Kansas City 1968, sec. 1971, pres. 1975-76), Pi Kappa Lambda. Home: 4322 Rockhill Rd Kansas City MO 64110

HOYLE, KAREN NELSON, univ. librarian; b. Boston, Jan. 8, 1937; d. Arthur Frederick and Ruth Paula (Rasmussen) Nelson; B.A., St. Olaf Coll., 1958; M.L.S., U. Calif., Berkeley, 1964; M.A., U. Minn., 1971, Ph.D. in Library Sci., 1975; m. Robert John Hoyle, Apr. 12, 1975; children—Rebecca Anne, Natalie Ruth. Asst. librarian, tchr. English John Marshall Sr. High Sch., Rochester, Minn., 1961-63; librarian Am. High Sch., Augsburg, Ger., 1964-65; tchr. children's lit. U. Sask., Regina, Can., Summers 1966, 67; librarian Anoka-Hennepin Sch. Dist., Minn., 1966-67; assoc. prof. U. Minn., 1980—, librarian, curator Children's Literature Research Collections, 1967—; tchr. storytelling St. Cloud State U., Summer 1980. George C. Marshall fellow, 1969, 72; Children's Literature Assn. fellow, 1981. Mem. Am. Library Assn., Internat. Research Soc. for Children's Lit., Danish-Am. Heritage Soc., Soc. Advancement Scandinavian Studies, Children's Literature Assn. Contbr. articles to profl. jours. Office: CLRC 109 Walter Library University of Minnesota Minneapolis MN 55455

HOYT, ANNE KELLEY, librarian; b. Muskogee, Okla., Mar. 31, 1919; d. Frank and Helen (Pyle) Kelley; B.A., U. Ark., 1942, M.Ed., 1962; M.S. in Library Sci., La. State U., 1964; m. Don L. Hoyt, June 8, 1945. Tchr., high sch., Winslow, Ark., 1942; br. librarian Muskogee (Okla.) Pub. Library, 1942-43; librarian Bacone (Okla.) Coll., 1943-45, Washington County Library, Fayetteville, Ark., 1946-47, Okla. State Tech. Coll., Okmulgee, 1948-50, jr. high sch., Springdale, Ark., 1957-64; librarian, Ednl. Div. Library, N.Mex. State U., University Park, 1965-66; asst. librarian, instr. library sci. Northeastern Okla. State U., Tahlequah, 1966-69; asst. prof. library sci. Okla. State U., Stillwater, 1969-75, assoc. prof., 1975—, dir. curriculum materials lab., 1974—. Mem. ALA, Southwest Library Assn., Okla. Library Assn. (sec. 1968-69, chmn. library edn. div. 1974, 79), Delta Gamma. Democrat. Episcopalian. Compiler: Bibliography of the Cherokees, 1969, Melt Down of the Melting Pot: Materials for Multicultural Education, 1980. Home: 625 S Monroe St Stillwater OK 74074 Office: Library Okla State U Stillwater OK 74078

HOYT, PATTY JO, hosp. exec.; b. St. Joseph, Mo., Oct. 28, 1945; d. George William and Julia Irene May (Walkup) McClain; B.S. in Art, N.W. Mo. State Coll., 1967; cert. med. record adminstrn. (Ga. State scholar 1971-72), Emory U. Hosp., Atlanta, 1972; m. Stephen Max Hoyt, Feb. 5, 1977; 1 dau., Elizabeth Patricia. Caseworker, Buchanan County Welfare Office, St. Joseph, 1968-70; tchr. Thomas County Schs., Thomasville, Ga., 1970-71; dir. records adminstrn. City-County Hosp., La Grange, Ga., 1972-75, W. Central Ga. Regional Hosp., Columbus, 1975, Doctors Hosp., Columbus, 1975—; cons. in field. Mem. Am. Med. Record Assn., Ga. Med. Record Assn. Methodist. Home: 4 Cayenne Ct Columbus GA 31904 Office: 616 19th St Columbus GA 31993

HOYT, SUSAN SILODOR, retail store exec.; b. Phila., Mar. 12, 1944; d. Sidney and Elizabeth Knox (Collins) Silodor; B.A., Randolph Macon Woman's Coll., Lynchburg, Va., 1965; M.A.T. (NDEA fellow), Washington U., St. Louis, 1967; m. H. Phillips Hoyt, Jr., Sept. 10, 1966. Tchr., University City (Mo.) Schs., 1967; tng. dir. Famous-Barr, St. Louis, 1969-75, dir. exec. devel., 1975-77; v.p., dir. personnel The Emporium, div. Carter Hawley Hale, San Francisco, 1977-80, v.p. personnel Emporium-Capwell, 1980—. Mem. Nat. Retail Mchts. Assn., Am. Mgmt. Assn., Am. Soc. Tng. and Devel., Phi Beta Kappa. Home: 2525 Larkin St San Francisco CA 94109 Office: The Emporium 835 Market St San Francisco CA 94103

HOYT-FAULKENBURG, DOROTHY MARIE, career counselor; b. Greeley, Colo., Sept. 16, 1943; d. Edwin G. and Edna W. (Borchardt) Hoyt; B.S., U. No. Colo., Greeley, 1976; m. Samuel George Faulkenburg, Feb. 24, 1963; children—Christina Rose, Michelle Denise. Personnel mgr. Met. State Bank, Commerce City, Colo., 1970-75; ops. mgr. Jefferson Bank and Trust Co., Lakewood, Colo., 1976-77; pres. Hoyt-Faulkenburg and Assos., Arvada, Colo., 1978—. Area rep. Youth for Understanding Fgn. Exchange Program, 1978-80; bd. dirs., mem. devel. com. KHUM Community Radio Sta., 1980; mem. Arvada adv. council Jefferson County Mental Health, 1977-78; chmn. fund raising com. Homemakers for ERA, 1976; vol. probation counselor Pathways, 1975-77; active local Democratic Party. Mem. Nat. Assn. Female Execs., Rocky Mountain Career Planning Assn., Arvada Bus. and Profl. Women's Assn. Mem. Unity Ch. Home: 9105 Oberon Rd Apt 5 Arvada CO 80004 Office: 7850 Vance Dr Suite 220 Arvada CO 80003

HREHA, ALYCE MARY, botanist; b. Trenton, N.J., Apr. 15, 1948; d. George Joseph and Alyce Catherine (Bertothy) H.; B.A. in Biology, Trenton State Coll., 1970; M.S. in Botany, Brigham Young U., Provo, Utah, 1978. Research asst. Trenton State Coll., 1968-70; high sch. sci. tchr., Burlington, N.J., 1970-71; teaching asst. Brigham Young U., 1976-77; research technician U.S. Forest Service, 1977-78; sr. botanist Meiiji Resource Cons., Layton, Utah, 1978—; vol. State Arboretum Utah, 1981-82. mem. speakers bur. Utah Women's Math.-Sci. Network, 1981-82. Mem. Am. Bot. Soc., Southwestern Assn. Naturalists, Calif. Native Plant Soc., Colo. Native Plant Soc., Utah Native Plant Soc. Roman Catholic. Home: 625 S Main St Bountiful UT 84010 Office: 38 N Main St Layton UT 84041

HU, CHI YU, educator; b. Szchwan, China, Feb. 12, 1933; d. T.C. and P.S. (Yang) Hu; came to U.S., 1956, naturalized, 1974; children—Marcia, Mark, Albert, Han Chin. Asst. prof. physics Calif. State U. at Long Beach, 1963-68, asso. prof., 1968-72, prof., 1972—. NSF grantee; Long Beach State U. Found. summer grantee. Mem. Am. Phys. Soc., United Profs. Calif. Contbr. articles to profl. jours. Office: Dept Physics Calif State U Long Beach CA 90840

HUBBARD, DELORES LABELLE, telecommunication technician; b. Ottawa, Kans., Nov. 10, 1938; d. Francis Henry and Alice Ruby (Alcorn) H. Daugherty, B.A. with honors in Biology, U. Kans., 1973; postgrad. (NIH trainee, USPHS grantee) in radiation biophysics, 1973-75. Chief nuclear med. tech., instr. dept. radiology Kans. U. Med. Center, Kansas City, 1960-67; instr., tech. program coordinator Nuclear Medicine Inst., Cleve., 1967-70; research asst. U. Kans., Lawrence, 1970-71, 73; nuclear medicine technician Meml. Hosp., Topeka, 1974-75, VA Center, Leavenworth, Kans., 1975-77; telecommunication technician ARCO Pipeline Co., Independence, Kans., 1979—; mem. guest faculty Cuyahoga Community Coll., Cleve., 1969-70; cons., lectr. nuclear medicine. Mem. Am. Registry Radiologic Technologists, Soc. Nuclear Medicine (asso.), Am. Soc. Clin. Pathologists. Home: 1106 N 10th St Independence KS 67301 Office: ARCO Place Independence KS 67301

HUBBARD, GLORIA KENDRICK, mfg. co. exec., advt. co. exec.; b. Folkston, Ga., Sept. 24, 1939; d. Grover Lee and Mildred Elizabeth (Wildes) Kendrick; A.B., Jacksonville U., 1959; B.S., Fla. State U., 1961; m. Samuel Walter Hubbard, Jr., June 10, 1967 (dec. 1976); children—Samuel Walter, Whitney Alexander. Vice-pres., Hubbard Co., Atlanta, 1977—; pres. J & J Advt., Inc., Atlanta, 1980—. Republican. Methodist. Office: 7N319A 250 Spring St Atlanta GA 30303

HUBBARD, ISABEL JANICE, educator; b. LaCrosse, Wis., June 18, 1935; d. Frank Peter August and Janice May (Grutzmacher) Erichsen; B.S. with honors, U. Wis., Madison, 1957, M.S., 1979, postgrad., 1980; m. Allan Paterson, Apr. 4, 1959; children—Jane Isabel, John Allan. Tchr., Kenosha (Wis.) Bd. Edn., 1957-60; tchr., supr. Madison (Wis.) Bd. Edn., 1968—; pvt. piano and vocal coach, 1950—; choir dir. St. Mary's Lutheran Ch., Kenosha, 1959-61. Program chair YWCA, 1961-65; chmn. UNICEF, 1960, Coop. Nursery Sch., 1960; info. chmn. Am. Cancer Soc., Dane County, 1960-68; active Methodist Women's Soc., United Ch. Women, Madison Civic Assn., Opera Buffs, Wis. Exec. Mansion Guides, Cherokee Homeowners Assn. Recipient Carol award Madison Jaycette Club, 1966, 3d grand prize Wis. State Jour. Cookbook, 1971. Mem. Am. Ednl. Research Assn., NEA, Wis. Edn. Assn., Madison Tchrs., Inc., Lafollette Area Lang. Arts Cadre, U. Wis. Alumni Assn. (life), Sigma Alpha Iota (Sword of Honor), Chi Omega (dir., Alumni dir.), Phi Lambda Theta, Pi Kappa Delta. Methodist. Clubs: Cherokee Country, Jr. Golf (dir. 1974-75), Eastern Star, Elks Aux. Author: Reading Techniques Using the Newspapers, Magazines, 1975; Spell It Again Sam, 1978; Hidden Curriculum, 1979; contbr. to Kenosha Kindergarten Teacher's Handbook, 1958. Home: 5321 Namekagon Ln Cherokee Park Madison WI 53704 Office: 2421 E Johnson St Madison WI 53704

HUBBARD, KRISTIN KUHNS, press officer, public relations co. exec.; b. Dayton, Ohio, July 15, 1946; d. James Edward and Faith (Colgan) Kuhns; B.A., Sweet Briar Coll., 1968. Editor, Harcourt Brace, N.Y.C., 1969-70; editor pub. relations dept. C.I.T. Fin. Corp., N.Y.C., 1970-73; news reporter TV Channel 13, N.Y.C., 1973-74; press officer Champion Internat.-U.S. Plywood, 1975-76; writer House Beautiful mag., 1976-77; press officer Govt. of P.R., N.Y.C., 1977—, also cons.; pres. Kristin Hubbard Public Relations, 1980—. Active Jr. League, Environ. Action Coalition. Democrat. Episcopalian. Contbr. articles to Town and Country, Ingenue, Christian Sci. Monitor, House Beautiful, Dayton Jour. Herald. Club: City of N.Y. Home: 517 E 82d St New York NY 10028

HUBBARD, MARGARET ELEANOR, broadcasting co. exec.; b. New Glasgow, N.S., Can., Nov. 8, 1931; d. Percil Cameron and Harriet Ellen (Wilson) Munsie; student R.I. Sch. Broadcasting, 1978, Providence Coll., 1976, 78; m. Lincoln W. Hubbard, Apr. 13, 1957; children—Cameron M., Harriet K. With Brown & Sharpe Co., Providence, 1951-55, Auto Mut. Ins. Co., Providence, 1955-60; with Edgewood Electronics Co., Warwick, R.I., 1960-76; news dir., dir. public affairs Sta. WARV, Warwick, 1976—. Deacon, 1st Presbyterian Ch., Providence, 1969—; mem. communications dept. R.I. State Council Chs., 1973—; mem. exec. bd. R.I. Assn. Evang. Chs. 3d class engr., FCC. Mem. R.I. Press Club, R.I. Advt. Club. Club: Rebekah (past noble grand). Home: 52 Park View Ave Warwick RI 02888 Office: 19 Luther Ave Warwick RI 02886

HUBBARD, MARYJOANNE CHRISTINE, psychologist; b. Benton Harbor, Mich., Jan. 12, 1939; d. Harvey Howard and Vivian (Wolford) Halsey; B.A., Calif. State U., Fullerton, 1970, M.S., 1976; Ph.D., U.S. Internat. U., San Diego, 1981; children—Kim Rene, Craig Martin, Nicole Elizabeth. Counselor, Orange County Juvenile System, 1967-69; psychometrist San Diego State U., 1970-71; grad. asst. dept. psychology Calif. State U., Fullerton, 1974-75, lectr., 1976-78; intern Olive-Vista Psychiat. Hosp., Pomona, Calif., 1975, Met. State Hosp., Norwalk, Calif., 1975-76; marriage, family and child counselor, Fullerton, Calif., 1976—; juvenile diversion psychologist Santa Ana (Calif.) Police Dept., 1976-80, police psychologist, 1980—; psychol. asst. Town and Country Psychol. Services, Orange, Calif., 1981—; instr. Orange County Sheriffs Acad., 1980—. Bd. dirs. Mariposa Women's Center, 1981—, COPES, 1979. Mem. Acad. Criminal Justice Scis., Soc. Police and Criminal Psychology, Calif. Assn. Marriage and Family Counselors, Calif. Psychol. Assn., Am. Psychol. Assn., Psi Chi. Contbr. articles to profl. jours. Office: Santa Ana Police Dept 24 Civic Center Plaza Santa Ana CA 92701

HUBBARD, RUTH, biologist, educator; b. Vienna, Austria, Mar. 3, 1924; d. Richard and Helene (Ehrlich) Hoffman; B.A., Radcliffe Coll., 1944, M.A., 1941, Ph.D., 1950; m. George Wald, June 11, 1958; children—Elijah, Deborah Hanna. Technician Tenn. Pub. Health Service, Chattanooga, 1945-46; USPHS fellow Univ. Coll. Hosp. Med. Sch., London, Eng., 1948-49; research fellow Harvard U., Cambridge, Mass., 1951-58, research assoc., 1958-73, lectr., 1969-73, prof. biology, 1974—; vis. prof. M.I.T., Cambridge, 1971. Active Women's Health Movement, Nat. Women's Health Network, Sci. for People, Cambridge Civic Assn., ACLU. Guggenheim fellow, 1952-53; recipient Paul Karrer medal Swiss Chem. Soc., 1967. Mem. AAAS, Soc. Biol. Chemists, Nat. Women's Studies Assn. Contbr. articles to profl. jours. Home: 21 Lakeview Ave Cambridge MA 02138 Office: 16 Divinity Ave Cambridge MA 02138

HUBBARD, SUSAN DEE, nurse; b. Hereford, Tex., Dec. 2, 1954; d. John Robert and Joyce Marie (Lewis) Hickman; B.S.N., West Tex. State U., 1978; m. Charles Bruce Hubbard, Aug. 11, 1978; children—Christopher Todd, Toby Brannon. Microbiology lab. instr. West Tex. State U., Canyon, 1975-76; clin. asst. and R.N., Northwest Tex. Hosp., Amarillo, 1976-78; R.N., Midland (Tex.) Meml. Hosp., 1978-79; service coordinator, R.N., Upjohn Healthcare Services, Midland, 1979-80, service dir., 1980-81; surg. nurse St. Anthony's Hosp., Amarillo, Tex., 1981—. Vol., Jr. Baseball Assn. Midland, 1979-80, PTA, 1978-82, Midland Soccer Assn., 1978-79. Named Miss Teenage Hereford, 1972, Miss Hereford, 1974; recipient vocal awards. Mem. Critical Care Nurses Assn., Tex. Nurses Assn., Sigma Theta Tau, Tri Beta. Republican. Baptist. Home: 3704 Montague Amarillo TX 79110 Office: St Anthony's Hosp Amarillo TX 79102

HUBER, ANN KATHLEEN, educator; b. Ann Arbor, Mich., May 30, 1948; d. Robert Daniel and Jean Anna (Murray) H.; B.E., Seattle U., 1970; postgrad. U. Wash., summers 1971-74, also U. San Francisco. Tchr., Willapa Valley Sch. Dist., Wash., from 1970; tchr., Forestville, Calif., now vice prin. Bd. dirs. Caring Connection. Mem. Forestville PTA, Sonoma County Sch. Adminstrs. Assn., Assn. Sch. Adminstrs. Calif., Delta Kappa Gamma. Republican. Office: 6321 Hwy 116 Forestville CA 95436 *

HUBER, BEVERLY JEAN, human services systems specialist; b. Minot, N.D., Mar. 30, 1932; d. Fred William and Bernice Lorrayne (Cooley) Buchwitz; B.S. in Edn. cum laude, Minot State Coll., 1951; B.M. in Piano, Am. Conservatory Music, Chgo., 1953; M.S.W., U. Calif., Berkeley, 1967; diploma Computer Learning Center, Los Angeles, 1981. Pvt. music tchr., pianist, accompanist, N.D. and Chgo., 1947-58; tchr. high sch. music, English and sci., N.D. and Calif., 1951-52, 59-63; med. caseworker Los Angeles County Bur. Med. Social Service, 1963-65, clin. social worker, summer 1966, 67-72; dir. social service St. Vincent Med. Center, Los Angeles, 1972-80; programmer Tower, Perrins, Forster & Crosby, Los Angeles, 1982—; field work supr. UCLA Grad. Sch. Social Work, 1979-80. VA grad. fellow in psychiat. social work, 1966-67; NSF summer fellow in botany and chemistry, 1961; lic. clin. social worker Calif. Acad. Certified Social Workers. Mem. Soc. Clin. Social Workers, Nat. Assn. Social Workers, Town Hall. Roman Catholic. Home: 750 E Carson St Space 25 Carson CA 90745 Office: 1925 Century Park E Los Angeles CA 90067

HUBER, JOAN ALTHAUS, sociologist; b. Bluffton, Ohio, Oct. 17, 1925; d. Lawrence and Hallie (Althaus) H.; B.A., Pa. State U., 1945; M.A., Western Mich. U., 1963; Ph.D., Mich. State U., 1967; m. William Form, Feb. 2, 1971; children—Nancy Rytina. Steven Rytina. Asst. vis. prof., asst. prof. U. Notre Dame (Ind.), 1969-71; asst. prof. U. Ill., Urbana-Champaign, 1971-73, assoc. prof., 1973-78, prof., 1978—, head dept. sociology, 1980—. NSF research grantee, 1978-81. Mem. Am. Sociol. Assn. (council 1975-78, v.p. 1980-83), Population Assn. Am. Author: (with W. Form) Income and Ideology, 1973; (with Paul Chalfant) Sociology of American Poverty, 1974; editor: Changing Women in a Changing Society, 1973. Office: 702 S Wright St 326LH Urbana IL 61801

HUBER, JOAN MACMONNIES, frozen food co. exec.; b. N.Y.C., Dec. 15, 1927; d. Wallace and Marguerite Adele (Searing) MacMonnies; B.S. in Chemistry, Northwestern U., 1949; student specialized courses; m. Don Lawrence Huber, June 23, 1951. Research chemist, then research supr. Continental Baking Co., Jamaica, N.Y., 1949-57; co-owner, asst. mgr. Sta. KALE, Richland, Wash., 1957-59; with Southland Frozen Foods Co., Gt. Neck, N.Y., 1959—, mktg. mgr., 1969-72, v.p. distbn. and corp. planning, 1972—. Bd. overseers Adelphi U. Cert. fin. planner. Mem. Inst. Food Technologists, Am. Chem. Soc., Am. Mgmt. Assn., Internat. Assn. Fin. Planners, Am. Frozen Food Inst. Distbn. Council (chmn. council 1979-80, chmn. warehousing com. 1977-78, past chmn. steering com.). Home: 24 Rolling Dr Brookville NY 11545 Office: 1 Linden Pl Great Neck NY 11021

HUBER, JOAN MARIE, nurse, naval officer; b. Boston, Sept. 15, 1951; d. Fred Robert and Catherine Mary (Donovan) Huber; B.S. in Nursing, Villanova U., 1973; M.S. in Nursing, U. Calif., San Francisco, 1982. Commd. in USN, 1971, advanced through grades to lt. comdr., 1980; staff nurse surg. ICU, Naval Regional Med. Center, Phila., 1973-76; head nurse critical care areas Naval Submarine Med. Center, Groton, Conn., 1976-78; head nurse surg. ICU, Naval Regional Med. Center, Okinawa, Japan, 1978-80; head nurse surg. unit Naval Regional Med. Center, Gt. Lakes, Ill., 1982—. Decorated Navy Commendation medal, Nat. Def. medal. Mem. Am. Assn. Critical Care Nurses, Assn. Mil. Surgeons U.S., Nat. League Nursing, Am. Nurses Assn., Am. Assn. Nephrology Nurses and Technicians, Bus. and Profl. Womens Club (named Groton Young Career Woman of Yr. 1978), Sigma Theta Tau. Roman Catholic. Home: 1431 Henry Pl Waukegan IL 60085 Office: Nursing Service Naval Regional Med Center Great Lakes IL 60088

HUBER, RITA NORMA, civic worker; b. Cin., July 16, 1931; d. Andrew Elwood and Mary Gertrude (Hille) Stewart; student Cin. Coll. Conservatory Music, 1949-50, Berlitz Sch., Cin., 1951-52; m. Justin G. Huber, July 17, 1954; children—Monica Ann, Sarah Marie, Rachel Miriam Tchr. Russian lang. for officers' wives Ft. Sill, Okla., 1955-56; bd. dirs. United Community Services, Cedar Rapids, Iowa, 1969; founder, chairperson Linn County Consumers League, 1969-70; founder, public relations dir. Cedar Rapids Rape Crisis Services, 1974—; chairperson Linn County Democratic Womens Club, 1966-67, Linn County Com., Eugene McCarthy for Pres., 1967-68; campaign mgr. Delores Cortez for Iowa Legislature, 1968, Jan V. Johnson for Iowa Legislature, 1970, Stanley Ginsberg for county supr. Linn County, 1974, E.L. Colton for Cedar Rapids pub. safety commr., 1977; chairperson Linn County Dem. Central Com., 1976-77; state coordinator Jerry Brown for Pres., 1976; chairperson Pat Kane for Linn County Recorder, 1982; mem. Iowa and Nat. Women's Polit. Caucus; chmn. Linn County Bd. Health; instr. parliamentary procedures Cedar Rapids Women's Community Leadership Inst., 1975-77; lectr. local colls. and service orgns.; tchr. conversational Russian, Pierce Elementary Sch., Cedar Rapids, 1976; instr. Russian, Community Edn. div. Kirkwood Community Coll. Roman Catholic (extraordinary minister of Eucharist). Composer: She is Risen, 1973. Home: 2050 Glass Rd NE Cedar Rapids IA 52402

HUBERT, THERESA AILENE, social worker; b. Brunswick, Maine, Sept. 7, 1930; d. Alfred W. and Gladys A. (Hart) Mackay; B.A., Keuka Coll., 1952; M.S.W., Barry Coll., 1977; children—Nancy, Lisa, James, Robert, Jeanne. Grad. asst. U. Miami, 1953, 54; supr. pregnancy counseling and adoption Cath. Service Bur., Ft. Lauderdale, Fla., 1977-79; mediator, counselor, family conciliation unit 17th Jud. Circuit Ct. of Fla., Ft. Lauderdale, 1979—; adj. prof. Ft. Lauderdale Coll. Bd. dirs. Cath. Service Bur., 1959-63, 80—; bd. dirs., past mem. budget com. United Way. Mem. Nat. Assn. Social Workers (exec. com.), Assn. Family Conciliation Courts. Democrat. Roman Catholic. Home: 1110 SE 5 Ct Fort Lauderdale FL 33301 Office: Family Conciliation Unit 305 S Andrews Ave Fort Lauderdale FL 33301

HUCKABONE, ELIZABETH FRIED, real estate mgmt. exec.; b. Buffalo, June 13, 1947; d. Martin B. and Isabel (Peek) Fried; A.B., SUNY, Coll. at Buffalo, 1979; postgrad. SUNY, Buffalo 1979-81; m. Darrell A. Huckabone, July 1, 1981. Mgr., Belmont Mgmt. Co., Inc., Buffalo, 1976—; pres. Belmont Shelter Corp., Buffalo, 1977—; partner Belmont Housing Assos., Buffalo, 1981—. Registered apt. mgr. Mem. Nat. Leased Housing Assn. (dir., asst. sec.), Niagara Frontier Bldrs. Assn. (chmn. apt. council edn. com., dir.). Office: 661 Delaware Ave Buffalo NY 14202

HUCKEBY, KAREN MARIE, graphic arts exec.; b. San Diego, June 4, 1957; d. Floyd Riley and Georgette Laura (Wegimont) H.; student Coll. of Alameda, 1976; student 3-M dealer tng. program, St. Paul, 1975. Staff Huck's Press Service, Inc., Emeryville, Calif., 1968—, v.p., 1975—.

Mem. East Bay Club of Printing House Craftsman (treas. 1977-78), San Francisco Mus. Soc. Home: 509 Civic Center Richmond CA 94804 Office: 1311A 63d St Emeryville CA 94608

HUCKENPAHLER, VICTORIA, dance historian, educator; b. Washington, Oct. 7, 1945; d. Charles August and Lisa (Naefe) Cerami; student George Washington U., 1963-64; m. James G. Huckenpahler, Sept. 12, 1964; 1 son, Bernard James, Jr. Tchr., Nat. Ballet Acad. Sch., Washington, 1968-72; lectr. Georgetown U., Washington, 1972—, Smithsonian Instn., 1974—; curator exhbn. America Dancing Onstage, Library of Congress, 1980; mem. faculty Grad. Sch. Arts & Scis., George Washington U., 1981—; bd. dirs. Modern Dance Council Washington, 1973—. Mem. Dance Critics Assn., Am. Dance Guild. Episcopalian. Author: (cassette tape series) History of Ballet, 1974; Ballerina (biography of Violette Verdy), 1978; contbr. articles to profl. mags. Home: 2122 California St NW Washington DC 20008 Office: Georgetown U 38th and Prospect Sts Washington DC 20007

HUCKSTADT, ALICIA ANNETTA, nurse; b. Garden City, Kans., Dec. 30, 1949; d. Allen Gilbert and Emma Catherine (Arends) Cole; B.S. in Nursing, Wichita (Kans.) State U., 1975, M.Nursing, 1978; Ph.D. in Edn., Kans. State U., Manhattan, 1981; m. Loren D. Huckstadt, Jan. 30, 1970. Staff nurse surg. ICU, St. Francis Hosp., Wichita, 1975-76; project coordinator, instr. alcohol edn. and tng. Wichita State U., 1975-76, instr. nursing, 1976-81, asst. prof., coordinator continuing edn., 1981-82; asst. Prof., 1981—; cons., speaker in field. Mem. Am. Nurses Assn., Kans. Nurses Assn., Task Force Continuing Edn. Nurses, Sigma Theta Tau (chpt. pres. 1982—), Phi Kappa Phi. Roman Catholic. Author articles in field. Office: Dept Nursing Box 41 Wichita State U Wichita KS 67208

HUDDLES, LINDA SUE, psychotherapist; b. Balt., July 5, 1939; d. Louis Cyrus and Beatrice (Freedman) Schwartz; B.S. summa cum laude, U. Md., 1962; M.S., Loyola Coll., Balt., 1980; m. Gary Huddles, Dec. 16, 1961; children—John David, Kirk. Jr. exec. trainee Williams & Wilkens Med. Pubs., Balt., 1958-59; elem. tchr., Balt., 1962-63; vol. worker Sinai Hosp., Balt., 1970-71, Asso. Jewish Charities, Balt., 1970-75; counselor Planned Parenthood of Md., Balt., 1977-79; psychologist Northwestern Community Mental Health Center, Randallstown, Md., 1981—; pvt. practice psychotherapy, Towson, Md., 1981—. Former mem. Balt. County Arts Council; former chmn. div. Asso. Jewish Charities, award for service. Mem. Am. Psychol. Assn., Md. Psychol. Assn., Am. Personnel and Guidance Assn., Phi Kappa Phi, Kappa Delta Pi. Democrat. Jewish. Oil painter, works exhibited Balt. area, 1976-77. Home: 7 Swanhill Dr Baltimore MD 21208 Office: 104 W Pennsylvania Ave Towson MD 21204

HUDDLESTON, EMMA JEAN, ednl. adminstr.; b. Knoxville, Tenn., Dec. 2, 1931; d. Robert Lewis and Bertie Annabell (Scoggins) Leek; B.S. in Edn., U. Tenn., 1954, M.S. in Guidance, 1965; postgrad., 1966-75; m. William Newman Huddleston, Apr. 10, 1965. Tchr., guidance counselor Christenberry Jr. High Sch., Knoxville, 1954-60, Whittle Springs Jr. High Sch., Knoxville, 1960-65, Tyson Jr. High Sch., Knoxville, 1969-71; librarian Whitwell (Tenn.) High Sch., 1965-69; guidance counselor Gresham Jr. High Sch., Knoxville, 1971-76; prin. Tyson Middle Sch., Knoxville, 1976—. Mem. Polit. Action Com. for Edn., 1974—. Named Citizen of the Yr., Christenberry Jr. High Sch., 1964. Mem. Knoxville Edn. Assn., Tenn. Edn. Assn., NEA, AAUW (pres. Knoxville br. 1978-80, corr. sec. Tenn. div. 1981-83), Delta Kappa Gamma, (Zeta Chapter Pres., 1964-65, 70-72), Phi Delta Kappa, Pi Lambda Theta, Delta Zeta. Democrat. Episcopalian. Home: 3401 Fountain Park Blvd Knoxville TN 37917 Office: 2607 Kingston Pike Knoxville TN 37919

HUDGENS, ANNA FAYE, social worker; b. Cleburne, Tex., Nov. 29, 1932; d. Jimmie Powell and Ethel Mae Hudgens; B.A., N. Tex. State U., 1963; M.S.W. (Tex. Dept. Human Resources fellow), La. State U., 1967. Regional tng. specialist Tex. Dept. Human Resources, Ft. Worth, 1968-71, regional dir. for social services programs, Waco, 1972-74, mgr. budget control and analysis div., Austin, 1975-77, adminstr. needs assessment div., 1978-79, budget analyst budget and planning div., 1980—, mem. bd. Fed. Credit Union, 1979—, pres., 1982—. Mem. Am. Public Welfare Assn., Nat. Assn. Social Workers, Acad. Cert. Social Workers, N. Tex. State U. Alumni Assn. Baptist. Home: 4159 Steck Ave #150 Austin TX 78759

HUDGINS, CATHERINE HARDING (MRS. ROBERT SCOTT HUDGINS, IV), business exec.; b. Raleigh, N.C., June 25, 1913; d. William Thomas and Mary Alice (Timberlake) Harding; B.S., N.C. State U., 1929-33; grad. tchr. N.C. Sch. for Deaf, 1933-34; m. Robert Scott Hudgins, IV, Aug. 20, 1938; children—Catherine Harding, Deborah Ghiselin, Robert Scott V. Tchr., N.C. Sch. for Deaf, Morganton, 1934-36; sec. Dr. A. S. Oliver, Raleigh, 1937; tchr. N.J. Sch. for Deaf, Trenton, 1937-39; sec. Robert S. Hudgins Co., Charlotte, N.C., 1949-60, v.p., sec., treas., 1960—, also dir. Mem. Jr. Service League, Easton, Pa., 1939; project chmn. ladies aux. Profl. Engrs. N.C., 1954-55, pres., 1956-57; pres. Christian High Sch. PTA, 1963; program chmn. Charlotte Opera Guild, 1959-61, sec., 1961-63; sec. bd. Hezekiah Alexander House Restoration, 1949-52, mem. Hezekiah Alexander Found., 1975—, also aux., 1980—. Mem. N.C. Hist. Assn., English Speaking Union, Mint Mus. Arts (pres. drama guild 1967-69), Daus. Am. Colonists (N.C. chmn. nat. def. 1973-74), DAR (chpt. regent 1957-59, state program chmn. 1961-63, state chmn. nat. def. 1973-76, state rec. sec. 1977-79, state regent 1979-81, N.C. chmn. 1963-66, N.C. sr. pres. Children Am. Revolution 1963-66, nat. bd. mgmt. 1963—, sr. nat. corr. sec. 1966-68, sr. nat. 1st v.p. 1968-70, sr. nat. pres. 1970-72, sr. nat. chmn. fin. com., pres. nat. officers club 1979-82), Presbyterian (past chmn. home missions, annuities and relief Women of Ch., past pres. Sunday Sch. class). Club: Carmel Country (Charlotte). Home: 1514 Wendover Rd Charlotte NC 28211 Office: PO Box 220217 Charlotte NC 28211

HUDGINS, MARY DENGLER, writer; b. Hot Springs National Park, Ark., Nov. 24, 1901; d. Jackson Wharton and Ida (Dengler) Hudgins; B.A., U. Ark., 1924; student U. Wis., 1941, U. Chgo., 1940, Emory U., 1952, Rice Sch. of Spoken Word, 1925. Tchr., Waldo (Ark.) High Sch., 1924-25; free-lance writer, 1925-39, 60—; librarian Hot Springs Public Library, 1939-43; med. and gen. librarian Army and Navy Gen. Hosp., Hot Springs, 1943-59; articles pub. in encys., hist., lit., profl. and popular publs., radio, TV. Dir., Hot Springs Writer's Workshop, 1960-61, rep. to Fine Arts Council, Hot Springs, 1960—. Historian YWCA, Hot Springs. Mem. Ark. Hist. Assn. (dir. 1964-71, v.p. 1971-80), Ark. Geneal. Soc. (dir. 1965-73), D.A.R., Garland County Hist. Soc. (pres. 1962-63, program chmn. 1960, 61), ALA, Ark. Library Assn. (sec. spl. libraries div. 1959-60), Med. Library Assn., Southwest Library Assn., (Ark. reporter 1955), Ark. Folklore Assn. (1st v.p. 1958-59), AAUW (Ark. 1st v.p. 1929-30, pres. Hot Springs br. 1927, Ark. fellowship chmn. 1957-61, rep. to Fine Arts Council 1961-62), Med. Library Assn., Fine Arts Center (dir., incorporator 1961). Presbyterian. Clubs: Altrusa Internat. (pres. 1980-81), Sabina (pres. 1935), Current Book (pres. Hot Springs, 1952, 64, 68, 74). Author numerous mag. articles in field of Ark. composers and lyricists. Collector, donor to colls. and univs. Arkansiana in all fields; donor endowments for Ark. composers and hist. researchers U. Ark. Address: 1030 Park Ave Hot Springs AR 71901

HUDGINS, PATRICIA MONTAGUE, physiologist; b. Buckhannon, W.Va., Jan. 31, 1938; d. Richard Wells and Clella Mae (Barger) Montague; B.S., W.Va., U., 1959, M.S., 1960, Ph.D., 1966; m. Guy Hugh Bond, June 30, 1975; children—Audrey Dale, Monica Sue. Instr. Med. Coll. Va., Richmond, 1966-68, asst. prof., 1968-72, assoc. prof., 1972-75; assoc. prof. Kirksville (Mo.) Coll. Osteo. Medicine, 1975-80, prof. physiology, 1980—. Bd. dirs. Planned Parenthood Northeast Mo., 1976-82, Adair County Nursing Home, 1977—; mem. research com. Mo. affiliate Am. Heart Assn., 1981—. Mem. Am. Physiol. Soc., Am. Soc. Pharmacology and Exptl. Therapeutics. Home: 301 Hillcrest Dr Kirksville MO 63501 Office: Dept of Physiology Kirksville Coll of Osteopathic Medicine Kirksville MO 63501

HUDSON, DOROTHY MORGAN, businesswoman; b. Omaha, May 23, 1928; d. Glover and Maria Elizabeth Morgan; student U. Colo., 1967-68, Metropolitan State Coll., 1974-75; cert. EEOC Acad., 1975; m. Harrison Hudson, Aug. 29, 1964; 1 dau., Ronnette Marie Marshall Davis. Owner, propr. D.M.H. Enterprises; investigator, conciliator EEOC Denver, 1974-75, pay audit technician Air Force Fin. Center, Denver, 1956-74; pres. City Park Sundries. Committeewoman, Democratic party; neighborhood task force rep. Denver City Council. Recipient cert. of honor City of Denver, 1976, Colo. Centennial-Bicentennial Archivist Pin, 1976; named Colo. Outstanding Woman of Yr., 1979. Mem. Nat. Profl. Writers Club, Nat. Fedn. Bus. and Profl. Women's Clubs, Nat. Assn. Female Execs. (rep. Nat. Ind. Bus. Assn.), LWV (dir. 1977-78, spl. events chmn. 1982, editor newsletter), Colo. Press Assn., Adult Edn. Council Met. Denver, Greater Park Hill Community, Inc., Nat. Council Negro Women, Colo. Black Women for Polit. Action, NAACP, Nat. Assn. Ret. Fed. Employees, Sigma Gamma Chi. Baptist. Clubs: Denver Jane Jefferson, Denver Century.

HUDSON, ELIZABETH BAUMBERGER, lawyer, govt. ofcl.; b. Asheville, N.C., Sept. 1, 1924; d. John Ernest and Lucy (Cowan) Baumberger; scholar Va. Intermont Coll., 1940-42; spl. student, U. N.C., 1944; A.B. in Psychology cum laude, Queens Coll., Charlotte, N.C., 1960; M.A. in Public Adminstrn. with honors, U. Va., 1976; postgrad. in law Am. U., 1977-79; J.D., Emory U., Atlanta, 1981; widow; children—John Henry Palmer, James Thomas Hudson, Jr. Sci. tchr., Charlotte, 1960-61; real estate profl. various firms, Washington, 1963-66; stockbroker Bache & Co., Washington, 1966-68; various positions HEW and HUD, Washington and Atlanta, 1968—; admitted to Ga. bar, 1981, since practiced in Atlanta; cons. law and estate planning. Former sect. chmn. United Appeal, award 1956; chmn. Status of Women, Woman's Soc. Christian Service, Methodist Ch., 1957. Mem. Am. Bar Assn., Young Lawyers Bar Assn., Decatur-DeKalb Bar Assn., State Bar Ga., Sigma Nu, Phi Rho Pi.

HUDSON, GRACE ALBERTA POWERS, editor, writer, artist; b. Ramer, Tenn., July 9; d. James Ernest and Sallie Verdelle (Jones) Powers; A.B., Union U., 1923, diploma in violin, 1925; postgrad. U. Tenn., summer 1923; M.S., Iowa State U., Ames, 1928; studied Corcoran Sch. Art, Washington, 1930-31, 59-60; m. Print Hudson, July 17, 1926. Dean dept. home econs. Union U., 1926-30; asst. prof. home econs. Iowa State U., 1930-31, 32-34; specialist in child devel. and family relations hdqrs. staff Am. Home Econs. Assn., Washington, 1934-38; research in child devel. and nursery sch. edn., 1929-40; mem. Nat. Commn. on Edn., Athens, Greece, 1945-48; adviser FAO, ECA, Athens, 1947-49, Lisbon, Portugal, 1949-51; editor-writer Leaves mag., Washington, 1972-78, Goodwill Guild Newsletter, 1978—; lectr. on art, travel. Mem. governing bd. YWCA, Washington, 1958-62; Sibley Hosp. Guild, Washington; founder, pres. Fgn. Friends of Creche, Athens, 1953-57; founding mem. Hellenic-Am. Club, Athens, 1953; pres. Am. Opera Scholarship Soc., 1973-79; mem. women's benefit com. Wolf Trap Farm Assos., Nat. Symphony Orch.; mem. benefit com. Am. Cancer Assn. Recipient Emily Gates Nat. Leadership award, 1938; Unselfish Service citation Union U., 1958; award (and life pres.) Nat. Bd. Children's Shelter, Athens, 1957; Service award YWCA Bd., Washington, 1962; Unselfish Service award Salvation Army, 1976; Distinguished Achievement citation Iowa State U., 1978. Mem. Nat. League Am. Pen Women (nat. officer; nat. corr. sec. 1976-78, v.p. 1978-82; v.p. Washington br. 1974-78, 1st prize award for non-fiction 1975, for water-color 1977, nat. award public relations-publicity 1978), Am. Assn. Fgn. Service Women (chmn. bd.), Assn. Hist. Preservation, Nat. Soc. Colonial Dames, D.A.R., P.E.O., Pi Gamma Mu, Chi Omega. Clubs: Am. Newspaper Women's of Washington (governing bd. 1978-83), Nat. Press, Capital Speakers (pres. 1978-79, governing bd.), Garden, Art and Book of Spring Valley, Wesley Heights. Author: Goodwill Guild Embassy Tour Book. Editor-writer: (prospectus) Research in Home Economics, 1937-40; author bulls. on Kitchen planning and equipment for high schs. and colls. Home: 5109 Upton St NW Washington DC 20016

HUDSON, JACQUELINE, artist; b. Cambridge, Mass.; d. Eric and Gertrude (Dunton) H.; student Columbia U., Art Students League. One-woman shows: Burr Gallery, N.Y.C., Rockport (Mass.) Art Assn., Present Day Club, Princeton, N.J., Maine Art Gallery, Wiscasset, Moulson Union, Bowdoin Coll., 1979; group shows: NAD, Pa. Acad. Fine Arts, Library of Congress, Cin. Mus., Riverside Mus., Portland (Maine) Mus. Art, Dayton Art Inst., Bixler Mus., Colby Coll., Maine Art Gallery, Wiscasset, Bowdoin Coll., Farnsworth Mus., Rockland, Maine, Vallombreuse Gallery, Palm Beach, Fla., many others; represented permanent collection Library of Congress; pvt. collections. Recipient Pennell Purchase prize Library of Congress, 1951; Allen Kander Found. award Rockport Art Assn., 1957, Edith Wengenroth Meml. prize, 1971, 75; Alice Standish Buell Meml. prize Nat. Assn. Women Artists, 1968, Helen Turner Graphic prize, 1974. Mem. Art Students League, Nat. Assn. Women Artists (Donna Miller Meml. prize 1980), Rockport Art Assn., Lincoln County Cultural and Hist. Assn., Monhegan (Maine) Assos. (chmn. mus. com. 1963-67). Home: Monhegan Island ME 04852

HUDSON, JANE SMITHER, furniture mfg. co. adminstrv.; b. Altavista, Va., July 5, 1937; d. Victor Nelson and Elois Reynolds Smither; A.A.S. summa cum laude in Mgmt., Central Va. Community Coll., 1978; m. J. Lee Hudson, May 15, 1954; 1 son, Michael Edward. Adminstrv. asst. Altavista (Va.) High Sch., 1954-55; with Lane Co., Inc., Altavista, 1956—, exec. sec. to chmn. bd., 1976-81, exec. sec. to chmn. exec. com., 1981—; realtor R. B. Carr & Co., Altavista, 1980—. Mem. town council Town of Altavista, 1980—; sec. Altavista Community Improvement Council, 1981-82; mem. bd. deacons First Bapt. Ch., Altavista, 1981—. Mem. Profl. Secs. Internat., Va. Assn. Realtors, Nat. Assn. Realtors. Corr. Lynchburg (Va.) News., 1966-72. Home: 1102 Commonwealth Dr Altavista VA 24517 Office: Lane Co Inc Franklin Ave Altavista VA 24517

HUDSON, MARY SUMMERLIN, ins. co. exec.; b. Duplin County, N.C., Oct. 30, 1935; d. McCoy Stephen and Nannie (Grady) Summerlin; A.A., Pineland Coll., 1955; children—Mary Allen, Joseph McCoy. Agy. coordinator Pa. Life Ins. Co., Santa Monica, Calif., 1972-79; pres., gen. mgr. United Underwriters, Inc., Mt. Olive, N.C., 1979—. Bd. dirs. Sleepy Creek Club, Inc., 1981—. Recipient Pacesetters award Puritan Life Ins. Co., 1980. Mem. Mt. Olive C. of C., Nat. Assn. Female Execs. (network dir. 1980-81). Methodist. Home: Sleepy Creek PO Box 227 Mount Olive NC 28365 Office: 710 N Church St Mount Olive NC 28365

HUDSON, ROSETTA ANN, editor; b. Springfield, Ill., June 6, 1937; d. Loren Austin and N. Naomi (Combs) Perry; student public schs., Springfield; 1 son, Keith Austin. Clk., Ill. State Archives, 1955-60; circulation clk., then editorial asst. Farmland Industries, Kansas City, Mo., 1960-73, editor Inside Farmland, 1973-81; asso. editor Farmland News, 1982—. Mem. Reach to Recovery program Am. Cancer Soc. Recipient Writing awards Nat. Council Farmer Coops., 1971-80. Mem. Nat. Fedn. Press Women (Writing awards 1975, 80), Coop. Editorial Assn. (Writing awards 1973, 77-81), Mo. Press Women (Writing awards 1974-80), Kansas City Bus. Communicators (Writing awards 1976, 79, 81). Club: Toastmaster. Home: Kansas City MO Office: PO Box 7305 Kansas City MO 64116

HUDSON, WANDA LEE, ednl. cons.; b. Hamilton, Tex., Nov. 29, 1924; d. John Henry and Allie Mae (Tubbs) Bollier; A.A., Clifton Jr. Coll., 1945; B.S., U. Tex., 1949, M.Ed., 1957; postgrad. U. Houston, 1962; Ph.D., Kans. State U., 1974; m. Sumner Hudson, Jr., Sept. 6, 1964. Progressed through teaching, counseling, advising, adminstrn. and curriculum devel. in public schs. and univs. at city and state level, also U.S. Dept. Def. Overseas Schs., 1943-74; asst. coordinator, chief academic officer Univ., European div. under contract with USAF-EUROPE, 1975-78, coordinator Mediterrean Area, 1978-79; cons. asso. McFann, Gray & Assos., Inc., San Antonio, 1979-81, Dept. Def. Lang. Inst., 1981—. Recipient Outstanding Performance award, 1962, Sustained Superior Performance award, 1963 (both Dept. Army Dependent Edn. Sch. System); named Outstanding Instr., English Lang. Inst; only female to be promoted to high sch. prin. Dept. Army, 1963; cert. life supt., prin., counselor, elementary and secondary tchr., Tex. Mem. Am. Mgmt. Assn., Am. Assn. U. Adminstrs., AAUP, AAUW, Am. Personnel and Guidance Assn. (past mem. council European br., senator N. Atlantic region), Nat. Assn. for Women Deans, Adminstrs. and Counselors, Am. Psychol. Assn., Nat. Council Adminstrv. Women in Edn., NEA, Phi Delta Gamma, Phi Delta Kappa. Democrat. Writer ednl. bulls., reports, tng. handbooks, others. Home: 120 Tuxedo San Antonio TX 78209

HUDSPETH, DONNA GALASSI, psychologist; b. Springfield, Ill., Sept. 18, 1943; d. Vincent and Mary Elizabeth (Foykier) Galassi; A.A., Springfield Coll., 1963; B.A., Ill. Coll., 1965; M.A., Bradley U., 1967; m. Lionel Mark Hudspeth, July 24, 1970. With public relations dept. Disney Prodns., Burbank, Calif., 1966-67; tng. supr. Bullock's, Los Angeles, 1966-67; clin. psychologist Baumann Clinic, Springfield, Ill., 1973-80; staff psychologist Sch. Dist. 186, Springfield, 1976—; clin. psychologist Psychol. Assos., Springfield, 1980—; part-time instr. Sangamon State U., 1976—, Lincoln Land Coll., 1969-79; cons. Ill. Dept. Public Aid, Springfield, 1973-77; mem. Ill. Status Offender Bd., 1978—. Registered psychologist, Ill.; cert. sch. psychologist, Ill. Mem. Nat. Health Service Providers, Assos. in Psychol. Services, Am. Psychol. Assn., Ill. Psychol. Assn., Springfield Edn. Assn. (sec. 1980—), NEA. Contbr. articles to profl. jours. Office: 444 W Reynolds St Springfield IL 62702 also Univ Med Bldg 901 North First Springfield IL 62704

HUEBNER, MILDRED HARRIET, educator; b. Buffalo, Dec. 6, 1913; d. Harrington Warner and Gertrude (Weber) H.; B.S., Edinboro State Tchrs. Coll., 1939; M.A., Western Res. U., 1947, Ed.D., 1955. Tchr. public schs., Girard Twp., Pa., 1937-41, Erie, Pa., 1941-51; asst. prin. various schs., Erie, 1951-53; asst. prof. edn. Western Res. U., Cleve., 1953-59; asso. prof. edn. So. Conn. State Coll., New Haven, 1959-61, prof. edn., 1961-79, dir. Reading Center, 1959-79, chmn. reading dept., 1971-79, prof. emeritus, 1979—. Dir. NDEA Spl. Reading Insts., summers 1965-67. Mem. Internat. Reading Assn., NEA, Conn. Assn. Reading Research, AAUW. Author: (with Mary C. Austin and Clifford L. Bush) Reading Evaluation 1961; (with C. L. Bush) Strategies for Reading, 2d edit., 1979. Contbr. articles to profl. jours. Home: 15 Santa Fe Ave Hamden CT 06517

HUEY, MARY EVELYN BLAGG, univ. adminstr.; b. Wills Point, Tex., Jan. 19, 1922; d. Henry H. and Melissa Evelyn (Manning) Blagg; B.S., Tex. Woman's U., 1942, M.A., 1943; M.A., U. Ky., 1947; postgrad. Harvard U., 1950; Ph.D., Duke U., 1954; Litt.D. (hon.), Baiko Jo Gakuin, Shimonoseki, Japan, 1981; m. Griffin B. Huey, Aug. 21, 1954; 1 son, Henry Griffin. Instr. English, Tex. Woman's U., Denton, 1943-45, dean Grad. Sch., 1971-76, prof. govt., 1971-76, pres., 1976—; asst. dir. Bur. Public Adminstrn. U. Miss., 1946-47; instr. govt. North Tex. State U., 1947-51, asst. prof., 1954-63, asso. prof., 1963-66, prof., 1966-71. Bd. Adjustment, City of Denton, 1962-68, chmn., 1963-68; mem. regional exec. bd. N. Central Tex. Planning Council for Hosp. and Related Health Services, 1969-70; mem. exec. bd. N. Central Tex. Council Govts., 1970-71, pres. Tex. Women's U. Demonstration Sch. PTA, 1970-71; exec. v.p. Fine Arts Soc. Tex., 1977, pres., 1977-79; mem. Denton Area War on Drugs Adv. Bd., 1981—; mem. exec. com. Def. Adv. Com. on Women in the Services, 1981-84; active First Presbyn. Ch., Denton, ruling elder, 1973-75, 81—. Recipient Disting. Alumna award Tex. Women's U., 1974; Otis Fowler award Denton C. of C., 1980; Women Helping Women award, Soroptimist Internat., 1980. Mem. AAUW (pres. Denton br. 1962-63, chmn. internat. cuisine and customs study group 1967-69) Am. Council Edn., Am. Polit. Sci. Assn., Am. Soc. Public Adminstrn. (v.p. N. Tex. chpt. 1968-69, pres. 1969-70), Assn. Tex. Coll. and Univs. (mem. exec. bd. 1977-80), Am. Assn. State Colls. and Univs.), So. Polit. Sci. Assn., Southwestern Polit. Sci. Assn., Southwestern Social Sci. Assn., Tex. Acad. Sci., Tex. Assn. Coll. Tchrs., Tex. Found. Women's Resources, Nat. Acad. Public Adminstrn., Nat. Commn. Coop. Edn. (trustee 1978—), Phi Alpha Theta, Delta Kappa Gamma, Phi Delta Gamma, Phi Kappa Phi, Pi Sigma Alpha, Sigma Alpha Iota. Republican. Contbr. in field. Office: PO Box 23925 Texas Women's U Station Denton TX 76204

HUFF, PRISCILLA ROWE, social worker; b. Atlanta, Aug. 7, 1943; d. Robert Jackson and Fannie (Head) Rowe; B.A., Spelman Coll., 1962; M.S., Simmons Coll. Sch. Social Work, 1965; m. Ronald R. Huff, Nov. 25, 1965; children—Valerie, Rochelle, Michelle. Social worker birth defects Johns Hopkins Hosp., Balt., 1965, social worker comprehensive child care program, 1966-69; social worker Children's Guild, Balt., 1969-70; social worker adolescent center Sinai Hosp., Balt., part-time, 1969-70, coordinator adolescent center, 1970-76, family planning coordinator dept. ob-gyn, 1976—; mem. faculty Sch. Social Work, U. Md., Planned Parenthood of Md.; cons., faculty workshops on adolescent sexual behavior, task force on adolescent pregnancy Am. Coll. Obstetricians and Gynecologists. Recipient longevity service certificate Sch. Social Work and Community Planning, U. Md., 1980. Mem. Nat. Assn. Social Workers (dir. Md. chpt. 1980—), Sex Edn. Coalition Met. Wash. Home: 3716 Marmon Ave Baltimore MD 21207 Office: Sinai Hosp Dept Ob-Gyn Belvedere and Greenspring Aves Baltimore MD 21215

HUFFMAN, LOIS ROYALL (MRS. MONROE HUFFMAN), banker; b. Wilkes County, N.C., May 25, 1935; d. William Quincy and Cora Lee (Holbrook) Royall; student U. N.C., Greensboro, 1953; m. Thomas Monroe Huffman, Nov. 12, 1960; 1 son, Thomas Mark. With Northwestern Bank, Sparta, N.C., 1953-56; with Northwestern Bank, North Wilkesboro, N.C., 1956-73, 78—, asst. treas., 1970-73, v.p. br. adminstrn. dept., 1978—; asst. treas. Northwestern Fin. Corp., North Wilkesboro, N.C., 1973-74, asst. v.p., 1974-75, v.p., 1975-78; sec., dir. Western Investment Corp., North Wilkesboro, 1960-79, Northwestern Finance Co., North Wilkesboro, 1973-75, N.W.B. Bldg. of Asheville, Inc., 1975-79. Baptist. Office: Northwestern Bank 420 Brushy Mountain Rd Wilkesboro NC 28697

HUFFMAN, NANCY ANNE, city ofcl.; b. McAlister, Okla., Dec. 26, 1942; d. Eustace Wright and Margaret Marcelle (Miller) Carlton; B.S., Spring Hill Coll., 1965; student Pensacola Jr. Coll., 1968-69; m. William Eugene Huffman, Nov. 26, 1966; children—Eugenia Anne, Carlton Eugene. Claims examiner Social Security Payment Center, Birmingham, Ala., 1965-68; mem. Springboro (Ohio) Village Council, 1974-77, 78-81, pres. council, 1978, dep. mayor, 1979—, past mem. street com., now legal com.. fin. com., salary and wage com., rep. to Warren County HUD Rehab. Bd., 1976-78, chmn. fin. com. 1976—. Joint mem. Ohio Mcpl.

League of Cities and Villages. Republican. Methodist. Author: One Chance for Happiness, 1963. Home: 165 Pinecone Ln Springboro OH 45066 Office: Springboro Mcpl Bldg 280 W Central St Springboro OH 45066

HUFFORD, FRANCES MARCHMAN, educator; b. Dale County, Ala., Aug. 12, 1907; d. Robert Lee and Eleanor Rowena (Paris) Marchman; B.S., U. Cin., 1937; postgrad. U. Fla., 1952, 55, 57, U. South Fla., 1970; m. Edwin W. Hufford, Dec. 27, 1927; children—Kay Hufford Ruff, Dee Hufford Burnette. Tchr. English and phys. edn. Wauchula (Fla.) High Sch., 1927-29; tchr. English, Hernando High Sch., Brooksville, Fla., 1930-32; tchr. elem. schs., Tampa, Fla., 1932-40, 46-70; instr. humanities Morgan Woods Elem. Sch., Tampa, 1970-76, St. Mary's Sch., 1976-81; instr. U. South Fla., summer 1969. Bd. dirs. Hillsborough County (Fla.) Mental Health Assn., 1957-63; pres. Tampa Jr. Mus., 1967-68; pres. Tampa Woman's Club, 1978, 3d v.p., 1980; pres. Friends of Library, Tampa, 1971, 78; 2d v.p. Women of the Church, 1980. Recipient Meritorious Tchr. award Hillsborough County, 1963; Cultural award Fla. Ballet Theatre, 1969; Freedoms Found. award, 1972; named Tchr. of Yr., Tampa Jr. Woman's Club, 1971. Mem. Hillsborough County Assn. Childhood Edn. (pres. 1961), Joint Adv. Group Hillsborough County, Hillsborough County Classroom Tchrs. Assn., Hillsborough County Council PTA, Tampa Preservation Soc., AAUW (1st v.p. 1979), Delta Kappa Gamma (pres. Chi chpt. 1963). Democrat. Presbyterian. Clubs: Tides Bath, MacDill Officers. Author articles on humanities programs in elem. schs. Home: 110 S New Jersey Ave Tampa FL 33609

HUFSTEDLER, SHIRLEY MOUNT (MRS. SETH M. HUFSTEDLER), lawyer; b. Denver, Aug. 24, 1925; d. Earl Stanley and Eva (Von Behren) Mount; B.B.A., U. N.Mex., 1945, LL.D., 1972; LL.B., Stanford U., 1949; LL.D., U. Wyo., 1970, Gonzaga U., 1970, Occidental Coll., 1971, Tufts U., 1974, U. So. Calif., 1976, U. Pa., 1976, Georgetown U., 1976, U. Pacific, 1977, Columbia U., 1977, U. Mich., 1978, Rutgers U., 1981, Yale U., 1981, Claremont U. Center, 1981; H.H.D., Hood Coll., 1981; m. Seth Martin Hufstedler, Aug. 16, 1949; 1 son, Steven Mark. Admitted to Calif. bar, 1950, pvt. practice Los Angeles, 1961; mem. firm of Beardsley, Hufstedler & Kemble, Los Angeles, 1951-61; mem. staff Stanford U. Law Rev., 1947-49, article and book rev. editor, 1948-49, judge Superior Ct., County Los Angeles, 1961-66; justice Calif. Ct. Appeal for 2d dist., 1966-68; circuit judge U.S. Ct. Appeals, 9th Circuit, 1968-79; U.S. sec. of edn., Washington, 1979-81; partner firm Hufstedler, Miller, Carlson & Beardsley, Los Angeles, 1981—. Bd. councilors Law Center U. So. Calif.; trustee Calif. Inst. Tech., Occidental Coll., Aspen Inst. Humanistic Studies, Colonial Williamsburg Found., Constnl. Rights Found. Named Woman of Yr., Los Angeles Times, 1968, Ladies Home Jour., 1976; recipient UCLA medal, 1981. Mem. Am., Los Angeles bar assns., Women Lawyers Assn. (pres. 1957-58), Am. Judicature Soc., Am. Law Inst., Inst. Jud. Adminstrn., Town Hall, Order of Coif. Office: 700 S Flower St Los Angeles CA 90017

HUGGARD, LINDA ANN, remfg. co. exec.; b. Ardmore, Okla., July 6, 1948; d. Paul Wilton and Carlene Louvaine (Saunders) Howard; student Central State U., 1968-69, South Oklahoma City Jr. Coll., 1974; m. Art Huggard, Feb. 14, 1974. Long distance operator Southwestern Bell Telephone Co., Oklahoma City, 1967-68; apprentice Bill Merritt Funeral Service, Bethany, Okla., 1969-70; reservations mgr. Skirvin Hotel, Oklahoma City, 1969-70, front office mgr., 1970-71, asst. mgr. house ops., 1971-73; v.p. adminstrv. ops. Diesel Casting Service, Inc., Tulsa, 1975—, also dir. Mem. Okla. Maintenance Suprs. Council (sec. 1979-80), Automotive Engine Rebuilders Assn., Asso. Motor Carriers Okla., Nat. Royalty Owners Assn., Nat. Fedn. Ind. Bus. Republican. Office: 6039 S Newport Tulsa OK 74105

HUGGINS, CANNIE MAE COX HUNTER, former educator; b. Belton, Tex., July 16, 1916; d. Jesse Daniel and Mary Alice (Hamilton) Cox; B.S., Mary Hardin Baylor Coll., 1940; M.S., San Marcos Tchrs. Coll., 1942; postgrad. U. Tex., 1946-47, Tex. Tech U., 1956-70, U. San Diego, 1975, St. Mary's U., 1976; m. William Dudley Hunter, June 5, 1938 (div. 1967); children—Darline, Bob Roy; m. 2d, Bertrand Huggins, Aug. 4, 1979 (dec. July 19, 1980). Tchr. pub. schs., Belton, 1935-38, Galveston, Tex., 1938-42; mem. staff testing dept. U. Ariz., 1942-43; reading cons. Phoenix Pub. Schs., 1943-45; tchr.-counselor pub. schs., Killeen, Tex., 1946-54; classroom tchr., Lubbock, Tex., 1954-74; tchr. first grade bilingual lang. devel. Posey Elementary Sch., Lubbock, Tex., 1974-82; pres. CM Corp. First aid chmn. ARC, Lubbock County, 1960-63, first aid instr., 1956—; area dir. March of Dimes, 1958-63; tchr. high sch. dept. First Bapt. Ch., Lubbock, 1960—. Recipient Outstanding Service award ARC, 1966. Cert. educator, Tex. Mem. Assn. Childhood Edn. Internat., NEA, Tex. Tchrs. Assn., Tex. Classroom Tchrs. Assn., Nat. PTA, Tex. Edn. Assn., Lubbock Educators Assn., Lubbock Classroom Tchrs. Assn., AAUW, Am. Bus. Women's Assn., S. Plains Writers Guild, YWCA, Lubbock, Killeen chambers commerce. Baptist. Club: University City (Lubbock). Home: 4626 30th St Lubbock TX 79410

HUGGINS, CHARLOTTE SUSAN HARRISON, educator; b. Rockford, Ill., May 13, 1933; d. Lyle Lux and Alta May (Bowers) H.; student Knox Coll., 1951-52; A.B. magna cum laude, Radcliffe Coll., 1958; M.A., Northwestern U., 1960, postgrad, 1971-73; m. Rollin Charles Huggins, Apr. 26, 1952; children—Cynthia Charlotte, Shirley Ann, John Charles. Asst. editor Hollister Publs., Inc., Wilmette, Ill., 1959-65; tchr. advanced placement English New Trier High Sch. East, Winnetka, Ill., 1965—, asst. sponsor Echoes, 1981, Trevia, 1982; pres. Harrison Farm, Inc., Lovington, Ill., 1976—. Mem. women's bd. St. Leonard's House, Chgo., 1965-75; Central Sch. PTA Bd., Wilmette, 1960-64; mem. jr. bd. Northwestern U. Settlement, Chgo., 1965-75. Recipient DAR Citizenship award, 1953, Phi Beta Kappa award, 1957; Am. Legion award, 1959; named Master Tchr., New Trier High Sch., 1979. Mem. NEA, Ill. Edn. Assn., New Trier Edn. Assn., Nat. Council Tchrs. English, Ill. Assn. Tchrs. English, MLA, Northwestern U. Alumni Assn., Jr. Aux. Chgo. Cancer Research Bd., Mary Crane League, Pi Beta Phi. Clubs: Nat. Huguenot Soc., Ill. Huguenot Soc., Womans' of Wilmette, Univ. of Chgo., Mich. Shores, Knox Coll., Radcliffe Coll. of Chgo. Author: A Sequential Course in Composition Grades 9-12, 1979; A History of New Trier High School, 1982. Home: 700 Greenwood Ave Wilmette IL 60091 or Ptarmigan Meadows Creede CO 81130 Office: 385 Winnetka Ave Winnetka IL 60093

HUGGINS, KAE PARKS, nurse; b. Seward, Nebr., Feb. 5, 1948; d. Herschel Keith and Lavilda Louise (Richters) Parks; diploma nursing, Immanuel Hosp., Omaha, Nebr., 1969; B.S. in Nursing, Loretto Heights Coll., Denver Colo., 1972; M.S., U. Ariz., Tucson, 1978; m. Jerold Delmore Huggins, Nov. 4, 1978; children—Darin Lauren, Megan Diane. Staff nurse hosps. in Nebr. and Colo., 1969-73; staff nurse Panama Canal Govt., 1973-75; instr., Gorgas Hosp., Ancon, 1975-77; nursing edn. coordinator health bur., Ancon, 1979; chief nursing edn. and tng. service U.S. Army MEDDAC, Panama, 1979—; instr.-trainer CPR, 1979—; lectr. in field. Vice pres. Redeemer Lutheran Women, Balboa, 1980; fin. sec. Redeemer Luth. Ch., 1980—. Recipient Outstanding Service award Gorgas Hosp., Canal Zone, 1976. Mem. Am. Nurses Assn. Republican. Home: 1013-A Fort Clayton Republic Panama Office: USA MEDDAC Panama Gorgas Army Hosp APO Miami FL 34004

HUGGINS, MISSIE WILLIAMS, clubwoman; b. Crystal Springs, Miss., Feb. 14, 1902; d. Thomas Jefferson and Mary Belle (Millsaps) Spencer; B.A., Blue Mountain Coll., 1923; postgrad. U. Ala., 1926; m. Charles DuBuisson Williams, Apr. 27, 1927; 1 son, Charles DuBuisson; m. 2d, Will Zack Huggins, Apr. 16, 1977. Tchr., Blue Mountain Coll. High Sch., 1923-25, Yazoo City Public Sch., 1925-27, 45-75. Bd. dirs. Miss. Tb Assn., 1953-80; v.p. Miss. Easter Seal Soc., 1961-63; membership chmn. Miss. Women's Cabinet Public Affairs, 1963-64; vol. VA Hosp., 1946-60; county vol. chmn. Miss. Assn. Mental Health, 1960-64; chmn. Adv. Council to Miss. Children's Code Commn. Day Care Center, 1953-59; girl's state dir. Am. Legion Aux., 1955, 58, 72-79, girl's state chmn., 1955-64, 79; mem. Yazoo County Democratic Com., 1956-80; pres. Millsaps Family Assn., 1959-64; mem. Yazoo County Cancer Com., 1936-64; publicity chmn. Yazoo County Polio, 1960; bd. mem. Yazoo County United Givers. Mem. NEA, Miss. Edn. Assn., DAR (vice-regent 1963-64), UDC (pres. gen. 1978-80), Yazoo Hist. Assn. Baptist. Editor-in-chief UDC mag., 1979-80. Home: 517 Campbell St Yazoo City MS 39194

HUGGINS, ROSE ELAINE, health center exec.; b. Charleston, S.C., Jan. 21, 1951; d. James Franklin and Mabel Thearse H.; B.A., Johnson C. Smith U., 1973; M.S., L.I. U., 1977; M.P.A., C.W. Post Coll., 1978. Tchr., Community Sponsor Day Care Center, Bklyn., 1975-79; personnel dir. Charles Drew Neighborhood Health Center, Bklyn., 1979-80; vice-chmn. bd. Project Teen Aid Inc./Cumberland Hosp., Bklyn., 1980—. Mem. Am. Personnel and Guidance Assn., NAACP. Home: 288 Crown St Apt 2N Brooklyn NY 11225 Office: 51 Saint Edwards St Brooklyn NY 11205

HUGHES, ANN HIGHTOWER, economist; b. Birmingham, Ala., Nov. 24, 1938; d. Brady Alexander and Juanita Whitfield (Pope) Hughes; B.A., George Washington U., 1962, M.A., 1969. Internat. economist Dept. Commerce, Washington, 1963-77, dep. asst. sec. for trade agreements, 1981, dep. asst. sec. for western hemisphere, 1982—; mgr. U.S. tariff negotiations during multilateral trade negotiations for U.S. Trade Rep., Exec. Office of Pres., 1977-79; asst. U.S. Trade Rep. for Interagy. Coordination, 1979-80. Office: Dept Commerce 14th and Constitution Ave NW Washington DC 20230

HUGHES, AUDREY CLAYRE, lab. dir.; b. Cambridge, Mass., Oct. 27, 1924; d. Arthur E. and Clara J. (Walther) Hughes; B.A., Coll. Notre Dame, 1945; M.A., Boston U., 1950; postgrad. Tufts U., 1950-54, Rensselaer Poly. Inst., 1952. Med. technologist Sacred Heart Hosp., Manchester, N.H., 1945-46, St. John's Hosp., Lowell, Mass., 1946-48, instr. anatomy, physiology and microbiology, 1952-56, chief med. technologist, 1956-74, lab. coordinator, 1974—; instr. advanced biology Mt. St. Mary Coll., Hooksett, N.H., 1948-52, Lowell Gen. Hosp., 1952-56; asst. prof. biology and math. Lowell State Coll., 1952-56; adj. clin. instr. U. Lowell, 1977. Mem. Mass. Gov.'s Council Adv. Com. on Clin. Labs. Mem. Mass. Assn. Med. Technologists, Am. Assn. Blood Banks, Mass. Assn. Blood Banks, Am. Assn. Clin. Chemists, New Eng. Clin. Radioassay Soc., New Eng. Med. Lab. Sci. Edn. Forum, New Eng. Cath. Hosp. Assn., Am. Soc. Clin. Pathologists, Clin. Lab. Mgmt. Assn., AAAS, Tri Beta. Democrat. Roman Catholic. Home: PO Box 297 Tyngsboro MA 01879 Office: 1 Hospital Dr Lowell MA 01852

HUGHES, BARBARA ANN, dietitian, public health adminstr.; b. McMinn County, Tenn., July 22, 1938; d. Cecil Earl and Hannah Ruth (Moss) Farmer; B.S. cum laude in Home Econs. Carson Newman Coll., Jefferson City, Tenn., 1960; M.S. in Instl. Mgmt., Ohio State U., Columbus, 1963; M.R.E. (Adonarium Judson scholar), So. Bapt. Theol. Sem., 1968; M.P.H. in Public Health Adminstrn., U. N.C., Chapel Hill, 1972; postgrad. in nutrition U. Iowa, 1974, U. N.C., 1975—, Case Western Res. U., 1979; m. Carl Clifford Hughes, Oct. 13, 1972. Dietitian, instr. Riverside Meth. Hosp., Riverside Whitecross Sch. Nursing, Columbus, 1963-66; consulting dietitian eastern region N.C. Bd. Health, Raleigh, 1963-73; head Nutrition and Dietary Services br., div. Health Services, N.C. Dept. Human Resources, Raleigh, 1973—; cons. dietitian Mt. Holly Nursing Home, Louisville, 1967-68; adj. asso. prof. dept. nutrition Sch. Public Health, U. N.C., Chapel Hill; mem. adv. bd. Hospitality Edn. program N.C. Dept. Community Colls., 1974—, adv. com. Ret. Senior Vol. Program, Raleigh and Wake County, N.C., 1975-79, N.C. Network Coordinating Council for End-Stage Renal Disease, 1975, Nat. Adv. Council on Maternal, Infant, and Fetal Nutrition, Spl. Supplemental Food Program for Women, Infants, and Children, Dept. Agr., 1976-79, adv. com. Nutrition Edn. and Tng. program N.C. Dept. Public Instruction, 1978-80; coordinator undergrad. program in gen. dietetics East Carolina U.; adv. council N.C. Gov.'s Office Citizen Affairs; lectr., cons.; cons. dietitian Augusta Victoria Hosp. and Jerusalem (Israel) Crippled Childrens Center, 1968; witness U.S. congressional and Senate hearings in field. Active edn. programs Pullen Memorial Bapt. Church, Raleigh, deacon, 1976-80, area ministry capt., 1977-78, personnel com., 1978-80; dietitian/dir. food service archeol. expedition to Israel, 1978; bd. dirs. N.C. Literacy Assn. 1978—, pres., 1981-83; trustee Gardner-Webb Coll., Boiling Springs, N.C., 1979—, chmn. curriculum com., 1981-82. Named Woman of Yr., Wake County, 1975, N.C. Outstanding Dietitian of Yr., 1976, N.C. Outstanding Dietitian, Southeastern Hosp. Conf. for Dietitians, 1978. Mem. AAUW (life, pres. Raleigh br. 1971-75, pres. N.C. div. 1978-80, dir. 1980-82, mem. numerous coms.), Am. Dietetic Assn. (del. 1971-74, pres. N.C. state assn. 1976-77, N.C. network legis. coordinator 1978-81, nat. nominating com. 1979-80, chmn. elect council on practice 1981-82, chmn. 1982-83), Am. Public Health Assn. (exec. com. So. br. 1977—, sec.-treas. 1979-80, 1st v.p. 1980-81), So. Health Assn. (pres. 1982-83), Assn. State and Territorial Public Health Nutrition Dirs. (pres. 1977-79, dir. 1981—), N.C. Council Foods and Nutrition (dir. 1976-78, chmn. membership 1975, nominating com. 1979). N.C. Council Women's Orgns., Am. Acad. Health Adminstrn., Soc. Nutrition Edn., Nutrition Today Soc., N.C. Acad. Public Health, AAUW (area rep. 1980-82), Ohio State U. Alumni Assn., U. N.C. Gen. Alumni Assn., U. N.C. Public Health Alumni Assn., Altrusa Internat. (pres. Raleigh club 1973-74, dir. 1976-78, 1st vice gov. 1978-79, chmn. nomination com. 1980-82, gov. dist. Three, 1979-80, internat. vocat. services chmn. 1977-79), Women's Forum N.C. Co-author: Diet and Kidney Disease, Assn. for N.C. Regional Med. Program, 1969; contbr. numerous papers, articles to symposia, periodicals in field, vol. areas. Home: 4208 Galax Dr Raleigh NC 27612 Office: PO Box 2091 Raleigh NC 27602

HUGHES, BARBARA ELIZABETH, speech pathologist; b. Passaic, N.J., Dec. 22, 1942; d. Frank Edward and Barbara Marion (Trouve) H.; B.A., Paterson State Coll., 1964, also postgrad.; M.A., No. Mich. U., 1973; postgrad. Farleigh Dickinson U. Speech pathologist, N.J., 1964-65, West Milford Twp. (N.J.) Bd. Edn., 1965—; negotiations cons. N.J. Edn. Assn. Mem. Am. Speech and Hearing Assn. (cert.), West Milford Edn. Assn. (legis. chairperson 1966-72, pres. 1968-71, v.p. 1972—), N.J. Speech and Hearing Assn. (public sch. affairs com.), Passaic County Speech and Hearing Assn. (pres. 1980-81), NEA (del. rep. assembly 1972—), N.J. Edn. Assn. (past mem. state nominating com., mem. affiliates com.), Passaic County Edn. Assn. Author: Articulation Disorders: An Outline of Diagnosis and Therapy, 1973. Home: 1263-A Valley Rd Wayne NJ 07470 Office: West Milford Bd Edn Arnold Rd West Milford NJ 07480

HUGHES, BLANCHE ROBERTS, social work adminstr.; b. Okla.; d. Walter and Levolia (Nobel) Roberts; B.S., Talladega County Coll., 1943; M.S., Simmons Coll., 1949; Ph.D., N.Y. U., 1973; m. Julius Hughes, June 6, 1957; 1 dau., Elizabeth. Social worker Bronx VA Hosp., 1950-56; cons. N.Y.C. Health Dept., 1956-64; asso. dir. social work Bronx Lebanon Hosp. Center, 1964—; adj. prof. Sch. Bus. and Fin., Mercy Coll., 1977—. Mem. N.Y. State Bd. Social Work, 1977—, chmn., 1982-83; chmn. Commn. on Abuse of Elderly, 1981-83. Mem. Nat. Assn. Social Workers (treas. 1975-77, exec. bd. 1975-77), Phi Delta Kappa. Home: 555 Kappock St Riverdale NY 10463

HUGHES, CASEY, psychologist; b. Angola, La., Feb. 19, 1943; d. John Alexander and Barbara Eileen (Bolin) Jensen; B.S., La. Stte U., 1964; M.S., U. Ga., 1966, Ph.D., 1970; children from previous marriage—Howard Hampton, Halane Hedra. Asst. prof. psychology Va. Commonwealth U., Richmond, 1969-71; psychologist Prince Georges County (Md.) Public Schs., 1971-73; nat. legis. dir. NOW, Washington, 1974-76; pvt. practice as psychologist, Annapolis, 1976—. Democratic state senatorial candidate, 1974, Ho. of Reps., 1976. Mem. NOW, Women's Polit. Caucus, Am. Psychol. Assn., Anne Arundel Psychol. Assn., Assn. Advancement Psychology, Assn. Women in Sci., Biofeedback Soc. Am., Md. Psychol. Assn., Psi Chi. Democrat. Office: 63 West St Annapolis MD 21401

HUGHES, DOROTHY ANN, mfg. co. ofcl.; b. Montgomery, Ala., May 10, 1948; d. James William and Gladys (Boatner) H.; student Meridian Jr. Coll., 1966-67, Northwestern State U. La., 1976—. Exec. sec. to pres., chief exec. officer So. Pipe & Supply Co. Meridian (Miss.), 1966-71; exec. sec. to chmn. and chief exec. officer AFCO Industries, Inc., Alexandria, La., 1971-81, adminstrv. asst. to chmn.-chief exec. officer and v.p. adminstrn., 1980—; mem. nat. adv. bd. Today's Sec. mag., 1981-82. Mem. bus. adv. council Bolton High Sch., Alexandria, 1980-82. Cert. profl. sec.; Nat. Secs. Assn. scholar, 1966-67. Mem. La. Talent Bank Women, Nat. Secs. Assn. (officer LaPine chpt., Sec. of Yr. 1980), La. Assn. Cert. Profl. Secs. Democrat. Pentecostal Ch. Composer: Close to Thee, 1969, One Touch of the Master's Hand, 1970. Home: PO Box 5191 Alexandria LA 71301 Office: PO Box 5085 Alexandria LA 71301

HUGHES, ELAINE MARIE, social worker; b. Seattle, Dec. 29, 1925; d. Arthur Thorvald and Magda Josefine (Mikaelsen) Kjellmann; A.A., Imperial Valley Coll., 1964; B.A., San Diego State Coll., 1966; postgrad Calif. State U., Long Beach, 1966; M.S.W., U. So. Calif., 1977; m. Hugh Hugo Hughes, May 5, 1972. Sec., Bethlehem Steel Co., 1944-46, Nat. Auto Ins. Co., 1947-48, Zurich Inst. Co., 1948-49; clk. Home Indemnity, 1950-51; med. sec. U.S. Navy Hosp., Oceanside, 1952-54, VA Hosp., 1956; salesperson Turner Investment Co., 1962; sec. U.S. Dept. Agr., 1962-63; social worker adoption div. Imperial County Welfare Dept., El Centro, Calif., 1966-68, Orange County Dept. Social Service, Santa Ana, Calif., 1968-75; clin. social worker Human Services Agy., Orange County, Calif., 1977-79; social work Cons., Santa Ana, 1980—, U.S. Navy Family Services, Long Beach, Calif., 1982—. mem. East Orange County Child Abuse Task Force, 1979. Cert. tchr., Calif. Mem. AAUW, Nat. Assn. Social Workers. Democrat. Lutheran.

HUGHES, ELINOR LAMBERT, drama editor, critic; b. Cambridge, Mass., Mar. 3, 1906; d. Hector James and Elinor (Lambert) H.; ed. Buckingham Sch., Cambridge, 1915-20, May Sch., Boston, 1920-23; A.B., Radcliffe Coll., 1927; m. David D. Jacobus, July 14, 1957; stepchildren—David P. Jacobus, John H. Jacobus. Asst. in drama dept. Boston Herald-Traveler, 1929-34, drama and film editor and critic, 1934-66; lectr. on drama and film criticism. Mem. Soc. Preservation New Eng. Antiquities, Inst. Contemporary Art. Republican. Unitarian. Clubs: Women's City (Boston); Harvard (N.Y.C.). Author: Famous Stars of Filmdom (Men) and Famous Stars of Filmdom (Women), 1932; Passing Through to Broadway, 1948. Blank verse rev. of Shakespearean prodns. included in Best News Stories of 1937-38. Home: 24 Academy Ln Bellport NY 11713

HUGHES, EMILY KARLA VOLLMAR, food scientist, nutritionist; b. Kansas City, Kans., Jan. 31, 1951; d. Emil Karl and Mildred (Harker) Vollmar; B.S. (Martha S. Pittman scholar 1972), Kans. State U., 1972, M.S., 1974; Ph.D., U. Tenn., Knoxville, 1978; m. L.H. Hughes, III. Grad. research asst., foods and nutrition, Kans. State U., Manhattan, 1973-74, asst. prof., state extension specialist, foods and nutrition, 1979; instr. human nutrition and foods Va. Poly. Inst. and State U., Blacksburg, 1974-76; grad. research asst. in food tech. and sci. U. Tenn., Knoxville, 1976-78; asst. prof., state extension specialist, human nutrition, foods, food systems mgmt. U. Mo., Columbia, 1980—, coordinator computer activities Home Econs. Extension, 1981—, mem. Mo. Coop. Extension Computer Com., 1982—. Adv. com. home econs. curriculum Columbia Public Sch. System, 1981-82; mem. Super Shopper program Columbia-U. Mo. Columbia Chpt. Vet. Wives, 1980. Mem. Inst. Food Technologists, Am. Dietic Assn. (registered), Mo. Dietetic Assn., Central Mo. Dietetic Assn. (chmn. community nutrition com. 1980), Am. Home Econs. Assn., Mo. Home Econs. Assn., Assn. for Devel. of Computer-based Instructional Systems, Sigma Xi, Phi Kappa Phi, Phi Upsilon Omicron, Omicron Nu, Phi Tau Sigma (sec. U. Tenn. chpt., 1979), Gamma Sigma Delta. Contbr. papers to profl. confs.; coordinator com. for revision of Handbook of Food Preparation, Am. Home Econs. Assn., 1979; contbg. author to videotape and slide programs in field, articles to publs. in field. Home: 401 Lexington Sq Columbia MO 62201 Office: 308 Gwynn Hall Univ Mo Columbia MO 65211

HUGHES, JUDITH ANN, chemist; b. Denver, Dec. 27, 1941; d. William Leonard and Alice (Buckley) Reichwein; B.A. in Chemistry, Loretto Heights Coll., Denver, 1964; postgrad. U. Colo.; m. Roy A. Hughes, Oct. 15, 1971. With Public Service Co. of Colo., Denver, 1967—, supt. chemistry, 1974-81, dir. fuel forecasting and utilization, 1981—; mem. exec. bd. Women and Bus. Conf., 1982—. Mem. Edison Electric Inst. (exec. com.), Am. Chem. Soc., Am. Entrepreneurs Assn., Nat. Assn. Female Execs., Exec. and Profl. Women's Council (co-founder, pres. 1980-81). Democrat. Home: 8097 Brook Dr Littleton CO 80123 Office: PO Box 840 Denver CO 80201

HUGHES, LINDA ELLEN, businesswoman; b. Noble County, Ohio, Mar. 15, 1938; d. Charles Franklin and Verna Ellen (King) Dotson; m. Clair Hughes, Aug. 27, 1955; children—Edward Wayne, Scott Anthony, Daniel Steven. Office mgr., realtor Reed Realty, Caldwell, Ohio, 1969—; v.p., treas. Clair Hughes Trucking, Inc., Caldwell, 1972—; v.p., treas. Hughes Discount Truck Parts, Inc., 1978—. Republican. Roman Catholic. Home: 811 Main St Caldwell OH 43724 Office: 810 Main St Caldwell OH 43724

HUGHES, LINDA GAYLE, banker; b. East Chicago, Ind., Sept. 6, 1946; d. Walter O. and I.B. Pierce; B.A., UCLA, 1968; postgrad. Calif. State U., Los Angeles, 1970-72; M.B.A., Pepperdine U., 1974. Adminstrv. asst. Energy Scis., Inc., 1968-70; sales rep. E.R. Co., Inc., 1971; product mgr. Creative Sound, Inc., 1972; sr. mktg. rep. Dun & Bradstreet, Inc., 1973-75, dist. sales mgr., 1976-80; corp. mktg. mgr. Kirk Paper Co., Inc., Los Angeles, 1981-82; asst. v.p. Wells Fargo Bank, Los Angeles, 1982—. Mem. Sales and Mktg. Execs. Assn., Direct Mail Mktg. Assn., Assn. Retail Mgmt. Info. Systems, Am. Mktg. Assn., NOW, Beverly Hills Bd. Realtors. Republican. Home: 6121 Shoup Ave Apt 12 Woodland Hills CA 91367 Office: 6550 E Washington Blvd Los Angeles CA 90040

HUGHES, LOIS JUNE HULME, home economist; b. Grand Island, Nebr., June 15, 1941; d. Orville George and Erna Lena-Marie (Kruse) Hulme; B.S. (Union Pacific Carl Raymond Gray scholar), U. Nebr., 1961, M.Ed., 1968; Ph.D. (Home Econs. Edn. fellow), U. Mo., 1970; m. Harlan Gene Hughes, July 23, 1961; children—Pamela Sue, Patricia Ann. Home econs. and sci. tchr. Ceresco (Nebr.) Pub. Schs., 1961-62, Newhawka (Nebr.) Consol. Schs., 1962-64, Washington Twp. Schs.,

Centerville, Ohio, 1966-67; grad. asst. home econs. edn. U. Mo., Columbia, 1967-70; conversational English tchr. Sch. English for Brazilians, Sao Paulo, Brazil, 1970-71; asst. prof. home econs. edn. U. Wis., 1973-78; prof., head div. home econs. U. Wyo., Laramie, 1978-81, prof., 4-H home econs. specialist, 1981—; cons. Wyo. State Dept. Edn., 1981-82. Bd. dirs. Sexual Assault and Family Violence Ednl. Project, 1979-82, mem. personnel com., 1981-82. Mem. Am. Home Econs. Assn., Am. Vocat. Assn. (life), Home Econs. Edn. Assn., Phi Upsilon Omicron, Pi Lambda Theta. Lutheran. Home: 2416 Skyview Ln Laramie WY 82070 Office: Box 3354 University Station University of Wyoming Laramie WY 82071

HUGHES, LYRIC MERRIE, mktg. exec.; b. Denver, Mar. 28, 1953; d. James Clifford and Meladee Ann (Annes) H.; student Northwestern U., 1970-74; A.B. in Near Eastern Langs. and Civilizations, U. Chgo., 1976; m. James R. Liebling, Dec. 24, 1980. Instr. figure skating Northwestern U. and Winnetka Park Dist. (Ill.), 1968-74; pres. Trans-Lingual Communications, Inc., Chgo., 1977—; permanent guest lectr., exec. in residence Harper Coll., Palatine, Ill., 1981—. Chmn., Cook County New Voters, 1972-73. Rotary scholar, Sendai, Japan, 1969-70; Ill. Gov.'s internship program, 1972; Am. Cancer Soc. summer grantee, 1969. Mem. Lang. and Internat. Studies Network (chmn. 1982—), Women in Internat. Trade (pres. 1981—), Internat. Bus. Council Mid-Am., Internat. Advt. Assn., Japan Am. Soc., Asia Soc., Rotex. Office: 8 S Michigan Ave Chicago IL 60603

HUGHES, MADELON GRACE, accountant; b. Seattle, July 21, 1926; d. Lawrence Christopher and Thelma May (McKay) Prentice; student public schs., Seattle; m. James Robert Hughes, Apr. 29, 1967; children—Robert, Kathleen, Teresa, Linda. With Pacific Iron & Metal Co., Seattle, 1965-66; acct. Judson Park Retirement Home, Des Moines, Wash., 1966-69, Budget Rent A Car of Tacoma, Medved Auto Parks, Inc., 1969-72; self employed bookkeeping service and Tax acct., Torrance, Calif., 1972—. Treas., St. James Women's Council, 1974-75. Mem. Nat. Assn. Enrolled Agts. (sec. 1974-78; pres. Los Angeles chpt. 1977-78, dir. 1978-80), Calif. Soc. Enrolled Agts. (sec. 1977, 80-81, pres. South Bay chpt. 1981-82, dir. 1982-83), Southwood Homeowners Assn. Home and Office: 5227 Lillian St Torrance CA 90503

HUGHES, MARGARET CYRENA, ret. assn. exec.; b. Springfield, Ill.; d. Thomas Patrick and Elizabeth (Donelan) Hughes; student Springfield Jr. Coll., U. Ill. Campaign chmn. Community Fund Assn., 1947-51; exec. dir. Sangamon County Tb Assn., Springfield, 1951-70; exec. dir. Lincoln Land Tb and Respiratory Disease Assn., 1970-76. Pres. Friends of Library, 1956. Exec. com. Sangamon County Council Social Agys., 1940-41; pres. Ill. State Assn. Women's Divs. Chambers of Commerce; bd. dirs., sec. Springfield Safety Council, 1978—, trustee, 1976, now treas.; bd. dirs. Sangamon County Mental Health, 1948-53, R.S.V.P., Sr. Citizens of Sangamon County; Cath. adv. com. Girl Scouts U.S.A., 1946-51, nat. resettlement adv. com. 1948-53; bd. dirs. St. John's Sanitorium Aux. Recipient Pro Ecclesia at Pontifice medal. Mem. Assn. Commerce and Industry (pres. women's div. 1961-62), Ill. C. of C. (v.p. women's div.), Ill. Conf. Tb Workers (pres. 1961-62), Dioceasen Council Cath. Women (past pres.; dir.), Nat. Council Cath. Women (past provincial dir.; chmn. youth com. 1944-51), Louise de Marillac Guild, Sacred Heart Acad. Alumni Assn. (past pres.), Cathedral Altar Soc. (pres. 1956-57), Symphony Guild. Clubs: Zonta (pres. Springfield 1962, area dist. dir. 1963-64); Cotarle (dir. 1943-44); Springfield Women's (dir., chmn. safety com., v.p. 1971—, pres. 1973-75, membership chmn.). Home: 417 E Canedy St Springfield IL 62703

HUGHES, MARIJA MATICH, law librarian; b. Belgrade, Yugoslavia; d. Zarija and Antonija (Hudowsky) Matic; B.A. in Music, Mokranjac, Belgrade; B.A. in English, U. Belgrade and Calif. State U. Sacramento; M.L.S., U. Md.; McGeorge Sch. Law. Counselor, gen. mgr. Career Counseling Service, Sacramento, 1963-64; sec. to mgr. Sacramento State Coll. Food Service, 1965-66; student librarian "High John", Program U. Md., Fairmont Heights, 1967-68; reference librarian Calif. State Law Library, Sacramento, 1968-69; head reference librarian U. Calif. Hastings Coll. Law, San Francisco, 1969-72; head law librarian AT&T, Washington, 1972-73; chief law librarian Nat. Clearinghouse Library, U.S. Commn. on Civil Rights, Washington, 1973—. Mem. Assn. Am. Law Libraries, ALA, Nat. Women's Polit. Caucas, Federally Employed Women, Soc. for Internat. Devel., Advisors for Women, Spl. Libraries Assn., Assn. Internat. Law Libraries, Women in Legal Edn., Nat. Orgn. Women, Women's Equity Action League (sec.). Author, compiler: The Sexual Barrier: Legal and Economic Aspects of Employment, 1970-72; The Sexual Barrier: Legal, Medical, Economic and Social Aspects of Sex discrimination, 1977. Contbr. articles to profl. jours. Home: 500 23d St NW Apt B 203 Washington DC 20037 Office: Nat Civil Rights Library US Commn on Civil Rights 1121 Vermont Ave NW Washington DC 20425

HUGHES, MARTHA HANNAH, educator; b. Pitts., Nov. 25, 1939; d. Jesse and Ethel May Foreman; B.S., Chgo. State U., 1972; postgrad. Pepperdine U., 1979, Calif. State U., Dominguez Hills, 1979-81; m. John D. Thompson (dec.); m. 2d, Virgil Hughes, Nov. 27, 1971; children—Jewell Lee Golliday, Jawanna Lynn Thompson, Virgil Hughes. Sec., Allied Radio Corp., 1965-70; tchr. Chgo. Bd. Edn., 1972-78; tchr. Los Angeles Unified Sch. Dist., 1978—; receptionist Los Angeles County Sheriff's Dept., 1981—. Mem. Psi Alpha Theta. Roman Catholic. Office: 450 Grand St Los Angeles CA 90054

HUGHES, MICHELE JOAN, mgmt. cons.; b. Natick, Mass., Nov. 1, 1945; d. Harry G. and Mildred (Goldstein) Feldman; B.A. in English, U. Mass., 1967; postgrad. Oxford (Eng.) U., 1967; M.A. in English/Edn., Hofstra U., Hempstead, N.Y., 1972; m. Justin Peter Hughes, June 16, 1968. Secondary sch. tchr., Boston and N.Y., 1967-72; pres. Scott Parker Anderson, Inc., exec. search consultants, San Francisco, 1972-74, dir., 1973-74; pres. M.J. Hughes & Co., exec. search cons., San Francisco, 1974-76; partner William H. Clark Assos., exec. search cons., San Francisco, 1976-78; partner, shareholder, dir. Ward Howell Internat., San Francisco, 1978—; co-anchor cable TV show; producer radio series Sta. KSFO. Mem. bus. adv. bd. North Shore Community Coll. Sch. Bus.; mem. Bay Area Council, Internat. Hospitality Center. Named One of 25 Fastest Rising Execs. in San Francisco Bay Area, 1980, One of Top Ten Profl. Women, Glamour mag., 1980. Mem. Women's Forum West (dir. 1977-78), Nat. Jr. Tennis League (dir., hon. trustee 1975—), San Francisco C. of C., Am. Mgmt. Assn., Am. Conservatory Theatre, Am. Mktg. Assn. (lectr.), Women in Bus. (speaker), Chi Omega. Club: Tiburon Peninsula. Home: 6 Rolling Hills Tiburon CA 94920 Office: 3 Embarcadero Center Suite 1060 San Francisco CA 94111

HUGHES, PAULA D., investment exec.; b. N.Y.C., Sept. 25, 1931; 1 dau., Catherine H. Benton. With Brown & Bigelow, N.Y.C., 1953-61; account exec. Shields & Co., N.Y.C., 1961-72; v.p. Thomson McKinnon Securities Inc., N.Y.C., 1972—, 1st. v.p., dir., 1979—; gov. U.S. Postal Service, 1980—; allied mem. N.Y. Stock Exchange; life trustee Cargenie-Mellon U., mem. fin. and exec. compensation coms.; dir. Com. for Corp. Support of Pvt. Univs.; lectr.-instr. Personal Investment Mgmt., N.Y.U.; lectr. various schs. and colls. including Vassar Coll.; speaker New Sch., N.Y.C., panel mem. Wall St. Conf., 1979, 82; speaker Securities Industry Assn. Conf., Wharton Sch., U. Pa., 1977. Panelist N.Y. State Casino Gambling Study, 1979; gov. Greenwich House, N.Y.C., 1961—. Recipient AMITA Golden Lady award in Fin., 1975; named Bus. Woman of Yr., Calif. Bus. Women, 1976. Mem. Women's Forum (dir. 1979—), Sales Execs. Club N.Y. (treas. 1977-79, dir. 1977—), Fin. Women's Assn., Am. Arbitration Soc., Internat. Assn. Fin. Planners. Republican. Clubs: Duquesne (Pitts.); Shenorock Shore (Rye); Yale (N.Y.C.). Featured cover articles in Fin. World, 1975, 78; featured articles in publs. including Fortune mag., Wall St. Jour., Pitts. Press, Ariz. Republic, N.Y. Times, N.Y. Post, Indpls. Star; guest on Wall St. Week. Office: Thomson McKinnon Securities Inc 200 Park Ave New York NY 10166

HUGHES, RUTH PIERCE, home economist; b. Utica, N.Y., Sept. 2, 1919; d. Gilbert Davis and Elizabeth Bertha (Bennett) Pierce; B.S., Cornell U., 1941, M.S., 1949, Ph.D., 1969; divorced; children—Betty Ann, Carol Ellen. Secondary sch. tchr. N.Y. State, intermittently, 1941-65; grad. asst., research assoc. Cornell U., 1965-68; asso. prof. home econs., dir. div. family resources W.Va. U., 1968-71; prof. home econs. Iowa State U., Ames, 1971—, head dept., 1971—, Mary B. Welch disting. prof., 1980—; cons. in field. Chmn. edn. work area First United Methodist Ch., Ames, 1980—. Served with USNR, 1944-46. Mem. Am. vocat. Assn., Am. Home Econs. Assn., Am. Ednl. Research Assn., Am. Vocat. Edn. Research Assn., Nat. Soc. Study Edn. Clubs: Ames Golf and Country, Order Eastern Star. Author papers in field. Editor Jour. Vocat. Edn. Research, 1980—. Home: 3425 Ross Rd Ames IA 50010 Office: 219 MacKay Hall Iowa State U Ames IA 50011

HUGHES, SARAH TILGHMAN, fed. judge: b. Balt., Aug. 2, 1896; d. James Cooke and Elizabeth (Haughton) Tilghman; A.B., Goucher Coll., 1917, LL.D. (hon.), 1950; LL.B., George Washington Law Sch., 1922, LL.D., 1977; LL.D. (hon.), So. Methodist U., 1967, Ind. State U., 1967, Iowa Wesleyan Coll., 1969, Mary Hardin Baylor, 1974; L.H.D. (hon.), Clarkson Coll., 1975; m. George Ernest, Mar. 13, 1922. With Met. Police Dept., Washington, 1919-22; admitted to D.C. bar, 1922, Tex. bar, 1922; practice law, Dallas, 1922-35; mem. Tex. Ho. of Reps., 1931-35; judge 14th Dist. Ct., Dallas, 1935-61; judge U.S. Dist. Ct., No. Dist. of Tex., Dallas, 1961—. Faculty, So. Methodist U. Law Sch., Dallas, 1942-43. Mem. nat. commn. UNESCO, 1953-56, 64-70. Mem. Nat. Fedn. Bus. and Profl. Women's Clubs (pres. 1950-52), Internat. Fedn. Bus. and Profl. Women's Clubs (v.p. 1953-62), Dallas UN Assn. (pres. 1953-55, 62-63). Mem. Am., Inter-Am., Dallas bar assns., State Bar Tex., Nat. Assn. Women Lawyers, Am. Judicature Soc., Phi Beta Kappa, Kappa Beta Pi, Delta Sigma Rho, Delta Kappa Gamma. Democrat. Episcopalian. Office: Federal Bldg Dallas TX 75242 *

HUGHES, SUE MARGARET, librarian; b. Cleburne, Tex., Apr. 13; d. Chastain Wesley and Sue Willis (Payne) H.; B.B.A. with highest honors, U. Tex., Austin, 1949; M.L.S., Tex. Woman's U., 1960, postgrad. Sec.-treas. several privately owned corps., Waco, Tex., 1949-59, asst. in pub. services Baylor U. Moody Library, Waco, 1960-64, acquisitions librarian, 1964-79, dir., 1980—, mem. univ. senate. Mem. AAUP (pres. Baylor chpt. 1979-80), AAUW (pres. Waco br. 1974-76, state bylaws and resolutions chmn. 1977-79), Am., (sec. RTSD Reprinting com., past chmn. duplicates exchange union com.), Southwestern, Tex. (local chmn. dist. 3 meeting, 1975) library assns., Library Club (Waco), Sigma Delta Pi, Beta Gamma Sigma, Delta Kappa Gamma (chmn. research com. 1976-78, rec. sec. 1978-80), Beta Phi Mu. Methodist. Clubs: Altrusa; Baylor Round Table (treas. 1974-75, sec. 1977-78). Office: PO Box 6307 Waco TX 76706

HUHTA, MARY FOYE, civic worker; b. Phila., Sept. 20, 1936; d. Arthur Wesley and Anna Rebecca (Potterfield) Perry; B.S. in Edn., Baldwin-Wallace Coll., 1958; postgrad., Middle Tenn. State U., 1976—; m. James Kenneth Huhta, Dec. 28, 1958; children—Rebecca Foye, Mary Suzanne. Tchr. public schs., Lakewood, Ohio, 1958-59, Durham, N.C., 1959-63; civic vol. LWV, Murfreesboro, Tenn., 1966—, pres., 1971-73, land use co-chmn., 1973—, fin. chmn., 1976, 77; chmn. Murfreesboro Beautification Commn., 1977-82; mem. Rutherford County Bd. Zoning Appeals, 1974—, Murfreesboro Bikeways Com., 1976—, Murfreesboro City Council, 1982—, Murfreesboro Neighborhood Parks Com., 1976—; house restoration chmn. Oaklands Assn., 1979—; mem. landscaping com. Cannonsburgh Mus. Village, 1977-78; bd. dirs. Sack-Up Saturday, 1978, 79, Rutherford County Arts and Humanities Council, 1978-79; mem. Murfreesboro City Council, 1982—. Mem. Ladies Hermitage Assn., Rutherford County Hist. Soc., Tenn. Mus. Assn., Nat. Trust for Hist. Preservation, LWV. Home: 507 E Northfield Blvd Murfreesboro TN 37130

HUIZENGA, ANN HARRIET, ret. public health cons.; b. Englewood, N.J., June 6, 1913; d. Lee Sjoerdt and Matilda (Van Dyken) H.; A.B., Calvin Coll., 1933; M.D., Rush Med. Coll. U. Chgo., 1937; M.P.H., U. N.C., 1969; M.A., U. Conn., 1973. Intern, Presbyn. Hosp., Chgo., 1937, Chgo. Mcpl. Contagious Disease Hosp., 1938, San Francisco Children's Hosp., 1938-39; resident Margaret Hague Hosp., Jersey City, 1944-45, Women's Coll. Pa. Hosp., 1945, Evang. Deaconess Hosp., Detroit, 1957; missionary med. practice, China, N.Mex. and Ariz., 1939-50; practice medicine specializing in ob-gyn., Greenville, N.C., 1950-62; cons. in maternal health and family planning N.C. Bd. Health, Raleigh, 1962-79. Recipient Reynolds award N.C. Public Health Assn., 1978. Mem. Am. Coll. Ob-Gyn, AMA, N.C. Med. Soc., Nat. Council Family Relations, N.C. Public Health Assn., N.C. Family Life Council. Home: 2474 32d St SE Grand Rapids MI 49508

HULA, KAY BOCOX, sch. psychologist; b. Perry, Okla., Aug. 28, 1942; d. George H. and Mary E. (Kirtley) Bocox; B.A., Okla. State U., 1971, M.S., 1974; children—Roger, Rachel. Jr. high spl. edn. tchr., Ponca City, Okla., 1971-73; teaching asst. Okla. State U., Stillwater, 1973-74; prescriptive tchr. Regional Edn. Service Center, Cushing, Okla., 1974-75, prescriptive tchr., psychometrist, 1975-76, ednl. cons., 1976-77; psychometrist Tulsa Vocat.-Tech. Sch., 1977—; dir. Okla. State Vocat. Occupational Skills Fair, 1981. Mem. Nat. Assn. Female Execs., Nat. Tchrs. Assn., Okla. Tchrs. Assn., Okla. Psychol. Assn., Delta Kappa Pi. Democrat. Mem. Christian Ch. Club: Buttons and Bows. Home: 10128 E 34th St Tulsa OK 74145 Office: Tulsa Vocational-Technical School 3802 N Peoria St Tulsa OK 74106

HULEN, MARJORIE JANE, assn. exec.; b. Denver, Sept. 23, 1921; d. Perry E. and Garnet W. (Doty) Kellogg; student public schs., Redondo Beach, Calif.; m. Ray Romaine Hulen, June 10, 1950; 1 son, Lynn Robert. With A.O. Smith Corp., Los Angeles, 1948-60, sec., 1956-60; exec. sec. Sterling Electric Motors, Los Angeles, 1960-61; research sec. Pasadena (Calif.) Found. for Med. Research, 1961-65; exec. sec. Profl. Staff Assn., Los Angeles County/U. So. Calif. Med. Center, Los Angeles, 1965-70, office mgr., 1970-74, bus. mgr., 1974—, exec. dir., 1980—. Instl. rep. Los Angeles Regional Family Planning, 1977—. Mem. Nat. Secs. Assn., Soc. Research Adminstrs. (pres. So. Calif. chpt. 1982-83), Nat. Assn. Accts. (nat. pub. relations award 1979), Am. Soc. Assn. Execs., Nat. Assn. Female Execs. Democrat. Home: 2311 El Paseo St Alhambra CA 91803 Office: Los Angeles County/U So Calif Med Center 1739 Griffin Ave Los Angeles CA 90031

HULL, BETTY JANE, dir. guidance; b. Fremont, Nebr.; B.A. in English, French and Latin, Luth. Midland Coll., Fremont, 1942; student in bus. Katharine Gibbs Coll., N.Y.C., 1943; M.A. in Guidance and Counseling, Case Western Reserve U., Cleve., 1960; married; 4 children. Tchr. social studies Bay Village (Ohio) City Schs., 1957-58, tchr., chmn. bus. dept., 1958-60, guidance counselor, 1960-68, dir. guidance, 1968—. Mem. Ohio High Sch. Advisory Bd. Admissions Registration Services, 1974—. Mem. Ohio, Northeastern Ohio, Am. personnel guidance assns., Am., Ohio (exec. bd. 1974—), Cuyahoga County sch. counselors assns., Ohio Assn. Coll. Admissions Counselors (past pres.), NEA, Ohio Edn. Assn., Bay Tchrs. Assn., Delta Kappa Gamma. Contbr. articles to profl. jours. Certified in pupil personnel, Ohio. Home: 28924 Lake Rd Bay Village OH 44140 Office: Bay High Sch 29230 Wolf Rd Bay Village OH 44140

HULL, DIANA, psychologist; b. Lawrence, N.Y., Aug. 13, 1924; d. Louis Albert and Rosalyn (Diamont) Jaffer; B.A., City U. N.Y., 1946; M.S.W., U. Mich., 1954; Ph.D., Sch. Public Health, U. Tex. Health Scis. Center, 1975; children—Marcy Ross Burton, Allison Langdon Boomer; m. 2d, David P. Hull, Dec. 27, 1969. Mem. clin. faculty Baylor Coll. Medicine, Houston, 1964-80; mem. Task Force Guidelines for Media Psychologists; cons. cons. Tex. Inst. Family Psychiatry, Children's Psychiat. Clinic of Baylor Coll. Medicine. Fellow Am. Group Psychotherapy Assn. (nat. faculty), Houston Group Psychotherapy Soc. (pres. 1967, adv. bd. 1967-80); mem. Am. Psychol. Assn., Calif. Psychol. Assn., AAAS, N.Y. Acad. Scis., Assn. Media Psychology (sec.), Sierra Club. Unitarian. Club: Birnam Wood Golf. Contbr. articles to profl. jours. Home: 815 Cima Linda Ln Santa Barbara CA 93108

HULL, JANE LAUREL LEEK, nurse, adminstr.; b. Ontario, Calif., July 4, 1923; d. William Abram and Susan Bianca (Pethick) Leek; R.N., Columbia Presbyn. Sch. Nursing, 1944; B.A., Redlands U., 1977; ; m. James B. Hull, Oct. 10, 1944 (dec.); children—James W., William P., Kenneth D. Supr. obstetrics Sch. Nursing, Mid-Valley Hosp., Peckville, Pa., 1945-46; surg. nurse acute nursing Scranton (Pa.) State Hosp., 1947-52; nurse San Antonio Community Hosp., Upland, Calif., 1953-55; office nurse H.L. Archibald, Upland, 1965; vis. nurse Pomona West End Inc., continuity of care coordinator, Montclair, Calif., 1968-73, exec. dir., 1973—; tchr. ARC nursing course to high sch. students. Treas. PTA, Pomona, Calif.; vol. exec. dir. Inland Hospice Assn., 1979-80. Mem. Calif. Nurses Assn. (pres. dist. 53 1958), Calif. Assn. for Health Services at Home (dir.), Calif. League Nursing, Nat. Homecaring Council (dir.). Republican. Club: Zonta (Ontario, Upland, pres., 1976). Organizer Homemaker Dept. in Vis. Nurse Assn., 1972; developer (with Don Baxter Corp.) plugs for in-dwelling Foley catheters, 1963. Home: 543 W F St Ontario CA 91762 Office: 5156 Holt Blvd Montclair CA 91763

HULL, JOAN CAROL, soc. adminstr.; b. Newark, Apr. 31, 1938; d. Milton O. and Cemelia (Molitor) H.; B.A., St. Lawrence U., 1954; M.A., Montclair State Coll., 1962; degree in mus. adminstrn. Columbia U. Tchr., Butler High Sch., 1958-63; dir. jr. hist. socs. N.J. Hist. Soc., Newark, 1963-69, asst. dir., 1969-79, acting dir., 1979, exec. dir., 1979—. Recipient Montclair State Coll. Alumni Bicentennial award; N.J. Hist. Commn. Pitcher. Mem. AAUW (1st v.p. Essex county br.). Clubs: Skytop, Downtown, Soroptomists (Newark). Office: 230 Broadway Newark NJ 07104 *

HULL, LOIS A. WINEFORDNER, social worker; b. Detroit, Aug. 12, 1932; d. J. Guy and Cora B.(Daoust) Winefordner; student Black Hawk Jr. Coll., Moline, Ill., 1966-70; B.A., Marycrest Coll., Davenport, Iowa, 1972; M.S.W., U. Iowa, 1975; m. Ward K. Hull, Aug. 11, 1951; children—Richard W., Randall L., Russell J., Daniel A., Jonathon A. Nurse's aid Hillcrest Home, Geneseo, Ill., 1965-72; dir. social services Hammond Henry Hosp., Geneseo, 1972—; mem. bd. Clinic on Alcohol and Other Drugs, 1976-77; tchr. biofeedback Black Hawk Jr. Coll., Moline, Ill. Mem. founding bd. Growth Inc. Day Care Center, Geneseo, 1974-76, Geneseo Marriage and Family Counseling Services, 1975-80; founding bd. Good Shepherd Found. of Henry County, 1977—, sec., 1977-78, 80—, v.p., 1979; treas. Henry County Mental Health Assn., 1973-75. Cert. social worker, alcoholism counselor. Mem. Am. Hosp. Assn. Social Work Dirs., No. Dist. Hosp. Social Work Dirs. (del.-at-large), Nat. Assn. Social Workers, Ill. Alcohol and Drug Dependence Assn., Ill. Welfare Assn. (sub-com. edn. and tng.), Am. Assn. Biofeedback Clinicians (cert. asso.), Ill. Biofeedback Soc., Biofeedback Soc. Am., Ill. Assn. for Prevention Child Abuse, Ill. Mental Health Assn., Ill. Fedn. Women's Clubs (pres. Geneseo jr. women's club 1966-67). Roman Catholic. Club: Geneseo Columbian. Writer children's poetry. Home: Rural Route 4 Geneseo IL 61254 Office: 210 W Elk St Geneseo IL 61254

HULL, MONA CUTLER, educator; b. N.Y.C., Dec. 6, 1912; d. Frederick John and Anna (Dunham) Cutler; A.B., Mount Holyoke Coll., 1933; M.Nursing, Yale U., 1937; Ph.D., Boston U., 1962; m. Gordon Ferrie Hull, II, June 24, 1937; children—Gordon Ferrie, Mona Jerusha, David Berney, Jonathan Cutler, Berney Elizabeth. Founder, prin. Advent Sch., Boston, 1961-65; asst. dir. overseas ednl. inst. Brown U., 1965-66; asso. prof. Boston U. Grad. Sch., 1969-73; asso. prof. Lowell (Mass.) State Coll., 1973-75, prof. health service adminstrn., 1977—, dir. Gerontology Resource Center, 1977—; nurse practitioner, 1976—; dir. Hull Assos., Multinat. Learning Center, Rockport, Mass. Adv. com. Mass. Dept. Social Services, 1980—; Mass. rep. Housing Authority, Rockport, 1979—; pres. bd. dirs. Vis. Nurse Assn. N. Shore, 1978-80; treas. Cape Ann Project for Elders, 1975-79; project dir. Project Connect, Mass. Dept. Elder Affairs, 1976-80. Boston U. Human Relations Center fellow, 1969-72; Ella Lyman Cabot Found. grantee, 1962-65. Mem. Am. Nurses Assn., Nat. League Nursing, Am. Coll. Nursing Home Adminstrs., Am. Public Health Assn., Mass. Nurses Assn., Mass. Tchrs. Assn., Sigma Theta Tau, Mt. Holyoke Coll. Alumnae Assn. Clubs: Sandy Bay Yacht, Soc. St. Francis. Contbr. articles to profl. jours. Home: 2 Jewett St Rockport MA 01966 Office: Weed Hall U Lowell Lowell MA 01854

HULL, OLLIE SYKES, nurse anesthetist; b. Delhi, La., Apr. 17, 1935; d. Elbert and Eunice (Garrett) Sykes; grad. Vicksburg Hosp. Sch. Nursing, 1955; B.S. in Anesthesiology, U. Miss., 1975; m. Sherman Cody Hull, Jr., May 14, 1955; children—Sherman Cody, Steven Earl. Surg. asst. Vicksburg (Miss.) Hosp., 1959-65; pvt. duty nurse Vicksburg area hosps., 1965-67; sch. nurse Vicksburg Public Schs., 1970-73; staff anesthetist Bapt. Med. Center, Jackson, Miss., 1975—. Bd. dirs. Am. Cancer Soc., Vicksburg, 1976; mem. adv. bd. Salvation Army, 1972—. Named Miss. Woman of Achievement, 1976. Mem. Miss. Assn. Nurse Anesthetists (bd. dirs., pres. 1982), Nat. Fedn. Bus. and Profl. Women's Clubs, Am. Assn. Nurse Anesthetists, Miss. Fedn. Bus. and Profl. Women's Clubs (pres. 1981—), Nat. Assn. Female Execs., Miss. Women's Polit. Caucus (charter). Democrat. Baptist. Home: Route 2 Box 185T Terry MS 39170 Office: 1225 N State St Jackson MS 39201

HULL, PHILLIS MAY ANDREWS, educator; b. Dallas, Dec. 13, 1919; d. John Fidelos and Lula Ann (Parvin) Andrews; B.S., Tex. A&I U., 1957, M.S., 1960; postgrad. Baylor U., Waco, Tex., 1973; m. James Beaird Hull, Apr. 5, 1941; children—James Beaird, Linda Kay Hull Adrian, Mary Ann Hull Smith. Elem. sch. tchr. in Tex., 1955—; tchr. Woodville Ind. Sch. Dist., 1969—. Mem. NEA, Nat. PTA, Tex. Tchrs. Assn. (dist. chmn. human relations com. 1973, instrl. services com. 1974), Tex. Classroom Tchrs. Assn., Tyler County Tchrs. Assn. (pres. 1972), Internat. Reading Assn., Tex. Reading Assn., Nat. Ret. Tchrs. Assn., Woodville Ind. Sch. Dist. Sch. Service League, Nat. Bus. and Profl. Women's Club, Woodville Bus. and Profl. Women's Club (pres. 1973; Woman of Yr. award 1974), Federated Women's Club (pres. Woodville 1974; Outstanding Leadership Resolution 1974) AAUW, Delta Kappa Gamma Soc. Internat. (scholarship 1974, Achievement award 1978, 79, v.p. Delta Epsilon chpt. 1978, pres. 1980-82). Democrat. Baptist. Clubs: Cheswood Lake, Woodville Woman's Reading. Address: 30 Lake Dr Woodville TX 75979

HULSEY, RUTH LENORA, state ofcl.; b. Athens, Ga., Nov. 28, 1927; d. Joseph Alonzo and Frances Rebecca (Bell) Johnson; student Pasadena Jr. Coll., 1938-40, San Bernardino Valley Coll., 1963-65; m. William A.

Hulsey III, Mar. 28, 1958; children—William A., Stephen G., Alicia A. With State of Calif. Employment Devel. Office, 1960—, supr., San Bernardino Field Dept. Office, 1969-75, So. Region Office, Riverside, 1975-78, employment program mgr., asst. mgr. Ontario Field Office, 1979-80, employment program mgr., mgr. Fontana Field Office, 1980—; dir. Calif. State Employees Credit Union, 1972-75, mem. employer adv. council, 1978—. Mem. edn. com. Urban League, 1965, mem., 1965—; mem. Arrowhead Allied Arts Council, 1966-72; mem. Social Lites, 1963—, pres., 1964-66, 80-81, bd. dirs., 1980—, rec. sec., 1981—. Mem. Internat. Assn. Personnel in Employment Security, Calif. State Employees Assn., Bloomington C. of C., Fontana C. of C., Rialto C. of C., San Bernardino C. of C. Democrat. Methodist. Home: 1246 E Shamrock Ave San Bernardino CA 92410 Office: State of Calif Employment Devel Dept Office 17590 Foothill Blvd Fontana CA 92335

HULTINE, HILDRETH MARION, mental hosp. exec.; b. Clay Center, Nebr., Dec. 26, 1923; d. Oscar Vernon and Myrtle Nora Belcher; R.N., Mary Lanning Meml. Hosp., 1946; B.A., Hastings Coll., 1965; M.A., U. Nebr., 1970; cert. in mental health adminstrn. U. Minn., 1979; m. Dale Hultine, Oct. 4, 1944; children—Barton, Brian, Bruce. Head nurse dept. pediatrics Mary Lanning Meml. Hosp., Hastings, Nebr., 1952-53, night nurse supr., 1953-60; instr. psychiat. nursing program Hastings Regional Center, 1960-70, dir. nursing, 1970-73, chief exec. officer, 1973-79; supt. Larned (Kans.) State Hosp., 1979—. Mem. Nat. League Nursing, Am. Acad. Med. Adminstrs., Assn. Mental Health Adminstrs. Democrat. Lutheran. Home and Office: Rural Route 3 PO Box 89 Larned KS 67550

HULUBEI, MONICA ELENA, architect; b. Bucharest, Romania, Aug. 29, 1943; came to U.S., 1976, naturalized, 1979; d. Theodor and Florica (Botez) Balaban; diploma architecture, Ion Mincu Inst. Architecture, Bucharest, 1970; m. Valeriu Hulubei, Feb. 8, 1969; children—Horatius, Victoria, Hugh-Adrian, Monica. Researcher, Inst. Art History, Bucharest, 1971; architect, then design engr. firm in W. Ger., 1971-76; engr. R.A. Hanson Co., Spokane, Wash., 1976-77, Western Nuclear, Inc., Wellpinit, Wash., 1978—; painter portraits and religious works. Diplom-Engr., Land Hessen, W. Ger., 1980. Home: E 1717 16th Ave Spokane WA 99203 Office: Western Nuclear Inc PO Box 392 Wellpinit WA 99040

HUME, GWENNE, state legislator, educator; b. Bridgeport, Conn., June 13, 1942; B.S. in Phys. Edn.; M.A. in Dance; Ed.D. in Exercise Physiology and Gerontology; m. Sandy Hume; child, Marcia. Mem. faculty U. Colo., Boulder, now asst. prof.; tchr. public schs., N.J. and Mass.; mem. Colo. Ho. of Reps., vice chmn. appropriations com., mem. edn. com. Chmn. Gov.'s Council on Phys. Fitness, 1975-80. Republican. Office: Colorado House of Representatives State Capitol Denver CO 80203 *

HUME-THARP, SANDRA JEAN, interior designer; b. Seattle, Dec. 25, 1949; d. Ora Lester and Frances Mae (Apple) Hume; B.A. in Interior Design, San Jose (Calif.) State U., 1973; m. Michael John Tharp, Sept. 2, 1979. Interior designer Dohrmann Contract, Menlo Park, Calif., 1973-74, Edwards Bldgs. Co., Beaverton, Oreg., 1975-77, Villard Design, Beaverton, 1978—. Mem. Am. Soc. Interior Designers (asso.), Nat. Assn. Homebuilders. Club: Multnomah Athletic (Portland, Oreg.). Home: 15738 NW Sunningdale St Beaverton OR 97006 Office: 4905 SW Griffith Dr Beaverton OR 97005

HUMMEL, ALICE H., ednl. co. exec.; b. Bklyn., July 23, 1939; d. Samuel and Ethel (Beitchman) Holtz; C.L.A., Boston U., 1958; postgrad. N.Y. Inst. Fin., 1967, U. New Haven, 1972-79; m. Kurt Hummel, Nov. 30, 1957; children—Karen, Stephanni, Eric. Acct. exec. Blair & Co., Inc., New Haven, Conn., 1966-73; ter. mgr. Bradford Sch. Corp., New Haven, 1973-77, mgr. Time Sharing Resources, Stamford, Conn., 1977-79; pres. Ednl. Career Devel. Corp., New Haven, 1979—; cons. in field. Mem. exec. bd. New Haven County (Conn.) March of Dimes, 1975—. Mem. Nat. Bus. Educators Assn., Conn. Bus. Educators Assn., Network N.H., Conn., Concerned Woman Colleagues. Republican. Club: Farms Country. Home: 24 Crestview Dr North Haven CT 06473 Office: 900 Chapel Sq Upper Mall New Haven CT 06510

HUMPHREY, KATHARINE LYNN, mining co. exec.; b. Akron, Ohio, Mar. 19, 1951; d. Edwin Murray and Diane (Zabiegalski) H.; B.A., Johns Hopkins U., 1973. Dir. public affairs council Electronic Industries Assn., Washington, 1974-75; pension cons. Proskauer, Rose, Goetz & Mendelsohn, N.Y.C., 1976-77; sr. mktg. cons. The Equitable Life Assurance Soc., N.Y.C., 1977-79; dir. advt., asso. dir. public affairs St. Joe Minerals Corp., N.Y.C., 1979-82, mgr. communications projects, 1982—. Recipient Nicholson award, 1980, 81. Mem. Am. Mgmt. Assn., Am. Mining Congress, Bus. and Profl. Advt. Assn. Club: Airline Theater Wing. Home: 1076 Miramar St Laguna Beach CA 92651 Office: 250 Park Ave New York NY 10017

HUMPHREY, LOUISE IRELAND (MRS. GILBERT W. HUMPHREY), civic worker, horsewoman; b. Morehead City, N.C., Nov. 1, 1918; d. R. Livingston and Margaret (Allen) Ireland; ed. pvt. schs.; m. Gilbert W. Humphrey, Dec. 27, 1939; children—Margaret (Mrs. K. Bindhart), George M. II, Gilbert Watts. Nurse's aide ARC, 1944—; trustee Musical Arts Assn., mem. exec. com.; hon. trustee, past pres. Vis. Nurse Assn.; hon. trustee Lake Erie Coll., Cleve. Zool. Soc., United Way Cleve., Archbold Hosp., Thomasville, Ga.; hon. trustee Case Western Res. U.; bd. dirs. Thomas County (Ga.) Hist. Soc., Monticello (Fla.) Opera House; mem. Cuyahoga and Lake County Republican Exec. Com.; mem., past trustee, 2d v.p. Jr. League; bd. dirs. Met. Opera Assn., pres. nat. council; bd. dirs. Thomas County Entertainment Found.; pres., trustee No. Ohio Opera Assn.; former master foxhounds Chagrin Valley Hunt, Gates Mills, Ohio; dir., zone v.p. U.S. Equestrian Team, Inc.; mem. Ohio Arts Council, Garden Club Cleve.; bd. dirs., past pres. Nat. Homecaring Council; treas., trustee Wildlife Fedn. Fund Am., mem. adv. bd. Tall Timbers Assn. Home: Woodfield Springs Plantation Miccosukee FL 32309

HUMPHREY, PATRICIA ANN, nurse, educator; b. Craven County, N.C. Mar. 28, 1942; d. James Allen and Sally Elizabeth (Maine) H.; diploma Watts Hosp. Sch. Nursing, 1963; B.S.N., U. N.C., 1967, M.P.H., 1972; cert. family nurse practitioner U. N.C., 1980. Staff nurse Craven County Hosp., N.C., 1963-64; nurse Watts Hosp., Durham, N.C., 1963-64, head nurse, 1964-65; pub. health nurse Durham County Health Dept., 1967-71; asst. prof. nursing Duke U., Durham, 1972—; vis. prof. U. N.C., Chapel Hill, summer 1978. USPHS trainee, 1965-67, 71-72. Mem. Am. Nurses Assn., Sigma Theta Tau. Republican. Methodist. Club: Durham Jr. Women's. Co editor: Human Growth and Development Throughout Life, 1982. Home: 1606 University Dr Durham NC 27707 Office: Sch Nursing Duke U Durham NC 27710

HUMPHREYVILLE, THERESA RUTH, coll. dean; b. New Philadelphia, Ohio, Jan. 28, 1918; d. Charles King and Dana Edna (Orr) H.; B.S. in Bus. Adminstrn., Ohio State U., 1940; M.Sc. in Retailing, N.Y. U., 1941; Ed.D. in Psychol. Service, Columbia U., 1953. Research asst. Nat. Retail Dry Goods Assn., 1940-41; personnel officer Johns-Manville Corp., N.Y.C., 1941-46; psychologist Coll. Human Ecology, Cornell U., 1946-68; dir. Caudell div. applied arts and scis. N.Y. State Univ. Coll., Buffalo, 1968-73, prof. human devel., 1973-76; asst. dean Coll. Home Econs., Va. Poly. Inst. and State U., Blacksburg, 1976—; exec. com. home div. Erie County (N.Y.) Coop. Extension Service, 1969-76; chmn. com. child/day care services Erie County Dept. Social Services, 1972-75. Pres. bd. dirs. Camp Fire Girls Buffalo and Erie County, 1973-76. Mem. Am. Psychol. Services, Am. Home Econs. Assn., AAUW, NOW, Nat. Council Aging, Common Cause, Va. Home Econs. Assn. Republican. Author: Futures for Home Economists, 1963; reviewer Jour. Home Econs., 1976-78. Office: 216 Wallace Hall Va Poly Inst and State U Blacksburg VA 24061

HUMPHRIES, BEVERLY NELL (MRS. DONALD R. HUMPHRIES), librarian; b. Gatesville, Tex., July 3, 1930; d. E.B. and Nora H. (Nelson) Harris; A.A., Clifton Jr. Coll., 1946-48; B.S., N. Tex. State U., 1950; M.S., So. Ill. U., 1971; m. Donald R. Humphries, May 27, 1951; children—Brett, Joel. Elem. tchr. Balmorhea (Tex.) Public Schs., 1948-49; res. librarian Tex. Technol. U., Lubbock, 1950-51; elem. tchr. Fairbanks (Alaska) Sch. Dist., 1952-54; serials and documents librarian Tex. A. and M. U., College Station, 1954-57; periodicals librarian Davenport (Iowa) Public Library, 1957-59; librarian Monticello Coll., Godfrey, Ill., 1965-71, Lewis and Clark Community Coll., Godfrey, 1971—. Bd. dirs. Greater Alton Concert Assn., 1968-80, 81—. Mem. Am., Ill. library assns. Club: Zonta. Home: 4810 Chateau Dr Godfrey IL 62035 Office: Lewis and Clark Community College Godfrey IL 62035

HUMPHRIES, JOAN ROPES, psychologist, educator; b. Bklyn., Oct. 17, 1928; d. Lawrence Gardner and Adele Lydia (Zimmermann) Ropes; B.A., U. Miami, Coral Gables, Fla., 1950; M.S., Fla. State U., 1955; Ph.D., La. State U., 1963; m. Charles C. Humphries, Apr. 4, 1957; children—Peggy Ann, Charlene Adele. Instr. dept. psychology U. Miami, 1964, 65; mem. faculty dept. psychology Miami-Dade Community Coll., Miami, Fla., 1966—, now asso. prof. Bd. dirs., v.p. Inst. Evaluation, Diagnosis and Treatment, Miami; bd. dirs. Profl. Community Services, Miami. Mem. Am. Psychol. Assn., Internat. Platform Assn. (gov., com. chmn.), Fla. Psychol. Assn., Dade County Psychol. Assn., AAUP. Clubs: Coral Gables Country, Jockey, Colonial Dames. Contbr. articles to profl. jours. Home: 1311 Alhambra Circle Coral Gables FL 33134 Office: 11380 NW 27th Ave Miami FL 33167

HUMPHRIES, MARTHA JEAN, learning resources dir.; b. Camden, N.J., July 19, 1950; d. William Harry and Mary Catherine (Aust) Nethery; B.A., Alma (Mich.) Coll., 1972; M.A., Mich. State U., East Lansing, 1977; M.A.M., U. Phoenix, 1981; m. James David Humphries, III, June 8, 1974. Music tchr. Stockbridge (Mich.) Community Schs., 1972-74; media librarian Mich. Law Enforcement Officers Tng. Council, Lansing, 1976; media librarian, dir. learning resources No. Ariz. U., Flagstaff, 1976-78; dir. learning resources Embry-Riddle Aero. U.-West, Prescott, Ariz., 1978—. Vol., A.R.C., 1965-76. Mem. Assn. Ednl. Communications and Tech., Am. Assn. Aerospace Educators, Am. Aviation Hist. Soc., Univ. Aviation Assn., Flight Safety Found., Future Airline Profls. Am., ALA, Soaring Soc. Am. (dir. aerospace edn. resource center), Am. Mgmt. Assn., Exptl. Aircraft Assn., Ariz. Library Assn. Presbyterian. Author bibliographies. Office: 3200 N Willow Creek Rd Prescott AZ 86301

HUNDERE, MYRIAM GOLDSMITH SPRINKLE, pub. cons., writer; b. St. Louis, Nov. 3, 1933; d. Orlando Thomas and Rua Ollie (Hargus) Goldsmith; grad. Rhodes Secretarial Sch., 1953; student Trinity U., 1957, St. Mary U., San Antonio, 1958, Incarnate Word Coll., 1982; m. John Sprinkle, Feb. 1, 1952; 1 son, Davis Harrison; m. 2d, Al Hundere, July 27, 1964 (div. 1971); children—Herman Lars, Wendy Jane, Guy Alan. Legal sec. to sr. partner Roberts, Baker, Richards, Elledge & Cunningham, Houston, 1953-56; exec. sec. to partner George, Thrift & Cockrell (name now changed to Ernst & Ernst), San Antonio, 1956-58; exec. sec. and adminstrv. asst. to pres. Texstar Corp., San Antonio, 1959-61; sec.-treas. Alcor, Inc., San Antonio, 1961-81, co-chmn. bd., corp. sec., 1981—; corp. sec. MIZAR Internat., Inc.; pres., owner Myriad Moods, San Antonio; pres. M3O Industries, San Antonio; founder Top Drawer Services, 1971. Active Cursillo Movement; founder Crystal Cathedral, Garden Grove, Calif.; bd. dirs. YMCA Camp Flaming Arrow; mem. exec. bd. PTA, San Antonio, 1967, 68, 75, 76. Named Boss of Yr., Am. Bus. Women's Assn., 1977. Mem. Poetry Soc. Tex., Manuscript Club San Antonio, Speech Arts Assn. San Antonio (exec. bd.), Acad. Am. Poets, DAR, Am. Bus. Women's Assn., C. of C., Internat. Platform Assn., Am. Mktg. Assn., Am. Mgmt. Assn., Nat. Audubon Soc. Republican. Episcopalian. Club: Altrusa. Home: 1530 Larkspur St San Antonio TX 78213 Office: 10130 Jones-Maltsberger San Antonio TX 78216

HUNG, AILEEN WU, social worker; b. Hong Kong, July 9, 1938; d. Henry and Helen (To) Wu; came to U.S., 1969; B.A. with honors, U. Hong Kong, 1959; M.S.W., McGill U., 1965; postgrad. Columbia U. Sch. Social Work, 1970-72, D.Social Welfare, 1976; m. Craig Chi-Sze Hung, Mar. 1, 1967; 1 dau., Lyris. Psychiat. social worker Med. Dept., Hong Kong, 1960-63, Provincial Guidance Clinic, Calgary, Alta., Can., 1965-66; med. psychiat. social worker Jewish Gen. Hosp., Montreal, Can., 1966-68; acting chief social worker Royal Ottawa Hosp., Can., 1968-69; chief psychiat. social worker Dubois Day Treatment Center, Stamford, Conn., 1970, social work cons., 1970-72; instr. Columbia U. Sch. Social Work, 1972; exec. dir. N.Y. Chinatown Found., N.Y.C., 1972-73; social work research specialist Neurol. Inst., N.Y.C., 1973-75; v.p. Sysdyne Corp., Stamford, 1975—; sec., newsletter editor Chinese Assn. Fairfield County, Conn., 1976-78. Laidlaw Found. scholar, Toronto, Can., 1963-65; NIMH fellow, 1970-71. Mem. Nat. Assn. Social Workers, Acad. Certified Social Workers, Chinese Assn. of Fairfield County. Home: 30 Apple Tree Ln Stamford CT 06905

HUNGERINK, MARCINE, credit union adminstr.; b. Holland, Mich., Feb. 22, 1953; d. Gordon Henry and Zola Mae (Lander) H.; B.B.A., U. Wis., Madison, 1974. Mgr., MAT Employees Credit Union, Omaha, 1971-74; asst. treas., acting mgr. Blue Cross Employees Fed. Credit Union, Los Angeles, 1974-75; sr. fin. counselor Gen. Telephone Employees Fed. Credit Union, 1975-76; asst. treas., mgr. Operating Engrs. Local Fed. Credit Union, Los Angeles, 1976-77; mgr. credit union Hughes Helicopters div. Summa Corp., Culver City, Calif., 1977-78; fin. cons. to credit unions, Glendale, Calif., 1978—; owner Perfectly Balanced-Acctg. and Cons. Services, 1978—. Republican. Address: 4807 Clybourne Ave Toluca Lake CA 91602

HUNKER, EDITH MAE, sec., bookkeeper; b. Union City, Okla., June 1, 1930; d. Clarence Pearly and Grace DeEtte (Ricketts) Hambay; student Blackwood Bus. Coll., Oklahoma City, 1950, Calif. State U., Northridge, 1969; m. James Edward Hunker, Oct. 12, 1952; children—Edward Palmer, Steven Mark, James Warren. Asst. bookkeeper Bapt. Book Store, Oklahoma City, 1948, Downtown Chevrolet Co., Oklahoma City, 1950-52; acctg. clk. Universal Comml. Investment Trust, Oklahoma City, 1948-50; bookkeeper Eason Oil Co., Oklahoma City, 1953-54; sec. 1st Bapt. Ch., Amarillo, Tex., 1961-64; ednl. sec., bookkeeper 1st Bapt. Ch., Clovis, N.Mex., 1968-73; fin. sec. 1st Bapt. Ch., Lubbock, Tex., 1973-76; office mgr. John O. Goodman and Co. of Tex., Lubbock, 1976-79; instr. sign lang. 1st Bapt. Ch. Amarillo, 1963-66, Clovis, 1967-73, Glorieta (N.Mex.) Bapt. Conf. Center, 1967-68, 77-78, Tex. Tech. U., Lubbock, 1975; instr. sign lang. Oakwood Bapt. Ch., Lubbock, 1976—, fin./records sec., 1982—; workshop leader deaf ministries. Recipient Interpreter award So. Bapt. Conv., 1966; named Mother of Yr., Oakwood Bapt. Ch., 1981. Mem. Tex. Soc. Interpreters Deaf (bd. dirs. 1966, 2d v.p. 1978, editor 1978, sec. 1979-80, pres. local chpt. 1974), N.Mex. Registry Interpreters of Deaf, Nat. Assn. Deaf, Nat. Sign Instrs. Guidance Network, Registry Interpreters of Deaf, Baptist. Author: Simplified Sunday School Lessons, 1974. Home: 6002 Ave Q Lubbock TX 79412

HUNKING, LOILA GRACE BELCHER, educator, polit. ofcl.; b. Milw., Aug. 21, 1939; d. Harold Alvin and Lois Marie (Bigler) Belcher; B.A., Jamestown (N.D.) Coll., 1960; M.Ed. (Charles Wiseman award), S.D. State U., 1979; m. Floyd R. Hunking, Dec. 30, 1961; 1 son, Jeffrey Scott. Tchr., N.D., Minn., 1960-63; reporter, editor Sioux Falls Argus Leader, 1964-67; classroom tchr., English dept. chmn. Brandon (S.D.) Valley High Sch., 1967—; chmn. S.D. Democratic party, 1980—. Mem. S.D. Ho. of Reps., 1973-76, S.D. Commn. on Indian Affairs, 1975-76; mem. S.D. Commn. on Status of Women, 1973-80, chmn., 1978-80; chmn., S.D. state meeting Internat. Women's Year, S.D. del. Nat. Women's Conf., Houston, 1977. Named YWCA Woman of Year for Govt., Sioux Falls, 1980; Title IV-C grantee, 1979-80. Mem. NEA, S.D. Edn. Assn. (dir. 1971-73), Brandon Valley Edn. Assn., NOW, Nat. Women's Polit. Caucus, LWV. Mem. Ch. of Christ. Supr., researcher, editor Conspiracy of Silence, 1979. Home: 2309 S Stephen Ave Sioux Falls SD 57103 Office: Brandon Valley High Sch Brandon SD 57005

HUNLEY, ANN BERNICE SUGGS, ednl. counselor; b. Balt., July 17; d. Isaac and Mary Elizabeth (Jones) Suggs; A.B., Morgan State Coll., Balt., 1954; M.S., Johns Hopkins U., 1975, Advanced Degree in Clin. Therapy, 1978. With Balt. County Sch. System, 1955—, ednl. counselor Parkville Middle Sch., 1973—; vol. div. instructional TV, Md. Dept. Edn., 1969. Past mem. bd. Md. div. Am. Lung Assn.; incorporator, past treas. Bar Belle-Field Neighborhood Assn.; pres. Our Lady of Lourdes Roman Cath. Ch. Parish Council, 1975—; v.p. women's com. Balt., United Negro Coll. Fund, 1973; adv. world youth affairs UN, 1966; pres. aux, Echo House, 1975, pres. bd. dirs. Echo House Found., Inc., 1981—; mem. exec. com., bd. trustees Morgan Christian Center, Morgan State U.; mem. Md. Task Force for Grad. Nursing Edn., 1975. Recipient citations for vol. work United Negro Coll. Fund, 1973, 74, Disting. Leadership award, 1980. Mem. NEA, Md. Tchrs. Assn., Tchrs. Assn. Balt. County, Balt. County Sch. Counselors Assn., Am. Personnel and Guidance Assn., Md. Personnel and Guidance Assn., Balt. Urban League, NAACP (life), Mental Health Assn., YWCA, Md. League Women's Clubs, Nat. League Nursing, Md. League Nursing, Alpha Kappa Alpha (chpt. plaque 1973), Phi Delta Gamma (1st v.p. Gamma chpt. 1976-77, pres. 1979-80), Pi Lambda Theta. Roman Catholic. Home: Baltimore MD Office: Avondale and Hiss Ave Baltimore MD 21234

HUNNEWELL, GERALDINE GROSVENOR, poet; b. Oakland, Calif., Aug. 21, 1918; d. William Bennett and Lavinia Ruth (Lay) Grosvenor; hon. doctorate World U.; D.Litt. (hon.); m. Lester Arthur Hunnewell, Mar. 8, 1940; children—Larry Dennis, Richard Lynn. Formerly sec. Physicians and Surgeons Underwriters Corp. Mem. United Republican Fin. Com. Recipient certificate of merit Acad. Polit. Sci., Columbia U., Am. Judicature Soc.; Bronze medal, named hon. fellow Harry S. Truman Library for Scholarly Research; numerous other awards. Fellow Internat. Biog. Assn. (hon.); mem. AAAS, Nat. Space Inst. Author: The Etude of Agamemnon-Zeus, A Saga; The Song of Elatra, 1977; Tales from King Arthur's Court, 1977; The Mountain Song, 1978; contbr. poetry to mags. and anthologies. Address: Oakdale Mobile Park 10799 Sherman Grove Ave Space 39 Sunland CA 91040

HUNSBERGER, RUTH PEDERSEN, assn. exec.; b. Forest City, Iowa, Apr. 22, 1911; d. Nils and Emily (Johannson) Pedersen; A.B. in Psychology, Antioch Coll., 1934; M.A. in Am. History, U. Rochester, 1961; m. Warren S. Hunsberger, Apr. 17, 1942; children—Peter, David, Ellen Hume. Research analyst, Mil. Intelligence, War Dept., Washington, 1941-45; writer Library of Congress, 1961-63; mem. Fulbright Commn., Kuala Lumpur, Malaysia, 1963-66; country rep. Am. Field Service, Malaysia, 1966; 3d v.p. Overseas Edn. Fund, LWV, Washington, 1972-74; vice chmn. exec. com. Japan Am. Soc., Washington, 1979—; lectr. on U.S. women's movement, India, N.Z., Japan, 1974. Recipient Meritorious Civilian Service commendation Office Sec. of War, 1945. Mem. LWV, Woman's Nat. Dem. Club, Unitarian. Home and office: 3606 35th St Washington DC 20016

HUNSTIGER, CYNTHIA ANN, nurse; b. St. Cloud, Minn., Aug. 24, 1948; d. William Henry and Patricia Jane (Fisher) H.; grad. St. Marys Sch. Nursing, 1969. Staff nurse St. Marys Hosp., Rochester, Minn., 1969-73, health services supr., 1973-77, asst. dir. materials mgmt.-central service, 1977-80, dir. central service, 1980—. Co-chairperson Olmsted County Public Edn. Com., Am. Cancer Soc.; cons. Minn. Program for Victims of Sexual Assault. Mem. Am. Soc. Hosp. Central Service Personnel, Am. Hosp. Assn., Am. Assn. Occupational Health Nurses, NOW, St. Mary's Sch. Nursing Alumni Assn. (past pres.). Roman Catholic. Office: 1216 2d St SW Rochester MN 55901

HUNT, ACACIA GRAHAM, cons., former trade assn. exec., lobbyist; b. Washington, Aug. 21, 1951; d. William Vincent and Mary Evelyn (Turner) Graham; B.A., Vanderbilt U., 1973; m. Frederick Talley Drum Hunt, Jr., Dec. 4, 1976; 1 son, Andrew Graham. Legis. rep. Am. Bakers Assn., Washington, 1974-81; asst. treas. Bread Polit. Action Com., 1974-81; cons., 1981—. Mem. Westmoreland Citizens Assn. Mem. Women in Govt. Relations, Pi Beta Phi (v.p. 1973). Republican. Presbyterian. Club: George Washington U. Home and office: 5308 Blackistone Rd Westmoreland Hills Bethesda MD 20816

HUNT, BERNICE KOHN, author; b. Phila., June 15, 1920; d. Joseph Bernhardt and Sarah (Freedman) Herstein; B.A., SUNY, Empire, 1982; M.S., L.I.U., 1983; m. Morton Hunt, Sept. 10, 1971; children—Barbara Adler, Judith Wolman, Eugene Kohn. Children's sci. editor Coward-McCann & Geoghegan, 1964-67; adj. prof. creative writing Southampton Coll., L.I.U., 1976-78; editor-in-chief Dandelion Press, 1978-81; guest lectr. Notre Dame U., Tex. A&M U., U. Iowa, U. Conn., others; author over 60 books, 1960—, including The Beachcomber's Book, 1970; (with Clifford Sager) Intimate Partners, 1979; (with Morton Hunt) The Divorce Experience, 1977; Great Bread!, 1977; also articles.

HUNT, ELIZABETH CHRISTINE MULLEN, ednl. adminstr.; b. Long Beach, Calif., Dec. 16, 1912; d. William and Anna Christine Mullen; B.A., Occidental Coll., 1934; M.A., U. So. Calif., 1939; postgrad. U. Tex., 1940; Adminstrs. cert. U. Houston, 1955; m. Andrew W. Hunt, Sept. 3, 1941; children—Lacy H., II, Andrew W., William T. C. Tchr., Calif. Public Schs., 1934-41; lectr. speech, radio, debate Stephen F. Austin U., 1947-49, Hardin Simmon U., 1949-50, McMurry Coll., 1950-55; tchr. Houston Ind. Sch. Dist., 1955—; producer, dir. dramatic prodns., writer Centennial Mus., 1976; prin. Grissom Elem. Sch., Houston, 1967—; drama cons., curriculum cons., lectr. children's creative activities. Recipient Am. Educator medal Freedoms Found. at Valley Forge, 1964. Mem. Nat. Assn. Elem. Suprs. and Prins., Nat. Assn. Supervision and Curriculum, Am. Assn. Sch. Adminstrs., NEA, Tex. Assn. Elem. Suprs. and Prins., Tex. Assn. Supervision and Curriculum, Tex. Tchrs. Assn., Houston Prins. Assn., Delta Kappa Gamma. Episcopalian. Club: Freedoms Found. Author numerous children's plays, operattas and ednl. articles. Home: 5154 Jackwood St Houston TX 77035 Office: 4900 Simsbrook St Houston TX 77045

HUNT, ELIZABETH HOPE, psychologist; b. Hattiesburg, Miss., Oct. 14, 1943; d. Emory S. and I. Elizabeth (Burkette) H.; A.B., Sweet Briar (Va.) Coll., 1965; M.S.W., U. Pa., 1971; Ph.D. (fellow 1974), U.Oreg., Eugene, 1980; m. John Volney Allcott, III, Sept. 9, 1978; 1 son, John Volney. Vol., Peace Corps, Santiago, Chile, 1967-69; civil rights specialist HEW, Region III, Phila., 1971-74; doctoral fellow Rehab. Research & Tng. Center in Mental Retardation, U. Ore., Eugene,

1974-77; intern, Phila. Child Guidance, U. Pa., Phila., 1977-78; psychologist in pvt. practice Oreg. Family Center, Eugene, 1980—; lectr., workshop presenter, 1975—. Co-chmn., speakers bur., Physicians for Social Responsibility, Eugene, 1982—. Bd. dirs. Lane County Relief Nursery for Abused and Neglected Children, 1981—. Grantee, Nat. Inst. Handicapped Research, 1977-79, U. Oreg., 1978. Mem. Am. Psychol. Assn., Oreg. Psychol. Assn., Lane County Psychologists Assn. Club: Profl. Women's Network of Oreg. Author articles in field.

HUNT, GERTRUDE LOYOLA, wire mfg. co. exec.; b. Central Falls, R.I., Feb. 16, 1925; d. John Francis and Gertrude Elizabeth (Daley) H.; student pub. schs., Central Falls. Accountant, Royal Electric Co., Inc., Pawtucket, R.I., 1943-48, exec. sec., 1948-56, sec. retirement bd., 1951-64; adminstrv. asst. ITT Royal Electric Corp., Pawtucket, 1956-61, asst. sec., 1961-64; asst. sec. ITT Wire and Cable Div., Pawtucket, 1964-69; bd. dirs. ITT Royal Fed. Credit Union, Pawtucket, 1963-72, asst. treas., 1963-65, v.p., 1965-69, chmn. bd. dirs., pres., 1969-72, hon. mem. bd. dirs., 1972—; asst. sec. ITT Caribbean Indsl. Products, San Juan, P.R., 1967-80, ITT Royal Electric Div., Pawtucket, 1969—; pres. New Eng. regional chpt. Royal Electric div. ITT Quarter Century Club, 1978-82. Mem. perpetual com. for implementation and continued devel. Library for Capt. G. Harold Hunt Elementary Sch., Central Falls. Home: 6 Rolling Acres Dr Cumberland RI 02864 Office: 95 Grand Ave Pawtucket RI 02862

HUNT, GLADYS MAE, writer; b. Moline, Mich., Oct. 23, 1926; d. Wilbur J. and Clara Jeanette (DeWeerd) Schriemer; B.A. in Journalism, Mich. State U., 1948, postgrad., 1958-59; m. Keith L. Hunt, Oct. 9, 1948; 1 son, Mark Earl. Author books: Does Anyone Here Know God?, 1967, Honey for a Child's Heart, 1969, Listen to Me, 1969, Focus on Family Life, 1970, How-to Bible Study, 1971. Don't Be Afraid to Die, 1971, Ms Means Myself, 1972, also Bible study guides; contbr. numerous articles for periodicals; asso. dir. Cedar Campus, a univ. student tng. center, 1954—; editorial bd. Today Mag., 1970—, Leadership Mag., 1979—. Mem. AAUW, Authors Guild. Baptist. Home: 1710 Saxon St Ann Arbor MI 48103

HUNT, IRMGARD, consumer organization exec.; b. Berchtesgaden, Ger.; came to U.S., 1958, naturalized, 1968; d. Max and Albine (Poehlmann) Paul; B.A. in Polit. Sci. and German Lit., Columbia U.; children—Peter Alan, Karen Ingrid. Founding mem. Consumer Action Now, Inc., 1970, editorial head, project dir., 1970-75, exec. dir., 1977—; lectr. Mem. aux. bd. Bloomingdale House of Music; bd. dirs. Center Renewable Resources, Inst. Ecol. Policies; adv. bd. Survival Inst. Can. Mem. Assn. Female Execs., AAUW, Solar Energy Industries Assn., Phi Beta Kappa. Club: Rome. Office: 110 W 34th St New York NY 10001

HUNT, JANELL ELODIE, radio broadcaster, florist; b. Thief River Falls, Minn., Jan. 4, 1950; d. John A. and Eleanor C. (Hall) Ness; A.A., Northland Community Coll., 1971; student Bemidji State U., 1971-72, Cliff Mann Sch. Floral Design, 1979; m. Donald L. Hunt, Feb. 14, 1975; children—Donald L., John, Daniel. Exec. dir. Red River Valley Hist. Soc., Fargo-Moorhead, 1975-76; reporter, layout Montevideo (Minn.) Am.-News, 1978; coordinator Minn. Valley Sr. Fedn., Montevideo, 1978-79; florist, owner Hunt's Riverside Floral, Montevideo, 1979—, also radio news dir. Sta. KDMA, 1980—. Chmn. Chippewa County Democratic Farmer Labor Party, 1980-81, exec. com. 6th Dist., 1980-81, mem. State Central Com., 1980-81; ambassador Montevideo Fiesta Days, 1981; mem. Montevideo City Energy Com., 1982; chmn. Montevideo Chamber Tourism, 1982; bd. dirs. Chippewa County Hist. Soc., 1982, Montevideo Fiesta Celebrations, Inc., 1982. Mem. North Central Florists Assn., Soc. Am. Florists, North Central Broadcasters, Montevideo Area C. of C., Minn. Assn. Radio-TV News Dirs. Home: 302 N 6th St Montevideo MN 56265 Office: KDMA Radio Box 738 Montevideo MN 56265

HUNT, JUDITH WAHNITTAH, fashion editor; b. Phila., June 2, 1940; d. Carlee Gordon and Norma Ethlyn (Coe) Hunt; B.A. in Journalism, U. Wash., 1962; m. Neil C. Modie, Aug. 8, 1964 (div. 1975); children—Jonathan N., Claire E. Agrl./schs. reporter Lewiston (Idaho) Morning Tribune, 1963-64; gen. assignment reporter, makeup editor Vancouver (Wash.) Columbian, 1965-69; feature writer Seattle Post-Intelligencer, 1970—, furnishings editor, 1978—. Winner, Spl. award, Penney-Mo. award, 1975; winner 14 state awards, Wash. Press Assn., 1974-81; 3d Pl. Nat. Hearst Papers award, 1977, others. Mem. Pacific N.W. Newspaper Guild (pres. 1979—), Wash. Press Assn., Nat. Press Women (3d place award 1979), Theta Sigma Phi, Kappa Delta. Democrat. Episcopalian. Club: Mazamas. Home: 13614 SE 232 St Kent WA 98031 Office: 521 Wall St Seattle WA 98121

HUNT, MYRTLE EVA, career devel. services exec.; b. Elberfeld, Ind., Jan. 20, 1927; d. John W. and Eva E. (Besing) Wilkison; B.A., U. Evansville, 1957; M.Ed., Colo. State U., 1964; m. Talmadege Hunt, Oct. 3, 1943; 1 son, Torrence L. Tchr. Evansville (Ind.)/Vanderburgh Sch. Corp., 1957-65; supr. Pinellas County Schs., Clearwater, Fla., 1965-71, dir., 1971—. Mem. Am. Assn. Sch. Adminstrs., Am. Vocat. Assn., Am. Home Econs. Assn., Fla. Assn. Sch. Adminstrs., Fla. Assn. Career Devel., Fla. Vocat. Assn., Fla. Home Econs. Assn., Am. Personnel and Guidance Assn., Fla. Personnel and Guidance Assn., Fla. Assn. Supervision and Curriculum Devel., Am. Personnel Assn., Fla. Personnel Assn., Pinellas Personnel Assn., Nat. Assn. Female Execs., Am. Assn. Supervision and Curriculum Devel., Bus. and Profl. Women, Program to Increase Minority Engring. Grads. (bd. dirs.). Democrat. Club: Elks. Contbr. articles to profl. jours. Home: 1036 McCarty St Dunedin FL 33528 Office 1895 Gulf-to-Bay Blvd Clearwater FL 33515

HUNT, PATRICIA STANFORD, judge; b. Dunn, N.C., June 9, 1928; d. Lewis Knox and Florence Hibbette (Cooper) Denning; student Sweet Briar Coll., 1946-48; A.B., U. N.C., 1950, M.A., 1966, J.D., 1978; m. Donald M. Stanford, June 30, 1949 (dec. May 1970); children—Donald M., Randolph Lewis, Charles Ashley, James Cooper; m. Thomas M. Hunt, June 17, 1972. Tchr., Chapel Hill (N.C.) Carrboro Schs., 1963-69, counselor, 1969-73; admitted to N.C. bar, 1978; practiced in Chapel Hill, 1978—; mem. N.C. Gen. Assembly, 1972-81; dist. ct. judge, 15B Judicial Dist., Hillsborough, N.C., 1981—. Pres., Jr. Service League, 1960. Recipient Cert. of Appreciation, N.C. Autistic Soc., 1981, N.C. Assn. Attys., 1981, N.C. Acad. Trial Lawyers, 1981; Rockerfeller scholar, 1968-70; R. J. Reynolds fellow, 1970. Mem. Conf. Dist. Judges, N.C. State Bar Assn., N.C. Acad. Trial Lawyers, N.C. Assn. Women Attys. Democrat. Presbyterian. Co-author: (with Hugh Lefler) N.C. History, Geography and Government, 1970. Home: 100 Northwood Dr Chapel Hill NC 27514 Office: Clk Superior Ct Hillsborough NC 27278

HUNT, SHIRLEY ANNE, seminar instr.; b. Worcester, Mass., July 30, 1941; d. Fozy G. and Lillian B. (Borack) Tokla; student Salter Secretarial Sch.; m. Emery Newell Hunt, Oct. 10, 1964; 1 child, Shelli Anne. Operator, New Eng. Tel. & Tel., 1957-62; saleswoman Marquis China Co., Springfield, Mass., 1960-62, regional sales mgr., 1963-67, designer commerative plates, 1967-72, exec. v.p., 1973-75; co-founder Marquise Commeratives and Marquise Acceptance, 1976-77; dir. mktg., lectr., instr. advanced ednl. seminars PSI World, Larkspur, Calif., 1977—. Roman Catholic. Author manuals in field. Home: 46 Calypso Shores Novato CA 94947 Office: 1601 Larkspur Landing Circle Larkspur CA 94943

HUNT, SUSANNE CAROL KRAFT, nurse; b. Plainfield, N.J., Dec., 25, 1943; d. Rudolph A. and Helen A. (Thomas) Kraft; diploma East Orange Gen. Hosp. Sch. of Nursing, 1964; m. Kenneth G. Hunt, Oct. 29, 1965; children—Kenneth G., Kristen S. Nurse, Overlook Hosp., Summit, N.J., 1965-67; head nurse Woodbine Nursing Home, Alexandria, Va., 1967-68; staff nurse Circle Terrace Hosp., Alexandria, 1969-70; head intensive care Manassas (Va.) Manor Nursing Home, 1976-77, dir. nurses, 1977-79; charge nurse Martin Meml. Hosp., Stuart, Fla., 1979—. Cert. intravenous therapy technician; cert. chemotherapy nurse. Mem. Va. Nurses Assn., No. Va. Dirs. of Nursing Assn., United Meth. Women. Home: 1464 NE 24th St Jensen Beach FL 33457 Office: Hospital Dr Stuart FL

HUNTER, BEVERLY JUNE, banker; b. Abilene, Tex., May 16, 1939; d. Grover Knox and Dora Mae (Meeks) Beall; extension student U. Tex., Austin, also student various banking courses; m. Archie Dee Hunter, Nov. 23, 1977; children—Jamie, Rusty, Rodney. With credit dept. Thornton's Dept. Store, Abilene, 1967-71; receptionist, collector Abilene Credit Control, 1971-72; credit mgr. Cox Meml. Hosp., Abilene, 1972-74; asst. v.p., loan officer in charge installment loan dept. Permian Bank & Trust, Odessa, Tex., 1974—; author, dir., adv. Golden Connextion Program for Sr. Citizens. Bd. dirs. Odessa chpt. Am. Heart Assn., sec., 1979—; vol. Odessa United Way, 1981; bd. dirs. Better Bus. Bur., 1982—. Recipient Service award Am. Heart Assn. Mem. Nat. Assn. Bank Women, Am. Inst. Banking, Banks of Odessa (dir.). Democrat. Baptist. Home: 1400 Tanglewood St Odessa TX 79761 Office: 2710 N Grandview St Odessa TX 79761

HUNTER, DIANNE MARY, health care products co. exec.; b. Mansfield, Ohio, July 29, 1946; d. William George Brooker and Helen B. (Hickey) Dickson; student in biology Mt. Union Coll., 1969. Asst. product mgr. Technicon Instruments subs. Revlon, Tarrytown, N.Y., 1976-77, product mgr. hematology, 1977-79; mktg. mgr. Ortho Instruments subs. Johnson & Johnson, Westwood, Mass., 1979-80; v.p. mktg./sales Genetic Diagnostics, Gt. Neck, N.Y., 1980—; mktg. and mgmt. cons.; co. dir. Mem. Biomed. Mktg. Assn., Nat. Assn. Female Execs., Pelham C. of C. Home: New Rochelle NY 10805 Office: 160 Community Dr Great Neck NY 11021

HUNTER, EDNA J., research psychologist; b. Danville, Ill., Mar. 25, 1923; d. John William and Nettie (Lee) Shank; B.A., U. Calif., Berkeley, 1946; M.S., San Diego State U., 1967; Ph.D., U.S. Internat. U., 1970; m. Daniel Bear Hunter, Apr. 28, 1924; children—Daniel, Robert, Ninah, Barbara. Tchr. adminstr. public schs., Stafford, Va., 1946-49; teaching asst., lectr. San Diego State U., 1964-67; clin. research psychologist Naval Health Research Center, San Diego, 1967-71; acting dir., adminstrv. dir. and head Family Studies Center for POW Studies, Naval Health Research Center, San Diego, 1971-78; chmn. marriage and family therapy programs, dir. Family Research Center, U.S. Internat. U., San Diego, 1978—; owner Hunter Publs.; cons. San Diego Navy Regional Med. Center dept. psychiatry; mem. Nat. Adv. Bd. of Mil. Family Resource Centers; cons. Mark H. Saipe Psychology Corp., Westinghouse Corp., William Beaumont Med. Ctr.; mem. Task Force on Families of Catastrophe; mem. Speakers' Bur.-Scientists in the Schs. Program. Fellow Am. Psychol. Assn., Interuniv. Seminar on the Armed Forces; mem. Am. Assn. Marriage Family Therapy, Nat. Council on Family Relations, Internat. Assn. Applied Psychology, Am. Women in Sci., Am. Bar Aux., Internat. Platform Assn., Internat. Council Sex Therapy. Republican. Club: Lioness. Author/editor 7 books; contbr. articles to profl. jours. Home: PO Box A-81391 San Diego CA 92138 Office: US Internat U 10455 Pomerado Rd San Diego CA 92131

HUNTER, ILENE IOLA (DONNER), educator; b. Ft. Hall, Idaho, June 28, 1921; d. William and Daisy M. (Whipple) Donner; B.A., U. Ariz., 1943; M.S., U. Calif., Davis, 1969; m. Robert L. Hunter, Feb. 16, 1944; children—Jean, Richard, Joanne, Janet. Tchr. elem. public schs., Tucson, 1943-45; tchr. lab. sch. U. Mich., 1962-63, Big Nursery Sch., Stanford U., 1968-69, Davis Presch. U. Calif., 1968-70; instr. Sacramento City Coll., 1971-73; instr. in child devel., music for tchrs. Solano Community Coll., 1973—; Head Start tchr. and cons.; cons. music. Mem. Nat. Assn. Edn. Young Children, NEA, Sigma Alpha Iota, Pi Lambda Theta. Episcopalian. Author: Simple Folk Instruments to Make and to Play, 1977; research in child rearing and value systems of N. Am. Hutterites, 1976—. Office: PO Box 246 Suisun Valley Rd Suisun City CA 94585

HUNTER, JANET BONINE, nurse; b. Los Angeles, Oct. 16, 1944; d. Elwood Thomas and Hazel Mae (Wood) Bonine; B.S. in Nursing, Calif. State U., Los Angeles, 1967; M.A. in Adminstrn. and Pupil Personnel, Point Loma Coll., San Diego, 1978; postgrad. U. Calif., San Diego, 1974-79; m. Ralph Ames Hunter, Jr., July 8, 1967; 1 dau., Michelle Lynn. Public health nurse Vis. Nurses Assn., San Diego County, 1967-70; sch. nurse, sch. nurse practitioner San Deigo City Schs., 1971—, sch. nurse practitioner spl. edn., 1979—; instr. Regional Occupational Program, 1979-80. Public Health grantee, 1966-67. Mem. Nat. Soc. Autistic Children, Calif. Sch. Nurse Assn., San Diego Tchrs. Assn., San Diego County Assn. Retarded, Sigma Theta Tau. Republican. Methodist. Office: 3401 Clairemont Dr San Diego CA 92117 also 2716 Marcy Ave San Diego CA 92113

HUNTER, JUDITH PITT, social services adminstr.; b. Roanoke, Va., Aug. 19, 1939; d. Maynard H. and Malena Ann (Burwell) Law; B.A. in Sociology, Fisk U., 1961; M.S.W., N.Y.U., 1964; children—Eric M. Pitt, Lori A. Hunter. Social worker Bklyn. Child Care Assn., 1965-66; clin. social worker VA Med. Center, Salem, Va., 1966-71, social work educator, 1971-73; asst. prof. social work Hollins (Va.) Coll., 1973-74; dir. social work services Burrell Meml. Hosp., Roanoke, Va., 1972-74; dir. mental health asso. tng. program Brentwood VA Med. Center, Los Angeles, 1974-78; coordinator in-patient unit staff social work services Wadsworth VA Med. Center, Los Angeles, 1978—; adj. prof. Los Angeles City Coll., 1974-78; mem. adv. bd. Roanoke City Dept. Public Welfare, 1970-74; investigator EEO, 1980-82, chmn. adv. com., 1980-82; chmn. Intra-Agy. Exchange Com., Fed. Exec. Bd. Assos., 1980-81. Chmn. Combined Fed. Campaign, VA Med Center, 1980-81. Recipient VA Hosp. Dir.'s Spl. award, 1968. Mem. Nat. Assn. Social Workers, Acad. Cert. Social Workers, Nat. Assn. of Black Social Workers (pres., founder Roanoke chpt. 1971-74), Family Service Assn. (dir. 1972-74), Delta Sigma Theta. Presbyterian. Home: 3836 Ridgeley Dr Los Angeles CA 90008 Office: Wadsworth VA Med Center Wilshire/Sawtelle Blvds Los Angeles CA 90073

HUNTER, KIM (JANET COLE), actress; b. Detroit, Nov. 12, 1922; d. Donald and Grace Mabel (Lind) Cole; ed. pub. schs.; student acting with Charmine Lantaff Camine, 1938-40, Actors Studio; m. William A. Baldwin, Feb. 11, 1944 (div. 1946); 1 dau., Kathryn Emmett; m. 2d, Robert Emmett, Dec. 20, 1951; 1 son, Sean Emmett. First stage appearance, 1939; played in stock, 1940-42; Broadway debut in A Streetcar Named Desire, 1947; appeared in Two Blind Mice (tour), 1950; Darkness at Noon (N.Y.C.), 1951; The Chase, 1952 (N.Y.C.), They Knew What They Wanted (tour), 1952; The Children's Hour (revival) (N.Y.C.), 1952; The Tender Trap (N.Y.C.), 1954; Write Me a Murder (N.Y.C.), 1961; Weekend (N.Y.C.), 1968; The Penny Wars (N.Y.C.), 1969; And Miss Reardon Drinks a Little (tour), 1971-72; The Glass Menagerie (Atlanta), The Women (N.Y.C.), 1973; In Praise of Love (tour), 1975, The Lion in Winter (N.J.), 1975; The Cherry Orchard (N.Y.C.), 1976; The Chalk Garden (Pa.), 1976; Elizabeth The Queen (Buffalo), 1977; Semmelweiss (Buffalo), 1977; The Belle of Amherst (N.J.), 1978; The Little Foxes (Mass.), 1980; To Grandmother's House We Go (N.Y.C.), 1981, Another Part of the Forest (Seattle), 1981, When We Dead (N.Y.C.), Awaken, 1982, Ghosts (Garden City and Tarrytown, N.Y.), 1982; frequent appearances summer stock and repertory theater, 1940—; appeared Am. Shakespeare Festival, Stratford, Conn., 1961; film debut in The Seventh Victim, 1943; other motion pictures include: Tender Comrade, 1943, When Strangers Marry (re-released as Betrayed), 1944, You Came Along, 1945, A Canterbury Tale, 1949, Stairway to Heaven, 1946, A Streetcar Named Desire, 1951, Anything Can Happen, 1952, Deadline U.S.A., 1952, Storm Center, 1956, Bermuda Affair, 1957, The Young Stranger, 1957, Money, Women, and Guns, 1958, Lilith, 1964, Planet of the Apes, 1968, The Swimmer, 1968, Beneath the Planet of the Apes, 1970, Escape from the Planet of the Apes, 1971, Dark August, 1975; made TV debut on Actor's Studio program, 1948; numerous TV appearances include: Requeim for a Heavyweight, 1956, The Comedian, 1957 (both on Playhouse 90), Give Us Barabbas on Hallmark Hall of Fame, 1961, 63, 68, 69, Love, American Style, Colombo, Cannon, Night Gallery, Mission Impossible, The Magician, 1972-73, Marcus Welby, Hec Ramsey, Griff, Policy Story, Ironside, Med. Center, Bad Ronald, Born Innocent, 1974, Ellery Queen, 1975, Lucas Tanner, This Side of Innocence, Once an Eagle, Baretta, Gibbsville, Hunter, 1976, The Oregon Trail, 1977, Project: U.F.O., Stubby Pringle's Christmas, 1978, Backstairs at the White House, 1979, Specter on the Bridge, 1979, Edge of Night, 1979-80, F.D.R.'s Last Year, 1980, Skokie, 1981; rec. From Morning 'Til Night (and a Bag Full of Poems), RCA Victor, 1961, Come, Woo Me: Unified Audio Classics, 1964; lectr. High Sch. for Performing Arts, N.Y.C., Friends Sem., N.Y.C., 1961, S.D. U., 1965, Lehigh U., 1965, ANTA In-Tchrs.-Service, N.Y.C., 1965, High Sch. Music and Art, N.Y.C., 1968, Brigham Young U., Provo, Utah, 1978. Recipient Donaldson award for best supporting actress in A Streetcar Named Desire, 1948, also on Variety N.Y. Critics Poll, 1948, for film, version, 1952; winner Acad. award, LOOK award, Hollywood, Fgn. Corrs. Golden Globe award; Emmy nominations for Baretta, 1977, Edge of Night, 1980. Mem. Acad. Motion Picture Arts and Scis., ANTA, A.E.A. (council 1953-59), Screen Actors Guild. AFTRA. Author: Kim Hunter—Loose in The Kitchen, 1975.

HUNTER, MARLENE SELF, chamber of commerce exec.; b. Morganton, N.C., Feb. 9, 1934; d. Richard James and Azalee (Ritchey) Self; comml. cert. U. N.C., 1953; student U. Del.; m. Bill Roper Hunter, Nov. 28, 1953; children—Pamela Dawn, Charles Phifer, Gregory Scott, Susan Azalee. Adminstrv. asst. Charles County C. of C., La Plata, Md., 1974-78, mgr., 1978, exec. dir., 1978—. Pres. Charles County Democratic Club, 1976-78; bd. dirs. Charles County Handicapped and Retarded Citizens, 1978-80, sec., 1982; mem. Charles County Career Edn. Adv. Council. Mem. Am. C. of C. Execs. (chmn. chpt. 1982), Md. C. of C. (legis. com.), Md. Assn. C. of C. Execs. (scholarship 1978), Bus. and Profl. Women, Md. Council Small Bus. Execs. Methodist. Clubs: Crescent Cities Jaycee-Ettes (pres. 1972); Zonta (pres. 1982-83) (Charles County). Home: Hunter Hill Farm Route 232 Box 148 Bryantown MD 20617 Office: Route 301 Box 593 La Plata MD 20646

HUNTER, MILDRED CECILIA, health care adminstr.; b. Pensacola, Fla., Dec. 6. 1947; d. Cecil Thomas and Gloria Juanita (James) H.; A.B., Fisk U., 1969; M.S.W. Washington U., 1971; M.P.H., U. Ill., 1976. Caseworker, Ill. Children's Home and Aid Soc., Chgo., 1971-74; med. social worker Cook County Hosp., Chgo., 1974-75; program dir. STEA, Inc., Chgo., 1976-77; health and social services cons. Kirschner Assos., Chgo., 1976—; program mgr. Ill. Family Planning Council, Chgo., 1978—; field instr. U. Chgo. Sch. Social Service Adminstrn. Mem. community adv. bd. Chgo. Heart Assn., Chgo. Area Women Infants and Children's Program Task Force; bd. dirs. Zion's Hill, A Community for Unwanted Children, 1977—. Mem. Caucus on Teenage Pregnancy, Nat. Council Negro Women, Am. Public Health Assn. (Midwest regional chmn. Black Caucus Health Workers 1979—), Nat. Assn. Health Services Execs., Chgo. Fisk U. Assn., U. Ill. Sch. Public Health Alumni Assn. (v.p.), Alpha Kappa Alpha, Delta Omega. Roman Catholic. Home: 1649 E 50th St Chicago IL 60615 Office: 401 N Wabash St Suite 500 Chicago IL 60611

HUNTER, SUE PERSONS, state agy. ofcl.; b. Hico, Tex., Aug. 21, 1921; d. David Henry and Beulah (Boatwright) Persons; B.A., U. Tex., 1942; m. Charles Force Hunter; children—Shelley Hunter Richardson, Mary Hunter McCullough, Margaret Hunter Brown. Air traffic controller CAA (now FAA), San Antonio and Houston, 1942-52; writer Bissonet Plaza News, 1969-72; coordinator Goals for La., 1971-74; adminstrv. dir. Jeff Pubs. Inc., 1974; press sec. Jefferson Parish Dist. Atty., 1972-75, communications cons., 1975-78; adminstr. Child Support Enforcement Div., 1979—; contbg. editor The Jeffersonian, 1975-76. Pres. United Ch. Women East Jefferson (La.), 1958-59, LWV Jefferson Parish, La., 1961-64; pres. LWV La., 1967-71, also bd. dirs., 1962-67; mem. probation services com. Community Services Council, Jefferson, 1966-73, v.p., 1970-72; mem. Library Devel. Com. La., 1967-71, Nat. Com. for Support of Public Schs., 1967-72; mem. Goals Found. Council Met. New Orleans, 1969-75, sec. 1970, 72; mem. Goals La. Task Force State and Local Govt., 1969-70; pres. MMM Investment Club, 1969-72; bd. mem. New Orleans Area Health Planning Council, 1969-75; mem. adv. council La. State Health Planning, 1971-76; title I adv. council La. State Dept. Edn., 1970-72; vice chmn. Jefferson Women's Polit. Caucus, 1977-78, chmn., 1979, treas., 1980; bd. dirs. New Orleans Area/Bayou-River Health Systems Agy., 1978-82, pres., 1980, 81; mem. Task force for La. Talent Bank of Women, 1980; exec. bd. La. Child Support Enforcement Assn., 1980—, pres., 1982. mem. La. Statewide Health Coordinating Council, 1980—. Recipient Outstanding Citizens award Rotary Club, Metairie, La., 1962; River Ridge award, 1976. Mem. New Orleans Panhellenic (pres. 1956-57), Alpha Xi Delta. Presbyterian (elder). Home: 210 Stewart Ave River Ridge LA 70123

HUNTLEY, ALICE MAE, mfg. exec.; b. Atoka, Okla., May 9, 1917; d. Joseph LaHay and Lula May (Stapp) Howe; B.A., U. Okla., 1939; m. Loren Clifford Huntley, Nov. 7, 1942; children—Loren Lee, Marcia Lynn. Reporter, McAlester (Okla.) News Capital, 1939-41; sec., asst. to pres. and chmn. bd. N.Am. Aviation, Los Angeles, 1941-63; v.p., co-owner Tubular Specialties Mfg., Inc., Los Angeles, 1966—. Former sec. 1st Baptist Ch. of Westchester; sec. Westchester-Del Rey Republican Women, 1959-60; asso. mem. Rep. State Central Com., 1973. Cert. profl. sec.; named Outstanding Sec. in So. Calif., So. Calif. chpt., 1954, Internat. Sec. of Year, 1955 (both Nat. Secs. Assn.). Home: 8238 Calabar Ave Playa del Rey CA 90291 Office: 13011 S Spring St Los Angeles CA 90061

HUNTLEY, HELEN, see Stambaugh, Helen Huntley

HUNTLEY, HELEN LOU, rehab. cons.; b. Scottdale, Pa., Nov. 8, 1925; d. Issac Newton and Josie Louisa (Hellein) Huntley; B.A., Muskingum Coll., 1946; M.A., U. Hawaii, 1951; Ed.D. (Dept. Health, Edn. and Welfare scholar), U. Ariz., 1972; certificate occupational therapy Tex. Womens' U., 1957; certificate sheltered workshop adminstrn. (Dept. Health, Edn. and Welfare scholar), U. San Francisco, 1968. Apprentice machinist Altec Lansing Radio Corp., Los Angeles, 1947-49; dir. Central Command Craft Shops, Japan, 1953-55; dir. occupational therapy dept. Mahelona Hosp., Kapaa, Kauai, Hawaii, 1957-67; project dir. Statewide Planning Rehab., Guam, 1968-69; project dir. Planning for New Vocational Rehab. Services Program, Trust Territory of the Pacific Islands, 1971-73; cons. Nat. Iranian Soc. for Rehab. of the Disabled, Iran, 1974-75; maj. prof. grad. program in rehab. adminstrn. Sch. Rehab. Sci., Tehran, Iran, 1974-75. Cons. Pub. Health Service, Kauai, Hawaii, 1965-67, also various hosps. on the Island of Kauai. State dir. at-large Hawaii Tb. Assn., 1966-69; charter mem., pres., sec. Rehab. Unltd., Kauai, 1957-67. Mem. World Fedn. Occupational Therapists, Rehab. Internat., Nat. Rehab. Assn., Am. Occupational Therapy Assn., U. Hawaii Alumni Assn., U. Ariz. Alumni Assn., Pi Lambda Theta. Home: 5393 Poola St Honolulu HI 96821 also 3000 Silverleaf Dr Austin TX 78757

HUNTRESS, BETTY ANN, former music store propr.; b. Poughkeepsie, N.Y., Apr. 29, 1932; d. Emmett Slater and Catherine V. (Kihlmire) Brundage; B.A., Cornell U., 1954; m. Arnold Ray Huntress, June 26, 1954; children—Catherine, Michael, Carol, Alan. Tchr. high sch., Bordentown, N.J., 1954-55; part-time asst. to prof. Delta Coll., Northwood Inst., Midland, Mich., 1958-71; part-time tchr. Midland Pub. Schs., 1968-79; owner, mgr. The Music Stand, Midland, 1979-82. Bd. dirs. Midland Center for Arts, 1978—, v.p., 1981-82; mem. charter bd. mgrs. Matrix Midland Ann. Arts and Sci. Festival, 1977-80; cons. Girl Scouts U.S.A., 1964-76; mem. Mich. Internat. Council, 1975-76. Named (with husband) Midland Musician of Yr., 1977. Mem. Music Soc. Midland Center for Arts (dir. 1971—, chmn. 1976-79), AAUW (dir. 1962-73, pres. 1971-73, mem. Mich. state dv. bd. 1973-75, outstanding woman as agt. of change award 1977, fellowship grant named in her honor 1976), Midland Symphony League Soc, Community Concert Soc., Kappa Delta Epsilon, Pi Lambda Theta, Alpha Xi Delta. Republican. Presbyterian. Home: 5316 Sunset Dr Midland MI 48640

HUPALO, MEREDITH TOPLIFF (MRS. NICHOLAS HUPALO), artist, illustrator; b. Tarpon Springs, Fla., Apr. 28, 1917; d. Walter and Maurine (Martin) Topliff; cert. in design Pratt Inst., 1938; m. Nicholas Hupalo, July 13, 1940 (dec. Sept. 1977); children—Walter Topliff, John Nicholas. One-woman shows: Tarpon Springs Public Library, 1945, Valley Stream (N.Y.) Mus., 1962, Contemporary Arts, Inc., N.Y.C., 1966, Jet Clubs Internat., N.Y.C., Henry Waldinger Library, Valley Stream, N.Y., 1977, East River Savs. Bank, Valley Stream, 1978; represented in permanent collection Valley Stream Public Library, Tarpon Springs (Fla.) Public Library, Eastern Airlines Exec. Offices, N.Y.C.; tchr. printmaking Nassau County (N.Y.) Home Extension Service; art adviser Valley Stream Mus., 1962-64; illustrator Eastern Airlines, 1964-68; artist Shell Oil Co., 1968-70; designer Continental Can Co., N.Y.C., 1970-73; art tchr. Astor (Fla.) Community Center, 1980-82. Recipient spl. award oil painting 34th Nat. Spring Exhbn. Nat. Art League L.I., 1964, gold medal in oil painting 35th Membership Show, 1965; 1st pl. fine art Fla. Silver Springs Arts & Crafts Festival, 1980. Mem. Nat. Art League L.I. (treas. 1959-60), Am. Watercolor Soc. (asso.), Astor Area C. of C. (dir. 1981-82). Methodist. Works included Paintings with Markers, 1972. Home: Lot 37 Holiday Haven Astor FL 32002

HUPPER, DOROTHY WALLACE HEALY, civic worker; b. Michigan, N.D., Sept. 13, 1899; d. Henry Herbert and Mary Maud (Wallace) Healy; B.A., U. N.D., 1921; m. Roscoe H. Hupper, June 13, 1923; children—John R., Roger W., Joel H. Pres. James Lenox House Corp., 1973-77, 80—, James Lenox House Assn., 1980—, Presbyn. Home for Aged Women Corp., 1971-76; chmn. auditions com. YWCA, N.Y.C., 1955-79, chmn. com. mgrs., 1966-67. Recipient Sioux award U. N.D., 1977. Mem. Phi Beta Kappa, Kappa Alpha Theta, Sigma Alpha Iota. Republican. Presbyterian (elder). Clubs: Nat. Arts, Colony, Cosmopolitan. Home: 36 E 72d St New York NY 10021

HURAJ, HELEN ICEA, social worker; b. Montreal, Que., Can., July 13, 1926; B.A., Concordia U., Montreal, 1956; M.S.W., Smith Coll., Northampton, Mass., 1966. Chief social worker St. Thomas Psychiatric Hosp., 1975—; instr. St. Lawrence Coll. Applied Arts and Tech.; divisional supt., instr. St. John Ambulance, 1944-56. Life mem. Montreal Boys Club, Buenavista on the Rideau; bd. dirs., rep. United Way, Provincial Ministerial Assn. of Province of Que.; pres. Park Extension Recreation Assn., 1969, Buena Vista-on-the-Rideau, Merrickville, 1974-76, Mental Health Assn. of Brockville, 1974-76; mem. Coping with Cancer (Can. Cancer Soc.), 1980—, New Horizons Sr. Citizens Steering Com., 1981—; chmn. Telecare Elgin (Contact), 1981-82, now adv. bd. Recipient Venerable Order of the Hosp. of St. John of Jerusalem, The Priory in Can., 1956, Order of Can. medal, 1974, Queen's Silver Jubilee Medal, 1978, Mental Health/Elgin plaque for outstanding and selfless service, 1977, cert. of appreciation St. Thomas Jaycees, 1976; spl. award City of St. Thomas, 1979; Lifestyle award medal, 1982. Mem. Can. Mental Health Assn. (v.p. Elgin, dir. 1975, pres. 1981), Mental Health Assn. of Ont. (v.p. 1975-77), Acad. Cert. Social Workers, La Corporation Professionnelle des Travailleurs Sociaux Professionnells de la Province de Que., Nat., Can., Ont. assns. social workers, Can. Soc. Forensic Sci., Am. Assn. Marriage and Family Therapists, Lutheran Women's Missionary League. Lutheran. Clubs: Can. Univ. Women's (Brockville, Ont.), St. Thomas Quota. Home: 55 Bailey Ave Saint Thomas ON N5R 4Z8 Canada

HURD, MAGGIE PATRICIANNE, electron microscopist; b. Atlanta, Mar. 6, 1940; d. Oscar James and Rubye (Chunn) Hurd; B.A., Spelman Coll., 1962; M.A., Atlanta U., 1967, Ph.D., 1976. Tchr. sci. Atlanta Public Schs., 1962-75; electron microscopist DeKalb (Ga.) County Sch. System, Fernbank Sci. Center, Atlanta, 1975—; adj. prof. Ga. State U., 1977—; adviser coop. ind. study program Agnes Scott Coll., 1978; adviser coop. grad. biology program Emory U., 1978; cons. sci. career seminar Spelman Coll., 1977; cons. NSF Workshop on Techniques in Preparing Sci. Projects for Sci. Tchrs., 1979; guest lectr. Malcolm X Coll., Chgo., 1980; participant Internat. Electron Microscopy Meeting, Hamburg, W.Ger., 1982; lectr. Janssen Pharmaceutica Research Lab., Beerse, Belgium, 1982. Mem. Ga. Acad. Sci., NEA, Am. Inst. Biol. Scis., AAAS, Assn. of Southeastern Biologists, Nat. Sci. Tchrs. Assn., SE Electron Microscopy Soc., Am. Phytopath. Soc., Electron Microscopy Soc. Am. (arrangements chairperson meeting southeastern chpt. 1981), Minority Women in Sci. (charter mem. Atlanta chpt. 1980), Phi Delta Kappa, Alpha Kappa Alpha, Beta Kappa Chi. Contbr. articles in field to profl. jours. Office: 156 Heaton Park Dr Atlanta Ga 30307

HURD, MERNA MARIE, civil engr.; b. Lexington, Nebr., Dec. 3, 1941; d. William Franklin and Edna Marie (Goodsell) Prettyman; B.S.C.E., U. Nebr., 1964, M.S. in San. Engring., 1969; m. Michael Frankel, Jan. 1, 1979. Design engr. Harold Hoskins & Assos., Lincoln, Nebr., 1965-69; dir. water and sewer mgmt. New Castle County, Del., 1970-77; dir. water planning EPA, Washington, 1977-80, asso. dep. asst. adminstr. water program ops., 1980, asso. asst. adminstr. Office of Water, 1980-82; v.p. hazardous waste and engring. Clements & Assos., Arlington, Va., 1982—. Named Del. Outstanding Public Adminstr., 1977. Mem. Am. Waterworks Assn., Water Pollution Control Fedn., Nat. Soc. Profl. Engrs., Sigma Tau, Chi Epsilon, Pi Mu Epsilon. Office: 1515 Wilson Blvd Suite 700 Arlington VA 22209

HURDLE, BESSIE M., civic worker; b. Reading, Pa., May 17, 1945; d. Frelton and Bessie Walker; student Reading Area Community Coll., 1975-78; m. James Hurdle Jr., Aug. 14, 1965 (separated); children—James W., Obai. Exec. dir. Berks County Welfare Rights Orgn., Reading, Pa., 1978-81; com. mem. Pa. State Food and Nutrition Com., 1979-81; Pa. coordinator Black Women in Polit. Action, 1979—; a coordinator Vol. Clearing House, Washington, nat. st. law program for adult edn. Shilo Bapt. Ch., nat. conv. Nat. Women of Color; active Wider Opportunities for Women, Birth Right; Women in Crisis. Bd. dirs. Berks Youth Counseling Center. Mem. Health Maintenance Orgn., NOW, Female Exec. Club, Internat. Readers Assn. (D.C. council). Home: 1338 Levis St NE Washington DC 20002

HURLBURT, SARAH WORLEY, mariculture specialist, author; b. Williamson, W.Va., Feb. 16, 1925; d. Douglas Fleming and Virginia (Miller) Worley; student Peace Coll., 1945, U. N.C., 1947; m. C. Graham Hurlburt, Feb. 10, 1956; children—Sarah, C. Graham III, Cynthia, Leeds. Condr. research on mariculture, Europe, Harvard U., 1973-74; v.p., dir. Blue Gold Sea Farms, Cambridge, Mass., 1977—; lectr. on mariculture to mems. U.S. Congress. Recipient Nat. Taste Maker award, 1978. Mem. Authors Guild, Authors League Am., Inc. Clubs: Harvard Faculty; Harvard (Boston). Author: Blue Gold, 1974; The Mussel Cookbook, 1977; Underutilized Sea Foods, 1978. Home: 28 Linden Ln Duxbury MA 02332

HURLEY, ANN MARIE, mcpl. ofcl.; b. N.Y.C., July 13, 1925; d. Timothy Charles and Mary Frances (Lacey) O'Neill; ed. N.Y.C. public schs., bus. courses and seminars; m. John D. Hurley, Jr., Aug. 24, 1947; children—John Edward, Patty Ann Hurley McGovern. Clk., bookkeeping supr. Guaranty Trust Co., N.Y.C., 1942-47; bookkeeping supr. Continental Bank & Trust Co., N.Y.C., 1947-48, N.Y. Trust Co., N.Y.C., 1948-49; head bookkeeper, prin. clk., dep. receiver of taxes Town of Huntington, N.Y., 1960-67, receiver of taxes, 1967—; spl. com. revision Suffolk County Tax Act, mem. Blue Ribbon com. to revise Suffolk County Tax Act, 1982; mem. adv. bd. N.Y. State Community Affairs. Pres. Heatherwood Civic Assn., South Huntington Democratic Club; exec. bd. Suffolk County Dem. Party; Dem. zone leader, Huntington Station, N.Y.; committeeperson Dem. Party, 1960—; parish council St. Elizabeth Roman Catholic Ch.; grand marshal Huntington ann. St. Patrick's Day Parade, 1976. Mem. N.Y. State Receivers and Collectors of Taxes Assn. (v.p. 1979-82, pres. 1982), Suffolk County Receivers of Taxes Assn. (pres. 1969—). Home: 2 Coe Pl Huntington Station NY 11746 Office: Huntington Town Hall 100 Main St Huntington NY 11743

HURLEY, CAROL REYNOLDS, mktg. cons. co. exec.; b. Stamford, Conn., Sept. 21, 1932; d. Walter Buxton and Esther (Nelson) Reynolds; grad. Katharine Gibbs Sch., N.Y.C., 1951; m. Edward Daniel Hurley, Sept. 5, 1964. Exec. sec., public relations dir. Interchurch Center, N.Y.C., 1957-63; editor Combined Book Exhibit, N.Y.C., 1963-64; sec.-treas. Hurley Assos., Los Angeles, 1964—; exec. sec. Associated Rehab. Centers, Evanston, Ill., 1967-69; asst. to pres. Intercole Inc., Brentwood, Calif., 1974-78; asst. to chmn. Donegal Internat. Machinery Ltd., Ballyshannon, Ireland, 1977—; v.p. Lodestar Prodns., Los Angeles, 1978—; mgr. adminstrn. Hesburgh Internat., Inc., Pacific Palisades, Calif., 1978—. Founder, Pacific Palisades Hunger Walk orgn., 1975, Pacific Palisades Hospice Vols. orgn., 1980. Mem. Nat. Assn. Female Execs., Am. Bonsai Soc., Sunset Succulent Soc. Home: 1330 Monument St Pacific Palisades CA 90272 Office: Hesburgh Internat Inc Suite 200 15135 Sunset Blvd Pacific Palisades CA 90272

HURLEY, CHERYL JOYCE, pub. co. exec.; b. Pitts., Oct. 30, 1947; d. John and Violet Dernorsek; cert. de langue et de litt, Universite de Lyon, France, 1968; A.B., Ohio U., 1969; M.A., U. Mich., 1971; m. Kevin Hurley, July 27, 1974. Research asso. Modern Lang. Assn. Am., N.Y.C., 1972-74, dir. spl. programs, 1974-79; exec. dir. Lit. Classics of U.S., N.Y.C., 1979—; cons. in field. Rackham fellow, 1969-70. Mem. Phi Beta Kappa, Alpha Lambda Delta, Phi Sigma Iota, Phi Kappa Phi. Contbr. articles to profl. jours. Home: 105 W 13th St New York NY 10011 Office: 1 Lincoln Plaza New York NY 10023

HURLEY, MARGARET (MRS. JOSEPH E. HURLEY), state senator; b. Winnebago, Minn.; B.A., Holy Names Coll.; m. Joseph E. Hurley (dec.); 4 children. Mem. Wash. State Senate. Home: Spokane WA

HURLEY, MARY KATHERINE, sch. system food service dir.; b. Oakman, Ala., Mar. 27, 1933; d. William Isaiah and Abbie Eugenia (Carter) Allen; B.S., Blue Mountain (Miss.) Coll., 1955; M.S., U. Tenn., Martin, 1980; m. Lee L. Hurley, Jan. 30, 1970; 1 son, James. Food service supr. F. W. Woolworth Co., 1955-75; dir. food service Jackson (Tenn.) City Schs., 1975—. Mem. NEA, Tenn. Edn. Assn., Jackson Edn. Assn., Am. Sch. Foodservice Assn., Tenn. Sch. Foodservice Assn. (pres.-elect 1982-83), Jackson City Sch. Foodservice Assn. Republican. Baptist. Home: 529 North Pkwy Jackson TN 38301 Office: 201 E Deaderick St Jackson TN 38301

HURLEY, MIRIAM GREENE (MRS. DONALD J. HURLEY), civic worker; b. Cambridge, Mass., Dec. 24, 1910; d. William John and Catherine Marie (Dooley) Greene; A.B. cum laude, Radcliffe Coll., 1931; m. Donald Joseph Hurley, Aug. 28, 1937; children—Cornelia Hurley McPeek, Donald, Stephen Nash, Rosamond Hurley Shugrue. Chmn. Boston Day Care Nursery Centers, 1941-44; v.p. Boston Council Camp Fire Girls, 1944-59; chmn. nat. alumnae fund Radcliffe Coll., Cambridge, Mass., 1957-59, trustee coll., 1961-65; mem. vis. com. Harvard Bd. Overseers, 1960-64; trustee Martha's Vineyard Hosp., 1970-76; mem. ladies com. Boston Mus. Fine Arts; mem. bd. overseers Martha's Vineyard Open Land Found.; bd. mgrs., now hon. bd. mgrs. Boston Vis. Nurse Assn.; hon. v.p. Boston Children's Service Assn.; pres. Boston League Women Voters, 1939-41; v.p. Mass. League Women Voters, 1941-45; bd. dirs. Asso. Harvard Alumni, 1965-67. Club: Radcliffe (pres. 1942-44). Home: 41 Aberdeen Rd Weston MA 02193

HURNEY, KATE, concert and opera soprano; b. Quincy, Mass., Sept. 14, 1940; d. Michael Joseph and Nora Magdalen (Carr) Hurney; B.A., Tufts U.; student New Eng. Conservatory, Juilliard Sch. Music, Internat. Opera Center, Zurich, Accademia Cuigrand, Siena, Italy; m. Robert Braverman, Dec. 31, 1964; children—Samuel, Amy Carr. Soprano, Dallas Civic Opera, 1974, Houston Grand Opera, 1975, Boston Opera, 1974, Theatre Monnaie, Brussels, Freiburg Orch.; orchestral engagements include Marlboro, Tanglewood, Miami, Houston, Buffalo, Boston Arts Festivals; rec. artist Decca, Poseidon, Sudwest, others; pres. Public Opera Theatre Co., N.Y.C., 1973-75. Rockefeller grantee, 1962, 63, 73; Avalon Found. fellow; Internat. Bach Soc. fellow. Mem. Actors Equity Assn., Am. Guild Musical Artists. Address: 235 W 76th St New York NY 10023

HURREY, KATHARINE CARR, librarian; b. Washington, Jan. 5; d. William Arthur and Katharine Louise (Eckloff) Carr; A.B. in Psychology, Hollins (Va.) Coll., 1949; M.L.S., U. Md., 1967; m. Charles Lauder Hurrey, Feb. 21, 1951; children—Peter Laird, Earl Telford, Robert McGregor, Virginia Lee, Patrick Carr. Bookmobile librarian Calvert County (Md.) Public Library, 1962-65; adminstrv. asst., then children's coordinator So. Md. Regional Library Assn., LaPlata, 1965-68, dir., 1968—; mem. Library Practitioners, cons.; instr. Charles County Community Coll. Mem. Calvert County Bd. Edn., 1966-72, pres., 1968-72. Mem. ALA, Am. Mgmt. Assn., World Future Soc., Md. Library Assn. (Disting. Service award 1978). Republican. Episcopalian. Home: Hurry Ln Port Republic MD 20676 Office: PO Box 1069 LaPlata MD 20646

HURST, GWENDOLYN FELS, nurse; b. Lancaster, Pa., July 31, 1949; d. John Richard and Hazel May (Butzer) Fels; B.S.N., U. Va., 1971; m. Jon Tucker Hurst, May 4, 1974; children—Alexander Michael. Staff nurse Hershey (Pa.) Med. Center, 1971-74; staff nurse Lancaster (Pa.) Gen. Hosp., 1974-75, nursing instr., 1975-77; part time staff nurse St. Joseph Hosp., Lancaster, 1981-82; hosp./home care coordinator Vis. Nurse Assn., Lancaster, 1982—. Mem. Jr. League Lancaster, U. Va. Alumni Assn. Presbyterian. Home: 817 Janet Ave Lancaster PA 17601 Office: 630 Janet Ave Lancaster PA 17601

HURST, LINDA LOUISE, constrn. exec.; b. Oakland, Calif., Mar. 9, 1941; d. John Frederick and Doris Ethel McGregor; student San Francisco public schs.; m. Timothy J. Hurst, May 18, 1968. Computer clk. U.S. Govt., San Francisco and Oakland, 1959-68; corp. sec. C & H Engrng. Corp., Redwood City, Calif., 1968-71, Compass Engring. Corp., Phoenix, 1971-74; v.p. Hurst Constrn., Inc., Scottsdale, Ariz., 1974—; works include: preservation and conversion of hist. home to profl. office bldg., rehab. hist. home in Hist. Alvarado Area of Phoenix. Steering com. Hist. Alvarado Assn., 1981—, Scottsdale 5th Ave. Assn., 1980—. Recipient Environ. award City of Phoenix, 1975; named Miss Zero Defects, Oakland Army Terminal, 1966. Mem. Nat. Assn. Homebuilders, Smithsonian Instn. Republican. Club: Plaza (Phoenix). Home: 2233 N Alvarado Rd Phoenix AZ 85004 Office: 6840 E Indian School Rd Scottsdale AZ 85251

HURST, TRICIA ANN, writer; b. Manhattan, N.Y., Apr. 2, 1926; d. Alfred Dickson and Dorothy Kinnie (Vanderbilt) H.; student Finch Jr. Coll., N.Y.C., 1944-46, Columbia U., 1946-48; m. John Alan Richards; children—Farmington Dickson, Hamish Peabody; m. 2d, Arthur Alan Allen-Jones; children—Augusta Alexandra Allen-Jones, Omega. Feature writer N.Y. Jour. Am., 1944, N.Y. Publicist, 1945-51; dir. publicity Stork Club, 1952; public relations dir. El Rancho Vegas, Las Vegas, 1952-53; freelance writer contbg. to Look, Readers Digest, Esquire, TV Guide and others; interviewer, feature writer, columnist New Mexican, Santa Fe, Taos Mag., Southwest Art, New Mexico Mag., 1960-80, Washington Post, Los Angeles Times, Chgo. Sun Times, Albuquerque Jour., Ariz. Republic, 1981—; asso. editor Taos Mag. Recipient awards for writing. Mem. Nat. Fedn. Press Women, N.Mex. Press Assn., N.Mex. Press Women, Writers Guild of Am. Author: R.C. Gorman-The Posters. Democrat. Episcopalian. Home and Office: Ranchos de Taos NM 87557

HURST-BERNADT, GAIL MIHRICAN, social worker; b. Fairmont, Minn., Sept. 11, 1946; d. Muzzafer Ahmet and Mary Jane (McKee) Gokbora; A.A., William Woods Coll., Fulton, Mo., 1966; B.S.W., U. Mo., 1971, M.S. in S.W., 1973; m. William Hurst, 1967 (div. 1973); 1 son, Brad; m. 2d, William F. Bernadt, Jr., July 21, 1979. Dir. off grounds residential programs St. Catherines Center for Children, 1973-76; foster care tng. specialist N.Y. State Div. Youth, 1976-77; psychiat. social worker La Salle Sch., Albany, N.Y., 1978—; field instr. Sch. Social Welfare, State U. N.Y., 1974-76. Ford Found. scholar, 1965; NIMH grantee, 1971-73. Mem. Nat. Social Workers, Acad. Cert. Social Workers. Episcopalian. Home: 919 Sacandaga Rd Scotia NY 12302 Office: 391 Western Ave Albany NY 12203

HURTT, MARTHA WESSON, congressional asst.; b. Lawrenceville, Va., Nov. 21, 1930; d. Murray Powell and Martha (Elliott) Wesson; secretarial diploma Madison Coll., Harrisonburg, Va., 1949; A.B., Pfeiffer Coll., Misenheimer, N.C., 1965; M.R.E., Wesley Theol. Sem., Washington, 1969; M.Ed., Am. U., 1972; m. Richard L. Hurtt, Nov. 18, 1972; 1 stepson, Leslie Elliott. Various clerical and secretarial positions, 1949-63; ednl. asst. Bon Air United Meth. Ch., Richmond, Va., 1965-67; coordinator community center Calvary Bapt. Ch., Washington, 1968; student placement asst. Am. U., 1970-73; exec. sec. U.S. Telephone Assn., 1973-75; staff asst. to U.S. Congressman McClory of D.C., 1975-81, adminstrv. asst., 1981—. Tchr. jr.-sr. high youth, mem. United Meth. Women, Faith United Meth. Ch., Accokeek, Md., 1975—. Recipient H. Q. Schisler award, 1968; grantee United Meth. Ch., 1967. Mem. Adminstrv. Assts. Assn., Congressional Staff Club. Office: 2109 Rayburn House Office Bldg Washington DC 20515

HUSS, PATRICIA ANN, oil and gas co. exec.; b. Paris, Ark., Apr. 22, 1934; d. Coy Burl and Marjorie Lois (Pearson) Cobb; B.S. in Bus. Edn., U. Tulsa, 1956; m. Albert Lee Huss, Apr. 22, 1968; children by previous marriage—Kathryn Lynn Andress, Elizabeth Ann Andress. Sec. subs. Standard Oil N.J., Tulsa, 1956-65; secondary sch. tchr., Tulsa, 1966-67; prodn. clk./sec. Reading & Bates Offshore Drilling Co., Tulsa, 1967-69; exec. sec., asst. W.J. Wiseman, D.D., Tulsa, 1975-76; prodn. clk. Helmerich & Payne, Tulsa, 1976-77; office mgr. Roy M. Teel Cos., Tulsa, 1977-79, corp. sec.-treas., mgr. Okla. div., 1979—; v.p. Adams Petroleum Enterprises Corp., Tulsa, 1981—. Vol., St. Francis Hosp., 1970; chmn. polit. edn. com. Republican Women's Club, 1971; asst. leader Girl Scouts U.S.A., 1972-73; active PTA, Women's Assn. of Tulsa Philharm. Delta Delta Delta scholar, 1954-55. Mem. Desk and Derrick, Phi Gamma Kappa, Pi Gamma Mu, Sigma Alpha Sigma, Delta Delta Delta Alumnae Assn. Presbyterian. Club: Candlewood Tennis and Swimming. Home: 5614 S Gary Pl Tulsa OK 74105

HUSSELMAN, GRACE, educator; b. Paterson, N.J., July 24, 1923; d. Edward and Lydia (Kliphouse) Van Allen; B.A., William Paterson Coll.; m. Samuel Husselman, June 3, 1944; children—Samuel Glenn, Howard Lloyd. With personnel office Wright Aero. Corp., Fairlawn, N.J., 1942-45; library asst. Wyckoff (N.J.) Public Library, 1964-66; library dir. Allendale (N.J.) Public Library, 1967-81; elem. sch. tchr., asso. ednl. media specialist, 1981—. Reading Merit Badge counselor Boy Scouts Am.; pioneer guide Pioneer Girls, nat. youth v.p., sec. friendship circle; sec. bookstore com. Christian Growth Ministries. Mem. N.J., Bergen-Passaic library assns., Kappa Delta Pi. Mem. Christian Reformed Ch. Club: Captains and Mates Yacht. Home: 3 Hillside Ave Midland Park NJ 07432

HUSSELMAN, JANET, ret. accountant; b. Hawthorne, N.J., July 21, 1924; d. William and Clara Yeskoo; student public schs., Hawthorne; m. John Husselman, May 3, 1947; children—John W., Janice Husselman VanderPyl. Sec., Erie R.R., N.Y.C., 1942-49; customer service supr. Alesco, Paramus, N.J., 1965-73; accounts payable adminstr. APC Corp., Hawthorne, N.J., 1973-81, ret., 1981; notary public, 1977—. Mem. Passaic County (N.J.) Election Bd. Republican. Mem. Christian Ref. Ch.

HUSSEY, MARIANNE C., advt. agy. exec.; b. N.Y.C., Oct. 27, 1946; d. James Richard and Edythe (Kennedy) H.; B.A. in Math., Ladycliff Coll., 1968; M.B.A., Fordham U., 1972. Various positions including Dancer Fitzgerald Sample, N.Y.C., 1968-76; account supr. Waring & LaRosa, N.Y.C., 1976-78; v.p., mgmt. supr. SSC & B, N.Y.C., 1978-81; v.p. Cunningham & Walsh, N.Y.C., 1981—; participant internat. seminars. Democrat. Office: 260 Madison Ave New York NY 10016

HUSSEY, NORA W., supt. mint, Denver; b. N.Y.C., Mar. 26, 1915. Organizer, Meade County Federated Republican Women, S.D.; Republican precinct committeewoman; vice-chmn. Meade County Republican Party, formerly, chmn., 1964-72; Rep. Nat. Committeewoman, S.D., 1972-81; supt. USS. Mint, Denver, 1981—. Mem. ARC (home nursing chmn.), PEO (chpt. treas.), Toastmistress Club. Episcopalian (pres. ch. women). Address: Office of Supt U S Mint Denver CO 80225 *

HUSSIN, JEAN HELENE, investment co. exec.; b. Chgo., May 14, 1911; d. Giles Edward and Eva Marie (Tomczak) Ratkowski; m. Floyd Joseph Hussin, June 19, 1937 (dec. 1979). Legal sec. Marcus Rabwin & Nash, Los Angeles, 1927-33; office mgr. Moulding Supply Co., Alhambra, Calif., 1933-59, pres., 1979—; pres. Fremont Service Co., Alhambra, 1967—; v.p. Sequoia Mgmt. Corp., Alhambra, 1965—; dir. Progressive Savs. and Loan Assn., Alhambra. Mem. Alhambra City Planning Commn., 1970-80; 1t. Women's Ambulance and Def. Corps Am. organist San Gabriel Mission, 1935—.

HUSTED, JUNE ROSE, psychologist; b. Highland Park, Mich., Dec. 10, 1934; A.B., UCLA, 1962, M.A., 1967, Ph.D., 1972. Staff psychologist Long Beach VA Med. Center, 1971-73, chief Day Treatment Center, 1973—; clin. asso. prof. U. So. Calif., 1973—; clin. asso. prof. Fuller Theol. Sem., 1977—; clin. asst. prof. U. Calif., Irvine, 1979—, UCLA/Harbor Med. Center, 1980—; regional gov., dir. Who's Who Internat. Recipient Superior Performance award Long Beach VA Hosp., 1975, 81. Mem. Am. Psychol. Assn., Western Psychol. Assn., Am. Soc. Clin. Hypnosis, So. Calif., Soc. Clin. Hypnosis, Phi Beta Kappa. Contbr. chpts. to books, articles to profl. jours. Office: 5901 E 7th St Long Beach CA 90822

HUSTON, JANE FITZSIMONS, state agy. adminstr.; b. Salem, Oreg., July 22, 1926; d. Oliver Bruce and Florence (Challoner) H.; B.A., Willamette U., 1946; M.B.A., U. Pitts., 1976; children—Patrick, Anne, James, Jane. With State System of Higher Edn. State of Oreg., 1966-71; program dir., div. mgr., supr. Dept. Community Devel., Salem, 1971-74; with Abt Assos., Inc., Cambridge, Mass., 1974-79; dir. Oreg. Dept. Commerce, Salem 1979—. Mem. Am. Soc. Public Adminstrs., Oreg. Econ. Recovery Council. Republican. Presbyterian. Office: 428 Labor and Industries Bldg Salem OR 97310

HUSTON, LESLIE A., mgmt. cons. co. exec.; b. Sharon, Pa., July 25, 1947; d. Charles B. and Betty J. Fickes; B.S., Pa. State U., 1969; M.S., Bryn Mawr Coll., 1977. Legal asst. firm Pepper, Hamilton & Scheetz, Phila., 1973-75; research asst. Crozer-Chester Hosp., Chester, Pa., 1976-77; dist. mgr. Fogel & Assos., Inc., Phila., 1977-80, v.p., 1980—; pres. Logistics Support Group, Phila., 1978—. Mem. Nat. Assn. Female Execs., Nat. Assn. Women in Constrn., Project Mgmt. Inst., Assn. Profl. Planners and Schedulers, Phila. Women's Network, Am. Mgmt. Assn. Contbr. articles to profl. jours. Office: Fogel & Assos Inc 1420 Walnut St Philadelphia PA 19102

HUSTON, MARGO, journalist; b. Waukesha, Wis., Feb. 12, 1943; d. James and Cecile (Timlin) Bremner; student U. Wis., 1961-63; A.B. in Journalism, Marquette U., 1965; m. James Huston, Dec. 9, 1967 (div.); 1 son, Sean Patrick. Editorial asst. Marquette U., Milw., 1965-66; feature editor, reporter Waukesha Freeman, 1966-67; feature reporter Milw. Jour., 1967-70; reporter Spectrum, women's and food sections, 1972-79, editorial writer, 1979—. Recipient Penney-Mo. award for consumer abortion series, 1975, Pulitzer Prize for investigation into plight of elderly, 1977, Clarion award, 1977, Knight of Golden Quill award, Milw. Press Club, 1977, Wis. AP writing award, 1977, special award Milw. Soc. Profl. Journalists, 1977, Penney-Mo. Paul Myhie award for excellence, 1978; By-Line award Marquette U. Coll. of Journalism, 1980. Mem. Nat. News Council (dir.), Investigative Reporters and Editors, Sigma Delta Chi. Club: Milw. Press. Home: 4825 W Townsend St Milwaukee WI 53216 Office: 333 W State St Milwaukee WI 53201

HUSUM, BARBARA MOFFET, paper co. exec.; b. Evanston, Ill., Nov. 25, 1954; d. Howard F. and Marjorie M. (Moffett) H.; B.A. in Psychology and Econs. magna cum laude, Wheaton (Mass.) Coll., 1976; M.B.A., Northwestern U., 1981. Sales trainee Folding Carton and Label div. Internat. Paper Co., Chgo., 1976, jr. sales rep., 1977, sales rep. nat. accounts, 1978, regional sales adminstr., 1979-80, sr. sales rep., 1980-81, new product mgr., N.Y.C., 1982—. guest lectr. Ill. Inst. Tech. Mem. Wheaton Coll. Alumnae Assn. (treas. Chgo. chpt. 1979-80). Office: 77 W 45th St New York NY

HUSZAGH, ELENIE KOSTOPOULOS (MRS. RICHARD W. HUSZAGH), lawyer; b. Portland, Oreg., May 1, 1937; d. Peter V. and Mary C. (Birou) Kostopoulos; A.B., U. Chgo., 1957; J.D., John Marshall Law Sch., 1963; m. Richard W. Huszagh, July 1, 1962; 1 son, Peter. Admitted to Ill. bar, 1963; house counsel Liberty Loan Corp., Chgo., 1964; asso. A.J. Geokaris, atty., Zion, Ill., 1965; partner Huszagh & Huszagh, Glenview, Ill., 1965-70; pres. Miller & Huszagh, Ltd., attys., Glenview, 1970-78, Miller, Forest, Downing, Rodman & Huszagh, Ltd., 1978—. Mem. caucus com. Village of Northbrook (Ill.), 1971; mem. exec. com., bd. govs. Nat. Council of Chs., 1979—. Mem. Chgo. Bar Assn. (uniform comml. code com., fin. instns. com., sec. consumer credit com., bankruptcy and reorgns. com.), Women's Bar Assn. Ill., Hellenic Bar Assn. (dir.), U. Chgo. Alumni Assn. Greek Orthodox (pres. bd. trustees 1973, 74, mem. archdiocesan council 1976—, adv. bd. Orthodox Observer, chmn. constn. and bylaws com. 1982-84). Home: River Ridge Northbrook IL 60062 Office: 800 Waukegan Rd Glenview IL 60025

HUTCHERSON, BARBARA FAYE, ct. clk.; b. Tyler, Tex., July 4, 1944; d. Alfred and Lorine Isabell Hackett; B.A., U. Nebr., 1966; med. sec. cert. C. E. Sch. Commerce, 1965; IBM keypunch cert. Tyler Comml. Coll., 1968; computer programming cert. Computer Careers Inst., Dallas, 1971. Med. sec. Nebr. Psychiat. Inst., Omaha, 1965-66; steno-clk. No. Natural Gas Co., Omaha, 1965-67, U.S. Atty., Tyler, Tex., 1967-69, VA Hosp., Dallas, 1969-76; grants clk. HEW Office Edn., EEO, 1975-76; fed. women's program mgr./program ops. clk. ACTION, Dallas, 1976-77; legal clk. U.S. Atty., Tyler, Tex., 1977-79; dep. clk. U.S. Dist. Ct., Tyler, Tex., 1979-81, supervising dep. clk., Marshall, Tex., 1981—; instr. Operation LIFT, Dallas, 1975-77. Mem. Profl. Secs. Internat., Federally Employed Women, Am. Woodmen, Fed. Ct. Clks. Assn., Tyler Legal Secs. Assn., Dallas Downtown Noon Bus. and Profl. Women (sec. 1974-75, Woman of Yr. award 1977, Woman on Move award 1976), Tyler Evening Bus. and Profl. Women (rec. sec. 1981-82, Woman of Yr. award 1981). Baptist. Home: 1619 N Ross St Tyler TX 75702 Office: 100 E Houston St Room 125 Marshall TX 75670

HUTCHINS, BARBARA ANN, Realtor; b. Fort Wayne, Ind., Apr. 19, 1937; d. Spencer and Ila Christeen (Spencer) Chase; student Ind. U., 1955-57; children—James, David, Scott, Eric. Policyholders service rep. Lincoln Nat. Life Ins., Fort Wayne, 1957-59; asst. claims mgr. Teamsters Security Fund, San Francisco, 1965-75; claims supr. Prudential Life Ins. Co., San Mateo, Calif., 1977; realtor asso. McGinnis & Assos., Colorado Springs, Colo., 1980—. Home: 5952 Del Paz Dr Colorado Springs CO 80918 Office: 4828 Flintridge Colorado Springs CO 80918

HUTCHINS, JEANNE BAHN, town ofcl.; b. Rochester, N.Y., Mar. 12, 1922; d. Carl E. and Marie (Hall) Bahn; B.A., Wells Coll., 1943; M.P.A., SUNY, Brockport, 1980; m. Frank McAllister Hutchins, Aug. 24, 1945; children—Katharine H. Welling, Virginia H. Valkenburgh, Patricia H. Murphy, Constance H. Mills. Bacteriologist/chemist Manhattan Project Atomic Energy U. Rochester/Strong Meml. Hosp., 1943-45; library asst. Fort Benning, Ga., 1946-47, Dartmouth Coll., Hanover, N.H., 1947-48; town bd. legislator Town of Brighton, Rochester, N.Y., 1976—; trustee Monroe Savs. Bank, 1978—. Trustee, Wells Coll., 1977—; vestrywoman St. Paul's Episcopal Ch., 1977—; bd. dirs. United Way of Greater Rochester, 1974—; trustee Center for Govt. Research, 1979—; pres. Jr. League Rochester, 1957-59; bd. dirs. Vis. Nurse Service, Northaven Adoption Agy., 1965-69, Genesee Region Health Planning Council, St. Ann's Home, 1982—; pres. bd. dirs. Council Social Agys., 1969-70; bd. dirs. Nat. Commn. on Social Work Careers, 1964-65, Monroe County Human Resources Council, 1975-81; v.p. bd. dirs. Family Service Rochester, 1962-69, Planned Parenthood, 1960-69; mem. women's council Rochester Inst. Tech., 1970—, N.Y. State Communities Aid Assn., 1970—. Recipient Forman Flair award, 1973; Grant Garvey award Am. Soc. Public Adminstrn., 1980. Mem. Brighton C. of C., LWV Found., Rochester Female Charitable Soc. Republican. Clubs: Mid Town Tennis, Rochester Dist. Golf, Western N.Y. Golf Assn. Home: 75 Indian Spring Ln Rochester NY 14618 Office: Brighton Town Hall 2300 Elmwood Ave Rochester NY 14618

HUTCHINS, MAUDE, artist, author; b. N.Y.C.; d. Warren Ratcliffe and Maude (Phelps) McVeigh; B.F.A., Yale U., 1926; m. Robert Maynard Hutchins, 1921 (div.); children—Mary Frances, Joanna Blessing, Clarissa Phelps. Painter, sculptress; ann. exhbns. Quest Art Galleries, Chgo., 1930-39, Roullier Art Galleries, Chgo., 1942-48; one-woman exhbns. include Grand Central Art Galleries, Renaissance Soc., U. Chgo., St. Louis Mus., Wildenstein Galleries, San Francisco Mus. Art, Toledo Mus. Art; sculpture exhbn. Am. Fine Arts Soc. Galleries 3d ann. nat. exhbn.; author: (novels) Georgianana, 1948, A Diary of Love, 1950, The Memoirs of Maisie, 1955, Victorine, 1959, Honey on the Moon, 1964, Blood on the Doves, 1965, The Un-Believers Downstairs, 1967; (stories and plays) Love is a Pie, 1952; My Hero, 1953; co-aurthor: Diagmammatics, 1932; rep. in anthologies, contbr. articles to profl. jours., mags. Episcopalian. Address: 1046 Pequot Rd Southport CT 06490

HUTCHINSON, ANGELYN NELSON, journalist, public relations exec.; b. Salt Lake City, Oct. 31, 1948; d. Claron Eschler and Jennie Janie (Williams) Nelson; B.A., U. Utah, 1971; M.S. in Journalism, Northwestern U., 1972; m. Jerry Boyce Hutchinson, June 19, 1981. Feature writer, Chgo. Today, 1972; writer, public relations Ariz. State U., 1972-73; med. editor, gen. assignments reporter, night city editor Salt Lake Tribune, 1973-81; writer, editor, public relations Latter-day Saints Hosp., Salt Lake City, 1981—. Recipient award Utah Optometric Assn., 1974, Utah Med. Assn., 1977, Salt Lake County Med. Soc., 1977, 79. Mem. Sigma Delta Chi (v.p. 1980, dir. 1981-82, awards 1978, 79), U. Utah Young Alumni Bd. Home: 225 6th Ave Salt Lake City UT 84103 Office: 325 8th Ave Salt Lake City UT 84143

HUTCHINSON, ANN, banker; b. Davenport, Iowa, Sept. 3, 1948; d. Sloan and Mabel Iona (Brown) H.; student U. Colo., 1966-67; B.A. in Psychology, Augustana Coll., 1973; postgrad. U. Iowa Grad. Studies Center, Rock Island, Ill., 1979—, Grad. Sch. Banking, U. Wis., 1981. With Security State Trust & Savs. Bank, Bettendorf, Iowa, 1974—, cashier, 1976-77, asst. v.p., cashier, 1977-78, v.p., cashier, 1978-81, exec. v.p., cashier, 1981—; instr. Am. Inst. Banking. Mem. Adminstrv. Mgmt. Assn., Nat. Assn. Bank Women, Am. Inst. Banking, Am. Mgmt. Assn., Bettendorf C. of C. Office: Security State Trust & Savs Bank 1710 Grant St Bettendorf IA 52722

HUTCHINSON, BARBARA BETHUNE, labor union ofcl., lawyer; b. Braddock, Pa., Nov. 23, 1946; d. Clifton Blaine and Annabelle Leah (Bush) Bethune; B.A., U. Pitts., 1968; J.D., Dickinson Sch. Law, 1972; m. Harry Lane Hutchinson, Nov. 25, 1972; children—Harry Lane, Brian David. Admitted to Pa. bar, Ga. bar, D.C. bar; asst. atty. gen. Pa. Bur. Occupational Injury and Disease Compensation; mem. firm Hames, Bethune & Oakley, Atlanta, 1974-77; trial atty. U.S. EEO, Washington, 1977-80; dir. women's dept. Am. Fedn. Govt. Employees, 1980—; v.p. exec. council AFL-CIO. Mem. Coalition Labor Union Women, Alpha Kappa Alpha. Office: American Federation of Government Employees 1325 Massachusetts Ave NW Washington DC 20005

HUTCHINSON, BARBARA CARLEEN BRICE, speech pathologist; b. Tama, Iowa, June 22, 1915; d. Carl Sturdevant and Alice (Bracken) Brice; B.A., Cornell Coll., Mt. Vernon, Iowa, 1938; M.A., State U. Iowa, 1947, Fla. State U., 1950; Ph.D., U. Utah, 1965; m. Albion Knight Hutchinson, July 6, 1952; children—Lynn Hutchinson Merry, Constance. Dir. Children's Speech Correction Clinic, Jacksonville, Fla., 1951-52; asst. prof. U. Ga., Valdosta, 1958-61, U. Okla., 1965-66; prof. speech pathology and audiology Ill. State U., Normal, 1966—; pres. Conlyn, Inc., mktg. speech and lang. tests. Mem. Am. Ednl. Research Assn., Am. Speech, Lang. and Hearing Assn., Ill. Speech and Hearing Assn., Phi Kappa Phi. Episcopalian. Co-author: Diagnostic Handbook of Speech Pathology, 1979. Originator Children's Lang. Processes Inventory. Home: Rural Route 4 Lake Vue Knolls Bloomington IL 61701 Office: Speech and Hearing Clinic Ill State U Fairchild Hall Normal IL 61761

HUTCHINSON, ELEANOR LOUISE, nurse; b. Mpls., Nov. 9, 1928; d. Paul Carl Theodore and Amanda Marie (Doell) Ewert; R.N., Swedish Hosp., Mpls., 1951; B.S. in Nursing Edn., U. Minn., 1956; m. Richard Westervelt Hutchinson, Mar. 6, 1965; children—David Henry, Susan Elizabeth. Instr., clin. supr. pediatrics Hennepin County Gen. Hosp., Mpls., 1956-60; supr. pediatric and young adult unit Fairview Hosps., Mpls., 1961-67; dir. nursing, staff devel. coordinator Indianola (Iowa) Long-Term Care Facility, 1973-80; dir. nursing Madison County Meml. Hosp., Winterset, Iowa, 1980—. Mem. Nat. League Nursing, AAUW, Madison County Nurses Assn., Simpson Coll. Guild. Presbyterian. Club: Order Eastern Star. Home: Box 397 Indianola IA 50125 Office: 300 Hutchings St Winterset IA 50273

HUTCHISON, FLORENCE MELINDA, genealogist; b. Chgo., June 20, 1911; d. George and Nancy Melissa (Baker) Dressel; B.S. in Home Econs., Okla. State U., 1936; postgrad. U. Mo., 1949, So. Ill. U., 1957, Sangamon State U., Springfield, Ill., 1978-79; m. Sanford Elijah Hutchison, 1936; children—Nancy Ann, Richard Lee, Judy Margaret, Mary Ruth, Linda Kay. Tchr. home econs. and art in Mo. and Ill., 1949-59; founder, pres. Jacksonville (Ill.) Area Geneal. and Hist. Soc., 1972—; editor Jacksonville Geneal. Jour.; chmn. Morgan County Records Preservation Com., 1976—; lectr. on genealogy, heraldry and flag history; legis. promoter new Ill. state flag, 1964-70, re-designer 1970 flag. Mem. Morgan County Bicentennial Commn., 1975-77, Jacksonville Bicentennial Commn., 1975-77; adv. bd. Morgan County Cemetery, 1980—. Recipient award merit Ill. Hist. Soc., 1969, Jacksonville Mayor's disting. service award, 1982. Mem. AAUW, N.Am. Vexillological Assn. (corr. sec. 1978-80), Ill. Geneal. Soc. (Geneal. Service award 1975), Augustan Soc., Societas Octavianus, Colonial Daus. of XVII Century (John Rolfe chpt.), U.S. Daus. of 1812 (Sangamon River chpt.), Palatines to Am., Gen. Fedn. Women's Clubs (First Ladies recognition 1974). Methodist. Clubs: Morgan County Garden, Order Eastern Star, Jacksonville Women's. Author, pub.: Basics of Heraldry for Ancestral Knowledge, 1973, Constellatory Origins of the National Flag and Great Seal of the U.S.A., 1973, Helpful Hints for Genealogical Hopefuls, 1974, Am I May Mother's and Father's Lineage Keeper?, 1977, 800 G.A.R. Posts in Illinois, 1977. Address: 629 S Diamond St Jacksonville IL 62650

HUTCHISON, JANIE RUTH, broadcaster, songwriter; b. Shreveport, La., Aug. 31, 1943; d. Rufus and Josephine (McGinthy) Martin; B.A., Columbia Coll., 1975; m. William E. Hutchison (dec.); children—William, Natalie Roxanne, Tamara Renee. Dir. Nightline, sales sec. Sta. WBBM-FM, Chgo., 1974-76; adminstrv. asst., communications dir. Chgo. Met. Council on Alcoholism, 1976-77; public affairs dir. Sta. WLOO-FM, Chgo., 1977-81. Chairperson adv. com. North Chgo. Sch. Dist. 64, 1974; office mgr. Jack Benny Center for Arts, Waukegan, Ill., 1968-70. Recipient Outstanding YWCA Leader award, Lake County, 1980; Spl. Recognition award Ill. State Rep. John Matijevich, 1980. Mem. ASCAP. Baptist. Club: Publicity (Chgo.).

HUTSON, GENEVA, refining co. exec.; b. Tyler, Tex., Nov. 6, 1923; d. Lonnie Frederick and Sylvia Louise (Allen) Wallace; student Sam Houston Tchrs. Coll., 1946, U. Houston, 1973, 74; m. Walter Murphy Hutson, May 23, 1941; children—Wayne Murphy, Mark Farrell. Stenographer Lone Star Def. Corp., Texarkana, Tex., 1942, Montgomery & Ward, Denver, 1943; sec.-bookkeeper William Steinkamp Lumber Co., Groveton, Tex., 1944-45; sec. to plant mgr. Continental Can Co., Houston, 1948-49; sec.-bookkeeper Wherry & Green Ind. Oil Co., Houston, 1951-59; exec. sec., bookkeeper, office mgr. Holmes Drilling Co., Houston, 1961—; sec., treas. Hartcap Refining Corp., Houston, 1974—. Lic. real estate broker, Tex.; cert. profl. sec. Mem. Profl. Secs. Assn. Republican. Episcopalian. Home: 4302 Sarong Dr Houston TX 77096 Office: 1912 Bank of SW Bldg Houston TX 77002

HUTT, PATRICIA ELLEN, home appliance demonstration cons.; b. Chgo., Feb. 10, 1927; d. Thomas Joseph and Anne Marie (Carney) Coe; student Oakland Community Coll., 1963, Wayne State U., 1945-47; m. Albert Edward Hutt, Apr. 23, 1948; children—Ann Marie, Ellen Clare, John Albert, Thomas Joseph, Patricia Ann. Credit mgr. Laulas Jewelry, Highland Park, Mich., 1945-48; with Curtis Publs., 1965; Detroit demonstrator coordinator Sharp Electronics, 1970-73; pres., dir. Mid-West Home Appliance Demonstrators, 1973-79, Mid-West Demonstrators, Inc., Royal Oak, Mich., 1979—; cons. maj. appliance mfrs. Recipient hon. home economist award Gen. Electric Co., 1981. Mem. Internat. Assn. Cooking Schs., Internat. Microwave Power Inst., Hardware Houseware Assn., Exec. Women, Royal Oak C. of C. Author: Mid-West Demonstrators Seminar Recipe Book, rev. ed., 1981; Microwave Cooking Starts Here, 1982. Home: 130 E Sunnybrook Rd Royal Oak MI 48073 Office: 4314 Rochester Rd Royal Oak MI 48073

HUTTO, BETTE BRASWELL, ednl. adminstr.; b. Parchman, Miss., Feb. 14, 1942; d. Grover O. and Agnes (Young) Braswell; B.S., U. So. Miss., 1963; m. Fred Kent Hutto, July 21, 1971; 1 dau., Ramona. Home economist La. Power and Light Co., Gretna, 1963-66; tchr. Gretna Jr. High Sch., 1968-69, Aurora Gardens Acad., New Orleans, 1969-72, Baylake Pines Pvt. Sch., Virginia Beach, Va., 1973; asso. dir. Profl. Bus. Inst., Norfolk, Va., 1973-74, exec. dir., 1975—, bd. dirs. 1976—; dir. Theta Kappa House Corp., 1971-73, Epsilon Mu House Corp., 1971-72. Mem. Am., Va. vocat. assns., Va. Assn. Student Fin. Aid, Va. Assn. Pvt. Schs., Tidewater Va. Delta Zeta Alumnae Assn. (pres.). Home: 52 Odd Rd Poquoson VA 23662 Office: Profl Bus Inst Bel-Aire Bldg Norfolk VA 23510

HUTTON, BEVERLY ANN, county ofcl.; b. Cleve., Oct. 6, 1939; d. Steve T. and Ann M. Galias; A.S. in Secretarial Sci., Dyke Coll., 1981, student, 1981—; 1 dau., Karen. Exec. sec. to sr. v.p. Atlantic Fed. Savs. & Loan Assn. of Ft. Lauderdale (Fla.), 1971-79; exec. sec. to pres. Work Wear Corp., Cleve., 1979; office mgr. Cuyahoga County Mental Health Bd., Cleve., 1980—. Mem. Profl. Secs. Internat. (cert.). Club: Women's City (Cleve.). Home: 8519 Bears Den Ln Broadview Heights OH 44147 Office: Cuyahoga County Mental Health Bd 112 Hamilton Ave Cleveland OH 44114

HUTTON, GINGER (VIRGINIA CAROL HUTTON), journalist; b. Phoenix, Aug. 30, 1940; d. Don M. and Ellen Louise (Martins) Wiley; A.A., Phoenix Coll., 1960; student Ariz. State U., 1960; children—Kimberly Rose, Richard Dean. Reporter, UPI, Phoenix, 1959, Glendale News, Phoenix, 1961, Phoenix Gazette, 1962-65; columnist, reporter Ariz. Republic, Phoenix, 1969-73, asst. editor women's sect., 1973-77, women's editor, 1977-80, daily columnist, feature sect., 1975—; free lance writer for various mags. and newspapers including: Ariz. Hwys., Us Mag., Cosmopolitan; collected book of columns Reflections—Thoughts on Love and Living, 1980. Recipient various state and nat. writing competition awards Ariz. Press Club. Mem. Sigma Delta Chi (pres. Valley of Sun chpt. 1975). Club: Ariz. Press. Office: Ariz Republic 120 E Van Buren St Phoenix AZ 85004

HUTTON, LINDA GREY, psychiat. social worker; b. Washington, Aug. 8, 1949; d. Howard V. and Georgette A. Hutton; B.A. with honors, U. Fla., 1972; M.S.W., Fla. State U., 1974. Clin. social worker Greenville (S.C.) Mental Health Center, 1974-78; coordinator child and adolescent services South Greenville Mental Health Center, 1978-80, Greenville Intrafamily Sexual Abuse Project, 1980—; profl. adv. Rape Crisis Council of Greenville, 1978—. Mem. Nat. Assn. Social Workers, Acad. Cert. Social Workers. Home: 2413 Wade Hampton Blvd Greenville SC 29615 Office: 715 Grove Rd Greenville SC 29603

HUTTON, MARGARET MACSTEVEN, physician; b. Owensound, Ont., Can.; d. Arthur Ernest and Helen (MacSteven) Hutton; B.A., U. Alta., 1937, M.D., 1942. Intern Royal Jubilee Hosp., Victoria, B.C. and U. Alta. Hosp., Edmonton; specialist in obstetrics and gynecology. Fellow A.C.S., Royal Soc. Arts, Royal Coll. Surgeons of Can., Am. Coll. Obstetricians and Gynecologists; mem. Soc. Obstetricians and Gynecologists Can., Delta Kappa Gamma, Pi Beta Phi. Address: 4551 Parry Rd Rural Route 1 Victoria BC V8X 3W9 Canada

HUTTON, MARY MAGDELENE BOONE (MRS. RICHARD HUTTON), educator; b. Brownsville, Tenn., Nov. 1, 1925; d. George Alexander and Helen (Jones) Boone; student Wayne U., 1945-49, Tenn. Agrl. and Indsl. State Coll., 1946, Territorial Coll. Guam, 1954; A.A., Merritt Coll., 1962; student Laney Coll., 1967-68; B.A., Calif. State Coll. at Hayward, 1969; M.A. (Grad. Minority Program grantee), U. Calif. at Berkeley, 1971; Ph.D., Ind. U., 1975; m. Richard Hutton; children—Cozzette (Mrs. Richard Davis), Larry Keith, Jacqueline Yvonne. Timekeeper, Govt. Service, Agana, Guam, 1955-56; clk. typist Health Dept., Oakland, Calif., 1957-58, clk. III, 1958-59; clk.-typist Oakland (Calif.) Police Dept., 1960-64, div. sec. to capt. police, 1964-69; asst. instr. speech Ind. U., Bloomington, 1971-74; instr. Afro-Am. Studies, Milw., 1974-75; asst. prof. speech communication U. Ga., 1975-77, coordinator Black studies program, 1976-77; chairperson communications dept. Ala. State U., Montgomery, 1977-80, asso. prof. speech communication, 1980—. Bd. dirs. Rose St. Child Care Center, Berkeley, Calif., 1970-71. Served with WAVES, 1950-51. Econ. Opportunity fellow, 1971-72; Ford Found. fellow, 1973-74. Mem. Pi Kappa Delta, Pi Lambda Theta. Mem. Disciples of Christ. Home: 3126 S Perry St Montgomery AL 36105 Office: Dept Communications Ala State Univ Montgomery AL 36101

HUXLEY, CAROLE CORCORAN, state ofcl.; b. Evanston, Ill., Jan. 1, 1938; d. Harold Francis and Angela Mary (Dawson) Corcoran; B.A., Mount Holyoke Coll., 1960; M.A. in Teaching, Harvard U., 1961; m. Michael Remsen Huxley, Mar. 27, 1971; children—Samuel Dawson, Ian Matthew Remsen. Tchr., Woodbury (Conn.) High Sch., 1961-62; area supr. to divisional dir. Am. Field Services, N.Y.C., 1962-71; program officer Nat. Endowment for the Humanities, Washington, 1971-79, dep. dir. state programs, 1979-80, dir. spl. programs, 1980-82; dep. commr. cultural edn. N.Y. Dept. Edn., Albany, 1982—. Trustee, Mount Holyoke Coll., 1982—. Mem. Am. Assn. for Advancement of Humanities. Roman Catholic. Office: State Education Dept Albany NY 12234

HUXTABLE, ADA LOUISE, architecture critic; b. N.Y.C.; d. Michael Louis and Leah (Rosenthal) Landman; A.B. magna cum laude, Hunter Coll.; postgrad. N.Y. U.; hon. degrees Yale U., N.Y. U., Washington U., U. Pa., Radcliffe Coll., Oberlin Coll., Smith Coll., Skidmore Coll., Md. Inst., Mt. Holyoke Coll., Trinity Coll., LaSalle U., Pace Coll., Pratt Inst., Colgate U., Hamilton U., Williams Coll., Rutgers U., Bard Coll., Emerson Coll., C.W. Post Coll. at L.I. U., Cleve. State U., others; m. L. Garth Huxtable. Asst. curator architecture and design The Museum of Modern Art, N.Y.C., 1946-50; Fulbright fellow for advanced study in architecture and design, Italy, 1950, 52; free-lance writer, contbg. editor to Progressive Architecture, Art in America, 1950-63; Guggenheim fellow for studies in Am. architecture, 1958; architecture critic N.Y. Times, N.Y.C., 1963-73, mem. editorial bd., architecture critic, 1973-82; Cook lectr. in Am. instns. U. Mich., 1977. Mem. vis. com. Sch. Architecture and Planning, Mass. Inst. Tech.; bd. overseers Grad. Sch. Design Harvard, Grad. Sch. Fine Arts, U. Pa.; mem. council Rockefeller

U., Smithsonian Instn.; bd. dirs. N.Y. Landmarks Conservancy, N.Y. Council for Humanities. Recipient 1st Pulitzer prize for disting. criticism, 1970; Spl. award Nat. Trust for Historic Preservation, 1971; Am. Inst. Interior Designers Elsie de Wolfe award, 1969; Archtl. Criticism medal AIA, 1969; medal for lit. Nat. Arts Club, 1971; Diamond Jubilee medallion City N.Y., 1973; Woman of Year award AAUW, 1974; Sec.'s award for conservation U.S. Dept. Interior, 1976; Thomas Jefferson medal U. Va., 1977, others; MacArthur prize fellow, 1981—. Fellow Am. Acad. Arts and Scis.; mem. Am. Acad. and Inst. Arts and Letters, AIA (hon.), Soc. Archtl. Historians. Author: Pier Luigi Nervi, 1960; Classic New York, 1964; Will They Ever Finish Bruckner Boulevard?, 1970; Kicked a Building Lately?, 1976. Office: NY Times 229 W 43d St New York NY 10036

HUZAR, ELEANOR GOLTZ, educator; b. St. Paul, Minn., June 15, 1922; d. Edward Victor and Clare (O'Neill) Goltz; B.A., U. Minn., 1943; M.A., Cornell U., 1945, Ph.D. (George Boldt fellow 1947-48), 1948; m. Elias Huzar, June 21, 1950 (dec.). Instr. history Stanford U., Palo Alto, Calif., 1948-50; asst. prof. classics U. Ill., Urbana, 1951-55; assoc. prof. history Southeast Mo. State Coll., Cape Girardeau, 1955-59; assoc. prof. classics Carleton Coll., Northfield, Minn., 1959-60; chmn. program in classical studies, prof. history Mich. State U., East Lansing, 1960—. George Boldt fellow, 1947-48. Mem. Am. Philol. Assn., Am. Hist. Assn., Archaeol. Inst. Am., Classical Assn. Middle West and South, Assn. Ancient Historians, Am. Cath. Hist. Assn., Am. Sch. Classical Studies Athens Am. Acad. Rome (adv. council). Roman Catholic. Author: Mark Antony: A Biography, 1978. Contbr. articles to profl. jours. Home: 289 Gunson St East Lansing MI 48823 Office: Dept History Michigan State U East Lansing MI 48824

HYDE, ENID ANGELINE GRISWOLD, art historian; b. Montclair, N.J., Feb. 14, 1924; d. Frederick and Enid (Hall) Griswold; B.A., Smith Coll., 1945; postgrad. Northwestern U., Columbia U., Middlebury (Vt.) Coll. Lang. Sch.; M.A., Am. U., 1981; m. James F.C. Hyde, Jr., Oct. 25, 1952; children—James F.C., III, Leslie Dunham, Andrew Griswold. Founder, 1975, since pres. Nat. Fine Arts Assos., Inc., art tour service, Washington; prof. art history U. Va. Sch. Continuing Edn., 1970—; lectr. art history Fgn. Service Inst.; ednl. cons. to schs. and univs.; lectr. and tour leader fgn. art tours; trustee com. on Art Sch., Corcoran Gallery Art, also chmn. coms., mem. women's com. Club: Smith (past pres.) (Washington). Address: 5402 Duvall Dr Bethesda MD 20816

HYDE, JANET SHIBLEY, psychologist, educator; b. Akron, Ohio, Aug. 17, 1948; d. Grant Ohio and Dorothy Mae (Reavy) Shibley; B.A., Oberlin Coll., 1969; Ph.D., U. Calif., Berkeley, 1972; m. Clark Hyde, June 2, 1969; children—Margaret, Luke. Asst. prof., assoc. prof. psychology Bowling Green (Ohio) State U., 1972-78; assoc. prof. psychology, Denison U., Granville, Ohio, 1979—; NIMH grantee, 1975-78. Mem. Am. Psychol. Assn., Behavior Genetics Assn., Am. Assn. Sex Educators, Counselors and Therapists. Episcopalian. Author: Understanding Human Sexuality, 1982; (with B. G. Rosenberg) Half the Human Experience: The Psychology of Women, 1980. Home: 98 W Central Ave Delaware OH 43015 Office: Psychology Dept Denison U Granville OH 43023

HYDE, JO ANN MARIE, computer scientist; b. Grand Rapids, Mich., Oct. 6, 1946; d. Joseph Charles and Lucille Irene (Lambers) Russo; B.A. magna cum laude in Lit., Central Mich. U., 1968; M.S. magna cum laude in Stats., U. Mich., 1970; m. Thomas W. Hyde, Feb. 17, 1979. Customer service rep. Westinghouse Elec. Co., 1968-69; with IBM Corp., 1969—, plans and controls asst., 1979-80, br. mgr. field engring. div., East Lansing, Mich., 1980-82, mgr. div. field ops., White Plains, N.Y., 1982—. Mem. Assn. Profl. and Exec. Women, Lansing C. of C. Republican. Methodist. Home: 60 Cannonball Rd Wanaque NJ 07465 Office: 360 Hamilton Ave White Plains NY 10601

HYDE-BAKER, KAREN JOAN, community assn. exec.; b. Fargo, N.D., Nov. 14, 1936; d. Ervin William and Josephine E. (Ugelstad) Edinger; B.S., N.D. State U., 1958; children—Leslie Ann, Steven Charles, Todd M. Tchr. biology St. John's Acad., Jamestown, N.D., 1958-61; spl. program dir. Mid-Penisula YWCA, Palo Alto, Calif., 1967-71, exec. dir., 1971-75; exec. dir. Jonathan Assn., Chaska, Minn., 1976—. Vice pres. Minn. Dance Theatre and Sch., 1976-80; bd. dirs. Neighbor Abroad, 1973-75. Recipient Outstanding Service award Social Planning Agy., 1975. Mem. Community Assn. Inst. (v.p. 1979, pres. 1980), Assn. United Fund Agys. Santa Clara County (chmn. 1974-75), Kappa Kappa Gamma. Office: Jonathan Assn 11100 Bavaria Rd Chaska MN 55318

HYER, MARTHA (MRS. HAL WALLIS), actress; b. Ft. Worth, Aug. 10; d. Julien C. and Agnes (Barnhart) Hyer; student Fairfax Hall Jr. Coll., 1943-45; B.A., Northwestern U., 1947; m. Hal Wallis, Dec. 31, 1966. Featured in movies with RKO Studios, Hollywood, Calif., 1950-55, Universal Studios 1955-60; starred in movies including Some Came Running, Carpetbaggers, Sons of Katie Elder, The Happening, The Chase, others. Trustee Northwestern U., Eisenhower Med. Center, Palm Springs Desert Mus., Natural History Mus. Found. Los Angeles; v.p. Blue Ribbon 400 of Los Angeles Music Center. Nominated for Acad. award, 1959. Mem. Pi Beta Phi. Home: 515 S Mapleton Dr Los Angeles CA 90024 Office: 9200 Sunset Blvd Los Angeles CA 90069

HYETT, EVANGELINE SHEIBLEY, emeritus educator; b. Ottawa, Ohio, Aug. 27, 1906; d. Albert Franklin and Agnes Elizabeth (Preisendorter) Sheibley; A.B. summa cum laude, Marygrove Coll., 1929; M.A., Cath. U. Am., 1930; M.S.S.A., Case Western Res. U., 1943; postgrad. U. Mich., 1930-49, Wayne State U., 1933-45. With Bur. Cath. Welfare, Detroit, 1930-31, Children's Center, Detroit, 1931-32, Cath. Home Bur., N.Y.C., 1933-34, Detroit Orthopedic Clinic, 1934-36; psychiat. social services dir. Wayne County Gen. Hosp. and Psychiat. Clinic, Detroit, 1936-45; exec. dir. Family Services of Montgomery County, Dayton, Ohio, 1945-48; sec. family and child welfare services United Community Services of Met. Detroit, 1948-52; asst. prof. Wayne State U. Sch. Social Work, Detroit, 1952-54, assoc. prof., 1954-69, acting dean, 1963-64, dir. admissions and placement, 1954-69, prof. emeritus, 1969—. Mem. Mich. Mental Health Commn., 1951-61, chmn., 1956, 61. Recipient award of merit Met. Detroit chpt. Nat. Assn. Social Workers, 1958; Mother Domitilla award Marygrove Coll., 1958. Mem. Nat. Assn. Social Workers (nat. bd. 1952-56, nat. exec. com. 1953-55), Marygrove Coll. Alumni Assn., Cath. U. Am. Alumni Assn., Case Western Res. U. Alumni Assn., Kappa Gamma Pi. Roman Catholic. Contbr. articles to profl. jours. Address: 630 Merrick St Detroit MI 48202

HYLAND, ANGELA MUSALO, fin. publs./debt ratings co. exec.; b. N.Y.C., Apr. 16, 1947; d. Raymond M. and Angelina M. (Corrado) Musalo; B.A. in Econs., Bklyn. Coll., 1968; m. Thomas S. Hyland, Jr., Oct. 8, 1972; children—Thomas Raymond, Matthew Sheridan. Mcpl. bond analyst Dun & Bradstreet, N.Y.C., 1968-70; mcpl. analyst Standard & Poor's Corp., N.Y.C., 1971-74, asso. mgr., 1974-76, asst. v.p., 1976-79, v.p. mcpl. bond dept., 1979—, chairperson mcpl. rating criteria com., 1981—. Office: Standard & Poor's Corp 25 Broadway New York NY 10004 *

HYLAND, KATHLEEN NOLAND, steel co. exec.; b. Long Beach, Calif., July 3, 1945; d. Richard Lee and Grace Irene Noland; B.A., U. Wash., 1967; m. Arthur Walter Hyland, Aug. 26, 1967. Asso. editor Kaiser News, Kaiser Aluminum & Chem. Corp., Oakland, Calif., 1968-73; dir. communications Kaiser Engrs., Oakland, 1973-74; mgr. internal communications Kaiser Industries Corp., Oakland, 1975-77; dir. public relations and advt. Kaiser Steel Corp., Oakland, 1977—, now v.p. Recipient award for Excellence, Am. Advt. Fedn., cert. of distinction N.Y. Art Dirs.; Merit award Fin. World. Mem. Public Relations Soc. Am., World Affairs Council, Oakland C. of C., Mortar Bd., Gamma Phi Beta. Club: Sea Ranch Assn. Author: (with Don Fabun) Dimensions of Change, 1971, Children of Change, 1970. Office: 300 Lakeside Dr Oakland CA 94666 *

HYMAN, SHEILA BERKS, travel cons.; b. San Francisco, July 12, 1931; d. Irving and Rose Berke; student City Coll. San Francisco, 1949-50, U. Calif. Extension, 1952-53, Can. Coll., 1977-78; cert. travel cons.; m. Bernard Hyman, Apr. 10, 1954; children—Marc Steven, David Alan, Robert Craig. Agt., United Travel Service, 1971-74, br. mgr., 1975—; pres., partner Profl. Resource Opportunities; partner Destinations in Depth. Mem. Pacifica City Park Beach and Recreation Commn., 1959-72; mem. San Mateo Commn. Aging. Mem. Calif. Assn. Park and Recreations Commrs., Bus. and Profl. Women, Am. Soc. Travel Agts., San Francisco Travellarians (edn. chmn.), Peninsula Travel Agts. Assn., Bon Vivants. Republican. Jewish. Home: 223 Stanley Ave Pacifica CA 94044 Office: 401 Tanforan Park San Bruno CA 94066

HYMEL, FRANCES M., physician; b. White Castle, La., Dec. 3, 1914; d. Lulovic Paul and Agnes (LeGlue) Hymel; M.D., La. State U., 1949. Head nurse Charity Hosp., New Orleans, 1935-36; staff nurse La. State Dept. Health, New Roads and Franklin, 1936-42; intern Charity Hosp., New Orleans, 1949-50, resident, 1950-51; practice gen. medicine, New Orleans, 1951—; mem. staff Hotel Dieu, New Orleans. Charter fellow Am. Acad. Family Physicians; mem. Am., Can. med. women's assns., Orleans Parish, La. med. socs., AAUW, Am. Legion Aux., Alpha Epsilon Iota. Home: 1241 N Hagan Ave New Orleans LA 70119 Office: 1239 N Hagan Ave New Orleans LA 70119

HYTIER, ADRIENNE DORIS, educator; d. Jean and Katharine (Matson) H.; B.A. summa cum laude, Barnard Coll., 1952; M.A., Columbia U., 1953, Ph.D., 1958. Instr. Vassar Coll., Poughkeepsie, N.Y., 1959-61, asst. prof., 1961-66, assoc. prof., 1966-70, Louis Boyd Lichtenstein Dale prof. French, 1970—; vis. assoc. prof. Columbia U., 1966, U. Calif., 1968-69. Guggenheim fellow, 1967-68. Mem. MLA, Am. Assn. Tchrs. French, Am. Soc. 18th Century Studies, Internat. Soc. 18th Century Studies, N.E. Soc. 18th Century Studies, Middle Atlantic Soc. 18th Century Studies, Phi Beta Kappa. Author: The 18th Century: A Current Bibliography Two Year of French Foreign Policy: Vichy 1940-42, 1958, 2d edit., 1974; Les Depeches diplomatiques du Comte de Gobineau en Perse, 1959; La Guerre, 1975; contbr. articles to profl. jours. Home: 71 Raymond Ave Poughkeepsie NY 12601 Office: Vassar Coll Poughkeepsie NY 12601

IACHETTI, ROSE MARIA ANNE, educator; b. Watervliet, N.Y., Sept. 22, 1931; d. Augustus and Rose Elizabeth Archer (Orciuolo) Iachetti; B.S., Coll. St. Rose, 1961; M.Ed., U. Ariz., 1969. Joined Sisters of Mercy, Albany, N.Y., 1949-66; tchr. various parochial schs. Albany (N.Y.) Diocese, 1952-66; tchr. Headstart Program, Troy, N.Y., 1966; tchr. fine arts Watervliet Jr. and Sr. High Sch., 1966-67; tchr. W.J. Meyer Sch., Tombstone, Ariz., 1968-71, Colonel Johnston Sch., Ft. Huachuca, Ariz., 1971-78; tchr. Myer Sch., Ft. Huachuca, 1978—, coordinator program for gifted and talented, 1981-83. Ann. chmn. Ariz. Children's Home Assn., Tombstone, 1973-74; trustee Tombstone Sch. Dist. #1, 1972-80; active Democratic Club; mem. Bicentennial Commn. for Ariz., 1972-76, Tombstone Centennial Commn., 1979-80; pres. Tombstone Community Health Services, 1978-80; mem. Tombstone City Council, 1982—. Mem. Ariz. Edn. Assn. (so. regional dir. 1971-73), Ft. Huachuca Edn. Assn., Tombstone Dist. 1 Edn. Assn. (pres. 1969-71), Ariz. Sch. Bd. Assn., NEA (del. 1971-73), Ariz. Classroom Tchrs. Assn. (del. 1969-71), Internat. Platform Assn., Tombstone Bus. and Profl. Womens Club, Pi Lambda Theta, Delta Kappa Gamma, (pres. 1982-84), Phi Delta Kappa (historian 1979-82). Home: Round Up Trailer Ranch Box 725 Tombstone AZ 85638 Office: Myer School Fort Huachuca AZ 85613

IADAVAIA, MARIE GRACE PATRICIA, psychologist; b. Bronx, N.Y., Aug. 13, 1947; d. Vincent A. and Rosaria (D'Angelo) I.; B.A. cum laude, Coll. Mt. St. Vincent, 1969; Ed.M. (NDEA fellow) Boston U., 1970. Counselor, Boston Coll., Chestnut Hill, Mass., 1969-70; counselor, trainer of vols. Dial Help, New Rochelle, N.Y., 1971-73; asst. psychologist Echo Hills Mental Health Clinic, Dobbs Ferry, N.Y., 1972—. N.Y. State regents fellow, 1969. Mem. Am. Psychol. Assn. (asso.), Am. Orthopsychiat. Assn. (asso.). Home: 17 Archer Dr Bronxville NY 10708 Office: Echo Hills Mental Health Clinic Children's Village Dobbs Ferry NY 10036

IALEGGIO, EDITH CAYOT, pub. relations cons.; b. West New York, N.J., Sept. 21, 1925; d. Paul Peter and Anna E. (Vanson) Cayot; B.A., N.Y.U., 1947; m. Victor M. Ialeggio, Aug. 21, 1949; children—Victor George, James Christopher, Patricia Anne, Donna Marie. Photo editor CARE, Inc., N.Y.C., 1947-51; freelance publicist, 1954-69; dir. pub. relations sta. WLIW-TV, Garden City, N.Y., 1969-81; pres. ECI Public Relations, Plainview, N.Y., 1981—; mem. adj. faculty Nassau Community Coll.; mem. media adv. com. N.Y. Inst. Tech., Old Westbury; adv. council Nassau Council Office Vols. Recipient Larry Brennan Meml. award N.Y. Province Newman Clubs, 1951, Liberty Bell award Nassau Bar Assn., 1979; named Woman of Yr. in Pub. Relations on L.I., Internat. Women's Yr., 1976. Mem. Internat. Assn. Bus. Communicators (chmn. 1981 conf.), Pub. Relations Soc. Am. (past chpt. v.p.), Am. Women in Radio and TV, Internat. Radio and TV Soc., L.I. Women's Network, Press Club of L.I. Roman Catholic. Address: 44 Forest Dr Plainview NY 11803

IBA, BARBARA JEAN YOUNG, govt. ofcl.; b. Ellwood City, Pa., Oct. 18, 1937; d. Robert Harold and Ellen Lucille (Newton) Young; R.N., Presbyn.-Univ. Hosp., Pitts., 1958; student Bethany (W.Va.) Coll., 1958-59; B.S. in Nursing, U. Pitts., 1961; postgrad. Am. U., 1980; m. Edward Toshikatsu Iba, Oct. 23, 1965; children—Jennifer Emi, Robert Yoshio. Staff nurse Presbyn.-Univ. Hosp., 1958-59, Bethany Coll., 1958-59; nursing instr. Presbyn.-Univ. Hosp., 1959-64; nurse, population genetic researcher Nat. Inst. Dental Research, NIH, Bethesda, Md., 1964-74, equal opportunity coordinator, 1974-80, acting fed. women's program mgr., 1980—, chief of staff Equal Opportunity Evaluation Task Force, 1979-80; mem. Woodside Child Care Program Task Force, Silver Spring, Md., 1973-79; vice chmn. NIH Child Care Program Adv. Coms., 1973-74. Chmn., Parents of Preschoolers, Inc., 1974-75; mental retardation adv., Washington. Fed. nurse trainee, 1960; recipient Equal Opportunity Achievement award Nat. Inst. Dental Research, 1978; Dir.'s award NIH, 1980. Mem. Women's Equity Action League, Federally Employed Women. Home: 8716 Milford Ave Silver Spring MD 20910 Office: Bldg 31 Room 2B 41 NIH Bethesda MD 20205

IBBOTSON, PATRICIA ANN, nurse; b. Detroit, Nov. 17, 1940; d. Russell Edward and Sophia Mary (Nigbor) Ibbotson; grad. cum laude Mercy Sch. Nursing, 1961; student Eastern Mich. U., 1971-77. Staff nurse County of Wayne (Mich.), 1961-65, head nurse med. unit, 1965-70, clin. nursing supr., 1974—. Vol. Juvenile Diabetes Found., 1975—; mem. founder's soc. Detroit Inst. Arts, 1971—. Mem. Am., Mich. (chmn. editorial subcom. Detroit dist.) nurses assns., Mich. League Nursing, Perinatal Assn. Mich., Profl. Nurse Council Eloise (rec. sec. 1971-76), Wayne County Profl. Nurse Council (dir., trustee 1977—, v.p. 1977-80, pres. 1980—). Home: 22036 Nowlin St Dearborn MI 48124

ICHINO, YOKO, ballerina; b. Los Angeles; student of Mia Slavenska, from 1967. Mem. City Center Joffrey Ballet, N.Y.C., 1973-75, Stuttgart Ballet, W. Ger., 1975-76, Am. Ballet Theatre, N.Y.C., 1977—; internat. guest artist and tchr., including 2d World Ballet Festival, Japan, 1979. Recipient Bronze medal Moscow Competition, 1977. Office: Am Ballet Theatre 890 Broadway New York NY 10019

IDDINS, MILDRED, ret. librarian; b. Fountain City, Tenn.; d. Joseph Franklin and Lucy (Chandler) I.; A.B., Carson-Newman Coll., 1936; B.S., George Peabody Coll., 1941. Tchr., Bell House Sch., Knoxville, Tenn., 1936-37; tchr. Roane County High Sch., Kingston, 1937-41; librarian Dandridge (Tenn.) High Sch., 1941-43; Army librarian, Ft. Oglethorpe, Ga., 1943-44; librarian Carson-Newman Coll., Jefferson City, Tenn., 1944-81. Mem. ALA, Southeastern, Tenn. library assns., AAUW (br. treas. 1964-66). Baptist. Clubs: Monday Literary, Modern Literary. Home: 403 Russell St Jefferson City TN 37760

IDEMA, MARIAN JOYCE, public relations exec.; b. Faribault, Minn., June 22, 1934; s. Robert Edward and Martina Caroline Oelschlager; B.A., Antioch Coll., 1957; m. James Mead Idema, Aug. 26, 1967. Dir. public relations Denver Symphony Orch., 1965-70, N.J. Symphony Orch., Newark, 1971-73, Nat. Symphony Orch., Washington, 1973-80, Chgo. Symphony Orch., 1980—. Ford Found. grantee, 1965. Mem. Am. Symphony Orch. League, Am. Women in Radio and TV. Office: Chgo Symphony Orch 220 S Michigan Ave Chicago IL 60604

IGGERS, WILMA ABELES, educator; b. Mirkov, Czechoslovakia, Mar. 23; d. Karl and Elsa (Ornstein) Abeles; came to U.S., 1943, naturalized, 1954; B.A. with honours, McMaster U., Hamilton, Ont., Can., 1942; A.M., U. Chgo., 1943, Ph.D., 1952; m. Georg F. Iggers, Dec. 23, 1948; children—Jeremy, Daniel, Jonathan. Mem. faculty U. N.B. (Can.), 1946, U. Akron (Ohio), 1949-50, U. Ark., 1950-56, Dillard U., New Orleans, 1957-60, Tulane U., 1962-63, Loyola U., Chgo., 1963-65; mem. faculty Canisius Coll., Buffalo, 1965—, prof. German, 1976—, acting chmn. modern lang. dept., 1976, dir. Office Grad. Fellowships and Scholarships, 1975—; seminar speaker, 1982—. Mem. MLA (chmn. Western Slavic sect. N.E. sect. 1982, pres. sect. 1969-70), AAUP (treas., exec. bd. N.Y. State conf. 1975-77), Czechoslovak Soc. Arts and Scis., NAACP, Urban League, ACLU, Women's Internat. League Peace and Freedom (pres. Buffalo br. 1968-69). Democrat. Jewish. Author: Karl Kraus, A Viennese Critic of the Twentieth Century, 1967. Contbr. revs. to books and jours. Home: 100 Ivyhurst St Buffalo NY 14226 Office: 2001 Main St Buffalo NY 14208

IHDE, JANET KAY, surgeon; b. Barstow, Calif., July 13, 1952; d. Ralph H. and Jean Holderby (Laidley) I.; B.S., Loma Linda U., M.D., 1977. Resident in surgery Loma Linda U., to 1982; mem. faculty Oral Roberts U., 1983—. Recipient Harold J. Hoxie award, 1977, Sandoz award, 1976-77. Mem. Alpha Omega Alpha. Office: Oral Roberts U City of Faith Surgery Dept Tulsa OK 74136

IKEDA, DONNA R., state legislator; b. Honolulu, Aug. 31, 1939; B.A. in Speech Communications, U. Hawaii; 3 children. Substitute tchr.; legis. researcher; supr. tax sheltered annuities; mem. staff House Republican Research Office, 1971-74; mem. Hawaii Ho. of Reps., 1975—, asst. minority floor leader, 1976—. Del. Rep. State Conv., 1971-80; pres. Kamiloiki PTA, 1972-73; bd. dirs. Kaiser Boosters Club. Mem. Na Hoaloha (historian univ. extension chpt. 1978-79). Office: State Capital Room 424 Honolulu HI 96813 *

IKERD, DARLENE GAY, metals service center exec.; b. Bell, Calif., Feb. 21, 1941; d. Kelly and Valentine (Hait) Petillo; student UCLA, 1958-60; B.S., Pepperdine U., 1976; m. Lloyd Ray Ikerd, Sept. 14, 1960; children—Cheri Lynn and Terri Anne (twins), Sandra Raye. With Parco Specialty, Bell, 1970-71; office sec. Ducommun Metals Co., Los Angeles, 1971-72, personnel rep., 1972-78, personnel mgr., 1978—; notary public, 1971-78. Republican. Office: 4890 S Alameda St Los Angeles CA 90058

ILDSTAD, SUZANNE T., surgeon; b. Mpls., May 20, 1952; d. Lee A. and Jane E. I.; B.S. summa cum laude, U. Minn., 1974; M.D., Mayo Med. Sch., 1978; m. David J. Tollerud, Dec. 19, 1971. Clin. fellow in surgery Mass. Gen. Hosp., Boston, 1978—; med. staff fellow immunology br. Nat. Cancer Inst., Bethesda, Md., 1982—. Mem. Am. Med. women's Assn., Mass. Med. Soc. Contbr. articles to profl. jours.; research on transplantation and tumor immunology. Office: Bldg 10 Room 4B-17 National Cancer Institute Bethesda MD 20205

ILLMER, RUTH, psychologist; b. Festus, Mo., May 31, 1918; d. Joseph B. and Bertha H. (Martin) Landau; A.A., Flat River Jr. Coll., 1937; B.A., U. Mo., Kansas City, 1959, M.A. (Univ. fellow), 1966, Ph.D., 1974; m. Norman Rousseau, July 17, 1976; children—Richard, Paul Illmer West. Tchr. public schs., Jefferson County, Mo., 1937-38, Prairie Village, Kans., 1959-64; teaching fellow U. Mo., 1964-66, instr. elem. edn., 1966-68, lectr. elem. edn. 1966-68; elem. counselor public schs., Grandview, Mo., 1966-68, ednl. cons., 1968-70; ednl. cons. dept. hearing and speech Menorah Med. Center, Kansas City, Mo., 1970-72; ednl. cons., dir. Ruth Illmer Assos., Kansas City, Mo., 1972—; chmn. dept. edn. Park Coll., 1974-79; project dir. Title VI; cons. psychologist Crittenton Center, Kansas City, Mo., 1979—; cons. in field. Lic. psychologist, cert. psychol. examiner, Mo.; Title VI grantee, 1968-69, 1969-70, 1971-71. Mem. Prairie Village PTA (life). AAUW (chmn. local chpt.), Sch. Edn. Alumni Assn., Assn. Children With Learning Disabilities (profl. adv. bd. Kansas City Council), Am. Sch. Counselor Assn., NEA, Mo. Tchrs. Assn., Am. Personnel and Guidance Assn., Profl. Counselors Assn., Am. Psychol. Assn., Council Exceptional Children, Orton Soc. (dir.). Unitarian. Author: (with Jack Katz) Auditory Problems in Children With Learning Disabilities, 1972; contbr. articles to books, profl. jours. Home: 9671 Reeder St Overland Park KS 66214 Office: 11201 Colorado Ave Kansas City MO 64137

IMBODEN, MARY ELLEN, civic worker; b. Centerville, Iowa, Mar. 26, 1927; d. Francis Lazelle and Almira (Baker) Sawyers; B.A., Vassar Coll., 1949; m. John B. Imboden, Apr. 10, 1950 (div.); children—John B., Connie Ellen. Bd. trustees Goucher Coll., 1975-81, Community Found. Greater Balt., 1978—, William G. Baker Found., 1973—; trustee Fellowship of Lights, 1979—, pres., 1982—; treas. Md., Nat. Soc. Colonial Dames Am., 1968-73, v.p., 1977-79, pres., 1979-80; co-founder Balt. Council Hist. Sites, 1980; founding mem. Sheppard Pratt Hosp. Woman's Aux., 1969. Clubs: L'Hirondelle, Mt. Vernon. Home: 6610 Darnall Rd Baltimore MD 21204

IMBODY, NORMA CARROLL, ins. exec.; b. Fort Wayne, Ind., July 3, 1936; d. Francis Leroy and Esther Leeannie (Kniss) Bennett; student public schs. Fort Wayne; m. 2d, Louis C. Imbody, July 22, 1978; children by previous marriage—Merle E. LeMay, Gary A. LeMay, Richard D. LeMay, Carol M. LeMay, Franklin E. LeMay; stepchildren—Lora M., Shaun C. Clk. typist, Lincoln Nat. Life Ins. Co., Fort Wayne, 1954-56; legal sec. firm Hayes & Hayes, Fort Wayne, 1956-60, firm Hoffman, Moppert & Solomon, 1960-62; terminal and claim sec. Expressways Freight Co., Fort Wayne, 1962-67; sec. Robert's Mobile Ins. Agy., Fort Wayne, 1967-81, v.p., 1976-81, mgr. underwriting, 1976-81; owner Ins. Agy. Execs., Inc., 1982—; mgr. casualty dept. Gregory Assos., 1982—; sec. treas. Andromeda Nat. Investment Corp., Fort Wayne, 1974-76. Mem. Fort Wayne Bicentennial Commn., 1976; mem. Democratic Precinct Com., 1972-76, 80—. Mem. Profl. Ins. Agts., Ins. Women's Assn. Fort Wayne, Nat. Assn. Female Execs., Am. Bus. Women's Assn. Club: Rebeccas. Home: 1005 Milton St Fort Wayne IN 46806

IMPERI, LILLIAN LOUISE, psychiatrist; b. Grand Rapids, Mich., Jan. 16, 1924; d. Eggidio Louis and Mabel Phena (McConnell) I.; B.S., Marygrove Coll., 1950; M.D., U. Mich., Ann Arbor, 1955; 1 son, William John Rumbos, Jr. Intern, St. Joseph's Hosp., Pontiac, Mich., 1955-56; resident Wayne County Gen. Hosp., Detroit, 1956-59; fellow student mental hygiene Yale U. Dept. Psychiatry, Dept. Mental Hygiene, New Haven, 1965-67; fellow forensic psychiatry U. So. Calif. Med. Center, Inst. Psychiatry and Law, Los Angeles, 1981-82; pvt. practice psychiatry, Detroit, 1959-65; dir. outpatient dept. Undercliff Mental Health Center, Meriden, Conn., 1967-72; dir. Calif. Mental Health Center, Thousand Oaks, 1972-76; pvt. practice psychiatry, Yuma, Ariz., 1978-81; forensic psychiatrist Inst. Psychiatry and Law, U. So. Calif. Med. Center, Los Angeles, 1981—. Served to lt. col. M.C. USAF, 1976-78. Mem. AMA, Am. Psychiat. Assn. Roman Catholic. Home: 1509 Fair Oaks Apt P South Pasadena CA 91030 Office: 235 Graduate Hall 1935 N Hospital Pl Los Angeles CA 91030

IMPERIAL, BOLYN RAMOS, psychologist; b. Davao City, Philippines, June 19, 1926; came to U.S., 1951, naturalized, 1969; d. Mauricio C. and Felicidad B. (Balatero) Ramos; B.A. magna cum laude, Beaver Coll., 1955; M.A., Ohio Wesleyan U., 1956; A.B.D., Pa. State U., 1960; m. George R. Imperial, June 23, 1956; children—Beth, Gina, Carla. Asst. prof. psychology Silliman U., Philippines, 1963-64; clin. psychologist Wayne County Mental Health Center, Lyons, N.Y., 1972-74; service psychologist Newark (N.Y.) Devel. Center, 1974-79; psychologist Assn. for Help Retarded Children Orange County, 1980-81, Letchworth Day Treatment Center, 1981—. Bd. dirs. Rochester (N.Y.) br. Hemophilia Assn., 1976-78; elder United Presbyn. Ch., Webster, N.Y., chairperson Christian edn., 1972-76; vol. TWIG, Arden Hill Hosp. Aux., Monroe, N.Y., Orange County Mental Health Center Help-Line; elder 1st Presbyn. Ch., Monroe, 1980—, gen. mission treas., 1980—. Recipient Outstanding Woman award United Presbyn. Women, Webster, 1973. Mem. Am. Psychol. Assn., Genesee Valley Psychol. Assn., Beaver Alumni Assn. (pres. Rochester br. 1970-71, fund chmn. class of '55, 1981-83), Pa. State Alumni Assn., Orange County Classic Chorale Soc., Lambda Delta Alpha, Alpha Kappa Alpha, Psi Chi, Pi Delta Epsilon. Republican. Club: United Presbyn. Women's Assn. (pres. 1970-71).

IMREY, HARRIET HALL, health care researcher; b. Indianola, Miss., June 14, 1945; d. Edward Moody and Juanita (Chapman) Hall; B.A., Southwestern U. at Memphis, 1966; Ph.D. (NIMH fellow) Louis Harris fellow), U. N.C., 1976; m. Peter Bert Imrey, Mar. 30, 1969; 1 son, Lee Jeremy. Research assoc. dept. health adminstrn. U. N.C. Sch. Pub. Health, Chapel Hill, 1973-75; research assoc. population dynamics group U. Ill., Urbana, 1977-78; adminstrv. asst. to dean Schs. Basic Med. Scis. and Clin. Medicine, U. Ill., 1979-80, dir. research Regional Health Resource Ctr., 1980—, vis. asst. prof. Sch. Clin. Medicine, 1980—. Mem. Soc. Prospective Medicine (research com.), Am. Pub. Health Assn., Am. Assn. Pub. Opinion Research, Phi Beta Kappa. Office: 1408 W University Ave Urbana IL 61801

INCLÁN, HILDA MARIANNE, mag. editor; b. Havana, Cuba, June 4, 1946; came to U.S., 1960, naturalized, 1976; d. Clemente and Rosa Blanca (Guas) Inclán; B.A. cum laude in Mass Communications, U. Miami, 1969; m. Marcos Galigarcia, Sept. 2, 1967; 1 son, Marcos Clemente. Reporter, Hollywood (Fla.) Sun-Tatler, 1966-67, Ft. Lauderdale (Fla.) News, 1968-70; Latin community writer, daily columnist Miami (Fla.) News, 1970-78; editor-in-chief Intimidades Mag., Virginia Gardens, Fla., 1978—. Mem. Republican Presdl. Task Force, 1981—. Recipient community service awards from civic orgns. and local schs., local awards for maj. stories on Latin lifestyle and investigative pieces on corruption. Mem. Women in Communication, Nat. Assn. Female Execs., Mental Health Assn. Dade County, Phi Beta Kappa. Roman Catholic. Club: Coconut Grove Sailing. Home: 10371 SW 44th St Miami FL 33165 Office: 6355 NW 36th St Virginia Gardens FL 33166

INFANTE, MARIE CATHERINE, nurse; b. Woodbury, N.J., Apr. 25, 1949; d. John Angelo and Blanche (Gale) I.; R.N., B.S.N., U. Md., 1972, M.S., 1980; M.B.A., Loyola Coll., 1982; m. Gerald Davis Schuster, June 4, 1978. Nurse clinician U. Md. Hosp., Balt., 1972-75; clin. coordinator Doctors Hosp., Prince George's County, Lanham, Md., 1975-77; clin. coordinator Associated Pain Cons., Silver Spring, Md., 1976-79; exec. dir., 1979—, also dir., sec.-treas. Mem. task force on consumer edn. Md. State's Atty. Gen. Kellogg Found. grantee, 1971-72; U. Md. Sch. Nursing grantee, 1976-78. Mem. Am. Nurses Assn. (council nursing adminstrn., council specialists in psychiat. and mental health nursing), Am. Congress Rehab. Medicine, Nat. Assn. Orthopedic Nursing (nat. edn. com.), Md. Nurses Assn., Am. Pain Soc., Internat. Assn. Study Pain, Am. Heart Assn., Nat. Assn. Female Execs., Alpha Chi Omega, Sigma Theta Tau, Phi Kappa Phi. Home: 10233 Holly Hill Pl Potomac MD 20854 Office: 8830 Cameron St Silver Spring MD 20910

INFINGER, GLORIA ALTMAN, nurse; b. Charleston, S.C., Feb. 16, 1941; d. Norman Bainister and Gladys Viola (Risher) Altman; diploma Med. U. S.C., 1962; m. Norman Marion, May 21, 1961; children—Robert Mark, Michael Scott. Staff nurse Med. U. Hosp., Charleston, S.C., 1962-68; office nurse John Aycock, Jr., M.D., Mount Pleasant, S.C., 1968-69; asst. head nurse, acting head nurse, charge nurse Charleston County Hosp., 1969-73; supr. Med. U. Hosp. South Charleston, Charleston, 1973-74, asst. dir. evenings, 1974—. Chmn., PTA Com. for Prevention Substance Abuse for Brentwood Middle Sch., 1981—, com. mem. for adv. council, 1981—. Mem. Med. U. S.C. Alumnae Assn. Baptist. Clubs: Order Eastern Star (chpt. worthy matron 1976-77), Order Rainbow Girls (majority mem.). Home: 4512 Paramount Dr Charleston SC 29405 Office: 171 Ashley Ave Charleston SC 29405

INGALSBE, LILLIAN CAROLINE (MRS. CHARLES KREIGER), real estate broker, judge; b. Donald, Washington, Mar. 27, 1932; d. Wiley Claude and Lillian (Graham) Close; student Centralia Jr. Coll., 1970—; m. Charles Kreiger, Sept. 22, 1947; children—Sherry, Charles E., Roger, Tony, Shane. Justice peace, Morton, Wash., 1961-67; police judge, 1963-75; real estate salesman Rainier Real Estate, 1966-67; broker, br. mgr. Forrester Realty, Morton, after 1968; now owner, broker Mountain Realty, Morton. Sec., Eastern Lewis County Democratic Club. Agt., Dept. Licensing, Dept. Transp. Mem. Women of Moose. Home: Box 130 Morton WA 98356 Office: 2d St and Airport Way Morton WA 98356

INGE, ROSALIND ROBERTSON, mgmt. cons.; b. Danville, Va., July 15; d. Richard Lindbergh and Arimentha (Irby) Robertson; B.A., Howard U., 1972, M.A. (NIMH fellow 1972-74), 1974; postgrad. Am. U.; m. Willie Hugh Inge, Feb. 5, 1972; 1 son, Rashaad Robertson. From statis. asst. to sr. research asst. Nat. Urban League, 1972-76; research asso., then asso. project dir. Social Systems Intervention, Washington, 1977; dir. research Washington Urban League, 1977-78; sr. asso. A.L. Nellum & Assos. Inc., Washington, 1979—; freelance cons., 1977, 80-81. Mem. Am. Soc. Public Adminstrn., Nat. Assn. Female Execs., Lamond Riggs Civic Assn. Democrat. Asso. editor Urban League Rev., 1974-76. Home: 516 Oneida St NE Washington DC 20011 Office: 1990 M St NW Washington DC 20036

INGERSOLL, FAY ESTELLE, nurse, ednl. adminstr.; b. Manokin, Md., Dec. 7, 1933; R.N., Milford Meml. Hosp. Sch. Nursing, 1954; B.S., U. Maine, 1969, M.Ed., 1974; m. Norris E. Ingersoll, Jan. 21, 1956; 1 dau., Debora A. Staff nurse Peninsula Gen. Hosp., Salisbury, Md., 1954-55, USPHS Hosp., Salisbury, 1955-56; head nurse Deer's Head State Hosp., Salisbury, 1956-57; staff nurse Central Maine Gen. Hosp., Lewiston, 1957; instr. nursing sci. Central Maine Gen. Hosp. Sch. Nursing, 1957-72, asst. dir. nursing edn., 1973-76, dir., 1976—. Bd. dirs. Am. Cancer Soc., 1979—, pub. health edn. com. Androscoggin Unit, 1979—; mem. council Maine High Blood Pressure Council, 1981—; C.M.M.C. liaison rep. in Fed. Relations, Am. Council on Edn.; adv. com. B.S.N. program U. New Eng., 1981—. Mem. LWV, Maine Nurses Assn., Nat. League Nursing, Milford Meml. Hosp. Sch. Nursing Alumni Assn., U. Maine Alumni Assn., Phi Kappa Phi, others. Roman Catholic. Home: 13 Highland Ave Lisbon Falls ME 04252 Office: 300 Main St Lewiston ME 04240

INGERSON, HELEN G. KNAPP (MRS. JOSEPH P. INGERSON), dietary mgmt. cons., co. exec.; b. West Winfield, N.Y., Oct. 24, 1922; d. Marion R. and Geraldine (Smith) Knapp; B.S., Cornell U., 1944; M.Ed., U. Rochester, 1969; m. Joseph P. Ingerson, Feb. 24, 1950; children—Terrence V., Charles Joseph, Joanne Carol. Dietetic intern Eastman Kodak Co., Rochester, N.Y., 1945, ednl. dir. for dietetic internship, asst. supr. nutrition services, 1951-71, supr. nutrition services, 1971-72, dir. dietetic internship, 1971-72; asso. prof. dept. human nutrition and food Coll. Human Ecology, Cornell U., 1972-74; asst. dir. clin. dietetics and edn. U. Rochester Med. Center, 1974-80; v.p. and sec. Joseph P. Ingerson Assos., Inc., Rochester, 1980—; dietary mgmt. cons., dietitian Strong Meml. Hosp., Rochester, 1944, Bausch Lomb Optical Co., Rochester, 1945-47, Western Electric Corp., Chgo., 1947; chief dietitian Rochester Gen. Hosp., 1947-51; mem. adv. com. Community Savs. Bank, 1976-79. Vice chmn. Rochester and Monroe County Nutrition Com., 1954-56, chmn., 1956-58; health chmn. Iron-dequoit Parent Tchrs. Council, 1958-60; area E rep. women's N.Am. sailing com. N.Am. Yacht Racing Union, 1958-75, chmn., 1974-75, sec. Lake Yacht Racing Assn., 1975-81, pres., 1980—; chmn. women's sailing, women's coordinating com. U.S. Yacht Racing Union, 1976—, bd. dirs., 1976-79, 80—; cert. sr. judge, 1978—; mem. U.S. Yacht Union; mem. women's sailing com. Internat. Yacht Racing Union, 1977-78, vice chmn., 1977-78, chmn. organizing com. World Women's Sailing Championship, 1978; internat. judge Internat. Yacht Racing Assn., 1981—; trustee U.S. Internat. Sailing Assn., 1979—. Mem. Am. (sec. council 1963-66, chmn. public relations com. 1960-62, del.-at-large 1963-66, mem. adminstrv. com. dietetic internship council 1966-69, chmn. adminstrv. com. 1966-68, mem. ednl. practices com. 1969-71), N.Y. State (pres. 1958-59, editor bull. 1949-57), Genessee (pres. 1949-51) dietetic assns. Am. Soc. Parenteral and Enteral Nutrition, Soc. Nutrition Edn. Home: 1600 Islamorado Blvd Apt 71-C Punta Gorda FL 33955 also 299 Rock Beach Rd Rochester NY 14617 Office: 299 Rock Beach Rd Rochester NY 14617

INGLE, PATTY POLEN, social worker; b. Dubois County, Ind., Dec. 10, 1954; d. Samuel Donald and Irene Leota (Lichlyter) Polen; B.S. in Sociology, Ind. State U., Evansville, 1977; M.A. in Counseling, gerontol. specialist cert., U. Evansville, 1980; m. Donnie Ingle, June 30, 1979. Social dir. Village Health Care Center, Washington, Ind., 1978-79; social worker, dir. social work Northwood Good Samaritan Home. Jasper, Ind., 1979—; lectr. Ind. U.; instr. Vincennes U., Jasper; appearances on radio and TV. Bd. dirs. Pike County Assn. Retarded Citizens, 1981—. Recipient Ind. Community Service award, 1981; Ind. Health Care Recipient award, 1982. Mem. Jasper Bus. and Profl. Women's Club, Pike County Mental Health Assn. Methodist. Club: Jasper Bus. and Profl. Women's (v.p.). Author resource directory, booklets, newspaper columns. Office: 2515 Newton St PO Box 459 Jasper IN 47564

INGLE, PAULINE STEPHANIA, nurse; b. Sevier County, Tenn., June 1, 1916; d. Charles Henry and Martha (Dodgen) Hoffman; R.N., Knoxville (Tenn.) Gen. Hosp., 1939; m. Ronald J. Ingle, Oct. 13, 1945 (dec. 1963); children—LeAnne, Elizabeth K. Staff nurse hosps. in Ky. and Ohio, 1939-40; supr. Gibson Hosp., Richmond, Ky., 1940-45; public health nurse Sevier County (Tenn.) Health Dept., 1946; mem. nursing staff Sevier County Med. Center, Sevierville, 1965-79, asst. dir. nurses med. center and nursing home, 1977-79; chmn. health com. Sevier County Elem. Sch. PTA, 1955-59. Pres. Sevier County Library Bd., 1952, Sevierville Garden Club, 1947; vol. meml. chmn. Am. Cancer Soc., tri-county ednl. chmn. Mem. Tenn. Nurses Assn., Beta Sigma Phi (past pres. exemplar chpt.). Republican. Presbyterian. Home: 127 Main St Sevierville TN 37862

INGLETON, FAYE ALEXANDRA, nurse; b. Australia, June 16, 1947; came to U.S., 1970; d. William Roy and Sheila Frances (Cunningham) Ingleton; grad. Wimmera Base Hosp., Victoria, Australia, 1967, Royal Womens Hosp., Melbourne, Victoria; B.A., Redlands U., 1977. Various mgmt. positions, N.Y.C., Los Angeles, since 1970; now asst. dir. nursing recruitment Marina Mercy Hosp., Marina Del Rey, Calif. Mem. Nat. Assn. Female Execs. Office: 4650 Lincoln Blvd Marina Del Rey CA 90291

INGLIMA, JUNE KING, govt. ofcl.; b. Knoxville, Tenn., Nov. 27, 1925; d. Arthur Emery and Gladys (Prestwood) King; degree in voice Juilliard Sch. of Music, 1948; B.Music Edn., Mt. Union Coll., 1958; M.A. in Music and English, Kent State U., 1960; certificate in bus. Canton Bus. Coll., 1961; m. John M. Inglima, May 12, 1968; 1 son, Michael. Singer on Broadway stage, model, N.Y.C., 1948-53; tchr. English, Lakewood (Ohio) High Sch., 1962-65; cons., program dir. in tng. and devel. Office of Personnel Mgmt., Washington, 1965-68; dir. sales tng. and communication Soc. for Savs. Bank, Hartford, Conn., 1968-69; sr. tng. specialist Citibank, N.Y.C., 1969-71; sr. tng. specialist Royal Globe Ins. Co., N.Y.C., 1971-74; regional tng. dir. U.S. Customs Service, Los Angeles, 1974—; profl. singer. Recipient cert. of recognition Los Angeles C. of C. and Los Angeles Unified Sch. Dist.; 1976. Mem. Am. Soc. for Tng. and Devel., Nat. Soc. Arts and Letters (nat. music chmn.), Am. Mgmt. Assn., Wilshire Bus. and Profl. Women, Ebell of Los Angeles, Adrians of Ebell, Phi Beta Kappa, Mu Phi Epsilon. Democrat. Office: US Customs Service 300 N Los Angeles St Los Angeles CA 90012

INGRAHAM-PARSON, VIVIAN JUNE LOWELL, fed. program adminstr.; b. Omaha, June 1, 1922; d. John Calvert and Pearl Mabel (Whitscell) Lowell; student schs. Omaha; m. Clarence Parson, Sept. 7, 1969; children—Richard D. Ingraham, Leroy Lowell Ingraham, John Edwin Ingraham, Jeffrey Scott Ingraham. Supr. customer service Met. Utilities Dist., 1940-46; news reporter Sta. KBON, Omaha, 1962-67; med. transcriber VA Hosp., Omaha, 1971-73; exec. dir. Gt. Plains council Girl Scouts U.S.A., Omaha, 1973-75; job developer City of Omaha, 1976-81; employment coordinator Iowa CETA, 1981—. Exec. com. Mid-Am. council Boy Scouts Am., 1960—, Fontenelle Dist. Boy Scouts Am., 1958-76; youth coordinator Douglas County ARC, 1965-70; dist. II dir. Nebr. State PTA, 1964-68; v.p. Omaha PTA Council, 1966-68; pres. Walnut Hill Sch. PTA, 1958-60, Monroe Sch., 1965-67, Fontenelle Schs., 1962-64; dist. del. Republican Party. Recipient hon. life membership award, nat. and state PTA, 1972; Good Neighbor award Ak-Sar-Ben, 1970; Brotherhood Week-Good Neighbor award NCCJ, 1967; Service award ARC, 1968; nat. officer (Stewards) Nat. Presbyn. Mariners, 1960-66; hon. adm. Nebr. Navy. Mem. Profl. Assn. Girl Scout Execs. Presbyterian. Panelist: Discrimination and Its Effect on Children, 1970; author booklet: A Look at PTA, 1966; contbr. articles to religious mags. Office: 521 S Main St Council Bluffs IA 51501

INGRAM, ARBUTUS BOYD, envelope mfg. co. exec.; b. Ferrum, Va., Mar. 29, 1930; d. Ted Lee and Gladys (Spencer) Boyd; student Ferrum Coll., 1947, Cornett Bus. Sch., 1947-48; m. Alexander Fountin Ingram, Jr., Nov. 16, 1948. Sec. to v.p. Clover Creamery, Roanoke, Va., 1948-50; sec. to pres. Double Envelope Corp., Roanoke, Va., 1954-75, v.p., asst. to pres., 1975-78, asst. to chmn., 1977—. Sec. North Roanoke Civic League. Mem. Profl. Secs. Internat. (dir.). Episcopalian. Clubs: Jefferson, Alpine Garden (pres.). Home: 7823 Alpine Rd Roanoke VA 24019 Office: 7702 Plantation Rd Roanoke VA 24019

INGRAM, DOROTHY EUGENE, mgmt. info. system exec.; b. Smithfield, N.C., June 16, 1934; d. Edward Imory and Georgianna (Brasuell) Blackman; student N.C. Coll., 1952-53, Dover Bus. Sch., 1967-68, Morris County Coll., 1974-75, St. Elizabeth Coll., 1980-81; m. Oeglaire Ingram, Feb. 20, 1954; 1 dau., Garney Yvette. Accounts receivable clk. Silver Burdette Co., Morristown, N.J., 1966-69; keypunch operator Keuffel & Esser Co., Morristown, N.J., 1969, invoice control clk., 1970-72, keypunch group leader, 1972-75, keypunch supr., 1975-80, mgmt. info. system supr., 1980—. Pres., Carettes Inc. of No. N.J., 1976-77, 81—; pres. sr. usher bd. A.M.E. Ch. Mem. NAACP, Data Entry Mgmt. Assn. Democrat. Address: 24 Cottage Pl Morristown NJ 07969

INGRAM, HELEN MOYER, polit. scientist; b. Denver, July 12, 1937; d. Oliver Weldon and Hazel Margaret (Wickard) Hill; B.A., Oberlin Coll., 1959; Ph.D., Columbia U., 1967; children—Mrill, Maia, Seth. Lectr., asst. prof. polit. sci. U. N.Mex., Alburquerque, 1962-69; staff polit. scientist, cons. Nat. Water Commn., Washington, 1969-72; assoc. prof. polit. sci. U. Ariz., 1972-77, prof., 1979—; sr. fellow Resources for the Future, Washington, 1977-79, cons., 1979—; mem. bd. agr. and renewable resources Nat. Acad. Scis., 1977-80. Mem. Ariz. Council Humanities, Policy Studies Orgn. (council, exec. com. 1978—), Am. Polit. Sci. Assn., Western Polit. Sci. Assn. (v.p., program chmn.). Author: (with Dean Mann) Why Policies Fail, 1980, (with N. Laney and J. R. McCain) A Policy Approach to Political Representation: Lessons from the Four Corners States, 1980. Home: 3244 E Waverly St Tucson AZ 85716 Office: Dept Polit Sci U Ariz Tucson AZ 85721

INGRAM, LOIS SWINTON, pharmacist; b. Galesburg, Ill., Oct. 13, 1934; d. Wayne and Hope Gurnee (Giddings) Swinton; B.S., St. Louis Coll. Pharmacy, 1963; m. William Ingram, Mar. 21, 1954; children—Susan, William Scott. Pharmacist, Bakers Rexall Drug Store, Keokuk, Iowa, 1963-69; dir. pharacy Graham Hosp., Keokuk, 1969-74; pharmacist Osco Drug Store, Keokuk, 1974-75; dir. pharmacy St. Lukes Hosp. West, Chesterfield, Mo., 1975—. Mem. Am. Soc. Hosp. Pharmacists, St. Louis Soc. Hosp. Pharmacists. Republican. Episcopalian. Home: 710 Wild Walnut St Manchester MO 63011 Office: 232 Woodsmill Rd Chesterfield MO 63017

INGRAM, MILDRED ELIZABETH, state legislator; b. Wabash, Ind., Nov. 27, 1906; d. Charles Sylvester and Emma May (Wilbur) Seavey; ed. Lulu Compton Sem., Birmingham, Ala., 1912-24; m. John Colvin Ingram, Sept. 15, 1925; children—Wilbur, Patricia Ann, Jean Eugene. Actress, 1927-34; with Socony Vacuum Co., N.Y.C., 1940-42, N.Y. Times, N.Y.C., 1942-45, N.Y.U., N.Y.C., 1945-53; mem. N.H. State Legislature, 1977—; active local Republican Party; chmn. Acworth (N.H.) Bicentennial Com., 1975-76; deacon Acworth Community Congl. Ch., 1976—. Mem. DAR (regent), Acworth Hist. Soc. (pres.), Mass. Soc. Mayflower Descs., Magna Charta Dames (life), Order Women Legislators. Home: Dreams Landing Acworth NH 03601 Office: State House Concord NH 03301

INGWERSEN, FAITH CHARLENE, educator; b. Santa Monica, Calif.; d. Urmson and Anna May (Boswell) Sloniger; B.A., U. Wyo., 1955, M.A., 1957; postgrad. U. Oslo, 1958-59, U. Copenhagen, 1959-61, 62-65; Ph.D. in Comparative Lit., U. Chgo., 1974. Tchr., English and history Chugwater (Wyo.) High Sch., 1956; guest lectr. U. Wis. extension, Madison, 1974-81; lectr. comparative lit. U. Wis., Milw., 1977-79; lectr. Scandinavian studies U. Wis., Madison, 1980. Am. Studies scholar, 1955-56. Mem. MLA, Internat. Assn. Scandinavian Studies, Soc. for Advancement Scandinavian Study. Co-author: Martin A. Hansen, 1976; author: The Scandinavian Experience in the New World, 1979; translator of Norwegian and Danish works.

INMAN, CHRISTINE L., personnel exec.; b. Long Beach, Calif., June 12, 1947; d. Charles W. and Doris L. (Hathaway) Shepard; student Harbor Coll., UCLA; cert. Sawyer Bus. Sch., 1968; 1 son, William Henry Inman IV. With Noble, Cooke div. Gregory & Sons, Los Angeles, 1967-69; personnel mgr. Wedbush, Noble, Cooke, Inc., Los Angeles, 1969-80; asst. v.p., dir. personnel Morgan, Olmstead, Kennedy & Gardner, Los Angeles, 1981—. Mem. Spring Street Brokers. Democrat. Presbyterian. Club: Magic Kingdom (membership dir.). Office: 606 S Olive St Los Angeles CA 90014

INMAN, LUCY DANIELS, psychologist, author; b. Durham, N.C., Mar. 24, 1934; d. Jonathan Worth and Lucy (Cathcart) Daniels; B.A. in Psychology, U. N.C., 1972, Ph.D., 1977; m. Thomas P. Inman, July 2, 1957 (div.); children—Patrick, Lucy, Jonathan, Benjamin. Psychol. services dir. Lee-Harnett Mental Health Center, Sanford, N.C., 1977-80; pvt. practice clin. psychology, Raleigh, N.C., 1977—. Guggenheim fellow in lit., 1957. Mem. Am. Psychol. Assn., N.C. Psychol. Assn., Phi Beta Kappa. Democrat. Author: Caleb My Son, 1956; High on a Hill, 1961; contbr. articles to profl. jours. Home: 5113 Shamrock Dr Raleigh NC 27612 Office: Glenwood Profl Village 3041 Essex Circle Raleigh NC 27608

INNIS, PAULINE, author, newspaper co. exec.; b. Devon, Eng.; student U. Manchester, U. London; m. Walter Deane Innis, Aug. 1, 1959; came to U.S., 1954. Author: Hurricane Fighters, 1962; Ernestine or the Pig in the Potting Shed, 1963; The Wild Swans Fly, 1964; The Ice Bird, 1965; Wind of the Pampas, 1967; Fire from the Fountains, 1968; Astronumerology, 1971; Gold in the Blue Ridge, 1973, 2d edit., 1980; My Trails (transl. from French), 1975; (with Mary Jane McCaffery) Protocol, 1977; Prayer and Power in the Capital, 1982. Bd. dirs. Washington Goodwill Industries Guild, 1962-66; membership chmn. Welcome to Washington Club, 1961-64; co-chmn. Internat. Workshop Capital Speakers' Club, 1961-64; pres. Children's Book Guild, 1967-68; dir. Ednl. Communications; bd. dirs. Internat. Conf. Women Writers and Journalists; mem. criminal justice com. D.C. Commn. on Status of Women; founder vol. program D.C. Women's Detention Center; chmn. women's com. Washington Opera, 1977-79; mem. Liaison Com. for Med. Edn., 1979—; nat. trustee Med. Coll., 1980—. Pa. Named Hoosier Woman of Yr., 1966. Mem. Soc. Woman Geographers, Authors League, Smithsonian Assos. (women's bd.), English-Speaking Union (dir.), Spanish-Portuguese Group D.C. (pres. 1965-66). Clubs: Am. Newspaper Women's (pres. 1971-73), Nat. Press. Home: 2700 Virginia Ave NW Washington DC 20037 also Skipper's Row Gibson Island MD

INSELMAN-TEMKIN, BARBARA RUTH, clin. psychologist; b. Bklyn., Apr. 7, 1948; d. Alexander M. and Rae C. (Bloom) Inselman; A.B. magna cum laude with honors in Psychology (N.Y. State Regents Coll. scholar), Barnard Coll., 1968; M.S. in Psychology (Rice Meml. grad. fellow, NSF fellow), Yale U., 1972, Ph.D. in Psychology, 1973; m. Lawrence P. Temkin, June 6, 1971; 1 son, Joshua Michael. NIMH trainee, 1968-70; teaching fellow Yale U., 1971, NIMH postdoctoral fellow dept. psychiatry, 1973-74; VA clin. trainee, 1972-73; clin. psychologist Stamford (Conn.) Hosp., 1974-77; pvt. practice clin. psychology, Tucson, 1977—; adj. faculty U. Ariz. Health Scis. Center, 1981—; speaker, cons., 1974—. Cert. psychologist, Ariz.; lic. clin. psychologist, Conn. Mem. Am. Psychol. Assn., So. Ariz. Psychol. Assn.

(treas. 1979-80, v.p. 1981—), Ariz. Psychol. Assn., AAAS, Tucson Forum for Alcoholism Profls., Family Life Council Tucson, Pima County Med. Soc. Aux., Tucson C. of C., Nat. Register Health Service Providers in Psychology, Phi Beta Kappa, Sigma Xi. Contbr. articles to profl. jours.; also editorial referee. Home and Office: 3444 N Camino Esplanade Tucson AZ 85715

INTONS-PETERSON, MARGARET JEAN, psychologist; b. Mpls., Oct. 3, 1930; d. Wilfrid Wesley and Ruth Margaret (Maxwell) Lowther; B.A., U. Minn., 1951, Ph.D., 1955; M.A., U. Denver, 1953; m. Lloyd Richard Peterson, Dec. 28, 1953; children—Stephen, Laryn, Bruce, Celia. Teaching asst. U. Minn., 1953-54; research assoc., lectr. Ind. U., Bloomington, 1956-67, vis. assoc. prof., 1967-69, prof. psychology, 1969—, assoc. dean Coll. Arts and Scis., 1972-74, acting dean faculties, 1974-77; vis. scientist U. Calif., Berkeley, 1965-66; vis. scientist Stanford U., 1977-78. Grantee NIMH. Fellow Am. Psychol. Assn., AAAS; mem. Assn. Women Scientists, Psychonomic Soc., Midwestern Psychol. Assn., Sigma Xi. Democrat. Author papers in field. Acting editor Jour. Exptl. Psychology: Human Perception and Performance. Home: 2200 E Maxwell Ln Bloomington IN 47401 Office: Dept Psychology Ind U Bloomington IN 47405

IORFIDA, ISABELLA MARIA, newspaper pub.; b. Pitts., Nov. 28, 1941; d. John and Natalie (Bonacci) Camillo; m. Iorfida; children—Vincent, Victor, Margaret, Anthony. Owner, mgr. The Paper Doll Boutique, Pitts., 1965-68; accounts exec. The Beacon Newspapers, Romeoville, Ill., 1969-74; advt. dir., promotional dir. Old Chicago Town Partners, Bolingbrook, Ill., 1974-75; account exec. Herald News, Joliet, Ill., 1975-79; owner, pub., pres. The Beacon Newspapers, Romeoville, Ill., 1979—. Bd. dirs. United Cerebral Palsy, Joliet, 1982. Mem. Ill. Press Assn., Romeoville C. of C. (dir.), Bolingbrook C. of C. Office: Beacon Newspapers 759 Luther Dr Romeoville IL 60441

IRACI, ANTOINETTE ANGELA, educator; b. Jersey City, July 8, 1923; d. Louis Alexander and Rosalia (Celauro) Caldiero; B.A. in Edn., N.Y. U., 1944; m. John Iraci, June 24, 1945; children—Donna Maria Iraci DeBlasis, Judith Ellen Iraci Manni. Circulation mgr. Wise Pub. Co., N.Y.C., 1943; worker with prisoner of war mail U.S. Office of Censorship, N.Y.C., 1944-45; tchr. Annunciation Roman Cath. Sch., Paramus, N.J., 1955-73; ret., 1973. Mem. Paramus P.T.A., 1951-60; mem. Rosary Soc. Annunciation, Paramus, 1952-80, sec., 1953-55; mem. Midland Sch. P.T.A., 1954-56; mem. Valley Hosp. Aux.; mem. Bd. Edn. Archdiocese of Newark, 1971-74, parish council Annunciation Roman Cath. Ch., 1977-80. Mem. AAUW (pres. 1976-78). Home: 179 Arundel Rd Paramus NJ 07652

IRBY, BETTY ROTH, freight forwarding, customhouse brokering co. exec.; b. Toledo, Ohio, Jan. 18, 1925; d. Ralph DeZang and Myrtle L. (Burkholder) Rupp; student Toledo Conservatory Music, 1941-43; m. Arthur C. Roth, Dec. 21, 1943 (div. 1958); children—William C., Michal H., Jon A. and Cheryl A. Roth; m. 2d, Clarence N. Irby, July 17, 1961. Sec. internat. reservations/tours Trans World Airlines, Toledo, Columbus, Ohio, and Atlanta, 1957-62; mgr. Arlington Travel Service, Columbus, 1962-64; cons. Edlow Cons.'s., Columbus, 1964-69; pres. Brie Internat. Inc., Columbus, 1970—; cons. in field. Mem. Columbus Internat. Trade Com., 1969—; mem. Internat. Council Mid-Ohio, 1977—. Mem. Nat. Def. Transp. Assn. Club: Zonta Internat. Office: Brie Internat Inc 494 W Johnston Rd Columbus OH 43230 *

IRBY, LEILANI JUNE, nursing educator; b. Idaho Springs, Colo., Feb. 26, 1939; d. Robert C. and Bernice M. (Reimer) McClain; R.N., Grace-New Haven Sch. Nursing, New Haven, 1958; B.S.N., U. Okla., 1967, M.S., 1974, doctoral candidate, 1977-82; m. Michael Eugene Irby, Aug. 27, 1966; children—Michelle, Michael. Staff nurse/supr. Presbyn. and Mt. Sinai hosps., N.Y.C., Good Samaritan Hosp., Phoenix and Cedars-Sinai Hosp., Los Angeles, 1958-66; chief nurse Central Okla. Mental Health Center, Norman, 1967-72; nurse epidemiologist, asst. dir. nursing St. Anthony Hosp., Oklahoma City, 1974-77; instr. Central State U., Edmond, Okla., 1977-81, asst. prof., 1981—. Active public edn. and screening for diabetes and hypertension; resource person Redlands council Girls Scouts U.S.A., local PTA; Sunday sch. tchr. New Convenant United Methodist Ch., 1968—. Mem. Am. Nurses Assn., Okla. Nurses Assn., Phi Delta Kappa, Sigma Theta Tau. Democrat. Clubs: Edmond Garden, Edmond Soccer. Home: 2713 Kenwood Ct Edmond OK 73034 Office: 100 N University Dr Edmond OK 73034

IREDALE, NANCY LOUISE, lawyer; b. Pasadena, Calif., Nov. 27, 1947; d. Richard J. and Lois (Cashman) I.; B.S. summa cum laude, Georgetown U., 1969; J.D., Yale U., 1972; m. Clifton Cates, Nov. 26, 1976; 1 son, Clifton B. IV. Admitted to D.C. bar, 1973, Calif. bar, 1977; asso. firm Ivans, Phillips & Barker, Washington, 1972-76; tax counsel to Senator William Brock, U.S. Senate Finance Com., Washington, 1976; partner firm Paul, Hastings, Janofsky & Walker, Los Angeles, 1976—; mem. faculty Haile Sellassie U., Addis Ababa, Ethiopia, 1971; speaker in field. Mem. Am. Bar Assn. (chmn. spl. task force on expatriation), Calif. Bar Assn. (exec. com., tax sect. 1978-81), Los Angeles County Bar Assn. (chmn. fgn. tax subsect., tax sect.), Internat. Fiscal Assn., Am. Soc. Women Accts., Town Hall Calif. (chmn. taxation and public fin. sect.), Yale Law Sch. Assn. (exec. com., v.p.), Phi Beta Kappa. Office: 555 S Flower St 22d Floor Los Angeles CA 90071

IREY, CHARLOTTE YORK, educator; b. Oklahoma City, Arp. 29, 1918; d. Charles William and Annie Charlotte (Upsher) York; B.S. with honors, U. Wis., 1940; M.A., U. Colo., 1965; m. Eugene Floyd Irey, June 10, 1942; 1 dau., Susan Gail. Instr. dance Stephens Coll., Columbia, Mo., 1940-43; prof. dance U. Colo., Boulder, 1945—, chmn. dance div., dept. theatre and dance, 1973—. Recipient Robert L. Steans award U. Colo., Boulder, 1973, Thomas Jefferson award, 1980; Mem. Nat. Dance Assn. (pres. 1975-76, Scholar of Yr. 1982-83), AAHPERD, Am. Coll. Dance Festival, Council Dance Adminstrs., Congress Dance Research, Am. Dance Guild. Episcopalian. Author: (with Frances Bascom) Costume Cues, 1952. Office: 970 Aurora St Boulder CO 80309

IRHAZY, MARIA ELIZABETH, ins. co. ofcl.; b. N.Y.C., Nov. 13, 1944; d. Daniel and Maria (Schali) I.; B.A. in English and Philosophy, Elmira (N.Y.) Coll., 1966. Underwriter, Equitable Life Assurance Soc., N.Y.C., 1967-75, underwriting supr., 1975-76, mgr. underwriting, Fresno, Calif., 1976-78, chief underwriter Western Service Center, Fresno, 1978-81, mgr. planning, N.Y.C., 1981—. C.L.U.; cert. Health Ins. Assn. Am. Fellow Life Office Mgmt. Assn. (with distinction); mem. Acad. Life Underwriting (asso. with distinction), No. Calif. Underwriters Assn., Western Home Office Underwriters Assn. Home: 75 Cherokee Ave Allendale NJ 07401 Office: 1285 Ave of Americas New York NY

IRVINE, ANNA WILKES, clubwoman; b. Pitts., Dec. 7, 1915; d. Harry Edward and Estella Dorothy (Starner) W.; m. Paul Edgar Irvine, Feb. 15, 1937; children—Paul Edgar, Daryl Lynn, Harry Edward. Chmn., Quarry Park neighborhood Lake Erie Girl Scout Council, 1961-62; pres. Christian Fellowship League, 1962-63; trustee Forest Hill Presbyn. Ch., 1964-66; coordinator mission Western Res. Presbyterial Assn., 1968-74; hon. mem. Bd. Nat. Missions, Presbyn. Ch. U.S., 1967; parliamentarian Ch. Women United Greater Cleve., 1973-76; pres. Western Res. Women's Republican Club, South Euclid, Ohio, 1975-77; mem. bd. mgmt. Ohio Fedn. Republican Women, 1978-79, sec. Lakeside Fedn., 1978-79. Mem. Nat. Assn. Parliamentarians (sec. Nellie M. Cooley unit 1977-78), Ohio Fedn. Women's Clubs (health div. chmn., 1976-78), Fedn. Women's Clubs Greater Cleve. (pres. 1978-80). Clubs: Women's (pres. 1966-68, recognition 1977) (South Euclid), Women's City (Cleve.). Home: 3799 Princeton Blvd South Euclid OH 44121

IRVINE, EILEEN MARIE, biologist, computer simulation specialist; b. Sandia Base, N.Mex., Nov. 22, 1948; d. James and Mildred (Jones) I.; B.A. in Math. with honors, U. Calif., Santa Barbara, 1970, M.A. in Biology, 1972; student U. Birmingham (Eng.), 1969-70; Engrng. aide Fed. Electric Corp., Vandenberg AFB, Calif., summers 1967, 68, 69, 71; jr. math. analyst Dynalectron Corp., Point Mugu, Calif., 1972-72; asso. engr. Raytheon Co., Santa Barbara, 1972-74; research scientist Environ. Research and Tech., Inc., Westlake Village, Calif., 1977-81; cons., 1981—. Mem. Ecol. Soc. Am., Bot. Soc. Am., Nat. Women's Hon. for Coll. Sophomores (nat. officer 1967-68), Women's Hon. for Coll. Jrs. (chpt. pres. 1968-69), Mortar Bd. Contbr. articles to profl. jours. Address: 3040 Gibraltar Rd Santa Barbara CA 93105

IRVING, AMY, actress; b. Palo Alto, Calif., Sept. 10, 1953; student Am. Conservatory Theatre, London Acad. Dramatic Art. Films include Carrie, The Fury, Honeysuckle Rose, The Competition; TV appearances include: I'm A Fool; Dynasty; Voices; Once An Eagle. Office: care Rifkin-David Agy 7319 Beverly Blvd Suite 1 Los Angeles CA 90036 *

IRVING, JUANITA JOAN, nurse; b. St. Paul, Alta., Can., Nov. 27, 1940; came to U.S., 1960, naturalized, 1970; d. Walter W. and Marie Melashenko; B.Sc. in Nursing, Walla Walla (Wash.) Coll., 1962; diploma in interior design La Salle U., Chgo., 1974; now postgrad. in bus. adminstrn. Calif. Western U.; m. Russell Irving, Sept. 2, 1962; children—Lynette, Trevor. Indsl. nurse Birds Eye div. Gen. Foods Corp., Walla Walla, 1962-63; employee health nurse Gen. Hosp., Medicine Hat, Alta., Can., 1963-64; sch. health nurse, instr. Can. Union Coll., College Heights, Alta., 1964-65; mgr. Doctors Clinic, Oshawa, Ont., 1966-68; asst. dir. nurses Parkview Hosp., Chattanooga, 1970-72; asst. adminstr. nursing Loma Linda (Calif.) Community Hosp., 1979—; guest lectr. E. Los Angeles Coll.; adv. bd. Loma Linda (Calif.) U. Sch. Nursing, Registered Nurses Bd. Examiners. Mem. Calif. Dirs. Nursing Council, Calif. Soc. Nursing Service Adminstrs., Inland Area Dirs. Nursing Council. Home: 15604 Pintura Dr Hacienda Heights CA 91745 Office: 25333 Barton Rd Loma Linda CA 92354

IRVING, TRAVILLA DARLENE, clothing store exec.; b. Mt. Ayr, Iowa, Apr. 30, 1928; d. Truman Wallace and Lola Blanche (Greenrod) Dulany; m. David Julian Irving, Dec. 27, 1945; children—Patrick, Timothy, Victoria, Jean. Clk., Irving Clothing Store, Mt. Ayr, 1950-66, owner, mgr., 1966—, partner, Osceola, Iowa, 1973—, Indianola, Iowa, 1976—. Mem. Bus. and Profl. Women, Gray Ladies, Hosp. Aux. Republican. Methodist. Home: Rural Route 2 Mount Ayr IA 50854 Office: Box 160A Rural Route 1 Mount Ayr IA 50854

IRWIN, CONSTANCE FRICK, author; b. Evansville, Ind., May 11, 1913; d. Herman Christian and Minnie Constanze (Lauenstein) Frick; A.B. with distinction, Ind. U., 1934, M.A., 1941; B.S. in L.S. with high honors, Columbia U., 1947; m. William Robert Irwin, June 15, 1954; 1 stepson, William Andrew. Librarian, tchr. journalism, Beech Grove, Ind., 1936-37; librarian Reitz High Sch., Evansville, 1937-42, 47-54, U. Evansville, 1946; book editor Columbia U. Press, 1947-50; asst. prof. library sci. U. Iowa, 1961-67; author: (as Constance Frick) The Dramatic Criticism of George Jean Nathan, 1943; (as C. H. Frick) Tourney Team, 1954, Five Against the Odds, 1955, Patch, 1957, The Comeback Guy, 1961; (as Constance Irwin) Jonathan D., 1959, Fair Gods and Stone Faces (Black Hawk award Midland Booksellers Assn. 1964, Dobbs award 1965), 1963, Gudrid's Saga, 1974, Strange Footprints on the Land, 1980. Served with USNR, 1942-45. Named Disting. Pen Woman, 1982. Mem. AAUW (past chpt. pres.), Authors League Am., Nat. League Am. Pen Women (past br. pres.), Jr. League Am., Phi Beta Kappa, Delta Kappa Gamma, Pi Lambda Theta, Alpha Chi Omega. Address: 415 Lee St Iowa City IA 52240

IRWIN, MARTHA LEE, nurse; b. Portland, Oreg., Jan. 29, 1935; d. Henry and Helen (Gaffney) I.; B.S.N., U. Wash., 1957; postgrad. State U. Iowa, 1963. Pub. health nurse Seattle-King County Pub. Health Dept., 1957; psychiat. nurse Langley Porter Neuropsychiat. Inst., San Francisco, 1958-61; head nurse Mendocino State Hosp., Ukiah, Calif., 1962; asst. dir. nursing Western State Hosp., Steilacoom, Wash., 1963; clin. nurse USPHS div. Indian Health, Wagner, S.D., 1964-68; dir. nursing Rivercrest Manor, Pierre, S.D., 1968-70; psychiat. supr. VA Med. Center, Ft. Meade, S.D., 1970-74, asst. chief nursing service, Leavenworth, Kans., 1974-76, chief nursing service, Reno, 1976-78, chief nursing service, Chillicothe, Ohio, 1978—; adj. faculty Humboldt State Coll., 1962, St. Mary's Sch. Practical Nursing, Pierre, 1968. Contbg. mem. Democratic Nat. Com., 1970—. Recipient Dirs. commendation VA, 1978, Service award, 1976, 81. Mem. Am. Nurses Assn., Ohio Nurses Assn., Nat. Orgn. Chief Nurses, AAUW. Presbyterian. Clubs: Lake White Country, Soroptimists, Bus. and Profl. Women's. Home: 60 Delaware Dr Chillicothe OH 46601 Office: Veterans Administration Medical Center Chillicothe OH 45601

IRWIN, STORMY G., paper co. ofcl., editor; b. Melrose Park, Ill., Sept. 4, 1929; d. Don W. and Mary E. (Worthley) I.; student pub. schs., North Sacramento, Calif. With reprodn. dept. Zellerbach Paper Co., Sacramento, 1952-70, with customer service dept., 1971-73, credit control adminstr., 1974-81, saleswoman, 1982—; editor, contbg. writer Women in Sports mag. (name changed to Women in Softball 1972) (award for Best Continuous Coverage of Softball for non-daily publ. under 50,000 circulation Nat. Softball Broadcasters and Writers Assn. 1965, 67, 69, 71, 74), 1957-78. Coach, mgr. Sacramento City Recreation League, 1950-75 (team winners of 24 championship awards). Named to Sacramento Softball Assn. Hall of Honor, 1980. Address: Golden Palms MH Estates 8181 Folsom Blvd #258 Sacramento CA 95826

ISAAC, MARGRETHE GLORIA, educator; b. Chgo., May 6, 1927; s. Merle J. and Margrethe D. (Lehmann) I.; B.E., Chgo. Tchrs. Coll., 1947; M.A., Northwestern U., 1950, Ph.D., 1962. Tchr., Chgo. Pub. Schs., 1947-58; instr. TV Tchrs. Coll., WGN-TV, Chgo., 1958-59; asst. prof. Chgo. Tchrs. Coll., 1959-61; assoc. prof. Northeastern Ill. U., Chgo., 1961—, assoc. chmn. dept. early childhood edn., 1968-71, 73-80, chmn., 1980—; vis. faculty Northwestern U., summer 1964. Mem. exec. com. elem. sch. sect. Nat. Safety Council, 1972-81, vice-chmn., 1975-76, chmn., 1976-77, mem. exec. com. sch. and coll. div., 1976-81, bd. dirs., 1977-80; book reviewer Ill. Reading Service, 1971-76; mem. adv. com. Child Safety Club, 1977—. Recipient Outstanding Service award Nat. Safety Council, 1977. Mem. Chgo. Pub. Schs. Kindergarten-Primary Assn. (pres. 1954-56), Ill. Edn. Assn. (pres. Chgo. div. 1964-65, Disting. Service award 1967), Ill. Assn. Higher Edn. (pres. 1968-69), Assn. Childhood Edn. Internat. (chmn. various coms. 1954—, v.p. Chgo. area br. 1973-77), NEA, AAUP, AAUW, Assn. Tchr. Educators, Nat. Assn. Edn. Young Children, Alpha Delta Kappa (Pres. Ill. Alpha Epsilon chpt. 1957-59, Ill. historian 1958-60, Ill. rec. sec. 1964-66), Pi Lambda Theta (rec. sec. Alpha Zeta chpt. 1965-67, corr. sec. Chgo. area chpt. 1973-77, pres. Chgo. area chpt. 1977-81), Delta Kappa Gamma (chpt. music chmn. 1972-76), Phi Delta Kappa (chpt. historian 1977-79). Research on profl. problems of beginning tchrs. Home: 700 Victoria Rd Des Plaines IL 60016 Office: Northeastern Ill U Bryn Mawr at St Louis Ave Chicago IL 60625

ISAACS, ARLINE, author, photojournalist; b. N.Y.C., Mar. 20, 1927; d. Louis and Fay (Durst) Goldberg; student N.Y. U. and Parsons Sch. Design, 1945-48, UCLA, Calif. State U. (Fullerton), 1966-68; m. A. David Isaacs, Jan. 7, 1950; children—Ellen, Dean. Interior designer Henry Roth, N.Y.C., 1947-50; freelance author, photojournalist newspapers, 1950—; publicist, public relations ofcl., photojournalist Bullocks Realty, Santa Ana, Calif., 1966-70; owner, operator SunBox Press, Laguna Beach, Calif., 1979—. Commr., sec.-treas. Laguna Beach Arts Commn., 1979-80, recipient award; bd. dirs. Laguna Beach Mus. Art, 1979—, Orange County Arts Alliance, 1980—; chmn. 1st Ann. Beaux Arts Ball, Laguna Beach, 1978, recipient placque. Mem. Nat. Fedn. Press Women, Orange County Press Women, Women's Nat. Book Assn., Orange County Arts Alliance, Am. Council for the Arts, Women in Communications, Am. Soc. Mag. Photographers, Author: Who's Cooking in Laguna Beach, 1980; one woman show of photographs, Laguna Niguel, Calif., 1975. Home and Office: 750 Alta Vista Way Laguna Beach CA 92651

ISAACS, HELEN COOLIDGE ADAMS (MRS. KENNETH L. ISAACS), artist; b. Flushing, N.Y., Jan. 17, 1917; d. Thomas Safford and Martha (Montgomery) Adams; student Miss Hewett's classes, N.Y.C., Miss Porter's Sch., Farmington, Conn., Fontainbleau (France) Sch. Art and Music, 1935, Art Students League, 1936; m. Kenneth L. Isaacs, Mar. 10, 1949; children—Kenneth Coolidge, Anne Isaacs Merwin. Agt., Child's Gallery, Boston; one-woman shows at Child's Gallery; exhibited in group shows Allied Artists, N.Y., Boston Arts Festival; portraits of various prominent persons; murals in various public bldgs., Boston, Rochester, N.Y., Pittsfield, Mass., Daytona, Fla. Mem. Colonial Dames Am. Clubs: Colony (N.Y.C.); Chilton (Boston). Home: 68 Beacon St Boston MA 02108

ISAACS, MARLA B., psychologist; b. N.Y.C., Apr. 5, 1945; B.A. with honors, U. Wis., 1966; M.A. in Indian Studies (NDEA fellow), 1967; M.Ed. in Counseling Psychology (VA trainee), Columbia U., 1969; Ph.D. (Soroptimist Fedn. Am. fellow 1971-72), U. Calif., Berkeley, 1974; married; 1 son, Aaron. NIMH postdoctoral fellow Mt. Zion Hosp., San Francisco, 1974-76, research fellow in clin. psychology, 1975-76; research asso. San Francisco Psychoanalytic Inst., 1975-77; dir. divorce counseling service for children and families Phila. Guild Guidance Clinic, 1978—, dir. families divorce project, 1979—; asst. prof. psychiatry, asso. faculty U. Pa. Lic. Psychologist, Calif., Pa. Mem. Am. Psychol. Assn., Am. Orthopsychiat. Assn. Author papers, revs. in field. Office: 2 Children's Center 34th St and Civic Center Blvd Philadelphia PA 19104

ISAACS, MARY JO, ednl. adminstr.; b. Winston-Salem, N.C., June 27, 1931; d. James Spurgeon and Era (Brookshire) Isaacs; student Mars Hill Jr. Coll., 1949-51; A.B. cum laude, Meredith Coll., 1953; M.Ed., U. N.C. at Greensboro, 1958. Tchr., Sedge Garden Elem. Sch., Winston-Salem/Forsyth County Schs., 1953-59, supr. elem. edn., 1959-71, prin. Diggs Intermediate Sch., 1971-76, Brunson Elem. Sch., 1976—; tchr. Western Carolina U., Cullowhee, N.C., summers 1964, 65. Pres. Winston-Salem Maids of Melody, 1957; v.p. Winston-Salem Altrusa Club, 1967-68, pres., 1968-69; bd. dirs. Forsyth Singer's Guild, 1959, 60, Group Homes Forsyth County, 1976—, Children's Theatre, 1977-81. Mem. Assn. for Childhood Edn., N.C. (pres. div. suprs. and dirs. instrn. N.C. 1970-71), Winston-Salem/Forsyth County (pres. 1959-61) edn. assns., Forsyth County Elem. Prins. Assn. (sec.-treas. 1973-74), Forsyth County Prins. Assn. (sec. 1974-75), N.C. Assn. Educators (div. prins.), N.C. Prins./Asst. Prins. Assn., N.C. Assn. Sch. Adminstrs., N.C. Assn. for Childhood Edn. (sec. 1965-67), Assn. Supervision and Curriculum Devel., Phi Delta Kappa, Delta Kappa Gamma. Democrat. Baptist. Home: 4240 Mashie Dr Grandview Route 1 Pfafftown NC 27040 Office: 155 N Hawthorne Rd Winston-Salem NC 27104

ISALY, SHARON MARTIN, interior designer, constrn. and land devel. exec.; b. Columbus, Ohio, July 31, 1946; d. John W. and Patricia M. Martin; student in edn. No. Ariz. U., 1964-66; m. Charles W. Isaly, Nov. 5, 1966; children—Jeffrey Scott, Bradley William. Interior designer John Martin Constrn., Phoenix, 1967-72; v.p., interior designer Martin Devel. Co., Missoula, Mont., 1972-79; v.p., partner Security-West Devel. Co., Missoula, 1979—, also dir.; pres., owner SMI Interiors, Missoula, 1979—; sec.-treas. Prospect Assos./Devel. Co., Missoula, 1979—, also dir. Vice pres. Missoula Civic Symphony, 1977-78; bd. dirs. Missoula Children's Theatre, 1977-78. Mem. Am. Soc. Interior Designers, LWV, Delta Delta Delta. Republican. Methodist. Home: 2 Elk Ridge Ct Missoula MT 59801 Office: 2806 Garfield St Missoula MT 59801

ISBELL, VIRGINIA, state legislator; b. Chinook, Mont., May 8, 1932; d. Domenico Renda and Bessie M. (Newton) Renda; cert. med. sec. No. Mont. Coll., 1953; m. Donald D. Isbell, Aug. 11, 1953; children—David, Daniel, Maheolani, Iwalani, Richard. Tchr., Kona (Hawaii) Schs., 1962-72; mgr. Wilmot Boone, M.D., Allan Nubacker, M.D., Kona Coast Med. Group, Inc., Kailua, Kona, Hawaii, 1978—; mem. Hawaii Ho. of Reps., 1980—. Bd. dirs. Kona Family YMCA; active ARC. Named Woman of Yr., Mayor's award, 1980. Republican. Mem. Ch. of Jesus Christ of Latter-day Saints. Club: Soroptimist (pres.).

ISELI, CLAIRE EDNA, advt. cons.; b. Altantic City, Sept. 2, 1944; d. Charles Edward and Edna (Henderson) Hartman; B.S., Am. U., 1966; m. Carl O. Iseli, Aug. 20, 1966; children—Christopher, Curtis. Budget analyst U.S. Dept. Agr., Washington, 1966-67; market research specialist, advt. copywriter Nat. Acad. Scis. Printing and Pub. Office, Washington, 1967-71, mktg. mgr., 1971-74; spl. asst. cons. for mktg., 1974—; cons. membership recruitment and product sales AAAS, 1974-76; v.p. Creative Images, 1976—; advt., circulation and bus. mgmt. cons. to publishers of sci. and scholarly books and jours. Republican. Editor: A Guide for Preparing Manuscripts, 1970. Home and Office: 2108 Kingshouse Rd Silver Spring MD 20904

ISHAM, BERNICE JEAN, musician, educator; b. Salem, Oreg., Mar. 30, 1929; d. Earl and Tillie Charlotte (Kildahl) I.; B.Mus., Willamette U., 1950; M.Mus., U. Oreg., 1957, D.M.A., 1976. Tchr. music Taft (Oreg.) High Sch. and Elem. Sch., 1950-56, Beaverton (Oreg.) High Sch., 1956-59, Elmhurst Jr. High Sch., Oakland, Calif., 1959-60; instr. music West Hills Community Coll., Coalinga, Calif., 1960—; condr.; ch. choir dir.; dir. opera workshop; dir. ann. Christmas madrigal feast. Musician, various community orgns. Recipient disting. services citation Sec. Treasury, 1944, community services award Masons, 1974. Mem. Music Assn. Calif. Community Colls. (state sec. 1965-66, v.p. 1966-67), Am. Choral Dirs., Music Educators Nat. Conf., Nat. Assn. Tchrs. of Singing, Delta Kappa Gamma. Lutheran. Home: PO Box 752 Coalinga CA 93210 Office: 300 Cherry Ln Coalinga CA 93210

ISHEE, JUDITH HARBAUGH, computer analyst; b. Mobile, Ala., Jan. 11, 1947; d. Elmer Aaron and Mary (Rabby) Harbaugh; B.S. in Math., U. S. Ala., 1969; M.S. in Stats., U. Ga., 1971, postgrad. in Mgmt. Sci., 1976-78; m. Lonnie J. Ishee, Aug. 30, 1969; children—Thomas, Michael, Charles, Kathryn. Tchr. math. Clarke Central High Sch., Athens, Ga., 1972-74; computer analyst Agrl. Expt. Stas., U. Ga., Athens, 1978-80, dir. nat. computerized mgmt. info. system for Small Bus. Devel. Centers, 1980—. Mem. Urban and Regional Info. Systems Assn., Inst. Mgmt. Sci. (treas. 1977-78). Episcopalian. Home: Route 1 Box 207 Danielsville GA 30633 Office: SBDC Brooks Hall U Ga Athens GA 30601

ISHERWOOD, ELIZABETH MAYNARD, advt. and public relations co. exec.; b. New Bedford, Mass., Apr. 6, 1951; d. Norman Bigelow and Janice (Braley) Maynard; B.B.A. cum laude, U. Mass., 1973; M.B.A., Southeastern Mass. U., 1980; m. Steven William Isherwood, May 29, 1971; 1 dau., Allison. Acct. exec. Moore & Slater, Inc., New Bedford,

Mass., 1975-76, v.p., asst. treas., 1976—; pres., treas. Moore/Isherwood, Inc. Public Relations, 1980—; vis. lectr. Southeastern Mass. U., 1980—. Mem. town meeting Town of Fairhaven (Mass.), 1976—; vice chmn. Fairhaven Indsl. Devel. Fin. Authority, 1979—. Mem. Bedford Area C. of C. (dir. 1981—), Southeastern Mass. Advt. Club (dir. 1981—), Am. Mktg. Assn., Public Relations Soc. Am. (accredited). Home: 38 Pleasant St Fairhaven MA 02719 Office: 222 Union St New Bedford MA 02740

ISON, GEORGIE LOU (JOY), ins. agy. exec.; b. Bryn Mawr, Pa., June 4, 1949; d. Malvin Harland and Georgie Lou (Easterling) I.; B.S. in Mktg., U. Ala., 1971. Sr. asst. buyer Mercantile Store, Inc., N.Y.C., 1971-72; rep. coordinator Coll. Mktg. & Research, Inc., Chgo., 1972-74; sales rep. Revlon, Inc., Chgo., 1974-76; v.p. Ison Ins. Agy., Mobile, Ala., 1976—. Tutor, Mich. Ave. Presbyn. Ch., Chgo., 1975. Mem. Internat. Platform Assn., Nat. Assn. Female Execs., Ins. Women Mobile (edn. chmn., by-laws chmn., mem. exec. bd., Rookie of Yr. 1979), U. Ala. Alumni Assn. Baptist. Club: Career. Home: 57 Byrnes Blvd Mobile AL 36608 Office: PO Box 6623 Mobile AL 36660

ISRAEL, MARGIE OLANOFF, psychotherapist; b. Atlantic City, Apr. 30, 1927; d. Herman and Mary (Salter) Olanoff; student U. Miami, 1945-46, 50, Am. Acad. Dramatic Arts, 1946-47; B.A. in Psychology cum laude, Hunter Coll., 1970; M.S.W. with honors in fieldwork, Hunter Sch. Social Work, 1972; psychoanalytic tng. N.Y. Soc. Freudian Psychologists, 1965-70, Manhattan Center for Advanced Psychoanalytic Studies, 1972-74, 76; m. Allan Edward Israel, Sept. 20, 1953; 1 dau., Janet. Celebrity interviewer Lunchin' with Marge radio show Sta. WFPG, Atlantic City, 1947-48; co-host Steel Pier Midnight radio show, 1949; publicity writer Hy Gardner Astor Hotel, N.Y.C., 1948; writer theatrical interviews Miami (Fla.) Daily News, 1950-51; sec. to exec. dir. Hebrew Old Age Center, Atlantic City, 1951-55; sec. to dir. TV-films and radio Nat. Office, Am. Cancer Soc., N.Y.C., 1959-66, asst. to dir. TV-films and radio, 1966-70; social worker Bellevue Hosp., N.Y.C., 1972-76; field instr. social work N.Y. U., 1975-76; practice psychotherapy, N.Y.C., 1973—. Certified social worker, N.Y. Fellow N.Y. State Soc. Clin. Social Work Psychotherapists; mem. Nat. Assn. Social Workers, Acad. Certified Social Workers, Am. Orthopsychiat. Assn., Psi Chi. Office: 201 E 28th St Suite 1F New York NY 10016

ISROFF, LOLA KOVENER (MRS. EMANUEL R. ISROFF), artist, writer; b. N.Y.C.; d. Wolf and Hannah (Levin) Kovner; m. Emanuel R. Isroff, June 9, 1961 (dec. Apr. 4, 1975). One man shows at Cushman and Wakefield, N.Y.C., Lord and Taylor, N.Y.C., Dime Bank for Savs., N.Y.C., Akron (Ohio) Jewish Center, Village Theatre Gallery, Akron, Akron Pub. Library. Summit County Hist. Soc., Akron, Packard Gallery, Akron, Massillon (Ohio) Mus. Art, Canton (Ohio) Art Inst., Rudolph Galleries, Coral Gables, Fla., Caravan House Gallery, N.Y.C., Boston Safe Deposit & Trust Co., Mansfield (Ohio) Art Center, Akron Art Inst., Gallery on Square, Lexington, Mass., French Library, Boston; exhibited in group shows at Salmagundi Club, N.Y.C., Village Art Center, N.Y.C., Nat. Acad. Art, N.Y.C.; asso. Am.'s Folk Art Heritage Gallery, N.Y.C., Gallery Folk Art, Cambridge, Mass.; rep. on UNICEF Calendar, 1976; represented in pvt. collections, N.Y.C., Coral Gables, Fla., Milw. Beverly Hills, Calif., Lisbon, Portugal, Hawaii, Westport, Conn., Denver, Kent, Akron, musee d'Art Naif de L'Ile de France, Vicq; commd. to paint New Eng. town halls and country scenes by Wheelabrator-Frye Corp., 1980-81. Mem. exec. bd. Friends Akron U. Library; cultural arts chmn. Akron Jewish Center; co-chmn. citizens adv. com. Akron U. Inst. for Civic Edn.; trustee Western Res. Archtl. Historians. Recipient Merit award Art News Nat. Amateur Painters, 1950. Mem. Nat. Soc. Lit. and Arts, Authors League (founder mem.), Soc. Archtl. Historians. Author: Mama and Papa Livnok, 1949; A Different Kind of Saturday, 1950; Old Houses of New York, 1952; I'll Call You at 10, Doll, 1957; Christmas is a Gift, 1957; Tender Deception, 1957. Contbr. articles, illustrations on nat. landmarks of archtl. interest to mags. Home: 275 N Portage Path Akron OH 44303

ISSER, NATALIE, historian; b. Phila., July 12, 1927; d. David and Frances Judith Kleinman; B.A., U. Pa., 1947, M.A., 1948, Ph.D., 1962; m. Leonard David Isser, June 15, 1947; children—Raymond, Miriam, Steven, Edward. Mem. faculty Ogontz campus Pa. State U., 1962—, assoc. prof. history, 1975—. Mem. Am. Hist. Assn., Soc. French Hist. Studies, Assn. Jewish Studies, Ethnic Studies Assn. Del. Valley. Author: The Second Empire and the Press, 1974; also articles. Home: Cedarbrook Hill Apts A507 Wyncote PA 19095 Office: Pa State U Ogontz Campus Abington PA 19001

ISTOMIN, MARTA, performing arts adminstr.; b. P.R., Nov. 2, 1936; d. Aguiles and Angelica (Martinez) Montanez; student Mannes Coll. Music, 1950-54; hon. degrees World U., P.R., 1972, Marymount Coll., 1975; m. Pablo Casals, Aug. 3, 1957 (dec. 1973); m. 2d, Eugene Istomin, Feb. 15, 1975. Prof. cello Conservatory Music, San Juan, P.R., 1961-64; vis. prof. Curtis Inst. Music, 1974-75; co-chmn. bd. dirs., music dir. Casals Festival, 1974-77; artistic dir. John F. Kennedy Center for Performing Arts, Washington; dir. Harcourt Brace Jovanovich, Inc., N.Y.C. Trustee Marlboro Sch. Music and Festival, Marymount Sch., N.Y.C., World U. Recipient award P.R. Fedn. Women's Clubs, 1967, Cultural Achievements award City San Juan,1975, Nat. Conf. Puerto Rican Women award, 1975, Casita Maria medal, N.Y.C., 1978. Roman Catholic. Office: 700 New Hampshire Ave NW Washington DC 20037 *

ITTLEMAN, LEONA R(UTH), lawyer; b. Malden, Mass., Nov. 4, 1947; d. Isidore and Grace (Horowitz) I.; B.A. in English, Am. Internat. Coll., 1969; J.D., Western New Eng. Sch. Law, 1977. Admitted to Mass. bar, 1978, U.S. Dist. Ct. bar, 1979; employee relations specialist Honeywell Info. Systems, Waltham, Mass., 1972-75, mgr. EEO, 1975-79, employee relations atty., 1978-79, employee relations mgr. and asso. employee relations counsel, 1979—. Mem. nominating com. of bd. dirs. Boston YWCA, 1979-80. Mem. Am. Bar Assn., Mass. Bar Assn., Boston Bar Assn., Mass. Assn. Women Lawyers, AAUW, Alumni Assn. Am. Internat. Coll. (pres. Boston chpt. 1971-73, pres. assn. 1980-81, dir.). Home: 72 Nicholas Rd Framingham MA 01701 Office: 200 Smith St Waltham MA 02154

IVENS, VIRGINIA RUTH, educator; b. Decatur, Ill., July 27, 1922; d. John Raymond and Dessie Lenora (Underwood) I.; B.S., U. Ill., 1950. Tracer blueprints Caterpillar Mil. Engine Co., Decatur, 1941-45; mem. faculty Coll. Vet. Medicine, U. Ill., Urbana, 1950—, asso. prof. vet. parasitology, 1979—, chmn. curriculum com. dept. vet. pathobiology, 1976-78; chmn. 9th Ann. Conf. Coccidiosis, 1972. Mem. Am. Soc. Parasitologists (transl. com. 1963-71, 80-82), Soc. Protozoologist, Am. Inst. Biol. Scis., Entomol. Soc. Am., LWV, Sigma Xi, Phi Zeta. Translator Russian articles on parasitology; contbr. articles to profl. jours. and co-author 4 monographs; sr. author: Principal Parasites of Domestic Animals in the U.S., 1978, 81. Home: 608 S Edwin St Champaign IL 61820 Office: 303 Veterinary Medicine Annex U Ill 1101 W Peabody Dr Urbana IL 61801

IVERSON, ANN HAVEN CUMMINGS, advt. agy. exec.; b. N.Y.C., May 23, 1941; d. Barton Arthur and Regina Haven (Pugh) Cummings; A.A., Briarcliff Coll., 1963; student London Sch. Econs., 1963-65; m. Clifton Iverson, Jr., Aug. 1, 1970; 1 dau., Haven Cummings. Mktg. researcher Garland-Compton, London, 1963-65; supr. corp. communications BBDO, N.Y.C., 1965-68, acct. exec., 1968-70; with Ogilvy & Mather, N.Y.C. and Houston, 1970—, sr. v.p., dir. client services, 1981—, also mem. operating com., dir. Bd. dirs., mem. exec. com. San Jacinto council Girls Scouts U.S.A., 1982—. Mem. Houston Advt. Fedn., (dir. 1980—), Houston Bus. Forum, Forum of Houston. Episcopalian. Clubs: Houston Country, Heritage. Office: 1 Allen Center Houston TX 77002

IVERSON, EVELYN MAE, social worker; b. Toronto, S.D., Dec. 7, 1926; d. Ingvald John and Lena Marie (Mathison) Iverson; state cert. Augustana Coll., Sioux Falls, S.D., 1950; B.S. with honor, S.D. State Coll., 1960; M.A., State U. Iowa, 1962. Tchr. rural schs., Brookings County, S.D., 1944-48; tchr. rural village sch. Lester (Iowa) Ind. Sch. Dist., 1950-52; research asst. rural sociology dept. S.D. State Coll., Brookings, 1958-60; caseworker, coordinator overseas program for child placement and support program in Korea, Luth. Social Service Minn., Mpls., 1962—. Mem. council Beth. Luth. Ch., Mpls., 1978-80; vol. Kidney Found. Upper Midwest, 1979-80, Am. Cancer Soc., 1979-80. Mem. Nat. Assn. Social Workers, Acad. Cert. Social Workers. Home: 5545 Chicago Ave Apt 306 Minneapolis MN 55417 Office: 2414 Park Ave Minneapolis MN 55404

IVERSON, VIRGINIA RUTH, nurse; b. Bailey, Okla., Apr. 11, 1937; d. Norvin W. and Harriet Louise (Pittman) Whitehead; A.A. in Nursing, Casper Coll., 1971; cert. Harrisburg Sch. Enterostomal Therapy, 1974; m. Robert A. Sharp, Feb. 15, 1965; children—Deborah, Marcia, Marva, Laurie, Sheila; m. 2d, Leo Leslie Iverson, Apr. 17, 1979. Staff nurse Meml. Hosp. of Natrona County (Wyo.), Casper, 1971-73, nursing supr., 1974-79, enterostomal therapist, 1974-79; dir. seminars on ostomy care for State of Wyoming Health Care Facilities, 1974-79; enterostomal therapist Holy Family Hosp., Spokane, Wash., 1979—. Mem. Am., Wash. State nurses assns., Internat. Assn. for Enterostomal Therapy. Mem. Christian Ch. Home: Route 1 Box 152C Valley WA 99181 Office: N5633 Lidgerwood Spokane WA 99207

IVES, RITA JOY, educator; b. Pitts., Dec. 4, 1931; d. Samuel and Nettie (Blau) Klein; B.A. in Primary Edn., U. Pitts., 1953, M.A. in Elem. Edn., George Washington U., 1957, Ed.S. in Spl. Edn., 1967, Ed. D. in Spl. Edn., 1971; m. Jerry J. Ives, Oct. 28, 1950; children—Sandi Bee, Samuel, Nettie. Tchr. elem. schs., Prince George's County, Md., 1953-59, resource spl. edn., tchr. mildly handicapped children, various adminstrv. and supervisory positions, 1959—; instr. Towson (Md.) State U., 1960-61; tchr., Montgomery County, Md., 1960-67, Washington, 1967-68; dir. Day Treatment Center for Learning Disabled Children, 1968-69; instr. George Washington U., Washington, 1970-73, asst. prof., 1970-73, asso. prof., 1973-75, prof., 1975—, chmn. dept. spl. edn., 1979—. Mem. Council for Exceptional Children, Nat. Assn. for Edn. of Young Children, AAUP, Am. Edn. Research Assn., Phi Delta Gamma, Phi Lambda Theta. Democrat. Jewish. Contbr. articles in field to profl. jours. Home: 9912 Hall Rd Potomac MD 20854 Office: 2201 G St NW Washington DC 20052

IVEY, GERALDINE BOLDUC, chem. engr.; b. Wilmington, Del., Dec. 1, 1950; d. Albert Ernest and Irene Theresa (Miner) Bolduc; B.S. in Chem. Engring., U. Houston, 1978; student St. Edwards U., 1969-71; m. Shawn Dolan Ivey, Jan. 9, 1971; 1 son, Kevin Michael. Coop. engr. M.W. Kellogg Co., Houston, 1974-75, 76-77; asst. process engr. Fluor E&C Inc., Houston, 1978-79, asso. process engr., 1979-82, process engr., 1982—. Republican. Roman Catholic. Home: 4701 Hummingbird St Houston TX 77035

IVEY, MONTEENE CORRINE, computer programmer; b. Little Rock, June 16, 1940; d. Gordon Beecham and Dorothy Corrine (Evans) I.; student Ft. Smith Jr. Coll., 1958-59, Rio Hondo Coll., 1972-73, Citrus Coll., 1973-74. Communications supr. Dept. of State, Paris, 1964-65, statis. asst., 1965-67; statis. clk. U.S. Army Behavioral Sci. Research Lab., Arlington, Va., 1967-68, digital computer systems operator, 1968, statis. asst., 1968-70, lead computer operator, 1970-73, computer systems jr. specialist, 1973-77, computer systems analyst, 1977-79; computer programmer, software specialist Nat. Test Adminstrn. Center, U.S. Postal Service, Los Angeles, 1979—. Bd. dirs. Two-Thirds Outreach, Inc., Pasadena, 1981. Democrat. Club: Ind. Order Foresters. Home: 12177 Hemlock St El Monte CA 91732 Office: 300 N Los Angeles St Room 2001 Los Angeles CA 90012

IVEY, PATRICIA MELGIE, author/photographer; b. Omaha, Mar. 5, 1941; d. Wilbur and Mabel Gertrude (Morton) Ward; student Colo. State U., 1959, U. Alaska, 1976-80; children—Perry Gene Vaughn, Jr., Stephen Michael Vaughn. Various secretarial positions, 1966-69; exec. asst. to v.p. indsl. mktg., sales div. Spartan Mills Inc., Spartanburg, N.C., 1969-74; freelance writer, photographer, 1976—; profl. model, 1977-78; sec., then adminstrv. sec. Alaska Coop. Extension Service, U. Alaska, Fairbanks, 1975—; condr. workshops, speaker, lectr. in field. Public relations chmn. Fairbanks chpt. Am. Heart Assn., 1978. Mem. Am. Film Inst., Nat. Fedn. Press Women, Alaska Press Women (pres. No. region 1977-79), Alaska Heritage Writers Assn. (exec. sec.). Home: PO Box 60634 Fairbanks AK 99706

IVORY, GOLDIE LEE, educator; b. Chgo., Apr. 19, 1926; d. Percey Carr and Edna M. (Scott) Carr Williams; B.S., Ind. U., 1949; M.A., U. Notre Dame, 1956; M.S.W., Ind. U.-Purdue U., Indpls., 1977; m. Sam Ivory, Aug. 7, 1947; children—Kenneth L., Kevin D. Juvenile probation officer St. Joseph County Juvenile Probation Dept., South Bend, Ind., 1949-56, intake supr., 1956-59; psychiat. social worker Beatty Meml. Hosp., Westville, Ind., 1960; instr. sociology Ind. U., South Bend, 1960-67; relocation rep. Urban Redevel. Commn., South Bend, 1960-62; social worker Elkhart (Ind.) Community Schs., 1962-66, supr. social services, 1966-69, dir. human relations, 1970—; mem. faculty Goshen (Ind.) Coll., 1971—, asst. prof. social work, 1975-81, adj. prof. social work, 1981—; instr. sociology and social work St. Mary's Coll., 1967-69, dir. Upward Bound program, 1970. Recipient Human Service award Acad. Human Services, 1974-75, Merit award Indpls. Public Schs. Dept. Social Work, 1977; plaque for community services Mayor of Elkhart, 1981; State chpt. Delta Kappa Gamma scholar, 1969-70. Registered clin. Social worker. Mem. Nat. Assn. Social Workers, Nat. Assn. Black Social Workers, Acad. Cert. Social Workers, Delta Kappa Gamma, Delta Sigma Theta. Methodist. Club: Altrusa. Author articles in field. Home: 1309 E Bissell St South Bend IN 46617 Office: 2720 California Rd Elkhart IN 46514

IVY, MARGARET ONEIDA, assn. acct.; b. Dallas, May 31, 1947; d. Fred and Mary Lou (McGowan) May; m. Jess Lawrence Ivy, Aug. 4, 1974; 1 son, James Daniel. Sec., office mgr. Security Realty, Irving, Tex., 1965-68; bldg. mgr. Carpenter Freeway Med. Center, Irving, 1968-69; office mgr. Runaway Bay, Bridgeport, Tex., 1970-71; v.p., corp. sec. Metro Warehouse, Carrollton, Tex., 1971-81; dir. fin. Airline Passengers Assn., Irving, Tex., 1981—. Mem. Am. Warehousemen's Assn., Nat. Assn. Exec. Secs. Mem. Ch. of Christ. Home: 3302 Pritchett Irving TX 75061 Office: 1725 Hayden Rd Carrollton TX 75006

IWAMASA, FUMIKO, state ofcl.; b. Honolulu; d. W.G. and Sho (Muraoka) Kimura; B.A., U. Hawaii, 1933; m. Haruto W. Iwamasa, Apr. 2, 1937. Social work Dept. Social Services, Hilo, Hawaii, 1939-47, asst. supr., 1947-54, supr., 1954-62, Hawaii br. adminstr., 1962-75, ret., 1975. Adviser, Big Island Presch. Assn., 1965-75. Mem. disaster council County of Hawaii, 1960-75; mem. eviction com. Hawaii Housing Authority, 1962—; mem. county com. Children and Youth, 1954-75; mem. Gov.'s Com. Mental Health, proceedings chmn., 1962-63, mem. Com. Aging, 1962—; mem. Big Island Council on Addiction, 1963-75; mem. Big Island adv. com. Law Enforcement Adv. Agy., 1969-75; exec. com. Hawaii County Comprehensive Health Planning Advisory Council, 1968-75. Bd. dirs. ARC, Hilo, 1962-78, Am. Cancer Soc., 1962-77, Salvation Army, Hilo, 1963-80, YMCA, 1963-70, Hawaii County Econ. Opportunity Council, 1965-75, Hawaii Fed. and State Employees Fed. Credit Union, 1966-71, Hawaii Island United Way, 1975—; mem. Hawaii County Rural Devel. Com., 1970-75. Mem. Am. Public Welfare Assn. Club: Zonta. Home: 52 Puuko St Hilo HI 96720

IYER, HOLLY HENDERSON, telephone co. ofcl.; b. Glen Cove, N.Y., Jan. 11, 1949; d. George Devine and Genevieve (Manning) Henderson; B.A. in Math., Bucknell U., 1971; M.Stats., U. Fla., 1973; M.B.A., Pace U., 1981; m. Harihar K. Iyer, Apr. 14, 1974; 1 dau., Janna. Asst., U. Fla., 1971-73; engr. So. Bell Tel. & Tel. Co., 1973-77, forecaster, Atlanta, 1982—; corp. planner AT&T, Basking Ridge, N.J., 1977-82. Coordinator fund raising drive Bucknell U. Mem. Nat. Assn. Female Execs. Office: 29Q71 So Bell Center 675 W Peachtree Atlanta GA 30375

IZZI, JOYCE ANN, township govt. ofcl.; b. Detroit, Apr. 14, 1935; d. George Raymond and Agnes Hazel (Selman) Jenkins; student Oakland County (Mich.) Community Coll., Mercy Coll., Detroit, Wayne County Community Coll., Detroit; m. Peter A. Izzi, Sept. 29, 1956; children—Donna, John, Nancy, James, Ronald. Clk., Highland (Mich.) Twp., 1976—; mem. Highland Twp. Planning Commn. and Zoning Bd. Mem. parish council Holy Spirit Roman Cath. Ch., Highland; bd. dirs. Alvord Acres Subdiv. Assn.; trustee Milford-Highland Democratic Club; Dem. precinct del. Mem. Internat. Inst. Mcpl. Clks., Nat. Assn. Female Execs., Mich. Soc. Planning Ofcls., Oakland County Mcpls. Clks. Assn., LWV, Huron Valley Arts Council, Nat. Trust for Hist. Preservation. Home: 3755 Kingsway Dr Highland MI 48031 Office: 205 N John St PO Box 249 Highland MI 48031

IZZO, PATRICIA MARIE, coll. ofcl.; b. N.Y.C., Oct. 25, 1949; d. Patrick I. and Louise Rose (Gammello) I.; B.A. in English Lit., George Washington U.; M.A. in Communications, U. Iowa. Editorial asst. Electronics Industries Assn., Washington, 1971; newscast editor, reporter Iowa Ednl. Broadcasting Network, 1971-72, Bklyn. Network News, 1972-73; researcher, adminstrv. asst. to gen. news editor AP, N.Y.C., 1972-75; reporter, polit. analyst Daytona Beach (Fla.) News Jour., 1974-77; asst. dir. community affairs Daytona Beach Community Coll., 1977—; cons. in field. Mem. AAUW, Women's Am. Orgn. Rehab. and Tng., Fla. Assn. Community Colls., Council Advancement and Support Edn., Nat. Council Community Relations, Am. Assn. Community and Jr. Colls., Nat. Assn. Female Execs., Phi Delta Kappa, Sigma Delta Chi. Democrat. Roman Catholic. Author papers in field.

JABLONSKI, WANDA MARY, pub. co. exec.; b. Czechoslovakia; d. Eugene and Mary J.; came to U.S., 1938, naturalized, 1945; B.A., Cornell U., 1942; postgrad. Columbia U., 1943; L.H.D. (hon.), St. Lawrence U., 1978. Oil editor Jour. Commerce, N.Y.C., 1943-54; sr. editor Petroleum Week, McGraw-Hill, N.Y.C., 1954-61; founder, owner, editor, pub. Petroleum Intelligence Weekly, N.Y.C., 1961—. Mem. Oxford Energy Policy Club, Council Fgn. Relations, Middle East Inst., Fgn. Policy Assn. Club: Nat. Press. Contbr. articles to Colliers, other mags. Home: 575 Park Ave New York NY 10021 Office: Suite 805 49 W 45 St New York NY 10036 also 25 E 86th St New York NY 10028

JABLONSKI-POLK, TERESA LYNN, social worker; b. Madison, Wis., Nov. 18, 1951; d. Stanley Florian and Marian Grace (Ostroski) Jablonski; B.A., U. Ky., 1972; M.S.W., Washington U., St. Louis, 1977; m. Dion Thomas Polk, Feb. 14, 1976; children—Derrell, Demone, Shannon Dion. Sch. social worker, Lexington, Ky., 1972-74; asst. camp dir. Loughborough YMCA camp, St. Louis, 1975; social worker St. Louis Mcpl. Ct., 1976-77; vis. lectr. So. Ill. U., Edwardsville, summer 1977, winter 1980, 81; instr. human services St. Louis Community Coll., Florissant Valley, 1977—. Vol., Women's Self-Help Center, 1978-81, Victim Service Council, 1980-81; resource person 4-State Minority Adoption Network. Mem. Nat. Assn. Social Workers, Mo. Assn. Social Welfare, Mo. Vocat. Assn., Washington U. Alumni Assn. Roman Catholic. Home: 1308 Waldron Saint Louis MO 63130 Office: 3400 Pershall Rd Saint Louis MO 63135

JABS, PAULA MAE, ins. co. exec.; b. New Prague, Minn., May 21, 1951; d. Raymond Andrew and Irma Martha Frances (Beuch) Grassman; B.A., U. Minn., 1975; grad. Am. Coll., Bryn Mawr, Pa., 1982; m. Bernhard Jabs, Oct. 20, 1971; 1 son, Damon. Public relations asst. Minn. Mut. Life, St. Paul, 1975-77, public relations asso., 1977-80, mgr. public relations, 1980-82, mgr. external communication and video prodn., 1982—. Soprano sect. leader White Bear Community Chorus, 1981. C.L.U. Mem. Women in Communications, Inc., Internat. TV Assn. Lutheran (Wis. Synod). Office: 400 N Robert St Saint Paul MN 55101

JACKER, CORINNE LITVIN, author; b. Chgo., June 29, 1933; d. Thomas Henry and Theresa (Bellak) Litvin; student Stanford U., 1950-52; B.S. (Lovdedale scholar, Univ. scholar), Northwestern U., 1954, M.A., 1955, postgrad., 1955-56; m. Richard Jacker, July 1, 1956 (div. Apr. 1959). Asso. editor Liberal Arts Press, 1959-60, trade sci. dept. Macmillan Co., 1961-63; asst. editor sci. book dept. Charles Scribner's Sons, N.Y.C., 1963-65; writer, researcher NET Playhouse, WNET, 1971-73; story cons. CBS Playhouse 90, 1973-74; script editor Bicentennial Minutes, CBS, 1974-75; head writer Best of Families, PBS, 1976-77, Another World, NBC, 1981—; vis. asst. prof. Yale U., 1979-81. Recipient Obie award, 1974, 75, Link Golden Eagle, 1975, Ciné Golden Eagle; Rockefeller fellow, 1979-80. Mem. Authors League, Dramatists Guild, Writers Guild Am., Zeta Phi Eta. Author: (books) Man, Memory, and Machines, 1964; Window on the Unknown, 1966; Black Flag of Anarchy, 1968; The Biological Revolution, 1971; (off-Broadway and regionally produced plays) Pale Horse, Pale Rider, 1958; A Happy Ending, 1959; Terminal; Jennifer, Jemima and the Machine, 1970; Scientific Method, 1970; Project Omega, Lillian, 1971; Bits and Pieces, 1973; Travellers, 1974; Night Thoughts, 1974; Harry Outside, 1974; My Life, 1976; Other People's Tables, 1976; Later, 1978; After the Season, 1979; Domestic Issues, 1981; In Place, 1982; (TV plays) Actors Choice Series, 1970; The Anatomy of Love; When This You See, Remember Me; A Singular Man; Brewsie and Willie, 1972; Boxes, 1972; Secrets, 1973; The Adams Chronicles, 1976; Best of Families, 1977; Loose Change, 1978; The Jilting of Granny Weatherall, 1979; various poems published in Spectrum, Fiddlehead, Carleton Miscellany, Riverside Poetry III, Mutiny. Office: 110 W 86th New York NY 10024

JACKMAN, MARY RUTH REBECCA, sociologist, educator; b. Guernsey, Gt. Brit., May 1, 1948; came to U.S., 1968, naturalized, 1980; d. Edward and Lily (Aaronson) Peretz; B.A., U. Auckland (N.Z.), 1968; M.S., U. Wis., Madison, 1970, Ph.D., 1972; m. Robert W. Jackman, Sept. 12, 1968; 1 dau., Rachael Peretz. Asst. prof. sociology Mich. State U., East Lansing, 1972-73; asst. prof. U. Mich., 1973-79; asso. prof., 1979—, faculty asso. Inst. Social Research, 1975—. NSF grantee, 1975-81, NIMH grantee, 1975—; NIMH research scientist devel. awardee, 1980-84. Mem. Am. Sociol. Assn. Author: (with R. W. Jackman) Class Awareness in the United States, 1982. Office: Dept Sociology U Mich Ann Arbor MI 48109

JACKS, ELIN BECKMAN, psychotherapist; b. Ft. Smith, Ark., July 1, 1940; d. James S. and Pauline Triplett Beckman; student Tufts Coll., 1959-60; B.A., U. Ark., 1964; M.S.S.W., U. Tex., Arlington, 1973; m. Dan Meredith Jacks, July 31, 1971; children by previous marriage—Carmen Elizabeth Hill, Robert Beckman Hill. Social worker Fresno County Dept. Public Welfare, Fresno, Calif., 1968-70; social worker protective services Tex. Dept. Human Resources, Ft. Worth, 1970-71; family counselor Family and Individual Services Assn., Ft. Worth, 1973-77; pvt. practice psychotherapy, Arlington, 1977—; tchr. continuing edn. dept. U. Tex., Arlington; coordinator Plays for Living Program, 1979-80. Bd. dirs. New Ways of Being Inst. of Dallas, 1978-80; v.p. Metroplex Assn. for Gifted and Talented. Recipient award First Presbyn. Ch., 1979, United Way, 1979. Mem. Nat. Assn. Social Workers, Acad. Cert. Social Workers, Assn. Humanistic Psychology, Humane Soc. U.S., Inst. for Noetic Scis., ACLU, Network of Exec. Women, Internat. Trade Assn. Dallas, Dallas Council World Affairs, Arlington C. of C., NOW, Sierra Club. Office: 2313 W Arkansas Ln Arlington TX 76013

JACKSON, ANN HOWARD, state ofcl.; b. Durant, Miss., Feb. 1, 1925; d. John McCullen and Modena Lowery (Cargill) Howard; B.S.C., U. Miss., 1946; m. Chatwin M. Jackson, Jr., June 14, 1947; children—Sara Cargill Jackson Sutterfield, Dena Fair, Chatwin M. III. Social worker Attala County (Miss.) Welfare Dept., 1968-76; mental health cons. Region VI Mental Health Center, Kosciusko, Miss., 1976-78; mem. Miss. Bldg. Commn., 1980—; mem. Miss. Health and Human Services Block Grant Adv. Bd., 1981—. Sec., Attala County Democratic Com., 1964-68; del. Dem. Nat. Conv., 1980; officer Prairie council Girl Scouts U.S.A., 1961; pres. PTA, Kosciusko Schs., 1956-57; chmn. March of Dimes Dr. of Kosciusko and Attala County, 1956-57. Mem. Chi Omega. Home: 310 E Jefferson St Kosciusko MS 39090

JACKSON, ANN(IE LOU STINGLEY, librarian; b. Blevins, Ark.; d. William Henry and Nina (Duke) Stingley; A.B., Henderson State Tchrs. Coll., 1951; M.L.S., Tex. State Coll. for Women, Denton, Tex., 1954; m. Joseph Jackson, Sept. 4, 1922; children—Joseph Lyle, Andrew Stingley, Kenneth Edwin. Tchr., librarian Washington (Ark.) High Sch., 1940-46; asst. librarian Ouachita Coll., Arkadelphia, Ark., summer 1944; head librarian Arkadelphia City and Clark County Library, 1946-53; cons. for high sch. and public libraries Ark. Library Commn., 1953-65; state sch. library supr. Ark. Dept. Edn., 1965-72; library cons., 1972-74; dir. Elem. and Secondary Edn. Act, Title II; mem. adv. bd. Southwest Ark. Regional Archives, 1977-78. Active Community Chest Bd., Arkadelphia, UN Speakers Bur. in Ark.; mem. adult edn. coordinating bd. YWCA. Mem. Commr. Edn.'s Adv. Com. on Sch. Libraries; chmn. state com. on sch. library study So. States Work Conf. on Edn., 1957-60; vol. chmn. library services Second Bapt. Ch. in Little Rock, 1979—; sec. Pulaski County Chapter UN, 1964; exec. dir. Nat. Library Week for Ark., 1963. Recipient cert. merit, Ark. Jaycees, 1956; cert. merit for disting. service to library sci. Mem. Am. Assn. Sch. Libraries (state pres., rep. for Nat. Library Week 1959-60), Am. (chmn. Ark. membership com. Audio-Visual div. 1956), Ark. Student (librarian's council), Ark. library assns., Nat. Adult Edn. Assn., Ark. Hist. Assn., Nat. Assn. State Sch. Library Suprs. (pres. 1972-73), AAUW (1st v.p. 1970-72), Vets. World War I Aux. (state conductress 1973-74, chaplain 1974-75, state pres. 1976-77), UN Assn. (pres. state div. USA for Ark. 1969-70), Clark County Hist. Soc., NEA, Ark. Edn. Assn., Nat. Soc. Arts and Letters (pres. Little Rock 1974-76, asso. nat. chaplain 1976), Internat. Platform Assn., Women's Nat. Book Assn. (chmn. U. Ark. Personal Library Contest 1972-73, chpt. pres. 1976-77), Greater Little Rock Fedn. Womens Clubs (sec. 1974-75), Ark. Geneal. Soc., Delta Kappa Gamma (2d v.p. Gamma chpt. 1966-68), Kappa Delta Pi, Alpha Chi, Alpha Beta Alpha. Democrat. Baptist. Mem. Order Eastern Star. Clubs: Altrusa (bd. dirs. Little Rock 1965-74, 1st v.p. 1968-69, pres. 1971-72, internat. relations chmn. internat. dist. 8 1970-72), Fine Arts. Mem. ALA editorial subcom., compiling Basic Book Collection for High Schs., 1957; adviser and assisted editing Handbook for the Student Assistant in the School Library, 1959; rev. bibliography Arkansiana for High Schools, 1960, 1964; editorial com. for bibliography Ethnic Groups: Their Cultures and Contbns.; chmn. com. compiling bibliography on Black Ams. Contbr. World Book Ency., 1960, 72. Home: 321 East 7th St Little Rock AR 72202

JACKSON, BETTY RUTH, nurse, educator; b. Maypearl, Tex., Oct. 12, 1930; d. William Roy and MaryAnne (Underwood) Hutchins; student Tex. Christian U., 1948-49; grad. Harris Coll. Nursing, 1951; B.S.N., W. Tex. State U., 1975; M.S. in Nursing, U. Tex. at Austin, 1977, postgrad., 1978—; m. James Robert Jackson, Jan. 27, 1952; children—Jamie Beth, Julie Anne, George Robert. Charge nurse Harris Hosp., Fort Worth, Tex., 1951-52; office nurse, Lubbock, Tex., 1953; staff nurse Deaconess Hosp., Oklahoma City, 1954-55; Midland Meml. Hosp., Midland, Tex., 1957-59; indsl. nurse Shell Oil Co., Midland, 1962; charge nurse, head nurse, nursing supr. Midland Meml. Hosp., 1962-74; asso. prof. nursing program Odessa (Tex.) Coll., 1974—. Mem. Am. Nurses Assn., Nat. League Nursing, Tex. Nurses Coalition Action Politically, AAUP, Tex. Jr. Coll. Tchrs. Assn., Sigma Theta Tau, Phi Kappa Phi. Lutheran. Home: 1907 Ward Midland TX 79701 Office: PO Box 3752 Nursing Dept Odessa TX 79760

JACKSON, BETTY ZAN, banker; b. Commerce, Okla., Mar. 24, 1935; d. John Roupert and Thelma Lucille (Stinnett) Cowen; student UCLA, 1972-73, Calif. Inst. Tech., 1972-74, San Jose U., 1975-76; married, 1953 (div. 1958); children—Pamela Lynn, Paulie Ann, Lester Wade; m. 2d Donald Hugh Jackson, Aug. 24, 1980. With Goodner Van Co., Tulsa, Okla., 1951, Record Club of Am., 1958-59; sec. Fletcher Aviation, Rosemead, Calif., 1960-61; with First Western Bank (now Lloyds Bank Calif.), Sierra Madre, Calif., 1962—, asst. v.p., mgr., 1975-80, v.p. mgr., 1980—, dir. adv. bd., 1972—. Bd. dirs. Sierra Madre Community Hosp., 1975-80. Mem. Sierra Madre C. of C. (v.p. 1973-74, pres. 1975-76), Am. Inst. Banking, Western Bankers Assn., Nat. Assn. Bank Women. Republican. Baptist. Office: 100 W Sierra Madre Sierra Madre CA 91024

JACKSON, BEVERLY JUNE, real estate broker; b. Grenora, N.D., June 28, 1933; d. Jens Clemens and Mabel Luetta (Sather) Hansen; student public schs., also jr. coll. night classes; m. David Jackson, 1950; children—David, Marta D., Monica Turner, Katheryn Scott; m. 2d, Charles Shubin, 1963 (div. 1974); 1 dau., Shelly L. Engaged in real estate, 1952—; partner Orangefair Realty, Buena Park, Calif., 1955-59; owner Beverly Jackson Realty, Stanton, Calif., 1959—, Calif. Castles, Inc., loan brokerage, Anaheim, Calif., 1971—; lectr. on real estate foreclosures. Recipient award City of Garden Grove (Calif.), 1973. Mem. Women's Econ. and Career Advancement Network (affiliate), Anaheim Bd. Realtors, Anaheim C. of C. Republican. Lutheran. Clubs: Women's Civic (past pres., hon. mem.) (Garden Grove); Mannequin Charity, Los Coyotes Country. Office: 806 S Beach Blvd Anaheim CA 92804

JACKSON, BRENDA LOUISE, utility co. home economist; b. Aberdeen, Md., Oct. 27, 1950; d. Henry Taylor and Annie Marie (Ellison) Jackson; B.S. in Home Econs., Prairie View A & M U., 1972. With Dallas Power and Light Co., 1973—, home service advisor, 1973-78, supr. consumer services, 1978-81, community programs mgr., 1981—. Vol. Tom Paukins Campaign for Congress, 1978; bd. dirs. Dallas County chpt. Am. Heart Assn.; bd. visitors Mus. Afro-Am. Life and Culture, Bishop Coll., 1979—. Recipient Award of Merit Am. Heart Assn., 1978. Mem. Dallas Black C. of C., Am. Home Econs. Assn., Tex. Home Econs. Assn., North Tex. Home Economist in Bus., Am. Assn. Blacks in Energy. Baptist. Author: (with Charlene Clark) The Children's Help Your Heart Cookbook, 1978. Home: 4621 Avondal St Dallas TX 75219 Office: Dallas Power and Light Co 1506 Commerce St Dallas TX 75201

JACKSON, CLETA NELL, counselor, family therapist; b. Dunn, N.C., June 15, 1935; d. James and Ellen (Williams) Patterson; B.S., Fayetteville State U., 1956; M.S., Ind. U., 1963; counseling cert. Colgate U., 1971; postgrad. Azusa Pacific Coll., Coll. St. Rose; children—Keith Deon, Sandra Rochelle, Angela M. Tchr., Goldsboro, N.C., 1956-57, 60-65, Tachikawa, Japan, 1958-60, Rome, N.Y., 1965-70; sch. counselor, Rome, 1970—; family therapist, Rome, 1976—; field instr. LaVerne Coll., 1977—. Chmn., Internat. Relations Group, 1969-71; bus. mgr. Rome United Way, 1976; bd. dirs. Girl Scouts Am., 1970-77; committeewoman Democratic Party, 1977—; pres. Rome chpt. ARC, 1977-78. Named Outstanding Young Educator, N.Y. State, 1967; Edn. Achievement award Lambda Kappa Mu, 1979. Gladys Mersereau scholar, 1977; named Woman of Yr., Rome, 1980. Mem. NAACP (exec. bd. 1978—), NEA (life), Nat. Counselors Assn., Internat. Reading Assn., Classroom Tchrs. Assn., Community Concert Assn., AAUW, N.Y. State Personnel and Guidance Assn., Oneida County Personnel and Guidance Assn., Rome Tchrs. Assn., Ind. U. Alumni Assn., Alpha Kappa Mu, Delta Kappa Gamma (chpt. sec. 1975-79), Alpha Kappa Alpha (grad. adv. 1976-79). Democrat. Mem. Ch. of Christ. Office: 500 Turin St Rome NY 13440

JACKSON, CONSTANCE CORDICE, reading cons.; b. Winchester, Mass.; d. Conrad and Florence (Smith) Cordice; B.S. in Elem. Edn., Boston U., 1963, M.Ed. in Reading, Lang., Elem. Edn., 1966, Ed.D. in Reading, Elem. Edn., 1974; m. Eugene B. Jackson. Tchr. Scituate (Mass.) Public Schs., 1963-64; tchr. Marshfield (Mass.) Public Schs., 1964-68, reading cons., 1968—; teaching fellow Boston U., 1972. Dir. Marshfield Right to Read Effort, 1973-76. Mem. NEA, Internat. Reading Assn., Mass., Marshfield tchrs. assns., Pi Lambda Theta. Home: PO Box 126 North Marshfield MA 02059 Office: Eames Way Sch Marshfield MA 02050

JACKSON, DORIS CARSON, personnel exec.; b. Hicksville, N.Y., Dec. 24, 1940; d. Clarence and Mary E. (Myers) Carson; B.A. cum laude, Hunter Coll., N.Y.C., 1970; M.A., N.Y.U., 1975; m. Melvin K. Jackson, July 11, 1959; children—Mark, Sheila, Matthew. Tchr. high sch. English, 1970-77; editor sch. dept. lang. arts Holt, Rinehart and Winston, 1977-79; mgr. communications and planning, personnel benefits dept. CBS, Inc., N.Y.C., 1979, mgr. tng. and devel., personnel, edn. and tng. dept., 1979—; mem. Commn. on Writing, Council for Basic Edn., Washington, 1977-78. Trustee, sec. Pelham (N.Y.) Public Library, 1974-76; bd. dirs. Pelham Family Service, 1975-77, chmn. public relations, 1975-77. Mem. Am. Soc. Tng. and Devel., Young Woman's League, Phi Beta Kappa, Delta Kappa Gamma. Baptist.

JACKSON, DORIS MAMIE MOZELLE ADAMS, health professions rep.; b. Vicksburg, Miss., Jan. 13, 1940; d. James Henry and Thelma Irma (Shelton) Watson; A.A., J.P. Campbell Coll., 1960; student Alcorn State U., 1961-63; m. Van Lester Jackson, Mar. 12, 1978; 1 son, James L. Adams. Sec. to comptroller Jackson (Miss.) State U., 1969-73; asst. coordinator minority student affairs U. of Miss. Med. Center, 1973-76, field rep., Sch. Health Related Professions, Jackson, 1976—; instr. Opportunities Industrialization Center, Jackson, 1971-73; co-founder Minority Med. Edn. Found., Inc. Mem. NEA, Found. Negro Affairs, Iota Phi Lambda. Mem. African Meth. Episcopal Ch. Office: 500 S Main St Suite 1205 Orange CA 92668

JACKSON, DOROTHY LOUISA GREENLEE, ct. reporter; b. Hamburg, Iowa, Feb. 19, 1911; d. Henry Oliver and Mattie (Landreth) Greenlee; student public schs.; m. Fred Knox Jackson, Oct. 3, 1944 (dec.). Asst. county ct. reporter, Auburn, Nebr., 1927-29; sec. local atty., 1927-29; sec. Berksons, Kansas City, Mo., 1929-33; corr. A.A.A., Washington, 1933-36. sec. Intelligence Unit, Kansas City, St. Louis, 1936-40; free-lance ct., conv. reporter, St. Louis, 1940-44; free-lance ct. reporter, Prattville, Ala., 1948—; contract reporter Ala. Public Service Commn., Montgomery, 1967-80; co-owner, operator Prattville (Ala.) Quick Freeze, 1948-63. Chmn., Autauga County Operation Santa Claus, State Christmas Card. Bryce Mental Hosp., Tuscaloosa, Ala., 1963-70; active Birmingham Opera Guild, 1960-70. Mem. Nat. League Am. Pen Women (br. pres. 1964-68, 72-74, 76-78, state pres. 1972-74, state v.p. 1982—), Ala. Writers Conclave, Montgomery Creative Writers Club, Autauga County Creative Writers Club, Montgomery Press and Authors Club (pres. 1971-72), Ala. Shorthand Reporters Assn., Montgomery Assn. Legal Secs., Nat. Shorthand Reporters Assn., Ala. Poetry Soc., Autauga County Bus. and Profl. Women's Club (County Woman of Achievement 1972). Author: (poetry) Fallen Leaves, 1968; Poody, 1970. Home: 856 Gillespie St Prattville AL 36067

JACKSON, ELEANOR GERTRUDE ALEXANDER, microbiologist; b. N.Y.C., July 1, 1904; d. Jerome and Gertrude E. (Hammerslough) Alexander; B.A., Wellesley Coll., 1925; M.A., Columbia U., 1928; Ph.D., N.Y.U., 1934; m. William R. Jackson, Nov. 1, 1934 (div. 1947); 1 son, Togwell A. Research asst. U. Mich. Hosp., 1928-30; lab. asst. Med. Coll. N.Y.U., 1935-36; research N.Y. State Br. Lab., 1936-39; research fellow Med. Coll., Cornell U., 1941-50; research bacertiologist Cancer Research Lab., 1950-54; Ind. research, 1954-60; guest investigator Inst. Comparative Medicine, Columbia U., 1960-65; cons. research microbiologist, N.Y.C., 1965—; research asso. U. San Diego, 1968-73. Recipient A. Cressy Morrison prize N.Y. Acad. Scis., 1944, Grant-in-aid award Sigma Delta Epsilon, 1965. Fellow AAAS, N.Y. Micros. Soc., N.Y. Acad. Medicine (asso.); mem. Am. Soc. Microbiology, U.D.C., Sigma Xi, Sigma Delta Epsilon (pres. Kappa chpt.). Clubs: Altrusa, Women's City (N.Y.C.). Contbr. articles to profl. jours. Discovered L forms of Mycobacterium tuberculosis, 1944, M leprae, 1945; cultured M leprae in cell-free broth, 1951-74; found DNA in Rousvirus, 1969; research on cancer and other proliferative diseases. Home: 390 Riverside Dr New York City NY 10025

JACKSON, ESTELLE SHARPE, journalist; b. Kalamazoo, Dec. 29, 1924; d. Leason and Edith J. (Nelson) Sharpe; student U. Ill.; grad. U. Chgo.; M.A., U. Mich., 1948; m. Auzville Jackson, Jr., Sept. 12, 1953; children—Robert, Sarah. Reporter, copyreader, feature writer Battle Creek (Mich.) Enquirer-News, 1948-51, Washington Post, 1951-55, Louisville Courier-Jour., 1955-56; instr. journalism Va. Commonwealth U., 1967-69; consumer columnist Richmond (Va.) Times-Dispatch, 1969—. Pres., Va. Assn. Emotionally Disturbed Children, 1965-66. Mem. Va. Press Women, Washington Press Club. Presbyterian. Club: Fishing Bay Yacht. Home: 115 Santa Clara Dr Richmond VA 23229 Office: 333 E Grace St Richmond VA 23219

JACKSON, ETHEL CURRY (MRS. RAYMOND T. JACKSON), civic worker; b. Mineral Point, Wis.; d. William Jenkin and Adeline (Argall) Curry; student Northwestern U.; m. Raymond T. Jackson, Sept. 30, 1918. Adv. mem. Marquis Biol. Library Soc.; mem. Cleve. Council on World Affairs, Cleve. Museum Art, Cleve. Health Museum, Cleve. Mus. Natural History, Musical Arts Assn., Garden Center of Greater Cleve., Women's Com. Cleve. Orch., Cleve. Inst. Music, Playhouse Women's Com., Cleve. Zool. Soc., UN Assn. U.S.A., Friends of Cleve. Pub. Library, Smithsonian Assos., Met. Mus. Art, N.Y.C., Nat. Trust Historic Preservation, Citizens League Cleve., U.S. Olympic Soc., Am. Bible Soc., Nat., Cleve. hist. socs., Shaker Heights Western Res. Women's Rep. Club. Mem. Northwestern U. Alumni Assn. Republican. Methodist. Clubs: Country, Union, Women's City. Home: 13901 Shaker Blvd Cleveland OH 44120

JACKSON, FREDA LUCILLE, ch. adminstr., editor; b. Sikeston, Mo., Sept. 15, 1928; d. Jesse Freda and Ruby Lucille (Carter) Andres; student Three Rivers Jr. Coll., 1969, Central Bible Coll., Springfield, Mo., 1973; B.S., Drury Coll., 1980; postgrad. Assemblies of God Grad. Sch., 1981—; m. Thomas Lowell Jackson, Oct. 2, 1947; children—Stephen Andres, Elizabeth Ann, Thomas Dean. Bookkeeper, Aduddel Wholesale Auto Parks, Sikeston, 1947-48; pvt. sec. to v.p. So. Ice & Coal Co., Memphis, 1948-49; sec. firm Bailey & Craig, Sikeston, 1950-56, firm Blanton & Blanton, 1956-57; lic. to ministry Assemblies of God Ch., 1964; promotions coordinator, editor deferred giving and trusts dept., gen. council Assemblies of God, Springfield, Mo., 1974—. Mem. Alpha Sigma Lambda, Womens Ministries, Maranatha Aux. Editor: New Dimensions, 1979—, Maranatha newsletter, 1977; contbr. articles to denominational publs. Home: 1513 N Hillcrest St Springfield MO 65802

JACKSON, GAIL ELISABETH, social worker; b. Phila., July 11, 1944; d. Elmore and Elisabeth (Averill) J.; B.A., Wellesley Coll., 1966; M.S.W., U. Wis., Madison, 1974. Program asst. N.Y. State Council on Arts, N.Y.C., 1967-68, acting program dir., 1968; sec. to adminstr., dir. Child Devel. and Mental Retardation Center, U. Wash., Seattle, 1968-72; clin. social worker Southwestern Mental Health Center, Luverne, Minn., 1974-78, coordinator mental health consultation and edn. program, 1978-80, asst. to dir., 1980-82; dir. Five County Mental Health Center, Braham, Minn., 1982—. Chmn. personnel com. Sch. Dist. 518 Community Edn. Adv. Council, Worthington, Minn., 1977-81; bd. dirs., chmn. personnel com. SW Action Council, Worthington, 1977-78; chmn. Worthington Social Service Agys., 1980. Mem. Nat. Assn. Social Workers, Acad. Cert. Social Workers, Nat. Assn. Rural Mental Health (dir. 1979—, Chmn. 1981-82). Quaker. Home: 406 Park St Mora MN 55051 Office: Five County Mental Health Center PO Box 287 Braham MN 55006

JACKSON, GLENDA, actress; b. Birkenhead, Cheshire, Eng., May 9, 1936; d. Harry and Joan Jackson; ed. West Kirby County Grammar Sch. for Girls; m. Roy Hodges; 1 son, Daniel. Made stage debut as student in Separate Tables, Worthing, Eng., 1957; first appeared on London (Eng.) stage at Arts as Ruby in All Kinds of Men, 1957; appeared in Hammersmith, 1962, The Idiot, 1963, Alfie, 1963; joined Royal Shakespeare Co. and appeared in exptl. Theatre of Cruelty season L.A.M.D.A., 1964, Stratford season, 1965, played Princess of France in Love's Labour's Lost, Ophelia in Hamlet, at Aldwych played Eva in Puntila, 1965; reader in The Investigation, 1965; appeared as Charlotte Corday in Marat/Sade, 1965, and repeating performance in N.Y. debut at Martin Beck, 1965 (Variety award as most promising actress); appeared in U.S. at Aldwych, 1966, as Masha in Three Sisters at Royal Ct., 1967, as Tamara Fanghorn in Fanghorn at Fortune, 1967, Katherine Winter in Collaborators, 1973, as Solange in The Maids, 1974, as Hedda Gabler, 1975, as Vittoria Corombona in The White Devil, 1976, appeared on stage in Rose, N.Y.C., London, 1980-81; appeared in numerous films, 1968—, including Women in Love (Acad. award for Best Actress 1970), Sunday, Bloody Sunday, The Music Lovers, Marat-Sade, Negatives, Mary Queen of Scots, Triple Echo (being reissued as Soldier in Skirts), The Nelson Affair, A Touch of Class (Acad. award for Best Actress 1973), The Maids, The Romantic Englishwoman, The Incredible Sarah, Nasty Habits, House Calls, Lost & Found, 1979, Heath, 1980, Hopscotch, 1980, Stevie, 1981; numerous TV appearances, 1960—, including series Elizabeth R. Office: care Robinson & Assos 132 S Rodeo Dr Beverly Hills CA 90210 *

JACKSON, HARRIET MARIE, fin. exec.; b. Washington, Jan. 16, 1957; d. Harry Thomas and Dorothy Marie (Jenkins) Jackson; B.S. in B.A., U. Dayton, 1979. Asst. controller Marriott Hotels, Lincolnshire, Ill., 1979, Somerset, N.J., 1979-80, Washington, 1980-82, controller, 1982—. Mem. Nat. Assn. Female Execs., Zeta Phi Beta. Office: PO Box 17450 DIA Washington DC 20041

JACKSON, HAZEL BRILL, sculptor; b. Phila.; d. William Henry and Lizabeth Lee (Stone) Jackson; student Friends Select Sch., Phila., Boston Mus. Sch. Fine Arts, Scuola Rosatti, Florence, Italy, with Angelo Zanelli, Rome, Italy. Exhibited Nat. Mus. Modern Art, Rome, Trieste and Florence, Royal Acad. Scotland, Nat. Acad. N.Y.C., Guild Boston Artists; represented mus., pvt. collections, including Brookgreen Garden, S.C., Newburgh Pub. Library, bronzes at Wellesley, Vassar, Dartmouth colls., Springfield (Mass.) Art Mus. Recipient Ellen Spayer Meml. award Nat. Acad., 1945, 48, 60, 65; Allied Artists prize Smithsonian Instn., 1963; other awards. Fellow Nat. Sculpture Soc.; mem. NAD (Young Meml. prize 1965), Guild Boston Artists, Soc. Animal Artists, Am. Artists Profl. League. Clubs: American Alpine, Italian Alpine. Home: Old Balmville Rd Newburgh NY 12550

JACKSON, HELEN, army nurse; b. Cleve., Dec. 22, 1925; d. James and Idell (Hann) J.; R.N., Cleve. City Hosp., 1948; B.S. in Nursing, Boston U., 1957. From staff nurse to supr. communicable disease sect. Cleve. City Hosp., 1948-55; commd. capt. Nurse Corps, U.S. Army, 1957, advanced through grades to col., 1977; service in Korea, W. Ger. and Vietnam; asst. chief dept. nursing Letterman Army Med. Center, San Francisco, 1977-80, ret., 1980. Decorated Army Commendation medal with oak leaf cluster, Meritorious Service medal; Republic of Vietnam Cross of Gallantry with palm, Bronze Star, Legion of Merit. Mem. Am. Nurses Assn., Nat. League Nursing, Assn. Mil. Surgeons, Am. Legion (comdr. San Francisco nurses' post 452, historian 7th dist. council Calif., rec.-corr. sec. Calif., women's post comdr. 1981-82, historian 2d area Calif. 1981-82, other offices), Honor Soc. Women Legionnaires (v.p. 1981-82, pres.-elect 1982-83). Address: 100 Font Blvd Apt 11C San Francisco CA 94132

JACKSON, JACQUELYNE JOHNSON, sociologist, educator; b. Winston-Salem, N.C., Feb. 24, 1932; d. James Albert and Beulah Naomi (Crosby) Johnson; B.S., U. Wis., 1953, M.S., 1955; Ph.D., Ohio State U., 1960; postgrad. U. Colo., summer 1961, Duke U., 1966-68, U. N.C., 1977-78; m. Frederick A.S. Clarke, Aug. 26, 1955 (div. 1959); m. 2d, Murphy Jackson, May 15, 1962; 1 dau., Viola Elizabeth. Prof., So. U., Baton Rouge, 1959-62, Jackson (Miss.) State Coll., 1962-64, Howard U., Washington, 1964-66, 78—; asst. to asso. prof. med. sociology Duke U., Durham, N.C., 1968—; prof. sociology St. Augustine's Coll., Raleigh, N.C., 1969-80; cons. and speaker on aging, families and public policies. Exec. dir. Nat. Council on Black Aging, Inc., 1975—; mem. Nat. Council on Equality of Ednl. Opportunity, 1973-78. Life mem. Tuskegee (Ala.) Civic Assn. Trustee Carver Research Found., Tuskegee Inst. Recipient Pres.'s award Assn. Homes for Aging, 1972, Black Women's award in edn. Clark Coll., 1975; Solomon Fuller award Am. Psychiat. Assn., 1978; Ford fellow, summer 1957, John Hay Whitney fellow, 1957-59, NSF fellow, 1961, NIH fellow, 1966-68. Mem. Am. Sociol. Assn. (editor Jour. Health and Social Behavior 1972-75), Assn. Social and Behavioral Scientists (pres. 1969-72, pres.'s service award 1973, W.E.B. Du Bois award 1980), AAAS, Nat. Council on Family Relations, Gerontol. Soc., So. Sociol. Soc. Democrat. Episcopalian. Author: These Rights They Seek, 1962; Minorities and Aging, 1980; also numerous articles; editor: Aging Black Women, 1975; Jour. Minority Aging, 1975—. Address: PO Box 8522 Durham NC 27707 *

JACKSON, JOY JUANITA, educator; b. New Orleans, Oct. 8, 1928; d. Oliver Daniel and Oneida Christina (Drouant) Jackson; student La. State U., 1946-49; B.A., Tulane U., 1951, M.A., 1958, Ph.D., 1961. Feature writer New Orleans Times-Picayune, 1951-56; instr. Nicholls State Coll., Thibodaux, La., 1961-62, asst. prof., 1962-66; asst. prof. Southeastern La. U., Hammond, 1966-68, asso. prof., 1968-73, prof. history, 1973—, dir. Center for Regional Studies and univ. archives, 1982—. AAUW Irma E. Voight fellow, 1960-61. Mem. Am., La. (dir.

1966-68, pres. 1977-78), So. S.E. La. (pres. Hammond 1978) hist. assns., Oral History Assn. Author: New Orleans in the Gilded Age, 1969. Home: 1411 University Dr Hammond LA 70401

JACKSON, LAURA (RIDING), writer; b. N.Y.C., Jan. 16, 1901; d. Nathaniel S. and Sarah (Edersheim) Reichenthal; student Cornell U., other univs.; m. Schuyler Brinckerhoff Jackson, June 20, 1941 (dec. 1968). Mem. The Fugitives, mid 1920's; mng. partner Seizin Press, 1927-38; collaborator, 1st author: A Survey of Modernist Poetry, 1927, A Pamphlet Against Anthologies, 1928; (critical essays) Contemporaries and Snobs, 1928; Anarchism Is Not Enough, 1928; Four Unposted Letters to Catherine, 1930; (essays and poems) Though Gently, 1930; (essays and stories) Experts Are Puzzled, 1930; (under pseudonym Madeleine Vara) Convalescent Conversations, 1935; (collected stories) Progress of Stories, 1935, 2d edit., 1982; (hist. novel) A Trojan Ending, 1937; (hist. stories) Lives of Wives, 1939; (with Harry Kemp) The Left Heresy, 1939; Collected Poems from 9 preceding vols., 1938; Selected Poems: In Five Sets, 1973; (discourse on human destiny) The Telling, 1972; (with husband) Rational Meaning: A New Foundation for the Definition of Words, in press; also articles and pamphlets, 1925—; editor, contbr. (gen. criticism) Epilogue, Vols. I-III, 1935-37; editor, commentator The World and Ourselves, 1938; Selected Writings, Published, Unpublished, book issue, Chelsea 35, 1976; Collected Poems, new edit., 1980, Description of Life, 1980. Recipient Fugitive poetry prize, 1925; appreciation grant Mark Rothko Found., 1971. Guggenheim fellow, 1973. Home: Box 35 Wabasso Fl 32970

JACKSON, LEE, psychiatrist; b. Cleve., Nov. 29, 1922; d. William Leo and Jessie Irene (Austin) J.; A.B. magna cum laude, Ohio U., 1944; M.D., U. Rochester, 1950; m. John Robert Carruth, Oct. 6, 1962; 1 son, Bruce Douglas. Civilian lab. technician Crile Gen. Army Hosp., Cleve., 1944-45; jr. chemist Standard Oil Co. (Ohio), Cleve., 1945-46; pediatric intern U. Minn. Hosps., Mpls., 1950-51; resident in pediatrics Strong Meml. Hosp., Rochester, N.Y., 1951-52; resident in pediatrics and child psychiatry Univ. Hosps., Cleve., 1953-54; fellow in psychiatry Mass. Gen. Hosp., Boston, 1956-57; clin. fellow in psychiatry McLean Hosp., Belmont, Mass., 1957-59; fellow in child psychiatry Judge Baker Guidance Center, Boston, 1959-61; practice medicine specializing in psychiatry and child psychiatry, Rochester, N.Y., 1974—; staff psychiatrist Orleans County Mental Health Center, Albion, N.Y.; cons. psychiatrist Rochester Rehab. Center; instr. pediatrics Western Res. U., Cleve., 1954-56; asst. prof. pediatrics and child psychiatry U. Rochester, 1974-77. Docent, U. Rochester Meml. Art Gallery. Diplomate Am. Bd. Pediatrics. Mem. Am. Psychiat. Assn., Rochester Acad. Sci., Genesee Ornithol. Soc., English-Speaking Union, Phi Beta Kappa. Club: Midtown Tennis. Office: 122 Danbury Circle N Rochester NY 14618

JACKSON, LORA RUTHE THOMPSON, parliamentarian, corp. exec.; b. Ft. Worth, Oct. 29, 1920; d. John Lyle and Florence (Ector) Thompson; student Ft. Worth Christian Coll., 1960, Christian Coll. of Southwest, 1969, bus. courses; m. Vernon Jackson, Sept. 10, 1944; children—Xanna Yvonne Jackson Young, Jorja Annette Jackson Clemson. Mail and advt. clk. Mut. Benefit Ins. Co., 1940-42; clk. to exec. sec. N. Am. Aviation, 1942-45; exec. sec. TEMCO Mfg., 1945-47, Luscombe Aircraft, 1947-50; sec., gen. office supr. SA-SO Sign Mfg. Co., 1950-53; co-owner All-Quality Sign Co., 1953-59; co-owner, v.p., office supr., public relations dir. Jackson Vending Supply, Inc., Grand Prairie, Tex., 1959—; dir. DeSoto First Nat. Bank; tchr., judge parliamentary law. Mem. Dallas County Sch. Bd., 1974—, Dallas County Hist. Commn., 1974—; chmn. Grand Prairie Arts and Hist. Preservation Commn., 1976—; chmn. Grand Prairie Bi-Centennial, 1974-76; mem. Grand Prairie Civil Def. Commn., 1959—; mem., past chmn. Grand Prairie Community and Home Improvements Commn., 1964—; mem. spl. funds com. Grand Prairie Ind. Sch. Dist.; active local, council and dist PTA's; regional v.p. Tex. PTA. Recipient Mrs. Lyndon B. Johnson environ. award Keep Am. Beautiful, 1977; hon. life mem. Nat. Congress Parents and Tchrs., Tex. Congress Parents and Tchrs.; recipient Tex. Bluebonnet state award Beautify Tex. Council, 1978, award in conservation Tex. Forest Service, 1976; named Woman of Yr., Grand Prairie Daily News, 1979. Registered profl. parliamentarian. Mem. Grand Prairie Friends of the Library (pres. 1978-80), Grand Prairie C. of C. (Women of Year Women's div. 1967, Citizen of Year, 1969, pres. chamber 1982—), Tex. Assn. Parliamentarians (state pres. 1974-75), Nat. Assn. Parliamentarians, Beautify Tex. Council (state pres. 1976-78), Grand Prairie Hist. Orgn., (life, sec., founding pres.), Grand Prairie Hosp. Aux. (life). Democrat. Mem. Ch. of Christ. Clubs: Grand Prairie Bus. and Profl. Women's (treas., Woman of Year 1976, 82, pres.-elect 1982-83), Grand Prairie Garden (pres., Woman of Year 1975), Soroptimist of Grand Prairie (corr. sec.), Soroptomist Internat. (regional parliamentarian). Contbr. articles on parliamentary law, beautification and community improvement, and cultural arts to mags.; co-host, co-dir. cable TV show It's Happening in Grand Prairie, 1981—. Home and Office: 200 Meyers Rd Grand Prairie TX 75050

JACKSON, LORRAINE MORLOCK, counseling psychologist; b. Phila., Mar. 11, 1939; d. Jacob and Sophie Morlock; B.Sc., Bloomsburg State Coll., 1960; M.Ed., Pa. State U., 1961, Ph.D., 1982; postgrad. Temple U., 1962, U. Western Ont., 1976; m. Douglas Northrop Jackson, July 28, 1962; children—Douglas Northrop III, Lorraine D., Charles Theodore VI. Tchr. math. and English, San Carlos (Calif.) Bd. Edn., 1962-64; co-founder Research Psychologists Press, Inc., Port Huron, Mich., and London, Ont., Can., 1964—, dir., 1977-82; psychometrist Middlesex Bd. Edn., 1970-71, 78; learning specialist Lawrence Twp. Bd. Edn. and N.J. State Dept. Edn., 1971-72; research and assessment staff London Bd. Edn., 1972-73; cons. U. Western Ont., 1976-77. Pres. Parents Assn., White Hills Montessori Sch., 1969-70; pres. Ont. Assn. Children with Learning Disabilities, 1976-77. Recipient Gold Service award key, 1960. Mem. Am. Psychol. Assn., Am. Personnel and Guidance Assn., Ont. Psychol. Assn., Phi Kappa Phi. Club: Toastmasters. Contbr. to Personality Research Form and Jackson Vocat. Interest Survey, 1964-78; editor London French Sch. Newsletter, 1970-71; contbr. articles to profl. jours. Home: 911 Ashton Rd Cornwell Heights PA 19020 Office: Pennsylvania State University Div of Counseling and Educational Psychology 327 Cedar Bldg University Park PA 16802

JACKSON, LYDIA OCTAVIA, poet; b. Grafton, N.D., Mar. 5, 1902; d. Karl Olaf and Inga (Schellstad) Svarte; student pub. schs., N.D.; m. Arthur F. Jackson, Dec. 20, 1920; 1 dau., Elizabeth Marjean (Mrs. Leonard Fagerholt). Author: Rhymes for Every Season, 1943; Selected Poems, 1962; Pardon My Gaff (book verse), 1965; compiler: Peace Garden of Verses, 1967; also numerous poems in various publs. Publicity chmn. Poetry Day, 1950. Treas. Grafton Sch. Dist. 22, 1931-62. Recipient Nat. Writers award Farmers Union Ednl. Dept., 1950; named co-poet laureate State N.D., 1979. Mem. Walsh County Sch. Officers Assn. (treas. 1945-62), Am. Poets Fellowship Soc., (Poet Laureate V), World Poetry Day Assn. (past membership chmn. N.D. and S.D.), Centro Studie Scambi Internazionali Rome (Bronze medal 1965, Silver medal 1967), Midwest Fedn. Chaparral Poets (state regent 1950-51), Nat. League Am. Pen. Women, N.D. Pen Women, Am. Poetry League, World Poetry Soc. Inter-continental, Poetry Soc. of London. Presbyterian. Mem. Order Eastern Star. Clubs: Riverside Woman's (v.p. 1957-59, sec. 1955-57, 59-61); Sigma Rho Study (sec.-treas. 1958—, pres. 1952-54). Home: Route 2 Grafton ND 58237

JACKSON, MARIA VERONICA, educator; b. N.J., July 17, 1941; d. Archie Lee and Audrey Veronica (Salley) Parker; B.S., Jersey City State U., 1973; M.A., Seton Hall U., 1976; children—Robert, Tyrone, Alfred, Jonessa. Asst. buyer Arthur Mandel Assos., N.Y.C., 1959-61; account expediter Bell Telephone Labs., 1961-64; research coordinator Jersey City CANDO and Community Orgn., 1964-69; tchr. elem. sch., Newark, 1973-80; tchr. math. Vailsburg High Sch., Newark, 1978-80, coach cheerleaders; mem. athletic staff Kean Coll.; owner Woman's Friend, Inc., career and fin. counseling bus., tutorial service. Mem. Nat. Assn. Female Execs., N.J. Math. Assn., Jersey City State Coll. Alumni Assn., Internat. Platform Assn., 100 Black Women of Am., Alpha Kappa Alpha. Democrat. Home: 1423 Hiawatha Ave Hillside NJ 07205

JACKSON, (MARY) RUTH, orthopaedic surgeon; b. Jefferson, Iowa, Dec. 13, 1902; d. William Riley and Carolyn Arabelle (Babb) J.; B.A., U. Tex., 1924; M.D., Baylor U., 1928. Gen. intern Meml. Hosp., Worcester, Mass., 1928-29, resident in orthopaedic surgery, 1930-31; intern in orthopaedic surgery Univ. Hosps., U. Iowa, 1929-30; resident in orthopaedic surgery Tex. Scottish Rite Hosp. for Crippled Children, Dallas and asst. at Carrell-Driver-Girard Clinic, Dallas, 1931-32; pvt. practice medicine specializing in orthopaedic surgery, Dallas, 1932—; clin. instr. in orthopaedic surgery Baylor U., Dallas, 1936-43; hon. cons. orthopaedic surgeon Baylor U. Med. Center, Dallas, Parkland Meml. Hosp., Dallas; hon. asst. clin. prof. orthopaedic surgery Southwestern Med. Sch. of U. Tex., Dallas; lectr. in field. Diplomate Am. Bd. Orthopaedic Surgery. Fellow ACS, Internat. Coll. Surgeons; mem. Dallas County Med. Assn., Tex. Med. Assn., So. Med. Assn., AMA, Tex. Orthopaedic Assn., Tex. Rheumatism Assn., Southwestern Surg. Congress, Am. Acad. Orthopaedic Surgeons, Am. Orthopaedic Foot Soc., Am. Assn. for Study Headache, Am. Trauma Soc., Am. Assn. Automotive Medicine, Am. Soc. Contemporary Medicine and Surgery, Western Orthopaedic Assn., Law-Sci. Acad. Am., Pan-Am. Med. Assn. (diplomate sect. orthopaedic surgery), Rayve Soc. Medicine (assoc.), Nat. Assn. Disability Examiners, Dallas C. of C., North Dallas C. of C., Kaufman C. of C. Republican. Methodist. Club: Zonta Internat. Author monograph: The Cervical Syndrome, 1956, 4th edit., 1977, Japanese transl, 1967; contbr. articles to profl. jours. Office: 3629 Fairmount Dallas TX 75219

JACKSON, MARZETTA MARY, social worker; b. Phila., Jan. 6, 1949; d. Thomas James and Susie Viola (Johnston) Frazier; A.A., Ellen Cushing Jr. Coll., 1968; B.S. in Sociology, St. Joseph's Coll., 1970; M.S.W., U. Pitts., 1974. Instr. orientation and assessment Concentrated Employment Program, Pitts., 1971-72; med. social worker Clouster County Vis. Nurses Assn., Woodbury, N.J., 1975-77; caseworker Family and Community Service, Media, Pa., 1977-79; tchr. Camden (N.J.) Bd. Edn., 1975; psychiat. social worker So. Home for Children, Phila., 1979—. Ch. sch. sec. Brights Hope Bapt. Ch., Phila., 1980. Mem. Nat. Assn. Social Workers, Nat. Assn. Christians in Social Work, Nat. Assn. Blacks in Social Work. Home: 245 S Barber Ave Woodbury NJ 08096

JACKSON, MURIEL GRACE, univ. adminstr.; b. Wood-Ridge, N.J., Apr. 21, 1929; d. John David and Lillian Grace (Rogers) Kappeler; B.A., Keuka Coll., 1950; M.S., Columbia U. Sch. Journalism, 1952; grad. U. Mich. Inst. Acad. Adminstrv. Advancement, 1973, Oreg. Mgmt. Devel. Program, 1974; m. Rudolph Lorenz, Mar. 27, 1955 (dec. Nov. 1965); children—John Martin, Tracy Ann, Andrea Grace; m. 2d, Ross E. Jackson, June 10, 1967. Pub. relations asst. St. Lawrence U., 1950-51; editorial asst. Ridgewood (N.J.) News, 1952-53; reporter Binghamton (N.Y.) Press, 1953-56; adminstrv. asst. to pres. San Jose State Coll., 1966-69; asst. to pres. U. Oreg., 1969-75, dir. univ. relations, 1974-79, asst. for adminstrn., 1979—, dir. univ. bookstore, 1977-78. Troop leader Western Rivers Council Girl Scouts U.S.A., 1973-74; troop treas. Oreg. Trails Council Boy Scouts Am., 1973-74; sr. warden Episcopal Ch. of the Resurrection, Eugene, Oreg., 1973-74; chmn. Central Convocation Episcopal Diocese of Oreg., 1974-76; spl. events chmn. Lane County (Oreg.) United Way, 1976, 77; bd. dirs. Lane County Cancer Soc., 1978-80, Lane Meml. Blood Bank, 1979—. Recipient Disting. Alumna award Keuka Coll., 1975. Mem. Council Advancement and Support of Edn., Eugene C. of C. (chmn. univ. affairs com. 1978, 81, 82), Lane County Rubicon Soc. Republican. Home: 401 Brae Burn Dr Eugene OR 97405 Office: Office of Pres U of Oreg Eugene OR 97403

JACKSON, NORVELL, univ. adminstr.; b. Springfield, Mass., Nov. 30, 1945; d. James Herbert and Irma Lee (Washington) Hamer; B.A. magna cum laude, U. Mass., 1975; M.Ed., U. Mass., 1979, postgrad., 1979—; m. L. Van Allen Jackson III, Mar. 27, 1965; children—Rhonda R. G., L. Van Allen IV. Adminstrv. asst. W. E. B. DuBois Dept. Afro-Am. studies U. Mass., Amherst, 1971-77, asst. to dean student and alumni affairs, 1977—; asst. prin. Amherst Regional High Sch., 1979-80. Chmn. personnel com. ABC, Inc., Amherst, 1977—; mem. Tri-County Youth Program, Northampton, Mass., 1977—. Mem. Nat. Assn. Female Execs., Inc., NAACP, U. Mass. Profl. Assn., Phi Delta Kappa, Mortar Bd. Home: 34 Pomeroy Ct Amherst MA 01002 Office: 125 Sch Edn U Mass Amherst MA 01003

JACKSON, PAMELA MARIE, ins. agy. exec.; b. Snyder, Tex., May 30, 1952; d. Mitchell Ferguson and Doris Marie (Jones) Jackson; student Tex. Tech. U., 1970-74. Service rep. William Rigg Ins. Co., Arlington, Tex., 1976-77; patient account rep. Parkland Hosp., Dallas., 1977; sales and service rep. TBA Ins., Inc., Dallas, 1977-79, br. mgr., El Paso, Tex., 1979—. Mem. Ins. Women's Assn., Nat. Assn. Female Execs., Profl. Referal Orgn., Exec. Womens Council. Home: 734 Mesa Hills St Apt 80 El Paso TX 79912 Office: 300 E Main St Suite 618 El Paso TX 79901

JACKSON, PATRICIA LEE (MRS. CLIFFORD L. JACKSON), psychologist; b. N.Y.C.; d. Albert George and Lisbeth P. (Lee) Scharf; B.A., Barnard Coll.; M.A., Ph.D., Tchrs. Coll. Columbia U.; m. Clifford L. Jackson. Dir. psychol. testing R. H. Macy & Co., Inc., 1941-49; employment dir. Alexander's Dept. Stores, Inc., Bronx, N.Y., 1949-52; asst. prof. psychology Hunter Coll., N.Y.C., 1951-66, asso. prof., 1966-77, coordinator of counseling services, 1959-71; research dir. Klein Inst. for Aptitude Testing, Inc., N.Y.C., 1953-59, asst. v.p., 1957-59; pvt. practice in psychotherapy, 1964—. Trustee Alfred Adler Inst.; v.p. bd. trustees Ch. of Healing Christ (Emmet Fox Ch.), N.Y.C. Mem. AAAS, Am. Personnel and Guidance Assn., Am. Psychol. Assn., Am. Statis. Assn., Am. Group Psychotherapy Assn., N.Y. Soc. Clin. Psychologists. Author articles in field. Home: 129 E 35th St New York NY 10016

JACKSON, POLLY B., bank officer; b. Tigerville, S.C., Feb. 26, 1925; d. William Leroy and Nannie (Wallace) Adams; student public schs. Cope, S.C.; m. Clyde Fletcher Jackson, Sept. 30, 1951; children—James William Dempsey, Clyde Jonathan Jackson. Teller, Ohio Nat. Bank, Columbus, 1952-58; with Bank One of Columbus (Ohio), 1962—, student loan adminstr., 1977-81, adminstrv. officer, student loan dept., 1981—; mem. adv. council Ohio Student Loan Commn., 1975—. Recipient Gov's award, 1979. Mem. Nat. Assn. Bank Women, Columbus Credit Women Internat. (pres. 1977). Club: Women of Moose. Home: 776 Galloway Rd Galloway OH 43119 Office: Bank One of Columbus Dept 0398 Columbus OH 43271

JACKSON, RUTHIE FAY, govt. ofcl.; b. Wynne, Ark., June 2, 1948; d. Tyree and Ruth (Perry) Weaver; A.A.S. in Secretarial Sci., Seattle Community Coll., 1968; student U. Wash., 1971; m. Charles M. Jackson, July 6, 1974; children—Vanessa Marie, Casey Nathaniel. Receptionist Mobil Oil Corp., Seattle, 1969; clk., stenographer HEW (now Dept. Health and Human Services), Seattle, 1970-74, equal opportunity specialist, 1974-78, child support specialist, 1978-80, dep. regional rep. child support office, 1980-81, regional rep. Office Child Support Enforcement, Region X, Seattle, 1981—. Recipient Cert. of Merit, Dept. Health and Human Services, 1980. Mem. Nat. Assn. Female Execs., Seattle Urban League, NAACP. Mem. Church of God in Christ. Home: 12734 SE 73d St Renton WA 98056 Office: 2901 3d Ave M/S 415 Seattle WA 98121

JACKSON, SARAH EVELYN, educator; b. Selma, Ala., Mar. 26, 1929; d. Thomas Jeremiah and Cola Barr (Craig) J.; A.B., King Coll., Bristol, Tenn., 1951; M.A., U. N.C., Chapel Hill, 1953; Ph.D., Emory U., 1959. Registrar, instr. English, King Coll., 1953-55; instr. Emory U., Atlanta, 1959-60; instr. Agnes Scott Coll., Decatur, Ga., 1960-61; instr. Ga. State U., Ga. Inst. Tech., Atlanta, 1961-62; asst. prof. Ga. Inst. Tech., 1962-76, asso. prof., 1976—. Elder, Eastminster Presbyn. Ch., Stone Mountain, Ga.; mem. Council of Atlanta Presbytery, Presbyn. Ch. U.S., 1980—. Mem. Am. Name Soc., MLA, South Atlantic MLA, Am. Dialect Soc., AAUP, Am. Folklore Soc., N.C. Folklore Soc., Appalachian Writers Assn., Coll. English Assn., Ga.-South Carolina Coll. English Assn. Democrat. Contbr. in field. Home: 1836 Silver Hill Rd Stone Mountain GA 30087 Office: Georgia Inst of Tech North Ave Atlanta GA 30332

JACKSON, SHIRLEY WHIPPO, speech pathologist; b. Wilkinsburg, Pa., Dec. 11, 1923; d. Harrison Morton and Anna Belle (Wedemyer) Whippo; B.S., U. Pitts., 1945; M.A., Columbia U. Tchrs. Coll., 1961; m. Merrick Taylor Jackson, Nov. 27, 1953. Engrng. asst. Westinghouse Electric Corp., Pitts., 1945-47; office adminstr. Hill and Knowlton, Inc., Pitts. and N.Y.C., 1950-53; sr. speech pathologist St. Barnabas Hosp., N.Y.C., 1961-67, dir. speech pathology, audiology dept., 1969—; pvt. practice speech pathology, N.Y.C., 1967-69; clin. supr. Adelphi U., Garden City, N.Y., 1977—. Vol., ARC, 1954-59. Licensed Speech Pathologist, N.Y. Mem. Am. Speech, Lang. and Hearing Assn., N.Y. State Speech and Hearing Assn., Council Hosp. Hearing and Speech Dirs. (pres. 1979-80), Kappa Kappa Gamma. Republican. Episcopalian. Home: 19 Stoneleigh Close Scarsdale NY 10583 Office: St Barnabas Hosp 4422 3d Ave New York City NY 10457

JACKSON, THELMA HARRISON, mgmt. tng. cons.; b. Prichard, Ala., Jan. 14, 1946; d. Charles L. and Myrtle (Holmes) Harrison; B.S. in Biochemistry, So. U., Baton Rouge, 1968; m. Nathaniel Jackson, Sept. 7, 1965; children—Debrena Faye, Ericka Devette. Sr. research technician Battelle Northwest, Richland, Wash., 1968-71; project coordinator, work options for women, YWCA, Olympia, Wash., 1975-78; tng. cons. Jackson & Assos., Olympia, 1979—. Pres. North Thurston Sch. Bd., 1976—; chmn. Wash. State Adv. Council on Vocat. Edn., 1977—; trustee Evergreen State Coll., 1981—; mem. Wash. State Sch. Dirs. Assn.; founder Black Women's Caucus Wash. State, 1977, state pres., 1977-80, pres. Thurston County chpt., 1980—, service award, 1980; co-chmn., Olympia, White House Conf. on Families, 1980; Republican chmn. Fleetwood Precinct, 1980; co-chmn. various polit. campaigns, 1980; mem. Thurston Regional Planning Council, 1976-80; del. to Nat. Women's Conf., Houston, 1977; mem. Wash. state coordinating com. for Internat. Women's Yr., 1977; pres. Lydia Hawk Elementary Sch. PTA, 1974-76, Golden Acorn award, 1977; bd. dirs. YWCA, 1974-76, Pacific Peaks council Girl Scouts U.S.A., Olympia, 1970-74, Mid-Columbia Council Girl Scouts U.S.A., Richland, 1971-74, Benton-Franklin ARC, 1974; vol. counselor social and health services Maple Lane Sch. for Girls, 1971-74. Recipient awards, Odessa Brown Benefit Guild Assn., 1979, Pacific Peaks Council Girl Scouts U.S.A., 1974, East Pasco Neighborhood Council, 1971. Mem. Wash. State Bus. League (sec. to bd. dirs.) NW Conf. Black Public Ofcls., Nat. Caucus Black Sch. Bd. Mems., Thurston County Urban League, NAACP, Wash. State Women's Polit. Caucus, Elected Wash. Women, So. U. Alumni Assn. Contbr. writings to various publs. Home: 7533 Steilacoom Rd SE Olympia WA 98503 Office: 208 W Bay Dr Olympia WA 98502

JACKSON, WILMA (DARCY DEMILLE), journalist, public relations cons.; b. Chgo., Dec. 17; d. R.L. and Sophia O. Littlejohn; B.S. in Urban Studies/Sociology, U. Mich., 1977; cert. in urban studies Mich. State U., 1977; m. Gordon Chester Jackson, July 1, 1959; children—Carole Lynn Jackson Harris, Linda Kathryn Jackson Woodall, Jill Jackson Grandts, Alshaya Bethay Alexis Lewis. Shelley Susanne Jackson Bethay. Feature writer and columnist Sepia Mag., Fort Worth, 1961—; columnist Hip Mag., 1963—, Soul-Teen Mag., 1973—, Bronze Thrills Mag., 1957—, also feature writer, 1956—, Chgo. Daily Defender, 1959-61; syndicated columnist Associated Negro Press, 1959-64, women's editor, 1959-61; reporter and feature writer Negro Press Internat., 1964-65; market research interviewer Barlow Survey Service, Chgo., 1958-59; owner, mgr. Medi-Rary Lit. Agy., 1963—; asso. editor Vines mag., 1980—; guest lectr. creative writing U. Mich., Flint, 1977-78; adv. Black Fashion Mus., N.Y.C., 1979-80; public relations dir. The Links, Inc., 1979—; evaluation specialist and instr. The Kennedy Center, Flint, 1979—; cons. Manulife Ins., Timeshares, Inc. Mem. public affairs com. YWCA. Recipient numerous writing awards. Mem. Nat. Assn. Media Women (Woman of Yr. award 1978, pres. 1978-80), Flint Writers Club (v.p. 1973-74), AAUW, Nat. Bus. and Profl. Women, U. Mich. Alumni Assn. Democrat.

JACOB, DELIA LEGGETT, law firm adminstr.; b. Los Angeles, Sept. 16, 1950; d. Charles William and Delia (Marin); B.A. with honors, Stanford U., 1972; M.A., U. Mich., 1975; student U. So. Calif., 1968-70; m. John Edward Jacob, Feb. 14, 1979; 1 son, Jonathon Michael. Study coordinator Soc. Psychol. Study of Social Issues-Am. Psychol. Assn., Ann Arbor, Mich., 1973; teaching fellow U. Mich., Ann Arbor, 1974, 75-76; research asso. Survey Research Center, Ann Arbor, 1977-78; adminstrv. mgr. Rackham Grad. Sch., U. Mich., 1979-80; personnel asst. Martec Services, Los Angeles, 1981; asst. dir. personnel Cox, Castle & Nicholson, Los Angeles, 1981-82. Mem. career mktg. bd. Mademoiselle mag. Ford Found. fellow, 1972-77; Calif. State scholar, 1970-72; recipient Book award Calif. State Employees Assn., 1968-69; Gov.'s scholar, Calif., 1968. Mem. Am. Psychol. Assn., Women in Communication, Chicano Student Psychol. Assn., Theta Sigma Phi. Democrat. Contbr. articles to profl. jours.

JACOB-BENNETT, MELISSA ROSE, lexicologist; b. Bedstede, Belgium, May 9, 1926; d. Karl Gustav and Nina Christina (Seger) Bennett; came to U.S., 1955, naturalized, 1961; M.A. Harcourth Coll., Cambridge (Eng.) U., 1951; m. Yan de Zware, May 1, 1944 (div. Dec. 1950); children—Yan, Peter; m. 2d, Peter de Lichte, Feb. 4, 1952 (div. Aug. 1958); children—Astrid, Carita; m. 3d, Everett E. Jacob, Jan. 17, 1960; children—Sonya, Cassandra, Anne. Raconteur, Dutch Radio Network, 1944-48; research in royal history, 1948-54; lexicologist Cheese Coll. Assn. Internat., Denmark, 1954-55, Henk Newenhouse, Inc., 1950-77; raconteur Perennial Edn. Inc., Northfield, Ill., 1970—; dir. First Nat. Bank, Aspen, Colo., Bulla, Inc., Copenhagen, Ferrari Works U.K. Recipient Helene Waldorf award Daus. of Christina (Copenhagen), 1968, 72, 73. Fellow Danish Lexicology Assn.; life mem. Raconteur Registry Am.; mem. Alumni Assn. Harcourth Coll. (pres. 1974-76), Ravinia Rock Protection Found. (pres.). Mem. Socialist Workers Party. Author: Prince Bernhard-Crown or Crook?, 1955; Lexicon of Danish Cheese Collections, 1964; Perennial Education, A Lifetime of Learning, 1972; Queen Nan of Flanders: Early Feminist or Fraud?, 1980. Address: 477 Roger Williams Ave Highland Park IL 60035

JACOBOZZI, VIVIAN MARIE, wholesale co. exec.; b. Montenero, Italy, Apr. 24, 1933 (parents Am. citizens); d. Andrea and Adelia Z. (Tornincasa) Iacobozzi; student public schs., Lorain, Ohio. Acct., Caravan Inn, Phoenix, 1963-67; office mgr. AME Food Service, Scottsdale, Ariz., 1967-70, v.p., 1970-78, pres., 1978—, also dir.; treas.

Arcos Dress Shop, Sun City, Ariz., 1973—. Recipient plaque March of Dimes, 1978. Mem. Nat. Assn. Meat Purveyors (dir.), Livestock Mktg. Assn. (trustee). Republican. Roman Catholic. Home: 2836 N 76th Pl Scottsdale AZ 85251 Office: 8705 E McDowell Scottsdale AZ 85257

JACOBS, ALMA SMITH, librarian; b. Lewistown, Mont., Nov. 21, 1916; d. Martin Luther and Emma Louise (Riley) Smith; B.A., Talladega Coll., 1938; B.S. in L.S., Columbia U., 1942; Litt.D., Mont. State Coll., 1962; L.H.D., Mt. Holyoke Coll., 1968; m. Marcus Jacobs, July 18, 1945. Catalog librarian Great Falls (Mont.) Public Library, 1946-54, librarian, 1954-73; state librarian Mont., Helena, 1973-81. Mem. Am. (exec. bd. 1964-68), Pacific N.W. (pres. 1957), Mont. (pres. 1960) library assns., Delta Kappa Gamma. Home: 1205 Highland Helena MT 59601

JACOBS, DEBORAH EDITHE BLACKMAN, psychologist; b. Tel Aviv, Israel, Feb. 1, 1937 (parents Am. citizens); d. Jerome and Ruby (Freeman) Blackman; B.A., City U.N.Y.-Bklyn. Coll., 1959; M.Ed., Northeastern U., 1970, C.A.G.S., 1971; Ed.D., Boston U., 1975; married; children—Cheryl Lee, J. David, Lauryl Anne, Daniel Bradford. Tchr., N.Y.C. public schs., 1958-59; with Therapeutic Tutorial Services, 1961-69, faculty Peabody Sch. for Emotionally Disturbed, Newton (Mass.) public schs., 1969-70; with counseling dept. Brookline (Mass.) public schs., 1970-71; psychotherapist in pvt. practice Waban (Mass.) Psychol. Assos., 1971—; psychologist/counselor Dover-Sherborn Regional Schs., Dover, Mass., 1972—; mem. adv. bd., cons. in psychotherapy Sudbury (Mass.) Clin. and Cons. Assos., 1980—; faculty Boston Emotionally Disturbed, Newton public schs., 1969-70; faculty Boston U. Med. Center-Smokers Control Center Group Therapy, 1965-69, Medfield State Hosp. Art Therapy, 1969-71, Walden Mental Health Clinic, 1971-72; cons. North Shore Campfire Girls, Multi-Service Center, Newton, Wellesley, Weston; parent advocate cons. Office for Children. Mem. Mass. Psychol. Assn., Am. Psychol. Assn., Mass. Tchrs. Assn., NEA, Mass. Sch. Psychologists, Mass. Personnel and Guidance Assn., Women Counselors and Therapists of Mass., Am. Assn. Family Therapists and Counselors, Parent Counseling Assn. New Eng., LWV, NOW, Am. Assn. Coll. Women, Phi Delta Kappa, Kappa Delta Pi. Author: A Practical Application of Play Therapy in the Public School Setting; Debby and the Sharing Club, A Child's Introduction to Play Therapy in the Group Setting, 1973; Helping Children: Readings in the Practice of Working Therapeutically with Children, 1974. Home: 50 Roslyn Rd Waban MA 02168 Office: 137 Farm St Dover MA 02030 also 50 Roslyn Rd Waban MA 02168

JACOBS, ELEANOR ALICE, clin. psychologist; b. Royal Oak, Mich., Dec. 25, 1923; d. Roy Dana and Alice Ann (Keaton) Jacobs; B.A., U. Buffalo, 1949, M.A., 1952, Ph.D., 1955. Chief psychology service VA Med. Center, Buffalo, 1954—, equal employment opportunity counselor, 1962-79; clin. prof. SUNY, Buffalo, 1950—. Speaker on psychology to community orgns., clubs, 1952—. Past mem. adult devel. and aging com. NICHD, Dept. Health, Edn. and Welfare. Recipient Outstanding Superior Performance award Buffalo VA Hosp., 1958; Spl. Recognition award State U. N.Y. at Buffalo, 1971; Adminstrs. commendation VA, Washington, 1974; Dirs. commendation VA Med. Center, Buffalo, 1978; named Woman of Year, Bus. and Profl. Women's Club Buffalo, 1973. Mem. Am., Eastern, N.Y. State psychol. assns., Am. Group Psychotherapy Assn., Am. Soc. Group Psychotherapy and Psychodrama, Nat., Western N.Y. leagues nursing, Psychol. Assn. Western N.Y. (Disting. Achievement award 1976), Group Psychotherapy Assn. Western N.Y., Undersea Med. Soc., N.Y. Acad. Sci., Assn. Advancement Women in Sci. Research and publs. on hyperbaric medicine, hyperoxygenation effect on cognitive functions in aged. Home: 221 Pleasant Ave N Ridgeway ON L0S 1N0 Canada Office: VA Hosp 3495 Bailey Av Buffalo NY 14215

JACOBS, GLORIA MARGARET, state ofcl.; b. Colfax, Wash., July 28, 1924; d. Merle Haley and Kathryn Lois (Shoemaker) Price; A.A., Western Wash. U., 1972; m. Nile Harvey Vande Mark, July 3, 1941 (div. 1951); children—David B., Cassandra Mae Van de Mark Lown, William Nile, Kathryn Rose Van de Mark Binkley; m. 2d, George Henry Jacobs, Sr., Oct. 16, 1954 (dissolved 1981); children—Lois A. Jacobs McKee, Alice Lynne Jacobs Baxter, Mildred Bernice Jacobs Baxter, George Henry. Checker, Chroma-Crystalike Photo Finishing Co., Tacoma, 1961-63; community counselor trainee Community Mental Health Clinic, Tacoma, 1966; community counselor Make Opportunity Rehab. Econs. Inc., Puyallup, Wash., 1966-67; br. mgr. Rural Econ. Opportunity Inc., Parkland, Wash., 1967-68, acting dir., 1968, field rep., asst. to dir., 1968-70; social service asst. III, Office of Econ. Opportunity State of Wash., Olympia, 1970-73, community affairs asst., 1973-74, community affairs cons. I, 1974-80, community program developer II, 1980—. Baha'i. Home: 4401 Saratoga Pl NE #1 Olympia WA 98506 Office: Planning and Community Affairs Agency 9th St and Columbia Bldg Olympia WA 98504

JACOBS, JIMMIE SPARKMAN, owner, mgr. real estate; b. Gainesboro, Tenn., Sept. 13, 1932; d. James Merlin and Evelyn Christine (Roberts) Sparkman; B.S., Middle Tenn. State U., 1960; M.A., George Peabody Coll. for Tchrs., 1964, Ed.S., 1968; m. Harold Thomas Jacobs, July 5, 1980; children—Steven M., Victoria C., Teresa J. Tchr. public schs., Nashville, 1960-72; realtor Baker-Harwell Realtors, Inc., Nashville, 1974-76; owner, mgr. real estate, Nashville, 1966-78, Bonita Springs, Fla., 1978—. Originator team teaching program public schs., Nashville, 1969. Mem. NEA, Tenn. Edn. Assn., Middle Tenn. Edn. Assn., DAR. Republican. Baptist. Author: Eighty-eight Years with Sarah Polk, 1972; The River's Course, 1974. Home: 26897 Hickory Blvd Bonita Springs FL 33923

JACOBS, JOAN FELICIA DIPANGRAZIO, pharmacist; v. Dennison, Ohio, July 10, 1925; d. Serafino Ernesto and Concetta (DiGiacinto) diPangrazio; B.Sc. in Pharmacy, Ohio State U., 1948; cert. health facility adminstr., Indpls. Med. Center, 1975; D.Pharm., Ind. Bd. Pharmacy, 1980; m. Forest Robert Jacobs, Sept. 18, 1948; 1 son, Forest Robert. Engaged in retail pharmacy mgmt., 1948-55; dir. pharmacy Clark County Hosp., Jeffersonville, Ind., 1956-60; staff pharmacist VA Med. Center, Louisville, 1960—; securities dealer, 1968-72; propr. Healthfax, health care cons. pharmacy, 1977—; cons., speaker in field. Fellow Am. Soc. Cons. Pharmacists; mem. Am. Soc. Hosp. Pharmacists, Am. Soc. Parenteral and Enteral Nutrition, Nat. Intravenous Therapy Assn., Am. Heart Assn., AAUW (Disting. Service award Ky. chpt. 1970), Nat. Assn. Female Execs., Ky. Pharm. Assn., Ky. Soc. Hosp. Pharmacists, Ind. Pharm. Assn., Jefferson County Acad. Pharmacy, Ohio State U. Alumni Assn. (life, bd. govs. Louisville chpt. 1982—), Ohio State U. Devel. Fund. Roman Catholic. Club: Louisville Arts. Home: 409 Springwood Ln Louisville KY 40207 Office: 800 Zorn Ave Louisville KY 40202

JACOBS, JUDITH BULA, psychiat. social worker; b. Lyons, Kans., Nov. 29, 1949; d. Ralph Elmer and Fay Elizabeth (Haeckel) Bula; B.Social Work with honors, Kans. U., 1972, M.S.W., 1973; Ph.D., Bryn Mawr Coll., 1982; m. James Stephen Jacobs, May 23, 1971. Asst. dir. psychiat. social services Carrier Clinic Found., Belle Mead, N.J., 1973-76; pvt. practice marital counseling, lectr., cons. marital and family services, Jenkintown, Pa., 1976-80; mem. faculty Westchester Inst. for Tng. in Counseling and Psychotherapy, Mt. Kisco, N.Y., 1981—; mem. staff Hudson River Counseling Service, Mt. Kisco, 1981—. Mem. Acad. Cert. Social Workers, Nat. Assn. Social Workers, Nat. Council Family Relations, Soc. Psychol. Study Social Issues, Internat. Human Learning Resources Network, NOW, Conn. Assn. Social Workers. Address: 40 Glen Hill Rd Wilton CT 06897

JACOBS, JUDITH H., health adminstr.; b. Boston, Apr. 20, 1948; d. Leonard and Marion L. (Izen) J.; B.S., U. Mass., 1970; M.P.H., U. N.C., 1971, Dr.P.H., 1974. Dir. edn. Planned Parenthood League of Mass., Newton Centre, 1972-73; asst. prof. U. Mass., 1973-74, dir. devel. disabilities program, 1973-74; research asso. Harvard U., 1974-76; asst. prof. dept. health edn. Temple U., 1976-77; compliance officer, then asst. chief Community Mental Health Services Support br. NIMH, Rockville, Md., from 1977, acting chief until 1982, research scientist div. biometry and epidemiology, 1982—; mem. faculty Johns Hopkins U., Balt., 1981—. Mem. Am. Public Health Assn. Club: Washington Women's Art Collective. Contbr. articles to profl. publs. Office: NIMH 5600 Fishers Ln Rockville MD 20857

JACOBS, KAREN LOUISE, lab. adminstr.; b. Kingston, N.Y., May 7, 1943; d. William Charles and Vera Elizabeth (Kelly) Jacobs; B.S. in Applied Tech., Empire State Coll., 1976; M.S. in Public Service Adminstrn., Russell Sage Coll., 1982. Sr. lab. technician, hosp. lab. supr. City of Kingston (N.Y.) Labs., 1962-68; sr. research asst. Dudley Obs., Albany, N.Y., 1972-75; lab. adminstr. Albany Med. Coll., 1976—, mem. faculty, 1982—. Active Sierra Club. Mem. Clin. Lab. Mgmt. Assn., Blood Banks Assn. of N.Y. State, Am. Soc. Clin. Pathologists. Home: 37B Picotte Dr Albany NY 12208 Office: Albany Med Coll Div Oncology 47 New Scotland Ave Albany NY 12208

JACOBS, LILLY, import-export co. exec.; b. Mexico City, Aug. 22, 1936; came to U.S., 1970; d. Horace H. and Luz G. J.; ed. in computer sci. IBM Sch., Mexico City, 1966-68; children—Alfonso, Lilly Ann, Carlos, Alex. Sales mgr. Bellavista Real Estate Devel., Mexico City, 1968-70, San Antonio Shores, Rosarito Beach, Baja, California, Mex., 1971-78; dir. Playas De Tijuana (Mex.), 1978-80; mgr. Improcosa, Tijuana, 1980-82; pres. Indsl. Exports, La Jolla, Calif., 1982—; v.p. Fratel, S.A., Panama Corp., Alejandrina, Inc. Mem. Sales and Mktg. Execs. (public relations officer chpt. 1970-82), Advt. Assos. Mex., San Diego Mus. Art, Club Madrugadores Tijuana. Roman Catholic. Club: Cuernavaca Country. Home: Coral Tree Plaza Apt 4A 3634 7th Ave San Diego CA 92103 Office: 8950 Villa La Jolla Dr Suite 2230 La Jolla CA 92037

JACOBS, LINDA LEE, hosp. adminstr.; b. Lincoln, Nebr., Apr. 18, 1949; d. Jacob and Darleen Rose (Worster) J.; B.S., U. Nebr., 1971. Gastrointestinal asst. Bryan Meml. Hosp., Lincoln, Nebr., 1972-78, chief gastrointestinal asst., 1978-81, supr. gastrointestinal lab., 1981—, mem. employee adv. com., 1973-74; dir. Jacobs Constrn. Co., Inc., Lincoln. Active Vols. in Probation. Mem. Nat. Soc. Gastrointestinal Assts. (pres. 1980-81, chmn. nominating com. 1981-82, ex officio dir. at large 1981—, editor jour. 1981—). Nat. Assn. Female Execs., Am. Legion Aux., Gamma Phi Beta Alumnae (corp. bd.). Republican. Club: Does (Lincoln, Nebr.). Home: 2624 Austin Dr Lincoln NE 68506 Office: 4848 Sumner St Lincoln NE 68506

JACOBS, MARIAN BECKMANN, geologist; b. Teaneck, N.J., Dec. 20, 1935; d. Frederick J. and Marguerite J. (Thoma) Beckmann; B.A. cum laude (Grace Potter Rice fellow), Barnard Coll., 1957; M.A. (Columbia scholar, Quincy Ward Boese fellow, James Furman Kemp fellow), Columbia, 1959, Ph.D., 1963; m. Warren R. Jacobs Jr., Sept. 5, 1959 (dec.); children—Laura Diane, Anita Michelle; m. 2d, Donald H. Norman, Jan. 9, 1975 (dec.). Research asst. mineralogy dept. Columbia, N.Y.C., 1960-63; research asso. Lamont-Doherty Geol. Obs. of Columbia, Palisades, N.Y., 1963—; asst. prof. oceanography Ramapo Coll. of N.J., Mahwah, 1974-76; sr. analyst market and industry research for polyolefins and spl. chems. ARCO Chem. Co., Inc. subs. Atlantic Richfield Co., 1976—. NSF grantee, 1965-66, 66-67, 69-71, 71-72, 72-73. Mem. Am. Geophsy. Union, Am. AAAS, Mineral. Soc. Am., Geol. Soc. Am., Clay Minerals Soc., N.J. Acad. Sci., Hudson River Environmental Soc., Phi Beta Kappa, Sigma Xi. Contbr. articles to profl. jours. Research X-ray diffractions and fluorescence studies deep-sea sediments and particulate matter in sea water. Home: 7 Robin Rd PO Box 572 Mahwah NJ 07430 Office: Arco Chem Co 1500 Market St Philadelphia PA 19101

JACOBS, MARY SHARRON, librarian; b. Endicott, N.Y., June 19, 1947; d. John Arnold and Evelyn Grace Jacobs; student U. Buffalo, 1965-68, M.L.S., SUNY, Geneseo, 1971. Dir., David A. Howe Public Library, Wellsville, N.Y., 1972—. Librarian, The Little Ch., 1978—. Mem. Allegany County Library Assn. (v.p. 1981-83), N.Y. State Library Assn., ALA. Republican. Office: 155 N Main St Wellsville NY 14895

JACOBS, PATRICIA DIANNE, trade assn. exec.; b. Camden, Ark., Jan. 27, 1950; d. Felix H. and Helen M. (Tate) J.; B.A., Lincoln U., 1970; J.D., Harvard U., 1973. Asst. dir. fin. aid Lincoln U., Pa., 1970; admitted to N.Y. State bar, 1973, D.C. bar, 1979; tax counsel Exxon Corp., N.Y.C., 1973-74; partner firm Pickett & Jennings, Newark, 1974-75; asst. prof. John Jay Coll. Criminal Justice, N.Y.C., 1974-75; asst. minority counsel U.S. Senate Small Bus. Com., Washington, 1975-77; chief adminstrv. officer Am. Assn. of Minority Enterprise Small Bus. Investment Cos., Washington, 1977—. Bd. dirs. Rockefeller Found., 1977—, Council on Founds., 1980—, Center for Youth Affairs, 1980—. Mem. Nat. Bar Assn., Am. Bar Assn., Ark. Bar Assn., D.C. Bar Assn., Nat. Assn. Minority Trade Assn. Execs., Potomac Fiscal Soc., Coalition of 100 Black Women of D.C., Assn. Black Found. Execs. (dir. 1979—), AAUP, LWV, Alpha Kappa Alpha.

JACOBS, RUTH HARRIET, sociologist, educator; b. Boston, Nov. 15, 1924; d. Samuel J. and Jane G. Miller; B.S., Boston U., 1964; Ph.D., Brandeis U., 1969; m. Neal Jacobs, Aug. 1948 (div.); children—Eliha, Edith. Reporter, feature writer Herald-Traveler, Boston, 1943-49; tchr. Mass. Bay Community Coll., Northeastern U., 1961-69; mem. faculty Boston U., 1969-82, prof. sociology, 1969-82; prof., chmn. dept. sociology Clark U., Worcester, Mass., 1982—; cons. in field. Grantee NIMH, 1972-75; postdoctoral fellow NSF, 1977-78. Mem. Am. Sociol. Assn., Soc. Sci. Study Social Problems, Clin. Sociology Assn., Eastern Sociol. Assn., Mass. Sociol. Assn. (v.p. 1979), Boston Soc. Gerontol. Psychiatry. Jewish. Author: Life After Youth; Female, Forty, What Next, 1979; also articles, chpts. in books; co-author: Re-engagement in Later Life: Re-employment and Re-marriage, 1979. Home: 75 High Ledge Ave Wellesley MA 02181 Office: Dept Sociology Clark U Worcester MA 01610

JACOBS, SHERRY RAPHAEL, lawyer; b. Weehawken, N.J., June 29, 1943; d. Leon L. and Fay (Silverstein) Raphael; B.A., Fairleigh Dickinson U., 1967; J.D., Loyola U., Chgo., 1970; m. Stephen E. Jacobs, Jan. 4, 1976; children by previous marriage—Jeremiah Raphael and Deborah Feinsmith. Admitted to Ill. bar, 1970, N.Y. State bar, 1974; asso. firm Weil, Gotshal & Manges, N.Y.C., 1972-75, Wachtel, Lipton, Rosen & Katz, N.Y.C., 1975-76; asso. counsel Este Lauder, Inc., N.Y.C., 1976-77; v.p. legal R.H. Macy & Co., Inc., N.Y.C., 1977-79; v.p., gen. counsel Saks Fifth Ave., N.Y.C., 1979—. Co-chmn. New Leadership div. State of Israel Bonds, 1980-81. Mem. Am. Bar Assn., N.Y. State Bar Assn., N.Y. County Bar Assn., Assn. Bar City N.Y. Home: 180 East End Ave New York NY 10028 Office: 611 Fifth Ave New York NY 10022

JACOBSEN, DOROTHY HELEN CALDWELL, occupational therapist; b. Algona, Iowa, Aug. 19, 1935; d. Harry Vincent and Beulah Ramona (Larsen) Caldwell; B.A. in Occupational Therapy, U. Iowa, 1957; m. Eric Kasner Jacobsen, Mar. 30, 1957; 1 son, Steven Keith. Occupational therapist St. Louis County (Mo.) Spl. Dist. of Edn. for Severely Handicapped Children, Brentwood, 1960-64; dir. occupational therapy St. Luke's Hosp., St. Louis, 1964-69; instr. U. Kans., 1970-71; pvt. practice occupational therapy, phys. dysfunction and sensory dysfunction, Chagrin Falls, Ohio, 1971—; cons. in field. Lic. profl. therapist. Mem. Am., Ohio occupational therapy assns., Center for the Study of Sensory Integrative Dysfunction. Presbyterian. Home: 16 Louise Dr Chagrin Falls OH 44022

JACOBSEN, JULIA MILLS, ednl. adminstr.; b. Princeton, N.J., July 26, 1923; d. Alan Balch and Mary (Handlan) Mills; A.B., Sweet Briar (Va.) Coll., 1945; m. Lawrence Jacobsen, Sept. 7, 1945; children—John Lawrence, Mary Mills. Tchr., dir. alumnae and devel. Holton-Arms Sch., Washington, 1954-62; pres. Baker, Jacobsen and Sanders Inc., Washington, 1962-65; exec. v.p. Edutech, Inc., Washington, 1965-67; dir. govt. relations and sponsored programs Sweet Briar Coll., 1967—; spl. asst. research/contracts and grants Washington office U. So. Calif., 1979—; v.p., dir. Assn. Affiliated Coll. and Univ. Offices, 1978—; mem. Nat. Adv. Council Edn. Professions Devel., 1973-76, Va. Adv. Council Community Service and Continuing Edn., 1977-80; mem. adv. com. Va. Council Higher Edn., Research and Devel., 1972-80; cons. in field. Mem. D.C. Med. Care Adv. Council, 1973-76; mem. public relations adv. bd. USO, 1978—; bd. dirs. Vis. Nurse Assn., Washington, 1970—, pres., 1973-76. Mem. Nat. Council Univ. Research Adminstrs. (sec.-treas. 1973-77), Soc. Research Adminstrs. (exec. com. 1981-82), Council Advancement and Support Edn., Jr. League Washington. Republican. Episcopalian. Clubs: Sulgrave, Fed. City. Author papers, reports, directories in field. Office: 1701 K St NW Suite 701 Washington DC 20006

JACOBSEN, NANCY EILEEN, fabric designer, educator; b. Menominee, Mich., Nov. 1, 1948; d. Jesse J. and Helen N. (O'Hara) J.; student Barat Coll. of Sacred Heart, 1966-67; B.S. in Related Arts, U. Wis., 1970. Mgr. art needlecraft dept. Ruhama's Yarn and Fabric Co., Milw., 1970-71, mgr., 1970-71; instr. needlecrafts and quilting Emily Griffith Opportunity Sch., Denver, 1972-77; instr. needlecrafts U. No. Colo., Greely, 1977—; instr. Am. Sch. Needlework, 1979, Elsa Williams Sch. Needle Art, 1981-82; free lance sales in quilting and clothing, Chgo., 1973-74, N.Y.C., 1972-74, Milw., 1974, Denver, 1972—; Learning for Living instr. Adult Edn. Program, Met. State Coll., Denver, 1973-76; cons. in restoration of antique quilts Molly Brown House, Denver, 1974-75; designer of Colo. Centennial Needlepoint Tapestry, 1975; mem. Fashion Group, Inc., 1976; co-chmn. Denver lectr. series, 1978; clothing, needlepoint designer Nancy Jacobsen Designs. Mem. jr. advisory bd. Bonfils Theatre, Denver. AIA grantee, 1975. Mem. Am. Needlepoint Guild (pres. Colo. chpt. 1978, instr.), Jr. League Denver, Denver Art Mus., Delta Gamma Alumnae (pres. 1975-77). Office: PO Box 6479 Denver CO 80206

JACOBSEN, PHEBE R., archivist; b. Balt., Mar. 24, 1922; d. Orris Gravenor and Dorothy (Medders) Robinson; A.B., Western Md. Coll., 1943; m. Bryce DuVal Jacobsen, Oct. 16, 1943; children—Eric Gravenor, Kristin Bryce. Tchr., Clifton Forge (Va.) High Sch., 1943, Chestertown (Md.) High Sch., 1943; jr. asst. research technician, archivist IV, Div. Public Records, Harrisburg, Pa., 1955-58; profl. researcher Historic Annapolis (Md.), Inc., 1958-60; jr. archivist Md. Hall Records, Annapolis, 1960-63, archivist II, 1964-66, archivist III, 1967-73, archivist IV, head research room and spl. collections, 1973—; mem. Md. Gov's. Commn. Afro-Am. History and Culture, vice chmn., 1980—. Mem. Soc. Am. Archivists, Mid-Atlantic Regional Archives Conf., Swarthmore Coll. Peace Collection (mem. adv. council), Md. Hist. Soc. (mem. geneal. com.). Author: (with Morris L. Radoff and Gust Skordas) The County Courthouses and Records of Maryland, Part II, The Records, 1963; Quaker Records in Maryland, 1967; (with Gregory Stiverson) William Paca, A Biography, 1976. Office: Box 828 Annapolis MD 21404

JACOBSON, DEBRA ANN, lawyer; b. Kingston, N.Y., Mar. 20, 1952; d. Charles and Esther (Tasker) Denkensohn; B.A. summa cum laude in Environ. Studies, U. Rochester (N.Y.), 1974; J.D. with honors, George Washington U., 1977; m. David Edward Jacobson, Aug. 10, 1975. Admitted to N.Y. bar, 1979; congressional legis. asst., 1977-79; counsel subcom. on oversight and investigations, com. energy and commerce U.S. Ho. Reps., 1979—; dir.-at-large Women's Council Energy and Environ., 1981—. Recipient award Delta Labs., 1972. Mem. Nature Conservancy. Office: 2323 Rayburn House Office Bldg Washington DC 20515

JACOBSON, GLORIA NADINE, coll. adminstr.; b. Jewell, Iowa, July 12, 1930; d. Christian Frederick and Amanda M. (Englebart) Larson; B.B.A., U. Iowa, 1974; m. Richard T. Jacobson, July 22, 1951; children—Richard Thomas, Douglas L., William Andrew. Mem. adminstrn. staff U. Iowa, Iowa City, 1950—, asst. to the dean Coll. of Pharmacy, 1981—. Mem. Phi Gamma Nu, Kappa Epsilon. Republican. Lutheran. Home: 415 Ridgeview Iowa City IA 52240 Office: U of Iowa Coll of Pharmacy Iowa City IA 52242

JACOBSON, HELEN G. (MRS. DAVID JACOBSON), civic worker; b. San Antonio, Tex.; d. Jac Elton and Rosetta (Dreyfus) Gugenheim; B.A., Hollins Coll.; m. David Jacobson, Nov. 6, 1938; children—Elizabeth, Dorothy (Mrs. Sam Miller). News, spl. events staff NBC, N.Y.C., 1933-38. First v.p. San Antonio, Bexar County council Girl Scouts U.S.A., 1957-63; Tex. State rep. UNICEF, 1964-69; bd. dirs. U.S. com. UNICEF, 1970-80, hon. bd. dirs., 1980—; bd. dirs. Nat. Fedn. Temple Sisterhoods, 1973-77, Temple Beth-El Sisterhood; v.p. Youth Alternatives, Inc.; bd. dirs. United Way of Tex.; bd. dirs. Community Guidance Center, chmn. bd., 1960-63; bd. dirs. Sunshine Cottage Sch. for Deaf Children, chmn. bd., 1952-54; pres. Community Welfare Council, 1968-70; pres. bd. trustees San Antonio Pub. Library, 1957-61; trustee Nat. Council Crime and Delinquency, 1964-70, San Antonio Mus. Assn., 1964-73; bd. dirs., sec. Cancer Therapy and Research Found. South Tex., Tex. Council Crime and Delinquency, Am. Inst. Character Edn.; pres. S.W. region Tex. Coalition for Juvenile Justice, 1977-79; chmn. Mayor's Commn. on Status of Women, 1972-74; del. White House Conf. on Children, 1970; mem. Commn. on Social Action of Reform Judaism, 1973-77; chmn. Foster Grandparent project Bexar County Hosp. Dist., 1968-69; sec. Nat. Assembly for Social Policy and Devel., 1969-74; pres. women's com. Ecumenical Center for Religion and Health, 1975-77; mem. criminal justice planning com. Alamo Area Council of Govts., chmn., 1975-77; mem. Tex. Internat. Women's Yr. Coordinating Com., 1977; co-chmn. San Antonio chpt. NCCJ. Recipient Headliner award for civic work Theta Sigma Phi, San Antonio chpt., 1958; named Vol. Woman of Yr., Express-News, 1959; honoree San Antonio chpt. NCCJ, 1970, Nat. Jewish Hosp., 1978; Nat. Humanitarian award B'nai B'rith, 1975; Hannah G. Solomon award Nat. Council Jewish Women, 1979, others. Mem. San Antonio Women's Fedn., Nat. Council Jewish Women, Symphony Soc. (women's com.). Club: Argyle. Home: 207 Beechwood Ln San Antonio TX 78216

JACOBSON, JUNE, psychotherapist; b. Worcester, Mass., June 6, 1929; d. James Allen and Agnes May (Cunningham) Fusca; B.A., Mich. State U., 1965, Ednl. Specialist, 1976; children—David, Matthew, Paul. Coordinator, Listening Ear Crisis Center, East Lansing, Mich., 1969-72; counselor Mich. State U. Counseling Center, East Lansing, 1973-76; social worker Psychol. and Behavioral Consultants, East Lansing,

1976—; cons. Child Abuse and Neglect Council. Recipient public service citation East Lansing City Council, 1972. Mem. Am. Psychol. Assn. (asso.), Am. Personnel and Guidance Assn., Phi Kappa Phi. Office: 5020 Northwind Dr Suite 201 East Lansing MI 48823

JACOBSON, LILLIAN ESTHER, ret. radiol. physicist; b. N.Y.C.; d. Lazar Benjamin and Betty (Blumberg) Jacobson; B.A., Cornell U., 1925; M.A., Columbia, 1932; m. William V. Tenzel, Oct. 26, 1933; children—Joan Louise Davis, James Henry. Physicist, Crile Clinic, Cleve., 1925-28, physicist to Dr. Gustave Bucky, N.Y.C., 1928-31; radiation physicist Montefiore Hosp., Bronx, N.Y., 1931-55; biophysicist Presbyn. Hosp. unit United Hosps. of Newark, 1956-66; radiation physicist L.I. U. Hosp., 1968-78; cons. radiol. physicist; tchr. physics, N.Y.C. Mem. AAAS, Am. Assn. Physicists in Medicine, Health Physics Soc. (pres. Greater N.Y. chpt. 1965-66), Radiation Research Soc., Biophys. Soc., Soc. Nuclear Medicine (founding mem., pres. N.Y. chpt. 1959-60), Radium Soc., Radiol. Soc. N. Am., Cornell Women's Club N.Y. (sec. 1934-35), Phi Beta Kappa. Contbr. papers to teach lit. Address: 3964 46th St Long Island City NY 11104

JACOBSON, NITA JEAN GROSSMAN (MRS. IRWIN ROBERT JACOBSON), educator; b. Boston; d. Joseph Arthur and Sadie (Feldberg) Grossman; student Syracuse U.; B.S., Boston U.; M.Ed., Northeastern U.; m. Irwin Robert Jacobson, Mar. 20, 1955; children—Lisa Faye, Barry Steven. Tchr., Plympton Sch., Waltham, Mass., 1952-55; dean of women Emerson Coll., Boston, 1965-68; cons., dir. edn. research Spl. Legislative Commn. on Drug Abuse State Mass., Boston, 1968-70; pres. Nat. Ednl. Evaluation Services, Inc., 1971—; dir. employee edn. Faulkner Hosp., Jamaica Plain, Mass., 1976-79; cons. mgmt. skills and human resources to health industry. Mass. commr. Edn. Commn. of States, 1971-73; cons. div. occupational and vocat. edn. Mass. Dept. Edn., 1976. Trustee Parker Hill Med. Center, 1961—, rec. sec., 1963-64, asst. sec. bd. trustees, 1969-74, sec. to bd. trustees, 1975-77, v.p., 1977—; mem. exec. bd. Womens Scholarship, 1969-70; mem. exec. bd. Friends League Sch. Boston, 1968—. Mem. Nat., Mass. assns. women deans and counselors, NEA, Nat. Assn. Adminstrv. Women, Am. Ednl. Research Assn., AAUW, Am., Mass., Boston personnel and guidance assns., Am. Assn. Higher Edn., Nat. Vocational Guidance Assn., Child Study Assn. Am., Am. Counselor Edn. Suprs., Brookline Mental Health Assn., Brookline Chamber Music Soc., Internat. Child Study Assn., Pi Lambda Theta, Kappa Delta Pi, Phi Kappa Phi. Mem. B'nai B'rith, Hadassah. Home: 152 Beverly Rd Chestnut Hill MA 02167

JACOBSON, PATRICIA OLENCHALK, mortgage co. exec.; b. Luzerne, Pa., Oct. 17, 1939; d. John Joseph and Mary Ann (Skerut) Olenchalk; student pvt. and pub. schs., New Britain, Conn.; m. Nicholas Jacobson, Jan. 11, 1975; 1 son, Albert J. Moseley; stepchildren—Karla Pelletier, Kris Jacobson. Clk. typist Household Fin. Corp., New Britain, Conn., 1956-70, asst. mgr., 1970-71, mgr., Nashua, N.H., 1971-74, Atlanta, 1974; inventory clk. Montgomery Ward, Newington, N.H., 1974; mgr. Burgher Haus Restaurant, Manchester, N.H., 1976-77; loan counselor Manchester Bank, 1977-78, mcht. devel. rep., 1978-79, sr. loan counselor and personal banking officer, 1979; mgr. mortgage processing Bank East Mortgage Corp., Manchester, 1979-82, asst. v.p. ops., 1982—. Mem. Greater Manchester Bus. and Profl. Women's Club (treas.), Nat. Assn. Bank Women, Nat. Assn. Female Execs., YWCA. Republican. Congregationalist. Home: 35 N Reading St Manchester NH 03104 Office: 1138 Elm St Manchester NH 03105

JACOBSON, ROVENA FURNIVALL (MRS. CALHOUN E. JACOBSON), educator, writer; b. Los Angeles, Oct. 21; d. Joseph Walter and Florence (Gieson) Furnivall; B.Ed., U. Calif. at Los Angeles, 1940; M.Ed., Loyola U., Los Angeles, 1965; Ed.D., U. So. Calif., 1969; m. Calhoun E. Jacobson, Aug. 6, 1941; children—Denise Rovena (Mrs. Jeremy Ferris), Eric Calhoun. Tchr. Mojave (Calif.) Elem. Sch., 1941-42; adult edn. classes in art and home econ. Downey, Rivera, and Bellflower, Calif., 1944-52; tchr., counselor Santa Monica City, Calif., 1952—; psychol. cons. film Runaway, Runaway, (released in Eng. as You Can't Run Away From Sex); producer Interchange, KCRW-FM radio sta., Los Angeles; dir. Malibu programs Santa Monica Coll., 1975; moderator unit 4, KTTV, 1976; cons. film For The Very First Time, Hillcrest Prodns. Pres., chmn. bd. dirs. Assn. for Women's Active Return to Edn., 1965—. Recipient Minerva award Avare Internat., 1975. Mem. Nat. Assn. Bus. and Profl. Women, Calif. Tchrs. Assn., Nat. Assn. Pub. Sch. Adult Edn., AAUW (Status of Women award Santa Monica br. 1967), Calif. Coll. Personnel Assn. (sec. 1973-74), Cal. Personnel and Guidance Assn., Am. Women in Radio and TV, Phi Mu, Pi Lambda Theta. Presbyn. Club: Malibu Woman's. Author: (with Denise Ferris) It's Your Baby, Baby. Community coll. editor Open Channels quar. Home: 6804 Zumirez Dr Malibu CA 90265 Office: 1900 Pico Blvd Santa Monica CA 90403

JACOBSON, RUTH ANNETTE KRAUSÉ, public relations counselor; b. Watertown, N.Y., June 30, 1925; d. Thomas Murray Russell and Ruth Elizabeth (Parmelee) Krausé; B.S. in Journalism, Northwestern U., 1947; postgrad. U. Chgo.; 1 dau., Anne Heyliger Jacobson (Mrs. Jules Rosen). Guest editor Mademoiselle mag., N.Y.C., 1945; with Howard G. Mayer & Assos., Chgo., 1947-48; Midwest area rep. CARE, Inc., Chgo., 1948-50; account exec. Harshe-Rotman & Druck, Chgo., 1950-51; counselor, sr. partner, dir. spl. events Fleishman-Hillard, Inc., St. Louis, 1957—. Community adv. bd. Sta. KWMU, U. Mo., 1978—; bd. dirs. Gateway chpt. Cystic Fibrosis Found., 1981—; 2d v.p., bd. dirs. Chatillon-DeMenil House Found., 1965—; bd. dirs. Downtown St. Louis, Inc., 1975—; pres.'s adv. cabinet Greater St. Louis council Girl Scouts U.S.A., 1980—; bd. dirs. Grace Hill Episcopal Settlement House, 1976—; bd. dirs. Vis. Nurse Assn., 1965-71, Vocat. Counseling and Rehab. Services, Inc., 1973—. Jr. Achievement Miss. Valley, 1975—, St. Louis Soc. for Blind, 1978-80, Miss. Vanderschmidt's Secretarial Sch., 1978—, YWCA, 1979—, St. Louis Conservatory and Schs. for the Arts, 1979—, St. Louis U. Assos. of the Libraries, 1979, St. Louis Ambassadors, 1981—, St. Louis Assn. Retarded Children, 1981—; trustee Mary Inst., 1979—, Mo. Hist. Soc., 1981; counselor-at-large to bd. dirs. on public relations Landmarks Assn. St. Louis, Inc., 1976-77; public relations adv. bd. Nat. Park Service of Dept. of Interior, 1965-70. Mem. Public Relations Soc. Am. (sec. St. Louis chpt. 1962-64), Dance St. Louis, Women in Communications, Friends of City Art Mus., Nat. Trust Hist. Preservation (public relations com.), Assn. Churchill Fellows (Winston Churchill Meml. and Library in U.S., Westminster Coll., Fulton, Mo.), St. Louis Pinch-Hitters, Inc., St. Louis Symphony Soc. Women's Assn., Media Club. Episcopalian. Clubs: Media, Noonday (dir.). Home: 5 Little Ln Saint Louis MO 63124 Office: 1 Memorial Dr Saint Louis MO 63102

JACOBSON, SELMA MARIA ELIZABETH, educator; b. Joliet, Ill., Oct. 10, 1906; d. Albin August and Bertha (Thorsson) Jacobson; student Chgo. Tchrs. Coll., 1924-26; Ph.B., DePaul U., Chgo., 1933; M.A., Northwestern U., 1943; student arts and crafts, Sweden, 1950-51. Tchr. home econs. Chgo. Bd. Edn., 1926-33, 2d through 8th grade, 1933-38, tchr. home mechanics, 1938-69, home mechanics curriculum cons., 1943-48; tchr. spl. courses, Södertalje, Sweden, 1951-53, 56-58; creator Comparative Edn. Study tours in Scandinavia, 1960-66, Scandinavian Pioneer Trails midwestern tours, 1969-73; creator Swedish Pioneer Archives, Chgo., 1960, now archivist, curator; asst. dir. Swedish Mus. of Chgo. Area; narrator Viking Myths and Home Life, Mus. Sci. and Industry, Chgo., 1982; exhibitor Holiday Folk Fair, Chgo., 1959—. Hon. pres. Central Swedish Commn. Chgo. Area, 1969-79; mem. Chgo. and Ill. commns. for Bicentennial, 1974-76. Decorated knight Royal Order Vasa (Sweden), comdr. Royal Order of No. Star; named one of Chicagoland 100, 1971, Citizen of Yr., Lerner News, 1979; recipient Charlotta medal Swedish Emigrant Inst. Mem. Textiles, Clothing and Related Arts Forum, Inter-Ethnic Consultation, World Edn. Fellowship, PTA, Chgo. Tchrs. Union, Am. Daus. Sweden, Swedish Pioneer Hist. Soc. (Carl Sandburg medal 1980), Swedish Cultural Soc., Chgo. Hist. Soc., Art Inst. Chgo., Home Econs. Club of Chgo., Am. Assn. State and Local History, Nat. Trust Historic Preservation, Delta Kappa Gamma. Lutheran. Club: Friendship. Author: Gör Det Av Plast. Producer several films on Swedish arts and crafts. Home: 5641 Warwick Ave Chicago IL 60634

JACOBSON, SHERYL FRAN, psychologist; b. Bklyn., Dec. 2, 1948; s. David and Betty (Simon) Jacobson; B.A., Bklyn. Coll., 1969; M.A. in Coll. Counseling, Hunter Coll., 1971; Ph.D. in Counseling Psychology, N.Y. U., 1977. Psychol. research asst. Downstate Med. Center, SUNY, Bklyn., 1967-69; counseling intern Hunter Coll., 1970-71; research asst. Grad. Center, CUNY, N.Y.C., 1971-72; career counselor Hunter Coll., N.Y.C., 1973-75; career counselor Rutgers U., Newark, 1976-77, asso. dir. counseling and career devel., 1977-79, acting dir. career devel., 1979, dir. career devel., 1980—; pvt. practice clin. psychology, 1977—; cons. for corps., 1978—. Cert. in clin. and counseling psychology, N.Y. State. Mem. Am. Psychol. Assn. (com. on women div. counseling psychology, com. on mentoring div. psychology of women), N.Y. State Psychol. Assn. Editor: Met. N.Y. Coll. Placement Officers Assn. Metro News, 1977-79; book reviewer Jour. Coll. Placement, 1980—, Am. Personnel and Guidance Jour.; research on sex-role variables and women's achievement motivation. Home: 150 E 69th St New York NY 10021 Office: Rutgers U Newark NJ 07102

JACQUES, SHIRLEY PETERSON, vocat. rehab. program specialist; b. Jamestown, N.Y., May 6, 1937; d. Glenn John and Anne G. Peterson; B.A. cum laude in Sociology, U. West Fla., 1974, M.P.A., 1981; m. M. Allan Jacques, Jr., Dec. 29, 1956; children—Scott Allan, Renee Elizabeth, Tami Lynn. File clk. Jamestown Mut. Ins. Co. (N.Y.), 1955-56; secretarial positions Times-Star Newspaper, Cin., 1956-58, Advance Mortgage Corp., Cin., 1958-60; legal sec., Rochester, N.Y., 1961-63; food stamp eligibility specialist Fla. Dept. Health and Rehab. Services, Pensacola, also social worker, research and devel. coordinator, vocat. rehab. counselor, staff devel., tng. specialist, 1974—. Bd. dirs. Escambia County Mental Health Assn.; mem. woman's com. YWCA. Recipient Peggy Dodson Leadership award Pensacola Jr. Woman's Club, 1970. Mem. Am. Soc. Public Adminstrs., Fla. Assn. Health and Social Services (coms.), Aux. ASME, Phi Kappa Phi, Beta Sigma Phi (rec. sec., corr. sec.). Democrat. Methodist. Home: 3865 Hwy 297A Cantonment FL 32533 Office: 160 Government Center Pensacola FL 32501

JAE, sculptress; b. Bklyn., Jan. 9, 1947; d. Benjamin and Shirley Shareff; student Pace U., 1964-68, Inst. dell Arte, Pietrasanta, Italy, 1971-72. Apprentice under Bruno Lucchesi, N.Y.C., 1970-72, Jacques Lipchitz, Italy, 1972-73, Evangelos Moustakis, Greece, 1973, Manola, Spain, 1973; exhbns. include: N.Y. Film Festival, 1972, Artists Showroom, N.Y.C., 1972, 74 Am. Hellenic Soc., Athens, 1973, Marguttiana-Forte dei Marme, Italy, 1973, Gallery Artworks, N.Y.C., 1974, L.I.U., Bklyn., 1975, Del Valentino Gallery, 1975, Nat. Arts Club, 1976, Met. Mus. Art, N.Y.C., 1976, Bklyn. Mus., 1977, Dorothy Rosenthal Gallery, Chgo., 1977, U.S. Naval Acad., Annapolis, 1977, Salmagundi Club, N.Y.C., 1977, Walton-Gilbert Gallery, San Francisco, 1977, Galeria Paco, N.Y.C., 1978, Shayne Gallery, Mont, 1980, Hansen Gallery, 1981, Anton Gallery, Washington, 1981, H. H. Leonard Gallery, Washington, 1982, Patricia Judith Gallery, Ltd., Boca Raton, Fla.; sculpture for Piero Alessandro Giusti, Massa, Italy; tchr. Inst. dell Arte, Pietrasanta, 1973-74. Mem. Artists League Bklyn., Salmagundi Club, Artists Equity. Home: 300 E 54th St New York NY 10022 Studio: 6 E 30th St New York NY 10010

JAEGER, INA CLAIRE, musician, music educator b. Ashtabula, Ohio, July 18, 1929; d. Norman Clare and Vivien Elizabeth (Cole) Burlingham; Mus.B., Eastman Sch. Music, U. Rochester, 1952, Mus.M., 1955; m. Marc Jules Jaeger, June 23, 1973; children—David, Dominic, Olivia. Violinist, Rochester Philharm. Orch., 1953-54; violinist Fla. String Quartet, U. Fla., Gainesville, 1963-66; violinist New Orleans Philharm. Orch., 1966-67; asso. prof. music U. Fla., Gainesville, 1967—. Research grantee U. Fla., 1970 granted research sabbaticals, 1973, 75, 80-81. Mem. Music Educators Nat. Conf., Fla. Music Educators Assn., Sigma Alpha Iota. Lutheran. Author: (with Clementine White) Fundamentals of Music Theory, 1973; Basic Elements in Music Theory: A Modular Program of Instruction, 1976. Home: 519 NW 19th St Gainesville FL 32603 Office: Dept Music U Fla Gainesville FL 32611

JAFFA, AILEEN RABY, ret. librarian, poet, artist; b. Oakland, Calif., Apr. 26, 1900; d. Myer Edward and Adele Rosa (Solomons) J.; A.B., U. Calif., Berkeley, 1922, cert. in librarianship, 1928; m. Milton Jerome Katzky, June 21, 1922 (div.); children—Lawrence Marvin, Joan Elizabeth (dec.). Jr. asst. U. Calif. Library Agrl. Reference Service, Berkeley, 1928-33, agrl. librarian, 1933-62; head Agr. Library, U. Calif., Berkeley, 1956-62, ret., 1962; poet, artist; books include: Three Sonnets, 1939; Trondheims, 1960; Three Dragons Easily, 1963; Word Out of Time, 1965; Tiptoe To the Wind, 1967; Let the Star Shine, 1973; The Forty-First Day, 1978; paintings and sculpture exhibited in Berkeley, Richmond, Modesto and San Francisco, Calif., New Eng. Mem. Calif. Writers Club, Calif. Poetry Soc., Calif. Fedn. Chaparral Poets, Central Calif. Art League, Ina Coolbrith Circle (pres. 1971-72), Nat. League Am. Pen Women, San Francisco Browning Soc., San Francisco Mus. Soc., Modesto Arts Adv. Council, Am. Assn. Ret. Persons, Ret. State Govt. Employees Assn. Calif., U. Calif. Berkeley Sch. Librarianship Alumni Assn., Phi Beta Kappa. Republican. Club: U. Calif. Berkeley Women's Faculty. Home: 1105 Wellesley Ave Modesto CA 95350

JAFFE, MARY SCHUSTER, chemist; b. Bklyn., Jan. 6, 1917; d. Edward and Mary Merritt (Crawford) Schuster; A.B. in Chemistry, Cornell U., 1937; postgrad. N.Y.U., 1942-45; m. Hans Jaffe, Sept. 6, 1947; children—Ann, John. Electron microscopist Interchem. Corp., N.Y.C., 1942-47; chemist Gen. Electric Co., Cleve., 1947—. Founder, bd. dirs., sec. Youth Enrichment Services for Educable Retarded, Cleve. Mem. Am. Chem. Soc., Electron Microscopy Soc. Am., N.Y. Micros. Soc., Soc. Coatings Tech., Kappa Kappa Gamma. Democrat. Unitarian. Patentee in field. Office: Lighting Research and Tech Service Operation 1364 Nela Park Cleveland OH 44112

JAFFE, NORA, visual artist; b. Urbana, Ohio, Feb. 25, 1928; d. Harry Jefferson and Margaret Elizabeth (McNab) Miller; m. Joseph Jaffe, Jan. 19, 1951; children—Lenore A., Kenneth A. One woman shows: Village Art Center, N.Y.C., 1963, A.M. Sachs Gallery, N.Y.C., 1965, Gallery Lasson Modern Art, London, 1970, Open Studio Gallery, Rhinebeck, N.Y., 1978, Vassar Coll., Poughkeepsie, N.Y., 1978; exhibited in group shows at Mus. Modern Art, N.Y.C., 1961, 63, Balt. Mus. Art, 1963, Pa. Acad. Fine Arts, 1964, 67, 68, L.I. U., 1966, A.M. Sachs Gallery, N.Y.C., 1967, Finch Coll. Mus., 1967, New Sch. Art Centre, N.Y.C., 1969, 73, Va. Mus. Fine Arts, Richmond, 1970; represented in permanent collections Pa. Acad. Fine Arts, Phila., Finch Coll. Mus., N.Y.C., Univ. Art Mus., U. Calif., Berkeley, Bklyn. Mus. Recipient 2d prize Gymnasium Show I, 1964; MacDowell Colony Residence, 1969, 70. Mem. N.Y. Artists Equity Assn., MacDowell Colony (fellow). Address: 285 Central Park W New York NY 10024

JAFFE, NORA CROW, educator; b. Los Angeles, Feb. 12, 1944; d. Thomas J. and Helen E. (Beshears) Crow; A.B. magna cum laude in English (Univ. scholar, Ford Found. fellow), Stanford U., 1965; A.M., Harvard U., 1968, Ph.D. (Grad. Prize fellow), 1972; m. Arthur M. Jaffe, July 24, 1971. Tutor, teaching fellow Harvard U., 1968-70; asst. prof. English, Smith Coll., Northampton, Mass., 1971-79, asso. prof., 1979—. Ford Found. fellow, 1965; Harvard U. travel grantee, 1969; Hyder Rollins Found. grantee, 1975. Mem. Am. Soc. 18th-Century Studies, MLA, Phi Beta Kappa. Author: The Poet Swift, 1977; (with Patricia L. Skarda) The Evil Image. Two Centuries of Gothic Short Fiction and Poetry. The Literary Art of Terror from Daniel Defoe to Stephen King, 1981; contbr. articles to profl. jours., chpts. in books. Home: 27-Lancaster St Cambridge MA 02140 Office: English Dept Smith College Northampton MA 01063

JAFFE, RONA, author; b. N.Y.C., June 12, 1932; d. Samuel and Diana (Ginsberg) J.; B.A., Radcliffe Coll., 1951. Sec., N.Y.C., 1952; asso. editor Fawcett Publs., N.Y.C., 1952-56; author: The Best of Everything, 1958, Away From Home, 1960, The Last of the Wizards, 1961, Mr. Right is Dead, 1965, The Cherry in the Martini, 1966, The Fame Game, 1969, The Other Woman, 1972, Family Secrets, 1974, The Last Chance, 1976, Class Reunion, 1979; Mazes and Monsters, 1981. Office: Ephraim London & Buttonweiser 10 E 40 St New York NY 10016

JAFFE, SHARON BRICKMAN, speech pathologist; b. Washington, Mar. 13, 1946; d. Robert and Hilda Rena (Ashman) Brickman; B.A. cum laude, U. Md., 1967, M.A., 1969; m. Howard A. Jaffe, June 29, 1968; children—Elisabeth Joy, Amanda Gabrielle. Speech pathologist Valley Stream (N.Y.) Central High Sch. Dist., 1968-75, speech cons. com. on handicapped, 1980—; pvt. practice speech pathology, Atlantic Beach, N.Y., 1975—. Mem. Assn. for Help of Retarded Children (v.p. Atlantic Beach chpt. 1975—), Am. Speech, Lang. and Hearing Assn., N.Y. State Speech, Lang. and Hearing Assn., Soc. Gifted and Talented Children, Am. Speech and Hearing Assn., LI. Speech and Hearing Assn., Sigma Alpha Eta. Home: 1585 Bay Blvd Atlantic Beach NY 11509

JAFFE, SYLVIA SARAH, art collector, former med. technologist; b. Detroit, May 16, 1917; d. Sam and Rose (Rosmarin) Turner; B.S. in Med. Tech., U. Wis., 1940; m. David Jaffe, Nov. 8, 1942. Med. technologist Watts Hosp. Lab., Durham, N.C., 1940-45; research hematology technologist in leukemia Sloan Kettering Meml. Hosp. Lab., N.Y.C., 1946-47; chief med. technologist in hematology Arlington (Va.) Hosp. Lab., 1948-55; chief technologist in diagnostic hematology Georgetown U. Hosp., Washington, 1959-70; self employed, collector 19th century art, 1970—. Mem. Am. Soc. Med. Technologists, Am. Soc. Clin. Pathologists (affiliate), Am. Women in Sci., Smithsonian Assocs. Democrat. Jewish. Club: Pioneer Women. Contbr. articles to profl. socs. Address: 1913 S Quincy St Arlington VA 22204

JAHN, BILLIE JANE, research and devel. co. exec., nurse; b. Byers, Tex., Dec. 12, 1921; d. Thomas Oscar and Molly Verona (Kennemer) Downing; student Scott and White Sch. Nursing, 1941-42, U. Mich., 1973-75; B.S. in Nursing, Wayne State U., 1971; M.S., East Tex. State U., 1976, Ph.D., 1982; m. Edward L. Jahn, Dec. 6, 1942; children—Antoinette R., James T., Thomas L., Edward L., Janette E. Staff nurse Warren Meml. Hosp., Centerline, Mich., 1957-61; supr. nursing service Mich. Dept. Mental Health, Northville, 1962-71, Franklin County (Tex.) Hosp., 1972-74; instr. nursing Paris (Tex.) Jr. Coll., 1975-80; nurse educator VA, Waco, Tex., 1981-82; exec. v.p., dir., sr. nursing cons. Dos Cabezas, Inc., Mt. Vernon, Waco and Temple, Tex., 1981—; cons. East Tex. State U., Texarkana, 1978—. Vol., ARC, 1971—; den mother Boy Scouts Am., 1960-62; sec. PTA, Warren, Mich., 1960-62, v.p., Temple, Tex., 1957-58. Mem. AAAS, Nat. League Nursing, Tex. League Nursing, AAUP, Nat. Assn. Female Execs., Am. Assn. Curriculum and Supervision, Phi Delta Kappa, Kappa Delta Pi. Home: PO Box 594 Mount Vernon TX 75457 Office: PO Box 340 Mount Vernon TX 75457 also 2024 S 15th St Temple TX 76501

JAI, JONI, automatic tube cleaner mfg. co. exec.; b. Des Moines, Feb. 15, 1936; d. Mahlon Alonzo and Mary Jane (Cooper) Baldwin; student Orange Coast Coll., U. Minn.; m. Ken Jai, Apr. 24, 1967; children—Robert, Cindy, Troy, Aubrey, Mitchell, Tonya. Owner tax cons. and bookkeeping service, Calif., 1969; owner Global Heat Exchanger Inc., Beaumont, Tex., 1970—, sec.-treas., chmn. bd., 1970—; developer Riverside Marina seminar leader boiler maintenance. Mem. Republican Nat. Com. Mem. Tex. Assn. Bus., U.S. Automobile Club, Nat. Assn. Stock Car Autoracing. Roman Catholic. Patentee automatic tube cleaner, clean and brush cleaning tool. Address: PO Box 1127 Beaumont TX 77704

JAIN, PUSHPA RANI, radiation oncologist; b. Jabalpur, India, July 5, 1935; came to U.S., 1973; d. Beharilal and Rama Devi (Narad) J.; B.Sc., U. Saugor, Sagar, India, 1955; M.B.B.S., U. Nagpur (India), 1960. Asst. surgeon Kastuiba Hosp., Bhopal, India, 1962-73; fellow in solid tumors U. Wis., Madison, 1974-75; resident in radiation therapy SUNY, Syracuse, 1975-77; clin. asso. clin. cancer edn. program, clin. research fellow Meml. Slan Kettering Cancer Center, 1978-80; asst. prof. radiation oncology W.Va. U. Med. Center, Morgantown, 1980—; participant edn. program Am. Cancer Soc. Diplomate Am. Bd. Radiology. Mem. Am. Soc. Therapeutic Radiologists, Radiol. Soc. N.Am., Am. Coll. Radiology, AMA, W.Va. Med. Soc., Monongahela County Med. Soc. Office: WVa U Med Center Morgantown WV 26506

JAKAB, IRENE, psychiatrist, educator; b. Oradea, Rumania; came to U.S., 1961, naturalized, 1966; d. Odon and Rosa A. (Riedl) Jakab; M.D., Ferencz Jozsef U., Kolozsvar, Hungary, 1944; lic. in Psychology, Paedagogy, Philosophy cum laude Hungarian U., Kolozsvar, 1947; Ph.D. summa cum laude in Psychology, Paedagogy, Gen. Lit., Pazmany Peter U., Budapest, 1948. Rotating intern Ferencz Jozsef U., Kolozsvar, 1943-44; resident in psychiatry Univ. Hosp., Kolozsvar, 1944-47, resident in neurology, 1947-50; resident in internal medicine Univ. Hosp. of Internal Medicine, Pecs, Hungary, 1950-51; chief physician Univ. Hosp. for Neurology and Psychiatry, Pecs, 1951-59; staff neuropath. research lab. Neurol. Univ. Clinic, Zurich, Switzerland, 1959-61; sect. chief Kans. Neurol. Inst., Topeka, 1961-63; dir. research and edn., 1966; resident psychiatry Topeka State Hosp., 1963-66; asst. psychiatrist McLean Hosp., Belmont, Mass., 1966-67, asso. psychiatrist, 1967-74; prof. psychiatry U. Pitts. Med. Sch., 1974—, dir. John Merck program, 1974-81; mem. faculty dept. psychiatry Med. Sch., Pecs, 1951-59; asst. Univ. Hosp. Neurology, Zurich, Switzerland, 1959-61; asso. in psychiatry Harvard Med. Sch., Boston, 1966-69, asst. prof. in psychiatry, 1969-74, lectr. psychiatry, 1974—; dir. planning Children's Treatment and Ednl. Center, John Merck Found., 1970; program dir. grad. course in mental retardation NIMH, 1970—. Fellow Menninger Sch. Psychiatry, Topeka, 1963-66. Recipient Prinzhorn prize, 1967, Ernst Kris prize, 1973. Diplomate Am. Bd. Psychiatry. Mem. AMA, Am. Psychol. Assn., Am. Psychiat. Assn. (Gold award for sci. exhibit 1980), Société Medico Psychologique de Paris, Internat. Rorschach Soc., Internat. (v.p. 1959—), Am. (chmn. 1965—) socs. psychopathology of expression, Internat. Soc. Child Psychiatry and Allied Professions, Deutschsprachige Gesellschaft fur Psychopathologie des Ausdrucks (hon.). Author: Dessins et Peintures des Alienes, 1956; Zeichnungen und Gemalde der Geisteskranken, 1956. Editor: Art and Psychiatry, Proceedings of the Fourth International Colloquium of Psychopathology of Expression, 1968, Art Interpretation and Art Therapy, 1969; Conscious and Unconscious Expressive Art: Theories, Methodology and Pathographies, 1971; Transcultural Aspects of Psychiatric Art, 1975; co-editor:

Dynamische Psychiatrie (Berlin), 1968; mem. editorial bd. Confinia Psychiatrica (Basel), 1968, now editor-in-chief. Reviewer, Annales Medico-Psychologiques, 1957—, Acta Paedo Psychiatrica, 1963—. Contbr. articles to publs. Home: 228 Parkman Ave Pittsburgh PA 15213 Office: 3811 O'Hara St Pittsburgh PA 15261

JAKOBI, SHARON MARIE, ins. brokerage exec.; b. Berwyn, Ill., Mar. 7, 1940; d. Arthur H. and Christine A. J.; C.P.C. U. cert. Am. Inst. Property and Casualty Underwriters, 1976; asso. in risk mgmt. cert. Ins. Inst. Am., 1979; student in ins. Golden Gate U. Sec., personnel asst. Ceco Steel Corp., Chgo., 1959-65; with Dinner Levison Co., San Francisco, 1965-78, account coordinator, 1973-77, dept. mgr./ednl. coordinator, 1977-78; v.p., dept. mgr., tng./ednl. coordinator Andreini and Co., San Mateo, Calif., 1977, 78-80; v.p., account exec. Poulton Assos., Oakland, Calif., 1981—. Sec. Meadowland Homeowners Assn., Fairfax, Calif., 1977-79; sec. Montcarle Townhouse Homeowners Assn., 1981-82, pres., 1982-83. Mem. Soc. C.P.C.U.s (columnist The Retro 1977-79, ednl. v.p., candidate devel. No. Calif. chpt. 1978-79, sec. chpt. 1979—, v.p. ops. 1980, chmn. bylaw com. 1981-82, chmn. internship com. 1981-82), Ins. Ednl. Assn. (C.P.C.U. rep. to industry liaison com. 1980-82), Ins. Forum San Francisco (ednl. chairperson 1978-79), Golden Gate Alumni Assn. (council, mem. chpt. devel. com. Peninsula-South Bay chpt. 1980-82). Office: 220 W 20th Ave San Mateo CA 94403

JAKUBOWSKI, BETTE JEANNE, mktg. exec.; b. Tulsa, Mar. 20, 1950; d. William Charles and Betty (Howell) Medley; grad. with distinction Inst. Fin. Edn., 1978; 1 dau., Tanya Ann. Teller, Hawaii Thrift & Loan, Honolulu, 1970-71; savs. supr. Am. Savs., Tucson, 1972-73; asst. br. mgr. Albuquerque Fed. Savs., 1973-78, asst. sec.; asst. v.p. Am. Savs., Albuquerque, 1978; solicitor, underwriter Van Schaack Mortgage, Albuquerque, 1978-79; real estate and fin. mgr. Nu-West, Inc., Phoenix, 1979-82; mktg. dir. Fausett Mgmt. Co., Little Rock, 1982—; lectr. in field. Mem. Am. Bus. Women's Assn., Inst. Fin. Edn. (dir. 1973-78). Republican. Episcopalian. Club: Civitan (Duke City 1977, 78). Home: 9th and Ferry Sts Apt 10A Little Rock AR 72202

JALLU, OFA, artist; b. Alameda, Calif., May 5, 1907; d. Wilbur Oliver and Minnie Jean (Mead) Hayes; A.B. with honors in Art, U. Calif., Berkeley, 1928, M.A. in Art, 1931; student summer sessions univs., adult classes, workshops, pvt. tchrs.; m. Frank Marcel Jallu, Apr. 8, 1972; children by previous marriage—Gaylan John Hayes, Vivian Hayes, James Hayes Irvine. Artist in oils, watercolors, drawing, etchings, acrylics; works exhibited extensively in Central Calif., 1954-72, in San Diego, La Jolla, Los Angeles, Redlands, and Del Mar, Calif., 1972-80; one-person shows: La Jolla Art Assn. Gallery, 1973, 75, 77, Foothills Art Assn., La Mesa, Calif., 1976, H. Hery Gallery, San Diego, 1978, First Unitarian Ch., San Diego, 1976, R.J. Software Systems, La Mesa, 1978-80, Glendale Fed. Savs., Pacific Beach, Calif., 1978; two-person show: La Jolla Art Assn. Gallery, 1979; tchr. art and home econs. Calif. schs., 1931-71; judge Ramona Art Guild Show, 1976, Nat. Fedn. Women's Club Art Show, 1976; demonstrator collage techniques, figure drawing techniques. Recipient numerous awards. Mem. Nat. League Am. Pen Woman (Woman of Achievement award 1977, pres. San Diego br. 1976-78), San Diego Art Guild, San Diego Art Inst., Spanish Village Art Center, San Diego Watercolor Soc., Artists Equity Assn., Foothills Art Assn., La Jolla Art Assn., Central Calif. Art League (past pres.), Rosicrucian Order. *

JALOVAAVA, ROSEMARY ANN HAUGER, psychologist; b. Brainerd, Minn., Sept. 4, 1936; d. Joseph and Pauline Sophia Hauger; B.S. with honors, Mich. State U., 1960; M.S., Queens Coll., City U. N.Y., 1965, profl. diploma in Psychology, 1975; m. Harri K. Jalovaara, Dec. 20, 1969; 1 son, Erik. With Bd. Coop. Ednl. Services, Huntington, N.Y., 1960-79; psychologist, lang. cons. Headstart, Saginaw, Mich., 1980-81; psychologist, speech and lang. pathologist Planning For Living, Bay City, Mich., 1980—. Mem. Am. Psychol. Assn., Am. Speech and Hearing Assn., Am. Assn. Sex Educators Counselors and Therapists. Democrat. Office: 2355 Delta Rd Bay City MI 48706

JAMES, AMY, real estate broker; b. Tsingtao, China, Apr. 8, 1936; came to U.S., 1955, naturalized, 1956; d. K. and Florentine Richter; student U. Idaho, 1958-60; B.A., U. Mass., 1979; m. Charles F. James, Mar. 3, 1955; children—Debbie June, Dwight Douglas, Dana Van der. Sec. to post comdr. Ft. Richardson, Alaska, 1964-68; real estate agt. Northside Realty, Atlanta, 1972-76; real estate broker Re/Max North Atlanta, 1980—. Mem. Atlanta Bd. Realtors, Million Dollar Club. Republican. Roman Catholic. Office: 1705 Mount Vernon Rd Dunwoody GA 30338

JAMES, EMMOGENE, editor; b. Brinkley, Ark., Apr. 6, 1946; d. Herman Lee and Elsie Ree (Harris) J.; B.A., Hofstra U., Hemspstead, N.Y., 1974. Various positions in business, 1965-74; editor Grumman Aerospace Corp., Bethpage, N.Y., 1974—, sr. tech. editor, 1979—. Mem. Nat. Assn. Female Execs., NAACP. Club: Sno-Burners Ski. Home: 15 Scherer Pl Roosevelt NY 11575 Office: Grumman Aerospace Corp Bethpage NY 11714

JAMES, GENEVA BEHRENS, educator; b. Marietta, Minn., Mar. 23, 1942; d. Siegfried and Dora (Schoenrock) Behrens; B.S., Mankato State U., 1963; m. Howard James, Aug. 2, 1963; children—Scott, Dawn. Tchr. English high schs., Minn., 1964-65; instr. acctg., Adult Continuing Edn., Bellevue, Nebr., 1971-75, dir. Adult Basic Edn. Center, 1974—. Mem. exec. com. Boy Scouts Am., 1974-80. Mem. AAUW, Nat. Assn. Public and Continuing Adult Edn., Adult and Continuing Edn. Assn. Nebr., NEA. Republican. Lutheran. Home: 1314 Hansen Ave Bellevue NE 68005 Office: 2221 Main St Bellevue NE 68005

JAMES, JANE EMERSON, psychologist; b. Creston, Iowa, Oct. 5, 1920; d. Stephen Ray and Meta Florence (Raney) Emerson; B.A., U. Mo., Kansas City, 1968, M.A., 1970; Ph.D., Union Grad. Sch., Ohio, 1977; m. Fred Allen James, Sept. 15, 1945; children—John William, Meta Elizabeth. Surveyor, freelance writer Kansas City (Mo.) Star, 1971-72; counselor Nevada (Mo.) State Hosp., 1972, Nat. Council on Alcoholism, Kansas City, 1972-77; cons. Midwest Research Inst., Kansas City, 1976—; founder, pres. Task Force for Women Alcoholics, Inc., 1975-76; dir. Jan Clayton Center, 1977-79; trustee Kansas City area Nat. Council on Alcoholism. Mcpl. judge City of Lake Winnebago (Mo.), 1977-78. Recipient award N.Am. Women's Commn. on Alcohol and Drug Abuse, 1979. Mem. PEO, U. Mo. Kansas City Alumni Assn., Mensa. Author: Alcoholism in the Future - Views from Four Delphis, 1978; editorial referee Jour. of Studies on Alcohol, 1972—. Home: 432 Winnebago Dr Lake Winnebago MO 64034

JAMES, JEANNIE HENRIETTA, educator; b. Greenville, S.C., Dec. 5, 1921; d. Portice J. and Essie Virginia (Ross) J.; B.S., Berea (Ky.) Coll., 1945; M.S., U. N.C., 1949; postgrad. Iowa State U., 1955-56; Ed.D., Pa. State U., 1965. Tchr. home econs. Stowe (Vt.) High Sch., 1945-48; asst. prof., asso. prof. home econs. Lincoln Meml. U., Harrogate, Tenn., 1949-59; asst. prof., asso. profl. Ill. State U., Normal, 1959-75; asso. prof. early childhood edn. U. S.C., Columbia, 1975-79, Spartanburg Meth. Coll., 1980; mem. Ill. White House Conf. on Children and Youth, 1969-70. Mem. Nat., S.C. assns. for edn. young children, Soc. for Research and Child Devel., AAUP, World Orgn. for Edn. Children, S.C. Home Econs. Assn., So. Highlands Handicraft Guild, Am. Home Econs. Assn. (program chmn. sect. 1977-79), AAUW, Phi Kappa Delta, Zeta Tau Alpha. Contbr. articles to profl. jours. Home: Belmont Estates Route 2 Box 538 Fountain In SC 29644

JAMES, JUNE MARION, physician; b. Trinidad, W.I., June 17, 1939; came to Can., 1960, naturalized, 1969; d. Carlston Ethelbert and Elaine Frances (Patterson) James; B.Sc., U. Man., 1963, M.D., 1967; m. Ralph Eric James, Dec. 21, 1966; children—Roger Eric, Robert Eliot. Interne Health Scis. Center, Winnipeg, Man., 1967-68; hematology fellow, 1970-71; resident in pediatrics Children's Centre, Winnipeg, 1968-70; chief resident children's Hosp., 1971-72, clin. fellow in allergy and immunology, 1972-73, research fellow, 1974—; clin. lectr. U. Man., 1975-80, asst. prof., 1980—; cons. in field. Chmn. multicultural com. Internat. Centre, Winnipeg, 1974-75; bd. dirs. Can. Citizenship Council Winnipeg, 1976—; mem. pub. affairs com. YWCA; mem. Man. Action Com. Status Women; pres. Citizen Council Man., Dante Day Nursery Inc., Winnipeg Mayor's Adv. Com. on Race Relations. Recipient Woman of Yr. award, 1981. Mem. Royal Coll. Physicians and Surgeons Can., Can. Pediat. Soc., Can. Soc. Allergy and Clin. Immunology, Am. Assn. Clin. Allergy and Immunology, Am. Acad. Allergy, Man. Med. Soc., Nat. Congress Black Women in Can. (v.p., program dir.). Winnipeg). Club: Caribbean-Can. Assn. Winnipeg. Co-editor Caribbean Can. Newsletter, 1975-78, editor, 1978—; co-editor Caribbean Cuisine, 1975. Home: 63 Lake Park Dr Winnipeg MB R2J 3A7 Canada Office: Winnipeg Clinic 425 St Mary Rd Winnipeg MB R3C ON2 Canada

JAMES, MARY KATHERINE, ins. co. exec.; b. Bellevue, Ohio, June 12, 1944; d. Kent Fleet and Charlotte Mitchel (Seltzer) D.; B.A., Western Res. U., 1966; student Smith Coll., 1962-63, Case Western Res. U., 1981—; m. Richard Carl James, Sept. 10, 1966; children—Carl, Daniel. Personnel asst. Fisher Foods, Inc., Cleve., 1966-69, payroll asst., 1973-75, asst. tax mgr., 1975-76, accounts payable supr., 1977; acct., C.P.A., Cohen & Co., Cleve., 1977-80; bus. mgr. Hathaway Brown, Shaker Heights, Ohio, 1980-82; fin. ops. mgr. Progressive Casualty Ins. Co., Cleve., 1982—. C.P.A., Ohio. Mem. Am. Inst. C.P.A.s, Nat. Assn. Ednl. Buyers, Ohio Soc. C.P.A.s, Nat. Assn. Female Execs., Ohio Assn. Ind. Sch. Bus. Mgrs. Republican. Episcopalian. Club: Pine Lake Trout. Home: 824 Nautilus Trail Aurora OH 44202 Office: 19600 N Park Blvd Shaker Heights OH 44122

JAMES, NONA FAYE, ins. agt., civic worker; b. Konawa, Okla., Aug. 13, 1939; d. Fred and Dora Gertrude (Mosley) Snell; student Okla. Bapt. U., 1963-64, East Central State Coll., 1964-66, Seminole Jr. Coll., 1978; m. Vernon James, June 25, 1965. Bookkeeper, Haynes Shoe Store, Seminole, Okla., 1958-60; underwriter Sullivan-Dollar, Inc., Seminole, 1960-69; part owner, office mgr., sec.-treas. Dacus Ins., Seminole, 1969—; adv. bd. Gordon-Cooper Vocat.-Tech. Sch. Former pres. Seminole Bus. and Profl. Women's Club, dist. dir. Dist. 11, 1979-80, chmn. state conv., 1980-81, named Woman of Year, 1979-80. Mem. Okla. Ind. Ins. Agts. Assn., Nat. Assn. Ins. Agts. Mem. Assembly of God. Home: 1723 W Strothers St Seminole OK 74868 Office: 312 E Broadway Seminole OK 74868

JAMES, PAULINE, court reporter; b. Chgo.; student Roosevelt U., 1951-53, 65-66, 76-78, Chgo. Coll. Commerce, 1958-60, 63-64; m. Goldwyn James, Feb. 10, 1952; children—Pamela M., Goldwyn H., Karen L., Keith Edward. Sec. to head dept. pedodontics U. Ill. Dental Sch., 1958-60; sec. U. Chgo. Law Sch., 1960-61; sec. to Luis Kutner, internat. law specialist, 1961-63; office mgr. Ill. Inst. Tech. Research Inst., 1963-66; owner James Sec. Service, 1966-72; ct. reporter, office mgr. U.S. Dist. Ct., 1969-72; owner Pauline James, Inc., Chgo., 1972-74, Pauline James & Assos., Ct. Reporters, Chgo., 1975—. Active Nat. Urban League. Mem. Nat. Women Bus. Owners (ednl. seminars com.), LWV, Ill. Ct. Reporters Assn. (editor newsletter), Nat. Assn. Shorthand Reporters, Ill. C. of C. (exec. com.). Club: Order Eastern Star. Home: 2218 E 99th St Chicago IL 60617 Office: 219 S Dearborn St Chicago IL 60604

JAMES, SUSAN OLIVIA, mfg. co. exec.; b. Balt., Apr. 14, 1951; d. Joseph Edward and Frances Marleen (Kolodziejski) Schmidt; student Community Coll. R.I., 1977—; m. Alan R. James; children—Eileen, Karen. With Victor Corp., West Warwick, R.I., 1971—, cost estimator, 1973-76, process engr., 1976-79, applications engr., 1979-81, process engring. supr., 1981-82, process engring. mgr., 1982—. Mem. Wire Assn. Mem. Soc. Friends. Home: 19 Levalley St West Warwick RI 02893 Office: 618 Main St West Warwick RI 02893

JAMESON, DOROTHEA, sensory psychologist; b. Newton, Mass., Nov. 16, 1920; d. Robert and Josephine (Murray) Jameson; B.A., Wellesley Coll., 1942; M.A. (hon.), U. Pa., 1973; m. Leo M. Hurvich, Oct. 23, 1948. Research asst. Harvard, 1941-47; research psychologist Eastman Kodak Co., Rochester, N.Y., 1947-57; research scientist N.Y.U., 1957-62; vis. scientist Venezuelan Inst. Sci. Research, 1965; research asso. to prof. Psychol. and Inst. Neurol. Scis., U. Pa., 1962-74, Univ. prof. U. Pa., 1975—; vis. prof. Center Visual Sci., U. Rochester, 1974, Columbia U., 1974-76; cons. in field. Mem. Nat. Acad. Sci.-NCR Commn. on Human Resources, 1977-80, chmn. com. on vision, 1980-80. Recipient I.H. Godlove award Inter-Soc. Color Council, 1973; Alumnae Achievement award Wellesley Coll., 1974; fellow Center for Advanced Study in the Behavioral Scis., 1981-82. Mem. Soc. Exptl. Psychologists (Howard Crosby Warren medal 1971), Am. Psychol. Assn. (Distinguished Sci. Contbn. award 1972), Nat. Acad. Scis., Am. Acad. Arts and Scis., AAAS, Assn. Research in Vision and Ophthalmology, Biophys. Soc., Internat. Research Group Color Vision Deficiencies, Optical Soc. Am. (Tillyer medal 1982), Psychonomic Soc., Soc. Neurosci., Sigma Xi. Co-author: The Perception of Brightness and Darkness, 1966; co-author introduction and English translation: (E. Hering) Outlines of a Theory of the Light Sense, 1964. Co-editor, author chpt.; Visual Psychophysics: Handbook of Sensory Physiology, vol. VII/4, 1972. Contbr. articles to profl. jours. Home: 286 St James Pl Philadelphia PA 19106 Office: 3815 Walnut St Philadelphia PA 19104

JAMESON, PATRICIA MARIAN, govt. ofcl.; b. Pitts., Mar. 17, 1945; d. Vernon L. and Dorothy Leam (Wilson) J.; B.A., Northwestern U., 1967; M.A., Ohio State U., 1969, with HUD, 1970—, project mgr., Detroit, 1976-77, acting dir. housing mgmt., 1978, dep. area mgr. Milw. Area office, 1978—, acting area mgr., 1979-80, 82. Counselor, Women's Crisis Line. Recipient Quality Performance award HUD, 1973, 75, 80, Outstanding Performance award, 1980; NDEA fellow, 1967-69. Mem. Am. Mgmt. Assn., Nat. Assn. Female Execs., NOW, ACLU, Phi Beta Kappa, Pi Sigma Alpha. Office: 744 N 4th St Milwaukee WI 53203

JAMESON, PHYLLIS ANN, psychologist, educator; b. LaJolla, Calif., Sept. 12, 1942; d. Hubert E. and Mary Elizabeth (Rodolf) Brooke; B.A., Stanford U., 1964; M.A., U. Wis., Madison, 1974, postgrad. (NSF fellow 1963, NIMH fellow 1967-70); m. Kenneth P. Jameson, Jan. 5, 1965; children—Rex Meredith, John Matthew. Tchr. math. and sci. Peace Corps, Jamaica, 1964-66; asst. prof. psychology St. Mary's Coll., Notre Dame, Ind., 1971-74, prof., 1975—; cons. Inst. Internat. Edn., Peru, 1974-75; project leader Am. Friends Service Com., Oaxaca, Mex., summer 1981. Bd. dirs. Fitchburg Montessori Sch., 1968-73, Early Childhood Devel. Center, 1971—, Brown Starr Sch., 1972-76, Community Coordinated Child Care, 1976-80, 1st Methodist Ch. Infant and Toddler Care, 1977-79, Child Abuse and Neglect Coordinating Com., 1977-80; needs assessment chmn. Title XX Citizens Adv. Com., 1979; mem. Bishop's Adv. Council, 1980-82; overseas selection chair Holy Cross Assos., 1980—. NSF undergrad. teaching grantee, 1982; St. Mary's research grantee, 1982; recipient Maria Pieta teaching award, 1982. Mem. Am. Psychol. Assn. Roman Catholic. Club: St. Mary's Coll. Soccer. Home: 412 Lamonte St South Bend IN 46616 Office: 156 Madeleva Saint Mary's College Notre Dame IN 46556

JAMISON, DARLENE MARY, univ. adminstr.; b. Kansas City, Mo., Nov. 24, 1928; d. Joseph and Caroline E. Broyles; B.A. in Sociology, U. Mo., Kansas City, 1963, M.A., 1969; m. Homer C. Jamison, Feb. 12, 1971; 1 dau., Carolyn Suzanne Love. Mem. adminstrv. staff U. Mo., Kansas City, 1967-74, dir. affirmative action-academic, 1973-74; adminstrv. asso., affirmative action officer Sch. Optometry, U. Ala., Birmingham, 1974-81, asst. to dean, 1981—. Mem. Am. Soc. Personnel Adminstrs., Coll. and Univ. Personnel Assn., Nat. Council Adminstrv. Women in Edn., Ala. Assn. Women Deans, Adminstrs. and Councelors, Personnel Assn. Birmingham, Nat. Conf. Women in Chambers of Conf. (del. 1979-81), Women's Jr. C. of C. Birmingham (pres. 1981-82), Birmingham Met. Bus. and Profl. Women's Club (v.p. 1979-80), Am. Bus. Women's Assn. Club: Birmingham Soroptimists. Editor various univ. publs. Home: 3586 Rockhill Rd Birmingham AL 35223 Office: Sch Optometry U Ala Birmingham AL 35294

JAMISON, JUDITH, dancer; b. Phila., 1944; d. John Jamison; student Fisk U., Phila. Dance Acad. Debut with Am. Ballet Theatre, 1965; prin. dancer Alvin Ailey Am. Dance Theater, N.Y.C., 1965, 67-81, now appearing on Broadway with Musical Sophisticated Ladies, Harkness Ballet, 1966; guest appearances with Am. Ballet Theatre, San Francisco Ballet, Dallas Ballet. *

JAMISON, JUDITH JAFFE, judge; b. Phila., Aug. 19, 1924; d. Selig and Mary (Salit) Jaffe; B.A., Antioch Coll., 1946; postgrad. (fellow) Law Sch., U. Chgo., 1946-47; J.D., Temple U., 1948; m. I.I. Jamison, June 23, 1957; children—Seth, Sara. Admitted to Pa. bar, 1949; individual practice law, Phila., 1949-73; asst. atty. gen. Commonwealth of Pa., 1956-63, 71-73; spl. hearing examiner Office U.S. Atty., 1959-63, judge Ct. Common Pleas, Phila., 1974—; mem. faculty Pa. Coll. Judiciary; lectr. Law Sch. Temple U., Children's Hosp. Democratic committeewoman, 1954-73, vice chmn. exec. com. 8th ward, 1969-73; bd. dirs. aux. Children's and Grad. hosps., 1965-74, Antioch Coll. Assn., 1973-76, Elizabeth Blackwell Health Center for Women, 1978-80, Fox Chase Cancer Center and Inst. Cancer Research, 1980—, women's council Fedn. Jewish Agys. Greater Phila.; mem. exec. com. Bus. and Profl. Women's Coalition, 1980; bd. dirs. Girls' Coalition Southeastern Pa., 1980—, Offender Aid and Restoration, 1980; mem. Settlement Music Sch., Phila. Orch. Assn., parents com. Wesleyan U. Mem. Nat. Coll. Probate Judges, Pa. Bar Assn., Phila. Bar Assn., Pa. Prison Soc., Pa. Conf. State Trial Judges (exec. com.). Jewish. Clubs: Women's Way, B'nai B'rith (dir.), Justice Lodge, Sisterhood Rodeph Shalom. First woman apptd. judge Orphans Ct. Pa. Home: 2119 Delancey St Philadelphia PA 19103 Office: 1302 One E Penn Sq Bldg Philadelphia PA 19107

JAMISON, LEILA DUNCAN, state ofcl.; b. Denmark, S.C., Nov. 6, 1932; d. Johnnie and Lillie (Thomas) Duncan; A.A., Voorhies Jr. Coll., 1953; B.S., S.C. State Coll., 1955; M.P.A., Am. U., 1979; m. Norman Jamison, Jr., Sept. 12, 1954. Sec., Office Acad. Dean, Office Bus. Office, Voorhees Coll., Denmark, S.C., 1957-66; instr., bus. edn., 1966-67, alumni affairs, asso. devel. officer, public relations officer, 1967-75; ops. mgr. Howard U., Washington, 1976-79; community cons. div. rural devel. and spl. econ. assistance Office Gov. S.C., Columbia, 1980—. Recipient Alumni Service award Voorhees Coll., 1974. Mem. AAUW. Democrat. Baptist. Home: PO Box 573 Holly Ave Denmark SC 29042

JAMISON, LILLIAN ELIZABETH, nurse, educator; b. Smiths Creek, Mich., Aug. 31, 1938; d. Michael and Lillian Alice (Lacey) Mayer; A.S., Port Huron (Mich.) Jr. Coll., 1958; ordination Salvation Army Sch. for Officers, 1960; R.N., St. Clair County Community Coll., 1968; B.S., Coll. St. Francis, 1974; M.A., U. Mich., 1980, doctoral candidate, 1981—; m. Gary Jamison, Aug. 9, 1958; children—Susan, Robert and Mark (twins), Tracy. Corps officer Salvation Army, Iowa, S.D., Ill., 1960-67; R.N., asst. dir. nursing Good Samaritan Home, Ethan, S.D., 1968; nurse ICU and CCU units Peoples Hosp., Peru, Ill., 1969-73; sub. tchr. Yale, Mich., also nurse CCU, Port Huron (Mich.) Hosp., Yale Hosp., Port Huron, 1974; tchr. vocat. edn. Sanilac County Career Center (Mich.), 1975-77, tchr. adult edn., 1979-80; instr. practical nursing St. Clair County Community Coll., 1977-78; dir. nursing Yale Med. Care (Mich.), 1978; mem. part-time nursing faculty Saginaw Valley (Mich.) State Coll., 1981; dir. nursing Sanilac Med. Care Facility, Sandusky, Mich., 1979—. Marysville Alumni Assn. scholar, 1956-57; HEW fellow, 1978-80; State of Ill. scholar, 1973-74, grantee, 1980-82. Mem. AAUW, Mich. Med. Care Facilities Assn. (parents adv. council). Presbyterian. Clubs: Jr. Woman's of Ladd (Ill.) (pres., 1973), United Presbyn. Women. Home: 8401 Wildcat Croswell MI 48422 Office: Sanilac Med Care Facility 137 N Elk Sandusky MI 48471

JAMISON, VIRGINIA WRAY, environ. microbiologist; b. Phila., Oct. 11, 1924; d. Robert Weir and Elizabeth (Wray) J.; student Juniata Coll., 1942-44; B.S., U. Pa., 1969. Technician, Sun Oil Co., Marcus Hook, Pa., 1944-63, asst. scientist, 1964-69, asso. scientist, 1969-75, scientist Sun Tech, Inc. subs., 1975-81, sr. research scientist, 1981—. Recipient Charles Porter award Soc. Indsl. Microbiology, 1975. Mem. Am. Chem. Soc., ASTM, Am. Soc. Microbiology, Soc. Indsl. Microbiology. Republican. Baptist. Contbr. articles to profl. jours.; patentee in field. Office: PO Box 1135 Marcus Hook PA 19061

JANES, JEANENE MARIE, social work adminstr.; b. Ft. Worth, Feb. 27, 1939; d. Melvin Joseph and Thelma Marie (Golden) J.; B.E., U. Ala., 1959; M.S.W., Fla. State U., 1969. Choral dir. Disque Jr. High Sch., Gadsden, Ala., 1959-61, Plant City (Fla.) High Sch., 1961-62; social worker Plant City Dept. Public Welfare, 1962-66, social work supr., 1967-69; casework supr., asst. region dir. Tampa (Fla.) Dept. Public Welfare, 1969-71; state program coordinator Div. Family Services, Jacksonville, Fla., 1971-75, adminstr. planning and evaluation, 1975-76; dist. program coordinator State Dept. Health and Rehab. Services, Jacksonville, 1976-80, service network mgr., 1980—; mem. adv. com. Fla. Diagnostic and Learning Resources System, 1979-80; field work instr. Fla. State U. Sch. Social Work, 1971-72, 76-77; vol. Spl. Olympics. Mem. Children's Home Soc., Jacksonville Zool. Soc., Nat. Assn. Social Workers (nat. dir.), Acad. Cert. Social Workers, Am. Public Welfare Assn., Fla. Assn. Health and Social Services, Mental Health Assn. United Methodist (mem. adminstrv. bd., council on ministries). Club: Quota Club Internat. (chpt. treas. 1977-78, pres. Jacksonville chpt. 1978-80). Home: 3932 Raintree Rd Jacksonville FL 32211 Office: PO Box 52239 Jacksonville FL 32201

JANEWAY, ELIZABETH (HALL), author; b. Bklyn., Oct. 7, 1913; d. Charles H. and Jeannette F. (Searle) Hall; student Swarthmore Coll.; A.B., Barnard Coll., 1935; D. Litt., Simpson Coll., 1972, Cedar Crest Coll., 1974, Villa Maria Coll.; D.H.L., Russell Sage Coll., 1981; m. Eliot Janeway; children-Michael, William. Author: The Walsh Girls, 1943; Daisy Kenyon, 1945; The Question of Gregory, 1949; The Vikings, 1951; Leaving Home, 1953; Early Days of the Automobile, 1956; The Third Choice, 1959; Angry Kate, 1963; Accident, 1964; Ivanov Seven, 1967; Man's World, Woman's Place, 1971; Between Myth and Morning: Women Awakening, 1974; Powers of the Weak, 1980; Cross Sections from a Decade of Change, 1982; contbr.: Comprehensive Textbook of Psychiatry, 2d edit., 1980; Harvard Guide to Contemporary American Writing, 1979; also short stories and critical writing in periodicals and newspapers. Judge, Nat. Book Award, 1955, Pulitzer Prize Com., 1971. Trustee Barnard Coll. Named Disting. Alumna, Barnard Coll.; recipient Medal of Distinction Barnard Coll., 1981. Mem. Authors Guild Inc. (council), Authors League Am. (council), PEN, Phi Beta Kappa (hon.). Home: 15 E 80th St New York NY 10021

JANIAK, BETTY PAYNE, psychologist; b. Janesville, Wis., Dec. 29, 1925; d. James Richard and Lella Mary (Tibbals) Payne; B.S. with distinction, U. Wis., 1950, M.S., 1964; Ph.D., Utah State U., 1975; m. Matthew Anthony Janiak, Dec. 21, 1943; children—Leilandi Joy, Karyn Keolani. Tchr. home econs. dept. pub. instrn., Adult Community Sch., Honolulu, 1950-51; tchr., prin. Palau (Western Caroline Islands) Dependents' Sch., 1957-61; instr. English U. Wis., Stout, 1962; guidance counselor Intermountain Indian Sch., Brigham City, Utah, 1962-66; instr. spl. edn. Utah State U., Logan, 1967-69; generalist Weber Sch. Dist., Ogden, Utah, 1969-75; psychologist Bear River Mental Health Center, Brigham City, 1975-78, asst. dir., 1978-80; pvt. practice psychology, Brigham City, Utah, 1980—; adj. asst. prof. psychology Utah State U., Logan, 1979—. Bd. dirs. Honolulu Child and Family Service, 1955-57; sr. warden St. Michael's Episcopal Ch., 1973, 1980, treas., 1975, organist, 1962—. Recipient NDEA fellowship, 1966-67. Mem. Am. Psychol. Assn., Utah Psychol. Assn., Rocky Mountain Psychol. Assn., Am. Orthopsychiat. Assn., Utah Psychologists in Pvt. Practice, AAUW (v.p. 1976-78). Episcopalian. Club: Soroptimist. Home: 624 Shamrock Dr Brigham City UT 84302 Office: 118 E First North Brigham City UT 84302

JANICKE, PATRICIA ANN, tech. writer, logistics analyst; b. Milw., Aug. 28, 1932; d. John Harold and Dorothy Ellen (Lappen) Carney; student U. Wis., 1950-51; B.A. in Speech, Radio and Dramatics, Mt. Mary Coll., 1954; postgrad. Moorpark Coll., 1974-76; m. Joseph E. Janicke, Jan. 13, 1962 (dec. 1976); 1 dau., Julia Ellen. Exec. sec. Acad. Motion Picture Arts and Scis., Beverly Hills, Calif., 1959-63; computer operator Litton Industries, Van Nuys, Calif., 1969-72; acct. Vetek Computer Systems, Inc., Westlake Village, Calif., 1974-75, Datex, Oxnard, Calif., 1975-76; tech. writer, editor Vitro Labs., Oxnard, 1976-80; tech. writer, logistics analyst Raytheon Service Co., Ventura, Calif., 1980-82; tech. writer Two-D Corp., Oxnard, 1982—. Pres. Westlake Village (Calif.) chpt. One Again, Inc., 1977-79, bd. dirs., 1977-79; bd. dirs. Am. Contract Bridge League, Oxnard, 1978-80; v.p. Raytheon Activities Club, 1980-82. Recipient Masque and Gavel award Mt. Mary Coll., 1954. Mem. Am. Soc. Women Accts., N.W. Indsl. Editors Assn. Republican. Roman Catholic. Club: Sweet Adelines. Home: 42 Margarita Camarillo CA 93010 Office: 555 Hueneme Rd Oxnard CA 93034

JANIS, LUCILLE GOLDFEDER, communications adminstr.; b. N.Y.C., Aug. 7, 1933; d. Max and Helen (Orlinsky) Goldfeder; B.A., N.Y.U., 1954; m. Howard K. Janis, May 22, 1955 (dec.); children—Pamela Ruth, Caroline Sara, Michele Grace, Gordon Ariel. Research librarian Paramount Newsreels, 1954-56; tchr. Stamford (Conn.) Schs., 1962-73; bus. researcher Ambassador Arthur K. Watson, 1973-74; adminstr. IBM, Mt. Pleasant, N.Y., 1976-77; communications adminstr. Satellite Bus. Systems, McLean, Va., 1977—. Recipient Person of Yr. award Brotherhood of Temple Sinai, Stamford, Conn., 1980. Mem. LWV (fgn. policy chmn. 1962-70), Smithsonian Assos. Jewish. Home: 8350 Greensboro Dr McLean VA 22102 Office: 8283 Greensboro Dr McLean VA 22102

JANJIGIAN, HANNAH M. (MRS. EDWARD R. JANJIGIAN), broadcasting exec., civic worker; b. Edinburg, Ind., Dec. 7, 1911; d. W. Alfred and Elsie (Meier) McEwen; student (AAUW scholar), Franklin Coll., 1930-31; B.S. in Home Econs. (4-H scholar), Purdue U., 1934; postgrad. U. Chgo., 1933-34, Ohio State U., 1934-35, Coll. of Misericordia, 1964, Pa. State U., 1965-66, Mansfield State Coll., 1968; m. Edward R. Janjigian, Aug. 22, 1937; children—Jessie, Hannah, Edward R. Instn. mgmt. work U. Chgo., 1933-34, Carson, Pirie Scott & Co., Chgo., 1934, Ohio State U., 1934-35; nat. range home economist Westinghouse Electric Co., Mansfield, Ohio, 1935-36; home demonstration agt. U.S. Dept. Agr., 1936-37; owner, mfr. Feather Brand Cakes, Kingston, Pa., 1947-54; originator med. TV series Sta. WILK-TV, Luzerne County Med. Soc., Kingston, 1956, co-producer Safeguard Your Health series, 1956—. Pres. Nebbitt Hosp. Aux., Kingston, 1951-53, fund raiser, 1958-68; conferee Working with Disadvantaged Youth, HEW, 1965; publicity chmn. Luzerne County Nutrition Com. Dept. Agr., 1965-66; vol. dir. YMCA Tutorial, Wilkes-Barre, Pa., 1969—; mem. adv. com. Upward Bound Wilkes Coll., Wilkes-Barre, 1972—. Recipient Governor's award for safety Commonwealth of Pa., 1965; citation Nat. Safety Council, 1965; Benjamin Rush award Luzerne County Med. Soc., 1972; 1st award in ednl. programming Pocono N.E. Community Awards of Econ. Devel. Council N.E. Pa., 1981. Mem. Woman's Aux. Luzerne County Med. Soc. (TV-radio-press chmn. 1959-65, pres. 1955-56, 64-65) Woman's Aux. Pa. Med. Soc. (pub. relations chmn. 1956-58, mental health chmn. 1958-59; editor newsletter 1961-63), VFW Aux., Am. Home Econs. Assn., Aux. Am. Acad. Neurology, DAR (treas. Wyoming Valley 1956—). Methodist. Home: 22 Pierce St Kingston PA 18704

JANKOWSKI, JANET MARIE, speech pathologist; b. Worcester, Mass., Nov. 5, 1949; d. Chester Joseph and Sophie Mary (Modzelewski) Jankowski; B.A. in French, Anna Maria Coll., 1971; M.S. in Speech, Emerson Coll., 1974; m. John Paul Chmielowiec, May 16, 1981. Tchr. French, St. Mary's High Sch., Worcester, Mass., 1974; vol. speech pathologist Mercy Center, Worcester, 1974; speech and lang. pathologist Stamford (Conn.) Public Schs., 1974—. Mem. Am. Speech and Hearing Assn. (cert. clin. competence), Alpha Mu Gamma. Christian Ch. Home: 1425 Bedford St Stamford CT 06905

JANNEY, MARY DRAPER, social and ednl. service orgn. adminstr.; b. Bklyn., May 28, 1921; d. Ernest Gallaudet and Mary White (Childs) Draper; B.A. in Sociology, Vassar Coll.; M.A. in Sociology, Yale U.; m. Frederick Wistar Morris Janney, Jan. 15, 1944; children—Peter Wistar, Christopher D. Tchr. Am. history Potomac Sch., McLean, Va., 1961-64, head history dept., student adviser, 1961-64; founder, pres. Wider Opportunities for Women, Inc., Washington, 1966—; exec. dir. Planned Parenthood of Met. Washington. Mem. Washington Commn. on Status of Women, 1973—; bd. dirs. The Madeira Sch., Greenway, Va., 1969-72, Potomac Sch., McLean, 1966-72; trustee Vassar Coll., 1975—, chmn., 1981—; trustee Fed. Woman's Award. Named One of 1975's Washingtonians of Year. Home: 2960 University Terr Washington DC 20016 Office: 1108 16th St NW Washington DC 20016

JANNUCCI, GLORIA ISABELLA, psychologist; b. Elizabeth, N.J., Jan. 16, 1929; d. Louis and Anna Carmella (Vitale) J.; A.B. cum laude, U. So. Calif., 1953; M.A. in Guidance, Columbia U., 1954; Ed.D. in Sch. Psychology, Rutgers U., 1964. Intern in psychology N.J. Dept. Instns. and Agys., 1954-55; clin. psychologist II, Marlboro (N.J.) State Hosp., 1955-58, clin. psychologist, then sr. clin. psychologist, 1960-65, prin. clin. psychologist, 1969-70; staff psychologist Middlesex Mental Health Clinic, New Brunswick, N.J., 1958-60; sch. psychologist various local sch. systems, 1965-69; lectr. psychology Monmouth Coll., Brookdale Community Coll., Keene Coll., 1969-70; sch. psychologist Colts Neck (N.J.) Public Schs., 1970—; cons. psychologist Monmouth Sch. Exceptional Children, Eatontown, N.J., part-time 1970-77; pvt. practice clin. and sch. psychology, West Long Branch, N.J., part-time, 1977—. Mem. Am. Psychol. Assn., N.J. Psychol. Assn., Monmouth-Ocean County Psychol. Assn. (membership chmn.), N.J. Assn. Sch. Psychologists, N.J. Assn. Clin. Psychologists, NEA, N.J. Assn. Children with Learning Disabilities. Office: 265 Monmouth Park Hwy West Long Branch NJ 07764

JANNUZZI, JOAN MARIE, seminar prodn. co. exec.; b. Dayton, Ohio, Dec. 1, 1935; d. Thomas Harold and Marie Louise (Truax) Foos; student Los Angeles City Coll., 1953-54, Pierce Coll., 1954-55, Valley Coll., 1962-63; m. James J. Jannuzzi, Mar. 1956 (div. July 1958); 1 son, Michael. Sec., So. Calif. Gas Co., 1954-63; real estate saleswoman Stroud Realty, 1963-64; sec. N.Am. Rockwell, Downey, Calif., 1964-66; exec. sec., adminstrv. asst. Computer Measurements Co., Sylmar, Calif., 1966-69, Data Instruments, Sepulveda, Calif., 1969-71, Circulation Sales, Westlake Village, Calif., 1972-75; office mgr. Nat. Assn. Accts., Los Angeles, 1975-76; office mgr. Circuit-Stik, Torrance, Calif., 1976-77; mgr. Profl. Bus. Services, secretarial service, Woodland Hills, Calif., 1977-79; v.p., treas. Universal Seminars Corp. Am., Tarzana, Calif., 1979-81; pres. Unicom Internat. Tarzana, 1981—; condr. personal devel. and profl. growth workshops; sec. Interdel Ltd., 1980—; sec., treas. Sonja Karon Corp., 1980—. Cert. profl. sec. Mem. Profl. Secs. Internat. (2d v.p. chpt. 1973, 80-82, pres. chpt. 1974, numerous chairmanships 1967—, San Fernando Valley chpt. Sec. of Yr. 1972, Satellite chpt. Mem. of Yr. 1981), Women in Mgmt., Nat. Assn. Female Execs., Am. Soc. Profl. Exec. Women. Republican. Baptist. Office: 18455 Burbank Blvd Suite 409 Tarzana CA 91356

JANOWITZ, DORIS, pub. co. exec. With Farrar, Straus & Giroux Inc., N.Y.C., 1954—, asst. to mgr. prodn., 1954-59, mgr. prodn., 1959-72, art dir., dir. prodn., 1972—, v.p., 1973—, also dir. Office: care Farrar Straus & Giroux Inc 19 Union Sq W New York NY 10003 *

JANSEN, CATHERINE SANDRA, artist, educator; b. N.Y.C., Dec. 14, 1945; d. George G. and Catherine Jansen; B.F.A., Cranbrook Acad. Art, 1968; M.F.A., Temple U., 1973; m. William G. Larson, Feb. 14, 1973; 1 dau., Erika. Instr., Phila. Mus. Art, 1973-75; asst. prof. dept. art Bucks County Community Coll., Newtown, Pa., 1975—; artist-in-residence Art Park, Lewiston, N.Y., summer 1975; guest lectr. Internat. Center for Photography, N.Y.C., 1979, U. Md., Balt., 1980, N.Y. U., N.Y.C., 1980, Corcoran Sch. Art, Washington, 1980, Rutgers U., 1980; one-woman shows sculpture and/or photography include: Photopia Gallery, Phila., 1978, U.S.D., Vermillion, 1978, Temple U., Phila., 1979; numerous group shows include: Del. Art Mus., Wilmington, 1978, Syracuse (N.Y.) U., 1979, Honolulu Acad. Art, 1979, Beaver Coll., Phila., 1980, Acad. Fine Arts, Warsaw, Poland, 1980, De Cordova Mus. Art, 1981, Santa Barbara Mus. Art, 1982; represented in permanent collections: Phila. Mus. Art, Honolulu Acad. Art, Center for Creative Photography, Tucson. Pa. Council on Arts grantee, 1980; Nat. Endowment for Arts grantee, 1982. Mem. Soc. Photog. Edn. Contbr. illustrations and photographs to various books. Address: 152 Heacock Ln Wyncote PA 19095

JANSEN, ISABEL, civic worker; b. Phlox, Wis., May 26, 1906; d. Mose A. and Clara K. J.; R.N., Marquette U., Milw., 1927. Surg. asst. to prof. oral and maxillofacial surgery Marquette U., 1927-52; ret., 1954; pres. Citizens Action Program for Safe Wis. Water, 1972—; chmn. Antigo Freedom Com., 1960—. Recipient Liberty award Congress of Freedom, Inc., annually 1972-78, Keeper of the Flame award Woman Constitutionalist, 1974, cert. of appreciation Nat. Police Officers Assn. Am., 1973. Roman Catholic. Research on heart deaths in Antigo, Wis., 1974; inventor Jansen Ray Pen, 1947. Home: 608 Gowan Rd Antigo WI 54409

JANSEN, JENELLE LORRAINE, personnel dir.; b. Harvey, Ill., Oct. 28, 1948; d. James Charles and Genevieve Alberta (Wing) Blatt; B.S. in Criminal Justice, Fla. Internat. U., 1979; m. Gregory Wayne Jansen, Sept. 10, 1977; 1 son, Michael James. Sec., stenographer U.S. Govt., Phila., 1966-68, Balt., 1970-71, Miami, Fla., 1972-73; flight attendant Northeast Airlines, Boston, 1969-70; personnel asst. Miami-Dade Gen. Hosp., Miami, 1974-78; dir. personnel Coral Gables (Fla.) Hosp., 1979—. Mem. NOW, So. Fla. Hosp. Personnel Dirs. Assn., Am. Soc. Personnel Adminstrs.

JANSEN, MARGARET JOSEPHINE, nurse; b. Milo, Iowa, Oct. 6, 1928; d. August John and Flossie Mary (Clanton) Heinen; student Ottumwa Heights Coll., 1946-48, St. Joseph Hosp. Sch. Nursing, diploma, 1960; m. Joseph Bernard Jansen, Aug. 1, 1964; children—Patrick Joseph, Ronald Gerard. Staff nurse Univ. Hosp., Omaha, 1963, Sacred Heart Hosp., Yankton, S.D., 1976-79; adminstr., nurse Sunshine Nursing Home, Yankton, S.D., 1979—, also dir. nursing. Mem. S.D. Nurses Assn., S.D. Adminstrs. Long Term Care. Roman Catholic. Home: Box 132 Fordyce NE 68736

JANSEN, PATRICIA GAIL, cable TV exec.; b. Bronxville, N.Y., July 3, 1946; d. Patrick Frank and Rita (Twohig) Curry; B.A. in Journalism/Broadcasting, Fordham U., 1968. Exec. producer Skyline series WNET, N.Y.C., 1978-79; coordinating producer Alexander the Great, Time-Life Films, N.Y.C., 1979-80, FYI with Hal Linden, ABC/Network, N.Y.C., 1980-81; asso. dir. documentary programming HBO Cable, N.Y.C., 1981—. Bd. dirs. Am. Video Inst., N.Y.C., 1979-82. Recipient Emmy award FYI series ABC-TV, 1980. Mem. Am. Video Inst. (bd. dirs.), Women in Film, Am. Acad. TV Arts and Scis. Home: 430 W 24th St New York NY 10011 Office: HBO Time Life Bldg New York NY 10020

JANSON, SANDI, psychotherapist; b. Phila., Mar. 6, 1938; d. Samuel and Pauline (Epstein) J.; B.S. in Home Econs., Drexel U., 1959; M.A., Lindenwood Coll., 1976; m. Marvin Robert Stern, June 15, 1958 (div. Nov. 1972); children—Judith Anne, Susan Marie. High sch. tchr., Suitland, Md., 1959-61; supervising dietitian Sheridan Sch., Washington, 1969-76; psychotherapist Colo. N.W. Mental Health Center, Steamboat Springs, 1976-78, Pastoral Counseling Center, Steamboat Springs, 1978-79, Project PPEP, Tucson, after 1979; mem. faculty Colo. N.W. Community Coll., Steamboat Springs, 1978-79; cons. curriculum devel. Tucson Unified Sch. Dist., 1980; cons. industry, community agencies. Founder Yampa Valley chpt. NOW, 1977; adv. com. EEO, Colo. Edn. Commr.; bd. dirs. Woodstock House, Tucson, Pima County Collaborative for Youth, Tucson. Mem. Assn. Humanistic Psychology, Colo. Assn. Sex Therapists, Nat. Honor Soc. Home Econs., So. Ariz. Biofeedback Assn., Tucson Family Life Council, Tucson Holistic Health Assn. Democrat. Home: Box 7874 San Diego CA 92107

JANSZEN, PEARL POLLARD (MRS. ARTHUR A. JANSZEN), psychologist; b. Boston, Sept. 20, 1929; d. David and Rebecca (Bell) Pollard; B.S., State Coll. Boston, 1949, M.Ed., 1964; postgrad. Harvard U., Tufts U., Boston U., U. Tex.; m. Arthur A. Janszen, June 20, 1953; children—David, Karen, Eric. Tchr. pub. schs., Boston, 1949-54; asst. mgr. Janszen Lab., Inc., Cambridge, Mass., 1954-56; intern, clin. counselor, cons. Eastern Middlesex Guidance Center, Reading and North Reading, 1964-69, psychologist, Melrose, Mass., 1969—; psychol. services Lesley Coll. Schs., Cambridge, 1968-69; pvt. practice psychotherapy, cons., 1974—; co-dir. Community Counseling Collaborative, 1977. Active various civic and cultural groups, including Common Cause, Friends Belmont Library. Mem. Bd. Registration Psychologists, Nat. Register Health Services Providers in Psychology. Mem. AAUW, Soc. Family Therapy and Research, Northeastern Soc. Group Therapy, Am., Mass. psychol. assns., NOW, Mus. Fine Arts (Boston), Mus. Mod. Art (N.Y.C.), Smithsonian Assocs. Home: Belmont MA 02178

JANVEJA, MARIA ANNETTE, nursing home adminstr.; b. Haslach, W. Ger., Apr. 4, 1951; came to U.S., 1951, naturalized, 1956; d. William and Thersia Maria Keit; A.A., Delta Coll., 1971; B.A. with honors, Mich. State U., 1973; postgrad. U. Mich., 1979—; m. Subhash C. Janveja, July 24, 1981. Hostess, cashier, mgr. Theresa's Restaurant, Bay City, Mich., 1960-74; adminstr. Chesaning (Mich.) Nursing Home, Inc., 1974—, social worker designee, activity dir., 1974-76. Recipient cert. St. Paul's Parish of Owosso, 1976. Mem. Am. Coll. Nursing Home Adminstrs., Health Care Assn. Mich. (corr. sec. N.E. region 1976-81), Phi Beta Kappa. Republican. Roman Catholic. Home: 3681 Christyway Saginaw MI 48603 Office: 201 S Front St Chesaning MI 48616

JANZEN, NORINE MADELYN QUINLAN (MRS. DOUGLAS MACARTHUR JANZEN), med. technologist; b. Fond du Lac, Wis., Feb. 9, 1943; d. Joseph Wesley and Norma Edith (Gustin) Quinlan; B.S., Marian Coll., 1965; med. technologist St. Agnes Sch. Med. Tech., Fond du Lac, 1966; M.A., Central Mich. U., 1980; m. Douglas MacArthur Janzen, July 18, 1970; 1 son, Justin James. Supr. med. technologist Mayfair Med. Lab., Wauwatosa, Wis., 1966-69, Drs Mason, Chamberlain, Franke, Klink & Kamper, Milw., 1969-76; supr. med. tech. Parkview Med. Assos., Ltd., 1976—. Substitute poll worker Democratic com., Fond du Lac, 1964-65; mem. Dem. Nat. Com., 1973—. Mem. Wis. South Eastern Suprs. Groups (co-chmn. 1976-77), Milw. Soc. Med. Technologists (pres., 1971-72; dir. 1972-73), Wis. Assn. Med. Tech. (treas. 1977-81, chmn. awards com. 1976-77, dir. 1977, pres.-elect 1981-82, pres. 1982—, Med. Technologist of Yr. award 1982), Am. Soc. Med. Tech., Alpha Delta Theta (nat. dist. chmn., 1967-69; nat. alumnae dir. 1969-71). Methodist. Home: N 98 W 17298 Dotty Way Germantown WI 53022 Office: 1004 E Sumner St Hartford WI 53027

JAPAR, SUSAN ELIZABETH, nurse, obstet. nurse practitioner; b. Bronx, N.Y., Jan. 8, 1949; d. Romeo and Susan (Kuklish) Japar; B.S. in Nursing, Hunter Coll., 1970; ob/gyn nurse practitioner cert. U. Kans. Med. Center, 1975; M.S., U. Calif., San Francisco, 1977. Med.-surg. staff nurse Albert Einstein Hosp., Bronx, 1970-72; staff nurse USAF Hosp., 1972-74; nurse practitioner, Grand Forks AFB, N.D., 1974-75; USAF Hosp., Clark AFB, Philippines, 1977-78; course supr. USAF, 1978—; vis. lectr. U. Okla. Health Scis. Center. Served with USAF, 1972—. Lutheran. Author: Diagnosis and Treatment of Vulvovaginitis, 1982. Office: SHLS/MSOM Sheppard AFB TX 76311 *

JARABICA, RAI LYNNE, real estate broker; b. New Orleans, July 30, 1937; d. Fernand William and Dorothy Marie (Hereford) Sanchez; m. George Albert Jarabica, Apr. 19, 1954 (div.); children—Donna Gayle (Mrs. Ernest L. Bonnoitt, Jr.), Gerard Peter, Aaron Lloyd, Craig Christopher. Real estate sales Bienville Assos., Inc., 1971-72; pres. Rai Lynne Realty, Inc., Gretna, La., 1972—; mem. La. Real Estate Commn., 1980—. Republican. Roman Catholic. Columnist: West Bank Guide, Gretna, 1971-79. Home: 2180 Carol Sue Gretna LA 70053

JARAMILLO, FLORENCE POULIN, restaurant propr.; b. Hartford, Conn., Dec. 23, 1930; d. Albert and Florida Poulin; student schs. Hartford; m. Arturo Jaramillo, June 27, 1953; 1 dau., Laura Ann. Filing clk. Curtis 1000, Inc., Hartford, Conn., 1947-51; bookkeeper Frank A. Blesso Inc., Hartford, 1951-63; acct. Houston Lumber Co., Santa Fe, N.Mex., 1963-71; mgr. Nina's Dress Shop, Santa Fe, 1971; tax acct. Sisneros-Stuart-Hallquist C.P.A.'s, Santa Fe, winters 1972-74; owner, operator Rancho de Chimayo, Chimayo, N.Mex., 1965—. Bookkeeper Holy Family Ch., 1966-75, chmn. fin. com., mem. parish council, 1975—; bd. dirs., fin. com. McCurdy Schs., 1979—; voting state del. for presdl. elections, 1976. Mem. N.Mex. Restaurant Assn. (dir. 1978—, 2d v.p. 1980—, pres. 1981-82, chmn. bd.), Nat. Restaurant Assn. (com.), Nat. Assn. Female Execs. Democrat. Roman Catholic. Home and Office: PO Box 11 Chimayo NM 87522

JARAMILLO, MARI-LUCI, former diplomat; b. Las Vegas, N.Mex., June 19, 1928; d. Maurillo and Elvira (Ruiz) Antuna; B.A. magna cum laude, N.Mex. Highlands U., 1955, M.A. with honors, 1959, Ph.D., 1970; m. J. Heriberto Jaramillo, Jan. 3, 1969. Prof., chmn. dept. elem. edn. U. N.Mex., 1972-74, prof. edn., 1974-77; A.E. and P. to Honduras, 1977-80; cons. in field, keynote conf. speaker. Recipient N.Mex. Disting. Public Service award, 1977. Mem. Mex. Am. Women's Assn. Democrat. Roman Catholic. Author chpts. in books, articles, filmstrips. Address: UNMex Albuquerque NM 87131

JARDINE, ELLEN ALEXANDER, artist; b. Eng., Nov. 26, 1909; d. William and Ellen (Smith) Alexander; came to U.S., 1910, naturalized, 1918; student Hillyer Coll., U. Hartford, 1942-47, Hartford Coll. Ins. and Law, 1946, U. New Haven, 1958, Madison Art Sch., 1970-71; m. William Leslie Jardine, Aug. 6, 1949 (dec. May 1979); children—Barbara Hick Warner, Ronald B. Hick. Tool insp. Colt Patent Firearms, Hartford, Conn., 1942-45; tool designer Pratt & Whitney Aircraft, East Hartford, Conn., 1947-51, Marlin Firearms, North Haven, Conn., 1952-56; product designer Control Circuits, Inc., Portland, Conn., 1957-58; designer checker Cramer, div. Conrac Corp., Old Saybrook Conn., 1958-68, Blu-Ray, Inc., Essex, Conn., 1968-70; group exhbns. include: Pinch Penny Gallery, House of Rubens, both Essex, Conn., 1978, Schofield & Vose Gallery, Branford, Conn., 1978, Madison (Conn.) Art Soc., 1978; represented in permanent collections: Madison Med. Center, Madison Public Health Nursing Assn., Madison Public Schs.; also represented in many pvt. collections. Dir. South Central Commn. on Aging, 1976-77; dir. Madison Art Soc., 1975-76. Mem. Clinton Art Soc. (asso.), Nat. League Am. Pen Women, Lyme Art Assn. Republican. Home: 15 Hamilton Dr Madison CT 06443

JARONITZKY, JUNE, state legislator; b. Edmonton, Alta., Can., June 9, 1938; student U. Alta., Alta. Coll.; B.A., Mac Tavish Coll., 1960. Former tchr., cost acct.; mem. Wis. Ho. Reps., 1980—, mem. biennial com., 1981—, children and human devel. com., commerce and consumer affairs com., small bus. and econ. Devel. com., mem. tourism and recreation com. Membership chmn. Bayfield County Republican Com. Mem. Iron River Bus. Assn., Iron River Speedway Assn., Bayfield County Recreation Assn. Office: Wis Ho Reps Room 304 W State Capitol Madison WI 53702

JARRATT, MARY CLAIBORNE, govt. ofcl.; b. Clifton Forge, Va., Oct. 29, 1942; bus. cert. Katharine Gibbs Sch., Boston, 1965; B.A., Mary Baldwin Coll., 1964. Asst. to prof. Harvard U. Grad. Sch. Bus., 1966-67; exec. asst. to Rep. Richard H. Poff of Va., 1967-72; exec. sec. to William R. Haley, mem. Nat. Transp. Safety Bd., 1972-75; mem. profl. staff Com. on Agr., U.S. Ho. of Reps., Washington, 1975-82; asst. sec. of agr. for food and consumer services Dept. Agr., Washington, 1981—. Office: Dept Agr 14th and Independence Ave SW Washington DC 20250

JARRETT, JOYCE CRISCOE, editor; b. Greensboro, N.C., Oct. 13, 1938; d. Langester Clayton and Lillian Louise (Joyce) Criscoe; A.A., Guilford Coll.; married; 1 dau., Patti Lee Jessup Thomas. Tech. publs. writer Celanese Corp., Asheville, N.C., 1962-65; exec. sec. Lorillard Co. div. Loews Theatres Inc., Greensboro, 1965-75, mng. editor employee publs., also public relations, 1975—. Del. N.C. Gov.'s Conf. for Women, 1982. Mem. Internat. Assn. Bus. Communicators (compleat communicator awards 1981, 1982). Carolinas Assn. Bus. Communicators, Quill and Scroll. Republican. Baptist. Home: 2416 Lawndale Dr Greensboro NC 27408 Office: 2525 E Market St Greensboro NC 27401

JARVIS, BARBARA ANNE, former mem. Democratic nat. com., lawyer; b. Kansas City, Mo., Apr. 14, 1934; d. Herman Edward and Marjorie Maude (Graber) Spitzenfeil; A.A., Kansas City Jr. Coll., 1953; B.S. in Polit. Sci. magna cum laude, Ariz. State U., 1976, J.D., 1979; m. Thomas B. Jarvis, Sept. 9, 1965; 1 son, Kenneth Mark. Technologist Menorah Med. Center, Kansas City, Mo., 1955-56, Ariz. State U. Student Health Service, 1960-62, Scottsdale (Ariz.) Bapt. Hosp., 1962-65; chief technologist Skyline Lab., Globe, Ariz., 1967-72; practice law, Phoenix, 1979—. Sec. Globe Planning and Zoning Commn., 1970-75; asso. coordinator Women's Polit. Caucus Ariz.; 1st vice chairperson Ariz. Democratic Com.; mem. Dem. Nat. Com. from Ariz.;

chmn. neighborhood rehab. com. Phoenix Urban Form, 1976-77, mem. steering com., 1976-79; mem. Phoenix Bd. Adjustment, 1977—, chmn., 1980-81; chmn. Village 4 Planning Com., City of Phoenix; bd. dirs. Salvation Army, Globe, Gila Pueblo campus Eastern Ariz. Coll., Gila County Guidance Clinic. Mem. Am. Bar Assn., State Bar Ariz., Maricopa County Bar Assn. (co-chmn. alternatives to sentencing com. 1980-81), Ariz. Women Lawyers, Women in Law (chmn.), Pi Sigma Alpha, Phi Kappa Phi. Address: 7015 N 4th Pl Phoenix AZ 85020

JAUCHEN, BELLE, publishing co. exec.; b. Greenport, N.Y., May 31, 1947; d. Edward and Belle (Clark) J.; B.A., Syracuse (N.Y.) U., 1969. Public relations rep. Yardley of London, 1969-70; advt., publicity and fashion coordinator Berkshire Hosiery div. Vanity Fair Corp., 1970-73; advt. and mktg. mgr. for Forecast mag. Scholastic Mags., 1973-79; regional sales mgr. Ladycom mag. Downey Communications, 1979-81; advt. mgr. Runner mag. Ziff-Davis Publs., N.Y.C., 1981—. Mem. Home Economists in Bus. (dir. 1979), Advt. Women N.Y. Republican. Club: Sandbar Beach. Office: 1 Park Ave New York NY 10016

JAVA, JUDITH JANET JONES, editor, video program dir.; b. Warren, Ohio; d. Philip Ford and Florence (Hoagland) Jones; B.A., Ohio State U.; children—Veronica Anne, Kelley Lynne, Jeffrey Richard. Reporter, Contra Costa (Calif.) Times, 1965-66; spl. sections editor Oakland (Calif.) Tribune, 1966-67; reporter Pitts. Post Dispatch, 1967-69; editor Lafayette (Calif.) Sun, 1970-72; city editor Valley Times, Pleasonton, Calif., 1972-75; spl. sections editor Tri-Valley Herald, Livermore, Calif., 1975-80; news editor, video program dir. Contra Costa Times, Walnut Creek, Calif., 1980—. Chmn. Alameda County Commn. Women, 1975-77. Recipient 1st pl. feature writing East Bay Press Club, 1977; Suburban Newspapers Assn. Community Service award, 1980; AP 1st pl. award, 1980; Pulitzer Prize nominee, 1981. Mem. Soc. Profl. Journalists, Mensa, Nat. Assn. Female Execs. Author: The Java Principle, 1971, also articles. Office: 2640 Shadelands Dr Walnut Creek CA 94598

JAVONS, JOANN, real estate devel. co. personnel exec.; b. Rochester, Pa., Apr. 17, 1945; s. Joseph and Rose Marie Javonovich; B.A. in Psychology, Indiana U. Pa., 1967; postgrad. in counseling Northeastern U., 1970-71; M.A., Goddard Coll., 1973. Asso. dean students Scripps Coll., Claremont, Calif., 1973-76; asso. dir. Women's Center, Calif. State U., Fullerton, 1976-78; asst. dir. Career Planning Center, U.So. Calif., Los Angeles, 1978-80; personnel mgr. Goldrich and Kest Industries, Los Angeles, 1980—. Mem. Am. Soc. Tng. and Devel. (dir. Los Angeles chpt. 1980-81), Personnel and Indsl. Relations Assn. Home: 13900 Panay Way M Bldg #104 Marina del Rey CA 90291 Office: 5150 Overland Ave Culver City CA 90230

JAVORS, IRENE ROSENBERG, psychotherapist; b. Bklyn., Aug. 31, 1948; d. Philip and Miriam (Kopilow) Rosenberg; A.B., Hunter Coll., 1970; M.Ed. in Guidance and Counseling, State U. N.Y. at Buffalo, 1972, M.A. in History, 1973; M.Philosophy, U. City N.Y., 1979; m. Bruce R. Javors, June 20, 1970. Tchr., counselor, Work Incentive Program, Buffalo, 1970-71; youth worker, N.Y. State Div. for Youth, Buffalo, 1971-72; adminstrv. liason, Inst. for Study of the Older Adult, N.Y.C. Community Coll., 1973; tchr., counselor, Kings County Hosp., Ct. Referred Project, Alt. Programs, N.Y. Bd. Edn., 1975-76; pvt. practice psychotherapy, N.Y., 1973—; co.-dir., co-founder Feminist Center for Human Growth and Devel., Inc., N.Y.C., 1977-78; instr. labor history Cornell U. Sch. Labor and Indsl. Relations, N.Y.C. Chmn. mental health sub-com. Health Task Force for Albany Women's Conf., 1977; chmn. N.Y. psychology com. NOW, 1974-76. Mem. Am. Hist. Assn., Coordinating Caucus of Women in the Hist. Profession, Am. Humanistic Psychology Assn., Assn. Women in Psychology (panelist Copenhagen conf. UN World Conf. on Women 1980), Am. Studies Assn., Am. Platform Assn., Internat. Primal Assn. Democrat. Jewish. Participant Women at the Crossroads program, Sta. WNBC, 1977; contbr. paper, Am. Hist. Assn. conf., 1975. Home: 300 Mercer St New York NY 10003

JAYARAM, SUSAN ANN, profl. sec.; b. Stockton, Calif., Nov. 23, 1930; d. George Leroy and Violet Yvonne (Rushing) Potter; student Pasadena Coll., 1951-52; Woodbury Coll., 1961; A.A., Long Beach City Coll., 1979; m. M. R. Jayaram, July 2, 1960. Sec. to mgr. First Western Bank, Los Angeles, 1953-56; sec. to pres. Studio City Bank (Calif.), 1957-60; sec. to exec. v.p. Union Bank, Los Angeles, 1962-81; with Amex Systems, Inc., Hawthorne, Calif., 1981-82; with W.M. Keck Found., Los Angeles, 1982—. Sec., bd. advisors Citizens for Law Enforcement Needs, 1972-74; dir. Los Angeles, Bombay Sister City Com. Cert. Profl. Sec. Mem. Nat. Secs. Assn., DAR, Assistance League So. Calif., Windsor Square/Hancock Park Hist. Soc., League of Ams. (dir.). Republican. Club: Los Angeles Club (dir., sec. 1967—). Editor: Los Angeles Club Panorama, 1979-80; California Clarion, 1978-80. Office: 555 S Flower St Los Angeles CA 90071

JEAN, BARBARA, mfg. co. mktg. exec.; b. Akron, Ohio, Apr. 22, 1941; d. Edwin William and Eva Margaret (Hoffman) Jauchem; student Ohio State U., 1959-60, Rochester Inst. Tech., 1964, U. Rochester, 1967; m. Paul Kuzniar, May 29, 1968; 1 son, Scott Headley. With Eastman Kodak Co., 1963—, sales rep. bus. systems markets div., 1975-77, sales mgr., 1977, coordinator nat. accounts, Rochester, N.Y., 1978, dist. sales mgr., N.Y.C. 1979—; bd. dirs. Kodak Camera Club, 1967-68. Bd. dirs. Planned Parenthood Rochester, 1973-74. Named to 21 Club, Kodak Bus. Systems Div., 1977; recipient N.Y.C. Professionalism award Eastman Kodak Co., 1978. Mem. Exec. Women Internat., Nat. Assn. Profl. Saleswomen, Nat. Account Mktg. Assn. (dir. 1979-80), Advt. Women N.Y., Nat. Microfilm Soc., Photog. Soc. Am. Unitarian. Author: How to Make Good Pictures, 1968; Creative Darkroom Techniques, 1973. Home: 432 E 85th St New York NY 10028 Office: 1133 Ave of Americas New York NY 10036

JEBSEN, JOAN HELENE, med. office systems cons.; b. Bklyn., May 16, 1932; d. Henry William and Helene (Hastedt) Dannevig; student Hunter Coll., 1951-52, Bklyn. Coll., 1953-56, Tex. Christian U., 1962-63; B.A., U. Cin., 1975; postgrad. Wright State U., 1976-77; children—Eric Richard, James Mark, Lawrence Bradford. Adminstrv. sec. Allied Chem. and Dye Corp., N.Y.C., 1953-56; office mgr. Physiatrist Assos., Cin., 1971-74; state coordinator Urban Appalachian Council, Cin., 1975-78; pres./owner Women Assos., Cin., 1978-79; asst. adminstr. U. Cin. Med. Center, 1979-80; owner, cons. Med. Systems Mgmt., Radford, Va., 1980—. Active PTA, 1964-70. Recipient Golden Acorn Lifetime award PTA, 1965. Mem. LWV (chmn. 1974-76), Women in Communications, Bus. and Profl. Women, Med. Group Mgmt. Assn. Unitarian.

JEFFERDS, MARY LEE, environ. edn. assn. exec.; b. Seattle, July 16, 1921; d. Amos Osgood and Vera Margaret (Percival) Jefferds; A.B., U. Calif. at Berkeley, 1943, gen. secondary teaching certificate, 1951; M.A., Columbia, 1947; certificate Washington and Lee U., 1945. Sec., Fair Play Com. Am. Citizens Japanese Ancestry, 1943-44; adminstrv. asst. U.C. Alumni Assn. book Students at Berkeley, 1949; dir. Student Union Monterey Jr. Coll., 1949-50; mgr. Nat. Audubon Soc. Conservation Resource Center, Berkeley, 1951-66; dir. Nat. Audubon Soc. Bay Area Ednl. Services, 1966-71; curriculum cons. Project WEY, U. Calif. Demonstration Lab. Sch., Berkeley, 1972-81; cons. Berkeley Sch. Dist., Alameda County Schs. Mem. land use com., environ. edn. com. East Bay Mcpl. Utility Dist., 1968—; mem. steering com. Nat. Sci. Guild, Oakland Mus., 1971-77; adv. com. Natural History Series, U. Calif. Press, 1972—; community adviser Jr. League of Oakland and East Bay, 1973-77; mem. Cornell Lab. Ornithology, Berkeley Bay Front Council, 1977—. Mem. Berkeley Women's Town Council, 1970—; bd. dirs. East Bay Regional Park Dist., 1972—, v.p., 1976-78, pres., 1979-81; bd. dirs. Save San Francisco Bay Assn., 1969—, Calif. Natural Areas Coordinating Council, 1968—, People for Open Space, 1977—, Living History Center, 1982—, Bay Area Environ. Edn. Alliance, 1982—; bd. dirs. Friends U. Calif. Bot. Gardens, 1976-80, v.p., 1977-80; mem. Calif. Land Use Commn. Served with USAAF, 1944-46. Recipient merit award Calif. Conservation Council, 1953, Woman of Achievement award Grizzly Peak council Camp Fire Girls, 1976; Merit award Am. Assn. Landscape Architects, 1978. Mem. Prytanean Alumnae, Inc. (pres. 1969-71, chmn. adv. council 1971-73), AAUW (mem. Calif. com. 1970-73), Nature Conservancy (chmn. no. Calif. chpt. 1970-71), LWV, U. Calif. Class of 1943 (permanent sec.), Regional Parks Assn., Calif. Assn. Recreation and Park Dists. (dir. 1976—, v.p. No. Calif. 1977-81), Nat., Golden Gate Audubon socs., Nat. Assn. Environ. Edn., Planning and Conservation League, Calif. Native Plant Soc., Nat. Women's Polit. Caucus, Internat. House (N.Y.C.), Urban Care, Citizens for Urban Wilderness Areas, Stiles Hall, U. Calif. Art Council, U. Calif. Alumni Assn., Costeau Soc., Inst. Calif. Man in Nature, NAACP, Mortar Board, Gavel (pres.), Pi Lambda Theta. Democrat. Clubs: Soroptimist (Berkeley), Berkeley Democratic, Commonwealth. Contbr. articles to environ. publs. Home: 2932 Pine Ave Berkeley CA 94705

JEFFERIES, CAROL BROCK, nurse; b. Portsmouth, Va., June 26, 1952; d. Hills Dewitte and Hope Cecil Brock; R.N., Norfolk Gen. Hosp. Sch. Profl. Nursing, 1973; m. Kirk Young Jefferies, Sept. 22, 1973. Staff nurse emergency dept. Portsmouth (Va.) Gen. Hosp., 1973-74; mgr. internists office T. C. Mascarinas, Virginia Beach, Va., 1974-79; charge nurse emergency dept. Portsmouth (Va.) Gen. Hosp., 1976-79, asst. dir. nursing service, 1979-81, head nurse emergency dept., 1981—. Club: Churchland Jaycettes, Sweetbriar Garden Club. Home: 5228 Amherst Dr Portsmouth VA 23703 Office: 850 Crawford Pkwy Portsmouth VA 23703

JEFFERS, MARY GRACE, communications co. exec.; b. Phila., Dec. 2, 1952; d. Harry W. and Helen (Haliday) Jeffers; student Pace U. Mktg. rep. Bell of Pa., 1972-79; market adminstrn. AT&T Long Lines, 1979-81, nat. account exec., 1981—. Recipient numerous sales awards. Mem. Am. Chem. Soc., Nat. Restaurant Assn., Carnegie Hall Soc. Club: Woodbridge Thespian Soc. Pub., editor Woodbridge Commons Newsletter. Home: 1211 Woodbridge Commons Way Iselin NJ 08830 Office: 32 Ave of Americas Rm 1131 New York NY 10013

JEFFERS, SUZANNE MIDDLETON, media cons.; b. Apr. 10, 1949; d. A.H. and Rita Eileen Middleton; B.S., Calif. State Poly. U., 1970; M.A., U. Calif., Berkeley, 1976; m. Michael B. Jeffers, Aug. 14, 1977. Flight attendant TWA, 1970-75; instr. Marymount Manhattan Coll., N.Y.C., also ind. bus. cons., 1974-75; TV journalist, also cons. to corps. in tng. and devel., 1976-79; pres. Corp. & Media Cons., Inc., N.Y.C., 1979—; lectr. in field. Chmn. bd. Children's Oncology Soc. N.Y., 1977—. Named an outstanding working woman of U.S., 1981. Mem. Nat. Acad. TV Arts and Scis., Nat. Acad. TV Program Execs., Assn. Women Bus. Owners, U. Calif. Alumni Assn., Jr. League N.Y. Episcopalian. Clubs: West Side Tennis, River (N.Y.C.). Address: 993 Park Ave New York NY 10028

JEFFERSON, GERALDINE, communications cons.; b. N.Y.C., June 4, 1951; d. Frank Linwood and Bessie (Andrews) Hailstolk; student Hunter Coll., 1970, Bklyn. Coll., 1969; B.S., Empire State Coll., 1982; m. Herbert T. Jefferson, July 19, 1975; 1 dau., Lisa Lynn. Prodn. coordinator Great Am. Dream Machine, Feeling Good Health Show, N.Y.C., 1972, 75; program supr. ABC-TV Entertainment Div., N.Y.C., 1973-74; features editor Soap Opera Digest, N.Y.C., 1977-79; writer/producer Law and the Disabled radio series, N.Y.C., 1979-80; radio cons. Center for Ind. Living, N.Y.C., 1981—; consumer columnist Elan Mag., 1982—; grants evaluator U.S. Dept. Edn., 1980-81; panel mem. Nat. Acad. TV Arts and Scis. Emmy Awards, 1980. Crisis Counselor, N.Y. Women Against Rape Center, 1978. Recipient Award for Excellence in TV Prodn., Bklyn. Coll./Central Bklyn. Model Cities, 1971, Nat. Acad. TV Arts and Scis., 1972. Mem. Authors Guild, Nat. Acad. TV Arts and Sci. Club: N.Y. Press. Contbr. articles to profl. and consumer jours.; also poetry. Address: 35 Midwood St Brooklyn NY 11225

JEFFERSON, MARY KILBOURN, nurse; b. St. Clair Shores, Mich., Sept. 19, 1949; d. Robert Chester and Mary Elizabeth (Yundt) Kilbourn; R.N., Good Samaritan Hosp., 1970; B.S. in Nursing, U. Ky., 1981; children—Dale Matthew, Jennifer Beth. Office nurse Vicente B. Chiong, M.D., Homestead, Fla., 1970-72; asst. head nurse Hayswood Hosp., Maysville, Ky., 1972-75; office, surg. asst. Douglas E. Ott., M.D., Maysville, 1975-79; staff nurse Hayswood Hosp., Maysville, 1979-81; dir. staff devel. Maysville Hosp., 1981—; instr. prepared childbirth classes, basic cardiac life support Am. Heart Assn. Residential chmn. Mason County Heart Fund, 1982; dist. chmn. Cub Scouts, Zanes Trace Dist., Scioto Area council Boy Scouts Am., 1980-82, dist. rep., council exec., 1981—, council tng. chmn., 1982-83. Mem. Am. Nurses Assn., Ky. Nurses Assn. ARC, Buffalo Trace Cancer Council, Sigma Theta Tau. Episcopalian. Home: 904 E 2d St Maysville KY 41056 Office: 8 W 4th St Maysville KY 41056

JEFFREY, MARGIE SUE, transp. co. exec.; b. Evansville, Ind., June 19, 1935; d. James Andrew and Eula Madeth (Tucker) Baughn; student McHenry County Coll., 1977-79, Coll. Advanced Traffic, Chgo., 1977; m. Joseph W. Jeffrey, Nov. 28, 1981; children from previous marriage—Dan Market, Tony Market, Lee Ann Market. With Market Produce Trucking, Evansville, 1959-70; gen. ops. mgr. Farm Service & Supplies Inc., Marengo, Ill., 1970—, v.p., 1980—; pres. MLB Mktg. Services, Marengo 1981—; admitted to practice transport law ICC, 1977. Mem. Marengo Union C. of C., Am. Soc. Traffic and Transp., Assn. ICC Practitioners (nat. com. motor fleet supr. tng.), Am. Assn. Handwriting Analysts, Women's Traffic Club Evansville, Delta Nu Alpha, Traffic Clubs Internat. Home: 9505 Elm Ln Crystal Lake IL 60014 Office: 21606 W Railroad St Marengo IL 60152

JEFFRIES, COUNTESS PEASE, lawyer; b. Washington, Nov. 24, 1948; d. Lincoln and Daisy Pease; B.S.E.E., Howard U., 1969; M.B.A., N.Y. U., 1974; J.D., Harvard U., 1977; 1 son, Brandon. Elec. engr. Underwriter's Labs., Melville, N.Y., 1969; market analyst Hay Fales, N.Y.C., 1972-73; exec. v.p. Urban Bus. Assistance, N.Y.C., 1973; corp. fin. asst. Salomon Bros., N.Y.C., 1975; law clk. firm Graham & James, San Francisco, 1976; admitted to Calif. bar, 1977; mem. firm Manatt, Phelps, et. al., Los Angeles, 1977-78; partner firm Evans, Manpearl & Harter, Los Angeles, 1979-81; asst. prof. Calif. State U., Los Angeles, 1980. Mem. Los Angeles County Bar Assn., Los Angeles C. of C., Inglewood C. of C., Am. Soc. Internat. Law, Inter-Am. Bar Soc., Fgn. Trade Assn., Brazil-Calif. Trade Assn., Harvard Internat. Law Soc., Los Angeles Trial Lawyers Assn., Los Angeles World Affairs Council, Council of Americas, Beverly Hills C. of C. Clubs: Am. Brazilian, Harvard Radcliffe of So. Calif. Office: 400 S Beverly Dr Suite 102 Beverly Hills CA 90212

JELTEMA, JUDITH LOUISE, constrn. co. exec.; b. Grand Rapids, Mich., Oct. 9, 1946; d. Wesley G. and Maxine C. (Datema) J.; B.S., Western Mich. U., 1969; postgrad. Mich. State U., 1974-76. Tchr., girls athletic dir. Lakeview Schs., Battle Creek, Mich., 1969-74; dir. edn. and safety Asso. Gen. Contractors, Lansing, Mich., 1974-76; corporate mgr., human resources and safety Townsend & Bottum, Inc., Ann Arbor, Mich., 1976—. Mem. Am. Soc. Personnel Adminstrs., Am. Soc. Safety Engrs., Constrn. Personnel Execs., Gamma Phi Beta. Home: 2200 Fair St Ann Arbor MI 48103 Office: Townsend & Bottum Inc 2245 S State St Ann Arbor MI 48106

JENKINS, ANNE ELIZABETH GREEN, pediatric therapist, ednl. adminstr.; b. Richmond, Va., May 18, 1944; d. John P. and Dorothy Mae (Williams) Green; B.S., (Rehab. Service Adminstrn. scholar), N.Y.U., 1972; M.A. (Minority Student grad. fellow), Columbia Tchrs. Coll., 1975, Ed.M., 1976; Ph.D., U. N.C.-Greensboro, 1983; m. Earnest Jenkins, June 1, 1964; children—Frederick Anthony, April Kaché, August Kali. Occupational therapist Harlem Hosp., N.Y.C., 1972-74, Blythedale Children's Hosp., Valhalla, N.Y., 1974-77; developmental disabilities specialist Amos Cottage Bowman Gray Sch. Medicine, Winston-Salem, N.C., 1977; dir. Early Intervention Program, Forsyth/Stokes counties, Winston-Salem, 1977-80, learning disabilities specialist, 1980—; mem. faculty N.Y.U. Sch. Edn., N.Y.U. Med. Sch., U. N.C.-Chapel Hill. cons. pre-schools and developmental day-care centers. Mem. Am. Occupational Therapy Assn., Smithsonian Instrn., Assn. Retarded Citizens (dir.), Center Study Sensory Integrations, Am. Burn Assn. Liberal. Roman Catholic. Designer hand orthotics, adaptive equipment for the handicapped. Home: 2931 Springhaven Dr Winston-Salem NC 27103

JENKINS, CAROLE JEAN, banker; b. St. Joseph, Mo., Apr. 11, 1930; d. Leroy Jasper and Lois Mae Speer; student Tyler Jr. Coll., 1965-68, Am. Inst. Banking, 1975, El Centro Jr. Coll., 1976; m. Elmer B. Jenkins, Dec. 4, 1948; 1 dau., Susan K. Jenkins Dodson. Mem. staff Credit Bur. Service, St. Joseph, Mo., 1958-61; mem. credit dept. staff 1st Bank & Trust Co., Richardson, Tex., 1962-65; mem. staff loan dept. 1st Nat. Bank Richardson, 1969-70; asst. cashier Promenade Nat. Bank, Richardson, 1971-74; v.p., cashier Richardson Nat. Bank, 1974-79; v.p., cashier Liberty Nat. Bank, Dallas, 1979-81, sr. v.p., cashier, 1981—. Mem. Bankers Adminstrn. Inst., Assn. Women Bankers, Am. Inst. Bankers. Democrat. Methodist. Club: Soroptimist (treas. 1978-80, pres. 1981). Home: 416 Fairview St Richardson TX 75081 Office: 10501 N Central Expy Dallas TX 75231

JENKINS, CLARA BARNES, educator; b. Franklinton, N.C.; d. Walter and Stella (Griffin) Barnes; B.S., Winston-Salem State U., 1939; postgrad. N.Y.U., 1947-48, U. N.C., 1963; M.A., N.C. Central U., 1947; Ed.D., U. Pitts., 1965; postgrad. N.C. Agrl. and Tech. State U., summer 1971; m. Hugh Jenkins, Dec. 24, 1949 (div. Feb. 1955). Tchr. pub. schs., Wendell, N.C., 1939-43, Wise, N.C., 1943-45; mem. faculty Fayetteville State U., 1945-53, Rust Coll., Holly Spring, Miss., 1953-58; asst. prof. Shaw U., 1958-64; prof. edn. and psychology St. Paul's Coll., Lawrenceville, Va., 1964—; vis. prof. edn. Friendship Jr. Coll., Rock Hill, S.C., summer 1947, N.C. Agrl. and Tech. State 1966-82. Former mem. bd. dirs. Winston-Salem State U. Notary pub., N.C.; United Negro Coll. Fund Faculty fellow, 1963-64; Am. Bapt. Conv. grantee, 1963-64. Mem. AAUP, Nat. Soc. for Study Edn., NEA, AAUW, Am. Hist. Assn., Va. Edn. Assn., Am. Acad. Polit. and Social Sci., AAAS, Internat. Platform Assn., Assn. Tchr. Educators, History Edn. Soc., Doctoral Assn. Educators, Am. Assn. Higher Edn., Acad. Polit. Sci., Am. Psychol. Assn., Soc. Research in Child Devel., Marquis Biog. Library Soc., Jean Piaget Soc., Philosophy of Edn. Soc., Soc. Profs. Edn., Phi Eta Kappa, Zeta Phi Beta. Episcopalian. Home: 920 Bridges St Henderson NC 27536 Office: St Paul's Coll Lawrenceville VA 23868

JENKINS, E. CYNTHIA, librarian; b. Nashville, July 21, 1924; d. Stephen Alexander and Mayne Hampton (Young) Burnley; B.A., U. Louisville, 1945; M.L.A., Pratt Inst., 1966; postgrad., Columbia U.; m. Joseph D. Jenkins, Apr. 17, 1949; 1 son, Joseph D. Librarian, Bklyn. Public Library, 1960-62; br. librarian Queensborough Public Library, Jamaica, N.Y., 1962—. Founder, Social Concern Vendor Agy., Social Concern Home Attendant Program; elected Dem. dist. leader 29th Assembly Dist., 1978—; founder SE Queens Regular Dem. Club: charter mem. Queens chpt. Top Ladies of Distinction. Recipient service citation Negro Bus. and Profl. Women, Jamaica chpt. Mem. N.Y. Black Librarians Caucus (founder), ALA (council), N.Y. Library Assn., Alpha Kappa Alpha (award, Epsilon Pi Omega chpt.). Methodist. Editor, contbr. Forum mag.; contbr. to Handbook on Black Librarianship. Home: 174-63 128 Ave Jamaica NY 11434

JENKINS, ELAINE BROWN, cons. firm. exec.; b. Butte, Mont., Apr. 2, 1916; d. Russell S. and Floy Z. (Zelema) Brown; B.A. in Edn., U. Denver, 1937; M.A. in Philosophy of Edn., Ohio State U., 1938; m. Howard Jenkins, Jr., June 24, 1940; children—Judith E., Howard Jenkins, III, Lawrence C. Tchr. pub. schs., Denver; lead tchr. pub. schs., Washington; pres., founder One America Inc., Washington, 1969—; dir. Women's Nat. Bank; cons. Republican Nat. Com., 1960-69. Chmn. exec. recruitement com. Council of 100 Black Republicans, 1980—; vice chmn. D.C. Central Com., 1962, interim chmn., 1963-64; mem. Commn. of Orgn. Govt. of D.C., 1975; mem. Nat. Vol. Service Adv. Council, 1982, Nat. Adv. Council for Edn. Disadvantaged Children, 1974—. Recipient Eartha N. M. White Women's Achievement award Nat. Bus. League, 1973; Appreciation award Nat. Council Disadvantaged Children, 1973; Appreciation award Oral Roberts, 1976; Service award Las Amigas, Inc., 1978. Mem. Nat. Bus. League, D.C. Bd. Trade, Nat. C. of C., D.C. C. of C., Nat. Assn. Women Bus. Owners, Black President's Roundtable, Delta Sigma Theta. Congregationalist. Home: 3333 University Blvd W Apt 1101 Kensington MD 20795 Office: 1523 L St NW 7th Floor Washington DC 20005

JENKINS, GLORIA DELORES, airline ofcl.; d. David and Johnnie Sue (Smith) Barnes; extension student City U. N.Y.; cert. fund raising N.Y. U., 1982; m. John Elmo Jenkins, 1960 (dec.); children—Gloria Susan Rosario, Melanie Yvette Jenkins Treadwell, Carol Lynn, Jonathan Edward. With Pan Am. World Airways, 1955—, mgmt. prodn. planning aircraft service control maintenance and engring. John F. Kennedy Airport, N.Y.C., 1979-82, mgmt. powerplant planning A/C engine maintenance and engring., 1982—; speaker. Exec. bd. Hansel & Gretel Inc., 1977-79; pres. Addisleigh Park Civic Orgn., 1960; mem. John E. Jenkins Meml. Scholarship Fund, 1980. Recipient various service awards. Mem. Nat. Assn. Female Execs. (network dir.). Mem. A.M.E. Ch. Clubs: Hansel and Gretel (past nat. pres.), Toastmistresses. Office: Pan Am Jet Center Bldg 208 Room 1305 Jamaica NY 11430

JENKINS, JANIE MARIE, beauty cons.; b. Hazen, N.D., Jan. 4, 1950; d. John and Gertrude Ima (Buschbacher) Y.; grad. high sch. Grooming supr. Air Calif., Orange County, 1969-71; home office mgr. Merle Norman Cosmetic Co., Los Angeles, 1971-74; dir. fashion and beauty Carr & Assos. Internat., Los Angeles, 1974-76; owner, pres. Spl. Effect Co., Long Beach, Calif., 1976—; cons. Barbizon Internat., Sun Life Pharms.; originator Formula-J Cosmetics. Active Long Beach Meml. Hosp. Aux. Mem. Nat. Speakers Assn., Marina Pacifica Profl. Women's Assn. (Golden Woman award 1978). Club: Health and Beauty Spa for Women. Author: Build A Better You, 1980. Office: 8211 Marina Pacifica Dr N Long Beach CA 90803

JENKINS, MYRA ELLEN, historian, educator; b. Elizabeth, Colo., Sept. 26, 1916; d. Lewis Harlan and Minnie (Ackroyd) Jenkins; B.A. cum laude, U. Colo., 1937, M.A., 1938; Ph.D., U. N.Mex., 1953. Instr. pub. schs., Climax, Colo., 1939-41, Granada, Colo., 1941-43, Pueblo, Colo., 1943-50; fellow U. N.Mex., 1950-52, asst., 1952-53; free-lance historian and hist. cons., Albuquerque, 1953-59; archivist Hist. Soc.

N.Mex., Santa Fe, 1959-60; archivist, state historian N.Mex. Records Center and Archives, 1960-80; ret., 1980; prof. history Coll. of Santa Fe, 1981-82. Mem. Soc. Am. Archivists, Western History Assn., Hist. Soc. N.Mex., Phi Beta Kappa, Phi Kappa Phi, Phi Alpha Theta, Kappa Delta Pi. Democrat. Episcopalian. Author: The Baltazar Baca Grant, History of an Encroachment, 1961; Guide and Calendar to the Spanish Archives of New Mexico, 1968; Guide and Calendar to the Mexican Archives of New Mexico, 1970; Guide and Calendar to the Territorial Archives of New Mexico, 1974; (with A.H. Schroeder) Brief History of New Mexico, 1975; also articles to profl. jours. and book reviews. Home: 1022 Don Cubero St Santa Fe NM 87501

JENKINS, PHYLLIS ANN, mktg. exec.; b. Washington, Jan. 25, 1946; d. Felix W. and Viola T. (Rumsey) Stevenson; B.Mgmt. and Tech., U. Md., 1979; m. James Arthur Jenkins, May 27, 1972; children—Phyllis Renee, Ronald George, Jelani Akil. Adminstrv. asst. Congressman Richard Schweiker, Congressman Donald Fraser and Congressman Parren Mitchell, Washington, 1968-71; budget analyst/program analyst Consumer Product Safety Commn., EPA, HEW, Washington, 1971-79; maj. account mktg. rep. Xerox Corp., Arlington, Va., 1980—; cons. Info. Processing Center & Public Relations, Washington, 1978—; v.p. info. mgmt. Unique Enterprises, 1978-82. Recipient Superior Performance award U.S. Govt., 1978; Cert. for outstanding contbn. to Mid-Atlantic Conf., Balt., 1981. Democrat. Roman Catholic. Address: 7213 24th Pl Hyattsville MD 20783

JENKINS-LEGGETTE, SEBETHA LEE, ednl. adminstr.; b. Learned, Miss., Sept. 29, 1939; d. Eunice Lee Nelson; B.A., Jackson State U., 1960; M.Ed. (NEH grantee), Delta State U., 1970; Ed.D., Miss. State U., 1978; m. Clyde Leggette, Sept. 19, 1981; 1 dau., Jennifer. Instr., English Clarksdale (Miss.) City Schs., 1960-64, Madison County (Miss.) Schs., 1964-66; instr. English, dept. head Coahoma Jr. Coll., Clarksdale, 1966-75; sex equity cons. Title IX Miss. State U., 1975-79, asst. univ. v.p., 1979—; cons. Miss. Ednl. Services Center. Bd. dirs. Big Bros./Big Sisters Inc.; pres. Scholarship Commn.; active Commn. on Status of Women. Mem. AAUW, Nat. Assn. Women Deans, Adminstrs. and Counselors, Nat. Hook-Up of Black Women, Miss. Assn. for Women in Higher Edn., NAACP (dir. Oklibbeha County chpt.), Orgn. for Profl. Women Devel. (charter mem.), Delta Sigma Theta. Home: PO Box 43 Starkville MS 39759 Office: PO Box J Mississippi State MS 39762

JENKS, EDITH CHARLOTTE, personnel corp. exec.; b. St. Paul; d. Jonas G. and Betsy (Erickson) Engquist; student extension courses U. Minn. and Oakland Community Coll. various years; m. Wilbur R. Jenks, Apr. 20, 1935 (div.). Personnel counselor Los Angeles Comml. Service, 1947-48, supr. female div., 1948-51; with Graebner and Co., Mpls., 1951-53, Detroit, 1953-54; Pres. Dorothy Day Personnel, Inc., Detroit, Dearborn, Livonia, Warren and Royal Oak, Mich., 1953—; owner Hill Personnel, Mpls., 1965—, St. Paul Employment Service, 1968—, Dorothy Day Office Service, 1965—, Hill Office Service, 1975—, Golden Lion Antiques, Long Lake, Minn., 1976-78. Active Franklin Mich. Community Assn., Birmingham, centennial commn. Excelsior, Minn., Hist. Soc.; fund raiser Am. Cancer Soc.; active Republican presdl. elections, Franklin, Birmingham, Excelsior. Mem. Nat. Assn. Personnel Cons., Mich. Assn. Personnel Cons., Detroit Employment Assn. (sec. 1958-60), Nat. Assn. Female Execs., Detroit C. of C. Clubs: Minnetonka Country, Order Eastern Star (officer Los Angeles 1947-58). Home: 26175 Wild Rose Ln Excelsior MN 55331 Office: 950 Buhl Bldg Detroit MI 48226

JENKS, SARAH ISABEL, nursing adminstr.; b. Springfield, Mo., May 5, 1913; d. George S. and Mary (Laing) Cuckie; diploma St. Joseph Mercy Hosp., 1934; student U. Calif. Extension, 1959-70, West Coast U., 1974, 78; m. Dean F. Thompson, June 16, 1936 (dec. 1949); 1 son, Dean F.; m. 2d, Kermit Jenks, June 17, 1951. Staff nurse Calif. Hosp., Los Angeles, 1936-37, head nurse, 1937-38, supr., 1938-40; indsl. nurse May Co., Los Angeles, 1941-43; office nurse, Burbank, Calif., 1944-45, Fort Dodge, Iowa, 1946-57; office mgr. Inglewood Med. Clinic (Calif.), 1957-58; occupational health nurse, Hawthorne, Calif., 1958-72; supervising nurse Occupational Health Service, Los Angeles County, 1972-75; chief occupational health nurse Naval Regional Med. Center, Long Beach, Calif., 1975-81; adminstrv. nurse Occupational Health Center, U. Calif., Irvine, 1981—; nursing chmn. ARC, 1964-70. Recipient Schering Occupational Health Nurse award, 1979. Mem. Am. Nurses Assn. (chmn. occupational health nurse forum 1968-72), Calif. State Nurses Assn. (pres. Centinela Valley 1963-65), Calif. State Occupational Health Nurses Assn., Am. Assn. Occupational Health Nurses, United Scottish Soc. Democrat. Presbyterian. Home: 17700-88 Avalon Blvd Carson CA 90746 Office: Southern Occupational Health Center Univ Calif Irvine 19722 MacArthur Blvd Irvine CA 92717

JENNERICH, ELAINE ZAREMBA, librarian; b. New Castle, Pa., Apr. 17, 1947; d. Casimir Paul and Regina Anna (Wajert) Zaremba; B.A., Syracuse U., 1968; M.S. in Library Sci. (H. W. Wilson Co. scholar), Drexel U., 1970; Ph.D. in Library Sci., U. Pitts., 1974; m. Edward John Jennerich, May 27, 1972. Library asst. Syracuse U. Library, 1964-68; grad. asst. Drexel U. Grad. Sch. Library Sci., 1968-70; cataloger German Soc. Phila., 1969; cataloger Grace Library, Carlow Coll., 1971-73, reference librarian, 1973-74; instr., asst. in reference services Moody Library, Baylor U., Waco, 1974-75, asso. prof., head reference services Moody Library, 1975—. Recipient award in librarianship Spl. Libraries Council Phila., 1970. Mem. ALA (chmn. reference and adult services div. standards com. 1977-81, reference tools adv. com. 1981—), Library Adminstrn. and Mgmt. Assn. (dir. personnel adminstrn. sect. 1979-81), Chi Omega (v.p. Syracuse U. chpt.), Beta Phi Mu. Book reviewer Library Jour., 1973-75; book reviewer RQ, 1976-78, editorial bd., 1979—. Home: 3306 Cliffdale Waco TX 76708 Office: Baylor U Moody Meml Library Box 6307 Waco TX 76706

JENNINGS, ANNE M., counseling psychologist; b. Nashville, July 26, 1931; d. Richard H. and Mollie E. (Smith) Young; B.A., Neumann Coll., 1977; M.A., Bowie State Coll., Adler-Dreikurs Inst. Human Relations, 1979; m. William B. Jennings III, Sept. 1, 1950; children—Jennifer, Jeannine, Jeffrey. Pvt. practice psychol. counseling, Wilmington, Del., 1978—; adv. com. Family Ct. of Del. Restitution project, 1979-80, guardian ad litem., 1981—; counselor, supr. Family Edn. Center of Del., Inc., 1974-77. Mem. Am. Personnel and Guidance Assn., Nat. Employment Counselors Assn., Nat. Vocat. Guidance Assn., N.Am. Soc. Individual Psychology. Republican. Unitarian. Address: 4 Broadbent Rd Wilmington DE 19810

JENNINGS, CAROL RAYMOND, former sch. psychologist; b. Buffalo, Apr. 24, 1929; d. Morris Thomas and Dorothy Cushing (Whitridge) Raymond; student Cazenovia Jr. Coll., 1947-49; B.A., Denison U., 1951; M.A., Fairfield U., 1970; student So. Conn. State Coll., 1976; m. Irving Callander Jennings, June 25, 1977; children—William M. Salmons, Jr., Elizabeth D. Salmons. Dir. teen-age program YWCA, Greenwich, Conn., 1951-54; sch. psychologist Norwalk (Conn.) Bd. Edn., 1970-81, coordinator psychol. services, 1974-77. Treas., Farm Creek Com. of Nature Conservancy, 1976-77, chmn., 1977-78, sec., 1978-79; mem. Norwalk Land Trust, 1979-82. Mem. Conn. Assn. Sch. Psychologists.

JENNINGS, MADELYN PULVER, communications co. exec.; b. Saratoga Springs, N.Y., Nov. 23, 1934; d. George Joseph and Martha (Walsh) Pulver; B.A. in Bus. and Econs., Tex. Woman's U., 1956. Asst. mgr. pub. relations Slick Airways, Dallas, 1956-58; asst. dir. radio-TV promotion VIP Service, Inc., N.Y.C., 1958-60; bus. mktg. planning Gen. Electric Co., Bridgeport, Conn., 1960-68, mgr. manpower planning, 1968-71, mgr. environ. support operation, 1971-73; v.p. human resources Standard Brands, Inc., N.Y.C., 1976-79; v.p. human resources Gannett Co., Rochester, N.Y., 1979-80, sr. v.p. personnel and adminstrn., 1980—. Trustee Russell Sage Coll. Mem. AAUW, Adv. Council Mgmt. and Personnel, Human Resources Planning Soc., Human Resources Roundtable; Am. Soc. Profl. and Exec. Women (adv. bd.), Newspaper Personnel Relations Assn., Am. Soc. Personnel Adminstrs., Human Resources Execs. Steering Com. Office: Gannett Co Lincoln Tower Rochester NY 14604

JENNINGS, MARCELLA GRADY, rancher, investor; b. Springfield, Ill., Mar. 4, 1920; d. William Francis and Magdalene Mary (Spies) Grady; student pub. schs.; m. Leo J. Jennings, Dec. 16, 1950 (dec.). Pub. relations Econolite Corp., Los Angeles, 1958-61; v.p., asst. mgr. LJ Quarter Circle Ranch, Inc., Polson, Mont., 1961-73, pres., gen. mgr., owner, 1973—; dir. Giselle's Travel Inc., Sacramento; fin. advisor to Allentown, Inc., Charlo, Mont.; sales cons. to Amie's Jumpin' Jacks and Jills, Garland, Tex. investor. Mem. Internat. Charolais Assn., Los Angeles County Apt. Assn. Republican. Roman Catholic. Home and office: 509 Mt. Holyoke Ave Pacific Palisades CA 90272

JENNINGS, MYRA FERN, savs. and loan assn. exec.; b. Alton, Ill., Mar. 15, 1941; d. Henry Martin and A. Mae (Nixon) J.; A.Acctg., So. Ill. U., 1975, B.S. in Bus. Adminstrn.- Acctg., 1978; grad. diploma Inst. Fin. Edn., 1972. Teller Citizens Savs. and Loan Assn., East Alton, Ill., 1959-70, treas., 1970—, head acctg. dept., 1969—, dir., 1977—; instr. Lewis and Clark Coll., Godfrey Inst. Fin. Edn. Organist 1st United Meth. Ch., East Alton, 1976—. Mem. Fin. Mgrs. Soc., Women in Savs. Assn. State of Ill. (formation com.) Republican. Home: 620 Valley Dr East Alton IL 62024 Office: 700 Berkshire Blvd East Alton IL 62024

JENNINGS, TONI, state ofcl.; b. Orlando, Fla., May 17, 1949; d. Jack and Margaret J.; B.A., Wesleyan Coll., 1971; postgrad. Rollins Coll., 1972-73. Tchr., Orange County Public Schs., 1971-73; corp. officer Jack Jennings & Sons, Inc., Orlando, 1973—; mem. Fla. Ho. Reps., 1976-80; mem. Fla. Senate, Orlando, 1980—. Recipient Spl. Commendation, Fla. Restaurant Assn., 1970; Meritorious Service award Fla. Fedn. Humane Socs., 1979; named Legislator of Yr., Associated Builders and Contractors of Fla., 1978, Orange County Young Republican Club, 1980-81; Freedom award for excellence in state govt. Women for Responsible Legislation, 1982. Mem. Orlando-Winter Park Bd. Realtors, Associated Builders and Contractors, Central Fla. Builders Exchange, Delta Kappa Gamma, Phi Kappa Phi, Kappa Delta Epsilon. Republican. Episcopalian. Office: 1032 Wilfred Dr Orlando FL 32803

JENSEN, ANNE TURNER, automobile service co. exec.; b. Upper Providence Twp., Pa., Sept. 15, 1926; d. Ellwood Jackson and Elizabeth Addis (Downing) Turner; student Hood Coll., 1944-45, Phila. Coll. Pharmacy and Sci., 1945-46, 47-48; m. Harry Frederick Jensen, Jr., Apr. 13, 1946; children—Frederick Howard, Richard Jordan, Peter Hielm. Legal sec. Robertson & Turner, Media, Pa., 1950-51; sec. Luncheon-is-Served, Media, 1951-53; asst. sec., treas. Delvale Realty Corp., Media, 1955-59; bookkeeper Turner Realty Co., 1960-64, William H. Turner, Atty., 1960-64, Media Auto Service, 1957-74; sec. Media Auto Service, Inc., 1957-72. Capt. Heard Fund Dr., 1958-60. Republican. Presbyterian. Clubs: DAR (chpt. regent 1971-74, state corr. sec. 1977-80, nat. chmn. 1974-77), Daughters of Am. Colonists, Daughters of Colonial Wars (state treas. 1974-77, 80-83), Magna Carta Soc., Daus. of 1812, Navy League U.S. (N.Y. Council). Home: 401 Gayley St Media PA 19063

JENSEN, BARBARA WOOD, interior designer; b. Salt Lake City, Apr. 30, 1927; d. John Howard and Loretta (Sparks) Wood; student public schs.; m. Lowell N. Jensen, June 26, 1947; children—Brent Lowell, Robyn Lynn, Todd Wood. Bookkeeper, 1945-47; interior decorator paint and wallpaper co., 1947-49; cons. interior designer, 1950-60; pres., treas. Barbara Jensen Interiors, Inc., Salt Lake City, 1960-79, interior designer, 1979—; dir. 1st Women's Bancorp. Utah. Ball chmn. Utah Legis. Republican Ball, 1970, Utah Symphony Ball, 1979. Fellow Inst. Profl. Designers (London); mem. Assistance League, Com. Fgn. Affairs, Interior Design Soc. (assoc.). Mem. Ch. Jesus Christ of Latter-day Saints. Clubs: Ft. Douglas Country, Knife and Fork, Hi-Steppers Dance, Ladies Lit., Pres. of U. Utah, Elks. Office: 3265 S 1100 E Salt Lake City UT 84106

JENSEN, ELEANOR GRACE, psychologist; b. Bklyn., May 25, 1946; d. Charles Joseph and Jane Elizabeth (Moore) Rifenberg; A.A.S., N.Y.C. Community Coll., 1967; B.A., Richmond Coll., 1970; M.Ed., U. Ariz., 1973; m. Richard Alan Jensen, Aug. 8, 1970; 1 dau., Jennifer Ann. Behavior analyst Chandler Public Schs., 1973; counselor Mesa Community Coll., 1972-73; behavior analyst Tucson Elem. Schs., 1973; research asst. organic chemistry dept. U. Heidelberg (W. Ger.), 1967-68; sci. asst. chemistry dept. Bklyn. Coll., 1965-70; sci. tchr. Bel-Air Middle Sch., 1970-71; tech. recruiter Dunhill of Phoenix, 1973-75; instr. E. Central Community Coll. Service Center, Cambridge, Minn., 1978-81, Mesa (Ariz.) Community Coll., 1982—; behavior analyst Cambridge State Hosp., 1979-80. Mem. Am. Psychol. Assn. (asso.), Minn. Psychol. Assn., Minn. Women Psychologists Assn., Minn. Assn. Behavior Analysts. Republican. Lutheran. Address: 2548 W Keating Mesa AZ 85202

JENSEN, HELEN, musical artists mgmt. co. exec.; b. Seattle, June 30, 1919; d. Frank and Sophia (Kantosky) Leponis; student public schs., Seattle; m. Ernest Jensen, Dec. 2, 1939; children—Ernest, Ronald Lee. Co-chmn., Seattle Community Concert Assn., 1957-62; sec. family concerts Seattle Symphony Orch., 1959-61; hostess radio program Timely Topics, 1959-60; gen. mgr. Western Opera Co., Seattle, 1962-64, pres. 1963-64; v.p., dir., mgr. public relations Seattle Opera Assn., 1964—, preview artists Coordinator, 1981-83; bus. mgr. Portland (Oreg.) Opera Co., 1968, cons., 1967-69; owner, mgr. Helen Jensen Artists Mgmt., Seattle, 1970—. First v.p. Music and Art Found., 1981-83. Recipient Cert., Women in Bus in the Field of Art, 1973. Mem. Am. Guild Mus. Artists, Music and Art Found., Seattle Opera Guild (pres.), Ballard Symphony League (sec.), Seattle Civic Opera Assn. (pres. 1981-83), Portland Opera Assn., Portland Opera Guild, Seattle Civic Opera Assn., 200 Plus One, Aria Preview, Lyric Preview Group, Past Pres. Assembly (pres. 1977-79) North Shore Performing Arts Assn. (pres. 1981). Clubs: Helen Jensen Hiking, Kenmore Community. Home: 19029 56th Ln NE Seattle WA 98155 Office: 716 Joseph Vance Bldg Seattle WA 98101

JENSEN, JACKSIE ANN, nurse, artist; b. Robersonville, N.C., Mar. 4, 1932; d. Floyd Oscar and Annie Elizabeth (Warren) Whitehurst; A.B. cum laude, Free Will Baptist Bible Coll., 1957; grad. Met. Nashville Gen. Hosp. Sch. Nursing, 1960; m. Roy Stanley Jensen, Sept. 4, 1960; children—Chris Stanley, Timothy Floyd, Rebecca Louanne. Staff nurse, head nurse pediatrics Norfolk (Va.) Gen. and Children's Hosp., 1960-61; staff nurse Met. Nashville Gen. Hosp., 1961-65; head nurse Jesse Holman Jones Hosp., Springfield Tenn., 1965; psychiat. nurse instr. Ky. Dept. Vocat. Edn., 1966-69; charge nurse CCU, Jennie Stuart Hosp., Hopkinsville, Ky., 1970; charge nurse and supr. Jesse Holmon Jones Hosp., 1970-74, dir. coronary ICU, 1974—; exhibited at Robertson County Fair, 1981, 82 (1st pl. in oils), Creek Falls State Park, 1982. Mem. Am. Assn. Critical Care Nurses, Tenn. Hosp. Assn., Am. Heart Assn. (nursing edn. com.). Republican. Baptist. Home: Route 2 Cedar Hill TN 37032

JENSEN, JANET IRMA, accountant; b. Salt Lake City, Sept. 24, 1948; d. Orville A. and Irma H. (Kortesoja) J.; B.S. in Bus., U. Hawaii, 1974, postgrad., 1974-75. Self-employed accountant, 1970-73; part-time real estate saleswoman, 1973; accountant firm Laventhol & Horworth, Honolulu, 1974-76; pvt. practice public acctg., Honolulu, 1976—; cons. in field. Bd. dirs., treas., chmn. fund raising Big Bros./Bis Sisters Honolulu, 1977-80. C.P.A., Hawaii. Mem. Nat. Assn. Accts., Small Bus. Mgmt. Assn., Nat. Fedn. Ind. Bus., Hawaii Soc. C.P.A.'s (edn. chmn. 1979-80), Honolulu Bd. Realtors, Honolulu C. of C. Mem. Minya Konka climbing expdn., Tibet, 1980. Home: 3121 Paulei Circle Honolulu HI 96815 Office: Suite 1220 Grosvenor Center 733 Bishop St Honolulu HI 96813

JENSEN, JULIE MAE, educator; b. Hutchinson, Minn., Dec. 6, 1943; d. Axel M. and Mae A. (Hoodecheck) J.; B.S., U. Minn., 1965, M.A., 1968, Ph.D., 1970. Classroom tchr. Mpls. Public Schs., 1965-67; instr. U. Minn., 1967-70; mem. faculty U. Tex., Austin, 1970—, prof. edn., 1981—; vis. prof. U. Tenn., 1975, U. Minn., 1977; cons. in field. Recipient award of excellence for profl. journalism Ednl. Press Assn. Am., 1982; NDEA fellow, 1967-70. Mem. Nat. Council Tchrs. English (research award in teaching English 1970), Nat. Conf. Research in English. Author: and Evaluation in the English Language Arts, 1975; (with Petty) Developing Children's Language, 1980; (with Fagan and Cooper) Measures for Research also revs., articles, chpts. in books; editor Lang. Arts, 1976—. Office: 406 Edn Bldg U Tex Austin TX 78712

JENSEN, LINDA SMERNOFF, human resource cons., fin. and estate planner; b. Bingham Canyon, Utah, Sept. 23, 1942; d. Hyman and Norrene (Andreason) Smernoff; student U. Utah, 1960-63; m. Frank Jensen, Mar. 28, 1973; 1 son, Gary Bryan Fessenden. With Prudential Fed. Savs. & Loan Assn., Salt Lake City, 1965-68; office mgr. Knight Adjustment Bur., Salt Lake City, 1968-73; owner, mgr. LDR Profl. Billing, Salt Lake City, 1973-79; asst. dir. Padaux Inst., 1982—; v.p. Septre Group Ltd., Salt Lake City, 1980—; owner, operator Yes I Will, Inc., Sale Lake City, 1979—. Assoc. dir. Phoenix Transition Center, 1982. Mem. Nat. Assn. Female Execs., Sales and Mktg. Execs. Salt Lake (dir.), Life Underwriters Assn. Salt Lake, Women's Life Underwriters Conf., Internat. Assn. Fin. Planners, Inst. Cert. Fin. Planners, Salt Lake Area C. of C., Women's Info. Network (founder, past pres.). Club: Soroptimists Internat. (v.p. Salt Lake chpt.). Office: 383 S 6th E Salt Lake City UT 84102

JENSEN, LO KATHRYN, precious metal co. exec.; b. Richmond, Calif., Mar. 22, 1946; d. Charles Augustus and Vera Violet (Peterson) Bailey; student Merit Coll., U. Calif., Berkeley; m. Lin Clifford Jensen, Feb. 14, 1964 (div.); 1 dau., Lisa Kristina. Exec. sec. to regional mgr. TRT Telecommunications, N.Y.C., 1974; asst. to sr. vice-pres. Minemet Trading Corp., N.Y.C., 1974-75; asst. to pres. Commodity Finance Corp., N.Y.C., 1975; asst. to pres. Krohn Industries, Inc., Carlstadt, N.J., after 1975, now v.p.; dir. CSI, Inc., Caribbean Supply Internat. Inc., Surtidos Caribe Internat. Inc. Mem. NOW. Republican. Office: Krohn Industries Inc 303 Veterans Blvd Carlstadt NJ 07072

JENSEN, LUELLA MAXINE, business exec.; b. Lusk, Wyo., Mar. 23, 1946; d. Harold A. and Catherine A. (Brunckhorst) Wilson; B.S. in Bus. Edn., Chadron State Coll., 1968, M.S., 1973; postgrad. Central Mo. State U., 1978; m. Ronald R. Jensen, Aug. 14, 1971. Tchr. bus. Sandhills Public High Sch., Halsey, Nebr., 1968-71; grad. asst. Chadron (Nebr.) State Coll., 1971-72, instr. bus., 1973-77, asso. prof. bus., 1978-80, EPDA vocat. in-service grant dir., 1974-75, faculty facilitator Title III Instl. Planning Team. Adult vol. Dawes County 4-H program, 1975-77, 80-81; sec., co-owner, bus. mgr. Ron's Repair Shop, Chadron, 1980—. Active Chadron Walking Blood Bank, 1975—. Mem. Nat. Bus. Edn. Assn., Nebr. Bus. Edn. Assn., NEA, Nebr. Edn. Assn., Chadron State Coll. Edn. Assn., Council for Advancement Exptl. Learning (Nebr. state coordinator 1980—), Phi Kappa Phi, Phi Beta Lambda. Republican. Methodist. Contbr. articles to profl. jours. Home: Route 1 Box 126 Chadron NE 69337 Office: 227 Morehead St Chadron NE 69337

JENSEN, MAGDELINE EILEEN, probation officer; b. Oakland, Calif., Sept. 4, 1949; d. Thorwald B. and Editha P. J.; A.B. in Criminology with honors (Phoebe A. Hearst scholar 1967-68, Univ. Alumni scholar 1967-68, 69-70, 70-71), U. Calif., Berkeley, 1971, M.Criminology, 1972, postgrad. in criminology, 1972-73, 74. Pharmacy clk. Eden Hosp., Castro Valley, Calif., 1967-72; teaching asst. U. Calif., 1972; dep. probationofficer Contra Costa County (Calif.), 1973—; lectr. Calif. State U., Hayward, 1978—; mem. Women's Work Furlough Adv. Com., 1976; mem. Contra Costa County Women's Detention Facility Task Force, 1977; Bd. dirs. Friends Outside, Martinez, Calif., 1977—, pres., 1982—. Mem. Calif. Probation, Parole and Correctional Officer's Assn. (exec. bd. Transbay chpt.), Sigma Kappa. Democrat. Office: 938 Main St Martinez CA 94553

JENSEN, MARGARET FOSTER, bldg. and contracting co. exec.; b. Norfolk, Va., May 6, 1938; d. Walter Herrick and Dorothy Louise (Ellis) Foster; student public schs., Norfolk; m. George C. L. Jensen, June 22, 1974 (dec. 1978); children—Stephen L. Annarino, Donna A. Gilbert. Sec., George Jensen (became George Jensen Inc. 1968), Norfolk, 1962-68, corp. sec., 1968-78, pres.-treas., owner, 1978—. Active Tidewater and Va. chpts. Assn. for Retarded Children. Mem. Builders and Contractors Exchange (dir. 1981-83). Presbyterian. Club: Daus. of Nile (Queen 1965). Home: 369 W Princess Anne Rd Norfolk VA 23517 Office: 3334 Marne Ave Norfolk VA 23509

JENSEN, MARGIT STRANDER, educator; b. Copenhagen, Aug. 8, 1934; came to U.S., 1953, naturalized, 1956; d. Herman Strander and Marie Hoff (Tofft) J.; B.A., Purdue U., 1975; M.S., Butler U., Indpls., 1977; children—Gregory, Karen, Kirsten. Tchrs. aide Gary (Ind.) Community Sch. Corp., 1965-75; media specialist Lebanon (Ind.) Community Sch. Corp., 1975-78, Duneland Sch. Corp., Chesterton, Ind., 1978—. Mem. NEA, Ind. Tchrs. Assn., Ind. Media Educators, Duneland Tchrs. Assn. (past negotiator). Compiler bibliography for nutrition manual State of Ind., 1978. Home: 1507 Monticello Park Dr Valparaiso IN 46383 Office: 100 Beam St Porter IN 46304

JENSEN, MARILYN ELLEN, practical nurse; b. Kenosha, Wis., Mar. 31, 1949; d. Donald J. and Ellen June (Tjepkema) Bosman; student Concordia Coll., Moorhead, Minn., 1967-69; lic. practical nurse, Kenosha Tech. Inst., 1971, cert. early childhood devel., 1978; m. Robert Dean Jensen, Aug. 9, 1969; 1 son, Jason Ryan. Practical nurse Kenosha Meml. Hosp., 1971-76, 79—; presch. tchr. Kiddie Kollege, Kenosha, 1977—. Mem. Jane Vernon Sch. Assn. (dir.), Gen. Fedn. Women's Clubs, Kenosha Meml. Hosp. Aux. (dir.). Lutheran. Clubs: Kenosha Jr. Women's (hon. past pres.). Address: 8312 23d Ave Kenosha WI 53140

JENSEN, MYRTLE TAYLOR, accountant; b. Kelso, Wash., July 20, 1917; d. Perry Edward and Ada May (Hubbard) Taylor; student U. So. Calif., U. Calif. at Los Angeles; m. Walter P. Jensen, May 20, 1936. Prin., M.T. Jensen, C.P.A., Los Angeles, 1947—. C.P.A., Calif. Mem. Am. Inst. C.P.A.'s, Calif. Soc. C.P.A.'s Soc. Calif. Accountants, Nat. Soc. Pub. Accountants. Republican. Home: 912 E Windsor Rd Glendale CA 91205 Office: 4201 Wilshire Blvd Suite 218 Los Angeles CA 90010

JENSEN, SENTA HELLA, speech pathologist, translator, writer; b. Hamburg, Ger., Sept. 17, 1920; d. John Henry and Martha Erna (Wiering) Poock; cert. Webster Bus. Coll., Jersey City, 1938; B.A., Hunter Coll., 1950; M.A. in Speech Pathology, 1953; m. Christian T. Jensen, June 26, 1943 (dec.); children—Lenore Christina Jensen Simon. Fgn. lang. sec., N.Y.C., 1938-42; co-owner John Poock Constrn. Co., Ridgefield Park, N.J., 1942-52; pvt. practice speech pathology, N.Y.C., 1958-61; dir., owner Bergen Speech Clinic, Ridgefield Park, 1953-61; speech pathologist Cornell U., N.Y. Hosp., dir. plastic surgery cleftpalate speech clinic, 1953-61; chief speech clinician Einstein Med. Center, Phila., 1964; speech pathologist Pennsauken (N.J.) Public Schs. and Bucks County (Pa.) Public Schs., 1965-68; speech pathologist, hearing clinician De La Warr Sch. Dist., New Castle, Del., 1968-72; free-lance learning disability cons., 1972-74; coordinator, cons. N.J. Dept. Mental Retardation, 1974-75; adminstrv. dir. Betty Bacharach Rehab. Hosp., Pomona, N.J., 1975-78; founder, dir. 1st cleftpalate speech clinic and aphasia clinic in S. Jersey, 1976-78; speech pathologist CORA Youth Services, Phila., 1982—; mem. Legis. Task Force Com. Am. Speech and Hearing Assn., Washington, 1978-80. Fund raiser Easter Seals. Lic. speech pathologist, Md., Del. Mem. Am. Speech, Lang. and Hearing Assn. (cert.), N.Y. Acad. Scis., Lit. Soc. Found. (hon.), Am. Scandinavian Found., Internat. Council Exceptional Children, Delta Phi Alpha, Sigma Epsilon Phi.

JENSEN, SHERRIE JEAN, sch. dist. personnel adminstr.; b. Enumclaw, Wash., Sept. 15, 1949; d. Gomer and Marie Ann (Barnes) Evans; student Seattle City U., 1981—; m. Kenneth Albert Jensen, Oct. 2, 1979; children— Jennifer, Bradley Jensen, Michael Armstrong. Exec. sec. Kent (Wash.) Sch. Dist., 1971-76, personnel mgr., 1976, supr. personnel, 1977—; cons./trainer for tchr. hiring practices. Mem. Wash. Assn. Sch. Personnel Adminstrs., Am. Assn. Sch. Personnel Adminstrs., Wash. Assn. Sch. Adminstrs., N.W. Women in Ednl. Adminstrn., King County Personnel Adminstrs. Assn., Maple Valley Athletic Assn., Maple Valley C. of C. (parade chairperson 1978). Democrat. Presbyterian. Clubs: Maple Valley Jr. Football (sec.), Internat. Order of Rainbow (lifetime mem.). Home: 17604 SE 292d Pl Kent WA 98031 Office: 12033 SE 256th St Kent WA 98031

JENSEN, SHIRLEY WULFF, bus. exec.; b. Kingsbury County, S.D., Jan. 12, 1925; d. Ferdinand and Karen Margaret (Jensen) Wulff; honor grad. Chillicothe Bus. Coll., 1943; m., Nov. 23, 1975; 1 son, Fred Monroe Smith, Jr. Legal sec., New Port Richey, Fla., 1959-63; sec. to pres. Huron (S.D.) Coll., 1947-50; ins. agt., bd. dirs., mgr. Farm Mut. Fire Ins. Co. of Kingsbury County, De Smet, S.D., 1972-75; exec. sec. Beresford (S.D.) C. of C. and Beresford Bus. and Indsl. Devel. Corp., 1976-78; partner, office mgr., sales asst. Black Angus Ranch and Jensen Appliances, Beresford, 1979—. City commr. De Smet, 1974-75; Kingsbury County chmn. Easter Seal Soc., 1973-75; mem. S.D. Women's Caucus, Women's Action for Nuclear Disarmament, S.D. Peace and Justice Center. Mem. S.D. Assn. Mut. Ins. Cos. (1st woman dir.), Beresford C. of C. Club: Christian Women's. First woman city commr. De Smet. Home and Office: Route 3 Box 11 Beresford SD 57004

JENSEN, WILMA MARY WESTBURG, assn. exec.; b. Hopkins, Minn., June 11, 1916; d. Andrew Herman and Ida (Anderson) Westburg; B.A., Gustavus Adolphus Coll., 1938; B.L.S., U. Minn., 1940; m. Emmanuel T. Jensen, Aug. 15, 1947. Asst. librarian reference library, U. Minn., Mpls., 1940-43; counsellor for students Nat. Lutheran Council, U. Calif., Berkeley, 1943-47, Iowa State U., Ames, 1947-48; librarian, sec. Donovan-Lovering-Boyle, Contractors, Pickstown, S.D., 1951-56; sec. Lutheran World Fedn., Mpls., 1957; sec. bd. Am. missions, Augustana Lutheran Ch., Mpls., 1957-62; exec. sec. Lutheran Ch. Library Assn., Mpls., 1963—. Nat. del. Lutheran Ch. Am., 1966; nat. adv. Lutheran Student Assn. Am., 1946-47; mem. Minn. Adv. Council on Library Scis., 1973-78. Bd. dirs. Com. Am. Missions, Minn., Lutheran Ch. in Am., Minnetonka (Minn.) Music Assn., Gustavus Library Assos., 1977—. Named World Brother, World Brotherhood Exchange, 1962; recipient Distinguished Alumni citation Gustavus Adolphus Coll., 1974. Mem. Lutheran Ch. Library Assn. (nat. v.p., 1962, nat. pres., 1963), Ch. and Synagogue Library Assn. (nat. dir. 1967-77, v.p. 1970-71, pres. 1971-72), Am., Minn. library assns., Council of Nat. Library and Info. Assns. (councillor 1979—), United Lutheran Ch. Women (life), Alpha Phi Gamma, Iota Beta. Republican. Lutheran. Home: 3620 Fairlawn Dr Minnetonka MN 55343 Office: Luth Ch Library Assn 122 W Franklin Ave Minneapolis MN 55404

JERNIGAN, DORIS BYRD, nursing home adminstr.; b. Bunnlevel, N.C., June 13, 1922; d. Almond Stewart and Geneva (Jones) Byrd; student bus. Campbell Coll., Buies Creek, N.C., 1955, spl. courses, 1955-77; A.A. in Social Work, William Carter Coll., 1977; m. Theodore N. Jernigan, Apr. 16, 1942; children—John Ronald, James Donald, Michael Douglas. Bookkeeper, Dunn (N.C.) Prodn. Credit Assn., 1955-61; chief acct. Sampson County Meml. Hosp., Clinton, N.C., 1962-74, patient rep., 1974-76; adminstr. Guardian Care, Kenansville, N.C., 1976-77, Harborview Nursing Home, Morehead City, N.C., 1977—; v.p., treas. Jernigan Nursing Home Services, Inc.; sec. Plain View Twp.-Democrat. Del. N.C. Democratic Conv., 1951-76; active Sampson County Cancer Dr., Heart Assn. Sampson and Carteret Counties; bd. dirs. Southea. Dist. Easter Seal Soc., Neuse River Council Govts., Ea. Carolina Emergency Med. Systems, Inc., Ea. N.C. Health Systems Agy.; mem. Carteret Tech. Coll. Adv. Com., Carteret-Craven Sch. Nursing; mem. Morehead City Employment Security Commn. Recipient William G. Follmer award, 1978. Fellow Am. Coll. Nursing Home Adminstrs.; mem. N.C. Health Care Facilities Assn., Carteret County C. of C., Hosp. Fin. Mgmt. Assn. (past dir., statis. sec.). Democrat. Presbyterian. Club: Careteret Bus. and Profl. Women's. Home: Route 4 Box 297 Newport NC 28570 Office: 812 Shepard St Morehead City NC 28557

JERNIGAN, JEAN ALLEN, business ofcl.; newspaper reporter; b. Brookline, Mass., May 26, 1923; d. Langdon and Dorothy (Talbot) Allen; A.A., Garland Jr. Coll., 1942; m. Roger R. Jernigan, May 31, 1943; children—Roger, Jeffrey, Bruce, Linda. Fashion and beauty editorial asst. Boston Herald Traveler, 1942-44; news editor Sun Newspapers, Contra Costa County, Calif., 1958-64; aide to county supr. Contra Costa County, 1964-66; dir. public relations Children's Hosp. Med. Center, Oakland, Calif., 1966-68; women's editor, feature writer Berkeley (Calif.) Gazette, 1968-78; dir. public relations, asst. exec. dir. Berkeley-East Bay Humane Soc., 1978-81; adminstrv. asst. to v.p. fin Cetus Corp., Berkeley, 1981—; freelance reporter Contra Costa Suns, Lafayette, Calif., 1979-80. Mem. Women in Communication, East Bay Press Club, Contra Costa Press Club. Republican. Office: 600 Bancroft Way Berkeley CA 94710

JERNIGAN, MARY YOUNGER, educator; b. McKinney, Tex., Jan. 23, 1916; d. Isham Henry and Ada Udorah (Hill) Younger; B.A. cum laude, Baylor U., 1937, M.A., 1956; postgrad. San Francisco State U., 1949-52, S.W. Tex. State U., 1956-58, Tex. A&M U., 1968-73; m. Jesse Stewart Jernigan, Sept. 30, 1939; children—David Stewart, Susan Jernigan Gibbs. Tchr., McKinney pub. schs., 1937-39, Collin County (Tex.) pub. schs., 1939-42; instr. English, Okla. State U., Stillwater, 1946-48; tchr. Oakland (Calif.) pub. schs., 1948-52; dir. spl. edn. program Bryan (Tex.) Ind. Sch. Dist., 1952-76; summer prof. edn. Baylor U., Waco, Tex., 1966—; profl. cons. in field; mem. profl. adv. bd. Brazos Valley Mental Retardation Center, 1966—; adviser dept. spl. edn. Tex. A&M U., 1968—, mem. adv. bd. spl. edn. Region VI Ednl. Service Center, 1966-74; mem. Tex. planning com. Vocat. Rehab. Services, 1970-71, Regional Devel. Disabilities Task Force, 1973-74, Regional Forum on Early Childhood Devel. in Tex. 1974-75. Chmn. vol. com. citizens adv. council Brazos Valley Mental Health Center, 1973—; vice chmn. Brazos County Child Welfare Bd., 1970—; chmn. personnel Shelter Arms, 1975-77; bd. dirs. St. Michael's Acad., 1975—; co-chmn. Youth Concerts Series, 1976—; mem. med. adv. com. Brazos Valley March of Dimes; chmn. Women of St. Andrews, 1981—; chmn. bd. St. Michael's Episcopal Sch., 1981—. Recipient Outstanding Community Contbn. award Brazos Valley Arts Council, 1978. Mem. NEA, Bryan Edn. Assn., Am., Tex. speech and hearing assns., Nat., Tex. councils adminstrs. spl. edn., Nat., Tex. councils for exceptional children, Nat., Tex., Brazos Valley council for retarded, Tex., Brazos Valley assns. for learning disabilities, Tex. Assn. for Supervision and Curriculum Devel., Tex. Soc. for Crippled Children and Adults, Brazos Valley Soc. for Crippled Children, Tex. Tchrs. Assn., Brazos Valley Arts Council, Opera and Performing Arts Guild (pres. 1976—). Republican. Episcopalian. Club: Woman's (treas. 1978-79, community service chmn. 1981). Author: Handbook for Special Edn., 1956, Instructional Guide for Mentally Retarded, 1965, Five Year Plan for Special Education, 3d edit., 1975. Home: 3210 Link St Bryan TX 77801

JERNIGAN, SARAH LEONARD, newspaper editor; b. Reidville, S.C., Apr. 22, 1920; d. Paul Holland and Eunice Ruth (Harper) L.; student Converse Coll., Spartanburg, S.C., 1937-39; B.A., U. S.C., 1941, M.A., 1980; postgrad. spl. courses U. S.C., U. Ga.; m. Martin L. Jernigan, Oct. 4, 1947; children—Sarah Holland, Jan Leonard. Reporter, Charleston (S.C.) News & Courier, 1941-44; radio editor Office of Agr., Washington, 1945-46; editorial asst. Collier's Mag., Washington, 1946-47; feature writer Richmond (Va.) Times-Dispatch, 1949-55; art and copy dept. writer Richmond Newspapers, 1949-52; editor S.C. Mag., 1955-57; exec. sec. S.C. Assn. Real Estate Bds., 1957-64; asst. to v.p. public relations Citizens & So. Nat. Bank, 1964-65; exec. v.p. S.C. div. Am. Cancer Soc., 1965-68; sales rep. Bollin & Co., Roy Little Co., 1968-71; public relations dir. Mid-Carolina Council on Alcoholism, 1977-78; press sec. Raymon Finch gubernatorial campaign, 1978; exec. dir. S.C. Fedn. Older Ams., 1978-80; editor Columbia Star-Reporter, 1980-82. Public Relations Soc. Am. grantee, 1978-80. Mem. Caroliniana Soc., UDC, DAR (past dist. dir., chpt. regent), Am. Legion Aux., Huguenot Soc., Daus. Am. Colonists (state regent 1979-82), S.C. Hist. Soc., Columbia Mus. Art and Sci., S.C. Network Female Execs., Media Club Columbia, Sigma Delta Chi, Kappa Tau Alpha. Episcopalian. Clubs: Richland County Republican Women's, Dianthus Garden. Home: 900 Laurens St Columbia SC 29201

JEROME, BETTE, actress, speaker; b. Newport News, Va.; d. Elias and Sophie (Harris) J.; m. Samuel M. Bialek, June 26, 1960; children by previous marriage—Alan Craig Rafel, Lisa Rafel Himelfarb. Stage and radio actress, concert artist, choral condr., TV producer/moderator, writer, 1953—; narrator govt. and industry tng. films; actress, spokes-voice commls.; pres., exec. dir. BJB Prodns., Ltd.; producer radio programs including Mind's Eye Theatre, Foggy Bottom, Interact; tchr. dynamic speech for TV and radio newscasters, announcers; condr. speech and spokespersons workshops. Recipient Emmy award, AAUW award, Dept. Indian Affairs award, Gold Mike award McCalls. Mem. Am. Women in Radio and TV (pres. Washington chpt. 1971-72), AFTRA (pres. Washington/Balt. local 1973-75), Nat. Acad. TV Arts and Scis., Screen Actors Guild, Internat. Platform Assn., Advt. Club Met. Washington. Office: 322 W 57th St PH 50 E New York NY 10019

JEROME, SISTER, MARY, librarian; b. Chgo., Dec. 14, 1914; d. Sidney M. and Anna (Ryan) Heyman; B.A., Rosary Coll., 1937; M.S. in L.S., U. Ill., 1947. Tchr., librarian Trinity High Sch., Bloomington, Ill., 1939, Cathedral High Sch., Sioux Falls, S.D., 1940; librarian Visitation High Sch., Chgo., 1940-50, Catholic High Sch., Oklahoma City, 1950-53, Edgewood Coll. of Sacred Heart, Madison, Wis., 1953—. Mem. adv. bd. for library cooperation Dane County, Wis., 1968-72; rep. Madison Area Library Council, 1974-76, 78-80. Mem. Am., Cath., Wis. State (membership chmn. 1958-60, sec. 1962-63, dir. 1967-70, mem. com. on faculty status and tenure, acad. div. 1971-72) library assns. Contbr. articles to profl. jours. Home: 855 Woodrow St Madison WI 53711 Office: Edgewood Coll of Sacred Heart Madison WI 53711

JESSE, MARY JANE, pediatric cardiologist; b. Owensboro, Ky., Jan. 8, 1918; d. Joseph Preston and Ethel (May) J.; A.B., Nazareth Coll., 1939; M.D., Columbia U., 1959. Dir. radio and TV publicity Young and Rubicam Advt., N.Y.C., 1947-54; intern Bronx Mcpl. Hosp., Albert Einstein Med. Center, N.Y.C., 1959-60; resident in pediatrics Babies Hosp., Columbia-Presbyn. Med. Center, N.Y.C., 1960-62, resident in pediatric cardiology, 1962-64; mem. faculty Coll. Physicians and Surgeons, Columbia U., 1960-70; prin. investigator Specialized Center of Research in Atherosclerosis, U. Miami, 1970-73, Berenson prof. pediatric cardiology, 1973-76; dir. div. heart and vascular disease Nat. Heart, Lung and Blood Inst., NIH, Bethesda, Md., 1976-79; prof., vice chmn. dept. pediatrics, prof. dept. medicine U. Miami, 1979—. Fellow Am. Acad. Behavioral Medicine, Internat. Soc. Epidemiology; mem. Am. Acad. Pediatrics, Am. Coll. Cardiology, Am. Pediatric Soc., Am. Heart Assn. (pres.-elect 1981-82, pres. 1982—). Democrat. Roman Catholic. Contbr. articles in field to profl. jours. Home: 1 Grove Isle Apt 205 Coconut Grove FL 33133 Office: U Miami Sch Medicine Dept Pediatrics PO Box 016960 Miami FL 33101

JESSEE, SALLEY SUE, psychiatrist; b. Huntington, W.Va., Sept. 12, 1948; d. James Robert and Maxine (Fletcher) Jessee; student Emory U., 1969, M.D. cum laude, 1973. Resident, Emory U. Affiliated Hosps., 1973-76; practice medicine specializing in psychiatry, Atlanta, 1976—; asst. prof. psychiatry, Emory U., Atlanta, 1976—; med. dir. psychiat. emergency services, asso. dir. div. emergency and stablzn. psychiatry Grady Meml. Hosp., Atlanta, 1979—; cons. SSA. Mem. Phi Beta Kappa, Alpha Omega Alpha. Presbyterian. Home: 1429 Bubbling Creek Rd Atlanta GA 30319 Office: 3340 Peachtree Rd NE Atlanta GA 30326

JESSEN, SHIRLEY AGNES, artist; b. Bklyn., Jan. 23, 1921; d. Arnold Peter and Agnes Veronica (Maguire) Hemmersbach; student (scholar) N.Y. Sch. of Applied Design for Women, 1939, Fashion Inst., 1944; m. Albert Vern Jessen, Nov. 23, 1944; 1 son, Gregory Vern. Paintings exhibited in 23 solo shows including: Nassau County Office of Performing and Fine Arts, 1971, N.Y. State Council on Arts, 1972, Wantagh Library, 1972, Locust Valley Art Show, 1972, 73, Community Arts Show, 1973, Garden City (N.Y.) Library, 1975, Artists Equity Assn. N.Y., 1976, Union Carbide Gallery, 1977, Reynold Securities Inc. Gallery, 1977, Garden City Hist. Soc. Mus., 1978, Salmagundi Club Show, 1978, Nat. Acad. Gallery, Soc. Painters in Casein and Acrylics, 1978, Roslyn Mus. Fine Arts, 1979, PBS-TV, 1980, 81, Adelphi U., 1980, 81, 82, SOHO Nat. Art Center, 1980, Galerie D'Art Helof, Paris, 1980, Long Beach Mus., 1980, Town of Oyster Bay Div. Cultural and Fine Arts, 1981, Bryant Library, 1981, GEICO Gallery, 1981, Cathedral of Incarnation Sem. Library, 1981, North Merrick Library, 1982, Roslyn Mus. Fine Art, 1982, Freeport Arts Council Exhibit, 1982; participant 106 juried shows; works represented in permanent collections in six states. Bd. dirs. Cerebral Palsy Aux., 1955-76, pres., 1959-62; bd. dirs. Pro-Arte Symphony Orch. Hofstra U., 1968-71; bd. dirs. Nassau County Med. Soc. Aux., 1958-83, pres., 1961-62, artist, 1959-83; publicity chmn. Garden City Hist. Soc. ann. dance, 1981. Winner Grumbacher award Am. Artist Mag. nat. competition, 1978; prize winner Suburban Art League ann. juried competition, 1981, Lincoln Center exhibit, 1981-82; recipient various awards and certs. of recognition; disting. service award Nassau County Med. Soc. Aux., United Cerebral Palsy Assn.; Academie delle Arte e del Lavoro with Gold medal. Mem. Artists Equity Assn. N.Y., Garden City Community Club Art Studio, Audubon Asso. Artists, Nat. Soc. Painters in Casein and Acrylics, Suburban Art League, South Shore Art League (publicity chmn., 1st prize 1981), Village Art Club, Ind. Art League, L.I. Artists Alliance, Soc. N.Am. Artists, Gavel Club (hon. life, pres., 1981-84, sec.-treas. 1963-66). Roman Catholic.

JESSUP, MARSHA EDWINA, med. illustrator; b. Washington, Nov. 8, 1944; d. Elmer Stanley and Georgia (Mills) J.; B.S. in Zoology (univ. tuition scholar 1965-66), Howard U., 1966; M.S. in Med. and Biol. Illustration (Nat. Med. Assn. scholar 1969, 69-70, univ. scholar 1970-71), U. Mich., 1971. Asst. med. illustrator Howard U., 1968-69; free-lance sci. illustrator Smithsonian Instn., 1967-68; med. illustrator Walter Reed Army Med. Center, 1972; mem. faculty Dept. Agr. Grad. Sch., 1971-74; med. illustrator NIH, 1972-74; adj. asst. prof., chief med. illustrator, dir. med. resources U. Medicine and Dentistry N.J.-Rutgers U. Med. Sch., Piscataway, 1975—; mem. task force re-evaluating illustrator series for fed. govt. career classification system CSC, 1974; mem. gen. adminstrn. bd. Dept. Agr. Grad. Sch., 1973-74. Named Young Career Woman, Silver Spring (Md.) Bus. and Profl. Women's Club, 1973. Mem. Assn. Biomed. Communications Dirs., Health Scis. Communications Assn., Health Edn. Media Assn., Assn. Ednl. Communications and Tech., Assn. Med. Illustrators, Guild Natural Sci. Illustrators. Office: CMDNJ-Ruters Med Sch Piscataway NJ 08854

JESTER, LINDA R., state ofcl.; b. Indpls., June 30, 1944; d. Edwin A. and Lula M. (Richardson) J.; B.A., Ind. Central U., 1966. Dir. for Indpls. div. tourism Ind. Dept. Commerce, 1973-76; dir. pub. relations Hilton Hotels, 1976-77; dir. econ. devel. Ind. Dept. Commerce, 1977-81; exec. dir. Ind. Office Occupational Devel., 1981—; bd. dirs. Ind. Tng. and Ednl. Stata Service, Ind. Staff Devel. Inst.; exec. bd. Assn. Ind. Employment and Tng. Adminstrs. Republican. Methodist. Home: 4273 Woodsage Trace Indianapolis IN 46227 Office: 150 W Market St 7th Floor ISTA Bldg Indianapolis IN 46204

JETER, KATHERINE LESLIE BRASH (MRS. ROBERT MCLEAN JETER, JR.), lawyer; b. Gulfport, Miss., July 24, 1921; d. Ralph Edward and Rosa Meta (Jacobs) Brash; B.A., Tulane U., 1943, J.D., 1945; m. Robert McLean Jeter, Jr., May 11, 1946. Admitted to La. bar, 1945; asso. mem. Montgomery, Fenner & Brown, New Orleans, 1945-46, Tucker, Jeter & Jackson, and predecessor firms, Shreveport, La., 1947-79, mem., 1980—judge pro-tem Dist. Ct., Caddo Parish, 1982; hon consul of France, Shreveport, 1982. Pres., Little Threatre Shreveport, 1966-67, YWCA, 1963, LWV, 1950-51; treas. Am. Nat. Theatre and Acad., Shreveport, 1963; pres. Shreveport Art Guild, 1974-75; mem. council La. State Law Inst., 1980—; adv. com. La. Civil Code Revision, 1973; trustee Public Affairs Research Council, 1976-81, exec. com., 1981—. Mem. Am. Bar Assn., La. Bar Assn., Shreveport Bar Assn., Nat. Assn. Women Lawyers, La. Law Inst., Jr. League Shreveport, Order of Coif, Phi Beta Kappa. Editor: Tulane Law Rev., 1945. Home: 3959 Maryland Ave Shreveport LA 71106 Office: 1300 Beck Bldg 400 Travis St Shreveport LA 71101

JETT, JOYCE LENORA, mfrs.' rep.; b. Johnston City, Tenn., Oct. 10, 1935; d. David Milford and Ruth Leota Sadler; course certs. Illuminating Engring. Soc., Houston, 1966, Thomas Industries Lighting Center, Chgo., 1968; children—Melody Lynn, Kirby Alan, John David. Outside salesperson M & M Lighting, Houston, 1961-65; pres. J. J. Lighting Co., Houston, 1970-72; mgr. BASCO, Houston, 1965-70; dir. sales, columnist Houston Mag., 1972-73; dir. sales Med. Center-Holiday Inn, Houston, 1974-77; rep. Bill Teiber Agy., Dallas, 1978—. Recipient award Houston Fire Dept., 1976; letter of appreciation Nat. Easter Seal Soc., Houston, 1976, Muscular Dystrophy Assn., Houston, 1976; cert. recognition El Consulado de Mexico, Houston, 1976; cert. appreciation City of Houston, 1978, Key to City, 1979; letter of recognition and award Cruz Roja Mexicana, 1978, cert. appreciation Shriners Hosp. for Crippled and Burned Children, Houston, 1981; named hon. fire marshall City of Houston Fire Marshal, 1981. Home: 11614 Southlake Dr Houston TX 77077 Office: 1301 Dallas Trade Mart Dallas TX 75207

JETT, MILDRED SUNDAY, nurse, adminstr.; b. Bessmer, Ala., July 1, 1947; d. Jimmie and Inez (Norwood) Sunday; B.S.N. magna cum laude, U. Mich., 1975; L.P.N. diploma No. Mich. U., 1967; m. Arthur Robert Jett, Aug. 15, 1970; children—Nataki Elissar, Kanye Kamo. Lic. practical nurse Providence Hosp., Southfield, Mich., 1968-70; nurse St. Luke's Hosp., Marquette, Mich., 1970-72; lic. practical nurse Univ. Hosp., Ann Arbor, Mich., 1972-74, staff nurse, 1976-77; inservice instr. Kirwood Gen. Hosp., Detroit, 1976-77, dept. head, ednl. dir. hosp. staff devel., 1977—; tchr. CPR to sr. citizens. Mem. Detroit Black Nurses Assn. (2d v.p. 1978-80, 80-82), Am. Nurses Assn., Nat. Black Nurses Assn., Met. Detroit Health Edn. Council, Met. Detroit Coalition for Blood Pressure Control, Delta Sigma Theta, Sigma Theta Tau (membership com. 1975-76). Mem. Christian Ch. Office: 4059 W Davison Detroit MI 48238

JEUNETTE, LYNN MARIE, public relations exec.; b. Arlington, Va., June 18, 1954; d. William Carl and Barbara Ann J.; grad. public schs. Personnel mgr. W. & J. Sloane, Washington, 1973-75; public relations adminstr. Computer Scis. Corp., Falls Church, Va., 1975—. Mem. Air Force Assn., Assn. U.S. Army, Nat. Space Club, Navy League, Nat. Energy Resources Orgn., Public Relations Soc. Am., Armed Forces Communications and Electronics Assn. Lutheran. Home: 7616 Shelly Ln Manassas VA 22111 Office: 6565 Arlington Blvd Falls Church VA 22046

JEVNE, LOUISE PRISCILLA ARMSTRONG, genealogist; b. Ward County, N.D., Jan. 1, 1910; d. Joseph Robert and Valentine Emma (Butterfield) Armstrong; grad. Minot State Tchrs. Coll., 1964; m. Harry Oscar Jevne, Mar. 21, 1932; children—Henry Eugene, Vallie Ann, Donald Harry, Terry Byron. Tchr., Van Buren 3, Lansford, N.D., 1929-31, 49-54, Clay Center Consol. Sch., Lansford, 1931-32, Mercer County Rural Sch., Hazen, 1937-39, Nedrose Rural Sch., Minot, N.D., 1954-58, Minot (N.D.) pub. schs., 1958-71; writer biographies, tchr. family history, 1971-80. Dir. Van Buren Sch. Dist., 1948-49. Mem. N.D. Congress Parents and Tchrs. (life), Nat. Ret. Tchrs. Assn., Renville County Hist. Soc. (dir., life mem.), N.D. Hist. Soc., Red River Valley Hist. Soc., Valdres Samband, DAR (past state registar and chmn. geneal. records 1972-80; regent Pierre Verendrye chpt. N.D. 1980-81, N.D. state regent 1981-83), Drane Family Hist. and Geneal. Soc., Garrett County (Md.) Hist. Soc., Soc. of Mareen Duvall Descendants, Red River Valley Genealogy Soc., Wis. State Geneal. Soc., Mouse River Loop Genealogy Soc., Erie County (Pa.) Soc. for Geneal. Research, Delta Kappa Gamma. Mem. Ch. of Nazarene. Club: Vansign Homemakers. Author: Drane Families of Maryland, 1973; Teachers and Pupils, 1979; compiler: Methodist Church Records of Renville County, North Dakota, 1980. Home: Route 1 Box 17 Lansford ND 58750

JEWELL, IRMA FAY, educator; b. Springfield, Ohio, Apr. 17, 1920; d. Lloyd D. and Lela Fay (Edwards) Browne; B.S.N., Valdosta State Coll., 1975; M.S.N., Med. Coll. Ga., 1976; postgrad. Valdosta State Coll., Ga. State U.; m. Everett L. Jewell, Nov. 16, 1941; children—Eunice Elnora, Lloyd Burton. Tchr./health worker Luz Mission, Luso, Angola, West Africa, 1942-50; co-worker, counselor Nova Lisboa, Angola, 1950-69; sec./translator Pub. House, Euro-Africa div., Seventh-Day Adventists, Bern, Switzerland, 1969-72; asst. prof. nursing Valdosta (Ga.) State Coll., 1976—. Mem. Ga. Citizens Council on Alcoholism, 1978-79; pres. Welfare and Disaster Services, 1950-68; active Ga.

Sheriff's Boys' Ranch, ARC. Mem. Am. Nurses Assn., Seventh-Day Adventist So. Tchrs. Assn., Epsilon Pi, Sigma Theta Tau.

JEWETT, MARSHA EFFNER, securities co. exec.; b. Fitchburg, Mass., May 30, 1941; d. Walter Leonard and Ida (Gosselin) Mossey; B.S., Boston U., 1962; m. W. S. Effner, Jr., Nov. 10, 1962 (div. June 1980); children—Stephen, Megan; m. 2d, David M. Jewett, July 11, 1981. Acct., Marcus & Nocka Architects & Engrs., 1962; pvt. practice acctg., Ipswich, Mass., 1973-76; asst. trust officer Shawmut Bank, Boston, 1976-77; acct., office mgr. Newbury House Pubs., Rowley, Mass., 1977-78; controller First New Eng. Securities Corp., Boston, 1978-82; v.p. fin. and ops. First Commonwealth Investment Corp., Boston, 1982—; cons. Yankee Oil & Gas Inc., 1978-82. Chmn., Fund Raising for Public Library, Ipswich, 1975-78. Recipient Scholarship, Boston U., 1959-62. Mem. Nat. Assn. Female Execs. Republican. Episcopalian. Clubs: Manchester Yacht, Newburyport Maritime Soc. Home: 145 Garden St West Newbury MA 01985 Office: Boston MA

JEZYK, ELISABETH, controller; b. Northampton, Mass., Jan. 9, 1941; d. George F. and Mary M. Chandler; B.S., Va. Commonwealth U., 1971; postgrad. U. Pa., 1973; m. Peter Jezyk, Oct. 28, 1959 (div.); children—Andrea, Brenda. Credit mgr. Mass. Electric Co., Northampton, 1959-61; spl. edn. tchr., Richmond, Va., 1971-72; adminstrv. asst. student health U. Pa., 1972-74; bus. mgr. Drs. Kroungold, Bortin, Weiss, Bala Cynwyd, Pa., 1974-80; acct. Allen Speiser, C.P.A. cons., Bala Cynwyd, 1979—; controller Summit Group Travel, Phila., 1980—. Mem. Nat. Assn. Female Execs., Am. Hist. Soc. Democrat. Lutheran. Home: 4919 Larchwood Ave Philadelphia PA 19143

JILEK, ANITA GAIL, mktg. and sales promotion exec.; b. Oak Park, Ill., Sept. 20, 1951; d. Robert and Elsie Ruth (Rosenfeld) J.; B.S., U. Ill., Urbana-Champaign, 1973, M.A., 1974. Product sales mgr. Zenith Radio Corp., Chgo., 1975-77; div. dir. House of Vision Inc., Chgo., 1977-80; area mgr. Twentieth Century Fox Video, Detroit, 1980-81; gen. mgr. Feldman Assos., Chgo., 1981—; pres. A Neater Co., mktg. services agy., Oakbrook Terrace, Ill., 1981—; mem. career adv. com. Northwestern U.; tchr. French cooking Lyons Twp. (Ill.) High Sch. Adult Edn., 1977-78. Mem. blood assurance program Hinsdale (Ill.) Hosp., 1977—; mem. Oak Brook (Ill.) Park Dist. Com., 1980—. Mem. Nat. Assn. Female Execs., U. Ill. Alumni Assn. (life), Alpha Xi Delta Alumna Assn. Home: 425 W Belmont Ave Chicago IL 60657 Office: 213 W Institute #703 Chicago IL 60610

JILEK-AALL, LOUISE MATHILDE, psychiatrist, anthropologist; b. Oslo, Norway, Apr. 21, 1931; d. Anathon August and Lily Elisabeth (Weiser) Aall; came to Can., 1963, naturalized, 1969; philosophicum exam., U. Oslo, 1950; student Med. Schs., Univs. Tuebingen, Saarland, Zurich, 1951-58; M.D., U. Zurich, 1958; diploma in tropical medicine U. Basel (Switzerland), 1959; diploma in psychiatry McGill U., 1965; M.A. in Anthropology, U. B.C., Vancouver, 1972; m. Wolfgang George Jilek, May 11, 1963. Clin. asst., research fellow in Africa, 1960-62, Switzerland, 1962-63, Can., 1963-66; cons. psychiatrist Chilliwack Gen. Hosp., 1966-74, Vancouver Gen. Hosp., 1975—, U. B.C. Health Scis. Centre, 1975—; founder clinic for Epileptics, Mahenge, Tanzania, 1960; pediatric asst. to Dr. Albert Schweitzer, Lambarene, Gabon, 1961; UN and Internat. Red Cross med. officer, Congo, 1960-61; transcultural psychiatric research in E. Africa, Congo, Haiti, S.Am., New Guinea, with Canadian Indians; asst. prof. dept. psychiatry U. B.C., 1975—; cons. Istituto di Studi Transculturali Milan, Italy, Institut fuer Interkulturelle Forschung, Heidelberg, Germany, Recipient citation Congo medal League Red Cross Socs., Geneva, 1961. Fellow Royal Coll. Phys. and Surgs. of Can.; mem. Canadian Psychiat. Assn. (sect. on Can. native peoples mental health), Canadian, B.C. med. assns., Colloque Franco-Canadien sur l'Analyse de Systemes Idéologiques (Paris), Peruvian Psychiat. Assn. (corr.), Assn. African Psychiatrists (corr.), Nat. Assn. Underwater Instrs. (certificate in scuba diving). Permanent rev. author Transcultural Psychiatric Research Rev.; author (autobiography) Call Mama Doctor—African Notes of a Young Woman Doctor. Contbr. articles to sci. publs. Home: 571 English Bluff Rd Tsawwassen Delta BC V4M 2M9 Canada

JILES, PATRICIA RUTH, nurse; b. Kent, Ohio, May 17, 1933; d. Jerry and Zola Fay (Warburton) Kane; A.S., Antelope Valley Coll., 1976; student Victor Valley Coll., 1969-71; m. Herman N. Jiles, May 13, 1956 (div. 1971); children—Coral, Shannon, Darin, Starr, Gavin. Nurse, Saddleback Community Hosp., Laguna Hills, Calif., 1976-77, Nurses Registries, and Med. Staffing Services, Costa Mesa, Calif., 1977-80; mem. staff Kimberly Nurses, Santa Ana, Calif., 1978-81, Buena Park (Calif.) Community Hosp., 1981—; pres. Golden Dream Enterprises, 1980—; mem. Medox Nurses' Registry, 1980—. Mem. Nat. Critical Care Inst. Edn., Am. Heart Assn., ARC. Assn. Humanistic Psychology, Parents Without Partners. Methodist. Club: Sierra Singles. Concert tour with Lake Hills Chancel Choir, Europe, 1981. Home: 1715C Normandy Pl Santa Ana CA 92705

JIMENEZ, BEATRICE CAROLYN, educator; b. Stockton, Calif., Nov. 12, 1943; d. Louie and Dolores (Vasquez) J.; A.A., San Joaquin Delta Coll., 1964; B.A., San Jose State Coll., 1966; M.A., Calif. State U., Fresno, 1975; Ph.D., Ohio State U., 1977. Social worker, Los Angeles County, 1969-74; dir. Saturday speech and hearing clinic Ohio Dept. Health, Bellefontaine, 1976; speech pathologist Humphrey Homes, Columbus, Ohio, 1976-77; asst. prof. speech communication Allegheny Coll., Meadville, Pa., 1977-80; asst. prof. speech pathology Calif. State U., Chico, 1980—. Mem. Am. Speech, Lang. and Hearing Assn., Internat. Assn. Logopedics and Phoniatrics, Calif. Speech, Lang. and Hearing Assn., Council Univ. Suprs. of Praticum in Speech-Lang. Pathology and Audiology, Internat. Assn. for Study Child Lang., Ohio State U. Alumni Assn., Phi Kappa Phi. Home: 20 Fremont St Chico CA 95926 Office: 112D Amer J Hamilton Bldg Calif State U Chico CA 95929

JIMENEZ, ESTHER EVE, liquified petroleum gas co. ofcl.; b. San Antonio, July 19, 1955; d. Jose Guadalupe and Esther (Garza) J.; B. in Chem. Engring., Ga. Inst. Tech., 1977. Plant engr. Warren Petroleum div. Gulf Oil Co., Lovington, N.J., 1977-79, project engr., Tulsa, 1979-80, process engr., 1980, engr. gas supplies and new projects, Tulsa, 1980-81, dir. new projects so. area, Tulsa, 1981—. Project bus. cons. Marquette Sch.; adv. Jr. Achievement, 1980—. Mem. Soc. Women Engrs., Soc. Petroleum Engrs., Am. Inst. Chem. Engrs., Alpha Gamma Delta (treas. 1975-77). Democrat. Roman Catholic. Office: PO Box 1589 Tulsa OK 74102

JNAH, EDWIGE CLAUDIA, designer; b. Paris, Sept. 26, 1946; came to U.S., 1965, naturalized, 1974; d. Marian and Christine Janina (Piekarski) Babeluck; B.A., Art Inst. Chgo., 1971; divorced; 1 son, N. Eric. Designer, Rydertpes, Chgo., 1966-67; freelance designer, 1967-72; art dir. Ladd/Wells/Presba, Chgo., 1972-75; graphic art coordinator U.S. League Savs. Assns., Chgo., 1975-78; exec. v.p. Chott & Jnah Design, Chgo., 1978—. Vol., N.W. Neighborhood Fedn. Mem. Nat. Assn. Women Bus. Owners (program chmn.), Nat. Assn. Future Women (communications chmn.), Soc. Typographic Art, Women in Design, Alliance Francaise, Polish Nat. Alliance. Democrat. Roman Catholic. Home: 5215 W Newport Ave Chicago IL 60641 Office: 222 N Dearborn Pkwy Chicago IL 60601

JOBE, ALICE, transp. co. exec.; b. Little Rock, Nov. 24, 1935; grad. high sch., Sheridan, Ark.; student industry spl. transp. Long Beach City Coll., 1960-61; m. K.L. Jobe, Mar. 12, 1957; 1 dau., Cathy. With Nat. Equity Life Ins. Co., Little Rock, 1954-55, Cash Wholesale Co., Little Rock, 1956-57; with Bekins Internat., subs. Bekins Co., Wilmington, Calif., 1959-77, v.p., 1971-77; exec. v.p. Imperial Internat., Inc., Torrance, Calif., 1977-80, dir., 1977-81, pres. Imperial Van Lines Internat., Inc., 1980-81; industry cons., 1981-82; founder, pres. Caddo Internat., Los Alamitos, Calif., 1982—. Mem. Household Goods Forwarders Assn. (exec. com. 1977-78), Nat. Def. Transp. Assn. (life), Am. Soc. Profl. Women. Republican. Office: PO Box 666 Los Alamitos CA 90720

JOFFE, EUNICE CLAIRE, educator, director, performer, writer; b. Chgo., July 1, 1933; d. Louis Eliezer and Mascha (Tolchinova) Gershman; B.E., Nat. Coll. Edn., 1953; postgrad. UCLA, summer 1950, U. Wis., summer 1951, U. Minn., summer 1952, Hunter Coll., summer 1953; m. Jerome Morton Joffe, June 28, 1953; children—Lora Ellyn Joffe, Shari Michelle Joffe. Tchr. Dewey Sch., Evanston, Ill., 1953-56; tchr. dramatics Skokie (Ill.) YMCA, 1954-60; producer, writer, actress children's programming Sta. WNMP, Evanston, 1954-55; author programs Twinkle Time, WEAW, Evanston, 1955-56, Happy Helpers Club, 1956; producer, writer, actress WTTW-TV, Chgo., 1957-59; author, performer The Magic Door, CBS-TV, Chgo., 1961; dir. tchr. Children's Theater, Highland Park, Ill., 1962-75; founder, dir. Playmakers, 1968—; exec. dir. Imagination Theater, Chgo., 1975—, exec. bd., pres., 1975-76, bd. dirs., 1977; condr. tchr. insts., 1973—; creator participatory prodns. for major shopping centers, Mus. Contemporary Art, Chgo., 1976-77; cons., panelist Arts and Handicapped Conf., Chgo. Council on Fine Arts and Rehab. Center of Chgo., 1977; producer, creator, dir. programs and workshops for emotionally, physically and mentally handicapped, 1976-77. Chmn. cultural enrichment Indian Trail PTA Bd., Highland Park, 1965-67; bd. dirs. Elm Place Jr. High Sch. PTA, Highland Park, 1968-71, Chgo. League Theaters, 1981-83. Recipient Alumni Achievement award Nat. Coll. Edn., 1980; Gov.'s award for achievement and enrichment in arts in Ill., 1982; Ill. Arts Council grantee 1973, 74, 77; Comprehensive Employment Tng. Act grantee, 1976, 77; Continental Bank grantee, 1976, 77; Mayor's Office grantee, 1981-82; Ill. Arts Council grantee, 1980, 81, 82; Nat. Endowment Arts grantee, 1981; Ill. Dept. Mental Health grantee. Mem. Am. (governing regional bd., sec. treas. 1976), Ill., Children's theatre assns., Ill. Theatre Assn. (childrens theatre rep.), Chgo. Alliance for Performing Arts, Ill. Dance Co. (asso.). Jewish. Author: A Manual for Participatory Theater, 1976; Creative Dramatics in the Classroom; Manual on Drama Activities for the Developmentally Disabled, 1982. Address: 353 2W Park Ave Highland Park IL 60053

JOFFE, ZERLINE CHARLOTTE HESS, designer; b. N.J., July 25, 1936; d. Richard Hess and Dorothy Kaye (Newman) Hess; student Hunter Coll., 1954-57; cert. Parsons Sch. Design, N.Y. Sch. Interior Design, 1972; m. Martin Lee Joffe, Oct. 8, 1958; children—Paul, Simeon. With Robert Caigan Assos., 1974-77; prin. firm Zerline Joffe Interiors, 1977-82; cons. archtl. firms. Mem. Allied Bd., Am. Soc. Interior Designers. Home and Office: 300 Central Park W New York NY 10024

JOHN, CAROLINE CARLTON, newspaper exec.; b. Winston-Salem, N.C., Dec. 22, 1944; d. Romulous Lancaster and Caroline (Cheney) Carlton; B.A., Duke U., 1967; postgrad. Radcliffe Coll., 1967; m. David Vaughn John, Aug. 31, 1968; children—Matthew Ian, Caroline Elizabeth. Dir. info. services and publs. Guilford Coll., Greensboro, N.C., 1967-68; asst. editor alumni publs. Duke U., 1968-70; account exec., creative dir. Farnan Advt., Atlanta, 1970-74; with Atlanta Jour.-Constn., 1974—, mktg. dir., 1981—. Mem. Am. Mktg. Assn. (dir. 1980-82), Internat. Newspaper Promotion Assn. (dir. 1980—), Atlanta Advt. Club, Newspaper Research Council. Democrat. Club: Ad 2 (Atlanta). Home: 1065 Mount Paran Rd Atlanta GA 30327 Office: 72 Marietta St Atlanta GA 30303

JOHN, FLORENCE MAE, accountant; b. Morgantown, W.Va., July 1; d. George B. and Margaret H. (Barker) Flegal; diploma in acctg. Chaparral Career Coll., 1973; children—Marta S., David A., Paul S. Bookkeeper, R.C. Still Co., 1973-75, Baron's Restaurant, 1976-77; office mgr. Dresser Industries, 1977-82; owner, operator Florence John Co., Tucson, 1982—. Mem. Ariz. Soc. Practicing Accts., Nat. Soc. Practicing Accts., Women in Mining, Nat. Secs. Assn., Fraternal Order Police (asso.). Office: 4909 E Broadway Suite 290 Tucson AZ 85711

JOHN, MARTHA TYLER, educator; b. Saranac, Lake, N.Y., Apr. 22, 1930; d. Albert C. and Helen E. (Moss) Tyler; A.B., Eastern Nazarene Coll., 1951; M.S., Purdue U., 1958; Ed.D., Stanford U., 1966; m. Floyd John, Aug. 8, 1952; children—Floyd, Bruce, David. Asst. prof., asso. prof. Boston U., 1967-74; asso. prof. Bowie State Coll., Bowie, Md., 1974-77; research asso. U. Dar-es-Salaam, Tanzania, 1978—; asso. prof., chmn. div. edn. and psychology, phys. edn. Mid-Am. Nazarene Coll., Olathe, Kans., 1977—; Fulbright grantee U. Botswana, 1979. Active Youth Diversion Group, 1982. Mem. Internat. Reading Assn., Nat. Council for Social Studies, Kans. Assn. for Aging in Higher Edn., Assn. Supervision and Curriculum Devel. (reader nat. sci. found. div. internat. program), Internat. Assn. Cross Cultural Psychology, Pi Lambda Theta, Kappa Delta Pi, Phi Delta Kappa. Author: A Guide for Elementary Social Studies Teacher, 1978; Using Media in the Elementary Classroom, 1979; Teaching and Learning: Philosophical, Psychological and Curricular Applications, 1975; Practice in Research and Study Skills, 1974; The Research Project, 1981; Teaching and Loving the Elderly, 1981; contbr. articles to profl. jours. Home: 1629 Sunvale Dr Olathe KS 66062 Office: 2030 Collegeway Olathe KS 66062

JOHN, PATRICIA SPAULDING, harpist, composer; b. Canton, Ill., July 16, 1916; d. Alfred Morgan and Grace (Spaulding) J.; student Mills Coll., Calif., 1935, Curtis Inst. Music, Phila., 1936; B.A., Rice U., 1941; m. Frank Geoffrey Keightley, Mar. 1, 1957; children—Patricia Keightley Bolding, Pamela Keightley Hughes. Prin. harpist Springfield (Ill.) Civic Symphony, 1947-48, Galveston (Tex.) Civic Symphony, 1952-55; asso. harpist Houston Symphony orch., 1955-56; mem. faculty dept. music Houston Bapt. U., 1976—, Stowe Summer Sch. Music, Buckinghamshire, Eng., 1978; solo recitals at Clifton Hill, Trinidad, B.W.I., 1957, Eduard van Beinum Found., Queekhoven, Breukelen, Netherlands, 1973, Rice U., Houston, 1974, 76, U.K. Harpists Assn., Brit. Inst. Recorded Sound, London, 1975, Contemporary Arts Mus., Houston, 1975, Sta. KPFT, Houston, 1975, Music Guild, Houston, 1976, Ysgol Y Delyn, Wales, 1977, Internat. Harpcentrum Nederland, Rolduc, Kerkrade, Netherlands, 1977, U. Houston, Clear Lake, 1979, Rothko Chapel, Houston, 1979, Houston Bapt. U., 1980, Houston Public Library, 1980; dir. Harp Ensemble, 1981-82; dir., pub. Pantile Press. Mem. Am. Harp Soc. (public relations dir. N.Y.C. 1969, editor Harpists in N.Y. 1969-70, founder Houston chpt. 1966, pres. San Jacinto chpt., Houston, 1975, v.p. 1979), U.K. Harpists Assn., Welsh Harp Soc., Association International des Harpists, Musicians Club N.Y.C., Nat. Assn. Am. Composers and Condrs., Curtis Inst. Music Alumni Assn. (sec. region XIV-Tex. 1975), Galveston Mus. Club (pres. 1954). Composer: Sea Changes (suite), Fog off Pelican Spit, Summer Squall, Surf, 1968, Mnemosyne, Aprille, 1969; Tachystos, 1971; Henriette, 1974; Let's Play Series: Clown Dance, Arithmetic, Canoe, 1975; Americana (suite): Preamble, Time of Snow, Imago Ignato, 1978; Serenata, 1981; Sea Anemones, 1982; contbr. articles to mus. publs. Home: 1414 Milford Ave Houston TX 77006

JOHNS, CAROL JOHNSON, physician, educator; b. Balt., June 18, 1923; d. Ashmore Clark and Elsie Greacen (Carstens) Johnson; B.A., Wellesley Coll., 1944; M.D., Johns Mem. U., 1950; D.H.L. (hon.), Coll. Notre Dame of Md., 1981; m. Richard James Johns, June 27, 1953; children—James Ashmore, Richard Clark, Robert Shanard. Intern, Johns Hopkins Hosp., 1950-51, asst. resident in medicine, 1951-53, fellow, 1953-54, physician outpatient dept., 1953-64, dir. Sarcoid Clinic, 1962—, active staff, 1964—, dir. med. clinic, 1967-76, dir. hosp. quality assurance, 1974-79, mem. hosp. med. adv. bd., 1971-79; asst. in medicine Johns Hopkins U., 1951-58, instr., 1958-67, asst. prof., 1967-71, assoc. prof., 1971—, adv. bd. Applied Physics Lab., 1974-78; Coll. pres. Wellesley Coll., 1979-81, asst. dean, dir. continuing edn., 1981—; chmn. bd. Balt. City PSRO, 1975-79; pres. Internat. Sarcoid Conf., 1984; mem. pulmonary allergy adv. com. FDA, 1973-75; faculty adv. editorial bd. Johns Hopkins U. Press, 1981. Mem. vestry Ch. of Redeemer, 1967-70, sr. warden, 1976-79, layreader; bd. trustees Calvert Sch., 1968-72; bd. trustees Wellesley Coll., 1971—, exec. com., 1971-80, chmn. nat. devel. fund, 1975-80, trustee fin. com., 1979—; bd. trustees St. Paul's Sch. for Girls, 1973-75. Named Med. Woman of Yr. Med. Coll. Pa., 1984. Mem. Am. Clin. Climatol. Assn., Am. Thoracic Soc., Balt. City Med. Soc., Johns Hopkins Med. Surg. Assn. (sec.-treas. 1981), Johns Hopkins Women's Med. Alumni Assn. (pres. 1957-59, dir.), Md. Med. Chirurg. Faculty (council 1978-79), Soc. Med. Coll. Dirs. Continuing Edn., Phi Beta Kappa, Sigma Xi, Alpha Omega Alpha. Episcopalian. Clubs: Johns Hopkins, Wellesley Coll., Mt. Vernon. Contbr. articles med. jours., chpts. in textbooks. Home: 203 E Highfield Rd Baltimore MD 21218 Office: 17 Turner 720 Rutland Ave Baltimore MD 21205

JOHNS, CECILY ANN, librarian; b. Wichita, Kans., Oct. 5, 1939; d. Fred Ben and Beth (Means) J.; B.A., U. Kans., 1961, M.A., 1967; M.L.S., UCLA, 1968. Reference librarian U. Tex., Austin, 1968-70, UCLA, summer 1970; instr. English, Ferris State Coll., Big Rapids, Mich., 1970-71; asst. prof., reference librarian Central Mich. U., Mt. Pleasant, 1971, asst. to dir. Library, 1972-79; head reference/bibliographic services Central Library, U. Cin., 1979-81, dir. collections and info. services, 1981—. Mem. ALA, Mich. Library Assn., NOW (v.p. Mt. Pleasant chpt. 1976-77). Author: (with Doris Miller) Introduction to the Library: Unit Study Guide and Supplemental Reading, 1975; editor Reference Services Rev., 1977-80; contbr. to Magazines for Libraries, 3d edit., 1978; contbr. articles to profl. library jours. Home: 1158 Herschel Ave Cincinnati OH 45208 Office: Central Library U Cin Cincinnati OH 45221

JOHNSEN, KAREN KENNEDY, writer, adminstrn. and media cons.; b. Easton, Pa., June 28, 1939; d. Charles E. and Gladys S. (Swensen) Kennedy; B.S. cum laude in Bus., Russell Sage Coll., 1961; M.S., SUNY, Albany, 1970; m. Henry L. Johnsen, May 26, 1962; children—Erik Lehmann, Elisa Beth. Sec. account service dept. McCann-Erickson, Inc., N.Y.C., 1961-62; exec. sec. public relations Johnson & Johnson, New Brunswick, N.J., 1962-65; sec., staff writer investment div. Glens Falls Ins. Co. (N.Y.), 1965-66; exec. sec. to pres. and sec.-treas. Glens Falls Portland Cement Co., 1966-69; fund raiser, public relations dir., audience developer Lake George Opera Festival, Glens Falls, 1970-73; freelance writer, cons. adminstrn. and media, Summit, N.J., 1974—; sales exec. Lifelines, N.Y.C., 1981—; publicity dir. fund raising campaign Glens Falls YMCA; membership developer, fund raiser Vasa Order of Am. Former bd. dirs. Plainfield Symphony Soc.; pres., sec. Jaycees, Glens Falls, 1965-73; sec. Lake George Opera Guild, 1970-73; treas. AAUW, Glens Falls, 1972; club directory chmn., bull. editor Welcome Wagon Newcomers Club, 1974-75. Mem. Nat. Assn. Female Execs., AAUW, Scandinavian Am. Heritage Soc., Am. Scandinavian Found., Vesterheim Norwegian Mus., Delta Pi Epsilon. Presbyterian. Clubs: Fortnightly (Summit), Eastern Star, Vasa Order Am. (past N.J. dist. sec., past chmn. Linne lodge). Home and Office: 15 Kendrick Rd Summit NJ 07901

JOHNSON, ANITA LORRAINE, nurse practitioner; b. San Bernardino, Calif., July 24, 1942; d. Adam and Ursula Lorraine (Evans) Jones; A.A. in Nursing, San Bernardino Valley Coll., 1975; student U. Calif., San Francisco, 1977, Harbor Gen. Hosp. UCLA Sch. Medicine, 1978; B.A. in Bus., U. Redlands, 1983; m. Morsell Johnson, Dec. 26, 1977; children—Ursula Ballard, Dawna Ballard. R.N., San Bernardino County Gen. Hosp., 1975; nurse practitioner San Bernardino County Health Dept., 1977-82, West End Women's Med. Group, 1982—; realtor asso., co-owner Morsell Johnson Real Estate, 1979—. Nursing trainer Nat. Council Negro Women, 1976-79. Mem. NAACP (chmn. Freedom Fund), Nat. Assn. Nurse Practitioners in Family Planning, Inland Empire Nurse Practitioner Assn., Nat. Assn. Realtors, San Bernardino Valley Bd. Realtors, Calif. Assn. Realtors, San Bernardino Bus. and Profl. Women. Democrat. Baptist (supt. jr. dept. Sunday sch. 1981—). Home: 1558 N Chestnut St Rialto CA 92376 Office: 5050 San Bernardino St Montclair CA 91763

JOHNSON, ANNABELL, author; b. Kansas City, Mo., June 18, 1921; d. Burnam R. and Estelle (Ball) Jones; student William and Mary Coll., 1939-40; m. Edgar R. Johnson, Sept. 14, 1949. Author (with husband): As A Speckled Bird, 1956, The Big Rock Candy, 1957, Torrie, 1960, The Secret Gift, 1961, A Golden Touch, 1963, The Grizzly, 1964, A Peculiar Magic, 1965, The Burning Glass, 1966, Count Me Gone, 1968, The Last Knife, 1971, Finders, Keepers, 1981; An Alien Music, 1982; others. Recipient Friends of Am. Writers award, 1961; William Allen White award, 1967; Western Writers Am. award, 1968. Mem. Gamma Phi Beta. Home: 2925 S Teller St Denver CO 80227

JOHNSON, ARLENE LYTLE, govt. agy. ofcl.; b. Pitts., Jan. 20, 1937; d. Willis and Minnie Lee (Blackman) Neal; student various profl. courses; m. William Dalois Johnson, Aug. 27, 1971; children—Robin Gerome Lytle, Cheryl Rose Lytle Campbell. Clk.-typist, Pa. Dept. Revenue, Harrisburg, 1955; office sec. Akron (Ohio) Jewish Center, 1956-57; clk.-stenographer Pa. Employment Service, Pitts., 1960-61; Dept. Treasury, Washington, 1961; sec.-stenographer HEW, Washington, 1961-70, exec. sec. to dir. Bur. Community Health Services, Health Services Adminstrn., Rockville, Md., 1970-81; exec. sec. to dep. asst. sec. human devel. services Dept. Health and Human Services, 1981—. Recipient Spl. Recognition award USPHS, 1976, Superior Service award Health Services and Mental Health Adminstrn., 1973. Jehovah's Witness. Home: Capitol Heights MD 20743 Office: 305-F Hubert Humphrey Bldg Washington DC 20201

JOHNSON, BARBARA BEE, investments cons.; b. Larned, Kans., Dec. 15, 1921; d. Thomas Kilburn and Hattie Leara (Fisher) Balman; student schs., Neosho, Mo.; m. Eddie Jack Johnson, Jan. 28, 1942 (dec.); children—Judith Ann, Jackie Carolee (dec.). Farm mgmt., Brawley, Calif., 1942—; mgr., owner riding stable, Descanso, Calif., 1960-65; office sec., Imperial Valley, Calif., 1965-75; owner, mgr. rental complex, Brawley, 1965-73; owner, operator real properties, money mgmt. Barbara Bee Johnson Investments Co., Palm Desert, Calif., 1973—. Democrat. Office: PO Box 2406 Palm Desert CA 92261

JOHNSON, BARBARA COE, med. librarian; b. Detroit, Jan. 19, 1923; d. Harrison Thomas and Ann (Mack) Coe; B.A., Bryn Mawr Coll., 1944; B.S. in Library Sci., U. Calif., Berkeley, 1951. Patients' librarian VA Hosp., Palo Alto, Calif., 1951-53, med. librarian, 1953-56; dir. Libraries Harper Hosp., Detroit, 1956—; mem. biomed. library rev. com. Nat. Library, 1978-82. Mem. Med. Library Assn. (dir. 1968-71, pres. 1974-76), Spl. Libraries Assn. (profl. cons. 1959—). Quaker. Contbr. articles on med. library sci. to profl. jours. Office: 3990 John R St Detroit MI 48201

JOHNSON, BARBARA JANE, sales rep.; b. Chgo., Aug. 19, 1946; d. Sidney and Norma Mona Shaffer; B.A. in Sociology and Psychology, U. Ill., 1968; postgrad. M.B.A. program, Roosevelt U., 1971-72; m. Gary Johnson, Aug. 25, 1968. Asst. personnel dir. Assoc. Mills, Chgo., 1967-69, Scholl Mfg. Co. Inc., Chgo., 1969-71; nurse recruiter Cook County Hosp. Governing Com., Chgo., 1971-73; recruiter Mt. Sinai Hosp., Chgo., 1973-76; sales rep. Stryker Corp., Kalamazoo, 1976-81, area trainer; sales rep. Physio Control Corp., Schaumberg, Ill., 1982—; founder Chgo. Area Nurse Recruiters; cons. positions as nurse recruiter. Vice pres. Budlong Community Action Group, 1979—; advisor Jr. Achievement, 1969-72; auction com. Ednl. TV. Recipient Lee Stryker sales award, 1979. Mem. Assn. of Operating Room Nurses (sponsor). Recipient first place Recruitment Brochure for Chgo. Area Bus. Communicators, 1975; salesman of year, 1979; first woman to achieve nat. award, 1979. Office: 935 N Plumgrove Rd Schaumberg IL 60195

JOHNSON, BARBARA LOUISE, budget officer; b. Louisville, Aug. 28, 1946; d. Rodman Patton and Dorothy Louise (Wise) Oldham; student U. Ga., 1964, Massey Bus. Coll., 1965, Ga. State U.; m. Hugh Samuel Johnson, Oct. 11, 1979; children—Robert David, Douglas Alan, Brian Patrick, Sarah Iona. Bookkeeper, Massey Bus. Coll., Jacksonville, Fla., 1964-65; exec. sec. Smith Container Corp., Atlanta, 1971-74; exec. sec. Atlanta Housing Authority, 1974—, fin. asst., 1974, fin. analyst, 1974-75, investment officer, 1975, auditor, 1976—, budget officer, 1976—; tchr. budgeting various seminars, 1976—; cons. to various orgns., 1976—. Mem. LWV (sec. 1964-65), Nat. Assn. Female Execs., Nat. Assn. Housing and Redevel. Ofcls., Mcpl. Fin. Officers Assn. Home: PO Box 240 Palmetto GA 30268 Office: 739 W Peachtree St NE Atlanta GA 30365

JOHNSON, BARBARA POWELL, speech-lang. pathologist; b. Washington, Sept. 19, 1941; d. Leroy and Clara Louise (Perry) Powell; B.S., D.C. Teachers Coll., 1963; M.S., U. D.C., 1978; m. Burley Edward Johnson, May 23, 1964; children—Terrance Powell, Christopher Shaw. Speech/lang. pathologist regular edn. program D.C. Public Schs., 1964-79, Sharpe Health Sch., state sch., 1979—; guest lectr.; instr. grad. communication sci. courses; participant workshops, convs. Clk., Bapt. Ch., 1977-78; treas. Brightwood Elem. Parent-Tchr.-Student Assn., 1979—. Mem. Am. Speech/Lang./Hearing Assn. (cert.), D.C. Speech/Lang./Hearing Assn. (public sch. com.), Nat. Black Assn. Speech/Lang./Hearing (membership com.), Council for Exceptional Children. Democrat. Club: Delta Sigma Theta. Address: 1628 Nicholson St NW Washington DC 20011

JOHNSON, BETTY JANE, advt. agy. exec.; b. Watertown, N.Y., Oct. 3, 1926; d. Edward and Loleta Mary (Wiswell) Roux; student Fashion Inst. Tech., R.I. Sch. Design; m. George E. Johnson, July 16, 1949; children—Linda, Scott, Brett. Tracer, tech. illustrator Gen. Electric Co., Schenectady, 1946-55; freelance artist The Little Studio, Schenectady, 1956-62; mgr., art dir., saleswoman Johnson's Little Studio Inc., 1962-79; exec. mgr. Johnson's Visual Arts, Ltd., Schenectady, 1979—. Mem. Ad Club Albany (N.Y.). Republican. Club: Order Eastern Star. Home: 1210 Godfrey Ln Schenectady NY 12309 Office: 128 Erie Blvd Schenectady NY 12305

JOHNSON, BETTY LOU GUGE, dietitian; b. St. Louis, May 19, 1924; d. Lee Brown and Louise Susanna (Reitz) Guge; B.S. in Home Econs., U. Mo., 1945; m. Harold Arthur Johnson, Oct. 1, 1954; children—Christopher Arthur, Stephen Paul. Dietetic intern Michael Reese Hosp., Chgo., 1945; dietitian VA Hosp., Van Nuys, Calif., 1945-49, Portland, Oreg., 1949-51; relief cons. dietitian Md. Dept. Health and Mental Hygiene, 1972, 76; dept. head, dir. dietary services Pineview Gardens Nursing Home, Clinton, Md., 1967-70; instr. U. Md. Adult Edn. Center, College Park, 1977; cons. dietitian to 6 health care facilities Washington area, 1977—; mem. H.I.E.F.S.S. Cert. Bd. for Dietetic Assts. and Dietetic Technicians; mem. dietetic curriculum adv. com. No. Va. Community Coll.; mem. food mgmt. programs adv. com. Montgomery County Community Coll. (Md.). Active PTA; den mother Cub Scouts, 1963-70; mem. Republican Nat. Com. Served with USAF, 1951-55; Korea. Mem. Am. Dietetic Assn. (registered; chmn. Cons. Dietitians-Health Care Facilities 1980-81, treas. 1978-79), Md. Found. Health Care, Md. Dietetic Assn., Nutrition Today Soc. Lutheran. Club: Officers' Wives Andrews AFB. Editor cookbooks for service orgns.; cons. editor Today's Nursing Home, 1980—. Home and Office: 9303 Gwynndale Dr Clinton MD 20735

JOHNSON, BETTY MARIE, nurse, assn. exec.; b. Rockford, Ill., Mar. 5, 1931; d. Martin Carl and Hildur Marie (Tinberg) J.; diploma Swedish-Am. Hosp. Sch. Nursing, 1951; B.S. in Nursing Edn., U. Minn., 1955; M.S., U. Colo., 1962; Ph.D., U. Wis., Madison, 1970. Staff nurse Swedish Am. Hosp., Rockford, Ill., 1951-52, ednl. dir., 1955-61; staff nurse Swedish Hosp., Mpls., 1952-54; instr. Case Western Res. U., Cleve., 1962-64, asst. prof. nursing, 1964-66; coordinator of advisement U. Wis., Madison, 1969-70, asst. prof. nursing, 1970-74; dean, prof. nursing U. S.C., Columbia, 1975-80; vis. prof. nursing U. Va., Charlottesville, 1980-81; project dir. Am. Assn. Colls. Nursing, Washington, 1981—; mem. nat. arthritis adv. bd. NIH; mem. S.C. Task Force on Nursing Edn.; bd. dirs. Three Rivers Health Service Agy., 1978-79. Bd. dirs. S.C. Partners of Ams., 1978-81. Am. Jour. of Nursing Co. fellow, 1967-68; R.N., Va., S.C. Mem. Am. Nurses Assn., Nat. League Nursing, Am. Assn. Colls. of Nursing, Sigma Theta Tau. Office: 11 Dupont Circle Washington DC 20036

JOHNSON, BEVERLEY BEAUCHAMP BROWN, career cons.; b. Atlanta, Oct. 9, 1917; d. Carl Lewis and Carolyn Beatrice (Bird) Brown; A.B., Fla. State U., 1938; M.A., Columbia U., 1947; Ph.D., U. N.C., 1959; m. Victor Bernhard Johnson, Dec. 24, 1966 (dec. Sept. 1968); 1 dau., Carolyn S. Parlato. Residence counselor Fla. State U., 1943-45; personnel interviewer ARC, 1945-46; asst. personnel dir. NAM, 1948-49; asst. dean women U. Miami, 1952-53; dist. dir. Girl Scouts U.S.A., 1954-57; tchr. preparation program U. N.C., 1957-59; cons. guidance and sch. psychology Fla. State Dept. Edn., 1959-67; dir. Occupational Info. Center for Edn.-Industry, Atlanta, 1967-72; dir. career guidance Atlanta Pub. Schs., 1972-82; dir. Career Decisions Cons., 1982—. Mem. Am. Psychol. Assn., Am. Personnel and Guidance Assn., Assn. Counselor Edn. and Supervision, Nat. Vocat. Guidance Assn., So. Assn. Counselor Edn. and Supervision (pres. 1973-74). Contbr. articles to profl. jours., encys. Home: 3488 Paces Pl NW Atlanta GA 30327 Office: 2380 Peachtree Rd NW Atlanta GA 30305

JOHNSON, BONNIE LEE, ins. co. adminstr.; b. Green Bay, Wis., Nov. 5, 1954; d. Arthur Arnold and Gladys Eleanor (Little) Hooyman; B.B.A., U. Wis., Eau Claire, 1978. Mgr. meetings and convs. Am. Bankers Ins. Group, Miami, Fla. Mem. Meeting Planners Internat. Office: 600 Brickell Ave Miami FL 33131

JOHNSON, BUFFIE, painter; b. N.Y.C., Feb. 20, 1912; B.A., UCLA, 1936; student Art Students League, N.Y., 1927-28, Academie Julien, Paris, 1938; studied with Hayter Atelier, 1938-39, Francis Picabia, 1939; m. Gerald Sykes, May 30, 1950 (div. 1973); 1 dau., Jenny. One-woman shows include: Ringling Mus., Sarasota, Fla., 1947, Betty Parsons Gallery, N.Y.C., 1950, Galerie Bing, Paris, 1960, Max Hutchinson Gallery, N.Y.C., 1973, Stamford (Conn.) Mus., 1977, retrospective Landmark Gallery, N.Y.C., 1981; group shows include: Carnegie Internat., 1939, Whitney Mus., Le Salon Internat. de la Femme, Nice (2d prize), 1972, Gedok, Hamburg Mus.; executed murals Astor Theatre, N.Y.C., 1959. Bollingen Found. grantee, 1954, Nat. Archives grantee, 1973. Address: 102 Greene St New York NY 10012

JOHNSON, CAROL ANN (WILSON), real estate asso.; b. Pasadena, Calif., May 7, 1942; d. Aubrey Dean and Flora Eva (Mitchell) Wilson; B.A., San Diego State Coll., 1964; m. David Arthur Johnson, July 3, 1964; children—James David, Darrin Robert, Dayna Lynn. Tchr. spl. edn. mentally retarded San Diego city schs., 1964-68; realtor asso. Annen & Busse Realtors, Schaumburg, Ill., 1974-77, dir. corp. devel., 1981—; realtor asso. Thorsen Realtors, Schaumburg, 1977-81; asso. dir. N.W. Suburban Bd. Realtors, 1982—; chmn. Ill. Realtors Polit. Pact, 1980-81; mem. NW Bd. Realtors Polit. Action Com., 1979. Bd. dirs. Lord of Life Luth. Ch., Schaumburg, 1976-79, Clearbrook Center Handicapped, Rolling Meadows, Ill., 1979; bd. dirs. Community Counseling Center, Salvation Army, NW Area, 1976-80, chmn. Do-Nut Day, Schaumburg-Hoffman Estates, 1976-79. Life mem. Real Estate Two Million Dollar Club; voted Realtor-Asso. of Yr. for State of Ill., 1981. Mem. Nat. Assn. Realtors, NW Suburban Bd. Realtors (v.p. women's council 1982—), Women's Council Realtors, NW Suburban Assn. Commerce and Industry, Timbercrest Homeowners Assn. (pres. 1976), LWV (charter mem., dir., 1st chmn. fin. Schaumburg-Hoffman Estates area). Republican. Clubs: Meadows, Jobs Daus. Office: 821 W Higgins Rd Schaumburg IL 60195

JOHNSON, CAROL HANCOCK, telephone co. ofcl.; b. Flushing, N.Y., Mar. 21, 1947; d. Carl and Ophelia Lucille (Balkcom) Hancock; B.A., Radford U., 1969; 1 dau., Heather Lynn Johnson. Service rep. Ohio Bell Telephone Co., Cleve., 1969-72, S. Central Bell, Birmingham, Ala., 1972-77; service rep. So. Bell, Atlanta, 1977-79, asst. mgr. residence service center, Decatur, Ga., 1979—. Active Heart Fund, Am. Cancer Soc. Republican. Episcopalian. Home: 3811B Brockett Trail Clarkston GA 30021 Office: 200 Swanton Way Decatur GA 30030

JOHNSON, CAROLE EILEEN, human resource devel. specialist; b. Elizabeth, N.J., Apr. 29, 1939; d. Cecil and Rebecca Shirley (Tate) Fleming; degree in bus. edn. Trenton (N.J.) State Coll., 1960; degree in philosophy Pace U., 1972; degree in human behavior New Sch. for Social Research, 1976; m. Norman H. Johnson, Jr., July 23, 1960; children—Mark Norman, Nicole Kendall. Asst. children's fashion editor N.Y. Times, 1960-66; spl. projects coordinator Chem. Bank, N.Y.C., 1970-72; mgr. employee career devel. Philip Morris, Inc., N.Y.C., 1972-77; cons. Boyle-Kirkman Assos., N.Y.C., 1977-78; dir. tng. and devel. Sandoz, Inc., East Hanover, N.J., 1978—. Mem. Nat. Assn. Female Execs., Am. Soc. Tng. and Devel., Links, Inc., Black Profl. Women's Network. Home: 182 Lake Rd Morristownship NJ 07960 Office: Route 10 East Hanover NJ 07936

JOHNSON, CAROLE SCHULTE, educator; b. Ft. Madison, Iowa, Sept. 11, 1935; d. William Albert and Mary Josephine (Lawlor) Schulte; student Clarke Coll., 1953-55; B.A., U. Iowa, 1957, M.A. 1963, Ph.D., 1967; m. Roy A. Johnson, Oct. 14, 1967; children—Jennifer Lynn, Mark Andrew. Tchr. Longfellow Sch., Jackson, Mich., 1957-60, Glen Oak Sch., Peoria, Ill., 1960-62; reading cons. Supt. Pub. Instruction, Des Moines, 1966-67; asst. prof. Wash. State U., Pullman, 1968-73, assoc. prof., 1973-77, prof. edn., 1977—; lectr. Wis. State U., Platteville, 1966, U. Wash., Seattle, 1967. Mem. Am. Ednl. Research Assn., Internat. Reading Assn., Nat. Council Tchrs. English, Phi Beta Kappa, Phi Delta Kappa. Contbr. articles to profl. jours. Home: SE732 Ridgeview St Pullman WA 99163 Office: Dept of Edn Washington State Univ Pullman WA 99164

JOHNSON, CATHERINE COMMON, newspaper exec.; b. Watertown, N.Y., Feb. 12, 1914; d. James Allison and Minna (Anthony) Common; B.A., St. Lawrence U., 1935; M.S. in Journalism, Columbia U., 1937; m. John Brayton Johnson, June 21, 1941; children—John Brayton, Ann Catherine, Deborah Jane, Harold Bowtell. Reporter, editor Watertown (N.Y.) Daily Times, 1937-41, editorial and spl. features writer, 1950—; v.p., sec. Johnson Newspaper Corp., owners Watertown Daily Times, Batavia Daily News; dir. N.Y. Casualty Ins. Co., Watertown, Creg Systems Corp., Watertown. Vice chmn. Thousand Islands State Park Commn. Recipient Alumni citation St. Lawrence U., 1972. Mem. Nat. League Am. Pen Women, North Country Artists Guild, AAUW (pres. Jefferson br. 1981-82). Republican. Presbyterian. Club: Coll. Women of Jefferson County (pres. 1954-56). Home: 221 Flower Ave Watertown NY 13601 Office: 260 Washington St Watertown NY 13601

JOHNSON, CECILE RYDEN (MRS. PHILIP JOHNSON), artist; b. Jamestown, N.Y.; d. Ernest Edwin and Agnes E. (Johnson) Ryden; A.B., Augustana Coll.; postgrad. Am. Acad. Fine Arts, Art Inst. Chgo., U. Wis., U. Colo., Pa. Acad. Fine Art, Scripps Coll.; m. Philip Arthur Johnson; children—Pamela Cecile, Stevan Philip. One-woman shows Grand Central Gallery, N.Y.C., 1965, 67, 69, 71, 73, 75, TWA Paris, 1973, Greenville Mus. Art, Remington Mus., 1980; exhibited with Am. Watercolor Soc., Washington Watercolor Soc., Artist Guild of Chgo., Art Dirs. Annual, Nat. Acad., N.Y.C., Soc. of Illustrators; designed and executed stained glass windows for Nursery Chapel, Augustana, Chgo., 12 paintings on Bermuda for collection Bank of Bermuda, 1964, mural for Bermuda Airport, 1966, 32 paintings for U.S. Naval Art Collection on women in naval service, ofcl. lithographs, nat. fine art com. Lake Placid Olympic Organizing Com., 1980; traveling solo exhibit, Am. Univs., 1964, 65, 66; designed covers Ford Times, Chgo. Tribune Sunday Mag., others; designed Am. UNICEF Christmas card for 1968; illustration in Motor Boating, Ford Times, Lincoln Mercury Times; designed and executed Memorable Mountains series for skiing mag., 1965-74, folios of ski prints for Aspen, Vail, Snowbird, Lake Tahoe, series of 16 prints for TWA on Paris, London, Rome, 1973, series of paintings and folio prints for Napa Valley Vinters, 1975, Broadmoor Hotel, Colorado Springs, 10 originals and 450 signed prints for Broadmoor West, 1976, mural for 1st Fed. Savings and Loan, St. Paul, Bicentennial painting of St. Paul's Fed. Courts Bldg., silk screen for U.S. Hockey Team, 1976 Olympics; represented in permanent collections Augustana Coll., Gen. Mills, Minn. Mining, Ford Motor Co., Nat. Safety Council, Henderson Coll., Wagner Coll., Skiing mag., Davenport Municipal Art Gallery, others; affiliation Grand Central Galleries, N.Y.C., others. Recipient awards All Ill. Watercolor, 1953, Ill. Fedn. Music Clubs, 1955; Outstanding Achievement award Alumni Assn. Augustana Coll., 1962; Woman of Achievement award in Art Nat. League Pen Women, 1962, named 1st Woman Artist by USN and NACAL com. Salmagundi Club; Catherine Lorillard Wolffe gold medal for watercolor, 1965; Disting. Citizen citation Macalester Coll., 1979. Mem. Am. Watercolor Soc., Soc. Illustrators. Lutheran. Featured in film Creating in Watercolor; featured ABC Wide World of Sports, 1977, 79. Studio: One W 67th St New York NY 10023

JOHNSON, CHARLENE ELIZABETH, lang. arts cons.; b. Aurora, Ill., June 7, 1933; d. Floyd Clark and Marion Priscilla Smith; B.S.E., Butler U., 1960, M.S.E., 1968, Ed.S., 1982; m. Bennett F. Johnson, July 25, 1955 (div. 1961): children—Roderick Julian, Marshall Floyd. Classroom tchr. Indpls. Public Schs., 1960-68, reading tchr., 1968-71, lang. arts cons., 1971—; condr. parent workshops in reading Flanner House, 1980. Instrumentalist Butler U. Orch., C 2d Christian Ch. String Ensemble; trainer reading tutors Public Housing Authority. Mem. Internat. Reading Assn., Indpls. Reading Assn., Ind. Reading Assn., Nat. Council Negro Women, Indpls. Assn. Adminstrs., Suprs. and Consultants, NAACP, Delta Sigma Theta, Sigma Alpha Iota. Mem. Christian Ch. Author: Parent Primer, 1979. Research on Unifon, 1972.

JOHNSON, CHARLOTTE HOPE, psychologist; b. Moniteau County, Mo., Sept. 24, 1927; d. Nugent Clifford and Edna Edith (Hunziker) J.; A.A., Kansas City Jr. Coll., 1947; B.A., U. Mo., 1949, postgrad. in spl. edn., 1960, 61, 63, 66; M.A., U. Kansas City (Mo.), 1965; cert. mental retardation U. So. Calif., 1967. Sch. psychologist, public schs., Overland Park, Kans., 1959-64, Leavenworth, Kans., 1965-66; spl. edn. cons., instr. pediatrics and edn. U. Mo., Columbia, 1966-72; psychometrist Columbia Public Schs., 1972-81; job devel. Specialist missions and refugee resettlement Catholic Diocese of Jefferson City (Mo.), 1981—. Chairperson Far East refugee resettlement com. First Presbyterian Ch., Columbia, 1979—, mem. missionary com., 1981—; mem. Tulsa 1980 Com. For Human Rights; supt. primary dept., mem. bd. Religious Edn. Country Club Congregational Ch., Kansas City, Mo.; adv. bd. Voluntary Action Agys., 1981—; mem. Columbia Community Refugee Resettlement Com., 1981—. Gregory fellow, 1950; Spl. Edn. Fed. fellow, 1964. Mem. AAUW, Mo. Assn. Sch. Psychologists, LWV, Christian Crusade, Phi Beta Kappa, Pi Lambda Theta, Sigma Pi Alpha. Home: 105 W Broadway Apt 24 Columbia MO 65201 Office: 1130 E Elm St Jefferson City MO

JOHNSON, CONSTANCE A., ins. agt.; b. S. Fayston, Vt., Apr. 16, 1934; d. Guy Boyce and Harriet (Spooner) Folsom; student U. Vt., 1951-52; student Goddard Coll., 1966; m. Larry W. Johnson, Aug. 17, 1952; children—Russell Kendall, Lauren Jeanne, Erika Leigh, Kerrick Lance, Robin Winona, Marilyn Margaret. Owner, mgr. Johnson's Inc., Barre, Vt., 1970-79; sales agt. Union Mut. Ins., Barre, 1980—. Justice of the Peace, Vt., 1971—; mem. Washington County Republican Com., 1965—; mem. Vt. Rep. State Com., 1969—, vice chmn., 1971-77; mem. New Eng. Rep. Council, 1973—; del. to nat. convs., 1968-72, alt. del., 1976. Mem. Vt. Federated Bus. and Profl. Women's Clubs Inc. (state pres. 1979-80, del. to nat. conv., 1978-79), VFW Aux., Am. Legion Aux., Barre Tones, Burlington Assn. Life Underwriters, Barre Bus. and Profl. Women's Club (pres. 1982—), Nat. Assn. Female Execs., Vt. Center Performing Arts. Republican. Congregationalist (deacon 1977-79). Home: 18 Bridgeman St Barre VT 05641

JOHNSON, CORNELIA JANE, state agy. ofcl.; b. Atlanta, Nov. 16, 1951; d. Paul and Lula (Bell) Johnson; B.S. in Bus. Edn., Fort Valley State Coll., 1975. Accounting and inventory control clk. Baker Motors, Atlanta, 1975-76; clk. Ga. Dept. Revenue, Atlanta, 1977-78, asso. ops. analyst, computer operations mgr., 1978—. Mem. Digital Equipment Computer Users Soc., Atlanta Local Users Group, Nat. Assn. Female Execs., Am. Mgmt. Assn. Home: 3243 S West St Covington GA 30209 Office: 270 Washington St Atlanta GA 30334

JOHNSON, DEANNA GILMORE, social welfare adminstr.; b. Junction City, Kans., Mar. 8, 1942; d. William Edward and Helen Walters (Jones) Gilmore; B.A. cum laude, Washburn U. 1964; M.S.W., U. Kans., 1966; m. John M Johnson, Oct. 20, 1962; 1 son, Jeffrey Marc. Cons., Cons. welfare div. Kans. Dept. Social Welfare, Topeka, 1966-79; child welfare unit chief San Joaquin County Dept. Public Assistance, Stockton, Calif., 1973-79, mgr. staff devel., quality control and affirmative action, 1973—; mem. steering com., Hispanic cultural tng. materials project Sch. Social Work, San Jose State U., 1979-81; mem. San Joaquin County Affirmative Action Adv. Bd., 1980-82 . Sec., Kans. Com. on Fair Housing Legis., 1966-67. Mem. LWV, SEIU Local 535 (state treas. 1973, 74), Nat. Assn. Social Workers, County Welfare Dirs. Assn., Bay Area Staff Devel. Suprs. Exchange. Democrat. Home: 3343 Meade Ct Stockton CA 95209 Office: 133 E Weber Ave Stockton CA 95202

JOHNSON, DENA NANCEAN, real estate co. exec.; b. Des Moines, May 31, 1944; d. William W. and Genevieve Garland (Myrick) den Hartog; student Central Coll., Pella, Iowa, 1962-65, Coe Coll., summer 1965; B.A., Central Mo. State U., 1968; student Dijon (France) U., summer 1967; postgrad. Fla. State U., 1969; interior design cert. Griffith Opportunity Sch., 1975; m. Richard K. Johnson, Jan. 9, 1965; children—Scot Richard, Kurt William. Tchr., Gadsen County Sch. System, Quincy, Fla., 1969; with Junction Realty, Evergreen, Colo., 1977-79; salesman Pine Ridge Realty, Evergreen, 1979—; v.p. Tamarac Ltd., Evergreen, 1978-82; salesman, treas. Tamarac Homes, Ltd., Evergreen, 1974-82. Pres. Bear Mountain Homeowners' Assn., 1980-82. Lic. real estate salesman, Colo. Mem. Nat. Assn. Realtors, Colo. Assn. Realtors, Jefferson County Bd. Realtors, Evergreen Bd. Realtors, AAUW (charter mem. Lakewood), PEO. Mem. Unity Ch. Office: PO Box 1567 Evergreen CO 80439

JOHNSON, DOROTHY MARY BAKERJIAN, nurse, coll. dean; b. Cambridge, Mass., Aug. 5, 1944; d. Yervant Harry and Rose Mary (Bakerjian) Hadidian; B.S.N., Boston U., 1966; M.S., U. Calif., San Francisco, 1967; postgrad. W.Va. U., 1977—; m. Willard F. Johnson, Sept. 6, 1969; 1 son, Brendan Yervant. Instr. nursing U. Calif., San Francisco, 1967-69, San Diego State U., 1970-71, Coll. St. Benedict, St. Joseph, Minn., 1971-73; chmn. div. health occupations So. W.Va. Coll., Williamson, 1974-76; chmn. dept. nursing Davis & Elkins Coll., Elkins, W.Va., 1976-81; asst. dean Sch. Nursing. W.Va. U., Morgantown, 1981—; mem. adv. bd. Appalachian Med. Services. Am. Orthopsychiat. Assn. fellow, 1977—; Masters and Johnson Inst. fellow, 1978-80. Mem. Am. Nurses Assn., Nat. League Nursing, Council Nurse Specialists in Psychiat. Mental Health Nursing, Am. Assn. Allied Health Professions, Phi Delta Kappa, Sigma Theta Tau. Office: Sch Nursing W Va U Morgantown WV 26505

JOHNSON, EDNA DECOURSEY, educator; Balt., June 1, 1922; d. Jacob Garfield and Rosa Felicia (Wilson) De Coursey; B.S., Coppin State Coll., 1944; postgrad. Rutgers U., 1950, 56, Johns Hopkins, 1952, U. Md., 1959-63, U. Wis., 1966; m. Laurence Harry Johnson, Sept. 30, 1956. Tchr. pub. schs., Balt., 1944-63; asso. dir. Family Life Project Balt. Urban League, 1963-65, project dir. consumer protection program Community Action Agy., 1965-68, dir. consumer services, 1968-78; exec. dir. NW Balt. Corp., 1978-79; consumer edn. cons., tchr. Area Community Colls., 1979—; program planner Md. Food Bank, 1980-82. Mem. faculty U. Dayton, 1967; cons. Sears, Roebuck and Co. Sec., Md. Council on Family Relations, 1976—; mem. Commn. on Status Women, 1968-78, Pres.'s Consumer Adv. Council, 1974-77, Md. Gov.'s Energy Adv. Commn., 1974—. Bd. dirs. Consumers Union U.S., Balt. Area Council on Alcoholism; consumer adv. Am. Egg Bd.; public mem. Nat. Advt. Rev.; mem. consumer adv. council Fed. Res. Bd., 1976-79. Named Tchr. of Week Afro-Am. Newspapers, 1947; recipient outstanding community service awards Pi Beta Sigma, 1958, Balt. Club Nat. Assn. Negro Bus. and Profl. Women's Clubs, 1968, Nat. Negro Coll. Fund, 1970, Tau Gamma Delta, 1971, Lambda Kappa Mu, 1972. Mem. Nat. Assn. Negro Bus. and Profl. Women's Clubs (Mid-Atlantic gov. 1965-69, 73-75, nat. corr. sec. 1971-73; pres. Balt. Club 1970-73, Sojourner Truth award Balt. 1974), Am. Council on Consumer Interests, Md. Conf. Social Concerns, Am. Bus. Women's Assn., Coppin State Coll. Alumni Assn., Zeta Phi Beta, Pi Beta Sigma. Mem. United Ch. of Christ. Home: 3655 Wabash Ave Baltimore MD 21215

JOHNSON, ELLA BERNIECE, educator; b. Minatare, Nebr., Mar. 28, 1933; B.S. in Edn., Concordia Tchrs. Coll., Seward, Nebr., 1968; postgrad. U. No. Colo., Greeley, 1966-67, Chadron (Nebr.) State Coll., 1970-77, Kearney (Nebr.) State Coll., 1978-79, U. Nebr., Lincoln, 1980; m. Walter F. Johnson, Aug. 8, 1954; children—Jon Ray, Mark Lee. Tchr., Zion Luth. Sch., Plainview, Nebr., 1952-54; tchr. St. Paul's Luth. Sch., Sidney (Nebr.) Public Schs., 1960-64, 66-78, instr., facilitator for gifted, 1978—; cons. gifted edn. Panhandle area, 1979—. Pres., Nebr. Aux. to Letter Carriers, 1969-70; pres. Luth. Women's Missionary

League, St. Paul's Luth. Ch., 1975-77. Mem. NEA, AAUW (treas. 1969-70), Nebr. State Edn. Assn. (dist. sec. 1977-79, pres.-elect 1980-81, pres. 1981-82), Sidney Educators Assn. (pres. 1978-79, chief negotiator 1980-82), Delta Kappa Gamma (pres. 1976-78). Home: 1550 20th Ave Sidney NE 69162

JOHNSON, E(LLA) DOLORES, telecommunications co. mktg. exec.; b. Buffalo, Feb. 2, 1948; d. Charles Roosevelt and Merna Elizabeth (Lewis) J.; B.S. (fellow), Howard U., 1970; M.B.A. (Congress Grad. Mgmt. Edn. fellow), Harvard U., 1972; m. Luther M. Johnson, Dec. 15, 1973; 1 dau., Jennifer. Fin. analyst Fed. Home Loan Bank Bd., Washington, 1971-72; bus. office mgr. N.Y. Telephone, Bronx, 1972-73; sales mgr. So. Bell, Greenville, S.C., 1974-75, South Central Bell, Baton Rouge, 1975-77; dist. mktg. mgr. AT&T, Basking Ridge, N.J., 1977—. Christian bd. cons. Union Baptist Ch., Morristown, N.J.; bd. dirs. Career Workshops, Morristown. Named Black Achiever in Industry, Harlem br. YMCA, 1981; recipient Dash-Thompson award AT&T, 1981. Mem. Harvard Bus. Sch. Black Alumnae Assn., Howard U. Alumni Assn., Delta Sigma Theta. Home: 44 Kahdena Rd Morris Twp NJ 07960 Office: 295 N Maple Ave Basking Ridge NJ 07920

JOHNSON, ELLA MARIA, nurse; b. Pensacola, Fla., Mar. 20, 1950; d. Tom Allen and Inell Teresa (Evans) J.; B.S. in Nursing, Barry Coll., Miami, Fla., 1972; cert. ICC, St. Francis Cabrini Hosp., Alexandria, La., 1974; 1 child, Angelo Nicholi. Nurse technician VA Hosp., Miami, 1970-72; ICC head nurse Osteo. Hosp., Miami, 1972-73; med.-surg. relief head nurse CCU, St. Francis Cabrini Hosp., Alexandria, 1973-75; staff nurse ICU, Oschner Found. Hosp., New Orleans, 1975—. Address: 4211 S Broad St New Orleans LA 70125

JOHNSON, ETHEL LOUISE WHITE, retail exec.; b. Washington, Jan. 7, 1924; d. Arthur Belmore and Ethel Irene (Schulz) White; student Columbia Tech., 1943; m. Bernard Lee Johnson, Nov. 24, 1942; children—Bruce, Nancy. Control supr. Dept. Commerce, Suitland, Md., 1943; acct. GI Market, Suitland, 1950-67; treas. G.I. Liquors, Inc., Morningside, Md., 1967—; dir. White Enterprises, Morningside, 1975—. Mem. Nat. Council Churches; pres. United Churchwomen Prince Georges County, 1963. Republican. Club: Tantallon Country. Home: 300 Rexburg Ave Oxon Hill MD 20022 Office: GI Liquors Inc 6712 Suitland Rd Morningside MD 20023

JOHNSON, EVA MAYNE, educator; b. Balt.; A.B., George Washington U., 1949, M.A., 1951, Ph.D., 1957; m. Edwin Joseph Johnson. Office mgr. Dept. Agr. Grad. Sch., Washington, 1936-43; adminstrv. asst. UN Relief and Rehab., U.S., Greece, Italy, 1944-46; research psychologist D.C. Child and Welfare Dept., 1951-52; prof. dept. psychology George Washington U., Washington, 1952—, prof. Emeritus Reading Center, 1976—. Lic. psychologist, Washington. Mem. Am. Psychol. Assn., Eastern Psychol. Assn., D.C. Psychol. Assn., D.C. Assn. for Retarded Citizens (past pres., dir.), Nat. Assn. for Retarded Citizens (past v.p.). Research into psychol. effects of purulent meningites, 1959-60; author: Code of Behavior for Teenagers, 1967. Home: 3232 Woodstream Ln Ellicott City MD 21043

JOHNSON, EVANGELINE CAROLYN, accountant; b. Carteret, N.J., Feb. 16, 1925; d. William Douglas and Fannie Page (Howard) Dewberry; A.A.S. in Bus. Adminstrn., Camden County Coll., 1974; B.S. in Bus. Adminstrn. summa cum laude, Glassboro State Coll., 1982; m. Lonnie E. Johnson, Oct. 11, 1947; children—Lonnie, Anita, Enoch, Marcelia. Asst. underwriter Ins. Co. N.Am., Phila., 1966-68; faculty sec. English dept. Camden County Coll., Blackwood, N.J., 1968-74, purchasing agt., 1975-81; acct. Ins. Co. N.Am., Phila., 1981—; lectr. in field. Troop leader Girl Scouts U.S.A., Lawnside, N.J.; mem. scholarship com. Kaighn Ave. Baptist Ch. Mem. Am. Mgmt. Assn., Minister Wives Assn. So. N.J., NAACP, Colored Women's Civic Assn., Nat. Acctg. Assn., AAUW, Lawnside Master Choral Soc. Democrat. Club: Lawnside Scholarship. Home: 46 E Oak Ave Lawnside NJ 08045

JOHNSON, EVELYN BRYAN, flying service exec.; b. Corbin, Ky., Nov. 4, 1909; d. Edward William and Mayme Estelle (Fox) Stone; grad. Tenn. Wesleyan Jr. Coll., 1929; student U. Tenn., 1930-32; m. Wyatt J. Bryan, Mar. 21, 1931 (dec. 1963); m. 2d, Morgan N. Johnson, Feb. 25, 1965 (dec. 1977). With Morristown (Tenn.) Flying Service, Inc., 1947-82, chief flight instr., 1949—, sec.-treas., 1949-62, pres., 1962-82; mgr. Moore Murrell Airport, 1962—. Recipient Carnegie Hero medal, 1958, Service to Mankind award Morristown Sertoma Club, 1981; named Flight Instr. of Yr., Nashville dist., 1973, 79, So. region, 1979, Nat., 1979 (all FAA); Outstanding Alumnus, Tenn. Wesleyan Coll., 1981. Mem. Morristown Area C. of C., Nat. Assn. Flight Instrs. (dir.), Ninety-Nines, Whirly Girls, Aircraft Owners and Pilots Assn., CAP, Univ. Aviation Assn., Silver Wings (Woman of Yr. 1981). Republican. Baptist. Home: Route 1 Osage Hills Jefferson City TN 37760 Office: PO Box 1013 Morristown TN 37814

JOHNSON, EVELYN MARIE MARSH, ednl. cons., resource specialist; b. Erath, La., July 6, 1935; d. Donald and Evelyn N. (Lee) Marsh; B.A., So. U., 1956; M.Ed., Bowie State Coll., 1972, Loyola Coll., 1975; Ph.D., Walden U., 1981; m. W. Haywood Johnson, Dec. 24, 1956; 1 dau., Donna Marie. Tchr. public schs., La., 1956-58, Tex., 1960-61, Washington, 1963-67; spl. edn. tchr. Prince George's County Schs., Upper Marlboro, Md., 1967-70, ESL tchr., 1970-74, spl. edn. resource specialist, 1970—; cons. Walden U.-Walden Assos., Naples, Fla., 1982—. Mem. bd. dirs. Citizens Against Spousal Abuse, Columbia, Md., 1974-75; mem. bd. Christian edn. St. John Baptist Ch., Columbia, 1981-83, mem. youth adv. council, 1981-83; mem. Md. Bd. Examiners of Psychologists, 1982-85; precinct capt. Democratic Nat. Com., Columbia, Md., 1976-77, voter registration leader, 1979-80; del. Dem. Nat. Conv., 1980. Mem. Prince George's Tchrs. Assn. (Cert. of Recognition 1981), Nat. State Tchrs. Assn. (del. 1978-81, mem. legis. com. 1981—), Nat. Council Negro Women, Patuxent Bus. and Profl. Women Group, Nat. Hook Up of Black Women, NOW, LWV, NAACP, Md. State Tchrs. Assn., NEA, Alliance Toward Active Community, Alpha Kappa Alpha, Kappa Delta Phi. Home: 11067 Iron Crown Ct Columbia MD 21044 Office: 13710 Laurel-Bowie Rd Laurel MD 20708

JOHNSON, EVELYNE CLAIRE LEVOW, artist, author; b. N.Y.C., Jan. 20, 1922; d. David William and Rose (Geiger) Levow; student NAD, 1936-39; cert. in mktg. and advt. N.Y. U., 1941, postgrad., 1947; postgrad. CCNY, 1951; m. Frank A. Johnson, Jr., Oct. 10, 1942; 1 son, Barry Ellis. Pres., Evelyne Johnson Assos., N.Y.C., 1964—; works include: The Elephants Ball, 1977, The Cookie Cookbook, 1979, I Am A Baby, 1979, Beddybye Baby, 1979, Fun in the Tub, 1979, Baby's Farm, 1979, Peek-A-Boo, 1979, My Animal Friends, 1979, My Favorite Toys, 1979, The Coloring Cookbook, 1982, The Cow in the Kitchen, 1983. Mem. Nat. Arts Club, Soc. Illustrators, Soc. Photographers and Artists Reps., Graphic Artists Guild, Met. Mus. Art. Democrat. Jewish. Home and Office: 201 E 28th St New York NY 10016

JOHNSON, FLORA, accountant; b. S.C., Nov. 2, 1943; d. Will and Lauretta Takeall; B.B.A., Bernard Baruch Coll., 1972; M.B.A., L.I. U., 1976; children—Rodney, Omar, Malik. Tax acct., Price Waterhouse, N.Y.C., 1977-80; instr. taxation Malcolm-King Coll., 1980. Recipient Dirs. award Manhattan Dist. IRS, Dept. Treasury; Outstanding Profl. Achievement award Bernard M. Baruch Coll. Mem. Nat. Assn. Black Accts. (v.p. N.Y. chpt. 1979-80), Coalition 100 Black Women, Bernard M. Baruch Coll. Alumni Assn. Republican. Contbr. articles to profl. jours.; pub. Your Monthly Tax-Tips. Home: PO Box 1034 Stuyvesant Station New York NY 10009

JOHNSON, FRANCES DELL, nursing supr.; adminstr.; b. Bolivar, Tenn., Jan. 4, 1941; d. Ernest R. and Estelle Frances (Granger) McLain; A.D. in Nursing, Barton County Community Jr. Coll., 1971; student Kans. State U. Extension, 1966-70; children by previous marriage—Mary Deborah, Linda Dell. Psychiat. technician Western Mental Health Inst., Bolivar, Tenn., 1961-62, Tenn. Psychiat. Inst., Memphis, 1962-64, Larned State Hosp., Larned, Kans., 1964-71; R.N. supr. Western Mental Health Inst., Bolivar, 1972—; staff nurse Meth. Hosp., Memphis, 1973-82. Mem. Tenn. State Employees Assn., Am. Heart Assn. Republican. Baptist. Home: PO Box 356 Bolivar TN 38008 Office: Western Mental Health Inst Bolivar TN 38074

JOHNSON, FRANCES RUTH STEEN, record adminstr.; b. N.D., Jan. 17, 1921; d. Oscar W. and Liddia Mae (Hrabe) Steen; B.S. in Med. Record Adminstrn., Coll. St. Scholastica, Duluth, Minn., 1943; m. James S. Johnson, Jr., Sept. 24, 1972; children—William A. Cross, Nancy C. Langston. Med. record adminstr. Deaconess Hosp., Grafton, N.D., 1942, Jewish Hosp., Louisville, 1943, Good Samaritan Hosp., West Palm Beach, Fla., 1943, Charlotte (N.C.) Meml. Hosp., 1944; office mgr. Fla. Hosp. Service Corp., 1944-46; exec. sec. ITT Kellogg, Raleigh, N.C., 1961-65; dir. med. record services Dorothea Dix Hosp., Raleigh, 1965-75; chief med. record adminstr. N.C. Div. Mental Health, 1974-77; dir. Quality Assurance Project (NIMH grant), N.C. Div. Mental Health and Mental Retardation Services, Raleigh, 1977-78, chief program revs., 1978—; cons. New York Dept. Mental Hygiene, 1970-73, La. Office Mental Health and Substance Abuse, 1980—; chmn. adv. com. Sch. Med. Record Adminstrn., E.Carolina U., Greenville, N.C., 1975—; cons. NIMH, Washington, 1976—. Mem. Am. Med. Record Assn. (del. from N.C. 1969, 75, 76, bd. dirs. 1977—), N.C. Med. Record Assn. (pres. 1967-68), Southeastern Conf. Med. Record Adminstrs. Republican. Presbyterian. Contbr. articles to profl. jours. Home: Route 1 Box 341 Raleigh NC 27614 Office: NC Div Mental Health Mental Retardation and Substance Abuse Services 325 N Salisbury St Raleigh NC 27611

JOHNSON, GERTRUDE L., accountant; b. Freeport, N.Y., May 29, 1924; d. Harold Post and Sadie Bernice (Grover) J.; children—John Frank, Joan Frances. Owner, mgr. Gertrude Johnson Bookkeeping, Orlando, Fla., 1959-62; partner Garst Bookkeeping & Tax Service, Winter Park, Fla., 1962-66; owner, mgr. Gertrude Johnson Acct., Orlando, 1966-69; partner Gardner & Johnson, Accts., Orlando, 1969-81, owner, 1981—. Served with AUS, 1944-47. Mem. Fla. Accts. Assn., Nat. Soc. Public Accts., Nat. Assn. Enrolled Agts., Fla. Soc. Enrolled Agts. (pres. Orlando chpt.), Am. Legion. Club: Odd Fellows. Home: 835 N Primrose Dr Orlando FL 32803 Office: 2316 N Orange Blossom Trail Orlando FL 32804

JOHNSON, GLORIA YVONNE, telephone co. exec.; b. Wytheville, Va., Oct. 22, 1950; d. George Edward and Bertha Mae (Dandridge) J.; B.S. in Bus. Adminstrn. and Econs., Fisk U., Nashville, 1972. With Chesapeake & Potomac Telephone Co., Washington, 1972—, advt. mgr., sales promotion coordinator, 1977-81, corp. contbns. mgr., dir. community and ednl. relations, 1981—, also lectr. Mem. Youth Motivation Task Force; mem. exec. bd. Howard U. Cluster. Mem. Nat. Trade Show Exhibitors Assn., Advt. Club Met. Washington, Washington Urban League, Fisk U. Alumni Assn. (chmn. fundraising activities 1976, 78, 79), Nat. Assn. Female Execs., Delta Sigma Theta. Democrat. Baptist. Home: 12518 Winexburg Manor Dr Silver Spring MD 20906 Office: 2055 L St NW Suite 765 Washington DC 20036

JOHNSON, GLORYA J., cardiovascular technician; b. Toledo, Aug. 13, 1944; d. Walter W. and June S. (Totzke) J.; B.S. in Edn., Bowling Green State U., 1968; spl. cert. in respiratory therapy Washtenaw Community Coll., 1971. Health and phys. educator Elmwood Local Schs., Bloomdale, Ohio, 1966-70; respiratory therapist, cardiopulmonary technician Flower Hosp., Sylvania, Ohio, 1970-79; cardiovascular technician Columbia Hosp., Milw., 1981—. Bd. deacons Christ Presbyterian Ch., Toledo, 1974-76; mem. session, fin. sec. Tippecanoe Presbyn. Ch., Milw. Mem. Nat. Soc. Cardiopulmonary Tech., Nat. Women's Health Network, Am. Assn. Female Execs., AAAS. Club: Order Eastern Star. Contbg. author to tng. book. Home: 121 W Saveland Ave Milwaukee WI 53207 Office: 2025 E Newport Ave Milwaukee WI 53211

JOHNSON, HAZEL WINIFRED, nurse, army officer; b. West Chester, Pa., Oct. 10, 1927; d. Clarence Lemont and Garnett (Henley) J.; R.N. diploma Harlem Hosp., N.Y.C., 1950; B.S.N., Villanova U., 1959; postgrad. Columbia U., 1963; Ph.D. in Nursing Edn., Catholic U. Am., 1978. Commd. 1st lt. U.S. Army Nurse Corps, 1955, advanced through grades to brig. gen., 1979; mem. staff U.S. Army Med. Research and Devel. Command, Washington, 1967-73; dir. Walter Reed Army Inst. Nursing, Washington, 1976-78; asst. for nursing Office of Surgeon, Med. Command, Korea, 1978-79; chief Army Nurse Corps, Office Surgeon Gen., Dept of the Army, Washington, 1979—; cons. edn. com. Operating Room Nurses Assn. Decorated Legion of Merit, Meritorious Service medal, Army Commendation medal; recipient Evangeline G. Bovard Army Nurse of Yr. award Letterman Army Med. Center, San Francisco, 1964, Dr. Anita Newcomb McGee award DAR, Washington, 1971. Mem. Assn. Mil. Surgeons U.S., Am. Nurses Assn., Chester County (Pa.) Nurses Assn., Nat. League Nursing.

JOHNSON, HELEN SHOSHANAH, fashion designer, mfr.; b. Chgo., July 22; d. Albert Johnson and Teary Watson-Johnson; student Art Inst. Chgo., 1972, U. Chgo., 1972; cert. Cosmopolitan Sch. Bus., 1973. Designer apprentice Stanley Korshak, Chgo., 1971; with Eucos, Inc., Evanston, Ill., 1972-73, Fureal, Ltd., Skokie, Ill., 1973-74; tchr. Chgo. State U., 1974-75; fashion designer, coordinator Pier 1 Imports, Ft. Worth, 1975-77; designer Revere Sportswear, Chgo., 1977-79; pres. Helen Johnson Collectibles and Helen Johnson Originals, Chgo., 1979—; founder adult edn. fashion design program Olive-Harvey Coll., Chgo. State U.; faculty adviser Acad. Fashion and Merchandising, 1981, Ray-Vogue Sch. Fashion Design, 1982. Active Girl Scouts U.S.A. Chgo. Public Sch. Art Soc.-Sch. Art Inst. grantee, 1971; Stanley Korshak awardee and grantee, 1971; Oscar Arronson grantee, 1970. Mem. Chgo. Fashion Group Guild, Chgo. Fashion Exchange, League of Black Women, Fashion Group. Jewish. Office: 30 E Division St Lobby Chicago IL 60610

JOHNSON, JACQUELINE BETTY, banker; b. N.Y.C., Oct. 11, 1926; d. Claybourne and Ruthe K. (Baker) Robinson; diploma Wilberforce U., 1946; divorced; children—Yolando Miller, Deidre Sabe, Herbert, Tina. With Chase Manhattan Bank N.A., 1966—, asst. treas., br. mgr., Ridgewood, N.Y., 1966—. Adv. Bd. Salvation Army, 1979. Recipient Black Achievers award YMCA, 1981. Mem. Fresh Pond Rd. C. of C. Democrat. Methodist. Office: 66-60 Fresh Pond Rd Ridgewood NY 11385

JOHNSON, JANET H., Egyptologist; b. Everett, Wash., Dec. 24, 1944; d. Robert A. and Jane N. (Osborn) J.; B.A., U. Chgo., 1967, Ph.D., 1972; m. Donald Whitcomb, Sept. 2, 1978. Instr., U. Chgo., 1971-72, asst. prof., 1972-79, asso. prof., 1979-81, prof. Egyptology, Oriental Inst., 1981—. Grantee Nat. Endowment Humanities, 1978-81; 81-83, Smithsonian Instn., 1977-82, and Nat. Geographic, 1978, 80, 82. Mem. Egypt Exploration Soc., Am. Research Center Egypt (bd. govs. 1979—). Author: The Demotic Verbal System; (with Donald Whitcomb) Quseir al-Qadim: Preliminary Report, 1978, 1980. Office: 1155 E 58th St Chicago IL 60637

JOHNSON, JANET WRAE, publishing co. exec.; b. San Pedro, Calif., Jan. 19, 1948; d. John Warren and Janet (White) J.; student U. Calif., Sacramento, Am. River Coll., Sacramento, Sacramento City Coll. Asst. to pres. Master Mfg., Inc., Sacramento, 1966-72; partner Sacramento Area Bowling News, Sacramento, 1972-77; partner, mgr. Jan-L Enterprises, Incline Village, Nev., 1977-78; nat. sales mgr. Dynacom, Chgo., 1978-80; pres. J.W.J. Enterprises, Inc./Big Apple Guide Inc., N.Y.C., 1980—. Mem. Am. Mgmt. Assn., Am. Mktg. Assn., Sales Execs. Club N.Y. Address: 345 E 81st St Suite 14B New York NY 10028

JOHNSON, JANETTE, lawyer; b. Rochester, N.Y., Mar. 28, 1949; d. Arthur Daniel and Florence Cecilia (Vollmer) J.; B.A. in English, UCLA, 1971; J.D., Antioch Sch. Law, Washington, 1976. Legal intern subcom. labor U.S. Senate, 1975; pension hearing officer health and retirement fund United Mine Workers, summer 1975; admitted to Calif. bar, 1977, D.C. bar, 1980; atty. div. advice NIRB, 1976—. Bd. dirs., sec. 14th and U Sts. Coalition. Mem. D.C. Bar Assn. (co-chmn. labor relations div. 1981-82), Women's Bar Assn. D.C., Nat. Assn. Women Execs., ACLU, NOW, Logan Circle Community Assn. Democrat. Home: 1339 Wallach Pl NW Washington DC 20009 Office: 1717 Pennsylvania Ave Suite 865 Washington DC 20570

JOHNSON, JANNETTA FAIRES, social worker; b. McNairy County, Tenn.; d. R.F. and Ethel W. Faires; B.A., Blue Mountain (Miss.) Coll.; M.S.W., Fla. State U., 1965; divorced; children—Thomas A., Richard M. With Ga. Dept. Human Resources, 1948—, dist. social services dir., Lawrenceville, 1973—; dist., state rep. Title XX Social Service Planning Com.; workshop leader, cons. in field. Chmn. planning com. United Way Gwinnett County, bd. dirs. Mental Health Assn. Met. Atlanta; ch. tng. dir. 1st Bapt. Ch., Lawrenceville. Mem. Nat. Assn. Social Workers, LWV (pres. Gwinnett County chpt. 1980), Lawrenceville Bus. and Profl. Women's Club (Woman of Achievement award 1979). Democrat. Home: 168 King Arthur Dr Lawrenceville GA 30245 Office: 134 S Clayton St Suite 2 Lawrenceville GA 30245

JOHNSON, JEAN HART, art dir.; b. Mineola, N.Y., Nov. 25, 1931; d. Frank Ernest and Isabelle Tayor (Ellis) Hart; student Peace Jr. Coll., Raleigh, N.C., 1950-51, Queens Coll., Charlotte, N.C., 1951-52; m. William I. Herendeen, Aug. 22, 1952; m. 2d, Louis H. Johnson, Jan. 31, 1959; 1 dau., Jennifer Taylor. With Storer Broadcasting Co., Miami, Fla., 1956-57; with Southeast Banks N.A., Miami, Fla., 1974—, art dir., 1981—; mem. Gov. Fla. Panel Visual Arts, 1980, Dade County Art in Public Places, 1979-81; art cons., 1974—. Bd. dir. Viscaya Museum, Miami, 1963, Beaux Arts, U. Miami, 1968, Theatre Art Patrons, Miami, 1965. Recipient Gov. Fla. award art, 1976, 79, Miami Dade Public Library award, 1978, Bus. Com. for Arts award, 1975-79, WPBT Public TV award, 1976, 77, 80, Lowe Gallery, U. Miami cert. recognition, 1980, Dade County Art in Public Places cert. recognition, 1981. Democrat. Address: 600 Biltmore Way Apt 618 Coral Gables FL 33143

JOHNSON, JEANNE LOUISE, mgmt. cons.; b. Kenosha, Wis., Nov. 14, 1928; d. Byron Simpson and Amanda (Zeitler) Knight; B.S. cum laude, U. Dubuque, 1949. Head editing dept. Film Prodn. unit Ia. State U., 1954-56; head Continuity dept. WICS-NBC TV, Springfield, Ill., 1958-59; home service adv. Central Ill. Light Co., Springfield, 1959-61; instr. home economics Centralia (Ill.) City Schs., 1962-66; v.p. Tallman Robbins & Co., Springfield, 1967-77; v.p. Delta Business Forms, Cairo, Ill., 1971-77; mgmt. cons., 1977-80; v.p. Adminstrv. Techs. Inc., Springfield, Ill., 1980—. Mem. Data Entry Mgmt. Assn. Data Processing Mgmt. Assn., Internat. Orgn. Women Execs., Internat. Word Processing Assn., Zeta Phi. Address: 7667 Callaghan Rd #701 San Antonio TX 78229

JOHNSON, JOAN BLONDELL, town ofcl.; b. West Palm Beach, Fla., Nov. 29, 1933; d. Christopher C. and Cora (Winn) Maloney; M.S.W., SUNY, Stony Brook, 1977; m. Cleveland Johnson, Apr. 20, 1957; children—Keith, Genevieve, Kelly, Cleveland. County Head Start dir. Union Free Sch. Dist. 13, Central Islip, N.Y., 1967-69; dir. Head Start, Central Islip (N.Y.) Sch., 1970-77; dir. Econ. Opportunity Council Suffolk, Patchogue, N.Y., 1977; dir. human devel. Town of Islip, 1978—; field instr. SUNY, Stony Brook. Bd. dirs. Victim Info. Bur. Suffolk, Suffolk County Police Athletic League; chmn. adolescent pregnancy cons. com. Bd. Coop. Ednl. Services 1969. Recipient Outstanding Achievement award Central Islip Community Action Com., 1970, named Woman of Year, 1969. Mem. Nat. Assn. Social Workers, Nat. Assn. Black Social Workers, Nat. Assn. Black Alcoholic Counselors, Nat. Council Black Family and Child Devel. Republican. Home: 52 Miller Ave Central Islip NY 11722 Office: 401 Main St Islip NY 11751

JOHNSON, JOAN BRAY, ins. co. adminstr.; b. Kennett, Mo., Nov. 19, 1926; d. Plas Green and Mary Scott (Williams) Bray; student Drury Coll., Springfield, Mo., 1949-51, Central Bible Inst. and Coll., Springfield, 1946-49; m. Frank Johnson, Jr., Nov. 6, 1955; 1 son, Victor Kent. Staff writer Gospel Pub. Co., Springfield, 1949-51; sec. Kennett (Mo.) Sch. Dist. Bd. Edn., 1951-58; spl. features coor. Memphis Press-Scimitar, 1959-60; sec. to v.p. Cotton Exchange Bank, Kennett, 1959-60; proposal analyst Aetna Life Ins. Co., El Paso, 1960-64, pension adminstr., El Paso, 1964-71, office mgr. Brokerage div., Denver, 1971-78, office adminstr. Life Consol. div., Oakland, Calif., 1979—; instr. classes Life Office Mgmt. Assn.; tole artist. Officer, PTA, 1964-71; pres. Wesley Service Guild, 1968-71; den mother Boy Scouts Am. Recipient life service award Tex. PTA, 1970. Fellow Life Office Mgmt. Assn.; mem. Bus. and Profl. Women. Democrat. Methodist. Clubs: Last Monday, Opti-Mrs. Home: 1284 Marlboro Ct Concord CA 94521 Office: 1330 Broadway Suite 830 Oakland CA 94612

JOHNSON, JOAN D., educator; b. Wyandotte, Mich., Oct. 10, 1929; d. Joel C. and Emily Carla (Timm) J.; student W. Mich. Coll., 1947-49; B.S., U. Wis., 1951; M.S., U. So. Calif., 1955, Ph.D., 1965; student U. Mich., 1958. Instr. phys. edn. Bloom Twp. High Sch., Chicago Heights, Ill., 1951-53; teaching asst. U. So. Calif., Los Angeles, 1953-55, vis. prof., 1960; asst. prof. phys. edn. Calif. State U., Los Angeles, 1955-65, asso. prof. 1965-70, prof. 1970—, asso. chmn. dept. phys. edn. and athletics, 1969-77, chmn. 1977-80; vis. prof. Tex. Woman's U., Denton, 1973; coach, U.S. Women's Tennis Team, World U. Games, Sofia, Bulgaria, 1977; chmn. tennis com. Assn. Intercollegiate Athletics for Women, 1976-79. Recipient Women's Tennis Leadership award, U.S. Lawn Tennis Assn., 1970; Outstanding Prof. award Calif. State U., Los Angeles, 1977-78. Mem. Calif. Assn. Health, Phys. Edn., Recreation and Dance, AAHPERD, Western Soc. Phys. Edn. Coll. Women (sec. 1967-68, treas. 1972-73, pres. 1977-78, exec. bd. 1980—), Nat. Assn. Phys. Edn. Higher Edn., So. Calif. Tennis Umpires Assn., Phi Kappa Phi. Club: Soroptimist Internat. of Los Angeles (pres. Found. bd. 1982—). Author: (with P.J. Xanthos) Tennis, 4th edit., 1981; (with D.F. Kelley) A Workbook for Tests and Measurements in Physical Education, 1967. Office: Dept Phys Edn/Recreation/Leisure Studies Calif State U at Los Angeles 5151 State U Dr Los Angeles CA 90032

JOHNSON, JOANNE MARIE, nurse; b. Windsor, Ont., Can., Nov. 17, 1954; d. Maurice C. and Bernadine L. (Campeau) Tisdelle; came to U.S., 1967; B.S. in Nursing, U. So. Miss., 1977; m. Randy Johnson, Aug. 28, 1976; 1 son, Christopher. With Forrest Gen. Hosp., Hattiesburg, Miss., 1977-78, staff nurse med.-surg. unit, 1978-80, patient care supr., med.-surg. instr. dept. edn., 1981—. Mem. Am. Nurses Assn., Miss.

Nurses Assn., U. So. Miss. Alumni Assn., U. So. Miss. Sch. Nursing Alumni Assn. (nursing research com.). Roman Catholic. Office: PO Box 1897 Hattiesburg MS 39401

JOHNSON, JORENE KATHRYN, community orgn. adminstr.; b. Rockville Centre, N.Y., Jan. 6, 1931; d. Adam and Kathryn Lillian (Schoen) Freitag; B.F.A., Pratt Inst., 1952; M.P.A., U. Cin., 1975; student Mt. St. Joseph Coll., 1977-78; m. Roland E. Johnson, Oct. 10, 1954; children—Lorin, Melissa. Furniture designer Jacques Bodart, Inc., N.Y.C., 1952-54; interior decorator Albert Parvin Co., Los Angeles, 1955-57, Maria Bergson Assos., N.Y.C., 1957-61; office mgr., research asst. The Cin. Inst., 1973-74, research mgr., 1974-75; exec. dir. Friends of Cin. Parks Inc., 1975-77; community coordinator College Hill Forum, Cin., 1977—; sec., insp. Green Twp. Zoning Bd., 1982—. Mem. Cin. Mayor's Energy Policy Com., 1982—; vice-chmn. Monfort Heights Civic Assn., 1977, chmn., 1978; mem. Leadership Cin. Class III, 1979-80; mem. planning com. Community Chest, 1982—; mem. planning com. Program for Cin., 1982-83. Mem. Met. Exchange of Cin., AAUW, Bus. and Profl. Women. Clubs: Woman's City, Green Twp. Democratic. Home: 5200 Race Rd Cincinnati OH 45239 Office: 1805 Larch Ave Cincinnati OH 45224

JOHNSON, JOY NELSON, social worker, educator; b. Bluefield, W.Va., Aug. 14, 1926; d. James T. and Besse Marie (Liddle) Nelson; A.B. in Sociology, Franklin Coll. of Ind., 1947; m. Howard A. Johnson, July 19, 1947; children—Howard Arthur, Kraig N. Social case worker Ind. Public Welfare Dept., 1947-48; nursery sch. tchr., Middletown, Conn., 1949-50; substitute public sch. tchr., Middletown, 1948-49, Ft. Walton Beach, Fla., 1968-71; social case worker Child Guidance Service, Lexington, Ky., 1966-67; mem. Okaloosa County (Fla.) Textbook Evaluation Com. for Public Schs., 1974-80. Mem. Citizens Adv. Council for Operation Outreach, 1972-73. Cert. social worker, Conn., Ind.; cert. substitute tchr., Fla. Mem. AAUW (dir. Fla. div. 1971-73, br. pres. 1971-73, br. dir. 1968—), Hist. Soc. Okaloosa and Walton Counties, Panhellenic Assn. Ft. Walton Beach Area, Fla. Fedn. Women's Clubs, Delta Delta Delta, Psi Iota Xi. Presbyterian. Club: Order Eastern Star. Home: 309 Yacht Club Dr NE Ft Walton Beach FL 32548

JOHNSON, JOYCE MARIE BETTS, stockbroker, columnist; b. East Chicago, Ind., Jan. 18, 1938; d. Hobart and Mattie (Upshaw) Betts; B.S., U. Md., Magna Cum Laude, 1976; m. Emmitt Johnson, July 6, 1959; children—Roderick, Terence. Tchr. shorthand Universal lang. Center, Taipei, Taiwan, 1963; adminstrv. asst., exec. sec. U.S. Army Intelligence, Munich, Germany, 1969-73; tchr. McArthur Jr. High Sch., Ft. Meade, Md., 1974-75; bus. mgr. The Reading Center, Gary, Ind., 1976-77; stockbroker A.G. Edwards Co., Merrillville, Ind., 1977—; columnist Dollars and Sense mag., Chgo., 1979—, Info Newspaper, Gary, 1979—, Post Tribune, Gary, 1981—, Chgo. Defender, 1981—. Bd. dirs. Women's Assn. NW Ind. Symphony Soc., 1978, NW Ind. Opera Theatre, Friends Lake County Library, 1978; adv. bd. CEDCO Businesswomen's Ednl. Forum; mem. Northwest Ind. chpt. Nat. Kidney Found. Mem. Nat. Council Negro Women, (dir. Gary-Merrillville br. 1977—), Am. Soc. Women Accts., League of Black Women, YWCA, Nat. Soc. Registered Reps., Bus. and Profl. Women's Club, NAACP, PUSH, Civitan Internat., Am. Symphony Orch. League (vol. council),Group. Phi Kappa Phi, Alpha Sigma Lambda, Delta Sigma Theta. Home: PO Box 63 Gary IN 46402 Home: 1400 Lake Shore Dr Chicago IL 6061

JOHNSON, JUANITA ANN, nurse; b. Centralia, Mo., Aug. 21, 1942; d. George Benjamin and Madge Karettia (Woods) Dixon; A.A., Penn Valley Community Coll., 1978; student U. Mo.; children—Charles M., Alesha K., Mark N. Lic. practical nurse Wayne Miner Health Center, Kansas City, Mo., 1968-78; registered profl. nurse surg. floor VA Hosp., Kansas Coty, Mo., 1978—; mem. retention and recruitment com. VA Hosp., 1979, mem. audit com., 1981. Mem. Nat. Orgn. Orthopedic Nursing. Home: 2036 E 77th St Kansas City MO 64132 Office: VA Hosp Kansas City MO 64132

JOHNSON, JUDITH ANN, mfg. co. exec.; b. Providence, Mar. 3, 1943; d. Lyman A. and Virginia (Briggs) Draper; student Valencia Community Coll., 1972-73; m. Donald R. Johnson, Oct. 8, 1976; children—Denise Ann, Tina Ann, Donald R. Sec. to dept. mgr. Pershing subcontracts Martin Marietta Corp., Orlando, Fla., 1961-64; sec. Lawrence Condict, Realtor/Appraiser, Orlando, Fla., 1973-74; legal sec. Nichols & Tatich, Orlando, 1974-76; exec. sec., office mgr., corp. sec. and partner Forms Mfrs. Equip., Inc., Orlando, 1976—, dir., 1977—. Mem. Nat. Assn. Female Execs., Internat. Bus. Forms Industries. Republican. Office: 1423 W Long St Orlando FL 32805

JOHNSON, JUDITH LAWSON, commodity broker; b. Memphis, Jan. 12, 1943; d. David Voss and Julia (Larkey) J.; B.A., Smith Coll., 1965; M.A.T., Duke U., 1966. Sales asst. Howard, Weil, Labouisse, Friedrichs, Inc., New Orleans, 1969-72, analyst, Chgo., 1975-77, 1st v.p., commodity sales mgr., New Orleans, 1977—. Mem. Chgo. Bd. Trade, Chgo. Bd. Options Exchange, Chgo. Mercantile Exchange, N.Y. Futures Exchange, New Orleans Commodity Exchange, Futures Industry Assn. Presbyterian. Home: 3009 Constance St New Orleans LA 70115 Office: Howard Weil Labouisse Friedrichs Inc 211 Carondelet St New Orleans LA 70130

JOHNSON, JUDY WHITE, psychologist; b. Langley, Ark., Apr. 7, 1946; d. Warren G. and Olive Earnestine (Vaught) White; B.A., U. Ark., 1971, M.A. (NIMH fellow), 1974, Ph.D., 1976; 1 son, Dana Warren. With Ark. Women's Reformatory, 1971, U. Ark. Counseling Center, 1973-74, Little Rock State Hosp., 1974, U. Ark. Student Health Services, 1974-75; intern U. Okla. Health Scis. Center, 1975; dir. diagnostic services Ark. Div. Youth Services, Little Rock, 1976; staff psychologist VA Hosp., North Little Rock, Ark., 1977-79; clin. psychologist Ark. Psychology Assos., Little Rock, 1976—; mem. adj. faculty U. Central Ark.; mem. cons. staff St. Vincent Hosp., Bapt. Med. Center, Leo N. Levi Nat. Arthritis Hosp. Worcester State Hosp. research grantee, 1973. Mem. Am. Psychol. Assn., Internat. Neuropsychol. Soc., Ark. Psychol. Assn., Ark. Assn. Profl. Psychologists, Ark. Behavior Therapy Assn. (pres. 1979), Assn. of Women in Psychology. Home: 2212 N Garfield St Little Rock AR 72207 Office: 8500 W Markham Suite 200 Little Rock AR 72205

JOHNSON, JULIE M(ARIE), lawyer; b. Aberdeen, S.D., Aug. 7, 1953; d. Howard B. and Jerauldine M. J.; B.A., U. S.D., 1974, J.D., 1976, M.A., 1976; m. Terry J. Sherman, June 17, 1977. Admitted to S.D. bar, 1977; legal intern S.D. Atty. Gen.'s Office, 1975; assoc. firm Siegel, Barnett, Schutz, O'Keefe & Jewett, Aberdeen, 1976, 77; assoc. firm Maloney, Kolker, Fritz, Hogan & Johnson, Aberdeen, 1978-81, partner, 1981—; law clk. Fifth Jud. Circuit Ct., Aberdeen, 1977-78; pres. Shogon, Inc. doing bus. as Brown County Abstract Co.; treas. Johnson Motor Co., Inc. Bd. dirs. Aberdeen Resource Center for Women, 1978-82, Aberdeen Area Child Protection Team, 1978—; sec. bd. dirs. YWCA, Aberdeen, 1978-80, 1st v.p., 1980-81, pres., 1981—, chairperson 1979 Fantasy of Trees; loaned exec. Brown County United Way, 1979, co-chmn. profl. div., 1980, campaign worker small bus. div., 1981-82; co-chairperson Aberdeen Arts Festival Com., 1978-81; mem. Aberdeen Area Arts Council, S.D. Found. of the Arts; co-chmn., spokesperson S.D. Polit. Action Com., Taxpayers Against Dakota Proposition, 1980. Mem. S.D. Bar Assn. (title ins. com., com. on model rules for profl. conduct 1980—), S.D. Trial Lawyers Assn., Am. Bar Assn., Nat. Assn. Women Lawyers (assembly del. 1982-84), Aberdeen Bus and Profl. Women (pres. 1979-80, parliamentarian 1980-81, legis. chmn. 1981-82, PAC coordinator 1982—), S.D. Bus. and Profl. Women (bylaws chairperson 1979-80, rec. sec. 1980-81, 2d v.p. 1981-82, 1st v.p. 1982—), S.D.C. of C. (com. on state taxation 1981—, dir. 1982—), S.D. Women's Caucus (pres. 1978-79), AAUW (topic chairperson 1979-81, legis. chmn. 1981—), Aberdeen Area C. of C. (state govt. chmn. 1980-82, dir. 1982—), N.E. S.D. Women's Caucus (coordinator 1977-79), LWV (sec., dir. 1982—), Brown County Republican Women (pres. 1980-81). Lutheran. Clubs: Zonta (dir. 1980-82, v.p. 1982—), Moccasin Creek Country (dir. 1979—). Home: 4138 Greenwood Ln Rural Route 1 Aberdeen SD 57401 Office: 205 Berkshire Plaza 405-8th Ave NW Aberdeen SD 57401

JOHNSON, KATHARYN PRICE (MRS. EDWARD F. JOHNSON), civic worker; b. Smyrna, Del., Mar. 24, 1897; d. Lewis M. and Jennie Cairl (Smithers) Price; grad. Centenary Coll., 1915; student Goucher Coll., 1915-18; m. Edward F. Johnson, Nov. 16, 1920; children—Edward A., Jane Cairl Johnson Kent. With Liberty Loan Com. for Md. and Liberty Loan Assn. of Balt., 1918-20; pres. Women's Guild Hitchcock Meml. Ch., 1930-32; dir. Scarsdale Woman's Club, 1933-36; dir. White Plains Thrift Shop, 1930-43, pres, 1936-43; mem. exec. com. Scarsdale Community Fund, 1934-38; active Scarsdale council Girl Scouts, 1937-53, commr., 1939-41, now hon. mem. Scarsdale-Hartsdale council, 1953-69; mem. region 2 com. Girl Scouts U.S.A., 1942-56, mem. nat. bd., exec. com., 1947-55, chmn. orgn. and mgmt. dept., 1952-55, mem. nat. field com., 1943-55, mem. equipment service com. 1956-69, mem. internat. com., 1956-60, mem. meml. gifts com., 1974-81; mem. Bd. Edn., Scarsdale, N.Y., 1943-46; disaster chmn. Scarsdale chpt. ARC, 1942-45; mem. Commn. Human Rights, 1958-69, Commn. Status of Women, 1957-69; rep. World Assn. Girl Guides and Girl Scouts to UN, 1957-71, mem. NGO com. on UNICEF, 1965-72, sec., 1968-70; participant World Confs., World Assn. Girl Guides and Girl Scouts, Greece, 1960, Denmark, 1963, Japan, 1966, Finland, 1969, Can., 1972, Eng., 1975, Iran, 1978. Recipient Juliette Lowe World Friendship medal Girl Scouts. U.S.A., 1981. Mem. Nat. Council Women U.S., Scarsdale Hist. Soc., Pi Beta Phi. Republican. Presbyterian. Clubs: Scarsdale Woman's (life), Village of Scarsdale; Nat. Women's Republican. Home: 165 Brewster Rd Scarsdale NY 10583

JOHNSON, KATHERINE, lab. technician; b. Fillmore, Utah, Mar. 27, 1955; d. Earl Teeples and Mary Katherine (McBride) J.; A.A.S. in Med. Tech., Weber State Coll., 1975; B.S., U. Utah, Salt Lake City, 1983. Med. lab. technician Physicians Clin. Lab., Salt Lake City, 1975-76, Primary Children's Med. Center, Salt Lake City, 1976-77, 78—, Uinta County Meml. Hosp., Evanston, Wyo., 1977-78. Mem. Am. Soc. Clin. Pathologists. Mormon. Home: 947 E 400 S Salt Lake City UT 84102 Office: 320 12th Ave Salt Lake City UT 84103

JOHNSON, KATHERINE M. KING (MRS. NORMAN F. JOHNSON), art gallery dir., artist, real estate exec.; b. Lincoln, Nebr., 1906; d. John Ray and Clara (Plamondon) King; student U. Nebr. Coll. Fine Arts, 1923-24, U. Vt. Extension, 1941-42, Coll. of Desert, 1965-66; m. Norman F. Johnson, Sept. 4, 1925 (dec.); children—Raymond E., Lyman W., Carlene King (Mrs. Don C. Holloway) (dec.). Land devel. designer, contractor Eastridge Acres, Piedmont Devels., Rutland, Vt., 1957—; corporator Marble Savs. Bank, Rutland; one man show Chester (Vt.) Art Guild, 1970; participant in three man art show, Shadow Mountain Club, Palm Desert, Calif., 1964; exhibited with So. Vt. Artists in major U.S. cities, 1950, N.Y. World's Fair with Mid Vt. Artists, 1964; exhibited one man show Chaffee Art Gallery, Rutland, 1967, 74, retrospective, 1980, Weston (Vt.) Playhouse, 1969; represented in permanent collections; displayed painting 1967 Nat. Christmas Tree from Vt. in Washington, 1967, painting now in permanent collection Lyndon B. Johnson Meml. Library, Austin, Tex. Co-chmn. Vt. Com. for Nat. Art Week, 1940; dir. bicentennial exhibit Rutland (Vt.) Mus. Arts, 1961; founder Chaffee Art Gallery, Rutland, bd. dirs., 1962—, pres., 1962-74; mem. Vt. Council on Arts 1963—, art com. Manchester (Vt.) Art Center, 1961-66, Rutland Hosp. Aux., 1958-72. Bd. dirs. Desert Art Center, Palm Springs, Calif., 1963. Recipient award merit Vt. Council Arts, 1977, recognition award AAUW, 1977. Mem. Mid Vt. Artists (pres. 1941-49), Rutland Area Art Assn. (pres. 1962-74, chmn. bd. 1977-80, dir., chmn. bd. trustees 1980-82, sr. exec. 1983), Nat. League Am. Pen Women (pres. So. Vt. br., state art chmn. 1964-65, 74-75, state pres. 1972-73, exhibitor nat. show 1974, Vt. State awards 1973, 75), Shadow Mountain Palette Club, Sigma Kappa. Congregationalist. Home: 40 Piedmont Pkwy Rutland VT 05701 Office: Chaffee Art Center 16 S Main St Rutland VT 05701 also PO Box 403 Rutland VT 05701

JOHNSON, KATHRYN WEISNER, librarian; b. Karnack, Tex., Nov. 29, 1938; d. James and Thelma (Thomas) Weisner; B.S. magna cum laude (Univ. scholar), Prairie View A&M U., 1957; M.S. in L.S., Atlanta U., 1967; m. Clifton Johnson Jr., Aug. 21, 1961; children—Clifton III, Carl James, Christopher Joseph, Craig Jerome, Curt Johans. Asso. librarian Jarvis Christian Coll., Hawkins, Tex., 1964-66; reference librarian So. U., Shreveport, La., 1968-70, Baton Rouge, 1972—, acquisitions librarian, 1978—; broker Hometown Real Estate, Baton Rouge, 1981—. Rockefeller Found. grantee, Atlanta U., 1967. Mem. La. Library Assn. Home: 311 Lakecrest Ave Baton Rouge LA 70807 Office: So Univ Library So Br Post Office Baton Rouge LA 70813

JOHNSON, KATRINA MICHELLE PEKARCHICK, nuclear engr.; b. Ft. Knox, Ky., Sept. 16, 1955; d. Thomas Michael and Brenda Mae (England) Pekarchick; B.S. in Nuclear Engring. with honors, U. Tenn., 1978, M. Engring. in Nuclear Engring., 1982; m. Jeffrey Oscar Johnson, Sept. 8, 1979. Coop. edn. student TVA, Knoxville, Tenn., 1974-77, nuclear engr., 1978; grad. research asst. U. Tenn., Knoxville, 1978-80; systems engr. JBF Assocs., Inc., Knoxville, 1980—. Recipient U. Tenn. Bookstore award, 1978. Mem. Am. Nuclear Soc., Alpha Chi Sigma. Roman Catholic. Office: 1630 Downtown West Blvd Knoxville TN 37919

JOHNSON, LADY BIRD (CLAUDIA ALTA) (MRS. LYNDON BAINES JOHNSON), wife former pres. U.S.; b. Karnack, Tex., Dec. 22, 1912; d. Thomas Jefferson Taylor; B.A., U. Tex., 1933, B.Journalism, 1934, D.Letters, 1964; LL.D., Tex. Woman's U., 1964; D.Letters, Middlebury Coll., 1967; L.H.D., Williams Coll., 1967, U. Ala., 1975; H.H.D., Southwestern U., 1967; m. Lyndon Baines Johnson (36th Pres. U.S.), Nov. 17, 1934 (died Jan. 22, 1973); children—Lynda Bird Johnson Robb, Luci Baines Johnson Nugent. Mgr. husband's congl. office, Washington, 1941-42; owner, operator radio-TV sta. KTBC, Austin, Tex., 1942-63, cattle ranches, Tex., 1943—. Hon. chmn. Nat. Headstart Program, 1963-68, Town Lake Beautification Project. also cotton and timberlands, Ala. Mem. Advisory council Nat. Parks, Historic Sites, Bldgs. and Monuments; bd. regents U. Tex., 1971-77, mem. internat. conf. steering com., 1969; trustee Jackson Hole Preserve, Am. Conservation Assn., Nat. Geog. Soc. Recipient Togetherness award Marge Champion, 1958; Humanitarian award B'nai B'rith, 1961; Businesswoman's award Bus. and Profl. Women's Club, 1961; Theta Sigma Phi citation, 1962; Distinguished Achievement award Washington Heart Assn., 1962; Industry citation Am. Women in Radio and Television, 1963; Humanitarian citation Vols. of Am., 1963; Peabody award for White House TV visit, 1966; Eleanor Roosevelt Golden Candlestick award Women's Nat. Press Club; Damon Woods Meml. award Indsl. Designers Soc. Am., 1972; Conservation Service award Dept. Interior, 1974; Distinguished award Am. Legion, 1975; Woman of Year award Ladies Home Jour., 1975; Medal of Freedom, 1977. Life mem. U. Tex. Ex-Students Assn. Episcopalian. Author: A White House Diary, 1970. Address: LBJ Library 2313 Red River Austin TX 78705 *

JOHNSON, LATRELL SMITH, educator; b. Palestine, Tex., Feb. 4, 1936; d. Douglas and Vanneter (Williams) Smith; B.S., Huston Tillotson Coll., 1953; postgrad. Tex. So. U., 1960-62, Tex. A&I U., 1966, U. Tex., 1975, 79; M.Ed., Prairie View U., 1968; m. Edgar Johnson, June 27, 1954; children—Janet Lynn, Duane Edgar. Team leader Nat. Tchr. Corps, HEW, 1966-68; coordinator Ella Austin Community Center, San Antonio, 1971-76; tchr. home econs. San Antonio Ind. Sch. Dist., 1976-78, coordinator early childhood edn. program, 1978—. Pres. bd. dirs. Cowan Day Care Center, 1975—; bd. dirs. Head Start Edn. Com., 1978-80; chmn. adminstrv. bd. United Meth. Ch., also tchr. Sunday sch., trainer tchrs., mem. fin. com. Recipient Acad. Achievement award Huston-Tillotson Coll., 1981. Mem. San Antonio Bus. and Profl. Women's Club (pres. 1979—), Huston Tillotson Coll. Alumni Assn. (v.p. 1974-78), NAACP, Nat. Assn. Edn. Young Children, Tex. Tchrs. Assn., NEA, Adminstrs. and Suprs. Assn. San Antonio, Nat. Assn. Female Execs., Zeta Phi Beta. Democrat. Home: 2415 Tyne Dr San Antonio TX 78222

JOHNSON, LEANNE MARY, home economist; b. Forest Grove, Oreg., Nov. 2, 1950; d. James W. and Mary Jo (Fearn) J.; B.S., U. Wyo., 1973, M.S., 1976; Tchr. home econs., Farson (Wyo.) High Sch., 1973-75; 4-H and home econs. agt. U. Wyo., Afton, 1976—. Lic. emergency med. technician. Mem. Wyo. Assn. Extension Home Economists (treas. 1979), Nat. Assn. Extension Home Economists. Baptist. Clubs: Order Eastern Star, Daus. of Nile, Jolly Neighbors. Home: 267 E 6th St Afton WY 83110 Office: Box 308 Afton WY 83110

JOHNSON, LEE, educator, publisher; b. Richmond, Va., May 11, 1931; d. Mildred Simms Wible; B.A., Pa. State U., 1950; postgrad. Trinity Coll., Hartford, Conn., Columbia U., New Sch., N.Y.C.; m. J. Jay Johnson, June 3, 1950. Pub., editor Kids' Stuff mag., 1960—; tchr. Malverne (N.Y.) Jr. High Sch., 1971-74, Jr. Acad., Bklyn., 1973; book critic Richmond Times-Dispatch, 1965-71; tchr. Roger Ludlow High Sch., Fairfield, Conn., 1962-65, Central High Sch., Bridgeport, Conn., 1963; founder, asso. librarian Calvary Jr. Library, Bridgeport, 1965-68; mgr. Treasure-trove, rare books and records, Avondale, Ga.; psychol. counselor Alpha Psi Omega. Sec., Fed. Grand Jury Assn., 1965-75. Mem. AAUW (ways and means chmn. 1963), Nat. League Am. Pen Women, DeKalb Hist. Soc., Avondale Hist. Soc. Episcopalian. Clubs: N.Y. Classical, Avondale Estates Woman's (archivist 1978-80, publicity chmn. 1978—), Stone Mountain Woman's, Avondale Estates Garden (student judge). Home: 7 Exeter Rd Avondale Estates GA 30002

JOHNSON, LINDA FRANCES, telephone co. exec.; b. Detroit, Dec. 27, 1951; d. Robert and Mildred Eloise Johnson; B.A., Eastern Mich. U., 1973. Media buyer Ross Roy, Inc., 1974-76; market adminstr. Mich. Bell Telephone Co., 1977-78; account exec. Tate Communication, 1978-79; account exec. fin. New Eng. Telephone Co., Boston, 1979—. Fundraiser mobilization com. Citizens for Handgun Control, 1980-81; founder Spirit II Found. for Handgun Control, 1981; founders com. Free Breakfast Program for Sch. Children, 1970; vol. Big Sister/Little Sister Orgn., 1970, Jr. Achievement, 1977, Mich. Opera Theatre, 1978, Music Hall-Dance Center Detroit, 1978, Boston Shakespeare Co., 1979. Democrat. Home: 194 Marlborough St Boston MA 02116 Office: 6 Saint James Ave Boston MA 02116

JOHNSON, LINDA LEE, mfg. sales exec.; b. Buffalo, Apr. 5, 1947; d. Fred Richard and Lorraine (Gross) J.; B.A. in Sociology, U. Mich., 1969; A. Archtl. Constrn., Henry Ford Community Coll.; 1982. Program dir. U. Mich. tutorial project, 1968; research asst. U. Mich., 1969; employment counselor Wayne County Dept. Social Services, 1969-74; sales mgr., dir. Johnson Products Co., Taylor, Mich. 1975—. Bd. dirs. Detroit chpt. U.S.-China Friendship Assn., 1980—; producer, co-founder Women's Radio of WDET-FM, 1971—; mem. Detroit Welfare Reform Coalition, 1972-74. Recipient award Sta. WWJ, Detroit, 1972; Detroit and Mich. Council for the Arts grantee, 1979. Mem. Nat. Assn. Female Execs. Exhibitor fiber work Gallery of Contemporary Crafts, Detroit, 1979. Home: 58 W Buena Vista St Highland Park MI 48203 Office: 23593 Van Born Rd Taylor MI 48180

JOHNSON, LORNEVA, automotive interior accessories mfg. co. exec.; b. Hector, Ark., Aug. 23, 1921; d. Reece Allen and Ruth (Churchill) Dixon; m. Howard S. Johnson, Oct. 19, 1953; children—Willette, Dennis, Lura, Loretta. Area supr. Hospitality Hostess Service, Inc., San Diego, 1958-70; pres. H & L Products, Inc., National City, Calif., 1970—. Mem. Automotive Parts and Accessories Assn., Am. Research Merchandising Inst. Republican. Presbyterian. Home: 830 J Ave Coronado CA 92118 Office: 500 W 16th St National City CA 92050

JOHNSON, LOU AVAH PEVLOR, writer; b. Springfield, Ky.; d. C.L. and Edith (Long) Pevlor; B.A., U. Ky., 1947, postgrad., 1948-49; postgrad. U. Calif., Berkeley, 1968; m. John Riley Johnson Jr., Sept. 22, 1945; children—Jenefer, Cindy, John Riley III. Mem. The Writer's Center, Glen Echo, Md., 1976—. Mem. Women's Com. for Nat. Symphony Orch., Washington Met. Area, 1976—. Mem. Internat. Poetry Soc., Internat. Platform Assn., Nat. League Am. Pen Women, Songwriters Assn. Washington, No. Va. Literacy Council, AAUW, MLA, Poetry Soc. Va., Washington Ind. Writers, World Affairs Council Washington, Gen. Fedn. Women's Clubs. Contbr. articles and poetry to various newspapers, poetry mags. and anthologies. Home: 2009 Kirby Rd McLean VA 22101

JOHNSON, LOUISE CLAYTON, educator; b. Kansas City, Mo., June 15, 1923; d. John R. and Susan J. (Thresher) Clayton; B.A., Utica Coll., Syracuse U., 1958; M.S.W., U. Conn., 1962; children—Nancy, Charlotte. Exec. dir. Waterbury (Conn.) Girls Club, 1962-64; supervising psychiat. social worker Connecticut Valley Hosp., Middletown, 1964-68; asst. prof. Sch. Social Work, U. Iowa, Iowa City; 1968-74; asso. prof. social work U. S.D., Vermillion, 1974—; cons. to S.D. Dept. Health, S.D. Dept. Social Service, 1976—. Mem. Sr. Citizens Outreach Com., Vermillion, 1981—; chmn. bd. deacons First Bapt. Ch., Vermillion, 1981—; bd. dirs. United Campus Ministries, U. S.D., 1979—. S. D. Dept. Social Service grantee, 1978-81. Mem. Nat. Assn. Social Workers, Council on Social Work Edn., Am. Public Welfare Assn., LWV, Assn. Undergrad. Program Dirs., Delta Kappa Gamma, Alpha Kappa Delta. Democrat. Author: Social Work Practice, A Syllabus, 1971; contbr. articles on social work edn. to profl. jours. Home: 220 Sycamore Apt 20 Vermillion SD 57069 Office: Social Work Program U SD Vermillion SD 57069

JOHNSON, MARGARET ANN KIEFT, marquetry mfg. co. exec.; b. Chgo., Nov. 25, 1939; d. Charles Samuel and Betty Marie (Fridrich) Kieft; B.S. in Edn., No. Ill. U., 1961, postgrad., 1963-67; postgrad. Western Ill. U., 1962-63, (NDEA grantee) Northeastern U., 1967; m. Dale L. Johnson, Aug. 19, 1961; 1 son, Jeffrey Kieft. Tchr., Frew Elem. Sch., Aledo, Ill., 1961-62; tchr. English, Aledo High Sch., 1962-63; tchr. English, head dept. Hiawatha High Sch., Kirkland, Ill., 1963-72; sec.-treas., office mgr. Inlaid Woodcraft Co., Kirkland, 1973—. Mem. adv. bd. Kirkland Parent-Tchr. Orgn., 1977-78; mem. steering com. Sycamore Parent-Tchr. Orgn., Sycamore, Ill., 1980-81; mem. membership com. DeKalb County (Ill.), Ben Gordon Mental Health Center, 1980-81; den leader Sycamore Pack #118, Three Rivers council Cub Scouts, Boy Scouts Am., 1981-82. Mem. Marquetry Soc. Am., Nat. Fedn. Ind. Bus., Nat. Small Bus. Assn., Beta Sigma Phi (Order of Rose 1980). Club: Order Eastern Star. Home: Ellen Dr PO Box 497 Genoa IL 60135 Office: 140 W North St Kirkland IL 60146

JOHNSON, MARGARET HILL, ednl. adminstr.; b. Dundee, Scotland, June 26, 1923; d. John Barnet and Isabella Rae (Watson) Hill; came to U.S., 1946, naturalized, 1957; student Inverness (Scotland) Royal Acad., 1940, Edinburgh (Scotland) Royal Coll. Art, 1940-43; doctoral candidate U. Mass., Amherst, 1980—; m. Peter Dyer Johnson, Nov. 22, 1965; children—Ann Hill Doughty, James Appleton Doughty, Joanna Elizabeth Johnson. Latin and remedial English tutor Harvey Sch., N.Y.C., 1947-52; tchr. athletics Pingree Sch. for Girls, Hamilton, Mass., 1959-61; tchr. Shore Country Day Sch., Beverly, Mass., 1952-59; asso. dir. Theodore S. Jones & Co., design mgmt. cons., Milton, Mass., 1961-72; dir. career planning and placement Mass. Coll. Art, 1972—, coordinator human services; design cons. Theodore S. Jones & Co.; speaker Lesley Coll., 1977, Cambridge (Mass.) Community Schs., 1977—. Served with Brit. Women's Royal Naval Service, 1943-46. Mem. Coll. Placement Council, Mass. Assn. Women Deans and Counselors, Nat. Assn. Women Deans, Adminstrs. and Counselors, Am. Assn. Higher Edn., Coll. Art Assn. Am., Eastern Coll. Placement Officers, Arts Dirs. Club Boston, Graphic Artists Guild. Author: (with others) Your Future in Art and Design, 1977. Home: Box 75 Off Summer St Marshfield MA 02051 Office: 364 Brookline Ave Boston MA 02115

JOHNSON, MARGARET KATHLEEN, educator; b. Baylor County, Tex., Oct. 30, 1920; d. George W. and Julia Rivers (Turner) Higgins; B.S., Hardin-Simmons U., 1940; M.Bus. Edn., N.Tex. State U., 1957, Ed.D., 1962; m. Herman Clyde Johnson, Jr., July 27, 1949 (dec.); 1 dau., Carolyn Kay. Clk., Farmers Nat. Bank, Seymour, Tex., 1940-41; adminstrv. sec. U.S. Navy, Corpus Christi, Tex., 1941-46; adminstrv. asst. Hdqrs. 8th Army, Yokohama, Japan, 1946-49; instr. Coll. Bus. Adminstrn., U. Ark., 1957-60; teaching fellow Sch. Bus. Adminstrn., N.Tex. State U., 1960-62, instr., 1962-63; asst. prof. bus. tchr. edn. and secondary edn. Tchrs. Coll., U. Nebr., Lincoln, 1963-65, asso. prof., 1966-70, prof., 1970—; guest lectr. U. N.Mex., 1967, Curriculum Devel. in Bus. Edn., N.S. Dept. Edn., 1969, N.Tex. State U., 1970, E.Tex. State U., 1972. Recipient United Bus. Edn. Assn. award as outstanding grad. student in bus. edn. N.Tex. State U., 1957; award for outstanding service Nebr. Future Bus. Leaders Am., 1968; Mountain-Plains Bus. Edn. Leadership award 1977. Mem. Nat. (exec. bd. 1975, 76-79, policies commn. for bus. and econ. edn. 1979—), Mountain-Plains (exec. sec. 1970-73, pres. 1975), Nebr. (pres. 1966-67, Service award 1979) bus. edn. assns., Nebr. Council on Occupational Tchr. Edn., Delta Pi Epsilon. Author: Standardized Production Typewriting Tests series, 1964-65; National Structure for Research in Vocational Education, 1966; Introduction to Word Processing, 1980. Editor: the Changing Office Environment, 1980; Introduction to Business Communication, 1981. Home: 7300 South St Lincoln NE 68506 Office: 303 Tchrs Coll U Nebr Lincoln NE 68588

JOHNSON, MARIE C. BELLAMY, lawyer; b. Boley, Okla., Nov. 25, 1911; d. Louis Cecil and Bertha (Watson) Taylor; LL.B., John Marshall Law Sch., 1947, J.D., 1970; m. Wesley Maurice Johnson, Aug. 17, 1944 (div. 1974); children—Harold Bellamy, Viola Cecile, Marie Christine. Admitted to Ill. bar, 1948; practice law, Chgo., 1948-58, 75—; atty. IRS U.S. Treasury, Chgo., 1958-62; hearings supr. Unemployment Compensation div. Ill. State Dept. Labor, Chgo., 1963-82. Mem. Ill. State Bar Assn., Am. Bar Assn., Chgo. Bar Assn., Nat. Assn. Women Lawyers, Women's Bar Assn. of Ill. Club: Executi.e (Chgo.). Home: 300 N State St Chicago IL 60610 Office: 910 S Michigan Ave Room 706 Chicago IL 60605

JOHNSON, SISTER, MARIE INEZ, librarian; b. Mitchell, S.D., June 2, 1909; d. Charles and Inez L. (Williams) Johnson; B.A. in English, Coll. St. Catherine, 1929, B.S. in L.S., 1939; M.S. in L.S., Columbia U., 1940; postgrad. U. Denver, 1951-52, U. So. Calif., 1953-54. Joined Sisters St. Joseph Carondolet, 1926; tchr. elementary schs. St. Paul, 1930-38; librarian Coll. St. Catherine, St. Paul, 1940-42, head librarian, 1942—. Mem. steering com. U. Minn. Workshop for Librarians, 1956; library cons. survey Mt. Mercy Coll., Cedar Rapids, Iowa, 1963-64; bldg. cons. Fontbonne Coll., St. Louis, 1964—. Mem. Conf. Am. Folklore for Youth, St. Paul Speakers Bur., com. standard catalog for high sch. Cath. Support, Children's Lit. TV Series. Butler Fgn. Study fellow Coll. St. Catherine, 1958. Named Minn. Librarian of Year, 1967. Mem. Am. (various coms.), Cath. (various coms.) library assns. Editor column Cath. Library World, 1954—. Contbr. articles to profl. jours. Address: Coll St Catherine St Paul MN 55105

JOHNSON, MARILYN, obstetrician, gynecologist; b. Houston, May 7, 1925; d. William Walton and Marilyn (Henderson) J.; B.A., Rice Inst., 1945; M.D., Baylor U., 1950. Intern, New Eng. Hosp. Women and Children, Boston, 1950-51; resident Meth. Hosp., Houston, 1951-53; resident in gynecology M.D. Anderson Tumor Inst., Houston, 1954, fellow, 1955; fellow in gynecol. pathology Harvard Med. Sch., 1952-53; practice medicine specializing in ob-gyn, Houston, 1954-81, Fredericksburg, Tex., 1981—; mem. staffs St. Joseph's, Meml., Meth., Park Plaza, Hill Country Meml. Rosewood hosps.; clin. instr. ob-gyn Coll. Medicine, Baylor U., 1954—, Postgrad. Sch. Medicine, U. Tex., 1954—; gynecologist De Pelchin Faith Home, Houston, 1954—, also Rice U., Richmond State Sch.; med. dirs. Birthright, Inc., Houston, 1973—; pro-life public speaker. Bd. dirs. Right to Life, Houston, Found. for Life. Sandoz Labs. grantee, 1973, 75, Delbay Pharm. Co. grantee, 1977. Fellow Am. Coll. Obstetricians and Gynecologists; mem. AMA, Tex. Med. Assn., Am. Med. Women's Assn., Internat. Infertility Assn., Harris County Med. Soc., Postgrad. med. Assembly S. Tex., Houston Ob-Gyn Soc. Republican. Baptist. Clubs: Zonta; Fredericksburg Rockhounds. Home: 205 S Orange St Fredericksburg TX 78624 Office: 204 W Schubert St Fredericksburg TX 78624

JOHNSON, MARILYN P., ambassador; b. Boston, June 19, 1922; B.A., Radcliffe Coll., 1944; M.A., Middlebury Coll., 1952; grad. Sr. Seminar in Fgn. Policy, 1975; student in Russian lang. 1975-76. Tchr. French, public high schs., 1952-59; tchr. English as fgn. lang., Cameroon, Mali, 1962-64; commd. fgn. service officer Dept. State, 1964; cultural affairs officer, Bamako, French W.I., 1964, Tunis, Tunisia; public affairs officer, Niamey, 1971; dep. asst. dir. Info. Centers Program, 1971-74; cultural affairs officer U.S. embassy, Moscow, 1976-78; U.S. ambassador to Togo, Lome, 1978-81; with ICA, Washington, 1981—. Served with USN, 1944-46. Office: ICA 3710 Corey Pl Washington DC 20016 *

JOHNSON, MARJORIE TIPPINS, civic worker; b. Pitts., Sept. 26, 1922; d. Leon Hampton and Marie Connolly Tippins; B.A., Agnes Scott Coll., 1944; m. William Austin Johnson, Sept. 18, 1945; children—Christine, Edward, Carolyn. Tchr. organ Orange High Sch., 1957—. Co-founder Orange Community Arts Council, Pepper Pike, Ohio, 1968, sec., 1968-71, v.p., 1971-73, pres., 1973-75, treas., 1975—; census coordinator Orange Sch. Dist., 1957—, central registrar, 1967—; sec.-trustee Pepper Pike Civic League, 1969-72; elder United Presbyterian Ch., 1971-77, organist, 1961—. Mem. Am. Guild Organists, English Speaking Union. Republican. Club: Landerwood Swim (pres.-trustee). Home: 3745-1 Lander Rd Chagrin Falls OH 44022 Office: 32000 Chagrin Blvd Pepper Pike OH 44124

JOHNSON, MARLENE, advt. and public relations co. exec.; b. Braham, Minn., Jan. 11, 1946; d. Helen M. Nelson; B.A., Macalester Coll., 1968. Community organizer Ramsey Action Program, St. Paul, 1968-70; program dir. YMCA, St. Paul, 1970-71; pres., founder Split Infinitive Inc., St. Paul, 1971—. Vice-chmn. Minn. Task Force on Small Bus., 1978; mem. small bus. adv. com. U.S. Treasury Dept., 1978-80; co-chmn. Minn. del. White Ho. Conf. on Small Bus., 1980; mem. adv. bd. Sch. Mgmt., U. Minn.; bd. dirs. Spring Hill Center, Landmark Center, Minn. Public Programming Corp. Mem. Nat. Assn. Women Bus. Owners (pres.), Nat. Women's Polit. Caucus, Minn. Women's Polit. Caucus (chmn. 1974-77), Com. of 200 (charter 1982). Democrat. Clubs: Minnesota, St. Paul Athletic. Office: 46 E 4th St Suite 812 Saint Paul MN 55101

JOHNSON, MARNETTE MOLES, computer systems specialist; b. Norfolk, Nebr., Nov. 18, 1939; d. James Jerimiah and Evelyn Augusta (Preuss) Moles; B.A., MacMurray Coll., 1961; postgrad. U. Mich., summers, 1970, 73, U. Ky., summer, 1978, Def. Intelligence Sch., 1978, Western U.; m. Orval E. Johnson, June 26, 1966; 1 son, Bryan. Computer programmer U.S. Dayton A.F. Depot, Dayton, Ohio, 1961-64; mathematician U.S. Naval Electronics Lab., San Diego, 1964-80; sr. systems analyst/exec. engr. CALSPAN Field Services, Inc., Arlington, Va., 1980-81; computer systems specialist East Coast ops. Systems Devel. Corp., McLean, Va., 1981-82; staff engr. Martin Marietta Denver Aerospace, Denver, 1982—; FY78 1st woman profl. exchange for U.S. NEL(NOSC) to NISC (NAVINTCOM), Washington, 1977-78. Mem. Digital Equip. Corp. Users Soc., Assn. Computing Machinery, Computer Soc. of IEEE, Amway Distbrs. Assn. Republican. Mem. Assemblies of God. Club: Toastmasters. Contbr. articles to profl. jours. Office: PO Box 179 Denver CO 80201

JOHNSON, MARY CATHERINE, ins. co. mgr.; b. Hillsboro, Wis., June 18, 1942; d. John James and Alice Irene (Ennis) Sebranek; B.Ed., U. Wis.-Whitewater, 1969, M.S., 1974; m. Kenneth Lee Johnson, Oct. 13, 1962; children—Jeffrey Lee, Peggy Marie, Shelli Kay. Tchr., chmn. bus. edn. dept. Kettle Moraine High Sch., Wales, Wis., 1970-77; underwriting services supr. Comml. Union Assurance Cos., Milw., 1977-78, underwriter, underwriting services analyst, 1978-79; tng. mgr. Northwestern Nat. Ins. Co., Milw., 1979-81, tng. and organizational devel. mgr., 1981—. Mem. Wis. Bus. Edn. Assn., Ins. Co. Edn. Dirs. Soc., Internat. Assn. Personnel Women, Am. Soc. Tng. and Devel., Profl. Dimensions. Roman Catholic. Home: 7075 W. Southridge Dr Greenfield WI 53220 Office: 731 N Jackson Milwaukee WI 53201

JOHNSON, MARY ELIZABETH, music educator, pianist; b. Tyler, Tex., Mar. 29, 1933; d. Robert Edward and Mamie Oberia (Walters) Spaulding; B.F.A., So. Methodist U., 1955; pvt. study with Bomar Cramer, Dallas, 1964-69; m. George Devereaux Johnson, Mar. 31, 1955; children—Bradford D., Robin Elizabeth. Music tchr. Dallas Country Day Sch., 1955; tchr. Dayton (Ohio) pub. schs., 1956-57; pvt. tchr. piano Dallas, 1962—; profl. accompanist, Dallas, 1965—; duo-pianist, Dallas, 1965-78; sponsor-tchr. creative and performing arts program Dallas Ind. Sch. Dist., 1981-82. Named to honor roll Nat. Guild Piano Tchrs., 1971, Hall of Fame, Am. Coll. Musicians, 1981. Mem. Nat. Guild Piano Tchrs. (cert.), Tex. Fedn. Music Clubs (historian 1974-76, state chmn. music service in the community 1971-73, dist. jr. counselor 1971-78, dist. chmn. music service in the community 1971-78; rec. sec. 5th dist. 1975-76, 1st v.p. 1977-78, jr. festival chmn. 1977-80, dist. chmn. Jr. Gold Cup awards 1980, asst. chmn. North Dallas div. 5th dist. jr. festival 1981-82), Music Tchrs. Nat. Assn., Tex., Dallas music tchrs. assns., Music Study Club Dallas (chmn. piano program 1981-82), Schubert Study Club, Dallas Fedn. Music Clubs (del. 1969-78, 1st v.p. 1977), Daus. Republic Tex. (1st v.p. Bonham chpt. 1975-76), Alpha Delta Pi. Clubs: Melodie (pres. 1969-71, 3d v.p. 1977—, choral accompanist, counselor jr. club, historian, press sec. 1981-82), Kalista, Jr. Melodie, Jr. Harmonie. Home: 3848 Cedarbrush Dr Dallas TX 75229

JOHNSON, MARY HOLMAN, interior designer; b. Troy, Ala., Nov. 10, 1946; d. Manuel Holman and Ethel Lorraine (Jordan) J.; student Troy State U., 1965-66; B. Interior Design, Sch. Architecture, Auburn U., 1969. Interior designer Stevens Wilkinson, Architects and Engrs., Atlanta, 1968-71; dir. interior design Hauser Assos., Atlanta, 1971-72; exec. designer airport facilities Dobbs Houses, Inc., Memphis, 1972-73; pres. Interior & Graphic Designers, Memphis, 1973-76; prin., owner Mary Johnson & Assos., Memphis, 1976—; vis. critic, sr. adviser, interior design dept. Memphis State U., 1975—; designer Memphis Area Planning and Design Center, 1976—; cons. Downtown Council, 1976, Center City Commn., 1977—; instr. continuing edn. Shelby State Community Coll., 1976; guest speaker Southwestern U., 1977, U. Tenn., 1977, 79, 80. Council mem., co-chairperson Japanese and Am. events Memphis-In-May Internat. Festival, 1977; planner Downtown Neighborhood Assn., 1978; mem. Bus. Dist. Design Rev. Bd., Memphis, 1980; pres. d'arts Brooks Meml. Art Gallery, 1979-80; co-chmn. opera ball Guild of Opera Memphis, 1979; archtl. advisor Symphony Ball, 1979; del. Memphis Jobs Conf., 1981; chmn. image task force Leadership Memphis. Recipient Tenn. award of excellence for creative use of paper in graphic communications Beckett Paper Co., 1976; award Inst. Bus. Designers-Interior Design Mag., 1979; citation Cook Conv. Center Com., 1978; others. Mem. Inst. Bus. Designers. Home: 99 N Main St 2201 Memphis TN 38103 Office: 263 Court Ave Memphis TN 38103

JOHNSON, MARY LEONA, city ofcl.; b. Greenville, N.C., Sept. 21; d. Lewis and Leona (Anderson) Blow; B.A. in Sociology, Wayne State U., 1974; M.A., Antioch Sch. Law, 1982; 1 son, Reginald B. Johnson. With U.S. Treasury Dept., Washington, 1944-46; receptionist U.S. Army Tank Automotive Center, 1952-56; supr. Tb Registry, Detroit Dept. Health, 1956-71; Affirmative Action adminstr. Detroit Human Rights Dept., 1977—, cons. women's issues, 1975-77. Mem. Mich. State adv. council vocat. edn., 1980-83; bd. dirs. Selective Service Com., 1982—. Recipient Christian Service award. Mem. Nat. Assn. Human Rights Works of Mich. (v.p. 1982—), Mich. Coalition for Human Rights, Nat. Assn. Exec. Women, Detroit Round Table of Christian and Jews Detroit Women's Forum, Women's Econ. Club. Democrat. Mem. Ch. of Christ. Home: 4039 Clements St Detroit MI 48238 Office: 226 Michigan Ave 4th Floor Detroit MI 48226

JOHNSON, MARY STEPPE, educator; b. Marion, N.C., Nov. 2, 1945; d. Donald Carol and Thurley Anne (Franklin) Steppe; B.S., Western Carolina U., 1967, M.Ed., 1969; Ed.D., Duke U., 1980; m. Michael Lynn Johnson, Apr. 12, 1970; children—Brady Albert, Clinton James. Tchr. schs. in N.C., 1967-77; asst. prof. edn. Meredith Coll., Raleigh, N.C., 1980—; pres. Cons. Unltd., ednl. cons., 1980—. Bd. dirs. Swift Creek Sch. PTA, 1981-82. Mem. Internat. Reading Assn. (exec. com. N.C. chpt.), Delta Kappa Gamma, Kappa Delta Pi. Democrat. Methodist. Co-author: Success in Kindergarten Reading and Writing, 1980; Success in Reading and Writing Grade 3, 1980; also articles, tchr.'s guide. Home: Route 4 Box 711 Raleigh NC 27606 Office: Hillsborough St Raleigh NC 27611

JOHNSON, MARYANN ELAINE, ednl. adminstr.; b. Franklin Twp., Pa., Nov. 1, 1943; d. Mary I. Sollick; B.S. in Elementary Edn., Mansfield State Coll., Pa., 1964; M.S. in Elementary Edn., U. Alaska, College 1973; Ed.D., Wash. State U., Pullman, 1981; married. Tchr. Nayatt Sch., Barrington, R.I., 1964-66, North Sch., N. Chgo., Ill., 1966-67, Kodiak (Alaska) On-Base Sch., 1967-71; reading coordinator Eastmont Sch. Dist., East Wenatchee, Wash., 1971-77, now asst. supt. Sec. Parent Advisory Com., 1974-76. Mem. Assn. Supervision and Curriculum Devel., Wash. State Assn. Supervision and Curriculum Devel. (Educator of Yr. 1981), NEA, Wash. Assn. Sch. Adminstrs. (bd. dirs., chmn. curriculum and instrn. Job-Alike, profl. devel. com.), Delta Kappa Gamma (pres. 1982-84), Phi Delta Kappa, Phi Kappa Phi. Named Eastmont Tchr. of the Yr., 1973-74. Office: 460 N E 9th St East Wenatchee WA 98801

JOHNSON, MAXINE FRAHM, banker; b. Mason City, Iowa, Dec. 18, 1939; d. Peter and Emily Marian (Bistline) Frahm; B.A., Grinnell Coll., 1961; M.B.A., U. Pitts., 1976; grad. Nat. Grad. Trust Sch., 1980; m. Robert W. Johnson, June 3, 1962; children—Brenda Lynn, Janine Suzanne. Ins. contract writer Bankers Life Co., Des Moines, 1961-62; music tchr. Haworth (N.J.) public schs., 1962-63; pvt. tchr. music, substitute tchr. public schs., N.Y., Ill., Pa., 1963-75; gen. services specialist Pitts. Nat. Bank, 1976-78, sr. gen. services specialist, 1978-79, trust adminstr., 1979-80, trust officer, 1980-82; sr. trust officer Bank of New Eng., Boston, 1982—. Former treas., bd. dirs. Women's Center and Shelter of Greater Pitts.; former mem. North Pittsburgh Civic Symphony; advance solicitor United Way, 1979; former alumni rep. Grinnell Coll. Mem. Nat. Acctg. Assn., Nat. Assn. Female Execs., Nat. Assn. Bank Women, Pi Kappa Lambda, Beta Gamma Sigma. Contbr. articles to profl. publs. Office: Trust Div Bank of New Eng 28 State St Boston MA 02109

JOHNSON, NANCY ANN, educator; b. Southampton, N.Y., July 10, 1934; d. Charles and Julia (Malone) Mosley; B.A. in Polit. Sci., Kean Coll., 1981; children—Barbara, Donna, Regina. Researcher, United Community Orgn., Newark, 1967-72; comprehensive planner City of Newark Mayor's Policy Devel. Office, 1973-78; elem. sch. tchr., Newark, 1979—. Mem. South Ward Civic Assn., South Ward Community Health Center; mem. Beth Israel Community Council, 1968-72, Newark Health Planning Adv. Bd., 1976-78, Newark Task Force on Drugs, 1973-75. Mem. N.J. Bus. Women's Assn. Baptist (corr. sec.). Home: 170 Union Ave Irvington NJ 07111 Office: Bergen Street Sch 715 Bergen St Newark NJ 07108

JOHNSON, NANCY LEE, former state senator; b. Chgo., Jan. 5, 1935; d. Noble Wishard and Gertrude Reid (Smith) Lee; B.A., Radcliffe Coll., 1957; postgrad. U. London, 1957-58; m. Theodore H. Johnson, July 16, 1958; children—Lindsey Lee, Althea Anne, Caroline Reid. Vice chmn. Charter Commn. New Britain, 1976-77; mem. Conn. Senate from 6th Dist., 1977-82; Congl. Candidate, 1982. Bd. dirs. United Way New Britain, 1976-79, New Britain Symphony Soc., 1975-77, Plainville Group Home, 1975-76; pres. Friends of Library, New Britain Pub. Library, 1973-76; lectr. Am. art New Britain Mus. Am. Art, 1968-71; pres. Radcliffe Club No. Conn., 1973-75; bd. dirs., pres. Sheldon Community Guidance Clinic, 1974-75; pres. Unitarian Universalist Soc. New Britain, 1973-75, dir. religious edn., 1967-72. Grantee English Speaking Union, 1958-59; recipient Outstanding Vol. award United Way, 1976. Republican. Home: 141 S Mountain Dr New Britain CT 06052

JOHNSON, NORINE GOODE, psychologist; b. Indpls., Dec. 3, 1935; d. Frank and Marie (Collins) Goode; B.A., DePauw U., 1957; Ph.D., Wayne State U., 1972; postgrad. Harvard Med. Sch., 1975-77; m. Charles W. Johnson, Aug. 23, 1958; children—Cammarie, Kathryn Carroll, Margaret Ellen. Psychology cons. to pediatrics Univ. Hosps. Cleve., 1968-69; asso. clin. prof. dept. neurology Boston U. Med. Sch., 1976—; adj. prof. psychology Boston Coll., 1978—; dir. psychology Kennedy Meml. Hosp., Brighton, Mass., 1970—. Pres. area bd. Mental Health and Retardation, 1973, regional bd., 1974; mem. Gov.'s Adv. Council Mental Health and Mental Retardation, 1974-76, chairperson children's subcom., 1976. NIMH scholar, trainee. Mem. Mass. Psychol. Assn. (pres. elect 1980, pres. 1981-83, dir., bd. profl. affairs 1977—, chairperson 1977-78, liaison to Mass. Psychiat. Soc. 1978), Am. Psychol. Assn., Psi Chi. Club: Milton Hoosic. Home: 138 Central Ave Milton MA 02187 Office: 50 Warren St Brighton MA 02135

JOHNSON, NORMA HOLLOWAY, fed. judge; b. Lake Charles, La.; d. H. Lee and Beatrice M. (Williams) Holloway; B.S., D.C. Tchrs. Coll., 1955; J.D., Georgetown U., 1962; m. Julius A. Johnson. Admitted to D.C. bar, 1962; trial atty. U.S. Dept. Justice, Washington, 1963-67; asst. corp. counsel Office of Corp. Counsel D.C., 1967-70; judge Superior Ct. D.C., 1970-80; judge U.S. Dist. Ct., Washington, 1980—. Bd. dirs. Nat. Children's Center, Council for Ct. Excellence; past chmn. adv. com. Nat. St. Law Inst. Mem. Am. Judicature Soc. (dir.), Nat. Assn. Women Judges, Nat. Assn. Black Women Attys., Women's Bar, Nat. Bar Assn., Am. Bar Assn., D.C. Bar. Office: US Courthouse 3d and Constitution Ave NW Washington DC 20001

JOHNSON, NORMA JEAN WILSON, state ofcl.; b. Frankfort, Ky., Sept. 4, 1935; d. Henry Jack and Mable Frances (Jones) Wilson; student Murray State U., 1951, Columbia U., 1967, Morehead State U., 1973, Ky. State U., 1969-75, Upper Iowa U., 1977—; children—Teresa Ann, Martin. Council rep. Nat. Found.-March of Dimes, 1966-67; chief vol. coordinator vol. services Ky. Dept. Mental Health, Frankfort, 1967-69; state vol. coordinator dept. econ. security, Frankfort, 1969-73; supr. vol. adminstrn. Ky. Dept. Human Resources, Frankfort, 1973-75; exec. dir. Gov.'s Office of Vol. Services, Frankfort, 1975—. Bd. dirs. ARC, 1965-67, instr., 1957-67; pres., bd. dirs. Bur. Vol. Services, 1977-78; bd. dirs. Franklin County United Fund; chmn. Vol. Task Force Commonwealth of Ky.; exhibits chmn. Ky. Welfare Assn. Recipient numerous awards, latest including citations Am. Bus. Woman Assn., 1975, Ky. Fedn. Women's Clubs, 1975, Bur. Vol. Services, 1978, Ky. Council on Crime and Delinquency, 1979. Mem. Assn. Vol. Adminstrs. (dir. 1978-80), Am. Mgmt. Assn., The Assembly. Democrat. Baptist. Clubs: Heritage Woman's, Ky. Fedn. Woman's (dir.). Home: 249 Juniper Dr Frankfort KY 40601 Office: 903 Collins Ln Frankfort KY 40601

JOHNSON, NORMA JEANETTE, specialty wool grower; b. Dover, Ohio, Aug. 30, 1925; d. Jasper Crile and Mildred Catherine (Russell) J.; student Heidelberg Coll., 1943; cert. drafting techniques Case Sch. Applied Sci., 1944; student Western Res. U., 1945-47, Ohio State U., 1951, Muskingum Coll., 1965; A.A., Kent State U., 1979; m. Robert Blake Covey, Oct. 7, 1951 (div. 1960); 1 dau., Susan Kay. Instr. arts and crafts Univ. Settlement House, Cleve., 1944; mech. draftswoman Nat. Assn. Civil Aeros., Cleve., 1944-46; mfrs. rep. nat. spice house, 1947-49; tchr. econs., English, math, history, high sch., Tuscarawas County Sch. System, New Philadelphia, Ohio, 1962-69; owner, mgr. Sunny Slopes Farm, producer of splty. spinning wools, Dover, Ohio, 1969—. Tchr., Meth. Sunday Sch., 1956-61; chaplain Winfield PTA, 1960; program dir. Brandywine Grange, 1960-62; troop leader Girl Scouts, U.S.A., 1961-70; mem. Tuscarawas County Jail Com., 1981. Recipient Ohio Wildlife Conservation award Tuscarawas County, 1972. Mem. Mid States Wool Growers, Select-Sires Inc., Am. Angus Assn. Club: Nat. Grange. Home and Office: Route 1 Box 398 Dover OH 44622

JOHNSON, PATRICIA ELIZABETH, village ofcl.; b. Muskegon, Mich., Jan. 27, 1943; d. Francis William and Marjorie Ilene (LaRue) J.; student public schs. Whitehall, Mich. With Howmet-Misco Corp., Whitehall, 1965—, injection press operator, 1969—; trustee Village of Lakewood Club, 1968—, pres. pro tem, 1977-82, chmn. fin. and planning coms., legis. adminstr., grantsperson Village Council, 1980—; mem. Muskegon County Leaf Disposal Adv. Com., 1980, Muskegon County Solid Waste Disposal Steering Com., 1981; mem. Lakewood Union Chapel. Mem. UAW Local 1243 (exec. bd., fin. sec., editor local newsletter), UAW CAP Council (exec. bd. Muskegon County). Democrat. Bd. dirs. Muskegon County Big Bros./Big Sisters Agy., 1979-80. Club: Lakewood Civic Builders. Home: 96 W Ashland St Route 2 Twin Lake MI 49457 Office: 1116 S Mears Ave Whitehall MI 49461

JOHNSON, PATRICIA LYNN, ins. co. exec.; b. Columbus, Ohio, Oct. 22, 1943; d. James I. and Rosetta (Jacobs) Duren; B.S., Ohio State U., 1965; postgrad. Calif. State U., Long Beach, 1970, UCLA extension, 1975, U. Redlands, 1980; m. Harold Johnson, Dec. 25, 1965; 1 dau., Jill

N. Tchr. pub. schs., Columbus, Ohio, 1966-67, Cin., 1965-66, San Bernardino, Calif., 1969-70, Long Beach, Calif., 1970-72, Thetford, Eng., 1967-68; account rep. ITT, Hartford, 1973; tng. adminstr. Blue Cross Calif., Los Angeles, from 1975, now mgr. provider services. Vol. Women's Career Planning Center, Los Angeles. Mem. Am. Soc. Tng. and Devel., Am. Soc. Hosp. Educators and Trainers, Am. Hosp. Assn., So. Calif. Hosp. Assn., Am. Mgmt. Assn., Women's Exec. Workshop, Delta Sigma Theta. Home: 551 Hill St Inglewood CA 90302 Office: Box 70000 Van Nuys CA 91367

JOHNSON, PATRICIA MARY, interior designer; b. Evanston, Ill., Mar. 14, 1937; d. Harold W. and Florence M. (Miller) J.; Interior Design degree LaSalle U., Chgo., 1972; student Art Inst., Chgo., 1970-73; m. Dirk G. Swart, Feb. 13, 1980; children—William, Nancy, Richard. Various office mgmt. positions, Chgo., 1957-72; owner Decor Interior Design, Chgo., 1972-76; interior design communicator, producer/host weekly syndicated cable TV program on interior design Diversified Prodn. Resources, Newfield, N.J., 1980—; owner/pres. Design Communications, 1976—. Div. chmn. United Way, 1979, Achievement certificate, 1979. Mem. Nat. Home Fashions League, Inc. (Image Maker 1979, nat. dir. consumer affairs), Nat. Writers Club, Women in Communications, Inc., Am. Soc. Interior Designers, Nat. Fedn. Press Women, C. of C. (communications com. 1976—). Columnist, Jersey Woman, 1979—; contbr. articles to profl. jours. and consumer mags.; also radio broadcaster. Home: PO Box 381 Rosenhayn NJ 08352 Office: PO Box 296 Rosenhayn NJ 08352

JOHNSON, PATRICIA R., biologist; b. Waco, Tex., Feb. 28, 1931; A.B., Baylor U., 1952, M.A., 1958; Ph.D. in Biochemistry, Rutgers U., 1967. Health physicist Rocky Flats Plant, Dow Chem. Corp., 1952-53; analytical chemist Va. Carolina Chem. Corp., Tex., 1953-54; tchr. high sch., Tex., 1956-60; instr. biology and chemistry Malone Coll., 1960-61; research asst. Bur. Biol. Research, Rutgers U., 1961-64; from instr. to assoc. prof. biology Vassar Coll., 1964-75, prof., 1975—, chmn. dept., 1975—, William R. Keenan prof., 1981—; adj. assoc. prof. Rockefeller U., 1971-75, adj. prof., 1975-80. Mem. AAAS, N.Y. Acad. Scis., Am. Inst. Nutrition. Office: Dept of Biology Vassar College Poughkeepsie NY 12601 *

JOHNSON, PAULETTE DEJOIE, social worker; b. New Orleans, Aug. 3, 1925; d. Paul H.V. and Thelma Thersa (Epps) DeJoie; B.A., Chapman Coll., 1947; M.S.W., U. Pa., 1960; m. Turner C. Johnson, Dec. 26, 1948; 1 son, T. Kevin. Social worker Health and Welfare Council, Phila., 1967-73, social worker, 1948-65, asst. project dir., 1965-67; asso. regional dir. Planned Parenthood Fedn. of Am., Phila., 1974-78; lectr. Black studies dept. psychology St. Joseph's U., 1971-74; exec. dir. Girls Clubs of Southeastern Pa., Phila., 1978-81; appointed Pa. State Bd. Edn., 1978—; trustee Chestnut Hill Acad., Children's Aid Soc., Women's Way, Planned Parenthood Southeastern Pa. Recipient Salute to Educators award, 1972. Mem. Nat. Assn. Social Workers, Acad. Cert. Social Workers, Nat. Assn. State Bds. Edn., Community Leadership Assos. Democrat. Roman Catholic. Clubs: Cosmopolitan, Links, Inc., Circle-Lets, Inc. Home: 6807 Lincoln Dr Philadelphia PA 19119

JOHNSON, PENELOPE LAGIOS, ballet artistic dir., choreographer; b. San Francisco, Apr. 21, 1939; d. George Demetre and Eugenia Georgia (Kolias) Lagios; m. Kelly Grant Johnson, Aug. 23, 1970; 1 dau., Leda Meredith. Understudy for Alicia Alonso, Ballet de Cuba, 1959-60; prin. dancer Am. Concert Ballet, 1960-64; soloist San Francisco Opera and San Francisco Ballet, 1965-68; artistic dir., choreographer, tchr. San Francisco Dance Theater, 1969—; coach to prins. San Francisco Ballet; adv. to numerous local dance tchrs. Recipient award of merit Mayor Feinstein and Suprs., City of San Francisco, 1982; NEA grantee; CAC grantee; San Francisco Found. grantee. Home: 2217 Fillmore San Francisco CA 94115 Office: 1412 Van Ness San Francisco CA 94109

JOHNSON, PHYLLIS JUNO, merchant; b. Tomahawk, Wis., Aug. 20, 1936; d. Phillip F. and Juno K. (Stillings) Glines; student Rosemary Bishoff Modeling Sch., 1958, Waukesha Tech., 1965; m. William A. Johnson, July 11, 1955; children—James M., Jeff J., Dawn R. Typist, sec. Title Guarantee Co., Milw., 1954-55; free-lance profl. model, 1958-65; owner, mgr. Gidgets Beauty Salon, Menomonee Falls, Wis., then Lannon, Wis., 1965-74; owner, buyer Tomahawk (Wis.) Woolen Store, 1974—. Home: 805 E Kings Rd Tomahawk WI 54487 Office: Tomahawk Woolen Store Hwy 51 N Tomahawk WI 54487

JOHNSON, RAYNA PEEVEY, banker; b. Dallas, Dec. 23, 1943; d. Ray M. and Mary Elizabeth (Peevey) J.; A.A., Navarro Jr. Coll., 1964; student North Tex. State U., 1964-65, 66-67. Bookkeeper, Miller-Johnson Grocery Co., Dallas, 1960-62; receivables clk. accounts payable/receivable Republic Nat. Bank Bldg. Co., Dallas, 1965-66; asst. cashier credit dept. Preston State Bank, Dallas, 1967—. Mem. Am. Inst. Bankers, Robert Morris Assocs., Dallas Assn. Credit Mgmt. Presbyterian. Home: 405 Lois Ln Richardson TX 75081 Office: PO Box 12000 Dallas TX 75225

JOHNSON, REBECCA MCGEORGE, home economist; b. Roanoke, Va., Aug. 10, 1948; d. Gilbert Wesley and Pauline (Brooks) McGeorge; A.A., Lees McRae Coll., 1968; B.S. in Home Econs. Edn., Mars Hill Coll., 1971; m. James Edin Johnson, Apr. 3, 1971. Home Economist Va. Poly. Inst. & State U. Extension div., Appomattox, 1971-73, home economist, Hanover, 1974—; tchr. Campbell County (Va.) Schs., 1973-74; cons. in field. Mem. Criminal Justice Adv. Com., Lynchburg, Va., 1971-73, mem. consumer health adv. com., 1971-73; sec. Hanover Cannery Adv. Com., 1979—. Mem. Nat. Assn. Extension Home Economists, Va. Assn. Extension Home Economists (state public relations chmn. 1980-82), AAUW, Epsilon Sigma Phi, Va. Guild Needlewomen. Presbyterian. Contbr. in field. Home: Route 2 Box 328-F Mechanicsville VA 23111 Office: Wickham Office Bldg Hanover VA 23069

JOHNSON, REGENA FIX, musician, educator; b. Shenandoah, Va., Apr. 2, 1911; d. Henry Arthur and Beatrice (Mills) Fix.; B. Music, Cin. Conservatory Music, 1932; postgrad. U. Cin., Madison Coll., summer 1937, U. Va. extension, 1965-67; m. Albert Dunston Johnson, June 15, 1940. Pvt. tchr. music, 1933—; tchr. music Shenandoah, 1936-37, Nansemond County (Va.) Pub. Sch., 1937-40; substitute tchr. Windsor (Va.) High Sch., 1941; music dir. Windsor Bapt. Ch., 1940—. Vice pres. Tidewater Music Tchrs. Forum, 1977-79; sr. adviser Windsor Jr. Women's Club, 1959—. Mem. Music Tchr. Nat. Assn. (cert. tchr.), Va. Music Tchrs. Assn. (cert. tchr., bylaws chmn. 1980-82, former parliamentarian, chmn. Eastern Dist. Levels, I, II auditions 1974—), Nat. Guild Piano Tchrs., Southside Dist. Va. Fedn. Women's Clubs (pres. 1952-54), Delta Kappa Gamma, Phi Beta. Democrat. Baptist. Clubs: Windsor Women's (pres. 1941-42), Order of Eastern Star (worthy matron Sinai chpt. 18 1951-52). Home: POB 325 Windsor VA 23487

JOHNSON, ROBERTA, constrn. co. exec.; b. N.Y.C., Dec. 22, 1914; d. Louis and Lillian (Lowenthal) Sollisch; student CCNY, 1931-33, U. Miami, 1967; m. Bernard C. Johnson, Aug. 31, 1935; children—Laurence R., Laraine R. Sec., 20th Century Freight Forwarding Co., N.Y.C., 1931-33; model, sec. Trachtenberg Furs, N.Y.C., 1934-39; dancer Sammy Kaye Orch., 1933-34; payroll clk., U.S. Navy, various locations, 1939-46; constrn. contracting sec./acct. E.I. DuPont De Nemours & Co., North Augusta and Aiken, S.C., 1951-54; corporate officer Gust K. Newberg Constrn. Co., North Miami, Fla., 1955—; tchr. State of Fla., 1973—. Mem. Miami Shores Planning and Zoning Bd., 1974—. Cert. constrn. asso. Mem. Nat. Assn. Women in Constrn. Club: Miami Shores Women's. Home: 1089 NE 91st Ter Miami Shores FL 33138 Office: 12200 NE 14th Ave North Miami FL 33161

JOHNSON, ROBERTA MILLER, assn. exec.; b. Los Angeles, Jan. 24, 1939; d. Robert Theodore and Edith Gertrude (Swain) Miller Eckhardt; student UCLA, 1957-59; B.A., Calif. State U., Northridge, 1969; M.S., Azusa Pacific Coll., 1975; m. Sept. 25, 1959; children—Kathryn Ann, Karen Jeannette. Social worker, Los Angeles County Dept. Public Social Services, Glendale, 1969-72; asst. registrar Southwestern U. Law Sch., Los Angeles, 1972-74; asst. dir. admissions and records Northrop U., Inglewood, 1974-75; program specialist Inst. Internat. Edn., Los Angeles, 1975-77; coordinator job tng. United Way, Van Nuys, Calif., 1979—. Lic. marriage, family and child counselor, Calif. Mem. AAUW (1st v.p. 1978-80), NOW, Women in Mgmt., ACLU, UCLA Alumni Assn., Nat. Assn. Female Execs. (network dir. 1978-80). Democrat. Unitarian. Club: Westside Bruin (bd. dirs.). Office: 6851 Lennox Ave Van Nuys CA 91405

JOHNSON, RUTH BUHL, newspaper corp. exec.; b. Richland Center, Wis., Sept. 19, 1949; d. Walter Roland and Dorothy Ida (Wegner) Buhl; B.A., Macalester Coll., 1971. Personnel staffing specialist Fed. Govt., St. Paul, Mpls., 1971-73; publicity dir. Cricket Theatre, Mpls., 1973-74; asso. producer, researcher, writer Minn. Public TV, Mpls., 1974-76; project coordinator Minn. State Bicentennial Commn., St. Paul, 1976; promotion dir. Minn. Public Radio Network, St. Paul, 1976-77; promotion copy coordinator Mpls. Star & Tribune Newspapers, 1977-79, circulation tng. mgr., 1979-82, circulation sales mgr., 1982—. Pres., Assn. St. Paul Communities, 1976-78; chmn. Merriam Park Dist. Planning Com., 1975-77, mem. Merriam Park Community Council, 1976-77. Recipient Recognition cert. Bicentennial Commn., 1976, Bell award for edn. series on non-comml. TV, Minn. Edn. Assn., 1976, Merit awards, 1975, 76. Mem. Am. Soc. for Tng. and Devel. (program com. 1980), Minn. Assn. Continuing Adult Edn., Assn. for Ednl. Data Systems, Am. Mgmt. Assn., Central States Circulation Mgrs. Assn. Home: 371 Old Grandy Rd Stanchfield MN 55080 Office: Mpls Star & Tribune Newspapers 425 Portland Ave Minneapolis MN 55488

JOHNSON, SAMMYE LARUE, educator; b. Dallas, Oct. 8, 1946; d. Sam S. and Poppy (Hammond) Malosky; B.S. in Journalism with distinction, Northwestern U. Medill Sch. Journalism, 1968, M.S. in Journalism, with highest distinction, 1969; m. William H. Johnson, Aug. 1, 1970. Asst. editor Where Mag., Chgo., 1969; feature writer Chicago Today newspaper, Chgo., 1969-71, Sunday mag. editor, 1971-73; asst. dir., public relations mgr. W. O. Darby Library, Nurnberg, W.Ger., 1974-75; editor San Antonio Mag., 1976-79; communications dir. VIA Met. Transit System, San Antonio, 1979; asst. prof. journalism William Allen White Sch. Journalism, U. Kans., Lawrence, 1979-80, Trinity U., San Antonio, 1980—; cons. public relations I. Mehren of Tex., Inc., San Antonio, 1979—; cons. JRJ Enterprises, San Antonio, 1979—. Cons. communications Leukemia Soc. Am., South/Central Tex. chpt., 1981—; United Way San Antonio, 1981—; publicity com. young art patrons Mus. Art, San Antonio, 1981—. Named Today's Woman of Achievement, San Antonio Light Newspaper, 1981. Mem. Women in Communications (bd. dirs. 1978-80, Proliner award 1981), Internat. Assn. Bus. Communicators (bd. dirs. 1979, Gold Quill award 1979, named Communicator of Yr. 1981, numerous other awards 1976-79), Kappa Tau Alpha. Home: 16934 Turkey Point San Antonio TX 78232 Office: Box 225 Trinity Univ 715 Stadium Dr San Antonio TX 78284

JOHNSON, SANDRA ANN, personnel exec.; b. Detroit, July 14, 1943; d. LaFayette and Edna Marie (Clayborne) Miller; student Broome Community Coll., 1972-75; B.S., SUNY, 1982; m. Frederick E. Johnson, Nov. 2, 1963; children—Frederick E., Seth Harris. Outreach worker N.Y. State Dept. Labor, Binghamton, 1972-73; job placement counselor Broome County C. of C., Binghamton, 1973-74; assoc. buyer N.Y. State Electric & Gas Corp., Binghamton, 1974-76, profl. employment specialist, 1976-78, equal employment coordinator, Binghamton, 1978—; cons. in field; oral examiner N.Y. State Dept. Labor Civil Service Exams., 1974—. Mem. allocations panel United Way of Broome County, 1980—; mem. Vocat. Tech. adv. com. Binghamton City Sch. Dist., 1980—; bd. dirs. Broome County Urban League, 1978-80, Binghamton Boys/Girls Club, 1975-79; v.p. Broome County Adv. Com. to N.Y. State Div. Human Rights, 1969-71; mem. Mayor's Com. on Human Rights, 1968-69; pres. CORE, 1965-68. Mem. Am. Assn. Affirmative Action, Am. Assn. of Blacks in Energy, Broome County Urban League, NAACP, Nat. Assn. Female Execs., Pluralistic Women's Concern Group, So. Tier Personnel Assn., Women's Network of Broome County. Home: 501 Winston Dr Vestal NY 13850 Office: 4500 Vestal Pkwy E Binghamton NY 13902

JOHNSON, SHARON SLITER, writer, producer; b. Midland, Tex., July 22, 1950; d. Warren Greenlee and Barbara Jean (Hayslip) Sliter; B.A., DePaul U., 1976; m. Stephan Glenn Johnson, Nov. 7, 1981. Sec., adminstrv. asst. to chmn. bd. Ency. Brit. Ednl. Corp., Chgo., 1972-77, writer, producer, 1977—; freelance script cons., researcher, writer, 1978—. Democrat. Methodist. Home and office: 5124 W Dakin St Chicago IL 60641

JOHNSON, SHIRLEY (MRS. ASHER LANS), economist, educator; b. Wichita, Kans., Mar. 27, 1934; d. Howard and Kathryn (Wiebe) J.; B.A. magna cum laude, Radcliffe Coll., 1956; M.A. with 1st honors, U. Edinburgh (Scotland), 1957; Ph.D., Columbia U., 1966; m. Asher Lans, June 28, 1969; 1 dau., Andrea Elisabeth. Mem. faculty Mt. Holyoke Coll., 1958-59, City U. N.Y., 1959-62, Barnard Coll., 1962-65, N.Y.U., 1965-67; researcher Nat. Bur. Econ. Research, 1959-61; prof. Vassar Coll., Poughkeepsie, N.Y., 1967—, chmn. dept. econs., 1981—; bd. dirs. N.Y. State Mortgage Agy., 1978-85, dept. chmn., 1980—. Mem. vestry Calvary and St. George's Episcopal Ch., N.Y.C. Marshall scholar, 1956-58; Woodrow Wilson fellow, 1956-57. Mem. Am. Econ. Assn. Mem. adv. bd. Partisan Rev., 1981—; contbr. articles to profl. jours. Office: Box 378 Vassar Coll Poughkeepsie NY 12601

JOHNSON, SONDRA LEE, mcpl. bond specialist; b. Youngstown, Ohio, Apr. 12, 1940; d. Paul D. and Betty L. (Clawson) Smith; student Hiram Coll., 1958-60; B.A., U. Ariz., 1962, M.Ed., 1965; postgrad. UCLA, 1968-69, Calif. State U., Long Beach, 1968, Coll. Fin. Planning, 1981—; m. Everett L. Johnson, Mar. 28, 1975. Social studies curriculum guide com. mem. Flowing Wells Sch. Dist., Tucson, Ariz., 1962-67; English curriculum guide chmn., yearbook adv. Palos Verdes (Calif.) Unified Sch. Dist., 1967-78; instr. English dept. Long Beach (Calif.) City Coll., 1976-78; account exec. Merrill Lynch, Long Beach, 1978-81; investment specialist Sutro & Co., Inc., Newport Beach, Calif., 1981-82; mcpl. bond funds wholesaler, dist. sales rep., John Nuveen & Co., Inc., 1982—; invitee bd. dirs. meeting Internat. Investors, Johannesburg, S.Africa, 1981. Mem. exec. council and fin. com. YWCA. Recipient Exec. Club award Merrill Lynch, 1980. Mem. Internat. Assn. Fin. Planners, Am. Bus. Women's Assn., Pi Lambda Theta. Office: 1900 Avenue of the Stars Los Angeles CA 90067

JOHNSON, SUSAN MARJAMAA, educator; b. Newark, Jan. 16, 1945; d. Robert Oscar and Jane Albertina (Long) Marjamaa; B.S. with honors in Biology, Bates Coll., 1966; M.A., Johns Hopkins U., 1968; Ph.D., U. Tex., Austin, 1975; m. Lathrop Park Johnson, Aug. 4, 1973. Tchr., Balt. County pub. sch. system, 1967-69; instr. Essex Community Coll., Balt., 1968-69; teaching asst. U. Tex., Austin, 1972-73; asst. prof. curriculum research and devel. U. Fla., Gainesville, 1974-79, asso. prof., 1979-80, edn. cons., 1980—; cons. in field. Recipient Lyman and Am. Assn. Colls. Pharmacy, 1978. Mem. Am. Assn. Colls. Pharmacy, Health Edn. Media Assn., Nat. Assn. for Research in Sci. Teaching, Fla. PLATO Users Group, Phi Kappa Phi. Author: An Astronomy Bibliography-Selected and Annotated for the Layman and the Sci. Teacher, 1972; (with M.W. McKenzie) The Medication History Interview, a Self-Instructional Module, 1976; contbr. articles to pharm. jours. Home: 1002 Shellbark Rd Muncie IN 47304

JOHNSON, SYBIL ANN, banker; b. Wickes, Ark., Apr. 26, 1938; d. John Andrew and Annie Marie (Smith) Lewey; student Southwestern Oreg. Community Coll.; m. George Raymond Johnson, Sept. 6, 1956; children—Robert George, Jeffrey Jay, Raymond Scott. Teller, U.S. Nat. Bank of Oreg., Salem, 1955-57, proof operator, teller, 1957-61, ops. supr. Coos Bay br., 1972-73, various positions Cottage Grove br., 1962-72, ops. officer N. Bend br., 1973-76, br. mgr. Lakeside, 1976-82, br. officer ops., Springfield, 1982—. Chmn. City of Lakeside Budget Com., 1980-81, 1981-82. Mem. Bank Adminstrn. Inst., Am. Inst. Banking, Nat. Assn. Bank Women. Republican. Office: 437 Main St PO Box 149 Springfield OR 97477

JOHNSON, VERONICA ANN WILKERSON, librarian; b. Detroit, Aug. 5, 1952; d. James Henry and Alberta (Dixon) Wilkerson; B.A., Wayne State U., 1975; M.A., U. Mich., 1977; m. Melvin Lee Johnson, Nov. 3, 1973; 1 dau., Dichondra Rosalyn. Lab. technician Wayne County Health Dept., Project Prescad, 1978-79; children's librarian Inkster (Mich.) br. Wayne Oakland Library Fedn., 1979, head community librarian, 1979—; City of Inkster adviser Vol. Tng. for Youth Leadership Devel., Sister Cities Internat. Mem. City of Inkster Cable TV Task Force, 1981—; chmn. workshop com. Inkster Internat. Friendship Force Exchange, 1981—; sec. Inkster Community Project Pride, 1979-80. U. Mich. Sch. Library Sci. fellow, 1976-77. Mem. NAACP, ALA, Med. Library Assn., Women's Nat. Book Assn. (asst. membership chmn. Detroit chpt.), Mich. Library Assn., Gamma Phi Delta. Mem. Ch. of Christ. Home: 22732 Cambridge St Detroit MI 48219 Office: 2005 Inkster Rd Inkster MI 48141

JOHNSON, VICKI R., ins. co. ofcl.; b. Glens Falls, N.Y., June 19, 1952; d. Leonard H. and Rose (Petrosky) J.; A.B., Franklin and Marshall Coll., 1974; postgrad. U. Portland, 1979—; m. Robin James Johnson, Nov. 24, 1979. Mgr., Prudential Ins. Co. Am., Woodland Hills, Calif., 1974—; mem. Oreg. Accident and Health Claim Assn., 1976-81. Pres., Ridgeview Condominium Assn., 1978-81. Mem. Los Angeles Accident and Health Claim Assn. Home: 21931 Burbank Blvd Woodland Hills CA 91367 Office: 5800 Canoga Ave Woodland Hills CA

JOHNSON, VICTORIA CHARLOTTE, music educator; b. N.Y.C., Feb. 21, 1951; d. Arthur Henry and Nathalie Young; B.Mus., Boston U., 1972, Ed.M., 1978; m. William M. Johnson, June 25, 1972. Tchr. music pub. schs., Abington, Mass., 1972—; adj. clin. instr. Boston U. Mem. Mass. Music Educators Assn., Music Educators Nat. Conf. (past sec. S.E. dist.), Mass. Tchrs. Assn., NEA, Pi Lambda Theta. Home: 29 Liane Way Pembroke MA 02359

JOHNSON, VILMA TERESA, nurse; b. Panama, June 14, 1944; d. Clayton Fitzgerald and Hilda Rosebelle (Rogers) Osborne; grad. Meth. Hosp. of Bklyn. Sch. Nursing, 1966; B.S., St. Francis Coll., 1977; M.P.A. candidate N.Y. U.; children—Michelle Ann, Nicole Marie. Head nurse adult psychiatry Meth. Hosp. of Bklyn., 1968-70; nursing coordinator Leviton Mfg. Co., Bklyn., 1970-73; head nurse L.I. Coll. Hosp., Bklyn., 1974-76; investigator Patient Adv.'s Office, N.Y. State Dept. Health, N.Y.C., 1976—. Mem. Am. Nurses Assn. N.Y. State Nurses Assn., Nat. Assn. Female Execs., St. Francis Coll. Alumni Assn. Home: 568 Beach 65 St Arverne NY 11692 Office: 1 Penn Plaza New York NY 10007

JOHNSON-COUSIN, DANIELLE PAULETTE, educator; b. Geneva, Nov. 7, 1943; came to U.S., 1964; d. Edouard Henri and Suzanne Louise (Maurer) Cousin; certificat de maturite cum laude Coll. de Geneve, 1962; B.A., U. Alaska, 1966; M.A., Purdue U., 1968, Ph.D., U. Ill., 1977; postgrad. Oxford U., Eng., Northwestern U., U. Munich, Ger.; m. Harry M. Johnson, Jan. 25, 1970; 1 dau., Eliza Suzanne. Vis. lectr. U. Ill. 1976-77; asst. prof. French, Amherst Coll. 1979-82; asst. prof. French, Vanderbilt U. 1982—, also Andrews W. Mellon fellow. Inst. Advanced Studies in Humanities U. Edinburgh fellow, summer 1979. Mem. MLA, Assn. suisse de Litt comp et gén, Soc. des Etudes Staëliennes Paris, AAUP, AAUW, Soc. Suisse des Ecrivains, Soc. Genevoise des Ecrivains, Hist. Soc. Pa., Soc. des Etudes Romantiques; South Atlantic Modern Lang. Assn., Am. Assn. Tchrs. French, Am. Comparative Lit. Assn., Internat. Comparative Lit. Assn. Contbr. articles to profl. jours. Office: Department of French and Italian Furman Hall 222 Vanderbilt University Nashville TN 37235

JOHNSON-JENSEN, KAREN SUE, computer systems analyst; b. Springfield, Mo., Mar. 7, 1955; d. E.E. Johnson and Jean Alice Cain. B.A., U. Tex. at Austin, 1977; postgrad. So. Meth. U., 1979—; m. John C. Jensen, Mar. 24, 1979. Lab. research asst. II Applied Research Labs., 1976-77; software design engr. Tex. Instruments Inc., 1977—. Campaign vol. Austin City Council, 1980-81, 82-83; blood fund co. coordinator Central Tex. Regional Blood Center, 1978—. Recipient Lifegiver award Central Tex. Regional Blood Center, 1979. Mem. Assn. Computing Machinery, IEEE, Mortar Bd., Alpha Chi Sigma, Pi Mu Epsilon. Presbyterian. Home: 11503 Santz Cruz Austin TX 78759 Office: Tex Instrument PO Box 2909 Austin TX 78769

JOHNSON-LEE, DONA RUTH, psychiat. social worker; b. Gilbertsville, Ky., Sept. 7, 1941; d. O. D. and Ruth (Russell) Johnson; B.A., So. Meth. U., 1963; M.S.W., Columbia U., 1966; m. William S. Lee, Apr. 14, 1979; 1 dau., Jennifer Catherine Lee. Casework aide in adoption Meth. Mission Home, San Antonio, 1963-64; social worker Children's Village, Dobbs Ferry, N.Y., 1966-68; psychiat. social worker St. Vincent's Hosp., N.Y.C., 1968—; field instr. Fordham U., 1974-77; pvt. practice psychiat. social work, N.Y.C., 1972—. Mem. Nat. Assn. Social Workers, Acad. Cert. Social Workers. Democrat. Methodist. Home: 792 Columbus Ave Apt 1-R New York NY 10025 Office: St Vincent's Hosp 144 W 12th St New York NY 10011

JOHNSON-MASTERS, VIRGINIA E., sex therapist, inst. adminstr.; b. Springfield, Mo., Feb. 11, 1925; d. Harry H. and Edna (Evans) Eshelman; ed. U., Mo. Columbia, Washington U., St. Louis; D.Sc. (hon.) U. Louisville, 1978; m. William H. Masters, Jan., 1971; children by previous marriage—Scott F. Johnson, Lisa E. Johnson. Editorial writer, adminstrv. sec. St. Louis Daily Record, 1947-50; mem. advt. dept. CBS, St. Louis, 1950-51; mem. research staff div. reproductive biology dept. ob-gyn Washington U., St. Louis, 1957-64, research asst., 1960-62, research instr., 1962-64, lectr. in human sexuality dept. psychiatry Sch. Medicine, 1981—; research asso. Reproductive Biology Research Found. (now Masters & Johnson Inst.), St. Louis, 1964-69, asst. dir., 1969-73, co-dir., 1973-80, dir., 1981—. Recipient Paul H. Hoch award Am. Psychopath. Assn., 1971; Biomed. Research award World Assn. Sexology, 1979; Rotary Internat. Paul Harris fellow, 1976. Edward Henderson Lecture award Am. Geriatrics Soc., 1981; Mem. AAAS, Am. Assn. Sex Educators, Counselors and Therapists, Author's Guild, Inc., Colombian Sexological Soc., Eastern Assn. Sex Therapy, Eastern Assn. Sex Therapy, Eastern Mo. Psychiat. Soc., Internat. Acad. Sex Research (treas. 1975-76), Internat. Platform Assn., Soc. Sci. Study Sex. Episcopalian. Author: (with William H. Masters), Human Sexual Response, 1966, Human Sexual Inadequacy, 1970, The Pleasure Bond, 1975;

Homosexuality in Perspective, 1979; Ethical Issues in Sex Therapy and Research, 1977, Volume 2, 1980; (with others) Textbook on Sexual Medicine, 1979; Textbook of Human Sexuality for Nurses, 1979; Human Sexuality, 1982; mem. editorial bd. Science Digest, 1982—; contbr. numerous articles in field. Office: 4910 Forest Park Blvd Saint Louis MO 63108

JOHNSON-SADUR, KRISTINA, cons.; b. Elmhurst, Ill., June 23, 1953; d. Harry William and Frieda (Bartolme) Johnson; A.A., Coll. DuPage, 1973; B.A., Marquette U., 1975; m. Allan Edward Sadur, Aug. 31, 1980. Mem. research staff Ill. House Democratic Staff, 1975-77; staff coordinator Conf. Women Legislators, also women's adv., Springfield, Ill., 1978-81; mgmt. cons., fund raiser politics, Schaumburg, Ill., 1981—; mem. family com. Ill. Commn. on Status of Women, 1979—. Women's adv. for Ill. House of Reps., 1977-81; del. Democratic Nat. Conv., 1980; bd. dirs. Life-Span, domestic violence shelter, Des Plaines; bd. dirs. Nantucket Cove Homeowners Assn., Schaumburg, also v.p. Mem. Nat. Abortion Rights Action League, Ill. Dem. Women's Caucus, Ill. Women's Polit. Caucus (Legis. Support award 1980), NOW. Contbr. articles to Ill. Women's Agenda Newsletter, 1979-81; pub. Rev. of Legis. Women's Issues bimonthly newsletter, 1979-82. Home and Office: 222 Nantucket Harbour Schaumburg IL 60193

JOHNSTON, DEE SHELY, mfg. co. ofcl.; b. Anderson County, Ky., Feb. 6, 1937; d. Tyler Gilbert and Sarah Eliza (Crooke) Shely; student George Peabody Coll., 1956-58; grad. Campbellsville Coll., 1956; student Jackson State U., 1974, Lord Fairfax Community Coll., 1981, Shenandoah Coll., 1982—; m. Ronald E. Johnston, Aug. 13, 1957; children—Steven Christopher, Michael David, Kevin Eugene, Russell Desha. Dir. music and edn. First Bapt. Ch., Front Royal, Va., 1965; announcer, advt. copywriter Sta. WFTR, Front Royal, 1965-66; sec. Berryville (Va.) Primary Sch., 1967-70; fund raising staff United Way of Louisville, 1970-72; dir. music St. Andrew's Episcopal Ch., Kokomo, Ind., 1973; sec. ITT, Milan, Tenn., 1973-74; with O'Sullivan Corp., Winchester, Va., 1976—, purchasing mgr., 1979—. Mem. Nat. Assn. Female Execs., Nat. Assn. Purchasing Mgrs., Purchasing Mgrs. Assn. of the Old Dominion (editor newsletter 1980—, dir. 1982-83). Episcopalian. Home: Route 2 Box 376-A2 Berryville VA 22611 Office: PO Box 603 Winchester VA 22601

JOHNSTON, DOLORES MAE MASCIK (MRS. ROBERT EDGAR JOHNSTON), clubwoman; b. Conneaut, Ohio, May 26, 1927; d. Michael Morris and Roberta Mary (Jacobs) Mascik; B.S., Ohio State U., 1949; m. Robert Edgar Johnston, Mar. 19, 1950; children—Kirk, Christine, Mark. Researcher, hematology Ohio State U., Columbus, 1949-54; med. technologist Youngstown (Ohio) Hosp. Assn., 1954-55, Eli Lilly Clin. Research Labs., Indpls., 1955-57, Green Bay, Wis., 1958-60. Mem. Green Bay Community Chorus, 1966-70, Bach Choir of Green Bay, 1970-80; mem. St. Norbert Coll. Collegiate Chorale, 1980—; pack officer Boy Scouts Am., 1970-71; co-chmn. ARC Blood Bank, 1970-72, mem. Lakeland chpt. steering com., 1974-76, 78-79, vol. chmn. blood bank vols., 1976-80; bd. dirs. Lakeland chpt. ARC, 1980—, rep. to Badger Region blood services com., 1979-81, 82—, rep. to Pere/Marquette div. council, 1980-82; vol. worker Mobile Meals, 1971—; pres. Brown County Med. Soc. Aux., 1969-70, dir., 1973-78; mem. Brown County Republican Women's Club, 1969—; bd. dirs. Wis. Polit. Action Com., 1972-73; bd. dirs. Curative Workshop Rehab. Center, 1975—, sec., 1976-78, pres., 1980-82; chmn. Ind. Living Program Council, 1982—; sec. bd. dirs. Brown County United Way Council of Agys., 1975-76. Recipient Brown County Med. Aux. outstanding mem. award, 1973-74; named YWCA Woman of Yr., 1977; Vol. of Yr. award Lakeland chpt. ARC, 1981; Med. Services award Brown County Med. Soc., 1982. Mem. Woman's Aux. State Med. Soc. Wis. (pres. 1973-74, parliamentarian 1981—), AMA Aux. (N.C. regional family health chmn. 1974-75, N.C. regional area counselor Project Bank, 1975-76, 76-77, nat. project bank coordinator 1977-78, nat. rec. sec. 1979-80, chmn. nat. health projects 1978-79, nat. historian, 1980-81), Aesculapian Soc. (charter), P.E.O. (chpt. treas. 1970-72, state conv. treas. 1976), Alpha Lambda Delta, Alpha Chi Omega. Lutheran. Mem. Order Eastern Star. Clubs: Federated Women's, Junior Women's. Home: 3285 Waubenoor Dr Green Bay WI 54301

JOHNSTON, ELIZABETH (EMMERETTA) BOOTH, educator; b. Billings, Mont., Mar. 8, 1930; d. Edwin Sherman and Mary Katherine (Maier) Booth; B.A., U. Mont., 1952; M.S., U. Oreg., 1958; Ed.D., U. Cin., 1978; m. Andrew Vance Johnston, Dec. 23, 1952; children—Denis Andrew, Paula Maureen, Mark Edwin. Tchr., English and speech George Washington High Sch., Agana, Guam, 1952-56; speech and hearing therapist Children's Hosp. Sch., Eugene, Oreg., 1958-60; itinerant speech and hearing therapist Washoe County (Nev.) Sch., 1962-67; tchr. Talawanda Sch., Oxford, Ohio, 1967-68; therapist Hamilton (Ohio) Sch., 1968-69; instr., supr. speech and hearing clinic Miami U., Oxford, Ohio, 1969—; cons. in field. Lic. in speech pathology, Ohio. Mem. Am. Speech, Lang. and Hearing Assn. (cert. clin. competence), Ohio Speech, Lang. and Hearing Assn., Southwestern Ohio Speech, Lang. and Hearing Assn., Ohio Council Sch. Supts. Speech and Hearing, Internat. Reading Assn., Nat. Assn. Edn. Young Children, Delta Gamma, Delta Kappa Gamma. Republican. Roman Catholic. Author: (with A. Johnston) The Piagetian Language Nursery, 1983. Home: 6424 Contrearas Rd Oxford OH 45056 Office: 20 Bachelor Hall Miami U Oxford OH 45056

JOHNSTON, GLENDA ANNE, educator, mktg. specialist, choreographer; b. Covington County, Ala., Mar. 3; d. Carl Leland and Doris L. (Kirkpatrick) Joyner; B.A. in Health and Phys. Edn., Northeastern Ill. U., 1969; M.Ed. in Adminstrn. and Supervision (Gwen Brooks scholar), Ga. State U., 1976; student real estate sales Atlanta Area Tech. Sch., 1977; m. Allen Leo Johnston, Apr. 24, 1971; 1 son, Corey Jamal. Instr. phys. edn., student tchr. supr., dir. curricular activities Chgo. Public Schs., 1969-73; gymnastics specialist Fulton County (Ga.) Sch. System, 1976-78; dir. gymnastics S.W. Montessori Schs., 1978—; mktg. specialist Southland Realty, Century 21; health instr. Atlanta Bd. Edn.; cons. Nutralite Weight Reduction Program, Amway Products; dance dir. Kuumba Workshop, Chgo., 1971-73; founder, dir. Afro-Am. Dance Troupe, Chgo., 1971-73; choreographer and performer; works include: Heritage, 1971; Love Song, 1971; Jazz 'n' Tazz, 1972; Deliverance, 1974. Asst. sec. William Cousins polit. campaign, 1970, 73. Recipient Appreciation award Chgo. Fisk Alumni Assn., 1973. Mem. Ga. Assn. Health, Phys. Edn. and Recreation, Eta Phi Beta. Unitarian. Club: Eastern Star.

JOHNSTON, HELEN BRIDGET, advt. co. exec.; b. N.Y.C., Sept. 17, 1934; d. Dominick and Bridget (Carroll) J.; ed. Hunter Coll., With Grey Advt. Inc., N.Y.C., 1957—, v.p., dir. media research, asso. media dir., 1970—. Mem. Agy. Media Research Council (past pres.), Radio TV Research Council (past pres.). Office: 777 3d Ave New York NY 10017

JOHNSTON, JANE ELLEN, social worker; b. Stillwater, Minn., June 3, 1949; d. Glenn D. and Kathleen B. (Drury) J.; B.A. in Philosophy magna cum laude, U. Minn., 1972, M.S.W., 1976. Chief social worker dept. oncology Mayo Clinic Med. Social Services, Rochester, Minn. 1976-79, chief social worker home parenteral nutrition program, 1976-79; psychiat. social worker Zumbro Valley Mental Health Center, Rochester, 1977-78; team leader mental health team Olmsted County Dept. Social Services, Rochester, 1979-80; community program specialist Sch. Social Work, U. Minn., Mpls., 1980-81; asst. dir. social service North Meml. Med. Center, Mpls., 1981-82; pvt. practice, Mpls., 1982—; cons. med. social worker, Mpls.-St. Paul, 1980-81; mem. cancer rehab. com. Mayo Comprehensive Cancer Center, 1976-79; mem. home health care adv. com. Public Health Dept., Rochester, 1979-80. Mem. Acad. Cert. Social Workers, Nat. Assn. Social Workers. Home: 511 S Owens St Stillwater MN 55082 Office: Shea and Assocs 1219 Marquette Ave Minneapolis MN 55403

JOHNSTON, MARGUERITE, journalist, author, lectr.; b. Birmingham, Ala., Aug. 7, 1917; d. Robert C. and Marguerite (Spradling) Johnston; A.B., Birmingham-So. Coll., 1938; m. Charles Wynn Barnes, Aug. 31, 1946; children—Susan, Patricia, Steven, Polly. Reporter, Birmingham News, 1939-44; Washington corr. Birmingham News, Birmingham Age-Herald and London Daily Mirror, 1945-46; columnist Houston Post, 1947-69, fgn. news editor, mem. editorial bd., 1969—, asso. editor editorial page, 1972-77, asst. editor editorial page, 1977—. Lectr., 1947—; instr. creative writing U. Houston, 1946-47, lectr. feature writing, 1965-66; lectr. Baker Coll., Rice U., 1977-78. Del. Asian-Am. Women Journalists Conf., Honolulu, 1965, 1st World Conf. Women Journalists, Mexico City, 1969. Bd. dirs. Tex. Bill of Rights Found., 1962-64, Planned Parenthood, 1953-55, Homes St. Mark, 1962-63, Rice Center, 1980—; mem. Municipal Art Commn., 1971-76. Recipient Theta Sigma Phi Headliner award, 1954; 1st ann. award of merit Houston Com. Alcoholism, 1956; Am. Soc. Safety Engrs. certificate of merit Gulf Coast chpt., 1960; Agnese Carter Nelms award Planned Parenthood, 1968; Sch. Bell award Tex. State Tchrs. Assn., 1974, 75; Gold Key award Nat. Council Alcoholism, 1975; Population Action Council award, 1981. Mem. Tex. Soc. Architects (hon.), Mortar Bd., Tex. Soc. Architects (hon.), Phi Beta Kappa, Pi Beta Phi. Author: Public Manners, 1957; A Happy Worldly Abode, 1964. Office: Houston Post Houston TX 77001

JOHNSTON, MARGUERITE KULP, ednl. adminstr.; b. Los Angeles, Mar. 11, 1920; d. C. Stanley and Marguerite (Winter) Kulp; B.A. in Polit. Sci. and Public Adminstrn.. U. Calif., Berkeley, 1943, M.A. in Polit. Sci., 1950; m. Ted D. Johnston; children—Michael, Stanley, Marguerite. Sec. office of pres. and gen. mgr. Bechtel Corp., San Francisco, 1938-39; field time-checker Kaiser Shipyards, Richmond, Calif., 1943-44; with U. Calif., Berkeley, 1953-58, social sec. Office of Chancellor, also Office of Pres., 1958-68, adminstrv. asst. Centennial Office, 1967-69, asst. for social events Pres.'s Immediate Office, 1968; cons. numerous colls. and orgns.; seminar speaker, discussion leader Presidents' Inst., Am. Council Edn., 1974, 75, ann. meeting Assn. Am. Univs., 1978. Mem. adv. com. on edn. of women Berkeley Unified Sch. Dist., 1966-67, mem. master plan com., 1967-69; mem. spl. com. for 100th concert Cazadero Music Camp, City of Berkeley, 1975; mem. Univ. Art Mus. Council, 1975—, pres., 1977-79; mem. spl. adv. com. Faculty Club, U. Calif., Berkeley, 1977-81; mem. exec. com. People for Open Space, 1979—; pres. Gavel, 1943—. Mem. Prytanean Soc., Mortar Bd. (v.p. 1942-43), U. Calif., Berkeley Alumni Assn., Pi Sigma Alpha. Club: Commonwealth of California. Office: President's House 70 Rincon Rd Kensington CA 94707

JOHNSTON, MARY HOLLIS, clin. psychologist; b. Woodward, Okla., Oct. 19, 1946; d. James Quincy and Mary Alda (Neighbor) Johnston; A.B. summa cum laude, Carleton Coll., 1968; M.A., U. Chgo., 1970, Ph.D. (NDEA fellow), 1975; m. Randall Roy Rowlett, Mar. 20, 1976; 1 son, Nathan Aaron. Research asst. U. Chgo. Hosp., 1970-74; research psychologist Michael Reese Hosp., Chgo., 1974-75; asst. prof. psychology and psychiatry U. Ill. Med. Center, Chgo., 1975-81; mem. faculty Erikson Inst. Early Edn., Chgo., 1976—; psychol. cons. Virginia Frank Child Devel. Center, Chgo., 1974—. Registered psychologist, Ill. Mem. Am. Psychol. Assn., Soc. Personality Assessment, Chgo. Assn. Psychoanalytic Psychology, Phi Beta Kappa, Sigma Xi. Author: Assessing Schizophrenic Thinking, A Clinical and Research Instrument for Measuring Thought Disorder, 1979. Home and office: 5404 S Kimbark Ave Chicago IL 60615

JOHNSTON, MARY ROSELIND, accountant; b. Harlingen, Tex., Apr. 16, 1944; d. Aaron and Lucy (Salinas) J.; B.B.A., U. Tex., Austin, 1966. Personal acct. to Fred J. Heyne, Jr., Houston, 1966-70; sr. and mgr. level acct. G.C. Branum & Co., C.P.A.s, Houston, 1970-79; pres. Roselind Johnston, P.C., Houston, 1979—, Nicholson Co., Inc., 1981—; mng. partner Johnston, Reinhardt & Assos., 1982—. C.P.A., Tex. Mem. Am. Inst. C.P.A.s, Tex. Soc. C.P.A.s. Roman Catholic. Home: 5801 Lumberdale St Townhouse 124 Houston TX 77092 Office: 720 N Post Oak Rd Suite 344 Houston TX 77024

JOHNSTON, MARY WILL, manpower/mgmt. analyst, assn. exec.; b. Newell, Ala.; d. David Eugene and Mamie Heptinstall Johnston; B.A. in Bus. Adminstrn., Jacksonville State U., 1972. Sec., office mgr. Boy Scouts Am., 1947-51; sec., edn. technician U.S. Army Chem. Center and Sch., 1951-73; sec./clk., directorate of indsl. ops. Ft. McClellan, Ala., 1973-75; sec., program/budget analyst U.S. Army M.P. Sch., Ft. McClellan, 1975—, program budget/manpower analyst, 1980—. Past pres. Nat. Secs. Assn. Cert. profl. sec. Mem. Beta Sigma Phi (pres. 1976-77, sec. Anniston city council 1979-80). Home: 1130 Christine Ave Apt 15 Anniston AL 36201 Office: Mgmt Office US Army Mil Police Fort McClellan AL 36205

JOHNSTON, PATRICIA VEITCH, food scientist; b. Liverpool, Eng., Mar. 15, 1932; d. Sidney Herbert and Lilian (Veitch) J.; came to U.S., 1968, naturalized, 1979; MRIC (King George VI Meml. fellow 1954-55), Liverpool Poly., 1954; M.S. (Grad. Coll. fellow 1954-55), U. Ill., 1956, Ph.D., 1957. Asst. prof. food sci. U. Ill., 1958-61, vis. asst. prof., 1966-71, asso. prof., 1971-78, prof. food sci. and nutritional scis., 1978—; hon. lectr. dept. anatomy Univ. Coll., London, 1962-66. Mem. Am. Inst. Nutrition, Royal Soc. Chemistry, Soc. Neurochemistry, Soc. Neurosci., Sigma Xi. Author articles in field. Asso. editor Lipids, 1974—. Office: 1208 W Pennsylvania St Rm 205 U Ill Urbana IL 61801

JOHNSTON, RUBY CHARLOTTE, nurse; b. Freedom, Nebr., Oct. 6, 1918; d. William Murray and Delia Isabel (Morgan) Phillips; student Nebr. Sch. Agr., Curtis, 1932-36, U. Colo., Boulder, summer 1938; R.N., Denver Gen. Hosp., 1945; m. Gerald William Johnston, Sept. 19, 1943; 1 son, Leo F. Rural sch. tchr., 1936-41; sec. supt.'s office Nebr. Sch. Agr., 1941-42; staff nurse Denver Gen. Hosp., 1945-46; office nurse, Cambridge, Nebr., 1946-47; staff nurse St. Catherine's Hosp., McCook, Nebr., 1947-56, LaGrange County Hosp., LaGrange, Ind., 1956-58; obstet. supr. LaGrange County Hosp., 1958-68, dir. nurses, 1968-70; dir. nurses Miller's Merry Manor, LaGrange, 1970-76; county health nurse LaGrange County Health Dept., LaGrange, 1976—; chmn. exec. com. Ind. Nurses Assn. Geriatric Conf., 1975-77. Bd. dirs. Mental Health Assn. LaGrange County, 1979—, N.E. Ind. chpt. Am. Lung Assn., 1981—; Co-coordinator Focus on Health, LaGrange, 1982. Registered Mem. Ind. Nurses Assn., Nurses Assn. Am. Coll. Obstetricians and Gynecologists, Ind. Public Health Assn., Am. Legion Aux. Republican. Presbyterian. Clubs: Bus. and Profl. Women's, New Century, Eastern Star. Home: Rural Route 2 Box 107C Howe IN 46746 Office: 100 N Detroit St LaGrange IN 46761

JOHNSTON, SUSAN HOLYOKE, social worker; b. Evanston, Ill., Mar. 22, 1948; d. Robert Harold and Audra Winifred (McLean) Holyoke; B.A. with high honors, Mich. State U., 1970; M.S.W., San Diego State U., 1973; m. Charles Richard Johnston, Jr., Aug. 22, 1970; children— Kylie McLean, Ryan Holyoke. Counselor emotionally disturbed adolescents Town House Found., San Diego, 1972-73; social worker Cambridgeshire County Council, Cambridge, Eng., 1973-74; family counselor Family Services Assn., San Diego, 1975-76; mental health therapist Mt. Vernon Center for Community Mental Health, Alexandria, Va., 1976-80; regional counselor Youth for Understanding, Washington, 1977-79; pvt. practice clin. social work, Alexandria, 1977—. Charter mem. mgmt. com. Women's Room and Resource Center, Alexandria Community Y, 1979; v.p. Growing Women Inc., Silver Spring, Md., 1978-79; co-founder Potomac Psychol. Resources, 1981. Cert. social worker, Md.; lic. clin. social worker, Va.; lic. marriage, family and child counselor, Calif. Mem. Nat. Assn. Social Workers, Acad. Cert. Social Workers, NOW, Phi Beta Kappa, Phi Kappa Phi, Alpha Lambda Delta, Tau Sigma. Home: 2820 S Abingdon St Apt C-1 Arlington VA 22206 Office: 1225 Martha Custis Dr Suite Z Alexandria VA 22302

JOHNSTON, VIRGINIA EVELYN, editor; b. Spokane, Wash., Apr. 26, 1933; d. Edwin and Emma Lucile (Munroe) Rowe; student Portland Community Coll., 1964, Portland State U., 1966, 78-79; m. Alan Paul Beckley, Dec. 26, 1974; children—Chris, Denise, Rex. Proofreader, The Oregonian, Portland, 1960-62, teletypesetter operator, 1962-66, operator Photon 200, 1966-68, copy editor, asst. women's editor, 1968-80, spl. sects. editor (UPDATE), 1981—; editor (FOODday/UPDATE), 1982—; pres. Matrix Assos., Inc., Portland, 1975—, chmn. bd., 1979—; cons. Democratic party Oreg., 1969, Portland Sch. Dist. No. 1, 1978. Mem. Women in Communications, Inc., Inst. Profl. and Managerial Women, Nat. Assn. Female Execs. Democrat. Editor Principles of Computer Systems for Newspaper Mgmt., 1975-76. Home: 4140 NE 137th Ave Portland OR 97230 Office: 1320 SW Broadway Portland OR 97201

JOINER, VIVIAN NADINE WILKERSON, ins. co. exec.; b. Little Rock, Dec. 29, 1941; d. Robert Edward and Ora Vivian (Greene) Wilkerson; student public schs., Little Rock; m. Ralph Phillip Joiner, May 30, 1959; children—Phillip Wayne, Kelli Nicole. Asst. sec. Am. Found. Life Ins. Co., Little Rock, 1975-77, sec.-asst. treas., 1977-79, sec.-treas., Birmingham, Ala., 1979-81, v.p., sec.-treas., 1981—. Fellow Life Mgmt. Inst., Life Office Mgmt. Assn.; mem. Am. Soc. Personnel Adminstrs. Home: 5057 Pinehurst Terr Birmingham AL 35243 Office: Am Found Life Ins Co 530 Beacon Pkwy W Birmingham AL 35209

JOLLEY, MARGIE TOWNSEND, lawyer, clin. psychologist; b. Atlanta, Nov. 8, 1947; d. Warner Leon and Margaret (Chapman) Townsend; B.A., Emory U., 1970; M.S., Fla. State U., 1972, Ph.D., 1974; J.D., U. Miami, 1979. Clin. psychology intern W.Va. U. Med. Center and Robert F. Kennedy Youth Center, Morgantown, 1973-74; research asso. U. South Fla., Tampa, 1975-76; admitted to Fla. bar, 1979, N.Y. State bar, 1980; mem. firm Cadwalader, Wickersham & Taft, N.Y.C., 1979-80, Gunster, Yoakley, Criser & Stewart, Palm Beach, Fla., 1980-81; pvt. practice law, 1981—; pvt. practice clin. psychology, 1981—. Mem. Am. Psychol. Assn., Fla. Psychol. Assn. (Palm Beach chpt. ethics com.), Broward County Soc. Profl. Psychologists, Dade County Psychol. Assn., Am. Bar Assn., Soc. Psychol. Study Social Issues. Democrat. Methodist. Contbr. articles to profl. jours. Home: 5460 N Ocean Blvd Apt 1-C Singer Island FL 33404 Office: Law Bldg 315 3d St West Palm Beach FL 33401 also Community Profl Bldg 2151 45th St Suite 302 West Palm Beach FL 33407

JONA, MARJORIE HELEN PUGH, city ofcl.; b. Mansfield, Ohio, July 18, 1917; d. Walter C. and Hasel (Kennedy) Pugh; student Richland County Jr. Coll., 1934-35, Mansfield Bus. Coll., 1935-36. div. 1956; 1 son, Robert P. K. Clk., Reese Optical Co., Mansfield, 1936-43; sec. P & E. Tile Co., Los Angeles, 1953-54, Hamilton Realty, Mansfield, 1951-52, 55; sales rep. Mid-Ohio Realty, Mansfield, 1955-56; X-ray technologist Mansfield Gen. Hosp., 1956-57, registered X-ray technologist Madison Hosp., Mansfield, 1957-60; with Richland County Welfare Dept., 1960-69, social worker intake dept., food stamp dept., 1967-69; probation officer Domestic Relations div. Richland County Ct. Common Pleas, 1969-74; income maintenance worker Richland County Dept. Welfare, 1975-76; probation officer City of Mansfield Municipal Ct., 1976—. Sec. adv. bd. Richland County Welfare, 1969-74. Treas., Malabar Music Parents Club, 1967-68. Mem. Am. Registry Radiol. Technologists. Methodist. Clubs: Order Eastern Star, Rebekah Lodge. Home: 207 S Mulberry St Mansfield OH 44903 Office: Mansfield Municipal Ct City Bldg 30 N Diamond St Mansfield OH 44902

JONAS, ANA MASIULIS, biochemist; b. Rokiskis, Lithuania, Nov. 24, 1943; came to U.S., 1962, naturalized, 1967; d. Antanas and Stefania (Paalksnis) Masiulis; B.S. (scholar), U. Ill., Chgo., 1966; Ph.D., U. Ill., Urbana, 1970; m. Jiri Jonas, June 1, 1968. Hematology lab. technician Presbyn. St. Luke's Hosp., Chgo., 1964-66; research and teaching asst. chemistry U. Ill., Urbana, 1966-70, postdoctoral trainee NIH in biochemistry, 1970-73, asst. prof. biochemistry, 1974-79, assoc. prof., 1979—; cons. NIH, Ill. Heart Assn.; public speaker, TV appearances. Recipient B.B. Freud award in chemistry, 1973; NATO postdoctoral fellow in sci., 1973; investigator Am. Heart Assn., 1974-79; Fogarty Internat. fellow, 1981; grantee NIH, Am. Heart Assn. Fellow Council Arteriosclerosis Am. Heart Assn.; mem. Am. Soc. Biol. Chemists, Am. Heart Assn., Ill. Heart Assn., N.Y. Acad. Scis. Roman Catholic. Clubs: U. Ill. Tennis, Naples Bath and Tennis. Contbr. articles, revs. and abstracts to profl. jours. Home: 2202 Grange Circle Urbana IL 61801 Office: University of Illinois 506 S Mathews Ave Urbana IL 61801

JONAS, HILDA, harpsichordist, pianist; b. Duesseldorf, Ger., Jan. 21, 1913; came to. U.S., 1938, naturalized, 1943; d. Moritz and Ann (Lilienfeld) Klestadt; student Hochschule Musik, Cologne, 1932-33; diploma Gumpert Conservatory, Duesseldorf, 1934; pupil of Rudolf Serkin, Wanda Landowska; m. Gerald Jonas, Jan. 30, 1938; children—Susanne Leilani, Linda Irene. Owner pvt. piano studio, Honolulu, 1938-42, Cin., 1942-75; soloist maj. orchs. throughout world, 1932—; solo recitalist throughout world, 1932—; founder Put-in-Bay Harpsichord Festival, 1965, dir., 1965-75; rec. artist Educo, Sanjo Music; harpsichordist for rec. Johann Kuknau: Six Biblical Sonatas. Life mem. Brandeis Hadassah. Jewish. Author articles in field. Address: 50 Chumasero Dr San Francisco CA 94132

JONAS-CLUFF, MARY THELMA RAY, bus. analysis cons.; b. Lenoir, N.C., Jan. 16, 1915; d. Robert Lee and Jennie Estelle (Keller) Ray; student Lenoir Bus. Coll., Phoenix Coll., Mesa Community Coll.; m. John Kaiser Jonas, July 5, 1931 (div. 1941); 1 son, John Kaiser; m. 2d, David Lamar Cluff, Sept. 8, 1956 (div. 1969). Accountant, Smith Ford Motor Co., Lenoir, 1936; owner, mgr. apt. bldg., Atlanta, also credit mgr. Sherwin-Williams Co., 1943-48; owner, mgr. jewelry concession Newberry's, Montgomery, Ala., 1948-49, fashion shop Thelma Jonas, Charlotte, N.C., 1950-51; buyer for splty. fashion stores, 1952-56; engaged in acctg., Phoenix, 1956-74; bus. analyst cons., Tempe, Ariz., 1975—. Mem. Ariz. Soc. Practicing Accountants (pres. 1980-81), Nat. Soc. Public Accts. Mormon. Home: 231 N Robson St Apt 3 Mesa AZ 85201 Office: 201 E Southern St Suite 100 Tempe AZ 85282

JONES, ALICE HANSON, economist; b. Seattle, Nov. 7, 1904; d. Olof and Agatha Marie (Tiegel) Hanson; A.B., U. Wash., Seattle, 1925, M.A., 1928; postgrad. U. Chgo., 1928-29, 32-34, Ph.D., 1968; m. Homer Jones, Apr. 21, 1930; children—Robert Hanson, Richard John, Douglas Coulthurst. Teaching fellow U. Wash., 1927-28; fellow, research asst. U. Chgo., 1928-29, 32-34; asst. editor Ency. Social Scis., N.Y.C., 1930; economist, asst. chief Cost-of-Living div. U.S. Bur. Labor Stats., Washington, 1934-44, other fed. agys., 1945-48, 58-61; econs. lectr. to prof. Washington U., St. Louis, 1963-77, prof. emeritus, 1977—; adj. econs. prof. Claremont Men's Coll., 1973-74; research writer Pres.'s Com. on Social Trends, N.Y.C., 1931; econ. adv. Bank of Korea, U.S.

AID, 1967-68. Research grants panelist Nat. Endowment for Humanities, 1974-75. NSF research grantee, 1969-75; Nat. Endowment for Humanities research grantee, 1970-76; named Woman of Achievement, St. Louis Globe Democrat, 1980. Mem. Am. Econ. Assn. (asso. mem. com. on status of women in econs. profession, 1972-76), Econ. History Assn. (pres. 1982-83), Internat. Assn. for Research in Income and Wealth, Orgn. Am. Historians, Inst. Early Am. History and Culture (asso.), Social Sci. History Assn., Soc. Profs. Emeriti Washington U. (pres.-elect, sec. 1982), Mortar Board, Phi Beta Kappa, Omicron Delta Epsilon, Beta Phi Alpha (nat. pres., 1932-34), Delta Zeta (Woman of Yr. 1981). Contbr. articles to encys., govt. and profl. publs.; author: American Colonial Wealth: Documents and Methods, 3 vols., rev. ed., 1978; Wealth of a Nation to Be, 1980. Home: 404 Yorkshire Pl Webster Groves MO 63119 Office: Dept Econs Washington Univ Saint Louis MO 63130

JONES, ALYCE HONORE, communications specialist; b. Prairie View, Tex., May 19, 1948; d. John Clayborne and Priscilla Carrie (Jackson) Honore; B.A., Prairie View A&M U., 1969; M.Ed., Tex. So. U., 1976; postgrad. U. Houston, 1977—; m. Robert J. Jones, Dec. 21, 1979; 2 sons, 1 dau. Research supr. reservoir behavior Exxon Co. U.S.A., Houston, 1970-76; word processing coordinator Vinson & Elkins Law Firm, Houston, 1977—. Vol. guidance counselor; polls vol. registration and sr. citizens transp.; vol. Julia C. Hester House; advisor Young People's Aux. of Mt. Horem Baptist Ch.; counselor Concerned Teens, Big Sister Exxon Vol. Program, 1974-76; bd. dirs., word processing advisor Houston Community Coll. Recipient VIP Profl. service award Exxon, 1975. Mem. Internat. Word Processing Assn., Am. Bus. Women's Assn., Nat. Assn. Negro Bus. and Profl. Women, Nat. Assn. Female Execs., Urban League, Nat. Council Negro Women, Operation Breadbasket, Nat. Assn. Black Women in Bus. and Industry, Eta Phi Beta. Democrat. Methodist. Club: Eastern Star. Home: 4635 Smooth Oak Ln Houston TX 77053 Office: 7135 Ardmore St Houston TX 77001

JONES, ANN BREWSTER, priest; b. Portland, Oreg., Dec. 10, 1952; d. Howard Richard and Marjean Eleanor (Erickson) J.; B.S., U. Rochester, 1974; M. Div., Va. Theol. Sem., 1977. Ordained priest Episcopal Ch.; asso. rector St. John's Ch., Washington, 1977-80, St. James's Ch., N.Y.C., 1980—; lectr. in field. Mem. Hyde Sch. Neighborhood Council, Washington, 1978-80; exec. alumni council, fund raiser Kent Sch., 1978—; mem. exec. alumni council Va. Theol. Sem., 1982—. Mem. Washington Episcopal Clergy Assn., Evang. Edn. Soc. Contbg. author: Prayer Book Manual, 1981. Office: 865 Madison Ave New York NY 10021 *

JONES, A(NNE) ELIZABETH, fgn. service officer; b. Munich, W. Ger., May 6, 1948 (parents Am. citizens); d. William Charles, III, Sara Demarest (Ferris) J.; B.A., Swarthmore (Pa.) Coll., 1970; diploma advanced Arabic lang., Am. U., Cairo, 1977; m. Thomas A. Homan, Apr. 9, 1977; children—Todd William, Courtney Anne. Joined U.S. Fgn. Service, 1970; services in Cairo, Kabul, Afghanistan and Amman, Jordan; dep. prin. officer, polit. officer diplomatic mission, Baghdad, Iraq, 1979-80; country officer for Lebanon, Dept. State, Washington, 1981-82, dep. dir. office for Jordan, Syria, Iraq, Lebanon, 1982—. Bd. dirs. Am. Fgn. Service Protective Assn. Recipient Meritorious Honor award Dept. State, 1975. Mem. Am. Fgn. Service Assn., Dept. State Women's Action Orgn., NOW. Address: 4425 Brandywine St NW Washington DC 20016

JONES, ANNE HUDSON, educator; b. El Dorado, Ark., Nov. 14, 1944; d. Thomas Jefferson Hudson and Ethel May (Sprankle) Hudson Bonner; B.A. magna cum laude (Nat. Merit Scholar), La. State U., 1965; Ph.D., (NDEA fellow), U. N.C., Chapel Hill, 1974; m. Robert Leslie Jones, Mar. 19, 1971. Asst. prof. English, Va. Wesleyan Coll., Norfolk, 1970-71; instr., asst. prof. Va. Poly. Inst. and State U., Blacksburg, 1973-78, asst. dir. Center for Programs in Humanities, 1978; asst. prof. lit. and medicine Inst. Med. Humanities, U. Tex. Med. Br., Galveston, 1979—; mem. nat. bd. cons. Nat. Endowment Humanities, 1977—. Co-convenor, treas. NOW, Blacksburg, 1976. Mem. Galveston Hist. Found., Galveston County Cultural Arts Council, Am. Comparative Lit. Assn., MLA, Womens Caucus for Modern Langs., Soc. Health and Human Values, Inst. Society, Ethics and Life Scis., Sci. Fiction Research Assn., Soc. Tech. Communication, Am. Med. Writers Assn. Editorial bd. The Comparatist, 1977—, Tex. Reports on Biology and Medicine, 1979—, Lit. and Medicine, 1979—; contbr. articles to profl. jours. Office: Inst Med Humanities U Tex Med Br Galveston TX 77550

JONES, ARTENCER CLAY, indsl. relations exec.; b. Bklyn., Feb. 6, 1932; d. Addison and Henrietta Jenkins; student N.Y.C. Community Coll., 1972-73; B.A., Bklyn. Coll., 1979; m. Ben Jones, Nov. 12, 1961; 1 son, Keith. Personnel coordinator employment and tng. Western Union Telegraph, N.Y.C., 1970-73, mgr. customer service Internat. Bur., 1973-74; ops. mgr. Opportunities Industrialization Center, N.Y.C., 1974-76, mgr. job devel., 1976—. Adviser Jr. Achievement, 1971-73; mem. exec. bd. Crispus Attucks polit. club, 1971-76; mem. Community Planning Bd., 1974-76. Recipient Outstanding Service award Opportunities Industrialization Center, 1970. Democrat. Baptist. Club: Order Eastern Star. Office: 460 Park Ave S New York NY 10016

JONES, AUDREY HOWARD, utility exec.; b. Bklyn., May 13, 1928; d. Edward Richard and Venie Ednora (Jacobs) Howard; B.A., Hunter Coll., 1949; M.S. in Marine Sci., L.I.U., 1969; m. Farrell Jones, June 16, 1951; children—Joanne Kathryn and Jacqueline Elinor (twins). Research biochemist Manhattan Eye, Ear and Throat Hosp., 1949-51, Downstate Med. Coll., SUNY, Bklyn., 1952-58; instr. biology Nassau Community Coll., Garden City, N.Y., also cons. Environ. Assos. and Urban Edn., Inc., 1970-73; environ. scientist, then EEO mgr. L.I. Lighting Co., Hicksville, N.Y., 1972-79, personnel policies and services mgr., 1979—; adj. asst. prof. N.Y. Inst. Tech., 1979-80; field faculty adv. Goddard grad. program Norwich U.; lectr. SUNY, Farmingdale; mem. career services adv. bd. Adelphi U., 1981—. Mem. citizens adv. com. N.Y. State Coastal Zone Mgmt. Program; mem. L.I. regional adv. com. N.Y. State External High Sch. Diploma Program; del. 10th Jud. Dist. Democratic Conv. Recipient various service awards, certs. appreciation. Mem. Am. Gas Assn. (urban affairs com.), Edison Electric Inst. (tng. and mgmt. devel. com.), L.I. Assn. (chmn. personnel dirs. council 1980-81), LWV, NAACP, 110 Center for Bus. and Profl. Women (pres.), Delta Sigma Theta. Democrat. Unitarian-Universalist. Clubs: Zonta, 100 Black Women of L.I. Home: 22 Driftwood Dr Port Washington NY 11050 Office: LILCO 175 E Old Country Rd Hicksville NY 11801

JONES, BARBARA, pediatricians; b. Salt Lake City, Feb. 8, 1928; d. George M. and Helen J.; A.B., Stanford U., 1949; M.D., U. Utah, 1952. Intern, St. Louis Children's Hosp., 1952-53, resident in pediatrics, 1953-55; asst. in pediatric research Washington U., St. Louis, 1955, instr., 1955-57, research fellow in pediatrics, 1957-58, asst. prof., 1958-61; mem. faculty W.Va. U., Morgantown, 1967—, prof., 1968—, asso. chmn. dept., 1979-82, chmn., 1982—; mem. clin. cancer project, cancer center rev. com. Nat. Cancer Inst. Mem. Am. Acad. Pediatrics (alt. dist. chmn. dist. III), Am. Pediatric Soc., Soc. Pediatrics Research, Am. Acad. Pediatrics, Am. Soc. Hematology, Am. Soc. Clin. Oncology, Am. Assn. Cancer Research, Soc. Internat. Oncology Pediatrics. Episcopalian. Contbr. articles to profl. jours.; author: Acute Lymphoblastic Leukemia in Cancer Medicine, 1982. Home: 667 Bellaire Dr Morgantown WV 26505 Office: Dept Pediatrics W Va U Med Center Morgantown WV 26506

JONES, BARBARA LOUISE, legal asst.; b. Steubenville, Ohio, Nov. 11, 1942; d. David LaDomus and Dorothy (Kottnauer) Huestis; B.A., Denison U., 1963; M.A., U. Mich., 1965. Tchr., Garden City, Mich., 1963-64, Milan, Mich., 1965-68, Saugus, Mass., 1968-71; asst. to planner-coordinator N.H. Gov.'s Commn. on Crime and Delinquency, summer 1971; adminstrv. legal asst., exec. sec. to sr. partner law firm Stebbins, Bradley, Wood & Harvey, Hanover, N.H., 1971—. Mem. City Council Lebanon, 1975-82, dep. mayor, 1979-81, chmn. city mgr. selection com., 1979, mem. charter revision commn., 1976-77, council rep. to recreation commn., 1981, Lebanon rep. to Upper Valley Lake Sunapee Council, 1982—, ward clk., 1973-75; bd. govs. W. Central N.H. Community Mental Health Services, 1981—; pres. Terrace View Condominium Assn.; trustee Lebanon Coll., 1976—. NDEA Inst. postgrad. fellow Eastern Mich. U. summer 1967. Mem. NEA, Nat. Assn. Legal Secs., Women's Network Upper Valley, LWV. Clubs: Appalachian Mountain, Trout Unltd. Address: 16 Terrace View Lebanon NH 03766

JONES, BECKY LOU, optical products co. mgr.; b. Minden, La., Jan. 28, 1937; d. James Lemiel and Jennie Margaret (Searles) J.; B.S., La. Tech. U., 1959. Tchr. sci. public schs., Heflin, La., 1959-60; home service advisor Gulf States Utilities, Port Arthur, Tex., 1960-69; publicist Corning Glass Works, N.Y.C., 1969-73, supr. product info., 1973-76, advt. mgr., 1977-78, sales mgr. N.W. region, 1979, sales and mktg. mgr. optical products, Corning, N.Y., 1980—. Trustee COREPAC, 1977-78. Recipient Nktg. Excellence award Pres.'s Mktg. Council Corning Glass Works. Mem. Am. Women in Radio and TV, Public Relations Soc. Am., Am. Home Econs. Assn., Home Economists in Bus. (nat. dir. 1976). Republican. Methodist. Home: 4 Timber Ln Painted Post NY 14870 Office: Rt 17 Corning NY 14831

JONES, BETTY ANN, art publisher; b. Clarksdale, Miss., Mar. 31, 1943; d. Meade Merrill and Frances Lou (Pirtle) Goode; B.S., Ala. Coll., 1965; postgrad. U. Ala., 1970, Massey Coll., 1966-69; children—Robert Benford, Michael Edwin. Editor, mng. editor, prodn. mgr. Oxmoor House, Birmingham, Ala., 1969-75, advt. mgr., sales promotion mgr., 1976-77, dir. mktg. program mgr., 1978-80; mgr. So. Living Gallery, art and collectible pub., Birmingham, 1981—; guest lectr. U. Ala. Active PTA, Boy Scouts Am., Jr. Achievement. Mem. Nat. Assn. Female Execs., Direct Mail Mktg. Assn. (cert. of creative recognition 1975), Am. Mgmt. Assn. Democrat. Baptist. Home: 5121 Selkirk Dr Birmingham AL 35243 Office: PO Box 2262 Birmingham AL 35201

JONES, BETTY CHEYNE, social worker; b. Chateaugay, N.Y., Nov. 1, 1928; d. Clayton T. and Amelia (Richey) Cheyne; B.A., Hartwick Coll., 1953; M.S. in Social Work (AAUW fellow), Columbia U., 1955; m. Rees Jones, Dec. 4, 1971. Social worker Big Sisters, N.Y.C., 1955-56, N.Y.C. Youth Bd., 1956-59; research caseworker Community Service Soc., N.Y.C., 1959-61; dir. permanency services Edwin Gould Services for Children, N.Y.C., 1961-75; asst. exec. dir. Brookwood Child Care, Bklyn., from 1975, now acting exec. dir.; cons. N.Y. State legis. coms., 1973—; mem. adv. com. Puerto Rican Family Inst., 1979—, bd. dirs., 1954-64; condr. workshops and seminars for profl. groups, 1969—. Elder, 1st Presbyn. Ch., N.Y.C., 1971-73, 75-78; bd. dirs. Presbyn. Sr. Services, 1975-78, sec. 1975-78. Mem. Acad. Cert. Social Workers, Nat. Assn. Social Workers, Columbia U. Sch. Social Work Alumni Assn., Hartwick Coll. Alumni Assn. Home: 3 Stuyvesant Oval New York NY 10009 Office: 363 Adelphi St Brooklyn NY 11238

JONES, BETTY HARRIS, educator; b. St. Louis, May 25, 1937; d. Homer and Pearl (Fulgham) Harris; A.B., Rutgers U., 1967; M.A., Bryn Mawr Coll., 1968, Ph.D., 1972; m. Calvin Walter Jones, Dec. 2, 1954; children—Christopher Walter, Nicholas Alexander. Instr. in English, Rutgers U., Camden, N.J., 1969-72, asst. prof., 1972—; bd. dirs. Burlington County Opportunities Industrialization Centers. Grad. collector in English, Bryn Mawr Coll., mem. bd. cons., 1974-76. Danforth Found. fellow, 1967-68; Danforth Found. asso., 1972; Rutgers U. summer fellow, 1975, faculty fellow, 1977; nominee Lindback award for excellence in coll. teaching, 1970, 77. Mem. MLA, AAUP, N.J. Coll. English Assn., Contbr. articles to profl. jours. Home: 42 Norman Ln Willingboro NJ 08046 Office: Rutgers U Camden NJ 08102

JONES, BILLIE JUNE HAND, nurse; b. St. Louis, Jan. 23, 1925; d. William G. and Robbie Omega (Taylor) Day; R.N., U. Tex., 1946; m. Alfred P. Jones, May 8, 1949. Pvt. duty nursing, Houston, 1946-47; supr. nursing, Dayton, Tex., 1947-48; staff nurse St. Joseph Hosp., Houston, 1948-49, Hermann Hosp., Houston, 1950-51; head nurse Bataan Meml. Hosp., Albuquerque, 1952-55; head nurse, relief supr. VA Hosp., Albuquerque, 1955-66; relief nurse Student Health of U. N.Mex., 1966-67; nursing instr. Job Corps for Women, Albuquerque, 1968; inservice nursing instr. Univ. Heights Hosp., Albuquerque, 1969-73; staff nurse BCMC Hosp., Albuquerque, 1973-74; med. claims rev. and claims auditor Blue Cross-Blue Shield of N.Mex., Albuquerque, 1974—; relief nurse Presbyn. Hosp. Mem. N.Mex. Nurses Assn. (pres. Dist. 1 1967). Methodist. Clubs: Nat. Appaloosa Horse, N.Mex. Appaloosa Racing Assn., N.Mex. Appaloosa Horse (treas. 1970-76). Home: 117 Diers Rd NW Albuquerque NM 87114 Office: 12800 Indian School Rd NE Albuquerque NM 87112

JONES, BONNIE ALLEN, florist, floral designer; b. Daytona Beach, Fla., Apr. 29, 1940; d. Myron Lewis and Violet E. (Hogg) Allen; student public schs., Greenville, S.C.; children—Joni Sue, Steven Larry, Martin Allen. Co-owner, v.p., sec. La Bon Greens, Inc., Pierson, Fla., 1960-76; owner, mgr. Bonnie Jones Fernery, Pierson, 1977-80; owner, operator Le Bon Greens, 1980—; owner, operator Town N Country Florist & Gifts, 1981—. Mem. adv. bd. Human Resource Center, 1981—; mem. West Volusia Zoning Bd., 1982—. Mem. Nat. Assn. Female Execs., Am. Bus. Womens Assn., Fla. Fern Growers Assn., Wholesale Florists and Floral Suppliers Am., U.S. C. of C., Soc. Am. Florists. Democrat. Lutheran. Office: 628 Minshew Rd Pierson FL 32080

JONES, CAROLYN JANE, clergywoman; b. Grove City, Pa., Jan. 28, 1937; d. Hester Clark and Winifred Eleanor (Hoag) J.; B.A., Westminster Coll. (Pa.), 1958; M.A. in Edn., Syracuse U., 1963; M.Div., Pitts. Theol. Sem., 1977. Tchr., Am. Coll. for Girls (now Ramses Coll.), Cairo, Egypt, 1958-61, Bethel Park (Pa.) High Sch., 1963-68; asst. dean of women Syracuse (N.Y.) U., 1968-71, dir., asst. dir. activities and orgns. Office Student Affairs, 1971-74; asso. in Christian edn. Pebble Hill Presbyn. Ch., DeWitt, N.Y., 1971-74; dir. Christian edn. Newlonsburg United Presbyn. Ch., Murrysville, Pa., 1975-77; ordained to ministry United Presbyn. Ch., 1977; asso. pastor Glenshaw (Pa.) Presbyn. Ch., 1977—; bd. dirs. Pitts. Theol. Sem.; bd. mgrs. New Wilmington Missionary Conf. Thomas Jamison scholar, 1977; Sylvester S. Marvin Meml. fellow, 1977. Mem. Cleric of Pitts., Assn. Presbyn. Ch. Educators. Home: 103 Calmwood Dr Glenshaw PA 15116 Office: 300 Glenn Ave Glenshaw PA 15116

JONES, CATHERINE ANN DELANTY, librarian; b. Conneaut, Ohio, Apr. 30, 1936; d. Leo Joseph and Mary Louise (McGinty) Delanty; B.A., U. Ala., 1965; M.S. in Library Sci., Cath. U. Am., 1969; M.A. in Govt., George Washington U., 1980; m. Thomas Michael Jones, May 18, 1957; 1 son, Michael S. Library chief reference and loan Office of Mgmt. and Budget, Exec. Office of Pres., Washington, 1967-72; asso. dir. Washington office ALA, 1972-73; asst. univ. librarian for reader services George Washington U., Washington, 1973-78; chief congressional reference div. Congressional Research Service, Library of Congress, Washington, 1978—. Mem. ALA, D.C. Library Assn. (pres. 1977-78), Cath. U. Library Sci. Alumni Assn. (pres. 1977-78), Spl. Libraries Assn. (pres.-elect 1981), Am. Soc. Public Adminstrs. Roman Catholic. Office: Congressional Research Service Library of Congress 10 First St SE Washington DC 20540

JONES, CLARICE RHODES, educator; b. Houston, Dec. 31, 1925; d. Charles Benton and Fannie Lillian (Bailey) Rhodes; B.A., Tex. State U., 1949; M.S. in Edn., U. So. Calif., 1969; 1 dau., Iverne Clarice. Profl. dancer with Carmen Jones, 1943-44, with Katherine Dunham, 1945-46; tchr. phys. edn., public schs., Houston, 1951-54; recreation dir., dance specialist City of Los Angeles, 1955-62; tchr. spl. edn., public schs., Duarte, Calif., 1963-69; tchr. 4th grade, public schs., Inglewood, Calif., 1970—; chairperson parent participation Sch. Adv. Council, Clyde Woodworth Sch., Inglewood; mem. consold. application adv. com. Project Invest. Mem. Calif. Tchrs. Assn., NEA, NAACP, Nat. Council Negro Women, YWCA, Los Angeles Urban League, Inst. Religious Sci., Delta Sigma Theta, Chi Kappa Rho. Democrat. Home: 7818 S Harvard Blvd Los Angeles CA 90047 Office: 3200 w 104th Inglewood CA 90303

JONES, CORINNE MALMIN, writer; b. Mary's Igloo, Alaska, Nov. 14, 1918; d. Cornelius Knutson and Christine (Skillingstad) Malmin; student Pacific Luth. U., 1936-38; children—Jan W. Sande, Christine Jones Chagnon, Rebecca Jones Murphy. Rewriter, Alaska Sportsman mag., Ketchikan, 1938-42; office worker, Seattle, 1942-46; saleswoman, 1946-48; office worker, Fairbanks, Alaska, 1948-50, St. Louis, Houston, 1950-52; with direct sales, Valdez, Alaska, 1953-58; editor, writer This Alaska mag. and Our Alaska Bus. & People mag., 1971-78; news and feature writer Anchorage (Alaska) Daily News, 1976; corp. sec. Gallagher-Jones & Assos., Inc., Anchorage, 1973—; writer Alaska Industry mag., Wien Air Alaska mag. Recipient certs. Am. Soc. Safety Engrs., 1979, Mine Safety and Health, U.S. Dept. Labor, 1978. Mem. Am. Soc. Safety Engrs., Nat. Fedn. Press Women (award 1972), Alaska Press Women (17 awards 1971-78). Republican. Lutheran. Club: Pioneers of Alaska.

JONES, DIANNE CHRISTINE, univ. athletic exec.; b. Hamilton, Ohio, Dec. 13, 1951; d. Earl Francis and Barbara Jean (Pheneger) J.; B.S. with distinction, Eastern Ky. U., 1974; M.S., Western Ill. U., 1975; Ed.D., W.Va. U., 1979. Asst. prof., women's basketball coach U. Wis., Whitewater, 1975—; camp counselor, 1966-70; basketball camp dir., 1975-82, mem. Wis. Women's Intercollegiate Commn., 1979—, Midwest Regional Basketball Com., 1981-82. Mem. N.Am. Soc. for Psychology of Sport and Phys. Activity, AAHPER and Dance, Midwest Assn. Health, Phys. Edn., Recreation and Dance, Wis. Assn. Health, Phys. Edn., Recreation and Dance (chmn. elect for coll. div. 1982-83), Midwest Assn. Phys. Edn. for Women, Nat. Assn. Phys. Edn. for Higher Edn., Women's Athletic Caucus, N.Am. Soc. for Sociology of Sport, Assn. Intercollegiate Athletics for Women (div. III nat. basketball com. 1980—, chmn. 1981-82), Wis. Women's Intercollegiate Athletic Conf. (ethics and eligibility com. 1979-80), Nat. Women's Basketball Coaches Assn., Delta Psi Kappa, Eta Sigma Gamma, Kappa Delta Pi. Contbr. articles in field to profl. jours. Home: Route 3 Kettle Moraine Dr Whitewater WI 53190 Office: Dept Athletics 117 Williams Center U Wis Whitewater WI 53190

JONES, DONNA MAE, trucking terminal exec.; b. Chgo., Apr. 12, 1948; d. William C. and Juanita Jones; A.S., Moraine Valley Coll., 1975; A.M., John Marshall Law Sch., 1967. With P-I-E Trucking, 1966-81, office mgr., Chgo., 1974-78, terminal mgr., Grand Rapids, Mich., 1978-81; Valuliner mgr. and office mgr. Assoc. Truck Lines, Chgo., 1981-82, terminal mgr. Aurora, Ill., 1982—; terminal mgr. Assoc. Truck Lines/ANR Freight System, South Holland, Ill., 1982—; Mem. Grand Rapids Motor Carriers Assn., Grand Rapids Transp. Club, Kalamazoo Transp. Club, Holland (Mich.) Traffic Club, Fox Valley Traffic Club, South Suburban Traffic Club, Ladies Transp. Club Chgo., Am. Trucking Assn., Delta Nu Alpha. Home: 7553 W 62d Pl Argo IL 60501 Office: ANR Freight System Route 2 Box 174 Aurora IL 60504 also ANR 605 W 172d St South Holland IL 60473

JONES, DORIS DUTCHER, polit. party ofcl.; b. Center Moriches, N.Y., Aug. 22, 1920; d. Howard C. and Mildred A. (Tooker) Dutcher; B.S., State U. N.Y., Buffalo, 1942; M.S. in Edn., State U. N.Y., Oswego, 1961, certificate of advanced studies, 1971; m. Kenneth G. Jones, Apr. 20, 1965; children—Judith Lee, Stuart Craig, Tchr., adminstr. schs. in B.C., N.Y. and Maine, 1942-73; adminstr. Emerson J. Dillion Sch., Phoenix, N.Y., 1968-71; vice chmn. Maine Democratic Party, 1976—; sec., treas. Eastern Region Caucus, Dem. Nat. Com., 1977—. Mem. Gov.'s Com. on Children and Youth, 1973-75, Conservation Commn., 1973-78; mem. exec. bd. State Chmns. Assn. Mem. NEA, AAUW, Nat. Ret. Tchrs. Assn., League Women Voters, Kappa Delta Pi. Methodist. Author: Problems of Beginning Teachers-with Implications for Teacher Education, 1971. Home: Great Bay Rd Sebago Lake ME 04075

JONES, ELIZABETH ANDREWS JONES, banker; b. Bourbon County, Ky., Sept. 1, 1919; d. Robert G. and Elizabeth Dudley Andrews Jones; student Stephens Coll., 1939, U. Ky., 1942; m. William M. Jones, Jr., Mar. 4, 1945; 1 son, William Thomas. Cashier North Middletown Deposit Bank (Ky.), 1958-74, exec. v.p., 1974-76, dir., 1958-76; v.p. Bourbon Agrl. Bank & Trust Co., Paris, Ky., 1976—. Mem. North Middletown City Council, 1974-81; commr. Zoning Bd. Bourbon, 1977-81; chmn. drives ARC, United Way, Cerebral Palsy; deaconess, bd. dirs. North Middletown Christian Ch.; bd. dirs. Paris (Ky.) YMCA. Named hon. Ky. col. Mem. Christian Women's Fellowship, Delta Delta Delta (state alumnae pres. 1952). Democrat. Club: North Middletown Women's (past pres.). Office: Bourbon Agrl Bank 4th and Main Sts Paris KY 40361

JONES, ELIZABETH BROWN, writer; b. Kansas City, Mo., Sept. 27, 1907; d. James Riley and Agnes Julia (Gammage) Brown; student U. Mo., Kansas City, 1946, Mid-Am. Nazarene Coll., 1981; m. Clare Hartley Jones, June 4, 1929; children—Elizabeth Ann, Sara Denise, David Hartley, Phyllis Elaine. Free-lance writer, 1940-62, 78—; author numerous books, including: Teaching Primaries Today, 1974; Because God Made Me, 1975; Stories of Jesus, 1977; When We Share the Bible with Children, 1977; Let the Children Come, 1978; contbr. numerous stories, poems to children's publs.; author song lyrics; editor, curriculum planner, writer Nazarene Pub. House, Kansas City, Mo., 1962-78; workshop leader; speaker at writers' confs.; mem. nat. com. for planning Sunday sch. curriculum; book reviewer; speaker at parent's groups. Mem. Ch. of the Nazarene.

JONES, ELIZABETH RIEKE (MRS. WAYNE VAN LEER JONES), club woman; b. Chgo., Oct. 15, 1903; d. Henry Edward and Vina Genevieve (Coulter) Rieke; A.B., Northwestern U., 1925; m. Wayne Van Leer Jones, Jan. 14, 1926; 1 son, Wayne Van Leer II. Dir. Houston Grand Opera Assn., 1956-77, mem. pres.'s council, 1977—. Charter mem. Assistance Guild Houston, 1966-68, Assistance League, 1968—, nat. finance com., 1970. Mem. Houston U. Women's Alliance (pres. 1951-53, scholarship chmn. 1963-65, meml. scholarship chmn. 1965—), Houston Geol. Aux. (parliamentarian, 1950-51, 60-61, 63-64), Kappa Kappa Gamma, Theta Sigma Phi. Republican. Presbyterian. Home: 5672 Longmont Dr Houston TX 77056

JONES, FAY ELLEN, nurse; b. Black Brook, Wis., July 24, 1930; d. Neil Robert and Mabel Christine (Bjorgum) J.; R.N., Milw. Hosp., 1951; diploma Moody Bible Inst., Chgo., 1955; m. Roger Milton Jones, June 12, 1955; children—Nathan Jerome, Natalie Mae. Staff nurse hosps. in Wis., Ill. and Ind., 1951—; staff nurse Student Health Center, Moody Bible Ins., Chgo., 1953-55; mem. nursing staff St. Mary's Med. Center, Racine, Wis., 1961—, patient edn. instr., 1968—; speaker on diabetes. Mem. Am. Diabetes Assn. Mem. Ind. Bible Ch. Office: 3801 Spring St Racine WI 53405

JONES, FLORENCE THOMPSON, account exec., tax investment specialist; b. Charleston, W.Va., Nov. 5, 1952; d. Estil Forrest and Ruth Mary (Thompson) J.; student U. London, 1974; B.A. in Econs., Mary Baldwin Coll., 1975; postgrad. in Bus. Adminstrn., U. N.C., Chapel Hill, 1975-76. Teller, Kanawha Valley Bank, Charleston, W.Va., summer 1976; account exec., tax investment specialist Merrill Lynch, Pierce, Fanner & Smith Inc., Charleston, 1976-80, sr. mktg. specialist tax shelter dept., nat. mktg. mgr. for real estate net leasing and venture capital, N.Y.C., 1980-81, account exec., tax investment specialist, asst. v.p., Houston, 1982—, research coordinator, 1977-78, tax shelter coordinator, 1979-80. Elected del. to state Democratic conv., W.Va., 1972, 76, 80, del. to state jud. conv., 1972, 76, 80; vol. Charleston Area Med. Center, 1967-79; docent W.Va. Cultural Center 1978; active United Way, 1967-79, Jr. Achievement, 1978, Chamber Commerce and Devel., 1978, W.Va. Surface Mining and Reclamation Assn., 1977-80. Recipient various sales and prodn. awards. Mem. Greater Houston Alliance of Bus. Club: Jr. League. Guest speaker various civic orgns. and convs. Office: 3330 One Allen Center 500 Dallas Houston TX 77002

JONES, FLORESTA DELORIS, educator; b. Hopewell, Va., Dec. 24, 1950; d. William Abner and Florine (Brown) Jones Martin; B.A. cum laude, Berry Coll., 1972; M.A., Mich. State U., 1975; postgrad. Rutgers U., 1981—. Grad. teaching asst. Sch. Journalism, Mich. State U., East Lansing, 1975; edn. specialist, Petersburg, Va., 1976-78; adj. journalism faculty Sch. Lang. and Lit., Va. State U., Petersburg, also adj. faculty skills devel. dept., English dept., 1979-82; assoc. dir. Edn. Opportunity Fund Program, Georgian Ct. Coll., Lakewood, N.J., 1978-82; writing team faculty English dept. Brookdale Community Coll., Lincroft, N.J., 1982—. Mem. Commn. on Status of Women, 1980-81; active NAACP, YWCA of Lakewood. Recipient Cert. of Appreciation, Ocean County Women's Commn., 1980, 81; Mich. State U. grad. fellow, 1972, 74. Mem. NOW, LWV, Ednl. Opportunity Fund Profl. Assn., Assn. for Equality and Excellence in Edn., Internat. Communication Assn., Women in Communications, N.J. Tchrs. English to Speakers of Other Langs., Bilingual Educators N.J., Nat. Council Tchrs. English, N.J. Coll. and Univ. Coalition on Women's Edn., AAUW, Sigma Delta Chi. Baptist. Contbr. articles to profl. jours. Home: 32 Chelsea Rd Jackson NJ 08527 Office: Brookdale Community Coll Lincroft NJ 07738

JONES, FRANCES SYLVIA, educator; b. Mangham, La., July 30, 1934; d. Harvel Traylor and Eva Dee (Weems) Jones; B.S., N.E. La. U., 1956; M.S., La. Tech. U., 1970. Chief technologist E.A. Conway Hosp., Monroe, La., 1956-62; staff technologist to supr. VA Med. Center, Shreveport, La., 1962-72; edn. coordinator Sch. Med. Tech., VA Med. Center, Shreveport, 1972—. Chmn., VA Fed. Employees Credit Union credit com., 1972-79, dir., 1978—. Recipient Superior Performance award, VA Med. Center, 1971, 79; La. Heart Assn. grantee, 1953-54. Mem. Am. Soc. Clin. Pathologists, Am. Bus. Women's Assn., La. Soc. Med. Tech., Am. Soc. Med. Tech. Democrat. Baptist. Home: 1823 Pluto Dr Bossier City LA 71112 Office: 510 E Stoner Ave Shreveport LA 71130

JONES, GERALDINE WARE, govt. ofcl.; b. Chgo., Sept. 14, 1931; d. Clim Christopher and Helen Mildred (Francis) Slaughter; B.A., Roosevelt U., Chgo., 1980; widow; children—Geoffrey Reginald, Erica Danice. Keypunch operator Peoples Gas, Light & Coke Co., Chgo., 1950-55; with Fed. Crop Ins. Corp., Dept. Agr., 1961-62; claims rep. Markham (Ill.) dist. office Social Security Adminstrn., 1962—; examiner CSC, 1975—. Chmn. Haco Anti-Crime Com., 1974-81. Recipient Cert. of Achievement, Community Edn. on Law and Justice. Recipient Service award HEW, 1971, 81; award merit Human Action Community Orgn., 1974, 77, 81. Exec. bd. Human Action Community Orgn. Mem. Am. Fedn. Govt. Employees (union steward), Internat. Platform Assn., Sadie Waterford Manor (dir.), Nat. Assn. Female Execs., Fed. Women's Program, Nat. Writers Club. Baptist. Home: 14930 Marshfield Ave Harvey IL 60426

JONES, GLENOWYN LORRAINE, educator; b. Muskegon, Mich., June 30, 1922; d. Dudley Van Gorden and Iva Bertha (Chaffee) Tice; B.S., Central Mich. U., 1952; M.A., U. Mich., 1956; m. William Louis Jones, June 20, 1949; children—Dennis, Denise, Deanna. Tchr. elem. schs., Lake City, Mich., Farwell, Mich., Pinconning, Mich., 1946-50, Davison, Mich., 1950-53; prin. elem. schs., Burton, Mich., 1953-60; lectr. edn. U. Mich., Flint, 1960-63; cons. reading and gifted edn. Genesee Intermediate Sch. Dist., Flint, 1963—; mem. faculty Oakland U., Rochester, Mich., 1970-76, U. Mich., Ann Arbor, 1975-77. Mem. NEA, Mich. Edn. Assn., Genesee Intermediate Sch. Dist. Edn. Assn. (past pres.), Flint Area Reading Assn. (past pres.), Mich. Reading Assn. (dir., membership chmn.), Internat. Reading Assn. (state coordinator 1975-82), Assn. of Tchrs. of Academically Talented, Delta Kappa Gamma, Phi Delta Kappa. Mem. Ch. of Christ. Home: 10484 Leann Dr Clio MI 48420 Office: 2413 W Maple Flint MI 48507

JONES, IRMA JEWEL, social worker; b. Alton, Ill., Apr. 6, 1934; d. Damon and Willie Ann Jones; student So. Ill. U., Carbondale, 1952-54, San Francisco-Columbia Sch. Broadcasting, St. Louis, 1969-72. With Madison County (Ill.) Dept. Public Aid, 1956-72, 76—, social worker, caseworker, 1976—; adminstrv. sec., clk. III, So. Ill. U., Edwardsville, 1973-76; religious music radio announcer, producer, coordinator Sta. WOKZ, Alton, 1974—. Mem. Nat. Assn. Colored Women's Clubs (past 2d and 3d v.p.), Fedn. Methodist Women, Nat. Gospel Announcers Guild, Gospel Music Workshop Am. Mem. A.M.E. Ch. Author: Irma's Kreative Book of Religious and Kontemporary Works of Art, 1975—. Office: 2745 E Broadway Alton IL 62002

JONES, JACQUELINE MARIE, consumer products sales exec.; b. Detroit, July 4, 1949; d. Benjimen G. and Ava Jane (James) Jones; B.S., Eastern Mich. U., 1971; M.B.A., Pepperdine U., 1977; postgrad. (Coll. scholar) Detroit Presbytery Coll., 1967-71. Mgmt. trainee Sears & Roebuck Inc., Livonia, Mich., 1971-72; asst. buyer May Co., Los Angeles, 1972-74; pharm. sales rep. Hoffman-La Roche Co., Beverly Hills, Calif., 1974-79; mktg. mgr. Johnson Products Co., Chgo., 1979-80; dist. sales mgr. McNeil Consumer Products, Ft. Washington, Pa., 1980—. Active fund raising campaigns for local elected ofcls. Mem. Nat. Assn. Market Developers, Nat. Black M.B.A. Assn., Am. Mktg. Assn., Pharm. Reps. Assn. Democrat. Club: Four Seasons West Ski. Home: 5625 Windsor Way Apt 105 Culver City CA 90230

JONES, JACQUELINE RAE MCBRIDE, city ofcl.; b. Cumberland County, N.J., Oct. 3, 1950; d. James Elwood and Lucy Mae (Coursey) McBride; B.S., Howard U., 1972; M.A., Fairleigh Dickinson U., 1976; postgrad. Am. U., 1978, U. Mich., 1979; m. Norman Preston Jones, Oct. 19, 1974; children—D'Andre, Pheon, Coyuca, Matoya. Asst. dir. social services, psychol. and sociol. cons. NARCO, Atlantic County, N.J., 1972-75; therapist Seabrook House, Cumberland County, N.J., 1976-77, Alternatives, Atlantic County, 1978; project dir. Mental Health Assn., Atlantic County, 1978; cons., program dir. Jacobs Youth Shelter, Atlantic County, 1979; pres. Sanctuary Assn., Atlantic County, 1979-80; pension fund supr. City of Atlantic City, 1980—. Bd. dirs. Empire State Coalition for Youth & Family Services, 1979—, Nat. Network Runaway and Family Services, 1979—; bd. dirs., v.p. Garden State Coalition for Youth and Family Services, 1979—; Pension fund supervisor Atlantic City 1980—. Mem. Nat. Assn. Female Execs., Atlantic County Juvenile Officers Assn., N.J. Assn. Alcoholism Counselors, Mainland C. of C., Greater Atlantic City C. of C. Democrat. Methodist. Home: 9A Powder Mill Springs Mays Landing NJ 08330 Office: PO Box 44 Atlantic City NJ 08404

JONES, JEANNE BARNHILL, horticulturist; b. Pomona, Calif., June 11, 1946; d. Paul B. and Esther Maurine (Westfall) Barnhill; B.A. in Botany, U. Calif., Riverside, 1968, M.S. in Plant Sci., 1970; postgrad. in bus. adminstrn. So. Methodist U., 1980—; m. William Clay Jones, Sept. 26, 1970; 1 son, William Bryce. Staff research asso. dept. plant sci. U. Calif., Riverside, 1969-74; dir. research Paul Ecke Poinsettias, Encinitas, Calif., 1974-80; prin. Hort. Evaluation and Rev. Service, Dallas, 1980—; nat. and internat. cons. Vol. librarian The Lamplighter Sch., 1981. Mem. Am. Soc. Hort. Sci., Internat. Assn. Plant Tissue Culture, Ohio Florist Assn., Tissue Culture Assn. Republican. Methodist. Contbr. articles in field. Office: 4247 Brookview Dr Dallas TX 75220

JONES, JO BOOT, psychologist; b. Visalia, Calif., Nov. 10, 1914; d. Edgar S. and Josephine A. (Westlake) Boot; B.A. in Art and French, U. Calif., Berkeley, 1939; M.A., San Francisco State Coll., 1951, postgrad., 1952, 55, 56, 57; postgrad. Claremont Grad. Sch., 1952-53, U. San Francisco, Mallorca, Spain, 1970, Centrodes Artes y Lenguas Espanoles, Mex., 1971; m. William Sammons, June, 1939 (div. 1972); children—Toni, Sheri Bea Sammons Schulster; m. 2d, Mark Wade Jones, July, 1976. Cons. psychology Norwalk City Schs., 1953-56; psychotherapist Deveraux Found., Santa Barbara, Calif., 1956-62, clin. adminstr., 1956-62, chmn. dept. psychotherapy, 1958-62; cons. psychologist Warner Child Guidance Center, Palm Springs, Calif., 1962, dir. 1963-64; dist. psychologist Palm Springs Unified Sch. Dist., 1963-64, supervising psychologist psychol. services, 1964-68; cons. psychologist Human Devel. Tng. Inst., San Diego, 1967-70; dist. psychologist Sequoia (Calif.) Union Sch. Dist., 1968-79; supr. doctoral and masters candidates clin. psychology State U. Hayward, Calif., also Calif. Sch. Profl. Psychology, San Francisco, 1968—; pvt. practice clin. psychology, 1950—; guest panelist spl. edn. Calif. Dept. Edn., 1967; cons. El Dorado County Schs., 1980—; one woman shows of paintings include: U. Calif., Berkeley, 1935, 38, Mills Coll., Oakland, Calif., 1941, 44, San Francisco Adult Schs., 1950; group shows include: Oakland Art Mus., 1941, Los Angeles County Art Mus., 1954, Calif. Assn. Sch. Psychologists and Psychometrists, Los Angeles and San Francisco, 1970, 72, 73, 74, Placerville Art Club (Merit award oil), 1981; represented in pvt. collections. Recipient Outstanding Service award Sequoia Union High Sch. Dist., 1979. Mem. Am. Psychol. Assn., Calif. Psychol. Assn., Assn. Calif. Sch. Adminstrs., Delta Kappa Gamma, Placerville Art Club. Democrat. Contbr. articles to psychology jours.; art editor Calif. Sch. Psychology, 1972-74. Home: PO Box 117 River Cliff Coloma CA 95613

JONES, JOAN VERNITA, social worker; b. Washington, Jan. 12, 1941; d. George M. and Alice A. Ford; A.B., Morgan State U., Balt., 1963; M.S.W., Howard U., 1969; m. Leland R. Jones, Apr. 22, 1961; children—Sharon R., Deborah L. Social services rep. Washington Dept. Public Welfare, 1965-69; social worker, then supervisory social worker Washington Dept. Human Resources, 1969-73, social welfare specialist, then exec. asst., 1973-78, asst. to dir. for social services, 1978—; mem. vis. com. Howard U. Sch. Social Work, 1976—, chmn. program com., 1978—. Pres., Benjamin Stoddert Jr. High Sch. PTA, Hillcrest Heights, Md., 1975-76, G. Gardner Shugart Jr. High Sch. PTA, Hillcrest Heights, 1977-78. Mem. Nat. Assn. Social Workers, Acad. Cert. Social Workers, NAACP, Nat. Assn. Realtors, So. Md. Bd. Realtors, Prince Georges County Bd. Realtors. Democrat. Methodist. Home: Route 1 Box 1042B Valley Rd LaPlata MD 20646 Office: 801 N Capitol St NE Washington DC 20002

JONES, JOANNE E., nurse; b. Dayton, Ohio, Jan. 15, 1930; d. Pascal Hale and Lydia Martha (Mankat) Kessler; B.S. in Nursing, U. Cin., 1951; M.S. in Edn., Ind. U., 1979; m. Jack A. Jones, Nov. 15, 1958; children—Laurence Martin, Gayle Anne. Staff nurse, then head nurse Cin. Gen. Hosp., 1951-54; office nurse, Dayton, 1954-58; public health nurse and Health and Hosp. Corp., Indpls., 1958-60; staff nurse Home Care Agy., Indpls., 1971-73; instr. health occupations J. Everett Light Career Center, Indpls., 1973—, dir. Sch. Practical Nursing, 1979—. Mem. Am. Vocat. Assn., Ind. Vocat. Assn., Ind. Citizen League Nursing, Ind. Fedn. Lic. Practical Nurses, PEO, Buick Club Am. Republican. Presbyterian. Club: Riviera. Home: 8632 El Rico Rd Indianapolis IN 46240 Office: 1901 E 86th St Indianapolis IN 46240

JONES, JOYCE FLORENCE, social worker; b. Lake Charles, La., Apr. 25, 1927; d. Joseph and Edna (Geyen) Wilson; B.A. cum laude, U. San Francisco, 1972; M.S.W., U. Calif., Berkeley, 1974; cert. Ethel Percy Andrus Sch. Gerontology, U. So. Calif., 1975; m. Alton Joseph Jones, Nov. 16, 1946; children—Ronald, Stephen (dec.), Michele, Brian, Kenneth. Part-time substitute tchr., tchr.'s aide All Hallows Sch., San Francisco, 1965-67; social worker Bayview Hunter's Point Health Service, San Francisco, 1967-72; dir. info. and referral services, asst. to exec. dir. San Francisco Commn. on Aging, 1974—; speaker in field; coordinator workshops on elderly. Lic. social worker, Calif. Mem. Acad. Cert. Social Workers, Nat. Assn. Social Workers. Democrat. Roman Catholic. Home: 1775 Palou Ave San Francisco CA 94124 Office: 1360 Mission St 4th Floor San Francisco CA 94103

JONES, JULIA HUGHES, state auditor; b. Camden, Ark., Sept. 9, 1939; d. James Harvey and Alice Olivia (Chandler) Rumph; student Tex. U. Ark., Little Rock, 1978-79; State and Local Govt. Program, John F. Kennedy Sch. Govt., Harvard U., 1981; m. James H. Jones, Aug. 26, 1979; children by previous marriage—C. David Hughes, Anne Elizabeth Hughes, Alice Lori Hughes. Chief investigator Office of Pros. Atty., Little Rock, 1973-76; circuit clk. Pulaski County, Little Rock, 1977-78; project dir. Assn. Ark. Counties, Little Rock, 1979-80; auditor State of Ark., Little Rock, 1980—. Woman's U., 1957-58, U. Ark., Fayetteville, 1958-61, Mem. Am. Mgmt. Assn., Ark. Assn. Circuit Clks., Nat. State Auditors Assn., Nat. Assn. State Auditors, Comptrollers and Treas., Jr. League Little Rock, Delta Delta Delta Alumnae Assn. Democrat. Roman Catholic. Office: Office of Auditor of State 230 State Capitol Little Rock AR 72201

JONES, JUNE SHIRLEY THOMPSON, dancer; b. Hammond, La., Sept. 17, 1921; d. Lewis Russell and Mamie Ola (Arbuthnot) Thompson; B.S. in Bus. Adminstrn., Southeastern La. U., Hammond, 1943; m. Roy Jackson Jones, Sept. 9, 1940; children—Judith Maudeen, Stephanie Lew, Roylynn, Melissa June (dec.). Various clerical and civil service positions, 1936-39, 44-45; dancing tchr., 1945—; propr. Jones Sch. Dance, Golfport, Miss., 1946—; choreographer Gulfport Little Theatre, Biloxi Children's Theatre. Sunday sch. tchr. for United Methodist Ch. Mem. Nat. Assn. Dance Masters (past dist. dir.), Broadwater Ladies Aux. (past pres.), DAR (past regent, Corr. sec. chpt. 1971-74, vice regent chpt. 1980—, state chmn. 1974—). Address: 218 Milner Ave Gulfport MS 39501

JONES, LAURIE LYNN, editor; b. Kerrville, Tex., Sept. 2, 1947; d. Charles Clinton and Jean Laurie (Davidson) Jones; B.A., U. Tex., Austin, 1969; m. C. Frederick Childs, June 26, 1976; children—Charles Newell, Cyrus Trevor. Asst. to dir. coll. admissions Columbia U., N.Y.C., 1969-70, asst. to dir. Office Alumni, 1970-71; asst. advt. mgr. Book World, Washington Post/Chgo. Tribune, 1971-72; editorial asst. N.Y. Mag., N.Y.C., 1972-74, asst. editor, 1974, sr. editor, 1974-76, mng. editor, 1976—. Mem. Am. Soc. Mag. Editors, Women in Communication, Advt. Women N.Y. Republican. Methodist. Home: 40 Great Jones St New York NY 10012 Office: 755 2d Ave New York NY 10017

JONES, LE-NORA, educator; b. Bklyn., Jan. 4, 1951; d. Herman Wellington and Augusta Leslie (Dore) Jones; diploma Bank St. Coll. Edn., 1980; M.F.A., Howard U., 1974. Tchr., N.Y.C. Public Schs.; art tchr. Model Cities summer academies. Chmn. local sch. devel. program Urban Coalition, 1980-81. Mem. Alpha Kappa Alpha. Adventist. Illus.: Writing: A Manual for Teachers, 1982. Home: 240 Cozine Ave Brooklyn NY 11207 Office: 1137 Herkimer St Brooklyn NY 11233

JONES, LINDA NELL, real estate broker; b. Bonham, Tex., Sept. 17, 1939; d. Lowell Curn and Elta Agnes (Ridings) Shuler; student U. Mich., 1969; m. John David Jones, Sept. 6, 1957 (div. 1980); children—Angela Kay, Randal David. Salesperson, Arbor Oaks Realtors, Ann Arbor, Mich., 1969; salesperson Larson & Gillies, Ann Arbor, 1970-72; partner/broker Gillies Co., Ann Arbor, 1972-75; owner, broker Century 21-Arbor Homes, Inc., Ann Arbor, 1975—. Sec., bd. dirs. met. council Century 21 of Mich., 1977—. Cert. residential specialist. Mem. Am. Soc. Profl. and Exec. Women, Nat. Assn. Female Execs., Ann Arbor Networks; Ann Arbor Bd. Realtors (pres. women's council 1976) Mich. Assn. Realtors, Nat. Assn. Realtors. Baptist. Club: U. Mich. Faculty Womens (dir. 1970). Home: 4345 Crestline St Ann Arbor MI 48103 Office: 1829 W Stadium Blvd Ann Arbor MI 48103

JONES, LOIS MAILOU (MRS. VERGNIAUD PIERRE-NOEL), artist, educator; b. Boston; d. Thomas Vreeland and Carolyn (Adams) Jones; diploma Boston Mus. Sch., 1927; cert. Boston Normal Art Sch., 1928, Designers Art Sch., 1928, Academie Julian, Paris, France, 1938, Academie de la Grande Chaumiere, 1962; A.B. magna cum laude, Howard U., 1945; student Harvard U., 1927, Columbia U., 1934-36; Ph.D., Suffolk U., 1981; m. Vergniaud Pierre-Noel, Aug. 18, 1953; H.L.D., Suffolk U., 1981. Exhibited one man shows Vose Galleries, Boston, Studio Mus. in Harlem, N.Y.C., Barnett Aden Gallery, Washington, Howard U. Gallery Art, Washington, Los Angeles County Mus. Art, High Mus. Art, Atlanta, Pan Am. Union, Centre d'Art, Port au-Prince, Haiti, Galerie Internationale, N.Y.C., Mus. Fine Arts, Dallas, Lincoln U., Pa., Hampton Inst., Va., Cornell U., Ithaca, N.Y., W.Va. State Coll., Galerie Soulanges, Paris, France; retrospective exhbn. Howard U. Gallery Art, 1972, Boston Mus. Fine Arts, 1973, Acts of Art Gallery, N.Y.C., 1973, Phillips Collection, Washington, 1979; exhibited group shows Salon des Artistes Francais, 1938, 39, 66, Biennial exhbn. Corcoran Gallery Art, Nat. Acad. Design, N.Y.C., Nat. Mus., Pa. Acad., Balt. Mus., Oakland Art Mus. (Calif.), Seatle Mus., Wash. State, A.C.A. Galleries, N.Y.C., Grand Central Art Galleries, San Francisco Mus. Art, Princeton U., Mus. Modern Art, N.Y.C., Fisk U., San Jose Mus. Art, Smith Coll., Carnegie Inst., Ill. State U., FESTAC, Nigeria, Galerie Jean Charpentier, Paris, Galerie de Paris, Salon des Independents, Paris, Rhodes Nat. Gallery, S. Rhodesia, King George VI Gallery, Port Elizabeth, Republic S. Africa, Smith Coll., Harmon Found., Pa. U. Mus., Am. Embassy, Tanzania, Nat. Collection Fine Art and Nat. Potrait Gallery; represented permanent collections Phillips Collection, IBM Corp. Palais Nationale, Haiti, Howard U. Gallery Art, Atlanta U., Barnett Aden Gallery, Bklyn. Mus., 135th St. Public Library, Rosenwald Found., Retreat for Fgn. Missionaries, Washington, U. Panjab, Pakistan, Internat. Fair Gallery, Izmir, Turkey, Walker Art Mus., Am. Embassy, Luxembourg, Ebony hdqrs., Chgo., Boston Mus. Fine Arts, Met. Mus. Art, N.Y.C., Hirshhorn Mus., Nat. Collection Am. Art, designed stained glass window Andrew Rankin Meml. Chapel, Howard U. Prof. design and watercolor painting Coll. Fine Arts Howard U., Washington; lectr. Afro-Am. Artists, Contemporary Haitian Artists. Conducted 5 week Around the World Tour, summers 1966, 67; Howard U. Research grantee study tour 17 African countries, 1970, 71. Recipient many awards and prizes, including Robert Woods Bliss award, 1st Luban Watercolor award, 1958; Franz Bader award, 1962; 1st hon. mention for oil painting Societe des Artistes Francais, Paris, 1966; Howard U. Alumni award, 1978; diplome and decoration de l'Ordre Nat. D'Honneur et Merite Haitian Govt., 1954; Candece award Met. Mus., 1982; citation Mass. Ho. of Reps., 1982. Fellow Royal Soc. Arts; mem. Nat. Art Dirs. Club, Washington Soc. Artists, Am. Watercolor Assn. (asso.), Washington Watercolor Assn., Alumni Assn. Boston Mus. Sch., Artists Equity, Nat. Conf. of Artists (1st v.p.), Blenfalteur, Foyer Montparnasse, Paris, Alpha Kappa Alpha. Author: Peintures, Lois Mailou Jones, 1937-51, Presses Georges Frere, Tourcoing, France, 1952. Home: 4706 17th St NW Washington DC 20011

JONES, LOIS MONAHON, educator; b. Germantown, Ky., Apr. 28, 1933; s. Harry and Calma (Case) Monahon; B.A. magna cum laude, Georgetown Coll., 1955; M.A., George Peabody Coll. for Tchrs., 1958; m. Robert Hopkins Jones, Aug. 8, 1959. Elem. sch. tchr., Malaga Sch., Wolfe County Sch. System, Campton, Ky., 1955-57, Crieve Hall Sch., Nashville, 1958-63; supervising tchr. third grade Peabody Demonstration Sch., George Peabody Coll., Nashville, 1963-66, substitute tchr., 1966-70; instr. edn. Belmont Coll., Nashville, 1970-73, asst. prof. edn., 1973—; dir. third grade Sun. sch. dept. First Bapt. Ch., Nashville, 1966—. Mem. Sunday sch. council First Bapt. Ch., 1966—, mem. edn. adv. com., 1975-77, mem. spl. com. on renovation of ednl. facilities, 1976-79, mem. long-range planning com., 1982—; mem. Davidson County/Nashville City Schs. Ednl. TV com., 1961-62; mem. Friends of Public Library, Nashville, 1978—; bd. dirs. Children's Internat. Edn. Center, Nashville, 1982—. Ford Found. fellow, summer 1956, 57-58. Mem. NEA, Assn. Tchr. Educators, Assn. Supervision and Curriculum Devel., Assn. for Childhood Edn. Internat., Internat. Reading Assn., Delta Kappa Gamma (pres. 1976-78), Kappa Delta Pi, Sigma Alpha Iota. Clubs: Adelicia Acklen Woman's (pres. 1974-75). Office: Belmont Coll Nashville TN 37203

JONES, LORA LEE SIMS, nurse; b. Burbank, Calif., Aug. 24, 1942; d. Marion Dodd and Lora Beatrice (Clark) Sims; Asso. in Nursing, Grayson County Coll., Sherman, Tex., 1972; student Ardmore (Okla.) Higher Edn. Center; m. David Duke Jones, June 18, 1960; children—Gregory David, Kimberly Ann, Amy Lee. Sec.-treas. Jones Meat Packing Co., Inc., Old Fashioned Meat Market; dir. nurses Brookside Manor Nursing Home, Madill, Okal., 1972-73; supr., charge nurse Love County Health Center, Marietta, Okla., 1973-74; supr. Marshall Meml. Hosp., Madill, 1974-76; nurse Marshall County Pub. Health Dept., 1976-77; cons. nurse Texoma Health Care Facility, 1977-80; sch. nurse Kingston (Okla.) Public Schs., 1977-80; indsl. nurse UniRoyal Tire Co., Ardmore, Okla., 1981; public health nurse, Carter County Public Health Dept., 1981-82; sr. nurse Love County Public Health Dept., Marietta, 1982—. Mem. adminstrv. bd. First United Methodist Ch., 1975-76; co-founder Wildcat Teen Town, Inc., pres., 1977-78; bd. dirs. Madill Day Care Center, 1974-76. Mem. Okla. Pub. Health Assn., PTA, Am. Sch. Health Assn., Am., Okla. Nurses Assn., Okla. Public Employees Assn. Democrat. Clubs: Eastern Star, Madill All Sports Booster (sec.-treas. 1977-78), Madill Round-Up, Madill T.M. (sec. treas. 1977-78). Home: 410 S 11th Ave Madill OK 73446 Office: 200 Medical Dr West Route B Box 5 Marietta OK 73448

JONES, LORETTA ANN, sales exec.; b. Kansas City, Kans., June 1, 1946; d. Robert G. and Elizabeth Margaret (Schneider) Jones; B.A., Kans. State U., 1973; m. Richard L. Green; 1 dau., Stephanie Leigh Jones. Mktg. rep. Service Bur. Corp., Kansas City, Mo., 1973-75; territorial mgr. Prince Matchabelli, Kansas City, 1975-78; life ins. agt., estate planner Mass. Mut., 1978-79; dist. sales mgr. G.A.F. Pictoral Products, Kansas City, 1979-80; sales rep. Houbigant, Inc., Kansas City,

1981—. Republican. Roman Catholic. Address: 6360 W 49th St Mission KS 66202

JONES, LYNN ALLYSON, family planning agys. exec.; b. San Francisco, Sept. 17, 1954; d. Calvin Samuel and Eulalia (Childers) J.; B.A. in Psychology with great distinction, San Jose State U., 1976; postgrad. in Bus. Adminstrn., Coll. of Notre Dame, 1979-82. Public speaker Planned Parenthood, San Jose, Calif., 1975-77; counselor Pregnancy Consultation Center, San Jose, 1977-78, dir., 1978—. Designer and implemented human sexuality program Elmwood Rehab. Center. Mildred Grote scholar, 1972-76, Beta Sigma Phi scholar, 1972—; recipient cert. of appreciation for vol. service, 1976. Mem. Nat. Assn. Female Execs., San Jose State Alumni Assn. Producer TV program Sex Education in High Schools, 1976; dir. TV show Pandora's Box, 1975. Home: 75 San Benito Way San Francisco CA 94127 Office: 5150 Graves Ave Suite 5B San Jose CA 95129

JONES, MAE DAVIS, former seafood co. exec., oil co. exec.; b. Pitt County, N.C., Nov. 2, 1938; d. Horance Gibbs and Marjorie Ann (Williams) Davis; student Flora Macdonald Coll., 1956-58; cert. N.C. Oil Jobbers Mgmt. Inst. at U. N.C., 1979; m. W. Lawrence Jones, Feb. 16, 1980; children—Susan Ann, Bruce R. Mgr., Bruce's Drug Store, Ayden, N.C., 1961-66; advt. mgr. Beaufort Hyde News, Belhaven, N.C., 1968-69; mgr., sec.-treas. Bateman Oil Co., Belhaven, 1969-80; sec.-treas. Sea Safari, Ltd., Belhaven, 1975-80. Vice pres. John A. Wilkerson Sch. PTA, Belhaven, 1967-68; pres. Pungo Acad. PTA, Belhaven, 1972-73; pres. United Methodist Women, Belhaven, 1969-71. Cert. notary public, N.C. Mem. N.C. Oil Jobbers Assn., Sea Grant Coll. Program N.C., N.C. Fisheries Assn. Belhaven C. of C., Nat. Assn. Female Execs. (dist. dir.). Democrat. Home: Oakwood Dr Prestwould Estates Clarksville VA 23927 also 500 Pacific S Apt 1111 Virginia Beach VA 23451

JONES, MALLORY MILLETT, actress, photographer; b. St. Paul; d. James Albert and Helen Rose (Feely) Millett; B.A., U. Minn., 1961; 1 dau., Kristen Vigard. Active with N.Y. Theatre, 1971-80, mem. original cos. of Annie and The Best Little Whorehouse in Texas, 1977; appeared in Dodsworth, Berkshire Theatre Festival, 1978; also on Love of Life, CBS-TV, 1978-79, NBC Movie of the Week, Eischied: Only the Pretty Girls Die, 1979; Edward Albee's Everything in the Garden (dir. Shelley Winters), Actors' Studio, 1980—, also Another World, New Line Cinema: Alone in the Dark; appeared in House of Blue Leaves, Berkshire Theatre Festival, 1981; exhibitor of photography: Third Eye Gallery, N.Y.C., 1974-75, Modernage Discovery Gallery, N.Y.C., 1976-79, Gallery of St. Clement's, N.Y.C., 1979.

JONES, MARJORIE BERTHA, fin. and loan broker; b. Mpls., Feb. 5, 1924; d. Vincent L. and Kathryn C. (McIntosh) J.; B.S. in Polit. Sci., UCLA, 1950; student U. Minn., 1942-43. Mgmt. trainee Coast Fed. Savs. & Loan Assn., Los Angeles, 1950-56; treas., controller Lytton Savs. & Loan Assn., Los Angeles, 1956-65; sr. v.p. Hemet Fed. Savs. & Loan (Calif.), 1965-75; pres., dir. Adobe Mortgage, Inc., Escondido, Calif., 1975—; cons. in fin. Bd. dirs. Riverside-San Bernardino Better Bus. Bur., 1978-80. Served with USAAF, 1944-46; PTO. Decorated Army Commendation Medal. Mem. Am. Soc. Women Accts. Republican. Episcopalian. Clubs: Zonta Internat., Eastern Star. Home: 44604 Adobe Dr Hemet CA 92343

JONES, MARJORIE RUTH, aluminum co. ofcl.; b. New Kensington, Pa., Mar. 29, 1919; d. Roy LaTelle and Alice Edith (Tweed) J.; student Grace Martin's Secretarial Sch., Pitts., 1937-38, U. Pitts., 1953-54. Stenographer, Harrison Twp., 1938-39; sec. Larkin Constrn. Co., 1939, Met. Club Pitts., 1939-40, Union Nat. Bank, Tarentum, Pa., 1940; sec. Aluminum Co. of Am., 1940-56, adminstrv. asst., sec. to asst. dirs. basic materials labs. and metal prodn. labs. Alcoa Labs., Alcoa Center, Pa., 1956-81, adminstrv. asst. sec. to tech. dirs. refining and smelting, research and devel., 1981—; lectr. Mem. Pa. Alcoans Polit. Action Com. Mem. Profl. Secs. Internat. (pres. Allegheny Valley chpt. 1953-54, 61-66, 77-79). Republican. Methodist. Club: River Forest Country. Home: New Kensington PA 15068 Office: Alcoa Laboratories Alcoa Center PA 15069

JONES, MARY CLAIRE, cytotechnologist; b. Atlanta, Nov. 12, 1939; d. James Lamar and Lucia Annette (Lindsey) Martin; B.S., U. South Ala., Mobile, 1973, M.S., 1982; m. Edward Eugene Joes, Feb. 28, 1964; children—Donna Claire, Kaaren Annette, Shelley Gene, Gene Lamar. Clin. cytologist, 1960-74; ednl. coordinator cytology program U. South Ala., 1974-76, chmn. dept., 1976-81; dir. ednl. services St. Joseph's Hosp., Atlanta, 1981—. Mem. So. Assn. Cytotechnologists, Am. Soc. Cytology (assoc.; Cytotechnologist award 1978), Am. Soc. Clin. Pathologists. Home: 4009 Bowen Rd Stockbridge GA 30281 Office: 5665 Peachtree Dunwoody Rd NE Atlanta GA 30342

JONES, MARY DAILEY (MRS. HARVEY BRADLEY JONES), clubwoman; b. Billings, Mont.; d. Leroy Nathaniel and Janet (Currie) Dailey; student Carleton Coll., 1943-44, U. Mont., 1944-46, U. Calif. at Los Angeles, 1959; m. Harvey Bradley Jones, Nov. 15, 1952; children—Dailey, Janet Currie, Ellis Bradley. Owner Mary Jones Interiors. Founder Jr. Art Council, Los Angeles County Mus., treas., 1953-55, v.p., 1955-56, mem. Pasadena (Calif.) Philharmon. com., Costume Council, co-founder Art Rental Gallery, 1953, chmn. art and architecture tour, 1955; founder mem. Art Alliance, Pasadena Art Mus., sec., 1955-56; benefit chmn. Pasadena Girls Club, 1959, bd. dirs., 1958-60; chmn. Los Angeles Tennis Patron's Assn. Benefit, 1965; sustaining Jr. League Pasadena; mem. docent council Los Angeles County Mus.; mem. costume council Los Angeles County Mus. Art., program chmn. 20th Century Greatest Designers; mem. blue ribbon com. Los Angeles Music Center; benefit chmn. Venice com. Internat. Fund for Monuments, 1971; co-chmn. benefit Harvard Coll. Scholarship Fund, 1974, Otis Art Inst., 1975; mem. adv. bd. Estelle Doheny Eye Found., 1976, chmn. benefit, 1980; bd. dirs. Founders Music Center, Los Angeles, 1977-81; mem. nat. adv. council Sch. Am. Ballet, N.Y.C., nat. co-chmn. gala, 1980; bd. dirs. Los Angeles Ballet; mem. Los Angeles Olympic Com. for 1984. Mem. Kappa Alpha Theta. Clubs: Valley Hunt (Pasadena); California (Los Angeles). Home: 260 Hillside Rd South Pasadena CA 91030

JONES, MARY GARDINER, lawyer, educator, communications co. exec.; b. N.Y.C., Dec. 10, 1920; d. Charles Herbert and Anna Livingston (Short) Jones; B.A., Wellesley Coll., 1943; J.D., Yale U., 1948. Intern tchr. George Sch., Newtown, Pa., 1943-44; research analyst, research and analysis br. Internat. Law sect. OSS, Washington, 1944-46; admitted to N.Y. bar, 1949; asso. firms Donovan, Leisure, Newtown and Irvine, 1948-53, Webster, Sheffield, Fleischmann, Hitchcock & Chrystie, 1961-64 (both N.Y.C.); trial atty. antitrust div. Dept. Justice, N.Y.C., 1953-61; commr. FTC, Washington, 1974; prof. Coll. Commerce and Bus. Adminstrn. and Coll. Law, U. Ill., Urbana, 1973-75; now v.p. for consumer affairs Western Union Telegraph Co., Washington; pres. Consumer Interest Research Inst., Washington, mem. Consumer Research Found. dir. MCA, Inc., Universal City, Calif., Safeway Stores, Oakland, Calif. Mem. com. on sci. and tech. Fed. Council Sci. and Tech.; non-trustee mem. research and policy com.; chmn. bd. Council Econ. Priorities, 1976—, Inst. Future, 1977—; dir. Council Better Bus. Bureaus. mem. Pres.' Panel on Antitrust Laws, 1977-78. Trustee Wellesley Coll., 1971—; nat. adv. council Hampshire Coll.; Mem. Fed. Bar Assn. Internat. Law Assn., Assn. Bar City N.Y., Am. Arbitration Assn., Yale Law Sch. Assn. (v.p. D.C. 1969-70, exec. com. 1971—), AAUW (2d v.p. Washington br. 1968-69, adv. council). Bd. editors Jour. Consumer Affairs; editorial rev. bd. Jour. Consumer Interest; contbr. articles law jours. Home: 1631 Suter's Ln NW Washington DC 20007 Office: 1828 L St NW Washington DC 20036

JONES, MARY JANE, interior designer; b. Terre Haute, Ind., Apr. 1, 1934; d. Robert F. and Lillian H. (Shook) Scherer; student MacMurray Coll. Women, 1951-53, Ind. State U., 1955-57; diploma N.Y. Sch. Interior Design, 1974; student U. Tex., Arlington, 1978-79; m. Marvin D. Jones, Sept. 1, 1962; children—Valerie, Don, Mike, Karen. Exec. sec. dir. research Comml. Solvents Corp., 1956-57; exec. sec. to program mgr. Honeywell Corp., Mpls., 1960-61; tchr. bus. Met. Bus. Coll., Galveston, Tex., 1958-59, Ft. Worth Sch. Bus., 1980-81; owner, mgr. MJ Jones Interior Design, Ft. Worth, Tex., 1977—. Active Circle T council Girl Scouts U.S.A., Ft. Worth, 1972-82. Mem. Nat. Assn. Women in Constrn., Ft. Worth C. of C., Nat. Assn. Historic Trust, Exec. Women Internat. Republican. Methodist. Home: 5617 Wonder Dr Fort Worth TX 76133 Office: 4232 McCart St Fort Worth TX 76115

JONES, MARY VIRGINIA, mech. engr.; b. Roanoke, Va., Sept. 19, 1940; d. James Bernard and Evangeline (Jamison) Jones; B.S. in M.E., Va. Poly. Inst. and State U., 1962; M.S. in M.E., George Washington U., 1972, postgrad. 1972. Design engr. Atlantic Research Corp., Alexandria, Va., 1962—, head design engrng. sect., Gainesville, Va., 1981, chief mech. design group, 1982—; research scholar asst. George Washington U., Washington, 1972. Recipient Tau Beta Pi Woman's Badge, 1961; registered profl. engr., Commonwealth of Va. Mem. ASME, Soc. Women Engrs. (Balt./Washington v.p. 1981, pres. 1982), Soc. Plastics Engrs., Tau Beta Pi, Pi Tau Sigma, Phi Kappa Phi, Omicron Delta Kappa. Methodist. Home: 9718 Kingsbridge Dr Apt 3 Fairfax VA 22031 Office: 7511 Wellington Rd Gainesville VA 22065

JONES, MARY VIRGINIA WALTERS, newspaper editor; b. Dothan, Ala., Apr. 10, 1923; d. Thomas Jackson and Rachel Irell (Etheridge) Walters; B.A., in Journalism, U. Bridgeport, 1973; postgrad. in pub. communications Fordham U., 1975, U. Bridgeport, 1976-77; m. Raymond C. Jones, Dec. 3, 1943; children—Virginia Ann, Thomas Christopher, Edward William. Airways radio operator CAA, 1942-44; reporter, bur. chief Bridgeport Post-Telegram, 1960-73; editor Fairfield (Conn.) Citizen News, 1973-76, Westchester-Rockland Newspapers, White Plains, N.Y., 1976-77, Fairfield County Morning News, Trumbull, Conn., 1977—, Pensacola (Fla.) News Jour., 1978—. instr. journalism U. Bridgeport, 1974-78. Rep. Trumbull Town Council, 1955-59; vice chmn. Trumbull Democratic Town Com., 1959-61. Recipient editorial award New Eng. Press Assn., 1976. Mem. Women in Communications, Inc., Deadline Club N.Y.C., Soc. Profl. Journalists. Episcopalian. Club: Nat. Press (Washington).

JONES, MELBA JOHNSON, public accountant; b. Winnsboro, La., Jan. 24, 1933; d. Malcolm Malone and Lillie (McKaskle) Johnson; student N.E. La. U., 1951-52; grad. Sch. Acctg., Internat. Accts. Soc., 1967; m. Aubrey Jones, Oct. 11, 1952; children—Michael Aubrey, Gregory Alan. Office mgr. C.P.A. firm, Monroe, La., 1969-72; owner, operator Melba Jones, Acct., Ruston, La., 1972-79; C.P.A., Ruston, 1980—; dir. United Banker Ins. Co. Adv. bd. N.E. La. Vocat. Sch. Recipient Citizenship award Am. Legion, 1952; C.P.A., La. Mem. Am. Inst. C.P.A.s, La. Soc. C.P.A.s, Bus. and Profl. Women's Club (named Outstanding Bus. Woman 1966), Ruston C. of C. Republican. Baptist. Address: 1221 Farmerville St PO Box 96 Ruston LA 71270

JONES, MILDRED JEAN, librarian; b. Algoma, W.Va., Jan. 5, 1946; d. Dan Sanders and Eva Mae (Pilson) Price; B.S. in Behavioral Scis., Grand Canyon Coll., Phoenix, 1979, B.S. in Tng. and Devel., 1979; M. Higher and Adult Edn., Ariz. State U., 1982; divorced; children—Jeri Lynn, Alton James, Justin Sanders. With Motorola Inc., 1967-75; tng. and devel. mgr., tech. librarian. Unidynamics/Phoenix, Inc., 1979—. Mem. Am. Soc. Tng. and Devel., NAACP (youth adv., dir.), Phoenix Urban League, Phi Beta Lambda, Phi Lambda Theta. Democrat. Baptist. Home: 6521 W Camelback St Phoenix AZ 85033 Office: PO Box 2990 Phoenix AZ 85062

JONES, NANCY ANN, home economist; b. Princeton, Ky., Jan. 3, 1944; d. Frank Urey and Marie Elizabeth (Blackburn) Young; B.S. in Home Econs., Murray State U., 1966, M.S., 1970; m. Virgil Wayne Jones, Apr. 22, 1966; children—Brian Keith, Anita Marie. Tchr. vocat. home econs. Carlisle County High Sch., Bardwell, Ky., 1966-67, home living tchr. Outwood Hosp. and Sch., Dawson Springs, Ky., 1968-73; home econs. agt. Webster County Extension Service, Dixon, Ky., 1974—. Sunday Sch. tchr. Victory Bapt. Ch., 1975-79, active Woman's Missionary Union. Mem. Am. Assn. on Mental Deficiency, Am. Home Econs. Assn., Nat. Assn. Extension Home Economists. Club: Dixon Bus. and Profl. (pres. 1978-80). Home: 606 Church Providence KY 42450 Office: Courthouse Main St Dixon KY 42409

JONES, NANCY TAYLOR, parliamentarian; b. Salt Lake City, Apr. 10, 1921; d. Arthur Dunham and Priscilla (Jennings) Taylor; B.S., U. Utah, 1942, M.A., 1947; postgrad. U. Wash., 1947-51; m. Earl Jones, June 16, 1947 (dec. May 1980); children—Christopher Taylor, Candace Elisabeth, Dana Michele. Tchr., elem. sch.; jr. clin. psychologist U. Wash. Child Guidance Clinic, Seattle, 1948-51; pres. Calif. Assn. Parliamentarians, 1980-81; dir. Dist. VIII, Nat. Assn. Parliamentarians, 1981—; instr. parliamentary procedure local community colls. Pres. local PTA, also Loma council PTA; pres. Point Loma Assembly; officer Elections Bd. Precinct. Served to 2d lt. WAC, 1942-46. Mem. Delta Gamma (pres. So. Calif. coordinating council, nat. constns. chmn.). Republican. Home: 3020 Goldsmith St San Diego CA 92106

JONES, PATRICIA, educator; b. Cin., May 29, 1953; d. John Hoyt and Eva Mae (Perry) J.; B.S. magna cum laude, Cumberland Coll., 1975; M.Ed., Xavier U., 1975. Tchr. physically handicapped Yealey Elem. Sch., Florence, Ky., 1975-76; tchr. 2d grade Sharpsburg Primary Sch., Norwood, Ohio, 1976—. Mem. NEA, Ohio Edn. Assn., Norwood Tchr. Assn., PTA, Women's Missionary Union. Baptist. Home: 2254 Hanaford Ave Norwood OH 45212 Office: Sharpsburg Primary Sch Forest and Smith Rds Norwood OH 45212

JONES, PATRICIA ANN LEE, microbiologist; b. Smithfield, N.C., Nov. 18, 1950; d. Elbert and Lillie M. (Mitchener) Lee; B.S. in Microbiology, Howard U., 1975; m. Donald A. Jones, Feb. 22, 1974. Staff asst. U.S. Geol. Survey, Dept. Interior, Washington, 1970-73, staff asst. Fish and Wildlife Service, 1973-75; pesticide specialist EPA, Washington, 1975-77; microbiologist, regional mgr. Nabisco, Inc., East Hanover, N.J., 1978—. Career awareness conf. cons. Nat. Urban League; mem. Randolph (N.J.) Environ. Bd., 1981—. Recipient award U.S. Geol. Survey, 1970; EPA, 1977. Mem. Am. Inst. Biol. Scis., Soc. Indsl. Microbiology, Environ. Mgmt. Assn., Assn. Women in Sci., N.J. Assn. Environ. Commns. (adj. mem.), Food Sanitation Inst. (treas. N.Y.-N.J. chpt. 1979-80). Asst. editor: Endangered Birds and Mammals of South America, 1975. Office: Nabisco Brands Inc Quality and Environ Systems East Hanover NJ 07936

JONES, RAMONA LEE CHILDS, state agy. exec.; b. Milw., Oct. 8, 1940; d. Lorenzo Will and Lucille Campbell Childs; B.S., Winona State U., 1962; M.Ed., Northeastern Ill. U., 1969; 1 dau., Nadená Wenonáh. Tchr. public schs., Kenosha, Wis., 1962-63, Waukegan, Ill., 1963-64, Mpls., 1964-67, Chgo., 1967-72; instr. Northeastern Ill. U., Chgo., 1969-74, Bemidji (Minn.) State U., 1974-79; govt. civil rights and research specialist HEW, 1972-74, Desegregation Inst., 1972-74; co-dir. Independent Consultings, nat., regional and local, Welch, Minn., 1967-79; Indian and rural housing devel. specialist Minn. Housing Fin. Agy., St. Paul, 1979—. Bd. dirs. Community Program for Arts and Scis., St. Paul, 1977—; bd. dirs. Prairie Island Project Inc., 1979—; commr. City of Red Wing Adv. Planning Commn., 1977-78; bd. dirs. Minn. Women of Color, 1977—. Mem. AAUW, Minn. Planning Assn., United Indian Planners Assn., Internat. City Mgrs. Assn., Nat. Congress Am. Indians. Nat. Assn. Female Execs., Nat. Urban Indian Council, Dakota Tribe. Home: Route 2 Box 72 Welch MN 55089 Office: 333 Sibley St Suite 200 Saint Paul MN 55101

JONES, ROBIN ROHRBOUGH, audiologist, educator; b. Weston, W.Va., Jan. 15, 1951; d. Otto Alonzo and Jo Ann (Gump) R.; B.S. magna cum laude, W.Va. U., 1972, M.S., 1973; 1 dau., Megan Nicole. Clin. audiologist Fairmont (W.Va.) Ear, Nose and Throat Assos., 1973-75; instr. audiology W.Va. U., Morgantown, 1975-79, asst. prof., 1979—, clin. dir., asst. chmn., 1976—. Mem. Am. Speech-Lang.-Hearing Assn., Am. Auditory Soc., W.Va. Speech-Lang.-Hearing Assn. Home: Route 2 Box 47-B Morgantown WV 26505 Office: 805 Allen Hall W VA U Morgantown WV 26506

JONES, RUBY DARLENE, home health agy. adminstr.; b. Tahoka, Tex., Nov. 19, 1940; d. Arthur Benjamin and Renda Clementine (Mullings) Jones; student Lamar U., 1965, U. Tex., Austin, 1974; 3 children. Nurse, Orange, Tex., 1966-69; charge nurse Jones Rest Home, Inc., Orange, 1969-74; partner England (Ark.) Flying Service, Inc., 1970-74, Delmar's Aerial Service, Kans. and Okla., 1970-74; Del Mar, Inc., Little Rock, 1975-76; charge nurse Bayshore Nursing Home, Inc., La Porte, Tex., 1976-80; regional adminstr. Home Health-Home Care, Inc., San Antonio, Tex., 1976-80, community relations dir., Orange, 1980-82, dir. community relations and devel. Tex. region, 1982—. Mem. Tex. Home Health Agys. Assn., Nat. Home Health Agys. Assn., Tex. Nursing Home Assn., LWV, Nat. Assn. Female Execs., San Antonio Women's Credit Union. Home: 1001 28th St Orange TX 77630 Office: 904 28th St Orange TX 77630

JONES, RUBYE, labor union ofcl.; b. Millen, Ga., Nov. 16, 1938; d. Paul and Julia (Jacob) Jones; B.A., Empire State Coll., 1982; children—James Paul, Harry, Eileen. Vice pres. exec. bd. Local 99, Internat. Ladies Garment Workers Union, N.Y.C., 1964-74, edn. dir. Local 91, 1974—. Del., N.Y. State AFL-CIO Conv., 1974-80; chmn. labor caucus N.Y. State Conf. for Internat. Women's Yr., 1977; mem. N.Y.C. Aux. Police Force, 1980—; vol. cons. labor ARC, 1979—. Named Woman of the Yr., N.Y.C. chpt. Soroptimist Internat., 1979; recipient Susan B. Anthony award NOW, 1980. Mem. Coalition of Labor Union Women (chpt. pres. 1976-80), NAACP, Bapt. Tng. Union. Democrat. Baptist. Home: 302 W 79 St New York NY 10024 Office: 100 E 17 St New York NY 10003

JONES, RUTH ELIZABETH, county govt. probation ofcl.; b. Houston, Oct. 5, 1943; d. Benjamin Bowman and Elizabeth Angeline (Freeman) J.; B.A., Tex. So. U., 1967; m. Thaddies Jones, Jr., Sept. 9, 1967 (dec) 1 son, Thaddies III. Juvenile probation officer Bexar County Juvenile Probation Dept., San Antonio, 1975-80, community assistance program coordinator, 1980-82, juvenile commn. coordinator, 1982—. Bd. dirs. Ella Austin Community Center, 1974—, pres., 1978-82; mem. Democratic Women of Bexar County, 1971—, pres., 1974, mem. Tex. State Dem. Exec. Com. Women, 1980—; mem. City of Antonio Planning Commn., 1978—. Recipient Outstanding Community Service citation City of San Antonio, 1980; Disting. Public Service citation Tex. Ho. of Reps., 1973; Outstanding Contbn. toward Good Govt. citation Tex. State Senate, 1975; commd. Yellow Rose of Tex., Gov. of Tex., 1978. Mem. Tex. Probation Assn., Tex. Corrections Assn., Delta Sigma Theta. Roman Catholic. Club: Top Ladies of Distinction. Home: 4226 Redstone San Antonio TX 78219 Office: Bexar County Juvenile Probation Dept 203 W Nueva San Antonio TX 78285

JONES, SALLY DAVIESS PICKRELL, author; b. St. Louis, June 4, 1923; d. Claude Dildine and Marie Daviess (Pittman) Pickrell; student Mills Coll., Oakland, Calif., 1941-43, U. Calif., Berkeley, 1944, Columbia, 1955-58; m. Charles William Jones, Sept. 2, 1943; 1 son, Matthew Charles. Author: (novel) The Lights Burn Blue, 1947. Mem. UN Women's Guild (hospitality chmn.), Fgn. Policy Assn., Nat. Council Women, Asia Soc., English-Speaking Union, Met. Mus. Art. Episcopalian. Address: 311 E 58th St New York NY 10022

JONES, SANDRA YVONNE, judge; b. Chgo., July 13, 1952; d. Fred Alexander and Luenettie (Joiner) J.; B.S. in Psychology and Polit. Sci., U. Ill., Urbana, 1975; J.D., Valparaiso U., 1977; diploma Nat. Jud. Coll., 1981. Admitted to Ill. bar, 1978, U.S. Supreme Ct. bar, 1982; legal intern Porter County (Ind.) Prosecutor's Office, 1977; staff atty., then sr. litigation atty. Office Cook County (Ill.) Legal Assistance, 1978-81; adminstrv. law judge Human Rights Commn., Chgo., 1981—. Recipient Janet Trisch Meml. award, 1975. Mem. Am. Bar Assn., Chgo. Bar Assn., NAACP, Chgo. Urban League, Black Alumni Assn. U. Ill., Phi Alpha Delta. Methodist. Home: 3316 S Calumet Ave Chicago IL 60616 Office: 32 W Randolph St Chicago IL 60601

JONES, SHARON COLNAR, graphic designer; b. Quincy, Ill., Mar. 18, 1943; d. Frank George and Jean (Morris) Colnar; B.A., UCLA, 1966; M.A., San Diego State U., 1975; m. Richard Dennis Jones, Aug. 24, 1968; children— Bradley McKennon Colnar, Darren Mitchell Colnar. Asst. art dir. Needham, Harper & Steers, Chgo., 1966; graphic designer Robert Lipman Design, Chgo., 1966-68; design cons. Med. Coll. Ga., Augusta, 1970-71; publs. dir. U. Ga., Athens, 1968-73; art instr. San Diego State U., 1974-75; project dir. San Diego Dept. Edn., 1977; pres. Graphicshop-a Graphic Design and Cons. Service, San Diego, 1973—; instr. graphic design Southwestern Coll., 1981-82. Mem. Univ. and Coll. Designers Assn. (treas. 1973-74, pres. 1976, dir. 1977—, design awards 1971-76), Am. Coll. Pub. Relations Assn. (design awards 1971-76). Contbr. design work Communication Arts Mag. Home: 4752 Mission Bell Ln La Mesa CA 92041

JONES, SHERYL BLANCHE, entertainment co. exec.; b. Memphis, Dec. 19, 1947; d. Hozell (Johnson) Frizell; B.A., So. Ill. U., 1968; A.A., U. Ill., 1976; m. W.L. Jones, Apr. 4, 1965; 1 son, Antoney Renard. Code enforcement specialist City of Carbondale, Ill., 1975-78; personnel dir. Madison County Econ. Opportunity Commn., Alton, Ill., 1979—, also pres. Do-Mayn Enterprises, Chgo., 1981—. Active Urban League, NAACP; bd. dirs. Alton LWV. Recipient NAACP Youth award, 1960, Civic award YWCA, 1961, Social Service award Jacqueletts Social Club, 1962. Mem. Black Music Assn., Media Assn. media Women, Nat. Assn. Female Execs. Methodist.

JONES, SHIRLEY FORBES, univ. comptroller; b. Camden, N.C., May 31, 1938; d. Lawrence and Gladys Equilla (Spence) Forbes; B.S. in Bus. Adminstrn. cum laude (study grantee), Elizabeth City (N.C.) State U., 1975; m. Vernon W. Jones, June 21, 1958; children—Constance V., Kevin W. Mem. adminstrv. staff Elizabeth City State U., 1962—, comptroller, 1980—; cons. in field. Bd. dirs. Northeastern N.C. Tomorrow Project, 1982-84; past v.p. Camden County PTA, 1975-76. Mem. NAUW, Nat. Assn. Coll. and Univ. Bus. Officers, Elizabeth City State U. Alumni Assn., Alpha Chi, Alpha Kappa Mu, Alpka Kappa Alpha. Democrat. Baptist. Club: Order Eastern Star. Home: Route 1 Box 252 Camden NC 27921 Office: 1001 Parkview Dr Elizabeth City State U Elizabeth City NC 27921

JONES, STANCIE LINDLEY, med. technologist; b. Mexico City, July 24, 1948; d. Paul Webster and Dorothy-Nell (Lindley) Jones; B.A. in

Biology and History, Trinity U., 1970; M.A. in Allied Health Adminstrn., Central Mich. U., 1979. Med. technologist Tex. Children's Hosp., Houston, 1971-72, Meth. Hosp., Houston, 1972-74, supr. Foundren Stat. Lab., 1974-78; asst. dir. tech. services, pathology Bexar County Hosp. Dist., San Antonio, 1978-81, adminstrv. dir. pathology dept., 1981—; mem. clin. faculty U. Tex. Health Sci. Center. Active Sierra Club. Mem. Am. Soc. Clin. Pathologists, Am. Soc. for Med. Tech. (pres. local chpt.), Clin. Lab. Mgmt. Assn., Brit. Interplanetary Soc., Smithsonian Assos. Presbyterian. Home: 6323 Viva Max San Antonio TX 78238 Office: 4502 Medical Dr San Antonio TX 78284

JONES, SUSAN LANGFORD, consumer economist; b. Richmond, Va., Dec. 29, 1945; d. E. Langford and Mildred Turnley (Howerton) J.; cert. U. d'Aix-Marseille (France), 1965; B.A., Vanderbilt U., 1967; M.B.A., N.Y.U., 1979; m. James Robert Scala, Feb. 28, 1981. Cons., ISIS Systems Inc., N.Y.C., 1976-79; fin. analyst CBS TV Network, N.Y.C., 1979-80, mgr. sales analysis devel., 1980—; guest lectr. N.Y. U., 1979—. Mem. Nat. Assn. Bus. Economists, N.Y. Assn. Bus. Economists, Am. Statis. Assn., Beta Gamma Sigma. Republican. Episcopalian. Guest on MoneyLine show, Cable News Network, 1981. Home: 1641 3d Ave New York NY 10028 Office: 51 W 52d St New York NY 10019

JONES, SUSAN LYNN, nurse, sociologist; b. Iowa City, Feb. 11, 1945; d. John Charles and Ada Loraine (Johnson) Organ; B.S. in Nursing, Marycrest Coll., 1968; M.A. in Psychiat. Nursing (NIMH fellow), U. Iowa, 1971; M.A. in Sociology, Case Western Res. U., 1973, Ph.D. in Sociology (NIH fellow), 1975; m. Paul K. Jones, Dec. 30, 1971. Staff nurse Mercy Hosp., Burlington, Iowa, 1968-69, Psychopathic Hosp., Iowa City, 1969-71; student health nurse Case Western Res. U., Cleve., 1971-72, asst. prof. nursing Frances Payne Bolton Sch. Nursing, Case Western Res. U., 1975-77, asso. prof., 1977-78; asso. prof. Kent State U., 1978—, coordinator nursing research, 1978—. Mem. residence governing bd. Cleve. YWCA, mem. gender identity program; chmn. task force on health and sch. desegregation Ohio Nurses Assn.; trustee Woodruff Hosp., Cleve. Mem. Am. Nurses Assn., Am. Sociol. Assn., Assn. for Family Therapy, Council for Nurse Researchers, Sigma Theta Tau. Democrat. Roman Catholic. Editor Case Western Res. U. Jour. Sociology, 1974-75; contbr. articles in field to profl. jours. Home: 2307 S Belvoir Blvd University Heights OH 44118 Office: Sch Nursing Kent State U Kent OH 44242

JONES, SUSAN SUTTON, ednl. adminstr.; b. Nanticoke, Md.; d. Douglas Judson and Emma Jerona (Evans) Sutton; B.S., Fisk U., 1946; M.Edn., Johns Hopkins U., 1965; postgrad. Temple U., 1978-82; m. Clifton Ralph Jones, Apr. 2, 1978; 1 son, George Henry Miles, Jr. Caseworker Dept. Pub. Assistance, Phila., 1946-49; tchr. Balt. City Pub. Schs., 1949-63, counselor, 1963-67, adminstr., 1967—; prin. Edmondson Sr. High Sch., Balt., 1975—. NSF grantee, 1967-68. Mem. NAACP, Nat. Assn. Secondary Sch. Prins., Pub. Sch. Adminstrs. and Suprs. Assn. Balt., Continental Soc. Disadvantaged Youth, Delta Sigma Theta, Pub. Service Sorority. Democrat. Episcopalian. Home: 1190 W Northern Pkwy Baltimore MD 21210 Office: 501 Athol Ave Baltimore MD 21229

JONES, SUZANNE (TAFFY) (MRS. DONALD S. JONES), writer, playwright; b. Binghamton, N.Y., Sept. 27, 1922; d. Frank William and Villo (Latcher) Taft; student Finch Coll., N.Y.C., 1942, Am. Acad. Dramatic Arts, N.Y.C., 1942, Bread Loaf Writer's Conf., Vt., 1966, Chautauqua Writer's Workshop; m. Donald S. Jones, June 17, 1944; children—Ronald, Laurie. Photographer's model Ansco film, 1935-41; fashion model, 1940-62; dancing and drama tchr. Knox Sch. for Girls, Cooperstown, N.Y., 1943-44; dir. Aquacades and Ballets Sidney Recreation Center, winters 1959-69; writer, commentator TV show Show Window, WNBF-TV, 1953-55; syndicated column Frazzles, 1966-68, also Columns Bedtime Stories, Grandma's Delite; dir. Birmingham Children's Theatre, 1975-76; writer, dir., producer Whistle-Stop Children's Theatre, 1976—; mem. St. Dunstin's Theatre, Cranbrook, 1976-77; lectr. on writing Bloomfield Hill Lasher High Sch., artist in residence summer and winter programs Bloomfield Hill Schs., 1979—; instr. drama and play prodn. Farmington Community Center, 1977-80; drama dir. Kirk in the Hills; condr. Creative Seminars for Tchrs. and Librarians, 1980—. Pres. Sidney Service Council, 1961-67; bd. dirs. Camp Brace, Masonville, N.Y. Mem. Nat. Assn. Penwomen, Fashion Group Detroit Inc. Mem. Women's Nat. Book Assn. (editor The Bookwoman). Presbyterian. Author childrens plays: Pompous Digs Ecology, Scat, Scat's Monster, Peas, Gold Watches, Christmas Pie, Indian Disco, Friends on Farmington Road, Crazy Cards, Pompous in the Pumpkin Patch, Professor Pompous in the Potato Patch, 1975, Rag-A-Pac and Ragg-A-Bagg Dolls, 1976; author: Whistle-Stop Puppet Plays; contbr. articles to profl. jours. Designer Taffy doll; creator Ecology Coloring Book. Home: 1601 Thumb Point Dr Fort Pierce FL 33450

JONES, SUZETTA JEAN, word processing co. exec.; b. Wheeling, W.Va., Jan. 18, 1949; d. Harold Stuart and Eva Jean J.; B.S. in Home Econs. Edn., W.Va. U., 1970. Sales rep. Wang Labs., San Jose, Calif., 1973, CPT Corp., San Francisco, 1974-77; sales rep. NBI, Inc., San Jose, Calif., 1977, br. mgr., 1978—; bd. dirs. Word Processing/Office Equipment Trade Shows, 1978—. Mem. Internat. Word Processing Assn., Santa Clara Valley Word Processing Assn. Office: 4040 Moorpark Ave San Jose CA 95117

JONES, TALOVA LANE, real estate agy. adminstrv. asst.; b. Henryetta, Okla., Dec. 27, 1925; d. Everett Ray and Ruby Mae (Tarwater) Lane; student Muskogee Jr. Coll., 1943, Baldwin-Wallace Coll., 1956-58, Fairleigh Dickinson U., 1959-60; children—Karen Jones Nolan, Marta Jones Briscoe, Marygaye Jones Franklin. Sec. various firms, 1955-68; sales asso. Boehmer Hedlund Realtors, Barrington, Ill., 1969-70, The Country Squire, Realtors, Barrington, 1970-72; sales mgr. Bob Turner Inc., Realtors, Edmond, Okla., 1972-75; sales mgr. Red Carpet Realtors, Edmond, 1975-76, broker, owner, 1976-78; mgr. Abide, Inc., Realtors, 1978-82, adminstrv. asst. to pres., 1982—; dean Okla. Realtors Inst., 1977—; cons. in field. Active, Drug and Narcotics Com., Barrington, Ill., 1971-72, Environ. Affairs Com., Edmond, Okla., 1974. Elected to Million Dollar Club, Ill. Assn. Realtors, 1971. Mem. Oklahoma City Met., Edmond (Realtor of Yr. 1975), bds. realtors, Okla. Assn. Realtors (designated Graduate Realtors Inst., 1972, dir. 1977, regional v.p. 1978), Women's Council Realtors, Realtors Nat. Mktg. Inst., Nat. Assn. Realtors, Edmond C. of C. (v.p., residential council 1982), Epsilon Sigma Alpha. Republican. Methodist. Clubs: Republican Women's, Order Eastern Star. Contbr. articles in field to newspapers, profl. jours. Home: 2112 Tall Oaks Trail Edmond OK 73034 Office: 7908 N May Ave Oklahoma City OK 73120

JONES, TERRI LYNN, advt. co. exec.; b. Wagoner, Okla., Feb. 18, 1950; d. George R. and Dorothy Louise (Burress) J.; B.S. with honors in Communications, Phillips U., 1972; postgrad. Richland Coll., 1974-75, Brookhaven Coll., 1977-78; m. W. Cleveland Smith, May 28, 1977; stepchildren—April Amber, W. Cleveland III. Media buyer Greene-Webb Assos., Dallas, 1972-73; writer, public relations exec. McCrary-Powell, Inc., Dallas, 1973-74; account service and research adminstr. Crume & Asso., Dallas, 1975; account supr. and stockholder KCBN, Inc., 1975-79; v.p. Preston Square, Inc., 1978-79; pres. Terri Jones Advt., Inc., Dallas, 1979—; exec. v.p., dir. Fun Corp. Am., 1979—; guest instr. U. Dallas, Arlington, Tex., 1977-78. Vol., Am. Cancer Soc., 1976-77, Am. Heart Assn., 1977-78; bd. dirs. Big Bros. and Sisters Met. Dallas, 1979, Campfire, Inc. Recipient Spl. Judges award Southwest VTR and TV Festival, 1975; Golden Pyramid award Internat. Assn. Splty. Advt., 1977; 1st pl. advt. award (2) Savs. Instns. Mktg. Soc. Am., 1978, 8 Gold medals, 1981; Golden Radio award Olney Savs., 1979; 3 Gold medals, 2 certs. of merit Wichita Falls Ad Club, 1981; named Saleswoman of Year, Big Bros. and Sisters of Met. Dallas, 1979. Mem. Am. Women in Radio and TV (pres. 1978-79, dir. 1979-80), Tex. Public Relations Assn. (Best of Tex. award, Cert. of Merit 1980, 2 Gold medals 1981) Assn. Broadcasting Execs. of Tex., Dallas Communications Council, Nat. Assn. Female Execs., Dallas Ad League (recipient 2 Gold medals, Cert. of Merit 1980). Republican. Mem. Disciples of Christ Ch. Home: 6306 Clubhouse Circle Dallas TX 75240 Office: 3116 Hood St Dallas TX 75219

JONES, VERNA NEWCOMB, Realtor; b. Bakersfield, Calif., July 14, 1931; d. Verne Elliott and Ruth Blanche (Henry) Newcomb; A.A., Santa Fe Community Coll., 1973; student U. Fla., 1974—; m. Herbert John Jones, Jan. 13, 1951; children—Jonathan Herbert, H. Christopher, Linda Leigh. Mgr., Hammond Organ Studios, Gainesville, Fla., 1967-70; broker-salesman Greene & Rowe, Gainesville, 1975-80, RE/MAX Profls., Inc., Gainesville, 1980; broker-salesman Comml.-Investment div. Metroplex, Inc., Gainesville, 1980—. Mediator Citizens Dispute Settlement program, Gainesville, 1977—, Juvenile Arbitration Settlement program, Gainesville, 1980. Mem. Gainesville Bd. Realtors, Fla. Assn. Realtors, Nat. Assn. Realtors, Realtors Nat. Mktg. Inst., Soc. Real Estate Appraisers, Nat. Assn. Female Execs. Office: 5200 Newberry Rd Bldg C Gainesville FL 32607

JONES, VICKI BRINEGAR, fin. exec.; b. Winston-Salem, Jan. 25, 1938; d. Don Orton and Mayme Elaine (Dowell) Brinegar; student Wake Forest U., 1956-57; children—Craig Thomas, Brett Alan, Scott Patrick, Derek Charles. Free lance advt. exec. in real estate field for Lambe-Young Inc., Lambe-Young-Jones, Inc., McNames-Sparks Realty, Inc., Frank E. Rhodes, Inc., 1961-71; sales asso. Lambe-Young Gallery of Homes, Winston-Salem, 1971-76; sales mgr. Heather Realty, Winston-Salem, 1976-77, Cagle Realty Co., Winston-Salem, 1977; sales asso. Hunt Realty & Investment Co., Winston-Salem, 1978; loan officer The Lomas & Nettleton Co., Winston-Salem, 1978—; tchr. Tech. Inst. Alamance, N.C., 1975-80, Forsyth Tech. Inst., 1974-81, others. Mem. Winston-Salem Bd. Realtors, N.C. Assn. Realtors, Nat. Assn. Realtors, Mortgage Bankers Assn. Democrat. Presbyterian. Office: 1530 B Martin St PO Box 15107 Winston-Salem NC 27103

JONES, VIRGINIA A., state agy. adminstr.; b. Trumbull, Conn., Jan. 3, 1947; d. Raymond C. and Mary (Walters) J.; student Marywood Coll., 1977—. With Sikorsky Aircraft, Stratford, Conn., 1966-70; with Micro-Tech, Inc., New Orleans, 1970-71; with Dikewood Corp., Albuquerque, 1971-76; micrographic specialist State Records Center, Santa Fe, 1976-80, chief records mgmt. div., 1980-81, chief micrographics services div., 1981—. Mem. Nat. Assn. Female Execs., Am. Bus. Women's Assn., Nat. Micrographics Assn., Assn. Record Mgrs. and Adminstrs., Internat. Micrographics Congress. Democrat. Episcopalian. Home: 707 Agua Fria Santa Fe NM 87501 Office: 404 Montezuma St Santa Fe NM 87503

JONES, VIRGINIA IRENE, electronics mfg. co. exec.; b. Brighton, Mass., May 29, 1935; d. Carl Andrew and Virginia Irene (Dowd) Bigham; student public schs., Reading; children—David Robert, Debra Irene, Donna Irene, Doreen Tammy, Denise Martha, Darryl Roy. Vice pres. E J Systems, Inc., Lawrence, Mass., 1978, Tru-Con, 1979, E J Realty Trust, 1981—; dir. E J Systems, Tru-Con; partner E J Realty. Active ARC; Water Safety instr. Mem. Am. Electronic Assn. Home: 124 Chestnut St North Reading MA 01869 Office: 601 S Union St Lawrence MA 01843

JONES, VIRGINIA SMITH, social worker; b. Atlanta, July 1, 1943; d. Edward Charles and Ida (Cary) Smith; A.B., Wilson Coll., 1965; M.S.W., Ohio State U., 1967; M.P.H., Johns Hopkins U., 1973; m. Philip Clark Jones, Aug. 24, 1968. Social work intern Menninger Found., Topeka, 1967-68; clin. social worker maternal and child health div. Health Dept., Washington, 1968-72; public health social worker Montgomery County Health Dept., Rockville, Md., 1973-74; mental health research specialist Mental Health Adminstrn., Dept. Human Resources, Washington, 1975-76, psychiat. social worker Area A Community Mental Health Center, 1977—; instr. U. Md. Grad. Sch. Social Work, 1979, 80. Vol. counselor D.C. jails, 1971-72; vol. foster parent D.C. Runaway House Program, 1975-76; vol. S.O.M.E. Soup Kitchen, 1981—. NIMH grantee, 1965-66, 67-68, 66-67, HEW grantee, 1972. Mem. Am. Public Health Assn., Nat. Assn. Social Workers, Acad. Cert. Social Workers. Home: 5515 Broad Branch Rd NW Washington DC 20015 Office: 4820 Howard St NW Washington DC 20016

JONES-LUKÁCS, ELIZABETH LUCILLE, flight surgeon, air force officer; b. Norfolk, Va.; d. Oliver C. and Gertrude (Layden) Jones; B.S., Oglethorpe U., 1955; m. Michel J. Lukacs (dec.); children—Amanda, Laurel, Angelique, Klara. Intern, Beth Israel Hosp., N.Y.C., 1964-65; gen. practice medicine, Goshen, N.Y., 1965-73, Buckingham, Va., 1973-78; commd. maj. U.S. Air Force, 1978; flight surgeon, Andrews AFB, Md., 1978—. Diplomate Am. Bd. Family Practice. Mem. Am. Med. Womens Assn., Assn. Aerospace Physicians, Aerospace Med. Assn., Md. Thoroughbred Breeders. Episcopalian. Author: The Curies Radium & Radioactivity, 1962; The Golden Stamp Book of Flying Animals, 1963. Home: Star Route Box 56 Rattle N Snap Farm Buckingham VA 23921 Office: Flight Surgeon's Office Andrews AFB MD 22331

JONES-PARKER, JANET ELIZABETH (MRS. THOMAS G. PARKER), gen. mgmt. cons.; b. Berkeley, Calif., Dec. 27, 1942; d. Elmo Dewey and Audrey May (Johnson) Jones; student Brigham Young U., 1960-61, Université de Dijon (France), 1961-62; B.A., Drew U., 1965; student London Sch. Econs., 1965; m. Thomas Garcin Parker, Mar. 24, 1976; children—Jessica Elizabeth Lynn, Thomas Garcin. Group ops. mgr. in-flight services Trans World Airlines, 1969-73; chmn. Mgmt. Woman and Parker Hyde Inc., N.Y.C., 1973—; cons. Commn. of Status of Women, N.Y.C.; speaker on women in bus., dual career marriages, and human resources problems. Mem. Women's Forum (dir.), Assn. Exec. Recruitment Cons.'s (dir. 1980—). Mormon. Contbr. articles to publs. Office: 151 Railroad Ave Greenwich CT 06830

JONES-WILSON, FAUSTINE CLARISSE, educator; b. Little Rock, Dec. 3, 1927; d. James Edward and Perrine Marie (Childress) Thomas; A.B., Ark. A.M.&N. Coll., 1948; A.M., U. Ill., Urbana, 1951, Ed.D., 1967; m. James T. Jones, June 20, 1948 (div. June 1977); children—Yvonne Dianne, Brian Vincent; m. 2d, Edwin L. Wilson, July 10, 1981. Tchr., sch. librarian, Gary (Ind.) Public Schs., 1955-62, 1964-67; asst. prof. Coll. Edn., U. Ill., Chgo., 1967-69; asst. prof. adult edn. Fed. City Coll., Washington, 1970-71; prof. edn., grad. prof. Howard U., Washington, 1969-70, 1971—. Recipient Frederick Douglass award, Nat. Assn. Black Journalists, 1979. Mem. Am. Ednl. Studies Assn., John Dewey Soc., Soc. of Profs. of Edn., Adult Edn. Assn. of Met. Washington, Washington Women's Forum, NAACP. Democrat. Editor Jour. Negro Edn., 1978—; author: The Changing Mood in America: Eroding Commitment, 1977; A Traditional Model of Educational Excellence: Dunbar High School of Little Rock, Arkansas, 1981. Home: 908 Dryden Ct Silver Spring MD 20901 Office: Sch Edn Howard U 2400 Sixth St NW Washington DC 20059

JONG, ERICA MANN, author, poet; b. N.Y.C., Mar. 26, 1942; d. Seymour and Eda (Mirsky) Mann; B.A., Barnard Coll., 1963; M.A., Columbia U., 1965. Faculty, English dept. CUNY, 1964-65, 69-70, overseas div. U. Md., 1967-69; m. Allan Jong (div. Sept. 1975); m. Jonathan Fast, 1977; 1 dau., Molly. Mem. lit. panel N.Y. State Council on Arts, 1972-74. Recipient Bess Hokin prize Poetry mag., 1971, Alice Faye di Castagnola award Poetry Soc. Am., 1972; Nat. Endowment for Arts grantee, 1973. Mem. Authors Guild (dir. 1975), Writers Guild Am.-West, PEN, Phi Beta Kappa. Author: Fruits & Vegetables (poems), 1971; Half-Lives (poems), 1973; Fear of Flying (novel), 1973; Loveroot (poems), 1975; How to Save Your Own Life (novel), 1977; At the Edge of the Body (poems), 1979; Fanny, Being the true History of the Adventures of Fanny Hackabout-Jones (novel), 1980; Witches (art, fiction, poetry), 1981. Office: care Sterling Lord Agy 660 Madison Ave New York NY 10021 also care New American Library 1633 Broadway New York NY 10019

JORDAN, BARBARA C., congresswoman; b. Houston, Feb. 21, 1936; d. Ben and Arlyne Jordan; B.A. magna cum laude, Tex. So. U., 1956; LL.B., Boston U., 1959; Admitted to Tex. bar; adminstrv. asst. to county judge, Harris County; mem. Tex. Senate, 1966-72, pres. pro tem, 1972, chmn. labor and Mgmt. Relations Com. and Urban Affairs Study Com.; mem. 93d-95th Congresses from 18th Dist. Tex., mem. Com. on Judiciary, Com. Govt. Ops., Spl. Task Force on 94th Congress; mem. steering and policy com. House Democratic Caucus; Lyndon B. Johnson Public Service prof. L.B.J. Sch. Public Affairs, U. Tex., Austin, 1979—. Named One of 10 Most Influential Women in Tex., One of 100 Women in Touch With Our Time, Harpers Bazaar mag.; A Woman of Year, Time Mag., 1975. Mem. Am., Houston, Mass. bar assns., State Bar Tex., NAACP. Baptist. Office: Lyndon B Johnson Sch Public Affairs U Tex Austin TX 78712

JORDAN, BARBARA SCHWINN, painter; b. Glen Ridge, N.J.; d. Carl Wilhelm Ludwig and Helen Louise (Jordan) Schwinn; grad. N.Y. Sch. Fine and Applied Art (Parsons), N.Y. and Paris; student Grand Central Art Sch., Art Students League, Grand Chaumiere, Academie Julien-Paris, Columbia U., NAD; m. Frank Bertram Jordan, Jr.; children—Janine Jordan Newlin, Frank Bertram III. Illustrator mags. including Vogue, 1930's, Ladies Home Jour., Saturday Evening Post, Colliers, Good Housekeeping, Cosmopolitan, McCall's, American, Town and Country, 1940's-50's. Woman's Jour., Eng., Hors Zu, Germany, Marie Claire, France, other fgn. publs., 1950's-60's; portrait painter, including Queen Sirikit, Princess Margaret, Princess Grace; free lance painter, 1970—; one-man shows include Soc. of Illustrators, 1940, 50, Barry Stephens Gallery, 1950, Bodley Gallery, N.Y.C., 1971, 80, Community Coll., West Mifflin, Pa., 1973, Duquesne U., 1973; exhibited in group shows including NAD, 1955, Royal Acad., London, Guild Hall, N.Y., 1981, Summit N.J. Art Center, 1981; works represented Holbrook Collection, Ga. Mus. Art, various pvt. collections; lectr., instr. illustration Parsons Sch., 1952-54; founder adv. council Art Instrn. Sch., 1956-70. Chmn. art com. UNICEF greeting cards, 1950-61 mem. com. Spence Chapin Sch., Philharm. Soc., 1950's-60's. Winner prizes Art Dirs. Club, 1950, Guild Hall, 1969. Asso. mem. Guggenheim Mus. Episcopalian. Club: Cosmopolitan N.Y. Author: Technique of Barbara Schwinn, 1956; World of Fashion Art, 1968. Home and office: RFD 550 Mecox Rd Water Mill NY 11976

JORDAN, BETTIE ELLA NICHOLSON, savs. and loan exec.; b. Brenham, Tex., May 4, 1913; d. William Henry and Bettie Holcomb Nicholson; student Massey Bus. Coll., 1932, U. Houston extension, 1972-75, U. Tex., summers 1963, 64; m. William Henry Jordan, Sept. 13, 1936; children—Henry Carl, William John, Anna Elizabeth Jordan Khalili. Clerical and secretarial positions Houston Assn. of Credit Men, 1932-33, Gen. Electric Supply Corp., Houston, 1933-38, War Chest, 1944-45, United Fund, intermittently, 1955-57, Depelchin Faith Home, Houston, 1957-59; with Heights Savs. Assn., Houston, 1959—, loan officer, 1961-65, sec.-treas., 1965-75, sr. v.p., sec., 1975—; sec. to bd. dirs., 1965—. Mem. Presdl. Task Force, Heritage Found. Recipient Outstanding Woman award YWCA, 1978. Mem. Nat. Forum for Exec. Women of Nat. Savs. and Loan League, Fin. Officers Soc. of U.S. Savs. and Loan League, Washington Legal Found. Republican. Lutheran. Club: Senatorial. Home: 4727 Orange St Bacliff TX 77518 Office: 204 W 19th St Houston TX 77008

JORDAN, BILLIE JOYCE, telephone co. exec.; b. Memphis, July 29, 1938; d. Booker T. and Katherine (Johnson) Moore; B.A., Roosevelt U., 1973, postgrad., 1973-79; postgrad. Syracuse U., 1981-82; m. Andrew H. Jordan, Dec. 14, 1958 (div.); 1 dau., Sharon R. With Ill. Bell, 1957-79, course developer non-mgmt. tng., 1972-74, tng. specialist for mgmt. tng., Chgo., 1974-77, instructional technologist for mgmt. tech. tng., Lisle, 1977-79; staff mgr. systems devel. AT&T, Parsippany, N.J., 1979-82; with Ill. Bell Telephone Co., Chgo., 1982—; editor various Bell System publs., including Quar. Systems Newsletter, 1981-82. Recipient cert. recognition, V award Vol. Service Corps, Vol. Bur., Welfare Council Met. Chgo., 1966. Mem. Roosevelt U. Alumni. Club: Cedar Knolls Racquetball. Coordinator assistance in planning and implementation of computerized system throughout Bell System. Office: 225 W Randolph St HQ7D Chicago IL 60606

JORDAN, CAROLYN DAVIS, lawyer; b. Ft. Worth, Mar. 7, 1941; B.A., Fisk U., 1963; LL.B., Howard U., 1966. Admitted to D.C. bar, 1967, Calif. bar, 1969; dep. city atty., Compton, Calif., 1969; individual practice law, Los Angeles, 1970-72; senatorial legis. asst., 1972-74; counsel banking com. U.S. Senate, 1974-80, minority counsel, 1980—. Commr., D.C. Ed. Labor Relations, 1975, Commn. Real Estate D.C., 1979, D.C. Tax Revision Commn., 1978, D.C. Condominium Commn., 1979; bd. dirs. Capital East Neighborhood Housing Center, 1979—; mem. adv. bd. Howard Hosp., 1970. Recipient various service awards. Office: Room 5300 Dirksen Senate Office Bldg Washington DC 20510

JORDAN, LILLIAN, Ariz. state legislator; b. Belen, N.M.; d. Joseph Curtis Julien and Kathryn Seymour J.; student Phoenix Coll.; m. Roy Martin Jordan, 1945; children—Martin Curtis, Royann. Dep. county sch. supt. Maricopa County, Ariz., 1973; mem. Ariz. Ho. Reps., 1977—. Hon. life mem. Ariz. PTA; mem. Am. Legis. Exchange Council, Ariz. Council Republican Women, Freedoms Found. Valley Forge, Roadrunner Republican Women. Baptist. Office: State Capitol Ho Reps Wing Phoenix AZ 85007 *

JORDAN, PATRICIA EUBANK, psychologist; b. Detroit, Feb. 9, 1944; d. Richard Grewig and Ruth (Koch) Eubank; B.A., Denison U., Granville, Ohio, 1965; M.Ed., U. Pitts., 1967, Ph.D. in Edn. (univ. fellow 1973-75), 1975; m. Raymond E. Jordan, Jr., Aug. 6, 1966; children—Christopher Reed, Raymond Ellsworth, III. Tchr. English and German, North Allegheny schs., Pitts., 1965-67; counselor Allegheny Intermediate Unit, 1967-71; grad. asst. U. Pitts., 1973-75; psychologist Wheeler Sch., Pitts., 1976—, Ednl. Tng. Corp., Warrendale, Pa., 1981—; ind. practice psychotherapy, Baden, Pa., 1977—; tng. cons., tchr. in field. Bd. dirs. Bellwood Sch., Ingomar, Pa., 1981-82. Mem. Am. Personnel and Guidance Assn., Am. Psychol. Assn., Assn. Humanistic Psychology, Commonwealth Prevention Alliance. Home: Sleepy Hollow Farm RD 1 Baden PA 15005 Office: Ednl Tng Corp Box 87 Warrendale PA 15086

JORDAN, PATRICIA JANE, Can. provincial ofcl.; b. Vernon, B.C., Dec. 7, 1931; d. John William and Eva Maud (Wiseman) Laidman; student U. B.C., Vancouver Gen. Hosp. Sch. Nursing, San Antonio State Coll., U. Minn.; m. Malurance Theodore Jordan, Sept. 4, 1954; children—James David Edward, Laurance Henry Phillips. Minister without portfolio, B.C., Can., now minister of tourism for B.C.; 19 —;

B.C. rep. for Fed. Govt. Fashions Canada; post-trainee open heart surgery ward St. Mary's Hosp., Rochester, Minn.; tchr. Aldridge Meml. Nursery Sch., Rochester; instr. psychiat. nursing Rochester State Hosp. (Mayo Clinic). Hon. mem. 4-H Club; mem. Vancouver Art Gallery, Vernon Arts Soc. Club: Mayo Clinic-Fellow Wives Assn. (pres.). Anglican. Author: Laws and Rights of Women in British Columbia. Office: Parliament Bldgs Victoria BC V8V 1X4 Canada *

JORDAN, SHARON ANN, social worker; b. Detroit, July 22, 1953; d. Benneal and Myrtice Marie J., A.B. in Journalism, U. Mich., 1975, M.Urban Planning, 1977, M.S.W., 1979. Intern, research asst. City of Ann Arbor (Mich.), 1976-77; caseworker asst. Ann Arbor Community Center, 1977-78; caseworker aide ARC, 1978-79; parent orientation coordinator U. Mich., 1978, resident dir. housing, 1975-79; adminstrv. intern City of Ann Arbor, 1979; social worker, counselor, staff devel. coordinator U. Mich. opportunity program, 1979—. U. Mich. fellow, 1976-77. Mem. Nat. Assn. Social Workers, Acad. Cert. Social Workers, Phi Beta Kappa. Home: 1000 W Huron St Apt 4A Ann Arbor MI 48103 Office: 1415 Mason Hall Ann Arbor MI 48109

JORDETH, ELLA JOYCE, home economist; b. Morrill, Nebr., Nov. 2, 1931; d. James William and Mary Gertrude (Altig) Croft; A.A., Graceland Coll., 1951; B.S., Iowa State Coll., Ames, 1954, M.S., 1959; m. Olaf M. Jordeth, Apr. 16, 1977. Tchr. 5th grade Sunflower Schs., Mitchell, Nebr., 1951-52; home demonstration agt. Niobrara County, Lusk, Wyo., 1954-58; home demonstration agt. Carbon County, Rawlins, Wyo., 1959-61; asso. state 4-H Club leader U. Wyo., Laramie, 1961-70; 4-H youth specialist Colo. State U., Fort Collins, 1970—. Tchr. Sunday Sch., Reorganized Ch. Jesus Christ Latter-day Saints. Mem. Colo. Home Econs. Assn., Am. Home Econs. Assn., Colo. Assn. Extension 4-H Agts., Nat. Assn. Extension 4-H Agts., Epsilon Sigma Phi, Extension Specialist Group, Omicron Nu. Club: Sons of Norway. Home: 632 Endicott St Fort Collins CO 80524 Office: Aylesworth Hall Colo State U Fort Collins CO 80523

JORDON, PEARL, psychotherapist, educator; b. N.Y.C., July 24, 1926; d. Max and Clara (Pineus) J.; B.A., Bklyn. Coll., 1959; M.S., Yeshiva U., 1960; M.S.W., Hunter Coll., 1963. Sr. social worker Manhattan State Hosp., Wards Island, N.Y., 1959-66, psychiat. cons. social service dept., 1967-68; psychiat. cons. Kings County Psychiat. Social Service Dept., Bklyn., 1969-71; asso. dir. dept. social services Montefiore Hosp. & Med. Center, Bronx, N.Y., 1971-79; asst. prof. N.Y.U., N.Y.C., 1969-71; lectr. Hunter Coll., N.Y.C., 1975, adj. clin. asso. prof., 1976—; clin. asso. prof. SUNY, Stony Brook, 1979—, chmn. integrated practice concentration, 1980—; pvt. practice psychotherapy, N.Y.C., 1968—. Mem. social service adv. com. March of Dimes, Jericho, N.Y., 1980-81; guest speaker Nassau and Suffolk Health Systems Assn., Melville, N.Y., 1980; mem. com. Suffolk/Nassau Health Systems Agy., 1980-81. Fellow Soc. Clin. Social Work Psychotherapists, Am. Orthopsychiat. Assn., Council Social Work Edn.; mem. Nat. Assn. Social Workers, Soc. Hosp. Social Service Dirs., State Assn. Gerontology Educators, Council on Social Work Edn. Contbr. articles in field to profl. pubs. Office: Sch Social Welfare SUNY Stony Brook NY 11794

JORGENSEN, ALICE ELIZABETH, mfg. co. exec.; b. Chgo., Nov. 30, 1936; d. Clarence William and Elva Mae (Edmunds) Jorgensen; R.N., B.S., Boston U., 1964; children—Paul Robert, Ann Margaret. With Superior Fastener Corp., Chgo., 1965—, pres., 1974—; with Gates Washer & Mfg. Co., Chgo., 1974—, v.p., 1975-76, pres., 1976—. Office: 9536 W Foster Ave Chicago IL 60656

JORGENSEN, JUDITH ANN, psychiatrist; b. Parris Island, S.C., Aug. 31, 1941; d. George Emil and Margaret Georgia Jorgensen; B.A., Stanford U., 1963; M.D., U. Calif., 1968; m. Ronald Francis Crown, July 11, 1970. Intern, Meml. Hosp., Long Beach, 1969-70; resident County Mental Health Services, San Diego, 1970-73; staff psychiatrist Children and Adolescent Services, San Diego, 1973-78; practice medicine specializing in psychiatry, La Jolla, Calif., 1973—; staff psychiatrist County Mental Health Services of San Diego, 1973-78; psychiat. cons. San Diego City Coll., 1973-78; asst. prof. dept. psychiatry U. Calif., 1978—; chair med. quality rev. com. Dist. XIV, State of Calif. Mem. Am. Psychiat. Assn., San Diego Psychiat. Soc. (chmn. membership 1975-77, v.p. 1978-80), Am. Soc. Adolescent Psychiatry, San Diego Soc. Adolescent Psychiatry (pres. 1981-82), Soc. Sci. Study of Sex, San Diego Soc. Sex Therapy and Edn. Club: Rowing. Office: 470 Nautilus St Suite 211 La Jolla CA 92037

JORGENSEN, KAY SUSAN, state legislator; b. Winner, S.D., May 25, 1951; d. Arnold and Twyla Vivian J.; B.S. in Edn., Black Hills State Coll., 1974; m. Michael R. Pangburn, July 5, 1975. Auctioneer, 1968—; page adv., tchr. S.D. Legislature, Pierre, 1975-78; co-owner, mgr. Bell Boy Drive Inn, Spearfish, S.D., 1976-77; mgr. food concession Passion Play, Spearfish, 1976-80; exec. dir., trustee High Plains Heritage Soc., Spearfish, 1979—; mem. S.D. Ho. of Reps., 1978—, mem. tax and state affairs coms. Mem. Black Hills State Coll. Alumni Assn. (pres. 1978-79), S.D. Restaurant Assn., AAUW, Bus. and Profl. Women's Club, Epilepsy Found., Am. Quarter Horse Assn., Community Concert Assn., Delta Kappa Gamma (hon.). Republican.

JORGENSEN, LOU ANN BIRKBECK, social worker; b. Park City, Utah, May 14, 1931; d. Robert John and Lillian Pearl (Langford) Birkbeck; student Westminster Coll., 1949-51; B.S., U. Utah, 1953, M.S.W., 1972, D.S.W., 1979; m. Howard Arnold Jorgensen, June 9, 1954; children—Gregory Arnold, Blake John, Paul Clayton. Social work adminstr. nursing home demonstration project, dept. family and community medicine U. Utah Med. Center, Salt Lake City, 1972-74; mental health ednl. specialist Grad. Sch. Social Work, U. Utah, 1974-77, 77-80, asst. prof., 1974-80, asso. prof., 1980—; regional mental health cons. Bd. dirs. Info. and Referral Center, 1975—, United Way of Utah, 1976—, Pioneer Trail Parks, 1977—; pres. Human Services Conf. for Utah, 1979-80. Mem. Council on Social Work Edn., Nat. Assn. Social Workers (pres. Utah chpt. 1978-79), Adminstrs. of Public Agys. Assn., Human Services Assn. Utah, Jr. League of Salt Lake City, Phi Kappa Phi. Republican. Episcopalian. Clubs: Ft. Douglas Country, Town, Eastern Star. Author: Explorations in Living, 1978; Social Work in Business and Industry, 1979; Handbook of the Social Services, 1981; contbr. articles to profl. jours. Home: 3442 East Oaks Dr Salt Lake City UT 84117 Office: Grad Sch Social Work U Utah Salt Lake City UT 84112

JORGENSEN, VIRGINIA TRIEST, psychiatrist; b. New Orleans, Mar. 22, 1923; d. Kenneth G. and Luise (Schiele) Triest; B.A. cum laude, Hofstra U., 1951; M.D., U. Copenhagen, 1957; postgrad. N.Y. Sch. Psychiatry, 1963; m. Eric Jorgensen, Aug. 5, 1951; children—Ellen Verena, Nina. Intern, Flushing (N.Y.) Hosp., 1957-58; resident in psychiatry Creedmore State Hosp., Queens, N.Y., 1959-62, sr. psychiatrist, 1962-64; practice medicine specializing in psychiatry, Garden City, N.Y., 1963—; psychiat. cons. Sch. for Emotionally Disturbed Children, Nassau County, N.Y., 1962-71, Children's Village, Dobbs Ferry, N.Y., 1964-65; asst. attending physican N. Shore Hosp., Manhasset, N.Y., 1980—; clin. instr. psychiatry Cornell U. Coll. of Medicine, 1981. Mem. med. adv. bd. Planned Parenthood of Nassau County, 1966—; bd. dirs. Family Life Center, Garden City, 1981. Diplomate Am. Bd. Psychiatry. Mem. Am. Psychiat. Assn., Am. Med. Women's Assn., Nassau County Psychiat. Soc. Club: Garden City Ski. Office: 520 Franklin Ave Garden City NY 11530

JORGENSON, AVIS EVELYN (KNUDSEN), ednl. adminstr.; b. Albert Lea, Minn., Aug. 1, 1923; d. Holger Frederick and Evangeline Sophia (Larsen) Knudsen; B.S., U. Colo., 1966; Ed.M. (fellow), U. Ill., 1969; postgrad. Pacific Oaks Coll., 1977-78; doctoral candidate U. No. Colo.; children by previous marriage—Robert Alan Jorgenson, Kristine Raye Godecker, Peter Lowell Jorgenson. Presch. tchr. Littleton (Colo.) pub. schs., 1960-65; Head Start kindergarten tchr. Denver pub. schs., 1966-69; follow through dir. Trinidad (Colo.) pub. schs., 1969-70; curriculum coordinator of child care aide tng. program Community Coll./North, Denver, 1970-71; instr. Aims Coll., Greeley, Colo., 1971-72; dir. early childhood edn. U. So. Colo., Pueblo, 1972—, also mem. Women's services bd.; mem. Colo. Dept. Edn. Task Force on Early Childhood, 1975—, Colo. Dept. Edn. Task Force on Cert. for Early Childhood Spl. Edn., 1978. Bd. dirs. Pueblo Infant Toddler Center. Recipient Outstanding Service award Head Start, 1972, 73, 74, 75, 76, 77, 78, 79, 80. Mem. Nat., Colo. (pres. 1977-79), Alianza (co-founder) assns. edn. young children NEA, Colo. Edn. Assn., Colo. Coalition for Child Care, Women's Caucus U. So. Colo., NOW, Colo. Women's Polit. Caucus, Delta Kappa Gamma. Home: 15 Villa Dr Pueblo CO 81001 Office: Education Dept Belmont Campus Pueblo CO 81001

JORIAN, PAULINE ANNETTE, nursing adminstr.; b. North Providence, R.I., Aug. 29, 1935; d. Romeo William and Edith Frances (Driscoll) Lambert; A.D.N., R.I. Jr. Coll., 1970; student R.I. Coll., 1970; m. Franklin T. Kennedy, Mar., 1982; children—Paul C. Ward, Barbara E. Ward, Donna Hernandez. Staff nurse various hosps., R.I., until 1977, Calif., 1977-81; nurse, dir. nurses Broadway Convalescent Hosp., San Gabriel, Calif., 1981—; charge nurse Brea (Calif.) Community Hosp., 1982—. Home: 16040 Leffingwell Rd Apt 39 Whittier CA 90603 Office: Broadway Convalescent Hosp 112 E Broadway San Gabriel CA 91776

JORSS, EMMA BARBARA, univ. pres.; b. Odessa, Russia; foster dau. Jacob and Wilhelmina Bauman; student Dakota Wesleyan Coll., 1930-31, U. Calif., Berkeley, 1931-32, U. So. Calif., 1932-37, U. Omaha, 1964-65; J.D., Lincoln U., 1950; LL.D., Am. Acad. Asian Studies, 1977, Lincoln Law Sch., 1982; m. Harry Charles Jorss, 1932; 1 dau., Margaret. Mgr., Eversharp Inc., San Francisco, 1939-45; bus. mgr. YWCA, San Francisco, 1945-53, exec. v.p. Lincoln U., San Francisco, 1953-78, pres., 1978—, sec.-treas. bd. trustees, 1953-80, founding mem., dir. Lincoln U. Found., founder Lincoln U. Law Sch., Sacramento. Mem. Nat. Assn. Women Deans, Adminstrs. and Counselors, Am. Assn. Higher Edn., AAUP. Republican. Episcopalian. Club: Commonwealth. Exec. producer cable TV series This Is Your Law, 1974. Office: Lincoln U 281 Masonic Ave San Francisco CA 94118

JOSE, PHYLLIS ANN, librarian; b. Detroit, Mar. 15, 1949; d. William Henry and Isobel Eleanor (Mundle) J.; B.A., Mich. State U., 1971, M.A., 1972; M.A. in Library Sci., U. Mich., 1975. Library aide audio-visual div. Dearborn (Mich.) Dept. Libraries, 1973-76, librarian gen. info. div., 1976-77; reference library dir. Oakland County (Mich.) Library, 1977—. Officer Southfield Economic Devel. Corp., 1980—; mem. Southfield Tax Increment Fin. Authority, 1981—. Mem. ALA, Mich. Library Assn., Spl. Library Assn., LWV Southfield, Lathrup Village and Oak Park (officer). Presbyterian. Office: 1200 N Telegraph Rd Pontiac MI 48053

JOSEFF, JOAN CASTLE, jewelry rental co. exec., mfg. exec.; b. Alta., Can., Aug. 12, 1922; naturalized U.S. citizen, 1945; d. Edgar W. and Lottie (Coates) Castle; B.A. in Psychology, UCLA; widow; 1 son, Jeffrey Rene. With Joseff-Hollywood, jewelry rental, Burbank, Calif., 1939—, chmn. bd., pres., sec.-treas., 1948—; exec., aircraft components mfg. co. Mem. Burbank Salary Task Force, 1979—, Los Angeles County Earthquake Fact-Finding Commn., 1981—; bd. dirs. local chpt. Am. Cancer Soc. Hon. life mem. Women of Motion Picture Industry. Mem. Nat. Fedn. Republican Women (regent), Calif. Rep. Women (dir.), N. Hollywood Rep. Women (pres. 1981-82). Home: 10060 Toluca Lake Ave Toluca Lake CA 91602 Office: 129 E Providencia Ave Burbank CA 91502

JOSELYN, JO ANN, space scientist; b. St. Francis, Kans., Oct. 5, 1943; d. James Jacob and Josephine Felzien (Firkins) Cram; B.S. in Applied Math., U. Colo. 1965, M.S. in Astrogeophysics, 1967, Ph.D. in Astrogeophysics, 1978. Research asst. astrogeophysics U. Colo., 1964-67; research asst. NASA/Manned Space Center, Houston, 1966; physicist NOAA/Space Environ. Lab., 1967-78, space scientist 1978—. Recipient NOAA unit citation 1971, 80. Mem. Am. Geophys. Union, Union Radio Sci. Internat., Internat. Union Geodesy and Geophysics, Assn. Geomagnetism and Aeronomy, AAAS, AAUW, Assn. Fed. Profl. and Adminstrv. Women, Sigma Xi, Tau Beta Pi, Sigma Tau. Republican. Methodist. Club: PEO. Office: 325 Broadway St Boulder CO 80303

JOSEPH, EDNA WHITEHEAD (MRS. LAWRENCE J. JOSEPH), bank exec.; b. Everett, Mass., Feb. 4, 1924; d. Alfred Edward and Mary Kathleen (Butler) Whitehead; attended Boston U., Am. Inst. Banking; m. Lawrence James Joseph, May 30, 1958. With Nat. Shawmut Bank (name now Shawmut Bank of Boston, N.A.), 1941-55, 57—, asst. tax officer, 1965-69, tax officer, 1969-79, sr. trust officer, 1979—; income tax mgr. Sam C. Charlson, Manhattan, Kans., 1955-57. Bd. dirs. Found. of Hope, Boston; mem. Republican Nat. Com., Women's Rep. Club Essex County, Nat. Fedn. Rep. Women. Mem. Fiduciary Tax Assos., Mass. Bankers Assn. (vice chmn. taxation com. 1971-72, chmn. 1972-73, tax cons. com. 1975—), Nat. Assn. Bank Women, Am. Inst. Banking, Nat. Early Am. Glass Club, North Shore Antique Assn., Soc. Preservation New Eng. Antiquities, Friends of Sandwich Mus., Woman 76 (Boston organizing com.), Soc. Jesus in New Eng. (liaison com. 1974-75, exec. com. 1975-76), Mus. Fine Arts, Bostonian Soc., Victorian Soc., Essex Inst., Peabody Mus., Jones Gallery Glass and Ceramics. Home: 8 Laurel Rd Lynnfield MA 01940 Office: Shawmut Bank of Boston NA One Federal St Boston MA 02110

JOSEPH, GERI MACK, journalist, former ambassador to The Netherlands; b. St. Paul, June 19, 1923; d. Samuel S. and Edith E. Mack; B.A. magna cum laude, U. Minn., 1946; m. Burton M. Joseph, Apr. 2, 1953; children—Shelley Joseph Kordell, I. Scott, Jonathan. Staff writer for health, edn. and welfare Mpls. Tribune, 1946-53, contbg. editor and columnist, 1972-78; ambassador to Netherlands, The Hague, 1978-81; dir. Honeywell, George A. Hormel Co., Twin City Barge Co., Northwestern Nat. Bank; mem. adv. council NIMH, 1962-67; mem. adv. bd. Rutgers U. Center Am. Women and Politics, 1970-75; mem. vis. com. dept. govt. Harvard U., 1973-78; mem. adv. com. Women's Equity Action League, 1975-80; mem. Pres. Kennedy's Com. on Youth Employment, 1962-63; mem. Pres. Johnson's Commn. on Income Maintenance Programs, 1967-69; mem. task panel on public attitudes of media Pres.'s Commn. on Mental Health, 1977-78. State chairwoman Minn. Democratic-Farmer-Labor Party, 1958-60, nat. committeewoman, 1960-72; del. Dem. Nat. Conv., 1960, 64, 68; mem. exec. com. Dem. Nat. Com., 1960-71; vice-chmn. United Democrats for Humphrey, 1968; vice chmn., dir. women's activities Dem. Nat. Com., 1968-70; mem. Dem. Policy Council, 1969-71; Pres. Nat. Assn. Mental Health, 1968-69; bd. dirs. U. Minn. Found., 1973-78, Carleton Coll., 1975—. Recipient Disting. Service award Minn. Jr. C. of C., 1952, Sigma Delta Chi award, 1952, award for writing Am. Newspaper Guild, 1947, 48, 49, 50, 51, Outstanding Achievement award U. Minn., 1974. Mem. U. Minn. Alumni Assn. (dir. 1971-75).

JOSEPH, JOY DEE, ednl. adminstr.; b. Jeanerette, La., Jan. 28, 1930; d. Louis and Addie W. J.; B.S., So. U., 1954, M.Ed., 1972. Tchr., head bus. dept. C. M. Washington High Sch., Thibodaux, La., 1954-66; tchr., Coop. Office Edn. coordinator, head bus. dept. Thibodaux High Sch., 1966-72, 72-74; supr. bus. and office edn. La. Dept. Edn., Baton Rouge, 1974-77, supr. sex equity, 1977—. Sec., 7th dist. La. Interscholastic, Athletic and Lit. Orgn., 1954-63; sec. Lefeda Fed. Credit Union, 1963-71. Named Hon. Citizen New Orleans, 1981. Mem. Vocat. Edn. Equity Council (sec.-treas. 1982), Am. Vocat. Assn., Am. Soc. Curriculum Devel., La. Bus. Edn. Assn., La. Assn. Sch. Execs., La. Vocat. Assn., Women in Politics, YWCA. Democrat. Baptist. Club: Order Eastern Star. Home: 1718 Blvd DeProvince Baton Rouge LA 70815 Office: 224 North St Baton Rouge LA 70804

JOSEPH, JUDITH ROSE, editor; b. Newark, Sept. 18, 1948; d. Siegmund and Yolanda (Klein) J.; B.A. with honors, N.Y.U., 1970; M.A., U. Va., 1973; m. Alan M. de Vries, June 1982. Sales rep. Prentice-Hall Pub., Inc., 1973-75; pub. social sci. and humanities texts D. Van Nostrand Co., Inc., N.Y.C., 1975-79, v.p., publs. dir., 1979-81; sr. editor vocat. and tech. texts John Wiley & Sons, Inc., N.Y.C., 1981—. Recipient Cert. of Honor, Offender Aid and Restoration Charlottesville, Va., 1973. Mem. Am. Assn. Pubs. (mem. student relations com.), Nat. Assn. Female Execs., NOW. Office: 605 3d Ave New York NY 10158

JOSEPH, NORMA, nursing cons.; b. Miami, Fla., Sept. 20, 1949; d. Norman and Marjorie (Martindale) J.; R.N., Jackson Meml. Hosp., Miami, Fla., 1970; postgrad. Fla. Internat. U., 1974-76; B.S., Willmington Coll., 1980. Staff nurse Jackson Meml. Hosp., Miami, Fla., 1970-71; asst. head nurse, Am. Med. Internat., Parkway Gen. Hosp., N. Miami, Fla., 1971-72, head nurse, 1972-76, quality assurance supr., 1976-80, pre-planning supr., 1980-81; nursing service adminstr. Palm Beach Gardens (Fla.) Hosp., 1981-82; nursing cons. So. Region Am. Med. Internat., Atlanta, 1982—; adv. bd. nursing program Palm Beach Jr. Coll., 1981-82. Participant AMI mgmt. course, 1981, nursing mgmt., 1980; cert. hosp. mktg., 1981, hosp. fin., 1981, public relations, 1981. Mem. S.Fla. Nursing Service Adminstrs., Am. Hosp. Soc. for Nursing Adminstrs., Am. Nurse Assn., Am. Heart Assn., Am. Mgmt. Assn. Office: 6400 Powers Ferry Rd Atlanta GA 30339

JOSEPH, PATRICIA DORA, fin. exec.; b. Springfield, Mass., Sept. 2, 1944; d. Phillip Jay and Doris (Ferris) J.; B.F.A., Ohio U., 1966; M.A., N.Y.U., 1975. Vice pres., co-owner House of Tapes, Toledo, Ohio, 1961-77; tchr. United Cerebral Palsy, N.Y.C., 1971-72, asst. dir., 1973, dir., 1974-80; account exec. Merrill Lynch, N.Y.C., 1981—. Mem. Internat. Assn. Fin. Planners. Eastern Orthodox. Home: 185 E 85th St New York NY 10028 Office: 345 Park Ave New York NY 10154

JOSEPH-FELDMAN, DIANE, appraiser; b. Chgo., May 21, 1933; d. Wilfried Elmer and Rose (Kopca) Davis; ed. Am. Acad. Art, Art Inst. Chgo., Stone-Camryn Sch. Ballet; m. Z. Albert Joseph, 1957 (div. 1969); m. 2d, Hy Feldman, Feb. 14, 1979; children—Diana Jill Joseph, John Alan Joseph. Soloist, tchr. ballet Interlochen (Mich.) Nat. Music Camp, 1954-55; soloist in Brigadoon, N.Y.C. Center, 1956, My Fair Lady, other musicals; dancer WGN-TV and Lyric Opera Ballet, Chgo., 1955-58; founder, pres. Heritage Appraisal Service, Inc., Wilmette, Ill., 1971-82. Mem. Simon Wiesenthal Center, Democratic Nat. Orgn. Mem. Internat. Soc. Appraisers (rec. and corr. sec. Chgo. chpt.), ACLU, NOW, Audubon Soc. Address: 2201 Crestview Ln Wilmette IL 60091

JOSEY, LERONIA ARNETTA, lawyer, govt. exec.; b. Norfolk, Va., May 21, 1942; d. Embri and Carrie Arlene (Darden) Stokes; B.A., with honors, Spelman Coll., 1965; M.S.W., U. Md., 1973; M.P.A., Maxwell Sch. Citizenship and Public Affairs, 1977; J.D. cum laude (Afro-Am. fellow 1975-76), Syracuse U., 1977; m. 2d William N. Mason, Aug. 15, 1979; 1 son, Quenton Christopher Josey. Caseworker, Balt. City Welfare Dept., 1965-66, 67-68; center dir. Balt. Community Action Agy., 1969-72; dir. work study program Regional Planning Council, Balt., 1972-73; adv. specialist Sch. Dist. Phila., 1973-74; tchr. public schs., Norfolk, Va., 1966-67, Balt., 1968-69; legal honors intern Office Gen. Counsel, HUD, Washington, 1977; atty.-adv. block grants project br., 1978-79, atty.-adv. consumer protection br., 1979—, coordinator legal honors program; admitted to Pa. bar, 1978; mem. Md. Parole Commn. Mem. legal redress com. Balt. County NAACP, 1978—; bd. dirs. Echo House Found., Balt., 1978—, Med. Eye Bank. Recipient Senate award Syracuse U. Law Sch., 1977, Spl. Achievement award HUD Gen. Counsel, 1979; Ford Found. Minority Adminstrs. grantee, 1975. Mem. Nat. Bar Assn., Nat. Assn. Black Women Attys., Balt. County League Women Voters, Nat. Assn. Blacks in Criminal Justice, Nat. Assn. Social Workers, Assn. Minority Attys. at HUD, Democrat. Mem. African Methodist Episcopal Ch. Clubs: Syracuse U. Law Coll. Alumni, Spelman Coll. Alumnae. Home: 3700 Lochearn Dr Baltimore MD 21207 Office: Suite 601 1 Investment Pl Towson MD 21204

JOSHI, SMITA KEDARNATH, physician, pathologist; b. Ahmedabad, India, Mar. 11, 1945; came to U.S., 1969, naturalized, 1978; d. Ramanlal Narctamdas and Bhanumati Ramanlal (Mahadevia) Magiawala; M.B., B.S., B.J. Med. Coll., 1975. Resident in pathology Mt. Carmel Mercy Hosp., Detroit, 1971-75; asso. pathologist Deaconess Hosp. and Doctors Hosp., Detroit, 1976—. Diplomate Am. Bd. Pathology. Mem. Coll. Am. Pathologists, Am. Soc. Clin. Pathologists, Mich. Soc. Pathologists, Mich. Soc. Cytology, S. Central Soc. Microbiology, Am. Soc. Cytology, Internat. Soc. Pathologists. Home: 3151 Walnut Ln W Bloomfield MI 48033 Office: 3245 E Jefferson Detroit MI 48207

JOURE, SYLVIA ANN, psychologist; b. St. Clair, Mich., Oct. 15, 1945; d. Patrick Louis and Martha Ann (McDonald) J.; B.S., Memphis State U., 1966, M.S., 1969, Ph.D., 1970. Teaching and research asst. Memphis State U., 1967-70; asst. prof. psychology U. Ark., Little Rock, 1970-71; organizational/indsl. psychologist Frye/Timmons and Assos., Memphis, 1968—, operating v.p., 1973—; founder and sr. partner Frye/Joure & Assos., Memphis, 1972—; cons. numerous public and pvt., nat. and internat. orgns. Patron, Theatre Memphis, Memphis Opera Theatre, Memphis State Univ. Theatre; vol. Women's Bur., Pres.'s Council on Phys. Fitness; bd. dirs. Girls Clubs Memphis. U. Ark. grantee, 1970; Am. Soc. Plastic and Reconstructive Surgeons grantee, fall 1977, spring 1979. Diplomate Am. Bd. Profl. Psychology. Mem. Am. Psychol. Assn., Internat. Assn. Applied Psychology, Southwestern Psychol. Assn., Tenn. Psychol. Assn., AAAS, N.Y. Acad. Sci., Am. Soc. Tng. Dirs., Am. Soc. Personnel Adminstrs., Am. Mgmt. Assn., Southeastern Psychol. Assn., Sales and Mktg. Execs. Internat., Memphis C. of C., Houston C. of C., Mus. of Modern Art, LWV, NOW (Memphis task force chmn.: sexual harassment project), Psi Chi. Contbr. articles to profl. publs. Home: 367 Caraway Cove Memphis TN 38117 Office: 5580 Murray Rd Memphis TN 38117

JOURNEY, MARTHA JANE GRAY, psychologist; b. Marshall, Mo., July 13, 1950; d. Cecil Eric and Martha Louise (McQuitty) Gray; B.A., Central Mo. State U., 1972, M.S., 1974; M.Ed., U. Mo., Columbia, 1976. Psychologist, Fulton (Mo.) State Hosp., 1973-74; clin. psychologist Higginsville (Mo.) State Sch. and Hosp., 1976-81; instr. psychology Raytown (Mo.) Adult Edn., 1977-81; sch. psychologist Comprehensive Mental Health Services, Independence (Mo.) Sch. Dist., 1981—. Mem. Am. Psychol. Assn., Am. Assn. Mental Deficiency, Am. Personnel and Guidance Assn., Mo. Psychol. Assn., Sigma Sigma Sigma. Club: Kansas City Ski. Home: 3517 Blue Ridge Blvd Independence MO 64052 Office: Oldham Edn Center 14220 E 35th St Independence MO 64055

JOY, PEGGY MARGARET, artist; b. Boston, Jan. 4, 1926; d. George Horther and Margaret Mary (Culhane) Joy; B.A., Cedar Crest Coll., 1948; postgrad. Los Angeles Art Center, 1948-51; student Ray Ellender, N.Y.C., 1964-66, Miles Batt, Ft. Lauderdale, Fla., 1968-69. Mech. artist Universal Publs., N.Y.C., 1951; prodn. artist Norcross Greeting Cards, N.Y.C., 1953-58; art dir., record cover designer Joy Music & Select Records, N.Y.C., 1958-66; group shows include: Fort Lauderdale Mus. Arts, Broward Art Guild, Boca Raton Center for Arts. Mem. Broward Art Guild (v.p. 1974-75, mural com. 1977—), Gold Coast Water Color Soc. Democrat. Roman Catholic. Inventor, designer Zodiac Game, 1971. Home and Office: 801 S Federal Hwy Pompano Beach FL 33062

JOYCE, BERNITA ANNE, U.S. Dept. Interior adminstr.; b. Omaha, Aug. 11, 1927; d. Albert A. and Margaret C. Joyce; B.A., Duchesne Coll.; M.B.A., U. Santa Clara, 1968, Ph.D., 1974; m. Kenneth B. Lucas, Aug. 2, 1975. Adminstr., Soc. of Sacred Heart, Menlo Park, Calif. and Seattle, 1957-71, regional adminstr., San Francisco, 1969-71; with Wolfe & Co., C.P.A.s, Washington, 1971-72; fin. dir. Nat. Forest Products Assn., Washington, 1972-74; budget fiscal officer ICC, Washington, 1974-77, Office Mgmt. and Budget, 1977-80; asst. dir. mgmt. services Bur. Mines, Dept. Interior, 1980—. Mem. Am. Inst. C.P.A.s, Am. Mgmt. Assn., AAUW, Beta Gamma Sigma. Home: 6001 Bradley Blvd Bethesda MD 20817

JOYCE, FLORENCE V. MIENERT (MRS. GEORGE T. JOYCE), civic worker; b. Fosston, Minn., Feb. 13, 1923; d. William P. A. and Clara (Lindfors) Mienert; R.N., Ancker Hosp. Sch. Nursing, St. Paul, 1944; student U. Minn., 1944-45; m. George T. Joyce, Aug. 8, 1946; children—Roberta Eileen, Elizabeth Anne. Bd. dirs. N. Central Iowa chpt. ARC, 1960-66, 67-73, nursing services chmn., 1967-75; pres. Vols. Service League, St. Joseph Mercy Hosp., Mason City, Iowa, 1959-61; leader Girl Scouts U.S.A., 1948-66; bd. dirs. YWCA, 1963-66, Community Achievement award, 1979; precinct chmn. Cerro Gordo County Republican Central Com., 1974-82. Mem. Am. Nurses Assn., Iowa Nurses Assn., Iowa Dist. 10 Nurses Assn. (dir. 1981—), Nat. Trust for Historic Preservation, Cerro Gordo County Med. Aux., Ancker (Hosp.) Alumni Assn., Charles H. MacNider Art Guild (pres. 1972-73, mems. council 1973-80). Club: Mason City Womans (dir. 1965-75, pres. 1969-70). Roman Catholic. Home: 259 N Crescent Dr Mason City IA 50401

JOYNER, GAIL EILEEN HARRISON, social worker; b. Scranton, Pa., Mar. 22, 1944; d. Merrit Franklin and Doris Helen (Ferguson) Harrison; B.S., Methodist Coll., 1966; M.S.W., U. N.C., Chapel Hill, 1970; m. Worth Basil Joyner, Jr., Dec. 15, 1974. Social worker, Cumberland County Dept. Social Services, Fayetteville, N.C., 1966-68, Southeastern Mental Health Center, Lumberton, N.C., 1970, Caswell Center, Kinston, N.C., 1970-74; juvenile project mgr. Youth Services Bur., Winston Salem, N.C., 1974; supr. children protective services unit Mecklenburg County Dept. Social Services, Charlotte, N.C., 1974-75; cons. adult protective services N.C. Div. Social Services, Raleigh, N.C., 1975-79; mgr. patient and family services Wake County Med. Center, Raleigh, 1979—. Bd. dirs. Meth. Coll., Fayetteville, N.C., 1978—; mem. N.C. Cancer Control Task Force, 1977, N.C. Task Force on Battered Women, 1977-78. Mem. Acad. Cert. Social Workers, Nat. Soc. Hosp. Social Work Dirs., N.C. Soc. Hosp. Social Work Dirs., N.C. State Council Social Legis., N.C. Social Services Assn., Nat. Assn. Social Workers (past social action chmn. N.C. chpt.). Methodist. Home: 6312 Secret Dr Raleigh NC 27612 Office: 3000 New Bern Ave Raleigh NC 27610

JOYNER, JUDITH REBECCA, educator; b. Meggett, S.C., Aug. 14, 1920; d. Ernest Luther and Lena Rebecca (Butler) J.; B.A., Appalachian State U., Boone, S.C., 1942, M.A., 1957; Ph.D., U. S.C., 1960; postgrad. U. N.C., Temple U., Phila. Civilian with Dept. Def., 1948-54, mgmt. analyst Frankfort Arsenal, Phila., 1952-54; mem. faculty U. S.C., 1958—, prof. history and philosophy of edn., 1971—, dean Grad. Sch., 1974, chmn. dept. social founds. edn. Coll. Edn., 1965; vis. prof. U. Ala., Birmingham, 1975-76; cons. Choice, 1970—. Served to 1st lt. WAC, 1954-56; Korea. Mem. Nat. Soc. Study Edn., John Dewey Soc., History Edn. Soc., S. Atlantic Philosophy Edn. Soc. (pres. 1968-70), S.C. Soc. Social, Hist. and Philos. Study Edn. (pres. 1980-81), So. History Edn. Soc., S.C. Hist. Soc., LWV (dir. S.C. 1964-71), Phi Delta Kappa, Omicron Delta Kappa. Home: 57 Churchill Circle Columbia SC 29206 Office: Coll Edn U SC Columbia SC 29208

JOYNER, SYLVIA PETTIS, fundraiser; b. Galveston, Tex., Sept. 12, 1946; d. Louis James Pettis and Florence Gloria Lawton Cody; B.A., Tuskegee Inst., 1968; 1 son, Michael Pettis. Social service advisor Prichard (Ala.) Housing Authority, 1973-74; community rep. McDonald's of Mobile (Ala.), 1974-76; nat. VISTA worker, VISTA Spl. Project, Fedn. So. Coops., Epes, Ala., 1978; area devel. dir. United Negro Coll. Fund, Inc., Birmingham, Ala., 1978—. Bd. dirs. Vol. and Info. Center, 1980—, Birmingham Creative Dance Co. Mem. Ala. Soc. Fund Raising Execs. (exec. com. 1980—), Urban League, NAACP, Nat. Assn. Young Children, Nat. Soc. Fundraisers, Alpha Kappa Alpha (Omicron Omega chpt.). Office: 1728 3rd Ave N Birmingham AL 35203

JUDD, INGE, mgmt. cons.; b. Vienna, Austria, Mar. 5, 1936; d. Ludwig and Margit (Silberstein) Voss; came to U.S., 1938, naturalized, 1944; B.A., Bard Coll., 1958; postgrad. Rutgers U., 1964-65; m. Eugene Judd, May 14, 1965; 1 dau., Heidi. Dir. adminstrn. E.F. Shelly, N.Y.C., 1966-69; co-founder, chmn. exec. com., chief operating officer, exec. v.p. Judd-Falk, Inc., N.Y.C., 1969—; co-founder, pres., chmn. bd., chief exec. officer Judd-Falk, Inc., Chgo., 1977—; dir. Woodstock Communications, Cornucopia, Ltd.; chairperson Merriewold Park; cons. Peace Corps, Reef Resorts, Ltd., Falcon Co., Privateers Bay. Active Murray Hill Com. Mem. Am. Mgmt. Assn. Home and office: 124 E 37th St New York City NY 10016

JUDGE, JEAN FRANCES, journalist; b. Fall River, Mass., Mar. 18, 1930; d. James Edward and Dolores Veronica (Dunn) J.; B.A. magna cum laude in English Lit., Salve Regina Coll., Newport, R.I., 1951. Mem. staff Fall River Herald News, 1951—, editor woman's page, 1972-80, lifestyle editor, 1980—. Named Woman of Achievement Greater Fall River Bus. and Profl. Women's Club, 1982. Home: 716 Broadway Fall River MA 02724 Office: 207 Pocasset St Fall River MA 02722

JUDISCH, JANIFER MANN, pediatric hematologist/oncologist; b. Ames, Iowa, Mar. 25, 1939; d. Louis H. and Clara (Mann) J.; student Iowa State U., 1956-58, Grinnell (Iowa) Coll., 1958-59; M.D., State U. Iowa, 1963. Straight pediatric intern, Children's Hosp. of Buffalo (N.Y.), 1963-64, asst. chief resident, 1965-66, chief resident, 1966-67; sr. resident Children's Hosp. of Phila., 1964-65; asst. attending pediatrician Children's Hosp. Buffalo, 1970-75, asso. dir. hematology, 1970-75, acting dir. hematology, 1974-75, dir. clin. labs., 1974-75; asso. prof. pediatrics, head sect. pediatric hematology/oncology U. South Fla., Tampa, 1975—, asst. dean equal opportunity and affirmative action, 1976—, asso. dean extramural affairs, 1981—, exec. dir. Children's Center Cancer and Blood Diseases, 1976—, coordinator pediatric clerkship, 1975-80; mem. regional oncology tech. com. Fla. Gulf Health Systems Agy., Inc., 1979—. Diplomate Am. Bd. Pediatrics. Named 1 of 10 Outstanding Young Women in Fla., Redbook mag., 1977; recipient Edn. award Tampa Lakes Jr. Woman's Club, 1978; Disting. Service award Tampa Jaycees, 1981. Bd. dirs. Hillsborough County unit Am. Cancer Soc., 1976-77, mem. com. leukemia, lymphoma and childhood cancer Fla. div., 1976—; bd. dirs. Fla. State Sickle Cell Found., Inc., 1980—; mem. steering com. Fla. Women's Network, 1978—; chairperson patient care com. Leukemia Soc. Am., 1979—. Mem. Am. Acad. Pediatrics, Am. Assn. Med. Colls. (minority affairs officer, women's liaison officer), Am. Soc. Hematology, Fla. Assn. Pediatric Tumor Programs (chairperson psychosocial task force), Fla. Cancer Council, Fla. Med. Assn., Fla. Pediatric Soc., Fla. Soc. Clin. Oncology, Hillsborough County Med. Assn., Hillsborough County Pediatric Soc., Pediatric Oncology Group, Athena Soc., C. of C., South Fla. Cancer Found., Alpha Omega Alpha, Alpha Lambda Delta. Democrat. Contbr. chpt.: Reticuloendothelial Studies in Pediatrics, 1974; contbr. articles to profl. jours. Home: 1354 Eckles Dr Tampa FL 33612 Office: 12901 N 30th St Box 37 Tampa FL 33612

JUERGENSEN, ILSE DINA, poet; b. Frankfurt/Main, Ger.; d. Alfred and Martha T. Loebenberg; came to U.S., 1940, naturalized, 1945; diploma Frankfurt/Main High Sch., 1938; postgrad. U. So. Fla., Tampa; m. Hans Juergensen, Oct. 27, 1945; 1 dau., Claudia Jeanne Juergensen Noble. Poet-in-schs., Tampa, 1973—; author: The Second Time, 1972; I Don't Want a Thunderbird Anymore, and New Poems, 1977, 2d rev. edit., 1980; represented in 5 anthologies; editor: (anthology children's poems) From Feather to Feather, 1976; co-editor Gryphon mag. Recipient award Fla. Poetry Rev. Mem. Nat. Fed. State Poetry Socs. (sec. 1968-70, 1st prize poems 1970, 71), Friends of Poetry, Poetry Soc. Am. Democrat. Jewish. Address: 7815 Pine Hill Dr Tampa FL 33617

JUERGENSMEYER, JESSICA JANE STUART (JANE STUART), author, translator; b. Ashland, Ky., Aug. 20, 1942; d. Jesse Hilton and Naomi Deane (Norris) Stuart; student Am. U., Cairo, 1960-61, U. Ky., 1962-63; A.B. magna cum laude, Case-Western Res. U., 1964; M.A. in Greek and Latin, Ind. U., 1967, M.A. in Italian, 1969, Ph.D. in Italian, 1971; m. Julian Conrad Juergensmeyer, Aug. 20, 1963; children—Conrad, Erik. Author (as Jane Stuart) collections of poetry: A Year's Harvest, 1957, Eyes of the Mole, 1967, White Barn, 1973; novels: Yellowhawk, 1973, Passerman's Hollow, 1974, Land of the Fox, 1975, Gideon's Children, 1976; contbr. poems and short stories to mags., newspapers, and jours., including: Ariz. Quar., Minn. Rev., Louisville Courier Jour., Ladies' Home Jour., Kans. Mag., Nat. Wildlife, Chgo. Tribune, Pegasus, Dublin Rev., Playgirl, others, also anthologies; contbr. transl. to Hartwick Rev., Kans. Mag., others; teaching assoc. dept. classics Ind. U., 1965-67; lectr. Italian, Haile Sellassie I U., Ethiopia, 1968-69; instr. creative writing U. Fla., 1972-75. Mem. Am. Pen Women, Phi Beta Kappa, Eta Sigma Phi. Home: 5726 NW 91st Blvd Gainesville FL 32606

JUHASZ, ANNE MCCREARY, ednl. psychologist; b. Stratford, Ont., Can., Jan. 19, 1922; came to U.S., 1962; d. John Harold and Edythe Selina (Staines) Phillips; B.Sc., Cortland (N.Y.) Coll., 1958; M.Ed., Cornell U., 1959, Ph.D., 1961. Asso. prof. ednl. psychology U. B.C. (Can.), 1962-67; mem. faculty Loyola U., Chgo., 1967—, prof. ednl. psychology, 1971—. Can.-Scandinavian postdoctoral research fellow, 1961-62. Mem. Am. Assn. Orthopsychiatry, Nat. Council Marriage and Family, Groves Conf. Family, Am. Assn. Sex. Educators, Couselors and Therapists (pres. Ill. sect. 1981). Author: Adolescents in Society, 1969; Language Experience Reading Program, 1970; Sexual Development and Behavior, 1978; asso. editor Family Therapy, Jour. Early Adolescence. Home: 4300 Marine Dr Chicago IL 60613 Office: 820 N Michigan Ave Chicago IL 60611

JUKOSKI, MARY ELLEN, educator; b. Massena, N.Y., May 17, 1949; d. Joseph and Helen (Oroszi) Jukoski; A.A., Mater Dei Coll., 1970; B.A. in English and Secondary Edn., Coll. of St. Rose, 1973, M.A. in English, 1979; M.S. in Curriculum Planning and Devel., SUNY, Albany, 1974. Tchr. 6th grade Holy Family Sch., Watertown, N.Y., 1970-71; English tutor Albany (N.Y.) City Schs., Teenage Mothers Program, 1972-74; chemistry lab. receptionist Albany Med. Center Hosp., 1973-74; secondary English tchr. Acad. of Holy Names, Albany, 1974-77; asst. dean Center for Statewide Programs, Empire State Coll., Saratoga Springs, N.Y., 1977-80; asst. to exec. dean World U., Miami, Fla., 1979-80; grad. asst. Center for Study of Higher Edn., Memphis State U., 1980, program asst. Inst. for Acad. Improvement and Higher Edn. for Adult Mental Health Project, NIMH, 1980-81, asso. dir., 1981—. Mem. Am. Assn. for Higher Edn., Assn. Students in Higher Edn. (pres. 1981-82), So. Coll. Personnel Assn., Tenn. Personnel Guidance Assn., AAUW, Kappa Gamma Pi. Clubs: Brook Meml. Art Gallery, Dixon Art Gallery and Gardens. Author: A Study of Selected Accredited Nontraditional Institutions and Programs, 1981-82. Home: 3341 Southern Ave #28 Memphis TN 38111 Office: Memphis State U Ball Edn Bldg #409 Memphis TN 38152

JULIANO, PATRICIA, city ofcl.; b. E. Orange, N.J., Dec. 8, 1930; d. John and Mildred (Petoia) Tricoli; A.S., Essex County Coll., 1975; B.A., Rutgers U., 1980; m. Carmen Juliano, May 10, 1952; children—John, Frank, Carmen, Angelo, Kathy, Michael, Joseph. Tchrs. aide Oakwood Ave. Sch., Orange, N.J., 1973-75; mem. Orange City Council, 1976—. Pres., PTA, Orange, 1960-61; v.p. Essex County Council PTA, 1963-65; vol. N.J. Assn. Retarded Children, 1965—; sec. to Parents of Orange PAL, 1962; co-founder Parents' Groups for Exceptional Children, 1975—, Orange Parents of Exceptional Children, 1978; mem. Community Service Council, United Way, 1976—; lobbyist for better edn. for exceptional children; mem. Essex County Community Action Bd., 1980—; mem. governing bd. Community Mental Health Center, Region II, 1982—; mem. adv. bd. Women in Support of Essex; co-ordinator Central Jersey Telephone Bank, Floria for Gov., N.J. Dem. Com., 1981; Orange chmn. Mother's March, March of Dimes Found., 1982. Recipient Outstanding Vol. award Community Services Council of United Way, 1977; Achievement award Essex council N.J. State Civil Service Assn., 1982. Mem. N.J. League of Municipalities (legis. com. 1980—), N.J. Assn. Elected Women Ofcls. (treas. 1981), Orange LWV, Am. Mus. Natural History, N.J. Fedn. Dem. Women, Rutgers U. Alumni Assn. Roman Catholic. Home: 390 Tremont Pl Orange NJ 07050 Office: 29 N Day St Orange NJ 07050

JULIOUS, KISSIE MAE, mfg. co. ofcl.; b. Yazoo County, Miss., Jan. 27, 1951; d. John and Luella (Berry) J.; B.S. in Bus. Adminstrn., Roosevelt U., 1977; 1 dau., Zaneta. File clk. Union Carbide Corp., Chgo., 1969, 71-72, order entry clk., 1972-73, order service rep., 1973-76, office sales rep., 1976-79, application rep., Parma, Ohio, 1979-81, sales rep., Detroit, 1981, account mgr., 1981—. Democrat. Baptist. Home: 38745 Golfview W Mount Clemens MI 48044 Office: 120 S Riverside Plaza Chicago IL 60606

JULIUS, JOYCE LEWIS, public relations exec.; b. New Kensington, Pa., June 26, 1942; d. John William and Geraldine Elizabeth (Markland) Lewis; B.S., Ohio State U., 1965, postgrad., 1965-68; children—Cindy, Lori. Toxicology researcher Ohio State U. Coll. Vet. Medicine, 1965-67; microbiologist Mich. State U., 1969-70; head research and devel. Aultman Hosp., Canton, Ohio, 1971-73; supr. microbiology Flint (Mich.) Osteo. Hosp., 1973-75; nat. promotions dir. Project Concern Internat., San Diego, 1978-82; cons. fund raising, 1981-82; dir. public relations Domino's Pizza, Ann Arbor, Mich., 1982—. Recipient Outstanding Service awards Kidney Found., 1978, Multiple Sclerosis Soc., 1979; named Outstanding Young Woman of Mich., Bus. and Profl. Women's Assn., 1980. Mem. Nat. Soc. Fundraising Execs., U.S. Jaycettes (parlamentarian 1979-80), Nat. Speakers Assn., NOW. Republican. Methodist. Club: Toastmasters. Home: 8699 B-3 Spinnaker Way Ypsilanti MI 48097 Office: 1968 Green Rd Ann Arbor MI

JUNEAU, JO ANN PHYLISS, splty. mdse. retailer; b. Hazleton, Pa., July 3, 1935; d. Phillip and Florence Lucille (De Lash) Manganaro; m. J. D. Juneau, June 19, 1959; children—Emory Kapral, Deborah, Kevin. Quality control exec. Rochester (N.Y.) Products div. Gen. Motors, 1967-74; realtor Town Crier Properties, Rochester, 1977; owner, mgr. Juneau's Grocery, Juneau's Restaurant, Marion, N.Y., 1975-79, Something Different Family Restaurant, Berwick, Pa., 1979-80; founder, owner, mgr. Gift World Home Party Plan, Gift World Boutique, Penfield, N.Y., 1980—, Candles by Candlelights, Penfield, 1982—. Mem. Internat. Entrepeneur's Assn., Nat. Assn. Female Execs., Nat. Specialty Merchandise Assn., Wayne County Sheriff's Assn., Real Estate Bd. Rochester N.Y. Home: 136 Holyoke St Rochester NY 14615 Office: Penn-Fair Plaza 2200 Penfield Rd Penfield PA 14526

JUNG, DORANNE, educator, public relations counsel; b. Los Angeles, June 11, 1948; d. Harry Gordon and Frances (Wong) J.; B.A., Mills Coll., 1970; postgrad. U. Calif., Berkeley, 1969, Fla. Presbyn. Coll., London, 1970-72; M.S., Boston U., 1972. Media asst. Young & Rubicam Internat., N.Y.C., 1970; communications coordinator New Eng. Spl. Edn. Instrnl. Materials Center, Boston, 1972-73; media dir./account exec. Harcomm Assos., Cambridge, Mass., 1973-76; promotion, advt. and public relations mgr. Westinghouse Broadcasting, WBZ Radio, Boston, 1976-79; pres. Corcoran & Doranne, Inc., Cambridge, 1979—; asst. prof. Boston U. Sch. Public Communication, 1980—; producer/dir. video TV and radio shows; cons. Mem. public affairs com. Boston chpt. ARC, 1979—; mem. public relations com. Am. Heart Assn., 1978; mem. corp. com. United Way Mass. Bay, 1979-81; mem. Hale House/Back Bay Aging Concerns Benefit Com., 1981—. Recipient award Ohio State Inst. Edn. by Radio/TV award, 1978, Broadcast Promotion Assn., 1978; Clarion award Women in Communications, 1978. Mem. Press Club Boston, Broadcast Promotion Assn., New Eng. Broadcasters Assn., Nat. Assn. TV Program Execs. Presbyterian. Contbg. author: Teaching About Funerals, 1980; author/dir. radio series Fishing and Our Law, 1979-80. Office: 640 Commonwealth Ave Boston MA 02215

JUNG, DORIS, opera singer, voice tchr.; b. Centralia, Ill., Jan. 5, 1924; d. John Jay and May (Middleton) Crittenden; student U. Ill., 1945-46, Manne Coll. Music, 1950, Vienna Acad. Performing Arts, 1954; pvt. voice studies with Julius Cohen, Emma Zador, Luise Helletsgruber, Winifred Cecil; m. Felix Popper, Nov. 3, 1951; 1 son, Richard Dorian. Debut as Vitellia in Mozart's Clemenza di Tito, Zurich Opera, 1955; appeared with Hamburg State Opera, Munich State Opera, Vienna State Opera, Royal Opera Copenhagen, Royal Opera Stockholm; appeared in Marseille, Strasbourg, France, Naples and Catania, Italy, with N.Y.C. Opera, Met. Opera, Washington, Portland, Oreg. and Aspen, Colo; soloist Wagner concert conducted by Leopold Stokowski, 1971; soloist with Syracuse Symphony, 1981; voice tchr.; condr. opera workshop.

JUNGERS, MARY BLANCHE, ednl. adminstr.; b. Grayson, Ky., May 27, 1927; d. Arthur R. and Phebe Edith (Horton) Huff; B.A., Ky. Christian Coll., 1948; B.S. in Edn., Washington U., St. Louis, 1959; M.S. in Edn., So. Ill. U., 1968; Ph.D., St. Louis U., 1972; m. Jack R. Jungers, Jan. 1, 1978; children—Arthur Jordan, Carla Jordan, John Jordan, Jim Jordan. Mem. staff Alton (Ill.) Community Unit Sch. Dist. 11, 1959—, prin. Central Jr. High Sch., 1974-75, asst. supt. pupil personel services, 1976-80, asst. supt. for elementary edn. services, 1980—; condr. workshops. NEXTEP fellow, 1967-68; Ford Found. grantee, 1978. Mem. Am. Assn. Sch. Adminstrs., Met. East Women's Polit. Caucus, League Women Voters, Phi Delta Kappa, Pi Lambda Theta, Delta Kappa Gamma. Mem. Christian Ch. Author articles, short stories. Home: 4321 Wedgewood St Alton IL 62002 Office: 1854 E Broadway Alton IL 62002

JUNIEL, EUNICE KIMBROUGH, clergywoman; b. Magnolia, Ala., Sept. 12, 1931; d. Joseph and Emma Lee (Jenkins) Kimbrough; B.A. in Sociology, Calif. State U., 1969, M.A., 1974; D. Metaphysical Sci., U. Metaphysics, Los Angeles, 1981; children—Josephus, Cheryl, Michael, Kathleen. Psychiat. technician State of Calif., Walnut, 1962-64; tchr. Los Angeles public schs., 1971-81; founder weekly program Patterns for Living, Sta. KTYM, Los Angeles, 1982—. Founder, pres. Universal Truth Found., 1982—. Mem. Phi Delta Kappa, Psi Gamma Mu. Democrat. Office: PO Box 11088 Marina Del Rey CA 90291

JUNZ, HELEN B., economist; d. Samson and Dobra Bachner; B.A., U. Amsterdam; M.A., New Sch. Social Research, 1956. Research officer Nat. Inst. Econ. and Social Research, London, 1958-60; economist Bur. Econ. Analysis, Dept. Commerce, Washington, 1960-62; adv. div. internat. fin. bd. govs. Fed. Res. System, Washington, 1962-77; adv OECD, Paris, 1967-69; sr. internat. economist Council of Econ. Advs., The White House, Washington, 1975-77; dep. asst. sec. Office of Asst. Sec. for Internat. Affairs, Dept. Treasury, Washington, 1977-79; v.p., sr. adv. First Nat. Bank Chgo., 1979-80; v.p. Townsend-Greenspan & Co., Inc., N.Y.C., 1980-82; Sr. adv. Internat. Monetary Fund, Washington, 1982—; dir. Securities Group Money Fund, Inc., N.Y.C. Mem. Am. Econ. Assn., Downtown Econs., Internat. Econs., Women's Econ. Roundtable, Council Fgn. Relations, Nat. Women's Polit. Caucus. Contbr. articles in field to profl. publs. Home: 50 E 10th St New York NY 10003 Office: 1 New York Pl New York NY 10004

JURAN, SHELLEY HOMNICK, psychologist; b. N.Y.C., Mar. 10, 1946; d. Jack and Henrietta Homnick; B.A., Bklyn. Coll., 1966, M.A., 1973; Ph.D. (fellow), CUNY, 1979; m. Barry Juran, June 13, 1965; 1 son, Brian. Youth counselor N.Y. State Dept. Labor, 1966, Tex. Neighborhood Youth Corps, 1967; bd. dirs. Bklyn. Coll. Day Care Center, 1970; group therapist Jellinik Clinic, Amsterdam, 1973; psychologist Am. Insternat. Sch. Rotterdam (Netherlands), 1973; adj. instr. Bklyn. Coll., 1973-75; asst. prof. St. Francis Coll., Bklyn., 1976-77, 78; vis. instr. Pratt Inst., 1978; adj. asst. prof. Bklyn. Coll., 1979; asst. prof. psychology Coll. Mt. St. Vincent, Riverdale, N.Y., 1980, Pratt Inst., 1980—; staff psychologist, clin. instr. Clinic for Study Sexual Devel., N.Y. U. Med. Center, 1978-81; pvt. practice psychotherapy, 1979—. Lic. psychologist, N.Y. Mem. Am. Psychol. Assn., Assn. Women in Psychology, Women Polit. Caucus, NOW, Psi Chi. Home: 101 Clark St Brooklyn NY 11201 Office: Psychology Dept Pratt Inst Brooklyn NY 11205

JURGEVICH, NANCY JEAN, army officer; b. Stoystown, Pa., July 20, 1940; d. Peter and Ruth Leone (Kimmel) Jurgevich; student U. Ky., 1965-67; B.B.A., George Washington U., 1973; M.S., U. Utah, 1977; grad. U.S. Army Command and Staff Coll., 1976; postgrad. Cath. U. Am., 1981. Joined U.S. Army, 1958, advanced through grades to lt. col., 1981—, communications operator, U.S., Ger., and France, 1958-62, communications supr., Ft. Benning, Ga., 1962-65, personnel ops. officer Ft. Knox, Ky., 1966-67, comdr., WAC Detachment, White Sands (N.Mex.) Missle Range, 1967-68, Long Binh, Vietnam, 1968-69, personnel mgr. Saigon Support Command, 1969-70, personnel staff officer U.S. Army Forces Command, Atlanta, 1973-75, U.S. European Command, Vaihingen, W.Ger., 1976-79, insp. gen. U.S. Army Insp. Gen. Agy., Pentagon, Washington, 1979—; instr. U. Md., 1978—, Park Coll., 1980—; cons. policies for women in army Dept. Army, 1981; lectr. in field. Decorated Bronze Star medal, Army Commendation medal. Mem. Non-Commd. Officers Assn., Am. Mgmt. Assn., Nat. Assn. Female Execs., Am. Legion. Contbr. articles to profl. jours. Home: 3023 White Birch Ct Fairfax VA 22031 Office: Dept of Army Office Inspector General Washington DC 20310

JURKAT, MAYME PORTER, urban planner; b. Mt. Home, Ark., June 27, 1934; d. Charles and Victoria (Porter) Rhine; student Earlham

Coll., Richmond, Ind., 1952-54; B.A., U. N.C., 1959; M.U.P., Hunter Coll., 1972; m. M. Peter Jurkat, May 31, 1958; children—Martin Alexander, Susanna, Maria. Dir., Ridgewood (N.J.) Housing Authority, 1973-76; with Center Mcpl. Studies and Services Stevens Inst. Tech., Hoboken, N.J., 1976—, intern dir., 1981—; mem. Hoboken Mayor's Adv. Com. on Waterfront Devel. Mem. Am. Planning Assn., Nat. Council Urban Econ. Devel., Sigma Xi. Democrat. Mem. Soc. of Friends. Contbr. in field. Home: 706 Hudson St Hoboken NJ 07030 Office: Castle Point Station Hoboken NJ 07030

JURZYKOWSKI, MILENA CHRISTINE, film producer; b. N.Y.C., Sept. 25, 1949; d. Alfred and Milena J.; B.A., Boston U., 1968. Editor, Nat. Assn. Broadcast Employees and Technicians, N.Y.C., 1973-80; prodn. mgr., exec. producer Neal Marshad Assos., N.Y.C., 1973-76; pres. Cinetudes Film Prodns. Ltd., N.Y.C., 1976—; founder Atelier Cinema Video Stages and Cinetudes Cable Programming Assocs. Mem. N.Y. Women in Communications, Nat. Assn. Broadcast Employees and Technicians, Internat. Indsl. TV Assn., Assn. Ind. Film and Video Makers, Info. Film Producers Am., Soc. Motion Picture and TV Engrs., N.Y. Women in Film. Office: 295 W 4th St New York NY 10014

JUSSAWALLA, FEROZA FRAMJI, educator; b. Hyderabad, India, Jan. 14, 1953; came to U.S., 1973, naturalized, 1979; d. Framji Jehangir and Meheroo (Dalal) Jussawalla; B.A. with honors, Osmania U., India, 1973; M.A., U. Utah, 1975, postgrad. 1975—. Teaching fellow U. Utah, Salt Lake City, 1974-80; lectr., U. Tex., El Paso, 1980—; tech. writer Eimco Mfg. Utah, 1976-77. Jack H. Adamson dissertation fellow, 1979-80; Clarice Short cert. excellence in teaching, 1978. Mem. MLA, Nat. Council Tchrs. English, Lambda Iota Tau. Zorastrian. Contbr. articles to profl. jours. Office: 307 Hudspeth Hall Dept English U Tex El Paso TX 79968

JUST, ANN, state legislator; b. Washington, May 2, 1937; student Corcoran Sch. Art, Washington, U. Madrid (Spain). Mem. Vt. Ho. Reps., 1977—. Chmn. Washington County Democratic Com.; mem. Warren Planning Commn., 1975-77; mem. Central Vt. Regional Planning Commn., 1975-77; auditor Warren Town, 1975-76; mem. Warren Scenery Preservation Council, 1976-77; bd. dirs. Vt. Natural Resources Council. Mem. Vt. Hist. Soc., Warren Grange, Women in Bus., Valley Area Assn. Democrat. Office: Vt Ho Reps State Ho Montpelier VT 05602

JUST, BARBARA MARION, nurse; b. Boston, Mar. 8, 1935; d. Frederick George and Dorothea Elizabeth (Burke) Aschenneller; R.N. (scholar), Bklyn. Hosp., 1956; student St. John's U.; B.S.P.A., St. Joseph's Coll.; m. Joseph Just, Sept. 6, 1958 (dec.). Mem. nursing staff Bklyn. Hosp., 1956—, asst. dir. nursing, 1973—. Mem. N.Y. State Nurses Assn., Nurses Assn. Counties L.I., Bklyn. Hosp. Sch. Nursing Alumnae Assn., Aux. Bklyn. Hosp. Republican. Roman Catholic. Home: 9201 Shore Rd Brooklyn NY 11209 Office: 121 DeKalb Ave Brooklyn NY 11201

JUST, FAYE JORDAN, antique restoration co. exec.; b. Carthage, Miss., June 6, 1925; d. Neadham Guice and Ethel (Doude) Jordan; student UCLA, 1943-62, U. So. Calif., 1950-52; A.A. in M.E., Pierce Coll., 1965; B.S. in B.A. and Math., U. Calif., Northridge, 1969; m. Virgil Louis Just, May 2, 1970; children—Babetta, Sandra, Audrey. Loftswoman/flying wing Northrope Aircraft, Hawthorne, Calif., 1943-45; with Rockwell Internat., Los Angeles and Canoga Park, Calif., 1947-70, sr. research engr. rocket engines, to 1970; Co-owner Just Marine Engring. Cons., 1972-77, Just Enterprises, Ventura, Calif., 1977—. Office: 2790 Sherwin Ave #10 Ventura CA 93003

JUST, GEMMA R., advt. agy. exec.; b. N.Y.C., Nov. 29, 1921; d. Philip and Brigida (Consolo) Rivoli; B.A., Hunter Coll., N.Y.C., 1943; m. Victor Just, Jan. 29, 1955. Copy group head McCann Erickson, N.Y.C., 1958-62; copy. supr. Morse Internat., N.Y.C., 1962-67; v.p., dir. creative services Deltakos div. J. Walter Thompson, N.Y.C., 1967-75; v.p., copy dir. Sudler & Hennessey, div. Young & Rubicam, N.Y.C., 1975—. Mem. Women of St. Bartholomew's Episcopal Ch., also ch. altar guild. Named Best Writer, Art Dirs. Club N.Y., 1979, Modern Medicine mag., 1980, Young & Rubicam, 1981. Mem. Council Communications Socs., Pharm. Advt. Council, Am. Med. Writers Assn. (exec. com. 1973). Home: 155 E 38th St New York NY 10016 Office: 292 Madison Ave New York NY 10017

JUSTICE, PATRICIA KALLBERG, community coll. dean; b. St. Helens, Oreg., Mar. 17, 1944; d. Leroy Arthur and Johanna (Schuring) Kallberg; B.S., Portland State Coll., 1966, M.S. (Alpha Chi Omega fellow 1968), 1970; Ed.D. (EDPA fellow 1978), Oreg. State U., 1978. Public sch. tchr., 1967-68; teaching asst. Portland State U., 1968-70; instr. speech and communications Mt. Hood Community Coll., Gresham, Oreg., 1970-73, dir. staff devel., then dir. instructional resources, 1973-79; dean occupational programs Highline Community Coll., Midway, Wash., 1979-81; dean instrn. Fort Steilacoom Community Coll., Tacoma, Wash., 1981—. Trustee Trinity Lutheran Ch., Gresham, 1978-79; mem. Wash. State Criminal Justice Tng. Law Enforcement Edn. Adv. Com. Mem. Nat. Council Staff Profl. Orgn. Devel., Am. Assn. Community and Jr. Colls., Am. Vocat. Assn., Wash. Vocat. Assn., Nat. Council Local Adminstrs., Speech Assn. Am., Am. Soc. Tng. and Devel., Am. Soc. Curriculum and Devel., Lakewood Area C. of C., Alpha Chi Omega, Phi Delta Kappa, Pi Kappa Delta. Democrat. Author articles in field. Home: 1812-D SW 318th Pl Federal Way WA 98003 Office: 240 Pacific Hwy S Midway WA 98031

JUSTINIAN, SHARON LEE, social worker; b. Highland Park, Mich., Jan. 20, 1949; d. Ernest Harold and Helen Catherine (Wade) Richards; cert. d'etudes, Coll. Ste Anne de la Pocatiere, Quebec, Can., 1971; A.B. with distinction, U. Mich., 1970, M.S.W., 1977; m. Leonard Donald Justinian, June 3, 1977. Tchr., English as fgn. lang., Spanish tchr. U.S. Peace Corps, Obala, Cameroun, 1971-73; editor, proofreader Fuji Nat. City Cons. Ltd., Tokyo, 1973-74; 67 English tchr. Exec. Lang. Schs., Tokyo, 1973-74; resources cons., tchr. trainer Peace Corps, Phila., 1975; eligibility worker Alexandria (Va.) Dept. Social Services, 1978-79; adoption/foster care social worker Fairfax County Dept. Social Services, Fairfax, Va., 1979—; vol. cons. M.A. linguistics program U. Mich., 1975-76. Mem. Speakers' Bur., Returned Peace Corps Vols., 1977—. Recipient Gold Key, Detroit News, 1967; Cert. of Appreciation, Peace Corps, 1973. Mem. Nat. Assn. Social Workers (listed in Register of Clin. Social Workers, 3d edit.), Acad. Cert. Social Workers.

JUSTISON, HELEN ELIZABETH, nurse; b. Crawford County, Ill., Jan. 13, 1940; d. Paul Allen and Frances B. (Hanover) Kent.; R.N., Meml. Med. Center, Springfield, Ill., 1961; B.S. in Health Careers, Eastern Ill. U., 1978; m. Rolland E. Justison, Apr. 16, 1961; children—Tracey Lynn, Lisa Lynnae, Michelle Lynnette. Pediatric nurse Meml. Med. Center, Springfield, 1961-64; nurse St. Johns Hosp., Springfield, 1964-72; sch. nurse Community Unit 5, Chatham, Ill., 1972—; v.p. TLM Services Inc. Coordinator Outreach Program; tchr. first aid to youth groups. Mem. Ill. Assn. Sch. Nurses. Methodist.

JUZAK, TATANIA, psychologist; b. Willimantic, Conn.; d. Pafnuty and Constance Juszczak; B.S., Willimantic State Tchrs. Coll., 1942; M.A., U. Minn., 1944; Ph.D., N.Y.U., 1953. Psychologist, Kings County Hosp., Bklyn., 1946-49; sr. psychologist Bellevue Hosp., N.Y.C., 1953-59; chief psychologist New Rochelle (N.Y.) Guidance Center, 1959-60, Westchester County (N.Y.) Med. Center, 1960—; asst. prof. psychiatry N.Y. Med. Coll., N.Y.C., 1972—; cons. psychology Health Ins. Plan, N.Y. State Bus. Disability Determinations. Served with U.S. Army, 1944-46. Diplomate Am. Bd. Profl. Psychology; lic. psychologist, N.Y. State, Conn. Mem. N.Y. Acad. Sci., N.Y. State Psychol. Assn., Am. Psychol. Assn., Internat. Council Psychologists, N.Y. Soc. Clin. Psychologists, Contbr. articles in field to profl. jours. office: 108 E 91 St New York NY 10028

KABACK, ELAINE, career counselor-cons.; b. Phila., Feb. 22, 1939; d. Sol and Evelyn Zitman; student Pa. State U., 1956-58; B.A., Temple U., 1960; M.S., Calif. State U., 1977; children—Douglas, Stephen, Michelle. Tchr. English, Sayre Jr. High Sch., Phila. Public Schs., 1960-62; tchr. English and history Beth Rfiloh Pvt. Day Sch., Balt., 1968-72; mgmt. cons., trainer Sandra Winston Assos., Palos Verdes, Calif., 1975—; counselor Career Planning Center and Mid-Life Center, Long Beach City Coll., 1977-78, instr. in assertion tng. coll. extension; dir. program devel. Univance Career Centers, Inc., Los Angeles, 1978-80; pvt. practice career counseling, 1980—; coordinator career planning program, trainer/presenter UCLA Extension. Pres. Palos Verdes chpt. NOW, 1974-76, chairperson, lectr. Speaker's Bur., 1977—; treas. S.W. chpt. Nat. Women's Polit. Caucus, 1973, 78; bd. dirs. STEP Adult Edn. Programs, Palos Verdes, 1974—, cert. community coll. life counselor, Calif.; cert. tchr., Pa. Mem. Calif. Personnel and Guidance Assn., Calif. Career Guidance Assn., Am. Soc. Tng. and Devel., Am. Personnel and Guidance Assn., Nat. Assn. Female Execs., Phi Kappa Phi. Home: 2813 Via Barri Palos Verdes Estates CA 90274 Office: 24222 Hawthorne Blvd Suite B Torrance CA 90505

KABEL, BARBARA, civic worker; B.A., Northland Coll., 1951; postgrad. U. Wis.; m. Jerome R. Kabel. Former educator, librarian; curator Rhinelander (Wis.) Mus., 1961-75. Com. mem. Am. Indian Fund of Assn. on Am. Indian Affairs, 1967—; historian Rhinelander Am. Revolution Bicentennial Commn.; mem. Wis. Landmarks Commn.; trustee Rhinelander Library Bd., 1964-66, Wis. Valley Library Assn., 1964-66; mem. women's programs adv. bd. Nicolet Coll., 1978—; mem. Nicolet Coll. Women's Resource Bur., 1980; Oneida County coordinator Wis. State Old Cemetery Assn., 1978—; enumerator U.S. Census, 1980; mem. Wausau Women's Community, Oneida County Humane Soc., ACLU, Wis. Civil Liberties Union; historian Rhinelander Centennial Com., 1982. Recipient cert. of appreciation Employers Ins. Wausau, 1975, award of appreciation City of Rhinelander, 1976, cert. of recognition, 1977. Mem. Wis. Geneal. Soc. (dir. 1971-77), Wis. Library Trustees Assn., Wis. Hist. Soc. (award of merit 1968, mem. women's aux.), Northland Hist. Soc. (dir., pres. 1973-75), Nat. Trust Hist. Preservation, Wis. Hist. Survey Commn., Wis. Arts Found. and Council, Am. Assn. Museums, Am. Assn. State and Local History, Wis. Fedn. Museums, German-Am. Nat. Congress (charter mem.), Inst. Noetic Scis. (charter), Inst. Study Women in Transition, Northland Coll. Alumni Assn. (life), Northland Coll. Student Union Assn. (life), Wis. Acad. Sci., Arts and Letters, Internat. Platform Assn. Clubs: Eastern Star, Shrine Women's Aux., White Shrine of Jerusalem. Author: Northwoods Anthology, 1970; History of the Rhinelander Logging Museum—1932 to 1972, 1971; editor: rev. edit. (original 1902): Fearsome Creatures of the Lumberwoods (Cox), 1968; producer record Lumberjack Songs from Hodagland, 1969. Office: Rhinelander Museum Rhinelander WI 54501

KABESCHAT, ANN MARY, controller; b. Plymouth, Pa., Mar. 13, 1924; d. Gustav and Martha Ann (Mraz) K.; student Wharton Sch., U. Pa., 1947-53. Beautician, tchr. Empire Beauty Sch., Wilkes-Barre, Pa., 1945-46; with acctg. areas Sears, Roebuck & Co., 1947—, controller, Oakdale Mall, Johnson City, N.Y., 1980—. Active Broome County Status of Women Council. Mem. Am. Mgmt. Assn. Democrat. Roman Catholic. Clubs: Zonta Internat., Bus. and Profl. Women's (nat. and internat.). Home: Apt 1E 378 Prospect St Binghamton NY 13905 Office: Sears Roebuck & Co Oakdale Mall Route 17 Johnson City NY 13790

KABRIEL, MARCIA GAIL, psychotherapist; b. El Reno, Okla., Jan. 8, 1938; d. Gail Frederick and Katherine (Marsh) Slaughter; B.A., U. Okla., 1965, M.S.W., 1968, also postgrad. Am. U.; m. J. Ronald Kabriel, May 25, 1957; children—Joseph Charles, Jeffrey Gail, Jae B. Psychiat. social worker Dept. Mental Hygiene, N.Y.C., 1968-69; psychiat. social worker Washington Hosp. Center, 1970-72, asso. mem. dept. psychiatry, 1972-75, sr. psychotherapist Counseling Center, 1972-75; psychotherapist Md. Inst. Pastoral Counseling, Annapolis, Md., 1972—; chief dept. social services Washington Hosp. Center, 1979-82, cons. spl. projects, 1974-82; field instr. Cath. U., Washington, 1973-75, U. Md., 1976-78. Active Amberly Community Assn., 1979-80. Mem. Nat. Assn. Social Workers, Acad. Cert. Social Workers. Democrat. Presbyterian. Home: 844 Holly Drive S Annapolis MD 21401 Office: 104 Forbes St Suite F Annapolis MD 21404

KACHIROUBAS, DIMITRA IRENE, bus. and law pub. exec.; b. Chgo., Nov. 11, 1918; d. Constantine John and Stella (Rigas) K.; B.A. in Law, U. Chgo., 1942, postgrad. Law Sch., 1940-42. With Commerce Clearing House, Inc., Chgo., 1942—, asst. sec., mgr. spl. editorial projects dept., 1975-79, asst. v.p., mgr. utilities law dept., 1979—. Democrat. Mem. Greek Orthodox Ch. Office: 4025 W Peterson Ave Chicago IL 60646

KACIR, BARBARA BRATTIN, lawyer; b. Buffalo, July 19, 1941; d. William James and Jean (Harrington) Brattin; B.A., Wellesley Coll., 1963; J.D., U. Mich., 1967. Admitted to Ohio bar, 1967, D.C. bar, 1980; practiced in Cleve., 1967-79, Washington, 1980—; asso. firm Arter & Hadden, Cleve., 1967-74, partner, 1974-79; partner firm Jones Day Reavis & Pogue, Washington, 1980—; asso. prof. law Case Western Res. U., 1974-78. Mem. nat. fund raising com. U. Mich. Law Sch., 1973-79, mem. nat. com. visitors, 1980—. Mem. Am., Ohio (counsel dels. 1972-79), Cleve. (continuing legal edn. com. 1969-74, vice chmn. 1973-74, 77—, trustee 1974-77, mem. young lawyers com. 1968-72, arbitration com. 1971-74; mem. budget com. 1974-79, chmn. 1978-79, treas. 1978-79), D.C. bar assns., Am. Arbitration Assn. (Cleve. regional council 1972-79). Home: 6601 Sulky Ln Rockville MD 20852 Office: 1735 I St NW Washington DC 20006

KACZANOWSKA, WIESLAWA, psychiatrist; b. Poland, Sept. 27, 1925; came to U.S., 1968, naturalized, 1977; d. Alfred and Janina (Chmielinska) Kozaczewski; M.D., Warsaw Sch. Medicine, 1952; Ph.D. in Psychiatry, Warsaw U., 1964; m. Mieczyslaw Kaczanowski, Dec. 6, 1951; 1 son, Peter. Staff psychiatrist, chief of in-patient services, adj. prof. in psychiatry Neuropsychiat. Inst., Poland, 1952-66; registrar in psychiatry, Eng., 1966-68; resident Beth Israel Hosp., N.Y.C., 1969-72, staff psychiatrist, Brookdale Med. Center, Coney Island Hosp., Brooklyn, N.Y., 1972-74; faculty mem. U. Pa., Phila., 1974-77; psychiatrist Community Mental Health, Phila.; faculty mem. Jefferson Med. Coll., 1977—; cons. psychiatrist, social-vocat. programs Horizon House. Polish Govt. fellow. 1965. Mem. Am. Psychiat. Assn., Am. Med. Women's Assn., Pa. Psychiat. Soc. Research on psychiat. patients' response to antipsychotic medicine. Home: 728 Lombard St Philadelphia PA 19147

KADEN, MAXINE MEARS, jr. coll. counselor; b. Ft. Lauderdale, Fla., Oct. 10, 1926; d. Walter Marion and Annie Blanche (Gilbert) Mears; B.A., Stetson U., Deland, Fla., 1946; M.Ed., U. Fla., 1955; m. T. David Kaden, Aug. 4, 1972; children—Jerome Loren Williams, Sharon Elizabeth Williams. Tchr., Fla. public schs., 1947-67; counselor Fla. Jr. Coll., 1967—; cons. in field. Bd. dirs. YWCA, Jacksonville, Fla., 1974—. Gen. Electric Co. fellow, 1970; named Bus. Woman of Year, Jacksonville, 1973. Mem. Nat. Assn. Community Colls., Am. Bus. Women's Assn. (chpt. pres. 19), Fla. Assn. Community Coll., Fla. Personnel and Guidance Assn., So. Assn. Colls., Fla. Assn. Colls., Fla. Adult Edn. Assn., Fla. Employment Counselors Assn., Fla. Vocat. Council. Republican. Home: 59 Swimming Pen Dr Middleburg FL 32068 Office: 101 W State St Jacksonville FL 32020

KAEL, PAULINE, movie critic, author; b. Petaluma, Calif., June 19, 1919; d. Isaac Paul and Judith (Friedman) Kael; student U. Calif., Berkeley, 1936-40; LL.D., (hon.), Georgetown U., 1972; Litt.D. (hon.), Smith Coll., 1973, Allegheny Coll., 1979; L.H.D. (hon.), Kalamazoo Coll., 1973, Reed Coll., 1975, Haverford Coll., 1975; D.F.A. (hon.), Sch. Visual Arts, N.Y.C., 1980; 1 dau., Gina James. Movie critic New Republic mag., 1966-67, New Yorker mag., 1968—. Author: I Lost it at the Movies, 1965; Kiss Kiss Bang Bang, 1968; Going Steady, 1970; Deeper into Movies, 1973; Reeling, 1976; When the Lights Go Down, 1980; 5001 Nights at the Movies, 1982; contbg. author: The Citizen Kane Book. Recipient Polk award in criticism, 1970; Nat. Book award, 1974; Front Page award Newswomen's Club N.Y., 1974; Guggenheim fellow, 1964. Address: care The New Yorker 25 W 43d St New York NY 10036

KAFER, ENID ROSEMARY, acad. physician; b. Sydney, Australia, May 27, 1937; came to U.S., 1971; d. David and Edna Anne Kafer; B.Sc. with honors in Medicine, U. Sydney, 1959, B.S. with honors, 1962, M.D. (Australian and N.Z. Life Ins. med. research fellow), 1970. Registrar, Royal Prince Alfred Hosp., Sydney, 1962-64; research fellow in medicine U. Sydney, 1965-69; sr. anesthesiol. registrar Royal Postgrad. Med. Sch., London, 1969-71; asst. prof. anesthesia U. Calif., San Francisco, 1971-73; asso. prof. anesthesiology and physiology U. N.C., Chapel Hill, 1973—; research rev. com. Am. Heart Assn., 1975-79; physician Outward Bound, Australia, 1966-69. Recipient Peter Bancroft prize U. Sydney, 1970; grantee NIH, 1973-81, Heart Assn., 1973-74; U. Sydney postgrad. fellow, 1969, 71. Fellow Royal Australasian Coll. Physicians, Faculty Anesthetics of Royal Coll. Surgeons; mem. AAAS, Am. Soc. Anesthesiologists, Am. Thoracic Soc., Am. Physiol. Soc., N.Y. Acad. Scis., Assn. Univ. Anesthesiologists, Soc. Cardiovascular Anesthesiologists, Assn. Advancement Med. Instrumentation, Sigma Xi. Home: 108 Saddle Ridge Rd Chapel Hill NC 27514 Office: Dept Anesthesiology 225 Burnett Womack Bldg 229H Chapel Hill NC 27514

KAFKA, MARIAN ADELE STERN, physiologist; b. Richmond, Va., Mar. 30, 1927; d. Henry S. and Adele (Lewit) Stern; A.B. in Zoology, Conn. Coll., 1948; Ph.D., U. Chgo., 1952; m. John S. Kafka, Oct. 3, 1952; children—David Egon, Paul Henry, Alexander Charles. Research asst. dept. biol. chemistry Emory U., 1952-53; research asso. dept. psychiatry U. Ill., 1953-54; research asso. dept. medicine Yale U., 1954-57; USPHS fellow Nat. Heart Inst., NIH, Bethesda, 1965-68, physiologist Hypertension-Endocrine br., 1968-74; physiologist Biol. Psychiatry br. NIMH, Bethesda, 1974-82, Clin. Neurosci. br., 1982—; chmn. ad hoc com. to study impact of intramural program on men and women, mem. clin. research rev. com. Mem. Am. Physiol. Soc. (chmn. public info. com. 1981), Endocrine Soc., Biophys. Soc., Soc. Neurosci., AAAS. Contbr. chpts. to books, articles to profl. jours. Home: 7834 Aberdeen Rd Bethesda MD 20814 Office: Clin Neurosci Br NIMH 9000 Rockville Pike Bethesda MD 20205

KAGAN, MARCIA PESSIN, social worker; b. Hartford, Conn., Jan. 4, 1922; d. Israel George and Gussie Elizabeth (Marcus) Pessin; A.A., Hillyer Coll., 1943; B.A., U. Miami, 1947; M.S.W., U. Conn., 1969; m. Nathaniel D. Kagan, May 9, 1948; children—Larry H., Jeffrey M. With Dept. Children and Youth, Conn. State Dept. Welfare, Hartford and Torrington, 1947-74, program supr., 1969-74; sr. staff social worker Hartford Rehab. Center, 1974-80; pvt. practice social work, West Hartford, Conn., 1980—. Bd. dirs. CAC 18, North Central Regional Mental Health Bd., 1979-82, Capital Region chpt. Mental Health Assn., 1980-82, Sunshine Group, Inc., 1980-82; bd. trustees Sisterhood Temple Beth Israel, 1982-83; mem. consumer adv. bd. Div. Vocat. Rehab., 1982-83. Mem. Nat. Assn. Social Workers, Acad. Cert. Social Workers, Conn. Assn. Human Services. Democrat. Jewish. Clubs: Cliffside Country; B'nai B'rith (v.p. 1964-65). Home: 43 Whitehill Dr West Hartford CT 06117 Office: 1010 Farmington Ave West Hartford CT 06107

KAHLER, CAROL, educator; b. Rochelle, Ill., May 25, 1921; d. John Francis and Adah (Sullivan) K.; B.S., Northwestern U., 1941, M.S. in Edn., 1943; Ed.D., N.Y. U., 1956. Tchr., Glencoe (Ill.) Pub. Schs. 1941-43, Grosse Pointe (Mich.) Pub. Schs., 1943-45, Walden Sch., N.Y.C., 1945-47; resource tchr. Schenectady (N.Y.) Pub. Schs., 1947-48; curriculum and teaching aids cons. Endicott (N.Y.) Pub. Schs., 1948-52; asst. prof. edn. SUNY, Buffalo, 1952-55; prof. St. Louis U. 1955—; cons. project Teaching and Tng. Films Teheran, Iran Syracuse U., 1953-54; dir., cons. Citizenship Edn. Clearing House. Bd. dirs. Nursery Found., St. Louis, 1965-70, 72-75, pres., 1973-74; chmn. Mo. Foster Child Care Com., St. Louis, 1971-72. Cert. tchr., Ill., N.Y., Mich. Mem. Assn. Supervision and Curriculum Devel., State Council Social Studies, Pi Lambda Theta. Democrat. Roman Catholic. Contbr. articles in field. Office: 221 N Grand St Saint Louis MO 63103

KAHLIFF, MARGARET WARE, govt. bank adminstr.; b. Cecil, Ark., July 11, 1961; d. William Rufus and Lattie E. (Jones) Bumpers; student Coll. Ozarks, H.H.D. (hon.), 1972; student Baldwin Wallace Coll., Western Res. U.; H.H.D. (hon.) Defiance (Ohio) Coll., 1982; m. William T. Kahliff, Mar. 27, 1959 (dec.); children by previous marriage—Linda Ware Smith, William B. Ware, David E. Ware. Founder Ware Vending Co. (merged into Servomation Corp.), 1950, group pres., 1961-72; pres. Majestic Molding Co., Elyria, Ohio, 1970-75, also chmn. bd.; Republican mem. bd. dirs. Export-Import Bank of U.S. Washington, 1976—. Mem. Elyria C. of C., Council Smaller Enterprises of Cleve. Growth Assn. Congregationalist. Clubs: Elyria Country; Aqua Marine (Avon Lake, Ohio). Musician for radio and TV. Home: 4200 Massachusetts Ave NW Apt 104 Washington DC 20016 Office: 811 Vermont Ave NW Washington DC 20571

KAHN, ANNA LEE, food co. exec.; b. Henryetta, Okla., Aug. 15, 1923; d. Ernest Claude and Alice Pomesa (Gantt) Vaughn; student Am. Bus. Coll., 1942, Christopher Newport Coll., 1963-65, Coll. William and Mary, 1966-69; m. Edward E. Kahn, June 13, 1942; children—Dianne Kahn Haley, David. Profl. model, St. Louis, Cin., Norfolk and Newport News, Va., 1950-61; pres., fashion show coordinator and commentator Lee Kahn Sch. Beauty, Newport News, Va., 1961-63; gen. mgr. Guaranteed Foods of Va., Inc., Newport News, 1963—; mng. partner Huntington 30, 1965—. Bd. dirs. Jewish Fedn., 1979—; past pres. Hidenwood PTA, Heritage council Girl Scouts U.S.A.; nat. bd. dirs. Girl Scouts U.S.A., 1981—; trustee Peninsula United Fund, 1977—; pres. bd. trustees Temple Sinai, 1979—. Recipient Thanks badge Girl Scouts U.S.A., 1972; Shofar award Boy Scouts Am., 1974 citation NCCJ, 1982. Mem. Peninsula C. of C. (dir. 1979-81). Democrat. Author: How to Write Advertising that Sells, 1960. Office: Guaranteed Foods of Virginia Inc 3001 Huntington Ave Newport News VA 23607

KAHN, ARLENE JUDY MILLER, nurse, educator; b. Chgo., Dec. 16, 1940; d. Fred and Sophie (Schelbe) Miller; R.N., A.B., U. Ill., Chgo., 1963, M.S. in Nursing, 1970; m. Roy M. Kahn, Oct. 25, 1968; 1 dau., Jennifer M. Head nurse psychiat. unit Grant Hosp., Chgo., 1966; supervising nurse Ill. Psychiat. Inst., Chgo., 1967; instr. psychiat. nursing Calif. State U., San Francisco, 1968-70; mem. faculty Calif. State U., Hayward, 1974—, asso. prof. nursing, 1980—; cons. in field.

Research grantee Calif. State U., Hayward, 1980-81. Fellow Am. Assn. Psychiat. Nursing; mem. United Profs. Calif., Calif. Nursing Assn., Sigma Theta Tau. Author articles in field. Home: 95 Sonia St Oakland CA 94618 Office: Hayward State U Sch Sci Hayward CA 94542

KAHN, BLOSSOM, motion picture exec.; b. N.Y.C., Aug. 16, 1936; d. Jules Franklin and Anita Beatrice (Arkin) K.; B.A. in English, Hofstra Coll., Hempstead, N.Y., 1958; postgrad. Columbia U. Sch. Journalism, N.Y.C. Exec., story dept. Universal Pictures Corp., N.Y.C., 1963-64; head motion picture, TV and play depts. Curtis Brown Lit. Agy., N.Y.C., 1964-68; pres. Kahn-Penney Lit. Agy., Los Angeles, 1968-77; dir. creative affairs First Artists Prodns., Los Angeles, 1977-78; exec. in charge creative projects Avco-Embassy Pictures, Los Angeles, 1978-82; head prodn. Zupnick Curtis Enterprises, Inc., Los Angeles, 1982—; lectr. Sherwood Oaks Coll., Marymount Coll., Los Angeles. Mem. Women in Film, Women in Communication. Office: 9229 Sunset Blvd Los Angeles CA 90069

KAHN, ETHEL, social psychologist, psychotherapist; b. N.Y.C., Apr. 1, 1923; d. Jesse T. and Bertha (Resnikoff) Dubin; B.A. cum laude, U. Wis., 1944; M.A., N.Y. U., 1966, Ph.D., 1974; postgrad. Inst. Behavior Therapy, 1978-80; m. Bernard Kahn, Aug. 13, 1944; children—Edward, Paul, Elissa. Dir. liberal arts N.Y. U. Extension, N.Y.C., 1958-65; dir. adult edn. Ft. Lee (N.J.) Bd. Edn., 1965-68; asso. prof., extension specialist in human relations and community devel. Rutgers U., New Brunswick, N.J., 1968-71, asso. prof. Grad. Sch. Social Work and Grad. Sch. Applied and Profl. Psychology, 1974—; chmn. dept. edn. Finch Coll., N.Y.C., 1971-72; asso. prof. Cornell U., Ithaca, N.Y., 1972-74; pres. TEAM (Tng. for Edn. and Mgmt.) Assos., tng. firm for corp. personnel and public service agy. professionals; cons. CATALYST, 1976-78; staff team trainer in diagnosis and treatment planning for psychiat. patients Hudson County Mental Health Bd., 1979. Named Woman of Achievement, Bus. and Profl. Women, 1966; Contbr. articles to profl. jours.; editor: (with William Phillips) Trouble in Our Community; The Issue in Black and White. Mem. Am. Psychol. Assn., Nat. Assn. Social Workers, Council on Social Work Edn., NOW, Nat. Women's Polit. Caucus. Home: 1530 Palisade Ave Suite 22-B Fort Lee NJ 07024 Office: Rutgers U CN 5059 New Brunswick NJ 08903

KAHN, FAITH-HOPE, nurse, adminstr., writer; b. N.Y.C., Apr. 25, 1921; d. Leon and Hazel (Cook) Green; R.N., Beth Israel Med. Center, N.Y.C., 1942; student N.Y. U., 1943; m. Edward Kahn, May 29, 1942; children—Ellen Leora, Faith Hope II, Paula Amy. First scrub operating room Beth Israel Hosp., N.Y.C., 1942; supr., operating room Hunts Point Gen. Hosp., 1942; gynecol. reconstrn. procedures researcher Phoenixville (Pa.) Gen. Hosp., 1943, Sydenham Hosp., N.Y.C., 1945; supr. ARC Disaster Field Hosp., Queens, N.Y., 1950-51; adminstr., mgr. team coordinator Dr. Edward Kahn, FACOG, Queens Village, N.Y., 1945—; inventor; Publicity chmn. Girl Scouts U.S.A., 1953; exec. dir. publicity Woodhull Schs., 1956-60, pres., 1961-62; exec. dir. publicity N.Y. Dept. Parks Figure Skating, 1956-70; exec. dir. publicity and applied arts St. John's Hosp., Smithtown, N.Y., 1965-66; state advisor N.Y., U.S. Congressional Adv. Bd., Washington, 1981—; nat. adv. bd. Am. Security Council, 1978—; founder Am. Security Found. Recipient citation A.R.C., 1951, Am. Law Enforcement Officers Assn.; Bronze medal Am. Security Council Ednl. Found., 1978; cert. of appreciation Am. Police Acad., 1979; spl. recognition award Center Internat. Security Studies, 1979; Meml. Plate, Patriots of Am. Bicentennial, 1976; Great Seal of U.S.A. Plate. Mem. Am. Acad. Ambulatory Nursing Adminstrn., Nurses Assn., Nat. League Nursing, Am. Coll. Obstetricians and Gynecologists, Nat. Assn. Physicians' Nurses, Nat. Critical Care Inst., Assn. Operating Room Nurses, AAAS, N.Y. Acad. Scis., Am. Police Acad., Internat. Platform Assn., Security and Intelligence Fund, Nat. Rifle Assn. Clubs: Tiyospaye, Paul Revere, Sterlingshire Woman's. Author, editor: The Easy Driving Way for Automatic and the Standard Shift, 1954; (with Edward Kahn) The Pelvic Examination, Outline and Guide for Residents, Internes and Students, 1954; (with Edward Kahn) Traction Hysterosalpingography for Uterine Lesions, 1949; contbr. articles profl. and lay jours. Home: 213 16 85th Ave Hollis Hills NY 11427 Office: 213 16 85th Ave Queens Village NY 11427

KAHN, JULIANNA B., fin. analyst; b. Chgo., Aug. 17, 1953; d. Leroy Hirschfield and Esther (Levine) Blumenthal; B.S. in Acctg., U. Ill., Urbana, 1975; m. Frederick J. Kahn, Sept. 6, 1981. Auditor, B. L. Rosenberg & Co., Chgo., 1975-76; acct. Bankers Life & Casualty Co., Chgo., 1977-78, fin. analyst, 1978-81; prin. fin. analyst Chgo. Bd. Edn., 1981—. C.P.A., Ill. Home: 2020 Lincoln Park W Chicago IL 60614 Office: 228 N LaSalle St Chicago IL 60601

KAHN, LINDA MCCLURE, actuary; b. Jacksonville, Fla.; d. George Calvin and Myrtice Louise (Boggs) McClure; student Jacksonville U.; B.S. with high honors, U. Fla.; M.S., U. Mich., 1964; m. Paul Markham Kahn, May 20, 1968. Actuarial trainee N.Y. Life Ins. Co., N.Y.C., 1964-66, actuarial asst., 1966-69, asst. actuary, 1969-71; v.p., actuary USLIFE Ins./Calif., Pasadena, 1972-74; mgr. Coopers & Lybrand, Los Angeles, 1974-76, sr. cons., San Francisco, 1976-82; dir. program mgmt. Pacific Maritime Assn., 1982—. Sec.-treas. Heights Residents Assn., 1981. Enrolled actuary. Fellow Soc. Actuaries, Conf. Actuaries in Public Practice; mem. Internat. Actuarial Assn., Internat. Assn. Cons. Actuaries, Actuarial Studies in Non-Life Ins., Am. Acad. Actuaries, Western Pension Conf., Actuarial Club Pacific States, San Francisco Actuarial Club (pres. 1981). Clubs: Met., Soroptimist (v.p. 1973-74), Commonwealth. Home: 2430 Pacific Ave San Francisco CA 94115 Office: 635 Sacramento St San Francisco CA 94111

KAHN, MARY VIRGINIA, real estate appraiser; b. Vernon, Tex., Jan. 4, 1925; d. John Edward, Jr. and Juanita (Mercer) Lutz; tchr.'s cert. English, North Tex. Agrl. Coll.; m. Harry B. Kahn, Jr., Mar. 19, 1949 (div.); children—Jon Eric, Kandyce Virginia. Owner Virginia Kahn Appraisals, Ft. Worth, 1969—; spl. commnr. condemation all dist. cts. Tarrant County (Tex.); tchr. real estate classes. Del. numerous state and county Republican convs. Served as aircraft communicator in Civil Aeros., Air Corps U.S., World War II. Cert. rev. appraiser. Mem. Nat. Assn. Real Estate Bds., Ft. Worth Real Estate Bd., Arlington Real Estate Bd., N.E. Real Estate Bd., Nat. Inst. Real Estate Appraisers, Internat. Inst. Valuers. One of 1st women in field of real estate appraisal. Address: 3628 Chaffin Fort Worth TX 76118

KAHN, PHYLISS, state legislator; b. Bklyn., 1937; B.A. in Physics, Cornell U.; Ph.D. in Biophysics, Yale U.; m. Donald Kahn; children—Tamar, Jeremy. Former genetics researcher; mem. Minn. Ho. of Reps., St. Paul, 1972—, chairperson state depts. div. appropriations com., mem. energy, environ. and natural resources coms. Mem. Minn. Women's Polit. Caucus, Democratic-Farmer-Labor Feminist Caucus, NOW, Sierra Club, AAAS, Fedn. Am. Scientists, Citizens League, Ams. for Democratic Action. Office: 237 State Office Bldg Saint Paul MN 55155 *

KAHN, SUSAN BETH (MRS. JOSEPH KAHN), artist; b. N.Y.C., Aug. 26, 1924; d. Jesse B. and Jenny Carol (Peshkin) Cohen; student Parsons Sch. Design, 1945; pupil Moses Soyer, 1950-57; m. Joseph Kahn, Sept. 15, 1946 (dec. 1979); m. 2d, Richard I. Rosenkranz, Feb. 1, 1981. One-man shows at Sagittarius Gallery, 1960, A.C.A., Galleries, 1964, 68, 71, 76, 80, Charles B. Goddard Art Center, Ardmore, Okla., 1973, Albrecht Gallery Mus. Art, St. Joseph, Mo., 1974, N.Y. Cultural Center, N.Y.C., 1974, St. Peter's Coll., Jersey City, 1978; exhibited in group shows at Audubon Artists, N.Y.C., Nat. Acad., N.Y.C., Springfield (Mass.) Mus., City Center, N.Y.C., A.C.A. Galleries, N.Y.C., Nat. Arts Club, N.Y.C.; represented in permanent collections at Tyler (Tex.) Mus., St. Lawrence U. Mus., Canton, N.Y., Fairleigh Dickinson U. Mus., Rutherford, N.J., Syracuse U. Mus., Sheldon Swope Gallery, Terre Haute, Ind., Montclair (N.J.) Mus. Fine Arts, Butler Inst. Am. Art, Youngstown, Ohio, Reading (Pa.) Mus., Albrecht Gallery Mus. Art, St. Joseph, Cedar Rapids (Iowa) Art Center, U. Wyo., Laramie, Joslyn Mus., Omaha, S.A.I.S., Washington, Edwin A. Ulrich Mus., Wichita, Kans., Wichita State U. Recipient Knickerbocker prize for best religious painting, 1956, Edith Lehman award Nat. Assn. Women Artists, 1958, Knickerbocker Artists award, 1961, Simmons award Nat. Assn. Women Artists, 1961, Nat. Arts Club award, 1967, Knickerbocker medal of Honor, 1964, Famous Artists Sch. award, 1967. Mem. Nat. Assn. Women Artists (Anne Barnett Meml. prize 1981), Artists Equity, Knickerbocker Artists, Met. Mus., Mus. Modern Art. Home: 870 United Nations Plaza New York NY 10017

KAHOA, VIRGIE NINA, civic worker; b. Grimes, Okla., July 1, 1912; d. George Elgin and Mary Stella (Morris) Stevens; teaching cert., Southwestern Okla. State U., 1933; m. William Conward Kahoa, Nov. 18, 1933; children—Naomi Faye, A.A., Connie Mae, George Michael. Local pres. Extension Homemakers, 1946—, county v.p., 1962-64, dist. rep., 1974-76; mem. state coms., 1972—, parliamentarian, 1966-69; local pres. Okla. Fedn. Women's Clubs, 1956—, dist. pres., 1970-72, state chmn., 1970—; chmn. public affairs and safety Home Life, 1978—; pres. Pioneer Club, 1973-76. Recipient public service achievement awards, citation disting. service Gen. Fedn. Women's Clubs, 1979-80. Democrat. Mem. Ch. of Christ. Writer essays and short stories. Home: Route 1 Cheyenne OK 73628

KAHUMOKU, MARY ANN, travel agt.; b. Tuscarawas County, Ohio, Feb. 4, 1932; d. Robert Floyd and Wilma Iona (Haueter) Vollmer; ed. Strasburg (Ohio) public schs., travel mgmt. course; m. Rex R. Kahumoku, June 26, 1979. Mgr. world wide travel Tuscarawas County Am. Automobile Assn., 1960-62, dir. world wide travel, Canton, Ohio, 1962-76; pres., gen. mgr. Trip & Travel, Canton, 1976—. Mem. Am. Soc. Travel Agts. Republican. Mem. Cathedral of Life. Home: 170 Fromm St NW Canton OH 44708 Office: 4050 W Tuscarawas St Canton OH 44708

KAICHEN, LISA MERIDETH, assn. exec.; b. South Bend, Ind., Feb. 19, 1951; d. John Arnold and Elizabeth Joyce (McGuire) Kaichen; B.A. summa cum laude, U. Detroit, 1972; M.S.W., U. Mich., 1975. Coordinator, The Applied Social Research Project, Birmingham, Mich., 1974-75; dir. The Sanctuary Runaway Program, Pleasant Ridge, Mich., 1975-79; instr. criminal justice dept. Wayne State U., Detroit, 1976—; exec. dir. Children's Charter Cts. of Mich., Inc., Pontiac, 1980—. Bd. dir. Mich. Com. for Prevention of Child Abuse, 1980—, Mich. Assn. Youth Service Burs., 1980—, United Community Services, Oakland, 1980—, Met. Detroit United Community Services, 1981—; others. Mem. Nat. Council Juvenile and Family Ct. Judges, Mich. Probate and Juvenile Ct. Judges Assn., Juvenile Justice Assn. Mich., Mich. Coalition to Prevent Shoplifting, Acad. Cert. Social Workers, Nat. Assn. Social Workers (pres. Oakland unit 1978-80, Nat. Assn. Female Execs., Nat. Assn. Women in Criminal Justice, Mich. Profl. Women's Network. Author: Citizen Participation in Juvenile Cts., 1980; Applied Social Research (manuals), 1975. Home: 303 Highland St Rochester MI 48063 Office: 2893 Dixie Hwy Pontiac MI 48055

KAISER, RUTH HARTER (MRS. ROBERT M. KAISER), sociologist; b. Perryton, Ill.; d. Harold M. and Winifred (Osborn) Harter; B.A., U. Calif., Berkeley, 1943; postgrad. fellow Stanford U., 1960-61; M.S., San Jose State Coll., 1968; m. Robert M. Kaiser, Dec. 15, 1945. Exec. sec. Newman Hall, U. Calif., Berkeley, 1943-44; program dir. USO Club, Nat. Catholic Community Services, Bremerton, Wash., 1944-45; exec. dir. Calif. Fedn. Civic Unity, 1948-52, Calif. Assn. Health and Welfare, San Francisco, 1953-59, Santa Clara County Assn. Mental Health, San Jose, 1961-65; project dir. Comprehensive Mental Health Planning Com., San Jose, 1965-68; exec. dir. Comprehensive Health Planning Assn. Santa Clara County, San Jose, 1968-76; prin. Kaiser/Satten Assos., San Francisco-San Jose, 1977—; mem. nat. expectations study group Comprehensive Health Planning Services, Health Services and Mental Health Adminstrn., HEW, 1971-72. Mem. Regional Med. Programs Area Adv. Council, 1971; mem. San Jose Adv. Commn. on Health; bd. dirs. Social Planning Council Santa Clara County, 1968-71; v.p. Mexican-Am. Community Services Agy., San Jose, 1968, bd. dirs., 1967-72; bd. dirs. Calif. Social Welfare Heritage, 1980—. Mem. Nat. Assn. Social Workers (chmn. grad. sch. social work 1968-72), Acad. Cert. Social Workers, AAUW. Am. Public Health Assn., Lawyer's Wives of Santa Clara County, Alpha Kappa Delta. Home: 1989 Adele Pl San Jose CA 95125 Office: 1989 Adele Pl San Jose CA 95125

KAKASCIK, RITA MARIE, computer services co. ofcl.; b. Bayonne, N.J., Sept. 21, 1948; d. Anthony Thomas and Florence Joan (Zafian) K.; B.A., St. Peter's Coll., Jersey City, 1970; grad. Dale Carnegie course, 1979. With Atlantic Richfield, 1970-72, Paine Webber Jackson & Curtis, N.Y.C., 1972-81, v.p., systems cons., 1976-81; ADP mgr. customer services Fin. Timesharing Service, N.Y.C., 1981—; lectr. career planning Seton Hall U., S. Orange, N.J. Pres. Wall St. Women's Bowling League, 1968-70. Mem. Nat. Assn. Female Execs., Women in Data Processing. Address: 101 W 15th St Apt 5HS New York NY 10011

KALB, BARBARA, psychologist; b. N.Y.C., Mar. 23, 1935; d. Joseph and Ruth Fliederbaum; B.A. summa cum laude with high honors in Psychology (acad. scholar), Hofstra U., 1973, Ph.D. in Psychology, 1978, postgrad. in public adminstrn., 1980—; children—Austin, Rodney, Todd. Counselor, Tempo Drug Rehab. Center, Woodmere, N.Y., 1969-71; cons. Biofeedback Research Inst., Los Angeles, 1971-76; research analyst Nassau County Dept. Sr. Citizens Affairs, Carle Place, N.Y., 1973-76; research cons., 1976—; research scientist Nassau County Dept. Mental Health, Mineola, N.Y., 1977-80; pvt. practice biofeedback, clin. psychology, 1978—; psychologist Beverly Hills Community Clinic, 1980—; clin. psychologist Martin Luther King Hosp., Los Angeles, 1980—; adj. asso. prof. Grad. Sch., C.W. Post Coll., L.I.U., 1978-80, Profl. Sch. Humanistic Psychology, 1980—. Sec., Long Beach Republican City Com.; Long Beach del. Nassau County Fedn. Rep. Women; committeewoman Long Beach Election Dist. 16. Cert. biofeedback clinician. Mem. Am. Psychol. Assn., Biofeedback Soc. Am., Am. Assn. Biofeedback Clinicians (charter), New Eng. Biofeedback Soc., Psi Chi. Jewish. Club: Hofstra U. Home and Office: 418 Calle Miramar Redondo Beach CA 90277

KALEDO, GRACE LUCILLE, public relations exec.; b. Adrian, Mich., Dec. 17, 1928; d. Everett Ray and Ethel (Moore) Deken; student Adrian schs.; m. Charles Gordon Kaledo, June 22, 1946; children—Mary Lou Kaledo Mitchell, Kathryn Sue Kaledo DeMeritt, Larry Michael. Lic. practice nurse, 1959-68; editor, publisher Lenawee Tribune, Adrian, 1968-74; public relations with community services dept. City of Adrian, 1975-79; dir. Croswell Opera House, Adrian, 1975—, bd. dirs., 1978—. Mem. continuing edn. com. Adrian Coll.; past bd. dirs. Fine Arts Assn. Adrian; pres. Greater Adrian Inter Club Council; active Trenton Hills United Brethren Ch. Recipient Outstanding Community Service award Adrian Kiwanis, 1971, Service to Youth award, 1973. Mem. Nat. Fedn. Press Women, Mich. Women's Press Club. Clubs: Lenawee Civitan, Adrian Zonta. Home: 124 W Hunt St Adrian MI 49221 Office: PO Box 306 Adrian MI 49221

KALEY, MAUREEN MCARDLE, psychologist; b. N.Y.C.; B.S., Hunter Coll., N.Y.C., 1964; M.S. in Child Devel., and Family Relationships, U. Tenn., Knoxville, 1965; Ph.D. in Psychology, City U. N.Y., 1977; m. Jack Kaley; 1 dau., Amanda. Asso. research sci. Inst. Devel. Studies, N.Y.U., N.Y.C., 1965-68; research asso. Downstate Med. Center, N.Y.C., 1968-73; adj. lectr. Hunter Coll., N.Y.C., 1970-75; psychotherapist Great Neck Consultation Center, L.I., N.Y., 1974-78; div. dir. Profl. Exam. Service, 1977-79, v.p., 1979—. Mem. Am., N.Y. State (pres.-elect personnel psychology div.), Nassau County psychol. assns., IPMAC. Contbr. articles to profl. jours. Research in competency assessment, female devel., presch. edn., alcohol, cancer. Office: 65 Stillwater Ave Massa NY 11758

KALIK, BARBARA FAITH, travel agt., state legislator; b. Bronx, N.Y., Nov. 8, 1936; d. Albert and Lydia (Cohen) Benowitz; student CCNY, 1953-55; children—Darcie Lynn, Andrew Jay, Lance Jon. Owner, operator Jolie Travel Center, Inc., Willingboro, N.J., 1968—; mem. N.J. Gen. Assembly, 1978—. Council mem. Willingboro, 1971-75; mayor, Willingboro, 1974, 77; pres. Willingboro Democratic Club, 1967; Dem. committeewoman Willingboro 16th Dist., 1965-77; vice chmn. Burlington County Dem. Com., 1970-77; adv. bd. Burlington County Community Coll.; bd. dirs. United Way Burlington County; bd. dirs. Spl. Services Sch. Mem. Burlington County C. of C. (treas., bd. dirs.). Jewish. Office: Country Club Plaza Beverly-Rancocas Rd Willingboro NJ 08046 also Laino Bldg Route 130 N Delran NJ 08075

KALIN, MARCIA FAY, physician; b. N.Y.C., Sept. 12, 1954; d. Milton and Marilyn (Kravitz) Kalin; B.A. cum laude, Brandeis U., 1976; M.D., Mt. Sinai Sch. Medicine, 1980; m. Edward C. House, Oct. 12, 1980. Resident in internal medicine Overlook Hosp., Summit, N.J., 1980-81; editor Sci. Am., N.Y.C., 1981—. Home: 16 E 98th St 2C New York NY 10029 Office: 415 Madison Ave New York NY 10017

KALINA, FRANCES AUDREY, retailer; b. Valley Falls, Kans., Sept. 4, 1916; d. Charles Fredric Earl and Maude E. (McCracken) Jackson; student pub. schs., Valley Falls; m. Louis Kalina, Jr., Nov. 21, 1937; children—Dennis A., Sherman, Jerry. Owner, partner Kalina Apts., Malin, Oreg., 1940-76; partner Kalina's Food Market & Hardware, Malin, 1947-61, Kalina's Hardware, Malin, 1962-78; bookkeeper all cos., 1953—. Mem. West Malin Election Bd., 1944—, chmn., 1969—; mem. Parents and Patrons Club, 1947-70, treas., 1947, pres., 1957; den mother Modoc area council Cub Scouts, Boy Scouts Am., 1950-57; bd. dirs. Order Rainbow for Girls, 1957-78, mother advisor, 1957, 58. Recipient Community Service award, 1965. Club: Order of Eastern Star (worthy matron 1960, 67, 77, grand com. mem. Oreg. 1961, grand officer 1962). Address: PO Box 6 Malin OR 97632

KALINA, JO ANN, nursing adminstr.; b. Pawnee City, Nebr., Mar. 7, 1939; d. Edward George and Libbie Edna (Findeis) K.; R.N., St. Elizabeth Hosp. Sch. Nursing, 1960; B.S., Nebr. Wesleyan U., 1962; M.S. in Nursing, Washington U., St. Louis, 1964; B.A., Doane Coll., 1981. Nursing instr. St. Joseph Sch. Nursing, Phoenix, 1966-67; indsl. nurse Campbell Soup Co., Tecumseh, Nebr., 1967-68; dir. nursing service York (Nebr.) Gen. Hosp., 1968-70; asst. dir. nursing edn. Lincoln (Nebr.) Gen. Hosp. Sch. Nursing, 1970-73, dir. nursing edn., 1973-76; dir. nurses Crete (Nebr.) Mcpl. Hosp., 1976—; instr. Coll. Nursing U. Nebr., Lincoln, 1982; nursing home cons. USPHS grantee, 1962-64. Mem. Am. Nurses Assn., St. Elizabeth Alumni Assn., Table Rock Hist. Soc., Am. Legion Aux. Mem. Christian Ch. Home: 1505 Code St Crete NE 68333 Office: 15th and Grove Sts Crete NE 68333

KALINS, DOROTHY, mag. editor; b. Westport, Conn., Oct. 9, 1942; d. Joseph M. and Gil G. Kalins; student Skidmore Coll., 1960-62, Sorbonne U., Paris, 1962-63; B.A., Columbia U., 1965. Design writer Home Furnishings Daily, N.Y.C., 1965-68; freelance writer, 1969-74; exec. editor Apartment Life mag. (now Met. Home mag.), N.Y.C., 1974-78, editor-in-chief, 1978—. Mem. Am. Soc. Mag. Editors. Author: Researching Design in New York, 1968; Cutting Loose, 1972; The Apartment Book, 1979; The New American Cuisine, 1981; contbg. editor N.Y. mag. Contbr. articles to various mags. including Cosmopolitan, N.Y. Mag. Office: Metropolitan Home Magazine 750 3d Ave New York NY 10022

KALISCH, LEONORA LIPH (MRS. GERHARD K. KALISCH), social worker; b. Chgo., May 14, 1919; d. Samson and Rose (Fein) Liph; B.A., U. Chgo., 1939, M.A., 1957; m. Gerhard K. Kalisch, Nov. 28, 1942; children—John M., Peggy J. Caseworker, supr. Childrens Home Soc. Minn., St. Paul, 1947-51, Jewish Family Service, Mpls., 1957-62; sch. social worker Mpls. Pub. Schs., 1964-67; social worker Childrens Home Soc., Santa Ana, Calif., 1967-72; psychol. cons. Head Start Program, La Habra, Calif., 1972; social worker psychiatry and neurosurgery Long Beach (Calif.) VA Hosp., 1972-77, social work coordinator, 1977—; field work instr. UCLA, U. So. Calif. Chmn., LWV, Mpls., 1956-58. Mem. Nat. Assn. Social Workers, Acad. Cert. Social Workers, (lic. clin. social worker), Faculty Wives U. Calif. at Irvine. Home: 4530 Roxbury Rd Corona Del Mar CA 92625

KALISH, RUTH ANN, assn. exec., psychologist; b. Bridgeport, Conn., July 30, 1939; d. George and Francis Weissman; B.A., Boston U., 1961, M.A., 1964; postgrad. Emory U., 1968-71; Ph.D., Ga. State U., 1976; postgrad. Program for Health Systems Mgmt., Harvard U., 1980; 1 dau., Deborah Leslie. Chief phys. therapist Leonard Morse Hosp., Natick, Mass., 1962; instr. Sargent Coll., Boston U., 1961-65; asst. prof. phys. therapy Tufts U., 1964-68; asso. prof. and dir. grad. programs phys. therapy Emory U., 1969-81, asst. to exec. dean Sch. Medicine, 1981—; dir. legal and regulatory affairs Am. Hosp. Assn., 1982—; pres. Health and Edn. Designs, Inc., 1979—; chmn. Spl. Edn. Adv. Panel Ga., 1978-81; cons. in field. Active Com. Drug Abuse, Met. Atlanta Com. Alcohol and Drug Abuse. Recipient various govt. grants. Mem. Am. Phys. Therapy Assn., Am. Congress Rehab. Medicine, Soc. Behavioral Kinesiology. Author: Therapy in Educational Environments for Handicapped Children, 1980; also manuals, articles in field. Office: 840 N Lake Shore Dr Chicago IL 60611

KALISTY, DOLORES FEROL, mgmt. cons.; b. Beacon, N.Y., Apr. 25, 1932; d. Walter S. and Inez D. (Reed) K.; ed. Poughkeepsie (N.Y.) public schs., spl. courses Vassar Coll., Cornell U., Pace Coll., U.S. Navy. Successively floor mgr., asst. toy mgr., asst. millinery buyer Luckey Platt & Co., Poughkeepsie, 1948-53; operator N.Y. Telephone Co., Poughkeepsie, 1953-55, supr., 1968-70; instr., mgr. IBM, Owego, N.Y., 1956-59; supr. Diversified Elec. Co., Poughkeepsie, 1959-62; dist. mgr. New Bedford Hosiery, Brockton, Mass., 1962-68; owner Mahdy's Accessories, Poughkeepsie, 1969-70; supr. Petrie Stores, N.Y.C., 1970-73; mgr. Braunstein's Dept. Store, Prices Corner, Del., 1973; unit v.p. Integrated Control Systems, Litchfield, Conn., 1974-80, also mem. exec. com.; mgmt. analyst WOFAC, Bridgewater, N.J., 1980—. Served with USNR, 1955-56. Mem. Assn. Productivity Specialists. Mem. Bahai Faith. Home: 24 Raintree Dr New Castle DE 19720

KALLEK, SHIRLEY, govt. ofcl.; b. Roselle, N.J., Nov. 23, 1928; d. Louis and Pauline (Rosenzweig) K.; B.A., Hunter Coll., 1947; M.A., N.Y.U., 1949. Statis. analyst Port of N.Y. Authority, 1949-50; analyst Air Transport Assn., Washington, 1950-52; pvt. practice econ. cons., Washington, 1952-55; statistician, div. chief U.S. Bur. Census, Washington, 1955-74, assoc. dir., 1974—. Recipient gold medal U.S. Dept. Commerce, 1974. Fellow Am. Statis. Assn. (dir. 1972-75); mem. Am.

Econ. Assn., Nat. Economists Club, Internat. Assn. Survey Statisticians, Nat. Assn. Bus. Economists. Office: Bldg 3 Washington DC 20233

KALMAR, ROBERTA, assn. adminstr.; b. N.Y.C., Mar. 19, 1944; B.A., Bklyn. Coll., 1969; M.S.W., N.Y. U., 1971; M.P.A., John Jay Coll., City U. N.Y., 1976; cert. fund raising mgmt. Adelphi U., Garden City, N.Y., 1976; m. Jack Kalmar. Social worker Bklyn. Bur. Community Services, 1971-74; dir. adminstrn. Sphere Community Center Arts, Bklyn., 1976-77; program coordinator Buckingham Sch., Queens, N.Y., 1975-78; social worker Com. Handicapped, Bklyn., 1977-79; dir. Graham-Windham Family Services, Bklyn., 1979-81; exec. staff Nat. Fedn. Temple Sisterhoods, N.Y.C., 1982—; adoption cons. lectr. Adelphi U., 1977. Mem. Nat. Assn. Social Workers, Am. Soc. Public Adminstrn., Am. Soc. Tng. and Devel. Author study guide, articles in field. Home: 571 8th St Brooklyn NY 11215

KALSEM, MILLIE E., investment co. exec.; b. Huxley, Iowa, Dec. 12, 1896; d. Ole J. and Anna (Nelson) Kalsem; B.S., Iowa State Coll., 1921; dietetic study Michael Reese Hosp., Chgo., 1922-23; postgrad. U. Ill. Med. Sch., 1935-36. Tchr. home econs. and physiology Monticello (Iowa) High Sch., 1921-22; hosp. dietitian Beaver Valley Gen. Hosp., New Brighton, Pa., 1923, Iowa Meth. Hosp., Des Moines, 1923-27, Ill. Tng. Sch. Nurses and Cook County Sch. Nursing, 1927-38; chief exec. dietitian Cook County Hosp., 1938-62; registered rep. All Am. Mgmt., investment broker, Chgo. Bd. govs. Iowa State U. Selected by Carrie Chapman Catt as one of 100 Women, Women's Centennial Congress, 1940; recipient Alumni merit award Iowa State Coll., 1946, alumni medal, 1956. Mem. Am. (v.p. 1946-47), Ill. (organizer and 1st pres.), Chgo. (past pres.) dietetic assns., Women's Finance Forum Am. (research chmn. 1954-57, regional dir. 1960—), Art Inst. Chgo. (life), Order of Knoll, Omicron Nu, Phi Kappa Phi, Chi Omega. Club: Altrusa (pres. Chgo. 1959-61). Home: 111 Lynn Ave Ames IA 50010 Office: 11 S LaSalle St Chicago IL 60603

KAMAN, CAROL KATZEN, county ofcl.; b. Phila., Feb. 23, 1929; d. Wolf W. and Sylvia Katzen; B.A., U. Pa., 1950; postgrad. U. Rochester, 1966-68; m. Jack A. Kaman, Aug. 6, 1950; children—Cathy E., Karen J., John B. Research asst., Rochester Inst. Tech., 1970-74, Rochester Area Colls., 1974; assessment specialist Empire State Coll., Rochester, 1974-80; clk. Monroe County Legislature, Rochester, 1980—; tchr. BOCES 1, 1966-70. Mem. Town Council Pittsford, 1972-80; mem. Pittsford Rep. Town and County Com., 1965-79; del. Nat. Women Polit. Conf., Aspen, Colo., 1977. Republican. Jewish. Club: Faculty U. Rochester. Home: 65 Alpine Dr Rochester NY 14618 Office: County Office Bldg 39 W Main St Room 406 Rochester NY 14614

KAMELHAIR, NORA BRANTLEY, advt. co. exec.; b. Miami, Fla., Aug. 23, 1948; d. Allen Emmett and Sue Editha (Horton) Brantley; student Jacksonville U., 1966-68; B.A., U. South Fla., 1971; m. Bruce Ira Kamelhair, Aug. 13, 1972. Asst. traffic dir. Sta. WBMG-TV, Orlando, Fla., 1972-75; account exec. Sta. WSIR, 1975-76; sales service dept. Sta. WFTV-TV, 1976-77; media dir. Gilpin, Peyton & Pierce Advt., 1977—. Recipient Effie award Pepsi-Cola Co., 1981. Mem. Orlando Area Advt. Fedn. (dir. 1982-83, sec. 1982-83). Democrat. Home: 4085 Anthony Ln Orlando FL 32807 Office: Gilpin Peyton & Pierce Advertising 1601 W Colonial Dr Orlando FL 32804

KAMENSTEIN, CAROL LANDY, T-shirt mfg. co. exec.; b. Phila., Jan. 6, 1943; d. Benjamin H. and Pauline (Dobkin) Landy; B.A., Boston U., 1963; m. David Kamenstein, Sept. 19, 1963; children—Tracy D., Sloan G. Owner, operator U Name It and U Name It Travel, Harrison, N.Y., 1973—. Active Little League, Harrison, 1977—, United Way, Harrison, 1977—. Recipient service awards, United Way, Little League. Office: 225 Harrison Ave Harrison NY 10528

KAMERMAN, SHEILA BRODY, educator, social worker; b. U.S. Jan. 7, 1928; d. S. Lawrence and Helen (Golding) Brody; B.A., N.Y. U., 1946; M.S.W., Hunter Coll., 1966; D.Social Welfare, Columbia U., 1973; m. Morton Kamerman, Sept. 11, 1947; children—Nathan Brody, Elliot Herbert, Laura Kamerman-Barouch. Social worker N.Y.C. Dept. Social Services, 1966-68; social work supr. Bellevue Psychiat. Hosp., N.Y.C., 1968-69; research asso., sr. research asso. Columbia U. Sch. Social Work, 1971-73, co-dir. Cross Nat. Studies, 1973—; asso. prof. social work Hunter Coll., City U. N.Y., 1977-79; asso. prof. social policy and social planning Columbia U. Sch. Social Work, 1979-81, prof., 1981—; mem. adv. coms. and bds. in social welfare field; cons. founds., internat. orgns., govtl. agys., social welfare programs. Recipient (1st) Hexter award Alumna Hunter Coll. Sch. Social Work, 1977. Mem. Nat. Assn. Social Workers, Am. Public Welfare Assn., Am. Soc. Public Adminstrn., Gerontol. Soc., Phi Beta Kappa. Author books including: (with Alfred J. Kahn) Not for the Poor Alone, 1975, Social Services in the United States, 1976, Social Services in International Perspective, 1977, Government and Families in Fourteen Countries, 1978; Parenting in an Unresponsive Society, 1980; Child Care, Family Benefits and Working Parents, 1981; Helping America's Families, 1982; Maternity Policy and Working Women, 1983; contbr. numerous articles to profl. publs. Home: 1125 Park Ave New York NY 10028

KAMINSKY, ALICE R., educator; b. N.Y.C.; d. Morris and Ida (Spivak) Richkin; B.A., N.Y.U., 1946, M.A., 1947, Ph.D., 1952; m. Jack Kaminsky. Mem. faculty dept. English, N.Y.U., 1947-49, Hunter Coll., 1952-53, Cornell U., 1954-57, 59-63, Broome Community Coll., 1958-59; mem. faculty dept. English, SUNY, Cortland, 1963—, prof., 1968—. Mem. MLA, Chaucer Soc., Am. Soc. Aesthetics. Author: George Henry Lewes as Critic, 1968; Logic: A Philosophical Introduction, 1974. Editor: Literary Criticism of George Henry Lewes, 1964; Chaucer's Troilus and Criseyde and the Critics, 1980; contbr. articles to profl. jours. Office: Dept English SUNY Cortland NY 13045

KAMINSKY, PHYLLIS, govt. ofcl.; b. Montreal, Que., Can., Dec. 1, 1936; came to U.S., 1945, naturalized, 1958; d. Julius and Betty (Shapiro) Levitt; B.A. in Polit. Sci., U. Mich., 1957; postgrad. Columbia U., 1957-58; m. I. Samuel Kaminsky, June 24, 1971; children—David, Glenn. Sec. speakers bur. Fgn. Policy Assn., N.Y.C., 1957-58; editor disarmament procs. UN, Geneva, 1958; secretarial supr. McKinsey and Co., Geneva, 1963-64; adminstrv. asst. Chrysler Internat. S.A., also Internat. Research Cons. S.A., Geneva, 1959-63, Grey Advt. Internat., N.Y.C., 1965-67; exec. asst. Lee Burdick Advt., Inc., N.Y.C., 1967-68; bi-lingual press attache S.B.M. Resort Complex, Monte Carlo, 1968-69; public relations asst. Mayor's Com. for 25th Anniversary of UN, N.Y.C., 1970-71; consular corps liaison officer N.Y.C. Dept. Public Events, 1967-68; media cons., public relations adv. United Jewish Appeal, N.Y.C., 1971-80; media cons. Bush for Pres. Campaign, Pa. and Ill., 1980; dep. dir. communications Coalition for Reagan-Bush, 1980; press sec. to sr. fgn. policy adv. Office of President-Elect, 1980-81; press liaison Nat. Security Council, 1981; dir. Office of Public Liaison, U.S. Info. Agy., 1981—; mem. U.S. ofcl. del. 29th session UN Commn. on Status of Women, 1982. Co-founder Jerusalem Women's Seminar, 1979—. Mem. Washington Women's Network, Public Relations Soc. Am., AAUW, Nat. Assn. Female Execs., Women in Communications; Exec. Women in Govt. Clubs: Washington Press (bd. dirs.), Celebrate Women Inc., Washington Women's Forum, Am. News Women's. Office: 1750 Pennsylvania Ave Washington DC 20547

KANAVY, MARGARITA GUADALUPE, educator; b. El Paso, Tex., Feb. 22, 1939; d. Jose Cruz and Maria G. (Fernandez) Burciaga; B.A. in English, Tex. Western Coll., 1963; M.A., U. Tex., 1969; m. Cletus C. Kanavy, Nov. 28, 1963; children—Patricia, Catherine. Librarian, U. Tex., El Paso, 1972-73; tchr. English, El Paso (Tex.) public schs., 1963-64, 73-79; lectr. English, U. Tex., El Paso, part-time, 1978—; communicative arts instr. U.S. Army Air Def. Sch., Ft. Bliss, Tex., 1979—; lectr. El Paso Community Coll. Bd. dirs. Mujeres de El Paso, 1980—; EEO counselor Ft. Bliss, Tex., 1980—. Named Woman of the Yr., Mujeres de El Paso, 1981. Mem. Pan Am. Roundtable, Nat. Council Coll. Tchrs. English, Loretto Acad. Alumnae Assn. Democrat. Roman Catholic. Office: Tactics USAADS Fort Bliss TX 79916

KANDARAS, CHRISTINE STEVICK, psychotherapist; b. Detroit, Dec. 10, 1946; d. Doyle Odell and Harriet Wilta (Fenstermaker) Stevick; B.A., No. Mich. U., 1969; M.A. (NIMH grantee 1969-71), U. Chgo., 1971; cert. Chgo. Inst. Psychoanalysis, 1980; m. Kenneth Kandaras, May 30, 1976; 1 dau., Ashley Elizabeth. Staff social worker, dir. intake, chmn. community services Children's Meml. Hosp., Chgo., 1971-74; child therapist Community Mental Health Center, Ravenswood Hosp., Chgo., 1975-77; cons. Mary Crane Nursery Sch., Chgo., 1975—; psychotherapist Lutheran Gen. Hosp., Chgo., 1978—; vis. lectr. Jane Addams Coll. Social Work, 1978; pvt. practice psychotherapy, 1978—; cons. in field. Mem. Assn. Child Psychotherapists, Nat. Assn. Social Workers. Lutheran. Office: Lincoln-Peterson Med Center 5962 N Lincoln Ave Chicago IL 60659

KANDARIAN, FAY, utility co. exec.; b. Manchester, Conn., June 16, 1947; d. Everett H. and Thelma D. (Dibble) K.; B.A., George Washington U., 1971. With So. New Eng. Telephone, 1969—, dist. mgr.-residence, Bridgeport, Conn., 1979, now dist. mgr. interconnection and bus. relations; New Haven; pres. Self Mgmt. Systems Inc. Mem. exec. bd. Milford United Way, 1977-79; mem. Milford Fine Arts Council, 1977—, vice chmn., 1979-80; pres. Poor People's Fedn., Inc., 1977-79. Mem. Bridgeport C. of C. (bd. dirs.), Kappa Kappa Gamma. Club: Algonquin. Contbg. author: Management Handbook, 1981. Home: 20 Daggett St Milford CT 06460 Office: 1227 Church St New Haven CT 06506

KANDZARI, JUDITH CAROL HIGHTOWER, nurse; b. Gary, W.Va., Dec. 25, 1943; d. George Edward and Ruby Jewel (Slone) Hightower; B.S.N., W.Va. U., 1965, M.A., 1973; now postgrad. in health edn.; m. Stanley J. Kandzari, Jan. 17, 1966; children—Pamela, David. Staff nurse U. N.C. Hosp., Chapel Hill, 1965-66; mem. faculty W.Va. U., Morgantown, 1973-78, instr., 1978-81, asst. prof. nursing, 1981—; nurse practitioner Med. Group Practice Clinic, W.Va. U., 1982—. Mem. Am. Nurses Assn., W.Va. Nurses Assn. (dir.), Am. Public Health Assn., W.Va. Diabetes Assn. (sec.), Mental Health Assn., Soc. Public Health Educators, W.Va. Public Health Assn., Ladies Aux. AMA, Sigma Theta Tau. Methodist. Club: Order Eastern Star. Author: (with J. R. Howard) The Well Family-A Developmental Approach to Development, 1981. Office: Sch Nursing W Va U Morgantown WV 26506

KANE, ARIADNE MARIA, orgn. exec.; b. N.Y. State, Jan. 12, 1936; d. Maurice Andre and Sylvia Phyllis (Sophias) K.; B.S., CCNY, 1958, M.Ed., 1959; Ph.D., U. Buffalo, 1962. Tchr. math. acads. and colls., New Eng. and Europe, 1963-69; ednl. cons. Endl. Dynamics, Boston, 1969-72; adminstr. Beth Israel Hosp., Boston, 1972-74; tng. and devel. specialist Gen. Radiation Corp., Concord, Mass., 1974-76; appraiser, realtor La Vaux Realty, Cambridge, Mass., 1976-79; exec. dir. Outreach Inst., Boston, 1979—; cons. pre-retirement planning. Mem. Am. Soc. Tng. and Devel., Am. Assn. Sex Educators, Counselors and Therapists, Assn. Humanistic Psychology, Soc. Sci. Study Sex, Nat. Assn. Female Execs. Unitarian-Universalist. Office: Kenmore Station Box 368 Boston MA 02215

KANE, CAROL, actress; b. Cleve., June 18, 1952. Appeared with touring co. of play The Prime of Miss Jean Brodie, 1966; with Joseph Papp's Pub. Theatre; with Charles St. Playhouse, Boston, appearing in Arturo Ul; film appearances include: Carnal Knowledge, 1971; Desperate Characters, 1971; The Last Detail, 1974; Dog Day Afternoon, 1975; Hester Street (Acad. award nomination for Best Actress), 1975; Harry and Walter Go to New York, 1976; Annie Hall, 1977; Valentino, 1977; The World's Greatest Lover, 1977; When a Stranger Calls, 1979; The Muppet Movie, 1979; La Sabina, 1979; Les Jeux, 1980; stage appearances include: The Effect of Gamma Rays on Man in the Moon Marigolds, 1978; Tales From the Vienna Woods, 1979; Benefit of a Doubt, 1979; The Tempest and MacBeth at Lincoln Center, 1980; Sunday Runners in the Rain, 1980; A Midsummer Nights Dream 1981, appeared in TV films: Those Girls in Their Summer Dresses, Many Mansions; appeared in TV Series, Taxi. Office: care William Morris Agy Inc 151 El Camino Beverly Hills CA 90212 *

KANE, FLORA, investment cons.; b. Lyon, France, Apr. 2, 1948; d. Henry Greenbaum and Rochelle (Selmanowicz) Greenbaum; dental technician degree with honors, UCLA, 1967; m. Alan Steven Kane, Mar. 15, 1969 (div. Apr. 1977); 1 dau., Dawn Elizabeth-Marie. Fin. coordinator for physician, 1968-69; owner, office mgr. Ditto of Calif., Inc., clothing mfrs., 1969-75; cons. in fin. and investments, Woodland Hills, Calif., 1975—; notary public, 1980—. Active Orphans Aid Soc., Tel Aviv, 1975-77. Mem. Exec. Female, Internat. Assn. Med. Assistance to Travellers, Save Children Fedn., Am. Entrepreneurs Assn., Acad. Magical Arts, Am. Platform Assn., Nat. Notary Assn. Republican. Jewish. Address: 3410 San Martin Circle Palm Springs CA 92262

KANE, JACQUELINE ANNE, ednl. adminstr.; b. N.Y.C., Aug. 27, 1946; d. Philip and Jacqueline (Jones) K.; A.B., Morgan State Coll., 1968; M.S., SUNY Coll., Oneonta, 1974; postgrad. in sociology SUNY, Albany, 1980—. Caseworker, Dept. Social Services N.Y.C., 1968-70; counselor SUNY Coll., Oneonta, 1970-71, coordinator counseling and acad. advisement, 1971-75; asso. in higher edn. opportunity N.Y. State Edn. Dept., Albany, 1975—. Bd. dirs. Albany County Big Brothers/Big Sisters, 1977-80. Mem. Am. Council Edn. (nat. identification project, N.Y. state planning com.), Black Profl. Womens Network (dir. 1978—), N.Y. State Assn. Non-White Concerns in Personnel and Guidance (pres.), Assn. Black Women in Higher Edn. (pres. 1978-81, conf. chmn. 1978—), Delta Sigma Theta (chmn. program com. alumnae chpt. Albany, 1979-81, rec. sec. 1981-83). Lutheran. Office: CEC 5A55 Empire State Plaza Albany NY 12230

KANE, JEAN CAROLINE, interior design fabricator; b. N.Y.C., May 2, 1941; d. James Alfred and Theresa Miriam (Schulz) Amoroso; A.S., Endicott Coll., 1961; m. John Francis Kane, May 2, 1964; 1 dau., Cathleen Theresa. Free-lance model with Candy Jones Modeling Agy., N.Y.C., 1950-8; asst. dept. mgr. Lord & Taylor, Scarsdale, N.Y., 1959, multi-br. mdse. mgr., N.Y.C., 1961-62; asst. advt. mgr. Van Raalte, Inc., N.Y.C., 1962-64; free-lance promotion coordinator for Van Raalte, Inc., 1965-68; free-lance interior design fabricator Mamaroneck, N.Y., 1969—; cons. Eye of the Needle, Larchmont, N.Y., 1965—; Prentis Hall Media on Upholstery teaching Viedo tapes 1982—; tchr. upholstery Bd. Coop. Ednl. Services, Yorktown, N.Y., 1979. Sec., Rye Neck Sch. Bd.; trustee Selection Com., Mamaroneck, 1976-77, pres., 1977-78; chairwoman club activities F.E. Bellos Sch. Parent Tchr. Student Assn., Mamaroneck, 1977-79, co-chairwoman book and art show, 1980; active Girl Scouts U.S.A., Mamaroneck community dir., 1978—, del. ann. meeting Sackerah Path council, 1978-79, Westchester/Putnam council, 1979-82; active campaign for mayor of Mamaroneck, 1979. Roman Catholic. Designs include: 2 rooms of Larchmont Shore Club; fabric design for Bloomingdale Mansion, YWCA house tour; 3 rooms of 16th century replica French castle; members' needlpoint for doors of Temple Israel, Scarsdale. Home and Office: 116 Lawn Terr Mamaroneck NY 10543

KANE, LORRAINE L., state legislator; b. Providence, July 28, 1944; student Annhurst Coll.; m. Stephen Kane; children—Colin, Brendan, Michaela. Former condominium specialist; mem. R.I. Ho. of Reps., 1978—. Exec. sec. Vols. of Warwick (R.I.) Schs.; exec. bd. Am. Cancer Soc.; adv. bd. Women in Govt.; mem. Young Polit. Leaders (Soviet del.). Democrat. Office: Rhode Island State House Providence RI 02903 *

KANE, MARGARET BRASSLER, sculptor; b. East Orange, N.J., May 25, 1909; d. Hans and Mathilde (Trumpler) Brassler; student Packer Collegiate Inst., 1920-26, Syracuse U., 1927, Art Students League, 1927-29, N.Y. Coll. Music, 1928-29, John Hovannes Studio, 1932-34; Ph.D., Colo. State Christian Coll., 1973; m. Arthur Ferris Kane, June 11, 1930; children—Jay Brassler, Gregory Ferris. Work has appeared at Jacques Seligmann Gallery, N.Y., Whitney Ann. Exhbns., All Sculptors Guild Museum and Outdoor Shows, 1980, Nat. Sculpture Soc. Ann. Bas-Relief Exhbn., 1938, Whitney Mus. Sculpture Festival, 1940, Bklyn. Mus. Sculptors Guild, 1938, Bklyn. Soc. Artists, 1942, Lawrence (Mass.) Art Mus., 1938, N.Y. World's Fair, 1939, Sculptors Guild World's Fair Exhbn., 1940, Robinson Gallery, N.Y., 1939, Traveling Mus. and Instns., 1938, Lyman Allyn Mus., 1939, Met. Mus., Internat. Exhbns., 1940, 1949, Roosevelt Field Art Center, N.Y.C., 1957, Phila. Mus., N.Y. Archtl. League, Nat. Acad., Pa. Acad., Chgo. Art Inst., Am. Fedn. Arts, Riverside Mus., Montclair Mus., Grand Central Art Galleries, Lever House, N.Y.C., 1959-82, Rye (N.Y.) Library, 1962, Lever House Sculptors Guild Ann. Exhbn., 1977—, and exhbns. of nat. scope, 1938—; executed plaque for Burro Monument, Fairplay, Colo.; solo sculpture exhibit Friends of Greenwich Library, 1962; exhibited N.Y. Bank for Savs., 1968, Mattatuck Mus., 1967, Lamont Gallery, N.H., 1967. Head craftsman for sculpture, arts and skills unit ARC, Halloran Gen. Hosp., N.Y., 1942-43. Jury mem. Brooklyn Mus., 1948, Am. Machine & Foundry Co. Art Exhibit, Greenwich, Conn., 1957; com. mem. Am. Group, Inc. Slide lectr. and sculpture demonstrator for art socs. and orgns. Recipient Ann Hyatt Huntington award, 1942; awards Am. Artists Profl. League, Montclair Art Assn., 1943; 1st Henry O. Avery prize, 1944; sculpture prize Bklyn. Soc. Artists, Bklyn. Mus., 1946, John Rogers award, 1951; Lawrence Hyder prize, 1952, 54; David Zell Meml. award, 1954-63; hon. mention U.S. Maritime Commn., 1941; A.C.A. Gallery Competition, 1944; medal of honor for sculpture, 1951, Nat. Assn. Women Artists, Nat. Acad. Galleries, N.Y.; prize for carved sculpture, 1955, animal sculpture, 1956, Ann. New Eng. Exhbns., Silvermine, Conn.; 1st award for sculpture Greenwich Art Soc., 1958, 60; award for creative work in sculpture Am. Biog. Inst., 1982. Fellow Internat. Inst. Arts and Letters; mem. Nat. Trust for Hist. Preservation, Sculptors Guild (sec. to exec. bd. 1942-45, chmn. exhbn. com. 1942, 44), Nat. Assn. Women Artists (2d v.p. 1943-45), Artists Council, U.S.A., Bklyn. Soc. Artists, Greenwich Soc. Artists (council mem.), Pen and Brush, Silvermine Guild Artists. Contbr. articles to mags.; sculpture reproduced in books Contemporary Stone Sculpture, Contemporary American Sculpture; featured in Am. Artist mag., 1970. Home and Studio: 30 Strickland Rd Cos Cob CT 06807

KANG, BANN, physician; b. Kyungnam, Korea, Mar. 4, 1939; d. Daeryong and Buni (Chung) K.; came to U.S., 1964, naturalized, 1976; A.B., Kyungpook Nat. U., 1959, M.D., 1963; m. U. Yun Ryo, Mar. 30, 1963. Intern, L.I. Jewish Hosp.-Queens Hosp. Center, Jamaica, N.Y., 1964-65, resident in medicine, 1965-67; teaching asso. Kyungpook U. Hosp., Taegu, Korea, 1967-70; fellow in allergy and chest Creighton U., Omaha, 1970-71; fellow in allergy Henry Ford Hosp., Detroit, 1971-72; clin. instr. medicine U. Mich. Hosp., Ann Arbor, 1972-73; asst. prof. Chgo. Med. Sch., 1973-74; chief allergy-immunology Mt. Sinai Hosp., Chgo., 1975—; asst. prof. Rush Med. Sch., Chgo. 1975—; cons. allergy-immunology Edgewater Hosp., Chgo., 1976—, St. Anthony's Hosp., Chgo., 1976—. Recipient NIH award U. Mich., 1972-73. Diplomate Am. Bd. Internal Medicine, Am. Bd. Allergy-Immunology. Fellow ACP, Am. Acad. Allergy; mem. Am. Fedn. Clin. Research, AMA, Inter-Asthma Assn. Contbr. over 40 articles to profl. jours. Home: 1555 N Astor St Chicago IL 60610 Office: Mount Sinai Hosp Chicago IL 60608

KANIN, DORIS MAY, Democratic nat. committeewoman; b. Somerville, Mass.; d. Sidney J. and Ida Gloria (Gelbsman) Small; B.A. in Govt., Boston U., 1966, M.A., 1970, now doctoral candidate; m. Irving Lynwood Kanin; children—Dennis, Erik, Lisa. Legis. and exec. asst. to Congressman Joe Moakley of Mass., 1973-75; dir. fed.-state relations Mass. Secretariat of Human Services, Boston, 1979-82; dir. public affairs Physicians for Social Responsibility, 1982—; pres. Lynwood Labs. Inc.; mem. Norwood (Mass.) Human Rights Steering Com.; mem. state steering com. Mass. PAX, 1970-73; mem. state exec. bd. Citizens for Participatory Politics, 1971-72; del.-at-large Dem. Nat. Conv., 1972; mem. presdl. campaign staff, 1972, coordinator urban ethics div., head Concerned Clergy for McGovern-Shriver, 1972; mem. Dem. Nat. Com. from Mass., 1972—, mem. nat. edn. and tng. council, 1976-80; nat. legis. chmn. Ams. for Dem. Action, 1973—; mem. nat. legis. com. Nat. Women's Polit. Caucus, 1973—; nat. dep. polit. dir. Senator Frank Church for Pres. campaign, 1976; spl. asst. Tsongas for Senate campaign, 1977-78 mem. adv. bd. Mass. chpt. ACLU, 1979; mem. nat. exec. com. New Dem. Coalition. Mem. Am. Polit. Sci. Assn., Dem. Nat. Committeewomen's Caucus, Capitol Hill Women Polit. Caucus, Federally-Employed Women, LWV (pres. chpt. 1957-59). Patentee chem. products. Home: 1 Longfellow Pl Boston MA 02114 also 25 Buckingham Rd Norwood MA 21062 Office: 639 Massachusetts Ave Cambridge MA

KANIN, FAY, writer, producer; b. N.Y.C.; d. David and Bessie Mitchell; student Elmira Coll., 1933-36; B.A., U. So. Calif., 1937; m. Michael Kanin; children—Joel (dec.), Josh. Writer screenplays including: (with Michael Kanin) Teacher's Pet, Rhapsody, The Opposite Sex; writer for Broadway, including: Goodbye My Fancy, (with Michael Kanin) His and Hers, (with Michael Kanin) Rashomon; writer, co-producer Friendly Fire, ABC-TV (Emmy award for best TV film, San Francisco Film Festival award for best TV film); writer TV spls.; Hustling (Writers Guild award for best original drama), Tell Me Where It Hurts (Emmy award, Christopher award); producer-writer; mem. western regional exec. bd., judge Am. Coll. Theatre Festival, 1975-76; dir. Filmex. Mem. Writers Guild Am., West (pres. screen br. 1971-73, Val Davies award 1975) Am. Film Inst. (trustee), Acad. Motion Picture Arts and Sci. (pres. 1979—). Jewish. Address: care Acad Motion Picture Arts and Scis 8949 Wilshire Blvd Beverly Hills CA 90211

KANOVSKY, HELEN RENEE, lawyer; b. Warren, Pa., Mar. 4, 1951; d. Hershel and Rose (Gernstat) K.; A.B. cum laude, Cornell U., 1973; J.D. cum laude, Harvard U., 1976; m. Marc Bernard Dorfman, Aug. 8, 1976. Dir. vols. Biden for Senate, Wilmington, Del., 1972; legis. aide to U.S. Senator Joseph R. Biden, Washington, 1973; admitted to D.C. Ct. Appeals bar, 1976, U.S. Dist. Ct. bar for D.C., 1977, U.S. Ct. Appeals bar for D.C., 1977; asso. firm Dickstein, Shapiro and Morin, Washington, 1976-79; spl. asst. to sec. HUD, Washington, 1979; spl. asst. to sec. HEW, Washington, 1979-80, spl. asst. to the sec., asso. exec. sec. to HHS and exec. asst. to under sec., Dept. Health and Human Services, 1980-81; asso. firm Dickstein, Shapiro & Morin, Washington, 1981—. Bd. dirs. Women's Legal Def. Fund, 1981—. Recipient cert. spl. achievement Sec. HUD, 1979. Mem. Am. Bar Assn., D.C. Bar, Bar Assn. D.C. (chairperson ethics com. sect. young lawyers 1978-79), Phi Beta Kappa. Democrat. Jewish. Editor Harvard Civil Rights—Civil Liberties Law

Rev., 1975-76. Home: 7004 Winslow St Bethesda MD 20817 Office: 2101 L St NW Washington DC 20037

KANTOR, JUDITH AULD, molecular biologist; b. Pitts., Apr. 5, 1942; d. Howard Stanley and Elizabeth (Hanlon) Auld; B.S., Allegheny Coll., Meadville, Pa., 1964; M.Sc. in Hygiene, U. Pitts., 1967; Ph.D., George Washington U., 1975; m. Falk Kantor, Sept. 7, 1969. With molecular hematology br. Nat. Heart, Lung and Blood Inst., 1972-75; postdoctoral fellow Georgetown U., 1975-77; expert cons. clin. hematology Nat. Heart, Lung and Blood Inst., 1977-81; research assoc. prof. biochemistry, Lombardi fellow Georgetown U. Med.-Dental Schs., 1981—; instr. Found. Advanced Edn. Scis., 1978—. Mem. AAAS, N.Y. Acad. Scis., Assn. Women in Scis. Sigma Xi. Author numerous articles in field. Patentee reverse transcriptase from human milk. Office: Div Molecular Genetics Lombardi Cancer Ctr Georgetown U Washington DC 20007

KANTOR, MICHELE JEAN, audiologist; b. Utica, N.Y., Apr. 13, 1954; d. Theodore Joseph and Doris Sage (Cahill) K.; B.A. magna cum laude, Elmira Coll., 1975; M.A., George Washington U., 1976. Audiology trainee VA Hosp., Washington, 1976; audiology research asst., 1976; clin. audiologist Rome (N.Y.) Devel. Center, 1977—; audiology cons. nursing home, psychiat. hosps. Cert. clin. competence in audiology; lic. in audiology, N.Y. State. Mem. Am. Speech Lang. and Hearing Assn., N.Y. State Speech and Hearing Assn., Mohawk Valley Speech and Hearing Assn., Assn. Speech Pathologists and Audiologists in Mental Hygiene, Am. Research Found., Landmarks Soc., George Washington U. Alumni Club, Elmira Coll. Alumni Club. Home: 18 Arlington Rd Utica NY 13501 Office: 550 S James St Rome NY 13440

KANUK, LESLIE LAZAR, educator; b. N.Y.C.; d. Charles and Sylvia (Hoffman) Lazar; M.B.A., Baruch Coll., 1964; Ph.D., CUNY, 1973; Ph.D. (h.c.), Mass. Maritime Acad., 1981; m. Jack Lawrence Kanuk; children—Randi Ellen, Alan Robert. Research dir. Skill Advancement, Inc., N.Y.C., 1966-68; pres. Leslie Kanuk Assos., mgmt. consultants, 1968-78, 81—; prof., dept. chmn. mktg. dept. Baruch Coll., N.Y.C., 1967-78, Lippert Disting. prof., 1981—; adj. prof. dept. command communications U.S. Army Signal Sch., Ft. Monmouth, N.J., 1967-69; adj. prof. U.S. Mcht. Marine Acad., Kings Point, N.Y., 1970-71; Commr., vice chmn., then chmn. Fed. Maritime Commn., Washington, 1978-81; cons. U.S. Maritime Adminstrn., N.Y. State Dept. Edn., Revlon, Ergonomics Inc., AT&T, N.Y.C. Human Resources Adminstrn., Merc. Dept. Stores, Curtis-Wright Corp., Skill Achievement, Inc., Universal Transistor Corp., others; mem. Maritime Transp. Research Bd. Nat. Acad. Scis., 1975-78; panelist NRC, Nat. Acad. Scis.; chmn. adv. panel maritime trade and tech. Office of Tech. Assessment, 1982; bd. dirs. Nat. Maritime Resource Center, 1982, Containerization and Intermodal Inst., 1981—. Recipient Diamond super woman award, 1980; Person of Yr. award Containerization and Intermodal Inst., 1980, Fgn. Freight Forwarders and Brokers Assn., 1981; Fgn. Trade Soc., 1981. Mem. AAAS, Acad. Mgmt., Am. Mktg. Assn., Am. Assn. for Public Opinion Research, Beta Gamma Sigma. Author: Upgrading the Low Wage Worker: An Ergonomic Approach, 1968; Environmental and Behavioral Study of U.S. Merchant Marine Officers, 1971; Improving the Efficiency of Maritime Personnel, 1972; Consumer Behavior, 1978, 83; also numerous articles. Contbg. editor Breaking Barriers of Occupational Isolation, 1966; editor The American Seafarer monographs: Occupational Hazards in the U.S. Merchant Marine, 1972; editor: Management of a Seaport, 1972; mem. editorial review bd. Jour. Mktg., 1978. Office: 809 Watergate S Washington DC 20573

KANY, JUDY C., state legislator; B.B.A., U. Mich., 1959; postgrad. U. Maine; m. Robert H. Kany, 1958; children—Kristin, Geoffrey, Danny. Mem. Maine Ho. Reps., 1975—. Alt. del. Democratic Nat. Conv., 1976. Mem., Commn. Maine's Future, ACLU. Office: Maine Ho Reps State Capitol Augusta ME 04330

KANZLER, MAUREEN BYRNE, research scientist; b. N.Y.C., Sept. 10, 1916; d. Richard Michael and Mary Agnes (Colligan) Byrne; B.A., Hunter Coll., 1938; M.S., 1960; M.A., N.Y.U., 1940; M.A., Fordham U., 1962, Ph.D., 1968; m. Robert Edward Lee, Oct. 21, 1972. Guidance counselor Yorktown Heights (N.Y.) High Sch., 1956-59 research scientist dept. biol. psychiatry N.Y. State Psychiat. Inst., N.Y.C., 1965—; asst. prof. clin. psychology Coll. Physicians and Surgeons, Columbia U., N.Y.C., 1971—. Nat. Inst. Drug Abuse grantee, 1978-82. Mem. Am. Psychol. Assn., Nat. Register Health Service Providers in Psychology, Sigma Xi. Roman Catholic. Contbr. articles in field to profl. jours. Office: 722 W 168 St New York NY 10032

KAPILOFF, HELEN BELL, social worker; b. Houston, Oct. 13, 1915; d. Wolf B. and Lena (Robinowitz) Bell; B.A., Rice Inst., 1935; M.A., U. Chgo., 1937; m. Gerald Kapiloff, Nov. 2, 1943 (div., dec.); 1 son, David. Med. social worker Johns Hopkins Hosp., 1937-38; social worker Com. for Care Jewish Tb, 1938-41; Caseworker ARC, 1941-43; supr. Harris County chpt., 1943-46; chief social worker VA Regional Office, Houston, 1946-49, VA Med. Center, Houston, 1949—; mem. adv. com. adj. faculty, lectr. U. Houston Grad. Sch. Social Work; social work adminstr. trainer VA, 1972-77. Mem. Nat. Assn. Social Workers (bd. dirs. 1974-77, past pres. Tex. council, pres. Houston unit 1980-82), Am. Soc. Hosp. Social Work Dirs., Tex. Soc. Hosp. Social Work Dirs. (past pres.). Office: VA Med Center 2002 Holcombe Blvd Houston TX 77211

KAPLAN, ALINE, religious orgn. ofcl.; b. N.Y.C., June 23, 1923; d. Morris and Dora (Zeresky) K.; B.A., Hunter Coll., 1943; LL.B., Columbia U., 1946; postgrad. Sch. Edn. Yeshiva U., 1959-62. Admitted to N.Y. bar, 1946; pvt. practice in N.Y.C., 1946-52; dir. Nat. Jr. Hadassah, 1952-64; asst. dir. Hadassah, Women's Zionist Orgn. Am., 1964-71, exec. dir., 1971—; Hadassah rep. Am. Israel Pub. Affairs Com., 1971—; Hadassah del. World Zionist Congress in Jerusalem, 1956, 64, 72, 78, 82, Convs. of World Fedn. United Zionists, 1956, 64, 72, 78; mem. tribunal World Zionist Orgn., 1978—. Bd. dirs. United Israel Appeal, 1971—. Mem. Am. Zionist Fedn., Delta Phi Epsilon. Jewish. Contbr. articles to Zionist ency. Office: 50 W 58th St New York NY 10019

KAPLAN, ANNE JOHNSON, legal sec.; b. Rockford, Ill., June 25, 1950; d. Donald Briggs and Shirley (Levis) Johnson; B.A., Converse Coll., 1972; cert. in legal secretarial studies N.Y. U., 1978, cert. in bus. mgmt., 1979, cert. in law office mgmt. 1980, paralegal diploma, 1981; m. Bruce Frederick Kaplan, Dec. 22, 1978. Exec. sec. to pres. Internat. House, N.Y.C., 1974-76; legal sec. to gen. counsel Cantor Fitzgerald, N.Y.C., 1977; legal sec. to sr. partner Rogers & Wells, N.Y.C., 1978-79, asst. supr., 1979-80; legal sec. to mng. partner firm Carb, Luria, Glassner, Cook & Kufeld, N.Y.C., 1980—; rec. sec. to bd. trustees Internat. House, 1974-76; rec. sec. bd. dirs. Morningside Heights Housing Corp., N.Y.C., 1974-76. Vol., Daytop Village, N.Y.C., 1974-76, Phoenix House, N.Y.C., 1974-76; bd. dirs., sec. Schneider Village, Inc., Monticello, N.Y., 1981-82. Mem. Nat. Assn. Legal Secs., N.Y.C. Assn. Legal Secs. (rec. sec. 1979-80, 2d v.p. 1980). Jewish. Clubs: Columbia U. Orch. (violinist 1979-80), Jr. League Bklyn. Home: Brooklyn NY

KAPLAN, ARLENE LAVENDER, banker; b. N.Y.C., Mar. 4, 1928; d. Michael and Leah Lavender; B.A. in Math. cum laude, SUNY, Albany, 1948; M.A. in Math., Columbia U., 1966; m. Bernard Kaplan, Aug. 23, 1952; children—Lee Michael, Jonathan Harris. Actuarial asst. G.B. Buck, Cons. Actuary, 1948-54; programmer Bankers Trust Co., N.Y.C., 1966-68, mgmt. scientist, 1968-72, asst. treas., asst. v.p. retail planning, 1972-79, v.p., head mgmt. info. systems in strategic planning dept., 1979—. Home: 27 Pryer Manor Rd Larchmont NY 10538 Office: 280 Park Ave New York NY 10015

KAPLAN, DOROTHY ANNE, clin. psychologist; b. N.Y.C., May 7, 1954; d. Milton and Madeleine (Hundert) Kaplan; B.A. with highest honors in Psychology, SUNY at Stony Brook, 1975; Ph.D. in Clin. Psychology (NIMH fellow), U. Vt., 1979. Asst. prof. psychology SUNY Coll. at Brockport, 1979—; cons. clin. psychologist Orleans County Mental Health, Job Corps., Bur. Disability Determination; lectr. U. Vt., 1978-79. Lic. psychologist, N.Y. Mem. Assn. for Advancement of Behavior Therapy, Am. Psychol. Assn., N.Y. State Psychol. Assn., Gennesee Valley Psychol. Assn. (v.p.), Soc. for Study of Social Issues, Phi Beta Kappa. Contbr. articles to profl. jours. Home: 108 Bryan St Rochester NY 14613 Office: Dept Psychology SUNY Coll Brockport NY 14420

KAPLAN, ERNA F., clin. social worker; b. N.Y.C., Feb. 25, 1925; d. Adolph and Rose (Herson) Fox; B.S., Cornell U., 1944; M.S.W., Columbia U., 1960; m. Alan William Kaplan, June 17, 1945; children—Elisabeth K. (Mrs. Richard Boas), Michael, David, Jonathan, Barbara. Clin. social worker U. Health Service, SUNY, Stony Brook, 1969—, asst. prof. field work, 1980, 81, field work supr. Sch. Social Welfare, 1971—. Pres., Family Service League of Suffolk County, 1963-65, Community Devel. for Youth, 1963, 64; bd. dirs. Huntington Youth Bd., 1964, Huntington Twp. Mental Health Clinic, 1956-58. Mem. Nat. Assn. Social Workers, Acad. Cert. Social Workers, Nat. Assn. Social Workers Clin. Register. Democrat. Jewish. Home: Box 377 Northport NY 11768 Office: Univ Health Service State Univ NY Stony Brook NY 11790

KAPLAN, FLORA S., educator; b. N.Y.C., Aug. 28, 1930; d. Harry H. and Sarah (Golder) Siegel; B.A. cum laude, Hunter Coll., 1951; M.A., Columbia U., 1958; Ph.D., City U. N.Y., 1976; m. George L. Kaplan, May 27, 1956; children—Elizabeth Rose, Jonathan Todd. Acting curator dept. primitive art and New World cultures Bklyn. Mus., 1954-57, asst., 1951-54; adj. lectr. City U. N.Y., 1970-73, lectr., 1973-74, grad. fellow, 1974-76; asst. prof. anthropology N.Y.U., 1976—, dir. mus. studies program, 1976—; research asso. Mus. Am. Indian, N.Y.C. Mem. spl. adv. bd. S.I. Hist. Soc.; committeewoman Democratic Party, County of New York, 1979. Grantee in field. Fellow Am. Anthrop. Assn., N.Y. Acad. Sci.; mem. Am. Assn. Mus., Council for Mus. Anthropology, Internat. Council Mus., Internat. Com. on Museology, Soc. Am. Archeology, Soc. Visual Communication. Author: Una Tradición Alfarera: Conocimiento y Estilo, 1980; Art of the Royal Court of Benín: Images of Power, 1981. Home: Gansett Ln Amagansett NY 11930 Office: NYU 19 University Pl New York NY 10003

KAPLAN, HELEN SINGER, psychiatrist; b. Vienna, Austria, Feb. 6, 1929; d. Phillip Sigmund and Sophie (Lanzi) Singer; came to U.S., 1940, naturalized, 1947; B.F.A., Syracuse U., 1949; M.A., Columbia U., 1951, Ph.D., 1955; M.D., N.Y. Med. Coll., 1959; m. Harold I. Kaplan, June 20, 1953 (div. 1970); children—Phillip, Peter, Jennifer. Intern, Bronx (N.Y.) Hosp., 1960-61; resident N.Y. Med. Coll., 1961-64; practice medicine specializing in psychiatry, N.Y.C., 1964—; asso. vis. psychiatrist Met. Hosp.; asso. prof. psychiatry N.Y. Med. Coll.; asso. clin. prof. psychiatry Cornell U. Med. Coll.; head sexual treatment and study program, coordinator student teaching of psychiatry, asso. attending psychiatrist N.Y. Hosp., N.Y.C., Nat. Inst. Mental Health career teacher in psychiatry, 1964-66. Fellow Am. Psychiatric Assn., Am. Psychol. Assn., Acad. Psychoanalysis; mem. Sigma Xi, Alpha Omega Alpha. Co-editor: Progress in Group and Family Therapy, 1972. Asst. to editors: Comprehensive Textbook Psychiatry, 1967, New Sex Therapy, 1974, The Illustrated Manual of Sex Therapy, 1975, Making Sense of Sex, 1979, Disorders of Sexual Desire, 1979. Co-editor Jour. Sex and Marital Therapy. Contbr. articles to profl. jours. Home: 912 Fifth Ave New York NY 10021 Office: 30 E 76th St New York NY 10021

KAPLAN, HELENE FEUERMAN, speech-lang. pathologist; b. Bklyn., Feb. 22, 1936; d. Abraham David and Dorothy (Ehlin) Feuerman; B.A., Bklyn. Coll., 1956; M.S., Pa. State U., 1957; m. Sidney Kaplan, Feb. 28, 1960; children—David Brian, Randi Sue. Speech and lang. pathologist Northampton County Crippled Childrens Soc., Easton, Pa., 1958-61, Easton Area Head Start, 1966-67; pvt. practice speech pathology, 1967-77; dir. speech and hearing center Warren Hosp., Phillipsburg, N.J., 1977—. Bd. dirs. Easton Area Jewish Fedn., 1977—; pres. Easton Area Jewish Community Center, 1975—; sec. to bd. dirs. B'Nai Abraham Synagogue, 1971-77; charter mem. Palmer Twp. Hist. Soc., 1977. Mem. Am. Speech, Lang. and Hearing Assn., AAUW, N.J. Speech and Hearing Assn., Hadassah. Republican. Club: B'nai B'rith Women. Author articles in field. Home: One Sutton Pl Easton PA 18042 Office: Warren Hosp 185 Roseberry St Phillipsburg NJ 08865

KAPLAN, HELENE L., lawyer; b. N.Y.C., June 19, 1933; d. Jack and Shirley (Jacobs) Finkelstein; A.B. cum laude, Barnard Coll., 1953; J.D., N.Y. U., 1967; m. Mark N. Kaplan, Sept. 7, 1953; children—Marjorie Ellen, Sue Anne. Admitted to N.Y. bar, 1967; individual practice law, N.Y.C., 1967-78; mem. firm Webster & Sheffield, 1978—. Trustee N.Y. Council for Humanities, 1976—, chmn., 1978-81; trustee N.Y. Found., 1976—; trustee Barnard Coll., 1973—, vice chmn., 1975—; trustee Columbia U. Press., 1977-80, John Simon Guggenheim Found., 1981—; trustee Carnegie Corp. N.Y., 1979—, vice-chmn., 1981—; Mt. Sinai Med. Center Hosp. and Sch., 1977—, MITRE Corp., 1978—; dir. Toys "R" Us, Inc., 1978-80, Verde Exploration Ltd., 1978—; trustee N.Y.C. Public Devel. Corp., 1978—, v.p., 1979-81; mem. Women's Forum, 1982—. Mem. Assn. Bar City N.Y. (com. philanthropic orgn. 1978-81, com. profl. responsibility, com. problems concerning recruitment of new lawyers), Am., N.Y. State bar assns., Am. Arbitration Assn. (dir. 1980—). Club: Cosmopolitan. Home: 146 Central Park W New York NY 10023 Office: One Rockefeller Plaza New York NY 10020

KAPLAN, JOAN ELLEN, art cons., curator; b. N.Y.C., Dec. 30, 1943; d. Henry and Frieda (Peck) Goldman; B.A. with honors, Conn. Coll., New London, 1964; m. Stephen L. Kaplan, Aug. 14, 1966 (div.); 1 son, Craig Robert. Dir. Adria Art Gallery, N.Y.C., 1966-68; pres. Joan Kaplan Fine Art, N.Y.C., 1968—; cons., curator numerous corps; cons. Organizing Com. XIV Olympic Games, Sarajevo, 1984. Mem. Assn. Profl. Art Advisors.

KAPLAN, JUDITH HELENE, business exec.; b. N.Y.C., July 20, 1938; d. Abraham and Ruth (Kiffel) Letich; B.A., Hunter Coll., 1960; postgrad. New Sch. Social Research, 1960-61; m. Warren Kaplan, Dec. 31, 1958; children—Ronald Scott, Elissa Ann. Registered rep. Herzfeld & Stern, N.Y.C., 1963-64; agt. N.Y. Life Ins. Co., N.Y.C., 1964-69; registered rep. Scheinman, Hochstin & Trotta, 1969-70; v.p. Alpha Capital Corp., N.Y.C., 1970-73; pres. Tipex, Inc., N.Y.C., 1966—; v.p. Alpha Public Relations, N.Y.C., 1970-73; pres. Utopia Recreations Corp., 1971-73, Howard Beach Recreation Corp., 1972-73; chmn. bd. Alpha Exec. Planning Corp., 1970-72, Life Underwriter N.Y. Life, 1974-75; co-chmn. Congressman Lester Wolff's Equal Rights Com.; cons. woman suffrage State of Wyo., 1979; co-convenor Central Fla. People of Faith for ERA; co-chairperson Ocala ERA Countdown Campaign. Mem. NOW (v.p. N.Y.; co-founder Ocala/Marion County chpt. 1982; creator, cachet dir. NOW-N.Y. Women's History Series of First Day Covers 1976—), Women's Equity Action League, Women Leaders Round Table, Nat. Assn. Life Underwriters, Bus. and Profl. Women, Assn. Feminist Cons., Nat. Women's Polit. Caucus, Manhattan Women's Polit. Caucus, Am., L.I. (dir.) stamp dealers assns., Am. Philatelic Soc., Am. Topical Assn., Bus. and Profl. Women, AAUW, Internat. Assn. Philatelic Journalists, Am. First Day Cover Soc. Author: Woman Suffrage, 1977; contbg. editor Stamp Show News. Home: 577 Silver Course Circle Ocala FL 32672 Office: 344 Cypress Rd SSS Industrial Park Ocala FL 32672

KAPLAN, KAREN ORLOFF, health care researcher; b. N.Y.C., June 9, 1941; d. Arthur Eugene and Molly (Jaffe) Orloff; A.B., Goucher Coll., 1963; M.S.W., Ohio State U., 1966; M.P.H., Johns Hopkins U., 1976, postgrad.; m. Kenneth Lawrence Kaplan, June 22, 1969; children—Ian Stuart, Andrew David. Social worker Long View State Hosp., Cin., 1964-66; instr. dept. psychiatry Sch. Medicine, U. Cin., 1966-68; clin. social worker dept. medicine Johns Hopkins Hosp., Balt., 1968-69; clin. instr. in medicine Sch. Medicine, Tufts U., Medford, Mass., 1969; asst. dir. dept. social work Tufts-New Eng. Med. Center, Boston, 1969, supr. med./surg. social services, 1969-71; clin. social worker Psychiat. Inst., Washington, 1971-75; sr. asso., project mgr. Kappa Systems, Inc., Arlington, Va., 1975-77; exec. dir. Rockburn Inst., Elkridge, Md., 1977-79; pres. Corbin Assos., McLean, Va., 1979—, also chmn., cons., clin. faculty Joint Commn. Accreditation of Hosps.; cons. com. spl. housing Ind. U. Sch. Law, 1967-71, Adminstrv. Mgmt. Tng. Center, Indian Health Service, 1978, Regional Med. Edn. Centers, VA, 1979, In the Public Interest, Can., 1977—; spl. staff advisor div. edn. and publs. Joint Commn. Accreditation of Hosps., 1978. Sec., bd. dirs. Langley Sch., 1981—. Research grantee Health Care Financing Adminstrn., 1978—. Mem. Am. Assn. Profl. Standards Rev. Orgns., Am. Public Health Assn., Nat. Assn. Social Workers, Acad. Cert. Social Workers. Author: The Quality Assurance Guide - A Manual for Hospitals, 1980; contbr. chpt. to book, articles to profl. publs. Office: 1210 Corbin Ct McLean VA 22101

KAPLAN, SUSAN, lawyer; b. Jamaica, N.Y., Oct. 28, 1949; d. Murray and Miriam B. (Loewenthal) K.; B.A. summa cum laude (scholar), Hofstra U., 1971; J.D. (Harlan Fiske Stone scholar), Columbia U., 1974. Admitted to N.Y. bar, 1975; asso. firm Patterson, Belknap & Webb, N.Y.C., 1974-76; asst. dist. atty. Nassau County (N.Y.), 1976-81; asst. chief of prosecution Office Profl. Discipline State of N.Y., 1981—. Chmn. legal aid com. Meml. Sloan-Kettering Cancer Center, 1975-78, mem. adminstrv. bd., 1975-78; mem. exec. bd. Nassau County council Boy Scouts Am., 1977—, v.p., 1981—; mem. UN Hospitality Com., 1974-76; bd. dirs. North Shore div. Am. Jewish Congress, 1977—; senator alumni coll. senate of Hofstra U., 1978; sec., bd. dirs. Harkness Ballet Found., 1980—, chmn. fund raising com., 1982. Mem. N.Y. State Bar Assn. (com. internat. law 1975-78, com. public health 1975-78), Citizens Union City N.Y. (legis. com.), Columbia U. Law Sch. Alumni Assn. (treas.), Soc. Internat. Law, Phi Delta Phi. Home: 237 Fairhaven Blvd Woodbury NY 11797 Office: 622 Third Ave New York NY 10017

KAPLAN, SUSAN D., mental health agy. exec.; b. Los Angeles, Apr. 28, 1953; d. Ira and Gloria (Tishler) Hirsch; B.A., UCLA, 1975, M.B.A., 1979; m. Alan D. Kaplan, Dec. 30, 1976. Co-dir., Women's Resource Center, Berkeley, Calif., 1972-73; research analyst Calif. Dept. Mental Health, Van Nuys, 1973-74; adminstr., chief fin. officer Friends of the Family, Inc., Van Nuys, 1974—; v.p. Kaplan Assos., mgmt. cons. and orgn. devel. firm. Mem. Am. Mgmt. Assn., Nat. Assn. Female Execs., OD Network. Office: 14522 Kittridge St Van Nuys CA 91405

KAPLAN, SYLVIA YALOWITZ KAPLAN (MRS. MILTON I. KAPLAN), librarian, educator; b. Chgo., May 23, 1921; d. Max and Gertrude (Yalowitz) K.; Ph.B., Northwestern U., 1956; M.A. in L.S., Rosary Coll., 1961, postgrad., 1962; postgrad. U. Ill., 1965-69, HEA Inst. on Reclassification, Rosary Coll., 1969, DePaul U., 1970; postgrad. in L.S. (scholar) U. Pitts., 1980-81; m. Milton I. Kaplan, Apr. 5, 1959. Asst. librarian Argonne Nat. Lab., U. Chgo., 1943-50; chief med. librarian Mcpl. Tb Sanitarium, Chgo., 1953-57; sch. librarian, Gary, Ind., 1957-59; librarian Inst. Applied Research, U. Chgo., 1961-62; chief librarian, instr. med. bibliography Chgo. Med. Sch., 1960-64; librarian Michael Reese Hosp. Sch. Nursing, Chgo., 1964-66, Ill. Dept. Mental Health, 1967-70; instr. library sci. Northeastern Ill. State Coll., 1970—; asst. prof. library sci. Eastern Ill. U., Charleston, 1970—. Mem. AAUW, AAUP (officer), Catholic, Med. (cert.) library assns., Assn. Am. Library Schs., Assn. Acad. Librarians, Internat. Assn. Semantics, Hadassah, Internat. Platform Assn. (hon.), Delta Kappa Gamma (hon.; scholar 1979). Democrat. Jewish. Contbr. revs. to profl. jours. Office: Eastern Ill U Dept Library Sci Charleston IL 61920

KAPLAN, VIOLA MARGUERITE, state ofcl.; b. Chgo., July 26, 1919; d. Charles J. and Rae Vesta (Pike) Epstein; A.A. in Math., UCLA, 1949; B.S. in Bus. Adminstrn., Rutgers U., 1973; m. Herbert G. Kaplan, Aug. 24, 1947; children—Ronna, Debra, Michael, Clifford. Research mathematician Forrestal Helicopter Lab., Princeton, N.J., 1954-55; tchr. math. and German, State Coll. (Pa.) Area High Sch., 1966-68; research asst. Pa. State U., University Park, 1967; bus. mgr. Ceramic Finishing Co., State College, Pa., 1968-69; asst. controller Atmos Tech. Corp., Edison, N.J., 1969-71; auditor Div. Mental Health and Hosps., State of N.J., Trenton, 1972-73; acct. and budget supr. Northwestern U., Chgo., 1973-75, asst. dir. adminstrv. and fin. services Med. Sch., 1975-78; adminstrv. analyst N.J. Commn. for Blind, Newark, 1978—. Vice pres. Samuel Everitt Sch. PTA, 1959-60; bd. dirs. Solomon Schechter Day Sch. of Somerset County. Mem. Am. Assn. Med. Colls., Nat. Assn. Accts., Hosp. Fin. Mgmt. Assn., Bus. and Profl. Women of North Shore, Hadassah (founder 1974, pres. 1974-76, pres. Somerset chpt. 1980-82). Club: Penn Valley Women's (pres. 1956-57), Toastmasters. Office: 1100 Raymond Blvd Rm 108 Newark NJ 07102

KAPLAN, VIVIAN KLINE, constrn. co. exec.; b. Pitts., June 2, 1936; d. Lowry Adam and Esther Mary (Wamsley) Kline; student U. Pitts., 1964-69; m. Fred L. Kaplan, Dec. 4, 1969; children—Linda, Todd, Teri, Judy. Saleswoman, West Real Estate Agy., Gibsonia, Pa., 1966-71; with Tectonics Inc. Miami, Fla., 1972-82, San Antonio, 1982—; v.p., owner, mgr.; partner, project mgr. fed. contracts Fortec Constructors, San Antonio, 1973—. Mem. San Antonio Home Builders Assn., San Antonio Builders Exchange. Office: 10942 Wye Dr Suite 205A San Antonio 78217

KAPPA, MARGARET MCCAFFREY, resort hotel exec.; b. Wabasha, Minn., May 14, 1921; d. Joseph Hugh and Verna Mae (Anderson) McCaffrey; B.S. in Hotel Mgmt., Cornell U., 1944; grad. Dale Carnegie course, 1978; m. Nicholas Francis Kappa, Sept. 15, 1956; children—Nicholas Joseph, Christopher Francis. Asst. exec. housekeeper Kahler Hotel, Rochester, Minn., 1944; exec. housekeeper St. Paul Hotel, 1944-47, Plaza Hotel, N.Y.C., 1947-51; exec. housekeeper, personnel dir. Athearn Hotel, Oshkosh, Wis., 1952-58; dir. housekeeping The Greenbrier, White Sulphur Springs, W.Va., 1958—; tchr. housekeeping U.S. and Fgn. countries; cons.; vis. lectr. Cornell U. Pres. St. Charles Borromeo Parish Assn., White Sulphur Springs, 1962, v.p., 1980, 82. Recipient diploma of honor Société Culinaire Philanthropique, 1961. Mem. Cornell Soc. Hotelmen (pres. 1980-81, exec. com. 1981-82), Nat. Exec. Housekeepers Assn. (pres. N.Y. chpt. 1950), N.Y.U. Hotel and Restaurant Soc. (hon. life). Republican. Roman Catholic. Clubs: Nat. Woman's; Quota (charter mem. Greenbrier County). Home and Office: The Greenbrier White Sulphur Springs WV 24986

KARAGULLA, SHAFICA, psychiatrist; b. Mardin, Turkey, 1914; came to U.S., 1956; d. Abdul-Karim and Bedour (Murad) K.; B.M., Am. U. Beirut, 1946, M.D., 1940; diploma in psychol. Medicine, Royal Coll. Physicians London and Royal Coll. Surgeons Eng., 1948. Tng. in psychiatry Royal Edinburgh (Scotland) Hosp. for Mental and Nervous

Disorders; research fellow U. Edinburgh, 3 yrs.; research fellow dept. neurology and neurosurgery McGill U., Montreal, Que., Can., Montreal Neurol. Inst., from 1952; cons. psychiatrist, 3 1/2 yrs.; asst. prof. dept. psychiatry SUNY, from 1957; pres. Higher Sense Perception Research Found., Los Angeles; lectr. numerous univs., Calif. Mem. Royal Coll. Physicians (Edinburgh). Author: Breakthrough to Creativity—Your Higher Sense Perception, 1967 (transl. into Danish, Italian, Icelandic); contbr. articles to profl. jours. Address: PO Box 49435 Los Angeles CA 90049

KARAKEY, SHERRY JOANNE, aerospace mfg. co. exec.; b. Wendall, Idaho, Apr. 16, 1942; d. John Donald and Vera Ella (Frost) Kingery; student Ariz. State U., 1960; m. James Joseph Dalgleish, Oct. 6, 1973 (div.); children—Artist Roxanne, George Wayne II, Kami JoAnne, Launi JoElla. Secretarial positions D-Velco Mfg. of Ariz., Phoenix, 1959-62, exec. v.p., 1972—, also dir.; with AiResearch Mfg. Co., Phoenix, 1962-63; corp. sec.-treas. Karbel Metals Co., Phoenix, 1963-67; sec. to pub. Scottsdale (Ariz.) Daily Progress, 1969-72. Mem. Nat. Tool and Die Assn. Republican. Office: D-Velco Mfg of Ariz 401 S 36th St Phoenix AZ 85034

KARAS, RENEE, psychotherapist; b. N.Y.C., Nov. 21, 1934; d. Valentine and Irene Naftali; B.S., Simmons Coll., 1956; M.S., Columbia U., 1976; m. Donald A. Karas, Feb. 18, 1956; children—Jon, Robin, Steven, James. Social worker, County of Westchester, N.Y., 1957-58; psychiat. social worker Rockland Mental Health Center, 1974-75, Hillside Hosp., 1975-76; psychotherapist Postgrad. Center for Mental Health, N.Y.C., 1977—. Mem. Soc. Clin. Social Work Psychotherapists, Nat. Assn. Social Workers. Home: 200 Delhi Rd Scarsdale NY 10583 Office: 124 E 28th St New York NY 10016

KARASIK, GITA, concert pianist; b. San Francisco, Dec. 14, 1949; d. Monia and Bereni Karasik; student San Francisco Conservatory Music; pupil of Lev Shorr, Rosina Lhevinne, Karl Ulrich Schnabel. Debut as soloist, San Francisco Symphony, 1958; N.Y.C. debut Carnegie Hall, 1972; solo recitalist, pianist with major orchs. throughout world, 1955—; tchr. master classes, 1970—; 1st Am. pianist to make ofcl. concert tour of China, 1980; mem. music adv. panel solo artists Nat. Endowment Arts, 1980; interdisciplinary panel 1st D.C. Arts Commn., 1981; mem. Artists for Nuclear Disarmanent, Artists to End Hunger. Recipient Solo Artists award Nat. Endowment Arts, 1981-82, Artists award and commd. concerto Ford Found., 1976, Musicians award Rockefeller Found., 1982, 1st prize Xerox/Affiliated Artists Internat. Piano Competition, 1982, 1st prize Pacific Mus. Soc., 1961; winner Young Concert Artists Internat. Auditions, 1969; Solo Artist sponsorship Pro Musicis Fedn., 1978. Address: 670 West End Ave Suite 11D New York NY 10025

KAREN, RUTH, pub., research, and cons. firm exec.; b. Germany, Feb. 18, 1922; came to U.S., 1940, naturalized, 1947; d. David and Paula (Freudenthal) Karpf; B.Sc., London Sch. Econs.; M.A., New Sch. Social Research, 1944; m. S. A. Hagai, Apr. 1962. Fgn. and war corr., 1947-60, Reporter mag., Toronto (Ont., Can.) Star, 1947-60; columnist World Wide Press corr. Latin Am. Times, Bus. Abroad, 1960-66; with Bus. Internat. Corp., N.Y.C., 1966—, editor, 1973, v.p. corp. public policy div., 1976—; cons. in field. Recipient Mitchell prize, 1982. Democrat. Club: Town Tennis. Author: The Land and People of Central America, 1965; Hello Guatemala, 1967; The Seven Worlds of Peru, 1968; Song of the Quail, 1969; Brazil Today: A Case History of Economic Development, 1972; Kingdom of the Sun, 1975; Featherred Serpent 1979; Questionable Practices, 1980. Home: 360 E 55th St New York NY 10022 Office: 1 Dag Hammarskjold Plaza New York NY 10017

KARGER, JUNE ELAINE, speakers bur. exec.; b. Lexington, Mass., June 24, 1931; d. Irving and Lillian (Friedman) Wermont; student Northeastern U., Boston Coll.; children—Janet, Richard, Nancy. Dir. adminstrn., regional sales mgr. Holidair Ltd., Boston, 1972-76; v.p., gen. mgr. Am. Program Bur., Inc., Chestnut Hill, Mass., 1976—; founder Sch. for Speakers, Boston. Mem. Internat. Platform Assn., Nat. Speakers Assn., Meeting Planners Internat., Nat. Assn. Female Execs., Exec. Club Boston C. of C., Women's Network Boston, Publicity Club Boston, Am. Soc. Assn. Execs., Nat. Acad. TV Arts and Scis. Home: 22 Chestnut Pl Brookline MA 02146 Office: 850 Boylston St Chestnut Hill MA 02167

KARIN, GLORIA SUSAN, educator; b. Bklyn., Dec. 16, 1941; d. Martin and Estelle (Kelban) Berkowitz; B.A. cum laude, Queen Coll., 1962, M.S. in Edn., 1964; Ed.D., Columbia U., 1971; m. Steven Norman Karin, Nov. 21, 1964; children—Janice Michelle, Lori Felicia, Marcy Lynn. Tchr., East Meadow (N.Y.) Public Schs., 1962-63, Public sch. 88, Queens, N.Y.C., 1963-66; guidance cons. Cert. Tutor Service, Flushing, N.Y., 1966-73; adj. asst. prof. C.W. Post Center, L.I.U., 1971-77; adj. instr. Reading Area Community Coll., 1978; lectr. in field. Active women's div. Children's Med. Center, L.I. Jewish Hosp., 1974-76; mem. Jewish Women's League of Pottsdown, Pa., 1977—, exec. bd. 1982—; exec. bd. local Parent-Tchr. Orgn., 1979—, pres. 1979-81, bd. dirs. Montessor Assn., 1981-82, Cornerstone of the Arts, 1979-82. Cert. guidance counselor, Pa., N.Y. Mem. Am. Personnel and Guidance Assn., Assn. Counselor Edn. and Supervision, Assn. Measurement and Eval. in Guidance, Pa. Personnel and Guidance Assn., Pa. Assn. Counselor Edn and Supervision Edn. (fund-raising chmn. 1979-80, sec.-treas. 1980—, exec. bd. 1977—), Pa. Assn. Measurement and Eval. in Guidance, N. Atlantic Regional Assn. Counselor Edn. and Supervision (exec. bd. 1979-83), Nat. Soc. Study Edn., AAUW, Phi Beta Kappa, Kappa Delta Pi. Contbg. author texts; contbr. articles to profl. jours. Home: RD 1 Box 300 Elaine Dr Boyertown PA 19512

KARKUT, ANN LOUISE, editor; b. Bellwood, Ill., June 30, 1924; d. Walter and Anna (Jacobs) Knippenberg; student LaSalle U.; m. Edward Karkut, Mar. 20, 1943; children—Patricia, Edward, Stanley, Susan, Christopher. Asst. editor, Lockport (Ill.) Herald, 1960-63, editor, 1963-69; asst. editor Naperville (Ill.) Sun, 1969-70; editor Joliet (Ill.) Circle, 1970; editor Pointer Publs., Riverdale, Ill., 1970-72; asst. editor Lisle (Ill.) Sun, 1972-74; asst. editor Big Farmer mag., Frankfort, Ill., 1974-81. Sec., Homer Fire Dept. Aux., 1962, Dist. 92 Band Parents, 1967; mem. Homer Republican Precinct Com., 1976—; Homer Twp. clk., 1981—; bd. dirs. Will County Hist. Soc. Mem. Lockport Bus. and Profl. Women's Club (charter mem., past pres., named Woman of Yr. 1979), Ill. Bus. and Profl. Women's Club, Ill. Fedn. Bus. and Profl. Women's Clubs Found. (chmn.), Ill. Press Women's Assn. Roman Catholic. Club: Waa-Shee Riders (pres.). Home: Rt 2 Box 26 Gougar Lockport IL 60441 Office: 143d St Lockport IL 60441

KARLE, ISABELLA LUGOSKI, scientist, govt. ofcl.; b. Detroit, Dec. 2, 1921; B.S., U. Mich., 1941, M.S., 1942, Ph.D. in Phys. Chemistry (Rackham fellow, AAUW fellow), 1944, D.Sc. (hon.), 1976; D.Sc. (hon.), Wayne State U., 1979; married, 1942; 3 children. Asso. chemist U. Chgo., 1944; instr. U. Mich., 1944-46; physicist U.S. Naval Research Lab., Navy Dept., Washington, 1946-59, head X-ray sect., 1959—; mem. U.S. Nat. Com. on Crystallography; adv. bd. Office Chemistry and Chem. Tech., NRC; mem. bd. internat. orgns. and programs Nat. Acad. Scis. Mem. adv. bd. M.I.T. Corp. Vis. Com. Recipient Superior Civilian Service award Navy Dept., 1965; ann. Achievement award Soc. Women Engrs., 1968, Hillebrand award, 1970, Fed. Woman's award, 1973; Capt. Robert Dexter Conrad award Office Naval Research, 1980. Mem. Am. Phys. Soc., Nat. Acad. Scis., Am. Biophys. Soc., Am. Crystallographic Assn. (pres., 1976), Am. Chem. Soc. (Garvan award, 1976). Mem. editorial bd. Internat. Jour. Peptide and Protein Research; mem. adv. bd. Biopolymers. Research in application of electron and x-ray diffraction to structure problems in chemistry and biology. Office: Naval Research Lab for Structure of Matter Code 6030 Washington DC 20375

KARLL, LAURA HISS, interior designer; b. Balt., Dec. 26, 1922; d. John Bosley and Amy Louisa (Beck) Hiss; B.A., Smith Coll., 1944; B.F.A., Md. Inst. Coll. Art, 1972; m. William Richard Karll, June 2, 1947; children—Barbara, Nancy, Sandra, Pamela, Laurie, Claudia. Interior decorator Glenmar Estates Corp., model homes, Balt., 1952-65, Stewart & Co., Balt., 1971-72, Karl Graf & Co., Balt., 1972-73; propr. Laura Designed Interiors, Balt., 1973—; v.p. Chesapeake Village, Inc., 1963—. Trustee, Univ. Baptist Ch., Balt., 1977-78; reunion chmn. Smith Coll. class of 1944, 1979. Served to 2d lt. Phys. Therapy Corps, WAC, 1944-46. Mem. Am. Inst. Interior Designers, Am. Soc. Interior Designers. Republican. Clubs: Zonta, Smith Coll. (past pres.) (Balt.). Address: 703 Benston Pl Baltimore MD 21210

KARLSON, KAREN LOUISE, radiologist; b. N.Y.C., May 6, 1950; d. Loyd Alfred and Antoinette Sifua (Petersen) Bolling; B.A., CCNY, 1971; M.D., Columbia U., 1975; m. Thomas J. Karlson, May 19, 1971; 1 dau., Aurora. Intern, St. Vincent's Hosp., N.Y.C., 1975-76; resident Columbia Presbyn. Med. Center, 1976-79; fellow, 1979-80, asst. prof., 1980-81; attending radiologist St. Barnabas Med. Center, Livingston, N.J.; asst. prof. Cornell U. Med. Center-N.Y. Hosp. Mem. Columbia U. Coll. Physicians and Surgeons, Black and Latin Students Orgn., Am. Coll. Radiology, Radiol. Soc. N.Am. Lutheran. Contbr. articles to profl. jours. Home: 6 Orchard Ln Livingston NH 07039 Office: Dept Radiology St Barnabas Med Center Livingston NJ 07039

KARLSON, MARGARET VERCELLOTTI, health care adminstr.; b. Joliet, Ill., Dec. 15, 1941; d. Joseph Francis and Mary Therese (Walowski) Vercellotti; B.S., Joliet Jr. Coll., 1962; B.S. in Adminstrn., U. Ill., 1973; grad. in asso. long-term care adminstrn., George Washington U., 1979; m. Bud Carter, July 26, 1981; children by previous marriage—Greg, Cyndie, Todd, Teri. Asst. dir. public relations St. Joseph Hosp., Joliet, 1975-76; asst. adminstr. Americana Healthcare Center, Joliet, 1976-79, v.p., adminstr., Decatur, Ga., 1981-82; adminstr. Beverly Enterprises, Glenwood Manor, Decatur, Ga., 1982—; v.p., adminstr. Family Tree Care Center, Peoria, Ill., 1979-81; seminar condr.; TV panelist. Mem. Quad County Task Force on Aging, 1978; ednl. adv. com. Ill. Dept. Public Health; ednl. adv. com. Ill. Central Coll.; bd. dirs. Ill. Valley Health Systems Agy., 1979-81. Lic. nursing home adminstr., Ga., Fla., Ill. Fellow Am. Coll. Nursing Home Adminstrs.; mem. Ga. Healthcare Assn., Am. Healthcare Assn., Continuity of Care Assn., Ga. Gerontology Soc., DeKalb C. of C. Club: Atlanta Bus. and Profl. Women's. Editor: The Growing Concern, 1980-81; The Voice of Experience, 1981-82. Home: Alpharetta GA 30201

KARMAZIN, JOSEPHINE ROSE, Realtor; b. N.Y.C., Feb. 9, 1922; d. John and Rose Marie (Mares) Karmazin; grad. Bradford Jr. Coll., 1941. Personnel mgr. Kline's Store, Detroit, 1945-53; asst. buyer and advt. Hutzel Store, Ann Arbor, Mich., 1953-55; v.p. personnel and labor relations Karmazin Products Corp., 1955-69; now co-owner So. Wayne Realty, Inc. Chmn. bd. mgmt. Downriver YWCA, 1970-73; chmn. Camp Cavell com. YWCA Met. Detroit, 1974, chmn. expansion com., 1975-78, 3d v.p., 1978—, mem. planning and devel. com., 1980-81; bd. mgmt. Family Neighborhood Services, 1958-68; deacon Grosse Isle Presbyterian Ch., mem. ch. in world service com., 1980-81, also adminstrn. com.; Republican precinct del., 1978, 80. Clubs: Grosse Ile Yacht; Soroptimist (pres. 1961, 63) (Wyndotte, Mich.). Home: 22085 Thorofare Grosse Ile MI 48138 Office: 3010 Van Horn Rd Trenton MI 48138

KARMEL, BARBARA MARBUT, bus. exec., educator; b. Denver, Dec. 13, 1932; d. George Carlton and Charlotte Baldwin (Reed) Marbut; B.A., Cornell U., 1954; M.S., Purdue U., 1969, Ph.D., 1970; m. Kenneth Edward Karmel, Aug. 25, 1955 (div. 1969); children—Kelly Anne, Clayton Reed. Grad. instr. Purdue U., West Lafayette, Ind., 1969-70; mem. faculty Sch. Bus., Oreg. State U., Corvallis, 1970-75; Sch. Bus. U. Wis., Madison, 1975-78; prof., asso. dean Atkinson Grad. Sch. Mgmt. Willamette U., Salem, Oreg., 1979—; mgmt. cons., mgmt. auditor Reed & Co., pres., 1982—; dir. U.S. Bancorp., U.S. Nat. Bank of Oreg., Mem. Suislaw Nat. Forest Adv. Council, 1971-74; Gov.'s Mgmt. Devel. Steering Commn., Oreg., 1972-75; Oreg. Adv. Council on Occupational Health and Safety, 1980—, Oreg. Econ. Recovery Council, 1982. Mem. Acad. of Mgmt. (gov. 1974-76), Am. Psychol. Assn., Women Entrepreneurs of Oreg. (dir. 1979—), Internat. Assn. Applied Psychology, Organizational Behavior Teaching Soc. (dir. 1979-81). Author: Point and Counterpoint in Organizational Behavior, 1981; mem. editorial bd. Acad. of Mgmt. Rev. 1974-81; contbr. articles in field to profl. jours. Home: 6610 Huntington Circle SE Salem OR 97306 Office: Grad Sch Mgmt Willamette U Salem OR 97301

KARMEL, ROBERTA S., lawyer; b. Chgo., May 4, 1937; d. Jacob H. and Eva (Elin) Segal; B.A. cum laude, Radcliffe Coll., 1959; LL.B. (Florence Allen scholar) cum laude, N.Y. U., 1962; m. Paul Karmel, June 9, 1957; children—Philip, Jonathan, Solomon, Miriam. Admitted to N.Y. State bar, 1962, U.S. Supreme Ct. bar, 1968; asst. regional adminstr. SEC, N.Y.C., 1962-68, commr., Washington, 1977-80; assoc. firm Willkie Farr and Gallagher, N.Y.C., 1969-72; partner firm Rogers and Wells, N.Y.C., 1972-77, 80—; adj. prof. Bklyn. Law Sch., 1973-77, N.Y.U. Sch. Law, N.Y.C., 1980-81; adviser Am. Law Inst., 1980—; mem. legal adv. com. N.Y. Stock Exchange, 1980—; dir. International Minerals & Chemical Corp., Northbrook, Ill. Recipient Woman of the Year award Ladies Home Jour., 1978. Mem. ABA (mem. com. on securities regulation 1980—), Am. Judicature Soc., Fed. Bar Assn., Assn. of Bar of N.Y.C. (com. on profl. responsibility 1976-77, com. on adminstrv. law 1970-73), Fin. Women's Assn. of N.Y., N.Y. Women's Bar Assn., Econ. Club of N.Y., U.S. C. of C. (govt. affairs com. 1980—), Order of Coif. Democrat. Jewish. Author: Regulation By Prosecution, 1982. Contbr. articles to legal jours. Home: 26 Hopke Ave Hastings on Hudson NY 10706 Office: 200 Park Ave New York NY 10166

KARNES, SUSAN MCKEAGUE, symphony society exec.; b. Harvey, Ill., Mar. 31, 1954; d. Gordon Clark and Louise Marea (Jones) McKeague; student Tulsa U., 1971-77; m. Sam Bryant Karnes, Dec. 30, 1978; 1 son, Bryant. Tng. dir. Renberg's Inc., Tulsa 1977, personnel dir., 1978-79; v.p., dir. personnel Republic Bancorp, Inc., Tulsa, 1979-81; dir. fund raising, bd. dirs., mem. exec. com. N. Ark. Symphony, Fayetteville, 1982—. Bd. dirs. Mgmt. Devel. Center U. Tulsa. Mem. Am. Soc. Tng. and Devel. (treas. 1979), Am. Soc. Personnel Adminstrn., Am. Soc. Tng. and Devel., Nat. Assn. Bank Women. Home: 1818 Viewpoint Dr Fayetteville AR 72701

KARNIOL, HILDA HUTTERER (MRS. FRANK KARNIOL), artist, educator; b. Vienna, Austria, Apr. 28, 1910; d. Simon and Josephine (Weisman) Hutterer; student Acad. for Women, Vienna, 1926-30, Mrs. Olga Konetzny-Maly and A. F. Seligman, Vienna, 1925-28; m. Frank Karniol, June 25, 1933; 1 son, William George. Over 100 one-man shows, including Susquehanna U., 1952-73, Pa. State Mus., Harrisburg, 1954, Neville Mus., Green Bay, Wis., 1958, Addha Artzt Gallery, N.Y.C., 1960, Cornell Library Gallery, Ithaca, N.Y., 1960, Drexel Inst. Tech., Phila., 1960, Farnsworth Mus., Rockland, Maine, 1960, Mary Buie Mus., Oxford, Miss., 1960, Columbus (Ga.) Mus., 1962, Rutgers U., 1965-66, Laurel (Miss.) Rogers Mus., 1962; La Salle Coll., Phila., 1964; Hallmark Art Gallery, Kansas City, Mo., 1967, U. Ill., Urbana, 1968, U. Minn., St. Paul, 1969, U. Mich., 1969, U. Ky., Elizabethtown, 1970, La. State U., New Orleans, 1971, Kans. State Coll., Pittsburg, 1972, Purdue U., 1973; represented in permanent collections at St. Vincent Arch Abbey, Latrobe, Pa., Susquehanna U., Selinsgrove, Pa., Lincoln Sch., Honesdale, Pa., Del. Art Center, Wilmington, HEW, Lycoming Coll., Williamsport, Pa., Bloomsburg (Pa.) State Coll., Lewisburg (Pa.) Art Council; instr. fine arts Susquehanna U., 1959-75; lectr., artist-in-residence Fed. Govt. Cultural Enrichment Program for Clearfield, Clinton, Centre and Lycoming counties, Pa., 1967; art adviser Sunbury Bicentennial Com., 1972; demonstrator, exhibitor Laurel State Festival, Wellsboro, Pa., 1975. Recipient 1st prize in portraiture Berwick (Pa.) Arts Center, 1965; purchase prize Lewisburg Arts Festival, 1975, 1st prize, 1978. Mem. Nat. Forum Profl. Artists, Art Alliance Central Pa., Société d'Honneur Française, Pi Delta Phi, Sigma Alpha Iota. Club: Alliance Française (Tampa, Fla.). Home: 960 Race St Sunbury PA 17801

KARP, ANNE, advt. exec.; b. N.Y.C., Mar. 26, 1938; d. Harold I. and Helen P. (Spiegel) Halperin; B.A., Vassar Coll., 1959; 1 son, Clifford. Advt. supr. Montgomery Ward, N.Y.C., 1963-69; publs. officer Community Coll. of Balt., 1978-79; advt. account mgr. Mass Mktg. Systems Internat., N.Y.C., 1982—; v.p. Md. Pub. Relations Affiliates, 1979. Bd. dirs. Md. New Directions for Women, 1977; mem. fed. funds grant com. Md. Displaced Homemakers, 1977. Recipient Wards Outstanding Performance award, 1967; Mead Award of Merit, 1979. Mem. Direct Mktg. Assn., Women's Direct Response Group. Home: 219 E 69th St New York NY 10021 Office: 475 Park Ave S New York NY 10016

KARP, JEAN MARY HORSEMAN, media generalist; b. Balt., July 31, 1932; d. Ezard Hamilton and Anna Elsie (Curry) Horseman; B.S., Towson State Coll., 1953; M.S., Johns Hopkins, 1958; M.S. in L.S., Cath. U., 1964; m. Paul William Karp. Tchr. William Paca Sch., Balt., 1953-54, Montebello Sch., 1954-58; librarian Glenmount Sch., Balt., 1958-65, Roland Park Sch., Balt., 1965-68, Herring Run Sch., Balt., 1968—. Mem. Phi Delta Gamma, Beta Phi Mu, Pi Lambda Theta. Home: 7915 Roseland Ave Baltimore MD 21237 Office: 5001 Sinclair Ln Baltimore MD 21206

KARP, JUDITH ESTHER, oncologist; b. San Diego, July 15, 1946; d. Louis Moses and Bella Sarah (Perlman) K.; B.A. in Chemistry, Mills Coll., Oakland, Calif., 1966; M.D., Stanford U., 1971; m. Stanley Howard Freedman, Sept. 21, 1975. Intern medicine, jr. resident in medicine Stanford Hosps., 1971-72; asst. resident in medicine Johns Hopkins Hosp., 1972-73; clin. and research fellow oncology Johns Hopkins Med. Sch., 1973-75, instr. oncology and medicine, 1975-78, asst. prof., 1978—; speaker Internat. Congress Chemotherapy, Vienna, Austria, 1983. Recipient Aurelia Henry Reinhardt prize Mills Coll., 1966, Cancer Research award Washington chpt. Awards for Research Coll. Scientists, 1975; San Diego Heart Assn. grantee, 1965-67; Am. Cancer Soc. Jr. clin. faculty fellow, 1976-79. Diplomate Am. Bd. Internal Medicine. Mem. Am. Soc. Hematology, Am. Soc. Clin. Oncology, Cell Kinetics Soc., Internat. Soc. Exptl. Hematology, Nat. Bd. Med. Examiners, Phi Beta Kappa. Democrat. Jewish. Home: 15 Farmhouse Ct Baltimore MD 21208 Office: Oncology Center Johns Hopkins Hosp 601 N Broadway Baltimore MD 21205

KARP, RUTH HARRIS, ednl. adminstr.; b. Bklyn., Apr. 10, 1923; d. Joseph and Fannie (Cohen) Harris; A.A. with distinction, Newton Jr. Coll., 1963; A.B. magna cum laude in Govt. and History, Boston U., 1963-66; M.A., Northeastern U., 1968; postgrad. Inst. Ednl. Mgmt., Harvard U., 1974, div. higher edn. Boston Coll.; m. Harvey Karp, May 23, 1943; children—Bruce Lawrence, Marcia Susan. Reporter, The News-Tribune, Waltham, Mass., 1963-64; teaching asst. Northeastern U., 1966-68, lectr. in history, 1968-74, asst. to dean liberal arts, 1968-70, asst. dean liberal arts, 1970-73, asso. dean, 1973-78; asso. dean students, 1978—; cons. Women's Studies Adv. Bd., Coop. Edn. Pres., LWV Waltham (Mass.), 1952-54, numerous chairmanships, 1949-52; sec., adv. new groups Mass. LWV, 1954-56; edn. chmn. bulletin editor, group leader Newton (Mass.) LWV, 1954-62; den mother Boy Scouts Am., 1954-56; brownie and troop leader Girl Scouts U.S.A., 1957-62; bull. editor, public relations chmn., program Newton PTA, 1954-64. Recipient Disting. Alumna Award, Newton Jr. Coll., 1966, 74. Mem. Mass. Assn. Women Deans, Adminstrs. and Counselors (conf. program com. 1982-82), Nat. Assn. Coll. Personnel Adminstrs. (conf. pub. com. 1980), AAUW (conf. panelist Mass. 1982), Nat. Assn. Student Personnel Adminstrs., NE Assn. Student Personnel Adminstrs., Nat. Assn. Women Deans, Adminstrs., Counselors, Northeastern U. Profl. Women, Phi Beta Kappa, Phi Kappa Phi (pres. 1973-75), Phi Alpha Theta. Home: 32 Warren Rd Waban MA 02168 Office: Northeastern U 360 Huntington Ave Boston MA 02115

KARPEL-FREILICH, ANNE RENEE, speech pathologist; b. Bklyn., Feb. 27, 1952; d. Leonard and Elaine (Malin) Karpel; B.S. in Speech, Emerson Coll., 1973; M.S., Columbia U., 1975; m. Leib Freilich, Dec. 17, 1978; children— Avraham Nir, Adir Joshua. Speech pathology cons. nursing homes, N.Y.C., 1975-76; speech pathologist Vis. Nurse Service of N.Y., 1976-78; pvt. practice speech pathology, N.Y.C., 1978—; speech pathology cons. Forest Hills (N.Y.) Nursing Home, 1979-80. Lic. speech pathologist, N.Y. State. Mem. Am. Speech, Hearing and Lang. Assn. (cert. clin. competence). Address: 88 Bleecker St Apt 1D New York NY 10012

KARPEN, MARIAN JOAN, fin. exec.; b. Detroit, June 16, 1944; d. Cass John and Mary Jay Karpen; A.B., Vassar Coll., 1966; postgrad. Sorbonne, Paris, N.Y. U. Grad. Sch. Bus., 1974-77. New Eng. corr. Women's Wear Daily Fairchild Publs.-Capital Cities Communications, 1966-68, Paris fashion editor, TV and radio commentator Capital Cities Network, 1968-69; fashion editor Boston Herald Traveler, 1969-71; nat. syndicated newspaper columnist and photojournalist Queen Features Syndicate, N.Y.C., 1971-73; account exec. Blyth Eastman Dillon, N.Y.C., 1973-75, Oppenheimer, N.Y.C., 1975-76; v.p., mcpl. bond coordinator Faulkner Dawkins & Sullivan (merged Shearson Hayden Stone), N.Y.C., 1976-77; mgr. retail mcpl. bond dept. A.G. Becker (Warburg, Paribas, Becker Group), N.Y.C., 1977-79, prin., v.p., lectr., 1979—. Mem. Nat. Assn. Securities Dealers, N.Y. Stock Exchange, English Speaking Union, Women's Econ. Roundtable. Clubs: Vassar, Skating (N.Y.C. and Boston). Contbr. numerous articles and photographs to newspapers and mags., 1966—. Home: 233 E 69th St New York NY 10021 Office: 55 Water St New York NY 10041

KARR, DEBORAH NAVAS, editor; b. Providence, Feb. 22, 1943; d. Joseph and Dorothy (Hunt) Navas; A.B. in English literature, Brown U., 1971; m. Harlan E. Karr, Jr., Mar. 21, 1981; children by previous marriage—Sarah, Elizabeth, Benjamin. Asst. editor Yankee Mag., Dublin, N.H., 1975, sr. editor, 1979-82, fiction editor, 1977—; freelance writer, 1974—. Treas. Democratic Party Town of Dublin, 1968. Office: Yankee Magazine Dublin NH 03444

KARRAS, DONNA CIRIPOMPA, dental hygienist, educator; b. Wheeling, W.Va., Aug. 1, 1951; d. George Henry and Eleanor Jane (Nyles) Ciripompa; A.S./B.S., W. Liberty State Coll., 1973; M.A. in Community Health, W.Va. U., 1978; m. Donald George Karras, Mar. 6, 1982. Dental hygienist, Morgantown, W.Va., 1973-78; asst. prof. dental hygiene U. S.D., Vermillion, 1979-80, asst. prof., 1980-82, assoc. chmn. dept. dental hygiene, 1980-82; dental hygienist in pvt. practice, Aurora, Colo., 1982—; instr. CPR various schools, univs. and orgns. Vol., Clay County (S.D.) Ambulance Dept., 1979-82. Cert. emergency med. technician, CPR instr., dental hygienist. Mem. Nat. Dental Hygienist Assn., S.D. Dental Hygienist Assn., Sioux Falls Dental

Hygienist Assn., Am. Assn. Dental Schs., Nat. Emergency Med. Technician Assn., Clay County Ambulance Assn., Am. Raquetball Assn., Delta Zeta. Home: 3673 S Lewiston St Aurora CO 80013

KARRENBAUER, BEVERLY WOLFORD, elem. sch. adminstr.; b. Marion Center, Pa., Aug. 5, 1938; d. Clarence Frederick and Thelma Pearl (MacArthur) Wolford; B.S. in Edn., Indiana (Pa.) U., 1959; M.Ed., U. Pitts., 1963; m. Raymond Joseph Karrenbauer, Jr., Aug. 20, 1960; 1 son, Raymond Joseph, III. Supr. perceptual devel. Keystone Oaks Sch. Dist., Pitts., 1967-69; supr. early childhood edn. Dade County (Fla.) public schs., 1969-80; adminstr. Miami Gardens Elem. Sch., Opa-Locka, Fla., 1980—; ednl. cons. children's programming WTVJ-TV, 1981-82; sr. cons. early childhood program Scholastic Mag. Inc. Recipient Internat. Year of Child award, 1979, Kiwanis Appreciation award, 1963; Frick Found. scholar 1962. Mem. Assn. Children Learning Disabilities, Elementary Prins. Assn., Dade County Adminstrs. Assn., PTA, N.E. Improvement Assn., Delta Kappa Gamma. Democrat. Author: Perpetual Development Correction, 1968. Home: 1040 NE 82d St Miami FL 33138 Office: 4444 NW 195th St Opa-Locka FL

KARSEN, SONJA PETRA, educator; b. Berlin, Germany, Apr. 11, 1919; d. Fritz and Erna (Heidermann) K.; came to U.S., 1938, naturalized, 1945; Titulo de Bachiller, Colombia, 1937; student Nat. U., Bogotá, Colombia, 1937-38; B.A., Carleton Coll., 1939; M.A. (scholar in French 1939-41), Bryn Mawr Coll., 1941; Ph.D., Columbia U., 1950. Instr. Spanish, Lake Erie Coll., Painesville, Ohio, 1943-45; instr. modern langs. U. P.R., 1945-46; instr Spanish, Syracuse U., 1947-50, Bklyn. Coll., 1950-51; asst. to dep. dir. gen. UNESCO, 1951-52, Latin Am. desk, tech. asst. dept., 1952-53, mem. tech. assistance mission Costa Rica, 1954; asst. prof. Spanish, Sweet Briar Coll., 1955-57; asso. prof., chmn. dept. Romance langs. Skidmore Coll., Saratoga Springs, N.Y., 1957-61, prof. Spanish and chmn. dept. Romance langs., 1961-65, prof. Spanish, 1961—, chmn. dept. modern langs. and lits., 1965-79; Fulbright lectr. Free U. Berlin, 1968. Decorated chevalier Ordre des Palmes Academiques, 1964; recipient Leadership award N.Y. State Assn. Fgn. Lang. Tchrs., 1973, 79, Nat. Disting. Fgn. Lang. Leadership award, 1979; Spanish Heritage award, 1981; Alumni Achievement Award Carleton Coll., 1982; exchange student auspices Inst. Internat. Edn. at Carleton Coll., 1938-39; Buenos Aires Conv. grantee for research in Colombia, 1946-47; faculty research grantee Skidmore Coll., summer 1959, 61, 63, 65, 67, 69, 70, 73. Mem. AAUP, MLA (mem. del. assembly 1976-78), Am. Assn. Tchrs. Spanish and Portuguese, AAUW, Nat. Geog. Soc., Instituto Internacional de Literatura Iberoamericana, Asociación Internacional de Hispanistas, Nat. Assn. Self-Instructional Lang. Programs (treas. 1973-77, dir. 1978-81, v.p. 1981-82, pres. 1982-83), UN Assn. of U.S.A., Phi Sigma Iota (chmn. nat. scholarship com. 1980-81). Author: Guillermo Valencia, Colombian Poet, 1951; Educational Development in Costa Rica with Unesco's Technical Assistance, 1951-54, 1954; Jaime Torres Bodet: A Poet in a Changing World, 1963; Selected Poems of Jaime Torres Bodet, 1964; Versos y prosas de Jaime Torres Bodet, 1966; Jaime Torres Bodet, 1971; advisory bd. Modern Lang. studies, 1977—; editor: Lang. Assn. Bull., 1980-83; contbr. articles to profl. jours. Office: Skidmore Coll Saratoga Springs NY 12866

KASEL, JANE MARIE, pub. co. exec.; b. Bay City, Mich., June 19, 1947; d. Vincent A. and Jenotte Marie Curtis (Lipan) Emeott; B.A., U. Calif., Santa Barbara, 1970; postgrad. Calif. State U., Fullerton, 1972-73; m. Richard S. Kasel, Jr., Dec. 12, 1981. Salesperson, bookkeeper Heth Hardware, Baldwin Park, Calif., 1962-66; mgrs. asst. univ. approved housing U. Calif., Santa Barbara, 1968-70; exec. sec. contracts div. Aerojet Gen., Azusa, Calif., 1966-71; tchr. English, yearbook adv., adv. council Walnut (Calif.) High Sch., 1971-77; yearbook specialist Taylor Pub. Co., Covina, Calif., 1977—, mem. pres. adv. council, 1980-82, mem. sales adv. council, 1981-82. Mem., guide for communication seminars House of White Shell Woman. Named Woman of Yr., Bank Am., 1967; recipient Mktg. awards Taylor Pub. Co., 1979, Pacesetter award, 1979, also named Rookie of Yr. Mem. Journalism Educators Assn., So. Calif. Journalism Educators Assn., Alpha Gamma Sigma. Office: 562 Laguna Canyon Way Brea CA 92621

KASE-POLISINI, JUDITH BAKER, educator; b. Wilmington, Del., Dec. 13, 1932; d. Charles Robert and Elizabeth Edna (Baker) Kase; B.A., U. Del., 1955; M.A., Case Western Res. U., 1956; m. James F. Polisini; children—James, Elizabeth, John, Katherine, Ann. Tchr., dir. children's theatre Agnes Scott Coll., 1956, U. Tenn., 1957, U. Md., Germany, 1958-60, Denver Civic Theatre, Denver U., Kent Sch. for Girls, 1960-61; dir. children's theatre U. N.H., Durham, 1962-69; dir. theatre resources for youth, Somersworth, N.H., 1966-69; asso. prof. edn. U. S. Fla., Tampa, 1969—; project dir. Hillsborough County Artists-in-Schs. Evaluation and Inservice Project, 1980-82. Bd. dirs. Fla. Alliance for Arts Edn., sec., 1976-77, vice-chairperson, 1979-82, chairperson, 1982—; mem. theatre adv. panel Arts Council Tampa-Hillsborough County; chmn. Wingspread Conf. on Theatre Edn., 1977; drama adjudicator Nat. Arts Festival, Ministry of Edn., Bahamas, 1975, 76, 79, 80; cons. theatre edn. and prodn. Mem. Children's Theatre Assn. Am. (pres.-elect 1975-77, pres. 1977-79, chmn. symposia planning com.), Am. Theatre Assn. (chief div. pres.'s coordinating council 1977-78 commn. on theatre edn. 1982—), Speech Communication Assn., Southeastern, Fla. theatre confs., Internat. Assn. Theatres for Children and Youth, Fla. Conf. Tchrs. English, United Faculty Fla., Tampa Mus. Democrat. Episcopalian. Club: Carrollwood Village. Contbr. articles to profl. jours.; pub. playwright; dir. plays. Home: 5311 Taylor Rd Lutz FL 33549 Office: Dept Arts Edn U S Fla Tampa FL 33620

KASH, (FRANCYS) KAYGEY, banker, civic worker, service orgn. exec.; b. Sioux City, Iowa, Feb. 25, 1921; d. Jacob David and Ida (Schwab) Maron; student pub. schs., Sioux City; m. Louis Kash, Dec. 17, 1939; 1 dau., Leslie Jo. Dir., Columbia Savs. and Loan Assn., Beverly Hills, Calif., 1976-81; v.p. 1st Pacific Bank, 1981—. Vice pres. B'nai B'rith Women, Washington, 1965-76, mem. exec. bd., 1958, treas., 1963-65, internat. pres., 1976-78, also chmn., then vice chmn. Anti-Defamation League, mem. fund raising cabinet, now life mem., also active Hillel, B'nai B'rith Youth Orgn.; guest lectr. U. Calif. Extension, Los Angeles, 1977; mem. exec. com. western region, U.S. Com. for UNICEF, 1966; mem. Los Angeles City Human Relations Commn. Adv. Com., 1963—; mem. Calif. Atty. Gen. Constl. Rights Adv. Com., 1962-64; bd. govs., life mem., exec. com. B'nai B'rith. Named Woman of Achievement, N.Y. Women's Div. of Anti-defamation League, 1976; recipient Outstanding Service award State of Israel, 1973, Los Angeles Mayor award, 1976-77. Mem. Jewish Fedn. Council (bd. dirs. 1958-76, pres. women's conf. 1960-61), Sisterhood Congregation Mogen David (life). Home: 9311 Alcott St Los Angeles CA 90035

KASHDIN, GLADYS SHAFRAN, painter, educator; b. Pitts., Dec. 15, 1921; d. Edward M. and Miriam P. Shafran; B.A. magna cum laude, U. Miami, 1960, M.A., 1962; Ph.D., Fla. State U., 1965; m. Manville E. Kashdin, Dec. 11, 1942 (dec.). Photographer, N.Y.C. and Fla., 1938-60; tchr. art, Fla. and Ga., 1956-63; asst. prof. humanities U. S. Fla., Tampa, 1965-70, assoc. prof., 1970-74, prof., 1974—; works exhibited in 33 one-woman shows, 38 group exhbns.; maj. touring exhibits include: The Everglades, 1972-75; Aspects of the River, 1975-80; Processes of Time, 1981—; represented in permanent collections: Taiwan, Peoples Republic of China, Columbus Mus. Arts and Sci., LeMoyne Art Found., Tampa Internat. Airport, Tampa Mus. Art, Council of 100; lectr.; adv. bd. Hillsborough County Mus., 1975-83. Mem. U. S. Fla. Status of Women Com., 1971-76, chmn., 1975-76. Recipient Women Helping Women in Art award Soroptimist Internat., 1979. Mem. AAUW (1st v.p. Tampa br. 1971-72), Assn. Gen. and Liberal Studies, Phi Kappa Phi (chpt.-pres. 1981-83). Home: 441 Biltmore Ave Temple Terrace FL 33617 Office: U S Fla Tampa FL 33620

KASLICK, JESSICA HELLINGER, psychiat. social worker; b. N.Y.C., Nov. 9, 1945; d. Joshua and Joan (Nathan) Hellinger; student Elmira Coll., 1963-65; B.A., N.Y. U., 1967; M.S., Columbia U., 1969; m. Ralph S. Kaslick, Oct. 24, 1976. Staff, Mt. Sinai Med. Center, N.Y.C. - Dept. Social Wk., Child and Adult Psychiatric Service, 1969—, preceptor of med. students, 1970—, preceptor of social work students, 1978—, psychiatric social worker, 1969—. Bd. dirs. Columbia U. Sch. Social Work Alumni Assn., 1977-79. Recipient Alpha Delta Kappa award in sociology, 1967; Vol. Service award, United Hosp. Fund, 1968; D.A.R., Citizenship award, 1963, others. Mem. Nat. Assn. Social Workers, Acad. Cert. Social Workers, Soc. Clin. Social Workers. Office: 100 St and 5th Ave New York NY 10029

KASLOW, FLORENCE WHITEMAN, psychologist; b. Phila., Jan. 6; d. Irving and Rose (Tarin) Whiteman; A.B., Temple U., 1952; M.A., Ohio State U., 1954; Ph.D., Bryn Mawr Coll., 1969; children—Nadine Joy, Howard Ian. Pvt. practice psychology and family therapy, West Palm Beach, Fla., 1981—; chief forensic psychology/psychiatry sect. Hahnemann Med. Coll., Phila., 1973-80, mem. faculty U. Pa. Grad. and Med. Sch.; dean, prof. Fla. Sch. Profl. Psychology, Miami, 1980-81; cons. family therapy Psychiatry Residency Tng. Program, Dept. Navy, San Diego, Portsmouth, Phila., Center for Pastoral Counseling, Ft. Lauderdale, Fla. Mem. Am. Psychol. Assn., Fla. Psychol. Assn., Am. Assn. Marital and Family Therapists, Am. Acad. Forensic Psychologists, Am. Family Therapy Assn., Am. Psychology-Law Soc., AAAS, Internat. Council Psychologists, Temple U. Gen. Alumni Assn. (dir. 1965-80). Contbr. articles in field to profl. jours.; editor-in-chief Jour. Marital and Family Therapy, 1976-81; mem. editorial bd. Jour. Sociology and Social Welfare, 1974-77, Jour. Divorce, 1977—, Terapia Familiare (Italian Jour. Family Therapy), 1978—, Jour. Sex and Marital Therapy, 1980—, Terapia Familiar (Argentenian Jour. of Family Therapy), 1980—, Family Therapy Quar., 1981—, Jour. Family Relations, 1982—, Conciliation Cts. Rev., 1982—. Home: 1900 Consulate Pl Apt 1903 West Palm Beach FL 33401 Office: 2617 N Flagler Dr Suite 404 West Palm Beach FL 33407

KASSEBAUM, NANCY LANDON, U.S. Senator; b. Topeka, July 29, 1932; d. Alfred M. and Theo Landon; B.A., U. Kans., 1952; M.S. in Diplomatic History, U. Mich., 1956; m. Philip Kassebaum, 1955 (div. 1979); children—John Philip, Linda Josephine, Richard Landon, William Alfred. Vice pres. Stas. KFH-KBRA-FM, Wichita, Kans.; staff asst. Sen. James B. Pearson, Washington, 1975-76; mem. U.S. Senate from Kans., 1978—, mem. banking, housing and urban affairs com., commerce, sci. and transp. com. Recipient Matrix award Women in Communications. Republican. Episcopalian. Office: US Senate 304 Senate Russell Office Bldg Washington DC 20510 *

KASSEL, VIRGINIA WELTMER, TV producer; b. Omaha; d. Tyler and Inez (Willard) Weltmer; B.A., Bryn Mawr Coll., 1954; Producer Sta. WGBH-TV, Boston, 1959-63; producer NET, N.Y.C., 1964-68, coordinator nat. programs, 1968-70; creator, producer The Adams Chronicles, PBS, 1970-76; mgr. spl. projects Sta. WNET, N.Y.C., 1976-79, exec. producer humanities programs, 1979-80; sr. producer CBS Cable, N.Y.C., 1980—. Recipient George Foster Peabody award, 1977, Ohio State award, 1977; Nat. Assn. Ednl. Broadcasters Spl. Achievement award, 1977. Mem. Nat. Acad. TV Arts and Sci. (4 awards), Writers Guild of Am. Contbr. articles to profl. publs. Home: 4 E 89th St New York NY 10028 Office: CBS Cable 1211 6th Ave New York NY 10036

KASSEWITZ, RUTH EILEEN BLOWER, hosp. exec.; b. Columbus, Ohio, May 15, 1928; d. E. Wallett and Helen (Daub) Blower; B.S. in Journalism-Mgmt., Ohio State U., Columbus, 1951; m. Jack Kassewitz, July 28, 1962; 1 step son, Jack. Copywriter, Ohio Fuel Gas Co., Columbus, 1951-55, Merritt Owens Advt. Agy., Kansas City, Kans., 1955-56; account exec. Grant Advt., Inc., Miami, Fla., 1956-59; account supr. Venn/Cole & Assos. (now Venn Corp.), Miami, 1959-67; dir. communications Ferendino/Grafton/Candela/Spillis Architects & Engrs., Miami, 1967-69; dir. communications Dade County Dept. Housing and Urban Devel., Miami, 1969-72; dir. communications Met. Dade County Govt., 1972-78; adminstr. community relations and communications U. Miami/Jackson Meml. Med. Center, 1978—. Pres., U. Miami Women's Guild, 1973-74; bd. dirs. Girls Scouts Tropical Fla., 1974-76, 81—, Lung Assn. Dade-Monroe Counties, 1976—; 1st v.p. Mental Health Assn. Dade County, 1978—; mem. Miami Ecol. and Beautification Com., 1978—; bd. govs. Barry U., Miami, 1981—; trustee Nat. Humanities Faculty, 1981—. Recipient Disting. Service award Plymouth Congl. Ch., Miami, 1979; Mem. Public Relations Soc. Am. (pres. S. Fla. chpt. 1969-70, nat. chmn. govt. sect. 1973-74, nat. dir. 1974-78; Silver Anvil award 1973), Women in Communications (pres. Greater Miami chpt. 1962-63; Clarion award 1973), Fla. Hosp. Assn., S. Fla. Hosp. Public Relations Assn., Miami Forum. Conglist. Home: 1136 Aduana Ave Coral Gables FL 33146 Office: Jackson Meml Hosp 1611 NW 12th Ave Rm 0118 Miami FL 33136

KASTER, BARBARA JEANNE, filmmaker; b. El Paso, Tex., June 27, 1934; d. James Jay and Louize (Beeman) K.; A.B., Tex. Western Coll., 1957; M.A., U. Tex., 1967, Ph.D., 1970; 1 dau., Kimberly Chris. Tchr., El Paso Public Schs., 1957-66; asst. prof. U.S. Fla., 1967; teaching asst. Ind. U., 1968, U. Tex., 1968-70; asst. prof. Fla. Atlantic U., 1970-73; asso. prof. communication Bowdoin Coll., Brunswick, Maine, 1973-75, Harrison King McCann prof., 1975—; pres. Dunster Films, Brunswick, 1970—; cons. audio visual dept. Maine Med. Center, 1976—; cons. Media Design, Inc., Portland, Maine, 1976—; films include Making Policy, Not Coffee, 1972, Flo!, 1975; Green Seas, White Ice, 1978; Poggio Civitate, 1979; The Treasure, 1981. Bd. dirs. El Paso chpt. LWV, 1966; v.p. Palm Beach (Fla.) County chpt. NOW, 1972; mem. Palm Beach County Democratic Com., 1973. Grantee Mell Found., 1974, Ford Found., 1976. Mem. Nat. Speech Communication Assn., So. Eastern Speech Communications Assn., Assn. Am. Film Inst. Democrat. Roman Catholic. Contbr. articles to profl. jours. and text books. Home: RFD 2 Box 2112 Brunswick ME 04011 Office: Bowdoin Coll Brunswick ME 04011

KASWER, BARBARA ANNE, nurse; b. Stamford, Conn., Dec. 22, 1939; d. Stanley Jacob and Irene Elizabeth (Kovacs) Kaswer; diploma, St. Vincent's Hosp. Sch. Nursing, 1957-60; Student, SUNY, 1978-81. Staff nurse med., surg. unit St. Joseph Hosp., Stamford, 1960-65, sr. charge nurse ICU/CCU, 1965-71, head nurse ICU/CCU, 1971-81, instr. inservice edn. dept., 1981—, coordinator coronary care course, 1971—, also editor Info. Mat hosp. newspaper. Cert. critical care nurse. Mem. Am. Assn. Crit. Care Nurses, Democrat. Roman Catholic. Office: 128 Strawberry Hill Ave Stamford CT 06904

KATHURIA, NIRMAL BHATIA, physician; b. New Delhi, India, May 23, 1948; came to U.S., 1973, naturalized, 1980; d. Banarsi Das and Chander (Kanta) Bhatia; M.D., Lady Hardinge Med. Coll., New Delhi, 1969; m. Mineshwar Kathuria, Jan. 14, 1973. Intern, Lady Hardinge Med. Coll. and Hosp., 1970-72; resident in psychiatry Fairfield Hills Hosp., Newtown, Conn., 1974-77, staff psychiatrist, 1977-88; resident in psychiatry Yale-New Haven Hosp., Stamford (Conn.) Hosp., 1974-77; dir. outpatient clinic Charlotte Hungerford Hosp., Torrington, Conn., 1978-80, dir., chmn. psychiat. services, 1980—; cons. Country Place, Litchfield, Conn., 1979-82, bd. govs., 1979—; mem. adv. bd. Regional Health Services, Winsted, Conn., 1979-81; program chmn., mem. exec. com. Assn. Psychiat. Clinics Conn., 1981-82. Diplomate Am. Bd. Psychiatry and Neurology. Mem. Am. Psychiat. Assn., Conn. Psychiat. Soc. Home: Beach St Goshen CT 06756 Office: 778 E Main St Torrington CT 06790

KATSON, ROBERTA MARINA, economist; b. Albuquerque, Oct. 5, 1947; d. Robert V. and Penelope (Papafrangos) Katson; student Emory U., 1966-67, Ga. State U., 1967-69; B.A., U. N.Mex., 1974, M.A., 1977; m. Cyrus Butner, 1980; 1 child, Justin Cyrus. Gen. mgr. Window Rock (Ariz.) Motor Inn, Navajo Reservation, 1972-73; research asst. dept. econs. U. N.Mex., Albuquerque, 1974-75, research asso. Resource Econ. Group, 1975-77; economist program analysis Econ. Devel. Adminstrn., Dept. Commerce, Washington, 1977-79; economist Dept. Energy, Washington, 1979—. Mem. Phi Kappa Phi, Omicron Delta Epsilon. Democrat. Contbr. articles to profl. jours. Home: 3111 N 20th St Apt C443 Arlington VA 22201 Office: Dept Energy Forrestal Bldg Washington DC 20585

KATZ, ANN LEHMAN, psychologist; b. Washington, June 5, 1948; d. Milton and Mildred (Kharfen) Lehman; B.S., U. Mich., 1970; M.Ed., Boston Coll., 1971; Ed.D., Boston U., 1977; m. Howard M. Katz, May 16, 1970; children—Amanda Lehman, Gregory Milton. Asst. psychologist McLean Hosp., Belmont, Mass., 1977—; instr. psychology Harvard U. Sch. Medicine, 1977—; pvt. practice psychology, Belmont, Mass., 1979—. Lic. psychologist, Mass. Mem. Am. Psychol. Assn., Mass. Psychol. Assn. Office: 115 Mill St Belmont MA 02178

KATZ, ANNETTE SARA, editor, journalist; b. Miami, Fla., Jan. 25, 1948; d. Harold Orville and Jean (Bulafkin) Van Dam; B.S. in Journalism, U. Fla., 1970; m. Stephen K. Katz, Feb. 26, 1978; 1 son, Matthew R. Reporter, Coral Gables (Fla.) Times, also The Guide, Coral Gables, 1970-71, women's editor, 1971-72, edn. editor, 1972-74; dir. communications United Tchrs. Dade County (Fla.), 1974—, publs. specialist, 1980—, editor UTD Today (named best union newspaper in Fla. 1981-82). Mem. Fla. Women's Polit. Caucus, 1970-71. Recipient Sch. Bell award Fla. Edn. Assn., 1973, 74; Number Two Suburban Journalist in U.S. award Suburban Newspapers Am., 1973; resolution City of Coral Gables, 1973; 1st pl. feature writing Union Press, 1975; State Union Press award, 1976, 77; award for disting. journalism Fla. Tchr. Press Assn., 1980, others. Mem. Women in Communications (corr. sec. 1972-73, rec. sec. 1973-74), Fla. Press Club, Sigma Delta Chi. Democrat. Jewish. Office: 2929 SW 3d Ave Miami FL 33129

KATZ, HILDA (HULDA WEBER), artist, poet; b. N.Y.C.; d. Max and Lina (Schwartz) Katz; student N.A.D. (New Sch. Social Research scholar), 1940-41. One-woman shows: Bowdoin Coll. Art Mus., 1951, Calif. State Library, 1953, Print Club of Albany (N.Y.) Inst., 1955, U. Maine, 1955, 58, Jewish Mus. N.Y., 1956, Pa. State Tchrs. Coll., 1956, Masillon (Ohio) Mus., 1957, Ball State Tchrs. Coll., 1957, Springfield Art Mus., 1957, U. Maine, 1958, Miami Beach (Fla.) Art Center, 1958, Art Assn. Richmond (Ind.), 1959, Old State Capitol Mus. La., La. Art Commn., others; group shows include: Corcoran Bienniale Library Congress, Am. in the War (26 museums) Pa. Acad. Fine Arts, Soc. Am. Graphic Artists, Phila. Water Color Club, Audubon Artists, Print Club Albany, Albany Inst., Bklyn. Mus., Delgado Mus. Art-U.S.A., 1959, Jewish Mus., Boston Printmakers, Massillon Mus., Springfield Art Mus., NAD, Met. Mus. Art, Italian Fedn. Women in Art, Italy, Venice Biennial, Italy, Conn. Acad. Fine Arts, Congress Jewish Culture, Calif. State Library, Bowdoin U., State Tchrs. Coll. Pa., Art Assn. Richmond, Boston, N.Y. public libraries, Miami Beach Art Center, Children's Mus., Hartford, Conn., Washington Printmakers, Miniature Painters, Engravers and Sculptors Soc., Peoria Art Center, Engrs. Club. Phila., La. Art Commn., also numerous others in U.S., Eng., France, Italy, Israel, S.Am., S.E. Asia, Middle East; represented in permanent group collections Library of Congress, Balt. Mus. Art, Fogg Mus., Franklin D. Roosevelt Collection, Santa Barbara Art Mus., Colo. Springs Fine Arts Center, Soc. Am. Graphic Artists, U.S. Nat. Mus., Met. Mus. Art, Bezalel Nat. Mus., Jerusalem, Addison Gallery Am. Art, Springfield (Mo.) Art Mus., Newark Public Library, N.Y. Public Library, Calif. State Library, Pa. State Library, U. Minn., Print Club Albany, Safed Mus., Bat Yam Museum (both Israel), Peoria (Ill.) Art Center, St. Margaret Mary Sch. Art, State Mus. Albany, Jewish Mus. N.Y., Archives Am. Art, Smithsonian Instn., numerous others, including several colls. and univs.; pictures represented in spl. collections U.S. Nat. Mus., 1965-72 U. Maine, 1965, Library Congress, 1965, 71, Met. Mus. Art, 1965, 80, Nat. Gallery Art, 1965, Nat. Collection Fine Arts, 1966, 71, 78, Nat. Air and Space Mus., 1970, N.Y. Public Library, 1971, 78, New Britain Mus. Am. Art, 1978, Mus. City N.Y., 1979, Jewish Mus., N.Y.C., 1979, A. Hyatt Mayor Collection Met. Mus. Art, 1980, Ft. Lewis (Colo.) Coll., 1980, Israel Mus., Jerusalem, 1980, Boston Public Library, 1980, others. Recipient award graphic Nat. Assn. Women Artists, 1945, water color, 1947, Am. artists group prize Soc. Am. Graphic Artists, 1950; best painting in landscape Soc. Miniature Painters, Sculptors, Gravers, 1959, print award Peoria Art Center, 1960, Library of Congress Purchase Prizes; Purchase award Print Club of Albany, 1964, Peoria (Ill.) Art Center, 1964, U. Minn., Calif. State Library, Met. Mus. Art, State Tchrs. Coll. Pa., Art Assn. Richmond, N.Y. Public Library, Newark Public Library, St. Margaret Mary Sch. Art Coll., plaque of honor Hall Fame, 1966, also life mem.; poetry awards, including James Joyce Poetry award Poetry Soc. Am. life fellow Met. Mus.; named Dau. of Mark Twain. Fellow-founder Internat. Acad. Poets; mem. Nat. Assn. Women Artists, Soc. Washington Print-makers, Am. Color Print Soc., Audubon Artists, Soc. Am. Graphic Artists, Internat. Platform Assn., Hunterdon Art Center, Conn. Acad. Fine Arts, Phila. Watercolor Club, Boston Print-makers (award 1955), Hunterdon County Art Center, Print Club Albany, Print Council Am., Marquis Biog. Library Soc. (adv. mem.), Poetry Soc. Am., Accademia di Scienze, Lettere, Arti (hon. consigliere), Classe Storia Letteratura Americana (Milan, Italy). Author (under pen name Hulda Weber) poems included in numerous anthologies. Contbr. numerous poems and short stories to mags. Address: 915 West End Ave Apt 5D New York NY 10025

KATZ, IRIS LEVINE, speech pathologist; b. Bklyn., Aug. 8, 1949; d. Sidney and Beatrice Levine; A.A., Montgomery Coll., 1970; B.S. cum laude, Towson State Coll., 1971; M.A., U. Md., 1972; m. Dec. 30, 1972. Speech and lang. pathologist Baltimore County (Md.) Bd. Edn., Reisterstown, 1972—; trained student clinicians Towson State U., 1974—, lectr. dept. speech pathology, 1974—. Obedience instr. Canine Coll., Balt., 1976-81, Carroll Kennel Club, Westminster, Md., 1979—. Mem. Am. Speech and Hearing Assn. (cert. clin. competence), Md. Speech and Hearing Assn., Cavalier King Charles Spaniel Clubs U.S.A., Can. and Gt. Britain, Cavaliers of N.E., Phi Theta Kappa, Sigma Alpha Eta. Democrat. Jewish. Office: Franklin Elementary School Cockeysmill Rd Reisterstown MD 21136

KATZ, JANE, educator; b. Sharon, Pa., Apr. 16, 1943; d. Leon and Dorothea (Oberkewitz) K.; B.S. in Edn., Coll. City N.Y., 1963; M.A., N.Y. U., 1966; M.Ed., Columbia Tchrs. Coll., 1972, Ed.D., 1978. Mem. faculty Bronx Community Coll., City U. N.Y., 1964—, prof. phys. edn., 1972—; mem. U.S. Round-the-World Synchronized Swim Team, 1964; synchronized swimming solo tour of Eng., 1969; founding co-organizer, coach 1st Internat. Israeli Youth Festival Games, 1970; mem. winning U.S. Maccabiah Swim Team, 1957; vice chmn. Metro Master AAU Swim Team, 1974—; mem. AAU Nat. Masters All-Am. Swimming

Team, 1974—, synchronized swimming solo champion, 1975; speaker, judge in field. Trainee Fed. Adminstrn. Aging, 1971-72; mem. Internat. Hall. of Fame, Ft. Lauderdale, Fla. Mem. U.S. Com. Sports for Israel (dir., co-chmn. women's swimming com. 1970—), AAHPER, Nat. Jewish Welfare Bd., Internat. Aquatics. Author Swimming for Total Fitness, 1981 papers in field. Address: 400 2d Ave New York NY 10010

KATZ, JUDITH KAPUSTIN, counseling psychologist; b. Phila., Apr. 22, 1939; d. David and Belle (Erfer) Kapustin; A.B., Temple U., 1960; M.A., U. Mich., 1961; Ed.D., U. Pa., 1975; m. Solomon Hertz Katz, June 21, 1964; children—Noah, Rachael. Psychologist, Norristown (Pa.) State Hosp., 1961-66; psychol. counselor Harverford (Pa.) Coll., 1965-70; founder, dir. Options for Women, Phila., 1970-72; dir. Career Planning and Placement, Swarthmore (Pa.) Coll., 1970—; counseling psychologist Phila. Coll. Art, 1974—; partner Divorce Mediation & Counseling Service, Plymouth Meeting, Pa., 1981—. Mem. Am. Psychol. Assn., Mid-Atlantic Placement Assn., Pa. Psychol. Assn., Phila. Soc. Clin. Psychologists, Am. Personnel and Guidance Assn., Am. Coll. Personnel Assn. Home: 519 N Wynnewood Ave Narberth PA 19072 Office: Career Planning and Placement Swarthmore Coll Swarthmore PA 19087

KATZ, JUDITH TERRY, food mktg. specialist; b. N.Y.C., Apr. 17, 1946; d. Morris and Beatrice (Miller) K.; B.A., Bklyn. Coll., 1966, M.A., 1968; grad. Chef's Cert., Le Cordon Bleu, 1977. Public relations dir., catering mgr. TWTF Restaurant Group, N.Y.C., 1972-76; exec. chef Ashleys, N.Y.C., 1977, LaGriglia, N.Y.C., 1977-78; dir. food service prodn. Macy's, N.Y.C., 1977-78; mgr. Marine Midland Food Service, Service Systems Corp., N.Y.C., 1978-79, Veggies Park Restaurants, N.Y.C., 1979; dir. mktg. and food standards Corp. Food Services Inc., N.Y.C., 1980-82; free-lance restaurant cons., guest lectr. Restaurant Sch., Nassau Community Coll.; guest lectr. New Sch. Culinary Arts. Fund raiser Kennedy Found. Spl. Olympics, 1981—. Mem. Am. Soc. Profl. and Exec. Women, Nat. Assn. Female Execs., Food and Beverage Mgrs. Assn., Mensa. Club: N.Y. Roadrunners. Home and office: 222 E 93d St New York NY 10028

KATZ, LILIAN GONSHAW, educator; b. London, June 7, 1932; came to U.S., 1947, naturalized, 1953; s. Joseph and Eva (Freidine) Gonshaw; B.A. cum laude, San Francisco State Coll., 1964; Ph.D., Stanford U., 1968; m. Boris I. Katz, Nov. 8, 1952; children—Daniel, Stephen, Miriam I. Tchr., Redwood Parents Nursery Sch. and Parent Educator Sequoia Adult Sch., Redwood City, Calif., 1962-64; asst. prof. early childhood edn. U. Ill., Urbana-Champaign, 1968-70, asso. prof., 1970-73, prof., 1973—, dir. ERIC Clearinghouse on elem. and early childhood edn., 1970—, chmn. dept. elem. and early childhood edn., 1979-81, co-chmn. research unit on tchr. edn., 1979—; vis. prof. edn. Macquarie U., Sydney, Australia, 1975; vis. lectr. St. Mary's Coll., Cheltenham, Gloucestershire, Eng., 1976; vis. prof. U. Hamburg (W.Ger.), 1981. Mem. Ill. Gov.'s Adv. Council to Dept. Children and Family Services, 1974; mem. early childhood task force Corp. Pub. Broadcasting, 1974; pub. rep. Child Devel. Assos. Consortium Bd., 1975; pres. U.S. nat. com. Orgn. Mondiale pour l'Educational Prescholaire, 1980; chmn. Nat. Task Force Child Devel., 1980-81; co-chmn. pre-primary project Internat. Evaluation Assn., 1980—. Schoolmaster's fellow Coll. St. Matthias, Bristol, Eng., 1975; Fulbright fellow U. Baroda (India), 1983. Fellow Am. Psychol. Assn.; mem. Soc. Research Child Devel., Am. Ednl. Research Assn., Nat. Assn. Edn. Young Children (editorial adv. bd. 1969-71), AAUP, Nat. Soc. Study Edn., Assn. Supervision and Curriculum Devel., Orgn. Mondiale pour l'Education Prescholaire. Author: Talks with Teachers: Reflections on Early Childhood Education, 1977; editorial bd. Children in Contemporary Soc., 1981; contbr. articles to profl. jours. Office: 805 W Pennsylvania Ave Urbana IL 61801

KATZ, LILLIAN MENASCHE, mail order sales exec.; b. Leipzig, Germany, Mar. 18, 1927; came to U.S., 1937, naturalized, 1942; d. Herman and Erna (Feiner) Menasche; student N.Y.U.; m. Robert Katz, Oct. 24, 1970; children by previous marriage—Fred P. and David C. Hochberg. Pres., founder Lillian Vernon Corp., Mt. Vernon, N.Y., 1951—, subs. Country Gourmet, Gramatan Advt. Co., Provender, The New Co.; lectr. N.Y.U. Sch. Continuing Edn.; dir. Better Bus. Bur. of Westchester. Bd. dirs. Westchester County Assn., Westchester Mental Health Assn. Recipient awards Westchester County Med. Center (Valhalla, N.Y.), Mt. Vernon Hosp. Mem. Direct Mail/Mktg. Assn., New Eng. Mail Order Assn., Direct Mktg. Idea Exchange, Third Class Mail Assn., Catalog Leaders, Women's Forum. Contbr. articles Direct Mktg. Mag. Office: 510 S Fulton Ave Mount Vernon NY 10550

KATZ, SUSAN LEE, writer; b. N.Y.C., Nov. 10, 1943; d. Freda (Friedman) K.; B.A., Hunter Coll., 1964. Advt., public relations copywriter various agys., 1964-72; mng. editor Silver Screen mag., N.Y.C., 1972-74; exec. editor Modern Screen mag., N.Y.C., 1974-78; freelance writer, 1978—. Mem. Women in Communications. Author: Zabar's Deli Book, 1979; Just Desserts, 1978; The Yogurt Book, 1977; Dieters' Desserts, 1981; TV Superwomen's Scrapbook, 1978; Superwomen of Rock, 1979; Where Have They Gone, 1980; Frampton Comes Alive, 1979; various features in nat. and local mags. and newspapers. Home and Office: 247 W 76th St New York NY 10023

KATZ, VERA, state legislator; b. Germany, Aug. 3, 1933; d. Lazar and Reissa (Goodman) Pistrak; B.A., Bklyn. Coll., 1954, M.A., 1956; m. Melvin Katz, 1954; 1 son, Jesse. Mem. Oreg. Ho. of Reps. from 8th Dist., 1972—; mem. State Health Coordinating Council, 1977; mem. Task Force on Sunset Legislation, Oreg. Liquor Control Commn. Agy., 1978; mem. Task Force on Mental Health, 1978; mem. Mayor's Task Force on Downtown Housing, 1978; mem. Nat. Urban Policy Roundtable, 1978. Recipient Service to Mankind award Rose City Sertoma Club, 1970; Oreg. Environ. Council award, 1973, 77; Oreg. Women's Polit. Caucus award for Outstanding Pub. Service, 1977; Outstanding Legislative award, 1977. Office: Oreg Ho Reps State Capitol Salem OR 97310 *

KATZEL, JEANINE ALMA, journalist; b. Chgo., Feb. 20, 1948; d. LeRoy Paul and Lia Mary (Arcuri) Katzel; B.A. in Journalism, U. Wis., 1970; M.S. in Journalism, Northwestern U., 1974. Publs. editor U. Wis. Sea Grant Program, Madison, 1969-72; editor research div. agrl. sch. U. Wis., Madison, 1972; research editor Prism mag. AMA, Chgo., 1972-73; free-lance writer, 1974-75; lit. editor Plant Engring. mag. Tech. Pub. Co., Barrington, Ill., 1975-76, news editor, 1976-77, asso. editor, 1977-79, sr. editor, 1979—. Eucharistic minister Saints Peter and Paul Roman Cath. Ch.; mem. Circle Ch. Spirit Singers. Recipient Elsie Bullard Morrison prize in Journalism, U. Wis., 1969. Mem. Women in Communications, Soc. Profl. Journalists, Am. Soc. Bus. Press Editors (pres. Chgo. chpt. 1977-78), Am. Inst. Plant Engrs., Assn. Energy Engrs., Nat. Fire Protection Assn. (tech. com. on fire pumps), Am. Soc. Safety Engrs., Soc. Fire Protection Engrs., Phi Kappa Phi. Club: Chgo. Headline. Home: 16 Boxwood Ln Cary IL 60013 Office: 1301 S Grove Ave Barrington IL 60010

KATZEN, SALLY, lawyer, former govt. ofcl.; b. Pitts., Nov. 22, 1942; d. Nathan and Hilda (Schwartz) K.; B.A. magna cum laude, Smith Coll., 1964; J.D. magna cum laude, U. Mich., 1967. Congressional intern Senate Subcom. on Constl. Rights, Washington, summer, 1963; legal research asst. civil rights div. Dept. Justice, Washington, summer 1965; law clk. to Judge J. Skelly Wright, D.C. circuit U.S. Ct. Appeals, 1967-68; admitted to D.C. bar, 1968, U.S. Supreme Ct. bar, 1971; asso. firm Wilmer, Cutler & Pickering, Washington, 1968-74, partner, 1975-79; gen. counsel Council on Wage and Price Stability, 1979-80; dep. dir. Council Wage and Price Stability, 1980-81; partner firm Wilmer Cutler and Pickering, 1981—; Mem. com. visitors U. Mich. Law Sch., 1972-82; mem. Jud. Conf. for D.C. Circuit, 1972-81. Mem. Am. Bar Assn. (house of dels. 1978-80, council adminstrv. law sect. 1979—; governing com. forum com. communications law), D.C. Bar Assn., FCC Bar Assn., Women's Legal Def. Fund (pres. 1977, v.p. 1978), Order of Coif. Editor-in-chief U. Mich. Law Rev., 1966-67. Home: 1825 Que St NW Washington DC Office: 1666 K St NW Washington DC 20006

KAUFF, CYNTHIA ANN, personnel specialist; b. New Brunswick, N.J., June 7, 1944; d. Harold Clinton and R. Virginia (Jameson) Harris; B.S., U. Md., 1966; M.A. in Edn., George Washington U., 1977; m. Robert B. Kauff, Apr. 20, 1968 (dec.). Dir. women and girls programs, dir. pub. relations Silver Spring (Md.) YMCA, 1966-71; coordinator adult social programs, patient activity dept. NIH, Bethesda, Md., 1971-75, supr. mental health programs of dept., 1975-80, NIH health mgmt. intern, 1981—. Bd. dirs. Alliance, Washington, 1977—; charter mem. Colonial Women, George Washington U., 1981—; vol. Montgomery County Mental Health Assn., 1982—. Mem. Am. Soc. Pub. Adminstrn., Am. Soc. Profl. and Exec. Women, Md. Recreation and Parks Soc. (exec. council 1979, sec. 1980). Episcopalian. Clubs: Washington Ski, Potomac Tennis. Contbr. (with Naral) The Federal Resource File, 1976. Home: Apt 405 10320 Westlake Dr Bethesda MD 20817

KAUFFMAN, MARY ANN MCNEMAR, banker; b. Wilmington, Del., Dec. 11, 1929; d. Leslie Haines and Bessie Ratcliffe (Narvel) McNemar; B.S. in Mgmt., Simmons Coll., 1980; student U. Del., 1968-80; m. Harold B. Kauffman, Dec. 29, 1948; children—Robert, Jeffrey, Mark. With Wilmington Savs. Fund Soc., 1960—, asst. br. mgr., 1966-70, br. mgr., asst. sec., 1970-72, br. mgr., asst. treas., 1972-74, asst. treas., tng. officer, 1974-79, asst. v.p. tng. officer, 1979—; seminar leader; instr. Am. Inst. Banking. Internat. Yr. of Women workshop leader Del. State Coll., 1979. Nominee Trailblazer award Wilmington Women in Bus., 1981; honoree Tribute to Women and Industry, 1979; cert. model-netics mgmt. instr. Mem. Nat. Assn. Bank Women, Wilmington Women in Bus., Am. Soc. Tng. and Devel., Am. Inst. Banking. Episcopalian. Home: 111 Denn Pl Wilmington DE 19804 Office: 838 Market St Wilmington DE 19801

KAUFMAN, BEL, author, educator; b. Berlin; d. Michael J. and Lala (Rabinowitz) Kaufman; B.A. magna cum laude, Hunter Coll.; M.A. with highest honors, Columbia U.; LL.D., Nasson Coll., Maine; div.; children—Jonathan Goldstine, Thea Goldstine. Asst. prof. English, City U. N.Y.; lectr. New Sch. for Social Research; tchr. English, N.Y.C. high Schs.; lectr. throughout country, also appearances on TV and radio. Mem. Commn. Performing Arts; bd. dirs. Shalom Aleichem Found.; mem. adv. council Town Hall Found. Recipient plaque Anti-Defamation League; award and plaque United Jewish Appeal; Paperback of Yr. award; Bell Movie award; Nat. Human Resource award; awards for best articles on edn. Ednl. Assn. Am.; named to Hall of Fame Hunter Coll. Mem. Author's Guild (council), Dramatists Guild, PEN (exec. bd., membership com.), English Grad. Union, Phi Beta Kappa (editorial bd. Phi Delta Kappan). Author: Up the Down Staircase, 1965; Love, Etc., 1979; also short stories, translations of Russian, lyrics for musicals.

KAUFMAN, BONNIE LOU WATSON, mfg. co. exec.; b. Winchester, Ind., July 29, 1930; d. Reece Lorris and Lulu Willette (Shouse) Watson; student Ind. Bus. Coll., 1965-67, Ball State U., 1970-72; children—Bonita Lee Streetman, Stephen Wayne, Dane Constantine. With Westinghouse Electric, Inc.. Union City, Ind., 1958-64, J. Cody Longnecker C.P.A., Winchester, 1965-66; with Overmyer Mould Co., Winchester, 1966—, sales and prodn. scheduling coordinator, traffic mgr., now inventory and material controller. Republican. Home: 403 S Olive St Farmland IN 47340 Office: Overmyer Mould Co One Omco Sq Winchester IN 47394

KAUFMAN, CAROLYN CHAMBERS, accountant, fin. planning co. exec.; b. Erie, Pa., Mar. 6, 1941; d. Lawrence C. and Freda Ruth (Lusk) Chambers; B.S. in Bus. Adminstrn., Dyke Coll., 1962; M.B.A., Cleve. State U., 1974; 1 son, David Kaufman. Asso. prof. acctg. Dyke Coll., Cleve., 1962-74; vis. prof. acctg. Cleve. State U., 1974-75, asst. prof. acctg., 1975-79; tax specialist Peat, Marwick and Mitchel Co., Cleve., 1975; prin. Carolyn C. Kaufman, acct., Cleve., 1975-78, cons. to govt. agys. and bus. corps., 1975-80; partner Spero-Kaufman Fin. Planning, Beachwood, Ohio, 1979—; adj. prof. acctg. Lake Erie Coll., Painesville, Ohio, 1979—; adj. prof. arts mgmt. Ohio State U., Columbus, 1980—; appeared on various radio and TV shows, 1979-82. Named Outstanding Prof. of Acctg., Cleve. State U. Acctg. Assn., 1977-78; recipient Outstanding Educator of the Year citation Dyke Coll. Delta Club, 1970; C.P.A., Ohio; cert. fin. planner, Ohio. Mem. Inst. of C.P.A.s, Am. Acctg. Assn., Ohio Soc. C.P.A.s, Am. Inst. Decision Scientists, Inst. Internat. Fin. Planners, Am. Bus. Women's Assn., Beta Alpha Psi, Beta Gamma Sigma, Phi Gamma Nu. Republican. Contbr. articles on acctg. to profl. jours. Home: 4622 Greenwold South Euclid OH 44121 Office: 3355 Richmond Rd Beachwood OH 44122

KAUFMAN, CHARLOTTE KING, ednl. adminstr.; b. Balt., Dec. 5, 1920; d. Ben and Belle (Turow) King; A.B., Goucher Coll., 1969; M.P.H., Johns Hopkins U., 1972, M.Ed., 1976; m. Albert Kaufman, July 22, 1945; children—Matthew King, Ezra King. Dir. public relations Balt. Jewish Community Center, 1962-67; research and editor Johns Hopkins U. Sch. Hygiene and Public Health, Balt., 1969-72, admissions officer, 1972-74, dir. admissions and registrar, 1974—. Mem. Am. Pub. Health Assn., Am. Assn. for Higher Edn., Am. Assn. Collegiate Registrars and Admissions Officers. Democrat. Jewish. Home: 1 E University Pkwy Baltimore MD 21218 Office: 615 N Wolfe St Baltimore MD 21205

KAUFMAN, CLAIRE BEHRENS, personnel recruitment exec.; b. S.C., Sept. 5, 1947; d. Max and Jean Behrens; B.A., U. Miami (Fla.), 1969; m. Peter Hart Kaufman, July 27, 1980; children—Robert Todd, Wendy Jeanne, Ethan Hart. Mgr. health care recruitment Pacific Recruiting Offices, Inc., Beverly Hills, Calif., 1977-80; mgr. internat. recruiting Nat. Med. Enterprises, Santa Monica, Calif., 1980-81; dir. internat. recruiting Am. Med. Internat., Beverly Hills, 1981—; cons. in field. Mem. Profl. Women Los Angeles, LWV. Democrat. Author tng. manuals, seminar materials. Home: 629 29th St Manhattan Beach CA 90266 Office: Am Med Internat 9465 Wilshire Blvd Beverly Hills CA 90212

KAUFMAN, JOYCE JACOBSON, chemist; b. N.Y.C., June 21, 1929; d. Abraham and Sarah (Seldin) Deutch; B.S. with honors, Johns Hopkins U., 1949, M.A., 1959, Ph.D. in Chemistry, 1960; D.E.S. (tres Honorable) in Theoretical Physics, Sorbonne, Paris, 1963; m. Stanley Kaufman, Dec. 26, 1948; 1 dau., Jan Caryl. Analytical research chemist Army Chem. Center, Md., 1949-52; mem. chemistry research staff Johns Hopkins U., Balt., 1952-60; head quantum chemistry group Research Inst. Advanced Studies, Balt., 1960-69, staff scientist, 1965-69; prin. research scientist dept. chemistry Johns Hopkins U., asso. prof. dept. anesthesiology Sch. Medicine, 1969—, asso. prof. dept. surgery div. plastic surgery Johns Hopkins U. Sch. Medicine, 1977—; mem. sci. adv. com. Dept. Def., 1977; mem. rev. panel for undergrad. chemistry edn. NSF, 1977; Fogarty Internat. Exchange specialist NIH-USSR Ministry of Health, 1978; mem. internat. organizing com. for Internat. Conf. Theoretical Biophysics and Biochemistry Tata Inst. Fundamental Research, Bombay, India, 1981. Recipient Garvan medal as outstanding woman chemist Am. Chem. Soc., 1974; Md. Chemist award Am. Chem. Soc. Md. sect. 1974. Fellow Am. Phys. Soc., Am. Inst. Chemists; mem. Am. Chem. Soc. (chmn. Md. sect. 1972, councilor phys. chemistry div. 1971—, councilor Md. sect. 1968-71, chmn. subdiv. theoretical chemistry div. phys. chemistry 1979-80), Am. Soc. Pharmacology and Exptl. Therapeutics, European Acad. Scis., Arts and Letters (corr. mem.), Internat. Soc. Quantum Biology, Am. Soc. Anesthesiology, AAUP, Phi Beta Kappa, Sigma Xi. Mem. editorial adv. bd. John Wiley and Intersci. Pubs., 1965—, Molecular Pharmacology, 1970—, Internat. Jour. Quantum Chemistry, 1967—; editor Benchmark Book Series in phys. chemistry-chem. physics, 1975—, overall chemistry editor, 1977—; contbr. numerous articles to profl. jours. Office: Dept Chemistry Johns Hopkins U Baltimore MD 21218

KAUFMAN, LOUISE SUSAN, pharm. co. ofcl.; b. Staten Island, N.Y., Dec. 4, 1952; d. Santo Michael and Selma Mary (Sidoti) Repage; B.S., Wagner Coll., 1975, M.S., 1978; postgrad. St. John's U., 1979—; m. Peter Joseph Kaufman, Sept. 18, 1976. Vet. technician Hylan Animal Hosp., Staten Island, N.Y., 1972-75; vet. abstractor Merck & Co., Inc., Rahway, N.J., 1975-78, regulatory affairs asst., 1978-79, sr. regulatory coordinator, 1979-82, mgr. registration, 1982—. Mem. Drug Info. Assn. (publicity dir. 1980-82, treas. 1982-84), Nat. Soc. Microbiology, Am. Vet. Med. Assn. Aux., N.Y.C. Soc. Microbiology. Home: 13 Foote Ave Staten Island NY 10301 Office: PO Box 2000 Rahway NJ 07065

KAUFMANN, RISE ARLENE, psychologist; b. N.Y.C., Feb. 25, 1943; d. Sol and Sylvia (Silverman) Jacobson; B.A., CCNY, 1963; Ph.D., Columbia U., 1970; m. Yoram Kaufmann, Oct. 8, 1972. Staff psychologist, child and adolescent outpatient dept. Payne Whitney Clinic, N.Y. Hosp., 1968-69; staff psychologist, adult outpatient dept., 1969-71; asst. prof. CUNY, 1971-77; pvt. practice psychotherapy, N.Y.C. and Ramsey, N.J., 1970—. Mem. Am. Psychol. Assn. Jewish. Home and office: 159 Deer Trail N Ramsey NJ 07446 also 257 Central park west New York NY 10024

KAUFMANN-HORWITZ, SUSAN BABETTE SNELL, engr., architect; b. Aurora, Ill., Oct. 7, 1952; d. Robert Donald and Carole Marie (Lizer) Snell; B.S. with distinction, Purdue U., 1972; M.Arch., U. Ill., 1979; cert. with honors U. Aberdeen (Scotland), 1968; postgrad. (M.A. equivalency) No. Ill. U., 1975; m. Richard Lyon Horwitz, Apr. 30, 1982. Designer, Holland House, Inc., Ann Arbor, Mich., 1972-73; mgr. Prange & Co., Madison, Wis., 1975-76; staff architect, structural engr. Caterpillar Tractor Co., Aurora, Ill., 1978—. Mem. Aurora Preservation Commn., 1977—; v.p. Paramount Arts Center Assn., Aurora, 1977-80; v.p. Waubonsee Child Devel. Center, Sugar Grove, Ill., 1979-81; pres. Fox Valley Symphony Guild, 1981—; bd. dirs. YWCA Aurora, 1980—, Aurora Hist. Soc., 1979-81; v.p. Ill. Preservation Commn., 1982—. Recipient Aurora Mayor's award, 1979; Ill. Senate Resolution, 1980; Woman of Year award YWCA, 1980. Mem. Am. Inst. Plant Engrs., Landmarks Preservation Council Ill., Nat. Trust Hist. Preservation, AAUW (dir., 1977-79), Women in Mgmt. (dir. 1980-82), Madison Panhellenic Alumnae Council (pres. 1975-76), Zeta Tau Alpha. Republican. Episcopalian. Contbr. articles to profl. jours. Home: Towerview 503 W Downer Pl Aurora IL 60506 Office: Caterpillar Tractor Co Box 348 Aurora IL 60507

KAUNITZ, RITA DAVIDSON, religious orgn. ofcl.; b. N.Y.C., Apr. 18, 1922; d. David and Bessie (Golden) Davidson; B.A. magna cum laude, N.Y. U., 1942; M.A., Columbia U., 1946; Ph.D., Radcliffe Coll., 1951; m. Paul E. Kaunitz, Aug. 10, 1947; children—Victoria Moss, Jonathan Davidson, Andrew Moss. Adminstrv. asst. OPA, Washington, 1943-44; columnist planning and housing Progressive Architecture mag., N.Y.C., 1944-46; editor Plan for Rezoning, 1st year's studies, N.Y.C., 1948-49; asso. editor bull. housing and town and country planning UN Secretariat, 1950-52; cons. Center Housing, Bldg. and Planning, UN Secretariat, 1960-66; research asso. grad. program in city planning Yale U., 1955-57; policy and program specialist Model Cities Program, Bridgeport, Conn., 1969; project dir. Conn. Issues and Answers, Regional Plan Assn., N.Y.C., 1976-78; sci. adv. L.I. Sound Regional Study, New Eng. River Basin Commn., New Haven, 1972-75; cons. individual risk-taking and health care N.Y. U. Law Sch., 1978—; asst. to dir. N.Y. chpt. Am. Jewish Com., N.Y.C., 1980—; vis. lectr. U. R.I., 1967-69; cons. in field, condr. seminars, planning cons., 1965—. Mem. Conn. Clean Air Commn., 1969-71; chmn. reorgn. task force Conn. Public Utilities Control Authority, 1976-77; chmn. Conn. com. public info. Commr.'s Council on High Blood Pressure, 1978—; chmn. com. housing and urban affairs Nat. Council of Women, N.Y.C., 1968-70; bd. dirs. Woman's Place, Darien, 1976-80. Recipient service citation Fulbright-Hayes Fellowships, 1975. Mem. Am. Soc. Planning Ofcls. (dir. 1973-76), Am. Inst. Planners. Democrat. Club: Lower Fairfield County Radcliffe. Author articles. Address: 14 Red Coat Rd Westport CT 06880

KAUS, MARGARET ELIZA, ednl. cons.; b. Stillwater, Minn., July 9, 1934; d. Clarence Daniel and Beulah Mae (Nicol) Shingledecker; B.S., Evergreen State Coll., Olympia, Wash., 1973; m. William Kaus, Dec. 17, 1968. Office mgr. Hoerner Waldorf Corp., St. Paul, 1961-68; career planning placement dir. Green River Coll., Auburn, Wash., 1970-74, asso. dean instrn.-continuing edn., 1974-82; cons. in field. Served with USAF, 1955-61. Mem. Nat. Career Devel. Assn., Nat. Identification Women in Higher Edn., N.W. Adult Edn. Assn., Wash. Continuing Edn. Dirs. Assn. Republican. Episcopalian. Office: 12401 SE 320th St Auburn WA 98002

KAUSKAY, ROBERTA LAURA, librarian; b. Buffalo, July 14, 1916; d. Robert Allen and Emma Barbara (Keil) Bork; B.A., Washington U., St. Louis, 1937; M.L.S., U. Okla., Norman, 1965; m. Stanley Stuart Kauskay, Jan. 11, 1946; children—Karen Leola, Linda Christine. Case worker Erie County Dept. Social Work, Buffalo, 1939-42; adminstrv. asst. USAAF, Buffalo, 1942-47; tchr., Rome, N.Y., 1957-64; grad. asst. Sch. Library Sci., U. Okla., 1965, social scis. librarian, 1965-66, dir. Library Center, Office Research Adminstrn., 1966-76, dir. Media Resources and Guidance Center, 1976—. Mem. ALA, Internat. Assn. Sch. Librarianship (charter), Am. Assn. Sch. Libraries, Assn. Ednl. Communications and Tech., Assn. Supervision and Curriculum Devel., NEA, AAUP, Southwestern Library Assn., Okla. Library Assn., Okla. Assn. Sch. Librarians and Media Specialists, Okla. Assn. Ednl. Communications and Tech. Home: PO Box 665 Norman OK 73070 Office: 1808 Newton Dr Norman OK 73069

KAUSS, ROBERTA CRAIG, investment banker; b. Pitts., Feb. 12, 1938; d. Robert Martin and Esther Mabel (Johnson) Craig; bus. degree Robert Morris Coll., Pitts., 1957; postgrad. U. Pitts., 1957, 58, N.Y. Inst. Fin., 1975; children—Kimberly, Robert, Lee. Petro-chem. demonstrator Consol. Natural Gas Co., Clarksburg, W.Va., 1966-68; stockbroker Moore, Leonard & Lynch, Indiana, Pa., 1975-80; fin. planner, v.p. Parker/Hunter, Inc., Indiana, 1980—; mem. Pa. Gov.'s Task Force Team for Schs. Bd. dirs. Vis. Nurses Assn. Indiana County, Indiana County Guidance Center, Pitts. Episcopal Diocese; lay reader Episcopal Ch.; mem. deferred gifts com. Indiana U. of Pa. Mem. Nat. Assn. Securities Dealers. Republican. Club: Zonta (pres. 1981). Home: 528 Chestnut St Indiana PA 15701 Office: 20 S 6th St Indiana PA 15701

KAUTENBURG, LOUISE MARIE, real estate broker; b. Burlington, Wis., July 9, 1945; d. Edward Raymond and Mary Ann (Johns) Kober; grad. Wis. Sch. of Real Estate, 1977; m. Loren L. Kautenburg, Jan. 11, 1964; children—Paul Alan, Keven Garrett. Retail sales, Nat. Foods, Kenosha, Wis., 1967-77; sales asso. Stanich Realty, Inc., Kenosha,

1977-78, br. sales mgr., 1978—. Mem. Nat. Assn. Realtors, Wis. Realtors Assn., Kenosha Bd. Realtors (ad hoc com., profl. standards com., bd. dirs.), Realtors Nat. Mktg. Inst., Wis. Realtors Honor Soc. Lutheran. Home: 8210 22 Ave Kenosha WI 53140 Office: 7520 39th Ave Kenosha WI 53142

KAWECKI, JEAN MARY, sculptor, gallery dir.; b. Liverpool, Eng., June 24, 1926; came to U.S., 1951, naturalized, 1961; d. Donald McRae and Doris (Hankey) Cameron; ed. Lowther Coll., Wales, Liverpool Coll. Art; m. Wladyslaw Kawecki, May 26, 1951; 1 son, Tim Stefan. Freelance artist, London, 1947-51; freelance illustrator Mitchell Pub. Co., N.Y.C., 1951-53, Tobias-Mayer-Nebenzahl, N.Y.C., 1958-66; sculptor, 1970—; one-man show Bergen Mus., 1981; exhibited widely in N.Y. and N.J.; represented in numerous corp. collections including Hoffman-LaRoche, Crum & Forster Ins. Co., Wolf Design Techniques, also over 250 pvt. collections; co-founder Doubletree Coop. Gallery Fine Art, 1974; judge art shows; organizer community shows. Recipient numerous sculpture awards, including Audubon Artists N.Y., 1978, Hudson Artists Bergen Mus., 1977, Short Hills Tri-State Show, 1976, Art Centre N.J., 1974, AAUW Ann., 1972. Mem. Artists Equity Assn. N.J., Artists Equity N.Y. Home: 28 Mountainside Park Terr Upper Montclair NJ 07043

KAY, ELIZABETH CAMP, writer, dir., producer media materials; b. San Jose, Calif.; d. Edwin Lee and Helen (Boyd) Camp; student Whittier Coll., 1928-29; B.A., U. So. Calif., 1933; M.A., 1965; children—Sharon, Debriana; m. Joseph Vernor Voorhees, II, Sept. 4, 1982. Tchr., Los Angeles City Sch. Dist., 1958-73; writer, dir., producer film-multi-media prodns. Mich. State U., 1973-78; ind. film-media prodns., 1978-80; writer, 1980—; writer, dir., producer Lizbeth Camp Communications, La Canada, Calif., 1965—. Mem. Am. Soc. Profl. and Exec. Women, AAUW, Women in Communications, Nat. Assn. Edn. Young Children, Edn. Assn. Alumni U. So. Calif., Pi Lambda Theta, Delta Kappa Gamma. Republican. Presbyn. Home: La Canada CA 91011

KAY, HERMA HILL, educator; b. Orangeburg, S.C., Aug. 18, 1934; d. Charles Esdorn and Herma Lee (Crawford) Hill; B.A., So. Meth. U., 1956; J.D., U. Chgo., 1959. Admitted to Calif. bar, 1960; law clk. to Justice Roger Traynor, Calif. Supreme Ct., 1959-60; asst. prof. law U. Calif. , Berkeley, 1960-62, asso. prof., 1962, prof., 1963—, dir. family law project, 1964-67, chairperson acad. senate, 1973-74; co-reporter uniform marriage and divorce law Nat. Conf. Commrs. on Uniform State Laws, 1968-70; vis. prof. U. Manchester (Eng.), 1972, Harvard U., 1976; mem. Gov.'s Commn. on Family, 1966. Trustee Russell Sage Found., chmn. bd. trustees, 1980—; chmn. bd. dirs. Equal Rights Advs., Inc., 1977—. Fellow Center for Advanced Study in Behavioral Scis., Palo Alto, 1963-64. Mem. Calif. State Bar Assn. (mem. family law com. 1964-67), Calif. Women Lawyers (bd. govs. 1975-77), Order of Coif (nat. v.p. 1980, nat. pres. 1983-85). Democrat. Club: Zonta (pres. 1980-81) (Berkeley). Contbg. author: Law in Culture and Society, 1969; co-author Text, Cases and Materials on Sex-Based Discrimination, 1974, author 2d edit., 1981; Conflict of Laws: Cases, Comments, Questions, 2d edit., 1975, 3d edit., 1981; contbr. articles to profl. jours. Office: Sch Law U Calif Berkeley CA 94720

KAY, KARYN MARCIA, filmaker, writer; b. Chgo., Aug. 31, 1948; d. Henry and Miriam (Zinman) K.; B.A. in English, U. Wis., Madison, 1973; M.A. in Film, Northwestern U., 1977; teaching fellow Columbia U., 1977-79. Editorial staff, Northwestern Film Reader, 1974; script cons., prodn. asst. WHA-TV, Madison, 1973; asst. editor, research asso. History of Wisconsin (Alice Smith), 1972; asst. editor Close-ups: The Movie Star, 1978; instr. film and English, Livingston Coll. of Rutgers U., 1975-79; script cons. Empty Suitcases (Bette Gordon), 1979-80; instr. film Columbia U., 1977-80; instr. film and English SUNY, Old Westbury, 1980-81; theater and media tchr. Learning to Read Through the Arts, N.Y.C. Bd. Edn., 1981—, also instr. English Bklyn. Coll., 1981— and instr. film C.W. Post U., Greenvale, N.Y., 1981—; lectr.; selection com. N.Y. Women's Film Festival, 1976; retrospective com. UN Festival of Women in the Arts, 1975; festival com. Films by Women: The Chgo. Women's Film Festival, 1974; organizing com. Midwest Women's Film Conf., Madison, 1973; mem. N.J. Women's Writing Workshop, 1977-79, union film com. U. Wis., 1972-73; writer; books include: Myrna Loy, 1977; books edited include: (with Gerald Peary) Women and the Cinema: A Critical Anthology, 1977; editorial bd. The Velvet Light Trap, 1972-73; fine arts editor The Daily Cardinal, 1973; filmaker; films include: The Fruit at the Bottom of the Bowl, 1974; She (Overlooking, Overworking) While..., 1979; Someone Else's Clothes, 1980; 149, 1981. Bd. dirs. Dayton House, Madison, 1969. Home: 58 Middagh St Apt 6 Brooklyn NY 11201

KAY, LISAN, dancer, dance tchr.; b. Conneaut, Ohio, May 4, 1910; d. Jay Clyde and Lisbeth Maude (Pond) Hathaway; student public schs., Conneaut; m. Yeichi Nimura, Nov. 29, 1964. Mem. Chgo. Civic Opera Co. Ballet, 1926-27; soloist Pavley-Oukrainsky Ballet, 1928-31; Am. scholar to 1st Internat. Dance Congress, Buxton, Eng., 1932; partner of Yeichi Nimura in tours of Europe, Palestine, Egypt, U.S., Can., Cuba and Hawaii, 1932-40; instr., asso. Ballet Arts Sch., Carnegie Hall, N.Y.C., 1940—, Ballet Arts of Carnegie Hall in Tokyo, 1969; tchr., dance cons., 1938-64; tchr. master class, Tokyo, 1980. solo concerts, N.Y.C., 1941-43; lead dancer mus. Lute Song, 1945-46, Desert Song, 1946-47; dance dir. Republic Pictures-N.Y. Times Style Show, 1943-44. Universalist. Author: Biography of Nimura, 1971.

KAY, M. JANE, utility exec.; b. Detroit, Aug. 31, 1925; d. Albert A. and Celia R. (Betzing) K.; B.S., U. Detroit, 1948; M.A., Wayne State U., 1952; M.B.A., U. Mich., 1963. Sr. personnel interviewer employment Detroit Edison Co., 1948-60, personnel coordinator for women, 1960-65, office employment adminstr., 1965-70, gen. employment adminstr., 1970-71, dir. personnel services, 1971-72, mgr. employee relations, 1972-77, asst. v.p. indsl. relations, 1977-78, v.p. employee relations, 1978-82, v.p. adminstrn., 1982—; tchr. U. Detroit Evening Coll. Bus. and Adminstrn., 1964-75; seminar leader div. mgmt. edn. U. Mich., 1968-74, Waterloo Mgmt. Edn. Centre, 1972-76. Mem. Mich. Employment Security Adv. Council, 1967—; chmn. bd. dirs. Detroit Inst. Commerce, 1976-79. Recipient Alumni Tower award U. Detroit, 1967; Headliner award women Wayne State U., 1970, Wayne State U. Alumni Achievement award, 1974, Career Achievement award Profl. Panhellenic Assn., 1973; named one of Top Ten Women of Detroit, 1970; Alumnus of Yr., U. Detroit, 1981; cert. Adminstrv. Mgmt. Soc., Am. Soc. Personnel Adminstrn. Mem. Internat. Assn. Personnel Women (pres. 1969-70), Women's Econ. Club (v.p. 1971-72, pres. 1972-73), Personnel Women Detroit (pres. 1960-61), U. Detroit Alumni Assn. (pres. 1964-66), Phi Gamma Nu (nat. v.p. 1955-57). Office: 2000 2d Ave Detroit MI 48226

KAY, MARY ELLEN CROXTON, brokerage exec.; b. Sewickley, Pa., June 21, 1947; d. Edmond and Virginia (Stueber) Kay; student Point Park Jr. Coll., 1964-65, Carnegie-Mellon U., 1965-69, N.Y. Inst. Fin., 1970-73; m. Randolph Rudisill Croxton, Apr. 19, 1969. Stockbroker, Dupont-Walston, N.Y.C., 1971-73, Shearson-Am. Express, N.Y.C., 1973-75; v.p. A.G. Becker, N.Y.C. 1975—; pres. K & W Music, N.Y.C., 1980—, Easy Street Music Prodns., N.Y.C., 1979—; mus. performer, writer 1978-81; cons. in field. Adv. bd. First Women's Bank, N.Y.C., 1974-75. Recipient Lyric Competition award Internat. Am. Song Festival, 1981. Mem. Am. Soc. Composers Authors and Publs. Author: A Time to Remember, 1980. Home: 16 E 84th St Apt 3-B New York NY 10028 Office: 55 Water St New York NY 10041

KAY, M(ARY) PATRICIA, bank exec.; b. Pitts., Oct. 13, 1953; d. Edward W. and Mary Margaret (Dixon) K.; B.A., Syracuse U., 1975, M.B.A., Ind. U., 1978; postgrad. U. Wis., 1979-80. Student tchr., Syracuse, N.Y., 1974; mgmt. trainee 1st Wis. Nat. Bank, Milw., 1978, loan officer, 1980; asst. v.p. Md. Nat. Bank, Washington, 1980—. Adv. to United Way Campaign, Milw., 1979; fund raiser YMCA, 1979-80, Girl Scouts U.S.A., 1979; mem. Republican Nat. Com., 1976—. Mem. MBA Assn., Alumni Assn. of Syracuse U., Ind. U. Alumni Assn., Delta Gamma (v.p. 1974-75), Phi Sigma Iota. Roman Catholic. Club: Congressional Country. Home: 4200 Massachusetts Ave NW #608 Washington DC 20016 Office: Md Nat Bank 1110 Vermont Ave NW Suite 1000 Washington DC 20016

KAY, PATRICIA M., educator; b. Bklyn., June 22, 1934; d. Lawrence Peter and Helena Frieda (Seifert) McGoldrick; B.S., Cornell U., 1956; Ed.D., Rutgers U., 1969; m. Morris I. Kay; children—Mary Katherine, Andrew Stephen. Asst. prof., coordinator research and evaluation, div. tchr. edn. CUNY, 1970-73; asst. prof., assoc. prof., prof. edn. and ednl. psychology Baruch Coll. and Grad. Center, 1973—; cons. in field; mem. N.Y. State Tchr. Edn., Cert. and Practices Bd., 1980—. Mem. Metuchen (N.J.) Bd. Edn., 1971-77; trustee Chamber Symphony N.J., 1976-78, N.J. Youth Symphony, 1980—. Mem. Am. Ednl. Research Assn., Nat. Council on Measurement in Edn., Am. Psychol. Assn., Kappa Delta Pi. Cons. editor Jour. Exptl. Edn., guest editor Jour. Tchr. Edn.; contbr. articles to profl. jours. Home: 5 Mark Circle Metuchen NJ 08840 Office: 17 Lexington Ave New York NY 10010

KAYE, CELIA ILENE, physician; b. Highland Park, Mich., June 12, 1943; d. Mitchell and Mary (Lazarecky) Kaye; B.S., Wayne State U., 1965, M.S., 1968, M.D., 1969; Ph.D. in Biochemistry, Northwestern U., 1975; m. Tod B. Sloan, June 26, 1973; children—Gwendolin Kaye, Heather Aieleen. Dir. div. genetics Cook County (Ill.) Hosp., 1975-80; dir. med. genetics U. Ill.-Chgo. Center Craniofacial Anomalies, 1975—; asso. prof., 1977—; dir. sect. genetics Luth. Gen. Hosp., Park Ridge, Ill., 1980—. Chmn. health profl. adv. com. Chgo. Met. chpt. March of Dimes-Birth Defects Found., 1980—, mem. exec. bd., 1980; mem. exec. bd. El Valor Corp. for Handicapped Citizens, 1980-81. NIH fellow, 1974. Mem. Am. Soc. Human Gnetics, Am. Acad. Pediatrics, Soc. Pediatric Research, Soc. Inherited Metabolic Disease, Phi Beta Kappa, Alpha Omega Alpha. Congeregationalist. Contbr. articles to profl. jours. Home: 102 5th St Wilmette IL 60091 Office: 1775 Dempster Park Ridge IL 60068

KAYE, JUDITH SMITH (MRS. STEPHEN RACKOW KAYE), lawyer; b. Monticello, N.Y., Aug. 4, 1938; d. Benjamin and Lena (Cohen) Smith; B.A., Barnard Coll., 1958; LL.B. cum laude, N.Y. U., 1962; m. Stephen Rackow Kaye, Feb. 11, 1964; children—Luisa Marian, Jonathan Mackey, Gordon Bernard. Admitted to N.Y. bar, 1963; atty. firm Sullivan & Cromwell, N.Y.C., 1962-64; staff atty. IBM, N.Y.C., 1964-65; mem. firm Olwine Connelly Chase O'Donnell & Weyher, N.Y.C., 1969—; v.p., bd. dirs. Legal Aid Soc., 1976—. Trustee, vice chmn. Clients Security Fund, State of N.Y.; mem. Pres. Carter's Nominating Commn. for 2d circuit judges, 1979-80. Mem. Am. (litigation sect.), N.Y. State (internat. law com. 1962-63, vice chmn. ethics com. 1977—) bar assns., Assn. Bar City N.Y. (adminstrv. law com. 1972-75, ethics com. 1975-78, fed. cts. com. 1978-79, exec. com. 1979—), Am. Judicature Soc. (dir. 1980—). Home: 101 Central Park W New York NY 10023 Office: 299 Park Ave New York NY 10017

KAYE, LORI, publishing co. exec.; b. N.Y.C.; d. Eldin Bert and Katherine Angeline Onsgard; student Detroit Inst. Art, 1951, 56, U. N.Mex., 1960. Actress, radio and TV commls., 1951-82; actress Warner Brothers, 1960-64; dir., v.p. John Robert Powers Schs., Los Angeles, 1961-71; v.p. Electron Industries, Torrance, Calif., 1963-65; owner, v.p., Lawrence Leon Photography Studio, Los Angeles, 1964-68; pres. Lori Kaye Cosmetics, Hollywood, Calif., 1964-70; co-owner, v.p. K and S Employment, Calif. Fashion Mart, 1965-67; dir., internat. cons. Airline Schs. Pacific, Van Nuys, Calif., 1972-74; dir. Caroline Leonetti Ltd. Sch., Hollywood, 1976-79; internat. cons. Internat. Career Acad., Van Nuys, 1978—, Glendale Coll. Bus. and Paramed. (Calif.), 1980—, Acad. Pacific, Hollywood, 1981—; pres. Molori Publs., Studio City, Calif., 1981—; cons. A&T Inst. Travel and Tourism, 1982; lectr., 1969—. Dir. project Camarillo State Hosp., 1963-69; cons. Job Corps. Recipient Mental Health Achievement award, 1967. Mem. Nat. Assn. Female Execs., AAU, Screen Actors Guild, AFTRA, U.S. Masters-Internat. Swim Club, Nat. Geog. Soc. Paintings included in UNICEF collection, 1957; hostess TV talk show The New You, KTTV, Hollywood, 1964-65. Office: Molori Publs 11684 Ventura Blvd Suite 134 Studio City CA 91604

KAYE, MARGARET HENRY, public relations ofcl.; b. Miami, Fla., Oct. 29, 1927; d. William Bryan and Helen Rita (Toomey) Brewer; student Palm Beach (Fla.) Jr. Coll., 1945-46, Emory U., 1947-49; B.A., Agnes Scott Coll., 1949; postgrad. Atlanta div. U. Ga., 1950, Miss. U. for Women, 1974-75; m. John Robertson Henry, May 14, 1955 (dec. Nov. 1978); children—John Robertson, Taylor, Margaret Mary, Bryan; m. 2d, John Morgan Kaye, July 24, 1981. Asst. news editor Atlanta Suburban Reporter, 1949-50; staff corr., White House corr. Internat. News Service, Atlanta and Washington, 1950-54; copywriter radio sta. WGST, Atlanta, 1954; woman's editor Jackson (Miss.) State Times, 1955; news columnist, feature writer Birmingham (Ala.) News, 1957-63; spl. writer pub. relations Miss. U. for Women, Columbus, 1970-75, asst. dir. pub. info., 1975-80, dir., 1980—; guest script writer, master of ceremonies WCBI-TV, Columbus, 1971; dir. Mchts. and Farmers Bank, Columbus. Publicity chmn. Nat. Assn. Jr. Auxs., 1962-63. Named Public Relations Practitioner of Yr., Public Relations Assn. Miss., 1981. Mem. Nat. Fedn. Press Women (nat., state winner writing contests), AAUW (pres. Columbus br. 1960-62), Miss. Press Women (v.p. 1972-74, Woman of Achievement 1975), Women in Communications (sponsor Miss. U. for Women chpt. 1972—, v.p. region 8, 1975-78, dir. Miss. U. for Woman Centennial 1984-85), Am. Coll. Public Relations Assn., Public Relations Assn. of Miss. (dir. 1982—), Columbus-Lowndes C. of C. (dir., mem. mil. affairs com. 1979—). Club: Soroptimists (charter mem., dir. Columbus 1973-74). Home: 416 7th St N Columbus MS 39701

KAYE, NORA (NORA KOREFF), choreographer, dancer, ballet co. artistic adminstr.; b. N.Y.C., student at Met. Opera Ballet Sch.; m. Herbert Ross, 1959. Ballet debut with Met. Opera's children's ballet; joined Am. Ballet Theatre, N.Y.C., 1939; with N.Y.C. Ballet, 1951-54; returned to Am. Ballet Theatre, 1954-60, asso. artistic dir., 1977—; co-founder, prima ballerina Ballet of the Two Worlds, 1959-60; ret. as dancer, 1961; asst. to Herbert Ross on films, including: Funny Lady, Play It Again, Sam, The Seven Percent Solution, The Sunshine Boys; producer film The Turning Point, Nijinsky, Pennies from Heaven. Address: care Am Ballet Theatre 890 Broadway New York NY 10003

KAYSER, JUNEROSE JOAN, transp. co. exec.; b. Chgo., Oct. 27, 1924; d. Fred E. and Rose Barbara (Reikowski) Maynard; student public schs., Chgo.; m. Harold Melvin Kayser, Nov. 26, 1943; children—Harold Melvin, Kathaleen Rose Kayser McConathy. Sec., Bandy & Yeoman Co., Merchandise Mart, Chgo., 1942-43, Blue Cross/Blue Shield, Chgo., 1943-45; sch. sec. Sch. Nursing, Bryan Meml. Hosp., Lincoln, Nebr., 1955-69, Coll. Home Econs., U. Nebr., Lincoln, 1968-73; partner, v.p., sec. Melro Transport, Inc., Lincoln, 1973—; part owner Kayser Farms, 1946—; partner Kayser Ins. Agy., Palmyra, Nebr., 1965—. Health chmn. Lancaster County (Nebr.) Extension Council, 1959-61, chmn., 1964-66; rep. for extension council Nebr. Heart Council, 1961-62. Recipient Homemaker's award Ladies C. of C., 1963; certs. of appreciation Heart Fund, 4-H, Extension Service. Mem. Nebr. Fedn. Bus. and Profl. Women's Clubs (dist. II dir. 1979-81). Lutheran. Clubs: Lincoln Bus. and Profl. Women's, Ladies Aid and Luth. Women's Missionary League (zone pres. 1980-82), Busy Belles Extension (organizer). Address: Route 8 10171 Old Cheney Rd Lincoln NE 68506

KAYWOOD, MIRIAM, city ofcl.; b. N.Y.C., Dec. 14, 1922; d. William and Sandra (Seldin) K.; grad. high sch., 1940; m. Richard Kaywood, Feb. 28, 1941; children—Barry Gordon, Judith Loren. Legal and exec. sec., N.Y.C., N.Mex., 1940-47, Anaheim, Calif., 1961-65; city councilwoman City of Anaheim, 1974—, mayor pro tem, 1978-79, mem. Park and Recreation Commn., 1974—, chmn. storm drain bond com., 1980; mem. Sanitation Dist. Orange County, 1974-77; mem. So. Calif. Assn. Govts. exec. com., 1975-79. Planning commr., Anaheim, 1970-73, chmn. pro tem, 1972-73; resdl. chmn. United Way, Anaheim, 1973; mem. City Bond Com., 1970-71; mem. Citizens Capital Improvement Com., 1968; pres. Joint Fire Tng. Tower; chmn. Orange County Subregional Planning Council. Recipient award Cypress Coll., 1977. Mem. Am. Soc. Public Adminstrn., LWV, Calif. Elected Women's Assn. for Edn. and Research, Anaheim C. of C. (life women's div., award 1967), Anaheim Beautiful, Anaheim Art Assn., Anaheim Hist. Mus., Found. Culture and Arts, Friends of Library, Orange County Performing Arts Center. Republican. Clubs: Ebell (Anaheim); Calif. State U. Faculty Wives (Long Beach). Office: City Hall 200 S Anaheim Blvd Anaheim CA 92805

KAZANJIAN, WENDY COFFELT, educator, assn. exec.; b. Hollywood, Calif., Aug. 21, 1946; d. R. Wendell and Dolores (Storm) Coffelt; B.A., U. So. Calif., 1968, M.S. in Edn., 1970; m. Phillip Kazanjian, Feb. 5, 1972. Tchr., Los Angeles Unified Sch. Dist., 1970—; dir. Project Cold, ESEA Title IV-C Fed. Grant, Los Angeles, 1980-81; master/demonstration tchr. U. So. Calif., Los Angeles and Calif. State U., Los Angeles, 1972—; exec. dir. Polar Regions Soc., Inc., 1982—. Dir. youth programs United Fedn. Republican Women, 1980—; mem. exec. council law student sect. Los Angeles County Bar Assn., 1980—; active Am. Heart Assn., 1975—. Recipient Nat. Tchrs. medal Freedoms Found. Valley Forge, 1976; U.S. Congl. Record Tribute, 1977; Freedoms Found. scholar, 1978; Robert A. Taft scholar, 1979. Mem. U. So. Calif. Educare, Alpha Phi Alumni Assn. Republican. Office: 617 W 7th St Suite 300 Los Angeles CA 90017

KAZLO, MARTHA PEYTON, psychologist; b. Cumberland, Md., Nov. 18, 1945; d. Orvel Patrick and Henrietta Maria (Peyton) K.; B.S., U. Md., 1967; M.Ed., 1972, Ph.D., 1975. Asst. dir. commuter services U. Md., College Park, 1973-74, psychol. intern Counseling Center, 1974-75; psychologist Calif. State Coll., San Bernardino, 1975—; mgmt. cons. in assertiveness tng., 1976—. Bd. dirs. YWCA, 1977-79; pres. NOW, Riverside, Calif., 1977. Mem. Am. Psychol. Assn., Am. Personnel and Guidance Assn., Am. Coll. Personnel Assn., Am. Assn. Sex Educators, Counselors and Therapists, Nat. Women's Polit. Caucus. Home: PO Box 321 Cedarpines Park CA 92322 Office: Counseling Center Calif State Coll San Bernardino CA 92407

KAZO, CHRISTINE MARIE, computers corp. ofcl.; b. Derby, Conn., Dec. 8, 1946; d. Frank Charles and Ann Marie (Malec) K.; B.A., So. Conn. State Coll., 1972; M.B.A., Babson Coll., 1982. Mgr. Elderly Services, Concord, N.H., 1976-77; central revenue acctg. supr., promotion, mktg. specialist II Digital Equipment Corp., Marlboro, Mass., 1977—; with Kazo Consultants. Contbr. mktg. articles in field to publs. Home: 10 Westwood Rd Lexington MA 02173

KEALIINOHOMOKU, JOANN WHEELER, anthropologist, educator; b. Kansas City, Mo.; B.S.S., Northwestern U., 1955; M.A., 1965; Ph.D., Ind. U., 1976; 1 child, Halla K. Mem. faculty No. Ariz. U., Flagstaff, 1970-72, 75—, asso. prof. anthropology, 1980—; mem. faculty World Campus Alfoat, fall 1972, 73; resident scholar Sch. Am. Research, Santa Fe, 1974-75; vis. faculty U. Hawaii, Hilo, spring 1973, summer 1973, 74. Bd. dirs. Native Americans for Community Action, Flagstaff Indian Center, 1977—, sec., 1980-82. Grantee, Am. Philos. Soc. Wenner Gren Found.; Weatherhead fellow Sch. Am. Research, 1974-75; research fellow East-West Center, 1981. Fellow Current Anthropology; mem. Soc. Ethnomusicology (councilor; co founder Southwestern chpt.), Dance Research Center (charter), Cross Cultural Dance Resources (founder 1981). Contbr. articles to profl. jours. Home: 518 S Agassiz St Flagstaff AZ 86001 Office: CU Box 15200 No Ariz U Flagstaff AZ 86011

KEAN, OPAL NORRIS MELLOWAY, social worker; b. Columbia, Mo., Nov. 19, 1906; d. John Franklin and Dottie May (Maupin) Melloway; A.B., U. Mo., 1932; M.S.W., Washington U., 1948; m. Robert E. Kean, June 14, 1933. Caseworker, Family Service, Kansas City, Mo., 1932-45; med. social worker Jewish Family and Children Service, Kansas City, 1947-55; dir. social service dept., psychiat. social worker Menorah Med. Center, Kansas City, 1955-66; pvt. practice as psychiat. social worker, Kansas City, 1966—. Mem. Nat. Assn. Social Workers, Acad. Cert. Social Workers (field work instr. 1950-54), Phi Beta Kappa, Alpha Kappa Delta. Methodist. Home and Office: 631 E 74th St Kansas City MO 64131

KEANE, MICHELLE ANNE, broadcasting exec.; b. Pitts., Sept. 10, 1955; d. John Edgar and Janet Marie (Mackall) K.; B.A. in Urban Affairs, U. Pitts., 1977, M.B.A., 1982. TV account exec. sta. KDKA-TV2, Pitts., 1977—. Anna R.D. Gillespie scholar, 1976-77; Pa. Senatorial scholar, 1976-77. Mem. Am. Women in Radio and TV, Pitts. Radio and TV Club, Pitts. Turkish-Am. Assn., Omicron Delta Kappa, Chi Omega, Rho Lambda. Club: Pitts. Press. Home: 2247 Manor Ave Pittsburgh PA 15218 Office: 1 Gateway Center Pittsburgh PA 15222

KEARBY, NORMA LOU, physician; b. Dallas, Nov. 14, 1930; d. John Gallatin and Julia Vivian (Drew) Kearby; student Rice U., 1948-49; B.S., Baylor U., 1952; M.D., U. Tex., 1955. Intern Hotel Dieu Hosp., New Orleans, 1955-56; resident otolaryngology Charity Hosp., New Orleans, 1956-59; fellow Ochsner Found. Hosp., 1957; practice medicine specializing in otolaryngology Browne-McHardy Clinic, New Orleans, 1959—; mem. exec. com Eye, Ear, Nose and Throat Hosp., 1967-71, v.p. staff, 1969-70, sec.-treas. staff, 1973-74; chief dept. otolaryngology and mem. exec. com. East Jefferson Hosp., Metairie, La., 1973-74; asso. prof. dept. otolaryngology La. State U. Med. Sch., 1968—. Bd. dirs. St. Marks Community Center, New Orleans Speech and Hearing Center. Diplomate Am. Bd. Otolaryngology. Fellow Am. Acad. Ophthalmology and Otolaryngology; mem. Pan-Am. Assn. Otolaryngology, So., Jefferson Parish med. assns., La. Med. Soc., La.-Miss. Ophthalmology and Otolaryngology Assn., Centurion Club Deafness Research, Am. Council Otolaryngology, Am. Assn. Phys. and Surg., DAR, La. Landmarks Soc., Vieux Carre Property Owners Assn., NOW, Nat. Gay Task Force, Am. Med. Women's Assn. Methodist (mem. council on ministry 1970—,

Commn. on Status and Role of Women, La. Conf.). Home: 1235 Decatur St New Orleans LA 70116 Office: 4315 Houma Blvd Metairie LA 70002

KEARIN, ANITA MARCELLA, bank pub. relations ofcl.; b. Chgo., July 24, 1924; d. Dennis A. and Anne M. (Brophy) K.; student pvt. schs., Chgo. Auditor, tax technician U.S. Treasury Dept., IRS, Chgo., 1943-68; clerical asst. Marshall Field & Co., Chgo., 1956-67; sales staff William Y. Gilmore & Sons, Oak Park, Ill., 1967; dir., sec. Triangle Mfg. Co., Clifford Peterson Tool Co., Chgo., 1968-71; mgr. Fed. Info. Center, GSA, Region V, Chgo., 1968-81; communications and pub. relations staff No. Trust Bank, Chgo., 1982—; coordinator Midwest Women and Bus. Conf., 1979, Twin Cities Women and Bus. Conf., 1980. Mem. Mayor's Com. for a Cleaner Chgo., Chgo. Beautiful Riverfront Com., 1958-64; mem. exec. bd. Chgo. Beautiful Com., 1964-77; v.p. Loretto Hosp. Women's Aux., 1965-66; asso. mem. Chgo. Policemen's Benefit and Welfare Assn., 1967-68; sec., dir. Chgo. Boosters League, 1968-77; mem. Mayor's Com. for Neighborhood Pride and Beautification, 1977; v.p. Beautiful Chgo. Com., 1978, mem. women's vol. bd., 1979; co-chmn. Chgo. Beautiful Awards Com., 1978; mem. Chgo. Outdoor Art League, 1978, Chgo. Council Fgn. Relations, 1978. Recipient Superior Work Performance awards U.S. Dept. Treasury, IRS, GSA, 1964, 71, 75, 80; First Lady of Day award Sta. WAIT, 1968; Pile of Gold award Chgo. Boosters League, 1971; Exceptional Service award GSA, 1981. Mem. Chgo. Press Club. Roman Catholic. Club: Chgo. and Cook County Democratic Women's. Office: 50 S LaSalle St Chicago IL 60675

KEARNEY, LOUISA DANIELS, mag. publisher; b. N.Y.C., Dec. 19, 1950; d. Henry and Virginia M. (Kaboolian) Daniels; B.A., Queens Coll., 1972; m. Stephen M. Kearney, June 2, 1973. Asst. controller Harper's Mag., N.Y.C., 1972-76, adminstrv. coordinator, 1976-79, asso. pub., 1980-82, pub., 1982—; fin. analyst Charter Pub. Co., N.Y.C., 1980; treas. Harper's Mag. Found. Recipient Citation of Accomplishment Nat. Council of Women, 1982. Office: 2 Park Ave New York City NY 10016

KEARNS, BESSIE JEAN RULEY, univ. ofcl.; b. Bell City, La.; d. Eugene Elvis and Bessie (Hebert) Ruley; B.S., McNeese State U., 1957; M.S., U. Ariz., 1958; Ph.D., Fla. State U., 1966; m. Desmond Patrick Kearns, Sept. 21, 1968. Instr., McNeese State U., Lake Charles, La., 1958-59; prof. U. Ariz., Tucson, 1959-78, chmn. div. child devel., 1975-76, asst. exec. v.p. U. Ariz., 1978—, dir. Foster Parents Tng. Project, on-site in-service tng. for paraprofls. Bur. Indian Affairs; AID design team mem. to Yemen Title XII Project; vis. prof. Philippine Women's U., Manila, 1960, U. B.C., 1962; Fulbright prof. Singapore Tchrs. Tng. Coll., 1967-68; summer prof. Fla. State U., 1966, Ohio U., 1966; vis. disting. prof. N.Mex. State U., 1982; cons. Bur. Indian Affairs. Mem. Mayor's Com. on Employment of Handicapped. Recipient John Henry Cardinal Newman faculty award, 1966; research grantee U. Ariz., 1976-80; recipient various grants Dept. Econ. Security. Mem. Nat. Assn. Edn. of Young Children, Ariz. Assn. Edn. of Young Children, Pima Council on Aging, Chinle Agy. Planning Com., Royal Soc. Medicine, Western Assn. Gerontology. Roman Catholic. Mem. sex edn. com. Tucson Sch. Dist. I; researcher multicultural childrearing practices and menopause perceptions; author manuals for nonprofls. working with children. Office: Adminstrn Bldg Rm 503 U Ariz Tucson AZ 85721

KEARSE, AMALYA LYLE, fed. judge; b. Vauxhall, N.J., June 11, 1937; d. Robert Freeman and Myra Lyle (Smith) K.; B.A., Wellesley Coll., 1959; J.D. cum laude, U. Mich., 1962. Admitted to N.Y. State bar, 1963, U.S. Supreme Ct. bar, 1967; asso. firm Hughes Hubbard & Reed, N.Y.C., 1962-69, partner, 1969-79; judge U.S. Ct. Appeals 2d Circuit, 1979—; lectr. evidence N.Y. U. Law Sch., 1968-69; bd. dirs. NAACP Legal Def. and Endl. Fund, 1977-79, Am. Contract Bridge League Nat. Laws Commn., 1975—; mem. Pres.'s Com. on Selection of Fed. Jud. Officers, 1977-78. Mem. Lawyers Com. for Civil Rights Under Law, 1970-79. Mem. Am. Law Inst., Assn. Bar City N.Y., Am. Bar Assn. Author: Bridge Conventions Complete, 1975; Bridge at Your Fingertips, 1979; translator, editor: Bridge Analysis, 1979; editor Ofcl. Ency. of Bridge, 3d edit., 1976. Nat. Women's Pairs Bridge Champion, 1971, 72. Mem. Charles Goren Editorial Bd., 1974—. Office: US Ct Appeals Foley Sq New York NY 10007

KEAS, JEAN HALE, YWCA exec.; b. Dallas, Sept. 8, 1943; d. Arthur Kenneth and Ruth (Price) Hale; B.A., Tex. Wesleyan Coll., 1965; m. William Wesley Keas, Jr., Nov. 17, 1973; children—Alisa Christine, Nathan Reuel. Dir. religious edn. First United Methodist Ch., Hurst, Tex., 1964-66; curriculum coordinator Dos Mundos Sch., Corpus Christi, 1970-72; dir. intervention center, law enforcement spl. project Corpus Christi YWCA, 1972-74, exec. dir. YWCA, 1974—. Adv. bd. Martineau Juvenile Hall, Corpus Christi, 1976—. Mem. S. Tex. Women's Forum (sec. 1979), Leadership Corpus Christi Alumni. Presbyterian. Clubs: Zonta, Order Rainbow Girls, Order Eastern Star. Office: 401 N Carancahua St Corpus Christi TX 78401

KEATING, ANNE ELIZABETH, social worker; b. Washington, Sept. 14, 1946; d. Louis Clark and Lucille Elizabeth (Tate) K.; student U. Ky., summer 1964, Instituto Tecnológico y de Estudios Superiores, Monterrey, Mex., summer 1965, Hamilton Coll., France, 1966-67; B.A., Coll. William and Mary, 1968; postgrad. U. Calgary (Alta., Can.), 1969-70; M.S.W. (NIMH scholar), U. Minn., 1972. Out-patient therapist, med. social service cons. Aroostook Mental Health Center, Ft. Kent, Maine, 1972-74; sr. caseworker Women and Infants Hosp. R.I., Providence, 1974-75; sr. social worker U. Ky. Med. Center, Lexington, 1975-79; child protective services specialist Youth Services Div., Bur. Social Services, Ky. Dept. Human Resources, Frankfort, 1979—; instr. med. knowledge for social professions U. Ky., fall 1978. Cert. social worker, Ky. Mem. Acad. Cert. Social Workers, Nat. Assn. Social Workers, Am. Public Welfare Assn., AAUW (br. v.p., program planning, chmn. hearing on needs of displaced homemakers, Lexington, 1979). Democrat. Presbyterian. Home: 608 Raintree Rd Lexington KY 40502

KEATING, BARBARA HELEN, marine geologist; b. Brooksville, Fla., Dec. 25, 1950; d. William Bernard and Rosabea (Hendricks) Keating; B.S., Fla. State U., 1971; M.S., U. Tex., 1975, Ph.D., 1976. Geophysicist, U. Hawaii, Honolulu, 1976—, asst. prof. oceanography, 1981—. NSF grantee, 1976—, Office Naval Research, 1978—, Geol. Soc. Am., 1974-75. Mem. Internat. Assn. Geomagetism and Aeronomy Working Groups, UNESCO, Soc. Exploration Geophysics (mem. com.), Geol. Soc. Am., Am. Geophys. Union, European Geophys. Soc. Soc. Econ. Paleontologists and Mineralogists, Internat. Assn. Geomagnetism and Aeronomy. Republican. Co-author: Initial Reports of the Deep Sea Drilling Project; contbr. articles to profl. jours. Home: 2432 Halenoho Pl Honolulu HI 96816 Office: 2525 Correa Rd Hawaii Inst of Geophysics Honolulu HI 96822

KEATING, GLADYS BROWN, state legislator; b. N.Y.C., Aug. 1, 1923; student Queens Coll., N.Y., Weatherford Coll., Tex., U. Va., George Mason U.; m. John A. Keating; children—John A., Lawrence P., Michael L., Margaret E. Jones, Eileen P. Mem. Va. Ho. Reps., 1978—. Exec. bd., v.p. Va. Citizens Consumer Council; state affairs chmn. Fairfax County Democratic Com., 1974-77; mem. Va. State Central Democratic Com., 1980—; mem. Consumer-Industry Telephone Solicitation Panel. Mem. Brookland-Bush Hill Citizens Assn. (past pres.), Bus. and Profl. Women's Club. Democrat. Club: Toastmistress. Office: Va Ho Dels State Capitol Richmond VA 23219 *

KEATING, RITA BERTHA, med. technologist; b. Franklin, N.H., Apr. 5, 1932; d. Thomas Joseph and Bertha Sarah (Welters) K.; B.S. in Biology, Mt. St. Mary Coll., 1955; postgrad. Rivier Coll., 1979—. Intern in med. tech. Bishop De Goesbriand Hosp., Burlington, Vt. 1955, med. technologist 1955-60, asst. chief med. tech., head blood bank 1961-62; head technologist bacteriology lab. Suburban Clin. Lab., Silver Spring Md., 1962-68; supr. blood bank, Instr. St. John's Hosp., Lowell, Mass. 1971—; supr. blood bank, instr. U. Lowell 1971—. Mem. Am. Assn. Blood Banks, Mass. Assn. Blood Banks, Am. Soc. Clin. Pathologists. Roman Catholic. Club: Catholic Daughters Am. Home: 657 Robbins Ave Apt 58 Dracut MA 01826 Office: Hospital Dr Lowell MA 01852

KEATON, DIANE, actress; b. Calif.; student Neighborhood Playhouse, N.Y.C., 1968. Appeared on New York stage in Hair, 1968, Play It Again Sam, 1971, The Primary English Class, 1976; appeared in numerous films, including Lovers and Other Strangers, 1970, Play It Again Sam, 1972, The Godfather, 1972, Sleeper, 1973, The Godfather Part 2, 1974, Love and Death, 1975, I Will-I Will-For Now, 1975, Harry and Walter Go To New York, 1976, Annie Hall, 1977, Looking for Mr. Goodbar, 1977, Interiors, 1978, Manhattan, 1977, Reds, 1981, Shoot the Moon, 1982. Recipient Best Actress award N.Y. Film Critics Circle, 1977, Nat. Soc. Film Critics, 1977; Golden Globe award, 1978; Acad. award for best actress, 1978. Office: care Arlyne Rothberg Inc 145 Central Park W New York NY 10023 *

KEATZ, HERTA ELIZABETH HOPFENSITZ, ins. co. exec.; b. N.Y.C.; d. William and Laura (Hindle) Hopfensitz; B.S., Drexel U.; m. W. Martin Keatz, Jan. 8, 1969. With Equitable Life Assurance Soc. of U.S., 1970—, C.L.U.; cert. ins. cons. Mem. Southwestern Conn. Assn. Life Underwriters (dir.) Fairfield County C.L.U.s Assn., AAUW (dir. Greenwich chpt.). Republican. Roman Catholic. Home: 198 Milbank Ave Greenwich CT 06830 Office: Equitable Life Assurance Soc US 25 Valley Dr Greenwich CT 06830

KEBBEL, PAULETTE ANITA, educator; b. Collinsville, Ill., Feb. 23, 1922; d. Peter Thomas and Katherine (Holst) Pruetzel; student So. Ill. U., Edwardsville, 1964-67; m. Albert W. Kebbel, Apr. 20, 1941 (dec. Sept. 1963); children—Janice, Beverly, Nancy; m. 2d, Herschel B. Malvin, June 29, 1981. Tchr. kindergarten, Holy Cross Luth. Sch., Collinsville, 1961-64; owner, dir., tchr. Kebbel's Kiddy Garden, Collinsville, 1964—. Club: Soroptimist (pres. 1978-79). Home and Office: 715 Lillian St Collinsville IL 62234

KEEBLER, CATHERINE MARTHA, cytologist; b. Chgo., Dec. 15, 1929; d. Robert Ernest and Cecilia Pauline (Braun) K.; R.N., St. Luke's Hosp., Chgo., 1951; diploma Sch. Cytotech., U. Chgo., 1957; B.A., Mundelein Coll., Chgo., 1981; Sc.D. (hon.), Thomas Jefferson U., Phila., 1981. Staff nurse Wesley Meml. Hosp., Chgo., 1951; head nurse St. Luke's Hosp., 1952; research asst., then cytotechnologist U. Chgo., 1953-58, edn. coordinator, chief cytotechnologist, 1958—, lab. mgr., 1960—; cons. in field. Recipient Merit award U. Chgo., 1972. Fellow Internat. Acad. Cytology (registrar 1970—); mem. Am. Soc. Cytology (editor bull. 1963-73; Cytotechnologist of Yr. award 1966), Am. Assn. Allied Health Profls., Am. Soc. Clin. Pathology (asso.), Ill. Soc. Cytology (pres. 1969, hon. mem. 1976—). Color Camera Club. Roman Catholic. Author articles in field. Editor: Manual of Cytotechnology, 1975—; Compendium in Cytopreparatory Techniques, 1971—; mng. editor Compendium on Clin. Cytology, 1981—. Home: 1640 E 50th St Chicago IL 60615 Office: 5841 S Maryland Ave Chicago IL 60637

KEEFAUVER, BARBARA ATKINS, arts adminstr.; b. N.Y.C., June 13, 1928; d. Henry John and Emma (Fayen) Atkins; B.A. in Bus. Adminstrn., Pa. State U., 1949; postgrad. Rutgers U., 1968-69; m. William Lloyd Keefauver, July 9, 1949; children—Bruce Lloyd, Elizabeth Ann. With Equitable Life Assurance Co., N.Y.C., 1949-52; bd. dirs. Colonial Symphony, 1962-72; tchr. dramatics George Washington Sch., Morristown, N.J., 1971-72; with Arts' Council Morris Area, Drew U., Madison, N.J., 1972—, dir., 1973-82, exec. dir., 1982—. Dir. childrens plays, 1962—; bd. dirs. Jr. League Morristown, 1962-66; chmn. Arts Council N.J. Jr. Leagues, 1967-69, chmn. exec. council, 1969-71. Recipient Vol. of Yr. Award Jr. League Morristown, 1966. Mem. Nat. Assembly Community Art Agys., Am. Council for Arts, Jr. League Morristown, Delta Gamma. Republican. Episcopalian. Office: Arts Council Morris Area Drew Univ Madison NJ 07940

KEEFE, DIANE MARIE, cons. co. exec.; b. Columbus, Ohio, June 19, 1949; d. Dale Francis and Virginia Irene (Ashenfelter) Buckenmeyer; B.S. in Home Econs. Edn., Ohio State U., 1971; m. May 15, 1976. Mem. sales staff high volume mail equipment Cheshire/A Xerox Co., Houston, 1976-78; mktg. rep. word processing equipment Lexitron/A Raytheon Co., Dallas, 1978; market support rep. shared logic systems Basic Four Corp./Wordstream, 1978-79; word processing support specialist, shared logic systems and communications Digital Equipment Corp., Dallas, 1980-81; pres. D.K. Assos., office systems cons., Carrollton, Tex., 1981—. Mem. Internat. Word Processing Assn., Dallas Local Word Processing Assn. Club: Racquetball. Contbr. articles to word processing publs.

KEELE, REBA LOU, ednl. adminstr., educator; b. Emery, Utah, Oct. 28, 1941; d. Frederick Manning and Pearl Valentine (Peterson) K.; B.S., Brigham Young U., 1963, M.A., 1966; Ph.D., Purdue U., 1974. Asst. prof. communications, debate coach Brigham Young U., 1967-68, coordinator ednl. psychology, 1969-74, asso. dir. honors program, 1974-77, dir. honors program, 1977-78, asso. prof. orgnl. behavior, 1979—; dir. Title III project; cons. numerous sch. dists.; vis. scholar Purdue U., 1978-79. Pres., Stake Relief Soc., Mormon Ch., Provo, Utah, 1975-77; speaker community, ch. groups; mem. advisory bd. women's history archives Harold B. Lee Library, 1976-81; exec. dir. Consortium for Utah Women in Higher Edn., 1977-78, 79-82; state facilitator Higher Edn. Resource Service W., 1979-82; bd. regents Utah System Higher Edn., 1981—; mem. Democratic Central Com., 1977-78; del.-at-large Internat. Women's Yr., 1977. Past Brigham Young U. fellow, Purdue U. fellow. Mem. Speech Communication Assn., Western Speech Communication Assn., Acad. Mgmt., Utah Women in History Assn. (adv. bd. 1977-78), Am. Mgmt. Assn., Phi Eta Sigma, Phi Kappa Phi. Club: Alice Louise Reynolds. Author: Let's Talk: Adults and Children Sharing Feelings, 1977; contbr. articles to profl. publs.; writer, instr. TV programs: Helping Your Child to Read, 1974. Home: 459 E 800 North Orem UT 84057 Office: 1074 SWKT Brigham Young U Provo UT 84602

KEELER, MIRIAM BROWN, writer, lectr.; b. Cleburne, Tex., June 12, 1902; d. Emmett and Sally Canary (Harper) Brown; B.A., U. Tex., 1922, M.A., 1927; postgrad. Tulane U., 1929-31, U. Poitiers (France), 1929; m. George Eldridge Keeler, July 14, 1932; children—George Eldridge III, Harper B., Emmett B. Tchr. public high schs., Austin, Tex., 1922-24, Del Rio, Tex., 1924-25, Wilson, N.C., 1925-26, C.Z., 1931-32; prin. post sch., Corregidor, Philippines, 1937-39; tchr., chmn. English dept. public schs., Fairborn, Ohio, 1954-59; tchr. Ashley Hall, Charleston, S.C., 1960-67; instr. English, Tulane U., 1927-31; prof. English, Coll. of Charleston, 1968-71, chmn. dept., 1969-70; contbr. articles to numerous mags., newspapers, acad. quars., including Sewanee Rev., S.W. Rev.; author book: The Vigorous Hearts, 1974; lectr., slide-show lectr. travel and lit. Recipient 1st Pl. award S.C. Women's Clubs Creative Writing Contest, 1974; Univ. fellow, 1926-27. Mem. Carolina Arts Assn. (life), Charleston Preservation Soc. (life), Phi Beta Kappa, Alpha Phi. Episcopalian. Clubs: Century (pres. 1973-75), Charleston Women's (dir.), English-Speaking Union (dir. club). Home: 704 North Shore Rd Charleston SC 29412

KEELER, RUBY, actress; b. Halifax, N.S., Can., Aug. 25, 1910; d. Ralph and Elnora (Leahy) Keeler; D.F.A. (hon.), Providence Coll., 1971, Saint John's U., 1974; m. Al Jolson, 1928 (div. 1939); 1 son; m. 2d, John Lowe, Oct. 29, 1941; 1 son, 3 daus. Debut in N.Y.C. in chorus The Rise of Rosy O'Reilly, 1923, later appeared in Bye-Bye, Bonnie, 1927, Lucky, 1927, The Sidewalks of New York, 1927, Show Girl, 1929 (all N.Y.C.), Hold Onto Your Hats, Chgo., 1940; appeared in films including 42nd Street, 1933, Gold Diggers of 1933, Footlight Parade, 1933, Dames, 1934, Flirtation Walk, 1934, Go Into Your Dance, 1935, Shipmates Forever, 1935, Colleen, 1936, Ready, Willing and Able, 1937, Mother Carey's Chickens, 1938, Sweetheart of the Campus, 1941; star No No Nanette!, 1970; appeared on TV in Jackie Gleason Show, This Is Your Life, Jerry Lewis Show, The Greatest Show on Earth. Mem. Actors Equity Assn., Screen Actors Guild. Address: care Gloria Safier 667 Madison Ave New York NY 10021 *

KEELER, VIRGINIA MARY, univ. ofcl.; b. San Antonio, Aug. 24, 1932; d. Thomas Love and Margaret Therese (Conway) K.; A.B., Chestnut Hill Coll., Phila., 1953. Sec. to Office of Pres., Georgetown U., 1953-54, sec. to pres., 1954-74, asst. sec. of univ., 1968-74, sec. of univ., 1974—. Recipient Vicennial medal Georgetown U., 1973. Mem. Am. Assn. Higher Edn., Assn. Governing Bds. Roman Catholic. Home: 2712 Wisconsin Ave NW 811 Washington DC 20007 Office: Georgetown University Washington DC 20057

KEEN, CHARLOTTE ELIZABETH, geophysicist; b. Halifax, N.S., Can., June 22, 1943; d. Murray Alexander and Elizabeth Randall (Cobb) Davidson; B.Sc. in physics with honors, Dalhousie U., 1964, M.Sc., 1966; Ph.D. in Geophysics, Cambridge U., 1970. Research scientist Atlantic Oceanographic Lab. Bedford Inst. Oceanography, Dartmouth, N.S., Can., 1970-73, Atlantic Geoscience Centre, 1973—; chmn. Canadian Com. on the Lithosphere. Fellow Royal Soc. Can., Geol. Assn. Can.; mem. Am. Geophys. Union, Commn. Marine Geology. Editor: Crustal Properties Across Passive Margins, 1979; contbr. numerous articles in field. Office: Atlantic Geoscience Centre Bedford Institute of Oceanography Dartmouth NS B24 4A2 Canada

KEEN, MARIA ELIZABETH, educator; b. Chgo., Aug. 19, 1918; d. Harold Fremont and Mary Eileen Honore (Dillon) Keen; A.B., U. Chgo., 1941; postgrad. U. Wyo., summer 1943, U. Mich., 1957; M.A., U. Ill., 1949. Tchr. high sch., Wyo., 1942-43, Mich., 1943-44; tchr. Am. Coll. for Women, Istanbul, Turkey, 1944-47; mem. faculty U. Ill., Urbana, asst. prof. English as 2d lang., asst. prof. ednl. adminstrn., 1967—. Mem. Champaign Community Devel. Com.; coms. YWCA, YMCA. Mem. AAUP (treas.), Animal Protection Inst., Defenders of Wildlife, LWV, Nat. Assn. Fgn. Student Advs., Am. Inst. Biol. Scis., Nat. Council Tchr. Educators, U. Ill. Athletic Assn. (sec., dir.), Ont. Geneal. Soc., AAAS, Phi Kappa Epsilon. Baptist. Home: 608 S Edwin St Champaign IL 61820 Office: 3054 Fgn Langs Bldg U Ill Urbana IL 61801

KEEN, MARY FRANCES, nurse, educator; b. Lancaster, Pa., June 8, 1949; d. Robert Hess and Mary Carolyn (Greider) K.; diploma in nursing Johns Hopkins Hosp. Sch. Nursing, Balt., 1970; B.S.N., U. Md., 1973, M.S., 1976; D.N.Sc. (HEW profl. nurse trainee), Catholic U. Am., 1981; Instr. Johns Hopkins U. Sch. Health Services, 1976-79, nursing curriculum researcher Sch. Hygiene and Pub. Health, 1979-80; asst. prof. nursing U. Md., 1979-81; assoc. prof. U. N. Miami, Coral Gables, Fla., 1981—; cons. Pan Am. Health Orgn.; health fair vol. HEW research grantee, 1977-80; NIH grantee, 1981—. Mem. AAUP, Am. Assn. Critical Care Nurses, Am. Nurses' Assn., Nat. League Nursing (test item writer in med. nursing), Nat. Council Internat. Health, Arthritis Found., Johns Hopkins Nurses' Alumni Assn. (treas. 1977-79, pres. 1980-81), Am. Field Service, Phi Kappa Phi, Sigma Theta Tau. Research, publs. in field. Office: PO Box 248106 Coral Gables FL 33124

KEENAN, LOUISE, psychologist; b. Pittsfield, Mass., July 10, 1914; d. Joseph James and Margaret Jane (Coleman) K.; A.B., Emmanuel Coll., Boston, 1938; Ed.M., Harvard U., 1943; Ed.D., Boston U., 1963. Dir. adult civic edn., 1941-46; dir. testing and remedial reading, 1946-49; sch. psychologist, Everett, Mass.; part-time lectr. R.I. Coll. Edn., 1956-59; part-time lectr., psychologist Cardinal Cushing Coll., Brookline, Mass., 1965-70; prof. psychology, assoc. dean students, Fitchburg, Mass., 1968-76; ret., 1976; diagnostic psychologist Watertown (Mass.) Pub. Schs., part-time, 1977—; chmn. steering com. Everett Mental Health Assn.; mem. profl. com., sec. North Central Mental Health Assn. Cert. psychologist and sch. psychologist, Mass.; diplomate in sch. psychology Am. Bd. Profl. Psychology. Fellow Mass. Psychol. Assn. (life mem.); mem. Am. Psychol. Assn., New Eng. Psychol. Assn. (charter), Mass. Sch. Psychologists Assn. (past pres.), Mass. Adminstrs., Deans and Counselors Assn. (dir.), Tri City Mental Health Assn., Pi Lambda Theta. Roman Catholic. Club: Harvard (Boston). Contbr. to profl. publs. Home: 10 Sheraton Park Arlington MA 02174

KEENAN, MARY LOU, hotelier; b. Oklahoma City, Jan. 19, 1931; d. Richard and Lulua (Plowman) Stewart; student Napa Community Coll.; m. Robert Millard Keenan, June 21, 1952; children—Deborah Jean, Valerie Lynn, Robert Stuart, Ralph Edward. Propr., Burgundy House Antiques, 1971-75; pres. Burgundy House Inc., Bordeaux House, hotels, 1975—. Mem. adv. bd. Calif. Health Care Delivery Services. Recipient award Upper Napa Valley Assn. Mem. Napa C. of C., Yountville C. of C., Calif. Hotel and Motel Assn., Disting. Inns and Historic Hotels. Republican. Office: 6600 Washington St and 6711 Washington St Yountville CA 94599

KEENAN, RETHA VORNHOLT, nurse; b. Solon, Iowa, Aug. 15, 1934; d. Charles Elias and Helen Maurine (Konicek) V.; B.S.N., State U. Iowa, 1955; M.S.N., Calif. State U., Long Beach, 1978; m. Roy Vincent Keenan, Jan. 5, 1980; children from previous marriage—Scott Iverson, Craig Iverson. Public health nurse City of Long Beach, 1970-73, Hosp. Home Care, Torrance, Calif., 1973-75; patient care coordinator Hillhaven, Los Angeles, 1975-76; mental health cons. InterCityHome Health, Los Angeles, 1978-79; instr. Community Coll. Dist., Los Angeles, 1979-83; instr. nursing El Camino Coll., Torrance, 1981-83, NIMH grantee, 1977-78; instr. nursing Chapman Coll., Orange, Calif., 1982—. Cert. nurse practitioner adult and mental health, 1979. Mem. Phi Delta Gamma, Phi Kappa Phi, Delta Zeta. Lutheran. Home: 27849 Longhill Dr Rancho Palos Verdes CA 90274 Office: Dept Nursing West Los Angeles Coll Culver City CA 90230

KEENE, RUTH FRANCES, army ofcl.; b. South Bend, Ind., Oct. 7, 1948; d. Seymour and Sally (Morris) K.; B.S., Ariz. State U., 1970; M.S., Fairleigh Dickinson U., 1978. Inventory mgmt. specialist U.S. Army Electronics Command, Phila., 1970-74, U.S. Army Communications-Electronics Materiel Readiness Command, Ft. Monmouth, N.J., 1974-79; chief inventory mgmt. div. Crane (Ind.) Army Ammunition Activity, 1979-80; supply systems analyst Hdqrs. 60th Ordnance Group, Zweibruecken, W.Ger., 1980—. Mem. Federally Employed Women (chpt. pres. 1979-80), Nat. Assn. Female Execs., Soc. Logistics Engrs., Assn. Computing Machinery, Am. Soc. Public Adminstrn., Soc. Profl. and Exec. Women, Internat. Info./Word Processing Assn., AAAS, NOW. Democrat. Jewish. Home: 4916 W Pinchot Ave Phoenix AZ 85031 Office: Hdqrs 60th Ordnance Group Attn AEROD-MS APO NY 09052

KEER, JANET S., fin. exec.; b. N.Y.C., June 8, 1936; d. Martin and Ada (Karnig) Katz; B.B.A., Baruch Sch. Bus. and Public Adminstrn., City U. N.Y., 1956; m. Howard Keer, Apr. 8, 1962; children—Jennifer,

Elizabeth. Asst. to advt. dir. WNEW-TV, N.Y.C., 1959-62; comptroller/ins. sales Joel Katz & Assos., Inc., Roslyn, N.Y., 1969-75; comptroller Am. Bus. & Profl. Program, Inc., Manhasset, N.Y., 1975—; sec.-treas. Arrandale Mgmt. Co., N. Shore Mgmt. Co., Roslyn Cons. Ltd., Melville Equities, Ltd., 1975—; mng. gen. partner Pueblo Sq. Assos., Manhasset, 1978—. Office: 1205 Northern Blvd Manhasset NY 11030

KEESEE, MARGARET POLLARD, state legislator; b. Greensboro, N.C., Jan. 6, 1945; d. Charles Rogers and Margaret Lena (Kersey) Keesee; B.A., Guilford Coll., 1967; postgrad. Radford Coll., 1967. Former tchr. Greensboro (N.C.) Pub. Schs.; mem. N.C. State Adv. Com. to U.S. Commn. on Civil Rights, 1974—; mem. N.C. Ho. Reps., 1973-74, 79-80, 81—, mem. various coms. Mem. N.C. Assn. Educators, Assn. Classroom Tchrs., Nat. Edn. Assn., AAUW, N.C. Women's Polit. Caucus (state sec. 1975-76), Greensboro Women's Profl. Forum. Methodist. Office: NC Ho Reps State Capitol Raleigh NC 27602 *

KEESEE, PATRICIA ANN, bank exec.; b. Elkins, W.Va., Mar. 1, 1943; d. Jesse Paul and Effie Louise (Basil) Kniley; grad. W.Va. Sch. Banking, 1979; m. K. Harrison Keesee, May 25, 1963. With Davis Trust Co. Bank, Elkins, W.Va., 1963—, proof operator, 1968-74, supr. bookkeeping dept., 1974—, asst. treas., 1974-80, asst. v.p., 1980—. Mem. Nat. Assn. Bank Women. Democrat. Mem. Ch. of Christ. Home: Route 1 Box 306B Elkins WV 26241 Office: PO Box 1429 Elkins WV 26241

KEEVER, NANCY HART, govt. ofcl.; b. Albany, Ga., Oct. 28, 1939; d. Russell William and Goldie Elizabeth (Kelleher) Hart; student Mills Coll., 1957-59; B.A., U. Ky., 1963; M.L.S., Fla. State U., 1964; m. Dale Keever. Reference librarian N.Y. Public Library, 1964-65; br. head librarian San Mateo (Calif.) Public Library, 1965-68; instr. div. librarianship Emory U., 1968-69; coordinator outside services and resources Atlanta Public Library, 1968-69, librarian III, head br., 1969-74, head Sandy Springs Regional Library, 1974-79; prodn. asst. Cable News Network, 1980-81, asso. producer, 1981-82; dep. dir. Region IV, Dept. Health and Human Services, 1982—; guest lectr. div. librarianship Emory U., 1971-72. Chmn., Orpheon Concert, Hillbarn Little Theater, San Mateo County, Calif., 1967; judge Jr. Miss Pageant, Smyrna (Ga.) Jr. C. of C., 1969. Mem. Calif. State Republican Central Com., 1967-69; del. Rep. Nat. Conv., 1980; v.p. San Mateo County Fedn. Rep. Women's Club, 1966-67; sec. San Mateo County Young Reps., 1967-68, Fulton County, Atlanta, 1969; co-chmn. 19th biennial conv. Nat. Fedn. Rep. Women, 1977; mem. women's aux. Atlanta Humane Soc., 1976-83. Mem. ALA, Southeastern, Ga., Met. Atlanta, Peninsula (sec.-treas. 1966-67) library assns., Atlanta Women's Network, Ga. Fedn. Rep. Women (1st v.p. 1979-81), Alliance Française, DAR (Cherokee chpt.), Woman's Place, Mems. Guild of Young Careers of the High Mus. Art, Spiritual Frontiers Fellowship, Atlanta Backgammon Soc., Braves 400 Club, San Mateo Employees' Assn. (v.p. 1966-67), Delta Gamma. Club: Greater Atlanta Rep. Women's (pres. 1976-78), Atlanta Press (bd. dirs. 1982-83). Producer, hostess TV series Explore Your Options: Women and Work, 1981-83. Home: 4613 Club Circle NE Atlanta GA 30319 Office: HHS Region IV 101 Marietta GA 30323

KEGEL-FLOM, PENELOPE SHARON, psychologist, educator; b. Milw., Sept. 17, 1938; d. Paul William and Volga (Linken) Kegel; M.A., Ind. U., 1962; Ph.D., U. Calif., Berkeley, 1970; m. Mert Flom, 1968; children—Caitlin, Megan. Research asso. U. Calif., Berkeley, 1972-80; asso. prof. U. Houston, 1980—. USPHS grantee, 1974-79. Mem. Am. Psychol. Assn., Assn. for Women in Sci., Phi Beta Kappa, Sigma Xi. Contbr. numerous articles in field to profl. jours.; mem. editorial council Jour. Optometric Edn., sci. referee Am. Jour. Optometry and Physiol. Optics. Office: Coll Optometry U Houston Houston TX 77004

KEGLEY, CLAUDIA ALLEN, food service exec.; b. Wenona, N.C., Oct. 17, 1939; d. Lewis Fairfield and Estelle Mae (Williams) Allen; student Roanoke Bible Coll., 1958; 1 dau., Linda Diane. Receptionist, Hastings-Raydist, Inc., Hampton, Va., 1960-62; clk., typist Newport News (Va.) Shipbldg., 1962-69; mgr. Carrols of Va., Newport News, 1969-73; owner, mgr. Claudia's Drive-In, Keysville, Va., 1973—. Mem. Nat. Assn. for Female Execs., Va. Restaurant Assn. Republican. Mem. Ch. of Christ. Home: PO Box 43 Keysville VA 23947

KEHR, DEBERA JUANITA, former head start dir.; b. Chgo., Apr. 15, 1950; d. Richard Alfred and Eleanor (Nagel) Kehr; student U. Barcelona, 1971-72; B.A. in Spanish Edn., U. Ill., 1973. Tchr. aide Head Start program N.W. Opportunity Center, Mt. Prospect, Ill., 1974, family devel. coordinator, 1975-76, dir., 1976-81. Named Staff Person of Yr., Ill. Parent Policy Action Council, 1975. Mem. Nat. Assn. Edn. of Young Children, Chgo. Assn. Edn. of Young Children, Am. Assn. Tchrs. of Spanish and Portuguese, N.W. Suburban Council of Community Services, Harper Coll. Child Care Council. Lutheran. Club: Friendship Sport. Home: 804 S Owen St Mount Prospect IL 60056

KEIM, AMY LOU, assn. exec.; b. Latrobe, Pa., Dec. 10, 1954; d. Floyd Frederick and Ruth Marian (Boggio) Keim; B.S. in Psychology, Slippery Rock State Coll., magna cum laude, 1976; postgrad. Pa. State U., 1978. Resident advisor Adelphoi Village, Inc., Latrobe, Pa., 1976-77; staff Pre-Sch. Opeining, St. John's Luth. Ch., Latrobe, 1977-78; behavior specialist Assn. for Retarded Citizens, Westmoreland, Pa., 1978-80; legis. coordinator-advocate, 1980—. Bd. dirs. Health & Welfare Council, Westmoreland County, 1980—. Mem. ACLU, Psi Chi. Contbr. articles to profl. jours. Home: 27 E Madison St Latrobe PA 15650 Office: 15 W 3d St Greensburg PA 15601

KEIR, ANNA LUCILLE, educator; b. Presho, S.D., Oct. 7, 1923; d. Zee Lloyd and Mary Ruth (Vawter) Ritchie; student Ohio State U., 1969-75; cert. med. asst., No. Ill. U., 1975, Ind. U., 1977; m. Willard James Keir, Aug. 17, 1946; children—Willard, John, Glen. Various positions as med. asst., 1952-69; vocat. med. asst. instr. Columbus (Ohio) public schs., 1969—; cons. in field. Parliamentarian, Clintonville Commn., 1978—. Served with USNR, 1945-46. Registered parliamentarian. Mem. Nat. Vocat. Assn., NEA, Vocat. Indsl. Clubs Am., Nat. Assn. Parliamentarians, Am. Inst. Parliamentarians, Am. Assn. Med. Assts., DAR. Club: Toastmistress. Author handbook on parliamentary procedure. Home: 119 W Dunedin Rd Columbus OH 43214 Office: 546 Buckingham St Columbus OH 43215

KEIRS, KAREN MARIE, warehousing co. exec.; b. Springfield, Ill., Aug. 19, 1953; s. John Cornelius and Betty L. (Timmons) Burtle; student bus. mgmt. Lincoln Land Coll., Springfield; m. Kevin L. Keirs, July 7, 1973; children—Brian L., Jason M. Distbr., Shoreline Trailer Sales, Inc., Arlington, Tex., 1976-82; v.p., sec.-treas. Marine Warehouse, Inc., Virden, Ill., 1982—. Named Distbr. of Year, Shoreline Trailer Sales, Inc., 1978. mem. Nat. Fedn. Ind. Bus., U.S. C. of C. Roman Catholic. Home: 109 Bob-O-Link Dr Virden IL 62690 Office: 229 E Holden St Virden IL 62690

KEIRSTEAD, BILLIE HINES, inst. exec.; b. Oak Park, Ill., Aug. 21, 1943; d. Victor John and Shirley (Powell) Marasa; A.A., U. Fla., 1963; B.A. in English, U. South Fla., 1965, postgrad. 1974-80; m. Earle Cline Keirstead, Aug. 5, 1978; 1 dau., Aimee Elizabeth. Tchr. English and journalism Cypress Lake High Sch., Ft. Myers, Fla., 1972-76; mem. exec. bd. Fla. Scholastic Press Assn., Gainesville, 1973-76; ednl. coordinator, asst. dir. Modern Media Inst., St. Petersburg, Fla., 1976—; mem. adv. bd. So. Interscholastic Press Assn., U. S.C., Columbia, 1980-81; condr. workshops state, regional, nat. levels in prodn. techniques and graphics, 1977—; prodn. coordinator, designer Am. Soc. Newspaper Editors Best Newspaper Writing, 1981, 82, Newspapers and Videotex: How Free A Press?, 1981. Mem. Women in Communications (com.), Soc. Newspaper Design, Phi Kappa Phi. Office: 556 Central Ave Saint Petersburg FL 33701

KEISS, SISTER, ISABELLE, coll. pres.; b. N.Y.C., Dec. 11, 1931; d. Walter and Sara (Boyle) K.; B.A., Villanova U., 1960; M.A., Cath. U., 1966; Ph.D., Notre Dame U., 1972; postgrad. Harvard Grad. Sch. Edn., 1972. Joined Religious Sisters of Mercy, 1952; tchr. English, Bishop Egan High Sch., Levittown, Pa., 1960-63; chmn. English dept. Walsingham Acad., Williamsburg, Va., 1963-65; teaching asst. U. Notre Dame (Ind.), 1967-71; pres. Gwynedd-Mercy Coll., Gwynedd Valley, Pa., 1971—; mem. com. on personnel affairs Pa. Assn. Colls. and Univs., 1975—, chmn., 1978; mem. instl. survey com. Commn. Ind. Colls. and Univs., 1976-79, chmn., 1977, mem. exec. com., 1977-80; mem. adv. bd. Nat. Cons. Network, Council Advancement Small Colls., 1976-80; mem. exec. com. Found. Ind. Colls. Pa., 1978-81; mem. exec. com. Conf. Small Pvt. Colls., 1978—; bd. dirs. Compact for Lifelong Ednl. Opportunities, 1982—. Bd. dirs. Mercy Cath. Med. Center, 1975—, Coll. Misericordia, 1979—. Recipient award Rotary Club, 1980. Home and Office: Gwynedd-Mercy Coll Gwynedd Valley PA 19437

KEITH, ELIZABETH MILLER, civic worker; b. Wayne, Pa., July 23, 1911; d. Edgar T. and Norah (Schweyer) Miller; grad. Baldwin Sch., 1930; B.A., Vassar Coll., 1934; postgrad. Maria Ouspenskaya Sch. Acting, 1934-36; cert. N.Y. Sch. Design, 1972; m. George R. Vila, Oct. 4, 1941 (div. Feb. 1970); children—John Desmond, Richard Lawrence; m. 2d, Percival Cleveland Keith, Jan. 17, 1976 (dec. July 1976). Actress, Essex (N.Y.) Summer Theatre, 1937, Barter Theatre, Abingdon, N.Y., 1938-39, Drove Players, Greenwich Village, N.Y.C., 1939-41, Canton Workshop (Conn.), 1941, Woonsocket (R.I.) Theatre, 1940. Nurse's aide ARC, Waterbury Hosp., 1942-48; chmn. Planned Parenthood; pres. Woodbury (Conn.) PTA, 1951-53; mem. Citizens Com. to Evaluate Pub. Sch. and Tchr. Tng., 1954; mem. restoration com. Wallace House, Somerville, N.J., 1966-68; chmn. decorating, seminar coms. Wykeham Rise Sch. Festival, 1972-73, mem. public relations com.; edn. chmn. N.Y. Bryant Park Flower Show, 1976-77, 77-78; bd. dirs. Vis. Nurse Assn., Somerset Hills, N.J., 1962-68, Washington, Conn., 1972-74; trustee Gunnery Sch., Washington, Conn., 1973-76. Episcopalian (vestry 1973-76). Clubs: Garden of Am. (hort. zone rep. 1974-76, flower show zone rep. 1978-80, nat. flower show chmn. 1980-82, dir. 1982—), Somerset Hills Garden (historian 1967-69); Vassar, Cosmopolitan (N.Y.C.); Washington (Conn.) Garden (hort. chmn. 1971-73, program chmn. 1973-75, vis. garden chmn. 1978-79, v.p. 1982—); Washington (Washington). Home: Meadow Wind Washington Depot CT 06794

KEITH, GINNI, orch. mgr.; b. Seattle, Oct. 1, 1949; d. George Dunlap and Elizabeth Emma (Patz) Paynton; B.A., U. Wash., 1973, B.Mus. cum laude, 1973; m. David Keith, July 5, 1972. Mgr., dir. devel. Los Angeles Mozart Orch., Los Angeles, 1975—; mem. London Symphony Orch. Chorus, 1973-74, Roger Wagner Chorale, 1975-77, Los Angeles Master Chorale, 1975-77. Mem. Phi Beta Kappa. Clubs: Am. Fedn. Aviculture, Nat. Wildlife Fedn.

KEITH, IRENE BEATRICE, airline dispatcher; b. Derry, N.H., Dec. 16, 1919; d. Ernest Talmage and Monica-Julia (Pitt) K.; student public schs., also numerous flying and airline courses. With Pan Am. World Airways Inc., 1948—, dispatcher, load master, Johannesburg, South Africa, 1975-76, dispatcher Kennedy Airport, N.Y.C., 1956—; guest speaker. Served with Women's Aircraft Maintenance Squadrons, 1942-44, Air Transp. Command (alert crew mechanics badge), 1944-45. Recipient Lady Hay Drummond Hay trophy Women's Internat. Assn. Aeros., 1960. Mem. Transp. Workers Union, Air Force Assn. (past state v.p.), Ninety-Nines (Amelia Earhart medal 1958; past gov. N.Y.-N.J. sect.), Women's Internat. Assn. Aeros. (treas.), Fedn. Airline Dispatchers. Republican. Home: 84-20 Austin St Kew Gardens NY 11415 Office: Hangar 14 2d Floor Flight Control Office Kennedy Internat Airport Jamaica NY 11430

KEITH, JOCELYN SULLIVAN FREER, realty co. exec.; b. Boston, Sept. 24, 1927; d. Harold Wardsworth and Alice Elizabeth (Barry) Sullivan; student George Washington U., 1945-47; children—Quentin Barry, Jonathan Chilton, Jocelyn Deborah. Interviewer program Diplomatic Debs, Sta. WBBC, 1947, 58; bd. dirs. Ch. Farm Sch., 1954-67, Children's Convalescent Hosp., 1958-75; assoc. A.S. Gardiner & Co., Inc., Washington, 1968—. Clubs: Chevy Chase (Md); Sulgrave (Washington). Home: 5407 Moorland Ln Bethesda MD 20814 Office: 7923 Eastern Ave Silver Spring MD 20910

KELL, VENETTA BYNUM, educator; b. Cyril, Okla.; d. William McKinley and Ada Mae (Attaway) Bynum; B.S., Okla. Coll. Women, 1940; M. Bus. Ed., U. Okla., 1947, Ed.D., 1961; postgrad. So. Meth. U., U. Pa., 1957, San Diego State U., 1958; m. Ernest Kell; 1 dau., Ann. Tchr. bus., high schs., Okla., 1940-55; vis. prof. Utah State U., summer 1964, Central Wash. U., summer 1967, U. Wis., summer 1968, Okla. Coll. Women, summers 1952-54, Phoenix Coll., summer 1972; mem. faculty No. Ariz. U., Flagstaff, 1961—, prof. bus. edn., 1965—. Delta Kappa Gamma scholar, 1959-60. Mem. Bus. and Profl. Women's Club (pres., regional dir. 1973-75), Am. Bus. Communicators Assn., Nat. Bus. Edn. Assn., Western Bus. Edn. Assn., Ariz. Bus. Edn. Assn., AAUW, Delta Kappa Gamma, Phi Kappa Phi, Delta Pi Epsilon. Democrat. Home: 332 E David Dr Flagstaff AZ 86001 Office: Coll Bus Adminstrn No Ariz U Flagstaff AZ 86001

KELLEHER, MARIE BARBARA, assn. exec.; b. Sandwich, Mass., Dec. 6, 1921; d. James Henry and Alice Cecelia (Montague) K.; B.S., U. Mass., 1942; A.M., Stanford U., 1958. Commd. ensign U.S. Navy, 1942, advanced through grades to capt., 1967; assigned to Naval Tng. Center, San Diego, 1958-62, Bur. Naval Personnel, 1962-71, ret., 1971; v.p. personnel U.S. Auto Assn., San Antonio, 1972—. Bd. dirs. Children's Hosp., 1977—, Greater San Antonio Safety Council, 1979—; mem. Def. Adv. Com. on Women in Service, 1980-82. Mem. Nat. Assn. Ind. Insurers, Am. Soc. Personnel Adminstrn., Am. Mgmt. Assn., Bus. and Profl. Women. Roman Catholic. Clubs: Army Navy Country, Fair Oaks Country. Home: 4218 Laurel Trail San Antonio TX 78240 Office: USAA Bldg Fredericksburg Rd San Antonio TX 78288

KELLER, LOUCILLE ELEANOR, nurse; b. Columbus, Ohio, June 2, 1913; d. Clarence and Della Romayne (Erwin) Wagner; R.N., Meml. Hosp., 1934; tchr.'s diploma, Life Bible Coll., 1963; m. Clarence M. Keller, May 25, 1963; children—Bill, Donna, James; stepchildren—Barbara, Tom, Donald. Indsl. nurse B.F. Goodrich, Akron, Ohio, 1948-52; anesthesia nurse Oral Surgeons office, Akron, 1953-55; dir. nursing Lakewood Manor, Los Angeles, 1958; admitting clk. Doctor's Hosp., Los Angeles, 1959; office nurse, Los Angeles, 1960-62; staff nurse dept. surgery New Hollywood (Calif.) Community Hosp., 1963-66, Black W. Adams Hosp., Los Angeles, 1971-72, Title 22 P.E.O. Home, Alhambra, Calif., 1975; nurse Eisenhower Med. Center, Palm Springs, Calif., 1976—; dir. nursing Sparr Convalescent Hosp., Los Angeles, 1978-80, Country Villa Westwood, Beverly Hills, Calif., 1980; nursing supr. Chandler Facility, North Hollywood, Calif., 1981—. Mem. Am. Nurses Assn. Republican. Contbr. articles to profl. jours. Home: 6000 Hillandale St Apt 1 Los Angeles CA 90042 Office: 5335 Laurel Canyon Blvd North Hollywood CA 91607

KELLER, MARGARET GILMER (MRS. GEORGE HENRY KELLER III), educator; b. Harrisburg, Pa., July 11, 1911; d. Charles Greenwalt Gilmer and Mary Ellen (Sullivan) Gilmer; A.B., Trinity Coll., 1933; A.M., Columbia, 1934, cert., 1942; cert. State Tchrs. Coll., Bloomsburg, Pa., 1934; m. George Henry Keller, III, July 13, 1940; children—Mary Ellen, Margaret Marie, George Henry, IV. Acting chmn. dept. history Trinity Coll., Washington, 1935-36; chmn. classical dept. Convent Sacred Heart, 1936-37, Steelton (Pa.) High Sch., 1937-41; adj. prof. English dept. Univ. Coll., Rutgers U., 1946—, mem. dean's adv. com. Univ. Coll., 1968—, also advisor to women's clubs Univ. Coll.; chmn. classical dept. Glen Rock (N.J.) High Sch., 1956-59, chmn. fgn. lang. dept., 1959—; curriculum cons. Glen Rock Sch. Dist., 1980—. Mem. Sch.-Community Adv. Com. to Ridgewood (N.J.) Public Sch., 1956—, TV adv. bd., 1955—; active Am. Cancer Soc., United Fund, ARC, Girl Scouts U.S.A.; mem. nominating bd. Ridgewood Nursing Service, 1959-60; chmn. Trinity Coll. Devel. Fund Drive N.J.; trustee Trinity Coll., 1963-67, 74—81, life trustee, 1981, nat. chmn. 75th anniversary fund, 1975-76; committeewoman Republican County Com. Cited by Rutgers U., 1953, 61, 64, 65, 66, 71, 82, for disting. service to student activities, 1978, named to coll. honor soc., 1982; cited by Newman Province of N.J., 1963; recipient Robert Ax award for disting. teaching, 1971; Outstanding Educator award Jr. C. of C., 1973; Alumnae Service award Trinity Coll., 1977; citation Middle States Assn. Colls., 1979; U.S. Presdl. Achievement award, 1982; Pres.'s medal Trinity Coll., 1982; others. Mem. NEA, N.J. Edn. Assn., Am. Classical Soc., AAUW (past dir.), Met. Assn. Coll. Tchrs. English, Chaplain's Aid Assn., Trinity Coll., Alumnae Assn. (nat. pres. 1963-67), Phi Chi Theta. Clubs: Newman (adv. Rutgers U.), Univ. Coll. Women (hon. Rutgers U.). Home: 200 Phelps Rd Ridgewood NJ 07450 Office: Rutgers U New Brunswick NJ 08903

KELLER, MARY ELLEN, ednl. adminstr.; b. St. Clair, Pa., July 4, 1916; d. Andrew and Julia (Balazik) Antal; student Bowling Green State U. Extension, 1963-65; m. William Owrey Keller, Oct. 4, 1941; children—Maria Elena, Susan Bliss (dec.), Janis Ann Keller Wotiz, William Ontal. Tchr., Erie County (Ohio) Council of Parents and Friends of Exceptional Citizens, Sandusky, 1955-67, exec. sec., 1967—. Leader, Erie Shores council Girls Scouts U.S.A.; mem. Community Council of Sandusky; mem. Community Bd. Mental Health and Mental Retardation of Erie and Ottowa Counties, 1968-74, sec., 1968, vice chmn., 1973; bd. deacons Zion Lutheran Ch., Sandusky, 1974-76, chmn., 1975; co-chmn. bd. trustees for organizing Citizens Council Domestic Violence, 1981—. Recipient Vocat. Services award Sandusky Area C. of C., 1974; named Citizen of Week, Channel 7, Sandusky, 1974. Mem. Nat. Assn. Retarded Citizens, Ohio Assn. Retarded Citizens, Ohio Council Exec Dirs, Pres.'s Horizon Club. Republican. Clubs: Altrusa (pres. 1977-79) (Sandusky); Eagles Aux., United Comml. Travelers Ladies Social (sec. 1977—). Home: 624 E Washington St Sandusky OH 44870 Office: 416 Columbus Ave Sandusky OH 44870

KELLER, TRUDY THAL, sales exec.; b. Fairfield, Calif., Feb. 16, 1944; d. Warren Adolph and Sybil (Wessendorf) Thal; A.A., Stephens Coll., 1963; student U. Mo., 1963-64; B.S., Black Hills State Coll., 1966; M.A., Calif. State U., Los Angeles, 1979; children from previous marriage—Pete Heyden, Kristen Cosette. Instr. art Mountain Home (Idaho) Sch. Dist., 1966-69; sales rep. Art et Decor, Mission Viejo, Calif., 1976-77; sales rep. Kraft Food Service, Carson, Calif., 1977-79; account exec. Sta. KWAV-FM, Monterey, Calif., 1979-81; pres. Keller Enterprises; instr. sales Cabrillo Coll., Aptos, Calif., 1980-81. Vol., Hotline for Youth Salt Lake City, 1972-74. Hudson Rousher scholar, 1975. Mem. Nat. League Am. Penwomen, Am. Soc. Tng. and Devel., Nat. Assn. Profl. Saleswomen. Home: 1612 Escalona Dr Santa Cruz CA 95060 Office: PO Box 1136 Santa Cruz CA 95060

KELLERMAN, SALLY CLAIRE, actress; b. Long Beach, Calif., June 2, 1937; d. John Helm and Edith Baine (Vaughn) K.; student Los Angeles City Coll., Actor's Studio, N.Y.C.; m. Richard Edelstein, Dec. 19, 1970; 4 step-daus.; m. 2d, Jonathan Krane, 1980. Stage appearances include Breakfast at Tiffany's, Singular Man, N.Y.C.; films include MASH, Brewster McCloud, Last of the Red Hot Lovers, Reflection of Fear, Slither, Lost Horizon, Rafferty and the Gold Dust Twins, The Big Bus, The Boston Strangler, The April Fools, Welcome to L.A., A Little Romance, 1979, Foxes, Head On, Loving Couples, Serial; also TV roles Mannix, It Takes a Thief, Crysler Theatre; TV film Verna; USO Girl, 1978. Nominee Acad. and Golden Globe awards for MASH. Mem. Actor's Equity, AFTRA. Home: 7944 Woodrow Wilson Rd Los Angeles CA 90368 Office: care Robert Littman Keith Addis Co 409 N Camden Beverly Hills CA 90210 *

KELLETT, DEBORAH SHARON, psychologist; b. DeKalb, Ill., Sept. 22, 1944; d. Harry Bernard and Frances Rose (Lomas) K.; B.A., U. So. Calif., 1966; M.A., Harvard U., 1968, Ph.D., 1973. Teaching fellow Harvard U., 1970-72; clin. psychologist and chief mental health unit VA Outpatient Clinic, Worcester, Mass, 1972—; cons. Chandler St. Center, Worcester, 1976-78; asst. prof. psychology Clark U., 1975—; cons. U. Mass. Med. Sch. Dept. Family and Community Medicine, 1978—. Lic. Psychologist, Mass. Mem. Am. Psychol. Assn., Eastern Psychol. Assn., New Eng. Psychol. Assn., Mass. Psychol. Assn. Office: 595 Main St Worcester MA 01601

KELLEY, DELORES GOODWIN, coll. dean; b. Norfolk, Va., May 1, 1936; d. Stephen Cornelius and Helen (Jefferson) Goodwin; B.A., Va. State U., 1956; M.A., N.Y.U., 1958, Purdue U., 1972; Ph.D., U. Md., 1977; m. Russell Victor Kelley, Dec. 26, 1956; children—Norma Delores, Russell Victor, III, Brian Todd. Instr. English, Morgan State Coll., Balt., 1966-70; grad. teaching fellow Purdue U., 1970-72; chmn. dept. lang., lit. and philosophy Coppin State Coll., Balt., 1976-79, dean lower div., 1979—; panelist, reviewer Nat. Endowment Humanities; mem. Md. Dept. Edn. evaluation com. for Hood Coll., 1978—, Md. Commn. Values Edn., 1980—; dir. Harbor Bank Md., Balt., 1980—; chmn. Adv. Council Gifted and Talented Edn. Balt. City Schs., 1980—. Mem. Mayor Balt. Adv. Council Mental Health, 1981-84; v.p. Cross Country Improvement Assn., 1980-82. Grantee Md. Com. Humanities and Public Policy, 1977. Mem. Nat. Assn. Women Deans, Adminstrs. and Counselors, Nat. Council Tchrs. English, Md. Collegiate Honors Council (sec.-treas. 1981-82), Md. Assn. Higher Edn., Alpha Kappa Mu, Alpha Kappa Alpha. Democrat. Lutheran. Home: 3400 Olympia Ave Baltimore MD 21215 Office: 2500 W North Ave Baltimore MD 21216

KELLEY, JUDITH ANN, real estate broker; b. Hamburg, N.Y., Feb. 14, 1938; d. Howard Banks and Elsie Agnes (Funk) Nixon; real estate cert., Grossmont Coll., LaMesa, Calif., 1974; cert. real estate exchanging, Anthony's Schs., San Diego, 1976; m. William T. Kelley, July 5, 1958; children—David, Sherrie, Tina. Engaged in real estate sales, 1974—; owner Kelley & Assos. Real Estate Co., El Cajon, Calif., 1975—; co-owner Kelley Enterprises; dir., fin. adv. Cajon Corp. Sec. bd. dirs. Lexington Sch. PTA, El Cajon, 1968-69; coach Jr. League Bowling, 1969-71. Mem. Nat. Notary Assn., Women's Council Realtors (bd. dirs., membership chmn. East San Diego County chpt. 1977-78), E. San Diego County Bd. Realtors. Methodist. Address: 1048 Stoneridge Rd El Cajon CA 92021

KELLEY, KAY KENNEDY, state ofcl.; b. Montgomery, Ala., Apr. 2, 1942; d. Bart F. and Geneva Kennedy; B.A., Huntingdon Coll., 1964; student U. Montevallo, 1960-63; postgrad. Jones Law Sch., 1967-69, Nat. Mortgage Sch., Ohio State U., 1967-68; m. E. Jerome Kelley, June 23, 1963. Mortgage loan officer 1st Ala. Bank, Montgomery, 1968-74, v.p., 1974-80; exec. dir. Ala. Commn. on Aging, 1980—. Chmn. bd. Ala. Health Planning and Devel. Agy., 1979—. Recipient Outstanding Young Banker award Ala. Bankers Assn., 1979. Mem. Huntingdon Coll. Alumni Assn. (sec. 1979—), Nat. Assn. Bank Women, Am. Inst. Banking, Nat. Assn. Ins. Women, Greater Montgomery Home Builders Assn. Baptist. Club: Altrusa. Office: 2853 Fairlane Dr Bldg G Montgomery AL 36130

KELLEY, ONETIA MAY, artist; b. Groesbeck, Tex., May 27, 1909; d. Walter Thistle and Bessie Anna (Currey) Nettles; B.A., U. So. Calif., 1942; postgrad. U. N.Mex., 1950-51, 63; m. David Otis Kelley, June 29, 1930; children—Onetia Jean Leonard, Robert Otis. Tchr. math. Harwood High Sch., Albuquerque, 1959-63; one-woman shows include Mus. Fine Arts, Santa Fe, 1952, Four Hills Country Club, Albuquerque, 1968, Lovelace Clinic Gallery, Albuquerque, 1980; exhibited in group shows Ann. Art Exhibit, Ouray, Colo., 1975, N.Mex. 100 Invitational, Albuquerque, 1974; represented in pvt. collections. Mem. AAUW, Nat. League Am. Pen Women (pres. Yucca chpt. 1982-84, hon. mention State Fair Gallery exhbn. 1981), Nor Este Art Assn., N.Mex. Art League, Democrat. Mem. Ch. of Christ. Home: 3417 Groman Ct NE Albuquerque NM 87110

KELLEY, ROSELEE COOK, educator; b. Benton Harbor, Mich., July 26, 1924; d. Wooda and Carrie S. (Herdeg) Cook; B.A., Nazareth Coll.. Kalamazoo, 1945; M.A., Marquette U., Milw., 1949; Ed.D., Nova U., 1981; m. John E. Kelley, June 17, 1950 (div.); children—John L., Paul J., James E., Mary C. Grad. asst., instr. Marquette U., 1945-48; instr. communications St. Petersburg (Fla.) Jr. Coll., Clearwater campus, 1965—; Fla. adv. Phi Theta Kappa, 1969—; pres. Kelley Internat. Mktg. Treas. Dunedin chpt. Am. Field Service, 1981—. Mem. Nat. Council Tchrs. of English, Southeastern Conf. English in Two-Year Colls., Fla. Assn. Community Colls., Fla. Devel. Edn. Assn., World Future Soc. Home: 1608 San Roy Dr Dunedin FL 33528

KELLISON, SYLVIA EILEEN, govt. ofcl.; b. Norfolk, Va., Apr. 22, 1952; d. Raymond Guy and Patricia Ann (Pedrotty) K.; student U. Calif., 1970-71; B.S., San Diego State U., 1975; student in Acctg., Loyola Law Sch., 1980—. Internal revenue agt. IRS, Los Angeles, 1973—; chief steward, chmn. local negotiating com. Nat. Treasury Employees Union, 1976—, mem. nat. bargaining team, 1978-80, pres. chpt. 015, 1979—, mem. nat. resolutions com. nat. conv., 1981, chairwoman Los Angeles Joint Council, 1981-82; cons. Fed. Sector Labor Relations. Active gen. com. Combined Fedn. Campaign Los Angeles County. Mem. Am. Soc. Women Accts., IRS C.P.A.s and Public Accts., Am. Bar Assn. (law student div.), Nat. Assn. Female Execs., Am. Arbitration Assn., Phi Alpha Delta. Democrat. Office: 300 N Los Angeles St Room 4014 Los Angeles CA 90012

KELLNER, CYNTHIA ANN, credit union exec.; b. Milw., Nov. 4, 1948; d. Robert Q. and Alice (Barcz) K.; student U. Wis., Milw., 1970-72, Mt. Mary Coll., 1979—. Sec., Marquette U. Sch. Dentistry, 1966-68; sec., receptionist Edwards Advt. Agy., Inc., Milw., 1969-70, name changed to Edwards Commo-Net, Inc., sec. to pres., 1970-71, asst. to pres., 1971-73, v.p. charge ops., dir., 1973-80; mktg. dir. State Central Credit Union, Milw., 1980-81, sr. v.p. mktg., 1982—; speaker. Mem. Nat. Assn. Female Execs., Nat. Assn. Exec. Secs., Am. Mktg. Assn., Am. Soc. Profl. and Exec. Women. Home: 5250 N Shoreland Ave Whitefish Bay WI 53217 Office: 10015 W Greenfield Ave Milwaukee WI 53214

KELLOGG, DOROTHY MARIE, state legislator; b. Mpls., July 26, 1920; d. Carl H. and Marie M. (Mundhenke) Sorteberg; student public schs.; m. Lawrence S. Kellogg, June 16, 1940; children—Larry, Ralph, Jean Kellogg Jostad. Various secretarial positions, 1938-39, 65-68; mem. S.D. Ho. of Reps. from 4th Dist., 1980—. Bd. dirs. Jenkins Home, Watertown, S.D., 1981—. Mem. Nat. Order Women Legislators, Watertown C. of C., Women's Resource Center, Women in Mgmt., LWV, Bus. and Profl. Women, Peace and Justice Center, Farmers Union. Democrat. Methodist. Clubs: H.O.A., Sweet Adelines (dir.).

KELLY, CECILIA MARY, artistic dir., choreographer; b. Beckenham, England, Mar. 22, 1922; d. James Robert and Emily Monica (Hewitt) Ellis; came to U.S., 1946, naturalized, 1949; student Ballet Sch., LaScala Theatre, Milan, Italy, 1931-36; m. Eugene Joseph Kelly, May 22, 1945; children—Eugene James, Chinta Monica (Mrs. Alvin Tucker). Mem. LaScala Co., Milan, 1936-38; concerts in Far East, Bombay, Cape Town, Penang, Singapore, 1938-41; mem. Sadler's Wells Ballet, England, 1941-46; guest chr., lectr. N.H., 1946-54; master classes, Taiwan, 1955-59; founder, dir. ballet, Ark. Arts Center, Little Rock, 1960-63; founder, dir. Shreveport (La.) Symphony Ballet, 1966-72, El Dorado Civic Ballet (Ark.), 1967-70, Twin City Civic Ballet, Monroe, La., 1970—; guest artist So. Methodist U., Dallas, 1968; artist in residence Shreveport Symphony Ballet, 1974-75. Chmn., Save the Whale Com. La.; benefit performances March of Dimes, 1954, 70. Recipient award Gov. Faubus. Mem. Nat. Soc. Arts and Letters (nat. dance chmn. 1970-72, 74-76, nat. career award chmn. 1976—). Roman Catholic. Home: PO Box 171 Greenwood LA 71033

KELLY, DOROTHY ANN, coll. pres.; b. Bronx, N.Y., July 26, 1929; d. Walter David and Sarah (McCauley) Kelly; B.A., Coll. New Rochelle, 1951; M.A., Catholic U., Washington, 1958; Ph.D., U. Notre Dame, 1970; Litt.D. (hon.), Mercy Coll., Dobbs Ferry, N.Y., 1976; LL.D. (hon.), Nazareth Coll. of Rochester (N.Y.), 1979; D.H.L., Coll. St. Rose, 1981, Manhattan Coll., 1979. Mem. faculty Coll. New Rochelle (N.Y.), 1957—, chmn. dept. history, 1965-67, acad. dean, 1967-72, acting pres., 1970-71, pres., 1972—. Trustee, vice chmn. Commn. Ind. Colls. and Univs. of State of N.Y., 1977-78, chmn. bd. trustees, 1978-80, mem. govt. relations com., 1980—; chmn. Com. Higher Edn. Opportunity, 1977; mem. commr. edn. Adv. Council on Higher Edn. for N.Y. State, 1975-77, subcom. on postsecondary occupational edn., 1975-77; exec. com. Empire State Found. Ind. Liberal Arts Colls., 1975—, vice chmn., 1977-81, chmn., 1981—; trustee, mem. exec. com. Assn. Colls. and Univs. of State of N.Y., 1976—; mem. exec. com. Assn. Colls. Mid-Hudson Area, 1976—, pres., 1979-81; mem. com. on purpose and identity Assn. Cath. Colls. and Univs., 1975-80, mem. Neylon Conf. steering com., 1978—, mem. bishops and presidents com., 1979—; mem. adv. council on fin. aid to students Office Edn., HEW, 1978—; chmn. Women's Coll. Coalition, 1980—; trustee United Student Aid Funds, 1980—; chmn. govt. relations adv. com. Nat. Assn. Ind. Colls. and Univs., 1981—; bd. dirs. Westchester County Assn., 1977-80, 81—. Mem. AAUP, Am. Hist. Assn., AAUW, Nat. Fedn. Bus. and Profl. Women, Am. Assn. Higher Edn., Nat. Assembly Women Religious. Address: Coll New Rochelle New Rochelle NY 10801

KELLY, DOROTHY MARGARET, mgmt. cons.; b. Jamaica, N.Y., Apr. 29, 1925; d. Charles Frank and Mary (Emken) Lehner; A.Bus., Kaupert Jr. Coll., 1945; student Katherine Gibbs Mgmt. for Women, 1974-75; m. George M. Kelly, June 25, 1944; children—Karen P. Kelly Dehncke, Kathleen M. Kelly Devlin, Richard C., Virginia D. Staff asst. to pres. Maxson Electronics, Great River, N.Y., 1962-66; exec. asst. to chmn. Eltra Corp., N.Y.C., 1966-74, Studebaker Worthington, Inc., N.Y.C., 1974-75; exec. asst. to pres. United Mchts., N.Y.C., 1975-77; exec. asst./adminstrn. group v.p., mem. pres.'s panel Equitable Life Assurance Soc. U.S., N.Y.C., 1977-79; asso. mgmt. cons. G L Staff Cons., N.Y.C., 1979—; lectr., cons. Mem. Nat. Assn. Female Execs. Roman Catholic. Clubs: Indian Hills Country, Brightwaters Yacht. Home: 415 Ackerson Blvd Brightwaters NY 11718 Office: Suite 906 15 Columbus Circle New York NY 10023

KELLY, ELIZABETH NICHOLS, editor; b. Oklahoma City, Feb. 22, 1940; d. DeOwen and Margaret Lee (Roberts) Nichols; B.A., U. Mich., 1962; m. Joseph F. Kelly, Jr., Feb. 21, 1970; children—James Hamilton, Elizabeth Lee. Asst., New Yorker mag., 1962; editor Bus. Equipment Mfrs. Assn., N.Y.C., 1963; asso. editor Dell Pub. Co., Inc., N.Y.C., 1964-68; sr. editor Bobbs-Merrill Co., N.Y.C., 1968-74; sr. editor, exec. editor Delacorte Press, N.Y.C., 1974-82; fiction and book editor Cosmopolitan mag., 1982—. Mem. Womans Media Group. Republican. Editor: Understanding Pregnancy, 1972; Magic, 1976; Americans, 1978; Paris One, 1977; The New Assertive Woman, 1976; Your Two, Three and Four Five and Six Year Old, 1976; Redbook Report on Sexuality, 1977; The Family Money Book, 1978; Women and Anxiety, 1978; Scott Was Here, 1978; Green Ice, 1978; Tinsel, 1978; Everyone's Money Book, 1979; Random Winds, 1980; contbr. articles to popular jours. Home: 1088 Park Ave New York NY 10028 Office: 1 Dag Hammarskjold Plaza New York NY 10017

KELLY, ELIZABETH SLUSSER, librarian; b. Kalamazoo, Mich., Jan. 24, 1938; d. Herbert and Lois E. (Maher) Slusser; B.A., Coll. St. Catherine, 1958; J.D., So. Ill. U., 1978; m. Matthew J. Kelly, Aug. 30, 1958; children—Michael, Sarah, Margaret, Mark. Librarian colls. Ind., Ill., Calif., 1958-72; tech. services librarian So. Ill. U. Sch. Law Library, Carbondale, 1973-75, reader services librarian, 1975-77, law library dir., 1978—. Ford Found. scholar, 1953. Mem. Am. Assn. Law Libraries (dir. 1981 Inst.), Mid-Am. Assn. Law Libraries (pres. 1980-82), Chgo. Assn. Law Libraries, Phi Beta Kappa. Roman Catholic. Articles editor So. Ill. U. Law Jour., 1976; mem. editorial adv. bd. Oceana Group, 1981—. Office: Lesar Law Bldg So Ill U Carbondale IL 62901

KELLY, GAIL VANESSA WILKERSON, mktg. exec.; b. N.Y.C., Mar. 29, 1947; d. Ezekiel Bill and Lorraine Luella (Cole) Wilkerson; B.S., Coll. Notre Dame, 1968; M.B.A., Golden Gate U., 1977; m. John Kelly, Jan. 17, 1981; 1 son, John Ashley III. Adminstr., San Francisco Neighborhood Legal Assistance Found., 1971-77; sales mgr. Southland Corp., Cupertino, Calif., 1977-80; mktg. analyst Crown Zellerbach, San Francisco, 1980—; cons. Project Bus., Jr. Achievement, 1980—. Mem. Nat. Assn. Female Execs., Nat. Assn. Black M.B.A.s, Assn. M.B.A. Execs. Baptist. Home: 7833 Greenly Dr Oakland CA 94605

KELLY, GRACE DENTINO, sci. educator; b. Peoria, Ill., Mar. 30, 1934; d. Michael and Arnita Balagna (Barto) Dentino; cert. med. technology, St. Francis Sch. Med. Tech., 1955; B.S., Bradley U., 1971, M.S., 1973; m. Robert N. Kelly, Aug. 31, 1957; children—Susan, James, Stephen, Patrick. Tchr. sci. St. Mark Sch., Peoria, asst. prin., 1980—, chmn. jr. high sch. curriculum com. for drug edn. Mem. ednl. adv. bd. Peoria Jour. Star Newspaper, 1973—. Mem. Nat. Sci. Tchrs. Assn., Am. Soc. Clin. Pathologists, Ill. Sci. Tchrs. Assn. (dir. region III, presenter papers), Ill. Jr. Acad. Sci. (dir. region I), AAUW. Roman Catholic. Home: 1815 W High St Peoria IL 61606 Office: 711 N Underhill Peoria IL 61606

KELLY, HELEN ZOELLNER, lawyer; b. La Crosse, Wis., Mar. 18, 1943; d. Paul William and Grayce (Hartung) Zoellner; B.S. in Polit. Sci. with highest honors, U. Wis., 1976, J.D., 1980. Sales clk. Zoellner's Bakery, La Crosse, 1957-61; dental asst., La Crosse, 1961-62; teletype typist Trane Co., La Crosse, 1962-63; relocation interviewer OEO, Topeka, 1965; keypuncher Trane Co., La Crosse, 1967-69, Profl. Bus. Service, La Crosse, 1969-71; admitted to Wis. bar, 1980; law clk. Donald J. Harman, Ltd., La Crosse, 1978-80; practice law, La Crosse, 1980; guest lectr. U. Wis., La Crosse, 1976, Western Wis. Tech. Inst., 1980-82. Leader Riverland council Girl Scouts U.S.A., 1972-75; 19th dist. alderman La Crosse, 1975-79; city planning commr. La Crosse, 1976-78; mem. adv. bd. Cath. Social Service, 1975-78; bd. dirs. La Crosse Citizens Coalition for Rape Counseling, 1974-77, Western Wis. Legal Services; treas. Up Your Income Investment Club; treas., mem. exec. bd. La Crosse County Democratic party. del. to White House Conf. on Domestic and Fgn. Affairs, 1973. Recipient Friends of La Crosse Public Library award, 1978. Mem. Nat. Lawyers Guild, Wis. State Bar, La Crosse County Bar, La Crosse Polit. Sci. Assn., Women's Polit. Caucus, ACLU, NOW (pres. La Crosse 1973-76), Wis. League Municipalities, Ratom, Eta Phi Alpha. Home: 1213 Madison St La Crosse WI 54601 Office: 304 Exchange Bldg PO Box 455 La Crosse WI 54601

KELLY, JOAN BERLIN, clin. psychologist; b. Sewickley, Pa., Aug. 24, 1939; d. Allison and Louise (Porter) Berlin; B.A., Bucknell U., 1961; M.S., Yale U., 1963, Ph.D., 1965; m. James Montgomery Kelly, III, Oct. 7, 1967; children—Andrew James, Sarah Elizabeth. Lectr., instr. U. Mich., Ann Arbor, 1965-68; chief So. Marin children's team Marin Community Mental Health Center, San Rafael, Calif., 1968-71, dir. child and youth div., 1970-71, co-prin. investigator children of divorce research project, 1971-80; dir. No. Calif. Mediation Center, Greenbrae, 1981—; sr. staff psychologist dept. psychiatry Mt. Zion Hosp. and Med. Center, San Francsco, 1970-74, faculty continuing edn. program, 1974-76; instr. U. Calif. at Berkeley Extension, 1973-76; pvt. practice psychology, cons., Greenbrae, Calif., 1974—; clin. dir. Project COPE, Marin Mental Health Assn., 1975-78; sr. cons. Child and Family Divorce Counseling Service, Children's Hosp. San Francisco, 1977-80; sr. cons. children of single parent families project Mill Valley (Calif.) Schs., 1977-78; mem. dissertation coms. Calif. Sch. Profl. Psychology, 1977-82; adv. panel Am. Insts. for Research project, 1979. Mem. alumni adv. council Bucknell U., 1979—; bd. dirs. Tamalpais Nursery Sch., Mill Valley, 1975-78, Marin Mental Health Assn., 1980—. Fellow Am. Orthopsychiat. Assn.; mem. Am. Psychol. Assn., Calif. Psychol. Assn., Marin Psychol. Assn. Author: Surviving the Breakup: How Children and Parents Cope with Divorce, 1980; also numerous articles. Office: 900 S Eliseo Dr Greenbrae CA 94904

KELLY, JOAN MARIE, psychologist; b. Plymouth, Mass., Dec. 31, 1940; d. Martin Edward and Margaret Mary (Roche) K.; B.A. in English and Edn., Boston Coll., 1968; M.A. in Sch. Psychology (NIMH fellow 1968-72), Columbia U., 1970, Ph.D., 1972; divorced; 1 son, Jon. Elem. sch. tchr. Mass. and Conn., 1961-66; sch. psychologist N.J. and N.Y., 1970-74; sch. psychologist, chmn. com. handicapped Greenwood Lake (N.Y.) Sch., 1974—; workshop presenter, cons. in field. Mem. Am. Psychol. Assn., Nat. Assn. Sch. Psychologists, Assn. Children with Learning Disabilities, Commn. Gifted Edn., ABC Reading Council, Mensa. Club: Middletown Scrabble (co-dir.). Author articles in field. Home: 53 Sarah Ln Middletown NY 10940 Office: Greenwood Lake Sch Waterstone Rd Greenwood Lake NY 10925

KELLY, MARGARET MARY, phys. therapist; b. Whitman, Mass., May 16, 1947; d. Martin Edward and Margaret Mary (Roche) K.; B.S. in Phys. Therapy, Boston U., 1969. Staff phys. therapist Norwood (Mass.) Hosp., 1969-72; chief phys. therapist, founder dept. Worcester (Mass.) Hahnemann Hosp., 1972-74; asso. partner Rehab. Services, Inc., Walpole, Mass., 1974—; adv. bd. phys. therapist asst. program Becker Jr. Coll. Mem. Am. Phys. Therapy Assn. (chmn. Central Mass. dist. 1975-78), Comprehensive Health Planning Council of Central Mass. Office: 290 Main St Walpole MA 02081

KELLY, MARGARET RICAUD (MRS. THOMAS W. KELLY), educator; b. Dillon, S.C., Mar. 22, 1910; d. Robert Barry and Lulu Mowry (Crosland) Ricaud; A.B., Winthrop Coll., 1931; postgrad. Duke U., 1931, U. Miami, 1937, U. Fla., 1938, U. N.C., 1950, 52, 53, U. S.C., 1954, Coker Coll., 1954-55; m. John Quinton Maynard, Jan. 1, 1936; m. 2d, Thomas W. Kelly, Sept. 12, 1950. Prin. Ebenezer Sch., Marlboro County, S.C., 1932-35; tchr. public schs., Homestead, Fla., 1937-39; tchr. Fletcher Meml. Sch., McColl, S.C., 1940-46, 67-69, prin., 1942-45; attendance tchr. Marlboro County Schs., Bennettsville, 1946-50; tchr. elem. sch., Tabor City, N.C., 1950-51; tchr. pub. schs., Cordova, N.C., 1951-56, Society Hill, S.C., 1956-67; tchr. spl. edn. Blenheim (S.C.) primary schs., 1970-73; individual tutor, Bennettsville, 1973—. Mem. Marlboro Arts Council. Registered genealogist. Mem. Nat., S.C. edn. assns., Nat. Assn. Women Deans, Adminstrs. and Counselors, Marlboro County Tchrs. (chmn. public relations 1940-45), Colonial Dames 17th Century (registrar 1979-81), Magna Charta Dames, Soc. Decs. Most Noble Order of Garter, Geneal. Soc. London, French Huguenot Soc., Colonial Order of Crown, DAR, UDC, Nat. Geneal. Soc., S.C., Marlborough hist. socs., D.A.R., Nat. Poetry Soc., Marlborough Arts Council. Author: Jack and the Flying Saucer, 1973; Poems by Margaret Ricaud Kelly, 1974; The Ricaud Family, 1976; A Short History of Marlboro County, S.C., 1600-1979, 1979; contbr. poetry to anthologies, articles to various local newspapers. Home: 402 Fayetteville Ave Bennettsville SC 29512

KELLY, SISTER, MARY JULIA, welfare found. adminstr.; b. Muscatine, Iowa, May 16, 1927; d. Edward James and Freda Helen (Schrempf) K.; student Mercy Hosp. Sch. Nursing, Marshalltown, Iowa, 1945-47. Joined Order of St. Francis, Roman Catholic Ch., 1948-50, Order of St. Benedict, 1958—; nurse Rock Island (Ill.) Franciscan Hosp., 1956; mem. staff Good Shepherd Shelter, Mill Bay, B.C., Can., 1959—, now dir., acting pres. Editor: The Shepherd's Crook, 1977—. Address: Route 1-2500 Mill Bay V0R 2P0 Canada

KELLY, MATTIE CAROLINE MAY, business woman; b. Vernon, Fla., Mar. 12, 1912; d. William W. and Mary Alice (Russ) May; student Rollins Coll., 1944-46, 48-49; A.B., Fla. State U., 1952, postgrad., 1970-71; m. Coleman Lee Kelly, Mar. 26, 1932 (div. June 1971); children—Carnera Lee, Lila Bernarr, Imogene (Mrs. H.J. Toole), Carol Kelly Adams, Cecelia Kelly Sims; m. 2d, Paul Sims, July 13, 1973 (div. May 1979). Tchr. public schs., Fla., 1928-33, 37; pres. Kelly Boat Service, Inc., 1980—, Kelly Homes, Inc., Destin, Fla., to 1978; co-owner, trustee Coleman L. Kelly Trust; co-organizer, co-owner, sec.-treas. Radio Sta. WMMK-FM, Destin. Mem. Okaloosa County Democratic Com., 1958—, exec. adv. bd., 1956-72; mem. State Dem. Exec. Com., mem. adv. bd., 1966-70, del. nat. conv., 1968, 72. Bd. dirs. Destin Library, 1956—, Fla. League Arts, 1980-81; bd. dirs. Okaloosa County chpt. ARC, 1954-60, chmn., 1957-58; adv. bd. diversified coop. tng. Choctawhatchee High Sch., 1960—; camp counsellor Senior Hi, Camp Weed, 1964; patron Stagecrafters; promoter, supporter Mattie M. Kelly Fine Arts Center, Destin. Mem. coordinating council for arts Okaloosa-Walton Jr. Coll., 1965—, rep. to Fla. Arts Council, 1966—; patron Okaloosa County Symphony, Ft. Walton Beach Ballet Assn.; adv. bd. Okaloosa County Mental Health Assn., 1978—, Women's Theatre Workshop Okaloosa-Walton Jr. Coll., 1978—; chmn. Historic Sites Commn., Okaloosa-Walton. Recipient award ARC, 1960; award for arts for Northwest Fla., Gov. Fla., 1982. Mem. Am. Camellia Soc., Nat. Writers Club, Geneal. Soc. Okaloosa County, N.Y. Bot. Gardens Club, Okaloosa County Concert Assn., Nat. Hist. Soc., Nat. Trust for Historic Preservation, Pensacola Little Theatre, Playground Poets Assn. (coordinator 1977—), Ft. Walton Beach C. of C. (edn. com., mem. host com.), Fla. Boatsmen's Assn. (sec. 1972—), Hist. Soc. Okaloosa and Walton Counties, Ft. Walton Beach Woman's Club (chmn. fine arts com. 1957-58), Woman's Club (v.p. 1958-59), Gulf Coast Dem. Women's Club, AAUW (charter, legis. com. 1971—), Asso. Council Arts, Okaloosa County Community Concert Assn. Mem. Protestant Episcopal Ch. (adminstr., supt. ch. sch. 1953-60, br. chmn. Christian edn. 1955-60, dist. chmn. Christian edn. 1958-61, asst. organist, tchr., del. adult conf. 1957, 59, del. religious TV programming workshop 1955-56; dist. v.p. 1961-64; pres. church-women Diocese Fla. 1965-68). Author: Songs and Sonnets From the Sea (poetry), 1964; donor land and funds for Mattie M. Kelly Fine Arts Center. Address: PO Box 425 Indian Bayou Destin FL 32541

KELLY, MOIRA J., indsl. relations exec.; b. Stuttgart, Germany, Aug. 30, 1952; d. Francis John and Margaret Genevieve (Casserly) K.; B.A., Marquette U., 1974; student U. Wis., 1977. Employment cons. MS Employment Service, Milw., 1974; hospitality mgr. Big-Boy-Marcus Corp., Milw., 1974-75; asst. personnel dir. T. A. Chapman Co., Milw., 1975-76; asst. personnel mgr. Grede Foundries Inc., Milw., 1976-80; corp. labor relations specialist Wis. Electric Power Co., Milw., 1980-82; plant indsl. relations mgr. Vulcan Materials Co., 1982—. Producer, Wis. Electric Employee Talent Show, 1982; mem. local bd. SSS, 1982—; chmn. candidates and campaigns com. Milw. County Republican Com., 1982—, vice-chmn. Milw. County Republican Com., 1981-82; treas. Milw. County Bd. Suprs., 1978—; co-chmn. 5th Congl. Dist., George Bush Presdl. Campaign, 1980; state precinct coordinator, asst. fin. dir. Sen. R. W. Kasten, 1980; campaign mgr. State Rep. Mordecai Lee, 1976; mem. adv. panel Adult Edn. and Tech. and Vocat. Schs., Reedsburg, Wis., 1977. Mem. Am. Soc. Personnel Adminstrn., Wis. Soc. to Prevent Blindness (treas. jr. bd.), Personnel and Indsl. Relations Assn. Wis. Home: 2423 E Belleview Pl Milwaukee WI 53211 Office: 9100 S 5th Ave Oak Creek WI 53154

KELLY, MONICA LOUISE, personnel exec.; b. Osaka, Japan, Oct. 8, 1949; parents Am. citizens; d. George Richard and Helen Frances (Christman) K.; student U. Wis., 1967-69; B.A. with distinction, George Washington U., 1980. Personnel mgmt. intern Dept. Navy, U.S. Naval Acad., 1977-79; position classification specialist Dept. Air Force, Andrews AFB, Washington, 1979-80, employee relations specialist, 1980-82; employee relations specialist Hdqrs. Dept. Air Force, 1982—. Recipient Spl. Achievement award Andrews AFB, 1981. Mem. Classification and Compensation Soc., Internat. Personnel Mgmt. Assn., Alpha Sigma Lambda. Episcopalian. Home: 2106 Old Fort Hills Ct Friendly MD 20744 Office: AF/MPKE Room 4D229 The Pentagon Washington DC 20330

KELLY, NANCY MONROE, med. technologist; b. High Point, N.C., May 9, 1932; d. Clayton Lee and Ellen Dorothy (Ridgill) Monroe; B.S. in Med. Scis., Wake Forest U., 1954; cert. med. tech. Bowman Gray Sch. Med. Tech., 1954; M.A. in Edn., E. Tenn. State U., 1979; children—David Monroe, Kevin Lee, Shannon Elizabeth. Med. technologist City Hosp., Winston-Salem, N.C., 1954-56, Bowman Gray Sch. Medicine, 1956-57, 1960-63, Hoback Clin. Labs., Bristol, Tenn., 1971-76, United Intermountain Pathology Med. Lab., Bristol, 1980, Bristol (Tenn.) Meml. Hosp., 1977—; mem. Nat. Certification Agy. rev. bd.; chmn. U. Eastern Tenn. Nat. Lab. Week; mem. Tenn. Lab. Adv. Com. Active PTA, 1963-80, former sec., v.p., pres., mem. city ednl. bd.; chmn. ARC Vol. Sch. Clinic; mem. bd. Band Boosters; sec., pres. Child Study Club; former sec., pres. v.p. Va. Parrish Study Club; chaperone swim team booster club, recipient parent appreciation award; mem. altar com. State St. Meth. Ch.; active Jr. League, 1965-72, sec., v.p., nominations and membership com. chmn., chmn. by-laws, edn.; vol. in gen. and heart clinics, Bargain Box, swimming instr. Girls Club. NSF Scholar, 1978. Mem. Upper E. Tenn. State Med. Technologists (pres., sec., state task force on communications and public relations, conv. com., mem. state bd.), Am. Soc. Clin. Pathologists (affiliate mem., cert. med. technologist), Am. Soc. Med. Tech., Beta Beta Beta, Gamma Sigma Epsilon, Phi Delta Kappa. Clubs: Beta, Doctors Wives (past pres.). Home: 100 Walnut Circle Bristol TN 37620 Office: Bristol Meml Hosp Bristol TN 37620

KELLY, PATRICIA ANN, banker; b. Bay Shore, N.Y., Nov. 4, 1944; d. Roger Michael and Dorothy Clark (Morrell) K.; B.A. in History, Coll. Notre Dame, Balt., 1966. Actuarial analyst Pension Planners Balt., 1966-68; with First Nat. Bank Md., Balt., 1969—, v.p. comml. loans, 1977—. Mem. hosp. aux. Greater Balt. Med. Center. Mem. Nat. Assn. Bank Women, Robert Morris Assos. Club: Towson Golf and Country. Office: 25 S Charles St Baltimore MD 21203

KELLY, PATRICIA DUCY, civic worker; b. Pueblo, Colo., Nov. 11, 1923; d. Damian Patrick and Ruth Russell (Taylor) Ducy; B.A., U. Colo., 1948; m. Bret Kelly, Mar. 25, 1944; children—Eric Damian, Kate Kelly Schweitzer. Dir., Steel City Agys., Inc., 1973—; mem. Fed. Home Loan Bank Bd. of Topeka, 1977—. Mem. Colo. Council on Arts and Humanities, 1967-71; mem. Pueblo City Council, 1970-78, v.p., 1972-73, chmn. exec. com., 1974-75, 77; mem. exec. bd. Colo. Mcpl. League, 1970-74, v.p. exec. bd., 1972-73; mem. So. Colo. Econ. Devel. Dist. Exec. Bd., 1975-77; mem. steering com. Colo. Front Range Project, 1979—; bd. dirs. Pueblo Conservancy Dist., 1977—, chmn., 1977-79; mem. Pueblo Energy Commn., 1975—, chmn., 1975-77; mem. environ. steering com. Nat. League of Cities, 1971-76; mem. consumer affairs/spl. impact adv. com. Fed. Energy Adminstrn., 1976-77; mem. energy extension adv. com. Dept. Energy, 1978—; mem. citizens adv. com. Colo. Office of Energy Conservation, 1978—; mem. Colo. Bicentennial Commn., 1972-74; trustee Sangre de Cristo Arts and Conf. Center, 1971-77; bd. dirs. Project Colo., 1982—. Recipient Disting. Woman award U. So. Colo., 1970; outstanding achievement in arts award Pueblo C. of C., 1970; Disting. Citizen award Pueblo Rotary Club, 1976; Energy Conservation award Denver Fed. Exec. Bd., 1977. Mem. Women's Forum of Colo. (founding mem., dir. 1977-78). Democrat.

KELLY, PATRICIA SUE HAGGERTY, chem. co. exec.; b. Pitts., June 12, 1950; d. Bernard Anthony and Helen Rita (Pellegrini) Haggerty; student Duquesne U., 1968-69; B.S. with highest honors, W. Liberty State Coll., 1972; M.B.A. magna cum laude, U. Pitts., 1974; m. Robert E. Kelly, Apr. 21, 1979. Sales clk. Gimbels Dept. Store, Pitts., 1969-70; supr. Mktg. Services Center, Pitts., 1973; market research analyst Koppers Co., Pitts., 1974-78; planning asso. Mobil Chem. Co., Pitts., 1978—; tchr. indsl. mktg. research Carnegie-Mellon Grad. Bus. U., 1977-78; cons. A. O. Smith Co., Pitts. Nat. Bank, Darlington Clay Products div. Gen. Dynamics. Bd. dirs., public notary animal care and welfare Soc. Prevention Cruelty to Animals, 1974—; adv. Explorers Program, 1974-78. Recipient Phi Chi Theta award U. Pitts. Grad. Sch. Bus., 1974. Mem. Assn. Time Share Users (sec.-treas.), Nat. Assn. Female Execs., Am. Mktg. Assn. (v.p. intercollegiate chpt.), Beta Gamma Sigma, Delta Mu Delta (sec.-treas.). Republican. Roman Catholic. Home: 422 Mueller Ave Pittsburgh PA 15205 Office: 2000 Westhall St Pittsburgh PA 15233

KELLY, VIANNA BARKER, antique dealer; b. Moscow, Idaho, Feb. 6, 1910; d. George Refus and Martha Julia (Schultz) Hodge; student Success Bus. Coll., Seattle, 1930; m. Virgil G. Kelly, Oct. 28, 1961; 1 son, John Barker. Propr., Barkers Antique Shop, Seattle, 1941—; tchr. antique classes, 1956—. Mem. Appraisers Assn. Am., Am. Soc. Appraisers, Gemol. Inst. Am., Seattle Ceramic Soc., Associated Antique Dealers Am. Democrat. Roman Catholic. Club: Wash. Athletic (Seattle). Address: 22456 Pacific Hwy S Seattle WA 98188

KELM, CAROL HELENA, museum curator; b. Spokane, Wash., Aug. 28, 1929; d. Carl Delano and Ellen Minnesota (Keyes) Raney; B.A. in History, Wash. State Coll., 1952; B.Library Sci., U. Calif., Berkeley, 1953; m. Raymond Louis Kelm, Oct. 24, 1971. Library cataloger U. Calif., Davis, 1953-56; subject cataloger, serials div. head Yale U. Library, 1956-65; asst. catalogue librarian joint bank/fund library IMF, 1965-66; chief catalogue dept. Smithsonian Instn. Library, 1966-69; exec. resources and tech. services div. ALA, Chgo., 1969-77; curator Hist. Soc. Oak Park and River Forest, Ill., 1981—, bd. dirs., 1980-81. Sec., Unity Temple Restoration Found., 1979-82. Mem. ALA, Ch. and Synagogue Library Assn., Am. Soc. Indexers, Phi Beta Kappa, Phi Kappa Phi, Phi Alpha Theta. Home: 432 N Elmwood St Oak Park IL 60302

KELMAN, JUDITH ANN, writer; b. N.Y.C., Oct. 21, 1945; d. George Joseph and Flora (Underberg) Edelstein; B.S., Cornell U., 1967; M.A. (Fed. fellow), N.Y. U., 1968; M.S., So. Conn. State Coll., 1977; m. Edward Michael Kelman, June 28, 1970; children—Matthew Steven, Joshua Kenneth. Tchr. educable mentally handicapped Valley Stream (N.Y.) Public Schs., 1968-71; recreation supr. Camp A.N.C.H.O.R., extracurricular activities for handicapped children, Town of Hempstead, (N.Y.), 1968-71; speech pathologist Greenwich (Conn.) public schs.; spl. edn. cons. Area Cons., Inc., N.Y.C.; freelance writer, 1981—. Bd. dirs. Stamford (Conn.) Aid for Retarded, 1973-74; founder Touch, Inc., orgn. for parents of handicapped, Stamford, 1975, pres., 1975-76; asso. Am. Acad. Cerebral Palsy. Mem. Am. Speech and Hearing Assn., Conn. Speech and Hearing Assn., NEA, Conn. Edn. Assn., Council Exceptional Children. Democrat. Jewish. Club: Cornell of Fairfield County (Conn.) (sec. 1979—). Home: 60 Thornwood Rd Stamford CT 06903

KELNE, NANCY (ESTHER TEIN), educator; b. Rochester, N.Y.; d. Benjamin and Pearl (Hyde) Tein; B.S., N.Y. State Tchrs. Coll., Albany, 1943; M.S., Adelphi U., Garden City, N.Y., 1969; m. Nathan Kelne, Sept. 7. 1946; 1 dau., Elizabeth. Asst. to dir. edn. Inst. Life Ins., N.Y.C., 1948-50; tchr. Mineola (N.Y.) High Sch., 1952-55, 64-67; prof. secretarial sci. Nassau Community Coll., Garden City, 1967—; lectr., cons. in field. Recipient Chancellor's award excellence in teaching Nassau Community Coll., 1974. Mem. Am. Arbitration Assn., Am. Soc. Profl. and Exec. Women, Nat. Bus. Edn. Assn., N.Y. State Occupational Edn. Assn. Club: N.Y.U. Mem. editorial bd. Insight. Home: 58 Tara Dr East Hills NY 11576 Office: Nassau Community Coll Stewart Ave Garden City NY 11530

KELSEY, BARBARA HELEN, mfg. co. exec.; b. Olean, N.Y., Aug. 18, 1926; d. Bruce Douglas and Mary (Kelsey) Clover; student U. Louisville, 1944-45; m. Frank I. Kelsey, Sept. 28, 1957 (dec., 1974). Exec. sec. with Bethlehem Steel Corp., Lackawanna, N.Y., 1951-69; adminstrv. asst. Lincoln Sch., Shelbyville, Ky., 1969-70; sect. to v.p. fin. Vt. Am. Corp., Louisville, 1970-76, asst. sec., asst. treas., 1976-80, corp. sec., asst. treas., 1980—. Mem. Nat. Assn. Female Execs., Am. Bus. Women's Assn. Republican. Episcopalian. Club: Order Eastern Star. Home: 403 N Birchwood Ave Louisville KY 40206 Office: 100 E Liberty St Louisville KY 40202

KELSEY, KAREN ASHLEY, energy co. exec.; b. San Angelo, Tex., Apr. 18, 1944; d. Percy Eugene and Ivy Alice (Riu) Arthur; student U. Houston, 1962-65; m. John Wilson Kelsey, Dec. 26, 1977; 1 dau., Kelly Elizabeth. Office adminstr. Dr. John McCutcheon, Houston, 1965-67; legal sec. Hyer & Eickenroht, Houston, 1967-69; asst. to v.p./office office mgr. Ogilvy & Mather, Advt., Houston, 1970-72; exec. sec. to pres. and sr. v.p. Browning-Ferris Industries, Houston, 1972-74, part-time, 1974-76; exec. asst. to chmn. Transco Energy Co., Houston, 1977—, adminstr. contbns., 1982—. Co-chmn. commemorative plate sales Mus. Fine Arts, 1981; asst. to fin. dir. John Connally for Pres. campaign, 1980; asst. to chmn. YMCA campaign, 1979. Named YWCA Outstanding Woman for Transco Cos., Inc., 1981. Episcopalian. Clubs: Univ., River Oaks Tennis, Bayou, Maxim, Bus. and Profl. Women's (program dir. 1980). Home: 4007 W Main St Houston TX 77027 Office: PO Box 1396 Houston TX 77251

KELSEY, SHARA LYNN, govt. ofcl.; b. Sacramento, July 15, 1943; d. Rollin Eastman and Thelma Amelia (Dreith) K.; B.A. in Social Psychology, Calif. State U., Sacramento, 1976, M.A. in Quantitative Psychology, 1982; student Minn. Outward Bound Sch., 1967, 75. With Calif. State Service, Sacramento, 1965—, account clk. Dept. Edn., Div. Hwys., 1965-69, sr. computer operator, sr. data processing technician Dept. Motor Vehicles, 1969-78, social and behavioral research analyst, 1978—; research cons. to Motorcycle Safety Found., Sacramento Safety Council, Energy Commn. Recipient Luis Leon Meml. blood donor award. Mem. Am. Statis. Assn. (Sacramento); Western Psychol. Assn., Mensa. Clubs: Sierra, Ind. Order Foresters, Ten Gallon. Contbg. author to publs. in field, presentations to profl. confs. Office: 2415 1st Ave Sacramento CA 95818

KELSOE, LYNDA CAROL, computer analyst; b. Birmingham, Ala., Apr. 5, 1943; d. Johnny Willard and Marjorie Nanette (Wallace) Simmons; B.S., U. Montevallo, 1966; student U. Ala., 1968; B.S., Stevens Inst. Bus. Tech., 1971; M.A., U. Houston, 1977, M.A., 1979; m. Neal Marshall Kelsoe, July 18, 1981. Tchr. English, Birmingham (Ala.) Public Schs., 1966-70; programmer Bell Telephone Labs., Whippany, N.J., 1971-74; sci. programmer Lockheed Electronics, Houston, 1973-74; programmer analyst IBM, Houston, 1974-76, Lockheed Electronics, Houston, 1977-78; sr. analyst Computer Scis. Corp., Houston, 1978-82; corp. staff Jefferson Assocs., Inc., Houston, 1982—. Lic. pvt. pilot. Mem. Assn. Computing Machinery, Nat. Mgmt. Assn., Nat. Assn. Female Execs., Graphics Exchange. Home: 206 Yacht Club Ln Seabrook TX 77586 Office: 1640 Nasa Rd One Suite 200 Houston TX 77058

KELTY, MARION KUECHLE, nurse; b. Rego Park, N.Y., Oct. 14, 1931; d. Eugene E. and Esther M. (Boecler) Kuechle; B.A. summa cum laude, Jersey City State Coll., 1976; postgrad. Rutgers U., 1976-77; R.N., Orange Meml. Hosp. Sch. Nursing, 1951; children—Jeff, Kathy, Barbara, Sue. Staff nurse Somerset Valley Nursing Home, Bound Brook, N.J., 1965-69, supr., 1969-73, dir. nursing, 1973—; charter mem. Somerset County Hospice. Bd. mgrs. Am. Cancer Soc., 1971—; pres., co-founder Somerset County chpt. Make Today Count. Diplomate Am. Coll. Nursing Practice; cert. gerontol. nurse. Mem. Am., N.J. nurses assns., Alumni Assn. Orange Meml. Hosp., Gerontol. Soc., N.J. Soc. for Cert. Gerontol. Nurses (sec. 1975-77). Republican. Lutheran. Home: 14 Oak Ridge Rd Basking Ridge NJ 07920 Office: 1621 Route 22 Bound Brook NJ 08805

KELVER, ANN ELKINS, librarian; b. Delaware City, Del., Sept. 6, 1915; d. Dennie and Carrie Ridgeway (Cox) Elkins; B.A. with honors, Goshen (Ind.) Coll., 1964; M.A. in Secondary Edn., U. Denver, 1966, M.A. in L.S. (Colo. State Library scholar 1967-69), 1969; m. Gerald O'dell Kelver, Aug. 24, 1938. Cost accountant Miles Labs., Elkhart, Ind., 1944-62; librarian Jimtown (Ind.) High Sch., 1964-65; library dir. Arapahoe Regional Library Dist., Littleton, Colo., 1966—. Pres. Elkhart council Girl Scouts, 1959-61. Recipient Nell I. Scott award Friends of Library, Denver, 1978. Mem. ALA, Colo. Library Assn., Mountain Plains Library Assn., U. Denver Alumni AAUW. Republican. Methodist. Contbr. articles to profl. publs. Home: 13490 Kennedy Ave Brighton CO 80601 Office: 2305 E Arapahoe Rd Littleton CO 80122

KEMBLE, CAROLINE MARY, businesswoman; b. Bklyn., Dec. 4, 1916; d. Louis Aloysius and Antoinette (Nespoli) Coccaro; student St. John's Sch. Nursing, 1937-39; m. Harold Kemble, Oct. 29, 1939 (div.); children—Patricia, Elizabeth, Valerie. Trademark searcher partner Robert A. West, Inc., N.Y.C., 1952-63; owner, pres. Trademark Service, Baldwin, N.Y., 1964—. Home: 2363 S Grand Ave Apt 13C1 Baldwin NY 11510

KEMP, SUZANNE LEPPART, educator, clubwoman; b. N.Y.C., Dec. 28, 1929; d. John Culver and Eleanor (Buxton) Leppart; grad. Ogontz Jr. Coll., 1949; B.S., U. Md., 1952; m. Ralph Clinton Kemp, Apr. 4, 1953; children—Valerie Gale, Sandra Lynn, John Maynard, Renee Alison. Elem. sch. tchr. Bd. dirs. Dulaney Valley Symphony Soc. Mem. Nat. Soc. Women Descs. of Ancient and Hon. Arty. Co., Nat. Soc. Daus. of Founders and Patriots of Am. (corr. sec.), Nat. Soc. Dames of Court of Honor, Nat. Soc. Sons and Daus. of Pilgrims, Nat. Soc. U.S. Daus. of 1812 (chpt. organizing pres. 1977-79; state 2d v.p., chpt. v.p., 1979—), Nat. Soc. New Eng. Women (colony pres. 1978-80), Nat. Soc. Coloniel Dames XVII Century (state chmn. heraldry and coats of arms 1977-79), Nat. Soc. DAR (chpt. regent 1970-73, chpt. v.p.; Md. soc. chmn. transp. 1976-79), Md. State Officers Club, Md. Hist. Soc., Friends of Animals, Defenders of Animal Rights, Inc., U. Md. Alumni, English Speaking Union, Star Spangled Banner Flag House Assn., Kappa Delta Alumni. Christian Scientist. Clubs: Baltimore Country; Lago Mar Country. Editor: The Spinning Wheel, 1973-76. Home: 1206 Doves Cove Rd Towson MD 21204

KEMPER, DORLA DEAN (EATON), real estate broker; b. Calhoun, Mo., Sept. 10, 1929; d. Paul McVey and Jesse Lee (McCombs) Eaton; student William Woods Coll., 1947-48; B.S. in Edn., Central Mo. State U., 1952; m. Charles K. Kemper, Mar. 1, 1951; children—Kevin Keil, Kara Lee. Tchr. pub. schs., Twin Falls, Idaho, 1950-51, Mission, Kans., 1952-53, Burbank, Calif., 1953-57; real estate saleswoman Minn., 1967-68, Calif., 1971-73; Deanie Kemper, Realtor (name changed to Deanie Kemper, Inc. Real Estate Brokerage 1976), Loomis, Calif., 1974-76, pres., 1976—, also dir. Pres. Battle Creek Park Elem. Sch. PTA, St. Paul, 1966-67; mem. Placer County (Calif.) Bicentennial Commn., 1976; mem. real estate adv. com. Sierra Coll., 1981—. Named to Masters Club (lifetime) Sacramento and Placer County bds. Realtors, 1978; cert. resdl. specialist Realtors Nat. Mktg. Inst. Mem. Nat., Calif. assns. Realtors, Sacramento, Placer County bds. Realtors, Grad. Realtors Inst., Auburn Travel Study Club (pres. 1978-79), DAR (chpt. regent 1971-73, organizing chpt. regent 1977—, dist. dir. Calif. 1978-80, vice-chmn. nat. def. com., registrar Calif. 1980-82, state vice regent Calif. 1982-84). Republican. Mem. Christian Ch. Clubs: Auburn Travel Study (pres.), Hidden Valley Women's (pres. Loomis club 1970-71). Republican Mem. Christian Ch. Home: 8165 Morningside Dr Loomis CA 95650

KEMPIN, LINDA JEANNE, account exec.; b. Chgo., June 5, 1951; d. Emil August and Margaret Mary (Pierorazio) K.; student (James scholar) U. Ill., 1969-71; B.F.A., No. Ill. U., 1974; postgrad. in bus. adminstrn. Keller Grad. Sch. Mgmt., 1979—. Layout editor, asst. prodn. mgr. No. Star, DeKalb, Ill., 1972-74; advt. and promotional dir. Group Travel Enterprises, Chgo., 1973-74; design asst. 3M Nat. Advt., Chgo., 1974; designer, asso. art dir. R.R. Donnelley & Sons, Chgo., 1975-79; communications cons. Saga Communications Group, Greenwich, Conn., 1979-81; sr. project mgr. PCS Reports, Ltd., Oak Brook, Ill., 1981-82; account exec. Nexus, Inc., Chgo., 1982—. Past v.p., publicity chmn. Southeast Lakeview Neighbors; cons. Internat Resource Dynamics, Chgo., 1981. Mem. Soc. Typog. Arts, Nat. Assn. Female Execs., Bus. and Profl. Women Chgo., Women in Design. Home: 517 W Oakdale Ave Apt 303 Chicago IL 60657 Office: 233 E Erie St Suite 708 Chicago IL 60611

KEMPNER, RUTH LYDIA (BENEDICTA MARIA) (MRS. ROBERT M.W. KEMPNER), author, social worker; b. Geislingen, Germany; d. Hermann and Marie-Luise (Spring) Hahn; diploma social work Sch. Social Work, Berlin, 1930; postgrad. Pa. Sch. Social Work, Phila., 1940-41; m. Robert M. W. Kempner; children—Lucian K., Andre K. Social worker City of Berlin, 1929-33; dean women Fiorenza Coll., Florence, Italy and Nice, France, 1936-39; social-work agys. in Phila., 1941-45; M-project, Pres. F. D. Roosevelt, 1944-45; research analyst U.S. Army, Nuremberg War Crimes Trials, 1947-48; work on claims for health damage Catholic and Jewish Nazi victims, 1953-63; researcher martyr priests, 1963—, TV, radio documentations, Rome, Germany, U.S. Docorated Pro Ecclesia et Pontifice, Pope Paul VI; Cross of Merit, Govt. German Fed. Republic; recipient Golden Honor award Austrian Govt. Mem. Am. Assn. Social Workers, Am. Acad. Social Work, Internat. Pen Club Am. Author: (under pen name Benedicta Maria) Women in Nazi Germany, 1944; Priester before Hitler's Tribunals, 1966; Nuns under the Swastika, 1979; contbr. to Catholic mags. Home: 112 Lansdowne Court Lansdowne PA 19050

KEMPTON, GRACE FICKLING ARRINGTON (MRS. WILLETT MAIN KEMPTON), realtor, journalist; b. Rome, Ga., June 26; d. Homer Newell and Grace (Fickling) Arrington; A.B., Shorter Coll.; B.A. in Journalism, U. Ga., 1940; m. Willett Main Kempton, Aug. 5, 1939 (dec. Nov. 1962); children—Willett Main, Grace Arrington (dec. May 1973), John Houston. Soc. columnist Athens (Ga.) Banner Herald, 1940-41; with Clark County Draft Bd., Athens, 1941; spl. writer Atlanta Constn., 1942; reporter Army Public Relations, Atlanta, 1942-43; owner, mgr. Embassy Service Bur., Washington, 1946-47; adminstrv. asst. Congressman Henderson Lanham, Ga., 1947-48; Washington soc. columnist Palm Beach (Fla.) Life, 1947; social news columnist Providence Jour., McLean, Va., 1952-53; columnist Courier of George Washington U. Med. Sch., 1952-57; owner, realtor Grace A. Kempton Realty Co., McLean, 1955—. Mem. women's bd. George Washington U. Hosp., Washington, 1953—; life mem. Athens Jr. Assembly; dir. McLean Horse Show Assn., 1950-70. Served from 2d lt. to capt., WAC, 1943-45. Mem. Nat., No. Va. bds. Realtors, Va. Real Estate Assn., Am. News Women's Club, Nat. Trust Historic Preservation, Ga. State Soc. (pres. 1975), Women in Communications, Chi Omega. Methodist. Clubs: Capitol Speakers, The Washington. Home: 1313 Rockland Terr McLean VA 22101 Office: 8112 Old Dominion Dr McLean VA 22102

KENDALL, CHARLOTTE KALIKOHOU, contract adminstr.; b. Honolulu, Jan. 25, 1940; d. Charles Russel and Mililani Rose (Lucas) Kendall; student Colo. State Coll., 1959-60; children—Rhonda McKeague, Alex McKeague, Charles McKeague. Bookkeeper, So. Md. Oil, LaPlata, 1972-73; accounts payable, shipping-receiving mgr. Mammoth Mart Inc., Waldorf, Md., 1974-77; purchasing agt., contract adminstr. Plessey Micro Sci., Mountain View, Calif., 1977-81; subcontract adminstr. FMC Corp., San Jose, Calif., 1981—. Recipient outstanding achievement award Girls Club of Mid-Peninsula, 1978. Mem. Am. Electronics Assn., Am. Prodn. and Inventory Control Soc., Nat. Contract Mgmt. Assn., Purchasing Mgmt. Assn. No. Calif. Home: 1340 Jonathan St #2 Santa Clara CA 95050 Office: 1105 Coleman Ave Box 1201 San Jose CA 95108

KENDALL, DOLORES DIANE, artist, direct mail mktg. exec.; b. Newark, June 1, 1946; d. Dominick Pisapia and Ann Fanfone K.; student Berkeley Bus. Coll., 1964-65, Middlesex County Coll., 1966-67, Rutgers U., 1967-69, Art Inst. Boston, 1976, Sch. Visual Arts, N.Y.C., 1978. Proofreader, supr. N.J. State Diagnostic Center, 1965-74; apprentice Graham Art Studio, Boston, 1975-77; dir. direct mktg. Boardroom Reports, Inc., N.Y.C., 1977-82; pres., chief operating officer Roman Managed Lists, Inc., N.Y.C., 1982—; exhibited in group shows including city and county shows in Middlesex and Somerset Counties (N.J.), 1965-74, Greenwich Village Art Show, N.Y.C., 1972, Graham Art Studio, Boston, 1975-77; represented in pvt. collections. Recipient Desi award for promotion package, 1980. Mem. Direct Mail Mktg. Assn., Nat. Bus. Circulation Assn., Nat. Mail Order Soc., NOW, Direct Mktg. Creative Forum, Copley Art Soc. Author: (poems) My Eyes Are Windows, 1972. Home: 530 2d Ave New York NY 10016

KENDEL, DORLA DEAN (MRS. ROBERT LEWIS KENDEL), former mfrs. rep. co. exec., artist; b. Los Angeles, Apr. 16, 1930; d. Thomas Weston and Lois May (Oliver) Hall; grad. high sch.; m. Robert Lewis Kendel, Aug. 13, 1949; children—Robert L., Michael L., Richard L. Tchr. oil painting, LaCrescenta, Calif., 1960-62; with Air Conditioning Spltys. Co., Inc., mfrs. rep., LaCrescenta, 1962-79, corp. sec.-treas., 1970-79; artist, 1979—. Active Scouting, sch. and sport activities, 1956-70. Mem. ASHRAE. Address: 46-058 Verba Santa Palm Desert CA 92260

KENDER, DOROTHY, trade assn. pub. exec.; b. Bklyn., Feb. 12; d. Emil and Mary (Schenone) Perosio; B.S., Duquesne U., 1950; m. Joseph Kender, Apr. 15, 1948; children—Karen, Scott. Adminstr., Ring Engring., Pitts., 1950-53, Tom Mistick, Inc., Monroeville, Pa., 1953-57; with Bldg. Stone Inst., N.Y.C., 1958—, exec. asst., 1960-75, exec. v.p., 1975—, researcher, producer Stone Catalog, 1962—, Stone Info. Manual, 1974, editor-pub. Building Stone News, 1970—, pub. Building Stone Mag., 1979—. Home: 65 Tappan Landing Tarrytown NY 10591 Office: 420 Lexington Ave New York NY 10017

KENDRICK, DOLORES THERESA, poet, educator; b. Washington, Sept. 7, 1927; d. Robert Eldridge, Jr. and Josephine (Merriweather) K.; B.S., Miner Tchrs. Coll., 1949; M.A.T., Georgetown U., 1970. Tchr. public schs., Washington, 1953-72; Fulbright Exchange tchr., No. Ireland, 1963-64; instr. English, Phillips Exeter Acad., Exeter, N.H.; poet, tchr.-in-residence various schs. U.S. Recipient Experienced Tchr. Fellowship award Georgetown U., 1969-70. Mem. Poets and Writers, Inc. N.Y.C., Poetry Soc. N.H. Author: (poetry) Through the Ceiling, 1975, Women of Plums, 1982; poems include Freddie (Deep South Writers' award 1966); author short stories; contbr. poems to various anthologies, poetry mags.; poems recorded in Contemporary Poets' Series, Library of Congress; poems read at Coolidge Auditorium, Library of Congress, 1981; play, Pavane for a Dead Princess, produced at Fisher Theatre, Phillips Exeter Acad., 1981. Address: Phillips Exeter Acad Exeter NH 03833

KENDRICK, MAURINE LAJUINE, ednl. cons.; b. Magna, Utah; d. Herbert John and Minnie (Bellows) Taylor; B.A. in Edn., LaVerne (Calif.) Coll., 1943; M.S. in Edn., Purdue U., Hammond, Ind., 1971. Jr. high sch. reading tchr. Ben Franklin High Sch., Kenmore, N.Y., 1963-65; elementary reading specialist Dist. 149, Dolton, Ill., 1965-66; tchr. English, Thornton Fractional Twp. Dist. 215, Lansing, Ill., 1967-70, dist. reading cons., Calumet City, 1970—, also coordinator competency based testing and edn. program; community dir. Right to Read; mem. Right to Read Adv. Council, Developmental Task Force, Ill. State Supts. Literacy Program, 1974-76. Trustee, Community Council Greater Hammond, 1975—. Mem. Internat., Suburban (corr. sec.) reading assns., Ill. Tchrs. of English Assn. Cert. tchr. and supr. lang. arts. Ill.; cert. adminstr. Home: 325 Belden Pl Munster IN 46321 Office: Adminstrv Center 1601 Wentworth Ave Calumet City IL 60409

KENEL, MARY ELIZABETH, psychologist; b. N.Y.C., Feb. 19, 1940; d. Raymond Frederick and Mary Josephine (McCaffrey) K.; B.S. M.T., St. John's U., 1963; Ph.D., Cath. U. Am., 1976. Psychologist, Potomac Center, Alexandria, Va., 1975-78, Fred B. Ugast Center, Washington, 1976-77, Child Guidance Clinic, Superior Ct. Washington, 1977—; instr. pastoral counseling div. Loyola Coll. Mem. Am. Psychol. Assn., Assn. for Advancement Psychology, D.C. Psychol. Assn. Roman Catholic. Vol. abstractor service, 1977-81. Home: 901 Perry Pl NE Washington DC 20017 Office: 409 E St NW Washington DC 20001

KENLEY, ELIZABETH SUE, chem. co. exec.; b. Kansas City, Mo., Oct. 4, 1945; d. Ralph Raymond and Josephine Allen (Wells) Cummins; B.S.. Kans. U., 1968, M.P.A., 1972. Asst. city mgr. Winfield (Kans.),

1968-70; adminstrv. asst. Kansas City (Mo.) Police Dept., 1970; cons., 1973; with E.I. DuPont Co., Kingwood, Tex., 1974—, regional tech. buyer, 1977-79, cons., plant start up, 1979, regional tech. buyer, 1980-82; internat. project buyer Aramco, Houston, 1982—. Mem. Houston C. of C., Am. Mgmt. Assn. Home: 811 D Timberline St Humble TX 77338 Office: 1200 Smith Houston TX 77002

KENNA, PEGGY TROWER, exec. search and human devel. cons. co. exec.; b. Billings, Mont., Sept. 21, 1930; d. Jewel W. and Irene S. (Alpaugh) Trower; B.A., U. Mont., 1958, M.A., 1960; postgrad. Mont. State U., Bozeman, 1974-76; m. Howard F. Kenna, Apr. 14, 1951 (dec. 1971); children—Julie Kenna Killorn, Mary Pat, Teresa Joan. Clinician in communication disorders U. Mont., 1958-60, Mont. Bd. Health, 1960-61, Center for Handicapped Children, 1962-64, Elks Speech and Hearing Clinic, Livingston, Mont., 1962-64; partner retail bus., Livingston, 1964-71; cons., 1965-70; dir. spl. services Livingston public schs., 1970-73; clin. coordinator, dept. communication disorders U. Mont., Missoula, 1973-74; adj. prof. Mont. State U., Bozeman; internal cons. Easter Seals, 1974-76; internal cons. Easter Seals of Minn., also MDAC, Inc., St. Paul, 1976-78; owner, pres. Women's Career Service, Tempe, Ariz., 1978—. Mont. Health grantee, 1967; HEW grantee, 1969. Mem. Nat. Assn. Female Execs., Am. Speech and Hearing Assn. Club: All The Good Old Gals (Mpls.). Home: 1525 E Baseline Rd Apt 115 Tempe AZ 85283

KENNAN, ELIZABETH TOPHAM, coll. pres.; b. Phila., Feb. 25, 1938; d. Frank and Henrietta (Jackson) Topham; B.A. summa cum laude, Mt. Holyoke Coll., 1960; M.A. (Hon. Woodrow Wilson fellow, Marshall scholar), St. Hilda's Coll., Oxford (Eng.) U., 1962; Ph.D., U. Wash., 1966; L.H.D. (hon.), Trinity Coll., Washington, 1978, Amherst Coll., 1980; m. 2d, Martin L. Budd, July 26, 1977; 1 son by previous marriage, Frank Alexander Kennan. Asst. prof. history Catholic U. Am., 1966-70, asso. prof., 1970-78, dir. medieval and Byzantine studies program, 1970-78, dir. program in early Christian humanism, 1974-78, mem. pres.'s emergency adv. bd. on univ. fin., 1976-77; pres. Mt. Holyoke Coll., 1978—; lectr. in field; dir. Summer Inst. for Basic Skills, 1974, Andrew W. Mellon Fellowships in Early Christian Humanism, 1974-78; mem. bd. advs. Hill Monastic Microfilm Library, 1976-78; mem. bd. cons. Nat. Endowment for Humanities, 1975—; dir. T.N.B. Fin. Corp., Springfield, Mass., N.E. Utilities, Hartford, Conn., Berkshire Life Ins. Co., Pittsfield, Mass.; cons. to colls. Bd. dirs. Assn. Am. Colls., 1980—, Women's Coll. Coalition, 1979—; mem. commn. on govt. relations Am. Council on Edn., 1979—; mem. Pres.'s Emergency Adv. Bd. on Univ. Fin., 1976-77. Named Tchr. of Year, Cath. U. Am., 1977. Mem. Mediaeval Acad. Am. (chmn. com. on centers and regional assns. 1975—, dir. books-out-of-print project 1976-77), Phi Beta Kappa. Translator, author introduction and notes: (with John D. Anderson) On Consideration (St. Bernard of Clairvaux), 1976; contbr. articles to profl. publs. Home: Pres's House Mt Holyoke Coll South Hadley MA 01075 Office: 265 Barbourton Rd Canton CT 06019

KENNEALLY, CONSTANCE, med. electronic equipment co. exec.; b. San Francisco, June 27, 1953; d. William and Wanda Kenneally (guardian: Mary J. Patterson); student London Sch. Econs., 1975; B.S., U. Pitts., 1976. Rep., Sandoz Pharms., Indpls., 1976-77, tech. rep., Chgo., 1977-78; dist. mgr. Ivac Corp., Rochester, N.Y., 1978—. Mem. Nat. Tax Limitation Com., Chgo. Council Fgn. Relations. Mem. Am. Mgmt. Assn., Nat. Assn. Female Execs. Republican.

KENNEDY, ANGELA GALLION, mental health adminstr.; b. Charleston, W.Va., June 23, 1944; d. John W. and Sylvia Elizabeth (Turner) Gallion; B.A., W.Va. State Coll., 1964; M.S.W., Wayne State U., Detroit, 1966; Ph.D., Clayton U., St. Louis, 1977; m. Harry James Kennedy, Nov. 5, 1962; 1 dau., Carmen Gallion. Caseworker, then supr. Wayne County Dept. Social Services, Detroit, 1966-69; cons. Mayor Detroit Com. Human Resource Devel., 1969-70; instr. sociology Wayne County Community Coll., 1970-71; asst. prof. social work U. Detroit, 1971-73; dir. social services Detroit Gen. Hosp., 1973-74; successively unit coordinator, outpatient services div., exec. dir. Northeast Guidance Center, Detroit, 1974-79; exec. dir. New Center Community Mental Health Services, Detroit, 1979—; bd. dirs. Downtown Sr. Center, Neighborhood Services Orgn. Fellow Claude Worthington Benedum Found., 1961-64, John Hay Whitney Found., 1964-66. Mem. Acad. Cert. Social Workers, Nat. Assn. Social Workers, Assn. Black Social Workers, Am. Public Health Assn., AAUP, Alpha Kappa Alpha. Mem. Unity Ch. Author papers in field. Home: 20011 St Marys St Detroit MI 48235 Office: 2990 W Grand Blvd Suite 300 Detroit MI 48202

KENNEDY, CATHRYN IRENE, state govt. adminstr.; b. Manhattan, Kans., June 4, 1953; d. Thomas Joseph and Mable Elizabeth (Andrews) Claydon; B.S. magna cum laude in Journalism, Kans. State U., 1975; m. James Griffin, Sept. 18, 1976. Reporter, Olathe (Kans.) Daily News, 1975; reporter Red Wing (Minn.) Republican Eagle, 1975-77; media dir. Republican Caucus, Minn. Ho. Reps., 1977-79; press aide to gov. State of Minn., St. Paul, 1979-81, dir. communications, press sec., 1981—. Recipient 1st pl. feature writing, 2d pl. investigative reporting awards, Minn. Newspaper Assn., 1977. Mem. Twin Cities Women in Communications (chmn. award dinner 1982), Minn. Press Club, Gamma Phi Beta. Office: State Capitol Saint Paul MN 55155

KENNEDY, CECILIA ROKUSEK, home economist, nutritionist; b. Yankton, S.D., June 27, 1953; d. John C. and Alice T. (Fiala) R.; B.A. (Presdl. scholar), Mt. Marty Coll., Yankton, 1975; M.S. (Regents scholar), U. Nebr., Lincoln, 1976; postgrad. in adult and higher edn. U. S.D., Vermillion, 1977—; m. Kevin C. Kennedy, Sept. 20, 1980. Grad. asst. dept. edn. Sch. Food Services, U. Nebr., 1976; asst. clin. prof. dental hygiene U. S.D., Vermillion, 1977—, asst. prof. allied health, 1979—, now also cons. nutritionist Center for Developmentally Disabled; asst. prof. home econs. Mt. Marty Coll., 1976-81, internship dir. for hotel/restaurant interns, 1979-81; nutritionist Headstart, Vermillion and Elk Point, S.D.; cons., adv. in field. Campaign worker Century of Service Nat. Fund Dr., Mt. Marty Coll. Named Outstanding Young Woman Am., Jaycees, 1977, 78, 79, 80, state winner, 1981, Yankton winner, 1982; recipient Alumni Merit award Mt. Marty Coll., 1979. Mem. Mt. Marty Coll. Alumni Assn. (chpt. pres. 1978-79, nat. pres. 1979-80), Am. Dietetics Assn., Am. Home Econs. Assn., Soc. Nutrition Edn., Nat. Center Sci. in Public Interest, S.D. Nutrition Council (state pres. 1980-81), S.D. State Dietitians Assn., Czech Heritage Preservation Soc. Republican. Roman Catholic. Clubs: Catholic Sokol Social, Catholic Workmen Lodge, Bus. and Profl. Women's Yankton (pres. 1978-79, state 1st v.p. 1979-80, state pres.-elect 1981-82), Federated Women's (edn. chairperson 1977-79), Am. Legion Aux. (fgn. relation chairperson 1978—). Home: Apt 10 600 W 6th St Yankton SD 57078 Office: 1100 W 5th St Yankton SD 57078

KENNEDY, CHARLOTTE BANKS, investment analyst; b. Dallas, Mar. 28, 1948; d. Robert Marion and Hazel Bernice (Hearne) Banks; B.A. magna cum laude, U. Tex., 1969, M.B.A., 1973; m. Douglas Lee Kennedy, Jan. 2, 1971 (div. 1980). Investment analyst tchr. Retirement System Tex., Austin, 1973-76; trust investment officer Republic Nat. Bank of Dallas, 1977-78, trust officer 1978-80; v.p. New Court Capital Mgmt., N.Y.C., 1980-81; v.p. Morgan Guaranty Trust Co. N.Y., 1981-82; v.p. J. and W Seligman and Co., Inc., N.Y.C., 1982—. Investment Bankers Assn. scholar, 1969-70, Mosle scholar 1972-73, College of Bus. admn. scholar 1972-73; CPA; chartered fin. analyst. Mem. Fin. Analysts Fedn., Inst. Chartered Fin. Analysts, Am. Inst. C.P.A.s, Tex. Soc. C.P.A.s, N.Y. Soc. Security Analysts, Alpha Delta Pi, Phi Beta Kappa, Alpha Lambda Delta, Kappa Delta Pi, Phi Kappa Phi, Pi Lambda Theta, Beta Gamma Sigma. Republican. Methodist. Office: 1 Bankers Trust Plaza New York NY 10006

KENNEDY, CORNELIA BLANCHE GROEFSEMA, (MRS. CHARLES S. KENNEDY, JR.), judge; b. Detroit, Aug. 4, 1923; d. Elmer H. and M. Blanche (Gibbons) Groefsema; A.B., U. Mich., 1945, J.D. with distinction, 1947; LL.D., No. Mich. U., 1971, Eastern Mich. U., 1971, Western Mich. U., 1973, Detroit Coll. Law, 1980; m. Charles S. Kennedy, Jr., Mar. 5, 1960; 1 son, Charles S. III. Law clk. Harold M. Stephens, U.S. Ct. Appeals, Washington, 1947-48; admitted to Mich. bar, 1947; atty. Elmer H. Groefsema, Detroit, 1948-52; practiced in Detroit, 1952-54; mem. firm Markle & Markle, Detroit, 1954-66; judge Wayne County Circuit Ct., Detroit, 1967-70; U.S. dist. judge Eastern Dist. Mich., 1970-79, chief judge, 1977-79; judge U.S. Ct. Appeals 6th Circuit, 1979—; bd. dirs. Fed. Jud. Center Bd.; mem. Supreme Ct. Fellows Commn.; chmn. Nat. Conf. Fed. Trial Judges. Fellow Am. Bar Found.; mem. Phi Beta Kappa. Office: 744 Federal Bldg Detroit MI 48226

KENNEDY, DEMA ELIZABETH, orgn. exec.; b. Indpls., Aug. 19, 1903; d. John H. and Elsie Marie (Hoyt) K.; A.B., Butler U., 1925; postgrad. U. Wis., 1927, DePauw U., 1930; M.A., Bread Loaf Sch. English, Middlebury, Vt., 1932. Tchr., dean girls Plymouth (Ind.) High Sch., 1925-37; exec. sec. Girl Scouts U.S.A., Peoria, Ill., 1937-39, mem. nat. staff, 1939-47, staff adviser Western Hemisphere Encampment, 1941; asst. head Ferry Hall Sch., Lake Forest, Ill., 1947-51, acting head, 1947-48; field cons. Nat. Congress Parents and Tchrs., Chgo., 1951-68; librarian Chgo. Lake Shore Club, 1970-78; mem. exec. bd. New Eng. sect. Am. Camping Assn., 1941-43; mem. Mass. Gov.'s Com. for Emergency Preparedness, 1941-43; staff adviser N.E. Girl Scout Mariner Gams, 1940-43. Mem. Nat. Assn. Parliamentarians (chmn. edn. com. Ill.), Boston Women's Republic Club (council fgn. relations), DAR, Chgo. Duplicate Bridge Club, Chgo. Geog. Soc., Chimes, Pi Beta Phi, Phi Kappa Phi, Delta Phi (pres.). Episcopalian. Clubs: Altrusa (Chgo.); Cambridge Boat. Editor: Ferry Hall News, 1949-51; Council News and Comment, 1960-68. Home: 211 E Delaware Pl Chicago IL 60611

KENNEDY, EVELYN SIEFERT, found. exec.; b. Pitts., Nov. 11, 1927; d. Carmine and Assunta (Iacobucci) Rocci; B.S. magna cum laude, U. R.I., 1969, M.S. in Textiles and Clothing, 1970; m. George J. Siefert, May 30, 1953 (div. 1974); children—Paul Kenneth, Carl Joseph, Ann Marie; m. 2d, Lyle H. Kennedy, II, Oct. 12, 1974. With Pitts. Public Schs., 1945-50; with Goodyear Aircraft Corp., Akron, Ohio, 1950-54; clothing instr. Groton (Conn.) Dept. Adult Edn., 1958-68; pres. Sewtique, Groton, 1970; v.p. Kennedy Capital Advisors, Groton, 1973, Kennedy Mgmt. Corp., Groton, 1974, Kennedy InterVest, Inc., Groton, 1975; pres., exec. dir. P.R.I.D.E. Found., Inc., Groton, 1978—; clothing cons. Coop. Extension Service, Dept. Agr.; adj. faculty U. Conn., Eastern Conn. State Coll., St. Joseph Coll.; fed. expert witness Care Label Law, FTC, 1976. Regional adv. council SBA active corps Execs., Hartford; bd. dirs. Easter Seal Rehab. Center Southeastern Conn.; bus. adv. council U. R.I.; active LWV; mem. Groton Vocat. Edn. Adv. Council. Recipient award of distinction U. R.I., 1969. Mem. Better Sleep Council (consumer affairs rep.), Nat. Assn. Bedding Mfrs., Conn. Home Economists in Bus. (founder 1977), Nat. Home Economists in Bus. (chmn. internat. relations), Am. Home Econs. Assn., Coll. and Univ. Bus. Instrs. of Conn., Omicron Nu, Phi Kappa Phi. Democrat. Roman Catholic. Clubs: New London Zonta, Bus. and Profl. Women's (Outstanding Women of Year 1977). Author: Dressing With Pride, 1980. Office: Kennedy Bldg 1159 Poquonnock Rd Groton CT 06340

KENNEDY, FRANCES MIDLAM, advt. agy. exec.; b. Wilmington, Del., Feb. 26, 1913; d. Edward West and Annie Elizabeth (Bullen) Midlam; student Wilmington public schs.; m. Joseph Conrad Kennedy, Sept. 4, 1937; children—Edward Carter, Stephen Dandridge, Katharine Kennedy Treadway. Writer, Compton Advt., N.Y.C., 1939-47; v.p., copy chief, then v.p. creative group head Dancer Fitzgerald Sample, Inc., Chgo. and N.Y.C., 1947-69; sr. v.p., creative dir. Chair Creative/Mgmt. Rev. Bd., N.Y.C., 1969-81; exec. v.p. Chair Creative Rev. Bd., 1981—. Recipient Emma Proetz award, 1954, Golden 30 award Chgo. Copywriters Club, 1958; named Chgo. Advt. Woman of Yr., 1960. Mem. Fashion Group. Episcopalian. Club: Cosmopolitan (N.Y.C.). Home: 517 E 84th St New York NY 10028 Office: 405 Lexington Ave New York NY 19917

KENNEDY, JANE ANNETTE, dietitian; b. Vancouver, Wash., Dec. 31, 1939; d. Wilbert P. and Grace E. (Woolf) K.; B.S., Wash. State U., 1961. Intern in dietetics U. Oreg. Med. Sch. and Hosp., 1961-62; commd. 2d lt. U.S. Air Force, 1961, advanced through grades to capt.; dietitian Andrews AFB, Md., 1962-63, Amarillo, Tex., 1963-65, Dover, Del., 1965-67, Wichita Falls, Tex., 1967-70, U.S. Air Force Hosp., Lakenheath, Eng. 1971-75; commd. health service officer USPHS, HEW, 1975; diet dir., pub. health service officer USPHS Hosp., Carville, La., 1975—. Treas., Stop Rape Task Force, Baton Rouge, La., 1975-76; bd. dirs. YWCA, Baton Rouge. Mem. Am., Baton Rouge Dist. dietetic assns. Lutheran. Home: 3030 Congress Blvd Baton Rouge LA 70808 Office: NHDC Hosp Carville LA 70721

KENNEDY, JEAN THRASHER, writer, poet, educator; b. Atlanta, Aug. 5, 1932; d. Barton Edmonds and Winnie H. (Ham) Thrasher; A.B., Wesleyan Coll., Macon, Ga., 1954; M.A., Northwestern U., 1956; m. Victor N., June 30, 1956; children—Philip, Elaine, Laura. Staff writer Atlanta Constitution newspaper, 1952-54; tech. manuscript editor Jour. AMA, Chgo., 1956-57, Jour. ADA, Chgo., 1957-58; asst. to editorial page editor Waterloo (Iowa) Courier, 1972-76; writing tchr. Waterloo Recreation Commn., Iowa Arts Council and Waterloo YWCA, 1980-81; instr. in English lang. and lit. U. No. Iowa, 1981—; contbr. fiction, non-fiction, poetry to various publs. Bd. dirs. Waterloo-Cedar Falls Jr. League, 1967-68; pres. Waterloo Reciprocity, PEO Sisterhood, 1981-82; mem. adult program com. YWCA, Waterloo. Recipient prizes for poetry. Mem. Nat. League Am. Pen Women (v.p. Waterloo-Cedar Rapids br. 1980-82), AAUW, Iowa Council Tchrs. English, Nat. Council Tchrs. English. Presbyterian. Home: 857 Sunrise Blvd Waterloo IA 50701 Office: Dept English Lang and Lit U No Iowa Cedar Falls IA 50614

KENNEDY, JEANNE BONNEAU, state legislator; b. Lebanon, N.H., July 10, 1942; grad. U. Vt., Montpelier, 1962; postgrad. Trinity Coll.; m. Mark H. Kennedy; 2 sons. Pres. Mem. Vt. Ho. of Reps., 1981—. Chittenden County Democratic Women, 1977-79; active Chittenden County Democratic Women's Club; Vt. del. White Ho. Conf. on Families, 1980; bd. dirs. Northeast Conf. Rural Ministry; mem. South Burlington Sch. Bd., 1974-78; exec. bd. Vt. Dental Care Program Inc., 1972-77. Mem. Vt. Dental Hygienists' Assn. (pres. 1963-65, 68-69). Office: Vt Ho Reps State Ho Montpelier VT 05602 *

KENNEDY, KATE (KITTY) PEARCE, assn. exec.; b. Poplarville, Miss., Jan. 27, 1935; d. Oscar Knox and Johnnie Rose (Gates) Pearce; grad. Jackson (Miss.) Comml. Coll., 1953; student Millsaps Coll., 1955-56, U. Miss., 1956-57; m. William David Kennedy, July 23, 1953; 1 son, David Keith. Asst. exec. sec. Miss. Med. Assn., 1954-60; exec. sec. Central Med. Soc., Jackson, 1960-65; budget commitment and expenditure ofcl. Boeing Co., Bay Saint Louis, Miss., 1965-69; exec. sec. to plant mgr. Price Bros Co., Hattiesburg, Miss., 1975-79; exec. officer Hattiesburg Bd. Realtors, also Realtors Multiple Listing Service, Inc., Hattiesburg, 1979—, also dir. Mem. Jackson Soc. Med. Assts. (charter pres.), Miss. Assn. Med. Assts. (charter pres.), Nat. Sec. Assn., Miss. Assn. Execs. Forum, Nat. Assn. Realtors Exec. Officers, Nat. Assn. Female Execs., Am. Soc. Assn. Execs., Miss. Soc. Assn. Execs., Miss. Assn. Realtors Exec. Officers Council (charter chmn.). Methodist. Club: Elks Aux. (sec. 1980). Contbr. articles to profl. jours. Home: 2601 Clayton Pl Hattiesburg MS 39401 Office: 201 S 26th Ave Suite 114 Hattiesburg MS 39401

KENNEDY, KAY J., researcher-writer; b. S.D.; d. Edward James and Marie Amelia (Bowman) K.; B.A. in Geology, U. Wyo., 1931. Reporter, Gt. Falls (Mont.) Leader, 1944-45, Denver Post, 1945, Alaska Daily Empire, Juneau, 1950-51, Fairbanks (Alaska) Daily News-Miner, 1952-56; chief news bur. Alaska Visitors Assn., Seattle, 1957-60; news bur. chief Alaska Travel Promotion Assn., 1961-62; public relations exec, Qien Alaska Airlines, Fairbanks and Anchorage, 1966-70; freelance research-writer, 1936—; producer 1st 2 Alaska Travel manuals, 1957-58; 68; author original copy Alaska Sunset Discovery Book, 1963, Wien Brothers Story, 1967. Recipient Lulu award Los Angeles Advt. Women, 1958; named Wash. Woman of Achievement, Wash. Press Women, 1978. Mem. Outdoor Writers Assn. Am., Alaska Press Women (founder, pres. 1961; awards 1969, 71), Wash. Press Women (award 1959), Soc. Am. Travel Writers. Clubs: Alaska Press (award 1959). Address: PO Box 106 Loomis WA 98827

KENNEDY, LEA MCGOVERN, veterinarian; b. Jenkintown, Pa., Feb. 12, 1928; d. Joseph F. and Katherine M. (Reilly) McG.; B.S., Chestnut Hill Coll.; V.M.D., U. Pa., 1955; m. Thomas Livingstone Kennedy, Sept. 18, 1982. Owner, dir. Newtown Square (Pa.) Animal Hosp., 1955-74; public health veterinarian Chester County Health Dept., West Chester, Pa., 1974-76; staff veterinarian Smith, Kline & French Labs., Phila., 1976-79; chief animal feed safety br. Bur. Vet. Medicine, FDA, Washington, 1979—; mem. vet. career devel. com. USPHS. Past mem. Council Govts., Washington; docent Phila. Zool. Soc. Mem. Am. Coll. Vet. Toxicologists, AVMA, Nat. Assn. Fed. Veterinarians, U.S. Animal Health Assn. Roman Catholic. Clubs: Pinehurst (N.C.) Country; Bay Hills Golf (Annapolis, Md.). Office: 5600 Fishers Ln Rockville MD 20857

KENNEDY, LEILA MAY (MRS. ROY KENNEDY), lawyer; b. Marysville, Ind., Nov. 9, 1895; d. John Conrad and Katharine Elizabeth (Reis) Hartling; LL.B., Benjamin Harrison Law Sch., 1936, Ind. U., 1944; m. Roy Kennedy, May 14, 1913 (dec.); children—Roy Albert, Dorothea Leila (Mrs. James W. Powers). Sec., Herbert Foltz & Sons, Indpls., 1933-37; admitted to Ind. bar, 1940; registrar Ind. Law Sch., Indpls., 1937-44; law librarian Ind. Supreme Ct. Library, Indpls., 1944-50; referee Juvenile Ct., Indpls., 1950-53; real estate broker Irvington Realty Co., Indpls., 1953-60; pvt. practice law, Indpls., 1960—. Mem. Bus. and Profl. Woman's Club, Ind. U. Alumni Assn., Ind. U. Women's Assn., Mutual Service Assn., Phi Alpha Delta. Club: Pilot (pres. Indpls. 1940). Presbyn. Mem. Order Eastern Star. Home and Office: 1314 N Emerson Ave Indianapolis IN 46219

KENNEDY, MARITA JEAN, psychologist; b. Branch, Mo., Aug. 23, 1933; d. John Walter and Hazel Arymintha (McClanahan) Huber; A.A., Met. Jr. Coll., 1969; B.A., U. Mo., 1971, M.A. in Psychology, 1975, M.A. in Counselor Edn., 1976; m. Sammy O'Neal Kennedy, June 26, 1956; children—Jimmy Lynn, Sharon Kay, Karen Ann, Gina Renee, Angela Diane, John O'Neal. Research asst. U. Mo., Kansas City, 1969-72; alcohol/drug counselor Western Mo. Mental Health Center, Kansas City, 1973-78; psychologist N.E. Jackson County Mental Health Center, Independence, Mo., 1977-79; mental health coordinator Mo. Dept. Mental Health, Jefferson City, 1978—; instr. psychology U. Mo., Kansas City, 1972; therapist Project Re-direction, Mcpl. Ct., Kansas City, 1975. Social sec. Jackson County Assn. for Retarded Citizens, 1975; trustee Kansas City Nat. Council on Alcoholism, 1975—; active Good Govt. League, Independence, 1978—. Lic. psychologist, Mo. Mem. Women's Polit. Caucus (communications officer 1977-78), Am. Psychol. Assn., Am. Psychology Law Soc., Greater Kansas City Assn. Mental Health, Nat. Assn. Female Execs., Psi Chi. Presbyterian. Contbr. articles to profl. jours. Address: 600 E 22d St Kansas City MO 64108

KENNEDY, MARY ELLEN, librarian; b. Pitts., Feb. 28, 1939; d. Joseph Michael and Stella Marie (Kane) K.; B.A., Villa Maria Coll., 1961; M.L.S., U. Pitts., 1970, Ph.D., 1980. Tchr., Pitts. Catholic Schs., 1962-65; tchr., Anne Arundel County Schs., Annapolis, 1965-67; legal sec., firm Joseph M. Kennedy, Pitts., 1967-70; cataloger Newport News (Va.) Library System, 1970-71; reference librarian Glenville (W.Va.) State Coll., 1971-80; asst. prof. library sci. Ball State U., Muncie, Ind., 1980—. Sec. women Glenville Presbyn. Ch., 1973-74, pres., 1974-76, bd. deacons, 1979-80; chmn. library com. Presbyn. Ch. Muncie, 1981—; mem. belle com. W.Va. Folk Festival, 1973-80. Recipient Title III advanced study grant, 1977-78. Mem. ALA, Ind. Library Assn., Assn. Ind. Media Educators, Assn. Am. Library Schs., AAUW (corr. sec. 1981-82), Delta Kappa Gamma, Sigma Sigma Sigma. Democrat. Home: 808 Riverside Ave Apt 210 Muncie IN 47303 Office: Dept Library Sci Ball State U Muncie IN 47306

KENNEDY, MAUREEN NORA JANE, investing co. exec.; b. Pitts., May 20, 1950; d. Harry Joseph, IV and Frances Lydia (Flynn) K.; B.S. in Edn., Duquesne U., Pitts., 1973. Tchr. math. St. Winifred Sch., Pitts., 1973-76; tchr. reading St. Peter Sch., Pitts., 1976-77; broker-dealer Federated Investors, Inc., Pitts., 1977-78, office services supr., 1978-82, dir. office services, 1982—; tchr. math., evening div., Community Coll. Allegheny County. Recipient Ecology award Duquesne Light Co., 1974, 75. Mem. Internat. Word Processing Assn., Postal Customers Council. Roman Catholic. Club: 550. Home: 414 Jamaica Ave Pittsburgh PA 15229 Office: 421 7th Ave Pittsburgh PA 15219

KENNEDY, MELANIE SPROUL, pathologist; b. Lima, Ohio, Oct. 21, 1942; d. James Wesley and Clellah Leola (Stotts) Sproul; B.A., Ohio No. U., 1964; M.D., Ohio State U., 1968; m. Bruce H. Kennedy, Feb. 20, 1965; 1 dau., Melita L. Intern, Mt. Carmel Hosp., 1969-70; asst. med. dir. Central Ohio Red Cross Blood Center, Columbus, 1969, acting med. dir., 1970-71, med. dir., 1971-76; mem. faculty Ohio State U., Columbus, 1973—, asst. prof. pathology, 1979—; asst. dir. blood bank Univ. Hosps. Ohio State U., 1977-79, asso. dir., 1979-82, dir., 1982—; mem. adv. com. hemophilia program Ohio Dept. Health, 1973—, chmn. center criteria com., 1979-81. Am. Cancer Soc. grantee, 1979-80. Fellow Coll. Am. Pathologists, Am. Soc. Clin. Pathology; mem. AMA (Physicians Recognition award 1972, 76, 79), Am. Assn. Blood Banks, Ohio Med. Assn., Acad. Medicine Columbus and Franklin County, AAAS, Am. Med. Women's Assn., Ohio Assn. Blood Banks, Sigma Delta Epsilon. Club: Ohio State U. Faculty. Editor newsletter Ohio Assn. Blood Banks, 1973-79; contbr. articles to profl. jours. Office: Dept Pathology Ohio State U Columbus OH 43210

KENNEDY, NANCY KETRING, optometrist; b. Bonne Terre, Mo., Feb. 9, 1953; d. Collman Howard and Naomi Janet (French) Ketring; student U. Mo., Rolla and Columbia, 1971-73; B.S. magna cum laude, U. Houston Coll. Optometry, 1975, O.D. summa cum laude, 1977; m. William F. Kennedy, Jr., Aug. 10, 1974. Teaching asst. U. Houston Coll. Optometry, 1976-77; exec. dir. Optometric Center of St. Louis, nonprofit orgn., 1977-78, bd. dirs., 1980—; vision cons. St. Louis Spl. Sch. Dist., 1978—; speaker local Lions Clubs. Mem. adv. com. Sch. Optometry, U. Mo., St. Louis, 1980, chmn., 1981. Mem. Am., Mo. optometric assns., St. Louis Optometric Soc., Optometric Extension Program, Heart of Am. Contact Lens Soc., Am. Public Health Assn.,

Mo. Public Health Assn., Beta Sigma Kappa, Phi Kappa Phi, Zeta Tau Alpha. Methodist. Author: (with Rocky Kaplan) Helping the Learning Disabled, 1977. Home: 2409 Hiddenmeadow Ln Manchester MO 63011 Office: 621 S New Ballas Rd Saint Louis MO 63141

KENNEDY, ROSE FITZGERALD (MRS. JOSEPH P. KENNEDY), mother of former Pres. of U.S.; b. Boston, July 22, 1890; d. John Francis and Josephine Mary (Hannon) Fitzgerald; ed. New Eng. Conservatory, Blumenthal Acad., Netherlands; LL.D. (hon.), Manhattanville Coll., Georgetown U., 1977. m. Joseph P. Kennedy, 1914 (dec.); children—Joseph (dec.), John Fitzgerald (Pres. of U.S. 1961-63, dec.), Rosemary, Kathleen (dec.), Eunice (Mrs. Robert Sargent Shriver), Patricia, Robert Francis (dec.), Jean (Mrs. Stephen Smith), Edward M. Named Papal Countess, Pope Pius XII. Roman Catholic. Author: Times to Remember, 1974. *

KENNEDY, SHEILA SUESS, lawyer; b. Indpls., Oct. 20, 1941; d. Joseph S. and Annette (Marcus) Simkin; A.A., Stephens Coll. Women, 1960; B.S., Ind. U., 1964, J.D., 1975; m. Robert N. Kennedy, Mar. 2, 1980; children—Michael Suess, Stephen Suess, David Suess. Admitted to Ind. bar, 1975; asso. firm Baker & Daniels, Indpls., 1975-77; corp. counsel City of Indpls., 1977-80; ptnr. firm Treacy Cohen Mears & Crawford, Indpls., 1980—. Instr. bus. law Ind. Central U., 1978. Republican candidate U. S. Ho. Reps., Ind. 11th Dist., 1980; mem. nat. bd. govs. Am. Jewish Com.; chmn. Cable Franchise Bd., City of Indpls., 1982—; mem. environ. mgmt. bd. State of Ind., 1982—. Mem. Indpls. Bar Assn., Ind. Bar Assn., Am. Bar Assn., Nat. Inst. Mcpl. Law Officers. Republican. Jewish. Club: Columbia. Mng. editor Ind. U. Law Rev., 1974-75. Home: 628 Lockerbie St Indianapolis IN 46202 Office: 1135 Market Square Center Indianapolis IN 46204

KENNEDY, SUSAN JOANNE, vocational placement specialist; b. Coatesville, Pa., Mar. 5, 1943; d. Lloyd F. and Alice Mae (Jackson) K.; A.A., Brevard Community Coll., 1977, A.S. in Human Service Tech., 1977; B.S. in Social Sci., Rollins Coll., 1979; postgrad. Stetson U., 1980-81; M.S. in Counseling Psychology, Nova U., 1982. Various positions with hotels and restaurants, Ill., Miss., Fla., 1965-74; social worker Brevard Achievement Center, Rockledge, Fla., 1977, vocat. placement specialist, 1978—; mem. Brevard Equal Opportunity Com., 1980—; mem. Brevard Community Coll. Equal Access/Equal Opportunity Adv. Com., 1979—; mem. Brevard County Job Developers Com., 1981; mem. Forum on Info., Community Schs. and Agts. Com., 1979—; mem. Community Agts. and Schs. South Brevard, 1979—, chmn. 1980-81; mem. human service tech. adv. bd. Brevard Community Coll., 1980—. Sec. exec. com. Family Service Bur., 1976-77; scouting coordinator Boy Scouts Am., 1981—; loaned exec. United Way, 1980, 81. Recipient Community Service award Brevard Community Coll., 1977. Mem. Nat. Rehab. Assn., Fla. Vocat. Evaluation and Work Adjustment Assn., Brevard Vocat. Assn., Brevard Assn. Human Service Agys., Brevard Personnel Assn., Nat. Assn. Human Service Technologists, Am. Rehab. Counseling Assn., Fla. Personnel and Guidance Assn., Nat. Assn. Female Execs., VFW Aux. Democrat. Episcopalian. Home: 921 O'Hara Dr Rockledge FL 32955 Office: 1845 Cogswell St Rockledge FL 32955

KENNELLY, BARBARA BAILEY, Congresswoman; b. Hartford, Conn., July 10, 1936; d. John Moran and Barbara (Leary) Bailey; B.A. in Econs., Trinity Coll., Washington, 1958; grad. Harvard-Radcliffe Sch. Bus. Adminstrn., 1959; M.A. in Govt., Trinity Coll., Hartford, 1971; hon. doctorate Sacred Heart U., Bridgeport, Conn., 1981; m. James J. Kennelly, Sept. 26, 1959; children—Eleanor Bride, Barbara Leary, Louise Moran, John Bailey. Mem. Hartford Ct. of Common Council, 1975-79; sec. of state State of Conn., Hartford, 1979-82; mem. U.S. Ho. of Reps., 1982—, mem. com. transp. and public works, com. govt. ops.; Hartford rep., sec. exec. com. Capitol Region Council of Govts., 1975-79; Conn. rep. Nat. Adv.'s Com. on Fine Arts, Washington, 1975-79; chmn. applications for Pres.'s Friendship Flight Com., 1978; mem. Conn. Commn. Human Services, 1972-73. Bd. dirs. Hartford Architecture Conservancy, Hartford Riverfront Recapture, Inc.; chair Conn. Elected ofcls. for Soviet Jewry; mem. alumnae bd. dirs. Trinity Coll., Washington; mem. Conn. bd. dirs. Catholic Family Services, Inc.; trustee Trinity Coll., Washington, Hartford Coll. for Women. Mem. Internat. Inst. Mcpl. Clks. Democrat. Roman Catholic. Office: 450 Main St Hartford CT 06103 also 1630 Longworth House Office Bldg Washington DC 20515

KENNELLY, KAREN MARGARET, religious order adminstr.; b. Graceville, Minn., Aug. 4, 1933; d. Walter John and Clara Stella (Eastman) Kennelly; B.A., Coll. St. Catherine, 1956; M.A., Cath. U. Am., 1959; Ph.D., U. Calif., Berkeley, 1962. Entered Sisters of St. Joseph Carondelet, Roman Catholic Ch., 1954; faculty Coll. St. Catherine, St. Paul, 1956-79, asso. acad. dean, 1970-71, acad. dean, 1970-79; adminstrv. intern Wayne State U., Detroit, 1969-70; exec. dir. Nat. Fedn. Carondelet Colls., 1979-82; province dir. Sisters of St. Joseph of Carondelet, St. Paul, 1982—. Trustee, sec. bd. trustees St. Mary's Hosp., Mpls., 1972—; trustee, v.p. bd. trustees Derham Hall High Sch., 1977—; trustee St. Mary's Jr. Coll., Mpls., 1979—, Coll. St. Catherine, 1982—; commr. N. Central Assn., 1978-82; Woodrow Wilson fellow, 1961-62; chmn. bd. St. John's Hosp., Fargo, N.D., 1982—; St. Mary's Hosp., 1982. Am. Council Learned Socs. fellow, 1964-65; Fulbright fellow, Spain, 1964-65. Mem. Am. Hist. Assn., Am. Cath. Hist. Assn., Medieval Acad. Am., Women Historians of Midwest, Acad. Research Historians on Medieval Spain, Leadership Conf. Women Religious, Phi Beta Kappa. Democrat. Contbr. articles to profl. jours. Home: 1890 Randolph Ave Saint Paul MN 55105 Office: 1884 Randolph Ave Saint Paul MN 55105

KENNER, MARY ELLEN, utility ofcl.; b. Darlington, Wis., Jan. 7, 1941; d. Horace James and Adean Elizabeth (McDonald) Smith; B.S., Marquette U., 1963, M.S. in Bus. Adminstrn., 1966; m. John Miller Kenner, Sept. 27, 1975. Fashion dir. spl. events Federated Store, Milw., 1962-63; mktg. ofcl. Ohio Bell and Wis. Telephone Cos., 1963-66; coll. mktg. instr. Milw. Inst. Tech., 1966-67; advt. positions AT & T and Wis. Telephone Co., 1967-78; advt. dir. No. States Power Co., Mpls., 1978—; pres. Kenner Enterprises. Steering com. 1st Conf. Consumerism. Recipient Clio award, 1974, Effy award, 1978. Mem. Minn. Advt. Fedn., Minn. Center Arts, Milw. Advt. Club (dir. 1969-72, sec. 1973-76), Edison Electric Inst., Marquette U. Alumni Assn. Roman Catholic. Club: Belleek Collectors. Home: 909 Santa Rosa Blvd Fort Walton Beach FL 32548 Office: 2d Floor 414 Nicollet Ave Minneapolis MN 55401 also 909 Santa Rosa Blvd Fort Walton Beach FL

KENNEY, ALICE PATRICIA, historian; b. Schenectady, May 1, 1937; d. Ralph Burch and Marjorie Frances (Waite) K.; B.A., Middlebury Coll., 1958; M.A., Columbia U., 1959, Ph.D., 1961. Instr., Cedar Crest Coll., Allentown, Pa., 1961-63, asst. prof., 1963-69, assoc. prof., 1969-76, prof., 1976-79, chmn. interstudies, 1970-72, chmn. dept. history, 1975-79; research asso. Albany (N.Y.) Inst. History and Art, 1979—; vis. prof. N.Y. State Hist. Assn., Cooperstown, N.Y., 1972-73; dir. Mus. Access, 1977—. Recipient Am. Assn. State and Local History award of merit, 1976; Holland Soc. N.Y. fellow, 1979. Mem. Am. Assn. Mus., Am. Assn. State and Local History, AAUW, Am. Hist. Assn., Hymn Soc. Am., N.Y. State Hist. Assn., Victorian Soc. Am., Phi Alpha Theta, Phi Beta Kappa. Presbyterian. Author: Gansevoorts of Albany, 1969; Stubborn for Liberty, 1975; Albany: Crossroads of Liberty, 1976; Access to the Past, 1980; contbr. articles in field to profl. jours. Home and Office: 78 Salisbury Rd Delmar NY 12054

KENNEY, ELSIE CARLSON, nurse; b. New Milford, Conn., May 14, 1935; d. Gustaf A. and Signe E. (Carlson) Carlson; R.N., Meriden Hosp. Sch. Nursing, 1956; A.S., Northwestern Community Coll., 1976; B.S., St. Joseph Coll., 1980; m. Robert G. Kenney, June 15, 1957. Staff nurse New Milford (Conn.) Hosp., 1956-57; head nurse Lahey Clinic, Boston, 1957-61; dir. nurses Tranquil House Convalescent Hosp., Warren, Conn., 1968-71, Skilled Nursing Facility, Watertown, Conn., 1971—, Watertown (Conn.) Convalrium, 1971—. Recipient Most Sympathetic Nurse award Meriden Hosp. Sch. Nursing, 1956. Mem. Com. of Geriatric Nursing Edn. Congregationalist (chmn. service com.). Home: North St Morris CT 06763 Office: 560 Woodbury Rd Watertown CT 06795

KENNEY, ESTELLE KOVAL, artist; b. Chgo., Feb. 15, 1928; d. Hyman English and Florence (Browman) Koval; B.F.A., Art Inst. Chgo., 1976, M.F.A., 1978; postgrad. Yale U., 1980; m. Herbert Kenney, Feb. 6, 1948; children—Carla, Robert. Art therapist Grove Sch., Lake Forest, Ill., 1973-78, New Trier High Sch. and Central High Sch., Winnetka, Ill., 1978-79, Mosely Sch., Chgo., 1979, Cove Sch., Evanston, Ill., 1979-82; dir. art therapy program; instr. painting and drawing Loyola U., Chgo., 1981—; one woman shows: Evanston (Ill.) Library, 1971, Zaks Gallery, Chgo., 1977, 79, 82, Renaissance Soc.-Bergman Gallery, U. Chgo., 1980; group shows include: Ill. State Mus., 1975, Women Artists, Here and Now, 1976, Chgo. Connections travelling exhbn., 1976-77, Nat. Women's Caucus for Art, 1977, Nancy Lurie Gallery, 1978, Marycrest Coll. Gallery, Davenport, Iowa, 1982, Chgo. Internat. Art Expo, 1981, 82, Notre Dame U. Gallery, South Bend, Ind., 1982; represented in permanent collections: Ill. State Mus., Springfield, Union League Club of Chgo. Mem. Am. Art Therapy Assn., Ill. Art Therapy Assn. (pres. 1979—), Coll. Art Assn. Home: 3830 N Clark St Chicago IL 60613 Office: Loyola University of Chicago Dept Fine Arts 6525 N Sheridan Rd Chicago IL 60626

KENNY, ALFREIDA BELLINDA, lawyer; b. Richmond, Va., Mar. 12, 1950; d. Emanuel Joseph and Lucille H. Kenny; A.B., Syracuse U., 1972; J.D., Columbia U., 1975; m. Dana Jon Harrell, June 27, 1970. Admitted to Pa. bar, 1975, N.Y. State bar, 1976, U.S. Supreme Ct. bar, 1981; staff atty. Fed. Res. Bank of N.Y., N.Y.C., 1975-76; asst. gen. counsel Harper & Row, Publs., Inc., N.Y.C., 1976-80; asso. firm Weil, Gotshal & Manges, N.Y.C., 1981—. Named to Outstanding Young Women Am., U.S. Jaycees, 1978. Mem. Assn. Bar City N.Y. (labor and employment com. 1980—), Nat. Assn. Black Women Attys. (pres. N.Y.C. chpt. 1978-80), Alumni Assn. Columbia U. Sch. Law (Class of 1975 treas. 1975-80, v.p. 1980—), Alumni Assn. Columbia U. Sch. Law (treas. 1980-81), Friends of Syracuse (v.p. Black Alumni Assn.), Nat. Bar Assn., Am. Bar Assn. Democrat. Baptist. Home: 225 W 106th St New York NY 10025 Office: 10 E 53d St New York NY 10022

KENNY, BETTIE ILENE CRUTS (BIK), artist, author, lead-crystal engraver; b. Longmont, Colo., June 5, 1931; d. Lester Arthur and Ruby Doris Cruts; B.A., U. Wash., cum doctorus monere honoris; m. Donald Keith Kenny, Nov. 20, 1951. Adminstrv. asst. Boeing Co.; partner Bettie Kenny Diamond Point Engraving Co., Seattle, 1971—; works in permanent collections in White House, at Corning Museum of Glass, Smithsonian Instn., Pioneer Mus., Longmont, Colo., Mus. History and Industry, Seattle, Seattle Art Mus., Wash. State Hist. Mus., Tacoma, also pvt. collections. Mem. Internat. Platform Assn., Psychology Forum. Address: 5610 44th Av SW Seattle WA 98136

KENNY, LISA ANN, artist, sculptor, author; b. Mineola, N.Y.; d. Thomas Henry and Patricia Anne (Flowers) K.; M.F.A., Ohio Christian Coll., 1974. Exhibited in one man show Mus. Modern Art, Miami, Fla., 1971; exhibited in group shows including: Mus. Modern Art, Miami, Wooster Coll., 1971, U. Mo. Mus. Art, 1972, Newark Public Library, 1972, Firehouse Gallery, 1971; represented in permanent collections including: Mus. Modern Art, Miami, Madison (Wis.) Art Center, Phila. Pub. Library. Clk., Bd. of Elections Village of North Hills (N.Y.), 1975-77. Mem. Assn. Am. Artists, Am. Fedn. Art, Inst. Contemporary Arts (London), Visual Artists and Galleries Assn. Author: How Brandy Saved Mill Neck, 1975; A Collection of Letters, 1976; A Scrapbook On Understanding Art, 1977. Home: 3920 Catamarca Dr San Diego CA 92124 Office: Box 3337 Wall St La Jolla CA 92037

KENSINGER, MILDRED LOUISE, paralegal asst.; b. Centerville, Iowa, July 30, 1921; d. Perry Wilson and Fay Elizabeth (Jarman) Porter; student Kirksville (Mo.) State Tchrs. Coll., 1939-41, Merritt Coll., Oakland, Calif., 1973-74, N.Tex. State, Denton, 1965; children—Jesse Porter, Chari Louise. Music tchr. public schs., Troy, Mo., 1941-42; art tchr. public schs., Livonia, Mo., 1942-43; sec. U.S. Govt., Kansas City, Mo., 1943-45; legal sec. State of Calif., Oakland, 1970-72, firm Spencer, Fane, Britt & Browne, Kansas City, 1972-73; sec. for U. Calif., Berkeley, 1973-74; free lance legal sec., Dallas, 1974-78; legal asst., office mgr. Winikates & Curtis, Dallas, 1978-81; v.p. Associated Services, Inc., 1981—. Bd. dirs. Dallas Minority Repertory Theatre, 1975-78, sec., 1976-78. Mem. Dallas Assn. Legal Assts., Am. Bridge Assn., Internat. Order Kings, Daus. and Sons (dir. Ala. br.), Dallas Jazz Soc., Mensa. Presbyterian. Address: Route 1 Box 356 Quinlan TX 75474

KENSINGTON, NITA LILLIAN, banker; b. Bristol, Eng., Jan. 22, 1947; came to U.S., 1954, naturalized, 1973; d. Nicholas and Moira Esther (Peacock) Ktoris; B.A., Rutgers U., 1972; postgrad. N.Y.U. Real estate analyst Tchrs. Ins. & Annuity Assn., N.Y.C., 1972-76; v.p. charge real estate acquisitions for domestic pension funds and fgn. clients Morgan Guaranty Trust Co., N.Y.C., 1976—. Office: 9 W 57th St New York NY 10019

KENT, ALLEGRA, dancer; b. Los Angeles, Aug. 11, 1937; ed. Sch. Am. Ballet; children—Trista, Susannah, Bret. Mem. N.Y.C Ballet Co., 1953—; prin. ballets include Seven Deadly Sins, 1958, Swan Lake, Bugaku, 1964, Afternoon of a Swan, Night Shadows, 1962, Episodes, Brahms-schoenberg-Quartet, 1966, Dances at a Gathering, 1969, Dumbarton Oaks, 1972. Address: care NYC Ballet Lincoln Center Plaza New York NY 10023 *

KENT, GRACE TEED, restaurant cons.; b. Ann Arbor, Mich., July 16, 1929; d. Reed Wallace and Florence (Schleicher) Teed; student Wheaton Coll., 1947-49; B.S., Mich. State U., 1951; m. Nov. 2, 1957 (div.); 1 dau., Deborah Grace. Home service adv. Detroit Edison Co., 1952-57; range specialist Kelvinator Corp., Detroit, 1954-56; asst. dir. home service RCA Whirlpool Corp., St. Joseph, Mich., 1956-57; dir. home econs. Leo Burnett Corp., Chgo., 1957-59; account exec. Ted Sills, Inc., N.Y.C., 1960-63; dir. home econs. Colgate Palmolive Co., 1963-64; dir. World Fair public relations Restaurant Assos., Inc., N.Y.C., 1964-66; v.p. advt. mktg. Longschamps Inc., N.Y.C., 1966-76; restaurant cons. Media Communications, Inc., N.Y.C., 1976—; instr. Berkeley (N.J.) Secretarial Sch., 1974-77, New Sch., N.Y.C., 1979-80. Pres., Young Republican Club, Mich. State U., 1950; treas. Easter Seal Soc. N.Y. State, 1976-78. Mem. Advt. Club. N.Y. (officer), Les Dames d' Escoffier (officer), Woman's Ad Club N.Y., Home Economists in Bus., Am. Home Econs. Assn., Milton Halpern Library for Forensic Medicine, Alpha Chi Omega. Methodist. Contbr. articles to profl. jours. Home: 245 E 63d St Apt 502 New York NY 10021 Office: Media Communications Inc 660 Madison Ave New York NY 10021

KENT, JOAN GAY, bus. exec., writer; b. Mineola, L.I., N.Y.; d. William Lewis and Helen (Remsen) Gay; B.A., Colby Coll. Vice-pres., mng. editor Missiles and Space, NATO Jour., Manhasset, N.Y., 1956-63; editor The Manhasset Mail, The Port Mail, Manhasset, 1964-66; editor United Tech. Publs., Garden City, N.Y., 1967, writer, advt. cons., 1968-78; prin. Kent Creative Services, Sands Point, N.Y., 1978—. Trustee, Port Washington Library; bd. dirs. Sands Point Civic Assn.; v.p. Cow Neck Hist. Soc. Mem. Pi Gamma Mu, Sigma Kappa. Club: N.Y. Colby Coll. Alumni. Home and Office: Sycamore Dr Sands Point NY 11050

KENT, LOIS SCHOONOVER, geologist; b. Marietta, Ohio, Dec. 1, 1912; d. Draper Talman and May Haines (Bowen) Schoonover; A.B., Oberlin Coll., 1934; M.A., Cornell U., 1936; Ph.D., Bryn Mawr Coll., 1940; m. Louis R. Kent, May 5, 1943; 1 dau., Katherine Louise Kent Kloss. Jr. geologist, asst. geologist U.S. Geol. Survey, 1941-45; instr. U. Ill., Urbana, 1954-55; asst. geologist Ill. State Geol. Survey, Champaign, 1956-59, asso. geologist, 1959—, curator paleontol. collections, 1956—. Mem. Geol. Soc. Am., Paleontol. Soc., Soc. Econ. Geologists and Paleontologists, Paleontol. Research Instn. Home: 1003 Lincolnshire Dr Champaign IL 61820 Office: Ill Geol Survey 615 E Peabody Dr Champaign IL 61820

KENT, MARY LOUISE, state legislator; b. Quincy, Ill., Oct. 3, 1921; d. Frank M. and Myrtie M. (Booth) McFarland; student Nat. Coll. Edn., 1939-41; m. Laurence S. Kent, Oct. 4, 1941; children—Curtis, Roger Hathaway, Laura Louise. Asst. exec. Quincy (Ill.) C. of C., 1960-72; mem. Ill. Ho. of Reps., Springfield, 1972—; dir. Quintron Corp., Quincy. Pres. PTA, 1950, Quincy Service League, 1959. Republican. Methodist. Club: Altrusa (pres. 1971). Office: 2071 Stratton Bldg Springfield IL 62706

KENT, PAULA (MRS. STANLEY J. LLOYD), lectr., public relations exec., mgmt. and mktg. cons.; b. N.Y.; d. John and Estelle (Frye) Smith; B.S., State Tchrs. Coll., Worcester, Mass., 1939; Master's degree, Grad. Sch., Coll. Bus. Adminstrn., Boston U., 1941; m. Stanley J. Lloyd, Jan. 23, 1943; children—Diane Adrienne Noel, Robin Michele Cheri, Kevin Christopher Kent, Gisele Nicolette Jolie. Methods engr. IBM, 1941-42; personnel dir. Daily Jour., San Diego, also Sta. KSDJ, 1946-48; fashion editor San Diego Union, 1949; promotion dir. San Diego Union and Evening Tribune, 1950-70; v.p. La Jolla Clin. Labs., Inc., 1972—. Public speaker, master of ceremonies in U.S.; seminar speaker, Paris, Brussels, Madrid, 1960—. Formerly active ARC, Am. Cancer Soc., Gray Ladies, Med. Aux., San Diego, Fiesta Del Pacifico, U. San Diego Aux.; dir. San Diego's Ann. Giant Sales Rally, 1953, 56, 65; chmn. Advt. Recognition Week Campaign, San Diego, 1953-54; dir. San Diego Ann. Soap Box Derby, 1951-59, Bowl Down Cancer, 1963, San Diego Ann. Golden Gloves Boxing Tournament, 1961-68, San Diego Ann. Metro Tennis Championships, 1952-70, San Diego Ann. Model Yacht Regatta, 1952-70, San Diego Ann. Power Boat Regatta, 1950-62, San Diego Ann. Hole-in-One Tournament, 1951-70; producer San Diego Ann. Investment Clinic, 1962-70; public relations cons. Mrs. Am. Pageant, San Diego, 1966, Unlimited Hydroplane Races, San Diego, 1964; producer Ann. Gentleman of Distinction awards, 1967, 68, 69, San Diego Advt. SalesRama, 1971, Woman of Year awards, 1967, 68, 69 (both San Diego), others. Commd. ensign, Women's Res., USNR, 1942, transferred USCG, served from ensign to lt., 1943-46. Recipient 158 awards 1950—, including 39 nat., 18 western states and Hawaii, 100 Calif. state awards, 1 local resulting from ann. competitions sponsored by Los Angeles Advt. Women's Club, Nat. Newspaper Assn. Mgrs., Calif. Newspaper Pubs. Assn., Calif. Press Women, Nat. Fedn. Press Women; named one of San Diego's Women of Achievement, 1958, 59, 64, One San Diego's Women of Valour, 1958, one of San Diego's Advt. Men of Distinction, 1972; recipient San Diego Outstanding Citizen award, 1961; Outstanding Service plaque Sales and Mktg. Execs. Club, 1963, 66, 67, 68, 71; San Diego Woman of Yr. award, Council Women's Service and Bus. Clubs, 1965; Los Angeles Man of Year award Sales Promotion Execs. Assn., 1965; Golden Spear award Twin Cities Sales Promotion Execs. Assn., Mpls., 1965; Woman of Achievement award Nat. Fedn. Bus and Profl. Women, 1966; Jeanne Hoffman Unique Coverage award, 1968, Don award Legion of Portola, 1968, Disting. Service award Investment Edn. Inst., Detroit, 1969, many others. Mem. Sales Promotion Execs. Assn. Los Angeles, Advt. and Sales Club San Diego (dir., former editor monthly bull). Sales and Marketing Execs. Club San Diego (dir., bull. editor, pres. 1970-71), Internat. Newspaper Promotion Assn. (pres. western region 1965, Disting. Service award 1971) Calif. Press Women, Nat. Fedn. Press Women (del. Russia 1973), Sales and Mktg. Execs. Internat. (internat. dir.-at-large 1971-73), Am. Mgmt. Assn., Soc. Advancement Mgmt. Am. Advt. Fedn. (western states edn. chmn. 1970-71). Roman Catholic. Home: 515 Bon Air St La Jolla CA 92037 Office: PO Box 2243 La Jolla CA 92038

KEON, PEGGY LUMPKIN, sales/mktg. cons.; b. Chgo., Sept. 10, 1931; d. Richard Adamson and Mary Hart (Green) Lumpkin; B.A., Wellesley Coll., 1952; children—Pamela Ryan, Lisa Anne, Susan Tamara, Margaret Lynley, Joseph John, Katherine Stoddert. Career counselor Peggy Keon & Assocs., San Francisco, 1978-80; owner Careers for Women, San Francisco, 1980—; dir. Utility Bond & Share Co. Active, San Francisco Women for Pete Wilson, 1977. Mem. San Francisco C. of C. (mem. Women's Council), Women Entrepreneurs. Republican. Episcopalian. Clubs: Wellesley Coll. of No. Calif., Union Sq. Bus. and Profl. Women's. Home: Belvedere CA 94920 Office: 1 Hallidie Plaza Suite 750 San Francisco CA 94102

KEOPPEL, DENEESE MONTGOMERY, med. technologist; b. Ogden, Utah, May 6, 1932; d. Lorenzo Vermont and Melba Eleanor (Montgomery) Colvin; B.S. cum laude in Med. Tech., Weber State Coll., 1972; m. Russell Joel Keoppel, June 23, 1950; children—Paul Joel, Jean, Dale Russell (dec.), Kent Ren. Blood bank supr. St. Benedict's Hosp., Ogden, Utah, 1972-76, supr., ednl. coordinator, 1979—; blood bank asst. supr. Latter Day Saints Hosp. Salt Lake City, 1976-79; mem. clin. faculty Weber State Coll. Allied Health, 1973—. Mem. Am. Assn. Blood Banks, Am. Soc. for Med. Tech. (rep.), (recipient outstanding service award 1981), Utah Soc. for Med. Tech. (pres. no. chpt. 1983-84), Am. Soc. for Clin. Pathologists (affiliate mem., cert. med. technologist, specialist blood bank), Utah Immunohematology Soc. (pres. 1978-79), Phi Kappa Phi, Omicron Sigma. Mormon. Home: 4511 S 1975 W Roy UT 84067 Office: 5475 S 500 E Ogden UT 84403

KEPNER, RITA MARIE, sculptor; b. Binghamton, N.Y., Nov. 15, 1944; d. Peter Walter and Helena Theresa (Piotrowski) Kramnicz; student Elmira Coll., 1962-63, U. Wash., 1974-75; B.A., Harpur Coll., SUNY, 1966; m. John C. Matthiesen; 1 son, Stewart John. One-woman shows include: Willoughby Wallace Meml. Gallery, Branford, Conn., 1967, Penryn Gallery, Seattle, 1970, 73, 76, Haines Gallery, Seattle, 1975, Zoliborz Gallery, Warsaw, Poland, 1981; group shows include: SUNY, Binghamton, 1966, Manawath Art Gallery, Palmerston North, N.Z., Modern Art Mus., Seattle, 1976, Portland (Oreg.) Art Mus., 1976; major works include: Peace Pipe, Zalalgerszeg, Hungary, Human Forms in Balance, City of Seattle, 1975, Unity, City of Znin, Poland, 1976; visual arts ambassador between U.S. and Poland, 1976—; artist-in-residence City of Seattle, 1975, 77-78; del. Internat. Sculptors Conf., Toronto, Ont., Can., 1978; VISTA vol., 1982. Paramedic, bd. dirs. Aradia Med. Clinic, Seattle, 1972-74. Kosciuszko Found. grantee, 1975, 76, 79, 81. Mem. Internat. Artists Assn. of UNESCO, Paris Artists Equity Assn., Internat. Artists Cooperation (Edewecht, W. Ger.), N.W. Multihull Assn. (commodore 1974). Contbr. articles to Northwest Arts, Seattle Post Intelligencer, Leonardo mag., Polska Panorama, Poland mag. Home and Office: 2231 Post Alley Seattle WA 98121

KEPPEL, MARILYN DEANS, account exec.; b. Dallas, Oct. 1, 1926; d. Herbert Ambrose and Marie Emma (Cooke) Deans; B.A., Randolph-Macon Woman's Coll., Va., 1947; M.Humanities, U. Richmond (Va.), 1970; m. Ernest L. Keppel, Oct. 3, 1947; children—Marilyn Deans, Ernest Merritt, Margot Derring, Mark Alexander, John Gwaltney. Part-time tchr. French and dramatics Collegiate Schs., Richmond, 1954-63; with First & Mchts. Nat. Bank, Richmond, 1970-81, asst. v.p., consumer services mgr., 1976-78, dir. community relations, community reinvestment officer, 1979-81; account exec. Merrill Lynch, Pierce Fenner & Smith, Richmond, 1981—; dir. First & Mchts. Corp. Art Collection, 1973-80; sec.-treas. F&M Found., 1979-81; lectr. in field, dir. fin. edn. seminars. Vice pres., bd. dirs. Jr. Achievement Richmond, 1977-80; chmn. residential div. Richmond United Way, 1971; mem. council Va. Mus. Recipient Gold Coin award Bank Mktg. Assn., 1979. Mem. Nat. Assn. Bank Women (chmn. public relations com. Richmond chpt. 1974-77), Inst. Contemporary Art, Kappa Alpha Theta. Republican. Episcopalian. Clubs: Tuckahoe Woman's, Country of Va. Home: 8911 Norwick Rd Richmond VA 23229 Office: Merrill Lynch Pierce Fenner & Smith F&M Center Pavillon 12th and Main Sts Richmond VA 23215

KEREW-SHAW, DIANA, producer; b. Hackensack, N.J., Oct. 3, 1942; d. Samuel William and Esther (Freed) Kerew; student State U. Iowa, 1960; B.F.A. magna cum laude, Boston U., 1964; m. Steven Shaw, Aug. 5, 1973. Mem. prodn. staff N.Y. Shakespeare Festival and Public Theater, 1965-70; asst. to dir. creative affairs Paramount Pictures, N.Y.C., 1970-72; v.p. creative affairs, exec. producer Talent Assos./Time-Life Films, N.Y.C., 1972-80; exec. producer, sr. v.p. TV Highgate Pictures, N.Y.C., 1980-82. Recipient Christopher awards, 1978, 81; Emmy award for Outstanding Children's Entertainment Spl., 1982. Mem. N.Y. Women in Film (dir. 1980-81, v.p. 1981-82). Democrat. Jewish. TV shows produced: Breaking Up, 1977, Lovey, 1978, The Bunker, 1981, The Wall, 1982. Home: 520 E 90th St New York NY 10028

KERMOND, CAROLYN CONWAY, author; b. Boston, Oct. 2, 1927; d. John Edward and Evelyn L. (Canty) Conway; A.B., Trinity Coll., Washington, 1949; m. William L. Kermond, Jan. 23, 1954; children—Ellen, Peter, Richard, Justin, Louise. Author: Little Ways, 1962; More Little Ways, 1963; Little Ways to Heaven, 1983. Mem. CCD bd. St. Mary's Ch., Winchester, Mass.; bd. dirs. Middlesex East Dist. Med. Assn. Aux., Mass. Med. Assn. Aux. Roman Catholic. Home: 7 Sheffield St W Winchester MA 01890

KERN, CORALEE SMITH, maid service co. exec.; b. Milw., Dec. 3, 1932; d. Quentin Van Doozer and Ida Marie (Blank) Smith; student public schs., Hartland, Wis.; children—Kendra Lynn, Kevin Robert. Adminstrv. mgr. Workman Diversified Enterprises, Chgo., 1956-60; nat. franchise coordinator Labor Pool Am., Chgo., 1960-62; with Lake Shore Mgmt. & Romanek Golub, Chgo., 1962-64; owner Key Girl, Chgo., 1964-68; owner, pres. Maid-to-Order, Inc., Chgo., 1971—; pub., editor-in-chief newsletter for small bus. Mind Your Own Bus. at Home. Mem. Ill. Commn. on Status of Women, Nat. Com. on Household Employment. Mem. Nat. Assn. Temporary Services, Nat. Assn. Women for Home Based Bus., Newsletter Assn. Am., Chgo. Women in Pub., WOMAN, New Women's Network. Office: 224 S Michigan Ave Chicago IL 60604

KERNALEGUEN, ANNE PAULE, educator; b. St. Brieux, Sask., Can., Feb. 15, 1926; d. Pierre P. and Marguerite S. Kernaleguen; B.H.Sc., U. Sask., 1948; B.Ed., U. Alta., 1957; M.A., Mich. State U., 1963; Ph.D., Utah State U., 1968. Dist. home economist Ont. Agr., 1948-51, Alta. Agr., 1951-54; tchr. high sch., Red Deer, Alta., 1954-60; Can. bilingual ednl. rep. McCall's Corp., N.Y.C., 1960-62; mem. faculty Mich. State U., 1963-64, U. Sask., 1964-66, Utah State U., 1968-70; mem. faculty U. Alta., Edmonton, 1970—, prof., chmn. clothing and textiles div., 1970-80. Bd. dirs. Handicapped Housing Soc., 1978-79, Handicapped Communication Soc., 1978-79; bd. dirs., merchandising program Olds Coll., 1975—; sec. Westcliffe Arms Owners Condominium, 1978-79. Mem. Am. Home Econs. Assn., Am. Psychol. Assn., Assn. Coll. Profs. of Texiles and Clothing and Apparel Studies Can., Can. Assn. Gerontology, Am. Gerontol. Assn., Soc. for Color in Art Industry and Sci., Alta. Home Econs. Assn., Can. Home Econs. Assn., Edmonton Home Econs. Assn., Can. Psychol. Assn., Phi Kappa Phi, Omicron Nu, Phi Upsilon Omicron. Roman Catholic. Author: Clothing Designs for the Handicapped, 1978; research editor Can. Home Econs. Jour., 1973-75, 77—; contbr. articles to various profl. and popular jours. Office: Faculty of Home Econs U Alta Edmonton AB T6G 2M8 Canada *

KERNER, FRANCINE JUDY, lawyer; b. Bronx, N.Y., Jan. 5, 1950; d. Seymour L. and Ruth T. (Glick) K.; B.A., Queens Coll., 1971; J.D., N.Y.U., 1974. Admitted to N.Y. bar, 1975; asst. dist. atty. Kings County (N.Y.) Dist. Atty.'s Office, 1974-79; counsel to insp. gen. Dept. Commerce, Washington, 1979—. Office: Insp Gen Dept Commerce Washington DC 20230

KERNESS, BONNIE GAY, social worker; b. N.Y.C., Oct. 27, 1942; d. Edward Joseph and Jeanne Ullger; B.Social Work (Social Work Student of Year award 1975), Kean Coll., Union, N.J., 1975; M.S.W., Rutgers U., 1977; divorced; children—Paul, Lauren, Stacey, Jonathan. Civil rights worker in Tenn. and Fla., 1960-70; with Am. Friends Service Com., 1970—, asso. dir. Newark justice program, 1977—; cons. in field. Mem. Nat. Assn. Social Workers, Am. Assn. Humanistic Psychology, N.J. Assn. Corrections. Author papers in field. Home: 186 Keats Ave Elizabeth NJ 07208 Office: 40 Walnut St Newark NJ 07102

KERNS, GERTRUDE YVONNE, psychologist; b. Flint, Mich., July 25, 1931; d. Lloyd D. and Mildred (Ter Achter) Brewer; B.A., Olivet Coll., 1953; M.A., Wayne State U., 1958; Ph.D., U. Mich., 1979. Psychologist, Roseville (Mich.) public schs., 1958-68, also instr. psychology Macomb Community Coll., part time; psychologist Grosse Pointe (Mich.) public schs., 1968—. Mem. Mich. Psychol. Assn., Am. Psychol. Assn., Mich. Edn. Assn., NEA, Psi Chi. Home: 28820 Grant St St Clair Shores MI 48081 Office: 389 St Clair St Grosse Pointe MI 48230

KERR, CATHERINE EARL BAILEY, artist, music educator; b. Montgomery, W.Va., July 4, 1928; d. Alonzo K. and Lyn (Wilson) Bailey; degree in teaching of art, Mason Coll. Music and Fine Arts, Charleston, W.Va., 1953; postgrad. in art Art Student League (N.Y.C.); m. J. Kenneth Kerr, May 26, 1962. Owner, Kerr Internat. Sch. Art and Music for handicapped, Roswell, N.Mex., 1977—; internat. artist; piano and organ tchr.; designer architect; exhibited works at Ligoa Duncan Gallery, N.Y.C., Raymond Duncan Galleries, Paris, David's Gallery, Roswell, numerous others; represented in permanent collections in U.S. and fgn. countries including White House. Recipient awards Assn. Belgo-Hispanica, 1973, 74, Raymond Duncan Gallery, 1975, 76, Luxembourg Mus., 1979, numerous others. Mem. Roswell Fine Arts League (corr. sec., dir., historian, 1st place award). Republican. Presbyterian. Address: 1412 W Hendricks St Roswell NM 88201

KERR, DEBORAH, actress; b. Helensburgh, Scotland, Sept. 30, 1921; d. Arthur Kerr-Trimmer; student Helensburgh schs., Northumberland House Sch., Bristol; m. Anthony C. Bartley, Nov. 28, 1945 (div. 1959); children—Melanie, Francesca; m. 2d, Peter Viertel, July 23, 1960. Began motion picture career in England in Major Barbara, 1940; appeared in Love on the Dole, Hatter's Castle, The Day Will Dawn, The Avengers, Perfect Strangers, Colonel Blimp, I See a Dark Stranger; came to U.S., 1947; appeared in Black Narcissus (N.Y. Critics award), The Hucksters, Edward, My Son, King Solomon's Mines, Quo Vadis, Thunder in the East, Prisoner of Zenda, Julius Caesar, Dream Wife, Young Bess, From Here to Eternity, The End of the Affair, 1955, Proud and Profane, 1956, The King and I, 1956, Heaven Knows Mr. Alison (N.Y. Critics Award), 1956, Bonjour Tristesse, 1958, Count Your Blessings, 1959, The Journey, 1959, Beloved Infidel, 1959, The Grass is Greener, 1960, The Sundowners (N.Y. Critics award), 1960, The Naked Edge, 1961, Chalk Garden, 1964, Night of the Iguana, 1964, Marriage on the Rocks, 1965, Casino Royale, 1967, The Gypsy Moths, The Arrangement, Witness for the Prosecution, 1982; appeared on stage in Heartbreak House, 1943, Gaslight (for Brit. troops in Europe), 1945, Tea and Sympathy, 1954-55, The Day After the Fair, London, 1972-73, U.S. tour, 1973—; appeared in U.S. tour of Seascape, 1975, Long Day's Journey into Night, Los Angeles, 1977, Candida, London, 1977, The Last of Mrs. Cheney, U.S. and Can., 1978-79, The Day After the Fair, Australia, 1979; appeared on London stage in Overheard, 1981. Recipient Sarah Siddons award as Chgo. actress of yr. Office: care Jess S Morgan 6420 Wilshire Blvd 19th Floor Los Angeles CA 90048

KERR, DIANNE SIMPSON, legal office adminstr.; b. South Gate, Calif., Dec. 2, 1943; d. Maurice Everard and Irene Ethel (Chaplar) Simpson; student South Gate public schs.; divorced; children—Deborah Dianne, Daniel Gerard. Various secretarial and adminstrv. asst. positions, 1971-75; legal sec., 1975-78; office mgr. firm Booth, Mitchel, Strange & Smith, Los Angeles and Costa Mesa, Calif., 1979-80; dir. personnel Adams, Duque & Hazeltine, Los Angeles, 1980-81, dir. adminstrn., 1981—. Mem. Assn. Profl. Law Firm Mgrs., Assn. Legal Adminstrs., Am. Bar Assn., Calif. Bar Assn. (law office mgmt. sect.). Roman Catholic. Home: 20749 Martha St Woodland Hills CA 91367 Office: 523 W 6th St Los Angeles CA 90014

KERR, ELIZABETH MARGARET, educator, author; b. Sault Ste Marie, Mich., Jan. 25, 1905; d. John Arthur and Katherine Dorothy (Hirth) Kerr; B.A., U. Minn., 1926, M.A., 1927, Ph.D., 1941. Instr. English, Tabor Coll., Hillsboro, Kans., 1929-30, U. Minn., Mpls., 1930-37, 38-43, Coll. of St. Catherine, St. Paul, 1937-38; asst. prof. Rockford (Ill.) Coll., 1943-45; instr. Milw. State Coll., 1945-55; asso. prof. U. Wis., Milw., 1956-59, prof., 1959-70, prof. emeritus English, 1970—. MLA research grantee, 1942; Summer Salary Support grantee U. Wis., Milw., 1959, 1961. Mem. MLA, Dickens Studies, Soc. for Study So. Lit. Democrat. Congregationalist. Author: Bibliography of the Sequence Novel, 1950; Yoknapatawpha: Faulkner's Little Postage Stamp of Native Soil, 1969; William Faulkner's Gothic Domain, 1979; William Faulkner's Yoknapatawpha: —A Kind of Keystone in the Universe,— 1982. Home: 4259 N Sercombe Rd Milwaukee WI 53216

KERR, JEAN, writer; b. Scranton, Pa., July 1923; d. Thomas J. and Kitty (O'Neill) Collins; M.F.A., Cath. U. Am., 1945; L.H.D., Northwestern U., 1962, Fordham U., 1965; m. Walter Kerr, Aug. 16, 1943; children—Christopher, John and Colin (twins), Gilbert, Gregory, Katharine. Author: (play) Jenny Kissed Me, 1949; Touch and Go, 1950; (play) King of Hearts (with Eleanor Brooke), 1954; Please Don't Eat the Daisies, 1957; The Snake Has All The Lines, 1960; (play) Mary, Mary, 1961; (play) Poor Richard, 1964; Penny Candy, 1970; (play) Finishing Touches, 1973. Recipient Campion award, 1971; Laetare medal, 1971. Mem. Nat. Inst. Arts and Scis. Democrat. Roman Catholic. Home: 1 Beach Ave Larchmont NY 10538 *

KERR, MABEL DOROTHEA, physician; b. Toronto, Ont., Can. (parents Am. citizens); d. George Houston and Mabel (Wark) Kerr; B.S., Ohio State U., 1944; M.D., Columbia, 1950. Intern dept. medicine St. Luke's Hosp., N.Y.C., 1950-51, resident, 1951-52; psychiat. resident Payne Whitney Clinic, N.Y. Hosp., 1952-57; practice medicine, specializing in psychiatry, N.Y.C., 1954—; asso. attending psychiatrist N.Y. Hosp., 1979—; clin. asst. prof. psychiatry Cornell U. Med. Coll., 1968-79, clin. asso. prof., 1979—; asst. med. examiner, officer chief med. examiner City of N.Y., 1957-66. Pres., Elmora Found. Fellow N.Y. Acad. Medicine; mem. AMA, Am. Psychiat. Assn., Nat. Assn. Med. Examiners, Pan Am. Med. Assn., Women's Med. Soc. N.Y. State, Am. Med. Women's Assn. Address: 20 E 68th St New York NY 10021

KERR, MURIEL KAYE, psychologist, educator; b. Niagara Falls, N.Y., Oct. 18, 1941; d. Russell Barrs and Helen (Jeffords) Stephenson; B.A., U. Minn., 1963, M.A., 1967, Ph.D., 1976; m. Ian Kerr. Asso. prof. history Mid-Mo. Mental Health Center, Columbia, 1968; asso. prof. psychology U. Winnipeg (Man., Can.), 1969—; asst. prof. psychiatry U. Man., 1980—. Mem. canadian Assn. Univ. Tchrs. (dir. 1974-82), Canadian Mental Health Assn., Canadian Psychol. Assn., Am. Psychol. Assn., Soc. Research in Child Devel., Canadian Soc. Study of Edn., Anthrop. Assn. Study of Play, Delta Kappa Gamma. Office: 515 Portage Ave Winnipeg MB R3B 2E9 Canada

KERRAN, JANIS LOUISE, lubricants mfg. co. exec.; b. Oklahoma City, Mar. 11, 1949; d. Cameron L. and Joanne P. Kerran; B.A. in Math. Edn., Okla. State U., Stillwater, 1972. With Double Eagle Lubricants, Inc., Oklahoma City, 1971—, office mgr., comptroller, sec.-treas., 1972—; sec.-treas. Double Eagle Refining Co., Waste Oil Service Co., CAM-ML Enterprises, Inc. Republican. Home: 1301 NW 85th St Oklahoma City OK 73114 Office: PO Box 11257 Oklahoma City OK 73136

KERSCHNER, VELMA LINOLA, health careers educator; b. Gonzales County, Tex., June 27, 1923; d. Daniel Madison and Clara Olive (Lincecum) Handley; R.N. diploma Brackenridge Hosp. Sch. Nursing, Austin, Tex., 1944; student U. Tex., 1943-45; B.S.N., Incarnate Word Coll., 1961; postgrad. in edn. Trinity U., 1970—; m. Harrison F. Kerschner, Sept. 14, 1947; children—Harrison Frederick III, Olivia Ann. Asst. nursing arts instr. Brackenridge Hosp. Sch. Nursing 1944-45; supr. operating room San Antonio State Chest Hosp., 1956-58; dir. nurses Southton Convalescent Hosp., San Antonio, 1958-60; dir. nurses Santa Rosa Med. Center, San Antonio, 1960-61; instr. San Antonio Sch. Vocat. Nursing, 1962-66, San Antonio Coll. asso. nursing program, 1969-72; asst. prof. health careers St. Philips Coll., San Antonio, 1972—; Served with Nurses Corps, U.S. Army, 1945-46, 46-48. Mem. Am. Nurses Assn., Tex. Jr. Coll. Tchrs. Assn., Nat. Assn. Health Unit Clks-Coordinators (rep. on bd.), Nat. Assn. Female Execs. Author: Nutrition for Practical Nurses, 1969, 3d edit., 1982. Home: Route 1 Box 211 Lavernia TX 78121 Office: 2111 Nevada San Antonio TX 78203

KERSH, ELEANOR RUTH, home economist; b. Columbus, Ohio, Dec. 30, 1924; d. Earl Francis and Ruth Frances (Killilea) Marquette; B.S., St. Mary of Spring Coll., 1947; M.S., Ohio State U., 1976; m. Robert B. Kersh, Feb. 27, 1954; children—Valerie Ann, Jill E. Tchr. home econs. St. Mary's Acad., Columbus, 1947-49; home service adv. Ohio Fuel Gas Co., 1949-51; regional home economist Amana Refrigeration Co., 1951-54; home economist Columbus and So. Ohio Electric Co., 1955-60; cons. in field, 1961-70; condr. cooking schs. Sta. WCOL, Columbus, 1965-67; home econs. agt. Coop. Extension Service, Delaware, Ohio, 1970—; mem. bd. Delaware Meals on Wheels, Delaware Homemaker Home Health Aides Service. Mem. Delaware County Social Agy., 1972—. Mem. Nat. Agts. Home Econs. Assn., Am. Home Econs. Assn., Ohio Home Econs. Assn. (award of merit 1982), Ohio Coop. Extension Agts. Assn., Delaware County Home Economists, Epsilon Sigma Phi. Republican. Catholic. Club: Delaware Altrusa. Home: 1425 Clubview Blvd S Worthington OH 43085 Office: 110 N Franklin St Delaware OH 43015

KERSHAW, BEULAH FRANCES (MRS. BRYAN IVERSON KERSHAW), music tchr., poet; b. Cloride, Mo., Jan. 9, 1914; d. William Washington and Esther Matilda (Bone) Warren; student public schs.; m. Bryan Iverson Kershaw, July 10, 1965; children—Georgia Carolyn Manchette, Sandra Kay Gentry. Tchr. piano, organ, guitar and drums, 1962—; writer poetry, 1942—; rec. artist. Vol. worker in rest homes. Mem. Republican Party, Evansville, Ind., Carmi, Ill., 1967—. Author: Poems by Beulah, Vol. I, 1968, Vol. II, 1973. Composer: It Hurts To Be Hurt, 1939; Your Woman, 1964; Santa Kissed Me; A Woman in Love. Home: Route 1 Crossville IL 62827

KERSHAW, GERALDINE SALVIN, educator; b. New London, Conn., July 16, 1935; d. John Henry and Julia Irene (Ustic) Salvin; B.S., Framingham Coll., 1956; M.Sc., Rivier Coll., 1978; m. Joseph R. Kershaw, June 14, 1958; children—Sandra Lee, Benjamin David. Therapeutic dietitian New Eng. Bapt. Hosp., Boston, 1957-58; adminstrv. teaching dietitian Leominster Hosp., Mass., 1958-60; cons. dietitian Nashua, N.H., 1964-73; instr., adv. Rivier Coll., Nashua, N.H., 1973—; Contbr. articles in field. Mem. Am. Dietetic Assn., Am. Home Econs. Assn. Address: Rivier Coll Nashua NH 03060

KERSHAW, LANA JO, mfg. co. mktg. exec.; b. Minot, N.D., May 18, 1950; d. Martin Oscar and Josephine Constance (Boklep) Blestrud; student Mesa Community Coll., 1970-71; m. Ronald A. Kershaw, May 21, 1978; children—Lawrence C. Forsythe, Lariana Jo Marchelle Forsythe. Hostess, S.W. Restaurant Systems, Phoenix, 1972, supr., 1972, asst. mgr., 1973; sales rep., asst. food and beverage mgr. Camelback Sahara, Phoenix, 1974-75; supr. Windjammer Restaurant, Phoenix, 1975; sales sec. United Mobile Homes, Inc., Phoenix, 1975; mktg. dir. Roker, Inc., Phoenix, 1975-80; pres. Taries Assocs., Inc., Tempe, Ariz., 1976-77; adminstrv. asst. MS & Co., Sarasota, Fla., 1981—; pres. Taries Assos., Inc., 1976-77. Mem. Sarasota Bd. Realtors. Democrat. Lutheran.

KESSEL, ELSIE IRENE, mcpl. fin. exec.; b. Finland, Mar. 5, 1910; came to U.S., 1916, naturalized, 1926; d. Matt Leander and Marie Sophia Anderson; student public schs.; m. June 22, 1929 (dec.); children—David, Joy, Rosalind, Dianne, Barbara. In farming, Lake County, Irons, Mich., 1938-71; twp. treas. Eden Twp., Lake County (Mich.), 1935-38, 40—. Address: Route 1 Irons MI 49644

KESSINGER, BETTY B., health care exec.; b. Radford, Va., Aug. 6, 1950; d. Thomas Spencer and Bessie Lee (Furrow) Brookfield; student Bluefield State Coll. Exec. sec., dispatcher Colonial Natural Gas Co., Pulaski, Va., 1968-74; exec. sec. to exec. v.p. and cashier Princeton (W.Va.) Bank & Trust Co., 1975-79; adminstrv. sec. Glenwood Park United Meth. Home, Inc., Princeton, 1979-80, adminstrv. asst., 1980-81, asst. adminstrv. officer, 1981—. Bluefield dist. del. W.Va. Ann. Conf., United Meth. Ch., 1982, also dist. health and welfare rep. Named Sec. of Yr., Princeton chpt. Nat. Secs. Assn., 1979; named Young Career Woman, Bus. and Profl. Women's Club Pulaski County, 1974. Mem. Nat. Secs. Assn. (chpt. charter pres. 1978-79). Home: Route 1 Box 464 Princeton WV 24740 Office: Route 1 Box 463 Princeton WV 24740

KESSLER, ANN ELIZABETH, social sci. educator, nun; b. Aberdeen, S.D., Jan. 28, 1928; d. George William and Elizabeth Marcella (Sahli) K.; B.A., Mt. Marty Coll., 1953; M.A., Creighton U., 1957; Ph.D. (grad. fellow 1960), Notre Dame U., 1963. Joined Order St. Benedict, Roman Catholic Ch., 1945; tchr. parochial schs., S.D. and Nebr., 1949-56; vis. prof. Marquette U., Milw., 1969-70; acad. dean Mt. Marty Coll., Yankton, S.D., 1963-65, prof. social sci., 1962—. Mem. S.D. State Criminal Justice Commn., Pierre, 1977-82, S.D. Council of Humanists, Sioux Falls, 1980-82; chmn. bd. dirs. Sojourn House for Troubled Youth, Yankton, S.D., 1981—; chmn. (S.D.) Gov.'s Council on Aging., 1980-81. N.W. Area Found. grantee, 1969-72. Mem. Acad. Polit. and Social Sci., Am. Hist. Assn., LWV, S.D. Social Sci. Assn. (pres. 1976-77). Contbr. articles in field to profl. publs. Home: 1103 W 8th St Yankton SD 57078 Office: Mount Marty Coll Yankton SD 57078

KESSLER, DEBORAH SHARON, audiovisual co. exec.; b. Chgo., Jan. 10, 1947; d. Max and Leah (Jacobson) K.; B.S., U. Mich., 1968; M.A., Columbia, 1969; m. Kenneth Butler, Sept. 5, 1978. Sr. research technician U. Chgo. Med. Sch., 1969-70; research technician Northwestern U. Med. Sch., Chgo., 1970-71; editor med. dept. Harper and Row Pub. Co., N.Y.C., 1971-72; prodn. editor Academic Press, N.Y.C., 1972; project dir. IntraMed Communications, N.Y.C., 1973-74, creative supr., 1974-76; pres. Biosci. Communications, Inc., N.Y.C., 1976-77, sec.-treas., 1977—; free-lance writer and editor, N.Y.C., 1971-76. Mem. Phi Beta Kappa. Contbr. articles to profl. jours. Home: Mill Hill Rd Jacksonville VT 05342 Office: PO Box 379 Jacksonville VT 05342

KESSLER, DORIS HENRIETTA, army officer; b. New Kensington, Pa., Sept. 19, 1935; d. Francis Arthur and Dora Mary Molinari; B.S., Pa. State U., 1957; m. Otto F. Kessler, June 1958 (div.). Tchr., Duquesne (Pa.) High Sch., 1958-68; commd. 1st lt. U.S. Army, 1968, advanced through grades to lt. col. Adj. Gen.'s Corps, 1983; chief staff support sect., command, control and communications, Camp Smith, Hawaii, 1980—. Committeewoman, Allgheny County, Pitts., 1963-67. Decorated Meritorious Service medal, Army Commendation medal (2). Mem. Nat. Assn. Female Execs., Assn. U.S. Army. Club: Mil. Dist. Washington Officers. Office: US Army Readiness Group Fort Sheridan IL 60037

KESSLER, JEAN S., profl. sec., ins. co. exec.; b. New Brunswick, N.J., Oct. 20, 1954; d. John S. and Henrietta Marguerite (Pasquier de Lumeau) Kessler; Assoc. in Applied Sci. with highest honors, Middlesex County Coll., 1981; postgrad. Rutgers U., 1981—. Sec. to dir. Carter-Wallace, Inc., Cranbury, N.J., 1977-78, exec. sec. to corp. v.p., 1978-80; exec. sec. to v.p. Continental Ins. Co., Piscataway, N.J., 1981, exec. sec. to sr. v.p., 1981—. Recipient Sec. of Yr. award Profl. Secs. Internat., 1981-82. Cert. profl. sec. Mem. Profl. Secs. Internat. (chmn. civic com. New Brunswick chpt. 1980-81, sec. of yr. com. 1981-82; mem. nominating com. 1981, audit com. 1982, ways and means com. 1981-82), Nat. Assn. Female Execs., Nat. Christian Secs. Assn., Mensa, Nu Tau Sigma. Office: Two Corporate Pl S Piscataway NJ 08854

KESSLER, JOAN F., U.S. atty.; b. Alexandria, Va., June 25, 1943; d. Hoyt and Joan (Lloyd) Fowler; B.A., U. Kans., 1965; postgrad. U. Wis. Law Sch., 1965-66; J.D. cum laude, Marquette U., 1968; m. Frederick P. Kessler, Sept. 11, 1966; children—Elizabeth, Anna. Law clk. Marquette Inst. on Poverty and Law, summer, 1966, 67, Milw. County

Bd. Judges, summer 1967, Quarles, Herriott, Clemons, Teschner, 1967-68; U.S. Dist. Ct., Eastern Dist. Wis., 1968-69; asso. firm Warschafsky, Rotter & Tarnoff, 1969-71; partner firm Kessler & Kessler, Milw., 1971-74; asso. firm Cook & Franke, S.C., Milw., 1974-78; U.S. atty. for Eastern Dist. of Wis., Milw., 1978-81; mem. firm Foley and Lardner, 1981—; lectr. U. Wis. Milw.; chmn. labor standards adv. comm. Wis. Dept. Industry, Labor and Human Relations. Vice-pres. Legal Aid Soc., 1978, bd. dirs., 1974-78; bd. dirs. Michael's Community Sch., 1970-73; mem. adv. bd. St. Michael's Hosp., 1975-77; mem. Selective Service Appeals Bd., Eastern Dist. Wis., 1971-76; mem. Met. Milw. Criminal Justice Council, 1972-75; bd. dirs. Milw. Forum, 1978. Recipient public service award Wis. Jr. Womens Clubs, 1978; named Outstanding Woman in Govt., Milw. YWCA, 1978. Mem. Fed. Bar Assn., Am. Acad. Matrimonial Lawyers, Milw. Bar Assn., Milw. Jr. Bar Assn. (bd. dirs. 1972-77, sec. 1973-74, v.p. 1974-75, pres. 1975-76), Lawyers Assn. for Women, Am. Bar Assn. (state del. to young lawyers sect. 1975-76). Democrat. Office: Foley and Lardner First Wisconsin Center 777 E Wisconsin Ave Milwaukee WI 53202 *

KESSNER, DELORES ELAINE, social worker; b. Waukesha, Wis., Sept. 13, 1928; d. Ervin and Elara (Wiese) Schroeder; B.S., U. Wis., Madison, 1950; m. Edward Kessner, Aug. 23, 1952; children—Alan, Jean. Public welfare caseworker Marinette County (Wis.), 1950-52; home tng. specialist Portal Programs, Inc., Grafton, Wis., 1970-73, case mgr./counselor-home trainer, 1973-75, devel. disabilities intervention/outreach-home trainer, 1976-79, profl. services coordinator, 1979—. Mem. Nat. Rehab. Counselors Assn., Am. Assn. Mental Deficiency, Wis. Assn. Home Trainers. Home: 207 W Washington St #30 Port Washington WI 53074 Office: 420 10th Ave Grafton WI 53024

KESTER, PATRICIA ANNETTE, clin. psychologist; b. Colorado Springs, Colo., Aug. 9, 1945; d. James Douglas and Lucille Erma (Townley) K.; B.A., U. Tex., Austin, 1967; M.Ed., U. Houston, 1973; Ph.D., U.S. Internat. U., 1978. Social worker Okla. Dept. Public Welfare, Oklahoma City, 1967-68, Tex. Dept. Public Welfare, Houston, 1968-69, Harris County Child Welfare, Houston, 1969-71; tchr. Houston Ind. Sch. Dist., 1971-72; counselor Tex. Research Inst. for Mental Sci., Houston, 1973-74; research asso. dept. psychiatry SUNY, Stony Brook, 1974-76; psychol. intern Mercy Hosp., San Diego, 1977-78; lectr. dept. psychology U. Calif., San Diego, 1979; postdoctoral fellow Garrard Center for Psychology, La Mesa, Calif., 1979-80; pvt. practice clin. psychology, La Mesa, Calif., 1980-82, Orange, Calif., 1980—, La Jolla, Calif., 1982—; adj. asst. prof. Chapman Coll., Orange, 1979—. Bd. dirs. Who Cares, community mental health center, Houston, 1973-74. NIH fellow, 1974-76; NIMH grantee, 1975-76. Mem. Am. Psychol. Assn., Calif. Psychol. Assn., Nat. Assn. Social Workers, Calif. Assn. Marriage and Family Therapists, Running Psychologists, San Diego Soc. Sex Therapists and Educators (treas. 1982—), Soc. for Personality Assessment. Club: City (San Diego). Contbr. articles to profl. publs. Home: PO Box 278 La Jolla CA 92038 Office: 8950 Villa La Jolla Dr Suite 2200 La Jolla CA 92037 also 1485 N Tustin St Suite 230 Orange CA 92667

KESTLER, ROBERTA PAULINE, chiropractor; b. Torrance, Calif., Oct. 4, 1954; d. Robert A. and Pauline (Stolle) Kestler; A.S., Santa Rosa Jr. Coll., 1974; B.S., Los Angeles Coll. Chiropractic, 1978, D.C., 1978; m. Russell R. Tobias, Dec. 30, 1978. Practice chiropractic medicine, 1979—. Diplomate Nat. Bd. Chiropractic Examiners, Calif. State Bd. Chiropractic Examiners. Mem. Am. Chiropractic Assn., Calif. Chiropractic Assn. Contbg. author: Biochemistry Lab. Manual, Procedures and Practices. Office: 1061 2d St Santa Rosa CA 95404

KETCHUM, KIMBERLY JANE, controller; b. Normal, Ill., Sept. 13, 1949; d. Lovell D. and Cleo J. (Roush) Warrick; student Ill. State U., 1967-68, 82—; m. Bill R. Ketchum, Dec. 27, 1967; children—Todd, Doug, Jason. Various positions Nat. Bank, Bloomington, Ill., 1971-78, supr. asst., 1978; supervising bookkeeper Prairie State Bank, Bloomington, Ill., 1978-79, asst. cashier in charge ops., 1979-81; controller Lowell Supply Co., Bloomington, 1981—. Bd. dirs., den leader Cub Scouts Am., 1981-82; mem. Oakdale Sch. Bd., Normal, Ill., 1982—. Mem. Nat. Assn. Female Execs. Methodist. Office: Lowell Supply Co PO Box 2635 Bloomington IL 61701

KETCHUM, SHARON JOYCE, apparel mfg. co. exec.; b. Johnson City, N.Y., Mar. 15, 1948; d. William Burlew and Elleen Loretta K.; A.A., Stephens Coll., Columbia, Mo., 1968; postgrad. Calif. State U., Los Angeles, 1970-71, Fullerton, 1972-73; m. Gary D. New, July 25, 1981; 1 son by previous marriage, Damion Joel. Asst. mgr. for female singers, Paul Simmons Artist Mgmt., Toronto, Ont., Canada, 1968-69; writer Mallets & Brass TV show, CBC, Toronto, 1969; advance publicist Disney on Parade, NBC/Disney Roadshow, 1969-70; prodn. asst. Bing Crosby Christmas Spl., NBC, Burbank, Calif., 1970, Pearl Bailey Show, ABC, Los Angeles, 1970; account exec. Commercial Uniform Co., Los Angeles, 1974-79; nat. account exec. Action Line Uniform Co., Dallas, 1979-81. Recipient script award World Peace Fund, 1967, 68. Mem. Nat. Assn. Female Execs., NOW. Republican. Mem. Ch. Religious Sci. Home: 1236 Cornerbrook Pl Mississauga ON L5C 3J4 Canada

KETKAR, INDIRA SHARADCHANDRA PANCHANADIKAR, audiologist; b. Naregal, India, Aug. 8, 1927; came to U.S., 1967, naturalized, 1972; d. Chintaman Bhalchandra and Laxmi Chintaman (Kelkar) Panchanadikar; B.A., Bombay U., 1950; M.Ed., Poona (India) U., 1958; M.S., Syracuse U., 1968, Ph.D., 1972; m. S.V. Ketkar, Dec. 17, 1951; children—Charulata, Umesh. Tchr. high schs., India, 1950-55; tchr. V.R. Ruia Sch. for Deaf, Poona, India, 1957-60; insp. women's and children's instns., India, 1960-65; dir. social welfare, insp. spl. edn. instns., Maharashtra, 1965-67; dir. Dr. K. Gruppe Hearing and Speech Center, Children's Hosp. and Rehab. Center, Utica, N.Y., 1970—; adj. faculty Utica Coll., Syracuse U. Mem. adv. council Vis. Nurse Assn., 1974-75, 76, mem. health adv. com., 1974—, mem. adv. bd., 1975—; mem. adv. bd Oneida County Bd. of Coop. Ednl. Services; mem. health adv. bd. Headstart; mem. N.Y. State Com. on Sch. Audiology. Smith-Mundt, Fulbright tchr. devel. grantee, 1961-62; Office of Aging grantee, 1976—. Mem. Am. Speech and Hearing Assn. (com. on internat. affairs 1976—), N.Y. State Hearing and Speech Assn., N.Y. State Educators of Deaf (editor newsletter 1977-79), Am. Schs. for Deaf, India Assn. of Mohawk Valley (pres. 1979). Contbr. articles to profl. jours. Home: 1752 Burrstone Rd New Hartford NY 13413 Office: Dr K Gruppe Hearing and Speech Center Children's Hosp and Rehab Center 1675 Bennett St Utica NY 13502

KETOVER, HARRIET ARLENE, state legislator; b. Portland, Maine; d. Morris and Lillian Lerman; m. Jay Ketover, Aug. 14, 1966; children—Jill, Kimberly. Moderator, People Talk, Channel 6, Portland, 1980—; mem. Maine Ho. of Reps., 1980—. Bd. dirs. Parents of Learning Disabled Students, Shaarey Tphiloh Synagogue, Portland. Mem. Nat. Assn. Jewish Legislators. Democrat. Office: State House Augusta ME 04333

KETTELHACK, ALICE VIRGINIA, artist; b. Bklyn., Dec. 24, 1917; d. Henry Gerald and Elizabeth (Stonehouse) Blake; student Art Students League, 1934-39; m. Carl Herman, July 25, 1943; children—Robert Alan, Guy Blake. Art dir. G. Schirmer, Music Pubs., N.Y.C., 1942-45; staff artist Norcross, N.Y.C., 1967-68; art dir. South Shore Record, Hewlett, N.Y., 1969-71; group exhbns. include: Nat. League Am. Pen Women, Sacramento, 1978, Salmagundi Club, N.Y.C., 1979—. Mem. Nat. League Am. Penwomen, Art Students League N.Y. (life). Club: Salmagundi. Home: 5 Cottage Pl Amityville NY 11701 Office: PO Box 286 Amityville NY 11701

KETTERING, CARROL LUCILLE SIPLE, civic worker; b. Montpelier, Ohio, Aug. 4, 1903; d. Clyde Lavonius and Fannie Hope (Allman) Siple; cert. Edinboro (Pa.) Tchrs. Coll., 1923; B.S.E., Kent State U., 1954, M.A., 1957; m. Lester W. Kettering, June 27, 1928; children—Paul Siple, Neil Lester. Tchr. English and social studies jr. high sch., Erie, Pa., 1923-28, Canton, Ohio, 1941-71, Canton High Ability Program, 1960-71, ret., 1972; chmn. Protective Services for Ret. Tchrs. Regent DAR, 1977-79, recipient 2 gold medal awards; congl. intern on behalf of sr. citizens, 1979. Recipient service award Eastern Ohio Edn. Assn., 1967, Ohio Bd. Edn., 1972. Mem. Stark County Ret. Tchrs. Assn. (past pres.), Canton Profl. Educators Assn. (past pres.), NEA (life), Ohio Edn. Assn. (life, Doer award 1972), Delta Kappa Gamma, Kappa Delta Pi. Clubs: Eastern Star (past dep. grand matron), Masonic Women's Aux. of the Grotto (past high officer of the caldron), Canton Sorosis, Canton Woman's (bd. dirs.). Editor: Wind Chill Factor (Paul A. Siple), 1965-67; contbr. articles to edn. mags. Home: 839 Columbus Ave NW Canton OH 44708

KEVORKIAN, LOUANNA FERN, acct.; b. Salinas, Calif., Apr. 11, 1938; d. Sylvester Ernest and Hazel (Rossiter) Todd; B.B.S. summa cum laude, Calif. State U., Fresno; m. LeRoy Kevorkian, Nov. 16, 1963. Bookkeeper, W. W. Annin, Tulare, Calif., 1956-62; office mgr. Occidental Chem., Fresno, Calif., 1962-70; acct. Bagdasarian Farms, Fresno, 1970—, sec.-treas., 1980—; sec. Lodi Vintners, Ltd., Acampo, Calif., 1975-79. Mem. Nat. Assn. Accts. (v.p. 1975-79, pres. Fresno area 1979-80), Soc. Calif. Accts. Office: 6382 E North Ave Fresno CA 93725

KEWIN, NANCY ANN, sales/mktg. exec.; b. Wyandotte, Mich., June 26, 1953; d. Arthur L. and Virginia M. (Lapham) Kewin; B.Music, U. Ariz., 1975; postgrad. Pepperdine U., 1981—. Keyboard dept. mgr. W. Los Angeles Music, 1976-78; electronic merchandising specialist Norlin Corp., Lincolnwood, Ill., 1978-79; Western region sales/mktg. mgr. Moog Music/Norlin Corp., Los Angeles, 1979—. Gen. Music scholar, 1971-72; Albert A. Haldeman Fine Arts scholar, 1972-75; recipient Moog Music Sales Achievement awards, 1980-82. Mem. Nat. Assn. Female Execs., Nat. Assn. Profl. Saleswomen. Republican. Home: 22040 Gault St Apt 47 Canoga Park CA 91303 Office: 2500 Walden Ave Buffalo NY 14225

KEY, MARY RITCHIE (MRS. AUDLEY E. PATTON), linguist, author, educator; b. San Diego, Mar. 19, 1924; d. George Lawrence and Iris (Lyons) Ritchie; student U. Chgo., summer 1954, U. Mich., 1959; M.A., U. Tex., 1960, Ph.D., 1963; postgrad. UCLA, 1966; children—Mary Helen Key Ellis, Harold Hayden Key, Thomas George Key. Asst. prof. linguistics Chapman Coll., Orange, Calif., 1963-66; asst. prof. linguistics U. Calif., Irvine, 1966-71, asso. prof., 1971-78, prof., 1978—, chmn. program linguistics, 1969-71, 75—; cons. Am. Indian langs., Spanish, in Mexico, 1946-55, S. Am. and Easter Island, 1955-62, 75, English dialects, 1968-74, U.S. Office Edn., 1969-72, Calif. State Dept. Edn., 1966-75; cons. Center Applied Linguistics, Washington, 1967, 69; lectr. in field. Fulbright-Hays grantee, 1975; U. Calif. Regents acad. grantee, 1974-75; recipient Friends of Library Book award, 1976. Mem. AAUW, Linguistic Soc. Am., MLA, Am. Dialect Soc. (exec. council; regional sec. 1974—), Internat. Reading Assn. (dir. 1968-72), Delta Kappa Gamma (local pres. 1974-76). Author numerous books, including: Male/Female Language, 1975; Paralanguage and Kinesics, 1975; Nonverbal Communication: A Research Guide and Bibliography, 1977; The Grouping of South American Indian Languages, 1979; Catherine the Great's Linguistic Contribution, 1980; founder, editor newsletter Nonverbal Components of Communication, 1972-76; editorial bd. Forum Linguisticum, 1976—, Language Sciences, 1978—, La Linguistique, 1979—; editor (with others) Organization of Behavior in Face-to-Face Interaction, 1975; contbr. articles to profl. jours. in field. Office: Program in Linguistics U Calif Irvine CA 92717

KEY, ZADIE BOWLING, ednl. adminstr.; b. Murfreesboro, Tenn., Oct. 20, 1921; d. John William and Nancy Beatrice (Kelton) Bowling; B.S., Middle Tenn. State U., 1941; postgrad. U. Houston, 1955-56; m. Edward Key, Jan. 10, 1948; children—John Matthew, Edward Huey, James Bowling. Sec. to pres. W.S. Bellows Constrn. Co., Houston, 1953-61, Tenn. Aircraft, Inc., Nashville, 1961-66; asst. to dean Sch. Basic and Applied Scis., Middle Tenn. State U., Murfreesboro, 1971—. Chmn. Rutherford County (Tenn.) Democratic Com., 1978—, treas., 1974-78; mem. bd. dirs. United Way, Murfreesboro, 1980—. Mem. Tenn. Fedn. Dem. Women (v.p. 1978, corp. sec. 1976-77), Murfreesboro-Rutherford County C. of C. (v.p. 1980, dir. 1978-80)., Tenn. Assn. Ednl. Secs., Profl. Secs. Internat. Mem. Ch. of Christ. Home: 304 4th Ave Murfreesboro TN 37130 Office: Peck Hall 101 Middle Tenn State Univ Box 83 Murfreesboro TN 37132

KEYES, MARGARET FRINGS, social worker; b. Butte, Mont., Aug. 8, 1929; d. John Matthew and Mary Ellen (Dyer) Frings; B.A. in Psychology, U. Calif., Berkeley, 1951; M.S.W., Cath. U. Am., 1953; postgrad. U. Chgo., 1961. Med. social worker U. Calif. Med. Center, San Francisco, 1955-61; postgrad. fellow U. Chgo. Sch. Social Service Adminstrn., 1961-62; dir. profl. services. Cath. Social Services of Marin County, San Rafael, Calif., 1962-69; pvt. practice psychotherapy, San Francisco, 1969—; assoc. prof. psychology Lone Mountain Coll., San Francisco, 1972-78; cons. to psychotherapists, 1969—. Pres. bd. dirs. Berkeley Center Human Interaction, 1978-79. NIMH fellow U. Chgo., 1960-61. Fellow Soc. Clin. Social Workers. Democrat. Roman Catholic. Author: The Inward Journey: Art as Psychotherapy, 1974, 2d edit., 1982; Staying Married, 1975; also chpts. in books. Home: 75 Sunset Way Muir Beach CA 94965 Office: 613 Wisconsin St San Francisco CA 94107 also 736 Bay St San Francisco CA 94109

KEYS, MARTHA ELIZABETH, former congresswoman; b. Hutchinson, Kans., Aug. 10, 1930; d. S.T. and Clara (Krey) Ludwig; student Olivet Coll., Kankakee, Ill., 1946-48; A.B., U. Mo. at Kansas City, 1952; children—Carol, Bryan, Dana, Scott. Co-chairperson Manhattan (Kans.) Riley County United Way Dr., 1973; mem. spl. commn. for Manhattan recreational needs, 1973; mem. 94th-95th Congresses from 2d Kans. Dist.; spl. adviser to sec. HEW, 1979; asst. sec. of edn., 1980; exec. dir. Friends of the Family, 1981; vis. prof. Am. U., SUNY. Oswego, Sangamon State U., Chatham Coll., U. Oreg., Mt. Vernon Coll.; politician-in-residence Wells Coll., 1982. Kans. coordinator McGovern for Pres. campaign, 1972; del. dist. and state Dem. conv., 1972, alt. del. nat. conv., 1972; chmn. Riley County Dem. Club, 1973; co-chmn. Manhattan Arts Council, 1973. Mem. AAUW, Common Cause, Am. Council on Ger. (bd. dirs.), Former Mems. Congress, Women's Compaign Fund, Ind. Action, Civic Music Club, Sigma Alpha Iota. Home: 6423 Lakeview Dr Falls Church VA 22041 Office: 1733 Connecticut Ave Washington DC 20009

KEYSER, MARIEATHA MADONNA, cable TV exec.; b. Ashland, Ky., June 10, 1935; d. Garland Patrick and Lillian Fern (Haney) Booth; student public schs.; m. James William Keyser, Jan. 2, 1950; children—Candice J. Keyser Reed, Cindy M., James D., George W. Engaged in TV service bus., 1957-75, in cable TV and earth stas. bus., 1975—; corp. sec.-treas., owner C-K Video, Inc., Mar-Key Satellite Prodns. Inc., Jamar Investments, Keyser Cable Installations, Key-White Video, Satellite Prodns., Inc. Pres. Kenova PTA, 1960, Wayne County PTA, 1962; life mem. W.Va. PTA. Mem. Women in Cable (charter). Democrat. Baptist. Club: Order Eastern Star. Office: 901 Chestnut St Suite 1-A Kenova WV 25530

KEYSERLING, HARRIET HIRSCHFELD, state legislator; b. N.Y.C., Apr. 4, 1922; d. Isador and Pauline (Steinberg) Hirschfeld; B.A. cum laude in Econs., Barnard Coll., 1943; m. Ben Herbert Keyserling, June 24, 1944; children—Judith, William, Paul, Beth. Asst. employment mgr. Eagle Pencil Co., N.Y.C., 1943-44; mem. Beaufort (S.C.) County Council, 1974-76; mem. S.C. Ho. of Reps. from Beaufort dist., 1976—; mem. Adv. Panel on Nuclear Wastes, Office of Tech. Assessment, U.S. Congress, 1978—. Chmn., S.C. Task Force on the Arts; active Concert Assn., Little Theatre, PTA, Planned Parenthood, Synagogue Aux. Mem. Nat. Conf. State Legislatures (exec. com., arts task force), LWV, Bus. and Profl. Women. Democrat. Jewish. Home: PO Box 1108 Beaufort SC 29902 Office: SC Ho of Reps Columbia SC 29211

KHEEL, ANN SUNSTEIN, civic worker; b. Pitts., Nov. 5, 1915; A.B. with honors, Cornell U., 1936; m. Theodore Woodrow Kheel, July 1, 1937; children—Ellen Margaret (Mrs. Arnold S. Jacobs), Robert Jeffrey, Constance Elizabeth, Martha Louise, Jane Meredith, Katherine Emily. Columnist, Ithaca (N.Y.) Jour., asso. editor Cornell Alumni News, 1936-37; asst. editor Tide Mag., N.Y.C., 1937-39; info. specialist Dept. Agr., Washington, 1939-43, editor Land Policy Rev.; dir. Play Schs. Assn., 1944-55; founder, chmn. Riverdale Community Forums, Riverdale/Bronx, N.Y., 1954-64, dir., 1953-65, v.p., 1958-60; mem. steering com. Riverdale Com. on Intergroup Relations, 1958—; del. to President's Com. on Equal Employment Opportunity, Washington, 1963, 64; spl. corr. N.Y. Herald Tribune, 1957; sec., bd. dirs. N.Y. Urban League, 1965—, founder, chmn. ann. Frederick Douglass Awards Dinners, 1966—; corp. mem., trustee Schomburg Center for Research in Black Culture, 1971—; mem. Mayor's Screening Panel for Bd. of Higher Edn. of N.Y.C., 1964-66; trustee Rand Inst. of N.Y.C., 1973-76; mem. Coop. Edn. Commn., N.Y.C. Bd. Edn., 1968—; appointee Regents Regional Coordinating Council for Post-secondary Edn., N.Y.C., 1974-76; chmn. State Parks and Recreation Commn. for N.Y.C., 1977—. Home: 407 W 246th St Bronx NY 10471

KIBLER, RUTHANN, immunologist, educator; b. Mansfield, Ohio, Dec. 1, 1942; d. Orville David and Elizabeth June (Hale) K.; B.S., Marietta (Ohio) Coll., 1964; M.S., Purdue U., 1967; Ph.D., U. Calif., Berkeley, 1973. Research asso. Inst. Virology, U. Wurzburg (W.Ger.), 1973-76; research scientist U. Ariz., Tucson, 1976-79, asst. prof. microbiology Coll. Medicine, 1980—. Mem. Am. Assn. Immunologists, Am. Soc. Microbiology, Reticuloendothelial Soc., Sigma Xi. Author articles in field. Home: 429 1/2 S 5th Ave Tucson AZ 85701 Office: Dept Microbiology U Ariz Med Sch Tucson AZ 85724

KIBRE, PEARL, historian, ret. educator; b. Phila.; d. Kenneth and Jane (du Plone) Kibre; student UCLA, 1920-22; A.B., U. Calif. at Berkeley, 1924, M.A., 1925; Ph.D., Columbia U., 1936. Instr. history Pasadena (Calif.) Jr. Coll., 1925-28; research asst. Columbia U., 1929-37; instr. history Bklyn. Coll., 1937-38; mem. faculty Hunter Coll., N.Y.C., 1938-71, prof. history, 1957-71, prof. emeritus, 1971—; doctoral faculty Grad. Center City U. N.Y., 1964-71; co-chmn. Columbia Seminar in Polit. and Legal Thought, 1971-73. Research fellow N.Y. Acad. Medicine, Nyon, Switzerland, 1938-39; Guggenheim fellow, 1950-51; recipient Charles Homer Haskins medal, 1964. Fellow Mediaeval Acad. Am. (v.p. 1964-67, pres. Fellows 1975-78); mem. History Sci. Soc., AAUP, Renaissance Soc., Medieval Club N.Y.C., Am. Hist. Assn., Acad. Internationale d'histoire des sciences (corr.), Phi Beta Kappa. Author: The Library of Pico della Mirandola, 1936; (with Lynn Thorndike) A Catalogue of Incipits of Mediaeval Scientific Writings in Latin, 1937, 2d edit., 1963; The Nations in the Mediaeval Universities, 1948; Scholarly Privileges in the Middle Ages, 1962; Hippocrates Latinus: Repertorium of Hippocratic Writings in the Latin Middle Ages: Traditio, 1975-82; co-editor: Osiris, vol. XI, 1954; contbr. to New Catholic Ency., Dictionary Sci. Biography, also to books, profl. jours. Home: 1100 Madison Ave New York NY 10028

KICHLU, ALICE LUTHER, educator; b. Muskogee, Okla., May 3, 1920; d. George Monroe and Eva Jane (Leopold) Luther; B.S. magna cum laude in Elem. Edn., Villa Maria Coll., 1967; M.Ed., Edinboro State Coll., 1969; m. Kunj Behari Kichlu, Sept. 3, 1952 (dec. July 1980); children—Marilyn Ann O'Meara, David Luther. Profl. dancer, 1937-39; sec. Gen. Telephone Co. of Pa., Erie, 1950-52; primary tchr. Erie Sch. Dist., 1967-75, reading specialist, 1975—. Bd. dirs. PTA, 1954-68, sec., 1962-63, historian, 1963-64; supr. cradle roll dept. Elmwood Presbyn. Ch., 1954-57; bd. dirs. Internat. Inst., 1957. Mem. NEA, AAUW, Pa. Edn. Assn., Erie Edn. Assn., Erie County Med. Aux., DAR, Internat. Dancers of Erie, Exchange Club Aux. (pres. 1960-62). Republican. Home: 1324 South Shore Dr Apt 108 Erie PA 16505

KICKLIGHTER, ALMA LOUISE, nurse, county adminstr.; b. Live Oak, Fla., Jan. 12, 1933; d. Eugene and Mary Bell (Ashley) Young; B.S. in Nursing, Fla. A&M U., 1958; m. Samuel Kicklighter; children—Carletta Ophelia, Harrell Alonzo, Samuel, June Renee. Tchr., Columbia County (Fla.) Schs., 1955; charge nurse, med., surg. and obstet. ward Mercy Hosp., St. Petersburg, Fla., 1958-62; public health nurse, sch. cons. Pinellas County (Fla.) Health Dept., 1959-63, public health nurse supr., 1964—, supr. epidemiology, 1979—; cons. on health careers for high sch. students. Chairperson equal employment com. HRS Dist. 5, St. Petersburg; bd. dirs. Latchkey, St. Petersburg; 2d v.p. St. Petersburg Citizen's Council on Crime; pres. PTA of Boca Ciega High Sch., St. Petersburg; organizer Open Door Bible study, 1980. Recipient plaque Equal Employment Com., 1979. Mem. Am. Nurses Assn., Fla. Nurses Assn., Fla. Public Health Assn., Am. Bus. Women's Assn. (Woman of Yr. 1978-79), Staff Assn. Community Nursing Service, Chi Eta Phi. Democrat. Club: Registered Nurses. Home: 2137 19th St S Saint Petersburg FL 33712 Office: 500 7th Ave S Saint Petersburg FL 33701

KIDD, BARBARA JEAN, nursing and athletics adminstr.; b. Ft. Wayne, Ind., Aug. 30, 1941; d. Matthew Jackson and Margaret Eileen Barnes; A.S., Ind. U., 1974, B.S., 1980, grad. student, 1980—; m. James Charles Kidd, Nov. 19, 1960; children—Stephanie, Susan, Sarah. Staff nurse, St. Joseph's Hosp., Fort Wayne, Ind., 1974-75; office nurse, Fort Wayne, 1975-76; office nurse C. G. McEachern, Fort Wayne, 1976—; pharmacology tutor Ind.-Purdue U., Ft. Wayne, Ind., 1979-80, nurse, athletic trainer, 1980—, staff nurse Univ. Health Service, 1980—, health and tng. coordinator, 1981—. Instr. CPR, Am. Heart Assn., 1981; instr. blood pressure screening ARC, 1979. Treas., Northwood Jr. High Sch. PTA, 1978-79, mem. parent adv. com., 1979; vice-pres. Northcrest Sch. PTA, 1970-71, sec., 1969-70. Mem. Ind. State Nurses Assn. (mem. membership com. 1980), Am. Coll. Sports Medicine, Purdue Alumni Assn. (pres. 1981-82). Republican. Lutheran Mo. Synod. Home: 5201 Northcrest Dr Fort Wayne IN 46825 Office: Ind-Purdue U 2101 Coliseum Blvd E Fort Wayne IN 46805

KIDD, CATHERINE JUNE, social worker; b. Baton Rouge, May 25, 1943; d. Cecil Clyde and June Sylvia (Gregory) K.; student So. Meth. U., 1961-62; B.A., La. State U., 1965. Researcher, Project on Head Start Program, Baton Rouge, 1965; kindergarten tchr. Kingsley House, also New Orleans Day Nursery Assn., New Orleans, 1965; tchr. Data Service Center, Shell Oil Co., 1967; social caseworker Charity Hosp. of La., New Orleans, 1967—. Mem. Nat. Assn. Social Workers (assoc. mem. state bd.), Assn. for Care of Children in Hosps., Children's Council of New Orleans, Mental Health Assn. Greater New Orleans. Home: 4317

Dryades St New Orleans LA 70115 Office: Charity Hosp of La 1532 Tulane Ave New Orleans LA 70140

KIDD, MARGARET ANN, univ. adminstr.; b. Kansas City, Mo., Dec. 10, 1942; d. Louis H. E. and Myrtle Ida (Nolte) Schlickelman; B. Music Edn., Tex. Christian U., 1964; M.A. in Interdisciplinary Studies, U. Tex., Dallas, 1981; m. Richard D. Kidd, Apr. 17, 1963; children—Sara Ann, Robert Matthew. Fgn. student adv. U. Tex., Austin, 1965-72, asst. dir. internat. office, 1972-74; dir. internat. and spl. services U. Tex., Dallas, 1974—; Coordinating Council N.Am. Affairs grantee, Republic of China, 1981; profl. devel. grantee Workshop on Students and Scholars from People's Republic of China, 1979, Seminar on Middle East/Arab World and Iran, 1978; recipient Sr. Fulbright award Project for Ednl. Experts, Fulbright Commn. Fed. Republic Germany, 1980. Mem. Tex. Assn. Internat. Edn. Adminstrs., Nat. Assn. Fgn. Student Affairs (govt. regulations adv. com. 1979—, cons. Council Advs. to Fgn. Students and Scholars 1978—), Assn. Handicapped Student Services Programs in Post-Secondary Edn., Fulbright Alumni Assn. Home: 3815 Duchess Tr Dallas TX 75229 Office: PO Box 688-GR 21 Richardson TX 75080

KIDD, MARY VIRGINIA LOVE (MRS. W.J. KIDD), geol. analysis co. exec.; b. Monroe, La., Nov. 16, 1940; d. Ocie Ray and Eunice Eullar (Reppond) Love; student Northeast U., Monroe, La., 1959-60; m. Willis James Kidd, Aug. 10, 1974; 1 son, Stephen Willis; children by previous marriage—James Randall Bryant, Karen Eileen Bryant. Sec., Phillips, Phillips & Harrop, ophthalmologists, Monroe, 1967-69; sec., nurse asst., Monroe, 1969-71, Monroe, Mich., 1971-72; sec., office mgr. Morris Enterprises, Monroe, La. and Gulfport, Miss., 1972-74; bookkeeper Pepsi Cola Bottling Co., Greenville, Miss., 1974-75; office mgr., sec., bookkeeper So. Mud Logging, Inc., West Monroe, La., 1976—. Mem. Monroe Desk and Derrick Club (v.p.), Nat. Assn. Female Execs. Democrat. Baptist. Club: Eastern Star. Home: PO Box 115 Eileen Rd Swartz LA 71281 Office: 104 Ozone St W Monroe LA 71291

KIDD, REBECCA (LOUISE) MONTGOMERY, artist, illustrator; b. Muncie, Ind., Nov. 29, 1942; d. Joe Buckley and Mary Marguerite (Mark) Montgomery; corr. student comml. art, Famous Artists Schs.; m. Ben Roy Kidd, Apr. 10, 1964; children—Daniel Ben, Diana Piper. Portrait painter and drawer, 1962-81; now painter in oils, pastels, watercolors, acrylics, inks; character painter, 1966—; outdoor scene, still life, floral painter, 1969—; children's story illustrator, 1972-74; archtl. restorer houses, 1972-81; adaptor of master's paintings, 1974—; miniature painter, 1974—; film illustrator, 1975; Am. Indian painter, 1975-81; trading pin designer, 1977, 78; lithograph printmaker, 1977; monotype printmaker, 1978— ; one woman show: Roadside Gallery, Melfa, Va., 1982; group shows include: Roadside Gallery, 1977—, The Gallery, Ct. Plaza, Salisbury, Md., 1977—; Shipmate Gallery, Ononcock, Va., 1981—, Queens Coll., Cambridge U., 1982. Mem. Quality Edn. Accomack County (Va.), Exec. Com., 1979-80; mem. Arts Council Eastern Shore. Mem. Eastern Shore Art League (constn. and bylaws chmn. 1979, dir. 1982), Visual Artists and Galleries Assn., Internat. Platform Assn. Subject of articles in several news publs. Address: 9 Lake St Onancock VA 23417

KIDD, SUSAN MARIE, broadcast journalist; b. San Antonio, Oct. 18, 1950; d. Richard D. and Mary B. (Bullock) K.; B.A., Albion Coll., 1972; m. Stanley W. Reid, Mar. 4, 1982. Anchorwoman, producer, reporter Sta. WFMY-TV, Greensboro, N.C., 1973-80; anchorwoman evening newscasts Sta. KTVI-TV, St. Louis, 1980—. Bd. dirs. Coro Found., St. Louis Black Repertory Theatre. Mem. Greater St. Louis Black Journalists Assn., Alpha Kappa Alpha. Office: 5915 Berthold St Saint Louis MO 63112

KIDDER, PRISCILLA, fashion designer, clothing mfr.; b. Quincy, Mass., Dec. 14; student New Eng. Art Sch.; m. James Kidder, 1940. Asst. buyer White's Dept. Store, Boston; founder bridal shop, Boston, 1945, founder Priscilla of Boston, wholesale bridal bus., 1950—. Office: care Priscilla of Boston 498 7th Ave New York NY 10018 *

KIDNEY, JULIET FISHER, govt. ofcl.; b. Richmond, Ind.; d. Edgar Andrew and Florence (Corwin) Fisher; B.A. (Class of 1905 fellow), Mt. Holyoke Coll., 1934; M.A., Radcliffe Coll., 1937; m. Daniel M. Kidney, July 6, 1946; children—James Andrew, Stephen Corwin. Instr. econs. Mt. Holyoke Coll., 1937-40, 41-43; economist OPA, 1943-46; instr. U. P.R., 1944-45; with CIA, 1951-55; with Dept. of Labor, 1960—, chief div. tng. Bur. Labor Stats., 1972-80, asst. commr. field ops., 1980—. Recipient Disting. Career Service award Dept. Labor. Mem. Indsl. Relations Research Assn. Democrat. Clubs: Nat. Press, Mt. Holyoke Alumnae (pres. Washington). Office: 441 G St NW Washington DC 20212

KIEHL, JANET K., communications exec.; b. Akron, Ohio, June 7, 1945; d. Arthur and Katherine Kiehl; B.S., Bucknell U., 1967; student U. Pa., 1968-69, U. N.H., 1974-75; M.B.A., Pace U., 1979. Systems engr. IBM, Phila., 1967-70, mktg. rep., 1971-74; market mgr. strategic planning AT&T, Basking Ridge, N.J., 1975-80; asst. v.p. sales Ill. Bell Telephone Co., Chgo., 1980-82, area v.p., 1982—. Mem. M.B.A. Adv. Bd., Lewis U. Mem. Atty.-Exec. Forum of Women's Bar Assn. Ill., Office: HQ 17F 225 W Randolph St Chicago IL 60606

KIELSMEIER, CATHERINE JANE, sch. adminstr.; b. San Jose, Calif; d. Frank Delos and Catherine Doris (Sellar) MacGowan; M.S., U. So. Calif., 1964, Ph.D., 1971; m. Milton Kielsmeier; children—Catherine Louise, Barry Delos. Tchr., Pub. Schs. Maricopa (Calif.); sch. psychologist Campbell (Calif.) Union Sch Dist., 1961-66; asst. prof. edn. and psychology Western Oreg. State Coll., Monmouth, 1966-67, 70; asst. research prof. Oreg. System Higher Edn., Monmouth, 1967-70; dir. spl. services Santa Rosa (Calif.) Pub. Schs., 1972—. Bd. dirs. Sonoma County Council Community Services, 1976—, Sonoma County Orgn. for Retarded. Mem. Council Exceptional Children. Home: 7495 Poplar Dr Forestville CA 95436 Office: 211 Ridgeway Ave Santa Rosa CA 95402

KIELY, MARGARET CLARE, clin. psychologist, educator; b. Tacoma; d. John Roach and Isabella (MacLean) K.; B.A., Central Coll. Edn., Wash., 1956; B.Sc. (hon.), U. Montreal, 1961, M.A. (hon.), 1963, Ph.D. (hon.), 1970. Prof. psychology Marianopolis Coll., Montreal, Que., Can., 1967-72; clin. psychologist Centre d'Orientation, Montreal, 1970-77; research psychologist Mental Hygiene Inst., Montreal, 1967-77; asso. prof. clin. and community psychology U. Montreal, 1972—; cons. Montreal Diocesan Theol. Coll., 1972-75, Centre des Services Sociaux-Gaspe, 1976-79. Health and Welfare of Can. grantee, 1979—. Mem. Am. Psychol. Assn., Que. Corp. Psychologists, Internat. Council Psychologist, Internat. Assn. Applied Psychology, Nat. Register of Health Providers in Psychology of the U.S., Orthopsychiat. Assn. Roman Catholic. Editorial bd. Essence, 1976—, Can. Jour. Community Mental Health; contbr. articles to profl. jours. Office: Psychology Dept Univ Montreal Case Postale 6128 Montreal PQ H3C 3J7 Canada

KIENITZ, LADONNA TRAPP, librarian; b. Bay City, Mich., Sept. 27, 1930; d. Orlin D. and Mary (Stanford) Trapp; B.A., Westmar Coll., LeMars, Iowa, 1951; M.A. in Library Sci., Rosary Coll., River Forest, Ill., 1970; postgrad. U. Calif., Berkeley, 1970-73; children—John, James, Rebecca, Mary, Timothy, David. Instr., Waukegan (Ill.) Public Schs., 1956-57, Pirmasens Am. Schs. (Germany), 1960-63; head librarian Woodlands Acad., Lake Forest, Ill., 1973-77; project librarian Lincolnwood (Ill.) Library Devel. Project, 1977-78; dir. Lincolnwood Library, 1978—; mem. Regional Librarians Adv. Council, 1978—, mem. exec. com., sec., 1979—. NDEA grantee, 1966-67. Mem. ALA, Ill. Library Assn., Glencoe LWV (legal observor local govt. 1979—). Methodist. Home: 361 Madison Ave Glencoe IL 60022 Office: 4100 Pratt Ave Lincolnwood IL 60646

KIER, MARY ALICE, literary agt.; b. Los Angeles, May 13, 1943; d. Thomas Nelson and Mary Elizabeth (LaChasse) Kier; A.A., Orange Coast Jr. Coll., 1963; B.A. in English, Calif. State Coll., Fullerton, 1965. Advt. copywriter Hixson & Jorgensen, Los Angeles, 1966-67; free lance writer/photographer, Europe, Greece, U.S.A., 1968-73; asso. producer, dir. devel. for documentaries and features EMC Corp., Cobra Prodns., Ltd., also ind. producers, Los Angeles, 1974-76; lit. agt. for TV and motion pictures Bloom, Beckett, Levy & Shorr, Beverly Hills, Calif., 1977-79; dir. lit. dept. STE Representation Ltd., 1980—. Bd. dirs. Internat. Children's Sch. Mem. Women in Films (sec., pub. relations Los Angeles). Contbr. photographs to newspapers, mags. and books. Office: 211 S Beverly Dr Suite 201 Beverly Hills CA 90212

KIERNAN, CONNIE BEHRENDS, fast food exec.; b. Springfield, Ill., July 12, 1946; d. Elmer G. and Bernice M. (Harms) Behrends; B.A., Eastern Ill. U., 1977; m. Tony Kiernan, Sept. 15, 1979. Employment counselor Betty Gray Employment, Washington, 1968-70; customer rep./sr. customer rep. Xerox Corp., Honolulu, 1970-73; mgr., buyer The Nautical Boatique, Honolulu, 1973-75; merchandising/promotion dir. Heftel Broadcasting, Honolulu, 1975-77; advt., promotion mgr. WGMS AM/FM, Washington, 1977-79; with Metroplex Communications, Washington, 1979-80; v.p. advt. Mut. Broadcasting System, Arlington, Va., 1981-82; co-owner Slices Pizza and Subs, Honolulu, 1982—. Ill. rep. St. Cloud U. Art Sch., 1968. Named Xerox Nat. Employee of Yr., 1972; WGMS Employee of Yr., 1978; RKO Promotion Dir. of Yr., 1978. Clubs: The Prodn., Ad of Washington, Art Dirs. Home: 1912 Wilhelmina Rise Honolulu HI 96816 Office: 870 Kapahulu Ave Honolulu HI 96816

KIEVMAN, BEVERLY STEIN, mktg., public relations and sales tng. agy. exec.; b. Atlanta, Nov. 21, 1937; d. Jack Clarence and Bess (Segal) Stein; student Rollins Coll., 1954-56; A.B. in Journalism, U. Ga., Athens, 1958; m. Michael Kievman, Apr. 30, 1977; children—Mark, Steve; stepchildren—Chris, Carson, Michele, Corin. Founder, pres. Atlanta Models & Talent, Inc., 1960-71; pres. Beverly Anderson & Assos., Atlanta, 1972-74; dist. mgr. Research Inst. Am., Atlanta, 1975-76, dir. mgmt. services, 1976-77, regional dir., 1977-78; founder, pres. Mktg. Innovations Corp., Atlanta, 1979—; dir. Nat. Bank of Ga., 1981—. Pres. Ga. chpt. Leukemia Soc. Am., 1981-82. Mem. Women's Forum, Inc. (nat. bd. dir. 1980-82), Women's Commerce Club Am. (dir. 1981—), Com. of 200, Sales and Mktg. Execs. (dir. 1980-81), Atlanta Advt. Club (dir. 1971-74), Women in Film (dir. 1974-76), Women Bus. Owners (dir. 1980-81), Am. Mktg. Assn., Am. Soc. Tng. and Devel., Nat. Speakers Assn. Author: The Complete Success Workbook for Today's Saleswoman, 1982. Home: 573 Tara Tr NW Atlanta GA 30327 Office: 1953 Piedmont Circle Atlanta GA 30324

KIKAWADA, AGNES MITSUE, banker; b. Osaka, Japan, Feb. 22, 1941; came to U.S., 1963, resident, 1970; d. Naokichi and Kazue (Isoda) Kurihara; B.S., Kohnan U., Kobe, 1963; postgrad. Baldwin-Wallace Coll., Berea, Ohio, U. Calif., Berkeley; m. Isaac Mitsuru Kikawada June 1965 (div. Oct. 1978). Teller, clk. Calif. First Bank, San Francisco, 1970-72, ops. officer, loan officer, Oakland, 1973-78, asst. mgr., then mgr., asst. v.p., San Mateo, 1978—; consumer loan clk. Bank of Calif., Berkeley, 1972-73. Bd. dirs. Sakai City and Berkeley Sister City Assn., 1977. Mem. San Mateo C. of C., San Mateo County Devel. Assn., U. Calif. Alumni Assn. Club: Circlon. Office: 400 S El Camono Real San Mateo CA 94402

KILBOURNE, JEAN, lectr., advocate, media analyst, writer; b. Junction City, Kans., Jan. 4, 1943; d. W. Wallace and Lillian (Brazier) K.; B.A. (Pendleton scholar, BBC fellow), Wellesley Coll., 1964; M.Ed., Boston U., 1972, Ed.D., 1980. Prodn. asst. BBC, London, and Transatlantic Prodn., Paris, 1964-66; tchr. English Norwell (Mass.) High Sch., 1969-72; instr. Emerson Coll., Boston, 1972-75; media analyst, lectr., writer, cons., Boston, 1975—; films and slide shows include: The Naked Truth: Advertising's Image of Women, 1970; Killing Us Softly: Advertising's Image of Women, 1979; Under the Influence: The Pushing of Alcohol Via Advertising, 1979; Calling the Shots: The Advertising of Alcohol, 1982; dir. Advt. Analysis, Inc.. Bd. dirs. Nat. Center Women in the Performing and Media Arts, 1978-80; adv. bd. Mass. Women's Polit. Caucus, 1981—. Ednl. Found. Am. grantee, 1978. Mem. New Eng. Screen Edn. Assn. (asst. dir.), Women's Inst. Freedom of the Press (assoc.), Action For Children's TV, Am. Council Consumer Interests, Amnesty Internat., Feminist Writers Guild, Nat. Citizens Com. for Broadcasting, NOW, Nat. Women's Polit. Caucus, Nat. Women's Studies Assn., Nat. Writers Union, Nine to Five, Women Against Violence Against Women, Women Against Violence in Pornography and Media, Women's Inst. Freedom of the Press, Women's Media Network. Office: 51 Church St Boston MA 02116

KILBURN, MARY BROWN, psychologist; b. Conway, Ark., Feb. 2, 1934; d. Doyne DeWitt and Mary Marie (Ruble) Brown; B.S. cum laude, Memphis State Coll., 1956; M.S. in Psychology, N.C. State U., Raleigh, 1969, Ph.D. in Clin./Community Psychology, 1977; m. Stanley Collins Kilburn, Mar. 24, 1957 (separated June 1982); children—Katherine Marie, Amanda Caroline. Asst. dir., office mgr. Girl's Club Memphis, 1955-56; gen. agt. Trans-Continental Life Ins. Co., Little Rock, Ark., 1956-57; adminstrv. sec. div. med. psychology dept. psychiatry Duke U. Med. Center, Durham, N.C., 1957-58; ltd. pvt. practice psychology, Raleigh, N.C., 1965-80, full-time, 1980—; pres. Mary Kilburn, Ph.D. and Assocs. Psychol. Services of Raleigh P.A., 1980—; research asst. cognitive tng. project N.C. State U., Raleigh, 1965-66, teaching asst. dept. psychology, 1966-67; mem. faculty Peace Coll., Raleigh, 1969-70; psychologist N.C. Div. Social Services, Raleigh, 1970-73; clin. psychologist Mental Health Center, N.C. Dept. Corrections, Raleigh, 1973; asst. dir., chief clin. services Developmental Evaluation Center, Raleigh, 1973-77; psychol. services dir. Div. Social Services, N.C. Dept. Human Resources, Raleigh, 1977—, div. rep. State Adv. Council on Wilderness Camping for Emotionally Disturbed Children; affiliate staff Holly Hills Psychiat. Hosp., 1982—. Chmn. steering com. N.C. Consumer's Council, 1966-68; mem. N.C. Adv. Bd. Small Bus. Service Bur., 1982—; mem. exec. bd. Life Enrichment Center, 1980-82. Cert. sch. psychologist, lic. practicing psychologist, N.C. Mem. Am., N.C. (mem. exec. bd. 1969, 81—, chmn. ins. com.) psychol. assns., N.C. Group Behavior Soc., Wake County Mental Health Assn. (dir. 1983—), Phi Kappa Phi, Psi Chi, Tau Kappa Alpha. Author research papers. Office: 229 Bryan Bldg Cameron Village Raleigh NC 27605

KILESKY, FLORENCE ANN, nurse; b. Scranton, Pa., Aug. 23, 1924; d. William and Anna Kilesky; R.N., Moses Taylor Hosp., Scranton, 1946; B.S. in Nursing Edn., Coll. Misericordia, Dallas, Pa., 1969; M.A. in Counseling, Marywood Coll., Scranton, 1981. Mem. nursing staff Moses Taylor Hosp., 1946—, dir. nursing, 1969—; adv. bd. nursing dept. Marywood Coll.; bd. dirs. Northeastern Pa. Nurse Adminstrn. Forum, Moses Taylor Hosp. Aux.; cons. in field. Asso. Hosp. Linens scholar, 1965. Mem. Nat. League Nursing, Am. Soc. Nursing Service Adminstrs., Am. Nurses Assn., Am. Personnel and Guidance Assn., Nat. Fedn. Bus. and Profl. Women, Pa. Nurses Assn., Lackawanna County Nurses Assn., Moses Talor Hosp. Alumnae Assn., Marywood Coll. Alumnae Assn., Coll. Misericorida Alumnae Assn. Club: Quota. Home: 2032 Price St Scranton PA 18504 Office: 700 Quincy Ave Scranton PA 18510

KILEY, SUSAN WRIGHT, social worker; b. Montreal, Que., Can., May 8, 1946; d. Thomas Fleming and Lexie (Johnson) Wright; brought to U.S., 1947, naturalized, 1954; B.A., Cornell U., 1968; M.S.W., Portland State U., 1975; m. John E. Kiley, Aug. 10, 1968; children—Christopher John, Jessica Susan. Social worker Stark County Child Welfare, Canton, Ohio, 1969-70, Dept. Instns., Social and Rehab. Services, Lawton, Okla., 1970-72, Oreg. Health Scis. U., Portland, 1975—; field instr. Portland State U. Sch. Social Work, 1976—; social worker Rosenfeld Center for Study, Prevention and Treatment of Child Abuse, 1975-80. Bd. dirs. Crisis hotline, Lawton, 1971-72. Mem. Acad. Cert. Social Workers, Nat. Assn. Social Workers. Home: 2734 NE Bryce St Portland OR 97212 Office: Oreg Health Scis U Social Service Dept 3181 SW Sam Jackson Park Rd Portland OR 97201

KILGARIN, KAREN, state legislator; b. Omaha, Mar. 12, 1957; student Kearney State Coll., 1975-79. Sales asso. Bill Morrison Real Estate, 1981—; mem. Nebr. Legislature, 1980—. Past pres., past charter mem. Kearney Young Democrats; mem. Douglas County Dem. Central Com.; co-chmn. Legis. Dist. 7 Democrats. Mem. Omaha Jaycees, Omaha Women's C. of C. Office: PO Box 34638 Omaha NE 68134

KILGORE, ELAYNE STATTON, trade assn. exec.; b. Chgo., Mar. 7, 1921; d. Harry William and Harriet Margaret (Gordon) Statton; grad. Thornton Twp. (Ill.) Jr. Coll., 1938-40; postgrad. U. Ill., Northwestern U.; m. Charles A. Kilgore, Sept. 29, 1956. Mem. staff Bldg. Mgrs. Assn. Chgo., 1953—, asst. sec., 1961-72, exec. sec., 1972—; exec. sec. Bldg. Owners and Mgrs. Assn. Suburban Chgo., 1971-82; sec.-treas. N. Central Regional Conf. Bldg. Owners and Mgrs., 1967-77; pres. asso. execs. Bldg. Owners and Mgrs. Assn. Internat., 1973-75. Mem. Chgo. Bldg. Mgrs. Club, Chgo. Assn. Commerce and Industry, Execs. Club Chgo., Chgo. Soc. Assn. Execs., Am. Soc. Assn. Execs., Chgo. Real Estate Bd., Chgo. Bldg. Supts. Assn. (hon.). Club: Monroe. Home: 175 E Delaware Pl Chicago IL 60611 Office: 135 S LaSalle St Chicago IL 60603

KILGORE, MARGARET ANN, govt. orgn. adminstr.; b. Stilwell, Okla., July 18, 1939; d. Julius Henry and Margaret Eileen (Snodgrass) Thomas; B.S. in Microbiology, Okla. State U., 1969, postgrad., 1971-74; m. Lary M. Kilgore, June 3, 1962; children—Katheryn, Linda, Lance. Ednl. specialist Bur. Indian Affairs, Ft. Defiance Agy., 1974-77, employee devel. specialist Navajo Area Tng. Center, Continental Divide, N.Mex., 1977-79; tng. dir. USPHS Indian Health Service, Navajo area, Window Rock, Ariz., 1979—; instr. ARC, N.Mex., 1978; lectr. nutrition U. N.Mex., Gallup, 1979-80. Comdr., CAP, Tohatchi, N.Mex., 1975-78, Gallup, N.Mex., 1978-79. Mem. Am. Soc. Microbiologists, Am. Soc. Tng. and Devel., N.Mex. Personnel and Guidance Assn., Phi Delta Kappa. Democrat. Home: 506 Stagecoach Rd Gallup NM 87301 Office: Indian Health Service Box G Window Rock AZ 86515

KILGORE, MARY LEE, advt. exec.; b. Houston, June 19, 1947; d. Jack Edgar and Ruby Lee (Dickerson) K.; B.F.A., So. Meth. U., 1969, M.F.A., 1979. Radio producer Glenn Advt., Dallas, 1969-71; regional media supr. Batton, Barton, Durstine & Osbourn Advt., N.Y.C. and Dallas, 1971-73; nat. media supr. Clinton E. Frank Advt., Dallas, 1973-75; media dir., v.p. to sr. v.p., dir. media services KCBN Advt. and Public Relations, Dallas, 1975-81; field advt. mgr. Southland Corp., Dallas, 1981—; adj. prof. So. Meth. U.; instr. Dallas County Community Colls. Advt. and pub. relations steering com. United Way of Dallas; chmn. Soaring Spirits Project of Tex. Children's Hosp. Mem. Assn. Broadcasting Execs. of Tex. (pres. 1980), Am. Women in Radio and TV (pres. Dallas chpt. 1975), Dallas Advt. League, 500, Inc., Gamma Phi Beta, Alpha Epsilon Rho, Zeta Phi Eta. Office: 2828 N Haskell Ave Dallas TX 75221

KILKELLY, SHIRLEY HOFFMAN, systems engr.; b. Bklyn., Nov. 27, 1922; d. Frank George and Lillian Mae (Kehlenbeck) Hoffman; B.S.M.E., U. Miami, 1952; m. Daniel J. Kilkelly, Feb. 14, 1956 (dec. May 1963). Jr. engr. patent law Worthington Corp., Harrison, N.J., 1952-54; mech. engr. Bendix Corp., Teterboro, N.J., 1954-56, 60-63; system test engr. Grumman Aerospace, Bethpage, N.Y., 1963-72; sr. systems engr. Raytheon Corp., Bedford, Mass., 1973-75; systems engr. space div. Am. Sci. & Engring., Inc., Arlington, Mass., 1975-81, sr. systems engr. internat. solar polar mission program, 1981; systems engr. Sikorsky Aircraft, Stratford, Conn., 1982—. Served with Women's Res. USMC, 1943-45. Recipient Achievement awards NASA, 1977, 78, 80. Mem. AIAA. Home: 24 Woodward Ave Apt 37 New Haven CT 06512

KILLEA, LUCY LYTLE, city ofcl.; b. San Antonio, July 31, 1922; d. Nelson and Zelime (Pettus) Lytle; B.A., Incarnate Word Coll., San Antonio, 1943; M.A. in History, U. San Diego, 1966; Ph.D. in History, U. Calif., San Diego, 1975; m. John F. Killea, May 11, 1946; children—Paul, Jay. Research analyst for Western Europe, Army Intelligence, Spl. Br., Washington, 1944-48; adminstrv. asst. Dept. State, London, 1946; econ. officer Econ. Coop. Adminstrn., The Hague, Netherlands, 1949; research analyst CIA, Washington, 1948-56; part time book reviewer USIS, 1956-60; teaching and research asst. U. Calif., San Diego, 1967-72; exec. dir., exec. v.p. Fronteras de las Californias, San Diego, 1974-78; mem. City Council, San Diego, 1978—, dep. mayor, 1982—, mem. planning commn., 1978, public services and safety com., 1979—, chmn., 1980-81, rules, legis. and intergovtl. com., 1981—, housing authority, 1978—, redevel. agy., 1978—; lectr. Socioeconomics of Baja, Calif., and Mex., Southwestern Coll., Chula-Vista, 1976; lectr. dept. history San Diego State U., 1976-77; participant, organizer, panelist, moderator confs. in field, U.S., Mex.; mem. Palm City Sanitation Dist., 1978—, Met. Transit Devel. Bd., 1978—. Regional Employment and Tng. Consortium Bd., 1978-80, City-County Reinvestment Task Force, 1978-80, Transp. and Land Use Com., 1978-80, Public Facilities and Recreation Com., 1979-80. Bd. trustees San Diego Zool. Soc., 1976-78; mem. San Diego County Cultural Heritage Com., 1971-78, vice chmn., 1973-75; mem. Hist. Site Bd., City San Diego, 1968-75, vice chmn., 1971-75; bd. dirs. San Diego Hist. Soc., 1971-77; chmn. Internat. Com. Conv. and Visitors Bur., 1978, host com., 1976-77; adv. bd. Sharp Hosp.; bd. dirs., com. mem. Friends of Library, U. Calif., San Diego; founding mem. Caridad Internacional; mem. community adv. bd. of program in U.S.-Mex. Studies, U. Calif., San Diego, 1981—; mem. James S. Copley Library Adv. Council, U. San Diego, 1981—; active community orgns. including LWV, Fine Arts Soc. San Diego, YWCA, San Diego Mus. Art, San Diego Chpt. ARC, Dimensions, Aardvarks Ltd., Pacific Beach Hist. Soc., San Diego Symphonic Assn. Research grantee, Justice Found., 1965, U. Calif., San Diego, 1971; recipient awards, Conf. Calif. Hist. Socs., 1966, Inst. for Protection of Children, City of Tijuana and Tijuana Com., 1966, Alice Paul Award, Nat. Women's Polit. Caucus, 1982; named one of 12 Women of Valor, Beth Israel Sisterhood of Temple Beth Israel, San Diego, 1966, Woman of Accomplishment, Bus. and Profl. Clubs. San Diego, 1979, Woman of Yr., San Diego Irish Congress, 1981; honored Leukemia Soc., 1980; named alumna of distinction Incarnate Word Coll., San Antonio, 1981. Mem. Nat. Women's Polit. Caucus, Calif. Women in Govt. (bd. dirs.), Mid City C. of C., San Diego C. of C., Nat. League of Cities, World Affairs Council, Am. Fgn. Service Assn., Incarnate Word Alumnae Assn., U. San Diego Alumni Assn., U. Calif., San Diego Alumni and Friends (career adv. panel), Calif. Elected Women's Assn. for Edn. and Research (bd. 1980—, sec., treas., 1980-81, v.p. 1982—). Democrat. Roman Catholic. Clubs: Catfish, Army-Navy (Arlington, Va.), Ducks

Unlimited. Contbr. writings to publs. in field. Office: 202 C St San Diego CA 92103

KILLEBREW, ELLEN JANE (MRS. EDWARD S. GRAVES), cardiologist; b. Tiffin, Ohio, Oct. 8, 1937; d. Joseph Arthur and Stephanie (Beriont) K.; B.S. in Biology, Bucknell U., 1959; M.D., N.J. Coll. Medicine, 1965; m. Edward S. Graves, Sept. 12, 1970. Intern, U. Colo., 1965-66, resident 1966-68; cardiology fellow Pacific Med. Center, San Francisco, 1968-70; dir. coronary care, Permanent Med. Group, Richmond, Calif., 1970—; asst. prof. U. Calif. Med. Center, San Francisco. Robert C. Kirkwood Meml. scholar in cardiology, 1970; recipient Physician's Recognition award continuing med. edn. Diplomate Am. Bd. Internal Medicine. Mem. ACP, Fedn. Clin. Research, Am. Heart Assn. (research chmn. Contra Costa chpt. 1975—, v.p. 1980, pres. chpt. 1981-82), Home: 30 Redding Ct Tiburon CA 94920 Office: 280 W MacArthur Blvd Oakland CA 94611

KILLEBREW, MIRIAM CLAIRE (SHARPE), mcht.; b. Indpls., Oct. 25, 1920; d. Randle and Lucille (Horton) Sharpe. A.A., Placer Coll., 1940; m. James Artell Killebrew, Sept. 14, 1940; children—Dorothy Jean, Deborah Jean. Vice pres. K & H Sales, 1946-76, pres., 1976—. Home: 18397 Magee Way Castro Valley CA 94546 Office: 1800 Williams St San Leandro CA 94577

KILLEBREW, RACHEL ELKINS, data processing cons.; b. McMinnville, Tenn., Aug. 9, 1942; d. Joseph E. and Emma (Henderson) Elkins; B.S., Tenn. Technol. U., 1964; M.B.A., Rockhurst Coll., 1980; div.; 1 son, Winston G. Denton. Analyst, IBM Corp., Kennedy Space Center, Fla., 1966-69; data processing specialist Mgmt. Sci. Am., Atlanta, 1969-71; cons. Stockholders System, Inc., Atlanta, 1971-73; mgr. data systems devel. TWA, Kansas City, Mo., 1973—; v.p. RS Computing Assos., Inc., Kansas City, Mo., 1981—. Data processing seminar leader Career Crossroads for Women, 1980-81. Mem. Data Processing Mgmt. Assn. (dir. 1980-81), Trans World Airlines Mgmt. Club, Rockhurst Exec. Fellows Soc., Kappa Mu Epsilon. Clubs: Kansas City Ski, Assn. Research and Enlightenment, Friends of Art, Silva Mind Control, Erhardt Seminar Tng., Audubon Club. Home: 6520 W 49th St Mission KS 66202 Office: TWA PO Box 21026 1-310 MCI Kansas City MO 64195

KILLENS, THERESE ROLANDE, M.P.; b. Trois-Rivieres, Que., Can., June 29, 1927; d. Omer Joseph and Cecile Marie (Thelland) Gauthéer; student St. Agele de Laval Convent Boarding Sch.; m. Raymond Lowes Killens, Sept. 3, 1945; children—Francena, Doreen, Joanne, Daniel, Louise. Commnr., mem. exec. com. Montreal Catholic Sch. Commn., 1973-79; bd. dirs. Vanier CEGEP Coll., 1975, mem. exec. com. 1978, vice-pres. 1977-79; M.P., Saint-Michel, 1979—, parliamentary sec. to Hon. Judy Erola, Minister of State and Minister Responsible for Status of Women. Mem. Canadian Catholic Sch. Trustees Assn. (bd. govs. 1973-78), Spera Found. for Drug Addicts. Liberal. Roman Catholic. Home: 10305 St Charles Ave Montreal PQ H2C 2L2 Canada Office: Ho of Commons Center Block 535S Ottawa K1A 0A6 Canada

KILLGORE, KAY, counselor; b. Selma, Ala., July 16, 1948; d. Brack and Polly Latham; B.S. in Psychology, Bethany Nazarene Coll., 1975; M.Ed. in Psychology, Central State U., 1977. Owner, operator Woman to Woman Counseling, Oklahoma City, 1977—, Women's Work Shop, Oklahoma City, 1979—. Mem. Women's Polit. Caucus. Office: 527 NW 23d St Oklahoma City OK 73103

KILLIAN, JUDY ANNE, psychiat. social worker; b. New Holland, Pa., Dec. 21, 1940; d. Allen B. and Pauline K.; B.A., Millersville State Coll., 1972; M.S.W. cum laude, U. Pitts., 1976. Sec., Armstrong Cork Co., Lancaster, Pa., 1963-67; mgr. income maintenance Dept. Public Assistance, Lancaster, 1967-74; psychiat. social worker Crisis Intervention, Lancaster Guidance Center, 1976—; also pvt. practice psychotherapy, Lancaster. Steinman scholar, 1975. Mem. Acad. Cert. Social Workers, Nat. Assn. Social Workers. Methodist. Club: Soroptimists Internat. Home: 104 Pearl St Lancaster PA 17603 Office: 227 E Orange St Lancaster PA 17602 also 18 S Duke St Lancaster PA 17602

KILLICK, KATHLEEN ANN, biochemist; b. Chgo., Jan. 22, 1942; d. Orson Smyth and Maori Madeline (Maloney) K.; B.S. in Biology (NSF undergrad. fellow, Pullman scholar), Ill. Inst. Tech., 1964, M.S. in Microbiology, 1966, Ph.D. in Biochemistry, 1969; cert., U. Uppsala, 1977; postgrad. Argonne (Ill.) Nat. Lab., U. Chgo., 1969-70. Postdoctoral fellow Boston Biomed. Research Inst., 1970-76, staff scientist dept. devel. biology, 1976-82; asst., prof., dept. of biol. scis., St. John's Univ., N.Y., 1982—; lectr. dept. microbiology and molecular genetics Harvard U. NSF trainee, 1968-69, spl. fellow, 1972-74, grantee, 1978—; AEC postdoctoral fellow, 1969-70; Selznick fellow Hereditary Disease Found., 1978. Mem. N.Y. Acad. Scis., AAAS, Am. Soc. Microbiology, Northeastern Soc. Microbiology, Am. Chem. Soc., Am. Soc. Biol. Chemistry, Gerontology Soc., Electrophorosis Soc., Carbohydrate Soc., Sigma Xi. Democrat. Roman Catholic. Office: Grand Central Utopia Parkways New York NY 11439

KILLINGBECK, JANICE LYNELLE (MRS. VICTOR LEE KILLINGBECK), journalist; b. Flint, Mich., Nov. 11, 1948; d. Leonard Paul and Ina Marie (Harris) Johnson; B.A., Mich. State U., 1970; postgrad. Delta Coll., 1971-72; m. Victor Lee Killingbeck, Sept. 26, 1970; children—Deeanna Dawn, Victor Scott. Tourist counselor Mich. Dept. State Hwys., Clare, 1969; copy editor Mich. State News, East Lansing, 1969-70; gen. reporter Midland (Mich.) Daily News, 1970; tchr. Saginaw (Mich.) Pub. Schs., 1971; pub. relations teller 1st State Bank of Saginaw, 1971-75; crew leader spl. census in Buena Vista Twp., Detroit Regional Office, U.S. Bur. Census, 1976, interviewer ann. housing survey-standard met. statis. areas, 1977-78, interviewer on-going health surveys, 1979—. Mem. Women in Communications, Sigma Delta Chi. Methodist. Home and Office: 4946 Hess Rd Saginaw MI 48601

KILMER, MARIE CARLYLE BECKWITH, nurse; b. Omaha, Feb. 26, 1917; d. Edward Simpson and Mary Letitia (Carlyle) Beckwith; R.N., Kahler Sch. Nursing, Rochester, Minn., 1942; B.S. in Nursing, U. Omaha, 1944; M.S. in Psychiat. Nursing and Counseling, U. Nebr., Lincoln, 1965; m. Lloyd Warren Kilmer, June 28, 1945. Instr., Nebr. Methodist Sch. Nursing, Omaha, 1945, ARC, 1946; counselor Nebr. Nurses Assn., 1947-49; instr., counselor Immanuel Sch. Nursing, Omaha, 1963-74, dir., 1974-76; chmn. div. nursing Coll. St. Mary, Omaha, 1976—; mem. Nebr. Nursing Home Adv. Council, 1981—. Mem. Am. Nurses Assn., Nat. League Nursing, Nat. Nurses Holistic Health Assn., Omaha League Nursing, Dist. Two Nurses Assn., Coll. St. Mary Faculty Assn. and Faculty Forum, PEO, Nebr. Nurses' Assn., Nebr. League Nursing, Am. Legion Aux., Sigma Theta Tau. Republican. Methodist. Clubs: Rotary Anns, Daus. Nile. Home: 682 S 84th St Omaha NE 68114 Office: 1801 S 72d St Omaha NE 68124

KILMER, SALLY JEAN, educator; b. Woodhull, N.Y., Feb. 26, 1936; d. Percy Ellsworth and Marion Leona (Whiteman) Kilmer; B.S., Pa. State U., 1958, M.S., 1961; Ph.D., Stanford U., 1974. Instr., U. Minn., Mpls., 1960-67, coordinator Center for Early Edn. and Devel., 1972-73; child devel. specialist, Inst. for Interdisciplinary Studies, Mpls., 1970-72; child devel. cons., Minn. Planning Agy., St. Paul, 1973-74; child devel. specialist Ramsey County Family Day Care Tng. Project, St. Paul, 1973; asst. prof., dir. day care supr. tng. program, Inst. for Child Behavior and Devel., U. Ill., Champaign, 1975-79; asso. prof., dir. Child Devel. Center, Bowling Green (Ohio) State U., 1979—; cons. Minn. Higher Edn. Coordinating Commn., Minn. Early Learning Design, 1973-75; chmn. subcom. on tng., Ill. Statewide Day Care Adv. Com.; adv. com. Parkland Community Coll. Child Devel., 1977-79; mem. adv. com. Ohio White House Conf. on Children and Youth, 1981. Charter mem., chmn. Champaign County (Ill.) Women's Polit. Caucus, 1977-79; bd. dirs. Ill. Women's Polit. Caucus, 1977-79; chmn. Champaign County United Way Day Care Study Com., 1978. NDEA Fellow, 1967-70. Mem. Soc. for Research in Child Devel., Am. Psychol. Assn., Am. Ednl. Research Assn., Nat. Assn. Edn. Young Children, Ohio Assn. Edn. Young Children (treas. 1981—), Organisation Mondiale pour L'Education Prescholaire (Ohio liaison U.S. nat. com. 1979—), LWV (dir. Bowling Green 1980-82). Author: (with Shirley Moore) Contemporary Preschool Education: A Program for Young Children, 1973. Editor: Advances in Early Education and Day Care, Vol. 1, 1980, Vol. 2, 1981. Home: 828 Normandie Blvd Bowling Green OH 43402 Office: Bowling Green U Bowling Green OH 43403

KILPATRICK, CAROLYN CHEEKS, state legislator; b. Detroit, June 25, 1945; d. Marvell and Willa Mae (Henry) Cheeks; A.S., Ferris State Coll., 1965; B.S., Western Mich. U., 1972; M.S., U. Mich., 1977; children—Kwame Malik, Ayanna Monifa. Tchr., Detroit Pub. Schs., 1972-79; mem. Mich. Ho. of Reps., Lansing, 1978—, majority whip, majority vice chairperson com. constl. revision, majority vice chairperson liquor control. Recipient Disting. Legislator award U. Mich., 1981, Anthony Wayne award Wayne State U., 1982. Mem. Nat. Orgn. 100 Black Women, Nat. Conf. Black State Legislators, Nat. Order Women Legislators. Home: 7445 LaSalle Blvd Detroit MI 48206 Office: 114 1/2 State Capitol Lansing MI 48909

KILPATRICK, DIANE CORNELIA, psychologist; b. Newport News, Va., Dec. 7, 1943; d. Claude Cornelius and Anne Eloise (Jones) K.; A.B., U. Ala., 1966, M.Ed., 1967; Ph.D., U. Ill., Champaign-Urbana, 1976. Head resident-coordinator U. Ill., 1967-69, acad. adviser and adminstr. Coll. Liberal Arts and Scis., 1969-72; asst. dean of coll. Dartmouth Coll., Hanover, N.H., 1972-73, instr. dept. psychiatry Med. Sch., 1973-76, asst. prof. clin. psychiatry, 1976—, psychologist student health service, 1973—. Mem. bd. student affairs A Better Chance Program, Hanover, 1973-75; vol. Hanover-Dartmouth Daycare Center, 1974-75. Cert. psychologist N.H. Bd. Examiners Psychologists. Mem. New Eng. Coll. Health Assn. (mem. exec. com.), Am. Coll. Health Assn., Am. Psychol. Assn., Eastern Psychol. Assn., Am. Assn. Suicidology, Am. Assn. Higher Edn. Home: 26 E Wheelock St Hanover NH 03755 Office: Dartmouth Coll Health Service 7 Rope Ferry Rd Hanover NH 03755

KILPATRICK, PATRICIA BALDWIN, univ. ofcl.; b. Cleve., May 19, 1927; d. Leland Stanford and Agnes Mildred (Sweeney) Baldwin; student Ohio Wesleyan U., 1945-47; A.B., Case Western Res. U., 1949, M.A., 1951; m. Rufus Hall Kilpatrick, June 9, 1951; children—Timothy Leland, Catherine Louise, Rufus Hall III. Tchr., Lorain (Ohio) High Sch., 1951-52; instr. Case Western Res. U., Cleve., 1962-65, asst. prof. phys. edn., 1965-72, chmn. dept., 1970-72, asst. dean Flora Stone Mather Coll., 1965-72, asso. dean univ., 1972-77, asst. sec. univ., 1977-79, sec., 1979—. Layreader, Episcopal Ch., 1972—, mem. council Ohio Diocese, 1977, v.p. council, 1979, mem. various coms. Mem. Nat. (profl. standing com.), Ohio (treas. 1965-67, 79-81) assns. women deans, adminstrs. and counselors, AAHPER, Kappa Alpha Theta (coll. dist. pres. 1965-67). Contbr. sect. to Ency. Edn., 1970. Home: 33 Division St Hudson OH 44236 Office: Case Western Res U 2040 Adelbert Rd Cleveland OH 44106

KILSON, MARION DUSSER DE BARENNE, educator; b. New Haven, May 8, 1936; d. Joannes Gregorius and Emily Lockwood (Greene) Dusser de Barenne; B.A., Radcliffe Coll., 1958; M.A., Stanford U., 1959; Ph.D. (NIMH fellow), Harvard U., 1967; m. Martin L. Kilson, Aug. 8, 1959; children—Jennifer Greene, Peter Dusser de Barenne, Hannah Laws. Instr., asst. prof. U. Mass., Boston, 1966-68; fellow Radcliffe Inst., 1968-70; asso. prof. Simmons, Boston, 1969-73; prof. Newton Coll., Mass., 1973-75; dir. research Radcliffe Inst., Cambridge, Mass., 1975-77; dir. Bunting Inst., Cambridge, Mass., 1977-80; acad. dean Emmanuel Coll., Boston, 1980—. Mem. Am. Folklore Soc., Nat. Assn. Women Deans (dir. coll. sect. 1982—), AAUW, Am. Assn. for Higher Edn., Radcliffe Grad. Soc. (chmn. 1981—). Author: Kpele Lala: Ga Religious Songs and Symbols, 1971; African Urban Kinsmen, 1974; Royal Antelope and Spider: West African Mende Tales, 1976. Home: 4 Eliot Rd Lexington MA 02173 Office: 400 The Fenway Boston MA 02115

KIM, SARAH, businesswoman; b. Seoul, Korea, Oct. 1, 1938; d. Bong Hyun and Sang Rim (Nam) Choi; B.A., Ehwa Women's U., 1961; M.Ed., Northeastern U., 1973; m. John Kim, Oct. 26, 1961; children—Stewart, Teddy. Realtor, Lexington, Mass., 1973-77; ownerHouse of Kim, Inc., Lexington, 1974-79; treas. Supertek, Lexington and Los Angeles, 1975—; pres. JKK Enterprises, Inc., Los Angeles, 1979—; sec. Kim-Supertek, Inc., 1979—. Mem. AAUW. Republican. Methodist. Contbr. articles to Korean Women's mags. Home: 1670 Carla Ridge Beverly Hills CA 90210 also 24300 Malibu Rd Malibu CA 92465 Office: 2320 Cotner Ave Los Angeles CA 90064

KIMBALL, OLIVE MAE, educator, univ. adminstr.; b. Laurium, Mich., Aug. 19, 1930; d. William Verran and Jennie (Oliver) Cornish; B.S., Mich. Technol. U., Houghton, 1952; M.S., No. Ill. U., 1969, Ed.D., 1973; postgrad. Bryn Mawr (Pa.) Coll., 1976; m. Clyde W. Kimball, Oct. 11, 1952; children—Karen Lee, Paul Gordon. Sr. bio-med. research technologist Bio-Med. div. Argonne (Ill.) Nat. Lab., 1952-53; med. technologist St. Marks Hosp., Salt Lake City, 1953-55, Clin. Labs., St. Louis, 1955-56; guidance counselor Waterman Community Sch. Dist. 431, 1970-71; self employed cons. in individual ednl. diagnosis, 1973; asst. prof. dept. elem. Coll. Edn., No. Ill. U., DeKalb, 1973-74, asst. prof. Sch. Allied Health Professions, Coll. Profl. Studies, 1974-79, assoc. prof., 1979—, asst. dean Coll. Profl. Studies, 1975, acting assoc. dean, 1980-81, dir. Sch. Allied Health Professions, 1975—; accreditation survey evaluator for allied health edn. AMA. Cert. med. technologist. Mem. Am. Soc. for Allied Health Professions (dir. 1979-81, sec.-treas. council individual mems.), Am. Soc. for Med. Tech., Ill. Med. Tech. Assn. (edn. chmn., coordinator Sci. Assembly), Am. Ednl. Research Assn., Nat. Council on Measurement in Edn., Women Educators, Am. Assn. Higher Edn., Am. Pub. Health Assn., AAUP, Health Edn. Resource Council of Northeastern Ill. (vice chmn.). Contbr. articles to profl. jours. Office: Sch Allied Health Professions Northern Ill U DeKalb IL 60115

KIMBALL, VERA F., editor, writer; b. Seward, Alaska, Feb. 8, 1903; d. Irving L. and Della (Carpenter) Kimball; A.B., Columbia U., 1929; m. William T. Castles, Jr., Dec. 2, 1942. On clerical staff Legislature of Ty. of Alaska, 1923; with Alaska R.R., Anchorage, 1923-24, N.A. Newspaper Alliance, Met. Mus. Art, Gen. Foods Corp., Todd-Robertson & Todd (all N.Y.C.), part time 1924-29; asst. to sec. Am. Inst. Chemists, 1929-35; editor Chemist, N.Y.C., 1935-68, asso. editor, 1968-70; sec. S.C. Inst. Chemists, 1970—. Mem. N.Y. Acad. Scis., Am. Inst. Chemists (hon. life), AAAS, Cook Inlet Hist. Soc., Alaska (charter), Chester County Hist. Soc. Club: Barnard College (N.Y.C.). Author: (with W. T. Castles) Firearms and Use, 1942; (with M. R. Bhagwat) Your Future in Chemistry, 1943. Contbr. to Am. Chemists and Chem. Engrs., World Scope Ency. Ency. of Chemistry, Herbert Ives Papers, 1979, year books, profl. and popular mags. Home: Magnolia Apts Chester SC 29706 Office: Route 2 Box 491 Chester SC 29706

KIMBER, FRANCES ROBERTSON, state ofcl.; b. Charleston, S.C., May 18, 1940; d. Richard Harleston and Marguerite Anna (Mears) Robertson; B.S., Fla. A&M U., 1963; M.S., Tenn. State U., 1964; m. Charles M. Kimber, July 30, 1964; children—Chinene Michaelyn, Carlos Miguel, Chawne Monique. Psychol. examiner George Peabody Coll. for Tchrs., Nashville, 1964; staff psychologist Diagnostic and Evaluation Center, Frankfort, Ky., 1968-70, asst. facility dir., 1969-71; project coordinator, developmental disabilities program Dept. Mental Health-Mental Retardation, Frankfort, 1971; personnel examiner, Dept. of Adminstrn., State of Fla., Tallahassee, 1973-74; aging program specialist Dept. Health and Rehab. Services, State of Fla., Tallahassee, 1974-76, mental health program analyst, 1976—. Mem. adv. com. Foster Grandparents Program, 1974-75; bd. dirs. Grandpeople, Inc., 1976-78. Mem. Knit and Crochet Circle. Methodist. Home: 1401 Oldfield Dr Tallahassee FL 32312 Office: 1323 Winewood Blvd Tallahassee FL 32301

KIMBERLEY-CHAMPLIN, YETIVE, accountant; b. Brandon, Vt., Feb. 1, 1917; d. Elroy Edward and Avis Maude (Ives) Kimberley; cert. Bryant Coll., 1936; m. John L. Champlin, June 3, 1950; children—John Roy, Charles Jay. Asst. sec. R.I. Mut. Ins. Co., Providence, 1940-50; accountant Forum Ins. Co., Providence and Safety Casualty Co., Providence, 1964-66; sr. accountant Inst. Mental Health State of R.I., Cranston, 1979—. Mem. Children of Am. Revolution (sr. state pres. 1968-71), Sigma Iota Chi. Club: Bridge of R.I. Home: 171 Wendell Rd Warwick RI 02888

KIMBLE, GLADYS AUGUSTA LEE, nurse, civic worker; b. Niagara Falls, Can., June 28, 1906; d. William and Florence Augusta Baker (Buckton) Lee; R.N., Christ Hosp., Jersey City, 1929; B.S., Columbia U. Tchrs. Coll., 1938, M.A., 1948; m. George Edmond Kimble, Jan. 5, 1952. Nurse, Willard Parker Hosp., N.Y.C., 1931; asst. and supervisory relief nurse Margaret Hague Maternity Hosp., Jersey City, 1931-37; staff nurse, relief supr. Manhattan Eye, Ear and Throat Hosp., 1937-38; sr. staff, asst. nurse supr. Vis. Nurse Service, N.Y.C., 1938-41; sr. public health nurse USPHS, Little Rock, 1941-43; public health supr. Providence Dist. Nursing Assn., 1943-46; edn. dir. Jersey City Public Health Nursing Service, 1946-49, also instr. Seton Hall U., 1947-48; public health nurse cons. U.S. Inst. Inter-Am. Affairs, Brazil, 1949-51; dir. public health dept. Englewood (N.J.) Hosp., 1951-53; nurse coordinator exchange visitor nurse program Overlook Hosp., Summit, N.J., 1964-71. Recipient Appreciation award for service rendered Providence Hosp.; Woman of Yr. award Essex County Bus. and Profl. Women, 1968. Fellow Am. Public Health Assn.; mem. Manasota Geneal. Soc., Sarasota Geneal. Soc. (charter), AAUW. Episcopalian. Club: Ladies Oriental Shrine of N. Am. (SAR-I Ct. 79). Home: 4540 Bee Ridge Rd Villa 12 Sarasota FL 33583

KIMBLE, LAURA LOURDES, beauty salon owner; b. Habana, Cuba, July 5, 1945; d. Manuel and Catalina Eulalia (Delgado) Amandi; student Carousel Beauty Sch., 1965; 1 dau., Deborah A. Hairstylist, Dayton, Ohio, 1965-71; owner, mgr. Madison Ave. Beauty Salon, Burlington, Iowa, 1971-73, Robert's Hairdressers, Pitts., 1975—. Mem. Nat. Assn. Women Bus. Owners, NOW, Nat. Assn. Female Execs. Republican. Club: Senatorial Leadership. Home: 237 Quail Run Rd Venetia PA 15367

KIMBRELL, JANET ILLEEN, educator; b. Duncan, Okla., Apr. 9, 1945; d. Chester and Hazel Ozel (Buckmaster) K.; B.S. in Math., Southeastern Okla. State U., 1968; M.P.A., U. Tex., Arlington, 1976; Ph.D. in Acctg. (Haskins and Sells fellow 1977, univ. summer grantee 1976-78), Okla. State U., 1979; m. James Robert Boatsman, Aug. 18, 1978; children—Richard, Sean Adam. Tchr. math. Durant (Okla.) Public Schs., 1968-69, Louisville (Tex.) Public Schs., 1969-70; research asso. U. Tex., 1973-75; instr. Okla. State U., 1975-79, asst. prof. acctg., 1979—. PMM Research Opportunities grantee, 1979; Okla. State U. Dean's Excellence Fund grantee, summer 1980; Arthur Young & Co. grantee, summers 1981-82; Amoco Outstanding Tchr. award nominee, 1982. C.P.A., Tex. Mem. Am. Acctg. Assn. (Fellowship award 1977), Am. Inst. C.P.A.s (tech. reviewer, course author), Beta Alpha Psi, Beta Gamma Sigma, Kappa Delta Pi. Contbr. articles to various jours. Office: Coll Bus Adminstrn Okla State U Stillwater OK 74078

KIMBROUGH, EMILY (EMILY KIMBROUGH WRENCH), writer; b. Muncie, Ind., Oct. 23, 1899; d. Hal Curry and Charlotte Emily (Wiles) Kimbrough; B.A., Bryn Mawr Coll., 1921; student The Sorbonne, Paris, 1922; m. John Wrench, Dec. 31, 1926; children—Margaret Achsah and Alis Emily (twins). Editor Fashions of the Hour, Marshall Field & Co., Chgo., 1922-27; fashion editor Ladies' Home Jour., 1927, mng. editor, 1927-29; writer, 1932—. Author: (with Cornelia Otis Skinner) Our Hearts Were Young and Gay, 1942; We Followed Our Hearts to Hollywood, 1943; How Dear to My Heart, 1944; It Gives Me Great Pleasure, 1948; The Innocents from Indiana, 1950; Through Charley's Door, 1952; Forty Plus and Fancy Free, 1954; So Near and Yet So Far, 1955; Water, Water Everywhere, 1956; And a Right Good Crew, 1958; Pleasure by the Busload, 1961; Forever Old, Forever New, 1964; Floating Island, 1968; Now and Then, 1972; Time Enough, 1974; Better Than Oceans, 1976. Home: 11 E 73d St New York NY 10021

KIMBROUGH, EVELYN SUE, environ. engr.; b. Nashville, Aug. 30, 1954; d. George Robert and Irene K.; A.A., Martin Coll., 1974; B.S., Vanderbilt U., 1976. Environ. scientist U.S. EPA, Research Triangle Park, N.C., 1977—. Methodist. Club: Order of Eastern Star. Home: 700 Morreene Rd R-8 Durham NC 27705 Office: MD-14 Research Triangle Park NC 27711

KIMBROUGH, FRANCES HARRIETT, counseling psychologist; b. Bryan, Tex., Sept. 10, 1947; d. Wallace M. and Frances (James) K.; B.A. with honors in Modern Langs., Tex. A&M U., 1969, M.Ed., 1971, Ph.D. in Ednl. Psychology (Counseling), 1981. Head sportswear dept. Townshire, Lester's Clothing Store, Bryan, 1970-71; tchr. Spanish, head fgn. langs. dept. S.F. Austin High Sch., Bryan, 1971-77, counselor, 1982—; counselor Bryan High Sch., 1977-78; counseling psychology intern Acad. Counseling Center of Tex. A&M U., 1981, counseling psychology intern personal counseling service, 1981-82; Tex. real estate broker, 1975-82; conf. presenter. Adminstrv. bd. 1st United Meth. Ch. of Bryan, 1974-75, sec. bd.; sch. curriculum council Bryan Ind. Sch. Dist., 1974-77; faculty adv. com. S.F. Austin Sch., 1975-76; sr. high counselor United Meth. Youth Fellowship, 1978-81. Named Disting. Student, Tex. A&M U., 1966-69; A&M Former Students Assn. grantee, 1980-81. Mem. Tex. Personnel and Guidance Assn., Am. Personnel and Guidance Assn., Am. Coll. Personnel Assn., Nat. Vocat. Guidance Assn., Am. Psychol. Assn., Tex. Psychol. Assn., Brazos Valley Psychol. Assn., Brazos County Citizens Historic Preservation, Phi Kappa Phi. Club: Brazos County A&M. Research on effects of group career/life planning counseling model on sex role and career self-concept of female undergrads. Home: 501 E 29th St Bryan TX 77801

KIME, CAMILLE DAVIS, govt. ofcl.; b. Frederick, Md., June 17, 1943; d. Theodore David and Johanna Marie (Riordan) Davis; student Frederick Community Coll.; children—Traci Sue, Deani Ann. Sec., AEC, Washington, 1961-71; adminstrv. asst. Office Environ. Affairs, AEC, 1972-73; adminstrv. officer Nuclear Regulatory Commn., 1973-75, br. chief adminstrv. br. Office Nuclear Regulatory Research, 1975-81, br. chief adminstrn. br. Office Insepction and Enforcement, 1981—. Tchr., St. John's Roman Catholic Ch., Frederick, 1969—. Recipient numerous awards AEC and Nuclear Regulatory Commn.

Republican. Editor: AEC Aerways Newsletter, 1968-73. Home: 5921 Quinn Orchard Rd Frederick MD 21701 Office: US Nuclear Regulatory Commn NRC-66-14 Washington DC 20555

KIMES, BEVERLY RAE, editor, writer; b. Aurora, Ill., Aug. 17, 1939; d. Raymond Lionel and Grace Florence (Perrin) K.; B.S., U. Ill., 1961; M.A. in Journalism, Pa. State U., 1963. Dir. publicity Mateer Playhouse, Neff's Mills, Pa., 1962, Pavillion Theatre, University Park, Pa., 1963; asst. editor Automobile Quar. Publs., N.Y.C., Princeton, N.J., 1963-64, asso. editor, 1965-66, mng. editor, 1967-74, editor, 1975-81; editor The Classic Car, 1981—. Recipient Cugnot award Soc. Automotive Historians, 1978, 79. Mem. Internat. Motor Press Assn., Soc. Automotive Historians. Author: The Classic Tradition of the Lincoln Motor Car, 1968; (with R.M. Langworth) Oldsmobile: The First Seventy-Five Years, 1972; The Cars That Henry Ford Built, 1978; editor: Great Cars and Grand Marques, 1976; Packard: History of the Motor Car and the Company, 1979; Automobile Quarterly's Handbook of Automotive Hobbies, 1981.

KIMMEL, ELLEN BISHOP, psychologist, educator; b. Knoxville, Tenn., Sept. 16, 1939; d. Archer W. and Mary Ellen (Baker) Bishop; B.A., U. Tenn., 1961; M.A., U. Fla., 1962, Ph.D., 1965; div.; children—Elinor, Ann, Jean, Tracy. Asst. prof., research asso. Ohio U., 1965-68; research asso. U. South Fla., 1971-72, asst. prof., 1971-72, asso. prof., dir. Univ. Studies Coll., 1972-73, prof. psychology and ednl. psychology, 1975—; disting. vis. prof. psychology Simon Fraser U., Vancouver, B.C., Can., 1980-81; cons. numerous sch. systems, bus. and govt. Mem. Fla. Blue Ribbon Task Force on Juvenile Delinquency, 1976-77; mem. Fla. Gov.'s Commn. on Women, 1979—; mem. adv. bd. Stop Rape, Good Govt., Inc. Recipient Outstanding Teaching award U. South Fla., 1978. Fellow Am. Psychol. Assn. (governing council 1982—); mem. Am. Ednl. Research Assn., Am. Personnel and Guidance Assn., Assn. Women in Psychology, Women in Edn., Psychonomic Soc., Southeastern Psychol. Assn. (pres. 1978-79), So. Soc. Philosophy and Psychology, Athena Soc., Sigma Xi, Delta Kappa Gamma, Omicron Delta Kappa. Democrat. Contbr. articles to jours., chpts. to books. Home: 8643 Lake Isle Dr Tampa FL 33617 Office: FAO 268 U South Fla Tampa FL 33620

KIMMEL, MARJORIE ANNE, health care exec.; b. Ft. Wayne, Ind., July 11, 1936; d. Edward Henry and Marie Virginia (Woodworth) Ernst; student Ind. State U., Ohio U.; m. Kenneth Robert Kimmel, Nov. 24, 1955; children—Kathleen Marie Zonar, Cynthia Louise Sniff. Sec. bd. trustees, then acting dir. Washington County Council Alcoholism, Marietta, Ohio, 1978-79, exec. dir. 1979—; adv. bd. Washington County Dept. Welfare; treas., trustee Eve, Inc., shelter battered women. Cert. alcoholism counselor. Mem. Assn. Labor, Mgmt., Adminstrs. and Cons. Alcoholism, Ohio Task Force Women and Alcohol, Nat. Council on Alcoholism/Ohio, Nat. Assn. Female Execs. Office: 300 Wooster St MArietta OH 45750

KIMMERLING, CONSTANCE BELL, sculptor, former social services adminstr.; b. Franklin, Pa., Aug. 20, 1895; d. William M. and Mary Alice (Ladds) Bell; B.A., Vassar Coll., 1916; postgrad. social work Western Res. U., 1918-20, U. Pitts., 1935, U. Chgo., 1936-37, 40-41; student art Carnegie Mus. and Pitts. Art Inst., 1968-69, Laguna Beach Sch. Art, 1969, 71, 72, 74, Otis Inst., 1971-72, Calif. State U., Long Beach, spring 1976, 77, Orange Coast Coll., 1976; m. Lloyd E. Kimmerling, Jan. 3, 1925 (div. Jan. 1944). Tchr. high schs., Pa., 1916-18; social worker, Ohio, Nebr., 1918-23; exec. Internat. Inst., Honolulu, 1923-24; social worker, Pa., 1931-37; mem. Oral Bds., Pa. Social Service Exams, 1938-39; mem. adminstrv. rev. staff Pa. Pub. Welfare Dept., 1939-40; home service field rep. ARC, Miss., W.Va., 1942-45; reorganizer casework dept. Japanese Relocation Center, Twin Falls, Idaho, 1945, mem. relocation staff, Los Angeles, 1945-46; with HEW, Oregon, 1947-48; child welfare field rep. Calif. Welfare Dept., Sacramento, 1948-57; social worker Family and Child Service, Franklin, Pa., 1957-58, Erie, Pa., 1958-60; exec. dir. Children's Aid and Family Service, Beaver (Pa.) County, 1960-66; exhibited in group shows: Internat. Platform Assn. anns., 1970-76, Kennerdell (Pa.) Music and Art Festival, 1970—, Nat. League Am. Pen Women, 1976, 78. Mem. Nat. Assn. Social Work, Nat. Conf. Social Work, Internat. Council Social Welfare, Social Work Vocat. Bur., AAUW, Internat. Platform Assn., Nat. League Am. Pen Women, UN Assn., Bus. and Profl. Women's Club, LWV. Presbyterian. Club: Quota. Home: 1347 Otter St Franklin PA 16323

KIMSEY, CAROLYN JOHNSTON, county ofcl.; b. Clay County, N.C., Nov. 30, 1939; d. Robert Lee and Cora (Matheson) Johnston; student W. Ga. Coll., 1968-70, Young Harris Coll., 1969-70, Western Carolina U., 1971-72; m. L.E. Kimsey, Jr., Mar. 27, 1956; children—Benny Lee, Donald Kent, Denise Michele. Head start tchr. Towns County Bd. Edn., Hiawassee, Ga., 1967-74; dir. child care programs Ga. Mountain Planning and Devel. Commn., Gainesville, 1974-76; dir. child care programs Upper Hiawassee Watershed Med. Programs, Inc., Hiawassee, 1976-80; dir. Towns County Child Devel. and Outreach Programs, Hiawassee, 1980—. Ga. liaison person, legis. com. Appalachian Regional Commn., 1978-80; dir. Child Care Policy Adv. Bd., 1967-80; Dist. rep. 9th Dist. Opportunity Com., 1963-80. Mem. Nat. Assn. Edn. Young Children, Ga. Title XX Dirs. Assn., So. Assn. Children Under Six. Home: PO Box 34 Bell Creek Hiawassee GA 30546 Office: PO Box 472 Berrong Hiawassee GA 30546

KIMURA, LILLIAN CHIYEKO, human service agy. exec.; b. Glendale, Calif., Apr. 7, 1929; d. Homer and Hisa (Muraki) Kimura; B.A., U. Ill., 1951, M.S.W., 1954. Program dir. Olivet Community Center, Chgo., 1954-68; dir. Olivet Service Area, Chgo. Commons Assn., 1968-71; program cons., dir. mid states region Nat. Bd. YWCA, 1978-80, exec. field services, 1980—. Pres., Japanese Am. Service Com., 1973-79; bd. dirs. Nat. Japanese Am. Citizens League, 1972-79; gov., 1974-79. Mem. Acad. Cert. Social Workers, Assn. Social Workers, Nat. Conf. Social Welfare, Nonprofit Mgmt. Assn. Office: 135 W 50th St New York NY 10020

KINARD, ALICE DANIELSEN, public sch. tchr.; b. Newberry, S.C., 1650 16, 1930; d. John Theodore and Mary Jane (Enlow) Danielsen; B.A. summa cum laude, Newberry Coll., 1975; M.A., Winthrop Coll., Rock Hill, S.C., 1977, M.Ed., 1980; m. Hubert Vernon Kinard, Jan. 14, 1951; children—Daniel Hubert, John Luther. Various positions in bookkeeping, 1949-68; tchr. social studies Newberry County schs., 1975—, head social studies dept. Newberry High Sch., 1979—, master tchr., 1981—. Mem. exec. bd. S.C. Lutheran Ch. Women, 1979-81, historian, 1980—. Mem. Nat. Council Social Studies, Nat. Hist. Soc., Orgn. Am. Historians, Assn. Supervision and Curriculum Devel., S.C. Palmetto Tchrs. Assn., Newberry Coll. Alumni Assn. (adv. com. Newberry County 1976-79), Phi Kappa Phi, Phi Alpha Theta. Republican. Author curriculum materials. Home: 1044 Tanglewood Ct Newberry SC 29108 Office: Newberry High Sch Hwy 219 Newberry SC 29108

KINCAID, BETSY STRAUSE, wholesale co. exec.; b. Richmond, Va., Jan. 12, 1949; d. Bernard Halle and Elizabeth Hope (Curry) Strause; student Univ. Coll., Richmond, 1970-71, Westhampton Coll., 1971; m. James Wheeler Kincaid, Jr., June 1, 1971; children—Steven, James. Exec. sec. Kincaid Distbg. Co., Inc., Suffolk, Va., 1973—, also dir. Mem. Nat. Assn. Female Execs., Nat. Neurofibromatosis Found. (chpt. pres.), Virginians for Horseracing. Methodist. Democrat. Home: 1212 River Rd Suffolk VA 23434 Office: 324 N Main St Suffolk VA 23434

KINCHELOE, MAXINE CAROL, state legislator; b. Austin, Tex., Aug. 14, 1929; d. Walter and Blanche (Pegram) Miller; student U. Phillipines, 1963; grad. Am. Inst. Banking, 1966-69; m. Lawrence Reed Kincheloe, Jan. 3, 1949; children—Cheryl, Teresa, Lawrence Reed. With Bank of Am., 1965-71; tax cons. H & R Block, from 1974; cons. taxes, Choctaw, Okla.; now mem. Okla. Ho. of Reps. Mem. Nat. Order Women Legislators. Republican. Baptist. Office: State Capitol Bldg Room 544 Oklahoma City OK 73105

KINDLE, MARY ETHEL SMYERS (MRS. CECIL HALDANE KINDLE), librarian; b. Aplin, Ark., Sept. 24, 1913; d. Dan Taylor and Ruby Robb (Neale) Smyers; B.S., U. Ark., 1936; M.S. in L.S., Columbia U., 1941, postgrad. Tchrs. Coll., 1941, 54-57, 69—; postgrad. Fordham U., 1962-63; m. Cecil Haldane Kindle, Jan. 26, 1941; children—Mary Anne (Mrs. Roger Alan Stafford) (dec.), Elizabeth Lee (Mrs. Burke Baker III), Cecil Haldane, Millicent Robb. Asst. children's and adult depts. Little Rock Public Library, 1930-34; librarian elem. schs., Fort Smith, Ark., 1936-39, Liberty St. Elem. Sch., Nyack, N.Y., 1940-41; librarian young people's dept. Bloomingdale br. N.Y. Public Library, 1954, Nyack High Sch., 1954-57, Hilltop Jr. High Sch., Nyack, N.Y., 1957-68, Valley Cottage Elem. Sch., 1968-75. Cons. Bethlehem (Conn.) Public Library, 1958; sec. bd. dirs. Rockland Fed. Credit Union, Nyack, 1976-77. Mem. Vols. for Internat. Tech. Assistance, 1965-69; mem. search com. for supt. Nyack Public Schs., 1977-78, mem. citizens budget adv. com., 1978-79, mem. facilities com., 1979-80; pres. guild First Reformed Ch., Nyack, 1981—; pres. Rockland/Westchester Classis of N.Y. Synod, Ref. Ch. Women, 1981—. Recipient Martha Washington medal SAR, 1971. Mem. NEA (co-chmn. membership Rockland County, N.Y. 1967-69), ALA, N.Y. Library Assn., Rockland County Sch. Librarians Assn. (rec. sec. 1963), N.Y. State, Rockland County (rec. sec. 1968-72), Nyack (v.p. 1974-75) tchrs. assns., Am. Security Council, Little Rock Jr. Fedn. Women's Clubs (charter), Kappa Delta Pi, Delta Kappa Gamma (charter mem. Eta chpt. 1940, co-installer Epsilon chpt. N.Y.C. 1944, chmn. publicity and publs. com. Alpha Eta chpt. 1972—). Editor: Authors of Rockland County, 1960. Home: 332 N Midland Ave Upper Nyack NY 10960

KINDLER, BEVERLY LOUISE, home economist; b. Esbon, Kans., Oct. 29, 1930; d. Glenn Edward and Edna M. (Willson) K.; B.S. in Home Econs., Kans. State U., 1952; M.A. in Adult Edn. (J.C. Penney fellow, 1966), Mich. State U., 1967. County extension home economist Decatur County Extension Council, Oberlin, Kans., 1952-60, Norton County Extension Council, Norton, Kans., 1960—; trainer agt. Kans. Coop. Extension Service. Sec. Norton chpt. Am. Cancer Soc., 1966, crusade chmn., 1968-70; pres. Norton County Mental Health Assn., 1976. Horace Moses scholar, extension summer sch. Colo. State U., 1960. Mem. Am. Home Econs. Assn., Kans. Home Econs. Assn. (pres. elect 1982, past dist. pres.), Nat. Assn. Extension Home Economists (2d v.p. 1972-73, pres. 1979, Grace Frysinger fellow 1961, disting. service award 1964), Kans. Assn. Extension Home Economists (pres. 1961-63), AAUW, Epsilon Sigma Phi. Methodist. Clubs: Mid Century Federated Study, PEO. Home: 1108 1/2 Nixon Norton KS 67654 Office: PO Box 407 Norton KS 67654

KINDRED, ELIZABETH MATHENY, former educator; b. Sarasota, Fla.; d. Charles Woodburn and Virginia (Yates) Matheny; student Ringling Jr. Coll., 1933-34; A.B. in Edn., Fla. State U., 1937; postgrad. U. Fla., 1939; M.Ed. in counseling, U. Va., 1967; postgrad. George Mason U., summer 1970, Gallaudet Coll., 1971, 72; M.Ed. in Deaf Edn., Western Md. Coll., 1974; postgrad. Boston U., U. Wyo., Radford U., Marymount Coll. of Va.; m. Worth Lytton Kindred, Mar. 5, 1949; children—Tari Kindred Morgan, Julia Elizabeth. Tchr. secondary schs., Sarasota, 1937-44; clk. Arty. Sch. Book Dept., Fort Sill, Okla., 1944-48; guidance counselor Herndon (Va.) Intermediate Sch., 1967-69; substitute tchr. public schs. of Fairfax and Arlington Counties, Va., 1969-70; tchr., coordinator hearing impaired program in secondary sch., Arlington, Va., 1970-80, secondary spl. edn. tchr., 1979-82. Credit union dir. Arlington Sch. Fed. Credit Union, 1980-83. Mem. NEA, Va., Arlington edn. assns., Tchrs. Assn., Council for Exceptional Children (past pres. suburban council, Jennie Brewer award 1978), Am. Speech and Hearing Assn., Internat., Va. reading assns., Greater Washington Reading Council, A.G. Bell Assn. for Deaf (Va. FLAG coordinator 1977-79), Conv. Am. Instrs. of the Deaf (Howard M. Quigley award 1981), Am. Deafness and Rehab. Assn., Assn. for Edn. of Hearing Impaired Children No. Va. (v.p.), Nat. Assn. of Deaf, Internat. Assn. Parents of Deaf, Am. Orgn. for Edn. of Hearing Impaired (Tchr. of Year 1979), Va. and Arlington County Assn. Children with Learning Disabilities, Am., Va., No. Va. personnel and guidance assns., Gen. Fedn. Women's Clubs, DAR, AAUW, Phi Delta Kappa, Phi Delta Gamma. Episcopalian. Home: 6213 N 12th St Arlington VA 22205

KINDRED, JOAN HOVER, actress, civic worker, home economist; b. Poughkeepsie, Nov. 28, 1930; d. Ernest William and Florence (Christiansen) Hover; B.S., U. Md., 1953; m. John Joseph Kindred, III, Aug. 25, 1956 (div. Aug. 1980); 1 dau., Drewry Ann. Promotion and speech writer Sta. WTOP, Washington, 1953-54; producer, star daily TV women's culinary arts show Sta. WRC, Washington, 1955-56; home economist Potomac Electric Power Co., 1956; producer, star indsl. and comml. film for TV, 1956-59; pres. Snark, Ltd., repertory group, N.Y.C., 1969-72. Vice pres., bd. dirs. Twilight Park Assn., 1971-75; bd. dirs. Sheltering Arms Children's Service, 1974—, treas. aux., 1975-77. Republican. Presbyterian. Address: 1070 Park Ave New York NY 10028

KINER, SUSAN LOUISE, advt. exec.; b. Blue Island, Ill., Feb. 9, 1954; d. Donald Raymond and Billie Sue (Adams) Kiner; B.S. in Communications, U. Ill., 1976; m. Jack Modzelewski, May 19, 1978. With Benton & Bowles, Inc., N.Y.C., 1976-78, Chgo., 1978-79, Tatham-Laird & Kudner, Chgo., 1979-80; account supr. D'Arcy-MacManus & Masius, Chgo., 1981—; cons. for Chgo. comedian, Tim Cavanagh, 1980—. State fundraiser John Anderson Presdl. campaign, 1980; exec. com. Nat. Unity Party, Ill., 1981; bd. dirs. Towers Condominium Assn. Recipient Chgo. YWCA Leadership award, 1981. Mem. Am. Advt. Fedn. (6th dist. conf. chmn. 1982—). Club: Chgo. Advt. (co-chmn. seminars 1981, social chmn. 1981-82). Home: 1221 N Dearborn Pkwy 1001 N Chicago IL 60610 Office: 200 E Randolph Dr 71st Floor Chicago IL 60601

KING, ANITA HELENE ROBINSON (SULTANA SAADET), dancer, tchr.; b. Sandhoven, Germany, Dec. 11, 1956; d. James Lee and Erika (Rubenschuh) Robinson; student public schs., Kans.; m. Michael Scott King, Dec. 13, 1973. Pvt. dance tchr., Newport, Mich., 1976—; tchr. belly dancing Monroe (Mich.) YMCA, 1976, Michelle's Dance Acad., Monroe, 1981—; tchr. Orchard Community Adult Edn. Program, Monroe, 1976—, Monroe Public Schs., 1976—, Airport Sch., 1977-78; tchr. Green's Dance Studio, Monroe, 1979—. dancer various local groups and orgns.; appeared at Monroe County Fair, 1981, The Tigris night club, Romulus, Mich., 1980, 81. Mem. Belly Dancers Guild Am. (dancer/performer cert.), Tchrs. Assn. Middle Eastern Dance Mich., Calif. Belly Dance Assn., Middle Eastern Cabaret Dancers Assn. Contbr. poetry to several mags.

KING, BARBARA JEAN, nurse; b. Cape Girardeau, Mo., June 28, 1941; d. Otto Samuel and Goldie Elizabeth (Clover) Fowler; student Weatherford Jr. Coll., 1965; R.N., John Peter Smith Hosp. Sch. Profl. Nursing, 1969; m. Charles Basil King, Jr., Sept. 4, 1972; children—Otto Samuel, Christopher Lee. Head nurse pediatrics and isolation County Hosp., also intensive care and coronary care units Small Gen. Hosp., Ft. Worth, 1969-75; dir. nursing service Jarvis Heights Nursing Center, Ft. Worth, 1976-77; dir. nursing services Ft. Worth Rehab. Farm, 1978—; instr. vocat. nursing Cooke County Coll., Gainesville, Tex., 1981; cons. convalescent centers and hosps. Chmn. child care com. Women of Moose, 1977—; ch. organist Zion Valley Cumberland Presbyterian Ch.; asso. organist St. Matthew Cumberland Presbyn. Ch. Served with M.C., USN, 1962-65. Mem. Dirs. Nursing Homes Assn. Tarrant County (v.p.). Democrat. Home: Rt 1 Box 90-A Alvord TX 76225

KING, BARBARA SUE, tchrs.' assn. exec.; b. Huntingburg, Ind., June 7, 1938; d. William Anthony and Lydia Catherine Miller; B.S. in Elementary Edn., Ind. Central U., 1960; M.S., Ind. U., 1966. Elementary tchr. Perry Twp., Indpls., 1960-78; dir. profl. devel. Ind. State Tchrs. Assn., Indpls., 1978—; organizer, participant workshops. Active Indpls. Southside Symphony Group. Mem. NEA (life), Ind. State Tchrs. Assn., AAUW, Alpha Delta Kappa. Republican. Methodist. Contbr. articles to profl. publ. Home: 4955 Rue Vallee Apt 52 Indianapolis IN 46204 Office: 150 W Market St Indianapolis IN 46204

KING, BILLIE JEAN MOFFITT, profl. tennis player; b. Long Beach, Calif., Nov. 22, 1943; d. Willard J. Moffitt; student Calif. State U., Los Angeles, 1961-64; m. Larry King, Sept. 17, 1965. Amateur tennis player, 1958-67, profl. 1968—; singles champion tournaments Wimbledon, 1966-68, 72, 73, 75, U.S. Open, Forest Hills, N.Y., 1967, 71, 72, 74, U.S. Hardcourt, 1966, Italian Open, 1970, West German Open, 1971, Australian Open, 1968, South African Open, 1966-67, 69, U.S. Indoor, 1966-68, 71, U.S. Clay Court, 1971, French Open, 1972; doubles champion at Wimbledon, 1961, 62, 65, 67, 68, 70-73, 79, U.S. Open, 1965, 67, 74, 78, 80, French, 1972, Italian, 1970, South African, 1967-70, Bridgestone, 1976, 78, 80, Va. Slims, 1974; mixed double champion at Wimbledon, 1967, 71, 73, 74, U.S. Open, 1967, 71, 73, 76, French, 1967, 70, South African, 1967, 70, Australian, 1968; winner 29 Va. Slims singles titles, 1970-77, 4 Colgate titles, 1977. Fedn. Cup, 1963-67, 76-79, Wightman cup, 1961-67; 70, 77, 78; World Tennis Team All-Star, 3 times; mem. Tennis Challenge Series, 1977, 78; host Colgate women's sports TV spl. The Lady is a Champ, 1975; co-founder, dir. Kingdom, Inc., San Mateo, Calif.; sports commentator ABC-TV, 1975-78; mem. U.S. Team which won Fedn. Cup, 1976; co-founder, pub. WomenSports mag., 1974—. Named Sportsperson of Yr., Sports Illus., 1972, Woman Athlete of Yr., A.P., 1967, 73; Top Woman Athlete of Year, 1972, Woman of Yr., Time mag., 1976, One of 10 Most Powerful Women in Am. Harper's Bazaar, 1977, One of 25 Most Influential Women in Am., World Alumanac, 1977. Author: Tennis to Win, 1970; (with Kim Chapin) Billie Jean, 1974. Address: care IMG 1 Erieview Plaza Cleveland OH 44207 *

KING, BILLIE JO, computer programmer/analyst; b. Port Arthur, Tex., May 31, 1938; d. Joseph Richard and Ida Ann (Daigle) Barrows; A.A., Lamar U., 1958; postgrad. Tex. A&I U., 1963-64, 74-75, Southeastern La. U., 1966-67; B.B.A., Eastern Ky. U., 1976, M.B.A., 1978; children—Kelly Lynn, Kevin Wayne. Service rep. Southwestern Bell Telephone Co., Port Arthur, Tex., 1958-61, Kingsville, Tex., 1972-75; sec. Gen. Mills, Inc., Houston, 1961, Continental Oil Co., Houston, 1961-62, Mobile Oil Co., Victoria, Tex., 1962-63; teletype operator Union Carbide, Seadrift, Tex., 1963; receptionist, teletype operator, PBX operator Alcoa, Point Comfort, Tex., 1963; sec. Humble Oil & Refining Co., Kingsville, 1964; sec. English dept. Southeastern La. U., Hammond, 1965, Miss. State U., Starkville, 1968; instr. electronic data processing Eastern Ky. U., Richmond, 1978; computer programmer analyst Sq. D Co., Lexington, Ky., 1978-81; programmer/analyst First Security Nat. Bank & Trust, Lexington, 1981—. Mem. Nat. Mgmt. Assn., Data Processing Mgmt. Assn., Nat. Assn. Female Execs., Mensa. Democrat. Methodist. Home: 604 Severn Way Lexington KY 40503 Office: First Security Nat Bank & Trust One First Security Plaza Lexington KY 40507

KING, BRENDA W., pub. co. exec.; b. Farmington, Maine, July 18, 1949; d. Lawrence B. and Shirley (Perkins) Williams; B.S., Husson Coll., 1972; m. Stephen S. King, July 9, 1977; children—Kristin Jean, Tory Preston. Office mgr. Community Broadcasting Service, Bangor, Maine, 1972-74; chief acct. Diversified Communications, Camden, Maine, 1974-79; acctg. supr. Internat. Marine/Nat. fisherman, Camden, Maine, 1979-81, bus. mgr. Internat. Marine Pub. Co., 1981—. Staff mem., bd. dirs. Dirigo Girl's State. Mem. Am. Legion Aux. Democrat. Congregationalist. Home: West St Ext W Rockport ME 04865 Office: 21 Elm St Camden ME 04843

KING, CAROL LOUISE, city ofcl.; b. Detroit, Dec. 10, 1948; d. William Albert and Mary Theresa (Simon) K.; B.A. in English and Speech, Western Mich. U., 1971. Sales rep. Am. Can Co., Detroit, 1973-76; employment counselor, account exec. New Options, In., Detroit, 1976-78; congressional aide, 1978-79; pres. Mich. conf. NOW, 1979-80; placement coordinator Displaced Homemaker Project, Warren, Mich., 1980-82; adminstrv. asst. to Detroit City Councilwoman Maryann Mahaffey, 1982—; legis. liaison, cons. in field. Vice pres. Mich. conf. NOW, 1978-79, pres. Macomb County (Mich.) chpt., 1976-78, nat. chmn. reproductive rights com. 1978-79, nat. bd. dirs., 1980—; bd. dirs. Planned Parenthood Detroit, 1980—; founding mem., mem. steering com. Democratic Citizens Caucus, 1980. Mem. ACLU, Nat. Abortion Rights Action League, Voice of Reason, Older Women's League, Women's Econs. Club Detroit, Detroit Women's Forum. Democrat. Home: 13610 Cedargrove St Detroit MI 48205

KING, CAROLYN MAE, educator; b. Fond du Lac, Wis., Oct. 23, 1946; d. John Francis and Adina Elnora (Bahr) K.; B.S., Wis. State U., Oshkosh, 1970; M.S., Niagara U., 1974. Tchr. phys. edn. Public Schs. Niagara Falls (N.Y.), 1970—; women's swim coach Niagara (N.Y.) U., 1975-76. Water safety instr. ARC; mem. Nat. Ski Patrol. Recipient award Joseph P. Kennedy Jr. Found., 1972. Mem. Niagara Falls Tchrs., N.Y. State United Tchrs., Am. Fedn. Tchrs., Alpha Kappa Delta. Democrat. Lutheran. Club: College. Home: 360 S 4th St Lewiston NY 14092 Office: Trott Vocat High School Niagara Falls NY

KING, CATHRYN TEER, social worker; b. St. Louis, June 17, 1944; d. Cornelius and Catherine (Allen) Teer; student S.D. State U., Brookings, 1961-63, Central State Coll., Wilberforce, Ohio, 1963-64, Ind. U.-Purdue U., Indpls., 1979-82; m. Richard L. King; children—Troy A., Traci A. Caseworker, Douglas County Social Services, Omaha, 1969-70, eligibility technician, 1970-71; caseworker Mo. Dept. Welfare, St. Louis, 1971-73, casework supr. I, 1973-74; diagnostic counselor Community Addiction Services Agy., Indpls., 1974-76; field services specialist Ind. Office Occupational Devel., Indpls., 1976-77, program assessment supr., 1977-79, evaluation specialist, 1979—. Bd. dirs. Day Care Center for Elderly; vice-chmn. Adv. Com. on Sex Discrimination, Ind. Civil Rights Commn., 1977-80. Mem. Nat. Assn. Black Social Workers, Nat. Assn. Female Execs., Inc., Lawrence Glenn Community Assn. Mem. Christian Ch. (Disciples of Christ). Office: 150 W Market St Indianapolis IN 46204

KING, CLYMATHES BERNICE, educator; b. Claiborne County, Miss., Mar. 6, 1922; d. Rufus Daniel and Nettie Berthena (Chambliss) K.; A.B., Alcorn A. and M. Coll., 1943; M.A. in Elem. Edn., Hampton Inst., 1950; M.A. in Bus. Edn., Columbia U., 1957, postgrad., 1974, 78. Elem. tchr. Jackson (Miss.) Public Sch. System, 1943—; U.S. rep. Ednl. Conf., Caux, Switzerland and London, 1969. Active Progressive Voters League, YWCA, YMCA; mem. United Christian Ch. (Disciples of Christ), sec., 1962-64, pres. Dist. III, 1963-66, sec., 1977—, del. Miss. Christian Missionary Conv., 1966-72, 72-73, 76; del. Internat. Conv.

Christian Chs., 1963-69, mem. Black Caucus for Christian Chs. U.S. and Can., United Missionary Soc., Indpls., 1974—, Black & Hispanic Concerns Com., 1979—; editor, pub. ch. news bull.; mem., prin. various coms. Recipient citation Nat. Council Negro Women, 1968; named Elem. Tchr. of Year, Jacksonians for Public Edn., 1976. Mem. Am. Tchrs. Assn. (trustee 1961-64, life mem.), Miss. Tchrs. Assn. (life, del. 1950-73, del. MTA-NEA 1974-78, award for human understanding 1970, Tchr. of Year 1972), Miss. Classroom Tchrs. Assn. (founding pres. 1966-68, dir. 1968—, award for outstanding leadership 1969), Classroom Tchrs. Assn. (dir. 1963-65, pres. 1965-67, del. NEA-ACT 1965-73, adv. council 1965-68, conv. del. 1965-73, del. study conf. 1965, mem. nat. conf. 1965-68, del. White House Conf. 1966), NEA (life, leader SE regional confs., rep. Am. Assn. Sch. Adminstrs. 1965-68, bd. behavioral sci. Nat. Tng. Labs. 1968-71, human relations adv. council 1968-71, disting. service award Council Human Relations 1971), Miss. Eighth Ednl. Dist. Assn., Jackson Tchrs. Assn. (pres. 1960-62, dir. 1962-64, bldg. rep. 1970—). Clubs: Hampton Alumni (pres. Central Miss. chpt. 1973—, nat. exec. com. 1973—), Nat. Alcorn Assn. (life), Internat. Platform Assn., Bus. and Profl. Women (publicity chmn.), Jackson Alcorn Alumni (pres. 1973—). Home: 935 Eastview St Jackson MS 39203 Office: PO Box 3355 Jackson MS 39207

KING, CORETTA SCOTT (MRS. MARTIN LUTHER KING JR.), lectr., writer, concert singer; b. Marion, Ala., Apr. 27, 1927; d. Obidiah and Bernice McMurray) Scott; A.B., Antioch Coll., 1951; Mus.B., New Eng. Conservatory Music, 1954, Mus. D., 1971; L.H.D., Boston U., 1969, Marymount-Manhattan Coll., 1969, Morehouse Coll., 1970; H.H.D., Brandeis U., 1969, Wilberforce U., 1970, Bethune-Cookman Coll., 1970, Princeton, 1970; LL.D., Bates Coll., 1971; m. Martin Luther King, Jr., June 18, 1953 (dec. Apr. 1968); children—Yolanda Denise, Martin Luther III, Dexter Scott, Bernice Albertine. Concert debut, Springfield, Ohio, 1948, numerous concerts throughout U.S.; concerts India, 1959; performances Freedom Concert; voice instr. Morris Brown Coll., Atlanta, 1962; lectr., writer. Del. to White House Conf. on Children and Youth, 1960; sponsor Sane Nuclear Policy, Com. on Responsibility, Inc., Moblzn. to End War in Viet Nam, 1966, 67, Margaret Sanger Meml. Found.; pres. Martin Luther King Jr. Meml. Center for Social Change, 1968—, comentator Cable News Network, 1980—, Martin Luther King Found., co-chairperson Nat. Com. for Full Employment; mem. exec. bd. Nat. Health Ins. Com.; mem. So. Rural Action, Inc.; bd. dirs. So. Christian Leadership Conf., Martin Luther King Jr. Found. Gt. Britain; trustee Robert F. Kennedy Meml. Center, Ebenezeer Baptist Ch. Recipient Outstanding Citizenship award Montgomery (Ala.) Improvement Assn., 1959, Merit award St. Louis Argus, 1960, Woman of Year award Utility Club N.Y.C., 1962, Distinguished Achievement award Nat. Orgn. Colored Women's Clubs, 1962, 73, Louise Waterman Wise award Am. Jewish Congress Women's Aux., 1963, Myrtle Wreath award Cleve. Hadassah, 1965, Wateler Peace prize, 1968, Martin Luther King Meml. medal City Coll. N.Y., numerous others; named Woman of Year, Nat. Assn. Radio and TV Announcers, 1968. Mem. Nat. Council Negro Women (ann. Brotherhood award 1957), Women Strike for Peace (del. disarmament conf. Geneva, Switzerland 1962, citation for work in peace and freedom 1963), Women's Internat. League for Peace and Freedom, United Ch. Women (bd. mgrs.), Links, Inc. (Human Dignity and Human Rights award Norfolk chpt. 1964), Alpha Kappa Alpha (hon). Baptist (mem. choir, guild adviser). Author: My Life With Martin Luther King, Jr., 1969. Contbr. articles to mags. Address: care Martin Luther King Jr Center for Social Change 449 Auburn Ave NE Atlanta GA 30312 *

KING, ELAINE A., art historian; b. Oak Park, Ill., Apr. 12, 1947; d. Casimir S. and Catherine (Camele) Czerwien; B.A., No. Ill. U., 1968, M.A., 1974; postgrad. Northwestern U., 1979—. Tchr., Morton West High Sch., Berwyn, Ill., New Trier High Sch., Wilmette, Ill., 1970-74; supr. craft studio Northwestern U., Chgo., 1974-75; dir. Artemisia Gallery, 1976-77; asso. dir. Pallas Photographica, 1977; instr. art Northwestern U., Evanston, 1977-81, curator photography and contemporary art, 1975-81; asst. prof. art history Carnegie Mellon U., Pitts., 1981—. Capt., Democratic Precinct Com. Evanston, 1978, ward election judge, 1977-78. Recipient Hunt award Chgo. Art Awards, 1977; intern George Eastman House, Rochester, N.Y., summer 1977. Mem. Coll. Art Assn., Soc. Photog. Edn., Chgo. Artist Coalition. Contbr. articles to photog. publs. including New Art Examiner. Home: 5604 Fair Oaks St Pittsburgh PA 15217 Office: Coll Fine Arts Carnegie Mellon U Pittsburgh PA 15213

KING, ELLEN HALL, nursing adminstr.; b. Drewfield, Fla., Mar. 21, 1944; d. William A. and M. Carolyn (Anderson) K.; student U. Ga., 1962-64; B.S. in Nursing, Emory U., 1967, M.N., 1968; Ph.D., Tex. Women's U., 1979. Instr. pediatric nursing Univ. Hosps. of Cleve., 1968-69; asst. prof. pediatric nursing Jacksonville (Ala.) State U., 1970-71; instr. pediatric nursing Case Western Res. U., Cleve., 1971-72, asst. prof., 1972-76, coordinator undergrad. pediatric nursing, 1973-76; pediatric nurse U. Hosps. Cleve., 1972-73; chief of nursing Nisonger Center for Mental Retardation/Developmental Disability, Columbus, Ohio, 1979—; asst. prof. nursing Ohio State U., Columbus, 1979—; project dir. nat. workshop 1981-82. Mem. Denton Community Chorus, Chagrin Valley Little Theater, Ohio, 1970-74. Mem. Am. Nurses Assn., Public Health Assn., Am. Assn. Child Health, Midwest Nursing Research Soc., NOW, Phi Mu. Contbr. articles on pediatric nursing to profl. publs. Office: The Nisonger Center 1580 Cannon Dr Columbus OH 43210

KING, JANET, social services adminstr.; b. Washington, Dec. 5, 1950; d. Johnnie Curtis and Ruth Mathelda (Amos) Bradley; student Morgan State Coll., 1974-76; m. Aug. 4, 1972; children—John Kenneth, Christopher Alexander. Counseling specialist Cath. U. Am., 1971-76; researcher Grantsmanship Center, Washington, 1977-80; adminstrv. officer Citizen's Communications Center, Washington, 1980—, asst. adminstr. mental health law project, 1980-82; cons. Youth Employment Project, Washington. Vol., D.C. Dept. Corrections, Lorton Correctional Facility. Mem. Nat. Assn. Female Execs., Legal Services Corp. Nat. Clients Council. Home: 14 47th St SE Apt D Washington DC 20019 Office: 2021 L St NW Suite 800 Washington DC 20036

KING, JANET FAYE, nurse; b. Bellefontaine, Ohio, Aug. 11, 1947; d. Robert Lee and Wanda Beatrice (Shields) Swartz; diploma Community Hosp. Sch. Nursing, Springfield, Ohio, 1968; student Southwestern Okla. State U., 1979; m. Dwayne King, Jan. 11, 1969; children—Michael Dwayne, Valerie Lynn. Staff nurse Doctors Hosp., Columbus, Ohio, 1968; head nurse Southwestern Meml. Hosp., Weatherford, Okla., 1970-73; substitute clin. instr. Western Okla. Area Vocat. Tech. Sch., Burns Flat, Okla., 1973-77; asst. dir. nursing, inservice dir. Cordell Christian Home (Okla.), 1977—. Chmn. med. personnel ARC blood drive, Burns Flat, 1977—, instr., 1979—; chmn. Am. Cancer Soc., Burns Flat; tchr. Sunday Sch., Bapt. Ch., also mem. nursery com. Mem. Young Homemakers (treas. 1975-77). Clubs: New Direction Extension (treas. 1980-81). Home: 203 Potomac St Burns Flat OK 73624 Office: 1400 N College St Cordell OK 73632

KING, JEANNE SNODGRASS, mus. registrar; b. Muskogee, Okla., Sept. 12, 1927; d. Chester Alba and Mabel Ethel (Etheridge) Owens; student Northeastern State Coll., 1944-46, U. Okla., 1947-49; m. Morris Eugene King, Apr. 16, 1977. Curator, asst. dir. Philbrook Art Center, Tulsa, 1955-68; mng. editor Ednl. Dimensions, Inc., Shaker Heights, Ohio, 1969-71; registrar Thomas Gilcrease Inst. Am. History and Art, Tulsa, 1973—; researcher, lectr. in field; art cons.; juror art competitions. Recipient award Indian Arts and Crafts Bd., Dept. Interior, Washington, 1966. Mem. Am. Assn. Mus., Native Am. Art History Assn. Author: American Indian Painters, A Biographical Directory, 1968; (catalogs) Native American Painting, 1981, Fred Beaver & Solomon McCombs/Meml. Exhbn., 1981; coordinator, author Oscar Howe Retrospective Exhbn. Catalog, 1982; contbr. articles to mags. Home: 3931 S Madison Tulsa OK 74105 Office: 1400 N 25th W Ave Tulsa OK 74127

KING, JOAN HONE, writer, art dealer, book researcher; b. N.Y.C., Nov. 27, 1929; d. John Hone and Frederica (Stevens) Auerbach; cert. of studies Inst. Polit. Scis., Paris, 1950; B.A. cum laude, Bryn Mawr Coll., 1951; m. Nicholas LeRoy King, Feb. 19, 1955; children—Sarah, Bayard, Ledyard. Cons. J. Walter Thompson, Paris, 1951-52; researcher, librarian Time-Life Inc., Paris, 1952-54; mgr. Ohrbach Dept. Store, N.Y.C., 1956-57; housing locator Am. embassy, Paris, 1963-69; spl. asst. for book and art research to Cass Canfield, Harper & Row, N.Y.C., 1971—; art dealer, N.Y.C., 1973—; cons. in field. Active fund raising Bryn Mawr Coll., 1970-72, Sr. Citizens' Center, Newport, R.I., 1975. Mem. Colonial Dames Am. Club: Byrn Mawr Club (N.Y.C.). Republican. Episcopalian. Illustrator: The Incredible Pierpont Morgan (Cass Canfield), 1974; researcher, illustrator: Sam Adam's Revolution, 1976; Outrageous Fortunes, 1980; author: Passages: The Iron Will of Jefferson Davis, 1978; author hist. and fictional works. Home: 39 E 79th St New York NY 10021 Office: Harper & Row Pubs Inc 10 E 53d St New York NY 10022

KING, JUDITH JOANN, med. technologist; b. Sioux Falls, S.D., Feb. 15, 1940; d. Francis James and Verda Agnes (Simon) Sheridan; M.T., McKennan Hosp., 1961; A.A., S.D. State U., 1960; m. William W. King, Aug. 2, 1962; children—Richard W., Steven P., Mark T. Bench technologist McKennan Hosp., Sioux Falls, S.D., 1961-63, Sioux Valley Hosp., Sioux Falls, 1963-69, DCL Labs., Denver, 1970-71; supr. hematology Met. Labs., Denver, 1971—. Mem. Am. Soc. Clin. Pathologists. Democrat. Roman Catholic. Home: 5465 Flower Ct Arvada CO 80002 Office: 2137 S Birch St Denver CO 80222

KING, LAURA JANE, librarian, former home economist; b. Pemberville, Ohio, Jan. 19, 1947; d. Richard D. and Jessie Florence (Brown) Zepernick; B.A., Bowling Green (Ohio) State U., 1969, M.Ed., 1976; m. Bruce William King, June 17, 1972; 1 son, Christian Andrew. County extension agt. home econs. Ohio Coop. Extension Service, Paulding County, 1970-77; librarian Pemberville Elem. Sch.; mem. PRIDE com., vocat. home econs. dept. Paulding Exempted Village, 1975—; instr. genealogy Office Continuing Edn., Bowling Green State U. Mem. Paulding County Bicentennial Commn., 1975-77; organist 1st Presbyn. Ch., Pemberville, ruling elder. Recipient Tenure award Coop. Extension Service, 1975; cert. geneal. record searcher. Mem. Ohio, Wood County hist. socs., Ohio Geneal. Soc. (pres. Wood County chpt. 1978-80, chmn. public relations chmn. 1982-83), Berks County Geneal. Soc., Va.-N.C. Piedmont Geneal. Soc., Palatines to Am., Pa. German Soc., DAR (vice regent chpt. 1975-77, regent 1979-83; state vice chmn. pages 1978-80, state chmn. lineage research 1980-83, state and div. outstanding jr. mem. 1980), U.S. Daus. of 1812, First Families Ohio, Daus. Union Vets., Daus. Am. Colonists, Bus. and Profl. Women's Club (pres. Paulding 1975-76, v.p. 1974-75). Club: Order Eastern Star. Author monthly geneal. column Sentinel-Tribune, Bowling Green; corr. docent DAR Mus., Washington. Home: 14553 N River Rd Pemberville OH 43450

KING, LEATHA VANCE, designer; b. Los Angeles, Aug. 30, 1932; d. Quinn Merida and Mable Krien (McBride) Vance; A.A. in Fashion Design, Los Angeles Trade Tech. Coll., 1961, cert. in photography, 1963; B.S. in Psychology, Calif. State U., 1972; children—Ruby Carol, Adrian, William, Ronald, Katriena, Katauna. Vocat. nurse White Meml. Hosp., Los Angeles, 1951-53; jewelry appraiser Watts Jewelry and Loan, Los Angeles, 1958-63; tchr., dir. playground Gompers Jr. High Sch., Los Angeles, 1963-69; tchr. Saugus (Calif.) Sch. Dist., 1976-81; designer Laur's, Semi Valley, Calif., 1981—; partner Corner Boys TV, Los Angeles, 1976-81. Vice pres. West Valley Democratic Coalition, 1979-81; mem. exec. bd. Nat. Women's Polit. Caucus, 1979-81; mem. Los Angelinos, 1974-81; active Cancer Soc., Sickle Cell Anemia, Arthritis Found., others. Mem. NAACP (exec. bd.), Nat. Assn. Female Execs., Urban League. Home and Office: 21913 Gresham St Canoga Park CA 91304

KING, LINDA JOHNSON, TV anchor, producer, reporter; b. Columbia, S.C., Sept. 11, 1947; d. Bertel Rudolf and Florence Ola (Daniel) Johnson; B.A., Winthrop Coll., 1969; postgrad. U. S.C., 1970; m. Robert Hughes King, Jr., June 19, 1971; 1 dau., Kristin Elizabeth. TV talk show host, radio announcer WNOK-TV-Radio, Columbia, S.C., 1970-72; asso. producer news S.C. ETV Network, Columbia, 1972-73; anchor/producer-reporter WFBC-TV, Greenville, S.C., 1973-74, Today's Woman, Newsweek Video, Inc., N.Y.C., 1974-79; anchor Newsweek Woman ABC Hearst Cable, 1982—; free-lance producer, 1979—. Recipient gold medal N.Y. Internat. Film Festival, 1975; bronze medal V.I. Film Festival, 1976; Detroit Vanguard award, 1981. Mem. Women in Communications. Home and Office: 18475 San Quentin Dr Lathrup Village MI 48076

KING, LIS SONDER, pub. relations co. exec.; b. Roskilde, Denmark; d. Carl Otto and Gerda Vohnsen (Soender) Petersen; grad. Roskilde Katedralskole; m. T. A. Pace; 1 dau., Dorte King; came to U.S., 1956, naturalized, 1961. Feature writer Berlingske Tidende, Copenhagen, 1956-58; reporter, editor Moreau Pub. Co., Bloomfield, N.J., 1957-59; reporter, editor St. Thomas (V.I.) Daily News, Island Times, San Juan, P.R., 1962-63, Advance, Dover, N.J., 1963-64; v.p. pub. relations Keyes, Martin & Co., Springfield, N.J., 1964-69; pres. Lis King Pub. Relations, Mahwah, N.J., 1969—. Mem. Internat. Platform Assn. Author: St. Thomas Directory, 1961; Furniture: Make-Do, Make-over, Make Your Own, 1977; contbr. articles to various publs. Address: 30 Dundee Court Mahwah NJ 07430

KING, LYNDA ANNE WHITLOW, psychologist, educator; b. Danville, Va., Aug. 7, 1947; d. Detlef F. and Doris F. (Van Hook) Whitlow; student Coll. of William and Mary, 1965-67; B.S., U. Md., 1969; M.A., U. Washington, 1975, Ph.D., 1979; m. Daniel Walter King, Nov. 29, 1969. Research asst. Bur. of Sch. Service and Research, U. Washington, Seattle, 1975-76, research asso., 1976-77; instr. City Coll., Seattle, 1976-78; asst. prof. psychology Central Mich. U., Mt. Pleasant, 1979—. Vol., ARC, 1981—. Served with Nurse Corps, U.S. Army, 1969-72. R.N., Wash. Mem. Am. Ednl. Research Assn., Midwestern Psychol. Assn., Am. Psychol. Assn., Common Cause, Phi Delta Kappa, Sigma Theta Tau, Phi Kappa Phi. Contbr. articles on psychology to profl. jours. Home: 414 Pine St Mt Pleasant MI 48858 Office: Sloan Hall Central Mich Univ Mt Pleasant MI 48859

KING, MARCIA LOWELL, librarian; b. Lewiston, Maine, Aug. 4, 1940; d. Daniel Alden and Clarice Evelyn (Curtis) Barrell; B.S., U. Maine, 1965; M.S.L.S., Simmons Coll., 1967; m. Howard P. Lowell, Feb. 15, 1969 (div. 1980); m. 2d, Richard G. King, Jr., Aug. 1980. Reference, field advisory and bookmobile librarian Maine State Library, Augusta, 1965-69; dir. Lithgow Public Library, Augusta, 1969-72; exec. sec. Maine Library Adv. Com., Maine State Library, 1972-73; dir. Wayland (Mass.) Free Public Library, 1973-76; state librarian State of Oreg., Salem, 1976-82; dir. Tucson Public Library, 1982—. Mem. ALA, Oreg., Pacific N.W. Library Assn., Chief Officers of State Library Agys., Oreg. Hist. Soc. Unitarian. Address: Tucson Public Library 111 E Pennington PO Box 27470 Tucson AZ 85726 *

KING, MARY ELIZABETH, mfg. co. exec.; b. Hardin County, Tenn., Apr. 21, 1937; d. Charlie Richard and Artie Mae (Alexander) Ganus; student U. Tenn., 1968-70, Nashville State Tech. Inst., 1972—; m. William Barthel King, Sept. 26, 1956. With Howard, Nielsen, Lyne, Batey & O'Brien, Inc., Engrs.-Architects, Nashville, 1956-65, I.C. Thomasson & Assos., Inc., Nashville, 1965-77; with Cummings, Inc., Internat. Sign Service, Nashville, 1977—, now v.p. adminstrn., corp. sec.; fellow Inst. Women Execs., U. Ala. Bd. dirs. Martha O'Bryan Community Center, 1977-80. Cert. profl. sec. Mem. Exec. Women Internat. (bd. dirs. 1979-80), Am. Soc. Corp. Secs., Exec. Women Internat. Presbyterian. Home: 706 Desmond Dr Nashville TN 37211 Office: 200 12th Ave S Nashville TN 37203

KING, MARY KATHLEEN, nursing educator; b. Milton, Ont., Can., June 30, 1925; d. John Leslie and Maude (Partridge) King; B.A., U. Toronto, 1947, B.Sc. in Nursing, 1951; M.S. in Nursing, Yale U., 1959. Gen. staff nurse, instr. Kitchener-Waterloo Hosp., Kitchener, Ont., Can., 1951-54; successively lectr., asst. prof., asso. prof., asso. dir., 1954-72, dean faculty nursing U. Toronto, 1972-79, prof., 1979—; Rockefeller grantee, 1962; WHO fellow, 1965. Mem. Registered Nurses Assn. of Ont., Can. Nurses Assn., Internat. Council Nurses, Canadian Public Health Assn. Presbyterian. Contbr. articles in field to jours.; gen. editor Lit. Rev. Series (monographs). Office: 50 St George St Toronto ON M5S 1A1 Canada

KING, NANCY RUBIN, educator; b. Bklyn., June 28, 1936; d. Israel and Ruth (Kurinsky) Rubin; B.S., SUNY, Cortland, 1957; M.A., U. Del., 1968; 1 son, Lance Richard. Tchr. phys. edn., dance, Swedish gymnastics, movement, Providence, 1958-64; dir. dance and movement Arden (Del.) YWCA, 1964-67; founder, dir. Magic Circle Players, Wilmington, Del., 1965-67; tchr. theatre dept. U. Del., Newark, 1968-75, asso. prof., 1975—; dir. Title III Project, Del., 1967-68; theatre cons. Am. Coll. Theatre Festival, Kans., 1976, Idaho, 1977, Mont., 1978; condr. workshops, Sweden and Denmark, 1980. Fellow, U. Wis., 1957, Conn. Coll. Sch. Dance, 1957; Faculty research grantee, 1974, 78. Mem. Am. Theatre Assn. (v.p. theatre edn. UCTA div.), Ednl. Arts Assn., Internat. Assn. Theatre for Children and Young People. Author: Theatre Movement: The Actor and His Space, 1971; Giving Form to Feeling, 1975; Protecting Students from Body Abuse, 1977; The Development of Critical Thinking in Movement and Drama, 1977; A Movement Approach to Acting, 1980; From Literature to Drama to Life, 1980; Moving into Drama, 1980; Music and Dance for the Actor, 1981; A Management Approach to Acting, 1981; Silent Song, 1981; Helping Students to Shape Their Learning Experience, 1981. Experience, 1981; A Collision of Voices, 1982. Office: Dept Theatre U Del Newark DE 19711

KING, PATRICIA, tng. cons.; b. Paterson, N.J., Mar. 17, 1941; d. Salvatore Francesco and Anna Marie (Psacane) Puglise; A.B., Coll. St. Elizabeth, 1963; m. David Jay Clark, Sept. 7, 1974; 1 dau., Kerry Ann King. With Equitable Life Assurance Soc., N.Y.C., 1963-65; personnel officers Bankers Trust Co., N.Y.C., 1965-72; founder, pres. Patricia King Assos., N.Y.C., 1972—. Mem. Nat. Assn. Italian-Am. Women. Contbg. author: Affirmative Action for Women, 1983; author: Productive Performance Appraisal. Office: 275 W 12th St New York NY 10014 *

KING, PATRICIA ZANNIE, govt. ofcl., artist; b. Rochester, N.Y., Mar. 17, 1941; d. Sabatino and Elissa Mary (Aschettino) Zannie; B.S. in Social Studies, LeMoyne Coll., Syracuse, N.Y., 1963; m. Simon T. King, Nov. 17, 1964; 1 son, Teddy. With Dept. Labor, 1963—, tech. info. officer U.S. Employment Service, Employment and Tng. Adminstrn., Washington, 1974-76, manpower analyst, job search info. project 1976—, office rep. Affirmative Action Council, EEO, 1978—; exhibiting artist, 1955—; group exhbns. include: Humanities Found., Harper's Ferry, W.Va. (cert. of merit), 1980, Brazilian-Am. Cultural Inst., 1980, Can. Embassy, 1980, Art World V (catalogue editor, graphic designer), 1981; one-woman shows: Fact and Fantasy, 1981, The Human Form, 1982. Recipient Superior Performance award Dept. Labor, 1968, 80, letter of commendation, 1981. Mem. Cultural Alliance D.C., Washington Woman's Art Center, Rockville Art League. Democrat. Roman Catholic. Home: 10843 Bucknell Dr Wheaton MD 20902 Office: 601 D St NW Room 8431 Washington DC 20213

KING, PEARL COQUEECE, nurse; b. Drumright, Okla., Dec. 21, 1936; d. Alonzo Cottrol and Marjorie Opal (Price) Alexander; degree Long Beach City Coll., 1961; R.N., Asso. Sci., 1971; student Calif. State U., Long Beach, 1977—; m. Carl Dee King, Dec. 8, 1951; children—Carl Dee, Crystal, Michael (dec.), Marcus. Office nurse for gen. practitioner, Long Beach, Calif., 1961-66; nurse VA Hosp., Long Beach, 1966-69; nursing supr. outpatient alcoholism treatment and rehab. center Long Beach Gen. Hosp., 1971-78; dir. nursing Viewpark Community Hosp., Los Angeles, 1978-81; asst. nursing dir. Augustus F. Hawkins Psychiat. Facility, Los Angeles, 1981—; mem. So. Calif. Women's Substance Abuse Task Force; tchr. Long Beach City Coll., 1975. Rotary Club scholar, 1970-71; Cert. of Honor, Long Beach City Coll., 1971. Mem. Am., Calif. nurses assns., Los Angeles County Sub Area Health Council. Democrat. Baptist. Office: 1720 E 120th St Los Angeles CA

KING, PEGGY SUE, banker; b. Marengo, Iowa, Dec. 25, 1950; d. Marvin Clark and Eunice Mildred (Jordan) Morse; B.A. magna cum laude in History, Trinity Coll., Deerfield, Ill., 1973; M.A. in European History, U. Iowa, Iowa City, 1974; postgrad. Drake U., Des Moines, 1981—; m. Merrill Jack King, June 26, 1976. Asst. head teller Iowa-Des Moines Nat. Bank, 1975-77; head teller Bankers Trust Co., Des Moines, 1979, consumer banker, 1980, asst. mng. officer, 1981-82, mng. officer, 1982—. Mem. Nat. Assn. Bank Women, Robert Morris Assocs., Women's C. of C. Greater Des Moines. Home: 1070 35th St Des Moines IA 50311 Office: 3905 Merle Hay Rd Des Moines IA 50310

KING, RACHEL HADLEY, educator; b. Leavenworth, Kans., Apr. 27, 1904; d. Frank Campbell and Georgianna May (Brackett) King; B.A., Smith Coll., 1926; M.A., U. Chgo., 1927, U. Colo., 1931; Ph.D., Yale, 1937. Bible tchr., then head dept. Northfield (Mass.) Sch. Girls, 1928-31, 35-66; tchr. English, Kobe Coll., Japan, 1937-38; adj. prof. Bibl. studies Barrington (R.I.) Coll., 1972—; vol. tchr. underprivileged children N.Y.C. Pub. Schs., summers 1969-71. Mem. Kobe Corp., 1960—; alumni council Yale Div. Sch., 1968-75. Recipient citation Council Religion in Ind. Schs., 1967. Mem. Am. Acad. Religion, Nat. Assn. Bible Instrs. (chmn. curriculum com. 1946-64), Am. Sch. Oriental Research, So. Bibl. Lit. Presbyterian. Author: George Fox and The Light Within 1650-1660, 1940; God's Boycott of Sin, 1946; Theology You Can Understand, 1956; The Omission of the Holy Spirit from Reinhold Neibuhr's Theology, 1964; The Creation of Death and Life, 1970. Home: The 60 Broadway Providence RI 02903 Office: Barrington Coll Middle Hwy Barrington RI 02806

KING, RITA ANN, ins. co. exec.; b. Waterville, Maine, Oct. 1, 1949; d. Allen Richard and Nellie Mable (Trask) K.; B.A., SUNY, Albany, 1973; M.Ed., Springfield (Mass.) Coll., 1976. Dir. rehab. services Springfield (Mass.) Mcpl. Hosp., 1975-76; sr. vocat. counselor Mass. Rehab. Commn., Holyoke, 1976-77; ins. sales rep. Mass. Mut. Life Ins. Co., Dallas, 1977-80; career supr. New Eng. Mut. Life, Dallas, 1980—. Mem. Dallas Assn. Life Underwriters, Nat. Assn. Life Underwriters, Tex.

Leaders Roundtable, Tex. Lone Star Leaders, Million Dollar Roundtable, Bus. and Profl. Women's Club, Women's Leaders Roundtable, Signum Laudis. Republican. Roman Catholic. Home: 10219 Regal Oaks Dr Dallas TX 75230 Office: One Main Pl Suite 730 Dallas TX 75250

KING, ROSALIE ROSSO, educator; b. Tacoma, May 22, 1938; d. Stanley and Gertrude Emma (Conrad) Rosso; B.S., U. Wash., 1960, Ph.D., 1975; M.Ed., Mass. State Coll., Framingham, 1965; m. Indle Gifford King, Sept. 10, 1960; children—Indle Gifford, Paige Phyllis. Product devel. Lyndens (Wash.) State Coop., 1960; home economist Seattle Times, 1961; acad. adv. U. Wash., Seattle, 1965-67, asso. and lectr., 1967-75, chmn. div. textile sci. and costume studies, 1975—; mem. flammable fabrics adv. com. Consumer Product Safety Commn., 1977-79; cons. textile flammability litigation. Pres., Mercer Island Sch. PTA, 1972-73; active Cub Scouts, Girl Scouts. Denney fellow, 1973-74. Mem. Am. Assn. Textile Chemists and Colorists, ASTM, Am. Chem. Soc., Nat. Assn. Coll. Profs. Textiles and Clothing, Fashion Group, Pi Beta Phi, Omicron Nu (nat. v.p. 1978-80, pres.-elect 1980, pres. 1981-83), Clubs: Women's Univ., U. Wash. Faculty (dir.). Contbr. articles to profl. jours.; participant fiber art exhbns. Home: 5075 W Mercer Way Mercer Island WA 98040 Office: U Wash Seattle WA 98195

KING, RUTH ALLEN, mgmt. cons.; b. Providence, Oct. 8, 1910; d. Arthur S. and Wilhelmina H. (Harmon) Allen; grad. Tefft Bus. Inst., Providence, 1929; 1 dau., Phyllis King Dunham. Sec. to atty., Providence, 1929; stenographer N.Y. Urban League, N.Y.C., 1929; with Nat. Urban League, 1929-75, asst. dir. placement services New Nat. Skills Bank, to 1975; cons. to chmn. EEOC, Washington, 1976; mgmt. cons. Hazeltine Corp., Greenlawn, L.I., N.Y., 1976—; mgmt. cons., Bklyn., 1976—. Founder, sec. THE EDGES GROUP, INC., 1969—. Named Affirmative Action Pioneer, Met. N.Y. Project Equality, 1975; Ruth Allen King Scholarship Fund established, 1970; EDGES Ruth Allen King Ann. Excalibur award established, 1978; recipient Ann Tanneyhill award for commitment to Urban League Movement, 1975; Recognition award NCCJ, 1975; spl. citation Gov. of R.I. and Providence Plantations, 1981; Woman of Yr. award Suffolk (N.Y.) chpt. Jack and Jill of Am., 1982. Mem. N.Y. Personnel Mgmt. Assn., Council Concerned Black Execs., Julius A. Thomas Soc. (charter). Home: Willoughby Walk Apts Suite 1715 185 Hall St Brooklyn NY 11205

KING, SALLY TAYLOR (MRS. CHARLES ALBERT KING), former coll. dean, businesswoman; b. Alhambra, Calif., Jan. 19, 1926; d. Ezra Felton and Margaret Cunningham (Rae) Taylor; B.A., Pomona Coll., 1948; M.A., Stanford U., 1950; m. Charles Albert King, June 17, 1961 (div. Oct. 1964). Asst. prof. Pomona (Calif.) Coll., 1950-61; tchr. Tulare (Calif.) High Schs., 1961-63; dean girls Desert Sun (Calif.) Sch., 1963-64; dean students Bradford (Mass.) Coll., 1964-68; dean students Christian Sci. Nurses Tng. Sch., Chestnut Hill, Mass., 1969-71, Endicott Coll., Beverly, Mass., 1971-79; partner The Country Cook, San Clemente, Calif., 1979—. Pres., 1st Ch. of Christ, Scientist, Beverly, 1975-76, 1st reader, 1976-79; pres. Palisades Plaza Mchts. Assn. Former mem. Nat. (mem. nominating com. 1973-74), Mass. (membership chmn. 1972-74) assns. women deans, adminstrs. and counselors, Eastern Assn. Coll. Deans and Advisors of Students; mem. Pomona Coll. Alumni Assn., Stanford U. Alumni Assn. (life), San Clemente C. of C., Phi Theta Kappa (hon.). Republican. Christian Scientist. Home: 385 Calle Guaymas San Clemente CA 92672 Office: 380 Camino de Estrella San Clemente CA 92672

KING, SANDRA JENKINS, aviation co. ofcl., pilot, ins. co. exec.; b. Jackson, Ga., Mar. 23, 1946; d. Richard Lamar and Margaret Lucille (Pugh) Jenkins; student Jackson public schs. Sec., salesperson Spencer Ins. Agy., Jackson, 1964-66; sec., dispatcher, office mgr. Atlanta Air Taxi, 1966-69; mgr. office and ops., pilot Mobley Aviation, Inc., Atlanta, 1969—; real estate sales rep., asso. broker Thompson Group Realtors, Mableton, Ga.; v.p. Thompson Group Insurors. Mem. Aircraft Owners and Pilots Assn. Baptist. Home: 463 Landmark Way Austell GA 30001 Office: PO Box 43352 Atlanta GA 30336

KING, SARAH MCKELLEY, civic worker; b. Murfreesboro, Tenn., Nov. 7, 1921; d. James Dudley and Lutie Jameson (Osborn) McKelley; student Vanderbilt U., 1939-41; m. Walter Hughey King, May 10, 1941; children—Walter Hughey, Susan Carmine King Jordan, Newton Dudley, Sallie King Norton. Regent, Oaklands Assn., Murfreesboro, 1959-61; pres. chpt. V11, Colonial Dames Am., 1965-68; regent Tenn. soc. DAR, 1968-71, curator gen. nat. soc., 1971-74, nat. chmn. museum, 1971-74; regent Sam Davis Meml. Assn., 1971-75; nat. chmn. Constn. Week Com., 1977-80; trustee Kate Duncan Smith, also Tamassee schs.; regional adv. Tenn. Commn. Status Women, 1980-81; mem. Tenn. State Mus. Commn., 1974-75, Tenn. Bicentennial Commn., 1975-76. Recipient Disting. Service award VA, 1971, Outstanding Citizen award Rutherford County (Tenn.) chpt. Am. Bus. Women's Assn., 1978. Mem. Tenn. Hist. Soc., Ky. Hist. Soc., N.Y. Soc., Daus. Cin., New Eng. Women, Am. Legion Aux., Daus. Am. Colonists, Daus. Colonial Wars, Sons and Daus. Pilgrims, U.S. Daus. of 1812, Daus. of Founders and Patriots of Am., Huguenot Soc. Methodist. Address: 2107 Greeland Dr Murfreesboro TN 37130

KING, VALARIE GREENE, psychologist, counseling cons.; b. Hawthorne, Fla., Oct. 29, 1946; d. James Randolph and Mildred Beatrice (Barlow) Greene; B.A., Spelman Coll., 1967; M.Ed., N.C. Central U., 1970; Ph.D., Am. U., 1977; 1 son, Steven Randolph. Counselor, Bethune-Cookman Coll., Daytona Beach, Fla., 1969-74, asso. prof. psychology, 1971-74, dir. Counseling Center, 1977-79, dir. Office Instnl. Research, 1979-81; commd. capt. U.S. Army, 1981; with psychology service William Beaumont Army Med. Center, El Paso, Tex., 1981—; ednl. and career devel. cons., 1977—; mem. Fla. Edn. Task Force on Standardized Testing, 1977-78; mem. adv. com. Volusia County Crisis Bd., 1977-78; mem. Fla. Bd. Ind. Colls. and Univs., 1979—. Mem. Volusia County Drug Council, 1977—. Rockefeller fellow; Am. Colls. and Univs. for Internat. Intercultural Studies, Inc., grantee, 1972; Educators to Africa, Inc. grantee, 1973; Inst. for Services to Edn. fellow, 1974-75; Am. Personnel and Guidance Assn. grad. fellow, 1975; Cokesbury Fellow, 1975-77. Mem. Am. Psychol. Assn., Fla. Ethnic Counselors Assn., Delta Sigma Theta. Democrat. Methodist. Office: Psychology Service Dept Psychiatry William Beaumont Army Med Center El Paso TX 79920

KING, VERNA LORENE, radio sta. exec.; b. Casper, Wyo., June 26, 1941; d. Verner Arnold and Lillie Elizabeth Hendricksen; Asso. Bus., Central Bus. Coll., Denver, 1960; m. Sidney King, Mar. 14, 1969; children—Joel, Robert Christopher, Randall Allen. Co-owner Sta. KCIN, Victorville, Calif., 1978—; partner Broadcast Software & Services Co.; computer installer. Exec. sec. Wyo. Republican State Com., 1968-74. Methodist. Club: Soroptomist Internat. Office: KCIN PO Box 1428 Victorville CA 92392

KING, VERNA ST. CLAIR, sch. counselor; b. Berwick, La.; d. John Westley and Florence Ellen (Calvin) St. C.; A.B., Wiley Coll., 1937; M.A., San Diego State U., 1977; m. Alonzo Le Roy King, Aug. 27, 1939; children—Alonzo Le Roy (dec.), Joyce Laraine, Verna Lee Eugenia King Bickerstaff, St. Clair A., Reginald Calvin (dec.). Tchr., Morgan City, La., 1939-40; tchr. San Diego Unified Sch. Dist., 1955-67, parent counselor, 1967-78, counselor grades 1-9, 1978—; cons. Tucson Sch. Dist., 1977—. Mem. Calif. Democratic State Central Com., 1950—, Dem. County Central Com., 1974—, del. nat. conv., 1976; mem. San Diego County Sander Adv. Commn., 1982; hon. life mem. PTA. Recipient Key to City, Mayor C. Dail, 1955, cert. United Negro Coll. Fund dr., 1980, Urban League Pvt. Sector award, 1982, 4th Ann. Conf. on Issues in Ethnicity and Mental Health Participants award, 1982. Mem. NEA (women's council 1980-82), AAUW, Calif. Tchrs. Assn. (state council 1979—), San Diego Tchrs. Assn. (dir. 1958, 64, sec. 1964-67), Nat. Council Negro Women, Pres. Women, Inc., Alpha Kappa Alpha (pres. 1978-80), Delta Kappa Gamma. Methodist. Clubs: Women's Inc., Order Eastern Star. Home: 5721 Churchward St San Diego CA 92114 Office: San Diego Unified Sch Dist 2850 Logan Ave San Diego CA 92113

KING, VERNE LORENE, apparel co. exec.; b. Danbury, Conn., Oct. 20, 1921; d. Vernon J. and Mildred M. (Roswell) Elsenboss; B.S. in Journalism, Boston U., 1943; m. Gerald G. King, Aug. 5, 1944 (dec. Feb. 1950); children—Gerald G., Susan V. Editor, Chance Vought Aircraft Co., Stratford, Conn., 1944-45, Columbia Record Co., Bridgeport, Conn., 1951-61; publs. editor Olin Co., New Haven, 1961-62; mgr. employee communication Warnaco Inc., Bridgeport, 1962-77, mgr. communications and community relations, 1977-79; pres., treas. Warnaco Fund, Inc., 1978—, dir. corp. communications, 1979—; trustee Mechanics & Farmers Savs. Bank; trustee Conn. Pub. Expenditure Council, 1978—, exec. com., 1982; lectr. employee communication, 1965—. Chmn. employee publs. United Way, Bridgeport, 1958-73, mem. public relations com., 1958-73, chmn., 1974; mem. Bridgeport Pvt. Industry Council, 1979-81; mem. assessment task force Conn. Dept. Children's and Youth Services. Bd. dirs. Easter Seal Rehab. Center, Bridgeport Econ. Devel. Corp., Vis. Nurse Assn. Bridgeport, 1975-78, Jr. Achievement, 1977-80; bd. assos. U. Bridgeport Center Policy Issues, Sacred Heart U. (chmn. 1982-83). Mem. Barnum Festival Soc. (hist. 1972-73, gov. 1971-73), Conn. Assn. Profl. Communicators (pres. 1966-67), Internat. Assn. Bus. Communicators (dir. chpt. affairs 1967-69), Bridgeport Bus. Industry Council (dir. 1976-81, v.p. 1976—, 1st vice chmn. 1978, chmn. 1979). Home: 1 Barrows St Stratford CT 06497 Office: 350 Lafayette St Bridgeport CT 06601

KING, VICTORIA VAN BEUREN, otolaryngologist; b. St. Louis, Jan. 16, 1953; d. Willard Van Beuren and Frances Howell (Lewis) K.; B.A. in Human Biology with honors, Stanford U., 1975; M.D., U. Mo., Columbia, 1979. Resident in otolaryngology Stanford U. Hosp., 1980—, now chief resident. Mem. U.S. Olympic Swimming Team, 1968, U.S. Swimming Teams to Australia, Tahiti, Can. and Eng., 1969-72. U.S. Nat. Swimming Champion, 1969; recipient award for scholastic achievement Am. Med. Women's Assn., Mem. AMA, Am. Acad. Facial Plastic and Reconstructive Surgery, Am. Acad. Otolaryngology/Head and Neck Surgery, Alpha Omega Alpha. Office: Stanford U Hosp Dept Otolarynogology Stanford CA 94305

KING, YVONNE ARNOLD, coll. adminstr., lawyer; b. Norton, Va.; d. Henry and Bessie (Thomas) Arnold; diploma Reid Bus. Coll., 1946; student Spelman Coll., 1946-48; LL.B., Atlanta Law Sch., 1973, LL.M., 1974; m. William Price King, June 26, 1946; children—Carl Victor, William Price, Janette Yvonne, Carole Patricia. Asst. to dir. public relations and publicity Atlanta U., 1952-69; staff asst. Morehouse Coll., Atlanta, 1969, adminstrv. asst. to pres., 1971, exec. asst. and legal advisor to pres., 1980—, asst. sec. to bd. trustees, 1972—, sec. to faculty, 1970—. Active Grad. Leadership Atlanta Inc. Program, 1978; mem. License Rev. Bd. Atlanta, 1979—, Atlanta Clean City Commn., 1977—, Friends of S.W. Community Hosp.; mem. steering com. Urban Life Assocs., Ga. State U. Recipient cert. YWCA, 1976, Ga. Assn. Study of Life of Black Georgians, 1981. Mem. Assn. Study and Life of Black Georgians (exec. com. 1980—), Atlanta Urban League (dir. 1981—), NAACP (exec. com. 1980—), Metro. Atlanta Crime Commn. (dir. 1979—), Ga. Assn. Woman Lawyers, Gate City Bar Assn., Ga. State Bar, Am. Bar Assn. Democrat. Baptist. Clubs: Girl Friends, Inc., Gate City Day Nursery Aux. Home: 704 Aline Dr Atlanta GA 30318 Office: Morehouse Coll Atlanta GA 30314

KINGDON, LORRAINE BRADY, ednl. adminstr.; b. Minot, N.D., Feb. 11, 1927; d. Leo Frances and Margaret Amanda Brady; B.S., N.D. State U., 1948; M.S., U. Del., 1974; m. Frederick W. Kingdon, June 22, 1948 (div., 1970); children—Frederic W., Alice Marie Kingdon Labay, Susan Ellen Kingdon Lovelace, Leo F. Columnist, Newark (Del.) Weekly, 1965; public relations cons. Webb Assos., Newark, 1967; asst. agrl. editor U. Del., Newark, 1965-72; consumer info. specialist Wash. State U., Pullman, 1972-79; head dept. agrl. communications U. Ariz., Tucson, 1980—, communications instr. Farm Press Inst., Winter Sch.; communications cons. Mem. Agrl. Communicators in edn. (regional dir. 1976-78, nat. pres. 1981, nat. communicators award 1971, nat. profl. award 1976), Women in Communications, Ariz. Agri-Press Club, Phi Kappa Phi. Author: Urban Opinions of Agriculture: Farm Press Institute Survey, 1970; Manual for Extension Radio Broadcasting, 1973, editor; New Directions: Proceedings National Extension Home Economics Communications Workshop, 1975. Office: 314 Agriculture Univ Ariz Tucson AZ 85721

KINGMAN, ELIZABETH YELM, librarian; b. Lafayette, Ind., Oct. 15, 1911; d. Charles Walter and Mary Irene (Weakley) Yelm; B.A., U. Denver, 1933, M.A., 1935; m. Eugene Kingman, June 10, 1939; children—Mixie Kingman Eddy, Elizabeth Anne. Asst. in anthropology U. Denver, 1932-34; mus. asst. Ranger Naturalist Force, Mesa Verde Nat. Park, Colo., 1934-38; asst. to husband in curatorial work, Indian art exhibits Philbrook Art Center, Tulsa, 1939-42, Joslyn Art Mus., Omaha, 1947-69; tutor humanities dept. U. Omaha, 1947-50; asst. to husband in exhibit design mus. of Tex. Tech. U., 1970-75, bibliographer Internat. Center Arid and Semi-Arid Land Studies, 1974-75; librarian Sch. Am. Research, Santa Fe, 1978—. Mem. Archeol. Inst. Am. (v.p. Santa Fe chpt. 1981—), N.Mex. Library Assn., LWV, Santa Fe Hist. Soc. (sec. 1981-83), Council Internat. Relations. Presbyterian. Home: 604 Sunset St Santa Fe NM 87501 Office: 660 Garcia St Santa Fe NM 87501

KING-SHAW, ETHEL MARGUERITE, educator; b. Vancouver, B.C., Can., June 16, 1927; d. Walter and Mildred Laura (Mason) King; B.Ed., U. Alta., 1949; M.A., U. Iowa, 1950, Ph.D., 1963; m. John Charles Shaw, Aug. 15, 1981. Tchr., Edmonton (Alta., Can.), Public Schs., 1950-53; asst. prof. Meml. U., Newfoundland, Can., 1953-55; successively lectr., asst. prof., asso. prof., prof. U. Calgary, Alta., Can., 1955—, now prof. curriculum and instrn. Fellow Can. Coll. Tchrs.; mem. Organisation Mondiale pour l'Éducation Préscolaire (sec. Can. com.), Can. Assn. Young Children, Assn. for Childhood Edn. Internat., Alta. Assn. for Young Children, Early Childhood Edn. Council, Internat. Reading Assn., Can. Soc. for Studies in Edn., Can. Ednl. Research Assn., Am. Ednl. Research Assn., Nat. Council Tchrs. of English, Can. Council Tchrs. of English, Nat. Conf. on Research in English. Anglican. Club: Altrusa (Calgary). Editor: Can. Tests of Basic Skills, 1966-82; contbr. numerous articles in field to profl. jours. Home: 3620 6th St SW Calgary AB T2S 2M7 Canada Office: Dept Curriculum and Instrn Faculty Edn U Calgary Calgary AB T2N 1N4 Canada

KINGSLEY, ELLEN, TV news reporter; b. N.Y.C., Oct. 1, 1951; d. Theodore Kingsley and Judith Kingsley Fitting; B.A., Sarah Lawrence Coll., 1973; M.A., N.Y.U., 1977. Speech writer for Elinor Guggenheimer, N.Y.C. Commr. Consumer Affairs, 1974-76, for John Sawhill, Pres. of N.Y.U., 1976-77; consumer affairs reporter, anchor WJZ-TV, Balt., 1977-80; consumer affairs reporter WDVM-TV, Washington, 1980—. Mem. AFTRA. Contbr. articles to newspapers, mags. Office: WDVM-TV 400 Brandywine St NW Washington DC 20016

KINGSLEY, ROSALIND KATZ, psychologist; b. Valley City, N.D., Apr. 13, 1929; d. Jay P. and Sadie H. Katz; B.A., Mich. State U., 1952; M.A. in Psychology, Hofstra U., 1976, Ph.D., 1978; children—Jeffrey, Paul. Music therapist, Manteno (Ill.) State Hosp., 1952; advt. saleswoman N.Y. Times, N.Y.C., 1955-57; tchr. music Levittown (N.Y.) Sch. Dist., 1962-68; profl. artist, 1968-74; sch. psychologist Milford (Del.) Sch. Dist., 1978-81; pvt. practice clin. psychology, Milton, Del., 1981—; cons. in field; family ct. psychologist, Sussex County, Del. Named Wonder Woman, Del. chpt. NOW, 1979. Mem. Am. Psychol. Assn., Del. Psychol. Assn., Del. Psychologists in Pvt. Practice, Phi Delta Kappa. Home: 648 Evans Dr Eastman Heights Milford DE 19963 Office: 424 Mulberry St Milton DE 19968

KINGSTON, MAXINE HONG, author; b. Stockton, Calif., Oct. 27, 1940; d. Tom and Ying Lan (Chew) Hong; B.A., U. Calif., Berkeley, 1962; m. Earll Kingston, Nov. 23, 1963; 1 son, Joseph Lawrence. Author: The Woman Warrior: Memoirs of a Girlhood Among Ghosts (Nat. Book Critics Circle award for non-fiction, 1976; cited by Time mag., N.Y. Times Book Rev. and Asian Mail as one of best books of year); China Men (Am. Book award, 1981; citated by Time mag., N.Y. Times Book Rev. and Asian Mail as one of best books of 1980); contbr. short stories, articles and poems to mags. and jours., including N.Y. Times Mag., New West, New Dawn, Hawaii Review, Viva, English Jour., Am. Girl, Ms., Am. Heritage, New Yorker, Iowa Rev.; tchr. English, Sunset High Sch., Hayward, Calif., 1965-66, Kahuku (Hawaii) High Sch., 1967, Kahaluu (Hawaii) Drop-In Sch., 1968, Kailua (Hawaii) High Sch., 1969, Honolulu Bus. Coll., 1969, Mid-Pacific Inst., Honolulu, 1970-77; asst. prof. English, vis. writer U. Hawaii, Honolulu, 1977—. Recipient Mademoiselle Mag. award, 1977, Anisfield-Wolf Race relations award, 1978; Stockton (Calif.) Arts Commn. award, 1981; NEA writing fellow, 1980; Living Treasure of Hawaii, 1980. Address: care Alfred A Knopf Inc 201 E 50th St New York NY 10022 *

KINKER, KANDACE LEE LIBKA, med. technician; b. Indpls., July 25, 1951; d. James Curtis and Jacqueline Jean (Wright) Libka; B.A. in Microbiology, Ind. U., 1973; m. Carl Joseph Kinker, Aug. 21, 1976. Med. technician infectious diseases U. Louisville, 1974-76; med. technician Drs. C.W. McClary and J.W. LaFollette, Bloomington, Ind., 1977—. Vol. tutor Vols. in Tutoring Adult Learning, 1979—. Mem. Bloomington Jaycee Women (charter pres. 1979-80), Ind. Hist. Soc., Monroe County Hist. Soc., Am. Soc. Microbiology, Ind. U. Alumni Assn., AAUW, Bus. and Profl. Women. Club: Bloomington Community Band. Home: 3432 Valley View Dr Bloomington IN 47401

KINLEIN, M(ARY) LUCILLE, nurse; b. Ellicott City, Md., Dec. 17, 1921; d. Julius Augustus and Mary Teresa (Plantholt) K.; B.A., Coll. Notre Dame, Balt., 1943; B.S. in Nursing Edn., Catholic U. Am., 1947, M.S., 1953. Asst. prof. nursing Cath. U. Am., 1947-69, dir. masters program in cardiovascular disease nursing, 1962-69; mem. faculty Georgetown U. Sch. Nursing, 1970-74; pres. D.C. Profl. Nurses Exam. Bd., 1955-61, D.C. Practical Nurses Exam. Bd., 1961-67; cons. HEW, 1964-74; ind. general nurse, 1971—; partner Détente Manor, McLean, Va., 1978—; vis. prof. U. So. Miss., Hattiesburg, 1975-78, also coordinator Center Nursing Edn., Practice and Research; vis. lectr. univs. Wis., Va., Alaska Pacific U.; mem. Washington Nursing Devel. Conf. Group. Recipient Alumni Achievement award Coll. Notre Dame, 1973, Cath. U. Am., 1974; Linda Richards award Nat. League Nursing, 1977; Nat. Center for Kinlein founded, 1979, 1st issue Jour. Kinlein, 1982. Mem. Am. Nurses Assn., Nat. League Nursing, Am. Heart Assn., Sigma Theta Tau, Kappa Gamma Pi. Roman Catholic. Author: Independent Nursing Practice with Clients, 1977; co-author: Concept Formalization in Nursing, 1973. Home: 7015 Highview Terr W Hyattsville MD 20782 Office: 6525 Belcrest Rd Hyattsville MD 20782

KINNE, KATHARINE (MRS. CHARLES E. SIGETY), home economist; b. Herkimer, N.Y., Nov. 23, 1921; d. Cornelius Harry and Katharine (Kinne) Snell; B.S., Cornell U., 1944; m. Charles Edward Sigety, July 17, 1948; children—Charles Birge, Katharine Kinne, Robert Griswold, Cornelius, Elizabeth. Tng. squad J.L. Hudson Co., Detroit, 1944; overseas recreation work ARC, 1945-46, nat. fund campaign speaker, 1947; publicity work Union Carbide and Carbon Corp., 1947-48; dist. sales mgr. Berger Bros., New Haven, 1948-50; European tour condr. Olson Travel Orgn., 1950; TV home economist Sally Smart's Kitchen, WOR-TV, 1951-53; on camera food editor Home Show, NBC-TV, 1953-56; owner, dir., gen. mgr. Video Vittles, Inc. N.Y.C., 1953—; food service cons. Florence Nightingale Health Center, N.Y.C., 1967—; sec. Piper Hill Operating Co., Inc. (Pa.); mgr. Cucumber's Restaurants, Piperhill, Pa.; dir. Profl. Med. Products, Inc., Greenwood, S.C. Co-chmn. nat. parents com. Bates Coll., Lewiston, Maine; bd. dirs. Parents League N.Y., Trinity Sch. Mothers Orgn., Grace Ch. Sch. Parents Orgn., 1966-67. Recipient scholarships N.Y. State Fedn. Women's Clubs, D.A.R. Home Econ., Women in Bus., Mortar Bd., Delta Delta Delta. Mem. Am. Home Econs. Assn., Am. Women in Radio and TV, AFTRA, Screen Actors Guild. Presbyterian. Address: 175 E 96th St New York NY 10028

KINNEAR, ALICE TAYLOR, telephone co. exec.; b. Buffalo, June 16, 1949; d. Floyd Davidson and Marie Alice (Thomas) Taylor; B.S. cum laude, U. Bridgeport, 1971. Account rep. N.Y. Telephone, Manhattan, 1971-73; communications cons. So. New Eng. Telephone Co., New Haven, 1973-75, staff asst., 1975-76, staff mgr., 1976-77, account exec. II, 1977-79, staff mgr., 1979—. Mem. Am. Mgmt. Assn., DAR. Democrat. Methodist. Club: North Salem Bridle Trails Assn. Office: 367 Orange St New Haven CT 06511

KINNEAR, ANN BONNEY HALL YOUNG, advt. exec.; b. Somerville, N.J., Sept. 18, 1929; d. Robert Rodenbaugh and Irma Ione (Apgar) Hall; ed. public schs.; m. Robert Kinnear, June 17, 1967; 1 son, Richard H. Cole. Classified ad-taker Newark Star Ledger, 1950-52; asst. account exec. Halpern Advt. Agy, N.Y.C., 1952-58; account exec. Gottesmann, Baader, & Frank Advt. Agy., Newark, 1958-66; v.p. in charge recruitment advt. Lewis Advt. Agy., Newark, 1966—. Public relations dir. Hunterdon County Goldwater Assn., 1962-64. Republican. Presbyterian. Home: 1225 Evergreen Rd Morrisville PA 19067 Office: 17 Academy St Newark NJ 07102

KINNEY, MARJORIE SHARON, fin. exec.; b. Gary, Ind., Jan. 11, 1940; d. David Harrison and Florence Clara Dunning; student El Camino Coll., 1957-58; D.H.L., West Coast U., 1982; m. Daniel Dean Kinney, Dec. 31, 1958 (div. 1973); children—Steven Daniel, Michael Alan, Gregory Lincoln, Bradford David. Partner, Kinney Advt., Inc., Inglewood, Calif., 1958-68; pres. Greeters of Am., Inglewood, 1967-69; chmn. bd. Person to Person, Inc., Cleve., 1969-72; pres. Kinney Mktg. Corp., Encino, Calif., 1972-80; sr. v.p. Beverly Hills Savs. and Loan Assn., 1980—; dir. Safeway Stores Inc., Chubb/Pacific Indemnity Co.; adv. bd. Marine Nat. Bank; lectr. profl. groups, univs. Bd. dirs. ARC, 1976-81, United Way, 1979-81; trustee West Coast U.; adv. bd. U.S. Human Resources. Mem. Savs. Inst. Mktg., Calif. Savs. and Loan League, Women of Wall St. West (adv. bd.). Republican. Presbyterian. Office: 27271 Las Ramblas Mission Viejo CA 92629

KINSELLA, FRANCES, former home designer; b. Chillicothe, Mo., July 1, 1915; d. Charles Henry and Appollonia (Martin) Moylan; student N.W. Mo. State Tchrs. Coll., also N.E. Mo. State Tchrs. Coll.; m. Joseph L. Kinsella, May 2, 1936; children—Joseph R., Frances Kinsella Hayes, Lawrence, Kathryn Kinsella Reece. Tchr., Livingston County Schs., 1933-36, 39-40, 46-50; tchr. English, USAF, Chillicothe Bus. Coll.,

1950-51; bookkeeper, contracting firm, 1951-59; city clk. City of Chillicothe, 1959-63; designer for contracting firm, 1963-70; youth specialist Mo. State Tng. Sch. for Girls, Chillicothe, 1970-79. Mem. publicity com. Chillicothe Fine Arts Council, 1967; pres. Livingston County Health Assn., 1957-59. Mem. Am. Contract Bridge League (dir. Chillicothe 1958-59), Nat. League Am. Pen Women (br. pres. 1950-54), Bus. and Profl. Women's Club (chmn. radio com.), Hedrick Med. Center Aux. (life). Democrat. Roman Catholic. Home: 42 10th St Chillicothe MO 64601

KINSEY, MATTIE (MRS. GLAUCUS E. KINSEY), club woman; b. Milan, Tenn.; d. Ezekiel Jessie W. and Martha M. (McGee) Armstrong; student pub. schs., Bonham, Tex.; m. Glaucus Edward Kinsey, May 10, 1917; children—Martha Dell Kinsey Carpenter, Margaret Louise Kinsey Brown. Asso. mem. Los Angeles Music Center for Performing Arts; life mem. Braille Inst. Aux., also mem. exec. bd.; mem. UDC, Opera Guild Calif.; life mem. Assistance League, Calif. Mus. Scis. and Industry (charter). Mem. Town and Gown (life). Clubs: Ebell (life), Los Angeles Country, Jonathan (Los Angeles); Balboa Bay (Newport Beach). Home: 450 N Rossmore Ave Los Angeles CA 90004

KINSEY-CALORI, JOANNE, broadcasting firm exec.; b. McKeesport, Pa., Sept. 3; d. George Morris and Pauline Vivian (Anderson) Kinsey; B.A., M.A. Ohio State U., 1976; Ph.D., Harvard U., 1982; m. Dan John Calori, June 6, 1952 (div.); children—Paula Christine, Kevin Kinsey. Reporter, Sta. WOSU, Ohio State U., Columbus, 1969-70; communications asst. dept. continuing edn. Ohio State U., 1970-72, pub. relations dir. Coll. Adminstrv. Sci., 1974-75, acting asst. prof. communications, psychology, 1971-76; editor Columbus region Internat. Harvester Corp., 1973-77; pres., co-owner Profl. Broadcasting Services, Redondo Beach, Calif., 1976—. Pres. PTA, Marburn, Ridgeview, Whetstone schs., Columbus, 1965-70; campaign mgr. Republican party, Franklin County, 1965-68. Recipient spl. award for outstanding community service Columbus Pub. Schs. Mem. Nat. Acad. TV Arts and Scis., Women in Communications (Los Angeles chpt.), Pacific Pioneer Broadcasters, So. Calif. Wine Writers (charter mem.), Archaeology Soc. Columbus, Jr. League, Mirrors and Chimes, Phi Beta Kappa, Phi Kappa Phi. Presbyterian. Clubs: Worthington Music, Clintonville Women's, Columbus Players. Office: Suite 10 625 Esplanade Redondo Beach CA 90277

KINSTREY, PATRICIA ANN MUTH, health educator; b. Phila., Jan. 31, 1941; d. Stephen Anthony and Ruth Cecilia (Bade) Muth; B.S., SUNY, Plattsburgh, 1962; M.S., Russell Sage Coll., 1977; Cert. Advanced Study, SUNY, New Paltz, 1977-79; m. Lawrence Kinstrey, July 7, 1962; children—Michael, Holly. Adminstrv. nurse Wiltwyck Sch. for Boys, Esopus, N.Y., 1963-65; sch. nurse tchr. Kingston (N.Y.) City Schs., 1965-70; health educator, 1970—. Mem. Esopus Zoning Bd. Appeals, 1978-80; vice-pres. MJM Jr. High Sch. PTSO, 1977-79. Mem. N.Y. State United Tchrs., N.Y. State Profl. Health Educators, Nat. Assn. Female Execs., Friends of Kingston Area Library, SUNY Plattsburgh Alumni Assn., Russell Sage Alumni Assn., N.Y. State Public Health Assn., AAUW (br. chairperson ednl. founds. 1981-82), Opus 40, Delta Kappa Gamma Soc. Internat. Home: PO Box 204 Main St Esopus NY 12429 Office: MJM Jr High Sch Andrews St Kingston NY 12401

KINTNER, JANET IDE, mcpl. judge; b. Dayton, Ohio, Feb. 25, 1944; d. Herbert A. and Marian G. (Hetzler) Ide; B.A., U. Ariz., 1966, J.D., 1968; m. Charles F. Kintner, Sept. 14, 1968; children—Zachary Ide, Darien Ide. Admitted to Calif. bar, 1969; atty. Legal Aid Soc. of San Diego, 1969-70; dep. city atty., San Diego, 1971-74; individual practice law, San Diego, 1974-76; apptd. judge Mcpl. Ct., San Diego, 1976—, elected to San Diego Mcpl. Ct., 1978—; spl. assignment to San Diego Superior Ct., 1978—; mem. faculty Calif. Jud. Coll., 1980-81; Jud. Studies Program, 1980-82. Ct. liaison to San Diego Community Child Abuse Coordinating Council, 1978-81; bd. dirs. New Entra Casa Halfway House, 1982; bd. dirs. Tradition One Alcohol Rehab. Facility, 1979; mem. adv. council Nat. Council on Alcoholism, 1979; mem. adv. Council Clairemont Neighborhood Recovery Center, 1980-81. Mem. Psychology and the Law (adv. bd.), Calif. Judges Assn., Ariz. State Bar (hon.), Am. Judges Assn., Nat. Assn. Women Judges (charter), San Diego County Judges Assn. (chmn. ethics com. 1982), San Diego County Bar Assn. (v.p. 1976, dir. 1973-76, del. chmn. for state bar conv. 1976), Bus. and Profl. Women's Club. Club: Lawyers. Contbr. articles in field to profl. jours.; asso. editor: Cts. Commentary, 1980-82; mem. planning com. Evidence Benchbook, 1981, Small Claims Ct. Benchbook, 1981-82. Office: 220 W Broadway San Diego CA 92101

KINZIE, JEANNIE JONES (MRS. JOSEPH KINZIE), physician; b. Gt. Falls, Mont., Mar. 14, 1940; d. James Wayne and Lillian Alice (Young) Jones; B.S., Mont. State U., 1961; M.D., Washington U., St. Louis, 1965; m. Joseph Kinzie, Mar. 25, 1965; 1 son, Daniel Joseph. Intern in surgery U. N.C., Chapel Hill, 1965-66; resident in radiology (radiation therapy) Washington U. Sch. Medicine, St. Louis, 1968-71, instr. radiology, 1971-73; Am. Cancer Soc. advanced clin. fellow, 1971-74; asst. radiologist Barnes Hosp., St. Louis, 1971-73; cons. radiology Homer G. Phillips Hosp., St. Louis, 1971-73; mem. med. records com., asst. prof. radiology Med. Coll. Wis., 1973-74; asso. attending staff Milw. County Gen. Hosp., 1973-74; head radiation therapy dept. Wood (Wis.) VA Hosp., 1973-74; cons. in radiology Community Meml. Hosp., Menomonee Falls, Wis., 1974; radiology staff West Allis (Wis.) Meml. Hosp., 1973-74; asst. prof. radiology U. Chgo., 1975-78, asso. prof., 1978-80; asso. prof. radiation oncology Wayne State U., Detroit, 1980—; mem. radiation studies sect. NIH, 1981—. NIH grantee, 1974-76. Diplomate Am. Bd. Radiology. Mem. AMA, Am. Coll. Radiology (com. on edn.), Wayne County Med. Soc., Am. Soc. Therapeutic Radiologists, AAAS, AAUP, Am. Soc. Clin. Oncology, N.Y. Acad. Scis., Alpha Lambda Delta, Phi Kappa Phi, Mortar Bd., Sigma Xi. Republican. Lutheran. Home: 436 Lakeland Grosse Pointe City MI 48230 Office: Radiation Oncology Center 4201 St Antoine St Detroit MI 48201

KIONKA-HEINRITZ, SANDRA SELLERS, interior architect, constrn. mgr.; b. Tuscola, Ill., Feb. 24, 1939; d. Thomas Wesley and Janice Meridith (Morrison) Sellers; student U. Ill., 1957-60; B.A. in Tchr. Tng. and Social Studies, So. Ill. U., Carbondale, 1974, B.S. in Interior Design, 1973; m. Edward James Kionka, Aug. 17, 1958; children—Thomas Edward, Meridith Ann, David James; m. 2d, Robert G. Heinritz, Jr., July 30, 1977. Social studies tchr. Rantoul Twp. (Ill.) High Sch., 1960-62, Springfield (Ill.) High Sch., 1965-66, St. Hilda's and St. Hugh's, N.Y.C., 1972-73; interior designer Centerre Bank, St. Louis, 1975-77, facilities planning officer, 1977—, project mgr. hdqrs. bldg. constrn., 1978-82, asst. v.p., 1982—; guest lectr. Washington U., St. Louis, 1977, 78. Steering com. YWCA; leader Lunch for Women, 1981, chmn. awards com., 1981-82. Recipient cert. of appreciation Purdue U., 1980. Mem. Am. Soc. Interior Designers (pres. Mo. East chpt. 1980, nat. dir. 1981-82), Inst. Real Estate Mgrs., Mo. Assn. Realtors. Office: One Centerre Plaza Saint Louis MO 63102

KIPNEES, MARCIA (DARYL), pub. co. advt. sales exec.; b. N.Y.C., Oct. 29, 1950; d. Jerome J. and Pearl B. (Brown) K.; A.B., U. Pa., 1970; M.A., Tufts U., 1972. Mktg./editorial rep. div., Prentice-Hall Inc., N.Y.C., 1976-77, asso. editor acquisitions, med. book div., 1977-79; advt. sales rep., med. jours. div. Appleton-Century-Crofts, N.Y.C., 1979—. Mem. Pharm. Advt. Council, Health Care Bus. Women's Assn., Ad Women N.Y., Nat. Assn. Female Execs. Club: N.Y. Tufts. Home: 60 E 8th St New York NY 10003 Office: 292 Madison Ave New York NY 10017

KIPNIS, NORMA CARLIN, civic worker; b. Bklyn., July 4; d. Joseph Melvin and Ruth (Streifler) Carlin; ed. U. Miami (Fla.), Penland (N.C.) Sch. Crafts, N.Y. Inst. Fin.; m. Jerome Leon Kipnis; children—Daniel, David (dec.), Douglas, Donald, Diane. Account exec. Smith Barney, Harris-Upham Co., Inc., Miami. Trustee, U. Miami; chmn. Dade County Sch. Vol. Adv. Bd.; pres. Friends of Dade County Sch. Vol. Program; bd. dirs. Nat. Children's Cardiac Hosp.; past sec.-treas., bd. dirs., exec. bd. Greater Miami Jewish Fedn.; bd. dirs. women's div. United Jewish Appeal, Council Fedns. and Welfare Fund, Joint Distbn. Com.; del. White House Conf. Nat. Sch. Vol. Program; on assignment to New World Festival of Arts, until 1982. Recipient numerous awards, certs. of appreciation. Address: 248 Ashdale Pl Los Angeles CA 90049 also 555 NE 15th St Apt 28A Miami FL 33132

KIRATZOPOULOS, WANDA BORGES, lawyer; b. Bronx, N.Y., Aug. 29, 1950; d. Jaime Nemesio Borges and Ada C. (Pujadas) Borges Mady; B.A., Mercy Coll., 1972; m. George Kiratzopoulos, July 23, 1977. Legal sec., firm Jules Teitelbaum, N.Y.C., 1972, law clk., 1972-79, assoc., 1979-82; assoc. firm Teitelbaum & Gamberg, P.C., N.Y.C., 1982—; admitted to N.Y. State bar, 1979, U.S. Dist. Ct. bar, 1979. Bd. dirs. Home Studies, Inc. Mem. Nat. Assn. Female Execs., Am. Bar Assn., Fed. Bar Council, N.Y. State Bar Assn., N.Y. Women's Bar Assn., Bankruptcy Lawyers Bar Assn., Mercy Coll. Alumni Assn. Roman Catholic. Club: Fairfield County Chorale (bd. dirs.). Home: 1096 Main St Stamford CT 06902 Office: 121 E 18th St New York NY 10003

KIRBY, DEBORAH MACDONALD, rehab. psychologist; b. Washington, May 19, 1948; d. Robert Angus and Margarett Mary (Harrison) MacDonald; B.A., George Washington U., 1970; M.Ed., Am. U., 1972; m. Stephen Edward Kirby, Sept. 6, 1980. Psychiat. asst. Chestnut Lodge Psychiat. Hosp., Rockville, Md., 1969-70; research psychologist Dept. Army, 1970; clin. intern Am. U. Counseling Center, 1972; clin. psychologist Bay County Guidance Clinic, Panama City, Fla., 1972-73; rehab. counselor State of Fla., Panama City, 1974; rehab. psychologist Woodrow Wilson Rehab. Center, Fisherville, Va., 1975—; pvt. practice Shenandoah Counseling Assos., 1978—. Mem. Am. Psychol. Assn., Va. Counselors Assn., Va. Mental Health Counselors Assn., Kappa Alpha Theta. Democrat. Club: Charlottesville-Albemarle Kennel (past dir.). Author papers in field. Office: Psychol Services WWRC Fisherville VA 22939 also Shenandoah Counseling Assos PO Box 500 Churchville VA 24421

KIRBY, DIANA CATHERINE, nurse, army officer; b. Guttenberg, Iowa, Jan. 22, 1951; d. Albert Edward and Bernadette Lucretia (Berns) Cherne; B.S. in Nursing, U. Iowa, 1973; M.S. in Edn., U. So. Calif., 1977; m. Fred W. Kirby, Nov. 24, 1981. Mem. nursing staff Mercy Med. Center, Dubuque, Iowa, 1973-74; commd. 1st lt. Nurse Corps, U.S. Army, 1974, advanced through grades to capt., 1976; service in W. Ger.; community health nurse William Beaumont Army Med. Center, 1978-80, Ft. Leonard Wood, Mo., 1980-82, 24th Med. Detachment, Schweinfurt, W.Ger., 1982—. Mem. Am. Nurses Assn., Am. Fedn. Nurses, Am. Philatelic Soc. Roman Catholic. Address: 24th Medical Detachment APO New York NY 09033

KIRBY, ELLEN IRENE, nurse; b. Petersburg, W.Va., Aug. 28, 1947; d. Earl A. and Neva Ellen (Ours) Groves; R.N., Rockingham Meml. Sch. Nursing, 1968; diploma registered nurse therapist Phys. Modalities Inst., 1970; postgrad. Shepherd Coll., 1977-79, Tex. Woman's U., 1970; m. Wilford Cline Kirby, Sept. 9, 1973; 1 son, Edward Earl. Head nurse Grant Meml. Hosp., Petersburg, 1970-71, staff nurse, 1968-69, supr. phys. therapy dept., 1971-73, instr. inservice edn., 1971; public health, sch. nurse Grant County Health Dept., Petersburg, 1973—. Mem. Internat. Four-H Exchange to Norway, 1971; active Grant County Heart Assn. fund raising campaign, 1979-80, chmn., 1979-82; mem. Nat. Commn. on Observance of Internat. Women's Yr., 1975-77; mem. W.Va. State Coordinating Com. for Women's State Meeting, 1977; bd. dirs. Internat. 4-H Youth Exchange, 1975-80; sec. Maysville Elem. Sch. Parent Tchrs. Orgn., 1979; mem. South Branch Charge Choir, 1978—. Mem. Am. Nurses Assn., W.Va. Nurses Assn., W.Va. Public Health Assn., W.Va. Health Systems Agy., W.Va. Heart Assn. (county fund chmn. 1979—), Internat. 4-H Youth Exchange Alumni Assn. (v.p. 1978-79, pres. 1979-80), Rockingham Meml. Hosp. Nurses Alumni Assn., Bus. and Profl. Womens Club (various coms.). Republican. Methodist. Clubs: Grant Meml. Hosp. Aux., W.Va. Garden, Petersburg Garden, Bus. and Profl. Women's, Internat. 4-H Youth Exchange Assn., W.Va. 4-H All Stars. Home: PO Box 211 Petersburg WV 26847 Office: PO Box 326 Petersburg WV 26847

KIRBY, JUDITH HELEN, public relations co. exec.; b. Paterson, N.J., Dec. 9, 1948; d. Harry George and Ruth Evelyn Estes (Wood) DeKeukelaere. With Conti Advt., Ridgewood, N.J., 1966-68; flight attendant United Air Lines, Newark, 1969; exec. sec. Owens & Assos. Advt., Phoenix, 1970-71; public relations dir. Waller & Assos. Advt., Tucson, 1971-72; owner, founder, pres. Kirby & Assos. Public Relations, Tucson, 1972—; instr. U. Ariz., Tucson, 1978-82. Pres. bd. dirs. Guardian Ad Litem, Tucson, 1981-82; v.p. bd. dirs. Jr. Achievement, Tucson, 1980-82; bd. dirs. Ronald McDonald House, Tucson, 1981-82, So. Ariz. council Boy Scouts Am., 1981-82, Tucson YMCA, 1981-82; chmn. bus. com. Udall for U.S. Congress in 1982, 1980; public relations vol. NAACP, Phoenix, 1971, 72; Girl Scout leader, Glendale, Ariz., 1971-72. Recipient cert. of Appreciation March of Dimes, 1979, United Way of Tucson, 1979, 80, Jr. Achievement, 1980. Mem. Exec. Women's Council, Women's Polit. Caucus, C. of C., Tucson Trade Bur., Tucson Art Mus. Clubs: Old Pueblo, Tucson Advt., Ariz. Daily Star Sportsmen (dir. 1979-81). Author: Woman-Endings & Beginnings, 1979; contbr. articles to profl. publs. Office: 620 N Country Club Rd Tucson AZ 85716

KIRBY, MARY XAVIER, coll. dean; b. Newark, Mar. 7, 1917; d. Alfred Lyndon and Helen Agnes (Murphy) K.; A.B., Coll. New Rochelle (N.Y.), 1938; M.A., Cath. U. Am., 1949; Ph.D., U. Pa., 1965; D.H.L., Chestnut Hill Coll., Phila., 1980. Joined Sisters of St. Joseph, Roman Catholic Ch., 1940; mem. faculty Chestnut Hill Coll., 1959—, prof. English, 1959-68, pres., 1968-70, dean grad. studies, 1980—; mem. nominating panel of bd. dirs. Phila. Community Coll., 1968-80. Bd. dirs. Chestnut Hill Community Assn. Named Woman of Yr., Bus. and Profl. Women's Assn. Chestnut Hill, 1978. Mem. AAUW, Assn. Advancement Humanities, Del. Valley Regional Assn. Colls. and Univs. (exec. com.). Democrat. Office: Chestnut Hill Coll Philadelphia PA 19118

KIRBY, RITA MAYE, real estate mgmt. co. exec.; b. Dalhart, Tex., Sept. 10, 1941; d. Luby F. and Jonnie Reta Knowles; student Frank Phillips Jr. Coll., Borger, Tex.; children—Michael, Daniel. Property mgr. Villa France Apts., Irving, Tex., 1971-72; mgmt. v.p. First Property Mgmt. Corp., Chgo. and Dallas, 1972-80; v.p. ops. S & S Properties, Inc., Dallas, 1980; exec. v.p., partner Capital Concept Mgmt. Corp., Dallas, 1980—; mem. Nat. Apt. Mgmt. Accreditation Bd., 1979-81, chmn., 1980-81; nat. public speaker, 1978—. Mem. Dallas Apt. Assn. (dir. 1979-82, sec. 1981-82), Tex. Apt. Assn. (dir. 1979-82, edn. chmn. 1980-81), Nat. Apt. Assn. (dir. 1978-82). Baptist. Author: Community Directors Guide, 1975; co-author: Property Operating Procedures, 1981; Professional Leasing Program, 1981; Property Evaluation and Acquisition, 1982. Home: 2112 Rocky Cove Irving TX 75060 Office: Dallas TX

KIRIAS, SUSAN HERNEY, public relations exec.; b. San Diego, Aug. 27, 1942; d. Albert F. and Dorothy Ann (Charleson) Herney; B.A., U. Calif., Berkeley, 1964; m. Christopher H. Kirias, July 20, 1979; 1 son, Ross Royer Veal. Staff asst. U.S. Senator Thomas Kuchel, Washington, 1964; communications officer spl. projects Loyola U. New Orleans, 1965-68; planning coordinator community relations New Orleans Public Schs., 1968-70; conf. coordinator U. Utah, Salt Lake City, 1970-71; freelance communications cons., 1972-75; sr. cons. Osoro & Assos., Denver, Phila., 1975-81; sr. planner HSA of N.E. Pa., 1980-81; public relations dir. United Gilsonite Labs., Scranton, Pa., 1981—; lectr. U. Denver Grad. Sch. Social Work, 1979. Chmn. human resources task force, citizens adv. com. Denver Regional Council Govts., 1974-77; bd. dirs. Big Sisters Colo., 1976-77, Planned Parenthood of Lackawanna County, 1982—; mem. Gov.'s Commn. Utah Environ. Conf., 1971; mem. Scranton Women's Coalition, 1980-82. Mem. Women in Communications, Am. Soc. Tng. and Devel., Internat. Assn. Bus. Communicators, Advt. Club N.E. Pa., NOW. Editor: Service Directory for Veterans in Colorado, 1977. Office: UGL PO Box 70 Scranton PA 18501

KIRK, COLLEEN JEAN, educator, condr.; b. Champaign, Ill., Sept. 7, 1918; d. Bonum Lee and Anna Catherine (Hoffert) K.; B.S. with high honors, U. Ill., 1940, M.S., 1945; Ed.D., Columbia U., 1953. Tchr. music Public Schs., Danvers (Ill.), 1940-44, Watseka (Ill.), 1944-45; instr. Univ. High Sch., Urbana, Ill., 1945-49; asst. prof. edn. and music U. Ill., 1949-58, asso. prof., 1958-64, prof., 1964-70; prof. Fla. State U., Tallahassee, 1970—, condr. choral union, 1970—; dir. music Wesley United Methodist Ch., Urbana, 1947-70; dir. jr. chorus Ill. Summer Youth Music, Urbana, 1963-71; choral clinician, condr. adjudicator. Recipient Fla. State U. Pres.'s award, 1979. Mem. Am. Choral Dirs. Assn. (pres. So. div. 1971-75, nat. pres.-elect 1979-81, nat. pres. 1981—), Music Educators Nat. Conf., Fla. Music Educators Assn., AAUP, Coll. Music Soc., Fla. Vocal Assn., Fla. Coll. Music Educators Assn., Pi Kappa Lambda, Kappa Delta Pi, Sigma Alpha Iota. Author: (with others) Modern Methods in Elementary Education, 1959. Contbr. to Choral Jour., 1978—. Home: 2028 Wildridge Dr Tallahassee FL 32303 Office: Sch Music Fla State U Tallahassee FL 32306

KIRK, HELEN WHITE (MRS. KENNETH BURSON KIRK), club woman; b. Detroit; d. William John and Grace (Ramsay) White; B.A., U. Mich.; m. Kenneth Burson Kirk; children—Cynthia Grace, Helen Victoria. Sec.-treas., dir. Kirk Dial Corp., Beverly Hills, Calif.; bd. dirs. Beverly Hills Women's Club, 1936-37, Palm Springs (Calif.) Women's Club, 1953-54; pres. Lifelighters, 1955-56, 71-72, Palm Springs chpt. W.A.I.F., 1958-59; chmn. Bookworms of Assistance League So. Calif., 1967-68; mem. adv. bd. Los Angeles Women's chpt. Freedom's Found., 1972-77; mem. women's com. Los Angeles Philharmonic Orch., Opera Guild Soc. Calif.; gen. chmn. ladies div. Rotary Internat. Conv., 1962; pres. Palm Springs chpt. Nat. Charity League, 1965; v.p. women's aux. Desert Hosp., 1965; mem. adv. council Los Angeles County women's chpt. Freedoms Found. at Valley Forge; bd. dirs. Children's Hosp., 1981-82. Mem. Internat. Platform Assn. Clubs: Beverly Hills Garden (pres. 1978-80), Ebell, Beverly Hills Women's. Home: 702 N Bedford Dr Beverly Hills CA 90210 also 155 S Belardo Rd Palm Springs CA 92262

KIRK, MARY CAMPBELL, govt. agy. statistician; b. Mooresville, N.C., May 23, 1945; d. Isaac Lewis and Mamie Laura (Murray) Campbell; student Elizabeth City State U., 1962-63; B.A., N.C. A&T U., 1966; postgrad. Am. U., 1971-72, Southeastern U., 1972-73; student Prince Georges Community Coll., 1979-80; m. Albert Lee Kirk, June 4, 1966; 1 son, Albert Lee. With IBM at N.C. Nat. Bank, Charlotte, N.C., 1966-68, Celanese Corp., Charlotte, 1968-69, Dept. Fin. Revenue, Washington, 1970; personnel mgmt. specialist D.C. Army Nat. Guard, 1975-81; survey statistician Bur. of Census, Washington, 1970—, population technician, 1980—, EEO counselor, 1978-81; realtor asso. Latter and Blum Real Estate Agy., New Orleans, 1982—. Mem. EEO adv. com., 1979; treas. Commerce Com. for Black Concerns, 1978-79; mem. Suitland Commerce Com. for Women, 1979—. Mem. Enlisted Assn. of N.G., Am. Fedn. Govt. Employees. Club: Toastmistresses.

KIRK, VIRGINIA, psychologist; b. Kirksville, Mo., Dec. 22, 1895; d. Sherman and Harriet Rose (White) Kirk; B.A., Drake U., 1917; postgrad. U. Nanking (China), 1921-22; B.N., Yale U., 1927, M.S., 1930; Ph.D., U. Chgo., 1949. Research asst. Yale Psycho-Clinic, New Haven, 1930-31; dir. nursing Emma Pendleton Bradley Home, Riverside, R.I., 1931-35; asst. in ednl. psychology Columbia U., N.Y.C., summer 1935; research asso. Williamson County Child Guidance Study, Franklin, Tenn., 1935-42; instr. Sch. Medicine, Vanderbilt U., Nashville, 1943-47, asst. prof., 1947-53, asso. prof., 1953-60, asso. clin. prof. emerita, 1961—; pvt. practice clin. psychology, 1948-73, part-time, 1973—; cons. psychologist Specialized Center of Research, Vanderbilt U. Hosp., 1963-73; cons. clin. psychologist Family and Children's Service, Nashville, 1953-73; mem. childhood and adolescence com. Nashville Mental Health Assn., 1975-76. Recipient Disting. Alumni Service award Drake U., 1965; lic. psychologist, Tenn.; cert. clin. psychologist, Va.; diplomate in clin. psychology Am. Bd. Profl. Psychology. Fellow Am. Psychol. Assn.; mem. Tenn. (honors award 1976), Midwestern, Southeastern psychol. assns., Am. Assn. Mental Deficiency, N.Y. Acad. Scis., Tenn. Acad. Sci., AAAS. Club: Univ. (Nashville). Author: (with E.S. Robinson) Introduction to Psychology, 1935; also articles. Address: 666 Timber Ln Nashville TN 37215

KIRKHAM, DIANE JANICE, biologist, toxicologist; b. Kansas City, Mo., Feb. 11, 1952; d. Van Chaffin and Thelma Lorraine (Mckinley) Jones; B.S. cum laude (Honor scholar), William Woods Coll., 1974. Research asst. U. Kans. Med. Center, Kansas City, 1974; biologist in drug safety research, research and devel. dept., sr. clin. research asso. corp. med. affairs Marion Labs., Inc., Kansas City, Mo., 1974; unit leader, cons. Deco Plants, Inc. Chmn. young marrieds class, local United Meth. Ch., 1974-75. Recipient Cockrell award William Woods Coll., 1974; cert. lab. animal technician. Mem. Am. Assn. Lab. Animal Sci., Drug Info. Assn., William Woods Coll. Alumnae (dir.), Soc. Centennial Fellows William Woods Coll., Am. Bus. Woman's Assn. (historian), YMCA, Dachshund Club Am., Nat. Miniature Dachshund Club, Corvette Corps Club, Beta Beta Beta, Chi Omega. Home: 6702 E 99 Terr Kansas City MO 64134 Office: 10236 Bunker Ridge Rd Kansas City MO 64137

KIRKHART, KAREN EILEEN, educator; b. Pomona, Calif., Jan. 6, 1948; d. Harry Burdell and Mabel Eileen (Reinhardt) K.; B.A., Pomana Coll., 1970; M.S.W., U. Mich., 1972, Ph.D., 1979. Community service worker Community Action Center, Adrian, Mich., 1970-71; therapist Family Service Agy. of Genessee County, Flint, Mich., 1971; therapist Family and Sch. Consultation Project, Ann Arbor, Mich., 1971-72; teaching asst. Psychology Dept., Sch. Social Work, U. Mich., 1974-77; asso. dir. evaluation curricul devel. project Inst. Labor and Indsl. Relations, U. Mich.-Wayne State U., 1976-78; asst. prof. ednl. psychology U. Tex., Austin, 1979—; mem. epidemiologic and services research com. Nat. Inst. Mental Health, 1981—; research product evaluator NSF, 1980—. Mem. adv. bd. Office of Research and Evaluation, Austin (Tex.) Ind. Sch. Dist. Mem. Am. Psychol. Assn., Assn. for Advancement of Behavior Therapy, Evaluation Network (pres. 1981), Evaluation Research Soc., Nat. Council Community Mental Health Centers, S.W. Psychol. Assn., Tex. Psychol. Assn., Am. Ednl. Research Assn., Soc. Psychol. Study of Social Issues, Nat. Orgn. Women. Home: 1703 A Summit View Austin TX 78703 Office: Dept Ednl Psychology (EDB 504) Univ Tex Austin TX 78712

KIRKLAND, BERTHA THERESA (MRS. THORNTON CROWNS KIRKLAND, JR.), engr., estimator; b. San Francisco, May 16, 1916; d. Lawrence and Theresa (Kanzler) Schmelzer; m. Thornton Crowns Kirkland, Jr., Dec. 27, 1937; (dec. July 1971); children—Kathryn Elizabeth, Francis Charles. Supr. hosp. ops. Am. Potash & Chem. Corp., Trona, Calif., 1953-54; office mgr. T.C. Kirkland, elec. contractor, 1954-56; sec.-treas., dir. T.C. Kirkland, Inc., San Bernardino, Calif., 1956-72; design and build estimator Add-M Electric, Inc., San Bernardino, 1972-82, v.p., 1974-82; estimator, engr. Corona Indsl. Electric, Inc., 1982—. Episcopalian. Club: Arrowhead Country. Home: 526 E Sonora St San Bernardino CA 92404

KIRKLAND, GELSEY, dancer; b. Bethlehem, Pa., 1953; student Sch. Am. Ballet. With N.Y.C. Ballet, 1968-74, soloist, 1969-72, prin. dancer, 1972-74; ballerina Am. Ballet Theatre, 1974—; appeared TV show The Nutcracker, 1977; created roles in ballets, including: Firebird, 1970, The Goldberg Variations, Scherzo fantastique, An Evening's Waltzes, The Leaves are Fading, Hamlet: Connotations, others. Office: care Dube Zakin Mgmt Inc 1841 Broadway New York NY 10023* *

KIRKLAND, IRIS MCWHERTER, social worker, govt. personnel ofcl.; b. East St. Louis, Ill., June 29, 1946; d. James Washington and Artie Irene McWherter; B.A., Central State U., Wilberforce, Ohio, 1966; M.S.W., St. Louis U., 1969; m. Jack A. Kirkland, Jan. 5, 1979. Sch. social worker Sch. Dist. 189, East St. Louis, Ill., 1969-70; instr. social work Grambling (La.) Coll., 1971; dir. Air Force Alcohol Rehab. Program, Scott AFB, Ill., 1975-78; position classification specialist Dept. Army, St. Louis, 1978—; cons. social work and personnel mgmt. Baptist. Contbr. articles to profl. publs. Home: 8514 Old Bonhomme Saint Louis MO 63132 Office: 4300 Goodfellow Saint Louis MO 63120

KIRKLAND, KATHLEEN, speechwriter; b. Evanston, Ill., Oct. 18, 1947; d. William Stevens and Bernice J. (Bauman) K.; student Chaffey Jr. Coll., Alta Loma, Calif., 1965-66. Asst. editor Weight Watchers mag. 21st Century Communications, N.Y.C., 1967-72; editor Tiger Beat mag., Los Angeles, 1972-80; speechwriter, asst. to Edward Asner, 1980—. Mem. Am. Film Inst., Nat. Assn. Female Execs. Baptist. Club: Hollywood (Calif.) Women's Press (treas. 1980-82). Office: 3855 Lankershim Blvd North Hollywood CA 91604

KIRKLAND, MARJORIE LOVE HAMAKER, social worker; b. Washington, Sept. 22, 1917; d. John Irvin and Ray (Parker) Hamaker; A.B., Randolph-Macon Woman's Coll., 1938; M.A. in Psychology, Syracuse U., 1939; M.S.C.W., Richmond Profl. Inst., Coll. William and Mary, 1957; m. Charles Henry Kirkland, May 11, 1940 (div. 1963); children—Archie Howard, Richard Gish, Ray Love. Asst. prof. Lynchburg (Va.) Coll., 1948-49; social worker Lynchburg Tng. Sch. and Hosp., 1951-54, chief psychiat. social service, 1954-63; dir. social work edn. mental retardation Grad. Sch. Social Work, U. Tex., 1963-65; cons. social services mentally retarded children U.S. Children's Bur., Washington, 1965-67; cons. mental retardation Rehab. Services Adminstrn., HEW, Dallas, 1967-69; social work cons., Washington, 1969-72; dep. br. chief Univ. Affiliated Facilities, 1972-75; dep. dir. Devel. Disabilities Office, Office Human Devel. Services, HEW, Washington, 1975-77, div. dir., 1978-80; regional program dir. Region IX, Dept. HHS, San Francisco, 1980-82, dir. bd. and care coordinating unit, Washington, 1982—; lectr. in field. Fellow Am. Assn. Mental Deficiency (1st v.p. 1977-78, pres. elect 1978—); mem. Nat. Assn. Social Workers, Acad. Cert. Social Workers, Phi Beta Kappa, Psi Chi. Author: Retarded Children of the Poor, 1971. Home: 521 G St SW Washington DC 20024 Office: HHH Bldg Washington DC 20201

KIRKORIAN, KATHLEEN MARIE, restaurant owner; b. Milw., Mar. 25, 1950; d. Theodore Lewis and Lorraine Margaret (Narloch) Poplawski; B.A. in Psychology, Lawrence U., Appleton, Wis., 1972; m. Isaac Krikorian, Dec. 4, 1974; children—Isaac, Natasha. Writer, copy editor Wis. newspapers, 1969-75; public relations writer Hoffman-York, Milw., 1972-73; co-owner, mgr. Cafe La Boheme, Milw., 1975—; freelance writer, 1981—. Bd. dirs. Florentine Opera Club, 1978-80. Mem. Wis. Restaurant Assn., Milw. Symphony Women's League, Milw. Press Club, Zool. Soc. Milw., Roman Catholic. Office: 319 E Mason St Milwaukee WI 53202

KIRKPATRICK, DIANE MARIE, art historian; b. Grand Rapids, Mich., June 28, 1933; d. Myron Sanford and Alice Elizabeth (McBlain) K.; B.A., Vassar Coll., 1951; M.F.A., Cranbrook Acad. Art, Bloomfield Hills, Mich., 1957; M.A., U. Mich., 1965, Ph.D., 1969. Editor, Fideler Pub. Co., Grand Rapids, 1957-58; dir. children's edn. Grand Rapids Art Mus., 1961-63; teaching fellow U. Mich., 1965-66, mem. faculty, 1972—, asso. prof. history art, 1982—; Meadows disting. vis. prof. art history So. Methodist U., 1982. Recipient Innovation in Large Group Instrn. award U. Mich., 1973-74, Faculty Devel. Teaching award Center Research Learning and Teaching, 1977; Nat. Endowment Humanities grantee, 1977-78. Mem. Coll. Art Assn. Am. Author: Eduardo Paolozzi, 1970; also TV series, exhbns.; editor cinema and photography series U. Mich. Microfilms Research Press, 1981-82. Office: Dept History Art Tappan Hall U Mich Ann Arbor MI 48109

KIRKPATRICK, JEANE DUANE JORDAN, polit. scientist; b. Duncan, Okla., Nov. 19, 1926; d. Welcher F. and Leona (Kile) Jordan; A.A., Stephens, Coll., 1946; A.B., Barnard Coll., 1948; M.A., Columbia U., 1950, Ph.D., 1967; postgrad. (French govt. fellow) U. Paris Inst. de Sci. Politique, 1952-53; L.H.D. (hon.), Mr. Vernon Coll., 1978; m. Evron M. Kirkpatrick, Feb. 20, 1955; children—Douglas Jordan, John Evron, Stuart Alan. Research analyst Dept. State, 1951-53; research assoc. George Washington U., 1954-56, Fund for Republic, 1956-58; asst. prof. polit. sci. Trinity Coll., 1962-67; assoc. prof. polit. sci. Georgetown U., Washington, 1967-73, prof., 1973—, Leavey prof. in founds. Am. freedom, 1978— (on leave); resident scholar Am. Enterprise Inst. for Pub. Policy Research, 1977— (on leave); mem. cabinet, U.S. permanent rep. to UN, 1981—; co-chmn. task force presdl. election process 20th Century Fund; cons. Am. Council Learned Socs., Dept. State, HEW, Dept. Def., intermittently 1955-72. Mem. Democratic Nat. Com., vice chmn. com. on v.p. selection 1972-74, mem. nat. comnn. party structure and presdl. nomination, 1975—; mem. credentials com. Dem. Nat. Conv., 1976; mem. internat. research council Center for Strategic and Internat. Studies, Georgetown U.; trustee Helen Dwight Reid Ednl. Found., 1972—, Robert A. Taft Inst. Govt., 1978—; mem. bd. curators Stephens Coll. Recipient Disting. Alumna award Stephens Coll., 1978; Earhart fellow, 1956-57. Mem. Internat. Polit. Sci. Assn. (exec. council), Am. Polit. Sci. Assn., So. Polit. Sci. Assn., Midwest Polit. Sci. Assn. Author: Foreign Students in the United States; A National Survey, 1966; Mass Behavior in Battle and Captivity, 1968; Leader and Vanguard in Mass Society; The Peronist Movement in Argentina, 1971; Political Woman, 1973; The Presidential Elite, 1976; Dismantling the Parties: Reflections on Party Reform and Party Decomposition, 1978; editor, contbr.: Elections USA, 1956; Strategy of Deception, 1963; The New Class, 1978; The New American Political System, 1978; contbr. articles to Commentary, New Republic, Brit. Jour. Polit. Sci., Commonsense, Washington Quar., Publius, others. Office: 799 UN Plaza New York NY 10017 *

KIRKPATRICK, SUE WILSON, educator; b. Bellefontaine, Ohio, Dec. 5, 1944; d. W. Fremont and Anna Belle (Sidders) Wilson; B.Sc., Ohio State U., 1966, M.Sc., 1969, Ph.D., 1971. Tchr. family living and home econs. Olentangy High Sch., Delaware, Ohio, 1966-68; acting dir. Child Care pilot program Ohio State U., 1972; asst. prof. psychology and developmental learning U. Ala., 1972-79, asso. prof. 1979—. Mem. adv. bd. Parent-Child Services of Huntsville-Madison County Mental Health Center, 1977-80; mem. adv. and screening bd. Progress Pl., Huntsville Al; judge North Ala. Regional Sci. Fair. Danforth Found. asso. Mem. Am. Psychol. Assn., Groves Conf. on Marriage and the Family, Jean Piaget Soc., Soc. Research in Child Devel., Southeastern Psychol. Assn., Midwestern Psychol. Assn., Phi Upsilon Omicron, Omicron Nu, Alpha Lambda Delta. Democrat. Episcopalian. Contbr. to profl. jours. Office: U Ala Huntsville AL 35899

KIRKSEY, JEAN THERESA, advt., sales promotion co. exec.; b. Springfield, Mass., Nov. 19, 1926; d. James and Hilma (Malmgren) McCreanor; B.A., Trinity Coll., Hartford, Conn., 1946; m. Amos Harold, Nov. 12, 1949. Cosmetic cons. Albert Steiger Co., Springfield, 1947-49; regional sales mgr. Frances Denney Co., Phila., 1956-72, Revlon Co., N.Y.C., 1972-73; founder, exec. v.p. McKnight-Kirksey Inc., N.Y.C., 1973—; v.p. creative mktg. Calvin Klein Cosmetic Corp., 1980—. Mem. Fragrance Found., Foragers of Am., Cosmetic, Toiletries and Fragrance Assn., Cosmetic Career Women, Bus. and Profl. Women. Republican. Roman Catholic. Home: 167 Mountain Rd Ridgefield CT 06877 Office: 39th Floor 9 W 57th St New York NY 10019

KIRKWOOD, EL WANDA JO, ins. agt.; b. Midland, Tex., July 27, 1943; d. Louis Edwin and Lenora Maudine (Richters) Shields; student U. Ky.; m. Daniel Edward Kirkwood, Aug. 8, 1959; children—Kimberly Jo, Dana Lenora, Daniel Edwin. Sec., office mgr. State Farm Ins., Madisonville, Ky., 1965-68; agt. Allstate Ins., Madisonville, 1976—. Hon. Ky. col. Mem. Nat. Assn. Life Underwriters (pres.), Ky. Assn. Life Underwriters (bd. dirs. region 5), Nat. Fedn. Bus. and Profl. Women's Clubs, Working Women Am., Nat. Assn. Women's Club Am., Women's Conf. Life Underwriters, Internat. Platform Assn. Democrat. Home: 975 Chickasaw Dr Madisonville KY 42431 Office: Allstate Insurance Madison Sq Shopping Center Madisonville KY 42431

KIRPALANI, LAKSHMI ASSUDOMAL, educator; b. Hydersbad Sindh, Pakistan, Aug. 24, 1920; came to U.S., 1962, naturalized, 1972; d. Assudomal Shewakram and Hari Assudomal (Advani) K.; diploma Montessori Internat., 1946; B.A. with honors, U. Bombay, 1962; M.A., Iowa U. and Seton Hall U., 1966, cert. supr. and prin., 1976. Founder, headmistress New India Sch., 1943-47; founder Pawai Refugee Camp Sch. for Refugees, Bombay, India, 1947; head mistress Garrison Sch., Bombay, 1948-62; dir. Montessori Sch., Iowa City, 1962-64; founder Montessori Sch., Newark, 1964-65; founder. Montessori Center of N.J., 1966, now gen. dir.; internat. examiner Montessori Tchr. Tng. Centers; cons. in field. Mem. Assn. Supervision and Curriculum Devel., N.J. Edn. Assn., Nat. Assn. North Am. Montessori Tchr. Assn., Assn. Montessori Internat., Nat. Council Montessori Tchr. Trainers. Republican. Hindu-Unitarian. Contbr. in field. Home and Office: 79 Midland Ave Montclair NJ 07042

KIRSCHENBAUM, PAULENNE ROESKE, energy conservation co. exec.; b. Port Chester, N.Y., June 5, 1936; d. Paul John and Gertrude Frieda (Haefele) Roeske; A.A.S., Fashion Inst. Tech., 1956; student N.Y. Inst. Fin., 1960-61; m. J. Michael Kirschenbaum, May 17, 1968; children—Lisa L., Nina Sue, Jill M. Stockbroker Bache & Co., N.Y.C., 1964-67; stockbroker, br. mgr., gen. partner Bruns-Nordeman, N.Y.C., 1967-71; stockbroker, investment banker Adams & Peck, N.Y.C., 1972-73; registered investment adviser, Washington, 1974—; pres. Energystics, Inc., Bernardsville, N.J., 1975—. Bd. dirs. Westmont Sch., Chester, N.J., 1977-78. Mem. Women's Stockbrokers Assn. (dir. 1968-69), Internat. Platform Assn. Club: Roxiticus Country (Mendham, N.J.). Home: Bernardsville NJ 07924 Office: 80 Chapin Rd Bernardsville NJ 07924

KIRSCHSTEIN, RUTH LILLIAN, physician; b. Bklyn., Oct. 12, 1926; d. Julius and Elizabeth (Berm) K.; A.B. magna cum laude, L.I.U., 1947; M.D., Tulane U., 1951; m. Alan S. Rabson, June 11, 1950; 1 son, Arnold B. Intern, Kings County Hosp., Bklyn., 1951-52; resident in pathology VA Hosp., Atlanta, 1952, Providence Hosp., Detroit, 1952-54; Nat. Heart Inst. fellow, instr. Tulane U. Sch. Medicine, New Orleans, 1954-55; resident Clin. Center NIH, 1956, physician, 1960-72, 74—, chmn. grants peer rev. study team, 1975-76, dir. Nat. Inst. Gen. Med. Scis., 1974—; dep. asso. commnr. sci. FDA, 1973-74; mem. expert group internat. requirements for biol. substances WHO; cons. in field. Recipient Superior Service award HEW, 1971, USPHS, 1978; Presdl. Meritorious Exec. Rank award, 1980. Mem. Am. Assn. Immunologists, Am. Assn. Pathologists, Am. Soc. Microbiology. Author papers in field. Office: Bldg 31 Room 4A 52 NIH Bethesda MD 20205

KIRSHNER, JANET BERGER, public relations exec.; b. N.Y.C., Mar. 24, 1933; d. Elmer Steil and Elsie (Feinberg) Berger; student U. Calif.-Berkeley, 1951-53; B.S., UCLA, 1956; m. Lester Kirshner, Sept. 8, 1957; children: Elizabeth, Jonathan. Partner, H/K Communications, N.Y.C., 1974-78, pres., owner, 1981—; dir. public relations Branielle Assos., N.Y.C., 1978-79, Delphi Commodities, N.Y.C., 1979-80; v.p. public relations and adminstrn. Fahy Internat. Trading Corp., N.Y.C., 1980-81. Mem. Public Relations Soc. Am. Democrat. Jewish. Office: 500 Fifth Ave New York NY 10110

KIRSTEN, DOROTHY, opera singer; b. Montclair, N.J., July 6, 1919; d. George W. and Margaret (Beggs) Kirsten; mus. tng. U.S., France and Italy; Mus.D., Ithaca Coll.; D.F.A., Santa Clara U.; m. John D. French, July 18, 1955. Debut as Musetta in La Boheme, Chgo. Opera Co., Nov. 1940; debut Met. Opera Co., Dec., 1945; has sung roles of Violetta, Cho Cho San, Juliet, Marguerite, Manon Lescaut, Nedda, Micaela, Louise, Fiora, Tosa, Mimi, Massanet Manon, Cressida, Girl of Golden West, and many operettas; also appeared films The Great Caruso, Mr. Music. Episcopalian. Address: care Met Opera Lincoln Center New York NY 10023

KIRWAN, RHONDA SUZANNE, veterinarian; b. Lawrence, Kans., May 21, 1956; d. James Leonard and Patricia Anne (Myers) K.; D.V.M., Iowa State U., 1980. Veterinarian, Boulder Terrace Animal Hosp., 1980-81, Flossmoore Animal Hosp., 1981-82, Adair Gardens Pet Hosp., Belleville, Ill., 1982—. Mem. AVMA, Ill. Vet. Med. Assn., St. Louis Vet. Med. Assn. Democrat. Roman Catholic. Home: 250 Rayburn Dr Apt 10 Belleville IL 62223 Office: 1808 North Belt W Belleville IL 62223

KIRZ, STEPHANIE AGER, advt., public relations agy. exec.; b. Seattle, Apr. 28, 1946; d. Robert Lee and Jean (Purrington) Ager; B.A. in Art, U. Wash., 1969; m. Howard Lutz Kirz, Mar. 9, 1978. Promotion and public relations dir. Sta. KOL-AM & FM, Seattle, 1969-73, Channel 13 TV, Seattle, 1973-74; project dir. Ilium Advt., Seattle, 1974-75; prin. The Stephanie Ager Agy., Seattle, 1975—; syndicated daily radio show The Zodiac Lady. Pres., Wash. Panhellenic, 1967-68. Recipient Totem award Public Relations Soc. Am., 1980. Mem. Women in Communications (v.p. fin. 1981), Public Relations Soc. Am., Seattle C. of C., Women and Bus. 1980, Am. Fedn. Radio and TV Announcers, Kappa Kappa Gamma. Club: Women's University. Home: 705 McGilvra Blvd East Seattle WA 98112 Office: 100 S King St Suite 270 Seattle WA 98104

KISH, CARLA E., legis. asst.; b. Ann Arbor, Mich.; d. Leslie and Rhea (Kuleske) Kish; B.A., U. Mich., 1970, M.Sc., 1972; M.A., London Sch. Econs., Eng., 1974. Cons., Subcom. on Energy and Environment, Ho. Com. on Interior and Insular Affairs, 1976-80; Western rep. Western Orgn. Resource Councils, 1980; legis. asst. to Sen. Levin of Mich., 1980—. Office: Room 140 Russell Senate Office Bldg Washington DC 20510

KISH, PAULINE FISHER, nurse; b. Manchester, Eng., Feb. 13, 1942; came to U.S., 1970; d. Joseph and Mary Jane Elizabeth (Nicholson) Fisher; diploma Withington Hosp. Sch. Nursing, Manchester, 1966. Staff nurse operating rooms Diagnostic Hosp., Houston, 1971-73; supr. operating rooms and central supply Rosewood Hosp., Houston, 1973-74; asst. dir. operating rooms Park Plaza Hosp., Houston, 1974-76; dir. operating rooms Tulane U Med. Center Hosp., New Orleans, 1976-77; dir. surg. services Cape Coral (Fla.) Hosp., 1977—; sec., chmn.-elect operating room adv. com. Hosp. Shared Purchasing Program Fla. Sec., S. Pointe Condominium Assn. Recipient Bronze medal Withington Hosp. Sch. Nursing, 1965. Mem. Assn. Operating Room Nurses (nominating com. chpt.), Internat. Assn. Hosp. Central Service Mgmt., Assn. Advancement of Med. Instrumentation, Nat. Assn. Female Execs. Nat. Assn. Theatre Nurses (Eng.). Home: 6300 S Point #140 Fort Myers FL 33907 Office: 636 Del Prado Cape Coral FL 33904

KISHEL, PATRICIA GUNTER, mgmt. cons.; b. Los Angeles, Sept. 4, 1948; d. John Exum and Pauline Beatrice (Smith) Gunter; B.A., UCLA, 1970, M.F.A., 1972; M.B.A., Calif. State U., Long Beach, 1978; m. Gregory Francis Kishel, July 1, 1977. Script writer Salenger Ednl. Media, Santa Monica, Calif., 1972-79; traffic/pub. service coordinator Theta Cable TV, Santa Monica, 1973-74; adminstr. C.B.S., Inc., Los Angeles, 1974-78; partner K&K Enterprises, Marina del Rey, Calif., 1978—; instr. Calif. State U., Long Beach, 1978-81, Long Beach City Coll., 1979—, Brooks Coll., 1978—. Mem. Authors Guild, Womens Nat. Book Assn., Book Publicists Assn. So. Calif., Network Group, AAUW. Author: (with G.F. Kishel) How to Start, Run and Stay in Business, 1981; Student Survival Guide, 1979. Address: 4572 Via Marina Suite 309 Marina del Rey CA 90291

KISTER, JOAN CATHERINE, health planning cons.; b. Cadet, Mo., Feb. 11, 1929; d. Raphael George and Margaret Ann K.; diploma in nursing St. Elizabeth Hosp., Brighton, Mass., 1955; cert. midwifery Glen Gray Hosp., Lady Frere, South Africa, 1959; B.S. summa cum laude in Nursing, St. Louis U., 1970; M.S. in Health Service Adminstrn., SUNY, Stony Brook, 1975. Staff nurse Kennedy Meml. Hosp., Brighton, 1955-56, dir. nursing, 1956-57; matron St. Patrick's Hosp., Bizana, South Africa, 1958, Assunta Hosp. Petaling Jaya, Malaysia, 1960-65; staff nurse Gen. Hosp., Larenco Marques, Mozambique, 1958, L'Hôpital d'Enfants, St. Denis Ile de la Reunion, 1959-60; nursing supr. St. Francis Hosp., Roslyn, N.Y., 1967-68, project coordinator for hosp. constrn., 1970-73, chief exec. officer, 1973-78; health planning cons., pres. Heart Internat. Found., Inc., Queens, N.Y., 1978—; cons. for rehab. rural health facilities in Uganda; mem. adv. council on health to N.Y. State Senator Tarky Lombardi, 1976-81. Mem. legis. adv. council to Congressman Lester Wolff, 1976-79. Named Woman of Yr. in Sci., Nassau Press Assn., 1976, Woman of Yr., North Shore Bus. and Profl. Women's Club, 1977; recipient Heart medal St. Francis Hosp., 1977. Mem. Am. Acad. Med. Adminstrs. (regional v.p. 1978), Am. Public Health Assn. (exec. com. L.I. chpt. 1976-79), Am. Heart Assn. Roman Catholic. Office: PO Box 424 Little Neck NY 11363

KISTER, SUZON ELIZABETH, librarian; b. Danville, Pa., Jan. 20, 1937; d. Albert Bergstresser and Florence Louise (Beck) Ott; A.B., Wilson Coll., 1958; S.M., Simmons Coll., 1963, A.M., 1968; m. Kenneth F. Kister, Mar. 27, 1959 (div. 1975). Cataloguer, Smith Meml. Library, Chautauqua, N.Y., 1958-60; reference librarian, cataloguer Brookline (Mass.) Public Library, 1961-64; intern Nottingham and Nottinghamshire (Eng.) library systems, 1964-65; librarian Schlesinger Library on History of Women in Am., Radcliffe Coll., Harvard U., Cambridge, Mass., 1966-67; instr. English, Bryant & Stratton Sch., Boston, 1968-69; head librarian Chamberlayne Jr. Coll., Boston, 1969-70; reference librarian Agrl. and Tech. Coll., SUNY Canton, 1970-75, adminstrv. librarian, 1975-76; head librarian Jefferson Community Coll., Watertown, N.Y., 1976—; participant Inst. on Am. Indian in Higher Edn., St. Lawrence U., Canton, 1972; mem. chancellor's adv. com. on awards for excellence in librarianship SUNY, 1976-79. Trustee, North Country Reference and Research Resources Council, Canton, 1978—; bd. dirs. Family Counseling Service Jefferson County, Inc., 1979—; mem. Jefferson County Arts Council, 1979—. Mem. ACLU, NOW, N.Y. Library Assn., Simmons Coll. Sch. Library Sci. Alumni Assn. (founder, editor The Simmons Librarian 1968-70), Wilson Coll. Club of Greater Boston (pres. 1968-70). Democrat. Home: 522 Washington St Watertown NY 13601 Office: Melvil Dewey Library Jefferson Community Coll Outer Coffeen St Watertown NY 13601

KITAGAWA, EVELYN M., sociologist; b. Hanford, Calif., July 13, 1920; d. Frank F. and Erma Rose; B.A. with highest honors in Math., U. Calif., Berkeley, 1941; Ph.D. in Sociology, U. Chgo., 1951; m. Joseph M. Kitagawa, July 22, 1946; 1 dau., Anne Rose. Statistician, War Relocation Authority, Washington, 1942-46; research asso. to prof. sociology U. Chgo., 1951—, dir. Population Research Center, 1977—; bd. trustees Nat. Opinion Research Center, 1973—; mem. biometry and epidemiology contract rev. com. Nat. Cancer Inst., 1977—. HEW grantee, 1978—. Fellow Am. Statis. Assn. (dir. 1972-75); mem. Population Assn. Am. (pres. 1977), Am. Sociol. Soc., Internat. Union Sci. Study of Population, Sociol. Research Assn. (pres. 1976-77). Author: Differential Mortality in the United States, 1973; Suburbanization of Manufacturing Activity Within Metropolitan Areas, 1955; contbr. articles to profl. jours., chpts. to books. Office: Population Research Center University of Chicago 1126 E 59th St Chicago IL 60637

KITCH, DIANA LEBOSQUET, therapist; b. Wichita, Kans., July 1, 1941; d. John Rude and Florence Edith (Bergstresser) LeBosquet; B.A. in Philosophy and Religion, Southwestern Coll., 1963; M.A. in Psychology, Wichita State U., 1979; m. Paul Richard Kitch, Apr. 1, 1974; children—Mary Suzanne, William Russell Parlette. Staff counselor Wichita State U. Counseling Center, 1976—; cons. to chaplain VA Hosp., Wichita, 1980-81, psychology technician, 1979-80; cons. Developmental Vision Clinic, Wichita; vol. Suicide and Crisis Center, Honolulu, 1971-72. Acting chairperson Wichita Hospice, Inc., 1981-82. Mem. Am. Psychol. Assn., Nat. Hospice Orgn., N. Am. Soc. Adlerian Psychology. Clubs: Wichita Country, Wichita. Contbr. articles to profl. jours. and books. Home: 8316 E Central Ave Wichita KS 67206 Office: PO Box 91 Wichita State U Counseling Center Wichita KS 67208

KITCHELL, SHIRLEY BOUVY, food supplements co. exec.; b. Vincennes, Ind., Dec. 5, 1936; d. James Earl and Elizabeth Cecilia Carie) Bouvy; student parochial schs.; m. Robert Doyle Kitchell, June 20, 1959; children—Robert Douglas, Steven Paul. Stenographer, Western & So. Life Ins. Co., Vincennes, 1954-59, City Electric System, Key West, Fla., 1959-60, Wallace Process Piping Co., Norfolk, Va., 1960-61; pres. SKI Enterprises, Virginia Beach, Va., 1976—; cons. Fenton & Assos., 1979—. Organist, St. Johns Catholic Ch., Vincennes, 1948-59, Immaculate Conception Chapel, Norfolk Naval Air Sta., 1968-78. Mem. Assn. Female Execs. Home: 5404 Coventry Circle Virginia Beach VA 23462

KITCHO, CATHERINE ANN, geologist; b. Saginaw, Mich., Dec. 31, 1949; d. Peter and Mildred Marylin (Cepak) K.; B.S. in Geology, Mich. State U., 1970; postgrad. U. So. Calif., 1971-74. Geologist, Bechtel Inc., San Francisco and Norwalk, Calif., 1972-78; sr. staff geologist Woodward Clyde Cons., San Francisco, 1978-79, project geologist, 1980—; chmn. industry adv. panel Calif. Remote Sensing Task Force, 1979—. Mem. Am. Soc. Photogrammetry, Geol. Soc. Am., Assn. Engring.

Geologists, Assn. Women Geoscientists (pres. 1979). Contbr. articles to profl. jours. Specialist in remote sensing applications geology. Home: PO Box 584 Moss Beach CA 94038 Office: Woodward Clyde Cons 3 Embarcadero Center Suite 700 San Francisco CA 94111

KITE, VIVIAN GALLIHER, real estate sales rep.; b. Washington County, Va., Jan. 17, 1929; d. William Robinson and Blanche Campbell (Saunders) Galliher; cert. Va. Highlands Community Coll., 1973-77; m. George L. Kite, May 13, 1974; children by previous marriage—Carl Robinson Maiden, Donna Maiden, Ann Maiden. Sec., Farmers Mut. Fire Ins. Co., 1968-74; dep. commr. of revenue Washington County, Va., 1974-78; realtor Charles J. Lowry's Gallery of Homes, Bristol, Va., 1978—. Pres., Washington County Democratic Club, 1976-78, 9th Dist. Dem. Women, 1978-80. Mem. Bristol Va.-Tenn. Bd. Realtors, Washington County C. of C. Baptist. Club: Eastern Star (worthy matron 1972-73). Home: 104 Johnson Dr Abingdon VA 24210 Office: 3285 Lee Hwy Bristol VA 24201

KITT, EARTHA MAE, actress, singer; b. North, S.C., Jan. 26 1928; d. John and Anna Kitt; grad. high sch.; m. William McDonald, June 1960 (div.); 1 dau. Soloist with Katherine Dunham Dance Group, 1948; night club singer, 1949—, appearing in France, Turkey, Greece, Egypt, N.Y.C., Hollywood, Las Vegas, London, Stockholm; stage appearances in Dr. Faustus, Paris, 1951, New Faces of 1952, N.Y.C., Mrs. Patterson, N.Y.C., 1954, Shinbone Alley, N.Y.C., 1957, Timbuktu, 1978; motion pictures include New Faces, 1953, Accused, 1957, Anna Lucasta, 1958, Mark of the Hawk, 1958, St. Louis Blues, 1957, Saint of Devil's Island, 1961, Synanon, 1965, Up the Chastity Belt, 1971, also 2 French films; rec. artist for RCA Victor; numerous television appearances. Named Woman of Year, Nat. Assn. Negro Musicians, 1968. Author: Thursday's Child, 1956; A Tart is Not a Sweet: Alone With Me, 1976. Address: care Norby Walters Assos 1290 Ave of Americas Suite 264 New York NY 10019 *

KITTNER, SABRA CORBIN, media specialist; b. Federalsburg, Md., Nov. 1, 1922; d. George Edwin and Hilda Villars (Corbin) MacDorman; A.B., Western Md. Coll., 1944, M.Ed., 1966; postgrad. Cath. U., Johns Hopkins U.; m. Joseph Raymond Kittner, June 24, 1949 (div. Sept. 1965); children—Sabra Corbin, Jo Corbin. Tchr., Kenwood High Sch., 1944-49, Stemmers Run Jr. High Sch., 1949-50, Franklin High Sch., 1950-51; librarian North Carrol High Sch., 1957-66; supr. media services Carroll County, Md., 1966—, also asso. prof. Western Md. Coll., 1968—. Mem. Assn. Ednl. Communication and Tech., Md. Ednl. Media Orgn., Nat. Assn. Suprs. and Prins. Methodist. Home: 94 Willis St Westminster MD 21157 Office: 55 Court St Westminster MD 21157

KITTO, KATHLEEN LEONE, metall. engr.; b. Butte, Mont., Oct. 7, 1956; d. Howard Stanley and Elizabeth Mary (Murphy) K.; A.S., Mont. Coll. Mineral Sci. and Tech., 1976, B.S., 1978, M.S., 1981. Student engr. Hanna Mining Co., 1977; research engr. Mont. Coll. Mineral Sci. and Tech., Butte, 1978-81; cons. metall. engr. Mineral Research Center, Butte, 1981—; instr. dept. metallurgy Mont. Coll. Mineral Sci. and Tech., Butte, 1981—, also mem. human resources student experience com. Vol. judge high sch. sci. fair, Westinghouse Talent Search, 1974. Newmont scholar, 1974-78, Anaconda Sci. Fair scholar, 1972-74. Mem. Am. Soc. Metals, Am. Ceramic Soc., AIME, Alpha Sigma Mu, Mu Beta Pi. Republican. Roman Catholic. Contbr. articles to profl. jours. Home: 643 S Main St Butte MT 59701 Office: Mont Coll Mineral Sci and Tech 106 Metallurgy Bldg West Park St Butte MT 59701

KITTRELL, SARA JANE BAKER, educator; b. Paris, Tex., June 1, 1941; d. William Thomas and Ola Mae (Richetts) Milam; B.A., E. Central State U., 1961; M.S., Pepperdine U., 1982; m. Richard R. Baker, Aug. 18, 1973; m. 2d, Robert C. Kittrell, Apr. 4, 1982. Tchr. public schs., Okla., 1961-63, Kans., 1963-65; tchr. Fairfield (Calif.) Elem. Sch., 1965-66, Stockton (Calif.) Elem. Sch., 1966-69, Maraga Ln. Elem. Sch., Santa Ana, Calif., 1969—. Conceptual orginator Exploratory Learning Center, Santa Ana, 1979, 1st chmn., 1979-80, fund raiser, curriculum adv., 1981-82. Recipient Tchr. of Yr. award Santa Ana, 1973-75. Mem. Santa Ana Edn. Assn. (v.p. 1971, pres. 1972-73, negotiations rep. 1973-74), Calif. Tchrs. Assn. (state council rep. 1972-73), NEA (del. 1973), Phi Delta Kappa. Club: Santa Ana Jr. Women's. Photography exhbn. Newport Beach Sch., 1978-79; contbr. poems to various publs. Home: 2 Amberwood St Irvine CA 92714 Office: 3600 S Raitt St Santa Ana CA 92704

KITZINGER, GRACE MARIAN LIVENGOOD, editor; b. Hillsdale, N.J., Dec. 15, 1927; d. William Winfred and Dorothy Grace (Edmed) Livengood; B.A. cum laude, Bucknell U., 1949. Free-lance writer, 1949-50; with Am. Cyanamid Co., Wayne, N.J., 1951—, mgr. tech. publs. internat. agrl. products, 1968—. Recipient ann. award for excellence in tech. pub. N.Y. chpt. Soc. Tech. Writers and Editor, 1960, certificate of spl. merit Printing Industries Met. N.Y., 1962, 63, award of merit N.Y. chpt. Soc. Tech. Communication, 1972, hon. mention, 1973, Distinguished Publs. award, 1977, Achievement award, 1978, Internat. Publs. Achievement award, 1978. Mem. Am. Med. Writers Assn., Soc. Tech. Communication, Soc. Scholarly Publs., Nat., N.J. Audubon socs., Sierra Club, Phi Beta Kappa, Phi Sigma, Alpha Lambda Delta. Clubs: Ahdeek, Tenafly Tennis. Home: 471 Haworth Ave Haworth NJ 07641 Office: Am Cyanamid Co Wayne NJ 07470

KIVETT, VIRA RODGERS, researcher, educator; b. Augusta, Ga., May 18, 1933; d. James Hamilton and Mary Katherine (Rogers) Rodgers; student High Point Coll., 1951-52; B.S. in Home Econs., Woman's Coll. of U. N.C., 1955; M.S. in Home Econs., U. N.C., Greensboro, 1960, Ph.D., 1976; Gen. Foods fellow Med. Sch., Duke U., 1974-75; m. Allen Edward Kivett, Aug. 17, 1957; children—Mary Martitia, Allen Wyke. Tchr. vocat. home econs., Southern Pines, N.C., 1955-57; dietitian U. N.C., Greensboro, 1957-60, research instr. home econs., 1960-64, 68-76, asst. prof. child devel. and family relations, 1976-81, asso. prof., 1981—, grad. faculty, 1976—, developer, instr. workshops, dept. continuing edn., 1977—; asst. prof. Agrl. Research Service, N.C. State U., Raleigh, 1976—, vis. prof. social gerontology, summer 1973; developer, instr. inservice workshops for nursing home personnel, 1978—; cons. legis. com. div. of aging State Dept. Human Resources, Raleigh, 1976-77, Area Agy. on Aging, Piedmont Triad Council Govts., Greensboro, 1975-78, state resource person in social gerontology Duke Med. Sch., 1975—, Mountain Area Health Edn. Center, Asheville, 1980—, Greensboro Area Health Edn. Center, 1980—, N.C. Agrl. Extension Service, 1971—, faculty home econs. Helwan U., Cairo, Egypt, 1979; home econs. researcher, 1980—; del. 1981 White House Conf. on Aging. Bd. dirs. Share-a-Home of Guilford County, 1978—, chmn., 1979-80; home county rep. to Regional Aging Advisory Bd. Piedmont Triad Council of Govts., 1976-79, vice chmn., 1977-78; rep. Guilford County Coordinating Council on Aging, 1975-76; mem.-at-large bd. dirs. Greensboro Council on Aging, 1975-76; mem. Gov.'s steering com. White House Conf. on Aging, 1980; ad hoc com. Greensboro Family Life Council; bd. dirs. United Meth. Housing, Inc., 1975-79; mem. Greensboro Dist. Council Ministries of United Meth. Ch., 1976-78, exec. bd., 1972-78; task force religious edn. needs of exceptional, United Meth. Ch., 1977-79, exec. bd., 1977-78; spl. projects com. Mendenhall Jr. High Sch. PTA, 1977-78; counselling tchr. Nursery II West Market St. United Meth. Ch., 1969—. Recipient service award Piedmont Triad Council Govts., 1978; grantee HEW, 1975, CSRS, 1974-78, U. N.C., 1975, Title IV, 1975, USDA, 1979—. Mem. Am. Home Econs. Assn. (rep. to Nat. Council on Aging 1978—, mem. com. on aging 1977-78), N.C. Home Econs. Assn. (com. on aging 1976-78, chmn. coll. and univ. sect. 1977-79, exec. bd. 1977-78), So. Gerontol. Assn. (charter), Internat. Center Social Gerontology, Gerontol. Soc., Inst. Nutrition U. N.C., Nat. Council Aging, Internat. Fedn. Aging, Carolina Population Center (Chapel Hill), U. N.C. Greensboro Alumni Assn., U. N.C. Greensboro Home Econs. Alumni Assn., Omicron Nu. Clubs: Pinetop Tennis. Jefferson Country, Pilot Country. Author: Aging: A Home Economics Guide to Independent Living, 1980; Implications of a Stationery Population, 1975; co-author: Leisure and the Third Age, 1972; contbr. writings on aging to publs., papers to profl. confs.; traveler Yugoslavia, Italy, Switzerland, Greece, Egypt, Israel. Home: 1316 Clover Ln Greensboro NC 27410 Office: 400 Stone Bldg University NC Greensboro NC 27412

KIYABU, ELIZABETH LOUISE, govt. ofcl.; b. Junction City, Kans., Nov. 20, 1942; d. John Joseph and Elizabeth Louise (McManus) Yourick; student Woburn Sch. Bus., 1961, Andover Sch. Bus., 1967, Middlesex Community Coll.; m. Rodney T. Kiyabu, Oct. 20, 1967; children—Robin Albert, Cary Rickey. Procurement clk. U.S. Army Missile Command, Andover, Mass., 1965-68; export documentation clk. hdqrs. office Raytheon Co., Lexington, Mass., 1968-69; sec. to chief acct. Baird Atomic, Inc., Bedford, Mass., 1969-70; self-employed, 1970-72; clk.-stenographer Def. Civil Preparedness Agy., Maynard, Mass., 1972-77, regional field specialist, 1977-78; budget and fiscal asst. Region 1, Fed. Emergency Mgmt. Agy., Maynard, 1979-80, support coordination asst., Boston, 1980—; regional coordinator U.S. Savs. Bond Drive, 1976-78; rec. sec. Boston Fed. Exec. Bd. Women's Opportunity Com., 1977-78; mgr. Fed. Women's Program, 1977-78. Mem. Nat. Assn. Female Execs., Federally Employed Women, Bus. and Profl. Women's Club. Home: 111 Taylor St PO Box 2307 Harwood Station Littleton MA 01460 Office: Fed Emergency Mgmt Agy Region 1 John McCormack Post Office and Courthouse Bldg Boston MA 02109

KIZMAN, SUSAN LEE, ice cream franchising co. exec.; b. Chgo., Apr. 27, 1947; d. William F. and Violet A. (Brandenburg) Herod; student Wright Coll., 1965-66, Triton Coll., 1980, 82; children—Michael, Wendy. Sec. to v.p. mktg. Franchisng Co., Chgo., 1973-75, adminstrv. asst., 1975-77, dir. adminstrv. services, 1977-79, v.p., 1979—. Mem. Women in Mgmt., Nat. Assn. Female Execs. Home: 8507 W Gregory St Chicago IL 60656 Office: 4010 W Belden St Chicago IL 60639

KLAGES, CONSTANCE WARNER, mgmt. cons. exec.; b. N.Y.C., May 29, 1934; d. Ernest Frederick and Elsie (Roedler) Klages; B.A., Dickinson Coll., 1956; certificate personnel mgmt. and indsl. relations N.Y. U., 1959; m. R. James Lotz, Jr., Apr. 26, 1975. Asst. to personnel dir., personnel asst. Inst. Internat. Edn., N.Y.C., 1956-62; salary analyst, employment supr. Remington Rand div. Sperry Rand Corp., Univac Div., N.Y.C., 1962-65; research and survey mgr. Commerce and Industry Assn. N.Y., N.Y.C., 1965-66; asso. and research mgr. Battalia, Lotz, & Assos., Inc., N.Y.C., 1966-72, v.p., 1972-75; v.p., treas. Internat. Mgmt. Advisors, Inc., N.Y.C., 1975-77, exec. v.p., 1977—, also dir. Vol., Elmhurst (N.Y.) Gen. Hosp., 1957-62; bd. advisers Dickinson Coll., 1980—; membership com. Sutton Area Community. Mem. N.Y. Personnel Mgmt. Assn., Nat. Assn. Corporate and Profl. Recruiters (charter), Dickinson Coll. Alumni Council, Phi Mu (pres. N.Y.C. alumni chpt. 1962-63). Presbyterian. Office: 767 3d Ave New York NY 10017

KLAGSBRUNN, ELIZABETH RAMSEY (MRS. HANS A. KLAGSBRUNN), physician, placentologist; b. N.Y.C., Feb. 17, 1906; d. Charles Cyrus and Grace (Keys) Ramsey; grad. Bishop's Sch., LaJolla, Calif.; B.A., Mills Coll., 1928; fellow Inst. Internat. Edn., Hamburg, Germany, 1928-29; M.D., Yale U., 1932; D.Sc., Med. Coll. Pa., 1965; m. Hans Alexander Klagsbrunn, Jan. 27, 1934. Intern, asst. resident New Haven Hosp., 1932-34; asst. pathology Yale U., 1933-34; asso. pathology George Washington U., 1934-41, professorial lectr., 1941-55; asst. chief Office Med. Info., NRC, 1942-45; guest investigator dept. embryology Carnegie Inst., Washington, 1934-51, research asso. and pathologist, 1951-63, staff mem. placentalogy, pathology, 1963-71, research asso., 1976—; Mamie A. Jessup vis. prof. Ob-Gyn, U. Va. Sch. Medicine, 1972-76; Bartholomew Mosse Meml. lectr. Rotunda Hosp., Dublin, Ireland, 1970; professorial lectr. Georgetown U. Sch. Medicine. Bd. dirs. Nat. Symphony Orch., 1949—, 2d v.p., 1952-55, mem. exec. com., 1955-64, 67-68, 81—, chmn., 1955-61; trustee Cathedral Choral Soc., 1967-81. Recipient Alumna of Year citation Bishop's Sch., 1960, Lewis prize Am. Philos. Soc., 1970, diplome d'Honneur, Federation Internationale de Gynecologie Infantile et Juvenile, 1972. Hon. fellow Chgo. Gynec. Soc.; mem. Audubon Naturalist Soc. Central Atlantic States (dir. 1961-64), Am. Assn. Anatomists (exec. com. 1963-66, v.p. 1974-76), Am. Coll. Obstetricians and Gynecologists (hon. asso., recipient disting. service award 1976), Am. Gynecol. Soc. (hon.), Perinatal Research Soc. (charter), Soc. Gynecologic Investigation (hon.), AAAS, Acad. Med. Scis. (Cordoba, Argentina) (acad. fgn. corr.), Phi Beta Kappa, Sigma Xi. Episcopalian. Club: City Tavern. Author: The Placenta of Laboratory Animals and Man, 1975; (with Martin W. Donner) Placental Vasculature and Circulation, 1980; contbr. to profl. jours. Home: 3420 Q St NW Washington DC 20007 also Salem Farm Route 1 Box 157 Purcellville VA 22132

KLAICH, MICHELE ANN, steel co. communications exec.; b. Ely, Nev., Feb. 18, 1952; d. George Wayne and Jacqueline Avis (Shaver) K.; A.B. with distinction (Max C. Fleischmann Found. scholar), Stanford U., 1974. Claims rep. Social Security Adminstrn., San Francisco, 1974-76; account exec. Orsborn Group Public Relations, San Francisco, 1977-78; staff writer Newsmaking Internat., Inc., Santa Monica, 1978-79; publs. editor Kaiser Steel Corp., Oakland, Calif., 1979-81; public affairs rep. West Coast dist. U.S. Steel Corp., San Francisco, 1981—. Mem. public relations steering com. Big Bros. San Francisco; mem. Bay Area Pub. Affairs Council. Mem. Public Relations Soc. Am., Assn. Iron and Steel Engrs., Internat. Assn. Bus. Communicators, Contbns. Roundtable, Stanford U. Alumni Assn. Columnist Air Calif. mag., 1979. Office: 120 Montgomery St San Francisco CA 94106

KLAJBOR, DOROTHEA M., lawyer, state govt. ofcl.; b. Dunkirk, N.Y., Dec. 2, 1915; d. Joseph M., Sr., and Susan R. (Schrantz) K.; student George Washington U., 1949-52; J.D., Am. U., Washington, 1956. Admitted to D.C. bar, 1957; successively legal asst., legis. atty., atty., 2d asst. to Chief U.S. Marshal, civil rights compliance officer Dept. of Justice, Washington, 1938-70; supr. Town of Dunkirk, N.Y., 1973-76; mem. N.Y. State Liquor Authority, Buffalo, 1976—. Bd. dirs. Center for Women Govt., Albany, N.Y., 1978—; mem. Chautauqua County Task Force on Aging, 1972-73, Town of Dunkirk Indsl. Devel. Agy., 1972-76, Chautauqua County Planning Bd., 1973-76, No. Chautauqua County Intermcpl. Planning Bd., 1974-76, Chautauqua County Overall Econ. Devel. Planning Bd., 1974-76, Literacy Vols., 1972-76, Dunkirk Vol. Fire Dept., 1973—; adv. bd. Dunkirk Sr. Citizens, 1974-76; mem. women's div. N.Y. State Democratic Com. Mem. Am. Bar Assn., Fed. Bar Assn., Women's Bar Assn. D.C., AAUW, Nat. Lawyers Club, Cath. Daus. Am., Kappa Beta Pi. Democrat. Roman Catholic. Clubs: Chautauqua County Dem. Women's (treas. 1974-76), Town of Dunkirk Dem. Home: 5081 W Shorewood Dr Dunkirk NY 14048 Office: 125 Main St Buffalo NY 14203

KLASING, MARY LOU, telephone co. exec.; b. Okawville, Ill., Aug. 16, 1943; d. August Henry and Mary (Wernecke) Grefe; student Belleville Jr. Coll., 1971-72, Purdue U., 1977, 78; m. Lloyd William Klasing, Aug. 22, 1965. Clk. typist, ASCS, Nashville, Ill., 1961-62; cashier, bookkeeper Universal CIT, Centralia, Ill., 1962; sec. Okaw Comml. Telephone Co., Okawville, Ill., 1962-63; with Continental Telephone Co. Ill., Mascoutah, Ill., 1963-78, customer service mgr., 1977-78; region bus. office coordinator Continental Telephone Service Corp., St. Louis, 1978—. Mem. Ind. Telephone Pioneer Assn., Nat. Assn. Female Execs. Republican. Mem. United Ch. of Christ. Home: 109 S Sparta St Okawville IL 62271 Office: 600 Mason Ridge Center Dr St Louis MO 63141

KLASS, SHEILA SOLOMON, educator, author; b. Bklyn., Nov. 6, 1927; d. Abraham Louis and Virginia (Glatter) Solomon; B.A., Bklyn. Coll., 1949; M.A. in English, State U. Iowa, 1951, M.F.A. in Creative Writing, 1953; m. Morton Klass, May 2, 1953; children—Perri Elizabeth, David Arnold, Judith Alexandra. Tchr. English, Julia Ward Howe, Jr. High Sch., N.Y.C., 1951-57; mem. faculty Borough Manhattan Community Coll., CUNY, 1965—, prof. English, 1982—; USIS lectr., India, 1963-64; lectr. U. Conn., summers 1965, 79; vol. tchr., community resources person Leonia (N.J.) Alternative High Sch., 1972-75; author: (novels) Come Back on Monday, 1960, Bahadur Means Hero, 1969, A Perpetual Surprise, 1981; (memoir) Everyone in This Mouse Makes Babies, 1964; (juvenile novels) Nobody Knows Me in Miami, 1981, To See My Mother Dance, 1981, Amazin' Grace, 1983. Yaddo fellow, 1974. Mem. PEN, Poets and Writers, AAUP. Jewish. Home: 330 Sylvan Ave Leonia NJ 07605 Office: 199 Chambers St New York NY 10019

KLECKNER, JO'AN, avionic technician; b. East Chicago, Ind., Mar. 11, 1939; d. James Harold and Nina Maude (Davis) K.; student Coll. San Mateo, 1969, 73-75. With Gary-Hobart Water Corp., Gary, Ind., 1959-63; with TWA, San Francisco, 1965—, avionic technician, 1977-79; newscaster, program host, bd. operator, engr., past sec. Sta. KEAR-FM, San Francisco, 1976—; mechanic United Airlines, San Francisco Internat. Airport, 1979, now engr. technician. Mem. Internat. Assn. Machinists and Aerospace Workers, Fellowship Christian Airline Personnel. Club: Toastmasters. Office: 1234 Mariposa St San Francisco CA 94107

KLEEMAN, ROSSLYN ANETA (SHORE), govt. ofcl.; b. Mpls., Apr. 20, 1922; d. S. Louis and Tessa (Woolpy) Shore; student U. Minn., 1939-40, B.S., Univ. Coll., 1972; student U. Ariz., 1940-41; m. Richard Pentlarge Kleeman, Jan. 1, 1950; children—Nancy, Alice, Katherine, David. Bd. dirs., staff, Info. Center, Washington Opportunities for Women, 1966-69; dir. Women's Action Program, HEW, Washington, 1970-72; project dir. Pres.'s Adv. Council on Mgmt. Improvement, Office Mgmt. and Budget, Washington, 1973-80; group dir. U.S. GAO, Washington, 1973-80, asso. dir. Fed. Personnel and Compensation Div., 1981—. Active LWV, Women's Equity Action League; mem. Interdepartmental Task Force on Women, 1977-80. Recipient meritorious service award GAO, 1980. Mem. Am. Soc. Public Adminstrn. (bd. dirs. Nat. Capital Area chpt., 1978-80, mem. nat. fin. and adminstrn. com., 1980—), Internat. Personnel Mgmt. Assn., Washington Women's Network. Office: 4037 441 G St NW Washington DC 20548

KLEIDON, ROSE ANN OSTERMAN, educator, design studio exec.; b. Streator, Ill., Sept. 9, 1945; d. Theodore W. and Edyth C. (Hakes) Osterman; B.A. in English Lit., Ill. Wesleyan U., 1967; M.A.T.E., U. Ill., 1968; m. Dennis A. Kleidon, Aug. 19, 1967; 1 son, Kurtis Bradford. Tchr., Copley (Ohio) High Sch., 1969-70; instr. U. Akron, 1970-75, asst. prof. English, 1975—; co-owner, v.p., copywriter Kleidon & Assos., Inc., Medina, Ohio, 1975—; cons. PSI Designs, Boulder, Colo., 1979. Copywriter, Akron-Kent office McGovern Campaign, 1972; author brochure Unitarian-Universalist Ch., Akron, 1978. Recipient 10-Yr. Service award U. Akron, 1980. Mem. Nat. Council Tchrs. English, Coll. English Assn., Assn. Tchrs. Tech. Writing, Am. Bus. Communications Assn., Assn. Two-Yr. Colls., Kent Weavers Guild, Kappa Kappa Gamma. Club: Atwood Yacht. Author: A Stylesheet for Technical Reports, 1979. Home: 26 Waterside Dr Medina OH 44256 Office: Schrank Hall 210 Univ Akron Akron OH 44235

KLEIN, ARLETTE, mgmt. info. systems exec.; b. Egypt, Apr. 1, 1944; d. Chalom and Lily (Tammam) Haim; came to U.S., 1963, naturalized, 1969; M.S., Pratt Inst., 1976; B.A., CUNY Hunter Coll., 1968; m. Robert S. Klein, Mar. 3, 1963; 1 son, Jason D. Programmer analyst Ohrbach's and J. Walter Thompson, 1965-66; cons. in mgmt. info. systems services, various N.Y. and N.J. companies, 1966-72; dep. dir. systems and devel. Computer Center, Health Dept. N.Y.C., 1973-77; dir. systems and programming Bradford Adminstrv. Services, N.Y.C., 1977-81; dir. systems devel. Blue Cross Blue Shield Greater N.Y., N.Y.C., 1981—. Mem. Assn. Computing Machinery, Am. Mgmt. Assn., Profl. Women in Data Processing.

KLEIN, CAROL LYNNE, psychologist; b. Bklyn., Nov. 8, 1941; d. Jay J. and Rebecca (Perlman) Lehrman; B.S., SUNY, Cortland, 1962; M.Ed., Temple U., 1975, Cert., 1977, postgrad., 1977—; m. Robert L. Klein, Aug. 20, 1966; children—Alisa Beth, Matthew Douglas. Tchr. Bklyn. Elem. Schs., 1962-66; tchr. Knoxville (Tenn.) Elem. Schs., 1966-70; counseling psychologist B'nai B'rith Career and Counseling Service, Phila., 1977-78; psychologist Whitemarsh Psychol. Assos., Lafayette Hill, Pa., 1979—. Sec. LWV, Plymouth-Whitemarsh, Pa., 1973-75; bd. dirs. Whitemarsh Citizens Council, 1974-75. Mem. Am. Psychol. Assn., Am. Orthopsychiat. Assn., Nat. Assn. Sch. Psychologists, Mental Health Assn. Pa., Pa. Psychol. Assn., Phila. Soc. Clin. Psychologists, Delaware Valley Assn. Gifted Edn. Home and Office: 105 Hollyhock Dr Lafayette Hill PA 19444

KLEIN, EDITH IOLAMAY MILLER, lawyer, former state senator; b. Wallace, Idaho, Aug. 4, 1915; d. Fred L.B. and Edith (Gallup) Miller; B.S. in Bus., U. Idaho, 1935; J.D., George Washington U., 1946, LL.M., 1954; m. Sandor S. Klein, 1949 (dec. 1970). Teaching fellow Wash. State U., 1935-36; tchr. Grangeville (Idaho) High Sch., 1936-37; interviewer Idaho State Employment Service, 1940-41; tchr. Vocat. Sch., Weiser, Idaho, 1941-42; and personnel specialist War Labor depts., Washington, 1942-46; admitted to D.C. bar, 1946, Idaho bar, 1947, N.Y. bar, 1955, U.S. Supreme Ct., 1954; practice law, Boise, Idaho, 1947—; judge Mcpl. Ct., Boise, 1947-49; atty. FCC, Washington, 1953-54, FHA, N.Y.C., 1955-56; asso. firm Langroise, Sullivan & Smylie, Boise, 1957-67, partner, 1968—; mem. Idaho Ho. of Reps., 1949-50, 65-68; mem. Idaho Senate, 1968-82, chmn. judiciary com., 1971-82; legis. mem. Idaho Law Enforcement Planning Commn., 1972-81; mem. Idaho Gov.'s Commn. on Status of Women, 1965-79, 82—, chmn., 1965-71; mem. Idaho Endowment Investment Bd., 1979—; mem. Nat. Adv. Com. Regional Med. Programs, 1974-76, Idaho Gov.'s Council Comprehensive Health Planning, 1969-76. Bd. dirs. Harry W. Morrison Found., Inc., 1978—; past pres. Ada County Republican Women's Club; bd. dirs., past pres. Boise Civic Opera, Boise Philharm. Assn. Named Woman of Yr., Boise Altrusa Club, 1966, Greater Boise C. of C., 1970; Disting. Citizen, Idaho Statesman, 1970; Woman of Progress, Idaho Bus. and Profl. Women, 1978; Women Helping Women award Soroptimists, 1982. Mem. DAR, Bus. and Profl. Women's Club, Boise Art Assn., Greater Boise C. of C. (dir. 1976-78), AAUW, Am. Bar Assn., Am. Judicature Soc., Idaho Bar Assn., Internat. Bar Assn., LWV, Nat. Order Women Legislators, Kappa Beta Pi. Republican. Congregationalist. Club: Altrusa (past pres.) (Boise). Office: PO Box 2527 Boise ID 83701

KLEIN, ESTHER MOYERMAN (MRS. PHILIP KLEIN), publisher; b. Phila., Nov. 3, 1907; d. Louis and Rebecca (Feldman) Moyerman; B.S., Temple U., 1929; student U. London, 1954; m. Philip Klein, Apr. 26, 1930; children—Arthur, Karen Louise Klein Mannes. Reporter, Phila. Jewish Times, 1925, Atlantic City Times, 1927; feature writer Pub. Ledger Syndicate, 1928-29, Pub. Ledger, Evening Bull., Phila. Record,

1929-32; pub. relations counsellor, editor Art Alliance Bull., 1945-49; commentator Sta. WPEN, 1949-53; pub. Phila. Jewish Times, 1953-74; author, hist. researcher, 1974—; lectr. women's clubs, 1951—. Del. Internat. Conf. Residential Adult Edn., Holland, 1957, Germany, 1959; participant in first workshop Residential Adult Edn. for Adult Edn. Assn. U.S., 1954. Mem. Gov.'s Commn. on Charitable Orgns., 1969—; chmn. Rittenhouse Sq. Women's com. for Phila. Orch., 1957; organizer bicentennial women's com. Walnut St. Theatre; adv. com. Friends Nat. Independence Hist. Park; chmn. bicentennial program Beth Zion - Beth Israel Congregation; bd. dirs. Rittenhouse Found., Phila. Jewish Times Inst., also dir. ann. cooking festivals; exec. com. Long Beach Island Found. Arts and Scis., N.J. Named Distinguished Dau. Pa.; recipient Gimbel Phila. award, 1975; awards Alumnae Girls High Sch., Phila. Art Alliance, Temple U., City Council Phila., Colonial Hist. Soc.; Klein Recital Hall at Temple U. named in her honor. Mem. Pa. Newspaper Pubs. Assn., Temple U. Alumni (honored at 80th anniversary, 1964), Phila. High Sch. for Girls Alumnae, Hannah Penn House, Emergency Aid of Pa., Chgo. Art Mus., Mus. Modern Art N.Y., Pan Am. Assn. Club: Print. Author: A Guidebook to Jewish Philadelphia, 1965; International House Celebrity Cookbook, 1965; History and Guidebook of Fairmount Park, 1974. Address: 135 S 18th St Philadelphia PA 19103

KLEIN, JO ANN, journalist; b. Hattiesburg, Miss., Aug. 28, 1949; d. Jack Conrad and Minnie Louise (Worcester) K.; B.S., U. So. Miss., Hattiesburg, 1971, M.S., 1975. Copy editor Biloxi-Gulfport (Miss.) Daily Herald, 1971-73; reporter Montgomery (Ala.) Advertiser, 1973; asst. to dean continuing edn. U. So. Miss., 1973-75; public relations asst. So. Bell Telephone Co., Atlanta, 1976; polit. and state govt. reporter Jackson (Miss.) Clarion-Ledger, 1976-80; exec. dir. Miss. Democratic Com., Jackson, 1980—; instr. journalism Miss. Coll., Clinton, 1976. Public relations chair U. So. Miss. Alumni Assn., 1971. Mem. Miss. Press Women (writing and editing awards 1971-73), Edn. Writers Assn. Am. (Charles Stewart Mott award 2d place 1977), Miss. Assn. Educators (Sch. Bell award 1979), Nat. Fedn. Press Women. Baptist. Home: 327A Livingston St Jackson MS 39202 Office: PO Box 1583 Jackson MS 39205

KLEIN, JOYCE FISHMAN, former financial analyst; b. Albany, N.Y., Feb. 19, 1941; d. Hyman and Helen (Firsty) F.; student U. Buffalo, 1958-60; B.B.A., Russell Sage Coll., Albany, 1964; postgrad. U. Md., 1970-71; m. Richard H. Klein, June 17, 1979. Asst. ops. mgr. Merrill Lynch, Pierce, Fenner & Smith, Inc., Albany, 1960-64; customer service rep. Matthew Bender & Co., Inc., Albany, 1964-66; with credit card div. Am. Express Co., Washington, 1966-67; asst. treas. The Macke Co., Cheverly, Md., 1967-73; revenue supr. Washington Suburban San. Commn., Hyattsville, Md., 1973-77, trustee pension plan; asst. mgr. treasury div. Citibank, N.A., San Juan, P.R., 1977-79; sr. staff officer Citicorp U.S.A., Inc., Phila., from 1979. Mem. Washington Soc. Investment Analysts, Fin. Analysts of Phila.

KLEIN, JUDITH RUTH, psychotherapist, social worker; b. Bklyn., Jan. 8, 1945; d. Sidney and Carla Laufman K.; B.A. in Sociology, CCNY, 1966; M.S.W., U. Conn., 1968; m. Edmond Spencer Slatus, Oct. 6, 1974; 1 dau., Jessica Klein Slatus. Supr. Coney Island office Jewish Bd. of Family and Children Services, Bklyn., 1968-78; pvt. practice child and adult psychotherapy, N.Y.C., 1973—; chief social worker East Plains Mental Health Service, Hicksville, N.Y., 1978—. Vocat. Rehab. Adminstrn. scholar, 1966-68; cert. social worker, N.Y. State; cert. in child psychotherapy, N.Y. State. Fellow Soc. Clin. Social Work Psychotherapists; mem. Nat. Assn. Social Workers, Acad. Cert. Social Workers, Women's Psychotherapy Referral Service. Office: 100 W 12th St New York NY 10011

KLEIN, MARGRETE SIEBERT, physicist; b. Cleve., Feb. 28, 1938; d. Arthur Aloysius and Martha Margrete (Siebert) K.; B.S., Baldwin-Wallace Coll., 1960; M.S., U. Mich., 1964; Ph.D., Northwestern U., 1978; m. Jacques Paul Klein, Aug. 24, 1968; children—Christian Andre-Albert, Maia Margrete-Odile. Asst. prof. physics Chgo. City Colls., 1964-71; researcher, writer, cons. Berlin, Bonn, Germany, Washington, 1974-80; staff asso. NSF, Directorate Sci. and Engring. Edn., Washington, 1980, program mgr. info. dissemination sci. edn., 1980-82, staff asso. div. physics, 1982—; chmn. Citizens Adv. Com. Gifted and Talented Edn., Falls Church (Va.) City Schs., 1981—. Internat. Research and Exchanges Bd. grantee, 1982. Mem. exec. com. Citizens for a Better City, Falls Church, Va., 1980—. Mem. League Women Voters, AAAS, AAUP, Nat. Sci. Tchrs. Assn., Nat. Soc. Study Edn., Comparative and Internat. Edn. Soc. Author: The Challenge of Communist Education: A Look at the German Democratic Republic, 1980; editor: A Challenge for American Education: Science Literacy in Japan, the Two Germanies and the Soviet Union, 1982. Office: NSF Div Physics Washington DC 20550

KLEIN, MARJORIE HANSON, psychologist; b. Milw., Sept. 13, 1933; d. Norman Richard and Anna Adelia (Emery) Hanson; B.A., Wellesley Coll., 1955, M.A., 1957; Ph.D., Harvard U., 1964; m. Norman S. Greenfield, May 17, 1969; children—Jennifer, Susan; 1 stepdau., Ellen Greenfield. Research asst. NIMH, 1957-59, postdoctoral research fellow, 1966-67; mem. staff Wis. Psychiat. Research Inst., Madison, 1962-66, 67-72, research asso., 1967-72; mem. faculty U. Wis., 1972—, prof. psychiatry, 1980—, also prof. women's studies program. Grantee, Ford Found., NIMH, Alcohol, Drug Abuse and Mental Health Adminstrn., State of Wis., Nat. Library Medicine. Mem. Am. Psychol. Assn., Soc. Psychotherapy Research, Am. Psychopath. Assn., Phi Beta Kappa, Sigma Xi. Author numerous papers, reports in field. Office: 600 Highland Ave Madison WI 53792

KLEIN, NORMA, author; b. N.Y.C., May 13, 1938; d. Emanuel and Sadie (Frankel) K.; B.A., Barnard Coll., 1960; M.A. in Slavic Langs., Columbia U., 1963; m. Erwin Fleissner, July 27, 1963; children—Jennifer, Katherine. Author fiction; latest works include (for adults) Girls Turn Wives, 1976, Domestic Arrangements, 1981, Wives and Other Women, 1982; (for teenagers) Love is One of the Choices, 1978, Breaking Up, 1980, The Queen of the What Ifs, 1982; (for juveniles) Tomboy, 1978, A Honey of a Chimp, 1980, Robbie and the Leap Year Blues, 1981; (picture books) A Train for Jane, 1974, Dinosaur's Housewarming Party, 1974, Visiting Pamela, 1979; (novelizations) The Sunshine Years, 1975, Sunshine Christmas, 1977, French Postcards, 1979. Mem. PEN, Author's Guild, Women's Network. Address: 27 W 96th St New York NY 10025

KLEIN, RUTH B., civic worker, packaging co. exec., poet, author; b. Cin., Jan. 31, 1908; d. Samuel and Minnie (Schunke) Becker; student U. Calif. at Los Angeles, 1926-28, San Jose State Coll., 1928-29; m. Charles Henle Klein, Sept. 23, 1938; children—Betsy Klein Schwartz, Charles Henle, Carla Klein Fee III. Sec., Novelart Mfg. Co., Cin., 1960—, dir., 1960—. Vol. Aid to Visually Handicapped program Cin. sect. Nat. Council of Jewish Women, 1951-82, sec., 1954-56, 63-64, bd. dirs., 1952-70; bd. dirs. Civic Garden Center of Greater Cin., 1956-63, chmn. spl. services for aid to visually handicapped, 1952-82. Mem. Nat. Braille Assn., Greater Cin. Writers League, Verse Writers' Guild Ohio. Club: Contemporary Literary. Author: Latitude of Love; Longitude of Lust, 1979; contbr. poems to various anthologies. Home: 6754 Fair Oaks Dr Cincinnati OH 45237

KLEIN, VIRGINIA SUE, psychotherapist; b. Liberty, N.Y., Dec. 30, 1936; d. Abraham and Lillian Rose (Malin) Levine; B.S., Rutgers U., 1972, M.S.W., 1974, Ph.D., 1978; m. Andrew Klein, Mar. 29, 1969; children—Earl, Holly Jo. Social worker N.J. Correctional Instn. for Women, Clinton, 1972-74; pvt. practice clin. social work, Somerville, N.J., 1973—; co founder, developer Dynamic Workshops, Somerville, 1980—; instr. Somerset County Coll., Trenton State Grad. Sch., Rutgers U. NIMH fellow, 1972-80. Mem. Acad. Cert. Social Workers, Nat. Acad. Social Workers, Rutgers Alumni Assn. Address: 18 S Cadillac Dr Somerville NJ 08876

KLEINROCK, SUSAN NAOMI, psychologist; b. N.Y.C., Mar. 30, 1955; d. Martin and Ruth Lenore (Blum) K.; B.A., N.Y. U., 1976; M.S., Syracuse U., 1977, Ph.D., 1981. Regional assessor N.Y. State Div. Youth, 1977-78; indsl. cons., psychologist Crawford Rehab. Services, Syracuse, N.Y., 1979; personal and indsl. counseling, Bronx, N.Y., 1979—. Menninger fellow, 1979. Mem. Am. Psychol. Assn., Am. Assn. Psychiat. Services for Children, N.Y. Acad. Scis., Nat. Rehab. Assn., N.Y. Zool. Soc., Am. Soc. Prevention Cruelty to Animals, NOW, LWV. Home and office: 958 Brady Ave Apt 2 Bronx NY 10462

KLEMENT, GRACE MURPHY, geologist; b. El Paso, Tex., July 13, 1936; d. Herbert Leroy and June Dee Ellis (Glardon) Murphy; B.S. in Geology, U. Tex., El Paso, 1970; children—Paul, Bryan, Kevin, Tamie, Corie. Teaching asst. dept. geology U. Tex., El Paso, 1968-70; sr. geologist El Paso Natural Gas Co., 1970-76; dist. geologist St. Joe Am. Corp., Austin, Tex., 1976—. Pres. El Paso Pre-Sch. for Deaf and Hard of Hearing, 1964-65; v.p. bd. dirs. Meml. Park Sch. for Retarded Children, 1965-66; co-chmn. women's div. El Paso County United Fund Drive, 1965; bd. dirs. El Paso chpt. NCCJ, 1967, El Paso chpt. Pro-Am., 1967. Mem. Am. Assn. Petroleum Geologists, Soc. Mining Engrs. of AIME (pres. South Tex. minerals sect.), Am. Bus. Women's Assn., Austin Geol. Soc., Tex. Fedn. Women's Clubs (state chmn. jr. clubs dept. internat. affairs 1963), Sigma Gamma Epsilon. Episcopalian. Office: 8900 Shoal Creek Suite 440 Austin TX 78758

KLEMKE, JUDITH ANN, savs. and loan assn. exec.; b. Berwyn, Ill., July 22, 1950; d. John Stanley and Mildred Lucille (Baldwin) K.; B.S., U. Ill., Champaign-Urbana, 1972; m. Keith Michael Kurzeja, Nov. 6, 1976. With Ben Franklin Savs. Assn., Oak Brook, Ill., 1973-74, asst. v.p., Skokie, Ill., 1975; asst. v.p., then v.p. First Fin. Savs. & Loan Assn., Downers Grove, Ill., 1975-80, sr. v.p., 1981—. Mem. U.S. League Savs. and Loan Assn., Chgo. Council Savs. and Loan Assns., Savs. Inst. Mktg. Soc. Am., Nat. Assn. Female Execs., Am. Soc. Profl. and Exec. Women, AAUW, Ill. League Mktg., Bus. and Profl. Women, U. Ill. Alumni Assn. (life), Alpha Gamma Delta. Lutheran. Home: 18 W 206 Lathrop Ln Villa Park IL 60181 Office: 1048 Ogden Ave Downers Grove IL 60515

KLENE, MARY JEAN, educator; b. Hannibal, Mo., Sept. 8, 1929; d. Othmar Carl and Ada Blanch (Ridder) Klene; B.A., St. Mary's Coll., Notre Dame, Ind., 1959; M.A., U. Notre Dame, 1966; Ph.D., U. Toronto (Ont., Can.), 1970. Faculty dept. English, St. Mary's Coll., Notre Dame, Ind., 1966—, chmn. dept. english, 1972-77, 81—, regent, 1979—; tchr. parochial high schs., Flint, Mich. and South Bend, Ind., 1951-66. Mem. MLA, Chaucer Soc., Nat. Council Tchrs. English. Roman Catholic (Sisters of the Holy Cross). Author: Shakespeare: New Productions, 1975-80; Instructor's Guide for Slides of Royal Shakespeare Co.; contbr. articles to profl. jours. Address: Saint Mary's Coll Notre Dame IN 46556

KLIEBHAN, MARY CAMILLE, univ. pres.; b. Milw., Apr. 4, 1923; d. Alfred Sebastian and Mae Eileen (McNamara) K.; B.A., Cath. Sisters Coll., Washington, 1949; M.A., Cath. U. Am., 1951, Ph.D., 1955. Joined Order of St. Francis of Assisi, Roman Cath. Ch., 1945; legal sec. Spence and Hanley, Milw., 1941-45; instr. edn. dept. Cardinal Stritch Coll., Milw., 1955-62, asso. prof., 1962-68, prof., 1968—, head dept. of edn., 1962-67, dean of students, 1962-64, chmn. grad. div., 1964-69, v.p. acad. and student affairs, 1969-74, pres., 1974—, bd. dirs., 1974—; treas. Wis. Found. of Ind. Colls., 1974-79, v.p., 1979-81, pres., 1981—. Mem. program com. De Paul Rehab. Hosp. Mem. Am. Psychol. Assn., Wis. Assn. for Tchr. Educators, Phi Delta Kappa, Delta Epsilon Sigma, Psi Chi, Delta Kappa Gamma. Contbr. monograph to profl. publs.

KLIER, CONSTANCE MARIE, foods services exec.; b. Worcester, Mass., Dec. 15, 1941; d. Fred Anthony and Florence Mary (Cummins) K.; B.S. in Edn., State Coll. at Framingham (Mass.), 1964; M.S., Cornell U., 1966. Food standards supr. Marriott Corp., Washington, 1966-70; mgr. food standards Quality Motel Corp., Silver Spring, Md., 1970-71; home econs. tchr. Montgomery County Public Schs., Rockville, Md., 1972-73; mgr. Washington Food Services, Woodward & Lothrop, Washington, 1971-72, 73—. Mem. Washington Home Econs. Craft Adv. Council. Mem. Am. Home Econs. Assn., Home Economists in Bus., Am. Dietetic Assn. Roman Catholic. Home: 5401 Westbard Ave Apt 1312 Bethesda MD 20816 Office: 1025 F St NW Washington DC 20013

KLIMAN, SYLVIA MAY STERN, filmmaker, writer, editor, realtor; b. Boston, July 16, 1934; d. Edward I. and Bernice Stern; A.B., Vassar Coll., 1956; m. Allan Kliman, June 24, 1956; children—Gilbert Harrow, Douglas Hartley. Editorial asst. Harvard Law Sch. profs., Cambridge, Mass., 1956-58; editor Vassar Miscellany News, Poughkeepsie, N.Y., 1953-56; editor founder Park Parent, Brookline, Mass., 1968-73; pres. Sylvia S. Kliman Real Estate Brokerage, 1971—; pres. Dunewind Films, 1979—. Vol. Mass. ARC Blood program, 1970-73; polit. speechwriter, 1960—. Trustee Park Sch., Brookline, 1970—; bd. friends Peter Bent Brigham Hosp., 1970-75; bd. dirs. Spl. Com. to Restore Ogunquit Dunes, 1975—. Mem. Park Sch. Parents Assn. (pres. 1968-70), Norfolk Dist. Med. Soc. Womens Aux., Boston Museum Fine Arts. Unitarian. Club: Vassar (dir.) (Boston). Home: 40 Newton St Brookline MA 02146 also Dunewind Ogunquit ME 03907

KLINCK, PATRICIA EWASCO, state librarian Vt.; b. Albany, N.Y., May 13, 1940; d. Albert C. and Mary Ann (Sopko) Ewasco; B.A. in History, Smith Coll., 1961; M.S. in Library Sci., Simmons Coll., Boston, 1963; postgrad. in edn. SUNY, Albany, 1964-67; m. C. Hoagland Klinck, Jr., Sept. 12, 1970; 1 dau., Natalie Childs. Young adult worker Boston Public Library, 1961-63; library dir. Colonie Central High Sch., Albany, 1963-67; librarian Library/U.S.A., U.S. Pavilion, N.Y. World's Fair, summer 1965; library dir. Simon's Rock Coll., Gt. Barrington, Mass., 1967-70; regional dir. NW Regional Library, Vt. Dept. Libraries, Montpelier, 1970-72, dir. extension services div., 1972-73, 73-74, acting asst. state librarian, 1973, asst. state librarian, 1974-77, state librarian, 1977—; chmn. New Eng. Library Bd., 1979-81. Mem. Am., New Eng., Vt. library assns., Am. Soc. Public Adminstrs., Chief Officers of State Library Agys. (dir. 1978-80, vice chmn. 1980-81, chmn. 1981-82). Home: 47 Brewer Pkwy South Burlington VT 05401 Office: 111 State St Montpelier VT 05602

KLINE, BETTY HALTERMAN, psychologist; b. Harrisonburg, Va., Sept. 17, 1934; d. Blaine and Lois (Bowman) Halterman; B.A., Bridgewater Coll., 1955; M.A., U. Hawaii, 1957; m. Paul Miller Kline, June 20, 1953; children—Pamela Kline Wolfe, Debra Kline Murphy, Kristopher Miller. Staff psychologist Commonwealth Psychiat. Inst., Richmond, Va., 1957-59; asst. prof. dean of women Bridgewater (Va.) Coll., 1960-65; staff psychologist Valley Mental Health Center, Staunton, Va., 1965-69, dir., 1969-79; coordinator Children's Services Massanutten Mental Health Center, Harrisonburg, 1979—; cons. Staunton Girls Home; vice chmn. bd. dirs. Rivendale Home for Boys, Abraxis, Va. Del., Va. State Democratic Conv., 1981; mem. county Dem. Com., 1982—. Mem. Am. Psychol. Assn., Va. Assn. Mental Health Providers. Home: Rt 2 PO Box 245 Bridgewater VA 22812 Office: 1241 N Main St Harrisonburg VA 22812

KLINE, LINDA, personnel exec.; b. Boston, Aug. 8, 1940; d. George and Eva (Weiner) Kline; B.A. in Biology, Boston U., 1962. Personnel dir. Block Engring. Inc., Cambridge, Mass., 1964-66; brokerage mgr. Eastern Life Ins. Co. N.Y., Boston, 1966-68; mgr. direct placement Lendman Assos., N.Y.C., 1968-72; dir. women-in-mgmt. div. Roberts-Lund, Ltd., N.Y.C., 1972-77; pres. Kline-McKay, Inc., Exec. Search and Outplacement Cons., Maximus Cons., Inc., N.Y.C., 1978—; exec. dir. Majority Money, women's network, 1976—; tchr. fin. planning for women Marymount-Manhattan Coll., 1977; lectr. and/or cons. women's programs at several colls. and univs. and corps. Mem. Women Bus. Owners N.Y. (dir. 1978-82). NOW. Co-author: Career Changing: The Worry-Free Guide, 1982. Address: 16 E 98th St Apt 3B New York NY 10029

KLING, CANDACE, archtl. lighting design cons.; b . Phila., Oct. 30, 1945; d. Harry C. and Rosemary Roberta (McLaughlin) Wilson. Broadway Lighting designer Jean Rosenthal, N.Y.C., 1963-68, Howard Brandston Lighting Design, 1968-70; asos. Jules Horton Lighting Design, N.Y.C., 1970-72; with Marriott Hotel Corp., Washington, 1972-80; owner C. M. Kling Lighting Design, Falls Church, Va., 1980—; guest lectr. Mt. Vernon Coll., Cath. U. Am., U. Md. Design Schs. Recipient award of Merit, Chgo. Marriott Hotel Lighting Design. Mem. Illuminating Engrs. Soc., Internat. Assn. Lighting Designers, NOW. Office: Suite 100 113 Park Ave Falls Church VA 22046

KLINGE, VALERIE, clin. psychologist; b. N.Y., Feb. 14, 1940; d. Robert and Grace (Murray) K.; B.A. cum laude, Smith Coll., 1962; M.A., Conn. Coll. for Women, 1964; Ph.D., SUNY, Stonybrook, 1970; m. Phillip M. Rennick, Feb. 14, 1973 (dec. 1976). Research asso. Yale U., New Haven, 1964-67; instr. So. Conn. State Coll., 1965-66; adj. asst. prof. Wayne State U., Detroit, 1970-74, adj. asso. prof. Sch. of Medicine, 1973—, adj. asso. prof. dept. psychology, 1973—; adj. asso. prof. dept. psychology U. Detroit, 1974—; asso. chief div. psychology Lafayette Clinic, Detroit, 1974-76, chief psychologist, 1976-77, dir. Behavior Therapy Clinic, 1973—; site visitor various mental health care instns., 1975—, Thomas Jefferson Med. Coll., Phila., 1981. Recipient Disting. Psychotherapist award Internat. Soc. Disting. Therapists, 1981. Mem. Am. Psychol. Assn., Mich. Psychol. Assn., Midwestern Psychol. Assn., Biofeedback Research Soc., Soc. for Psychophysiol. Research. Episcopalian. Contbr. articles to jours. in psychology. Home: 1300 Lafayette East Detroit MI 48207 Office: Lafayette Clinic 951 E Lafayette Detroit MI 48207

KLINGENSMITH, THELMA HYDE (MRS. DON J. KLINGENSMITH), educator; b. Rauville, S.D., May 23, 1904; d. Eber Watson and Ida (Lebert) Hyde; B.A. magna cum laude, John Fletcher Coll., 1928; M.S. in Ed., U. N.D., 1962; m. Don Joseph Klingensmith, Sept. 11, 1930; children—Merle Joseph, Eunice Victoria (Mrs. Hilary Evans). Tchr. rural schs., Almont, N.D., 1922-24; exec. sec. Young People's Gospel League, Chgo., 1928-30; asst. supt. Ponca Meth. Indian Mission, Ponca City, Okla., 1936-43; tchr. English, Almont High Sch., 1951-54; supt. schs. Morton County, Mandan, N.D., 1959-73; mem. Am. Assn. Sch. Adminstrs. seminar to Russia, 1969. Dir. N.D. div. Am. Cancer Soc., 1958-72, chmn. pub. edn. com., 1958-60, sec., 1960-66; sr. v.p. N.D. Young Citizens League, 1959-63, sr. pres., 1963-65; legis. rep. N.D. Council County Supts. Assn., 1963-66; adviser Morton County Library Bd., 1960—, trustee, 1977—; sec.-treas. Heart River Gospel Assn., 1950-66, dir., 1950—; dir., treas. N.D. Action Com. for Environ. Edn., 1968-75; bd. dirs. Dickinson Coll. Found.; v.p. West Wis. Conf., Women's Soc. Christian Service, Methodist Ch., 1945-46; legis. rep. N.D. Woman's Christian Temperance Union, 1978—; Western dist. coordinator Christian Social involvement N.D. Conf., United Meth. Women, 1979—; Dakota area del. Internat. Conf. Christian Heritage in Govt., United Meth. Ch., London, 1981. Named N.D. Mother of the Yr., 1965; recipient citation for conservation edn. Nat. and N.D. wildlife fedns., 1974. Mem. Mandan Hosp. Aux., Rural Edn. Assn., ALA, Am. Library Trustees Assn., N.D. Assn. Sch. Adminstrs., Am. Bible Soc., Mountain Plains, N.D. (trustee citation award 1980, cert. of appreciation 1982) library assns., N.D. Library Trustees Assn. (v.p. 1967-68, 74-76, sec. 1971-73, dir. 1976-82, pres. 1979-81), N.D. Wildlife Fedn. (chmn. essay contest 1973-78), Marquis Library Soc. (adv. mem.). Clubs: Golden Grad of Vennard Coll. (pres. 1981—) (University Park, Iowa); Zonta (dist. VII chmn. pub. affairs com. 1968-70; del. internat. convs. 1968, 70, 72). Editor: Almont Jubilee History Book, 1956; Morton County Elementary Tchrs. Bull., 1959-73. Home: 206 Collins Ave PO Box 613 Mandan ND 58554

KLINGER, KAREN MARIE, journalist; b. Orange, N.J., July 2, 1946; d. George C. and Marie T. (O'Connor) K.; A.B. in English, U. Pa., 1968; postgrad. Stanford U. Staff writer San Jose (Calif.) Mercury News, 1971-74, 78—, sci. writer, 1980—; with English desk Agence France Presse, Paris, 1975; staff writer Ind. Jour., San Rafael, Calif., 1976-78. Fellow Centre de Formation des Journalistes, Paris, 1974-75. Mem. No. Calif. Sci. Writers Assn., N.Y. Acad. Scis., Sierra Club, Stanford U. Alumni Assn., U. Pa. Alumni Club. Office: 750 Ridder Park Dr San Jose CA 95190

KLIOT, CHERYL SUSAN, nurse, air force officer; b. Wadsworth, Ohio, July 11, 1946; d. Harry and Helen (Zwick) K.; B.S. in Nursing, Ohio State U., 1968; M.S., U. Calif., San Francisco, 1980. Intensive care, coronary care nurse Ohio State U., 1968-69; instr., staff orthopedic nurse Riverside Hosp. Sch. Nursing, Columbus, Ohio, 1969-71; commd. officer U.S. Air Force, advanced through grades to maj.; nurse surg. ward USAF Nurses Corps, Davis, Monthan AFB, Ariz., 1971-72, surg. ward U Tapao, Thailand, 1972-73, staff nurse, night supr., March AFB, Calif., 1973-75; pediatric asst. charge nurse, night supr. USAF Hosp., Wiesbaden, Germany, 1975-76, charge nurse pediatric clinic, 1976-78; pediatric nurse practitioner Sheppard AFB, Tex., 1980-82, course supr. USAF pediatric nurse practitioner course, 1982—. Mem. adv. council Explorer Scouts, 1976-78; bd. dirs. Wichita Falls March of Dimes. Mem. Internat. Soc. Prevention Child Abuse and Neglect, Am. Nurses Assn., Nat. Assn. Pediatric Nurse Assos. and Practitioners, Alpha Tau Delta, Sigma Theta Tau. Jewish. Contbr. articles to profl. jours. Home: 3309 Beechwood Ave Cleveland OH 44118 Office: 4833 Colleen St Wichita Falls TX 76302

KLIPSCH, LEONA KATHERINE, former newspaper publisher-editor; b. Vancouver, Wash., Feb. 24, 1914; d. Louis John and Marie Rosetta (Debitt) Hinkel; A.B., Smith Coll., 1935; student Sorbonne, Paris, 1934, Columbia U. Grad. Sch. Library Service, summers 1942-44; m. Robert Darius Klipsch, Nov. 25, 1937; children—Phyllis Marie Klipsch Smith, Katharine Klipsch Abbott, Marjorie Klipsch McCracken. Tchr. French and library sci. Marshall U., Huntington, W.Va., 1949-54; br. librarian Albuquerque Public Library, 1955-56; high sch. librarian, Gallup, N.Mex., 1963-65; co-owner, editor Defensor Chieftain, Socorro, N.Mex., 1965-82, pub., 1980-82. Bd. dirs. Socorro Gen. Hosp. Mem. N.Mex. Press Assn. (dir.), Nat. Investigative Reporters, PEO, Sigma Delta Chi. Republican. Presbyterian. Author: Treasure Your Love (Librarian prize for jr. novel 1958); (as Jean Kirby) A Very Special Girl, 1963. Home: 1304 Kitt Pl Socorro NM 87801 Office: 200 Winkler St Socorro NM 87801

KLOCK, MARY AGNES, telephone co. exec.; b. Drumright, Okla., July 16, 1948; d. Richard Noah and Mabel Clair (McNabb) K.; student Okla. State U., 1966-67, Southwestern Okla. State U., 68-69; B.S., U. Tulsa, 1982. With Southwestern Bell Tel. Co., 1974—, account exec., 1975-78, sr. account exec.-data, Tulsa, 1978, market mgr.-profl. services,

St. Louis, 1979-81, industry mgr.-profl. services, real estate, bus. services, Dallas, 1981-82, industry mgr.-profl. services and real estate, 1982—. Mem. Nat. Assn. Female Execs., Am. Soc. Profl. and Exec. Women. Home: PO Box 400842 Dallas TX 75240 Office: 5525 Lyndon Baines Johnson Freeway Dallas TX 75240

KLOCK, MARY EILEEN, social worker; b. Mpls., Apr. 4, 1929; d. Lester Joseph and Margaret (Dunn) K.; B.A., Hamline U., 1950; M.S.W., U. Denver, 1958, M.A., 1965, Ph.D., 1971. Social worker Olmsted County Welfare, 1950-52, Minn. Dept. Welfare, 1952-55; pediatric social worker Denver Gen. Hosp., 1958-61, U. Colo. Med. Center, 1961-63; costumier Palo Alto (Calif.) Children's Theatre, 1963-65; teaching fellow U. Denver, 1965-67; asst. prof., costumier So. U., 1967-71; social worker Adams County Mental Health Center, 1971-72; supr. Denver Dept. Social Services, 1972—; instr. Community Coll. of Denver. Mem. Nat. Assn. Social Workers, Am. Theatre Assn., AAUP, ACLU. Author: Creative Drama: a selected and annotated bibliography, 1975. Home: 2339 Downing St Denver CO 80205 Office: 1247 Santa Fe Denver CO 80204

KLOCK, SALLY JEAN, service orgn. exec.; b. Gloversville, N.Y., Dec. 13, 1948; d. Ward Carl and Florence (Pedrick) K.; B.A. magna cum laude in Psychology and Sociology, SUNY, Buffalo, 1971; M.Social Admistrn., Case Western Res. U., 1974; M.B.A., Cleve. State U., 1981; m. Michael M. Kleiman, Sept. 3, 1977. Bldg. mgr. Marc Equity Corp., Buffalo, 1971-72; community safety organizer Western Res. Area Agy. on Aging, Cleve., 1974-75, coordinator monitoring and evaluation, 1975-76; exec. dir. Lake County Council on Aging, Painesville, Ohio, 1976—; adv. bd. Ret. Sr. Vol. Program, 1976—; student field supr. Case Western Res. U., Cleve. State U., Bowling Green U., U. Mich. Mem. Ohio Citizens Council, 1977-78. N.Y. State Regents scholar, 1967; Ohio Manpower grantee, 1972; Social and Rehab. Services grantee, 1973. Mem. Am. Mktg. Assn., Nat. Council on Aging, Phi Beta Kappa, Beta Gamma Sigma. Home: 29051 Edgewood Dr Willowick OH 44094 Office: 105 Main St Painesville OH 44077

KLOPFLEISCH, STEPHANIE SQUANCE, social services agy. administr.; b. Rupert, Idaho, Dec. 21, 1940; d. William Jaynes and Elizabeth (Cunningham) Squance; B.A., Pomona Coll., 1962; M.S.W., UCLA, 1966; m. Randall Klopfleisch, June 27, 1970; children—Elizabeth, Jennifer, Matthew. Social worker, Los Angeles County, 1963-67; program dir. day care, vol. services Los Angeles County, 1966-71; div. chief children's services Dept. Public Social Services, Los Angeles County, 1971-73, dir. bur. of social services, 1973-79; chief dep. dir. Dept. Community Devel., Los Angeles County, 1979—; with Area 10 Devel. Disabilities, 1981-82. Mem. Calif. Commn. on Family Planning, 1976-79; mem. Los Angeles Commn. Children's Instns., 1977-78; bd. dirs. United Way Info., 1978-79; chmn. Los Angeles County Internat. Yr. of Child Commn., 1978-79; bd. govs. Sch. Social Welfare, UCLA, 1981—. Mem. Nat. Assn. Social Workers, Am. Public Welfare Assn., Calif. Welfare Dirs. Assn.

KLOSSNER, RUTH ANN, county extension agt.; b. New Ulm, Minn., Jan. 14, 1948; d. Hillard Albert and Edna Marie (Fischer) K.; B.S., U. Minn., 1970, M.Agr., 1979. Acting home economist U. Minn. Agrl. Extension Service, Watonwan County, 1970-71, extension home economist, Sherburne County, 1971-73, Sibley County, 1973-78, extension agt.-youth, 1978—, asso. prof., 1979—; mem. State horse adv. com. 4-H, 1974-80. Organizer, 1st capt. Sibley County Sheriff's Mounted Posse, 1976; officer, dir. Minn. Sheriff's Mounted Posse, 1977; county chmn. Pony Express Ride for Charity, 1975-77. Recipient Mindisa award Minn. Assn. Extension Home Economists, 1975; Disting. Service award Nat. Assn. Extension Home Economists, 1980. Mem. Minn. Assn. Extension Agts., Nat. Assn. Extension 4-H Agts., Epsilon Sigma Phi, Phi Kappa Phi. Lutheran. Author: Places to Go and Things to See in Central Minnesota, 1978; The First 50 Years of Sibley County 4-H, 1981. Home: Route 1 Box 123B Lafayette MN 56054 Office: Courthouse Box 207 Gaylord MN 55334

KLOSTER, GAYLE SANDRA, employment service ofcl.; b. East Grand Fork, Minn., Feb. 7, 1946; d. Glen and Hazel Virginia (Torgerson) Fowler; ed. Fargo (N.D.) pub. schs., corr. courses; m. Robert Enrest Kloster, Dec. 29, 1966; children—William Robert, Kathleen Gayle. Office mgr. Manpower Temporary Services, Inc., Edina, Minn., 1980—. Mem. Edina C. of C., Women in Bus., Am. Mgmt. Assn., Edina LWV, Word Processing Assn. Mpls., Working Opportunities for Women, Minn. Women's Network, Sales and Mktg. Execs. (Mpls. br. Women in Bus. Seminar). Republican. Lutheran. Office: 6750 France Ave S Edina MN 55435

KLOTZMAN, DOROTHY ANN, musical educator; b. Seattle, Mar. 24, 1937; d. Henry and Irva (Graham) Hill; B.S., Juilliard Sch., 1958, M.S., 1960. Prof., chmn. music Bklyn. Coll. 1971; condr. Bklyn. Coll. Symphonic Band, 1970—, Symphony Orch., 1980—; 1st women condr. Goldman Band, 1973; guest condr. Guggenheim Concerts Band, 1980, 81. Mem. citizens adv. bd. WNCN, 1976. Recipient N.Y. Philharmonic Young Composers' Contest 1st prize, 1953-54; Benjamin award in composition, 1955, 58; Fromm prize composition Aspen Music Sch., 1960; Danforth Found. E. Harris Harbison award, 1972. Mem. Am. Music Center, Am. Musicol. Soc., Coll. Music Soc., Music Library Assn., Am. Soc. Composers and Performers. Composer: Three Songs from Chamber Music; Sonatine for Piano; Poetical Sketches; Sonata for Trumpet and Two Trombones; Exulta filia Sion; Nothing Heavy and Nothing at Rest (symphonic band); Cantata; Good Day Sir Christmas (soprano solo, chorus and instrumental ensemble); Divertimento (chamber orch.); Concerto (saxaphone and orch.); Chimera (ballet); Variations (orch.); Overture for a Dedication; arranger: Grand Centennial March (Zeuner); President Garfield's Inauguration March (Sousa); Slavonic Dance No. 12 (Dvorak). Home: 543 E 24th St Brooklyn NY 11210

KLUCKHOHN, FLORENCE ROCKWOOD (MRS. GEORGE E. TAYLOR), educator; b. Ill., Jan. 14, 1905; d. Homer Garfield and Florence (McLaughlin) Rockwood; A.B., U. Wis., 1927; Ph.D., Radcliffe Coll., 1941; m. Clyde Kluckhohn, Oct. 15, 1932 (dec. 1960); 1 son, Richard Paul Rockwood; m. 2d, George E. Taylor, 1968. Tchr., Wellesley Coll., 1940-48; analyst OWI, Washington, 1944-45; lectr. dept. social relations, asso. in Lab. Social Relations, Harvard U., 1948-68, ret.; hon. affiliate prof. anthropology U. Wash., 1974. Mem. Am. Anthrop. Assn., Am. Sociol. Assn., Am. Acad. Polit. and Social Scis., Soc. Applied Anthropology, Phi Beta Kappa. Clubs: Harvard (Seattle); Radcliffe (Boston). Author: (with Fred L. Strodtbeck) Variations in Value Orientations, 1961; The American Family Past and Present and America's Women, 1952. Home: The Highlands Seattle WA 98177

KLUG, MARILYN JOAN, investor; b. Gt. Bend, Kans., Mar. 18, 1936; d. Walter Henry and Ressa Evelyn (Barrett) Otte; student Ft. Hays (Kans.) State Coll., 1954-56; m. Douglas Klug, Aug. 28, 1955; children—Bryce Karl, Brenda Lee, Bruce Allan. With C.E., 1956-61; head sec. Airports div. FAA, Alaska, 1965-68; mgr., owner investment property, Anchorage, 1968—. Recipient awards Fed. Govt., 4-H; lic. gen. contractor, real estate sales assoc., Alaska. Mem. Nat. Assn. Realtors. Republican. Methodist. Home and Office: 2853 W 100th Ave Anchorage AK 99502

KLUZEK, DIANE LEE, mgmt. cons.; b. Palo Alto, Calif., Oct. 29, 1954; d. Robert Miles and Lida Pearl (Loffel) Kluzek; B.A., U. Calif., Berkeley, 1975; M.Edn., U. San Francisco, 1978. Assessment specialist Inst. for Profl. Devel., San Jose, Calif., 1975-77; mgr. Assessment Center, U. San Francisco, 1977-79; mgmt. cons. Performex, San Francisco, 1979-81; prin. Spl. Events Prodns., San Francisco, 1981—; faculty Resource Center for Women, 1980-81. Peer forums coordinator Women Entrepreneurs, 1981; v.p. Embarcadero Center Forum, 1982—. Mem. Project Mgmt. Inst. (publs. chmn.), C. of C. Author: How To Run a High Volume Assessment Center, 1977. Office: The Hearst Bldg 5 3d St San Francisco CA 94104

KNAPE, ANNE SABRA (MRS. CLIFFORD S. KNAPE), librarian; b. San Angelo, Tex., Jan. 24, 1917; d. Sumner Morrison and Sonora Jane (Divers) Ramsey; B.S., U. Tex., 1938; postgrad. Tex. Woman's U., 1950; M.S., Baylor U., 1952; m. Clifford S. Knape, May 30, 1942; children—Mildred Anne (Mrs. Douglas Witte), Sabra Jane, Carl G. Librarian Austin (Tex.) Ind. Sch. Dist., 1939-44; librarian Manchester (N.H.) Pub. Library, 1944-45; library coordinator LaVega Ind. Sch., Waco, Tex., 1953-58; librarian Waco (Tex.) Ind. Sch. Dist., 1958-74; catalog cons. H.W. Wilson Co., 1970-74. Mem. Am., Tex. library assns., NEA (life), Tex. State Tchrs. Assn., Nat., Tex. mental health assns., Alpha Beta Alpha, Theta Sigma Phi, Delta Kappa Gamma. Home: 4319 Cedar Mountain Dr Waco TX 76708

KNAPP, MILDRED FLORENCE, social worker; b. Detroit, Apr. 15, 1932; d. Edwin Frederick and Florence Josephine (Antaya) K.; B.B.A., U. Mich., Ann Arbor, 1954, M.A. in Community and Adult Edn. (Mott Found. fellow 1964), 1964, M.S.W. (HEW grantee 1966), 1967. Dist. dir. Girl Scouts Met. Detroit, 1954-63; planning asst. Council Social Agencies Flint and Genessee County, 1965; sch. social worker Detroit Public Schs., 1967—; field instr. grad. social workers. Mem. alumnae bd. govs. U. Mich., 1972-75, scholarship chmn., 1969-70, 76-80, chmn. spl. com. women's athletics, 1972-75, class agt. fund raising Sch. Bus. Adminstrn., 1978-79; mem. Founders Soc. Detroit Inst. Art, 1969—, Friends Children's Museum Detroit, 1978—, Women's Assn. Detroit Symphony Orch., 1982—. Recipient various certs. appreciation. Mem. Nat. Assn. Social Workers, Acad. Cert. Social Workers, Nat. Community Edn. Assn. (charter), Outdoor and Edn. Camping Council (charter), Mich. Sch. Social Workers Assn. (pres. 1980-81), Detroit Sch. Social Workers Assn. (past pres.), Detroit Assn. U. Mich. Women (pres. 1980-82), Detroit Fedn. Tchrs. Methodist. Clubs: Detroit Boat, Detroit Women's City. Home: 14214 Jane St Detroit MI 48205 Office: 4300 Marseilles Detroit MI 48224

KNAPP, ROSALIND ANN, lawyer; b. Washington, Aug. 15, 1945; d. Joseph Burke and Hilary (Eaves) K.; B.A., Stanford U., 1967, J.D., 1973. Admitted to Calif. bar, 1973, D.C. bar, 1980; with Dept. Transp., Washington, 1974—, asst. gen. counsel legislation, 1979-81, dep. gen. counsel, 1981—. Mem. D.C. Bar Assn., Calif. Bar Assn. Office: 400 7th St SW Washington DC 20590

KNAPP, ROSALYN ROCHELLE, air force officer; b. Fredericksburg, Pa., Aug. 2, 1939; d. Herbert and Mabel May (Darkes) K.; B.S. in Music Edn., Lebanon Valley Coll., 1961; M.A. in Personnel Mgmt., Central Mich. U., 1975. Music tchr. East Orange (N.J.) Public Schs., 1961-62; commd. 2d lt. U.S. Air Force, 1963, advanced through grades to lt. col., 1979; personal affairs and family services officer Plattsburgh (N.Y.) AFB, 1963-65; WAF squadron sect. comdr. Westover (Mass.) AFB, 1965-67; officer-in-charge message distbn. br. Directorate Adminstrn., Hdqrs. SAC, Offutt (Nebr.) AFB, 1967-68; wing exec. officer 432 Tactical Reconnaissance Wing, Udorn Air Base, Thailand, 1968-69; dependent schs. liaison officer, chief quality control, chief processing div., asst. chief consol. base personnel office, Rhein-Main Air Base, Germany, 1969-73; chief career advancement, chief sr. officer mgmt. Hdqrs. Command, Bolling AFB, Washington, 1973-76; comdr. 3743 Basic Mil. Tng. Squadron, Lackland (Tex.) AFB, 1976-79; chief exec. services, chief of staff, manpower and personnel Hdqrs. USAF, Pentagon, 1979-80; mem. bd. Sec. Air Force Personnel Council, Rosslyn, Va., 1980—. Decorated Gallantry Cross with Palm (Republic of Vietnam). Mem. Nat. Assn. Female Execs., Air Force Assn. Republican. Mem. United Ch. of Christ. Home: 5422 Midship Ct Burke VA 22015 Office: Commonwealth Bldg Rosslyn VA

KNAPP, VIRGINIA ESTELLA, educator; b. Washington, May 11, 1919; d. Bradford and Stella (White) Knapp; B.A., Tex. Tech. U., 1940; M.A., U. Tex. 1948; postgrad. Sul Ross Coll., 1950, Stephen F. Austin U., 1964-68. Tchr. journalism, high schs., Silverton, Tex., 1940-41, Electra, Tex., 1941-42, Joinerville, Tex., 1942-60, Carthage, Tex., 1961-69; tchr. history and journalism Longview (Tex.) High Sch., 1969-80; instr. Trinity U., San Antonio, summer 1972; fellowship tchr. Wall St. Jour., Tex. A&M U., College Station, summers 1964-67. Chmn., Rusk County (Tex.) Hist. Commn., 1980—. Recipient Wall St. Jour. award Outstanding Journalism Tchrs. of Yr., 1965-66. Mem. Tex. State Tchrs. Assn., Classroom Tchrs. Assn., Tex. Assn. Jour. Dirs., Rusk County Heritage Assn., Rusk County Hist. Survey Com., Women in Communications (pres. Longview chpt. 1972-74, Service award 1975), Tex. Press Women, DAR. Episcopalian. Contbr. hist. writing to Ala. Rev., Progressive Farmer, Rusk County C. of C. Brochure, Rusk County Heritage, numerous others. Home: 321 College Ave Henderson TX 75652 Office: 325 Fairpark Henderson TX 75652

KNAPPENBERGER, ANGELA CORALIE, chem. co. sales ofcl.; b. Jamestown, N.Y., Sept. 1, 1951; d. Harold Lester and Faith Coralie (Whitaker) K.; B.A. in Chemistry, Ohio Wesleyan U., 1973. Systems chemist Gen. Public Utilities, Reading, Pa., 1973-74; with Am. Cyanamid Co., various locations, 1974—, sales mgr. South Pacific Dist. water treating dept. indsl. products div., Los Angeles, 1981, Azusa, Calif., 1982—. Mem. NOW (treas. chpt. 1980-81). Home: 600 California Riverside CA 92507 Office: 1001 N Todd Ave Azusa CA 91702

KNAPP-NIXON, BETTY LOU, educator; b. Fairmont, W.Va., Feb. 11, 1927; d. Earl Dale and Susie Belle (Bryne) Knapp; A.B. with honors, Fairmont State Coll., 1949; M.A. with high honors, W.Va. U., 1952, Ed.D., 1970; m. Henry Maltby Nixon, Sept. 18, 1965. Sponsor/chorus dir. Girls' State, Am. Legion Aux., Fairmont, W.Va., 1954-63; choral dir. Monongahela Power Co., Fairmont, 1955-60; choir dir. First Meth. Ch., Fairmont, 1951-63; elementary music specialist Marion County Bd. Edn., Fairmont, 1949-54, music tchr., tchr. English lit., music dir., 1954-63; spl. tchr. East Orange (N.J.) Bd. Edn., 1964-70; prof. Rutgers U. Grad. Sch. Edn., New Brunswick, N.J., 1977; prof. elementary/spl. edn. Rutgers Coll.-Rutgers U., New Brunswick, 1970-81; cons. U.S. Dept. Edn., Washington, 1982. Mem. exec. bd. Nat. Republican Women, N.Y.C., 1982-83, N.J. Coalition for Women, 1981; mem. Republican Presidential Task Force, 1982. Mem. Internat. Platform Assn., AAUP, Nat. Assn. Tchr. Educators (asst. chmn. com. on fiscal affairs 1979-85), N.J. Assn. Tchr. Educators (pres. 1981-82), N.J. Coll. and Univ. Coalition on Women's Edn. (vice-chmn.-mem. chmn. 1980-81), W.Va. U. Alumni Assn., Kean Coll. Profl. Women's Assn., Republican Women Union County, Soc. Educators and Scholars, Phi Delta Kappa, Kappa Delta Pi, Alpha Psi Omega. Methodist. Clubs: Echo Lake Country, Coll. Women (Westfield, N.J.), Westfield Women's Rep. Author: Student Teaching: A Time for Success. Home: 117 Linden Ave Westfield NJ 07090

KNAUER, BARBARA ANN, speech pathologist; b. Balt., Apr. 13, 1953; d. Richard James and Margaret Marie (Burton) K.; student Essex Community Coll., 1971-73; B.A., Loyola Coll., Balt., 1976; M.S. (Fort Howard VA fellow), 1977. Speech and lang. pathologist Bd. Edn. Balt., 1977—. Tchr. learning disabled children Christian Class in Doctrine, 1979—. Mem. Am. Speech and Hearing Assn., Md. Speech and Hearing Assn., Balt. Council Stutterers, Met. Balt. Assn. Children with Learning Disabilities. Clubs: Balt. Ski, Cub Hill Civic Assn. Home: 2910 Northwind Rd Baltimore MD 21234 Office: 2001 Sinclair Ln Baltimore MD 21206

KNAUER, VELMA STANFORD, savs. and loan assn. exec.; b. Pottstown, Pa., July 4, 1918; d. Chester Miller and Pearl Fretz (Miller) Stanford; student public schs.; m. Joseph Daniel Knauer, Feb. 17, 1940; children—Joseph Daniel, Susan Velma Knauer Metz. With U.S. Axle Co., Inc., Pottstown, 1936-45; with First Fed. Savs. & Loan Assn., Pottstown, 1953—, controller, 1953—, asst. treas., 1953-62, asst. sec., 1962-75, treas., 1976—. Mem. Am. Soc. Profl. and Exec. Women. Home: 970 Feist Ave Pottstown PA 19464 Office: Box 1 High and Hanover Sts Pottstown PA 19464

KNAUER, VIRGINIA HARRINGTON WRIGHT (MRS. WILHELM F. KNAUER), govt. ofcl.; b. Phila., Mar. 28, 1915; d. Herman Winfield and Helen (Harrington) Wright; B.F.A., U. Pa., 1937, LL.D. (hon.); postgrad. Pa. Acad. Fine Arts, Royal Acad. Fine Arts, Florence, Italy, 1938-39; LL.D., Phila. Coll. Textiles and Sci., Allentown Coll. St. Francis de Sales, Widener Coll., Chester, Pa., Tufts U.; Litt.D., Drexel U.; L.H.D., Russell Sage Coll., Pa. Coll. Podiatric Medicine; m. Wilhelm F. Knauer, Jan. 27, 1940; children—Wilhelm F., Valerie H. (Mrs. I. Townsend Burden III). Dir., Pa. Bur. Consumer Protection, 1968-69; spl. asst. consumer affairs to Pres., White House, 1969-77, 81—; dir. U.S. Office Consumer Affairs, 1971-77, 81—; pres. Virginia Knauer & Assos., Inc., Washington, 1977-81; chmn. Council for Advancement of Consumer Policy, 1979-81; U.S. rep., vice chmn. consumer policy com. OECD, 1970-77; mem. Council Wage and Price Stability, 1974-77. Councilman-at-large, Phila., 1960-68; vice-chmn. Philadelphia County Rep. Com., 1958-77; pres. Phila. Congress Rep. Women's Councils, 1958-77; dir. Pa. Council Rep. Women, 1963-80; founder N.E. Council Rep. Women, pres., 1956-64. Bd. dirs. Hannah Penn House, 1956—, v.p., 1971; former trustee Pa Coll. Podiatric Medicine; co-founder Knauer Found. Historic Preservation. Recipient Gimbel-Phila. award; named Disting. Dau. Pa. 1969. Mem. Nat. Trust Historic Preservation, Zeta Tau Alpha, Kappa Delta Epsilon (hon.) Episcopalian. Office: The White House Exec Office Bldg Washington DC 20500

KNAUF, JANINE BERNICE, educator; b. Rochester, N.Y., Apr. 10, 1945; d. William Charles and Ila May (Hauss) Knauf; S.B., M.I.T., 1967; M.B.A., Rutgers U., 1971; M.Ph., Columbia U., 1979, Ph.D., 1981; 1 son, Christopher Robert Burgess. Research engr. Northrop/Norair, Hawthorne, Calif., 1965-66; sci. research engr. Rockwell Internat., Los Angeles, 1967-68; acct. Knauf and Knauf, Rochester, 1968-69, 76, 78; lectr. mgmt. dept. Poly. Inst. N.Y., 1972-73; asst. prof. info. systems Rutgers U., Newark, N.J., 1973-79; asst. prof. acctg. Fla. State U., Tallahassee, 1980—. C.P.A., N.Y. State. Mem. Soc. Women Engrs., Internat. Platform Assn., AIAA, Am. Woman's, N.Y. State socs. C.P.A.s, Am. Acctg. Assn., AAUP, Aircraft Owners and Pilots Assn., Beta Gamma Sigma, Sigma Gamma Tau.

KNECHT, DENISE JEAN, lawyer; b. Akron, Ohio, Nov. 14, 1948; d. William H. and Rita (Poydock) Knecht; B.A., U. Akron, 1970; postgrad. U. Wis., 1976, Cleve. State U., 1975, J.D., Cleve. Marshall Coll. Law, 1981. Fashion coordinator O'Neils Co., Akron, 1970-72; freelance pub. relations and promotional mktg. N.Y., Fort Lauderdale, Miami, Cleve., 1972-74; program dir. Am. Cancer Soc., Cleve., 1974-76, exec. dir. Lorain and surrounding counties, 1977; dir. pub. relations Marcus Advt., Cleve., 1977-79; public relations cons., Cleve., 1979-81; practice law, 1981—; producer, moderator radio program Women's Connection, Stas. WBBG and WWWM-FM. Cons. pub. relations, senatorial and mayoral campaigns Ohio. Mem. Cleveland Women Lawyers Assn., Cuyahoga County Bar Assn., Women in Communications, NOW, Alpha Delta Pi. Club: Women's City of Cleve. (2d v.p.). Author, pub.: The Pocket Guide to Cleveland. Home: 1721 Fulton Rd Cleveland OH 44113 Office: 508 Park Bldg 140 Public Sq Cleveland OH 44114

KNEE, RUTH IRELAN (MRS. JUNIOR K. KNEE), social worker, health care cons.; b. Sapulpa, Okla., Mar. 21, 1920; d. Oren M. and Daisy (Daubin) Irelan; B.A., U. Okla., 1941, cert. social work, 1942; M.A., U. Chgo., 1945; m. Junior K. Knee, May 29, 1943 (dec. Oct. 21, 1981). Psychiat. social worker, asst. supr. Ill. Psychiat. Inst., U. Ill. at Chgo., 1943-44; psychiat. social worker USPHS Employee Health Unit, Washington, 1944-46, chief psychiat. social worker, 1946-49; psychiat. social work asso. Army Med. Center, Walter Reed Army Hosp., Washington, 1949-54; psychiat. social work cons. HEW, Region III, Washington, 1955-56; with NIMH, Chevy Chase, Md., 1956-72; chief mental health care adminstrn. br. USPHS, 1967-72, asso. dep. adminstr. Health Services and Mental Health Adminstrn., 1972-73, dep. dir. Office of Nursing Home Affairs, 1973-74; long-term mental health care cons.; mem. com. on mental health and illness of elderly HEW, 1976-77; mem. panel on legal and ethical issues Pres.'s Commn. on Mental Health, 1977-78; liaison mem. Nat. Adv. Mental Health Council, 1977-81. Bd. dirs. Hillhaven Found., 1975—. Fellow Am. Public Health Assn. (sec. mental health sect. 1968-70, chmn. 1971-72), Am. Orthopsychiat. Assn.; mem. Am. Assn. Psychiat. Social Workers (pres. 1951-53), Nat. Conf. Social Welfare (nat. bd. 1968-71, 2d v.p. 1973-74), Council on Social Work Edn., Nat. Assn. Social Workers (sec. 1955-56, nat. dir. 1956-57, chmn. competence study com., practice and knowledge com. 1963-71), Am. Public Welfare Assn., Gerontol. Soc., DAR, Phi Beta Kappa, Psi Chi. Editorial bd. Health & Social Work, 1979-81. Address: 8809 Arlington Blvd Fairfax VA 22031

KNEEDLER, JULIA ANNE, nurse educator; cons.; b. Martinez, Calif., Mar 27, 1938; d. John F. and Marge G. (Curl) Williams; B.S. in Nursing, Walla Walla Coll., 1961; M.S. in Nursing, Loma Linda U., 1967; Ed.D. in Adult Continuing Edn., U. No. Colo., 1976. Staff nurse Greater Bakersfield (Calif.) Meml. Hosp., 1961-63, Loma Linda (Calif.) U. Hosp., 1963-67; med.-surg. supr. Iowa Luth. Hosp., Des Moines, 1967-69; operating room supr. Porter Meml. Hosp., Denver, 1969-72, asst. dir. nursing service, staff devel., 1980—; asso. Operating Room Nurses Inc., Denver, asst. dir. edn./continuing edn., 1972-80; cons. Edn. Design, Inc.; leader seminars. R.N., Colo. Mem. Am. Nurses Assn., Colo. Nurses Assn. (dir. 1976-77, commn. on cert. 1973-74, ad hoc com. on C.E. 1974-78, commn. on nursing service and edn. 1976-78, del. Am. Nurses Assn. Conv. 1976, 78), Assn. Operating Room Nurses (regional joint rev. com. chmn. 1973-75), Am. Soc. Tng. and Devel., Adult Edn. Assn. U.S.A., Colo. Soc. Health Care Nursing Service Adminstrn., Sigma Theta Tau. Republican. Seventh-day Adventist. Contbr. numerous articles on nursing to profl. jours.; author: (with Diane F. Schoenrock) Operating Room Orientation Program for the New Graduate Nurse, 1974; (with Gruendemann et al) Nursing Audit: Challenge to the Operating Room Nurse, 1975; Speciality Nursing Courses: Operating Room, 1976; (with Ertl et al) Peer Review for Nursing Practice: Operating Room, 1977; (with Manuel and David) Surgical Experience: A Model for Professional Nursing Practice in the Operating Room, 1978; (with Lindeman et al) The Relationship Between Operating Room Nursing Activities and Patient Outcomes: An AORN-WICHE Report, 1978; (with Bradley J. Manuel) Design for Continuing Education Activities, 1979; (with Gwen H. Dodge) Perioperative Patient Care: The Nursing Perspective, 1983; compiler and editor: Guidelines for ORT Refresher Course, 1973; AORN Nat. Seminar Brochure, 1977-78, 1978-79, 1979-80; developed modular ind. learning system. Address: PO Box 31975 Aurora CO 80041

KNEELAND, SHARON ANNE, mfg. co. exec.; b. Westerly, R.I., Feb. 1, 1945; d. Andrew Henry and Althea (Reid) K.; B.S. in Edn., Worcester (Mass.) State Coll., 1972. Tchr., Brusett, Mont., 1973-74; personnel mgr. Marlboro Wire Goods Co. (Mass.), 1974-76; wage and salary adminstr. Boston U., 1976-77; compensation analyst Data Gen., Westboro, Mass., and Westbrook, Maine, 1977-79; mgr. human resources Gould/Modicon, Andover, Mass., 1979—; panelist, moderator Women in High Tech Careers workshops and seminars. Mem. Electronics Industry Personnel Assn., Computer Industry Personnel Assn., New Eng. Benefits Council. Office: PO Box 83 SVS Andover MA 01810

KNEER, MARIAN ELIZABETH, educator; b. Peoria, Ill., Mar. 8, 1924; d. Edwin and Gertrude Cecilia (Kelch) K.; B.S., Ill. State U., 1949, M.S., 1956; Ed.S., U. Mich., 1969, Ph.D., 1972. Tchr., head dept. East Peoria (Ill.) Community High Sch., 1949-68; prof. phys. edn. U. Ill., Chgo., 1969—, grad. dir., 1976—. Mem. AAHPER and Dance, Ill. Assn. Health, Phys. Edn., Recreation and Dance, AAUP, Assn. Tchr. Edn., Nat. Assn. for Sport and Phys. Edn. (editor Basic Stuff Series 1981). Roman Catholic. Author: (with Helen Heitmann) PE Instructional Techniques, 1975; (with McCord) Softball-Slow and Fast Pitch, 1980; contbr. articles to profl. jours. Home: 5731 Woodland Dr Western Springs IL 60558 Office: U Ill Chicago Circle Chicago IL 60680

KNEIP, CLOTILDE (COCO), civic worker; b. Milw., Aug. 18, 1937; d. William George and Glenn H. (Davidson) Patterson; student public schs.; m. Neal Charles Kneip, June 25, 1970; children—Alison, Jeffrey, Gregory, George. Co-producer, host Armed Forces TV, Ft. Greely, Alaska, 1964-65; dir. public relations Army Community Services, Tacoma, Wash., 1969-70, Spokane LWV, 1972-73; pres. Logan PTA, Spokane, 1973-74, Young Audiences, Inc., Spokane, 1974-75, Music for Youth, Spokane, 1975—; mem. election bd. precinct 322, Spokane County, 1973—; sec. Spokane County Republican Central Com., 1977-78, vice-chmn., 1978—; chmn. Juvenile Detention Facilities, 1977-78; mem. citizen's cons. com. Spokane County Juvenile Ct., 1978—; vol. coordinator auction KSPS-TV, public television, 1978; chmn. info. Western Art Show and Auction, Spokane, 1981; bd. dirs. Spokane Food Bank, 1981—; membership dir. Spokane Area Conv. and Visitors Bur., 1982. Home: 1123 Illinois Spokane WA 99207

KNELSON, NELDA LORAIN RIFE, mental health technician; b. Pierce County, N.D., June 16, 1915; d. Herbert Edward and Katie Marie (Christianson) Rife; student Sauk Valley Coll., 1968-75; m. Henry W. Knelson, Sept. 16, 1931; children—John Henry, Nelda May (Mrs. James W. Daley), James Douglas. Factory worker Brown Shoe Co., Dixon, Ill., 1937-45; waitress several locations, Dixon, 1945-47; survey worker, real estate salesperson Hurd Realtors, Dixon, 1948-50; mental health supr. and technician Dixon Devel. Center, 1964—. Pres. Lee County Home Extension, 1957-59; active Girl Scouts U.S.A., Boy Scouts Am., Dixon Writers Group Community Players. Mem. Lee County, Ill. hist. socs., Clubs: Dixon Women's (pres. 1959-61), Women of Moose, CROP, Travel. Author poetry: Out of the Inkwell, 1959; Out of the Fire, 1960; Out of the Mist, 1968; (juvenile) Tiger the Autobiography of a Cat, 1975. Home: 2016 W 1st St Dixon IL 61021

KNIGHT, ALICE D. TIERRELL, former state legislator; b. Manchester, N.H., July 14, 1903; d. Nathan Arthur and Clara (Stiles) Tirell; B.A., U. N.H., 1925, postgrad., 1933; postgrad. Boston U., 1941-42; m. Norman Knight, Nov. 15, 1952. Tchr., Newton Falls (N.Y.) High Sch., 1925-26; prin. Oswegatchie (N.Y.) Union Sch., 1926-27, Barrett Sch., Goffstown, N.H., 1932-35; home lighting specialist Public Service Co. N.H., Manchester, 1935-39; thcr. merchandising Mt. Ida Jr. Coll., Newton Centre, Mass., 1939-45; home service dir. Coyd Corp., Portland, Maine, 1945-47; dist. home economist Frigidaire Sales Corp., Boston, 1948-64; mem. N.H. Ho. of Reps., 1967-74, 76-78. Mem. budget com. Town of Goffstown, 1966-72; mem. Gov.'s Adv. Com. Alcoholism, 1972-73, 74—, Statewide Health Coordinating Council, 1977-78; past pres. bd. dirs. Hillsborough County North Cancer Soc.; bd. dirs. N.H. Cancer Soc. Recipient award N.H. Program on Alcohol and Drug Abuse, 1971, 75. Mem. Am. Home Econs. Assn., Nat. Home Fashions League (pres. 1957-58), Nat. Soc. State Legislators, Am. Women in Radio and TV, LWV, N.H. Council World Affairs, Nat. Grange, DAR (regent 1974-76), Nat. Order Women Legislators (pres. 1968-71), Manchester Bus. and Profl. Women (pres. 1972-74). Clubs: Republican. Episcopalian. Clubs: Order Eastern Star (life), Soroptomist (19fe) (Boston); Goffstown Unity, Goffstown Garden (pres. 1976-78), Goffstown Shirley (pres. 1977-78). *

KNIGHT, ATHELIA WILHELMENIA, journalist; b. Portsmouth, Va., Oct. 15, 1950; d. Daniel Dennis and Adell Virginia (Savage) K.; B.A. with honors in English, Norfolk State Coll., 1973; M.A. with honors in Journalism (Univ. fellow), Ohio State U., 1974. Aida, D.C. Coop. Extension Service, summers 1969-72; substitute tchr. Portsmouth Pub. Schs., 1973; reporter Virginian Pilot, Norfolk, 1973, Chgo. Tribune, 1974; met. desk reporter Washington Post, 1975-81, investigative reporter, 1981—; lectr. to high schs., colls. Cert. tchr., Va. Mem. Women in Communications, Washington-Balt. Newspaper Guild. Baptist. Home: 1535 C St SE Washington DC 20003 Office: 1150 15th St NW Washington DC 20071

KNIGHT, BARBARA JEAN, investments corp. exec.; b. Portland, Oreg., May 25, 1947; d. William Ralph and Jean (Boggs) K.; B.S. magna cum laude, U. So. Calif., 1969. Research asst., registered rep. First Calif. Co., San Francisco, 1970-72; sr. analyst, strategist Crocker Investment Mgmt. Corp., San Francisco, 1972-76; analyst, portfolio mgr. Wentworth Hauser & Violich, San Francisco, 1975-79; sr. research analyst, investments, Salomon Bros., N.Y.C., 1979; pres. Millbrook Advisors, Inc., Newport Beach, Calif., 1982—; investment advisor; cons. to major pension funds and individual clients. Chartered Fin. Analyst. Mem. Fin. Analyst Fedn., Phi Kappa Phi. Home: Laguna Niguel CA 92677 Office: 1300 Dove St Suite 200 Newport Beach CA 92660

KNIGHT, DIANE MARY, social worker; b. LaCrosse, Wis., Nov. 26, 1946; d. Charles Robert and Marcella Mary (Peterson) K.; student Clarke Coll., 1964-66; B.A., U. Wis., Milw., 1970, M.S. in Social Work, 1975. Social worker, Milwaukee County Dept. Social Services, Milw., 1970-79, casework supr., 1979—. Bd. dirs. United Meth. Children's Services of Wis., 1981—. Mem. Acad. Cert. Social Workers, Nat. Assn. Social Workers (treas. Wis. chpt. 1981—), Wis. Social Service Assn., NOW, Common Cause. Roman Catholic. Home: 1730 N 57th St Milwaukee WI 53208 Office: 1220 W Vliet St Milwaukee WI 53205

KNIGHT, GEORGINE MARIE, med. technologist; b. Hazleton, Pa., Feb. 22, 1954; d. George and Eleanor Marie (Subally) K.; B.S. in Med. Tech., Wilkes Coll., 1977. Med. technologist, asst. supr. chemistry Nesbitt Meml. Hosp., Kingston, Pa., 1977—. Winner Northeastern Pa. Philharm. Talent Competition, 1971. Mem. Am. Soc. Clin. Pathologists (affiliate, registered med. technologist). Home: 458 Monument Ave Wyoming PA 18644 Office: 562 Wyoming Ave Kingston PA 18704

KNIGHT, IVERY BANKS, educator, civic worker; b. Isle of Wight County, Va., Feb. 1, 1941; d. Willie James and Hattie Mae (Rawlings) Banks; B.S., Norfolk State U., 1965; M.A., Hampton Inst., 1972; postgrad. U. Md., summers 1973-77, Old Dominion U., 1978, Norfolk State U., 1979, Va. State U. Extension, 1968; m. Matthew C. Knight, Oct. 7, 1962; 1 dau., Dollicia Dimetria. Instr., Russell High Sch., 1965-67, East Suffolk Elem. Sch., 1967-72, Hampton Inst., 1972-73, Mallory Elem. Sch. and Tarrant Elem. Sch., 1974; instr. health and phys. edn. Eaton Jr. High Sch., Hampton, Va., 1974—; head basketball coach, softball coach for girls; drill team comdr. Conductress Order of Eastern Star Holland chpt. 162, 1979-80; pres. ch. choir, 1974-80; anti-basileus Zeta Epsilon Omega chpt. Alpha Kappa Alpha, 1978, basileus, 1979-80. Cert. instr. CPR and advanced first aid; nominee Tchr. of Year, 1977. Mem. Hampton Edn. Assn., Va. Edn. Assn., NEA, AAHPER and Dance, Va. High Sch. Coaches Assn., Va. Parent, Tchr. and Student Assn. Club: Smart Set Social and Savs. Home: 2207 Kentucky Ave Suffolk VA 23434

KNIGHT, LEONIA VONCELE, paper co. exec.; b. Tarboro, N.C., Sept. 22, 1948; d. Leon Knight and Annie Belle (Anthony) Johnson; B.S., Morgan State U., 1970; M.B.A., Howard U., 1975; advanced profl. cert. in fin. N.Y.U., 1979. Comml. lending trainee, sr. fin. analyst Bankers Trust, N.Y.C., 1975-76; credit rep. Internat. Paper Co., N.Y.C., 1976-78, credit mgr., 1978-80, sr. fin. analyst, 1980—. Mem. Riverside Bus. and Profl. Women's Club, Nat. Urban League, Alpha Kappa Alpha. Home: 253 W 72d St Apt 508 New York NY 10023 Office: 77 W 45th St New York NY 10036

KNIGHT, MARCEL VIOLA, computer services co. exec.; b. New Orleans, Aug. 25, 1923; d. Elijah Tucker and Marcella Viola (LaBiche) K.; B.S., George Washington U., 1945. Controller, Krupp Internat., Inc., New Orleans, 1969-78; treas., chief acct. Delta Com., Inc., New Orleans, 1979—, Delta Data Services, Inc., New Orleans, 1979—, UCI Services, Inc., New Orleans, 1979—. Mem. Am. Soc. Women Accts., Am. Acctg. Assn., La. Landmarks Soc., Jefferson Hist. Soc. La., Heraldry Soc. London, Nat. Geneal. Soc., La. Geneal. and Hist. Soc., Geneal. Research Soc. New Orleans, Richard III Soc. (London), Friends of Archives of La., Friends of Cabildo, La. Hist. Soc., River Rd. Hist. Soc., Soc. Genealogists (London). Republican. Roman Catholic. Home: 838 Bungalow Ct New Orleans LA 70119 Office: 723 Howard Ave New Orleans LA 70130

KNIGHT, MARCIA, clin. psychologist; b. N.Y.C., July 1, 1946; d. Murray M. and Ruth (Lynn) Knight; B.A., Brown U., 1968; M.A., Yeshiva U., 1975; Ph.D. (NIMH fellow), 1979. Adj. lectr. Bklyn. Coll., 1971-74; staff psychologist Met. Hosp., N.Y.C., 1974-80; pvt. practice psychology, N.Y.C., 1980—; cons. psychologist Gracie Sq. Hosp., N.Y.C., Sage Garden Acad., Bronx, N.Y.; supervising psychologist Child Devel. Center affiliated with Flower and Misericordia Hosps., Bronx; assoc. Dr. Karen Blaker Psychotherapy Center, N.Y.C. Mem. Am. Psychol. Assn., N.Y. State Psychol. Assn., NOW (psychology com.), Internat. Assn. for Human Relations Lab. Tng. (bd. advisors, editor Newsletter). Home: 224 E 18th St New York NY 10003 Office: 22 E 11th St New York NY 10003

KNIGHT, MARGARETT LEE, editor, lawyer, state ofcl.; b. Newtown, Ind., Jan. 3, 1923; d. Charles Oscar and Edna (Pace) Smith; LL.B., Ind. U., 1945, J.D., 1965; A.B., Mills Coll., 1953; LL.M., Yale U., 1955; m. Robert Cook Knight, June 20, 1961. Admitted to Ind. bar, 1945; now dep. atty. gen. Ind. Home: 1318 Hoover Ln Indianapolis IN 46260

KNIGHT, MARY ELAINE, nursing adminstr.; b. Cordele, Ga., May 29, 1946; d. Allen Edward and Lillian (Woodard) Roberson; diploma nursing Macon (Ga.) Hosp. Sch. Nursing, 1967; student Middle Ga. Coll., Cochran, Ga., 1973-74; m. Walter S. Knight, Oct. 7, 1972; 1 dau., Amber Elaine. Operating room staff nurse, relief nurse pediatrics and premature nursery Macon Hosp., 1967; operating room staff nurse St. Francis Hosp., Columbus, Ga., 1968; supr. Dodge County Hosp., Eastman, Ga., 1968-70; office nurse Dr. Wallace Lucas, Cochran, 1971-73; operating room supr. Laurens Meml. Hosp., Dublin, Ga., 1973-75; staff nurse Dublin VA Med. Center, 1975-78; relief supr. Tattnall Meml. Hosp., Reidsville, Ga., 1978-79; dir. nursing services John M. Meadows Meml. Hosp., Vidalia, Ga., 1979—; mem. adv. council Swainsboro Area Vocational-Tech. Sch., 1980-82. Vice-pres. 1st congressional dist. Ga. Peace Officers Assn. Ladies Aux. Mem. Am. Soc. Nursing Service Adminstrs., Am. Hosp. Assn., State Health Planning Devel. Agy., Southeastern Dist. Nursing Service Adminstrs. (pres. elect), Ga. Soc. Nursing Service (program com.), Ga. Hosp. Assn. Democrat. Baptist. Home: Route 5 Box 200 B-1 Lyons GA 30436 Office: PO Box 1048 Vidalia GA 30474

KNIGHT, MARY LUCILLE, convalescent center adminstr.; b. Enid, Okla., Dec. 5, 1938; d. Otis Stanley and Mary Ellen (Record) Kile; m. E. Harmon Knight, Apr. 30, 1962; children—Sherri, Fran, Cathy. Med. asst. Dr. Fred Thomas, Dallas, 1963-67; x-ray asst., physicians' asst. Prevost Meml. Hosp., Donaldsonville, La., 1967-72; asst. adminstr. Archusa Convalescent Center, Quitman, Miss., 1976—, sec. bd. dirs., 1976-78. Lic. adminstr. Mem. Miss. Nursing Home Assn. Republican. Baptist. Home: 10 Betty Circle Quitman MS 39355 Office: Hwy 511 E Quitman MS 39355

KNIGHT, PHYLLIS PRICE, mfg. co. exec.; b. Hamblen County, Tenn., Mar. 4, 1939; d. Amos Anderson and Flora Jane (Seals) Price; student public schs. Morristown, Tenn.; children by previous marriage—Larry Lee, Donna Carol. Co-buyer indsl. hardware Wallace Hardware Co., Morristown, 1965-72; v.p. mktg. ops. School Calendar Co., Morristown, 1972-81; mktg. dir., sales mgr. Huntington Industries, Chgo., 1981; pres. PK Creations, Inc. Chgo., 1982—. Mem. C. of C. Chgo., Am. Bus. Women's Assn., Nat. Assn. Women Bus. Owners, Nat. Assn. Female Execs. Clubs: East Bank, Lake Point Tower, Baneberry Golf/Racquet. Designer apparel accessories. Address: 505 N Lake Shore Dr Chicago IL 60611

KNIGHT, SHIRLEY, actress; b. Goessel, Kans., July 5, 1936; d. Noel J. and Virginia (Webster) K.; D.F.A. (hon.), Lake Forest Coll., 1979; m. John Hopkins; children—Kate, Sophie. Recipient numerous acting awards. Address: PO Box 157 Catchoque NY 11935

KNIGHT, YVONNE RICHMOND, educator; b. Phillips, Maine, Aug. 24, 1929; d. Russell C. and Maxine Hayden (Hoyt) Richmond; A.B., Colby Coll., 1955; M.B.A., Cornell U., 1957; m. Lawrence C. Knight, 1964; 1 son, Marc D. Fisher. Mem. faculty Colby Coll., 1958—, Waterville, Maine, now prof. adminstrv. sci.; dir. Canal Nat. Bank; cons. on taxes on bus. Past pres. Phillips C. of C.; pres. Phillips Hist. Soc., 1979—. Mem. Maine Snowmobile Assn. (past pres.), Phi Beta Kappa (treas. Maine Beta chpt.). Author cost study of rural hosp. for HEW, 1964; author various teaching manuals for fin., investment texts. Office: Colby Coll Waterville ME 04901

KNILL-CATTANEO, MARIAGNESE, educator, artist, psychotherapist; b. Schaffhausen, Switzerland, July 30, 1937; came to U.S., 1973; d. Mario and Emilia (Zanetti) Cattaneo; B.A. in Music Theory, Conservatory Winterthur, 1968, M.A. in Music Edn. and Performance, 1971. Tchr. kindergartens in Switzerland and Peru, 1958-63; mem. faculty Conservatory Winterthur, 1971-76, Conservatory Zurich, 1972-73; guest lectr. Tufts U., Medford, Mass., 1973-75; adj. prof. Swiss U. Adult Edn., 1972-75; pvt. practice art and music therapy, Switzerland and U.S., 1971-76; asst. prof. expressive therapies Lesley Coll. Grad. Sch., Cambridge, Mass., 1974—; cons. in field, concerts in Europe, U.S., Israel; exhibited art shows U.S. Cert. counselor State Dept. Health, Schaffhausen; cert. music therapist; cert. expressive therapist. Mem. Swiss Assn. Kindergarten Tchrs., Swiss Assn. Music Edn., Internat. Assn. Music Edn., Nat. Women's Studies Assn., Swiss Assn. Music Therapy, Assn. Expressive Therapies, Am. Assn. Artist Therapists. Author curriculum materials. Office: 11 Mellen St Cambridge MA 02138

KNIPE, BARBARA FORTUNE JANSSEN, reading specialist; b. Mankato, Minn., Dec. 14, 1938; d. Herman Girard and Lulu Elizabeth (Campbell) Janssen; B.S. in Elem. Edn., U. N.D., 1960, postgrad. (Hazel B. Neilson scholar), 1977—; m. Walter Harold Knipe, July 1, 1961; children—William Walter, Steven Girard, Anne Fortune. Tchr. public schs., Racine, Wis., 1960-61; tchr. public schs., Grand Forks, N.D., 1961-75, curriculum developer, 1972-73; post-secondary tchr. East Grand Forks (Minn.) Area Vocat. Tech. Inst., 1975-80, support services mgr., 1980—, supr. spl. needs, 1981-83, mem. state evaluation team spl. needs programs, 1980, 82; continuing edn. instr. U. N.D., 1977. Bd. dirs. Grand Forks County Hist. Soc., 1978-79, Community Input. Recipient individual recognition award for spl. needs personnel Mind, Inc., 1980-81; outstanding support to spl. needs award Minn. State Dept. Edn., 1981-82. Mem. Internat. Reading Assn., NEA, PEO, DAR, Delta Kappa Gamma, Alpha Phi. Presbyterian. Home: 717 S Fourth Grand Forks ND 58201 Office: Area Vocat Tech Inst Hwy 220 NE East Grand Forks MN 66721

KNISELY, SALLY, psychotherapist; b. Baraga, Mich., Mar. 17, 1917; d. Henry Samuel and Flora (Hagerman) Knisely; A.B., U. Mich., 1944; M.A., U. Chgo., 1946; Ed.D., Columbia U., 1964. Day nursery caseworker Bur. Family Service, Orange, N.J., 1946-49; caseworker to mentally ill vets. VA, N.Y.C., 1949-53; child psychotherapist Inter-Agy. Guidance Center, Yonkers, N.Y., 1953-58; child psychotherapist Monsey (N.Y.) Mental Health Clinic, 1957-58; child psychotherapist New Rochelle (N.Y.) Guidance Center, 1958-59; pvt. practice psychotherapy, Stamford, Conn., 1954—; cons. numerous nursery sch. and presch. programs; mem. profl. adv. bd. Early Childhood Programs, Martha's Vineyard, Mass. Fellow Conn. Soc. Clin. Social Workers; mem. Am. Orthopsychiat. Assn., Council Psychoanalytic Psychotherapists, Nat. Assn. Edn. Young Children, Soc. for Health and Human Values, Nat. Assn. Social Workers, Nat. Assn. of Deaf, Am. Deafness and Rehab. Assn., AAUW. Home and office: 69 Jordan Ln Stamford CT 06903

KNOBBE, MARY LOUISE SIEFER, library cons.; b. Cherryvale, Kans., Aug. 26, 1918; d. Clarence E. and Lula (Funkhouser) Siefer; A.B., Washburn U. 1940; postgrad. Sch. Library Sci. and Information U. Md., 1965-67; m. Ray H. Knobbe, Jan. 23, 1946; children—Ann, Jane. Library asst. Washburn U., Topeka, 1941-42; librarian Dept. Research, Kansas City, Mo., 1944-46; reference librarian Carnegie Library, Steubenville, Ohio, 1950-51; planning librarian Md. Nat. Capital Park and Planning Commn., Silver Spring, 1961-67; librarian Met. Washington Council Govts., 1967-79; library cons., 1979—; dir. Inter Library Users Assn., 1972-79. Mem. Council Planning Librarians, Spl. Libraries Assn. (chmn. social sci. div. D.C. chpt. 1967-68, chpt. dir. 1968-70; mem. govt. info. services com. 1971-75, chmn. urban affairs sect. 1975-76, chmn. govt. info. services com. 1975-77), Kans. Soc. Washington, Pi Gamma Mu. Episcopalian. Editor: Planning and Urban Affairs Library Manual, 3d edit., 1975; Planning, Building and Housing Libraries, 1969. Home and Office: 2300 Eccleston St Silver Spring MD 20902

KNOCK, FRANCES ENGELMANN (MRS. THEODORE EMANUEL KNOCK), surgeon, chemist; July 8, 1921; d. William Fred and Frances (Tietze) Engelmann; B.S., U. Chgo., 1940, Ph.D. (Swift fellow), 1943; M.D., U. Ill., 1954; m. Theodore Emanuel Knock, Oct. 23, 1943. Assoc. organic chemist Armour Research Found., Chgo., 1943-46, organic chemist, 1946-49, chem. cons., 1950-51; dir. Nat. Registry Rare Chems., Chgo., 1945-50; chem. cons. Merck Sharp & Dohme, Rahway, N.J., 1954-56; intern Evanston (Ill.) Hosp., 1954-55; resident Presbyn. Hosp., Chgo., 1955-59; practice medicine specializing in surgery, Chgo., 1959—; dir. Knock Research Found., Chgo., 1955—; staff Augustana Hosp., Chgo., 1961—, VA Hosp., Hines, Ill., 1961-74; mem. faculty U. Ill., Chgo., 1959—, clin. asst. prof. surgery, 1962—; lectr. in pharmacology Loyola, Hines, 1972—; cons. E.R. Squibb & Sons, New Brunswick, N.J., 1964-66. Diplomate Am. Bd. Surgery, Nat. Bd. Med. Examiners. Fellow AAAS, Am. Inst. Chemists, Am. Geriatrics Soc., Royal Soc. Health, Internat. Coll. Angiology, Sci. Council, Internat. Coll. Surgeons, Am. Coll. Med. Hypnotists; mem. AMA, Am. Chem. Soc., N.Y. Acad. Scis., Am. Inst. Chemists, Am. Coll. Angiology, Union Internat. Contra Cancer, Phi Beta Kappa, Sigma Xi, Alpha Omega Alpha. Author: Anticancer Agents, 1967. Contbr. over 100 articles to chem., biophysics, and med. jours.; showed common low electron spin resonance signals of all cancers (ESR) mask marked chem. heterogeneity of cancers, to negate any support for randomized protocols for cancer chemotherapy but to support precise chem. measurements to individualize human cancer chemotherapy. Patentee in field. Home: 416 Country Ln Glenview IL 60025 Office: 30 N Michigan Ave Chicago IL 60602 also Knock Research Found 6 N Michigan Ave Chicago IL 60602

KNOEBEL, BETTY LOU MARGARET, food service exec.; b. Hobart, Ind., July 12, 1931; d. Frank Orville and Louise Caroline (Sohn) Burnett; radiol. technician Meth. Hosp. Sch. Radiology, 1950; student Ind. U., 1952-54, St. Joseph's Hosp. Sch. Nursing, 1950-51, Calif. Western Res. U., 1976—; m. F. C. Knoebel, Apr. 27, 1974. Bookkeeper, Nash Agy., Gary, Ind., 1948-49; x-ray technician Gilfillan Clinic, Bloomfield, Ia., 1950-51; med. sec., x-ray technician Meth. Hosp., Gary, Ind., 1951-52; chem. lab. and indsl. x-ray technician Cast Armor Div., Am. Steel Foundry, East Chgo., Ind., 1952-53; med. sec., surg. asst., med. asst., R. G. Nilges, M.D., neurosurgeon, 1953-60; ins. sec., sales and claims sec. Farm Bur. Ins., Crown Point, Ind., 1960-63; med. sec., surg. and med. asst. M.R. Bernard, M.D., neurosurgeon, 1963-65; exec. sec. to v.p. mktg. and sales The Anderson Co., Gary, 1965-71; x-ray technician Melissa Meml. Hosp., Holyoke, Colo., 1971; corp. sec., adminstrv. asst. Nobel, Inc., Denver, 1971—; dir. Gen. Mgmt. Corp., Denver, 1974—, Capital Warehouse Corp., Denver, 1974—. Sec., Tolleston Ch. of Christ, Gary, 1940-48; pianist, tchr. Glen Park Assembly of God, Gary, 1948-71. Am. Cancer Soc. radiology grantee, 1949. Mem. Colo.-Wyo. Restaurant Assn. (chmn. 1978-79), Ind. Soc. Radiologic Technicians, Profl. Businesswomen's Assn., Nat. Secs. Assn., AAUW. Republican. Assemblies of God. Home: 5 Village Rd Englewood CO 80110 Office: 1101 W 48 Ave Denver CO 80217

KNOERLE, SISTER, JEANNE, coll. pres.; b. Cleve., Feb. 24, 1928; d. Harold and Bernedine (Seufert) Knoerle; B.A., St. Mary-of-the-Woods Coll., 1949; M.A., Ind. U., 1961, Ph.D., 1966, LL.D., 1975; LL.D., Rose Hulman Inst. Tech., 1971; LL.D., Ind. State U., 1972; D.D., Ind. Central U., 1978. Tchr. high schs., 1952-54; chmn. dept. journalism St. Mary-of-the-Woods Coll. (Ind.), 1954-63, asst. to pres., asso. prof. Asian studies, 1967-68, pres., prof., 1968—; vis. prof. Providence Coll., Taichung, Taiwan, 1966-67. Mem. Gov.'s Commn. Status of Women, 1973-75; pres. Ind. Conf. Higher Edn., 1973-74; dir. Fed. Home Loan Bank, Indpls., 1975—; mem. adv. council div. research resources NIH, 1975-79; mem. exec. com. Women's Coll. Coalition-Assn. Am. Colls.; mem. adv. council Acad. in Pub. Interest, Georgetown U. Grad. Sch. Bd. dirs. Union Hosp., Terre Haute, Ind., United Way of the Wabash Valley, 1971-75, Mental Health Assn. Vigo County, 1971-78, Wabash Valley Goodwill Industries, 1970-78, Terre Haute Med. Edn. Found. Mem. Assn. Cath. Colls. and Univs. (chmn. 1978-80), Am. Council Edn. (dir., mem. com. on women in higher edn.), Nat. Cath. Edn. Assn. (dir.), Assn. Am. Colls. (dir. 1976-80), Internat. Assn. Univ. Presidents (adv. council N. Am. council), Asso. Colls. Ind. (sec. 1970-72, v.p. 1978—), Council Advancement Small Colls. (dir. 1980-83), Ind. Conf. Higher Edn. (exec. com. 1972-73), Delta Kappa Gamma. Author: The Dream of the Red Chamber, a Critical Study, 1972. Contbr. articles to profl.

jours. Address: St Mary-of-the-Woods Coll St Mary-of-the-Woods IN 47876

KNOTT, CAROL REDE, interior designer; b. Weston, W.Va., Mar. 18, 1930; d. Marion Wyllys and Mary Warren Rede; student Rollins Coll., 1948-49; B.A., Northwestern U., 1966; m. Richard F. Knott, Nov. 26, 1949; children—Diana Despard, Richard F., Thomas Read, Sally Oliver. Designer, Betty Lotz Interiors, Winnetka, Ill., 1966-73; owner Carol R. Knott Interior Design, Kenilworth, Ill., 1973—; tchr. Wilmette Park Dist. Mem. Am. Soc. Interior Designers (dir.), Chgo. Designers Club, Colonial Dames, Desc. Signers Declaration of Independence. Republican. Episcopalian. Clubs: Farmington Country (Charlottesville, Va.); Mchts. and Mfrs. (Chgo.). Office: 430 Green Bay Rd Kenilworth IL 60043

KNOTT, MEREDITH LEE, computer scientist; b. Chgo., July 20, 1941; d. John Otis and Florence Margene (Lee) K.; B.A., Maryville (Tenn.) Coll., 1963; divorced; children—Shawn Charles, Laurel Lee. Instr., Colo. Mountain Coll., Glenwood Springs, 1970-71; IBM programmer, analyst Petro-Systems, Lakewood, Colo., 1980; tech. lead, computer graphics software engr. Martin Marietta Denver Aerospace, 1980—; tchr. computer sci. Founder, organizer, race sec., coach Buddy Werner Ski League, Glenwood Springs, 1973-74. Mem. Assn. Computing Machinery, Nat. Assn. Computer Graphics, Colo. Assn. Gifted and Talented. Republican. Home: 375 Ingalls St Lakewood CO 80226

KNOTT, TARA DAVIS, evaluation cons.; b. Alexandria, La., Dec. 5, 1943; d. Raoul Lynwood and Ruby Montez (Luneau) Brister; B.A. in Psychology, Memphis State U., 1971, M.A. in Speech Pathology, 1975; B.A. in Speech and Music, La. State U., 1961; Ph.D. in Evaluation Research, Clayton U., 1978; m. David Howard Knott, Aug. 6, 1978. Evaluator family practice dept. U. Tenn. Center for Health Scis., 1976-78; research cons. Deafness Found., 1978, Nat. Hearing Assn., 1978; evaluation cons. Covington Mental Health Center, 1978-79; head data collection Project WOMAN, 1978-79; evaluation cons. Mid South Hosp., 1979—, Jackson Splty. Hosp., 1980—; United Inns, 1981—, Memphis Mental Health Inst., U. Tenn. Center Health Scis., 1979—; cons., tchr. hosps., colls. and univs. Grantee in alcoholism and drug abuse. Mem. Evaluation Network, Evaluation Research Soc., Soc. Neurosci., Tenn. Evaluation Network. Democrat. Methodist. Contbr. articles to profl. jours. Home and Office: 4181 Chickasaw Rd Memphis TN 38117

KNOWLES, GLORIA BALL, personnel adminstr.; b. Magna, Utah, Mar. 14, 1937; d. Alfred Thomas and Virginia (Hatton) Ball; student public schs., San Francisco; m. Sanderson Llewellyn, Apr. 2, 1955; children—Douglas Llyn, Thomas Ross. Bookkeeper, Wells Fargo Bank, San Francisco, 1954-56; with Bank of Am., Richmond and Oakland, Calif., 1956-59, 60; credit/loan clk. Central Bank, Concord, Calif., 1972-73; sr. acctg. clk. produce div. Safeway Stores, Inc., Oakland, 1973-75, affirmative action rep., 1975-76, ERD Supply Dir., 1977-81, employee relations supr., 1981—. Contra Costa County regional occupation program adv. com., 1978—; mem. sci. adv. com., sec. Diablo Valley Coll., 1979-80, 80-81; United Way coordinator Safeway Stores, Inc., 1979-80. Recipient United Way Pacesetter Coordinator cert., 1980. Mem. Federated Employers Bay Area, Diablo Valley Indsl. Personnel Soc., Nat. Assn. Female Execs. Republican. Mem. Ch. Jesus Christ of Latter-day Saints. Office: 2800 Ygnacio Valley Rd Walnut Creek CA 94598

KNOWLES, MARJORIE FINE, lawyer, educator; b. Bklyn., July 4, 1939; d. Jesse J. and Roslyn L. Fine; A.B. magna cum laude (Dawes prize in govt. 1960), Smith Coll., 1960; postgrad. Radcliffe Coll., 1960-62; LL.B. cum laude (Joseph H. Beale prize 1965; teaching fellow, grad. asst.), Harvard U., 1965. Admitted to N.Y. bar, 1966, Ala. bar, 1975; law clk. to U.S. dist. judge, 1965-66; asst. U.S. dist. atty. So. Dist. N.Y., 1966-67; asst. dist. atty. Office Dist. Atty. N.Y. County, 1967-70; exec. dir. Joint Found. Support, Inc., N.Y.C., 1970-72; mem. faculty U. Ala. Law Sch., Tuscaloosa, 1972—, asso. dean, 1982—; Am. Council Edn. fellow, program asso. Office of President, 1976-77; asst. gen. counsel insp. gen. div. HEW, Washington, 1978-79; insp. gen. Dept. Labor, 1979-80; cons. Ford Found., N.Y.C., 1980; cons. in field. Mem. steering com. Washington Women's Network, 1978-80; bd. dirs. Ms. Found. Women, N.Y.C., 1975—, Women's Legal Def. Fund, 1980-81; mem. Nat. Commn. on Higher Edn. Issues, 1981—. Recipient Woman of Achievement award Tuscaloosa Bus. and Profl. Women's Club, 1974; named One of 10 Outstanding Young Women of Am., 1975; fellow Rockefeller Found. Aspen Inst., 1976. Mem. Am. Bar Assn., AAUW, ACLU, LVW, NOW, Women's Equity Action League, Ala. Bar Assn., Ala. Women's Poliy. Caucus. Contbr. articles legal publs.

KNOWLES, PATRICIA KAIRALLE, dancer, choreographer; b. W. Palm Beach, Fla., May 14, 1942; d. George E. and Mireille Sylvia (Cowan) Kairalla; B.A. in English, Fla. State U., Tallahassee, 1964, M.A. in Dance, 1966; m. Frank L. Knowles, June 26, 1966. Instr., choreographer, dancer U. Ga., Athens, 1966-70, Eastern Mich. U., Ypsilanti, 1970-73; dir. dance, choreographer, performer Brevard (N.C.) Music Center, summers 1968-70; head dept. dance U. Ill., Champaign-Urbana, 1973—; dancer, cons. in field.; mem. panel dance Ill. Arts Council, 1979-80; choreographer Ill. Dance Theatre, univ. and regional dance cos., others. Grantee Mich. Arts Council, Ill. Arts Council; 3 works commd. by Harbinger Dance Co. Mem. Council Dance Adminstrs., Am. Coll. Dance Festival Assn. (dir.), Nat. Assn. Schs. Dance (treas. 1982-83). Democrat. Roman Catholic. Home: 401 W Indiana St Urbana IL 61801 Office: 4-205 Krannert Center 500 S Goodwin St Urbana IL 61801

KNOX, BARBARA (RUTH) SNYDER, psychologist, adminstr.; b. Oklahoma City, Aug. 26, 1924; d. Chalmer Donaldson, Sr., and Ruth Margaret (Harbaugh) Snyder; student Park Coll., 1942-44; B.A. with distinction in Econs summa cum laude, Ohio State U., 1946; M.A. in Psychology, Towson State U., 1972; Ph.D., Cath. U. Am., 1975; m. June 8, 1946; children—Laura Elizabeth Knox Strong, Margaret Lela Knox Humanian, Robert Gaylord. Statistician, research asst. Ohio State Bur. Bus. Research, Columbus, 1946-47; social work asst. Anne Arundel County Dept. Social Services, Annapolis, Md., 1967-69; part time child psychologist Balt. City Hosps., 1971-73; psychology intern, 1973-74; coordinator adolescent services Spring Grove Hosp. Center, Catonsville, Md., 1974-76, staff psychologist, 1976-77, dir. Balt. City Unit Spring Grove, now Catonsville Unit of Walter P. Carter Community Mental Health Center, 1977-81; unit treatment coordinator, staff psychologist Taylor Manor Hosp., Ellicott City, Md., 1981—; adj. asst. prof. dept. psychology U. Balt., 1975-76; pvt. practice psychology, Balt., 1975—. Active LWV, 1951-58, 60-69, unit leader, resource person, sec. bd. Oklahoma City chpt., 1963-64, bd. dirs., newsletter editor Okla. state chpt., 1964-65. Recipient Ruth Strang Meml. Research award, Nat. Assn. Women Deans, Adminstrs. and Counselors, 1975. Mem. Am. Psychol. Assn., Md. Psychol. Assn. (rep.-at-large 1977-79), Exec. Women's Network, Assn. for Advancement of Psychology, Nat. Register of Health Service Providers in Psychology, Phi Beta Kappa. Democrat. Unitarian. Home: 404 George St Baltimore MD 21201 Office: Taylor Manor Hosp College Ave PO Box 272 Ellicott City MD 21043

KNOX, DOROTHY DEAN BRENT, police insp.; b. Jayess, Miss., Mar. 10, 1940; d. Robert Earl and Juanita I. (Jones) Brent; B.S. in Criminal Justice Adminstrn., Wayne State U., Detroit, 1975; m. Stanley R. Knox, Oct. 23, 1960. Apptd. to Detroit Police Dept., 1969—, sgt., 1974-77, lt., 1977-80, insp., 1980—, comdg. officer profl. standards sect., 1978—. Mem. Randolph W. Wallace Sr. Kidney Research Found.; vol. Am. Cancer Soc. Mem. Women Police Mich., Lts. and Sgts. Assn. (asso.), FBI Nat. Acad. Grads., Women's Econ. Club. Detroit. Office: 1300 Beaubien Detroit MI 48226

KNOX, ELISABETH ANN, nurse; b. Princeton, Ind., Dec. 31, 1936; d. Harry Dorsey and Mary Duncan (Fitzsimmons) Keneipp; B.S.N., Ind. U., 1958, M.S. Health Ed., 1968; M.S.N., U. Evansville, 1982; m. Lawrence J. Knox, Feb. 21, 1976; children—David L. Furr (dec.), Byron D. Furr (dec.). Staff nurse Riley Hosp., Indpls., 1958-59, VA Hosp., Indpls., 1959, Deaconess Hosp., Evansville, Ind., 1961; sch. nurse North Gibson Sch. Corp., Princeton, 1962-68; dir. asso. degree program Olney (Ill.) Central Coll., 1968-72; dir. asso. degree nursing program U. Evansville, 1972-76; cons. for asso. degree nursing programs, Olney, Ill., 1978—; vis. asst. prof. U. Evansville, 1982-83 Bd. dirs. Richland Meml. Hosp. Aux., 1977—, Olney Central Coll. Found., 1979—; mem. council ministries 1st United Meth. Ch., 1978—. bd. dirs. Fellow Am. Sch. Health Assn.; mem. Am. Nurses Assn., Ill. Nurses Assn. (awards com.), Dist. 12 Nurses Assn. (pres. 1978-80, dir. 1976-78, 80-82), Nat. League Nursing (visitor for asso. degree nursing programs 1973-76), Phi Kappa Phi. Club: Richland Country. Address: 1200 N East St Olney IL 62450

KNOX, JANICE ANN, banker; b. Chgo., Mar. 18, 1948; d. James W. and Lucy Olivia (Williams) Knox; B.A. in Math., Northeastern Ill. U., 1971; postgrad. Northwestern U. With First Nat. Bank Chgo., 1971—, programming instr., 1973-76, systems mgr., 1976—, systems officer, 1979—; programming instr. Malcolm X Coll., Chgo., 1974; tng. specialist urban skills City Colls. Chgo., 1978—. Grantee NSF, 1964-65. Mem. Assn. Computing Machinery, Pansophic Users Learning and Sharing Exchange, NAACP (1st v.p. women's aux. 1981—). Office: 1 First Nat Plaza Suite 0272 Chicago IL 60670

KNOX, LEILA CASANOVA, nursing adminstr.; b. San Pablo City, Philippines, May 13, 1951; came to U.S., 1972, naturalized, 1978; d. Pacifico Velasco Calinawan (stepfather) and Francisca Nohay Casanova; B.S. in Nursing cum laude, U. Sto Tomas, 1971; postgrad. U. Minn., 1981—; m. Gary Franklin Knox, Aug. 13, 1974. Charge nurse Community Hosp., San Pablo City, Philippines, 1971-72, Columbia Presbyterian Med. Center, N.Y.C., 1974; float nurse No. Dutchess Hosp., Rhinebeck, N.Y., 1973; hosp. supr., relief staffing coordinator Alaska Hosp., Anchorage, 1975-78; asst. dir. nursing services Nakoyia Health Care Center, Anchorage, 1978-79, dir. nursing services, 1979-80, adminstr. patient care services, 1981—. Mem. bd. dirs. Hospice of Anchorage, 1979—; v.p. bd. dirs. Mutt and Jeff, Inc., Wasilla, Alaska, 1979—; mem. adv. bd. RN/LPN program Anchorage Community Coll., 1979—. Mem. Alaskan Internat. Relief Fund. (v.p. 1981-82), Long Term Care Nurses Assn. (chmn. 1980—), Nursing Needs of Alaska (mem. analysis and planning task force 1980—), Am. Nurse's Assn., Nat. League Nursing, Nat. Assn. Female Execs., Am. Health Care Assn. Home: PO Box 411 Wasilla AK 99687 Office: Pouch 6617 4895 Cordova Anchorage AK 99502

KNOX, MARGARET ELLIOTT, newspaper editor; b. Norfolk, Va., Aug. 16, 1919; d. Roy and Mary (Upshur) Elliott; A.B. cum laude, U. Ala., 1941; m. Robert Bost Knox, Jr., Apr. 26, 1944 (dec.). With Raleigh (N.C.) Times, 1941, Raleigh News and Observer, 1942, Richmond (Va.) Times Dispatch, 1942-44, New Orleans States-Item, 1944-46, N.Y. World Telegram & Sun, N.Y.C., 1946-59, Norfolk Virginian-Pilot, 1962-63; founder, editor Leader, Research Triangle Park, N.C., 1966-81, editor emeritus, 1981—; editorial bd. adv. Capitol Broadcasting Co., Raleigh, 1981-82. Mem. public relations adv. com. N.C. State U., 1979. Recipient Best Series award N.Y.C. Newspaper Women's Club, 1951; Headliner award N.C. Women in Communications, 1981. Mem. N.C. Press Assn., Raleigh Fine Arts Soc. Episcopalian. Home: 2922 Wycliff Rd Raleigh NC 27607 Office: 10 Park Plaza Research Triangle Park NC 27709

KNOX, MARY SULLIVAN, banker; b. Trail, B.C., Can., Jan. 27, 1916; d. Michael Henry and Lucia Garrett (Merchant) Sullivan; B.S. in Home Econs., U. Idaho; m. William W. Knox, May 22, 1941 (dec.); children—William Ward II, Mary S. Knox Dickinson, Harry W. II, Ann Michael, Jane Kennedy Knox Potucek. Instr., Glenns Ferry (Idaho) High Sch.; owner, mgr. Pitchfork Ranch, King Hill; dir. Idaho State Bank, Glenns Ferry, 1945—, sec. to bd. dirs., 1950-70, v.p., 1967-69, pres., 1969-70, chmn. bd., 1970—; dir. Salt Lake City br. 12th Fed. Res. Dist. Bd. dirs. Valley Gallery; active Elmore County 4-H Council; precinct committeewoman Republican party. Recipient Outstanding 4-H award. Mem. Nat. Assn. Bank Women, Am. Bankers Assn., Ind. Bankers Assn., Banking Adminstrv. Inst., Western Ind. Bankers Assn. (mem. legis. com.), Idaho Bankers Assn., Am. Legion Aux., DAR, Nat. Home Econs. Soc. (hon. life). Republican. Roman Catholic. Clubs: Am. Nat. Cowbelles, Inc., North Bliss Cattle Assn. Home: River Ranch Glenns Ferry ID 83623 Office: Drawer AE Glenns Ferry ID 83623

KNUDSON, HELEN LOUISE, mfg. co. exec.; b. Stonecreek, Ohio, May 3, 1934; d. Paul Raymond and Dorothy Catherine (Bragg) Shank; student U. Wis., 1974-80; m. Keith Earl Knudson, Aug. 16, 1961; children—Lynda Lee, Raymond Riley, Keith Eric, Kristin Anna. With Slade Gas Co., Jacksonville, Fla., 1956-57, Cryovac div. W.R. Grace, Chgo., 1957-61; tchr. Edgerton (Wis.) Sr. High Sch., 1961-63; pres., owner Editions in Procelain, Inc., Edgerton, 1969—, Keili, Inc., Edgerton, 1978—; lectr. in field. Tchr. ceramics YWCA, 1967-68; bd. dirs. Albion Acad. Hist. Soc., 1973-77, Inner Peace Movement, 1975-79; govtl. appointee Wis. Dept. Vet. Affairs; mem. citizens adv. com. for raising venture capital Wis. Commn. Securities, 1981—; candidate for spl. election to Wis. Assembly, 1981. Served with USN, 1952-55. Mem. Nat. Assn. Female Execs., Nat. Assn. Women Bus. Owners, Wis. Mfrs. Assn. (dir. 1980—), VFW, Milw. Art Center. Republican. Mem. Unity Sch. Christianity. Clubs: Edgerton Country, Edgerton Garden (v.p. 1974-75). Home: 209 Bentley Pl Edgerton WI 53534 Office: 114 W Fulton St Edgerton WI 53534

KNUDSON, KATHRYN HELEN MALLOY, psychologist, army officer; b. St. Louis, Mar. 19, 1949; d. Albert Joseph and Julia (Kozar) Malloy; B.A. magna cum laude, U. Mo., St. Louis, 1971; M.A., U. Calif., Riverside, 1974, Ph.D. (NIMH fellow), 1978; m. Gregory Blair Knudson, Oct. 21, 1972; children—Todd Christopher. Commd. 2d lt. U.S. Army, 1971, advanced through grades to capt., 1979; research psychologist Walter Reed Army Hosp. Research Inst., Washington, 1979—. Mem. Am. Psychol. Assn., Assn. Women in Psychology. Home: 6621 Willis Ln Frederick MD 21701 Office: Dept Mil Psychiatry Walter Reed Army Inst Research Washington DC 20012

KNUDSON-COOPER, MARY S., clin. anthropologist; b. Cushing, Okla., Oct. 15, 1938; d. William H. and Elizabeth L. (Shogren) Sewell; B.A. with honors, U. Wash., 1960; Ph.D., U. Oreg., 1973; m. James O. Cooper, Jr., Dec. 16, 1979; children by previous marriage—Erik E. Knudson, Arne W. Knudson. Lectr. dept. anthropology U. Nev., Reno, 1972-73, asst. prof., 1973-75; asst. prof. dept. psychiatry U. Tex., Galveston, 1975—; chief, behavioral sci. div. Shriners Burns Inst., Galveston, 1975—. Mem. Am. Anthrop. Assn., Am. Burn Assn., Am. Psychol. Assn., Am. Soc. Clin. Hypnosis, Assn. for Care of Children in Hosps., Biofeedback Soc. Tex., Soc. Med. Anthropology. Office: Shriners Burns Institute Galveston TX 77550

KOBA, SISTER, MARY HILTRUDE, nun, coll. pres.; b. Phila., Feb. 8, 1916; d. Joseph and Agnes (Nowak) K.; B.S., Seton Hall U., 1955; M.A., Fordham U., 1960, Ph.D., 1974. Tchr. elem. schs.; prin. elem. sch.; tchr. high sch., guidance counselor, until 1958; registrar, dir. admissions Felician Coll., Lodi, N.J., 1958-60, registrar, instr. edn., dir. admissions, asst. prof. edn., 1964-67, dean acad. affairs, 1967-77, pres., 1977—. Named Most Disting. Alumna, Seton Hall U., 1978; recipient N.J. Senate Resolution, 1978. Mem. Assn. Ind. Colls. and Univs., AAUW, Am. Assn. Univ. Adminstrs., Nat. Assn. Women Deans, Adminstrs. and Counselors, N.J. Assn. Colls. and Univs. (chmn., dir.), Ind. Coll. Fund N.J., N.J. Coll. and Univ. Coalition Women's Edn., C. of C. No. N.J., Saddle River Sub-Basin Coordination Group. Roman Catholic. Home and office: 260 S Main St Lodi NJ 07644

KOBAYASHI, ANN, state senator, bus. exec.; b. Honolulu, Apr. 10, 1937; student Pembroke Coll., Northwestern U.; married; 3 children. Vice pres., sec. family corp.; adminstrv. asst. to Senator W. Yee, then legis. aide Senator E. Forbes; now mem. Hawaii Senate. Mem. Manoa Neighborhood Bd.; active Am. Cancer Soc., ARC, Boys' Club of Honolulu, Manoa Pop Warner League. Mem. Hawaii Dental Aux., C. of C. Office: Hawaii Senate State Capitol Honolulu HI 96813 *

KOBAYASHI, CHARLOTTE CHIYO, export co. exec.; b. Olaa, Hawaii, Sept. 2, 1942; d. Ginzo and Yukie (Horike) K.; B.A., U. Hawaii; M. Early Childhood Edn., Loyola U., Chgo., 1970; Paul A. Braga, June 15, 1980; 1 dau., Marissa Rike. Vice pres., mgr. Soken Trading Inc., Sausalito, Calif., also. dir. Contbr. articles to jours., mags.

KOBER, ARLETTA REFSHAUGE (MRS. KAY L. KOBER), civic worker; b. Cedar Falls, Iowa, Oct. 31, 1919; d. Edward and Mary (Jensen) Refshauge; B.A., U. No. Iowa, 1940, M.A., 1970; m. Kay Leonard Kober, Feb. 14, 1944; children—Kay Mary, Karilyn. Tchr. high schs., Soldier, Iowa, 1940-41, Montezuma, Iowa, 1941-43, Waterloo, Iowa, 1943-50; tchr. East High Sch., Waterloo, 1966—; head dept. coop. career edn. West High Sch., Waterloo Community Schs., 1966—. Mem. Waterloo Sch. Health Council; nominating com. YWCA, Waterloo; Black Hawk County chmn. Tb Christmas Seals; ward chmn. ARC, Waterloo; co-chmn. Citizen's Com. for Sch. Bond Issue; pres. Waterloo PTA Council, Waterloo Vis. Nursing Assn., 1956-57, Kingsley Sch. PTA, 1959-60; pres. Waterloo Women's Club, 1963-64, trustee bd. clubhouse dirs., 1957—; mem. Gen. Fedn. Women's Clubs, Nat. Congress Parents and Tchrs.; Presbyterial world service chmn. Presbyn. Women's Assn.; bd. dirs. Black Hawk County Republican Women, 1952-53, United Services of Black Hawk County; bd. dirs. Broadway Theatre League, v.p., 1963-65. Mem. AAUW (v.p. 1946-47), NEA, League Women Voters (dir. Waterloo 1951-52), Delta Pi Epsilon (charter mem. Alpha Delta chpt.), Delta Kappa Gamma. Club: Town (dir.) (Waterloo). Home: 1046 Prospect Blvd Waterloo IA 50702 Office: Baltimore and Ridgeway Waterloo IA 50702

KOBY, CONSTANCE AUDREY, investment co. ofcl.; b. Jacksonville, Fla., Feb. 25, 1944; d. John Stanley and Gloria (Christopher) Kirkland; grad. pvt. schs., Houston; 1 dau., Colette Marie. Various exec. secretarial positions, 1962-79; owner, operator Koby's Kiddie Korps, day care center, 1976-79; exec. sec., adminstrv. asst. to exec. v.p. Standard Metals, Houston, 1979-80; account exec. Byrd Internat., Houston, 1980-81; with oil and gas investments dept. Fin. div. Merrill Lynch White Weld, 1981—. Vol., St. Luke's Hosp. Mem. Nat. Assn. Profl. Saleswomen, Navy League U.S. Club: Space City Ski. Home: Merrill Lynch White Weld 2466 First City Tower 1001 Fannin Street Houston TX 77002

KOCH, JUNE QUINT, govt. dept. adminstr.; b. Bklyn., Jan. 18, 1933; d. Eli and Minnie Quint; B.A., Bklyn. Coll., 1954; M.A., Temple U., 1957; Ph.D., Columbia U., 1965; m. Noel Clinton Koch, Sept. 10, 1967; children—Justin, Monica, Jennie, Gabriel, Elias. Instr., Temple U. 1958-65; asst. prof. Widener Coll. 1965-68; asst. prof. Bryn Mawr Coll. 1968-73; dir. Fed. Liaison Phila. '76 Inc. 1973-75; v.p. Koch Assocs., Inc. 1976-80; dep. undersec. HUD, Washington 1981—. Dir. intergovernmental relations Reagan-HUD Transition Team, 1980-81. Nat. Endowment Humanities grantee, 1972-73. Mem. Republican Women's Forum, RNC Women's Network, Phi Beta Kappa. Jewish. Contbr. articles in field to profl. jours. Office: 451 7th St SW Washington DC 20410

KOCH, RUTH MARGUERITE, educator, artist; b. Hazleton, Pa., July 11, 1901; d. Henry George and Margaret (Zimmerman) Koch; grad. Bloomsburg State Tchrs. Coll., 1921; Ph.B., Muhlenberg Coll., 1931; M.A., Bucknell U., 1948; student Sch. Fine and Applied Arts, Chgo., 1923; postgrad. N.Y.U., 1925, 28, Pa. State U., 1935; visited art schs., galleries, Europe, 1952, 57, 65, 68, 71. One man shows: Penn. State U. Center, 1937, Hazleton Art League, 1948; exhibited annually in group shows Lehigh Art Alliance, Lehigh U., Muhlenberg Coll., nat. shows Miniature Painters Soc., Smithsonian Instn., Corcoran Gallery, also N.Y., N.J., Pa., Kans., Washington; represented in permanent collections at Lehigh U. Art Gallery, Call Chronicle Newspaper Art Collection, Allentown, Pa., also pvt. collections in U.S., P.R., Eng.; art tchr. elementary sch., Hazleton, 1921-39, jr. high sch., 1939-40, sr. high sch., 1940-67; designed, painted children's stories on glass lantern slides, 1930-35; lectr., demonstrator of art various religious and civic groups, clubs, schs., colls.; lectr. on travels. Recipient 1st place water color, Hazleton, 1938, 3d water color award, Harrisburg, 1940, 41. Mem. Pa. Edn. Assn. (pres. art group Scranton 1947) Nat., Pa., Luzerne County ret. tchrs. assns., Community Concert Assn., Lehigh Art Alliance, Hazleton Art League (purchase award 1968), Internat. Platform Assn., Delta Kappa Gamma. Author articles in art and other periodicals. Lutheran. Home and studio: 551 Lincoln St Hazleton PA 18201

KOCHANOWSKA, KRISTINA, physician; b. Warsaw, Poland, Jan. 12, 1933; d. Mieczyslaw and Janina (Krajewska) Kohn; came to U.S., 1969, naturalized, 1974; M.D., Med. Acad., Warsaw, 1956; m. John Kochanowski, Feb. 12, 1956; 1 son, Andrew Jack. Postgrad. tng., Univ. Hosp., Warsaw, 1956-60; staff Biel Hosp., Warsaw, 1960-65; vice-chmn. med. dept. Praski Hosp., Warsaw, 1965-67; staff Polish Ministry Health and Welfare Hosp., Warsaw, 1967-68; resident internal medicine Sinai Hosp. Detroit, 1969-72, staff, 1972—; staff Woodland Med. Group, also partner, Detroit, 1972—. Mem. Am., Mich., Wayne County med. assns., Am. Diabetes Assn. Jewish. Home: 4933 Lake Bluff Ct West Bloomfield MI 48033 Office: 22341 W 8 Mile Rd Detroit MI 48219

KOCHANOWSKI, VIVIAN FRENCH, nurse; b. Blue Mound, Kans., Mar. 1, 1939; d. Carlton Clyde and Vivian Electa (Squires) French; B.S.N., U. Kans., 1961; M.S. in Adult and Occupational Edn., Kans. State U., 1975; m. Glen Frederick Kochanowski, Nov. 30, 1963; children—Glenda Lynn, Patrick Eugene, Sean Andrew. Staff nurse Hempstead (N.Y.) Gen. Hosp., 1963-66; instr. nursing Asbury Hosp., Salina, Kans., 1966-79, dir. Sch. Nursing, 1979—; chmn. Kans. Assn. Hosp. Schs. of Nursing, 1980—. Served to lt. (j.g.), USNR, 1961-63. Mem. Am. Nurses Assn., Nat. League Nursing. Office: 400 S 7th St Salina KS 67401

KOCHARD, BEVERLY JOAN, coll. ofcl.; b. Plainfield, N.J., Oct. 25, 1951; d. John Hosking and M. Louise (Briden) Gaston; B.A. in English, Moravian Coll., Bethlehem, Pa., 1969-73; M.Ed. in Ednl. Adminstrn., Lehigh U., Bethlehem, 1978; m. Dale A. Kochard, Aug. 17, 1974. Reporter, copy editor Easton (Pa.) Express, 1973; dir. McShea Coll. Center, Allentown Coll., Center Valley, Pa., 1973-80; asst. dean students Moravian Coll., 1980—; cons.; workshop presenter. Bd. dirs. Big

Bros./Big Sisters of Northampton County, 1981—; chmn. Campus United Way Campaign, 1981. Mem. Pa. Coll. Personnel Assn., Pa. Assn. Student Personnel Adminstrs., Nat. Assn. Student Personnel Adminstrs., Assn. Coll. Unions Internat., Lehigh Valley Assn. Acad. Women, Bethlehem C. of C. (profl. women's com.). Home: 717 Hawthorne Rd Bethlehem PA 18018 Office: Moravian College Bethlehem PA 18018

KOCHTA, RUTH MARTHA, artist; b. N.Y.C., Jan. 5, 1924; d. Harry Joseph and Anna (Braun) Evers; student Art Students League, N.Y.C., 1965-69; m. Albert Kochta, Nov. 7, 1948; children—Alan, Carol. One-woman exhbns. include Ruth Green Gallery, Raleigh, N.C., 1977, 80, Ocean County Coll., N.J., 1978, Guild Gallery, N.Y.C., 1979; group exhbns. include Nat. Acad., Audubon Artists, Heckscher Mus., Elizabet Ney Mus., Wadsworth Atheneum, New Britain Mus., Tex. A&I U., Pan Am. Coll.; represented in permanent collections Philathea Mus., First & Mchts. Bank, Nat. Bank N.Am., Fairleigh Dickinson U.; art dir. Imperial Gallery, N.Y.C., 1980-81. Recipient numerous awards in competitions.

KOCZWARA, CHRISTINE JOY, artist; b. N.J., May 19, 1945; d. John Joseph and Sophie Ann K.; B.F.A., Ringling Sch. Art, 1967; M.A., William Paterson Coll. N.J., 1972. One-woman shows: Nat. Woman's Press Club, Washington, 1971, U.S. Naval Acad. Mus., Annapolis, 1972; exhibited in group shows: Pentagon, Smithsonian Instn. travelling shows, Nat. Gallery Art, The Residence, Salzburg, Austria, U. Tenn., Nat. Arts Club, Nat. Acad., N.Y.C., Seton Hall U., Jersey City Mus., Decatur House, Washington, Salmagundi Club, N.Y.C., others; represented in permanent collections U.S. and abroad; Navy combat artist, 1967-82; asso. prof. art and art edn. Tenn. Tech. U., Cookeville, 1972—. Recipient Grand prize Washington Sq. Outdoor Art Exhibit, N.Y.C., 1968; Outstanding Faculty award Tenn. Tech. U., 1981. Mem. AAUP, Am. Artists Profl. League, Nat. Art Edn. Assn., Nat. Arts Club, USMC Combat Artists, USMC Combat Corr. Assn., Tenn. Edn. Assn., Tenn. Art Edn. Assn., Navy Art Cooperation and Liaison Com. Episcopalian. Clubs: Salmagundi (N.Y.C.) Home: 775 Fisk Rd Box 05042 Cookeville TN 38501 Office: Dept Art Tenn Tech U Cookeville TN 38501

KODIS, MARY CAROLINE, retail and restaurant cons.; b. Chgo., Dec. 17, 1927; d. Anthony John and Callis Ferebee (Old) K.; student San Diego State Coll., 1945-47, Latin Am. Inst., 1948. Controller, div. adminstrv. mgr. Fed. Mart Stores, 1957-65; controller, adminstrv. mgr. Gulf Mart Stores, 1965-67; budget dir., adminstrv. mgr. Diana Stores, 1967-68; founder, treas., controller Handy Dan Stores, 1968-72; founder, v.p., treas. Handy City Stores, 1972-76; sr. v.p., treas. Handy City div. W.R. Grace & Co., Atlanta, 1976-79; founder, pres. Hal's Hardware and Lumber Stores, 1982—; retail and restaurant cons., 1979—. Treas., bd. dirs. YWCA Watsonville. Recipient 1st Tribute to Women in Internat. Industry, 1978. Republican. Home and Office: 302 Wheelock Rd Watsonville CA 95076

KODNER, PHYLLIS B., interior designer; b. St. Louis, Feb. 7, 1932; d. Norman and Mania (Gillerman) Mathless; student Washington U., 1949-50; m. Mike Kodner, Feb. 14, 1953; children—Karen, Susan, Jacqueline, Robert, Thomas. Pres., Phyllis Kodner Interior Designs, Inc., Creve Coeur, Mo., 1970—. Mem. Women's Info. Network, Mariam Found., Jewish Fedn., Nat. Council Jewish Women. Jewish. Mem. Hadassah. Home: 44 S Spoede Rd Creve Coeur MO 63141

KOEHLER, ISABEL WINIFRED, writer, artist; b. Boston, Feb. 5, 1903; d. George Wallace and Mary Elizabeth (Strout) Goodwin; student art courses Harvard U., M.I.T., others; m. Frederick Mills Koehler, Apr. 16, 1925; 1 son, Alden Goodwin. Contbr. articles to Boston Daily Post, Boston Herald-Traveler, poetry to Boston Daily Globe, Melrose Free Press, Everett Leader Herald, others; exhibited numerous galleries, festivals, ann. exhbns. Recipient first place for watercolor book illustrations Everett Bicentennial Arts Exhibit, 1976, 1st and 3d place awards in landscape oil, 1981; Diploma of Merit Università delle Arti (Italy) for cultural and profl. achievement, 1982; other awards, prizes. Mem. Mass. Poetry Soc., New Eng. Women's Press Assn., Agnes Carr Writers Club (pres., exec. bd.), Internat. Poetry Soc., N.Y. Poetry Forum, Everett Art Assn., Old Boston Soc. Ind. Artists, Am. Biog. Inst. Research Assn. (asso.), Centro Studi e Scambi Internazionali (Silver medal 1975, Gold medal in poetry 1976), Leonardo de Vinci Accademia (hon. rep., commemorative medal for art achievement 1973, Gold medal 1976, Poet of Month award 1980, Poet Laureate award 1980 Diploma of Honor for outstanding achievement in contemporary art 1982, v.p. 1982—). Author: Bouquets of Poems, 1974; Versified Variety, 1978. Address: 30 Fremont Ave Everett MA 02149

KOEHLER, MONIQUE SUZANNE, pharm. co. exec.; b. Bklyn., Jan. 5, 1944; d. Peter Nicholas and Madeleine Louise (Agnoux) Sfakianos; A.A.S., Nassau Community Coll., 1963; B.S., Hofstra U., 1966; student Wharton Sch., U. Pa., 1976-77; m. W. Peter Koehler, Jr., May 8, 1966; 1 son, Peter John. Chem. technician, Pvt. Formulations, Inc., 1963-64, inventory control, purchasing staff, 1965-68, v.p. purchasing, 1968-72, v.p. purchasing, mktg., 1972-77; v.p. mktg. Koehler Iversen Inc., N.Y.C., 1978—, also dir.; pres. MSK Assos., 1978—; dir., cons. Celestial Seasoning Inc., Boulder; cons. Athena Products, Ltd., Margate, Fla., AKM Industries, Inc., Dallas. Bd. dirs. Thoroughbred Retirement Found. Mem. Female Exec. Club, Bus. and Profl. Advt. Assn., Sales Execs. Club, Nat. Assn. Purchasing Mgrs., World Future Soc., Nat. Assn. Purchasing Mgmt. Home: 174 Deepdale Dr Middletown NJ 07748 Office: 6 E 39th St New York NY 10016

KOEHN, CAROL ANN, educator; b. Bklyn., Nov. 13, 1936; d. William James and Anna Marie (Koletty) Butcher; B.A., Wellesley Coll., 1958; M.A., Columbia, 1962; m. Enno Koehn, Nov. 25, 1967; children—William Enno, James Frederick. Tchr., MacDuffie Sch. Girls, Springfield, Mass., 1959-61; sr. map researcher Time mag., 1961-67; tutor of disadvantaged, Lima, Ohio, 1968; lectr. geography Ohio No. U., Ada, 1968-71, lectr. history, 1974-76; lectr. geography Findlay (Ohio) Coll., 1973-74, 77; exec. dir. Ada chpt. ARC, 1975-79; exec. sec. Ada C. of C., 1975-77; feature writer Ada Herald, 1975-79; editorial researcher, writer Dean's Office, Engrng. Schs., Purdue U., West Lafayette, Ind., 1979—. Sec., Hardin County Bicentennial Commn., 1975-76; del. Ohio Council Chs. assembly, 1971-78. Mem. Nat. Council Geog. Edn., Assn. Am. Geographers, AAUW (chmn. world problems 1970, edn. chmn. 1975), Wellesley Coll. Alumni Assn., Alpha Xi Delta. Republican. Lutheran. Club: Order Eastern Star. Address: 911 Sunset Ct West Lafayette IN 47906

KOEHN-VAN ZWIENEN, ILSE CHARLOTTE, graphic designer; b. Berlin, Aug. 6, 1929; came to U.S., 1958, naturalized, 1976; d. Fritz Wilhelm and Charlotte Martha (Sckrabei) Koehn; grad. Hochschule Bildende Künste, Berlin, 1953; m. John H. Van Zwienen, May 24, 1969. Freelance illustrator, copywriter German mags. and cos., 1953-59; asso. art dir. J. Walter Thompson Co., N.Y.C., 1959-64; art dir. Campbell-Down Advt., N.Y.C., 1965-68; freelance designer, illustrator, Old Greenwich, Conn., 1968—; group exhbn. Lynn Kottler Galleries, N.Y.C., 1960. Recipient Boston Globe-Horn Book award for nonfiction 1978, honor award Jane Addams Peace Assn., 1978. Mem. Authors Guild, Graphic Artists Guild. Club: Old Greenwich Yacht. Author: Mischling, Second Degree, 1977; Tilla, 1981. Address: 50 Sound Beach Ave Old Greenwich CT 06870

KOELLER, SHIRLEY ANN, educator; b. Cin.; d. Maurice Lipian; A.B., U. Calif., 1959; M.A., U. Colo., 1971, Ph.D., 1975; 1 son, Kevin. Tchr., San Francisco Public Schs., 1966-67, Jefferson County Public Schs., 1967-69; teaching asso. U. Colo., 1971-74; coordinator elem. Tech. Center Sheridan (Colo.) Public Schs., 1974-75; lectr. State Coll., San Bernardino, 1975-78; asst. prof. Tex. Tech. U., 1978—. Mem. Am. Ednl. Research Assn., Assn. Childhood Edn., Assn. Supervision and Curriculum Devel., Internat. Reading Assn., Nat. Council Social Studies, Nat. Council Tchrs. English, S.W. Ednl. Research Assn., Kappa Delta Pi, Phi Delta Kappa. Contbr. articles in field to profl. jours. Office: PO Box 4560 Texas Tech U Lubbock TX 79409

KOELLNER, KATHERINE TARPLEY, hotel exec.; b. Geary, Okla., Jan. 2, 1912; d. William and Dona (O'Connor) Tarpley; B.A., UCLA, 1935; postgrad. Los Angeles City Coll., 1953, Los Angeles Pierce Coll., 1967; m. Henry Beverly Koellner, Oct. 8, 1948 (div. 1968). Sec. fgn. trade dept. Los Angeles C. of C., 1935-37; sr. payroll clk. UCLA, 1938-43; touring dir. Nat. Automobile Club, Los Angeles, 1943-49; office mgr. Reservation Services Inc. for Desert Inn and Stardust Hotels of Las Vegas in Beverly Hills, Calif., 1950-67; field underwriter Mut. Life Ins. Co. of N.Y., Van Nuys, Calif., 1967-68; reservation mgr. Hollywood Plaza Hotel (Calif.), 1968-72; dir. sales Hollywood Roosevelt Hotel, 1972—. Mem. Los Angeles Travellarians, Am. Soc. Travel Agts., Nat. Bus. and Profl. Women's Club, Los Angeles C. of C., Calif. Hotel and Motel Assn., Hotel Sales Mgmt. Assn. (internat.), UCLA Alumni Assn. (life). Episcopalian. Home: 17515 Cohasset St Van Nuys CA 91406 Office: 7000 Hollywood Blvd Hollywood CA 90028

KOENIG, JOAN FOSTER, real estate broker; b. Harrisburg, Ill., Feb. 15, 1930; d. William Jennings and Adria May Foster; B.S., Miami U., 1951; M.A., Ariz. State U., 1967; m. Alan Eastman Disbrow, June 26, 1978; children—William R., Theodore J. Airline stewardess Am. Airlines, Inc., 1951-52; research investigator Procter & Gamble Co., Cin., 1952-53; co-owner, v.p. Koenig Aviation, Inc., Casa Grande, Ariz., 1953-69; real estate sales assoc. Ed Post Realty, Scottsdale, Ariz., 1979-79; real estate broker Ariz. Devel. Corp., Casa Grande, 1980—. Bd. govs. Casa Grande Town Hall, 1972-75; bd. dirs. Hoemako Hosp. Aux.; vice-chmn. Pinal County Democratic Com., 1972-76, dist. 6 chmn., 1972-76, mem. state exec. com., 1972-76; pres. West Pinal County Dem. Women's Club, 1975. Recipient Women's Flight Achievement award Internat. Flying Farmers, 1964. Mem. AAUW, Women's Council Realtors, Casa Grande Valley Cotton Wives, Casa Grande Panhellenic (pres. 1970), Mortar Board, Kappa Kappa Gamma. Democrat. Episcopalian. Home: Route 1 Box 469 Casa Grande AZ 85222 Office: PO Box 432 Casa Grande AZ 85222

KOENIG, JUNE HOFFMAN, health care corp. exec.; b. Oakes, N.D., June 30, 1943; d. Walter Frederick and Alice Mae (Obenchain) Hoffman; A.A., W. Valley Jr. Coll., Saratoga, Calif., 1980; widow. Various clerical and secretarial positions, 1962-71; med. sec. II, Profl. Group-VMC, Inc., San Jose, Calif., 1971-78, asst. to bus. mgr., 1978—; mem. med. adv. com., regional occupational program Met. Adult Health Program, San Jose, 1978-79. Mem. Nat. Assn. Female Execs. Office: 751 S Bascom Ave San Jose CA 95128

KOENIG, RUTH, psychiatrist, psychoanalyst; b. Chgo., July 14, 1920; d. Nathan and Rose (Weinberg) Steinman; B.S., Lewis Inst., 1943; M.S., U. Pa., 1949; M.D., Chgo. Med. Sch., 1951; m. Harold Koenig, Feb. 11, 1945; children—Suzanne Lark, Ellen Leslie. Instr. anatomy U. Pa., 1947-49; staff physician Chgo. State Hosp., 1951-53; instr. psychiatry U. Ill., 1955-57; candidate Chgo. Inst. for Psychoanalysis, 1958-65; asso. dept. neurology and psychiatry Northwestern U. Med. Sch., Chgo., 1958-75; cons. psychiatrist Ill. State Psychiat. Inst., 1965-67; pvt. practice psychiatry, 1957—; attending in psychiatry Northwestern Meml. Hosp., 1970-75; attending Gen. Med. Research (Neurology), VA Lakeside Hosp., 1975—. Mem. Chgo. Med. Soc., AMA, Am. Psychiat. Assn., Soc. Adolescent Psychiat., Soc. Liaison and Psychosomatic Psychiat. Author: articles on neurology, psychiatry, book: Manpower Problems in Mental Hosptials (A Consultant Team Approach), 1977. Home and Office: 45 E Elm St Chicago IL 60611

KOENIGSBERG, SUZANNE CUYLER HAEFELE, mfg. co. exec.; b. Wilkes-Barre, Pa., Nov. 20, 1946; d. Earl C. Haefele and Virginia (Jones) Haefele Ehalt; B.A., U. N.C., 1971; M.A.T. in Edn., Winthrop Coll., 1973; M.Librarianship. U. S.C., 1975; m. Nathan Koenigsberg, July 13, 1977. Instructional TV producer Charlotte-Mecklenburg (N.C.) Schs., 1970-72; teaching asst. Winthrop Coll., 1973-74; info. specialist grad. program criminal justice U. S.C., Columbia, 1975-76; program evaluator U. Hawaii, Honolulu, 1975; controller Chesterfield (S.C.) Mfg. Corp. & Affiliates, 1976—, mgmt. exec. in charge ladies div., 1978—, dir., 1979—, sec., 1979—. Bd. dirs. Winthrop Coll. Found., 1980—. Mem. Mensa, Phi Kappa Phi, Phi Alpha Theta, Beta Phi Mu. Republican. Jewish. Clubs: Greater Charlotte Dance Guild (sec., dir. 1970-74), Davison (Duke U.). Office: 110 Davis St Chesterfield SC 29709

KOEPPEL, MARY SUE, educator; b. Phlox, Wis., Dec. 12, 1939; d. Alphonse and Emma Petronella (Marx) K.; B.A., Alverno Coll., 1962; M.A., Loyola U., Chgo., 1968; postgrad. U. Wis., St. Louis U., U. N.H., U. Calif., U. Fla. Tchr., St. Joseph High Sch, Milw., 1962-68, Pius XI High Sch., Milw., 1968-72; instr., head dept. communications, dir. learning center Waukesha County Tech. Inst., Pewaukee, Wis., 1972-80; pres., exec. bd. West Suburban Council Teaching Profession, 1976-80; adv. Waukesha chpt. Parents Without Partners, 1975-80; cons. Leaning Centers, 1976—; instr. communications Fla. Jr. Coll., Jacksonville, 1980—; instr. Inst. for Tchrs. of Writing, Westbrook Coll., Portland, Maine, Summers 1980-82, instr. master tchr. seminar, summer 1982; mem. Sherman Park Community Center, 1975-80. NDEA grantee, 1968. Mem. Fla. Edn. Assn., Adult Vocat. Assn., Am. Adult Edn. Assn., Nat. Council Tchrs. of English, Nat. Assn. Female Execs. Contbr. articles to profl. jours. Home: 8424 San Martarro Dr W Jacksonville FL 32117

KOERING, MARILYN JEAN, educator; b. Brainerd, Minn., Jan. 7, 1938; d. Clement J. and Vi K. (Holtkamp) K.; B.A., Coll. St. Scholastica, Duluth, 1960; M.S., U. Wis., Madison, 1963, Ph.D., 1967, postgrad., 1968. Instr. dept. anatomy U. Wis., 1963-64; asst. prof. George Washington U., 1969-73, assoc. prof., 1973-79, prof., 1979—; vis. assoc. div. biology Calif. Inst. Tech., 1976; affiliate scientist Wis. Primate Research Center, Madison, 1975-78; guest worker Pregnancy Research br. NICHD, 1977—. NIH fellow, 1967-68, NIH grantee, 1969—. Mem. Am. Assn. Anatomists, Soc. Study Reproduction, AAAS, Washington Assn. Electron Microscopists, Sigma Xi. Mem. editorial bd. Biology of Reproduction, 1974-78; contbr. in field. Home: 1200 N Nash St Arlington VA 22209 Office: Department of Anatomy George Washington University Medical Center 2300 I St NW Washington DC 20037

KOESTER, ARDIS WILLIAMS, educator; b. Muscatine, Iowa, Feb. 9, 1939; d. Ralph William and Pearl Christine (Rock) Williams; B.S., Oreg. State U., 1961; M.S., U. N.C., Greensboro, 1971, Ph.D., 1974; m. Jerrold Herbert Koester, Aug. 17, 1975. Home econs. tchr., Rio Vista, Calif., 1961-62, Yuba City, Calif., 1962-66, Fremont, Calif., 1967-69; summer sch. instr. Kans. State U., Manhattan, 1972; grad. research, teaching asst. U. N.C., Greensboro, 1969-74; textiles and clothing specialist Extension Service, Oreg. State U., Corvallis, 1974—. Recipient Oreg. Extension Assn. Newer Staff recognition, 1979. Mem. Oreg. Extension Assn., Am. Home Econs. Assn., Oreg. Home Econs. Assn., Assn. Coll. Profs. Textiles and Clothing, Am. Assn. Textile Chemists and Colorists. Lutheran. Contbr. articles to profl. jours. Office: 135 Milam Hall Ore State Univ Corvallis OR 97331

KOFF, GAIL JOANNE, lawyer; b. N.Y.C., May 15, 1945; d. Murray and Sylvia Joan (Winer) Koff; B.A., U. Calif., Berkeley, 1967; J.D., George Washington U., 1970; m. Ralph Brill, Oct. 8, 1978; 1 son, Micah. Asst. to dir. Tng. and Demonstration program, Legal Services Program, Washington, 1969-71; admitted to N.Y. Bar, 1972; asso. firm Gasperini & Savage, N.Y.C., 1972-76, Skadden, Arps, Slate, Meagher & Flom, N.Y.C., 1976-78; founder, partner firm Jacoby & Meyers, N.Y.C., 1978—; lectr. in field. Chmn., legal service program Community Action for Legal Services, N.Y.C., 1979-81; mem. Com. of 200. Mem. Assn. Bar City N.Y. (exec. com. 1979—), N.Y. Bar Assn. Jewish. Editor: Legal Delivery Systems, 1977. Office: 1457 Broadway New York NY 10036

KOFFMAN, EARLDENE JOHNS, citrus processing sales exec.; b. Monona County, Iowa, Sept. 3, 1927; d. Ira Vinton and Jessie Laverne (Montgomery) Johns; grad. various courses, seminars; m. James C. Koffman, Dec. 26, 1967; children—Sheila Jean Braune Pappas, Paula Jane Braune Schubert. Exec. sec., officer mgr. Ardaman & Assos., Orlando, Fla., 1961-67; agt. New York Life Ins. Co., Orlando, 1967; adminstrv. asst. to pres. So. Gold Citrus Products, Orlando, 1967-73; corp. sec. Albertson Internat., Inc., Orlando, 1973—; sec.-treas. D.A. Internat., Inc., Orlando, 1975—. Past v.p. Nela Isle Community Council, Orlando. Mem. Am. Bus. Women's Assn. (past pres. City Beautiful chpt., Woman of Yr. award 1980), Nat. Assn. Female Execs., Am. Bus. Assn., Delta Nu Alpha. Democrat. Club: Tohopekaliga Yacht (editor monthly newsletter 1978-79, chmn. ways and means 1977-78). Office: CNA Tower 255 S Orange Ave Suite 1814 Orlando FL 32801

KOFFORD, KAREN JEAN, glassblower, glass sculptor; b. Orem, Utah, May 25, 1946; d. Weston Meiling and Lenore (Pyne) K.; student Coll. So. Utah, 1967-68, Steven Henegars Bus. Coll., Salt Lake City, 1966-67, Brigham Young U., Provo, 1965-67. Owner, pres. Krystal Kreations Glassblowing, Orem, 1967—, Jackson, Wyo., 1969—; developer swirled kneading process. Republican. Mormon. Home: 15 West 300 North Orem UT 84057 Office: K-133 University Mall Orem UT 84057 also PO Box 2077 Jackson WY 83001

KOGA, RUTH KAMURI, retailing exec.; b. Honolulu, July 19, 1929; d. Nenichi and Mino (Ozama) Kamuri; B.A., Smith Coll., 1951; m. George Koga, Nov. 22, 1958; 1 dau., Suzanne. With Ritz Dept. Stores, Honolulu, 1951—, pres., 1975—, sales mktg. exec. mem. Bd. dirs. Am. Cancer Soc., 1972-80; trustee St. Louis High Sch., 1980—, Hawaii News Agy., Found., 1980—; fund raiser Kuakini Hosp. Aux., 1956-65; active fund raising for charity and scholarships. Recipient award Am. Cancer Soc., 1976. Mem. Nat. Retail Mchts. Assn., Honolulu C. of C., Honolulu Art Acad. Democrat. Clubs: Smith Alumni, Waialae Country. Home: 1254 Center St Honolulu HI 96816 Office: 1143 Fort St Honolulu HI 96813

KOGELSCHATZ, JOAN LEE, psychotherapist, psychologist; b. Detroit, Nov. 26, 1940; d. Edgar Rolfe and Helen Josephine (York) Kogelschatz; B.A., U. Fla., 1963; postgrad. Wayne State U., 1964-65; M.S.W., Fla. State U., 1967, Ph.D., 1975. Intern, VA Hosp., Bay Pines, Fla., 1966, Div. Child and Adolescent Psychiatry, Dept. Psychiatry, U. Fla. Med. Center, Gainesville, 1966; instr. psychiatry Dept. Psychiatry, Div. Child & Adolescent Psychiatry, U. Fla. Med. Center, Shands Teaching Hosp. & Clinics, Gainesville, 1967-72; field supr., instr. Fla. State U., 1973, field supr., instr., Sch. Social Work, 1973-74; pvt. practice psychology, Dothan, Ala., 1975—; guest lectr. Dept. Psychiatry, Div. Child & Adolescent Psychiatry, Shands Teaching Hosp. & Clinics, 1975; cons. Lyster Army Hosp., Ft. Rucker, Ala., 1975-78; guest lectr. Dept. Mental Health, Ft. Rucker, 1975; lectr. in field; asst. prof. U. Ala., 1976-77; cons. in field. Bd. dirs. Ala. Soc. for Crippled Children & Adults, 1981—; mem. Law Enforcement Planning Agy. adv. bd., Ala., 1980—; lic. profl. counselor, Ala.; lic. psychologist, Ala.; lic. clin. psychiat. social worker, Ala. Mem. Am. Psychol. Assn., Acad. Psychosomatic Medicine, Am. Orthopsychiat. Assn., Am. Assn. Psychiat. Services for Children, Am. Soc. Clin. Hypnosis, Am. Assn. Marriage and Family Therapists, Nat. Assn. Social Workers, Acad. Cert. Social Workers, Nat. Council on Family Relations, Southeastern Council on Family Relations, Am. Assn. Sex Educators, Counselors and Therapists, Gulf Coast Assn. for Marriage and Family Therapy, Alpha Kappa Delta. Contbr. articles to profl. jours.

KOGER, MILDRED EMMELENE NICHOLS, educator, counselor; b. Jacksonville, Fla.; d. Hugh Huntley and Edna (Snell) Nichols; student Rollins Coll., 1945-46; B.A., Fla. State U., 1949; Mus.B., B.Mus. Edn., Jacksonville U., 1955; M.Ed., U. Fla., 1966, Ed.D., 1970; m. Gerald L. Gamache, Dec. 1974. Tchr., Lakeshore Jr. High Sch., Jacksonville, Fla., 1949-56; choral dir., head music dept. Paxon Sr. High Sch., Jacksonville, 1956-65; lectr. voice Jacksonville U., 1955-66; grad. asst. music U. Fla., 1965-67; counselor, psychology faculty Fla. Jr. Coll., Jacksonville, 1967-68; staff psychologist Duval County Bd. Public Instrn., Jacksonville, 1968-69, chief psychologist, 1969, 70, counselor, psychologist, 1972-81; resident coordinator student teaching Fla. State U., 1970-71; prof. Edward Waters Coll., 1971-72; lectr. Jacksonville U., 1973-77; adj. asst. prof. U. North Fla., 1974-77; dir. counseling services NE Fla. Counseling Services, 1975-81; pvt. practice, 1975—; psychologist Old Dominion U. Counseling Center, 1979; grad. lectr. Golden Gate U., Norfolk, Va. Cert. facilitator Emerging Women in Mgmt. Workshop, Response & Assos., Castro Valley, Calif., 1976; lic. profl. counselor, Va. Mem. Nat. Assn. Tchrs. Singing, Am. Choral Dirs. Assn., Am. Personnel and Guidance Assn., Fla. Personnel and Guidance Assn., Va. Counselors Assn., Fla. Assn. Sch. Psychologists (standards of practice com. 1977), Council for Exceptional Children, Council for Children with Behavioral Disorders, Am. Psychol. Assn., NOW, Alpha Xi Delta, Sigma Alpha Iota. Contbr. article to textbook. Address: 6824 Orangewood Ave Norfolk VA 23513

KOH, EUNSOOK TAK, educator, researcher; b. Seoul, May 3, 1936; came to U.S., 1967, naturalized, 1975; d. Chang Jae and Chungsook Lee Tak; B.S., Seoul Nat. U., 1958; M.S., U. Md., 1970, Ph.D. in Nutrition and Chemistry, 1973; m. Jae-Kon Koh, Nov. 19, 1962; children—Kyung-Ho, Kyung-Run, Lucy Hea-Run. Tchr. Jung-Ang sr. high sch., Seoul, Korea, 1958-67; research asst. U. Md., College Park, 1968-73; research asso. Agrl. Research Service, USDA, Nutrition Inst., Beltsville, Md., 1973-74; asso. prof. Alcorn State U., Lorman, Miss., 1974-80; prof. U. Okla., Norman, 1981—; cons. in field. Mem. Am. Inst. Nutrition, Am. Socs. Clin. Nutrition, Nutrition Today Soc., Nutrition Ednl. Soc., Am. Home Econs. Assn., Miss. Acad. Scis., N.Y. Acad. Scis., Phi Sigma. Presbyterian. Club: Korean Christian Women's. Contbr. articles to profl. jours. Home: 412 Rosewood Dr Norman OK 73069 Office: Sch Human Devel U Okla 610 Elm Ave Norman OK 73019

KOHL, CHRISTINE NOEL, lawyer; b. Pitts., Sept. 5, 1948; d. William Peter and Berndett Louise (Noel) K.; A.B. in Polit. Sci., U. Mich. 1970; J.D., U. Pitts., 1973. Admitted to Pa. bar, 1973, D.C. bar, 1974, U.S. dist. ct. (we. dist.) Pa. 1973, U.S. Ct. Apls. (D.C. cir.), 1976, (2d cir.) 1979, (5th cir.) 1978, (9th cir.) 1976, (10th cir.) 1977, U.S. Ct. Mil. Apls. 1973, U.S. Sup. Ct. 1977. Dep. asso. gen. counsel ICC, Washington 1978-79; chief staff counsel U.S. Ct. Apls. for D.C. Circuit 1979-80; adminstrv. judge Atomic Safety and Licensing Appeal Banel Nuclear Regulatory Commn., Washington, 1980—. Mem. ABA, NOW. Office: Nuclear Regulatory Commission Washington DC 20555

KOHL, MARGUERITE C., corp. exec.; b. 1918; B.A., Coll. New Rochelle, 1940; student N.Y. U. Asso. editor Woman's Day mag., 1941-44; copy-writer Borden Co., 1944-45; free lance writer mag. articles and books, 1948-55; asso. editor Today's Woman mag., 1951-54; with Gen. Foods Corp., 1955—, mgr. consumer contacts, 1961-66, mgr. consumer info. services, 1966-69, asst. dir. Gen. Foods Kitchens, 1969-71, dir. Gen. Foods Kitchens, 1971-72, corporate v.p., 1972—, v.p. consumer affairs, 1974—. Office: Gen Foods Corp 250 North St White Plains NY 10625

KOHLER, RUTH DEYOUNG, arts center exec.; b. Chgo., Oct. 24, 1941; d. Herbert Vollrath and Ruth Miriam (DeYoung) Kohler; ed. Smith Coll., U. Hamburg (Ger.), Kunsthochschule, Hamburg, U. Wis. Instr. in fine arts U. Alta. (Can.), Calgary, 1964-66; printmaker, 1967-68; asst. dir. John Michael Kohler Arts Center, Sheboygan, Wis., 1968-71, dir., 1972—; chmn. Wis. Arts Bd.; mem. mus. adv. panel, crafts panel Nat. Endowment for Arts; dir., mem. Kohler Found., Inc.; mem. Wis. Am. Revolution Bicentennial Commn.; mem. Nat. Crafts Planning Bd., trustee Beloit Coll. Office: 608 New York Ave Sheboygan WI 53081

KOHLES, CYNTHIA ANN LEATHAM, psychotherapist; b. Chgo., Jan. 7, 1937; d. Chester Arthur and Ann Hansen (Walsh) Leatham; B.A., San Francisco Coll. Women, 1958; M.S.W., Tulane U., 1964; m. Gregory Thomas Kohles, Aug. 22, 1959; children—Kristin Kohles, Caroline Kohles, Elisa Kohles. Psychiat. social worker Charity Hosp., New Orleans, 1964-66; asst. prof. U. Md. Sch. Social Work and Community Planning, 1970-73; pvt. practice psychiat. social work, 1973-74; sr. psychiat. social worker Alcoholism Program, Santa Rosa, Calif., 1975-78; dir. adult day treatment Sonoma County Mental Health Dept., Santa Rosa, 1978-81; pvt. practice psychotherapy, 1978—. Lic. clin. social worker. Mem. Nat. Assn. Social Workers, Acad. Cert. Social Workers. Home: 4770 Petrified Forest Rd Calistoga CA 94515 Office: 2525 Cleveland Ave Santa Rosa CA 95401

KOHLMEYER, IDA RITTENBERG (MRS. HUGH BERNARD KOHLMEYER), artist; b. New Orleans, Nov. 3, 1912; d. Joseph and Rebecca (Baron) Rittenberg; B.A., Tulane U., 1933, M.F.A., 1956; student Hans Hofmann Sch. Art, Provincetown, R.I., 1956; m. Hugh Bernard Kohlmeyer, Mar. 15, 1934; children—Jane Louise (Mrs. Henry Lowentritt), Jo Ellen. One man shows: Delgado Mus. Art, New Orleans, 1957, 66, 67, Tulane U., 1959, 64, Sheldon Meml. Art Gallery, Lincoln, Nebr., 1967, Marion Koogler McNay Art Inst., San Antonio, 1968, Ft. Wayne (Ind.) Mus. Art, 1968, High Mus. Art, Atlanta, 1972, David Findlay Gallery, N.Y.C., 1976; group shows include: Knoedler Galleries, N.Y.C., Bertha Schaeffer Gallery, N.Y.C., Harvard, Yale, Toledo Mus. Fine Arts, Cleve. Inst. Art, Denver Art Mus., Va. Mus. Arts, Richmond, La Jolla (Calif.) Mus. Art, Moore Coll. Art, Phila., Pratt Graphics Center, N.Y.C., Ft. Worth Art Mus., La Jolla Mus. Contemporary Art; represented in permanent collections New Orleans Mus. Art, Milw. Art Center, Hunter Mus. Art, Chattanooga, Tenn., Rochester Meml. Art Gallery, Rochester, N.Y., Addison Gallery Am. Art, Phillips Acad., Andover, Mass., Okla. Art Center, Oklahoma City, Columbus (Ga.) Mus. Art, Tyler (Tex.) Art Inst., Centro-Artistico, Baranquilla, Colombia, Mus. Fine Arts, Houston, High Mus. Art, Atlanta, Sheldon Meml. Art Gallery, Lincoln, Nebr., Ind. State U., Terre Haute, Nat. Collection Fine Arts, Washington, Vincent Price Collection, Ill. State U., Emory U., Atlanta, Marion Koogler McNay Art Inst., San Antonio, Ind. State U., Terre Haute, Corcoran Gallery Art, Washington, Xerox Co., N.J., Birmingham (Ala.) Mus. Art; mem. faculty art dept. Newcomb Coll., Tulane U., New Orleans, 1956-64; vis. asso. prof. fine arts La. State U., New Orleans, 1973-74. Recipient award Artist's Ann., Delgado Mus., New Orleans, 1957, 58, 60, 65, 73, Chautauqua Nat. Exhbn., 1962, 28th Corcoran Biennial of Am. Art, Washington, 1963, 67, Artists Ann., High Mus. Art, Atlanta, 1963, 66. Address: 11 Pelham Ave Metairie LA 70005

KOHN, CAROLYN ROOT, trust co. exec.; b. Summit, N.J., Apr. 19, 1954; d. Edmund Root and Lynn (Ronci) K.; B.A., Dartmouth Coll., 1976. Trainee, Bankers Trust Co., N.Y.C., 1976, govt. securities salesman, 1976-77, asst. treas., 1977-78, asst. v.p., 1978-79, v.p., 1979—, also sr. salesman in West Coast. Trustee, Storm King Sch. Republican. Episcopalian. Clubs: Yale, Vertical, Gypsy Trail, Blue Hill Troupe Ltd. Office: 14 Wall St New York NY 10005

KOHN, JULIEANNE, travel agt.; b. Detroit, Apr. 15, 1946; d. Ralph Merwin and Jane Tacke (Meyers) K.; B.A., Heidelberg Coll., Tiffin, Ohio, 1968; postgrad. Eastern Mich. U., 1969-70; diploma Inst. Cert. Travel Agts., 1979. Travel agt. Am. Express Co., Detroit, 1970-73, Thomas Cook Inc., Detroit, 1973-75; mgr. Island Traveller, Grosse Ile, Mich., 1975-76; pres., owner Flying Suitcase, Inc., Grosse Ile, 1976—; dir. Kohn Engrng. Corp., Taylor Grinding Co. (both Taylor, Mich.). Cert. travel. cons. Mem. Am. Soc. Travel Agts., Pacific Area Travel Assn. Episcopalian. Club: Grosse Ile Golf and Country. Home: 27081 E River Rd Grosse Ile MI 48138 Office: 8205 Macomb St Grosse Ile MI 48138

KOHN, MARY LOUISE BEATRICE, nurse; b. Yellows Springs, Ohio, Jan. 13, 1920; d. Theophilus John and Mary Katharine (Schmitkons) Gaehr; A.B., Coll. Wooster, 1940; M.Nursing, Case Western Res. U., 1943; m. Howard D. Kohn, 1944; 1 dau., Marcia R. Nurse, Univ. Hosps., Cleve., 1943-44, Atlantic City Hosp., 1944, Thomas M. England Gen. Hosp., U.S. Army, Atlantic City, 1945-46, Peter Bent Brigham Hosp., Boston, 1947, Univ. Hosps., Cleve., 1946-48; mem. faculty Frances Payne Bolton Sch. Nursing Case Western Res. U., 1948-52; vol. nurse Blood Service, ARC, 1952-55; office nurse, Cleve., part time 1955—; free-lance writer. Bd. dirs. Aux. Acad. Medicine Cleve., 1970-72, officer, 1976—; mem. Cleve. Health Mus. Aux.; mem. women's com. Cleve. Orch., 1970; women's council WVIZ-TV. Mem. Am., Ohio nurses assns., alumni assns. Wooster Coll., Frances P. Bolton Sch. Nursing (pres. 1974-75), Assn. Operating Rm. Nurses, Antique Automobile Assn. Am., Western Res. Hist. Soc., Am. Heart Assn., Cleve. Playhouse Aux., U.S. Humane Soc., Friends of Cleve. Ballet, Smithsonian Instn., Council World Affairs, Orange Community Arts Council. Clubs: Cleve. Racquet, Women's City, Women's of Case-Western Res. U. Sch. Medicine. Author: (with Atkinson) Berry and Kohn's Introduction to Operating Room Technique, 5th edit., 1978. Asst. editor Cleve. Physician, Acad. Medicine Cleve., 1966-71. Home: 28099 Belcourt Rd Cleveland OH 44124

KOHNERT, JILL ILENE, bank ofcl.; b. Mpls., June 18, 1950; d. Carl Creighton and June Ilene K.; student So. Methodist U., 1968-69; student U. Tex., 1970; B.A., U. Houston, 1972. Exec. sec. real estate and archtl. firms, Houston, Dallas, Austin, Tex., 1972-75; exec. asst. to exec. dir. State Bar Tex., Austin, 1975-77; exec. dir. Tex. Lawyers Ins. Exchange, Austin, 1978-81; exec. asst. Tex. Commerce Bank, Austin, 1981—. Mem. Zachary Scott Theatre Guild, Austin, 1979-82, Laguna Gloria Art Mus. Guild, 1981; mem. Austin Bus. Forum, 1981. Lic. securities dealer, Tex. Mem. Exec. Women Internat., Nat. Assn. Female Execs., Am. Inst. Banking, PEO. Club: Pilot. Home: 6908 Moonmont St Austin TX 78745 Office: Tex Commerce Bank 700 Lavaca St Austin TX 78701

KOHNO, TOSHIKO, flutist; b. Tokyo, May 28, 1954; came to U.S., 1961; d. Shuntatsu and Sumiko (Bekku) K.; B.Mus., Eastman Sch. Music, U. Rochester, 1976. Second flutist Buffalo Philharm. Orch., 1973-76; asso. prin. flutist Montreal (Que., Can.) Symphony Orch., 1976-78; prin. flutist Nat. Symphony Orch., Washington, 1978—; mem. faculty McGill U., Montreal, 1976-78; recitals and concerto appearances, U.S., Japan, Europe. Recipient 1st prize in flute Geneva Internat. Competition, 1973. Office: care Nat Symphony Kennedy Center Washington DC 20566

KOHOWSKI, BIDDIANA MARIE, children's services adminstr., civic worker; b. Olean, N.Y., June 5, 1938; d. Albert Joseph and Marie Edith (Metcalf) Heil; B.A., Notre Dame Coll., 1960; postgrad. Edinboro (Pa.) State Coll., 1971-72; m. Bruno F. Kohowski, Nov. 11, 1961; children—Edith, Mary, Judith. Social worker Cath. Service League, Ashtabula, Ohio, 1960-61, Mahoning County Welfare Dept., Youngstown, Ohio, 1961-62; tchr. Ashtabula County Sch. for Retarded, 1963-64; social worker Cath. Service League, 1965-73; caseworker Ashtabula County Children's Services Bd., 1973-76, dir. residential services, 1976—. Fin. sec. Ashtabula County Council Retarded Citizens, 1970-71, treas., 1972-74, pres., 1975-77, bd. dirs., 1978-80; coordinator needs assessment, bd. dirs. Human Services Center, Conneaut, Ohio, 1978—; sec. Mahoning, Ashtabula, Columbia, Trumbull Counties Dist. 11 Bd. Mental Retardation and Devel. Disabilities, 1978-79; pres. adv. bd. Ohio Dept. Mental Health and Mental Retardation Youngstown Devel. Center, 1981; active Ashtabula County Health Forum. Roman Catholic. Clubs: Zonta, Cath. Daus. of the Americas (regent). Home: 878 Broad St Conneaut OH 44030 Office: 2036 E Prospect Rd Ashtabula OH 44004

KOHRING, HAZEL LOUISE ROBERTS (MRS. WALTER G. KOHRING), life ins. broker; b. Moberly, Mo.; d. Elmer P. and Ruby (Murphy) Roberts; student Moberly Comml. Coll.; m. Walter G. Kohring, Aug. 4, 1939; children—Dorothy (Mrs. Charles Chappell), William Halliburton. Gen. agt., Met. Life Ins. Co., 1942-46; fashion mgr. Sears Roebuck & Co., Alton, Ill., 1946-59; life ins. broker, 1959—; pres. Hazel L. Kohring, Assos., Inc., ins. agy. Finance chmn., chmn. public edn., mem. exec. com. Mo. Heart Assn., chmn. bd., 1975—. Bd. dirs. St. Louis Heart Assn., 1965—, membership chmn., 1965-66, co-chmn. raising heart fund campaign, 1965; mem. assembly planning com. Am. Heart Assn., 1978; bd. dirs. St. Louis Met. YWCA, 1970-76; nat. chmn. spl. gifts Nat. Fedn. Bus. and Profl. Women Found., 1976. Recipient Man of Year award St. Louis Gen. Agts. and Mgrs. Assn., 1962-65, 68-69, 77-78; Distinguished Salesman awards Sales and Marketing Execs. Assn.; award Heart Fund, 1965; named outstanding Woman in Bus. Achievements, Downtown St. Louis, 1968; named one of three outstanding women of Mo., Phi Chi Theta, 1968. CLU. Mem. Nat. Assn. Life Underwriters (nat. pres. womens roundtable 1971-72, I.H. Dublin Nat. award 1971, nat. pub. service chmn. 1973-74), Million Dollar Round Table (life, qualifying mem.), Mo. Fedn. Bus. and Profl. Women's Club (1st v.p. 1971, pres. 1974-75, Woman of Year dist. VIII 1973), Bus. and Profl. Women's Club St. Louis (pres. 1958-59). Republican. Baptist. Mem. Order Eastern Star. Club: Altrusa (dir. St. Louis, Woman of Distinction 1971). Home: 2160 Mason Lake Dr Manchester MO 63011 Office: 11147 Olive Rd St Louis MO 63141

KOHUT, A. LORENE, artist; b. La Port, Tex., Nov. 16, 1929; d. Patrick E. and Alma Severance; m. Mike Kohut, Jan. 6, 1950; children—Michael D., Karen M., Michelle A. Exhibited one-woman shows: Gallery 252, Phila., 1965, Carspecken-Scott Gallery, Wilmington, Del., 1975, Kalon Gallery, McLean, Va., 1974, Ogunquit (Maine) Art Center, 1969, McBride Gallery, Annapolis, Md., 1982, Touch of Glass Gallery, Alexandria, Va., 1982; exhibited group shows: Nat. Artclub, N.Y.C., 1969, NAD, 1969, Acad. Artists Assn., Springfield, Mass., 1970, 71, 72, 73, Am. Artist Profl. League, N.Y.C., 1981. Served with WAC, 1948-51. Mem. Artist Equity, Phila. Art Alliance, Am. Artist Profl. League. Address: Route 3 Andrews Lake Felton DE 19943

KOKKINOS, EFROSINI, psychologist; b. Greece, Jan. 26, 1950; came to U.S., 1966, naturalized, 1971; d. Euripidis and Irene Kokkinos; B.A., Queens Coll., 1975; M.S., Bklyn. Coll., 1977; postgrad. Fordham U., 1977—. Research asst. SUNY, Bklyn., 1977-78, John S. Helmbold Edn. Center, Corbin City, N.J., 1978-79; sch. psychologist Ocean City (N.J.) Schs., 1979—; cons. psychologist N.Y.C. Bd. Edn., Atlantic Mental Health Clinic, 1979—; instr. Stockton (N.J.) State Coll. Mem. Am. Psychol. Assn., Nat. Assn. Sch. Psychologists. Home: 1040 Asbury Ave Ocean City NJ 08226 Office: 6th St and West Ave Ocean City NJ 08226

KOLANSKY, ELSA HARWITZ, journalist; b. Scranton, Pa., May 17, 1927; d. Isaac Harold and Hilda (Heller) Harwitz; B.A. in Journalism, Pa. State U., 1948; postgrad. New Sch. Social Research, 1975, Phila. Writers Sch., 1977, Temple U. Grad. Seminars, 1978-80, Pa. State U. Real Estate Inst., 1978; m. Harold Kolansky, June 8, 1948; children—Jeffrey, Betta, Daniel. Freelance writer, editor, 1948—; reporter Phila. weeklies, 1950-54, Beth Sholom Congregation Newsletter, 1970-72, Jenkintown Times Chronicle Bi-Centennial Edition, 1975; feature editor Am. Acad. of Child. Psychiatry Newsletter, 1978—; contbg. author chpt. —Montgomery County-Second Hundred Years.— Active Pa. State U. fund raising; mem. Beth Sholom Congregation and Sisterhood Bd., co-chmn. Sisterhood Adult Edn., 1982—; mem. Faculty Wives Jefferson Med. Coll. and Hosp. Mem. Women's Com. Phila. Assn. Psychoanalysis (treas. 1970), AAUW, Phila. Geriatrics Center, Phila. Writers Conf., LWV. Republican. Clubs: Cheltenham Racquet, Hadassah.

KOLAR, MARY JANE, assn. exec.; b. Benton, Ill., Aug. 9, 1941; d. Thomas Haskell and Mary Jane (Sanders) Burnett; B.A. with high honors, So. Ill. U., 1963, M.A. with highest honors, 1964; m. Otto Michael Kolar, Aug. 13, 1966; children—Robin Lynn, Deon Michael. Tchr. pub. schs., Benton and Zeigler, Ill., 1960-63; grad. asst. and grad. fellow So. Ill. U., Carbondale, 1963-64; instr. Ridgewood High Sch., Norridge, Ill., 1964-67, Maine Twp. High Sch., Des Plaines, Ill., 1967-70; freelance writer, Chgo., 1970-71; cons. Contractor Promotions, Chgo., 1970-71; ednl. coordinator Am. Dietetic Assn., Chgo., 1971-72; dir. profl. devel. Am. Dental Hygienists Assn., Chgo., 1972-78; dir. Learning Center div. Am. Coll. Cardiology, Bethesda, Md., 1978-80; dir. edn. Nat. Moving and Storage Assn., Alexandria, Va., 1980-82; exec. dir. Women in Communications, Inc., Austin, Tex., 1982—; cons., speaker various profl. assns., ednl. instns. and fed. agys. Troopleader, Girl Scouts U.S.A., 1970-71; adminstrv. bd. mem. Prince of Peace Ch., Elk Grove Village, Ill., 1972-76; edn. com. mem. St. Paul's Ch., Chgo., 1977-79; mem. adv. council Accrediting Commn., Assn. of Ind. Colls. and Schs., 1980—. Fellow Am. Soc. Allied Health Professions (dir. 1978-79); mem. Am. Soc. Assn. Execs. (cert. assn. exec.; dir. edn. sect. 1977—, chmn. edn. com., ex-officio mem. bd. dirs. 1982—, Educator of Yr. award 1978), Greater Washington Soc. Assn. Execs. (edn. com. 1981-82), Am. Bus. Women's Assn., Ill. Hist. Soc., Kellogg Nat. Com. on Allied Health Edn., Women in Communications (newsletter editor, legis. and career reentry chmn., chmn. ERA task force, dir. Washington profl. chpt.), So. Ill. U. Alumni Assn. (bd. govs. 1977-80, pres.-elect Washington chpt. 1981), Phi Beta Kappa, Phi Kappa Phi, Kappa Delta Pi, Alpha Lambda Delta, Pi Lambda Theta. Clubs: Triton Wives Service Orgn. (program chair 1971-72), Nat. Women's Polit. Caucus, Tex. Women's Polit. Caucus, So. Christian Leadership Conf. Contbr. articles to profl. jours., chpts. to books. Home: 7117 Woodhollow Dr Apt 1621 Austin TX 78731 Office: PO Box 9861 Austin TX 78766

KOLIDA, SYLVIA ANNE, psychiat. mental health therapist; b. Hamilton, Ohio, Apr. 20, 1941; d. Walter Joseph and Mary Jeannette (Suldovsky) Harmon; student Ohio U., 1975; B.S. in Nursing, Miami U., 1980, Cert. Psychiat. Nursing, 1980; div.; children—Karen Gardner, Kim Gardner, Kelly Gardner. Acct., Mosler Safe Co., Hamilton, 1956-58; with Gen. Tel. Communications, Oxford, Ohio, 1969-72; public relations Elder Beerman Dept. Stores, Cin., 1972-75; dir. nursing service Emerson A. North Hosp., Cin., 1975-77, dir. quality assurance, 1977-79; outpatient individual therapist Lawrenceburg Community Mental Health Center, Lawrenceburg, Ind., 1979—; pvt. practice nursing. Mem. Ind. Task Force on Women's Issues, 1979—. Mem. Am. Nurses Assn., Ind. State Nursing Assn., Biofeedback Soc. Ind., Nat. Assn. Female Execs., Ind. Counselors Assn. Alcohol and Drug Abuse. Office: 344 Walnut St Lawrenceburg IN 47025

KOLKER, BONNIE LYNNE, telephone co. account exec.; b. Phila., Mar. 26, 1953; d. Lester and Sandra (Cantor) K.; B.S. summa cum laude, Fairleigh Dickinson U., 1976, M.B.A., 1980. Asst. supr. public affairs Babcock and Wilcox, N.Y.C., 1974-78, asst. to v.p. public affairs, 1979; account exec. AT&T Long Lines, N.Y.C., 1979—. Active Young Friends of Arts and Camerata (N.Y.C. Opera Guild), 1978—, Friends of Whitney Mus., 1977-78. Mem. Am. Mgmt. Assn., Am. Mktg. Assn., Assn. M.B.A. Execs., Nat. Assn. Female Execs., Lambda Sigma Tau, Phi Omega Epsilon. Home: 200 Winston Dr Cliffside Park NJ 07010 Office: 32 Ave of Americas New York NY 10013

KOLKO, NAOMI GREENWOOD, clin. social worker; b. Phila., Feb. 12, 1941; d. David Nisan and Emma (Morgenstern) Greenwood; B.A. in Sociology with honors, U. Pa., 1962; M.S.W., Smith Coll., 1964; m. Burton S. Kolko, June 17, 1962; children—David Joseph, Joshua Howard. Clin. social worker St. Elizabeths Hosp., Washington, 1964-69; social worker children's unit Psychiat. Inst., Washington, 1972-76, asso. dir. social work, 1976-79, acting dir., summer 1979; pvt. practice clin. social work Bethesda, Md., 1979—; cons. Community Psychiat. Clinic, Wheaton, Md., 1980—. Provisional vice chmn. Precinct 7-14, Montgomery County, Md., 1982—. Lic. clin. social worker. Mem. Nat. Assn. Social Workers, Greater Wash. Soc. Clin. Social Workers, Am. Orthopsychiat. Assn., Am. Assn. Sex Educators, Counselors and Therapists, Wash. Women's Network. Democrat. Jewish. Clubs: Plowman and Fisherman, Hadassah. Home and office: 8313 Beech Tree Rd Bethesda MD 20817

KOLLER, KAREN KATHRYN, credit bur. exec.; b. Lorain, Ohio, June 23, 1949; d. Harry Charles and Lavonne Rita (Ball) K.; B.A., Adrian Coll., 1971; M.B.A., Baldwin-Wallace Coll., 1977. Office mgr. Harry C. Koller, Acct., Lorain, 1974-79; mgr., sec.-treas. Credit Bur. of Lorain, Inc., 1971-79; sec.-treas. Haytcotter, Inc., Lorain, 1979-80; partner K & K Co., Lorain, 1979—; ops. mgr. Lorain br. Credit Bur. of Toledo, Inc., 1979—. Mem. fin. com. Erie Shores council Girl Scouts U.S.A., 1979—, mem. nominating com., 1981—, bd. dirs., 1982—; mem. citizens adv. bd. Heritage Studies, Lorain City Schs., 1979-80; mem. communications sub-com. Lorain Mayor's Com. on Handicapped, 1979-81, sec. Mayor's Com. on Handicapped, 1982—. Named Lorain's Bus. and Profl. Women's Young Careerist, 1978-79; recipient cert. of achievement YWCA Women of Achievement program, 1979. Mem. AAUW, Delta Mu Delta. Clubs: Quota (pres. 1979—), Lorain Bus. and Profl. Women (treas. 1979-80). Home: 1132 7th St Lorain OH 44052 Office: 314 9th St Lorain OH 44052

KOLMER, ELIZABETH, nun, educator; b. Waterloo, Ill., Dec. 11, 1931; d. Arthur Francis and Carmelita Frances (Vogt) Kolmer; B.A. magna cum laude, St. Louis U., 1961, M.A., 1962, Ph.D. (Ford Found. grantee), 1965. Joined Adorers of the Blood of Christ, Roman Catholic Ch., 1949; Prof. history St. Louis U., 1964—, dir. Am. studies program, 1969-81. Trustee, St. Clement Hosp., 1978—. Nat. Endowment Humanities grantee, 1969. Mem. Midcontinent Am. Studies Assn. (v.p. 1977-78 pres. 1978-79), Orgn. Am. Historians, Am. Studies Assn. Contbr. articles in field to profl. jours. Home: 3825 W Pine Blvd St Louis MO 63108 Office: St Louis U Dept History 221 N Grand St Louis MO 63103

KOLOSEUS, KAREN BERNADETTE, health care service accountant; b. Rock Island, Ill., Dec. 18, 1953; d. Bernard Thomas and Margaret Theresa (Tollenaer) K.; B.A. in Bus. Adminstrn., St. Ambrose Coll., Davenport, Iowa, 1975; M.B.A., Drake U., 1977. Collection mgr., asst. patient account mgr. Franciscan Med. Center, Rock Island, Ill., 1976-79; bus. office mgr. trainee Eastern region Am. Med. Internat., Atlanta, 1979; bus. office mgr., budget coordinator Parkway Gen. Hosp., North Miami Beach, Fla., 1979-82; fin. cons. Profl. Hosp. Services div. Am. Med. Internat., Los Angeles, 1982—; cons. in accounts receivables mgmt., 1982—. Cert. patient accounts mgr. Mem. Hosp. Fin. Mgmt. Assn., Am. Guild Patient Accounts Mgrs., Am. Mktg. Assn., Receivables Mgmt. Task Force, Gold Coast Exec. Women's Network, Nat. Assn. Female Execs., M.B.A. Execs. Assn. Home: 13900 Fiji Way Marina Del Rey CA 90291 Office: 12960 Coral Tree Pl Los Angeles CA 90066

KOLOTKIN, RONETTE LOGANZO, clin. psychologist, educator; b. Bklyn., Nov. 29, 1950; d. Alfred Joseph and Thelma Delores Loganzo; B.A. in Psychology, Trinity Coll., Hartford, Conn., 1972; Ph.D. in Clin. Psychology, U. Minn., 1978. Research staff Inst. Living, Hartford, 1971-72; research asst. psychiatry U. Minn. Hosps., 1972-73, research asst. dept. psychology, 1972-78, teaching asst., 1975-77, instr. 1976-78, therapy supr., 1977-78; practicum, in-patient unit Hennepin County (Minn.) Med. Center, 1973, out-patient unit, 1974, clin. psychology intern, 1974-75; crisis counselor Youth Emergency Service, Mpls., 1973-74; therapist Walk-In Counseling Center, Mpls., 1974-78; women's group facilitator Minn. Women's Center, Mpls., 1976-78; asst. prof. dept. psychology and social scis. Rush-Presbyterian-St. Luke's Med. Center, Chgo., 1978—, staff clin. psychologist, 1978—, asst. scientist, 1978—; asst. prof. dept. psychology and social sci. Rush U., Chgo., 1978—. Registered psychologist, Ill. Mem. Am. Psychol. Assn., Assn. Advancement of Behavior Therapy, Ill. Assn. Psychologists in Health and Rehab., Soc. Behavioral Medicine, Soc. Psychotherapy Research. Contbr. articles to profl. jours. Home: 1303 Maple Ave #1W Evanston IL 60201 Office: 1753 W Congress Pkwy Chicago IL 60612

KOMECHAK, MARILYN GILBERT, psychologist; b. Wabash, Ind., Aug. 28, 1936; d. Russell and Evelyn Georgianna (Snyder) Gilbert; B.S., Purdue U., 1954; B.S., Tex. Christian U., 1966, M.Ed., 1968; Ph.D., North Tex. State U., 1975; m. George J. Komechak, Aug. 23, 1958; children—Kimberly Ann, Gilbert Matthew. Tchr. elem. sch., Huntsville, Ala., 1959-60; counselor clin. staff Child Study Center, Ft. Worth, 1968-74; assoc. dir. Sch. for Community Service, North Tex. State U., Denton, 1974-77; pvt. practice psychology, Ft. Worth, 1977—; adj. prof. Tex. Christian U., U. Tex., Arlington; dir. Jon Pierce, Inc.; cons. to schs. and mgmt.; mem. adv. bd. Trinity Valley Mental Health/Mental Retardation, Mental Health Assn. Tarrant County, 1980; presenter to profl. groups, 1974—. Mem. Am. Psychol. Assn., Tex. Psychol. Assn., Tarrant County Psychol. Assn. (officer 1977), Am. Soc. Clin. Hypnosis, Psi Chi, Delta Gamma. Episcopalian. Author: Getting Yourself Together, 1982; contbr. articles on counseling and psychology to profl. jours. Home: 8109 Rush St Fort Worth TX 76116 Office: 5280 Trail Lake Dr Fort Worth TX 76133

KOMERSKA, SALLY ARLENE, microbiologist; b. Mpls., Dec. 16, 1930; d. Helmer William and Esther Ingeborg (Reinertsen) Kestila; student Pa. State U., 1949-51, U. Pitts., 1951-52, Montefiore Hosp. Sch. Med. Tech., Pitts., 1952-53; B.S., U. Ariz., 1970, M.S., 1979; m. Robert James Komerska, Aug. 19, 1955; 1 son, Steven. Med. technologist Sch. Public Health, U. Pitts., 1953-54, Pima County Hosp., 1954-55, Thomas-Davis Clinic, 1955-60; free-lance med. technologist St. Joseph's Hosp., Tucson, 1962-63; weekend supr., microbiologist St. Joseph's Hosp., Tucson, 1962-63; med. technologist Thomas-Davis Clinic, Tucson, 1966-68, head microbiologist, 1970—, lab. supr., 1974—; bd.

dirs., sec. St. Joseph's Hosp. Credit Union, 1977-78. Den mother Cub Scouts, 1971-73; mem. Altar Guild, Our Savior's Luth. Ch., 1975-78; active Heard Mus., Phoenix, Mus. No. Ariz., Flagstaff. Mem. Am. Soc. Clin. Pathologists (asso.), Am. Soc. Med. Tech. (pres., merit award 1972), Am. Soc. Microbiology, Nat. Assn. Female Execs., Ariz. Med. Lab. Assn. (pres. Tucson chpt.). Republican. Lutheran. Mem. profl. adv. panel Med. Lab. Observer mag., 1980—. Home: 3804 E Calle DeSoto Tucson AZ 85716 Office: Alvernon at 5th St Tucson AZ 85726

KOMISAR, DONNA MARIA, controller; b. Nashville, Mar. 19, 1933; d. James Robert Muratta and Eloise (Pitts) Muratta O'More; student LaSalle Extension U., 1954, U. Tenn., Nashville, 1967, IBM Corp. RPG Programming Sch., 1973, Belmont Coll., 1980; m. Max Komisar, Mar. 5, 1976; children—Jennifer Maria Parker, Thomas L. Campbell, Jr. Sec., bookkeeper Roberts Bailey, C.P.A., Fayetteville, Tenn., 1953-55; med. sec., bookkeeper Drs. Patterson and Pace, Nashville, 1955-58; sec., bookkeeper Rhoten Realty Co., Nashville, 1958-61; bus. mgr. Cosmopolitan Health Spa, Nashville, 1961-65; corp. controller Blanton Smith Corp., Nashville, 1965—; sec.-treas. bd. trustees O'More Sch. Design, also exec. asst. to adminstrv. staff. Home: 4400 Belmont Park Terr Nashville TN 37215 Office: PO Box 23123 Nashville TN 37202

KOMJATHY, NANCY CAROLYN MARSH, hosp. exec.; b. Detroit, July 27, 1942; d. George and Beatrice (Mallock) Marsh; diploma Providence Hosp. Nursing, 1963; student Wayne State U., 1969-70; B.A., U. Detroit, 1976; M.S., U. Mich., 1978; m. Louis A. Komjathy, II, Jan. 27, 1967; 1 son, Louis A., III. Staff nurse, charge nurse Detroit Gen. Hosp., 1963-65, nurse-in-charge, part-time, 1971-72; supr. operating rm. and recovery rm. Martin Place Hosp. West, Detroit, 1965-67; asst. dir. nursing Doctor's Hosp., Detroit, 1968-69; staff nurse Children's Hosp., Detroit, part-time, 1969; supr. Henry Ford Hosp., Detroit, 1973-74, day supr. med. nursing units, 1974-75, instr. dept. manpower devel., 1975, asst. dir. nursing in charge operating rm. and recovery rm., 1975-77, staff nurse, 1977-78, dir. nursing Div. III, 1978-80; asso. dir. nursing affairs Hurley Med. Center, Flint, 1980—. Mem. Am. Soc. Nursing Service Adminstrs., Am. Hosp. Assn., Providence Hosp. Alumni Assn., U. Mich. Alumni Assn., Am. Operating Rm. Assn., Sigma Theta Tau. Office: Hurley Med Center One Hurley Plaza Flint MI 48502

KOMOTO, SHIRLEY A., corp. strategic and project planner; b. Tokyo, July 21, 1950 (parents Am. citizens); d. Yasuro and Irene (Fujimoto) K.; B.A., Calif. State U., Long Beach, 1973, M.P.A., 1976; postgrad. U. So. Calif. Mgmt. cons. various cos., Los Angeles County, 1970—; NIMH fellow Asian Am. Mental Health Tng. Center, 1972-75, HUD fellow, 1974; program coordinator Orange County/Long Beach Health Consortium, Inc., Irvine, Calif., 1975-76; program analyst dept. ob-gyn Charles R. Drew Postgrad. Med. Sch., Los Angeles, 1976-79; sr. planner WED Enterprises div. Walt Disney Prodns., Glendale, Calif., 1979-80, project bus. adminstr., 1980—. Vice chmn. Asian Pacific Family Outreach, 1979-80; chmn. Long Beach Pioneer Project, 1972-73, mem., 1970—; mem. Long Beach Commn. on Econ. Opportunities, 1972. Recipient community service award Los Angeles County Dept. Health Services, 1976. Mem. Women in Mgmt., Research Coordinating Council of Los Angeles, Am. Soc. Public Adminstrn., World Future Soc. Democrat. Co-author: Source Book on Perinatal and Other Health Indicators, 1978; contbr. articles on edn. study and plans to profl. publs., papers to confs. Office: 1401 Flower St Glendale CA 91201

KONARSKI, ELIZABETH LOUISE, small bus. owner; b. Seymour, Wis., Aug. 5, 1938; d. Francis and Evelyn (Coonen) C.; B.Ed., U. Wis., 1960; M.Ed., U. Wash., 1966; m. Aug. 13, 1960; children—Scott Alan, Lee Ann. Tchr., operator Cedar Rapids, Iowa and Renton, Wash., 1960-65; owner, The Country Mouse and the Calico Cat, 1970-80, Cottage Wearing Ltd., Issaquah, Wash., 1979—; mgr., founder Gilman Village Shopping Center, Issaquah, 1973—. Bd. dirs. King County E. Conv. and Visitors Bur., 1979-82; co-chmn. bd. Bellevue Community Coll. Women's Center, 1975-82. Mem. Women and Bus., Seattle C. of C. (dir.), The Fashion Group (dir.), Women's Profl. and Managerial Network, Issaquah C. of C., Nat. Assn. Female Execs., Ind. Bus. Assn., Gilman Village Mchts. Assn. Author: Merchant Assn. Handbook/ Gilman Village, 1976. Home: 835 Mount Park Blvd SW Issaquah WA 98027 Office: Gilman Village Issaquah WA 98027

KONDOROSSY, ELIZABETH DAVIS, educator; b. East Canton, Ohio, Dec. 23, 1910; d. William David and Lottie Pearl (Hall) Davis; A.B., Oberlin Coll., 1934; postgrad. U. Chgo., 1940-42; M.Ed., Kent State U., 1968, spl. edn. degree, 1970; m. Leslie Kondorossy, Jan. 19, 1962. Tchr. elem. sch., East Canton, 1934-37, high sch., Brewster, Ohio, 1937-40; tchr. music, English, typing, social studies and math. Sunbeam Sch. for Crippled Children, Cleve., 1952—; solo performances on organ and piano Severance Chamber Music Hall, Cleve., Tokyo, Budapest, Hungary; lectr. music and typing to handicapped children; organized handbell choir of handicapped children and of geriatrics; lectr. nat. conv. Am. Guild Handbell Ringers; adjudicator Piano Tchrs. Guild. Organist, dir. music First Hungarian Reformed Ch., Cleve. Recipient Martha Holden Jennings Master Tchr. award, 1968, grantee, 1971; Newspaper Fund fellow, 1963; Tchr. of Yr. award Greater Cleve. chpt. Council Exceptional Children, 1979, Ohio chpt., 1979; resolution Ohio State Senate, 1980; award City of University Heights (Ohio). Mem. Am. Coll. Musicians, Am. Guild Organists, Council Exceptional Children, Music Educators Nat. Conf., Greater Cleve. Council Bus. Edn. Tchrs., Greater Cleve. Council Journals Advisers, Greater Cleve. Council English Tchrs. Contbr. articles to profl. jours. Home: 14443 E Carroll Blvd Cleveland OH 44118 Office: 11731 Mount Overlook Rd Cleveland OH 44120

KONDRACKA, ELIZABETH TERESA, physician; b. Warsaw, Poland, Apr. 15, 1945; came to U.S., 1975, naturalized, 1979; d. Antoni and Anna (Haszczyn) Cwiek; M.D., U. Warsaw, 1970; m. Alex Kondracki, Dec. 14, 1974; 1 son, Anthony Joseph. Resident in family practice Tex. Tech U., Lubbock, also Anniston, Ala., 1977-80; practice medicine specializing in family practice, Lewisville, Tex., 1980—; part-time attending staff St. Paul's Hosp., Dallas. Fellow Am. Acad. Family Physicians; mem. AMA, Tex. Med. Assn., Denton County Med. Assn. Home: 2012 Sequoia Circle Grapevine TX 76051 Office: 500 W Main St Lewisville TX 75067

KONDY, STEPHANIE MARY, psychologist; b. Miami, Fla., May 26, 1949; d. Matthew Frank and Alice (Jarosz) K.; B.A. in Psychology cum laude, U. Fla., 1972; M.A., U. Ala., 1975; postgrad. U. Ala., Birmingham, 1978-79, U. Fla., 1980—. Psychologist, Fla. Community Bases Diagnostic and Evaluation Team, Ft. Myers, 1975-77; psychologist, then dir. psychology, acting behavior supr. Sunland Center, Miami, 1977-79, dir. programs and services, 1979-81, dir. residential services, 1982—; sec.-treas. Star Cons.; cons. in field. Mem. Am. Assn. Mental Deficiency (asso.), Am. Psychol. Assn. (asso.), Nat. Assn. Retarded Citizens, Ladies Guild. Roman Catholic. Club: Civitan. Home: 993 W 79th Pl Hialeah FL 33014 Office: 20000 NW 47th Ave Opa Locka FL 33055

KONER, PAULINE, dancer, choreographer; b. N.Y.C.; d. Samuel and Ida (Ginsburg) Koner; student Columbia, 1928-31; ballet student of Michel Fokine; student ethnic dance with Michio Ito, also Angel Cansino; m. Fritz Mahler, May 23, 1939. Solo concerts in N.Y.C., 1930—, Near East, 1932, Russia, 1935, U.S., 1930—; guest artist Jose Limon Co., 1945-60; guest artist, tchr. Jacob's Pillow Dance Festival, intermittently, 1945-70; dir. Pauline Koner Dance Co., 1947-64; guest choreographer Nat. Sch. Dance, Rome, Italy, 1960-63, Nat. Ballet Chile, 1961, Batsheva Co., Israel; performer, tchr. Conn. Coll. Sch. Dance, 1948-60; pioneer TV dance in CBS, 1946; established modern dance program in Japan under auspices Fulbright Com., 1965; State Dept. tour of India, Singapore and Korea, 1967; mem. faculty Sch. Performing Arts, N.Y.C., N.C. Sch. Arts, Winston-Salem; adj. prof. Bklyn. Coll., 1975—; performed at White House, 1967; conducted choreography workshops Nat. Assn. Regional Ballets, 1968; staged ballet Dayton (Ohio) Civic Ballet, 1969, Alvin Ailey Co., 1969, Atlanta Ballet Co., 1969; guest tchr. modern dance Internat. Ballet Seminar, Copenhagen, 1971, 72, Am. Dance Center, N.Y.C., 1972; lectr. and guest artist many leading univs. in U.S.; performed under auspices State Dept. in Mex., S.Am., Europe; filmed TV broadcasts of numerous performances; artist-in-residence N.C. Sch. Arts, Winston-Salem, 1965-76; tchr. choreographer workshop Cultural Center of Philippines, 1973; premiere Solitary Songs, Am. Dance Festival, 1975, Pauline Koner Dance Consort, 1976, A Time of Crickets, Am. Dance Festival, 1976, Mosaic, Dance Umbrella Series, 1977, Cantigas, Am. Dance Festival, 1978, Flight, Riverside Dance Festival, 1980; nat. adjudicator Am. Coll. Dance Festival, Kennedy Center, 1981. Recipient Dance Mag. award, 1963. Nat. Endowment of Arts grantee, 1969, 75, 77-78, 79.

KONNER, JOAN WEINER, broadcasting exec., TV producer, writer; b. Paterson, N.J., Feb. 24, 1931; d. Martin and Tillie (Frankel) Weiner; student Vassar Coll., 1948-49; B.A., Sarah Lawrence Coll., 1951; M.S., Columbia U., 1961; children—Rosemary, Catherine. Editorial writer-columnist, asst. to editor The Record, Hackensack, N.J., 1961-63; producer, reporter WNDT Ednl. Broadcasting Corp., N.Y.C., 1963-65; writer, reporter NBC News, N.Y.C., 1965-68, producer, writer TV documentaries NBC, N.Y.C., 1968-73, dir. programs NBC Radio Network, N.Y.C., 1973-74, network documentary producer-writer NBC News, 1974-77; exec. producer nat. pub. affairs programs WNET/13, Pub. TV, N.Y.C., 1977-81, v.p., dir. met. programming, 1982—. Trustee Columbia U. Recipient Emmy award Nat. Acad. TV Arts and Scis. (4); award AP Broadcasting Assn., 1969, 70, 71; gold medal Atlanta Film Festival, 1970, 71; awards N.Y. Film Festival, 1970, 71, 73, San Francisco Environ. Film Festival, 1970, Ohio State award Ohio State U., 1973, 76; awards Cath. Broadcasters Assn., 1970, Council Chs., 1970, 72; Front Page award best documentary, Chgo. Film Festival award, 1975; Alumni award Columbia Grad. Sch. Journalism, 1975. Home: Snedens Landing Palisades NY 10964 Office: 304 W 58 St New York NY 10019

KONOPKA, MARY ANN STEPHANY, container mfg. co. supr.; b. Chgo., Jan. 30, 1933; d. Thomas Stephen and Mary Irene (Plucinski) Poltorak; student public schs., Chgo.; m. Louis Steven Konopka, Nov. 22, 1964 (dec. 1976); stepdaus.—Linda Marie Konopka Orseno, Lorraine Louise Konopka Capra. With Continental Group, Inc., West Chicago, Ill., 1952—, project control supr., 1978-81, supr. inventory control and repair parts inventory. Mem. Nat. Assn. Female Execs., U.S. CB Radio Assn. Democrat. Roman Catholic. Club: Northwest International Trade. Home: 526 E Pomeroy St West Chicago IL 60185 Office: Continental Group Inc 1700 Harvester Rd West Chicago IL 60185

KOOCK, MARY FAULK, banker; b. Austin, Tex., Nov. 7, 1910; d. Henry and Martha (Miner) Faulk; student U. Tex., 1929-30, So. Meth. U., 1931; m. Chester L. Koock, June 6, 1934; children—Kenneth, Karen, Gretchen, Bill, Timothy, Judy, Martha. Founder, owner Green Pastures restaurant, Austin, 1945-65; cons. Tex. Dept. Agr., Austin, 1969-71; food editor Tex. Star, 1971-73, Tex. Parade, 1971-73; with Bank of Austin, 1974-80, v.p. public relations, head dept. spl. services for women, 1979-80; v.p. Republic of Tex. Bank South, 1980—; lectr. in field; sec. to exec. bd. Center Stage, Inc., Austin, 1979—; anchorperson for network TV series The Rest of Your Life. Mem. Tex. Agrl. Products Bd., 1971—; bd. dirs. Wild Basin Wilderness Park, 1978—, also v.p.; mem. exec. bd. Center Stage, Inc., 1979—; bd. dirs. Travis County chpt. Am. Cancer Soc., 1978—. Named Tex. Press Woman of Achievement, 1972; Austin's Outstanding Woman, 1974; Successful Innovator, Tex. Woman Mag., 1979; AAUW Outstanding Woman in Bus. and Fin., 1979. Mem. Nat. Assn. Bank Women, Women in Communications, Am. Inst. Banking, Austin Women's Symphony League (pres. 1959-60), Pan Am. Round Table, Am. Banking Assn. Democrat. Roman Catholic. Clubs: Austin Women's, Woman's Forum, others. Author: Texas Cookbook, 1965; Cuisine of the Americas, 1976; Deaf Smith County Cookbook, 1973. Home: 1202 Wild Basin Ledge Austin TX 78746 Office: 2501 S Congress St Austin TX 78704

KOONTZ, WILMA RUTH, nurse; b. New Enterprise, Pa., Nov. 10, 1935; d. Park Otto and Roxie Ethel (Kagarise) Berkheimer; R.N., Altoona Hosp. Sch. Nursing, 1956; m. Bernard G. Koontz, June 23, 1956; children—Douglas E., Diane S. Staff nurse Okaloosa Meml. Hosp., Crestview, Fla., 1956-59, Hollidaysburg (Pa.) State Hosp., 1959-61, Carlisle (Pa.) Hosp., 1962-70; inservice coordinator Cumberland County Nursing Home, Carlisle, 1971-79; inservice coordinator Ch. of God Nursing Home, Carlisle, 1980-81, infection control nurse, health care officer, mem. safety com. 1980-81; staff nurse Blue Ridge Haven, West Camp Hill, Pa., 1981-82, Cumberland County Nursing Home, 1982—. Mem. Ch. of Brethren. Clubs: Cumberland County Nurses (pres. 1977-78), Carlisle Band Boosters. Address: 331 Wertz Run Rd Carlisle PA 17013

KOPACK, PAMELA LEE (MACMINN), bus. services exec.; b. Portland, Maine, July 25, 1951; d. Everett John Foye and Lois Florence (Loveland) MacMinn; student Sears, Roebuck Extension Inst., 1969-73, Newspaper Inst. Am., 1979—; m. Charles Thomas Kopack, Apr. 2, 1971. Sales staff J.C. Penney Co., Cleve., 1966-69, credit collector, 1972-75; positions with various cos., 1969-72; exec. sec., asst., Cole Nat. Corp., Cleve., 1976-79; various positions as employment counselor, travel cons., bridal cons., model, photographer, advt. aide; pres. Kopack Service Bur., Cleve., 1979—; author poetry pub. in Poetry-People, 1975, other publs., 1974—, lyrics for songs recorded on single records and albums, 1974-79; author greeting cards, articles, short stories. Mem. Career Guild (New Feature award 1982), Secs. Workshop, P.S. for Profl. Secs. (Bur. Bus. Practice, article award 1979), Internat. Platform Assn., Nat. Assn. Female Execs. Clubs: Homeowners Assn., Holiday Inn-Inmates, Women's Opportunity Workshop, Women's Monthly Get-Together, George Washington Exec. Recipient poetry award for Facets of a Housewife, pub. in Beyond Verse, 1977. Compiler Royal Doulton Manual for Collectors. Home and Office: 9383 Driftwood Dr Olmsted Falls OH 44138

KOPELMAN, SUSANNE TARTER, lang. service co. exec.; d. Clemens A. and Margaret Ann (McGann) Tarter; B.A., Trinity Coll., Washington, 1968; postgrad. Columbia U.; m. Manuel E. Kopelman, July 25, 1979. Field asso. producer CBS News, 1969-70; asso. producer, researcher Sta. WNET, N.Y.C.; producer mag. Cue mag., 1976; pres. Ampro Multilingua Inc., N.Y.C.; v.p. Ampro Prodns. Inc. Bd. dirs. benefit programs L'Hopital Americain a Paris, Am. Hosp., Neiully-sur-Seine, France, 1972. Roman Catholic. Home: 900 Park Ave New York NY 10021 Office: 150 Fifth Ave New York NY 10022

KOPENHAVER, JOSEPHINE YOUNG, painter, educator; b. Seattle, June 9, 1908; d. George Samuel and Blanche Cecilia (Castle) Young; A.B., U. Calif., 1928; M.F.A. (scholar 1936-37), U. So. Calif., 1937; spl. student Claremont Grad. Sch., 1951, 67, Chouinard Art Inst., 1946-47, Otis Art Inst., 1954-55; m. Ralph Witmer Kopenhaver, Apr. 11, 1931. Prof. art Chaffee Jr. Coll., Ontario, Calif., 1946-47, Los Angeles City Coll., 1948-73, Woodbury U., Los Angeles, 1973-76, summer sessions Calif. State U., Los Angeles, 1950, Pasadena City Coll., 1949, Otis Art Inst., Los Angeles, 1959, Pasadena Art Inst., 1948; profl. painter, exhibiting artist, 1933—; work included in exhibits mus. and pvt. galleries U.S. and Mex., 1933—, including Hatfield Galleries, Los Angeles; art juror. Winner first award in oil Los Angeles Art Festival, 1936, various art awards. Mem. Los Angeles Art Assn. (trustee), Nat. Watercolor Soc. (sec.), Audubon Artists, Artists for Econ. Action, Calif. Tchrs. Assn. Clubs: Los Angeles Athletic, Zeta Tau Alpha. Office: PO Box 10666 Glendale CA 91209

KOPENHAVER, PATRICIA ELLSWORTH, podiatrist; b. N.Y.C., Aug. 18; d. J. Emerson and Rose Ellsworth; A.B., George Washington U., 1954; M.A., Columbia U., 1956; Dr. Podiatric Medicine, SUNY, 1963. Practice podiatric surgery and sports medicine, Greenwich, Conn., 1964—; mem. staff Laurelton Convalescent Hosp., Greenwich. Mem. Greenwich Women's Club; v.p. Monmouth Opera Festival, 1964, trustee, 1966; mem. Greenwich Woman's Gardeners Club; mem. Philharmonia, Met. Opera Co., YWCA; chmn. dist. 7, Greenwich Women's Republican Club, 1977; bd. dirs. Monmouth Opera Guild, 1965; mem. Greenwich Art Council, Greenwich Exchange for Woman's Work. Recipient Hosp. Fund award for med. research translations ARC. Diplomate Nat. Bd. Podiatric Medicine Examiners. Mem. Am. (pres. 1970, com. library and archives 1982-83), Conn., Fairfield, podiatry assns., Am. Assn. Women Podiatrists (pres. 1969-78), Acad. Podiatry, Am. Podiatric Circulatory Soc., Am. Podiatry Council, Columbia U. Alumni Assn., UN Assn. U.S.A., George Washington U. Alumni Assn., Nat. Assn. Professions, AAUW (chmn. nominating com. 1981, chmn. programs 1982, 1st v.p. 1982), NOW. Clubs: Soroptimist, Greenwich Women's Republican, Woman's (internat. com. 1980-83, program com. 1981) Wings, Toastmasters. Home: 2 Sutton Pl S New York NY 10022 also 8 Dearfield Dr Greenwich CT 06830

KOPLAN, JUDITH ANNE, cosmetics co. exec.; b El Paso, Tex., May 16, 1950; d. William Edward and Sarah (O'Bryan) Thompson; A.B., Stanford U., 1972; postgrad. Northwestern U. Exec. asst. Nat. Assembly of Bahais' of U.S., Wilmette, Ill., 1974-76; dist. sales mgr. Avon Products, Inc., Morton Grove, Ill., 1976-78, mgr. shipments supr. mdse. control dept., 1978-79, communication services supr., 1980-81, rep. service dept. supr./trainer, 1981—. Mem. AAUW, Nat. Assn. Female Execs., Evanston Bus. and Profl. Women's Club. Office: 6901 Golf Rd Morton Grove IL 60053

KOPP, JENNIFER LEE, tech. illustrator; b. Phoenix, May 30, 1949; d. Leonard Owen and Gloria Belle (Shaffer) Kelly; student Los Angeles Pierce Coll., 1976-78, Moorpark Coll., 1981—; m. Glenn Robert Kopp, Sept. 7, 1969; children—M. Scott, G. Douglas. Supr., Volt Tech. Corp., Van Nuys, Calif., 1977-78, project coordinator, El Segundo, Calif., 1979-80; checker in drafting Mainstream Engring., Sherman Oaks, Calif., 1978-79; sr. tech. illustrator Dynaction Resources, Chatsworth, Calif., 1979; sr. tech. illustrator Litton Data Command Systems, Agoura, Calif., 1980—. Recipient Presdl. Sports award Pres.' Council on Phys. Fitness, 1973, 4 awards of Merit for sports L.A. Pierce Coll., 1977; Sportsmanship award Women's Internat. Motorcycle Assn., 1976, Citizenship award, 1978. Mem. Nat. Abortion Rights Action League, Nat. Women's Polit. Caucus, NOW, Calif. Abortion Rights Action League, Nat. Rifle Assn., Nat. Assn. Female Execs. Club: Litton Data Command Systems Rod and Gun pres. 1982-83). Home: 2209 N Carlsbad Ct Simi Valley CA 93063 Office: PO Box 5000 Agoura CA 91301

KOPP, NANCY KORNBLITH, state legislator; b. Coral Gables, Fla., Dec. 7, 1943; d. Lester and Barbara M. (Levy) Kornblith; B.A. with honors, Wellesley Coll., 1965; M.A., U. Chgo., 1968; m. Robert E. Kopp, May 3, 1969; children—Emily, Robert E. III. Instr. polit. sci. U. Ill. at Chgo., 1968-69; mem. profl. staff, spl. subcom. on edn. U.S. Ho. of Reps., Washington, 1970-71; legis. asst. Montgomery County delegation to Md. Gen. Assembly, Annapolis, 1971-74; mem. Md. Ho. of Dels., 1975—. Mem. Am. Polit. Sci. Assn., LWV, AAUW, Common Cause. Democrat. Jewish. Office: Lowex House Office Bldg Room 223 Annapolis MD 21401

KOPPER, ELIZABETH BARTON, med. technologist; b. Pocatello, Idaho, July 11, 1927; d. Edward Thomas and Mary Ellen (Davis) Barton; B.S. in Microbiology, U. Utah, 1949; m. Walter C. Kopper, June 11, 1948; children—Paul E., Steven A., Thomas F., Daniel N. Chief technologist Student Health Service U. N.Mex., Albuquerque, 1967-69; staff technologist Sequoia Dist. Hosp., Redwood City, Calif., 1969-73; staff technologist St. Luke's Hosp., Boise, Idaho, 1973-81, edn. coordinator Sch. Med. Tech., 1977-81; staff technologist VA Med. Center, Boise, 1981—. Mem. Idaho Soc. for Med. Tech. (past pres., mem. of yr. 1977), Am. Soc. for Med. Tech. (mem. of yr. region VIII 1977), Idaho Council for Continuing Med. Lab. Edn. (charter mem., past pres.). Republican. Methodist. Clubs: Ch. Couples', Order of Eastern Star. Home: 2003 Norcrest Dr Boise ID 83705 Office: VA Med Center Fifth at Fort Sts Boise ID 83702

KOPPUS, BETTY JANE, fin. corp. exec.; b. Toledo, Ohio, June 14, 1922; d. Carl Emerson and Hilda Sarah (Semlow) K.; student schs. Toledo. With United Savs. and Loan Assn., Toledo, 1940—, treas., 1962-64, v.p., asst. sec., 1964-73, v.p., sec., 1973-78, first v.p., 1978—. Trustee Luth. Social Service Northwestern Ohio. Named an Outstanding Bus. Woman of 1980, Tribute to Women and Industry (TWIN). Mem. Am. Soc. Personnel Adminstrn., Inst. Fin. Edn. (pres. Toledo chpt. 1961-62), Toledo Area C. of C. (trustee, treas. 1975-77), Toledo Area Govtl. Research Assn. (dir., treas. 1970-71), Toledo Area SBA, Beta Sigma Phi. Clubs: Zonta (dir. Toledo I, 1972-74), Brandywine Country. Home: 2541 Midland Ave Toledo OH 43614 Office: United Savings and Loan Assn 519 Madison Ave Toledo OH 43604

KOPROWSKI, HILARY, medi. scientist; b. Warsaw, Poland, Dec. 5, 1916; s. Paul and Sarah (Berland) K.; B.A., Mikolaj Rej Gymnasium of Luth. Congregation, Warsaw, 1933; M.D., U. Warsaw, 1939; grad. Warsaw Conservatory Music and Santa Cecilia Acad., Rome; Doctor honoris causa, Widener Coll., Phila., Ludwig-Maximilian U. (Ger.); m. Dr. Irena Grasberg, July 14, 1938; children—Claude Eugene, Christopher Dorian. Came to U.S., 1944, naturalized, 1950. Research asst. dept. exptl. and gen. pathology U. Warsaw, 1936-39; staff Yellow Fever Research Service, Rio de Janeiro, 1940-44; staff research div. Am. Cyanamid Co., 1944-46, asst. dir. viral and rickettsial research Lederle Lab., Pearl River, N.Y., 1946-57; dir. Wistar Inst., Phila., 1957—; prof. microbiology Faculty Arts and Scis., U. Pa., 1957—, Wistar prof. research medicine U. Pa., 1957—; research cell biology, virology and immunology; vaccine against poliomyelitis, hog cholera, rabies; cons. WHO, Nat. Cancer Inst., NIH, USPHS, 1962-70. Decorated Commandeur Ordre du Mérite pour la Recherche et l'Invention; Chevalier Order Royal De Lion, Belgium; recipient Alvarenga prize. Coll. Physicians Phila., 1959; Alfred Jurzykowski Found Polish Millenium prize, 1966; Felix Wankel Tierschutz prize, 1979; Alexander Von Humboldt Sr. U.S. Scientist award; Fulbright Scholar Max Planck Inst. Für Verhaltensphysiologie, Seewiesen, Germany, 1971. Fellow N.Y. Acad. Medicine, Phila. Coll. Physicians; mem. Am. Acad. Arts and Scis., Nat. Acad. Scis., N.Y. Acad. Scis. (pres. 1959, trustee 1960-72); Co-editor Methods in Virology, Virus and Immunity, Current Topics in Microbiology and Immunology, 1965—. Home: 334 Fairhill Road Wynnewood PA 19096 Office: Wistar Inst 36th and Spruce Streets Philadelphia PA 19104

KOREY, LOIS BALK, advt. co. exec.; b. N.Y.C., May 19, 1933; d. Samuel and Lillian (Rosenblatt) Balk; student N.Y. U., 1951-52; m. Stanton Korey, Jan. 12, 1958 (div.); children—Susan, Christopher. Writer TV shows including Steve Allen Tonight, Ernie Kovacs, Wide Wide World, Andy Griffith, Sunday Night Comedy Hour; jr. partner Jack Tinker & Partners Advt. Co., N.Y.C., 1964-66; jr. partner, copywriter McCann Erickson Advt. Co., N.Y.C., 1967-69; creative dir. Revlon, N.Y.C., 1972; exec. v.p., creative dir. Needham, Harper & Steers Advt., Inc. N.Y.C., 1973-82; pres. Korey, Kay & Partners, N.Y.C., 1982—. Recipient 18 Clios, Am. TV Comml. Festivals: 8 Andys, Advt. Club N.Y., Cannes Film Festival TV Comml. award, 1973; 10 Hollywood Film Festival awards. Mem. Writers Guild Am., Dramatists Guild. Contbr. articles to mags. and profl. jours. Home: 920 Park Ave New York NY 10028 Office: 15 E 75th St New York NY 10021

KORN, ELAINE DECKER, humane soc. exec.; b. Binghamton, N.Y., Mar. 18, 1906; d. Charles Simmons and Edith Violeta (Ferris) Decker; student Cornell U., 1925-27; student art Mildred Moffet White, Sumter, S.C., 1962; student interior decorating U. S.C., 1962; m. Matthew Farrington Korn, Dec. 29, 1927; 1 dau., Jane Ferris Korn Tisdale. Co-owner, co-operator The Korner Shop, Binghamton, 1932-37; interior decorator, founder showrooms Sumter Cabinet Co. bedroom furniture div. Korn Industries (S.C.), 1947-76; founder Soc. for Prevention Cruelty to Animals, Sumter and Humane Edn. Center, Sumter, 1969, exec. dir. and pres. soc., 1972-80, exec. dir., 1969—, also dir. soc. and center; founder My Buddy Boarding Inn, 1977 and Nearly Nu Shop, 1979, for income support of shelter; dir. Korn Industries. Grand marshal Iris Festival Parade, Sumter, 1980; mem. adv. bd. Nat. Security Council; mem. dean's council Carolina Law Soc. of U. S.C. Sch. Law, 1980; bd. dirs. Citizens to Preserve the Santee-Cooper, 1982, World's Largest Furniture Library, High Point, N.C., Sumter Little Theater, Sumter Gallery Art, Sumter-Shaw Community Concert Assn.; mem. Leadership Found.; sponsor Nat. Conservative Polit. Action Com., Rep. Presdl. Task Force. Named Career Woman of Yr., local chpt. Nat. Bus. and Profl. Women's Club, 1979; recipient Senator Strom Thurmond Friendship award; award Furniture div. Korn Industries, 1979; cert. appreciation Kiwanis Club, Key Group, 1981; appreciation plaque Soc. Prevention Cruelty to Animals, 1980; numerous others; guest of honor Hist. Women's Club, YWCA Group, Sumter, 1982. Mem. S.C. Humane Assn. (dir. info. for establishment new humane socs. and animal shelters), Friends of Animals, Humane Soc. U.S., Am. Humane Assn., Nat. Horse Protection Assn., Nat. Audubon Soc., Columbia (S.C.) Audubon Soc., Riverbanks Soc. Zoo, Religious Roundtable, Heritage Found., 700 Club, Moral Majority, Christian Voice, Animal Protection Inst., Fund for Animals, Nat. Wildlife Fedn., Jacques Cousteau Soc., Internat. Fund Amimal Welfare, Nat. Senatorial Inner Circle Republican Party (charter), Washington Legal Found., Sumter Artist Guild, Sumter Art Assn., Am. Conservative Union, Nat. Taxpayers Union, Kappa Kappa Gamma. Presbyterian. Clubs: Sunset Country, Elks (Women's Div.), Jr. Welfare League (hon. mem.; pres. chpt. 1939-40, silver plate award 1940), Altrusa (hon.), Current Lit. (hon.; pres. 1951-53, v.p. 1959-60, 63-64). Home: 10 Swan Lake Dr Sumter SC 29150 Office: 1140 Guignard Dr Sumter SC 29150

KORNBLITH, CAROL LEE, psychologist, educator; b. Chgo., Sept. 6, 1945; d. Jack and Florence Rena (Kohn) K.; A.B., U. Mich., 1966, A.M., 1968; Ph.D. (NIMH trainee), Calif. Inst. Tech., 1972. Spencer Found. postdoctoral fellow Princeton U., 1972-74; asst. prof. psychology U. N.C., Chapel Hill, 1974-80; Interdisciplinary fellow U. N.C. Med. Sch., 1980-81; asso. prof. Ill. State U., Bloomington, 1981—. NIMH grantee, 1976-77. Mem. Soc. Neurosci., AAAS, Sigma Xi. Office: Dept Psychology Ill State U Normal IL 61761

KORNBLUTH, FRANCES HELEN SCHACHTER (MRS. MARVIN HUBERT KORNBLUTH), artist; b. N.Y.C., July 26, 1920; d. Jacob and Sarah (Goodstone) Schachter; B.A., Bklyn. Coll., 1940; M.A.E., Pratt Inst., 1962; postgrad. Bklyn. Mus. Art Sch., 1955-59, Adelphi U., 1964-66, N.Y. U., 1940-41; m. Marvin Hubert Kornbluth, Nov. 21, 1942; children—Bruce Ian, Jane Allyse Cathy. One-woman shows: Bklyn. Mus. Art Sch., 1958, Rockville Centre (N.Y.) Pub. Library, 1960, Sunken Meadow Gallery Contemporary Art, King's Park, N.Y., 1961 Hofstra U., Hempstead, N.Y., 1961, Charcoal Gallery, Manhasset, N.Y., 1962, Pratt Inst., Bklyn., 1962, Guild Gallery, Hempstead, 1963, Hicks St. Gallery, Bklyn., 1964, Dowling Coll., Oakdale, N.Y., 1965, Mineola (N.Y.) Pub. Library, 1965, Baiter Gallery, Huntington, N.Y., 1968, Art Works Gallery, N.Y.C., 1970, Annhurst Coll., Woodstock, Conn., 1971, Community Gallery, Livermore Falls, Maine, 1972, Annhurst (Conn.) Coll. Cultural Center, 1974, Worcester (Mass.) Art Mus., 1975, Cambridge (Mass.) Art Assn., 1976, U. Conn. Women's Center, Storrs, 1978, Artworks Gallery, Hartford, Conn., 1981; group shows: Heckscher Mus., 1957, 58, Bklyn. Mus., 1960, Hofstra U., 1960, 61, Riverside Mus., 1959, Nat. Mus., Washington, 1961, Nat. Acad., 1961-70, Pa. Acad. Fine Arts, 1963, Whitehall Galleries, London, Eng., 1962, Royal Scottish Acad. Galleries, Edinburgh, 1963, Royal Birmingham Soc. Artists, 1964, Adelphi U., 1965, Norfolk Mus., 1961, Molloy Coll., 1965, Nassau Community Coll., 1964, 67, 68, Lever House, 1963, 65, 66, 67, William and Mary Coll., 1966, Senate Office Bldg., Washington, 1966, Maine Art Gallery, 1967, Albuquerque Pub. Library Galleries, 1964, East Chicago Libraries, 1964, State Capitol, Albany, N.Y., 1963, Worcester Art Mus., 1970, Mystic Seaport Gallery, 1970, Sturbridge Art Assn., 1970, Jewish Community Center, Hartford, Conn., 1975, Conn. Artists, Slater Meml. Mus., Norwich, 1975, Union Carbide Gallery, N.Y.C., 1975, Providence Art Club, 1975, Wauters Gallery, N.Y.C., 1977, Maine Coast Artists, Rockport, 1978, Wadsworth Atheneum, Hartford, Conn., also Sarah Lawrence Coll., 1979, Fed. Bldg., N.Y.C., 1980, 81, 82, Joan Whitney Payson Gallery, Portland, Maine, 1982, City Gallery, N.Y.C., 1981, Artworks Gallery, 1981 Brick House Gallery, Boothbay Harbor, Maine, 1972—, tchr. Mineola Pub. Schs., 1959-67, Mills Coll. Edn., 1967-68, Hofstra U., 1967-68, Dowling Coll., 1968, Adelphi U., 1968, U. Conn., 1970, Annhurst Coll, 1980. Recipient Medal of Honor and Catherine and Henry J. Gaisman prize for watercolor Nat. Assn. Women Artists Ann., 1961, Aileen O. Webb prize, 1964, Medal of Honor and Elizabeth Ringius Fulda award in oil, 1968 ann., Woodbury Meml. prize, 1975; also Spl. Mention award Norfolk Mus. Am. Drawing Ann., 1961, first prize in graphics Hofstra Coll. 12th Ann. L.I. Artists Exhbn., 1961, Honorable Mention for oil North Shore Ann. L.I., 1961, Honorable Mention for watercolor North Shore Ann., 1962, Henningsen Meml. prize, 1977. Mem. Monhegan Assos., Nat. Assn. Women Artists (Elizabeth Morse Gemius Found. prize 1982), Boothbay Regional Found. for the Arts, Asylum Hill Artists Coop. Home: North Grosvenordale CT 06255 also PO Box 72 Monhegan Island ME 04852

KORNEL, ESTHER, psychologist; b. Basel, Switzerland, Dec. 16, 1928; d. Salomon and Perla (Muhlrad) Muller; came to U.S., 1958, naturalized, 1970; B.A., Roosevelt U., 1971, M.A., 1973; Psy.D., Ill. Sch. Profl. Psychology, Chgo., 1980; m. Ludwig Kornel, May 27, 1952; children—Edward Ezriel, Amiel Mark. Research asst. Inst. Applied Social Research, Jerusalem, 1953-55; mgr. travel agy., Birmingham, Ala., 1963-64; substitute tchr., elem. public schs., Chgo., 1970-71; psychiat. program coordinator Lutheran Gen. Hosp., Park Ridge, Ill., 1973—, cons., therapist oncology unit, 1976—; clin. asso., dept. psychiatry Abraham Lincoln Sch. Medicine, Chgo., 1974—; psychologist in pvt. practice, 1978—; group leader mastectomy counseling project Northwestern U. Med. Sch., Chgo., 1981—. Mem. Am. Psychol. Assn. (asso.), Ill. Group Psychotherapy Soc., ORT, Hadassah. Home: 6757 LeRoy Ave Lincolnwood IL 60646 Office: 1775 Dempster St Park Ridge IL 60068

KORNER, HILDA, research lab. exec.; b. N.Y.C., June 2, 1931; d. Manuel and Sadie (Brookman) Troob; B.S. in Personnel Adminstn., Empire State Coll., SUNY, Rochester, 1974; children—David, Peter. Successively supr. personnel services, dir. women's recruitment and promotion, coordinator human resources devel. SUNY, Buffalo, 1970-77; mgr. employment and staff devel. Stanford Linear Accelerator Center, Stanford U., 1977—; cons., instr. in field. Mem. Am. Soc. Personnel Adminstrn., Am. Soc. Tng. and Devel. Office: PO Box 4349 Stanford CA 94305

KORNFELD, PHYLLIS LORRAINE SCHAUM, educator; b. Bklyn.; d. Max and Gussie (Goldberg) Schaum; B.A., Bklyn. Coll., M.S.; postgrad. CCNY; Ed.D., Columbia U., 1972; children—Keith D., Elise J. Tchr. public sch., Bklyn.; reading clinician Bklyn. Community Counsel Center, N.Y. Infirmary; sr. lang. disabilities therapist Coney Island (N.Y.) Hosp.; remedial edn. tchr. Children's Aid Soc.; lectr. grad. div. Bklyn. Coll.; asst. prof. lang. arts and reading Paterson Coll., Wayne, N.J., Bklyn. Coll., City U. N.Y.; asst. prof., co-dir. Reading Center Ferkauf Grad. Sch. Yeshiva U., N.Y.C.; asst. prof. Coll. New Rochelle; adj. asso. prof. C.W. Post Coll. Fellow Am. Orthopsychiat. Assn.; mem. Manhattan Council Internat. Reading Assn. (pres. 1969-70), Mensa, AAUP, Internat. Reading Assn., Phi Delta Kappa. Office: 6 Hunters Ln Roslyn NY 11576

KOROBOW, ALICE SCHUSTER, psychologist; b. N.Y.C., Feb. 29, 1920; d. William and Sadie (Suroff) Schuster; B.A., City U. N.Y.; M.A., CCNY; Ph.D., N.Y.U., 1957; m. Sidney Speil, June 17, 1979; 1 dau. by previous marriage—Karen. Instr., CCNY, 1955-59; chief psychologist New Hope Guild, N.Y.C., 1958-64; supervising psychologist Whitman Inst. Psychotherapy, N.Y.C., 1972-75; tng. cons. Kingsbrook Jewish Med. Center, N.Y.C., 1971-75; pvt. practice psychology, Denver, 1975—; clin. psychologist, prof. Psychiat. and Guidance Clinic, Denver, 1976-79; psychologist St. Luke's Hosp., Denver, 1977-81. Mem. Am. Psychol. Assn., Colo. Psychol. Assn. Address: 3425 S Race St Englewood CO 80110

KORP, PATRICIA ANNE, communications/public info. specialist; b. Lincoln, Nebr., Nov. 15, 1942; d. Theodore R. and Elizabeth Anne (Olson) Munn; B.S. in Journalism, U. Wyo., 1967, M.A., 1974; m. Vince L. Korp, Jan. 15, 1965; children—Kathleen Anne, Karen Lee. Women's editor Sheridan (Wyo.) Press, 1964-66; public info. and research asst. Wyo. Dept. Edn., 1967-69; dir. public relations and communications Wyo. Edn. Assn., 1969-71; coordinator info. services Mountain Plains Program, Glasgow, Mont., 1972-73; freelance public relations, Laramie, Wyo., 1973-74; public info. specialist Bur. Land Mgmt., Rawlins, Wyo., 1975-76, Cheyenne, Wyo., 1976—; communications specialist Wyo. Spl. Olympics, 1978—. Mem. Wyo. Council Children and Youth, 1976-77. Recipient All-Am. award Ednl. Press Assn. Am., 1st pl. award Nat. Fedn. Press Women, 1980. Mem. Nat. Fedn. Press Women, Federally Employed Women, Wyo. Press Women (sec.), Sigma Delta Chi. Democrat. Roman Catholic. Club: Cheyenne Quota (public relations chmn. 1979-80). Editor: Wyo. Edn. News, 1969-71; asst. editor Wyo. Horizons, 1976-80, editor, 1980—. Home: PO Box 10272 Cheyenne WY 82001 Office: 2515 Warren Ave Cheyenne WY 82001

KORTMAN, JOYCE ELAINE, graphic arts co. exec., civic worker; b. Holland, Mich., Dec. 24, 1935; d. Henry John and Jeanette (Van Kampen) De Ridder; ed. Davenport Coll., Hope Coll.; m. Harris Jay Kortman, May 15, 1956; children—David, Calvin, Lafon, Renee, Mark. Mem. Mich. Comprehensive Health Planning Advisory Council, 1972; mem. advisory council Nat. Inst. Arthritis, Metabolism, Digestive Disease, NIH, 1973-75; mem. West unit Health Systems' Agy. Bd., HEW, 1972—; active Mich. affiliate Am. Diabetes Assn., 1970-76, vice chmn. nat. coordinating com. for pub. activities, mem. com. on pub. affairs and Mich. del. Central council, 1972-75, nat. dir., 1974—; co-chmn. work group on nat. resources Nat. Commn. on Diabetes, 1975; cons., speaker, and consumer adv. in health; propr. DaCal Printing Co., Heritage Printing Service, Holland. Bd. dirs., bd. rep. Holland City Hosp. Aux. Recipient certificate of appreciation Am. Diabetes Assn., 1970, citation for outstanding contbn., 1973, Vol. of Yr. award, 1976, Meritorious award, 1976. Mem. Am. Bus. Women's Assn., Litho Club of Grand Rapids (Mich.), Holland C. of C., Holland Christian Schs. Parent-Tchr. Assn. (mother club), Calvinette Internat. (counselor, co-chmn. com. on curriculum revision). Office: 16935 Riley St Holland MI 49423

KOSH, LILLIAN ELIZABETH, computer educator, apparel designer; b. Waller, Tex., Sept. 17, 1942; d. Julian Marion and Mary Elizabeth (Urban) K.; B.S. in Home Econs. Edn., U. Tex., 1964; M.S. in Clothing and Costume Design, Tex. Women's U., Denton, 1978; m. Ronald T. Paschall. Div. home economist Tex. Electric Service Co., 1964-68; tchr. home econs., head dept. Dallas Ind. Sch. Dist., 1968-76; grad. asst. Tex. Women's U., 1976; instr. N. Tex. State U., 1977; tng. analyst, staff adv., computer systems tng. mgr., mktg. support mgr. CAMSCO Inc., Richardson, Tex., 1978—. Mem. Am. Field Service Mgrs. (sec. Dallas chpt. 1980), Am. Soc. Tng. and Devel., Am. Home Econs. Assn., Am. Coll. Profs, Textiles and Clothing, Nat. Assn. Female Execs. Office: 1200 N Bowser St Richardson TX 75081

KOSIK, LYNN ANN, mortgage ins. mktg. exec.; b. Dayton, Ohio, June 22, 1950; d. Richard Paul and Barbara Jean (McMahon) Weber; student U. Dayton. Supr., Credit Bur. Dayton (Ohio), 1969-75; dep. head documentation of conventional loans United Fed. Savs. & Loan Assn., Ft. Lauderdale, Fla., 1975-78; account exec. Investors Mortgage Ins. Co., Boston, 1978—; mem. personnel adv. bd. United Fed. Savs. & Loan Assn., 1976-77. Mem. mortgage and banking adv. bd. Sch. Bd. Broward County, 1976-77, adv. bd. fin. edn., 1978; mem. adv. bd. Big Bros.-Big Sisters. Mem. Mortgage Bankers Assn. Broward and Dade County, Mortgage Bankers Assn. Fla., Fla. Atlantic Builders Assn., Nat. Savs. and Loan League for Women. Clubs: Nat. Women's Exec., German Shepherd Dog (pres. 1978-79). Office: 290 NE 3rd Ave Fort Lauderdale FL 33310

KOSINSKI, ARMIDA, civic worker; b. Amsterdam, N.Y., May 12, 1931; d. Eusebio and Carmella (Ottati) DiBlasi; ed. public schs., spl. courses Fulton Montgomery Coll.; m. Leo Kosinski, May 3, 1953; children—Lenora Sue, Edward V., Jennifer Lee. Prodn. control Bigelow Sanford Carpet Mills, 1950-55; sec. adminstrs. office City Hall, Amsterdam, 1967-79; sec. to Chief of Police and Fire Chief, Amsterdam, 1980—; 1st pres. Montgomery County City Hall unit Civil Service Orgn.; pres. Bus. and Profl. Women's Club of Amsterdam, 1972-73; v.p. pro tem Mental Health Assn., 1974; mem. citizens com. for new high sch., Amsterdam, 1975; life mem. Nat. Congress Parents and Tchrs.; chmn. Am. Cancer Soc., recipient honors; recipient Silver award Leukemia Soc. Am., service award Nat. Cystic Fibrosis Research Found.; sch. rep. Amsterdam Area Council P.T.A.; bd. dirs. Montgomery County Cancer Soc.; charter mem. Theodore Roosevelt Jr. High Sch. Mem. St. Sofia's Soc. Roman Catholic. Co-chmn. Internat. Food Festival, City of Amsterdam 175th Anniversary. Home: 269 W Main St Amsterdam NY 12010 Office: Guy Park Ave Extension Amsterdam NY 12010

KOSKI, MARY BERNADETTE, educator; b. Rice Lake, Wis., Aug. 23, 1951; d. Florian Frederick and Joyce Elizabeth (Kennedy) Kleusch; B.A. magna cum laude, U. Minn., 1981, postgrad. 1982—; m. David John Koski, June 18, 1971; children—Sarah, John. Adminstr., The Welcome Home, Biwabik, Minn., 1975-77; grad. teaching asst. U. Minn., Duluth, 1981-82; acctg. instr. Arrowhead Community Coll., 1982—. Mem. audit com. St. Mark's Luth. Ch., Aurora, Minn., 1980-81, choir dir., 1977-80; bd. dirs., N.E. Adult Day Care Center, Virginia, Minn., 1977-78. Am. Aux. Univ. Women scholar, 1979. Mem. Minn. Acctg. Educators Assn., Nat. Acctg. Assn., Phi Theta Kappa. Office: Arrowhead Community Coll Mesabi Campus Virginia MN 55792

KOSLOV, MARCIA JEAN, law librarian; b. Granite City, Ill., Sept. 8, 1949; d. Martin S. and Terry (Cohen) K.; B.A. in Polit. Sci. and L.S., U. Mo., Columbia, 1971, M.A. in L.S., 1972. Asst. librarian, then head librarian Mo. Supreme Ct. Library, Jefferson City, 1971-74; state law librarian Wis. State Law Library, Madison, 1974—. Bd. dirs. Friends of WHA-TV, Tamarack Trails Community Services Assn. Mem. Am. Assn. Law Libraries (exec. bd. 1980-83), Wis. Library Assn. (chmn. public relations com. 1981), Madison Area Library Council (chmn. coms. 1977—), LWV. Author articles in field. Office: 310 E State Capitol Madison WI 53702

KOSOY, MARJORIE AXELROD, psychologist; b. Phila., Oct. 3, 1941; d. Bernard and Cynthia Axelrod; B.A., U. Pa., 1963; M.Counseling, Troy State U., 1972; Ed.D. in Counselor Edn., U. Houston, 1979; m. Jerome Kosoy, June 10, 1963; children—Shira Beth, Rachel Amy, Joshua David. Tchr. public high sch., Cheltenham, Pa., 1963-66; grad. asst. U. Houston, 1976; clin. psychology intern VA Hosp., Houston, 1977-78; pvt. practice, Houston, 1978—. Mem. Am. Psychol. Assn. (asso.), Am. Personnel and Guidance Assn. Home: 5214 Queensloch Houston TX 77030 Office: 7505 Fannin Suite 444 Houston TX 77025

KOSS, GRACE JOHNSEN, retail co. exec.; b. Sheboygan, Wis., May 13; d. Alfred H. and Mary J. (Holub) Johnsen; student Drake U., Des Moines, 1937-39; m. Joseph Donald Koss, Sr., Sept. 13, 1941; children—Joseph Donald, John, James. Tchr. speech, Green Bay, Wis., 1940-43; staff writer The Spirit, Green Bay, 1965-69, editor lay orgns. page, 1969-72, weekly topical columnist, 1965—; pres. The Cheese Hut, Inc., Green Bay, 1975—. Sec., Green Bay United Community Council, 1953-59; mem. Brown County Community Relations and Social Devel. Commn. Recipient numerous awards for writing. Mem. Nat. Fedn. Press Women (regional dir.), Council Wis. Writers (dir.), Wis. Regional Writers (dir.), Wis. Council Better Broadcasts (past v.p.), Nat. Press Club, LWV, Kappa Kappa Gamma, Zeta Phi Eta. Roman Catholic. Home: R4 Sunset Shores Luxemburg WI 54217 Office: 1123 Main St Green Bay WI 54301

KOSS, HELEN L., state legislator; b. N.Y.C., June 3, 1922; A.B., Bennington Coll., 1942; married. Mem. Md. Ho. of Dels., 1971—, mem. joint com. on legis. ethics, 1972-78, rules com., chmn. elections law subcom., 1973-78, chmn. constl. and adminstrv. law com., 1979—, mem. legis. policy com., 1979—, co-chmn. task force on election laws, 1979—; mem. ethics and elections com. Nat. Conf. State Legislatures, 1975—; mem. human resources com. Met. Council Govts., 1975-79; del. Constl. Conv. of Md., 1967-68; chmn. Com. on Suffrage and Elections; bd. visitors Bowie State Coll.; mem. Gov.'s Commn. on Reapportionment, Gov.'s Commn. on Crime and Delinquency; mem. Montgomery County Task Force on Community Edn., 1977. Recipient Ann London Scott award for legis. excellence NOW, 1978, NAACP cert. of merit, 1978, Hendrick Ibsen award Md. Conf. Social Concern, 1976. Mem. LWV (pres. Md. 1963-67), AAUW (outstanding mem. award Md. 1978), Nat. Women's Dem. Club. Address: 3416 Highview Ct Silver Spring MD 20902

KOSTERS, JEAN WESTON, edn. cons.; b. American Falls, Idaho, Jan. 16, 1935; d. Roy Alan and Marian Anita (Cathro) Weston; B.S., U. Idaho, 1956; M.A. in Counseling, Ariz. State U., 1968; student Def. Lang. Inst., Va., 1969; m. Howard C. Kosters, July 20, 1968; children—Paula Kay, Mary Jean. Tchr., Dover Spl. Sch. Dist., Del., 1963-66, Clark AFB, Philippines, 1961-63, Albuquerque Public Schs., 1959-61; counselor Ariz. Boys Ranch, 1967; counselor and career devel. coordinator Community Action Program, 1967-68; art tchr. art Brindisi Dependent Schs., San Vito Air Sta., Italy, 1969-74; supr., master tchr. Vacaville (Calif.) public schs., 1974-78; sales rep. Adventures in Achievement, Inc., Irvine, Calif., 1978-79; Calif. cons. for Bowmar/Noble Pubs., Los Angeles, 1979-80; area mgr. Scholastic Inc., Pleasanton, Calif., 1980—. Mem. mental health adv. bd. Solano County (Calif.), 1977-78; coordinator PTA Council Cultural Arts, 1974-78. Recipient Sustained Superior Performance award Dept. Def. Overseas Schs., 1973. Mem. Women's Nat. Book Assn., Calif. Mgrs. Assn., Women in Mgmt., AAUW (area rep. 1976-78), Delta Kappa Gamma. Home: 913 Calle Miramar Redondo Beach CA 90277 Office: 5675 Sunol Blvd Pleasanton CA 94566

KOSUB, SANDRA MILLER, social worker; b. Savannah, Ga., July 13, 1952; d. Arthur Irving and Ann Portman (Strother) Miller; B.A. cum laude, U. Tex., Austin, 1975, M.S., 1978; m. Curtis Anthony Kosub, July 19, 1975. Counseling asso. Crisis Intervention Center, Austin, Tex., 1974-77; mental health/mental retardation supr. Children's Psychiatric Unit, Austin, 1975-76; social worker Brackenridge Hosp., Austin, 1976-77; psychiatric social worker VA, Waco, Tex., 1977-78; dir. tng. in social work Child Devel. Div., U. Tex. Med. Br., Galveston, 1978—; cons. in field. Recipient Maternal and Child Health award, 1977; VA stipend, 1977-78. Mem. Nat. Assn. Social Workers (exec. bd. dirs. 1978-79, 80-82), Am. Assn. Marriage and Family Therapy, Assn. for Care of Children in Hosps., Phi Kappa Phi. Contbr. articles to profl. jours. Office: Child Devel Div Dept Pediatrics Univ Tex Med Br Galveston TX 77550

KOSZYK, M. MADELEINE, pre-retirement counselor; b. Phila., Jan. 27, 1926; d. James J. and M. Madeleine (Scannell) Webster; student Burlington County Coll., 1979, Thomas Edison Coll., 1980, New Eng. Gerontology Center, 1978, U. Mich., 1978; m. Frank X. Koszyk, May 10, 1947; children—James, Maura Anne Koszyk Collinsgru, Francis William. Coordinator, Inst. on Aging, Burlington County Coll., 1977-81; pres. Pretirement, Inc., Riverton, N.J., 1980—; adv. office on Aging. Mem. Greater Phila. C. of C., N.J. Assn. Women Bus. Owners, Women in Mgmt., Options for Women, Assn. Trainers and Developers, Career Planning and Adult Devel. Orgn., Internat. Soc. Pre-Retirement Planners, N.J. Gerontology Assn. Roman Catholic. Office: PO Box 192 Riverton NJ 08077

KOTOWSKI, DOLORES, nursing supr.; b. Charleston, W.Va., Aug. 16, 1931; d. Adolphus and Mary Inez (Hartzog) DeLopaz; B.S. in Nursing, U. Cin., 1952; M.P.A., Nat. U., San Diego, 1975; children—Ralph, Sheri I., Jon M. Nurse various hosps., 1951-58; social worker Dept. Public Welfare, 1958-67; dir. nursing San Diego Home Health Services, 1967-70; dir. nursing Alvarado Home Health, San Diego, 1970-75, acting dir. nurses, asst. dir. nurses, 1973; supr. spl. services Vis. Nurse Assn., San Diego, 1975-76; exec. dir. Vis. Nurse Assn./Homemaker Service, San Diego, 1976-80; supr. out-patient dept. emergency room Al Hada Hosp., Taif, Saudi Arabia, 1980—. Active, Area Agy. on Aging, Adult Protective Services, Dept. Human Services, Sr. Adult Services, Dept. Mental Health, Scripps Meml. Hosp. Mem. Nat. League Nursing (mem. Council of Home Health Agys. and Community Health Services), Nat. Assn. Home Health Agys., Am. Public Health Assn., Agy. Exec. Assn., Calif. Assn. Health Services at

Home, U. Cin. Alumni Assn., Nat. U. Alumni Assn. (life). Home and Office: Al Hada Hosp Box 1347 Taif Saudi Arabia

KOUNITZ, LINDA DARKES, writer; b. Trenton, N.J., Nov. 1, 1952; d. Curtis Harry and Nevonne (Griffin) Darkes; B.A., Rider Coll., 1974. Writer, N.J. Mfrs. Ins. Co., Trenton, 1975-77; promotional writer Donald F. Smith & Assos., Princeton, N.J., 1977-81; free-lance writer, Gomaringen, W.Ger., 1981—. Mem. Pi Delta Epsilon. Home and Office: Hauffstr 11 7413 Gomaringen Federal Republic of Germany

KOUPAL, JOYCE ANN, polit. cons. and analyst; b. Sacramento, Mar. 7, 1932; d. Cecil Wallace and Elizabeth Louise (De Ree) Nash; m. Edwin Augustus Koupal (dec.); children—Cecil Edwin, Christine Ann, Diane Marie. Nat. dir. People's Lobby, Inc., Los Angeles, 1976—; polit. cons. and analysis, San Rafael, Calif., 1981—. Mem., Los Angeles County Energy Commn., 1975-76. Co-author (with Faith Keating): Success Is Failure Analyzed, 1976. Office: 182 Belvedere St Suite 5 San Rafael CA 94901

KOURY, EVELYN MICHAEL, fin. exec.; b. Tripoli, Lebanon, Apr. 7, 1907; d. Michael and Zahie (Tager) Khoury; came to U.S., 1911, derivative citizenship; student U. New Haven, 19 - . Asst. to credit dept. Shartenberg's Inc., New Haven, Conn., 1938-41; asst. to controller New Haven Motor Sales, 1941-42; jr. indsl. analyst WPB, New Haven, 1942-45; clk. IRS, 1946; compliance aide Office Rent Stblzn., New Haven, 1946-47; chief stenographer Sales and Use Tax Div. State Conn., Hartford, 1947-48; office mgr. Effland Motors, New Haven, 1948-49; office mgr., legal sec. to J. W. Curran, New Haven, 1950; acct., materials buyer Beaver Pond Machine Co., New Haven, 1953—; pvt. practice acctg., 1960—; mgr. Tweedle Dee Realty, Hamden, Conn., 1975—; fin. mgr., acct. Jan A Van Loan, Hamden, 1975—. Served with CAP aux. USAF, 1945-46. Mem., Nat. Assn. Public Accts., Conn. Assn. Public Accts. Jehovah's Witness. Home: 1430 Dixwell Ave Hamden CT 06514 Office: 1432 Dixwell Ave Hamden CT 06514

KOUSIS, CONSTANCE, personnel cons.; b. Washington, Aug. 6, 1947; d. Ernest and Christina (Stavros) K.; B.F.A., SUNY and Parsons Sch. Design, 1970; cert. in fashion design (scholar) Parsons Sch. Design, 1970; postgrad. Am. U., 1965-67. Asst. buyer Woodward & Lothrop, Washington, 1970-73; asso. buyer Bonwit Teller, N.Y.C., 1974; freelance designer, N.Y.C., 1973-74; buyer Jelleff's, Arlington, Va., 1975; pres., owner Personnel Associates, Washington, 1976—. Mem. Better Bus. Bur., 1976—, Downtown Jaycees, 1981. Recipient Fashion Critic awards Parsons Sch. Design, 1968-70; mem. Mademoiselle Mag. Coll. Bd., 1966-70; hon. mention Young Am. Creates, 1970. Mem. Capital Area Personnel Services Assn. (dir. 1978—, sec. 1981), Met. Washington Bd. Trade, Nat. Assn. Personnel Cons., Nat. Assn. Women Bus. Owners, Washington Women's Network, Direct Mktg. Assn., Alpha Chi Omega. Office: 1725 K St NW Washington DC 20006

KOUTSOGIANNIS, MARIA, information systems mgr.; b. Skoura, Sparta, Greece, Mar. 20, 1953; came to U.S., 1964, naturalized, 1972; d. John and Aphrodite (Cholakis) K.; B.A. (scholar), Elmira Coll., 1975; postgrad. U. Moscow and Leningrad, 1973, La Sorbonne et L'Institut Politique, Paris, France, 1973-74; postgrad. in bus. N.Y. Inst. Tech., 1981—. Multi-lingual legal asst. firm Fried, Fragomen & Del Rey, N.Y.C., 1974-79, mgr. info. systems, 1979—; tutor English to foreigners, 1979—. Recipient scholarship award Am. Legion, 1965. Mem. Nat. Assn. Female Execs. Greek Orthodox. Clubs: Republican, Thespis Theatrical. Home: 128 S 5th St Lindenhurst NY 11757 Office: 515 Madison Ave New York NY 10022

KOVACH, EDITH M(ARIE) A(MALIA), educator; b. N.Y.C., Mar. 29, 1921; d. Eugene John and Hortense Marie (Telmany) K.; A.B., Wayne State U., 1942, M.Ed., 1942; M.A. in Latin, U. Mich., 1945, Ph.D. in Classical Studies (Univ. fellow 1945-46, AAUW fellow 1948-49, Fanny Burr Butler fellow 1949), 1950. Tchr., head fgn. lang. dept. Detroit Public Schs., 1942-65; asso. prof. classical langs. U. Detroit, 1965-72, prof. classics and edn., 1972—. Semple scholar Am. Acad. in Rome, summer 1948. Mem. Am. Classical League, Archeol. Inst. Am., Classical Assn. Middle West and South, Am. Philol. Assn., Nat., Mich. edn. assns., Nat. Humanities Faculty, Phi Beta Kappa, Phi Kappa Phi. Roman Catholic. Clubs: Detroit Boat, Women's City of Detroit. Author Macmillan test and tape programs 1st and 2d yr. Latin. Asso. editor Classical Outlook, 1972—. Contbr. to Brit. Rev. of Fgn. Lang. Edn., 1969. Home: 2400 Edison Ave Detroit MI 48206 Office: Briggs Bldg U Detroit Detroit MI 48221

KOVACHEVICH, ELIZABETH ANNE, circuit judge; b. Canton, Ill. Dec. 14, 1936; d. Dan and Emilie (Kuchan) Kovachevich; A.A., St. Petersburg Jr. Coll., 1956; B.B.A. magna cum laude, U. Miami, 1958; J.D., Stetson U., 1961. Admitted to Fla. bar, 1961, U.S. Supreme Ct. bar, 1968; research, adminstrv. aide Pinellas County legislative delegation Fla. Legislature, 1961; asso. DeVito & Speer, 1961-62; house counsel in credit dept. Rieck & Fleece Bldrs. Supplies, Inc., 1962; gen. practice, St. Petersburg, Fla., 1962; now circuit judge; legal adviser for women's residence com. YWCA, St. Petersburg,, adv. bd., mem. ho. com. Chmn. St. Petersburg profl. legal project Days In Court, 1967; producer, coordinator TV prodn. A Race to Judgment; dir. Sheraton Inn, St. Petersburg. Vice chmn., Fla. conf. publicity chmn. 18th Nat. Republican Women's Conf., Atlanta, 1971; mem. Def. Adv. Commn. on Women in the Services; mem. Pres.'s Commn. on White House Fellowships, 1973—; chmn. bicentennial com. 6th jud. dist. Fla. Supreme Ct., 1975-76. Bd. regents State of Fla. Life; active mem. Children's Hosp. Guild, St. Petersburg. Recipient Appreciation award St. Petersburg Panhellenic Assn., 1964, award St. Petersburg Bus. and Profl. Women, 1967; named Woman of Year, St. Petersburg, chpt. Beta Sigma Phi, 1970, Distinguished Alumnae, Stetson U., 1970. Mem. Am., Fla., St. Petersburg (sec. 1969-70) bar assns., Fla. Assn. Women Lawyers, Am., Pinellas County trial lawyers assns., Am. Judicature Soc., Internat. Platform Assn., Am. Acad. Polit. and Social Sci., Smithsonian Instn. Nat. Assos., Phi Delta Delta, Delta Delta Delta, Alpha Sigma Epsilon, Phi Kappa Phi. Roman Catholic.

KOVACS, ELIZABETH ANN, assn. exec.; b. N.Y.C., July 25, 1944; d. Henry Philipp and Toni Selby (Auspitz) Leitner; B.A., Conn. Coll., 1965; M.A.T., Yale U., 1967; m. Imre Kovacs, June 19, 1965; children—Tobin Philipp, Kathryn Michel. Exec. dir. Assn. Advancement of Behavior Therapy, N.Y.C., 1971-80, Soc. Behavioral Medicine, N.Y.C., 1978-80; exec. v.p. Public Relations Soc. Am., N.Y.C., 1980—. Cert. assn. exec. Mem. N.Y. Soc. Assn. Execs. (dir.), Am. Soc. Assn. Execs. Office: Public Relations Soc Am 845 Third Ave New York NY 10022

KOVAK, ELLEN B., public relations exec.; b. N.Y.C., Nov. 28, 1944; A.B., Skidmore Coll., 1966; postgrad Brown U., 1967; m. Stan Kovak, Apr. 20, 1969; 1 dau., Janet. Asst. dir. publs. and info. N.Y. Network/SUNY, N.Y.C., 1967-72; communications dir. Conn. CALM, Stamford, Conn., 1972-76; dir. public relations N.Y. Mgmt. Center, N.Y.C., 1976-77; sr. account supr. Creamer Dickson Basford, Inc., N.Y.C., 1977-81; exec. v.p. Lobsenz-Stevens, N.Y.C., 1981—. Ford. Found. summer intern, 1965; recipient 1st prize corp. award Blow the Whistle on Crime Program, Nat. Commn. on Crime, 1981. Mem. Ad Club. Home: 10 East End Ave New York NY 10021 Office: Lobsenz-Stevens 2 Park Ave New York NY 10016

KOVALIC, JOAN MARIE, lawyer; b. Pitts., Dec. 27, 1948; d. Francis Bernard and Margaret Dolores (Poyma) Kovalic; B.A., Carnegie Mellon U., 1970, M.S., 1972; J.D., George Washington U., 1979; m. Keith Earl Bernard, May 22, 1982. Water resources analyst Com. Environment and Public Works, U.S. Senate, Washington, 1971; manpower policy analyst Office Asst. Sec. for Policy and Evaluation, U.S. Dept. of Labor, 1972-73; asst. counsel for water and the environments Com. Public Works and Transp., U.S. Ho. of Reps., 1973-80; admitted to Pa. bar, 1979, D.C. bar, 1980; dep. dir. Office Water Program Ops., U.S. EPA, 1980-82; asso. firm Taft, Steffinius and Hollister, Washington, 1982—; exec. dir., gen. counsel Interstate Conf. Water Problems, 1982—. Mem. Am. Bar Assn., Pa. Bar Assn., D.C. Bar Assn., Women's Bar Assn., Water Pollution Control Fedn., Am. Public Works Assn., Women's Econ. Roundtable, Phi Kappa Phi, Phi Alpha Delta. Office: 1919 Pennsylvania Ave NW Suite 300 Washington DC 20006

KOVELESKI, KATHRYN DELANE, educator; b. Detroit, Aug. 12, 1925; d. Edward Albert Vogt and Delane (Bender) Vogt; B.A., Olivet (Mich.) Coll., 1947; M.A., Wayne State U., Detroit, 1955; m. Casper Koveleski, July 18, 1952; children—Martha, Ann. Tchr. schs. in Mich., 1947—; tchr. Garden City Schs., 1955-56, 59—, resource and learning disabilities tchr., 1970—. Mem. PTA, Council Exceptional Children, NEA, Mich. Edn. Assn., Garden City Edn. Assn., Bus. and Profl. Women (2d v.p. Garden City 1979-80, 1st v.p. 1981-82, pres. 1982-83). Congregationalist. Clubs: Wayne Lit. (past pres., past parliamentarian), Sch. Masters Bowling League, Odd Couples Bowling League (pres. 1982-83). Office: 33411 Marquette St Garden City MI 48135

KOVEN, JOAN FOLLIN HUGHES, designer, spl. events adminstr.; b. Washington, Nov. 9, 1937; d. John Rodgers and Viola Brockett (Pugh) Hughes; B.S., W.Va. U., 1959; postgrad. Scarritt Coll., 1959, U. Salisbury (Zimbabwe), 1961, Sorbonne, 1962, 63, Am. U., 1973, George Washington U., 1979; m. Ronald Pierre E. Koven, Mar. 29, 1965 (div. 1977); children—Michele Elise Josette, Martine Sarah Aimee. Tchr., dir. home econs. dept., art dept., library Old Umtali Schs., Zimbabwe, 1960-62; adolescent counselor, Dreux High Sch., France, 1962-65; freelance market researcher, Paris, 1965-66; dir. student recreation center, Dreux, 1966; v.p. Koven Freres jewelry, N.Y.C., 1971-75; designer, fabricator jewelry, home lighting, Washington, 1977—; exec. asst. in spl. events, adminstrv. mgmt. to M.B. Patterson, Washington, 1976—. Mem. zoning comm. Palisades Citizens Assn., 1974; mem. commn. on missions Met. Meml. Methodist Ch. Kroger scholar, 1955; cert. scuba diver. Mem. Omicron Nu, Phi Upsilon Omicron. Club: Nat. Capital Shell. Home: 4812 V St Washington DC 20007

KOWALCZEWSKI, DOREEN MARY THURLOW, communications co. exec.; b. London, May 5, 1926; came to U.S., 1957, naturalized, 1974; d. George Henry and Jessie Alice (Gray) Thurlow; B.A., Clarke Coll., 1947; postgrad. Wayne State U., 1959-62, Rossevelt U., 1968; m. Witold Dionizy Kowalczewski, July 26, 1946; children—Christina Julianna, Janet Alice, Stephen Robin. Agy. supr. MONY, N.Y.C., 1963-67; office mgr. J.B. Carroll Co., Chgo., 1967-68; mng. editor Sawyer Coll. Bus., Evanston, Ill., 1968-71; mgr. policyholder service CNA, Chgo., 1971-73; EDP coordinator Canteen Corp., Chgo., 1973-75; mgr. documentation and standards LRSP, Chgo., 1975-77; mktg. mgr. Computerized Agy. Mgmt. Info. Services, Chgo., 1977—; founder, chmn. Tekman Assos., 1982—. Pres., Univ. Park Assn., 1980—. Mem. Nat. Assn. Female Execs., Women in Info. Processing, Chgo. Orgn. Data Processing Educators, Women in Mgmt., Mensa. Home: 1400 E 55th Pl Chicago IL 60637

KOZA, JOAN LORRAINE, fabric mfg. co. exec.; b. Berwyn, Ill., Apr. 28, 1941; d. Frank Louis and Lorraine Frances (Thomas) K.; B.S. in Communications, U. Ill., 1963. Office mgr. Dwan Med. Center, Summit, Ill., 1959-64; law office mgr. firm Gordon, Reicin & West, Chgo., 1964-73; sales mgr. Ambassador Hotels, Chgo., 1973-76; v.p. sales and mktg. M. Putterman & Co., Inc., indsl. and recreational fabrics, Chgo., 1976—; owner, mgr. JK Advt., 1977—; pres. Chgo. Legal Secs. Assn., 1970-72; v.p. Ill. Assn. Legal Secs., 1970-73. Pres., chmn. bd. Children's Research Found., 1963-66. Named Chgo. Legal Sec. of Yr., 1972, Ill. Legal Sec. of Yr., 1972. Mem. Alpha Lambda Delta, Theta Sigma Pi. Roman Catholic. Office: 2221 W 43d St Chicago IL 60609

KOZLOFF, JUDITH BONNIE, lawyer; b. St. Louis, Mar. 4, 1926; d. Isador and Ruth (Gould) Friedman; B.S., Northwestern U., 1947; J.D., U. Denver, 1968; m. Lloyd M. Kozloff, June 16, 1947; children—James S., Daniel I., Joseph H., Sarah R. Law clk. Mr. Justice Day, Colo. Supreme Ct., Denver, 1969-70; admitted to Colo. bar, 1969, Calif. bar, 1981; asso. Holland & Hart, Denver, 1970-73; sec., gen. counsel Affiliated Bankshares Colo., Boulder, 1973-78; atty. Mountain States Tel.&Tel. Co., Denver, 1979-80, Pacific Tel.&Tel. Co., San Francisco, 1981—. Recipient award Pacific Telephone Employees for Women's Affirmative Action, 1981. Mem. Am. Bar Assn., Colo. Bar, Calif. Bar Assn. Home: 1750 Grant Ave San Francisco CA 94133 Office: 140 New Montgomery St San Francisco CA 94105

KRA, PAULINE SKORNICKI, educator; b. Lodz, Poland, July 30, 1934; came to U.S., 1950, naturalized, 1955; d. Edward and Nathalie Skornicki; student Radcliffe Coll., 1951-53; B.A., Barnard Coll., 1955; M.A., Columbia U., 1963, Ph.D., 1968; m. Leo Dietrich Kra, Mar. 10, 1955; children—David Theodore, Andrew Jason. Lectr., Queens Coll., City U. N.Y., 1964-65; asst. prof. French, Yeshiva U., N.Y.C., 1968-74, asso. prof. French, 1974-82, prof., 1982—. Mem. MLA, Am. Assn. Tchrs. French, Am. Soc. 18th Century Studies, Société française d'étude du XVIII siècle, Assn. for Computers and Humanities, Phi Beta Kappa. Club: Radcliffe. Author: Religion in Montesquieu's Lettres persanes, 1970; contbr. articles to profl. jours. Home: 109-14 Ascan Ave Forest Hills NY 11375 Office: 500 W 185 St New York NY 10033

KRACZKIEWICZ, MONICA ANN, banker; b. London, Mar. 14, 1945; came to U.S., 1948, naturalized, 1958; d. Karol and Helen Juliet K.; B.A., Brown U., 1967; m. Giovanni Teti, Sept. 20, 1980. Investigator, credit dept. Irving Trust Co., 1967-68; account asst., account officer Bank Am., N.Y.C., 1968-71; discount officer Mfrs. Hanover Trust Co., N.Y.C., 1971-78, v.p., rep., Rome, 1978—. Mem. Italian-Am. C. of C. Club: American (Rome). Office: Via Bissolati 76 Rome Italy

KRADITOR, AILEEN S., historian; b. Bklyn., Apr. 12, 1928; d. Abraham and Henrietta K.; B.A., Bklyn. Coll., 1950; M.A., Columbia U., 1951, Ph.D., 1962. Instr., R.I. Coll., Providence, 1962-63, asst. prof., 1963-67; vis. prof. history Sir George Williams U., Montreal, Que., Can., 1968-69; prof. history Boston U., 1973-80, prof. emerita, 1980—. Recipient Ansley award Columbia U., 1963; Nat. Endowment Humanities fellow, 1975-76; Guggenheim fellow, 1976-77; Radcliffe Inst. fellow, 1975-76. Mem. Orgn. Am. Historians, Soc. Am. Historians. Republican. Jewish. Author: The Ideas of the Woman Suffrage Movement, 1890-1917, 1965; Up from the Pedestal, 1968; Means and Ends in American Abolitionism, 1834-1850, 1969; The Radical Persuasion, 1890-1917, 1981. Home: 117 Brook St Wellesley MA 02181

KRADJIAN, CHRISTINE STEVENS, publishing co. exec.; b. Honolulu, May 1, 1944; d. Kenneth Eldon and Dorothy Bowron (Mitchell) S.; R.N., Kaiser Found., Oakland, Calif., 1965; student nursing, U. Calif. Extension, 1965-74; m. Robert Milton Kradjian, Feb. 3, 1968. Intensive care nurse Kaiser Found. Hosp., San Francisco, 1965-66; charge nurse coronary care Mt. Zion Hosp., San Francisco, 1966-67; intensive care nurse Hosp. Ship Hope, Sri Lanka and Tunisia, 1968-69; nurse and cardio-pulmonary unit Presbyterian Hosp., San Francisco, 1970-75, also pvt. duty nurse; mgr. mktg. Pas Publ. Co., Daly City, Calif., 1975-78, dir. mktg., 1979-81, corp. sec., 1979—, exec. dir. new product devel., 1982—, also dir. Mem. Am. Nurses Assn., Nurse Cons. Assn., Calif. Nurses Assn., Direct Mail Mktg. Assn., Am. Mktg. Assn., Nat. Assn. Female Execs., Med. Mktg. Assn., Soc. Public Health Educators, Health Care Exhibitors Assn. Democrat. Mem. Soc. Friends. Office: 345 G Serramonte Plaza Daly City CA 94015

KRAFT, ANITA RANKOW, speech and Lang. pathologist; b. N.Y.C., Feb. 27, 1937; d. Mark A. and Janet (Klarsfeld) Rankow; B.A., Hunter Coll., 1957; M.S., Pa. State U., 1959; M.A., Columbia U., 1977; postgrad. Fordham U.; m. David W. Kraft, June 29, 1958; children—Arthur, Mark, Jill. Speech and lang. cons. Mt. Kisco (N.Y.) Schs., 1966-68; speech and lang. supr. No. Westchester Med. Center Diagnostic Clinic, Valhalla, N.Y., 1968-75; speech and lang. cons. Assn. Retarded Children, White Plains, N.Y., 1972-75; speech and lang. pathologist/learning disabilities Briarcliff Manor (N.Y.) Sch. Dist., 1975-82; speech and lang. pathologist BOCES, 1982—; mem. staff speech and lang. program Fedn. Jewish Philanthropies Camp Rainbow. Bd. dirs. LWV, 1962-66; pres. Hillel, 1955-56; actress various orgns., 1971—. Mem. Am. Speech and Hearing Assn., N.Y. State Speech and Hearing and Lang. Assn., Westchester Speech, Hearing and Lang. Assn., Westchester Speech, Hearing and Lang. Assn. (dir. 1970—, pres. 1972-74), Council Exceptional Children, Am. Psychol. Assn., N.Y. Acad. Scis. Democrat. Jewish. Home: 46 Walnut Pl Briarcliff Manor NY 10510

KRAFT, ELAINE JOY, corp. communications ofcl.; b. Seattle, Sept. 1, 1951; d. Harry J. and Leatrice M. (Hanan) K.; B.A., U. Wash., 1973; M.P.A., U. Puget Sound, 1979; m. Lee Somerstein, Aug. 2, 1980; 1 son, Paul. Reporter, Jour. Am. Newspaper, Bellevue, Wash., 1972-76; editor Jour./Enterprise Newspapers, Wash. State, 1976; mem. staff Wash. Senate, 1976-78; mem. staff Wash. Ho. of Reps., 1978-82, public info. officer, 1976-80, mem. leadership staff, asst. to caucus chmn., 1980-81; pres. Media Kraft Communications; mem. corp. communications staff Weyerhaeuser Co., 1982—. Publicity chmn. Am. Diabetes Assn. S.W. Wash., 1978—. Recipient journalism awards. Mem. Nat. Fedn. Press Women, Women in Communications, Wash. Press Assn. Home: 1111 E John St Seattle WA 98102 Office: 417 Legislative Bldg Olympia WA 98504

KRAFT, JESSIE LOFGREN, poet; b. Lindsborg, Kans., Oct. 16, 1911; d. Oscar Austin and Julia Jessie (Parsons) Lofgren; B.A., Bethany Coll., 1934; m. Charles B. Kraft, July 24, 1943. Presenter of poetry-music programs with Charles Kraft to numerous colls., univs., chs. also radio and TV, 1946—. Mem. Kans. Authors Club, Kans. Optometric Assn. Aux., Sigma Alpha Iota. Methodist. Author: Overtone (poetry), 1946; Moods in Melody (poetry), 1961. Home: 512 W Waverly St Norton KS 67654

KRAFT, JOANNE KING, credit exec.; exec.; b. Balt., Aug. 23, 1942; d. Joseph William and Ida May (Rice) King; B.S. in Mgmt., Johns Hopkins U., 1979. With Dun & Bradstreet, Inc. 1958-74, dist. reporting mgr., Balt., 1970-74; corp. credit mgr. I.C. Isaacs & Co. Inc., Balt., 1974-82. Mem. Nat. Assn. Credit Mgmt. (chpt. dir. 1977-81, chmn. Industry Day com. for Credit Congress 1982), Male Apparel Credit Group, Medium Priced Women's Apparel Credit Group, Nat. Apparel Mfrs. Credit Assn. (bd. dirs. 1980—). Democrat. Roman Catholic. Home: 3738 Chestnut Rd Baltimore MD 21220 Office: IC Isaacs & Co Inc Bank and Grundy Sts Baltimore MD 21224

KRAFT, PATRICIA FRISCH, acct.; b. Pitts., Aug. 30, 1935; d. August W. and Ruth H. (Gourley) Frisch; student Bethany Coll., 1953-55; grad. in acctg. Robert Morris Sch. Bus. Adminstrn., 1957; m. Richard E. Kraft, Feb. 23, 1963. Bookkeeper, Sam Heppenstall & Assos., also Sam Heppenstall Sales Co., 1957-60; office mgr., bookkeeper Conomos Painting Co., 1960-65; staff acct. Bielau, Tierney, Coon & Co., C.P.A.'s, 1966-74; pvt. practice public acctg., Pitts., 1974—. Treas. Bethel Presbyn. Ch., 1975—. Enrolled to practice before IRS, 1973; registered practitioner, Pa. Mem. Pa. Soc. Enrolled Agts. (treas.), Pa. Soc. Public Accts., Nat. Soc. Public Accts., (accredited), Pa. Inst. C.P.A.s, Nat. Soc. Enrolled Agts., Nat. Assn. Women Bus. Owners. Republican. Club: Eastern Star. Office: 3734 Library Rd Pittsburgh PA 15234

KRAGULAC, OLGA GOLUBOVICH, interior designer; b. St. Louis, Nov. 27, 1937; d. Jovica Todor and Milka (Slijepcevich) Golubovich; A.A., U. Mo., 1958; cert. interior design UCLA, 1979. Interior designer William L. Pereira Assos., Los Angeles, 1977-80; asso. Reel/Grobman Assos., Los Angeles, 1980-81; pvt. practice comml. interior design, Los Angeles, 1981—. Mem. invitation and ticket com. Calif. Chamber Symphony Soc., 1980-81; vol. Westside Rep. Council, Proposition 1, 1971. Recipient Carole Eichen design award U. Calif., 1979. Mem. Am. Soc. Interior Designers, Inst. Bus. Designers, Phi Chi Theta, Beta Sigma Phi. Republican. Serbian Orthodox. Office and Home: 700 Levering No 4 Los Angeles CA 90024

KRAHENBUHL, DONNA L(OU) MUELLER, bus. cons., educator; b. Richland Center, Wis., Sept. 25, 1938; d. George Friederick and I. Bethine (Kolman) Mueller; student U. Wis., Stevens Point, 1956-58, U. Wis., Madison, 1957; B.S. summa cum laude, U. Wis., Superior, 1960; postgrad. U. Colo., 1969, U. N.Mex., 1973, U. Va., 1976; M.S. magna cum laude, U. Dayton, 1979-80, postgrad.; m. David W. Krahenbuhl, June 1, 1961; children—Shannon Dawn, Glen Allen. Tchr., Rice Lake (Wis.) High Sch., 1960-61; instr. U.S. Air Force, Minot, N.D., 1963-65; tchr. Air Force Acad. High Sch., Colorado Springs, Colo., 1969-62; tchr. West Mesa High Sch., Albuquerque, 1972-74, West Springfield (Va.) High Sch., 1975-79; cons. bus., Washington, 1979, Dayton, Columbus, Cin., 1979-81; instr. U. Dayton, 1980; instr. communication Miami U., Oxford, Ohio, 1981—; guest speaker/lectr. in field; seminar leader/cons., Midwest and East Coast. Broadcasting dir. VFW, 1971-79; 1977-79; dir. Nat. Anti-Smoking Pilot Program, Washington, 1980; active local polit. campaigns, pub. schs. Recipient Western Region Speech award Toastmistress Internat., 1965, Tchr. of Yr. award, Colorado Springs, 1972, Albuquerque, 1974, Service-to-Youth citation Kiwanis, 1972. Mem. Speech Communication Assn., Central States Speech Assn. (Communication Competitive Papers award 1980, vice chairperson women's caucus 1982-83, chairperson women's caucus 1983-84), Speech Communication Assn. Ohio, Internat. Communication Assn., Assn. Women Faculty, Women in Communication, Internat. Assn. Bus. Communicators. Clubs: Officers' Wives' (sec.-treas. 1961); Toastmistress (pres. 1964). Research in field; author profl. papers. Home: 3131 Southfield Dr Tara Estates-Beavercreek Xenia OH 45385 Office: Dept Communication 160E Bachelor Hall Miami U Oxford OH 45469

KRAINIK, ARDIS, opera co. exec.; b. Manitowoc, Wis., Mar. 8, 1929; d. Arthur Stephen and Clara (Bracken) K.; B.S., Northwestern U., 1951, postgrad. in music, 1953-54. Tchr. drama and pub. speaking Horlick High Sch., Racine, Wis., 1951-53; mezzo-soprano, appearing with Lyric Opera, Chgo., 1955-59, Ft. Wayne Philharmonic Orch., Tri City Symphony, Davenport, Iowa, Cameo Opera Co., Chgo., North Shore Symphony, Winnetka, Ill., Lake Forest (Ill.) Symphony, 1954—; appeared in oratorio performances throughout Mid-West on Artists Showcase, NBC-TV, in recitals throughout area; soloist Temple Isaiah Israel, 1960-65, 1st Ch. Christ Scientist, Hinsdale, 1967-69, 17th Ch. Christ Scientist, Chgo., 1969-77; exec. sec., office mgr. Lyric Opera of Chgo., 1954-59, asst. mgr., 1960-80, artistic adminstr., 1976-80, gen. mgr., 1981—; mem. Chgo. Council Fine Arts, 1976—. Bd. dirs. Chgo.

br. English-Speaking Union, 1963—; women's bd. Northwestern U., 1978—. Mem. Mortar Bd., Pi Alpha Lambda, Phi Beta, Chi Omega. Christian Scientist. Office: 20 N Wacker Dr Chicago IL 60606

KRAJCECK, BARBARA JESSIE, city ofcl.; b. South River, N.J., Sept. 27, 1939; d. Daniel Louis and Jessie (Lazarski) Garibaldi; student public schs., South River; m. Charles Joseph Krajceck, May 16, 1959; children—Sandra, Gail, Michele. Sec., Sperry & Hutchinson Inc., Metuchen, N.J., 1958-60; sec., receptionist Bonamici Co., P.A., Spotswood, N.J., 1978—; mem. Spotswood Boro Council, 1976—, pres., 1976—. Vice chmn. Spotswood Charter Study Commn., 1975; liaison mem. Spotswood Sch. Bd., 1976-82; mem. exec. bd. Spotswood PTA, 1971-74; past pres. Spotswood Twirlers; past v.p., pres. Spotswood Taxpayers Assn.; past sec. Spotswood Watchdog Com.; mem. Old Bridge Regional Hosp. Aux., Spotswood Boosters Club. Recipient cert. of award Rutgers U. Extension Div., 1976, citation of meritorious service Spotswood Pub. Schs., 1973. Republican. Roman Catholic. Home: 19 Gaskin Ave Spotswood NJ 08884 Office: 406 Main St Spotswood NJ 08884 also 77 Summerhill Rd Spotswood NJ 08884

KRAKOWER, SUE-ANN, personnel exec.; b. Bklyn., Dec. 17, 1942; d. Paul Lewis and Lillian (Bennett) Friedman; ed. U. Ill.; m. Ira Krakower, Sept. 4, 1965; children—Gregory, Douglas. Instructional programs, systems writer, dir. programming Appleton-Century-Crifts Pub., N.Y.C., 1964-68; dir. Programs Conf. Service Corp., N.Y.C., 1970-71; mgmt. cons., 1968-70, 71-73; mgr. orgn. devel., dir. employment, dir. compensation NBC, N.Y.C., 1973-69; regional personnel mgr. Digital Equipment Co., N.Y./N.J., 1979—. Mem. Conf. Bd., Am. Mgmt. Assn. Jewish. Co-author instructional programs. Home: 336 Central Ave Scarsdale NY 10583 Office: 1 Penn Plaza New York NY 10119

KRALJEVIC, SUSAN CURRY, gold mktg. publicist; b. Covington, Va., Oct. 6, 1946; d. Robert Wilton and Virginia Colaw Curry; student Concord Coll., 1964-67; B.S. in Clothing, Textiles, and Related Art (home econs. scholar), Va. Poly. Inst. and State U., 1969; m. Vladimir Kraljevic, Oct. 27, 1970; children—Vladimir Brando, Kristian Marko, Kimberley Susanna. Merchandising/mktg. asst. Glamour mag., N.Y.C., 1969-71, mktg. editor, 1972, press editor 1973-76, public relations dir., 1976-78; publicity supr. Internat. Gold Corp., Ltd., N.Y.C., 1978—; media spokesperson Gold Info. Center, 1980—. Sec./treas. N.Y. Upbeat, 1974-76. Mem. Public Relations Soc. Am. (public service com., 1974-78), Kappa Omicron Phi. Republican. Presbyterian. Contbg. editor Fodor's Mid-Atlantic, 1974. Home: 32 Grandview Ave Mount Vernon NY 10553 Office: 645 Fifth Ave New York NY 10022

KRALL, VITA, clin. child psychologist; b. New Haven, July 9, 1923; d. Moses Adam and Jennie Edith (Alper) Krall; B.A., Antioch Coll., 1944; M.A., U. Iowa, 1945; Ph.D., U. Rochester, 1951. Instr., Mich. State Coll., East Lansing, 1951-53; sr. psychologist Topeka (Kans.) State Hosp., 1953-57; project cons. Menninger Found., Topeka, 1958; acting dir. psychology Kans. Neurol. Inst., Topeka, 1959-61; staff psychologist Child Guidance Clinic of Greater Bridgeport (Conn.), Inc., 1961-62, The Juvenile Ct., Bridgeport, 1962; sr. clin. psychologist Michael Reese Hosp. and Med. Center, Chgo., 1963-68, chief child psychologist, 1968—, dir. tng. in clin. psychology, 1969—; research asso., asst. prof. U. Chgo., 1977—; cons. Community Guidance Clinic Mercy Hosp., Chgo. Diplomate Am. Bd. Clin. Psychology; recipient James Saft award for excellence in teaching, 1980. Mem. Conn. Psychol. Assn., Kans. Psychol. Assn., Ill. Psychol. Assn., Midwestern Psychol. Assn., Eastern Psychol. Assn., New Eng. Psychol. Assn., Am. Othopsychiat. Assn., Soc. for Research in Child Devel., Soc. for Personality Assessment. Jewish. Contbr. numerous articles in field to profl. jours. Home: 1716 E 55th St Chicago IL 60615 Office: Michael Reese Hosp and Med Center 29th St and Ellis Ave Chicago IL 60616

KRAMAR, MARILYNN MAE, missionary evangelist; b. Los Angeles, May 5, 1939; d. William John and Lorine Hulda (Cederquist) Roberts; ed. public schs., Spanish Lang. Inst. (Mex.). Minister, Assemblies of God, 1961-67, Colombia, S. Am., 1968-71; co-founder, pres. Charisma in Missions, Los Angeles, 1972—; pres. Catholic Missionary Evangelization; Spanish-speaking coordinator evangelization ministries; condr. daily Spanish-speaking radio program; mem. evangelization commn. Archdiocese of Los Angeles. Roman Catholic. Office: PO Box 506 La Puente CA 91747

KRAMER, BARBARA SUE, mfg. co. exec.; b. N.Y.C., June 15, 1941; d. Sidney I. and Belle Rose Kramer; B.A. in English Lit., Barnard Coll., 1963. Mem. advt. promotion staff McCall's Mag., N.Y.C., 1963-66; account exec. Peter Rothholz Assos., N.Y.C., 1969-72; pres. Bobbie Kramer Assos., N.Y.C., 1972-73; dir. public relations Stiefel/Raymond Advt., N.Y.C., 1974-81, Art Carved div. Lenox China Inc., N.Y.C., 1981—. Mem. LWV (chmn. Ga. chpt. 1967-68), Women in Communications. Club: Publicity (N.Y.). Home: 315 E 56th St New York NY 10022 Office: 450 W 33d St New York NY 10001

KRAMER, BESS, state ofcl.; b. Balt., Mar. 24; d. Philip Samuel and Gertrude K.; student George Washington U., 1933-38, Corcoran Art Gallery Sch., Washington, 1938-40. Treas., Sauls Lithograph Co., Washington, 1943-65; owner, mgr. Ogden Kramer Assos., Balt., 1965-68; with Md. Dept. Transp., Glen Burnie, 1968—, contbg. editor Directions, 1976—; publs. specialist Motor Vehicle Adminstrn., 1968—. Mem. Am. Advt. Fedn. (Crystal Prism award 1972), Women's Advt. Club Balt. (pres. 1964-66), Md. Assn. Communicators (v.p.), Balt. Public Relations Council, Md. Press Club, Md. Press Women (pres. 1979-80; 1st, 2d, 3d feature stories awards 1977, 78-79), Internat. Assn. Communicators. Editor: The Vehicle, 1971—. Home: 8005-C Mollye Rd Pikesville MD 21208 Office: 6601 Ritchie Hwy NE Glen Burnie MD 21062

KRAMER, CECILE EDITH, med. librarian; b. N.Y.C., Jan. 6, 1927; d. Marcus and Henrietta (Marks) K.; B.S., CCNY, 1956, M.S. in Library Sci., Columbia U. 1960. Reference asst. Health Scis. Library, Columbia U. 1957-60, sr. reference asst., 1960-61, asst. librarian 1961-75; dir. Med. Library Northwestern U., Chgo., 1975—; lectr. in field. Mem. Med. Library Assn. (chmn. med. sch. libraries group 1975-76, editor News 1974-77), Assn. Acad. Health Scis. Library Dirs. Office: 303 E Chicago Ave Chicago IL 60611

KRAMER, DIANA FLANDINA, advt. agy. exec.; b. N.Y.C., May 18, 1928; d. Anthony Alfred and Dorothy Vernon (Wilkins) Flandina; B.A., Barnard Coll., 1949; m. John H. Kramer, Apr. 3, 1948; children—Anthony, Laura. Jr. copywriter, then v.p., copy chief Mutch, Haberman, Joyce, N.Y.C., 1967-69; sr. copy writer Gaynor & Ducas, N.Y.C., 1969-76; v.p., asso. creative dir. Warwick Advt., N.Y.C., 1976—. Recipient Andy awards, Clio awards, CEBA awards, U.S. Film Festival award. Mem. Advt. Club N.Y. Republican. Roman Catholic. Author song lyrics. Home: 175 E 62d St New York NY 10022 Office: 875 3d Ave New York NY 10022

KRAMER, DOROTHY GLORIA, mfg. co. exec.; b. Providence, July 5, 1925; d. Morris and Bessie (Goldberg) Friedman; student Bryant Coll., 1943; m. Sidney Kramer, Jan. 2, 1955. With Taco, Inc., Cranston, R.I., 1943—, personnel dir., 1960, sec. of corp., 1970, sr. v.p., treas., 1977—; treas. Unipas, Inc., Cranston, R.I., 1975—; dir. Providence Gas Co., 1976—, mem. exec. com., 1981—. Corp. mem. Cranston Gen. Hosp. Osteopathic, 1975—, bd. dirs., 1975—, sec., 1978—, v.p., 1981—. Mem. Fin. Execs. Inst. (dir. 1980—), C. of C. Home: 15 Sunset Dr East Greenwich RI 02818 Office: 1160 Cranston St Cranston RI 02920

KRAMER, JOAN LOUISE, photo agt.; b. Phila., Oct. 21, 1937; d. Samuel and Ida (Perchick) Shuster; student New Sch. Social Research; m. Erwin Kramer, Dec. 24, 1956; children—Ilene, Lee Mitchell. Corr. sec. Sterling Warner Co., N.Y.C., 1957-60; pres. Joan Kramer & Assocs. Inc., N.Y.C., 1971—. Mem. Soc. Photographer and Artist Reps., Am. Soc. Mag. Photographers, Am. Soc. Picture Profls. Office: 720 Fifth Ave New York NY 10019

KRAMER, JOAN WYCOFF, advt. agy. exec.; b. Elkins, W.Va., July 16, 1942; d. William Ray and Betty Jo (Miller) Waller; student public schs., Elkins; children—Jymme Jodette, Jill Renee, Julia Beth, T. Curtis. Bookkeeper, sec. Elkins YMCA, 1968-70, Tyrone Kramer Enterprises, Inc., Marietta, Ga., 1973-78; founder, owner Smiling Unicorn Enterprises, Panama City, Fla., 1981—; founder Video Safeguard Enterprises, 1982. Leader Girl Scouts U.S.A., Ger., 1962-64, Marietta, 1971-74; active Band Parents, 1972-74, Jerry Lewis Muscular Dystrophy Dr., 1980-81, Cancer Soc., 1970-81. Served with U.S. Women's Army Corps, 1960-61. Republican. Methodist. Clubs: Nat. New Neighbors League of Atlanta, Pythian Sisters. Home: 3806-B E 9th St Panama City FL 32401

KRAMER, LENORE, lawyer; b. Bronx, N.Y., Dec. 7, 1951; d. Eugene and Florence Kramer; B.A., SUNY, Albany; J.D., Boston U. Admitted to bar; formerly asso. firm Copland & Tillem; now partner Copland, Tillem & Kramer. Mem. Med. Malpractice Eval. Panel, panel Am. Arbitration Assn.; arbitrator N.Y.C. Civil Ct., Nassau County Dist. Ct. Mem. Met. Women's Bar Assn. (pres.), Assn. Trial Lawyers City N.Y. (dir.), Network Bar Leaders (exec. council), ABA, Bronx County Bar Assn., Assn. Bar City N.Y., N.Y. County Lawyers, N.Y. State Lawers Assn., N.Y. State Bar Assn. Club: B'nai Brith Lawyers. Office: 3475 Boston Rd New York NY 10469

KRAMER, MARCIA GAIL, journalist; b. Greenfield, Mass., Dec. 30, 1948; d. Louis Aaron and Blanche Shirley (Weiner) K.; B.A. in Polit. Sci., Boston U., 1970. Reporter, Greenfield Recorder Gazette, 1969, N.Y. Daily News, 1970—; guest appearances various radio and TV programs; lectr. various colls. and univs., N.Y.C.; adj. prof. journalism Columbia U., 1980, N.Y.U., 1982-83. Mem. Gov.'s Adv. Com. on Drug Abuse, 1978. Recipient Public Service award Kings County Borough, 1974; Gold Typewriter award and Bobby Spellman Heart of N.Y. award N.Y. Press Club, 1979; Legis. Reform award Patrolman's Benevolent Assn., 1981; Ret. Detectives Ardee award, 1981. Mem. N.Y. Press Women (v.p. 1977-78), N.Y. Press Club (fin. sec. 1979-80, 1st v.p. 1980-81, 2d v.p. 1981-83). Office: NY Daily News 220 E 42d St New York NY 10017

KRAMER, MARILYN WENDY, educator, speech therapist; b. Bklyn., Feb. 4, 1950; d. Monroe K. and Vivian (Horowitz) Lachowitz; B.A., Queens Coll., 1972; M.A., Hofstra U., 1974; m. Robert Kramer, Aug. 23, 1970; children—Jennifer, Brian. Tchr., N.Y.C. public schs., 1972-74; speech pathologist Bklyn. Devel. Center, 1974-76; pvt. practice speech pathology, Queens, N.Y., 1976-77; speech cons. for nursing homes, Queens and Nassau, N.Y., 1977-78; tchr. spl. edn. Forest Hills (N.Y.) High Sch., 1978—, mem. com. on mental retardation and devel. disabilities, 1978-80. Mem. exec. bd. Whitestone Hadassah, 1976-80, Roslyn Hadassah, 1981—. Cert. speech pathologist, N.Y. Mem. Am. Speech and Hearing Assn., L.I. Speech and Hearing Assn. Office: 67-01 110th St Forest Hills NY 11375

KRAMER, MARY EVERIST, orthoptist; b. Bancroft, Iowa, Dec. 12, 1911; d. Francis Joseph and Gertrude Antoinette (Budde) K.; grad. St. Joseph's Sch. Nursing, Sioux City, Iowa, 1933; student Iowa U., 1936, George Washington U. Sch. Medicine, 1939-42; m. William Perry Reeves, Jan., 1939. Instr. orthoptics George Washington U. Sch. Medicine, 1944-53; med. orthoptist Ophthalmic Lab., Phoenix, 1956—. Mem. Am. Assn. Cert. Orthoptists, Phoenix Writers Club, Internat. Platform Assn. Roman Catholic. Author: Clinical Orthoptics, 2d edit., 1953. Contbr. articles to profl. jours. Home: 3432 N 12th Pl #25 Phoenix AZ 85014 Office: 323 Park Central N Med Bldg 555 W Catalina Dr Phoenix AZ 85013

KRAMER, MELINDA LINA GAMBLE, univ. ofcl.; b. Salem, Ohio, Sept. 1, 1946; d. Homer S. and Devona Elaine (Jackson) Gamble; B.A., Earlham Coll., 1968; M.A., Purdue U., 1970, Ph.D., 1975; m. Gary Wayne Kramer, June 9, 1968. Instr. dept. English, Purdue U., 1975, writing specialist Krannert Grad. Sch. Mgmt., 1976-80, dir. mgmt. communications, 1980—; asso. faculty dept. English, Ind. U.-Purdue U., Indpls., 1976-79; cons. in field. Mem. Women in Communications, Nat. Council Tchrs. English, Conf. Coll. Composition and Communication, Am. Bus. Communication Assn., Friends Assn. Higher Edn. Quaker. Author: Prentice-Hall Workbook for Writers, 2d edit., 1978, 3d edit., 1982; The Right Book: From Patterned Sentence Practice Through Model Essay Construction, 1980. Office: Krannert Graduate School of Management Purdue University West Lafayette IN 47907

KRAMER, NORA, author, sculptor, book cons.; b. Pendleton, Eng.; d. Harris and Rachel (Wolf) Atkins; student Beaux Arts Inst., N.Y., 1920-21, Sch. Mus. Fine Arts, Boston, 1929-30, City Coll. N.Y., 1939-43, sculpture and fine arts workshops New Sch. for Social Research, 1970—; m. Sidney David Kramer, Oct. 27, 1917 (dec. June 1955); children—Karl Robert, Virginia Kramer Stein, Joan Kramer Stoliar. Cons. (under name of Eleanor Brent) The Little Bookshop, Macy's, N.Y., 1943-53; creator The Bookplan, 1944, dir., 1944—; editorial cons. Scholastic's Arrow Book Club, 1958-75; leader juvenile writing workshop Colo. U., 1955; mem. Child Study Children's Book Commn., Bank Street Coll. Edn., 1934-74, NCCJ, 1947—, English-Speaking Union Books-Across-the-Sea, 1953—; judge for Herald Tribune spring book festival, 1947, 53, Thomas Edison Awards Com., 1950, Boys Clubs Am., 1952, 54, 57, Scholastic Ann. Jr. Article Writing Awards, 1958—; sculpted works include portrait busts of children and adults, figures in round; exhibited in shows including Catherine Lorillard Wolfe Art Club Show, N.Y.C., 1974, 75, 76, 78, 79, 80, 81; represented in pvt. collections. Recipient award for Young Dreamer, 1975, award for After the Ball, 1979, award for Friendship, 1980. Mem. Woman's Nat. Book Assn. (past 1st v.p. and mem. bd.), Author's League Am., English-Speaking Union, Child Study Assn. Am. (children's book com. 1934). Author: Nora Kramer's Storybook for Threes and Fours, 1955; Nora Kramer's Storybook for Fives and Sixes, 1956; The Cozy Hour Storybook, 1960; The Arrow Book of Ghost Stories, 1960; The Grandma Moses Storybook, 1961; Princess Tales, 1971; Tricky Tales, 1970; The Ghostly Hand and Other Haunting Stories, 1972; co-author: (with Karl Robert Kramer) Coppercraft and Silver Made at Home, 1958, paperback edit., 1972. Editor-in-chief The Bookwoman, 1954-56. Editor: Grimms' Fairy Tales, 1962; (abridged editions) Swiss Family Robinson, 1960, Hans Brinker, 1967, Dracula, 1971, Ramona, 1972, Journey To The Center of The Earth, 1973. Address: 46 Jane St New York NY 10014

KRAMER, RUTH, accountant; b. N.Y.C., June 20, 1925; d. Isidore and Sarah (Heller) Kleiner; B.A., Bklyn. Coll., 1946; m. Paul Kramer, Oct. 27, 1946; children—Stephen David, Lynne Adair. Tchr. elem. sch. N.Y.C. Bd. Edn., 1946-50; acct. Lichtenstein & Kramer, N.Y.C., Lynbrook, N.Y., 1954; jr. partner Paul Kramer & Co., Lynbrook, 1954-56, partner, 1956-65, mng. partner, 1965—; cons. Nassau County (N.Y.) Dist. Attys. Office, 1956-65; expert witness acctg. matters Nassau County Grand Juries, 1956-65; mem. IRS liaison com. Bklyn. Dist., 1965-76; mem. N.Y. State Bd. for Pub. Accountancy, 1982—; dir. Flinch & Bruns Funeral Home, Inc. Troop leader Girl Scouts U.S.A., 1947-48; chmn. Tri-Town sect. Anti Defamation League, 1952-53; active Heart Fund; pres. Lynbrook Women's Republican Club, 1956-58; treas. Assembly Candidates Campaign Com., 1964; mem. Nassau County Fedn. Rep. Women, Syosset Woodbury Rep. Club. Named Woman in Acctg., local TV channel, 1974. Registered public acct., N.Y. Mem. Nat. Soc. Public Accts. (del.), Empire State Assn. Public Accts. (Meritorious Service award, 2d v.p., 1975-76, 1st v.p. 1977-78, pres. 1978-79, Pres.'s award, 2d past pres. exec. bd. 1979-80, 1st past pres. exec. bd. 1981-82, pres. Nassau County chpt. 1962, 63, 75, 76, state dir. 1980—), Tax Inst. C.W. Post Coll., Acctg. Inst. C.W. Post Coll. Jewish. Clubs: Sisterhood North Shore Synagogue; Am. Jewish Congress, Lynbrook Pythian Sisters. (past chief). Home: 23 Hilltop Dr Syosset NY 11791 Office: 23 Hilltop Dr Syosset NY 11791

KRAMER, SUSAN ALICE, media prodn. co. exec.; b. Los Angeles, Oct. 23, 1950; d. Raphael and Lillian (Rabuchin) Kramer; B.A. summa cum laude, UCLA, 1971, M.Ed. with honors, 1973. Tchr., Los Angeles City Schs., 1971-76; tchr. Calif. State U., Dominguez Hills, 1975-76; free-lance writer, 1973-76; mng. product devel. Walt Disney Prodns, 1976-79; owner, pres. Walker/Kramer & Assos. Mem. Women in Bus., Info. Film Producers Assn., Phi Beta Kappa, Pi Lamda Theta. Office: 14429 Ventura Blvd Suite 117 Sherman Oaks CA 91423

KRAMER, SYLVIA WEISMAN ROSENTHAL (MRS. JACOB R. KRAMER), civic leader; b. Gulfport, Miss.; d. Joseph and Elisa (Berliner) Weisman; grad. Murphy High Sch., Mobile, Ala., 1927; student Telegraph Sch., Rome, Ga., 1929; m. Joseph Rosenthal, June 29, 1936 (dec. Nov. 1966); children—Alice (Mrs. Malcolm Brachman), Michael Jay, Judith Susan (Mrs. Steven Winter); m. 2d, Jacob R. Kramer, Sept. 20, 1979. Tchr. public relations; conv. sec., mgr. brs. Western Union at Mobile, Miami Beach, Fla., Coral Gables, Fla., Washington, 1929-36; chief communications dept. U.S. Resettlement Div., Washington, 1935-36; v.p. Ellenville Lumber Co. (N.Y.), 1962-68; tchr. beaded flowers S.S. Rotterdam and S.S. Statendam, 1970-73; asso. Asta Travel Sch., 1970, Saltaire Travel Agy., 1970-79, Choice-Travel SVC, Encinitas, Calif., 1975-77, North Country Travel, Encinitas, 1977—, Hallendale Travel, Encinitas, 1979—. Vice pres. So. Young Judea, 1934; conv. chmn. Jamaica (L.I., N.Y.) ARC, 1947; v.p. fund raising Kew Gardens (N.Y.) Hadassah, 1954-56; chmn. women's div. Queens (N.Y.) Fedn. Jewish Philanthropies, 1966-68, chmn. bd., 1969-70; chmn. advance gifts Hillcrest (N.Y.) United Jewish Appeal, 1968; vol. tchr. crafts local charities; sponsor Internat. Synagogue, 1968, also past chmn. Lincoln Center (N.Y.C.); active Garment Center Congregation and Sisterhood, elected brother congregation, 1937, trustee, 1968—, pres. sisterhood, 1942-46, hon. pres., 1946—, benefit theatre party chmn., 1950-70; past mem. bd. Jamaica Jewish Center and Bd. Edn., past pres. Sisterhood, founder vol. catering dept.; past mem. bd. Fedn. Jewish Women's Orgns.; former mem. youth activities bd. Hillcrest Jewish Center and Sisterhood; mem. Forest Hills Council Jewish Women; founding pres. Henley Sch. Parents Assn.; founder (with others) chair Hebrew culture N.Y. U. Pres. Myer and Joseph Rosenthal Meml. Found.; mem. women's bd. Queen's Coll. Speech and Hearing Center; past mem. Found. for Ileitus and Colitis; mem. Am. Cancer Soc.; mem. bd. Greater Flushing YM-YWHA, chmn. swimming pool devel. com., 1969-73. Recipient Citizen of Week award, Mobile, 1934, This is Your Life award Garment Center Congregation and Sisterhood, 1958, Woman of Yr. award Fedn. Jewish Women's Orgns., 1961. Democrat. Clubs: B'nai B'rith, Hadassah (life; chpt. fin. sec. and membership chmn. 1982—); N.Y. U., La Costa Country, Aquarius Social (social com.) (Hollywood, Fla.). Address: 2751 S Ocean Dr Hollywood FL 33019 also 70-20 108th St Forest Hills NY 11375 also 2505 Navarra Dr Rancho La Costa CA 92008

KRANK, ETHEL RITA ANNETTE, found. exec.; b. Dickinson, N.D., Nov. 24, 1938; d. John P. and Leona V. (Hedge) K.; cert. acctg. Dakota Bus. Coll., Fargo, N.D., 1957. Membership sec., bookkeeper, officer mgr. Greater N.D. Assn., Fargo, 1958-68; officer mgr. N.D. 4-H Club Found., 1969-70, exec. dir., 1970—. Mem. Gov. N.D. Commn. Status Women, 1973-75; chmn. Fargo div. Women's Day activities Fargo-Moorhead Centennial, 1975. Mem. Nat. Assn. Extension 4-H Agts. (local sec. 1975-77, local chmn. public relations com. 1975-82; Disting. Service citation 1981). Republican. Roman Catholic. Club: Zonta (pres. Fargo 1972-74, dist. area dir. 1978-80). Home: 2402 S 17th St Fargo ND 58103 Office: Box 5436 State University Station Fargo ND 58105

KRANKING, MARGARET GRAHAM, artist; b. Florence, S.C., Dec. 21, 1930; d. Stephen Wayne and Madge Williams (Dawes) Graham; B.A. summa cum laude (Clendenin fellow), Am. U., 1952; m. James David Kranking, Aug. 23, 1952; children—James Andrew, Ann Marie Kranking Eggleton, David Wayne. Asst. to head publs. Nat. Gallery Art, Washington, 1952-53; profl. artist, 1966—; tchr. art Ursuline Acad., Bethesda, Md., 1971-72, Woman's Club Chevy Chase (Md.), 1976—; one-man shows: Spectrum Gallery, Washington, 1974, 76, 78, 79, 81, Gallery Kormendy, Alexandria, Va., 1979; group shows include: Balt. Mus., 1974, 76, Corcoran Gallery Art, Washington, 1952, 72, USIA Traveling Exhibit, C. Am., 1978-79; represented in permanent collection U. Va., 1979. Recipient Don Harris award W. Tex. Watercolor Soc., 1979, Mobay award Pitts. Watercolor Soc., 1980. Mem. Spectrum Gallery Washington, St. John's Mus. Art (Wilmington, N.C.), So. Watercolor Soc., Artists Equity, Washington Watercolor Assn., Watercolor Soc. Ala., Potomac Valley Watercolorists (pres. 1981-83), Am. Watercolor Soc. (asso.). Roman Catholic. Club: Salmagundi (N.Y.C.). Home: 3504 Taylor St Chevy Chase MD 20015

KRASNER, LEE, painter; b. Bklyn; ed. Cooper Union, Art Students League, CCNY, NAD; studied with Hans Hofmann; m. Jackson Pollock (dec.). Exhibited paintings at Palazzo Graneri, Turin, Italy, 1959, Galerie Beyeler, Basel, Switzerland, 1961, Laing Art Gallery, Newcastle-upon-Tyne. Eng., 1961, Marlborough Fine Arts, London and N.Y.C., 1961, Yale Art Gallery, 1961-62, Mt. Holyoke Coll., 1962, Wadsworth Atheneum, Hartford, Conn., 1962, Guild Hall, East Hampton, N.Y., 1963-64; Mary Washington Coll., U. Va., Fredericksburg 1962, Queens Coll., N.Y.C., 1962, Howard Wise Gallery, 1962, Guggenheim Mus., N.Y.C., 1964, Gallery of Modern Art, N.Y.C., 1965, Southampton Coll. of L.I. U., 1965; exhibited shows Hans Hofmann and His Students, 1963, 64, Abstract Watercolors by 14 Americans, 1963-65 (both Mus. Modern Art, N.Y.C.), White House traveling exhbn., 1967, Jewish Mus., N.Y.C., 1967, Mus. Modern Art, 1969, Palazzo Reale, Milan, 1971, Lakeview Center, Peoria, Ill., 1972; group exhbns. Bklyn. Mus., 1977, Andrew Crispo Gallery, N.Y.C., 1977, Parsons Sch. Design, N.Y.C., 1977, Whitney Mus. Am. Art, N.Y.C., 1977, 78, Mus. Modern Art, N.Y.C., 1977, 78, Coopers Union, N.Y.C., 1977, Abstract Expressionism travelling show Cornell U.-Johnson Mus.-Seibu Mus. Art, Tokyo-Whitney Mus. Am. Art, 1978, Phila. Coll. of Art, 1978, Contre Culturel Americain, Paris, 1979, Met. Mus. Art, N.Y.C., 1979, Guggenheim Mus., N.Y.C., 1979, Heckscher Mus., Huntington, N.Y., 1979, Hirshhorn Mus., Washington, 1980, Guild Hall, East Hampton, N.Y., 1981, Nassau Mus. Fine Art, Roslyn, N.Y., 1981, Carnegie Inst., Pitts., 1982, others; solo shows: Betty Parsons Gallery, N.Y.C., 1951, Stable Gallery, N.Y.C., 1955, Martha Jackson Gallery, N.Y.C., 1958, Signa Gallery, East Hampton, 1959, Howard Wise Gallery, 1960, 62, Whitechapel Gallery, London, 1965, Arts Council of Gt. Britain, London, 1966, U. Ala. Gallery, 1967, Marlborough-Gerson Gallery, N.Y.C., 1968, 69, Reese Palley Gallery, San Francisco, 1969, Marlborough Prints and Drawing Gallery, N.Y.C., 1973, 75, Whitney Mus. Art, N.Y.C.,

1973-74, Miami-Dade Community Coll., 1974, Beaver Coll., Glenside, Pa., 1974, Corcoran Gallery, Washington, 1975, Pa. State U., 1975, Brandeis U., 1975, Pace Gallery, N.Y.C., 1977, 79, 81, Susan Hilberry Gallery, Mich., 1977, Janie C. Lee Gallery, Houston, 1978, 81, Tower Gallery, Southampton, N.Y., 1980, Robert Miller Gallery, N.Y.C., 1982; represented in numerous collections. Address: The Springs East Hampton NY 11937

KRASNOW, E. JUDITH LEVINE, mental health ofcl.; b. Stamford, Conn.; d. Harry Hirsh and Adele Rae (Steinhauer) Levine; A.B., Boston U., 1958; M.S., Sch. Social Work Simmons Coll., 1960; D.S.W., Cath. U. Am., 1969; m. Erwin G. Krasnow, Sept. 4, 1960; children—Michael Andrew, Catherine Beth. Caseworker Boston Children's Services Assn., 1960-61; psychiat. social worker, dep. dir. treatment unit Alexandria (Va.) Community Mental Health Center, 1962-69, dir. preventive services and tng., 1969-77, dir., 1978—; field instr. Cath. U., Howard U., George Washington U.; cons. various social agys. and schs.; examiner Va. Bd. Social Workers. Bd. dirs. Nat. Child Research Center, 1974-76; rep. Parents Assn. steering com. Sidwell Friends Sch., 1981—; mem. Social Welfare Adv. Com., U.S. Employment Service, 1966-68. NIMH tng. grantee in mental health, 1959-60. Mem. Nat. Assn. Social Workers (clin. register bd.), Acad. Cert. Social Workers, Am. Orthopsychiat. Assn., Mental Health Assn., Fedn. Clin. Social Workers, Nat. Assn. Community Mental Health Centers, Va. Assn. Mental Health Center Dirs. Editorial bd. Social Work Met. Washington, 1976-77; contbr. research articles to profl. publs. Home: 5604 Surrey St Chevy Chase MD 20815 Office: 206 N Washington St Alexandria VA 22314

KRATT, LAURA ANTOINETTE, lawyer; b. Charlotte, N.C., Jan. 18, 1943; d. Emil Jacob and Lucy Margaret (Failing) K.; A.B., Randolph-Macon Woman's Coll., 1964; M.A.T., U. N.C., Chapel Hill, 1968; J.D., Wake Forest U., 1974. Research asst. Harvard Med. Sch., Boston, 1964-66; high sch. biology tchr. Chesterfield County Public Schs., Richmond, Va., 1968-71; admitted to N.C. bar, 1974; pvt. practice law, Charlotte, 1974-81; asst. city atty. City of Charlotte, 1981—; instr. Central Piedmont Community Coll., 1975-76, 79, Queens Coll., Charlotte, 1978. Mem. ad hoc housing study com., Mecklenburg County, N.C., 1976-77, housing and devel. com., 1977-81; substance abuse council Mecklenburg County Area Health Mental Authority, 1979-80; bd. dirs. Charlotte br. AAUW, 1975-77; bd. mgrs. Johnston Meml. YMCA, 1977-78; sec., bd. dirs. Charlotte Rehab. Homes, Inc., 1976-79; sec. Charlotte Women's Polit. Caucus, 1981-82. Mem. Am. Bar Assn., N.C. Bar Assn. (sec. litigation sect.), N.C. Acad. Trial Lawyers, Mecklenburg County Bar assn. (sec-treas. 1980-82), Charlotte Women Execs. (dir. 1981-82). Clubs: Zonta (pres. 1981-82), PEO (pres. 1980-82). Home: 2753 Picardy Pl Charlotte NC 28209 Office: City Attorney's Office City Hall 600 E Trade St Charlotte NC 28202

KRATZER, ROSEMARIE FRIEDA (NICHELSON), bus. educator; b. Heidelberg, W.Ger., May 15, 1950; d. Duane Blodgett and Irmgard Paula (Reinmuth) Boczanski; B.S. in Bus. Edn., U. Nebr., 1972; M.Ed., 1980; m. Rick Kratzer, Oct. 24, 1981. Instr., Columbus Vocat. Tech., Columbus, Ga., 1975-76; exec. sec. to comdr. 1st Inf. Div., U.S. Army, Goeppingen, W.Ger., 1976-79; grad. asst. U. Nebr., Lincoln, 1979-80; instr. bus. occupations S.E. Community Coll., Lincoln, 1980—; curriculum developer. Mem. Info. Word Processing, Nat. Bus. Edn. Assn., Nebr. Assn. Ednl. Data Systems, S.E. Community Coll. Faculty Assn., Am. Vocat. Assn. Home: 6242 Briar Rosa Dr Lincoln NE 68516 Office: 8800 O St Lincoln NE 68520

KRAUK, ELSIE ALEXANDRIA, educator; b. N.Y.C., Oct. 28, 1919; d. Harry and Katherine Huczko Harasym; B.A., Hunter Coll., 1941; M.A., Tchrs. Coll., Columbia U., 1942; postgrad. Johns Hopkins U., 1949-56, Towson State U., 1949-50, U. Md., 1956-59; m. Pembroke Mitchell Krauk, July 18, 1943; 1 son, James Mitchell. Tchr. phys. edn. Thomas Johnson Elem. Sch., Balt., 1942-43; social caseworker Dept. Public Welfare, Balt., 1948-49; tchr. grade 4 and 5 Guilford Ave. Elem. Sch., Balt., 1949-52, Glenmount Elem. Sch., 1952-77, ret., 1977; tutor, vol. work, 1977—. Tchr. rep. exec. bd. PTA, 1956-58, 63-65, area tchr. representing Balt., 1961-63. Mem. Ret. Public Sch. Tchrs. Assn., Md. Ret. Tchrs. Assn., NEA. Home: 6216 Walther Ave Baltimore MD 21206

KRAUS, HELEN ANTOINETTE, educator; b. Bklyn., Aug. 25, 1909; d. Christian W. and Clara Helen (Langenberg) Janson; B.S. in Edn. (scholar), Boston U., 1929; m. Harold George Kraus, June 27, 1934; children—Harold Christian, George Robert, Phyllis Ann Kraus Hostetter. Tchr., Long Beach, N.Y., 1929-35; cons., editor Nassau County (N.Y.) Tb Assn., 1935-36; tchr. Baldwin (N.Y.) Public Schs., 1949-71; tchr. English as a second lang., Rockville Centre, N.Y., 1971—; co-chmn. Little White House Conf. Edn., Rockville Centre, 1954—. Mem. gen. council, synod com. ch. support L.I. Presbytery, United Presbyn. Ch., 1977—, vice moderator, 1980—; commr. to Gen. Assembly, United Presbyn. Ch. U.S.A., 1982—; vol. Rec. for Blind; bd. dirs. Rockville Centre Community Concert Assn.; co-sponsor L.I. Future Educators; chmn. Queen of Hearts contest Nassau chpt. Am. Heart Assn., 1960-70; trustee Rockville Centre Public Library, 1968-78, pres., 1975, 77-78, chmn. centennial essay contest; chmn. Rockville Centre Bicentennial Festival Com., 1976; pres. Friends Rockville Centre Public Library, 1978—; bd. dirs. Friends of Channel 21, Nassau Library System, 1981—; mem. L.I. Library Planning Bd., L.I. Library Resources Council, co-chmn. Mayor's Sr. Service Adv. Com., 1980—; v.p. Nassau Fedn. Republican Women, 1977—; dir. 10th jud. dist. Fedn. N.Y. State Rep. Women, 1978—; co-chmn. U.S. Senator's Sr. Council, 1981—. Recipient Disting. Service medallion Nassau chpt. Am. Heart Assn., 1971, Meritorious Service medallion, 1972. Mem. NEA, N.Y. State Tchrs. Assn., AAUW, N.Y. State Ret. Tchrs. Assn., Pi Lambda Theta, Delta Kappa Gamma (editor state newsletter 1970—), Alpha Delta Pi. Clubs: Fortnightly (past pres.), Republican (Rockville Centre); Order Eastern Star.

KRAUS, KATHY JANE, bus shelter co. exec.; b. Cleve., May 9, 1949; d. William J. and Alyce L. Kraus; B.A. in English, teaching cert., U. Mich., 1971; M.English, Case-Western Res. U., 1973. Tchr. English, Shaker Heights (Ohio) High Sch., 1971-76; account exec. Sta. WQAL, Cleve., 1976-78; v.p. advt. sales City Shelters, Inc., Cleve., 1978, v.p., gen. mgr., 1978—. Active Ohio Dist. 22 U.S. Congl. campaign, 1980. Mem. Greater Cleve. Growth Assn., Cleve. Advt. Club. Home: 3580 Warrensville Center Rd Shaker Heights OH 44122 Office: 1745 Rockwell Ave Cleveland OH 44114

KRAUS, LILI, pianist, educator; b. Budapest, Mar. 4, 1908; d. Victor and Irene (Bak) Kraus; student of Zoltan Kodaly, Bela Bartok; student Royal Acad. Music, Budapest, 1915-22, tchrs. diploma, 1925; student of Steuermann, New Acad., Vienna, Austria, 1925-27, M.A., 1927; student Artur Schnabel, Berlin, 1930-34; Mus.D. (hon.), Chgo. Mus. Coll., Roosevelt U., 1969, Williams Coll., 1975; D.H.L., Tex. Christian U., 1980; m. Otto Mandl, Oct. 31, 1930 (dec. Aug. 1956); children—Ruth Maria (Mrs. Fergus Pope), Michael Otto Patrick. Pianist with orchs. in Europe, 1926—, Dutch East Indies, 1940; formed Kraus-Goldberg duo with violinist Szymon Goldberg, 1930's; Japanese prisoner-of-war, 1941-45; pianist in Australia and N.Z., 1945—, Europe, N. and S. Am., Asia, 1949—; world tours, appearances with major orchs. and all major European music festivals, 1925—; gave concert in Eng.'s Canterbury Cathedral, 1st concert ever performed in Brasilia (Brazil); appeared with Salzburg Chamber Orch., Royal Moroccan Mozart Festival, orchestral concert honoring Bertrand Russell's 90th birthday, Royal Festival Hall, London; first to play all 25 Mozart piano concerti in N.Y., 1966-67; premiered newly-discovered Shubert Grazer Fantasy, CBS-TV, 1969; recorded all 25 Mozart piano concerti and complete Mozart piano sonatas for CBS; now recording complete Schubert piano repertoire; lectr. various univs., U.S. and Europe; head piano dept. Cape Town U., South Africa, 1949-50; artist-in-residence Tex. Christian U., 1967—; adjudicator Van Cliburn Internat. Piano Competition, Tex. Named hon. citizen N.Z., late 1940's; decorated Cross of Honor for Sci. and Art (Austria). Hon. mem. Music Tchrs. Assn. Calif., Sigma Alpha Iota. Author: The Complete Original Cadenzas by W.A. Mozart for His Solo Piano Concertos. Office: care Alix Williamson 1860 Broadway New York NY 10023

KRAUS, LORRAINE MARQUARDT, biochemist; b. Suffern, N.Y., Sept. 6, 1922; B.S., Mt. Mary Coll., 1943; M.S., U. Tenn., 1952, (Nat. Heart Inst. fellow) Ph.D., 1956; B.F.A., Memphis Acad. Arts, 1982; m. 1944; 2 children. Research technician, dept. endocrinology and metabolic diseases Michael Reese Hosp., Chgo., 1943-44, 48; instr. biochemistry, U. Indonesia, 1955-56; research asso. U. Tenn., Memphis, 1957-60, asst. prof. biochemistry Center for Health Scis., 1960-67, asso. prof., 1967-72, prof., 1972—, chmn. dept., 1982—; mem. adv. com. div. blood diseases and resources Nat. Heart, Lung and Blood Inst., 1979—. Mem. Internat. Soc. Hematology, Am. Soc. Hematology, Am. Chem. Soc., Am. Soc. Human Genetics, Am. Soc. Biol. Chemistry. Office: Dept Biochemistry Center for Health Scis U Tenn 894 Union Ave Memphis TN 38163

KRAUS, MARGERY, found. exec.; b. Franklin, N.J., May 20, 1946; d. Soland Lily (Cvern) Rosen; B.A. in Polit. Sci., Am. U., 1967, M.A. in govt., 1970; m. Stephen Kraus, Sept. 4, 1966; children—Lisa, Evan, Mara. With Close Up Found., Arlington, Va., 1971—, v.p., 1976—; dir., v.p. Intervest, Inc.; cons., speaker in field. Bd. dirs. Small World, 1979-80; fund raising chmn. Green Hedges Sch.; active local Girl Scout. Mem. Am. Assn. Female Execs., Am. Polit. Sci. Assn. Jewish. Editor Civic mag., 1975-77. Home: 9609 Whitecedar Ct Vienna VA 22180 Office: 1235 Jefferson Davis Hwy Arlington VA 22202

KRAUS, MOZELLE DEWITTE BIGELOW (MRS. RUSSELL WARREN KRAUS), psychologist; b. Vicksburg, Miss., Sept. 29, 1929; d. Raymond Demar and Henrietta (DeWitte) Bigelow; B.S., D.C. Tchr's. Coll., 1952; M.A., George Washington U., 1954; Ed.D., Am. U., 1965; m. Russell Warren Kraus, Sept. 30, 1961. Instr., Dept. Def., Washington, 1952-54; tchr. Wheaton (Md.) High Sch., 1954-55; grad. asst. Am. U., 1955-56; research asst., then asso. to Dr. Leonard Carmichael, former sec. Smithsonian Instn., Washington, v.p. Nat. Geog. Mag., 1956-72; pvt. practice, Washington, 1972—; asso. prof. psychology George Washington U., 1965—; instr. psychology USDA Grad. Sch., 1964—; vis. prof. U.S. Naval Sch. Hosp. Adminstrn., 1968-69; group therapy Social Service Agy., Washington, 1980—. Fellow Am. Orthopsychiat. Assn.; mem. AAAS, Am. Psychol. Assn., Va. Psychol. Assn., D.C. Psychol. Assn., Psychiat. Outpatient Clinics Am., DAR, Salvation Army Aux., Phi Delta Gamma, Sigma Xi, Psi Chi, Sigma Kappa, Kappa Delta Epsilon. Episcopalian. Contbr. articles to profl. jours.; author newspaper column Person to Person. Home: 4710 Bethesda Ave Bethesda MD 20014

KRAUS, PANSY DAEGLING, editor; b. Santa Paula, Calif., Sept. 21, 1916; d. Arthur David and Elsie (Pardee) Daegling; A.A., San Bernardino Valley Jr. Coll., 1938; student Longmeyer's Bus. Coll., 1940; grad. gemologist diploma Gemological Inst. Am., 1966, Gemmological Assn. Gt. Britain, 1960; m. Charles Frederick Kraus, Mar. 1, 1941 (div. Nov. 1961). Clk., Convair, San Diego, 1943-48; clk. San Diego County Schs. Publs., 1948-57; mgr. Rogers and Boblet-Art Craft, San Diego, 1958-64; part-time editorial asst. Lapidary Jour., San Diego, 1963-64, asso. editor, 1964-69, editor, 1970—; lectr. gems, gemology local gem and mineral groups; gem and mineral club bull. editor groups. Mem. San Diego Mineral and Gem Soc., Gemmol. Soc. San Diego, Gemmol. Assn. Great Britain, Mineral. Soc. Am., Epsilon Sigma Alpha. Editor, layout dir.: Gem Cutting Shop Helps, 1964; The Fundamentals of Gemstone Carving, 1967; Appalachian Mineral and Gem Trails, 1968; Practical Gem Knowlege for the Amateur, 1969; Southwest Mineral and Gem Trails, 1972; revision editor Gemcraft, 1977. Home: 6127 Mohler St San Diego CA 92120 Office: 3564 Kettner Blvd San Diego CA 92101

KRAUSE, KATHERINE M., nurse; b. Jackson Heights, N.Y., Apr. 27, 1949; d. Daniel A. and Florence (Miller) Buechs; student Marquette U., 1966-68, M.S.N. candidate, 1979—; B.S. in Nursing, U. Wis., Milw., 1976; m. David J. Krause, Nov. 6, 1982. Operating room technician Luth. Hosp. Milw., Inc., 1969-76, nurse clinician operating room, 1976-80; dir. surg. services Froedtert Meml. Luth. Hosp., Milw., 1980—; area instr. CPR, 1976-80; mem. pub. edn. com. North Milw. unit Am. Cancer Soc., 1976-78, mem. patient services com., 1977-78; active in traveling med. show giving 1st aid at concerts, 1976-81, personnel coordinator for medics, 1977-81. Mem. Assn. Operating Room Nurses (chmn. surgeon's fund com. S.E. Wis. chpt. 1978-79, dir. 1979-81, chmn. membership com. 1979-80, chmn. project Alpha 1980-81, v.p., program chmn. 1981-82, pres. 1982-83, del. to nat. congress 1979, 81, 83). Home: 4708 Sonseeahray Dr Hubertus WI 53033 Office: 9200 W Wisconsin Ave Milwaukee WI 53226

KRAUSE, KRISTINE MARY, civil engr.; b. Milw., Sept. 8, 1954; d. James Louis and Monica Helen K.; B.S. in Civil Engring., Mich. Tech. U., 1976; postgrad. Marquette U., 1980—. Insp., coop. student Wis. Dept. Transp., Milw. and Green Bay, 1973-75; design engr. Allegany Power Service Corp., Greensburg, Pa., 1976-78; project adminstr. power plant Wis. Electric Power Co., Milw., 1979-80, constrn. supr., 1980—. Mem. Nat. Ski Patrol, 1980—. Registered profl. engr., Wis. Mem. ASCE (S.W. br. Wis. newsletter editor 1980—), Exptl. Aircraft Assn., Aircraft Owners and Pilots Assn. Republican. Roman Catholic. Home: 10880 W Donna Dr Milwaukee WI 53224 Office: 231 W Michigan St Milwaukee WI 53201

KRAUSE, MARCELLA ELIZABETH MASON, ret. educator; b. Norfolk, Nebr.; d. James Haskell and Elizabeth (Vader) Mason; B.S., U. Nebr., 1934; M.A., Columbia U., 1938; postgrad. summers U. Calif. at Berkeley, 1950, 51, 65, Stanford U., 1964, Creighton U., 1966, Chico (Calif.) State U., 1967; m. Eugene Fitch Krause, June 1, 1945; 1 dau., Kathryn Elizabeth. Tchr., Royal (Nebr.) public schs., 1930-32, Hardy (Nebr.) public schs., 1933-35, Omaha public schs., 1935-37, Lincoln Sch. of Tchrs. Coll. Columbia U., 1937-38, Florence (Ala.) State Tchrs. Coll., summer 1938, Tchrs. Coll. U. Nebr., 1938-42, Corpus Christi public schs., 1942-45; head counselor, data processing coordinator Oakland (Calif.) public schs., 1945-75; house dir. sorority, 1976-77. Bd. dirs. U. Nebr. Womens Faculty Club, 1940-42; mem. Nebr. State Tchrs. Conv. Panel, 1940; mem. U. Nebr. Reading Inst., 1940; speaker Iowa State Tchrs. Conv., 1941; reading speaker Nebr. State Tchrs. Conv., 1941; lectr. Johnson County Tchrs. Inst., 1942; chmn. Reading Survey Corpus Christi public schs., 1943; chmn. Inservice Reading Meetings Oakland public schs., 1948-57. Mem. Gov.'s Adv. Commn. on Status Women Conf., San Francisco, 1966; service worker ARC, Am. Cancer Soc., United Crusade, Oakland Civil Def.; Republican precinct capt., 1964-66; v.p. Oakland Rep. Women. Ford Found. Fund for Advancement Edn. fellow, 1955-56; scholar Stanford, 1964; Calif. Congress PTA scholar U. Calif., 1965. Mem. Nat. Council Women, AAUW (dir.), Calif. Tchrs. Assn., Ladies Grand Army Republic, 1960 Ruth Assn., DAR (regent Sierra chpt., pres. Eastbay regents assn., Calif. state vice chmn. for membership), Oakland Museum Assn., PEO, No. Calif. Alumnae Pi Lambda Theta (past pres.), Alpha Delta Kappa. Methodist. Club: Order Eastern Star (past matron; pres. Eastbay past matrons-patrons 1974, pres. Martha assn. 1979). Contbr. articles to profl. jours. Home: 5615 Estates Dr Oakland CA 94618

KRAUSS, MICHELLE EAGLE, interior designer; b. N.Y.C., Oct. 26, 1944; d. Ralph I. and Florence Eagle; B.F.A., R.I. Sch. Design, 1966; M.A., Stanford U., 1967; m. Allen Krauss, July 9, 1971; children—Eric Bailey, Seth Lawrence. Interior designer Daniel Schwartzman & Assos., interior designers, N.Y.C., 1967-68, Copeland, Novak & Israel, 1969, Katzman & Assos., 1969-71; instr. interior design Meramec Community Coll., Kirkwood, Mo., 1976-77; interior designer Bensinger's Inc., St. Louis, 1978—; pres. M.E. Krauss Interiors, St. Louis, 1978—. Mem. exec. bd. PTO McKnight Sch., University City, Mo., 1981-82. Jewish. Home: 7827 Greensfelder Ln University City MO 63130 Office: 8543 Page Ave St Louis MO 63114

KRAUSZ, ADRIENNE EVA MATYAS, surgeon; b. Cluj, Roumania; d. Akos and Teresia Matyas; came to U.S., 1961, naturalized, 1966; M.D., Timisoara (Romania) Med. Sch., 1958; 1 dau., Mariette. Resident in surgery Fed. Hosp., Beer Yakov, Israel, 1959-61; intern Orange (N.J.) Meml. Hosp., 1961-62; resident in surgery Middlesex Gen. Hosp., New Brusnwick, N.J., 1962-65, now attending surgeon; practice medicine specializing in gen. and vascular surgery, New Brunswick, 1966—; attending surgeon Middlesex Gen. Hosp., St. Peters Hosp. Center, Somerset Hosp.; mem. clin. faculty Rutgers U. Med. Sch., Piscataway, N.J. Mem. Am. Soc. Abdominal Surgeons, Internat. Coll. Angiology, Am. Coll. Angiology, AMA, N.J. Med. Soc. Democrat. Jewish. Contbr. articles to profl. jours. Office: 111 Livingston Ave New Brunswick NJ 08901

KRAUT, JOANNE LENORA, computer programmer, analyst; b. Watertown, Wis., Oct. 29, 1949; d. Gilbert Arthur and Dorothy Ann (Gebel) K.; B.A. in Russian, U. Wis., Madison, 1971, M.S. in Computer Sci., 1973. Computer programmer U. Wis. Sch. Bus., Madison, 1969-72, Milw. Ins. Co., 1973-74; tech. coordinator Wis. Dept. Justice, Madison, 1974—. Mem. Lakewood Gardens Assn. (dir. 1981—), Phi Beta Kappa. Home: 53 N Lakewood Gardens Ln Madison WI 53704 Office: PO Box 2718 Madison WI 53701

KRAUTH, DOROTHY COLETTE, real estate broker; b. Boston, Oct. 26, 1938; d. Edward Vincent and Ethel May (Sanford) Walsh; B.S., Harvard U., 1960; m. Gerald C. McDonald, May 23, 1959; children—Gerald C., Deborah L., Gregory Christopher; m. 2d, Carl H. Krauth, Jr., Dec. 15, 1980; 1 stepson, Carl H. III. Various secretarial positions, 1958-59. model, 1958-75; model, personal shopper Filene's, Chestnut Hill, Mass., 1974-78; designer program covers Boston Red Sox, 1974-76; TV facts girl for TV comml. T.V. Facts mag., 1974-75; real estate broker Channing Assos., Inc., Wellesley, Mass., 1976-79, 81—; broker Boca Blossom Realty Co., Boca Raton, Fla., 1979-81. Roman Catholic. Home: 230 N Federal Hwy Deerfield Beach FL 33441 Office: 151 Hampshire Rd Wellesley MA 02181

KRAVAT, JUDITH LYNN, battery mfg. co. exec.; b. Kansas City, Mo., Feb. 17, 1943; d. Erwin Ray and Elaine Ruth (Galamba) Sackin; B.S. in Art and Art History, U. Wis., 1964; m. Jeffrey Laurence Kravat, Dec. 26, 1964; children—Stephanie Ann, Jennifer Beth. Trend analyst Marshall Co., 1964; computer programmer Survey Research Labs., 1964-65; customer contact person Univ. br. First Nat. Bank, Madison, 1965-67; spl. edn. tchr. Madison Met. Sch. Dist., 1978; v.p. Re-Nu Battery Corp., also Med. Systems Tech. Co., Madison, 1978—. Bd. dirs. Mental Health Assn. Dane County, 1971—, pres., 1979-80, cert. of appreciation First Friends Com., 1976. Mem. Lawyers Wives Dane County, Technion, ORT. Jewish. Club: B'nai B'rith. Office: 1220 S Park St Madison WI 53715

KRAVITCH, PHYLLIS A., fed. judge; b. Savannah, Ga., Aug. 23, 1920; d. Aaron and Ella (Wiseman) K.; B.A., Goucher Coll., 1941, LL.D., 1981; LL.B., U. Pa., 1943. Admitted to Ga. bar, 1943, U.S. Supreme Ct., 1948; gen. practice law, Savannah, 1944-76; judge Superior Ct. Eastern Jud. Circuit Ga., 1977-79; judge 5th Circuit U.S. Ct. Appeals, Atlanta, 1979-81, 11th Circuit, 1981—. Trustee, Inst. Continuing Legal Edn. in Ga., 1979—; mem. Bd. Edn. Chatham County (Ga.), 1949-55. Recipient Hannah G. Solomon award Nat. Council Jewish Women, 1978. Fellow Am. Bar Found.; mem. Am. Bar Assn., State Bar Ga., Savannah Bar Assn. (pres. 1976), Am. Law Inst., Am. Judicature Soc. Jewish. Office: PO Box 8085 Savannah GA 31412

KRAWCZYNSKI, MARY ANN HELEN, legal office adminstr.; b. Bristol, Conn., June 5, 1946; d. Steve and Helen (Dabkowski) K.; student Moody Sch. Commerce, 1966-67, Central Conn. State Coll., 1964-65, U. Hartford, 1968-69, Am. Mgmt. Assn., 1977, 79, George Washington U., 1980—. Legal sec. Conn. Gen. Life Ins. Co., Hartford, Conn., 1969-72; asst. sec. corp., sec. to pres. Input Applications, Farmington, Conn., 1972-73; legal/exec. sec. firm Day, Berry & Howard, Hartford, 1973-76; legal sec. bookkeeper firm McClure & Trotter, Washington, 1976-77; office services mgr. firm Howrey & Simon, Washington, 1977—. Active, Friends of Nat. Zoo, Washington; mem. liturgy com. St. Martin's Ch., Gaithersburg, Md. Mem. Purchasing Mgmt. Assn. Washington, Am. Mgmt. Assn., Nat. Assn. Female Execs., Md. NARAL, U.S. Judo Fedn. Club: Montgomery County Rep. Office: 1730 Pennsylvania Ave NW Washington DC 20006-4793

KRAWIEC, STELLA STANISLAWA, economist; b. Sloboda, Poland, May 7, 1942; came to U.S., 1972, naturalized, 1979; d. Jan and Janina (Miszuk) Byczko; M.S. in Indsl. Econs., Sch. Econs., Wroclaw, Poland, 1965; Ph.D., Sch. Planning and Stats., Warsaw, Poland, 1971; m. Frank Krawiec, Aug. 15, 1965; children—Marzena, Peter, Margaret. Asst. prof. dept. indsl. econs. Sch. Planning and Stats., Warsaw, 1966-71; economist Public Utility Commn., Harrisburg, Pa., 1973-74, corp. planning dept. Am. Natural Resources Co., Detroit, 1974-76; sr. research economist dept. labor and industry Office Econ. Research, Trenton, N.J., 1976-78; sr. planner, economist Solar Energy Research Inst., Golden, Colo., 1978-82; sr. research analyst dept. econs. and forecasting Public Service Co. Colo., Denver, 1982—; cons. Mem. Eastern Econ. Assn., Internat. Assn. Energy Economists, Am. Statis. Assn., AIAA. Contbr. numerous articles to profl. jours. Home: 11900 W 22d Pl Lakewood CO 80215 Office: Public Service Co Colo 550 15th St Denver CO 80202

KREBILL, LORRIE LEABO, corp. exec.; b. Davenport, Iowa, Apr. 20, 1949; d. Dorwin Norman and Maxine Deloris (Jacobs) Leabo; B.S. in Spanish, Iowa State U., Ames, 1970; m. Douglas Dwight Krebill, Nov. 28, 1970; children—Kelli Ann, Darin Douglas. Mgr., Joseph Spiess Co., Crystal Lake, Ill., 1977-78; bilingual asst. Precision Twist Drill & Machine Co., Crystal Lake, 1978-79; asst. ethanol cons., office mgr. Radiographics, Inc., Bloomingdale, Ill., 1979-80. Mem. Iowa State U. Alumni, Alpha Omicron Pi Alumni. Republican.

KREBS, MARGARET ELOISE, pub. co. exec.; b. Clearfield, Pa., Apr. 20, 1927; d. Henry Louis and Delia Louise (Beahan) K.; grad. high sch. With Progressive Pub. Co., Inc., Clearfield, 1945—, bus. office mgr., 1956-60, bus. mgr., 1960-63, asst. to pub., 1963-69, asso. pub., 1981—, dir., exec. v.p., 1969-77, pres., 1977—; pres., sec., dir. Indiana Broadcasters, Inc. (Pa.), stas. WDAD-AM and WQMU-FM, 1967—; sec. Clearfield Broadcasters, Inc., stas. WCPA-AM and WQUX-FM, 1965—, dir., 1971—; sec. Collier Broadcasting Co., stas. WMIB-AM and WRGI-FM, Naples, Fla., 1975—; sec. Centre Broadcasters, Inc., State College, Pa., 1977—; v.p., sec., dir. Valley Communications, Inc., Sta.

WAHT-AM, Lebanon, Pa., 1981—. Mem. Pa. Newspaper Women's Assn., Clearfield Bus. and Profl. Women's Club (pres. 1952-53, dist. membership chmn. 1952-53), Sigma Delta Chi. Democrat. Roman Catholic. Club: Lake Glendale Sailing (sec. 1966—). Home: 526 Ogden Ave Clearfield PA 16830 Office: 206 E Locust St Clearfield PA 16830

KRECEK, VICTORIA JEAN, assn. exec.; b. Seattle, Dec. 23, 1942; d. John Stewart and Jean Wanita (Morris) Elliott; B.A., U. Nebr., 1965; m. David Arthur Krecek, June 13, 1965; children—John Stewart, Mark Morris. Mgr. communications Omaha C. of C., 1965-68; freelance writer, Omaha, 1968-74, North Platte, Nebr., 1974-76; mgr. community devel. City of Omaha Dept. Housing and Community Devel., 1976-79; mgr. communications Greater Omaha C. of C., 1979—. Bd. dirs. Omaha Symphony Guild Bd., 1969-72; mem. Omaha Zoning Bd. Appeals, 1973-74; mem. Nebr. adv. com. U.S. Commn. on Civil Rights, 1976—; bd. dirs. Coll. World Series, 1980—; membership drive chmn. YWCA, 1981—. Mem. Public Relations Soc. Am., Nat. Assn. Housing and Redevel. Ofcls., Omaha Press Club, Nebr. News Women, Omaha Women's Network, Am. C. of C. Execs. (mem. communications council), Delta Gamma. Democrat. Home: 12839 Jones St Omaha NE 68154 Office: 1606 Douglas St Omaha NE 68102

KREGNESS, SHIRLEY JEAN, sch. nurse; b. Stephen, Minn., Apr. 6, 1937; d. Henry and Marie Alfreda (Anderson) Paulsen; B.S. in Nursing, Mont. State U., 1959; M.S. Ed., Pepperdine U., 1975; sch. nurse practitioner cert. San Diego State U., 1975; m. John Robert Kregness, June 14, 1958; children—Lisa, Sherri, Steven. Public health nurse I, Cascade County (Mont.), 1960-63, public health nurse II, 1965-69; research nurse Mont. State U., 1964-65, teaching asst., 1968-69; public health nurse II, San Diego County Health Dept., 1970-73; sch. nurse San Diego City Schs., 1973-75, sch. nurse practitioner, spl. edn., 1975-80, resource nurse, 1980—, instr. health aide trainees, 1979; instr. in community nursing, clin. instr. U. Calif., San Diego, 1977-78; part-time prof. San Diego State U., 1981; guest speaker, lectr. in field; nurse cons. to curriculum writing project. Active Boy Scouts Am., 1974-78. Mem. Calif. Sch. Nurse's Orgn. (sec. San Diego/Imperial County sect. 1982), San Diego Tchr.'s Assn., Calif. Tchr.'s Assn., NEA, Nat. Sch. Nurse's Assn., Sigma Theta Tau. Lutheran. Home: 5515 Noah Way San Diego CA 92117 Office: 2716 Marcy Ave San Diego CA 92113

KREITZBURG, MARILYN JUNE, librarian; b. Rockford, Ill.; d. A.E. and Margaret Louise (Harvey) K.; student Rockford Coll. for Women, 1948-50; A.B. magna cum laude, Knox Coll., 1954; M.A., U. Va., 1956; cert. philosophy U. Edinburgh (Scotland), 1960. Copywriter radio and TV, Black Hawk Broadcasting Co., Waterloo, Iowa, 1956-57; freelance promotion, N.Y.C., 1957; lectr. on Asia, women and fgn. affairs, Ill., Iowa, 1959-60; order librarian, asst. to coll. librarian Knox Coll., Ill., 1960-72; librarian, asst. prof. U. Pitts. at Johnstown, 1972—, reference librarian and head library instructional services, 1977—. Bd. dirs. Prairie Players Civic Theater, 1962-64; rescue vol. Richland Twp. Vol. Fire Dept., 1977, ARC Disaster Inquiry Service; mem. Inter-Service Club Council, 1976-80. Recipient medal DAR, 1948; Helen Lee Wessels fellow, 1954-55; Fulbright fellow at large, 1957-59. Mem. Women's Assn. U. Pitts. at Johnstown (pres. 1978-79, exec. bd.), Assn. Coll. and Research Libraries, ALA, Pa. Library Assn., Tri-county Library Assn., Inter Nos, Phi Beta Kappa, Delta Kappa Gamma, Pi Sigma Alpha, Sigma Alpha Iota, Pi Beta Phi. Clubs: Soroptimists (pres. 1978-80, exec. bd.), Sr. Citizens Hobby Show (publicity and hospitality com. 1977-78). Founder, editor: Ivory Tower Chronicle, 1961-64. Office: Library Univ Pittsburgh Johnstown PA 15904

KRELOFF, BEATRICE, painter; b. N.Y.C., Sept. 11, 1925; d. William and Celia (Singer) Magit; student Art Students League, 1942-45, Pratt Inst., 1945-47, Bklyn. Mus. Art Sch., 1950-54; children by previous marriage—Elliot, Charles. One-man shows include: Norwalk (Conn.) Art Gallery, 1963, Mitch Sewall Gallery, N.Y.C., 1974, Bklyn. Mus. Art Sch., 1960, 63, 65, 68, Bklyn. Mus., 1967, Rosenhouse Gallery, N.Y.C., 1975, Vestart Gallery, N.Y.C., 1972, Westbeth Gallery, N.Y.C., 1972; represented in permanent collections Joseph H. Hirshhorn Found., Washington, also pvt. collections; tchr. painting, N.Y.C., 1963—; instr. Children's Aid Soc., Rhinelander Community Center, 1970-73; chmn. art dept. Fieldston Sch., Bronx, N.Y., 1974—; artist feminist posters for Creative Women's Collective; mem. HEW video documentary for Youth and Adult Conf., Tarrytown, N.Y.; residency grantee Ecole Superieux des Beaux Arts de Athenes, 1978. Mem. Creative Women's Collective, Women in Arts, Women Caucus for Art. Home: 463 West St New York NY 10014 Office: Fieldston Sch Fieldston Rd Bronx NY 10471

KREMENITZER, JANET PICKARD, educator; b. Bklyn., Sept. 12, 1949; d. Leonard and Francine (Saltzman) Pickard; B.A., Queens Coll., City U. N.Y., 1971; M.A., Tchrs. Coll. Columbia U., 1972, Ed.M., 1974, Ed.D., 1977; m. Martin William Kremenitzer, Dec. 21, 1974; 1 dau., Rebecca Jolie. Instr., Barnard Coll. Columbia U., N.Y.C., 1971-73; tchr. Dalton Sch., N.Y.C., 1972-73; lectr. CCNY, 1973-75; asst. prof. Western Conn. State Coll., Danbury, 1977-79; mem. adj. faculty, 1982—; ednl. cons., Newtown, Conn., 1979—; research cons. Asso. Neurologists Danbury, 1982—; research asst. Rose F. Kennedy Center for Research in Mental Retardation and Human Devel., Albert Einstein Coll. Medicine, 1973-74. Vice pres. Maimonides Acad. Western Conn., Inc., 1978-80, bd. dirs., 1978—. Mem. Am. Psychol. Assn., Soc. Research in Child Devel., Internat. Soc. Devel. Psychobiology, Friends of Neot Kedumim, Pi Lambda Theta, AAPHER. Clubs: Hadassah, LaLeche League. Address: Brookwood Dr Newtown CT 06470

KREMENTZ, JILL, photographer, author; b. N.Y.C., Feb. 19, 1940; d. Walter and Virginia (Hyde) K.; student Drew U., 1958-59, Art Students League, Columbia; m. Kurt Vonnegut, Jr., Nov., 1979. With Harper's Bazaar, 1959-60, Glamour mag., 1960-61; pub. relations staff Indian Industries Fair, New Delhi, 1961; reporter Show mag., 1962-64; staff photographer N.Y. Herald Tribune, 1964-65, Vietnam, 1965-66; asso. editor Status-Diplomat mag., 1966-67; contbg. editor N.Y. mag., 1967-68; corr. Time-Life Inc., 1969-70; contbg. photographer People mag., 1974—; one-woman photography shows Madison (Wis.) Art Center, 1973, U. Mass., Boston, 1974, Nikon Gallery, N.Y.C., 1974, Del. Art Mus., Wilmington, 1975; represented in permanent collections Mus. Modern Art, Library of Congress. Photographer: The Face of South Vietnam (text by Dean Brelis), 1968; Words and Their Masters (text by Israel Shenker), 1974; photographer, author: Sweet Pea—A Black Girl Growing Up in the Rural South (foreword by Margaret Mead), 1969; A Very Young Dancer, 1976; A Very Young Rider, 1977; A Very Young Gymnast, 1978; A Very Young Circus Flyer, 1979, A Very Young Skater, 1979; The Writer's Image, 1980; How It Feels When A Parent Dies, 1981; How It Feels To Be Adopted, 1982. Mem. P.E.N., Am. Soc. Mag. Photographers (dir.), Women's Forum. Contbr. numerous U.S. and fgn. periodicals. Address: care Donald C Farber 600 Madison Ave Room 1600 New York NY 10022

KREMER, HONOR (NOREEN) FRANCES, business exec.; b. Ireland, Aug. 9, 1939; came to U.S., 1961; d. Patrick Joseph and Mary (Malone) Queally; B.S., City U. N.Y., M.S., Baruch Coll.; m. Manny Kremer, May 17, 1963; 1 son, Patrick David. Group sec. Bentalls, Ltd., Kingston-On-Thames, Surrey, Eng., 1954-58, Central Secondary Sch., Hamilton, Ont., Can., 1959-61; office mgr. Aschner Assos., N.Y.C., 1961-63; public relations asst. McMaster U., Hamilton, 1963-64; office mgr. Packaging Components, N.Y.C., 1965-67; head acctg. Shaller Rubin Assos., N.Y.C., 1967-72, v.p. fin. and adminstrn., 1972-79, sr. v.p., 1979-82, exec. v.p., mem. exec. com., 1982—, sec.-treas. multi-media div., 1972—, dir., 1975—. Mem. Nat. Fedn. Bus. and Profl. Women (dir., v.p.), Advt. Fin. Mgmt. Group. Roman Catholic. Office: 122 E 25th St New York NY 10010

KREPS, JUANITA MORRIS, economist; Lynch, Ky., Jan. 11, 1921; A.B., Berea Coll., 1942; M.A. (fellow), Duke U., 1944, Ph.D., 1948; m. Clifton H. Kreps, Jr., 1944; children—Sarah Blair, Laura Ann, Clifton H., III. Instr. econs. Denison U., Granville, Ohio, 1945-46, asst. prof., 1947-50; lectr. Hofstra U., Hempstead, N.Y., 1952-54, Queens Coll., N.Y., 1954-55; vis. asst. prof., Duke U., Durham, N.C., asst. prof., 1958-61, asso. prof., 1962-67, prof., 1967-77, dean Women's Coll., asst. provost, 1969-72, James B. Duke prof., 1972-77, v.p., 1973-77; U.S. sec. of commerce, Washington, 1977-79; dir. N.Y. Stock Exchange, 1972-77, AT&T, Armco, Inc., Citicorp., UAL, Inc., United Air Lines, R.J. Reynolds Industries, Eastman Kodak Co., J.C. Penney Co., Zurn Industries, Inc., Deere & Co.; trustee Duke Endowment, N.C. Bd. dirs. Ednl. Testing Service, 1971-77, Nat. Merit Scholarship Bd., 1972-77, Am. Assn. Higher Edn., 1974-77. Trustee, Berea Coll. Ford faculty fellow, 1963-64. Co-author: Principles of Economics; Contemporary Labor Economics, 1974; Sex, Age and Work, 1975; Women in the American Economy, 1975; author: Lifetime Allocation of Work and Income, 1971; Sex in the Marketplace: American Women at Work, 1971. Editor: Employment, Income and Retirement Problems of the Aged, 1963; Technology, Manpower and Retirement Policy, 1966. Office: 115 East Duke Bldg Duke U Durham NC 27708

KRESCH-HAGLER, SANDRA DARYL, mgmt. cons.; b. N.Y.C., Sept. 13, 1945; d. Howard and Jean (Goldsmith) Gleich; B.S., U. Pa., 1966; m. Samuel H. Hagler, Jan. 6, 1973. Research assoc. Simat, Helliesen & Eichner, Inc., N.Y.C., 1966-67; study dir. Nat. Analysts, Inc., Phila., 1968-69; pres. Sandra D. Kresch Cons. Services, Calif., 1969-70; v.p., mgr. market research Nat. Analysts, Inc., Chgo., 1970-75; v.p. Booz, Allen Venture Mgmt., N.Y.C., 1976-78; v.p. corp. devel. Booz Allen Hamilton, Inc., N.Y.C., 1980—. Bd. dirs. mgmt. cons. div. Vol. Urban Cons. Group; chmn. bd. Candidate Service Adv. Council; bd. dirs. Spence-Chapin Services to Families, also mem. personnel and pension com., policy rev. com.; bd. dirs. Jose Limon Dance Found., Inc. Recipient Tribute to Women in Internat. Industry award, 1978. mem. Am. Mktg. Assn., Nat. Assn. Female Execs., Fin. Woman's Assn., NOW. Democrat. Jewish. Club: Atrium. Home: 14 E 75th St New York NY 10021 Office: 101 Park Ave New York NY 10178

KRESSMAN, ANNABELLE CARNEY, youth assn. exec.; b. Pennsville, N.J., Dec. 6, 1932; d. Robert McKinley and Anna S. Carney; B.A. in Psychology, Glasboro State Coll., 1979; student Goldey Bus. Coll., 1950-51; children by previous marriage—Jay D. II, Pamela, Robert, Daphne. Exec. sec. E.I. du Pont de Nemours & Co., Newark, Del., 1951-55; substitute high sch. tchr. Salem (N.J.) City Schs., 1966-73; field adv. Holly Shores council Girl Scouts U.S.A., 1973-75, adult edn. dir., 1975-77, public relations and fin. devel. dir., 1977-79; exec. dir. Chesapeake Bay council, 1980—; workshop leader in communications skills, 1975—; cons. to Salem, Gloucester and Cumberland community colls. women's programs, Women's Center U. Del., 1976-81; team trainer Girl Scouts U.S.A., 1977. Bd. dirs. Appel Farm, Cultural Arts Center, Elmer, N.J., 1978-81, Internat. Women's Year; mem. Del. Gov.'s Commn. on Status of Women. Cert. trainer Parent Effectiveness Tng., Youth Effectiveness Tng. Mem. Women in Communications, Assn. Girl Scout Exec. Staff (dir. 1967—, 1st v.p. 1982—), Assn. Humanistic Soc. Am., AAUW, LWV, Nat. Soc. Fund Raising Execs., Wilmington Women in bus. dir., 1981—. Presbyterian. Author: Resource Manual for Finance Development, 1978. Home: 17 The Strand New Castle DE 19720 Office: Chesapeake Bay Girl Scout Council 1503 W 13th St Wilmington DE 19806

KRETCHMER, JOY DARLENE, govt. ofcl.; b. Great Falls, Mont., Nov. 5; d. Robert John and Jessie May (Connolly) Doran; student U. Va., SUNY, N.Y.C.; divorced; children—Linda May, Jo Ann. With U.S. Govt., 1960—, contract adminstr./contracting officer Washington Area Contracting Center, Andrews AFB, 1979-80, procurement analyst Def. Logistics Agy., Alexandria, Va., 1980—; workshop leader, cons. in field. Mem. housing hygiene bd. City of Alexandria, 1981—. Recipient various govt. awards. Mem. Nat. Contract Mgmt. Assn., NOVA (chpt. exec. bd.), Federally Employed Women, Nat. Assn. Female Execs. (network dir.), Nat. Council Career Women, LWV, Washington Women's Network, Am. Bus. Women Assn. (exec. bd.). Democrat. Roman Catholic. Clubs: MDW Officers, Washington Ski. Home: 2623 N Van Dorn St Apt 202 Alexandria VA 22302 Office: DFSC-SC Cameron Sta Alexandria VA 22314

KREUZER, LAURA LEA, temporary profls. service co. exec.; b. Santa Monica, Calif., Mar. 22, 1947; d. John William and Ruth Collingwood (Hamby) K.; student Scripps Coll., 1965-67; B.A. in Polit. Sci., Am. U., 1969. Asst. dir. research Nat. Assn. Wholesalers, Washington, 1969-72; mem. nat. staff McGovern Campaign, Washington, 1972; editor Army Times Pub. Co., Washington, 1973-76; mem. nat. and traveling staff Carter Campaign, Atlanta, Plains, Ga. and Washington, 1976; speech researcher White House, 1977; dir. Office Exec. Sec., AID, Washington, 1977-78, editor Agenda Mag., 1978-79; adminstrv. officer Nat. Commn. on Social Security, Washington, 1979-81; founder, pres. TimeService, Washington, 1981—; freelance writer, 1981—. Mem. Nat. Assn. Female Execs., Washington Women's Network, Assn. Part-Time Profls., Nat. Council Career Women. Democrat. Roman Catholic. Home: 1829 Monroe St NW Washington DC 20010 Office: 1302 18th St NW #203 Washington DC 20036

KREVOY, SUSAN BARBARA, clin. psychologist; b. Los Angeles, Dec. 6, 1944; d. Melvin Sigal and Minerva Harriet (Knell) K.; student U. Calif., Berkeley, 1962-63; B.A., UCLA, 1966, M.A., 1972, Ph.D., 1978; m. Sam Kahn, Aug. 5, 1979; children—Jennifer, Heather. Fellow, Wright Inst., Los Angeles, 1977-79, cons., 1981—; pvt. practice psychology, Beverly Hills, Calif., 1980—; cons. Beverly Hills Schs., 1982—, Help Anorexia, 1982—. Leader, Girl Scouts U.S., 1976—. Mem. Am. Psychol. Assn., Calif. Psychol. Assn., Women In Bus. (chmn. health profls.), Los Angeles Inst. Psychoanalytic Studies (pres. students assn. 1983—), UCLA Alumni Assn. Home: 1947 Prosser Ave Los Angeles CA 90025 Office: 360 N Bedford Dr Beverly Hills CA 90210

KRIBBS, JAYNE KATHRYN, univ. dean; b. Oil City, Pa., Aug. 3, 1946; d. A. Merle and Edna M. (Eisenman) K.; B.S., Clarion State Coll., 1968; M.A., Pa. State U., 1969, Ph.D., 1973. Instr. English, Pa. State U., 1969-73, asst. prof., 1973-75; asst. prof. Temple U., 1975-80, assoc. prof., 1980—, dir. Master of Liberal Arts program, 1979-82, asst. chmn. grad. English program, 1977-81, assoc. dean Grad. Sch., 1982—. Research Initiation grantee, 1974-75; Temple U. Research fellow, 1976. Mem. MLA, N.E. MLA, Shakespeare Soc. Am. Author: An Annotated Bibliography of American Literary Periodicals, 1741-1850, 1977; Critical Essays on John Greenleaf Whittier, 1980; editor: MLA Internat. Bibliography, 1974-76; contbr. articles to profl. jours. Home: 717 Pine St Philadelphia PA 19106 Office: Grad Sch Temple U Philadelphia PA 19122

KRIEG, REBECCA JANE, newspaper reporter, editor; b. Bloomington, Ill., Oct. 7, 1953; d. Russell Edward and Betty Ilena (Clesson) Krieg; B.A. summa cum laude in Christian Edn., Lincoln Christian Coll., 1977. Trainer self-help skills for retarded Lincoln (Ill.) Devel. Center, 1975-76; women's editor Lincoln Courier, 1977—. Vol. rep. Central Ill. chpt. Cystic Fibrosis Found. Mem. Lincoln LWV, Delta Epsilon Chi. Mem. Christian Ch. Club: Zonta (Lincoln). Office: Lincoln Courier Lincoln IL 62656

KRIEGER, DOROTHY TERRACE, internist; b. N.Y.C., Feb. 17, 1927; d. Morris Abraham and Esther (Marsh) Terrace; A.B. summa cum laude, Barnard Coll., 1945; M.D., Columbia U., 1949; m. C. Wayne Bardin, Aug. 11, 1978; children by previous marriage—James, Nancy. Intern, Mt. Sinai Hosp., N.Y.C., 1949-50, asst. resident in surgery, 1950-52, asst. resident in medicine, 1952-53, chief resident in medicine, 1954-55, now mem. staff; practice medicine specializing in endocrinology, N.Y.C.; mem. faculty Mt. Sinai Sch. Medicine, 1966—, prof. medicine, 1972—; dir. div. endocrinology Mt. Sinai Hosp. Endocrinology Lab., N.Y.C., 1973—; chmn. endocrinology study sect. NIH, 1980-82; mem. council Nat. Inst. Aging, 1982—; prin. investigator USPHS grants, 1972—. Diplomate Nat. Bd. Med. Examiners, Am. Bd. Internal Medicine. Fellow ACP; mem. Am. Soc. Clin. Investigation, Assn. Am. Physicians, Endocrine Soc. (v.p. 1974-75). Editor: Peptide Hormone Assay and Action, 1973—; ACTH and Related Peptides, 1977, Circadian Rhythms, 1979, Neuroendocrinology, 1980; editorial bd. Chronobiology, Endocrine Research Communications, Jour. Steroid Biochemistry, Jour. Mt. Sinai Med. Center, Ann. Rev. Physiology, Am. Jour. Physiology, Jour. Clin. Endocrinology and Metabolism; contbr. articles to profl. jours. Home: 1148 Fifth Ave New York NY 10028 Office: Mount Sinai Hospital Div Endocrinology Fifth Ave and 100th St New York NY 10028

KRIESE, FRANCES ANNE, med. technologist; b. Syracuse, N.Y., June 18, 1950; d. William Francis and Mathilda (Ineich) Kriese; B.S. in Biology, LeMoyne Coll., 1972; B.S. in Med. Tech. SUNY Upstate Med. Center, 1974. Biology lab. asst. LeMoyne Coll., Syracuse, N.Y., 1971-72; lab. technician clin. pathology Upstate Med. Center, Syracuse, 1973-74, med. technologist, research asst. dept. anesthesiology, 1975—; med. technologist Syracuse Clin. and Ref. Lab., 1974-75. Mem. Am. Soc. Clin. Pathologists (asso. mem., cert. med. technologist), Am. Heart Assn. Republican. Roman Catholic. Home: 110 Male Ave Syracuse NY 13219 Office: 750 E Adams St Syracuse NY 13210

KRIEWALD, JANET OWEN, banker; b. Greenwich, Conn., Mar. 29, 1938; d. Richard Mereidith and Elizabeth Owen; B.A., Endicott Coll., 1958; m. Peter Lawrence Kriewald, June 21, 1963. Asst. buyer Lord & Taylors, N.Y.C., 1958-60; teller Soc. for Savs., Hartford, Conn., 1960-61; head teller Peoples Savs. Bank, Bridgeport, Conn., 1961-69, br. mgr., 1973—, asst. v.p., 1976—. Sec., Westport Republican Town Com., 1974-81, mem., 1974—. Mem. Savs. Bank Women. Republican. Congl-ist. Club: Republican Women of Westport. Home: 36 Bauer Pl Westport CT 06880 Office: 58 Boston Ave Bridgeport CT 06610

KRINER, PHYLLIS ANNE, nurse, educator, adminstr.; d. Ernie V. and Theresa J. (Stella) Kriner; B.S. in Nursing, St. Ambrose Coll., Iowa, 1959; postgrad. Iowa State U., 1961, U. Ill., 1965. Clin. psychiat. nurse Mercy Hosp., Davenport, Iowa, 1958-60; tchr., counselor of student practical nurses Davenport Pub. Schs., 1960-64; tchr. practical nursing edn. Health Occupational Careers Program, Chgo. Pub. Schs., 1965-73, asst. coordinator practical nurses, lab. assts. and nurses aides sects. and faculty, 1966-68, head curriculum com., 1969-71; mem. nursing staff Columbus Hosp., Chgo., 1973-75, head nurse of med.-surg. and infectious unit, 1975-79, nurse epidemiologist, 1979-80; faculty human resource devel. Sch. Nursing, Cabrini Hosp., 1980—; tchr. nat. tchr. edn. inst. for new health occupations tchrs. U. Iowa 1968. Certified tchr. Chgo. Bd. of Edn. Mem. Am., Ill. nurses assns. Co-developer practical nursing course Davenport Pub. Schs. Home: 3100 N Lake Shore Dr Chicago IL 60657 Office: Cabrini Hospital Chicago IL

KRISS, DOROTHY JEAN, dialysis sales specialist; b. Pitts., Sept. 17, 1947; d. Joseph Frank and Dorothy Ann (Crowley) K.; R.N., St. Joseph's Hosp., Pitts., 1968; B.S. in Biology, Mercy Coll., Dobbs Ferry, N.Y., 1976; M.B.A., N.H. Coll., 1981. Asst. head nurse dialysis transplant units Montefiore Hosp., N.Y.C., 1968-71, Mt. Sinai Hosp., N.Y.C., 1971-72; nurse adminstr. Bronx Dialysis Center, 1973-76; profl. services coordinator Erika, Inc., Rockleigh, N.J., 1976-80, dialysis sales specialist New Eng., 1980—. Named Dialysis Sales Specialist of Yr. for Northeast Region, 1981. Mem. Am. Assn. Nephrology Nurses and Technicians. Office: Erika Inc One Erika Plaza Rockleigh NJ 07647

KRISTOF, FAITH MARILYN, banker; b. Tigerton, Wis., Mar. 22, 1951; d. Ralph O. and Violet V. Hermann; B.S. (scholar), U. Wis., Stevens Point, 1973; m. James D. Kristof, May 25, 1974; children—Jill Renee, Paul James. With Citizens State Bank of Wittenberg (Wis.), 1973—, asst. v.p., br. mgr., Eland, Wis., 1975—. Pres., Maple Hills Golf Course Women's League, 1977-78. Mem. Am. Women Bankers Assn. Lutheran. Club: Maple Hills Golf. Home: Rt 1 Box 91 Tigerton WI 54486 Office: Box A Eland WI 54427

KRIVAL, MOLLY PENSON, educator, speech pathologist; b. N.Y.C., Nov. 19, 1925; d. Michael and Cele Penson; B.A., U. Mo., 1947, M.A., 1949; Ph.D. (Office Vocat. Rehab. fellow 1961-62, VA fellow 1962-65), U. Wis., Madison, 1965; m. Arthur S. Krival, Dec. 25, 1947; children—David, Michael, Stephen, Catherine. Asst. instr. U. Mo., 1947-49; speech correctionist Boone county (Mo.), 1949-50, Chgo. public schs., 1950-51; asst. instr. U. Kans., 1951-53, Kans. State U., 1954-60; clin. supr. U. Wis., Madison, 1961-65; asso. prof. communicative disorders U. Wis., Whitewater, 1971—; chief speech pathology VA Hosp., Madison, 1965-67; lectr. Kenyatta Hosp., Nairobi, 1968-70; mem. Gov. Wis. Com. Study Spl. Needs of Deaf, 1978-79. Coordinator, Congl. Action Com. Wis., 1976-81. Undergrad. teaching grantee U. Wis., 1980-81. Mem. Am. Speech, Lang. and Hearing Assn., Wis. Speech, Lang., Hearing Assn. (pres. 1978-79), Council State Assn. Presidents (sec. 1979). Home: 1690 Red Oak Dr Stoughton WI 53589 Office: Center Comunicative Disorders U Wis Whitewater WI 53190

KROCH, CARLA TERESA, temporary employment service co. exec.; b. Bklyn., Oct. 23, 1936; d. Charles Carl and Renee T. (DeMarco) K.; B.A., Hofstra U., 1959. Vice-pres. pres. Tempositions, Inc., N.Y.C., 1962-71; gen. mgr. TAD, Inc., N.Y.C., 1971-72; gen. mgr. City Wide Temporary Service, N.Y.C., 1972-74; news corr. Bergen Even Record, Va. Cablevision, Pompton Lakes, N.J., 1974—; pres. Status Temporary Help Co., Palisades Park, N.J., 1981-82; nat. field service rep. Career/Temp Force, Inc., 1980-81 account exec./personnel mgr. Western Temporary Services, Inc. Mem. Nat. Assn. Female Execs., Am. Mgmt. Assn., Profl. and Bus. Women, Assn. Temporary Contractors, Internat. Assn. Personnel Women.

KRODY, NANCY EILEEN, editor; b. Cin., July 13, 1939; d. John L. and Anna Eileen (Anderson) K.; B.A. (Univ. scholar, Am. Bapt. scholar), Ohio State U., 1960, postgrad., 1960-62; postgrad. (Ohio Bapt. Edn. scholar) Crozer Theol. Sem., 1962-66. Library asst. Bucknell Library, Crozer Theol. Sem., 1962-64; adminstrv. sec. United Ch. Bd. for Homeland Ministries, Phila., 1964-73, mem. corp. bd., 1975-81; mng. editor Jour. Ecumenical Studies, Temple U., Phila., 1973—; pres. Ken-Kro Assos., fin. mgmt., 1980—. Bd. dirs. Christian Assn., U. Pa., 1973-78; mem. adv. commn. on women in church and society United Ch. of Christ, 1975-79; coordinator Phila. Task Force on Women in Religion, also editor Genesis III, 1973—; mem. commn. on women in ministry Nat. Council Chs., 1976-80; treas., co-coordinator United Ch. Coalition for Gay Concerns, 1975-79, ecumenical liaison, 1981—; cons. on gay concerns Kirkridge Retreat Center, 1977-79, New Wineskins Research Center, 1979. Mem. United Ch. of Christ. Contbr. articles to various jours. Home: PO Box 6315 Philadelphia PA 19139 Office: Jour Ecumenical Studies Temple U 022-38 Philadelphia PA 19122

KROEGER, MARGARET ROSE, sales and mktg. co. exec.; b. Portland, June 19, 1949; d. Donald W. Kroeger; B.S., U. Wis., 1972. Vice-pres. mktg. Nev. Hotel div. Towne Realty, Inc., 1978-79; corp. dir. sales R & B Interprises, Los Angeles, 1979-81; v.p. mktg. A/QUO/D Group Assos., Inc., Los Angeles, 1981—; pres. MK Enterprises, Los Angeles, 1982—. Mem. Los Angeles C. of C., Hotel Sales Mgmt. Assn. Internat. (dir. Los Angeles chpt. 1980—), Travel Research Assn., Sales and Mktg. Execs., Nat. Tour Brokers Assn., Am. Soc. Personnel Adminstrn., Am. Soc. Tng. and Devel. Office: 1964 Westwood Blvd Suite 405 Los Angeles CA 90025

KROGER, ALTHEA P., state legislator; b. Chgo., Oct. 9, 1946; B.A., St. Louis U., 1969; postgrad. St. Michael's Coll., Winooski, Vt., 1974; M.A. candidate U. Vt.; m. Joseph Kroger; 1 son. Mem. Vt. Ho. Reps., 1977-78, 79-80, 81—, ho. Democratic asst. leader, 1979-80, 81—. Mem. Essex Junction (Vt.) Bd. Civil Authority; mem. Essex Town Dem. Com., Chittenden County Dem. Com., Vt. State Dem. Com.; mem. Renal adv. bd. U. Vt.-Montpelier Med. Center; active Ret. Srs. Vol. Program; Church St. Community Center. Roman Catholic. Office: Vt Ho Reps State Ho Montpelier VT 05602 *

KROGER, LAURIE LOUISE RHODES, univ. ofcl.; b. Casper, Wyo., Jan. 22, 1953; d. Edwin and Dolly (Harman) R.; B.A., U. Wyo., 1976, M.A., 1977. Asst. dean students U. Wyo., Laramie, 1978; m. Kenneth J. Kroger. Mem. Colo./Wyo. Assn. Women Deans, Adminstrs. and Counselors, Assn. Fraternity Advisors, Pi Beta Phi, Phi Kappa Phi. Home: 1516 Grand Ave Apt 105 Laramie WY 82070 Office: University of Wyoming PO Box 3135 Laramie WY 82071

KROHN, ALBERTINE, chemist, educator; b. Toledo, Nov. 28, 1924; d. Albert Herman and Bertha Marie (Rath) K.; B.S. in Chemistry, summa cum laude, U. Toledo, 1946, M.S. in Chemistry, 1949; M.S. in Chemistry, U. Mich., 1951, Ph.D. in Phys. Chemistry, 1956. Research asst. Ill. State Geol. Survey, 1946; instr. math. and chemistry U. Toledo, 1947-51, asst. prof. chemistry, 1951-57, asso. prof., 1957-63, prof., 1963—; cons. in field. Chmn. music com. St. Paul's Lutheran Ch., Toledo, 1972-77, trustee, 1980—. Recipient Gold T award U. Toledo Alumni Assn., 1973. Fellow Ohio Acad. Sci.; mem. Am. Chem. Soc., Electrochem. Soc.; Sigma Xi, Phi Kappa Phi (nat. pres., chmn. bd. dirs. 1972-77, trustee Found. 1969-80, Disting. Mem. award 1977), Delta Kappa Gamma, Pi Mu Epsilon. Contbr. chpts. to books and articles to profl. jours. Home: 5679 Monroe St Apt 711 Sylvania OH 43560 Office: University of Toledo Toledo OH 43606

KROL, SUSAN AGNES, real estate broker; b. Lawrenceville, N.J., Dec. 11, 1948; d. Stephen Joseph and Rose Marie Krol; degree Rider Coll., Trenton, 1966, Trenton State U., 1973. Engaged in real estate bus., 1961—; broker, owner Krol Realtors, Princeton, N.J., 1971—; real estate broker, Fla. Recipient various sales awards. Mem. Nat. Assn. Female Execs., N.J. Assn. Comml. Realtors, N.E. Region Comml. Realtors, Somerset County Bd. Realtors, Mercer County Bd. Realtors, Hunterdon County Bd. Realtors, Middlesex County Bd. Realtors, Princeton Real Estate Group (exec. dir. 1978-80). Unitarian. Club: Princeton Women's Athletic Assn. Address: 1000 State Rd Princeton NJ 08540 also 3912 S Ocean Blvd PH-12 Highland Beach FL 33431

KROLL, EVELYN BRENNAN, sporting goods mfg. corp. exec.; b. Staten Island, N.Y., Oct. 5, 1927; d. John Cornelius and Evelyn May (Sanford) Maher; student Hunter Coll., 1949-57; m. John L. Kroll, Dec. 29, 1966; children by previous marriage—John and James Brennan; 1 stepdau., Sharon Kroll. Tchr. public schs., N.J., 1952-53; advt. rep. N.Y. Times, 1954-60, asst. dir. sch. and camp advt. dept., 1960-65; prin. Sanmarev Advt. Agy., Stamford, Conn., 1965-67; dir. advt. and public relations Jayfro Corp., Waterford, Conn., 1968-72, v.p. mktg. and public relations, 1972-79, pres., dir., 1979—; co-founder, dir. Nat. Catalog Distbn. Corp., Harbor City, Calif., 1973; co-founder, mng. editor Nat. Trade Newsletter, 1973—; founder Kroll Press, Pub. and Advt. Co., Waterford, 1978. Trustee, Eugene O'Neill Theater Center, Waterford and N.Y.C., 1974-79; corporation Southeastern Conn. YMCA, Norwich, 1982—. Mem. Nat. Sporting Goods Assn. (sustaining), Sporting Goods Mfrs. Assn. (steering com. ann. internat. conv. 1976-79), Nat. Sch. Supply and Equipment Assn. (com. equipment for handicapped 1977), Am. Sports Edn. Inst., Friends of Mitchell Coll. (New London, Conn.) Fundraising Orgn., SE Conn. C. of C. (dir. 1982—). Clubs: La Coquille (Palm Beach); Delray Beach (Fla.); N.Y.U. (N.Y.C.); 2001 (Dallas). Author: (with John L. Kroll and Frank Smith) It Doesn't Pay to Work Too Hard, 1977; pub., editor: Blueprint for Safety in Sports and Recreation, 1978; regular mktg. and salesmanship columnist The Sporting Goods Dealer mag., 1974-79; contbr. articles to other publs. in field. Home: 535 Pequot Ave New London CT 06320 also 4201 S Ocean Blvd Highland Beach FL 33431 Office: Jayfro Corp PO Box 400 Hartford Turnpike Waterford CT 06385

KROMHOUT, ORA MORLIER, instructional systems designer; b. New Orleans, Nov. 26, 1925; d. Dudley Hypolite and Wilhelmine Louise (Cooper) Morlier; B.A., Newcomb Coll., Tulane U., 1945; M.S., U. Ill., 1951; Ph.D., Fla. State U., 1975; m. Robert Andrew Kromhout, Dec. 21, 1950; children—Sharon, Brian, Ethan. Physicist U.S. Dept. Agr., New Orleans, 1945-50; research physicist Zenith Radio Corp., Chgo., 1952-56; ednl. research asso. Computer Assisted Instrn. Center, Tallahassee, Fla., 1966-72; project mgr. Center for Studies in Vocat. Edn., Tallahassee, 1974—. Mem. Tallahassee Mcpl. Code Enforcement Bd., 1981—; sec. LeMoyne Art Found., 1967-69. Mem. LWV Fla. (v.p., state legis. chmn. 1971-75), LWV Tallahassee (mem. bd. 1958-63, 1980—), IEEE (exec. bd. 1980—), Am. Ednl. Research Assn., Phi Kappa Phi, Phi Delta Kappa, Pi Mu Epsilon, Sigma Delta Epsilon. Home: 206 Westminster Dr Tallahassee FL 32304 Office: College of Edn Fla State Univ Tallahassee FL 32306

KROMINGA, LYNN, cosmetic co. exec.; b. Los Angeles, May 16, 1950; d. Dale E. and Phyllis M. Krominga; B.A. in German, U. Minn., 1972, J.D., 1974; m. Barry Fox, Feb. 26, 1981. Admitted to Minn. bar, 1974, N.Y. bar, 1976; asso. firms in Mpls. and N.Y.C., 1974-77; asso. counsel Am. Express Co., N.Y.C., 1977-80; internat. counsel Revlon, Inc., N.Y.C., 1981—. Mem. Am. Bar Assn., Assn. Bar City N.Y., Phi Beta Kappa. Home: 12 E 88th St New York NY 10028 Office: 1 Scarsdale Rd Tuckahoe NY 10707

KRONBERG, MARIE ANTOINETTE, ins. broker; b. Teaneck, N.J., Oct. 16, 1927; d. Joseph E. and Marie A. (Bloxsom) Quirk; student Georgian Ct. Coll., 1944-48, N.Y. U., 1950-51, Am. Acad. Fin. Mgmt., 1956-57, Northeastern U., 1972-74; children—Marie, Karen, Joanne, Ingrid, Stephen. Owner, Air Conditioning & Elec. Service Corp., Closter, N.J., 1953-59; mgr. Quirk Funeral Homes, Englewood, N.J., 1950-68; with Quirk Enterprises, Englewood, 1967-75; ind. ins. broker, Marblehead, Mass., 1975—. Pres., Children's Ward Jr. League, 1951-53; sec. CD, 1950; bd. dirs. Office for Children, Plymouth, 1974-76, Lynn Girls' Club, 1973-74. Mem. LWV, Nat. Assn. Female Execs. Republican. Roman Catholic. Address: PO Box 973 Marblehead MA 01945

KRONEBUSCH, PATRICIA LOUISE, state senator; b. Mpls., Mar. 17, 1927; d. James Raymond and Luella Louise (Anez) Keller; B.A., Coll. of St. Teresa, Winona, Minn., 1948; M.S., Winona State U., 1969; m. Paul J. Kronebusch, May 30, 1949; children—Paula, Anne, Carol, Mary, Barbara, James, Stephanie, Kathleen. Tchr., Rollingstone, Minn., 1971-80; mem. Minn. Senate, 1980—. Active LWV; mem. Winona Sch. Bd. Dist. 861, 1973-80. mem. Nat. Order of Women Legislators. Ind. Republican. Roman Catholic. Office: Room 133 State Office Bldg Saint Paul MN 55155

KRONEGGER, MARIA ELISABETH, educator; b. Graz, Austria, Sept. 23, 1932; came to U.S., 1962, naturalized, 1968; d. Karl and Josefine (Sparovitz) K.; grad. Karl-Franzens Universitat, Austria, 1960; postgrad. Sorbonne, Paris, 1953-55; M.A. in English and Am. Lit., Kans. U., 1958; Ph.D. in French and Humanities, Fla. State U., 1960. Instr. French, German and Humanities, Fla. State U., 1958-60; mem. faculty Internat. Coll., St. Gallen, Switzerland, 1961-62; asst. prof. Hollins (Va.) Coll., 1962-64; asst. prof. French and comparative lit. Mich. State U., East Lansing, 1964-67, assoc. prof., 1967-70, prof., 1970—. Bd. dirs. World Inst. of Phenomenology, 1980—. Fulbright scholar, 1957-60; Ford Found. grantee, 1965-66. Mem. MLA, AAUP, Am. Soc. Aesthetics, Am. Comparative Lit. Assn., Semiotic Soc. Am., Chinese Comparative Lit. Assn., S. Atlantic MLA, Société Jean Giraudoux, Brit. Comparative Lit. Assn., Internat. Assn. Philosophy, Fédération Internationale des Langues et Littératures Modernes, Société Paul Claudel. Roman Catholic. Author: James Joyce and Associate Image Makers, 1968; Impressionist Literature, 1973; contbr. numerous articles on 17th and 20th century French and English lit., lit. and phenomenology to scholarly publs. Home: 351 Oakhill Ave Apt 307 East Lansing MI 48823 Office: Wells Hall 502 Mich State U East Lansing MI 48824

KRONSCHNABEL, DARLENE MARY, author; b. Rushford, Wis., July 26, 1932; d. Charles Austin and Theresa Mary (Wesmarovich) Doughty; secretarial diploma Waukesha (Wis.) Tech. Inst., 1964; student various U. Wis. extension courses; m. Gerald Leo Kronschnabel, June 2, 1951; children—Robert, Patricia, Jean, Mary. Weekly news corr. Lake Country Reporter, Hartland, Wis., 1964-65; rural life editor The Spirit, Cath. diocesan newspaper, Green Bay, Wis., 1968-70, news editor, 1970-72; food columnist Brown County Pub. Co., Denmark, Wis., 1972—, North Central Asso. Pubs., Durand, Ill., 1974—, Ocooch Mountain News, Gillingham, Wis., 1978-81; tchr. classes in field, 1976—; author: The Country Kitchen Cookbook, 1975, The Cookie Cookbook, 1977, The Country Bread Cookbook, 1978, Diabetic Dining Cookbook, 1979, Low Calorie Cookbook, 1981; (weekly food-in-history column) Recipes From a Country Kitchen, 1972—, (column) From My Country Kitchen, Farm Wife News, 1973-76; also articles. Mem. Nat. Fedn. Press Women (1st place award personal column 1974, 75), Wis. Press Women (treas. 1976-78, 1st place award press women contest 1969-70, 72-80, 1st place award weekly column 1977-80), Wis. Regional Writers Assn. (pres. 1976—), Council Wis. Writers (dir. 1979—), Newspaper Food Editors and Writers Assn. Roman Catholic. Address: 1303 Lost Dauphin Rd De Pere WI 54115

KROON, PHYLLISS ELLAINE, county govt. ofcl.; b. Sioux Center, Iowa, Dec. 25, 1951; d. Richard H. and Anna (DeGroot) K.; B.A., Northwestern Iowa U., 1974. Mem. staff Sioux County Assessor's Office, Orange City, Iowa, 1974—, dep. assessor, 1977-78, assessor, 1978—; chmn. Computer Users Group Iowa Counties, 1981-82. Mem. Internat. Assn. Assessing Officers, Am. Soc. Appraisers (asso.), Inst. Iowa Cert. Assessors, Iowa Assessors Assn. (dist. vice chmn. 1981-82). Republican. Mem. Reformed Ch. Am. Club: Sioux Golf and Country. Home: 609 Florida Ave SW Apt 2 Orange City IA 51041 Office: 210 Central Ave SW Orange City IA 51041

KROSKA, RITA CAROLINE ANN, nurse, educator; b. Duelm, Minn., July 6, 1921; d. Anthony (Tony) John and Alma Mary (Herbst) Kroska; B.S. in Nursing, Cath. U. Am., 1945; M.S. in Nursing Edn., 1956; cert. nurse-midwife Cath. Maternity Inst., 1948; M.P.H., U. Minn., 1961, Ph.D. in Anthropology, 1965. Instr. in nurse-midwifery Cath. Maternity Inst., Santa Fe, 1948-57; asst. prof. Sch. Public Health U. Minn., Mpls., 1965-71; prof. nursing U. N.Mex., Albuquerque, 1971-72, Marquette U., Milw., 1972-74, Mankato State U., Minn., 1974-76, Coll. of St. Teresa, Winona, Minn., 1976-78; asso. prof. U. Tex., El Paso, 1978—; Disting. Vis. Sorrel prof., holder Anise J. Sorrell chair in nursing Troy (Ala.) State U., 1982-83; chairperson Luna Inst., Inc., Albuquerque. Mem. Am. Coll. Nurse-Midwives, Am. Anthrop. Assn., Am. Nurses Assn., Nurses Assn. Am. Coll. Ob-Gyn, Tex. Perinatal Assn. Roman Catholic. Contbr. articles in field to profl. jours. Home: 735 Calle del Ensalmo Green Valley AZ 85614

KROSSNER, RHONDA PARRELLA, psychologist; b. Mt. Vernon, N.Y., Dec. 29, 1951; d. Joseph and Ida (Cornacchia) Parrella; B.S. summa cum laude, Fordham U., 1973, M.A. (NIMH fellow), 1975, postgrad., 1975—; m. William J. Krossner, Jr., Sept. 4, 1977. Vice pres. Psy Minn. Corp., Duluth, 1977—. Mem. Nat. Acad. Neuropsychologists, Am. Psychol. Assn., Phi Beta Kappa. Home: PO Box 3047 Duluth MN 55803 Office: 915 E 1st St Duluth MN 55805

KRUCKEBERG, MARJORIE ANN WADDLE, social worker; b. Chuckey, Tenn., Nov. 18, 1931; d. Dana George and Lucy Ann (Squibb) Waddle; B.A., Tusculum Coll., 1950; M.S.W., Tulane U., 1958; m. Frederick Lloyd Kruckeberg, May 29, 1958; children—Lloyd Edward, Kenneth Albert. Child welfare worker Greene County, Greeneville, Tenn., 1954-57; caseworker Children's Bur., New Orleans, 1958-59; child welfare worker Orleans Parish Child Welfare, 1959-61, children's worker, 1961-62; caseworker Amarillo-Potter County Child Welfare, 1964-65, supr. I, 1965-66, supr. II, 1966-67; chief social worker, adminstr. support services Amarillo State Center for Human Devel., 1967-81, adminstr. clin. services, 1981—; adj. prof. social work dept. W. Tex. State U. Mem. benevolent com. Paramount Christian Ch.; mem. social work bd. W. Tex. State U. Lic. social psychotherapist. Mem. Acad. Cert. Social Workers, Nat. Assn. Social Workers (sec. 1967, unit dir. 1982—), Am. Assn. Retarded Citizens, Tex. Assn. Retarded Citizens, Am. Assn. Mental Deficiency, Social Services Forum (v.p. 1980), High Plains Women's Polit. Caucus, Tex. Public Employees Assn., Women's Internat. Bowling Congress (past league pres.). Democrat. Mem. Christian Ch. (Disciples of Christ). Home: PO Box 3489 Amarillo TX 79106 also 3909 Kileen Amarillo TX 79109 Office: PO Box 3070 Amarillo TX 79106

KRUCKEBERG, VICKY LEE, home economist; b. Alton, Ill., Nov. 13, 1951; d. Kenneth and Hertha May (Brewer) K.; B.S., So. Ill. U., Carbondale, 1974, M.S., 1975. Grad. teaching asst. So. Ill. U., 1974-75; saleswoman Paul Harris Stores, St. Louis, 1975; textile conservator U.S. Cav. Mus., Ft. Riley, Kans., 1979, N.Y. State Parks, Recreation and Historic Preservation Dept., 1980—; instr. clothing and textiles Kans. State U., Manhattan, 1975-80. Recipient Home Econs. Faculty Research award Kans. State U., 1977, Grad. Sch. Faculty Research award, 1978. Mem. Am. Assn. Mus., Am. Assn. State and Local History, Am. Inst. Conservation, Costume Soc. Am., Assn. Coll. Profs. Textile and Clothing, Am. Home Econs. Assn. Republican. Presbyterian. Author papers in field. Address: 89 B Carriage Hill Twin Lakes Apt Clifton Park NY 12065

KRUEGER, CHERYL LEE, fashion merchandiser; b. Bellevue, Ohio, Jan. 1, 1952; d. William Arthur and Audrey Jean (Warner) K.; B.A. (scholar), Bowling Green State U., 1974. Asst. sportswear buyer Burdines, Miami, Fla., 1974-75, mgr. jrs. dept., 1975, dress buyer, 1975-77; dress buyer Limited, Columbus, Ohio, 1977, dress mdse. mgr., 1977-80; v.p. Chaus Sportswear, Inc., N.Y.C., 1980—; pres. Cheryl's Cookies Inc., 1981—. Recipient Leadership award Bowling Green State U., 1972. Mem. Mortar Bd. (v.p.). Republican. Lutheran. Clubs: Ski, Tennis. Research in fashion fabric, Europe, 1978.

KRUEGER, DELORIS VERA, fin. co. exec.; b. Cedarburg, Wis., Feb. 16, 1922; d. Erwin John and Martha Helen K.; student U. Wis., Milw., 1947-48. With IBM acctg. dept. Wis. Electric Power Co., Milw., 1940-45; with cashier's cage Loewi Fin. Cos., Ltd., Milw., 1945-48, asst. cashier, 1948-53, legal cashier, 1953-69, with compliance dept., 1970-74, asst. sec., broker/dealer, 1974-79; v.p., asst. sec. Blunt Ellis & Loewi, 1979—, asst. sec. Loewi Fin. Cos., Ltd., 1977—, sec. five subs. corps. Mem. Beta Sigma Phi. Lutheran. Office: 225 E Mason St Milwaukee WI 53202

KRUEGER, DILYS ANN, ednl. cons.; b. Canton, Ohio, Aug. 27, 1946; d. Thomas Bedford and Mary Marconi Jones; B.A., Evangel Coll., Springfield, Mo., 1969; m. Dietrich Heinz Krueger, Sept. 11, 1971; children—Martin Dietrich, Karl Randolph. Ednl. cons. Discovery Toys, Inc. Treas., Perry Twp. Jaycees Aux., 1976, pres., 1977, chmn. bd., 1979-80; supt. Sunday sch. Bethel Temple, Canton, Ohio, 1970-74; mem. Canton Childbirth Assn., Canton Scholarship Found.; vol. Bloodmobile, ARC; mem. Voters Service, Networking, Inc. Mem. Evangel Coll. Alumni Assn., Ohio Jaycees Aux. (mgr. individual devel. program 1980, Spokette award 1978, Outstanding Local Pres. award 1979, Outstanding Regional Coordinator award 1979), LWV, Ohio Jaycee Women (G.L.O.W. award 1982, Outstanding Exec. Staff Officer award 1982), U.S. Jaycees (mgr. region IV individual devel. program 1982, named One of Top 10 Program Mgrs. in U.S. 1981), Delta Psi Omega. Home: 1433 Saxony Circle NW Canton OH 44708

KRUEGER, PATRICIA LYNN, sales exec.; b. Cleve., Sept. 3, 1952; d. James Stewart and Phyllis Juliet (Schanda) Harrison; student pub. schs., Ohio; m. Darrell Bernard Krueger, Sept. 16, 1972; 1 son, Eric Louis. With Republic Powdered Metal, Brunswick, Ohio, 1968-70, Gowe Printing, Medina, Ohio, 1970-71; With A.I. Root Co., Medina, 1971—, sales promotion/advt. mgr., asst. office mgr., 1975-82, office mgr., 1982—, Deco Candle sales mgr., 1982—; pvt. house painting contractor, 1978—. Mem. City Council, Creston, Ohio, 1978-81. Baptist. Author, illustrator: Busy Bee, 1976. Home: 151 N Main St Creston OH 44217 Office: 623 W Liberty St Medina OH 44256

KRUEGER, VICTORIA SKIDMORE, clin. psychologist; b. Columbus, Ohio, Nov. 6, 1942; d. James Earl and Catherine (Dolby) Skidmore; B.A. with honors in Psychology, Ohio State U., 1964, M.A., 1970, Ph.D. in Clin. Psychology, 1976. Psychologist, Berkeley (Calif.) Child Devel. Center, 1966-67; intern to staff psychologist U. Mich. Psychol. Clinic, 1970-73; staff psychologist to chief psychologist Harding Hosp., Worthington, Ohio, also pvt. practice psychology, 1973-80; pvt. practice clin. psychology, Santa Fe, 1981—; cons. Bur. Indian Affairs, Child Devel. Center, San Juan Mental Health Center. Lic. psychologist, Ohio, N.Mex. Mem. Am. Psychol. Assn., Ohio Psychol. Assn., N.Mex. Psychol. Assn., Nat. Register of Health Care Providers, NOW. Democrat. Club: Sierra. Author: Generalization of Desensitization Techniques, 1971. Home: Route 2 Box 276 Santa Fe NM 87501 Office: 818 Camino Sierra Vista Santa Fe NM 87501

KRUEGER, VIRGINIA C., art cons., educator; b. Batavia, N.Y., Feb. 18, 1933; B.S. in Edn., SUNY, Buffalo; M.S. in Edn., U. So. Calif.; postgrad. U. Calif., San Diego, UCLA Extension; m. Robert Blair Krueger; children—Lisa Carmichael, Paula Leah, Robert Blair. Tchr., Batavia, 1953-54, La Jolla, Calif., 1954-56, Los Angeles City Schs., 1956-57, South Pasadena (Calif.) Public Schs., 1957-62, Poly. Sch., Pasadena, 1966; docent Los Angeles County Mus. Art, 1967—, chmn. docent council, 1974-75; art cons. Los Angeles City Schs., 1976—; art cons., partner Contemporary Art Cons., 1979—. Bd. dirs. Pasadena Art Alliance, 1979-82, Nat. Head Injury Found., 1982—, So. Calif. Head Injury Found., 1981—, Vol. Bur. Pasadena, 1969-70, Los Angeles Jr. Tennis, 1971-72, Am. Field Service, 1973-74, Graphic Arts Council Los Angeles County Mus. Art; chmn. WWW Tennis Tournament, 1966-67; active Center Theatre Group Vols., 1967-69; chmn. docent council Calif. Design, 1976; founder Neurol. Learning Center, Pasadena, 1978, pres. bd. dirs., 1978-82. Mem. Pasadena Art Mus., La Jolla Mus. Modern Art, Mus. Modern Art, Met. Mus. Art. Home: 501 Vallombrosa Dr Pasadena CA 91107 also 9828 La Jolla Farms Rd La Jolla CA 92037

KRUG, ADELE JENSEN (MRS. WALTER JOHN KRUG), educator; b. Thief River Falls, Minn., Mar. 30, 1908; d. Anton Martin Hulbert and Tillie Manspand (Johnson) Jensen; B.A., Gallaudet Coll., 1930; M.S., Cath. U. Am., 1961; m. Walter John Krug, June 18, 1932 (dec. May 1962); children—Janice Krug Riley, Diana Krug Armstrong, Walter F., Warren J. Instr., R.I. Sch. for Deaf, 1930-32; instr. library sci. Gallaudet Coll., Washington, 1955-63, asst. prof., 1963-67, asso. prof., 1967-75. Pres., Stuart Jr. High Sch. PTA, Washington, 1954-56, McKinley High Sch. PTA, 1956-57. Mem. AAUP, ALA, Conv. Am. Instrs. Deaf, Nat. Assn. of Deaf, D.C. Women's Aux., Nat. Luth. Home, Phi Kappa Zeta (nat. alumnae pres. 1954-60). Contbr. to Am. Anns. of Deaf. Home: Crystal Sq W 511 1515 S Jefferson Davis Hwy Arlington VA 22202

KRUGER, BARBARA, audiologist, speech and lang. pathologist; b. Corpus Christi, Tex., Aug. 16, 1944; d. R. N. and Lee (Borden) Walter and Leonard Samelson; B.A. cum laude, Queens Coll., 1967, M.A., 1970; Ph.D., City U. N.Y., 1975; m. Frederick M. Kruger, June 19, 1966. Electroencephalography trainee Kew Gardens Gen. Hosp., 1964; research asst. dept. exptl. neurosurgery Queens Hosp. Center, Jamaica, N.Y., 1964, histologist, research asst., 1967; research asst. visual physiology lab., psychology dept. Queens Coll., 1964-65, speech pathologist Speech and Hearing Center, summer 1968, teaching asst., 1968-69; speech and lang. pathologist spl. edn. program Bklyn. Diocese, 1969-70, coordinator speech, lang. and hearing therapy, 1970-71, coordinator speech, lang. and hearing therapy, coordinator programmed learning, 1971-72, audiologist, 1972-73; research asst. Columbia U., summer 1973; researcher Fowler Meml. Lab. dept. otolaryngology Coll. Physicians and Surgeons, Columbia U., 1974-75; audiol. cons. Kings Park (N.Y.) Psychiat. Center, 1974-75, 77—; audiologist Suffolk Rehab. Center for Physically Handicapped, Commack, N.Y., 1973-75; asst. prof. audiology, dir. hearing research lab. Tchrs. Coll., Columbia U., 1975-78, adj. asst. prof. audiology, 1978—; asst. prof. otolaryngology, dir. audiology and speech lang. pathology dept. otorhinolaryngology Albert Einstein Coll. Medicine, Yeshiva U., Bronx, N.Y., 1978—. Am. Otol. Soc. Research grantee, 1977-79; Spencer Found. grantee, 1976-77; Rehab. Services Adminstrn. fellowship, 1972-74; Office of Edn. fellow, 1971-72; N.Y. State Regents scholar, 1962-67. Mem. Acoustical Soc. Am., Am. Speech-Lang.-Hearing Assn. (legis. council 1977—, chmn. legis. council com. on credentials 1979—, del. corr. 1978-81, chmn. legis. council com. on spl. rules 1982, mem. resolutions com. Region 2, 1981), Am. Nat. Standards Inst. (U.S. del. Internat. Electrotech. Commn. 1982), Audiology Study Group Greater N.Y., Hearing Sci. Study Group N.Y., L.I. Speech and Hearing Assn. (clin. councilor for audiology 1978-80), Met. N.Y. chpt. Acoustical Soc. Am., N.Y. State Speech and Hearing Assn. (mem. com. on audiologic matters 1978—, exec. bd., del. hosps. and agys. 1980-82), Phi Beta Kappa, Sigma Alpha Eta, Psi Chi. Contbr. articles to profl. jours. Home: 37 Somerset Dr Commack NY 11725 Office: Albert Einstein Coll Medicine 1300 Morris Park Ave Room 3C 37 Van Etten Hosp Bronx NY 10461

KRUGER, NORMA JANE, coll. ofcl.; b. Wisconsin Rapids, Wis., Oct. 31, 1924; d. Harrison Harland and Grace Helen (Staffon) Kruger;

student Wis. State Coll. at Stevens Point, 1942-43; B.S., Wis. State Coll. at LaCrosse, 1946; M.S., U. Oreg., 1966; postgrad. (fellow) U. Mo., 1967-68. Owner, mgr. Kruger Cranberry Co., Wisconsin Rapids, 1948-65; pub. sch. tchr., Wis., 1946-58, 59-60, Oreg., 1958-59, 63-64; tchr. Air Force Dependent Schs., Ankara, Turkey, 1960-61, Japan, 1961-62, Okinawa, 1968-69; counselor, instr. Central Oreg. Community Coll., Bend, 1966-67; dir. tchr. placement U. Oreg. Eugene, 1969-72; dir. career devel. placement Edmonds Community Coll., Lynnwood, Wash., 1972-75, dir. counseling, career devel., 1975—; career devel. cons. to bus. and industry. Mem. AAUW (chmn. edn. found.), Am. Assn. Higher Edn. (pres. chpt. 1973-74, 81-82), Am. Personnel and Guidance Assn., N.W. Community Coll. Placement Assn. (pres. 1974-75), N.W. Personnel Mgrs. Assn. (pres. chpt. 1975-76). Democrat. Congregationalist. Club: Soroptimist (chpt. v.p. 1980-81, pres. 1981-82). Office: 20000 W 68th St Edmonds Community College Lynnwood WA 98036

KRUIS, MARY JEAN, psychiat. social worker/adminstr.; b. Jamestown, Mich., Feb. 2, 1925; d. Rolland and Elizabeth Ida K.; student Reformed Bible Coll., 1946-49; A.B., Calvin Coll., 1960; M.S.W., U. Mich., 1962. Lay missionary Christian Reformed Ch.; missionary to Navajo Indians, Church Rock, N.Mex., 1949-57; social worker Midland (Mich.) Family and Children Service, 1962-67; psychiat. social worker Midland County Mental Health Center, Midland, Mich., 1967-72; psychiat. social worker, dir. vol. services for mental health Gratiot County Mental Health Center, Alma, Mich., 1972—. Mem. Nat. Assn. Social Workers. Republican. Mem. Christian Reformed Ch. Home: 201 Pineview Dr Alma MI 48801 Office: 320 Warwick Dr Alma MI 48801

KRULFELD, RUTH MARILYN, anthropologist, educator; b. N.Y.C., Apr. 15, 1931; d. Leon and Frances (Rosenberg) Pulwers; B.A. cum laude, Brandeis U., 1956; Ph.D., 1974; m. Jacob Mendel Krulfeld, Aug. 24, 1964; 1 son, Michael David. Field researcher micro-geographic research farms in Singapore, Malaya, 1951-53; anthrop. research in Jamaica, 1957, Costa Rica, Nicaragua, Panama, 1958, Lombok Indonesia, 1960-62; asst. prof. anthropology, dir. grad. students George Washington U., Washington, 1964-72, asso. prof., 1973-76, prof., 1976—, also dir. spl. grad. research degree program. Currier scholar Yale U., 1958; Found. for Study of Man grantee, 1957; Ford fellow, 1960-62; Am. Council Learned Socs. and Social Sci. Research Council grantee, 1963. Mem. Anthrop. Assn. of Washington, Am. Anthrop. Assn. Jewish. Contbr. articles in field to profl. jours. Home: 4012 N Woodstock St Arlington VA 22207 Office: Dept Anthropology George Washington U Washington 20052

KRUPA, THERESA MARIE, sales exec.; b. Youngstown, Ohio, July 3, 1921; d. Nicholas Anthony and Rose Julia (Cichon) DePaola; student public and pvt. schs., Youngstown; m. Alexander Krupa, Nov. 22, 1942; 1 dau., Theresa Rose Krupa Beggs. Sales clk. McCrory Corp., Youngstown, 1939-42, floor mgr., 1946-49, office mgr., head cashier, payroll clk., 1949-59; office mgr., personnel dir. Ben Franklin Store, Youngstown, 1959-62; sales dir. Goodwill Industries, Inc., Vocat. Rehab. Center, Youngstown, 1962-81, facility cons. and coordinator, 1981—. Dir., Youngstown Traffic Referral Sch., 1972-73. Mem. Internat. Fedn. Bus. and Profl. Women's Clubs, Inc., Nat. Fedn. Bus. and Profl. Women, Ohio Bus. Women's Assn., Youngstown Bus. and Profl. Women's Clubs, Inc. (pres. 1972-73). Democrat. Roman Catholic. Home: 3465 Shelby Rd Youngstown OH 44511 Office: 2747 Belmont Ave Youngstown OH 44505

KRUPNICK, JANICE LEE, psychiat. social worker; b. Newark, Mar. 7, 1950; d. Jacob and Betty (Katz) Krupnick; B.A., Oberlin (Ohio) Coll., 1972; M.S.W., U. Mich., 1974; cert. psychoanalytic psychotherapy (NIMH fellow 1975-77), Mt. Zion Hosp. and Med. Center, San Francisco, 1977; m. Richard Michael Suzman, July 21, 1976. Clin. social worker St. Elizabeth's Hosp., Washington, summer 1973, Long Beach (Calif.) Neuropsychiat. Inst., 1974-75; asst. clin. prof. psychiatry U. Calif., San Francisco, 1977-80, 81—; cons., program analyst NIMH, Rockville, Md., 1980-81; pvt. practice psychotherapy, 1977—. Mem. Nat. Assn. Social Workers, Langley Porter Alumni-Faculty Assn. (pres.), Soc. Psychotherapy Research, Am. Assn. Orthopsychiatry. Author papers in field. Office: 401 Parnassus San Francisco CA 94143

KRUPP, DOROTHY ALENE, ednl. adminstr.; b. Coeur d'Alene, Idaho, June 16, 1924; d. Ernest John and Mabel Willamena (Kettenbeil) Neighorn; M.A., Wayne State U., 1968, B.S.E., 1964; m. Roland Gerald Krupp, July 15, 1944; children—Charlene and Marilyn (twins), Janet, Robert. Dir. cultural enrichment pilot program Port Huron (Mich.) Area Schs., 1965-66; counselor Mich. Employment Service, Port Huron, 1966-77; v.p., dir. Port Huron Sch. Bus., 1977—; corp. v.p. Pontiac Bus. Inst. Schs., Inc., 1980—; pvt. counselor, 1970—; mem. Bd. Career Edn. Planning St. Clair County, 1969-74, Econ. Devel. Corp. City Port Huron, 1978—. Mem. Met. Planning Commn. St. Clair County, 1978—; bd. dirs. United Way, 1974—, Family Service Agy., 1974—, Info. and Referral Crisis Center, 1967—; elder 1st United Presbyn. Ch., 1965—; pres. bd. United Way, 1981, gen. campaign chmn., 1981. Mem. Am. Personnel and Guidance Assn., Nat. Assn. Social Workers, Mich. Coll. Personnel Assn., Mich. Bus. Edn. Assn., Mich. Orgn. Pvt. Vocat. Schs., Nat. Vocat. Counselors, Nat. Employment Counselors, Blue Water Psychology Assn., Port Huron/Marysville C. of C. (chmn. edn. com. 1980—), Nat. Assn. Female Execs., Am. Mgmt. Assn., Am. Soc. Profl. and Exec. Women, Beta Sigma Phi (life). Republican. Home: 3962 Gratiot St Port Huron MI 48060 Office: 511 Fort St Suite 430 Port Huron MI 48060

KRUPP, IRIS MARIE, physician; b. New Orleans, May 1, 1928; d. Philip Joseph and Ione Krupp; B.S. in Zoology, La. State U., Baton Rouge, 1948; M.S. in Parasitology, Tulane U., 1955, Ph.D., 1958, M.D., 1971. Research asst. Amebiasis Project, Tulane U., 1949-53, research and teaching asst. parasitology, 1954-58, instr., 1959-61, asst. prof., 1961-65, asso. prof. psychiatry and neurology, 1966-68, asso. prof. tropical medicine, 1966-76, clin. asso. prof. dermatology, 1976—; instr. vet. parasitology Mich. State U., 1953-54; instr. parasitology U. Mich., summers 1954-55; intern USPHS Hosp., New Orleans, 1971-72; resident dermatology Charity Hosp., New Orleans, 1973-76; research and edn. asso. VA Hosp., New Orleans, 1972-73; mem. ad hoc study group on parasitic diseases U.S. Army Med. Research and Devel. Command, Walter Reed Army Inst. Research, 1973-75, cons. parasitic diseases, 1975-76; pvt. practice medicine, specializing in dermatology, Metairie, La., 1976—; cons. tropical disease Surg. Gen., 1973-76. Mem. Fedn. Am. Socs. Exptl. Biology, Am. Soc. Tropical Medicine and Hygiene, A.C.P., Am. Assn. Immunology, Reticuloendothelial Soc., So. Med. Assn., La., Orleans Parish med. socs., Am. Acad. Dermatology, Dermatology Found., Internat. Soc. Tropical Dermatology, Am. Coll. Cryosurgery, Sigma Xi. Contbr. articles to med. jours. Home: 4357 Folse Dr Metairie LA 70002 Office: 3601 Houma Blvd Suite 410 Metairie LA 70002

KRUSE, ANN GRAY, computer programmer; b. Oklahoma City, Jan. 4, 1941; d. Floyd and Bernice Florence (Follansbee) Gray; A.B., Randolph Macon Woman's Coll., 1963; M.B.A., U. Chgo., 1973; m. Roy Edwin Kruse, Mar. 20, 1971 (dec.). Programming mgr. Ind. Info. Controls, Valparaiso, Ind., 1966-67; systems programmer Nat. Bus. Lists, Inc., Chgo., 1968-69, Am. Steel Foundries, Hammond, Ind., 1970-73; engr. applications programming Bell Helicopter Textron, Fort Worth, 1974-76; lead systems programmer Harris Data Communications, Dallas, 1976-81; sr. systems programmer Lone Star Gas Co., Dallas, 1981-82; sr. software specialist E-Systems, Dallas, 1982—. Republican. Episcopalian. Home: 6128 Blackberry Ln Dallas TX 75248 Office: PO Box 226118 Dallas TX 75266

KRUSE, MARCIA ANN, navy officer; b. Leavenworth, Kans., Aug. 9, 1951; d. Warren LeRoy and Margaret Ann (Inkman) K.; B.S. in Edn., Emporia State U., 1973; postgrad. U. Ark., 1973. High sch. tchr., debate coach U.S.D. 465, Winfield, Kans., 1973-74; commd. ensign U.S. Navy, 1974, advanced through grades to lt., 1978; oceanographic watch officer Naval Facility, Adak, Alaska, 1975-76; officer programs recruiter engrng. programs. Navy Recruiting Dist., Kansas City, Mo., 1976-80; course dir. Inst. Human Resources Mgmt. Sch., Naval Air Sta., Memphis, 1980-82, adminstrv. discipline officer Naval Tech. Tng. Center, Meridian, Miss., 1982—. Vol. Rape Crisis Center,Memphis, 1980-82; mem. Kans. Com. for Prevention of Child Abuse. Decorated Naval Achievement Medal (2). Mem. U.S. Naval Inst., Nat. Assn. for Female Execs., NOW, Federally Employed Women. Democrat. Roman Catholic. Home: 2441 37th Ave Meridian MS 39301

KRUSE-SMITH, MARKENE, magazine editor; b. Cedar Rapids, Iowa, May 8, 1951; d. Richard Walter and Joanne (Kruse) Smith; student U. Colo., 1969-73; B.F.A. in Design, Calif. Inst. Arts, 1974; postgrad. Art Center Coll. Design, 1974, UCLA, 1980. Copy girl Cedar Valley Daily Times, Vinton, Iowa, 1966-69; staff writer Colo. Daily, Boulder, 1970-73; coll. bd. mem. Mademoiselle mag., 1969-73; editorial asst. Multihull Sailing mag., 1973; editorial asst. Petersen's PhotoGraphic mag., 1973-74, asso. editor, then movie editor, 1974-79, sr. editor, 1979-82; editorial dir. VideoCom. mag., 1982—; contbg. editor Rolling Stone mag., 1978-81; cons. in field, also ind. filmmaker. Recipient Bronze medallion for directing and producing short film Clowning Around, V.I. Internat. Film Festival, 1977. Mem. Info. Film Producers Am., Am. Film Inst., Women in Communications, Sigma Delta Chi. Methodist. Office: 8490 Sunset Blvd Los Angeles CA 90069

KSIAZEK, MARILYNN CHRISTINE, nutrition cons.; b. Scranton, Pa., Mar. 15, 1950; d. Francis A. and Madelyn D. (Shander) K.; B.S. in Home Econs., Marywood Coll., 1972, M.S. in Nutrition, 1979. Dietetic intern Mass. Gen. Hosp., Boston, 1973; therapeutic dietitian Custom Food Mgmt. Systems, Kingston, Pa.; therapeutic dietitian Moses Taylor Hosp., Scranton, 1973-74, chief dietitian, 1975-77, coordinator nutritional services, 1977—, asst. dir. food services, 1979—; pvt. cons., Dunmore, Pa., 1979—; mem. faculty Worthington Campus, Pa. State U., Dunmore, 1980—; nutrition cons. Vis. Nurse Assn., Scranton, 1979—, Emergency and Safety Programs Inc., Wilmington, Del., 1981—, Patient Care Corp., Kingston, 1982—; mem. project council, bd. dirs. Meals on Wheels Program, Lackawanna County, Pa., 1979-80, adj. mem., 1980—. Recipient Cert. of Appreciation, Custom Food Mgmt. Systems, 1977, Mgr. of Month award, 1977. Mem. Am. Diabetes Assn. (Outstanding Dietitian award NE Pa. chpt. 1978), Am. Dietetic Assn., Pa. Dietetic Assn., NE Pa. Dietetic Assn., Nutrition Soc., Am. Soc. Enteral and Parenteral Nutrition, Am. Heart Assn. (mem. profl. planning com. Keystone chpt. 1979—), Nat. Fedn. Bus. and Profl. Women's Clubs (chpt. rec. sec.), Am. Biog. Inst. Research Assn. Republican. Roman Catholic. Club: Jr. Century (Scranton). Home: 302 Cleveland St Olyphant PA 18447 Office: 1416 Monroe Ave Dunmore PA 18509

KUBALE, CHRISTINE BRIGHT, clin. social worker; b. Danville, Ky., Apr. 28, 1929; d. Robert Harding and Katherine (Letcher) Bright; A.B., Centre Coll., Danville, 1950; M.S.W., U. Ky., 1974; m. Rube Travis Kubale, Sept. 28, 1950; children—Travis Laney, Jane Letcher. Social worker Ky. State Hosp., 1965-68; area team leader, drug coordinator, county coordinator Community Mental Health-Mental Retardation Bd., Danville, 1968-79, coordinator consultation and edn., 1979-82; pvt. practice psychotherapy, Danville, 1982—; mem. Ky. Mental Health Coalition, W. Bluegrass Dist. Health Bd. Mem. Assn. Creative Change in Religious and Other Social Systems, Ky. Soc. Clin. Social Workers, Am. Orthopsychiat. Assn., AAUW. Democrat. Presbyterian. Home: Lexington Rd Danville KY 40422 Office: 219 S 4th St Danville KY 40422

KUBES, L. KELLY, fin. planner; b. Hackensack, N.J., Oct. 8, 1946; d. Otto A. and Esther (Holden) Vollertson; A.A., St. Petersburg Jr. Coll., 1981; student U. S. Fla., 1964-66; div.; children—Jarrod Lee, Dennis Edward. Bookkeeper, Corsaire, Clearwater Beach, Fla., 1973-74; office mgr., bookkeeper Bramlett Mfg., Clearwater, Fla., 1974-76; office mgr. H & S Swanson Tool, Pinellas Park, Fla., 1977-78; adminstrv. v.p. Cert. Fin. Analysis, Inc., Clearwater, 1979—. Sec., Skycrest Highland Pines Civic Assn. Inc., 1981. Mem. Suncoast Network, Internat. Assn. Fin. Planners. Club: Turning Point.

KUBICKI, FRANCES LYNN, mktg. co. exec.; b. Wyandotte, Mich., Jan. 20, 1948; d. Francis Woodrow and Edna May (Bradley) Cartwright; student Wayne State U., 1974-75, Henry Ford Community Coll., 1975—, U. Mich., 1980; m. George T. Kubicki, Jan. 28, 1966 (div. 1973); children—Keith Allen, Eric Todd. Legal clk. Household Fin. Corp., Dearborn, Mich., 1968-69; secretarial position Uniroyal Inc., Allen Park, Mich., 1970-72, sales asst. Latex Fiber Industries div., 1972-74; adminstrv. asst. r.r. investigations Consol. Rail Corp., Detroit, 1974-79; v.p. Joyce-Roger, Inc., Birmingham, Mich., 1979—, Elcometer, Inc., Birmingham, 1979—, Met. North Counseling Assos., P.C., 1981—; dir. A-R Tech. Products, Inc., 1981—. Co-leader Divorced Women's Support Group, 1974-75, Downriver Women's Forum, 1975-77; bd. advs. Downriver Unity Ch., 1975-76. Recipient Howard C. Flynn award Fedn. Socs. Coating Tech., 1979. Mem. Soc. Mfg. Engrs., ASTM, Nat. Assn. Corrosion Engrs., Nat. Assn. Female Execs., NOW, Fedn. Orgns. for Profl. Women. Democrat. Home: 544 S Fox Hills Dr Bloomfield Hills MI 48013 Office: Elcometer Inc 155 S Bates St Birmingham MI 48011

KUBISTAL, PATRICIA BERNICE, elem. sch. prin.; b. Chgo., Jan. 19, 1938; d. Edward John and Bernice Mildred (Lenz) Kubistal; A.B. cum laude, Loyola U. of Chgo., 1959, A.M., 1964, A.M., 1965, Ph.D., 1968; postgrad. Chgo. State Coll., 1962, Ill. Inst. Tech., 1963, State U. Iowa, 1963, Nat. Coll. Edn., 1974-75. With Chgo. Bd. Edn., 1959—, tchr., 1959-63, counselor, 1963-65, adminstrv. intern, 1965-66, asst. to dist. supt., 1968-69, prin. spl. edn. sch., 1969-75, prin. Simpson Sch., 1975-76, Brentano Sch., 1976—; supr. Lake View Evening High Sch., 1982—; lectr. Loyola U. Sch. Edn., Nat. Coll. Edn. Grad. Sch., Mundelein Coll.; coordinator Upper Bound Program of U. Ill. Circle Campus, 1966-68. Active Crusade of Mercy; mem. com. Ill. Constl. Conv., 1967-69; mem. Citizens Sch. Com., 1969-71; mem. edn. com. Field Mus., 1971; ednl. adv. North Side Chgo. PTA Region, 1975; chmn. Pathfinder dist. Boy Scouts Am., 1978-80; bd. govs. Loyola U., 1961—, chmn. alumni scholarship com., 1982. NDEA grantee, 1963, NSF grantee, 1965, HEW Region 5 grantee for drug edn., 1974; recipient Outstanding Intern award Nat. Assn. Secondary Sch. Prins., 1966; named Outstanding History Tchr., Chgo. Public Schs., 1963, Outstanding Ill. Educator, 1970, Outstanding Women of Ill., 1970; St. Luke's-Logan Sq. Community Person of Yr., 1977. Mem. Ill. Personnel and Guidance Assn., NEA, Ill., Chgo. edn. assns., Am. Acad. Polit. and Social Sci., Aux. Chgo. Prins. Assn. (pres.), Chgo. Prins. Club, Nat. Council Adminstrv. Women, Chgo. Council Exceptional Children, Chgo. Council Fgn. Relations, Chgo. Urban League, Loyal Christian Benevolent Assn., Kappa Gamma Pi (pres. Chgo. chpt. 1979-80), Pi Gamma Mu, Phi Delta Kappa, Delta Kappa Gamma (editor-in-chief Lambda State Newscater), Delta Sigma Rho, Phi Sigma Tau. Book rev. editor of Chgo. Prins. Jour., 1970-76; editor-in-chief Chgo. Prins. Reporter, 1981—. Home: 5111 N Oakley Ave Chicago IL 60625 Office: 2723 N Fairfield St Chicago IL 60647

KUCHENBECKER, RUTH HELEN, constrn., carpet co. exec.; b. Neenah, Wis., Mar. 4, 1937; d. August Herman and Rose E. (Buss) Peapenburg; student public schs., Neenah; m. Alfred Paul Kuchenbecker, Nov. 16, 1957; children—Ann Marie, Mary Kay, Amy Lynn. Sec., bookkeeper Wis. Paper Group, Menasha, 1955-65, Towne, Inc., Mech. Contractors, Appleton, Wis., 1967-69; partner, sec.-treas. Kuchenbecker Builders, Neenah, 1968—; sec.-treas. Wholesale Builders Supply, Inc., 1970—; owner, pres. Kuchenbecker Carpets Inc., Neenah, 1975—; partner D&K Leasing, Neenah, 1979—, Kuchenbecker Custom Woodworking, 1981—. Mem. Nat. Right to Work Com. Mem. Nat. Assn. Women in Constrn. (past pres., bd. dirs. Fox Valley chpt.), Nat. Assn. Home Builders Women's Aux. Republican. Lutheran. Home: 2689 Oakridge Rd Neenah WI 54956 Office: 1573 N Deerwood Neenah WI 54956

KUCHNIR, FRANCA TAGLIABUE, physicist, educator; b. Russe, Bulgaria, July 18, 1935; came to U.S., 1960, naturalized, 1973; d. Luigi and Matilde (Perez) Tagliabue; B.S., U. San Paulo, 1958; M.S., U. Ill., 1962, Ph.D., 1965; m. Moyses Kuchnir, Aug. 6, 1960; children—Louis, Deborah. Research asst. U. Ill., 1960-65, asst. prof., 1969-70; fellow nuclear physics Argonne Nat. Lab., 1966-68, asst. physicist, 1970-71; fellow med. physics U. Chgo., 1971-73, asst. prof., 1973-74, assoc. prof., 1974—, dir. med. physics, 1980—. Mem. Am. Phys. Soc., Am. Assn. Physicists in Medicine, Radiol. Soc. North Am. Contbr. articles in field to profl. jours. Office: 950 E 59th St Chicago IL 60637

KUCK, MARIE ELIZABETH BUKOVSKY, ret. pharmacist; b. Milw., Aug. 3, 1910; d. Frank Joseph and Marie (Nozina) Bukovsky; Ph.C., U. Ill., 1933; m. John A. Kuck, Sept. 20, 1945 (div. Nov. 1954). Pharmacist, tchr. Am. Hosp., Chgo., 1936-38, St. Joseph Hosp., Chgo., 1938-40, Ill. Masonic Hosp., Chgo., 1940-45; chief pharmacist St. Vincent Hosp., Los Angeles, 1946-48, St. Joseph Hosp., Santa Fe, 1949-51; dir. pharm. services St. Luke's Hosp., San Francisco, 1951-76; pharmacist Mission Neighborhood Health Center, San Francisco, 1968-72; mem. peer rev. com. Drug Utilization Com., Blue Shield Calif. and Pharm. Soc. San Francisco. Recipient Bowl of Hygeia award Calif. Pharm. Assn., 1966. Mem. No., Calif. (legis. chmn. aux. 1967-69, chmn. fund raising luncheon 1953-71, pres. San Francisco aux. 1974), Nat., Am., No. Calif. (pres. 1955-56, pres. San Francisco aux. 1965-66, editor ofcl. publ. 1967-70), San Francisco (sec. 1977-79, treas. 1979-80, pres. 1982-83; Pharmacist of Yr. award 1978) pharm. socs., Am. Pharm. Assn. (pres. No. Calif. br. 1956-57, nat. sec. women's aux. 1970-72, hon. pres. aux. 1975—), Calif. Council Hosp. Pharmacists (organizer 1962, sec.-treas. 1962-66), Am. Soc. Hosp. Pharmacists, Assn. Western Hosps. (gen. chmn. hosp. pharmacy sect. conv. San Francisco 1958), Internat. Pharmacy Congress (U.S. del. Brussels 1958, Copenhagen 1960), Fedn. Internationale Pharmaceutique, Lambda Kappa Sigma. Home: 2261 33d Ave San Francisco CA 94116

KUCSERA, ABBIE KENT, author; b. Detroit, Mar. 14, 1916; d. Walter Green and Marion Ella (Szekrak-Miller) Kent; student Detroit Inst. Technology, 1954; m. Carl Coleman Kucsera, Oct. 17, 1936 (dec. Oct. 28, 1981); children—Lorraine Joan, Carl Walter. Journalist, editor Pontiac (Mich.) Press, 1947-57; mng. editor Inter-Lake News, Walled Lake (Mich.) Bur., 1959-61; promotion, publicity writer City of Sunrise (Fla.), 1961-62; writer-editor On-the-Go, mag., Fort Lauderdale, Fla., 1963; copywriter Fla. Advt. Inc., Fort Lauderdale, 1963; author: Prize Winning Watercolors, North America, 1964; Best of Show, Flower Arrangements, America, 1964; editor (as Jan Malcolm) Hell Turned Wrong Side Out, 1965-66. Recipient Appreciation cert. Palm Beach County Bar Assn., 1975; poet laureate SE Fla. Dairy Inst., 1965. Mem. Forest History Soc. Baptist. Home: Whispering Pines PO Box 209 Georgetown FL 32039

KUENZLER, WANDA FAYE, nurse; b. Celina, Ohio, Dec. 18, 1950; d. Sherman William and Lucretia Arlene (Bolenbaugh) Marsee; B.S.N. cum laude, Okla. Bapt. U., 1973; postgrad. Central State U., 1975, Ball State U., 1976; m. Wolfgang Kuenzler, Aug. 24, 1973; children—Heidi Samantha, Katie Arlene. Staff nurse Presbyn. Hosp., Oklahoma City, 1973-75; sch. nurse Doddseur, Spangdahlen Air Base, W.Ger., 1976-78; staff nurse Huerfano Meml. Hosp., Walsenburg, Colo., 1979-80, dir. nursing, 1980—. Adv. bd. nursing programs Otero and Trinidad State Jr. Colls., 1980—; mem. Child Abuse Bd., Spangdahlem Air Base, 1976-78; young adult minister United Ch. of Walsenburg, 1981; preceptor Rural Internship Program, 1980-81. Served with U.S. Army, 1971-73. Mem. Colo. Hosp. Soc. Nursing Service Adminstrs., Am. Nurses Assn., Assn. Infection Control Practitioners. Democrat. Contbr. articles to profl. jours. Home: PO Box 91 1 Saint Vrain Rio Cucharas Walsenburg CO 81089 Office: 900 E Indiana Ave Walsenburg CO 81089

KUGLER, IDA CAROLYN, mus. dir.; b. Bancroft, Nebr., Dec. 22, 1905; d. Herman and Petrine (Pedersen) Grunke; cert. Montevideo (Minn.) Tchr. Tng. Dept., 1925; A.A. with honors, St. Cloud (Minn.) State U., 1931; B.S. with distinction, U. Minn., 1941, M.A., 1956; Ph.D., Walden U., Naples, Fla., 1972; m. William John Kugler, Nov. 8, 1940. Tchr., Chippewa County, Minn., 1925-30, Rushford, Minn., 1930-31, Lakefield, Minn., 1931-35, St. Paul Public Schs., 1935-61; pioneering prin. Aiyepe High Sch., Ogun State, Nigeria, 1961-65; tchr. St. Paul Public Schs., 1965-74; v.p. Kugler Musical Instrument Mus., St. Paul, 1974—, also edn. dir., registrar. Chmn. Chippewa County Field Day, 1929; tchr. English to Chinese immigrants from Hong Kong, 1965—; nat. adv. bd. Am. Security Council; mem. Republican Nat. Com., U.S. Senatorial Club. Mem. St. Paul Ret. Tchrs. Assn., Nat. Ret. Tchrs. Assn., Am. Assn. Museums, OAS, Cath. Golden Age. Roman Catholic. Office: 1124 Dionne Ave Saint Paul MN 55113

KUH, CHARLOTTE VIRGINIA, economist; b. Chgo., Apr. 13, 1944; d. Peter Greenebaum and Frederica Angela (Coerr) K.; B.A. magna cum laude, Radcliffe Coll., 1967; M.Phil. (Univ. fellow), Yale U., 1969, Ph.D. (Dept. Labor grantee), 1976; m. Roy Radner, Jan. 22, 1978; children—Siobhan Frederica, Michael Edwin. Rec. sec.-treas. Econometric Soc., New Haven, 1970-75; acting asst. prof. engrng. econ. systems Stanford U., 1974-76; asst. prof. Harvard U. Grad. Sch. Edn., 1976-79; staff mgr. AT&T Corp., 1979-80, dist. mgr. long-term forecasting, New Brunswick, N.J., 1980-82, dist. mgr. integrated planning and analyses, Murray Hill, N.J., 1982—; mem. rev. panel NSF, 1979, 81, Nat. Inst. Edn., 1978—; mem. com. study nat. needs for biomed. and behavioral research personnel NRC, 1980—; cons. in field. Grantee Carnegie Council Higher Edn., Ford Found., Spencer Found. Mem. Am. Econ. Assn., Econometric Soc., AAUP. Club: Harvard (N.Y.C.). Author articles in field. Office: 430 Mountain Ave Murray Hill NJ 07974

KUHAR, JUNE CAROLYNN, fiberglass mfg. co. exec.; b. Chgo., Sept. 20, 1935; d. Kurt Ludwig and Dorothy Julia (Lewand) Stier; student William Rainey Harper Coll., Chgo., Ins. Inst. Am.; m. G. James Kuhar, Feb. 5, 1953; children—Kathleen Lee, Debra Suzanne. Engaged in fiberglass mfg., 1970—; sec.-treas. Q-R Fiber Glass Industries Inc., Elgin, 1970—. Mem. Mt. Prospect (Ill.) Bus. and Profl. Woman's Club. Home: 9723 Arthur Dr Algonquin IL 60102 Office: 701 N State St Elgin IL 60120

KUHL, MARGARET HELEN CLAYTON (MRS. ALEXIUS M. KUHL), banker; b. Louisville; d. Joseph Leonard and Maude (Mitzler) Clayton; student Loyola U. Home Study Div., Chgo., 1955—, Buena

Vista Coll., Storm Lake, Iowa, summer 1964-65, 66; m. Alexius M. Kuhl, Apr. 21, 1936; children—Carol Lynn Ford Wassmuth, James Michael (adopted). Sales lady, buyer Silverberg, Akron, Iowa, 1924-34; owner dress shop, Fonda, Iowa, 1934-40; librarian, Fonda, 1940-43; bookkeeper, teller First Nat. Bank, Fonda, 1943-44; tchr. speech and drama, librarian asst. Our Lady Good Counsel Sch., Fonda, 1963-69; pres., chmn. bd. Pomeroy State Bank, 1975—, also dir. Recipient Adult Leadership award Catholic Youth Orgn., 1967, Pro Deo Juventute award, 1969. Mem. Cath. Daus. Am. (dist. dep. 1964-70, state chmn. ecumenism 1970-72, state treas. 1970-72), Diocesan Council Cath. Women (chmn. orgn. and devel. 1964-65), Nat. Council Cath. Women (diocesan pres. 1968-70, diocesan sec. 1966-67; chmn. Women in Community Service Sioux City Diocesan Bd. 1971-72), Internat. Platform Assn., Women in Community Service (pres. Iowa bd. 1972-73), Legion of Mary (pres. curia 1964-66, 67-70). Club: Fonda Country. Home: 5th and Queen Sts Fonda IA 50540

KUHN, ALICE RUTH, sales exec.; b. Pleasant Hill, Mo., Aug. 14, 1915; d. William and Margaret (Edelin) Gulick; B.S., Kans. State U., 1940; postgrad. U. Pacific, 1958-60; m. Eugene J. Kuhn, July 2, 1941; children—Lydia, Peter. Home demonstration agt., Atchison County, Kans., 1940-41; sch. lunch supr., Topeka and Lawrence, Kans., 191-42; tchr. elem. sch., Stockton, Calif., 1955-60; sales rep. World Book-Childcraft, 1960—, dist. mgr., 1962—. First v.p. Friends of Fresno County Library, 1982-83. Recipient Flying Circus award, 1978. Mem. AAUW (treas. 1979-82), Navy League U.S. Presbyterian. Club: Zonta. Home: 665 W Escalon Fresno CA 93704 Office: 5070 N 6th St Fresno CA 93710

KUHN, ANNE NAOMI WICKER (MRS. HAROLD B. KUHN), educator; b. Lynchburg, Va.; d. George Barney and Annie (Hicks) Wicker; diploma Malone Coll., 1933, Trinity Coll. Music, London, 1937; A.B., John Fletcher Coll., 1939; M.A., Boston U., 1942; postgrad. (fellow) Harvard, 1942-44, 66-68, Boston U.; hon. grad. Asbury Coll., Seoul, Korea, 1978; m. Harold B. Kuhn. Instr., Emmanuel Bible Coll., Birkenhead, Eng., 1936-37; asst. in history John Fletcher Coll., University Park, Iowa, 1938-39; librarian Harvard U., 1939-44; tchr. adult edn. program U.S. Armed Forces, Fuerstenfeldbruck Air Base, Germany, 1951-52; prof. Union Bibl. Sem., Yeotmal, India, 1957-58; lectr. Armenian Bible Inst., Beirut, Lebanon, 1958; prof. German, Asbury Coll., Wilmore, Ky., 1962—, co-dir. coll. study tour to E. Ger. and W. Ger., 1976, 77, 78, co-dir. acad. tours, 1979, 80; dir. acad. tour, Russia, 1981, Scandanavia, 1982; tchr. Seoul Theol. Sem., fall 1978. Del. Youth for Christ World Conf., 1948, 50, London Yearly Meeting of Friends, Edinburgh, Scotland, 1948, World Council Chs., Amsterdam, 1948, World Friends Conf., Oxford, Eng., 1952, World Methodist Conf., Oslo, Norway, 1961, Deutscher Kirchentag, Dortmund, Germany, 1963, German Lang. Congress, Bonn, W. Ger., 1974; participant Internat. Congress World Evangelization, Lausanne, Switzerland, 1974. Recipient German Consular award, Boston, 1965, Thomas Mann award Boston U., 1967; named Ky. Col. Fellow Goethe-Institut fur Germanisten, Munich, 1966-68, 70-71; named Ky. col. Mem. AAUW, Am. Assn. Tchrs. German, NEA, Ky. Ednl. Assn., Lincoln Lit. Soc., Protestant Women of Chapel, Delta Phi Alpha (award 1963, 65). Quaker. Club: Harvard Faculty. Author: (pamphlet) The Impact of the Transition to Modern Education Upon Religious Education, 1950; The Influence of Paul Gerhardt upon Wesleyan Hymnody, 1960; contbr. articles to profl. jours. Home: 406 Kenyon Ave Wilmore KY 40390

KUHN, JEAN GERLINGER, civic worker; b. Dallas, Oreg., Dec. 6, 1910; d. George Theodore and Irene Strang (Hazard) Gerlinger; B.A., U. Calif., Berkeley, 1932; m. Robert C. Kirkwood, Aug. 30, 1933 (dec.); children—Anne Kirkwood Millis, Robert C., Jean Kirkwood Casey, John Hazard; m. 2d, Charles B. Kuhn, June 15, 1968. Numerous vol. activities in various orgns., San Francisco, Sacramento, Saratoga and San Jose, Calif.; bd. dirs. San Francisco Found., 1969-79, Addiction Research Found., 1977—, Filoli Center, 1978—; bd. dirs. Community Found. of Santa Clara County, 1975—, chmn. bd. dirs., 1981—; bd. dirs. Montalvo Center for the Arts, Saratoga, 1970—, World Affairs Council of No. Calif., 1968—; mem. bd. visitors Stanford U. Law Sch., 1979—, Pacific Med. Center; chmn. bd. dirs. Pacific Med. Found., 1981—. Mem. Order St. John of Jerusalem, Kappa Kappa Gamma. Republican. Episcopalian. Club: Town and Country of San Francisco.

KUHN, KATHLEEN JO, acct.; b. Springfield, Ill., Aug. 9, 1947; d. Henry Elmer and Norma Florene (Niehaus) Burge; B.S. in Bus., Bradley U., 1969; m. Gerald L. Kuhn, June 22, 1968; 1 son, Gerald Lynn. Controller, Byerly Music Co., Peoria, Ill., 1969-70; staff acct. Clifton Gunderson & Co., Columbus, Ind., 1970-71; acct. Dept. ot Transp., State of Ill., Springfield, 1972-76; acct. Gerald L. Kuhn & Assos., C.P.A.'s, Springfield, 1976-78, partner, 1979—. Recipient attendance award Continuing Profl. Edn. for Accts., 1977, 78, 79; notary public, Ill.; C.P.A., Ill. Mem. Am. Inst. C.P.A.'s, Ill. Soc. C.P.A.'s, Am. Woman's Soc. C.P.A.'s. Lutheran. Clubs: Olympic Swim, Metro. Federated Jr. Women's. Writer, editor Policy Guideline of Gerald L. Kuhn & Assos., 1979-80. Home: 2511 Westchester St Springfield IL 62704 Office: 323 S Grand Ave W Springfield IL 62704

KUHN, LUCILLE ROSS, naval officer; b. Washington, July 19, 1927; d. Lilburn Joseph and Flora Lee (Perry) K.; A.A. with distinction, George Washington U., 1959, B.A., 1960. Ins. clk. Southwestern Life Ins. Co., Richmond, Va., 1945-48; joined U.S. Navy, 1949, advanced through grades to capt., 1975; woman officer rep. 2d Navy Recruiting Area, Washington, 1963-65; U.S. Naval Security Group, Washington, 1965-68; dir. mil. personnel 12th Naval Dist., San Francisco, 1968-70; mem. staff Office Asst. Sec. Def. for Legis. Affairs, Washington, 1971-74; dir. Officer Candidate Sch., Newport, 1975-77; dir. pay/personnel adminstrv. support system Bur. Naval Personnel, Washington, 1977-79; comdg. officer Recruit Tng. Command, Orlando, Fla., 1979-81; dep. comdr. Navy Recruiting Command, Washington, 1981—. Aide de camp to Va. govs., 1960—. Decorated Legion of Merit Meritorious Service medal with gold star, Nat. Def. Service medal with bronze star. Mem. Am. Sailing Assn., Smithsonian Assos., Naval Inst., Psi Chi. Home: 2302 Kenmore Rd Richmond VA 23228 Office: Navy Recruiting Command Washington DC 20370

KUHN, MARGARET (MAGGIE), orgn. exec.; b. Buffalo, 1905. Formerly with YWCA, Cleve., Germantown, Pa.; former writer, editor social action jours. Unitarian Ch., Boston, United Presbn. Ch. U.S.A., Phila.; alt. observer for Presbyns. at UN; a founder Gray Panthers, now nat. convener; cons. nat. task force on women United Presbyn. Ch., past 3d v.p. health, edn. and welfare assn.; lectr. Office: care Gray Panthers 3635 Chestnut St Philadelphia PA 19104 *

KUHNER, SUSAN MARY, psychologist; b. Cleve., Aug. 16, 1947; d. Arthur and Mary Annetta (Franklin) K.; B.A., Case Western Res. U., 1969; M.A., U. Portland, 1971, Ph.D., 1973. Intern, Atascadero (Calif.) State Hosp., 1972-73; staff psychologist Calif. Youth Authority, 1973-74; pvt. practice psychol. counseling, Los Angeles, 1974—; asst. exec. dir. Gay Community Services Center, Hollywood, Calif., 1977-79; supr. adult outpatient and crisis evaluation programs Tri-City Mental Health Authority, Pomona, Calif., 1979-81; founder Kuhner Inst. for Multiple Personalities, 1980—. Bd. dirs. New Alliance for Gay Equality, 1978—. Mem. Nat. Assn. Female Execs., Nat. Women's Polit. Caucus, NOW, ACLU, So. Calif. Women for Understanding. Home: 3204 Bonnie Hill Dr Los Angeles CA 90068 Office: 6109 Riverton Ave North Hollywood CA 91606

KUIUMGIAN, ROSE, conglomerate govt. relations exec.; b. Bucharest, Romania, Feb. 28, 1955; d. Horen and Hosrofui Kuiumgian; B.A. in Biology with honors (Jonas Clark scholar), Clark U., 1976; M.S. in Nutrition with honors, Rutgers U., 1980. Teaching asst. Rutgers U., research asst., to 1980; cons. Nat. Child Nutrition Project, N.J., 1979-80; fellow Nat. Nutrition Consortium, Washington, 1980-81; Washington rep. CPC N.Am., Washington, 1981—. Mem. Women in Govt. Relations, Washington Nutrition Group, Inst. Food Technologists. Office: 1730 K St NW Washington DC 20006

KUKLIN, REBA MAGID, publisher, author; b. Nashville, Aug. 25, 1914; d. Victor and Becky (Frankel) Magid; B.S. with distinction in Edn., U. Nebr., 1955, M.Ed., 1962; m. Harry H. Kuklin, Dec. 25, 1939; children—Bailey Howard, Bonnie Irene, Victor Alan. Tchr. elem. schs., Lincoln, Nebr., 1955-57; tchr. jr. high sch. English and social studies, Lincoln, 1957-77; founder, pres. Mercantine Press, Lincoln, 1979—; author: Learn to Invest and Trade on Wall Street, 1979. Mem. NEA, Assn. Women Entrepreneurs, Nebr. Edn. Assn., Lincoln Edn. Assn., Hadassah. Address: 4351 Washington St Lincoln NE 68506

KUKLIN, SUSAN BEVERLY, legal educator, library dir.; b. Chgo., Nov. 25, 1947; d. Albert and Marion K.; B.A., U. Ariz., 1969, J.D., 1973; M.L.S., Ind. U., 1970; LL.M. in Taxation, DePaul U., 1981. Admitted to Ariz. bar, 1973, Ill. bar, 1981; asst. city atty. Phoenix, 1974-75; dep. county atty. Pima County (Ariz.), Tucson, 1975-76; polit. sci./law librarian No. Ill. U., DeKalb, 1976-78; head law librarian U. S.D., Vermillion, 1978-79; dir. law library, asst. prof. law DePaul U. Coll. Law, Chgo., 1979—. Mem. Am. Assn. Law Librarians (cert.), State Bar Ariz., State Bar Ill., Chgo. Assn. Law Libraries, Ill. Bar Assn. (council of patent, trademark, and copyright coms., co-editor newsletter on patent, trademark, and copyright), Chgo. Bar Assn., Phi Beta Kappa, Phi Kappa Phi, Alpha Lambda Delta, Phi Alpha Theta, Phi Delta Phi. Book reviewer Library Jour., 1976—, Am. Reference Books Ann., 1979—. Office: 25 E Jackson Blvd Chicago IL 60604

KUKLINSKI, JOAN LINDSEY, librarian; b. Lynn, Mass., Nov. 28, 1950; d. Richard Jay and M. Claire (Murphy) Card; B.A. cum laude, Mass. State Coll., Salem, 1972; M.L.S., U. R.I., 1976; m. Walter S. Kuklinski, June 17, 1972. Classified librarian U. R.I. Extension Div. Library, Providence, 1974-75, U. R.I. Cataloging Dept., Kingston, 1975-79; original cataloger Tex. A&M U. Library, College Station, 1979-82; cataloger Goldfarb Library, Brandeis U., Waltham, Mass., 1982—. Mem. Town of South Kingstown (R.I.) Women's Adv. Commn., 1977-79. Mem. ALA (mem. resources and tech. services div. edn. com. 1982—, problems of access and control of ednl. materials com., edn. and behavioral scis. sect. 1981—), Assn. Coll. and Research Libraries, On-Line Audiovisual Catalogers, Tex. Library Assn., Am. Contract Bridge League, Delta Tau Kappa. Office: Goldfarb Library Brandeis Univ Waltham MA 02154

KUKURISAS, ADA LUCILLE SILVERS, educator; b. Kansas City, Mo., June 29, 1923; d. Charles Ralph and Nora Ellen (Crowder) Silvers; A.B., Ind. State U., 1965, M.S., 1970, postgrad, 1977; m. 2d, John P. Kukurisas, July 25, 1964; children from previous marriage—John Kracy, Charles Ralph Kracy, Joyce Lee Kracy Steiger. Fusion weld supr. Twigg Industries, Brazil, Ind., 1951-61; mem. faculty Ind. State U., Terre Haute, 1965—, asso. prof. English, 1981—, dir. writing lab., 1980—. Recipient Caleb Mills Disting. Teaching award Ind. State U., 1980. Mem. Ind. Council Tchrs. English (dist. dir. 1973—), AAUP (sec. 1981-82), Nat. Council Tchrs. English, Phi Delta Kappa, Delta Kappa Gamma. Democrat. Roman Catholic. Clubs: University, Faculty Women, Hungarian Working Men's Assn. Contbr. articles to profl. jours. Home: RR 16 Box 319 Brazil IN 47834 Office: Dept English Ind State U Terre Haute IN 47809

KULHAN, ANN MARIE, educator; b. Nove Zamky, Czechoslovakia, Aug. 24, 1947; came to U.S., 1950, naturalized, 1957; d. John and Marta (Baluch) K.; B.A., Dominican Coll., 1969; M.A. in Teaching, Fordham U., 1971. Tchr. English, Tappan Zee High Sch., Orangeburg, N.Y., 1971—. Mistress of ceremonies Slovak-Am. Cultural Center; stage program chmn. N.J. Slovak Heritage Festival, 1979-80. Am. studies fellow, 1978. Home: 106 Birchwood Ave Upper Nyack NY 10960 Office: Tappan Zee High Sch Dutch Hill Rd Orangeburg NY 10962

KULIEKE, BARBARA NEWSOM, personnel specialist; b. Topeka, Aug. 3, 1947; d. Francis Carter and Mary Elizabeth (Varner) Newsom; B.A. in English, U. Kans., 1970, M.A. in Speech Communication and Human Relations, 1973; m. Mark Warren Kulieke, June 26, 1977. Instr. dept. speech and drama U. Kans., Lawrence, 1969-71, researcher div. continuing edn., 1970-72, continuing edn. rep., 1972-73, asst. dir. continuing edn. classes, 1973-74; communications and mgmt. cons. in pvt. practice, Berkeley, Calif., 1974-75, Chgo., 1975-78; asso. dir. supervisory and communications tng. U.S. Office Personnel Mgmt., Great Lakes Regional Tng. Center, Chgo., 1978—. Nat. extension exec. Family of God Found., Inc., Berkeley, 1975—; bd. dirs. Urantia Brotherhood Corp., Chgo., 1976—, publs. chmn., 1976—. Recipient award to outstanding new speech tchr. U. Kans., 1970. Mem. Am. Soc. Tng. and Devel., Speech Communication Assn., Ill. Tng. and Devel. Assn., Mortar Bd., Phi Beta Kappa, Kappa Kappa Gamma. Episcopalian. Home: 415 Birch St Winnetka IL 60093 Office: 230 S Dearborn 29th Floor Chicago IL 60604

KULPIT-GARVY, DENISE MARIE, banker; b. Chgo., Apr. 16, 1953; d. Eugene Adam and Claire Dolores (Rutkowski) Kulpit; B.S. in Edn. (Ill. State scholar), No. Ill. U., 1975; m. William John Garvy, Jr., Sept. 18, 1976. With Sears Bank and Trust Co., Chgo., 1975-80, tng. supr., 1978-80; dir. tng. Bank of Ravenswood, Chgo., 1980—; instr. Am. Inst. Banking. Mem. Am. Soc. Tng. and Devel., Am. Inst. Banking. Home: 6742 N Campbell Ave Chicago IL 60645 Office: Bank of Ravenswood 1825 W Lawrence St Chicago IL 60640

KUMAGAI, GLORIA LYNN, ednl. cons.; b. Mpls., Nov. 14, 1947; d. Hisashi and Terry (Ogasawara) K.; B.A. magna cum laude, U. Minn., 1969, M.S.W., 1971; m. Steven Lee Savitt, Oct. 20, 1974. Sch. social worker Lyndale Elementary Sch., Mpls., 1971-74; urban affairs cons. for staff devel. St. Paul Pub. Schs., 1974—. 2d v.p. Japanese Am. Citizens league, 1975-77; mem. bd. Minn. Asian Am. Project, 1975—; mem. Minn. adv. com. U.S. Commn. on Civil Rights, 1975—; state del. Internat. Women's Year Meeting, 1977; mem. sex bias adv. com. Minn. Dept. Edn., 1976—. Mem. Nat. Assn. Social Workers, Acad. Cert. Social Workers. Author: The Asian Woman in America, 1977. Home: 2724 Drew Ave S Minneapolis MN 55416 Office: 360 Colborne St St Paul MN 55102

KUMIN, MAXINE WINOKUR, writer; b. Phila., June 6, 1925; d. Peter and Doll (Simon) Winokur; A.B., Radcliffe Coll., 1946, M.A., 1948; m. Victor Montwid Kumin, June 29, 1946; children—Jane Simon, Judith Montwid, Daniel David. Free-lance writer, 1953—; mem. Poetry Soc. Am. Author: (poems) Halfway, 1961, The Privilege, 1965; (novel) Through Dooms of Love, 1965; (novel) The Passions of Uxport, 1968; (poems) The Nightmare Factory, 1970; Up Country, 1972 (Pulitzer prize for poetry 1973); (novel) The Designated Heir, 1974; (poems) House, Bridge, Fountain, Gate, 1975, The Retrieval System, 1978; (essays) To Make a Prairie, 1980; (poems) Our Ground Time Here Will Be Brief, 1982; (short stories) Why Can't We Live Together Like Civilized Human Beings, 1982; poetry cons. Library of Congress, 1981—; contbr. poems to nat. mags. Woodrow Wilson vis. fellow, 1979-80; recipient award Am. Acad. and Inst. Arts and Letters, 1980. Address: care Curtis Brown Ltd 575 Madison Ave New York NY 10022

KUMM, DORIS JEAN, state legislator; b. Watertown, S.D., Oct. 27, 1929; d. Earl Edward Lebert and Minnie Augusta (Schwanke) Lebert Richardson; grad. Cosmetology Sch., Watertown, S.D.; m. Vincent Jerald Kumm, May 29, 1949; children—Deborah, Kelly, Roxanne, Marty, Todd, Kathy. Mem. S.D. Ho. of Reps., 1978—, mem. natural resources, transp. and bonding coms. Mem. S.D. Republican Com., del. state conv., 1978; del. Rep. Nat. Conv., 1980; mem. exec. com. Codington County (S.D.) Rep. Com. Mem. LWV, Women In Mgmt., Roundtable Extension, Rep. Women, Nat. Order Women Legislators (regional dir.). Home: 521 6th St SE Watertown SD 57201 Office: State Capitol Pierre SD 57501

KUMMER, SHARON ANN, educator; b. Longmont, Colo., Apr. 19, 1947; d. Edward Matthew and Dorothy Lorene (Marr) K.; B.A., U. No. Colo., 1969; M.A., Calif. State U., 1977, M.A. in Speech Communication, 1982. Tchr., Whittier (Calif.) City Sch. Dist., 1970—; prof. speech communication Calif. State U., Los Angeles, 1975—; asst. project supr. Parker Research Corp., Irvine, Calif., 1979-80; partner Brain Child Publs., Pasadena and Whittier, Calif. Mem. Calif. Speech Assn., Calif. Tchrs. Assn., Nat. Assn. Female Execs., Inc., Calif. Assn. Gifted, Am. Soc. Tng. and Devel., United Profs. Calif. Home: 767 S Los Robles Ave Pasadena CA 91106 Office: 5151 State University Dr Los Angeles CA 90032

KUNDERT, ALICE E., state ofcl.; b. Java, S.D., July 23, 1920; d. Otto J. and Maria (Rieger) Kundert; elementary tchr.'s certificate No. State Coll., Aberdeen, S.D., state tchr. certificate. Tchr. elementary grades, 1939-43, 48-54; clk., mgr., buyer Gates Dept. Store, Beverly Hills, Calif., Clifton Dress Shop, Hollywood, Calif., 1943-48; dep. supt. schs. Campbell County, S.D., 1954; county cts. clk., 1955-60; register deeds, 1955-69; town treas. Mound City, 1965-69; auditor State of S.D., Pierre, 1969-79, sec. state, 1979—. Leader, 4-H Club, 1949-53, county project leader in citizenship, 1963-64; sec. Greater Campbell County Assn., 1955-7; organizer, leader Mound City Craft and Recreation Club, 1955-60; chmn. Heart Fund, March Dimes, Red Cross, Mental Health drives; mem. Gov.'s Study Commn., 1968—; mem. State and local adv. com. region VIII Office Econ. Opportunity; bd. mem., cmn. Black Hills Recreation Lab., 1956-61; exec. sec. Internat. Leaders Lab. Ireland, 1963. Polit. county vice chmn. Republican Com., 1964-69, sec.-treas. fin. chmn., 1968; mem. State Rep. Adv. Com., 1966-68; state and nat. counselor Tenn Age Rep. Club Campbell County, 1964—; named Outstanding Teenage Rep. advisor in nation, 1970, 71, 76. Recipient Distinguished Alumni award No. State Coll., 1975. Home: 407 N Van Buren St Pierre SD 57501 Office: State Capitol Bldg Office of Sec State Pierre SD 57501

KUNGLE, SANDRA, soprano, voice therapist, educator; b. Baker, Kans., Mar. 4, 1947; d. Arthur and Eva Lea K.; B.Mus., U. Ill., 1968; M.Mus., U. Mass., 1970; D.Music Arts, U. Colo., 1976; m. Gregory Scott Blimling, Aug. 17, 1979; 1 dau., Jennifer Vanessa Bird. Soprano soloist 1st United Ch. of Christ, Keene, N.H., 1968-74; teaching asst. U. Mass., 1968-70; instr. voice Keene State Coll., 1970-74; dir. jr. choir 1st Congl. Ch., Boulder, 1974-76; teaching asst. U. Colo., Boulder, 1975-76; asst. prof. music Colo. State U., Fort Collins, 1976-77; asso. prof. music La. State U., Baton Rouge, 1977—. Mem. Nat. Assn. Tchrs. Singing (chmn. So. region auditions), La. Music Tchrs. Assn. (state vocal chmn.), Mu Phi Epsilon, Pi Kappa Lambda. Congregationalist. Home: 1625 Leycester Dr Baton Rouge LA 70808 Office: Sch Music La State U Baton Rouge LA 70803

KUNICKI-TADMAN, KRYSTYNA MARY ANNE, lawyer; b. Edmonton, Alta., Can., Aug. 22, 1950; d. Joseph Henry and Stefania Helen Kunicki; B.A., U. Alta., 1971; LL.B., Dalhousie U., Halifax, N.S., 1974; m. Hugh Frederick Tadman, June 17, 1978. Called to Alta. bar, 1975; atty. City of Edmonton, 1974-76, Ogilvie & Co., barristers and solicitors, Edmonton, 1976-79, Grotski & Co., barristers and solicitors, Edmonton, 1979—. Vice chmn. bldg. com. Sisem Day Care Center, Edmonton, 1977. Mem. Internat. Commn. Jurists, Law Soc. Alta., Can., Edmonton bar assns., Am. Trial Lawyers Assn., Pi Beta Phi (adv. bd. 1975-76). Clubs: Royal Glenora, Canadian Progress (dir.), Edmonton Marigolds (dir.), Uncles at Large (dir.), Camp Warwa Soc. (dir.).

KUNIGONIS, DEBRA JANE, human performance analyst; b. Wichita, Kans., May 28, 1954; d. Aloysius Frank and Dora (Metzler) K.; B.S. in Nursing with honors, Wichita State U., 1976, M.Ed. in Student Personnel and Guidance, 1982. Staff nurse Wesley Med. Center, Wichita, 1976-77, instr. Sch. Nursing, 1977-81; instr. nursing Kans. Newman Coll., Wichita, 1982; human performance analyst Boing Mil. Airplane Co., 1982—; vol. counselor Women's Crisis Center, Wichita. Mem. Common Cause, NOW, Bus. and Profl. Women, Nat. Assn. Female Execs. Home: 5010 E Gilbert Ct Wichita KS 67218

KUNIN, MADELEINE MAY, lt. gov. Vt.; b. Zurich, Switzerland, Sept. 28, 1933; came to U.S., 1940, naturalized, 1947; d. Ferdinand and Renée (Bloch) May; B.A., U. Mass., 1956; M.S., Columbia U., 1957; M.A., U. Vt., 1967; L.H.D. (hon.), Norwich U., 1979; m. Arthur S. Kunin, June 21, 1959; children—Julia, Peter, Adam, Daniel. Newspaper reporter Burlington (Vt.) Free Press, 1957-58; guide Brussels Worlds Fair, 1958; TV asst., producer Sta. WCAX-TV, Burlington, 1960-61; freelance writer, instr. English, Trinity Coll., Burlington, 1969-70; mem. Vt. Ho. of Reps., 1973-78; lt. gov. State of Vt., Montpelier, 1978—; mem. Vt. Gov.'s Commn. on Children and Youth, 1973-77, Vt. Commn. on Adminstrn. of Justice, 1976-77, Vt. Joint Fiscal Com., 1977-78; mem. exec. com. Nat. Conf. Lt. Govs., 1979-80. Named Outstanding State Legislator, Eagleton Inst. Politics, Rutgers U., 1975. Democrat. Author: (with Marilyn Stout) The Big Green Book, 1976. Contbr. articles to various mags. and newspapers. Office: Lt Governors Office State House Montpelier VT 05602

KUNITZ, SELMA JOYCE, computer scientist; b. Albany, N.Y., Aug. 29, 1943; d. Julius Leo and Gertrude (Hoffman) Cohen; B.A. in Econs., U. Rochester, 1965; M.S., Am. U., 1976; postgrad. Johns Hopkins U., 1982—; m. Norman Kunitz, Dec. 11, 1971; children—Daniel, Michele. Computer programmer Met. Life Ins. Co., N.Y.C., 1965-66; programmer Colo. Interstate Gas Corp., Colorado Springs, 1967-69; cons. Hamilton Coll., Clinton, N.Y., 1969; computer specialist, systems analyst U.S. Census Bur., Washington, 1970-72; freelance cons., 1973; head mgmt. info. systems Health Resources Adminstrn., HEW, Washington, 1974-76; chief computer applications Office Biometry and Field Studies, Nat. Inst. Neurol. and Communicative Disorders and Stroke, NIH, Bethesda, Md., 1977—; lectr., cons.; seminar leader. Cert. in data processing Data Processing Mgmt. Assn. Fellow Soc. Advanced Med. Systems; mem. Am. Pub. Health Assn., Assn. Systems Mgmt., IEEE Computer Group. Home: 6406 Tilden Ln Rockville MD 20852 Office: 7550 Wisconsin Ave Bethesda MD 20014

KUNTZ, MARION LUCILE LEATHERS (MRS. PAUL G. KUNTZ), educator; b. Atlanta, Sept. 6, 1924; d. Otto Asa and Lucile (Parks) Leathers; B.A., Agnes Scott Coll., 1945; M.A., Emory U., 1964, Ph.D., 1969; children—Charles, Otto Alan (Daniels); m. 2d, Paul G. Kuntz, Nov. 26, 1970. Lectr. Latin, Lovett Sch., Atlanta, 1963-66; faculty Ga. State U., Atlanta, 1966—, asso. prof., 1969-73, prof. Latin and Greek, 1973—, chmn. fgn. lang. dept., 1975—, Regents' prof. classics, 1975—. Named Latin Tchr. of Yr., State Ga., 1965; Semple scholar, 1965; Am. Classical League scholar, 1966; Am. Council Learned Socs. grantee, 1970, 73, 78, 81. Mem. Am. Philol. Assn., Renaissance Soc. Am., Archaeol. Inst. Am., Classical Assn. Midwest and South (Semple award 1965), Medieval Acad., Soc. Medieval-Renaissance Philosophy, Am. Cath. Philos. Assn., Société Française des Seizimistes, Venetian Seminar, Am. Philos. Assn., Ch. History Soc., Am. Acad. Rome (sec., treas. 1970-72), Internat. Soc. Neo-Latin Studies, Am. Soc. Aesthetics, Internat. Soc. Neo-Platonic Studies, Center for Reformation Research, Italian Cultural Soc., Phi Beta Kappa. Roman Catholic. Club: Hellenic Study (pres. Atlanta 1974). Author: Colloquium of the Seven About Secrets of the Sublime of Jean Bodin, 1975; Guillaume Postel, Prophet of the Restitution of all Things: His Life and Thoughts, 1981. Home: 1655 Ponce de Leon Atlanta GA 30307

KUNTZ, NANNIE-ANA BERENDSON, import-export co. exec.; b. Cologne, Germany, Sept. 27, 1946; came to U.S., naturalized, 1977; d. Max Berendson A. and Nannie Inez Seminario; B.A./S. summa cum laude, Loyola U., 1974; M.S. in Applied Psychology (Univ. fellow), U. New Orleans, 1976; children—Louis Max Oze, Michael Berendson Kuntz. Sales and public relations rep. Neiman Marcus, Dallas, 1963-64; vice-consul of Peru for Texas, 1966-74; owner, pres. Peruvian Originals, Tex., with fgn. ops. in W. Ger. and Peru, 1968-75, 81—; researcher, author Jefferson Parish (La.), 1975-78; pvt. investor; chmn. boutique com. Inst. Internat. Edn., 1981. Recipient First Pl. award for outstanding exhibit State Fair Tex., 1968; cert. psychol. asso., Tex. Mem. Import-Export Club, Am. Psychol. Assn., Tex. Psychol. Assn., Houston Psychol. Assn., Am. Assn. Individual Investors, Houston Ballet Guild. Republican. Roman Catholic. Clubs: Club Nacional (Lima, Peru); Santa Maria, Club Regatas, Los Condores. Author: Water Purification Operator's Manual, 1978.

KUNZ, JEAN TUELLER, educator; b. Montpelier, Idaho, Jan. 9, 1919; B.S. in Edn., Child Psychology, U. Idaho, 1940; M.A. in Early Childhood Edn., George Peabody Coll., Nashville, 1956; Ph.D. in Human Devel., 1967; widowed; 2 children. Asst. prof., coordinator human devel. lab. Brigham Young U., Provo, Utah, 1957-61; dir. nursery sch. U. Md., College Park, 1961-67; dir. Mary B. Eyre Nursery Sch., prof. psychology Scripps Coll., Claremont, Calif., 1967-70; chmn. dept. family life, profl. child devel. Weber State Coll., Ogden, Utah, 1970-76, chmn. dept. child and family studies, 1976—. Mem. gov. bd. Children's Aid Soc., 1973-74. Mem. Am. Psychol. Assn., Nat., Utah assns., edn. young children, U.S. Congress of World Orgn. Early Childhood Edn., World Council Curriculum and Instrn. Specialist in child devel., early childhood edn. Home: 1618 Capitol St Ogden UT 84401 Office: 3750 Harrison Blvd Ogden UT 84408

KUNZ, SHARON ELIZABETH, utility co. exec.; b. Bklyn., May 25, 1945; d. Albert Valentine and Dorothy Lee (Jacobs) Kunz; student St. Johns U., 1978—. With Consol. Edison Co., 1963—, dist. office teller, 1967-69, acctg. clk., customer service area, 1967-72, asst. supr. Manhattan customer service, 1972-78, unit mgr. Br. III-Westside, Manhattan customer service, 1978-81, unit mgr. Lincoln Center Br., 1981-82, unit mgr. Yorkville Br., 1982—. Mem. Consol. Edison Engring. Soc., Nat. Rifle Assn., Aircraft Owners and Pilots Assn. (lic. pilot). Democrat. Home: 189 Newbrook Ln Bayshore NY 11706 Office: 1555 3d Ave New York NY 10028

KUO, ELAINE HSIAO-MEI, ednl. adminstr., librarian, bus. research ofcl.; b. Chekiang, China, Feb. 15, 1946; came to U.S., 1968, naturalized, 1979; d. Chu and R.I. (Chen) Hsu; B.A., Tunghai U., Taiwan, 1968; M.L.S., U. Ill., 1972; m. Peter Chih-Chao Kuo, Mar. 29, 1969; children—Alice, Katherine. Head librarian Value Engring. Co., Alexandria, Va., 1973-77; chief library services U.S. Ry. Assn., Washington, 1977-80; dir. research ops. Houze, Shourds & Montgomery, Inc., Los Angeles, 1980-82; acting prin. Yu-tsai Elem. Sch., Taipei, Taiwan, 1982—. Instr. South Bay Sch. of Chinese Culture and Lang. Mem. ALA, Spl. Library Assn., Calif. Library Assn. Home: 1716 Dalton Rd Palos Verdes Estates CA 90274 Office: Yu-tsai Elem Sch Fu-Ho Rd Yung-ho Taipei Taiwan

KUPCINET, ESSEE SOLOMON, TV producer; b. Chgo., Dec. 7; d. Joseph David and Doris (Schoke) Solomon; Ph.B., Northwestern U., 1937; m. Irv Kupcinet, Feb. 12, 1939; children—Karyn (dec.), Jerry S. Asst. to dir. psychology dept. Michael Reese Hosp., Chgo., 1939-41; exec. producer eight Jefferson Award Shows; producer 1st Literary Arts Ball, Cultural Center, Chgo., 1979; talent coordinator Kup's Show, Chgo., 1964—; producer for spl. events, 1978—. Co-chmn. Community Arts Found.; mem. exec. bd. Free Street Theatre; mem. adv. bd. Shakespeare Festival; mem. adv. com. Chgo. Pub. Library Cultural Center, 1977; mem. adv. bd., producer 1st Annual Community Arts Festival, 1978; mem. adv. bd. DePaul-Goodman Sch. Drama, Wisdom Bridge Theatre, Organic Theatre, Free St. Theatre, Stage Center at the Forum; League Chgo. Theatres, 1979. Decorated Knight of Orange Nassau (Netherlands); recipient Spl. award Jefferson Com., 1976; Cliff Dwellers award, 1975; Emmy award CBS, 1977, 79; Artisan award Acad. Theatre Arts and Friends, 1977; Prime Minister's medal for service to Israel, 1974; Woman of Yr. award Facets Multimedia, 1982, others. Mem. Nat. Acad. TV Arts and Scis. (mem. governing bd., program chmn. 1982—). Jewish. Club: Arts.

KUPER, BARBARA ROZALIA, chemist, sculptress; b. Czestochowa, Poland; d. Stanislaw and Franciszka (Lewenhoff) Meryn; M.S., Cracow, Poland, 1948; postgrad. McGill U., 1961-63, Sir George Williams U. Mus. Fine Arts, 1961-70, Saidye Bronfman Centre, Montreal, 1967-70; m. Anthony Kuper, 1947; 1 dau., Eva. Analyst Warnock Hersey, Montreal, Que., Can., 1950-55; with quality control and forumulating depts. Internat. Paints Co., Montreal, 1955-61; chief lab. Globe Fur Blending, Montreal, 1961—; also owner sculptor studio, Montreal. One-woman shows: Dominion Gallery, Montreal, 1975, 78, 80, Stuart Hall, Point Claire, Que., 82, Confrontration 1982, Montreal, Man and His World, Que. Pavillion, 1982, Arnot Art Mus., Elmira, N.Y., 1982, Fredericton, N.B., Can., 1982, Sarnia, Ont., Can., 1982; group shows include: Saidye Bronfman Centre ann. exhbns., 1968-73, Dominion Gallery, 1976, Artist Showcase, Montreal, Herman Abramowitz chpt. Hadassah, 1979; represented in permanent collections: Sculptors Soc. Can., Met. Mus., Coral Gables, Fla., Confedn. Center, Charlottetown, P.E.I., also pvt. collections. Mem. Assn. des Sculpteurs du Que., Societe d'Etudes et de Conferences de Montreal, Chem. Inst. Can., Order Chemists Que., Can. Soc. Chem. Engring., Sculptors Soc. Can. Home: 852 Berwick Crescent Montreal PQ H3R 2K9 Canada

KUPIEC, KAREN JEAN, audiologist; b. Rochester, N.Y., Apr. 30, 1952; d. Edward John and Clementine Kupiec; B.S., Nazareth Coll. Rochester, 1974; M.A., SUNY, Geneseo, 1975. Clin. audiologist William R. Mast, M.D., Dover, Del., 1977—. Mem. Am. Speech and Hearing Assn., Del. Speech and Hearing Assn., Arthritis Found., AAUW. Home: Country Club Apts M-22 Dover DE 19001 Office: 1093 E Governors Ave Dover DE 19901

KUPPER, MARJORIE LAKIN, ednl. technologist; b. Norfolk, Va., Nov. 28, 1943; d. Charles Thomas and Gloria (Patterson) L.; B.A. with honors, U. Fla. at Gainesville, 1964; M.Ed., U. N.C., Chapel Hill, 1972, postgrad., 1975—; div.; 1 son, Mark L. Kupper. Tchr. math. Newberry (Fla.) High Sch., 1965-66, Orange Jr. High, Hillsborough, N.C., 1967-68; music tchr. St. Thomas More Elem. Sch., Chapel Hill, N.C., 1969-70; cons. designer EPA, Chapel Hill, 1972; edn. media specialist Title III grant, Chapel Hill City Schs., 1972-73; research asst. Office of Med. Studies, Sch. Medicine, U. N.C., 1973, dir. instrnl. design, prodn. AID African Health Project, Office Med. Studies, 1973-77; supervisory ednl. technologist U.S. Army Engr. Sch., Ft. Belvoir, Va., 1977-79; sr. edn. specialist Nat. Tng. Center, IRS, Arlington, Va., 1979—; cons. workshop leader African countries, U.S., 1974-77, contracting officers' rep., 1977-78. Asst. cubmaster Boy Scouts Am., 1977—. Recipient Army Comdr.'s award for outstanding civilian performance, 1979. Mem. Assn. Ednl. Communications and Tech., Fed. Ednl. Tech. Assn. (sec.-treas. 1978-79, pres.-elect 1982-83), Am. Ednl. Research Assn., Nat. Soc. Performance and Instrn., NOW. Democrat. Author: Use Manual for Self-Instructional Materials, 1977; also articles in profl. jours. Office: IRS Nat Tng Center 2221 Jefferson Davis Hwy Arlington VA 22202

KUPPERMAN, HELEN SLOTNICK, lawyer; b. Boston; d. Morris Louis and Minnie (Kaplan) Slotnick; B.A., Smith Coll.; postgrad. Royal Acad. Dramatic Art, London; J.D., Boston Coll., 1966; m. Robert H. Kupperman, Dec. 23, 1967; 1 dau., Tamara. Admitted to Mass. bar, 1966; atty., advisor NASA, Washington, 1966-73, sr. atty., 1973-77, asst. gen. counsel for gen. law, 1977—, chairperson contract adjustment bd., 1974—, rep. on U.S. delegation to legal subcommittee of UN Com. on Peaceful Uses of Outer Space, 1977—. Recipient NASA Sustained Superior Performance award, 1977. Mem. U.S. Assn. of Internat. Inst. Space Law (sec. 1981), Am. Bar Assn., Fed. Bar Assn., Boston Bar Assn., Internat. Women Lawyers Assn., Mass. Bar Assn., Jewish. Bus. editor Boston Coll. Indsl. and Comml. Law Rev., 1965-66. Home: 2832 Ellicott St NW Washington DC 20008 Office: 400 Maryland Ave SW Washington DC 20546

KURAITIS, JOAN PARSONS, ednl. adminstr.; b. Altoona, Pa., Apr. 15, 1952; d. William Kantner and Florence (Gable) Parsons; B.S. cum laude in Spl. Edn., Kent State U., 1973; M.Ed. in Guidance and Counseling, U. Akron, 1975; Ph.D., Kent State U., 1980; m. Vytenis Kuraitis, Sept. 15, 1973; children—Kristina Kantner, Anne Parsons. Tchr., Cuyahoga Falls (Ohio) Sch. Dist., 1973-75; coordinator fin. aid Stark Tech. Coll., Canton, Ohio, 1975-78; planning specialist Dyke Coll., Cleve., 1979-82; cons., Cleve., 1982—. Chmn. edn. com. Cleve. Restoration Soc., 1981-82. Mem. Nat. Assn. Women Deans, Adminstrs., and Counselors, Am. Assn. Higher Edn., Higher Edn. Reps. Network (chmn. program com. 1981-82). Republican. Presbyterian. Club: Women's City (Cleve.). Home and Office: 11425 Edgewater Dr Cleveland OH 44102

KURETSKY, SUSAN DONAHUE, art historian; b. Charleston, S.C., Oct. 11, 1941; d. James Kenneth and Esther (Lawshe) Donahue; A.B., Vassar Coll., 1963; M.A. (Woodrow Wilson fellow), Harvard U., 1964, Ph.D. (Bernice Cronkhite fellow), 1971; m. Robert L. Kuretsky, July 17, 1969. Teaching fellow Harvard U., 1965-67; asst. prof. art Boston U., 1969-74; asso. prof. art Vassar Coll., 1975—; cons. pub. programs Nat. Endowment Humanities. Smith fellow in Dutch and Flemish art Nat. Gallery, Washington, 1974-75. Mem. Coll. Art Assn. Am. Author: The Paintings of Jacob Ochtervelt, 1979; (with others) Gods, Saints and Heroes: Dutch Painting in the Age of Rembrandt, 1980-81; contbr. articles and revs. to profl. jours. Office: Box 114 Vassar College Poughkeepsie NY 12601

KURIANSKY, JUDITH ANNE BRODSKY, psychologist, TV personality; b. N.Y.C., Jan. 31, 1947; d. Abraham I. and Sylvia (Feld) Brodsky; B.A., Smith Coll., 1968; student U. Geneva, 1967; Ed.M., Boston U., 1970; Ph.D., N.Y. U., 1980; m. Edward J. Kuriansky, Aug. 24, 1969. Sr. research scientist N.Y. State Psychiat. Inst., 1970-76; lectr. postgrad. sexuality courses Columbia U. Med. Center, 1975—; intern in psychology St. Luke's Hosp., 1978-79; sex therapy coordinator Nat. Inst. for Psychotherapies, N.Y.C., 1978-80; lectr. Insts. of Religion and Health, N.Y.C., 1979—; v.p. Quezon Corp., N.Y.C., 1978—; on-air psychologist Sta. WABC-TV, N.Y.C., 1980—, on air feature reporter on psychology, 1980-81, host nightly talk show, 1981—; on air feature reporter on psychology Sta. WBZ-TV, Boston, 1980-81; host Modern Satellite Network Series, 1981; cons. and lectr. in field. Bd. dirs. Scientists Com. for Public Info., 1977-79. Sloan Found. sci. research grantee, 1968. Mem. Am. Psychol. Assn., Soc. for Sex Therapy and Research (charter), N.Y. Soc. for Clin. Psychologists, Am. Psychiat. Assn. (com. on nomenclature), Am. Assn. Sex Educators, Counselors and Therapists (cert. sex therapist), Am. Women in Radio and TV, Women in Communications. Contbr. articles to profl. jours. and lay mags. Home: 8 Thomas St New York NY 10007

KURKA, BARBARA FLORENCE, broadcasting soc. ofcl.; b. N.Y.C., Dec. 10, 1950; d. John and Florence Eva (Bossert) K.; B.A., Hunter Coll., 1972. Sales promotion coordinator Aramis, Inc., N.Y.C., 1972-76, tng. mgr., 1976-77; dir. Internat. Radio and TV Soc., Inc., N.Y.C., 1978—; awards coordinator Internat. Emmy Awards, 1977-78. Chmn., Internat. Year of Child com. St. Bartholomew's Community Club, 1979; chmn. bd. trustees Good Shepherd Protestant Parish, 1979. Mem. Nat. Acad. TV Arts and Scis., Am. Women in Radio and TV. Democrat. Methodist. Club: St. Bartholomew's Community. Office: 420 Lexington Ave New York NY 10170

KURLANS, ALICE JOAN, research specialist; b. Phila., May 4, 1940; d. John Joseph and Tivia Marie (Scalella) Kateiva; B.A. in Microbiology, U. Pa., 1962; postgrad. Hahnemann Med. Coll., 1965; M.S. in Info. Sci., Drexel U., 1971; m. William H. Kurlans, June 22, 1968. Microbiologist, Campbell Soup Co., Camden, N.J., 1963, Hahnemann Med. Coll., 1963-65, 66-70, Med. Coll. Pa., 1966; chemist Inst. Sci. Info., Phila., 1966; research specialist U. Pa., 1975—; info. analyst sci. research documents Franklin Inst.; USPHS fellow, 1965. Mem. Am. Soc. Microbiology, Am. Inst. Biol. Scis., Am. Soc. Info. Sci., NOW, Beta Phi Mu. Contbr. articles to sci. jours. Home: 2601 Benjamin Franklin Pkwy Apt 1145 Philadelphia PA 19130

KURRIK, MAIRE, educator; b. Tartu, Estonia, Jan. 22, 1940; d. Richard and Hedda (Klaser) Jaanus; B.A., Vassar Coll., 1961; Ph.D., Harvard U., 1968; m. Edward W. Said, July 8, 1962 (div.); m. 2d, Juhan Kurrik, Apr. 30, 1970. Instr. Barnard Coll., Columbia U., N.Y.C., 1968-69, asst. prof., 1969-76, asso. prof., 1976-81, prof. English, 1981—. Author: Georg Trakl, 1974; Literature and Negation, 1979. Office: 422 Barnard Hall Columbia U New York NY 10027

KURTYKA, JULIA CAROLYN, musician, educator; b. Detroit, Sept. 14, 1943; d. Joseph and Mary (Krainiak) K.; B.Mus., U. Mich., 1965, M.Mus., 1967. Tchr. music Toledo Bd. Edn., 1962-78; prin. violinist Toledo Symphony, 1965-78, music librarian, 1970-75; 1st violinist Toledo String Quartet, 1971-78; founder, dir. Parochial Sch. String Program and Orch., 1969-71; tchr. music Frankfort Area Schs., 1978-81; instr. music Northwestern Mich. Coll., 1978—; tchr. violin, Traverse City, Mich., 1978—; dir., condr. Benzie Area Symphonette, 1979—; concertmistress Northwestern Mich. Symphony, Midland (Mich.) Symphony orchs., 1979-82; soloist N.W. Symphony, 1981; tchr. Suzuki violin class, Cadillac, Mich., 1982—; violinist Northwood Symphonette, 1979—, also librarian, personnel mgr., 1981; violinist Cass City Bach Festival Orch., 1978—, librarian, 1981—. Mem. Am. String Tchrs., Am. Suzuki Tchrs. Assn., Sigma Beta. Russian Orthodox. Address: Route 1 Box 231 Copemish MI 49625

KURTZ, WINIFRED MARY, club woman; b. Washington, Iowa, Aug. 28; d. Charles Sanford and Gertrude Josephine (Swift) Ragan; student Washington Jr. Coll., 1949-50, St. Ambrose Coll., Davenport, Iowa, 1950; m. Robert Kurtz, Sept. 12, 1951; 1 son, Michael R. Hostess, waitress Grand Lake Lodge, Colo., 1946; desk clk. Cosmopolitan Hotel, Denver, 1946; cashier Sears Roebuck & Co., Kansas City, Mo., 1947; tchr. Pleasant Hill Sch., Washington County, Iowa, 1950-51, Riverside Sch., Brighton, Iowa, 1952-53. Pres. dist. 11, Diocesan Council Cath. Women, 1972-74, 76-78, parish rep. dist. 11, 1970—, mem. Orgn. Services Commn., 1981-83, mem. nominating com., 1982— Sunday sch. tchr. St. Joseph's Ch., East Pleasant Plain, Iowa, 1960-70, v.p. Altar and Rosary Soc., 1980—; sec. Writers Round Table, 1966-80; asso. Citizens for Decency through Law, 1974—; pres. Pleasant Plain (Iowa) Sch. PTA, 1966-68; state historian Daus. Am. Colonists, 1966-68, state corr. sec., 1968-70, state 1st vice regent, 1972-74, state regent, 1974-76, chmn. nat. def., 1976-78, vice chmn. flag U.S.A., 1976—, chmn. state flag com., 1982—, chmn. state nominating com., 1981—; state chmn. flag of U.S.A., DAR, 1976-78, nat. vice chmn. flag U.S.A., 1976-80, chpt. regent, 1971-73, 81-83, vice regent, 1982-83; mem. Iowa Button Club. Republican. Home: Rt 2 Brighton IA 52540

KURTZWEIL, MARGARET JEAN, recreation co. exec.; b. Syracuse, N.Y., May 6, 1954; d. Terrence John and Jean Laura Kurtzweil; A.A., Lorain County Community Coll., 1974; B.A. in Psychology, Bowling Green State U., 1976; M.A., Eastern Mich. U., 1979. Sales rep. Cedar Point, Inc., Sandusky, Ohio, 1976-78, dist. sales mgr., 1978-81, sales mgr. Western region, 1981—. Mem. Assn. Female Execs., Ann Arbor Bus. and Profl. Women, Ann Arbor Networks, Bowling Green State U. Alumni Assn. Republican. Club: Ford Lake Sail. Home: 2151 Lakeview Apt 31 Ypsilanti MI 48197 Office: Cedar Point Inc Sandusky OH 44870

KUSHNER, EVA, educator, author; b. Prague, Czechoslovakia, June 18, 1929; d. Josef and Anna (Kafkova) Dubsky; B.Ph., Coll. Marie de France, Montreal, 1946; B.A., McGill U., 1948, M.A. in Philosophy, 1950, Ph.D. in French Lit., 1956; m. Donn Jean Kushner, Sept. 15, 1949; children—Daniel Peter, Roland Joseph, Paul Joel. Lectr. in French, McGill U., Montreal, Que., Can., 1952-55, instr. French Summer Sch., 1956, 58, 61, 62, 67, 68, 69, prof. French Lang. and Lit., McGill U., 1976—; sessional lectr. in philosophy Sir George Williams U., 1952-53; lectr. Univ. Coll., London, Eng., 1958-59; lectr. Carleton U., 1961, asst. prof., 1963, assoc. prof., 1965, prof. French and Comparative Lit., 1969-76, chmn. comparative lit., 1965-69, 70-72, 75-76, adj. prof. lit., 1976-79. Exec. com. Can. Council, mem. Council, 1975-81; mem. Comite-Conseil Dept. Edn. Que.; mem. Council d'administration, fond de soutien et aide a la recherche; adv. bd. Nat. Library Can.; pres. Humanities Research Council Can., 1970-72. Elected Academie Europeene des lettres, des science et des Arts. Fellow Royal Soc. Can. (v.p.); mem. Academie des lettres et sciences humaines (pres.), Am. Comparative Lit. Assn. (adv. bd.), Internat. Comparative Lit. Assn. (pres. 1979-82), MLA Am. (del. Assembly, chmn. 16th Century French Lit. div.), Assn. internat. des etudes francaises, Assn. des profs. de francais des univs. canadiennes, assn. canadienne de litterature comparee (v.p. 1969-71), Internat. Assn. Neo-Latin Studies, Soc. canadienne d'etudes de la Renaissance, Assn. des litteratures canadienne et quebecoise, Can. Soc. Semiotic Research. Mem. United Ch. Can. Author: Patrice de La Tour de Pin, 1961; Le mythe d'Orphee dans la litterature francaise contemporaine, 1961; Chants de Boheme, 1963; Rina Lasnier collections Ecrivains canadiens d'aujourd'hui, 1964, Poetes d'aujourd'hui, 1969; Saint-Denys Garneau, 1967; Francois Mauriac, 1972, Japanese transl. 1976; co-author anthology Que. poetry, transl. Hungarian; co-editor Proceedings of the VIIth Congress of Internat. Comparative Lit Assn.; Vol. IV (Evolution of the Novel) IX ICLA Congress; contbr. articles in field to publs.; co-dir. research Renaissance vols. Histoire comparee des litteratures de langes europeennes; editorial com. Canadian Comparative Lit. Rev.; internat. adv. bd. Comparative Lit. Studies. Office: 3460 McTavish St Montreal PQ H3A 1X9 Canada *

KUSMA, KYLLIKKI, lawyer; b. Tartu, Estonia, Dec. 8, 1943; came to U.S., 1951, naturalized, 1958; d. August and Helju (Traat) K.; B.F.A., Ohio U., 1966; M.A. (Vet.'s Rehab. Adminstrn. fellow), Ohio State U., 1967; J.D., Ohio No. U., 1976; M.L.T., Georgetown U., 1980. Speech and hearing therapist Lima (Ohio) Meml. Hosp., 1967-70, Tipp City (Ohio) Schs., 1970-74; admitted to Ohio bar, 1977, D.C. bar, 1978; atty.-adv. Office Chief Counsel, IRS, Washington, 1977-81; v.p., asso. tax counsel Security Pacific Nat. Bank, Los Angeles, 1981—; instr. Wright State U., 1972-76. Vol. local civic, polit. activities. Mem. Am. Bar Assn., D.C. Bar Assn., Ohio Bar Assn., Women Lawyers Los Angeles, Phi Kappa Phi. Democrat. Office: 333 S Hope St Corp Tax H20-12 Los Angeles CA 90071

KUSNITZ, ADELE LEVINE, state legislator, histologist; b. Bridgeport, Conn., Sept. 8, 1941; d. Isadore and Diane (Sugarman) Levine; student U. Bridgeport, 1960-62; m. Leland Warren Kusnitz, July 26, 1963; children—Jennifer Amy, Lisa Elaine. Research asst. solid state physics CBS Labs., Stamford, Conn., 1960-62; research asst. dept. pathology Mass. Gen. Hosp., Boston, 1962-63; sr. histology technologist Yale U., New Haven, 1979—, in charge research histology Med. Sch., 1981—, also mem. safety com. Mem. Conn. Gen. Assembly, 1981—; mem. Monroe Republican Town Com., 1970—, chmn., 1974-76; mem. Monroe Parks and Recreation Commn., 1970-72; mem., sec. Monroe Recreational Authority, 1972-73; justice of peace, 1974-76; mem. Charter Revision Commn., 1976-77. Mem. Nat. Order Women Legislators, Nat. Assn. Jewish Legislators, Nat. Rep Women's Club. Jewish. Home: 45 Twinbrook Terr Monroe CT 06468 Office: Room 111 State Capitol Hartford CT 06115

KUTCHINSKY, LEIGH ELENA, public health epidemiologist, educator; b. N.Y.C., Aug. 4, 1947; B.S., U. Calif., Berkeley, 1976, M.P.H., 1977, Ph.D., M.D., 1978; children—Buddy, Tad, Scott, Yaakov. Epidemiologist, Contra Costa (Calif.) VD Program, 1973-75; lectr. U. Calif., Berkeley, 1976-77; epidemiologist Colo. Dept. Health, Denver, 1977—; asst. prof. U. Colo. Med. Center, 1977—; pres. Medi-Search, Inc.; co-founder West Contra Costa Clinic; childbirth and Lamaze instr. Brighton Hosp. Chairperson, Contra Costa Childcare Adv. Bd., 1973-75; mem. Joint Strategy Action Com. on Medi-Cal Reform, 1975-77, Com. on Access to Health Care, 1975-78, Med. Com. for Human Rights, 1968—, U. Calif. Acad. Affairs Council, 1975-77. Chmn. issues com. Adams County Democratic Women's Caucus; mem. exec. bd. Adams County. Calif. State fellow, 1976-78, Regents fellow, 1976-78. A-CC/AMA scholar, 1975-76; HEW trainee, 1976-78. Mem. Am. Public Health Assn., Am. Med. Women's Assn., Colo. Public Health Assn., Am. Trauma Soc., Colo. Holistic Health Network, Am. Acad. Polit. Sci., EST, Mensa, Phi Beta Kappa, Alpha Gamma Sigma (Gold Pin award). Democrat. Jewish. Club: Am. Kennel. Research on herpes virus. Home and office: 2490 Channing Way Apt 503 Berkeley CA 94563

KUYKENDALL, PATRICIA ANNE, hosp. exec.; b. Kewanee, Ill., Mar. 27, 1935; d. Samuel Burton and Theresa Mary (McEnroe) Ensley; diploma nursing St. Anthony Hosp., Rock Island, Ill., 1960; B.S. in Nursing, Incarnate Word Coll., San Antonio, 1961; M.S., St. Louis U., 1965; m. James K. Kuykendall, Jan. 17, 1973. Dir. staff devel. Barnes Hosp., St. Louis, 1969-74; program dir. oncology nursing project U. Tex., Houston, 1974-77; mem. nursing staff U. Tex. Med. Br., Galveston, 1977—, dir. nursing surg. operating suite, ICU and sterile processing dept., 1980-81, exec. dir., dir. nursing surg. operating and acute care support services, 1981—; mgmt. cons. in field. Mem. lay adv. bd. Forest Park Community Coll., St. Louis, 1972-74. Mem. Am. Nurses Assn., Am. Hosp. Assn., Sigma Theta Tau (chpt. treas. 1977-79). Roman Catholic. Office: U Tex Med Br University and Mechanic Sts Galveston TX 77550

KUYKENDALL, RUTH JANE, real estate co. exec.; b. Jackson, Mich., Aug. 22, 1908; d. James Elwood and Nellie Bethune (Allen) Bartlett; student Mich. State U., 1927-28, Fla. State Coll. for Women, 1930-31; m. Hubert Paul Kuykendall, June 12, 1945. Mgr., Myakka Hotel, Venice, Fla., 1931-41; corp. sec. J.E. Bartlett & Sons, Inc., 1931-54, pres., 1955-56; owner, mgr. Kuykendall Real Estate Co., 1951—. Mem. Internat. Platform Assn., Am. Inst. Parliamentarians, Gulf Coast Parliamentarians (v.p. 1981—), DAR, Am. Legion Aux., Daus. Am. Colonists, V.F.W. Colonial Dames XVII Century, Desc. Mayflower, Magna Charta Dames. Republican. Methodist. Home: 261 Ponce de Leon Ave Venice FL 33595

KYES, HELEN (MRS. ROGER M. KYES), civic worker; b. Marion, Ohio, Dec. 28; d. Benjamin and Bess (Gilmore) Jacoby; B.A. Oberlin Coll., 1926; H.H.D. (hon.), Oakland U., 1980; m. Roger M. Kyes, June 5, 1931; children—Carolyn, Frances, Katharine, Anne. Mem. bd. Woman's Nat. Farm and Garden, 1943-56, sec., 1943-45, 54-55; bd. dirs. Children's Aid and Home for the Friendless, 1949-69; bd. dirs. Brookside Sch., Cranbrook, 1953-58; sec., 1957-58; charter mem. bd. trustees Mich. State U. Oakland Found., 1957-70; v.p. exec. bd. Oakland U. Found., 1958—; trustee U. Oakland; mem. Women's Assn. Detroit Symphony; mem. com. of 100 Detroit Met. Opera; capt. spl. gifts Detroit United Fund, 1959-61; mem. Detroit Mus. Art Founders Soc., mem. com. Detroit Foster Home Edn. and Recruitment Program, 1960—. Mem. DAR, AAUW. Presbyterian. (vice moderator deacons). Clubs: Detroit, Ocean of Fla., Gulfstream Bath and Tennis, Bloomfield Hills Country, Village Woman's.

KYLE, KATHY MARIE, accountant; b. Washington, Dec. 22, 1957; d. James and Dorothy Marie (Alexander) K.; B.S. in Bus. Adminstrn. cum laude, Shippensburg (Pa.) State Coll., 1979; m. Edward M. Wagman, Jan. 2, 1982. Staff acct. Laventhol & Horwath, Harrisburg, Pa., 1979-82, sr. acct., 1982—. Mem. Am. Inst. C.P.A.s, Pa. Inst. C.P.A.s, Kappa Delta Pi, Phi Beta Lambda. Republican. Lutheran. Clubs: Sailing, Needlepoint, Order Eastern Star, Internat. Rainbow for Girls. Home: 1315 Strafford Rd Camp Hill PA 17011 Office: Laventhol & Horwath 2101 N Front St Harrisburg PA 17105

KYLE, PATRICIA JEAN, magistrate; b. Los Angeles, Oct. 23, 1943; d. John Hamilton and Jean Gillespie (Booher) K.; student Stephens Coll., 1961-63; B.A., U. Hawaii, 1968; postgrad. World Campus Afloat, Chapman Coll., 1968; J.D. cum laude, U. Miami, 1974. Admitted to Fla. bar, 1974; staff writer Action Line, The Miami Herald, Broward Edit., 1968-69; legis. aide Fla. Ho. of Reps., 1969; asst. to Broward County solicitor, 1969-70; asst. to chief asst. state atty., 1970-71; asst. U.S. atty. civil div. Office U.S. Atty., Miami, 1974-77; litigation atty. Stroock & Stroock & Lavan, Miami, 1977; U.S. magistrate, U.S. Dist. Ct., so. dist. Fla., Ft. Lauderdale, 1977—. Recipient commendations criminal div. U.S. Dept. Justice, U.S. Drug Enforcement Adminstrn., spl. achievement award U.S. Dept. Justice, 1974-77, appreciation award Gold Key Club, Nova Law Center, 1979, appreciation cert. Broward County Bar Assn., 1981. Mem. ABA (vice chmn. criminal appellate issues com., sect. criminal justice), Fed. Bar Assn., Fla. Bar Assn., Broward County Bar Assn. (spl. com. on fed. appellate circuit transition). Episcopalian. Office: Suite 204 299 E Broward Blvd Fort Lauderdale FL 33301

KYLE, REGINA MARY, mgmt. cons. co. exec.; b. Rockland, Mass., June 16, 1936; d. Alfred James and Helen Veronica (Keane) K.; B.A., Regis Coll., 1963; M.A. (univ. fellow, Fulbright fellow, AAUW fellow), Harvard U., 1965, Ph.D., 1971. Elem. and secondary sch. tchr., 1957-64; faculty Harvard U., Cambridge, Mass., 1968-73; exec. dean for undergrad. studies U. Tex., Dallas, 1973-76; dir. planning and program devel. Assn. Am. Colls., Washington, 1976-78, v.p. planning and programs, 1978-80; pvt. practice cons., Washington, 1973—; v.p. dir. edn. services E.H. White & Co., Mgmt. Cons., Washington. Co-chmn. Goals for Dallas Com. on Elem. and Secondary Edn., 1975-76; trustee sta. KERA-TV, 1974-75, Richardson Symphony Orch., 1974-76. Canaday grantee in humanities, 1971; award Leadership Dallas, 1975. Mem. MLA. Roman Catholic. Club: Harvard of Washington. Exec. editor: Trends 2000, 1978-80. Home: 318 9th St SE Washington DC 20003 Office: 1025 Vermont Ave NW Washington DC 20005

KYLE, SHELIA MARIE, nurse; b. Huntington, W.Va., Dec. 5, 1945; d. Roy James and Welthie Marie (Evans) Manis; A.S.N., Marshall U., 1965, B.S.N., 1977, M.S., 1981; postgrad. Coll. Nursing, U. Ky., 1982—; m. Larry Dusten Kyle, Sept. 7, 1963; 1 dau., Kristina Maria. Charge nurse Cabell-Huntington Hosp., 1965-67; staff nurse Marshall U. Health Center, 1967-77; instr. pharmacology and nursing fundamentals St. Mary's Hosp. Sch. Nursing, Huntington, 1977—. Pres., Huntington Jaycee-ettes, 1971-72, state dir., 1972-73, 74-75, regional v.p., 1972-73; active Miller Sch. PTA. Mem. Am. Nurses Assn., W.Va. Nurses Assn., Nat. League Nursing. Home: 1418 Charleston Ave Huntington WV 25701 Office: 2900 1st Ave Huntington WV 25701

KYLER-HUTCHISON, PANELPHA LILLIAN, occupational therapist; b. Balt., Apr. 4, 1949; d. Leighton S. and Lois J. K.; A.A., Community Coll. Balt., 1969; B.S. in Occupational Therapy, Va. Commonwealth U., 1972; M.A., Towson State U., 1983. Residents hall coordinator Commonwealth of Va., 1970-72; staff therapist Johns Hopkins Hosp., Balt., 1973-75; chief of occupational therapy Mt. Wilson (Md.) Hosp. Center, 1975-78; occupational therapist Spring Grove Hosp. Center, 1978-80; asso. dir. rehab. services Springfield Hosp. Center, Sykesville, Md., 1980-82, dir. rehab. services, 1980—; cons. Md. Dept. Health and Mental Hygiene, 1982—, N.J. Health and Hosps. Service, 1976-78; mem. Md. Bd. Occupational Therapy Practice, 1979—; cons. div. vocat. rehab. Carroll County Health Dept., 1977-78; instr. Community Coll. Balt., 1976-78; mem. joint practices com. Med. and Chirurgical Faculty of State of Md. Recipient Leadership key Va. Commonwealth U. Hotline Crisis Intervention worker, 1971-72. Mem. Am. (past pres. student com.; housing com. 1979-80), Md. (Recognition award 1982; program chmn., adv. bd., pres. 1976-78) occupational therapy assns., World Fedn. Occupational Therapy, Alpha Sigma Chi. Roman Catholic. Home: 1221 Ramblewood Rd Baltimore MD 21239 Office: Springfield Hosp Center Sykesville MD 21784

KYRIAKOU, LINDA GRACE, chem. co. exec.; b. N.Y.C., Dec. 5, 1943; d. Frank Thomas and Dolores Helen (Coscia) LaGamma; B.A., Hunter Coll., 1965; m. Konstantinos Kyriakou, May 7, 1967; 1 dau., Christina Elena. Info. editor Nat. Bur. Econ. Research, N.Y.C., 1967-69; dir. research/account officer Booke & Co., N.Y.C., 1969-75; mgr. communications services C.I.T. Fin. Corp., N.Y.C., 1975-79; dir. corp. communications Sun Chem. Corp., N.Y.C., 1979—. Mem. Public Relations Soc. Am., Nat. Investor Relations Inst. (dir. N.Y. chpt. 1981-82), Women's Bond Club N.Y. (bd. govs. 1978-80), Econ. Club Detroit. Home: 300 E 59th St New York NY 10022 Office: 200 Park Ave New York NY 10166

KYZER, JOAN MAXEY, retail exec.; b. Newberry, S.C., Feb. 27, 1942; d. Thomas C. Maxey and Elsie (Ellisor) Maxey Meetze; cert. acctg. Internat. Corr. Schs., 1970; m. T. Edward Kyzer, June 3, 1959; 1 son, Clarke. With Bergen's Stores, Newberry, 1960—, office mgr., 1970-75, controller, 1975—. Pres., United Meth. Women, 1972; counsellor United Meth. Youth, 1973-79, youth coordinator O'Neal St. United Meth. Ch., 1975-79. Mem. Sec.'s Guild Am. Home: 2210 Evans Circle Newberry SC 29108 Office: 1202 Caldwell St Newberry SC 29108

LAATSCH, AUDREY FRIEDA, social worker; b. Milw., Aug. 4, 1929; d. Edwin David and Rose Margaret (Kurz) L.; B.A., U. Wis., 1953; M.S.W., U. Calif., 1956; Cert. in Child Psychotherapy, Chgo. Inst. Psychoanalysis, 1968. Social work trainee Dept. Public Welfare, State of Wis., 1953-54; caseworker, 1956-59; therapist Lakeside Children's Center (now Lakeside Child and Family Center), Milw., 1959-62, dir. therapy, 1962-70, asso. dir. therapy, 1970-77, asso. dir., 1977—. Mem. Am. Assn. Residential Treatment Centers (program chmn. 1972-73, treas. 1974-75, chmn. nominating com. 1976, 77, 78-79), Nat. Assn. Social Workers, Assn. Cert. Social Workers, Am. Orthopsychiatric Assn., Assn. Child Psychotherapists, Phi Beta Kappa. Democrat. Lutheran. Home: 1111 N Astor St Milwaukee WI 53202 Office: 2220 E North Ave Milwaukee WI 53202

LAATZ, MARY JANE, med. librarian; b. Indpls., Dec. 27, 1916; d. Jacob Philip and Nell (Carey) Laatz; A.B., Butler U., 1938; B.S. in L.S., Western Res. U., 1939. Librarian, Ind. U. Extension Div., Indpls., 1939-41; cataloger Ind. U. Sch. Medicine Library, 1941-51, reference librarian, 1951, 53-57, acting librarian, 1951-53, med. librarian, 1957—, asst. prof. med. lit., 1957-72, asso. prof. med. lit., 1973—. Chmn. Council of Midwest Regional Health Scis. Library and Coop. Information Services, 1968-70; participant Conf. on Interlibrary Communication Network, ALA and U.S. Office Edn., 1970, Nat. Adv. Com. Conf. on Networks for Networkers, 1979; Ind. U. rep. ednl. communications network study EDUCOM, 1966; mem. Midwest Health Sci. Library Network Assembly Resource Libraries, 1973—, chmn., 1975-76; rep.-at-large faculty council Ind. U.-Purdue U. at Indpls., 1974-76; mem. Ind. Health Scis. Librarians Assn. Council, 1981—. Mem. Spl. Libraries Assn. (chpt. pres. 1960-61), Med. Library Assn. (mem. scholarship com. 1972-74, chmn. 1973-74), John Shaw Billings History Medicine Soc. (sec.-treas. 1965-67), Indpls. Mus. Art, Delta Gamma. Presbyterian. Contbr. articles to profl. jours. Home: 6824 Willow Rd Indianapolis IN 46220 Office: Med Sci Bldg 122 Ind U Sch Medicine Library 1100 W Michigan St Indianapolis IN 46223

LA BAIR, ARLYN JOYCE, data processing corp. exec.; b. Pontiac, Mich., Aug. 24, 1951; d. Donald Thomas and Arlyne Mary (Steinbaugh) Green; A.A. in Bus. Mgmt., El Camino Coll., 1978; postgrad. Calif. State U., Dominguez Hills, 1979-81, U. Colo., Denver, 1982—; m. Patrick J. Diemert, Jan. 23, 1982. Programmer/analyst Coldwell Banker Mgmt. Corp., Los Angeles, 1972-74; sr. programmer/analyst MBA Systems, Los Angeles, 1974-76; group leader, mktg. analyst Carte Blanche Corp., Los Angeles, 1976-78; mgmt. cons. The Berton Group, Inc., Los Angeles, 1978-80; asst. v.p., div. mgr. First Interstate Services Co., Englewood, 1980—. Treas., Parker North Homeowners Assn. Mem. Nat. Assn. Female Execs., S.E. Denver Bus. and Profl. Women's Club (scholarship chmn.). Office: 111 Inverness Dr E Englewood CO 80112

LABARBERA, ELLEN, editor; b. Passaic, N.J., Oct. 17, 1948; d. Jack Howells, and Mary (Singer) Samson; B.A., Antioch Coll., 1971; m. Michael J. LaBarbera, May 20, 1973; 1 dau., Jessica Mary. Editor, Marcel Dekker, Inc., N.Y.C., 1971-73, Thomas Bouregy & Co., Inc., N.Y.C., 1973-76; sr. editing supr. McGraw-Hill Book Co., N.Y.C., 1976-78, sponsoring editor, 1978—. Office: 1221 Ave of the Americas New York NY 10020

LA BARGE, MARY JANE, business exec.; b. Ticonderoga, N.Y., Nov. 30, 1930; d. Albert J. and Marguerite D. LaB.; student Katharine Gibbs Sch., N.Y.C. Corp. sec. Martin Marietta Corp., Bethesda, Md., 1977—, Martin Marietta Aluminum Inc., Bethesda, 1977—. Mem. Am. Soc. Corp. Secs Inc. Office: 6801 Rockledge Dr Bethesda MD 20817

LABASTILLE, ANNE, wildlife ecologist; b. N.Y.C.; d. Ferdinand Meyer and Irma (Goebel) LaBastille; B.S. in Conservation, Cornell U., Ph.D. in Wildlife Ecology, 1969; M.S. in Wildlife Mgmt., Colo. State U.; Litt.D. (hon.), Union Coll., 1980. Asst. prof. natural resources Cornell U., Ithaca, N.Y., 1969-71; pres. West of the Wind Publs., Inc., 1971—; photographer EPA, Adirondacks, 1973; cons. Smithsonian Instn., Washington, 1973-75, Gulf & Western Ams. Co., Dominican Republic, 1973-75; hon. cons. World Wildlife Fund, Internat.; commr. Adirondack Park Agy.; dir.-at-large Nat. Wildlife Fedn.; juror J. Paul Getty wildlife conservation award, 1974-82. Recipient Gold medal for conservation World Wildlife Fund, 1974; Lit. award N.Y. State Outdoor Edn. Assn., 1977; registered Adirondack guide. Mem. Wildlife Soc., Am. Union Ornithologists, Soc. Women Geographers, Am. Women in Sci., Explorer's Club, Beta Sigma Phi (hon.). Author: Woodswoman, 1976; Assignment: Wildlife, 1980; Women and Wilderness, 1980; children's books; contbr. articles to popular and profl. jours., Nat. Geog.

LABAY, NANCY CAROLE, librarian; b. Chgo., Apr. 12, 1943; d. Linus and Mary (Kovach) Kruse; student Valley Coll., 1961-63; cert. John Robert Powers Modeling Sch., 1965; m. Warren Charles LaBay, June 1, 1968; 1 son, Edward Christian. Fashion coordinator Montgomery Ward, Panorma City, Calif., 1965; receptionist Kenneth Leventhal & Co., 1966; tech. info. asst., 1970-75, acctg. prin., auditing standards asst., 1975-80, research librarian, fin. coordinator, 1980—. Historian, Westdale Homeowners Assn., 1970—, sec., 1980-82. Mem. Nat. Consumer Panel. Republican. Office: 2039 Century Park E Century City CA 90067

LABEDZ, BERNICE R., state legislator; b. Omaha, Sept. 19, 1919; student parochial and public schs.; m. Stanley J. Labedz, May 9, 1942; children—Terry, Jeannette, Toni, Frank. Former exec. sec. to mayor of Omaha; formerly with Nebr. Dept. Revenue; former staff aide, regional office of Senator Exon, Omaha; mem. Nebr. Legislature, 1976—; dir. B C Dressed Beef Co. Mem. Q Street Mchts. Assn., South Omaha and Omaha Police and Fire Aux., Cath. Daus. Am. *

LABEN, JOYCE KEMP, educator; b. Elgin, Ill., Mar. 2, 1936; d. Berton John and Lois Elizabeth (Heath) Kemp; B.S.N., U. Mich., 1957; M.S.N., U. Calif., San Francisco, 1964; J.D., Suffolk U., 1969; m. Robert J. Laben, Feb. 27, 1971. Nurse, U. Calif. San Francisco Med. Center, 1957-59, 61-62; surg./office nurse, San Francisco, 1960-61; instr. Boston State Hosp., 1964-65; asst. prof. Sch. Nursing, Boston U., 1965-70; asso. prof. Sch. Nursing, Vanderbilt U., Nashville, 1970-78, prof., 1978—, chmn. behavioral scis. as applied to nursing, 1975-81, acting asso. dean undergrad. studies, 1981-82, asso. dean undergrad. studies, 1982—, pres. women's faculty orgn., 1980-81. Dir. forensic services sect. Tenn. Dept. Mental Health, Nashville, 1972-74; cons. Tenn. Dept. Mental Health/Mental Retardation, 1974—, others; mem. task force panel Pres.' Commn. on Mental Health, 1977. Bd. dirs., v.p. Opportunity House, Nashville, 1973-80; bd. dirs. Nat. Commn. on Confidentiality of Health Records, 1976-79. Recipient Cert. of Spl. Recognition, Tenn. Dept. Mental Health, 1974; Mem. Am. Nurses Assn. (spl. recognition award 1980), mem. council advanced practitioners in psychiat./mental health nursing), AAUP, Am. Soc. Law and Medicine. Contbr. articles to profl. jours. Office: 103 Godchaux Hall Vanderbilt U Nashville TN 37240

LABER, MARIAN ROBERTA OPPENHEIM, real estate broker; b. Hanford, Calif., Jan. 18, 1918; d. Leon and Isabelle (Estrada) Oppenheim; student San Francisco City Coll., 1966, Golden Gate Coll., 1969; m. Lawrence E. Laber, Feb. 22, 1941; children—Lawrence E., Pamela, Deborah (Mrs. Thomas McDermott), James Harrison. Telephone operator Pacific Tel.&Tel. Co., 1936-39, instr., 1940-42; mgr. office Press Wireless, Washington, 1942-43; owner Marian Lawrence, children's shop, San Francisco, 1945-48; owner, mgr. San Bruno 5-10, San Francisco, 1947-50; girl Friday, Lampley Realty, San Francisco, 1968-72, owner, real estate broker Century 21 Lampley Realty, 1972—. Active Boy Scouts Am., Girl Scouts U.S.A., Camp fire Girls; pres. local PTA, 1954-55; trustee Drew Coll. Prep. Sch., chmn. bd., 1975-76, 81-83. Mem. ARC, Am. Cancer Soc., San Francisco Real Estate Bd., Calif. Real Estate Assn. Roman Catholic (pres. ch. group 1950-51). Home: 2235 Laguna St Apt 405 San Francisco CA 94115 Office: Century 21-Lampley Realty 2101 Pine St San Francisco CA 94115

LABONTE, DOROTHY HAZEL, hosp. adminstr.; b. Springfield, Mass., Oct. 13, 1925; d. Albert Edward Ernest and Merle Evelyne (Richings) Ellett; diploma Waltham Hosp. Sch. Nursing, 1947; B.A., Simmons Coll. Sch. Nursing, 1970; M.A., Framingham State Coll., 1982; m. Edward W. LaBonte, Sr., Sept. 28, 1947; children—Michele Shea, Edward W. Staff nurse, head nurse Waltham (Mass.) Hosp., 1947-50; staff nurse, supr. Leonard Morse Hosp., Natick, Mass., 1950-56, asst. dir. nursing, 1956-63, dir. nursing, 1963-76, dir. patient care services, 1976-81, asst. to exec. v.p., 1981-82; dir. nursing Fairlawn Hosp., Worcester, Mass., 1982—. Corporator Framingham (Mass.) Union Hosp.; trustee Hospice at Home, Wayland, Mass.; hon. bd. mem. Adult Day Care. Mem. Am. Soc. Nursing Service Adminstrs., Nat. League Nursing, Am. Heart Assn., Mass. Soc. Nursing Service Adminstrs., Mass. League Nursing. Unitarian. Home: 57 Edgewater Dr Framingham MA 01701 Office: 67 Union St Natick MA 01760

LABORDE, GENIE ZYLKS, seminar trainer, author; b. Borger, Tex., Feb. 19, 1928; d. Floyd Weber and Molsie Lee (Lowery) Zylks; m. John Peter Laborde, July 2, 1949; children—John Tracy, Cliffe Floyd, Gary Lee, John Peter, Mary Adrienne, Kathryn Anne Griffin; m. 2d, George Davis Griffin, Feb. 21, 1981; B.A., La. State U., 1948; M.A., Tulane U., 1970; Ph.D., U. Calif., Santa Barbara, 1977. Dir., Confluent Edn. Research and Devel. Center, 1973-77; research dir. Berkeley Inst. Psychol. Research, 1977; neuro-linguistic programming practioner, Palo Alto, Calif., 1980; precision trainer, Palo Alto, 1980; pres. Syntony, Inc., Palo Alto, 1981, Grinder, Laborde Hill, Palo Alto and N.Y.C.; partner V.A.K. Newsletter, N.Y.C., 1975—. Mem. Am. Psychol. Assn., Assn. Humanistic Psychology, Am. Soc. Tng. and Devel. Author: (with others) Tranquilizers for His Cup, 1961; editor: Around the World the YPO Way, 1964. Home: 1431 Webster St Palo Alto CA 94301 Office: 1433 Webster St Palo Alto CA 94301

LABUA, JOANNE MICHELE, sch. dist. ofcl.; b. N.Y.C., June 23, 1934; d. John Joseph and Frances M. (Walsh) Moore; B.A. in Home Econs. and Early Childhood Edn., Hunter Coll., 1956, postgrad., 1958; m. Anthony Peter LaBua, July 11, 1959; children—Andrea Joan, Michelle Marie. Tchr., edn. dir. Happy Hours Nursery Sch., 1955-59; tchr. kindergarten Public Sch. 100, Queens, N.Y., 1956-62; dir. elem. sch. religion St. Parick's Ch., Bedford, N.Y., 1964-72; tchr. C.E. Tompkins Sch., Croton, N.Y., 1968; substitute tchr. Bedford Public Schs., 1970-74; edn. dir., staff devel. specialist Port Chester Head Start, 1974-78; dist. dir. sch. food services Somers (N.Y.) Central Sch. Dist., 1978—. Adult advisor Cath. Youth Orgn., St. Michael's Ch., Greenwich, Conn.; bd. dirs. Bedford PTA; fund raising v.p. Cancer Care of No. Westchester. Mem. Am. Sch. Food Service Assn., Hunter Coll. Alumnae Assn., Westchester Sch. Food Service Assn. (pres. 1981-82, 82-83), N.Y. State Sch. Food Service Assn. (conv. com. 1982), Nutrition Edn. and Tng. Council Westchester, Rockland and Putnam. Singer at Papal Mass in Yankee Stadium, 1979. Office: Somers Central School District Route 202 Somers NY 10589

LACAYO, CARMELA G., orgn. exec.; b. Chihuahua, Mex., June 28, 1943; d. Enrique Luis and Mary L. (Velazquez) L.; B.A. in Social Welfare, Immaculate Heart Coll., Los Angeles; B.A. in Psychology, Regina Mundi U., Rome. Mem. Sisters of Social Service, Los Angeles, 1961-71; prof. urban devel. and sociology U. San Buenaventura (Colombia), 1973-74; adminstrv. coordinator Office of Mayor, Los Angeles, 1974-75; pres., exec. dir. Nat. Assn. for Hispanic Elderly, Los Angeles, 1975—; pres. Nat. Hispanic Inst. of Public Policy, 1978—, Nat. Hispanic Research Center, 1980—; bd. dirs. Nat. Council on Aging. First vice chmn. Democratic Nat. Com., 1977—. Named Latina Woman of Yr., Los Angeles, 1976; Nat. Woman of Yr., Latin Am. Profl. Women's Assn., 1977. Fellow Gerontol. Soc. Am.; mem. Am. Public Health Assn., Western Gerontol. Soc. Roman Catholic. Office: Nat Assn for Hispanic Elderly 1730 W Olympic Blvd Suite 401 Los Angeles CA 90015

LACERTE, RITA C(ECILIA), computer services co. fin. exec.; b. Can., May 31, 1922; came to U.S., 1949, naturalized, 1956; d. Louis Philippe and Emma (Lapierre) Taillon; student voice St. Joseph's Coll., Winnipeg, Man., Can., 1938-39; m. Arcel J. Lacerte, Mar. 24, 1940; children—Claudette, Grant. Interior decorator Shipley's, Kansas City, Mo., 1950-51; acct., salesperson Superior Motors & Service, Stafford, Kans., 1952-56; cost acct. Snively Groves Co., Winter Haven, Fla., 1956-59; acct. Midland Sales Co., Winter Haven, 1959-62; systems analyst Data Corp. Am., Winter Haven, 1962-82, acct., controller, to 1982; sec.-treas., controller Lacorte Enterprises, Tampa, Fla., 1982—. Republican. Roman Catholic. Clubs: Las Damas De Arte; Art (Tampa, Fla.).

LACEY, PATRICIA BISHOP, supply co. adminstr.; b. Indianola, Miss., June 25, 1938; d. Clinton Jack and Velma Barron (Burns) Bishop B.S., U. Miss., 1959; m. Bill Smithson Lacey, June 18, 1960; children—Jeffrey, Lesli, Jennie. Tchr. Kosciusko (Miss.) City Schs., 1959-60, Thomastown (Miss.) Public Schs., 1964-65; office mgr. Central Office Supply, Kosciusko, 1968—. Bd. dirs. United Givers Fund, 1972-76; area chmn. Cystic Fibrosis, 1966-79; state sec. Miss. Chpt. Cystic Fibrosis, 1980-82. Mem. Nat. Assn. Female Execs., Nat. Office Products Assn., Miss. Assn. Pub. Accts. (bd. dirs. Central Miss. chpt. 1982—), Kosciusko C. of C. (membership and mchts. coms.), Phi Mu. Mem. Christian Church (Disciples of Christ). Clubs: Cosmopolitan, Kosciusko Golf, Ladies Golf Assn. Participant seminars in field. Office: Central Office Supply 127 E Jefferson PO Box C Kosciusko MS 39090

LACH, ALMA ELIZABETH, home econs. writer; b. Petersburg, Ill.; d. John H. and Clara E. (Boeker) Satorius; diplome de Cordon Bleu, Paris, 1956; m. Donald F. Lach, Mar. 18, 1939; 1 dau., Sandra Judith. Feature writer Children's Activities mag., 1954-55; creator, performer TV show Let's Cook, children's cooking show, 1955; performer TV show Over Easy, PBS, 1977-78; food editor Chgo. Daily Sun-Times, 1957-65; pres. Alma Lach Kitchens Inc., Chgo., 1966—; dir. Alma Lach Cooking Sch., Chgo.; lectr. U. Chgo. Downtown Coll., Gourmet Inst., U. Md., 1963, Modesto (Calif.) Coll., 1978, U. Chgo., 1981; resident master Shoreland Hall, U. Chgo., 1978-81; food cons. Food Bus. Mag., 1964-66, Chgo.'s New Pump Room, Lettuce Entertain You, Bitter End Resort, Brit. V.I. columnist Modern Packaging, 1967-68, Travel & Camera, 1969, Venture, 1970, Chicago mag., 1978, Bon Appetit, 1980, Tribune Syndicate, 1982. Recipient Pillsbury award, 1958; Grocery Mfrs. Am. Trophy award, 1959, certificate of Honor, 1961; Chevalier du Tastevin, 1962; Commanderie de l'Ordre des Anysetiers du Roy, 1963; Confrerie de la Chaine des Rotisseurs, 1964; Les Dames D'Escoffier, 1982. Mem. U. Chgo. Settlement League, Am. Assn. Food Editors (chmn. 1959), Internat. Platform Assn. Clubs: Tavern, Quadrangle (Chgo.). Author: A Child's First Cookbook, 1950; The Campbell Kids Have a Party, 1953; The Campbell Kids at Home, 1953; Let's Cook, 1956; Candlelight Cookbook, 1959; Weekly TV food show CBS, 1962-66; Cooking a la Cordon Bleu, 1970; Alma's Almanac, 1972; Hows and Whys of French Cooking, 1974. Contbr. to World Book Yearbook, 1961-75, Grolier Soc. Yearbook, 1962. Home and Office: 5750 Kenwood Ave Chicago IL 60637

LACHER, FRANCES RUTLAND, educator, advt. copywriter; b. Bklyn., June 1, 1921; d. Morris and Dora (Diamond) Rosen; B.B.A., CCNY, 1942; M.A., New Sch., 1982; m. Samuel Lacher, Feb. 23, 1947 (dec. Apr. 1982); children—Dorothy Alison, Irene Melanie. Group head Compton Advt., Inc., N.Y.C., 1953-59; v.p., creative supr. Dancer-Fitzgerald-Sample, 1959-63; group head Foote, Cone & Belding, 1964-65; creative dir. Hirsch, Tigler, Fried, 1967-68; copy supr. Schwab, Beatty & Porter, 1968-70; asst. prof. advt. and communications Fashion Inst. Tech., State U. N.Y., 1972—, also co-dir. Bklyn. Collector Gallery, 1975—; freelance writer; cons. in field. Recipient 3d pl. award Printers Ink, 1961; Best Grocery campaign award This Week, 1961, 3d pl. 10 Best Campaigns award Newsfront, 1961. Mem. Authors League Am., Advt. Women N.Y. (bd. dirs. 1976-77), Am. Advt. Fedn. (acad. com.), Authors Guild, Women in Communications, Am. Acad. Advt., Assn. Jr. Colls., Bklyn., Park Slope chambers commerce, Park Slope Civic Council. Jewish. Author: The Brides Book, 1949. Editor: Ad Libber, 1974-77. Contbr. articles on travel and art to N.Y. Times. Home: 47 Plaza St Brooklyn NY 11217 Office: 227 W 27th St New York NY 10001

LACHERT, HANNA, violinist; b. Poland, Nov. 25, 1944; came to U.S., 1969, naturalized, 1976; d. Zygmunt Adam and Hanna Katarzyna (Chrzanowska) L.; M.A. with honors, Warsaw Acad. Music, 1967; student Hannover Solistenklasse, 1968, Brussels Conservatory, 1969; M.A. with honors, U. Conn., 1971; m. David Segal, Dec. 7, 1978; children—Adi, Yaniv. Violinist with N.Y. Philharm. Orch., 1972—; soloist throughout world, including TV, radio, recs., TELARC. Recipient Premier Prix, Brussels Conservatory, 1969. Home: 50 Riverside Dr New York NY 10024 Office: Lincoln Center New York NY 10023

LACIAK, TERESE MARIE, chemist; b. Hammond, Ind., June 21, 1943; d. Harry P. and Maryann Makowski; B.S., Loyola U., 1965; m. John A. Laciak, Sept. 10, 1966; children—Christine Anne, John Justin. Research asst. Michael Reese Hosp., Chgo., 1965; project mgr., analytical lab. supr. Chgo. Bridge & Iron, Plainfield, Ill., 1966-75; lab. mgr. Arro Labs., Inc., Joliet, Ill., 1975—; pres., dir. FDP, Inc., Oak Forest, Ill., 1981—. Recipient Cert. of Leadership, YWCA, 1975, award ASTM, 1974. Mem. Am. Inst. Chemists, Theta Phi Alpha. Patentee in field. Office: PO Box 686 Caton Farm Rd Joliet IL 60434

LACK, DOROTHEA Z., psychologist; b. Winthrop, Mass.; B.S., Boston U., 1968; M.A., Syracuse U., 1971, Ph.D., 1975. Psychology trainee Syracuse (N.Y.) Mental Hygiene Clinic, 1969-70, VA Hosp., Syracuse, 1970-71; adminstrv. asst. Childrens Psychol. Services, Syracuse, N.Y., 1971-72; psychology intern San Francisco VA Hosp., 1973-74; asst. psychologist Lynn (Mass.) Community Health Center, 1974-75; pain unit dir., dir. psychology Lourdes Hosp., Binghamton, N.Y., 1975—; clin. asst. prof. Upstate Med. Center, 1980—. Mem. Am. Psychol. Assn., Am. Pain Soc., Internat. Assn. Study Pain. Contbr. articles to profl. jours. Office: Lourdes Hospital 169 Riverside Dr Binghamton NY 13905

LACK, RUTH VINN HENDLER, business exec.; b. Birzai, Lithuania, Nov. 18, 1932; came to U.S., 1938, naturalized, 1954; d. Nathan Samuel and Rae Kayla (Hendler) Hendler; B.J., U. Tex., 1953; m. Sanford I. Lack, May 3, 1953; children—Sharon, Barry, Stephen, Sandy, Jonathan Nathaniel. Exec. facilitator Lack's Inc. of Tex., Houston, 1977—. Pres., Sisterhood Temple Emanu El, 1965, Women's Public Relations Council, St. Joseph Hosp., 1968, Jewish Family Service, Houston, 1977-78; v.p. Jewish Fedn. Greater Houston, 1978—; active United Way Allocators, Houston, 1979—. Named Congregant of Yr., Temple Emanu-El, 1975; recipient Young Leadership award Jewish Fedn. Greater Houston, 1971, Vol. Activist award, 1975. Mem. Nat. Assn. Jewish Family and Children Agys. (dir. 1977-79), Nat. Bd. Hebrew Immigrant Aide Soc. Clubs: Hadassah, Women of Rotary, B'nai B'rith Women, Council of Jewish Women, ORT, Brandeis. Office: 6867 Wynnwood St Houston TX 77008

LACKENDER, GERALDINE SELMA, civic worker; b. Williamsburg, Iowa, Oct. 7, 1920; d. Julius J. and Anna M. (Wetjen) Buser; student public schs., Iowa; m. Glenn Lackender, Feb. 11, 1942; children—Sherry, Penny, Vicki, Cathy, Randy, Ronda. With high sch. cafeterias, Iowa City, 1970-78; bd. dirs. Am. Cancer Soc., Iowa City, 1968-82, crusade chmn., 1968, mem. state service and rehab. com., 1972-82; pres. PTA, Iowa City, 1968-72; bd. dirs. Agrl. Assn., 1978-82; chmn. fair entertainment com. 4-H, 1979-82, mem. county youth com., 1972-78; dist. chmn. Iowa Farm Bur. Women, 1974-82, county chmn., 1967-68, public relations chmn., 1979-82, mem. state resolutions com., 1979, county legis. com., 1970-82; pres. Zion Luth. Ch. Women, 1972-75, bd. dirs., 1972-82; mem. County Extension Home Econs. Com., 1978-82, County Extension Council, 1968-72; active Goodwill Industries of SE Iowa, 1968-82; community theatre vol., 1976-82. Recipient Iowa Master Farm Homemaker award Wallaces Farmer, 1968; Outstanding Citizen award Hills Town & Country, 1979; Farm Family award Iowa City C. of C., 1980; Johnson County Mother of Yr. award, 1981. Clubs: Porkettes, Cowbelles, Univ. Women. Address: Route 3 Iowa City IA 52240

LACKS, PATRICIA EVERETT, clin. psychologist; b. Ontario, Oreg., Feb. 22, 1941; d. Franklin A. and Viola L. (Chamberlain) Everett; B.A., Washington U., St. Louis, 1961, M.A., 1962, Ph.D. (USPHS trainee 1961-66), 1966; m. Paul Gawronik, Apr. 4, 1981; children by previous marriage—Jeffrey, Amy. Staff psychologist Malcolm Bliss Mental Health Center, St. Louis, 1966-70; dir. research Jewish Employment and Vocat. Service, St. Louis, 1970-72; asso. prof. clin. psychology Washington U., 1972—. NIH grantee, 1981-82. Fellow Mo. Psychol. Assn. (pres. 1976); asso. fellow Inst. Rational Emotive Therapy; Mem. Am. Psychol. Assn., AAUP, Assn. Advancement Behavior Therapy. Author papers in field. Office: Psychology Dept Washington U St Louis MO 63130

LACYE, LYN LAUFIK, radio sta. exec.; b. Washington, Oct. 17, 1948; d. Rudolph and Kay (Nadler) Laufik-Lacye; student Ohio State U., 1966-68, San Diego City Coll., 1970-71, Columbus Bus. Sch., 1968-69. Ordained to ministry Ch. of Gospel Ministry; with KGB-FM and 13K, San Diego, 1972—, community affairs dir., 1975-82, community services dir. Sta. KGB-FM and community network news dir. Sta. KCNN, 1982—; radio cons. Blood Banks So. Calif., 1978-79, Community Congress, 1978, Southwestern Coll., 1979. Bd. dirs. Concerned Over Offshore Oil Leasing, 1977-80, Youth Services Program, El Cajon, Calif., 1979—, Greenpeace, San Diego, 1979-80; mem. media dir. I Love a Clean San Diego; mem. adv. com. San Diego Community Coll. Dist.; active Girl Scouts U.S.A., United Way, Boys Town. Recipient Heart Assn. Good Guy award, 1978; Maharishe award, TM-Sidhi Program, 1978, Clio Personality award, 1981, others. Mem. NOW, Smithsonian Inst., Friends of Cats. Editor, pub. (with Greg Vick) The Other Side of Radio, 1979; researcher, producer LP series Cruisin' 1964, 65, 66, 67. Office: 7150 Engineer Rd San Diego CA 92111

LADD, CHERYL (CHERYL STOPPELMOOR), actress; b. Huron, S.D., July 12, 1951; d. Marion and Dolores (Katz) Stoppelmoor; ed. pub. schs.; m. David Alan Ladd, May 24, 1973; 1 dau., Jordan Elizabeth. Toured with singing group The Music Shop, 1968-70; singing voice on TV cartoon series Josie and the Pussycats, 1970-72, Josie and the Pussycats in Outer Space, 1972-74; appeared over 100 commls.; TV appearances include: The Rookies, Code R, The Tonight Show, Switch, Ironside, Happy Days, The Partridge Family, Police Woman; regular on TV series Charlie's Angels, 1977—; TV movies Satan's School for Girls, When She Was Bad; films include: Jamaica Reef, Marriage of a Young Stockbroker. Recipient of Photography Award, 1978. Mem. AFTRA, AGVA. Office: care William Morris Agy Inc 151 El Camino Beverly Hill CA 90212 *

LADD, KAREN LOUISE, psychologist; b. Niles, Mich., Feb. 26, 1948; d. Gemroe and Amy Jean (Thomas) Fletcher; B.Sacred Lit. (essay contest scholar, 1966), Gt. Lakes Bible Coll., 1970; M.Ednl. Psychology, Andrews U., 1974, postgrad.; m. S. Lee Ladd, June 29, 1969; children—Christopher Lee, Matthew Lee. Therapist, Christian Counseling Services, Indpls., 1973—; asst. prof. psychology and sociology, Ind. Christian U., 1978-79; chmn. psychology div. textbooks adoptions com. State of Ind., 1979. Mem. Am. Assn. Christian Counselors, Am. Personnel and Guidance Assn., Nat. Speakers Assn., Christian Assn. for Psychol. Studies. Mem. Christian Ch. (Disciples of Christ non-denominational). Composer song: Why, Lord?, 1973; author booklet: Meeting the Needs of the Inmate, 1976; contbr. articles to publs. in field. Home: 2233 Darlene Ct Greenwood IN 46142 Office: 528 Turtle Creek North Dr Indianapolis IN 46227

LADD, LOIS ANN BUCHTA, theatre exec.; b. Madison County, Ill., Jan. 15, 1951; d. Chester Edward and Carol Katherine (Staaf) Buchta; B.A. in Art/Art Studio, So. Ill. U., Edwardsville, 1982; m. Michael D. Ladd, Apr. 30, 1976. Asso. forum coordinator Stifel, Nicholaus & Co., St. Louis, 1971-75; theatre technician Meridian Hall, So. Ill. U., 1976-79, asso. mgr., 1977-79; house mgr. Mississippi River Festival Facility, Neiderlander Corp., Edwardsville, 1978-79; free-lance designer Martiz Communication Co., Fenton, Mo., 1978-82; theatre mgr. St. Louis Community Coll. at Meramec, 1979—; prodn. mgr. Mid Am. Dance Co., St. Louis; dir. telethon for Enablers Club of St. Louis Community Coll. Dist.; speaker in field; free-lance advt. artist. Active Eden Village Aux., Glen Carbon, Ill. Recipient Access Meramec award Enablers Club, St. Louis Community Coll., 1981; Service award Mo. Air N.G., 1980; named Madison County Dairy Princess, Ill. Dairy Assn., 1969-70, 70-71. Mem. Higher Edn. Council Greater St. Louis, U.S. Inst. Tech. Theatre, Mo. Assn. Community and Jr. Colls., NOW, LWV. Unitarian. Home: PO Box 443 Edwardsville IL 62025 Office: 11333 Big Bend Blvd Saint Louis MO 63122

LADD-KIDDER, LISA KATHERINE, clin. psychologist; b. Boston, July 13, 1944; d. Alexander Hackett and Eleanor Mary (Murphy) Ladd; B.A., U. South Fla., 1966; M.Ed. (Office Edn. fellow), U. Ga., 1970; M.S., Hahnemann Med. Coll., 1973; m. James Kidder, 1977. Geog. analyst C.I.A., Washington, 1967-69; dormitory dir., counselor Swarthmore Coll., 1971-72; clin. psychologist, asso. prof. dept. counseling and psychol. services Kutztown U. of Pa., 1972—; pvt. practice psychology, 1978—; workshop presenter. Recipient 1st prize Fla. Poetry Contest, 1966; lic. tchr. spl. edn., emotionally disturbed, Pa.; lic. for pvt. practice, Pa. Mem. AAUP, Am. Fedn. Tchrs., Am. Psychol. Assn., Assn. Pa. State Coll. and Univ. Faculties, Internat. Transactional Analysis Assn. (cert.) Pa. Psychol. Assn. Democrat. Author: Cartographic Analysis of Southeast Asia, 1966. Office: 206 Administration Bldg Kutztown U Kutztown PA 19530

LADNER, JUDITH SLEPPY, sch. adminstr.; b. Salt Lake City, Apr. 9, 1940; d. George S. and Bertha Annetta (Garrett) Sleppy; B.A., U. No. Colo., 1962; M.A., San Jose State U., 1976; Ed.D., U. Pacific, 1979; m. R.L. Ladner, Jr., Dec. 23, 1968. Primary and intermediate tchr. Union Sch. Dist., San Jose, Calif., 1962-67, intermediate and jr. high sch. tchr., 1968-76, coordinator media services, 1976-77; intermediate tchr. Colegion Nueva Granda, Bogota, Colombia, 1967-68; prin. Alta Vista Sch., Los Gatos, Calif., 1977-80; asst. supt. Mountain View (Calif.) Sch. Dist., 1980—. Mem. exec. bd. Mountain View United Way; mem. planning and allocations council United Way of Santa Clara County; sec. exec. bd. YMCA of Mountain View-Los Altos. Mem. Assn. Calif. Sch. Adminstrs., AAUW, North Valley Adminstrs. Assn., Delta Kappa Gamma (chpt. pres. 1978-80), Phi Delta Kappa, Pi Lambda Theta. Republican. Methodist. Home: 1025 Robinhood Ct Los Altos CA 94022 Office: Mountain View Sch Dist 220 View St Mountain View CA 94042

LADRILLONO, NIEVA EVANGELISTA, med. technologist; b. Manila, Philippines, Aug. 15, 1943; d. Lucrecio Sahagun and Dolores (Magsaysay) Evangelista; came to U.S., 1965, naturalized 1973; B.S., U. Santo Tomas, 1963, A.B., 1964; m. Conrado Pascual Ladrillono, Nov. 23, 1968; children—Jennifer Jo, James Paul. Sr. technologist Harford Meml. Hosp., Havre De Grace, Md., 1971-74; supr. blood bank Gulf Coast Community Hosp., Biloxi, Miss., 1976-78; chief technologist Children's Hosp., Norfolk, Va., 1979, lab. mgr., 1979—. Mem. Va. Soc. Med. Tech. (mem. of yr. 1982; dir., 1980-81), Clin. Lab. Mgmt. Assn. (v.p. Tidewater chpt. 1982), Am. Soc. Med. Technology Am. Soc. Clin. Pathologists, Am. Assn. Blood Banks, Am. Assn. Clin. Chemists, Nat. Assn. Female Execs. Roman Catholic. Club: Quota. Home: 1625 Kingsway Rd Norfolk VA 23518 Office: 800 W Olney Rd Norfolk VA 23507

LAFFAL, FLORENCE, artist; b. N.J., Jan. 3, 1921; d. Jacob and Sarah (Berman) Schultz; B.S. in Fine Arts Edn., So. Conn. Coll., 1957; M.A. in Fine Arts and Fine Arts Edn., Columbia, 1958; m. Julius Laffal, Aug. 24, 1943; children—Paul David, Kenneth. Tchr. art North Haven Sch. System, 1958-66; free-lance artist 1966—; owner gallery, 1969—; v.p. Gallery Press Inc., Essex, Conn., 1975—. Mem. Silvermine Guild Artists, Soc. Conn. Craftsmen (pres., dir. 1968-74), Paint and Clay Club Club, Conn. Book Pubs. Assn. Author: Artists-Craftsmen of Connecticut Datebook, 1971; Breads of Many Lands, 1975; editor: Folk Art Finder. Office: Gallery Press Inc 98 N Main Essex CT 06426

LAFFEY, MARTHAROSE F(ELICIA), assn. exec.; b. N.Y.C., Jan. 15, 1950; d. Raymond and Phyllis L.; B.A. summa cum laude, Catholic U. Am., 1971, postgrad. in urban anthropology, 1982—. Research asso. Nat. Planning Assn., Washington, 1972-76; research asso. Mcpl. Fin. Officers Assn., Washington, 1976-79; tax and fin. specialist Nat. Assn. Counties, Washington, 1979—. Mem. Phi Beta Kappa, Phi Alpha Theta. Author County News jour. supplements, 1980-81, also profl. reports. Home: 1006 Columbia Rd NW Washington DC 20001 Office: 440 1st St NW Washington DC 20001

LAFFIN, SHIRLEY ELEANOR, research lab. exec.; b. Goffstown, N.H., July 29, 1935; d. Harold Edward and Anna Mary (Greenwood) Duefield; student N.H. Vocat. Tech. Coll., 1976; m. Lester Belloir, 1954 (div. 1958); children—Lester, George; m. 2d, Thomas W. Laffin, Feb. 14, 1970; children—Colleen, Ray. Insp., Internat. Packing Co., Bristol, N.H., 1964-66; quality control in-process insp. GT & E Sylvania, Hillsboro, N.H., 1966—; comptroller Communications Systems Center, Hillsboro, 1970—. Lic. radio-telephone operator. Mem. Internat. Platform Assn. Clubs: Indian Motorcycle N.H., Citizen Band Radio. Home and office: PO Box 133 Bridge St Hillsboro NH 03244

LA FOLLETTE, MARIAN W., state legislator; b. Van Nuys, Calif., Sept. 19, 1926; d. Edmund Store and Bernice Amelia (Betts) Waddell; B.A., U. Calif., Berkeley, 1948; m. John Travis La Follette; children—Laurie, Curtis, Jackie, Philip. First woman trustee and pres. Los Angeles Community Coll. Bd., 1969-75; assemblywoman 38th Calif. Assembly Dist., 1980—; first woman dir. Fed. Home Loan Bank Bd., San Francisco. Founder, charter pres. Northridge Guild of Children's Hosp.; active New Dimensions, Calif. Luth. Coll. Named Woman of Achievement, Glendale Bus. and Profl. Women, 1975, Calif. Fedn. Republican Women, 1975; recipient award of honor for edn. Los Angeles County Bd. Suprs., 1971. Mem. Pepperdine U. Assocs. Republican. Office: 23241 Ventura Blvd Suite 209 Woodland Hills CA 91364

LAFONT, FRANCES MILLER, nutritionist, dietitian; d. Steve J. and Laura (Grubb) Miller; B.S. magna cum laude, U. Tenn., Martin, 1957; M.S., U. Ill., 1960; m. David H. LaFont; children—Robert A., James D. With Miss. Bd. Health, Coahoma County, 1939-41; mem. faculty U. Ill., Urbana, 1960—, asst. prof. foods and nutrition, 1967—. Recipient Outstanding Tchr. award Sch. Human Resources and Family Studies U. Ill., 1973-74, 76-77; registered dietitian. Mem. AAAS, Soc. Nutrition Edn., Nutrition Today Soc., Am. Home Econs. Assn., Am. Public Health assn., Am., Eastern Ill. dietetic assns., Ill. Nutrition Com., Inst. Food Tech., Sigma Delta Epsilon. Methodist. Registered author PLATO. Office: Dept Foods and Nutrition Univ Ill Urbana IL 61801

LAFONTANT, JEWEL STRADFORD, lawyer; b. Chgo., Apr. 28, 1922; d. Cornelius Francis and Aida Arabella (Carter) Stradford; A.B., Oberlin Coll., 1943; LL.D., U. Chgo., 1946; LL.D. (hon.), Chgo. Med. Sch. U. of Health Scis., 1982; 1 son, John W. Rogers III. Admitted to Ill. bar, 1947; asst. U.S. atty., 1955-58; partner firm Lafontant, Wilkins, Jones & Waren, P.C., Chgo.; dep. solicitor gen. U.S., Washington, 1972-75; dir. Trans World Airlines, Mobil Oil Corp., Continental Bank, Foote, Cone & Belding, Bendix Corp., Equitable Life Assurance Soc. U.S., Harte-Hanks Communications, Inc., Food Fair, Inc. Mem. U.S. Adv. Commn. Internat. Edn. and Cultural Affairs, Nat. Council Minority Bus. Enterprises, Nat. Council on Ednl. Research; mem. Pres. Regan's Transition Team, 1980, Pres. Commn. on Exec. Exchange, 1982; mem. exec. com. Pres.'s Pvt. Sector Survey on Cost Control, 1982; chmn. adv. bd. Civil Rights Commn. Trustee Lake Forest (Ill.) Coll., Oberlin Coll., Howard U., Tuskegee Inst. Mem. Chgo. Bar Assn. (bd. govs.). Bd. editors Am. Bar Assn. Jour. Office: 69 W Washington St Chicago IL *

LAFOREST, CATHERINE CALL, sch. psychologist; b. Detroit, Jan. 12, 1921; d. Fred Erneldo and Olive Marie (Marxson) Call; B.A. in Psychology, U. Mich., 1943; M.Clin. Psychology, 1944; m. Ralph LaForest, Jan. 12, 1957 (dec.); children—Ann LaForest Diaz, Carl Ulrick. Clin. psychologist Mich. Dept. Mental Health, Lansing, 1944-49, 60-62: personnel supr. Mich. Bell Telephone Co., Detroit, 1949-53; sch. psychologist Trenton (Mich.) Bd. Edn., 1964-69; resource sch. psychologist Dearborn (Mich.) Bd. Edn., 1969—. Mem. Detroit Bd. Edn., 1970-73; mem. Village Players, Birmingham, Mich., First Theater Guild, Birmingham; elder Presbyn. Ch., Detroit, 1968-71, Birmingham, 1978-81. Mem. Am. Orthopsychiat. Assn., Am. Psychol. Assn., Internat. Platform Assn. Home: 30535 Rock Creek Dr Southfield MI 48076 Office: 4824 Lois Ave Dearborn MI 48124

LAFORNIA, LORRAINE, profl. sec.; b. Alamosa, Colo.; d. Herman and Phyllis (Archuleta) Chavez; student SUNY, 1973, Niagara U., 1973-74, Niagara County Community Coll., 1973-76; children—Debra Lynn, Donna Marie. With The Carborundum Co., Niagara Falls, N.Y., 1961—, sec. Abrasives Mktg. Div., 1972-76, sr. sec. Refractories Div., 1976-79, exec. sec. human resources, 1979-81, exec. asst. internat. ops., 1981—; notary public 1977—; lectr. in field. Officer, Niagara Beautification Commn., City of Niagara Falls (N.Y.), 1978—; chmn. bd., chief exec. officer Niagara Council of Arts, 1979—; bd. dirs. The Place to Be, St. Peter's Episcopal Ch., 1978—; adv. bd. Niagara County Community Coll., 1970—, mem. presdl. search com., 1979; adv. bd. Rehab. Internat. U.S.A., N.Y.C. Named N.E. Dist. Sec. of Yr., Syracuse, N.Y., 1978, N.Y. State Sec. of the Yr., 1978; recipient Top Hat award Radio Sta. WHLD, 1978. Cert. profl. sec. Mem. Profl. Secs. Internat. (pres. 1976-79). Democrat. Roman Catholic. Home: 198 Carpenter Ave Buffalo NY 14223 Office: Carborundum Center 156 Niagara Falls NY 14302

LAFOUREST, JUDITH ELLEN, editor, publisher; b. Indpls., Jan. 10; d. Edward Elston and Dorothy Jeanette (Parker) LaFourest; B.A., Ind. U.-Purdue U., Indpls., 1972; M.A.T., Ind. U., 1980; divorced; 1 dau., Beth Anne Gruner. Lead pre-vocat. instr., ednl. adminstr. Opportunities Industrialization Center, Indpls., 1972-76; part-time English and human relations instr. Profl. Careers Inst., Indpls., 1975-78; editor, pub. Womankind, Indpls., 1977—; co-dir. Womankind Center, 1981—; editor, creative writer, photographer Bio-Feed-Back Bio Dynamics/BMC, Indpls., 1977-80; mem. asso. faculty, creative writing inst. Ind.U.-Purdue U., Indpls., 1979—; also lectr., free-lance editor. Ind. sec. NOW, 1978-80. Recipient Disting. Alumni award Ind. U.-Indpls., 1980. Mem. Nat. League Am. Pen Women, Internat. Assn. Bus. Communicators, Nat. Women's Studies Assn., Ind. U.-Indpls. Liberal Arts Alumni Assn. (pres. 1982), Ind. Adult Edn. Assn., Sigma Tau Delta. Office: Womankind 3711 N Sherman Dr Indianapolis IN 46218

LAGANGA, DONNA BRANDEIS, pub. co. cons.; b. Bklyn., June 27, 1949; d. Sidney L. and Sylvia (Herman) Brandeis; B.S. in Bus. Edn., Central Conn. State Coll., New Britain, 1972, M.S., 1975; m. Thomas LaGanga, Aug. 11, 1974. Various secretarial positions, 1969-72; tchr. bus. Lewis S. Mills Regional High Sch., Burlington, Conn., 1972-78; cons. Southwestern Pub. Co., Pelham Manor, N.Y., 1978—; co-owner Colonial Welding Service; seminar condr., 1980—. Adv. bd. secretarial sci. dept. LaGuardia Community Coll., Long Island City, N.Y., 1982—. EDPA grantee, 1973; cert. profl. sec. Mem. Am. Mgmt. Assn., Nat. Bus. Edn. Assn., Profl. Secs. Internat., Eastern Bus. Edn. Assn., Conn. Bus. Edn. Assn., New Eng. Bus. Edn. Assn., Profl. Secs. Assn. N.Y., Delta Pi Epsilon. Office: 925 Spring Rd Pelham Manor NY 10803

LAGARCE, MELINDA, mfrs. rep., interior architect and designer, inventor; b. Herrin, Ill., Dec. 22, 1946; d. Gilbert and Betty Engram; B.S. in Interior Design (Ill. Legislature scholar, Nat. Merit scholar), So. Ill. U., 1968; M.F.A. in Interior Design, Tex. Tech. U., 1972; m. Raymond LaGarce, Dec. 18, 1965. Exed. designer, mgr. Famous Barr Co., St. Louis, also Classique Interiors, Inc., Potomac, Md., 1972-79, sr. designer, 1979-80; cons. interior architecture and design Mudelein Coll., Chgo., 1980-81; archtl. and design rep. Lee Kaufman & Co., Chgo., 1980-81; design and sales cons. Contract Distbrs. Corp., Chgo., 1981—; instr. Tex. Tech. U.; cons. Mundelein Coll. Mem. Am. Soc. Interior Designers, Smithsonian Assocs., Phi Kappa Phi. Home: 6033 N Sheridan Rd Chicago IL 60660

LAGIUSA, BETTY JEAN, accountant; b. Eureka, Calif., Oct. 12, 1927; d. Earl Chancel and Ruby Jewel (Cox) Lackey; student Foothill Coll., 1967, San Jose State U., 1972, Golden Gate U. Taxation, 1976; children—Jere, Marla, Mario. Pvt. practice bus. and tax acctg. Campbell, Calif., 1975—. Am. Bus. Women's Assn., 1971-72, 1978-79. Mem. Am. Bus. Womens Assn. (chpt. pres., Women of Yr. award 1972, 79), Assn. Enrolled Agts. (chpt. pres.), Nat. Soc. Pub. Accts., Am. Bus. Women's Assn. Democrat. Roman Catholic. Office: 595 N Millich Dr Campbell CA 95008

LAGOWSKI, JEANNE WECKER MUND, chemist, ednl. adminstr.; b. St. Louis, Nov. 17, 1929; d. Ira Joseph and Josephine Emma (Wecker) Mund; B.S. (Univ. Scholar), Beadley U., 1951, M.S., 1952; Ph.D., U. Mich., 1957; m. Joseph John Lagowski, Feb. 24, 1954. Instr. chemistry Bradley U., Peoria, Ill., 1951-52; teaching asst. U. Mich., Ann Arbor, 1952-54; research chemist Mich. State U., East Lansing, 1956-57; postdoctoral fellow Cambridge (Eng.) U., 1957-59; research scientist zoology U. Tex., Austin, 1959-73, asst. dean gen. and comparative studies, 1972-78, asst. dean Coll. of Natural Scis., 1978-81, asso. dean Coll. of Natural Scis., 1981—, prof. zoology, 1981—, Blunk Meml. prof., 1981—. NIH grantee, 1964; Danforth grantee, 1977. Mem. Am. Chem Soc., Nat. Assn. Women Deans, Adminstrs., and Counselors, So. Assn. Advs. for Health Professions, Assn. Acad. Affairs Adminstrs., Am.

Personnel and Guidance Assn., Mortar Bd., Sigma Xi, Phi Kappa Phi, Sigma Delta Epsilon, Iota Sigma Pi, Omicron Delta Kappa. Author: (with A. R. Katnitzky) The Principles of Heterocyclic Chemistry, 1967; Heterocyclic Chemistry, 1960; Chemistry of the Heterocyclic N-Oxides, 1971; asso. editor: Advances in Heterocyclic Chemistry, 1963-65; contbr. articles in field to profl. jours. Office: Dept Zoology U Tex Austin TX 78712

LAGRONE, GAIL LILLEY, personnel exec.; b. Dallas, Apr. 15, 1953; d. Barnett and Fayna Arzella Lilley; Asso. Bus. Adminstrn., Stephen F. Austin U., 1973; postgrad. U. Tex., Dallas, 1978—. Personnel asst. U.S. Brass Corp., Plano, Tex., 1975-78; regional personnel dir. Suburban Coastal Corp., Dallas, 1978-80, asst. v.p./personnel, 1980—. Mem. Am. Soc. Personnel Adminstrn., Dallas Personnel Assn. Office: 12750 Merit Dr Suite 900 Dallas TX 75251

LAGRONE, LAVENIA WHIDDON, chemist, real estate broker; b. Conroe, Tex., Feb. 27, 1940; d. James Lewis and Cora Lee (DeLuish) Whiddon; A.A., Kilgore Coll., 1960; B.S., N. Tex. State U., 1962; grad. med. technology Baylor U. Med. Center, 1962; m. Doyle W. LaGrone, June 26, 1959 (div. Sept. 1965); 1 son, Russell Randal. Sr. technologist in spl. chemistry Baylor U. Med. Center, Dallas, 1962-63; research chemist, supr. labs., cardiovascular surgery Southwestern Med. Sch., Dallas, 1964-69, Upstate Med. Center, SUNY, Syracuse, 1969-70; research assoc., supr. lab., dept. surgery U. Tex. Med. Br., Galveston, 1970-74, research assoc., supr. labs., pediatric nephrology, 1974—; real estate broker DeLanney & Assocs., realtors, 1979—. Chmn. student activities PTA Galveston, Tex., 1976-77. Recipient Top Real Estate Sales award, Top Real Estate Producer award, DeLanney & Assocs., 1979, also Broker's Excellence award and Top Real Estate Commn. award, 1980, also Million Dollar Producer award, 1980-81. Mem. Am. Soc. Clin. Pathologists (registered med. technologist), Nat. Assn. Realtors, Tex. Assn. Realtors, Galveston Bd. Realtors, Phi Theta Kappa. Contbr. articles to chemistry and med. jours. Home: 142 San Fernando St Galveston TX 77550 Office: U Tex Med Br 301 University Blvd Galveston TX 77550

LAGUERUELA, EARLINE, advt. exec.; b. Rio Piedras, P.R., Apr. 8, 1952; d. Rafael F. and Lisette (Ortiz) Veve; B.A., Manhattanville Coll., 1973; student U. Geneva, 1971; m. Jan. 29, 1972. Vice pres. Velsweet Internat. Ltd., Laredo, Tex., 1973-75; v.p. Burgundy Woods, Inc., San Antonio, 1975-77; pres., dir. Sounds and Creations, Inc., Satelco, Inc., San Antonio. Mem. San Antonio Advt. Fedn., Am. Mktg. Assn. Republican. Office: 100 Taylor St Suite 305 San Antonio TX 78205

LAHAIE, EVELYN GLUSAC, owner charm and model sch.; b. Gary, Ind., Apr. 9, 1937; d. Edward and Stella Evans; grad. Estelle Compton Modeling Sch., Chgo., 1950; student Ind. U. N.W., Gary, 1962-63; grad. Silva Mind Control Inst., 1975; student Madson Music Sch., 1977; children—Laurie, Terri; three stepchildren. Profl. model, 1950-73; owner, operator Evelyn Lahaie Modeling Sch., Gary, 1957—; exec. dir. for Ind., Miss. U.S.A.-Universe Pageant, 1970—; producer, coordinator, commentator, fashion shows, Gary and Chgo., 1957—; judge nat. pageants including: Miss Black America, 1976, World's Little Miss Pageant, 1972; lectr. various schs., orgns., clubs. Past bd. dirs. Gary Players, Inc.; vol. worker various churches and civic orgns. Mem. Model Assn. Am. Internat. (past dir., past rec. sec.), World Modeling Assn. (Most Outstanding Sch. award 1977). Office: Evelyn Lahaie Modeling Sch 607 S Lake St Gary IN 46403

LAHLUM, ELLEN BODNAR, mfg. co. plant mgr.; b. Jersey City, June 7, 1942; d. Anthony and Adele (Macknowsky) Bodnar; B.A., Bradford Coll., 1976; M.B.A., Suffolk U., 1979; m. Robye Lahlum, Oct. 26, 1968. Trainee, supervisory devel. program Western Electric Co., North Andover, Mass., 1973-74, prodn. supr., 1974-76; prodn. supr. Parker Bros., Salem, Mass., 1976-77, dept. mgr., 1977-79, prodn. mgr., 1979-80, plant mgr., 1980—. Mem. corp. edn. program adv. com. North Shore Community Coll.; mem. adv. bd. Children's Express. Mem. Am. Prodn. and Inventory Control Soc., Internat. Assn. Quality Circles, Women's Exec. Network N. of Boston (founding mem.), NOW, Salem C. of C. (dir.), League N.H. Wheelmen, Boxford Hist. Soc. Club: Appalachian Mountain. Home: Brookview Rd Boxford MA 01921 Office: 190 Bridge St Salem MA 01970

LAIDLAW, KATHLEEN REID, historian; b. Westford, Mass., Dec. 27, 1906; d. Clarence Alman and Kathleen Elizabeth (Denovan) Reid; student New Eng. Conservatory, 1926-27; m. Elliot Clifton Laidlaw, Apr. 26, 1928; 1 dau., Martha Kathleen Laidlaw Wyllie. Tchr. pianoforte, 1926-48; lectr. on history of Scituate (Mass.) to various schs. and orgns.; demonstrator of hand weaving: restorer of hist. bldgs.; pres. Scituate Hist. Soc., 1966—, editor bull., 1968—. Dir. Plymouth County Devel. Council; dir. tng. Newton Girl Scouts, 1945-48; dir. vols. South Shore Hosp., Scituate; chmn. Scituate Bicentennial Commn., 1975-77. Recipient Citizen of Yr. award Town of Scituate, 1980, Scituate C. of C., 1980; citations, gov. Mass., Senate, and Ho. of Reps., 1980; Josiah Quincy Jr. award Quincy Coop. Bank, 1981. Mem. Bay State Hist. League, Bostonian Soc., Plimoth Plantation, Nat. Trust for Hist. Preservation. Soc. for Preservation of New England Antiquities. Club: Scituate Garden (pres. 1960-62) Green Thumb. Home: 121 Maple St Scituate MA 02066

LAIER, HATTIE JEAN (BARBARA FURBUSH) (MRS. CARL ROGERS LAIER), artist, poet, lectr., minister; b. Lynn, Mass., May 26, 1926; d. Kenneth Carlyle and Elizabeth Esdale (Mac Kiel) Furbush; student Sch. Practical Arts, Boston, 1946, Decordava Mus., Northeastern U., 1972, Leslie Jr. Coll., 1973, Quinsigamond Community Coll., 1973; m. Carl Rogers Laier, Jan. 31, 1947; children—Carl Peter, Eric Conrad, Frieda Elizabeth, Jane Ellen. Exhibited art in shows at Salem State Coll., Prestige Gallery, Peabody, Mass., Rockport, Mass., Am. Mut. Co., Wakefield, Mass.; with Forbes Lithograph Co., Chelsea, Mass., 1945-47; with Photo-Reflex Studio, 1957-58, Filene's, North Shore, Peabody, 1973; owner Whistling Swan Studio, comml. and residental murals, Lynnfield, Mass., 1972—; ordained to ministry United Spiritual Sci. Ch., 1978. Set designer, plays Playboy Club, Boston, 1972; coordinator Saugus (Mass.) Rotary Arts Festival, 1972; chmn. Children's Poetry Contest, Lynnfield, 1970-71, Lynnfield Poetry Festival, 1972; moderator Nat. Poetry Day Festival, Lynn, 1971; chmn. poetry therapy program Torchlighters of Danvers (Mass.) State Hosp., 1974-75; numerous poetry readings, Mass., Pa., N.H., Maine, N.Y., Wis., 1968—, Calif., 1976-77; tchr. color sound Middletown (N.Y.) Exptl. Coll., 1978—; lectr., workshop leader Internat. Parapsychology Conf., San Juan, P.R.; lectr. E.S.P., healing through color and vibration. Appeared in musical productions To America with Love, Bumps Blackwell, 1978. Bd. dirs. Unity in Diversity Center, 1977. Recipient 2d prize, nat. poetry contest Jacksonville, Fla. br. Nat. League Am. Pen Women, 1971. Mem. Nat. League Am. Pen Women, New Eng. Poetry Club, Mass. Poetry Soc., Poetry Soc. N.H., Listening Post, Internat. Coop. Council (dir., sec. Los Angeles chpt., mem. newage servers ministerial tng. program), Spotlighters of Lynnfield, Center of Light, Lynnfield Art Guild, Spiritual Frontiers Fellowship, Inst. Reality Awareness, Sierra Creek Health Center. Author: Understanding the Circle, 1974; A Walk in Time, 1976. Contbr. poetry to publs., including Quill, Zahir, Ghost Dance, Softball, Brown Sweater, Legend, Premiere, Pyramid, The Listener, New Age Calendar, Boston After Dark, Boston Phoenix, Manchester Union Leader, Echos, The Shore Review, others; to anthologies including Variations of Mulberry, Syllables in Stone, The Shore Poetry Anthology. Address: 725 Salem St Lynnfield MA 01940 also Box 27 River Rd Hiram ME 04041

LAINE, DOLORES MAE (DEL), photography co. exec., city ofcl.; b. Vallejo, Calif., Mar. 20, 1930; d. Leslie Merritt and Mabel Ysabel (Paulson) Wright; A.A., City Coll. San Francisco, 1950; B.A., Calif. State U., Berkeley, 1953; M.Sc., Calif. State U., San Francisco, 1960; m. Ed Laine, Mar. 30, 1962; children—Paul, Brooke, Alison, Paige. Supr. playgrounds and community centers, Calgary, Alta., Can., 1953-57, cons. pub. recreation and park planning, 1957-61; dir. Lake Tahoe (Calif.) Recreation Div., 1961-62; co-owner Laine Assocs. Advt. and Pub. Relations, South Lake Tahoe, Calif., 1961-72, Laine Assocs. Photography, South Lake Tahoe, 1962—; chmn. South Lake Tahoe Parks and Recreation Commn., 1974-76; councilwoman City of South Lake Tahoe, 1976—, mem. affirmative action task force, 1978-80, mayor pro-tem, 1976-77, mayor, 1977-78. Co-founder, producer Lake Tahoe Children's Theatre, 1962-72; chmn. Tahoe Regional Planning Agy. Urban Design Com., 1973-76; chmn. Tahoe Basin Transp. Authority, 1979—; chmn. Tahoe Regional Transp. Dist., 1981—. Mem. Nat. Women's Polit. Caucus, South Tahoe Women's Center (pres. 1980—, dir.), Lake Tahoe Hist. Soc. (pres. 1970-74). Presbyterian. Club: Soroptimist Internat. (regional gov. 1976-78). Office: Box 7322 South Lake Tahoe CA 95731

LAING, BETTY JEAN, nurse; b. Higgins, Tex., Jan. 29, 1925; d. Elic Garland and Lettie Emily (Cook) Sanders; R.N., N.W. Tex. Sch. Nursing, Amarillo, 1946; B.A., U. Redlands (Calif.), 1970; m. Robert William Laing, Aug. 10, 1945 (dec.); children—John Leslie, Mary Lou Laing Munnecke, Jo Ann. Mem. nursing staff hosps. in Tex., N.Mex. and Calif., 1962-76, Okla., 1980; dir. inservice St. Mary of Plains Hosp., Lubbock, Tex., 1976—. R.N., Tex., N.Mex., Calif. Mem. Am. Hosp. Assn. Educators, Tex. Soc. Hosp. Educators. Author curriculum material. Home: 408 S Avery Moore OK 73160

LAING, JOAN RAE, counseling psychologist; b. Delta, Iowa, Dec. 10, 1938; d. George and Dorothea Mae (Walker) Jones; B.A., Central Coll., 1958; M.A., U. Iowa, 1960; M.S., Iowa State U., 1977, Ph.D., 1979; children—Catherine, John, Patricia. Teaching asst. U. Iowa, 1958-60; tchr. University High Sch., U. Iowa, 1960-61; tchr. Mid-Prairie Schs., Wellman/Kalona, Iowa, 1961-62; tchr. Anamosa (Iowa) High Sch., 1963; research asst. U. Iowa, 1964-65, 66-67; counseling intern U. Cin., 1978-79; counselor Vassar Coll., 1979-80; program specialist Am. Coll. Testing Program, Iowa City, Iowa, 1980—. Mem. Action Council, Des Moines Center of Sci. and Industry, 1973-75. Mem. Am. Psychol. Assn., Iowa Psychol. Assn., Am. Personnel and Guidance Assn., Nat. Vocat. Guidance Assn., Am. Coll. Personnel Assn., Assn. for Measurement and Evaluation in Guidance. Democrat. Episcopalian. Office: ACT PO Box 168 Iowa City IA 52243

LAIR, HELEN MAY, poet; b. New Castle, Ind., Jan. 3, 1918; d. Harry and Loma D. (Delon) Humphrey; student Anderson Coll., U. Wis., John Herron Sch. Art; m. Marvin E. Lair, July 2, 1966; children—Michael Lucas, Joan Lucas Krueckegerg, Nancy Lucas (dec.). Author book of poetry; Lair Of The Four Winds, 1978, Earth Pilgrim, 1981; contbr. numerous poems to anthologies; author column New Castle Courier Times, 1982—. Pres. Henry County (Ind.) Art Guild. Recipient Farnell award, N.Y. Poetry Forum, Richard Miller award, Muncie (Ind.) Star 1st place award, Ind. State Fedn. Poetry 1st place award. Mem. Women in Communication, Acad. Women Poets, Nat. Fedn. Poets, Internat. Poets Achievement, N.Y. Poetry Forum, Epsilon Sigma Alpha. Roman Catholic. Office: 1202 Mourer St New Castle IN 47362

LAIRD, DOROTHY CAREL STEPHENS, educator; b. Cape Girardeau, Mo., Feb. 2, 1912; d. Ellis G. and Edith L. (Maika) Carel; student So. Coll., 1930-31, Fla. State Coll. Women, 1931-32; A.B., U. Ky., 1934; M.A.E., U. Fla., 1945, Ed.D., 1955; m. Dozier T. Laird, Aug. 31, 1947; children—Grady C. Stephens, Denver N. Stephens, Laura L. Laird. Tchr., Palm Beach (Fla.) public Schs., 1935-39; instr. Palm Beach Jr. Coll., 1945-47; demonstration tchr. P.K. Yonge Lab. Sch., 1944-47; instr. edn. U. Fla., Gainesville, 1947-51, asst. prof., 1951-56, asso. prof., 1956-63; prof. Fla. Atlantic U., Boca Raton, 1963—. Recipient Mark Twain award, 1950. Mem. Am. Psychol. Assn., Southeastern Psychol. Assn., Fla. Psychol. Assn., Fla. Research Assn., Nat. Council on Measurement, Am. Personnel and Guidance Assn., Phi Kappa Phi, Delta Kappa Gamma, Kappa Delta Pi, Pi Lambda Theta. Contbr. articles to profl. jours. Home: 400 NW 11th St Boca Raton FL 33432 Office: 193 Bldg 2 2 Florida Atlantic U Boca Raton FL 33432

LAIRD, HAZEL ALICE (WATKINS), writer, craft tchr.; b. Curtis, Okla., Dec. 29, 1905; d. John Elliott and Mary Louisa (Miller) Watkins; B.S. in Journalism, Okla. State U., 1932; postgrad. Okla. Coll. for Women, summer 1959; M.S. in Spl. Edn., U. Okla., 1963; postgrad. in Spl. Edn., Children's Med. Center, Tulsa, 1965; m. Virgil Dewitt Laird, Dec. 30, 1933 (dec.); children—Hainds Elliot, Pamela Victory. With Beatrice Creamery, Woodward, Okla., 1926, abstract offices Oklahoma City, 1928-29; sec. Okla. State U., 1930-40; bookkeeper, sec., co-owner A. & M. Termite Co. and Lairds of Lawton (Okla.), 1933-75; spl. edn. tchr. Duncan, Okla., 1959-60; substitute tchr., Lawton, 1967-70. Author: Railroad Ties, 1975; Percy the Persistent Persimmon, 1975; Gleanings in the Grub Basket, 1976, Hazel Talks Turkey, 1976; How To Recycle Insulin Syringes; contbr. columns: It Beats the Band, Something to Crow About, Adventuring with the Cub Scouts; tchr. feather craft nursing and sr. citizens homes; poetry reader; also radio, TV appearances. Officer youth groups United Brethren and United Meth. Churches, 1920-32. Recipient Good Egg membership, Nat. Poultry Bd., 1953; awards Okla. Writers Fedn., 1974, 75, 77, 78, 79, 80, 81. Mem. Nat. Fedn. Press Women, Okla. Press Women (3 awards, 1977, 2 awards 1980, 3 awards 1981), Gt. Plains Writers' Assn., Lawton Pioneer Women, Soc. Children's Book Writers, Chi Delta Phi (lit. merit award), Phi Zeta Kappa. Republican. Methodist. Club: Ret. Sr. Vol. Program. Speaker to civic and ch. groups; creator feather Christmas tree for U.S. Pres. and UN offices, styrofoam peanuts and Peace Dove for Pres. Carter. Author photo-journalism work: On the Wings of a Dove; (song) Heritage of Peace, 1967. Home: 1811 Euclid St Lawton OK 73501

LAIRD, JEAN ELOUISE RYDESKI (MRS. JACK E. LAIRD), author, educator; b. Wakefield, Mich., Jan. 18, 1930; d. Chester A. and Agnes A. (Petranek) Rydeski; Bus. Edn. degree, Duluth (Minn.) Bus. U., 1948; postgrad. U. Minn., 1949-50; m. Jack E. Laird, June 9, 1951; children—John E., Jane E., JoanAnn P., Jerilyn S., Jacquelyn T. Tchr., Oak Lawn (Ill.) High Sch. Adult Evening Sch., 1964-72, St. Xavier Coll., Chgo., 1974—. Writer newspaper column Around The House With Jean, A Woman's Work, 1965-70, Chicagotown News column The World As I See It, 1969, hobby column Modern Maturity mag., travel column Travel/Leisure mag., beauty column Ladycom mag., Time and Money Savers column Lady's Circle Mag. Mem. Canterbury Writers Club Chgo. (past. pres.), Oak Lawn Bus. and Profl. Women's Club, St. Linus Guild, Mt. Assisi Acad., Marist, Queen of Peace parents clubs. Roman Catholic. Author: Lost in the Department Store, 1964; Around The House Like Magic, 1968; Around The Kitchen Like Magic, 1969; How To Get the Most From Your Appliances, 1967; Hundreds of Hints for Harrassed Homemakers, 1971; The Alphabet Zoo, 1972; The Plump Ballerina, 1971; The Porcupine Story Book, 1974; Fried Marbles and Other Fun Things To Do, 1975; Hundreds of Hints for Harassed Homemakers; The Homemaker's Book of Time and Money Savers, 1979; Homemaker's Book of Energy Savers, 1981; also 248 paperback booklets. Contbr. articles to mags. Home: 10540 S Lockwood Ave Oak Lawn IL 60453 also Whitewood Ave Grand Beach MI 49118 also Lake Geneva WI 53147

LAKAH, JACQUELINE RABBAT, polit. scientist, educator; b. Cairo, Apr. 14, 1933; came to U.S., 1969, naturalized, 1975; d. Victor Boutros and Alice (Mounayer) Rabbat; B.A., Am. U. Beirut, 1968; M.Pd. (Rockefeller Found. scholar, Columbia Faculty fellow, NDEA Title IV fellow), Columbia U., 1974, cert. Middle East Inst. (fellow), 1975, Ph.D., 1978; m. Antoine K. Lakah, Apr. 8, 1951; children—Micheline, Mireille, Caroline. Adj. asst. prof. polit. sci. and world affairs Fashion Inst. Tech., N.Y.C., 1978—; asst. prof. grad. faculty polit. sci. Columbia U., N.Y.C., summer 1979, vis. scholar, 1982-83, also mem. seminar on Middle East; cons. on Middle East; faculty research fellow SUNY, summer 1982. Mem. Am. Polit. Sci. Assn., Acad. Polit. Sci. Roman Catholic. Home: 41-15 94th St Queens NY 11373 Office: 227 W 27th St New York NY 10001

LAKE, ANN WINSLOW, lawyer; b. Lowell, Mass., May 14, 1919; d. Frank and Helen Jablonski; B.S., Lowell State Coll., 1940; J.D., U. Detroit, 1946; M.A., Boston State Coll., 1964, Boston U., 1967; m. Thomas E. Lake, Sept. 5, 1942; children—Beverly Wilkes, Douglas, Warren. Tchr. schs. in Maine, Ga. and Detroit, 1940-43; admitted to Mass. bar, 1946; ind. practice, Dedham, Mass., 1946—; prof. law Salem (Mass.) State Coll., 1970—; mem. Mass. Commn. Study Labor Laws, 1972-74, Mass. Mental Health Legal Advisers Com., 1974-79. Mem. Mass. Adv. Commn. Acad. Talented Pupils, 1960-64, Mass. State Coll. Bldg. Authority, 1964-67, Mass. Com. to Recruit and Screen Candidates for Office Atty. Gen., 1974-78, U. Lowell Found., 1977-82. Recipient award Mass. State Coll. Alumni Assn., 1963, 64, 72, Mass. Assn. Mental Health, 1969, 72. Fellow Am. Bar Found., Mass. Bar Found.; mem. Nat. Assn. Women Lawyers (pres. 1980-81), Polish Bus. and Profl. Women's Club Greater Boston (pres. 1977-79), Norfolk Mental Health Assn. (pres. 1972-73), Mass. Assn. Women Lawyers (pres. 1972-73), Assn. Mass. State Colls. Alumni (pres. 1961-64), Riverdale Improvement Assn. (pres. 1959). Republican. Address: 40 Sawyer Dr Dedham MA 02026

LAKE, HELEN ADELE, assn. exec.; b. Butte, Mont., Nov. 1, 1934; d. Edward and Adele Helen (Stern) Aho; A.A., Skyline Coll., 1980; student in polit. sci., San Francisco State U., 1980—; children—Dana Augustine, Julie Augustine. Exec. sec. Fox West Coast Theatres, San Francisco, 1953-57; office mgr. State Farm Ins., San Francisco, 1957-60; owner, dir. Town and Country Personnel, Seattle, 1960-63; exec. sec. Bank Calif., Burlingame, 1964-66; assn. sec. Nat. Assn. Theatre Owners Calif., San Francisco, 1967-74; exec. asst. Theatre Assn. Calif., San Francisco, 1974-81, exec. dir., 1981—; San Francisco columnist Box Office mag., 1979—. Mem. Women of Motion Picture Industry (past dir.), Nat. Film Soc., Calif. Conf. Employer Assns., No. Calif. Soc. Assn. Execs., Colina Homeowners Assn. Clubs: Women of Variety. (dir., 1st v.p.), Variety of No. Calif. Office: 544 Golden Gate Ave San Francisco CA 94102

LAKIN, PHYLLIS RITA, clin. neuropsychologist; b. N.Y.C., June 7, 1951; d. Jack A. and Rose (Schneider) L.; B.A. magna cum laude, N.Y.U., 1973; Ph.D. in Psychology, Yeshiva U., 1979; m. Murray S. Las, Sept. 20, 1981. Research asst. Inst. Rehab. Medicine, N.Y.U. Med. Center, N.Y.C., 1973-75, clin. neuropsychologist, head trauma project, 1979—; clin. psychologist Jewish Bd. Family and Children's Services, N.Y.C., 1978-79; pvt. practice psychotherapy, cons. in neuropsychodiagnostics; condr. workshops in cognitive remediation. DeWitt Wallace fellow, 1973. Mem. Am. Psychol. Assn., Internat. Neuropsychol. Assn., N.Y. Neuropsychol. Group, Phi Beta Kappa. Contbg. author to articles in profl. publs. Home: 288 Mt Tabor Rd Morris Plains NJ 07950 Office: 400 E 34th St New York NY 10016

LAKOS, MARCILLE HARRIS, clin. psychologist; b. Ontario, Oreg., Dec. 10, 1917; d. Marvin and Una Leota (Smith) Hurst; B.S. in Psychology, U. Oreg., 1947, M.S. in Psychology, 1949; m. Eugene A. Lakos, Mar. 3, 1957; 1 son, John Stuart. Co-therapist, Nathan W. Ackerman, Family Inst., N.Y.C., 1955-60, 62-72; pvt. practice clin. psychology, N.Y.C., 1972—. Mem. Am. Psychol. Assn., Fedn. Am. Scientists, AAAS, N.Y. State Psychol. Assn., N.Y. Acad. Scis., Nat. Register Health Service Providers in Psychology (cert., council), Sigma Xi. Home and Office: 201 E 66th St New York NY 10021

LAKOSKY, IRENE MARYAN, nursing adminstr.; b. Chgo., Oct. 12, 1932; d. Adolf and Agnes Christine (Dorau) Heigl; R.N., Triton Jr. Coll., 1970; B.S. in Profl. Arts, St. Francis Coll., 1975; M.S. in Nursing Adminstrn., Columbia Pacific U., 1980, D.Sc. in Wholistic Health, 1981; children—Michael, Linda, Steven, James. Adminstrv. asst. Mich. Mut. Liability Co., Chgo., 1955-60; charge nurse Loyola Hosp., Maywood, Ill., 1970-72, 1972, Rush-Presbn.-St. Luke's Hosp., Chgo., 1972; staff nurse Cook County Hosp., Chgo., 1972-73; charge nurse Loretto Hosp., Chgo., 1973-75; night nursing adminstr. West Suburban Hosp., Oak Park, Ill., 1975—; dir. nursing Home Med-Care Found., Oak Park, 1977—; holistic health practitioner, cons. doing bus. as Wellness for Life; also sexual dysfunction therapist. Mem. bd. Head Start Program, 1966-68. Mem. Ill. Nurses Assn., Am. Nurses Assn. (cert. nursing adminstr.; council on nursing adminstrn.), Am. Nurses Found. Century Club, Am. Holistic Nurses Assn. (founding mem.), Women's Connection of Oak Park, Al Anon. Republican. Roman Catholic. Contbr. articles to profl. jours. Office: 6545 W North Ave Oak Park IL 60302

LALEMAN, IRENE MARIE, nurse; b. Marshall, Minn., Oct. 23, 1949; d. Joseph David and Theresa Ann (Bakker) L.; R.N., Iowa Lakes Community Coll., 1979; Lic. Practical Nurse, Sioux Falls Sch. Nursing, 1969. Nurse, Pipestone (Minn.) County Hosp., 1968-73, Rice Meml. Hosp., Willmar, Minn., 1973-79, Meeker Meml. Hosp., Litchfield, Minn., 1979-80; nurse, in-service dir. Augustana Homes, Inc., Litchfield, 1981—. Mem. Minn. Nurses Assn. Roman Catholic. Home: RR 1 Balaton MN 56115 Office: Augustana Homes Inc 600 S Davis St Litchfield MN 55355

LALLATIN, CARLA SUE, city ofcl.; b. Casper, Wyo., Apr. 27, 1946; d. Carl Dabney and Dorothy May (Stuart) Moulden; student U. Mo., 1971-72; A.A., Met. Jr. Coll., 1971; 1 dau., Natalie. Typesetting mgr. Allen Typesetting Co., Kansas City, Mo., 1967-69; publs. dir. United Computing Systems, Kansas City, Mo., 1969-74; purchasing state adminstr. State Wyo., Cheyenne, 1974-79; dep. commr. mcpl. supplies City of N.Y., 1979—; guest lectr. World Trade Inst., Mich. State U., Nat. Inst. Govtl. Purchasing, 1975—. Fin. adviser Girl Scouts U.S., 1977-79. Recipient Award of Merit and Award of Excellence, Internat. Assn. Bus. Communicators, 1974. Mem. Nat. Inst. Govt. Purchasing (bd. dirs., cert. of appreciation), Nat. Assn. State Purchasing Ofcls. (cert. of merit Cronin Club), Am. Bus. Women's Assn. (pres. 1978-79, Top Ten Bus Women of Year). Home: 61-15 97th St Apt 7A Rego Park NY 11374 Office: 1924 Municipal Bldg 1 Centre St New York NY 10007

LAM, AMY YUEN-HAR, fin. analyst; b. Hong Kong, June 23, 1954; came to U.S., 1973; d. Yin and Fung (Chan) Kwok; B.A. cum laude in Econs. (departmental honors), Yale U., 1977; M.S. in Mgmt., Purdue U., 1979; m. Michael Lam, Aug. 12, 1978. Actuarial analyst Aetna Ins. Co., Hartford, Conn., 1977-78; fin. analyst Internat. Harvester, Chgo., 1980; mfg. support analyst Xerox Corp., El Segundo, Calif., 1980-81, fin. analyst, 1981—. Group coordinator Internat. Assn. Students in Econs. and Bus., 1975; vol. Yale-New Haven Hosp., 1976. Mem. Nat. Assn.

Female Execs., Beta Gamma Sigma. Home: 21537 Craig Ct Carson CA 90745 Office: 701 S Aviation Blvd El Segundo CA 90245

LAMARR, HEDY (BORN HEDWIG KEISLER), motion picture actress; b. Vienna, Austria, Sept. 11, 1915; came to U.S., 1937; d. Emil and Gertrude Keisler; ed. by tutors and in pvt. schs., Vienna; m. Fritz Mandl; m. 2d, Gene Markey, 1939 (div. 1940); m. 3d, John Loder, May 1943 (div. 1947); m. 4th, Ernest Stauffer; m. 5th, Howard Lee; m. 6th, Lewis W. Bowles, Jr.; 1 adopted son, James. Appeared on stage, Vienna, in The Weaker Sex, Private Lives, and on screen in Storm in a Water Glass (1930), One Doesn't Need Money; starred in Ecstasy at age of 16 yrs.; on screen in U.S., in Algiers, 1938; Lady of the Tropics, 1939; Boom Town, 1940, Ziegfeld Girl, 1941, Crossroads, 1942, H. M. Pulham, Esq., 1941; White Cargo, 1942; The Conspirators, 1944; Her Highness and the Bellboy, 1945; Experiment Perilous, 1944, Dishonoured Lady, 1947, Samson and Delilah, 1949, A Lady Without Passport, 1950, My Favorite Spy, 1951, The Story of Mankind, 1957, The Female Animal, 1957, others. Author: Ecstasy and Me, 1967. Address: care Paul J Sherman 410 Park Ave New York NY 10022 *

LA MARRE, MILDRED HOLTZ, personal service co. exec.; b. Phila., May 10, 1917; d. Philip and Dora H.; student George Washington U., 1939-40; B.A., U. Md., 1966; m. Jack Understein, Dec. 25, 1938 (dec.); children—Robert, Norma, Norman, Gary; m. 2d, John La Marre, Feb. 14, 1981. With Jack Understein Co., Washington, 1960-71; exec. asst. Muskie for Pres., Washington, 1971-72; researcher Carnegie Endowment Internat. Peace, Washington, 1973-76; personal asst., adminstrv. asst. to Under Sec. Lucy Wilson Benson, U.S. Dept. of State, 1977-78; pres. Internat. Personal Shopping Service, Ltd., N.Y.C., 1980—. Bd. dirs. Hebrew Home Greater Washington, 1970—, Internat. Sickle Cell Anemia Research Inst., Washington, 1976—. Democrat. Address: 880 5th Ave Apt 7A New York NY 10021

LAMB, JEAN MARIE, govt. accountant; b. North Platte, Nebr., Apr. 24, 1933; d. James Ira and Catherine Isabell (Beckius) Wright; student in acctg. Boise State Coll., 1971; m. Harry Jack Lamb, June 4, 1950; children—Judy Marie, Jerrald Jack, Sandra Joan, Joy Elaine. Quality control technician Basic Vegetables Products Co., King City, Calif., 1967; prodn. control clk. Grandview Farms (Idaho), 1968-69; receptionist/bookkeeper Royal Lincoln Mercury, Boise, Idaho, 1970-72; index file clk. J. R. Simplot Food Processing Co., Caldwell, Idaho, 1972; bookkeeper/receptionist Happy Day Ford Inc., Caldwell, 1972-73; sec. Idaho Dept. Health and Welfare, Caldwell, 1973-77, sr. sec., word processing center supr., 1977-80, account clk. regional central collections unit, 1980—. Mem. Employee Devel. Assn. Republican. Baptist. Club: Order Eagles Aux. (pres. local aux. 1976-77). Home: 2814 S Illinois Ave Caldwell ID 83605 Office: 111 Poplar Caldwell ID 83605

LAMB, JOAN EUGENIA, govt. ofcl.; b. Phila., July 27, 1939; d. Joseph N. and Eugenia A. Juliano; B.A., George Mason U., 1973; postgrad. Am. U., 1974-75; m. James Patrick Lamb, Dec. 29, 1958; children—Joseph Julian, James Gerard. Public affairs officer Navy Office Info., The Pentagon, Washington, 1973-79, Naval Ordnance Sta., 1979-80; public affairs dir. Selective Service System, Washington, 1980—. Recipient Selective Service Silver medal for superior achievement, 1981. Mem. League Women Voters, Women in Communications, Pub. Relations Soc. Am., AAUW. Roman Catholic. Home: 4709 Newcomb Pl Alexandria VA 22304 Office: 1023 N St NW Washington DC 20435

LAMB, URSULA SCHAEFER, historian, educator; b. Esen, Germany, Jan. 15, 1914; came to U.S., 1935, naturalized, 1949; d. Waldemar Joachim and Maria Katharina (Hoffmann-Fallersleben) Schaefer; student U. Berlin, 1932-34, Smith Coll., 1935-36; M.A., U. Calif.-Berkeley, 1937, Ph.D., 1949; m. Willis E. Lamb, Jr., June 5, 1939. Lectr. history Barnard Coll., asso., 1949-51; tutor Brasenose Coll., lectr. Oxford, Eng., 1958, 60; lectr., research asso. Yale U., New Haven, 1962-74; prof. history U. Ariz., Tucson, 1974—. Am. Learned Socs. grantee, 1943, Soc. Sci. Research grantee Columbia U., 1947, Guggenheim fellow, 1968-69, Nat. Endowment Humanities fellow, 1972-73, Am. Philos. Soc. grantee, 1975, NSF grantee, 1978-79. Mem. Soc. History Discoveries (pres. 1976-79), Am. Hist. Assn. (council mem. Pacific br. 1977-79), Conf. Latin Am. History, Pan Am. Inst. Geography and History (mem. bibliography com.), Internat. Reunion Nautical Sci. (U.S. rep.), Colloque Internat. de l'Histoire Maritime (U.S. rep. 1979, 80, Soc. Spanish and Portuguese Hist. Studies. Author: Frey Nicolás de Ovando, Gobernador de las Indias, 1501-1509, 1956; A Navigator's Universe: The Libro de Cosmographía of 1538 (Pedro de Medina), 1972; The E. G. R. Taylor Lecture, 1981. Office: 215 Social Sci Campus U Ariz Tucson AZ 85721

LAMBERT, BELLE BRANHAM, shopping ctr. devel. co. exec.; b. Camden, S.C., Mar. 26, 1943; d. Arthur B. and Leila Mae (Ray) Branham; Asso. Sci., Piedmont Tech. Coll., 1981; m. C. Ronnie Lambert, Apr. 22, 1962; 1 dau., Nici Renee. Exec. sec. to pres. Neptune Internat., Greenwood, S.C., 1972-76; adminstrv. asst. Greenwood County Council on Alcohol and Drug Abuse, 1976-79, sec. bd. dirs., 1976—; gen. mgr., mktg. dir. Jim Wilson & Assocs., Greenwood, 1979—. Mem. Nat. Assn. Female Execs., Greenwood Forum (charter), Internat. Council Shopping Centers (asso., MAXI award 1981), Greenwood Bus. and Profl. Women (1st v.p. 1980-81, pres. 1981-82, named Career Woman 1981), Greenwood C. of C. Home: 130 Cherokee Rd Greenwood SC 29646 Office: Jim Wilson & Assocs Crosscreek Mall Office 420-22 ByPass NW Greenwood SC 29646

LAMBERT, LILLIE B., real estate broker; b. Washington, Jan. 19, 1928; d. Joseph Jefferson and Abbie Rose (Lloyd) Burns; ed. George Washington U., San Jose State Coll.; children—Rosemary, Shelly, Carl Jay, Keith. Health educator Prevention of Blindness Soc., Washington, 1964-69; founder, owner Tax Shelters, Inc., Carmel-by-The-Sea, Calif., 1977—, chmn. bd., 1977—; owner, broker Lillie Lambert Realty, Carmel, Calif., 1974—; cons. tax shelters, real estate investments. Mem. Internat. Real Estate Fedn., Am. Soc. Profl. Cons., Am. Soc. Profl. and Exec. Women, Nat. Assn. Realtors. Republican. Club: Order Eastern Star. Office: PO Box 3687 Carmel-by-The-Sea CA 93921

LAMBERT, MARIE M., judge; b. Cirella Reggio Calabria, Italy, Nov. 18, 1920; d. Nicola and Lucia (Bellasai) Macri; ed. Bklyn. Coll., N.Y.U.; m. Grady Lee Lambert, Aug. 18, 1946 (dec.); 1 son, Gregory L. Admitted to bar; mem. firm Chadbourne, Hunt, Jaeckle & Brown, 1944-46, Carroad & Carroad, 1946-49; individual practice, N.Y.C., 1949-74; partner Katz, Shandell, Katz & Erasmous, 1974-77; judge Surrogate's Ct. N.Y. County, 1978—; lectr. in field. Pres., Jr. Women's League; bd. dirs. Nyopia Research Found. Recipient awards Italian orgns.; Law Day award. Mem. Italian Execs. Am. (charter mem, dir.), St. Citizens Assn. (dir.), N.Y.C. Fedn. Women's Clubs, Women's Equity Action League, Women's Political Caucus, ABA, Nat. Coll. Probate Judges, Nat. Assn. Women Judges, N.Y. State Trial Lawyers Assn (past pres.), Met. Women's Bar, N.Y. Assn. Women Judges (v.p.), Am. Justinian Soc. Jurists, Nat. Probate Council, Am. Judges Assn., N.Y. Women's Bar Assn., Bklyn-Columbian Lawyers Assn., Internat. Fedn. Women Lawyers. Co-author: You May be Losing Your Inheritance. Home: 737 Park Ave New York NY 10021

LAMBERT, MARTHA LOWERY, state legislator; b. Douglasville, Ga., Mar. 27, 1937; d. Edmond Davis and Mary (Daniel) Lowery; m. Paul Dean Lambert, 1959; children—Melanie Lynn, Kurt Phillip, Brett Cameron, Matthew Dean. Mem. N.M. ex. Ho. Reps., 1981—. Pres. Albuquerque Fedn. Republican Women, 1975-76; alt. del. Rep. Nat. Conv., 1976. Office: N M Ho Reps State Capitol Santa Fe NM 87503

LAMBERT, NADINE MURPHY, psychologist, educator; b. Ephraim, Utah; d. Rulon E. and Maude Molla (Nielsen) Murphy; A.B. in Psychology, UCLA, 1948; M.A. in Edn., Los Angeles State U., 1955; Ph.D. in Psychology, U. So. Calif., 1964; m. Robert E. Lambert, Dec. 29, 1956; children—Laura Allan, Jeffrey Lambert. Sch. psychologist Los Nietos Sch. Dist., 1952-53, Bellflower Unified Sch. Dist., 1953-58; research cons. Calif. Dept. Edn., 1958-64; asst. prof. to prof., dir. sch. psychology program U. Calif., Berkeley, 1964—; cons. Calif. Dept. Justice. Fellow Am. Psychol. Assn. (Disting. Service award Div. Sch. Psychologists 1980), Am. Orthopsychiat. Assn.; mem. Calif. Assn. Sch. Psychologists and Psychometrists (pres. 1962-63), NEA, Am. Ednl. Research Assn., Coll. and Univ. Educators Sch. Psychologists. Author: Second Edition School Version Adaptive Behavior Scale, 1981; contbr. articles to profl. jours., chpts. to books; research on life histories of hyperactive children, adaptive behavior. Office: Sch Edn U Calif Berkeley CA 94720

LAMBERT, PATRICIA, photographer, painter, printmaker, educator; b. N.Y.C.; d. Robert K. and Maxine (Toch) L.; B.A. in Art and Chemistry, Mt. Holyoke Coll., 1958; postgrad. Pratt Inst., Art Students League, NAD, Columbia U. Sch. Painting and Sculpture; painting and scenic design for opera and theatre dept. grantee Juilliard Sch., 1959-60; asst. Photo-Graphics Workshop; exhibited group shows including NAD, N.Y.C., Allied Artists Am., N.Y.C., Painters and Sculptors Soc. N.J.; represented in permanent collection Stamford Mus., UNICEF 1967 collection, numerous pvt. collections; resident scenic artist Juilliard Sch., 1959-60; asst. to Ralph Mayer, Columbia U. Sch. Painting and Sculpture, to Dean Cornwell, Mural Workshop of Nat. Acad. Sch.; free-lance comml. and fine art work, 1965—; instr. Art Center, Summit, N.J., 1974, Photo-Graphics Workship, New Canaan, Conn., 1971, Parsons Sch. Design, N.Y.C., 1974—; mem. Bob Blakcburn's Printmakers Workshop, N.Y.C.; bd. dirs. Arts Tech. Research Inst. Mem. Artists Equity Assn. N.Y., Am. Chem. Soc., Asso. Conn. Theatre Artists, Contbr. articles on color, color theory and light in art, also lectr. Home: 356 Rockrimmon Rd Stamford CT 06903

LAMBERT, REBECCA FOTOUHI, assoc. dep. Sec. Commerce; b. Binghamton, N.Y., Jan. 31, 1947; d. Abol Hassan and Eleanor Margaret (Page) Fotouhi; student Williams Coll., 1968-69; B.A., Simmons Coll., 1969; Harvard U. Bus. Sch. Advanced Mgmt. Program, 1982. Vice pres., treas. Champlain Properties, Inc., Burlington, Vt., 1971-75; pres. Chardick Property, Inc., Southampton, L.I., 1973-74, Chatelian, Ltd., 1973-74; staff asst. U.S. Rep. James Jeffords, 1975; adminstrv. aide Nat. Republic Senatorial Com., Washington, 1975-76; cons. Wallop for Senate campaign, 1976-77; adminstrv. aide to Senator Malcolm Wallop, Washington, 1977-80; mem. Reagan Transition Team, 1980; dep. asst. sec. Dept. Energy, Washington, 1981-82; assoc. dep. sec. Dept. Commerce, Washington, 1982—. Fin. dir., mem. strategy com. Gov. Deane C. Davis reelection campaign, 1970; commr. Governor's Commn. on Status of Women, 1970-75, statewide chmn. presdl. campaign, 1972; sec.-treas. Grand Isle County Republican Com., 1973, vice chmn., 1972; mgr. senate campaign U.S. Rep. Richard Mallary, 1974; treas. Am. PAC, 1979-80. Presbyterian. Home: 813 Maryland Ave NE Washington DC 20002 Office: 14th and Constitution Ave NW Washington DC 20230

LAMBERT, SHEILA SONABEND, bus. info. co. exec.; b. N.Y.C., Feb. 13, 1947; d. David Howard and Roslyn G. Sonabend; B.A. magna cum laude, Miami U., Oxford, Ohio, 1968; M.A. with honors, U. Mich., 1969; postgrad. N.Y. U., 1974; m. July 26, 1970; 1 son. Personnel asst. Dun & Bradstreet, Inc., N.Y.C., 1971-72, personnel mgr., 1972-74, dir. employee relations, 1974-75, dir. personnel, 1976-77, v.p. personnel, 1977-79; v.p. human resources Moody's Investors Service, N.Y.C., 1980-81, sr. v.p., pub., 1981—. Mem. Am. Soc. Personnel Adminstrs., N.Y. Credit Mgmt. Assn., Phi Beta Kappa. Home: 140 Riverside Dr New York NY 10024 Office: Moody's Investors Service 99 Church St New York NY 10024

LAMBERTI, DEBORAH LOUISE, psychotherapist; b. New Haven, May 1, 1953; d. James Carmen and Eugenia Susan (Pascale) L.; B.A. magna cum laude in Psychology, Wheaton Coll., Norton, Mass., 1975; exchange student Trinity Coll., 1973-74; M.S.W., N.Y.U., 1977. Fellow, Greenwich Inst. for Psychoanalytic Studies, N.Y.C., 1976-79; psychotherapist community/clinic liaison Fifth Ave Center for Counseling and Psychotherapy, N.Y.C., 1976-79, asso. dir., 1979—; pvt. practice psychotherapy, 1979—; mem. Lower West Side subcom. N.Y. State Mental Health Assn.; mem. children's subcom. Lower West Side Mental Health Assn., 1976-77, mem. subcom acute care, 1977—, also assn. sec.; tng. supr. N.Y.U. Grad. Sch. Social Work, 1980—, Yeshiva U. Wurtzweiler Sch. Social Work, Hunter Coll., 1981—; mem. youth bd. Dist. II, N.Y.C., 1980—; cons. in field. Mem. Fedn. Mental Health Agys. (chmn.), Nat. Assn. Social Workers, Acad. Cert. Social Workers, Am. Orthopsychiat. Assn., Nat. Paraplegia Assn., Nat. Registry Cert. Clin. Social Workers. Clubs: Woodbridge Country, N.Y. Health and Racquet, N.Y.U. Alumni. Co-editor: Access: New York: An Accessibility Guide for the Disabled of East Midtown Manhattan Selected Facilities, 1976. Home: 141 Barrow St New York NY 10014 also 18 Ox Bow Ln Woodbridge CT 06525 Office: 10 W 10th St New York NY 10011

LAMBIRD, MONA SALYER, lawyer; b. Oklahoma City, July 19, 1938; d. B.M., Jr., and Pauline A. Salyer; B.A., Wellesley Coll., 1960; LL.B., U. Md., 1963; m. Perry A. Lambird, July 30, 1960; children—Allison Thayer, Jennifer Salyer, Elizabeth Gard, Susannah Johnson. Admitted to Okla. bar, 1968, also admitted to practice before Ct. Appeals Md., Supreme Ct. Okla., U.S. Dist. Ct., U.S. Supreme Ct.; atty. civil div. Dept. Justice, Washington, 1963-65; individual practice law, Balt. and Oklahoma City, 1965-71; mem. firm Andrews, Davis, Legg & Bixler, Milsten & Murrah, Inc., Oklahoma City, 1971—; cons. World Orgn. of China Painters; adv. Oklahoma City Media Council. Profl. liaison com. City of Oklahoma City, 1974-79; mem. Hist. Preservation of Oklahoma City, Inc., 1970—; del. Oklahoma County and Okla. State Republican Party Conv., 1971—; women's com. Okla. Symphony Orch., legal adv., 1973—, bd. dirs., 1973—; bd. dirs. RSVP Oklahoma County, 1978—, pres., 1982-83. Mem. Am., Md., Okla., Okla. County bar assns., Jr. League Oklahoma City (dir. 1973-76, Okla. County and State Med. Assn. Aux. (fin. adv., dir.), Friends of Okla. Libraries (dir. 1979—). Methodist (adminstrv. bd.). Club: Seven Colls. (pres. 1972-76). Editor, Briefcase of the Okla. County Bar Assn., 1976. Home: 419 NW 14th St Oklahoma City OK 73103 Office: 1600 Midland Center Oklahoma City OK 73102

LAMBSON, GLORIA MAE, assn. exec.; b. Russell, Mass., Oct. 1, 1921; d. Emmett Alderman and Lena Mae (Wood) Rogers; A.A.S. in Bus., Sch. Continuing Edn., N.Y. U., 1972, B.S. in Econs., Sch. Commerce, 1973, M.B.A. in Econs., Grad. Sch. Bus., 1976; m. Lorenzo D. Lambson, Dec. 7, 1939; 1 dau., Donna Mary. Alumni sec. Am. Internat. Coll., Springfield, Mass., 1953; asst. editor Hamilton Standard, Windsor Locks, Conn., 1957-58; editor Hampden County Improvement League, West Springfield, 1961-64; editor Episcopal Diocese of N.Y., N.Y.C., 1965-67; workshop mgr. Commerce and Industry Assn. of N.Y., N.Y.C., 1968; copywriter, account exec. CMC&C Advt., N.Y.C., 1969; part time sec. CC&C, N.Y.C., 1970; adminstrv. asst. Am. Inst. Chem. Engrs., N.Y.C., 1971-72, employment coordinator, econ. research mgr., 1973-79, staff dir. member activities and services, 1980—; instr. Sch. Continuing Edn., N.Y. U., 1976-77. Pres. Asso. Women, Mass. Farm Bur., 1948-49; chmn. Southwick (Mass.) Republican Town Com., 1954-64, alt. del. nat. conv., 1960, mem. Mass. Rep. state com., 1964-65; mem. Hoboken Environ. Com., 1979—. Recipient presiding bishop's prize, best diocesan Newspaper, 1967; univ. honors scholar N.Y. U., 1973. Mem. Nat. Assn. Bus. Economists, Women's Econ. Round Table, N.Y. Soc. Assn. Execs., Council Engring. and Sci. Soc. Execs., Am. Mensa, Beta Gamma Sigma Alumni of N.Y., Phi Chi Theta. Episcopalian. Contbr. reports, procs., surveys to profl. assn. Home: 539 Bloomfield St Hoboken NJ 07030 Office: 345 E 47th St New York NY 10017

LAMKE, LEANNE KAY, psychologist; b. Alamogordo, N.Mex., Mar. 18, 1954; d. Wayne E. and Edith E. (Washburn) L.; B.A. in Psychology, U. N.D., 1975; M.S. in Family Studies, Tex. Tech U., 1978, Ph.D., 1979. Instr. dept. child devel. and family relations Tex. Tech U., 1978-79; asst. prof. family relations Ariz. State U., Tempe, 1979-82, U. Ariz., Tucson, 1982—; cons. in communication skills and personnel mgmt. Tex. Tech. U. grantee, 1978, Ariz. State U. grantees, 1979—. Mem. Am. Psychol. Assn., Nat. Council Family Relations, Am. Assn. Marriage and Family Therapy, Minn. Couples Communication Program (certified instr.), Ariz. Home Econs. Assn. (dir. 1981-82), Am. Home Econs. Assn. Contbr. articles to profl. jours. Home: 444 W Orange Grove St Apt 915 Tucson AZ 85704 Office: Div Child Devel and Family Relations U Ariz Tucson AZ 85721

LAMLE, TAMMY, real estate broker; b. Wauseon, Ohio, Aug. 6, 1946; d. Clarance E. and Vesta M. (Champman) Planson; student public schs., Stryker, Ohio; 1 dau., Amy Jo. Clk., Empire Fire & Marine Co., Ft. Wayne, Ind., 1964-66; sec. Phelps Dodge, Ft. Wayne, 1966-68, Plant Instruments, Ft. Wayne and Calif., 1969-71; personnel asst. Spring Realty, Calif., 1971; sales asso., mgr. Graber Realty, Ft. Wayne, 1973-76; real estate broker, sales trainer Roth Wehrly Heiny, Inc., Ft. Wayne, 1976—. Vice precinct committeewoman Republican Party; active polit. campaigns. Lic. real estate broker, Ind.; lic. sales asso., Calif.; cert. residential specialist. Mem. Ft. Wayne Bd. Realtors, Grad. Realtors Inst., Nat. Assn. Realtors, Ind. Assn. Realtors. Republican. Home: 7531 Parliament Pl Fort Wayne IN 46815 Office: 6605 E State St Fort Wayne IN 46815

LAMMERS, JOYCE MARIE, hosp. adminstr.; b. Franklin County, Nebr., Feb. 15, 1951; d. Loyal Kenneth and Evelyn Marie (Johnson) H.; R.N., Asbury Sch. Nursing, 1971; student Colby Community Jr. Coll., 1968-69; m. Donald E. Lammers, Mar. 18, 1972; children—Donna Marie, Jason Lee. Staff nurse Asbury Hosp., Salina, Kans., 1971; asst. dir. nursing Windsor Estates Nursing Home, Salina, 1971-72; charge nurse Asbury Hosp., Salina, 1972-73; edn. coordinator, dur. nursing Smith County Meml. Hosp., 1973—. Vol. Ambulance Service person, 1977—; councilman Emergency Med. Services Region I, 1977. Mem. Kans. Nurses Assn., Kans. Emergency Med. Technicians Assn. Home: 416 East Ct Smith Center KS 66967 Office: 614 S Main St Smith Center KS 66967

LAMON, MARGARET RAE, educator; b. Chgo., May 29, 1935; d. Leonard Cletus and Beulah Martha (Lashbrook) Murray; B.A. in Speech and Drama, Rosary Coll., 1957; M.A. in English, No. Ill. U., 1973; m. John David Lamon, July 18, 1959. Tchr., Visitation High Sch., Chgo., 1957-58, Siena High Sch., Chgo., 1958-66, York Community High Sch., Elmhurst, Ill., 1966—. Mem. Hon. Thespian Soc., Sigma Tau Delta. Roman Catholic. Home: 107 W Central Ave Lombard IL 60148 Office: 355 W St Charles Rd Elmhurst IL 60126

LAMONT, FRANCES STILES (PEG), state senator; b. Rapid City, S.D., June 10, 1914; B.A., U. Wis., 1935, M.A., 1936; m. William Mather Lamont, Oct. 6, 1937; 4 children. Former journalist; mem. S.D. Senate, 1975—. Mem., chmn. S.D. Council on Aging; mem. Nat. Commn. on Status of Women, S.D. Commn. on Status of Women; bd. dirs. Nat. AAUW Ednl. Found.; mem. Nat. Mental Health Bd.; pres. Historic S.D., Inc. Named Aberdeen First Lady, 1954; recipient service award Sertoma Club, 1972; S.D. Mother of Yr. award 1974, 75; Disting. Alumni award U. Wis., 1975; Gerontologist of Yr. award, 1978; Gov.'s award, 1979; award State Aging Conf., 1979. Mem. Nat. Trust for Historic Preservation (trustee 1980—), S.D. Hist. Soc. (dir., award 1976), AAUW (br. and state awards 1969, 70, Nat. Centennial award 1981). Republican. Episcopalian. Office: South Dakota Senate Pierre SD 57501 *

LAMONTAGNE, NANCY HARTSHORN, info. systems specialist; b. Gardner, Mass., June 14, 1949; d. Charles and Pauline Flora (Blouin) Hartshorn; B.S. in Math. and Computer Sci., U. Mass., 1971; M.Mgmt., Simmons Coll., 1981; m. Stephen Paul Lamontagne, Mar. 1, 1980. Project evaluation specialist M.I.T., Cambridge, 1972-77; mfg. systems analyst USM Corp., 1977-79; fin. and mfg. systems sr. programmer Digital Equipment Corp., 1979-81; mgmt. info. systems mgr. The Gillette Co., Andover, Mass., 1982—; cons. data processing and office mgmt. Mem. Am. Mgmt. Assn., Data Processing Mgmt. Assn. Home: 7 Cole Rd Deerfield NH 03037 Office: 30 Burtt Rd Andover MA 01810

LAMONTE, GWYNNE ANN JERUS, systems engr.; b. Bklyn., Apr. 22, 1949; d. George R. and Margaret M. Jerus; B.A. cum laude, Marymount Coll., Tarrytown, N.Y., 1971; M.B.A., St. John's U., Jamaica, N.Y., 1980; m. Theodore N. LaMonte, June 5, 1971 (dec.). Programmer, analyst Bache Halsey Stuart Co., 1975-76; systems engr., then regional market support rep. IBM Corp., 1976-81, system engring. mgr., Cranford, N.J., 1981—. Bd. dirs. Tennis View Apts., 1977-79. Mem. Am. Mgmt. Assn., Beta Gamma Sigma. Office: 20 Commerce Dr Cranford NJ 07016

LAMPROS, ANGELIQUE, educator; b. West Orange, N.J., June 29, 1936; d. Nicholas and Vasiliki William (Kyriakarakos) Lampros; B.A., Montclair State Coll., 1958; M.A., George Washington U., 1973; postgrad. Seton Hall U., 1973-74, Fordham U., 1970-71, Kean Coll., 1960-63, Drakes Bus. Sch., 1955-56, Berlitz Sch. Lang., 1962-63. Tchr., Emerson High Sch., Union City, N.J., 1958-61; tchr. Jefferson Sch., Maplewood, N.J., 1961—, acting prin., 1971-81, chmn. faculty adv. bd., 1971-72; congl. legis. aide to Congressman Nicholas Galifianakis, Washington, 1972-73; chemistry lab. asst. Montclair State Coll., N.J., 1954-55. Supt. Religious project, Greek Orthodox Archdiocese of N. and S. Am., 1964-65; bd. dirs. ARC, 1967-69; chmn. bd. dirs. Met. Greek Chorale, Inc., 1979—. Mem. N.J. Edn. Assn., NEA, Nat. Assn. Female Execs., South Orange-Maplewood Edn. Assn. (dir. fund raising, scholarships 1970-73, chmn. profl. improvement 1981-82), Hellenic Heritage Found. Greek Orthodox. Clubs: Daus. of Penelope.

LANCASTER, ELAINE LAKIN, banker; b. Hennessey, Okla., July 20, 1935; d. Linley R. Krebs and Violet Elma Krebs Benson; B.S., U. Md., 1963; m. William Duval Lancaster, Apr. 30, 1977; children from previous marriage—Cameron Lakin, Jeffrey Lakin. Loan officer Am. City Bank, 1970-72; consumer fin. officer 1st Western Bank, 1972-73; regional loan officer Calif. Fed. Savs. and Loan, Los Angeles, 1973-77; mgr. consumer loans Coast Fed. Savs. and Loan, Hawthorne, Calif., 1977-78; regional consumer loan officer Glendale Fed. Savs. & Loan, Downey, Calif., 1978—. Mary Hardin Baylor Coll. scholar, 1955: Ford Found. fellow, 1965-66. Mem. Savs. and Loan League, Am. Inst. Banking, Nat. Notary Assn., AAUW, Coast Mgmt. Democrat. Club: Toastmistresses. Office: 9030 Stonewood St Downey CA 90241

LANCASTER, SALLY RHODUS, found. exec.; b. Gladewater, Tex., June 28, 1938; d. George Lee and Milly Maria (Meadows) Rhodus; B.A., So. Methodist U., 1960, M.A., 1979; postgrad. East Tex. State U.; m. Olin C. Lancaster, Jr., Dec. 23, 1960; children—Olin C. III, George Charles, Julie Meadows. Tchr. English, Tex. public schs., 1960-61, 78-79; exec. v.p., grants adminstr. Meadows Found., Inc., Dallas, 1979—, also trustee, dir. Trustee So. Meth. U., 1980-84. Mem. Am. Personnel and Guidance Assn., Phi Beta Kappa (chpt. pres. 1980-82), Kappa Delta Pi. Presbyterian. Office: 310 Meadows Bldg Dallas TX 75206

LANCASTER, VIRGINIA M., state legislator; b. N.Y.C., Feb. 17, 1929; d. student Florence, Italy; B.A., Goddard Coll.; postgrad. U. Vt.; m. John Lancaster; 3 sons, 1 dau. Mem. Vt. Ho. Reps., 1981—. Office: Vt Ho Reps State Ho Montpelier VT 05602

LAND, JANE MOODY, musician, educator; b. Richmond, Va., Dec. 7, 1923; d. Earle C. and Carrie M. (Franck) Moody; B.S. in Music Edn., Madison Coll., 1946; postgrad. U. Va., 1958, Va. Commonwealth U., 1968-69; m. Weldon Bell Land, Apr. 27, 1951; children—Carolyn Johnson, Susan. Dir. music Highland Springs Schs., Henrico County, Va., 1944-45; tchr. Richmond Bus. Sch., 1946-47; dir. music Chesterfield County (Va.) Public Schs., 1947-49, Manchester High Sch., 1950-51; dir. music Clarke County (Va.) Public Schs., 1950-51; social worker youth service Dept. Welfare and Instns., Richmond, Va., 1951-53; dir. music Spotsylvania County (Va.), 1958-61; pvt. tchr. piano, organ, voice, Richmond, 1946-50, St. Simons Island, Ga., 1956-58, Fredericksburg, Va., 1958-71, Richmond, 1976—; tchr., adminstr. Land Sch. Music, Richmond, 1971—; organist Madison Coll., 1941-45; organist, choir dir. Christ Episcopal Ch., Richmond, 1940-41; organist Scottish Rite, Christmas season, 1942-56, Christ Episcopal Ch., St. Simons Island, Ga., 1956-58; audition judge Bland Music Contests, Fredericksburg, 1969—. Mem. Am. Guild Organists, Nat. Guild Piano Tchrs. (area chmn., regional chmn.), AAUW, Duntreath Civic Assn. (treas. 1979-80). Democrat. Lutheran. Home: 906 Regester Pkwy Richmond VA 23226

LAND, LYNDA KAY, bus. cons.; b. Terre Haute, Ind., Aug. 26, 1940; d. William Paul and Sharon Eunice (McKee) Cherepkai; student Ind. State U., 1975; Ind.-Purdue U., 1977; children—Alan, Kim, Kendall. With Dept. Public Instrn., State Ind., 1969-77; trainee McDonalds Corp., Indpls., 1977-79, area supr., 1979-81, field cons., 1981-82, sr. tng. cons. for Europe, 1981—. Pres., Ind. Young Republicans, 1968-69; dist. dir., mem. state bd. Ind. PTA, 1965-70. Mem. NEA, Nat. Assn. Exec. Females. Republican. Home: 5958 Deerwood Ct Indianapolis IN 46254 Office: PO Box 50414 Indianapolis IN 46250

LAND, MARY ELIZABETH, author, composer; b. Benton, La., Sept. 28, 1908; d. Thomas T. and Elizabeth (Langford) Land; student Gulf Park Coll., Gulfport, Miss., 1924-25, Cheyney Trent Sch. Poetry, Calif., 1937, U. Chgo., 1938; m. Edward Timothy Kelly, 1925; 1 dau., Patricia Kelly Stevens; m. 2d, George T. Lock, 1931; 1 son, George T. Lock-Land. Mem. staff La. Conservation Rev., La. Dept. Conservation, New Orleans, 1940-41, Miss. Valley Sportsman, 1948, So. Outdoors Mag., Atlanta, 1959, 60, 61, West Bank Guide, New Orleans, 1962, Sportsman's News, Hot Springs, Ark., 1960; author (with Arthur Van Pelt) syndicated column, Outdoors South, for weekly newspapers Miss., La., 1947, 48; feature writer Fisherman Mag., 1954, R X Sports and Travel Mag., 1971, Down South Mag., 1964, Natchitoches Times, 1970. Named Co-Poet Laureate for Tenn., 1941; recipient Blue Ribbon award Gulf Coast br. Nat. League Am. Pen Women, Merit certificate Nash Motor Co., 1953, 1st Pl. award La. Press Assn., 1969-70, Merit certificate and 2 Keys to City Mayor New Orleans, 1954, Outstanding Contbn. certificate La. Soc. Colonial Dames, 1971, certificate Am. Bicentennial Research Inst., 1973. Mem. Nat. League Am. Pen Women (past br. pres.), Nat. Fedn. Am. Press Women, La. Press Women, Outdoor Writers Assn. Am., La. Outdoor Writers Assn. (charter), Fedn. Musicians. Author: Shadows of the Swamp (poetry), 1940, Mary Land's Louisiana Cookery, 1954 (So. Books award 1956), New Orleans Cuisine, 1968 (2d pl. award Fedn. Am. Press Women 1969), Abode (poetry), 1972, Dreams (poetry), 1977; contbr. conservation articles to mags., poetry to anthologies; composer: You Hang In My Heart, 1959, As Strange As You Are, 1959, Drink Deep, 1959, Piano Cho Cho Zarzosa, 1959, Voice-Allehandra Allegra, 1959. Address: 1314 Williams Ave Natchitoches LA 71457

LAND, PHYLLIS MARIE, state govt. ofcl.; b. Winona, Miss., Aug. 29, 1944; d. Sandy Kenneth and Ruth (Cottingham) L.; B.S., U. So. Miss., Hattiesburg, 1967; M.S. (Title II-B fellow 1968-69), U. Tenn., Knoxville, 1969; postgrad. Purdue U., Ind. U., Utah State U. Librarian, Natchez (Miss.)-Adams County schs., 1967-68; materials specialist Fulton County Bd. Edn., Atlanta, 1969-71; cons. div. instructional media Ind. Dept. Public Instrn., Indpls., 1971-74, dir. div., 1974—, dir. fed. resources and sch. improvement, 1982—; pres. bd. dirs. INCOLSA, mcpl. corp., 1980-82; mem. task force sch. Libraries Nat. Commn. Libraries and Info. Sci.; cons. in field. Mem. Gov. Inst. Conf. Children and Youth Task Force. Recipient citation Internat. Reading Assn., 1975. Mem. ALA, Nat. Assn. State Ednl. Media Profls., Delta Kappa Gamma. Adv. bd. Booklist. Office: Room 229 State House Indianapolis IN 46204

LANDA, BETH KIM, psychologist; b. Manhattan, N.Y., Oct. 18, 1954; d. Jay Myron and Ruth (Kaplan) L.; B.A. cum laude, Hofstra U., 1975, M.A. with distinction (Univ. fellow), 1977, Ph.D., 1980. Teaching asst. Hofstra U., 1975-76, research asst./assoc. 1977-78, mem. assoc. faculty, internship supr., 1980—; data analyst L.I. Jewish/Hillside Med. Center, Glen Oaks, N.Y., 1978, statistician psychiat. research, 1978-80, biostatistician divs. psychiatry and medicine, 1980—; instr. in child psychology, mem. adj. faculty C.W. Post Center, L.I. U., Greenvale, N.Y., 1982. Mem. Am. Psychol. Assn., Assn. Women in Computing, Psi Chi (pres. chpt. 1974-75). Home: 70 E 10th St New York NY 10003 Office: LI Jewish-Hillside Med Center Hillside Research Glen Oaks NY 11004

LANDA, ESTHER ROSENBLATT, civic worker; b. Salt Lake City, Dec. 25, 1912; d. Simon and Sylvia Gertrude (Liberman) Rosenblatt; B.A., Mills Coll., 1933, M.A., 1937, H.H.D. (hon.), 1980; LL.D. (hon.), U. Utah, 1978; m. Jerome Joseph Landa, Sept. 26, 1943; children—Carol Leslie, Howard Simon, Terry Ellen. Public relations Mills Coll. (Clif.), 1934-39, Bennington (Vt.) Coll., 1941; account exec. Constance Hope Assos., N.Y.C., 1941-42; info. specialist various agys. U.S. Govt., 1942-43; cons. burs. Community Devel. and Indian Services, U. Utah, 1962-65; dir. women's programs U. Utah, 1965-71; nat. pres. Nat. Council Jewish Women, 1975-79; mem. Pres.'s Adv. Com. Women, 1978-80, Pres.'s Commn. for Nat. Agenda for 80's, 1979-80; mem. Salt Lake City Bd. Edn., 1958-70, Utah State Bd. Edn., 1970-74; sec.-treas. Nat. Assn. State Bds. Edn., 1973-74; pres. Salt Lake County Community Action Program, 1968-70; pres. LWV Salt Lake City, 1956-58; chairperson task force on equal opportunity for women Nat. Jewish Community Relations Adv. Council, 1977-81, vice-chairperson, 1982—; mem. planning com. White House Conf. on Children, 1970; Utah del. White House Conf. on Families, 1980; U.S. del. World Conf. UN Decade for Women, Copenhagen, 1980. Named to Salt Lake Council of Women Hall of Fame, 1958; hon. life mem. PTA, 1963; recipient Libety Bell award Utah Bar Assn., 1963; Utah Woman of Year, AAUW, 1965; Woman of Year, B'nai B'rith, 1965; Man of Year in Utah Edn., Phi Delta Kappa, 1967; Civil Rights Worker of Year award NAACP, 1968; Disting. Service award Utah Sch. Bds. Assn., 1969, 72; U. Utah Alumni Merit award, 1976; Disting. Woman award U. Utah, 1978; Susa Young Gates award Nat. Women's Polit. Caucus, 1979; Citation Utah chpt. NCCJ, 1980. Mem. Nat. Council Jewish Women, LWV, NOW, Nt. Women's Polit. Caucus, ACLU, Phi Beta Kappa, Delta Kappa Gamma. Democrat. Jewish. Clubs: Hadassah, B'nai B'rith Women. Author Pres.'s column Nat. Council Jewish Women Jour., 1975-79. Home: 5006 S 1034 E Salt Lake City UT 84117 Office: 1130 Kennecott Bldg Salt Lake City UT 84133

LANDAU, EDYTHE, motion picture prodn. corp. exec.; b. Wilkes-Barre, Pa., July 15, 1927; d. Harry and Rose (Zatcoff) Rudolph; B.A., Wilkes Coll., 1948; J.D., U. West Los Angeles, 1981; m. Ely A. Landau, Mar. 13, 1959; children—Jon, Tina, Kathy. Exec. v.p. Nat. Telefilm Assos., Inc., 1953-60, Landau Prodns., 1960-70, Am. Film Theatre, 1970-75; producer, v.p. Edie & Ely Landau, Inc., Los Angeles, 1978—; producer films: Hopscotch, Beatlemania, The Chosen, The Deadly Game; admitted to Calif. bar, 1981. Awards given to films produced include: Long Days Journey Into Night (best acting award Cannes Film Festival, 1962, Katherine Hepburn Oscar nomination best actress); The Pawnbroker (Rod Steiger Oscar nomination best actor, 1965); King - A Filmed Record, Montgomery to Memphis (Oscar nomination best documentary, 1970); Man in the Glass Booth (Maximilian Schell Oscar nomination best actor, 1975); The Chosen (best picture Montreal World Film Festival, 1981, Rod Steiger best actor, 1981). Mem. Acad. Motion Pictures Arts and Scis., Women in Film, ABA, Calif. State Bar Assn., Beverly Hills Bar Assn.

LANDAU, GENEVIEVE MILLET, (MRS. SIDNEY LANDAU), editor; b. Dallas, June 17, 1927; d. Harry and Elsie (Lazarus) Hershson; B.A. summa cum laude, William Smith Coll., 1954; postgrad. Columiba U., 1954-55; m. Sidney Landau, Mar. 21, 1967; children—Elizabeth Millet, Jessica Millet. Asso. editor Parents' mag., 1958-60, articles editor, 1960-65, exec. editor, 1965-70, editor-in-chief, 1970—; v.p. Parents' Mag. Enterprises. Bd. dirs. Hasbro Center for Child Edn. and Devel., 1978—. Mem. Am. Soc. Mag. Editors, Phi Beta Kappa. Author, editor several books, articles. Office: Parents Magazine 52 Vanderbilt Ave New York NY 10017 *

LANDAU, SONIA, media cons.; b. Wichita, Kans., July 14, 1937; d. Sam William and Pearl Janet Sharmes; B.A., U. Denver, 1958; postgrad. U. Calif., 1959; m. John Corry, Apr. 18; children—Colette, Janet. Dir. radio and TV, Nat. Republican Congressional Com., Washington, 1969-72; formerly media cons. Roger Arles & Assocs., N.Y.C.; formerly dir. corp. affairs Dreyfus Corp.; now media cons., N.Y.C.; cons. J. Walter Thompson, London. Bd. dirs. Corp. for Public Broadcasting; exec. dir. N.Y. Republican State Fin. Com., N.Y.C.; Rep. nominee for U.S. Congress, N.Y.C., 1976; mem. Rep. County Com., N.Y.C. Club: City of N.Y. (trustee 1976-78).

LANDAU, SYBIL HARRIET, lawyer, educator; b. N.Y.C., Nov. 26, 1937; d. Sidney and Janice (Katz) Landau; B.A. with honors in history, Hunter Coll., 1958; LL.B. (Harlan Fiske Stone scholar 1961), Columbia U., 1961; B.C.L., Oxford (Eng.) U., 1963. Asst. prof. law Bristol (Eng.) U. Faculty Law, 1963-65; admitted to practice, U.K., 1965; admitted to N.Y. bar, 1965, U.S. Supreme Ct. bar, 1970; asst. dist. atty. New York County, 1965-72; asso. prof. law Hofstra U. Sch. Law, Hempstead, N.Y., 1972-74; cons. reporter N.Y. State Family Ct. Adv. and Rules Com., 1974-75; asso. prof. Benjamin N. Cardozo Sch. Law, N.Y.C., 1975-80, asst. dean, 1975-77; vis. adj. prof. law Bklyn. Law Sch., 1975; hearing examiner N.Y. State Family Ct., 1981-82. Mem. N.Y.C. Mayor's Task Force on Rape, 1974-77; lectr. on rape Nat. Confs. Women and the Law, 1973, 74, 76, 77, 81; mem. adv. bd. subcom. on juvenile delinquency Temporary State Commn. on Child Welfare. Named to Hall of Fame, Hunter Coll., 1974. Brookdale fellow Hunter Coll., 1977-78. Mem. Am. Law Inst., ABA, Assn., Bar Assn., N.Y. State Bar Assn., N.Y.C. Bar Assn., Met. Law Women Tchrs. (v.p. 1976-79), Honourable Soc. Middle Temple (Eng.), Alumni Assn. Hunter Coll. (dir. 1976-79, 80—), Phi Beta Kappa, Alpha Chi Alpha, Alpha Phi Theta. Club: N.Y.C. Women's. Office: 8 W 13th St New York NY 10011

LANDAZURI, COLLEEN ANN, public health nurse; b. Fond du Lac, Wis., Sept. 8, 1950; d. James Edward and Elizabeth Ann (Masloff) Flood; B.S. in Nursing, Marquette U., 1972, postgrad. (fed. nurse traineeship grant, 1976-77), 1976-77; m. Gabriel Landazuri, Oct. 26, 1974; children—Dario James, Patrick Xavier, Alexander Gabriel. Staff nurse Milw. Health Dept., 1972-76, dist. supr., 1976-80, program dir. prenatal edn. and assessment program, 1980—; coordinator-cons. interdisciplinary dental-nursing student assessment program Marquette U. Dental Sch. Ad hoc mem. Milw. Public Sch. Critical Health Problems Curriculum Adv. Com.; mem. Milw. Healthy Baby Coalition, Greater Milw. Com. Concerned with Unmarried Parents Services. Mem. Am. Public Health Assn., Am. Nurses Assn., Wis. Nurses Assn., Milw. Dist. Nurses Assn., Milw. Health Dept. Nursing Standards and Practice Com., Sigma Theta Tau. Roman Catholic. Office: 841 N Broadway Milwaukee WI 53202

LANDER, KATHLEEN GELCHER, writer, editor; b. Los Angeles, Apr. 24, 1923; d. Joseph and Grayce Clara (McCormick) Gelcher; B.A., U. So. Calif., 1944; postgrad. U. Calif. at Irvine, 1972-73, N.Y.U., 1977; m. Robert Frank Lander, Sept. 6, 1947 (div. 1974); children—Jeffrey, Richard, Lisa, Marc. Reporter, editor, San Marino (Calif.) Tribune, Inglewood (Calif.) Daily News, Rodgers-McDonald Newspapers, Los Angeles, 1944-47; owner public relations co., Inglewood, 1947-49; west coast editor High Fidelity Trade News, 1972-74, Consumer Electronic Product News, N.Y.C., 1974-77; free-lance writer-editor consumer and trade publs., N.Y.C., 1977—; sr. editor Leisure Time Electronics. Founding mem., pres. LWV, Santa Ana, Calif., 1961-63, chmn. Orange County Council, LWV, 1958; bd. dirs. Orange County Community Action Council, 1964-69. Mem. Women in Communications, Inc., Mortar Bd. Alumnae of So. Calif. (pres. 1945-46). Home: 144 E 36th St New York NY 10016

LANDERHOLM, ELIZABETH JANE, educator; b. Oak Park, Ill., Jan. 13, 1941; d. Daniel R. and Dorothy Thomkins (Ellis) LaBar; B.A., DePauw U., 1963; M.S.T., U. Chgo., 1966; Ed.D., No. Ill. U., 1980; m. Wayne A. Landerholm, June 6, 1964; 1 son, Arthur Scott. Group worker Marcy Newberry Center, Chgo., 1963-64; youth counselor Ill. State Employment Service, Chgo., 1964-65; tchr. Chgo. Public Schs., 1966-69; co-founder, dir. Ednl. Service Pool, 1971-72; mem. faculty Nat. Coll. Edn., Chgo., 1972-80, dir. student teaching, 1974-80, ednl. coordinator early childhood field based program, 1975-80; asst. prof. early childhood edn. Roosevelt U., Chgo., 1980—; cons. Theraplay Inst., Chgo. Mem. Ind. Precinct Orgn., Chgo. Roosevelt U. Dean's grantee, 1980-81, 81-82. Mem. Nat. Assn. Edn. Young Children, Council Exceptional Children, Pi Lambda Theta. Mem. Ch. of Christ. Author articles and monographs. Home: 325 N Humphrey Oak Park IL 60302 Office: 430 S Michigan Ave Chicago IL 60605

LANDERS, ANN (MRS. ESTHER P. LEDERER), columnist; b. Sioux City, Iowa, July 4, 1918; d. Abraham B. and Rebecca (Rushall) Friedman; student Morningside Coll., 1936-39, L.H.D., 1964; Hum.D., Wilberforce (Ohio) Coll., 1972; L.H.D., U. Cin., 1974; L.H.D., Am. Coll. Greece, Deree-Pierce Coll., 1975, LL.D., 1979; m. Jules W. Lederer, July 2, 1939 (div. 1975); 1 dau., Margo (Mrs. Ken Howard). Syndicated columnist Pubs.-Syndicate-Field Enterprises, Chgo., 1955—; pres. Eppie Co., Inc., Chgo. Chmn. Eau Claire (Wis.) Gray-Lady Corps, A.R.C., 1947-53; chmn. Minn.-Wis. council Anti-Defamation League, 1945-49; asst. Wis. chmn. Nat. Found. Infantile Paralysis, 1951-53; hon. nat. chmn. 1963 Tb Christmas Seal Campaign; bd. sponsors Mayo Clinic, 1970; mem. sponsors com. Mayo Found., nat. adv. bd. Dialogue for the Blind, 1972; adv. com. on better health services AMA. County chmn. Democratic Party of Eau Claire. Bd. dirs. Rehab. Inst. Chgo.; nat. bd. dirs. Am. Cancer Soc.; vis. com. bd. overseers Harvard Med. Sch.; trustee Menninger Found., Nat. Dermatology Found. Am. Coll. Greece, Deree-Pierce Coll., Athens, Meharry Med. Sch. Recipient award Nat. Family Service Assn., 1965; Adolf Meyer award Assn. for Mental Health, N.Y., 1965; Pres.'s Citation and nat. award Nat. Council on Alcoholism, 1966, 2d nat. award, 1975; Golden Stethoscope award Ill. Med. Soc., 1967; Humanitarianism award Internat. Lions Club, 1967; plaque of honor Am. Friends of Hebrew U., 1968; Gold Plate award Acad. Achievement, 1969; Nat. Service award Am. Cancer Soc., 1971; Robert T. Morse award Am. Psychiat. Assn., 1972; plaque recognizing establishment of chair in chem. immunology Weizmann Inst., 1974; Jane Addams Public Service award Hull House, 1977; Health Achievement award Nat. Kidney Found., 1978; Nat. award Epilepsy Found. Am., 1978; James Ewing Layman's award Soc. Surg. Oncologists, 1979; citation for distinguished service AMA, 1979; Thomas More medal Thomas More Assn., 1979; NEA award, 1979. Fellow Chgo. Gynecol. Soc. (citizen hon.); mem. League Women Voters (pres. 1948), Brandeis U. Women (pres. 1960). Author: Since You Asked Me, 1962; Teen-agers and Sex, 1964; Truth is Stranger..., 1968; Ann Landers Speaks Out, 1976; The Ann Landers Encyclopedia, 1978. Clubs: Chgo. Econs. (dir. 1975); Sigma Delta Chi. Address: Chgo Sun-Times 401 N Wabash Ave Chicago IL 60611 *

LANDERS, VERNETTE TROSPER, post office clk., author, ret. educator; b. Lawton, Okla., May 3, 1912; d. Fred Gilbert and LaVerne Hamilton (Stevens) Trosper; A.B. with honors, UCLA, 1933, M.A., 1935, Ed.D., 1953; m. Paul Albert Lum, Aug. 29, 1952 (dec. May 1955); 1 son, William Tappan; m. 2d, Newlin Landers, May 2, 1959; children—Lawrence, Marlin. Tchr. secondary schs., Montebello, Calif., 1935-45, 48-50, 51-59; prof. Long Beach City Coll., 1946-47; asst. prof. Los Angeles State Coll., 1950; dean girls 29 Palms (Calif.) High Sch., 1960-65; dist. counselor Morongo (Calif.) Unified Sch. Dist., 1965-72, coordinator adult edn., 1965-67, guidance project dir., 1967; clk.-in-charge Landers (Calif.) Post Office, 1962—. Vice-pres., sec. Landers Assn., 1965—; sec. Landers Vol. Fire Dept., 1972—; life mem. Hi-Desert Playhouse Guild, Hi-Desert Meml. Hosp. Guild; bd. dirs., sec. Desert Emergency Radio Service. Recipient internat. diploma of honor for community service award, 1973; cert. of merit for disting. service to edn., 1973; Creativity award Internat. Personnel Research Assn., 1972; named Soroptimist of Yr., 29 Palms Soroptimist Club, 1969; named Poet Laureate for 1981, Center of Internat. Studies and Exchanges, Italy. Lifefellow Internat. Acad. Poets (London); mem. Am. Personnel and Guidance Assn., Nat. League Am. Pen Women, Internat. Platform Assn., Intercontinental Biog. Assn., Nat. Ret. Tchrs. Assn., Montebello Bus. and Profl. Women's Club (pres.), Landers Area C. of C., Mortar Board, Phi Beta Kappa, Pi Lambda Theta, Sigma Delta Pi. Clubs: Soroptimist (sec. 29 Palms 1962); Whittier (Calif.) Toastmistress (pres. 1957); Homestead Valley Women's (Landers). Author: Impy, 1974; Impy's Children, 1975; Talkie, 1975; Nineteen O Four, 1976; Little Brown Bat, 1976; Slo-Go, 1977; Owls Who and Who Who, 1978; Sandy the Coydog, 1979; The Kit Fox and the Walking Stick, 1980; contbr. New Voices in American Poetry, An Anthology on World Brotherhood and Peace. Contbr. articles to profl. jours. Home: 905 Landers Ln Landers CA 92284 Office: 890 Landers Ln Landers CA 92284

LANDES, BARBARA LEVY, broadcasting co. exec.; b. N.Y.C., Jan. 11, 1950; d. David and Elizabeth (Kastan) Levy; B.A., Washington U., St. Louis, 1971; M.B.A., U. Pa., 1973; m. Mark A. Landes, June 4, 1978. Sr. fin. analyst CBS TV Network, N.Y.C., 1973-74, sr. planner CBS Records Group, 1974-75, mem. staff office of pres. CBS Inc., 1975-76, dir. fin. planning and analysis CBS News, 1976-78, asst. controller fin. planning and analysis, 1978-80; v.p. fin. planning and analysis NBC, Inc., N.Y.C., 1980—. Bd. dirs. Pan Asian Repertory Theatre, 1980—, Mgmt. Decision Simulation, N.Y. U. Grad. Sch. Bus., spring 1981. Office: NBC 30 Rockefeller Plaza New York NY 10020

LANDI, DIANE MARIE, designer; b. Paterson, N.J., Apr. 27, 1952; d. Mario Gustave and Josephine (Ryba) L.; student Sch. Visual Arts, N.Y.C., 1969-72. Chief designer Medallion Industries, 1971-76; designer, asst. art dir. Equitable Bag Co., L.I. City, 1977—; owner, art dir. Landigraphics Co., advt. art services, Queens, N.Y., 1977—; design cons., partner R-Art, Inc., N.Y.C. Mem. Nat. Assn. Female Execs., Am. Inst. Graphic Arts, Mensa, Beethoven Soc., Nat. Taxpayers Union, Amnesty Internat. Libertarian. Home: 75-12 35th Ave Jackson Heights NY 11372 Office: 50-20 70th St Woodside NY 11377

LANDIS, INGRID JOYCE, advt. exec.; b. Durham, N.C., June 25, 1946; d. Andrew Henderson and Alice Fatima L.; student Rutgers U., Maui (Hawaii) Community Coll., Honolulu Sch. Theology; divorced; 1 son, Song S. Sommer. Flight attendant United Airlines, 1967; project supr. manpower devel. and tng., Micronesia, 1970; advt. saleswoman Maui Sun Newspaper, 1974-75; advt. account exec. Pacific Bus. News, Hawaii, 1976-79, Fla. Trend mag., Tampa, 1979-80; advt. sales mgr. Tampa Bay Bus., 1980—. Founder, Christian Friends, Honolulu, 1978; pres. Single Christian Parents, Honolulu, 1978-79. Mem. Network Mktg. Women, Network Exec. Women (pres. Tampa 1980-81), NAACP, Tampa Advt. Fedn. (dir.). Democrat. Editor Christian newsletter Steps, 1977-79. Home: 4541 Tarpon Dr Tampa FL 33617 Office: 402 Reo St Suite 218 Tampa FL 33656

LANDIS, MARILYN ADAMSON, educator; b. Gallatin, Tenn., Nov. 11, 1948; d. John Thomas and Hester Mae (Curtis) Adamson; B.S. in Edn., Tenn. Tech. U., 1970; M.Ed., U. Tenn., Chattanooga, 1978; m. William Edmund Landis, Dec. 26, 1976; 1 dau., Abigail Christina. Various secretarial positions, 1966-72; adminstrv. asst. McCallie Devel. Fund, Chattanooga, 1972-74; tchr. typing and history McCallie Sch. for Boys, Chattanooga, 1974-78, tchr. typing, sch. counselor, 1978—. Mem. Am. Personnel and Guidance Assn., Am. Sch. Counselors Assn., Assn. Measurement and Evaluation in Guidance, Tenn. Personnel and Guidance Assn., Tenn. Sch. Counselors Assn. Presbyterian. Office: McCallie Sch Missionary Ridge Chattanooga TN 37404

LANDMAN, CHERYL MARSHALL, mfg. co. ofcl.; b. San Francisco, May 30, 1944; d. James Cecil and Alma Lois (Morris) Holmes; B.B.A., U. Tex., San Antonio, 1979, M.B.A., 1981. Owner, mgr. consumer products franchise, San Antonio, 1969-71; sales mktg. counselor, 1971-73; mil. mktg. sales rep. Bristol Myers Corp., N.Y.C., 1973-78; mktg. rep. Patient Care div. Johnson and Johnson, 1981—. Republican. Home: 5210 Newcome San Antonio TX 78229

LANDMAN, LIBBY GELLER LYNCH, librarian, educator; b. Springfield, Mass., Nov. 24, 1929; d. Isadore Loeb and Shirley (Bershatsky) Geller; student N.Y.U., 1958-68; B.A. in Russian Lit., Manhattanville Coll., 1973; M.A. in L.S., U. Wis., 1974; postgrad. Columbia U., 1974-77, Wright State U., 1977-78; Oxford U., 1981; M.Pub.Adminstrn., U. Okla., 1982; m. Jerome S. Lynch (dec.); children—Priscilla B. Lynch, Jonathan H. Lynch, Andrew S. Lynch; m. 2d, Nathan M. Landman, June 26, 1977. Public librarian Larchmont (N.Y.) Public Library, 1975-77; sch. librarian Scarsdale (N.Y.) and Mamaroneck Pub. Schs., 1975-77; info. cons. Netter Internat., N.Y.C., 1976-77; sch. librarian Fairborn (Ohio) Pub. Schs., 1978; European rep. NASCO Internat., Ft. Atkinson, Wis., 1979-81; public librarian Queens Borough Public Library, N.Y.C., 1981-82; public services librarian, instr. Coll. New Rochelle (N.Y.), 1982; lectr. in field. Mem. Bd. Edn., Larchmont

Temple, N.Y., 1968-70; treas. Officers' Wives 401st Combat Support Group, Spain, 1979-80; mem. PTA, 1969-74, ways and means treas., 1970; head librarian Larchmont Temple Library, 1967-70; chmn. victory luncheon United Jewish Appeal, 1974; librarian detention facility Juvenile Ct., Montgomery County, Ohio, 1977-78. Recipient Humanitarian Fellowship award, 1967; citation for religious leadership Union Am. Hebrew Congregations, 1971; cert. of appreciation U.S. Air Force, 1981; cert. librarian, N.Y., Ohio. Mem. ALA, Am. Soc. Public Adminstrs., Freedom To Read Found., Wis. Alumni Assn., Phi Beta Mu. Republican. Jewish. Clubs: Officers' Wives, Am. Women's (Madrid). Contbr. articles to profl. publs. Home: 15 Lookout Circle Larchmont NY 10538 Office: Gill Library Coll of New Rochelle New Rochelle NY 10801

LANDMAN, MARY DAVIS, real estate co. exec.; b. Windsor, Vt., Mar. 19, 1931; d. Michael Joseph and Margaret Mary (Healy) Walsh; m. Selwyn Landman, Aug. 13, 1971; children by previous marriage—Justin, Rebecca, Kathleen, Andrea, Kevin; stepchildren—David, Michael. Owner, pres. Mary W. Davis, Realtor and Assos., Inc., Ludlow, Vt., 1959—; vice chmn. Vt. Real Estate Commn., 1967-71, chmn., 1972-77; v.p. Ludlow Devel. Corp., 1975—; v.p., dir. Okemo Ski Area, 1978-81; dir. Vt. Nat. Bank. Trustee, Fletcher Meml. Library, Ludlow, 1965—. Mem. Nat. Assn. Real Estate Licensing Law Ofcls., Vt. Bd. Realtors, South Central Vt. Bd. Realtors. Roman Catholic. Home: Commonwealth Ave Ludlow VT 05149 Office: Ludlow Shopping Plaza Ludlow VT 05149

LANDON, HELEN JOSEPHINE, nursing center adminstr.; b. Delaware, Ohio, May 17, 1926; d. Thomas Albert and Rachel Savilla (Wood) Sartwell; student Bliss Coll., Columbus, Ohio, 1939-40, Ohio State U., 1975-77; L.P.N., Marion Gen. Hosp., 1965; m. Roy M. Landon, Dec. 7, 1944 (dec.); children—Delores A., Danny R., Michael L., Mary R., Janice S., Patrick A., Dennis D. Adminstr., Hillside Nursing Home, 1952-70; adminstr. Maplewood Nursing Center, Marion, Ohio, 1970-78, pres., 1977-78; adminstr. Village Care Center, Galion, Ohio, 1981—; pres. Lanjor House Inc., Marion. ARC vol. County Health Dept., Delaware, 1946-50; active Booster Assn., PTA, Girl Scouts U.S.A. Recipient Single Parent of Yr. award, 1973. Mem. Ohio Lic. Practical Nurses Assn. (sec. 1974-75), Nat. Nursing Home Assn. (dist. pres. 1962-65), Am. Coll. Nursing Home Adminstrs. Republican. Methodist. Home: 1166 Greenlea Dr Marion OH 43302 Office: 409 Bellefontaine Ave Marion OH 43302

LANDRE, DEBRA ANN, educator; b. Quantico, Va., Sept. 15, 1955; d. Thomas and Joy L. Landre; B.A., Bradley U., 1976, M.S., 1977; M.S., Ill. State U., 1979. Math. instr. Bradley U., 1976-78, Ill. State U., Normal, 1978-82; instr. computer sci. Lincoln Coll., Bloomington, Ill., 1981—; computer cons. Ill. Public Sch. System, 1980—. Mem. Math. Assn. Am., Nat. Council Tchrs. Math., Ill. Council Tchrs. Math., Ill. Math. Assn. Two-Year Colls., Phi Delta Kappa. Club: Apple User's Group (editor newsletter). Home: 1700 North School St Apt 29 Normal IL 61761 Office: Dept Edn Adminstrn Ill State U Normal IL 61761

LANDRENEAU, ELLEN RITA, nurse, educator; b. Ville Platte, La., Jan. 26, 1949; d. Joseph Otis and Clamie (Fusilier) L.; B.S., U. Southwestern La., 1971; M.S., U. So. Miss., 1978; m. A. Dale Thibodeaux, Feb. 21, 1981. Staff nurse Wuesthoff Meml. Hosp., Cocoa, Fla., 1971-72; pub. health nurse Brevard County Health Dept., Melbourne, Fla., 1972-74; day camp nurse Baton Rouge Assn. Retarded Citizens, 1974; staff nurse ICU, Earl K. Long Hosp., Baton Rouge, 1976; lab. asst. Southeastern La. U., 1974-77; instr. nursing Pearl River Jr. Coll., Poplarville, Miss., 1978; edn. cons. Acadiana Mental Health Center, Lafayette, La., 1979; asst. prof. U. Southwestern La., Lafayette, 1978—. Mem. Nat. League for Nursing, Am. Nurses Assn., La. Nurses Assn., AAUP, Alpha Lambda Delta, Phi Kappa Phi, Sigma Theta Tau. Roman Catholic. Home: 100 Edgebrook Circle Lafayette LA 70508 Office: University Southwestern Louisiana PO Box 40490 Lafayette LA 70504

LANDRETH, JANET, pianist, educator; b. Poplarville, Miss., Apr. 28, 1944; d. John and Margaret Morgan; B.Mus., U. Tulsa, 1965, M.Mus., 1967; D.M.A., U. Okla., 1980; children—Hobie Landreth, Phil Landreth; Instr., U. Tulsa, 1966-67; instr., head piano dept. Southwestern State Coll., Weatherford, Okla., 1967-71; coordinator piano div. Colo. State U., Ft. Collins, 1975—; performer, adjudicator. Pres., program chmn. Weatherford Fine Arts Council, 1968-70. Winner state piano competitions in Miss. and Okla., Bloch Young Artist award 5-state competition, 1967; Okla. Consortium Research Devel. grantee, 1969; U. Okla. Research Found. grantee, 1979-80. Mem. Nat. Music Tchrs. Assn., Sigma Alpha Iota, Pi Kappa Lambda. Democrat. Home: 701 Duke Sq Fort Collins CO 80525 Office: Colo State U Fort Collins CO 80523

LANDRUM, FRANCES ANN, dancer, educator; b. N.Y.C., Apr. 5, 1918; d. Edmund Charles and Mary Elizabeth (Lannon) Lourie; student Vestoff-Serova Sch. Dance, 1927-35, Tarasoff Sch. Dance, 1929-31, Martha Graham Sch. Dance, 1935-36; m. Robert Bascom Landrum, June 30, 1938; children—Elizabeth Ann (Mrs. J. Jesse Gwynn), Robert Bascom II; m. 2d, Theodore Wayne Brummund, June 17, 1979. Ballet dancer Russian Opera Co., 1930, Lee Schubert Prodns., 1931; mem. corps de ballet, soloist Radio City Music Hall, N.Y.C., 1933-42; founder, owner, dir. Landrum Sch. Dance, N.Y.C., 1948—; founder Young Peoples Dance Group L.I., 1964—; artistic dir. Ballet Repertory L.I., 1964—; produced, directed and choreographed dance recitals RKO Keiths Flushing Theatre, 1955—, Andre Eglevsky Co., 1960-61. Artistic dir. Bicentennial Com. College Point, N.Y., 1975—; active nat. council auxs. Am. Med. Center at Denver. Recipient Merit Cert., N.Y. State Com. on World's Fair, 1964. Charter mem. Assn. Am. Dance Companies, Concerned Citizens for the Arts in N.Y. State, N.Y. Dance Alliance. Presbyterian. Address: Route 2 Box 295B Elon College NC 27244

LANDRUM, GERRI FAYE, writer, lectr.; b. Lawton, Okla., Nov. 9, 1932; d. Brooks Lee and Velma Allene (Dixon) Truesdale; student Lawton public schs.; m. Wayne Merel Landrum, Jan. 1, 1950; children—Benjamin, Lori Richey. Freelance reporter, photographer Burkburnett (Tex.) Star, 1959-63; soc. editor Weatherford (Tex.) Democrat, 1963-65; retail advt. copywriter, 1965-78; freelance writer, lectr., 1978—; works include: The Creative Gift Guide for Uncreative People, 1980; pamphlets and booklets on club programming; program and spl. events cons. women's clubs. Mem. Tex. Press Women (2d v.p. Dist. 8 1979—), Internat. Platform Assn. Clubs: Internat. Toastmistress (pres. Council 5), Bammel Forest Home and Garden (pres. 1979-80). Baptist. Home: 2414 Bammel Timbers Houston TX 77068

LANDRUM, MARGO WADSWORTH, communications co. exec.; b. Washington, Dec. 14, 1940; d. Joseph Rodgers and Genevieve Frances (Folse) Wadsworth; B.A. in English, St. Mary's Dominican Coll., 1965; m. James F. Landrum, June 9, 1962; children—Courtney, Jay, Colin. Partner, Rent-A-Writer, San Jose, Calif., 1978—; pres. MS BS, Inc., San Jose, 1981—; cons. in field. Mem. San Jose C. of C. (publicity/historian chmn. 1980-81), Media Alliance, San Jose Women in Advt., Peninsula Women in Advt., South Bay Public Relations, Nat. Assn. for Profl. Sales Women. Democrat. Roman Catholic. Contbr. articles to profl. jours. Home: 6631 Mount Royal Dr San Jose CA 95120 Office: 1610 Blossom Hill Rd Suite 9 San Jose CA 95124

LANDRUM-BRUMMUND, FRANCES ANN, choreographer, dance instr.; b. N.Y.C., Apr. 5, 1918; d. Edmond Charles and Mary Elizabeth (Lannon) Lourie; student Vestoff-Serova Sch. of Dance, 1927-35, Tarasoff Sch. of Dance, 1929-31, Martha Graham Sch. Dance, 1935-36; m. Theodore Wayne Brummund, July 27, 1979; children by previous marriage—Elizabeth Ann Gwynn, Robert Bascom Landrum II. Ballet dancer Russian Opera Co., 1930, Lee Schubert Prodns., 1931; soloist Corps du Ballet, Radio City Music Hall, N.Y.C., 1933-42; founder, owner, dir. Landrum Sch. of Dance, N.Y.C., 1948—; founder Young People's Dance Group of L.I., 1964—; artistic dir. Ballet Repertory of L.I.; producer R.K.O. Keith's Flushing Theatre, 1960—, also Andre Eglevsky Ballet Co. Active, Concerned Citizens for the Arts. Recipient merit award N.Y. State Commn. on World's Fair, 1964. Mem. Am. Assn. Dance Cos., N.Y. Dance Alliance. Presbyterian. Office: 14 34 150th St Whitestone NY 11357

LANDRY, MARGARET AVET, med. technologist; b. Houma, La., Oct. 19, 1947; d. Philip Royce and Wilma (King) Avet; B.S., Nicholls State Coll., 1970, postgrad. 1977-78; M.S., La. State U., 1979; m. Jimmy John Landry, Sept 7, 1968. Med. technologist, Terrebonne Gen. Hosp., Houma, La., 1969, Bapt. Meml. Hosp., Memphis, 1970-71, Terrebonne Gen. Hosp., Houma, 1972—; research asst. La. State U., 1978-79, teaching asst., 1979. Mem. Am. Soc. Clin. Pathologists (affiliate mem.), La. Soc. Electron Microscopy. Clubs: Planetary Soc., L-5 Soc., Hist. and Cultural Soc. Terrebonne Parish, New Orleans Mus. Art, Friends of the Zoo. Office: Dept Pathology 936 E Main St Houma LA 70360

LANDSBERGER, BETTY HATCH, human devel. profl., educator; b. Tampa Aug. 9, 1918; d. Hugh Brenton and Margaret Lauder (Macdonell) Hatch; B.A. in Sociology, Fla. State U., 1939; M.A. Ed., U. Mich., 1940; Ph.D., Cornell U., 1951; m. Henry A. Landsberger, June 10, 1951; children—Margaret Ann, Samuel Ernest, Ruth Elizabeth. Mem. faculty edn. dept. Fla. State U., Cornell U., Roosevelt U., Chgo., 1941-54; program asso. evaluation research Learning Inst. N.C., Durham, 1969-71; mem. faculty U. N.C. Sch. Nursing, Chapel Hill, 1976—, asst. prof. nursing, 1979-81, asso. prof., 1981—; cons. N.C. Div. Health Services, public schs. Chmn. Orange County Sr. Citizens Bd., 1981—. Mem. N.C. Assn. Research in Edn. (pres. 1975-76), AAUP (pres. elect), Am. Public Health Assn., Phi Beta Kappa, Phi Kappa Phi, Pi Lambda Theta. Democrat. Contbr. articles to profl. jours. and textbooks. Home: 807 Kings Mill Rd Chapel Hill NC 27514 Office: Sch Nursing U NC Chapel Hill NC 27514

LANDSMAN, DIANE LYNN, public relations and advt. copywriter, cons.; b. Amsterdam, N.Y., Oct. 24, 1950; d. Joseph Raymond and Marion Leah (Aldrich) Frederick; B.A. magna cum laude, Houghton Coll., 1972. Adminstrv. intern. Dept. Interior, Washington, 1972-73; editorial asst. Smith, Bucklin & Assos., Chgo., 1973-74, account mgr. staff publicist, 1974-76; free-lance public relations/advt. copywriter/cons., Chgo., 1976—; co-founder, cons. Creative Events Services, Chgo., 1978-80; v.p. Connelly Design, Inc., 1980—. Ward coordinator 49th Ward, Thompson for Gov. Campaign, Ill., 1976; chmn. membership, dir. Upper North, Ind. Voters Ill., 1977-78, mem. state membership com., 1977-78. Mem. Women in Communications, Houghton Coll. Alumni Assn., Chgo. Council on Fgn. Relations, Chgo. LWV, Com. for Handgun Control, Internat. Platform Assn. Home: 820 Dobson St Evanston IL 60202 Office: 233 E Wacker Dr Suite 305 Chicago IL 60601

LANDVATTER, EDITH SUZANNE FORIS, chemist; b. Dayton, Ohio, Dec. 16, 1955; d. Peter Lazlo and Nancy Ellen (Walker) Foris; A.B., Carleton Coll., 1978; postgrad. U. Ill., Champaign-Urbana, 1978—; m. Scott White Landvatter, July 29, 1979. Lab. asst. gen. and organic chemistry Carleton Coll., Northfield, Minn., 1976-78; research asst. Monsanto Corp., St. Louis, summer 1978; teaching asst. U. Ill., Urbana, 1978—, research asst., 1979—. Mem. Am. Chem. Soc., Phi Lambda Upsilon, Iota Sigma Pi (treas. Iodine chpt. 1981—), Alpha Chi Sigma (sec. 1980). Office: Box 42 Noyes Lab U Ill 505 S Mathews St Urbana IL 61801

LANDY, SARAH EDITH, Sask. (Can.) edn. ofcl.; b. London, July 23, 1933; d. John Brodie and Louise Phyllis (Brodrick) Marshall; B.A. with honours, U. Western Australia, 1953; postgrad. Australian Nat. U., Canberra, 1970-73; M.A., U. Regina (Sask., Can.), 1976, Ph.D., 1981; divorced; children—Matthew, Alan. Jane. Vocat. guidance officer, Perth, W. Australia, 1960-65; research officer Dept. Territories, Australia, 1965-68; librarian Australian Nat. U., 1970-72; asst. chief librarian Regina Public Library, 1974-77; head profl. programs extension U. Regina, from 1977; now exec. dir. policy and program div. Dept. Continuing Edn., Province of Sask. Recipient President's award U. Rehina, 1979; Hackett scholar, 1953-54; Canadian Library Assn. scholar, 1967; Sask. Dept. Health bursary, 1979; Spinks scholar, 1979-80; Nat. Health and Welfare grantee, 1980-81. Mem. Can. Library Assn., Can. Psychol. Assn. Home: 3018 Gordon Rd Regina SK S4S 2T8 Canada Office: Sask Dept Continuing Edn Regina SK Canada

LANE, ALTA N(EWMAN), educator; b. Grand Bay, Ala., May 12, 1927; d. Alphia L. and Louella (Jones) Newman; B.S., Memphis State U., 1970; M.S., Okla. State U., 1971, Ph.D. (Univ. fellow), 1978; children—Sheila Kathryn Lane Williams, Belinda Michelle. Instr. home econs. Memphis State U., 1971-76; grad. fellow Okla. State U., 1976-78; asst. prof. U. No. Iowa, 1978-81; asst. prof. interior design Baylor U., 1981—; cons. interior design. Mem. Am. Home Econs. Assn., Am. Soc. Interior Designers, Assn. Am. Housing Educators. Baptist. Office: Dept Home Econs Baylor U Waco TX 76798

LANE, ANN BOYD, pub. co. exec.; b. Teaneck, N.J., Oct. 18, 1954; d. Douglas Lewis and Ann (Corcoran) Boyd; A.B., U. Calif., Berkeley, 1976; m. William Marcell Lane, Sept. 9, 1978. With mfrs. Hanover Trust Co., 1976-80; asst. treas. Harcourt Brace Jovanovich Inc., N.Y.C., 1981—. Mem. Corp. Cash Mgrs. Assn. N.Y. Democrat. Roman Catholic. Office: 757 3d Ave New York NY 10017

LANE, CHERYL ANN GROSS, nursing cons.; b. Pitts., Sept. 24, 1948; d. Charles N. and Maryalda (Freund) Gross; Asso. Sci. with honors, Jr. Coll. of Broward County, 1968; B.S. in Nursing, N.C. A. and T. U., 1981; m. Timothy Gerald Lane, June 20, 1969; children—Tamala Ann, Wendelyn Joy, Justin Bradley. Staff nurse Broward Gen. Hosp., Fort Lauderdale, Fla., 1968, asst. head nurse, 1969; oncology nurse clinician Bowman Gray Sch. Medicine, Winston-Salem, N.C., 1969-71, dir. cancer center nursing Oncology Research Center, 1971-81, oncology nursing cons., 1981—; mem. tumor registry com. N.C. Bapt. Hosp., 1980-81. Mem. N.C. Adv. Council on Cause and Control of Cancer Task Force, 1978. Mem. Am. Cancer Soc. (bd. dirs. N.C. div. 1980-81, chairperson nursing subcom. N.C. div. 1979-81), Oncology Nursing Soc., Piedmont Oncology Assn. (chairperson nursing com. 1979-81), Phi Theta Kappa. Roman Catholic. Author: (manual) Cancer Chemotherapy Guidelines, 1978; contbr. articles on nursing care to profl. jours. Home: 2025 Yorktown Dr Cape Girardeau MO 63701 Office: Oncology Center of Bowman Gray School Medicine 300 S Hawthorne Rd Winston-Salem NC 27103

LANE, CONSTANCE CARMICHAEL RENICK, sch. adminstr.; b. Rockford, Ill., Nov. 9, 1921; d. James Alexander and Nozella (Oda) Carmichael; B.S. magna cum laude in Edn., W.Va. State Coll., 1943; M.A., Northwestern U., 1962; m. Andrew J. Lane, June 20, 1964; children—Betty Anne Renick (Mrs. Flynn Jefferson), James Renick. Tchr., Rockford Public Schs., 1954-62, helping tchr. elem. math., 1962-63; prin. Henrietta Primary and Intermediate Schs., Rockford, 1963-66; prin. W. Ray McIntosh Sch., Rockford, 1966-79; Area IV coordinator Rockford Public Schs., 1971-79, asst. supt. for elem. edn., 1979—; part-time instr. Rockford Coll., evenings 1964-79. Mem. Taus, Inc. (pres. 1960-63, 74-78, treas. 1972-74), Ill., Rockford edn. assns., NEA, AAUW, Nat. Council Tchrs. Math., Assn. Supervision and Curriculum Devel., Rockford Prins. Assn., Nat. Elementary Prins. Assn., Ill. Women Adminstrs., Delta Kappa Gamma, Phi Delta Kappa. Episcopalian. Contbr. articles to profl. jours. Home: 2224 Clover Ave Rockford IL 61102 Office: Rockford Public Schs 201 S Madison St Rockford IL 61108

LANE, ELIZABETH ANN, ednl. adminstr.; b. New Orleans, Oct. 24, 1944; d. Jeremiah Lurry and Eunice Frances (O'Dwyer) L.; B.A., La. State U., New Orleans, 1966; M.Ed., Loyola U. of South, New Orleans, 1970; postgrad. in ednl. adminstrn. U. So. Miss. Tchr., C. F. Rowley Elem. Sch., St. Bernard Parish (La.) Sch. Bd., Chalmette, 1966-75, prin., 1975—; cons. So. Assn. Schs. and Colls. Named Outstanding Young Educator, St. Bernard Parish Jaycees, 1972, La. State Tchr. of Yr., 1972; Delta Kappa Gamma Soc. Internat. Epsilon State scholar, 1981. Mem. St. Bernard Parish Prins. Assn. (v.p. 1977-79), Nat. Sci. Tchrs. Assn., Nat. Assn. Elem. Sch. Prins., Delta Kappa Gamma Soc. Internat., Phi Delta Kappa, Kappa Delta Pi. Democrat. Roman Catholic. Editor newsletter St. Bernard br. AAUW, 1966-76.

LANE, EVELYN, employment agy. exec.; b. N.Y.C.; R.N., Met. Hosp., N.Y.C., 1945; M.A., Columbia U., 1948. Pres. Paragon Employment Agy., Inc., 1958—, Finchley Advt. Agy., N.Y.C., 1962—, Paragon Nurses Registry Inc., N.Y.C., 1972—, A Temp. Nurse, 1972—. Address: 300 Madison Ave Suite 1302 New York NY 10017

LANE, KATHLEEN WYER, mgmt. cons.; b. West Palm Beach, Fla., Aug. 7, 1945; d. Rolley Edward and Barbara Daly (Patterson) Wyer; B.A., SUNY, 1967, M.A., 1971; m. Sept. 2, 1967. Tchr., North Babylon (N.Y.) Schs., 1967-71; mktg. mgr. Xerox Corp., N.Y.C., 1971-79; mgmt. cons., N.Y.C., 1979—. Bd. dirs. East Harlem Career Counseling Center, 1969—, Open Housing Center, 1977—. Named YWCA Woman of Yr., 1975, 77. Mem. Black Profl. Women's Network (v.p. 1980—), Internat. Execs. Assn., Am. Mgmt. Assn. Club: Sales Exec. of N.Y.

LANE, MARGARET BEYNON TAYLOR, librarian; b. St. Louis, Feb. 6, 1919; d. Archer and Alice (Jones) Taylor; B.A., La. State U., 1939, J.D., 1942; B.A. in L.S., Columbia U., 1941; m. Horace C. Lane, Jan. 6, 1945; children—Margaret Elizabeth, Thomas Archer. Reference and circulation asst. Columbia Law Library, N.Y.C., 1942-44; law librarian, asst. prof. U. Conn. Sch. Law, Hartford, 1944-46; law librarian La. State U. Law Sch., Baton Rouge, 1946-48; recorder documents La. Sec. of State's Office, Baton Rouge, 1949-75; law librarian Lane & Clesi, 1976—. Mem. depository library council to Pub. Printer, 1972-77; mem. plan devel. com. La. Fed. Depository Library, 1982—. Treas. Delta Iota House Bd. of Kappa Kappa Gamma, 1965-68. Mem. ALA (interdivisional com. public documents 1967-74, chmn. 1967-70; govt. documents round table, state and local documents task force 1972—, coordinator 1980-82; James Bennett Childs award 1981), La. Library Assn. (Essae M. Culver Disting. Service award 1976; chmn. documents com. 1982—), La., Baton Rouge bar assns., Mortar Bd., Phi Delta Delta, Kappa Kappa Gamma. Club: Baton Rouge Library. Author: State Publications and Depository Libraries, 1981. Home: 7545 Richards Dr Baton Rouge LA 70809 Office: POB 3335 Baton Rouge LA 70821

LANE, MARILYN CLARE (MRS. ED GADINSKY), writer; b. Chgo.; d. Wallace Fredrich and Evelyn Marcele (Winters) Hurter; student U. Miami, 1963; m. S.R. Lane (div. 1968); 1 son, Glenn Edward; m. 2d, Ed Gadinsky, Mar. 9, 1969; stepchildren—Pamela, Brian, Seth. Reporter, photographer Miami News, 1960-66; dir. pub. relations E.J. Scheaffer Advt. Agy., Miami, Fla., 1966-69; free lance writer Miami (Fla.) Herald, 1970-74, Nat. Enquirer, 1973-75, House and Garden, 1972—, Family Circle, 1976—; writer Women on Way Up series Miami News, 1978; resource material for media course Sangamon State U.; originator Crime Watch, Channel 10-TV (Columbia-duPont award in broadcasting 1976, other awards). Recipient 6 awards for excellence for work with Miami News. Mem. Women in Communications. Home and Office: 5325 Pine Tree Dr Miami Beach FL 33140

LANE, MARY HELEN, educator; b. Milan, Tenn., Dec. 24, 1939; d. Burtran and Mary (Tolley) Lane; A.B. in English, Trevecca Coll., 1963; M.A. in Edn., Middle Tenn. State U., 1977, Ed.S., 1983. Elem. sch. tchr., Lorain, Ohio, 1964; tchr. Nashville Public Schs., 1966-75, mem. reading task force and program asst. to comprehensive communications/reading program Met.-Davidson County Schs., Nashville, 1975—. Recipient Outstanding Service award, Internat. Reading Assn./Middle Tenn. Council, 1981. Mem. Internat. Reading Assn. (pres. Middle Tenn. council), Tenn. Reading Assn., Middle Tenn. Reading Assn., Nat. Council Tchrs. English, Nashville Council Tchrs. English, Assn. Supervision and Curriculum Devel., NEA, Tenn. Edn. Assn., Met. Nashville Edn. Assn. Clubs: Pilot Internat., Delta Kappa Gamma. Editor, Middle Tenn. Newsletter, 1977-80; prodn. editor Tenn. Reading Tchr. Jour., 1980—. Home: 5000 Hillsboro Rd H3 Nashville TN 37215 Office: 3501 Byron Ave Nashville TN 37205

LANE, RUTH WINGATE, mining co. mgr.; b. Cave-in-Rock, Ill., Aug. 18, 1936; d. Clarence Henry and Nora (Douglas) Wingate; A.L.S., So. Ill. U., Carbondale, Southeastern Ill. Coll., Harrisburg, 1980; student Stephens Coll., 1981—; m. Arthur Lane, Oct. 8, 1954; 1 son, David. Bookkeeper, Eagle Supply Co., Fairfield, Ill. 1953-54; sec. H. L. Fyie, C.P.A., 1954-56; with Minerva Oil Co., Cave-in-Rock, 1956-75, flotation plant materials coordinator, 1956-75; acctg. dept., exec. asst. Allied Chem. Corp., Cave-in-Rock, 1975-80; sales and traffic mgr. Inverness Mining Co., Cave-in-Rock, 1980—. Chairwoman, Hardin County Republican party, 1978—. Mem. Profl. Secs. Internat., Assn. Mining Engrs., Profl. Secs. Internat. (v.p. Shawnee chpt.). Mem. Christian Ch. Home: Route 1 Box 221 Cave-in-Rock IL 62919 Office: Route 1 Box 119 Cave-in-Rock IL 62919

LANER, MARY RIEGE, sociologist, educator; b. Chgo., Dec. 9, 1927; d. Fred J. Granicher and Mary (Holasek) Vognsen; A.B., U. Chgo., 1966; M.A., U. N.Mex., 1969; Ph.D. (scholar), Va. Poly. Inst. and State U., 1976. Instr., No. Ariz. U., 1969-73; asst. prof. Ariz. State U., 1976-80, asso. prof. sociology, 1980—. U. Chgo. scholar, 1965-66. Grantee, Ariz. State U., summer 1978, 79; recipient Outstanding Faculty Woman award No. Ariz. U., 1971-72. Mem. Pacific Sociol. Assn. (sec.-treas. 1978-81), Am. Sociol. Assn., Nat. Council Family Relations, Soc. Personality and Social Psychology, Soc. Study Social Problems, Alpha Kappa Delta. Contbr. articles to profl. jours. Office: Dept Sociology Ariz State U Tempe AZ 85287

LANES, DENISE DEE, internat. trading co. exec.; b. Bklyn., Feb. 14, 1951; d. Irving and Sylvia (Maltz) L.; B.A., SUNY, Stony Brook, 1972; M.B.A., St. Johns U., 1977. Asst. gen. mgr. Mitsui & Co., Inc., N.Y.C., 1972—; owner, mgr. World Traders, Rego Park, N.Y., 1981—. Mem. N.Y. C. of C. and Industry, Sell Overseas Am., Women Bus. Owners N.Y., Am. Soc. Profl. Cons. Club: Appalachian Mountain. Office: World Traders 98-05 67th Ave Rego Park NY 11374

LANES, SELMA GORDON, critic, author, editor; b. Boston, Mar. 13, 1929; d. Jacob and Lily (Whiteman) Gordon; B.A., Smith Coll., 1950; M.S. in Journalism, Columbia, 1954; m. Jerrold B. Lanes, Nov. 21, 1959

(div. Mar. 1970); children—Andrew Oliver, Matthew Gordon. Asst. to publicity dir. Little Brown & Co., Boston, 1950-51; asso. editor Focus Mag., N.Y.C., 1951-53; travel page editor Boston Globe, 1953; spl. editorial asst., researcher Look Mag., 1956-60; children's entertainment editor Show Mag., 1961-63; critic children's books for Book World (N.Y. Herald-Tribune, later World Jour. Tribune, Wash. Post and Chgo. Tribune), 1965-71, N.Y. Times Book Rev., 1966—; articles editor Parents Mag., 1971-74; editor-in-chief Parents Mag. Press, 1974-78; cons. to Penguin Books, 1967, Starstream Books, 1980—. Lectr. New Sch./Parsons Sch. Design, 1975—, Del. Art Mus., 1979. Judge, Children's Spring Book Festival, 1970, dir., 1972; judge N.Y. Times Ten Best Illus. Children's Books, 1973, 79. Trustee Fund for Art Investment, N.Y.C. Mem. Phi Beta Kappa. Author (juvenile) Amy Loves Goodbyes, 1966; The Curiosity Book, 1968; Down the Rabbit Hole, A critical work for adults on children's literature, 1971, paperback, 1976; Maurice Sendak, a picture biography, 1980. Office: 26 E 91st St New York NY 10028

LANG, ALICE MARIE, hosp. pharmacy adminstr.; b. Mobile, Ala., Oct. 10, 1947; d. James Leslie and Sara Augusta (Pope) L.; B.S., Xavier U., New Orleans, 1970. Mgmt. trainee Osco Drugs, Chgo., 1970-72; chief pharmacist Williams Clinic, Chgo., 1972-73; pharmacy supr. Cook County Hosp., Chgo., 1973-76; chief pharmacist Truwick Pharmacy, Chgo., 1976-77; with Jackson Park Hosp., Chgo., 1977—, asst. dir. pharmacy, 1978-80, dir. pharmacy, 1980—. Mem. Am. Pharm. Assn., Nat. Pharm. Assn., Ill. Pharm. Assn., Chgo. Pharm. Assn., Am. Soc. Parenteral and Enteral Nutrition. Address: 6700 S Oglesby Ave Apt 401 Chicago IL 60649

LANG, BARBARA BETNER, investment exec.; b. Bryn Mawr, Pa., Apr. 21, 1947; d. Thomas Eugene and Harriet (DeMott) Betner; B.A., Finch Coll., 1969; postgrad. in banking and econs. N.Y. Inst. Fin., 1973-77; m. Richard W. Lang, Jr., May 1, 1980; 1 son, Richard W. III. With research dept. Lehman Bros. Inc., N.Y.C., 1972-73; v.p., investment mgr. instl. clients Fischer, Francis, Trees & Watts subs. Charter Atlantic Corp., N.Y.C., 1973—. Mem. N.Y. Jr. League. Republican. Episcopalian. Club: Bay Head Yacht. Office: 717 Fifth Ave New York NY 10022

LANG, DELORES ANNETTE, mfg. co. exec.; b. Roswell, N.Mex., Nov. 9, 1947; d. Richard Dow and Rose Lang; student Gulf Park Coll., 1965-66; A.A., Fullerton Coll., 1976; student Calif. State U., Fullerton, 1977—; 1 son, Scott. Adminstrv. asst. CBS Mus. Instruments, Fullerton, Calif., 1968-74; mem. inventory control and acctg. staff Sel-Rex Co., Santa Ana, Calif., 1974-76; Plessey EMD Co., 1976-77; inventory control leadperson Horiba Instruments Co., Irvine, Calif., 1978-79; analytical systems supr. BMF Foods, Fullerton, 1979-80; master scheduler Anaconda-Ericsson Inc., Orange, Calif., 1981—. Office: 303 W Palm Ave Orange CA 92688

LANG, DOE, communication specialist, author, actress, educator; b. N.Y.C.; d. Samuel Nathaniel and Florence Edith Caplow; B.A., Bennington Coll.; postgrad. (Fulbright fellow) U. Perugia (Italy), 1951, Acad. of St. Cecilia, Rome, 1951-52; postgrad. Julliard Sch. Music, 1961-63, New Sch. for Social Research, 1975-76; children—Andrea Ilona, Brian Simpson. Profl. actress in Broadway shows West Side Story, Mame, also numerous off-Broadway shows, numerous TV commls. and TV voice-overs; dubbed numerous fgn. films; appeared in day-time TV series: Edge of Night, Another World, appeared as Karen Adams in As The World Turns; pres. Charismedia, speaking services firm, N.Y.C., 1975—; author: The Charisma Book: What It Is and How To Get It, 1980, 2d edit., The Secret of Charisma, 1982; author books for Sears Roebuck: Voice, Image and Self-Confidence; contbr. articles to New Woman, Woman's Day, Good Housekeeping mags.; mem. faculty New Sch. for Social Research; lectr., cons. in field; TV, radio appearances. Founder, producer, dir. and mistress-of-ceremonies People Party to Save the N.Y. Public Library and the Performing Arts Library, N.Y.C., 1972; mem. Com. to Save Sta.-WNCN, N.Y.C., 1976; a founder, bd. dirs. Symphony Space Cultural Center, N.Y.C., 1976; mem. music com. Cathedral St. John the Divine, N.Y.C. Mem. Assn. Humanist Psychology, Assn. Transpersonal Psychology, DeToqueville Soc., Am. Psychol. Assn., Am. Lang. Assn., Actors Equity, Screen Actors Guild, AFTRA, Assn. Women Bus. Owners (dir. 1978-79), Subject of numerous articles; author memo to Pres. Carter on TV debates; author cassettes on stress mgmt., 1979-81. Office: 610 West End Ave New York NY 10024

LANG, GLORIA HELEN, tool engr.; b. N.Y.C., Mar. 15, 1932; d. Michael and Elizebeth (Snyder) L.; student Kent State U., 1957-61, Youngstown State U., 1977; A.A., SUNY, 1982. Retail salesman, 1947-51; owner, operator tax service, Tampa, Fla., 1954-55; tool and die maker Gen. Motors Corp., Warren, Ohio, 1955—; tool and die apprentice Ohio State U., 1972-76; tooling engr., cutting tool cons., pres., chief exec. officer Lang Industries, Inc., Warren, 1977—; lectr. on females in modern machine trades. Served with U.S. Army, 1951-54. Mem. Nat. Assn. Female Execs., Nat. Tool, Die and Precision Machining Assn., Nat. Small Bus. Assn., NOW, Internat. Platform Assn., Am. Soc. Bus. and Profl. Women, Am. Legion (past comdr. post 748 Warren). Home: 4793 Ardmore Ave Youngstown OH 44505 Office: Lang Industries Inc 2026 McMyler St NW Warren OH 44485

LANG, JEAN MCKINNEY, editor, educator; b. Cherokee, Iowa, Nov. 6, 1921; d. Roy Clarence and Verna Harvey (Smith) McKinney; B.S., Iowa State U., 1945; M.A., Ohio State U., 1969; postgrad. U. South Fla., 1972; 1 dau., Barbara Jean (Mrs. Michael L. Wilcox). Merchandiser, jewelry buyer Rike-Kumler Co., Dayton, Ohio, 1952-59, Met. Co., Dayton, 1959-64; tchr. DeVilbiss High Sch., Toledo, 1966-67; chmn. dept. retailing Webber Coll., Babson Park, Fla., 1967-72; asso. editor Wet Set Illustrated, 1972-75; sr. editor Pleasure Boating, Largo, Fla., 1975—; tchr. bus. adminstrn. St. Petersburg (Fla.) Jr. Coll., 1974—. Recipient recognition Nat. Retail Mchts. Assn., 1971, certs. of appreciation U.S. Power Squadron, 1976, Webber Coll., 1972. Mem. Fla. Women's Network, Greater Tampa C. of C., AAUW, Tampa Aux. Power Squadron, U.S. Coast Guard Aux., Sales and Mktg. Execs. of Tampa (pres.'s award 1973), Fla. Outdoor Writers Assn., Am. Mktg. Assn., Gulf Coast Symphony, Internat. Platform Assn., Fla. Council Yacht Clubs, Chi Omega. Republican. Presbyterian. Clubs: Toledo Yacht (hon.), Tampa Yacht and Country. First woman to cruise solo from Fla. to Lake Erie in single-engine inboard, 1969, to be accepted into Fla. Council Yacht Clubs; mem. Nat. Boating Safety Adv. Council; yachting accomplishments published in The Ensign, Lakeland Boating, Yachting, Boote mags. Office: PO Box 402 Largo FL 33540

LANG, LINDA JEAN, govt. ofcl.; b. Norwich, Conn., Apr. 25, 1948; d. Julius Harry and Sabina Lucille (Kubiak) Oettinger; student Pace U., 1979—. Group chief operator N.Y. Telephone Co., Bklyn., 1964-68; personnel mgr. Am. Stock Exchange, Inc., N.Y.C., 1969-81; asst. dir. adminstrn. and human resources N.Y. State Urban Devel. Corp., N.Y.C., 1981—; lectr. in field. Mem. Nat. Assn. Female Execs., Exec. Females, Internat. Assn. Personnel Women. Address: 78 15 83d St Glendale NY 11385

LANG, NANCY, govt. ofcl.; b. N.Y.C., Mar. 15, 1929; d. Carl and Annette Irma (Crystal) L.; B.M., Skidmore Coll., 1950; M.A., Columbia U., 1951. Tchr. vocal and string music, Sayville, N.Y., 1951-52; program guide, music info. supr. WQXR, 1952-59; asso. editor HiFi/Stereo Rev., 1959; dir. recorded music Heritage Stas., 1960-61; music dir. Sta. WTFM, 1961-62; publicity dir. Command Records, 1962-63; mail order supr. Record Centre Stores, 1963-65; music specialist Voice of Am., Washington, 1965—; condr. Nat. Symphony Orch. benefit concert, 1975. Pres., Washington chpt. Am. Jewish Com., 1978-80, nat. bd. dirs., 1976—. Ind. U. fellow, 1950. Mem. Music Critics Assn., Am. Women's Newspaper Club (past pres.), Am. Women in Radio and TV, Women in Communications, Am. Symphony Orch. League. Address: 5903 Frazier Ln McLean VA 22101

LANG, ROXANNE MARIE, speech-lang. pathologist; b. Kansas City, Mo., July 30, 1950; d. Anthony John and Elizabeth Anne (Maurer) L.; student Avila Coll., 1968-70; B.S., U. Kans., 1973; M.A., Kans. State U., 1974. Speech pathologist Hillsborough County (Fla.) Pub. Schs., 1974-77; lang. specialist Shawnee Mission (Kans.) Pub. Schs., 1977-80; instr. Kans. State U., 1980-81, dir. clin. services Speech and Hearing Center, 1982—; cons. in field. Mem. Am. Speech-Lang.-Hearing Assn. (cert. clin. competence), Kans. Speech-Lang.-Hearing Assn.

LANGDON, MARY, educator; b. Fall River, Mass., Apr. 9, 1919; d. Richard and Mabel Rebecca (Hanscom) Leather; student Hartt Coll. Music, 1952-54; m. Wilbur Spencer Langdon II, Aug. 27, 1938; children—Carol Langdon Kohankie, Wilbur Spencer III. Numerous concert, oratorio, orch. and opera performances, 1952—; pvt. voice tchr., Mystic, Conn., 1952—; faculty U.R.I., Kingston, 1974—, asst. prof. music, 1981—. Bd. dirs. Music Sch. of Westerly Center for the Arts, 1980—. Mem. Nat. Assn. Tchrs. Singing, Nat. Assn. Music Tchrs. Republican. Congregationalist. Home: 27 Gravel St Mystic CT 06355 Office: University of Rhode Island Music Dept Kingston RI 02881

LANGDON, THELMA NADINE PERSE, civic worker; b. Pueblo, Colo., May 15, 1925; d. Anthony Benedict and Helen (Olear) Perse; m. Joseph Raymond Langdon, Aug. 20, 1947; children—Stephen John, Patrick Sean, Margaret Ellen, Mary, Alexis. Mem. Alaska State Bd. Edn., 1975—, pres., 1978; mem. Alaska Post-secondary Commn., 1978—; bd. mgrs. Nat. PTA, 1971-75; pres. Alaska PTA, 1971-75; mem. White House Conf. on Children and Youth, 1970; bd. dirs. Office of Child Advocacy, Alaska, 1972-76; bd. dirs. Big Bros. of Anchorage, 1973—, sec., 1977, v.p., 1978-79; bd. dirs. AMA Aux., 1974-76; pres. Alaska State Med. Assn. Aux., 1970; pres. Anchorage Med. Soc. Aux., 1960-61. Address: 2363 Captain Cook Dr Anchorage AK 99503

LANGE, BARBARA HOLCOMB, public relations, video programming cons.; b. Akron, Ohio, June 13, 1936; d. Lynn Howe and Cathryn Marie (Wentsler) Holcomb; cert. Fontainebleau L'Ecole des Beaux Arts, 1957; B.F.A., Coll. of William and Mary, 1958; children—Scott Cameron, Christine Linwood. Exec. sec. to pres. Art Inst. Fort Lauderdale, Fla., 1974-75, dir. fin. aid, 1975-76, dir. community relations, 1976—; corporate dir. Community relations design schs. of art insts. of Pitts., Phila., Atlanta, Houston, Ft. Lauderdale, Seattle, also Colo. Inst. Art, Denver, 1978—; freelance public relations cons. Grifs Western, four western retail stores, Fla., 1979—; partner Point of View Prodns., Ft. Lauderdale, 1980—; writer, producer host weekly cable TV show, From a Women's Point of View, Ft. Lauderdale, 1980—; writer, producer montly cable TV show, Art Inst. Mag., Ft. Lauderdale, 1980—. Bd. dirs. Markham Park Zoo, Planned Preservation, Inc.; mem. task force on aging Broward County Commn. on Status Women; vol. counselor Sexual Assault Treatment Center, Broward County, 1978-79; exec. committeewoman Republican Party Broward County, 1975-76. Mem. Advt. Fedn. of Greater Ft. Lauderdale (chmn. community service task force 1981-82, 2d v.p. 1982), Women's Advocacy, Majority Minority (pres. 1982-83), C. of C., AAUW, Fla. Public Relations Assn., Public Relations Soc. Am., Women in Cable, Women in Communications (chpt. pres. 1981-82), Kappa Kappa Gamma. Republican. Author: Cablevision: the New Frontier, 1982. Home: 640 NW 19th St Fort Lauderdale FL 33311 Office: Art Institute of Fort Lauderdale 3000 E Las Olas Blvd Fort Lauderdale FL 33316

LANGE, CATHERINE LOUISE, book pub. ofcl.; b. Chgo., Oct. 18, 1949; d. Frank Michael and Irene Josephine (Kozak) L.; B.A. in Visual Arts, DePaul U., 1982; 1 dau., Jennifer C. Schmidt. Asst. to pub. Ragan Communications, Inc., Chgo., 1972-78, circulation and mktg. mgr., 1978-80, mng. editor The Ragan Report, 1978-81, editor The Reporter's Report, 1979-81, contbg. editor Speechwriter's Newsletter, 1980—; dir. Ragan Books; freelance photographer, designer, writer direct-mail promotional material. Mem. Chgo. Women in Pub., Soc. Typog. Arts, Internat. Assn. Bus. Communicators, Women in Communications, Children's Reading Round Table. Home: 200 N Lombard Ave Oak Park IL 60302 Office: 407 S Dearborn St Chicago IL 60605

LANGE, HOPE, actress; b. Redding Ridge, Conn., Nov. 28, 1938; d. John and Minnette (Buddecke) Lange; ed. Barmore Jr. Coll., Reed Coll. (Ore.); m. Don Murray; m. 2d, Alan S. Pakula, 1963 (div. 1971). Appeared as dancer Jackie Gleason TV program, also Kraft TV plays; motion pictures include: Bus Stop, The True Story of Jesse James, Peyton Place, The Young Lions, In Love or War, A Pocketful of Miracles, Love is a Ball, Jigsaw, Death Wish, Best of Everything, The Rivalry (TV), others; leading actress in TV series The Ghost and Mrs. Muir, New Dick Van Dyke Show. Recipient Emmy award, 1968, 69. Address: care Internat Creative Mgmt 8899 Beverly Blvd Los Angeles CA 90048

LANGE, JANE LOUISE, public health cons.; b. Platteville, Wis., Sept. 16, 1947; d. Ervin W. and Marian B. (Salzmann) L.; B.S. in nursing, Viterbo Coll., LaCrosse Wis., 1971; M.P.H., U. N.C., Chapel Hill, 1978; m. Robert John Phelan, Apr. 24, 1982. Charge nurse St. Joseph Meml. Hosp., Hillsboro, Wis., 1971-72; staff nurse Platteville (Wis.) Meml., 1973, St. Mary's Hosp., Madison, Wis., 1974-75; pub. health nurse Dane County Pub. Health Dept., Madison, 1975-77; instr. pub. health nursing Ariz. State U., 1978-81; pub. health cons. Dept. Health Services State of Ariz., Phoenix, 1981—. HEW trainee, 1977-78. Mem. Am. Nurses Assn., Ariz. Nurses Assn., Ariz. Pub. Health Assn., Am. Pub. Health Assn., Ariz. Nursing Network, Sigma Theta Tau. Office: 1740 W Adams St Phoenix AZ 85007

LANGE, VIRGINIA MORTON, franchise co. exec.; b. Charlottesville, Va., July 7, 1930; d. Charles Bruce and Virginia (Marshall) Morton; A.B., Vassar Coll., 1952; m. Peter Woldemar Lange, Nov. 29, 1952; children—Louise Virginia, Peter Bruce Augustus. Founder, chmn. Internat. Design Systems Ltd., Norwalk, Conn., 1978—. Fin. chmn. Albemarle County (Va.) chpt. LWV, 1953-56; bd. dirs. Children's Service Center, Charlottesville, Va., 1966-68, Conn. Soc. Prevention of Blindness, 1982—. Mem. Conn. Bus. and Industry Assn., Small Bus. Assn. New Eng., N.Y. Assn. Women Bus. Owners, Alumnae Assn. Vassar Coll., Am. Horse Show Assn. (life), U.S. Dressage Fedn., U.S. Combined Tng. Assn. Republican. Episcopalian. Club: Fairfield County Conn.) Hunt. Author articles on dressage and combined tng. in horse mags. Office: 2070 Belden St Norwalk CT 06852

LANGELIER, PAMELA ELIZABETH, cons. psychologist; b. Portland, Maine, June 10, 1946; d. Michael J. and Dorothy E. Maroon; B.A., Am. U., 1968; M.A., Calif. State U., Northridge, 1972; Ph.D. (Calif. State fellow), U. So. Calif., 1975; m. Régis Langelier, Aug. 5, 1978; 1 son, Charles. Pvt. practice marital, divorce, adult and child diagnostics, and forensic psychology; mem. faculty Assumption Coll., Worcester, Mass., 1980-81; dir. Psychol. Tng., Treatment and Research Center, Concordia U., Montreal, 1975-79, mem. faculty, 1975-78; mem. faculty McGill U., Montreal, 1975-82; psychol. cons. Villemarie Social Services, Montreal; staff U. Vt. Health Center, 1982—; condr. seminars in field. Grantee Que. Dept. Social Affairs, 1977-78; lic. psychologist, Vt. Mem. Am. Psychol. Assn., Can. Psychol. Assn., Que. Psychol. Assn., Am. Assn. Marriage and Family Therapists, Calif. Marriage, Family and Child Therapy Assn., Nat. Council Family Relations, Mass. Bd. Psychologists. Author research papers in field of divorce and family therapy. Home: Route 1 Box 325 South Hero VT 05486

LANGEMACH, ELEANOR RUTH, civic worker; b. Hinsdale, Ill., June 19, 1926; d. Walter Alva and Esther Ruth (Dillon) Peckenpaugh; B.J., U. Mo., Columbia, 1948; m. Vernon Rollin Langemach, Nov. 25, 1948; children—Susan Carol Langemach Brown, Paul Curtis. With advt. dept. St. Joseph (Mo.) News-Press, 1948-53; mgr. advt. dept. Hirsch's Dept. Store, St. Joseph, 1953; pres. Mo. PTA, 1975-77, public relations chmn., 1970-71; bd. dirs. Nat. PTA, 1975-81, mem. nat. commn. edn., 1977-79, mem. nat. commn. individual devel., 1979-81; Mo. trustee Caroline B. Ullmann scholarship, 1979-84; nat. chmn. Reflection Cultural Arts Project, 1980-81; dir. edn. Francis St. United Methodist Ch., St. Joseph, 1980-81; mem. curriculum council St. Joseph Sch. Dist., 1973-75, mem. tchr. evaluation com., 1979-80; adv. com. N.S. Hillyard vocat. ad hoc adv. com. Mo. Guide Children's Lit., 1979-80; exec. com. Area Council PTA's, 1966-81; bd. dirs. St. Joseph Public Library, 1981—. Named Lay Educator of Yr., Phi Delta Kappa, 1978; nat. accredited flower show judge, 1969—. Hon. life mem. Mo. PTA, Nebr. PTA, Nat. PTA; life mem. Federated Garden Clubs Mo., pres., 1981-83; Nat. Council State Garden Clubs (dir. 1981-83); mem. U. Mo. Alumni Assn., N.W. Dist. Flower Judges Council, United Meth. Women. Club: Bu-An-Co Gardeners (past pres.). Author articles in field. Home: 16 Carriage Dr N Saint Joseph MO 64506 Office: Francis St United Meth Ch 12th and Francis St Saint Joseph MO 64501

LANGENBACH, LISA GAYE, educator; b. Norfolk, Va., Aug. 10, 1958; d. Robert Warren and Gaye (Hilliard) L.; B.A., Mary Washington Coll., 1980; M.A., Purdue U., 1982, Ph.D. candidate, 1982—. Teaching asst. Purdue U., 1980-82, instr. polit. sci., 1982—. Mem. ACLU (chpt. pres.), NOW (treas. 1978), Women's Caucus for Polit. Sci., Am. Polit. Sci. Assn., Pi Sigma Alpha. Democrat. Unitarian. Home: 136 W State St Apt 12 West Lafayette IN 47906 Office: Purdue U West Lafayette IN 47907

LANGER, DOROTHY, computer mktg. exec.; b. Boston, Aug. 1, 1942; d. Harold Aaron and Goldie (Fineman) Potcherkoff; B.S. in Chemistry, Simmons Coll., 1964. Tech. librarian Shell Chem. Co., N.Y.C., 1964-65; research chemist Radiation Research Corp., Westbury, L.I., 1965-68; systems engr. IBM, 1968-71, mktg. rep., 1972-73, process industry rep., 1973-74, mktg. mgr., 1974-76, regional mktg. mgr., 1976-77, corp. mktg. cons., 1977-79, br. mgr., 1980-81; with Gartner Group, Inc., Stamford, Conn.; lectr. on women's issues. Trustee, Simmons Coll.; bd. dirs. Capital Dist. Jr. Achievement, 1980-82; chmn. Corp. Giving Simmons Coll. Pride II, 1981—. Clubs: Hudson River, Mensa. Office: Gartner Group Inc PO Box 10212 Stamford CT 06904

LANGER, SHIRLEY POLTORACK, educator; b. N.Y.C., July 7, 1922; d. Harry and Eva Poltorack; B.A., Hunter Coll., 1943; M.A., Columbia U., 1951; children—Elizabeth, Kenneth. Instr. psychology Hofstra U., Hempstead, N.Y., 1958-67, asst. prof., 1967-74, asso. prof., teaching fellow New Coll., 1974—; vis. asso. prof. psychology New Sch. for Social Research, N.Y.C., 1968-69; vis. prof. psychology Manhattan Sch. Music, fall 1973. Mem. Am. Psychol. Assn. Home: 82 Meadowbrook Rd Hempstead NY 11550 Office: New Coll Hofstra U Hempstead NY 11550

LANGEVIN, JUDITH BEVIS, lawyer; b. Tampa, Fla., Sept. 18, 1948; d. Harold Wayne and Colleen Beverly (Lunsford) Bevis; B.A., U. Calif., Berkeley, 1970; J.D., U. Minn., 1973; m. Steven Paul Lapinsky, June 1982; 2 children—Jacob, Joshua. Admitted to Minn. bar, 1973; social planner City of St. Paul, 1973, spl. asst. to mayor, 1973-74, asst. dir. dept. human rights, 1974-75; conciliator Minn. Dept. Human Rights, St. Paul, 1975-79, asst. commr., 1979-81; partner firm Horton and Langevin, Mpls., 1981—; mem. Hennepin County Legal Advice Clinic; adj. faculty William Mitchell Coll. Law, St. Paul. lectr., cons. on civil rights. Chmn., Mayor's Adv. Com. on Health, St. Paul, 1974. Mem. Am. Bar Assn., Minn. Bar Assn., Hennepin County Bar Assn., NAACP (exec. bd. St. Paul, 1975). Democrat. Office: 1625 Park Ave Minneapolis MN 55404

LANGFORD, ANNA RIGGS, lawyer, former alderwoman; b. Springfield, Ohio, Oct. 27, 1917; d. Arthur J. and Alice (Reed) Riggs; student Roosevelt U., 1946-48; J.D. with honors, John Marshall Law Sch., 1956; m. Lawrence W. Langford, Aug. 21, 1948 (div.); 1 son, Lawrence W. Clerk-typist Sec. State Ill., 1939-51; admitted to Ill. bar, 1956, since practiced in Chgo.; mem. firm Robinson, Farmer & Langford, and predecessor, 1959-69; alderwoman 16th Ward, Chgo., 1972-75. Mem. legal def. com. NAACP, Chgo. Urban League; mem. LWV, from 1969, West Englewood Improvement Assn., from 1969, Gov.'s Com. on Sr. Citizens, 1971-72, Com. on Ill. Govt., 1971-72, Gov.'s Ethics Com., 1976; del. World Congress of Peace Forces, Moscow, 1973; mem. commn. inquiry into conditions in Chili after Sept. 11 mil. coup, 1974; del. internat. prep. com. Internat. Commn. Inquiry into Crimes of Mil. Junta in Chili, Helsinki, Finland, 1974; bd. dirs. ACLU, 1970-71, Operation Breadbasket, 1971-72, Impact, Inc., Drug Abuse Program; nat. exec. bd., mem. Operation PUSH, 1972—; del. Nat. Dem. Conv., 1972, co-chmn. Ill. del. Recipient citation for service in cause interracial justice and brotherhood Cath. Interracial Council, 1970; Civil Rights award Cook County Bar Assn., 1968, Spl. Achievement award, 1971; Mahatma Ghandi Centennial Com. award Greater Chgo., 1969; IOTA Bus. Week award Alpha chpt. Iota Phi Lambda, 1969; James B. Anderson award for outstanding achievement in field politics Montford Point Marine Assn., 1971; Achievement award 7th Ward Ind. Orgn., 1971; award for outstanding service in govt. for human outstanding and equal justice in performance duties as alderwoman SCLC's Operation Breadbasket, 1971; Cert. award Internat. Travelers Assn., 1971; Humanist of Yr. award Ethical Humanist Soc. Chgo., 1977; Certs. of Appreciation, Kiwanis Club of Near North, Chgo., 1980, Christ United Meth. Ch., 1982, Mollison Local Sch. Council, Chgo., 1982; named Woman of Distinction, Etta Moten Civic and Ednl. Club, 1970. Mem. Nat., Cook County (dir. 1968-70, 74) bar assns., Def. Attys. Chgo., Internat. Platform Assn. Office: 1249 W 63d St Chicago IL 60636

LANGFORD, ELIZABETH HEGGE, civic worker; b. Oslo, Norway, May 19, 1921; came to U.S., 1929, naturalized, 1934; d. Hans Thorleif and Elise (Lerche) Grüner-Hegge; B.A. in Sociology, U. Mich., 1941; m. George Robert Langford, June 14, 1941; children—Nancy Langford Hague, George Lawrence. Chmn. Washtenaw County chpt. Nat. Found.-March of Dimes, 1949-52; bd. dirs. Ann Arbor (Mich.) Vis. Nurses Assn., 1949-52; founder, 2d pres. Univ. Hosp. Vol. Services Guild, 1952-53; pres. U. Mich. Alumnae Club, 1953-54; founder, 2d pres. Ann Arbor Women's City Club, 1953-54, 69-71; vice chmn. U. Mich. Alumnae Council, 1956-58; pres. Sorosis Club Mich., 1963-65; sec. U. Mich. Alumni Fund, 1958-60, vice chmn., 1960-61; sec. Barton Hills Charter Commn., 1973; bd. dirs. Sr. Citizens Guild, 1969-75; mem. Gov.'s State Health Planning Adv. Council, 1974-78; pres. Barton Hills Village, 1973—; chmn. Motor Meals of Ann Arbor, 1975—; mem. budget com. United Way, 1974-80. Republican. Presbyterian. Home: 859 Oakdale Rd Barton Hills Ann Arbor MI 48105

LANGFORD, NELL JOY, banker; b. Elk City, Okla., Dec. 30, 1931; d. Lloyd Leslie and Ollye Mae (Willis) Putman; ed. S.W. Tex. State Tchrs. Coll., San Marcos, Galveston Community Coll.; m. Andy Vernon

Langford, May 23, 1969; children by previous marriage—Larry Davis, Joy Anne Davis, Kelley Davis. Note teller State Nat. Bank, Corsicana, Tex., 1956, First Capitol Bank, West Columbia, Tex., 1956-59; collection and exchange teller Parkdale State Bank, Corpus Christi, 1961-62; note teller First State Bank, Hitchcock, Tex., 1962-64, asst. cashier, 1964-65, cashier, 1965-67, v.p., cashier, 1967-71; v.p. Am. Bank, Galveston, Tex., 1971-73, v.p., cashier, 1973-79, sr. v.p., dir., 1979—; dir. Am. Bank, Galveston. Trustee, South Tex. Girl Scout Council, 1965-74, chmn. fin. com., 1978-80, treas., 1980-82; Galveston County rep. Easter Seal Soc. Tex., 1978-80. Mem. Nat. Assn. Bank Women, Inc., Am. Bus. Women's Assn., VFW Ladies Aux. Episcopalian. Home: 2825 Palm Circle W Galveston TX 77550 Office: 2401 Broadway Galveston TX 77550

LANGHAM, NORMA, educator, author, composer; b. California, Pa.; d. Alfred Scrivener and Edith (Carter) Langham; B.S., Ohio State U., 1942; B. Theatre Arts, Pasadena Playhouse Coll. Theatre Arts, 1944; M.A., Stanford, 1956, postgrad. Summer Radio-TV Inst., 1960; student Pasadena Inst. Radio, 1944-45. Tchr. sci. California High Sch., 1942-43; asst. office pub. info. Denison U., Granville, Ohio, 1955; instr. speech dept. Westminster Coll., New Wilmington, Pa., 1957-58; instr. speech and drama dept. California State Coll., 1959, asst. prof., 1960-62, asso. prof., 1962-79, emeritus, 1979—, co-founder, sponsor, dir. Children's Theatre, 1962-79. Recipient award exceptional acad. service Pa. Dept. Edn., 1975; Appreciation award Bicentennial Commn. Pa., 1976. Henry C. Frick Ednl. Commn. grantee. Mem. Am. Ednl. Theatre Assn., Children's Theatre Assn., Internat. Platform Assn., California State Coll. Assn. Women Faculty (founder, pres. 1972-73), AAUW (co-founder California br., 1st v.p. 1971-72, pres. 1972-73), Alpha Psi Omega, Omicron Nu. Presbyn. Author: (play) Magic in the Sky, 1963; (text) Public Speaking; (play) John Dough (Freedoms Found. award 1968). Home: Box 455 California PA 15419

LANGHINRICHS, RUTH IMLER, public info., public edn. specialist; b. Chgo., Oct. 30, 1922; d. Roy Franklin and Susan Martha (Smith) Imler; B.S. cum laude, Northwestern U., 1944; student Wayne Sch. Social Work, 1958-59, Purdue U., Ft. Wayne, 1976; m. Richard Alan Langhinrichs, May 31, 1958; children—Julia, Jennifer. Mem. research staff Look mag., Cowles Pub. Co., N.Y.C., 1944-46; asst. editor Science Illustrated mag., McGraw Hill Pub. Co., N.Y.C., 1946-49; asst. feature editor Scholastic mag., Scholastic, Inc., N.Y.C., 1949-51; asso. editor Ladies' Home Journal mag., Curtis Pub. Co., Phila., 1951-58; instr. communication English dept. Purdue U., Ft. Wayne, 1966-76; writer-in-residence Ft. Wayne Fine Arts Found., Inc., 1977-79; public info., public edn. specialist mental Health Center at Fort Wayne, Inc., 1979—; cons. Unitarian Universalist Assn., Boston. Bd. dirs. Ft. Wayne Civic Youtheatre, 1973-77, Martin Luther King Montessori Sch., 1975-78, Citizens' Cable, 1981—. Mem. Women in Communication, Internat. Assn. Bus. Communicators, Ind. Council Community Comprehensive Mental Health Centers (public relations com. 1979—), Women's Caucus for Arts, Phila. Art Alliance. Unitarian Universalist. Club: Fortnightly. Co-author: Boy Dates Girl, 1949; You're Asking Me?, 1949; monthly columnist Sub-Deb, Ladies' Home Journal, 1951-58; contbr. poetry to Tomorrow mag., 1945, City Limits, 1979, Windless Orchard Lit. mag., 1972; author Mermaids in the Basement, dance drama, video tape prodn., 1977. Home: 459 Englewood Ct Fort Wayne IN 46807 Office: Mental Health Center at Fort Wayne 909 E State Blvd Fort Wayne IN 46805

LANGHOUT-NIX, NELLEKE, artist; b. Utrecht, Netherlands, Mar. 27, 1939; came to U.S., 1968, naturalized, 1978; d. Louis Wilhelm Frederick and Geertruida (Smits) Nix; M.F.A., 82, Ill. Fine Arts, The Hague, 1958; m. Ernst Langhout, July 26, 1958; 1 son, Klaas-Jan Marnix. Head art dept. Bush Sch., Seattle, 1969-71; dir. creative projects Project Reach, Seattle, 1971-72; artist-in-residence Fairhaven Coll., Bellingham, Wash., 1974, Jefferson Community Center, Seattle, 1978-82, Lennox Sch., N.Y.C., 1982; dir. NN Gallery, Seattle, 1970—; executed wall hanging for King County Courthouse, Seattle, 1974; one-woman shows: Nat. Art Center, N.Y.C., 1980, Gail Chase Gallery, Bellevue, Wash., 1979, Original Graphics Gallery, Seattle, 1981, Bon Internat. Gallery, Seattle, 1981; 3-man show Exhbn. Space, N.Y.C., 1982; group shows include: Cheney Cowles Mus., Spokane, 1977, Bellevue Art Mus., 1978, Renwick Gallery, Washington, 1978, Kleinert Gallery, Woodstock, N.Y., 1979, Artcore Meltdown, Sydney, Australia, 1979, Tacoma Art Mus., 1979, 82, Ill. State Mus., Springfield, 1979, Plener Sandomierz, Poland, 1980, Plener Kielce, Poland, 1980, Western Assn. Art Museums traveling show, 1979-80, Madison Square Garden, N.Y.C., 1981; represented in permanent collection: Plener Collection, Sandomierz, Poland; Bell Telephone Co. Collection, Seattle. Bd. dirs. Wing Luke Mus., Seattle, 1978-81; v.p. Denny Regrade Community Council, 1978-79; mem. Seattle Planning Commn., 1978—. Recipient Wallhanging award City of Edmonds (Wash.), 1974; numerous others. Mem. Denny Regrade Arts Council (co-founder). Allied Arts Seattle, Am. Craft Council.

LANGLEY, CAROL MARY, bus./office mgmt. exec.; b. Detroit, Mar. 22, 1945; d. Edson Carnegie and Ethel Helen (Hulett) L.; student Detroit Coll. Bus., Henry Ford Community Coll., Dearborn, Mich., U. Mich., Dearborn, U. Colo. Office mgmt., asst. to exec. and dep. dirs. Metro Fund and S.E. Mich. Council Govts., Detroit, 1967-70; asst. to exec. dir. and policy bd. dirs. Denver Regional Council Govts., 1970-80. Mem. exec. com. Heather Ridge Homeowners Assn. Mem. Nat. Assn. Female Execs., Women Bus. Owners Assn., Colo. Women's Network. Home: 13655B E Yale Ave Aurora CO 80014

LANGLEY, JANIE S., hotel exec.; b. Rosebud, Tex., Aug. 21, 1940; d. Ben R. and Leonor P. (Deleon) Salazar; student U. P.R., 1959-60, Cameron Comml. Coll., 1964, Central Tex. Coll., 1967, Newcomb Women's Coll., 1977, Delgado Coll., 1978; m. Charles E. Langley, June 19, 1972; children—Teretha, Eric, Melissa, Charles. Mgr., Cowhouse Motor Hotel, Killeen, Tex., 1961-71; chief acct. Tex. Hotel and Motel Assn., San Antonio, 1971-72; comptroller Rio Airways, Inc., Killeen, 1972-73; auditor, asst. controller Houston Club, 1973-74; controller Gunter Hotel, San Antonio, 1974-76; pres. Internat. Mktg. & Cons., Kenner, La. 1976-80, dir., 1980—; controller, cons. Sheraton Inn/New Orleans, 1980-81, North Park Inn, Dallas, 1981—; cons. in field. Mem. local bd. La. SSS, 1981—; chmn. bus. dist. Heart Fund Assn., Killeen, 1970. Lic. real estate agt., broker; cert. hotel adminstr. Mem. Am. Bus. Women's Assn. (pres. chpts. 1970, 80, sec. Nat. Conv. 1982, Quelles Nouvelles Woman of Yr. 1980, Inner Circle 1970, Gold Star award 1974, Emerald Star 1978, Golden Sapphire Star award North Dallas chpt. 1982), Tex. Hotel and Motel Assn. (2d v.p. 1969-70, 1st v.p. 1970-71), Am. Soc. Profl. Cons., Internat. Assn. Hospitality Accts., Am. Hotel and Motel Assn., New Orleans Assn. Hospitality Accts. Club: Propellor Ladies Aux. Home: 1714 Aurora Dr Richardson TX 75081 Office: 9300 N Central Expressway Dallas TX 75231

LANGLEY, LYNNE SPENCER, newspaper editor, columnist; b. West Palm Beach, Fla., June 4, 1947; d. George Hosmer and Elwa June (Harries) Spencer; B.A. with honors, Coll. of Wooster, 1969; student Glasgow U., Scotland, 1967-68; m. William A. Langley, Oct. 10, 1970. Feature writer, asst. women's editor Palm Beach Times, West Palm Beach, Fla., 1969-70; asst. editor Brunswick (Maine) Times Record, 1971; investigative reporter Maine Times, Topsham, 1971-75; asst. mng. editor York County Coast Star, Kennebunk, Maine, 1976-78; gardening editor, nature columnist, reporter Charleston (S.C.) Post-Courier, 1979—; editor Maine Audubon Soc. News, 1975-76; stringer Newsweek mag., 1971-75; freelance writer; speaker. Active Charleston Natural History Soc., Nat. Audubon Soc. Mem. Am. Hort. Soc., Garden Writers Assn. Am., PEO (sec. chpt. D Maine 1975-76). Home: 103 Gadsden St Summerville SC 29483 Office: 134 Columbus St Charleston SC 29401

LANGLEY, MARY LOLLIER, ednl. cons.; b. Upland, Calif., Mar. 24, 1939; d. Marshall L. and Rea Lollier; B.A., San Jose State U., 1963; postgrad. U. Calif., Santa Barbara, 1963-66; M.A., Calif. State Poly. U., 1968; m. Raymond M. Langley, Apr. 14, 1978. Instr., Orcutt, Calif., 1960-66; counselor, Atascadero, Calif., 1966-67; counselor, psychology instr. Cuesta Coll., 1967-68; cons. gifted edn. profl. inservice, child welfare and attendance Office of the San Luis Obispo County (Calif.) Supt. Schs., 1968—. Mem. Calif. Assn. Gifted, Assn. Calif. Sch. Adminstrs., Women's Network, Phi Delta Kappa. Club: Soroptimists Internat. of the Americas. Home: 2198 Pecho Rd Los Osos CA 93402 Office: Office of the San Luis Obispo County Supt Schs PO Box I Hwy One San Luis Obispo CA 93406

LANGLOIS, LAURIE YVONNE, govt. ofcl.; b. Holyoke, Mass., Apr. 9, 1947; d. Richard Adelard and Lorraine Alexina (Emery) L.; B.A., Tufts U., 1969; M. in Urban Affairs, Boston U., housing mgmt. officer, Boston, 1970-74, program analyst, 1974-80, regional mgr. Fed. women's program, 1975-80; chief loan mgmt. br., 1980—; nat. instr. housing mgmt. HUD Tng. Centers, 1973; chmn. Fed.-State Task Force on Pub. Housing Mgmt., 1973-74; pres. ODWIN-Health Careers, Inc., 1979-81, v.p., 1977-79, bd. dirs., 1974—; pres., Govt. Center Child Care Corp., 1979-81, v.p., 1978-79, sec., 1977-78. Recipient Spl. Achievement award HUD, 1977, 81, Outstanding Performance award, 1975, 79, 81, cert. of appreciation, 1973, 74, 78; cert. of appreciation Boston Fed. Exec. Bd., 1978; cert. secondary sch. tchr., Mass. Democrat. Office: Dept HUD Boston Area Office 15 New Chardon St Boston MA 02114

LANGSHAW, EDITH EMILY, accountant; b. Grand Ledge, Mich., Oct. 30, 1921; d. Leonard Martin and Margaret Irene (Taylor) Fishell; student Allegan Normal Coll., 1941, Western Mich. U., 1942, 43, Andrews U., 1943; m. James Everett Langshaw, Apr. 3, 1943; children—Margaret Langshaw Burdett, Douglas. Pvt. practice accounting, Allegan, Mich., 1954—; treas. Allegan Ambulance Service, Mich. Pipe Co., Allegan. Treas., Allegan Adventist Ch., 1950—, mem. bd., mem. elementary sch. bd., 1950—; vol. auditor Dollars for Scholars; mem. Monterey Twp. Zoning Commn. Named Woman of Yr., Allegan County, 1981. Mem. Allegan Bus. and Profl. Womens Club (treas. 1965-66, 70-71), Ind. Accts. Assn. (sec. 1964), Nat. Soc. Pub. Accts. Home: Route 5 Allegan MI 49010 Office: 3211 125th Ave Allegan MI 49010

LANGTON, JANE GILLSON, author; b. Boston, Dec. 30, 1922; d. Joseph Lincoln and Grace (Brown) Gillson; student Wellesley Coll., 1940-42; B.S., U. Mich., 1944, M.A., 1945; M.A., Radcliffe Coll., 1948; m. William Gale Langton, June 10, 1943; children—Christopher, David, Andrew. Books: The Majesty of Grace, 1961, The Diamond in the Window, 1962, The Transcendental Murder, 1964, The Swing in the Summerhouse, 1967, The Astonishing Stereoscope, 1971, The Boyhood of Grace Jones, 1972, Dark Nantucket Noon, 1975, Paper Chains, 1977, The Memorial Hall Murder, 1978, The Fledgling (named Newbery Honor book 1981), Natural Enemy 1982. Home: Concord Rd Lincoln MA 01773

LANGUM, W. SUE, civic worker; b. Kennett, Mo., Jan. 10, 1934; d. Howard S. and Lucille (Hubble) Walker; student Northwestern U., 1952-53, Crane Jr. Coll., 1953-54; m. John K. Langum, Dec. 28, 1972; 1 son, Kirby Walker Nelson. Receptionist, Chgo. Met. YMCA, 1952-56; service rep. Ill. Bell Tel. Co., 1956-57; receptionist Tri City Animal Hosp., 1967-69; research asst. Bus. Econs. Inc., Chgo., 1969-73, dir., 1973—; v.p. Elgin council PTA, 1969-73; bd. dirs., land use chmn., v.p. Elgin League Women Voters, 1965—; bd. dirs. OEO, 1972-73; vol. Fish, 1974-76; bd. dirs. Meals on Wheels, 1972—, Colloquy Coffee House, 1968-70, Elgin Womens Club, 1975-76, Judson Coll. Friends, 1976—, Elgin Hist. Soc.; bd. dirs., treas. Easter Seal Assn. for Crippled, Inc., Elgin, 1977—; bd. dirs., 1st v.p. Elgin Symphony League; pres. United Meth. Women; mem. Elgin Beautification Commn. Republican. Methodist. Clubs: Tuesday Morning Bible Study, Current History Forum. Home: 477 Oakhill Rd Elgin IL 60120

LANHAM, BETTY BAILEY, anthropologist, educator; b. Statesville, N.C., Aug. 12, 1922; d. Clyde B. and Naomi (Bailey) L.; B.S., U. Va., 1944, M.A., 1947; Ph.D., Syracuse U., 1962. Faculty, River Falls State Tchrs. Coll., 1948-49, U. Md., 1949-50, Randolph Macon Womens Coll., 1954-55, Oswego State Tchrs. Coll., 1956-58, Hamilton Coll., 1961-62, Ind. U., 1962-65, Western Mich. U., 1965-67, Albany Med. Coll., 1967-70; prof. anthropology Indiana U. of Pa., 1970—; vis. prof. Wakayama (Japan) U., 1951-52, U. Guyana, 1969-70. Werner-Gren Found. for Anthrop. Research fellow, 1951-52, AAUW research fellow, 1959-60. Mem. Am. Anthrop. Assn., Soc. for Applied Anthropology, Assn. for Asian Studies. Democrat. Methodist. Contbr. articles to profl. jours. Home: 121 Dolores Circle Indiana PA 15701 Office: Dept Sociology-Anthropology Indiana U of Pa Indiana PA 15705

LANIER, ALISON RAYMOND, author, intercultural specialist; b. N.Y.C., Apr. 1, 1917; d. Edward Holman and Isabel (Ashwell) Raymond; B.A. cum laude, Bryn Mawr Coll., 1938; m. Albert G. Lanier, Sept. 9, 1967. Asst. dir. pub. relations Bryn Mawr (Pa.) Coll., 1941-42; co-dir. N.Y. Office Internat. Child Welfare Union Geneva, N.Y.C., 1946-47; pub. relations dir. World Affairs Council Phila., 1947-51, Eastern area Pa. CD, Phila., 1951-55; exec. dir. Com. of Corr., N.Y.C., 1955-61; editor monthly publ. for UN personnel under Carnegie Endowment for Internat. Peace, N.Y.C., 1961-65; dir. meetings and programs Fgn. Policy Assn., N.Y.C., 1965-66; founder, pres. Overseas Briefing Assocs., N.Y.C., 1967-81; intercultural cons. to numerous multinat. corps., 1981—; lectr. New Sch. Social Research, N.Y.C., U.S. Dept. State Fgn. Service Inst., Washington, World Trade Inst., N.Y.C., Am. Mgmt. Assn., N.Y.C. Served with USN, 1942-46; comdr. Res. (ret.). Mem. Internat. Cons. Found., Soc. Internat. Edn., Tng. and Research, Am. Soc. Tng. Dirs., Soc. Internat. Devel., U.S. Nat. China Relations Com., Nat. Writers Club, Fgn. Policy Assn., Res. Officers Assn. Club: Bryn Mawr (N.Y.C.). Author 23 books including China Today: The Family and the Nation, 1974; Living in the U.S.A., 1975; Living in Europe, 1975; series of updates on countries including Update: Saudi Arabia, 1981, Update: Indonesia, 1982; contbr. numerous articles to mags. Home: 66 Little Brook Rd Wilton CT 06897 Office: 201 E 36th St New York NY 10016

LANNIN, BARBARA JOAN, county ofcl.; b. Traverse City, Mich., Jan. 12, 1932; d. Forrest Henry and Frances Louise (Germaine) Lannin; B.A., Rockford (Ill.) Coll., 1975; m. Armin Weng, Dec. 27, 1952 (div. Sept. 1981); children—Michael, Michelle. Reporter, freelance feature writer and photographer Rockford Morning Star and other No. Ill. newspapers, 1960-72; founder, exec. dir. Yellow Bird Sr. Citizens, Inc., Oregon, Ill., 1975—; exec. dir. Eastern Will County Sr. Services, Monee, Ill., 1979—. Mem. Ill. Press Woman's Assn. Democrat. Lutheran. Home: 4211 W 206th St Matteson IL 60443 Office: Route 1 Box 48 Monee IL 60449

LANNQUIST, BEVERLY CECELIA, finance exec.; b. Boston, Oct. 19, 1946; d. Arthur S. and Nancy (Hastings) Lannquist; B.A. cum laude, U. Mich., 1968; postgrad. N.Y.U. Grad. Sch. Bus., 1969-70. Research asst. acquisitions ITT, N.Y.C., 1968-69; trust officer Mfrs. Hanover Trust, 1970-72; v.p., prin. Auerbach, Pollak & Richardson, N.Y.C., 1972-75; v.p. Morgan Stanley & Co., N.Y.C., 1975-80; v.p. United Technologies, Hartford, Conn., 1980—. Trustee Hartford Coll. for Women. Recipient award of outstanding woman in bus. N.Y.C. YWCA, 1977; voted #1 or 2 Consumer Analyst in U.S., Instl. Investor Poll, 1974-79; nominated for Woman of Yr. in Bus., Ladies Home Jour., 1976. Mem. Fin. Womens Assn., Econs. Club N.Y. Home: 505 E 79th St New York NY 10021 Office: United Technologies Hartford CT 06101

LANPHERE, BETTY JOANNE, ct. reporter; b. Indpls., Mar. 26, 1938; d. Paul Sheldon and Doris Mae (Mathis) Furry; student Browning Bus. Coll., Albuquerque, 1967-68; m. James A. Lanphere, June 2, 1962; children—Michael, Lisa, Kristine, Scott, Jamie, Kimberly, Susan, Kevin, Julie, Jill, Kelly. Sec., Sandia Corp., Albuquerque, 1955-62, legal firm Jones, Gallegos, Snead & Wertheim, Santa Fe, 1967-68, firm Stephenson, Campbell & Olmsted, Santa Fe, 1968-69; ct. reporter Nye Reporting Service, Santa Fe, 1969, Lanphere Reporting Service, Santa Fe, 1969—; ofcl. reporter U.S. Dist. Ct., Santa Fe; mem. N.Mex. Ct. Reporting Bd., 1975—; mem. Nat. Audio-Video Com. on Electronic Rec., 1974—. Roman Catholic. Office: PO Box 449 58 S Federal Pl Santa Fe NM 87501

LANSBURY, ANGELA BRIGID, actress; b. London, Eng., Oct. 16, 1925; d. Edgar and Moyna (MacGill) Lansbury; student Webber-Douglas Sch. Drama (London), 1939-40, Feagin Sch. Drama, N.Y.C., 1940-42; m. Peter Shaw, Aug. 12, 1949; children—Anthony P., Deirdre A. Came to U.S., 1940, naturalized, 1951. Actress, Metro-Goldwyn-Mayer, 1943-50; free lance, 1950—; motion pictures include: Gaslight, 1944, Nat. Velvet, 1944, Dorian Gray, 1944, Harvey Girls, 1946, Till the Clouds Roll By, 1946, If Winter Comes, 1947, State of the Union, 1948, Samson and Delilah, 1949, Kind Lady, 1951, The Court Jester, 1956, The Long Hot Summer, 1957, Reluctant Debutante, 1958, Summer of the 17th Doll, 1959, A Breath of Scandal, 1959, Dark at the Top of the Stairs, 1960, Blue Hawaii, 1961, All Fall Down, 1962, In the Cool of the Day, 1963, World of Henry Orient, 1964, Out of Towners, 1964; appeared in plays Hotel Paradiso, 1957, A Taste of Honey, 1960, Anyone Can Whistle, 1964, Mame (on Broadway), 1966, Dear World, 1968, Something for Everyone, 1969, Bedknobs and Broomsticks, 1970, Death on the Nile, 1978, The Lady Vanishes, 1979, The Mirror Cracked, 1980; London debut R.S.C. prodn. Albee's All Over, 1972; appeared in Sondheim, A Musical Tribute, 1973; starred in Gypsy, London, 1973, N.Y.C., 1974; appeared in Hamlet, Nat. Theatre London, 1975, The King and I, N.Y.C., 1978, Sweeney Todd, N.Y.C., 1979 (on tour 1980). Recipient Antoinette Perry award, 1966, 69, 75, 79, Sarah Siddons award, 1975, Acad. award nominations, 1944, 45, 62. Address: care Uris Theatre 1633 Broadway New York NY 10019 *

LANSDOWNE, KAREN MYRTLE, educator; b. Twin Falls, Idaho, Aug. 11, 1926; d. George and Effie Myrtle (Ayotte) Martin; B.A. in English with honors, U. Oreg., 1948, M.Ed., 1958, M.A. with honors, 1960; m. Paul L. Lansdowne, Sept. 12, 1948; chilren—Michele Lynn, Larry Alan. Tchr., Newfield (N.Y.) High Sch., 1948-50, S. Eugene (Oreg.) High Sch., 1952; mem. faculty U. Oreg., Eugene, 1958-65; asst. prof. English, Lane Community Coll., Eugene, 1965—; cons. Oreg. Curriculum Study Center. Rep., Cal Young Neighborhood Assn., 1978—; mem. scholarship com. First Congl. Ch., 1950-70. Mem. MLA, Pacific N.W. Regional Conf. Community Colls., Nat. Council Tchrs. English, U. Oreg. Women, AAUW (sec.), Jaycettes, Pi Lambda Theta (pres.), Phi Beta Patronesses (pres.), Delta Kappa Gamma. Co-author: The Oregon Curriculum: Language/Rhetoric, I, II, III and IV, 1970. Office: 4000 E 30 St Eugene OR 97405

LANSING, SHERRY LEE, motion picture exec.; b. Chgo., July 31, 1944; d. Norton and Margot (Heimann) L.; B.S. cum laude in Theatre, Northwestern U., 1966. Tchr. math., public high schs., Los Angeles, 1966-69; appeared in motion pictures: Loving, 1970, Rio Lobo, 1970; exec. story editor Wagner Internat., 1970-73; head program devel. West Coast, Heyday Prodns., Universal City, Calif., 1973-75; exec. story editor Metro-Goldwyn-Mayer, Culver City, Calif., 1975-77, v.p. creative affairs, 1977; v.p. Columbia Pictures, Burbank, Calif., 1977-78, sr. v.p. prodn., 1978-80; pres. prodns. Twentieth Century-Fox, Beverly Hills, Calif., 1980—. Office: PO Box 900 Beverly Hills CA 90213

LANTERI, SOPHIE GRACE, assn. exec.; b. N.Y.C., May 15, 1950; d. Paul A. and Angelina F. (Rizzo) Lanteri; B.A. in Communications, Hunter Coll., 1980; cert. Conv. Mgmt., Am. Soc. Assn. Execs., 1980; cert. Hotel and Motel Mgmt., N.Y. Inst. Dietetics, 1980; cert. in Public Relations and Publicity, Publicity Club N.Y., 1971; postgrad. Pace U., 1982—; m. Frank Branciforte, Aug. 15, 1981. Bookkeeper, auditor's asst. Sirco Internat., Mt. Vernon, N.Y., 1966-69; adminstrv. asst. Soap and Detergent Assn., N.Y.C., 1969-74, asst. dir. consumer affairs, 1974-79, dir. indsl. and instl. info., 1980—, conv. coordinator, 1980—. Mem. Women in Communications, Inc., Am. Mgmt. Assn., Nat. Environ. Health Assn., Environ. Mgmt. Assn., Am. Soc. Assn. Execs. Office: 475 Park Ave South New York NY 10016

LANTRIP, KAY LYNN, civil engr.; b. Herrin, Ill., Aug. 25, 1953; d. Robert F. and Pauline K. Osowski; student So. Ill. U., 1971-73; B.S. in Civil Engring., U. Ill., 1975; m. Bruce M. Lantrip, Aug. 3, 1974. Civil engr., Old Ben Coal Co., Benton, Ill., 1975-77, Bechtel Power Corp., Gaithersburg, Md., 1977; civil engr. Ralph M. Parsons Co., Balt. Regional Rapid Transit System, Balt., 1977-80; project mgr. George Hyman Constrn. Co., 1980—. Registered profl. engr. Mem. Chi Epsilon. Home: 5704 Thunder Hill Rd Columbia MD 21045

LANTRY, MARILYN MARTHA, state senator; b. St. Paul, Oct. 28, 1932; d. Louis Leonard and Josephine Mary (Cermak) Kunz; student public schs., St. Paul; m. Jerome Horton Lantry, May 16, 1953; children—Jacqueline, Kathleen. Various secretarial and research, 1950-63; legislative aide St. Paul City Councilman, 1963-81; mem. Minn. State Senate, 1981—. Bd. dirs. YWCA; chmn. bd. dirs. Group Health Plan; bd. dirs. St. Paul-Ramsey Hosp. Democrat. Roman Catholic. Office: State Capitol St Paul MN 55155

LANTZ, ELIZABETH MARY, civic worker; b. Rawlins, Wyo., Feb. 13, 1915; d. Anthony and Margery (Walker) Stratton; student Lindenwood Coll., 1932-33; B.S., U. Wyo., 1936; m. Everett Delmer Lantz, Mar. 5, 1938; children—Phillip Edward, Keith William, George Everett, Barbara Elizabeth. Sec. to U. Wyo. Librarian, 1936-38. Pres. Ivinson Meml. Hosp. Aux., 1977-79, P.T.A., 1958-59; corr. sec., chaplain P.E.O.; pres. Kappa Kappa Gamma, 1934-36, alumnae pres., 1953-55, pres. house corp., 1946-52, 56-68, 76—; sec. Kiwivians, 1951; pres. Episcopal Women, 1966-69, 73-74, St. Anne's Guild, 1969-77; mem. vestry Episc. Ch., 1971-74; election bd. judge, 1965—; den mother Cub Scouts, 1947-49; registration chmn. Gov.'s Youth Conf., 1976, 78, 80, Youth Legis. Forum, 1977, 79; hostess statehouse briefing seminar Internat. Year of the Child, 1979. Mem. Phi Gamma Nu. Republican. Club: Rep. Women's. Home: 1614 Garfield St Laramie WY 82070

LANTZ, JOANNE BALDWIN, educator; b. Defiance, Ohio, Jan. 26, 1932; d. Hiram Joseph and Ethel Amanda (Smith) Baldwin; B.S., Ind. Central U., 1953; M.S., Ind. U., 1957; Ph.D., Mich. State U., 1969; m. Wayne Eugene Lantz, Oct. 22, 1955. Tchr. physics and math. Arcola (Ind.) High Sch., 1953-57; guidance dir. New Haven (Ind.) Sr. High Sch., 1957-65; asst. prof. psychol. scis. and coordinator acad. advising Ind. U.-Purdue U., Ft. Wayne, 1965-68, dir. counseling and testing, 1968-70, asst. dean student services adminstrn., asso. prof., 1970-75, asso. prof. psychol. scis., 1975-80, prof., 1980—, chmn. dept., 1982—; mem. St.

Joseph's Hosp. personnel adv. com. to bd. dirs., 1978—, chmn., 1980—; mem. adv. com. Samaritan Counseling Center, 1978—; dir. Anthony Wayne Vocat. Rehab. Center, mem. personnel com., 1969-75. Mem. Am. Psychol. Assn., AAUW (Am. women fellowship com. 1978-81), Southeastern Psychol. Assn., Delta Kappa Gamma (pres. Ind. 1975-77, exec. bd. 1975-77, research com. chmn. 1973-75, 1st v.p. 1971-73, gen. chmn. NE regional conf. 1976-77, internat. conv. rules com. 1978, leadership devel. com. 1978-80, chmn. 1980-82, NE regional dir. 1982-84). Democrat. Methodist. Club: Ind. Sch. Women's (v.p., program chmn. 1979-81). Bd. dirs. United Way of Allen County, 1974-80, sec., 1979-80. Contbr. numerous articles to profl. jours. Home: 3118 Eastbrook Dr Ft Wayne IN 46805 Office: Ind U-Purdue U 2101 Coliseum Blvd Ft Wayne IN 46905

LAO, ROSINA C., psychologist, educator; b. Hong Kong; came to U.S., 1962, naturalized, 1972; d. Cheng-Chein and Ching-chao (Soong) Chia; B.S., Nat. Taiwan U., 1962; M.A., U. Mich., 1963, Ph.D., 1969; m. Y. J. Lao, June 26, 1966; children—Eugene Y., Renee Y. Asst. study dir. U. Mich., Ann Arbor, 1965-69, instr., 1968-69; asst. prof. psychology, East Carolina U., Greenville, 1969-75, assoc. prof., 1975-78, prof., 1978—, chmn. dept. psychology, 1980—, spl. asst. to chancellor and univ. ombudsman, 1980-81; cons. to Govt. of Republic of China, 1981. Mem. Greenville Energy Commn., 1978-81; liaison Greenville Public Works Commn., 1980-81; bd. dirs. St. Peter's Sch., Greenville, 1978-81. Mem. AAAS, Am. Psychol. Assn., Southeastern Psychol. Assn., Assn. Asian Am. Psychologists (dir. 1979-82), Internat. Council Psychologists, Am. Edn. Research Assn. Roman Catholic. Contbr. articles in field to profl. publs. Office: East Carolina U Dept Psychology Greenville NC 27834

LAPHAM, EDNA VIRGINIA SHEPPARD, social worker, educator; b. Lincoln Park, Mich., June 13, 1931; d. Plato Lee and Nora Lee (Guthrie) Sheppard; B.A., Mich. State U., 1953; M.Ed., Wayne State U., 1965; M.S.W., Hunter Coll., 1974; m. Robert J. Lapham, Sept. 24, 1955; children—David, Susan, Frederick, Thomas, Timothy. Speech therapist, spl. edn. cons. Public Schs. County of Wayne (Mich.), 1953-55, 62-65, 67-68; internat. social worker Palestinian Refugees, Irbid, Amman, Hebron Jordan, 1955-62; founder, tchr. internat. kindergarten, spl. edn. cons. Rabat (Morocco)-Am. Sch., 1965-67; social worker, legis. specialist N.Y. Inst. for Edn. of Blind, N.Y.C., 1974-77, coordinator research, planning and devel., 1977—; adj. clin. instr. Hunter Coll., 1977-78; social work cons., Larchmont, N.Y. and Arlington, Va., 1978—. Bd. dirs. Methodist Fedn. for Social Action, S.I., N.Y., 1972—, co-pres., 1977—; bd. dirs. Clergy and Laity Concerned, N.Y.C., 1973-79, co-pres., 1976-79. Cert. social worker, N.Y. Lisle fellow, 1955. Mem. Acad. Cert. Social Workers, N.Y. State Sch. Social Work Assn. (dir. 1978—), N.Y. State Council Orgns. on Handicapped (dir. 1977-80), Nat. Assn. Social Workers, Council on Social Work Edn., Assn. Edn. Visually Handicapped, Assn. Spl. Educators, Council for Exceptional Children, Am. Assn. Psychiat. Services for Children. Author: Setting Our Sights: Educational Issues of Students With Visual Impairments, 1980; contbr. articles to profl. jours. Home: 6400 Lee Hwy Arlington VA 22205 Office: 999 Pelham Pkwy Bronx NY 10469

LAPIDUS, LEAH BLUMBERG, clin. psychologist, educator; b. Chgo., Apr. 6, 1938; d. Louis and Kay (Kahan) Blumberg; B.A., N.Y.U., 1960; Ph.D. in Clin. Psychology, 1968; M.A. in Developmental Psychology, Columbia U., 1961; m. Ivan Richard Lapidus, Feb. 28, 1959; children—Louise Diana, Lenora Michelle, Kyle Alexander Blumberg. Pvt. practice clin. psychology, N.Y.C., 1969—; instr. clin. psychology, psychologist-in-charge N.Y.U. Med. Center, Bellevue Hosp. dept. psychiatry, 1968-72, vis. asso. prof. Med. Center Lab. for Exptl. Medicine and Surgery in Primates and dept. psychiatry, 1979-80; asst. prof. Columbia U. Tchrs. Coll., N.Y.C., 1972-75, asso. prof., 1975—; vis. asso. prof. UCLA, 1980, 81; vis. research prof. SUNY Downstate Med. Center, 1979-81, U. Calif.-Davis Primate Research Center, 1980, 81; vis. lectr. U. London, U. Oxford (Eng.), 1982. Pres. bd. dirs. Shire Village Camp, Cumminton, Mass., 1970-74. Diplomate in Clin. Psychology, Am. Bd. Profl. Psychology; lic. psychologist, N.Y., N.J., Calif. Fellow AAAS, AAUP, Am. Orthopsychiat. Assn.; mem. Am. Psychol. Assn. (various divs.), Child Study Assn. Am., Internat. Soc. Psychosomatic Ob-Gyn, N.Y. Acad. Scis., N.Y. Soc. Clin. Psychologists (exec. bd. 1974-75), Psychologists for Social Action (nat. exec. bd. 1969-75), Nat. Register of Health Service Providers in Psychology, Phi Lambda Theta. Contbr. numerous articles in field to profl. jours. Office: 525 W 120th St New York NY 10027

LAPIN, SHARON JOYCE VAUGHN, interior designer; b. Lagrange, Mo., July 28, 1938; d. John Noland and Wilma Emma (Huebotter) Vaughn; B.A., U. Wash., Seattle, 1960; cert. in interior design, Maryville Coll., 1977; m. Byron Richard Lapin, Oct. 14, 1972. Appearing in various Broadway shows, TV commercials and TV shows, 1962-72; owner Sharon Lapin Designs St. Louis. Bd. dirs. St. Louis Conservatory and Schs. for the Arts, 1977—, v.p., 1982-83; chmn. bd. Studio Set, 1978-81, pres., 1975-78, bd. dirs., 1975—; bd. dirs. Friends of Sci. Mus., 1980-82, St. Louis Symphony Womens Assn., 1973-77. Mem. AFTRA, Screen Actors Guild, Actors Equity Assn., Am. Soc. Interior Designers, Pi Beta Phi. Republican. Baptist.

LAPINIG, STEPHANIE ANNA, home econs. cons.; b. Bklyn., July 25, 1923; d. Gaspare and Giovanna (Casella) Napoli; cert. in food mgmt. with honors, Pratt Inst., 1948; B.S., Fla. State U., 1955; M.S., Hunter Coll., 1967; m. Florencio Lapinig, Jan. 29, 1955; 1 dau., Sabina Johna-Ann. Successively co-dir. test kitchen Theodore R. Sills, Public Relations Agy., N.Y.C.; with Redbook Mag., N.Y.C.; home econs. cons., for day care centers, Agy. for Child Devel., N.Y.C., 1974—. Crew chief EMT, Queens Village, Hollis, Bellerose Vol. Ambulance Corps, 1972—; mem. N.Y. State Legis. Adv. Com., 1967—. Served with USAAF, 1943-45. Recipient Cert. of Appreciation, UNICEF, 1965, YMCA, 1967, 68, 69. Mem. Am. Home Econs. Assn., N.Y.C. Group Home Econs. in Bus., Food and Nutrition Council of Greater N.Y., Pratt Inst. Home Econs. Alumni Assn. (past pres., sec.), Fla. State U. Alumni Assn., Hunter Coll. Alumni Assn. Inventor of Pumpkin Pickle, 1972.

LAPPE, FRANCES MOORE, writer, educator; b. Pendleton, Oreg., Feb. 10, 1944; d. John and Ina Moore; B.A. in History, Earlham Coll., 1966; postgrad. Martin Luther King Sch. for Social Change, 1966, U. Calif.-Berkeley, 1968-69; L.H.D. (hon.), Starr King Sch. Religious Leadership, Berkeley, 1979; children—Anthony, Anna. Books: Diet for a Small Planet, 1971, rev. edit., 1981; (with Joseph Collins) Food First: Beyond the Myth of Scarcity, 1977, World Hunger: Ten Myths, 1977; (with Bill Valentine) What Can We Do?, 1980; (with Adele Beccar-Varela) Mozambique and Tanzania: Asking the Big Questions, 1980; (with Joseph Collins, David Kinley) Aid As Obstacle, 1980; (with Peter Sketchley) Casting New Molds: First Steps to Worker Control in a Mozambique Steel Factory, 1980; (with Joseph Collins) Now We Can Speak: A Journey Through the New Nicaragua, 1982; contbr. articles to mags.; co-founder Inst. Food and Devel. Policy, San Francisco, 1975; lectr. in field. Office: 1885 Mission St San Francisco CA 94103

LAPUZ-DE LA PENA, ERLINDA LARON, physician, pathologist; b. Manila, P.I., Nov. 26, 1933; d. Eriberto Mallari and Teodora Quiero (Laron) Lapuz; M.D., U. Santo Tomas, 1957; m. Cordell De La Pena, Apr. 1, 1957; children—Leslie, Nina, Cordell. Intern, St. John's Hosp., Lowell, Mass., 1959-60; attending physician Tewksbury (Mass.) Hosp., 1960-63; resident in pathology Mercy Hosp., Pitts., 1967-71; instr. pathology U. Pitts. Med. Sch., 1967-71; chief lab. service VA Hosp., Clarksburg, W.Va., 1971—; courtesy staff United Hosp. Center; asst. prof. pathology W.Va. U. Sch. Medicine, 1981—; asst. prof. Coll. Nursing, Salem (W.Va.) Coll., 1978, Coll. Nursing and Physician Assts., Alderson Broadus Coll., Phillipi, W.Va. Diplomate Am. Bd. Pathology. Fellow Coll. Am. Pathologists, Am. Soc. Clin. Pathology; mem. AMA, W.Va. Med. Assn., W.Va., Assn. Pathologists. Roman Catholic. Club: Clarksburg Country. Contbr. articles med. jours. Home: 209 Candlelight Dr Clarksburg WV 26301 Office: Veterans Administration Hospital Clarksburg WV 26301

LAREDO, RUTH, concert pianist; b. Detroit, Nov. 20, 1937; d Ben and Miriam (Horowitz) Meckler; diploma Curtis Inst. Music, 1960; m. Jaime Laredo, June 1, 1960 (div. Nov. 1976); 1 dau., Jennifer. N.Y.C. debut with Leopold Stokowski and Am. Symphony, 1962; debut with Boulez and N.Y. Philharmonic, 1974; soloist with major Am. orchs., including those in N.Y.C., Cleve., Detroit, Phila., and Nat. and Am. symphonies; performed at Aspen, Marlboro, Spoleto, Israel and Caramoor festivals; recordings with Columbia Records include Ravel's La Valse, 1967, piano sonatas of Alexander Scriabin, 1970-71, complete solo piano works of Rachmaninoff; asst. prof. Yale U. Sch. Music, 1974. Address: care Hillyer Internat Inc 250 W 57th St New York City NY 10019

LARIMORE, BETTY SHOLEY, civic worker; b. Muncie, Ind., June 29, 1931; d. Michael I. and Bessie Sholey; B.S. in Mktg., Ind. U., 1952; m. B.H. Larimore, Sept. 13, 1952; children—Deborah, Diane, Denise. Mdse. trainee L. S. Ayres Co., Indpls., 1952-53; swimming instr. YWCA, Muncie, 1952-56. Pres., Mental Health Assn. Delaware County, 1977, 78, mem. local exec. bd., 1980; pres. Ball Meml. Hosp. Aux. Bd., 1974, also hosp. vol.; mem. State Bd. Mental Health, 1976-80; active PTA, coms. Women's Symphony League; mem. steering com. Republican Party, also chmn. Vols. for Fall campaign, 1979. Recipient Gavel Plaque, Mental Health Assn., 1979, 10 Yr. pin for work with Girl Scouts U.S. Mem. Tri Kappa (pres. 1978), Beta Gamma Sigma. Methodist. Club: Elks. Home: 3400 Vienna Woods Dr Muncie IN 47304

LARKAM, BEVERLEY MCCOSHAM, clin. social worker; b. Vancouver, Can., Mar. 3, 1928; d. William Howard and Marjorie Isabel (Jerome) McCosham; came to U.S., 1951; asso. Royal Conservatory of Mus. of Toronto, U. Toronto, 1948; B.A., U. B.C., 1949, B.S.W., 1950, M.S.W., 1951; children—Elizabeth, Charles, Daphne, Peter, John. Psychiat. social worker Brackenridge Hosp., 1952-54; chmn. dept. sr. high sch. Univ. Presbyn. Ch., Austin, Tex., 1952-55, mem. Christian edn. com., 1961-67, mem. community orgn. to establish classes for mentally retarded children, 1966-68, bd. dirs. developing and organizing nursery sch., 1967-70; social worker Counseling-Psychol. Services Center U. Tex., 1971-72; psychiat. social worker, chief supr. adult mental health, children's mental health Human Devel. Center-South, Austin, 1972-79; pvt. practice marriage and family therapy, sex therapy and individual and group psychotherapy, Austin, 1975—; field supr. Sch. Social Work U. Tex.; cons. in field. Mem. City of Austin Commn. on Status of Women, 1978—. Lic. clin. social worker. Tex.; mem. Register of Clin. Social Workers. Mem. Am. Assn. Marriage and Family Therapy (approved supr.), Am. Assn. Sex Educators, Counselors and Therapists (cert. sex therapist), Soc. for Sci. Study of Sex, Am., Southwestern group psychotherapy socs., Am. Orthopsychiat. Soc., Acad. Cert. Social Workers, Nat. Assn. Social Workers, Nat. Council on Family Relations, Nat. Register Health Care Providers in Clin. Social Work, PEO. Presbyterian. Home and Office: 2102 Raleigh Ave Austin TX 78703

LARKIN, FLORENCE MARIE, home builder, real estate broker; b. Jefferson County, Kans.; d. Homer Joseph and Mae Rose (Reichart) Sloop; R.N., Stormont Vail Sch. Nursing, Topeka, 1952; m. Ford J. Larkin, Jan. 30, 1954 (dec. 1976); children—Michele Knight, Charlene, Janiece, Renee, John, Michael. Staff and operating rm. nurse VA, Leavenworth, Kans., 1952-68; home builder, 1966-82; real estate broker Larkin Co., Leavenworth, 1974—. Mem. Leavenworth C. of C. (Citizen of Yr. 1975), Leavenworth County Bd. Realtors (pres. 1978-79), Nat. Assn. Home Builders. Republican. Roman Catholic. Home and Office: 710 Ridge Rd Leavenworth KS 66048

LARKIN, GERTIE MAE, nurse; b. Tipton, Okla., Oct. 1, 1930; d. Urbane and Willie Mae (Linkous) Aaron; B.S. Nursing, Mary Hardin-Baylor Coll., 1975; postgrad. Tex. Woman's U., 1975—; m. William Clayton Larkin, Jr., Aug. 14, 1949 (dec. May 1970); 1 dau., Sue Ann. EKG technician Scott and White Hosp., 1951-52; elementary sch. tchr., Hampton, Va., 1954-55; sec. 1st Nat. Bank, Temple, Tex., 1956-58; staff nurse Santa Fe Hosp., Temple, 1976-80; charge nurse Cameron (Tex.) Community Hosp., 1980—. Mem. Am., Tex. nurses assns., Dist. 7 Nursing Assn., Scott and White Hosp. Sch. Nursing Alumnae Assn. Baptist. Home: 3716 Robinhood Dr Temple TX 76501 Office: Cameron Community Hosp Cameron TX 76520

LARKIN, MOLLY CHRISTINE, nursing adminstr.; b. Rochester, N.Y., May 4, 1953; d. Joseph W. and Jean A. (Judson) L.; diploma De Paul Sch. Nursing, 1975; B.S. in Nursing, Old Dominion U., 1980, postgrad., 1980—. Map evaluator State Hwy. Dept., Petersburg, Va., summer, 1972; WATS-line operator E.R. Carpenter Co., Richmond, Va., 1973; cashier Holiday Inn, Petersburg, Va., summer, 1974; staff nurse Norfolk (Va.) Gen. Hosp., 1975-79, asst. dir. nursing, 1979—; coordinator Skills Lab., Old Dominion U., Norfolk, 1982—. Mem. Am. Nurses Assn., Va. Nurses Assn. Roman Catholic. Home: 4495 Sir John's Ln Virginia Beach VA 23455 Office: 600 Gresham Dr Norfolk VA 23507

LAROCHE, MARIE-ELAINE A., investment banking exec.; b. N.Y.C., Aug. 17, 1949; d. Andre Brave and Madeleine E. (Hanin) LaR.; B.S. in Fgn. Service, Georgetown U., 1971; M.B.A. in Fin., Am. U., 1978. Staff asst. to Hon. Donald Rumsfeld, White House, Washington, 1970-72; staff asst. Office of Sec. of Treasury, Washington, 1972-73; instl. sales Wainwright Securities, N.Y.C., 1973-78; v.p. capital markets Morgan Stanley & Co., Inc., N.Y.C., 1978-81, v.p. corp. fin., 1982—. Mem. Fin. Women's Assn. (bd., 1979-82, v.p. 1982-83), Women's Dirs. Forum (bd. 1980-82). Republican. Roman Catholic. Office: 1251 Ave of Americas New York NY 10020

LAROCHE, SHIRLEY SUE, clin. psychologist; b. Fosterville, Tenn., June 21, 1936; d. Powell Maganan and Sophia Sue (Coop) Brothers; B.S., Middle Tenn. State U., 1958, M.A., 1965; Ph.D., U. N.Mex., 1973; m. Richard Frederick LaRoche, 1969; children—Norman Louis, Timothy, Shea. Tchr. public schs., Virginia Beach, Va., 1961-62; tchr., dir. Sch. for the Gifted, Murfreesboro, Tenn., 1965-68; psychol. counselor public schs., Albuquerque, 1968-74; adj. prof. U. Mex., 1974; staff clin. psychologist, chief psychology tng. Murfreesboro VA Med. Center, 1974—; adj. prof. Middle Tenn. State U., 1975—. Dir., Rutherford County Council for Rape and Sexual Abuse; dir. Am. League Women Voters, 1979—; personnel relations rep. Rutherford County Arts and Humanities Council. Mem. Am. Psychol. Assn., Southeastern Psychol. Assn., Tenn. Psychol. Assn., AAUW (pres. Murfreesboro br. 1975-77). Democrat. Roman Catholic. Home: Route 11 Betty Ford Rd Murfreesboro TN 37130 Office: VA Med Center Lebanon Rd Murfreesboro TN 37130

LAROCQUE, MARILYN ROSS ONDERDONK, bus. exec.; b. Weehawken, N.J., Oct. 14, 1934; d. Chester Douglas and Marion (Ross) Onderdonk; B.A. cum laude, Mt. Holyoke Coll., 1956; postgrad. N.Y.U., 1956-57; M.Journalism, U. Calif., Berkeley, 1965; m. Bernard Dean Benz, Oct. 5, 1957 (div. Sept. 1971); children—Mark Douglas, Dean Griffith; m. 2d, Rodney Clarence LaRocque, Feb. 10, 1973. Jr. exec. Bonwit Teller, N.Y.C., 1956; personnel asst. Warner-Lambert Pharm. Co., Morris Plains, N.J., 1957; editorial asst. Silver Burdett Co., Morristown, 1958; pub. relations cons., 1963-71, 73-77; pub. relations dir. Shaklee Corp., Hayward, Calif., 1971-73; dir. pub. relations Fidelity Savs. & Loan Assn., Oakland, Calif., 1977-78; exec. dir. No. Calif. chpt. Nat. Multiple Sclerosis Soc., 1978-80; v.p. public relations Cambridge Plan Internat., Monterey, Calif., 1980-81; sr. account exec. Hoefer-Amidei Public Relations, San Francisco, 1981-82; dir. spl. projects, asst. to chmn. Cambridge Plan Internat., Monterey, Calif., 1982—; instr. U. Calif. Extension, San Francisco, 1977-79. Mem. exec. bd., rep-at-large Oakland (Calif.) Symphony Guild, 1968-69; cabinet mem. Lincoln Child Center, Oakland, 1967-71, cabinet pres., 1970-71, 2d v.p. bd. dirs., 1970-71; pub. relations chmn. Oakland Mus. Assn., 1974; mem. Calif. Republican Central Com., 1964-66; bd. dirs. Calif. Spring Garden and Home Show, 1970-77, First Agrl. Dist. Calif., 1970-77; v.p. Piedmont council Boy Scouts Am., 1977. Mem. Pub. Relations Soc. Am. (dir. San Francisco Bay Area chpt. 1980-82), Women in Communications, Nat. Trust for Historic Preservation, U. Calif. Alumni Assn., Mus. Soc. San Francisco, Calif. Hist. Soc., Oakland Smithsonian Assos., AAUW, Clubs: Mt. Holyoke Coll. Alumnae, East Bay Press, East Bay Women's Press, Contra Costa Press; Commonwealth of Calif. Author: Maestro Baton and His Musical Friends, 1968; Happiness is Breathing Better, 1976. Address: 121 Alta Mesa Ct Moraga CA 94556

LAROE, DANNIE MARLENE, psychotherapist; b. Jasper, Tex., Jan. 14, 1931; d. charles Alton and Dovie Faye (DeShazo) LaR.; M.S.W., Smith Coll., 1953; m. DeWitt Shelton, Mar. 18, 1978; 1 son, Slater Vaugn Welte. Therapist in med. rehab. VA Hosp., Houston, 1953-55; asst. dir. social services Polio Found., Houston, 1955-57; with Family Service Bur., Houston, 1957-59; asso. prof. sociology Sam Houston State Coll., Huntsville, 1961-63; lectr. dept. sociology U. Houston, 1963-65, vis. lectr. Sch. Social Work, 1974-75; vis. lectr. U. Tex. Med. Sch., Houston, 1977-79; pvt. practice social psychotherapy, Houston, 1959—; lectr. in field; mem. State Bd. Examiners in Social Psychotherapy, Austin, 1980-81. Mem. Acad. Cert. Social Workers, Smith Coll. Alumni Assn., Author's Guild, Nat. Assn. Social Workers. Republican. Author: How Not to Ruin a Perfectly Good Marriage, 1979; contbr. articles to profl. jours. Office: 5005 Woodway St Suite 246 Houston TX 77056

LAROUNIS, MARY GEORGE, psychiat. social worker; b. Cefalonia, Greece, Dec. 21, 1934; came to U.S., 1953, naturalized, 1960; d. George P. and Stamatia O. (Razis) Efthymiatos; student Pierce Coll., Athens, Greece, 1951-53; B.A., Hunter Coll., 1955; M.S.W., Columbia U., 1957; m. George P. Larounis, Jan. 13, 1958; 1 dau., Daphne H. Case worker Community Service N.Y., 1957-60; caseworker Am. Aid Soc., Paris, 1964-66, asst. dir., 1966-79; asst. dir. Am. Student and Family Counselling Service, 1979—; mem. staff Internat. Counseling Service, Paris, 1979—. Mem. Nat. Assn. Social Workers, Acad. Cert. Social Workers. Clubs: Polo (Paris), Racing (France). Home: 9 Blvd du Chateau Nueilly-sur-seine France 92200 Office: 65 Quai D'Orsay Paris France 75007

LARRABEE, VIRGINIA ANN STEWART, educator; b. Jacksonville, Fla., Nov. 21, 1923; d. Edwin Homer and Clara Victoria (Anderson) Stewart; student Pine Manor Jr. Coll., 1941-43; B.A., Wellesley Coll., 1945; M.Ed., U. Vt., 1961; Ed.D., Boston U., 1969; m. Wesley Campbell Larrabee, May 4, 1947; children—Susan Ann, Diane Elaine, Linda Jane, Judith Ann. Asst. buyer B. Altman & Co., N.Y.C., 1945-46; tchr. public schs., Forest Dale, Vt., 1955-59, Shoreham, Vt., 1959-62; audiovisual dir., Shoreham, 1959-62; elem. supr., Castleton, Vt., 1962-64; instr., master tchr. Harvard, summers 1963-65; elem. supr. public schs., Rutland, Vt., 1964-66; asst. prof. edn. Castleton State Coll., 1966-68, asso. prof., 1969-74, prof., 1974—, chmn. dept. edn., 1972—, dir. grad. program in reading, 1974—; mem. adv. com. Right to Read, Vt., 1974—; mem. Vt. Edn. Commr.'s Forum, 1981—; owner, operator farm and orchard, 1953—. Sunday Sch. supt. Congregational Ch., Shoreham, 1948-60, choir dir., 1958-64. Mem. New Eng. (past dir.), Vt. (dir., pres. 1978—, editor newletter) reading councils, Internat. Reading Assn., Nat., Vt. (past pres.), New Eng. (past dir.) assns. supervision and curriculum devel., Phi Delta Kappa, Delta Kappa Gamma, Pi Lambda Theta. Clubs: Vt. Wellesley, Shoreham Hist. Home: RFD Box 56 Shoreham VT 05770 Office: Castleton State Coll Castleton VT 05735

LARSEN, BERNADINE MARGARET, educator; b. Penns Grove, N.J., Dec. 4, 1939; d. Joseph S. and Margaretta J. (Riley) Burke; B.S. in Edn., Coll. Notre Dame, Balt., 1969; children—Mary B., Kathleen A., Jimme J. Elem. edn. tchr., Md., N.J., Pa., Alaska, 1959-70; early childhood edn. tchr. rural Alaska, 1970—; dir. Head Start program Assn. Village Council Presidents, Bethel, Alaska, 1979—. Mem. Nat. Assn. Edn. Young Children, Nat. Indian Head Start Dirs. Assn., Alaska Head Start Dirs. Assn., Alaska Native Head Start Dirs. Assn. Co-author: Eskimos: Growing Up in a Changing Culture, 1977. Home: Box 178 Bethel AK 99559 Office: Box 219 Bethel AK 99559

LARSEN, DOROTHY HUNTINGTON HILL, ret. gerontol. cons.; b. Nora Springs, Iowa, Apr. 12, 1896; d. Charles and Emily (Huntington) Hill; A.B., U. Ill., 1922, M.A., 1925; M.A., Columbia, 1956, Ed.D., 1958; m. Harold Theodore Larsen, Jan. 26, 1924; 1 son, David Page. Tchr., Scornoway, Sask., Can., 1916-18; spl. lectr. Man. Ministery Agr., Winnipeg, 1920; instr. dept. English U. Ill., Urbana, 1922-27; counselor and gerontol. cons. Assn. Home for Women, N.Y.C., also Osborne Home, Harrison, N.Y., 1958-61; dir. Tower Leavue, Riverside Ch., N.Y.C., 1960-63; cons. gerontology Presbyn. Homes of N.J., 1965-80, Sisters of St. Dominic, Caldwell, N.J., 1971. Chmn. com. on exceptional child N.Y. State P.T.A., 1948-50; chmn. Rockland County (N.Y.) Mental Health Assn., 1952-53; mem. Rockland County Mental Health Bd., 1956-58; mem. N.J. steering com. White House Conf. on Aging, 1960-61; mem. Mercer County (N.J.) Council on Aging, 1969-71. Monmouth Presbytery Task Force on Aging, 1973—, East Windsor (N.J.) Bd. Health, 1973. Bd. dirs. N.Y.C. Bd. of Sr. Centers, 1965-74. Fellow Nat. Gerontol. Soc.; mem. Women in Communications, AAUW, Nat. Council Family Relations, Assn. for Community Edn. N.J., N.J. Gerontol. Soc., Kappa Delta Phi. Author: Dialogues on Aging, 1966. Home: 27-02 Meadow Lakes Hightstown NJ 08520

LARSEN, GRACE HUTCHISON, educator; b. Pomona, Calif., Dec. 4, 1920; d. Forest Glen and Pearl Carrie (Wolfe) Hutchison; B.A., U. Calif., Berkeley, 1942, M.A., 1945; Ph.D., Columbia U., 1955; m. Charles Edward Larsen, Nov. 27, 1943; children—Charles Eric, Douglas Edward. Instr., Rutgers U., Newark, 1947-49, 51-55; lectr. Bryn Mawr (Pa.) Coll., 1949-50; instr. Swarthmore (Pa.) Coll., 1949-51; asst. specialist in agrl. econs. U. Calif., Berkeley, 1955-62, asso. specialist, 1962-66; prof. history Holy Names Coll., Oakland, Calif., 1966—, acad. dean, 1970-80; mem. vis. teams Western Assn. Schs. and Colls., sr. commn., 1982—. Archbishop Riordan fellow in Am. History, 1942-43; Genevieve McEnerney fellow in history, 1945-46; Sigmund Martin Heller travelling fellow, 1946-47; Nat. Endowment for Humanities summer grantee, 1980. Mem. Am. Hist. Assn., West Coast Women Historians, Agrl. History Soc. Contbr. articles to profl. jours.; author: (with H.E. Erdman) Revolving Finance in Agricultural Cooperatives, 1965. Home: 4649 Meldon Ave Oakland CA 94619 Office: 3500 Mountain Blvd Oakland CA 94619

LARSEN, JANET JULIA, educator; b. St. Joseph, Mo., May 17, 1913; d. Harry Lee and Jessie Adelia (Armstrong) Seger; B.A. in Nutrition, U. Iowa, 1935; M.Ed. in Elem. Edn., U. Fla., 1957, Ednl. Specialist, 1967,

Ed.D. in Counselor Edn., 1969; m. Merwin John Larsen, Dec. 11, 1935; children—Mernet Larsen Palmer, Lyndell Larsen Millecchia, Janeen. Tchr. elem. schs., Gainesville, Fla., 1958-61; coordinator exceptional child program Alachua County Fla., mem. staff County Sch. Bd., 1962-65, sch. psychologist, 1966-69; asst. prof. English and counselor edn. U. Fla., Gainesville, 1969-74, asso. prof. arts and scis. Grad. Sch., 1974-80, prof. counselor edn. dept., 1981—, mem. interdisciplinary Child Help Center, J. Hillis Miller Health Center, 1971-75; nat. del. Internat. Fedn. Univ. Women, Japan, 1974; invited speaker 6th World Congress of Reading, Singapore, 1976, 7th, Manila, 1979, 8th, Dublin, 1980, 7th World Congress Internat. Assn. Advancement of Ednl. Research, Belgium, 1977. Mem. adminstrv. bd. 1st United Methodist Ch., Gainesville, 1973—. Mem. AAUW (nat. edn. found. 1973-75, nat. bd. dirs. 1973-76, 81-83, Fla. state pres. 1981-83), Am. Personnel and Guidance Assn., Internat. Reading Assn., Nat. Reading Conf. (exec. bd. 1979-82), Fla. Assn. Sch. Psychologists, Am. Psychol. Assn., Delta Kappa Gamma, Pi Lambda Theta (sponsor U. Fla., nat. long range planning bd. 1978-81). Author monograph: Developmental Individualized Reading in High School, 1973; contbr. articles on adult reading problems, acad. counseling and learning disabilities to profl. jours. Home: 805 NW 20th Terr Gainesville FL 32603 Office: Coll Edn 1209 Norman Hall Univ Florida Gainesville FL 32603

LARSEN, JEAN MAYCOCK, educator; b. Provo, Utah, Feb. 23, 1931; d. Lawrence S. and Lorna (Booth) Maycock; B.S., Brigham Young U., Provo, 1953, M.S., 1960; Ph.D., U. Utah, 1972; m. A. Dean Larsen, Feb. 14, 1958; children—David Lawrence, Paul Joseph, Ann, Charlotte. Tchr. schs. in Oreg. and Utah, 1953-55, 57-58; mem. faculty Brigham Young U., 1960—, assoc. prof. family scis., 1976—, coordinator early childhood edn. program, 1980—. Mem. Nat. Assn. Edn. Young Children, Assn. Childhood Edn. Internat., Utah Assn. Edn. Young Children (past pres., chmn. adv. bd.), Am. Ednl. Research Assn., Soc. Research Child Devel. Republican. Mormon. Author curriculum materials in field; also research. Home: 2678 North 880 East Provo UT 84604 Office: 1319-A SFLC Brigham Young U Provo UT 84602

LARSEN, JUDITH KAEDING, research inst. exec.; b. Fargo, N.D., Nov. 23, 1942; d. Harry C. and Helene E. (Carlson) Kaeding; B.A., Gustavus Adolphus Coll., 1964; M.A., Syracuse U., 1965; Ph.D., U. Calif., Santa Cruz, 1980. Engr., Philco-Ford, Palo Alto, Calif., 1965-67; sr. research scientist Am. Insts. for Research, Palo Alto, 1967-82, prin. research scientist, 1981-82; pres. Cognos Assos., 1982—; cons. to several nat., state govtl. orgns., 1972—. USPHS fellow, 1964-65. Mem. Am. Psychol. Assn., Evaluation Research Soc., Mental Health Assn., Nat. Council Community Mental Health Centers, Peninsula Profl. Women's Network, Women in Electronics. Office: Cognos & Assocs 111 Main St Suite 5 Los Altos CA 94022

LARSEN, LINDA FERMAN, auditor; b. Lehi, Utah, Dec. 27, 1945; d. Roy Leo and Adelaide (Anderson) Ferman; A.S., Snow Coll., 1965; B.S. magna cum laude, U. Utah, 1978; m. Grant K. Larsen, July 22, 1965; children—Rhett, Stephany, Julie. Internal auditor Utah Power & Light Co., Salt Lake City, 1981—. Vice chmn. Sanpete County (Utah) Democratic Party, 1972, sec. 27th Dist. Dem. Party, 1976. Mem. Am. Soc. Women Accts. (pres. Utah chpt. 1980-81), Beta Alpha Psi, Phi Kappa Phi, Phi Theta Kappa. Mormon. Home: 11078 Susan Dr Sandy UT 84092 Office: 1407 W North Temple Salt Lake City UT 84110

LARSEN, MARJORIE SUSAN, bus. woman; b. Reedley, Calif., July 12, 1916; d. William and Elizabeth Susan (Ario) L.; A.B., U. Calif., Berkeley, 1938; M.A., Coll. Pacific, 1947. Tchr., Orestimba High Sch., Newman, Calif., 1940-46; tchr., adminstr. Stockton (Calif.) Unified Sch. Dist., 1946-72; owner Bee Beauty Salon and Gift Shop, Stockton, 1967—; self-employed real estate asso., Stockton, 1971—. Recipient Others award Salvation Army, 1971, Disting. Service award Calif. Assn. Health, Phys. Edn. and Recreation, 1973, Susan B. Anthony award Women's Community Council, 1978; also various certs. of appreciation; life mem. PTA. Mem. Nat. Ret. Tchrs. Assn., Calif. Tchr. Assn. (life), Stockton Ret. Tchrs. Assn., Stockton Bd. Realtors, Delta Kappa Gamma. Republican. Club: Pacific Women's (pres. 1978-80). Author: Speed-a-way, A New Game for Boys and Girls, 3 edit., 1970 (also teaching film). Home: 1754 Middlefield St Stockton CA 95204 Office: 1904 Country Club Blvd Stockton CA 95204

LARSON, ANNA MCMANUS, magazine editor; b. Medford, Mass., Dec. 11, 1917; d. Charles A. and Margarida M. (DeAvellar) McManus; B.S. in Bus. Adminstrn., Simmons Coll., Boston, 1938; m. Conrad S. Larson, Aug. 5, 1967. Mem. staff Harvard U. Grad. Sch. Edn., 1938-73, adminstrv. asst. Center Internat. Affairs, 1971-73; asso. editor Yankee mag., Dublin, N.H., 1973—. Office: Yankee Pub Co Dublin NH 03444

LARSON, DONNA LOU, property mgr.; b. Rapid City, S.D., Mar. 15, 1939; d. Claude and Isma (Van Schiinhoven) Barton; ed. Foothill Coll.; m. Wayne Larson, May 23, 1959. Resdl. loan underwriter United Calif Bank; trustee, investment, loan processor Glendale Fed. Savs. & Loan, now property mgmt. supr. Lic. real estate broker. Mem. Inst. Real Estate Mgmt. Office: 5199 E Pacific Coast Hwy #301N Long Beach CA 90804

LARSON, DOROTHY JANE, nurse; b. Canby, Minn., Apr. 16, 1919; d. Hans H. and Olga Agnetta (Albrectson) Rastad; R.N., Fairview Hosp., Mpls., 1940; m. Selmer Edward Larson, Dec. 6, 1942; children—John, Katherine. Staff nurse hosps. in Minn. and Iowa, 1940-41, 42-51; pvt. duty nurse, 1941-42; supr. ob-gyn Lincoln (Nebr.) Gen. Hosp., 1957-69; sch. nurse Logan Fontenelle Jr. High Sch., Bellevue, Nebr., 1971—; tchr. prenatal classes. Mem. Am. Nurses Assn. Republican. Lutheran. Address: 1116 Tanglewood Ct Bellevue NE 68005

LARSON, EMILIE G., ret. educator; b. Northfield, Minn., Apr. 28, 1919; d. Melvin Cornelius and Frieda (Christiansen) Larson; A.B., St. Olaf Coll., 1940; M.A., Radcliffe Coll., 1946; student U. Chgo., 1951-52. Tchr. Hanska (Minn.) High Sch., 1940-42, Two Harbors (Minn.) High Sch., 1942-43; tchr. J. W. Weeks Jr. High Sch., Newton, Mass., 1946-56, guidance counselor, 1956-81; counselor Warren Jr. High Sch., Newton, 1979-81. Deacon, Univ. Luth. Ch., 1979. Mem. AAUW (state v.p. for program devel., topic chmn. Mass. div. 1975-76; past br. rep. for edn. Boston), Mass., Newton tchrs. assns., St. Olaf Coll. Alumni Assn. (dir. 1982-85), NEA, Virginia Gildersleeve Internat. Fund for Univ. Women Inc., Pi Lambda Theta. Lutheran. Club: Women's City (Boston). Contbr. articles to profl. jours. Address: 1110 W 1st St Northfield MN 55057

LARSON, JANE BALE, interior design firm exec.; b. Dickinson, N.D., Sept. 30, 1946; d. Stanley Walter and Hazel Eleanor (Barteau) Bale; B.S., N.D. State U., 1968. Home fashion coordinator Montgomery Wards, Mpls., 1968-69; staff interior designer McClain, Hedman & Schultz, St. Paul, 1969-72; sales, design mgr. Dayton's Contract Interiors, Mpls., 1972-73; v.p., contract mgr. Contemporary Designs, Inc., Mpls., 1973-79; pres., owner J.B. Larson Assos., Inc., Mpls., 1979—. Mem. adv. bd. design dept. U. Minn. Coll. Home Econs., 1982-84. Recipient Merit award Minn. Soc. of AIA, 1979, Architecture Minn. Pubs. Design award, 1980, Architecture Minn. Advt. award excellence, 1981. Mem. Inst. Bus. Designers, Mpls. C. of C. (cultural activities com. 1980). Home: 19255 Cedarhurst St Deephaven MN 55391 Office: J B Larson Assos Inc 1007 Harmon Pl Minneapolis MN 55403

LARSON, KALEN MARTELLE ACKLEY, public relations counsel; b. Pratt, Kans., Apr. 27, 1939; d. Lloyd Martel and Dorotha Madeline (Millspaugh) Ackley; B.S. in Tech. Journalism, Kans. State U., 1962; m. William R. Larson, Sept. 5, 1964; 1 son, William Martel. News editor Abilene (Kans.) Reflector-Chronicle, 1962-64; staff writer Las Vegas (Nev.) Rev.-Jour., 1964; adminstrv. asst. U.S. Air Force, Spangdahlem Air Base, W.Ger., 1965-67; freelance mag. article writer, Tampa, Fla., 1968; continuity dir., account exec. Parkinson & Assos., Inc., Wichita, Kans., 1968-72; freelance writer and editor, Met. Wichita, 1973-74; news editor, gen. mgr. Wichita Ind., Prairie Jour. Pub. Co., Wichita, 1974-75; columnist The Promoters column Wichita Jour., 1976-78; freelance public relations-advt. counsel, freelance writer, Met. Wichita, 1975—; public relations blood program Wichita region ARC Blood Services, 1978—; sec., dir. Wichita Aviation Inc., 1974-76. Hostess, Nat. Republican Conv., San Francisco, 1964; community service counsel Derby (Kans.) Police Reserves, 1975; precinct committeewoman Kans. Rep. Party, 1976-77. Recipient various communications and writing awards Kans. Press Women, Inc., Nat. Fedn. Press Women. Mem. Nat. Fedn. Press Women, Kans. Press Women (1st v.p. for membership 1972-74, 80-82, pres. 82-84), Wichita Press Women (sec. 1970), Women in Communications (pres. Wichita profl. chpt. 1975-76). Club: Order of Eastern Star. Home: 430 Mary Etta St Derby KS 67037 Office: Public Relations Office Midway-Kans Chpt ARC 707 N Main St Wichita KS 67203

LARSON, KAREN DIANE CRIPPEN, physician; b. Olympia, Wash., Nov. 23, 1949; d. Richard Eugene and Victoria Hildegard (Nelson) Crippen; B.S. summa cum laude, Utah State U., 1971; M.D., U. Ariz. Coll. Medicine, 1975; m. Jon Milton Larson, Nov. 1, 1975; 1 son, Ethan Erik. Med. research asst. Bell Aerospace, Tucson, Ariz., 1976; intern Ariz. Health Scis. Center, Tucson, 1976-77, resident in family practice, 1977-78; resident in phys. medicine and rehab. U. Calif., Irvine, 1978-80; pvt. practice medicine specializing in phys. medicine and rehab., Tucson, 1980—; asso. prof. family practice U. Ariz. Coll. Medicine, Tucson, 1980—; nat. surveyor Commn. for Accreditation Rehab. Facilities, Tucson, 1980—; team physician Pima County High Schs., Tucson, 1980—; mem. staffs St. Mary's Hosp., Ariz. Health Scis. Center, Tucson Med. Center, El Dorado Hosp., St. Joseph's Hosp. (all Tucson). Recipient Recognition award, U. Ariz. Faculty, 1980. Diplomate Am. Bd. Phys. Medicine and Rehab. Mem. AMA, Ariz. Med. Soc., Pima County Med. Soc., Ariz. Soc. Phys. Medicine and Rehab., Nat. Assn. Female Execs., Nat. Audobon Soc., Smithsonian Assos., Ariz. Sonoran Desert Mus. Lutheran. Home: 2111 N El Moraga Ridge Tucson AZ 85705 Office: 2001 W Orange Grove Rd Suite 612 Tucson AZ 85704

LARSON, MARGUERITE HELENE, public relations agy. exec.; b. Chgo., Jan. 12, 1918; d. Spero Peter and Catherine Annie (Heyden) Chevopulos; student Chgo. Pub. Schs.; m. Max E. Larson, Apr. 27, 1957. Various office, clerical and secretarial positions, 1936-57; beautician, beauty culture tchr., 1957-58; file supr. Am. Photocopy Co., Evanston, Ill., 1958-59; librarian Ronald Goodman Public Relations Counsel, Inc., Chgo., 1959-61; v.p., treas., dir. Daniel J. Edelman, Inc., Chgo., 1961—. Mem. Exec. Women Internat., Adminstrv. Mgmt. Soc. Office: 221 N LaSalle St Chicago IL 60601

LARSON, VALERIE ANN, educator; b. Melrose, Mass., May 7, 1953; d. Loring James and Marilyn June (Gascoigne) L.; A.S. in Hotel-Restaurant Mgmt. summa cum laude, Endicott Coll., 1974; B.S. in Hotel-Restaurant Adminstrn., Roosevelt U., 1980. Reservationist, Colonial Hilton Inn, Wakefield, Mass., 1974-75; personnel mgr., adminstrv. asst. to gen. mgr. Sheraton Inn and Conf. Center, Boxborough, Mass., 1975-76, rooms div. mgr., asst. mgr., 1976-77, asst. mgr., service mgr., 1977; instr. Endicott Coll., 1977—, head dept. hotel-restaurant-tourism, 1980—. Vol. supr./trainer 735 Hotline, Melrose, Mass., 1972-74; bd. dirs. Middlesex County (Mass.) Tourism and Devel. Council, 1976. Recipient Departmental award Endicott Coll., 1974 NIFI grantee, 1980-81. Mem. Council on Hotel, Restaurant, and Instl. Edn., Am. Hotel and Motel Assn., Phi Theta Kappa. Home: 53 Albion St Wakefield MA 01880 Office: Endicott Col 1 Hale St Beverly MA 01915

LARSON, VIRGINIA WING, social worker; b. Fort McPherson, Ga., June 2, 1929; d. Albert Gresham and Ida Frances (Oliver) Wing; B.A., U. Miss., 1952; m. Walter Richard Larson, Mar. 26, 1952; children—Laura L., Karen B. (dec.), Frances K., Virginia E. (dec.). Social worker, Augusta, Ga., 1968-69; with Health and Rehab. Services, State of Fla., Bradenton, 1969-80, supr. Childrens services and adoption services, 1972-80; case coordinator family protection team Community Council on Child Abuse and Neglect, Inc., 1980-81. Mem. Am. Public Welfare Assn., Nat. Com. for Prevention of Child Abuse, D.A.R. Democrat. Episcopalian. Home: 308 65th St Ct NW Bradenton FL 33529 Office: 2614 Manatee Ave W Bradenton FL 33529

LARVIN, LINDA ANN, personnel recruiter; b. Ft. Wayne, Ind., Jan. 11, 1954; d. William Charles and Ruth Ann (Miller) Green; B.S. Cum laude, No. Mich. U., 1976; m. Thomas Dixon Larvin, June 21, 1980. Mgr. client services Orgnl. Devel. Systems, Inc., Houston, 1977-78; with B & H Cons., Houston, 1978—, personnel recruiter, 1978—. Cert. personnel cons. Mem. Nat. Assn. Personnel Cons., Tex. Assn. Personnel Cons., Mortar Bd. Republican. Clubs: Desk and Derrick, Houston Area Assn. Personnel Cons. Office: 15835 Park Ten Blvd Suite 107 Houston TX 77084 Office: 15835 Park Ten Blvd Suite 107 Houston TX 77084

LARWOOD, LAURIE, psychologist; b. N.Y., 1941; Ph.D., Tulane U., 1974. Pres., Davis Instruments Corp., San Leandro, Calif., 1966-71, cons., 1969—; asst. prof. organizational behavior State U. N.Y. at Binghamton, 1974-76; asso. prof. psychology, chairperson dept., asso. prof. bus. adminstrn. Claremont (Calif.) McKenna Coll., Claremont Grad. Sch., 1976—; mem. western regional advisory council SBA, 1976-81; dir. The Mgmt. Team; pres. Mystic Games, Inc. Mem. Acad. Mgmt. (editorial rev. bd. Rev. 1977-82, past chmn. status of women interest group), Am. Psychol. Assn., Assn. Women in Psychology. Author: (with M.M. Wood) Women in Management, 1977; mem. editorial bd. Sex Roles, 1979-82, Group and Orgn. Studies, 1982—; columnist Exec. Suite, 1979-80; contbr. numerous articles, papers to profl. lit. Home: 9812 Lindero St Montclair CA 91763 Office: Dept Psychology Claremont McKenna Coll Claremont CA 91711

LARY, MARILYN SEARSON, educator; b. Walterboro, S.C., Sept. 3, 1943; d. Charles Baring and Julia Caroline (Rizer) Searson; A.B., Newberry Coll., 1964; M.S. in L.S., U. N.C., 1965; Ph.D., Fla. State U., 1975; m. Jahangir Lary, Oct. 27, 1975; children—Sara, Heidi. Young adult librarian Greenville County (S.C.) Library, 1965-66; library dir. U. S.C., Sumter, 1966-69; instr. Radford (Va.) Coll., 1969-70; asst. prof. East Carolina U., Greenville, 1970-72; reference librarian Clemson U., S.C., 1972-73; asst. prof. U. Mich., Ann Arbor, 1975-78, U. South Fla., Tampa, 1978—. Mem. ALA, Fla. Library Assn., Assn. Am. Library Schs. Methodist. Home: 1509 Warman Ct Tampa FL 33612 Office: University of South Florida HMS 448 Tampa FL 33620

LASCALA, LUCY BRADFIELD EVANS, abrasive mfg. co. ofcl.; b. Niagara Falls, Ont., Can., Feb. 22, 1927 (parents Am. citizens); d. John William and Sia Mona (Patience) Hudson; student public schs., Niagara Falls, N.Y.; m. Raymond W. Bradfield, July 23, 1949 (dec. Feb. 1963); children—William R., Robert L., Richard W.; m. 2d, William L. Evans, Aug. 7, 1971 (dec. Aug. 1972); children—Mary Beth Evans Finke, William L. III, JoAnn Evans Paris, Donald R.; m. 3d, Samuel S. LaScala, Sept. 10, 1976. Molder office services The Carborundum Co., Niagara Falls, N.Y., 1949-53, telephone/telegraph operator data processing and fin., 1966-69, scheduling sec., 1969-74, office mgr., flight ops. coordinator, 1974—. Vice-pres. children's activities Parents Without Partners, 1964-65, 72-75; active Cub Scouts, Cancer Soc., PTA, Ch. Sch. Riverside Presbyn., Little League Baseball. Named Single Parent of Year, Parents Without Partners, Internat., 1976. Republican. Presbyterian. Clubs: Carborundum Management, Women of Moose. Home: 6887 Joanne Circle Niagara Falls NY 14304 Office: PO Box 477 Niagara Falls NY 14304

LASCOE, MATTI, choreographer, educator; b. Bronx, N.Y.; d. Morris and Sarah (Timmons) New; A.A., Orange Coast Coll., Costa Mesa Calif., 1973; B.F.A., U. Calif. at Irvine, 1976; m. Gerald G. Lascoe, Dec. 18, 1960 (div. 1982); children—Cathy Leigh, Erika Cristine. Choreographer original prodn. Mother Earth at So. Coast Repertory Theatre, Costa Mesa, Calif., 1970, many other musicals; artistic dir., choreographer Matti Lascoe Dance Theater Co., 1972—; organizer 1st performing arts festival Huntington Beach, 1974; faculty Orange Coast Coll., Costa Mesa, 1975—; founder Afro-Haitian Dance Ensemble, 1982—; cons., lectr. in field. Mem. Allied Arts Commn. City of Huntington Beach, 1973-77; chmn. dance com., bd. dirs. Orange County Arts Alliance, 1977. Nat. Endowment for Arts choreography work fellow, 1975, 78; Calif. Arts Commn. grantee, 1975. Mem. Assn. Am. Dance Cos. (sec. So. Calif. chpt. Western div. 1975), Calif. Dance Educators Assn. Democrat. Choreographer: fiveforoctoberfive, 1974, Ellipsis, 1974, Deja Vu, 1974, Jubilatore, 1972, Little Green Box on Modale, 1974, Quasi, 1973, Thursday Between Three and Five, 1972, Hemidemisemiquaver, 1973, Marion's Garden, 1973, Synaptic Junction, 1972, Exit, 1973, The Great American Marble, 1975, Fourth/Street, 1976, Zero/Lot/Line, 1977, Nobody Ever Got a Ticket on the Bus, 1978; A Rainbow in Curved Air, 1978, Carnival, 1980, Witch Doctor, 1981, Possession, 1981, Highlife, 1982. Home: 1044-D Cabrillo Park Dr Santa Ana CA 92701

LASHLEE, JOLYNNE VAN MARSDON, army officer, nurse, adminstr.; b. Asheville, N.C., May 22, 1948; d. William Reid and Frances (Furey) Van Marsdon; B.S. in Nursing, U. Fla., 1971; M. Health Care Adminstrn., Baylor U., 1982. Team leader surg. specialties Shand Teaching Hosp., Gainesville, Fla., 1971; commd. lt. U.S. Army Nurses Corps, 1971, advanced through grades to maj., 1981; asst. head nurse organ transplant service unit Walter Reed Hosp., Washington, 1972; staff nurse surg. ICU, head nurse multi-service nursing unit Nurnberg, W. Ger., 1972-75; head nurse recovery room William Beaumont Army Med. Center, Ft. Bliss, El Paso, Tex., 1975-76, dep. dir. patient care specialist course, 1976-78; ednl. coordinator, project officer U.S. Lyster Hosp., Ft. Rucker, Ala., 1978; adminstrv. resident Madigan Army Med. Center, Tacoma, 1981-82; chief nurse methods div. Walter Reed Hosp., 1982—. Active Nat. Hospice Orgn.; Boy Scouts Am. Mem. Am. Hosp. Assn., Am. Coll. Hosp. Adminstrs. (affiliate), Am. Assn. Critical Care Nurses, Baylor U. Healthcare Adminstrs. Alumni. Home: 15635 Millbrook Ln Laurel MD 20707 Office: Directorate Resources Mgmt Walter Reed Army Med Center Washington DC 20012

LASKA, VERA ORAVEC, educator; b. Kosice, Czechoslovakia, July 21, 1928; Ph.D., U. Chgo., 1959; m. Andrew Josephus Laska, Nov. 5, 1949; children—Thomas Vaclav, Paul Andrew. Chmn. div. social scis. Regis Coll., Weston, Mass., 1966—, prof. Am. history, 1979—. Mem. Weston Hist. Commn., 1973-77, chmn., 1974-75; mem. adv. bd. Mass. Bicentennial Commn., 1974-77. Named Outstanding Tchr. of Am., 1972. Mem. Am. Hist. Assn., Pan Am. Soc., New Eng. History Tchrs. Assn. (v.p. 1981—), Nat. Assn. Fgn. Student Affairs, Czechoslovac Soc. Arts and Scis. in Am. Clubs: Masaryk (Boston and U. Chgo.). Author: Remember the Ladies, 1976; Czechs in America, 1633-77, 1978; Franklin and Women, 1979; Benjamin Franklin, Diplomat, 1982; Women in the Resistance and in the Holocaust, 1983. Home: 50 Woodchester Dr Weston MA 02193 Office: Regis Coll Weston MA 02193

LASKER, MARY (MRS. ALBERT D. LASKER), civic worker; b. Watertown, Wis.; d. Frank Elwin and Sara (Johnson) Woodard; A.B. cum laude, Radcliffe Coll.; LL.D., U. Wis.; postgrad. Oxford U.; L.H.D. (hon.), U. So. Calif., U. Calif., Berkeley, Bard Coll., Woman's Med. Coll. Pa., N.Y.U., N.Y. Med. Coll., Jefferson Med. Coll., Phila.; LL.D., Columbia U.; m. Paul Reinhardt (div.); m. 2d, Albert D. Lasker. Art dealer; connected with Reinhardt Galleries, N.Y.C., arranging benefit loan exhbns. outstanding old and modern French masters and selling pictures to collectors and museums; with husband established med. research found. Albert and Mary Lasker Found. which gives Albert Lasker awards for outstanding contbns. med. research, pub. health adminstrn., 1942. Trustee Research to Prevent Blindness; hon. chmn. bd. dirs. Am. Cancer Soc.; pres. bd. United Cerebral Palsy Research and Ednl. Found.; mem. adv. com. to dir. NIH; chmn. Nat. Health Edn. Com.; adv. council Ad Council; bd. dirs. Norton Simon Mus. Decorated chevalier, officer French Legion of Honor; recipient Presdl. Medal of Freedom, 1969. Office: 865 UN Plaza New York NY 10017 *

LASKY, LUCY, computer co. exec.; b. N.Y.C., Sept. 26, 1942; d. Frederick and Ethel Marjorie (Axelbaum) Kinzler; B.A. in Psychology and English, Queens Coll., 1964; M.S. in Psychology and Counseling, Hunter Coll., 1976; children—Nina Carole, Dara Suzanne. Supr., group leader Distritio Health and Drug Program, N.Y.C., 1972-75; pres. Photogram Ltd., N.Y.C., 1975-79; div. sales mgr. So. Pacific Communications, N.Y.C., 1978-81; sr. mktg. rep. Datapoint, N.Y.C., 1981-82; sales mgr. TDX Systems, N.Y.C., 1982—. Bd. dirs. Project Return, 1973—. Mem. Nat. Assn. Female Execs. Home: 290 Riverside Dr New York NY 10025 Office: TDX Systems 90 William St New York NY 10038

LASNIER, RINA, writer; b. St.-Gregoire d'Iberville, Que., Can., Aug. 6, 1910; d. Moise and Laura (Galipeau) Lasnier; Docteur Honoris Causa, U. Montreal (Que., Can.), 1977. Author 24 books of prose, poetry, and on theater; mem., v.p. Council of Arts Que. Recipient Prix Duvernay, 1957, Prix Molson, 1964, Smith prize U. Mich., 1974, Prix France-Can., 1974, Prix David, Province Que., 1974, Prix Edgar-Poe, France, 1979. Mem. Academie canadienne francaise, Societe royale du Canada, Institut Gracian, academie internationele. Roman Catholic.

LASSER, GAIL MARIA, psychologist, educator; b. Upper Saddle River, N.J., Feb. 29, 1952; d. Dominick A. and Genevieve M. Sanzo; B.A., Seton Hall U., 1971; teaching cert. William Paterson Coll., 1973; M.A., Montclair State Coll., 1975; cert. staff psychologist, N.J., 1977; m. Lloyd M. Lasser, Aug. 31, 1978; children—Michael, Jason. Public relations rep. European Health Spa, 1970-71; med. asst. Sci. Prevention and Rehab. Assn., 1973; grad. teaching and research asst. Montclair State Coll., 1973-74; clin. asst. Dr. Brower, 1974; instr. psychology Essex County Coll., 1976-77; clin. psychologist intern Community Mental Health Center, Mt. Carmel Guild, Newark, 1976-77; lectr. St. Michaels Med. Center-N.J. Coll. Medicine, 1977-80; instr. psychology Bergen Community Coll., Paramus, N.J., 1977—; asst. to ct. adminstr. Bergen County Cts., 1977-78. Mem. Am. Psychol. Assn., Am. Soc. for Psychical Research, Pi Lambda Theta, Psi Chi. Home: 75 Rolling Ridge Rd Upper Saddle River NJ 07458

LASSITER, HANNAH LOUISE, sch. adminstr.; b. Selma, Ala.; d. John Henry and Willie Ann (Givan) Edwards; B.S., Tuskegee Inst., 1959; M.S. in Spl. Edn. Adminstrn. and Supervision, Loyola Coll., Balt., 1966, M.S., 1976; m. E. Lee Lassiter, June 11, 1960. Tchr., Carver High Sch., Montgomery, Ala., 1959-61; successively tchr., dept. head, spl.

asst., summer sch. prin., asst. prin. Balt. City Sch. System, 1963—. Youth fellowship advisor, Sunday sch. tchr., Women's Day chair Mt. Ararat Baptist Ch. Recipient merit award Tuskegee Inst. Nat. Assn., 1975, Mayor's award for service, Balt., 1976, Nat. Sojourner Truth award for service Md. Ho. of Dels., 1980. Mem. Public Sch. Adminstrs. and Suprs. Assn., Phi Delta Kappa. Club: Balt. Tuskegee Alumni. Address: 7200 Seymour Pl Baltimore MD 21207

LASSITER, PATRICA ALFONSO, utility co. exec.; b. Balt., Oct. 13, 1945; d. Joaquin and Thelma O. (Overton) Alfonso; B.S. in Math., Morgan State U., 1972, M.B.A., 1976; postgrad. (Univ. fellow in organizational and community systems) Johns Hopkins U., 1981-82; m. Eric H. Lassiter, Mar. 11, 1979. With Group Hdqrs., Chesapeake & Potomac Telephone Co., Silver Spring, Md., 1973—, service counselor network ops./bus. services, 1975-79, asst. mgr. fin. and public affairs dept. div. cost analysis, 1979—; dir. Marketel, Inc., cons. firm, Columbia, Md., 1976-81; rep. for Career Seminar, Paris, 1976; designer, coordinator career devel. workshops Careerscope, Inc., Columbia, 1981-82. Named Outstanding Young Woman Am., U.S. Jaycees, 1978. Mem. Assn. M.B.A. Execs., Nat. Assn. Female Execs. Research on career/life planning. Home: 5368 Racegate Run Columbia MD 21045 Office: 8757 Georgia Ave Silver Spring MD 20910

LASSITER, RUBY FREEMAN, social worker, educator; b. Wilson, N.C., Feb. 5, 1930; d. Julius F. and Pattie (Hagan) Freeman; B.A., W.Va. State U., 1951; M.S.W., Ariz. State U., 1969; m. Harvey G. Lassiter, Nov. 22, 1952; children—Anthony, Harvey C., Honore D., Julius P. Dir. social services N.Mex. Dept. Human Services, 1962-71; asst. prof. social work N. Mex. State U., Las Cruces, 1971—. Grad. fellow N.Mex. Dept. Human Services, 1967. Mem. NAACP (br. pres. 1981—), Nat. Assn. Social Workers, Acad. Cert. Social Workers, Council Social Work Edn., Council Family Relations, N.Mex. Council Family Relations, Alpha Kappa Alpha. Home: 5638 Lassiter Rd Las Cruces NM 88001 Office: Box 35W N Mex State U Las Cruces NM 88001

LASSWELL, MARCIA, psychologist, educator; b. Oklahoma City; B.A., U. Calif., Berkeley, 1949; M.A. in Social Psychology, U. So. Calif., 1952; postgrad. U. Calif., Riverside, 1965-66, U. N.C., 1967; m. Thomas Lassell, May 29, 1950; children—Marcia Jane, Thomas Ely, Jr., Julia Lee. Lectr. Pepperdine Coll., Los Angeles, 1952-54, asst. prof., 1959-60; pvt. practice psychotherapy 1959—; vis. asso. prof. Scripps Coll., Claremont, Calif., 1968-69; spl. faculty Law Center, U. So. Calif., Los Angeles, 1969-75, vis. prof. summer 1971; vis. prof. Occidental Coll., Los Angeles, 1971-72; asso. clin. dir. marriage and family grad. program U. So. Calif., 1975—; asst. prof. dept. behavioral sci. Calif. State U., Pomona, 1960-64, asso. prof., 1964-69, prof., 1970—, chmn. dept. behavioral sci., 1964-69; lectr. U. Calif., Riverside, 1964-74; cons. to various schs., sch. dists. and legal agys., 1965-70; mem. staff spl. project for alcoholics and narcotics offenders Calif. State Prison System, 1970-73. Bd. dirs. Planned Parenthood, San Gabriel Valley, 1970-75, Pomona Counseling Service, 1970-80, Omega Found., 1975—, Taylor-Dimont Counseling Center, 1975—, Los Angeles Family Inst., 1978—; Menninger Found. fellow, 1979—; recipient Outstanding Tchr. award Calif. State U., 1971. Fellow Am. Assn. for Marital and Family Therapy (dir. 1970-72, chmn. public relations and publs. com. 1974-80); mem. Am. Sociol. Assn. (constitution revision com. 1978-79), Pacific Sociol. Assn. (chmn. counseling div. 1979-80), Am. Assn. Sex Educators, Counselors and Therapists, So. Calif. Assn. Marriage and Family Therapy (pres. 1972-73), AAAS, Phi Kappa Phi, Pi Gamma Mu, Alpha Kappa Delta. Author: College Teaching of General Psychology, 1967; Love, Marriage and Family, 1973; co-author; No-Fault Marriage, 1976; Styles of Loving, 1979; Marriage and the Family, 1982; contbr. articles to popular mags. and profl. publs.; monthly columnist McCall's Mag., 1977-80; editorial bd. Jour. Marital and Family Therapy, 1975—, Jour. of Divorce, 1981—. Home: 875 Hillcrest Dr Pomona CA 91768 Office: 1770 N Orange Grove Ave Suite 208 Pomona CA 91767

LASSWELL, SHIRLEY ANN BASSO SLEISINGER (MRS. FRED D. LASSWELL, JR.), lit. promoting co. exec.; b. Detroit, 1924; d. Michael and Clara (Leasia) Basso; grad. high sch.; m. Stephen Slesinger, Oct. 1949 (dec. 1953); 1 dau., Patricia Ann Slesinger; m. 2d, Fred D. Lasswell, Jr., June 1964. Appeared with Olsen & Johnson Show, 1941-49; pres. Stephen Slesinger, Inc., N.Y.C., Tampa, Fla., 1958—; pres. Red Ryder Enterprises, Inc., Hawley Publs., Inc., Tele-Comics, Inc.; owner U.S. and Canadian rights Winnie-the-Pooh Mdse., 1929—; owner comic strips Red Ryder, Little Beaver, King of the Royal Mounted, Ozark Ike; asso. Zane Grey, Inc. in motion picture field, promotion sales comic books based on famous Western stories. Mem. Tampa Aux. Power Squadron. Clubs: Krewe of Venus, St. Petersburg Yacht. Home: 5108 Longfellow Ave Tampa FL 33609 Office: 1111 N Westshore Blvd Tampa FL 33607

LAST, DIANNA LINN SCHNEIDER, electronics co. exec.; b. Canton, Ohio, Dec. 29, 1944; d. Ld Mervyn and Veronica Lee Schneider; B.A. in German, Ohio State U., 1977; m. David D. Last, Nov. 29, 1969. Research asst. physics Ohio State U., 1965-66; programmer, analyst RANCO, Inc., Columbus, Ohio, 1966-68; with Honeywell, Inc., 1968—, telecommunications cons., Orlando, Fla., 1978-79, mgr. networking edn. programs, Phoenix, 1979-82, mgr. distributed systems edn., Phoenix, 1982—; mem. exec. com., employment adv. com. Center Continuing Edn. Women, Orlando, 1972—; condr. bus. seminars Valencia Community Coll., Orlando, 1972-79, Am. Grad. Sch. Internat. Mgmt., Phoenix, 1982—; cons., speaker in field. Sunday sch. tchr., bishop's com. mem. St. John Baptist Episcopal Ch., Phoenix, 1980—; chmn. local adv. involvement Phoenix Coll.; bus. adv. Internat. Bus. Orgn., Am. Grad. Sch. Internat. Mgmt. Mem. IEEE (past vice chmn. programs), Soc. Data Educators. Home: 11611 N 30th Ln Phoenix AZ 85029

LAST, RUTH EDITH, actress, publicist; b. N.Y.C., May 31, 1934; d. Max A. and Fannie (Litt) L.; B.S., N.Y.U., 1954; 1 son, Adam. Creator, operator Singles Phone, telephone daily program of events for single people, N.Y.C., 1978—, also the Last Word, daily program of art events, concerts; actress appearing in films, including Fort Apache, Endless Love; appears in radio and TV commls., programs and narrations, N.Y.C. Mem. AFTRA (mem. nat. and local bd. 1979—), Nat. Acad. TV Arts and Scis., Screen Actors Guild, Actors Equity Assn. Democrat. Jewish. Home: 440 West End Ave New York NY 10024

LASTER, DEBORAH NANETTE, newspaper editor; b. Winona, Miss., Nov. 1955; d. Melvin Harris and Frances (Taylor) L.; student Holmes Jr. Coll., 1973-75, U. Miss., 1975-76. Sports writer, photographer Daily Sentinel-Star, Grenada, Miss., 1976, gen. assignment news reporter, photographer, 1977, acting mng. editor, 1978, mng. editor, 1979—. Mem. Nat. Fedn. Press Women, Sigma Delta Chi. Baptist. Home: PO Box 192 Duck Hill MS 38925 Office: 158 S Green Grenada MS 38901

LATHAM, ALICE FRANCES PATTERSON, pub. health nurse; b. Macon, Ga., Dec. 18, 1916; d. Frank Waters and Ruby (Dews) Patterson; R.N., Charity Hosp. Sch. Nursing, New Orleans, 1937; student George Peabody Coll. Tchrs., 1938-39; B.S. in Pub. Health Nursing, U. N.C., 1954; M.P.H., Johns Hopkins U., 1966; m. William Joseph Latham, July 21, 1940; children—Jo Alice (Mrs. Robert S. Solomon), Marynette, Lauruby Cathleen. Staff pub. health nurse assigned spl. venereal disease study USPHS, Darien, Ga., 1939-40; county pub. health nurse Bacon County, Alma, Ga., 1940-41; USPHS spl. venereal disease project, Glynn County, Brunswick, 1943-47; county pub. health nurse Glynn County, 1949-51, Ware County, Waycross, 1951-52; pub. health nurse supr. Wayne-Long-Brantley-Liberty Counties, Jesup, 1954-56 dist. dir. pub. health nursing Wayne-Long-Appling-Bacon-Pierce Counties, Jesup, 1956-70; dist. chief nursing S.E. Ga. Health Dist., 1970-79, organizer mobile health services, 1973—. Exec. dir. Wayne County Home Health Agy., 1968-80; exec. dir. Ware County Home Health Agy., 1970-79, mem. exec. com., 1978—; mem. governing bd. S.E. Ga. Health Systems Agy., 1975—; mem. governing bd. Health Dept. Home Health Agy., 1978—, also author numerous grant proposals. Bd. dirs. Wayne County Mental Health Assn., 1959, 60, 61, 81, 82, Wayne County Tb Assn., 1958-62; a non-alcoholic organizer Jesup group Alcoholics Anonymous, 1962-63; mem. adv. council Ware Meml. Hosp. Sch. Practical Nursing, Waycross, Ga., 1958; mem. Altar Guild, St. Paul's Episcopal Ch., 1979—, vestrywoman, 1981-82. Recipient recognition Gen. Service Bd., Alcoholics Anonymous, Inc. Fellow Am. Pub. Health Assn.; mem. Am., 8th Dist. (pres. 1954-58, sec. 1958-60, dir. 1960-62, 1st v.p. 1962), Ga. (exec. bd. 1954-58) nurses assns., Ga. Pub. Health Assn. (chmn. nursing sect. 1956-57), Ga. Assn. Dist. Chiefs Nursing (pres. 1976). Contbr. to state nursing manuals. Home: 115 Harper St Jesup GA 31545

LATHAM, CAROLINE JANET MACDONALD, state ofcl., home economist; b. Raymond, Wash., Jan. 9, 1917; d. John Richard and Alice Alzina (Campbell) MacDonald; A.A., Grays Harbor Coll., 1937; student U. Wash., 1938-39; B.S. in Home Econs., U. Idaho, 1956; M.S. in Home Econs. Edn., 1965; m. Charles A. Latham, Nov. 19, 1938 (div. June 1966); 1 son, Richard E. Buyer, Fredrick & Nelson, 1938; tchr. Buhl (Idaho) High Sch., 1943-64; grad. asst., vis. prof. U. Idaho, 1964-65; asst. state supr. home econs. Idaho Bd. for Vocat. Edn., Boise, 1965-72, acting state supr., 1972-73, state supr. home econs. edn., 1973—. Bd. dirs. Future Homemakers Am., 1966-68, 76-78; circle pres. First Methodist Ch., 1974. Recipient hon. chpt. degree Idaho Assn. Future Homemakers Am., 1955, hon. state degree, 1956; named Outstanding Buhl Bus. Women, 1958; Iowa State U. fellow, 1967; Mich. State U. fellow, 1969. Mem. Home Econs. Edn. Assn., Am. Vocat. Assn., Am. Home Econs. Assn., Nat. Assn. State Suprs. Home Econs. (pres. 1975), Idaho Home Econs. Assn. (pres. 1974-75), Boise C. of C. (sec. women's div. 1969), Bus. and Profl. Women, Phi Omicron Upsilon, Delta Kappa Gamma. Methodist. Office: Idaho Bd for Vocat Edn 650 W State St Boise ID 83720

LATHAM, EMILEIGH MAXWELL, communications exec.; b. Pink Hill, N.C., Oct. 26, 1923; d. Hugh Edgar and Emily (Turner) M.; student Woman's Coll., Univ. N.C., 1940-42; B.A. in Journalism, U. N.C., 1944; m. Herald Rowe Latham, May 26, 1951; children—Lynn Corbell, Diann, Herald Jeffrey. News dir. Sta WTAR-AM-FM-TV Norfolk, Va., 1947-51; public relations mgr., products div. Holiday Inns, Inc., Memphis, 1972-74; community relations dir. Sta. WKNO-TV-FM, Memphis, 1974-76; project coordinator Auction, Sta. WNET, N.Y.C., 1977; asst. dir. community relations L.I. Coll. Hosp., Bklyn., 1978; asst. dir. public affairs Fairfax Hosp. Assn., Springfield, Va., 1981—. Mem. Women in Communications, Inc., Methodist. Editor: Pacesetter, Holiday Inns, Inc., 1973; Healthline, L.I. Coll. Hosp., 1978. Home: 5303 Queensberry Ave Springfield VA 22151

LATHAM, MARY ELIZABETH, clergywoman; b. Cin.; d. Lawrence Lorenzo and Eugenia (Peters) Latham; B.A. cum laude, Asbury Coll., 1929. Tchr. math. and Latin, McAfee High Sch., Mercer County, Ky., 1929-32; entered ministry of evangelism Ch. of the Nazarene, 1933, ordained to ministry, 1937; traveled in work of evangelism and Christian edn., 1937-48; internat. dir. vacation Bible schs. Dept. Ch. Schs., Kansas City, Mo., 1948-67; dir. audiovisuals Ch. of the Nazarene, 1962-74; chmn. audiovisual com. Council of Chs. Greater Kansas City, 1955-58, chmn. com. on communications edn., 1966-67; chmn. Latham Communications, 1975—; also lectr. Recipient Albert F. Harper award Adult Ministries, Ch. of Nazarene, 1980. Author: Vacation Bible School, Why, What, and How, 1954, 9th rev. edit., 1968; Adventures with Jesus, 1948, rev. edits., 1951, 54, 57, 60, 63; Teacher, You Are an Evangelist, rev. edit., 1977; contbr. numerous covers and articles to periodicals; dir. prodn. films The Great Transition, motion picture of Nazarene Colls., 1964; Sing His Wonderful Name, 1965; Would You Believe It?, 1967; The Debtors and They Do Not Wait, 1968; The Way Out and God's Word for Today's World, 1969; Moving Ahead, 1970; Just for the Love of It, 1971; To Make a Miracle, 1972; To New Worlds, 1972; The Church of the Nazarene, 1974; The Alabaster Story, 1974; dir. filmstrips with cassettes How Young Is Our Welcome? and What Made the Orange Go Away?, 1976. Address: 10268 Cedarbrooke Ln Kansas City MO 64131

LATHEM, BETTY BROOKS, mgmt. cons. firm, exec.; b. Griffin, Ga., Aug. 16, 1931; d. Raymond England and Annie Ezelle (Chappell) Brooks; student public schs., Griffin, Ga.; m. Charles Malcolm Lathem, July 18, 1950; children—Charles Thomas, Richard Lee, Betty Kathryn. With So. Bell Telephone Co., Griffin, Ga., 1949-50, J.D. Jewell, Inc., Gainesville, Ga., 1950-54; part-time sec., various cos., Gainesville, 1954-59; with Jacobs, Matthews & Parker, Architects, Gainesville, 1959-69; self-employed ind. sec., Gainesville, 1969-70; adminstrv. asst. Internat. Mgmt., Gainesville, 1970—, specialist in orgn., research and preparation of bus. and profl. books and articles for publ. Active various charitable orgns. Bd. dirs. CONTACT, Hall County. Democrat. Baptist. Home: 599 Holly Dr NW Gainesville GA 30501 Office: Suite 120 So Bell Bldg 711 Green St NW Gainesville GA 30501

LATHROP, CHERYL ANN, electronics co. exec.; b. Santa Cruz, Calif., Feb. 7, 1947; d. A. Vernon and Joanne Elizabeth (Lovett) L.; A.B., Sacramento State U. with honors, 1968; M.B.A., Stanford U., 1973; m. Bernard Beecham, Apr. 1, 1977. Fin. adminstr. Recon Div., Watkins Johnson Co., Palo Alto, Calif., 1973-75, head fin. planning Recon Div., Palo Alto, 1975-76, head fin. planning CEI Div., Gaithersburg, Md., 1976-78, mgr. adminstrv. services internat., 1978—. Mem. Downtown North Neighborhood Assn., Palo Alto, 1979—. Recipient Bank of Am. Bus. award, 1966. Mem. Peninsula Profl. Women's Network. Democrat. Office: 3333 Hillview St Palo Alto CA 94304

LATHROP, GERTRUDE ADAMS, chemist; b. Norwich, Conn., Apr. 28, 1921; d. William Barrows and Lena (Adams) Lathrop; B.S., U. Conn., 1944; M.A., Tex. Womans U., 1953, Ph.D., 1955. Devel. chemist textiles Alexander Smith & Sons Carpet Co., Yonkers, N.Y., 1944-52; research asso. textiles Tex. Women's U., 1952-56; chief chemist Glasgo Finishing Plant div. United Mchts. & Mfrs., Inc. (Conn.), 1956-57, chief chemist Old Fort Finishing Plant div. (N.C.), 1957-63; research chemist United Mchts. Research Center, Langley, S.C., 1963-64; lab. mgr. automotive div. Collins & Aikman Corp., Albemarle, N.C., 1964-78; chief chemist, lab. mgr. Old Fort Finishing Plant div. United Mchts., 1979—. Recipient Disting. Alumni award U. Conn. Sch. Home Econs. and Family Studies, 1980-81. Mem. Am. Chem. Soc., Am. Assn. Textile Chemists and Colorists (sect. research chmn., treas., vice chmn. 1962-64; chmn. edn. com. Piedmont sect. 1977-78), ASTM (chmn. transp. fabrics on flammability com. 1973-75), Bus. and Profl. Womens Club (pres. chpt. 1974-76, Woman of Yr. 1979, 80), Iota Sigma Pi. Home: 301 Mountain St Black Mountain NC 28711 Office: Box 609 Old Fort NC 28762

LATHROP, JOYCE KEEN, civic worker; b. Los Angeles, Nov. 25, 1939; d. William Lavern Trewin and Therese (Wenig) Keen; student Russell Sage Coll., 1957-58, Goucher Coll., 1958-59; B.A., U. So. Calif., 1961; m. Mitchell Lee Lathrop, June 29, 1959 (div. 1977); children—Christin Lorraine, Alexander Mitchell, Timothy Trewin Mitchell. Dir. Assistance League Glendale, 1964-70, Pasadena (Calif.) Sr. Center, 1966-68; dir. jrs. Los Angeles Orphanage Guild, 1968-78, pres., 1974-75, treas., 1972-73, v.p., 1973-74; mem. Symphonians Los Angeles Philharm. Orch., 1969-73, Opera Assos. Music Center, 1965-77, Met. Opera Assos., 1967-78, Aux. Hosp. Good Samaritan, Los Angeles; mem. Nat. Council Met. Opera, N.Y.C., 1970-77; mem. Aux. Pasadena Sr. Center; bd. dirs. Los Angeles Music Center Opera Assn., 1973-74; bd. dirs. Calif. Mus. of Sci. and Industry Council, 1979—, pres., 1981-83, chmn. bd., 1983—. Recipient vol. service award Huntington Meml. Hosp., Pasadena, 1967; decorated officer Mil. and Hospitaller Order St. Lazarus of Jerusalem. Episcopalian. Clubs: Goucher of So. Calif. (treas. 1966-67, sec. 1964-66) (Los Angeles); Valley Hunt (Pasadena). Home: 1375 Inverness Dr Pasadena CA 91103

LATIMER, HEATHER, writer, lectr., photographer; b. Essex, Eng.; d. Robin and Jessie (Rose) Latimer; Pitman's Coll., London, Eng., 1943-45; m. Walther B. Neubauer, Aug. 24, 1957 (dec. Apr. 1976). Photographer's head and shoulders model, 1946-51; free lance writing and publicity projects, 1951-63; TV and radio publicity dir. Standard Reference Works Pub. Co., N.Y.C., 1963-65; asst. to pres. W. H. Schneider, Inc., advt., N.Y.C., 1965-67; patron relations to patrons Met. Opera, N.Y.C., 1968-70; asst. to dir. Bide-A-Wee Animal Protection Assn., N.Y.C., 1970-72; contbg. editor Dogs mag., N.Y.C., 1972-77; freelance writer, 1972—. Pres., Internat. League of N.Y., 1957-67. Recipient award for best nat. series Dog Writers' Assn. Am., 1972. Author: How to Make Money As A Professional Party Organizer in The Great New Leisure Time Market; Tidypet—How To Make Your Dog An Indoor Toilet and Teach Puppy or Grown Dog To Use It; One is Fun; Dogs: Everything You Need to Know to Care for Your Pet; Cats: Everything You Need to Know to Care For Your Pet; Louis Wain-King of the Cat Artists. Office: 155 Crary Ave Apt 1E Mount Vernon NY 10550

LATIMER, MARY JANE MITCHELL, banker; b. Morrilton, Ark., Feb. 11, 1949; d. William Moore, Jr., and Marie (Pledger) M.; B.S. in Math., U. Ark., Fayetteville, 1972; M.B.A. in Fin., Ind. U., 1975; grad. with distinction Southwestern Grad. Sch. Banking, 1981; m. David Anthony Latimer, Dec. 28, 1974. Instr. computer sci. E. Tex. State U., Commerce, 1972-73; credit analyst, loan asso. Am. Nat. Bank & Trust Co., Chgo., 1975-77, comml. loan officer, 1977-78, asst. v.p., br. loan coordinator, 1978-79, v.p., br. loan coordinator, 1979-81; v.p. comml. loans 1st Nat. Bank in Little Rock, 1981, Tex. Commerce Bank, Dallas, 1981—; instr. bus. U. Ark., Little Rock; grader, mem. faculty Southwestern Grad. Sch. Banking. Bd. dirs. Central Ark. YWCA, 1980-81, chmn. fin. com., 1981. Mem. Robert Morris Assos., Am. Soc. Tng. and Devel., Nat. Assn. Bank Women. Methodist. Club: Plaza Athletic (Dallas). Office: PO Box 222265 Dallas TX 75222

LATIMER, SUZANNE LOUISE, hosp. adminstr.; b. Albany, N.Y., Mar. 3, 1954; d. Olin Kenneth and Madeline Louise (Weeks) Latimer; R.N., Albany Med. Center Sch. Nursing, 1975; B.S.N., Russell Sage Coll., 1981, postgrad. 1981—. Gen. staff nurse labor and delivery Albany (N.Y.) Med. Center, 1975-81; physician's asst. Bellevue Maternity Hosp., Schenectady, 1979, interim dir. nursing, 1980, adminstrv. asst. to adminstr., 1980-82, dir. clin. support services, 1982—. Vol., educator Am. Cancer Soc., 1975—; vol., instr., ARC, 1980—. Mem. Nat. Commn. for Certification of Physician's Assts., Am. Acad. Physician's Assts., Nat. Assn. Female Execs., N.Y. Soc. Physicians Assts. Democrat. Roman Catholic. Home: 5M Fenimore Trace Apts Watervliet NY 12189 Office: 2210 Troy Rd PO Box 1030 Schenectady NY 12301

LATIOLAIS, MINNIE FITZGERALD, nurse, hosp. adminstr.; b. Vivian, La., Dec. 26, 1921; d. Thomas Ambrose and Mildred Surita (Nagle) Fitzgerald; R.N., Touro Infirmary, New Orleans, 1943; m. Joseph C. Latiolais, Jr., July 19, 1947; children—Felisa, Diana, Sylvia, Mary, Amelia, Joseph Clifton, III. Staff nurse Ochsner Clinic and Ochsner Found. Hosp., New Orleans, 1943-47; supr. Lafayette (La.) Gen. Hosp., 1960-64; adminstrv. asst., supr. operating room Abbeville (La.) Gen. Hosp., 1964-68; gen. mgr., neurol. surg. nurse J. Robert Rivet, neurol. surgeon, Lafayette, 1968-78; hosp. cons. asso. B.J. Landry & Assos., hosps. cons., Lafayette, 1979—; dir. nursing Acadia St. Landry Hosp., Church Point, 1981-82; supr. supplies, processing and distbn. Univ. Med. Center, Lafayette, 1982—; bd. dirs. S.W. La. Rehab. Assn., 1975—, pres., 1979-80; mem. Mid-La. Health Systems Agy., 1977-82, project rev. chmn., 1978-80; bd. dirs. Acadica Regional Clearing House. Mem. Am. Nurses Assn., Nat. League Nursing, La. State Nurses Assn., La. Hosp. Assn. Nurse Adminstrs., Lafayette Dist. Nurses Assn. (pres. 1967-69). Roman Catholic. Clubs: Lafayette Woman's, Lafayette Garden. Home: 1121 S Washington St Lafayette LA 70501

LATSHAW, FRANCES ELLEN, editor; b. Kansas City, Mo., Apr. 13, 1918; d. Lawrence Wallace and Ellen (Murphy) Latshaw; grad. high sch. Civilian employee narcotics div. Med. Depot, 1942-43; with Pratt-Whitney Co., Kansas City, 1944-45; auditor, recorder deed's office County Ct. House, Kansas City, 1946-59; mng. editor Record Newspaper Co., Kansas City, 1959—. Mem. County Grand Jury, 1967. Del., Nat. Democratic Conv., 1952; sec., v.p. Kansas City Women's Dem. Club, 1955-70; county clk. nominee on Dem. ballot, 1968. Mem. Kansas City Legal Secs. Assn. (corr. sec. 1966, Day in Ct. chmn. 1967-68, parliamentarian 1969), Nat. (del. 1971), Mo. (asst. finance chmn. 1971-72) assns. legal secs., Legal Assn. Kansas City (life). Home: 5925 Holmes St Kansas City MO 64110 Office: 3611 Troost St Kansas City MO 64109

LATSON, PATRICIA CORNETT, nurse, educator; b. Denver, Mar. 28, 1948; d. James A. and Florine Mae (Nemmers) Cornett; B.S., U. Colo., 1970; M.S., Tex. Womans U., 1976; postgrad. Rutgers U., 1983—; m. Harvey H. Latson III, June 6, 1970; children—Kimberly Marie, Keith Michael. Nurse, Cape Fear Valley Hosp., Fayetteville, N.C., 1970-71; instr. nursing Central Tex. Coll., Killeen, 1972-75; acting dir. nursing and inservice edn. St. Joseph's Hosp., Nogales, Ariz., 1976-77; ind. cons., community health nurse Army Regional Med. Center, Frankfurt, W.Ger., 1977-80; instr. U. Utah, Salt Lake City, 1980-82; pub. health nurse, dir. Sr. Citizens Health Screening Clinic, Tooele, Utah, 1981-82. Pack Health program cons. Boy Scouts Am., 1981—; troop leader Girl Scouts U.S., 1981—. Mem. Am. Nurses Assn., Am. Assn. Critical Care Nurses, Utah Nurses Assn., Am. Public Health Assn., Sigma Theta Tau. Democrat. Roman Catholic Office: 26 Hemphill Rd Eatontown NJ 07724

LATTANZIO, BETTY JANE, banker; b. West Grove, Pa., Aug. 31, 1934; d. John Mitchell and Zella Frances (Roberts) Vaughan; B.S. in Bus. Adminstrn., Marywood Coll.; m. Robert V. Lattanzio, Jr., June 17, 1956; children—Marianne, Robert V. III, Mark Stephen. Co-founder, sr. v.p., comptroller Jefferson Bank, Downgintown, Pa.; pres., chief exec. officer First Nat. Bank of Wilmington, Del., also dir.; regional v.p. community banking Am. Bank, Norristown, Pa. Bd. dirs. Bank Adminstrn. Inst., Del.; mem. adv. bd. U. Del. Women's Center; mem. Del. Gov.'s Commn. Status of Women. Recipient Tribute to Women & Industry award YWCA. Mem. Del. Bankers Assn. (chmn. fed. res. legis. com.), Nat. Assn. Bank Women, Robert Morris Assos., Greater Valley Forge C. of C. Baptist. Home: Box 389 Ellicott Rd Avondale PA 19311 Office: 1 Montgomery Plaza Suite 600 Norristown PA 19401

LATTIMER, AGNES DOLORES (MRS. FRANK BETHEL, JR.), physician; b. Memphis, May 13, 1928; d. Arthur Oneal and Hortense

(Lewis) Lattimer; A.B., Fisk U., 1949; M.D., Chgo. Med. Sch., 1954; m. Bernard Goss, Jan. 16, 1952 (div.); 1 son, Bernard C.; m. 2d, Frank Bethel Jr. Rotating intern Cook County Hosp., Chgo., 1954-55, resident pediatrics, 1955-56; resident pediatrics Michael Reese Hosp., Chgo., 1956-57, chief pediatric resident, 1957-58, dir. sect. ambulatory pediatrics, attending physician div. pediatrics; dir. div. ambulatory pediatrics Cook County Hosp. research fellow Chgo. Heart Assn., 1958-59, heart disease control program Chgo. Bd. Health, 1959-61; adj. physician Provident Hosp.; pediatric cons. Bethany Hosp.; mem. staff, chmn. dept. pediatrics Mary Thompson Hosp.; clin. instr. dept. preventive medicine U. Ill. Med. Sch.; asso. prof. dept. pediatrics Chgo. Med. Sch. Vice pres. bd. dirs. Greater Lawndale Conservation Commn. Diplomate Am. Bd. Pediatrics, Nat. Bd. Med. Examiners. Recipient Elsie and Phillip Tsang award, 1968; Disting. Alumni award Chgo. Med. Sch., 1971. Fellow Am. Acad. Pediatrics; mem. AMA, Ambulatory Pediatric Assn. (chpt. sec.-treas. 1974-80), Am. Public Health Assn. Contbr. articles to profl. publs. Office: 1825 W Harrison St Chicago IL 60612

LATTIN, JEAN MEREDITH, social worker; b. Scobey, Mont., Mar. 10, 1942; d. Clarence Leo and Adah Margaret (La Brant) L.; B.A. with highest honors, U. Calif., Santa Barbara, 1963; student U. Bordeaux (France), 1962-63; M.S.W., Calif. State U., 1975. Clin. social work apprentice in pvt. practice, Sacramento, 1975-77; pvt. practice clin. social work, Sacramento, 1977—; clin. social worker Sacramento County Social Services, 1967—; cons. in field; field placement supr. M.S.W. students Calif. State U., Sacramento, 1975-77; tng. coordinator Soc. Clin. Social Work, Sacramento area, 1979—. Coordinator, Organized North Area Emergency Food Closet, 1972; leader Divorce Adjustment Groups, 1976—; dept. chairperson Sacramento County Women's Affirmative Action Caucus, 1977-79. Recipient Outstanding Woman Student award U. Calif., Santa Barbara, 1962; award Bd. Suprs. for Achievements for Benefit of Women, 1978; Humane award North Shore Animal League, 1979-82; cert. of achievement Sacramento Chicano Alliance for Drug Abuse Treatment, 1975. Lic. clin. social worker, Nat. Registry Health Care Providers. Mem. Soc. for Clin. Social Work, Nat. Assn. Social Workers, Assn. Family Therapists No. Calif., Am. Orthopsychiat. Assn., Sacramento Apt. Owners Assn., U. Calif. Alumni Assn., Calif. State U. Alumni Assn., Sacramento County Women's Affirmative Action Caucus (dept. chmn. 1977-79), North Shore Animal League, Sacramento Pets in Need, Sacramento Rescue and Place Pets, Humane Soc., Defenders of Wildlife, Greenpeace, also other environ. protection memberships, Phi Kappa Phi. Club: U. Calif. Alumni Women's. Office: 3333 Watt Ave Suite 209 Sacramento CA 95821

LATTING, PATIENCE SEWELL (MRS. TRIMBLE B. LATTING), mayor; b. Texhoma, Okla., Aug. 27, 1918; d. Frank Asa and Leila (Yates) Sewell; A.B. magna cum laude, U. Okla., 1938; M.A., Columbia U., 1939; m. Trimble B. Latting, Aug. 23, 1941; children—Francelia Latting Wilson, Nancy Sewell Latting Spelman, James Trimble, Cynthia Longley. Asst. to research librarian Chase Nat. Bank, N.Y.C., 1938-39. Mem. Oklahoma City Council, 1967-71; mayor, Oklahoma City, 1971—. Legislation chmn. Okla. Congress Parents and Tchrs., 1960-67; mem. exec. com. Oklahoma City Council PTA's, 1960-62; pres. Edgemore PTA, Oklahoma City, 1963-64; mem. Okla. Gov's Reapportionment Com., 1960, Gov.'s Adv. Com. on Edn., 1964, Oklahoma City Citizens Emergency Fin. Com., 1965; trustee U.S. Conf. Mayors; apptd. officer of ct. to aid in reapportionment Okla. Legislature, 1964; Named Outstanding Sr. Woman, Theta Sigma Phi, U. Okla., 1938; recipient Amy B. Onken award to outstanding undergrad. mem. Pi Beta Phi, 1938, Phi Beta Kappa award to Outstanding Oklahoman, 1976; named Woman of Yr. in Civic Work, Oklahoma City chpt. Theta Sigma Phi, 1961, Outstanding Woman award, 1968; named Outstanding Woman of Okla., Soroptimists, 1969; named hon. col. Okla., 1960. Mem. LWV (mem. Oklahoma City bd. 1958-59), Oklahoma City Tennis Assn. (mem. bd. 1965—), Mortar Bd., Huguenot Soc. Founders of Manakin in the Colony Va., Phi Beta Kappa (v.p. Oklahoma City alumni, 1965—), Alpha Lambda Delta, Sigma Alpha Iota, Chi Delta Phi, Pi Mu Epsilon, Pi Beta Phi (pres. Oklahoma City alumni 1947-48), Delta Kappa Gamma (hon.). Clubs: 20th Century (sec. 1961-62), Oklahoma City Golf and Country, Altrusa (hon.). Instrumental in securing passage of state law permitting local sch. bds. to prohibit high sch. fraternities and sororities, 1953; author of amicus curiae brief filed on behalf of Okla. Congress Parents and Tchrs. dealing with reapportionment of state legislature, 1962. Office: City Hall 200 N Walker St Oklahoma City OK 73102 *

LAUBE, DIANA P., telephone co. exec.; b. Jersey City, June 29, 1934; d. Harold J. and Emily M. Pohl; grad. high sch.; m. Norman Laube, Oct. 3, 1952; children—Susan, Norma, Norman. With Vernon (N.Y.) Telephone Co., 1952—, treas., 1960-72, pres., treas., 1972—. Fin. chmn. United Methodist Ch. Mem. N.Y. State Telephone Assn. (dir. 1978-79), U.S. Ind. Telephone Assn., U.S. C. of C. Republican. Office: PO Box A Vernon NY 13476 *

LAUBE, JANICE RAE, corp. exec.; b. N.Y.C., June 4, 1952; d. Irwin and Arlyne Grace (Melton) Hirschlorn; B.A. in Theater Arts, Harpur Coll., 1974. Asst. personnel mgr. Ziff-Davis Pub. Co., N.Y.C., 1974-77; spl. markets mgr. Steyr Daimler Puch of Am., Secaucus, N.J., 1977—; v.p. Dickinson Rae & Co., Greenwich, Conn., 1981—. Mem. Nat. Assn. Female Execs., Am. Soc. Profl. and Exec. Women, NOW. Club: Heartbreakers (pres. 1981—). Home: 16 Highland Rd Greenwich CT 06830 Office: 85 Metro Way Secaucus NJ 07094

LAUBE, JERRI MARIETTA, ednl. adminstr.; b. Terre Haute, Ind., July 1, 1928; d. George J. and M. Martell (McBride) DeWald; B.S. in Nursing and Psychology, U. Tenn., 1961; M.S. in Nursing, U. Colo., 1969; Ph.D., Tex. Women's U., 1974; m. William B. Laube, Aug. 8, 1947 (dec. Feb. 2, 1979); children—Stephen William, Joan M. Instr., St. Joseph Sch. Nursing, Memphis, 1957-62, St. Paul Sch. Nursing, Dallas, 1962-67; asst. prof. Baylor U. Sch. Nursing, Waco, Tex., 1969-72, asso. prof., 1972-74; prof., chmn. dept. psychiat./mental health nursing Ind. U., Indpls., 1974-80; prof., dean Sch. Nursing, U. So. Miss., Hattiesburg, 1980—; adj. prof. psychology Purdue U. Sch. Sci., Indpls., 1977-80; project dir. psychiat. nursing grants NIMH, 1972-80. Fellow Am. Acad. Nurses; mem. Am. Assn. Marriage and Family Therapy, Am. Psychol. Assn., Am. Group Psychotherapy Assn., Am. Nurses' Assn., Council of Specialists in Psychiat./Mental Health Nursing, Sigma Theta Tau. Roman Catholic. Club: Altrusa Internat. Contbr. articles in field to profl. publs. Home: 611 Cox Ave Hattiesburg MS 39401 Office: U So Miss So Sta Box 5095 Hattiesburg MS 39406-5095

LAUBER, EVELYN GREMLI, real estate broker; b. Sarasota, Fla., July 8, 1917; d. Erwin and Mamie (Rewiss) Gremli; student Juilliard Sch. Music, 1940-42; grad. Realtor Inst.; m. Merritt Russell Lauber, July 28, 1940; children—Merritt Erwin, Douglas Ross. Owner, Erwin Gremli Real Estate, Inc., Sarasota, 1970—. Mem. Adelphi Opera Workshops. Cert. residential specialist, C.R.B. Mem. Sarasota Bd. Realtors, Women's Council Realtors (pres. 1976; Realtor of Year 1977), Multiple Listing Service Sarasota (sec.-treas.), Realtors Nat. Mktg. Inst., Fla. Assn. Realtors. Presbyterian. Club: Order Eastern Star. Home: 230 Scott St Sarasota FL 33580 Office: 1535 2d St Sarasota FL 33577

LAUBER, MIGNON DIANE, food processing co. exec.; b. Detroit, Dec. 21; d. Charles Edmond and Maud Lillian (Foster) Donaker; student Kelsey Jenny U., 1958, Brigham Young U., 1959; m. Richard Brian Lauber, Sept. 13, 1963; 1 dau., Leslie Viane. Owner, operator Alaska World Travel, Ketchikan, 1964-67; founder, owner, pres. Oosick Soup Co., Juneau, Alaska, 1969—. Treas., Pioneer Alaska Lobbyists Soc., Juneau, 1977—. Mem. Bus. and Profl. Women, Alaska C. of C. Libertarian. Club: Washington Athletic. Home: 120 W First St Juneau AK 99801 Office: PO Box 1625 Juneau AK 99802

LAUDER, ESTEE, cosmetics co exec.; b. N.Y.C.; m. Joseph Lauder; children—Leonard, Ronald. Chmn., Estee Lauder Inc., N.Y.C., 1946—. Created Adventure Playgrounds through Estee and Joseph H. Lauder Found., N.Y.C. Mem. N.Y. State Women's Council. Decorated chevalier Legion of Honor (France); recipient Neiman-Marcus Fashion award, 1962; Nat. Cancer Care Found. award, 1963; Spirit of Achievement award Albert Einstein Coll. Medicine, 1968; Kaufmann's Fashion Fortnight award, 1969; Bamberger's Designer's award, 1969; Gimbel's Fashion Forum award, 1969; Internat. Achievement award Frost Bros., 1971; Pogue's Ann. Fashion award, 1975; award Assn. Better N.Y., 1977; medaille de Vermeil de la Ville de Paris, 1979; 4th Ann. award for Humanitarian Service Girls Club N.Y., 1979; 25th Anniversary award Greater N.Y. council Boy Scouts Am., 1979; Ayres Look award, 1981; named one of top ten outstanding women in bus., 1970. Address: 767 Fifth Ave New York NY 10022

LAUDER, VALARIE ANNE, editor, educator; b. Detroit, Mar. 1, 1926; d. William J. and Murza Valerie (Mann) L.; A.A., Stephens Coll., Columbia, Mo., 1944; postgrad. Medill Sch. Journalism, Northwestern U. With Chgo. Daily News, 1944-52, columnist, 1946-52; lectr. Sch. Assembly Service, also Redpath lectr., 1952-55; freelance writer for mags. and newspapers, 1955—; editor-in-chief Scholasatic Roto, 1962; editor U. N.C., 1975-80, lectr. Sch. Journalism, 1980—; nat. chmn. student writing project Ford Times, 1981—; press rep. Am. Dance Festival, Duke U., 1982—. Mem. nat. fund raising bd. Kennedy Center, 1962-63. Recipient 1st place award Nat. Fedn. Press Women, 1981; 1st place awards Ill. Women's Press Assn., 1950, 1951. Mem. Public Relations Soc. Am. (treas. N.C. chpt. 1982), Women's Press Club N.C. (3d v.p. 1981-83; 1st place awards 1981, 82), Women in Communications (dir. N.C. Triangle chpt., chmn. freedom of info. com.), N.C. Press Women, DAR, Soc. Mayflower Desc. (dir. Ill. Soc. 1946-52), Chapel Hill Hist. Soc. (dir. 1981-83, chmn. publs. com. 1980—), Chapel Hill Preservation Soc. Clubs: Chapel Hill Woman's Order Eastern Star. Office: Howell Hall 021A U NC Chapel Hill NC 27514

LAUDICK, BONNIE BROUWER, social services adminstr.; b. Ft. Wayne, Ind., Sept. 20, 1943; d. Lester J. and Geraldine H. (Smith) Brouwer; B.S., Ind. U., 1965; children by previous marriage—William, Robert. Dir. recreational therapy and phys. edn. Ill. Children's Hosp. Sch., Chgo., 1965-68; supr. activity therapy day program Chgo. Read Mental Health Center, 1975-76; dir. recreational therapy and spl. services Orangegrove Rehab. Hosp., Garden Grove, Calif., 1976-78; dir. activity therapy Riveredge Hosp., Forest Park, Ill., 1978—; water safety instr. and life guard Syracuse (Ind.)-Wawasee Water Safety Council, summer, 1963, 64; guest speaker Chgo. radio talk show, 1966. Vol. fund raiser Nat. Cystic Fibrosis Research Found., No. Ill. chpt., 1968-76; vol. Ravenswood Mental Health Crisis Center, 1974-75. Recipient Plaque award Nat. Cystic Fibrosis Found., 1973, 74, 75, Letter of Commendation, President John F. Kennedy, 1963; named Employee of the Month, Orangegrove Rehab. Hosp., 1977; cert. tchr., Ill. Mem. Nat. Recreation and Park Assn., Nat. Assn. of Activity Therapy and Rehab. Program Dirs., Ill. Parks and Recreation Assn. (Outstanding Program award Therapeutic sect. 1980), Am. Vocat. Assn., Nat. Assn. Drama Therapy, Nat. Therapeutic Recreation Soc. Office: Riveredge Hosp 8311 W Roosevelt Rd Forest Park IL 60130

LAUDONE, ANITA H., lawyer, bus. exec.; b. 1948; B.A., Conn. Coll., 1970; J.D., Columbia U., 1973; married. Admitted to N.Y. State bar, 1973, practiced in N.Y.C., 1973-79; asst. sec. Phelps Dodge Corp., N.Y.C., 1979-80, sec., 1980—. Office: Phelps Dodge Corp 300 Park Ave New York NY 10022 *

LAUFER, BEATRICE, composer; b. N.Y.C.; d. Samuel and Fanny (Silverman) Laufer; student Juilliard Sch. Music, N.Y.C., 1944; m. Theodore Lassoff, Oct. 2, 1940 (dec. July 1955); 1 son, Samuel; m. 2d, Seymour H. Rinzler, Oct. 19, 1969 (dec. May 1970). Composer, Symphony No. 1 (performed by Eastman-Rochester Symphony Orch., 1945-46, performance Germany and Japan under auspices of State Dept., 1948, performed by Nat. Gallery Orch., Washington, 1982; Dance Festival (performed by Eastman-Rochester Symphony, 1946-47); choral compositions: Under the Pines, Spring Thunder performed Tanglewood, 1949, Song of the Fountain, Inter-racial Chorus, UN Freedom celebration, 1952; Small Concerto for Chamber Orch. performed McMillan Theatre, Columbia, 1949-50, Ile, opera, world premiere Royal Opera Co., Stockholm, Sweden, 1958; Second Symphony performed by Oklahoma City Orch., 1961; premiere concerto at Donnell Library Center, 1962; premiere performance Prelude and Fugue for Orch., Brevard (N.C.) Music Center, 1964, Cry! orchestral prelude, Orch. of Am., Town Hall, 1966, Lyric, string trio, Bowdoin Coll. Contemporary Music Festival, 1966; Cry, performed with Eastman-Rochester Symphony, 1968, Shreveport Symphony Orch., 1977, New Orleans Symphony Orch., 1978, N.C. Symphony Orch., 1978, Berkshire Symphony Orch., 1981; In the Throes performed Shreveport Symphony, 1980, New Orleans Symphony Orch., 1982; Conn. Found. of Arts grantee for performance And Thomas Jefferson Said, Norwalk Symphony Orch., 1976; master ceremonies Young Am. Artists, radio sta. WNYC; hostess The Conductor Speaks series Sta. WNYC. Mem. ASCAP, Am. Symphony Orch. League, Am. Music Center. Ile recorded at Yale U. Sch. Music by Nat. Pub. Radio and broadcast nationwide, 1980. Address: PO Box 3 Lenox Hill Sta New York NY 10021

LAUFFER, CAROLYN GIBSON, educator; b. Georgetown, S.C., Dec. 9, 1930; d. Robert James and Lydia (Ray) Gibson; A.B. in English, U. N.C., Greensboro, 1954; M.A., Glassboro (N.J.) State Coll., 1968; Ph.D., Duke U., 1977; m. Richard A. Lauffer, Apr. 9, 1955; children—Daniel, Lisa, Laura. Tchr. public high schs., Camp Lejeune, N.C., 1954-55, Lumberton, N.C., 1958-60, Glassboro, 1964-68; instr. in speech Pembroke (N.C.) State U., fall 1962; asst. prof. English, Campbell Coll., 1968-76, dir. student teaching, 1970-76; head dept. gen. studies Wilson County (N.C.) Tech. Inst., 1976-79; instr. English, Pitt Community Coll., Greenville, N.C., 1979—; mem. Edn. Professions Devel. Act. Inst. for Advanced Study in English (Applied Linguistics) for Trainers of Tchrs., summer 1969. Smith Reynolds grantee, 1970. Mem. Nat. Council Tchrs. English, South Atlantic MLA, Southeastern Conf. Teaching English in Two-Year Coll. Presbyterian. Home: 1600 Ridgeland Rd Raleigh NC 27607 Office: Dept English Pitt Community Coll PO Box 7007 Greenville NC 27834

LAUFFER, MARILYN HEATH BREWSTER, psychologist; b. Akron, Ohio, Mar. 18, 1935; d. Louis Caley and Irma (Brandes) Brewster; B.A. in Psychology cum laude, Allegheny Coll., 1957; M.A. in Psychology (scholar), Bucknell U., 1971; Ph.D. in Psychology, U. Del., 1975; m. James Lauffer, Feb. 9, 1957; children—William, Lori Lynn, Jeffrey. Asso. psychologist Danville (Pa.) State Hosp., 1972-76; asst. prof. psychology Bloomsburg (Pa.) State Coll., 1974-76; cons. psychologist Central Susquehanna Diagnostic and Rehab. Clinic., Sunbury, Pa., 1976-78; pvt. practice clin. psychology, Bloomsburg, 1977—. Bd. dirs., exec. com. Family Counseling and Mental Health Clinic, Bloomsburg, 1979—; bd. dirs. Women's Center, Bloomsburg, 1980—. Mem. Am. Psychol. Assn., Gestalt Inst. Cleve., Internat. Soc. Bioenergetics Analysis, Assn. Humanistic Psychology, Eastern Psychol. Assn., Phi Beta Kappa, Kappa Kappa Gamma (life). Office: 432 W Main St Bloomsburg PA 17815

LAUGHLIN, ALICE MARGARET, educator; b. Malone, N.Y., Feb. 19, 1918; d. John and Rose Ellen (Murray) L.; B.S., St. Joseph Coll., West Hartford, Conn., 1949; M.S., U. Vt., 1954; Ed.D., Columbia U., 1965; postgrad. Fordham U., 1971-76. Lab. technician S.I. Hosp., 1949-50; teaching asst. U. Vt., 1950-52; asst. biochemist Vt. Agrl. Expt. Sta., 1952-56; research chemist Nat. Biscuit Co., 1956-57; research asst. hematology and chemotherapy Columbia-Presbyn. Med. Center, N.Y.C., 1957-61; instr. sci. Sch. Nursing, St. Michael Hosp., Newark, 1961-62; asst. prof. Jersey City State Coll., 1962-67, asso. prof., 1967-74, chmn. dept., 1969-70, prof. chemistry dept., 1974—; resource mem. cons. meeting on chem. curriculum in jr. coll. NSF, 1969; resource mem. long range planning bd. Sch. Nursing St. Francis Hosp., Jersey City, 1963—. Mem. Am. Chem. Soc., Am. Microchem. Soc., Am. Assn. Cereal Chemists, Am. Inst. Chemists, Am. Assn. Clin. Chemists, Am. Soc. Med. Technologists, AAUP, N.J. Soc. Med. Technologists (sci. assembly person biochemistry 1976-78, 79-80), N.Y. Acad. Sci., N.J. Acad. Sci., Iota Sigma Pi. Revisor: Roe's Principles of Chemistry, 12th edit., 1976; mem. editorial panel Mosby's Comprehensive Review of Nursing, 8th edit., 1974. Home: 1225 76th St North Bergen NJ 07047 Office: Chemistry Dept Jersey City State Coll Jersey City NJ 07305

LAUGHLIN, JOAN MARIE, educator; b. Council Bluffs, Iowa, Sept. 11, 1940; d. Matthew John and Helen Frances (Roscoe) Laughlin; B.S., Coll. St. Mary, 1962; M.S., Iowa State U., 1965; Ph.D., Pa. State U., 1974. Tchr. public schs., Lake City, Iowa, 1962-65; chmn. dept. home econs. Mt. St. Clare Coll., 1965-69; asst. prof. U. N. Iowa, Cedar Falls, 1969-72; research asst. Pa. State U., University Park, 1972-74; asst. prof. U. Nebr., Lincoln, 1974-76, asso. prof., 1976-82, prof., dept. chmn. textiles, clothing and design, 1982—. Mem. nat. adv. council Consumer Product Safety Commn., 1978-82. Horton AHEA Found. fellow, 1973-74; EPA grantee, 1980-81, 81-82; N. Central Pesticide Impact Assessment grantee, 1981, 82; recipient Disting. Prof. award, 1982. Mem. Am. Home Econs. Assn. (dir. 1980, profl. sect. unit chmn. 1980-82), Assn. Coll. Profs. Textiles and Clothing (pres. 1979-80), Am. Assn. Textile Chemists and Colorists, ASTM, Internat. Fabricare Inst., Am. Council on Consumer Interests, N.Y. Acad. Sci., AAAS, Nebr. Acad. Sci., Nebr. Geneal. Soc., Lincoln-Lancaster Geneal. Soc., DAR, Sigma Xi, Sigma Delta Epsilon, Omicron Nu, Phi Upsilon Omicron, Sigma Phi Sigma, Gamma Sigma Delta. Democrat. Roman Catholic. Contbr. articles to profl. jours. Office: 234 Home Econs Bldg Lincoln NE 68583-0802

LAUGHLIN, JUDITH ANN, mgmt. devel. exec.; b. Buffalo, Dec. 13, 1947; d. Eugene M. and Catherine L. (Ryan) Larouere; B.S. in Nursing, D'Youville Coll., 1969; M.S. in Community Health Nursing, SUNY, Buffalo, 1972, Ph.D. in Orgnl. Communication and Policy, 1980; m. Daniel E. Laughlin, July 29, 1967. Public health nurse Erie County Health Dept., 1969-70; gen. duty nurse psychiatry E.J. Meyer Hosp., Buffalo, 1971; coordinator lead detection and prevention program Erie County Health Dept., 1972-73; public health nurse cons. Erie County Dept. Mental Health, 1973-75; dir. Erie County Dept. Anti-Rape and Sexual Assault, 1975-77; asst. prof., area dir. health planning and mgmt., nursing SUNY, Buffalo, 1977-81, now clin. asso. prof.; dir. human resources Am. Precision Industries, Inc., Buffalo, 1981-82; owner Mgmt. Devel. Group, Buffalo, 1982—; mgmt. cons. Chmn. Erie County Victim/Witness Coordination Bd., 1978—; bd. dirs. Buffalo chpt. ARC, 1978—, chmn. tng. and devel. com., 1979—; chmn. Erie County Sexual Assault Task Force, 1974; mem. Erie County Energy Com., 1973. Recipient awards for county programs, resolution for leadership in victim services Erie County Legislature, 1979. Mem. Am. Nurses Assn., Internat. Communications Assn., N.Y. State Public Health Assn., Nat. Orgn. Victim Assistance, Am. Soc. Tng. and Devel., Erie County Indsl. Relations Research Assn., Sigma Theta Tau, Pi Lambda Theta. Contbr. articles to profl. jours. Home: PO Box 211 Wales Center NY 14169 Office: 2775 Main St Buffalo NY 14214

LAUGHLIN, MARILYN JEAN, fin. services co. exec.; b. Chgo., Mar. 27, 1936; d. Herman William and Alice (Donahue) Bendig; B.A., Lake Tahoe (Calif.) U., 1959; diploma in reins., Coll. Ins., N.Y.C., 1977; m. Terry Laughlin, May 14, 1966. From sec. to reins. underwriter CNA Ins. Co., 1956-81; v.p. Laughlin Assos., Inc., Roselle, Ill., 1981—. Mem. Nat. Assn. Female Execs. Roman Catholic. Home: 56 N Salt Creek Rd Roselle IL 60172 Office: 100 E Irving Park Rd Roselle IL 60172

LAUGHLIN, MONIQUE MYRTLE, state ofcl.; b. Paton, Iowa, Aug. 30, 1924; d. Irving Leroy Weant and Ella Florence (Bauer) Blaylock; B.A., William Penn Coll., 1949; M.S., So. Ill. U., 1975; Ph.D., Okla. U., 1981; m. Gerald Laughlin, July 15, 1944 (div.); children—Roy Melvin, Owen Willard, James Byron. Asst. v.p., dir., mem. exam. and auditing com. 1st Nat. Bank, Higgins, Tex., 1962-74; dir., sec. bd., mem. exam. and audit com. 1st Bank & Trust Co., White Deer, Tex., 1970-74; alcohol and drug counselor Hill House, Carbondale, 1974-75; Mercy Health Center, Oklahoma City, 1975-76; public relations, staff therapist Community Counseling Center, Oklahoma City, 1977-79; pvt. tng. cons. and counselor, Oklahoma City, 1979-80; petroleum landman Johnco Inc., Oklahoma City, 1981; staff devel. coordinator div. instns. and community services to children Dept. Human Services, Oklahoma City, 1981—. Mem. Adult Edn. Assn., Okla. Adult and Continuing Edn. Assn., Am. Soc. Tng. and Devel., Assn. Labor Mgmt. Adminstrs. and Cons. on Alcoholism, Am. Correctional Assn., Am. Assn. Correctional Tng. Personnel, Am. Public Welfare Assn., Okla. Psychol. Assn., Oklahoma City Womens Forum. Home: 2704 N Meridian Pl Oklahoma City OK 73127 Office: Div Instns and Community Services for Children Sequoyah Bldg Capitol Complex Box 25352 Oklahoma City OK 73125

LAUGHREY, GLADYS, recreation exec.; b. Southport, Eng., May 16, 1924; came to U.S., 1946, naturalized, 1949; d. James Martland and Mary Almond; student Southport Tech. Coll., 1940-42; m. James C. Laughrey, Aug. 8, 1944; children—James S., Patrick A., Sharon A., Kathleen M. Sec., Toyad Corp., Latrobe, Pa., 1952-54; mgr. Laurel Mountain Express, Latrobe, 1957-68; office mgr. Latrobe Country Club, 1968-70, club mgr., 1970—. Served with Woman's Royal Navy Eng., 1942-45. Mem. Ladies Aux. Am. Legion (citizenship chmn. 1967), Club Mgrs. Assn. (dir., sec.-treas., edn. chmn. Pitts.), Nat. Assn. Female Execs., Am. Soc. Profl. and Exec. Women, Club Mgrs. Assn. Am. Club: Heritage Hill Racquet. Home: PO Box 629 Latrobe PA 15650 Office: PO Box 616 Latrobe PA 15650

LAUGHTER, MABEL YOUNG, educator; b. Fletcher, N.C., Jan. 22, 1941; d. Herman and Cora Carolyn (Hill) Young; B.S., Western Carolina U., 1963, M.A., 1970; Ed.D., U. Miss., 1972; m. Joseph Albert Laughter, June 29, 1963; children—Tara Charleen, Alexander Joseph. Tchr. Raleigh (N.C.) City Schs., 1963, Winston-Salem (N.C.)/Forsyth County Schs., 1964, Henderson County Schs., Hendersonville, N.C., 1966-70; social services caseworker Forsyth County Social Services, Winston-Salem, 1965; grad. teaching asst., supr. student tchrs. U. Miss., Oxford, 1970-72; prof. U. Southwestern La., Lafayette, 1972-74; prof., dir. remedial reading clinic for univ. students East Carolina U., Greenville, N.C., 1974—; maj. cons. exptl. middle sch. project Right to Read, Moore County, N.C. Chmn. Pitt County Task Force for Improvement of Middle Schs. Curriculum and Instructional Method. Mem. Internat. Reading Assn., Assn. Tchr. Educators, Phi Kappa Phi, Alpha Delta Kappa. Republican. Presbyterian. Club: Lake Ellsworth. Author: What Teachers Should Know About Reading, 1974; Parents, Too, Can Help Their Child Read, 1979; Shortage of Appropriate Level Reading Materials for Your Students?, 1979; Replacement for the Trusted Place Marker for Beginning and Remedial Readers, 1979; Rewriting Materials on a Lower Readability Level, 1979; Speed Reading for Faster, More Efficient Comprehension, 1982. Home: 3202 Ellsworth Dr Greenville NC 27834 Office: 246 Speight St Greenville NC 27834

LAURENCE, MARGARET, novelist; b. Neepawa, Man., Can., July 18, 1926; d. Robert Harrison and Margaret Campbell (Simpson) Wemyss; B.A., United Coll. (now U. Man.), 1947, hon. degree, 1966; D.Litt., McMaster U., 1970, Trent, 1971, Toronto, 1971, Carleton, 1974, Brandon, 1975, U. Western Ont., 1975, Mt. Allison, 1976, Simon Fraser, 1977, York, 1980; LL.D. (hon.) Dalhousie, 1971, Queen's U., 1975; others; m. John Fergus Laurence, 1947 (div. 1969); 2 children. Writer-in-residence U. Toronto, 1969-70; author: A Tree for Poverty, transl. This Side Jordan, 1960; The Prophet's Camel Bell, 1963; The Tomorrow-Tamer, 1963; The Stone Angel, 1964; A Jest of God (Gov. Gen. Award for fiction 1966), Long Drums and Cannons (essays on Nigerian lit.), 1968; The Fire Dwellers, 1969; Jason's Quest (children's fiction), 1969; A Bird in the House, 1970; The Diviners (Gov. Gen. Award for lit. 1974), 1974; Heart of a Stranger (essays), 1976; The Olden Days Coat (children's), 1979; Six Darn Cows (children's), 1979; The Christman Birthday Story (children's), 1980; contbr. short stories to publs. including: Prism. Tamarack Rev., Saturday Evening Post, Ladies Home Jour., Chatelaine, Atlantic Monthly, Argosy, Winter's Tales; contbr. articles to Holiday Mag. Recipient award best novel by Canadian, Beta Sigma Phi, 1960, best Can. short story award and Pres.' medal U. Western Ont., 1961, 62, 64, Molson Award, 1975; Periodical Distbrs.' award, 1977, award of merit City of Toronto, 1978; named Woman of Year Toronto women's br. B'nai B'rith, 1976; decorated companion Order of Can., 1971. Office: care Writers Union 24 Ryerson St Toronto ON Canada

LAURENTI, LUELLEN WATSON, educator; b. Charleston, W.Va., Aug. 27, 1939; d. Stephen Allen and Alice (Counts) Watson; B.A. in Spanish and French, Marietta Coll., 1961; M.A. in Spanish and Linguistics, U. Ill., Urbana, 1963, postgrad., 1969-72; m. Joseph Lucian Laurenti, June 10, 1967. Instr. Spanish, Ill. State U., Normal, 1963-69. instr. women's studies, 1978—; partner CAMCO Innovative Advt. Services, 1977-79; speaker, cons. in field. Campaign worker ERA Ratification, 1972—; chairperson ERA com. LWV, Bloomington-Normal, 1978-79; chairwoman, precinct committeewoman McLean County (Ill.) Democratic Central Com.; pres. NOW, Bloomington-Normal, 1976-77; co-chairperson Women's Polit. Caucus, McLean County, 1979-80; coordinator McLean County ERA Ratification Project; 44th Dist. coordinator ERA Ill.; bd. dirs. Ill. NOW Polit. Action Com.; alt. del. 1978 Dem. Mini-Conv. Mem. AAUW. Episcopalian. Co-author Illinois Women '77, report of Ill. Internat. Women's Year Conf. Home: 1407 Hanson Dr Normal IL 61761 Office: Dept Ethnic Studies Ill State U Normal IL 61761

LAURIE, GINI WILSON, editor; b. Pattonville, Mo., June 10, 1913; d. Robert Edward and Grace Marie (Cunningham) Wilson: B.A., Randolph Macon Women's Coll., 1934; m. Joseph Scott Laurie III, Feb. 26, 1938. Vol., vice chmn. canteen corps ARC, St. Louis, 1940-45, chmn. Chagrin Valley chpt., 1950-60; vol. Regional Respiratory Polio Center, Cleve., 1949-58; founder, editor, pub. Rehab. Gazette, Chagrin Falls, Ohio, 1958-71, St. Louis, 1971—. Bd. dirs. St. Louis chpt. Nat. Spinal Cord Injury Found. Mem. Nat. Rehab. Assn., Am. Coalition of Citizens with Disabilities, Mo. Press Women, Spinal Injuries Assn., Congress Orgns. Physically Handicapped, Can. Paraplegia Assn., Nat. Easter Seal Soc. (profl. adv. council 1979—), Phi Beta Kappa, Kappa Alpha Theta. Roman Catholic. Author: Housing and Home Services for the Disabled, 1977. Home and office: 4502 Maryland Ave Saint Louis MO 63108

LAURIE, MARILYN, public relations exec.; b. N.Y.C., Apr. 30, 1939; d. Abraham and Irene (Aberman) Gold; B.A., Barnard Coll., 1959; M.S. in Bus., Pace U., 1974; m. Robert Laurie, Nov. 11, 1962; children—Amy Laurie, Lisa Laurie. Writer, The Popular Sci. Pub. Co., N.Y.C., 1960-61; promotion mgr. Flamingo Films, N.Y.C., 1961-64, dir. advt./publicity, 1964-65; creative v.p. The Graphics Team, N.Y.C., 1965-68; co-founder, dir. public relations Environ. Action Coalition, N.Y.C., 1969-71; with AT & T, N.Y.C., 1971-80, environ. affairs supr., 1973-75, media relations supr., 1975-78, corp. info. mgr., 1978-79, advt. mgr., 1979-80; exec. dir. public relations Bell Labs., Short Hills, N.J., 1980—. Chmn. consumer affairs com. N.Y.C. Mayor's Council on Environ., 1970-72. Recipient Twin award Nat. Bd. of YWCA, 1981. Mem. Public Relations Soc. Am., Environ. Action Coalition (co-founder). Office: 150 J F Kennedy Pkwy Short Hills NJ 07078

LAURIE, MARY SHORROCK, mfg. co. ofcl.; b. Maricopa County, Ariz., Jan. 13, 1932; d. Herbert and Margaret (Ambrose) Shorrock; grad. McKee Vocat. and Tech. High Sch., 1950; children—Darlene, Gary, Richard, Burt. Cutter, Aetna Bookbindery, N.Y.C., 1948; duplicating operator Am. Sugar Refining Co., N.Y.C., 1950-53; typist Ace Press & Letter, N.Y.C., 1956-58; adminstrv. asst. Amstar Corp., N.Y.C., 1960—. Home: 604 Quincy Ave Staten Island NY 10305 Office: 1251 Ave of Americas New York NY 10020

LAURIE, PIPER (ROSETTA JACOBS), actress; b. Detroit, Jan. 22, 1932; student Los Angeles pub. sch.; m. Joseph Morgenstern, 1962; 1 child. Acted in sch. plays; motion picture debut in Louisa; other motion pictures include The Milkman, Francis Goes to the Races, Prince Who Was A Thief, Son of Ali Baba, Has Anybody Seen My Gal, No Room for the Groom, Mississippi Gambler, Kelly and Me, Golden Blade, Dangerous Mission, Johnny Dark, Dawn at Socorro, Smoke Signal, Ain't Misbehavin', Until They Sail, The Hustler, Carrie, 1976, Tim, 1978; TV appearances include Days of Wine and Roses, Playhouse 90, The Deaf Heart, The Ninth Day, G.E. Theatre, Play of the Week, Hallmark Hall of Fame, Nova: Margaret Sanger, The Woman Rebel, In the Matter of Karen Ann Quinlan, Rainbow, Skag; appeared Broadway play Glass Menagerie, 1965, off-Broadway plays Rosemary and The Alligators, 1961; Acad. award nominee for The Hustler, 1962, Carrie, 1976. Mem. Acad. Motion Picture Arts and Scis. Address: care Susan Smith & Assos 9869 Santa Monica Blvd Beverly Hills CA 90212 *

LAURISKI, SUSAN CATHERINE, banker; b. Detroit, Dec. 3, 1945; d. Charles Louis III and Eleanor Marie (Henchel) Roehm; A.S., Phoenix Coll., 1981; Data processing specialist Detroit Bank & Trust Co., 1963-66; with First Nat. Bank of Ariz. (name changed to First Interstate Bank of Ariz. 1981), Phoenix, 1970—, br. mgr., 1980—, asst. v.p., asst. div. v.p., 1982—. Mem. bd. dirs. Maricopa Camp Fire Council, Phoenix, 1981—; adv. Jr. Achievement, Phoenix, 1978-81; chmn. March of Dimes Walk-a-Thon, Phoenix, 1977-81. Nat. Assn. Bank Women Western Regional scholar, 1981-82. Mem. Nat. Assn. Bank Women (chmn. 1982-83). Republican. Roman Catholic. Club: Soroptimists. Home: 315 W Edgemont St Phoenix AZ 85003 Office: 114 W Adams St Phoenix AZ 85001

LAUTERBACH, KATHRYN HYDE, educator; b. Milw., Mar. 30, 1944; d. Henry Sebastian and Wilma Claire (Heath) Lauterbach; student Rollins Coll., 1962-64; student U. Seven Seas, 1965-66; B.S., So. Conn. State Coll., 1970; M.A., Fairfield U. with honors, 1972. Tchr., Danbury, Conn., 1972, Newtown Middle Sch., Conn., 1973-76; co-author Title IV grant, Model/Presch. Handicapped Children, 1976-78; founder, pres. exec. dir. Newbrook Acad., Watertown, Conn., 1979—, also bd. dirs. Bd. dirs. Dathar-Danbury Assn. to Help Handicapped and Retarded Citizens, 1978-79. Mem. Council for Exceptional Children (chpt. co-founder), Conn. Assn. Children with Learning Disabilities, Parents, Assn. Supervision and Curriculum Devel., Council Adminstrs. Spl. Edn., Children with Handicapping Conditions, Nat. Wildlife Assn., Audubon Soc. Contbr. articles to profl. jours. Home: Hydeaway Old Dodgingtown Rd Bethel CT 06801 Office: 25 the Green Watertown CT 06795

LAUVER, PATRICIA ELLEN, project engr.; b. Elizabeth, N.J., Oct. 22, 1951; d. Milton Renick and Edith Marie (Gedeon) L.; B.S. in Math. with honors, Mich. State U., 1973; M.B.A., Xavier U., 1978. Mem. tech. staff Rockwell Internat., Anaheim, Calif., 1974-75, Columbus, Ohio, 1975-78; project engr. Teledyne CAE, Toledo, 1978—; instr. U. Toledo Community and Tech. Coll., Owens Tech. Coll. Adviser Jr. Achievement, 1976-77, 78-79; sec. ch. council Luth. Ch. Mem. Nat. Mgmt. Assn. (treas Buckeye Council 1980-81, v.p. youth activities Rockwell Internat. Columbus chpt. 1976-77, pres. Teledyne CAE chpt. 1981-82), Soc. Women Engrs., Am. Soc. for Quality Control, Joint Tech. Coordinating Group/Aircraft Survivability, AAUW. Home: 3223 Knoll Ave Toledo OH 43615 Office: 1330 Laskey Rd PO Box 6971 Toledo OH 43612

LAVELLE, RITA MARIE, govt. ofcl., exec.; b. Portsmouth, Va., Sept. 8, 1947; d. Patrick James and Rita Adele (Raymond) L.; BA Coll. Holy Names, 1969, M.B.A., Pepperdine U., 1980. Publs. asst. Gov. Calif., 1969-71; info. officer, dir. consumer edn. Calif. Dept. Consumer Affairs, 1971-76; dir. mktg. Intercontinental and Continental Chems., Sacramento, 1976-78; dir. communications Cordova Chem. Co., Sacramento, 1978-79; dir. communications Aerojet Liquid Rocket Co., Sacramento, 1979-82; asst. adminstr. solid waste and emergency response EPA, Washington 1982—. Active Mercy Hosps., Sacramento; active No. Calif. council Girl Scouts U.S.A.; active Big Bros./Big Sisters. Mem. Rancho Cordova C. of C., Sacramento Met. C. of C., Sacramento Area Commerce & Trade Orgn., Navy League U.S., Air Force Assn., Internat. Assn. Bus. Communicators, NAM, Am. Chem. Soc., Calif. Council Environ. and Econ. Balance, Calif. Mfrs. Assn., AIAA, Aerospace Industry Assn., Am. Mgmt. Assn., Am. Soc. Aerospace Edn., Am. Nuclear Soc., Am. Soc. Chem. Engrs. Roman Catholic. Office: 401 M St SW Washington DC 20460

LAVENDELL, GIULIANA A., office products co. research info. exec.; b. Milan, Italy; d. Enzo G. and Isabelle Avanzini; D. Classics, U. Milan; M.L.S., Calif. State U., San Jose, 1972; m. Henry Lavendel; children—Laurence Andrew, Claire Maria. Asst. to cultural attache Italian embassy, N.Y.C., 1952-55; radio script writer Voice of Am., USIA, 1954-75; reference librarian, cataloger Xerox Palo Alto Research Centers (Calif.), 1971-74, mgr. tech. info., 1975—; tchr., lectr., research in field, U.S., Italy; bd. dirs. Coop. Info. Network, 1982-84. Mem. Am. Soc. Info. Sci., Spl. Libraries Assn. (chmn. publicity San Francisco Bay Area chpt. 1975-77, chpt. spl. rep. to CLASS 1978-79, cons. officer San Andreas chpt. 1979-80), IEEE, Assn. Computing Machinery. Republican. Roman Catholic. Author: A Decade of Research, Xerox Palo Alto Research Center 1970-1980, 1980; contbr. numerous articles, chpts. to profl. publs. Home: 1511 Hamilton Ave Palo Alto CA 94303 Office: 3333 Coyote Hill Rd Palo Alto CA 94304

LAVERGNE, MARY LOU, mfg. co. exec.; b. Detroit, Oct. 5, 1940; d. Bernard Clark and Lillian Bertha (Hackbart) Sherwood; student public schs.; divorced; 1 dau., Anita R. Secretary, 1958-60; office mgr. R.M. Richardson Co., Southfield, Mich., 1960-72; controller Seaman Mfg. Co., Pontiac, Mich., 1972-78; treas. Seamco Enterprises, Inc., steel rule die cutting, Kendallville, Ind., 1978—, also dir. Sec., Mich. Jr. Miss. Pageant, Pontiac, 1969-70, bd. dirs., 1975-76; pres. Pontiac Jaycee Aux., 1968, 70; co-chmn. residential area Pontiac United Fund drive, 1971. Named Pontiac Jaycette of Yr., 1969. Mem. Am. Mgmt. Assn., Nat. Assn. Female Execs., Am. Inst. Corp. Controllers. Home: 215 S Riley St Kendallville IN 46755 Office: 2525 Progress Dr Kendallville IN 46755

LAVERY, BEATRICE CANTERBURY, city ofcl.; b. Los Angeles, Jan. 20, 1926; d. Charles Milton and Bernice Mae (Peacock) Canterbury; A.B., U. So. Calif., 1948; m. Frederic William Wile, Jr., 1952 (dec. 1960); 1 son, Geoffrey; m. 2d, Emmet G. Lavery, Sept. 27, 1963; 1 child, Tracy. Editor Whittier (Calif.) Reporter, 1944; reporter Wave Publs., Los Angeles, 1944-45; with Publicity Pfd., Los Angeles, 1946-48; press rep. NBC, Hollywood, 1949-52; fashion dir. Bullocks Dept. Store, Los Angeles, 1960-63; advt. dir. Rose Marie Reid Swimsuits, Los Angeles, 1963-65; merchandising dir. Compton Advt., Los Angeles, 1966-67; freelance advt. and public relations cons., 1967-70; adminstrv. coordinator to mayor of Los Angeles, 1973—, now chief of protocol. Publicity Mannequins of the Assistance League of So. Calif., 1954-56; worker public relations UN Assn., Los Angeles, 1953-54, Encino Property Owners Assn., 1968-72; campaign worker Janice Bernstein candidate for Sch. Bd., Los Angeles, 1970; mem. Speakers Bur. Alan Cranston for senator campaign, 1968; public relations worker Tom Bradley for mayor campaign, 1969, 73. Bd. govs. U. So. Calif., 1973—. Decorated Order of Orange Nassau (Netherlands); recipient award Media Women Founder's, 1970, award Los Angeles City Human Relations Bur., 1970. Mem. Women in Communications (pres. 1949-51), Los Angeles Advt. Women (Lulu award 1965), Fashion Group (dir. 1958-63), Hollywood Women's Press Club, U. So. Calif. Journalism Alumni Assn. (pres. 1972-73), Am. Women for Internat. Understanding, Trusteeship for Betterment of Women. Club: Internat. (dir.) (Los Angeles). Home: 5120 Encino Ave Encino CA 91316 Office: 200 N Spring St Los Angeles CA 90012

LAVIN, LINDA, actress; b. Portland, Maine, Oct. 15, 1937; d. David J. and Lucille (Potter) Lavin; B.A., Coll. William and Mary, 1959. Off-Broadway debut in Oh, Kay!, 1960, Broadway debut in A Family Affairs, 1962; appearances in revues Wet Paint, 1965, The Game Is Up, 1965, The Mad Show, 1966; with nat. touring company On a Clear Day You Can See Forever, 1966-67; mem. acting company Eugene O'Neil Playwrights Unit, 1968; other stage appearances include It's a Bird... It's a Plane... It's Superman, 1966, Something Different, 1967, Little Murders, 1969, Cop-Out, 1969, The Last of the Red Hot Lovers, 1969, Story Theatre, 1970, The Enemy is Dead, 1973, Love Two, 1974, The Comedy of Errors, 1975, Dynamite Tonite!, 1975; star TV series Alice, 1976—; TV films: Like Mom, Like Me, 1972; The $5.20 An Hour Dream, 1979; other TV appearances on CBS Playhouse, Barney Miller, Rhoda, Harry O, Phyllis, also in The Beggar's Opera, Damn Yankees; nightclub appearances, also pvt. drama tchr. and rec. artist. Recipient Sat. Rev., Outer Critics Circle awards for Little Murders; Theater World award for Wet Paint; Golden Globe award, 1978, 79. Address: care CBS CBS Television City Los Angeles CA 90036 *

LAVITT, WENDY ADLER, antique dealer; b. N.Y.C., Nov. 28, 1939; d. Ralph M. and Eve Evelyn (Sperling) Adler; B.A., Finch Coll., N.Y.C., 1961; m. Mel S. Lavitt, Sept. 10, 1959; children—Kathy, John, Meredith. Copy editor Holt, Rinehart & Winston, N.Y.C., 1961-63; docent Mus. Am. Folk Art, 1978-79, guest curator Am. Folk Dolls show, N.Y.C., 1982; freelance mag. writer, 1979-81; antique dealer, 1978-81; owner Made in America, antiques, N.Y.C., 1981—; lectr. in field, 1980—. Author: American Folk Dolls, 1982; also articles. Home: 15 E 91st St New York NY 10028 Office: 1234 Madison Ave New York NY 10028

LA VOY, DIANE EDWARDS, mem. congl. staff; b. Caracas, Venezuela, Nov. 10, 1948; d. Edward Edwards and Margaret Lucille (Buchheit) Edwards Ross-Jones; B.A., Wellesley Coll., 1970; M.Pub. Affairs, Princeton U., 1977; m. David Wayne La Voy, Apr. 3, 1971; 1 dau., Sarah Edwards. Intern, Friends Com. on Nat. Legis., Washington, 1970-71; assoc. mgr. Quaker House, Washington, 1971-74, art dir., 1973-74; asst. editor Ams. mag. OAS, Washington, 1971-73; founder/dir. Washington Office on Latin Am., 1974; mem. profl. staff U.S. Senate Select Com. To Study Govtl. Activities with Respect to Intelligence, 1974-76; mem. profl. staff Subcom. Evaluation and Oversight of Ho. of Reps. Permanent Select Com. on Intelligence, 1977—; part-time freelance illustrator/designer. Founder, 1st pres. E St. Friends, 1979-80; active Am. Friends Service Com., 1971—; elder Presbyn. Ch., 1982—. Democrat. Author articles and reports in field. Home: 1614 E St SE Washington DC 20003 Office: The Capitol Room H-405 Washington DC 20515

LAVRIN, ASUNCIÓN ADELA, historian, educator; b. Havana, Cuba; M.A., Radcliffe Coll., 1958; Ph.D., Harvard U., 1963; m. David H. Lavrin, Aug. 30, 1958; children—Cecilia, Andrew. Lectr., Roosevelt U., Chgo., 1966-68, Rosary Coll., River Forest, Ill., 1968-70, Cath. U. Am., Washington, 1970-71, Georgetown U., Washington, 1975-76; vis. asst. prof. Columbia U., N.Y.C., 1974; asso. prof. dept. history Howard U., Washington, 1977—, dir. grad. program, 1981—. Recipient Robertson Meml. prize, 1967; Nat. Endowment for Humanities fellow, 1980-81; Am. Philos. Soc. fellow, 1972, 78. Mem. Am. Hist. Assn., Conf. on Latin Am. History, Berkshire Conf. of Women Historians, Middle Am. Conf. Latin Am. Studies, Sigma Delta Pi. Editor: Latin American Women: Historical Perspectives, 1978; editorial bd. Hispanic Am. Hist. Review, 1982—; contbr. articles to profl. jours. Home: 8501 Manchester Rd Silver Spring MD 20901 Office: Dept History Howard U Washington DC 20059

LAW, ARDITH ELAINE, pet shop owner; b. Spokane, Wash., Nov. 26, 1931; d. Charles Vernon and Mildred Maurene (Ricks) Steele; student Cascade Coll., Portland, Oreg., 1950-51, Wenatchee Bus. Coll., 1951-52; m. Noble Orin Law, Aug. 8, 1953; children—Stuart Dean, Keith DeWayne, Stanford William. Sec., Halstead & MacGregor, attys., Prosser, Wash., 1953-54, Prosser Jr. High Sch., 1954-55, Okanogan (Wash.) Elem. Sch., 1956-57, Hatcher & Son, Omak, Wash., 1957-60, James M. Greene Ins., Oroville, Wash., 1960-61, B.L. Schrader Co., 1964-65, D.A. Thorndike & Sons., Oroville, 1966-67; warehouse stamper, checker Stadelman Fruit Co., Oroville, 1967-71, Tonoro Fruit Co., Tonasket, Wash., 1971-78; owner, operator The Pet Net, Tonasket, 1979—. Pres., Presch. PTA, Oroville, 1964-65; pres. Kiwanis Ladies Aux., Oroville, 1965-66; organist United Methodist Ch., Oroville, 1961-69, Tonasket (Wash.) Community United Ch. of Christ, 1973—, United Ch. of Christ, 1974—. Mem. Wash. State Pet Industry Assn., (corr.). Mem. Ch. of Christ. Home: 31940 N Hwy 97 Tonasket WA 98855 Office: 414 S Whitcomb St Tonasket WA 98855

LAWHEAD, DORIS JEAN, educator; b. Bloomington, Ill., Aug. 13, 1927; d. Beryl C. and Mary (Krupp) Barber; student (Merit scholar) Western Coll. for Women, 1945-46; B.A., Ball State U., 1949, M.A., 1953; m. Victor B. Lawhead, July 11, 1953. Billing clk. Diamond Match Co., Chgo., 1948; records mgr. Time, Inc., N.Y.C., 1949; asst., grad. office Ball State U., Muncie, Ind., 1949-51, internat. curricular adviser, 1952-70, sr. acad. advisor, 1970—. Cert. tchr., Ind. Mem. Ind. Consortium for Internat. Edn. Democrat. Presbyterian. Home: 1408 W Neely Ave Muncie IN 47303 Office: Ball State U Muncie IN 47306

LAWLER, RUTH CURRY, judge; b. New Orleans, Feb. 13, 1900; d. Henry Thomas and Carrie Mary (Aycock) Lawler; B.Music, H. Sophie Newcomb Coll., 1921; B.A., Our Lady of the Lake Coll., 1931. Tchr. English and dramatics Castroville (Tex.) High Sch., 1951-61; owner, operator Landmark Inn, Castroville, 1942—; judge mcpl. ct., Castroville, 1965—. Councilwoman City of Castroville, 1964-72, mayor pro tem, 1969-72. Trustee, Medina County Hosp., 1961-63, Castroville Pub. Library, 1962-72, Castroville Pub. Sch., 1949-52. Recipient Woman of Yr. award C. of C., 1971; Ruth Lawler Day declared in her honor, Oct. 25, 1981. Mem. San Antonio Conservation Soc. Democrat. Roman Catholic. Club: Castroville Garden. Author: The Story of Castroville: Its People, Founder and Traditions, 1968. Donated Landmark Inn Complex to Tex. Park and Wildlife Commn. Home: PO Box 340 Castroville TX 78009 Office: Landmark Inn PO Box 340 Castroville TX 78009

LAWRENCE, DEAN GRAYSON, lawyer; b. Oakland, Calif.; d. Henry C. and Myrtle (Grayson) Schmidt; A.B., U. Calif., Berkeley, 1934, J.D., 1939. Admitted to Calif. bar, 1943, U.S. Tax Ct., 1944, U.S. Supreme Ct. bar, 1967; asso. with Pillsbury, Madison & Sutro, San Francisco, 1944, 1945; gen. practice, Oakland, 1946-50, San Jose, 1952-60, Grass Valley, 1960-63, 66—; county counsel Nevada County, 1964, 65, bd. suprs. 2d dist., 1969-73, chmn., 1971; sec. Nevada County Humane Animal Shelter Bd., 1966—; pres. Nevada County Humane Soc., 1974—; state humane officer, 1966—; mem. Nevada County Health Planning Council, 1973-79, Golden Empire Areawide Health Planning Council, 1974-75; mem. Nevada County Democratic Central Com., 1980—, sec., 1982—. Mem. Humane Soc. U.S., Fund for Animals, AAUW, State Bar Calif., Bus. and Profl. Women's Club, Phi Beta Kappa, Sigma Xi, Kappa Beta Pi, Pi Mu Epsilon, Pi Lambda Theta. Episcopalian. Office: PO Box 66 Grass Valley CA 95945

LAWRENCE, GLORIA EDITH, non-profit orgn. exec.; b. N.Y.C.; d. Victor R. and Mamie (Moss) L.; B.S., CCNY, 1956; postgrad. Columbia U., 1959, New Sch. Social Research, 1960-62. Dir. devel. So. Elections Fund, N.Y.C., 1969-70, Harlem Dowling Children's Center, N.Y.C., 1975-77; pub. relations exec. March of Dimes, N.Y.C., 1980—; dir. fin. devel. unit Nat. Bd. YWCA, N.Y.C., 1982—. Bd. dirs. Ams. for Democratic Action, 1977—; apptd. mem. Archives and Reference Research for N.Y.C., 1978—; mem. N.Y. County Com., 1973-78; del. Dem. Nat. Conv.; spl. asst. to pres. N.Y.C. Council, 1977. Episcopalian. Club: Women's City. Home: 165 West End Ave New York NY 10023 Office: 135 W 50th St New York NY 10020

LAWRENCE, MARY WELLS BERG, advt. exec.; b. Youngstown, Ohio, May 25, 1928; d. Waldemar and Violet (Meltz) Berg; ed. Carnegie Inst. Tech., 1949; LL.D., Babson Coll., 1970, Carnegie-Mellon U., 1974; m. Harding Lawrence, Nov. 25, 1967; children—James, State, Deborah, Kathryn, Pamela. Copywriter McKelvey's Dept. Store, Youngstown, 1951-52; fashion advt. mgr. Macy's, N.Y.C., 1952-53; copy group head McCann-Erickson, N.Y.C., 1953-56; v.p., asso. copy chief Doyle, Dane, Bernbach, N.Y.C., 1957-64; sr. partner, creative dir. Jack Tinker & Partners, N.Y.C., 1964-66; pres. Wells, Rich, Greene, Inc., N.Y.C., 1966-71, chmn. bd., chief exec. officer, 1971—; dir. Ralston Purina Co. Mem. N.Y. Commn. on Critical Choices for Ams., 1974, Pres.'s Council on Inflation; mem. council Rockefeller U.; bd. dirs. Multiple Sclerosis Soc.; nat. steering com. Spelman Coll. Named to Copywriters Hall of Fame, Copy Club, 1969; named Mktg. Saleswoman of Year, Sales Exec. Club N.Y., 1970, Advt. Woman of Year, Am. Advt. Fedn., 1971. Mem. Dallas Advt. Club. Office: 767 Fifth Ave New York NY 10022

LAWRENCE, PATRICIA ANN, broadcasting co. exec.; b. Pitts., Nov. 22, 1948; d. Edward and Helen (Campbell) Lawrence; B.S. in Journalism, W. Va. U., 1970. Copywriter DeSales Advt., Phila., 1970; publicity dir. Joseph Horne's Dept. Store, Pitts., 1970-72, KDKA TV, Pitts., 1972-75; promotion product on-air KDKA, 1975-76, dir. creative services, 1976-79; account exec. KYW-TV, Phila., 1979—. Mem. Am. Women in Radio and TV. Address: 200 Locust St Apt 3H Philadelphia PA 19106

LAWRENCE, PATRICIA ANNE, nurse; b. Worcester, Mass., Nov. 14, 1931; d. Ralph Seavey and Maude Irma (Haywood) L.; A.B., Bates Coll., Lewiston, Maine, 1954; M.A., Columbia U., 1960. Staff nurse Cornell U. Med. Center, 1954-57, Newton (Mass.)-Wellesley Hosp., 1957-58; instr. Cornell U.-N.Y. Hosp. Sch. Nursing, 1958-59, 60-61, Rutgers U. Coll. Nursing, 1961-64; asst. prof. Duke U. Sch. Nursing, 1964-70; ednl. dir. diabetes project N.C. Regional Med. Program, 1969-73; asso. prof.

U. N.C. Sch. Nursing, Chapel Hill, 1973—; site visitor, cons. diabetes research and tng. centers NIH, 1977-78, adv. bd. Nat. Diabetes Clearinghouse, 1978-80. Mem. Am. Nurses Assn., N.C. Nurses Assn., Am. Diabetes Assn. (dir. 1974-79, sec. 1976-77, v.p. 1977-79, dir. N.C. affiliate 1973-79, 81—), Internat. Diabetes Fedn., Am. Assn. Diabetes Educators (dir. 1973-75), Am. Kennel Club (tracking judge), Durham Kennel Club, Am. Belgian Tervuren Club, Co-author: Picture Pages for Diabetic Care, 1973; also numerous articles, chpts. in book. Co-editor: Educating Diabetic Patients, 1981; editorial bd. Diabetes care, 1977—. Home: 4711 Easley St Durham NC 27705 Office: Carrington Hall 214H Chapel Hill NC 27514

LAWRENCE, PAULINE W., food co. exec.; b. 1916. With Manning's Restaurant, prior to 1952; v.p., restaurant merchandiser, dir. Fred Meyer, Inc., Portland, Oreg., 1952—. Office: Fred Meyer Inc 3800 SE 22d St Portland OR 97202 *

LAWRENCE, RUTH BECKER, nurse; b. Bklyn., June 16, 1925; d. Edward F. and Lillian (Davis) Becker; B.S., nursing diploma Simmons Coll., 1947; m. W. Leland Lawrence, Feb. 8, 1948; children—Stoddard, Thomas, Jeffrey, Leland Davis, Leigh Anne, Richard. Instr. nursing, Simmons Coll., Boston, 1947; staff nurse Nassau Hosp., Mineola, N.Y., 1947-48; staff pediatric nurse Hartford (Conn.) Hosp., 1948-49; dir. nursing service Springfield (Vt.) Hosp., 1977—. Choir, tchr. Sunday Sch., Congl. Ch.; den mother Boy Scouts Am.; vol. ARC; bd. dirs. Springfield Sch. Bd., 1962-72. Mem. Am. Nurses Assn., Council Nursing Adminstrs., Vt. Hosp. Assn. Dirs. Nursing. Office: Springfield Hosp Springfield VT 05156

LAWRENCE, STELLA, elec. engr., educator; b. Montreal, Que., Can., Feb. 2, 1918; came to U.S., 1924, naturalized, 1945; d. M. and Fannie (Broide) Hertchikoff; B.A. magna cum laude, N.Y. U., 1938, M.S., 1941; B.E.E. summa cum laude, Poly. Inst. Bklyn., 1949, M.E.E., 1952. Devel. engr. Control Instrument Co., 1943-47; lectr. physics CCNY, 1958-70; mem. switching systems devel. dept. Bell Telephone Labs., 1947-60; asst. prof. Bronx Community Coll., 1960-65, asso. prof. elec. engring. tech., 1966-80, prof., 1980—; cons. advanced tech. dept. Ampex Corp., 1975—; cons. orbiting systems Aerospace Corp., summer 1978; cons. Jet Propulsion Lab., summer 1980; vis. scientist Lawrence Berkeley Lab., U. Calif., summer 1981, L.B. Johnson Space Center, summer 1982. Mem. Community Planning Bd. 7, Bronx, N.Y.C., 1970—. Faculty research fellow Argonne (Ill.) Nat. Lab., 1974, NASA Langley Research Center, summer 1976, NASA Marshall Space Flight Center, summer 1977, NSF fellow, 1977-80. Fellow Bklyn. Engrs. Club; mem. IEEE (sr., exec. com. N.Y. sect. 1956—, regional exec. com. 1975), Soc. Women Engrs. (sr., charter), Am. Soc. for Engring. Edn., N.Y. Acad. Scis., Phi Beta Kappa, Sigma Xi, Pi Mu Epsilon, Sigma Pi Sigma. Home: 3288 Reservoir Oval E Bronx NY 10467 Office: 181st and University Ave Bronx NY 10453

LAWRENCE, TELETÉ ZORAYDA, speech and voice pathologist, educator; b. Worcester, Mass., Aug. 5, 1910; d. James Newton and Cora Valeria (Hester) Lester; A.B. cum laude, U. Calif., Berkeley, 1932; M.A., Tex. Christian U., 1963; pvt. study voice with Edgar Schofield, N.Y.C., 1936-41, drama with Enrica Clay Dillon, N.Y.C., 1937-40; m. Ernest Lawrence, Oct. 9, 1939; children—James Lester, Valerie Alma. Mem. Am. Lyric Opera Co., 1939—; instr. speech Sch. Fine Arts, Tex. Christian U., Fort Worth, 1959-66, asst. prof., 1966-71, asso. prof., 1971-75, prof., 1975-76, emeritus, 1976—, speech pathologist specializing voice disorders Speech and Hearing Clinic, 1959—, faculty research leave, Gt. Britain, Western Europe, Hungary, 1968; pvt. practice speech and voice pathology, 1960—. Mem. bd. Sunshine Haven, home for retarded children, 1957-59; gen. chmn. Ft. Worth and Tarrant County, Nat. Retarded Children's Week, 1954; mem. family and child welfare div. Community Council Ft. Worth and Tarrant County, 1955-57, mem. health and hosp. div., 1959-60; mem. women's com. Ft. Worth chpt. NCCJ, 1956-59; exec. v.p. Fine Arts Found. Guild of Tex. Christian U., 1955-56, past exec. sec., past fin. sec. Recipient Faculty Research grant Tex. Christian U., 1961. Mem. Nat. Council Chs. (bd. joint com. missionary edn. Pacific Coast area, 1952-55), United Ch. Women of Ft. Worth (chmn. Christian world missions dept. 1955-57, pres. 1957-59). Ft. Worth Area Council Chs. (v.p. 1955-57, exec. com. 1957-59, bd. dirs. 1959-60), U. Calif. Alumni Assn. (life), Am. Speech-Lang.-Hearing Assn. (life; cert. clin. competence in speech pathology), Tex. Speech and Hearing Assn., Ft. Worth Council for Retarded Children, Speech Communication Assn. (sec. speech and hearing disorders interest group 1962-63, mem. com. 1961-64), Am. Dialect Soc., Internat. Assn. Logopodics and Phoniatrics, Internat. Soc. Phonetic Scis., Phonetic Soc. Japan, AAUP, Tex. Speech Assn., Lambda Ma'ams of Lambda Chi Alpha (pres. Ft. Worth 1962-63), Phi Beta Kappa Assn., Ft. Worth, Phi Beta Kappa (Alpha of Calif. chpt.; charter mem., v.p. Delta of Tex. chpt. 1971-73, pres. 1973-74), Delta Zeta, Psi Chi, Sigma Alpha Eta. Republican. Mem. Christian Ch. Clubs: Woman's of Fort Worth, Women of Rotary. Participant, 13th Congress of Internat. Assn. Logopedics and Phoniatrics, Vienna, 1965, 14th Congress, Paris, 1968, 15th Congress, Buenos Aires, 1971, 16th Congress, Interlaken, Switzerland, 1974, 17th Congress, Copenhagen, 1977, 18th Congress, Washington, 1980; participant 10th Internat. Congress of Linguists, Bucharest, 1967; participant 6th Internat. Congress of Phonetic Scis., Prague, 1967, 7th Internat. Congress, Montreal, 1971, 8th Internat. Congress, Leeds, Eng., 1975; participant 1st Congress Internat. Assn. Sci. Study Mental Deficiency, Montpellier, France, 1967, Semmelweis Ann. Week, Budapest Acad. Scis., 1968, 3d World Congress Phoneticians, Tokyo, 1976. Author: Handbook for Instructors of Voice and Diction, 1968; contbr. articles to profl. jours. Home: 3860 South Hills Circle Fort Worth TX 76109

LAWS, ETHEL, twp. ofcl.; b. Pitts., Sept. 12, 1918; d. John and Elizabeth (Toth) Pentek; student Olivet Nazarene Coll., 1957, U. Strasbourg (France), 1970; m. Byron Spencer Laws, Mar. 16, 1945 (dec.); children—Russell B., Janet E. Town clk., Twp. of Kankakee (Ill.), 1965—, judge of election, 1947-65; adminstrv. asst. Volkmanns Jewelers, 1965-78; acctg. clk. 1st Trust & Savs. Bank, 1979-81. Republican precinct committeewoman; mem. Riverside Hosp. Aux.; corr. sec. Kankakee Rep. Women's Fedn. Served to staff sgt. W.A.C., AUS, 1943-45. Mem. Ill. Twp. Ofcls. Assn., Am. Legion (post comdr. 1979-80, post dir. 1981—). Methodist. Clubs: Emblem, Zonta (pres. 1982-84, dir. 1969-72). Office: 187 S Schuyler Ave Kankakee IL 60901

LAWSON, ANN MARIE MCDONALD, librarian; b. Jersey City; d. William and Mary Agnes (Dolan) McDonald; student Columbia, 1947, N.Y. U., 1949, City Coll. N.Y., 1959, Pratt Inst., 1963; m. Philip James Lawson, Apr. 26, 1952. Methods analyst Rueben H. Donnelley Corp., N.Y.C., 1953-57; librarian chems. div. Union Carbide Corp., N.Y.C., 1957-65, Tatham Laird & Kudner, N.Y.C., 1965-67, Met. Transp. Authority, N.Y.C., 1967-80; cons., 1980—; active library tng. program Ballard Sch. (YWCA), 1949—; cons. WHO, Geneva, Switzerland, 1950; lectr. Pratt Inst. Grad. Library Sch., 1967. Mem. Assn. Records Mgrs. and Adminstrs. (pres. 1948-50); Spl. Libraries Assn. Republican. Contbr. articles to mags. Home and office: 119 Washington Pl New York NY 10014

LAWSON, BARBARA KAY, conservation services cons.; b. Columbus, Ohio, Apr. 15, 1950; d. Kirby and Frances (Rhodeback) Barrick; B.S., Ohio State U., 1972; m. Marple A. Lawson, Jr., Apr. 20, 1974; 1 son, Brett Matthew. Electric lighting cons. Public Service Ind., Seymour, 1973-78, sr. electric living cons., 1978-81, conservation services cons., Clarksville, 1981—. Mem. Ind. Home Economists in Bus. (legis. chmn. 1979-80; chmn. elec 1980-81, chmn. 1981-82), Am. Home Econs. Assn., Ind. Home Econs. Assn., Elec. Women's Round Table, Lambda Chi Omega (v.p. 1979-81). Mem. Christian Ch. Office: 1212 Eastern Blvd Clarksville IN 47130

LAWSON, CAROL, journalist; b. Chgo., Nov. 16, 1945; d. Peter and Jane (Weil) L.; B.S., Northwestern U., 1967, M.S., 1968; m. Daniel S. Arick, May 24, 1981. Editorial asst. McCall's mag., 1968-69; asst. news editor Sci. Research mag., 1969-70; asso. editor War/Peace Report mag., 1970-72; freelance writer, 1972-74; staff editor Arts and Leisure sect. N.Y. Times, 1974-77, reporter culture news staff, 1977—. Recipient Publisher's award N.Y. Times, 1976. Office: 229 W 43d St New York NY 10036

LAWSON, ELESA STEVES, pianist, educator; b. Riverside, Calif., Dec. 17, 1933; d. Richard Avery and Pauline (Smith) Steves; B.Mus. with distinction, U. Redlands (Calif.), 1955; M.A. in Adminstrn. and Edn., Azusa Pacific U., 1981; children—Steven, Mike, Cheryl. Public sch. tchr., 1962—; tchr., mem. counselling team and curriculum team Badillo Sch., Covina, Calif., 1968—; propr. Lawson Piano Studio, Covina, 1955—; dir. Covina Summer Theatre Music, 1969-79. Active local Boy Scouts Am. Mem. NEA, Music Tchrs. Assn. Calif. (dir. San Gabriel Valley chpt.), Calif. Tchrs. Assn., Charter Oak Educators Assn., PTA (life), Mortar Bd. (v.p. chpt. 1954), Mensa, Pi Kappa Lambda, Sigma Alpha Iota. Presbyterian. Author handbook, articles in field. Home: 5053 Arroway Ave Covina CA 91724 Office: PO Box 9 Covina CA 91723

LAWSON, ELLEN CAMPION, social worker; b. Nashville, July 11, 1929; d. John Evangelist and Ellen Fitzgerald (Shea) Campion; B.A. cum laude, Vanderbilt U., 1951; M.S.S.W., U. Tenn., 1976; m. Albert Robert Lawson, Nov. 22, 1958. Psychiat. social worker Middle Tenn. Mental Health Inst., Nashville, 1976-77, psychiat. social work supr., Nashville, 1977—; field instr. U. Tenn. Sch. Social Work, Nashville, 1977-79. Pres., Vanderbilt U. Med. Center Aux., Nashville, 1967-69, Nashville Symphony Guild, 1968-70. Women's Aux. of Nashville Acad. Medicine, 1971-72; bd. dirs. Nashville Symphony Assn., 1968-76, Nashville Acad. Theatre, 1972-73, Nashville Mental Health Assn., 1973-78, House of Friendship, 1976—, Ladies of Charity, 1960-66. Mem. Nat. Assn. Social Workers, Acad. Cert. Social Workers, Gamma Phi Beta. Roman Catholic. Club: Centennial. Home: 3940 Woodlawn Dr Nashville TN 37205 Office: Middle Tenn Mental Health Inst 1501 Murfreesboro Rd Nashville TN 37217

LAWSON, JOANNE FERRERO, ednl. cons., bus. exec.; b. Olympia, Wash., June 11, 1930; d. Benjamin P. and Gladys (Aronson) Ferrero; B.S. in Sociology, U. Oreg., 1979; m. Bud Lawson, July 24, 1947; children—Terry, Linda, Benjamin, Lisa, Steven. Co-founder, Women in Transition, U. Oreg., student coordinator lifelong learning; vocat. counselor, cons. in pvt. practice; co-owner, dir. Ferrero Equities, Eugene, Oreg.; instr. leadership tng. and communications skills; vocat. counselor. Mem. Eugene Apprenticeship Info. Center, Eugene Women's Commn. Women's Polit. Caucus, Mem. Phi Beta Kappa, Phi Theta Kappa. Democrat.

LAWSON, LOUISE QUARLES, savs. and loan assn. exec.; b. Port Gibson, Miss., Jan. 7, 1920; d. Harrison and Annie (Coleman) King; B.S. in Bus. Adminstrn., Alcorn A & M U., 1940; postgrad. John Marshall Law Sch., 1947-49; grad. diploma Am. Savs. and Loan Inst., 1961; m. H. Douglas Lawson, Oct. 18, 1969. Job analyst War Labor Bd., Chgo., 1945-46; with Ill./Service Fed. Savs. & Loan Assn., Chgo., 1946—, sec./treas., 1970-75, pres., chief exec. officer, 1975—, chmn. loan com., from 1975, also dir.; dir. N.C. Mut. Life Ins. Co., RESCORP. Bd. dirs., mem. women's benefit bd. Operation PUSH, Chgo.; mem. bldg. com. St. Bernard Hosp., Chgo.; mem. HUD Task Force on Future of FHA, from 1977; trustee Provident Hosp. Recipient Achiever's award CEDCO, 1974, Distinguished Mississippian award Gov. Miss., 1974; award for Outstanding Women, Am. Savs. & Loan League, 1975, award for outstanding service, 1975; Achievement award Nat. Council Negro Women, 1975, Cleve. chpt. award Black Econ. Union, 1975, Kansas City Kans. chpt., 1975; Achiever's award Black Book, 1975, Par Excellence award, 1977; honored by Black Enterprise Mag., 1974; named Woman of Yr., Beatrice Caffrey Youth Center, 1975, Cosmopolitan C. of C., 1975, Univ. Women, 1976. Mem. Exec. Club, Econ. Club Savs. and Loan Inst., Savs. Instns. Mktg. Soc., Ill., Am. (pres. 1973) savs. and loan leagues, Chgo. United (prin.), Chgo. Urban League, Alpha Gamma Pi. Democrat. Mem. United Ch. of Christ. Club: Monroe. Office: Ill/Service Fed Savs & Loan Assn 4619 S King Dr Chicago IL 60653 *

LAWSON, NANCY ANN, lawyer; b. Plainfield, N.J., May 25, 1948; d. Alexander E. and Nancy (Baker) Lawson; B.A., Skidmore Coll., 1970; M.Ed., Boston U., 1971; J.D., U. Toledo, 1975; m. Steven E. Simon, Sept. 16, 1973; 1 son, Andrew. Admitted to Ohio bar, 1975; atty. Advs. for Basic Legal Equality, Inc., Toledo, 1975-77; asso. John E. Lloyd Jr. & Assos., Cin., 1977-79; asso. firm Dinsmore & Shohl, Cin., 1979—; dir Gow-Mac Instruments Co., N.J. Bd. dirs. Cin. Legal Aid Soc. Mem. Am. Bar. Assn., Ohio Bar Assn., Cin. Bar Assn., Am. Assn. Trial Lawyers, Cin. Women Lawyer's Club. Home: 6171 Tulane Rd Cincinnati OH 45212 Office: 2100 Fountain Sq Plaza 511 Walnut St Cincinnati OH 45202

LAWSON, NANCY PARRISH, county ofcl.; b. Manassas, Va., Apr. 23, 1926; d. Edgar and Alverda (Jennings) Parrish; B.A. in Edn., Longwood Coll., 1947; m. Richard C. Haydon, Jr., 1948 (dec. 1964); children—Victoria Haydon Bonifant, Richard C. III, Geoffrey J.; m. 2d, G. Loyd Lawson, Sept. 15, 1979. Tchr., Prince William County, Va., 1947-48; gen. registrar of voting Prince William County, 1965—. Membership chmn. Prince William Hosp. Aux., 1964—; trustee Grace United Meth. Ch., Manassas, 1976—; mem. No. Va., Middle Md. and Washington areas elections com. Council of Govts., 1972—, co-chmn., 1979-81. Mem. Voter Registrars Assn. Va. (pres. 1973-76), Manassas Jr. Women's Club (pres. 1956-57). Democrat. Clubs: Sudley Swim and Tennis (pres. 1971-74), Everegreen Country. Home: 9007 Longstreet Dr Manassas VA 22110 Office: 9254 Lee Ave Manassas VA 22110

LAWTON, ALMA RHEA, home economist; b. Emory, Tex., July 29, 1918; d. Jesse Sylvester and Mary Viona (Smiley) Eades; B.S. in Home Econs. Edn., Tex. Tech. U., 1941; m. Carl William Lawton, Aug. 23, 1947; children—Sharon Lawton Cromwell, Carl William, Gary Lynn. Tchr. home econs. Patton Spring High Sch., Afton, Tex., 1941, Tulia (Tex.) High Sch., 1942, West Lafayette (Ind.) Jr. High Sch., 1947-48; supr. student tchrs. Purdue U., Lafayette, Ind., 1947-48, 50-56; free-lance tailoring tchr., Chattanooga, 1957-60; adult clothing and tailoring tchr. Farmington (Conn.) Park and Recreation, 1962-63, Hartford (Conn.) Bd. Edn., 1962-63; extension home economist Conn. Coop. Extension Service, U. Conn., Hartford, 1963-81, faculty emeritus, 1981—; coordinator Sand Home Orientation Program, Hartford, 1974-77, cons., 1978-79. Served with WAVES, USNR, 1943-46. Mem. Nat. Assn. Extension Home Economists (Cert., profl. improvement com.), Am. Home Econs. Assn. (sec. extension profl. sect. 1979-81), Quota Internat., Conn. Extension Home Economist Assn. (pres. 1977-79), Conn. Nutrition Council, Phi Upsilon Omicron, Omicron Nu, Epsilon Sigma Phi. Presbyn. Club: West Hartford Suburban Woman's (pres. 1980-82). Home: 52 Chapman Rd West Hartford CT 06107

LAWTON, BARBARA PERRY, public relations exec.; writer; b. Springfield, Mass., Aug. 26, 1930; d. Kenneth William and Elizabeth McGovern Perry; B.A., Mt. Holyoke Coll., 1952; m. Feb. 1952 (div.); children—William C., Cynthia Lawton Gilberg, Mark R. Editor, mgr. publs. Mo. Bot. Gardens, 1967-72; public relations cons. to various orgns., 1968—; partner Gary Ferguson, Inc., public relations, 1977-81, Wright & Manning, Inc., 1981—; columnist St. Louis Post-Dispatch, 1972—; contbr. articles to various publs., 1960—; instr. public relations/writing, 1971—. Recipient awards, state contests Mo. Press Women, 1976, 77, 78; 1st pl. award, black and white St. Louis Art Guild Photo Show, 1978. Mem. Nat. Fedn. Press Women (nat. awards for writing and photography), Women in Communications, Garden Writers Assn. Am. (nat. writing awards 1981, 82), Landscape and Nurserymen's Assn., Mensa. Home and office: 1430 Timberbrook Dr Kirkwood MO 63122

LAWTON, HELEN B., lecture agy. exec.; b. Indian Orchard, Mass., Dec. 6, 1912; d. John A. and Clara E. (Moren) Buckley; student N.Y. U., 1930-31; m. C. Herbert Lawton, Mar. 20, 1941. Asst. editor Funk & Wagnalls, N.Y.C., 1928-39; with W. Colston Leigh, Inc., exec. lecture agy., N.Y.C., 1939—, asst. treas., 1957-62, treas., 1962—. Mem. Nat. Council of Women of U.S. Roman Catholic. Home: 57 Broad St Matawan NJ 07747 Office: Colston Leigh Inc 49-51 State Road Princeton NJ 08540

LAWTON, JACQUELINE AGNES, communications co. exec.; b. Bklyn., June 9, 1933; d. Thomas Joseph and Agnes Rose (McLaughlin) Maguire; grad. N.Y.C. public schs.; m. George W. Lawton, Feb. 14, 1954; children—George, Victoria, Thomas. With Bell System, 1954—, mktg. mgr. N.Y. Telephone, 1978-81, mktg. mgr. health care, N.Y.C., 1981-82, AT & T dist. field market mgr. health care and lodging, N.Y.C., 1982—; lectr. in field. Mem. Sales and Mktg. Execs. Internat., Am. Mgmt. Assn., Nat. Assn. Female Execs. Republican. Roman Catholic. Home: 68 Oxford St New Hyde Park NY 11040 Office: 633 3d Ave 5th Floor New York NY 10036

LAWTON, MARICA JEAN, clin. psychologist; b. Pawtucket, R.I., May 21, 1937; d. Walter Lincoln and Jean Fraser (Baldwin) Lawton; A.B. magna cum laude in Psychology, Pembroke Coll., 1959; M.A. in Psychology, Northwestern U., 1961, Ph.D., 1963. Psychologist, inpatient coordinator Children's Unit, Nebr. Psychiat. Inst., Omaha, 1963-67, Arapahoe Mental Health Center, Englewood, Colo., 1968-70; pvt. practice psychology, Denver, 1970-73, Richmond, Va., 1977—; mgr. Women's Home, Arlington, Va., 1974-75; mem. faculty U. Nebr., 1963-67, Met. State Coll., 1970-71, Arapahoe Community Coll., 1972; asst. prof. rehab. dept. Va. Commonwealth U., Richmond, 1975—; mem. tech. panel health services area, Richmond, 1979-80; mem. Nat. Inst. of Alcohol Abuse and Alcoholism tng. grant rev. com., 1979-81; pres. Growth and Recovery Opportunites, Inc., 1981—; chmn. bd. Greater Richmond Council on Alcoholism and Drug Abuse, 1976-80, Richmond Aftercare, 1977-78. Mem. St. John's Adv. Com., 1981—. Mem. Am. Psychol. Assn., Va. Psychol. Assn., Va. Acad. Clin. Psychologists, Va. Assn. Alcoholism Counselors, Nat. Assn. Alcoholic Counselors, Soc. of Psychologists in Substance Abuse, Psychologists Helping Psychologists, Nat. Council on Alcohol Edn. (mem. rev. panel 1976, 1979—). Conglist. Clubs: Richmond Stamp, Appalachians Trail, Zonta. Contbr. articles in field to profl. jours. Home: 2430 Pineway Dr Richmond Va 23225 Office: Va Commonwealth U Alcohol and Drug Edn Rehab Program 812 W Franklin St Richmond VA 23284

LAWTON, MARY CECILIA, lawyer, govt. ofcl.; b. Washington, June 2, 1935; d. Frederick Joseph and Cecilia Alice (Walsh) L.; A.B. magna cum laude, Seton Hill Coll., 1957, LL.D. (hon.), 1972; LL.B., Georgetown U., 1960. Admitted to D.C. bar, 1960; atty.-advisor Office of Legal Counsel, U.S. Dept. Justice, Washington, 1960-72, dep. asst. atty. gen., 1972-79. counsel for intelligence policy, 1982—; gen. counsel Corp. for Public Broadcasting, Washington, 1979-80; adminstrv. law officer, White House, Washington, 1980-82. Trustee, Seton Hill Coll., 1970-77, 79—; dir. John Carroll Soc., Washington, 1979—. Recipient Atty. Gen.'s disting. service award, 1976. Mem. Am. Bar Assn., Fed. Bar Assn., D.C. Bar Assn. Roman Catholic. Co-editor: These Unalienable Rights, 1965, 68, 70. Office: 10th and Constitution Ave Washington DC 20530

LAX, FRANCES REINER, mfg. co. exec.; b. Steubenville, Ohio, July 16, 1922; d. Samuel and Minnie (Wigransky) Reiner: student Goucher Coll., 1940-42; B.A., Bryn Mawr Coll., 1944; M.A., Radcliffe Coll., 1946; m. June 1, 1947 (dec.); children—Jonathan Reiner, Stephen Girard, Andrew Reiner, Charles Reiner. Actuarial staff, John Hancock Life Ins. Co., Boston, 1946; econs. staff mem. Harvard U., 1947-48; dir. SGL Industries, Inc., Haddonfield, N.J., 1976—. Mem. LWV, 1950—, N.J. state dir., 1971-72, lobbyist, 1972-74; pres. Am. Field Service, Haddonfield, 1962-64, regional rep., 1964-69; mem. Phila. internat. adv. commn. Celebration Bicentennial, 1973-76; hostess Phila. Council Internat. Visitors, 1976—; bd. dirs. Glassboro State Coll., 1980—, vice chmn. bd. trustees, 1981—. Mem. Phila. Art Alliance, Bryn Mawr Club Phila., Goucher Club Phila., Radcliffe Club Phila., Harvard Club Phila. (dir.), Harvard Club N.Y. Democrat. Unitarian. Home: 130 The Mews Haddonfield NJ 08033

LAXTON, JUDY BRINKLEY, psychiat. social worker; b. Maryville, Tenn., Sept. 14, 1947; d. James Henderson and Alice Patricia (Hall) Brinkley; B.S., U. Tenn., 1969, M.S.S.W., 1971; m. Larry R. Laxton, Dec. 27, 1969; children—Natasha, Renea. Psychiat. social worker Searcy State Mental Hosp., Mount Vernon, Ala., 1971-77, dir. social services, 1977—, quality assurance coordinator, 1981—. Lic. Cert. Social Worker, Ala. Mem. Nat. Assn. Social Workers (co-chmn. continuing edn. com., chmn. nominating com. 1981, state nominating com. 1981), Acad. Cert. Social Workers. Home: 7855 Bardin Dr Semmes AL 36575 Office: Mount Vernon AL 36565

LAY, NANCY ANN, state ofcl.; b. Newton, Miss., Mar. 5, 1949; d. Robert Harold and Cherry (Pearson) Lay; B.S., U. So. Miss., 1971; postgrad. Miss. State U. Tchr., Sykes Elem. Sch., Jackson, Miss., 1972-73; mgr. Firestone Tire & Rubber Co., Jackson, 1975-76; supr. new bus. dept. Allstate Ins., Jackson, 1977-78; staff asst. U.S. Congressman G.V. Montgomery, Washington, 1979; state supr. indsl. tng. Miss. Dept. Edn., Jackson, 1980—. Mem. Nat. Employment and Tng. Assn., Miss. Employment and Tng. Assn. (v.p. 1981-82), Miss. Assn. Vocat. Educators, State Employees Assn. Miss., Nat. Assn. Female Execs., Delta Delta Delta. Roman Catholic. Office: PO Box 771 Jackson MS 39205

LAYCOCK, DEANE CLARK, banker; b. Lutherville, Md., Apr. 23, 1921; d. Robert Otto and Sadie (Robinson) Clark; student Balt. Coll. Commerce, 1937-38; m. Zane B. Laycock, Dec. 6, 1952. With Fiduciary Trust Co., Boston, 1962-68, 74—, trust officer, 1974—, v.p., 1981—; exec. asst. to pres. Yale U., 1969-74; asst. treas. Radcliffe Coll., 1975—. First v.p., chmn. fin. com. Boston YWCA, 1976-79, bd. dirs., 1976-79; exec. com., chmn. planning and evaluation com., trustee United Community Planning Corp., Boston, 1977—, asst. treas., 1981—; bd. dirs. Mass. chpt. Arthritis Found., 1981—; bd. dirs., mem. council, chmn. research com. YMCA of U.S.A., 1981—. Mem. Nat. Alliance Profl. and Exec. Women's Networks (pres. 1980—), Boston Luncheon Club Bus. and Profl. Women (founder, pres. 1975-80, exec. com. 1975—), Clubs: Harvard, Federal (Boston). Office: 175 Federal St Boston MA 02105

LAYMAN, ALICE BEDELL CONNOLLY (MRS. LESTER C. LAYMAN), journalist; b. New Haven; d. Edwin Greeley and Elizabeth (Degnan) Bedell; B.S. cum laude, N.Y. U., 1931; m. Roger A. Connolly,

Oct. 8, 1934 (dec. July 1953); m. 2d, Lester C. Layman, Oct. 31, 1959. Adminstrn. secondary schs., New Haven, 1931-54; asst. to dir. publicity ARC, New Haven, 1941-45; dir. pub. relations Quinnipiac council Boy Scouts Am., New Haven, 1953-54, New Haven Heart Assn., 1954-58, Nat. Found. for Infantile Paralysis, New Haven, 1953-57, Hosp. of St. Raphael, New Haven, 1954-58, Hosp. of Good Samaritan Med. Center, Los Angeles, 1959-69; mem. publicity com. New Haven Cancer Soc., 1957-58, Conn. Assn. for Blind, 1956-58; fashion and beauty editor Bridgeport (Conn.) Post, 1948-77. Bd. dirs. Neighborhood Music Sch., New Haven, 1949-58. Mem. Am. Hosp. Assn., Am. Soc. for Hosp. Pub. Relations (dir. 1965-67), Assn. Western Hosps., Hosp. Council So. Calif. (chmn. 1964-69), Charity League New Haven (life), New Haven Advt. Club (hon.), Fashion Group, Women in Communication, Kappa Delta Pi. Clubs: Desert Island Country, Desert Press, Palm Springs Women's Press. Address: 899 Island Dr E 405 Rancho Mirage CA 92270

LAYMON, EILEEN CAROL, advt. exec.; b. Englewood, N.J., Nov. 25, 1949; d. John William and Dorothy Patricia (Concannon) McIntyre; B.A. cum laude in Philosophy, Newton Coll. of Sacred Heart, 1971; M.S. in Broadcast Journalism, Boston U., 1973; m. Kent Davis Laymon, Sept. 18, 1976; 1 son, Jesse Davis. Communications dir. Eastern Mass. Public Interest Research Group, Boston, 1973; account exec. Earl Newsom & Co., N.Y.C., 1973-78, J. Walter Thompson, 1978—, account supr., 1980—, v.p., 1981—. Mem. mktg. adv. bd. Columbia U. Sch. Bus. Mem. N.Y. Women in Communications, Inc., Turtle Bay Neighborhood Assn. Office: 466 Lexington Ave New York NY 10017

LAYNE, LUCILE MONKS, YWCA exec.; b. Tipton, Mo., Nov. 10, 1932; d. Harry Ashley and Nell Lucile (Born) Monks; B.A., U. Mo., St. Louis, 1975; M.A., Webster Coll., 1976; m. William B. Layne, Jr., Sept. 19, 1953; children—Holly Jayne, Mark Lynn. Coordinator, U. Mo., St. Louis Women's Center, 1974-75; exec. dir. Alton (Ill.) YWCA, 1975—. Mem. Mo. Women's Polit. Caucus; treas. Women's Equity Action League, 1974-78. Mem. YWCA, NOW, ERA Coalition, Am. Assn. Social Studies. Home: 10099 Grosvenor Dr Saint Louis MO 63137 Office: 304 E 3d St Alton IL 62002

LAYTON, BRENDA SMITH, med. lab. technician; b. Spartanburg, S.C., June 1, 1941; d. Robert Paul and Agnes A. (White) Smith; M.T., Spartanburg Gen. Hosp., 1960; student U. S.C., 1973-74; m. Eugene Layton, June 8, 1963; 1 son, Clarence Eugene. Med. lab. technician Spartanburg (S.C.) Gen. Hosp., 1960-64, Dr. Otis M. Hill, Enoree, S.C., 1964-65, Dr. Otis Hill, Dr. Thomas Jenkins, Dr. Samuel H. Rankin, Laurens, S.C., 1965—. Pres. Cross Anchor Grade Sch. PTA, 1973-75; bd. dirs. Laurens Christian Women's Club, 1980-81. Mem. Am. Soc. Clin. Pathologists. Democrat. Baptist. Club: Homemakers. Address: Route 2 Enoree SC 29335

LAZANSKY, ELENORE MAY, psychologist; b. Manila, May 1, 1909 (parents Am. citizens); d. Milton William and Carrie May (Ward) L.; A.B., U. Calif., Berkeley, 1931, M.A., 1932. Tchr. math., counselor, testing chmn. Oakland (Calif.) Public Schs., 1935-74, organizer, evaluator gifted program, 1957-61; instr. Merritt City Coll., Oakland, 1956-57, 61-62; head dept. math. Castlemont High Sch., Oakland, 1968-69; tchr. U. Calif. summer demonstration secondary sch., 1943, 44, 51; pvt. practice ednl. psychology, Lafayette, Calif., 1975—; adviser, dir., treas. Calif. Scholarship Fedn., 1967-74; curriculum cons. NSF fellow, 1963-65. Fellow AAAS; mem. Nat. Council Tchrs. Math. (past dir.), Am. Ednl. Research Assn., Calif., Contra Costa (sec.-treas. 1976-77) psychol. assns., NEA, Calif. Tchrs. Assn., Internat. Platform Assn., Phi Beta Kappa, Sigma Xi, Pi Lambda Theta, Pi Mu Epsilon, Mt. Diablo Iris Soc. Republican. Presbyterian. Club: San Francisco Bay West Highland White Terriers. Author articles, reports, curriculum materials.

LAZAR, NANCY PADGETT, lawyer, librarian; b. Newberry, S.C., June 3, 1932; d. Price J. and Caroline (Weeks) P.; B.S., Northwestern U., 1953; M.L.S., U. Md., 1972; J.D., Georgetown U., 1977; m. David Lazar, Aug. 6, 1953. Admitted to D.C. bar, 1977; asst. librarian U.S. Ct. Appeals for D.C. Circuit, Washington, 1972-74, supervisory librarian, 1974—. Mem. D.C. Bar Assn., Am. Assn. Law Libraries, D.C. Law Librarians Soc., Am. Library Assn., D.C. Library Assn., Spl. Library Assn. Home: 5301 Duvall Dr Bethesda MD 20816 Office: United States Court House Washington DC 20001

LAZAROW, JANE KLEIN, state agency research analyst; b. Chgo., Jan. 18, 1919; d. Philip and Regina (Niederman) Klein; B.S., U. Chgo., 1939; M.S.L.S., U. Minn., 1970, now postgrad.; m. Arnold Lazarow, Dec. 15, 1940; children—Paul B., Normand H. Research asso. in hematology Michael Reese Hosp., Chgo., 1939-42; biochemist, war research, 1942-45; med. writer, editor, 1945-75; mem. staff info. retrieval project Diabetes Lit. Index, 1960-75; sr. research analyst Minn. Clearinghouse for Health Planning Info., Minn. Dept. Health, Mpls., 1975-77, sr. research analyst-med. info. systems, 1977—; research fellow/instr. health computer scis. U. Minn., 1974—, chmn. profl. women's sect., 1981-82. Mem. Minn. Mus. Art, Mpls. Inst. Arts, St. Paul Chamber Orch., Minn. Orch., St. Paul Sci. Mus.; chmn. bd. U. Minn. Meml. Found., 1977-80. Nat. Library of Medicine fellow, 1970. Mem. Am. Soc. Info. Sci., AAAS, AAUP, Am. Records Mgmt. Assn., Nat. Micrographics Assn., Soc. Computer Medicine, Med. Library Assn., Minn. Alumni Assn., LWV, Nat. Council Jewish Women, All Good Old Girls (Profl. Women's Network), Sigma Delta Epsilon, Phi Beta Mu. Jewish. Club: U. Minn. Faculty Women's (v.p. 1957-59). Home: 221 Woodlawn Saint Paul MN 55105 Office: 2829 University Ave SE Minneapolis MN 55414

LAZARUS, BARBARA BETH, coll. ofcl.; b. Chgo., Apr. 17, 1946; d. David and Betty (Rosenblatt) L.; A.B. cum laude (Univ. scholar), Brown U., 1967; M.A. (Doris Duke Found. fellow), U. Conn., 1969; Ed.D., U. Mass., 1973; m. Marvin Sirbu, Jan. 6, 1979. Instr. depts. anthropology U. Conn., Storrs, Waterbury and Hartford brs., Eastern Conn. State Coll., 1967-72, adminstrv./teaching staff U. Conn. Inner Coll., Storrs, 1969-72; dir. acad. advising U. Mass. Sch. Edn., Amherst, 1972-73; info. unit dir. career edn. project Ednl. Devel. Center, Newton, Mass., 1972-75; dir. Center for Women's Careers, Wellesley (Mass.) Coll., 1975—, dir. instl. programs, 1981—; coordinator/teaching teams Asian Women's Work Seminars, India, 1978, Singapore, 1979, Hong Kong, 1980, Manila, 1981; vis. staff mem. appts. com. St. Hilda's Coll., Oxford (Eng.) U., 1980. Mem. Council on Anthropology and Edn., Am. Assn. Higher Edn., Virginia Gildersleeve Internat. Fund for U. Women (dir. 1981—), Assn. N.Am. Cooperating Agys. of Overseas Women's Christian Colls. (cons. 1981—), Am. Council on Germany, Higher Edn. Resource Services (adv. bd. 1976—), Nat. Assn. Women Deans Adminstrs. and Counselors, Am. Personnel and Guidance Assn., Phi Kappa Phi. Democrat. Jewish. Contbr. articles to profl. jours. Office: Center for Women's Careers Wellesley Coll Wellesley MA 02181

LAZARUS, CAROL NUNES, clin. psychologist; b. Bethlehem, Pa., Oct. 27, 1929; d. Lee and Louise Adler (Comens) Nunes; A.B., U. Pitts., 1950, M.S., 1951; M.A., Adelphi U., 1975, Ph.D., 1978; m. Harold Lazarus, June 22, 1952; children—Mark, Eric. Social work asst. L.I. Jewish-Hillside Med. Center, 1973; instr., lectr. Hofstra U., 1955-65; asso. chief psychologist S.E. Nassau Guidance Center, 1977—; adj. prof. psychology Fla. Inst. Tech., 1980—. U. Pitts. scholar, 1950-51. Mem. Am. Psychol. Assn., Nassau County Psychol. Assn., ACLU, Adelphi Soc. Psychoanalysis and Psychotherapy, LWV (v.p. human resources Nassau County 1970-72; pres. Hempstead Central 1968-70). Home: 225 Wellington Rd Garden City NY 11530 Office: SE Nassau Guidance Counseling Center 3375 Park Ave Wantagh NY 11793

LAZARUS, JESSICA SLADKUS, educator; b. N.Y.C., Nov. 7, 1930; d. Louis Gene and Helen (Violante) Lombardi; B.S. in Retailing, L.I.U., 1950; m. Frank I. Lazarus, Apr. 14, 1962; children—Amy, Tracey, Trudi. Retail buyer Saks Fifth Ave., N.Y.C., 1955-58, Abraham & Straus, Bklyn., 1959-62; asso. prof. merchandising U. Cin., 1969—; cons. U.S. Shoe Corp., 1977-80; lectr. in field. Bd. dirs. Jewish Hosp., Cin., 1962-70. Mem. Fashion Group Internat., NOW. Clubs: Losantiville Country, U. Cin. Faculty. Home: 215 Hilltop Ln Cincinnati OH 45215 Office: U Cin Cincinnati OH 45220

LAZARUS, JUDY TOBIN, psychotherapist; b. Marion, Ohio, May 21, 1945; d. Harold Leo and Mary (Murphy) Tobin; B.A., Mt. St. Joseph on-the-Ohio, Cin., 1967; M.S.W. (Daus. of Isabella scholar), Cath. U. Am., 1972; m. Brian Lazarus, June 6, 1971; children—Kerry, Joshua, Devin. Child welfare worker, Cin., 1967-68; policewoman, Washington, 1968-69; alt. service youth worker runaway house, co-founder Second house, group foster home for adolescents, Washington, 1969-71; child therapist Prince George's County Community Mental Health, Cheverly, Md., 1972-76; pvt. practice psychiat. social work, Annapolis and Hyattsville, Md., 1976—; mem. Legal Def. Trust, 1980—, chmn., 1982—; cons. to YWCA Women's Center Counselling Service, 1978-79. Lic. cert. social worker, Md. Mem. Nat. Assn. Social Workers (chmn. legal def. trust, 1981—), Acad. Certified Social Workers. Democrat. Home: 1786 Generals Hwy Annapolis MD 21401 Office: Box 531 Route 1 Annapolis MD 21401

LAZARUS, ROCHELLE BRAFF, advt. agy. exec.; b. N.Y.C., Sept. 1, 1947; d. Lewis L. and Sylvia R. Braff; A.B., Smith Coll., 1968; M.B.A., Columbia U., 1970; m. George M. Lazarus, Mar. 22, 1970; children—Theodore, Samantha. Product mgr. Clairol Co., N.Y.C., 1970-71; with Ogilvy & Mather, N.Y.C., 1971—, account supr., 1973-77, mgmt. supr., 1977—, sr. v.p., 1981—; mem. career counseling bd. Smith Coll. Recipient Webster prize Columbia U. Bus. Sch., 1970. Clubs: Smith Coll., Columbia U. Bus. Sch. (N.Y.C.). Home: 530 E 86th St New York NY 10028 Office: Ogilvy & Mather 2 E 48th St New York NY 10017

LAZZARI, MARCELINE MARIE, social worker; b. Upland, Calif., Sept. 10, 1944; d. James and Louise Hortense (Biane) Lazzari; A.A., U. San Diego, 1965; B.A., Mt. St. Mary's Coll., 1968; M.S.W. (NIMH fellow, VA fellow), St. Louis U., 1971; postgrad. U. Denver, 1982—. Group worker Regis House Community Center, West Los Angeles, Calif., 1966-68; tchr. Spalding (Nebr.) Acad., 1968-69; social worker Boulder County Dept. Social Services, Boulder, Colo., 1972-76, Adams County Dist. 50 Schs., Westminster, Colo., 1976-77; social worker Boulder Valley Public Schs., 1977-81, chmn. sch. social workers, 1978-81; field instr. U. Denver, 1978-81; cons. Boulder Communications Clinic, Inc., 1980—. Lic. social worker, Colo. Mem. Nat. Assn. Social Workers, Acad. Cert. Social Workers, Colo. Sch. Social Work Assn., Boulder Valley Edn. Assn., NOW, ACLU, U.S. Volleyball Assn., Humane Soc. Home: 780 Grant Pl Boulder CO 80302 Office: PO Box 9011 Boulder CO 80301

LAZZARO, CHERYL ADELINA, personnel adminstr.; b. Norwalk, Conn., June 28, 1951; d. Joseph F. and Dorothy (Nottis) Manes; A.A., Cazenovia Coll. for Women, 1971; B.A., Sacred Heart U., 1983; m. Michael N. Lazzaro, Aug. 19, 1972; 1 son, Michael A. Asst. buyer Paul Zabin Children Shop, Westport, Conn., 1969-72; personnel rep. Roger William Hosp., Providence, 1973-74; sr. personnel rep. Gt. No. Nekoosa Corp., Stamford, Conn., 1974-78, benefit adminstr., 1977-78; personnel adminstr. GTE Satellite Corp., Stamford, Conn., 1978—. Active ARC, Am. Cancer Soc. Mem. Women in Mgmt., Am. Mgmt. Assn., Am. Soc. Personnel Adminstrn., Toastmasters Internat. (charter mem. local club). Roman Catholic. Home: 24 Mills St Norwalk CT 06850 Office: One Stamford Forum Stamford CT 06904

LEACH, ELIZABETH MOONEY, educator; b. New Haven, Jan. 19, 1932; d. William John and Elizabeth Mary (Duffy) Mooney; B.A., New Haven State Tchrs. Coll., 1953; M.S., U. Bridgeport, 1978; m. Clifford Leach, June 20, 1953; children—Clifford, Paul, Craig, Mary. Tchr., Jerome Harrison Sch., North Branford, Conn., 1953-56; dir. Head Start Program, New Haven, 1961-63; tchr. 6th grade Essex (Conn.) Elem. Sch., 1974—, asst. prin., 1978—. Mem. Essex Democratic Town Com.; mem. Conn. Dem. Central Com.; bd. dirs. Birthright of Greater Westbrook (Conn.). Mem. Valley Regional Tchrs. Assn. (dir.), NEA, Conn. Edn. Assn. Roman Catholic. Home: Dogwood Dr Centerbrook CT 06409

LEACHMAN, CLORIS, actress; b. Des Moines, ed. Northwestern U.; m. George England, 1953 (div. 1979); 5 children. Motion picture appearances include Kiss Me Deadly, Butch Cassidy and the Sundance Kid, The Last Picture Show, W.U.S.A., Dillinger, Daisy Miller, Young Frankenstein, 1974, Crazy Mama, High Anxiety, 1977, The North Avenue Irregulars, 1979, Scavenger Hunt, 1979, Herbie Goes Bananas, History of the World, Part I, 1981. TV appearances include Lassie, 1957, Route 66, Laramie, Trials of O'Brien, Mary Tyler Moore Show, Phyllis, 1975-77; appeared in TV movie Brand New Life, The Migrants, Death Scream, 1975, A Girl Named Sooner, 1975, Ladies of the Corridor (play), 1975. The New Original Wonder Woman, 1975, The Love Boat 1976, Recipient Oscar award as best supporting actress in The Last Picture Show, Nat. Acad. Motion Picture Arts and Scis., 1971; 4 Emmy awards for Mary Tyler Moore Show and others. Address: care Agy for Performing Arts 9000 Sunset Blvd Suite 315 Los Angeles CA 90069 *

LEAF, MARILYN GROSSMAN, clin. social worker; b. Detroit, Jan. 7, 1942; d. Sol C. and Pauline (Fried) Grossman; B.A., U. Mich., 1963; M.A., U. Chgo., 1965; div.; children—Matthew Aaron, Jeffrey Adam. Clin. social worker Psychiat. and Psychosomatic Inst., Michael Reese Hosp., Chgo., 1965-66, 67-68; clin. social worker, med. student preceptor Stanford U. Med. Center, Palo Alto, Calif., 1966-67; psychotherapist med. student supr. La Rabida Children's Hosp., Chgo., 1969-71; pvt. practice psychotherapy, Chgo., 1971-73; cons. Ancoma Montessori Sch., Chgo., 1971-72; asst. tchrs. profl. vol. Thalians Community Mental Health Center, Cheerful Helpers Nursery Sch.; Los Angeles, 1977-78; clin. social worker, instr., supr. Northridge (Calif.) Hosp. Found., 1978—; pvt. practice psychotherapy, Woodland Hills, Calif., 1978—; Mem. Community Relations Com., San Fernando Valley Region, Jewish Fedn. Council Greater Los Angeles, 1981—. NIMH grantee, 1964-65. Mem. Acad. Cert. Social Workers, Nat. Assn. Social Workers, Calif. Lic. Clin. Social Workers, Nat. Registry Health Care Providers, Soc. Clin. Social Work, Nat. Hospice Orgn. Office: 18401 Burbank Blvd Tarzana CA 91356

LEAHY, JEANNETTE (JEANNETTE OLIVER LEAHY TINEN KAEHLER), actress; b. Eau Claire, Wis., Sept. 9, 1927; d. Kenneth A. and Berthe Hortence (Borie) Oliver; student various acting workshops; m. Thomas J. Leahy (dec.); children—Denyse Leahy Karsten, Thomas J.; m. 2d, William J. Tinen, June 15, 1969 (dec.); m. 3d, Wallace W. Kaehler, Jan. 13, 1980. TV personality Jeannette Lee, Sta. WFBM-TV, Indpls., 1950-53; actress Peninsular Players, summer stock theatre, Door County, Wis., 1960—, also radio, TV, stage, film, commls. Vice-pres., Evanston Drama Club, 1961-62; dir. Wilmette Children's Theatre, 1960-65; bd. dirs. Easter Seal Soc., 1970-75. Mem. Actors Equity Union, SAG, AFTRA, Chgo. Unlimited. Republican. Roman Catholic. Clubs: North Shore Country, Wilmette-Kenilworth (pres. 1956-57), North Shore Assos. (pres. 1982-83).

LEAK, MARGARET ELIZABETH (PEGGY), ins. co. exec.; b. Atlanta, Sept. 9, 1946; d. William Whitehurst and Margaret Elizabeth (Whitsitt) L.; B.S. in Psychology, Okla. State U., 1968; postgrad. U. Okla., 1968-69, Cornell U., 1976-78. Editor, Communications, Eastern State Bankcard Assn., N.Y.C., 1969-71; sr. edn. specialist Citibank, N.Y.C., 1971-73; adminstr. orgn. devel. NBC, N.Y.C., 1973-74; mgr. tng. and devel. Atlantic Cos., N.Y.C., 1974-76, sec. human resources, 1976-78, v.p. human resources, 1978—. Mem. adv. bd., grad. mgmt. program for women Pace U., 1976-78. Mem. Am. Soc. Personnel Adminstrn., Am. Mgmt. Assn., Ins. Co. Edn. Dirs. Soc. (nat. v.p. 1978), Gamma Phi Beta. Presbyterian. Office: Atlantic Cos 45 Wall St New York NY 10005

LEAR, EVELYN, soprano; b. Bklyn.; vocal student in N.Y.C.; student N.Y.U., Hunter Coll.; children—Jan, Bonni; m. 2d, Thomas Stewart. Song recitals Phillips Gallery, Washington; mem. Juilliard Sch. Music Workshop; recital Town Hall, N.Y.C., 1955; lead in Marc Blitzstein's Reuben, Reuben; performed Strauss's Four Last Songs with London Symphony Orch., 1959; mem. Deutsche Opera, 1959; appeared in Lulu at Vienna Festival, 1962, The Marriage of Figaro at Salzburg Festival, 1962; appeared throughout world, 1962-66; debut Vienna State Opera, 1964, Frankfurt Opera, 1965, Covent Garden, 1965, Kansas City (Mo.) Performing Arts Found., 1965, Chgo. Lyric Opera, 1966, La Scala Opera, 1971, also in Brussels, San Francisco, Los Angeles, Buenos Aires; debut at Met. Opera, 1967, mem. co., 1967—; roles include Tosca, Manon, Marshallin; TV appearance in La Boheme, 1965; numerous solo appearances, 1960—; appeared in film Buffalo Bill, 1976; rec. artist Angel Records, Deutsche Grammophon. Recipient Concert Artists Guild award, 1955; Liederabend, Salzburg Festival, 1964; Grammy award for best operatic recording (Marie in Wozzeck), 1965. Fulbright scholar, 1957. Address: care Columbia Artists Mgmt Inc 165 W 57th St New York NY 10019

LEARNED, MICHAEL, actress; b. Washington, Apr. 9; ed. Austria, Eng.; m. Peter Donat (div.); children—Caleb, Christopher, Lucas; m. 2d, William Parker, Dec. 18, 1979. Apprentice, Conn. Shakespeare Festival; with resident and touring cos. Can. Stratford Shakespeare Festival, Am. Conservatory Theatre, also San Diego Shakespeare Festival; stage appearances include The Three Sisters, A God Slept Here, Antony and Cleopatra, Under Milkwood, Tartuffe, Deedle Dumpling, My Son, God, The Merchant of Venice, Private Lives, Importance of Being Earnest, Miss Margarida's Way, Dear Liar, Mary Stuart; TV appearances include Gunsmoke, Police Story, (movies) Hurricane, 1974, It Couldn't Happen to a Nicer Guy, 1974, Widow, 1976, Little Mo, 1978; appeared in film Apocalypse Now, 1977; appeared on TV series The Waltons, 1972-79, Christmas Without Snow, 1980; star CBS series Nurse, 1980-81; appeared in feature film Touched by Love; also numerous roles in Canadian Broadcasting Corp. prodns. Recipient Photoplay award, 1974; Emmy award Nat. Acad. TV Arts and Scis., 1973, 74, 76. Office: care Henderson / Hogan Agy Inc 247 S Beverly Dr Beverly Hills CA 90212 *

LEARY, MARY ELLEN (MRS. ARTHUR H. SHERRY), journalist; b. Salt Lake City, Apr. 21, 1913; d. William Henry and Alice Marie (Lynch) Leary; B.A., Duchesne Coll., Creighton U., 1934; M.A. in English, Stanford U., 1937; Nieman fellow Harvard U., 1945-46; m. Arthur H. Sherry, June 25, 1949; children—Suzanne, Judith, Virginia. Reporter, San Francisco News, 1937-44, polit. reporter, 1944-45, polit. editor, 1946-52, urban specialist-politics, 1952-56, asso. editor, 1956-64; West Coast corr. Scripps Howard papers, 1964-67; free lance writer and corr. The Economist of London, 1968—; project dir. Ford Found. study, Candidate Media Interaction, 1974-75; lectr. U. Calif., Berkeley and Irvine, U. So. Calif. Mem. advisory bd. San Francisco Human Rights Commn., 1966-68; mem. Oakland Catholic Social Justice Commn., 1968-74; bd. dirs. East Bay Activity Center; mem. advisory council U. Calif. Water Resources Center. Author: Phantom Politics, 1977. Contbr. articles to jours. and mags. Home: 319 El Cerrito Ave Piedmont CA 94611

LEASE, JANE ETTA, librarian; b. Kansas City, Kans., Apr. 10, 1924; d. Joy Alva and Emma (Jaggard) Omer; B.S. in Home Econs., U. Ariz., 1957; M.S. in Edn., Ind. U., 1962; M.S. in L.S., U. Denver, 1967; m. Richard J. Lease, Jan. 16, 1960; children—Janet (Mrs. Jacky B. Radifera), Joyce (Mrs. Robert J. Carson), Julia (Mrs. Earle D. Marvin), Cathy (Mrs. Edward F. Warren); stepchildren—Richard Jay II, William Harley. Newspaper reporter Ariz. Daily Star, Tucson, 1937-39; asst. home agt. Dept. Agr., 1957; homemaking tchr., Ft. Huachuca, Ariz., 1957-60; head tchr. Stonebelt Council Retarded Children, Bloomington, Ind., 1960-61; reference clk. Ariz. State U. Library, 1964-66; edn. and psychology librarian N.Mex. State U., 1967-71; Amway distbr., 1973—; cons. solid wastes, distressed land problems reference remedies, 1967; ecology lit. research and cons., 1966—. Ind. observer 1st World Conf. Human Environment, 1972. Mem. ALA, Nat., N.Mex. edn. assns., AAUP, Regional Environ. Edn. Research Info. Orgn., Nat. Assn. Female Execs., P.E.O., D.A.R., Internat. Platform Assn., Las Cruces Antique Car Club, Las Cruces Story League, N.Mex. Library Assn. Methodist (lay leader). Address: 2145 Boise Dr Las Cruces NM 88001

LEASK, BARBARA GLENN (WALLACE), educator; b. Fresno, Calif., Oct. 7, 1925; d. Joel Glenn and Doris Pearl (Childers) Wallace; A.A., Bakersfield Coll., 1945; B.A., San Jose State Coll., 1947; M.A., Pepperdine U., 1976; Ph.D., Pacific U., 1978; m. Richard Leask, Feb. 14, 1948; children—Jerelyn Leask Harrington, Larry, Wally. Tchr., Bakersfield City and Kern County Schs. (Calif.), 1945-65; tchr. Wingland Sch., Standard Sch. Dist., Oildale, Calif., 1965—. Public relations chmn. Assistance League Bakersfield; pres. Bakersfield Council PTA; mem. Calif. Visual and Performing Arts Rev. Coms. Recipient Outstanding Elem. Tchr. of Am. award, Washington, 1974. Mem. AAUW (past pres.; name grant award 1979; Barbara Leask award founded 1980), Standard Sch. Dist. Tchrs. Assn. (pres., 1978-79, Golden Apple award 1973-74), Freedoms Found. at Valley Forge (Tchr.'s medal 1975), Past Matrons Assn. Kern County, Kern County Matron's Assn. (pres.), Kern County Line Officers Assn. (pres.), Bakersfield Coll. Alumni Assn. (founder), NEA, Internat. Reading Assn. (bldg. rep. 1979-81), Freedoms Found. (chpt. pres. 1980-81), San Jose State Coll. Alumni Assn., Pepperdine Alumni Assn., Alpha Delta Kappa (pres. 1974-76), Delta Kappa Gamma. Republican. Presbyterian. Clubs: Order Eastern Star, Bakersfield Woman's (life). Home: 2907 Christmas Tree Ln Bakersfield CA 93306 Office: Wingland Sch 2000 Diane St Oildale CA 93308

LEATHERMAN, LINDA WILLOUGHBY, program analyst; b. Villa Rica, Ga., Sept. 28, 1939; d. William Robert and Mary Louise (Spinks) Willoughby; student Ga. State Coll. for Women, 1957-59; m. William James Leatherman II, July 7, 1961; children—Tammy, Cindy, William James III. Cost clk. Retail Credit Co., Atlanta, 1959-62; tax examiner IRS, Chamblee, Ga., 1963-64, analyst trainee, 1964-66, mgmt. analyst, 1966-67, computer systems analyst, 1967-69, mgmt. analyst, 1969-79, program analyst S.E. Regional Office, Atlanta, 1980—. Treas. Fairview Civic Club, 1976; treas. Fairview Athletic Assn., 1976, concession stand chmn., 1977-80. Club: Hidden Hollow Saddle (dir. 1977-80, treas., 1977, 78, 80).

LEATHERWOOD, LINDA ANN, illustrator; b. Evanston, Ill., Nov. 27, 1948; d. George Arthur and Margaret Ann (Schutz) Baumhardt;

B.A. in Botany, U. S.Fla., Tampa, 1971; m. Donald Howard Leatherwood, Sept. 27, 1975; 1 dau., Shelley Roxanne. Bot. illustrator U. S. Fla. Herbarium, 1970-71; comml. artist Gen. Telephone and Electronics Co., 1972; asst. U. S.Fla. Bot. Gardens, 1973-74; freelance illustrator, oil landscapist, 1974—; group exhbn. 4th Internat. Exhbn. Bot. Art and Illustration, Carnegie-Mellon U., Pitts., 1977-78; represented in permanent collections Hunt Inst. Bot. Documentation, Carnegie-Mellon U.; illustrator: A Flora of Tropical Florida, 1971; Marine Algae of the West Coast of Florida, 1974; Ferns of Florida, 1976; Marine Botany, 1981; editor newsletter NW Fine Arts League, Houston, 1977. Recipient Best of Media award, Best of Show award (oil-landscape class div.), N.W. Fine Arts League Group Show, 1977. Mem. Tex. Hort. Soc. Address: 28102 Side Saddle Way Magnolia TX 77355

LEAVELL, ALMA MALONE, educator; b. Clay County, Ala., Nov. 15, 1916; d. William Robert and Alice Swillie (Reagan) Ingram; B.S., Jacksonville State U., 1938; M.Ed., Hardin-Simmons U., 1950; Ed.D., George Peabody Coll., 1965; m. Clifton James Malone, May 7, 1941 (dec. 1959); m. 2d, James Berry Leavell, Dec. 22, 1972; children—Mary Carolyn Williams, Judith Anne Finch. Tchr. pub. schs., Clay County, Ala., 1934-41, Abilene, Tex., 1955-60; tchr. pub. edn. Hardin-Simmons U., Abilene, 1961-65; asst. prof. edn. Houston Baptist U., 1965-79, Disting. prof. edn., 1979—, chmn. dept. edn., 1973—, dean Coll. Edn. and Behavioral Studies, 1980—; cons. lang. arts Houston Area Schs. Mem. Am. Assn. Colls. Tchrs. Edn., Tex. Assn. Tchr. Educators, Tex. Assn. Coll. Tchrs. of Edn., Internat. Reading Assn., Delta Kappa Gamma, Kappa Delta Pi. Democrat. Baptist. Home: 8112 Fondren Houston TX 77074 Office: 7502 Fondren Houston TX 77074

LEAVITT, AUDREY FAYE COX, TV programming exec.; b. Old Hickory, Tenn., June 1, 1932; d. James Aubrey and Bernice (Hudnall) Cox; student David Lipscomb Secondary Sch. and Coll., 1947, Tenn. Sch. Broadcasting, 1949-50, Vanderbilt U., 1948-50; children—Jack, Teresa. Woman commentator, continuity chief radio sta. WGNS, Murfreesboro, Tenn., 1949-50; announcer, continuity chief, traffic dir. Sta. KDWT, Stamford, Tex., 1950-51; sales account exec. Sta. KMAC, San Antonio, 1952; continuity chief, announcer Sta. KEYL-TV, San Antonio, 1952-54, also firm dir.; film buyer, mgr. Sta. WOAI-TV, San Antonio, 1954-68, ops. mgr. film, video-tape traffic, continuity, 1968-71; film and videotape operations mgr., film buyer Sta. KENS-TV, San Antonio, 1972-79; exec. v.p. Jim Thomas & Assos., San Antonio, 1979-80; owner Communique Internationalé, TV programming syndication, 1981—; co-owner P.R. Inc., public relations cons.; exec. producer TV series The Lone Star Sportsman Show; writer, exec. producer and dir. TV series Weather or Not; writer, producer gourmet cooking show For Men Only. Republican. Home: 1009 Townsend St Apt 6 San Antonio TX 78209 Office: PO Box 1178 San Antonio TX 78294

LEAVITT, JOAN KAZANJIAN, state ofcl.; b. Boston, Jan. 14, 1926; d. Varaztad Hovannes and Marion V. (Hanford) Kazanjian; A.B., Radcliffe Coll., 1947; M.A., Smith Coll., 1949; M.D., Boston U., 1953; m. Don K. Leavitt. Intern in pediatrics Boston City Hosp., 1953-54, resident in pediatrics, 1954-55; resident in pediatrics Mass. Gen. Hosp., Boston, 1955-56, 57-58; pediatrician Comanche County (Okla.) Guidance Center, Lawton, 1959; pvt. practice medicine specializing in pediatric, Altus, Okla., 1959-64; med. dir. Jackson County (Okla.) Health Dept., 1960-67, Kay County (Okla.) Health Dept., 1967-75, Kay County and Payne County Health Depts., 1975-76; chief maternal and child health service Okla. Health Dept., 1976, dep. commr. for personal health services, 1976-77, commr. health, 1977—; mem. numerous bds., commns., councils and coms. in field. Mem. AMA, Okla. State Med. Assn., Okla. Public Health Assn., Oklahoma County Med. Soc., Assn. State and Territorial Health Ofcls., Sigma Xi.

LEAVITT, KATHLEEN JEAN, early childhood educator; b. San Francisco, Feb. 25, 1953; d. Malcolm M. and Jean (Chesley) Jacobs; B.A., Humboldt State U., 1974; M.A., Sonoma State Coll., 1977; m. Aug. 14, 1974; 1 dau., Julia Kathleen. Tchr. bilingual edn., Honolulu, 1973-74; tchr. elem. sch. and preschool, Erueka, Calif., 1974-75; dir. learning action Humboldt State U., 1975-76; dir. Tot Time program City of Rohnert Park (Calif.) Prescj., 1976-77; field work supr. early childhood edn. Mercy High Sch., Burlingame, Calif., 1981—; coordinator, dir., owner Parent Power Inc., San Mateo Calif., 1980—; coordinator, dir., owner Adopt-A-Grandparent Program, San Mateo, 1980—. Mem. Nat. Assn. Edn. Young Children, Calif. Assn. Edn. Young Children, Children's Advocacy, Profl. Assn. Childhood Education, Pvt. Nursery Sch. Assn., Nat. Assn. Gifted and Exceptional Democrat. Roman Catholic. Author numerous works in field. Office: 211 S Delaware St San Mateo CA 94402

LEAVITT, MARGARET MENTZER, editor; b. Bklyn., Sept. 12, 1921; d. John Kurtz and Mary Elsie (McKenrick) Mentzer; B.A., Smith Coll., 1943; cert. George Washington U., 1976; m. Howard Bliss Leavitt, June 9, 1944; children—Howard Huntington, Kenneth Read, John Bliss, Donald McKenrick. Instr. English and theater Westbrook Jr. Coll., Portland, Maine, 1943-46; producer, dir. Community Theater, DeKalb, Ill., 1951-55, Newton, Mass., 1958-62, Bethesda, Md., 1962-65, Rio de Janeiro, 1967: dir. Overseas Edn. Fund, LWV, Washington, 1973-76, dir. Asian program, 1973-76; editor in chief Clubwoman mag. Gen. Fedn. Women's Clubs, Washington, 1979—; asst. editor Single Parent Mag., Washington, 1977-79; U.S. del. Asian Women Community Leaders Conf., Kuching, Sarawak, E. Malaysia, 1976. Mem. Smith Coll. Alumnae Assn., AAUW (dir. State Coll. Pa., 1970-72, Bethesda, Md., 1973-74). Home: 8223 Lilly Stone Dr Bethesda MD 20817 Office: 1734 N St NW Washington DC 20036

LEAVITT, MARY JANICE DEIMEL, educator, civic worker; b. Washington, Aug. 21, 1924; d. Henry L. and Ruth (Grady) Deimel; B.A., Am. U., Washington, 1946; postgrad. U. Md., 1963-65, U. Va., 1965-67, 72-73, 78-79, George Washington U., 1966-67; m. Robert Walker Leavitt, Mar. 30, 1945; children—Michael Deimel, Robert Walker, Caroline Ann. Tchr., Rothery Sch., Arlington, Va., 1947; dir. Sunnyside, Children's House, Washington, 1949; asst. dir. Coop. Sch. for Handicapped Children, Arlington, 1962, dir., Arlington, Springfield, Va., 1963-66; tchr. mentally retarded children Fairfax (Va.) County Pub. Schs., 1966-68; asst. dir. Burgundy Farm Country Day Sch., Alexandria, Va., 1968-69; tchr., substitute tchr. specific learning problem children Accotink Acad., Springfield, Va., 1970-80; substitute tchr. learning disabilities Children's Achievement Center, McLean, Va., 1973—, Psychiat. Inst., Washington and Rockville, Md., 1976—, Home-Bound and Substitute Program, Fairfax, Va., 1978—; asst. info. specialist Ednl. Research Service, Inc., Rosslyn, Va., 1974-76; docent Sully Plantation, Fairfax County (Va.) Park Authority, 1981. Mem. edn. subcom. Va. Commn. Children and Youth, 1973-74. Den mother Nat. Capital Area Cub Scouts, Boy Scouts Am., 1962; troop fund raising chmn. Nat. Capitol council Girl Scouts U.S.A., 1968-69; capt. amblyopia team No. Va. chpt. Delta Gamma Alumnae, 1969; fund raiser Martha Movement, 1977-78. Recipient award Nat. Assn. for Retarded Citizens, 1975. Mem. AAUW (co-chmn. met. area mass media com. D.C. chpt. 1973-75, v.p. Alexandria br. 1974-76, fellowship co-chmn. Springfield-Annandale br. 1979-80, name grantee ednl. found. 1980, historian 1980-82), Assn. Part-Time Profls. (co-chmn. Va. local groups, job devel. and membership asst. 1981), Delta Gamma (treas. No. Va. alumnae chpt. 1973-75, pres. 1977-79, found. chmn. 1979-81). Roman Catholic. Club: Arlington Hall Officer's. Home: 7129 Rolling Forest Ave Springfield VA 22152

LEAVITT, NORMA MURIEL, educator; b. N.Y.C., July 27, 1911; d. Alvin Benton and Laura (Urquhart) L.; diploma Sargent Coll. of Boston U., 1930; B.S. in Edn., Boston U., 1931; M.A., Columbia U., 1933, Ed.D., 1948. Dir. women's phys. edn. and intramurals Tenn. Wesleyan Jr. Coll., Athens, 1931-32; instr. girls' phys. edn. Roger Ludlowe High Sch., supr. elem. sch. phys. edn., Fairfield, Conn., 1933-35; instr. phys. edn. U. Mo., Columbia, 1935-43, asst. prof., 1943-47, dir. women's intramurals, 1935-47; asst. prof. phys. edn. Ill. State Normal U., 1947-48, asso. prof., 1948-53; prof., head dept. phys. edn. U. Fla., Gainesville, 1953-62, prof. profl. phys. edn., 1962-81, prof. emeritus, 1981—. Sec. Kirkwood Environ. Improvement Assn., v.p., 1977-80. Recipient Twiness award Sargent Coll., 1970, Dudley Allen Sargent service award, 1953, Spl. Alumni award, 1980, Sargent Spirit Centennial award, 1981. Mem. AAHPER (life, honor award 1970, So. Dist. Honor award 1969), Fla. Assn. Health, Phys. Edn. and Recreation (honor award 1964), Fla. Assn. Phys. Edn. Coll. Women, So. Assn. Phys. Edn. Coll. Women, Nat. Assn. Phys. Edn. of Coll. Women. Republican. Presbyterian. Club: Gainesville Altrusa. Co-author 2 books; editor FAHPER Jour., 1965-67, 72-81; contbr. articles to nat. and state jours., chpts. to books. Home: 900 SW 21st Ave Gainesville FL 32601 Office: FLG 302 U Fla Gainesville FL 32611

LEBEDA, MILDRED RUTH, hosp. adminstr.; b. Sterling, Colo., Feb. 5, 1933; d. Frederick and Amalia Luft; student Northeastern Jr. Coll., U. No. Colo., St. Louis U., Colo. Women's Coll.; children—Valerie Jo Richards Hettinger, Renae Ruth Richards. Co-owner Fish's Profl. Pharmacy, Sterling, 1967-70: acct. Ceres Land & Cattle Co., Sterling, 1970-75; acct. Monfort of Colo., Greeley, 1975-77; adminstr. Meml. Hosp. of Greeley, 1977—, also bd. dirs. Trustee, No. Colo. Osteo. Hosp. Found.: active disaster com. City of Greeley. Mem. Am. Hosp. Assn., Am. Osteo. Hosp. Assn. (trustee 1981—, com. small and rural hosps. 1981—, pres. 1982, 83), Colo. Hosp. Assn., Colo. Osteo. Hosp. Assn. (sec.-treas. 1980—), N. Central Colo. Hosp. Adminstrs. Council (pres. 1982), Larimer/Weld Counties Hosp. Planning Council, Colo. Small and Rural Hosp. Task Force, TONACK (Osteo.) Assn., (People to People Internat./AHA goodwill ambassador to Australia and N.Z. 1981), Phi Sigma Alpha. Lutheran. Office: 928 12th St Greeley CO 80631

LEBEDEFF, DIANE ALEXIS, judge; b. Detroit, June 25, 1943; d. Alexis M. and Vera A. Lebedeff; B.A., U. Mich., 1965, J.D., 1968. Admitted to N.Y. bar, 1969, Mich. bar, 1969; asso. appellate counsel Legal Aid Soc., N.Y.C., 1968-71; atty. div. criminal justice services N.Y. State, 1971-73; atty. N.Y.C. Dept. Rent and Housing Maintenance, 1976-80, gen. counsel, 1976-80, also counsel N.Y.C. Rent Guidelines; housing judge N.Y. Civil Ct., 1980-82, judge, 1983—. Mem. Community Bd. 2, N.Y.C., 1979-80. Mem. Assn. Bar City N.Y., Am. Bar Assn., Nat. Assn. Women Judges, N.Y. State Bar Assn., N.Y. Women's Bar Assn., Delta Delta Delta. Clubs: Women's City, City (N.Y.C.). Address: 111 Centre St New York NY 10014 *

LEBENSON, ELIZABETH JANE, psychiat. social worker; b. N.Y.C., Mar. 17, 1943; d. Herbert and Charlotte (Springer) L.; B.A. magna cum laude, U. Wis.-Madison, 1963; M.S.W. (NIMH fellow), Columbia U., 1968. Vol. Peace Corps, Kabul, Afghanistan, 1963-65; social worker Gouverneur Health Services Program, N.Y.C., 1968-70, social work supr. Youth Services Agy., N.Y.C., 1970-71; mental health coordinator Provident Neighborhood Health Center, Bklyn., 1971-73; sr. social worker Aberdeen (Scotland) Assn. for Social Services, 1973-74; social work supr. St. Dominics Home, Blauvelt, N.Y., 1974-75; pvt. practice psychotherapy, N.Y.C., 1975—; chief social worker Internat. Center for Disabled, N.Y.C., 1975-81, dir. admissions dept., 1981—; adj. asst. prof. N.Y.U., N.Y.C., 1977—. Mem. rehab. com. Manhattan Mental Health Council, 1976—; mem. housing adv. com. Mayor's Office for Handicapped, N.Y.C., 1980—. Mem. Nat. Assn. Social Workers, Acad. Cert. Social Workers. Home: 245 E 25th St New York NY 10010 Office: 340 E 24th St New York NY 10010

LEBLANC, CAROLINE ANNE, nurse, psychotherapist; b. Worcester, Mass., Dec. 11, 1947; d. Leonard Eugene and Gertrude Rita (Plamondon) LeB.; B.S.N. cum laude, Boston Coll., 1969; M.S., U.Md., 1978; postgrad. Georgetown U., 1982—; m. Jon Ralph Hager, May 24, 1969; children—Keith Erik Hager, Brant William Hager. Public health and psychiat. staff nurse, 1969-71; occupational health nurse Def. Supply Agy., Boston, 1971-72; sr. asst. nurse officer USPHS, 1972-74; asst. prof. psychiat. nursing Bloomsburg (Pa.) State Coll., 1978-81; pvt. practice contractural services rural nursing and mental health, clin., ednl. and consultative services, Williamsport, Pa., 1977—; faculty adv. Bloomsburg State Coll. Campus Child Care Center, 1980-81. Founding mem. Balt. Nurses NOW Task Force; founding mem. Wellspring (Md.) Center Human Potential, 1974-75. Served with USPHS, 1972-74. Mem. Am. Nurses Assn., Am. Orthopsychiat. Assn., Pa. Nurses Assn., Phi Kappa Phi, Sigma Theta Tau. Home: 47 S 2d St Hughesville PA 17737

LEBLANC, KAREN MARIE, banker; b. Waltham, Mass., May 29, 1945; d. Moise S. and Mary E. (Murphy) LeB.; student pvt. schs., also various banking courses. With Bank of Watertown, 1964—, asst. v.p. lending div., 1979-80, v.p. mortage and consumer lending, 1980—. Mem. Savs. Bank Women Mass. (officer 1981-82), Watertown C. of C., Nat. Assn. Bank Women, Savs. Bank Officers Club. Address: Watertown Savs Bank Watertown MA 02172

LEBO, MARIE, mortgage broker; b. Newark, Jan. 22, 1941; d. Frank Joseph and Anna (Ferrara) Vumbaca; lic. in real estate Profl. Sch. Bus., Union, N.J., 1973; m. Richard Lebo, Apr. 4, 1959; children—Corey Allen, Linda Marie. Sec. to pres. J.I. Kislak Mortgage Co., Newark, 1962-77, mortgage loan originator sales dept., 1972-75, asst. v.p., 1974-77; partner, owner Mortgage Brokerage Services Co., East Orange, N.J., 1977-81; v.p. Supreme Fin. Services, Inc., Somerville, N.J., 1981—. Mem. Nat. Assn. Female Execs., Am. Soc. Profl. and Exec. Women. Home: 320 Eileen Way Bridgewater NJ 08807 Office: 45 Route 206 S Somerville NJ 08876

LEBOV, NANCY KAPLEAU, speech pathologist; b. New Haven, Dec. 30, 1951; d. Albert Davis and Janice S. (Boehm) Kapleau; B.A., U. Conn., 1973, M.A., 1975; m. Philip Lebov, July 20, 1978. Speech and lang. clinician East Hartford (Conn.) Bd. Edn., 1975-76, Monroe (Conn.) Bd. Edn., 1976-79; clin. supr. speech pathology So. Conn. State Coll., New Haven, 1979—; dir. speech and hearing services Laurel Hts. Hosp., Shelton, Conn., 1980—; cons. speech and lang. Monroe Bd. Edn., 1979—. U. Conn. fellow, 1974, 75. Mem. Am. Speech and Hearing Assn., Nat. Tchrs. Fedn., Conn. Speech and Hearing Assn., Conn. Health Assn. Clubs: Neighborhood Devel. Info., So. Conn. State Coll. Supervisory. Home: Knorrs Rd Oxford CT 06483 Office: 501 Crescent St New Haven CT 06515

LEBOVITZ, JOAN MOND, lawyer; b. N.Y.C., Feb. 23, 1933; d. Morris and Lilian (Socher) Mond; B.A., Hunter Coll., 1954; J.D., U. Conn., 1972; m. Robert Lebovitz, Aug. 29, 1954; children—Samuel, Joseph, Alisa. Tchr. public schs., Hartford, Conn., 1954-57; religious tchr. Beth Israel Synagogue, West Hartford, Conn., 1965-68; admitted to Conn. bar, 1972; atty. dist. counsel's office VA, Hartford, 1975-78, asst. dist. counsel, 1978—, mgr. fed. women's program, 1974—. Pres. Emanuel Synagogue Sisterhood, West Hartford, 1967-69. Mem. Fed. Bar Assn. (sec. Hartford County chpt. 1978-79, treas. 1979-80, v.p. 1980-81, pres. 1982-83), Conn. Bar Assn., Hartford County Bar Assn., Hartford Assn. Women Attys. Home: 574F Mountain Rd West Hartford CT 06117 Office: 450 Main St Hartford CT 06103

LEBOW, SUSAN M., lawyer; b. Bklyn.; d. Philip Jay and Anne (Benjamin) Weingard; B.A. magna cum laude, Bklyn. Coll., 1959; LL.B. cum laude, Bklyn. Law Sch., 1964; m. Marvin LeBow, Dec. 20, 1959; children—Adam, Douglas, Jacqueline, Philice. Admitted to N.Y. bar, 1964; staff atty. law dept. Port Authority N.Y.-N.J., 1964-70; editor Mathew Bender & Co. Legal Pubs., N.Y.C., 1970-73; partner firm Sarisohn, Sarisohn, Carner, Steindler & LeBow, Esqs., Commack, N.Y., 1973—; counsel Huntington chpt. NOW; former counsel to N.Y. State Assn. for Gifted and Talented. Bd. trustees Suffolk County council Girl Scouts U.S.A., 1975-81; Suffolk County liaison officer N.Y. State Lt. Gov., 1974-78. Recipient cert. of appreciation Suffolk County, 1977. Mem. Suffolk County Bar Assn., Nassau County Bar Assn., N.Y. State Bar Assn., Nassau-Suffolk Women's Bar Assn., L.I. Assn. Commerce and Industry (adv. bd.), Nat. Acad. TV Arts and Scis., Phi Beta Kappa. Office: 350 Veterans Memorial Hwy Commack NY 11725

LEBOWITZ, CHARLOTTE MEYERSOHN, social worker; b. Germany, Dec. 22, 1924; d. Franz and Magda (Wellisch) Meyersohn; came to U.S., 1938, naturalized, 1943; B.A., Brown U., 1946; M.S.W., Simmons Coll., 1948; m. Marshall Lebowitz, Aug. 7, 1949; children—Wendy Lebowitz Nowak, Marian, Mark. Psychiat. social worker Jewish Family and Children's Service, Boston, 1948-49, ARC Home Service Dept., Boston, 1949-53, Youth Guidance Center, Framingham, Mass., 1962-69, Brandon Sch., Natick, 1969-74, Natick Pub. Schs., 1975—; adj. clin. instr. Boston Coll. Sch. Social Work, 1981-82; mem. exec. bd. Natick Service Council, 1982—; cons. YWCA, 1970-71. Exec. bd. mem. PTA, 1955-71, chmn. pre-sch. unit, 1955-56, mem. council, 1956-70; trustee council Leonard Morse Hosp., 1976—. Mem. Acad. Cert. Social Workers, Nat. Assn. Social Workers, Sch. Adjustment Counselors Assn., Social Workers Employed Less Than Full Time, Assn. for Mentally Ill Children, Simmons Coll. Sch. Social Work, Brown U. alumni assns., LWV, Nonesuch Pond Improvement Assn. Jewish. Clubs: Walnut Hill Tennis, Rivers Sch. Tennis. Home: 2 Abbott Rd Natick MA 01760 Office: Natick Sch Dept Natick MA 01760

LEBRUN, VIVIAN LUCILLE DAVIS (MRS. DONALD EDWARD LEBRUN), theatre exec.; b. Ayersville, Ohio, Nov. 29, 1909; d. John Edgar and Nettie Ann (Eis) Davis; student pub. schs.; m. Donald Edward LeBrun, July 5, 1932; children—Suzanne LeBrun Cook, Donald Davis. Staff writer South Whitley (Ind.) Tribune, 1947-58, accounts exec., advt. dept., 1958; photographer, columnist Warsaw-Times-Union, Warsaw, Ind., 1947-72; co-owner, co-mgr. Kent Theatre, South Whitley, 1957—. Recipient award for oil painting Whitley County Art Guild Show, Columbia City, 1973. Mem. Gen. Fedn. Women's Clubs (county pres. 1941-42, dist. pres. 1956-58), Nat. League Am. Pen Women, Nat. Writers Club, Ft. Wayne Hist. Soc., DAR (chpt. regent 1972-74, 76, 78-82, organizing regent 1975, Ind. motion picture, radio and TV chmn. 1978—, Continental Congress house com. 1982, ret. state chmn. 1982), Ladies Aux. VFW (post pres. 1945, nat. vice-chmn. 1978—), Whitley County Artist Guild, Ind. Museum Soc. (dist. dir. 1973-75). Methodist. Clubs: Order Eastern Star (worthy matron 1944-45), Kendallville, White Shrine. Address: 106 N Maple St Box 495 South Whitley IN 46787

LECHTMAN, PAMELA JOY, travel writer; b. St. Paul, Apr. 29, 1943; d. Ben L. and Leona Betty (Cell) Price; B.S., U. Minn., 1965; m. Allen Lee Lechtman, June 16, 1967; children—Arthur Thomas, Anthony Grant. Tchr. art St. Paul Ind. Sch. Dist., 1966-67; tchr. Alameda (Calif.) Unified Sch. Dist., 1967-68; with public relations dept. Fitness, Inc., 1976-79; travel writer, 1979—; travel editor Shape mag., Woodland Hills, Calif., 1982—; travel columnist News Chronicle, Thousand Oaks, Calif., 1980; instr. tourism Ventura (Calif.) Coll., 1978-80; producer radio program Update, Sta. KUEN-AM, Ventura, 1974-80; author broadcasting guide You're On The Air, 1979. cert. travelcounselor, Inst. Cert. Travel Agts. Mem. Am. Women in Radio and TV, Public Info. Radio and TV Edn. Soc., AAUW (Grant fellow Ventura County br. 1976, individual grantee 1980). Home: 668 Camino Rojo Thousand Oaks CA 91360 Office: Shape Mag 21100 Erwin St Woodland Hills CA 91367

LECK, GLORIANNE MAE, educator; b. Tomahawk, Wis., July 28, 1941; d. Henry and Evelyn (Ratzburg) L.; B.S., U. Wis., Madison, 1963, M.S., 1966, Ph.D., 1968. Asst. prof. edn. Wis. State U., Oshkosh, 1967-69; asst. prof. cultural founds. of edn. Pa. State U., 1969-73; prof. philosophy and edn. Youngstown (Ohio) State U., 1974—. Chmn., East Wick Park Steering Com., Youngstown, 1981-82. Mem. Am. Ednl. Studies Assn. (mem. exec. council 1980-82), Philosophy of Edn. Soc., Am. Philos. Assn., Soc. Women in Philosophy, NEA, NOW (pres. Youngstown chpt. 1980). Editorial bd. Jour. Ednl. Studies, 1978-82. Home: 1330 Wick Ave Youngstown OH 44505 Office: Edn Bldg Youngstown State U Youngstown OH 44555

LE COCQ, RHODA PRISCILLA, author, educator; b. Lynden, Wash., Jan. 31, 1921; d. Ralph B. and Nellie O. (Straks) Le Cocq; B.A., Wash. State U., 1942; M.A. in Creative Writing, Stanford U., 1950; M.A. in Philosophy, U. Calif., Santa Barbara, 1967; Ph.D., Calif. Inst. Asian Studies, 1970. Radio writer and actress sta. KHQ, Spokane, sta. KOIN, Portland, Oreg., sta. KIRO, Seattle; owner LeCocq-Luray, N.Y.C., 1946-47; lit. scout Farrar, Straus & Cudahy, N.Y.C., 1948-53; public relations dir. art sch. Honolulu Acad. Arts, 1957-58; owner, propr. public relations counseling firm, Honolulu, 1958-61; info. officer Office CD City and County of Honolulu, 1961-63; info. and legis. officer Sacramento County (Calif.) Dept. Social Welfare, 1969-80; instr. U. Hawaii, 1960-61; asst. prof. philosophy extension dept. U. Calif., Davis, 1970-71; asso. prof. Calif. Inst. Asian Studies, 1972-81; lectr. Bombay, India, 1973, Cultural Integration Fellowship, 1975-80, Regional Assn. Transpersonal Psychology, 1977. Served to lt. USNR, 1942-46, ret. Res., 1970. Recipient cert. for contbn. to East-West Understanding, Cultural Internat. Fellowship, 1969, Author Aiding Inst. Understanding, London, 1973, photog. and pubs. awards NACID, 1974. Mem. Public Relations Soc. Am. (dir. Sacramento chpt.), Internat. Platform Assn., Smithsonian Assos., USNR Assn., Mensa, Armed Forces Writers League, Seattle Art Mus., Kappa Alpha Theta, Theta Sigma Phi. Clubs: San Francisco Press; Marines Meml. (life) (San Francisco). Author: Heidegger and Sri Aurobindo, 1972; Vision of Superhumanity, 1973; The Mother/Father Pair, 1977; short story Behold A Pale Horse included in several anthologies, dramatized TV, 1957. Mailing Address: Box 5025 Bellevue WA 98009

LE COUNT, VIRGINIA G., communications co. exec.; b. Long Island City, N.Y., Nov. 22, 1917; d. Clifford R. and Luella (Meier) LeCount; B.A., Barnard Coll., 1937; M.A., Columbia, 1940. Tchr. pub. schs., P.R., 1937-38; supr. HOLC, N.Y.C., 1938-40; translator Guildhall Publs., 1940-41; office mgr. Sperry Gyroscope Co., Garden City, Lake Success, Bklyn. (all N.Y.), 1941-45; billing mgr. McCann Erickson, Inc., N.Y.C., 1945-56; v.p., bus. mgr., bd. dirs. Infoplan Internat, Inc., 1956-69; v.p., bus. mgr. Communications Affiliates Ltd., Communications Affiliates (Bahamas) Ltd., 1968-71; bus. mgr. Jack Tinker & Partners, Inc., 1969-70; mgr. office services Interpublic Group of Cos., Inc., N.Y.C., 1970-72, corp. records mgr., 1972—, mktg. intelligence data mgr., 1978—. Mem. Alumnae Barnard Coll. (dir.). Mem. Marble Collegiate Ch. Club: Atrium. Home: 136 E 55th St New York NY 10022 Office: 1271 Ave of Americas New York NY 10020

LECOURS, ROSE MARY, taxi co. exec., city council woman; b. Boston, July 24, 1910; d. George and Julia (Assar) Haddad; student public schs., Boston; m. Harry Lecours, June 30, 1932; 1 son, Harry J. Owner, operator Rosie's Cab Co., Everett, Mass., 1942—; mem. Everett City Council, 1972—. Roman Catholic.

LECRONE-CHURCH, SALLY CAROLINE, educator; b. Wewoka, Okla., July 23, 1934; d. Elvis Avir and Geneva Cloe (Holmes) Miller; B.S., U. Okla., 1961, M.Ed., 1971; m. Gerlad D. Church, Feb. 14, 1981; children—David, Pamela (dec.), Greg, Jeffrey, Molly. Tchr. emotionally disturbed children in Okla., 1961-73; mem. psychology staff Phil Smalley Children's Center, Norman, Okla., 1973—, prin., 1976—; asso. prof. Oklahoma City U., 1974-76; instr. U. Okla., 1981—; cons., speaker, trainer in field. Adv. bd. Norman Alcohol Info. Center; bd. dirs. Wonder House Day Care Center, Norman, Cleveland County Mental Health Assn. Worry Clinic, 1978. Mem. Nat. Assn. Female Execs., Nat. Council Exceptional Children, NEA, Okla. Women in Edn. Adminstrn., Okla. Sch. Psychologists Assn., Okla. Group Process Soc., Okla. Edn. Assn., Nat. Council Children with Behavior Disorders, Nat. Council Adminstrs. Spl. Edn., Nat. Council Ednl. Diagnostic Services, Okla. Profls. for Emotionally Disturbed Profl. Educators Norman, Nat. Council Accreditation of Tchr. Edn. (evaluator), Hi-Noon Bus. and Profl. Women, Gamma Phi Beta, Phi Delta Kappa, Sigma Beta Phi. Democrat. Episcopalian. Home: 1429 Homeland St Norman OK 73069 Office: Box 1008 Norman OK 73070

LE CROY, BARBARA LOIS PEASE, govt. ofcl.; b. Boston, Apr. 27, 1923; d. Edmund Morris and Clara Hanson (Luscombe) Pease; B.S., Mass. Coll. Art, 1944; postgrad. Ark. State U., 1957-59; M.A., George Washington U., 1974; m. William Cecil LeCroy, Jan. 19, 1946 (dec.); 1 son, Edmund Deckard. Tchr., Portsmouth (N.H.) Sch., 1944-46; typist U.S. Navy, Corpus Christi, Tex., U.S. Marine Corps, Parris Island, S.C., 1946-49; tchr. Marine Corps Dependent Sch., Camp Lejeune, N.C., 1949-50; adminstrv. clk. U.S. Army, Boston, 1950-54; tchr. Lake City and Cash (Ark.) Schs., 1956-58; stenographer U.S. Army ROTC, State U. Ark., 1958-59; with Social Security Adminstrn., 1959—, supervisory employee devel. specialist, Balt., 1972-79, supervisory employee relations specialist, 1980—. Vol., Career Counseling Service, St. John's Episcopal Ch., Hagerstown, Md. Mem. Am. Soc. Tng. and Devel., Am. Soc. Public Adminstrs., Am. Mgmt. Assn., Am. Personnel and Guidance Assn., Vocat. Guidance Assn., Non-White Concerns Assn. Counselor Edn. and Supervision, AAUW, Am. Horse Council, Am. Quarter Horse Assn., Pa. Quarter Horse Assn., Md. Quarter Horse Assn., Va. Quarter Horse Assn., Tenn. Quarter Horse Assn., Am. Paint Horse Assn., Shenandoah Paint Horse Club, Pa. Paint Horse Club, Ohio Paint Horse Club, NOW, Women's Equity Action League, Federally Employed Women, Nat. Women's Party, Internat. Platform Assn. Episcopalian. Club: Blue Ridge Riding. Home: PO Box 45 Mount Airy MD 21771 Office: Social Security Administration Hdqrs 6401 Security Blvd Baltimore MD 21235

LEDBETTER, SANDRA GALE SHUMARD, educator; b. Little Rock, Oct. 18, 1948; d. Frank Ney and Mildred Elizabeth (Oldham) Shumard; B.A., U. Ark., 1971; m. Joel Yowell Ledbetter, Jr., Dec. 16, 1971; children—Elizabeth Talbot, Ann Shay, Mildred Myonne Mitzi. Tchr., Pulaski County (Ark.) Spl. Sch. Dist., 1970-72, Miss Selma's Sch., Little Rock, 1972-74, Pulaski Acad., Little Rock, 1976—. Mem. Pulaski County Democratic Com., 1976—, Dem. State Com., 1976—; co-chmn. Dem. State Adv. Com., 1981—; del. Dem. Nat. Conv., 1980. Mem. Jr. League Little Rock (dir. 1981-82). Methodist. Home: 7 Foxhunt Trail Little Rock AR 72207

LEDERER, ANNE TRACY (MRS. H. AUSTIN LEDERER), civic worker; b. Chgo., Nov. 4, 1917; d. Howard Van Sinderen and Ruth Alexander Tracy; A.B. with honors, Swarthmore Coll., 1938; A.M., Radcliffe Coll., 1940; m. William Rossmoore, June 24, 1938 (div.); 1 dau., Susan Tracy; m. 2d, H. Austin Lederer, Feb. 21, 1959; stepchildren—Meredith, Louise. Substitute tchr., Essex County, N.J., 1958-69. Organizer, first chmn. N.J. chpt. Parents Without Partners, Inc., 1958—; Swarthmore Coll. rep. to Barnard Forum, 1955-57; pres. North Jersey Swarthmore Coll. Alumni Assn., 1957, 69; sec. class of 1938 at Swarthmore, 1958—. Mem. LWV (mem. bd. Verona league 1971-74), Alliance Française. Clubs: Swarthmore; Radcliffe (dir. N.J. 1966-69, 75); Harvard of N.J. Contbr. articles to mags. Home: 32 Otsego Rd Verona NJ 07044

LEDERER, MARIE A., polit. campaign chmn.; b. Phila., Oct. 24, 1927; d. Donato and Edith (Vitacolonna) Panosetti; ed. Phila. Public Relations Inst., 1966-67, Temple U., 1973-76; m. William J. Lederer, June 17, 1950; children—Doneda M. Lederer Guyon, William M., Regina M. Instr. polit. sci. Temple U., Phila., 1976-77; exec. dir. Jackson for Pres. Com., 1976; del. Dem. nat. conv., 1976; voter registration chmn. Dem. exec. com., 1978-79; adminstrv. asst. to Congressman Joseph F. Smith, Pa., 1981-82. Dir. Southeastern Pa. Heart Assn., 1968-71; mem. bd. dirs. Balch Inst., ARC, U.S.S. Cruiser Olympia Ship; mem. Phila. Art Alliance. Recipient Pa. Ho. of Reps., 1974, certs. of merit U.S. Ho. of Reps., 1982. Roman Catholic. Clubs: Am. Legion Ladies Aux., Hist. Ships Assn., Mexican Soc. Home: 1237 Shackamaxon St Philadelphia PA 19125 Office: Congressman Joseph F Smith US Custom House 2d and Chestnut St Philadelphia PA 19106

LEDERMAN, MARIE JEAN, univ. dean; b. Bklyn., Dec. 28, 1935; d. Samuel and Gladys Candel; B.S. magna cum laude, N.Y.U., 1957, Ph.D. (teaching fellow), 1966; M.A., Bklyn. Coll., 1963; 1 son. Tchr. English, N.Y.C. Bd. Edn., 1957-59; instr. N.Y.U., 1965-66; from lectr. to asst. prof. English, N.Y.C. Community Coll., City U. N.Y. Center, 1966-68, asst. prof. SEEK program, 1968-69; from asst. prof. to prof. Baruch Coll., 1969-79; dean Office Acad. Affairs, City U. N.Y., 1979—; v.p. N.Y.C. Assn. Tchrs. English, 1979—; mem. minority affairs com. Coll. Composition and Communication, 1982-83; cons. in field. Recipient Faculty Research award City U. N.Y./PSC, 1976-78. Mem. Nat. Council Tchrs. English, MLA, Am. Com. Irish Studies, Internat. Reading Assn., Community Coll. Gen. Edn. Assn. (dir.). Jewish. Author articles in field. Contbr. profl. procs. Office: 535 E 80th St New York NY 10021

LEDFORD, PATRICIA ANN, state ofcl.; b. Kingsport, Tenn., Apr. 2, 1946; d. Loys Erwin Ledford and Avaleen Davis Ledford Anderson; student East Tenn. State U., 1964-65; student U. Tenn., Knoxville, 1976-79. Staff asst. Senator Bill Brock, Knoxville, 1970-71, 76-77, White House, 1971-72, Senator Howard Baker, Nashville, 1972-73; campaign coordinator Nat Winston for Gov., Nashville, 1973-75; asst. mgr. Hyatt Regency, Knoxville, 1975-76; account exec. Eric Ericson & Assos., Nashville, 1977-79; legis. liaison to Tenn. Gov. Lamar Alexander, Nashville, 1979-80, exec. dir. Tenn. Commn. on Status of Women, 1980, dir. Gov.'s Film and TV Prodn. Office, 1980—. Bd. dirs. Nashville Urban League, Matthew Walker Health Center, Nashville Women's Polit. Caucus; mem. council Am. Council Young Polit. Leaders; mem. aux. Hank Snow Found. Candidate for Met. Council-At-Large, Nashville, 1979; co-chmn. membership com. Nashville Women's Polit. Caucus; alt. del. Atlantic Alliance Young Polit. Leaders, 1979—; mem. adv. com. on human concerns Republican Nat. Com. Mem. CABLE, Tenn. Bus. and Profl. Women's Club, Nat. Assn. Female Execs. (dir.), Nashville Jr. C. of C., Alpha Delta Pi Alumnae Assn. (Alumnae award 1968). Presbyterian. Club: Tenn. Rep. Party Capitol. Office: State Capitol Nashville TN 37219

LEDMAN, LENORE ROSALIE, govt. ofcl.; b. N.Y.C., Oct. 29, 1946; d. Stephen Joseph and Stella Marina (Jurkiewicz) Ledman; B.A., Boston U., 1967; M.A. (hon.), Am. U., 1969. Intern, HUD Urban, N.Y.C., 1969-70, rep. multi-family housing, Newark, 1970-72; exec. dir. Fed. Exec. Bd. of Met. No. N.J., 1972-75; dir. intergovtl. relations Dept. Energy, N.Y.C., 1976-79, program coordinator Office of Fusion Energy, Washington, 1980—; exec. sec. Magnetic Fusion Adv. Com., 1982—; presdl. exchange exec. Grumman Corp., N.Y.C., 1979-80; adj. lectr. Lehman Coll., City U. N.Y., 1973-74. Mem. youth services com. ARC, N.Y. chpt., 1979-80. Mem. Federally Employed Women (v.p. N.Y. chpt. 1978-79). Editor-in-chief Fusion Forefront, 1981—. Office: Dept Energy ER-50 2 G0256 Washington DC 20545

LEE, ALISON ANN, med. technologist; b. Holyoke, Mass., June 30, 1950; d. Robert Keating and Audrey Ethel (Emery) L.; student Russell Sage Coll.; 1968-70; B.A., Mt. Holyoke Coll., 1973. Lab. technician Holyoke Hosp., 1969-72; research asst. U. Mass. Health Services, Amherst, 1972-73; med. technologist Wesson unit Baystate Med. Center, Springfield, Mass., 1973-78; cons. Tulsa City-County Health Dept., 1979-81, Moton Health Center, Tulsa, 1980—; lead med. technologist St. Francis Hosp., Tulsa, 1978—, vol. pediatric orientation program. Alumnae admissions rep. for Greater Tulsa, Mt. Holyoke Coll.; past public edn. chmn., mem. profl. edn. com., bd. dirs. Am. Cancer Soc.; vol. various community activities. Mem. Am. Soc. Clin. Pathologists, Am. Soc. Med. Tech., Okla. Assn. Med. Tech., Tulsa Jr. League (career edn. com.), Alumnae Assn. Mt. Holyoke. Home: 6370 H South 80 East Ave Tulsa OK 74133

LEE, AMY FREEMAN (MRS. FREEMAN LEE), artist, educator; b. San Antonio, Oct. 3, 1914; d. Joe and Julia (Freeman) Freeman; grad. St. Mary's Hall, 1931; student U. Tex., 1931-34; student Incarnate Word Coll., 1934-42, Litt.D. (hon.), 1965; m. Ernest R. Lee, Oct. 17, 1937 (div. Jan., 1941). Art critic San Antonio Express, 1939-41; staff art critic radio sta. KONO, 1947-51; lectr. on art humanities dept. Trinity U., San Antonio, 1954-56, San Antonio Art Inst., 1955-56; lectr. art Our Lady of Lake Coll., San Antonio, 1969-71, one man shows, 1947—, including U. Tex., 1970, 73, Tex. Tech. U., 1970, Del Mar Coll., Corpus Christi, Tex., 1970, Southwestern U., Georgetown, Tex., 1971, 79, Pioneer Meml. Library, Fredricksburg, Tex., 1971, U. Tex. Student Union, 1972, Ojo del Sol Gallery, El Paso, 1972, Shook-Carrington Gallery, San Antonio, 1972, 1st Repertory Theatre, San Antonio, 1974, Sol del Rio Galleries, San Antonio, 1976, Oakwell Library, San Antonio, 1976, U. Central Ark., Conway, 1977, NE La. State U., Monroe, 1978, Our Lady of the Lake U., San Antonio, 1978, Univ. Art Gallery, N. Tex. State U., Denton, 1979, L & L Gallery, Longview, Tex., 1980, Meredith Long Galleries, Houston, 1980, Incarnate Word Coll., San Antonio, 1981, St. Mary's Hall, San Antonio, 1981, others, Tex. and Calif.; exhibited works in numerous group shows U.S. and Europe, including Nat. Soc. Painters in Casein, N.Y.C., 1969-79, Tex. Watercolor Soc., San Antonio, 1974-77, Nat. Watercolor Soc., 1978, 79, Silvermine Guild, New Canaan, Conn., 1974-75, Art Mus. S. Tex., Corpus Christi, 1975-76, Nat. Tour Am. Drawings, Smithsonian Instn., 1965-66, S.W. Tex. Watercolor Soc., 1976, 79, Tex. Watercolor Soc., 1980, Silvermine Guild Artists, New Canaan, Conn., 1980, also ann. exhbns. nat. art socs., galleries, confs.; represented in permanent collections. Pres., mem. exec. bd. San Antonio Blind Assn.; jury mem. children's poetry contest San Antonio Library System; chmn. bd. trustees Incarnate Word Coll., San Antonio; bd. dirs., nat. sec., mem. adv. bd. Gulf States regional office Humane Soc. U.S.; corp. mem. Cambridge Sch., Weston, Mass.; bd. dirs. Madonna Neighborhood Centers, Animal Welfare Soc., West Kennebunk, Maine, Chamber Arts Ensemble, San Antonio, San Antonio Choral Soc., Man and Beast, Inc.; fine arts adv. council U. Tex.; pres. Friends San Antonio Public Library, 1969-70; mem. com. on grievance oversight Tex. State Bar, 1979; adv. bd. Council for Livestock Protection, Braintree, Mass.; mem. citizens' adv. bd. St. Peters-St. Josephs Children's Home, San Antonio, 1981—; mem. nat. adv. bd. Amigos de las Americas, Houston, 1981—; mem. adv. council Coll. Architecture and Environ. Design Tex. A&M U., 1981—; mem. Wild Canid Survival and Research Center, St. Louis. Recipient awards, 1960—, including: 1st prize Contemporary Artists Exhbn., San Antonio, 1973; Women in Art award San Antonio Bus. and Profl. Women's Club, 1975; Drought award Local Artists Exhbn., San Antonio, 1977, drawing award, 1978, M.J. Kaplan award Nat. Soc. Painters in Casein and Acrylic, 1978; numerous other art awards; Hon. Stagescrew award, drama dept. San Antonio Coll., 1975; Service award Providence High Sch., San Antonio, 1976; Gold medal Incarnate Word Coll., San Antonio, 1978; Disting. Alumna medal St. Mary's Hall, 1981; Spl. recognition award Tex. Ednl. Theater Assn., 1982; named Woman of Distinction, Baylor U., 1967; Amy Freeman Lee AAUW Ednl. Found. Fellowship named, 1973. Mem. Am. Fedn. Arts, Nat. Soc. Painters in Casein, Artists Equity Assn., Boston Soc. Ind. Artists (Smith Coll. purchase prize 1950), San Antonio Art League (adv. bd. of presidents, 6th v.p.), Nat. Soc. Arts and Letters, San Antonio Chamber Music Soc. (dir.), Philos. Soc. Tex., Defenders of Wildlife, Am. Anti-Vivisect. Soc. (life), World Fedn. for Protection Animals (life), Nat. Assn. for Advancement Humane Edn., Tex. Art Educators, Woman's Aux. Santa Rosa Hosp. (founder), St. Mary's Hall Alumni Assn., San Antonio Conservation Soc., Poetry Soc. Am., Am. Soc. for Aesthetics, Assn. Internationale des Critiques d'Art, Paris, Contemporary Artists Group San Antonio (dir.), Southwest Watercolor Soc. (purchase prize 1967, Harwood K. Smith award 1969), Tex. Watercolor Soc. (founder, pres., dir., purchase prize 1963, 64, 69, 74, 79, 80), Nat. Watercolor Soc. (Figure painting award 1967), Calif., Los Angeles, San Antonio watercolor socs., Tex. Art Edn. Assn., Coll. Art Assn. Am., Expts. in Art and Tech., Silvermine Guild Artists, S. Tex. Print Soc., Tex. Fine Arts Assn. (adv. council), Tex. Art Alliance, Artists Fellowship of N.Y., Assn. Governing Bds. Univs. and Colls., Internat. Platform Assn., Bus. and Profl. Women's Club (hon.), AAUP, AAUW, Internat. Soc. for Edn. Through Art, Cum Laude Soc. (hon.), Kappa Pi (hon.), Delta Delta Delta, Tau Sigma Delta (hon.), Delta Kappa Gamma (hon.), numerous other groups. Author: Hobby Horses, 1940; A Critic's Notebook, 1943; Remember Pearl Harbor, 1945. Contbg. editor S.A. mag. and Radio Sta. KTSA, San Antonio, 1977. Address: 127 Canterbury Hill San Antonio TX 78209

LEE, ANNE MAROLD, home economics educator; b. Buhl, Minn., Nov. 26, 1908; d. Anton and Maria (Hegler) Marold; B.A. (Shakespeare English award 1929), U. Minn., 1929; M.S. (Kellogg fellow 1929-30), Mich. State U., 1930; Ed.D., Ind. U., 1959; m. John Gordon Lee, Aug. 25, 1935; children—John Gordon, Mary Anne. Instr., then asst. prof., dir. home mgmt. Ind. State Tchrs. Coll., 1930-37; instr. Spokane (Wash.) City Schs., 1942-43; instr. English, U. Utah, 1943-44; mem. faculty Ind. State U., Terre Haute, 1930—, prof. home econs., 1938-75, prof. emeritus, 1975—, chmn. dept., 1938, dir. travel study in home econs., 1967—, dir. summer internship program working with disadvantaged, 1976-80. Bd. dirs. Wabash Valley chpt. ARC, 1965-67. Mem. Nat. Council Adminstrs. Home Econs. (pres. 1969-70), Coll. and Univ. Tchrs. of Food and Nutrition (chmn. central region 1979-80), Am. Home Econs. Assn., Am. Vocat. Assn., Ind. Home Econs. Assn. (pres. 1954-56; Outstanding Home Economist award 1973), Farrington's Grove Hist. Dist. (dir.), Phi Upsilon Omicron, Pi Lambda Theta, Omicron Nu. Home: 823 S 5th St Terre Haute IN 47807 Office: Ind State U Terre Haute IN 47803

LEE, ANNE NATALIE, nurse; b. Bklyn.; d. Taras Pavlovich and Maria (Jukovskaya) Dubovick; B.A., Hunter Coll., 1940; M.A., N.Y.U., 1948; R.N., McLean Hosp. Sch. Nursing, Waverly, Mass., 1946; M.S., Boston U., 1958; m. Henry Lee, Feb. 20, 1945; adopted children—Alice, Jennifer, Philip. Pvt. duty nurse, N.Y.C., 1946-48; staff nurse Vis. Nurse Service, 1947-48; staff nurse health dept. Schoharie Co., N.Y., 1948-51; supervising nurse N.Y. Dept. Health, Syracuse, 1951-53, cons. hosp. nursing, Albany, 1958-63, cons. nurse in service edn., 1963-75, dir. Bur. of Hosp. Nursing Services, 1975-80; cons. nursing services and adminstrn., 1980—; dir., coordinator nursing service instr. program co-sponsored N.Y. State Dept. Health, N.Y. State Hosp. Assn., N.Y. State League Nursing, N.Y. State Nurses Assn., 1954-57; sometimes lectr. Mem. Am. Nurses Assn. (cert. advanced nursing adminstrn.), Nat. League Nursing, Am. Hosp. Assn., Am. Soc. Tng. and Devel., Sigma Theta Tau. Contbr. articles to profl. jours. Home and Office: PO Box 414 Cobleskill NY 12043 also 1149 Hillsboro Mile Hillsboro Beach FL 33062

LEE, BETTY REDDING, architect; b. Shreveport, La., Dec. 6, 1919; d. Joseph Alsop and Mary (Byrd) Redding; student La. State U., 1936-37, 37-38, U. Calif. War Extension Coll., San Diego, 1942-43; student Centenary Coll., 1937; grad. Roofing Industry Ednl. Inst., 1980, 81, 82; m. Frank Cayce Lee, Nov. 22, 1940 (dec. Aug. 1978); children—Cayce Redding, Clifton Monroe, Mary Byrd (Mrs. Kent Ray). Sheetmetal worker Consol.-Vultee, San Diego, 1942; engring. draftsman, 1943-45; jr. to sr. archtl. draftsman Bodman & Murrell, Baton Rouge, 1945-55; sr. archtl. draftsman to architect Post & Harelson, Baton Rouge, 1955-60; asso. architect G. Ross Murrell, Jr., Baton Rouge, 1960-66; staff architect Charles E. Schwing & Assos., Baton Rouge, 1966-71, Kenneth C. Landry, Baton Rouge, 1971, 73-74; design draftsman Rayner & McKenzie, Baton Rouge, 1972-73; cons. architect and planner, div. engring. and cons. services, La. Dept. Health and Human Resources, Baton Rouge, 1974—; founding mem. La. Inst. Bldg. Scis., 1980—. Mem. La. Assn. Children with Learning Disabilities, 1970-71, Multiple Sclerosis Soc., 1963—, CPA Aux., 1960-69, PTA, 1953-66; troop leader Brownies and Girl Scouts U.S.A., 1959-60; asst. den mother Cub Scouts, 1955-57. Licensed architect, real estate counselor, La. Mem. AIA, La. Architects Assn., Found. Hist. La., Nat. Trust Hist. Preservation, Nat. Fire Protection Assn., Constrn. Specifications Inst. (charter mem. Baton Rouge chpt.), Miss. Roofing Contractors Assn. (hon.), Nat. Center Barrier-Free Environ., Jr. League Baton Rouge. Baton Rouge Caledonian Soc., DAR, La. Alliance Hist. Preservation, Kappa Delta. Democrat. Episcopalian. Clubs: Fais Do Do, Le Salon du Livre. Co-author: Building Owners Guide for Protecting and Maintaining Built-Up Roofing Systems, 1981. Designed typical La. country store for La. Arts and Sci. Center Mus. Home: 1994 Longwood Dr Baton Rouge LA 70808 Office: Box 44215 Capitol Station Baton Rouge LA 70804

LEE, CHUNHYE KIM, nutritionist, food chemist; b. Hiroshima, Japan, Mar. 31, 1941; came to U.S., 1964, naturalized, 1977; d. Key Tae and Sunghee (Sagong) Kim; B.S., Abilene Christian U., 1967; M.S., Ph.D., U. Utah, 1973; m. Sangmyung Lee, Dec. 28, 1968; children—Charles Chulsoo, Grace Youngey. Research asst. leukemia research dept. radiobiology U. Calif., Davis, 1967-69; research asst. microbiology and biochemistry Kennecott Research Center, Salt Lake City, 1969-71; research asst. human nutrition and physiol. chemistry U. Utah, Salt Lake City, 1970-72; asso. prof. food and nutrition sci. No. Ariz. U., Flagstaff, 1972—; clin. nutrition cons. to physicians, dietitians and allied health personnel. Mem. Am. Chem. Soc. (medicinal chemistry sect.), Am. Dietetic Assn., AMA (acad. mem.), Phi Kappa Phi. Home: 514 Charles St Flagstaff AZ 86001 Office: CU Box 6003 Northern Arizona University Flagstaff AZ 86011

LEE, DOROTHY DYE, educator; b. Pahala, Hawaii, Jan. 5, 1922; d. Harry Apau and Leo Tung Dye; Ed.B., U. Hawaii, 1945; M.S.A., Western Res. U., 1948; Ph.D., Case Western Res. U., 1975; m. Robert Mun Wah Lee, June 12, 1949; children—Darlene R. Lee Krenzke, Sherilyn M. Lee Twork, Marveen J., Bertman T. Lectr., U. Hawaii, Honolulu, 1948-49; psychiat. social worker Hawaii Dept. Health, Honolulu, 1966-74; researcher Hawaii State Legislature, 1975; asso. prof. Livingstone Coll., Salisbury, N.C., 1976-78; asso. prof. So. Ill. U., Carbondale, 1978-79; asso. prof. Western Carolina U., Cullowhee, N.C., 1979—; exec. dir., research asso. Asian-Pacific Services Inst., Honolulu, 1975—. NIMH fellow, 1970-71. Mem. Acad. Cert. Social Workers, Am. Public Health Assn. Democrat. Mem. United Ch. Christ. Editor Jour. Asian-Pacific and World Perspectives, 1977—. Home: 2115 Oahu Ave Honolulu HI 96822 Office: PO Box 2499 Cullowhee NC 28723

LEE, ELEANOR, Wash. state senator; b. Elgin, Ill., July 17, 1931; d. Earl Herbert and Catherine (Goldback) Selle; student Wash. State U., 1949-51; B.A. in Polit. Sci., Evergreen State Coll., 1973; m. David Hammond Lee, June 23, 1951; children—Virginia, Phyllis, Marcia. With Cooperative Ext. Service, Wash. Dept. Agr., 1949, 50; with Wash. State U. Food Service, 1951; bus. mgr. Fairman Lee Co., Seattle, 1965—; mem. Wash. Ho. of Reps., 1975-77, Wash. State Senate, 1977—. Commnr., Fire Dist. Civil Service, 1976-80; commnr. Wash. State Land Commn., 1971-73; chmn. CAP Adv. Council, 1976—; chmn. Puget Sound Air Quality Coalition, 1968-70; pres. Lake Burien PTA, 1964-65; pres. Ceders Jr. High Sch. PTA, 1966-67. Trustee, Highline Youth Found. Mem. Nat. Conf. State Legislators, Burien C. of C., Nat. Republican Legislators Assn., Am. Legislative Exchange Council, Wash. Women United, Wash. State Womens Polit. Caucus. Republican. Clubs: Soroptomist Internat., Elected Wash. Women (chmn.). Home: PO Box 66274 Burien WA 98166 Office: 404 Legislative Bldg Olympia WA 98504

LEE, ESTELLA ELIZABETH, social agy. adminstr.; b. Boston, Oct. 5, 1923; d. Marion Glen and Elaine Frances (Bivins) Halle; student Temple U., 1940-42; B.A., UCLA, 1946; postgrad. U. So. Calif.; m. Robert Wilson Lee, Feb. 13, 1949; children—Stephanie, Robert W. Social case worker Los Angeles County Bur. Public Assistance, 1946-52; real estate property mgr., ins. agt. Robert W. Lee Realty Co., 1955-65; acct. Delta Sigma Theta Head Start, Los Angeles, 1965-67, asst. project dir., 1967-71, exec. dir., 1971—; chairperson Pre Sch. Adminstrs. Forum, 1973-76; dir. So. Calif. Center Non Profit Mgmt., 1978—, Child Devel. Found., 1977-79; bd. dirs. Watts Model City Child Care Center. Mem. Los Angeles Mayor's Adv. Com., NAACP, Los Angeles Urban League. Recipient cert. for vol. services Delta Sigma Theta, 1971-79; Baha'i Human Rights award, 1978; award for service to children Women's Council Consol. Realty Bd., 1979. Mem. Nat. Assn. Edn. of Young Children, Black Child Devel. Inst., Nat. Head Start Dirs. Assn., Assn. Dirs. and Parents Together. Democrat. Methodist. Office: 4343 Crenshaw Blvd Los Angeles CA 90008

LEE, ESTHER FRANCES GABRIEL, ednl. adminstr.; b. Augusta, Ga., Jan. 21, 1936; d. James Alexander and Lola Ida (Cade) Gabriel; B.A. cum laude, So. U., Baton Rouge, 1954; M.A., Columbia U. Tchrs. Coll., 1959, postgrad. summer 1964; m. Robert A. Lee, July 9, 1965; children—James, Gloria. Tchr. public schs., Lincolnton and Augusta, Ga., Aiken, S.C., 1954-63; caseworker Ga. Dept. Family and Children's Services, Augusta, 1963-65, N.Y.C. Dept. Social Services, 1965-66; social worker, dir. social services Jersey City Child Devel. Centers, 1966-76, asst. dir. centers, 1976-78, exec. dir. Project Head Start, 1978—; mem. child care center div. infant and toddler care com. N.J. Bur. Licensing; exploring parenting trainer Nat. Head Start Bur.; cons. Nat. Contract Mgmt. Inst. Tng., N.J. Div. Youth and Family Services. Sec., Sr. Companion Program Adv. Bd., Jersey City, 1979—; mem. Foster Grandparent Adv. Com., Jersey City, 1980—. Recipient Vol. Service cert. Hudson County Cts. Juvenile Corrections Com., 1973-75; named Outstanding Mem. of Yr. Calvary Christian Methodist Episcopal Ch., Jersey City, 1978, Public Service award Sr. Companion Program, 1979, Vol. certs. Foster Grandparent Program, 1980-82, Mary McLeod Bethune award Com-Bin-Nations Civic Group, 1977. Mem. N.J. State Wide Head Start Dirs. Assn. (pres.), Nat. Assn. Edn. Young Children, Nat. Head Start Assn., Delta Sigma Theta. Home: 36 Bayview Ave Jersey City NJ 07305 Office: 514 Newark Ave Jersey City NJ 07306

LEE, FRANCES HELEN, editor; b. N.Y.C., Jan. 6, 1936; d. Murray and Rose (Rothman) Lee; B.A., Queens Coll., 1957; M.A., N.Y.U., 1962. Editorial asst. Christian Herald Family Bookshelf, N.Y.C., 1957-62; with Gordon and Breach Sci. Pubs., Inc., N.Y.C., 1964-66, Am. Electric Power Service Corp. AEP Operating Ideas, N.Y.C., 1966-69, Indsl. Water Engring. Mag., N.Y.C., 1969-71; directory editor Photographic div. United Bus. Publs., N.Y.C., 1971-80; editor Am. Druggist Blue Book, Hearst Books/Bus. Publs. Group, 1980-81, spl. projects coordinator motor manuals Hearst Book div., 1981-82, editor New Price Report, 1982—. Supr. Bronx div. N.Y. State CD, 1953-59. Mem. com. on N.Y.C. charter revision Citizens Union, 1975, com. on city personnel practices, 1975-76, com. on city mgmt., 1977—, bd. dirs., 1978—, co-chmn. com. on N.Y.C. Cultural Concerns, 1979—. Mem. Women's Equity Action League (chmn. research com.), N.Y. U. Alumnae Club (dir. 1976-78, rec. sec. 1978—, v.p. 1980-82, pres. 1982—). Home: 170 2d Ave New York NY 10003

LEE, HELEN MARJORIE, genealogist; b. Warrick County, Ind., Apr. 14, 1908; d. Dalton and Katheryn (Johnson) Wilson; B.Public Sch. Music, Ind. U., 1930; M.A., U. Miami, 1953; M.A., U. Boca Raton, Fla., 1963, M.A. in Edn., 1972; m. James K. Rice, Sept. 14, 1935; 1 dau., Katheryn Jean; m. 2d, Walter J. Lee, May 23, 1944. Tchr., Dade County (Fla.) public schs., 1954-75; ret., 1975. Mem. PACE Symphony, Opera Guild Miami; regent John McDonald chpt. DAR; chaplain Fleur de Lis chpt. Huguenot Soc. Fla.; pres. Lady Alice Needham br. Colonial Dames XVII Century; treas. Geneal. Children Am. Colonists; pres. Dames of Magna Carta, Col. William Carroll Lee chpt. Daus. 1812, Descs. of Colonial Clergy; sr. pres. Mockingbird chpt. Children Am. Revolution, also state v.p.; mem. Ancient and Hon. Arty. Recipient Outstanding Community Service award Phi Mu, 1971. Mem. Pi Lambda Phi. Republican. Episcopalian.

LEE, HELEN SHORES, psychologist; b. Birmingham, Ala., May 3, 1941; d. Arthur Davis and Theodora Helen (Warren) Shores; B.A., Fisk U., 1962; M.A., Pepperdine U., 1971; m. Robert Melvin Lee, Dec. 22, 1962; children—Robert Melvin, Arthur D. Shores, Keisha MaShaa. Counselor, Job Corps Center for Women, Los Angeles, 1969-71; counselor Lawson State Coll., Birmingham, 1971-72; instr. clin. psychology U. Ala., Birmingham, 1972-77; dir. cons. and edn. Jefferson County Health Dept. Western Mental Health Center, Birmingham, 1977—. Mem. Ala. Public TV Commn., 1979—; pres. bd. Jefferson County Child Devel. Council, 1978-80; mem. Ala. Community Edn. Adv. Council, 1979—; mem. Task Force on Child Abuse, 1977—; bd. dirs. Assn. Retarded Citizens Parents Anonymous Ala., Big Brothers-Big Sisters, YWCA; pres. PTA; mem. youth program services com. ARC. Recipient B.F. Sims Human Service award, 1975. Mem. Am. Psychol. Assn., Ala. Psychol. Assn., Internat. Assn. Applied Psychology, Internat. Soc. Prevention Child Abuse and Neglect, Nat. Com. for Mental Health Edn. Democrat. Congregationalist. Author: (with others) Medical Treatment of Delinquent Children, 1963, (with B. Shores) A Second Look at Educating the Disadvantaged Youth, 1974. Home: 1025 7th Pl W Birmingham AL 35204 Office: 1701 Ave D Ensley Birmingham AL 35218

LEE, JANICE SUSAN, broadcasting exec.; b. Cleve., Oct. 11, 1955; B.S. in Communication, Ohio U., 1976. Asst. program dir. Sta. ACRN-FM, Athens, Ohio, 1973-75; consumer info. production asst. Sta. WOUB-AM-FM-TV, Athens, 1974-76; producer, writer, Sta. QUBE-TV, Columbus, Ohio, 1977-78; entertainment critic Sta. QFM, Columbus, 1979; documentarian Sta. Bus. Systems, Greenwich, Conn., 1980-81; freelance writer, ind. film producer, 1978-80; promotion writer Warner Satellite Entertainment Corp., The Movie Channel, 1981; asso. dir. NBC Radio Network, N.Y.C., 1981—; student rep. for Ohio U., Nat. Assn. Broadcasters Conv., 1975; participant Nat. Outdoor Leadership Sch., 1976. Home: 50 B Oakridge St Greenwich CT 06830

LEE, JOAN COOK, lawyer, psychologist; b. Louisville, July 19, 1929; d. Byron and Ida (Mertinkate) Cook; B.A., U. Ky., 1951, Ph.D., 1961, J.D., 1975; m. Joe Lee (div.); children—Caroline, Caitlin, Annabel. Asst. prof. psychology Howard U., 1961-62; research psychologist Ky. Dept. Mental Health, 1962-64; pvt. practice psychology, Lexington, Ky., 1964-74; research psychologist Center Devel. Change, U. Ky., 1965-74; criminal justice planner Ky. Dept. Justice, 1974-75; staff atty., mng. atty. Legal Services Program, Nome, Alaska, 1976-81, 82—pvt. practice law, Covington, Ky., 1981-82; mem. faculty U. Ky., Transylvania U., Chase Law Sch., No. Ky. U., U. Cin. Bd. dirs. Lexington Deaf Oral Sch., 1965-68, Womens Crisis Center, Covington, Ky., 1976-79. Mem. Am. Psychol. Assn., Ky. Psychol. Assn., Ky. Bar Assn., Sigma Xi, Hardin County Bar Assn. Democrat. Unitarian. Contbr. articles to profl. jours. Office: PO Box 40 Nome AK 99762

LEE, JUNE BROWN, educator; b. Melber, Ky., June 15, 1933; d. Fred William and Mary Alice (Sperry) Brown; B.A., Baylor U., 1955; M.A., U. Louisville, 1979; m. William D. Lee, Jan. 24, 1958; children—Renee Shawn, William Douglass III, Kimberly Jane, Kelli Ann. Tchr., Williamsburg, Va., 1966-69, Hikes Elem. Sch., Louisville, 1969-75, Newburg Middle Sch., Louisville, 1975—; mem. exec. com. Ky. Gov.'s Edn. Task Force; mem. Edn. Commn. of States, 1980—; chairperson Tchr. Edn. and Certification Council; bd. dirs. Exceptional Equitation; del. Democratic Nat. Conv., 1980; mem. Louisville Mayor's Com. for Census Count, 1980. Recipient cert. merit City of Louisville, 1977; named Outstanding Social Studies Tchr., Social Studies Assn. of Ky., 1981. Mem. NEA (mem. polit. action com.), Jefferson County Edn. for Polit. Action (chairperson 1976-77), Ky. Edn. Assn. (pres. 1979, dir. 1980—), Jefferson County Edn. Assn. Jefferson County Tchrs. Assn. (pres. 1976, dir. 1970—), Nat. Council Tchrs. English. Baptist. Clubs: East End Dem., Honorable Order Ky. Cols. Lobbyist for Ky. Edn. Assn., NEA. Home: 3108 Cromarty Way Louisville KY 40220 Office: Newburg Middle Sch 5008 Indian Tr Louisville KY 40218

LEE, KAREN SONIA, govt. ofcl.; b. Cambridge, Minn., Apr. 11, 1939; d. Oscar M. and LaVerne Ruby (Erickson) L.; B.A., U. Minn., 1961, J.D., 1964. Admitted to Minn. bar, 1964; mgmt. intern, atty. guardianship service VA, 1964-67, mgmt. analyst Office Area Field Dir., 1967-68, atty. guardianship service, 1968-73; mgmt. analyst Office Mgmt. and Fin., U.S. Dept. Justice, Washington, 1973-75, dep. dir. mgmt. programs and budget staff, 1975-77, atty. office policy planning, antitrust div., 1977-78, spl. asst. to asst. atty. gen. antitrust div., 1978-79; dep. dir. Office Mgmt. Planning, asst. sec. adminstrn. U.S. Dept. Transp., Washington, 1980, dep. asst. sec. adminstrn., 1980—; mem. adv. council Center Telecommunications Studies, George Washington U., 1981—. Recipient Outstanding Performance award VA, 1967, 69; Outstanding Performance award Dept. Justice, 1975, 77, 78, Spl. Achievement award, 1974, 79; Congl. fellow, 1967-68. Mem. Fed. Bar Assn. (chmn. publs. bd., circuit v.p.), Women's Transp. Seminar, Armed Forces Communications and Electronics Assn. Office: 400 7th St SW Washington DC 20590

LEE, LENA K., state legislator; B.S., Morgan State Coll.; postgrad. Cheyney State Coll.; M.A., N.Y.U.; J.D., U. Md. Admitted to Md. bar, 1953; mem. Md. Ho. Dels., 1967—. Bd. govs. Lafayette Sq. Recreation Center. Mem. Women's Bar Assn., Monumental Bar Assn., Nat. Bar Assn., Nat. Order Women Legislators, Nat. Assn. Parliamentarians, Nat. Assn. Bus. and Profl. Women (past pres. Balt. Club), Cheyney Alumni Assn. (past pres. Balt. chpt.), Md. League Women's Clubs, NAACP, Internat. Platform Assn., Camp Mohawk Mothers of the YMCA, Herbert M. Frisby Hist. Soc. Office: 315 Lowe Bldg Annapolis MD 21401 *

LEE, LILLIAN VANESSA, clin. microbiologist; b. N.Y.C., June 1, 1951; d. Wenceslao and Ada (Otero) Cancel; B.S. in Biology, St. Johns U., 1972; M.S. in Microbiology, Wagner Coll., 1974; m. Thomas Christopher Lee, June 11, 1972; children—Tovan, John-Peter, Phillip-Michael. Grad. lab. asst. in microbiology Wagner Coll., S.I., N.Y., 1972-74; clin. microbiology technologist Queens Hosp. Center, Jamaica, N.Y., 1974-81, clin. microbiology supr., 1981—. Cert. registered microbiology and specialist microbiologist, clin. lab. specialist. Mem. Am. Soc. Clin. Pathologists, Am. Soc. Microbiology, Am. Acad. Microbiology, Med. Mycology Soc., N.Y., N.Y. Acad. Scis., Nat. Cert. Agy. Med. Lab. Personnel, Synergists Soc. Home: 150-11 86th Ave Jamaica NY 11432 Office: 82-68 164th St Jamaica NY 11432

LEE, LILY KIANG, sci. research co. exec.; b. Shanghai, China, Nov. 23, 1946; came to U.S., 1967, naturalized, 1974; d. Chi-Wu and An-Teh (Shih) Kiang; B.S., Nat. Cheng-Chi U., 1967; M.B.A. (scholar), Golden Gate U., San Francisco, 1967; m. Robert Edward Lee, July 12, 1969; children—Jeffrey Anthony, Michelle Adrienne. Acct., then acctg. supr. Am. Data Systems, Inc., Canoga Park, Calif., 1969-73; sr. acct. Pertec Peripheral Equipment div. Pertec Corp., Chatsworth, Calif., 1973-76; mgr. fin. planning and acctg., then mgr. program control and fin. analysis Sci. Center div. Rockwell Internat. Corp., Thousand Oaks, Calif., 1976—. Mem. Am. Mgmt. Assn., Nat. Mgmt. Assn., Nat. Property Mgrs. Assn., Nat. Assn. Female Execs. Republican. Baptist. Clubs: Fernando Valley Chinese, Foresters. Office: PO Box 1085 1049 Camino Dos Rios Thousand Oaks CA 91360

LEE, LYNDA LORAINE, educator; b. Eckert, Colo., June 23, 1941; d. Grant Eldon and Grace Hazel (Butler) L.; B.A. in Fgn. Langs., U.No. Colo., 1963; postgrad. Rice U., 1965, Ball State U., 1974-75; M.A. in Human Relations, Webster Coll., 1979. Tchr. high schs., Colo., Tex. and Maine, 1963-68; tchr., Dept. Def. Dependent Schs. European Region, Kaiserslautern, Germany, 1971-75, adminstr., Kenitra, Morocco, 1975-77; adminstrv. asst. external degree program So. Ill. U. at Carbondale, Tustin, Calif., 1977-80, program coordinator, asst. prof. aviation mgmt. and health care services, Tustin, Camp Pendleton, and Long Beach, Calif., 1980—; student adv. Webster Coll., 1981—; cons. tech. writing. Recipient letter of commendation Dept. Def., 1977. Mem. Calif. Colls. and Mil. Educators Assn., Adult Edn. Assn. U.S.A. Home: 169 W Avenida Cornelio San Clemente CA 92672 Office: PO Box 17166 Irvine CA 92713

LEE, MARGARET NORMA, artist; b. Kansas City, Mo., July 7, 1928; d. James W. and Margaret W. (Farin) Lee; Ph.B., U. Chgo., 1948; M.A., Art Inst. Chgo., 1952. Lectr., U. Kansas City, 1957-61; cons. Kansas City Bd. Edn., Kansas City, Mo., 1968—; one-man shows Univ. Women's Club, Kansas City, 1966, Friends of Art, Kansas City, 1969, Fine Arts Gallery U. Mo. at Columbia, 1972; exhibited in group shows U. Kans., Lawrence, 1958, Chgo. Art Inst., 1963, Nelson Art Gallery, Kansas City, Mo., 1968, 74; represented in permanent collections Amarillo (Tex.) Art Center, Kansas City (Mo.) Pub. Library, Park Coll., Parkville, Mo. Mem. Coll. Art Assn. Roman Catholic. Contbr. art to profl. jours. Home and studio: 4109 Holmes St Kansas City MO 64110

LEE, MARIA BERL, author; b. Vienna, Austria, July 30, 1924; d. Arthur Clemens and Gunda (Weisel) Berl; came to U.S., 1941, naturalized, 1948; B.A. magna cum laude (Pres.'s scholar), Nazareth Coll. of Rochester, 1946; M.A. (scholar), Fordham U., 1949; m. Ray Eaton Lee, Jr., Oct. 13, 1951. Asst. editor The Gleaner newspaper Nazareth Coll., 1945-46, editor Verity Fair lit. mag., 1946; bilingual sec. Eastman-Kodak Co., Rochester, N.Y., 1946-48; translator, interpreter USCOA and Am. embassy, Vienna, 1949-51; asst. placement dir. Georgetown U., 1951-53; rare books asst. John F. Fleming, N.Y.C., 1953-59; asst. to head Jacobus F. Frank, Indonesian Imports, N.Y.C., 1965-68; writer, editor Internat. Inst. Rural Reconstrn., N.Y.C., 1968—; lectr. Austrian Forum, 1972-78, Austrian Inst., 1975, 80, Nazareth Coll., 1974, Social Sci. Soc. for Intercultural Relations, 1975-81, St. John's U., 1980-81, Der Kreis, Vienna, Austria, 1980-81, Queens Coll., 1975-78, Literarischer Verein, 1977-80, others; collaborator tape program Dept. Interior's-Immigrants on Tape-for Statue of Liberty Mus. and Bicentennial, 1973. Recipient 2d prize Nat. Cath. Short Story Contest for Colls., 1945, lit. prizes for fiction and poetry Tempo, Can., 1970, Writers Digest, 1970, N.Am. Mentor, 1974, 80, 81, In a Nutshell, 1977, Outstanding Alumna award Nazareth Coll. of Rochester, 1979. Mem. PEN Club, Nazareth Coll. of Rochester Alumni Assn., Nat. Writers Club (lit. awards 1967, 69, 71), Soc. German-Am. Studies (citation of merit 1973), Soc. German-Am. Authors (Novella prize 1976), Austrian Forum (bd. dirs.), Kappa Gamma Pi. Roman Catholic. Author: (plays) Ein Tag Der Überraschungen, 1966-67, Bombe Im Tor, 1970, Don't Rock the Waterbed, 1975; The Case in Question, 1977; (poetry) Bitterroot, 1974-81, Second Coming, 1972, North American Mentor, 1974-81, Poet Lore, 1977, Community of Friends, 1974-76, Gusto, 1980, Echos, 1981, Pet Parade, 1981, Car Exchanges, 1981, Austrian Information, 1981, Driftwood East, 1975-78, Hyacinths and Biscuits, 1973-78, Spafaswap, 1971-79, Modus Operandi, 1977-80, Reach Out, 1972, Invictus, 1975, Tempo, 1969, Our Family, 1974, Eureka, 1974-75; (book) Schaumwein Aus Meinem Krug, 1974; (poetry) Oesterreichisches Aus Amerika (anthology), 1973, Amerika im Austro-Amerikanischan Gedioht 1938-1978 (anthology), 1978. Contbr. short stories, articles and poetry to mags., newspapers and jours. Home: 68-46 Ingram St Forest Hills NY 11375

LEE, MAYA, psychologist; b. Chgo., Sept. 30, 1937; d. Philip B. and Renee A. (Roll) Dispensa; B.A., Governors State U., Park Forest, Ill., 1974, M.A., 1975; Ph.D., U.S. Internat. U., San Diego, 1977; m. Lawrence R. Owens, Jan. 1, 1980; children by previous marriage—Barbara P., Elizabeth R., Renee M., Kelly A. Profl. artist, 1969-73; intern San Bernardino County (Calif.) Mental Health, 1977-78, psychologist, 1978-80; pvt. practice psychotherapy, San Bernardino, 1980—; mem. faculty Crafton Hills Coll., Yucaipa, Calif., Calif. State Coll., San Bernardino; one-woman art exhibit Monroe Gallery, Chgo., 1973. Bd. dirs. S. Suburban Women's Liberation Coalition, 1972-75, Park Forest YWCA, 1974-75, Rape Crisis Center, San Bernardino, 1980-81. Mem. Am. Psychol. Assn., Inland Psychol. Assn., NOW. Democrat. Unitarian. Address: 1797 N Arrowhead Ave San Bernardino CA 92405

LEE, MILDRED SCHIFF, art cons., art gallery exec.; b. Columbus, Ohio, Apr. 4, 1920; d. Robert W. and Rebecca (Lurie) Schiff; B.A., U. Wis., 1941; m. Herbert C. Lee, Oct. 21, 1941; children—Thomas H., Richard S., Jonathan. Owner, operator Lee Gallery, Belmont, Mass., 1970—; mem. art bd. overseers Brandeis U., 1963-72; mem. visitors com. Mus. Fine Arts, 1973-77; chmn. Com. to Rescue Italian Art, 1967; art history tchr. Belmont Hill Sch., 1965-68; modern art lectr. Adult Edn. Groups, 1960-68; co-chmn. art exhbns. and sales, bd. dirs. Friends of Art, Boston U., 1960-61; mem. council of friends, mem. acquisition com. Decordova and Dana Mus.; charge outdoor art exhbns. and music festivals Cape Cod Conservatory Music and Art, 1958-59. Pres., Friends of Rose Art Mus.; sec. bd. dirs. Assn. of Art of Music; bd. dirs. Boston U. Youth Symphony Orch., New Arts Orch., Young Audiences, Am. Jewish Com., Jewish Family and Childrens Service, League Women Voters of Brookline; trustee, adviser music com. Belmont Community Center; trustee womens com., Belmont area chmn. Combined Jewish Appeal; mem. womens com. Brandeis U., leader art study groups, mem. Extended Ednl. Program for Women; bd. overseers Met. Center. Clubs: Belmont Country, Belmont Hill. Home: 94 Juniper Rd Belmont MA 02178

LEE, NANCY ELLEN, med. technologist; b. Southington, Conn., Apr. 30, 1954; d. Joseph and Martha (Luty) Pellecchia; B.S. in M.T., U. Conn., 1976; m. Robert E. Lee, June 27, 1981; 1 dau., Sarah Ann. Bench technologist William W. Backus Hosp., Norwich, Conn., 1976-81, chemistry/spl. chemistry supr., 1981—. Bd. dirs. Northeastern Conn. Home Health Care Assn., 1980-81. Mem. Am. Soc. Clin. Pathologists. Home: 17 Ruth St Danielson CT 06239 Office: 326 Washington St Norwich CT 06360

LEE, NELDA S., art dealer, appraiser; b. Gorman, Tex., July 3, 1941; d. Olan C. and Onis L.; A.S. (Franklin Lindsay Found. grantee), Tarleton State U., Tex., 1961; B.A. in Fine Arts, N. Tex. State U., 1963; postgrad. Tex. Tech. U., 1964, San Miguel de Allende Art Inst., Mexico, 1965; 1 dau., Jeanna Lea Pool. Head dept. art Ector High Sch., Odessa, Tex., 1963-68. Bd. dirs. Odessa YMCA, 1970, bd. dirs. Am. Heart Assn., Odessa, 1975; fund raiser Easter Seal Telethon, Odessa, 1978-79; bd. dirs. Ector County (Tex.) Cultural Center, 1979—; bd. dirs., mem. acquisition com. Permian Basin Presdl. Mus., Odessa, 1978; bd. dirs., chairperson acquisition com. Odessa Art Mus., 1979—; pres. Ector County Democratic Women's Club, 1975. Recipient Designer-Craftsman award El Paso Mus. Fine Arts, 1964. Mem. Am. Soc. Appraisers, Appraisers Assn. Am., Appraisers of Fine Arts Soc., Nat. Soc. Lit. and the Arts, Tex. Assn. Art Dealers (pres. 1978-79), Odessa C. of C. Mem. Ch. of Christ. Contbr. articles to profl. jours. Home and Office: 2610 E 21st St Odessa TX 79762

LEE, PAMELA DIANE, phys. therapist; b. Milw., Dec. 14, 1946 d. Noble Ferdinand and Virginia Lorraine (Ihling) L.; student U. South Fla., 1964-65, Lake Sumter Community Coll., 1969-70; B.S. cum laude in Phys. Therapy, U. Fla., 1973; children—Tanya Sue Brookshire, Shelbi Nicole Brookshire. Staff phys. therapist Sunland Tng. Center, Fla. Health and Rehab. Services, Gainesville, 1973-75; owner, adminstr. Therapy, Inc., Gainesville, 1975—; owner/operator, pilot Club Aero, 1980—; owner, adminstr. P.E.R.T. of Daytona, Fla., Inc., phys. therapy, 1980—. Bd. dirs. United Cerebral Palsy, Arthritis Found. Mem. Am. Phys. Therapy Assn., Aircraft Owners and Pilots Assn., Beta Sigma Phi. Lutheran. Home: 8128 SW 44th Terr Gainesville FL 32601 Office: 301-A NW 1st Ave Williston FL 32696

LEE, PAULA DIANNE, former tech. sales rep.; b. Cin., July 12, 1954; d. Frank Lilburn and Miriam Loretta (Lahke) Boatright; B.A. in Psychology, U. Cin., 1976; m. Andrew Gilmore Lee, Aug. 9, 1975; 1 dau., Vanessa Erin. Sec., Fisher Sci. Co., Silver Spring, Md., 1976-77, tech. sales rep., 1977-81. Asso. mem. Am. Chem. Soc., Chem. Soc. Washington; mem. Kappa Kappa Gamma. Home: 2049 Washington Creek Ln Centerville OH 45459

LEE, PEGGY (NORMA DELORES EGSTROM), singer, actress; b. Jamestown, N.D., May 26, 1920; d. Marvin Engstrom; ed. high sch.; m. Dave Barbour, 1943 (div. 1951); 1 dau., Nicki; m. 2d, Brad Dexter, Jan. 4, 1955 (div. 1955); m. 3d, Dewey Martin, Apr. 25, 1956 (div. 1959); m. 4th, Jack del Rio, Mar. 1964 (div. Dec. 1964), Singer Sta. WDAY, Fargo, N.D.; various singing engagements, Mpls.; vocalist Will Osborne's band, Doll House, Palm Springs, Ambassador Hotel West, Chgo., Americana Hotel, Basin St. East, Benny Goodman's Band, 1941-43; concert with Benny Goodman at Melodyland Theatre, Anaheim, Calif., Circle-Star Theatre, San Carlos, Calif.; screen appearance in Mr. Music, 1950, The Jazz Singer, 1953, Pete Kelly's Blues, 1955; performer Revlon Revues CBS-TV, 1960, also mus. variety TV shows, dramatic role Gen. Electric Theater, 1960; composer mus. themes for motion pictures including Johnny Guitar, About Mrs. Leslie, musical score for cartoon feature Tom Thumb; lyricist, supplied several voices for Lady and the Tramp; numerous recs. Capitol Records, 1944, including Golden Earings, You Was Right Baby, It's A Good Day, Manana, and I Don't Know Enough About You, Is That All There Is, (album) I'm A Woman; A and M Records include Mirrors; conducted research, wrote program, performed The Jazz Tree, Philharmonic Hall Lincoln Center for Performing Arts, N.Y.C., 1963. Named Best Female Vocalist, Metronome, Downbeat mags., 1946; Most Popular Vocalist citation Billboard, 1950. Author: (verse) Softly, With Feeling, 1953. Address: care William Morris Agy 151 El Camino Dr Beverly Hills CA 90212 *

LEE, SHERYL LINETTE DUVONG, public health nutritionist; b. Oakland, Calif., Sept. 10, 1945; d. David Alvin and May Moytan (Hum) L.; A.A., Merritt Coll., 1965; B.S., U. Calif., Berkeley, 1967, M.P.H., 1970; postgrad. Ariz. State U., 1979—, U. Calif., Berkeley, 1971. Clin. dietitian, intern instr. Peter Bent Brigham Hosp., Boston, 1968-69; nutrition cons. maternal and child health Ariz. Dept. Health Services, Phoenix, 1971-76, regional nutrition coordinator, 1976-79; instr. dept. home econs. Ariz. State U., Tempe, 1981; chief Bur. Nutrition Services, Ariz. Dept. Health Services, Phoenix, 1979—; adj. prof. dept. home econs. Ariz. State U., 1979—; nutrition cons. Devel. Assos. Inc., Health Learning Systems, Gen. Foods Corp., Case Western Res. U., Ralston Purina Co. USPHS grantee, 1969-70. Mem. Soc. Nutrition Edn. (dir.), Am. Dietetic Assn., Ariz. Dietetic Assn., Central Ariz. Dist. Dietetic Assn., Am. Public Health Assn., Ariz. Public Health Assn., Nutrition Council Ariz., Assn. State and Territorial Public Health Nutrition Dirs. Democrat. Presbyterian. Clubs: Arizona Road Racers, Phoenix Chinese Tennis Assn., Tri-City Tennis Club, Phoenix Young Chinese Americans. Office: 200 N Curry Rd Tempe AZ 85281

LEE, SHIRLEY WILLIAMS, state senator; b. Bismarck, N.D., Jan. 8, 1924; d. John E. and Maude (Edgerton) Williams; student St. Olaf Coll., 1941-43; m. Warren T. Lee, 1942; children—Suzan (Mrs. John Fiberlstad), John W., Judy (Mrs. Leon Guenthner), Steven. Mem. N.D. State Senate from Dist. 8, 1973—. Vice-chmn. Burleigh County Young Republicans N.D., 1958-60; sec. Burleigh County Rep. Com., 1960-62; chmn. Burleigh County Rep. Orgn., 1962-64; chmn. N.D. State Rep. Orgn., 1964-66; vice-chairwoman N.D. State Rep. Com., 1966-68; trustee, Mercer-McLenn Regional Library; bd. dirs. Turtle Lake Community Chest. Mem. PEO, DAR. Lutheran. Club: Turtle Lake Study. Office: ND Senate State Capitol Bismarck ND 58501 *

LEE, VERA LOUISE, nurse; b. Jasonville, Ind., Jan. 28, 1930; d. Calude G. and Mary (Good) Gabbartl A.D.N., Vincennes U., 1965; B.S.N., U. Evansville, 1976, M.S.N., 1978; m. Charles E. Lee, June 15, 1946; children—Rogena, Suzie, Buddy, Marlene. Staff nurse Gibson Gen. Hosp., Princeton, Ind., 1965-69; dir. nursing Holiday Home, Petersburg, Ind., 1969-73; staff nurse Osteopathic Hosp., Oakland City, Ind., 1973-76; clin. nursing instr. U. Evansville, 1976-78; nursing inst., dir. nursing Ill. Eastern Community Coll. A.D.N. program, Mt. Carmel, Ill., 1978—. Mem. Am. Nurses Assn., Ind. State Nurses Assn., Gibson County Area Rehab. Center, Mental Health Assn. Address: 2200 College Dr Mount Carmel IL 62863

LEE, VIRGINIA FERN, med. records adminstr.; b. St. Paul, Mar. 14, 1921; d. Henry Orlando and Etta Lavina (Newstrand) L.; B.A., Coll. St. Scholastica, 1943; student UCLA, 1938-39, Stanford U., 1962, Dir. med. records, hosps. in Md., Iowa, Wis., Hawaii, Minn., Alaska, Nev., Ill., Calif., S. Am., 1943-60, 61-82; chief med. info. VA Med. Center, Palo Alto, Calif., area med. records adminstr., 1962-82. Registered med. records adminstr. Mem. Am. Med. Record Assn. (profl. publs. com.), Calif. Med. Record Assn. (past pres.), Central Calif. Med. Record Assn. (past pres.), Children's Health Council Mid-Peninsula (past pres. aux.),

Christian Bus. and Profl. Women. Republican. Episcopalian. Clubs: Singles Orgn. Bay Area, Good Bears of the World. Home: 433 Guinda Palo Alto CA 94301

LEECH, ALMA DAVENPORT CASE, assn. exec.; b. Mercer County, Ky., June 26, 1922; d. John Victor and Georgia Powell (Daveport) Case; student Northwestern U.; m. Stephen Kenneth Leech, Dec. 27, 1952; children—Stephen Kenneth, Darryl Case. Adminstrv. asst. ACS, Chgo., 1945-50; exec. sec. Internat. Coll. Surgeons, Chgo., 1950-52; mng. editor Fifth Dist. Dental Bull. N.Y., Dewitt, N.Y.C., 1955—, exec. dir. Fifth Dist. Dental Soc., 1956—. Bd. dirs. Hall of Health, N.Y. State Fair. Recipient Dental Editors award Ohio State U.-Am. Dental Assn., 1969; Disting. Service award Dental Soc. State of N.Y., 1981. Mem. Am. Soc. Assn. Execs., Dental Editors Assn., Assn. Component Soc. Execs. (pres. 1974-75), Public Relations Soc. Am., Women in Communications, Inc., Syracuse Execs. Assn. Episcopalian. Club: Syracuse Press. Home: 201 Lansdowne Rd Dewitt NY 13214 Office: PO Box 135 Dewitt NY 13214

LEEDY, EMILY L. FOSTER (MRS. WILLIAM N. LEEDY), state agy. ofcl.; b. Jackson, Ohio, Sept. 24, 1921; d. Raymond S. and Grace (Garrett) Foster; B.S., Rio Grande Coll., 1949; M.Ed., Ohio U., 1957; postgrad. Ohio State U., 1956, Mich. State U., 1958-59, Case Western Res. U., 1963-65; m. William N. Leedy, Jan. 1, 1943; 1 son. Dwight A. Tchr., Frankfort (Ohio) schs., 1941-46, Ross County Schs., Chillicothe, Ohio, 1948-53; elementary and supervising tchr. Chillicothe City Schs., 1953-56; dean of girls, secondary tchr. Berea City Schs., 1956-57; vis. tchr. Parma City Schs., 1957-59; counselor Homewood-Flossmoor High Sch., Flossmoor, Ill., 1959-60; teaching fellow Ohio U., 1960-62; asst. prof. edn., 1962-64; asso. prof., counselor Cuyahoga Community Coll., 1964-66; dean of women Cleve. State U., 1966-67, asso. dean student affairs, 1967-69; guidance dir. Cathedral Latin Sch., 1969-71; dir. women's service div. Ohio Bur. Employment Services, 1971—; cons. in edn. Mem. adv. com. S.W. Community Info. Service, 1959-60; youth com. S.W. YWCA, 1963-70, chmn., 1964-70, bd. mgmt., 1964-70; group services council Cleve. Welfare Fedn., 1964-66; chmn. Met. YWCA Youth Program study com., 1966, bd. dirs., 1966-72, v.p., 1967-68; chmn. adv. council Ohio State U. Sch. Home Econs., 1977-80. Named Cleve. area Woman of Achievement, 1969; named to Ohio Women's Hall of Fame, 1979. Mem. AAUW, Am., Northeastern Ohio (sec. 1958-59, exec. com. 1963-64, public relations chmn. 1962-64, newsletter chmn., editor 1963-64, del. nat. assembly 1959-63) personnel and guidance assns., Nat. Vocational Guidance Assn., Am., Ohio sch. counselors assns., Am. Rehab. Counseling Assn., Nat. (publs. com. 1967-69, profl. employment practices com. 1980—), Ohio (program chmn. 1967, editor Newsletter 1968-71) assns. women deans and counselors, Cleve. Counselors Assn. (pres. 1966), Women's Equity Action League, Zonta Internat. (exec. bd. 1968-70, treas. 1970-72, chmn. dist. V Status of Women 1980-81), Nat. Assn. Commns. for Women (dir. 1980-81, sec. 1981-83), Rio Grande Coll. Alumni Assn. (Atwood Achievement award 1975), Bus. and Profl. Women's Club (Nike award 1973), Delta Kappa Gamma. Clubs: Columbus Met.; Women's City (Cleve.). Home: 580 Lindberg Blvd Berea OH 44017 Office: 145 S Front St Columbus OH 43216

LEES, LYNNE SPENCER, social worker; b. Karuizawa, Japan, Aug. 17, 1918; d. Robert Steward and Evelyn (McAlpine) Spencer; B.A. with honors, Swarthmore Coll., 1940; M.S. in Social Sci., Boston U., 1952; m. Wayne Lowry Lees, Oct. 29, 1939; children—Diana Dorothy, Cynthia Carolyn. Jr. profl. asst. OSS, Washington, 1943-45; caseworker Family Service Assn., Boston, 1952-57; social worker Nashoba dist. Mass. Dept. Public Welfare, 1967-68, tng. specialist, Boston, 1968-70, supr. social services, 1970-77, dir. Cambridge area, 1977-80; dir. Cambridge-Somerville area Mass. Dept. Social Services, 1980—. Chmn. social concerns com. Follen Community Ch., Lexington, Mass., 1960, 61, 79-80, trustee, 1978—, mem. parish council, 1980-81; leader Camp Fire Girls, 1966-72. Mem. Nat. Assn. Social Workers, Acad. Cert. Social Workers, Am. Public Welfare Assn., LWV, Middlesex County Beekeepers Assn. Unitarian. Office: Mass Dept Social Services 51 Inman St Cambridge MA 02139

LEES, SALLY K., mfrs. rep.; b. Wichita, Kans., Apr. 17, 1926; d. August R. and Dena H. (Ellis) Krehbiel; B.A., Kans. U., 1947; m. Milton H. Lees, Nov. 16, 1969; children—Mary Catherine Kellett, Molly Ann. Mfrs. rep. children's wear, San Francisco, 1959—; pres. Sally Lees Inc. Mem. Children's Wear Assn. (dir. 1973-79). Mem. Kappa Kappa Gamma. Republican. Presbyterians. Club: Peninsula Golf and Country (San Mateo, Calif.). Home: 141 W Bellevue San Mateo CA 94402 Office: 833 Market St Suite 604 San Francisco CA 94103

LEESON, JANET CAROLINE TOLLEFSON, cake specialties co. exec.; b. L'Anse, Mich., May 23, 1933; d. Harold Arnold and Sylvia Aino (Makikangas) Tollefson; student Prairie State Coll., 1970-76; master decorator degree Wilton Sch. Cake Decorating, 1974; m. Raymond Harry Leeson, May 20, 1961; 1 son, Barry Raymond; children by previous marriage—Warren Scott, Debra Delores. Mgr., Peak Service Cleaners, Chgo., 1959; co-owner Ra-Ja-Lee TV, Harvey, Ill., 1961-66; founder and head fgn. trade dept. Wilton Enterprises, Inc., Chgo., 1969-75; tchr. cake decorating J.C. Penney Co., Matteson, Ill., 1975; office mgr. Pat Carpenter Assos., Highland, Ind., 1975; pres. Leeson's Party Cakes, Inc., cake supplies and cake sculpture, Tinley Park, Ill., 1976—; lectr. and demonstrator cake sculpture and decorating. Sec., Lutheran Ch. Women; active worker Boy Scouts Am. and Girl Scouts U.S.A., 1957-63; bd. dirs. Whittier PTA, 1962-70; mem. Bremen Twp. Republican Orgn.; councillor Calumet council Boy Scouts Am.; mem. Ingalls Meml. Hosp. Aux., 1963—. Recipient numerous awards for cake sculpture and decorating, 1970—. Mem. Am. Bus. Woman's Assn. (chpt. public relations dir.), Chgo. Area Retail Bakers Assn. (1st pl. in regional midwest wedding cake competition 1978, 80). Lutheran. Home: 6713 W 163d Pl Tinley Park IL 60477 Office: Leeson's Party Cakes Inc 6713 W 163d Pl Tinley Park IL 60477

LEFEBVRE, KAREN ANNE, optical co. ofcl.; b. Worcester, Mass., Sept. 12, 1953; d. Roland Joseph and Gladys P. (Czyzewski) Livernois; B.S. in Edn., North Adams State Coll., 1975; M.B.A., Nichols Coll., Dudley, Mass., 1982; m. William J. Lefebvre, July 2, 1977. Statis. analyst Am. Optical Corp., Southbridge, Mass., 1978-79, market analyst, 1979-80, market research analyst, 1980—. Statis. chmn. Am. Optical div. United Way, 1979-81; sec. Dudley Bicentennial Com., 1979. Mem. Am. Soc. Profl. and Exec. Women. Office: 14 Mechanic St Southbridge MA 01550

LE FEVRE, CAROL BAUMANN, psychologist; b. Pierron, Ill., Nov. 26, 1924; d. Berhard Robert and Eunice Leone Hoyt (Heston) Baumann; A.A., Stephens Coll., 1944; M.A. in Sociology, U. Chgo., 1948, M.S. Teaching in Edn., 1965, Ph.D. in Human Devel., 1971; m. Perry Deyo Le Fevre, Sept. 14, 1946; children—Susan Le Fevre Hook, Judith Ann, Peter Gerret. Tchr., Chgo. Theol. Sem. Nursery Sch., 1962-63, U. Chgo., Lab. Sch., 1965-66; asst. prof. psychology St. Xavier Coll., Chgo., 1970-74, asso. prof., 1974—, acting chmn. dept. psychology, 1970-71, chmn. dept. psychology, 1971-77, asst. dir. Inst. Family Studies, 1973-82, dir., 1982—; intern in clin. psychology with Adlerian pvt. practitioner, Chgo., 1973-75; pvt. practice clin. psychology, Chgo., 1975—; mem. staff Logos Inst. Chgo. Theol. Sem., 1973-76; speaker in field. Pub. Health Service tng. grantee NIMH, 1969; registered psychologist, Ill. Mem. Am., Ill. psychol. assns., Gerontol. Soc., N.Am. Soc. Adlerian Psychology, AAUP, Phi Beta Kappa. Mem. United Ch. of Christ. Research, publs. on subjects including returning women grad. students' changing self-conceptions, women's roles, inner city children's perceptions of sch., aging and religion. Home: 1376 E 58th St Chicago IL 60637 Office: St Xavier Coll 103d and Central Park Ave Chicago IL 60655

LEFF, ILENE JOAN, human resources exec.; b. N.Y.C., Mar. 29, 1942; d. Abraham and Rose (Levy) L.; B.A. cum laude, U. Pa., 1964; M.A. with honors, Columbia U., 1969. Statis. analyst McKinsey & Co., N.Y.C., 1969-70, research cons., 1971-74, mgmt. cons., N.Y.C. and Europe, 1974-78; dir. exec. resources Revlon, Inc., N.Y.C., 1978-81, dir. human resources, 1981—; research asst. U. Pa., Phila., 1964-65; employment counselor State of N.J., Newark, 1965-66; tchr., Newark, 1966-69; lectr. Grad. Program in Public Policy, New Sch. for Social Research, Coll. Mt. St. Vincent, Wharton Sch., Duke U.; chmn. com. on employment and unemployment, mem. exec. com. Bus. Research Adv. Council, U.S. Bur. Labor Stats., 1980. Ops. council Jr. Achievement Greater N.Y., 1975-78; cons. Com. for Econ. Devel., N.Y. Hosp., Regional Plan Assn., Am. Cancer Soc.; vol. for dep. mayor for ops. N.Y.C., 1977-78. Mem. Fin. Women's Assn. N.Y. (exec. bd., fund raising dir., 1977-78). Contbr. issue papers and program recommendations to candidates for U.S. Pres., U.S. Senate and Congress, N.Y. State Gov., mayor N.Y.C. Office: 767 Fifth Ave New York NY 10022

LEFF, JULIETTE, painter, educator; b. Rockville Centre, N.Y., Mar. 20, 1939; d. Samuel and Marie (Rosenberg) Simon; B.A. with honors in Art, CCNY, 1962; M.A., Hunter Coll., 1976; student (Max Beckmann Painting fellow), Bklyn. Mus. Art Sch., 1962-64; studied with Mark Rothko, Adolph Gottleib, Tony Smith, Eugene Goosen; children—Alexandra, Gabriela. Tchr., N.Y.C. Bd. Edn., 1962-82; art edn. coordinator Bronx Mus., 1976-77; artist-in-residence teaching grantee, 1977-82; adj. faculty Kingsborough Community Coll., 1979, Goddard Coll., 1981; one woman shows include: N.Y. Found. for the Arts, 1977, Paul Kessler Gallery, 1968, Loeb Center N.Y.U., 1971, L.I.U., 1972; exhibited in group shows: Purdue U., Occlectix, Columbia U., 1969, Butler Inst. Am. Art, Youngstown, Ohio, 1970, N.Y. U., 1971, Yr. of the Woman Reprise, Bronx Mus. Arts, 1976, What is Feminist Art? Writings of 200 Woman Artists, others; represented in permanent collections: Chase Manhattan Bank Art Collection, U.S.I.A. Print Collection, Aubrey Cartwright Mus. Religious Art, Cathedral of St. John the Divine, Jewish Bd. Guardians, others. Recipient Louis Comfort Tiffany Nat. award in painting, 1966-67; Change Artist's grantee, 1978. Mem. Coll. Art Assn., Women's Caucus for Art. Address: 98 Riverside Dr New York NY 10024

LEFF, MURIEL LERNER, civic worker; b. Bklyn., July 4; d. Leopold and Syril (Ruche) Lerner; student Packer Collegiate Inst., 1939; B.A., U. Wis., Madison, 1941; M.S., Columbia U., 1943; m. Walter Leff, Sept. 7, 1952; children—Ruth Leff Sigal, Alexander Leff. Family case worker, 1943-52; mem. staff, also bd. dirs. Jewish Family Service Agy., San Francisco, 1947-66; adminstr. Nat. Center Vol. Action, Western office, San Francisco, 1974-76; dir. self-employment program Displaced Homemaker Center, Mills Coll., Oakland, Calif., 1977-78. Mem. budget panel United Way Bay Area, 1976—; bd. dirs. San Francisco Urban Renewal Assn., 1962-66; pres. Arguello Park Community, Inc., 1960-66, Plays for Living of Greater Bay Area, 1963-73, Greater Bay Area Council Family Service Agys., 1963-73. Mem. Acad. Cert. Social Workers, LWV. Club: Stanford U. Womens.

LEFFERMAN, MICHAELE STRAUSS, mini-computer mfg. co. exec.; b. Balt., June 28, 1943; d. Kennard and Ruth (Grossman) Strauss; B.S. magna cum laude, Boston U., 1965; M.S., Stevens Inst. Tech., 1967; postgrad. N.Y.U., 1970—; m. Edward I. Lefferman, May 29, 1966; children—Matthew, Jessica. Mem. tech. staff Bell Labs., Whippany, N.J., 1965-69; sr. field systems analyst Xerox Data Systems, Hackensack, N.J., 1969-72; computer specialist Sandoz Pharms., East Hanover, N.J., 1972-73; sr. specialist Digital Equipment Corp., Fairfield, N.J., 1973-76; br. mgr. software services, Parsippany, N.J., 1976—. Jewish. Office: 4 Wood Hollow Rd Parsippany NJ 07054

LEFFLER, NELL FOUST, librarian; b. Humboldt, Tenn., Dec. 25, 1922; d. Asa Burnette and Lucile (Sinclair) Foust; student Vanderbilt U., 1942-43; B.A., Lambuth Coll., 1944; M.A., Fla. State U., 1951; m. John Edward Leffler, Nov. 26, 1952. Asst. librarian Fla. State U. Library, 1952, 65-72, head serials cataloging, 1970-74, univ. librarian, head dept. cataloging, 1974-79, univ. cataloging librarian, 1979—; asst. librarian Colquitt-Thomas County Regional Library, Moultrie, Ga., 1952; reference librarian Fla. Legis. Reference Bur., Tallahassee, 1954-63; research librarian Fla. Bd. Regents, Tallahassee, 1963-65. Mem. ALA, Southeastern Library Assn., Audubon Club, Beta Phi Mu, Pi Beta Phi. Democrat. Methodist. Club: Apalachee Yacht. Home: 2413 Miranda Ave Tallahassee FL 32304 Office: 165 Library Fla State U Tallahassee FL 32306

LEFKOWITZ, JUDITH HOPE, dance sch. owner; b. N.Y.C., d. David and Anna L.; B.A., Bklyn. Coll., 1974; postgrad. cert. in dance therapy N.Y. Med. Coll., 1976; M.A. in Dance Edn., N.Y. U., 1978. Asst. account exec. Ross Roy of N.Y., 1971-74; organizer, chmn. dance dept. Hebrew Ednl. Soc., Bklyn., 1968-71; dance tchr. Natalie Dance Studio, Bklyn., 1968-74; office mgr. Mfrs. Reps., Atlanta, 1974-75; owner, tchr. Sch. Dance, Bklyn., 1977—; dancer/actress summer stock theatre. Mem. Dance Educators Am. Office: 174 Ave S Brooklyn NY 11223

LEFOND, ANNE MAY, real estate broker; b. Ashland, Wis., Apr. 26, 1917; d. Charles and Anna (Erickson) Newman; B.A. cum laude, Northland Coll., Ashland, Wis., 1939; M.L.S., U. Wis., 1940; m. Stanley J. Lefond, Dec. 26, 1946; children—Dennis C., Robert E. Reference librarian Colgate U., Hamilton, N.Y., 1945-46, U. Mich., Ann Arbor, 1949-52; librarian Euclid (Ohio) Public Schs., 1953-66; sales asso. Lloyd C. Helgager Co., Woodland Hills, Calif., 1967-70; broker New Eng. Realty Co., Westport, Conn., 1970-72; broker-mgr. Crown Realty Co., Evergreen, Colo., 1972-75; broker-asso. Junction Realty Co., Evergreen, 1976—; v.p. Indsl. Minerals, Inc., Evergreen, 1976—. Mem. Evergreen Bd. Realtors (dir.), Colo. Assn. Realtors, Nat. Assn. Real Estate Brokers, Nat. Inst. Real Estate Brokers. C. of C. Lutheran. Clubs: Hiwan Country, Swedish of Denver. Home: 29983 Canterbury Circle Evergreen CO 80439 Office: PO Box 1867 Evergreen CO 80439

LEFRIANT, MARY ELIZABETH, real estate exec., educator; b. New Orleans, May 13, 1946; d. Urban Edwin and Cleo Thelma (Roig) Mathieu; B.A., La. State U., 1968; M.A., San Diego State U., 1971; m. Jacques Louis LeFriant, Jan. 27, 1968; children—Marc Louis, Christopher David. French tchr., Ganus Sch., New Orleans, 1965-68; real estate saleswoman, property mgr. Progressive Investors, San Diego, 1972—; v.p., sec. LeFriant Enterprises, Inc., DBA Scott's Porsche Parts, San Diego, 1976—; instr. French San Diego Community Coll., 1973—. Democrat. Roman Catholic. Club: Young Adult Group (coordinator 1981-82). Home: 1151 Hornblend St San Diego CA 92109 Office: Mesa Coll Room G 101 San Diego CA 92111

LEFTWICH, MERRY ANN, med. technologist; b. Seattle, July 6, 1917; d. Peter Hill and Esther (Redfield) Ottosen; student Goucher Coll., 1935-38; hon. alumnus U. Calif., San Diego, 1964; m. James A. Leftwich, Mar. 12, 1963; children by previous marriage—Edward Redfield Lewis, Peter Hill Lewis. Histologic technician Renton (Wash.) Hosp., 1952-57, Kings County Hosp., Seattle, 1957-59, Scripps Meml. Hosp., La Jolla, Calif., 1959-64; dir. tech. services Oral Pathology Service, La Jolla, 1964-81; dir. tech. services pathology lab. oral medicine dept. Scripps Clinic and Research Found., La Jolla, 1982—; lectr. in field. Mem. Am. Soc. Clin. Pathologists. Nat. Assn. Histotechnology, Colonial Dames Am., Gamma Phi Beta. Republican. Episcopalian. Club: La Jolla Beach & Tennis. Contbr. articles to profl. jours.; author: Pathology Careers for Tissue Technicians, 1971; A Pathology Lab Can Be Attractive, 1975; Historic Microscope Replicas, 1981, others. Home: 2056 Torrey Pines Rd LaJolla CA 92038 Office: 484 Prospect St LaJolla CA 92038

LE GALLIENNE, EVA, actress; b. London, Jan. 11, 1899; d. Richard and Julie (Norregaard) Le G.; ed. Collège Sévigne, Paris; M.A. (hon.), Tufts Coll., 1927; D.H.L., Smith Coll., 1930, Ohio Wesleyan U., 1959, Goucher Coll., 1960, U. N.C., 1964, Bard Coll., 1965, Fairfield U., 1966; Litt.D., Russell Sage Coll., 1930, Brown U., 1933, Mt. Holyoke Coll., 1937. Debut in The Laughter of Fools, Prince of Wales Theatre, London, 1915; N.Y. debut in The Melody of Youth, 1916; appeared in N.Y. and on tour in Mr. Lazarus, 1916-17; with Ethel Barrymore in The Off Chance, 1917-18; Not So Long Ago, 1920-21; Liliom, 1921-22; The Swan, 1923; Hannele in The Assumption of Hanele, by Hauptmann, 1923; Jeanne d'Arc, by Mercedes de Acosta, 1925; The Call of Life, by Schnitzler, 1925; The Master Builder, by Ibsen, 1925-26; founder, dir. Civic Repertory Theatre, N.Y.C., opening October 25, 1926; presented over 30 plays in 7 years including Three Sisters, Cradle Song, Inheritors, Peter Pan, Romeo and Juliet, Camille, Allison's House (Pulitzer prize), Alice in Wonderland; starred in Therese, 1945; co-founder with Margaret Webster of Am. Repertory Theatre, which produced (1946, 47), Shakespeare's Henry the Eighth, Barrie's What Every Woman Knows, Ibsen's John Gabriel Borkman, Shaw's Androcles and the Lion, Howard's Yellow Jack, Lewis Carroll's Alice in Wonderland, Ibsen's Hedda Gabler and Ghosts, 1948; toured in The Corn is Green, 1949-50; on Broadway in The Southwest Corner, 1955; as Queen Elizabeth in Schiller's Mary Stuart, N.Y.C., 1957, on tour, 1959-60; in Maxwell Anderson's Elizabeth the Queen, 1961-62; toured in Sea Gull, Nat. Repertory Theatre, 1963-64, in Madwoman of Chalilot and The Trojan Women; appeared with APA Repertory Theatre, N.Y.C. as Marguerite in Exit The King; also directed Chekov's The Cherry Orchard, 1967-68, Doll's House, Seattle Repertory, 1975; appeared as Countess in All's Well That Ends Well, Shakespeare Festival Theatre, Stratford, Conn., 1970, in The Dream Watcher, White Barn Theatre, 1975; The Royal Family, Helen Hayes Theatre, N.Y.C., 1976, nat. tour, 1976-77, To Grandmother's House We Go, Biltmore Theatre, N.Y.C., 1980-81; appeared in movie The Resurrection, 1979; dir., actress Alice in Wonderland revival Va. Theatre, 1982-83. Recipient Brandeis U. award for drama, 1966; winner of Pictorial Rev. Achievement award, 1926; gold medal Soc. Arts and Town Hall Club award, 1934; Am. Acad. Arts and Letters medal for good diction on the stage 1945; Outstanding Woman of Year award Women's Nat. Press Club, 1947; spl. award ANTA, 1964, award, 1977; Spl. Tony award Am. Theatre Wing, 1964; Handel medallion City N.Y., 1976; Emmy award, 1978; decorated cross Royal Order St. Olaf, 1961. Mem. Actors' Equity Assn., Dramatists Guild. Author: At 33 (autobiography), 1934; Flossie and Bossie, 1949 (London edit. 1950); With a Quiet Heart, 1953; The Mystic in the Theatre, a study of Eleonora Duse, 1966. Translator many works of Henrik Ibsen, Hans Christian Anderson. Home: Weston CT 06883

LEGAN, RITA FAYE, librarian; b. Humansville, Mo., Aug. 16, 1950; d. Floyd Lavern and Emma Lou (Rodgers) Farmer; B.A. in English and Speech, S.W. Baptist U., Bolivar, Mo., 1972; cert. in Library Sci., S.W. Mo. State U., 1980; m. Adolphus Kyle Legan, Dec. 31, 1969; children—Mark Allen, Amber Rachelle. Aide, S.W. Regional Library, Bolivar, 1968-69; tchr., librarian Wheatland (Mo.) Schs., 1972-73; tchr. English and speech high sch. Marion C. Early Sch. System, Morrisville, Mo., 1976-78; librarian Halfway (Mo.) R-3 Sch., 1978—. Sunday sch. tchr. Baptist Ch., 1982—. Mem. Mo. Tchrs. Assn., Halfway Classroom Tchrs. Assn. (sec. 1979, v.p. 1981), Halfway Young Farm Wives (sec. 1975, reporter 1979). Republican. Club: Fidelis Federated Women's. Address: Route 3 Bolivar MO 65613

LEGÉ, CYNTHIA VERRET, nurse; b. Lake Charles, La., Nov. 5, 1955; d. Robert Edgar and Eva Eugenia (Stewart) Verret; student U. Southwestern La., 1973-76; A.S. in Nursing, La. State U., Eunice, 1978; m. Larry Michael Legé, Mar. 1, 1980. Nurse, Am. Legion Hosp., Crowley, La., 1978-79; dir. nursing Lafayette (La.) Guest House, 1979-81; dir. nursing Crowley Town and Country Nursing Home (La.), 1981—. Mem. La. Health Care Assn. Dirs. of Nurses (pres. 1981—), An. Nursing Assn. Democrat. Methodist. Office: PO Box 1274 Crowley LA 70526

LEGG, LORRAINE OLIVERO, forest products co. exec.; b. Chgo., Oct. 12, 1939; d. John C. and Gisella M. (Nomellini) Olivero; B.A., U. Calif., Berkeley, 1960; J.D., Lincoln U., 1967; m. Kenneth G. Legg (div.). Vice pres. Bankers Mortgage Co. Calif., San Francisco, 1960-67, Fed. Nat. Mortgage Assn., Washington, 1967-70; with Boise Cascade Corp. (Idaho), 1970—, sr. v.p., gen. mgr., Boise Cascade Home & Land Corp., 1972—, dir. real estate and risk mgmt., 1979-80, treas., 1980—, v.p., 1982—; dir. L.B. Nelson Corp., Menlo Park, Calif., Terteling Mktg., Inc., Liquidity Fund for Thrifts, Inc. Pres. Women's Forum-West, 1978-79; commr. Idaho Housing Agy., 1979—; bd. dirs. Boise Civic Opera. Mem. Nat. Assn. Corp. Real Estate Execs., Fin. Execs. Inst., Treas. Club San Francisco. Democrat. Roman Catholic. Club: Hillcrest Country. Editor-in-chief Lincoln Law Rev., 1966-67. Office: 1 Jefferson Sq Boise ID 83728

LE GOFF, LOUISE DENISE, word processing corp. exec.; b. New Brunswick, N.J., June 21, 1951; d. John W. and Gertrude M. (Bergen) LeG.; B.A., Montclair State Coll., 1973; M.B.A., Seton Hall U., 1982. Editor Arthur Young & Co., Newark, 1973-75, 1975-79; sales promotion mgr. Exxon Office Systems, Florham Park, N.J., 1979-82; market mgr. Ohaus Scale Corp., Florham Park, 1979-82; word processing account exec. A.B. Dick Co., Springfield, N.J., 1982—. Mem. Am. Mktg. Assn., Lincoln Arts Center Film Soc. Office: 12 Edison Pl Springfield NJ 07081

LE GUIN, URSULA KROEBER, author; b. Berkeley, Calif., Oct. 21, 1929; d. Alfred Louis and Theodora (Kracaw) Kroeber; B.A., Radcliffe Coll., 1951; M.A., Columbia, 1952; m. Charles A. Le Guin, Dec. 22, 1953; children—Elisabeth, Caroline, Theodore. Recipient Boston Globe-Hornbook award for excellence in juvenile fiction, 1968; Nebula award, 1969, 75; Hugo award for best novel, 1969, 75, best novella, 1973, best short story, 1974; Newbery honor medal, 1971; Nat. Book award, 1973; Gandalf award, 1979; Fulbright fellow, France, 1953-54. Mem. Authors Guild, PEN, Phi Beta Kappa. Author: Rocannon's World, 1966; Planet of Exile, 1967; City of Illusion, 1967; A Wizard of Earthsea, 1968; The Left Hand of Darkness, 1969; The Tombs of Atuan, 1971; The Lathe of Heaven, 1971; The Farthest Shore, 1972; The Dispossessed, 1974; Wild Angels, 1975; The Wind's Twelve Quarters, 1975; A Very Long Way from Anywhere Else, 1976; Orsinian Tales, 1976; The Language of the Night, 1979; Malafrena, 1979; The Beginning Place, 1980; Hard Words, 1981; The Compass Rose, 1982.

LEHMAN, CLARA MAY HILEMAN, physician; b. Sharon, Pa., Oct. 30, 1901; d. Mayberry and Clara May (Keasey) Hileman; B.S., Pa. State U., 1924; postgrad. Columbia, 1927-28, Marine Biol. Lab., 1930-31; M.D., Woman's Med. Coll., Pa., 1935; m. Robert N. Lehman, Apr. 24, 1938; 1 dau., Mary Dorcas. Intern Lancaster (Pa.) Hosp., 1935-36, resident, 1936-37; practice gen. medicine, Pa., 1936-47; practice staff geriatrics U.S. Army Hosp., Ft. Meyer, Va., 1948-51, VA Hosp., Aspinwall, Pa., 1955-57, Woodville State Hosp., Carnegie, Pa., 1957-68. Mem. AMA, Pa., Allegheny County med. socs., Royal Soc. Health,

Alpha Omega Alpha, Alpha Epsilon Iota. Address: 801 Washington Ave Tyrone PA 16686

LEHMAN, ELYSE BRAUCH, psychologist, educator; b. N.Y.C., Apr. 5, 1952; d. John and Theresa (Kish) Brauch; A.B. in Psychology, Douglass Coll., 1962; A.M. in Clin. Psychology, George Washington U., 1967, Ph.D. in Developmental Psychology, 1970; m. Donald R. Lehman, Aug. 24, 1962. Research asso. George Washington U., 1970-76; asst. prof. dept. psychology George Mason U., Fairfax, Va., 1976-80, asso. prof., 1982—; cons. Nat. Inst. Neurol. Diseases & Stroke, 1972-75. Mem. Am. Psychol. Assn., Eastern Psychol. Assn., Soc. Research in Child Devel., Sigma Xi, Psi Chi. Democrat. Contbr. articles in field to profl. jours. Office: Dept Psychology George Mason U Fairfax VA 22030

LEHMAN, EVELYN JEANNE, lawyer; b. Ann Arbor, Mich., June 13, 1930; d. Arthur Conrad and Mildred Georgianna (Pearce) L.; B.A., Mt. Holyoke Coll., 1951; LL.B., U. Mich., 1954; m. Apr. 4, 1959; 1 son, Arthur Scott Long. Admitted to N.Y. State bar; assoc., then partner firm Gifford, Woody, Palmer & Serles, N.Y.C., 1957—. Pres., YWCA of City of N.Y., 1982—. Mem. Am. Bar Assn. Office: 14 Wall St New York NY 10005

LEHMAN, HYLA BEROEN, educator, performing artist; b. Story City, Iowa; d. Lewis Bernard and Helene Louise (Hagen) Beroen; student Waldorf Coll.; B.S. in Edn., Drake U., 1939; M.A., U. Iowa, 1947; postgrad. in classical theatre, Athens, Greece, 1978; m. Fredrick Bracken Lehman, Apr. 30, 1942; children—Rolfe Beroen, Rhea Helene. Tchr. theatre arts and English, LaPorte City, Iowa, Des Moines, Alexandria, Va., Los Angeles; mem. faculty dept. theatre Coe Coll., Cedar Rapids, Iowa, 1974— artistic cons. Dance Theatre of Hemispheres, 1979—; performing artist, 1967—, chmn. bd. dirs., 1981—; judge Am. Coll. Theatre Festival; performer, lectr. at various colls. and univs. Mem. Gov.'s Conf. on Edn.; mem. nat. alumni bd. Drake U.; chmn. Linn County unit Am. Cancer Soc.; mem. Public Health Nursing Bd. Recipient Disting. Alumni award Waldorf Coll., 1969. Mem. Am. Theatre Assn., AAUW (state pres. 1952-54, state arts chmn. 1950-52; fellowship named in her honor), Phi Mu Gamma (nat. alumnae dir. 1947-50, nat. pres. 1950-52), Phi Theta Kappa, Kappa Delta Pi. Lutheran. Home: 4347 Eaglemere Ct SE Cedar Rapids IA 52403

LEHMAN, PATRICIA MARCH, educator; b. Detroit, Aug. 15; d. Joseph A. and Beatrice March; B.A., Oakland U.; M.B.A., Central Mich. U.; m. William J. Lehman, Sept. 9, 1961; children—Jeffrey, Robert, Ann. Tchr. emotionally impaired, Utica (Mich.) Public Schs.; psychol. tester Merrill Palmer Inst., Detroit; profl. musician, Detroit; instr. bus., vocat. counselor Macomb County Community Coll., Clinton Twp., Mich. Probation counselor 41st Dist. Ct., Sterling Heights; bd. dirs., mem. citizens adv. bd. Utica Schs.; community relations dir. City of Sterling Heights. Mem. Nat. Assn. Female Execs. (Mich. dir.), Detroit Fedn. Musicians. Roman Catholic.

LEHMAN, SANDRA KAY, assn. exec.; b. Johnstown, Pa., Dec. 29, 1940; d. William O. and Helen M. (Blough) L.; B.S., Pa. State U., 1962; postgrad. U. So. Calif., Rensselaer Poly. Inst., spl. corp. courses. Procurement agt. Def. Fuels Supply Center, Alexandria, Va., 1964-67; programmer, analyst Def. Supply Ag., Alexandria, 1967-69; mgr. OCR services and ops. SDA Corp., Cheverly, Md., 1969-73; chief program devel. unit Assn. State and Territorial Health Ofcls., Washington, 1973-74; dir. composition and OCR services Informatics, Inc., Riverdale, Md., 1974-77; asso. dir. student services Assn. Am. Med. Colls., Washington, 1977-79, asso. dir. computer services, 1979—; mgmt. cons. Maine Dept. Health, 1979. Treas., fund raiser Alexandria Choral Soc., 1978—, rep. to Alexandria Performing Arts Council, 1978—. Mem. Mu Phi Epsilon, Gamma Phi Beta, Mensa. Home: 815 Church St Alexandria VA 22314 Office: 1 Dupont Circle NW Washington DC 20036

LEHMANN, RUTH PRESTON MILLER, emeritus educator; b. Ithaca, N.Y., Feb. 18, 1912; d. Ernest Allen and Lillian Allen (Phillips) Miller; B.A., Cornell U., 1932, M.A., 1934; scholar in English, Bryn Mawr Coll., 1935-36; Ph.D. (Annie Gorham research fellow), U. Wis., 1942; m. Winfred Philipp Lehmann, Oct. 12, 1940; children—Terry Jon, Sandra Jean Lehmann Hargis. Editor lang. texts U.S. Armed Forces Inst., 1943-44; instr. English, George Washington U., 1944-46, Washington U., St. Louis, 1946-47, Georgetown English Lang. Program, Ankara, Turkey, 1955-56; asso. prof. English, chmn. communications Huston-Tillotson Coll., 1956-58, lectr., 1963-67; asso. prof. English, U. Tex., Austin, 1967-72, prof., 1972-80, prof. emeritus, 1980—. Edwin Markham postdoctoral fellow, 1942-43; Kathryn McHale traveling fellow AAUW, 1953-54; grantee U. Tex. Research Inst. and Am. Council Learned Socs., 1972; recipient citation for outstanding teaching Grad. Sch., U. Tex., 1978; named Outstanding Woman in Scholarship, AAUW, 1979. Mem. MLA, Medieval Acad. Am., AAUW, Phi Beta Kappa, Phi Kappa Phi, Pi Lambda Theta. Democrat. Editor: Fled Duin na nGed Dublin, 1964; (with W.P. Lehmann) Introduction to Old Irish, 1975; transl., editor: Early Irish Verse, 1982. Home: 3800 Eck Ln Austin TX 78734 Office: English Dept U Tex Austin TX 78712

LEHMS, NELLIE ELLEN, real estate broker; b. Park City, Mont., Feb. 18, 1923; d. Richard Neil and Nellie Hazel (Nichols) Wright; student public schs.; m. Robert H. Osberg, Sept. 1, 1940 (div.); children—William R., Robert H., Barbara C. Osberg Smith; m. 2d, Richard Fred Lehms, Sept. 27, 1965. Real estate broker RSM, Inc., Kamuela, Hawaii, 1973-78, Waikoloa Home & Land Co., Kamuela, 1978-80, Ellen Lehms Realty, Kona, 1980—. Named Woman of Year in Cultural Arts, Kirkland (Wash.) Bus. and Profl. Club, 1957; past council chmn. Toastmistress Internat. Mem. Nat. Assn. Realtors, Kona Bd. Realtors, Waikoloa Village Assn. (pres. 1979-80), Lucy Henriques Med. Aux. (organizer, past pres.), Democrat. Home and Office: PO Box 4238 Kailua Kona HI 96740

LEHNER, EDITH ANNE, bldgs. mfg. co. exec.; b. Raleigh N.D., May 5, 1932; d. Daniel D. and Scholastica (Volk) Dirk; student Minot (N.D.) State Coll., 1949-50, Mt. Marty Coll., 1950-51, St. John's U., Summer 1959; B.A., Coll. St. Benedict, 1960; postgrad. State U. N.D., 1965, Marquette U., 1967, U. Pa., 1976; m. George F. Lehner, Feb. 17, 1975. Tchr. Bismarck (N.D.) Parochial Schs., 1949-55, 56-64; tchr. drama, speech Minot (N.D.) Public Schs., 1964-66; tchr. English, speech Upper Merion Sr. High Sch., King of Prussia, Pa., 1966-70; tchr. pvt. voice, piano, Minot, N.D., 1960-66; v.p. in charge field constrn., office mgmt. and fin. Bldg. Concepts, Inc., Douglassville, Pa., 1975—. Mem. Internat. Platform Assn., Nat. Real Estate Assn., Pa. Real Estate Assn., Pa. Manufactured Housing Assn., Bldg. Industries Exchange. Democrat. Roman Catholic. Home: 140 N Wall St Spring City PA 19475 Office: 236 Benjamin Franklin Hwy Douglassville PA 19518

LEHR, SALLY TYLER, psychotherapist, educator; b. New Orleans, Aug. 27, 1942; d. Thomas Bennett and Madeline (Moorman) Tyler; B.S.N., Emory U., 1965, M.Nursing, 1976; m. Ralph Ridgway Lehr, II, Aug. 14, 1965; children—Carolyn, Allison, Elizabeth. Staff nurse psychiat. unit Emory U. Hosp., Atlanta, 1965-67, head nurse, 1967-69; head nurse psychiat. unit Bexar County Hosp., San Antonio, 1969-71; part-time staff nurse Emory U. Hosp., Atlanta, 1971-73, Peachford Hosp., Dunwoody, Ga., 1974-75; nursing instr. (part-time) Nell Hodgson Woodruff Sch. Nursing, Emory U., Atlanta, 1977—; pvt. practice nurse psychotherapist Alliance for Counseling and Therapeutic Services, Atlanta, 1976—; lectr., workshop leader. Pres., Atlanta Dance Unltd., 1981—, Northside Red Runners Track Team, 1981—; youth leader Kingswood United Meth. Ch., 1975—; mem. adv. bd. So. Christian Home for Children, 1982; mem. com. sexuality N. Ga. Methodist Conf., 1976—; chmn. fin. Chesnut Elem. Sch. PTA, 1974—, pres., 1974-75. NIMH trainee, 1976. Mem. Emory U. Nurses Alumni Assn. (pres. 1979-80), Emory U. Alumni Assn. (v.p. 1979-80), Am. Nurses Assn., Ga. Nurses Assn. (psychology-mental health conf. group), Am. Orthopsychiat. Assn., Atlanta Group Psychotherapy Soc., Mental Health Assn. Met. Atlanta, Sigma Theta Tau. Club: Atlanta Track. Contbr. articles to books and profl. jours.; author: Sexual Counseling for Ostomates, 1980. Home: 2200 Spring Mill Cove Dunwoody GA 30338 Office: 174 W Wieuca Rd Atlanta GA 30342

LEHRER, ADRIENNE JOYCE, linguist, educator; b. Mpls., Jan. 16, 1937; d. Julius and Evelyn (Hill) Kroman; B.S., U. Minn., 1957; M.A., Brown U., 1960; Ph.D., U. Rochester, 1968; m. Keith Edward Lehrer, 1957; children—Mark, David. Instr., U. Rochester (N.Y.), 1967-68, asst. prof., 1968-74; asso. prof. U. Ariz., Tucson, 1974-79, prof., 1979—, chmn. dept., 1974-79. Fulbright-Hays fellow U Edinburgh, 1966-67; Center for Advanced Study in Behavioral Sci. fellow, 1973-74. Mem. Linguistic Soc. Am. Author: Semantic Fields and Lexical Structure, 1974; Wine and Conversation, 1983; co-editor: The Theory of Meaning, 1970. Contbr. articles to acad. jours. Home: 65 Sierra Vista Dr Tucson AZ 85719 Office: Dept Linguistics Univ Arizona Tucson AZ 85721

LEHTO, ARLENE LIONE, state legislator; b. Duluth, Minn., Sept. 14, 1939; student in speech and polit. sci. U. Minn., Duluth, 1968-71. 1959-67 Beauty salon mgr., hairstylist 1971-82, pres. ops. Lehto's Printing, Inc. 1970-74 editor, Lake Superior News; mem. Minn. Ho. of Reps., St. Paul, 1976-82, vice chairperson local and urban affairs com., mem. criminal justice, environ. and natural resources, govtl. ops. coms. Bd. dirs. United Devel. Achievement Center Duluth, 1974-82. Recipient Citizen award EPA Minn., 1974, Albert J. Chesley award Minn. Pub. Health Assn., 1975, Plaque of Appreciation, Minn. Chiefs of Police Assn., 1980. Mem. Save Lake Superior Assn., United No. Sportsmen, Minn. Women's Polit. Caucus, Democratic-Farmer-Labor Feminist Caucus, First United Church. Methodist. Clubs: East Hillside Community, Duluth Bus. and Profl. Women's Order Eastern Star. Duluth MN 55805 Office: 238 State Office Bldg Saint Paul MN 55155

LEIBOVICI, DOROTHEA, physician; b. Iasi, Romania, May 10, 1936; came to U.S., 1974; d. Leon S. and Ketty (Marcu) L.; M.D., Bucharest U., 1959. Physician, Romania, 1959-70, Kupat Houm, Ramat Gan, Mahoz Dan, Israel, 1970-74; practice medicine specializing in internal medicine and nephrology, N.Y., 1974—. Mem. AMA, Am. Soc. Internal Medicine (assoc.), ACP (assoc.), N.Y. State Soc. Internal Medicine (assoc.), N.Y. Acad. Scis. Research on preload and afterload reducing agts. Home: 42-49 Colden St Apt 16N Flushing NY 11355

LEIBOWITZ, REBECCA LEE FAUST, accountant; b. Tyler, Tex., Aug. 16, 1937; d. Clyde Wells and Cleo Emasue (Akins Clifton) Allen; A.A., LaSalle Extension U., Chgo., 1972; m. Guidell A. Faust, Sr., Mar. 5, 1959; children—Rebecca Ilene Taylor, Elizabeth Louise Guarisco, Cleo Denice Shuman, Wayne Maurice, Guidell A.; m. 2d, Richard M. Leibowitz, Nov. 7, 1981. Acctg. technician Appliance Buyers Credit Corp. div. RCA Whirlpool, 1958-65, Sears & Roebuck, 1965-67; acct. Greenfields Pvt. Sch., 1970-72; supr. acctg. dept. Estes Co., div. Singer Housing, Houston, 1972-77; office controller Elmer Fox Westheimer & Co., Tucson, 1977-79; adminstrv. asst. acctg. dept. Kelly Tyler Fed. Credit Union, Tyler, Tex., 1979-81; internal controller Air Power Tool & Hoist, Inc., Tyler, Tex., 1981—. Adv., Jr. Achievement, 1975-79; asst. campaign treas. Udall Election Com., 1977-79; treas. Girls Club, Inc., Tucson, 1978-79, So. Ariz. chpt. Muscular Dystrophy Assn., 1977-79, exec. bd. Tyler chpt., 1980—; mem. adv. com. higher edn. Ariz. Dept. Edn., 1978-79. Mem. Am. Soc. Women Accts. (pres. Tucson chpt. 1978-79), Am. Bus. Women's Assn., Nat. Assn. Accts., Bus. and Profl. Women, Council Profl. Orgns. Tucson (chmn. 1978-79). Democrat. Episcopalian. Home: Route 2 Box 236 J Lindale TX 75771 Office: PO Box 148 Tyler TX 75710

LEICHTMAN, SANDRA ROSE, psychologist; b. Detroit, Nov. 10, 1944; d. Alexander and Lillian (Siegel) L.; B.A., U. Mich., 1966; Ph.D., U. N.C., 1971. Postdoctoral fellow U. Colo. Med. Sch., Denver, 1971-72; pediatric psychologist Boston City Hosp., 1972-74; asst. prof. psychiatry and pediatrics U. Md. Med. Sch., Balt., 1974-80; sr. program analyst, planning, info. and evaluation Mental Hygiene Adminstrn., Md. Dept. Health and Mental Hygiene, Balt., 1980—; instr. Boston U. Med. Sch., 1972-74; cons. minority psychology tng. program Harvard U. Med. Sch., 1972-74. Mem. 4-C Com. on Early Identification, 1975. NASA fellow, 1966-68; USPHS fellow, 1968-70. Mem. Am. Psychol. Assn. (program chmn., rep.-at-large div. 37), Md. Psychol. Assn. (sec. 1975-76, rep.-at-large 1978-80). Jewish. Contbr. articles to profl. jours., chpts. to books. Office: 201 W Preston St Baltimore MD 21201

LEICK, MARYBELLE, hosp. adminstr.; b. Sheldon, N.D., May 8, 1921; d. George Henry and Mary Belle (McKinnon) L.; B.A. Coll. St. Scholastica, 1944; M.H.A., St. Louis U. 1957. Tchr. St. Timothy's Parochial Sch., Chgo. 1944-46, St. Joseph's Parochial Sch., Cloquet, Minn., 1947-49, Cathedral Sr. High Sch., Duluth, Minn., 1949-52; med. technologist intern St. Mary's Hosp., Duluth, 1952-53, chief med. technologist, 1953-55, pres. 1957—; dir. First Nat. Bank Duluth, Northwest Bancorp. Bd. dirs. Duluth Rehab. Center, 1965-68; trustee Coll. St. Scholastica, 1972-80. Recipient Am. Hosp. Assn. Trustees award, 1974; registered med. technologist. Fellow Am. Coll. Hosp. Adminstrs., St. Louis U. Alumni Assn., Am. Hosp. Assn. (trustee 1970-72, chmn. council on manpower and edn. 1969, chmn. council adminstrn. 1966-68), Upper Midwest Hosp. Conf. (pres. 1980-81), Minn. State Bd. Health, Minn. Hosp. Assn., Minn. Conf. Cath. Hosps., Duluth Area C. of C. (dir. 1977-80). Roman Catholic.

LEIDIG, MARJORIE WHITTAKER, clin. psychologist; b. Everett, Wash., Nov. 8, 1939; d. Norman Edson and Cleo Margie (Sahlinger) Whittaker; B.S., U. Wash., 1961, M.S., 1964; M.A., U. Colo., 1975, Ph.D., 1976; m. Raymond Leidig, June 19, 1971. Psychology trainee VA hosps., 1962-64; child psychologist Ryther Child Center, Seattle, 1964-66, Crisis Clinic, Seattle, 1964-66; sch. psychologist Shoreline Schs., Seattle, 1966-73; psychologist Denver Gen. Hosp., 1976-77; clin. dir. Battered Women Research Center, Boulder, 1977-79; pvt. practice clin. psychology, Boulder, 1976—; part-time faculty psychology dept. U. Colo., Boulder, 1976—; feminist theorist; mem. adv. bds., cons. govt. agys. on mental health needs of women; Colo. state coordinator feminist therapy; lectr., condr. workshops. Recipient Teaching Recognition award U. Colo., 1980. NIMH fellow, 1973-76; named Outstanding Profl., Shoreline Schs., 1976. Mem. Am. Psychol. Assn., Colo. Psychol. Assn., Wash. State Psychol. Assn., Assn. Women in Psychology, Nat. Assn. Feminist Therapists, others. Democrat. Contbr. articles to profl. jours.; contbr. chpt.: Female Psychology, 1980; Community Psychology, 1978. Office: 1911 11th St Suite 311 Boulder CO 80302

LEIFER, LAUREN RENEE, audio prodn. exec.; b. Chgo., Mar. 28, 1947; d. Maurice M. and Esther (Burkons) Leifer; B.S. in Edn., No. Ill. U., 1969; m. Steven Martin Goldman, Mar. 25, 1977 (div. 1981). Spl. edn. tchr. Lake County (Ill.) Public Schs., 1969-70; with Indsl. Audio Film Services, Morton Grove, Ill., 1970—, now exec. v.p. Bd. dirs. House of the Good Shephard, home for abused/battered women and children. Mem. Nat. Assn. Female Execs., Indsl. Audio/Film Services Assn. (pres. 1981—), Nat. Assn. Women Bus. Owners (dir.), Soc. Profl. and Exec. Women, Am. Mgmt. Assn., Am. Soc. Tng. and Devel., Chgo. Unltd. Office: 6228 W Oakton St Morton Grove IL 60053

LEIFERMAN, SILVIA WEINER (MRS. IRWIN HAMILTON LEIFERMAN), artist, civic worker, bus. exec., philanthropist; b. Chgo.; d. Morris H. and Anna (Caplan) Weiner; student U. Chgo., 1960-61; studied design and painting Chgo., Mexico, Rome, Madrid, Provincetown, Mass.; m. Irwin Hamilton Leiferman, Apr. 20, 1947. One woman shows include: D'Arcy Galleries, N.Y.C., 1964, Stevens Annex Bldg., Chgo., 1965, Hollywood (Fla.) Mus. Art, Schram Galleries, Ft. Lauderdale, Fla., 1966, 67, Miami Mus. Modern Art, 1966, 72, Contemporary Gallery, Palm Beach, Fla., 1966, Westview Country Club, 1968, Gallery 99, Miami Beach, Fla., 1969, Hall Gallery, Miami Beach; group shows include: Bryn Mawr Country Club, 1961, 62, Riccardo Restaurant Gallery, Chgo., 1961, 62, Covenant Club, 1963, D'Arcy Galleries, N.Y.C., 1965, 66, 67, Miami Mus. Modern Art, 1967, Baccardi Gallery, Miami, 1967, Internat. Platform Assn., 1967, Barry Coll., 1968, Gallery 99, Miami Beach, 1968, Hollywood Mus. Art, 1968, Lowe Art Mus., Beau Art Gallery Lowe Mus. at U. Miami; work represented in numerous pvt. collections; chmn. bd. Leiferman Investment Co., 1969-78, chmn. bd., 1968—; pres. Active Accessories by Silvia; v.p., sec. Silvia and Irwin H. Leiferman Found. Founder, Mt. Sinai Hosp., Miami Beach, 1969, Greater Technion Inst. Tech., Israel, 1972, Silvia and Irwin H. Leiferman Found.; organizer, met. chmn., charter mem. womens div. Hebrew U., Chgo., 1947; originator, met. Chgo. chmn. Ambassador's Ball, State of Israel, 1956, Presentation Ball, 1963, 64, 65; organizer women's div. Edgewater Hosp., 1954; chmn. salute to med. research met. campaign City of Hope, 1959; met. Chgo. chmn. Dior Israel Fashion Show, 1962; originator, chmn. presentation com. Ambassador's Ball, Bonds for Israel, 1963, 64, 65; originator, met. chmn. Paris in the Spring fashion show Nat. Council Jewish Women, also Alice in Fashion Land; originator met. chmn. Hawaii Holiday, Nathan Goldblatt Soc. Cancer Research; chmn. spl. sales and events Greater Chgo. Com. for State of Israel; met. chmn. opening gala luncheon, mem. bd. North Shore women's aux. Mary Lawrence Jewish Children's Bur.; internat. chmn. Bal Masque, Miami Ballet Soc., 1971, 72; patron Royal Ballet Soc. Miami, Lowe's lMus. Art, Greater Art Center Miami, Philharmonic Soc. Miami, Greater Miami Opera Guild; patron Greater Miami Cultural Arts Center, mem. hon. com. for gala, 1972; trustee, life mem. Nathan Goldblatt Soc. Cancer Research; trustee Jewish Fedn. Greater Miami; mem. bd. North Shore aux. Jewish Fedn. Chgo., Mary Lawrence chpt. Jewish Children's Bur., Nat. Council Jewish Women, Fox River Sanitorium, Temple Sholom, Edgewater Hosp., Orgn. Rehab. and Tng., women's guild Greater Miami Philharmonic Soc., numerous others; mem. nat. bd. govs. Bonds for Israel; hon. chmn. Miami Art Center. Named Woman of Valor, State of Israel, 1963; 73; recipient Achievement award State of Israel, 1963; keys of all 5 met. dists. Miami and surrounding counties, 1972; Pro Mundo Beneficio gold medal and diploma Brazilian Acad. Humanities, 1976; Donor award Miami Heart Inst., 1976; numerous plaques and citations. Fellow Royal Soc. Arts and Scis. (life); mem. Internat. Platform Assn. (The Club), Internat. Council Museums, Am. Fedn. Arts, Miami Beach Opera Guild, Artists Equity Assn., Miami Art Center, Greater Miami Cultural Art Center, Sculptors of Fla., Inc., Lowe Art Mus. (life), Friends of Lowe's Mus., Am. Contract Bridge League, Am. Friends of Hebrew Univ., Ft. Lauderdale Mus. Arts, Miami Mus. Modern Art (life), Art Inst. Chgo. (life), numerous others. Clubs: Internat., Whitehall, Key, Covenant, Standard, Bryn Mawr Country (Chgo.); Westview Country, Brickell (Miami); Greenacres Country (Northbrook, Ill.); Runaway, Jockey (Miami Beach). Address: 10155 Collins Ave Bal Harbour FL 33154

LEIGH, RUTH S, realtor; b. N.Y.C., Feb. 19; d. A. Lawrence and Anne (Frieder) Sokolski; student Hunter Coll., 1934-36, Wharton Sch., U. Pa., 1942; m. Murray Stuart Leigh, June 13, 1943; 1 dau., Leslie Susan Leigh Griffith. Sales dept. mgr., buyer Saks 34th St., N.Y.C., 1935-37; radio commls. WMCA, N.Y.C., 1936-39; interior decorator Roxberg, Inc., N.Y.C., 1937-40; broker Harold N. Sloane Co., Ins. brokers, N.Y.C., 1940-43; br. mgr. Manpower Inc., N.Y.C., 1952-53; interior designer Storr & Co., N.Y.C., 1949—; builder-broker Ruth S. Leigh, N.Y.C., 1965—. Dist. dir. Girl Scouts U.S.A., 1952-54; fund raiser N.Y. Heart Assn., 1955—, Salvation Army, 1960—, bd. dirs. Interfaith Neighbors, 1964-66; dist. liaison officer Black & White Assos. supporting Oddyssey House Drug Addicts, 1969-70; trustee Bloomingdale Ho. of Music, N.Y.C., 1970-71; mem. U.S. Senatorial Bus. Adv. Bd., mem. chmn.'s com., 1980. Recipient civic awards. Mem. Unitarian-Universalist Womens Fedn. (dist. pres. 1966—), Am. Unitarian Assn. (asst. non-govtl. orgn. rep. UN, nat. chmn. UN seminars 1958-62). Republican. Unitarian (v.p. bd. 1972, deacon 1974). Address: 945 Fifth Ave New York NY 10021 also 636 Lorna Ln Los Angeles CA 90049

LEIGHTON, ANNA BRUCE, nurse; b. Mulberry, Kans., Aug. 13, 1924; d. William Melvin and Hazel Ivy (Pettit) Bourland; diploma Queen of Angeles Coll. Nursing, 1947; m. Nephi Robert Leighton, Aug. 15, 1948; children—Patricia Ann, Sharon Eileen, James William. Nurse, Idarado Mining Hosp., Ouray, Colo., 1947, hosp. Fort Collins, Colo., 1948-51, Steamboat Springs, Colo., 1951-52, Richland Hosp., Sidney, Mont., 1952-55; nurse Pipestone (Minn.) Hosp., 1957-59, Paudre Valley Hosp., Ft. Collins, 1960-64; coronary care nurse Sutter Meml. Hosp., Sacramento, 1965-67, nurse intensive care and emergency care, 1968-75; home care evaluator Marion Home Health Agy., Sacramento, 1967-68; supr. emergency care Methodist Hosp., Sacramento, 1975—; now with Kaiser Permanente Med. Group Emergency Services. Mem. Sacramento Emergency Group; participant Flying Doctors program; instr. Fire Fighters Emergency Med. Tech. Program. Republican. Mem. Am. Nurses Assn., Calif. Nurses Assn. Mem. Reorganized Ch. Jesus Christ Latter-day Saints. Clubs: Papillion, Masons, Mothers (past pres.), Camillia (Sacramento). Home: 2651 Radcliffe Ct Sacramento CA 95826

LEIGHTON, CLARE, engraver, writer; b. London, Eng., Apr. 12, 1901; came to U.S., 1939, naturalized, 1946; student Slade Sch., U. London, 1921-23; D.F.A. (hon.) Colby Coll., 1940. Exhibited group shows Victoria and Albert Mus., London, Nat. Gallery, Stockholm, Nat. Gallery Can., Met. Mus., N.Y.C., others; commd. 33 stained glass windows St. Paul's Cathedral, Worcester, Mass.; mosaic, Convent Holy Family of Nazareth, Monroe, Conn.; windows, Lutheran Ch., Waterbury, Conn.; windows, Methodist Ch., Wellfleet, Mass. Mem. Royal Soc. Painters, Etchers and Engravers (London), Nat. Acad. Design, Soc. Am. Graphic Artists, Soc. Wood Engravers (London), Nat. Inst. Arts and Letters. Author, illustrator: The Farmer's Year, Four Hedges, Country Matters, Southern Harvest, Where Land Meets Sea, others. Address: Woodbury CT 06798

LEIGHTON, MARGARET CARVER, author; b. Oberlin, Ohio, Dec. 20, 1896; d. Thomas Nixon and Flora Frazee (Kirkendall) Carver; student pub. schs., Cambridge, Mass., Lycée Fenelon, Paris, France, Villa Rogivue, Switzerland; A.B., Radcliffe Coll.; m. James Herbert Leighton, May 5, 1921 (dec. Feb. 1935); children—James Herbert, Mary (Mrs. Carson F. Thomson), Thomas Carver, Sylvia (Mrs. Douglas Wikle). Former mem. bd. edn., Westfield, N.J. Served in Army Sch. of Nursing, World War I. Mem. Writers' Guild (Calif.), Authors League Am., PEN. Republican. Author: Junior High School Plays, 1938, The Secret of the Old House, 1941, Twelve Bright Trumpets (pub. in Eng. as The Conqueror), 1942; The Secret of the Closed Gate, 1944; The Singing Cave, 1945 (Jr. Lit. Guild selection, also received silver medal Commonwealth Club Calif.), 1946; Judith of France, 1948; Sword and the Compass, 1951; The Secret of Bucky Moran, 1952; The Story of Florence Nightingale, 1952; The Story of General Custer, 1954; Who

Rides By, 1955; Comanche of the Seventh, 1957; The Secret of Smuggler's Cove, 1959; Journey for a Princess, 1960; Bride of Glory, 1962; Voyage to Coromandel, 1965; The Canyon Castaways, 1966; A Hole in the Hedge, 1968; Cleopatra, 1969; The Other Island, 1971; Shelley's Mary, 1973. Contbr. to Child Life, American Girl, Portal, Target, Classmate, Girls Today, also anthologies and sch. readers. Address: 1053 20th St Santa Monica CA 90403

LEINER, MELISSA GAYLE, fin. planner and cons.; b. Salinas, Calif., Feb. 20, 1953; d. Fred B. and Helen G. (Gertner) L.; B.A., Skidmore Coll., 1975. Sales asst. Paine Webber Jackson & Curtis, N.Y.C., 1976, Kidder Peabody, Washington, 1977-78; fin. cons., fin. planner Shearson Am. Express, McLean, Va., 1978—. Active United Jewish Appeal, Nat. Council Jewish Women. Cert. fin. planner. Mem. Internat. Assn. Fin. Planners, Stockbrokers Soc., Skidmore Coll. Alumni Assn. Club: Skidmore Coll. Alumni (pres. Washington area). Office: Shearson 8260 Greensboro Dr McLean VA 22102

LEIPZIG, LIBBY (MRS. FRED LEIPZIG), state ofcl., automotive products co. exec.; b. Easton, Pa.; d. Benjamin and Mary (Bizar) Black; student Paterson Normal Sch., N.J., 1928, Rutgers U., 1943-44, Fairleigh Dickinson U., 1962; m. Fred Leipzig, Apr. 12, 1940; 1 dau., Marta Beth. With N.J. State Employment Service, Passaic, 1941—, supr. profl. comml. dept., Paterson, N.J., 1962-69, supr. indsl. services dept., Passaic, 1969-72; v.p. Major Automotive Products Co., Inc., Clifton, N.J. 1945-69, sec.-treas., 1969—. Home: Hills of Inverrary 5630 Hammock Ln Lauderhill FL 33319

LEIS, WINOGENE B. (MRS. HENRY PATRICK LEIS, JR.), nurse assn. exec.; b. Clay, W.Va., Feb. 27, 1919; d. Gruder L. and Daisy M. (Young) Barnette; R.N. cum laude, Kanawha Valley Hosp., 1939; m. Henry Patrick Leis, Jr., Jan. 8, 1944; children—Henry Patrick III, Thomas Federick. Nurse, Kanawha Valley Hosp., 1939-43. Decorated lady comdr. Equestrian Order Holy Sepulchre Jerusalem. Mem. Woman's Aux. Internat. Coll. Surgeons (corr. sec. N.Y. State surg. div. 1955-57, v.p. 1961-63, pres. 1963-67; pres. U.S. sect. 1970, dir. 1970-76), Flower Fifth Av. Hosp. Woman's Aux. (dir. 1956-59, 69—), Woman's Aux. N.Y. Acad. Scis., Woman's Aux. N.Y. State Med. Soc., Woman's Aux. Internat. Coll. Surgeons (corr. sec. 1972-74, pres. 1977-78, dir. 1978—). Republican. Roman Catholic. Home: 147-03 5th Ave Whitestone NY 11357

LEISER, BONNIE TERESA, bus. devel. officer; b. Salt Lake City, Aug. 7, 1947; d. Robert A. and Elinore C. McGregor; B.S. with high honors (Xerox scholar), Portland State U., 1980; m. Michael W. Leiser, Apr. 3, 1966; 1 son, Walker M. Acctg. mgr., cons. Component Resources, Inc., Portland, Oreg., 1978-80; fin. mgr. Far West Office Products, Inc., Portland, also pvt. practice fin. mgmt. cons., Portland, 1981; bus. devel. officer Barclays Am./Bus. Credit, Inc., Portland, 1982—. Recipient 1st Pl. in photography Lake Oswego Festival Arts, 1980. Mem. Am. Soc. Tng. and Devel. (treas. 1981), Inst. for Profl. and Managerial Women, Women in Fin. Mgmt., Phi Kappa Phi, Beta Gamma Sigma. Home: 10592 SW 63d Dr Portland OR 97219 Office: Barclays Am Bus Credit Inc 1001 SW 5th Ave Suite 1000 Portland OR 97204

LEISURE, RENEE PHILLIPPE, law firm adminstr.; b. Marion, Ind., Feb. 4, 1944; d. Charles Scutter and Geraldine Jacquette (Scheeler) Phillippe; grad. Croft Internat. Bus. Coll., 1964; student Purdue U., Lafayette, Ind., 1964-66; m. Ronald Jay Leisure, Sept. 3, 1966; 1 dau., Lori. Long distance telephone operator Bell System, 1964-66; program dir. Sta.-WTVD, Durham and Raleigh, N.C., 1966-68; scanner research on nuclear energy Duke U., Durham, N.C., 1967-68; documentation developer for field engring. IBM, Research Triangle Park, N.C., 1968-70; adminstr. firm Kramer and Brufsky, Stamford, Conn., 1970—; v.p. Barry Kramer Profl. Corp., Stamford, 1977—. Notary public, Conn. Mem. Greenwich Art Assn., DAR, Psi Iota Xi. Republican. Office: 898 Summer St Stamford CT 06905

LEITCH, ALMA MAY, city govt. ofcl.; b. Fredericksburg, Va., Nov. 24, 1924; d. Maurice Andrew Doggett and Nora May (Spicer) L.; grad. James Monroe High Sch., Fredericksburg; various specialized courses U. Va., Va. Poly. Inst. Dep. commnr. revenue City of Fredericksburg, 1946-49, commr. revenue, 1970—; mem. Va. Adv. Legis. Council, 1977-78; mem. subcom. Commonwealth Va. Revenue Resources and Econ. Commn., 1978. Bd. dirs. Fredericksburg chpt. ARC, 1960—, chmn., 1969; sec. Democratic Com. Fredericksburg, 1964; pres., bd. dirs. Rappahannock United Way for Fredericksburg, Spotsylvania, and Stafford counties, 1979. Recipient various service awards; Outstanding Citizenship award Fredericksburg Area C. of C., 1979. Mem. Commrs. Revenue Assn. Va. (pres. 1979-80), Va. Govtl. Employees Assn. (dir.-at-large 1979-80), League No. Va. Commrs. Revenue (pres. 1972), Va. Assn. Local Exec. Constl. Officers (exec. com.), Internat. Assn. Assessing Officers, Va. Assn. Assessing Officers, Hist. Fredericksburg Found., Bus. and Profl. Women's Club. Club: Ann Page Garden (pres. 1980-81, Mary B. Benoit award 1977), Altrusa. Home: 511 Hanover St Fredericksburg VA 22401 Office: City Hall Fredericksburg VA 22401

LEITER, BEULAH G. (MRS. ROBERT PAUL LEITER), lawyer; b. Chgo.; d. Jehiel D. and Rose (Rossman) Liebling; J.D., John Marshall U., 1945, LL.M., 1946; student U. Chgo., U. Ga., Emory U.; m. Robert Paul Leiter, May 10, 1936; children—Darryl J., Paula S. Admitted to Ga. bar, 1945, U.S. Supreme Ct.; since practiced in Atlanta; mem. firm Leiter & Leiter, 1946—; dep. sheriff, 1958—. Mem. Iota Tau Tau, 1951—, So. chancellor, 1955-57, Internat. supreme chancellor, 1955-59, mem. supreme council, 1955-63, supreme asso. dean, 1959-61, internat. supreme dean, 1961-63. Mem. nat. women's com. Brandeis U., 1961—. Mem. Internat. Fedn. Women Lawyers (legal edn. com. 1958, penal law, outer space law, UN com. coms. 1959-60), Nat. Assn Women Lawyers (mental health com.), Am. Trial Lawyers Assn., Internat. Platform Assn., Am. Judicature Soc., Com. Women in Pub. Service, Ga. Assn. Women Lawyers (past v.p., rec. sec., exec. com.), U. Ga. Alumni Soc., Nat. Sheriffs Assn., Ga. Bar Assn., Fulton County Lawyers Assn. (charter, trustee 1952, rec. sec. 1956—), Nat. Assn. Claimant Attys., Am. Bus. Women's Assn., PTA, Atlanta Art Assn., Phi Kappa Delta. Clubs: Equity (publicity com. 1959-60, 62—), Old War Horse Lawyers, Nat. Travel, Smithsonian Assos. Am. Mus. Natural History. Home: 1265 Poplar Grove Dr NE Atlanta GA 30306 Office: PO Box 1492 Atlanta GA 30301

LEITNER, ANITA J., mcpl. bond trader, co. exec.; b. Ft. Worth, Tex., Oct. 8, 1944; d. Louis E. and Alice H. (Hawkins) Reid; student U. Ark.; children—Jill Marie, Steven Jay. Mcpl. bond trader Hanifen, Imhoff, Inc., Denver. Mem. Colo. Mcpl. Bond Dealers Assn. Office: 6872 E Briarwood Dr Englewood CO 80212

LEITNER, SUSAN JANE, mgmt. cons., exec. recruiter; b. Albany, N.Y., June 28, 1947; m. Jerome Leitner; children—Staci, Allan, Kim. Vice pres. exec. search Richards Cons., N.Y.C., 1975-78; writer bus. art to major mags.; pres. Leitner Cons., Ltd., N.Y.C., 1978—. Office: 531 Main St New York NY 10044

LEIVISKA-WILD, NANCY LYNN, rec. co. exec.; b. Evanston, Ill., July 19, 1948; d. Laurie and Dorothy June (Sterner) L.; student Wis. State U., La Crosse, 1966-68, UCLA, 1968-70; m. Brian Wild, Sept. 26, 1980; 1 son, Stefan Kendall. Sec. to Sammy Davis, Jr., 1968-70; with Motown Records, Hollywood, Calif., 1970-71, editor Motown Newsletter, 1972-75, asst. to chmn. bd., 1976-78, dir. video ops., 1979-82, exec. dir. video prodn. film div., 1982—. Mem. Am. Film Inst., AFTRA, ASCAP, Archives Music Preservation (v.p. bd.), Orgn. Women in Music. Mem. Self-Realization Fellowship. Office: 6255 Sunset Los Angeles CA 90028

LEMASTER, SHERRY RENEE, ednl. adminstr.; b. Lexington, Ky., June 25, 1953; d. John William and Mary (Thompson) LeM.; B.S. in Food Sci. and Tech., U. Ky., 1975, M.S., 1982. Lab. technician Central Ky. Animal Disease Diagnostic Lab., Lexington, 1976-77; grant specialist and environ. specialist Ky. Dept. Natural Resources and Environ. Protection, Frankfort, 1977-78; residence hall program coordinator Murray (Ky.) State U., 1978-80; dean of students Midway (Ky.) Coll., 1980—, v.p. devel., 1981—. Mem. adminstrv. bd. First United Meth. Ch., Lexington, 1982—. Mem. Council Advancement and Support of Edn. (chmn. Ky. conf. 1982), Nat. Fedn. Bus. and Profl. Women's Clubs (young career woman program, chmn. com. 1982, former young career woman 1981), Ky. Assn. Women Deans, Adminstrs. and Counselors (newsletter editor 1981-82), Aircraft Owners and Pilots Assn., Greater Lexington Area C. of C. (accreditation com. 1982), U. Ky. Alumni Assn. (life), U. Ky. Coll. Agr. (ambassador), Order Ky. Cols., Alpha Kappa Psi Alumni Assn. (charter), Phi Beta Phi (alumni province pres. 1980-81). Home: 154 Louisiana Ave Lexington KY 40502 Office: Midway Coll Midway KY 40347

LEMASTER, SUSAN M., editor; b. Cody, Wyo., May 9, 1953; d. Floyd Morris and Virginia Kristena (Renner) LeM.; B.A., U. Wyo., Casper, 1979; A.A., Casper Coll., 1977. Reporter, night editor Casper Star Tribune, 1972-76; copy editor, editor In Wyo. mag., Casper, 1979; info. dir. Wyo. Rural Electric Assn., Casper, 1980-81; story editor Wyo. Horizons mag., Casper, 1981-82; freelance writer, 1982—. Recipient First Place News Story, Wyo. Press Assn., 1973. Mem. Nat. Fedn. Press Women, Wyo. Press Women (corr. sec., 1st Place Editing award 1980), NOW. Republican. Roman Catholic. Home: 645 E 16th St Casper WY 82601 Office: PO Box 90130 Casper WY 82609

LEMIEUX, LUCILLE CHENETTE, sch. prin.; b. Worcester, Mass., Dec. 16, 1935; d. Lionel Joseph and Dorothy May Ellen Chenette; B.A., Anna Maria Coll., 1958; M.Ed., State Coll. Worcester, 1967; M.S., Pepperdine U., 1975; postgrad. UCLA, 1977—; m. Bertrand Jean LeMieux, Nov. 22, 1958; children—Marc Kevin, Celeste Marie. Med. technologist Meml. Hosp., 1956-58; research asst. Surprenant Mfg. Co., Clinton, Mass., 1958-59; instr. math. Langford Jr. High Sch., Augusta, Ga., 1959-61; tchr. Worcester City Hosp., 1963-64; lectr. Anna Maria Coll., Paxton, Mass., 1962-65; tchr. sci. Arlington Sch., Torrance, Calif., 1970-72, instructional TV specialist, tchr., 1972-75, adminstr., 1975—; prin. Calle Mayor Middle Sch., 1976—. Vice pres. Torrance Hist. Soc., 1974, Torrance Sister City Assn., 1975; bd. dirs. Los Cancioneros, 1971-74; den leader, coach, merit badge counselor Boy Scouts Am., 1969-71. Recipient Yr. of Educator medallion Los Angeles County Bd. Suprs., 1982; Pi Lambda Theta scholar UCLA, 1980-81. Mem. Assn. Torrance Sch. Adminstrs. (pres. 1982-83), Assn. Calif. Sch. Adminstrs., Assn. Supervision and Curriculum Devel., Nat. Assn. Female Execs., Dean's Council UCLA, Torrance Area Reading Council, Torrance Friends of Library. Writer, producer, All Over This Lands TV series, 1972-74, also Step by Step (award Assn. Ednl. Communications and Tech.), 1974. Office: 4800 Calle Mayor Torrance CA 90505

LEMKE, SUSAN LUCILE, civic worker; b. Mpls., Aug. 2, 1941; d. George William and Irma Marie (LeTendre) Bergquist; B.A. cum laude, Gustavus Adolphus Coll., 1963; m. Lyle Thomas Lemke, July 3, 1965; children—Kirsten Lucile, Renée Christine. Instr. English and French, pub. schs. Little Falls, Minn., 1963-65; substitute tchr. Pub. Schs., Rochester, Minn., 1965-66. Leader Brownies, 1973-75, cons. River Trails council Girl Scouts U.S., 1975—; chmn. Rochester Com. on Urban Environ., 1973-74, sec. treas., 1975—; v.p. bd. dirs. Southeastern Minn. Recycling Corp., 1974-77; commr. Rochester Park and Recreation Bd., 1973—, chmn. park com., 1977—; mem. citizens adv. com. U.S. Army C.E. Zumbro Valley Flood Control Project, 1976-77; mem. Rochester Coordinating Com. for Women, 1972-73; chmn. Roster of Qualified Women, 1973; mem. auction com. Quarry Hill Nature Center, 1972-73; vol. Rochester State Hosp., 1970-76, Rochester Area Drug Abuse and Response Bd., 1972-73; mem., pres.-elect Rochester Area Citizens Adv. Council on Community Edn., Rochester Symphony Guild, chmn. gen. gifts United Way, 1978—; coordinator, chmn. Christian service groups, Christian Women's Club also bd. dirs.; dir. Gloria Dei's, Am. Lutheran Ch. Women. Mem. NEA, Minn. Edn. Assn., AAUW (chmn. ednl. found. program, v.p. Minn. div., legis. chmn. div., treas., v.p. membership, pres. br.), Internat. Fedn. U. Women (exec. bd. Rochester), U. Women Investment Club (chmn.), Rochester LWV, Rapport and Support Study Group, Families Facing Change Study Group, Reading with a Purpose Study Group, Women as Agts. of Change Study Group, Politics of Food Study Group, U.S. Fgn. Policy Study Group (chmn.), Redefining Goals of Edn. Study Group, Cultural Arts Club, Creative Arts Group, Issues in Edn. Group, Money Talks Group, Olmsted County Ind. Republican Women's Orgn. Clubs: Gourmet Food. Home: 620 20th St NE Rochester MN 55901

LEMMOND, MARY SHELDON, ednl. adminstr.; b. Chgo., Oct. 24, 1945; d. Clarence Eugene and Katherine (Wellens) Sheldon; B.S. in Speech and Hearing, U. Tulsa, 1967, postgrad. in ednl. adminstrn., 1977—; M.Ed. in Mental Retardation, Okla. State U., 1972; m. Charles Allen Lemmond, Dec. 24, 1977. Audiologist Hissom Meml. Center, Sand Springs, Okla., 1968-69; tchr. mentally retarded, Cushing (Okla.) Jr. High Sch., 1969-71, speech pathologist, 1971-76; dir. Project Speech Hearing, Lang. and Vision, four counties, Regional Resource Center, Cushing, 1976-79; tchr., speech pathologist, vice prin., prin. Developmental Center, Tulsa, 1976-80, asst. supt., 1980-82; dir. spl. services Jenks (Okla.) Pub. Schs., 1982—. Chmn. Tulsa Area Task Force on Edn. of Emotionally Disturbed/Behavior Disordered Children and Youth. Lic. pvt. pilot. Mem. Internat. Infant Mental Health Assn. (bd. dirs.), Am. Assn. Sch. Adminstrs., Coop. Council Okla. Sch. Adminstrn., Am. Assn. Sch. Bus. Ofcls., Okla. Speech and Hearing Assn., Council for Exceptional Children, Assn. for Severely Handicapped, Okla Dirs. Spl. Services, Nat. Assn. Female Execs., Assn. for Supervision and Curriculum Devel., Assn. for Children with Learning Disabilities, Nat. Soaring Soc., Epsilon Sigma Alpha, Phi Delta Kappa. Presbyterian. Republican. Speaker, participant workshops and profl. confs. Home: 813 N Forest Pl Jenks OK 74037 Office: 1st and B Sts Jenks OK 74037

LEMMONS, MIRIAM ELISE, nurse, social worker, rehab. counselor; b. New Orleans, Jan. 3, 1932; d. Walter Simpson and Ola Adele (Carruth) Weathersby; Asso. Nursing, Iowa Lakes Community Coll., 1977; B.A., Buena Vista Coll., 1978; M.S., Mankato State U., 1981; m. Ronald Lemmons, June 22, 1962; children—Robert, Linda, Mark, Kevin, Robin. R.N., Holy Family Hosp., Estherville, Iowa, 1977-82, dir. med. social services, 1981—, dir. home health dept., 1981—. Mem. Nat. Hospice Assn., Am. Nurses Assn., Nat. League Nursing, Assn. Rehab. Nurses, Nat. Rehab. Assn., NOW, Social Workers in Health Facilities, Am. Soc. Profl. and Exec. Women, Nat. Assn. Rehab. Profls. Democrat. Baptist. Home: 33 Manor Circle Estherville IA 51334 Office: 826 N 8th St Estherville IA 51334

LEMOINE, HELEN LOUISE, nurse; b. Millford, Tex., Feb. 20, 1929; d. Chester Randolph and Ina Louise (Dotson) Riddels; R.N., Parkland Hosp. Sch. Nursing, 1951; m. Louis M. Escude, Dec. 26, 1950; children—Annette, Escude, Michael Escude, Donna Escude McInnis; m. 2nd Albert L. Lemoine, Dec. 21, 1980. Staff nurse Wichita Falls Clinic Hosp., 1952, McConnell and Dupree Clinic and Hosp., Bunkie, La., 1955-65, Bayou Vista Manor Nursing Home, Bunkie, 1965; dir. nursing Avoyelles Manor Nursing Home, DuPont, La., 1966—. Mem. La. Health Care Asso. Dirs. of Nursing in Action (region rep.), Am. Legion Aux. Democrat. Roman Catholic. Club: Nurses Book, Altar Soc. Home: PO Box 115 Cottonport LA 71327 Office: Route 1 PO Box 215 Plaucheville LA 71362

LEMOS, GLORIA ELLIOTT, soft drink co. exec.; b. Royston, Ga., Apr. 29, 1946; d. Richard F. and G. Maxine (Brown) Elliott; A.A., Emmanuel Jr. Coll., 1966; student Oglethorpe U., 1966-68; 1 son, Joseph David. With Coca-Cola Co., Atlanta, 1967-77, Washington, 1977—, v.p. internat. govt. relations, 1979—. Bd. dirs. Community Found. Washington, 1980, Inst. Study of Diplomacy, Georgetown U., 1981—, Am. Com. East-West Accord; trustee Fed. City Council, 1978—, Meridian House Internat., 1981—. Mem. Washington Internat. Bus. Council, UN Internat. Bus. Council, Internat. Mgmt. and Devel. Inst., So. Center Internat. Studies. Club: Internat. Office: Coca-Cola Co 1627 K St NW Suite 800 Washington DC 20006

LENAHAN, MARIE, nun, med. center exec.; b. Phila., May 24, 1920; d. Michael and Rose (Burke) Lenahan; B.S., Villanova U., 1956; M.S. in Adminstrv. Medicine, Columbia U., 1970. Joined Sisters of Mercy, Roman Catholic Ch., 1939; bus. mgr. Thomas M. Fitzgerald Mercy Hosp., Darby, Pa., 1946-53, asst. adminstr., 1953-58, adminstr., 1958-68, asst. pres., 1968-72; pres. Mercy Cath. Med. Center, Darby, 1972—; trustee CHA, St. Louis; bd. dirs. Delaware Valley Hosp. Council. Bd. dirs. Gwynedd Mercy Coll., St. Francis Country House, Camillus Mercy Sch. Practical Nursing; bd. dirs., devel. com. Univ. City Sci. Center. Fellow Am. Coll. Hosp. Adminstrs. (examiner); mem. Hosp. Assn. Pa., Delaware Valley Hosp. Council, Inc. (dir., dir. Del. Valley Health Edn. and Research Found., exec. com. of Forum, Pa. voluntary health care cost containment com. Southeastern region), Pa. Conf. Cath. Hosps., Phila. Conf. Cath. Hosps., Cath. Health Assn. (dir. St. Louis). Home and office: Mercy Cath Med Center Lansdowne Ave and Baily Rd Darby PA 19023

L'ENGLE, MADELEINE (MRS. HUGH FRANKLIN), author; b. N.Y.C., Nov. 29, 1918; d. Charles Wadsworth and Madeleine (Barnett) Camp; A.B. with honors, Smith Coll., 1941; postgrad. Columbia U., 1960—; m. Hugh Franklin, Jan. 26, 1946; children—Josephine Morrison Franklin Jones, Maria Franklin, Bion Barnett. Appeared in Broadway plays Uncle Harry, 1944, The Cherry Orchard, 1945, The Joyous Season, 1946; appeared in summer stock, radio, TV, 1941—; tchr. St. Hilda's and St. Hugh's Sch., N.Y.C., 1960—; writer in residence Ohio State U., 1970; lectr. U. Minn., U. Mich., Ind. U., U. Rochester, Wheaton Coll., U. So. Mo., U. So. Miss., Kent State U., others; writer-in-residence Cathedral St. John the Divine; author: The Small Rain, 1945; Ilse, 1946; And Both Were Young, 1949; Camilla Dickinson, 1951; A Winter's Love, 1957; Meet the Austins, 1960; A Wrinkle in Time, 1962 (Newbery medal 1963; Sequoyah award 1965); The Moon by Night, 1963 (Austrian State Lit. award 1970); The Twenty-Four Days Before Christmas, 1964; The Arm of the Starfish, 1965; Camilla, 1965; The Love Letters, 1966; The Journey with Jonah, 1967; The Young Unicorns, 1968; Dance in The Desert, 1969; Lines Scribbled on an Envelope, 1970; The Other Side of the Sun, 1971; A Circle of Quiet, 1972; A Wind in the Door, 1973; The Summer of The Great-Grandmother, 1975; Dragons in the Waters, 1976; The Irrational Season, 1977; A Swiftly Tilting Planet, 1978; The Weather of the Heart, 1978; Ladder of Angels, 1979; A Ring of Endless Light, 1980; Walking on Water, 1980; author stories, poems, plays. Pres. Crosswicks Found.; bd. dirs. Author's Guild Found. Recipient Lewis Carroll Shelf award, 1965; Hans Christian Anderson Internat. Runner-up award; Sequoiah award; Austrian State prize for lit., 1969; medal U. So. Miss., 1978; Smith medal, 1981. Mem. Authors League (dir., children's book com., membership com., mem. council), Authors Guild (dir.), PEN, Internat. Platform Assn., Writers Guild Am. Mem. Anglican Ch. (choir dir. 1953-59).

LENGYEL, ELIZABETH ANN, editor; b. Waterbury, Conn., Mar. 16, 1939; d. John Francis and Margaret Dorothy (Dubiel) L.; B.A., Duke U., 1961. Reporter, sports writer Waterbury Am., 1957; social editor New Britain (Conn.) Herald, 1961-64; reporter, then feature writer New Haven Register, 1964-67; women's editor New London (Conn.) Day, 1967-70, religion editor, 1970—. Recipient various pub. service awards. Mem. Nat. Assn. Female Execs., LWV (chpt. dir.). Mem. Unity Ch. Club: Zonta. Home: 44 Georgiana St New London CT 06320 Office: 47 Eugene O'Neill Dr New London CT 06320

LENHER, IRENE K. (MRS. SAMUEL LENHER), artist; b. Rye, N.Y., Oct. 4, 1907; d. John Wilkinson and Elena (Hellmann) Kirkland; student Slade Sch. Art, U. Coll. (London), 1925-26, Grande Chaumiere, Paris, 1927-28; M.A. (hon.), U. Del., 1968; m. Samuel Lenher, Dec. 14, 1929; children—John K., Ann B., George V. Exhibited one-woman shows: Warehouse Gallery Arden, Decoy Gallery, Kennett Square, Pa., Hunter Gallery, 1965, Books, Inc., Wilmington, 1966, Grand Gallery, Wilmington, 1978; exhibited two and three man shows, also group shows: Wilmington (Del.) Soc. Fine Arts, Rehoboth (Del.) Art League, Cottage Tour Art, West Chester, Pa.; staff artist Cokesbury Courier; work represented in collections: Wilmington Trust Co., Hotel Du Pont, Del. Hosp. Sustaining mem. Everyman's Gallery; represented permanent collections: Wilmington Soc. Fine Arts, Copeland Purchase Fund, U. Del. Asso. mem. bd. Del. Hosp. Recipient 2d prize, best of show awards Nat. League Am. Pen Women shows, award of merit, 1962. Mem. Nat. League Am. Pen Women (state pres.), Colonial Dames Am., Am. Watercolor Soc. (asso.), Soc. Mayflower Descs. (past gov.), Wilmington Studio Group, Phila. Art Alliance. Episcopalian. Clubs: Greenville Country, Wilmington Country. Home: Cokesbury Village Box 50 Hockessin DE 19707 Studio: 1616 Rodney St Wilmington DE 19806

LENNON, DIANNE SAMPSON, educator; b. Clinton, N.C., Apr. 10, 1943; d. Ulysses Grant and Augusta Ollie (Hines) Sampson; B.S., N.C. Central U., 1965; M.A., Glassboro State Coll., 1977; m. Thayer Otis Lennon, Aug. 28, 1977. Asst. supr. Farmers Home Adminstrn., U.S. Dept. Agr., Mays Landing, N.J., 1965-70; extension home economist Coop. Extension Service, Atlantic and Cape May Counties, Mays Landing, N.J., 1970—; cons. in field; community nutrition educator, lectr. Recipient Rutgers U. Merit Increment for Superior Performance, 1971; Gold Star award, Cook Coll., Extension Home Econ., 1972; Stokley Van Camp Nutrition award, 1965; others; Outstanding Service award, Pin and Trophy, Ladies Aux. VFW, 1972; Florence Hall award, Disting. Service award, 1981. Mem. N.J. Home Econ. Assn. (pres. 1978-79), So. Counties Home Econ. Assn. (pres. 1974-75), Atlantic County Nutrition Council (v.p. 1978-79), Am. Home Econ. Assn., Nat. Assn. Extension Home Economists, VFW Aux. (pres. 1971-72), Epsilon Sigma Phi. Contbr. articles to profl. jours.; author leaflets on nutrition edn. Home: RD 4 PO Box 168 Tremont and West Jersey Aves Pleasantville NJ 08232 Office: 1200 W Harding Hwy Mays Landing NJ 08330

LENNON, THELMA CUMBO, state ednl. adminstr.; b. Raleigh, N.C., Apr. 12, 1928; d. Benjamin Franklin and Kittie (Glover) Cumbo; B.S.C., N.C. Central U., 1948; Ed.M., Boston U., 1953; m. John D. Lennon, Aug. 6, 1966. Dean of students Allen U., 1955-61; counselor-educator N.C. Central U., 1961-62; supr. guidance N.C. Dept. Pub. Instrn., Raleigh, 1962-70, spl. asst. in student services, 1970—; mem. bds. edn.

various guidance-related orgns.; speaker at numerous nat. guidance convs.; vol. pub. schs. Recipient Ella Stephens Barrett award N.C. Personnel and Guidance Assn., 1975; Disting. Vol. Service award Gov. N.C., 1979. Mem. Am. Personnel and Guidance Assn., Nat. Vocat. Guidance Assn. (Presdl. award 1978, Merit award 1982), Nat. Assn. Pupil Personnel Adminstrs., Internat. Assn. Pupil Personnel Workers, LWV, Alpha Kappa Alpha. Democrat. Baptist. Club: Civitan. Author: Counseling Persons of a Minority Culture, 1974; Guidance Needs of Special Populations, 1980; editor Jour. Non-White Concerns, 1982—. Office: Edn Bldg NC Dept Public Instruction Raleigh NC 27611

LENSMITH, BETTY, business exec.; b. Oconomowoc, Wis., Oct. 3, 1928; d. Alex F. and Vera (Zeiters) Henschel; m. Eugene A. Lensmith, Nov. 14, 1949; children—Lissa Kathleen, Larry Eugene. Receptionist, Schrader Studio, Milw., 1947; mgr. Tooley Myron Studios chain, 1948-49; owner, mgr. Country Studio, Oconomowoc, 1950—, Town and Country Studio, 1957—; founder, pres., treas. Photographers Specialized Services, Inc., Oconomowoc, 1968—; founder, pres. Ret. Persons Specialized Services, 1981—, Golden World Products, 1982—; instr. Winona Sch. Photography, 1975—, Miami and Traingle Inst. (Pa.), 1977, No. Ga. Sch. Photography, 1978. Recipient awards Kodak Co. Mem. Profl. Photographers Am. (cert. photographic craftsman, recipient various awards), Am. Soc. Photographers, Am. Mgmt. Assn., Studio Suppliers Assn., Female Execs., 700 Club, Presidents Club. Author: The Guide to Lighting, Posing and Composing, 1971, rev. edit., 1980; Selling, The Name of the Game, 1976; Profitable Promotions and Merchandising Techniques, 1977; The Basic Guide to Commercial Photography, 1979. Home: 612 Summit St Oconomowoc WI 53066 Office: 650 Armour Rd Oconomowoc WI 53066

LENSON, HILDA WOLK, civic worker; b. Cleve., July 22, 1907; d. Max and Lena (Sobul) Wolk; B.A., Western Res. U., 1928; cert., U. Grenoble, France, 1926; postgrad. Western Res. U., 1928, 57, Columbia U., 1930, U. N.C., 1932; m. Max Lenson, July 29, 1934; children—Larry Jay (dec.), Margery Carol (dec.), Betty Jane Lenson Katzner, Peggy Ann Lenson Weil. Instr., French Cleve. Coll., 1929; tchr. English New Hanover High Sch., Wilmington, N.C., 1930-32; instr. French Pa. State U., Altoona, 1957-63, 1964-67; adminstrv. asst., tchr. French Penn-Mont Acad., Altoona, 1963-64; asst. prof. French Pa. State U., Altoona, 1968-73, ret., 1973; pvt. tutor in French, 1973—. Discussion leader trainee Pa. State Bicentennial Project; pres. Friends of Altoona Area Public Library, 1976-77; bd. dirs. LWV of Altoona, 1977-82; vol. Recording for the Blind; active nursing home and vets. hosps., Blair County Sr. Service Center; pres. Temple Beth Israel Sisterhood, 1978-79; active Blair County Arts Found., Easter Seal Soc. Mem. AAUW, Hadassah, Pa. MLA (dir. 1960-63, pres. 1973-74), Altoona Campus Women. Democrat.

LENTNER, AUDREY M., med. office adminstr.; b. Detroit, June 26, 1936; d. Frank R. and Millicent M. (Kelley) L.; student parochial schs., Mich., Ohio, and Pa.; 1 dau., Janice Marie Simmerly Camerato. Sec., Union Savs. & Loan, Cleve., 1954-56, NASA, Cleve., 1956-57; sec., bookkeeper Cheton's Furniture, Canton, Ohio, 1958-59; sec. Frazier Mortgage Co., Canton, 1959-61; with public relations dept. Columbus (Ohio) Bd. Realtors, 1968-70; sec. Neurosurg. Cons., Inc., Columbus, 1970-76, office mgr., 1976—; owner Body Reflections East, European Body Wrap Salon, Reynoldsburg, Ohio, 1982—. Mem. Nat. Assn. Female Execs. Democrat. Roman Catholic. Club: Walnut Hills Country, Lions Aux. Home: 5721 Saranac Dr Columbus OH 43227 Office: Neurosurgical Consultants Inc 410 W 10th Ave Suite N-907 Columbus OH 43210

LENTS, PEGGY IGLAUER, mfg. co. mktg. exec.; b. St. Louis, Apr. 14, 1950; d. Hank S. and Elizabeth Ruth (Metzger) Iglauer; B.A. magna cum laude (univ. fellow), Jackson Coll., Tufts U., 1971; M.P.A. (fellow), Kennedy Sch. Govt., Harvard U., 1974; m. Don G. Lents, Aug. 27, 1972; 1 dau., Stacie Lee. Legis. aide Congressman Symington, Washington, 1971; adminstrv. mgr. May Co., London (Eng.) Hdqrs., 1974, buyer Famous Barr (May Co.), St. Louis, 1976-78; gen. mdse. mgr. Roman Co., St. Louis, 1978-80, mktg. dir., 1981-82, v.p., 1982—; cons. Human Resources Adminstrn., N.Y.C.; teaching fellow Tufts U., 1971-72. Bd. dirs. Lucky Lane Sch., 1980-81; chmn. NDC Nat. Leadership Program, 1974; cons., Washington, 1972, polit. campaigns N.D., Iowa. Mem. Am. Mgmt. Assn., Fashion Group, Pioneers, Direct Mail Club St. Louis, Women in Bus. Club: Westwood Country. Home: 570 Bedford Saint Louis MO 63130 Office: 1201 Hanley Ind Ct Saint Louis MO 63144

LENTZ, GLENDA FUTCH, educator; b. Plant City, Fla., Nov. 2, 1933; d. Hugh Jennings and Vera (Simmons) Futch; student Fla. State U., 1951-54; B.A., U. South Fla., 1963, M.A., 1972; m. Frank C. Lentz, June 18, 1954; children—Glenn Carver, Kevin John, Keith Hugh. Legal sec. Trinkle, Trinkle & Redman, Plant City, Fla., 1959-61; tchr. Hillsborough County Bd. Pub. Instrn., Tampa, Fla., 1963-68; coordinator coop. edn. U. South Fla., Tampa, 1968-70, asst. dir. student career and employment center, 1970-74, dir. coop. edn. and placement, 1974—. Mem. Am. Soc. Engring. Edn., Fla. Coll. Placement Assn., So. Coll. Placement Assn., Coop. Edn. Assn. Democrat. Presbyterian. Office: University South Florida Fowler Ave Tampa FL 33620

LENZ, KAY, actress; b. Los Angeles, Mar. 4, 1953; d. Ted and Kay Lenz; student public schs., Van Nuys, Calif.; m. David Cassidy, Apr. 3, 1977. Appeared in television films A Summer Without Boys, 1973, Unwed Father, 1974, The Underground Man, 1974, The FBI Story: Alvan Karpus, Public Enemy Number One, 1974, Journey from Darkness, 1975; appeared on television shows Love Story, Gunsmoke, Medical Center, Kodiak, McCloud, Nakia, Cannon, Petrocelli, Rich Man, Poor Man, Jigsaw John; appeared in motion pictures Breezy, 1973, White Line Fever, 1975, The Great Scout and Cathouse Thursday, 1976, Moving Violation, 1976. Recipient Golden Apple nomination, 1973, Hollywood Fgn. Press nomination, 1973, Emmy award, 1974-75, Emmy nomination, 1975-76. Address: care Creative Artist Agy 1888 Century Park E Suite 1400 Los Angeles CA 90067 *

LENZMEIER, MICHELLE STEPHANIE, civic worker, former govt. contractor; b. Fargo, N.D., Sept. 12, 1947; d. Frank Stephen and Marjorie (Miller) Lenzmeier; grad. Am. Acad. Dramatic Arts, 1972; B.A. in Arts, Stockton State Coll., 1976; M.A., Fairleigh Dickinson U., 1982; law student N.Y.U., 1982—. With Chevrolet Motor div. Gen. Motors Corp., Fargo, N.D., 1967-70; with Cheri Paul Modeling Sch., Fargo, 1968-70, Outlook Stores N.Y.C., 1970-73; partner developer LBL Devel. Co., West Fargo, N.D., 1973-82; project coordinator George T. Christine III Real Estate & Devel. Atlantic City, N.J., 1980-81; ind. cons., contractor, 1981-82. Trustee, Stockton State Coll., 1980—; bd. dirs. United Way of Atlantic County, 1981—, Miss Am. Pageant, 1975—; chmn., sect. leader fundraising campaigns Atlantic City Med. Center, 1973—; fin. rev. com./exec. bd. So. Jersey Human Services Council, 1980-81; founder Opera Co. of South Jersey, 1976-77; exec. com. N.J. League Municipalities, 1973-76; pres., head fin. com. Child Fedn. Atlantic City, 1978-82; coordinator Atlantic County Internat. Yr. of the Child Sept. Festival, 1979; pres. Friends of Stockton State Coll. Performing Arts Center, 1979-82. State Sch. of Sci. scholar, 1966-67; Am. Acad. Dramatic Arts scholar, 1970-72; named 1 of 9 Outstanding Polit. Women in Nation, 1968; recipient Outstanding Achievement award for serving as founding pres. Friends of Stockton Coll. Performing Arts Center, 1981; lic. pilot. Mem. AIAA, Aircraft Owners and Pilots Assn., Ninety-Nines Women's Internat. Pilots Assn., Whirly-Girls-Women's Internat. Helicopter Assn., Atlantic City/County Bd. Realtors, Nat. Assn. Female Execs., Legal Assn. of Women, Internat. Law Assn., Student Bar Assn., Criminal Law Soc. Clubs: Zonta, Porsche of Am., Brandywine River Mus. Conservatory. Roman Catholic. Address: 322 W 57th St Apt 40D New York NY 10019

LEON, DOROTHY SILVER, public relations exec.; b. Boston, Nov. 1, 1913; d. Louis and Sophia (Gerson) Silver; A.A., Los Angeles City Coll., 1950; m. Alfred Leon, Mar. 13, 1934; children—Marion, Richard, Dai, Boris, Leah. Public relations coordinator Los Angeles Unified Sch. Dist. Vol. Program, 1960-70; public relations coordinator Soc. Children's Book Writers, Hollywood, Calif., 1960-70. Recipient Minor awards. Mem. Women in Communications, Soc. Children's Book Writers (dir.), So. Calif. Council Lit. for Children and Young People. Author: One Eye, Two Eyes, Three Eyes, Four, 1980; By These Names I Am Known, 1980; Anybody Can Be Somebody, 1980; The Secret World of Underground Animals, 1982; also articles and stories. Home and Office: 7224 Hillside Ave Apt 18 Hollywood CA 90046

LEON, LINDA M., fin. co. exec.; b. Newark, Apr. 12, 1955; d. Gerard Anthony and Josephine (Bravoco) Montanino; B.S. in Acctg. (scholar), Georgetown U., 1977; m. Kenneth M. Leon, Sept. 20, 1981. Supr. acct. ops. and fin. Johnson & Johnson, Piscataway, N.J., 1977-78; internat. auditor Schering Plough Corp., Kenilworth, N.J., 1978-79; mgr. acctg. AT&T, N.Y.C., 1979-82; asst. controller Bankers Trust Co., 1979—. Democrat. Jewish. Home: 137 W Jersey St Elizabeth NJ 07202 Office: One Bankers Trust Plaza New York NY 10027

LEONARD, DARLENE RUTH, postmaster; b. Boone, Iowa, Dec. 19, 1924; d. Vernon Russell and Ruth Elizabeth (Carlson) Anderson; B.S., No. Mich. U., 1976; m. Clyde Edward Leonard, May 25, 1946; children—Donald, Clyde Edward. Adminstrv. clk. Briggs & Stratton Mfg. Co., Milw., 1956-57; cashier, operator Niagara Telephone Co. (Wis.), 1957-60; office mgr. Mich. Mfg. Co., Iron Mountain, 1960-62; postal service clk., Niagara, 1962-73, postmaster, 1973—; mgmt. sectional center coordinator Marinette County Post Offices. Active Vocat. Sch. Bd., Kingsford, Mich. Mem. Am. Bus. Women's Assn. (Boss of Yr. award Iron Mountain 1979), Nat. League of Postmasters (pres. Wis. br. 1982, postmaster of yr. award 1979, League Letter editor 1975-79), Nat. Assn. Postmasters, VFW Aux. (treas., 1965-70), Am. Legion Aux. (sec., 1975-78). Democrat. Methodist. Club: Niagara Women's. Home: 512 Washington Ave Niagara WI 54151 Office: 1181 Main St Niagara WI 54151

LEONARD, FLORENCE IRENE, educator; b. Trenton, Apr. 12, 1934; d. Esau and Alverine (Arnold) Courtney; B.A., Trenton State Coll., 1968, M.Ed., 1979, cert. in supervision, 1979; m. Henry L. Leonard, Feb. 21, 1953; children—Guy Anthony, Carl Henry, Celeste Alverine, Troy Courtney. Librarian asst. dept. edn. N.J. State Library, 1960-64; tchr. Harrison Elem. Sch., Trenton, 1968—, supr., 1981—, also part-time acting prin. Deaconess local ch. Chs. of God in Christ, Trenton. Mem. NEA, N.J. Edn. Assn., Trenton Edn. Assn., Mercer County Edn. Assn. Author: The Xerox Intermediate Dictionary, 1973; designer mural of the Crucifixion, Holy Trinity Ch. of God in Christ. Trenton, 1954, girls' dormitory for Chs. of God in Christ, Monrovia, Liberia, 1959. Home: 1015 Hughes Dr Apt 2 Trenton NJ 08690 Office: Harrison School Genesee St Trenton NJ 08611 also Trenton Bd Edn N Clinton Ave Trenton NJ 08609

LEONARD, FLORENCE JONES, educator; b. Camden, N.J., Oct. 10, 1933; d. John Henry and Florence May (Johnson) Jones; A.B., Rutgers U., 1955; M.Ed., Towson State U., Balt., 1972; m. Charles Brown Leonard, Jr., Aug. 26, 1955; children—Charles Brown, III, Bruce Joseph. Tchr., Moorestown (N.J.) public schs., 1955-56; dir. Mt. Hebron Presbyn. Presch. Center, Howard County, Md., 1964-72; dir. Student Day Care Center, Towson (Md.) State U., 1972-74, mem. faculty, 1974—, instr. early childhood edn., 1979—, also faculty dir. Aliza Brandwine Center Parent-Infant Devel.; bd. dirs. Md. Com. Children; cons. in field. Recipient Aethenaeum award Rutgers U., 1954. Grantee, Towson State U., 1979, 80, 4-C, 1979. Mem. AAUP, Orgn. Mondial Pour Edn. Prescholaire, Assn. Childhood Edn. Internat., Nat. Assn. Edn. Young Children, Phi Kappa Phi, Phi Delta Kappa. Mem. Ch. of Nazarene. Club: University at Towson. Home: 9202 Furrow Ave Ellicott City MD 21043 Office: Early Childhood Edn Dept Towson State U Baltimore MD 21204

LEONARD, FLORENCE MULLINS, adminstrv. asst.; b. Callaway, Va., Mar. 19, 1931; d. William Marshall and Fannie Lera (Prillaman) Mullins; student Coll. William and Mary, 1975, 78, Thomas Nelson Community Coll., 1974; m. Robert Warren Leonard, June 24, 1950; children—Susan Gail Leonard Little, William Ralph, Molly Marie. Sec., Newport News Public Sch. System, 1944-48; sec. to chief dynamic loads div. Nat. Adv. Com. Aeros., 1948-53; ednl. sec. guidance office Williamsburg James City County Public Sch. System, 1975-77; exec. sec. to exec. dir. Nat. Center State Cts., Williamsburg, Va., 1977-79, adminstrv. asst. to exec. dir., 1979—, asst. sec. bd. dirs., 1979-81, sec. bd. dirs., 1981—. Mem. Supt.'s Adv. Com. on Vocat. Edn., Williamsburg-James City County Public Schs., 1981—. Mem. Am. Soc. Profl. and Exec. Women, Nat. Assn. Female Execs., Inc., Exec. Secs. Club, LWV. Presbyterian. Clubs: Newport News Operatic Soc. (bd. dirs., exec. com.), Wednesday Morning Music (bd. dirs., exec. com.). Home: Riverview Plantation Route 4 Box 334 Williamsburg VA 23185 Office: 300 Newport Ave Williamsburg VA 23185

LEONARD, MICHELE TINSLEY, elec. products mfg. co. exec.; b. Bayshore, N.Y., Oct. 26, 1956; d. James Leonard and Martha Ann (Carle) Tinsley; student Dartmouth Coll., 1976; B.A., Wellesley Coll., 1977; m. Ronald Keith Leonard, June 9, 1979; children—Paul Vincent, Courtney Michele. Telephone interviewer Decision Research, Wellesley, Mass., 1977; staff asso. Western Electric, Inc., Boston, 1977-78, supr. prodn. control, North Andover, Mass., 1978—. Mem. Am. Soc. Profl. Women, Shinnecock Native Am. Cultural Coalition. Club: Merrimack Jr. Women's (rec. sec., 1980, chairperson membership, publicity and public affairs 1981). Home: Bean Rd Merrimack NH 03054 Office: 1600 Osgood St North Andover MA 01845

LEONARD, PATRICIA LYNN, univ. adminstr.; b. Rockville, Centre, N.Y., May 28, 1955; d. John Thomas and Grace Lillian (Foster) L.; B.A. in Social Work and Secondary Edn. in Social Studies, Coll. Misericordia, 1977; M.A. in Coll. Student Personnel Adminstrn., Mich. State U., 1979. Grad. resident adviser Mich. State U., 1977-79; residence coordinator U. N.C., Charlotte, 1979-80; area coordinator Miami U., Oxford, Ohio, 1980—, instr. in personnel and guidance, 1980—; cons. to student affair staff Coll. Misericordia. Mem. Am. Personnel and Guidance Assn., Am. Coll. Personnel Assn., Ohio Coll. Personnel Adminstrs., Phi Delta Kappa, Alpha Delta Mu. Office: 111 Warfield Miami U Oxford OH 45056

LEONARD, PHYLLIS G(RUBBS), novelist; b. Westerville, Ohio, Oct. 4, 1924; d. Maynard Lee and Lura McEwen (Steele) Grubbs; student Cleve. Coll., 1942-44; certificate U. San Carlos (Guatemala), 1948, Am. Grad. Sch. Internat. Mgmt., 1949; m. Walter Magruder Leonard, Jan. 31, 1948. Partner, Leonard Ins. Agy., Phoenix, 1952-63, pres., 1963-71; pres., treas. Leonard Corp., Phoenix, 1971-81; pres. Ins. Women Phoenix, 1956; author: Prey of the Eagle (1st prize fiction Ariz. Press Women, 2d prize adult fiction Nat. Fedn. Press Women), 1974; Phantom of the Sacred Well (1st prize fiction Soc. Southwestern Authors), transl. French, 1976; Warrior's Woman, 1977, English edit., 1978; Tarnished Angel, 1980; Mariposa, 1983; (as Isabel Ortega) Street of the Madwoman, 1978, German transl., 1982; Active, Tombstone Little Theatre, Tombstone Community Health Services Aux.; mem. Friends of Sierra Vista Library, Friends of Cochise County Library, Am. Legion Aux., Tombstone Restoration Commn., St. Paul's Episcopal Ch. Women's Guild. Mem. Authors Guild, Authors League Am., Ariz. Press Women, Nat. Fedn. Press Women, Soc. Southwestern Authors, Ariz. Hist. Soc., Ariz. Authors Assn., Tombstone Assn. Arts, Tombstone Vigilettes, Tombstone Small Animal Shelter (treas., editor newsletter). Address: PO Box 400 Tombstone AZ 85638

LEONARD HARKNESS, ELEANOR DELORIS, employment specialist; b. Due West, S.C., Sept. 1, 1946; d. John Joel and Edna Charlotte (Marshall) Harkness; A.A.S., Sullivan County Community Coll., 1966; B.S., L.I. U., 1973; M.B.A., Fordham U., 1976; m. Ronald Mace Leonard, Oct. 15, 1977; 1 dau., Antoinette Charlotte. Interviewer, salary adminstr., personnel asst. Bank of N.Y., N.Y.C., 1968-73; compensation analyst Exxon Internat., N.Y.C., 1973-75, fgn. assignments coordinator, 1975-77, employee relations analyst Exxon Chem. Co., N.Y.C., 1977-78, compensation and policy analyst Exxon Internat., 1978-80, employment specialist, 1980—; vis. prof. numerous univs. Bd. dirs. Manhattanville Community Centers, Inc., 1975-82, chairperson personnel com., 1978-82; employment adv. computer tech. adv. com. Opportunities Industrialization Center, 1982—, mem. tech. adv. com., 1980—. Mem. N.Y. Personnel Mgmt. Assn., Am. Mgmt. Assn., Council of Concerned Black Execs., NAACP, Fordham U. Grad. Sch. Bus. Alumni Assn., Fordham U. Women's Network. Home: 405 Westminster Rd Brooklyn NY 11218 Office: 1251 Ave of Americas New York NY 10020

LEONARDICH, CHRISTINE, lingerie mfg. co. ops. ofcl.; b. Watsonville, Calif., Nov. 14, 1951; d. Peter Paul and Agnes (Manfre) L.; B.A. in Philosophy, Coll. of Notre Dame, 1971; B.S. in Mech. Engring., U. Calif., Berkeley, 1972; A.A. in Criminology, Coll. of San Mateo, 1974. Mgr. legal records Utah Internat. Mining Corp., San Francisco, 1971-75; sr. tech. rep. Xerox, San Francisco, 1975-78; dir. operational improvements Sunset Designs, San Ramon, Calif., 1978-81; mgr. plant ops. and distbn. Victoria's Secret Designer Lingerie, San Francisco, 1981—. Active San Francisco Bay Area Spl. Olympics, Bay Area Big Sisters Program. Recipient spl. award, Xerox Corp., 1977; cert. Xerographic technician, Calif. Mem. Soc. Women Engrs., Nat. Women's Polit. Caucus, San Francisco Assn. Profl. Women, Nat. Newspaper Editors Assn. (award for contbns. as editor-in-chief, 1968). Home: 26 Fraser Dr Walnut Creek CA 94596 Office: PO Box 31442 San Francisco CA 94131

LEONE, ROSE MARIE, psychotherapist; b. N.Y.C., June 3, 1930; d. Peter and Mary (Marinelli) L.; B.R.E., Philathea Coll., 1967; M.A., N.Y. U., 1973; M.S.W., Hunter Coll., 1977; postgrad. Am. Inst. Psychotherapy and Psychoanalysis, 1974-79. Counselor, adminstrv. asst. So. Bronx Community Corp., 1966-70; drug abuse counselor Lincoln Hosp., Bronx, N.Y., 1970-74; placement and tng. coordinator Vera Inst. Justice Wildcat Service Corp., N.Y.C., 1974-75; dir. addiction services, sr. counselor N.Y. Med. Coll., 1975-77; coordinator Office Substance Abuse Services, N.Y.C., 1978; dir. women's services Project Return Found., N.Y.C., 1978-80; project coordinator Div. Substance Abuse Services, State of N.Y., N.Y.C., 1980-81, sr. drug abuse counselor, counselor assistance program, 1981—; pvt. practice psychotherapy, N.Y.C., 1975—; mem. Narcotic and Drug Research Instl. Rev. Bd., 1979—; cons. All Crafts Found., Inc., 1979—. N.Y.C., 1975—; lectr. in field. Cert. social worker, rehab. counselor; Mem. Nat. Rehab. Counselor Assn., Rehab. Counseling Assn. Contbr. articles to profl. publs. Home: 553 3d Ave New York NY 10016 Office: 201 E 15th St New York NY 10003

LEONG, PAMELA LUTTNER, home economist; b. Cleve., May 15, 1947; d. John H. and Louise R. (Steffen) Luttner; B.S., Kent State U., 1969, M.A., 1973; m. Kong Kwok Leong, May 15, 1976; children—Michelle Kum Soon, Mei Soon. Instr., U. Akron and Kent (Ohio) State U., 1973-74; copywriter Sta. WAKR and WAKR-TV, Akron, Ohio, 1973-74; instr. U. Pertanian, Serdang, Malaysia, 1974-76; copywriter Marklin Advt., Malaysia, 1975-76; asst. advt. dir. Bauer Enterprises, Stow, Ohio, 1977-78; county extension agent Ohio Coop. Extension Service, Sidney, 1978—. Recipient Nat. Newscolumn award, 1978-79. Mem. Am. Home Econs. Assn., Nat. Assn. Extension Home Economists, Kappa Omicron Phi. Contbr. articles to profl. jours. Office: Ohio Cooperative Extension Service Courthouse Sidney OH 45365

LEONHARDT, C. BARBARA, public relations mgr. b. Dunnville, Ky., Apr. 29, 1938; d. Lonzie Otis and Alice Beatrice (Propes) Patton; B.S., U. Cin., 1960; m. James Freeman Leonhardt, Jr., June 11, 1960; children—Scott Edward, Todd Michael. Home econ. technician Procter & Gamble, Cin., 1960-62; consumer corr. Drackett Co., Cin., 1969-70; bridal cons. Bride & Groom Showcase, Cin., 1974-77; public relations mgr. Stearns & Foster Co., Cin., 1977-80; freelance cons., 1980—. Mem. Am. Home Econs. Assn., Home Econs. in Bus. (sec.), Ohio Home Econs. Assn. Republican. Methodist. Address: 7391 Lake Pk Dr West Chester OH 45069

LEOPOLD, ESTELLA BERGERE, botanist, educator; b. Madison, Wis., Jan. 8, 1927; d. Aldo and Estella (Bergere) Leopold; Ph.B., U. Wis., 1948; M.S., U. Calif., Berkeley, 1950; Ph.D., Yale U., 1955. Asst. physiology and embryology Genetics Expt. Sta., Smith Coll., 1951-52; asst. biologist, then asst. animal ecology Yale U., 1952-54; botanist, paleontology and stratigraphy br. U.S. Geol. Survey, 1955-76; adj. prof. biology U. Colo., 1967-76; dir. Quaternary Research Center, prof. botany and forest research U. Wash., Seattle, 1976—. Co-recipient Conservationist of Year award Nat. Wildlife Fedn., 1969; award Keep Colo. Beautiful Inc., 1976; travel grantee NSF, Spain, 1957, Poland, 1961, Eng., 1977. Fellow AAAS; mem. Nat. Acad. Scis. (environ. studies bd. 1976-79). Ecol. Soc. Am. (climate research bd. 1979—), Internat. Quaternary Assn. U.S. Nat. Com., Am. Quaternary Assn. (pres.-elect 1980), Bot. Soc. Am. Inst. Ecology (dir.). Office: Quaternary Research Center Univ Wash Seattle WA 98195 *

LEPERE, GENE HARRIET, home furnishings industry cons.; b. N.Y.C., Oct. 16, 1926; d. Joseph Herman and Jennie (Berman) Hirshhorn; A.B., U. So. Calif., 1949; M.B.A. with honors, Pace U., 1977; m. Edward M. Kelley, Sept. 11, 1955; m. 2d James E. LePere, Mar. 15, 1963. Mgr., Los Angeles County Probation Dept., 1955-63; v.p., gen. mgr. LePere, Inc., antiques and fine arts, N.Y.C., 1966-75; mgr. mktg. info. Furniture div. Sperry & Hutchinson Co., N.Y.C., 1976-79; owner, pres. Gene LePere Assos., Mt. Kisco, N.Y., 1979—. Mem. Nat. Home Furnishings League, Nat. Assn. Exec. Women, Jewish. Contbr. articles to profl. publs.

LEPPELLERE, FREIDA ANNA, retail office products co. exec.; b. Altoona, Pa., Jan. 16, 1927; d. Leo A. and Anna (Cardinale) Martino; student public schs.; m. Anthony Leppellere, Oct. 5, 1946; children—Terrence, Allen, Annette, Anthony. Various secretarial positions, 1967-72; partner, store mgr., account exec., buyer The Gallery Stationers, Homewood, Ill., 1972—. Mem. Nat. Office Products Assn. Roman Catholic. Office: 18031 Dixie Hwy Homewood IL 60430

LEPSKY, HENRIETTA, nursing adminstr.; b. Cin., Sept. 27, 1938; d. Harry Oscar and Nellie (Molle) L.; R.N., B.S., U. Mich., 1956; M.S. in Community Health Planning, U. Cin., 1974; M.H.A., Xavier U., Cin., 1978; children—Stephanie, Steven. Mgmt. systems coordinator nursing dept. Cin. Gen. Hosp., 1971-74; dir. nursing Holmes Hosp., U. Cin.,

1974-76; asst. adminstr., dir. nursing Holmes div. U. Cin. Med. Center, 1976—; mem. faculty Edgecliff/Xavier U. Sch. Nursing, U. Cin. Coll. Nursing and Health; trustee Nurses Profl. Registry Cin. Kings Fund scholar, Eng., 1978. Cert. in advanced nursing adminstrn. Am. Nurses Assn. Mem. Am. Soc. Nursing Service Adminstrs. (bd. dirs. 1980-82), Am. Coll. Hosp. Adminstrs., Ohio Soc. Nursing Service Adminstrs. (pres. 1978-79), Greater Cin. Dirs. Nursing Service (pres. 1977-78). Jewish. Home: 9192 Peachblossom Ct Cincinnati OH 45231 Office: Holmes Div U Cin Med Center Eden and Bethesda Ave Cincinnati OH 45219

LERMAN, EILEEN R., lawyer; b. N.Y.C., May 6, 1947; d. Alex and Beatrice (Kline) L.; B.A., Syracuse U., 1969; J.D., Rutgers U., 1972; postgrad. U. Denver Grad. Sch. Bus., 1979—. Admitted to N.Y. State bar, 1973, Colo. bar, 1976; atty. FTC, N.Y.C., 1972-74; corp. atty. RCA, N.Y.C., 1974-76; corp. atty. Samsonite Corp. and consumer products div. Beatrice Foods Co., Denver, 1976-78, asso. gen. counsel, 1978—, asst. sec., 1979—; dir. Legal Aid Soc. of Met. Denver, 1979-80; guest lectr. Regis Coll., U. Denver, Colo. Women's Coll. Samsonite chmn. United Way, 1981; bd. dirs. Colo. Postsecondary Ednl. Facilities Authority, 1981—. Mem. Colo. Women's Bar Assn. (dir. 1980-81), Am. Bar Assn., Colo. Bar Assn., Denver Bar Assn., Rutgers U. Alumni Assn. Club: Soroptimist. Home: 1018 Fillmore St Denver CO 80206 Office: 11200 E 45th Ave Denver CO 80239

LERNER, GEORGIA BONITA, nurse; b. Hastings, Nebr., Dec. 5, 1922; d. Samuel and Emma Elizbeth (Tresenriter) Snell; B.S., U. Nebr. Sch. Nursing, 1945; m. Wilhelm A. Lerner, Apr. 4, 1946; children—Paul S., Mark W., Gretchen E. Staff nurse in obstetrics Meml. Hosp., North Platte, Nebr., 1958-60; dir. nursing Linden Manor Nursing Home, North Platte, 1960—. Grantee Kenny Rehab. Inst., 1972; U. Colo. grantee, 1976. Mem. Alumni Assn. U. Nebr. Sch. Nursing, Phi Sigma Alpha (Woman of Yr. 1972). Republican. Lutheran. Clubs: Order Eastern Star, Nebr. Extension. Home: 615 W 4th St North Platte NE 69101 Office: 420 W 4th St North Platte NE 69101

LERNER, GERDA, history educator; b. Vienna, Austria; B.A., New Sch. Social Research, 1963; M.A., Columbia U., 1965, Ph.D., 1966; m. Carl Lerner (dec. 1972). Lectr., New Sch. then instr. Social Research 1963-65; assoc. prof. L.I. U., 1964-68; faculty Sarah Lawrence Coll. 1968-80; Robinson-Edwards prof. history U. Wis., Madison, 1980—. NEH fellow, Lilly fellow, Ford fellow, Guggenheim fellow. Mem. Orgn. Am. Historians (pres. 1981-1982), AAUP, Authors League, PEN, Am. Hist. Assn. Author: The Grimke Sisters from South Carolina: Rebels Against Slavery 1967; The Women in American History 1971; Black Women in White America: A Documentary History 1972; The Female Experience: An American Documentary 1976; A Death of One's Son 1978; The Majority Finds Its Past 1979; Teaching Women's History 1981. Office: 5123 Humanities Bldg University of Wisconsin Madison WI 53706

LERNER, MILDRED SHERWOOD, clin. psychologist and psychoanalyst, counselor; b. N.Y.C., Mar. 29, 1929; d. Samuel Jerome and Rose (Malina) Sherwood; B.A. with honors, CCNY, 1951, M.A., 1952; Ph.D., N.Y.U. 1957; children—Andrew Roy, Julie Sue. Pvt. practice, N.Y.C., 1962—; supr. N.Y. Clinic Mental Health, N.Y.C.; instr. adult edn. CCNY, 1952-54; chief psychologist High Point Hosp., Port Chester, N.Y., 1954-61; dean student tng. Nat. Psychol. Assn. for Psychoanalysis, N.Y.C., 1968-73, pres. 1972-74; cons. Children's Aid Soc., N.Y.C., 1961-65; prof. Womanschool, N.Y.C., 1974-76; dir. grad. program in psychoanalysis Internat. Grad. U., Leysin, Switzerland, 1975-76. Alvin Johnson scholar, 1951; Psychology fellow CCNY, 1952-54, Fellow Am. Psychol. Assn.; mem. N.Y. State Psychol. Assn., N.Y. Soc. Clin. Psychologists, Am. Assn. Psychotherapy, Psychotherapists in Pvt. Practice, Am. Humanistic Psychol. Assn., Am. Group Psychol. Assn., Mcpl. Art Soc., Psi Chi. Contbr. articles to profl. jours. Address: 2 Fifth Ave New York NY 10011 also 23 Old Mill Westport CT

LERNER, SUSAN A., psychologist; b. N.Y.C., Sept. 6, 1946; d. Harry and Annette (Ober) Herbst; B.A. cum laude, Queens Coll., CUNY, 1973; M.A., St. John's U., 1975; Ph.D., Howard U., 1980; m. Daniel J. Lerner, June 2, 1974; 1 son, Scott Paget. Prisoner liaison Queens House of Detention, Forest Hills, N.Y., 1972-73; grad. asst. dept. psychology Howard U., Washington, 1976-78; research asst. Human Resources Research Orgn., Alexandria, Va., 1978; staff psychologist, coordinator student tng. Gt. Oaks Center, Silver Spring, Md., 1978-82; staff psychologist Patuxent Instn., Jessup, Md., 1982—; instr. dept. psychology Prince George's Community Coll., Largo, Md. NSF trainee, 1978-79. Mem. Am. Psychol. Assn. (div. 8), Md. Psychol. Assn., Eastern Psychol. Assn., Southeastern Psychol. Assn., Capitol Area Social Psychology Assn., Nat. Honor Soc. in Psychology. Contbr. to microfilms in field. Home: 12621 Red Pepper Ct Germantown MD 20874

LEROY, BARBARA ANN, ct. reporter; b. Kingsport, Tenn., Nov. 28, 1942; d. John, Jr., and Lucy Jane (Coffey) Winstead; grad. Jefferson Sch. Commerce, 1961; student Midway Jr. Coll., 1973-74; m. Walter Edward LeRoy, July 1, 1962; children—Melissa Ann, Timothy O'Brien. Sec. to engring. dept. Holston Def. Corp., Kingsport, 1961-63; sec. to civilian personnel officer Elmendorf AFB, Anchorage, 1963-64; sec. to forest engr. U.S. Forest Service, Tallahassee, Fla., 1964-66; legal sec. to Hon. William C. Jacobs, Lexington, Ky., 1967-74; free lance ct. reporter AN/DOR Reporting Service, 1974-78, half owner, 1978—. Mem. Nat. Shorthand Reporters Assn. (registered profl. reporter), Bluegrass Shorthand Reporters Assn. (v.p.), Ky. Shorthand Reporters Assn. Republican. Baptist. Clubs: Spring Lake Ladies Golf Assn. (past v.p.), Central Ky. Ladies Golf Assn. (1st v.p.). Home: 700 Cromwell Way Lexington KY 40503 Office: 201 W Vine St Lexington KY 40507

LESCH, ANN MOSELY, found. exec.; b. Washington, Feb. 1, 1944; d. Philip Edward and Ruth (Bissell) Mosely; B.A., Swarthmore Coll., 1962; Ph.D., Columbia U., 1973. Research asso. Fgn. Policy Research Inst., Phila., 1972-74; asso. Middl East rep. Am. Friends Service Com, Jerusalem, 1974-77; Middle East program officer Ford Found., N.Y.C., 1977-80, program officer, Cairo, Egypt, 1980—. Bd. dirs. Am. Near East Refugee Agy.; mem. Qauker UN Com., 199-70; mem. U.S. adv. com. Peace, 1978—. Fellow Catherwood Found., 1965; NDFL fellow, 1967-71. Mem. Middle East Studies Assn., Middle East Inst., Am. Polit. Sci. Assn. Unitarian. Author: Political Prescription of the Palestinians on the West, 1980; Arab Politics in Palestine, 1979; The Politics of Palestinain Nationalism, 1973; contbr. aticles to profl. jours. Office: 320 E 43d St New York NY 10017

LESH, HELEN ELEEN, civic worker; b. Portland, Oreg., June 22, 1925; d. Lawrence W. and Harriett M. (Alderson) Matthews; student Portland public schs.; m. Ralph Lesh, Apr. 4, 1947; children—Janet Lesh Yoh, William Arthur. Sec., Commerce High Sch., Portland, 1944-48, Lohr Office Equipment, Corvallis, Oreg., 1948-50, Lyle Glenn Engring., Roseburg, Oreg., 1951-55, Equifax Services, Roseburg, 1969-81. Recruitment chmn. ARC, 1955—, Vol. Service award for Bloodmobile, 1979; chmn. Douglas County Election Bd., 1960—; chmn. Douglas County Republican Precinct Com., 1976—, Roseburg City Election Bd., 1969—; pres. Roseburg Women's Bowling Assn., 1969-81, Inspirational Bowling award, 1969. Mem. Oreg. Women's Bowling Assn. (dir. Dist. 3). Presbyterian. Home: 2090 NW Excello Ave Roseburg OR 97470

LESHER, PHYLLIS ASENATH BAYERS, writer; b. Kaka, Alaska, May 19, 1912; d. Lloyd and Neenah Ivanovna (Sobeleff) Bayers; student U. Alaska, 1930-32, 56-60, Portland State U., 1970-73; m. Charles R. Lesher, May 19, 1936; children—Robert, Phillip, Victory, Ethyle. With Bur. Indian Affairs, Juneau, Alaska, 1951-53, Office of U.S. Marshall and Office of Dist. Atty., Juneau, 1953-56, Alaska Dept. Hwys., 1960-63, First Nat. Bank of Anchorage, 1964-67; freelance corr. Portland (Oreg.) Jour., 1973-76; poet-in-residence Lincoln County schs., 1972-74; freelance Photographer/Journalist; creative writing instr., continuing edn. programs NW Community Coll., Can., Lynn-Benton Community Coll., Oreg., 1980—; lectr. haiko workshops condr. poetry workshops, Wash., Oreg., Alaska. Recipient Citizen of Yr. award Lincoln County Vol. Community, 1975, 1st and 2d awards Alaska Press Women, 1975, Nat. Fedn. Press Women, 1975. Mem. Nat. Secs. Assn., Nat. Fedn. Press Women, Nat. League Am. Pen Women (Oreg. pres.), Central Oreg. Coast Writers (pres.), Wash., Alaska, Oreg. poetry assns. Author vols. of poetry: 99801, Juneau, 1968; Ah!-Ness of Things, 1970, rev. edit., 1978, 81; Forever Alaska, 1978; Intimately Oregon, 1980; editor Vol. Community, HEW newsletter, Lincoln County, 1972-76. Contbr. poetry to various publs. Home: PO Box 2033 Lincoln City OR 97367

LESIAK, AUDREY ANN, plastic co. exec.; b. Meriden, Conn., Oct. 14, 1941; d. James Vincent and Gertrude Mary (Lemke) Pontolillo; m. Donald A. Morrison. Vice pres., sec. Rowland, Inc., Berlin, Conn., 1972—; dir. Takiron-Rowland, Osaka, Japan, Rocel Sales div. Brit. Celanese, Spondon, Derby, Eng. Mem. Am. Soc. Corp. Secs. Inc. Home: 68 Davison Rd Moodus CT 06469 Office: Rowland Inc PO Box 176 Berlin CT 06037

LESNIAK, ANNA WASIL, ins. agt.; b. Akron, Ohio, Feb. 16, 1930; d. George and Christina (Ardelon) Wasil; diploma Hammel Actual Bus. Coll., Akron, 1951; B.B.A., Akron U., 1983; m. Chester Frank Lesniak, Feb. 11, 1950; children—Chester Frank, Kenneth J., Christine Marie. Adminstrv. sec., investigator Summit County Child Support Div., 1965-67; loan closing officer Akrons Savs. & Loan Bank, 1968-70; physician's asst., 1971-72; personnel counselor, 1973-74; fraud investigator II, CSC, 1978-79; agt. N.Y. Life Ins. Co., Akron, 1973-75, 82—; cons., lectr. in field. Mem. Am. Bus. Women's Assn., Exec. Female (chpt. dir.). Democrat. Roman Catholic. Home: 998 Dan St Akron OH 44310 Office: 3 Cascade Plaza Akron OH 44308

LESSARD, ELIZABETH CUNNINGHAM, dancer, educator; b. Camden, S.C., Jan. 16, 1943; d. John Edward and Catherine (Howell) Cunningham; B.S., Woman's Coll. Ga., 1964; M.A., Tex. Woman's U., 1965, Ph.D., 1980. Asst. prof. U. Fla., Gainesville, 1965-69; mem. faculty Ariz. State U., Tempe, 1969—, prof., 1982—, chmn. dance dept., 1977—; mem. Aludwigco (modern dance co.), 1981—; guest artist based Kelly Roth, N.Y.C., 1981; cons. Ariz. Commn. Arts, 1980-82. Recipient award Internat. Meditation Soc., Phoenix, 1981; State Tex. fellow, 1976-77. Mem. Council Dance Adminstrs. (sec.), Congress Research on Dance, Nat. Dance Assn., Nat. Assn. Schs. Dance, Ariz. Dance Arts Alliance, Ariz. Dance Guild, Ariz. State U. Faculty Women's Assn. Choreographer: By Reason of Connection, 1981; Avatar, 1980; A String of Pearls, 1981. Office: Dept Dance Ariz State U Tempe AZ 85287

LESSE, ETTA GORDON (MRS. S. MICHAEL LESSE), psychiat. social worker; b. Trenton, N.J.; d. H. Charles and Rose (Miers) Gordon; B.A., Beaver Coll.; M.Social Sci., Smith Coll.; postgrad. Bryn Mawr Coll. Sch. Social Economy; U. Pa. Sch. Social Work; m. S. Michael Lesse; children—Toni Gordon and Cathy Ross (twins). Exec. sec. Clinic for Child Psychiatry, Temple U. Med. Sch., Phila.; psychiat. social worker Bur. Family Service, Orange, N.J., Family Welfare Soc., Newport, R.I.; intake worker Bur. Family Service, Orange, N.J.; case supr., asst. to chief social worker VA, Phila.; consultant for social agys. and ct. Social and health counsellor to Draft Bd., Orange, N.J.; organizer steering com. for establishment case work sect. Council Social Agys., Newport, R.I.; chmn. Workshop for Profl. Social Workers Lehigh Valley; group chmn. regional conf. pub. edn. Gov.'s Commn. Pub. Edn., Pa. Gov.'s Commn. on Aging; cons. foster home devel. Northampton County Children's Aid Soc.; profl. participant in religion and psychiatry seminars, Easton, Pa.; interviewer Easton-Phillipsburg (Pa.) Commn. Human Relations; mem. adv. bd. Northeastern region Pa. Dept. Pub. Welfare. Lectr. to child study group PTA, Easton, Pa. Bd. dirs. Lehigh Valley Center Performing Arts Assn., v.p.; bd. dirs. Lehigh Valley Community Council, 1975—, Planned Parenthood of Northampton County; exec. bd. Am. Heart Assn., 1978—; mem. adv. bd. Jr. League of Lehigh Valley. Mem. Nat. Assn. Social Workers, Acad. Certified Social Workers, AAUW (past br. pres., dir. Eastern br.), Lehigh Valley Mental Health Assn. (dir., chmn. com. on personnel and nominating), Allentown Art Mus., Women's Com. Phila. Assn. Psychoanalysis, Northampton County Med. Soc. Aux., (dir. 1980—, v.p., pres., chmn. scholarships), Phila. Orch. Assn., Met. Opera Assn., Smith Coll. Alumni Assn. Contbg. author Two Hundred Years of Life in Northampton County, Pa. Home: 2768 Stephens St Easton PA 18042

LESSTRANG, BARBARA HILLS, pub. co. exec.; b. Grand Rapids, Mich., Jan. 24, 1935; d. John Henry and Ouida Louise (Russell) Hills; student U. Mich., 1951-52; m. Jacques LesStrang, Nov. 17, 1969; children—Steven, Linda, Christian; stepchildren—Michelle, Diane, Paul, David. Dir. sales and pub. relations Charter Hotels, Ann Arbor, Mich., 1967-69; v.p. advt. and sales, dir. Gt. Lakes Press, Traverse City, Mich., 1970—; dir. Gt. Lakes Mktg. Corp.; dir., vice chmn. Harbor House Pubs., pres., 1979—. Republican. Christian Scientist.

LESTER, IVA MARIA, accountant; b. Prague, Czechoslovakia, Nov. 22, 1927; came to U.S., 1951, naturalized, 1968; d. Karel and Anna (Hulka) Lisicky; B.A., U. B.C., 1950; M.B.A., N.Y. U., 1958. With UN, N.Y.C., 1951—, chief sect. accounts div. office fin. services UN Secretariat, 1974—; bd. dirs. UN Fed. Credit Union, UN Coop. Republican. Home: 433 E 56th St New York NY 10022 Office: United Nations Room 1921A 405 E 42d St New York NY 10017

LESTER, VIRGINIA LAUDANO, coll. pres.; b. Phila.; d. Edmund F. and Emily (Downes) Laudano; B.A., Pa. State U., 1952; M.Ed., Temple U., 1955; Ph.D., Union Grad. Sch., Cin., 1972; children—Pamela, Valerie. Tchr. primary grade Abington (Pa.) Twp. Public Schs., 1952-54, tchr. kindergarten, 1954-55; substitute tchr. 1st grade, Greenfield Center, N.Y., 1956; dir. ednl. research Skidmore Coll., Saratoga Springs, N.Y., 1967-68, instr. (part-time) dept. edn., 1962-64, asst. to pres. and dir. ednl. research, 1968-72; asst. dir. Capitol Dist. Regional Supplemental Edn. Center, Albany, N.Y., 1966-67; asst. prof. state-wide programs SUNY, Saratoga Springs, 1973-75, asso. prof., 1975-76, asso. dean, 1973-75, sr. asso. dean, 1975-76, acting dean, 1976; prof. interdisciplinary studies Mary Baldwin Coll., Staunton, Va., 1976—, pres., 1976—; cons. various colls. and ednl. instns., 1970—; vis. scholar Va. Poly. Inst. and State U., 1979; vis. faculty fellow Harvard U., 1976; v.p. Costume Collection, Inc., 1971-73; dir. So. Bank. Mem. citizen's adv. com. Saratoga Springs Bd. Edn., 1964-70; mem. Saratoga Springs Housing Bd. Appeals, 1966-76, Va. Gov.'s Adv. Com. Awards for the Arts, 1979; bd. dirs. Va. Found. for Ind. Colls., 1976—, Va. State Crime Commn., 1976-77, Saratoga Counties Planned Parenthood, 1970-74, v.p., 1972-74; bd. mgrs. Haverford Coll., 1981—, mem. fin. com., 1981-82, mem. Gov.'s Commn. to Study Future of Va., 1982. Recipient Disting. High Sch. Alumni award Frankford High Sch. Alumni Assn., 1977. Mem. Am. Assn. Higher Edn., Am. Acad. Polit. and Social Scis., Nat. Center Higher Edn. Mgmt. Systems (dir. 1978—), Council Advancement of Small Colls. (dir. 1978—), Am. Council Edn. (commn. women in higher edn. 1977-80, commn. govtl. relations 1982—), Assn. Va. Colls. (treas. 1978, v.p. 1979, pres. 1980), Council Ind. Colls. Va., Assn. Ch. Related Colls. and Univs. of South (v.p. 1982), Va. C. of C. (bd. dirs. 1982—), AAUP, Nat. Urban League (dir. 1979—), Pi Lambda Theta, Pi Gamma Mu. Quaker. Contbr. articles on edn. to profl. jours. Home: 240 Kable St Staunton VA 24401 Office: Mary Baldwin College Staunton VA 24401

LETICA, HELEN, advt. exec.; b. Belgrade, Yugoslavia, July 21, 1923; d. Charles and Renee Santich; came to U.S., 1941, naturalized, 1945; B.A. in Journalism, N.Y.U., 1945; postgrad. Columbia U., 1946; m. Jack W. Fine, Aug. 4, 1967; children—Gregory, Nicholas. Pres., Zeller & Letica, Inc., N.Y.C. Mem. Direct Mail Mktg. Assn., Mail Advt. Service Assn., 100 Million Club. Democrat. Club: Mill River (Upper Brookville, N.Y.). Contbr. articles in field of direct mail advt. to profl. jours. Office: 15 E 26th St New York NY 10010

LETTVIN, MARGARET B. (MAGGIE), author, educator; b. Phila., Mar. 15, 1927; d. Israel Warshavsky and Katherine Dietrich Brady; student public schs., Pa.; m. Jerome Ysroael Lettvin, Nov. 7, 1947; children—David Warren, Ruth Annalivia Lettvin McCambridge, Jonathan Democritus. Lectr. athletic dept. M.I.T., Cambridge, Mass., 1974—; nat. TV hostess Maggie and The Beautiful Machine, 1968—; author: Maggie and The Beautiful Machine, 1972; Maggie's Back Book, 1977; Maggie's Woman's Book, 1980; contbr. chpts., articles to profl. publs. Mem. AFTRA, Nat. Acad. TV Arts and Scis., Internat. Platform Assn. Address: MIT Athletics Dept MIT Br PO Box D Cambridge MA 02139

LEUTHOLD, JANE HORNADAY, economist, educator; b. Chgo., Dec. 31, 1941; d. Thomas F. and Helen M. Hornaday; B.A., Mich. State U., M.A., U. Wis., 1966, Ph.D., 1968; m. Raymond M. Leuthold, Aug. 20, 1966; children—Kevin, Gregory. Mem. faculty U. Ill., Urbana, 1967—, asso. prof. econs., 1973—. Ford faculty fellow, 1974. Mem. Am. Econ. Assn., Nat. Tax Assn. Author articles in field. Home: 2309 S Anderson St Urbana IL 61801 Office: 189 Commerce W Urbana IL 61801

LEVA, JEAN KATHRYN, psychotherapist; b. Vinton, La., Dec. 4, 1930; d. Lynn Levitt and Audrey Ethel (Reid) Walters; B.A. with honors, U. Tex., 1970, M.S.S.W., 1972; m. Dec. 6, 1952; children—Steven Lane, Michael Neil, Scott Andrew. Tchr. English, Collegio Pinson, Camaguey, Cuba, 1948-49; stewardess Pan Am. Airways, N.Y.C., 1951-52; adminstrv. asst. Hillcrest Children's Center, Washington, 1968-69; hosp. social worker Rancho Los Amigos, Downey, Calif., 1972-73; pvt. practice psychotherapy, Potomac, Md., 1973—; clin. social worker dept. psychiatry Alcohol Rehab. Unit, Nat. Naval Med. Center, Bethesda, Md., 1973-76; psychiat. social worker Psychiat. Inst., Washington, 1976-77; cons. Montgomery (Md.) County Sch. System, instr. transactional analysis; faculty mem. Gestalt Center of Washington; lectr. Howard U. Sch. Continuing Edn. Mem. Internat. Transactional Analysis Assn., Nat. Assn. Social Workers, Acad. Cert. Social Workers, Am. Assn. Marriage and Family Counselors. Author ednl. materials. Home: 11721 Beall Mountain Rd Potomac MD 20854

LE VECQUE, CHARLOTTE ROSE, psychiat. social worker, psychotherapist; b. Darby, Pa., Nov. 11, 1944; d. George Alfred and Charlotte Vivian (Bungart) Le V.; B.S., Western Mich. U., 1966; M.S.W., Adelphi U., 1968. Psychiat. social worker Patton State Hosp., Patton, Calif., 1968-71; sr. psychiat. social worker mental health unit San Bernardino (Calif.) County Hosp., 1971-74; licensed clin. social worker dept. psychiatry So. Calif. Permanente Med. Group, Fontana, Calif., 1974—. Lic. clin. social worker; cert. social worker, N.Y. Mem. Acad. Cert. Social Workers, Soc. Clin. Social Work, Nat. Assn. Social Workers, Nat. Registry Health Care Providers, Alpha Omicron Pi. Democrat. Clubs: American Fox Terrier, Western Fox Terrier Breeder's Assn. (gov. 1973, 78), Orange Empire Dog, San Bernardino Humane Soc., Santa Ana Valley Kennel, San Bernardino Horseman's Assn. Office: 9985 Sierra Ave Fontana CA 92335

LEVEEN, CORALIE KREINIK, interior designer, textile cons.; b. N.Y.C., Aug. 23, 1929; d. Harold Hyman and Jeanne Sophie Kreinik; grad. Ann-Reno Inst. N.Y., 1951; B.S. in Edn., Adelphi Coll., 1951; grad. N.Y. Sch. Interior Design, 1961; m. Irwin Arnold Leveen, Mar. 18, 1951; children—Harriet Sue, Judith May, Deborah Ann. Tchr., Les Coquelicots Nursery Sch., 1951-52; owner Coralie Leveen Interiors, Great Neck, N.Y., 1961—; v.p. E.F. Leveen Sales Corp; cons. textiles for interior decorating. Bd. dirs. various schs., 1957-75; pres. John F. Kennedy Sch., 1966-67; sec. United Parent Tchr. Council, 1965-67; bd. dirs. Gt. Neck (N.Y.) Edn. Assn., 1960-72, Citizens Sch. Com., 1965-73, Assn. Help of Retarded Children, 1972-78, Children's Med. Center of L.I. Jewish Hosp., 1975-78; mem. Sisterhood Temple Beth-El; membership chmn. North Shore chpt. Am. Technion; rec. sec. Lake chpt. Women's Am. ORT. Home: 97 Beach Rd Great Neck NY 11023 Office: 350 Fifth Ave New York NY 10018

LEVEN, ANN RUTH, bank exec.; b. Canton, Ohio, Nov. 1, 1940; d. Joseph J. and Bessie (Scharff) L.; A.B., Pembroke Coll., 1962; cert. with distinction program in bus. adminstrn. Harvard U. Radcliffe Coll., 1963; M.B.A., Harvard U., 1964. Asst. product mgr. household products div. Colgate-Palmolive, N.Y.C., 1964-66; asst. account exec. Grey Advt., N.Y.C., 1966-67; fin. asst. Met. Mus. Art, N.Y.C., 1967-69, asst. treas., 1970-72, treas., 1972-79; v.p., sr. corp. planning officer Chase Manhattan Bank, N.Y.C., 1979—; artist, awarded prizes for painting and graphic arts; adj. asst. prof. Grad. Sch. Bus. Columbia U., 1975-77, adj. asso. prof., 1977-79, adj. prof., 1980—; exec.-in-residence Amos Tuck Sch., Dartmouth Coll., winter 1976; dir. Alliance Capital Res., Inc., 1978-79. Mem. exec. bd. new leadership div. Fedn. Jewish Philanthropies, 1968-70; mem. council N.Y. Public Library, mem. exec. com., 1976-79; mem. mus. adv. panel N.Y. State Council on Arts, 1977-79; mem. staff Pres.'s Task Force on the Arts and Humanities, 1981; bd. dirs. Camp Rainbow, 1970—, v.p., 1976-78; bd. overseers Amos Tuck Sch., 1978—, chmn. ednl. affairs com., 1979—; trustee Artists Choice Mus., Twyla Tharp Dance Found., Carnegie Corp.; trustee Brown U., 1976—, also mem. fin. and budget com., student life com., devel. com., adv. and exec. coms.; mem. vis. com. Harvard U. Bus. Sch., 1979—. Recipient Young Leadership award Council Jewish Fedns. and Welfare Funds, 1968; named N.Y. State's Outstanding Young Woman, 1976. Mem. Harvard Bus. Sch. Alumni Assn. (exec. council 1976-79, v.p. 1978-79), Women's Fin. Assn., Women's Forum. Clubs: Cosmopolitan, Harvard Bus. Sch. (dir.), Radcliffe, Brown. Home: 1160 3d Ave New York NY 10021 Office: One Chase Manhattan Plaza New York NY 10081

LEVENE, PATRICIA JANIE GORICK, ct. reporter; b. Johnson City, N.Y., May 15, 1950; d. Alfred Frank and Stephanie (Petersen) Gorick; Applied Asso. Sci. Degree, Alfred State Coll., 1970; m. David Harry Levene, July 7, 1979. Ct. stenographer Jack W. Hunt & Assos., Buffalo, 1970-71; hearing reporter N.Y. State Dept. Labor Workers' Compensation Bd., Binghamton, N.Y., 1971-81; freelance ct. reporter, 1981—. Sec. Broome County Republican Com., Binghamton, 1975—; bd. dirs. Broome County Young Rep. Club, 1973-77, v.p., 1978-79; mem. adv. com. ct. reporting dept. Alfred State Coll., 1975-79. Mem. Nat. Shorthand Reporters Assn. (registered profl. reporter), N.Y. State Shorthand Reporters Assn., Broome County Rep. Women's Club. Home: 525 Midvale Rd Binghamton NY 13903

LEVENTHAL, RUTH LEE (MRS. BERNARD SENNET), sculptor; b. N.Y.C., Oct. 5, 1923; d. Isador H. and Ethel (Karp) Lee; student N.Y.U., Nat. Acad., Art Students League; m. Bernard Sennet, Feb. 19, 1972; children by previous marriage—Ricki (Mrs. Ivan Delbyck), Peter Leventhal. Exhibited sculpture in one-man shows at Lynn Kottler Galleries, N.Y.C., Chapman Sculpture Galleries, N.Y.C., Mus. Modern Art, Israel; exhibited in group shows at Nat. Acad. Galleries, N.Y.C., Nat. Arts Club, N.Y.C., Parke Bernet Galleries, N.Y.C., Met. Mus. Art, N.Y.C., 1979; represented in permanent collections at Mus. Modern Art, Israel, Tel Aviv (Israel) U., Riverside Meml. Chapel, N.Y.C., Goldsmith's Hall, London, Secular Sch., Bet Shean, Israel. Recipient Nat. 3M award, 1969; gold medal for sculpture Catherine Lorrilard Wolfe Arts Club, 1970, 81; Gold medal Nat. Arts Club, 1973; award Nat. Acad., 1978. Fellow Royal Soc.; mem. Nat. Soc. for Arts and Letters (dir.) Allied Artists Am. (sculpture award 1975), ASCAP, Am. Guild Authors and Composers. Clubs: Catherine Lorrilard Wolfe (dir.), Salmagundi (award 1975, 76, 78, 79, 81) (N.Y.C.). Patentee hosp. and home care equipment. Home: 425 E 58th St New York NY 10022

LEVERING, MARY BERGHAUS, lawyer, librarian, educator; b. West Palm Beach, Fla., June 1, 1940; d. Theodore Francis and Genevieve Valentine (Mahoney) Berghaus; B.A. maxima cum laude, U. Portland (Oreg.), 1965; M.L.S. with highest honors (Cath. Library Assn. nat. scholar), U. Wash., Seattle, 1966; J.D. (sr. editor law jour. 1975-77), Georgetown U., 1977; m. Robert John Levering, Oct. 16, 1976. Tchr. elem. and jr. high schs., Mass. and Wash., 1958-64; mgmt. intern Library of Congress, 1966-67, mem. staff, 1967—, chief network div. Nat. Library Service for Blind and Physically Handicapped, 1980—; adv. women career advisors program Georgetown U., 1981—; sec., pres. dir. Harbour Sq. Owners, Inc., 1981-83; admitted to D.C. bar, 1977. Bd. dirs. R.O.M.P. Sch., Wilmington, Del., (various offices and coms.), 1980—. Mem. ALA, Women's Nat. Book Assn. (chpt. v.p. 1979—), Fed. Bar Assn. D.C. Bar Assn., Women's Bar Assn. D.C., Nat. Assn. Women Lawyers, D.C. Library Assn., Delta Epsilon Sigma; Beta Phi Mu. Clubs: Cheverly Swim and Tennis, Congl. Underwater Explorers. Author articles in field. Home: 560 N St SW Apt N-502 Washington DC 20024 Office: NLS/BPH Library of Congress Washington DC 20542

LEVERTOV, DENISE, poet; b. Ilford, Essex, Eng., Oct. 24, 1923; d. Paul Philip and Beatrice A. (Spooner-Jones) Levertoff; ed. privately; Litt.D., Colby Coll., 1970, U. Cin., 1973; m. Mitchell Goodman, Dec. 2, 1947 (div. 1975); 1 son, Nikolai. Came to U.S., 1948, naturalized, 1955. Tchr. craft of poetry Poetry Center, YMHA, N.Y.C., 1964; vis. lectr. Drew U., 1965, Coll. City N.Y., 1965, Vassar Coll., 1966-67, U. Calif. at Berkeley, 1969; vis. prof. Mass. Inst. Tech., 1969-70; scholar Radcliffe Inst. Ind. Study, 1964-65, 65-66; artist-in-residence Kirkland Coll., 1970-71; Elliston lectr. U. Cin., spring 1973; vis. prof. Tufts U., 1973-74, 74-75, prof., 1975—. Guggenheim fellow, 1962; recipient Nat. Inst. Arts and Letters award, 1965, Longview award, 1961, Bess Hokins, Inez Boulton and Morton Dauwen Zabel prizes Poetry mag. Author: The Double Image, 1946; Here and Now, 1957; Overland to the Islands, 1958; With Eyes at the Back of Our Heads, 1960; The Jacob's Ladder, 1962; O Taste and See, 1964; The Sorrow Dance, 1967; Relearning the Alphabet, 1970; To Stay Alive, 1971; Footprints, 1972; The Poet in the World, 1974; The Freeing of the Dust, 1975. Translator: Selected Poems of Guillevic, 1969. Address: care New Directions 333 6th Ave New York NY 10014 *

LEVESON, NANCY GAIL, educator; b. Los Angeles, May 11, 1944; d. Charles Erwin and Betty Leveson; B.A., UCLA, 1965, M.S., 1967, Ph.D. in Computer Sci., 1980. Systems engr. IBM, 1967-70; cons. computer systems, 1972—; teaching asso. UCLA, 1976-80; asst. prof. computer sci. U. Calif., Irvine, 1980—; lectr. in field. Recipient UCI Career Devel. award. Mem. Assn. Computing Machinery, IEEE Computer Soc., Beta Gamma Sigma. Clubs: Del Rey Yacht (race fleet chmn), Songmakers. Contbr. numerous articles to profl. jours. Office: ICS Dept U Calif Irvine CA 92717

LEVESQUE, DEBORAH LEE PERKINS, nurse; b. Lynn, Mass., Jan. 22, 1950; d. Philip Walker and Grace Marilyn (Knapp) Perkins; R.N., New Eng. Bapt. Hosp. Sch. Nursing, 1970; student U. So. Calif., 1972, Tufts U., 1978, St. Joseph Coll., 1982; 1 dau.; Katherine Anne; m. Wilfred Philip Levesque, Dec. 19, 1982; stepchildren—Michelle Lyn, Christopher Todd. Pediatric staff nurse North Shore Children's Hosp., Salem, Mass., 1970-71; neonatal high risk charge nurse Kaiser Found. Hosp., Bellflower, Calif., 1971-73; head nurse Pilgrim House Rehab. and Skilled Nursing Facility, Peabody, Mass., 1973-75, supr. nursing, 1975-77, acting dir., 1977, dir. nursing service, 1977—. Mem. Nat. Forum for Adminstrs. of Nursing Service, Nat. League of Nursing, Mass. Nurses Assn., North Shore Dirs. Assn., New Eng. Bapt. Alumni Assn. Clubs: Lynnfield Art Guild, PTO. Office: 96 Forest St Peabody MA 01960

LEVI, MARY COX, ednl. adminstr.; b. Chattanooga, Dec. 24, 1929; d. Wilmer Walter and Gladys (Stafford) Cox; student Harvard U., 1950; B.S., U. Chattanooga, 1959; postgrad. U. Syracuse, 1960; M.S., U. Tenn., Knoxville, 1972; m. Lester Shirley Levi, Oct. 2, 1954; children—Mary Kathryn Mason Vaughn, Walter Lawrence, Christopher Harvey, Roger Scott, Milton Eric, Jefferson Stuart. Itinerant tchr., cons., curriculum specialist Chattanooga Public Schs., 1967-69; spl. edn. tchr. Judson Hill Spl. Edn. Sch., Morristown, Tenn., 1972-74; coordinator, cons. tchr., Meadowview and Lincoln middle schs., Morristown, 1975-77; coordinator, cons. spl. edn. Lincoln Heights Middle Sch., Morristown, 1977—; Easter Seals fellow Cove Schs., Evanston, Ill. and Racine, Wis., 1960. Chmn. constn. and by-laws, grant writer Bicentennial Commn. of Hamblen County, 1974-75; bd. dirs., mem. selections com. Rose Center for Arts, Morristown, 1975-80; bd. dirs., sec. Theatre Guild, Morristown, 1979-80, Utopia Services, Morristown. Bicentennial Commn. grantee, 1976. Mem. Council Exceptional Children, Morristown Edn. Assn., Eastern Tenn. Edn. Assn., Tenn. Edn. Assn., NEA. Club: Bridge. Home: Emerald Acres Route 10 Box 131 Deena Circle Morristown TN 37814 Office: Lincoln Heights Middle Sch 217 Lincoln Ave Morristown TN 37814

LEVI, SHEILA, bus. sch. ofcl.; b. Chgo.; d. Everett Van and Ida (Cabell) Overton; B.A., Roosevelt U., 1947; div. Caseworker, Ill. Dept. Public Aid, Chgo., 1947-69; supr., dir. Keyboard Tng., Chgo., 1969-70; with MSTA Bus. Sch., Chgo., 1970—, co-owner, 1973—; pres. Word Processing Trainers, Inc. Mem. Am. Personnel and Guidance Assn., Internat. Word Processors. Christian Scientist. Club: McCormick Inn Health. Office: 1307 S Wabash Ave Chicago IL 60605

LEVICK, MYRA FRIEDMAN, art psychotherapist, educator; b. Phila., Aug. 20, 1924; d. Louis and Ida (Segal) Friedman; B.F.A., Moore Coll. Art, 1963; M.Ed., Temple U., 1967; Ph.D., Bryn Mawr Coll., 1982; m. Leonard J. Levick, Dec. 26, 1943; children—Bonnie, Karen, Marsha. Art psychotherapist Albert Einstein Med. Center, Phila., 1963-67; dir. adjunctive therapies and dir. grad. tng. program in art therapy, Hahnemann Med. Coll. and Hosp., Phila., 1967-73, dir. masters creative arts in therapy tng. program, 1973—, prof. mental health scis. dept. Hahnemann U., 1977—; cons. affiliated clinics and instns. Recipient Outstanding Alumni award Moore Coll. Art, 1975; Humanitarian award Ronald Bruce Nippon Assn., 1976; NIMH grantee, 1975-78. Mem. Am. Art Therapy Assn. (founder, 1st pres. hon. life mem.), Family Inst. Phila. (exec. bd. 1982—), Am. Psychol. Assn., Pa. Psychol. Assn., Am. Ortho-Psychiat. Assn., Internat. Soc. Psychopathology of Expression, Am. Soc. Psychopathology of Expression. Contbg. author: Current Psychotherapies, 1975; Handbook of Innovative Psychotherapies, 1981; sr. editor The Arts in Psychotherapy, 1975-81, editor-in-chief, 1982—; contbr. articles to profl. lit. Home: 1901 Kennedy Blvd Apt 2623 Philadelphia PA 19103 Office: Hahnemann Med Coll and Hosp 230 N Broad St Philadelphia PA 19102

LEVIHN, KATHRYN ADELE, engring. co. exec.; b. Nouasseur, Morocco, Jan. 27, 1956 (parents Am. citizens); d. Paul and Nancy Levihn; B.S. in Civil Engring., Stanford U., 1978, A.B. in Internat. Relations, 1978. Constrn. engr. Harza Engring. Co., Chgo., 1978-79, asst. office engr., asst. field engr., Denver, 1979-81; office engr. Internat. Engring. Co., Wrangell, Alaska, 1981—. Mem. ASCE, Western Soc. Engrs. Address: PO Box 1501 Wrangell AK 99929

LEVIN, ANN ROCHELLE, county ofcl.; b. Phila., May 6, 1951; d. Morris and Sylvia (Moskowitz) L.; student Hofstra U., 1968-69; B.A., Temple U., 1972; M.A., U. Md., 1974; J.D., Marshall Coll. Law, 1979; m. Henry G. Mankowski. Nursery sch. tchr. YWCA of Montgomery County, Md., 1972-73; fiscal planner Mayor's Office Manpower Resources, Balt., 1973-74; program planner Cuyahoga County Office Employment and Tng. Adminstrn., Cleve., 1974-76, chief planner, 1976-78, research, planning and evaluation mgr., 1978-79, dep. dir., 1979, dir., 1979—. Trustee B'nai B'rith Youth Orgn., 1974-79, chairperson bd. trustees, 1980; trustee Jewish Community Center of Cleve., 1974-79. Ky. col., 1979; named to Ten Up and Coming, Cleve. Press, 1979; cert. in employment and tng. adminstrn. Harvard U., 1978. Mem. Ohio Manpower Assn., Ohio CETA Dirs. Assn., Nat. Assn. County Employment and Tng. Adminstrs. (dir.), Psi Chi. Author articles. Office: 1375 Euclid Ave Room 601 Cleveland OH 44115

LEVIN, BARBARA PATTERSON, state ofcl.; b. Akron, Ohio, Dec. 29, 1942; d. James Kenneth and Myrtle (Payne) Patterson; B.A., U. N.Mex., 1965; postgrad. U. N.Mex., 1972; m. Michael D. Levin, Oct. 25, 1970; children—David, Matthew. Mem. office staff Jordan's Co., Albuquerque, 1962-65, 67-68; caseworker Fla. Dept. Public Welfare, Pensacola, 1965-66; rate clk. Motors Ins. Co., Albuquerque, 1966-67; personnel analyst N.Mex. State Govt., Santa Fe, 1968-73, div. dir. personnel mgmt. services, 1973—. Co-chmn. parent adv. council Kearney Elem. Sch. PTA, 1976-77; mem. Gov.'s Reorgn. Task Force, 1977-78; mem. Human Services Mgmt. Oversight Com., 1977-78; co-chmn. Women's Career Devel. Conf., 1979; mem. Gov.'s Compensation Task Force, 1981. Mem. Internat. Personnel Mgmt. Assn., Am. Soc. Public Adminstrn., Data Processing Planning Council (personnel adv. bd. 1980—). Home: 2200 Ardor St Santa Fe NM 87501 Office: 130 S Capitol St Santa Fe NM 87501

LEVIN, EVANNE LYNN, laywer; b. Los Angeles, Nov. 6, 1949; d. Rose Levin; student U. Madrid, 1967; B.A. with honors, UCLA, 1971; J.D., Loyola U., Los Angeles, 1974. Admitted to Calif. bar; program atty. ABC, Century City, Calif., 1975-76; sr. atty. Paramount Pictures Corp., Hollywood, Calif., 1976-77; entertainment asso. firm Ervin, Cohen & Jessup, Beverly Hills, Calif., 1977-78; sr. partner firm Mason & Sloane, Beverly Hills, 1978—. Mem. Am. Bar Assn. (chmn. law and media com. 1978-79), Calif. Bar Assn., Los Angeles County Bar Assn., Beverly Hills Bar Assn. (gov. 1977—, panelist women and law com. 1981), Beverly Hills Bar Assn. Barristers (gov. 1976—, co-chmn. social com. 1977—, com. on arts 1978—), Women Lawyers of Los Angeles, Women in Entertainment Law (co-founder), Women in Film. Contbr. to profl. publs. Office: 9200 Sunset Blvd Suite 505 Los Angeles CA 90069

LEVIN, IRENE STAUB, librarian; b. Bklyn., Sept. 30, 1928; d. Harry and Regina (Klein) Staub; B.A., Hunter Coll., City U. N.Y., 1949; M.L.S., L.I., 1969; m. Harold E. Levin, Nov. 19, 1950; children—Alan, Leslie, Kim, Paula. Reference librarian and young adults Henry Waldinger Library, Valley Stream, N.Y., 1969—, program coordinator public relations, 1976—; cons. on Jewish books and libraries. Trustee, Sisterhood Temple B'nai Israel of Elmont, 1969-71, Temple B'nai Israel of Elmont, 1982. Recipient Library Public Relations Council award, 1973. Mem. Nassau County Library Assn., Assn. Jewish Libraries (editor Bull., 1973—, Newsletter, 1978—), Am. Mizrachi Women. Club: Hadassah. Contbr. to Contemporary Literary Criticism, Vol. 13, 1979. Office: Henry Waldinger Library 60 Verona Pl Valley Stream NY 11580

LEVIN, JEANETTE BROOKS, market researcher, travel agt., property mgmt. co. exec.; b. Buffalo, Aug. 5, 1930; d. Morris Jacob and Anna Pearl (Orzech) Brooks; student U. Buffalo, 1950-58, SUNY, Buffalo, 1965-70; cert. Guided Observation Tchr. Program, Cheektowaga (N.Y.) Schs., 1968; m. Frank Levin, July 11, 1954; children—Arnold, Robert, David, Susan. Adult edn. tchr. Cleveland Hill Sch., Cheektowaga, 1965-68; founder, owner, prin. Buffalo Survey & Research, Inc., 1965—; property mgmt. agt. Jackson Sq. Assos., Buffalo, 1978—; pres., mgr. Buffalo Survey Travel Tours, 1978—; cons. politics, image-making for candidates, 1974—. Pres., Temple Shaarey Zedek Sisterhood, Buffalo, 1977-78, Past Pres.'s Council, 1981-83. Honoree Temple Shaarey Zedek Ann. Ball, 1977; recipient citation for ch. worker of week Amherst Bee, 1978, citations for high degree of accuracy in polling Buffalo Evening News, 1971, 81. Mem. Mktg. Research Assn., Am. Assn. Public Opinion Research, Am. Mktg. Assn., Am. Contract Bridge League. Columnist Buffalo. Jewish Rev., 1976-80; media pollster Buffalo newspaper and TV; survey on U.S. tourism, 1973. Home: 324 Crosby Blvd Buffalo NY 14226 Office: 1255 Eggert Rd Buffalo NY 14226

LEVIN, LUBBE, univ. adminstr.; b. Wels, Austria; came to U.S., 1949, naturalized, 1955; d. Charles S. and Sonia Levin; student U. Nantes (France), 1966; A.B. with gt. distinction, Stanford U., 1967; M.A., U. Calif., Berkeley, 1968, Ph.D. in French, 1973; m. David Medlinsky Asst. prof. French, Washington U., St. Louis, 1973-75; mem. staff systemwide adminstrn. U. Calif., 1976—, dir. policy devel., spl. asst. to v.p., 1979—, dir. acad. and staff employee relations, 1982—; lectr. French, U. Calif., Berkeley, 1980—. Calif. State scholar, 1965-66; NDEA fellow, 1971-72; faculty Research grantee Washington U., 1974. Mem. Acad. Academic Personnel Adminstrn., NOW, MLA, Calif. Women in Govt., Phi Beta Kappa. Author articles in field. Office: 750 University Hall Univ Calif Systemwide Adminstrn Berkeley CA 94720

LEVIN, NANCY, retail mcht.; b. Pitts., Jan. 18, 1942; d. Albert Samuel and Elizabeth (Bloom) Sheffler; student public schs.; m. Marvin Lee Levin (dec.); children—Bonnie, Michael, Jack. With Deauville Hotel, Miami Beach, Fla., 1959-61; owner-mgr. Ft. Wayne Cigar Co., Pitts., 1972—. Bd. advs. Abraxis Found. Mem. Tobacco Action Network, Tobacco Inst., Pa. Tobacco Table (dir. 1978-81, sec. 1982—), North Side C. of C., South Side C. of C. Republican. Address: 619 E Ohio St Pittsburgh PA 15212

LEVIN, RUTH KAPLAN, social worker; b. Bklyn., Jan. 3, 1921; d. Samuel and Pauline (Korbenfeld) Kaplan; B.A. cum laude, Bklyn. Coll., 1940; postgrad. Bklyn. Coll., 1944-45, Hunter Coll., 1944-45; M.S.S.S., Boston U., 1955; postgrad. U. Mo., 1971-72; m. Barry Livingston Levin, Dec. 2, 1957; 1 dau., Susan. Student intern James Jackson Putnam Children's Center, also Family Service Assn., Boston, 1953-55; caseworker Jewish Family Service, N.Y.C., 1955-57; sr. caseworker Family Service Soc., Buffalo, 1958-60; psychiat. caseworker, after care and psychiat. out-patient clinics Fulton (Mo.) State Hosp., 1973-75; dir. family service dept. Toberman Settlement House, San Pedro, Calif., 1976-77; counselor, asst. to dir. Community Counseling Service, Salisbury, Mo., 1977-80; cons. social worker Sr. Services Council, Rolla, Mo., 1980—. Treas. PTA, 1969, mem. program com., 1973-75; sec. Deborah, 1971-73; bd. dirs., treas. Chariton County Mental Health Assn., 1977-79. NIMH fellow, 1954-55. Mem. Nat. Assn. Social Workers, Acad. Cert. Social Workers. Jewish. Home: 1021 Duke St Columbia MO 65201 Office: Sr Services Council Rolla MO

LEVIN, TOBE JOYCE, educator; b. Long Branch, N.J., Feb. 16, 1948; d. M. William and Janice M. (Metz) Levin; B.A. summa cum laude, Ithaca Coll., 1970; M.A., N.Y. U. in Paris, 1973; maîtrise, U. Paris, 1974; M.A., Cornell U., 1977, Ph.D., 1979; m. Stephen Edward Richards, Aug. 7, 1979. Teaching asst. Cornell U., Ithaca, N.Y., 1973-75; reader, reviewer fgn. publs. Frauen-offensive Verlag, Munich, W. Ger., 1977—; tchr. French, Munich elem. schs., 1977-79; lectr. Cornell U., 1979; lectr. dept. English, Univ. Coll., European div. U. Md., Heidelberg, W. Ger., 1979—. Active in W. Ger. women's movement. Recipient various scholarships and fellowships. Mem. MLA, Nat. Women's Studies Assn., African Studies Assn., Assn. Concerned Africa Scholars, West German Women's Studies Assn., ACLU, Fund for a Democratic Majority, Amnesty for Women, Terre des Femmes, Assn. for Women in Devel., Assn. Ams. Resident Overseas, NOW, Phi Kappa Phi. Democrat. Jewish. Co-editor: Materialien zur Unterstutzung von Aktionsgruppen gegen Klitorisbeschneidung, 1979; contbg. editor Women's Studies Quar.; contbr. articles to jours. Home: Rothschildallee 28 6 Frankfurt 60 Federal Republic of Germany Office: U Md European Div Im Bosseldorn 30 69 Heidelberg Federal Republic of Germany

LEVINE, BARBARA PEARLMAN, speech and lang. pathologist; b. Bklyn., Dec. 4, 1932; d. Murray and Sara (Wildansky) Pearlman; B.A., Bklyn. Coll., 1953, M.A., 1955; student Bklyn. Law Sch., 1979—; children—Allan Jeffrey, Michael Elliott. Speech therapist N.Y.C. Schs., 1954-55, Balt. City Schs., 1956-59, head dept. of speech, 1959-63; part time pvt. practice speech pathology, Balt., 1963-68; instr. Mt. St. Agnes Coll. and cons. Sheppard and Enoch Pratt Hosp., Balt., 1968-72; cons. Deaton Med. Center, Balt., 1973-75; clin. instr. psychiatry Downstate Med. Center, Bklyn., 1975—; speech pathologist, supr. Devel. Evaluation Clinic, Kings County Med. Center, Bklyn., 1976—. Mem. Am. Speech and Hearing Assn., Assn. Orthodox Jewish Scientists. Producer first ednl. TV series in speech improvement, Balt. City Schs., 1959-63, first head of dept. speech, author handbooks for tchrs. Home: 5520 15th Ave Apt 6C Brooklyn NY 11219 Office: DEC-KCH Box 26 451 Clarkson Ave Brooklyn NY 11203

LEVINE, ELLEN R., mag. exec.; b. Feb. 19; d. Eugene and Jean Jacobson; ed. Wellesley Coll.; m. Richard V. Levine; children—Daniel, Peter. Reporter, The Record Newspaper, N.J. 1964-70; formerly food and decorating editor Cosmopolitan mag., N.Y.C; now v.p., editor-in-chief Woman's Day mag., N.Y.C. Office: 1515 Broadway St New York NY 10036

LEVINE, ESTHER MAE, ins. agy. exec.; b. Walker, Minn., 1936; d. Ervin P. and Marjorie E. Hansen; student in ins. Broward Community Coll., 1975-77. Am. Inst. Property and Liability Underwriters, 1975-80, Ga. State U., 1978-80; m. J.J. Levine, 1973. Underwriter, J. Kenneth King Ins., Davie, Fla., 1964-67, Fast & Co., Ft. Lauderdale, Fla., 1967-72; agt. RISE/Paige Ins., Pompano, Fla., 1972-78, regional sales dir., 1976-78; regional sales rep. RISE/Warren & Welsh, Atlanta, 1978-82, resident v.p., 1981—. C.P.C.U. Mem. Ins. Women Broward County, Cars and Trucks Rental and Leasing Assn., Am. Car Rental Assn., Nat. Assn. Female Execs. (network dir.), Ga. Soc. C.P.C.U.s, Nat. Women's Automotive Assos. Republican. Contbr. articles to profl. jours.; sign lang. interpreter. Office: 340 Interstate N Pkwy Suite 140 Atlanta GA 30339

LEVINE, HELEN SAXON (MRS. NORMAN D. LEVINE), med. technologist; b. San Francisco; d. Ernest M. Saxon and Ann S. Dippel; A.B., U. Ill., 1939; m. Norman D. Levine, Mar. 2, 1935. Supr. lab. San Francisco Dept. Pub. Health Tb Sanatorium, 1944-46, U. Ill. Health Services, Urbana, 1952-65; research asso. in immunobiology, zoology dept. U. Ill., 1965—. Mem. AAUP, AAAS, Am. Heart Assn., Ill. Acad. Sci., Ill. Pub. Health Assn., Am. Soc. Med. Technologists, Am. Soc. Clin. Pathologists, Sigma Delta Epsilon. Research and publs. on devel. nematode antigens. Home: 702 LaSell Dr Champaign IL 61822 Office: Morrill Hall U Ill Urbana IL 61801

LEVINE, IRENE SHIFREN, psychologist; b. N.Y.C., Sept. 23, 1947; d. Joseph and Helen Waldman; B.A., Queens Coll., 1964; M.A., St. John's U., Jamaica, N.Y., 1971, Ph.D., 1981; married. Tchr., N.Y.C. Bd. Edn., 1968-72; psychologist, adminstr. Creedmoor Psychiat. Center, N.Y.C., 1973-75; assoc. dir. Transitional Services N.Y., Inc., 1975-77, exec. dir., 1977-78; HEW fellow, Washington, 1978-79; chief community support sect. NIMH, 1979-80, spl. asst. to dir., 1980-81; chief community services Los Angeles County Dept. Mental Health, 1981—; cons. in field. Mem. Am. Psychol. Assn., AAUW, N.Y. Acad. Scis., Assn. Humanistic Psychology, Eastern Psychol. Assn., Assn. Mental Health Adminstrs., Nat. Alliance Mentally Ill. Author papers, reports in field.

LEVINE, JANIS E., financial analyst; b. Akron, Ohio, Apr. 7, 1953; d. Paul and Sarah (Levin) L.; student U. Cin., 1971-73; B.S. in Acctg., U. Akron, 1975; M.B.A., Xavier U., 1978. Acctg. intern Price Waterhouse & Co., Cleve., 1974-75; systems acct. Mead Corp., Cin., 1975-77; internal auditor, capital expenditures analyst Champion Internat. Corp., Stamford, Conn., 1977—. Vol., Headstart and ARC; adv. Jr. Achievement; mem. Young Republicans. Recipient Young Citizens Achievement award Headstart, 1969. Mem. Women in Mgmt., Bus. and Profl. Women, Young Leadership Council, Nat. Assn. Female Execs., Stamford Council for World Affairs, Westport-Weston Arts Council, Assn. M.B.A. Execs., Nat. Assn. Accts. (community programs dir.), AAUW, Beta Alpha Psi (sec.). Office: Champion International Corp 1 Champion Plaza Stamford CT 06921

LEVINE, MARY ELIZABETH, music dir., pianist; b. Newark, May 1, 1924; d. Gwillym Llewelyn and Marian (Peck) Thomas; student St. Thomas More Coll., Covington, Ky., 1943-44, St. Mary Coll., Omaha, 1967-68; m. Joseph Levine, Feb. 16, 1945; children—Stephen, David. Repetiteur, Phila. Chamber Opera, 1946-50, Omaha Opera, 1958-69, Hawaii Opera Theatre, 1973-76; pianist Am. Ballet Theatre, N.Y.C., 1950-58; music dir. Omaha Playhouse, 1958-69, Omaha Regional Ballet, 1966-69, Honolulu Community Theatre, 1973-76, Honolulu City Ballet, also S. Pacific Dinner Theatre, 1975, Cirque Dinner Theatre, Seattle, 1977—; organist, choir dir. St. Andrew Episcopal Ch., Omaha, 1958-69, Ch. of Redeemer Episcopal, Seattle, 1969-73; mem. speakers bur. Seattle Symphony, 1969-73; public relations dir. Cornish Inst., Seattle, 1972-73, dir. mus. theatre workshop, 1976-79; public relations dir. Honolulu Symphony, also Hawaii Opera Theatre, 1974; pianist touring program, mem. speakers bur. Seattle Opera, 1977—; freelance corr./stringer for mus. tours; contbr. articles to nat. mags., newspapers. Recipient Dir.'s award Omaha Playhouse, 1960, Disting. Contbn. award Dana Coll., 1961. Mem. Nat. Fedn. Press Women, Nat. Soc. Arts and Letters, Nat. League Am. Pen Women, Am. Fedn. Musicians, Am. Guild Organists. Democrat. Episcopalian. Club: Ladies Musical (Seattle). Address: 2917 W Eaton St Seattle WA 98199

LEVINE, NATHALIE CHRISTIAN, ballet adminstr., educator; b. Las Animas, Colo., July 21, 1929; d. Fleming Vincent and Juanita Jeanne (Jobe) Christian; B.A. in Polit. Sci. magna cum laude, UCLA, 1958; ballet student Mia Slavenska, Vincenzo Celli, Rozelle Frey, Bronislava Nijinska, Valentina Pereyslavec, Michel Panaieff, Errol Addison and Pamela May (Royal Ballet Sch.), Nora Kiss (Paris); m. Victor T. LeVine,

July 19, 1958; children—Theodore Vincent, Nicole Jeanette. Soloist profl. dance cos. including Ballets de Los Angeles, 1948-49, Ballet Concerto, 1947-51, Radio City Music Hall, 1952-53, musical summer stock, Calif. and N.J.; dancer TV and theater prodns. and films including Greatest Show on Earth, Samson and Delilah; tchr. Wilcoxon Sch. of Dance, Los Angeles, 1946-48, Sutro-Seyler Studio, Los Angeles, 1949-51, Brown Gables Conservatory of the Arts, Los Angeles, 1952-61, Ecole de Danse, Yaounde, Cameroun, 1961-62, with Michael Simms, St. Louis, 1963-67, Dawn Quist Sch. of Dance, Accra, Ghana, 1969-70, Washington U., St. Louis, 1968-69, 70-71, Nathalie Le Vine Acad. Ballet, St. Louis, 1964—; guest tchr. Calif., Hawaii, Ind., 1955—; choreographer for prodns. including Ballet Concerto, Los Angeles, 1950, classical ballet groups Los Angeles and St. Louis, 1948—, St. Louis Dance Theater, 1966-72, Met. Ballet of St. Louis; co-founder, co-artistic dir. St. Louis Dance Theater, 1966-72; founder, artistic dir. Met. Ballet of St. Louis, 1974—. Organizer dance programs Montessori Sch., Chesterfield, Mo., Step-by-Step Pre-Sch., University City, 1973-78; participant planning and prodns. St. Louis Bicentennial, summer 1976, Dance Concert Soc. Dance Week, St. Louis, 1978, 79; organizer Dance Camp of the Arts, Jewish Community Centers Assn., St. Louis, 1977; co-planner, organizer Dance Workshops, St. Louis, 1977, 78; cons. Phelps County Dance Assn. and Rolla (Mo.) Bd. of Parks and Recreation, 1978—. Mem. Nat. Soc. Arts and Letters, Phi Beta Kappa. Office: 11607 Olive Blvd Saint Louis MO 63141

LEVINE, RHEA JOY COTTLER, educator; b. Bklyn., Nov. 26, 1939; d. Zachary Robert and Hildreth (Abramson) Cottler; A.B., Smith Coll., 1960; M.S., N.Y.U., 1963, Ph.D., 1966; postgrad. (fellow), Yale U., 1966-68; m. Stephen Maxwell Levine, June 16, 1960; children—Elizabeth, Michael Gordon, Zachary Thomas. Fellow dept. pharmacology N.Y.U., 1960; lab. instr., 1963-64; USPHS fellow, lab. instr. dept. anatomy Yale U., 1966-68; research asso. dept. neuropathology U. Pa., 1968-69; asst. prof. dept. anatomy Med. Coll. Pa., Phila., 1969-74, asso. prof., 1974-80, prof., 1980—; outside reviewer NSF, 1975—; mem. peer rev. group cardiovascular study sect. NIH, 1980—. Grantee in field. Mem. AAAS, Am. Assn. Anatomists, Histochem. Soc., Am. Soc. Cell Biology, Biophys. Soc., Soc. Gen. Physiology, Pa. Muscle Inst., Phi Beta Kappa, Sigma Xi. Jewish. Clubs: Woodcrest Country (Cherry Hill, N.J.); Phila. Myo-Bio Club, Phila. Smith Coll. Editor: (with Twarog and Dewey) Basic Biology of Muscles: A Comparative Approach; contbr. articles to profl. jours. Office: 3200 Henry Ave Philadelphia PA 19129

LEVINE, RUTH ROTHENBERG, educator; b. N.Y.C.; d. Jacob and Jeannette (Bandel) Rothenberg; B.A. magna cum laude, Hunter Coll., 1938; M.A., Columbia U., 1939; Ph.D., Tufts U., 1955; m. Martin J. Levine, June 21, 1953. Asst. prof. Tufts U. Sch. Medicine, 1955-58; asst. prof. pharmacology Sch. Medicine Boston U., 1958-61; asso. prof., 1961-65, prof., 1965—, univ. prof., 1972—, chmn. div. med. and dental scis. Grad. Sch., 1964—, asso. dean grad. biomed. scis. Med. Sch., 1981—; mem. sci. adv. bd. U.S. EPA. Fellow AAAS; mem. Am. Soc. Pharmacology and Exptl. Therapeutics (sec.-treas. 1975-76), Biophys. Soc., Am. Chem. Soc., Am. Pharm. Assn., Acad. Scis., Phi Beta Kappa, Sigma Xi. Office: Boston University Division Medical and Dental Sciences Boston MA 02118

LEVINE, SANDRA MARY, mfg. co. exec.; b. Newark, May 30, 1935; d. Samuel P. and Josephine E. (Sinisgalli) Marzano; B.A., Rutgers U., 1957; m. Sidney I. Levine, Apr. 5, 1973; children—Joseph B. Martinez, Samuel A. Martinez. Exec. v.p. Staflex Co., N.Y.C., 1968—. Mem. Women's Bus. Club. N.Y. (founder, pres.), B'nai B'rith, Hadassah. Office: Staflex Co 11 E 36th St New York NY 10016

LEVINSON, DOROTHY JANICE, jr. high sch. tchr.; b. Laurel, Miss., Feb. 1, 1918; s. Solomon Louis and Bessie Marian (Mindel) Wisenberg; B.A., Rice Inst., Houston, 1937; M.A., Northeastern Ill. U., Chgo., 1970, Northwestern U., 1974; m. Nathan Levinson, Jan. 11, 1945 (dec.); children—Irving Walter, Robert David. Tchr., Houston public schs., 1938-44, Edgewood Jr. High Sch., Highland Park, Ill., 1967—. Pres. Volta PTA, Chgo., 1959-61. Served with WAVES, 1944-45. Mem. Nat. Council Tchrs. English, NEA, Ill. Congress Parents and Tchrs. (dist. publs. chmn. 1961-62), Hadassah, Phi Beta Kappa. Jewish. Home: 8000 Foster Ln Niles IL 60648

LEVINSON, GAY MILNER, broadcasting co. exec.; b. Louisville, Apr. 6, 1950; d. Samuel Erlick and Betty Ann (Rieser) L.; A.A., Stephens Coll., 1970; B.A., U. Miami, 1972. Staff writer Fort Lauderdale News, 1971-74; dir. public relations Easter Seals for Crippled Children and Adults Broward County, 1974-75; project dir. Broward County Bicentennial, 1975-76; mktg. communications asso., Greenman Corp. Cons., Hollywood, Fla., 1977-78; promotion dir. Sta. WAXY-FM, Miami, 1978-80; promotion/creative services dir. Sta. WGBS/WLYF, Miami, 1980—. Bd. dirs. Big Bros. and Big Sisters Broward, Inc., 1977-80; chmn. adv. com. Women's Centers, Broward Community Coll., 1978-79. Recipient Freedom Found. award Broward County, 1976; Ky. col. Mem. Women in Communications (1st v.p. Atlantic Fla. chpt. 1978-79), Am. Women in Radio and TV. Republican. Jewish. Contbr. articles to profl. jours. Home: 1625 SE 10th Ave Fort Lauderdale FL 33316 Office: 710 Brickell Ave Miami FL 33131

LEVINSON, MEREDITH MOSS, writer; b. Youngstown, Ohio, Nov. 8, 1942; d. Jack and Shirley (Aaron) Moss; B.S. in Theatre, Northwestern U., 1964; M.A. in Communications, U. Pa., 1966; m. James Ross Levinson, Sept. 5, 1965; children—Stephen Jay, Joel Moss. Asso. editor Moderator mag., Phila., 1964-66; syndicated columnist Newspaper Enterprise Assn., 1964-66; public service dir./producer WTVN-TV, Columbus, Ohio, 1967-68; public service dir. WCPO-TV, Cin., 1968-69; publicity mgr. Avco Broadcasting Corp., Cin., 1970-73; promotion dir. Phil Donahue Show, Dayton, Ohio, 1974-75; spl. writer, columnist Dayton Daily News, 1976—. Bd. dirs. Covenant House, NCCJ, United Jewish Appeal Campaign. Recipient Dayton-Montgomery County Bicentennial award. Mem. Women in Communications, Jewish Fedn. of Women (dir., Young Leadership award), Jr. League Dayton, Hadassah. Nat. editor Columns of Alpha Epsilon Phi. Office: Dayton Daily News 4th and Ludlow St Dayton OH 45402

LEVINSON, RASCHA, psychotherapist; b. N.Y.C., Nov. 27, 1930; d. Frank Alfred and Goldye (Preiser) Cohen; B.A., N.Y.U., 1960; M.S., Sch. Social Work, Columbia U., 1962; 1 dau., Nadia Rachel. Therapist, trainee Washington Sq. Inst. and Clinic, N.Y.C., 1973-74; staff therapist Mid-Hudson Consultation Center, Wappingers Falls, N.Y., 1974-76, sr. staff, supr., 1976—; pvt. practice psychotherapy, N.Y.C., 1969—; intake person Women's Psychotherapy Referral Service, N.Y.C., 1973-77; instr. New Sch.; condr. seminars, workshops, lectr. on adult devel., especially role of women, N.Y.C., Poughkeepsie, Phila. Mem. Acad. Cert. Social Workers, Nat. Assn. Social Workers, N.Y. State Soc. Clin. Social Work Psychotherapists, Women's Psychotherapy Referral Service, Assn. for Humanistic Psychology, Am. Acad. Psychotherapists. Democrat. Contbr. article to newspaper. Home and Office: 506 E 87th St New York NY 10028

LEVINTON, PAULA HEICHLER, health care cons.; b. Washington, Oct. 30, 1952; d. Lucian and Muriel Ruth (Nordsiek) Heichler; student U. Chgo., 1970-72; cert. Institut Africain de Genève, Switzerland, 1973; m. Philip C. Levinton, Aug. 26, 1978; 1 son, Christopher. Asst. dir. agy. and tour sales Hilton Hotels, Washington, 1974-75; mem. staff communications group Am. Bankers Assn., Washington, 1975-76; cons. health care practice Arthur Young & Co., Washington, 1976-78; mgr. health systems documentation Libra Tech., Rockville, Md., 1978—; instr. public sector mktg., project planning. Mem. Assn. Computing Machinery. Lutheran. Research on computerized mental health info. systems, use of automated documentation aides for health care systems. Home: 8499 Hayshed Ln Columbia MD 21045

LEVISON, SHARRI CUTLER, paper co. ofcl.; b. Scranton, Pa., June 20, 1944; d. Jacob and Lucille Cutler (Levy) L.; B.F.A., Syracuse U., 1966; children—Kerry Sue, Jody Ann. Owner, v.p. Park Ave. Jeans Emporium, Ltd., Rochester, N.Y., 1975-77; freelance graphic designer, Rochester, 1977-78; with Economy Paper Co., Rochester, 1978—, dir. sales promotions, 1979—; cons. Graphic Careers, Rochester, 1979-82. Founder, Parent Group Affiliated/Rochester Sch. Dist., 1972-73; mem. Park Ave. Mchts. Assn., 1975-77. Mem. Rochester Club Printing House Craftsman, Mktg. Communications Execs. Internat., Women in Communications, Rochester Art Dirs. Club. Jewish. Home: 961 Harvard St Rochester NY 14610 Office: 1175 E Main St Rochester NY 14609

LEVIT, EDITHE JUDITH, physician; b. Wilkes-Barre, Pa., Nov. 29, 1926; B.S. in Biology, Bucknell U., 1946; M.D., Woman's Med. Coll. Pa., 1951; D.M.S., Med. Coll. Pa., 1978; m. Samuel M. Levit, Mar. 2, 1952; children—Harry M., David B. Grad. asst. psychology Bucknell U., 1946-47; intern, then fellow in endocrinology Phila. Gen. Hosp., 1951-53, clin. instr., asso. in endocrinology, then dir. med. edn., 1953-61, cons. med. edn.; asst. dir., then asso. dir., sec. bd. Nat. Bd. Med. Examiners, Phila., 1961-75, v.p., sec. bd., 1975-77, pres., dir., 1977—; cons. women in medicine Josiah Macy Jr. Found., 1966-76; evaluator in professions Law Sch. Adminstrv. Council, 1974, model med. practice in law Health Policy Center, Washington, 1976; mem. com. admissions to practice fed. cts. Jud. conf. U.S., 1977; mem. steering com. fgn. med. grads. Inst. Medicine, Nat. Acad. Sci., 1977; mem. bd. sci. counselors Nat. Library Medicine, 1981—. bd. mgrs. Germantown savs. Bank; dir. Phila. Electric Co. Bd. dirs. Phila. Gen. Hosp. Charitable Found., 1964-70. Recipient award for outstanding contbns. field med. edn. Commonwealth Com. of Woman's Med. Coll., 1970; Alumni award Bucknell U., 1978; Disting. Dau. Pa. award, 1981. Fellow Coll. Physicians Phila.; mem. A.C.P. (master), AMA, Pa. Med. Soc., Phila. County Med. Soc., Assn. Am. Med. Colls., AAUW (award outstanding grad. Woman's Med. Coll. 1951), Phi Beta Kappa, Alpha Omega Alpha, Phi Sigma. Contbr. articles to profl. jours. Office: 3930 Chestnut St Philadelphia PA 19104

LEVIT, LEONORE FRANK, psychologist; b. Frankfurt, Ger., 1926; d. Wiliam and Alma (Stern) Frank; B.A., N.Y. U., 1947, M.A., 1948; Ph.D., U. Chgo., 1963; m. Fred Levit, Mar. 15, 1947; children—Creon, Ted. Clin. psychologist Ill. Dept. Mental Health, Chgo., 1950-70; dir. crisis intervention Clark-Locust Mental Health Center, Chgo., 1970; conciliator Domestic Relations Div., Ill. Circuit Ct., Chgo., 1970—; pvt. practice family therapy, Chgo., 1969—; vis. prof. Inst. Family Studies, St. Xavier Coll., Chgo., 1973-76. Mem. South Shore Open House Com., 1966-70. Fellow Orthopsychiat. Assn; mem. Assn. Family Conciliation Cts. (dir.), Ill. Assn. Marriage and Family Therapists (legis. com.). Home: 250 Maple Ave Wilmette IL 60091 Office: 55 E Washington St Chicago IL 60602

LEVIT, SHERRY CHAMOVE, city ofcl.; b. San Francisco, June 3, 1942; d. Arnold and Elyse (Shirek) Chamove; A.B., Stanford, 1964; postgrad. San Francisco State U., 1974-77; m. Victor B. Levit, Feb. 25, 1962; children—Carson, Victoria. Mem. Belvedere (Calif.) City Council, 1974—, mayor, 1977-78; mem. exec. com. Assn. Bay Area Govts., 1975—; mem. San Francisco Bay Conservation and Devel. Commn., 1978—; mem. Marin County Council of Mayors and Councilmen, 1974—; chmn. Belvedere Parks and Recreation Commn., 1973-74; mem. Marin County Parks and Recreation Commn., 1977-79; dir. Tiburon Peninsula Adv. Com., 1976—; spl. asst. to San Francisco Mayor Joseph Alioto, 1968-70. Bd. dirs. Tiburon Peninsula Little League Baseball, 1974, coach, 1974-78; coach Tiburon Peninsula Soccer League, 1974-78; mem. women's pub. interest com. San Francisco Symphony Assn., 1966—. Mem. Florence Crittenton Home Women's Aux., San Francisco Lawyer's Wives, San Francisco Mental Health Assn., Calif. Acad. Sci., Tiburon-Belvedere Landmarks Soc., San Francisco Mus. Soc., San Francisco Mus. of Arts Soc. Clubs: Calif. Tennis, Metropolitan, Tiburon Peninsula. Home: 4 Embarcadero Ctr Ste 1800 San Francisco CA 94111

LEVIT, SUSAN RUTH, TV producer; b. Phila., May 2, 1947; d. Nathan and Tybie (Hershman) L.; B.S., Temple U., 1969. Documentary producer Westinghouse Broadcasting, Sta. KYW-TV, Phila., 1974-79, asso. program producer Evening Mag., Sta. WBZ-TV, 1979-80, exec. producer, Evening Mag., Boston, 1980—;tchr. Emerson Coll., 1979-80. Recipient Clarion award Women in Communications, 1977, 1st place award for TV for econ. understanding Amos Tuck Sch., Dartmouth Coll., 1978, Media award, 1979, award Freedoms Found., 1977, Gabriel award, 1981, Newsfeature first place award Mass. AP Broadcasters, 1982. Mem. Nat. Assn. TV Arts and Scis., Women in Film and Video (Boston chpt.), Sigma Delta Chi. Home: 7 Exeter St Boston MA 02116 Office: 1170 Soldiers Field Rd Boston MA 02134

LEVITAN, MARY CHRISTINA, mcht.; b. Milton, Pa., Nov. 19, 1915; d. Willard W. and Pearl E. (Golder) Remaly; student Pa. State U.; m. Paul M. Levitan, Oct. 26, 1938 (dec.); children—Jeffrey, David. Saleswoman Famous Dept. Store, Milton, Pa., 1938-42, buyer, dept. mgr., 1942-75, owner, gen. mgr., 1975—. Mem. bd. Am. Heart Assn., Pa. Assn. Blind, Temple Beth-El; area v.p. Eastern Pa. Hadassah. Recipient awards Fedn. Women's Clubs, 1976, Am. Heart Assn., 1969, State Israel Bonds, 1977. Mem. Merchants Assn. (v.p.), Milton Area C. of C. (pres. 1980-82, area v.p. Ea. Pa. Region 1980-82). Republican. Jewish. Clubs: Milton Woman's, Soroptimist, Lioness, Hadassah, Sisterhood Temple Beth-El, Evangelical Hosp. Aux., YMCA Aux., Country. Home: 62 1/2 S Front St Milton PA 17847 Office: 54-62 S Front St Milton PA 17847

LEVITT, ROCHELLE INEZ, mcht.; b. Memphis, Nov. 20, 1924; d. Max and Selma Florence (Henley) Myers; student Kansas City (Mo.) public schs.; m. Leo Levitt, Sept. 19, 1948; With Henry's, Inc., Wichita, 1950—, pres., 1978—; cons. Active Wichita C. of C. (award), Greater Downtown Wichita, Music Theatre of Wichita, Wichita Art Assn. Mem. Hall of Fame for Wichita State U. Sports Arena. Mem. Petroleum Club. Jewish. Clubs: Wichita, Crestview Country. Office: Henrys Broadway at William St Wichita KS 67201

LEVITZ, ELIZABETH JONES, air charter co. exec.; b. Baton Rouge, Apr. 12, 1941; d. Bob Reiley and Elizabeth Marguerite (Reeves) Jones; student Sophie Newcomb Coll., New Orleans, 1959-61, Sorbonne, 1961-62; 1 son by previous marriage, John S. Coulter II. With E.F. Hutton & Co. Inc., Baton Rouge, 1965-68; pres. Aero Charter, Inc., Miami, Fla., 1976—, also dir.; pres. Trophy Hunter Safaris; dir. Blairstown Land Inc. Bd. dirs. Miami chpt. Am. Heart Assn., 1972—; pres. women's com. Miami chpt. Big Bros., 1979-80, bd. dirs., 1978-80; charter mem. Children in Distress, 1980; mem. tower council, bd. advisers Pine Crest Sch., Ft. Lauderdale, 1979—. Fellow Royal Geog. Soc.; mem. Hakluyt Soc., Internat. Oceanographic Found., Internat. Game Fish Assn., Safari Club Internat., Game Conservation Internat., Ducks Unltd., Found. N.Am. Wild Sheep, Anglo-Am. Art Mus., Am Cancer Soc., Mzuri Safari Found., Kappa Alpha Theta. Methodist. Clubs: Cat Cay, Chub Cay (Bahamas); Les Ambassadeurs (London); Jockey, Palm Bay (Miami); Ocean Reef (Key Largo, Fla.); Surf (Bal Harbour, Fla.). Address: Tower I 1000 Quayside Terr Miami FL 33138

LEVITZKY, SUSAN LIPPERT, pediatrician; b. Bklyn., May 29, 1941; d. Robert and Pearl Marie (Bolduc) Lippert; B.A., U. Wis., 1963; M.D., U. Ill., Chgo., 1967; m. Munro Joseph Levitzky, May 11, 1968; children—Deborah Sheryl, Benjamin Evan. Intern, Bellevue Hosp. Med. Center, N.Y.C., 1967-68; resident, then chief resident Beth Israel Med. Center, N.Y.C., 1968-70, asso. attending pediatrician, 1968—, supr., tchr. pediatric house staff outpatient dept., 1970-78, chmn. subcom. utilization, 1979; sr. clin. instr. Mt. Sinai Sch. Medicine, 1973-81, asst. clin. prof., 1981—; physician reviewer Profl. Standards Rev. Orgn. Jewish. Home: 401 1st Ave Apt 18D New York NY 10010 Office: Beth Israel Med Center 10ND Perlman Pl New York NY 10003

LEVOKOVE, LINDA ANN, interior designer; b. Bklyn., Aug. 8, 1949; d. Irving and Rose (Winick) Gruber; grad. Wilsey Inst. Art and Interior Design, 1967; B.A. in Psychology cum laude, Marymount Coll., 1979; M.S. in Counseling/Human Resources, U. Bridgeport (Conn.), 1981; children—Shari, Jodi, Scott. Free lance interior designer, tchr. interior design, 1967—; owner Linda Levokove Interiors, Stamford, Conn., 1967—; leader dream appreciation workshops, 1978—; counselor, 1978—. Mem. Women's Place, Darien, Conn., Allied Bd. Trade, N.Y.C., 1967—. Home: 174 Butternut Ln Stamford CT 06903

LEVY, BARBARA MINA WEXNER, writer/pub., editor; b. Hot Springs, Ark., Jan. 30, 1927; d. Henry David and Helen Ruth (Loeb) Wexner; A.A., Lindenwood Coll., 1945; student U. Houston, 1958-59; m. Herbert E. Levy, July 25, 1945; children—Barbara Dian, Richard H., Lauren. Feature writer Houston Town, 1957-58; regional editor Boot & Shoe Recorder, Houston, 1958-65; with customer service Scholastic Mag., Englewood Cliffs, N.J., 1966-67; fashion shoe editor Window Shopping World, N.Y.C., 1967-68; women's fashion editor Boot & Shoe Recorder, N.Y.C., 1968-74; pub., editor Barbara's Report/Shoes and. . . , Miami, Fla., 1974—; lectr. in field. Mem. alumnae bd. Lindenwood Coll., 1967-68, v.p., 1969. Mem. Footwear and Accessories Council N.Y.C. (pres. 1973, chmn. bd. 1974, honored for creative contbn. to industry 1982), Fashion Group, Women in Communications. Club: Brown (N.Y.C.). Contbr. articles to profl. jours. Address: 1236 NE 92nd St Miami FL 33138

LEVY, BARBARA RIFKIN, theatrical exec. b. Schenectady, Apr. 25, 1941; d. Sam and Jane E. (Goodman) Rifkin B.S., U. Vt., 1962; postgrad. Ithaca (N.Y.) Coll. Music, Ohio U., U. Ariz.; m. Martin R. Levy, July 21, 1963; children—Douglas M., Mitchell B. Elem. sch. music tchr., Conn., Ohio, 1962-64; music therapist Athens (Ohio) State Hosp., 1964-66; dir. devel. Ariz. Opera, 1974-78; dir. devel. Ariz. Theatre Co., Tucson, 1978—; coordinator Tucson chpt. Arizonans for Cultural Devel. Mem. Nat. Soc. Fund Raising Execs., Devel. Exec. Round Table So. Ariz., Fund Raising Inst. Jewish. Office: 120 W Broadway Tucson AZ 85701

LEVY, CHARLOTTE LOIS, law librarian; b. Cin., Aug. 31, 1944; d. Samuel M. and Helen (Lowitz) L.; B.A., U. Ky., 1966; M.L.S., Columbia U., 1969; J.D., No. Ky. U., 1975; m. Herbert Regenstreif, Dec. 11, 1980; 1 dau., Cara Rachael. Law librarian No. Ky. U., 1971-75; admitted to Colo. bar, 1979; law librarian, asso. prof. law Pace U. Law Sch., 1975-77; mgr. Fred B. Rothman & Co., Littleton, Colo., 1977-79; law librarian, asso. prof. Bklyn. Law Sch., 1979—; adj. prof. Pratt Inst. Grad. Sch. Library and Info. Sci.; cons. in field. Mem. Am. Bar Assn., Am. Assn. Law Libraries, Law Library Assn. Greater N.Y. Democrat. Jewish. Author: The Human Body and The Law, 1975. Bd. editors No. Ky. U. Law Rev., 1974-75. Office: 250 Joralemon St Brooklyn NY 11201

LEVY, HELENE AIMEE, social worker; b. Bklyn., Sept. 29, 1908; d. David M. and Millie (Reichenbach) Levy; B.S., N.Y.U., 1931; M.S., Columbia U., 1945. Sec., 1935-38; social investigator N.Y.C. Dept. Welfare, 1938-44; asst. field dir. ARC, Luzon, Philippines, Yokohama, Japan, 1945-46, field dir. mil. hosps., New Eng., Stuttgart and Neurenberg, W. Ger., 1951-54; supr. 6 counties div. child welfare W.Va. Dept. Welfare, Elkins, 1946-51; case supr. Summit County Bd. Child Welfare, Akron, Ohio, 1954-58; cons. on protective services div. for children and youth Wis. Dept. Welfare, Madison, 1958-62; cons. on tng. UN, Iran, 1962-66; social sci. research analyst. Adminstrn. on Aging, Office Human Devel. Services, Dept. Health and Human Services, Washington, 1966—. Recipient supplemental award social and rehab. services HEW, 1977. Fellow Royal Soc. Health (Eng.); mem. Am. Public Welfare Assn., Am. Acad. Arts and Scis., Columbia U. Alumnae Assn. Home: 490 M St SW Washington DC 20024 Office: Adminstrn on Aging 330 Independence Ave SW Washington DC 20201

LEVY, JANET JACOBS, state govt. adminstr.; b. Oakland, Calif., Apr. 15, 1914; d. Herbert Alva and Jessie Adeline (Thiercof) Jacobs; B.A., San Francisco State Coll., 1957, M.S. in Gerontology and Rehab., 1959; postgrad. Columbia U., 1960-61, N.Y.U., 1961-62; m. Morrie Levy, Apr. 10, 1942 (dec.); 1 dau., Ellen Rae (dec.). Dir., Little House Sr. Center, Menlo Park, Calif., 1960-62; cons., exec. dir. Calif. State Commn. on Aging, Sacramento, 1962-68; asst. dir. Calif. Assn. Homes for Aging, 1968-71; cons. Calif. Legislature Joint Legis. Com. on Aging, 1971-75; dir. Calif. Dept. Aging, Sacramento, 1975—; mem. adv. bd. Calif. Council Geriatrics and Gerontology, UCLA/U. So. Calif. Long-term Care Gerontology Center. Bd. dirs. Hospice Care of Sacramento; bd. dirs. Marin County (Calif.) Hospice Program. Mem. Nat. Assn. State Units on Aging (dir.), Am. Assn. Ret. Persons, Calif. Specialists on Aging, Gerontol. Soc. Am., Western Gerontol. Soc., Nat. Council Sr. Citizens, Nat. Council Aging, Internat. Sr. Citizens Assn., Older Womens League. Democrat. Office: 1020 19th St Sacramento CA 95814

LEVY, JUDITH AMDUR, lawyer; b. Cleve., Mar. 28, 1940; d. Max and Frances Jane Amdur; B.S., Ind. U., 1962; postgrad. Purdue U., 1968-71; J.D., Valparaiso U., 1976; m. Joel C. Levy, June 4, 1961; children—Janice Ruth, Julie Ann. Admitted to Ind. bar, 1976; asso. firm Singleton, Levy, Crist and Johnson, Highland, Ind., 1976—; home bound tutor Munster (Ind.) Sch. System. Sec. Munster Human Relations Council, 1968-70; active Greater Hammond Community Services, 1977-79; mem. social services budget com. Lake Area United Way; mem. Lake County Task Force Calumet Women United Against Rape. Mem. Am. Bar Assn., Fed. Bar Assn., Ind. Bar Assn., Hammond Bar Assn. (public relations com.). Jewish. Home: 9124 Walnut Dr Munster IN 46321 Office: 9013 Indianapolis Blvd Highland IN 46322

LEVY, JUDITH MOSKOWITZ, clin. psychologist; b. Wilmington, Del., Oct. 8, 1934; d. Hugo and Florence (Kronfeld) Moskowitz; B.A. cum laude, Bklyn. Coll., 1955; M.A. (Univ. fellow), Tulane U., 1961; M.A., U. Fla., 1966, Ph.D., 1969; children—Thomas, Rachel, Jason. Teaching asst. in sociology Tulane U., New Orleans, 1956-57; research asst. U. N.C., Chapel Hill, 1959-60; psychologist Child & Parent Devel. Center, New Orleans, 1969-70; chief psychologist Childrens Mental Health Unit, U. Fla., Gainesville, 1970-75, asst. prof. psychology, 1970-75, adj. prof., 1976-78; dir. psychol. services Gainesville Womens Health Center, 1976-78; program dir. Birthplace, Inc., Gainesville, 1978—. Mem. Am. Psychol. Assn., Fla. Psychol. Assn., Phi Beta Kappa, Phi Kappa Phi. Contbr. articles in field to profl. jours. Home: 4610 NW 15th Pl Gainesville FL 32605 Office: Birthplace Inc 635 NE 1st St Gainesville FL 32601

LEVY, SUSANNA AGNES, hosp. exec.; b. Budapest, Hungary, Mar. 20, 1934; came to U.S., 1963; d. Joseph and Piroska (Puder) Konig; B.S.C., Poly. U. Budapest, 1956; M.S.C., Hebrew U., Jerusalem, 1961; Ph.D., Poly. Inst. N.Y., 1968; m. Ezra Levy, June 10, 1958; children—

Joseph, Uri. Asst. supr. Food Analysis Lab., Israeli Minstry Agr. and Industry, Jerusalem, 1957-60; chemist dept. nutrition Hadassah U. Hosp., Jerusalem, 1960-61; sr. research chemist Geol. Survey Israel, Jerusalem, 1961-63; chemist Kingsbrook Jewish Med. Center, N.Y.C., 1963-64, asst. chief clin. chemistry, 1968; teaching fellow, research fellow Poly. Inst. N.Y., 1964-68; chief clin. chemistry St. Vincent Hosp., N.Y.C., 1968-72, St. Barnabas Hosp., N.Y.C., 1972—; adj. asso. prof. Bridgeport U., Bronx Community Coll.; cons. diagnostic div. Abbott Labs., 1976-81; examiner N.Y.C. Bd. Health, 1972-79. Mem. Am. Assn. Clin. Chemistry (mem. exec. com. N.Y. Met. chpt. 1972—, chairperson chpt. 1979), Nat. Acad. Clin. Biochemists, N.Y. Acad. Sci., AAAS, Assn. Women Execs., Am. Chem. Soc., Assn. Clin. Scientists, Nat. Registry Clin. Chemistry. Democrat. Jewish. Home: 108-21 67th Ave Forest Hills NY 11375 Office: Saint Barnabas Hosp 183 St and 3d Ave Bronx NY 10457

LEVY, TIBBIE (MRS. ELI BENNETT LEVY), lawyer, painter; b. N.Y.C., Oct. 29, 1908; d. David and Minnie (Hoffman) Goldstein; A.B., Cornell U., 1929, postgrad., 1929-30; J.D., N.Y. U., 1931; studied with Arshile Gorky, Art Students League, Andre L'Hote, Academic de la Grande Chaumiere, Cornell U., also Vincenzo; m. Eli Bennett Levy, Nov. 19, 1931; children—Lynn (Mrs. Leland S. Zaubler), John Hoffman (dec.). Admitted to N.Y. bar, 1932; pvt. practice of law, N.Y.C., 1932—. Profl. painter under name of Lysan and Tibbie Levy; exhibited one-man shows in N.Y.C., Pa., Paris, Madrid, London, Tokyo; represented numerous permanent museum collections, Phoenix Mus. Art, Witte Mus., San Antonio, Jewish Mus. Hebrew Union Coll., Cin., Evansville (Ind.) Mus. Art and Sci., Boston U., Brandeis U., Cornell U., Ga. Mus., Jewish Mus., Cin., Mus. Modern Art, Miami, Witte Meml. Mus., Tex., George Peabody Mus., Tenn., Princeton, Palm Springs Mus., Barnard Coll., Fairleigh Dickinson U., N.J., Syracuse U., Colgate U., Rutgers U., N.Y. U., U. Notre Dame, Fashion Inst. Tech., Horace Mann Sch., Pace Coll., Drexel Mus., Pa.; also pvt. and indsl. collections. Pres. patrons council Barnard Sch. for Boys; mem. Speakers Bur., Anti-Defamation League; pres. Freedom chpt., mem. Speakers Bur., B'nai B'rith; pres. Parents Assn. Calhoun Sch.; bd. dirs. Hebrew Kindergarten and Infants Home, NCCJ. Home: 2 Sutton Pl S New York NY 10022

LEW, ALINE MAY, systems engr., cosmetics co. cons.; b. Los Angeles, Feb. 3, 1956; d. Gan Lew and Lai Sam Gee Wong; B.S. in Engring., UCLA, 1977; postgrad. in mgmt. U. Redlands, 1979—. Data entry operator Safecom Mgmt. Co., Panorama City, Calif., 1973-76; engring. analyst So. Calif. Edison Co., Rosemead, 1976-79, engring. planning engr., 1979-80; sr. systems analyst/engr. Exxon Co., U.S.A., Los Angeles, 1980—; cons. Mary Kay Cosmetics, Los Angeles, 1981—. Campaign aide to Calif. state senator, 1971-72; active United Way. Recipient cert. NSF, 1972; Calif. State scholar, 1973-77. Mem. Soc. Women Engrs., Women's Roundtable. Home: 7044 Atoll Ave North Hollywood CA 91605 Office: 1800 Ave of Stars Suite 1084 Los Angeles CA 90067

LEW, KAREN LESLIE, writer; b. Washington, Feb. 19, 1942; d. Lyman Littlefield and Betsy Mae (Dekema) Woodman; student San Francisco State Coll., 1960-61, El Camino Jr. Coll., 1966, UCLA, 1967, U. Alaska, Anchorage, 1971, 75, 77, Sheldon Jackson Coll., 1979, Anchorage Community Coll., 1980, 81, 82; m. Dan Wing Lew, Jan. 12, 1962 (div. 1970); children—Kent Charles, Danika Leslie, Mark Daren. Info. specialist ITT Arctic Services, Inc., Anchorage, Alaska, 1969-71; adminstrv. asst., Mike Ellis Advt., Anchorage, 1971; copywriter, continuity dir. sta. KYAK, Anchorage, 1971-72; copywriter, media buyer Graphix West, Anchorage, 1972-73; classified advt. mgr. Anchorage Daily News, 1973-74; media specialist Alaska Native Commn. on Alcoholism/Drug Abuse, 1974-75; copywriter, media buyer sta. KYAK/KGOT, Anchorage, 1976-77; advt. mgr. Alaska Advocate, Anchorage, 1977-78; advt. rep., writer Alaskafest mag., Anchorage, 1979; info. officer Dept. Natural Resources, State of Alaska, Anchorage, 1980—; free lance writer, 1969—; adj. lectr. composition Anchorage Community Coll., 1982; speaker in field ednl. and community groups. First v.p. Anchorage Council on Alcoholism, 1976-77; vol. arts writer. Recipient various state and nat. awards for writing, 1969-80. Mem. Nat. Fedn. Press Women, Alaska Press Women (v.p., 1973, rec. sec. 1982), Public Relations Soc. Am. Unitarian-Universalist. Clubs: Anchorage Chess, U.S. Chess Fedn., Theatre Guild, Anchorage Community Chorus. Editor newsletter Alaska State Council on the Arts; arts columnist Alaskafest Mag. Home: 3120 W 79th Ave Anchorage AK 99502

LEWELLEN, FLORENCE ORPHA, survey co. exec.; b. Sauk Centre, Minn., Apr. 9, 1914; d. Samuel Edward and Theresa (Spofford) Capkey; B.A., Hamline U., 1934; m. Floyd Lewellen, July 24, 1936; children—Frances, Foster. Free-lance entertainer, 1934-56; part-time staff asst. orgns. vols., 1957-59; field interviewer Burke Mktg., Cin., 1959-61; field interviewer Mid-Continent Surveys, Inc., Mpls., 1961-62, field supr., 1962-63, field dir., 1963-69, v.p. data collection, 1969—; cons. Normandale Community Coll., 1980—; career clinic cons. YWCA, Mpls., 1979; research cons., 1981—. Mem. Mktg. Research Assn. Inc., Internat. Soc. Gen. Semantics, Minn. Zool. Soc., Mpls. Soc. Fine Arts, Friends of Inst. Arts, Decorative Arts Council, YWCA, Help Our Wolves Live. Author: How To Handbook for Quality Interviewing, 1979. Home: 115 E Rustic Lodge Ave Minneapolis MN 55409 Office: 830 Midwest Plaza Minneapolis MN 55409

LEWIN, CAROLINE TOEPFER, clin. psychologist; b. Newark, Feb. 17, 1944; d. Chester Leon Throckmorton and Caroline Amanda Lange; B.A. in Psychology (Cleve. Found. scholar), Kent State U., 1965, M.A., 1967, Ph.D. (NIMH fellow), 1969; m. William Lewin II, Sept. 10, 1979; 1 son, Neil Norval. Social worker Fallsview Mental Health Center, 1965, Sagamore Hills Children's Psychiat. Hosp., 1966; psychologist Portage County Welfare Dept., 1966-68; intern Univ. Hosps., Case Western Res. U., 1968; asst. prof., dir. student interns Slippery Rock State Coll., 1969-75; pvt. practice clin. psychology Youngstown, Ohio, 1974-80, Columbus, Ohio, 1980—; cons. Bur. Disability Determination, Bur. Vocat. Rehab., St. Vincent's Children's Center; speaker, guest lectr.; condr. workshops; owner Snack Shack, Columbus. Mem. Selective Service Bd. 41. Lic. clin. psychologist, Ohio, Fla., Pa. Mem. Am. Psychol. Assn., Ohio Psychol. Assn., Psi Chi. Editor: Supplementary Readings in Applied Psychology and Human Behavior, 1970; (with Bicknell, Fox, Kirk and Sayre) Environmental Psychology, 1972. Home: 6473 Borr Ave Reynoldsburg OH 43068 Office: PO Box 2485 Columbus OH 43216

LEWIN, ELIZABETH SAMELSON, fin. planner; b. Bridgeport, Conn., Feb. 26, 1938; d. Lester and Edith Hecht Samelson; B.A., N.Y. U., 1959; A.S., Sacred Heart U., 1977; cert. fin. planner, Adelphi U., 1980; children—Valerie, Eric. With Hirsch Travel, 1974-76; founder, dir. Budget Adv. Service, Westport, Conn., 1977—; lectr. on money mgmt., fin. planning. Mem. Internat. Assn. Fin. Planners, Women's Pl., Nat. Assn. Female Execs. Contbr. articles to money mgmt. publs.

LEWIS, ANN FRANK, politician; b. Jersey City, Dec. 19, 1937; d. Samuel and Elsie (Golush) Frank; student Radcliffe Coll., 1954-55; children—Patricia Fay, Beth Ellen, Susan Jane. Asst. to mayor of Boston, 1968-75; dep. campaign mgr. Bayh for President, 1975-76; congl. adminstrv. asst., 1976-81; polit. dir. Democratic Nat. Com., 1981—; co-leader Mass. Women's Polit. Caucus, 1972-74; recorder Nat. Women's Polit. Caucus, 1972-75; mem. Newton (Mass.) Dem. City Com., 1972-75; mem. nat. bd., exec. com. Americans for Dem. Action, 1975—. Mem. Women's Equity Action League, NOW. Jewish. Office: 1625 Massachusetts Ave NW Washington DC 20036

LEWIS, ANNA ELIZABETH, writer; b. Salisbury, N.C., Oct. 24, 1946; d. Samuel Clee and Ruth Geraldine (Weaver) Laster, Sr.; A.A., Stratford Coll., 1966; postgrad. Wake Forest U., 1966-67; m. Jesse Ray Lewis, Jr., Mar. 14, 1970; children—Mary Elizabeth, Laura Ellen. Reporter, advt. saleswoman, photographer Myrtle Beach (S.C.) Sun News, 1967-70, spl. feature writer, 1972-76; freelance writer. Organizer, bd. dirs. Grand Strand Humane Soc., Myrtle Beach, 1969-70; bd. dirs. New Hanover Humane Soc.; vol. Services for the Aging. Mem. Beta Sigma Phi. Democrat. Episcopalian. Home: 214 W Wilson St Ridgecrest CA 93555

LEWIS, BARBARA ANN, psychologist; b. N.Y.C., Dec. 25, 1937; d. Robert Edward and Alice (Imholz) L.; student Wellesley Coll., 1955-57; A.B. in Psychology, U. N.C., 1959; M.A. in Counseling, Columbia U., 1960; Ph.D. in Psychology, Temple U., 1970. Clin. psychology intern Eastern Mental Health Center, Phila. Gen. Hosp., 1961-62, clin. psychologist, 1962; clin. psychologist Children's Hosp., Phila., 1963; clin. psychologist N.J. State Hosp., Trenton, 1965; research psychologist dept. exptl. psychology Walter Reed Army Inst. of Research, Washington, 1966-67; clin. psychologist N.Y. U. Med. Center, Bellevue Psychiat. Hosp., N.Y.C., 1967-70; clin. psychologist Bronx (N.Y.) State Hosp., 1970-72; family therapist Family Mental Health Clinic, Jewish Family Service, N.Y.C., 1972-74; therapist New Hope Guild Center, Bklyn., 1975-76; pvt. practice clin. psychology, N.Y.C., 1974—. Mem. Am. Acad. Psychotherapists (mem. ethics com., chmn. Eastern region 1981-83, exec. council 1982-85, chmn. 1983 summer workshop), N.Y. Soc. Clin. Psychologists, Am. Psychol. Assn., N.Y. State Psychol. Assn., Assn. Women in Psychology, NOW (coordinator psychology commn. 1977-79). Office: 315 Central Park W Suite 6W New York NY 10025

LEWIS, BARBARA JEAN, hosp. adminstr.; b.Chgo., Apr. 3, 1941; d. Frederick Henry and Florence Mary (Wachholz) Gauger; R.N., St. Mary's Sch. Nursing, 1962; B.A., Judson Coll., 1972; M.A., Webster Coll., 1979; 1 son, Kenneth John. Asst. head nurse Tucson (Ariz.) Med. Center, 1962-63; charge nurse St. Joseph's Hosp., Tucson, 1963-64, Santa Rosa Nursing Home, Tucson, 1965, VA Hosp., 1965-66; night supr. Deborah Hosp., 1967, McHenry (Ill.) Hosp., 1968; staff nurse Burlington County Meml. Hosp., Mount Holly, N.J., 1968-69; instr. Mercer Hosp. Sch. Nursing, Trenton, N.J., 1969-71; night supr. Warrensburg (Mo.) Nursing Home, 1972-73; office nurse J. M. Lederer, M.D., Warrensburg, Mo., 1973; dir. Conway Sch. Practical Nursing, Horry County Dept. Edn., Conway, S.C., 1973-78; dir. nursing/asst. adminstr. Conway Hosp., Inc., 1978-80; asst. exec. dir. nursing University Heights Hosp., Albuquerque, after 1980, now v.p. for nursing. Mem. vocat. edn. adv. com. N.Mex., S.C., 1976-77; mem. state planning com. curriculum revision practical nurse program S.C.; cons. Roper Hosp. Sch. Practical Nursing, Charleston, S.C., 1977, Richland County Sch. Practical Nursing, Columbia, S.C., 1977; mem. planning com. Gov.'s Conf. on Nursing in N.Mex., 1981-82; co-chmn. Forum Preparation-Practice, 1981-82. Recipient Cert. of Merit, Am. Cancer Soc., 1979. Mem. Nat. Council Hosp. and Related Facilities (interim exec. com.), Nat. League Nursing, Am. Hosp. Assn. Nursing Service Adminstrs., N. Mex. Hosp. Assn. (mem. edn. com.), N.Mex. Soc. Nursing Service Adminstrs. (pres. 1982), Nat. League Nursing Forum Nursing Service Adminstrs., Sigma Theta Tau. Roman Catholic. Home: 6217 Christy St NE Albuquerque NM 87109 Office: 1127 University Blvd NE Albuquerque NM 87102

LEWIS, BARBARA LYNN, mktg. exec.; b. Harlem, N.Y., Sept. 6, 1951; d. Thomas and Marjorie (Glegg) Lewis; B.A., Va. State U., 1974; 1 dau., Erica. Project coordinator Check Your Local Stations workshop Office of Communication, United Ch. of Christ, N.Y.C., 1975-77; mgr. Direct Mail Mktg. Assn., N.Y.C., 1977-81; dir. direct mail Roberts Proprietaries, Moonachie, N.J., 1981—. Mem. Nat. Assn. Female Execs., N.Y. Hundred Million Club, Direct Mktg. Minority Opportunities. Contbr. articles to profl. jours. Office: 1 Anderson Ave Moonachie NJ 07074

LEWIS, BERTHA ANN, biochemist; b. Lewisville, Minn., Oct. 21, 1927; d. Verne Elton and Lillian May (Halverson) L.; B.Chem., U. Minn., 1949, M.S., 1954, Ph.D., 1957. Postdoctoral research fellow U. Minn., 1957-65, research asso., 1965-67; asso. prof. dept. design and environ. analysis Cornell U., Ithaca, N.Y., 1967-80, asso. prof. div. nutritional scis., 1970—, asso. dean Coll. Human Ecology, 1973-80. Chmn., Tompkins County United Way, 1976; v.p. Finger Lakes Trail Conf., 1980-81. NIH grantee, 1972-77; NSF grantee, 1979—; Nat. Cancer Inst. grantee, 1978-79. Mem. Am. Chem. Soc., Inst. Food Technologists, Fiber Soc., Soc. Complex Carbohydrates, Am. Assn. Cereal Chemists, Sigma Xi, Sigma Delta Epsilon (nat. pres. 1979-80). Club: Zonta. Contbr. articles to profl. jours. Editor: Guide to Trails of the Finger Lakes Region. Home: 139 Snyder Hill Rd Ithaca NY 14850 Office: 254 Van Rensselaer Hall Cornell Univ Ithaca NY 14853

LEWIS, BETTE LOUISE, ednl. adminstr.; b. Chandler, Ariz., Dec. 24, 1931; d. Helm Elmo and Ella Margaret (Calley) Blythe; B.A., Marymount Coll., 1964; M.A., U. Md., 1970; postgrad. George Washington U., Loyola U., Balt., Appalachian State U., Boone, S.C.; m. Gladstone S. Lewis, Jr., Aug. 2, 1952; 1 son, Clinton Helm. Tchr. public schs., Calif. and Md., 1964-69; vice prin., then prin. Prince George's (Md.) County Public Schs., 1969—, prin. Roger B. Taney Jr. High Sch., Camp Springs, 1977—; treas. Md. Fall Ednl. Conf., 1980—; cons. Pres., Hillside (Calif.) Sch. PTA, 1962-63; v.p. Taney Sch. PTA, 1977—. Charles F. Kettering fellow, 1977—. Mem. Assn. Sch. Adminstrs. and Supts. (pres. 1977-78), Am. Assn. Sch. Adminstrs., Nat. Assn. Secondary Sch. Prins., NEA, Md. Assn. Sch. Adminstrs., Internat. Platform Assn., Alpha Delta Kappa, Sigma Sigma Sigma. Republican. Roman Catholic. Home: 4407 Weldon Dr Temple Hills MD 20748 Office: 4909 Brinkley Rd Camp Springs MD 20748

LEWIS, BETTY ANN, writer, historian, researcher; b. Fresno, Calif., June 1, 1925; s. Roy William and Dorothy Fredricka (Porter) Bagby; student Hartnell Coll.; m. Monte Randall Lewis, Jan. 11, 1946; children—Christine, Marci, Mike, Kelly. Author: Victorian Homes of Watsonville, 1974; Walking and Driving Tour of Historic Watsonville, 1975; Highlights in the History of Watsonville, 1975; Watsonville Memories That Linger, 1976; Monterey Bay Yesterday, 1977; Watsonville Yesterday, 1978; Watsonville Memories That Linger, Vol. II, 1980; speaker, cons. research radio programs. Mem. Watsonville Library Bd., 1982-85. Recipient SCOPE awards, 1977, 78; San Jose State U.-Sourisseau Acad. research grantee. Mem. Nat. League Am. Pen Women, Theatre Historians, Calif. Hist. Soc., Calif. Conf. Hist. Socs., (v.p. 1982), Pajaro Valley Hist. Assn. (pres. 1980-81, Hubert Wyckoff Meml. award 1979), Santa Cruz Soc. for Hist. Preservation. Republican. Presbyterian (elder). Club: Watsonville Woman's. Office: Mansion House 420 Main St Suite 204 Watsonville CA 95076

LEWIS, BETTY JANE, real estate exec., restaurant exec.; b. Grove City, Pa., May 22, 1920; d. George Franklin and Nancy Blanche (McGarvey) Weston; A.B.D., Grove City Coll., 1939; student Duquesne U., 1967-68, Carnegie Inst. Tech., 1965-68; m. Edward Denny, Feb. 7, 1942; children—Edward, Mark, William. Dist. supr. Comml. Labs., Newark, N.Y., 1960-65; owner Key Realty Co., Butler, Pa., 1971—; owner, operator Burger Hut, Butler, 1979—. Mem. Nat. Restaurant Assn., Butler County Bd. Realtors, Nat. Bd. Realtors, Mental Health Assn., Human Relations Assn. (pres.), Assoc. Artists (dir.). Republican. Methodist. Club: Women's. Home: 106 Randy Dr Butler PA 16001 Office: 1734 N Main St Extension Butler PA 16001

LEWIS, CHARLENE, financial exec.; b. Manson, Ark.; d. Robert Leo and Dorothy Donibee (Kidd) Lewis; B.S. in Acctg., San Diego State U., 1971; M.B.A., Nat. U., 1980. Gen. acct. Datagraphix, Inc., San Diego, 1970-73, adminstrv. acct., 1973-76, acctg. group leader, 1976-77, supr. acctg., 1977-79, sr. fin. analyst, 1979—. Mem. Mgmt. Club, Women in Data Processing, Clubs: San Diego Track; San Diego Marathon Clinic; Pacific Beach Tennis. Home: 10573 Greenford Dr San Diego CA 92126 Office: Datagraphix Inc PO Box 82449 San Diego CA 92138

LEWIS, CHERYL HOLCOMB, banker; b. Plainview, Tex., Dec. 20, 1955; d. James Reed and Tula Faye (Rose) Holcomb; B.S. in Bus. Edn., Baylor U., 1978; 1 dau., Tiffany. CD rep. Am. Bank, Waco, Tex., 1978-79; credit officer Parkdale Bank, Corpus Christi, Tex., 1979—. Co. coordinator United Way, 1981; active New Neighbor's League, 1979-81; vol. KEDT-TV, 1979-80, Apt. Assn. Trade Fair, 1980. Mem. Am. Inst. Banking (first v.p.), Bank Women Corpus Christi, NOW, C. of C., Nat. Assn. Female Execs., South Tex. Women's Forum. Baptist. Club: Aerobic Dancing. Home: 5202 Larcade St Corpus Christi TX 78415

LEWIS, DI ANN BARTEE, psychologist; b. Borger, Tex., May 2, 1941; d. Eddie Rex and Catherine Ann (Carruth) Bartee; B.S. cum laude, Miss. State U., 1968, M.Ed (NDEA fellow), 1969, Ph.D. (NDEA fellow), 1974; postgrad. La. Tech. U., 1975; m. Harvey Shelton Lewis, June 2, 1961; children—Jon Brian, Lauri Ann, Heather Ann. Dir. Project Gateway (spl. services), Title I supr. reading Lafayette (Miss.) County Schs., 1974-78; acting asst. prof. spl. edn. U. Miss., Oxford, 1975—, adj. asso. prof. psychology, 1979—; dir. dept. psychology N. Miss. Retardation Center, 1978—; cons. Miss. State Dept. Edn., Miss. State Commn. on Sch. Accreditation Coms. Bd. dirs. Leadership Miss. Named Outstanding Woman in Edn. Kappa Delta Pi, 1982. Mem. Miss. Psychol. Assn., Am. Psychol. Assn., Miss. Assn. Talented and Gifted, Nat. Assn. Gifted Children, Miss. Assn. for Retarded Citizens, Am. Assn. Mental Deficiency, Delta Kappa Gamma. Methodist. Clubs: Oxford Athletic Booster. Home: 221 Carol Ln Oxford MS 38655 Office: PO Box 967 Oxford MS 38655

LEWIS, DIANA, TV news anchorwoman; b. Coatesville, Pa., Mar. 17, 1943; d. James Davis and Doris Anna (Spann) Robinson; B.S., Central State U., Ohio, 1965; tchr.'s cert. West Chester State Coll., 1966; postgrad. Temple U., UCLA; m. Glenn Lewis, Feb. 25, 1973; children—Donna L'Vonne, Glenda Terrell. Psychol. social worker Embreeville (Pa) State Hosp.; tchr. sci. Devereaux High Sch., Devon, Pa.; tchr. English, Coatesville (Pa.) Public Schs.; anchorwoman/reporter Sta.-WPVI-TV, Phila., 1969-74, Sta.-KABC-TV, Los Angeles, 1974-77; news anchorwoman Sta.-WXYZ-TV, Detroit, 1977—; public speaker, Detroit area, nationally. Recipient Sojourner Truth award Nat. Assn. Negro Bus. and Profl. Women, Key to City Coatesville, 1979. Mem. NAACP, Women in Communications, Am. Women in Radio and TV (Outstanding Woman in News), Nat. Acad. TV Arts and Scis. (Phila. Emmy award, Los Angeles Emmy award, Detroit Emmy award. Office: 20777 W 10 Mile Rd Southfield MI 48075

LEWIS, DINAH LYNNE, lawyer, accountant; b. Denver, Oct. 27, 1952; d. James Robert and Martha Jean (See) Lewis; B.S.B.A., U. Denver, 1973, J.D., 1981; M.B.A., U. Colo., 1976; m. Don A. Childears, Apr. 18, 1981. Staff accountant Siecke, Newman & Co., Denver, 1974-75; agt. IRS, Denver, 1975-78, appeals officer, 1978-81; admitted to Colo. bar, 1981; atty. firm Hellerstein, Hellerstein & Shore, P.C., Denver, 1981—. C.P.A., Colo. Mem. Am. Inst. C.P.A.s, Colo. Soc. C.P.A.s, Am. Bar Assn., Colo. Bar Assn., Beta Alpha Psi, Alpha Lambda Delta. Office: 1050 17th St Denver CO 80265

LEWIS, DONNA JEAN IRENE, photojournalist; b. Spring Green, Wis., Oct. 27, 1940; d. Leslie and Irene Dorothy (Ziebarth) Cowley; m. Glenn LaVere Lewis, Oct. 4, 1958; children—Marie JoAnn, Rodney Wayne, Ronald Edward, Lori Lorraine. Reporter, feature writer Dodgeville (Wis.) Chronicle, 1968—; photographer Farm County Observer; free-lance writer Wis. State Jour., Milw. Jour., Rockford (Ill.) Morning Star, Farm Wife News Mag., various other pubs., 1969—; newsletter editor Madison (Wis.) Ostomy Assn., 1978—; corr. Sta. WMTV, Madison, 1978—; dir. homemaker public relations U. Wis. Extension. Recipient Carol award Iowa County Jaycettes, 1976. Mem. Iowa County Hist. Soc., Wis. Press Women, Wis. Regional Writers, Upland Writers Club (pres. 1979-80), Am. Agri-Women, South Central Photographers Assn., Wakefield Homemakers. Author: Ridgeway Host to the Ghost, 1976; Every One's Cookbook, 1978; One of A Kind Wedding, 1980. Contbr. articles to newspapers and mags. Home: RFD 3 Dodgeville WI 53533

LEWIS, DOROTHY ROE, journalist; b. Alba, Mo., May 18, 1904; d. Daniel Perkins and Anna Florence (Tibbs) Roe; B.J., U. Mo., 1924; m. John Bettington Lewis, July 4, 1937 (dec.); children—Judith Jennifer Lewis White, Jo Anne Lewis Schreiber. Reporter, Eldorado Daily News, 1924-25; shopping news columnist Los Angeles Examiner, 1926; feature writer Chgo. Herald-Examiner, 1927, Universal Service, 1927-37; free-lance feature writer N.Y. World, 1927-28; co-pub. Burlington (N.J.) Daily Enterprise, 1939-40; women's editor AP, N.Y.C., 1941-60; ghost writing assignments for celebrities in women's field Putnam, Lippincott, Prentice-Hall pub. cos., 1944-60; asst. women's editor King Features, 1940-41; columnist Chgo. Tribune-N.Y. News Syndicate, 1960-70; mem. journalism faculty U. Mo., Columbia, 1964-74; editor Mo. Republican, 1975-80; freelance writer for mags., newspapers, 1980—; judge Penney-Mo. Women's Page awards, 1962-74. Recipient Mo. medal for disting. service in journalism, 1958, Zonta Internat. Newswoman of Yr. award, 1958. Mem. Women in Communications. Republican. Mem. Christian Ch. (Disciples of Christ). Club: Fortnightly (U. Mo.). Author: (with Lilly Dache) Talking Through My Hats, 1946, Lilly Dache's Glamour Book, 1956; The Trouble with Women Is Men, 1962. Home: 2806 W Rollins Rd Columbia MO 65201

LEWIS, EILEEN FOWLER, social worker; b. Birmingham, Ala., Sept. 1, 1945; d. James Thomas and Thelma Annis (Taylor) Fowler; B.A. in Sociology and Psychology, Auburn U., 1967; student Sch. Alcohol Studies, U. Ga., 1972; m. Michael A. Lewis, Oct. 17, 1975. Social worker protective services child welfare div. Muscogee County Dept. Family and Childrens Services, Columbus, Ga., 1967-68; social worker with teenage girls Ala. State Tng. Sch. for Girls, Chalkville, 1968-70; social worker in service to mil. families, vets. and disaster services ARC, Birmingham, 1970—, instr., trainer ARC tng. system, 1978—. Sec., Jefferson County Human Service Club, 1978-79; mem. Jefferson County Child Abuse Task Force, Birmingham Civic Opera Chorus. Recipient service recognition for flood relief work ARC, 1978, 79; lic. social worker, Ala. Mem. Nat. Assn. Social Workers, Ala. Conf. Social Work, Ala. Council on Crime and Delinquency. Presbyterian. Home: 725 Abigail Ln Birmingham AL 35210 Office: 2225 3d Ave N Birmingham AL 35202

LEWIS, ELIZABETH NANCY, nurse adminstr.; b. St. Paul, Aug. 23, 1945; d. Clyde E. and Elsie I. (Larson) Hegman; R.N., St. Barnabas Hosp. Sch. Nursing, 1968; B.A.S., U. Minn., 1976; M.S., Ph.D., Columbia Pacific U. Staff nurse Mpls. St. Paul area hosps., 1968-74; asst. coordinator staff devel. and inservice edn. Midway Hosp., St. Paul, 1974-77; adminstrv. asst., dir. nursing NW Gen. Hosp., Milw., 1977-78; dir. nursing adminstrn. Sam Dimas (Calif.) Community Hosp., 1978-79; dir. nursing adminstrn. Doctors Hosp., Pinole, Calif., 1979—. Bd. govs.

St. Paul div. Minn. affiliate Am. Heart Assn.; mem. senate and student bd. U. Minn., 1977; mem. adv. com. Contra Costa County Regional Occupational Program. Mem. East Bay Nursing Adminstrs. Council, Flying Samaritans Internat., Calif. Soc. Nursing Service Adminstrs. Home: 6 Eagle Gap Rd Ignacio CA 94947 Office: Doctors Hosp 2151 Appian Way Pinole CA 94564

LEWIS, EVELYN LUCILE, home economist; b. Wichita, Kans., Jan. 25, 1923; d. James Walter and Edith May (Yoho) Rolf; B.S., Okla. Bapt. U., 1949; M.A., No. Ariz. U., 1967; Ed.D., Ariz. State U., 1979; children by previous marriage—Carol Diane, Milton Wayne. Tchr., Navajo Reservation, Ariz., 1946-48; tchr. elem. sch., high sch. home econs. Came Verde (Ariz.) Schs., 1952-57; tchr. Wellton (Ariz.) Elem. Sch., 1957-59; tchr. home econs. Antelope Union High Sch., Wellton, 1959-69; assoc. prof. home econs. No. Ariz. U., Flagstaff, 1969—; mem. adv. bd. Ariz. Future Homemakers Am., 1971-74. Mem. Gov.'s Conf. on Marriage and the Family, 1978. Delta Kappa Gamma scholar, 1976-77. Mem. Ariz. Home Econs. Assn. (Outstanding Tchr. award 1974), Am. Home Econs. Assn., Am. Vocat. Assn., Kappa Delta Pi, Delta Kappa Gamma, Phi Delta Kappa, Pi Lambda Theta, Phi Kappa Phi, PEO, Phi Upsilon Omicron. Baptist. Author: Housing Decisions, 1978, 80. Office: Box 6003 No Ariz U Flagstaff AZ 86011

LEWIS, FLORA, journalist; b. Los Angeles; d. Benjamin and Pauline (Kallin) Lewis; B.A., UCLA, 1941; M.S., Columbia U., 1942; LL.D., Princeton U., 1981; m. Sydney Gruson, Aug. 17, 1945 (div.); children—Kerry, Sheila, Lindsey. Reporter, Los Angeles Times, 1941, A.P., N.Y., Washington, London, 1942-46; free lance or contract for Observer, Economist, Financial Times, France-soir, Time Mag., N.Y. Times Mag., London, Warsaw, Berlin, Hague, Mexico City, Tel Aviv, 1946-54, Prague, Warsaw, 1956-58; editor McGraw-Hill, N.Y.C., 1955; bur. chief Washington Post, Bonn, London, N.Y.C., 1958-66; syndicated columnist Newsday, Paris, N.Y.C., 1967-72; bur. chief N.Y. Times, Paris, 1972-80, European diplomatic corr., 1976-80, fgn. affairs columnist, 1980—; Arthur D. Morse fellow in communications and society Aspen Inst. for Humanistic Studies, 1977. Decorated chevalier Legion d'Honneur; recipient awards for best interpretation fgn. affairs, 1956, best reporting fgn. affairs 1960 Overseas Press Club, Columbia Journalism Sch. 50th Anniversary Honor award, 1963; award for disting. diplomatic reporting George Washington U. Sch. Fgn. Service, 1978. Mem. Phi Beta Kappa. Author: Case History of Hope, 1958, Red Pawn, 1964, One of Our H-Bombs is Missing, 1967. Contbr. to anthologies, books, mags. Office: NY Times Foreign News Desk 229 W 43d St New York NY 10036 also NY Times 3 Rue Scribe Paris 9e France *

LEWIS, GLADYS SHERMAN, nurse, educator; b. Wynnewood, Okla., Mar. 20, 1933; d. Andrew and Minnie Elva (Halsey) Sherman; R.N., St. Anthony's Sch. Nursing, 1953; student Okla. Bapt. U., 1953-55; A.B., Tex. Christian U., 1956; postgrad. Southwestern Bapt. Theol. Sem., 1959-60, Escuela de Idiomas, San Jose, Costa Rica, 1960-61, Central (Okla.) State U., 1982—; m. Wilbur Curtis Lewis, Jan. 28, 1955; children—Karen, David, Leanne, Cristen. Mem. nursing staff various facilities, Okla., 1953-57; instr. nursing, med. missionary Bapt. mission and hosp., Paraguay, 1961-70; vice-chmn. edn. commn. Paraguay Bapt. Conv., 1962-65; sec. bd. trustees Bapt. Hosp., Paraguay, 1962-65; chmn. personnel com., handbook and policy book officer Bapt. Mission in Paraguay, 1967-70; trustee Southwestern Bapt. Theol. Sem., 1974—, chmn. student affairs com., 1976-78, vice-chmn. bd. 1978—; partner Las Amigas Tours; writer, conference leader, campus lectr., 1959—. Active Democratic party; leader Girl Scouts U.S.A., 1965-75; Okla. co-chmn. Nat. Religious Com. for Equal Rights Amendment, 1977-79; tour host Meier Internat. Study League. Mem. AAUW, Evang. Women's Caucus, Am. Nurses Assn., Internat., Am. colls. surgeons women's auxiliaries, Okla. State, Okla. County med. auxiliaries, Nat. Women's Polit. Caucus, Okla. Women's Polit. Caucus. Author religious instructional texts in English and Spanish; editor Sooner Physician's Heartbeat; contbr. articles to So. Bapt. and secular periodicals. Home: 14501 N Western Ave Edmond OK 73034

LEWIS, HARRIET BURLINGAME, state legislator, archaeologist; b. Lewiston, Maine, Feb. 7, 1951; d. William Burlingame and Joyce Elizabeth (Murphy) L.; B.A., Wellesley Coll., 1973; M.A., U.Minn., 1975, postgrad., 1975—. Grad. asst. U. Minn., 1974-78, staff mem. several archaeol. excavations, 1974—; mem. Maine Ho. of Reps., 1980—; tchr. Auburn (Maine) Sch. System. McMillian travel grantee, 1978; U. Minn. spl. grantee, 1978. Mem. Am. Inst. Archaeology, Am. Legis. Exchange Council, Maine Organic Farming and Gardening Assn. Republican. Home: Maple Hill Auburn ME 04210 Office: State House Augusta ME 04333

LEWIS, HELEN COALE, clin. social worker; b. Albany, Ga., Apr. 12, 1944; d. Allen Roberts and Louella (Meade) Coale; B.A. summa cum laude, Gettysburg Coll., 1966; M.S.W., U. Ga., 1969; m. David J. Lewis, Sept. 29, 1972; children—Shinae Karen, Myung. Clin. social worker Child Service and Family Counseling Center, Atlanta, 1969-72, Ga. Regional Hosp., Atlanta, 1972-73; dir. Central De Kalb Children's Center, Decatur, Ga., 1973-79; owner, dir. Atlanta Area Child Guidance Clinic, 1979—; mem. child and adolescent com. Gov.'s Adv. Council on Mental Health and Mental Retardation; adj. faculty U. Ga. Sch. Social Work. Vol. various positions Unitarian Ch. Mem Acad. Cert. Social Workers, Nat. Assn. Social Workers, Am. Assn. Marriage and Family Therapists (clin., approved supr.), Phi Beta Kappa. Democrat. Author: All About Families: The Second Time Around, 1980. Home: 1058 Rosewood Dr NE Atlanta GA 30306 Office: 2531 Briarcliff Rd NE Suite 215 Atlanta GA 30329

LEWIS, HELEN PHELPS HOYT, assn. exec.; b. Lakewood, N.J., Dec. 27, 1902; d. John Sherman and Ethel Phelps (Stokes) Hoyt; A.B., Bryn Mawr, 1923; M.A., Columbia, 1925; m. Bryon Stookey, May 11, 1929 (dec. Oct. 1966); children—John Hoyt, Lyman Brumbaugh, Byron; m. 2d, Robert James Lewis, Aug. 5, 1971. Mem. bd. mgrs. Christodora House Settlement, N.Y.C., 1927-38, 1st v.p., 1929-38; mem. nat. bd. YWCA, 1927-30; mem. womens adv. council N.Y. Bot. Gardens, 1952—; mem. nursing com. Columbia-Presbyn. Med. Center, 1944-54; trustee Columbia-Presbyn. Med. Center, 1969—; mem. women's aux. Neurol. Inst., 1939—, chmn., 1949-54; mem. womens exec. comn. United Hosp. Fund, 1951-64; vice chmn. womens campaign com., 1961-62, vice chmn. womens exec. com., 1963-64; pres. gen. Colonial Dames Am., 1953-56; pres. Darien Garden Club, 1935-38; pres. Millbrook Garden Club; bd. dirs. Met. Opera Guild, 1971—. Mem. Daus. of the Cincinnati. Republican. Presbyterian. Club: Colony (gov. 1954-76, sec. 1956-59, 69-71, v.p. 1969-71, pres. 1972-76, chmn. membership com. 1956-71). Home: 580 Park Ave New York City NY 10021

LEWIS, JANE ANN, mental health educator; b. Mpls., Jan. 16, 1933; d. Edwin H. and Gertrude (Kirby) L.; student Pa. State U., 1951-53; B.S., U. Ga., 1955; M.P.H., U. Minn., 1961; postgrad. Emory U., 1959. Tchr., St. Thomas More Sch., Decatur, Ga., 1955-59; pub. health edn. cons. Ga. Dept. Pub. Health, Atlanta, 1959-68; mental health educator San Francisco Dept. Pub. Health, 1968-69, Santa Clara County Dept. Pub. Health, 1970—; lectr. San Francisco State U., 1970—; cons. Mental Health Materials Center, N.Y., 1967-68. Fellow Am. Pub. Health Assn.; mem. AAUW, Am. Home Econs. Assn., Pub. Health Assn. No. Calif. (editor newsletter 1976—), Soc. Pub. Health Educators, No. Calif. Soc. Pub. Health Educators (nat. rep. 1977-8, pres.-elect 1982), Internat. Union Health Edn., Chimes, Phi Upsilon Omicron (treas. 1954-55), Chi Omega (sec. 1954-55), Phi Kappa Phi. Home: 4 Salt Landing Tiburon CA 94920 Office: 2220 Moorpark Ave San Jose CA 95128

LEWIS, JENNIFER ROSE, utility co. exec. lobbyist; b. Birmingham, Ala., Jan. 10, 1947; d. John Davis and Rose Louise (Twinn) Shacklett; B.A. in Bus. Adminstrn., Nat. U., 1979; m. Fred G. Lewis, Nov. 19, 1978; 1 stepdau., Lynn Ellyn. Mktg. rep. Pacific Telephone, San Diego, San Francisco, 1967-68; Master Charge rep. So. Calif. 1st Nat. Bank, San Diego, Orange, Los Angeles, 1968-71; customer service rep., teleprocessing design rep., customer info. supr., collections supr., customer service supr. San Diego Gas & Electric Co., 1971-80, bus. cons. and lectr. on oral communication-bus. and politics, sr. regulatory affairs rep., 1980—; sec., chief fin. officer Fred Lewis Prodns., Inc. Bd. govs. Arthritis Found., mem. exec. com., fed., state lobbyist, chmn. govt. affairs com., 1979-81, mem. speakers corps., 1978-81; mem. Mayor's Adv. Com., 1982; active United Way, 1979; bd. dirs. Nat. Friends of Arthritis Found. Mem. Nat. Alliance of Businessmen (active jobs campaign 1975-76), Alpha Phi Alumnae. Clubs: Balboa Tennis, San Diego Tennis Patrons. Home: 1413 Camino Zalce San Diego CA 92111 Office: 101 Ash St San Diego CA 92111

LEWIS, JO, travel agt.; b. Okla., Aug. 24, 1937; d. Lee Scott and Helen Julia (Kannon) Lewis; student psychology Tulsa U., 1955-56; 1 dau., Sydnie Pilkington Stingley. With Pacesetter Travel Service, Tulsa, 1969—, owner, pres., chief exec. officer, 1972—; mem. airline adv. bds. Pan Am., TWA, Brit. Caledonia, Frontier, Continental; an organizer curriculum for travel and tourism courses Tulsa Jr. Coll.; adv. bd. Norwegian Carribean Lines. Bd. dirs. Downtown Tulsa. Mem. Am. Soc. Travel Agts., Am. Mgmt. Assn., Tulsa C. of C. (dir. conv. and visitors div.), Internat. Visitors, Bon Vivants. Republican. Clubs: Tulsa, Shadow Mountain Tennis and Racquet, Williams Plaza Courte; Arts and Humanities. Author articles in field. Home: 2748 E 22d Pl Tulsa OK 74114 Office: William Center 2d St Level Tulsa OK 74103

LEWIS, LINDA DONELLE, neurologist, educator; b. Columbus, Ohio, Nov. 27, 1939; d. Donald Peter and Ann Elizabeth (Karn) Lewis; B.S., Bethany Coll., 1961, D.Sc. (hon.), 1981; M.D., W.Va. U., 1965; m. Gary Gambuti, Oct. 6, 1979. Practice medicine specializing in neurology, N.Y.C., 1971—; asst. prof. neurology Coll. Physicians and Surgeons, Columbia U., N.Y.C., from 1971, now assoc. clin. prof., assoc. dean student affairs, 1979—; cons. in field; mem. N.Y. State Bd. for Profl. Med. Conduct, 1979—. Recipient Outstanding Teaching award Columbia U., 1977. Mem. AMA (nat. com. on med. edn.), N.Y. State Med. Soc. (del.), New York County Med. Soc., N.Y.C. Med. Soc., Am. Assn. Med. Colls., Am. Assn. Neurology, AAAS. Contbr. articles to sci. jours. Home: 320 Central Park W New York NY 10025 Office: 710 W 168th St New York NY 10032

LEWIS, LORAINE RUTH, music tchr.; b. Vernal, Utah, July 22, 1921; d. Perrie Benjamin and Hazel (Bentley) Galbreath; B.S.L., Missionary Bible Coll., Tabor, Iowa, 1947; B.S. in Edn., Marion (Ind.) Coll., 1949; postgrad. Walla Walla Coll., 1967-70, Eastern Wash. State Coll., 1970-81, Central Wash. State Coll., 1970-81, Whitworth Coll., 1975 Seattle Pacific U., 1976-77, Ft. Wright Coll., 1980-81, Gonzaga U., 1980-81, Pacific Luth. U., 1980-81; m. Jesse Dale Lewis, Apr. 12, 1951; children—Nancy Loraine, Dale Delbert, Paul Jeffrey. Printer, linotype operator various printing and pub. cos., 1941-56; with Prosser Printing Co. (Wash.), 1956-66, 75-76; tchr. Prosser (Wash.) Consol. Sch. Dist., 1966—; pvt. music tchr. Named Outstanding Female Linotype Operator Bus. and Profl. Women's Orgn., 1960; named Outstanding Woman Prosser Ch. of the Nazarene, 1978. Mem. NEA, Wash., Prosser edn. assns. Specialist in edn. for migrant children. Home: 1914 Highland Dr Prosser WA 99350 Office: 832 Park Ave Prosser WA 99350

LEWIS, LORRI JENKS, psychotherapist, clin. social worker; b. Barrington, R.I., Jan. 21, 1952; d. Albert James and Joyce Marie (Kienzle) L.; A.S., Cazenovia Coll., 1972; B.A., Syracuse U., 1974, M.S.W., 1976. Counseling, therapist Catholic Charities, Syracuse, N.Y., 1976-78; coordinator residential program Elmcrest Children's Center, Syracuse, 1978-79; freelance artist, writer, psychotherapist, Syracuse, 1979; research asst. Syracuse U., 1980; pvt. practice psychotherapy, Syracuse, 1980—; dir. counseling services Epilepsy Found. Am., Syracuse, 1980; psychiat. social worker, outpatient psychiat. services Community Gen. Hosp., Syracuse, 1981—. Bd. dirs. Epilepsy Found. Am., 1975-79. Mem. Acad. Cert. Social Workers, Nat. Assn. Social Workers, Mental Health Assn., Holistic Health Assn., AAUW. Episcopalian. Author: A Child's Guide to Drugs, 1974. Office: Community Gen Hosp Outpatient Psychiat Services Broad Rd Syracuse NY 13215

LEWIS, LOUISE HOERMANN, photographer; b. Albuquerque, June 30, 1942; d. Clarence Ernest and Helen Louise (Beatty) Hoermann; B.S., U. N.Mex., 1964, M.A., 1970; m. Stewart A. Lewis, June 15, 1962. Caseworker, Bernalillo County Welfare Dept., Albuquerque, 1965-67; dist. sales mgr. Am. Photograph Corp., 1967-74; comml. photographer, custom black and white photo printer, Albuquerque, 1974—; co-owner Lewis Photographics, 1974—; ofcl. chpt. documentary photographer Albuquerque chpt. NOW, 1977—, N.Mex. Internat. Women's Year Conf., 1977; represented in permanent collections UN, Smithsonian Instn.; group exhbns. include N.Mex. chpt. Internat. Women's Year Conf. Art Show, 1977. Vol. counselor Albuquerque Suicide and Crisis Prevention Center, 1968; active numerous women's rights programs. Asso. mem. Profl. Photographers Assn. N.Mex. Club: Duke City React. Contbr. articles to nat. mags. Address: 1715 Solano St NE Albuquerque NM 87110

LEWIS, MARGUERITE GARBER, civic worker; b. nr. Bellville, Ohio, July 23, 1911; d. Horatio Seymour and Sylvia (Swank) Garber; B.A., Coll. of Wooster, 1933; M.A., U. Mich., 1936; postgrad. Northwestern U., 1937; m. William Leroy Lewis, June 16, 1937; children—Sylvia Jane, Thomas Leroy, David Garber, Catherine Carol, Linda Evelyn. Tchr., 1933-39. Troop leader Girl Scouts U.S.A., 1960-61, chmn. Am. Field Service, 1962-63; bd. mgrs. N.Y. State Congress Parents and Tchrs., 1962-65, Tex. Congress, 1973; mem. Larchmont-Mamaroneck Motion Picture Council, 1944—, pres., 1957-59; mem. Fedn. Motion Picture Councils, 1960—; nat. conf. chmn., 1961, nat. pres., 1965-67; radio and TV chmn. Ft. Worth City Council PTAs 1967-70; dir. communications Ninth Dist. PTA (Calif.), 1976-79, mass media chmn., 1979-81; moderator weekly TV program Parents in Action, KTVT, 1967-73; co-ordinator community services course, div. spl. courses Tex. Christian U., 1969-73; mem. exec. bd., editor newsletter San Diego State U. Women's Club, 1974-79, pres., 1977-79, publicity chmn., 1979-81; mem. Ams. Abroad selection com. Patrick Henry chpt. Am. Field Service, 1974-80, mem. area selection com., 1978; public TV vol. KPBS, 1976—; hon. life mem. N.Y. State Congress Parents and Tchrs., 1959, Tex. Congress, 1971, Nat. Congress, 1973. Recipient Disting. Alumni award Coll. Wooster, 1971. Mem. AAUW, Delta Sigma Rho, Pi Kappa Delta. Clubs: Wooster, Womans. Presbyterian Editor, Newsreel, 1965-67. Home: 6254 Cabaret St San Diego CA 92120

LEWIS, MARIAN ELIZABETH, systems analyst; b. Washington, June 6, 1939; d. Samuel and Margarette Ann (Simms) Jenifer; A.S.B.A., Southeastern U., Washington, 1975, B.S.B.A., 1976; M.B.A., City Coll., Seattle, 1981; children—Joe, Darwin Randolph, Roderick Michael, Yolanda Anita. Keypunch operator, supr. Bank of Am., San Francisco, 1961-64, Boeing Co., Seattle, 1964-66; data processing supr. Group Hosp., Washington, 1966-70; keytape operator Dept. Commerce, 1971-73, adminstrv. asst., 1973-77; systems analyst Boeing Co., Seattle, 1978—; pres. MAR-I-Gold; software cons.; tchr. Tng. dir. Boy Scouts Am., 1970-77; v.p. Bd. Edn. Catholic Sector, Washington, 1975-77; dir. Youth Choir, 1979—. Served with USAF, 1957-60, Res., 1976—. Mem. Am. Mgmt. Assn., Mark IV Systems Group (sec. 1979-80), Nat. Office Black Caths., Inner-City Youth (dir.). Roman Catholic. Club: Toastmistress (pres. 1975-76). Home: 1922 18th Ave S Seattle WA 98144 Office: Boeing Kent Benaroya Bldg 7-48-12 Kent WA 98031

LEWIS, MARILYN STOUGHTON, state legislator; b. Phila., July 19, 1931; d. Russell S. and Bernice (Bernard) Stoughton; student Harcum Jr. Coll.; m. Andrew L. Lewis, Jr.; children—Karen Lewis Sacks, Russell S., Andrew L. Mem. Pa. Ho. Reps., 1978—. Republican committeewoman; alt. del. Rep. Nat. Conv., 1976; den mother Boy Scouts Am.; bd. dirs. Sr. Adult Center. Lic. pilot. Office: Pa Ho Reps State Capitol Harrisburg PA 17120

LEWIS, MARY ANN, state legislator; b. Chgo., Nov. 6, 1916; m. Allen I. Lewis, Sept. 8, 1946; children—David I., Mark C. Complaint corr. Spiegel, Inc., Chgo., 1934-42; adminstrv. clk. Fed. Civil Service, U.S. Army, Chgo., 1942-45, USN, Honolulu, 1945; dist. loan asst. FHA, Concord, N.H., 1969-79; mem. N.H. Ho. of Reps., 1981—. Mem. Hopkinton Republican Com., 1964-69; del. Constl. Conv., 1964; fin. chmn. Contoocook Meth. Ch., lay leader, 1978-82. Republican. Methodist. Club: Owl's. Home: Cedar St Contoocook NH 03229

LEWIS, MARY ELLEN, psychotherapist, cons.; b. Green Bay, Wis., Nov. 17, 1948; d. Lawrence Edward, Jr., and Irene Marie (Mumm) L.; B.A. in Sociology, U. Wis., Madison, 1970, M.S.S.W., 1972; m. Thomas Duncan Nagel, May 8, 1976. Psychotherapist Central Comprehensive Mental Health Center, Centralia, Ill., 1972-75, clin. dir., 1975-76; psychotherapist Family Counseling, Aurora, Ill., 1977-80, dir. individual and family counseling div., 1980—; pvt. practice psychotherapy; counseling cons.; clin. instr. grad. students. Program chmn. Kane County NOW; adv. bd. YWCA, Aurora. Cert. sch. social worker, parent effectiveness tng. instr., Ill. Mem. Women in Mgmt., Women in Networking (adv. bd.), Nat. Assn. Social Workers, Acad. Cert. Social Workers, Am. Assn. Ethical Hypnotists, Am. Assn. Sex Educators, Counselors and Therapists (cert. sex counselor). Home: 1791 Lily St Aurora IL 60505

LEWIS, MARY THERESE, robotic engr.; b. Blue Island, Ill., June 21, 1951; d. Christian Henry and Marie Anne (Corcoran) Berns; B.S. in Math. with highest honors, U. Ill., 1975; M.S. in Physics, U. Chgo., 1978; m. Richard W. Lewis, Feb. 16, 1978. Lead engr. research and devel. robotics and artificial intelligence Boeing Mil. Airplane Co., Wichita, Kans., 1978—. Mem. Am. Assn. Artificial Intelligence, Robotics Internat. (sr.), Phi Kappa Phi. Home: 6359 S Clifton St Derby KS 67037 Office: 3801 S Oliver St Wichita KS 67210

LEWIS, MONICA, singer, actress; b. Chgo., May 5, 1930; d. Leon and Jessica Lewis; student Hunter Coll., N.Y.C., 1947; m. Jennings Lang, Jan. 1, 1956; 1 son, Rocky. Radio singer, 1940-50, film appearances, 1950—, including Charlie Varrick, 1974, Earthquake, 1976, Airport '77, 1978, Roller Coaster, 1979, Concorde/Airport '79, 1980, Zero to Sixty, 1980, Nunzio, 1981; rec. artist Capitol Records, Columbia Records, 1946—. Patron, Los Angeles Museum, Los Angeles Philharm. Mem. AFTRA, Screen Actors Guild, ASCAP, Musicians Union. Composer, lyricist: World of Slow, 1980. Office: 12214 Viewcrest Rd Studio City CA 91604

LEWIS, NANCY, publicist; b. Northampton, Mass., Aug. 29, 1948; d. Donald Alexander and Rena (Scogin) Lewis; student U. Mass., Amherst, 1966-69. Account exec. Osborne Assos., N.Y.C., 1977-80, Drucilla Handy Co., N.Y.C., 1980-81; owner, operator Nancy Lewis Public Relations, N.Y.C., 1981—. Mem. Women in Communications, Am. Soc. Interior Designers, Nat. Home Fashions League (chpt. v.p. Jour. Sales 1980, 81, 82). Episcopalian. Contbg. editor Budget Decorating and Remodeling, 1978-79; contbr. articles, photographs to nat. home furnishing and consumer mags. Home: 500 N Duke St Durham NC 27701 Office: 185 Hall St Suite 1612 New York NY 11205

LEWIS, NANCY HARVEY, social worker; b. Hackensack, N.J., Dec. 31, 1930; d. Chester and Lorena Grace (Harvey) L.; B.S., Marshall Coll., W.Va., 1952; M.A. in Social Work, U. Chgo., 1961. Child welfare worker, then child welfare asst. supr. W.Va. Welfare Dept., Huntington, 1956-62; casework supr. ARC, Womack Army Hosp., Ft. Bragg, N.C., 1962-63; hosp. field dir. Beauford (S.C.) Naval Hosp., 1963-64, Ft. Campbell (Ky.) Army Hosp., 1964-65; social worker U. Ky. Med. Center, Lexington, 1965, 66-68; hosp. field dir. ARC, U.S.S. Repose, Vietnam, 1965-66; asst. prof. U. Tenn. Sch. Social Work, Nashville, 1968-71; casework supr. Mobile County Dept. Pensions and Security, Mobile, 1971-75, supr. child welfare, 1975—; adv. com. Wilmer Hall, Mobile, 1979; mem. Child Abuse Workshop Com., 1978-79, Family Violence Com., 1979—; cons., speaker in field. Bd. dirs. Mobile Mental Health Assn., 1980—, Joe Jefferson Players, 1973-77, 81-82. Mem. Nat. Assn. Social Workers (unit chmn. 1979-81), Residential Care Assn. (exec. com. 1978-79), Child Welfare League Am. (conf. treas. 1972), Ala. Child Care Assn. Methodist. Home: 2104 Emogene St Mobile AL 36606 Office: PO Box 1906 Mobile AL 36633

LEWIS, ORA MAE ROBERTSON, assn. exec.; b. Hazen, Pa., Sept. 10, 1919; d. William Francis and Mattie Dallas (Penrod) Robertson; R.N., Sacred Heart Hosp. Sch. Nursing, 1940; m. William Charles Lewis, Sr., Apr. 5, 1942; 1 son, William Charles. Operating room asst. supr. Sibley Hosp., Washington, 1940-42; operating room supr. Church Home and Hosp., Balt., 1942-44; med.-surg. supr. Sacred Heart Hosp., Cumberland, Md., 1947-50; tchr.-trainer Md. Nurses Assn., 1950-55; exec. dir. Western Md. chpt. Am. Heart Assn., Cumberland, 1955—. Mem. Md. Gov.'s Com. on Phys. Fitness, Allegheny County Bd. Health; mem., past sec. region I, Md. Emergency Med. System Council. Registered nurse, Md. Fellow Nat. Soc. Heart Assn. Profl. Staff (sec.-treas. 1976), Mid-Atlantic Region Profl. Staff Conf. (past chmn., past sec.); mem. Soc. Md. Heart Assn. Profl. Staff (charter pres.), Sacred Heart Hosp. Alumnae Assn. (past sec.), Beta Sigma Phi (life; Woman of Yr. 1957; past pres.). Republican. Methodist. Home: 804 Elmwood Ln Cumberland MD 21502 Office: Western Md Chpt Am Heart Assn 551 N Centre St Cumberland MD 21502

LEWIS, PAULETTE MARY, tire co. exec.; b. Mt. Holly, N.J., Nov. 7, 1951; d. Paul Arthur and Marie Ann (Rizk) L.; B.S. in Broadcasting, U. Fla., 1973. With Paul Lewis Tire Centers, Inc., Jacksonville, Fla., 1974—, office mgr., 1976-78, advt. and public relations mgr., 1978-79, dir. mktg., 1979-81, gen. mgr., 1981-82, dir. ops., v.p., dir., 1982—; pres., dir. Lewis Internat.; del. Gov.'s Conf. on Small Bus., 1981. Mem. Nat. Tire Dealers and Retreaders Assn., Northside Businessmen's Club, Jacksonville Area C. of C., N.E. Fla. Better Bus. Council (pres. 1982), Nat. Assn. Women Bus. Owners, Jacksonville Women's Network, San Marco Mchts. Assn., Jacksonville Internat. Trade Assn., Arlington Council C. of C. (dir.). Office: 7621 Lem Turner Rd Jacksonville FL 32208

LEWIS, RITA HOFFMAN, plastic products mfg. co. exec.; b. Phila., Aug. 6, 1947; d. Robert John and Helen Anna (Dugan) H.; student Jefferson Med. Coll. Sch. Nursing, 1965-67; m. David J. Lewis, Oct. 4, 1981. Gen. mgr. Sheets & Co., Inc. (now Flower World, Inc.), Woodbury, N.J., 1968-72; dir., exec. v.p., treas. Hoffman Precision Plastics, Inc., Blackwood, N.J., 1973—; guest speaker various civic groups, 1974—. Mem. Com. for Citizens of Glen Oaks (N.J.), 1979—, Gloucester Twp. Econ. Devel. Com., 1981—. Recipient Winning Edge award, 1982. Mem. Sales Assn. Chem. Industry. Roman Catholic. Author: That Part of Me I Never Really Meant to Share, 1979; In Retrospect: Caught Between Running and Loving.

LEWIS, RUBY PAULINE, educator; b. Enfield, Ill., Aug. 8, 1922; d. Luther Rudolph and Clemie Jessie (York) Foley; B.S. in Edn., So. Ill. U., 1963; M.S. in Edn., Ind. State U., 1969; postgrad. So Ill. U., U. Hawaii, 1977; m. Merle Porter (dec. 1944); children—Merle Ann, Sharon Kay; m. 2d, William Lewis, June 24, 1947; children—William II, Brian David. Elem. tchr. Springerton (Ill.) Sch., 1942-43, Nubbin Ridge Sch., Enfield, Ill., 1945-46, Jefferson Sch., Carmi, Ill., 1946-47, Centerville Sch., Carmi, 1960-62, Washington Sch., Carmi, 1962-74, Washington Middle Sch., Carmi, 1974—; coordinator for gifted. Mem. Bus. and Profl. Women, Ill. Edn. Assn., NEA, Ill. Vocat. Home Econs. Assn., Carmi Edn. Assn. (pres. 1973-74, 81-82, negotiator 1981-82). Club: Federated Women's Spirit of Progress (pres. 1976-77). Home: RR 1 Box 206 Enfield IL 62835 Office: 201 W Main St Carmi IL 62821

LEWIS, SALLY BUTZEL (MRS. LEONARD THEODORE LEWIS), civic worker; b. Detroit, June 29, 1912; d. Leo Martin and Caroline (Heavenrich) Butzel; B.A., Vassar Coll., 1934; m. Leonard Theodore Lewis, Apr. 4, 1935 (dec. June 2, 1982); 1 son, Leonard Theodore. Mem. Women's City Club of Detroit, 1932-67, dir., 1935-38; dir., chmn. community services com. Village Club of Birmingham-Bloomfield; dir. Franklin-Wright Settlement, Inc., Detroit, 1939—, pres. 1959-60; trustee Oakland County Children's Aid Soc., 1950-64, Oakland U. Found., 1973-82; mem. exec. com. Detroit Fedn. Settlements, 1961; mem. steering com., women's orgn. United Fund, 1960-61; mem. Oakland planning div. United Community Services, Met. Detroit, 1959-70; membership chmn. Bloomfield Art Assn., Birmingham, Mich.; mem. scholarship com. Meadow Brook Sch. Music, Meadow Brook Festival, Rochester, Mich.; treas. Cranbrook Music Guild, Inc., 1959, dir., 1958-63, sec., 1960-61; mem. women's com. Cranbrook Galleries Art, Bloomfield Hills; mem. exec. com. Meadow Brook Festival, Rochester, Md., 1969-76; mem. Nat. Council Jewish Women, Am. Jewish Com., Women's Assn. Detroit Symphony, Friends Detroit Symphony. Mem. Women's Nat. Farm and Garden Assn. Club: Ibex. Home: 1421 Lochridge Rd Bloomfield Hills MI 48013

LEWIS, SHARI, ventriloquist, puppeteer; b. N.Y.C., Jan. 17, 1934; d. Abraham B. and Ann (Ritz) Hurwitz; student Columbia U.; m. Jeremy Tarcher, Mar. 15, 1958; 1 dau., Mallory. Recorded LP records, Fun in Shariland, Hi Kids, Shari in Storyland; star weekly NBC-TV show The Shari Lewis Show; star weekly TV show BBC, London, 1969-73, weekly TV show for ind. network in Gt. Britain, 1970; writer, producer, star NBC spl. A Picture of Us, 1971; command performance, London, 1970, 73, 78; performer, condr. symphony orchs. throughout U.S. and Can., including Rochester, Buffalo, Vancouver, Pitts.; star pay TV spl. Shari's Christmas Concert with Nat. Arts Center Orch. Can., 1982. Mem. nat. bd. dirs. Girl Scouts U.S.; internat. bd. dirs. Boy Scouts Am.; past pres. Am. Center Films for Children. Winner TV Emmy awards for best local program and outstanding female personality, 1957, for best children's show and outstanding female personality, 1958, 59, as outstanding children's entertainer, 1972-73; Peabody award, 1960; Monte Carlo Internat. TV award, 1961; Radio-TV Mirror award, 1960. Author: Shari Lewis Puppet Book; Fun for the Kids; Folding Paper Puppets; Folding Paper Toys; Dear Shari; Folding Paper Masks; Mcgraw Hill Headstart books (4); Making Easy Puppets; Be Nimble, Be Quick; Tell-It Make-It Book; Magic for Non-Magicians; The Kids-Only Club Book; How Kids Can Really Make Money; Toystore-in-a-Book; Impossible Unless You Know How; Spooky Stuff; Things Kids Collect; The Do It Better Book; Secrets, Signs, Signals & Codes; Magic Show in-a-Book; One Minute Bedtime Stories, 1982. Office: 603 Alta Dr Beverly Hills CA 90210

LEWIS, SUE BLASINGAME, polit. and public relations cons.; b. Miami, Fla., Dec. 3, 1933; d. Earnest LeRoy and Clara Louise (Collins) Blasingame; student public schs.; grad. Realtors Inst., 1973; m. James C. Lewis, Apr. 5, 1952; children—Susan C., James C. III, Douglas C. Saleswoman Claytons' Realty, Winter Park, Fla., 1972-76; polit. aide, 1976, 78, 79, 80; pres. Sue Lewis Cons., Inc., Winter Park, 1980—; speaker in field. Mem. Seminole County Planning and Zoning Commn., 1980—, Seminole County Land Planning Agy., 1981—. Republican. Club: Toastmistresses. Home: 280 Victor Ave Longwood FL 32750 Office: 609 Wymore Rd Winter Park FL 32789

LEWIS, TONI YVONNE, acct.; b. Chgo., Sept. 5, 1950; d. James Hutton and Evia (Earl) Young; B.S. in Acctg., N.Y.U., 1971; M.B.A. in Fin., Columbia U., 1973. From staff acct. to sr. acct. Touche, Ross & Co., C.P.A.s, N.Y.C., 1973-75; spl. asst. to dep. chancellor for bus. N.Y.C. Bd. Edn., 1975-77; ind. fin. cons., 1977-78; mgr. Mitchell/Titus & Co., C.P.A.s, N.Y.C., 1978-81; pvt. practice acctg., N.Y.C., 1982—. Treas., bd. dirs. Nigerian-Am. Friendship Soc. C.P.A., N.Y. Mem. Am. Inst. C.P.A.s, Assn. M.B.A. Execs., Nat. Assn. Black Accts., N.Y. State Soc. C.P.A.s, Delta Sigma Theta. Office: 392 Central Park W New York NY 10025

LEWIS, VIRGINIA ELNORA, mus. dir.; b. Sault Ste. Marie, Ont., Can., Apr. 7, 1907; d. Dan and Katherine (Barres) L.; A.B., U. Pitts., 1931, M.A., 1935; postgrad. Carnegie Inst. Tech., 1932-33. Proofreader, Carnegie Inst. Tech. Press, 1931-33; mem. faculty U. Pitts., 1934—, prof. fine arts, 1957-67, prof. emeritus, 1967—, acting head dept., 1954, 57-58, summers, 1940-63, curator exhbns. Henry Clay Erick fine arts dept., 1946—, head librarian Henry Clay Frick fine arts library, 1963-65, asst. dir. Henry Clay Frick fine arts bldg., 1965-67; dir. Frick Art Mus., Pitts., 1969—; researcher Helen C. Frick Found., 1967-69; dir. Dennis (Mass.) Art Gallery, 1953; cons., dir. Westmoreland County Mus. Art, 1954-56; adv. group 1981 Disting. Performance Awards, Chatham Coll., Pitts. Served as ensign USNR, 1941. Recipient salute Kaufmann's Dept. Store, Pitts., 1974; named Woman of Year, Pitts. Post Gazette, 1956, Disting. Dau. of Pa., 1977. Mem. Soc. Archtl. Historians (dir., chmn. Pitts. chpt. 1956), Coll. Art Assn. Am., Am. Assn. Mus., Pa. Hist. Soc., 100 Friends Pitts. (exec. bd.), Nat. Trust Hist. Preservation (chmn. session 14th ann. meeting), Print council Am., Pitts. plan Arts, Internat. Council Mus., Arts and Crafts Center Pitts., Pitts. Bibliophile Soc., Spl. Libraries Assn., Xylon. Clubs: Women's Press, Zonta, Monday Luncheon (pres. 1970—), Women's City (Pitts.), Author: Andrey Avinoff: The Man, 1953; Russell Smith: Romantic Realist, 1956; also articles, exhbn. catalogues, revs.; contbr. New Cath. Ency. Office: Frick Art Museum 7227 Reynolds St Pittsburgh PA 15208

LEWIS, VIRGINIA STOLPE (MRS. ELROY ROBERTSON LEWIS), home economist, educator, author; b. Topaz, Idaho, Mar. 20, 1919; d. Brady and Amelia (Feller) Stolpe; B.S., Utah State U., 1941; postgrad. U. Wyo., 1951, Mont. State U., Tex. Womens U., 1965; M.S., Oreg. State U., 1962; m. Elroy Robertson Lewis, June 24, 1943; children—Carolyn Lewis Kay, Stephen Stolpe, Marie Lewis Harward, Philip Stolpe, Kay Lewis Haueter and Kent Stolpe (twins). Home-economist Cowley (Wyo.) High Sch., 1941-43; tchr. home econs. public schs., Byron, Wyo., 1956-62; mem. faculty Utah State U., Logan, 1962—, asso. prof. home econs. and consumer edn., 1975—. Leader, 4H, 1943-50. Utah State U. grantee, 1974-76. Mem. Am. Home Econs. Assn., Utah Home Econs. Assn., Am. Assn. Housing Educators, Faculty Women's League, Am. Soc. Interior Design. Mormon. Author: Comparatave Clothing Construction Techniques, 1976; Consumer Buying and Design of Home Furnishings, revised, 1980. Home: 1776 E 1080 N Logan UT 84321 Office: 303C Coll Family Life Utah State U Logan UT 84322

LEWIS, WANDA ELLA, nurse; b Portsmouth, Ohio, June 12, 1927; d. George Frank and Emma Abigail (Rice) Jarrell; R.N., Christ Hosp. Sch. Nursing, 1951; m. Ramon Lamar Lewis, May 2, 1960 (div.); children—Kris, Gail Jean. Supr. nurses Clinton Meml. Hosp., Wilmington, Ohio, 1951-53; staff nurse Pima County Hosp., Tucson, 1953-55; field nurse Bur. Indian Affairs-Alaska Native Service, Bethel, 1955-58; stewardess Wien Airlines, Fairbanks, Alaska, 1958-61; admissions supr. Providence Hosp., Anchorage, 1972-75; staff nurse, charge nurse Spring View Center, Springfield, Ohio 1975-80; dir. nurses Good Shepherd Nursing Home, 1980-81; supr. St. John's Nursing Home, Springfield, 1981—. Active with mentally retarded, 1975-80; vol. instr. English, Udornthani, Thailand and Vientiene, Laos, 1965-67. Republican. Home: 1625 Avodire Dr Apt 6 Springfield OH 45504 Office: 3130 E National Rd Springfield OH 45505

LEWIS, WANDA FAYE, nurse, hosp. adminstr.; b. Osceola, Mo., Feb. 20, 1947; d. Chalmers and Viola Madge (Ralston) Howell; B.S. in Nursing, U. Mo., Columbia, 1977; M.S., Tex. Woman's U., 1979; m. Kenneth Ray Lewis, Dec. 19, 1976. Staff nurse CCU, U. Mo. Med. Center, 1971-72, U. Tex. Med. Center, Galveston, 1972; instr. in nursing edn. Galveston Coll., 1972-74; staff nurse CCU, St. Luke's Hosp., Houston, 1976-77, head nurse CCU, 1978-79; instr. in critical care Vet.'s Med. Center, Houston, 1977-81; dir. edn., infection control and quality assurance Raleigh Hills Gen. Hosp., Houston, 1981—; cons. Tex. Inst. Rehabilitative Medicine; tchr. trainer for cardiopulmonary resuscitation. Mem. Am. Heart Assn., Am. Assn. Critical Care Nurses. Republican. Research on effect of sleep-deprivation-post cardiovascular surgery, 1975. Home: 10407 Crescent Moon Houston TX 77064 Office: 6160 S Loop E Houston TX 77087

LEWIS, ZANNETTE ELOISE, hosp. personnel exec.; b. Richmond, Va., July 19, 1946; d. Otto Ellis and Gladys Elizabeth (Cooper) L.; B.A. in Sociology, Howard U., 1969; M.A. in Indsl. and Organizational Psychology, U. New Haven, 1981; m. Robert Johnson Moore, Mar. 9, 1969; 1 son, Tchad Jemahl. Project coordinator City of New Haven Redevel. Agy., 1970-72; personnel rep. Yale-New Haven Hosp., 1972—; organizational devel. cons. Episcopal Diocese Conn., 1980—. Bd. dirs. YWCA Greater New Haven, 1979—, Opportunities Industrialization Center Greater New Haven, 1978-80; mem. New Haven Sch. System Vocat. Edn. and Career Council, 1979-81. Recipient Women in Leadership Achievement award YWCA, 1979, Mut. Respect award Yale-New Haven Hosp., 1979, Service Above Self award Rotary Club, Hamden, Conn., 1979, William Spurgeon award Boy Scouts Am., 1980. Mem. Howard U. Alumni Assn. Episcopalian. Home: 32 Heather Rd Hamden CT 06518 Office: 330 Cedar St New Haven CT 06504

LEWIS-STONE, CAROLYN JEAN, psychiat. social worker; b. Lexington, Ky., May 4, 1948; d. George A. and Nannie M. (Lewis) Stone; B.A., Ky. State U., 1970; M.S.W., U. Mich., 1974. With Fayette County (Ky.) Public Schs., 1970-71, Ky. Dept. Child Welfare, 1971-72; counselor U. Mich. Office of Counseling Services, Ann Arbor, 1974—. Mem. Nat. Assn. Social Workers, Acad. Cert. Social Workers, Ann Arbor Civic Theatre. Roman Catholic. Office: 3100 Mich Union Bldg Ann Arbor MI 48109

LEWIS-UNDERHILL, ELIZABETH BETTYE, psychologist, educator; b. Port Washington, N.Y., Feb. 27, 1922; d. Llewellyn and Dorothy Guillette (Walter) Power; student Pa. State U., 1945, U. So. Calif., 1949; B.A., Chapman Coll., 1965, M.A., 1967; Ph.D., U.S. Internat. U., 1975; m. Bradford Burleigh Underhill, Dec. 18, 1943; children—Robert, Walter; m. 2d, William Horatio Lewis, June 22, 1949; children—Sanderson, William, Jacqueline, Terri-Bess; m. 3d, Bradford Burleigh Underhill, Sept. 16, 1979. Dir., Westview PreSch., Venice, Calif., 1952-54; tchr. LaPlaya PreSch., Culver City, Calif., 1956-59; dir. Tustin Community PreSch. Tustin, Calif., 1959-62; mem. publicity dept. World Campus Afloat, Chapman Coll., 1965, prof. psychology and edn., 1968; prof. sociology Orange Coast Coll., Coast Mesa, Calif., 1967; prof. psychology Santa Ana (Calif.) Coll., 1968—, coordinator child devel., 1969, chmn. child devel. dept., 1973—, pres. faculty senate; prof. early childhood edn. field div. LaVerne (Calif.) Coll., 1975-80; curriculum project mgr. Mass. State Coll. System, Worcester, 1980—; cons. in field. Served with U.S. Navy, 1942-45. Recipient spl. award Head Start, 1971—. Mem. Orange County Children's Services Council (past pres.), Am. Community Coll. Early Childhood Educators (pres.), Orange County Child Abuse Council, Nat. Assn. Edn. Young Children, AAUP, Am. Sociol. Assn., Calif. Articulation Conf., Early Childhood Task Force, Edn. Commn. States, Phi Delta Epsilon. Club: Toastmasters (dist. gov.). Pub., editor Early Childhood Edn. Options. Home: 255 North Rd #110 Chelmsford MA 01824 Office: Learning Center 15 Court Sq Boston MA 02108

LEWITZKY, BELLA, dance co. dir., choreographer; b. Los Angeles, Jan. 13, 1916; d. Joseph and Nina (Ossman) L.; student San Bernardino Valley Jr. Coll., 1933-34; m. Newell Taylor Reynolds, June 22, 1940; 1 dau., Nora Elizabeth Reynolds. Co-founder, co-dir. Dance Theatre, Los Angeles, 1946-50; founder, dir. Dance Assos., Los Angeles, 1951-55; founder, artistic dir. Bella Lewitzky Dance Co., Los Angeles, 1966—; choreographer, 1948—; choreographer numberous dances, most recent being: Game Plan, 1973, Spaces Between, 1974, Five, 1974, V.C.O., 1975, Greening, 1976, Inscape, 1976, Pas de Bach, 1977, Recesses, 1979, Rituals, 1979, Suite Satie, 1980, Changes and Choices, 1981, Confines, 1982, Continuum, 1982; chairperson contemporary dance dept. U. So. Calif., Idyllwild, 1956-72, mem. dept. adv. panel, 1972—; founder Sch. Dance, Calif. Inst. Arts, 1969, dean, 1969-72; mem. artists-in-schs. adv. panel Nat. Endowment for Arts, 1974-75, mem. dance adv. panel, 1974-77, vice chmn., 1974-77; mem. Joint Commn. on Dance and Theater Accreditation, 1979—; cons. Nat. Humanities Faculty, 1974—; mem. Nat. Adv. Bd. for Young Audiences, 1974—; mem. steering com., chairperson dance panel Nat. Arts Awards, Ednl. Testing Service, 1979—; trustee Joyce Theater Found., 1981—; bd. dirs. Center for Music, Drama and Art, 1982—. Recipient Dir.'s award Calif. Dance and Educators Assn., Dance Mag. award, 1978, YWCA Silver Achievement award, 1982; subject of mayoral proclamation, Los Angeles, 1976; Andrew W. Mellon Found. grantee, 1975, 81; John Simon Guggenheim Meml. Found. fellow, 1977-78; Nat. Endowment for Arts grantee, 1979— ; recipient State Senate resolution, 1982. Mem. Am. Arts Alliance (dir. 1977—), Arts, Edn. and Ams. (dir. 1978—), Calif. Assn. Dance Cos. (trustee 1976—), UNESCO Internat. Dance Council, Am. Research Inst.

LEWTER, CATHERINE JANE BOYTER, steel fabrication co. exec.; b. Kilgore, Tex., Nov. 15, 1944; d. Ralph E. and Johney F. (Scott) Boyter; student Cooke County Jr. Coll., 1963-65; degree in acctg. N. Tex. State Coll., 1969; m. Maxey G. Lewter, Jan. 8, 1976; 1 dau., Sherrie Kaye Coker. Acct., Chief Industries, Gainesville, Tex., 1969-70; controller Four Seasons, Inc., Dallas, 1970-73; asst. to controller Lincoln Properties, Dallas, 1973-78; controller Weaver Corp., Dallas, 1978—. Bd. dirs. United Fund, Cooke County, Tex., 1969-70; mem. adv. council Tejas council Girl Scouts U.S.A., Dallas, 1973-74. Mem. Nat. Builders Assn., Dallas County Assn. C.P.A.'s, Bus. and Profl. Woman's Club (sec.-treas. Dallas 1976-77), Beta Sigma Phi. Democrat. Methodist. Office: 3302 Pluto St Dallas TX 75212

LEWTON, KATHLEEN LAREY, hosp. public relations adminstr.; b. Bloomington, Ill., Feb. 27, 1948; d. Fred and Frances H. (White) Larey; B.A., Ill. Wesleyan U., 1970; M.S. in Journalism, Northwestern U., 1977; postgrad. Bowling Green State U., 1979—; m. John C. Lewton, Aug. 29, 1970. Reporter, editor Daily Pantagraph, Bloomington, 1966-71; asst. dir. news service Bowling Green (Ohio) State U., 1971-76; dir. public relations Flower Hosp.-Crestview Center, Sylvania, Ohio, 1977—; public relations cons. Acad. Medicine, Toledo, 1979—. Chmn. bd. dirs. Univ. br. YWCA; mem. project Twin com. Toledo YWCA; bd. dirs. Met. YMCA, 1980—; mem. public relations com. Task Force on Cost Effectiveness, 1979—. Recipient Spl. Achievement award Bowling Green State U., 1975; MacEachren award, cert. of merit Acad. Hosp. Public Relations, 1978; silver award Toledo Advt. Club, 1978; named one of Toledo's Ten Outstanding Young Women, 1979. Mem. Women in Communications Inc. (nat. dir. 1975—, nat. pres. 1980-81), Public Relations Soc. Am. (dist. awards 1978, 79, 80), Ohio Hosp. Assn. (mem. public relations com. 1979—), Ohio Soc. Hosp. Public Relations (dir. 1981—), Ill. Wesleyan U. Alumni Assn. (dir. 1976—, sec. 1979-80), Northwestern U. Alumni, Sigma Delta Chi, Sigma Kappa. Office: Flower Hosp-Crestview Center 5200 Harroun Rd Sylvania OH 43560

LEYDA, JEAN CRAVENS (MRS. VIRGIL WILLIAM LEYDA), author, editor, club woman; b. Granby, Mo., Jan. 15, 1903; d. William A. and Lois (Harmon) Cravens; A.A., Stephens Coll., 1920; B.A., Mt. Holyoke Coll., 1923; M.A. in English Lit., U. Wis., 1930; m. Virgil William Leyda, Aug. 10, 1945; 1 foster son, Leonard Breckler. Tchr. English, Freeport (Ill.) High Sch., 1923-26, head English dept., 1926-27; head English dept. Mishawaka (Ind.) High Sch., 1929-45, dir. English, Mishawaka Jr. and Sr. High Schs., 1938-45; co-author lit. anthologies Scott, Foresman Co., Chgo., 1940-50, editorial staff, after 1945; now ret. Pres., Chandler (Ariz.) Woman's Club, 1954-55, chmn. community service com., 1961-63; edn. chmn. Ariz. Fedn. Women's Clubs, 1955-57. Mem. founding adv. bd. Chandler Pub. Library. Recipient alumnae achievement award Stephens Coll., 1956. Former mem., past pres. Ind. Council Tchrs. English. Mem. Ind. Ret. Tchrs. Assn., Nat. Ret. Tchrs. Assn., DAR, Colonial Dames 17th Century, PEO, Phi Theta Kappa. Democrat. Presbyn. (trustee 1951-53, life elder). Mem. Order Eastern Star, Daus. of Nile. Club: Desert (past pres.). Author: (with others) Enjoying Life through Literature, 1951; Exploring Life through Literature, 1951. Address: 400 N Hartford St Chandler AZ 85224

LEYDEN, DIANE MONCHARSH, sales cons.; b. N.Y.C., Apr. 23, 1950; d. Bernard Jacob and Betty (Chock) Moncharsh Stone; B.S. cum laude, N.Y. U., 1972; postgrad. Adelphi U., 1972-74; m. Brian S. Leyden, Dec. 1, 1977; 1 dau., Lauren Helen. Tchr., N.Y.C. Bd. Edn., 1972-76, also remedial reading specialist; asst. sales promotion mgr. Seagram Overseas Sales Co., N.Y.C., 1977-78, mktg. analyst, 1978-79, sales promotion mgr., 1979-80; sales promotion cons., 1981—. Fund raising corporate capt. United Way, N.Y.C., 1978-79. Mem. Nat. Assn. Female Execs., N.Y. U. Alumni Assn.

LEYLAND, MARY FRANCES CAHILL, govt. ofcl.; b. Bennington, Vt., Aug. 20, 1936; d. John Francis and Mary Agnes (Wilson) Cahill; B.A., Newton Coll. Sacred Heart, 1958; M.Ed., State Coll. Boston, 1967; m. George Pearce Leyland, Oct. 21, 1961. Exec. officer EPA, 1972-77; acting dir. Peace Corps, Washington, 1978-79; asst. dir. adminstrn. and fin. ACTION, Washington, 1977-79; asst. dir. adminstrn. Internat. Devel. Coop. Agy., Washington, 1979—. Roman Catholic. Club: Hay Harbor (Fishers Island, N.Y.).

LEZEAU, GLADYS DAVIS, educator, evangelist; b. N.Y.C., July 25, 1937; d. Robert and Pearl Gertrude (Vaughan) Davis; B.S., State U. N.Y., 1960; M.S., Pace U., 1977; m. Lesly Lezeau, Sept. 10, 1976; 1 son, Leonel. Tchr. adult edn. Yonkers (N.Y.) Bd. Edn., 1960—; nat. evangelist Ch. of God in Christ, 1961-77; founder Women for Christ-Worldwide, 1970; founder Prayer and Praise, 1978, exec. dir., 1978-80; radio evangelist St. Paul's Ch., Westchester, 1968-80; founder, dir. Sun's of God, Inc., 1980—. Recipient award for dedicated service Women for Christ-Worldwide, 1968; Am. Studies fellow Eastern Bapt. Coll., summer 1970. Mem. N.Y. State Home Econs. Assn., Yonkers Fedn. Tchrs. Club: 700. Home: 105 Bruce Ave Yonkers NY 10705 Office: 145 Palmer Rd Yonkers NY 10701

LIANG, PEARL HO-CHENG (MRS. MICHAEL S. WEI), speech pathologist; b. Shanghai, China, Mar. 29, 1944; d. Monte V.C. and Marie (Tong) L.; came to U.S., 1956, naturalized, 1962; B.F.A., Ohio U., 1966; M.A., Tex. Woman's U., 1970; diploma Montessori teaching St. Nicholas Tng. Center, London, 1973; m. Michael S. Wei, Dec. 22, 1973. Speech pathologist Easter Seal Soc., Weston, W.Va., 1966; acting dir. speech, hearing and lang. clinic Montebello State Hosp., Balt., 1966-69; head speech and hearing therapist Suffolk State Sch., Melville, N.Y., 1970-74; speech pathologist Montgomery County Public Schs., Rockville, Md., 1974—; cons. Chinatown tutorial program Washington. Mem. Am. Speech Lang. and Hearing Assn., Council Exceptional Children, Internat. Montessori Soc., Assn. Children With Learning Disabilities, Nat. Assn. Chinese Americans, Kappa Phi, Sigma Alpha Eta. Home: 4505 N Chelsea Ln Bethesda MD 20814 Office: 850 N Washington St Rockville MD 20850

LIBASSI, PATRICIA CAMPBELL, writer; b. Mason City, Iowa, Sept. 29, 1929; d. David Lawrence and Mary Beatrice Campbell; R.N., St. Joseph Hosp. Sch. Nursing, South Bend, Ind., 1949; student Ind. U., U. Buffalo; m. Paul Joseph LiBassi, Aug. 12, 1950; children—Michael, Mark, David, J. Douglas, Patricia Ann, Suzanne. Staff nurse, then night William Coleman Hosp. for Women, 1952; staff nurse Ft. Leavenworth Army Hosp., 1954; with Call for Action, Sta. WIVB-TV, Buffalo, 1976—, co-dir., 1979, dir., 1980—, regional dir., 1980—, dir., Call for Action, Inc., 1980—. Mem. Nat. Writers Club, Action Line Reporters Assn., Am. Film Inst. Home: 4990 Pine Ledge Dr W Clarence NY 14031 Office: 2077 Elmwood Ave Buffalo NY 14207

LIBBY, JUDITH LYNN, lawyer; b. Elgin, Ill., Oct. 20, 1948; d. Jules Leon and Virginia Marie (Marshall) L.; B.A. in English Lit., Roosevelt U., 1970; J.D. with highest distinction (Scholar), John Marshall Law Sch., 1977; m. Richard J. Coffee, II, Feb. 14, 1981. Tchr. humanities Craigmore High Sch., Smithfield, South Australia, Australia, 1971-73; admitted to Ill. bar, 1977; asso. firm Taussig, Wexler & Shaw, Ltd., Chgo., 1977-78; chief counsel Ill. Dept. Ins., Springfield, 1978-80; partner firm Libby & Coffee, Springfield, 1981—. Vice pres. Evening Symphony Guild, Springfield, 1979-81; cons. Ill. Assn. for Deaf. Mem. Am. Bar Assn., Ill. State Bar Assn., Chgo. Bar Assn. Office: 522 E Monroe St Suite 703 Springfield IL 62701

LIBERSON, CATHRYN WALTERS, psychologist; b. Manly, Iowa; d. William George and Beulah Beatrice (Albert) Raftis; B.A., Oklahoma City U., 1960; M.S., U. Okla., 1968; Ph.D., Loyola U. Chgo., 1972; m. Frank Walters, 1941; 1 son; m. 2d, Wladimir T. Liberson, Aug. 31, 1964. Psychology technician VA Hosp., Oklahoma City, 1957-63; research and teaching asst. Loyola U. Med. Center, Maywood, Ill., 1964-69; clin. psychologist S. Fla. State Hosp., Pembroke Pines, 1973; dir. therapeutic services Hollywood (Fla.) Pavilion Psychiat. Hosp., 1974—. Lic. psychologist, Fla. Mem. Am. Psychol. Assn., Fla. Psychol. Assn., Broward and Dade County Psychol. Assn., Broward County Soc. Profl. Psychologists. Democrat. Contbr. articles to profl. jours. Home: 3262 NE 166 St North Miami Beach FL 33160 Office: 4020 Sheridan Rd Hollywood FL 33021

LIBERTY, SUSAN SPENCE, educator; b. Lincoln, Nebr., Sept. 15, 1937; d. William Morton and Catherine (Crancer) Spence; B.A. in Psychology (Regents scholar 1955-59), U. Colo., 1959; M.A. in English, Calif. State U., Northridge, 1971; div.; children—Jay Andrew, Joel Adrian, Jena Sue. Instr., English, Los Angeles Valley Coll., 1971-76, Calif. State U., Northridge, 1970-74; asso. UCLA, 1974-75; instr. directing Tutor Center, Fresno (Calif.) City Coll., 1976—; mem. exec. com. Acad. Senate Calif. Community Colls., 1981-83. Mem. MLA, Calif. Community Coll. Tutorial Assn. (pres. elect 1980, pres. 1981), Calif. Assn. Tchrs. English Speakers Other Langs., Mensa, NOW, Phi Beta Kappa. Democrat. Presbyterian. Author papers in field. Office: 1101 E University St Fresno CA 93741

LIBET, ALICE QUANTE, clin. psychologist; b. Savannah, Ga., Feb. 7, 1949; d. Albert Herman and Anita (Mahany) Quante; B.A. cum laude with gen. honors, (Ga. Regents scholar, Ga. State Tchrs. scholar), U. Ga., 1971, M.S., 1974, Ph.D., 1977; m. Julian Mayer Libet, Nov. 27, 1976; 1 son, Jared Quante. Instr. Ga. Retardation Center, Athens, 1974-75; research psychologist VA Med. Center, Charleston, S.C., 1978-81; clin. psychologist dept. pediatrics Med. U. S.C., Charleston, 1977—. Mem. Am. Psychol. Assn., Charleston Area Psychol. Assn., Psi Chi. Contbr. articles to profl. jours. Office: 171 Ashley Ave Charleston SC 29403

LICATA, LORRAINE, sch. psychologist, educator; b. N.Y.C., May 9, 1944; d. Paul Anthony and Lourdes (Hernández) Licata; B.A. in Sociology, Rutgers U., 1971; M.A. in Ednl. Psychology, Kean Coll. of N.J., 1975. Mental health counselor Coll. of Medicine & Dentistry, Newark, 1971-73; staff psychologist Middlesex County Youth Center, New Brunswick, N.J., 1974-77; sch. psychologist Monroe Twp. Sch., Jamesburg, N.J., 1974—; instr. psychology Georgian Ct. Coll., Lakewood, N.J., 1974—; cons. Middlesex County Ednl. Services, 1979—. Mem. Am. Psychol. Assn., N.J. Psychol. Assn., Sch. Psychologists Assn. N.J. Roman Catholic. Home: 58-02 Fox Run Dr Plainsboro NJ 08536 Office: Forsgate Dr Jamesburg NJ 07731

LICHT, JUDY CAROL, TV anchorwoman; b. N.Y.C.; d. Bernard and Eleanor (Abrams) L.; B.A. in History, Conn. Coll., 1966; M.S. in Broadcast Journalism, Syracuse U., 1967. Producer, writer, broadcaster Sta. WYNE-TV, N.Y.C., 1967-71; program co-host, reporter Sta. KMBC-TV, Kansas City, Mo., 1971-72; reporter Sta. WNEW-TV, N.Y.C., 1972-78, co-anchor, reporter 10 O'Clock News, after 1979; now with WABC-TV, N.Y.C.; reporter Sta. WCBS-TV, N.Y.C., 1978-79. Co-chmn., Mayor's Task Force on Rape, 1980. Recipient Ednl. leadership award Kappa Delta Pi, 1977; Young Women's Town Hall achievement award, 1975; Abraham & Strauss Woman of Year award, 1978; Our Town Otty award, 1977. Contbg. writer, columnist Soho Weekly News, N.Y. Mag. Office: WABC-TV 7 Lincoln Sq New York NY 10023

LICHTENDORF, SUSAN SIEGEL, sci. writer, author; b. N.Y.C., Jan. 16, 1941; d. Harry B. and Mildred (Sharfstein) Siegel; B.A., Queens Coll., City U. N.Y., 1962; postgrad. N.Y. U. Inst. Fine Arts, 1963-64; m. Arthur E. Lichtendorf, Dec. 14, 1969; 1 dau., Victoria Jane. Women's news feature writer L.I. (N.Y.) Press, 1962-66, gen. assignment news reporter, 1966-68; sci. writer nat. office Am. Cancer Soc., N.Y.C., 1968-80; freelance writer books and articles, 1970—; speaker nat. maternal and child health confs., 1979-80; vol. speechwriter ERAmerica, 1976. Mem. Nat. Assn. Sci. Writers, Women in Communications, Authors Guild, Women's Ink, Internat. Childbirth Edn. Assn., Nat. Women's Health Network. Co-author: (with Phyllis Gillis) The New Pregnancy: The Active Woman's Guide, 1979; author: Eve's Journey: The Physical Experience of Being Female, 1982. Contbr. numerous articles to various mags., newspapers. Home and Office: 141 E 89th St New York NY 10028

LICHTI, BARBARA JEAN, accountant; b. Corydon, Ind., Jan. 14, 1942; d. Lester and Evelyn Rose Ferguson; diploma acctg. Bryant and Stratton Bus. Coll., Louisville, 1962; m. Marvin Lichti, Dec. 20, 1963. Acct. sta. WLKY, Louisville, 1962-64; head dept. grain storage Dept. Agr., Champaign, Ill., 1964-68; acct. Larry Buhrmester, Champaign, 1968-73, Armstrong & Acord, C.P.A.s, Champaign, 1973-75; self-employed acct., Champaign, 1976—; sec.-treas., dir. HoHum, Inc., Champaign, 1973—. Mem. Twin Cities Bus. and Profl. Women's Club, Nat. Assn. Tax Practioners, Assn. Bus. Accts. Address: 909 Devonshire St Champaign IL 61820

LICKERMAN, CAROLYN ADLER, councilwoman; b. Cleve., Dec. 21, 1929; d. Emil Herman and Frances Lucille (Reiss) Adler; student Northwestern U., 1948-50; B.S. in Bus. Adminstrn., Ind. U., 1977; m. Howard Wayne Lickerman, Aug. 12, 1950; children—David Simon, Nancy Lickerman Halik, Jo Anne. 5th dist. rep. Columbus (Ind.) City Council, 1976—; dir. Irwin Union Bank & Trust Co.; mem. human devel. policy com. Nat. League Cities, 1979—. Pres. Columbus Redevel. Commn., 1975-76; mem. Columbus Human Rights Commn., 1967-70; founder, pres. Columbus LWV, 1961; bd. dirs. Columbus Pro Musica, 1978—; treas. Tulip Trace council Girl Scouts U.S.A., 1979—; div. chairperson United Way, 1974, vice chmn. fund drive, 1980; pres. Isabel Ritter chpt. Am. Field Service, 1971; mem. William R. Laws Found., 1968-76, pres., 1971; sec. nominating com. Sch. Bd. Nominating Assembly; chmn. Art in Public Places, Columbus City Hall, 1980. Mem. Columbus C. of C. (transp. com.), Beta Gamma Sigma. Democrat. Home: 3354 Woodland Pkwy Columbus IN 47201

LIDA, DENAH, educator; b. N.Y.C., Sept. 9, 1923; d. Haim David and Ephthimia (Semos) Levy; B.A., Hunter Coll., 1943; M.A., Columbia U., 1944; Ph.D., Universidad Nacional Autónoma de México, 1952; m. Raimundo Lida, Dec. 23, 1955. Asst. prof. Spanish, Smith Coll., Northampton, Mass., 1944-53, Sweet Briar Coll., Va., 1954-55, Brandeis U., Waltham, Mass., 1955-62, asso. prof., 1962-67, prof. Spanish and comparative lit., 1967—, chmn. Humanities Council; vis. prof. Harvard U., fall 1959, summer 1971. Bd. dirs. Am. Cancer Soc., Cambridge, Mass. Radcliffe fellow Bunting Inst., 1961-62. Mem. MLA, Renaissance Soc. Am., Internat. Assn. Hispanists, Asociación Internacional de Galdosistas, N.E. MLA. Contbr. articles in field to profl. jours.; editor: Benito Pérez Galdós, El Amigo Manso, 1963. Home: 19 Chauncy St-3A Cambridge MA 02138 Office: Shiffman Brandeis U Waltham MA 02254

LIDDELL, JANE HAWLEY HAWKES, civic worker; b. Newark, Dec. 8, 1907; d. Edward Zeh and Mary Everett (Hawley) Hawkes; A.B., Smith Coll., 1931; postgrad. Art History, Harvard U., 1933-35; M.A., Columbia U., 1940; Carnegie fellow Sorbonne, Paris, 1937; m. Donald M. Liddell, Jr., Mar. 30, 1940; children—Jane Boyer, D. Roger Brooke. Pres., Planned Parenthood Essex County (N.J.), 1947-50; trustee Prospect Hill Sch. Girls, Newark, 1946-50; adv. bd., mem. publicity and public relations com. N.J. State Mus., Trenton, 1952-60; sec., then v.p. women's br. N.J. Hist. Soc.; women's aux. prodn. chmn. Englewood (N.J.) Hosp., 1959-61; pres. Dwight Sch. Girls Parents Assn., 1955-57; v.p. Englewood Sch. Boys Parents Assn., 1958-60; mem. Altar Guild, women's aux. bd., rector's adv. council St. Paul's Episcopal Ch., Englewood, 1954-59; bd. dir. N.Y. State chpt. Nat. Soc. Colonial Dames, 1961-67, rep. conf. Patriotic and Hist. Socs., 1964—; regional v.p. Huguenot Soc. Am., 1979—; bd. dirs. Soc. Daus. Holland Dames, 1965-82; bd. dirs., mem. publs. com. Daus. Cin., 1966-72; bd. dirs. Ch. Women's League Patriotic Service, 1962—, pres., 1968-70, 72-74; bd. dirs., chmn. grants com. Youth Found., N.Y.C., 1974—; chmn. for Newark, Smith Coll. 75th Ann. Fund, 1948-50; pres. North N.J. Smith Club, 1956-58; pres. Smith Coll. Class 1931, 1946-51, 76-81, editor 50th ann. book, 1980-81. Recipient various commendation awards. Republican. Clubs: Colony, City Gardens, Church (N.Y.C.); Jr. League Bergen County; Needle and Bobbin, Nat. Farm and Garden; Englewood Woman's, Englewood Field; Hillsboro (Pompano Beach, Fla.). Editor: Maine Echoes, 1961.

LIDDY, MARIE THERESE, career cons. co. exec.; b. Newark, July 27, 1932; d. Joseph A. and Veronica Cecelia (Beston) L.; B.A. in English and Music, Chestnut Hill Coll., Phila., 1967; M.A. in English and Drama, St. Bonaventure U., Olean, N.Y., 1972, M.A. in Theology and Psychology, 1977. Tchr., counselor John Carroll High Sch., Bel Air, Md., 1968-70; instr. English, asso. in counseling St. Bonaventure U., 1970-72; lectr., career adv. Temple U., Phila., 1972-76; co-dir. campus community, counselor, adminstr. LaSalle Coll., Phila., 1977-78; research and devel. staff Am. Inst. Property and Liability Underwriters, 1978-80; pres., exec. dir. Mainstream Access, Inc., Phila., 1980—; seminar leader, 1968—. Mem. Interreligious Task Force Soviet Jewry, 1976-81, Phila. Human Relations Commn., 1972-76; co-sponsor Women's Inter Faith Dialogue on Middle East, 1976-78. Mem. Nat. Assn. Female Execs., Am. Soc. Tng. and Devel., Phila. Women's Network. Contbr., Insurance (Job Finder series), 1981; contbr. articles to profl. jours. Office: Western Savs Bank Bldg Philadelphia PA 19107

LIDE, NEOMA JEWELL LAWHON (MRS. MARTIN JAMES LIDE, JR.), poet; b. Levelland, Tex., Apr. 1, 1926; d. Charles Samuel and Juel (Yeager) Lawhon; Secretarial cert. Draughon's Bus. Coll., 1943; student U. Tex., 1944-46; R.N., Jefferson-Hillman Sch. Nursing, 1950; m. Martin James Lide, Jr., Nov. 12, 1950; children—Martin James, III, Brooks Nathaniel, Gardner Lawhon. Writer column Baldwin Times, Bay Minette, Ala., 1964-68, Shades Valley Sun newspapers, Birmingham, Ala., 1974-75; v.p., sec. Martin J. Lide Assos., Inc., Birmingham, 1977—. Mem. def. adv. com. Women in Services, for Ala., 1961-63; coordinator women's activities Nat. Vets. Day, Birmingham, 1961-68; mem. exec. com., 1968-70; poetry chmn. Women's Com. of 100 for Birmingham, 1974-75, historian, 1980—. Mem. Gorgas bd. U. Ala., Tuscaloosa, 1959. Recipient citation Merit, Muscular Dystrophy Assn. Am., 1961. Mem. DAR (chpt. program chmn. 1979-80). Club: The Club (Birmingham). Author: Instead of Sunset, 1973; Life of Service-These are My Jewels, 1979; Music in the Wind - The Story of Lady Arlington, 1980; Brother James Bryan-Hope Lives Eternal, 1981. Home: 3536 Brookwood Rd Birmingham AL 35223

LIDZ, CAROL SCHNEIDER, psychologist; b. Paterson, N.J., Feb. 27, 1941; d. Isadore Schneider and Elsie (Sussman) Berg; B.A., U. Mich., 1962; M.A., U. Tenn., 1964; Psy.D., Rutgers U., 1977; m. Howard Lidz, June 14, 1970. Sch. psychologist public schs., Monmouth County, N.J., 1965-70; pvt. practice psychology, Phila., 1970—; sch. psychologist, coordinator gifted edn. Montgomery County (Pa.) Intermediate Unit, 1970-73; psychologist pediatric unit Moss Rehab. Hosp., Phila., 1973-75; sch. psychologist Hall-Mercer Mental Health/Mental Retardation Center, Phila., 1975-80; dir. Headstart clinic team United Cerebral Palsy Assn., Phila.; mem. faculty Phila. Community Coll., Rutgers U., Camden, N.J. Lic. psychologist, Pa.; cert. sch. psychologist, Pa., N.J. Active, Hadassah. Mem. Am. Psychol. Assn., Phila. Soc. Clin. Psychologists, Del. County Assn. Sch. Psychologists, Nat. Assn. Sch. Psychologists, Assn. of Sch. Psychologists in Pa., Orgn. of Rehab. Through Tng. Democrat. Author: Improving Assessment of School Children, 1981; contbr. articles in field to profl. jours. Home: 2206 Lombard St Philadelphia PA 19146 Office: 4700 Wissahickon Ave Philadelphia PA 19144

LIEBELER, SUSAN WITTENBERG, lawyer, educator; b. New Castle, Pa., July 3, 1942; d. Sherman K. and Eleanor (Kilvans) Levine; B.A., U. Mich., 1963, postgrad. Law Sch., 1963-64; LL.B. (Stein scholar), UCLA, 1966; m. Wesley J. Liebeler, Oct. 21, 1971; 1 dau., Jennifer. Admitted to Calif. bar, 1967, Vt. bar, 1972; law clk. Hon. Gordon L. Files, Calif. Ct. of Appeals, 1966-67; asso. firm Gang, Tyre & Brown, 1967-68, firm Greenberg, Bernhard, Weiss & Karma, Los Angeles, 1968-70; asso. gen. counsel Republic Corp., Los Angeles, 1970-72; gen. counsel Verit Industries, Los Angeles, 1972-73; prof. of law Loyola Law Sch., Los Angeles, 1973—; spl. counsel, chmn. John S. R. Shad, SEC, Washington, 1981-82; vis. prof. U. Tex., summer 1982; cons. Office of Policy Coordination, office of Pres.-elect, 1981-82; cons. U.S. Ry. Assn., 1975, U.S. EPA, 1974, U.S. Price Commn., 1972. Mem. State Bar Calif., Los Angeles County Bar Assn. (bus. and corp. sect.), Women Lawyer's Assn. Los Angeles, Order of Coif. Republican. Jewish. Sr. editor UCLA Law Review, 1965-66; contbr. article to legal publ., 1978.

LIEBEL-WECKOWICZ, HELEN PAULINE GRIT, historian; b. N.Y.C., June 17, 1930; d. Emil Frederick and Anna Wilhelmina Johanna (Bonk) Liebel; B.A. summa cum laude, Bklyn. Coll., 1952; M.A., Northwestern U., 1953, Ph.D., 1959; m. Thaddeus E. Weckowicz, July 11, 1966. Asso. editor, Chgo. Consol. Ency., 1954-55; mem. Am. Hist. Assn. microfilming project of captured German war documents, 1958-59; Sessl lectr. Bklyn. Coll., 1959-62; mem. faculty U. Alta., Edmonton, Can., 1962—, prof. history, 1972—; mem. Can. nat. com. Internat. Hist. Congress, 1967-70, 77-78; research dir. Can. Council grants, 1969-71, 73-74; cons. in field. Fulbright grantee, W.Ger., 1955; scholar AAUW, 1956-57; grantee Carnegie Fund, 1957-58, U. Alta., 1962-82. Mem. Am. Hist. Assn., Am. 18th Century Studies Assn., Can. 18th Century Studies Assn., Can. Hist. Soc., Conf. Group Central European History, Internat. Econ. Hist. Soc., Internat. Soc. 18th Century Studies, Internat. Com. History Rep. and Parliamentary Instns. Democrat. Club U. Alta. Faculty. Author books, articles in field. Office: Dept History U Alta Edmonton T6G 2H4 Canada

LIEBEN, EILEEN BROOKS, univ. adminstr.; b N.Y.C., Jan. 23, 1916; d. Thomas and Margaret (Culkin) Brooks; B.A., Manhattanville Coll., 1937; M.A., Creighton U., 1962; m. Theodore J. Lieben, Dec. 13, 1941; children—Peter, John, Thomas Geoffrey. Asst. dean of women Creighton U., Omaha, 1962, instr. English, 1963-64, dean of women, asso. dean students, 1963—, acting v.p. student personnel, 1982—, coordinator fall honors program, 1978—. Bd. dirs. Performing Artists Omaha, 1981—. Recipient Creighton Disting. Adminstr. Service award, 1973, Mary Lucretia Creighton award for Advancement of Women, 1981; Sperry Hutchinson, Nebr. Com. Humanities grantee; Nebr. Arts Council grantee; Musicians Union grantee. Mem. Joslyn Mus. Women's Assn. Am. Assn. Higher Edn., Nat. Assn. Women Deans, Adminstrs. and Counselors, Assn. Am. Colls., AAUW. Roman Catholic. Home: 514 S 57th St Omaha NE 68106 Office: 2500 California St Omaha NE 68178

LIEBER, MIMI, sociologist; b. Detroit, Mar. 22, 1928; d. Theodore and Rhoda (Katzin) Levin; B.A., U. Chgo., 1951; M.A., Harvard U., postgrad., 1959-60; m. Charles D. Lieber, July 17, 1960; children—John Nathan, James Edmund, George Theodore, Ann Gabrielle. With Columbia Bur. Applied Social Research, N.Y.C., 1951-53; with Internat. Research Assos., 1953-55, Research Services Ltd., London, 1955-59; asso. creative research dir. Tatham-Laird, Chgo.; pres. Leiber Attitude Research, N.Y.C., 1960—. Trustee Jewish Bd. Guardians, 1968-75; mem. Community Planning Bd. #2, N.Y.C., 1975-82; trustee Soc. Advancement Judaism, 1971-73; mem. N.Y. State Bd. Regents, 1981—. Mem. Am. Sociol. Assn., Am. Mktg. Assn. Club: Harvard. Office: 1841 Broadway New York NY 10023 *

LIEBERMAN, CAROLYN BUCK, lawyer; b. St. Paul, Mar. 6, 1946; d. James H. and Eleanore C. (Schieber) Buck; B.A., U. Minn., 1968; J.D. cum laude, Nat. Law Center, George Washington U., 1971; m. Michael Lieberman, June 14, 1968. Admitted to Va. bar, 1971, D.C. bar, 1972, U.S. Supreme Ct. bar, 1975; atty. Office Gen. Counsel, HUD legal honors program, Washington, 1971-72, trial atty., 1973-79, asst. gen. counsel for litigation, 1980—. Recipient cert. spl. achievement HUD, 1979. Office: 451 7th St SW Washington DC 20410

LIEBERT, LUCILLE A., psychologist; b. Coffeyville, Kans., Feb. 10, 1934; d. Albert and Mamie (Jordan) L.; B.Mus., Kans. State Coll., Pittsburg, 1955; M.A., U. Notre Dame, 1968; postgrad. in Psychology, U. Mo., Kansas City, 1976-79. Pvt. music tchr., Coffeyville, 1955-67; tchr. Holy Name Jr. High Sch., Coffeyville, 1964-67; dir. counseling services Marymount Coll., Salina, Kans., 1968-71; psychologist Psychol. Services, Kansas City, Mo., 1971—; cons. Cath. Diocese of Kansas City-St. Joseph, 1971—, Cath. Diocese of Jefferson City, 1975—. Mem. Am. Psychol. Assn., Mo. Psychol. Assn., Kans. Psychol. Assn., Am. Personnel and Guidance Assn., Phi Kappa Phi. Roman Catholic. Home: 9100 Riggs Ln Overland Park KS 66212 Office: 1207 Grand Ave Kansas City MO 64106

LIEBIG, APRIL MAE, moving co. exec.; b. Indpls., Feb. 26, 1955; d. Herbert George and Rosemary Ann (Doran) Liebig; student Ind. State U., 1973-75, Ind. U. Purdue U., Indpls., 1976—. Dispatcher, sec. Nora Security Inc., Indpls., 1975-79; service coordinator Carleton Transit Co., Indpls., 1979—. Leader, Girl Scouts, 1974-75. Mem. U.S. Racquetball Assn., Nat. Assn. Female Execs., Smithsonian Assos., Indpls. Mus. Art, Nat. Trust Historic Preservation, Nat. Abortion Rights Action League, Police League Ind. Presbyterian. Club: Recreational Equipment Inc. Coop. Home: 8445 Evergreen Ave Indianapolis IN 46240 Office: 1333 E 86th St Indianapolis IN 46240

LIEBL, CATHERINE JEAN, chem. co. exec.; b. Portland, Oreg., Apr. 22, 1946; d. Charles and Iris Pauline (Mortimer) Liebig; B.B.A., CCNY, 1967; m. Hans Liebl, Feb. 19, 1967. With Arthur Young & Co., C.P.A.s, 1967-75, successive audit staff positions to audit mgr., N.Y.C., until 1975; mgr. fin. reports and consol. Mobil Corp., N.Y.C., 1975-77, mgr. fin. analysis, 1977-80, controller films div. Mobil Chem. Co., Pittsford, N.Y., 1981—. Mem. Am. Inst. C.P.A.s, Nat. Assn. Female Execs. Office: 1175 Pittsford-Victor Rd Pittsford NY 14534

LIEBMAN, JUDITH STENZEL, educator; b. Denver, July 2, 1936; d. Raymond O. and Mary Stenzel; B.A., U. Colo., 1958; Ph.D., Johns Hopkins U., 1971; m. Jon Charles Liebman, Dec. 27, 1958; children—Christopher, Rebecca, Michael. Engr., Convair Astronautics Co., San Diego, 1958-59; programmer Gen. Electric Corp., Ithaca, N.Y., 1963-64; programmer dept. chemistry Cornell U., Ithaca, 1964-65; research asst., mem. faculty Johns Hopkins U., Balt., 1965-72, asso. prof. depts. public health adminstrn., ops. research, and indsl. engring., 1971-72; asst. prof. civil, mech., and indsl. engring. U. Ill., Champaign-Urbana, 1972-77, asso. prof. ops. research, 1977—; trustee Engring. Info., 1979-85. Pres. bd. dirs. E. Central Ill. Health Systems Agy., 1980-82. Mem. Ops. Research Soc. Am. (chmn. health applications sect. 1978-79, mem. council 1980-83), AIIE, AAAS, AAUP, Assn. Women in Math., Soc. Women Engrs., Am. Public Health Assn., Am. Health Planning Assn., Sigma Xi, Sigma Pi Sigma, Alpha Pi Mu. Author articles in field; asso. editor Ops. Research Letters, 1980—; mem. editorial bds. profl. jours. Home: 2210 Fletcher St Urbana IL 61801 Office: 1206 W Green Mech Engring Bldg U Ill Urbana IL 61801

LIEBSON, ALICE RUTH, civic worker; b. Washington, Oct. 2, 1950; d. Sidney Harold and Jeannette (Burman) L.; B.A. in Journalism, Western Conn. State Coll., 1973. Mem. exec. bd. Young Jewish Adults of Fairfield County; chmn. driver recruitment Stamford chpt. ARC, 1976-77; chmn. young adult div. United Jewish Fedn., Stamford, 1976-77; justice of peace Conn., 1976—; notary public Conn., 1977—; pres. Young Democrats Stamford, 1976-77; sr. del. Young Dems. Club Conn., 1976-77; del. Conn. Dem. Conv., 1977, Nat. Conv., 1978, 82; mem. exec. com. Dem. City Com., 1976-78; mem. Dem. Women's Club Fedn. Conn., 1976—; mem. exec. bd. ex-officio North Stamford Dem. Club, 1977-78; Dem. candidate Stamford Bd. Reps., 1977; mem. state steering com. Common Cause Conn., 1979—; mem. Capital Region Forum, 1980—; mem. exec. com. Conn. Women's Polit. Caucus, 1981. Chief aide Ella Grasso campaign, 1978; commr.'s aide Conn. Dept. Housing, 1979; coordinator Barbara Kennelly for Congress, 1982; mem. budget and allocations com. United Way Capital Area. Recipient Outstanding Community Service award Gen. Electric Credit Corp., 1977; nominee Stamford Citizen of Yr., 1977. Ky. Col. Mem. AAUW (1st v.p. 1980, mem. Stamford Area Fine Arts Council), Hartford Women's Network. Originated first ann. Project-Munici-Pals, Stamford, 1977. Home: 712 Farmington Ave West Hartford CT 06119

LIEDMAN, JULIE, writer; b. Phila., Mar. 16, 1947; d. Samuel and Tybie (Marder) Moshinsky; B.A., Pa. State U., 1968; m. John Liedman, Nov. 23, 1969; children—Eli, Gabriel. Reporter, Phila. Bull., 1967-79; free lance writer, Phila. Recipient Smolar award, Jewish Fedn., 1981. Contbr. articles to profl. jours.

LIEF, INEZ, real estate exec.; b. Newark, Sept. 19, 1926; d. Jacob and Sophie (Levin) Hyatt; student public schs.; grad. Grad. Realtors Inst., 1974; m. Teddy Lief, Oct. 20, 1946; children—Linda, Barry (dec.), Scott. Engaged in real estate, 1967—; mgr. property mgmt. dept. Weichert Co., Realtors, Morristown, N.J., 1980—; partner Bernard Shub Real Estate; owner Century 21 Arbor House; mem. condemnation commn. Superior Ct. N.J., 1980—. Recipient Harry L. Schwarz award Morris County Bd. Realtors, 1975; cert. residential specialist, real estate brokerage mgr. Mem. Morris County Bd. Realtors (pres. 1981, 82), N.J. Assn. Realtors (3d dist. v.p. 1983), Nat. Assn. Realtors, Somerset County Bd. Realtors, Nat. Assn. Exec. Women, Nat. Mktg. Inst. Home: 15 Humphrey Rd Convent Station NJ 07961 Office: 6 Dumont Pl Morristown NJ 07960

LIENHARD, LORI ANNE, educator; b. Oak Park, Ill., June 30, 1956; d. John Hugo and Elizabeth Jean (Atkinson) Lienhard; B.A., Bard Coll., 1977; M.A. in English, U. Chgo., 1978. Permissions editor Winthrop Pubs., Inc., Cambridge, Mass., 1978-80; circulation mgr. Datek of New Eng., Newtonville, Mass., 1981; instr. English Auburn (Ala.) U., 1981—. Democrat. Home: 141A Maple St Auburn AL 36830 Office: Haley Center Auburn U Auburn AL 36830

LIESEN, DOROTHY ANN THIEL, epidemiologist, nurse; b. Milw., Dec. 13, 1944; d. Roman Aloise and Mary Ann Viola (Dorn) Thiel; R.N., St. Joseph's Hosp. Sch. Nursing, Marshfield, Wis., 1966; B.S., Carroll Coll., 1975; M.S., U. South Fla., 1979; postgrad. Nova U., 1982—; m. Richard Philip Liesen, Aug. 23, 1969 (dec. 1973). Med.-surg. nurse St. Michael's Hosp., Milw., 1966-67; instr. Sacred Heart Sch. Practical Nursing, Milw., 1967-73; infection surveillance officer Waukesha (Wis.) Meml. Hosp., 1973-76; nurse epidemiologist, lectr., cons. James A. Haley VA Hosp., Tampa, Fla., 1973—, also prin. research investigator; clin. assoc. prof. U. South Fla. Sch. Nursing, 1979—; faculty mem. continuing edn. Hillsborough Community Coll., 1979-81; lectr., cons., U.S.A., P.R., Bahamas, 1976—. Served to capt. U.S. Army Res., 1978-82. Mem. Fla. Practitioners Infection Control, Assn. Practitioners Infection Control (pres. Bay Area chpt. 1979-80), Am. Pub. Health Assn., U. South Fla. Pres.' Council (life), Phi Kappa Phi, Sigma Theta Tau. Roman Catholic. Contbr. chpts. to books. Home: 14101

Cherry Orchard Run Tampa FL 33618 Office: James A Haley Vets Hosp 13000 N 30th St Tampa FL 33612

LIFQUIST, ROSALIND CARIBELLE, ret. food economist, ret. govt. ofcl.; b. Henning, Minn., June 5, 1903; d. John D. and Frances Myrtle (Wilcox) Lifquist; B.S. with high distinction (Caleb Dorr scholar 1935), U. Minn., 1935, M.S., 1937; m. Milton H. Simon, May 25, 1927 (dec.). Tchr. home econs. public schs., Algoma, Gillett, and Shawano, Wis., 1921-26; dietetics intern U. Minn. Hosp., 1926, U. Wash., 1941; dietitian City Hosp., Lock Haven, Pa., 1926-33; instr. foods U. Minn., St. Paul, 1935-37; asst. prof. foods and nutrition Iowa State Coll., Ames, 1937-41; food economist Bur. Human Nutrition and Home Econs., U.S. Dept. Agr., Washington, 1946-55, Agrl. Mktg. Service, also Econ. Research Service, 1955-73. Served from lt. (j.g.) to lt. comdr. WAVES, 1942-46. Recipient cert. of merit U.S. Dept. Agr., 1961; Disting. Service award U. Wis., 1973. Mem. Nat. Fedn. Press Women, Omicron Nu, Pi Lambda Theta, Phi Upsilon Omicron. Club: Capital Press Women. Author several govt. publs. on food, consumer research, also numerous articles. Home: 1727 Massachusetts Ave NW Washington DC 20036

LIFSEY, MARY JANE, banker; b Raleigh, N.C., Apr. 18, 1938; d. Edwin Liles and Alma Vernon (Branson) Lassiter; A.A., Glendale Coll., 1968; B.S. in Bus. Adminstrn., Econs. and Social Sci., Rollins Coll., 1977; postgrad. Am. Inst. Banking, 1972-79; m. James Frank Lifsey, Oct. 24, 1954; children—Deborah Anne Lifsey Stapleton, April Elizabeth, Daniel Liles, David Vernon. With Barnett Bank of Central Fla., N.A., Cocoa, 1968—, lending officer, 1977-81, asst. v.p., 1981—. Mem. polit. action com. Barnett Banks of Fla., 1978—; dir. Merritt Island Dist. Library Bd., 1979-81; asso. mem. Brevard County Commn. on Status of Women, 1981. AAUW grantee, 1981. Mem. Calif. PTA (hon. life), Am. Bus. Women Assn. (Women of Yr. award Space Port Charter chpt. 1980), AAUW (internat. relations rep. Fla. div.), Fla. Bankers Assn. (installment credit com. 1980—), Omicron Delta Epsilon. Democrat. Methodist (asst. treas. 1980—). Home: 1460 Holly Ave Merritt Island FL 32952 Office: 430 Brevard Ave Cocoa FL 32922

LIGGET, FRANCES HAMMOND, civic worker; b. Phila., Oct. 28, 1901; d. Levi John and Frances Purves (Bernard) Hammond; ed. Agnes Irwin Sch., Phila., Phila. Sch. Design for Women (scholar); m. Robert Charles Ligget, Oct. 28, 1922 (dec. 1976); children—Frances Bernard (dec.), Audrey Hammond (Mrs. Frederick Robert Snyder). Chmn. ARC Camp and Hosp. Council Service Southeastern Pa., 1945-46; vice chmn. radio Emergency Aid Pa., World War II; sec. Women's Aux. Pa. Hosp., Phila., 1947; sec. house com. Presbyn. Hosp., 1937-39; organizing chmn. Valley Forge Hist. Soc. Mus. Aux., 1950. Recipient White Ribbon award Garden Club Fedn. Pa., 1952, community recognition award Chapel of Four Chaplains, Phila., 1974, citation Pa. Ho. of Reps., 1974. Mem. DAR, Am. Legion Aux., Women Nat. Farm and Garden Assn. (pres. Valley Forge br. Keystone div. 1935), Daus. Am. Colonists (flag chmn. 1970-73), Daus. of Colonial Wars (state chaplain 1974-77), Swedish Colonial Soc. (historian 1960-70), Nat. Soc. Colonial Dames XVII Century (state chmn. of insignia 1975-77), Dames of Loyal Legion State of Pa. (councilor, former chmn. of insignia), Nat. Soc. Descs. Early Quakers (founding). Republican. Presbyterian. Clubs: Acorn (Phila.); Merion Cricket (Haverford); Waynesborough Country. Compiler local history. Home: Valley Forge PA 19481

LIGHT, MARILYN HAMILTON, orgn. exec.; b. Troy, N.Y., July 6, 1930; d. George Howard and Harriet Euphemia (Pattullo) Hamilton; student Russell Sage Coll., 1950-51, Iona Coll., 1972-74; m. Edward W. Light, Feb. 1, 1955 (dec.); 1 son, Gregory Hamilton (dec.). Pvt. sec., dean women Russell Sage Coll., 1949-52; exec. sec., dist. mgr. Gulf Oil Corp., Albany, N.Y., 1952-55; exec. sec. regional exec. office Owens-Ill., Scarsdale, N.Y., 1965-67; with Hypoglycemia Found., 1967—, exec. sec., Scarsdale, 1967-69, exec. dir., 1969-71, pres., exec. dir. Adrenal Metabolic Research Soc. of found., Mt. Vernon, N.Y., 1971—; pres. Marilyn Light, Inc., 1979—, Samar Constrn. Inc., 1980—, Profl. Remodelers Inc., 1981—; cons. Paine Found., N.Y.C.; advisor N.Y. Inst. for Child Devel., N.Y.C. Vice chmn., bd. dirs. Troy Civic Devel. Assn. Mem. Mensa, Internat. Platform Assn., AAAS, N.Y. Acad. Scis., Hastings Center, Inst. Soc., Ethics and Life Scis., Nat. Assn. for Female Execs. Clubs: Troy, Troy Women's. Author: Hypoglycemia & Me, 1973; Homeostasis Revisited, 1981; Beleaguered Giant, 1982. Editor: Homeostasis Quar., 1971—. Contbr. articles to profl. publs. Home and Office: 153 Pawling Ave Troy NY 12180

LIGHTER, JESSICA ROYCE, psychologist; b. Bklyn., Sept. 27, 1944; d. Robert and Gertrude (Besmanoff) Wisch; B.A. in Sch. Psychology summa cum laude, Hofstra U., 1966, M.A. in Psychology, 1968; Ph.D. in Psychology, Fordham U., 1980; m. Gary Lawrence Lighter, June 22, 1968; children—Gwen Kimberly, Jennifer Lynn. Sch. psychologist Cherry Hill Public Schs., 1968-69; lectr. San Antonio Coll., 1970; psychologist Bd. Coop. Ednl. Services, N.Y.C., 1971-81; adj. asst. prof. doctoral program psychology Fordham U., 1980; dir. human resources Citizens Utilities, Stamford, Conn., 1981—; dir. Consultants Collaborative, Port Chester, N.Y., 1977—; Active ORT, Leukemia Soc. Am., PTA. Lic. psychologist, N.Y. Mem. Westchester County Psychol. Assn. (exec. bd.), Am. Psychol. Assn., Am. Soc. Personnel Adminstrs., Am. Ednl. Research Assn., Nat. Assn. Sch. Psychologists, N.Y. State Psychol. Assn., N.Y. State Assn. Sch. Psychologists, N.Y.C. Assn. Sch. Psychologists, Psi Chi. Contbr. articles to profl. jours. Home: 105 Country Ridge Dr Port Chester NY 10573 Office: High Ridge Park Stamford CT 06905

LIGHTFOOT, MARJORIE JEAN, educator; b. Oak Park, Ill., Apr. 24, 1933; d. Cecil Dane and Maybelle June (Doyle) Lightfoot; B.A. summa cum laude, Brown U., 1955; M.A., Northwestern U., 1956, Ph.D., 1964. Teaching asst. Northwestern U., Evanston, Ill., 1957-60; instr. U. Ariz., Tucson, 1960-63; asst. prof. Ariz. State U., Tempe, 1964-69, assoc. prof., 1969-74, prof. English, 1974—. Brown U. scholar, 1951-55, fellow, 1956-57; Northwestern U. scholar, 1955-57; recipient Speech prize Brown U., 1952, 53, English prize, 1955. Mem. NOW, Common Cause, Women's Caucus, Western Humor and Irony Assn., MLA, Rocky Mountain MLA, Ariz. State U. Faculty Women's Assn., Phi Beta Kappa, Phi Kappa Phi. Contbr. articles to profl. jours. Office: Dept English Ariz State U Tempe AZ 85821

LIGHTFOOT, REBEKAH TOLES, cable TV exec.; b. Rains County, Tex., Feb. 18, 1944; d. William Forest and Jamie Romine Toles; student Weatherford Coll., 1963-64; m. Donald C. Lightfoot, July 5, 1979; children—Robbie Suzan, James Russel, Devrus Charles Deal. Engring. sec. Antenna Products Co., Mineral Wells, Tex., 1965-68, Wilson Henderson Inc., yler, Tex., 1969-74; personnel/engring. adminstr. Poly-Am., Inc., Dallas, 1975-77; office adminstr. Longview Cable TV (Tex.), 1979—. Dir. youth and music Ch. of God, Tyler, 1970-75; pres. Chapel Hill Elem. Sch. PTA, 1974-75. Recipient Nat. Youth Leader award Chs. of God, 1974. Mem. Am. Bus. Women's Assn., League Am. Wheelmen. Republican. Club: Oak Forest Country. Home: 2108 Tryon Rd Longview TX 75601 Office: Longview Cable TV 200 N Frendonia St Longview TX 75606

LIGHTHALL, NANCY PEARMAN, educator, author; b. Sharon, Conn., Mar. 17, 1927; d. Earl O. and Jessie May (Batchelor) Pearman; B.A., Roosevelt U., 1962; M.A., U. Chgo., 1968; div.; children—Stephen, Alison. Tchr., counselor Central YMCA High Sch., Chgo., 1962-66; asst. prof. English, Olive-Harvey Coll., Chgo., 1968—; author: Point of View, 1968; Skiing for Women, 1978. Mem. Am. Fedn. Tchrs., Mensa. Office: 10001 S Woodlawn Ave Chicago IL 60628

LIGON, HELEN HAILEY, educator; b. Lott, Tex., Feb. 7, 1921; d. Rolla W. and Bobbye A. (Ruble) Hailey; B.S. in Bus. Adminstrn., Tex. Women's U., 1942, M.A. in Accounting and Econs., 1945; Ph.D. in Bus. Analysis, Tex. A. and M. U., 1976; m. William Grady Ligon, July 26, 1941; 1 son, William Grady III. Tutor in bus. adminstrn. Tex. Women's U., Denton, 1942-44; tchr. pub. schs., Lott (Tex.), 1947-52, Marlin (Tex.), 1952-55; exec. sec. Gen. Tire & Rubber Co., Waco, Tex., 1956-58; asst. prof. quantitative analysis Hankamer Sch. Bus., Baylor U., Waco, 1958-62, prof., 1962—, also dir. Casey Computer Center, 1962—. Named Most Popular Bus. Prof., Baylor U., 1964, 69, 78, Outstanding Woman Faculty Member, 1967, Outstanding Baylor U. Tchr., 1979. Mem. Soc. Mgmt. Info. Systems, Data Processing Mgmt. Assn., Am. Statis. Assn., Assn. of Computing Machinery, Delta Kappa Gamma, Beta Gamma Sigma, Sigma Iota Epsilon. Democrat. Presbyterian. Author: Changing Concepts in Management Information Systems, 1978; Successful Management Systems, 1978. Home: PO Box 388 Lott TX 76656 Office: PO Box 6278 Waco TX 76706

LILES, FRANCES ROSE, computer program mgr.; b. Richmond, Va., Jan. 4, 1943; d. Milford Kenyon and Helen Frances (Boston) L.; student Coll. William and Mary, 1961-63: B.A., U. Toledo, 1965. Adminstr., AID, Dept. of State, Washington, 1965-67; research analyst Def. Intelligence Agy., Lisbon, Portugal, Madrid and Washington, 1968-75; adminstr. Spanish programs Jet Engine Group, Gen. Elec. Co., Madrid, 1976; proposal mgr. corp. mktg. Atlantic Research Corp., Alexandria, Va., 1977-82; sr. mem. adv. staff Computer Scis. Corp., Falls Church, Va., 1982—. Chmn. youth com. Am. Embassy, Lisbon, 1968-70; active McLean (Va.) Center Theatre. Mem. Nat. Fedn. Bus. and Profl. Women (chmn.), Internat. Trade Assn., Women in Info. Processing, Nat. Assn. Female Execs., NOW, Mu Phi Epsilon, Sigma Delta Pi, Pi Beta Phi. Episcopalian. Home: 412 S Lee St Alexandria VA 22314 Office: 6565 Arlington Blvd Falls Church VA 22046

LILLIE, BEATRICE (LADY PEEL), actress; b. Toronto, Ont., Can., May 29, 1894; d. John and Lucie (Shaw) Lillie; ed. St. Agnes Coll., Belleville, Ont.; m. Sir Robert Peel (dec. 1934); 1 son, Robert (killed while with Royal Navy in Far East, 1942). Made first stage appearance in Not Likely, London, 1914; first N.Y. appearance at Times Square Theatre in Andre Charlot's Revue of 1924; has appeared in many plays in London and N.Y.; plays in N.Y. include Charlot's Revue of 1926, Oh, Please, 1926, She's My Baby, 1928, This Year of Grace, 1928, The Third Little Show, 1931, Too True To Be Good by George Bernard Shaw, 1932, Walk a Little Faster, 1932, At Home Abroad, 1935, The Show is On, 1936, Set to Music, 1939, Seven Lively Arts, 1944, Inside U.S.A., 1948-49, An Evening with Beatrice Lillie, 1952-53, Golden Jubilee edit. Ziegfeld Follies, 1957, High Spirits, 1964-65. Motion pictures: Exit Smiling, 1926, Doctor Rhythm, 1938, On Approval, 1943, Around the World in 80 days, 1955, Thoroughly Modern Millie, 1967, many others; numerous radio and TV appearances; during World War II entertained allied troops in England, Europe, Middle East and North Africa. Decorated by Gen. Charles de Gaulle; awarded African Star; other war citations and service ribbons; Donaldson award of 1944-45; 1948 citation by Nat. Conf. of Christians and Jews; citation as Greatest Comedienne of All Time, Am. Fedn. Women's Philanthropies, 1953; Spl. Antoinette Perry award for disting. contbn. to theatre, 1953; Sarah Siddons award, 1954, Outer Circle award, 1964. Author: (autobiography) Every Other Inch a Lady, 1972. *

LIN, HELEN TAI, educator; b. Ningpo, Chechiang, China, Mar. 29, 1929; d. Jen Chun and Yuan Chih (Ku) Tai; came to U.S., 1962; naturalized, 1972; student Nat. N.W. U., 1946-47; B.S., Nat. Taiwan U., 1950; m. Andrew W. Lin, Apr. 11, 1952; children—Catherine K., Vivian K. Teaching asst. dept. agrl. econs. Taiwan U., 1950-54; instr. Chinese lang. U.S. Fgn. Service Inst. Chinese Lang. and Area Tng. Center, Taiwan, 1957-62; inst. Chinese, Yale U. Far Eastern Inst., 1962-66; supr. Taipei Lang. Inst., Taiwan, 1964-65; asso. profl. dept. Chinese, Wellesley (Mass.) Coll., 1966-78, prof., 1978—, William R. Kenan Jr. Found. chair, 1979-81, chmn. dept., 1970—, co-dir. Chinese Studies Program, 1973—, curriculum designer, cons. study abroad program, 1982—; dir. Chinese Sch., Middlebury (Vt.) Coll., 1971-77; curriculum adv. Newton (Mass.) Chinese Sch., 1971-77; reviewer, panelist Nat. Endowment Humanities, 1979, 80, 82. NSF summer grantee, 1970, 71; Wellesley Coll. research awardee, 1975-76; Helen S. French Fund grantee, 1975-76. Mem. U.S. Chinese Lang. Tchrs. Assn. (exec. bd. 1972-75, editorial bd. of jour.), Assn. Asian Studies (com. on scholars of Asian descent 1979—), MLA. Author: (with Henry Fenn) Speak Mandarin Students, Workshop, 1967; Essential Grammar for Modern Chinese, 1981; A Survey of Common Expressions Used in Daily Life in People's Republic of China, 1982. Home: 22 Geraldine Dr Wellesley Hills MA 02181 Office: Central and Washington Stas Wellesley MA 02181

LIN, MEI-YING, librarian; b. Fukien Province, China, Dec. 9, 1944; d. Chen-Liu and Shu-Yu (Wu) L.; B.A., Nat. Cheng-Chi U., 1966; M.S. in Library Sci., Wayne State U., 1969. Asso. librarian Asia Library, U. Mich., Ann Arbor, 1969—; cons. Am. Chinese edn. and culture Center, Detroit, Detroit Bd. Edn. Contbr. articles to profl. jours. Home: 2663 Prairie St Ann Arbor MI 48105

LIND, MARILYN MARLENE, artist, writer, genealogist; b. New Ulm, Minn., Aug. 15, 1934; d. Fred S. and Emma L. (Steinke) Thiem; student pub. schs., Aitkin, Minn.; m. Charles R. Lind, Aug. 22, 1952; children—Michael, Bonnie, Vickie. Photographic asst., Aitkin, 1951-52; bookkeeper, office mgr. Rural Electric Assn., Aitkin, 1953-54; office mgr. N.E. Minn. Edn. Assn., Cloquet, 1970-77; pres. The Linden Tree, Cloquet, 1981-82; exhibited in one-woman show: Lake Superior Art Center, Duluth, 1972; group shows include: Lutheran Brotherhood Ctr. Gallery, Mpls., 1977. Precinct chmn. Ind. Republicans Minn., 1976-77, co-chmn. Carlton County/Senate Dist. 14, 1977-80, 8th Congl. Dist. Com., 1977-80, mem. Minn. state central com., 1977-82, county, dist. and state conv. del., 1976-83. Recipient Gallery awards, Duluth, 1972, Mpls., 1977. Mem. Geneal. Soc. Carlton County (bd. dirs. 1977-83, v.p. 1980-81) Sec., 1982-83. Lutheran. Author: Christoph and August, A Dream and a Promise, 1981. Home and Office: 1204 W Prospect St Cloquet MN 55720

LINDALL, JOAN DAGNY, social worker; b. Parkers Prairie, Minn., June 22, 1934; d. Oscar Regnar and Dagny (Hole) Lindall; B.A. magna cum laude, Gustavus Adolphus Coll., 1956; M.S.W. with honors, Washington U., 1959; m. James Byron Holcomb, June 1, 1962; children—Matthew, John, Peter. Clin. social worker Clin. Center, NIH, Bethesda, Md., 1959-62; asst. supr. Yakima (Wash.) Child Guidance Center, 1962-64; clin. social worker Univ. Hosp., Seattle, 1964-65; adoption worker Luth. Family and Child Service, Seattle, 1965-66; clin. social worker Artificial Kidney Center, Seattle, 1966-68; research asso. dept. nephrology U. Wash. Sch. Medicine, Seattle, 1968-71; exec. dir. Helpline/Fishline, Bainbridge Island, Wash., 1974—; practicum instr. U. Wash. Sch. Social Work, 1980—. Democratic precinct committeeperson, 1970-72; bd. dirs. Kitsap County YWCA. Served with USPHS, 1960-62. Danforth grad, 1956-57; NIH tng. grantee, 1957-59. Mem. Nat. Assn. Social Workers (Register Clin. Social Workers), Acad. Cert. Social Workers. Democrat. Episcopal/Lutheran. Home: 9596 Yew St NE Bainbridge Island WA 98110 Office: 533 Madison St N Bainbridge Island WA 98110

LINDBERG, ELAYNE VERNA, art appraiser; b. Browerville, Minn., Apr. 27; d. Leslie and Velma (Breighhaupt) Averill; M.Social Sci., U. Minn., 1967; m. Russell H. Lindberg; children—Gary, Bonnie Lindberg Carlson. With Dayton's Dept. Store, Mpls., 1965-71; pres., chief exec. officer Elayne Galleries, Inc., Mpls., 1971—; art restorer and appraiser, 1970—. Mem. Am. Soc. Appraisers (asso.), Internat. Soc. Appraisers, World Assn. Questioned Document Examiners, Internat. Graphoanalysis Soc. Club: Calhoun Beach (Mpls.). Composer verse, sacred music. Home: 2950 Dean Pkwy Minneapolis MN 55416 Office: 6111 Excelsior Blvd Saint Louis Park MN 55416

LINDBERGH, ANNE SPENCER MORROW (MRS. CHARLES AUGUSTUS LINDBERGH), author; b. 1906; d. Dwight Whitney and Elizabeth Reeve (Cutter) Morrow; grad. Miss Chapin's Sch., N.Y.C.; grad. Smith Coll., Northampton, Mass., 1928, M.A. (hon.), 1935; m. Charles Augustus Lindbergh, May 27, 1929 (dec.); children—Charles Augustus (dec.), Jon Morrow, Land Morrow, Anne Spencer, Reeve Morrow, Scott Morrow. Recipient two prizes for lit. work Smith Coll.; cross of honor for part in survey of trans-Atlantic air route U.S. Flag Assn., 1933; Hubbard gold medal for work as co-pilot and radio operator in flight of 40,000 miles over five continents Nat. Geog. Soc., 1934. Author: North to the Orient, 1935; Listen, the Wind, 1938; The Wave of the Future, 1940; The Steep Ascent, 1944; Gift from the Sea, 1955; Unicorn and Other Poems; Dearly Beloved, 1962; Bring Me a Unicorn, 1972; Hour of Gold, Hour of Lead, 1973; Locked Rooms and Open Doors, 1974; The Flower and the Nettle, 1976; War Within and Without, 1980. Home: Scotts Cove Darien CT 06820

LINDBLAD-GOLDBERG, MARION, psychologist; b. Akron, Ohio, Mar. 1, 1943; d. Alvar Willard and Marion Mitchell (MacLeod) Lindblad; B.A., Ohio Wesleyan U., 1965; M.A., U. Minn., 1967; Ph.D., Temple U., 1977; m. Martin Goldberg, May 26, 1978; 1 son, David. Psychologist, Phila. Psychiat. Center, 1967-73, Phila. Child Guidance Clinic, 1973-75, dir. clin. services, 1975-79; asst. prof. psychology, dir. Family Therapy Center, U. Cin. Med. Sch., 1979—; cons. Marriage Council, U. Pa., Sinai Hosp., Balt. HEW grantee, 1978-81. Mem. Am. Psychol. Assn., Am. Orthopsychiat. Assn., Am. Assn. Marriage and Family Therapists, Nat. Register, Am. Psychiat. Services for Children. Home: 2343 Vista Pl Cincinnati OH 45208 Office: 231 Bethesda Ave Cincinnati OH 45267

LINDEMAN, CONNIE LOUISE, retail chain personnel exec.; b. La Junta, Colo., Dec. 22, 1953; d. Arthur F. and Sarah Frances (Masters) L.; B.A., Colo. State U., 1975; postgrad. U. Colo., 1976-78. Counselor Careers Ltd., Denver, 1975-76; personnel coordinator Target Stores, Denver, 1976-78, regional personnel rep., St. Louis, 1978-82; regional personnel mgr. Target Stores div. Dayton Hudson Corp., Maryland Heights, Mo., 1982—. Active in alcohol and drug rehab. counseling Raleigh Hills Hosp., St. Louis; campaigner United Way of St. Louis. Mem. Am. Soc. Tng. and Devel., Nat. Assn. Female Execs., Assoc. Industrialists Mo., NOW. Republican. Lutheran. Home: 365 Towerwood Ballwin MO 63011 Office: 141 Progress Pkwy Maryland Heights MO 63043

LINDEMANN, ERIKA CAROLINE, educator; b. Valparaiso, Ind., Feb. 14, 1946; d. Richard and Charlotte (Bielefeldt) L.; B.A., U. Ga., Athens, 1968; M.A., U. N.C., Chapel Hill, 1969, Ph.D., 1972. Asst. prof. English, U. S.C., Columbia, 1972-76, asso. prof., 1976-80; vis. asso. prof. U. Tex., Austin, spring 1978; asso. prof. English, U. N.C., Chapel Hill, 1980—; cons. bd. Nat. Endowment Humanities. Mem. Council of Writing Program Adminstrs. (bd. cons. evaluators), Conf. Coll. Composition and Communication, Nat. Council Tchrs. English, MLA, Phi Beta Kappa. Author: A Rhetoric for Writing Teachers, 1982. Office: Dept English U NC Chapel Hill NC 27514

LINDEN, JANINE MAGER, public relations agy. exec.; b. N.Y.C., Oct. 2, 1946; d. Moses Fortune and Emma (Leo) Mager; B.A., U. Pa., 1968; divorced. Asst. buyer Bloomingdale's, N.Y.C., 1968-69; fashion credits editor Harper's Bazaar, 1969-72; publicity asso. Cotton Inc., 1972-73; press officer Harrods Ltd., 1973-74; project mgr. J. C. Penney Co., 1974-75; public relations dir. Kenyon & Eckhardt, Inc., 1975-77; v.p. corp. communications Compton Advt., Inc., N.Y.C., 1977—. Mem. Pres. Nixon's Women's Exec. Com., 1971. Mem. Advt. Women N.Y. Republican. Club: Cosmopolitan (N.Y.C.). Home: 433 E 51st St New York NY 10022 Office: 625 Madison Ave New York NY 10022

LINDEN, JUDITH MARSHA, symphony dir.; b. Bklyn., Nov. 17, 1951; d. Morton and Selma Samilow; B.A. cum laude, Ithaca Coll., 1973; postgrad. Renssalear Poly. Inst., 1976-78; m. Jay Linden, Sept. 2, 1973; 1 dau., Jessica Nicole. Placement dir. Mass. Med. Soc., 1973-74; public relations dir. Albany (N.Y.) Regional Med. Program, 1974-76; asso. dir. alumni relations Renssalear Poly. Inst., Troy, N.Y., 1976-78; exec. dir. Queens Symphony Orch., Rego Park, N.Y., 1978—, mem. bd. Queens Symphony, 1978—. Bd. dirs. Open Door Parenting Center. Mem. Am. Symphony Orch. League, Bus. and Profl. Women's Assn. Home: 170 Hillpark Ave Great Neck NY 11021 Office: 99-11 Queens Blvd Rego Park NY 11374

LINDEN, SONDRA R., housing fin. corp. exec.; B.B.A. in Polit. Sci., U. Miami, 1960, LL.B., 1962; postgrad. in Bus. Adminstrn., Loyola Coll., 1979. Real estate broker, Fla., 1958—; legal asst. in legislation gen. counselor' office FCC, 1962-63; admitted to Md. bar, U.S. Supreme Ct. bar, 1970, D.C. bar, 1972; individual practice law, 1964-69; atty. in gen. counsel's office HUD, Washington, 1969-72, in-house cons., 1972-74; asst. v.p. Valley Forge Corp., real estate subs. Certain-Teed Products Corp., 1972-74; asst. dir. govt. affairs Nat. Assn. Realtors, 1974-75; engaged in mortgage fin., equity financing, 1975-76; pres. Project Funding Corp., Washington and N.Y.C., 1976—; pres., chmn. Project Capital Corp., Washington, 1979—; cons. Occupational Safety and Health, Energy, Environ., Water and Sewer, EEO, Transp. and Fair Housing Washington Task Force, 1972-74; housing cons. Arlington County, Va., 1979—; mem. Housing Energy and Transp. Com., Nat. Urban Coalition, 1972-74; expert panelist in constrn. and real estate Am. Arbitration Assn., 1974—; bd. dirs. Nat. Housing Conf., 1976—; seminar panelist Nat. Assn. Home Builders, mem. multi-family and urban revitalization coms.; seminar panelist Nat. League of Insured Savs. and Loan Assns.; asst. housing com Mortgage Bankers Assn.; fin. adv. to tenant coop. groups.

LINDERHOLM, NATALIE WALKER, social work pub. relations cons.; b. Phila., June 5, 1892; d. John and Henrietta Harwood (Havey) Walker; A.B. magna cum laude, Radcliffe Coll., 1914; certificate Sch. Civics and Philanthropy (now Social Service Adminstrn.) U. Chgo., 1915; m. Ernest Arthur Linderholm, Mar. 2, 1918 (dec.); 1 dau., Elizabeth Linderholm Lustig. Sec. to dean Chgo. Sch. Civics and Philanthropy (now U. Chgo.), 1915-17; cons. pub. and/or program devel., Family Soc., Boston, 1930-37, Russell Sage Found., N.Y.C., 1937-39, Greater N.Y. Fund, N.Y.C., 1939-58, N.Y.C. Foster Care Commn., 1958-61, Fedn. Protestant Welfare Agys., N.Y.C., 1961-75, Woodycrest-Five Points Child Care, N.Y.C., 1972-77. Founder, bd. dirs. Vt. Children's Aid Soc., 1919-22, N.Y.C. Career Center for Social Service, 1953-73; mem. Sch. Com., Belmont, Mass., 1935-37. Recipient Ittleson award, 1970, Keystone award Fedn. Protestant Welfare Agys., 1971, award N.Y. State Welfare Conf., 1974, award Centennial Alumnae Recognition, Girls Latin Sch., Boston, 1978, Centennial award Radcliffe Alumnae Assn., 1979, Sch. Social Service award U. Chgo., 1979. Mem. Acad. Cert. Social Workers, Nat. Assn. Social Workers, N.Y. State

Welfare Conf., Radcliffe Coll. Alumnae Assn., U. Chgo. Alumni Assn., Phi Beta Kappa. Unitarian. Contbr. articles to profl. jours. Home: 1920 Collingwood Blvd Toledo OH 43624

LINDFORS, VIVECA, actress; b. Uppsala, Sweden; came to U.S., 1946, naturalized, 1950; d. Torsten and Karin (Dymling) L.; grad. Gymnasium, Stockholm; m. George Tabori, July 4, 1954; children—John, Lena, Kristoffer. Joined Royal Drama Theatre, Sweden, 1938; appeared in plays in Sweden including Twelfth Night, 1945, Bloodwedding, 1944, French Without Tears, 1942; Swedish films include: Think if I Marry the Minister, 1940, Anna Lans, 1941, The Two Brothers, 1941, In Death's Waiting Room, 1942; plays in the U.S. include: I've Got Sixpence, 1953, Anastasia (Drama League award), 1954, An Eve With Will Shakespeare, 1953, Miss Julie, 1955, King Lear, 1955, Brecht on Brecht, 1961, I Am A Women (co-producer, co-arranger, actress), Mother Courage, 1970, Dance on Death, 1971, Theatre of Space and Touring, 1973; toured in Far Country, coll. readings, 1964; films in U.S. include: Night Unto Night, 1947, Don Juan, 1947, No Sad Songs for You, 1948, Four Men in a Jeep (Berlin Film Festival award), 1948, Run for Cover, 1953, Captain Dreyfus, 1956, Weddings and Babies, 1956, No Exit (Berlin Festival Silver Bear award), 1960, Affair of the Skin, 1962, Sylvia, 1964, Brainstorm, 1965, The Stronger, The Jewish Wife, An Actor Works, The Way We Were, 1972, Welcome to LA, 1975, Tabu, 1975, The Wedding, 1977, Girlfriend, 1978; TV appearances include: The Bridge of San Luis Rey, 1958, The Idiot, 1958, Defenders, 1963, Naked City, 1963, Ben Casey, 1964, The Nurses, 1964, other weekly shows; theatre prodns. I Am a Woman, My Mother, My Son; prod. Strolling Players for coll. tours, 1966-69; artistic dir., founder Berkshire Theatre Festival; founder Berkshire Children's Theatre; tchr. acting workshop Sarah Lawrence Coll. Author: Viveha . . . Viveca, 1981. Address: care Bret Adams Ltd 36 E 61st St New York NY 10021 *

LINDHOLM, KATHRYN JEANNE, research psychologist; b Chgo., Aug. 3, 1954; d. Carroll Raymond and Sally Ann (Elmore) Lindholm; B.A., U. Calif., Santa Barbara, 1976; M.A., UCLA, 1977, PH.D., 1981; m. Amado Manuel Padilla, Aug. 1, 1981. Research asst. Edn. Devel. Center, Newton, Mass., 1974-76; research asst. Spanish Speaking Mental Health Research Center, UCLA, 1976-77, research asso., 1977-81, asst. research psychologist, 1981—, adj. lectr., 1981—; cons. to Calif. State Dept. Edn., Sacramento, 1979-80. Calif. State scholar, 1972-76; NSF grantee, 1974; NIMH grantee, 1981. Mem. AAAS, Am. Psychol. Assn., Am. Sociol. Assn., Research Com. on Sociolinguistics, Western Psychol. Assn., Am. Scandinavian Found., Sigma Xi. Author: Proposal Writing Strategies, 1981; contbr. chpts. to books. Home: 5139 Balboa Blvd Apt 1 Encino CA 91316 Office: Dept Psychology Univ Calif Los Angeles 90024

LINDLEY, JANE ANN, govt. adminstr.; b. Logansport, Ind., Oct. 2, 1942; d. Gerald Davis and Mary Jane (Beale) L.; B.A., Butler U., 1964; M.L.S., U. Md., 1973. With Library of Congress, Washington, 1964—, librarian, bibliographer, 1971-76, intern, 1975-76, congl. research adminstr. Congl. Research Service, 1976—; cons. Battelle Meml. Inst., 1970—. U.S. Internat. Communication Agy. grantee, 1981. Mem. Nat. Assn. Female Execs., Spl. Libraries Assn., Women in Info. Processing, Beta Phi Mu, Kappa Kappa Gamma. Baptist. Home: 2435 Mary Pl Fort Washington MD 20744 Office: Congressional Research Service Library of Congress Washington DC 20540

LINDLEY, JUDITH MORLAND, cat breeder; b. Burbank, Calif., Mar. 25, 1948; d. Howard Paxson and Hazel Mary (Morland) Conrow; student Calif. public schs.; m. William Ames, 1966; 1 dau., Pamela Irene; m. 2d, Jimmy McCoy Lindley, June 13, 1973; 1 son, Jimmy Joseph-Howard. Owner Tri-Color Ranch and Cattery, North Palm Springs, Calif., 1973—; pres.-founder Calico Cat Registry Internat., 1978—; operator Palm Springs Area Animal Helpline, 1979—. Mormon. Author: Calico Cat Registry Handbook, 1978. Address: 64406 Thumb Dr North Palm Springs CA 92258

LINDNER, CHARLOTTE K., librarian; b. N.Y.C., Feb. 28, 1922; d. Louis B. and Ada (Kreitman) Fisch; B.A., N.Y.U., 1942; M.L.S., Columbia U., 1959; children—Carol, Gregory, Amy. Asst. cataloger D. Samuel Gottesman Library, Albert Einstein Coll. Medicine, Bronx, N.Y., 1958-63, cataloger, 1963-76, asst. librarian, 1974-76, acting dir. library, 1976-78, dir. library, 1978—. Mem. Med. Library Assn.

LINDNER, ERNA CAPLOW, educator, choreographer, movement therapist; b. N.Y.C., May 26, 1928; d. Abraham Murray and Mildred T. (Farb) Caplow; A.B., Bklyn Coll., 1948; M.S., Smith Coll., 1950; m. Norman Lindner, June 18, 1950 (dec. Sept. 1981); 1 dau., Amy Beth. Instr. dance Brown U., 1950-54, Rutgers U., 1954-55; dance specialist Samuel Field YM—YWHA, Queens, N.Y., 1962-68; dance specialist N.Y.C. Bd. Edn., 1963-69; asst. dance dir., choreographer Martin de Porres Center, Queens, 1967-70; dir. Saturday Cultural Program, Rochdale Village Nursery Sch., Queens, 1964-73; dir.-choreographer Danceabouts Co., N.Y.C., 1966-80; prof. health, phys. edn. and recreation Nassau Community Coll. SUNY, L.I., 1968—; adj. prof. phys. edn. and dance Adelphi U., 1979—. Active Dance Library in Israel; charter mem. Queens Council on Arts, exec. bd. dirs., 1970-74; sec., mem. exec. com. Nat. Ednl. Council Creative Therapies. Mem. Am. Dance Guild (charter mem., past nat. pres., nat. exec. bd.), N.E. 4 State Region Dance Guild (officer), Queens Dance Guild (founding), Am. Dance Therapy Assn., Am. Assn. Sex Educators, Counselors and Therapists (cert. sex educator, sex counselor). Contbr. chpts. on dance to Fun for Fitness; interviewer on dance Sta. WHPC-FM; (with others) selected music and wrote manual for Special Music for Special People, Ednl. Act Rec. Co., 1977; Special Dancing on Your Feet and in Your Seat, 1982. Author: (with others) Therapeutic Dance/Movement, 1979; (monograph) Use of Dance in Sex Education and Counseling, 1974; also articles on geriatric dance therapy. Home: 4915 Skillman Ave Woodside NY 11377 Office: Nassau Community Coll Stewart Ave Garden City NY 11530

LINDQUIST, EDITH LORRAINE, educator; b. Duluth, Minn., Aug. 2, 1931; d. Andrew H. and Edith Margaret (Nordmark) Lindquist; B.S. (Calif. State scholar 1952), U. Calif., Santa Barbara, 1953; M.S., U. So. Calif., 1955; Ph.D. (teaching asst. 1962, 65), U. Mich., 1968. Instr. phys. edn. Los Angeles city schs., 1953-65; research grantee Horace R. Rackham Sch. Grad. Studies, U. Mich., 1968; prof. phys. edn. San Jose (Calif.) State U., 1966—; research chmn. Western Soc. Phys. Edn. Coll. Women, 1975-78, spl. projects chmn., 1975; cons. in field. Grantee HEW, 1971; spl. projects grantee Western Soc. for Phys. Edn. Coll. Women, 1977-78; Calif. State Dept. Edn. grantee, 1979-80. Mem. AAPHER (fellow Research Consortium), Calif. Assn. Health, Phys. Edn. and Recreation, Nat. Assn. Phys. Edn. in Higher Edn., Calif. Tchrs. Assn., N.Am. Soc. for Psychology of Sport and Phys. Activity, Can. Soc. for Psychomotor Learning and Sport Psychology, Alpha Delta Pi. Democrat. Author papers in field. Asso. editor Motor Skills: Theory into Practice, 1976—. Home: 4414 Thousand Oaks Dr San Jose CA 95136 Office: San Jose State Univ San Jose CA 95192

LINDQUIST, NANCY ELIZABETH, computer systems co. ofcl.; b. San Jose, Calif., Mar. 30, 1931; d. Alfred and Florence (Schroeder) Burnell; B.A. in Polit. Sci., U. Calif., Berkeley, 1951; m. Richard Morales, May 6, 1949; 1 son, Richard; m. 2d, John Lindquist, Dec. 21, 1974. Mem. acctg. staff United Airlines, 1951-58; dist. mgr. Tara Fifth Ave., 1958-66; head dept. accounts payable Sequoia Hosp., Redwood City, Calif., 1966-67; mgr. accounts payable Saga Corp., Menlo Park, Calif., 1967-79; mgr. dept. accounts payable Granger Assos., Santa Clara, Calif., 1979-82; acctg. mgr. Calif. Computer Systems, Sunnyvale, 1982—. Mem. Motivated Women's Network, Profl. Women's Network, Am. Soc. Profl. and Exec. Women, Smithsonian Instn., San Francisco Mus. Soc., Met. Mus. Art. Home: 602 Prune Way San Jose CA 95117 Office: 250 Caribbean Dr Sunnyvale CA 94086

LINDSAY, DIANNA M., ednl. adminstr.; b. Boston, Dec. 7, 1948; d. Albert Joseph and June (Mitchell) Raggi; A.B., Eastern Nazarene Coll., 1971; M.Ed., Wright State U., 1973, M.Ed., 1974; Ed.D., Ball State U., 1976; m. James William Lindsay, Feb. 14, 1981. Tchr., Wayne Twp. Schs., Dayton, Ohio, 1971-74, 75-77; instr. Ball State U., Muncie, Ind., 1974-75; state supr. for social studies and humanities Ohio Dept. Edn., 1977-78; asst. prin. Orange High Sch., Pepper Pike, Ohio, 1978-80; prin. N. Olmsted (Ohio) Jr. High Sch., 1980—; edn. cons. Sta. WCET-TV, Cin. Bd. trustees Glenn Oak Sch. for Girls. Mem. N. Olmsted Assn. Sch. Adminstrs. (pres.), Assn. Supervision and Curriculum Devel., Buckeye Assn. Sch. Adminstrs., Nat. Assn. Secondary Sch. Adminstrs., Ohio Assn. Secondary Sch. Adminstrs., Ohio Middle Sch. Assn., Ohio Sch. Bds. Assn., Phi Delta Kappa. Contbr. articles to profl. jours. Office: 27351 Butternut Ridge Rd North Olmsted OH 44070

LINDSAY, JUANITA, chem. co. exec.; b. Fort Worth, July 4, 1924; d. Clarence Hinton and Lavena Susan (Kennedy) High; student Brantley-Draughan Bus. Coll., 1948-49, Tex. Christian U., 1951; m. Kenneth E. Lindsay, May 21, 1976; children by previous marriage—Sherry Leonard Boatman, Pamela Sue Leonard Swift, Barbara Hefner. With Community Public Service Co., Fort Worth, 1947-50; owner, prin. bookkeeping service, Fort Worth, 1950-57; with Ridgewood Motor Hotel & Gift Shop, Beaumont, Tex., 1957-61; bookkeeper, office mgr. Beaumont Petroleum Club, 1957-61; with Green, McReynolds & Sherrell, C.P.A.s, Longview, Tex., 1962-65; with Delta Solvents & Chems. Co., Longview, Tex., 1968—, office mgr., 1969—, corp. sec., 1975—. Mem. Am. Bus. Womens Assn. Mem. Christian Ch. Clubs: Zonta of Longview, Lucky Squares. Office: Delta Solvents and Chemicals Co 610 Fisher Rd Longview TX 75604

LINDSAY, VAUGHNIE JEAN, univ. dean; b. Prague, Okla., Mar. 31, 1921; d. Irvin Frank and Cora Kennedy Garrette; B.S.E., Central State U., Edmond, Okla., 1940; M.B.E. with Spl. Distinction, U. Okla., 1959; Ed.D. with Spl. Distinction, Ind. U., Bloomington, 1966; m. Joseph D. Lindsay III, July 21, 1947 (dec.); children—Deborah Rogers, Sandra Doreson. Tchr., Guthrie (Okla.) High Sch., 1942-43; asst. prof. Southwestern State Coll., Weatherford, Okla., 1959-62; asso. prof. U. Okla., Norman, 1965-70; prof. Sch. Bus., So. Ill. U., Edwardsville, 1970—, dean grad. studies and research, 1973—. Recipient Teaching Excellence award So. Ill. U.-Edwardsville Sch. Bus., 1973; named Outstanding Bus. Educator, Delta Pi Epsilon, 1979; Danforth fellow, 1962-64. Mem. Ill. Assn. Grad. Schs. (pres.), Council Grad. Schs. (chmn. task force on women in higher adminstrn.), Nat. Council Univ. Research Adminstrn., Am. Council Edn., Nat. Assn. Bus. Tchr. Edn. (exec. bd.), Nat. Bus. Edn. Assn. (exec. bd.), Ill. Bus. Edn. Assn. (chmn. council affiliated pres.), Delta Pi Epsilon (nat. research com.) Editor: Nat. Assn. Bus. Tchr. Edn. Rev., 1972, Bus. Edn. Forum, 1971, Nat. Bus. Edn. Quar., 1971; contbr. articles to profl. jours. Office: So Ill U Box 46 Edwardsville IL 62026

LINDSEY, BARBARA ANN, pub. exec., polit. ofcl.; b. Corry, Pa., Sept. 11, 1940; d. Melvin C. and Madge Jeanette (Peterson) Gable; ed. U. Palm Beach, Indian River Jr. Coll.; children—Melody Layne, Merry Lee, Lorrie Ann, Jewel Lynne, Mona Louise. Head librarian, dept. sec. RCA, Palm Beach Gardens, Fla., 1960-63; legal sec. Thurlow & Thurlow, Stuart, Fla., 1963-64; v.p. R. C. Lindsey Plumbing, Inc., 1962-82; Amway distbr., dress designer Candi Lin, 1958—; pres. Lindsey, Gable, Conroy & Assos., Inc., Stuart, 1979-82; pres. Am. Advt. Agy.; editor, pub. Prominent People in Fla. Govt. Republican state committeewoman Martin County; exec. bd. Rep. Party of Fla., 1976-80; alt. vice chmn. 10th Congl. Dist.; mem. Rep. Nat. Com., Congl. Adv. Bd.; bd. advisors Am. Security Soc.; mem. Nat. Congl. Adv. Com. Named Sec. of Yr., Palm Beach Profl. Secs., 1968, Mem. of Yr., Treasure Coast Home Builders Aux., 1979. Mem. Profl. Secs. Internat., Nat. Home Builders Aux., Women for Responsible Legislation, Internat. Entrepreneurs Assn., Fla. Direct Markets Assn., Fla. Farm Bur., Stuart C. of C., Gold Coast Direct Mktg. Assn., Internat. Platform Assn. Baptist. Clubs: United Women's Rep. (pres.), Rep. of Fla., Women's Rep. of Martin, Fla. Fedn. Rep. Women. Home: 4108 SE Dixie Ross Rd Stuart FL 33494 Office: 6368 SE Held Ct Stuart FL 33494

LINDSEY, BEVERLY EILEEN, civic worker; b. Indpls., June 13, 1934; d. Elmer Allen and Gertrude Eileen (Snapp) Baldwin; B.S., Butler U. and John Herron Art Inst., 1956; postgrad. Toledo U., 1959-64; M.A., St. Francis Coll., 1974; postgrad. Ft. Wayne Art Sch., 1972-74; m. Hugh Makley Lindsey, Mar. 25, 1955; children—Pamela Eileen, Hugh Jeffrey, Matthew, Christopher. Tchr. elem. art Bryan (Ohio) City Schs., 1957-77, art supt., 1965-75; area adv. Ohio Art Edn. Assn., 1970-72. Pres., Williams County Panhellenic Assn., 1979, scholarship chmn., 1980; chmn., pres. Bryan Area Fine Arts Council, 1976; chmn., treas. Bryan Christian Women's Prayer Breakfast, 1980; deacon 1st Presbyn. Ch., 1979-81. Ohio Arts Council grantee, 1975-76. Mem. NEA, Ohio Edn. Assn., Ohio Arts Edn. Assn., Bryan Fine Arts Council, Delta Kappa Gamma. Republican. Club: Williams County Panhellenic Assn. Home: 925 Markey St Bryan OH 43506

LINDSEY, BEVERLY SUE, educator; b. Muncie, Ind., June 14, 1930; d. Rollin William and Merkel May (Ruckman) L.; diploma Meth. Hosp. Sch. Nursing, Indpls., 1952; B.S. in Nursing, U. Mo., 1962; M.S. in Nursing, U. Colo., 1972; postgrad. U. Kans., 1979-80, U. Mo., 1980—. Gen. duty nurse U. Kans. Med. Center, 1952-53; staff nurse med.-surg. intensive care unit VA Hosp., Kansas City, Mo., 1953-55, head nurse, 1957-60; instr. med.-surg. nursing U. Mo., Columbia, 1962-64; sch. nurse tchr. Kansas City (Mo.) Bd. Edn., 1964; med.-surg. coordinator Research Hosp. and Med. Center, Kansas City, Mo., 1964-65; instr. practical nurse program Kansas City Bd. Edn., 1965-66; nurse instr. cardiology Kansas City (Mo.) Gen. Hosp. and Med. Center, 1966-68, edn. coordinator programmed cardiovascular care project, 1968-71; asst. prof., U. Mo. Med. Sch., Kansas City, 1967-71; asst. prof. nursing Avila Coll., Kansas City, Mo., 1972-75, asso. prof., 1975—, acting chmn. dept. nursing, 1978-79, 80-82, asso. chmn., 1979-80, chmn., 1982—. reviewer grant projects HEW, 1974-75; lectr. in field. Served to col. Nurse Corp USAFR, 1960—. Mem. Am. Nurses Assn., Mo. Nurses Assn., Res. Officers Assn., Nat. League Nursing, Sigma Theta Tau. Club: Order Eastern Star. Contbr. articles to profl. jours. Office: 11901 Wornall Rd Kansas City MO 64145

LINDSEY, DOTTYE JEAN, educator; b. Temple Hill, Ky., Nov. 4, 1929; d. Jesse D. and Ethel Ellen (Bailey) Nuckols; B.S., Western Ky. U., 1953, M.A., 1959; m. Willard W. Lindsey, June 14, 1952 (div.). Owner, Bonanza Restaurant, Charleston, W.Va., 1965; tchr. remedial reading Alice Waller Elem. Sch., Louisville, 1967-75, tchr., 1953-67, 1975—, contact person for remedial reading, 1968—. Bn. sponsor ROTC Western Ky. U., 1950. Named Miss Ky., 1951. Mem. NEA, Ky. Edn. Assn., Jefferson County Tchrs. Assn., various polit. action coms., Internat. Reading Assn., Am. Childhood Edn. Assn., Met. Louisville Women's Polit. Caucus (treas. 1980—). Democrat. Baptist.

LINDSEY, LETHA HOBLEY, educator; b. Quincy, Fla., May 8, 1949; d. Joe Nathan and Luenez Bush Hobley; B.S., Bennett Coll., 1971; M.Ed., U. S. Fla., 1981. Reserve librarian Pilot Life Ins. Co., Greensboro, N.C., 1971; data analyst Ciba-Geigy Dyestuffs and Chemicals, Greensboro, N.C., 1972; tchr. math. Hillsborough County Schs., Tampa, Fla., 1972—; math. instr. Project Thrust, U. S. Fla., 1979—; Recipient Bennett Coll. Nat. Merit Scholarship award, 1967-70; City of Tampa Scholarship award, 1970-71; Grad. Ednl. Opportunity grantee, 1980-81. Mem. Nat. Council Tchrs. Math., Nat. Assn. Female Execs. Inc., Assn. for Supervision and Curriculum Devel., AAUW, Kappa Delta Pi. Baptist. Home: 1808 E Frierson Ave Tampa FL 33610

LINDSEY, RETHA, journalist, coll. ofcl.; b. Snyder, Tex., June 15, 1949; d. Joe William and Muriel Jean (Hammons) Vincent; student Tex. A&M Police Acad., 1972, Western Tex. Coll., 1980—; m. Johnny Marion Lindsey, July 15, 1967. Dispatcher, Snyder Police Dept., 1968; asst. librarian spl. services, USO, Aschaffenberg, W.Ger., 1970; dispatcher Sweetwater Police Dept., 1971-74; dep. sheriff Nolan County, Tex., 1974-75; reporter, asst. editor Sweetwater Reporter, 1976-79; corr. Abilene Reporter News, 1979-80; freelance writer, 1979—; reporter Odessa (Tex.) Am., 1981-82; dir. news/info. Odessa Coll., 1982—. Address: Star Route Box 58E Andrews TX 79714

LINDSEY-CRAIG, GRACE YVONNE, real estate devel. co. exec.; b. Wray, Colo., Nov. 4, 1935; d. Frank Robert and Vesta Mae (Rose) Allen; student Colo. Ohlone Coll., 1970-74; m. July 15, 1978; children—Linda Diane Lindsey, Debra Kaye Lindsey, Allen James Lindsey (by previous marriage). Bldg. mgr. J.M.B. Realty, San Mateo, Calif., 1973-75; property mgr. San Jose Gateway (Dillingham Corp.), 1975-78; gen. mgr. Copperfield Investment & Devel. Co., San Jose, 1978-82, v.p., 1982—; cons. in field. Lic. real estate broker, 1979; cert. property mgr. Mem. C. of C. Women in Bus. (exec. steering com. 1981), Public Relations Inst. of Real Estate Mgmt. (chmn. 1981), Peninsula Profl. Bus. Women's Network, Profl. Connections for Women, San Jose Bd. Realtors, South Bay Property Mgrs. Assn., South Bay Brokers Assn., Nat. Women's Polit. Caucus. Office: 2025 Gateway Place Suite 100 San Jose CA 95110

LINDSTROM, ANITA INGER, psychologist; b. Ranea, Sweden, May 7, 1940; came to U.S., 1972; d. Helge Eugene and Alice (Gunborg) Broms; B.Ed., U. Lulea, 1962; M. Ednl. Psychology, U. Stockholm, 1972. Tchr. various pub. schs., Sweden, 1962-71; resource tchr. Taby Schs., Ellagard, Sweden, 1965-69, ednl. program designer, 1969-71; program specialist for developmental disabilities Bd. Edn., Stockholm, 1971; sch. psychologist Taby Sch., 1972; exchange visitor UCLA Neuropsychiat. Inst., 1972-73; psychologist Children's Hosp. Regional Center, Los Angeles, 1973-75, St. John's Hosp., Kennedy Regional Center, Santa Monica, Calif., 1974-75, N. Los Angeles County Regional Center, Van Nuys, Calif., 1975-77, Exceptional Children's Found., Los Angeles, 1975-78; pvt. practice psychology, marriage, family and child counselor, Newhall, Calif., 1978—; cons. in field. King Gustav VI Found. grantee, 1972. Mem. Am. Psychol. Assn., Calif. Psychol. Assn., Calif. Soc. for Hypnosis in Family Counseling, Newhall C. of C. Home: 17349 Boswell Pl Granada Hills CA 91344 Office: 23560 Lyons Ave Suite 205 Newhall CA 91321

LINDVIG, ELISE KAY, ednl. psychologist; b. Sidney, Mont., Feb. 10, 1952; d. William F. and Katheryn E. (Taylor) L.; student Carroll Coll. (Mont.), 1970-71; B.A. in Psychology with honors, U. Mont., 1974; M.S. in Clin. Psychology with high honors, U. Idaho, 1979. Assoc. coordinator Dept. Community Affairs, State of Mont., Glendive, 1974-75; teaching asst. U. Idaho, Moscow, 1975-79; sch. psychologist Hamilton, Mont., 1979-82, diagnostician, cons. in field; bookkeeper, musician, 1975-79. Mem. Am. Psychol. Assn. (assoc.), Mont. Assn. Sch. Psychologists (cons.), Idaho Mental Health Assn., Am. Quarter Horse Assn., Am. Kennel Club, Nat. Hot Rod Assn. Republican. Roman Catholic. Clubs: Eagles Aux., Moose Aux. Condr. research on malnutrition in primates; author: Nutrition and Mental Health, 1979; Grade Retention: Evolving Expectations and Individual Differences, 1982. Home: PO Box 1358 Hamilton MT 59840 Office: 411 Daly Ave Hamilton MY 59840

LINEBERGER, MARILYN HAZZARD, psychologist; b. Abbeville, S.C., Dec. 10, 1952; d. Sanders and Louise (Lomax) Hazzard; B.A., U. S.C., 1975; M.S., U. Ga., 1977, Ph.D., 1979; m. Frank James Lineberger, Jr., Sept. 1, 1979. Counselor, Gleams Community Action Agy., Greenwood, S.C., summers 1973-75; asst. prof. psychology Kent (Ohio) State U., 1979-80; asst. prof. psychology and clin. psychologist Emory U., Atlanta, 1980—. Vol. various polit. campaigns; active Big Bro. and Big Sister orgns. Mem. Am. Psychol. Assn., Assn. Advancement Behavior Therapy, Assn. Black Psychologists, Council on Children, AAAS, Midwestern Psychol. Assn., Mortar Bd., Nat. Honor Soc., Phi Beta Kappa, Psi Chi. Democrat. Methodist. Club: Pre-Profl. Psychology (adviser). Contbr. research articles to profl. lit. Home: 1255 Muirforest Ln Stone Mountain GA 30088 Office: Dept Psychology Emory U Atlanta GA 30322

LINEHAN, MARSHA MARIE, psychologist, educator; b. Tulsa, Okla., May 5, 1943; d. J. Marston and Ella Marie (Bourg) L.; B.S. cum laude, Loyola U., Chgo., 1968, M.A., 1970, Ph.D., 1971; postgrad. (fellow) SUNY, Stony Brook, 1972-73. Lectr. psychology Loyola U., Chgo., 1969-71, adj. asst. prof. Inst. Pastoral Studies, 1973; adj. asst. prof. psychology State U. Coll., Buffalo, 1972; asst. prof. psychology Cath. U. Am., Washington, D.C., 1973-77; asst. prof. psychology U. Wash., Seattle, 1977—, adj. asst. prof. psychiatry, 1981—; clin. cons. Center for Psychotherapy and Human Devel., Washington, 1975-77; cons. Response Crisis Line, SUNY, Stony Brook, 1972-73, VA Hosp., Md., 1974-77; counselor St. Patrick's Roman Cath. Ch., Seattle, 1979-80. Psychology vol. Downtown Emergency Services Center, Seattle, 1981—; bd. dirs. Crisis Clinic, Inc., Seattle, 1980—. NIMH grantee, 1974-75, 77-79, 81—. Mem. Am. Psychol. Assn., Western Psychol. Assn., Soc. for Psychotherapy Research, Assn. for Advancement of Behavior Therapy (chmn. for membership 1974-77), Am. Assn. of Suicidology. Contbr. articles on clin. psychology to profl. jours.; editorial bd. Behavior Modification, 1978, Cognitive Therapy and Research, 1978; asso. editor Behavior Therapy, 1980-81. Home: 5234 Brooklyn St NE Seattle WA 98105 Office: Washington Dept Psychology NI-Z5 Seattle WA 98195

LING, BARBARA JOAN, bus. exec., cons.; b. Cedar Rapids, Iowa, Mar. 28, 1946; d. Calvin Herbert and Ellen (Hanson) Ling; B.A., U. Kans., 1968; certificate in med. tech. Ill. Masonic Med. Center, Chgo., 1969; M.B.A., Pepperdine U., 1980. Med. technologist U. Calif. Med. Center, San Francisco, 1970-72; tech. cons. Automated Health Systems, Wakefield, Mass., 1972-73; mktg. specialist, sr. bus. program analyst Digital Equipment Corp., Maynard, Mass., 1973-75; field systems sales engr. Applicon, Inc., Burlington, Mass., 1975-76; customer mktg. mgr., mktg. analysis mgr., bus. systems devel. mgr. Intel Corp., Santa Clara, Calif., 1976-81; mgr. advanced planning Corp. Info. Systems, Memorex Corp., Santa Clara, 1981—; mem. adv. bd. for small computing systems seminars and confs. Am. Inst. Indsl. Engrs. Bd. dirs. Dixon Landing Homeowners Assn., 1979—, pres., 1980. Mem. Children's Health Council Aux., Soc. Women Engrs., Am. Soc. Clin. Pathologists. Republican. Club: Peninsula Little (pres.). Home: 920 Peggy Ln Menlo Park CA 94025 Office: San Tomas

LINGARD, ANNE MARIE, ins. co. exec.; b. Fall River, Mass., Apr. 24; d. William Charles and Ann Cecilia (O'Brien) L.; student F.G. Allen Bus. Sch., 1942-43, New Eng. Conservatory of Music, 1950-52. Various sales and clerical positions with retail stores and mfg. firms, Fall River,

1940-68; personnel asst. Aetna Life & Casualty Co., Fall River, 1968-72, personnel dir., 1972—; instr. indsl. mgmt. evening div. Southeastern Mass. U., 1979—; mem. Fall River Indsl. Commn., 1979—. Mem. bd. bus. edn. Diman Regional Vocat. High Sch., Fall River, 1972-73; mgr. Deaconess Home Bd., 1979-81; pres. Cathedral Choristers, 1953-57; del. to Mass. Republican Conv., 1960-64; pres. Women's Rep. Club, 1964-66; bd. dirs. Fall River United Way, 1975-82, Fall River Arts Council, 1980—, Fall River Alcoholism Council, 1981—; v.p. Arts Unltd., 1980-82; mem. cathedral restoration com. St. Mary's Cathedral, 1979-80. Mem. Am. Soc. Personnel Adminstrs. (chpt. pres. 1982), Nat. Assn. Female Execs., Fall River Personnel Council (v.p. 1980-81, pres. 1981-82), Fall River Council on Arts (v.p. 1980), Internat. Platform Assn., Fall River C. of C. (dir. 1976-80), Am. Soc. Notaries, Fall River Pro Musica, Marine Mus., Fall River Symphony Soc. Clubs: Fall River Women's, Quequechan. Office: 299 S Main Fall River MA 02721

LINGREN, NANCY CARROLL, energy co. exec.; b. Woodland, Calif., Jan. 4, 1944; d. Charles Harvin and Eleanore Elizabeth (Doty) Carroll; B.A., Golden Gate U., 1981; m. Bill Wayne Lingren, Feb. 16, 1974; 1 son, Scott Kelly Morrison. With inventory, billing, mktg. depts. Ortho div. Chevron Chem. Co., San Francisco, 1970-73, field research, services, 1973-74, chem. buyer, purchasing, 1974-77, pub. affairs specialist youth and edn. Chevron U.S.A. Inc., San Francisco, 1977—. Chmn. nat. adv. bd. Distributive Edn. Clubs Am., 1982—; bd. dirs. Nat. Soc. for Internships and Exptl. Edn., 1981-82; bd. dirs. Yolo County Sheltered Workshop, 1971-73, sec., 1972-73. Mem. Nat. Fedn. Bus. and Profl. Women's Clubs, Pub. Affairs Women. Republican. Club: Commonwealth of Calif., Woodland Bus. and Profl. Women's (pres. 1973-74). Home: 4125 Barner Ave Oakland CA 94602 Office: Chevron USA Inc 595 Market St San Francisco CA 94105 also PO Box 7753 San Francisco CA 94120

LININGTON, BARBARA ELIZABETH, novelist; b. Aurora, Ill., Mar. 11, 1921; d. Byron Gerald and Ruth Cleveland (Biggam) L.; B.A., Glendale (Calif.) Coll., 1941. Author 73 mystery novels, 5 hist. novels, since 1955, including The Long Watch (Gold medal Calif. Commonwealth Club 1956). Republican. Address: 2715 Southview Ave Arroyo CA 93420

LINK, IRENE MAY AMMONS, educator, poet; b. Pueblo, Colo., Apr. 18, 1939; d. Elbert A. and Jennie D. (Panepinto) Ammons; B.A., N.W. Nazarene Coll., 1964; postgrad. U. Hawaii, 1968; m. Peter M. Link, Dec. 19, 1965. Feature writer, photographer Times-News, Twin Falls, Idaho, 1975—; instr. bus. dept. Coll. So. Idaho, Twin Falls, 1972—; instr. speech and English Twin Falls High Sch., 1965-70; v.p. Link Land and Livestock Co.; cons. image making, advt. and public relations; lectr. bus. women's seminars Mem. Idaho Edn. Assn., Idaho Assn. Bus. Tchrs., AAUW, NEA, Am. Soc. Profl. and Exec. Women, Nat. Assn. for Female Execs. Home: Route 1 Box 267 Hansen ID 83334 Office: Coll So Idaho PO Box 1238 Twin Falls ID 83301

LINK, MAE MILLS (MRS. S. GORDDEN LINK), space medicine research cons.; b. Corbin, Ky., May 14, 1915; d. William Speed and Florence (Estes) Mills; B.S., George Peabody Coll. for Tchrs., 1936; M.A., Vanderbilt U., 1937; Ph.D., Am. U., 1951; grad. Air War Coll., 1965; m. S. Gordden Link, Jan. 11, 1936. Instr. social sci. Oglethorpe U., 1938-39; instr. English, Drury Coll., 1940-41; asso. dir. edn. Ga. Warm Springs Found., 1941-42; mil. historian Hdqrs. Army Air Forces, 1943-45, Office Mil. History, Dept. of Army, 1945-51; spl. asst. to surgeon gen. and sr. med. historian U.S. Air Force, Washington, 1951-62; cons. in documentation and space medicine historian NASA, Washington, 1962-64, coordinator documentation and life scis. historian, 1964-70; research asso. Ohio State U. Found., 1970-72; trustee, dir. history fellows Koontz Meml. Center Advanced Studies, 1972—. Trustee, Univ. Press Fund, Amos R. Koontz Meml. Found. Recipient Meritorious Service award U.S. Air Force, 1955, Outstanding Performance awards, 1956-62; Friday Nighters cup, 1960; Outstanding Alumna award Sue Bennett Coll., 1977. Fellow Am. Med. Writers Assn. (past dir. Middle Atlantic region); mem. Aerospace Med. Assn. (standing com. on sci. communication in bioastronautics and space medicine), Am. Inst. Aeros. and Astronautics (hist. adv. com.), Air Force Hist. Found. (charter), Am. Assn. Med. History, Internat. Congress History Medicine, Soc. for History Tech., Societe International d'Histoire de la Medecine. Republican. Episcopalian. Clubs: Garden Va. Author: Medical Support of the Army Air Forces in World War II, 1955; Annual Reports of the U.S. Air Force Medical Service, 1949-62; Space Medicine in Project Mercury, 1965; (with others) Foundations of Space Biology and Medicine, 1976. Editor: U.S. Air Force Med. Service Digest, 1957-62. Contbr. to Ency. Brit., Collier's Ency., Funk & Wagnall's New Ency., Foundations of Space—Biology and Medicine (USA/USSR Joint Publ.). Contbr. articles to profl. jours. Home: Dellbrook Riverton VA 22651 Office: Koontz Center for Advanced Studies Riverton VA 22651

LINKE, FRANCES BAUR (NINA BARA), librarian; b. Buenos Aires, Argentina, May 3, 1924 (parents Am. citizens); d. George and Caroline (Cunioli) Baur; A.A., Los Angeles City Coll., 1962; B.S., Calif. State U., 1967; M.S. in L.S., U. So. Calif., 1972; m. Raymond J. Linke, Mar. 20, 1964; 1 dau., Cecillia. Appeared in TV series Space Patrol, 1950-54; librarian Minn. Mining & Mfg. Co., Los Angeles, 1960-64; librarian, writer library newsletter Blue Cross of So. Calif., Los Angeles, 1964—. Co-owner Nin-Ra Siamese Cattery, La Canada, Calif., 1967—. Mem. Calif. Library Assn. (pres. emeritus govt. publs. chpt. 1976—), Spl. Libraries Assn. (mem. subject heading com., ins. div. 1968-74), Med. Library Group So. Calif., Am. Cat Assn., Cat Fanciers Assn., Am. Cat Fanciers Assn., Screen Actors Guild, AFTRA. Author: Gone to the Cats, bibliography of cat books, 1973; Space Patrol-Memories, 1976; Space Patrol III, 1980; compiler: Space Patrol Comics, 1977; contbr. articles on cats, also sci. fiction, to publs. Office: PO Box 70000 Van Nuys CA 91470

LINKENHOKER, PATRICIA LOUISE LILLY, ednl. adminstr.; b. Athens, W.Va., Mar. 22, 1929; d. Paris I. and Tessie Fair (Ross) Lilly; B.S. in Music Edn., Concord Coll., 1949; M.A. in Supervision, Marshall U., 1973; m. George William Linkenhoker, Jr., June 3, 1949; 1 dau., Ruth Elizabeth Linkenhoker Boyles. Elem. music tchr. Mercer County, W.Va., and Thorn Sch., 1949-71; elem. supr. Mercer County, Princeton, W.Va., 1971—. Life mem. PTA; dir. youth and adult handbell choirs, mem. adult choir, Sunday Sch. worker, mem. Wesleyanna Sharing Group. Named tchr. of yr. Mercer County, 1969-70. Mem. NEA (life), W.Va. Edn. Assn., Mercer County Edn. Assn., Mercer County Elem. Prins. Assn., Assn. Supervision and Curriculum Devel., W.Va. Assn. Supervision and Curriculum Devel., Internat. Reading Assn., W.Va. Reading Council, Mercer County Reading Council, Phi Delta Kappa (pres.), Delta Kappa Gamma (pres. Zeta chpt., 1976-78, award, 1969), Sigma Sigma Sigma. Address: 1307 N Walker St Princeton WV 24740

LINKOUS, GARNETT SWENNEY, univ. ofcl.; b. Christiansburg, Va., Nov. 21, 1943; d. John Walker and Lelia Coleman (Lovern) Sweeney; student public schs.; m. Frederick T. Linkous, Sept. 14, 1961; children—Pamela Ann, Michael Thomas. Mem. adminstrv. staff Va. Poly. Inst. and State U., Blacksburg, 1962—, mgr. contract and grant adminstrn., 1978—, also advisor Mortar Bd. Bd. dirs. Women's Resource Center New River Valley, 1979—. Mem. Am. Assn. Women Accts. (pres.), Soc. Research Adminstrs., Am. Bus. Women's Assn. Lutheran. Home: 616 Owens St Blacksburg VA 24060 Office: 304 Burruss Hall Va Poly Inst and State Univ Blacksburg VA 24061

LINKSZ, JULIE FRAKNOI, psychologist; b. Budapest, Hungary, Feb. 12, 1915; came to U.S., 1956, naturalized, 1963; d. Isidor and Ethel (Weisz) Friedlander; diploma U. Budapest, 1938; Ph.D. summa cum laude, U. Szeged (Hungary), 1945; postdoctoral fellow Menninger Found., 1958-60; m. Arthur Linksz, May 5, 1978. Clin. psychologist Boys Indsl. Sch., Topeka, 1957-58, child and adult services, Dept. Psychiatry Med. Sch. U. Pa., Phila., 1960-62; sr. psychologist, dir. psychol. tng. Inst. Phys. Medicine and Rehab., N.Y.U. Med. Center, 1962-65; research cons. dept. child psychiatry, U. Pa., 1962-65, chief psychologist unit for autistic children, 1965-67, asso., then asst. prof. Med. Sch., 1960-75; cons. Child Study Center of Phila., 1967-70; dir. psychol. services Phila. Psychiat. Center Community Mental Health Program, 1967-75, dir. in service tng., 1971-74, Coping Clinic, 1973-75, mem. faculty tng. program for psychiat. residents, 1973-74; project mgr. personalized programs for sentenced offenders, Dade County (Fla.) Dept. Rehab., 1975-76; coordinator profl. supervision Middle Tenn. Mental Health Inst., Nashville, 1976-77, cons. and supr. Children and Youth Services and Drug and Alcohol Unit, Moccasin Bend Mental Health Inst., Chattanooga, 1977-78. NIMH grantee, 1960-75; lic. clin. psychologist, Tenn.; cert. clin. psychologist, Va., Hawaii, Wis. Fellow Pa. Psychol. Assn.; mem. Am. Psychol. Assn., Am. Group Psychotherapy Assn., Eastern Psychol. Assn., Tenn. Psychol. Assn., Phila. Soc. Clin. Psychologists, World Mental Health Assn., Menninger Sch. Psychiatry Alumni Assn. Democrat. Contbr. numerous articles in field to profl. jours. Address: 35 E 84th St New York NY 10028

LINLEY, MARILYN WILLIAMS, TV producer; b. Waukesha, Wis., Oct. 26, 1922; d. Arthur Joseph and Vivian Jeanette Marie (LaHaie) Williams; B.A., Carroll Coll., 1944; M.A., Marquette U., 1969; m. Herbert Laflin Linley, 1945 (div. 1963); children—Marilyn Margaret, Elizabeth Anne, Jane Milton. Tchr., Fort Atkinson (Wis.) High Sch., 1944-45; substitute tchr. Accelerated High Sch., Balt., 1945-46; tchr. public schs. Rahway, Long Branch, Eatontown and Oceanport, N.J., 1946-60; columnist Long Branch (N.J.) Daily Record, 1960; tchr. Long Branch Schs., 1960-61; tchr. Mukwonago (Wis.) Union High Sch., 1962-70, team tchr., 1970-71; cons., tchr. English Houston High Sch. for Performing and Visual Arts, 1971-73; tchr. Tng. Center Human Resources Devel. and Edn. Renewal, 1973-74; media staff devel. tchr. Continuing Careers Devel. Center, MacGregor, 1973-74; instr. TV specialist Instructional Media Services, Houston, 1974; instructional TV producer, Houston, 1977—. Former bd. dirs. Episcopal Churchwomen Diocese N.J., Rahway Service League (N.J.), Jr. League, Monmouth, N.J., Welfare Council, Monmouth, Long Branch (N.J.) Public Health Nursing Assn., PTA, Long Branch, N.J., Waukesha, Wis., Waukesha Symphony Orch., 1969; pres. Waukesha Symphony Aux., 1970, Friends U. Wis., Waukesha, 1963-71. Named Girl of Year, Monmouth Jr. League, 1959; recipient award of achievement Gulf Region Ednl. TV Affiliates, 1980. Mem. Women in Communications, Inc. (Headliner award 1980), Internat. TV Assn., Am. Women in Radio and TV, NEA (del. 1973), Cable TV Task Force (exec. bd. 1970-74), Tex. Assn. Ednl. Technologists, Tex. State Tchrs. Assn. (chmn. publicity 1973), Tex. Classroom Tchrs. Assn. (del. 1973, 74), Houston Tchrs. Assn. (faculty rep. 1972—), Tex. Ednl. TV Assn., Houston Area Sch. Librarians. Home: 5206 Memorial Dr Houston TX 77007 Office: 3830 Richmond Ave Houston TX 77027

LINNEHAN, ELIZABETH ANNE, educator; b. Bklyn., Sept. 10, 1917; d. Charles Andrew and Elizabeth Anne (Gerdes) Kratt; B.S., Coll. St. Elizabeth, 1939; m. John A. Linnehan, Nov. 28, 1946; children—John Joseph, Francis Xavier, Barbara Anne. Head dietitian Mary Imaculate Hosp., Jamaica, N.Y., 1942-46; nutrition instr. St. John's Hosp., Queens, N.Y., 1950-53, St. John's Episcopal Hosp., Bklyn., 1961-76; asst. prof. nutrition Molloy Coll., Rockville Centre, N.Y., 1968—. Mem. Am., N.Y., L.I. dietitic assns., AAUP, Nassau County Nutrition Council, Soc. Nutrition Today, Nassau Heart Assn. (diet therapy chmn., dir.). Roman Catholic. Home: 1304 Belmont Ave New Hyde Park NY 11040 Office: 1000 Hempstead Ave Rockville Centre NY 11570

LIPE, JEAN MARIE, home furnishings, apparel retail exec., design cons.; b. Los Angeles, Jan. 26, 1944; d. Charles Wilson and Marian Lucinda (Smith) Nibley; B.F.A., U. Denver, 1966; m. Gordon Clifford Lipe, May 14, 1975. Co-owner Mangy Moose Saloon & Steak House, Jackson Hole, Wyo., 1969-73; asst. to pres. Saffron House, Boston, 1973-74; asst. to fashion editor Skiing mag., 1975; v.p. Lipe Specialty Co., Inc., Jackson Hole, Wyo., 1975—; pres. Mountain House, Inc., Jackson Hole, 1977—; graphic artist Jackson Hole News, 1981—. Mem. Jackson Hole Fine Arts Guild, Jackson Hole Alliance For Responsible Planning. Home: PO Box 7 Teton Village WY 83025 Office: PO Box 435 Jackson WY 83001

LIPFORD, AUDREY HELENE, sports reporter; b. Buffalo, Aug. 30, 1956; d. Benjamin M. and Audrey Pauline (Hankins) Lipford; B.S. in Newspaper Journalism, Syracuse U., 1978. Proofreader, typesetter, news, society and features reporter, features editor The Amherst (N.Y.) Bee, 1978-80; sportswriter Hornell (N.Y.) Tribune, 1980; sports writer high sch. girls' and coll. women's athletics Buffalo Courier Express, 1981-82. Recipient Page One First Pl. award for developing news Buffalo Newspaper Guild, 1982. Mem. AAUW, Syracuse Alumni Club of Buffalo, Sigma Delta Chi. Office: 787 Main St Buffalo NY 14240

LIPINSKI, MARJORIE CAMPBELL, pub. relations cons.; b. Denver, Mar. 29, 1919; d. Earl Chester and Agnes Runyon (Herbert) Campbell; B.A., U. So. Calif., 1938; m. Joseph Eugene Lipinski, Aug. 3, 1946; 1 son, Gary Robert. Research asst. to author Gwen Bristow, 1938; sec. to pres. Mut. Don Lee Broadcasting System, Hollywood, Calif., 1939, film dir., mem. planning bd. Don Lee TV, W6XAO, Hollywood, 1940-48; publicist for Pi Beta Phi and Panhellenic of Hawaii Philanthropic Projects, 1954-63; coordinator The Advertiser Contemporary Arts Show for Pub. Relations Women of Honolulu, 1964; U. So. Calif. scholarship chmn. for State of Hawaii, 1964-68; opening night, day and event chmn. Flora Pacifica Ethno-Bot. Exhibit, 1965-68; mem. Honolulu Symphony Opera Com., 1968-70; gen. chmn. Honolulu Symphony Gt. Artists Recital Series, 1969; chmn. Speakers Bur. for Flora Pacifica Ethno-Bot. Expn., 1970-72; sec., mem. council Hawaii Opera Theatre, 1970—; bd. dirs. Honolulu Symphony Womens Assn., 1971—; head pub. relations, bd. dirs. Flora Pacifica, 1973—; incorporator dir. Citizens Com. for Community Cable Television in Hawaii, 1974-81; auction chmn. grand opening Hyatt Regency benefit Honolulu Symphony, 1976; franchise rep. Pacific Cable TV Network, 1976-81; spl. War Dept. tour of Army Air Force Post War Combat Labs. for Motion Picture and TV Personnel, 1945. Mem. AAUW, Am. Women in Radio and TV (provisional pres. Hawaii chpt. 1969-71), U. So. Calif. Pres.'s Circle, Internat. Platform Assn., Pub. Relations Women Honolulu, Hawaii Film Bd., Pi Beta Phi. Democrat. Christian Scientist. Home: 1408 Laamia St Honolulu HI 96821

LIPKIN, MARY CASTLEMAN DAVIS (MRS. ARTHUR BENNETT LIPKIN), former psychiat. social worker; b. Germantown, Pa., Mar. 4, 1907; d. Henry L. and Willie (Webb) Davis; student grad. sch. social work U. Wash., 1946-48; m. William F. Cavenaugh, Nov. 8, 1930 (div.); children—Molly C. (Mrs. Gary Oberbillig), William A.; m. 2d, Arthur Bennett Lipkin, Sept. 15, 1961 (dec. June 1974). Nursery sch. tchr. Miquon (Pa.) Sch., 1940-45; caseworker Family Soc. Seattle, 1948-49, Jewish Family and Child Service, Seattle, 1951-56; psychiat. social worker Stockton (Calif.) State Hosp., 1957-58; supr. social service Mental Health Research Inst., Fort Steilacoom, Wash., 1958-59; engaged in pvt. practice, Bellevue, Wash., 1959-61. Former mem. Phila. Com. on City Policy. Former diplomate and bd. mem. Conf. Advancement of Pvt. Practice in Social Work. Mem. Acad. Cert. Social Workers, Nat. Assn. Social Workers, Internat. Conf. Social Work, Menninger Found., Union Concerned Scientists, Physicians for Social Responsibility, Center for Sci. in Pub. Interest, Jr. League, Seattle Art Mus., Asian Art Council, World Fedn. Mental Health, Wing Lake Mus., Bellevue Art Mus., Pacific Sci. Center, Western Wash. Solar Energy Assn., Nature Conservancy, Wilderness Soc., Mcpl. League of Seattle-King County, Sierra Club, Am. Symphony Orch. League, Phila. Art Alliance, Common Cause, ACLU, Pa. Acad. Fine Arts. Clubs: Cosmopolitan, Cricket (Phila.); Women's University (Seattle). Home: 8230 SE 33d Pl Mercer Island WA 98040

LIPMAN, WYNONA M., state senator; b. Ga.; student Talledega Coll.; grad. Atlanta U.; Ph.D. (Rockefeller grantee), Columbia U.; Fulbright scholar, Sorbonne, U. Paris; children—Karen Anne, William. Tchr. Elizabeth Irwin High Sch., N.Y.C.; French instr. Morehouse Coll.; assoc. prof. div. bus. studies Essex County (N.J.) Coll.; mem. N.J. Senate; 1971—, vice chmn. instns. and welfare com., 1974, 75; vice chmn., then chmn. state govt. com.; vice chmn. edn. com., 1977-79; mem. Commn. to Study Sex Discrimination of Statutes; mem. Nat. Conf. State Legislatures, 1979-81; apptd. N.J. rep. Pres.' Fifty States Project on Women, 1981—; Essex County freeholder dir.; mem. steering com. NEW; mem. Bd. Public Welfare Assistance; bd. mgrs. Woodbridge State Sch., Regional Med. Program; bd. dirs. Interracial Council Bus. Opportunity. Life mem. NAACP (Newark br.), Nat. Council Negro Women; mem. Essex County Pvt. Industry Council, Order Women Legislators, Women's Polit. Caucus, Nat. Black Caucus of State Legislators. Office: New Jersey Senate Trenton NJ 08625 *

LIPP, MARILDA NOVAES, psychologist; b. Rio de Janeiro, Brazil; came to U.S., 1966; d. Moacyr Mendes and Gilda Emmanuel (Teixeira) Novaes; student (Univ. fellow) U. Brazil Law Sch., Rio de Janeiro, 1964-66; B.A. cum laude, Am. U., 1972; M.Phil., George Washington U., 1976, Ph.D., 1977; m. Abraham Lipp, Sept. 18, 1968; children—Daniel M. N., Louis M. N. Lang. instr. Dept. Def., Washington, 1970-72; research asst. George Washington U., 1976-77, asst. professorial lectr. in psychology, 1977-79; pvt. practice psychology, Md., 1978—; on leave as vis. prof. grad. psychology program Pontificia Universidade Catolica de Campinas, São Paulo, Brazil, 1980—, chmn. psychology dept., 1981—; vis. prof. Cath. U. Campinas, 1980—; psychologist Gt. Oaks Center, Silver Spring, Md., 1978-80; speaker in field. Sigma Xi research grantee, 1975; cert. psychologist, Md. Mem. Am. Psychol. Assn., Md. Psychol. Assn., Md. Ednl. Research Evaluation Assn., Brazilian Am. Cultural Inst., Sigma Xi. Democrat. Roman Catholic. Clubs: Bolling AFB Officers'; Author: Sex for the Mentally Retarded, 1981; dir. film A Beam of Light, The Behavioral Treatment of Mentally Retarded Children. Home: Ave Heitor Penteado 1653 CEP 13.100 Campinas São Paulo Brazil Office: care LTC A Lipp SAMS Ret Mail Sect Amcongen São Paulo APO Miami FL 34030

LIPPA, BARBARA JEAN, planning ofcl.; b. Rochester, N.Y., Sept. 3, 1952; d. Frank and Joan Patricia (Vitello) Lippa; B.S., SUNY, Brockport, 1974; M.A., George Washington U., 1977, M.S.A., 1982. Legis. intern Com. on Human Resources, U.S. Senate, Washington, 1974; edn. cons., 1974; cons. Nat. Adv. Council on Indian Edn., 1974; staff Nat. Adv. Council on Edn. of Disadvantaged Children, Washington, 1974-77; planning aide Fairfax County (Va.) Planning Commn., 1978-79; dep. exec. dir. Fairfax County Planning Commn., 1979—. Religious edn. tchr. Roman Cath. Ch., Alexandria, 1974-80, coordinator Bible sch., 1977. Recipient award for excellence HEW, 1975. Mem. Am. Planning Assn., Nat. Assn. Exec. Women. Home: 6419 Frenchmens Dr Alexandria VA 22312 Office: 10th Floor 4100 Chain Bridge Rd Fairfax VA 22320

LIPPERT, ANNE, educator; b. Seattle, Feb. 17; d. Raymond A. and Eva B. (Doran) L.; B.A., Coll. Holy Names, Oakland, Calif., 1959; M.A., U. Wash., Seattle, 1962; Ph.D., Ind. U., 1972; m. Jeffrey M. Schulman, May 7, 1977. Asst. prof. French, acad. dean Mt. Angel (Oreg.) Coll., 1959-68; asst. head residence halls, then head Ind. U., 1968-71; mem. faculty Ohio No. U., Ada, 1971—, prof. French, 1980—, chmn. dept. fgn. langs., 1971-82, asst. v.p. faculty personnel, 1982—; Fulbright lectr. U. Oran (Algeria), 1973-75. Dist. del. mid-term Ohio Democratic Conv., 1978; chmn. Saharawi Peoples Support Com., 1978—. Grantee Nat. Endowment Humanities, 1973, 81. Mem. African Studies Assn., Assn. Concerned African Scholars, African Lit. Assn., MLA, Am. Assn. Tchrs. Frech. Roman Catholic. Author: Inscription, 1970; also articles, chpt. in books. Office: Dept Fgn Langs Ohio No U Ada OH 45810

LIPPERT, FELICE M., weight loss firm exec.; b. N.Y.C., Feb. 9, 1930; d. Charles and Mollie (Weissblum) Mark; B.A., Hunter Coll., 1951; m. Mark Lippert, June 21, 1953; children—Randy S., Keith L. Tchr. elem. sch., Tuckahoe, N.Y., 1951-56; dir. food research Weight Watchers Internat., Inc., Manhasset, N.Y., 1963-71, treas., 1963-68, sec., dir., 1968-71, corp. sec., 1968-71, v.p. food research, 1971-81, cons., 1981—, also cons. food editor Weight Watchers mag., cons. Weight Watchers Cookbooks. Trustee, North Shore Hosp., 1979—; chmn. fund raising Mr. and Mrs. League, City of Hope, N.Y.C. Mem. Am. Parkinson's Disease Assn., Am. Home Econs. Assn., Home Economists in Bus. N.Y.C., Chi Omicron. Jewish. Clubs: Sands Point Golf; Hadassah (life); Sands Point Bath and Racquet; Lands of the President Golf. Office: Weight Watchers Internat Inc 800 Community Dr Manhasset NY 11050

LIPPITT, ELIZABETH CHARLOTTE, writer; b. San Francisco; d. Sidney Grant and Stella Lippitt; student Mills Coll., U. Calif., Berkeley. Writer, performer own satirical monologues; contbr. articles to 85 newspapers including Chgo. Tribune, Phoenix Republic, N.Y. Post, Los Angeles Examiner, St. Louis Globe-Democrat, Union Leader, Utah Ind., Pasadena Star-News, Jackson News, South W.Va. Enterprise, others. Recipient 7 Congress of Freedom awards. Mem. Nat. Assn. R.R. Passengers, Nat. Trust for Historic Preservation, Am. Security Council, Internat. Platform Assn., Com. for Free China, Am. Conservative Union, Guide Dogs for Blind, Amvets, Childrens' Village (Los Angeles), several humane socs. and antivivisection orgns. Clubs: Metropolitan, Olympic, Commonwealth. Pop singer, recorder song album Songs From the Heart. Home: 2414 Pacific Ave San Francisco CA 94115

LIPSCHUTZ, GERDI E., state legislator; b. Germany, Apr. 30, 1923; d. Isaac and Selma (Weil) Laemle; student public schs., Bronx, N.Y.; married; children—Peter J., Jamie M. Pres., Rockaway Park chpt. Hadassah, 1966-69; mem. state com. Democratic Party, 1970-72; mem. Queens County Dem. Exec. Com., 1972; exec. dir. Mayor's Vol. Action Center N.Y.C., 1974; mem. N.Y. State Assembly, 1976—. Mem. Orgn. Women Legislators. Democrat. Jewish. Office: 257 Beach 116th St Rockaway Park NY 11694

LIPSCHUTZ, ILSE HEMPEL, educator; b. Boennigheim, W.Ger., Aug. 19, 1923; came to U.S., 1946, naturalized, 1952; d. Joseph Martin Paul and Fanny (Wurzburger) Hempel; lic. ès lettres, Sorbonne, Paris, 1943, Diplôme d'Etudes Sup., 1944, Diplome Institut des Professeurs de Française ál'Etranger, 1945; Diploma de Estudios Hispánicos, U. Madrid, 1945; M.A., Radcliffe Coll., Harvard U., 1949, Ph.D., (AAUW fellow, N.Y. State, 1950-51, Anne Radcliffe fellow, 1950-51), 1958; m. Lewis D. Lipschutz, Feb. 6, 1952; children—Elizabeth, Marion, Marc, Margaret. Teaching fellow Radcliffe Coll.-Harvard U., 1947-51; instr. to prof. French, Vassar Coll., Poughkeepsie, N.Y., 1951—, dept. chmn., 1975—, Andrew W. Mellon Prof. in humanities, 1981—. Vassar faculty fellow, 1960, 67; research fellow Treatise of Friendship U.S.-Spain, 1979-80, summer 1981. Mem. AAUW, AAUP, Soc. Theophile Gautier. Democrat. Author: Spanish Painting and the French Romantics, 1972; co-author: La Imagen Romántica de España, 1981; contbr. articles in field to publs. Office: Vassar College Poughkeepsie NY 12601

LIPSCOMB, PEGGY ELAINE, pharmacist, real estate broker; b. Quitman, Tex., July 27, 1924; student Tex. Women's U., 1941-43; B.B.A., So. Meth. U., 1945; M.S., East Tex. State U., 1951; postgrad. U. Colo., 1953-54; B.S. in Pharmacy, U. Tex., 1959. High sch. tchr., Dallas, 1951-55; pharmacist, Dallas, 1959-63; pharmacist, owner Lipscomb's Pharmacy, Quitman, 1964-80; asso. realtor Fletcher's Realtors, Dallas, 1963—; asso. Tex-Lands Realty and Investment Co., Dallas, 1980—. Past chmn. Wood County chpt. Easter Seal Soc. for Crippled Children; mem. nat. voter adv. bd. Am. Security Council, Wood County del. to Tex. Democratic Conv.; Wood County precinct chmn. Mem. Am. Pharm. Assn., Nat. Assn. Retail Druggists, Tex. Pharm. Assn., Tex. Real Estate Assn., Dallas Bd. Realtors, Learning Labs. Corp., Internat. Traders, Mellinger Import-Export Assn., Bus. and Profl. Women's Club, Kappa Epsilon (past v.p.), Beta Sigma Phi. Clubs: Dallas Gun, United European Am. Address: PO Box 578 Clear Lakes Village Quitman TX 75783

LIPSCOMBE, BETTY JO, club woman; b. Austin, Tex., Feb. 17, 1926; d. Rowan Fuller and Mary Newman (Eby) Howard; student Mary Hardin Baylor Coll., U. Tex., Austin; m. Jack Wilfred Lipscombe, July 29, 1946; children—Marianne, Elizabeth, John Howard, William Charles. Pvt. investor, 1957—; sec., mem. exec. bd. St. Mary's Retirement Homes, Inc., Big Spring, Tex., 1967—, v.p., 1981—; Bd. dirs. W. Tex. council Girl Scouts, 1965-67, dist. chmn., 1965-67; sec. Malone-Hogan Hosp. Vols., Big Spring, 1965-77, pres., 1978-79, 2d v.p., 1982-83; bd. dirs. Tex. Assn. Hosp. Auxs., 1979—; vice chmn. Howard County Republican Com., 1966-70; del. Tex. Rep. Conv., 1966, 68, 70, 72; pres. Women of Ch., St. Mary's Episcopal Ch., 1965-67, 80. Mem. DAR (chpt. regent 1978-80), Tex. Hosp. Assn. (council on hosp. auxs. 1980—). Club: Austin Women's. Address: 2404 Allendale Rd Big Spring TX 79720

LIPSON, GRETA BARCLAY, educator; b. Toronto, Ont., Can., Jan. 6, 1925; d. Joseph and Rachel Barclay; B.S., Wayne State U., 1964, M.Ed., 1969, Ed.D. (grad. profl. scholar 1970, 71), m. William Allen Lipson, Mar. 12, 1942; children—Eric, Mark, Stefan. Tchr. elem. schs., Berkley, Mich., 1964-68; lectr. Wayne State U. Grad. Sch., Detroit, 1968-69; dir. student tchr. placement U. Mich., Dearborn, 1973-80, assoc. prof. edn., 1969—; coordinator Center for Alternative Teaching Strategies, Oak Park, Mich., 1973-75. Recipient Downer award for ednl. leadership, 1972. Mem. Nat. Council Tchrs. of English, Internat. Reading Assn., Assn. for Supervision and Curriculum Devel., Am. Newspaper Pubs. Assn., Nat. Assn. for Preservation and Perpetuation of Storytelling, NOW, Pi Lambda Theta (past pres.). Author: Fact, Fantasy and Folklore, 1977; It's A Special Day, 1978; Calliope, 1981; Extra! Extra!, 1981; Mighty Myth, 1982; Ethnic Me, 1983; contbr. articles to profl. jours. Home: 12740 Ludlow St Huntington Woods MI 48070 Office: U Mich Dearborn 4901 Evergreen Rd Dearborn MI 48128

LIPTON, MILDRED CERES, clin. child psychologist; b. Bklyn., May 21, 1921; d. Salvatore and Josephine (Nicotra) Ceres; B.A., Douglass Coll., 1943; M.A., State U. Ia., 1946; m. Edmond Lipton, Aug. 2, 1963. Psychol. intern SUNY, 1944; clin. psychologist children's unit Rockland State Hosp., Orangeburg, N.Y., 1945-48, VA Mental Hygiene Clinic, Bklyn., 1948-50, Erie (Pa.) Guidance Center, 1950-51; child clin. psychologist Westchester Children's Assn., White Plains, N.Y., 1951-63; psychologist Mills Coll. Edn., N.Y.C., 1963-67; pvt. practice clin. child psychology, Bklyn., 1967—. Mem. Am. Psychol. Assn., Council Nat. Register Health Service Providers in Psychology. Home: 132 Argyle Rd Brooklyn NY 11218

LIPTON, SONDRA MIRIAM (MRS. JACK SAHLMAN), painter, sculptor; b. N.Y.C., Apr. 24, 1929; d. Harry and Isabel (Koffman) Lipton; student art, N.Y. U., 1964-75; m. Jack Sahlman, July 23, 1952; 1 son, Michael David. Dancer, Broadway musicals, 1948-49; photographer's model, also fashion shows and TV commls., model and actress for TV, 1951-68; painter, sculptor; works exhibited N.Y.C., Palm Beach, Fla., Los Angeles, Dallas, Phoenix, Caracas, Venezuela, Dublin, Ireland; works rep. many pvt. collections including Pres. and Mrs. Lyndon B. Johnson, Jacqueline Kennedy Onassis, Lord and Lady Dunsany, Mrs. Vincent Astor, Gov. and Mrs. Winthrop Rockefeller, Mr. and Mrs. Richard Rodgers; co-founder Dining-In, 1975-78; rep. Knickerbocker Liquor Corp., 1978—. Mem. Sommelier Soc. Office: 99 Lafayette Dr Syosset NY 11791

LIS, YVONNE, mktg. exec.; b. Amsterdam, N.Y., June 14, 1957; d. Charles John and Rose Emily Lis; B.S. cum laude, SUNY, Albany, 1978; M.B.A., San Francisco State U., 1979; m. William D. Greenroad, Oct. 6, 1979. Adminstrv. asst. Office Lt. Gov. N.Y. State, Albany, 1975-78; price adminstrn. supr. Intel Corp., Santa Clara, Calif., 1979-80, customer mktg. engr., 1981-82; product mktg. mgr. Shugart Assocs., Sunnyvale, Calif., 1982—. Mem. Am. Mktg. Assn., Assn. M.B.A. Execs. Roman Catholic. Home: 651 E McKinley Ave Sunnyvale CA 94086 Office: 475 Oakmead Pkwy Sunnyvale CA 94086

LISBOA-FARROW, ELIZABETH OLIVER, pub. relations cons.; b. N.Y.C., Nov. 25, 1947; d. Eleuterio and Esperanza Oliver; student public schs., N.Y.C.; m. Jeffrey Lloyd Farrow, Dec. 31, 1980. With Harold Rand & Co. and various other public relations firms, N.Y.C., 1966-75; dir. public relations N.Y. Playboy Club and Playboy Clubs Internat., 1975-79; pres. Lisboa Assos., Inc., N.Y.C., 1979—; sec. Nat. Acad. Concert and Cabaret Arts; mem. nat. adv. council SBA, 1980-81. Mem. Nat. Assn. Female Execs. Club: Doubles Internat. Office: 3600 M St NW Washington DC 20007

LISS, MARY BETH, med. technologist; b. Peru, Ill., July 22, 1951; d. Maximillian Edmund and Mary Veronica (Wadas) Liss; B.S., U. Ill., 1973; cert. St. Francis Hosp. Sch. Med. Tech., 1974. Staff technologist St. Margaret's Hosp., Spring Valley, Ill., 1974—. Mem. Nat. Audubon Soc., U.S. Olympic Soc., Am. Soc. Clin. Pathologists (affiliate mem., cert. med. technologist), U. Ill. Alumni Assn. Democrat. Roman Catholic. Home: 715 E 12th St Peru IL 61354 Office: 600 E 1st St Spring Valley IL 61362

LISTON, HATTYE EILEEN, psychologist; b. Rocky Mount, N.C.; d. David Donald and T. Elizabeth (Parker) Hinton; B.S. in Bio. Sci., N.C. Coll.; M.S. in Psychology, N.Y. U., 1953; student Howard U., Yale, 1958, U. N.C., 1961-62; m. Hardy Liston, Jr., Sept. 7, 1943; children—Marsha Eileen Liston Wright, Marva Camille Liston McKinnon. Ednl. counselor and guidance specialist N.C. Agrl. and Tech. U., 1956-60, asst. prof. psychology, 1960-70, asso. prof., 1970—, asso. dir. nutrition and phys. fitness program for disadvantaged children, 1971, Univ. liaison to Black Coll. Initiative, NIMH grantee, 1972—. Cons. Upward Bound program Hampton Inst., 1967-68, 70, Westinghouse Health Systems; psychol. cons., O.P.O. Neighborhood Youth Corps, 1970, cons. staff, 1971-72; participant numerous mental health panels and confs.; coordinator Behavior Modification Inst., Beaufort, S.C., summer 1974; mem. N.C. Drug Authority Edn. Task Force, 1974—; mem. vis. women's program commn. on status of women Southeastern Psychol. Assn. Recipient award of Honor N.C. Agrl. and Tech. State U. Student Govt. Assn., 1970, plaque for outstanding services in Adult Edn. N.C. Agrl. and Tech. State U., 1973; cert. for outstanding services in corrections N.C. Dept. Corrections, 1975; lic. psychologist, biofeedback practitioner. Mem. Greensboro LWV, Family Life Council Greater Greensboro, AAAS, Am. Public Health Assn., Drug Action Council Guilford County (co-chmn. ednl. com.), AAUP, AAUW, Assn. Schs. Allied Health Professions, Internat. Assn. U. Women, Am. Personnel and Guidance Assn., Nat., N.C., Greensboro (bd. mem.) mental health assns., Am., Southeastern, N.C. psychol. assns., Greensboro Community Council, Alpha Kappa Alpha, Kappa Delta Pi, Psi Chi. Author: How to Study and Learn 1965; Basic Mathematical Statistics for the Behavioral Sciences and Techniques for Data Compilation in Ecological Studies, 1976; also other works in field. Home: 1213 East Side Dr Greensboro NC 27406 Office: 308 Gibbs Hall NC Agr and Tech State U Greensboro NC 27411

LITOFF, JUDY BARRETT, historian; b. Atlanta, Dec. 23, 1944; d. John and Dorothy Mae (Wooddall) Barrett; B.A., Emory U., 1967, M.A., 1968; Ph.D., U. Maine, 1975; m. Harold Lawrence Litoff, Sept. 30, 1966; children—Nadja, Alyssa. Teaching asst. U. Maine, Orono, 1971-75; asst. prof. history Bryant Coll., Smithfield, R.I., from 1975, now asso. prof.; chairperson or speaker several profl. confs. Mem. R.I. area com. Am. Friends Service Com., 1977—; bd. overseers Lincoln Sch.; session chairwoman R.I. Woman's Health Conf., 1976. Recipient honorariums Colby Coll., 1974, Salve Regina Coll., 1976, U. Maine, Farmington, 1975, Orono, 1978; Ford career scholar, 1965-67. Mem. AAUW, Am. Hist. Assn., Coordinating Com. on Women in Hist. Profession, Nat. Trust for Historic Preservation, Orgn. Am. Historians, So. Assn. Women Historians, Women Educators R.I., R.I. Com. for Humanities, R.I. Black Heritage Soc., Phi Kappa Phi, Phi Alpha Theta, Pi Sigma Alpha. Author: Recognition: A Source Book on Working Women in Maine, 1974; American Midwives Since 1860, 1970; also articles. Home: 248 Morris Ave Providence RI 02906 Office: Social Science Dept Bryant College Smithfield RI 02917

LITSKY, BERTHA YANIS, microbiologist; b. Chester, Pa., Jan. 2, 1920; d. Edward B. and Harriet (Howell) Meade; B.S. in Bacteriology, Phila. Coll. Pharmacy and Sci., 1942; M.S. in Hosp. and Nursing Home Adminstrn., N.Y. U., 1964; Ph.D. in Edn., Walden U., 1974. Supr. prodn. biol. products Nat. Drug Co., 1942-45; operator clin. lab., 1945-52; research microbiologist U. Pa., 1952-56; head clin. microbiology dept. S.I. Hosp., N.Y.C., 1956-63; research asso. U. Mass., Amherst, also nurse cons. Bingham Assos. Fund, 1963—; cons. environ. microbiology; mem. task force EPA; lab. researcher prevention of hosp. associated infections. Recipient Alumni award Phila. Coll. Pharmacy and Sci., 1979. Mem. Assn. for Advancement Med. Instrumentation (co-chmn. steam sterilization). Author: Hospital Sanitation: An Administrative Program, 1966; Food Service Sanitation, 1973; Central Service and the Prevention of Cross-Infection, 1981; editor Score, 1969—; contbr. numerous articles to profl. jours. Office: Dept of Environ Sciences Marshall Hall University of Massachusetts Amherst MA 01003

LITTELL, KATHERINE MATHER, fine arts research co. exec.; b. Seattle, June 5, 1936; d. Norman M. and Katherine M. (Maher) Littell; B.A. magna cum laude in English, Radcliffe Coll., 1958; postgrad. (German Exchange Service scholar) U. Munich, 1958-59; M.A. in German Lit., Harvard U., 1961; Ph.D. in Germanic Langs. and Lit., Columbia U., 1972. Instr. German, SUNY, New Paltz, 1965-66; instr. German lang. and lit. Tchrs. Coll., Columbia U., N.Y.C., 1966-69; instr. German and humanities SUNY, Stonybrook, 1968-69; asst. prof. Edinboro (Pa.) State Coll., 1969-70, assoc. prof., 1970-72, prof. methods of fgn. lang. teaching, German lit., 1972-76; asst. prof. dept. modern langs. Bucknell U., Lewisburg, Pa., 1976-78, research assoc., 1976-82; propr. Fine Arts Research Assocs., 1982—; lectr. on Jack London, Santa Rosa Jr. Coll., Yuba City Community Coll.; cons. to Central Susquehanna Intermediate Unit in Bilingual Edn., 1972-76, dir. Bilingual Program. Nat. Inst. of Edn. grantee, 1973, Bucknell U. grantee, 1975; Pro Helvetia grantee, 1978; grantee Ministry Edn., Republic of China. Mem. Pres' Assocs. of Sonoma State U. Republican. Lutheran. Author: Jeremiah Gotthelf's Die Käserei in der Vehfeude, A Didactic Satire, 1977; also articles in profl. jours., newspapers, mags. Clubs: Sulgrave, Harvard-Radcliffe of N.Y. Home: 1400 Heaven Hill Rd Sonoma CA 95476

LITTELL, PATRICIA L., contracting corp. exec.; b. Albuquerque, May 28, 1954; d. Birnie Glenn and Eleanor Marie (Maloney) Hammock; student U. N.Mex., 1972-73; m. E. Austin Littell, Nov. 24, 1979; 4 stepchildren. Exec. sec. to v.p. systems integration BDM Corp., Albuquerque, 1976-80; pres., treas., co-founder Littell and Assos., Albuquerque, 1979—; cons. small bus. firms. Recipient Corp. safety award Associated Gen. Contractors Am., 1980. Mem. Nat. Assn. Female Execs. Rebuplican. Methodist. Office: PO Box 5596 Kirtland AFB Albuquerque NM 87185

LITTLE, FLORENCE ELIZABETH, educator; b. Streator, Ill., July 7, 1911; d. Charles Arthur and Bertha (Schlachter) Herbert; B.A., Mich. State U., 1932; M.S.E., Drake U., 1962; m. Alfred Lamond Little, July 26, 1933 (dec.); children—Alan Rush, Barbara Jean Little Votaw. Accompanist, Mich. State U., 1930-32, 33-36, mem. faculty, 1930-32; tchr., pub. schs., Bridgeport, Ill., 1945, Holt, Mich., 1945-46, Hanover, Mich., 1949-50, Pittsford, Mich., 1950-53, Des Moines, 1953-73; now substitute tchr., tutor, public schs., La Place, La.; pvt. tchr. piano and voice, 1932-56. Active CD, Crime Watch, Am. Fedn. Police Nat. CB Posse. NSF grantee, 1963-64. Mem. Am. Bus. Women's Assn., Smithsonian Instn., NEA, Iowa Edn. Assn., Des Moines Edn. Assn., Orchid Soc. Jefferson, Kappa Kappa Iota, Mu Phi Epsilon. Republican. Presbyterian. Club: CB. Instituted elem. music programs, various schs.; hon. mem. editorial adv. bd. Am. Biographical Inst., 1980-82. Home: St James Pl 333 Lee Dr Apt 327 Baton Rouge LA 70808

LITTLE, GINA BOYD, computer consultant; b. Denver, Feb. 11, 1955; d. Edward Boyd and Sara Frances (Parrish) L.; student U. No. Colo., 1973-74, Met. State Coll., 1982. Lifeguard, instr., Swimland, Lakewood, Colo., summers, 1967-73; sales asso. Neusteters, Denver, 1974-75, Fashion Bar, Denver, 1975; sr. lease record cons. Scientific Software Corp., Denver, 1975-82; cons. software in oil and gas industry, 1982—. Recipient Most Improved Product award Sci. Software Corp., 1980, Outstanding Instr. award, 1980, others. Mem. Am. Assn. Petroleum Landmen, Nat. Assn. for Female Execs. Home and office: 5553 S Lowell Blvd Littleton CO 80123

LITTLE, MARTHA LOUISE, psychologist; b. Evansville, Ind., Mar. 28, 1914; d. Harry Wilson and Dora (Haussermann) L.; B.A., Wellesley Coll., 1935; M.A., Middlebury Coll., 1942; M.A., Cath. U. Am., 1959, Ph.D., 1967. Research asst. NIMH, Bethesda, 1955; trainee VA, Washington, and Balt., 1955-57; intern Columbus Psychiat. Clinic, Columbus, Ohio, 1957-58; staff psychologist Dayton (Ohio) State Hosp., 1958-59, Fairfax-Fall Church (Va.) Mental Health Center, 1961-63, Adult Psychiat. Clinic, Dayton, 1963-66; supervising clin. psychologist Oneida County (N.Y.) Dept. Mental Health, Utica, 1966-68; chief clin. psychologist Sinnissippi Mental Health Center, Dixon, Ill., 1968-70; pvt. practice psychology, Dixon, Ill., 1970-78, Sarasota, Fla., 1978—. Cert. Applied Psychiatry for Tchrs. Washington Sch. of Psychiatry, 1955; diplomate Am. Bd. Profl. Psychology. Mem. Am. Psychol. Assn., Am. Group Psychotherapy Assn., Internat. Assn. Group Psychotherapy. Unitarian. Club: Wellesley of Sarasota. Home: 800 Ben Franklin Dr Sarasota FL 33577 Office: 635 S Orange Ave Sarasota FL 33577

LITTLE, MARY ANN, clin. psychologist; b. Dallas, Dec. 2, 1952; d. John M., Jr., and Donna (Kaelson) L.; B.A., Smith Coll., 1974; Ph.D. in Clin. Psychology, U. Tex., Dallas, 1979; postgrad. U. Geneva (Switzerland), 1979-80. Clin. psychology trainee Child Psychiatry Clinic, Southwest Med. Sch., Dallas County Juvenile Dept., Children's Devel. Center, Scottish Rite Hosp., Terrell State Hosp., 1975-79; psychologist Callier Center Communication Disorders, 1980, adj. faculty spl. edn., 1980—; cons. Scottish Rite Hosp. Learning Disabilities Program, 1981; pvt. practice clin. psychologist, Dallas, 1982—; lectr. Bd. dirs. Big Bros. Assn. Dallas; Brainworks Sch., Inc.; cons. Scottish Rite Hosp. Lic. psychologist, Tex. Mem. Am. Psychol. Assn., Dallas Psychol. Assn., Orton Soc. (bd. dirs.), Tex. Psychol. Assn. Episcopalian. Clubs: Jr. League, Slipper, Cottilion, 500 of Dallas, Smith of Dallas. Author: Reasoning Strategies and Intellectual Skills in Learning Disabled and Normal Children; Assessment of the Special Vulnerabilities of Gifted Children; Ego Development and Creativity (with K. Karlson). Home: 3724 Villanova Dr Dallas TX 75225 Office: 5510 Abrams St Suite 116 Dallas TX 75214

LITTLE, SALLY SCHOPPERT, social worker; b. Seattle, July 22, 1948; d. Robert Keith and Fern Jane (Astell) Schoppert; B.A. in Sociology, U. Wash., 1970, M.S.W., 1973; m. William Henry Little, June 13, 1971; children—Rachel, Jessica. Coordinator Meals-On-Wheels, Chula Vista, Calif., 1973; social worker Child Protective Services, Dept. Public Welfare, San Diego, 1973-74; instr. Southwestern Oreg. Community Coll., Coos Bay, 1977; instr. family life Monterey Peninsula Coll., Monterey, Calif., 1978-80; social work cons. Family Advocacy program Naval Regional Med. Center, Guam, 1980-81. Mem. Monterey County Commn. on Status Women, 1979-80; mem. social services commn. Day Care Devel. Task Force Monterey County, 1979-80, chmn. ad hoc com. activities devel., 1980; active Girl Scouts U.S.A. Mem. Nat. Assn. Social Workers, Guam Assn. Social Workers, AAUW. Club: Family Resource Center Auxiliary (treas. 1978-80). Home: 4 Mount Tenjo Apra Heights FPO San Francisco CA 96630

LITTLE, SANDRA LYNN, educator; b. Wenatchee, Wash., July 30, 1941; d. Chester Leon and Yvonne Evelyn (Brandenburg) Bergeman; B.A., U. La Verne (Calif.), 1963; M.S., Ind. U., 1964; postgrad. Pa. State U., 1979-82; m. Larry J. Little, Dec. 21, 1968; 1 dau., Caroline A. Asst. dir. recreation Oak Park (Ill.) Recreation Dept., 1966-70; supt. recreation Elk Grove (Ill.) Park Dist., 1970-71; recreation supr., pre-sch. dir. Johnson County Park and Recreation Dist., Shawnee Mission, Kans., 1972-73; recreation coordinator Park Dist. Park Ridge (Ill.), 1973-75; instr. Triton Coll., River Grove, Ill., 1974; instr. recreation and parks Pa. State U., University Park, 1975—. Bd. dirs., sec. Civic Symphony of Oak Park-River Forest, 1964-71; bd. dirs. Oak Park Village Day Care Center, 1967-68; v.p. LWV, Kansas City, Kans., 1971-73; recreation and park commr. Borough of Shippensburg (Pa.), 1978-79. Mem. Nat. Recreation and Park Assn., Soc. Park and Recreation Educators, Pa. Recreation and Park Soc. Office: 267 Recreation Bldg University Park PA 16802

LITTLE, THELMA FORTUNE, social services exec.; b. Florence, S.C., Dec. 11, 1927; d. Herbert and Thelma (Cooper) Fortune; B.S., S.C. State Coll., 1947; M.S.W., Fordham U., 1972; m. Van Crawford Little, Oct. 1, 1955; 1 son, James C. McIntosh. With Dept. Social Services, N.Y.C. Human Resources Adminstrn., 1965—, program mgr., 1972-74, div. dir., 1974-75, dep. bur. dir., 1975—. Fin. sec. Bethany United Meth. Ch., 1968-72, chairperson social concerns, 1976-77, lay leader, 1981—; bd. dirs. United Meth. City Soc. Mem. Am. Soc. Profl. and Exec. Women, Am. Soc. Public Adminstrn., Nat. Assn. Social Workers, NAACP, Alpha Kappa Alpha. Democrat. Home: 666 Linden Blvd Brooklyn NY 11203

LITTLEDALE, FREYA LOTA BROWN, writer, editor; b. N.Y.C.; d. David Milton and Dorothy (Passloff) Brown; B.S., Ithaca Coll., 1951; postgrad. N.Y. U., 1952; 1 son, Glenn David. Tchr. English, Public Schs. Willsboro, N.Y., 1952-53; editor South Shore Record, L.I., N.Y., 1953-55; asso. editor Maco Mag. Corp., N.Y.C., 1960-61, Rutledge Books and Ridge Press, N.Y.C., 1961-62; juvenile book editor Parents' Mag. Press, N.Y.C., 1962-65; free-lance writer-editor, Wilton, Conn., 1965—; writer Silver Burdett div. Time-Life Corp., 1965; editor, anthologist Arrow Book Club div. Scholastic Book Services. Author: The Magic Fish, 1967; (with Harold Littledale) Timothy's Forest, 1969; King Fox and Other Old Tales, 1971; The Magic Tablecloth, the Magic Goat and the Hitting Stick, 1973; The Boy Who Cried Wolf, 1975; The Elves and the Shoemaker, 1975; Seven at One Blow, 1976; The Snow Child, 1978; I Was Thinking, 1979; The Magic Plum Tree, 1981; editor: A Treasure Chest of Poetry, 1964; Fairy Tales by Hans Christian Andersen, 1964; Aesop's Fables, 1964; Grimm's Fairy Tales, 1964; 13 Ghostly Tales, 1966; Ghosts and Spirits of Many Lands, 1970; Stories of Ghosts, Witches and Demons, 1971; Strange Tales from Many Lands, 1975; author plays: Stop That Pancake, 1975; The King and Queen Who Wouldn't Speak, 1975; The Giant's Garden, 1975; The Magic Piper, 1978; adaptor: Pinocchio, 1979; Snow White and the Seven Dwarfs, 1980.

LITTLEFIELD, NANCY, film producer, dir., writer; b. N.Y.C.; d. Benjamin George and Mildred Christine (Herndon) Kassel; student Coll. City N.Y., 1946-47, U. N.C., 1947-48; children—Joshua Christopher, Amy Joanna Littlefield. Adminstrv. asst. to v.p. Columbia Pictures, N.Y.C., 1950-51; exec. asst., then producer and casting dir. Screen Gems Inc., N.Y.C., 1951-59; asst. dir., then dir. and producer numerous films and TV shows, including: Naked City, The Defenders, The Patty Duke Show, Stakeout; asso. dir. Blood Sweat and Tears show, ABC-TV, 1970; producer indsl. film on alcoholism, 1971; dir. Mommy Where Are You? for Nat. Conf. Jews, 1972; stage dir. segment But Can She Type, NBC-TV; writer, producer, dir. And Baby Makes Two, documentary, 1978; also dir., producer numerous comml. and indsl. films; co-founder Transition Group, prodn. co., Los Angeles, 1977. Mem. Dirs. Guild Am., Women in Film. Office: Mayors Office Motion Picture and TV 110 W 57th St New York NY 10028 *

LITWIN, VALERIE DAWN PORTNOY, social worker; b. Bklyn., Aug. 16, 1954; d. Irving Leo and Kyla Anita (Einstein) P.; B.S.W., Adelphi U., 1975, M.S.W., 1977; m. Jeffrey H. Litwin, Aug. 23, 1980. Social worker N.J. Div. Youth and Family Services, 1975-76; social worker Samuel Field YW-MHA, Little Neck, N.Y., 1975; supr., social worker Angel Guardian Home, Bklyn., 1978-81; social worker N.Y.C. chpt. Multiple Sclerosis Soc., 1982—. Cert. social worker, N.Y. Mem. Nat. Assn. Social Workers, Acad. Cert. Social Workers. Home: 344 Beverly Rd Douglaston NY 11363

LITWOK, EVELYN, psychologist, distbn. co. exec.; b. N.Y.C., July 30, 1951; d. Zygmunt and Genia (Kohn) L.; B.A. in Psychology, U. Buffalo, 1969; M.A. in Psychology (research fellow 1973-75), Temple U., 1975. Dir. Child Devel. Research Lab., Temple U., Phila., 1973-75; dir. evaluation and research W. Phila. Community Mental Health Center, 1975-78; co-dir. Women's Resources, Inc., Phila., 1978—; exec. dir. Women's Resources Distbn. Co., 1981—; cons. in mgmt., fiscal planning, comprehensive fund-raising. Mem. Am. Psychol. Assn., Assn. Women in Psychology. Jewish. Contbr. articles in field to profl. publs. Home: 613 Lombard St Philadelphia PA 19147 Office: 623 Bainbridge St Philadelphia PA 19147

LIVAS, SAN JUANITA (JANIE), ednl. adminstr.; b. Comales, Tamps, Mexico, Jan. 20, 1949; naturalized citizen, 1960; d. Domingo and Angelina (Villarreal) Flores; B.S., Pan Am. U., 1971, M.Ed., 1979; m.

Arturo Livas, Dec. 18, 1971; children—Adrian Lee, Aliza Lynn, Annette Lorraine. Tchr., Edcouch-Elsa High Sch., Edcouch, Tex., then tchr. math. lab., coordinator reading/math. labs., sch. dist., now supr. Central Jr. High.; cons. Tex. Migrant Conf., 1980. Mem. Tex. State Tchrs. Assn. Classroom Tchrs. Assn., Assn. Supervision and Curriculum Devel., Assn. Compensatory Educators Tex., Rio Grande Valley Council Tchrs. Math., Tex. Assn. Bilingual Edn., Delta Kappa Gamma. Democrat, Roman Catholic. Home: 512 E 3d St Elsa TX 78543 Office: 501 E 2d St Elsa TX 78543

LIVENGOOD, ALICE MCCURDY, speech pathologist; b. Matawan, N.J., June 24, 1927; d. John S. and Elda K. (Seidel) McCurdy; B.A., Beaver Coll., 1949; postgrad. N.Y. U., 1950-52, U. Colo., 1955-56, Temple U., 1962-64. Speech pathologist Union (N.J.) public schs., 1949-61, Burlington (N.J.) public schs., 1961—; staff N.J. Speech Assn. Newspaper, 1951-52. Mem. South Jersey Speech and Hearing Assn. (1st pres. 1963-64), Burlington City Tchrs. Assn. (pres. 1972). Address: 301 Bridgeboro Rd Moorestown NJ 08057

LIVERANCE, DIANE EDLUND, nurse, cons.; b. Mpls., Apr. 6, 1944; d. Wallace Reid and Veda Loretta (Deits) Edlund; R.N., Bronson Meth. Sch. Nursing, 1965; A.S., Purdue U., 1977, B.S., 1978; postgrad. Ind. U., 1980—; children—Joseph, Kristin, Kerrin. Instr., Ind. Vocat. Tech. Coll., Lafayette, 1970-72; health services dir. Centralab Electronics, Lafayette, 1973-74; occupational health nurse Rea Magnet Wire, Ft. Wayne, Ind., 1975-76; dir. nursing and health services ARC, Ft. Wayne, 1976—, asst. exec. dir., 1980-82; supr. employee and community health edn. Wellness Center Parkview Meml. Hosp., 1982—; dir. Community Health Cons., 1978—. Active No. Ind. Health Systems Agy., 1977—, Ft. Wayne Area Consortium for Health Promotion, 1979—, chairperson, 1982-83; mem. Adolescent Pregnancy Awareness and Concern Task Force, 1979—, Ft. Wayne Women's Bur., 1978—, Purdue U. Alumni Bd., 1978—; adv. bd. Regional Vocat. Center, 1979—. Recipient Ft. Wayne Ednl. TV Found. public service award, 1982. Mem. Ind. State Nurses Assn. (pres. elect), Am. Nurses Assn., Am. Soc. Tng. and Devel. Methodist. Club: Ft. Wayne Track. Contbr. articles to profl. jours.; co-producer tv spl. Do You Know Where Your're Going to: A Journey into Wellness, 1982. Home: 15127 Hedgebrook Dr Huntertown IN 46748 Office: Total Life Center Parkview Meml Hosp 2200 Randolph Dr Fort Wayne IN 46505

LIVERPOOL, DEBRA LUDORA, bank exec.; b. Washington, June 13, 1955; d. Albert Walter and Pauline (Gadberry) Cook; B.A., George Washington U., 1977; m. Roland Harvey Liverpool, Feb. 14, 1981. Research surveyor George Washington U. Med. Center for Family Research, Washington, 1975-76; mgmt. trainee Citizens Bank & Trust Co. of Md., Riverdale, 1977-79, asst. mgr., Oxon Hill, 1979—. Child life vol. Children's Hosp. Nat. Med. Center, Washington, 1976-77. Mem. Am. Inst. Banking, Am. Bankers Assn., Alpha Kappa Alpha. Home: 448 Girard St Gaithersburg MD 20877 Office: Citizens Bank & Trust Co of Md 41 Audrey Ln Oxon Hill MD 20745

LIVINGSTON, MARGARET MORROW GRESHAM, civic leader; b. Birmingham, Ala., Aug. 16, 1924; d. Owen Garside and Katherine Molton (Morrow) Gresham; grad. The Baldwin Sch., Phila., 1942; A.B., Vassar Coll., 1945; M.A., U. Ala., 1946; m. James Archibald Livingston, Jr., July 16, 1947; children—Mary Margaret, James Archibald, Katherine Wiley, Elizabeth Gresham. Tutor in math., 1949-55; substitute elem., secondary sch. tchr., 1953-60; judge arts and crafts shows, founder edn. program Birmingham Mus. Art, 1962, acting dir., 1978-79, 81, chmn. bd. dirs., 1978—, sec. bd. dirs. 1978—, co-editor bulletin, 1970-75, pres. bd. dirs., 1971—, chmn. bd. Birmingham Mus. Art Edn. Council, 1968—; bd. dirs., past pres. Children's Aid Soc., 1959-81, treas., 1950, v.p., 1951; mem. arts com. Birmingham Civic Center Authority, 1970—; bd. dirs. U. Ala. Art Gallery, Birmingham, 1978—, Altamont Sch., Birmingham, 1959—, Greater Birmingham Arts Alliance, 1979-81. Mem. Am. Assn. Mus. (trustees com., edn. com., public relations com.), Internat. Com. of Mus. (edn. com. 1981—), Am. Fedn. Arts, So. Assn. Mus. Episcopalian. Clubs: Jr. League, English Speaking Union, Colonial Dames of Commonwealth of Va., Linly Heflin Unit, Ala. State Tennis Assn. Co-editor Spain Rehabilitation Arts Catalog, 1976-77. Home: 12 Country Club Rd Birmingham AL 35213 Office: Birmingham Mus of Art 2000 8th Ave N Birmingham AL 35203

LIVINGSTON, MARION GASKILL, b. Phila., June 28, 1924; d. Joseph Franklin and Marion Elizabeth (Cook) Gaskill; student Ohio State U.; m. N. B. Livingston, Jr., Jan. 9, 1946; children—John M., Peter G., William. C. Mem. Franklin County Bd. Elections, 1982—. Mem. screening com. Franklin County Republican Exec. Com.; committeeman Upper Arlington Ward 6; mem. women's bd. March of Dimes; mem. by-laws com. Aux. to Ohio State Med. Assn.; trustee Martha Kinney Cooper Ohioana Library; mem. County Bd. Visitors; mem. Planning Commn., City of Upper Arlington. Mem. Navy League U.S. (bd. dirs. Columbus council), Republican. Home: 4444 Langport Rd Upper Arlington Columbus OH 43220

LIVINGSTON, MYRA COHN, author; b. Omaha, Aug. 17, 1926; d. Mayer Louis and Gertrude (Marks) Cohn; B.A., Sarah Lawrence Coll., 1948; m. Richard Roland Livingston, Apr. 14, 1952; children—Joshua, Jonas, Jennie Marks. Profl. French horn player, 1941-48; book reviewer Los Angeles Daily News, Los Angeles Mirror and asst. editor Campus Mag., 1948-50; public relations staff, pvt. sec. to Hollywood personalities, 1950-52; tchr. creative writing Dallas Public Library, 1958-64; poet-in-residence Beverly Hills (Calif.) Unified Sch. Dist., 1966—; sr. instr. UCLA extension, 1973—; lectr. in field; cons. in field. Bd. dirs. Poetry Therapy Inst., 1975—; officer, mem. Beverly Hills PTA Council, 1966-75; pres. Friends of the Beverly Hills Pub. Library, 1979-81; bd. dirs. Reading is Fundamental, 1980—, Citizens Adv. Com. on Arts and Edn., Beverly Hills, 1982—. Recipient Honor award, N.Y. Herald Tribune Spring Book Festival, 1958; So. Calif. Council on Lit. for Children and Young People Comprehensive Contribution award, 1968, 72; Tex. Inst. Letters awards, 1961, 80; Excellence in Poetry award, Nat. Council Tchrs. English, 1980. Mem. Authors Guild, PEN Internat., Tex. Inst. Letters, Internat. Reading Assn., Soc. Children's Book Writers, So. Calif. Council on Lit. for Children and Young People. Author: Poems of Christmas, 1980; No Way of Knowing, Dallas Poems, 1980; How Pleasant to Know Mr. Lear, 1982; A Circle of Seasons, 1982; Why Am I Grown so Cold?, 1982, 26 others. Address: 9308 Readcrest Dr Beverly Hills CA 90210

LIVINGSTON, NORMA GROTH, psychologist; b. Villisca, Iowa, Mar. 2, 1929; d. Arthur Dale and Hester (Branan) Case; A.A., Stephens Coll., 1948; B.S., in Home Econs., U. Minn., 1951; postgrad. U. Houston, 1964-65; secondary teaching credential Calif. Luth. Coll., 1968; M.A. in Psychology, Calif. State U., Northridge, 1968; Ed.D. in Psychology, U. So. Calif., 1973; m. Joseph C. Groth, Jr., Sept. 2, 1950 (div. 1968); children—Rebecca Jean, Susan Kay, Kathleen Branan; m. 2d, Kenneth E. Livingston, Jr., Apr. 1, 1978. High sch. tchr. Newbury Park (Calif.), 1968-73; asst. prof. dept. psychology Ft. Lewis Coll., Durango, Colo., 1973-76; psychologist Colo. State Hosp., Pueblo, 1976—, alcohol treatment, 1976-79, forensic psychiatry, 1979—; psychologist Mental Health Clinic, Farmington, N.Mex., 1974-76, Pueblo, 1978. Active civic alcohol treatment center and half way house. Mem. Am. Psychol. Assn., Nat. Assn. Gifted Children (bd. dirs.), AAUW. Editor Gifted Child Quarterly; contbr. research writings under names Groth and Livingston to profl. publs. Office: Inst for Forensic Psychiatry Colorado State Hosp Pueblo CO 81003

LIVINGSTON, PAMELA ANNE, communications and mktg. mgmt. cons.; b. Richmond Hill, N.Y., Nov. 21, 1930; d. Paul Yount and Anna Margaret (Altland) L.; B.A., Adelphi U., 1951; postgrad. N.Y.U., 1952, Columbia U., 1959, Am. Acad. Dramatic Art, 1954, IBM Systems and Mktg. Schs., 1967-70, Brandon Sch. Electronic Data Processing, 1973. Personnel and public relations depts. Am. Can Co., N.Y.C., 1951-60; exec. sec. to pres. York (Pa.) div. Borg-Warner Corp., 1962-65; freelance writer, 1965-67; mktg. ofcl. IBM, 1967-70; research analyst, dir. new EDP bus. Ins. Co. N.Am., 1971-74; asst. to v.p. corp. affairs IU Internat., Phila., 1974-75, communications and mktg. mgmt. cons., specializing in devel. corp. identity and image programs and corp. repositioning programs for execs., 1975—. Recipient various journalism awards, award in mktg. and sales IBM, 1969-70, award for innovative product application, 1969. Mem. Sales/Mktg. Execs. Internat., Art Alliance, Public Relations Soc. Am., Econs. Club of York C. of C., Phila. Club Advt. Women, AAUW, Phila. Acad. Fine Arts, World Affairs Council, English-Speaking Union, Kappa Kappa Gamma. Contbr. articles to tech. jours. Home and Office: 108 S Rockburn St York PA 17402

LIVINGSTON, PATRICIA JANE, educator; b. St. Paul, Oct. 3, 1924; d. Walter William and Kathryn Frances (Seebold) Milbrath; B.A. in Psychology, U. Minn., 1946; M.A. in Ednl. Psychology, N.Y.U., 1954, Ph.D. in Rehab. Counseling, 1959; m. E. Arthur Livingston, Sept. 6, 1958. Rehab. counselor Bklyn. Tb and Health Assn., 1946-55; chief rehab. counselor and dir. sheltered workshop Bird S. Coler Hosp., N.Y.C., 1955-58; instr. edn. (rehab. counseling) N.Y.U., 1958-60, asst. prof., 1960-61, asso. prof., 1961-64, prof., 1964—, chmn. dept. rehab. counseling, 1960-74, head div. health, 1974—, program dir., disability determinations, 1979—; research cons. Just One Break, Inc., 1972-80; cons. and mem. bd. various agys.; trustee Internat. Center for Disabled, 1977—. Mem. Am. Personnel and Guidance Assn., Am. Psychol. Assn., Nat. Assn. Disability Examiners, Nat. Rehab. Assn., Nat. Rehab. Counseling Assn. (nat. bd. 1972), N.Y. Personnel and Guidance Assn. (pres. 1965), N.Y. Rehab. Assn. (pres. 1976), N.Y. Rehab. Counseling Assn. (pres. 1978). Office: 25 W 4th St New York NY 10013

LIVINGSTON, WANDA LOUISE, social worker; b. Kansas City, Mo., June 27, 1943; d. James W. and Juanita B. Walton; B.A. in History, U. Mo., 1966; M.S.W., U. Kan., 1972; m. Louis Dean Livingston, Mar. 28, 1964; children—Shawn R., Sharice D. Caseworker Mo. Div. Family Services, Kansas City, 1966-69, supr., 1969, psychiat. social worker Western Mo. Mental Health Center, Kansas City, 1972-74; med. social worker St. Joseph Hosp., Kansas City, Mo., 1974-76; pretrial services officer U.S. Dist. Ct., Kansas City, Mo., 1976—. First v.p. George Washington Carver Neighborhood Center Bd. Dirs., 1978-80. Mem. NAACP, Nat. Assn. Social Workers, Acad. Cert. Social Workers. Baptist. Home: 10600 Wenzel St Kansas City MO 64137 Office: 217 US Courthouse 811 Grand Ave Kansas City MO 64106

LIVINGSTONE, DIANE MARTIN, resource recovery systems specialist; b. Jacksonville, Fla., July 2, 1948; d. Douglas and Ruth (Kincart) Martin; A.B. in Social Scis., U. South Fla., 1972. Exec. v.p., cons. Cecoms, Inc., San Jose, Calif., 1978-81; exec. dir. Livingstone & Assocs., Santa Cruz, Calif., 1981—; chmn. Internat. Peacesat Satellite Conf., S. Pacific, 1982; co-originator NSF grant for conversion of anaerobic mcpl. wastewater sludges to fertile topsoil, 1978-81; U.S. rep. to UNESCO Conf., Paris, 1972; postgrad. instr. Bryn Mawr Coll. Extension, Avignon, France, 1972; lectr., researcher in field of vermicomposting (earthworm composting). Mem. Internat. Colloquium on Soil Zoology. Christian Scientist. Contbr. articles and reports to profl. jours. Address: Livingstone and Assocs PO Box 2910 Santa Cruz CA 95063

LIVSEY, JILL ELLEN, telecommunications co. exec.; b. Newark, Sept. 4, 1953; d. Howard David and Sandra Felice (Mandell) Taylor; B.A. cum laude, U. Miami, 1975; M.B.A., U. Ga., 1977; m. Richard Alan Livsey, Sept. 29, 1979; 1 son, Matthew Ross. Asst. product mgr. AT&T Long Lines, Bedminster, N.J., 1977-78, sales adminstrv. mgr., 1978-80, internal MBO cons., 1980-82, personnel mgr., 1982—. Home: 128 Chaucer Dr Berkeley Heights NJ 07922 Office: Route 202 Bedminster NJ 07921

LIZARDI, LINDA CAROL, mfg. co. exec.; b. San Diego, Aug. 27, 1954; d. Francisco Martinez and Jesse Marie (Snyder) L.; student San Diego State U., 1972-73; B.A., Calif. State U. Fresno, 1976. Community coordinator March of Dimes, Fresno, 1976; sec. Blue Thumb Co., Los Angeles, 1977, advt. mgr., salesperson, 1977-78, sales mgr., advt. mgr., 1978-79, pres., 1979—. Mem. Big Sisters Los Angeles, 1980—. Mem. Exhibit Designers and Products Assn. (v.p. Western chpt.), Calif. State U., Fresno Alumni Assn., AAUW, NOW, Women in Bus., Pres.'s Forum of Los Angeles. Home: 14823 Leadwell St Van Nuys CA 91405 Office: 5247 San Fernando Rd West Los Angeles CA 90039

LIZUT, NONA MOORE PRICE, state health ofcl.; b. Quay, N.Mex., Aug. 8, 1923; d. Charley W. and Alba Moore; student N.Mex. State U., 1941-42; m. Charles P. Price, Jr., 1944; 1 son, Charles P. III; m. 2d, William J. Lizut, May 27, 1970. Sec., N.Mex. Health Dept., Santa Fe, 1942-44: sec. environ. div., 1951-68; adminstrv. sec. environ. div. N.Mex. Health and Social Services Dept., Santa Fe, 1968-74, adminstrv. asst. to dep. dir., 1974-78; adminstrv. asst. to dep. sec. N.Mex. Health and Environ. Dept., Santa Fe, 1978-82, adminstr. health services div., 1982—. Mem. N.Mex. Water Pollution Control Assn. (life, adminstrv. officer 1956-71), N.Mex. Public Health Assn. (sec.-treas. 1962-68, pres. elect 1969), Nat. Secs. Assn. (v.p., program chmn. rec. sec., corr. sec.), Santa Fe C. of C. (women's div.), N.Mex. Round Dance Assn. (co-pres. 1981-82, newsletter editor 1979-82). Club: Capitol City Bus. and Profl. Women's (v.p., program chmn.). Home: 1408 Santa Rosa Dr Santa Fe NM 87501 Office: 809 St Michaels Dr Santa Fe NM 87503

LLOYD, ELIZABETH LEE, med. technologist; b. Charlotte, N.C., May 7, 1931; d. Harry Peachey, Jr. and Grace Elizabeth (Jackson) Murray; B.S., Queens Coll., Charlotte, 1954; m. Abbott Edward Lloyd, III, Oct. 15, 1955; 1 son, Abbott Edward, IV. Med. technologist Watts Hosp., Durham, N.C., 1953-58; chief technologist Med. Group Lab., Durham, 1958-65; supr. renal lab. Duke U. Med. Center, 1965-69, sr. med. technologist clin. hematology lab., 1973—. Cert. med. technologist, specialist in hematology, clin. lab. scientist, clin. lab. specialist. Mem. Am. Soc. Clin. Pathologists, Am. Soc. Med. Tech., LWV, Hillsborough Hist. Soc., DAR. Democrat. Episcopalian. Author papers in field. Home: Route 2 Box 43M Hillsborough NC 27278 Office: 3183 DUMC Erwin Rd Durham NC 27710

LLOYD, JUDITH ANN, nurse; b. Port Jefferson, N.Y., Mar. 26, 1942; d. Theodore Hulett and Irena Lenore (Coleman) Belden; student Adelphi U., 1960-61; grad. summa cum laude Cayuga County Community Coll., 1980; B.S. cum laude, SUNY, Albany, 1982; 1 dau., Erica Vollmar. Nurse, Huntington (N.Y.) Hosp., 1963-64; psychiat. nurse Central Islip (N.Y.) State Hosp., 1964-65; nurse ICU, Syosset, N.Y., 1966-69: asst. supr. Rochester (N.H.) Hosp., 1965-66; relief charge surg. ward nurse Auburn (N.Y.) Meml. Hosp., 1976-80; nurse Barnwell Health Facility, Valatie, N.Y., 1981—. Leader Girl Scouts U.S.A. Served to capt. USAF, 1969-72. Mem. Phi Theta Kappa. Lutheran. Home: Rural Delivery 1 Box 292 Valatie NY 12184

LLOYD, KATE RAND, editor, writer; b. Mpls.; d. Rufus Randall and Helen Starkweather (Chase) Rand; B.A. cum laude, Bryn Mawr Coll., 1945; m. John Davis Lloyd, Feb. 25, 1950; children—Kate Angeline, Ann Elizabeth, John Rand. Staff writer Vogue mag., N.Y.C., 1945-51, feature writer, 1951-54, sr. editor, 1963-67, feature editor, 1967-74, mng. editor, 1974-77; feature editor Glamour mag., 1954, mng. editor, 1954-63; editor-in-chief Working Woman mag., N.Y.C., 1977—; adj. lectr. Columbia U. Sch. Journalism, 1975—; adv. bd. First Women's Bank, N.Y.C. Mem. council Hunger Project, 1977—; mem. Nat. Commn. on Working Women; bd. dirs. Planned Parenthood Fedn. Am., 1978—, Nat. Black Theatre, 1980-82; mem. adv. bd. Inst. Women and Work, Cornell U., 1980—; adv. council Bus. and Profl. Women's Found.; mem. N.Y.C. Commn. on Status of Women, 1982. Recipient First prize Vogue Prix de Paris, 1945; named YWCA Woman of Achievement, 1978. Mem. Am. Soc. Mag. Editors, Women in Communications, Women's Forum (bd. dirs.), Advt. Women of N.Y. (bd. dirs.), UN Assn. (bd. dirs.) Democrat. Club: Colony (N.Y.C.). Editor: Glamour Mag. Party Book, 1965; Vogue Beauty and Health Guide, 1975, 76; editorial supr. Vogue's Book of Etiquette (rev. edit.), 1969; Vogue Real-Life Fashion Guide, 1976; mem. editorial bd. Bryn Mawr Coll. Bull. Office: 600 Madison Ave New York NY 10022

LLOYD, MARGARET ANN, psychologist, educator; b. Weiser, Idaho, Sept. 14, 1942; d. Laurance Henry and Margaret Jane (Patch) L.; B.A., U. Denver, 1964; M.S. in Edn., Ind. U., 1966; M.A., U. Ariz., 1972, Ph.D., 1973. Asst. dean of women Carroll (Wis.) Coll., 1966-68, instr. psychology, 1972-73; asst. prof. psychology Suffolk U., Boston, 1973-76, asso. prof., 1976-79, prof., 1979—, chairperson dept., 1981—. Mem. AAUP, Am. Psychol. Assn., Mass. Psychol. Assn. (sec. 1979-81, chairperson bd. acad. and sci. affairs 1981—). Home: 70 Abigail Adams Circle Weymouth MA 02191 Office: Suffolk U Beacon Hill Boston MA 02108

LLOYD, MARILYN ANN, personnel service agy. exec.; b. Frankfurt, Ind., Apr. 8, 1944; d. James Newton and Etta Jane (Hughes) Beaman; m. Michael James Lloyd, Sept. 16, 1972; children—Bridgena Ann, Terrina Leonne, Lisa Dawn. Owner Tex. Decorating, Dallas, 1962-78; co-owner, v.p., gen. mgr. Snelling Snelling, Dallas, 1979—. Mem. North Dallas C. of C. Home: 700 Pleasant View Hurst TX 76053 Office: 12900 Preston St Dallas TX 75230

LLOYD, NITA LORAINE, hotel exec.; b. St. Louis, Oct. 4, 1930; d. Harold Troester and Helen Elsie (Kohr) Bouligny; student public schs., University, City, Mo.; m. Jay Lloyd, Jr., Nov. 27, 1947; children—Sunny Lee Lloyd Cloud, Pamela Jayne Lloyd Deal, Laura L. Lloyd Riegler. Adminstrv. asst. to exec. v.p. Dairy Queen Nat. Devel. Co., St. Louis, 1959-67; sales mgr. Hilton Inn of St. Louis, 1967-68, dir. sales, 1968-73; dir. sales, corp. accounts Hilton Hotels Corp., St. Louis, 1973-75, dir. sales corp. accounts So. region, 1975—; lectr. in field. Cert. hotel sales exec. Mem. Hotel Sales Mgmt. Assn. (internat. pres. 1980-82), Sales and Mktg. Execs., Meeting Planners Internat. (charter mem. Ga. chpt.), Women's C. of C. of Atlanta. Republican. Lutheran. Club: Zonta. Author: Women's Opportunity in Hotel Sales, 1978; Three Faces of Eve...And How She Travels, 1979. Home: 4684 Shallowford Rd Roswell GA 30075 Office: 2070 S Park Pl Suite 200 Atlanta GA 30339

LOACH, JEAN CALANTHE, bus. cons.; b. Chgo.; d. George Winwood and Mary (Sipes) Loach; Mus.B., Mundelein Coll. Hostess Jean Loach TV Show, also women's editor Sta. WXYZ-TV, Detroit, 1950-60; pres. Jean Loach & Assos., Miami Beach, Fla., and N.Y.C., 1960-70, 72—; pres. Future Record Co., 1962—; dir. advt. and pub. relations Sheraton Park hotel, Sheraton Carlton hotel, Washington, 1971-72; chmn. bd. Jean Loach Assos. Corp., Washington, 1972—. Mem. adv. bd. Salvation Army, Miami, Fla., 1973; bd. dirs. Univ. Concert Series Seminars, 1970. Created dance Brit. Empire. Mem. AFTRA, ASCAP, Screen Actors Guild, Am. Fedn. Musicians, Am. Women in Radio and TV, Monarch Soc. Am. and Can. (dir.), Monarch Soc. Am. (founder, pres., dir.), Internat. Soc. Arts of Fla. Internat. U. (v.p.). Clubs: Order Eastern Star, Daus. Nile, Order White Shrine, Women's City (Detroit). Composer: Paree Still Seems the Same to Me, 1958; Where There's A Will There's A Way, 1966; Lucky, Lucky Me, 1973; A Mom Like Mine, 1973. Asso. editor Show Case mag. Address: 4925 Collins Ave Miami Beach FL 33140

LOBALZO, SUSAN VIRGINIA, interior designer; b. Wheeling, W.Va., Sept. 28, 1952; d. Nick and Grace (Hadjis) Karnell; student Ohio State U., 1970-72; B.A., Kent State U., 1974, M.A., 1979; student Parsons Sch. Design, 1981; m. Richard Lobalzo, July 21, 1973; children—Lisa, Dana. Successively mgr. custom drapery and bedspread dept., asst. buyer drapery dept., designer accessories, lamps and paintings Halle's Dept. Store, Cleve., 1975-78; grad. asst. Kent State U., 1978-79; freelance interior designer, Akron, Ohio, also instr. Kent State U., 1979—; conv. speaker. Cleve. Found. grantee, 1979; recipient Scalamandre award for hist. preservation, 1978, Presdl. citation Am. Soc. Interior Designers, 1980, 81. Mem. Am. Soc. Interior Designers (sec.), Nat. Trust Hist. Preservation, Nat. Center Barrier Free Environ., Akron Art Mus., Cleve. Art Mus. Democrat. Presbyterian. Home: 1190 Meadow Spur Akron OH 44313 Office: 103 Nixson Hall Kent State U Kent OH 44242

LOBL, MARYJANE, fin. planning exec.; b. Cleve., Jan. 19, 1939; d. Robert S. and Olive Belle (Weaver) Hall; student Western Res. U., 1957-59; m. Julian W. Lobl, May 17, 1980; children—D. Fletcher, Robert William, William, John. Adminstrv. asst. Allyne M. Gottlieb, Cleve., 1965-70; pvt. cons. on benefits, Cleve., 1970-75; asst. to pres. Empire Life Ins. Co., Cleve., 1975-77; v.p. N.E. Fin. Group, Inc., Cleve., 1977—. Cantorial soloist Brith Emeth Synagogue, Pepper Pike, Ohio, 1982. Mem. Am. Guild Organists. Dir. music Valley Luth. Ch., Chagrin Falls, Ohio, 1975—. Republican. Jewish. Home: 6922 Traymore Ct Mentor OH 44060 Office: 33 Public Sq Suite 250 Cleveland OH 44113

LOBNER, CORINNA DEL GRECO, educator; b. Florence, Italy, Feb. 22, 1927; came to U.S., 1946, naturalized, 1953; d. Francesco and Paola (Gatti) del Greco; B.A., Dominican Coll., 1965; M.A., U. Wis., 1968; Ph.D., U. Tulsa, 1981; m. Wesley Lobner, Nov. 7, 1945; 1 dau., Gloria Maria. Lectr. Italian art and culture, U. Wis. Art Centers, 1960-65; asst. prof. English and comparative lit. Dominican Coll., Racine, Wis., 1967-74; researcher for Am. Bicentennial, 1975-76; lectr. on Renaissance, Philbrook Art Center, Tulsa, 1979-81; asst. prof. Italian and comparative lit. U. Tulsa, 1982—. U. Wis.-Milw. fellow, 1968; U. Tulsa fellow, 1977-81, faculty research grantee, summer 1982; recipient Civic Recognition award for lecturing on Italian civilization, 1964. Mem. Wis. Acad. Arts, Scis. and Letters, U. Wis. Alumni Assn., MLA, James Joyce Found., Phi Kappa Phi, Lambda Iota Tau. Contbr. articles to profl. jours. Home: 7405 E 20th Pl Tulsa OK 74112 Office: Univ Tulsa 600 S College St Tulsa OK 74104

LO BOVES, JANET MARGARET, photog. equipment co. exec.; b. Jersey City, Mar. 11, 1950; d. Rudolph C. and Margaret (Campbell) LoBoves; B.A. in English, Ithaca (N.Y.) Coll., 1972. Quality control chemist Lever Bros. Co., Edgewater, N.J., 1972-73; photographer Graphic Reprodns. Lab., West New York, N.J., 1974-75; photo instr. New Hampton (N.H.) Sch., 1975-76; photog. instr. Fairleigh Dickinson U., Teaneck, N.J., 1976; photographer Ridgewood Newspapers (N.J.), 1976; demonstration/tng. coordinator 1 mil. sales cons. Ilford, Inc., Paramus, N.J., 1977-79; NE tech. rep. Bell & Howell/Mamiya Co., 1979; mktg. specialist Osawa & Co. (U.S.A.), N.Y.C., 1979-81; product specialist, 1981—. Staff Ridgefield Park Police Athletic League, 1970-72; notary public, N.J., 1972-77. Recipient hon. mention N.J. Press Photographers Assn., 1977, Bergen Community Mus. Photog. Contest,

1976. Mem. Nat., N.J. press photographers assns., Evidence Photographers Internat. Council. Photographs exhibited N.J. Press Photographers Touring Exhibit, 1977, Photo Mktg. Assn. Show, Chgo., 1978. Home: PO Box 1492 Kenner LA 70063 Office: 1 Mamiya Ct Kensington Center for Bus Mount Prospect IL 60056

LOBRON, BARBARA L., writer, editor, photographer; b. Phila., Mar. 19, 1944; d. Martin Aaron and Elizabeth (Gots) L.; student Pa. State U., 1962-63; B.A. cum laude, Temple U., Phila., 1966; student photography Harold Feinstein, N.Y.C., 1970, 79-80. Reporter, writer Camden (N.J.) Courier-Post, 1966-68; editorial asst. Med. Insight mag., N.Y.C., 1970-71; mng. editor Camera 35 mag., N.Y.C., 1971-75, also asso. editor photog. anns. for U.S. Camera/Camera 35, 1972, 73; freelance editor as Word Woman, N.Y.C., 1975-77, 79—; copy editor Camera Arts mag., N.Y.C., 1981—; contbg. editor Photograph; photographer, group exhbns. include: Photograph Gallery, N.Y.C., 1981, Rockefeller Center, N.Y.C., 1976, Internat. Women's Art Festival, N.Y.C., 1975; represented in collection Library of Calif. Inst. Arts, Valencia. Recipient 1st pl. honors Dist. 1, Internat. Assn. Bus. Communicators, 1977. Mem. Authors Guild, Editorial Freelancers Assn., Sigma Delta Chi. Copy editor: Camera Arts, 1981—, The Complete Guide to Cibachrome Printing, 1980; The Popular Photography Question and Answer Book, 1979; The Photography Catalog, 1976; Strand: Sixty Years of Photography, 1976; You and Your Lens, 1975; contbr. articles to comml. publs., chpts. to books. Home: 85 Hicks St Brooklyn NY 11201 Office: Ziff Davis Publishing 1 Park Ave New York NY 10016

LOBUONO, MARY AGNES, telephone co. ofcl.; b. Bayonne, N.J., Mar. 30, 1924; d. Arthur J. and Agnes F. (Malloy) Bonner; student Bayonne public and parochial schs.; m. Joseph J. LoBuono, Jan. 27, 1946; children—Joan, Joseph R. Per annum payroll clk. U.S. Army Base, Port Johnson, N.J., 1943-46; traffic mgr., spot announcements broadcasting Sta. WHN, N.Y.C., 1946-49; keypunch operator N.J. Bell Telephone Co., Newark, 1966-68, supr. data center, 1968-77, fin./comptroller deptl. rep., pensions, deaths and retirement, 1977—. Mem. ch. choir. Democrat. Roman Catholic.

LOCHAYA, ELLEN TEPER, mail order mktg. exec., public relations cons.; b. Albany, N.Y., Mar. 8, 1939; d. Eugene and Tilda Teper; B.S., Syracuse U., 1960; cert. teaching English as 2d lang. U. Mich., Ann Arbor, 1962; student Inst. Fund Raising, N.Y.C., 1977; 1 son, Ned. Copywriter, asst. to account exec. Grant Advt. Inc., Boston, 1960-61; publs. officer MIT, Cambridge, Mass., 1961-62; instr. English, Peace Corps, Thailand, 1962-64, Lang. Center, Bangkok, 1964-65; asst. to editor U.S. News & World Report, Bangkok, 1965-67; mng. editor, feature writer N.Y. State Dept. Health, Albany, 1969-70; sr. public info. specialist N.Y. State Dept. Commerce, Albany, 1970-72; public relations cons. N.Y. State Assembly, Albany, 1972-74; spl. projects asst. to indsl. commnr., N.Y. State Dept. Labor, Albany, 1974-76; upstate public relations dir. Group Health Inc., Albany and N.Y.C., 1976-77, public relations dir., 1977-78; owner Ellen Lochaya Public Relations, Albany, 1977—; pres. Asian Attic, Inc.; editor Flavors of Asia newsletter, 1981—; guest lectr. Union Coll., 1979. Bd. dirs. Point of Woods Condominium Homeowners Assn., 1977-79. Mem. Albany C. of C., Assn. Women Bus. Owners, Capital Dist. Press Club (dir.), Capital Dist. Ad Club, NAACP. Home and Office: 8 Briarwood Terr Albany NY 12203

LOCKARD, BETTY PINE, lawyer, educator; b. Kansas City, Mo., May 12, 1933; d. Gayles R. and Meda Marie (Burns) Pine; B.S. in Edn., Central Mo. State U., 1955, M.S. in Edn., 1956; J.D., U. Mo., Kansas City, 1961; m. Lawrence Allen Lockard, June 25, 1952. Tchr. elem. sch. Topeka Public Sch., System, 1955-56, Warrensburg (Mo.) Public Sch. System, 1956-58; admitted to Mo. bar, 1961; partner firm Pine, Welling, Jones and Lockard, Warrensburg, 1961-62, Pine & Lockard, Warrensburg, 1966-71; elected probate and ex-officio magistrate judge of Johnson County (Mo.), 1963-66; prof. criminal justice adminstrn. Central Mo. State U., Warrensburg, 1971—; cons., instr. Nat. Traffic Mgmt. Inst., 1971. Vol., Heart Fund, Cancer Fund, United Fund; campaign vol. various elections, Johnson County, 1978; asst. coordinator Johnson County, Republican Gubernatorial Primary election, 1980. Mem. Mo. Bar Assn., Johnson County Bar Assn., Am. Judicature Soc., Nat. Safety Council, Phi Kappa Phi (treas. Central Mo. State U. chpt.), Old Drum Humane Soc., Kappa Delta Pi, Alpha Phi Delta, Sigma Sigma Sigma (Emily Gates Alumni Achievement award 1977), Alpha Phi Sigma (hon.), Methodist. Club: Republican Women's (Johnson County). Home: Rt 7 Warrensburg MO 64093 Office: HUM 316A Central Mo State U Warrensburg MO 64093

LOCKE, DORIS WORTHEY, elec. co. exec.; b. Nettleton, Miss., June 30, 1941; d. John Albert and Amanda Mae (Johnson) Worthey; A.A., Itawamba Jr. Coll., 1961; m. Claude Douglass Locke, Jan. 11, 1973. Sec., Tombigbee Electric Power, Tupelo, Miss., 1961-65; sec. Paxson Electric Co., Jacksonville, Fla., 1965-70, adminstrv. asst., 1970—. Democrat. Club: Pilot (pres. 1979-80). Office: Paxson Electric Co 1050 Flagler Ave Jacksonville FL 32207

LOCKE, EDITH RAYMOND, editor; b. Vienna, Austria, Aug. 3, 1921; came to U.S., 1939, naturalized, 1944; d. Herman and Dora (Hochberg) Laub; student Bklyn. Coll., 1940-42, CCNY, 1942-45; m. A. Ralph Locke, Jr., May 29, 1963; 1 dau., Katherine Dee. Asst. to advt. dir. Harper's Bazaar, N.Y.C., 1945-46, asso. mdse. editor Jr. Bazaar, 1946-48; fashion dir. Abbott Kimball Advt. Agy., N.Y.C., 1948-49; asso. fashion editor Mademoiselle mag., N.Y.C., 1949-59, fashion editor, 1959-67, exec. editor, 1967-72, editor-in-chief, 1972-80; editor/producer/host weekly cable TV show for women You Magazine, 1981—; fashion and TV cons.; mem. Coty award jury Am. Fashion Critics, 1950—. Mem. Am. Soc. Mag. Editors, Fashion Group (pres. 1972-73). Author: The Red Door, 1965. Office: 1345 Ave of Americas Suite 4402 New York NY 10105

LOCKERY, DEBORAH HUMBLE, computer info. specialist; b. Burlington, N.C., Jan. 5, 1954; d. William Robert, Sr. and Ritchie (Sutton) Humble; B.S. in Computer Sci., N.C. State U., 1975; M.B.A., U. S.C., 1981; m. James Edward Lockery, Jr., May 23, 1980. Successively mgmt. trainee, sr. programmer, programmer analyst, functional analyst, sr. analyst, supr. Milliken & Co., Spartanburg, S.C., 1975-81; mktg. info. specialist Dowell div. Dow Chem. Co. U.S.A., Houston, 1981—. Mem. Alpha Lambda Delta, Pi Mu Epsilon, Upsilon Pi Epsilon. Methodist. Home: 11650 Trailmont Dr Houston TX 77077 Office: PO Box 4378 Houston TX 77010

LOCKETT, SANDRA A. JOHNSON BOKAMBA, librarian; b. Hutchinson, Kans., Nov. 18, 1946; d. Herbert Wales and Dorothy Bernice (Harrison) Johnson; B.S., U. Kans., 1968; M.L.S., Ind. U., 1973; m. J. Charles Lockett, May 26, 1979; children—Eyenga Marthe Bérénice Bokamba, Felicia Christine. Spl. assignments librarian Gary (Ind.) Public Library, 1973-74, Alcott br. librarian, 1974-76, asst. dir. public relations and programming, 1976-78, head extension services and public relations, 1978-79; head govt. documents dept. U. Iowa Law Library, Iowa City, 1979—. Pres., Iowa City Community Sch. Dist. Equity Com., 1980—; mem. Iowa City Com. Community Needs, 1981—; mem. Assn. Study Afro-Am. Life and History, 1976-78. Gary Public Library grantee, 1978. Mem. NAACP (sec. 1980-81), Am. Assn. Law Librarians, Mid-Am. Law Library Assn., Iowa Library Assn. (vice-chmn., chmn. elect govt. documents div. 1980—), Alpha Kappa Alpha. Democrat. Roman Catholic. Home: 2534 Bartelt Rd Apt 2-D Iowa City IA 52240 Office: U Iowa Coll Law Library Iowa City IA 52242

LOCKHART, DEBORAH ANN, computer programmer; b. Mineral Wells, Tex., Feb. 20, 1945; d. Joe Royce and Billie Louise (Crow) Williams; B.S., Tex. Christian U., 1967; postgrad. U. Tex., Arlington, 1971; m. Scott Charles Lockhart, June 17, 1976; children—Amy Louise, Adam Conan. Programmer aid Ling Temco Vought, Grand Prairie, Tex., 1966-67, 68-69; programmer analyst Trinity U., San Antonio, 1967-68; programmer analyst Info. Systems Tech., Dallas, 1969-71; systems engr. Optimum Systems Inc., Dallas, 1972-75; sr. programmer analyst Univ. Computing Co., Dallas, 1971-72, 75-81; mgr. CIF project Banking Systems, Inc., Dallas, 1981—. Mem. Mensa. Office: 5050 Quorum St Dallas TX 75234

LOCKHART, MADGE CLEMENTS, educator; b. Soddy, Tenn., May 22, 1920; d. James Arlie and Ollie (Sparks) Clements; student East Tenn. U., 1938-39; B.S., U. Tenn., Chattanooga and Knoxville, 1955, M.Ed., 1962; m. Andre J. Lockhart, Apr. 24, 1942; children—Jacqueline, Andrew, Janice, Jill. Elem. tchr. Tenn. and Ga., 1947-60, Brainerd High Sch., Chattanooga, 1960-64, Cleveland (Tenn.) City Schs., 1966-82; owner, operator Lockhart's Learning Center, Inc., Cleveland and Chattanooga, 1975—; co-founder Down Center, Hamilton County, Tenn., 1974, Hermes, residential, day care and workshops orgn., 1972. Pres., Cleveland Assn. Retarded Citizens, 1970, state v.p., 1976; pres. Cleveland Creative Arts Guild, 1980, Cherokee Easter Seal Soc., 1973-76; bd. dirs. Tenn. Easter Seal Soc., 1974-77, 80-83, recipient awards; chair Bradley County Internat. Yr. of Child; pres. Hermes, Inc., 1973-79. Recipient Service to Mankind award Sertoma, 1978. Gov.'s award for service to handicapped, 1979. Mem. NEA (life), Tenn. Edn. Assn., Am. Assn. Rehab. Therapy, Cleveland Edn. Assn., Council Exceptional Children, Tenn. Conf. Social Welfare, Bradley-Cleveland C. of C. Clubs: Byliners, Fantastiks. Mem. Ch. of Christ. Contbr. articles to profl. jours. and newspapers; writer poetry, short stories and fiction. Home: 3007 Oakland Dr Cleveland TN 37311 Office: 1212 Greenslake Rd Chattanooga TN 37412

LOCKRIDGE, KAREN SUE, motel exec.; b. Goshen, Ind., Nov. 23, 1948; d. Leslie Eugene and Rhea Jean (Reed) L.; B.A., Purdue U., 1971. With Allen & O'Hara, Inc., mgrs. Holiday Inns, 1967-82, sales dir., asst. gen. mgr. Holiday Inn, Tampa, Fla., 1975-82; corp. dir. sales Midway Motor Lodges, Brookfield, Wis., 1982—. Recipient Human Relations award City of Tampa, 1980. Mem. Am. Soc. Assn. Execs., Religious Conv. Mgrs. Assn., Nat. Tour Brokers Assn., Am. Bus. Assn., Fla. Soc. Assn. Execs., Tampa Bay Soc. Assn. Execs., Tampa Conv. and Visitors Bur. Episcopalian. Home: 2525 S Calhoun Rd Apt 104 New Berlin WI 53151 Office: 1025 S Moorland Rd Brookfield WI 53005

LOCKSLEY, ANNE, psychologist, educator; b. Ft. Riley, Kans., Apr. 12, 1951; d. Norman and Chrystene (Helm) L.; B.A., U. Mich., 1972, Ph.D., 1978. Asst. prof. psychology N.Y. U., N.Y.C., 1978-82, assoc. prof., 1982—. NSF grantee, 1979—. Mem. Am. Psychol. Assn., AAAS, N.Y. Acad. Scis., Phi Beta Kappa. Contbr. articles to profl. jours. Office: 6 Washington Pl Room 793 New York NY 10003

LOCKWOOD, BARBARA JORDAN, nurse adminstr.; b. Landshut, W. Ger., Aug. 23, 1948; d. Ernest Bob and Christa Barbara (Tilgner) Jordan (father Am. citizen); B.S. in Nursing with honors, U. Colo., 1970, M.S. in Med.-Surg. Nursing, 1973. Staff nurse Denver Gen. Hosp., 1970-72, Med. Personnel Pool, Denver, 1973; flight nurse St. Anthony Hosp. Systems, Denver, 1973-75, flight nurse supr., 1975-76, mgr. critical care services, 1976-79, systems dir. nursing services, 1979-81, asst. exec. dir. nursing services, 1981—; tchr. Am. Assn. Operating Room Nurses, 1976, Am. Assn. Critical Care Nurses, 1977, 78, Chautauqua confs. Colo. Assn. Nurses, 1977, 78, 79, 80, 81, Colo. Student Nurses Assn., 1979; vol. nurse Comitis Crisis Center, Aurora, Colo., 1970-73. Cert. critical care practitioner ACS. Mem. Am., Denver assns. critical care nurses, Nat. League for Nursing, Colo. League for Nursing (sec. 1982—), Sigma Theta Tau. Democrat. Lutheran. Contbr. chpt. on flight nursing to Critical Care Nursing, 1977; also articles. Office: St Anthony Hosp Systems 16th & Raleigh Sts Denver CO 80204

LOCKWOOD, BONNIE JEAN, librarian; b. Lincoln, Nebr., June 14, 1949; d. Carl Wallace and Maxana (Van Gundy) Simmons; B.S.Ed., U. Ga., 1971; M.Ed., 1973; m. David W. Lockwood, July 8, 1972; 1 dau., Allison Marie. Librarian, Beulah Elem. Sch., Douglasville, Ga., 1971-72; clk. typist U. Ga. Libraries, Athens, 1973; asst. librarian Bearden High Sch., Knoxville, Tenn., 1974; librarian Vestal Elem. Sch., Knoxville, 1974-77, Cedar Bluff Intermediate Sch., Knoxville, 1977-79, North Rose-Wolcott Middle Sch., Wolcott, N.Y., 1980—. Mem. ALA, N.Y. Library Assn., N.Y. Edn. Assn., NEA, Internat. Reading Assn., Phi Kappa Phi, Alpha Lambda Delta. Methodist. Home: 4256 Route 14 Lyons NY 14489 Office: North Rose-Wolcott Middle Sch Media Center New Hartford St Wolcott NY 14590

LOCKWOOD, HELSHI, advt. sales exec.; b. East Orange, N.J., May 18, 1941; d. Warren Sewell and Anne Frances (Gleason) Lockwood; B.A., Pa. State U., 1963; m. William B. Hewson, Jr., May 30, 1981; children by previous marriage—Bertram A. Tunnell III, Tory Lockwood Tunnell, Charles Warren Hewson. Promotion asst. Vogue mag., London, 1963-64; advt. sales rep. Brides mag., London, 1964-65; West Coast mgr. Status mag., Los Angeles, 1965-67, asst. advt. mgr., N.Y.C., 1968-69; advt. sales rep. Eye mag., N.Y.C., 1967-68; N.Y. mgr. Phila. and Boston mags., 1969-76; v.p., advt. sales mgr. Metro Mags., N.Y.C., 1976-78; v.p., partner Catalyst Communications, N.Y.C., 1978-80; account mgr. Dun's Bus. Month, N.Y.C., 1980-82, Eastern sales mgr., 1982—. Republican. Presbyterian. Home: 1133 Park Ave New York NY 10028 Office: 875 3d Ave New York NY 10022

LOCKWOOD, LINDA, fin. and mktg. cons., consumer economist; b. Evansville, Ind., July 13, 1942; d. Frank Roger and Elaine Williams Marriott; m. Sidney Irwin Bass, Sept. 7 1971 (div. 1978); children—Deana Gayle, Brent Leonard, William Allen, Daniel Charles, Stephen Howard. Internat. fin. cons., Beverly Hills, Calif., 1970—; pres. Lockwood & Assos., Inc., Beverly Hills, Calif., 1970—; bus. devel. exec. Calif. Real Estate Syndication Market, Beverly Hills, 1971; condr. money mgmt. seminars, 1973—; adv. to Prime Minister and cabinet ministers econs., edn. and welfare, Pau-New Guinea, 1973; cons. to Israeli Govt., 1972; mktg. dir. County Los Angeles, 1974; various appearances on TV shows including: Hour Mag. and NBC News, NBC Sunday Show, Steve Edwards Show, Toni Tenille Show, Mike Douglass Show, KHJ Midmorning Los Angeles, KTTV News; radio shows include: KOST, KLOS-FM, KISS, KMPC, K-EARTH, FM 100, KGO, San Francisco, Art Finley Show, K-Day Radio. First v.p. Easter Seal Soc. Crippled Children and Adults, Los Angeles, 1976, bd. dirs., 1976, chmn. exec. com., 1978, mem. fin. com. State of Calif. Bd.; founding pres. Continental Congress for Equal Rights, 1978; pres. State of Calif. Parent's Assn. Children's Centers, 1968, Youth Guidance League, 1969; bd. dirs. Reiss-Davis Child Study Center, 1969; founding pres. Equality Unlimited, 1978; mem. U.S. Democratic Senate Circle. Named Person of Yr. Easter Seal Soc., 1976. Mem. Nat. Soc. Fund Raisers, Aftra, Am. Women Radio and TV, Beverly Hills C. of C. (mem. com.). Democrat. Author: Money: What To Do With What You've Got, Then How To Get More, 1982. Office: 9025 Wilshire Blvd Beverly Hills CA 90211

LOCKWOOD, MOLLY ANN, communications co. exec.; b. London, Sept. 19, 1936; d. Warren Sewell and Ann Frances (Gleason) L.; B.S., Pa. State U., 1958. With exec. tng. program Lord & Taylor, N.Y.C., 1958-60; asso. merchandising editor House & Garden Mag., N.Y.C., 1960-65; advt. dir. Status Mag., N.Y.C., 1965-70; merchandising dir. Holiday Mag., N.Y.C., 1970; account mgr. Ladies' Home Journal Mag., N.Y.C., 1970-72; adv. dir. Girl Talk Mag., N.Y.C., 1972-74; mktg. dir./asso. pub. East/West Network Mag., N.Y.C., 1974-77; chief operating officer, v.p., treas., partner Catalyst Communications, Inc., N.Y.C., 1977—; mktg. and sales dir. Mus. mag., 1979—. Mem. Advt. Women N.Y., Am. Soc. Travel Agts., Caribbean Travel Assn., Kappa Kappa Gamma Alumnae Assn. Home: 1133 Park Ave New York NY 10028 Office: Catalyst Communications Inc 244 Madison Ave New York NY 10016

LODER, MARTHA KATHERINE, ret. educator; b. Bridgeton, N.J., July 12, 1914; d., LeRoy Ward and Maude (Woodruff) Loder; A.B., Dickinson Coll., 1934; A.M., U. Pa., 1937, Ph.D., 1943. Tchr., Bridgeton High Sch., 1935-38, 39-41, head dept. English, fgn. langs., 1943-57; tchr. Springfield Twp. High Sch., Chestnut Hill, Pa., 1941-43; supr. secondary instrn. Bridgeton Pub. Schs., 1957-71; ret., 1971. Bd. dirs. Bridgeton chpt. NCCJ, Bridgeton chpt. ARC; trustee Bridgeton Free Pub. Library. Recipient Am. Legion award for meritorious community service, 1950. Mem. DAR, AAUW, Nat. Ret. Tchrs. Assn., Alliance Francaise, Phi Beta Kappa. Author: The Life and Novels of Leon Gozlan, 1943. Home: 8 South Dr Bridgeton NJ 08302

LODGE, EDITH BENNETT (MRS. GEORGE TOWNSEND LODGE), poet; b. N.Y.C., Nov. 17, 1908; d. William Mason and Mary Evans (Umstead) Bennett; B.A., Oberlin Coll., 1929; M.A., Old Dominion U., 1970; m. George Townsend Lodge, June 18, 1929; children—Ann, David Townsend. Asst., Tchr.'s Coll. Library, Columbia U., N.Y.C., 1944-45; asst. Duke U. Library, Durham, N.C., 1955-58; lectr. English, Old Dominon U., Norfolk, Va., 1970-72; poems and prose segments pub. in Saturday Rev., N.Y. Times, Kaleidograph, Lantern, Arrows in the Air, Christian Century, Presbyn. Survey, Pulpit, Oregonian Verse, The Lyric, Imprints Quar., other mags. and newspapers; poems included in Golden Year, 1960, Diamond Anthologies of Poetry Soc. Am., 1971, Golden Anthology of Poetry Soc. Va., 1974, Sandwich Isles, U.S.A., Anthology of Hawaii Writers Club, 1973. Recipient 1st prize for sonnet Irene Leache Meml. Contest, 1964, 1st prize for lyric, 1965. Mem. Poetry Soc. Am., Acad. Am. Poets, Poetry Soc. Va., AAUW. Presbyn. Author: Song of the Hill, Selected Poems of Edith Lodge, 1964; Journey Through Noon (poems), 1974. Home: 3100 Shore Dr Apt 1230 Virginia Beach VA 23451

LOE, MADALYN ELLEN, interior designer; b. Mpls., Oct. 31, 1935; d. Frederick and Genevieve Catherine (Rooney) L.; student U. Minn., 1960-63. With Internat. Multifoods, Inc., Mpls., 1963-68, Microwave div. Litton Industries, Mpls., 1968-69, Ethan Allen, Inc., Minnetonka, Minn., 1969—. Active, Leadership-Mpls., 1976-79. Mem. Mpls. C. of C., Nat. Home Fashions League, Interior Design Soc. Home: 2321 Wildwood Trail Minnetonka MN 55343

LOEB, FRANCES LEHMAN (MRS. JOHN L. LOEB), club woman; b. N.Y.C., Sept. 25, 1906; d. Arthur and Adele (Lewisohn) Lehman; student Vassar Coll., 1924-26; L.H.D. (hon.), N.Y. U., 1977; m. John L. Loeb, Nov. 18, 1926; children—Judith Loeb Chiara, John L., Ann Loeb Bronfman, Arthur Lehman, Deborah Loeb Brice. N.Y.C. commr. for UN and Consular Corps, 1966-78. Exec. com. Population Crisis Com., Washington; life bd. dirs. Recreation Service for Children of Bellevue, 1974—; bd. dirs. N.Y. Landmarks Conservancy, Internat. Play Group, Inc.; chmn. bd. East Side Internat. Community Center, Inc.; mem. UN Devel. Corp., 1972—; life trustee Collegiate Sch. for Boys, N.Y.C.; trustee Cornell U., Inst. Internat. Edn.; mem. Council on Internat. Bus. Mem. UN Assn. (dir.). Clubs: Cosmopolitan, Vassar, Women's City (N.Y.C.). Home: 730 Park Ave New York NY 10021 also Anderson Hill Rd Purchase NY 10577

LOEB, HELEN WARD, educator; b. Rockville Center, N.Y., Mar. 19, 1933; d. Samuel Kemble and Mable Alma (Malmberg) Ward; student Hunter Coll., 1955-57; B.S.Ed., Glassboro State Coll., 1959; M.Ed., Temple U., 1961; Ph.D. (Coll. scholar), Bryn Mawr Coll., 1975; m. Paul Loeb; children—David, William. Tchr. nursery sch., Riverside Ch., N.Y.C., 1953-57; tchr. public schs., Mantua Twp., N.J., Haddon Twp., N.J., 1959-68; asst. prof. edn. and psychology Eastern Coll., 1969-75, asso. prof., 1975-80, prof., 1980—, chmn. dept. edn., 1978—; co-dir. Norris Sq. Neighborhood Project, Inc. Am. Baptist Chs. grantee, 1974-77. Mem. Am. Psychol. Assn., Nat. Council Tchrs. Math., Sci. Tchrs. Assn., Assn. Supervision and Curriculum Devel., Assn. Cooperation in Edn., Kappa Delta Pi. Contbr. articles to profl. publs. Office: Eastern Coll Saint Davids PA 19087

LOENING, SARAH ELIZABETH LARKIN, author; b. Nutley, N.J., Dec. 9, 1896; d. Adrian Hoffman and Katherine Bache (Satterthwaite) Larkin; student pvt. schs., N.Y.C., Paris; m. Albert Palmer Loening, Nov. 22, 1922; 1 son, Albert Palmer. Author: Three Rivers, 1934; The Trevals, a Tale of Quebec, 1936; Radisson, 1938; Dimo, French edit., 1940, 2d edit., 1978, English edit., 1979; Joan of Arc, 1950; The Old Master, 1958; Zulli, 1954; The Old Master and Other Tails, 1967; Mountain in the Field, 1972; The Gift of Life, 1978. Chmn. arts and skill corps ARC, Camp Upton, 1944, chmn. Hampton chpt. ARC, 1946; pres. Cathedral Guild St. John the Divine, 1961-64, 66-68, chmn. Bibl. Garden, 1972—, chmn. Gardeners of St. John, 1950-58. Mem. Am. Order St. John of Jerusalem (dame), Order St. Luke the Physician, Nat. Soc. Colonial Dames, Huguenot Soc. Episcopalian. Clubs: Colony, Pen and Brush, Hroswitha, Southampton Garden (past pres.). Home: PO Box 905 119 1st Neck Ln Southampton NY 11968

LOESCH, KATHARINE TAYLOR, educator; b. Berkeley, Calif., Apr. 13, 1922; d. Paul Schuster and Katharine (Whiteside) Taylor; student Swarthmore Coll., 1939-41, U. Wash., 1942; B.A., Columbia U., 1944, M.A., 1949; postgrad. Ind. U., 1953; Ph.D., Northwestern U., 1961; m. John George Loesch, Aug. 28, 1948; 1 son, William Ross. Instr. speech Wellesley (Mass.) Coll., 1949-52, Loyola U., Chgo., 1956; asst. prof. speech Roosevelt U., Chgo., 1957, 62-65; faculty U. Ill. at Chgo. Circle, 1968—, asso. prof. communication and theatre, 1970—. Recipient Golden Anniversary Prize award Speech Assn. Am., 1969. Am. Philos. Soc. grantee, 1970. Mem. Am. Soc. for Aesthetics, Linguistics Soc. Am., Speech Communication Assn. (chmn. interpretation div. 1979-80), MLA. Home: 2129 N Sedgwick St Chicago IL 60614

LOESER, NORMA MAINE, educator; b. Plattsburgh, N.Y., Aug. 1, 1922; d. James Wesley and Flora Maine (Coolidge) Laver; B.B.A., George Washington U., 1958, M.B.A., 1967, D.B.A., 1971; m. David John Loeser, Nov. 7, 1942 (dec.). Commd. 2d lt. WAC U.S. Army Air Force, 1945, advanced through grades to lt. col. U.S. Air Force, 1962; service in Eng., Germany and France; dep. dir. women in air force Hdqrs. USAF, 1964-66; ret., 1966; asst. dean Sch. Govt. and Bus. Adminstrn. George Washington U., 1971-73, asso. prof. bus. adminstrn., 1973-76, prof., 1977-78, dean, 1978—; mng. dir. CAB, 1976-77; commr. Def. Manpower Commn., 1974-76; dir. Thomas & Betts Corp., People's Life Ins. Co. Decorated Air Force Commendation medal with 2 oak leaf clusters; teaching fellow George Washington U., 1967-69. Mem. Acad. Mgmt., Am. Mgmt. Assn., Am. Econ. Assn., Aero Club Washington, Ret. Officers Assn., Nat. Aeros. Assn., Internat. Personnel Mgmt. Assn., World Futurist Soc. Republican. Author: Executive Leadership: The Art of Successfully Managing Resources, 1969. Home: 2707 Thyme Dr Edgewater MD 27037 Office: 710 21st St NW Washington DC 20052

LOEWY, BECKY WHITE, educator; b. Fountain Inn, S.C., July 24, 1931; d. James Ernest and Agnes (Roberts) White; student Mary Washington Coll., U. Va., 1948-50; B.A., Vanderbilt U., 1952; M.A., Ohio State U., 1953; Ph.D., U. Calif., Berkeley, 1957; m. Frederick Arnold Loewy, Aug. 28, 1962; children—Julia Anne, Caroline Marie. Residence counselor Ohio State U., Columbus, 1953-55; asst. prof. ednl. psychology, sr. counselor Duke U., 1957-59; asst. prof. San Francisco State U., 1959-63, asso. prof., 1963-69, prof. psychology, 1969—, program dir. gerontology, 1977—. Danforth Asso., 1979. Mem. Am. Psychol. Assn., Soc. Research in Child Devel., Am. Personnel and Guidance Assn., Western Gerontol. Soc., Psi Chi, Pi Lambda Theta. Home: 1275 Tuolumne Rd Millbrae CA 94030 Office: Psychology Dept San Francisco State U 1600 Holloway San Francisco CA 94132

LOFLAND, LYN HEBERT, sociologist; b. Everett, Wash., Dec. 2, 1937; d. Lisle F. and Estelle Mae (Hogan) Hebert; student Stanford U., 1955-56; B.A. in Sociology, Antioch Coll., 1960; M.A. in Sociology, U. Mich., 1966; Ph.D. in Sociology, U. Calif., San Francisco, 1971; m. John Lofland, Jan. 2, 1965. Acting asst. prof. U. Calif., Berkeley, 1970-71; asst. prof. sociology U. Calif., Davis, 1971-77, acad. dir. Women's Resources and Research Center, 1976-78, asso. prof., 1977—; cons. pubs. and jours. USPHS trainee, 1964-65; NDEA fellow, 1968-70. Mem. Internat., Am., Pacific sociol. assns., Soc. Study of Symbolic Interaction, Am. Hist. Assn. Democrat. Author: A World of Strangers, 1973; The Craft of Dying: The Modern Face of Death, 1978; (with John Lofland) Analyzing Social Settings, 1983; editor: Toward a Sociology of Death and Dying, 1976. Contbr. articles and revs. to profl. jours. Home: 523 E St Davis CA 95616 Office: Dept Sociology U Calif Davis CA 95616

LOGAN, GRACE ELEANOR MILLER, educator; b. Valencia, Pa., June 22, 1908; d. Alvah John and Lillian (Gibson) Miller; B.S., Temple U., 1930, M.S., 1931; postgrad., 1955-56; m. Henry Whittington Logan, Mar. 16, 1940; 1 son, Henry Whittington III. English instr. Temple U., 1930-33; asst. prof. to dept. head Moravian Coll., Bethlehem, Pa., 1933-42; asso. prof. edn. and philosophy Widener U. (formerly PMC Colls.), Chester, Pa., 1956-67, asso. prof. English and philosophy, 1969-70, prof. English, 1970—, dir. Coll. Reading Services, 1958—; dir. Fed. Office of Edn. Equal Opportunities Tng. Br. Insts., 1965—; cons., lectr.; only woman on faculty any mil. coll. U.S. for 8 yrs.; evaluator ESEA Title I project Chester Sch. Dist., 1968-69. Mem. adv. bd. Pa. Inst. Tech.; bd. dirs. Delaware County Hist. Soc.; mem. Emergency Aid of Phila. Mem. AAUP, Nat. Council Tchrs. English, Coll. English Assn., Internat. Platform Assn., Am. Assn. for Higher Edn., N.E.A., Coll. Reading Assn., Internat. Reading Assn., Pa. Council Tchrs., Am. Acad. Religion, Kappa Delta Epsilon, Pi Delta Epsilon. Presbyterian (elder). Club: Questers. Home: 201 Sykes Ln Wallingford PA 19086 Office: Widener U Chester PA 19013

LOGAN, KAYLEEN ANN, nurse; b. Rock Springs, Wyo., Jan. 18, 1954; d. Andrew Robert and Lois Ann (Lowe) Logan; B.S. cum laude, U. Utah, 1976. ICU nurse U. Utah Med. Center, Salt Lake City, 1976-77; charge nurse ICU, Holy Cross Hosp., Salt Lake City, 1977-78; public health nurse Sweetwater County, Rock Springs, Wyo., 1978-80; nursing dir. Miner's Respiratory Clinic, Rock Springs, 1980—; instr. cardio-pulmonary classes Am. Heart Assn., Sweetwater County, 1980—. Adv., Sweetwater Task Force on Sexual Assault, 1980—; adv. bd. Wind River Legal Services, 1981—. March of Dimes scholar, 1972-74. Episcopalian. Home: 674 Big Horn Rock Springs WY 82901 Office: PO Box 1359 Rock Springs WY 82901

LOGAN, REBECCA DE LOATCH POLLARD (MRS. JOHN A. LOGAN), civic worker, philanthropist; b. Port Norfolk, Va.; d. William Andrew and Daisy (De Loatch) Pollard; student Stuart Hall, Staunton, Va., Comstock Sch., N.Y.C., Grand Central Art Sch., 1926, Boston Sch. Mus. Fine Arts, 1931; m. William B. Van Lennep II, Sept. 6, 1926 (div. 1937); 1 son, Richard; m. 2d, M. Robert Guggenheim, Jan. 6, 1938 (dec. Nov. 1959); m. 3d, John A. Logan, Apr. 16, 1962. Exhibited art work Nat. Mus., Washington, 1948, Boston, 1931. Mem. women's bd. Washington Heart Assn., 1968—; mem. women's com. Corcoran Gallery Art, Washington, 1955—, trustee, 1973—, mem. art sch. com., 1973—; founder Art Barn, (name changed to Art Barn Assos. 1973), pres. Art Barn Assn. of Washington, 1971-73, pres. emeritus, 1973—; mem. Nat. Trust for Historic Preservation, Washington, 1966—; mem. nat. bd. Med. Coll. Pa., 1957—. Bd. dirs. Children's Hosp. Washington, 1945—, asso. mem., 1964—; bd. dirs. Washington Opera Soc. Guild, Washington Performing Arts, Capital Children's Mus., Nat. Symphony; hon. bd. dirs. Washington Ballet, 1980—; trustee Children's Speech and Hearing Center, Washington, 1969—. Recipient Golden award Smithsonian Instn. Mem. Am. Newspaper Women's Assn. (asso.), Nat. Soc. Arts and Letters (pres. 1958-60), Colonial Dames Am. (pres. chpt. III 1975-77, 1st v.p. 1977—), Huguenot Soc., DAR. Episcopalian. Clubs: Washington, Sulgrave, City Tavern, Chevy Chase 1925 F St. (Washington); Ha' Penny Pay Beach, Tennis (St. Croix). Home: 2230 S St NW Bellevue North Washington DC 20008

LOGAN, VICKI, writer; b. Oakland, Calif., Aug. 3, 1954; d. Robert Lee and Freida Elizabeth (Luckett) L.; B.S. in Bus. Adminstrn. magna cum laude, Pepperdine U., 1976; M.Internat. Mgmt., with honors, Am. Grad. Sch. Internat. Mgmt., 1979. Asst. to dep. dir. HUD, Washington, 1978; account exec. Doyle Dane Bernbach Advt., Inc., N.Y.C., 1979-81; writer Jordan Case & McGrath Advt., N.Y.C., 1981—; advt. cons. to CSC, Washington, 1978—. Office: 445 Park Ave New York NY 10022

LOGEMANN, JERILYN ANN, speech pathologist; b. Berwyn, Ill., May 21, 1942; d. Warren F. and Natalie M. (Killmer) L.; B.S., Northwestern U., 1963; M.A., 1964, Ph.D., 1968. Grad. asst. dept. communicative disorders Northwestern U., 1963-68; instr. speech and audiology DePaul U., 1964-65; instr. dept. communicative disorders Mundelein Coll., 1967-71; research assoc. depts. neurology and otolaryngology and maxillofacial surgery Northwestern U. Med. Sch., Chgo., 1970-74, asst. prof., 1974-78, dir. clin. and research activities of speech and lang., 1975—, assoc. prof. dept. neurology, otolaryngology and maxillofacial communicative disorders, 1978—, chmn. dept. communicative disorders, 1982—; mem. assoc. staff Northwestern Meml. Hosp., 1976—; assoc. dir. cancer control. Ill. Comprehensive Cancer Council, Chgo., 1980-82. Mem. rehab. com. Ill. div. Am. Cancer Soc., 1975-79, chmn., 1979—. Nat. Inst. Neurologic Disease, Communicative Disorders and Stroke postdoctoral fellow Northwestern U., 1968-70; Inst. Medicine Chgo. fellow, 1981—, Nat. Cancer Inst. grantee, 1975-84, Am. Cancer Soc. grantee, 1981-82. Fellow Am. Speech, Lang. and Hearing Assn.; mem. Internat. Assn. Logopedics and Phoniatrics, AAUP, Acoustic Soc. Am. (program com. Chgo. regional chpt.), Linguistic Soc. Am., Speech Communication Assn., Am. Cleft Palate Assn., Ill. Speech and Hearing Assn., Chgo. Heart Assn., Chgo. Speech Therapy and Auditory Soc. Author: The Fisher-Logemann Test of Articulation Competence, 1971; assoc. editor Jour. Speech and Hearing Disorders, 1978-82. Home: 1002 Greenleaf St Wilmette IL 60091 Office: Dept Otolaryngology Northwestern U Med Sch 303 E Chicago Ave Chicago IL 60611

LOGUE, LOIS JOAN, med. technologist; b. Mt. Pleasent, Mich., June 28, 1936; d. Daniel Edward and Thelma Margaret (Hanke) Hughes; student U. Tex., 1954-56; B.S., Incarnate World Coll., 1958; m. William J. Logue, Jr., Oct. 12, 1957; children—Kathleen Sue, William Joseph. Hematology supr. Meml. Hosp. of Chester County, West Chester, Pa., 1967-68; adminstrv. technologist Paoli (Pa.) Meml. Hosp., 1968-78; adminstrv. dir. Nat. Com. for Clin. Lab. Standards, Villanova, Pa., 1979—; key man State of Pa. for Am. Soc. Med. Technologists, 1977-82. Recipient Chi Omega award for outstanding service to the Profession, Am. Soc. Med. Technologists, 1980, 81. Mem. Am. Soc. Clin. Pathologists, Am. Soc. Med. Technologists, Clin. Lab. Mgmt. Assn. (nat. pres. 1978-79, dir. 1977—, pres. Del. Valley chpt. 1977-80), Clin. Ligand Assay Soc., Chi Omega. Republican. Roman Catholic. Mem. editorial bd. Lab. World, 1978-82. Home: 601 Waynesfield Dr Newtown Square PA 19073 Office: 771 E Lancaster Ave Villanova PA 19085

LOHAN, DIANE LEGGE, architect; b. Englewood, N.J., Dec. 4, 1949; d. Richard C. and Patricia (Roney) Legge; student Wellesley Coll. 1967-69, B.A. in Architecture, Stanford U., 1972; M.Arch., Princeton U., 1975; m. Dirk Lohan, Dec. 1, 1978. Draftsman various firms, N.Y.C. and Calif., 1970-75; designer The Ehrenkrantz Group, N.Y.C., 1975-77; Successively assoc., assoc. partner, now partner Skidmore, Owings & Merrill, Chgo. Mem. Met. Housing and Planning Council. Mem. AIA, Nat. Council Archtl. Registration Bds. Clubs: Racquet of Chgo., Arts, Tavern, Chgo. Yacht. Designs include: Ritz Carlton Hotel Addition, Boston, 1980, Chgo. Tribune Printing Plant, 1981. Office: 33 W Monroe St Chicago IL 60603

LOISELLE, DONNA FRANCES, social worker; b. Norfolk, Va., June 14, 1945; d. Donald William and Kathleen Elizabeth (O'Hayre) L.; A.B., Wilson Coll., Chambersburg, Pa., 1967; M.S.W., U. Conn., 1969. Social worker and adoption program coordinator Catholic Family Services Inc., New Britain, Conn., 1969—; field edn. instr. U. Conn. Sch. Social Work, 1979—. Mem. Nat. Assn. Social Workers, Acad. Cert. Social Workers, Conn. Council on Adoption, Archdiocese of Hartford Adoption Adv. Com. Home: 2301 Cromwell Hills Dr Cromwell CT 06416 Office: 90 Franklin Sq New Britain CT 06051

LOKER, ELIZABETH ST. JOHN, newspaper exec.; b. Leonardtown, Md., Jan. 1, 1948; d. William Meverell and June Whiting (Farner) L.; B.A. in Philosophy with distinction, George Washington U., 1969. Research asso. Planning Research Corp., Washington, 1971-72; analyst-programmer Met. Washington Council of Govts., 1972-74; analyst-programmer Washington Post, 1974-76, mgr. systems research, 1976, dir. data processing, 1977-79, planning dir. and asst. to publisher, 1979, v.p. planning and advanced systems, 1979—. Mem. Nat. Trust for Historic Preservation, George Washington U. Alumni Assn., Soc. for Mgmt. Info. Systems, Newspaper Systems Group, Assn. Computing Machinery. Office: 1150 15th St NW Washington DC 20071

LOMBARD, SUSAN, corp. exec.; b. Greenfield, Iowa, Oct. 4, 1942; d. Myron L. and Maudelln (Wallace) L.; B.A. in Polit. Sci., Grinnell Coll., 1964. Exec. sec. Coast Fed. Savs. & Loan Assn., Los Angeles, 1975-76; adminstrv. asst. to pres. Western Asset Mgmt., Los Angeles, 1977-78; adminstr. Baker Ancel & Hall, Los Angeles, 1979-80; corp. sec., adminstr. Dynasty Computer Corp., Dynasty Mfg. Co. and Dynasoft, Inc., Dallas, 1980—. Mem. Nat. Assn. Female Execs., Meeting Planners Internat. Republican. Home: 13354 Emily Rd Dallas TX 75240 Office: 14240 Midway Rd Dallas TX 75234

LOMONTE, LANECE POPE, educator; b. Trinity County, Tex., Sept. 4, 1934; d. Alton Lee and Bonnie Irene (Lawrence) Pope; B.S., Sam Houston State U., 1954, postgrad. 1961; M.Ed., U. Md., 1967; 1 dau., Emily Chandler. Asst. to dir. food services Dow Chem., Freeport, Tex., 1954-59; instr. Georgetown Visitation Coll., Washington, 1962-63; tchr. Anne Arundel County (Md.) public schs., 1963-70; asst. to dir. admissions St. John's Coll., Md., 1970-72; owner S:HE, Annapolis and Dallas, 1972-78; adminstrv. aide Hubbard & Assos., Dallas, 1977-80; contracts coordinator Community Health Computing, Houston, 1980-81; tchr. Spring Branch (Tex.) Public Schs., 1981—; cons. U. Md., 1964-70. Active, Nottingham W. Civic Assn., Houston, 1980—. Mem. AAUW, Am. Home Econs. Assn. Democrat. Episcopalian. Home: 14007 Myrtlea Houston TX 77079 Office: 1001 Kirkwood Houston TX 77043

LONCHARICH, MARY KATHY, TV sta. exec.; b. Milw., Apr. 25, 1947; d. Albert John and Helen (Bolich) L.; A.A. with honors, Mesa (Ariz.) Community Coll., 1967; B.S., Northwestern U., 1969. Sr. merchandising coordinator Seventeen mag., N.Y.C., 1971-74; dir. creative services for retail sales CBS, N.Y.C., 1975-77, account exec. Sta. WBBM-TV, Chgo., 1977-82; account exec. Sta. WNEW-TV, Metromedia, N.Y.C., 1982—. Mem. AFTRA, Phi Theta Kappa, Alpha Xi Delta, Phi Beta. Contbr. poetry to mags. Home: 4 Beaver Hill Rd Marlboro NJ 07746

LONDON, MARY ELLEN LEWIS, ednl. cons. and coordinator; b. Hutchinson, Kans., Apr. 3, 1927; d. Chester Iaasic and Edna Louise (Anderson) Lewis; grad. in Fine Arts/Edn., Kans. U., 1949; M.A. in Early Childhood Edn., Goddard Coll., 1973; m. Jesse London, Sept. 30, 1967; 1 son by previous marriage, Richard Norman Batie. Design engr. Boeing, Wichita, Kans., 1952-59; supr., trainer Parent Child Guidance Center Head Start, Los Angeles, 1968-74, Fedn. Head Start trainer, supr., 1974-78; pvt. practice cons. early childhood edn., Los Angeles, 1971—; dir. Creative Environment Learning Center, Los Angeles, 1971-73; instr., asst. prof. Long Beach (Calif.) State U., 1975-77; asst. prof. early childhood edn. Pepperdine U., Los Angeles, 1975-78, Calif. State U. Los Angeles, 1980—, Pacific Oaks Coll., 1980—, LaVerne (Calif.) U., 1975—; field coordinator state program career incentive program Inst. for Profl. Devel., 1978-80; dir. Assistance League Day Nursery, 1981—; adv. bd. on follow through Graham Elem. Sch.; adv. bds. on early childhood edn. S.W. Coll., Valley City Coll., Compton Coll., Dominguez Hills U., Calif. State U. Long Beach; adv. bds. Harbor Coll., El Camino Coll.; cons. assessor Urban Inst., Region IX ACYF-HEW, 1979—. Recipient awards Kans. Regional Art Exhibit, 1944, Head Start, 1968, 75, efficiency economy award Lockheed, 1962; tchr. tng. cert. OEO, 1966; Supr. of Yr. trophy Head Start, 1974, 78. Mem. So. Calif. Assn. for Edn. Young Children (Los Angeles v.p., 1976-78), Calif. Assn. for Edn. Young Children (chmn. Internat. Yr. of Child, 1978-79), Nat. Assn. for Edn. Young Children (governing bd., public policy task group, Washington, 1977—, local coordinator conf., Anaheim, 1976), Child Devel. Consortium (field rep., Washington 1975), Alpha Kappa Alpha (Black Heritage chmn., 1977-79, 25 year medalion, 1979, community service award, 1979, exhibit award, 1979), Black Women's Forum Los Angeles, Exec. Female, Methodist. Artist, organist, dress designer; participant art exhibit, Oakland, Calif., 1965; author: Creative Environment Learning Center, 1973. Home: 1235 Stearns Dr Los Angeles CA 90035 Office: 1375 St Andrews Pl Los Angeles CA 90028

LONDON, MICHELE LAKS, psychotherapist; b. Chgo., Apr. 12, 1951; d. Maurice and Sylvia (Singer) Laks; B.A., U. Calif., Berkeley, 1973; M.S.W., San Diego State U., 1975; m. Gary London, July 11, 1976. Dir. social services Clairemont Hosp., San Diego, 1975-77; clin. social worker Mercy Hosp. and Med. Center, San Diego, 1977-79; family counselor Family Service Assn., San Diego, 1979-81, Jewish Family Services, 1981—; field instr. Sch. Social Work, San Diego State U., 1976-79; sec., San Diego Community Child Abuse Coordinating Council, 1979; facilitator of pregnant minors therapy group Grossmont Union High Sch. Dist., 1980—. Lic. clin. social worker, Calif. Mem. Acad. Cert. Social Workers, Soc. Clin. Social Work, Nat. Assn. Social Workers, Internat. Yr. of Child Assn. Club: Hadassah. Office: 3355 4th Ave San Diego CA 92103

LONERGAN, JOYCE, state legislator; b. Benton County, Iowa, Mar. 5, 1934; d. Robert and Fannie Mary (Duda) Jacobi; student public schs.; m. Paul J. Lonergan (dec.); children—Patrick Joseph, Peter Thomas, Kathleen Ann, Staci Marie. Mem. Iowa Ho. of Reps. from 44th Dist., 1975—. Mem. Nat. Order Women Legislators, Am. Bus. Women's Assn. Democrat. Roman Catholic. Office: State House Des Moines IA 50319

LONG, BETTIE WOODS, adminstr. center for emotionally disturbed children; b. Tuscaloosa, Ala., Sept. 19, 1944; d. William Albert and Cora Lee Woods; B.A. in English, Stillman Coll., B.S. in Bus. Edn., 1966; M.A. in Counseling and Guidance, U. Cin., 1970; A.A., U. Ala., 1977; m. Fletcher James Long, Aug. 28, 1978. Tchr., Bradenton (Fla.) Jr. High Sch., 1967-68; instr. Cin. Tech. Coll., 1968-73; learning diagnostician Greene County (Ala.) Bd. Edn., 1973-74; unit dir. Brewer-Porch Children's Center, U. Ala., Tuscaloosa, 1974—; spl. scholar, project growth U. Ala. Inst. Higher Edn. Research and Services, 1979; tchr./psychotherapy therapist U. Ala. Affirmative Action Com., 1980-81; instr. Cin. Opportunities Industrialization Center, 1968-70, counselor, 1970-73; instr. Shelton State Community Coll., 1976, C.A. Fredd State Tech. Coll., 1978-80. Sec., Stillman Coll. Nat. Alumni Bd., 1978-80. Recipient cert. recognition Brewer-Porch Children's Center, 1978, cert. achievement, 1978; cert. in counseling and guidance, Ala. Mem. AAUW (chairperson scholarship com. Tuscaloosa br. 1978-79, br. chairperson marionette show 1980-81, pres. br. 1981—), Am. Assn. Psychiat. Services for Children, Ala. Personnel and Guidance Assn., Phi Delta Kappa. Democrat. Author: Diagnosis and Remediation of Reading Disabilities, 1974. Home: 5724 Kew Ln Tuscaloosa AL 35405 Office: PO Box 2232 University AL 35486

LONG, BETTY JANE, state legislator; b. Electric Mills, Miss., May 8, 1928. Admitted to Miss. bar; individual practice law, Meridian, Miss.; now mem. Miss. Ho. of Reps. Bd. dirs. Salvation Army, Cerebral Palsy; mem. Miss. Farm Bur. Mem. AAUW, Bus. and Profl. Women's Club, Pilot Club. Presbyterian. Office: Mississippi State House Jackson MS 39205 *

LONG, BEVERLY WHITAKER, educator; b. Memphis, July 16, 1936; d. Earl and Berniece (Price) Whitaker; B.A., Hendrix Coll., Conway, Ark., 1957; M.A., La. State U., 1962, Ph.D., 1967; m. William F. Long, Dec. 13, 1975. Dir. speech and drama Newport (Ark.) High Sch., 1957-60; teaching asst., instr. speech La. State U., 1966; instr. S.W. Tex. State U., 1962-65; mem. faculty U. Tex., Austin, 1967-76; adj. prof. DePauw U., Greencastle, Inc., 1976-77; prof. speech, chmn. dept. speech communication U. N.C., Chapel Hill, 1978—. Recipient Communication Teaching Excellence award U. Tex., 1971; grantee U. Tex. Research Inst., 1975, Pogue Research Inst., 1982. Mem. Speech Communication Assn., Assn. Communication Adminstrs., So. Speech Communication Assn., Nat. Council Tchrs. English, Am. Theatre Assn., Am. Soc. Aesthetics, Brit. Soc. Aesthetics, MLA, Modern Poetry Assn., N.C. Speech and Drama Assn. Democrat. Methodist. Clubs: Chapel Hill Country; U. N.C. Faculty. Co-author: Group Performance of Literature, 1977; Performing Literature, 1982. Editor Lit. in Performance, 1979—; co-editor: Contemporary Speech, 1977. Contbr. articles, revs. to profl. jours. Office: 115 Bingham Hall 007A U NC Chapel Hill NC 27514

LONG, CATHERINE ANN FRANTZ, health orgn. exec.; b. Wilkes-Barre, Pa., Oct. 31, 1940; d. Ralph William and Mary Elizabeth (Marley) Frantz; student public schs., Wilkes-Barre; m. Dec. 31, 1960 (div.); children—Thomas, Daniel. With Acme Warehouse Co., Forty-Fort, Pa., 1958-60, 7-11 Stores, Kendall Park, N.J., 1967-68; Scranton supr. Multiple Sclerosis, Wilkes-Barre, 1969-72; coordinator-supr. Cystic Fibrosis Found., Pittston, Pa., 1972-81. Democrat. Roman Catholic. Home: 23 Heather Highland Mobile Home Village Lot 23 Main St Jenkins Township Inkerman PA 18640

LONG, DEVONA ANDERSON, state legislator; b. Mpls., Apr. 5, 1939; d. Elder Carl and Emma Dorthea (Strom) Anderson; student Northwestern U., 1957-59; B.A. magna cum laude, U. Minn., 1961; m. Nicholas Kinsey Long, Aug. 27, 1966; children—Catherine Emma, Nicholas Kinsey Anderson. Instr., U. Minn., Mpls., 1962-66; research psychologist Am. Rehab. Found., Mpls., 1966-68; community faculty Met. State U., St. Paul, 1973—; mem. Minn. Ho. of Reps., 1979—. Mem. Alpha Gamma Delta. Democrat. Congregationalist. Club: Calhoun Beach. Office: State Office Bldg Saint Paul MN 55155

LONG, E. CLAUDINE, banker; b. Laurel, Miss.; d. William Andy and Ada Eunice (Clearman) Parrish; student Mundelein Coll., Chgo., 1979-80, Oklahoma City U., 1982—; m. Jack M. Long, Sept. 26, 1948; children—John R., Jaime E., Susan E., Mary E. Sr. v.p. Liberty Nat. Bank & Trust Co., Oklahoma City, 1982—; v.p., mgr. Liberty Found.; Gen. Motors Corp. arbitrator Better Bus. Bur. Mem. citizens adv. com. Jr. League Oklahoma City; bd. dirs. Daily Living Center, also hon. life mem. bd. Pathways Child Devel. Named Outstanding Sec. in Am., Manpower, Inc., 1964, one of Outstanding Ladies in the News, Okla. Hospitality Club, 1979; finalist for Corp. Woman of Yr., 1982. Mem. Nat. Assn. Female Execs., Nat. Assn. Bank Women, Am. Soc. Tng. and Devel., Okla. Bankers Wives, Oklahoma City C. of C. Clubs: Statesman's Toastmasters (officer, Leadership award 1982), Bus. and Profl. Women's (past pres. Town Club). Home: 423 NW 21st St Oklahoma City OK 73103 Office: 100 N Broadway Oklahoma City OK 73101

LONG, ERNESTINE MARTHA JOULLIAN, educator; b. St. Louis, Nov. 14, 1906; d. Ernest Cameron and Alice (Joullian) Long; A.B., U. Wis., 1927; M.S., U. Chgo., 1932; Ph.D., St. Louis U., 1975; postgrad. (NSF fellow) So. Ill. U., 1969-70. Tchr. scis. pub. schs. Normandy dist., St. Louis, 1927-66, Red Bud, Ill., 1966-70, St. Louis, 1970-75; coordinator continuing edn. U. Mo., St. Louis, 1976-79. Recipient Community Service award St. Louis Newspaper Guild, 1978-79. Mem. AAAS, Am. Inst. Physics, Am. Physics Tchrs. Assn., Am. Personnel and Guidance Assn. (treas. St. Louis br. 1954), Am. Chem. Soc., Central Assn. Sch. Sci. Math. Tchrs., Am. Soc. for Microbiology, LWV, St. Louis Symphony Soc. (women's div., docent), Am. Guild Organists, NEA, Nat. Sci. Tchrs. Assn. Home: 245 N Price Rd Ladue MO 63124

LONG, GERALDINE E., educator; b. Oceanside, N.Y., July 9, 1951; d. William Sidney and Geraldine Ann (Talcott) Kerridge; B.S. in Nursing, U. Miami, 1973, M.S.N., 1980; postgrad. U. Fla., 1980-82; 1 son, Lawrence John III. R.N., Mercy Hosp., Miami, Fla., 1973-77; childbirth educator Profl. Assn. Childbirth Edn., Miami, 1975-78; instr. U. Miami, Coral Gables, 1977-81, asst. prof., 1981—. Mem. Am. Nurses Assn., Am. Ednl. Research Assn., Profl. Assn. for Childbirth Edn., Phi Kappa Phi, Sigma Theta Tau, Delta Delta Delta. Roman Catholic. Home: 14034 SW 106th Terr Miami FL 33186 Office: Univ Miami Sch of Nursing 1540 Corniche St Coral Gables FL 33124

LONG, JANET TOKUNAGA, microbiologist; b. Amache, Colo., Aug. 4, 1945; d. Edward M. and Yaeko (Morishige) Tokunaga; B.A., B.S., U. Calif., Davis, 1968; m. Kenneth J. Long, Aug. 22, 1969; children—Roger, Steven, Michael. Staff technologist Ross (Calif.) Gen. Hosp., 1969; sr. technologist Woodland (Calif.) Meml. Hosp., 1970-76; supr. microbiology Kaiser Hosp., Walnut Creek, Calif., 1977—. Bd. dirs. Diablo Valley Japanese Am. Citizens League, 1982. Mem. Calif. Assn. Med. Technologists, Am. Soc. Microbiology, Am. Soc. Clin. Pathologists, Sierra Club. Lutheran. Office: 1515 Newell Ave Walnut Creek CA 94596

LONG, JOYCE MARALYN, govt. ofcl.; b. Seattle, Sept. 5, 1930; d. Gerald Paul and Blanche E. (Larsen) Lawrence; student Edmonds Community Coll., 1979, 80, Highline Community Coll., 1979; children —Suzi, Lisa Marie. With SBA, Seattle, 1971—, coordinator for women in bus. program, 1978—, dist. tng. officer, 1978—; vol. instr. Edmonds Community Coll., Highline Community Coll., Bellevue Community Coll.; lectr. in field. Recipient Nat. Public Contact of Yr. award, 1980; Spl. Achievement award SBA, 1981. Mem. Women Plus Bus. (dir. 1980-82). Contbr. articles to profl. jours. Office: 915 2d Ave Seattle WA 98174

LONG, LYNDA ANNE CAREY, govt. ofcl.; b. Kingston, Pa., Oct. 5, 1942; d. William Henry and Thelma Loretta (Tripp) Carey; A.B.A., Benjamin Franklin U., 1978; m. John Devlin Long, July 21, 1978; children by previous marriage—James Sinkavitch, Ned Sinkavitch; stepchildren—John Devlin, Douglas, Debra, Teri. Mgmt. analyst Def. Nuclear Agy., Washington, 1973-74; mgmt. analyst Dept. Army, Washington, 1977-78; stockpile mgmt. ops. officer, mgmt. analyst Def. Nuclear Agy., 1978—; mem. Nuclear Reporting Mgmt. Group, 1978—, Computer Measurement Group, 1981—. Pres., Our Savior Luth. Parent Tchrs. Assn., 1971. Recipient outstanding performance awards, 1980-81, 81-82; cert. of achievement Def. Nuclear Agy., 1975. Republican. Lutheran. Club: Pine Ridge Womens.

LONG, MADELEINE J., educator; b. N.Y.C., Apr. 13, 1938; s. Harry L. and Irma (Silverman) L.; B.A., Queens Coll., 1960; Ed.M., Harvard U., 1963; Ed.D., Columbia U., 1967. Tchr., Westbury (N.Y.) Sch. System, 1960-61; asst. prof. L.I. U., Bklyn., 1964-68, assoc. prof., 1968-71, prof. edn., 1971—, dir. div. edn. Bklyn. Center, 1978—, dir. edn. programs Westchester branch campus, 1975—, chmn. dept. edn., 1969-78; co-dir. NSF Pres-Coll. Tchr. Devel. in Sci. Program, Inst. Tng. High Sch. Tchrs. Math., 1978-82; assoc. dean grad. program in U.S., Universitas Internationalis Coluccio Salutati, Perscia, Italy; dir. curriculum workshops Dept. Def. Travis AFB, Calif., 1977. Mem. Assn. for Supervision and Curriculum Devel., Am. Assn. Higher Edn., Nat. Council Tchrs. Math., N.Y. Acad. Pub. Edn. Am. Assn. Colls. Tchr. Edn. Contbr. numerous articles to profl. publs. Office: Univ Plaza Long Island Univ Brooklyn NY 11201

LONG, MARIA-TERESA ELIZABETH, fin. exec.; b. St. Louis, July 10, 1947; d. Terry and Mary-Louise Katharyn (Madden) Butler; B.S., N.E. Mo. State U., 1972; M.A., Washington U., 1973; m. Ellery Long, Sept. 21, 1975; 1 child, Kortné. Dir. guidance Kinloch (Mo.) High Sch., 1973-74; vocat. counselor Ferguson-Florissant Sch. Dist., Ferguson, Mo., 1974-79; fin. planner Metro. Life Ins. Co., St. Louis, 1979—. Bd. dirs. Urban League Met. St. Louis, 1976—. Washington U. grantee, 1973. Mem. Am. Personnel and Guidance Assn., NEA (del., sec. 1976-77), Florissant-Ferguson Community Tchrs. Assn. (sec. 1976-77), Am. Vocat. Assn., Assn. Profl. Negotiations Teams, Delta Sigma Theta. Roman Catholic. Home: 3222 Hunterwood Dr Houston TX 77459 Office: 6601 Hillcroft Houston TX 77036

LONG, MARILYN LEONA, petroleum products and services co. ofcl.; b. Canton, Ill., Apr. 11, 1944; d. John Henry and Charlotte A. (Merrill) Bolender; B.S.B.A., U. Denver, 1968, M.B.A., 1974. Mgr. fin. ops. Info. Handling Services (Indianhead), Denver, 1976-78; fin. analyst Mountain Bell, Denver, 1978-80; mgr. cost and inventory control PAMCO (Research-Cottrell), Denver, 1980-81; field acctg. mgr. NL Baroid/NL Industries, Denver, 1981—. C.P.A., Colo. Mem. Am. Inst. C.P.A.s, Am. Woman's Soc. C.P.A.s, Colo. Soc. C.P.A.s. Home: 10879 E Powers Dr Englewood CO 80111 Office: 410 17th St Denver CO 80202

LONG, MAXINE CAMPBELL, microbiologist; b. Tazewell, Tenn., Jan. 27, 1929; d. Arthur L. and Elizabeth Grey (Ball) Campbell; B.A., U. Tenn., 1950; postgrad. Northwestern U., eves.; m. Robert H. Long, Mar. 31, 1951 (dec.); children—Russell L., Mary E. With Oak Ridge Health Dept., 1950-51; research asst., tissue technologist U. Chgo. Clinics, 1951-58; microbiologist Ill. Dept. Pub. Health, Chgo., 1958-70; microbiologist Ill. EPA, Chgo., 1970—, on detail to U.S. EPA Region V, 1976-80, quality assurance coordinator div. labs., Chgo., 1980—; speaker on quality assurance and lab. cert. to profl. groups. Sec., Harvard-St. George Sch. PTA, Chgo., 1971-72. Mem. Lake Michigan Water Analysts (pres. 1980), ASTM (mem. coms.), Am., Ill. (editor newsletter 1973-74) socs. for microbiology, Water Pollution Control Fedn. Mem. United Ch. of Hyde Park. Home: 945 S 4th St Apt 8 Springfield IL 62703 Office: 2121 W Taylor St Chicago IL 60612

LONG, RUTH STODDARD, ophthalmologist; b. Plainfield, N.J., Oct. 5, 1932; d. Rowland Hornshaw and Ruth (Way) Long; B.A., Clark U., 1956; M.D., N.Y.U., 1960. Intern, George Washington U. Hosp., Washington, 1960-61; resident ophthalmology Bellevue Med. Center, N.Y.C., 1962-65; fellow-research asso. dept. physiology Naval Med. Research Inst., Bethesda, Md., 1961-62; fellow retinal diseases and surgery NIH, Cornell U. Med. Coll., N.Y.C., 1965-66; prin. investigator diabetic retinopathy study N.Y. Clin. Center, Nat. Eye Inst., 1972-73; cons. retinal diseases USPHS Hosp., S.I., N.Y., 1966—; clin. instr. Cornell U. Med. Coll., N.Y.C., 1967-71; attending ophthalmology Flower and Fifth Ave. Hosps., N.Y.C., 1967-73; clin. asst. prof. N.Y. Med. Coll., N.Y.C., 1967-73, asso. prof. ophthalmology, 1972-73, acting chmn. dept. ophthalmology, 1973, clin. prof. ophthalmology, 1979—; dir. retina service Met. Hosp., Flower and Fifth Ave Hosps., N.Y.C., 1967-73, med. dir. Fluorescein Angiographic Lab., 1968-73; attending ophthalmology St. Vincent's Hosp. and Med. Center, N.Y.C., 1971—, dir. retina service, 1971—; chmn. dept. ophthalmology St. Clare's Hosp. and Health Center; sr. instr. Am. Acad. Ophthalmology, 1972—; attending ophthalmology Cabrini Med. Center, N.Y.C., 1973—, med. dir. Biomed. Photography and Fluorescein Angiographic Lab., 1973—, dir. retina service, 1973—. Recipient Award of Merit, Am. Acad. Ophthalmology, 1979. Mem. AMA, Am. Acad. Ophthalmology and Otolaryngology, Am. Retina Soc., Pan Am. Assn. Ophthalmology, Research to Prevent Blindness, Soc. Contemporary Ophthalmology, Retinitis Pigmentosa Found. (bd. dirs.), Ophthalmic Photographers' Soc., N.Y. County Med. Soc., N.Y. Soc. Clin. Ophthalmology, N.Y. Acad. Medicine, N.Y. Acad. Scis. Office: 737 Park Ave New York NY 10021

LONG, SHARON LEE, publisher, writer; b. Buckhannon, W.Va., July 15, 1938; d. Albert H. and Edna G. (Slaughter) Hicks; student W.Va. Bus. Coll., 1956, U. Ill., 1958, U. Pitts., 1964-65; m. C. Alvin Long, Nov. 1966 (dec. 1975); children—C. Alvin, Lori Ellen. Newspaper reporter The Clarksburg Telegram, Clarksburg, W.Va., 1956-58; continuity dir. Sta. WPDX, Clarksburg, 1960-61; adminstrv. asst. Fuller, Smith & Ross, Pitts., 1962-64; adminstrv. asst. to program mgr. Sta. WIIC-TV, Pitts., 1964-66; media buyer Campbell Ewald Advt. Co., San Francisco, 1966; media dir. Long Advt. Co., San Jose, Calif., 1966-67; pres. Lee Rothchild, Ltd. and subsidiaries, 1980—. Mem. Nat. Writers Club, Calif. Commonwealth Club, Internat. Platform Assn. Author: Love Has No Boundaries, 1982; Anyone Can Fall in Love, 1982.

LONGAN, LOUISE STEWART, librarian; b. Ft. Scott, Kans., Aug. 7, 1914; d. Lewis T. and Julia Elizabeth (Dodd) Stewart; student Fresno State Coll.; m. George Parsons Longan, Oct. 1, 1940; children—Patrick Bart, William Stewart, George Michael, Nancy Louise, John Edward (dec.). Reporter, bookkeeper Advance Register, 1934-39; milk technician Tulare County, Calif., 1941-48; library dir. Tulare Public Library, 1964—; co-owner The Central Calif. Implement Co.; v.p. Central Calif. Corp. Mem. Tulare/Inverell Sister City Assn.; active Tulare County Hist. Soc. Encor Theatre Group. Mem. Calif. Library Assn., Central Calif. Library and Media Assn. Republican. Roman Catholic. Clubs: Tulare Woman's, Tulare Palette. Home: 785 North M St PO Box 209 Tulare CA 93275 Office: 113 North F St Tulare CA 93274

LONGE, PATRICIA SHONTZ, economist, educator; b. Milw., Oct. 1, 1933; d. James Joseph and Erma (Graap) O'Donnell; B.S. summa cum laude, U. Detroit, 1955, M.B.A., 1956, LL.D. (hon.), 1977; Ph.D., Wayne State U., 1963; m. Patrick J. Longe, Nov. 24, 1977; 1 dau., Deborah Stevenson. Instr., dept. econs. U. Detroit, 1955-60; grad. asso. Wayne State U., 1960-63; asst. prof. econs. U. Windsor, Can., 1963-66; adj. prof. econs. U. Mich., Dearborn, 1966-67; economist, editorial writer, columnist Detroit News, 1966-73; syndicated columnist Universal Press Syndicate, N.Y., 1970-73; prof. bus. adminstrn., dir. publs. Grad. Sch. Bus. Adminstrn., U. Mich., Ann Arbor, 1973—; partner dir. econ. research R.A. Helling & Assos., Detroit, 1965-68; now sr. partner Imeco-Longe Co., econ. cons., Detroit; dir. Detroit Edison Co., Mfrs. Nat. Bank Detroit, Jacobson Stores, Inc., Kroger Co., Warner-Lambert Co., Am. Motors Corp.; cons. U.S. Treasury, 1973-76. Recipient G.M. Loeb award, nation's best financial column, 1970. Fellow Am. Statis. Assn.; mem. Am., Canadian econ. assns., Nat., Detroit (sec. 1966-67) assns. bus. economists, Detroit Bd. Commerce, Detroit Econ. Council (chmn.), Inst. Econ. Edn. (trustee), Sigma Sigma Sigma, Beta Gamma Sigma (chpt. sec. 1955-60). Home: 806 Bishop Rd Grosse Pointe Park MI 48230 Office: Grad School Business Adminstrn Univ of Mich Ann Arbor MI 48109 also 2950 E Jefferson Ave Detroit MI 48207

LONG-JOHNSON, CELESTE ANNE, mfg. co. exec.; b. Bulter, Ala., Sept. 4, 1931; d. Joseph Franklin and Erin Mason (Hearne) Long; R.N., Mobile Infirmary Sch. Nursing, 1952; student U. Ala., 1949-55, U. W. Fla., 1979-80; m. Leonard M. Johnson, 1954 (div.); 1 dau., Cynthia Rae. Instr. nursing Mobile Infirmary, 1952-55, Washoe Med. Center, Reno, Nev., 1955-57, staff nurse Marin Gen. Hosp., San Raphael, Calif., 1957-59; framing asst., Evreaux, France, 1961; with Maison Le Cel, Inc., Ft. Walton Beach, Fla., 1964—, pres., 1971—; instr. ARC, 1957; lectr. in field. Mem. Beautification-sign ordnance City of Ft. Walton Beach Council, 1980—; mem. Republican Exec. com., Okaloosa County, 1980-81. Recipient appreciation award Profl. Picture Framers Assn., 1979. Mem. Gulf Coast Picture Framers Assn. (pres. 1979-82), Ft. Walton C. of C., Profl. Picture Framers Assn. (S.E. regional dir. 1978-79), Nat. Art Materials Assn., Arts and Design Soc., Framers Guild Internat., Am. Fedn. Astrologers. Episcopalian. Clubs: Ft. Walton Beach Woman's, Women of the Ch. Office: 226 N Eglin Pkwy Fort Walton Beach FL 32548

LONGLEY, BERNIQUE (MRS. JAMES A. ORR), painter, muralist, sculptor; b. Moline, Ill., Sept. 27, 1923; d. Eli James and Effie Marie (Coen) Wilderson; grad. Art Inst. Chgo., 1945; postgrad. Instituto de Allende, Mex., 1971, Santa Fe Sch. Arts and Crafts, 1975; m. James Alexander Orr, Apr. 15, 1968; 1 dau., Bernique Longley Glidden. One-woman shows: Mus. N.Mex., 1947, 50, 52, 53, Little Shop, Santa Fe, 1952-58, Maurice Appleman Gallery, Denver, 1953-54, Van Dieman Lilienfield, N.Y.C., 1953, Rotunda-City Paris, San Francisco, 1955-56, Sanger-Harris Gallery, Dallas, 1968, Lars Laine, Palm Springs, Calif., 1963-69, Gallery A, Taos, 1966-69, Cushing Galleries, Dallas, 1977, Gov.'s Gallery, N.Mex. State Capitol, 1978, Santa Fe East, Austin, Tex., 1979, Woman's Bank of Denver, 1982; group shows include: Art Inst. Chgo., 1946, 48, Denver Art Mus., 1948-49, Mus. N.Mex., 1952, 53, 68, also Summer Gallery, Santa Fe, Blair Gallery, Santa Fe, Santa Fe Festival Arts, 1977-81, St. John's Coll., Santa Fe, others; retrospective exhbn. Santa Fe (N.Mex.) East, 1982; executed murals La Fonda del Sol restaurant, N.Y.C., home Alexander Girard, Santa Fe, 1960; represented in permanent collections of Red Skelton, Greer Garson, Mark Harris, Tex. Instruments, Dallas, First Nat. Bank Denver, Santa Fe Hilton Hotel, Dome Oil Exploration Co., San Francisco, Coll. Santa Fe, Mus. N.Mex., Santa Fe, Coll. Santa Fe, Colorado Springs Fine Arts Center, others; operator Summer Gallery, Santa Fe, 1973—. Bryan Lathrop fgn. traveling fellow, 1945. Mem. Art Inst. Chgo. Alumni Assn. Home: 427 Camino Del Monte Sol Santa Fe NM 87501

LONGLEY, MARJORIE WATTERS, newspaper exec.; b. Lockport, N.Y., Nov. 2, 1925; d. J. Randolph and Florence Lucille (Craine) Watters; B.A. with highest honors cum laude in English, St. Lawrence U., 1947; m. Ralph R. Longley, Oct. 1, 1949 (dec.). Sports editor, feature writer Lockport Union Sun & Jour., 1945; with N.Y. Times, N.Y.C., 1948—, asst. to v.p. consumer mktg., 1975-78, circulation sales mgr., 1978-79, sales dir., 1979-81, dir. public affairs, 1981—; mem. Nat. Newspaper Readership Council, 1979—; mem. adv. council API, 1980. Trustee, St. Lawrence U., 1969-75, 77—; bd. dirs. Global Perspectives in Edn., 1977—, Coro Found., 1980—; pres. N.Y. State Adult Edn. Council, 1974-77; mem. N.Y. State Adv. Council for Vocat. Edn., 1976-81, N.Y. State Adv. Council for Postsecondary Edn., 1978-81. Mem. Am. Mgmt. Assn. (Nat. Mktg. Council 1972—), Newspaper Pubs. Assn. (dir.). Democrat. Baptist. Club: Nat. Arts. Author: America's Taste, 1960. Office: 229 W 43d St New York NY 10036

LONGO, KATHRYN MILANI, pension cons.; b. Jersey City, N.J., July 22, 1946; d. Joseph John Baptiste and Kathryn (Sacco) Milani; B.A., Adelphi U., 1969; postgrad. N.Y. U., 1968-69, Hunter Coll., 1969-70; m. John Carmine Longo, Mar. 15, 1970. Pension cons. Laiken, Siegel & Co., N.Y.C., 1967—, partner, 1977—; pres., creative cons. Pinch-Hitters, Inc., N. Bergen, N.J., 1978—; Co-founder, co-chmn. Greater N.Y. Pension Cons. Workshop, 1974—; jazz dance tchr. Kay Marie Sch. Dance Arts, Hammonton, N.J., 1976—; guest choreographer Regis Drama Soc., Regis High Sch., N.Y.C., 1978-79. Adelphi U. scholar, 1964-68. Mem. Am. Soc. Pension Actuaries (asso.), N.J. Assn. Women Bus. Owners, Nat. Assn. Female Execs., Am. Soc. Profl. and Exec. Women. Roman Catholic.

LONSFORD, FLORENCE ELIZABETH HUTCHINSON, artist, designer, writer; b. Lebanon, Ind., Jan. 7, 1914; d. Frank Edwin and Jennie Cecelia (Pugh) Hutchinson; B.S. in Sci., Purdue U., 1936; student Nat. Acad. Fine Arts, 1956-58; M.A., Hunter Coll., 1963; student Art Students League, John Herron Art Inst., Barnard-NBC Inst. Radio-TV; m. Graydon Lee Lonsford, Dec. 18, 1938 (dec. Sept. 1958). Owner, operator greeting card design bus., 1966-69; tchr. fine arts N.Y. Public Schs., 1960-80; freelance artist and designer; freelance artist, copywriter Harper's Pub. House; illustrator Morningstar Prodns.; greeting card artist Curzart, Rust Craft Pubs., Dedham, Mass., Nat. Artcrafts, Detroit; paintings sold in decorating dept. Lord & Taylor; illustrator ch. publs.; art editor The Key of Kappa Kappa Gamma, 1947—; paintings shown nat. and regional shows, including: Hoosier Salon (Indpls.), Cooperstown, N.Y., Brockton, Mass., Mystic, Conn., Ind. State Fair, Jackson, Miss., N.Y., Ky., Ohio and Mich.; graphics rev. in Revue Moderne, Paris, 1967; writer Artists Equity; contbr. to Woman's Home Companion, Christian Sci. Monitor, Saturday Rev., N.Y. Times, Woman's Day, small verse and lit. mags. Recipient art prizes Ind. State Fair, Nat. Art League, Salmagundi, Hoosier Salon; named Outstanding Educator, Met. Mus. and N.Y. Center Arts and Humanities, 1977; recipient Prix de Honneur, Monaco, 1966; finalist Deauville and Cannes Grand Prix, 1973. Mem. Nat. Council Tchrs. of English, Women's Aux. N.Y. Acad. Scis., Am. Artists Profl. League, Nat. Art League, Cooperstown Art Assn., Artists Equity, Portrait Club N.Y., Greensward Found., Wilderness Soc., Kappa Kappa Gamma (nat. officer), Mortar Bd., Alpha Lambda Delta. Republican. Presbyterian. Home and Office: 311 E 72d St New York NY 10021

LONTOS, PAMELA KAY, radio sales exec.; b. Wichita, Kans., Feb. 28, 1945; d. Xenophon Steve and Mary (Leber) Congas; B.A. (Univ. scholar), So. Methodist U., 1967, M.L.A. (Univ. scholar), 1971; m. Ernest Tom Lontos, Sept. 19, 1965; children—Anna-Marie, Ryan Tom. Tchr. Highland Park (Tex.) Ind. Sch. Dist., 1967-71; sales and advt. dir. Nautilus Center, Dallas, 1975-77; account exec. Sta. KMGC, Dallas, 1977-79, local sales mgr., 1979-81; corp. sales trainer Shamrock Broadcasting, corp. v.p. sales, 1981—; pres. Pam Lontos, Inc., 1981—; sales cons., condr. seminars. Recipient awards, including Salesperson of Yr. award Sta. KMGC, 1978. Mem. Am. Broadcasting Execs. of Tex., Am. Women in Radio and TV. Greek Orthodox. Club: Toastmasters (Best Speech award 1979). Research on sales techniques and mktg. Author: Fundamentals of Broadcast Selling; Those Marvelous Mentors; also cassette series Persuaders. Office: 7055 Merriman Pkwy Dallas TX 75231

LOOBEY, PHYLLIS PRICE, city transp. ofcl.; b. Hoquiam, Wash., Dec. 3, 1937; d. Edward Paul and Ella Christine (Beck) Price; B.S., U. Oreg., 1974; diploma urban transp., Carnegie-Mellon U., 1977; 1 dau., Gonya Dyanne. Adminstrv. asst., then dir. adminstrv. services Lane Transit Dist., Eugene, Oreg., 1974-79, gen. mgr., 1979—, bd. dirs., 1972-74; mem. citizens adv. com. transp. and minority affairs Lane Council Govts., 1972-75. Mem. Eugene Human Rights Commn., 1971-72, Lane County Plan Adv. Commn., 1970-73; mem. tech. rev. com. Regional Transit Tng. Center, U. So. Calif., 1980. Mem. LWV (1st v.p. Central Lane County chpt. 1971-72), Am. Mgmt. Assn., Cascade Employers Assn. (dir. 1980), Oreg. Transit Assn. (pres. 1980-82), Am. Public Transit Assn. (v.p. mktg. 1981-82). Home: 5315 Nectar Way Eugene OR 97405 Office: Garfield St Eugene OR 97402

LOOMIS, BARBARA LEE, librarian; b. Cleve., Nov. 1, 1931; d. Guy Reuben and Florence Elizabeth (Lomnitz) Solomon; B.S., Ohio State U., 1956; M.S. in Library Sci. (scholarship 1970), Case Western Res. U., 1971; divorced. Reference librarian Lima (Ohio) Public Library, 1969-70; br. librarian Willoughby-Eastlake (Ohio) Public Library, 1971-72; dir. Mackenzie Meml. Public Library, Madison, Ohio, 1972-76; dir. Alaskan Air Command Library, also dir. Elemendorf AFB Library, 1977—; real estate broker Marshall & Assos., Inc., Anchorage, 1976—; adv. bd. Anchorage Mcpl. Library, 1978—; mem. Com. to Build New Library, Anchorage, 1981. Mem. curtain raisers Alaska Repertory Theater, 1976-78; mem. community resources program Anchorage Sch. Dist., 1980-81. Recipient cert. of appreciation Anchorage Sch. Dist., 1981; Sustained Superior Service award USAF, 1981. Mem. ALA, Pacific N.W. Library Assn., Alaska Library Assn., Nat. Library Assn., Nat. Assn. Female Execs., AAUW, Am. Mgmt. Assn., Fed. and Mil. Librarians Assn., Beta Phi Mu. Club: Order Eastern Star. Home: 3836 Telequana Dr Anchorage AK 99503 Office: Base Library FL5000 Elmendorf AFB AK 99506

LOONEY, KATHLEEN MITCHELL, nurse; b. Memphis, Aug. 4, 1943; d. David DeMint and Louise M. (McKinney) Mitchell; B.S.N., La. State U., 1976; m. James Holland, Feb. 11, 1979; children by previous marriage—Mary Ann King, Margaret Ann King. Night supr. Audubon Health Care Center, New Orleans, 1976, house supr., 1976, dir. nursing, 1976-77; div. mgr. nursing Taylor House, New Orleans, 1977—. Mem. Am. Nurses Assn., Council of Nursing Home Nurses, S.W. Soc. Aging, Acad. Gerontol. Nurses, Assn. La. State Nurses. Mem. Christian Ch. Office: 1421 General Taylor St New Orleans LA 70115

LOOS, DOROTHY SCOTT, translator; b. Savannah, Ga.; d. Duncan Jackson and Dolores Rachel (Price) Scott; A.B., Middlebury Coll., M.A. French; Ph.D. in Hispanic Langs., Columbia U., 1950; m. A. William Loos; 1 son, William Duncan Bradley Loos. Tchr. Spanish, Dalton Schs., New Lincoln Sch., The Brearley Sch.; asst. prof. Spanish, CUNY; free lance translator, Brattleboro, Vt., 1980—; scholar Vt. Council Humanities and Public Issues, 1980—. Pres., Brattleboro Unit Ch. Women United, 1980—; trustee Guilford Hist. Soc. Mem. Am. Assn. Tchrs. Spanish and Portuguese, Am. Lit. Translators Assn. Democrat. Author: The Naturalistic Novel of Brazil, 1963; translator: Dora, Doralina (by Rachel de Queiroz), 1983; contbr. articles to profl. jours.

LOPATE, KATHLEEN MARY, writer; b. Watsonville, Calif., Sept. 13, 1948; student Loyola/Marymount U., Los Angeles, 1968-69; B.A. in Journalism, Marquette U., 1975; postgrad. Mt. Mary Coll., 1977; 1 son, Lenny. Editor, Program mag., 1978-79, Metric News mag., 1977-78; free-lance writer, Brookfield, Wis., 1975-76, 77—; writer Post newspapers including Encore, 1975-77; worked toward devel. of 1st hospice in Wis., 1977—. Mem. pub. relations com. United Way Waukesha County, Waukesha, Wis., 1975; mem. pub. info. com. Kidney Found. Wis., 1973—; pub. relations intern Mt. Sinai Med. Center, Milw., 1974. Mem. Am. Med. Writers Assn., Loyola Marymount U. Calif. Writers, Nat. Writers Club, Profl. Writers Network, AAUW. Author: Lennie's Story, 1977. Home: 235 N Eastmoor Ave Brookfield WI 53005

LOPATYNSKI, SANDRA LEE, surg. products sales and mktg. exec.; b. Teaneck, N.J.; d. George, Jr., and Winifred Ruby (Shock) Torony; A.S. in Nursing (Nat. Meth. scholar), Vt. Coll., 1966; cert. in coronary care, N.Y. Hosp.-Cornell Med. Center, 1969; B.S. in Bus. Mgmt. with honors, Fairleigh Dickinson U., 1975—; m. Fred Lopatynski, Jr. Coronary care nurse Riverdell Hosp., Oradell, N.J., 1966-70; indsl. nurse Sherwin Williams Co., Newark, 1970-72; territorial sales mgr. Hollister, Inc., Chgo., 1972, asst. sales edn. mgr., 1975, N.E. dist. sales mgr., 1975-78; account rep. surg. products div. Minn. Mining and Mfg. Co., St. Paul, 1978-81; territory mgr. Am. Edwards Lab., Santa Ana, Calif., 1981—; grad. asst. Dale Carnegie course, 1969. Mem. Nat. Assn. Female Execs., Assn. Operating Room Nurses, No. N.J. Network Bus. and Profl. Women, Delta Mu Delta, Phi Theta Kappa. Home: 240 Essex St Oradell NJ 07649 Office: 17221 Red Hill Ave Santa Ana CA 92714

LOPER, JANET SWANSON, data processing exec.; b. Dunkirk, N.Y., Sept. 17, 1934; d. Ralph Edwin and Isabel Spencer (Emerson) Swanson; B.S. in Sales Mgmt., Syracuse U., 1956; m. Lyle C. Loper, Oct. 15, 1971. Systems engr. IBM, Rochester, N.Y., 1956-58, tech. writer, product planner, Endicott, N.Y., 1959-66, planner instruction systems devel. dept., Los Gatos, Calif., 1966-70, mem. R.B. Johnson fellow program, 1970-72, communications analyst, gen. systems div., 1972-79, application devel. cons., 1975-79; v.p., dir. communications Citibank, N.Y.C., 1979—; cons. U.S. Office Edn., 1970. Recipient Outstanding Contbn. award IBM, 1975. Mem. Am. Bus. Women's Assn. (pres. Binghamton chpt. 1964-66), Soc. Tech. Communications (past program dir.), Data Processing Mgmt. Assn. (past internat. dir.). Office: 399 Park Ave New York NY 10043

LOPER, MARILYN SUE, residential contractor; b. Detroit, June 7, 1944; d. Elmer Charles and Thelma Pearl (Haferkamp) L.; B.S. in Elem. Edn., Eastern Mich. U., 1967, M.A. in Guidance and Counseling, 1971. Elem. sch. tchr., 1967-73; supr. Office Vocat. Rehab., Fla. Dept. Health and Rehab. Services, 1973-81; pvt. practice marriage and family counseling, 1975-81; real estate salesperson Henry Dingus, Jr., Port Richey, Fla., 1977—; self-employed resident contractor and developer, 1976—. Masters and Johnson Inst. fellow. Mem. Nat. Rehab. Assn., Nat. Rehab. Counselor Assn., Nat. Assn. Social Workers, Fla. Rehab. Assn., Fla. Rehab. Counselor Assn., Fla. Bd. Realtors, Pasco Builders Assn., Suncoast Better Bus. Bur. (charter). Office: PO Box 64 Port Richey FL 33568

LÓPEZ, ALMA LAMAR, lawyer; b. Laredo, Tex., Aug. 17, 1943; d. Alejandro and Olivia (Roach) López; B.B.A., St. Mary's U., San Antonio, 1965, J.D., 1968. Admitted to Tex. bar, 1968; asso. firm Frank J. Greene, San Antonio, 1968-73; mem. firm Dilley, Ojeda, López, & Guzmán, San Antonio, 1973—. Mem. Immigration Adv. Com., 1978-79. Mem. San Antonio Bar Assn., Tex. Bar Assn. (com. laws relating to immigration and nationality), Am. Bar Assn., Immigration and Nationality Lawyers (Tex. chpt.), Nat. Assn. Immigration and Nationality, San Antonio C. of C. Address: 809 S St Mary's San Antonio TX 78205

LOPEZ, ANGELINA SILLER, social worker; b. San Antonio, Nov. 14, 1947; d. Rudy and Angelina (Siller) L.; A.A., San Antonio Jr. Coll., 1974; B.A., U. Tex., Austin, 1976; M.S.W. (Nat. Inst. Alcohol Abuse grantee), Our Lady of Lake U., San Antonio, 1977. Field surveyor Johns Hopkins U., Balt., 1977; aftercare coordinator Bexar County Mental Health-Mental Retardation, San Antonio, 1977-79, adult mental health caseworker III, 1979—. Allocation com. panelist United Way Agy. of San Antonio. Mem. Nat. Assn. Social Workers, Council of Social Work Edn. (dir. 1975-78), Alumni Assn. Worden Sch. of Social Services Our Lady of Lake U. San Antonio (pres.). Office: 434 S Main St San Antonio TX 78205

LOPEZ, CAROLYN ANN, bank exec.; b. Newark, June 6, 1953; d. Walter Francis and Nancy (Nicosia) L.; B.S., Salem State Coll., 1975; M.B.A., Suffolk U., 1983. Teller, mgmt. trainee Mut. Bank for Savs. (and predecessor co.), Boston, 1975-77, head teller, customer service rep., 1977-78, asst. br. mgr., 1978-80, br. mgr. 1980—; tchr. math. Mary Immaculate Jr.-Sr. High Sch., Marlboro, Mass., 1977. Recipient Marine Engrs. Beneficial Assn. Scholarship award, 1971-74. Mem. Savs. Bank Women of Mass., Nat. Assn. Bank Women, Savs. Bank Officers Assn. Home: 232 A Brandywyne Dr East Boston MA 02128 Office: 3 Center Plaza Boston MA 02108

LÓPEZ, GONZÁLEZ YADIRA, project architect; b. Piedras Negras, Coahuila, Mex., May 14, 1954; came to U.S., 1957; d. Jesus and Guadalupe (González) López; student U. Nacional Autonoma de Mexico, 1971, San Antonio Coll., 1973-75; B.S. in Environ. Design, Tex. A&M U., 1977. Draftsperson, Tuggle & Graves, Architects, San Antonio, 1978; in house architect San Antonio Ind. Sch. Dist., 1979; project architect Southwestern Bell Tel. Co., San Antonio, 1979—. Mem. Tex. Soc. Architects, AIA, Females Execs. Assn. Office: 3201 Cherry Ridge Suite 101A San Antonio TX 78230 also PO Box 2780 San Antonio TX 78299

LOPEZ, LILIAN MARRERO, mental health counselor; b. Havana, Cuba, Aug. 30, 1955; came to U.S., 1963, naturalized, 1971; d. Alberto and Tina (Puig) Marrero; B.A., U. Tex., El Paso, 1979, M.Ed., 1981; m. Luis Roberto Lopez, June 7, 1980. Grad. asst. U. Tex., El Paso, 1979-81; instr. Spanish, English, B. I. Lang. Service, El Paso, 1979-81; mental health counselor El Paso Mental Health and Mental Retardation, 1981—. Mem. El Paso Psychol. Assn., Zeta Tau Alpha. Home: 7321 Armistad El Paso TX 79912 Office: 9555 Diana St El Paso TX 79924

LOPEZ, LORETTA REBECCA, social worker; b. Wagon Mound, N.Mex., Oct. 4, 1943; d. Joe Arsenio and Amelia Lopez; B.A., U. Albuquerque, 1966; M.S.W., U. Denver, 1972. Caseworker, N.Mex. Dept. Public Welfare, Silver City and Belen, 1966-70; sch. social worker Albuquerque public schs.. 1972-73, sch. social work specialist, 1973—; guest lectr. Coll. Santa Fe, 1978—; mem. Albuquerque/Bernalillo County Child Abuse Council, 1978-81; mem. standards and goals task force Gov. N.Mex. Council Criminal Justice Planning; bd. dirs. Hogares Inc.; mem. Albuquerque Rape Crisis Adv. Bd., 1980-83 Grantee Children's Bur., HEW, 1970-72; named N.Mex. Social Worker of Yr., 1978. Mem. Nat. Assn. Social Workers (pres. N.Mex. chpt. 1979—), N.Mex. Youth Work Alliance, N.Mex. Trabajadores de la Raza, Hispanic Health Care Corp. (treas. 1979—), N.Mex. Human Services Coalition, Child Welfare League Am. (exec. com. S.W. region 1978), U. Albuquerque Alumni Assn. (dir. 1974-76). Roman Catholic. Author papers in field. Office: PO Box 25704 Albuquerque NM 87125

LOPEZ, NANCY, profl. golfer; b. Torrance, Calif., Jan. 6, 1957; d. Domingo and Marina (Griego) Lopez; student U., Tulsa, 1976-78. Profl. golfer, 1978—, first victor at Bent Tree Classic, Sarasota, Fla., 1978. Named AP Athlete for 1978. Mem. Ladies Profl. Golf Assn. (Player and Rookie of Yr. 1978). Republican. Baptist. Author: The Education of a Woman Golfer, 1979. Office: 1 Erieview Plaza Cleveland OH 44114

LOPEZ, NANCY MARY CEA, import co. exec.; b. N.Y.C., Jan. 8, 1944; d. Nunzio and Mary Cea; B.A., Hunter Coll., 1966; m. David Lopez, Aug. 29, 1964; children—David Charles, Jonathan Edward. Asst. buyer Bloomingdale's, N.Y.C., 1966-71; inventory mgr. Sigma Mktg., N.Y.C., 1971-75; pres. Nancy Lopez, Inc., N.Y.C., 1975—, also dir.; dir. Am. Temps, Inc. Club: Atrium (N.Y.C.). Home and Office: 111 E 85th St New York NY 10028

LOPEZ, SARA ISABEL, chem., indsl. engr.; b. Ocotal, Nicaragua, May 1, 1951; came to U.S., Dec. 4, 1978; d. Ricardo Andres and Emilia Mercedes (Barrios) Lopez; diploma chem. and indsl. engr. Universidad Centro Americana, 1975; m. John Kemink, Nov. 6, 1978 (div. 1982); 1 son, Ricardo. Plant engr. Polimeros Centroamericanos S.A., Managua, Nicaragua, 1975-76; mixing and baking supt. Nabisco Cristal S.A., Managua, 1976-77; prodn. and quality control mgr. Jaboneria Prego, S.A., Granada, Nicaragua, 1977-78; indsl. cons. tech. dept. Central Bank of Nicaragua, 1978; indsl. engr. Shaklee Corp., Hayward, Calif., 1979-80; chem. engr. system design Bechtel Petroleum, Inc., San Francisco, 1979—, also progress monitoring engr. Pal booster Activities League; mem. St. Stephen's Women's Guild. Cert. project engr. Mem. Indsl. Engrs. Assn., Calif. Alumni Assn., Fgn. Affairs Council. Republican. Roman Catholic. Club: Bechtel Employees. Home: 350 Arballo Dr 6J San Francisco CA 94132 Office: 50 Beale St San Francisco CA 94104

LOPEZ-ROMANO, SYLVIA ANNE, educator; b. Las Vegas, Nev., Dec. 11, 1937; d. Enrique A. Silva and Faustina Flores; B.A. in Social Welfare, Calif. State U., Chico, 1973, B.A. cum laude in Spanish, 1973, M.A. in Edn., 1981; m. 2d, Aldo Romano, Apr. 30, 1977; children—Peter John, Marie, Henry, Vincent, Renee. Migrant edn. community aide, 1968-70; case aide counselor Mental Retardation Service, Chico, Calif., 1970-72; elem. sch. tchr., 1973-75; instr., lectr. Calif. State U., Chico, 1975-78, coordinator Upward Bound project, 1976-80, dir. student affirmative action, 1980—; mem. adv. bd. Western Assn. Ednl. Opportunity Programs. Co-founder Hispanic Profl. Group. Mem. United Profs. Calif., NAACP, Nat. Assn. Female Execs., Concilio Mejicano de Chico, Delta Phi Upsilon, Delta Kappa Gamma. Democrat. Roman Catholic. Home: 10 Sunland Dr Chico CA 95926 Office: U Bldg 2d and Chestnut St Chico CA 95929

LORAN, MURIEL RIVIAN, pharmacologist; b. N.Y.C., Feb. 6, 1925; d. Morris and Anna Frances (Gavrin) L.; B.S. cum laude, Bklyn. Coll. Pharmacy, 1947; M.S. in Mfg. Pharmacy, Phila. Coll. Pharmacy and Sci., 1948; Ph.D. in Pharmacology and Electrochemistry, Ohio State U., 1951. Fellow, Am. Found. Pharm. Edn., 1947-48, 50-51; successively grad. asst., asst., instr. Ohio State U., 1948-51; asst. prof. pharmacy U. Mont., Missoula, 1951-54; from asst. research pharmacologist to asso. research pharmacologist, dept. medicine U. Calif. Med. Sch., San Francisco, 1954-66; research pharmacologist Children's Hosp. and Adult Med. Center, San Francisco, 1967-68, 69-71; prof. cell biology and pathology Tel Aviv U., 1968-69; dir. pharmacy Good Samaritan Hosp., Suffern, N.Y., 1971-72; supr. quality control pharmacy services Montefiore Hosp. and Med. Center, Bronx, N.Y., 1973-81; dir. SM Cons., N.Y.C., 1981—. Recipient Humanitarian award Epilepsy Soc. Social Service, N.Y.C., 1979. Fellow Am. Am. Inst. Chemists; mem. Am. Fedn. Clin. Research, AAAS, Am. Physiol. Soc., Am. Inst. Biol. Scis., N.Y. Acad. Scis., Am. Pharm. Assn., Acad. Pharm. Scis., Am. Soc. Hosp. Pharmacists, Am. Chem. Soc. Contbr. articles to profl. jours. Home: 200 Cabrini Blvd Apt 91 New York NY 10033

LORANGE, JOANNE, coll. adminstr.; b. Southbridge, Mass., Jan. 2, 1946; d. Albert Lucien and Lorraine Marguerite (Briere) Lorange; B.A., St. Elizabeth Coll., 1968; M.A., Columbia U., 1971, M.A. in Higher and Adult Edn., 1972; m. Ronald Davis Herron, May 18, 1974; 1 dau., Jocelyn Lorange-Herron. Dir. residential programming, adminstrv. asst. for housing Tchrs. Coll., Columbia U., 1969-72; dir. fin. aid Richmond Coll., CUNY, S.I., 1972-76; asso. dean students Barnard Coll., Columbia U., 1975-77; dir. admissions/external relations Antioch/New Eng. Grad. Sch., Keene, N.H., 1978—; instr. New Eng. Coll., Henniker, N.H., 1977-78, Sch. for Lifelong Learning, N.H., 1982; cons. Upward Bound, Keene State Coll., N.H., 1982—. Advisor, Women's Center, Richmond Coll., S.I., 1972-75; judge N.H. Jr. Miss Contest, 1980; fund-raising trainer United Way; bd. dirs. Grand Monadnock Arts Council. Mem. N.H. C. of C., N.H. Women in Higher Edn. (pres.), Nat. Assn. Women Deans, Counselors and Adminstrs., Nat. Assn. Student Personnel Adminstrs. Club: Kiwanis. Jour. reviewer Nat. Assn. Student Personnel Adminstrs. Region I, 1980. Home: 105 Bradford Rd Keene NH 03431 Office: Antioch NE Roxbury St Keene NH 03431

LORCH, BARBARA RUTH DAY, educator; b. Pendleton, Oreg., Sept. 30, 1924; d. George Washington and Ruth Irene (Spangler) Day; B.S., Wash. State U., 1946, M.A., 1947; Ph.D., U. Wash., 1956; m. Robert Stuart Lorch, Dec. 19, 1964; 1 son, John Day. Instr. sociology Ariz. State U., Tempe, 1947-48, Bowling Green (Ohio) State U., 1948-50; asst. prof. U. Ariz., Tucson, 1952-53; acting instr. U. Wash., Seattle, 1953-56; asst. prof. U. Mont., Missoula, 1956-57, asso. prof., 1957-59; faculty Calif. State U., Long Beach, 1959-69; prof. U. Colo., Colorado Springs, 1969—. Mem. Am. Sociol. Assn., Western Social Sci. Assn., Phi Beta Kappa, Delta Delta Delta, Phi Kappa Phi, Lambda Theta, Alpha Kappa Delta, Psi Chi. Episcopalian. Contbr. articles in field to profl. jours. Office: University of Colorado Austin Bluffs Pkwy Colorado Springs CO 80907

LORD, BETTE BAO, writer; b. Shanghai, China, Nov. 11, 1938; came to U.S., 1946, naturalized, 1964; d. Sandys and Dora (Fang) Bao; B.A., Tufts U., 1959, M.A., 1960, hon. doctorate, 1982; m. Winston Lord, May 4, 1963; children—Elizabeth Pillsbury, Winston Bao. Asst. to dir. East-West Cultural Center, Honolulu, 1961-62; program officer Fulbright Exchange Program for Sr. Scholars, 1962-63; dancer, tchr. modern dance, Geneva and Washington, 1964-73; conf. dir. Asso. Councils of the Arts, N.Y.C., 1970-71; writer, lectr. Leigh Bur., 1982—; author: (non-fiction) Eighth Moon (Readers' Digest Condensed Books; winner Nat. Graphic award for Photography), 1975; (novel) Spring Moon, a novel of China (Am. Book award nominee; Lit. Guild selection), 1982. Mem. selection bd. White House Fellows, 1979-81; bd. dirs. Nat. Com. U.S.-China Relations, Inc., N.Y.C., 1982. Named Woman of Yr., Chinatown Planning Council, 1982. Mem. Asia Soc. Address: 740 Park Ave New York NY 10021

LORD, EDITH ELIZABETH, psychologist, educator; b. Newark, Aug. 4, 1907; d. Arthur Herbert and Elizabeth Florence (Kemmerer) L.; B.S., U. Houston, 1935; M.A., U. Tex., 1938; Ph.D.. U. So. Calif., 1948; M.A., N.Y. U., 1954. Instr. to asso. prof. U. Houston, 1934-44; instr. U. S.C., 1946-48; mem. staff Hawaii Dept. Public Health, 1948-49; supr. mental hygiene State of Ariz., 1950-52; chief psychology tng. program VA, N.Y.C., 1952-54; human resources devel. officer Africa, U.S. Dept. State, 1954-68; prof. psychology U. Miami, 1968-76; behavioral psychologist Peace Corps, Jamaica, 1977; prof. psychology Sch. Profl. Psychology, Nova U. (formerly Fla. Sch. Profl. Psychology), Miami, 1979-81, adj. prof., 1981—. Served with WAC, 1944-46. Mem. Am. Psychol. Assn., Eastern Psychol. Assn., Am. Bd. Profl. Psychologists, Internat. Council Psychologists, Inter-Am. Assn. Psychologists, Fla. Psychol. Assn., Dade County Psychol. Assn. Club: Internat. of Washington. Author: Queen of Sheba's Heirs: Cultural Patterns in Ethiopia; contbr. chpts. to books, over 30 articles to profl. jours. Home: 880 NE 69th St Apt 1-A Miami FL 33138 Office: 8181 NW 36th St Suite 8 Miami FL 33166

LORD, EVELYN MARLIN, law firm adminstr.; b. Melrose, Mass., Dec. 8, 1926; d. John Joseph and Mary Janette (Nourse) Marlin; B.A., in Roman Langs., Boston U., 1948; M.A. in Polit. Sci., U. Del., 1957; J.D., U. Louisville, 1969; m. Samuel Smith Lord, Feb. 28, 1948; children—Steven A., Jonathan P., Nathaniel E., Victoria M., William K. Dir., Pvt. Urban Renewal Corp., Wilmington, Del., 1956-62; mem. Del. Senate, 1962-64; admitted to Ky. bar, 1969, U.S. Supreme Ct. bar, 1973; exec. dir. Community Improvement Dist., Louisville, 1969-70; columnist News Jour. Co., Wilmington, posted in No. Ireland, 1972-75; office adminstr. firm Orgain, Bell & Tucker, Beaumont, Tex., 1978—. Mem. Beaumont City Council, 1980—; pres., Wilmington chpt. LWV, 1957-60, Del. league, 1961-62; Beaumont chpt., 1977-79, Tex. league, 1979-80; Republican candidate for mayor, Wilmington, 1964; pres. Kentuckiana council Girl Scouts U.S.A., 1968-69; v.p. Three Rivers council Boy Scouts Am.; vice chmn. excellence com. Lamar U.; mem. budget com. United Way, Beaumont; trustee workmen's compensation and mcpl. liability joint self-ins. funds Tex. Mcpl. League, chmn. Mcpl. Leadership project; mem. exec. com. S.E. Tex. Regional Planning Com.; mem. com. community and econ. devel. Nat. League Cities. Named Outstanding Woman, U. Louisville Sch. Law, 1969; recipient Silver Beaver award Boy Scouts Am., 1979. Mem. Nat. Women in Mcpl. Govt. (dir.), Ky. Bar Assn., Assn. Legal Adminstrs., Beaumont Symphony Women's League, Beaumont Art Gallery Guild, Heritage Soc., AAUW, Phi Kappa Phi. Presbyterian. Club: S.E. Tex. Press. Editor: Jour. Family Law, 1968-69; weekly columnist Wilmington Morning News, 1972-75; free-lance journalist, 1972-75. Home: 1560 Continental Ln Beaumont TX 77706 Office: Orgain Bell & Tucker 470 Orleans St Beaumont TX 77701

LORD, MARION E. MANNS, educator; b. Fort Huachuca, Ariz., Dec. 17, 1914; d. George Wiley and Annie (Pellett) Manns; student R.I. State Coll., 1932; B.S., Northwestern U., 1936; postgrad. Breadloaf Coll., summer 1936; M.Ed., Harvard, 1962; M.A., Ph.D. (E.B. Fred fellow), U. Wis., 1968; m. William Shepard Lord, Apr. 29, 1938 (div. May 1965); children—Caroline B. (Mrs. Martin L. Gross), Marion F. (Mrs. Fred W. Steadman), Jane B. (Mrs. Chapin). N.H. State rep. Gen. Ct., Concord, 1957-62; dean women, dir. guidance New Eng. Coll., Henniker, N.H., 1962-64; edn. program specialist, asst. to dir. div. coll. support Bur. Higher Edn., Office Edn., Washington, 1968-71, project dir. for survey design to assess women's barriers in continuing edn. Nat. Center for Ednl. Statistics, 1971-75; dean faculty Borough of Manhattan Community Coll., City U. N.Y., 1975-78; dean of faculty Cottey Coll., Nevada, Mo., 1979—; prof. Central Mich. U., 1975; cons. N.H. U. and Coll. Council, 1974—; cons. Title VIII, U.S. Office Edn., 1977. Vice pres., dir. N.H. Council for Better Schs., 1957-64; county co-chmn. Nat. Found. Infantile Paralysis-March of Dimes, Laconia, N.H., 1958; dir. N.H. Council on World Affairs, 1957-63, Laconia Hosp. Mem. Am. Psychol. Assn., Am. Sociol. Assn., Am. Polit. Sci. Assn., D.C. Sociol. Soc. (com. on status women in professions, treas. 1974, 75), N.H. State Soc. in Washington, Nat. Assn. Women Deans and Counselors, Nat. Council Adminstrv. Women in Edn., Federally Employed Women, Am. Higher Edn. Assn., Order Women Legislators, League Women Voters, AAUW, Bus. and Profl. Womens Club, Phi Lambda Theta. Home: 929 W Cherry St Nevada MO 64772 Office: Cottey Coll Nevada MO 64772

LORD, PRISCILLA SAWYER (MRS. PHILIP HOSMER LORD), author; b. Woburn, Mass.; d. Frank Hayward and Emelyn (Strang) Sawyer; A.B., Boston U., 1933; m. Philip Hosmer Lord, Feb. 10, 1938; children—Beverly, Roberta (Mrs. William H. Moore, Jr.). Readers' adviser Woburn Public Library, 1933-38; story teller Book Reviewer, 1933—. Bd. dirs. Mass. Soc. Univ. Edn. for Women, 1965—; active Girl Scouts U.S.A.; vol. chmn. scholarship com., past v.p. Marblehead Hosp. Aid Assn. Named to Boston U. Collegium Disting. Alumni, 1975. Mem. Herb Soc. Am. (nat. bd., historian, chmn. New Eng. unit), Mass. Descs. of Mayflower, Nat. Soc. Colonial Dames Am., Alpha Gamma Delta. Clubs: Marblehead Garden (past pres.), Winter Garden (past pres.). Author: (with Daniel J. Foley) Easter Garland, 1963; The Folk Arts and Crafts of New England, 2d edit., 1975; The Eagle, 1968; Easter The World Over, 1970; (with Virginia Clegg Gamage) Marblehead: The Spirit of '76 Lives Here, 2d edit., 1975, The Lure of Marblehead, 1973, rev. edit., 1980; The History of the Herb Society of America, 1981-82. Contbr. articles to periodicals. Home: Dennett Rd Marblehead Neck MA 01945 Office: The Maritimes-C23 2051 NE Ocean Blvd Stuart FL 33494

LORE, HARRIET TERESA, acct.; b. Phila., Dec. 15, 1934; d. Harry Sheetz and Suzanne Elizabeth (Biringer) Sanders; B.B.A. cum laude, Temple U., 1980; children—Raymond, Denise, David. Controller, Marrakech Ltd., Horsham, Pa., 1973-76; asst. controller Barringer Knitting Mills, Phila., 1976-79; comptroller YWCA of Phila., 1980—. Com. chmn. bd. mgrs. Temple U. Bus. Sch. Alumni, 1981-82, recipient Bd. of Mgrs. award, 1978. Mem. Nat. Assn. Female Execs., Beta Alpha Psi. Office: 2027 Chestnut St Philadelphia PA 19103

LOREN, PAMELA JAN, telecommunications co. exec.; b. Paris, Jan. 11, 1944; d. Theodore and Mattie (Ephron) Loren; B.S., in Sociology, Columbia U., 1964; M.S. in Sociology, U. Madrid, 1968, M.S. in Langs., 1970; m. Morton P. Levy, June 2, 1963; children—Cristopher Aram, Stirling Brett, Cristina Sahula. Pres., Pamela Loren, Ltd., N.Y.C., 1964-74, Loren Communications Internat., Ltd., N.Y.C., 1972-74; chmn. bd. Loren Communications Internat., Ltd., Caracas, Venezuela, London, Milan, Italy and N.Y.C., 1974—; exec. v.p. Cinnamon World Trade Corp., 1974—; dir. Panda Internat. Export Corp., Durable Housing Internat., Crespi, Rosann & Ponti, Loren Group Constrn. and Mgmt., Danbury, Conn., 1981—; lectr. in field. Recipient Humanitarian award, Community Service Soc., 1972, Burden Center Aging, 1977, Soc. Order Helpers, 1978, 82. Mem. Am. Arbitration Assn., Am. Mgmt. Assn., Soc. Latin Am. Bus. Owners, N.Y. Assn. Women Bus. Owners, Women's Econ. Round Table. Club: Columbia. Author: The Generation In-Between Looking Ahead to Thirty-Five, 1978. Home: 1125 Park Ave New York NY 10028 Office: 235 E 57 St New York NY 10022

LOREN, SOPHIA, actress; b. Rome, Italy, Sept. 20, 1934; d. Riccardo Scicolone and Romilda Villani; student Sculoe Magistrali Superiori; m. Carlo Ponti, Sept. 17, 1957; children—Carlo Ponti, Edoardo. First appearance in Aida, 1951; leading role in Italian motion pictures including: The Gold of Naples, 1954, Woman of the River, 1954, Too Bad She's Bad, Luck of Being a Woman, 1955; actress in U.S. motion pictures, 1955—, including: Pride and Passion, Boy on a Dolphin, Legend of Lost, Desire Under the Elms, Houseboat, Black Orchid, The Key, That Kind of Woman, Heller with a Gun, Marriage Italian Style, Judith, Arabesque, The Countess from Hong Kong, Happily Ever After, The Verdict, Olympia, 1959, Bay of Naples, 1959, It Started in Naples, 1960, Heller in Pink Tights, 1960, The Millionaires, 1961, Two Women, 1962, Bocaccio 70, 1962, Five Miles to Midnight, 1963, Madame, 1963, More Than a Miracle, 1967, Ghosts-Italian Style, 1969, Sunflower, 1970, The Priests Wife, 1971, Man of La Mancha, 1972, Lady Liberty, 1972, White Sister, 1973, The Cassandra Crossing, 1977, A Special Day, 1977, Brass Target, 1978, Firepower, 1979. Recipient award for best film performances Festival of Venice, 1958; Oscar for best film performance, Japan, 1958; Acad. award for Best Actress, 1962; N.Y. Film Critics award, 1961; Gold Palm, Cannes Film Festival, 1961; named best fgn. actress Com. of Film Francais, and the Golden Donatello in Italy, 1958. Author: Sophia-Living and Loving: Her Own Story, 1979. Office: care Cinema 5 Ltd 595 Madison Ave New York NY 10022 *

LORENZ, BONNIE ELENITA, nurse; b. Murray, Ky., Jan. 19, 1929; d. Frank Tillson and Mary Helen (Altolf) Barker; B.S. in Nursing, Union Coll., Lincoln, Nebr., 1952; divorced; children—Terry, Wanda, Ted, Janice. Operating room nurse hosps. in Denver and Greeley, Colo., 1952-55; staff nurse surg. gynecology Weld County Hosp., Greeley, 1959—; staff nurse Bonell Health Care Facility, Greeley, 1970—; now staff nurse, relief supr. Weld County Gen. Hosp. Mem. Colo. Nurses Assn., Assn. Seventh-day Adventist Nurses. Republican. Home: 3405 16th St Greeley CO 80631 Office: Weld County Hosp Greeley CO 80631

LORENZI, NANCY M., univ. ofcl.; d. Louis L. and Mary A. Lorenzi; A.B., Youngstown (Ohio) State U., 1966; M.S., Case Western Res. U., 1968; M.A., U. Louisville, 1975; Ph.D., U. Cin., 1980; m. Robert T. Riley. Dir. med. library Saint Elizabeth's Hosp., Youngstown, 1963-67; reference librarian, head info. services U. Louisville Med. Center, 1968-71; dir. med. center libraries U. Cin., 1972—. Mem. Med. Library Assn. (pres. 1982-83), Am. Soc. Personnel Adminstrs., Cin. Personnel Assn., Ohio Acad. Scis. Contbr. articles in field to profl. jours. Office: University of Cincinnati 231 Bethesda Ave Cincinnati OH 45267

LORENZO, NORIS, educator; b. Ciego de Avila, Camaguey, Cuba, Jan. 22, 1939; came to U.S., 1966, naturalized, 1972; m. Fidel and Noema (Cossio) L.; B.A., Central U. Marta Abreu, Las Villas, 1963; M.S. in Bilingual Edn., CCNY, 1974; M.S. in Ednl. Adminstrn. and Supervision, Pace U., 1976. Bilingual program coordinator Am. Council Emigres in the Professions, N.Y.C., 1970-72; bilingual tchr., N.Y.C., 1972-73; chief examiner high sch. equivalency N.Y.C. Bd. Edn., 1973, dir. N.Y. State programs Sch. Dist. 6, 1973-81; instr. Passaic County (N.J.) Community Coll., 1981—, dir. English as 2d lang. and bilingual studies, 1982—; pres. Lor-Ca Assn., profl. service firm, 1981—; edn. columnist La Voz, 1979. Fellow Am. Council Emigres in Professions, 1969. Mem. United Fedn. Tchrs. (del.), Nat. Assn. Cuban-Am. Women, N.Y. State Reading Assn., Am. Assn. Tchrs. Spanish and Portuguese, Nat. Assn. Cuban Educators in Exile, Nat. Assn. Female Execs., CCNY Alumni Assn. (dir.), N.Y. State Educators in Compensatory Edn., Pace U. Alumni Assn., Assn. Supervision and Curriculum Devel. Author poems, articles in field. Editor books on Latin-Am. history and culture. Address: 416 8th St Union City NJ 07087

LORET DE MOLA, MARIA MATILDE, communications co. exec.; b. Habana, Cuba, Sept. 12, 1945; came to U.S., 1960, naturalized, 1966; d. Melchor Alberto and Angela Loreto (Molina) Loret de Mola; B.S., Fairleigh Dickinson U., 1966, M.S., 1969. Project engr. Bendix Corp., Teterboro, N.J., 1966-69; systems analyst ITT Data Services, Paramus, N.J., 1969-70; tech. rep. Gen. Electric Info. Services, East Orange, N.J., 1970-75, tech. mgr., N.Y.C., 1975, Eastern region support mgr., 1975-78; mgr. system analysis and support market devel. dept. ITT World Communications, Inc., N.Y.C., 1978-81, mgr. system analysis and support, market devel., 1981—; dir. mktg. info. Systems ITT United States Transmission Systems, Inc., Secaucus, N.J. Named Outstanding Tech. Rep., Gen. Electric Co., 1974. Mem. Nat. Assn. Female Execs.

Home: 380 Prospect Ave Hackensack NJ 07601 Office: 67 Broad St New York NY 10004

LOREY, PATRICIA JEAN, real estate broker and appraiser; b. Washington, Oct. 1, 1946; d. Richard Marshall and Ethel Louise (Brockman) Steinberg; student Coll. William and Mary, 1964-65; A.A. cum laude, No. Va. Community Coll., 1978; student George Mason U., 1978—; m. Ryan M. Lorey, June 18, 1966; children—Robert MacDowell, Deborah Angeline. Mem. staff property mgmt. div. Gulf-Reston, Inc., Reston, Va., 1966-68; mem. mktg. staff Dulles Indsl. Aerospace Park, Dulles Internat. Airport, Washington, 1968; comml./indsl. real estate agt. Wellborn Properties, Reston, 1968-71, Real Estate Assos., Falls Church, Va., 1971; cons. and educator in small bus. formulation and planning, Reston, 1971-75; broker, partner Land Sales/Asset Mgmt., Reston, Va., 1975-81; real estate appraiser, 1975-81; prin. broker Patricia S. Lorey, Realtor, 1981—; speaker, cons. real estate investments, small bus. formulation and fin. planning, personal estate planning, real estate portfolio mgmt.; sec. Com. for Dulles, 1970-71, treas., 1978-80, bd. dirs., 1981-83. Mem. Nat. Assn. Realtors (grad. Realtor's Inst.), Va. Assn. Realtors, No. Va. Bd. Realtors (editor Update 1979-81), Nat. Appraisers Inst. (sr. investment analyst), Nat. Assn. Ind. Free Appraisers (editor Appraiser-Gram 1978-79, cert. of appreciation for outstanding contbns. to chpt. 1978), Realtors' Nat. Mktg. Inst., Nat. Assn. Female Execs., NOW, No. Va. Women's Polit. Caucus. Democrat. Methodist. Editor: Aspire, 1975-77. Office: 11250-7 Roger Bacon Dr Reston VA 22090

LORIMER, PATRICIA ANN BLACKLIDGE, assn. exec.; b. Chgo., Feb. 7, 1944; d. William Harry and Josephine Alice (Mortimer) Blacklidge; student U. Dayton (Ohio), Loyola U., Chgo. Exec. sec. Shroyer and Cline, ins., Chgo., 1964-65; office mgr. Head and Valentine, attys. at law, Chgo., 1965-66; sr. sec. fin., then exec. asst. ednl. products Am. Soc. Clin. Pathologists, Chgo., 1974-77, dep. dir. ednl. products, 1978-79, dir. med. pub. div., 1979—. Mem. Am. Med. Writers Assn., Am. Mgmt. Assn., Chgo. Women in Pub., Chgo. Book Clinic. Home: 6223 N Magnolia Ave Chicago IL 60660 Office: 2100 W Harrison St Chicago IL 60612

LORTIE, LORENE, recording co. exec.; b. Youngstown, Ohio; d. Charles William and Ada Marguerite (Swimmer) Schrag; student Youngstown U., 1943-44; B.A. magna cum laude, U. Pitts., 1946; m. Donald Edward Lortie, Nov. 1, 1963. Radio, TV copywriter Stas. WFMJ/WFMJ-TV, Youngstown, 1946-53; advt. coordinator RCA Records, N.Y.C., 1954-58, copywriter, 1958-64, mgr. editorial packaging services, N.Y.C., 1964-78, mgr. RCA and A&M scheduling, 1978—. Recipient Grammy nomination Best Album Notes for Elvis Aron Presley Nat. Acad. Recording Arts and Scis., 1980. Mem. Women in Communications, Nat. Acad. Recording Arts and Scis. (N.Y. bd. govs. 1982-84), Country Music Assn., Acad. Country Music, NOW. Lutheran. Clubs: Toastmasters (adminstrv. v.p. Rough Riders 1981) (N.Y.C.). Home: 118 E 60th St Apt 30B New York NY 10022 Office: RCA Records 1133 Ave of the Americas New York NY 10036

LOSEE, MADELEINE WECKEL, adminstrv. librarian; b. Kenney, Ill.; d. John Conrad and Flossie Dale (McCullough) Weckel; B.S., U. Ill., 1933, M.S., 1936; postgrad. Catholic U., 1964; m. Gordon Carroll Losee, 1940; 1 dau., Carol Ann. Chief Am. law sect. Library of Congress, Washington, D.C., 1945-46, evaluation officer, 1946, chief Am. and Brit. Exchange, 1951; law librarian U.S. AEC, Washington, 1951-59, chief legis. reference service, 1951-61, chief hdqrs. library, 1961-62; chief legis. reference service NASA, Washington, 1962-63, asst. to dir. Tech. Services Div., 1963-64, dir. libraries, program coordinator, 1964—; U.S. del. Belgrade World Conf. World Peace through Law, 1971; participant ann. strategy seminar Dept. Army, 1973; del. White House Conf. on Libraries and Info. Services, 1979. Recipient outstanding performance award NASA, 1971, Apollo achievement award, 1969. Mem. Law Librarians Soc. (pres.), Fed. Council Sci. and Tech., League Women Voters (v.p. Arlington, Va. 1950-51), AAUW, Am. Soc. Info. Sci., Am. Assn. Law Librarians (chmn. com. on automation 1965-68), Spl. Libraries Assn., World Peace Through Law Assn., World Assembly of Judges. Author books and pamphlets in field. Contbr. articles to profl. jours. Home: 6166 Lessburg Pike D 401 Falls Church VA 22044 Office: 300 7th St Washington DC 20546

LOSSING, CRISTINE ELVIRA, book publisher; b. Ann Arbor, Mich., Mar. 5, 1946; d. Herbert Alfred and Ethel Louise (Winnai) L.; B.A., U. Mich., 1968; M.A., Western Mich. U., 1969. With Chilton Book Co., 1970-77, met. N.Y. sales rep., 1976-77; trade sales mgr. Berkley-Jove Pub. Group, 1977-79; mfrs. rep. Crissales Co., N.Y.C., 1980—; cons. in field. Named Editor of Year, Chilton Corp., 1975. Mem. Brotherhood Book Travellers. Address: 3236 Clubhouse Rd Merrick NY 11566

LOTAS, JUDITH PATTON, advt. co. exec.; b. Iowa City, Apr. 23, 1942; d. John Henry and Jane (Vandike) Patton; B.A., Fla. State U., 1964; children—Amanda Bell, Alexandra Vandike. Copywriter, Liller, Neal, Battle and Lindsey Advt., Atlanta, 1964-67; Grey Advt., N.Y.C., 1967-72; creative group head SSC&B Advt., N.Y.C., 1972-74, asso. creative dir., 1974—, v.p., 1975-79, sr. v.p., creative exec., 1979—. Bd. dirs. Samuel Waxman Cancer Research Found. Recipient Clio Venic Film Festival, 1969, Graphics award Am. Inst. Graphic Arts, 1969, 70. Mem. Advt. Women N.Y., Democrat. Home: 45 E 89th St New York NY 10028 Office: SSC&B Advt 1 Dag Hammarskjold Plaza New York NY 10017

LOTSTEIN, CAROLE SUE, tech. writer; b. Forest Hills, N.Y., Sept. 16, 1953; d. Raymond Sidney and Joan Barbara (Wolfe) L.; B.A. cum laude, Fairleigh Dickinson U., 1975. Asst. mgr. The Singer Co., Paramus, N.J., 1976-77, tech. writer instrn. manuals, Elizabeth, N.J., 1977-79, supr. instrn. manuals worldwide, 1979—. Mem. Home Economists in Bus., Phi Omega Epsilon. Club: Navigators. Home: PO Box 6513 Bridgewater NJ 08807 Office: 321 1st St Elizabeth NJ 07206

LOTZ, DOLLY IDELLA, banker; b. Blackfoot, Idaho, Dec. 22, 1918; d. William O. and Mollie Mary (McGinnis) Miller; student U. Idaho, 1936-37, Henager Bus. Coll., 1937-38, Idaho State U., 1964-65; m. George Lotz, Feb. 12, 1941; 1 dau., Frances. Sec., Taylor & Sandack, Salt Lake City, 1938-39; sec., clk. Western States Grocery Co., Pocatello, Idaho, 1939-40; clk., typist Civilian Conservation Corps, Pocatello, 1940-42; teller First Security Bank Idaho, Pocatello, 1949-50; teller, clk. Idaho Bank and Trust, Pocatello, 1950-71, asst. auditor, 1971, asst. cashier, 1972-78, asst. v.p., 1978-80, v.p., 1980—. Dir. YWCA, Am. Heart Assn., Attention Home. Mem. Nat. Assn. Bank Women (nat. dir., exec. com.), Am. Bus. Women's Assn., Idaho Bankers Assn. (edn. com.). Democrat. Roman Catholic. Home: Box 1613 Pocatello ID 83201 Office: Box 1788 Pocatello ID 83201

LOTZE, BARBARA, physicist; b. Mezokovesd, Hungary, Jan. 4, 1924; d. Matyas and Borbala (Toth) Kalo; came to U.S., 1961, naturalized, 1967; Applied Mathematician Diploma with honors, Eotvos Lorand U. Scis., Budapest, Hungary, 1956; Ph.D., Innsbruck (Austria) U., 1961; m. Dieter P. Lotze, Oct. 6, 1958. Mathematician, Hungarian Central Statis. Bur., Budapest, 1955-56; tchr. math., Iselsberg, Austria, 1959-60; asst. prof. physics Allegheny Coll., 1963-69, asso. prof., 1969-77, prof., 1977—, chmn. dept., 1981—; lectr. in history of physics; speaker to civic groups. Mem. Am. Phys. Soc., Am. Assn. Physics Tchrs. (sect. rep. Western Pa., chmn. nat. com. on women in physics), AAUP, AAUW, Am. Hungarian Educators Assn. (pres. 1980-82), Wilhelm Busch Gesellschaft (Hanover, Germany). Contbr. articles to profl. jours.; research in theoretical physics. Home: 462 Hartz Ave Meadville PA 16335 Office: Dept Physics Allegheny Coll Meadville PA 16335

LOUARD, AGNES ANTHONY, educator; b. Savannah, Ga., Mar. 10, 1922; d. Joseph and Agnes (Hollinger) Anthony; B.A., U. Pa., 1944; M.A., Fisk U., 1945; M.S., Columbia U., 1948; postgrad. N.Y.U., 1970—; m. Vernon Benjamin Louard, Sept. 2, 1950; children—Rita Jean, Diane Carole, Kenneth Anthony. Supr., Manhattonville Neighborhood Center, 1948-52; dir. recreation and edn. Union Settlement, N.Y.C., 1952-59; sr. caseworker Speedwell Services for Children, N.Y.C., 1959-61, Leake and Watts, 1961-63; recreation dir. Patterson Home for Aged, Uniondale, N.Y., 1963-65; field instr. Urban League, Columbia U., 1965-67; asst. prof. Sch. Social Work, N.Y.C., 1967-71, asso. prof., 1971—. Bd. dirs. Harriet Tubman Community Center, 1969—; bd. dirs. Pleasant Ave. Day Care Center, N.Y.C., 1970—, pres. 1968-70; bd. dirs., chmn. personnel com. Peninsula Counseling Center, 1971—, v.p., 1981—; mem. citizens adv. com. for mental health Town of Hempstead Supr., 1981—; mem. council N.Y. State Employment and Tng. Council, 1977-79. Recipient N.Y. State Employment and Tng. Council award, 1979; Headstart-Haryou Act award, 1968. Mem. ACLU, Common Cause, NAACP, Urban League, AAUP, Black Caucus Columbia, Nat. Assn. Social Workers. Home: 777 W Broadway Woodmere NY 11598 Office: 622 W 113th St New York NY 10025

LOUCKS, SANDRA, psychologist; b. New Orleans, Jan. 2, 1947; d. Frederick Chancey and Cornelia Cecilia (McCurdy) Loucks; B.A., La. State U., 1968; Ph.D., U. Tenn., 1974; m. Alvin George Burstein, Apr. 15, 1977. Research asso. La. State U., New Orleans, 1967-68; research asst. U. Tenn., Knoxville, 1968-69, clin. asst., 1970-71; sch. psychologist Knox County Sch. System, Knoxville, 1969-70; research asst. Stanford (Calif.) Research Inst., 1969-70; psychotherapist, cons. Adolescent Unit, Eastern State Psychiat. Hosp., Knoxville, 1969-70; psychology resident U. Tex. Health Sci. Center, San Antonio, 1971-72; jr. staff psychologist Regional Mental Health Center, Oak Ridge, 1972-73; cons. County Juvenile Ct., 1972-73; asst. prof. dept. psychiatry U. Tex. Health Sci. Center, San Antonio, 1974-78, 78-79, dept. psychiatry and pediatrics, 1979-80, asso. prof., 1980—; research dir., psychologist Therapeutic Community for the Treatment of Schizophrenia, 1974-76; staff psychologist Audie Murphy Meml. VA Hosp., San Antonio, 1974-78, staff psychologist Acute Psychiatric Admissions Unit, 1976-77, asst. dir. Day Hosp. Program, 1977-78; lectr., cons. in field; dir., asso. prof. Center for Personal and Ednl. Devel., Trinity U., San Antonio, 1980-82. Lic. psychologist, Tex. Diplomate Am. Bd. Profl. Psychology. Mem. Am. Psychol. Assn., Southwestern Psychol. Assn., Tex. Psychol. Assn. (liaison), Bexar County Psychol. Assn. Contbr. articles to profl. jours. Home: 6607 Adair Dr San Antonio TX 78238 Office: 715 Stadium Dr San Antonio TX 78284

LOUIE, JANICE MAUDE, nutritionist; b. Oakland, Calif., Aug. 4, 1949; d. Joseph Ong and Luella Frances (Chinn) L.; B.S., UCLA, 1971; M.A., Calif. State U., Los Angeles, 1976. Nutrition cons. Chinatown Community Children's Center, San Francisco, 1977; nutrition program coordinator div. outpatient and community services San Francisco Gen. Hosp., 1978—; field site supr., guest speaker U. Calif., Berkeley, Calif. State U., San Francisco. Adv. bd. S.E. San Francisco Area Health Edn. Center; mem. adv. bd. Food and Nutrition Program for Pregnant Teenage Women; mem. adv. com. coordinated program in dietetics U. Calif., Berkeley; chairperson com. on edn. and public info., mem. steering com. Asian/Pacific Islander Task Force on High Blood Pressure, Edn. and Control. Mem. Am. Dietetic Assn. (registered dietitian), Soc. Nutrition Today, Pub. Health Assn., Soc. Nutrition Edn., Am. Heart Assn., Am. Diabetes Assn. Office: San Francisco Gen Hosp 995 Potrero Ave San Francisco CA 94110

LOUISE, MELINDA, career coach, vocat. rehab. counselor; b. Tacoma, Nov. 19, 1947; d. John David and Ramona Joyce (Frazier) Wefler; B.A., Antioch U., 1978; M.A. in Career and Life Planning, Goddard Coll., 1980. Prin., Melinda Louise, Career Cons., Ventura and Los Angeles counties, Calif., 1979—; asso. Vocat. Counseling Assos., Santa Monica, Calif., 1982—. Mem. Mar Vista Bus. and Profl. Women's Club, Nat. Career Devel. Project, S. Coast Bus. Women's Network, San Diego Career Guidance Assn. Office: 1675 Edgemont Dr Camarillo CA 93010

LOURENÇO, SUSAN JANE LOEWENTHAL VALENTIM, educator; b. London, Dec. 8, 1935; came to U.S., 1959, naturalized, 1965; d. Hans E.H. and Ilse (Stenger) Loewenthal; B.A., Oxford U., 1957, M.A., 1961; M.A., Columbia U., 1960; Ph.D., U. Chgo. (NIMH tng. fellow), 1974; m. Ruy V. Lourenco, Jan. 18, 1960; children—Peter Edward, Margaret Philippa. Research asst. CCNY, 1962-66; asst. prof., program dir. Center for Teaching Professions, Northwestern U., Evanston, Ill., 1972-75; asso. prof. psychology George Peabody Coll., European div., Eng., 1975-76; vis. scientist Tavistock Inst. Human Relations, London, 1975-76; asso. prof. urban edn. research and health professions edn., asso. prof. Grad. Sch., U. Ill., Chgo., 1977-80, dir. organizational devel. Center Study Patient Care and Community Health, 1977-80, co-dir. urban health program, 1978-79 dir. Early Outreach program, 1980—, dir. community affairs, 1981—; cons. WMAQ-TV, NBC, Chgo., Area Health Edn. System, Chgo. Mem. Am. Psychol. Assn., Soc. Psychol. Study Social Issues, Am. Sociol. Assn., Am. Ednl. Research Assn. Mem. editorial bd. Am. Jour. Community Psychology, 1978—; contbr. articles to profl. jours. Home: 1000 N Lake Shore Dr Chicago IL 60611 Office: 1737 W Polk St Chicago IL 60612

LOUSIN, ANN MARIE, law educator; b. Chgo., Feb. 21, 1943; d. Max Bedros and Opal Marie (Anderson) L.; B.A., Grinnell (Iowa) Coll., 1964; postgrad. U. Heidelberg (Germany), 1964-65; J.D., U. Chgo., 1968. Admitted to Ill. bar, 1970, U.S. Dist. Ct. bar, 1974, U.S. Circuit Ct. Appeals bar, 1979; research asst. 6th Ill. Constl. Conv., Springfield, 1970; mem. staff Ill. 77th Gen. Assembly, 1971-73, 78th Gen. Assembly, also parliamentarian of House, 1973-75; asst. prof. John Marshall Law Sch., 1975-77, asso. prof., 1977-80, prof., 1980—. Chmn., Ill. State Civil Service Commn., 1977—. Recipient hon. mention Lincoln essay contest Ill. Bar Assn., 1975, 79. Mem. Am. Bar Assn., Ill. Bar Assn., Women's Bar Assn. Ill. (dir. 1975-77), Chgo. Bar Assn., Chgo. Council Lawyers.

LOVAS, DORINNE SUE TAYLOR, audiologist; b. East Orange, N.J., Mar. 29, 1949; d. William Henry and Evelyn Doris (Thorp) Taylor; B.A., Montclair State Coll., 1971, M.A., 1973; m. Patrick Andrew Lovas, May 2, 1970; children— Larissa Louise, Peter Alexander. Ednl. audiologist Morris County Coll., Dover, N.J., 1974-75, Kinnelon (N.J.) Bd. Edn., 1972—, Inst. for Career Advancement, Inc., 1980—. Cert. tchr. of hearing impaired, speech correctionist, tchr. speech and drama N.J. Dept. Edn. Mem. Am. Speech and Hearing Assn. (cert. of clin. competence in audiology), N.J. Speech and Hearing Assn., NEA, N.J. Edn. Assn., Morris County Edn. Assn., Kinnelon Edn. Assn. Methodist. Home: 4 Musconetcong Ave Stanhope NJ 07874 Office: Spl Services Kinnelon Bd Edn Kiel Ave Kinnelon NJ 07405

LOVE, ERIKA, librarian; b. Berlin, May 2, 1925; came to U.S., 1948, naturalized, 1953; B.A. cum laude, Ind. U., 1950, M.A. in L.S., 1953; m. Victor Lamar Love, Nov. 27, 1948. With Am. House, Darmstadt, W.Ger., 1947-48, Indpls. Pub. Library, 1950-51; asst. librarian Ind. U. Law Sch., 1951-53; chief librarian Carter Hosp., also Ind. Dept. Mental Health, 1953-67; librarian Bowman Gray Med. Sch., 1967-71; dep. assoc. dir. library ops. Nat. Library Medicine, also dir. Mid-Atlantic region, 1971-77; dir., prof. U. N.Mex. Med. Center Library, Albuquerque, 1977—, also mem. faculty Med. Sch.; mem. network adv. com. to librarian of Congress, 1978—; chmn. adv. council TALON Regional Med. Library Network, 1982—; cons. in field. Trustee, Cedar Lane Unitarian Ch., Bethesda, Md., 1976-77. Mem. Med. Library Assn. (pres. 1978-79), Am. Assn. History Medicine, Am. Soc. Info. Sci., Assn. Health Sci. Library Dirs, N.Mex. Library Assn. Author articles in field. Office: U NMex Med Center Library North Campus Albuquerque NM 87131

LOVE, JANE HAZELTON, media specialist, educator; b. N.Y.C., Sept. 24, 1931; d. Paul Higham and Mildred Mignon (Fay) Hazelton; B.A., U. Md., 1971; M.Ed., W.Va. U., 1974, Ed.D., 1977; m. Thomas McAdoo Love, June 5, 1952 (dec.). Mem. staff Anne Arundel County (Md.) Public Schs., 1959—, media specialist, 1972-77, media generalist, 1977—; adj. prof. Western Md. Coll., Westminster, 1981—; chmn. legis. com. ALA-Am. Assn. Sch. Librarians, 1980-82. Mem. Assn. Ednl. Communications and Tech. (council 1979-82, sec. steering com., bd. dirs. 1982-85), ALA, Md. Ednl. Media Orgn. (pres. 1979-80, conf. chmn. 1979, 80, 82, publs. chmn. 1981-83), Ednl. Media Assn. Anne Arundel County (pres. 1979-81), W.Va. U. Coll. Human Resources Alumni Assn. (pres.-elect 1981-82), Phi Delta Kappa (founds. chmn. U. Md. 1981-82). Home: 1736 Trent St Crofton Woods MD 21114 Office: Old Mill Media Center Shetland Ln Glen Burnie MD 21060

LOVE, KATHLYN, artist; b. Wilder, Vt., May 15, 1918; student Concord (N.H.) Coll., 1936-37; m. C.R. Love, Mar. 8, 1939 (dec.); children—Theodore J., Timothy R. Executed murals Central Maine Gen. Hosp., Lewiston, 1972, St. Mary's Hosp., Lewiston, 1973; exhibited in nat., state and regional exhbns., also U.K.; represented in permanent collection Senator George Mitchell; pres. Artists Equity Maine, 1971-73; mem. exec. bd. Artists Equity Assn., 1971-73, nat. bd. dirs., 1972-73, adv. bd., 1974-75; co-dir. art exhibits St. Mary's Hosp., 1974-75. Mem. Visual Artists Union, Lewiston-Auburn Arts Council, Western Maine Art Group, Nat. Soc. Lit. and Arts, Androscoggin Valley Art Assn. Democrat. Roman Catholic. Address: 12 Robinson Gardens Lewiston ME 04240

LOVE, LOIS, record co. exec.; b. New Haven; d. Kalil Bachara and Sara Louise (Magliola) Haddad; student Sacred Heart U., 1964-66, U. New Haven, 1966-67; m. Noel Love, Aug. 10, 1980; 1 dau., Krista Nicole. Traffic and public service dir. to asst. dir. music Sta. WNHC, New Haven, 1968-70; nat. sales service rep. Sta. WBZ-TV, Boston, 1970-71; mgr. Elizabeth Allen's Women's Health Club, 1972-73; local rep. Cin. region United Artist Records, 1973-74; regional dir. Chelsea Records, Detroit, Chgo., Cleve. and Cin., 1974-75; with Pvt. Stock Records, 20th Century Fox and Leber-Krebs Mgmt., Boston, 1975-78; N.E. regional mgr. Arista Records, Boston, 1978—; pres. Alternative Programming, Inc., Love Affair Mgmt. Chmn. Loring Sch. Vol. Com., 1980-81; mem. Sudbury Valley Trustees, 1981-82. Named Promotion Person of Yr., Confidential Report, 1977, 78; recipient gold and platinum records Rec. Industry Assn. Am. Columnist Lovenotes in Cosmic Muffin Newsletter., 1980—. Office: 6 W 57th St New York NY 10019

LOVE, MILDRED LEE, orgn. exec.; b. Ringold, La., Oct. 25, 1941; d. Willie B. and Irene B. (Walters) L.; B.S., So. U., Baton Rouge, 1963; postgrad. U. Pitts. Caseworker N.Y.C. Dept. Social Services, 1963-64; instr.-counselor Harlem Team Self Help, N.Y.C., 1965-71; with Nat. Urban League, 1971—, dir. Eastern regional office, 1976-79, dir. nat. dept. career tng. and econ. resources, 1979-81, v.p. program ops., 1981—; v.p. Nat. Youth Employment Coalition, 1981; mem. Nat. Commn. Fed. Unemployment Policy, 1979—. Chmn. program com. Harlem br. YMCA, 1981. Ford Found. fellow, 1968. Mem. NAACP, Nat. Council Negro Women, Am. Mgmt. Assn., So. U. Alumni Fedn. (chpt. sec. 1980-82), Delta Sigma Theta (chmn. chpt. social action com. 1980-82). Baptist. Address: Nat Urban League 500 E 62d St New York NY 10021

LOVE, MILDRED LOIS (JAN), public relations exec.; b. Iowa City, July 9, 1928; d. Joseph R. and Gladys M. (Parsons) Casey; B.S. in Bus. Adminstrn., U. Iowa, 1951; m. Gerald Dean Love, Apr. 4, 1952; children—Laura Anne Love Parris, Cynthia Love-Hazel, Gregory Alan, Linda Jayne, Geoffrey Dare. Vocal soloist Sta. KXEL, Waterloo, Iowa, 1944-46; sec. to lawyer, La Porte City, Iowa, 1944-46; adminstrv. aide Office of Supt., La Porte City High Sch., 1947-48; office mgr. Minn. Valley Canning Co., Iowa div. offices, LaPorte City, 1947-48; sec. dept. mktg. U. Iowa, 1948-51; asst. dept. public relations Chgo. Bd. Trade, 1949-51; exec. sec. patent dept. Collins Radio Co., Cedar Rapids, 1951-52; vol. VA Hosp., Albany, N.Y., 1965-73; adminstrv. dir. Tri-Village Nursery Sch., Delmar, N.Y., 1960-61; participant Internat. Lang. Teaching Exchange, Cambodia, 1961; vol. hosps. in Concord, N.H., 1963-64; vol. Chgo. Maternity Center, 1973-74; mgr. Wolf Trap Assos. Gift Shop, Vienna, Va., 1975-80; gen. mgr. Travelhost of Washington, 1980-81; cons. mgmt., 1980—; chair Nat. Cherry Blossom Festival, Washington. Participant community beauty pageants on local and dist. levels, Iowa, 1950-51; Sunday sch. tchr. Meth. Ch., 1941-61; mem. Flossmoor (Ill.) Planning and Zoning Commn., 1973-74, McLean (Va.) Planning and Zoning Commn., 1975—; precinct worker in Iowa, 1946-52, N.Y., 1956-61, N.H., 1963-64, Va., 1979—; pres. I.O.W.A. Inc., Washington, 1980-81; active various community fund raising drives. Mem. AAUW, Am. Mkgt. Assn., Nat. Assn. Female Execs., Nat. Conf. State Socs. (1st v.p. 1981—), LWV, Delta Zeta. Republican. Clubs: Princeton (Washington); Normandside Country, Olympia Fields Winter. Home: 1413 Celesta Ct Vienna VA 22180 Office: 180 Longworth Bldg Washington DC 20515

LOVE, RUTH B., supt. schs.; b. Lawton, Okla.; B.A. in Elem. Edn., San Jose State U.; M.A. in Guidance and Counseling, San Francisco State U.; Ph.D. in Human Behavior, U.S. Internat. U. Tchr., Oakland (Calif.) Unified Sch. Dist., 1954-59, counselor/cons. Ford Found. Project, 1960-62, tchr. adult edn., 1961-65, supr. schs., 1975-81; gen. supt. schs., Chgo., 1981—; Fulbright exchange tchr., Cheshire, Eng., 1960; project dir. Operation Crossroads, Ghana, summer, 1962; cons. Bur. Pupil Personnel Service, Calif. Dept. Edn., Sacramento, 1963-65, chief Bur. Compensatory Edn. Program Devel., 1965-71; dir. Right to Read Effort, Office Edn., HEW, Washington, 1971-75. Recipient numerous awards and citations. Mem. Assn. Supervision and Curriculum Devel., Guidance and Counseling Assn., Assn. Childhood Edn. Internat., World Council Tchrs., Internat. Reading Assn., Am. Personnel and Guidance Assn., NEA, Calif. Tchrs. Assn., Am. Acad. Polit. and Social Sci., Women's Forum, People to People Program World Orgn. on Early Childhood Edn., Am. Assn. Sch. Adminstrs., Calif. Assn. Sch. Adminstrs., Afro-Negro Internat. Travel Club, Delta Kappa Gamma, Alpha Kappa Alpha. Author: Strengthening Counseling Services for Disadvantaged Youth, 1966; Hello World, 8 book series, 1973; contbr. articles on edn. to profl. jours. Office: 228 N LaSalle St Chicago IL 60601 *

LOVE, SANDRA RAE, information specialist; b. San Francisco, Feb. 20, 1947; d. Benjamin Raymond and Charlotte C. Martin; B.A. in English, Calif. State U., Hayward, 1968; M.S. in L.S., U. So. Calif., 1969; m. Michael D. Love, Feb. 14, 1971. Tech. info. specialist Lawrence Livermore (Calif.) Nat. Lab., 1969—. Mem. Spl. Libraries Assn. (sec. nuclear sci. div. 1980-82), Beta Sigma Phi. Democrat. Episcopalian. Office: Lawrence Livermore Nat Lab Library PO Box 5500 Livermore CA 94550

LOVE, THOMASENIA, govtl. agy. adminstr.; b. Roxboro, N.C., Oct. 23, 1942; d. William Thomas and Roxie Anna (Collins) Clay; B.S., A&T State U., Greensboro, N.C., 1964; m. William L. Love, Aug. 28, 1964; children—Tonya D., Pamela M. Adminstrv. asst., sec. to execs. Dept. Labor, Office of Edn. and Nat. Adv. Commn. on Civil Disorders, Washington, 1964-68, employee devel. specialist Office of Edn. also EEOC, Washington, 1969-71, equal opportunity specialist EEOC, 1972-74, employee devel. specialist, 1975-76, position classification specialist, 1977-78, chief Employee Services and Career Counseling br., 1978-79, chief Spl. Programs br., Personnel div., 1979—. Corr. sec. Barnaby Manor Civic Assn., 1976-77. Mem. Am. Soc. for Tng. and Devel., NEA, Adult and Continuing Edn. Assn., Potomac Parent, Tchr., Student Assn. (bd. dirs.), Nat. Urban League, A & T State U. Alumni Assn. Democrat. Methodist. Clubs: Metropolitan Women's (mem. legislative and membership coms. 1978-81), Barnaby Manor Civic and Recreation Assn. Home: 1908 Deerfield Ct Oxon Hill MD 20745

LOVELACE, MARIAN ELIZABETH, social worker; b. Guthrie, Okla., Dec. 8, 1947; d. Murdock William and Margaret Estella (Burns) L.; B.A., Langston U., 1970; M.S. in Social Work, U. Mo.-Columbia, 1974. Benefit authorizer Social Security Payment Center, 1970-72; social worker Leavenworth (Kans.) VA, 1974-79; social worker Las Vegas VA Outpatient Clinic, 1979—; field instr. U. Kans. Sch. Social Work, 1977-78, Ariz. State U. Sch. Social Work, 1982—; chmn. Com. on Handicapped Employees VA Center, 1977-79; bd. dirs. Leavenworth Social Planning Council; bd. dirs., corr. sec. Center for Employment Tng., 1981—. Mem. Acad. Cert. Social Workers, Nat. Assn. Social Workers, Assn. Black Social Workers. Roman Catholic. Home: 3880 S Wynn Apt 117 Las Vegas NV 89103 Office: VA Outpatient Clinic 1703 W Charleston Blvd Las Vegas NV 89102

LOVELADY, GEORGIA NADINE, realtor, constrn. co. exec.; b. Sweetwater, Tex., May 23, 1917; d. Arthur Gabriel and Martha Ella (Gantt) Pool; student Lynchburg Bapt. Coll., 1976-80; m. John Travis Lovelady, Aug. 30, 1941 (dec. 1977); 1 son, Travis Gaylon. Mgr., Beverly's Dress Shop, Port Arthur, Tex., 1942-43; line instr. Reynolds Ammunition Plant, Macon, Ga., 1944-46; sales rep. Colonial Homes, 1957-63; owner Lovelady Realtor, Hobbs, N.M., 1960—; owner Lovelady Constrn., Hobbs, 1963—. Named Realtor of the Yr., Hobbs Bd. Realtors, 1971; Nat. Homes Blue Seal Builder award, 1974; cert. of appreciation City of Hobbs, 1973, cert. of recognition, 1979; cert. of appreciation Vocat. Industries Clubs Am., 1979; Nat. Homes Builders award, 1980; Mem. Hobbs Bd. Realtors (pres. 1970), N.Mex. Realtors Assn. (v.p. 1973), Nat. Assn. Realtors, Hobbs C. of C., Hobbs Trade Devel. Council, Am. Bus. Women, VFW Aux., Phi Sigma Alpha. Democrat. Baptist. Club: Women's Christian. Address: 2000 N Dal Paso Hobbs NM 88240

LOVELESS, JANE BRYAN, advt. exec.; b. Dallas, May 28, 1948; d. Lewis Calvin and Lucy Jane (Nunn) Bryan; B.A., So. Meth. U., 1970, M.L.A., 1974; m. Thomas Norman Loveless, May 17, 1980. Adminstrv. supr., legal librarian Jenkens, Spradley & Gilchrist, 1971-73; asst. to v.p., dir. mktg. Dallas Fed. Savs. & Loan, 1973-74; dir. communications, editor Alumni Mag., So. Meth. U. Alumni Assn., 1974-75; office mgr., recruitment coordinator Jenkens & Gilchrist, Dallas, 1975-77; salesperson Bonwit Teller, Boston, 1977; public info. supr. Dallas Fire Dept., 1977-79; salesperson Neiman Marcus, Dallas, 1979-80; press rep. Lone Star Gas, Dallas, 1979; mgr. product mktg. Tex. Fed. Savs. & Loan Assn., Dallas, 1979-82; advt. mgr. Mrs. Baird's Bakeries, Inc., 1982—; cons. Support Systems Inc., Dallas, 1981. Bd. dirs., public relations rep. Nat. Arthritis Found., N. Tex. chpt., 1981-84. Mem. Women in Communications (Matrix award Dallas chpt. 1980), Dallas Advt. League, So. Meth. U. Alumni Assn., Jr. League of Dallas, Dallas Press Club, Pi Beta Phi (dir., public relations rep. Dallas alumnae chpt.). Methodist. Club: Fencers League (Dallas). Home: 2833 Duval Dr Dallas TX 75211 Office: PO Box 417 Dallas TX 75221

LOVELL, C. HELEN, banker; b. New Rochelle, N.Y., June 3, 1933; d. Charles Howard and Loretto L.; B.A. in Math., Coll. Mt. St. Vincent, Riverdale, N.Y., 1955. With Morgan Guaranty Trust Co. of N.Y., N.Y.C., 1955—, asst. treas., 1963-69, asst. v.p., 1969-75, v.p., 1975—. Mem. Nat. Assn. Bank Women (chmn. Manhattan group), Alumnae Assn. Coll. Mt. St. Vincent. Republican. Roman Catholic. Office: Morgan Guaranty Trust Co of NY 522 Fifth Ave New York NY 10036 *

LOVELL, CORNEIDA DAVIDSON, mgmt. and career cons.; b. Charlotte, N.C., Feb. 8, 1932; d. Anderson E. and Priscilla (deVeaux) Davidson; student Fisk U., 1948-50; B.S. with honors, Johnson C. Smith U., 1952; M.A., Montclair State Coll., 1968; postgrad. U. Md., 1964, Millersville State Coll., 1965, Rutgers U., 1976-78; m. Walter R. Lovell, Jr., June 7, 1952; children—Michael deVeaux, Philip Alan. Instr. biology Montclair (N.J.) public schs., 1961-69; program asso. Bd. for Fundamental Edn., N.Y.C., 1969-70; curriculum cons. N.Y.C. Bd. Edn., 1970; asst. exec. dir. Newark (N.J.) Day Center, 1971, exec. dir., 1972-79; dep. commr. mgmt. services Ark. Social Services, Little Rock, 1979-80; interim dir. Family Service Agy. of Central Ark., Little Rock, 1980-81; cons. ednl. program design, career mgmt. and social agy. adminstrn., 1975—. Bd. dirs. Nutley (N.J.) Family Service Bur., 1968-74; mem. adv. com. to Commrs. of Health and Ins., N.J., 1974-75; mem. exec. com. N.J. State Health Planning Council, 1971-77; mem. Newark Health Services Commn., 1976-79; bd. dirs. Essex County Mental Health Bd., N.J., 1976-77, Essex County Heart Assn., 1976-79; chmn. adv. council Newark Ret. Srs. Vol. Program, 1976-79; pres. Little Rock Community Housing Resource Bd., 1982. Recipient Cert. Appreciation, Nat. Council of Black Child Devel., 1975, Leadership award N.J. Health Consumer's Union, 1978, Citizen of the Year award Coll. of Medicine and Dentistry of N.J., 1979, Outstanding Achievement award United Way of Essex County, 1979, Proclamation State of N.J., 1979, City of Newark, 1979. Mem. AAUW, LWV, Am. Public Health Assn., Minorities Caucus of Family Services Assn., Alpha Kappa Alpha. Club: Soroptimist Internat. (exec. bd. 1979-81), Nat. Epicureans. contbr. articles to profl. publs. Office: Personal and Profl Devel Services Suite 1260 Tower Bldg 4th and Center St Little Rock AR 72209

LOVELL, MARY ANN NORRIS, banker; b. Richmond County, Ga., June 2, 1945; d. Devayor Tompkins and Bertha (Caudill) Anderson; student Swainsboro Tech., 1968; student various banking schs.; m. Roger Bruce Lovell, Sr., Sept. 28, 1979; children—Natalie Jo Norris, Jeffrey Wesley Norris, Sonya Renee Norris, Stephen Edgar Norris. Office mgr. Wrightsville Loan Co. (Ga.), 1963-64; with Home Service Fin., Sandersville, Ga., 1965; cashier, ops. officer Citizens Bank of Washington County, Sandersville, 1965-73; with Bank of Perry (Ga.), 1973—, now v.p., personnel officer, compliance officer. Mem. Nat. Assn. Bank Women (chmn. Middle Ga. chpt. 1980-81), Ind. Bankers Assn. Ga. (young bankers sect., vice chmn. div. 3 1979-80), Ga. Bankers Assn. (personnel com. 1979-81). Democrat. Methodist. Clubs: Perry Bus. Women's, Perry Country. Office: Bank of Perry 1006 Main PO Drawer O Perry GA 31069

LOVETRI, JEANNETTE LOUISE, voice tchr.; b. Southampton, N.Y., Apr. 2, 1949; d. James John and Aline Rita (Zimmer) Lovetri; student Manhattan Sch. Music, 1967-68, Juilliard Sch., 1971-72; pvt. dance, piano and vocal study. Singer opera, cabaret, summer stock, oratorios, jazz, 1966-80; owner voice studio, Greenwich, Conn., 1970-75, N.Y.C., 1975—; tchr. voice music dept. Upsala Coll., East Orange, N.J., 1976-81; numerous appearances with Bklyn. Contemporary Chorus, Chapman Roberts Singers, Mid-Hudson Opera, others. Pres., Tenants of 212 W. 80th St., N.Y.C. Mem. N.Y. Singing Tchrs. Assn. (dir., treas.), Nat. Assn. Female Execs., Nat. Assn. Tchrs. Singing, Am. Guild Musical Artists, Women Bus. Owners N.Y. Home: 212 W 80th St New York NY 10024

LOVETT, CRISTINE LOUISE, electronics mfg. co. exec.; b. Las Animas, Colo., Aug. 8, 1951; d. Ivan Eugene and Rosalee (Pemberton) Brenton; BS. (Sch. of Journalism scholar, 1972, Scripps-Howard scholar, 1971-72, 72-73), Sch. Journalism, U. Colo., 1972, spl. studies Engring. Design and Econ. Evaluation, 1975, M.B.A., 1980; m. Daryle A. Lovett, May 19, 1972. Documentation supr. Valleylab, Inc., Boulder, Colo., 1973-74; nat. mktg. mgr. OWL Tech. Assos., Inc., Longmont, Colo., 1974—. Recipient Public Service award for article; U.S. Navy Community Service award, 1972. Cert. purchasing mgr. Mem. Colo. Mining Assn., M.B.A. Assn. (U. Colo.), Nat. Assn. Female Execs. (local dir.), Exec. and Profl. Women's Council. Polit. writer Tri-City Jour., Broomfield, Colo., 1977-78, Lafayette (Colo.) News, 1977-78. Home: 1260 Centaur Village Ct Lafayette CO 80026 Office: 1111 Delaware Ave Longmont CO 80501

LOVINGER, SOPHIE LEHNER, psychologist, educator; b. N.Y.C., Jan. 15, 1932; d. Nathan Harris and Anne (Rosen) Lehner; M.S., CCNY, 1959; Ph.D., N.Y.U., 1967; m. Robert Jay Lovinger, June 18, 1957; children—David Fredrick, Mark Andrew. Psychotherapy trainee Jamaica (N.Y.) Center for Psychotherapy, 1964-67; asst. prof. psychology Hofstra U., Hempstead, N.Y., 1967-70; prof. Central Mich. U., Mt. Pleasant, 1970—; mem. Psychology Bd. Licensing, State of Mich. Bd. dirs. A Child's World, Mt. Pleasant. Mem. Am. Psychol. Assn., Mich. Psychol. Assn., Am. Acad. Psychotherapists, Nat. Assn. Sch. Psychology, Soc. Personnel Assn. Author: Learning Disabilities & Games, 1978. Home: 714 S Main St Mount Pleasant MI 48858 Office: Central Michigan U Sloan 104 Mount Pleasant MI 48859

LOW, EDITH MCLEAN, newspaper editor; b. Wilmington, N.C., May 23, 1928; d. Cameron Moses and Sallie (Mason) McLean; student Bob Jones Coll., 1947-48, Palmer Sch. Writing, 1956-58, U. N.D., 1965-66, Central Piedmont Community Coll., 1981—; m. James Edgar Low, Aug. 2, 1953 (dec.); children—Cameron Lewis, Heidi Lynn, Jennifer McLean. Asst. buyer Maas Bros., Tampa, Fla., 1950-54; staff writer Cross Winds mag., Travis AFB, Calif., 1958-62, East Grand Forks (Minn.) Record, 1962-65; women's editor Wilmington (N.C.) Star-News, 1966-68; copy editor Charlotte (N.C.) News, 1968—, homemaking editor, 1969—; adult edn. tchr. food preparation Central Piedmont Community Coll., 1976-79. Active Charity League Charlotte, Sunshine Day Nursery, 1978—, mental health clinic project, 1971-73; treas. Cardiac Rehab. Program, 1973—; vol. elderly programs, 1976—; advisor cookbook div. to N.C. chpts. Am. Cancer Soc., 1981—. Recipient Golden Carnation for food writing, 1971, 73, 74, awards N.C. Press. Women, 1973, 74, Burlington House award, 1974, 75, Dallas Market Center award, 1974; named Food Writer of Yr., 1981. Mem. N.C. Press Women (pres. 1974), Am. Soc. Interior Designers, Sigma Delta Chi. Author: No Rank to Speak Of, 1965; The Love Yourself Cookbook—Easy Recipes for One or Two, 1982. Home: 3909 Woodbriar Trail Charlotte NC 28205 Office: 600 S Tryon St Charlotte NC 28201

LOWDON, JEANNIE ELIZABETH, educator, writer; b. Lincoln, Nebr.; d. Robert Harrison and Olive Esther (Bonar) Lowdon; B.A. cum laude, Hastings Coll., 1922; M.A., U. Nebr., 1928; postgrad. Middlebury Coll., summer 1945, U. Birmingham (Eng.) summers 1959, 61, 64. Script writer Radio KFAB-KFOR, Lincoln, Nebr., 1933-38; course writer, editor extension div. U. Nebr., Lincoln, 1938-52; chmn. dept. English, York Coll., Nebr., 1952-54; faculty English, Doane Coll., Crete, Nebr., 1954-55; asso. prof. English, Buena Vista Coll., Storm Lake, Iowa, 1958-62; prof. English, Aurora Coll., Ill., 1962-69; free lance writer, 1969—; editor Rho State Quar., 1945-52, Newsletter of Am. Guild Organists, Lincoln, 1973—. Mem. Am. Guild Organists, Nebr. Writers Guild, Musical Forum, Am. Guild Organists (hon. life), Sigma Tau Delta, Delta Kappa Gamma. Democrat. Congregationalist. Club: Tower. Contbr. articles to various mags. Address: 2232 S 15 St Lincoln NE 68502

LOWE, ADELE VIRGINIA (MRS. ALBERT ST. CLAIR LOWE), pharmacist; b. Indpls., June 27, 1919; d. Michael Angelo and Ivy Opal (Wilson) Lobraico; B.S. Indpls. Coll. Pharmacy, 1941; m. Albert St. Clair Lowe, Dec. 10, 1942; 1 dau., Judith A. (Mrs. Robert Frank Campbell). Chemist, E.I. duPont de Nemours & Co., Pryor, Okla., 1942-43; registered pharmacist Lobraico's Broad Ripple Pharmacy, Indpls., 1943—. Mem. Womens Orgn. Nat. Assn. Retail Druggists (pres. chpt. 20, 1977-79, chmn. legis. com.) Indpl. Assn. Retail Pharmacists, Broad Ripple Bus. and Profl. Womens Club, Lambda Kappa Sigma (mem. grand council, supr. Midwest region 1948-50, 66-68, supr. So. region 1958-60, 4th v.p. 1950-54, grand v.p. 1968-70, grand pres. 1970-74, mem.-at-large 1974-78, chmn. ednl. trust com. 1975—, hon. adv. 1978—, Disting. Service citation 1982). Clubs: Order Eastern Star, Daus. of Nile. Home: 6181 N Parker Ave Indianapolis IN 46220 Office: 902 E Westfield Blvd Indianapolis IN 46220

LOWE, ANNA EARLENE, nurse; b. Monroe County, Tenn., May 8, 1947; d. Arthur Earl and Anna Parlee (McJunkins) Beaty; Practical Nurse, 1966; R.N., Ft. Sander Presbyn. Hosp. Sch. Nursing, 1970; student U. Tenn., 1979—; m. David Lowe, Feb. 14, 1970; children—Michael David, Dianna Rene. Staff nurse ICU, U. Tenn. Meml. Hosp., Knoxville, 1970, staff nurse CCU, 1972, asst. head nurse, 1973, head nurse, 1973-79, critical care inservice coordinator, 1979—, instr. coronary care nursing workshop and arrhythmia identification, 1975—, ednl. coordinator for ambulatory care, 1982—. Cert. CPR instr. Mem. Am. Heart Assn. Baptist. Author: Arrhythmia Workbook, 1978. Office: U 40 1924 Alcoa Hwy Knoxville TN 37920

LOWE, CLAUDIA MARIE SANDERSON, psychiat. social worker; b. Memphis, Feb. 29, 1944; d. James Calhoun and Helen (Cone) Sanderson; B.A., Huntingdon Coll., 1965; postgrad. U. Mass., 1965-66, U. Tenn., 1970-71; M.S.W., U. Ill., 1976; m. Samuel Dennis Lowe, Apr. 4, 1966; children—Victoria, Clint. Psychiat. social worker Kankakee (Ill.) State Hosp., 1966-70; psychiat. social worker Riverside Med. Center, Kankakee, 1972-82, coordinator Riverside psychiat. day hosp. program, 1979-81, med. social worker, 1981-82; sch. social worker Kankakee Area Spl. Edn. Coop., 1982—. Registered social worker, Ill.; cert. social worker, Ill. Mem. Am. Assn. for Partial Hospitalization (editorial bd. 1982), Illiana Regional Assn. for Partial Hospitalization (chmn. 1981), Nat. Assn. Social Workers, Acad. Cert. Social Workers, Kankakee County Social Workers Assn. (corr. sec. 1978-79, mem. nominating com. 1980). Home: 764 Woodstock Ln Bourbonnais IL 60914 Office: Kankakee Area Spl Edn Coop Route 7 Box 339-A Kankakee IL 60901

LOWE, DOROTHY ANN, library technician; b. Gibson, N.C., Dec. 20, 1939; d. H. Bruce and Inez Campbell; B.S. in Media Tech., Fed. City Coll., 1975; M.S. in Media Sci., U. D.C., 1979; m. John Lowe, Jan. 18, 1958 (div. Dec. 1975); children—Donna, Steven, Inez. Personnel clk. FCC, 1972-76; microfilm photographer Library of Congress, Washington, 1976-77, personnel clk., 1977, library technician, 1977—. Pres., Pentecostal Ch. Missionaries, 1974—. Recipient letter of commendation FCC, 1976. Mem. Library of Congress Afro-Am. Culture Club, D.C. Library Assn., U. D.C. Alumni Assn. Democrat. Home: 923 Barnstable Ct Crofton MD 21114 Office: 10 1st St SE Washington DC 20540

LOWE, ETHEL BLACK, artist; b. Kiowa County, Okla., Jan. 30, 1904; d. Benjamin Alonzo and Harriet Ann (Heaton) Black; B.A., Central State U., Okla., 1926; M.A., U. Tulsa, 1937; postgrad. U. Okla., U. Colo., Columbia, U. Hawaii; m. William Glenn Lowe, June 5, 1939 (dec. 1942). Tchr. pub. schs., Okla., 1922-39, N.Y., 1942-49, 50-68, ret.; teaching prin. Dragon Sch., Sasebo, Kyushu, Japan, 1949-50; works exhibited 1945—; exhbns. include Nat. Assn. Women Artists, 1953, 55, 71, 75, 77, Terry Nat. Art Exhibit, 1952, Provincetown Art Assn., 1952-53, Nassau Community Coll., 1971. Reproductions of works in newspapers, mags. Mem. N.Y. State Ret. Tchrs. Assn., Nat. Assn. Women Artists, Am. Watercolor Soc., Nat. Ret. Tchrs. Assn., Delta Kappa Gamma. Home: 48-50 44th St Woodside NY 11377

LOWE, HELEN WINONA, educator; b. Weaverville, Calif., Feb. 21, 1936; d. Walter William and M. Winona (Starkey) Heffington; B.S., Tex. Woman's U., Denton, 1959; M.B.A., N. Tex. State U., Denton, 1965; children—Walter Richard, William Davis. Instr., Midwestern State U., Wichita Falls, Tex., 1962-65, Angelo State U., San Angelo, Tex., 1967-69; asst. prof. bus. edn. N.Mex. Highlands U., Las Vegas, 1972-75, Sul Ross State U., Alpine, Tex., 1977-79, founder Bus. Awards Program, 1978; asst. prof. bus. Eastern Oreg. State Coll., 1979—, also coordinator secretarial sci. bus. edn.; cons., guest lectr. in field. Hon. mem. Nat. Secs. Assn., Phi Chi Theta. Mem. Nat. Bus. Edn. Assn., Am. Mgmt. Assn., Am. Vocat. Assn., AAUP, Southwestern Adminstrv. Services Assn. (charter), Am. Records Mgmt. Assn., Nat. Assn. Female Execs., Nat. Assn. Bus. Tchr. Educators, Tex. Bus. Edn. Assn. (Dist. Post Secondary Bus. Tchr. of Year 1978), Tex. Assn. Coll. Tchrs., Tex. Bus. Tchrs. Edn. Council. Republican. Methodist. Clubs: Gourmet, Women's of Am., Garden. Author papers in field. Office: Sch Profl Studies La Grande OR 97850

LOWE, JEAN HOLMES, educator; b. Highland Park, Ill., Jan. 1, 1941; d. John Russell and Clara Jean (Bullard) Holmes; B.A. in Anthropology, U. Calif. Berkeley, 1963; M.Ed., U. Va., 1981; m. Pardee Lowe, Jr., Jan. 26, 1963; children—Alice Bailey, Andrew Russell, Edward Dickinson, Carol Brainerd. Social worker County of Contra Costa, Calif., 1963-65; research asst. depts. consumer econs., transp., and oral history Cornell U., Ithaca, N.Y., 1966-74; dir. adult edn. Fairfax County Adult Detention Center, Fairfax, Va., 1975-79; coordinator adult basic edn. Fairfax County, 1979—; vol. dir. edn. Woodbridge Correctional Unit, State of Va. Bd. dirs. Tompkins County (N.Y.) Co-op. Extension, 1969-74, Tompkins County LWV, 1968-74; bd. dirs. ACLU of Va., 1978—, pres. No. Va. chpt., 1980-82; counselor Offender Aid and Restoration of Fairfax, 1974—; founder, chmn. Support Group for Va. Prisoners. Mem. Literacy Council No. Va., Va. Assn. Children with Learning Disabilities, No. Va. Mental Health Assn. (treas., pres. 1981-82), Am. Correctional Assn., Va. Correctional Assn., Nat. Council Crime and Delinquency, Correctional Edn. Assn. Founder state orgn. to aid parolees. Contbr. articles to profl. jours. Home: 7803 Sycamore Dr Falls Church VA 22042 Office: 7423 Camp Alger Ave Falls Church VA 22042

LOWE, MARY JOHNSON, fed. judge; b. N.Y.C., June 10, 1924; B.A., Hunter Coll., 1952; J.D., Bklyn. Law Sch., 1954; LL.M., Columbia U., 1955; children by previous marriage—Edward H., Leslie H.; m. Ivan A. Michael, Nov. 4, 1961; 1 dau., Bess J. Michael. Admitted to N.Y. State bar, 1955; practiced law, N.Y.C., 1955-71; judge N.Y.C. Criminal Ct., 1972-73; acting justice N.Y. State Supreme Ct., 1973-77, justice, 1st Jud. Dist., 1978; judge U.S. Dist. Ct. for So. Dist. N.Y., 1978—. Recipient award for outstanding service to criminal justice system Bronx County Criminal Cts. Bar Assn., 1974, award for work on narcotics cases Asst. Dist. Attys., 1974. Mem. Women in Criminal Justice, Harlem Lawyers Assn., Bronx Criminal Lawyers Assn., N.Y. County Lawyers Assn., Bronx County Bar Assn., N.Y. State Bar Assn. (award for outstanding jud. contbn. to criminal justice Sect. Criminal Justice 1978), NAACP, Nat. Urban League, Nat. Council Negro Women, NOW. Office: US Dist Ct Foley Sq New York NY 10007 *

LOWENHERTZ, EDITH, social worker; b. N.Y.C., June 6, 1913; d. Samuel and Rose (Goldstein) L.; B.S., N.Y. U., 1951; M.S.W., U. Pa., 1953. Family caseworker Jewish Family Service Phila., 1953-55; field rep. Chatham (Pa.) Acres Convalescent Home, 1955-56; sr. caseworker Assn. Jewish Children, Phila., 1956-58; psychiat. casework supr. Pa. Eastern Diagnosis and Evaluation Center, Phila., 1959-61; spl. project caseworker Episcopal Community Services, Phila., 1962-63; casework supr. Children's Home Burlington County, Mt. Holly, N.J., 1963-66, Family Service, Camden, N.J., 1966-68, sch. social worker Deptford (N.J.) Spl. Services, 1968-72, Lenape Regional High Sch. Dist., Medford, N.J., 1973-80; ret., 1980; mem. Mt. Laurel Twp. Local Assistance Bd., 1970—. Served with WAC, 1943-46. Mem. Nat. Assn. Social Workers (unit treas. 1967), Acad. Cert. Social Workers, Council Sch. Social Workers, NEA, N.J. Assn. Sch. Social Workers (rep.), N.J. Edn. Assn., Burlington County Edn. Assn., Otto Rank Assn., Mt. Laurel Homeowners Assn. (chmn. membership com. 1965), Gray Panthers. Home: RD 2 Hartford Rd Mt Laurel NJ 08054

LOWENSTEIN, ARLENE JANE, nursing adminstr.; b. Phila., Oct. 10, 1936; d. Nathan M. and Rae (Greenburg) Needleman; diploma Hosp. U. Pa., 1957; B.S., Fairleigh Dickinson U., 1969; M.A., N.Y. U., 1974; m. Manfred Lowenstein, June 9, 1957; children—Jay David, Russell Scott. Instr. maternity and pediatric nursing Hosp. U. Pa., Phila., 1957-59; staff nurse Einstein Med. Center, Phila., 1959-69; instr. and staff nurse Albany (N.Y.) Med. Center, 1964-66; instr. Middlesex County Coll., Edison, N.J., 1970-72, Fairleigh Dickinson U., Rutherford, N.J., 1967-69; maternity supr. Middlesex Gen. Hosp., New Brunswick, N.J., 1972-74; acting dir. nursing Peter Bent Brigham Hosp., Boston, 1974—; asso. faculty Simmons Coll., 1977-81, also dir. adult nurse practitioner program, 1974-77, primary care grad. nursing program, 1977-81; asso. hosp. dir./dir. nursing service U. Ky. Med. Center, Lexington, 1981—. Mem. Am., Mass. nurses assns., Health Planning Council Greater Boston, Am. Public Health Assn., LWV (chpt. dir. 1977-78). Home: 500 Laketower Dr #90 Lexington KY 40502 Office: U Ky Med Center 800 Rose St Lexington KY 40502

LOWERS, PATRICIA ANN, data processing exec.; b. Detroit, Jan. 11, 1941; d. Louis and Frances (Wilder) Krakow; B.S. in Biology, Wayne State U., 1964; student in mgmt. tng. Lansing Community Coll., 1977-78; student various tech. data processing courses IBM, Burroughs, Univac, 1966—; m. James Allen Lowers, Feb. 24, 1973; 1 son, Randall. Lab. technician Detroit Inst. Cancer Research, 1964-65; programmer-systems analyst Detroit Data Processing Co., 1965-69; systems analyst Oakland U., 1969-71, instr. data processing, 1971-79; project mgr. data processing Mich. Supreme Ct., 1972-75; data processing mgr. Mich. Dept. Mental Health, Northville, 1976-79; mgr. data processing Flecto Co., Inc., Oakland, Calif., 1979—; instr. data processing Oakland Community Coll., Birmingham, Mich., 1976. Pres., Citizens for Survival, Oak Park, Mich., 1971-72. Mem. Nat. Assn. Female Execs., Am. Mgmt. Assn., Assn. Small Systems Users, ACLU, Calif. Save the Otters Assn., Smithsonian Inst., Jacque Cousteau Soc., Delta Phi Epsilon (pres. 1963). Home: 221 Daylight Pl Danville CA 94526 Office: 1000 45th St Oakland CA 94608

LOWERY, NANCY ALBRIGHT, educator; b. Monroe, La., Dec. 14, 1939; d. Ira Clay and Frances Adelia (Maxey) Albright; B.S., Northwestern State U., 1960; M.S., Emory U., 1964; m. Oliver Powell Lowery, Jr., July 9, 1966; children—Clay Patrick, Katherine Elise, John Oliver. Gen. staff nurse, La., N.J., 1961-63; faculty U. Tenn. Coll. Nursing, Memphis,

1964-66; faculty N.E. La. U. Sch. Nursing, Monroe, 1968—, mem. bd. nursing, 1976—, assoc. prof. nursing, pres. bd. nursing, 1981-82; item writer Nat. State Bd. Test Pool Exam, 1976, 77; lectr. in field. Officer, Riverfield Acad. Parents Club, 1980-81; trustee, catechism instr. Sacred Heart Cath. Ch., 1978—. Mem. La. Nurses Assn., Am. Nurses Assn., AAUW. Roman Catholic. Home: Route 5 Box 111 Rayville LA 71269 Office: NE La Univ Sch of Nursing Monroe LA 71201

LOWINGER, BARBARA BALLO, nurse; b. Ashtabula, Ohio, Nov. 2, 1943; d. Frank Edmond and Ellen Irene (Niemi) Ballo; grad. Fairview Park Hosp. Sch. Nursing, Cleve., 1964; student Kent State U., 1965, Case Western Res. U., 1967, U. Wis., Green Bay, 1982—; m. John A. Vincenzo, Nov. 20, 1965 (div.); children—Jonathon David, Ryan Michael; m. 2d, Terry A. Lowinger, June 7, 1980; 1 dau., Sara Ellen. Staff nurse Fairview Park Hosp., Cleve., 1964, Ashtabula Gen. Hosp., 1965, Euclid (Ohio) Gen. Hosp., 1965-66; staff nurse Mt. Sinai Hosp., Cleve., 1966-69, asst. head nurse kidney dialysis center, 1969-71, head nurse, 1971-81; research interviewer Nat. Hospice Study, Brown U., 1981-82; nursing supr. Bellin Meml. Hosp., Green Bay, 1982—; instr. Cleve. State U., 1973-74; mem. renal tech. adv. com. Kolff Found., Cleve., 1975-76. Mem. Am. Assn. Nephrology Nurses-Technicians, Transplant Soc. N.E. Ohio (membership chmn. 1977-78), Kidney Found. Ohio (mem. chpt. relations com. 1976-78, profl. edn. com. 1975-79, trustee 1975-79), Fairview Park Hosp. Alumni Assn. Lutheran. Author articles in field. Office: 744 S Webster Green Bay WI 54302

LOWMAN, MARY BETHENA HEMPHILL (MRS. ZELVIN D. LOWMAN), civic worker, realtor, former educator; b. Lewis, Kans., Feb. 10, 1922; d. Frederick William and Gladys (Follin) Hemphill; A.B., Western State Coll., Colo., 1945; m. Zelvin D. Lowman, Oct. 24, 1943; children—Freda Ruth (Mrs. Douglas Farr), James Fredrick, William Martin, Elizabeth June (Mrs. Joseph Herbst). Tchr., Stout Creek Sch., Colo., 1942-43, San Diego City Sch. Dist., 1944-45, Los Angeles City Sch. Dist., 1948-50; pvt. sch. tchr. So. Inst. Music, 1956-57. Troop leader Frontier council Girl Scouts U.S.A., 1957-70, mem. exec. bd., 1961-73, 2d v.p., 1962-63, pres., 1968-71, recipient Thanks Badge, 1964, chmn. established camp com., 1963-67, dir. Camp Foxtail, 1965, 67, mem. Girl Scouts U.S.A. Region VI Com., 1973-75, chmn. Region VI Com., mem. nat. bd., mem. exec. com. and councils com., 1975-78; mem. Am. Field Service Exchange Student Bd. So. Nev., 1961. Parliamentarian, West Chartleston PTA, 1957-59, Nev. Congress, 1960-61; chmn. Christian Edn. Commn., 1964-65; chmn. Commn. on Mission of Church, 1966; chmn. exec. com. Clark County Bicentennial Commn., 1974-76. Family chosen as Nev. All-Am. Family, 1960. Mem. Gen. Fedn. Women's Clubs (dir. 1958-60, 62-64, 72-78, chmn. scholarships and student aid 1974-76, chmn. family living div., 1976-78; treas. Western States Conf. 1968-70, sec. 1970-72, pres. 1972-74), Nev. Fedn. Women's, Clubs, (past pres.), Md. fedn. women's Clubs (past jr. dir.), Clark County Pan-Hellenic Assn., So. Nev. Alumni Club (pres. 1961-62), Internat. Platform Assn. Presbyterian (elder). Clubs: Las Vegas Mesquite (past pres.); Jr. Women's (past pres.) (College Park, Md.); Newcomers (past pres.), Nat. Presbyterian Mariners; (past pres.), Nevada-Sierra District Mariners; Las Vegas Nautilus Mariners. Home: 1713 Rambla Ct Las Vegas NV 89102

LOWRANCE, MURIEL EDWARDS, data analyst; b. Ada, Okla., Dec. 28, 1922; d. Warren E. and Mayme E. (Barrick) Edwards; B.S. in Edn., East Central State U., Ada, 1954; 1 dau., Kathy Lynn Lowrance Gutierrez. Accountant, adminstrv. asst. to bus. mgr. E. Central State U., Ada, 1950-68; grants and contracts specialist U. N.Mex. Sch. Medicine, Albuquerque, 1968-72, data analyst dept. orthopaedics, 1975—; asst. adminstrv. officer N.Mex. Regional Med. Program, 1972-75. Bd. dirs. Vocat. Rehab. Center, 1980—. Cert. profl. contract mgr. Nat. Contract Assn. Mem. Am. Bus. Women's Assn. (past pres. El Segundo chpt., Woman of Yr. 1974), AAUW, Amigos de las Americas (dir.). Democrat. Methodist. Club: Pilot (pres. 1979-80) (Albuquerque). Home: 3028 Mackland Ave NE Albuquerque NM 87106 Office: Dept Orthopaedics U NMex Sch Medicine Albuquerque NM 87131

LOWREY, SARA NELLE, writer, film producer; b. Gatesville, Tex., Oct. 6, 1949; d. Oliver Wendell and Nelle (Goodall) Lowrey; B. Journalism, U. Tex., 1971; postgrad. So. Meth. U., 1972-73; m. Donald J. Mackie, Apr. 6, 1974; 1 dau., Anna Kathleen. Gen. assignments reporter, anchorperson Sta. KDFW-TV, Dallas, 1972-74; gen. assignments reporter, 6 o'clock anchor person Sta. KPRC-TV, Houston, 1974-78, weekend anchorperson, 1979-80; prin. Lowrey Assos., Gatesville, 1978—. Cons. Tex. press office George Bush for Pres. Campaign, 1979; bd. dirs. Coryell Meml. Hosp. Aux., 1980-82. Recipient Addy award-1st place for TV comml., 1980; 1st place award for documentary on childbirth Tex. Public Health Assn., 1977; Sch. Bell award, Tex. State Tchrs. Assn., 1973. Mem. Soc. Profl. Journalists, Women in Communication, Chi Omega. Presbyterian. Home: Jonesboro Star Route Gatesville TX 76528 Office: 116 N Lutterloh Ave Gatesville TX 76528

LOWRY, BETTY HAMILTON, civic leader; b. Memphis, Nov. 15, 1923; d. Vaun C. and Myrtle Peterson Hamilton; student U. Tenn., 1942-43; m. C. C. Lowry; children—Duane, Conielyn. Research technician Vanderbilt Hosp., Nashville, 1943-45; sec.-treas. Calloway County Democratic Com., 1972-76, committeewoman 2d precinct, 1972-76; dist. chmn. Gubernatorial Dem. Campaign, 1972, Congl. campaign, 1974; mem. Ky. Dem. Central Com., 1980—; mem. Ky. Council on Higher Edn., 1962-66; chmn. Western Ky. Regional Mental Health and Mental Retardation Bd., 1972—, chmn. personnel com., 1964-66, mem. affiliate liaison com., 1962-64, chmn. exec. com., 1972-76, chmn. personnel com., mem. community relations com., 1977-78; mem. Murray (Ky.) City Council, 1970-72; sec. Murray Civic Music Assn., 1959-78; mother patroness Alpha Sigma Alpha Sorority, Murray State U., 1959-78; mem. Gray Ladies, ARC, 1946-62; chmn. U.S. for March of Dimes, 1974-76; vol. women's advisor Ky. March of Dimes, 1974-78; coordinator Calloway County Bicentennial, 1973-76; mem. Ky. Commn. on Human Rights, 1977—; mem. Ky. Children's Service Task Force, Council for Health Services, 1977-79; mem. Jackson Purchase Mus. Com., 1974-79; mem. Calloway County and Regional Devel. Disability Service Assn., 1970-72; mem. project rev. com. Health Systems Agy. W. Ky., 1980—. Named Ky. col., 1962, 69; recipient Ky. Mental Health Assn. award, 1966; Ky. Heart Assn. award, 1966; commd. Louisville Ambassador of Good Will, 1967, Lexington Ambassador of Good Will, 1967; named Citizen of Yr., Murray C. of C., 1977; recipient Lovey Raburn Meml. award Western Ky. Regional Mental Health and Mental Retardation Bd., 1979. Mem. Calloway County Med. Aux. (pres. 1952-57), Ky. Med. Assn. (dir. 1968), Ky. Med. Aux. (state communications chmn. 1974-76), Alpha Lambda Delta. Democrat. United Methodist (mem. choir 1963-78, dir. united campus ministry 1964-69, v.p. United Ch. Women, 1962, jr. high sch. Sunday sch. tchr. 1974-76, mem. council ministries, chmn. social concerns com. 1973-75). Clubs: Murray Country (sec. 1962-66), Murray Magazine (pres. 1972-74), Murray Woman's (pres. 1962-64, mem. adv. council 1964—), Ky. Fedn. Women's Clubs (1st v.p. 1965-66, pres. 1966-68, mem. past pres.'s council 1968—), Ky. State Golf Assn. (pres. 1968-72), Tri-State Golf Assn. (pres. 1962-66), Trans-Miss. Golf Assn. (Ky. rep. 1962-66), Murray Country Club Golf Assn. (chmn. 1976). Address: 1010 West Gate Dr Murray KY 42071

LOWRY, EVELYN BERNETTE NICHOLLS, bldg. contracting co. exec.; b. Cleve., Sept. 20, 1929; d. Albert William and Ruth Bernette (Whittaker) Nicholls; B.A., Western Res. U., 1952; cert. Acad. Computer Tech. 1968; m. Charles Glenn Lowry, Aug. 12, 1949; children—Kathleen Bernette Lowry Eaves, Linda Jeannette Lowry Lauderdale, Patricia Sue. Partner, Glenn Chem. Co., Inc., Cleve., 1955-63; pres. Comml. Property Exchange, Inc., Houston, 1963-74; dir. Nurses Aide Tng. Orgn., Inc., Houston, 1974-78; pres. Hit Products, Inc., Houston, 1978—. Fellow Nat. Inst. Credit; mem. Nat. Remodeling Assn. (housing adv. panel 1981), Houston Assn. Credit Mgmt., Houston Credit Women's Group, Tex. Farm Bur. Republican. Presbyterian. Home: 8200 Westview St Houston TX 77055 Office: PO Box 55075 Houston TX 77055

LOWRY, MARGARET ANN, accountant; b. San Francisco, May 6, 1925; d. David Frazer and Ovidia Ansbro (Strom) Bush; A.B., San Jose State Coll., 1948; 1 son, James Ansbro Young. Acct., office mgr. Kaiser Motors, Palo Alto and Oakland, Calif., 1949-51; asst. acct. Housing Authority County San Joaquin, 1951-58; planner Advance Planning Staff Stanislaus County, Modesto, Calif., 1958-60; planner City of Stockton (Calif.), 1960; sec.-treas. Henry Wolters & Son, Inc., Stockton, 1960—; v.p. Metalgraphics, Inc., Stockton. Sec.-treas., Stockton Police Youth Activities, 1974-78. Served with WAVES, 1945-46. Pub. acct., Calif. Republican. Methodist. Club: Soroptimist (past pres.; Loretta Doneux award 1976-77). Home: 17 W Pardee Ln Stockton CA 95207 Office: 888 E Lindsay St Stockton CA 95202

LOWRY, PATRICIA KATHLEEN, educator; b. Chgo., Apr. 29, 1928; d. Robert Beardsley Fredrick and Kathleen Cleola (Heilman) Hardy; B.A., Ball State U., 1951, M.A., 1964, Ed.D., 1968; postgrad. Bowling Green State U., Sam Houston State U.; m. Douglas Lowry, Aug. 23, 1948; children—Fredrick Robert Hugh, Patricia Marjorie. Tchr. English and social studies various elem. and high schs., Ind., Ohio, and Tex.; now mem. faculty Coll. of Edn., Sam Houston State U., Huntsville, Tex.; poetry judge, ednl. cons., lectr. in field. Leader Girl Scouts U.S.A., 4-H, Campfire Girls; bd dirs. Deep E. Tex. Council Govts., Huntsville Leadership Inst.; mem. citizens rev. com. Huntsville Item; asst. chaplain Tex. Dept. Corrections. Recipient Outstanding Alumnus award Ball State U./Kappa Delta Pi, 1977. Mem. Internat. Reading Assn., Assn. Supervision and Curriculum Devel., Early Reading Research Council, Tex. Assn. Profs. of Reading, NEA, Internat. Congress on Arts and Communication, AAUW, AAUP, Tex. Assn. Tchr. Educators, Tex. Assn. for Improvement Reading, NOW, Tex. Women for ERA, Am. Quarterhorse Assn., Am. Poultrymen, Bulldog Club Am., Audubon Soc., Delta Sigma Theta. Christian Scientist. Clubs: Order Eastern Star, Bus. and Profl. Women. Author: Handbook for Parents of Kindergartners, 1964; Teacher Evaluation, 1968; contbr. articles to profl. jours.; author reports on literacy edn. in Indonesia. Home: Lowry Ln Route 3 Box 13 Huntsville TX 77340 Office: Coll Edn Sam Houston State Univ Huntsville TX 77341

LOWTHER, ELOUISE LUCILLE, Realtor; b. Fairmont, W.Va., Dec. 17, 1928; d. Felix Lee and Minnie May (Jarrett) Springer; Grad. Realtors Inst., U. Va., 1974; m. Ermine Guy Lowther, 1948; children—Mark Alan, Timothy Lynn. Salesperson, Colborn Real Estate Agy., Inc., Fairmont, 1972-79; owner, broker Lowther Real Estate Fairmont, W.Va., 1979—; intr. real estate W.Va. Career Coll., 1976-77. Exec. sec. N. Central W.Va. Youth Assn., 1969—. Cert. residential specialist. Mem. Nat. Assn. Realtors (dir. 1982—), W.Va. Assn. Realtors (dir. 1979-80, Women's Council Realtors (gov. W.Va. 1979), Fairmont Bd. Realtors (pres. 1980), Omega Tau Rho. Republican. Baptist. Home and office: 1328 Jo Harry Dr Fairmont WV 26554

LOWY, BARBARA SUSAN, restaurant exec.; b. Lancaster, Pa., June 4, 1941; d. Hugh Marion and Edna Erna (Bair) L.; R.N., Lancaster Gen. Hosp., 1962. Staff nurse operating room Lancaster Gen. Hosp., 1962-64; supr. operating room Lancaster Osteo. Hosp., 1964-66; staff nurse Maynard McDougal Meml. Hosp., Nome, Alaska, 1967-68; head nurse, asst. dir. nursing USPHS Hosp. Kanakanak, Dillingham, Alaska, 1969-81; partner The Captain's Table restaurant, 1981—; instr. 1st aid, CPR; owner Su-ir Cake Top, cake decorating, 1970—. Councilwoman, Dillingham, 1976—, acting mayor, 1978. Mem. Assn. Operating Room Nurses, ARC, Alaska Heart Assn., Mcpl. League, Dillingham C. of C., Beta Sigma Phi. Republican. Mem. Moravian Ch. Address: Box 64 Dillingham AK 99576

LOY, MYRNA, actress; b. Helena, Mont., Aug. 2, 1905; d. David Franklin and Della Williams; grad. Venice (Calif.) High Sch., Westlake Sch. Girls. Appeared in numerous motion pictures, including Wife Versus Secretary, Petticoat Fever, The Great Ziegfeld, Libeled Lady, The Thin Man, After the Thin Man, Parnell, Double Wedding, Man Proof, To Mary-With Love, Test Pilot, Too Hot to Handle, The Rains Came, Best Years of Our Lives (award World Film Festival, Brussels), The Bachelor and the Bobby Soxer, Mr. Blanding Builds His Dream House, If This Be Sin, Cheaper by the Dozen, Airport 75, The End, Just Tell Me What You Want, others; appeared in stage plays Marriage Go Round, There Must Be A Pony, Dear Love, Good Housekeeping, Janus, Don Juan in Hell, The Women, Barefoot in the Park, Relative Speaking; TV appearances in Death Takes a Holiday, 1971, also Do Not Fold, Spindle or Mutilate, Indict and Convict, Columbo, Ironsides, Family Affair, The Virginian, The Couple Takes a Wife, It Happened at Lakewood Manor, Summer Solstice. Organizer, Hollywood Film com. U.S. Nat. Commn. for UNESCO, 1948, mem. commn., 1950-54; asst. head welfare activities ARC, N.Y. area, 1941-45. Mem. Am. Assn. UN, Nat. Commn. Against Discrimination in Housing. *

LOZANO, AMY SUE, violinist; b. Eugene, Oreg., Sept. 26, 1956; d. Arthur Hadley and Elizabeth Ann (Van de Visse) L.; Mus.B., San Francisco Conservatory Music, 1978. Mem. faculty prep. dept. San Francisco Conservatory Music, 1974-76; mem. 1st violin sect. Aspen (Colo.) Chamber Orch., 1975-76; prin. 2d violin N.Y. String Orch., N.Y.C., Christmas 1975, 76; concertmistress San Francisco Conservatory Orch., 1976-77; mem. violin sect. San Francisco Symphony, 1977—; 2d violinist Aurora String Quartet, San Francisco, 1979—; fellow Aspen Music Festival, 1975, 76; tchr.'s aide Antioch Fellowship Sch., South San Francisco. Recipient 1st Pl. award Coleman Chamber Music Competition, 1977; Julia Klumpkey Music award, 1975; Rockefeller scholar, 1974-75. Mem. Chamber Music Am., Internat. Conf. Symphony Orch. Mems., Am. Fedn. Musicians. Office: Davies Symphony Hall San Francisco CA 94102

LOZOWSKI, MARY, cytotechnologist; b. Bronx, N.Y., Oct. 9, 1953; d. William and Mary Charlotte (Kapustka) Lozowski; B.S., Fordham U., 1976; postgrad. Sch. Cytotechnology, Meml. Sloan-Kettering Cancer Center, 1974-75, Hofstra U., 1978. Staff cytotechnologist, cons., lectr. J.F. K. Meml. Hosp. and Med. Center, Monrovia, Liberia, 1976-77; cytology supr. dept. pathology Nassau Hosp., Mineola, N.Y., 1978—; lectr. in field. Mem. Internat. Acad. Cytology, Am. Soc. Clin. Pathologists, Am. Soc. Cytology, Greater N.Y. Assn. Cytotechnologists, AAAS. Clubs: Kosciuszko Found., Polish Am. Mus. Found. Contbr. articles to profl. jours. Address: Pathology Dept Cytology Div Nassau Hosp 259 First St Mineola NY 11501

LUA, MICHELLE ANN, govt. ofcl.; b. Paradise, Calif., Feb. 15, 1950; d. Raymond E. and Bettydean (Thomas) L.; B.A., Gonzaga U., 1972; postgrad. Calif. State U., Sacramento, 1973, Calif. State U., San Jose, 1975. Tchr. St. Mary's (Alaska) High Sch., 1972-73, San Juan Sch., Elk Grove Sch., Sacramento., 1973-74; office auditor IRS, San Jose, Calif., 1974-78, office exam. group mgr., Santa Rosa, Calif., 1978—. Recipient sustained superior performance awards IRS, 1980, 81. Mem. Nat. Assn. Female Execs., Kappa Delta Pi, Gamma Pi Epsilon. Office: 777 Sonoma Ave Room 112 Santa Rosa CA 95404

LUBCHENCO, LULA OLGA, pediatrician; b. Namangon, Turkestan, Russian, Apr. 21, 1915; d. Alexis Eleaser and Portia Mary (McKnight) L.; A.B., Denver U., 1936; M.D., U. Colo., 1939; m. Carl J. Josephson, Mar. 23, 1940; children—Patricia, Johanna, Karen, Gretchen. Rotating intern U. Colo. Health Scis. Center, Denver, 1939-40, intern in pediatrics Strong Meml. Hosp., Rochester, N.Y., 1940-41; resident in pediatrics Children's Hosp., Denver, 1941-42, 43-44, chief resident, 1942, 43-44, fellow in pediatric research, 1945; practice medicine specializing in pediatrics, Denver, 1942-43; assoc. dept. pediatrics U. Colo. Health Scis. Center, 1943-44, instr., 1944-51, asst. prof. pediatrics, 1951-61, assoc. prof., 1961-69, prof., 1969-77, prof. emerita, 1977—, pediatrician in charge Premature Infant Center, 1949-62, Newborn Services, 1962-65, co-dir. Newborn Service, Div. Perinatal Medicine, 1965-77, mem. Devel. Psychobiology Research Group dept. psychiatry, 1977—; mem. staff Univ. Hosp., Children's Hosp., Rose Med. Center, Denver Gen. Hosp.; med. adv. com. La Leche League, Denver, 1974—; med. assoc. La Leche League Internat., 1975—; mem. adv. com. Infant Devel. Program, United Cerebral Palsy Denver, 1977—; mem. adv. bd. Resources in Human Nurturing, 1977—; mem. task force Colo. Developmental Disabilities Council, 1979—; numerous vis. professorships, including U. Chile, Santiago, 1964, Pan Am. Health Orgn., Hospital Roberto del Rio, Santiago, 1968, U. Maracaibo (Venezuela), 1970, U. Autónoma, Guadalajara, Mex., 1974. Active, Girl Scouts U.S.A.; instr. in first aid, sailing ARC, Denver. Recipient 3d ann. Eleanor Roosevelt Meml. award Denver chpt. Hadassah, 1964; Women Physician of Yr. award Nat. Bd. Med. Coll. Pa., 1973; St. Scholastica Acad. award, 1975; Disting. Service award ARC, 1976, Children's Hosp. award in family health Mead Johnson Labs., 1976, 77, 78; Silver and Gold award U. Colo. Alumni, 1977; Hannah G. Solomon award Nat. Council Jewish Women, 1979; Weinstein-Goldenson award United Cerebral Palsy Assn., 1982; diplomate Am. Bd. Pediatrics. Mem. Am. Acad. Pediatrics, Am. Pediatric Soc., Soc. Pediatric Research, Western Soc. Pediatric Research, Rocky Mountain Pediatric Soc., AMA, Colo. Med. Soc. (Robbins award 1969), Denver Med. Soc., Soc. Research in Child Devel., Childbirth Preparation Assn. Colo., Alumni Assn. U. Colo. Health Scis. Center (exec. com. 1968—), Alpha Omega Alpha. Methodist. Author: The High-Risk Infant, 1976; contbr. numerous articles, chpts., abstracts to prof. publs.; mem. adv. bd. Keeping Abreast Jour., 1976—. Office: Newborn Service B-195 University Hosp 4200 E 9th Ave Denver CO 80262

LUBER, MARY LOU HATHAWAY, hotel exec.; b. Crestline, Ohio, Sept. 11, 1927; d. Sidney H. and Pearl (Yetter) Schoemer; A.A., Our Lady of Cin. Coll., 1945; student Orange Coast Coll., 1951; m. Herman P. Luber, June 16, 1979; children by previous marriage—Peter, Colleen, Maureen Hathaway. Controller, Milwaukee Inn, 1961-63; asst. mgr. Port O Call, St. Petersburg, Fla., 1964-69; food and beverage mgr. St. Petersburg Hilton, 1969-72; gen. mgr. Sheraton Lakeside Inn, Kissimmee, Fla., 1972-75; gen. mgr. Continental Services Corp. Miami, also Elizabeth, N.J., 1978-82, now v.p. ops.; advisor Essex Coll. Hotel Sch., 1978-80. Named Sheraton Mgr. of Yr., 1979; recipient Spl. award Internat. Geneve Assn., 1979. Mem. Union County C. of C., N.J. Hotel Motel Assn. (v.p.), Nat. Restaurant Assn. Democrat. Roman Catholic. Clubs: Soroptimists, Union County Women's. Office: 901 Spring St Sheraton Newark Airport Elizabeth NJ 07201

LUBIN, AMY, psychiat. social worker; b. N.Y.C., Oct. 24, 1935; d. Kevie and Vera (Issacs) Schwartz; B.A., Wellesley Coll., 1956; M.A., U. Chgo., 1975; m. Donald Gilbert Lubin, Feb. 2, 1956; children—Peter, Richard, Thomas, Alice. Tchr., Francis Parker Sch., Chgo., 1956-60, Senn High Sch., Chgo., 1960-62, Deerfield (Ill.) High Sch., 1970-71; psychiat. social worker div. psychiatry Children's Meml. Hosp., Chgo., 1975—. Governing life mem. Art Inst. Chgo.; women's bd. Field Mus., Northwestern U. Ford Found. grantee, 1960-62; Woodrow Wilson fellow, 1976. Mem. Nat. Assn. Social Workers, Acad. Cert. Social Workers. Author book revs. Home: 2269 Egandale Rd Highland Park IL 60035 Office: 710 Fullerton Pkwy Chicago IL 60614

LUBLINER, TAMARA EVA, social worker; b. Brussels, Belgium, May 5, 1948; came to U.S., 1951, naturalized, 1957; d. David and Helen (Laznowski) L.; B.A., Syracuse U., 1970; M.S.W., Cath. U., 1977; m. John Walters, June 20, 1976; children— Aaron Zvi, Avram Michel. Adminstrv. asst. Psychiat. Inst. Found., Center Group Studies, 1970-77, mem. faculty, 1972-77; group counselor Walden Resources, 1971-74; group psychotherapist Luth. Social Services, Washington, 1974-76; pvt. practice group, individual, and family psychotherapy, 1975—; clin. social worker Taylor Manor Hosp., Ellicott City, Md., 1977—; guest lectr. family therapy Cath. U., 1979; field supr. U. Md., 1980—. Mem. Nat. Assn. Social Workers, Acad. Cert. Social Workers. Office: Taylor Manor Hosp Ellicott City MD 21043

LUCAS, CAROL, gerontologist; b. Hewlett, L.I., N.Y., July 11, 1929; d. Irving William and Julia (Cutler) Lucas; B.S., Coll. William and Mary, 1949; M.A., Columbia U., 1951, Ed.D., 1953. Field dir. Greater N.Y. council Girl Scouts U.S.A., N.Y.C., 1949-51; recreation dir. Neponsit (N.Y.) Beach Hosp., 1951-53; cons. Nat. Council Jewish Women, N.Y.C., 1954-55; area coordinator Los Angeles County Heart Assn., Los Angeles, 1955-56; rehab. cons. City of Hope, Duarte, Calif., 1955-56, Los Angeles Tb and Health Assn., 1957-58; recreation cons. Fedn. Protestant Welfare Agys., N.Y.C., 1958-60; instr. Columbia, 1959—; dir. spl. pilot study in gerontology, N.Y.C., 1958-64; exec. dir. Five Towns Sr. Center; supr. adminstrn. on aging project Sr. Center of Nassau County, Uniondale, N.Y.; dir. services for aging Town of Hempstead (N.Y.), 1968—, commr., 1978—. Mem. Am. Recreation Soc., Nat. Assn. Social Workers, Nat. Recreation Assn., Acad. Cert. Social Workers, Royal Soc. Health (London), Kappa Delta Pi, Delta Psi Omega. Author: (with Josephine Rathbone) Recreation in Total Rehabilitation, 1958; Recreation Activity Development in Nursing Home, Homes for the Aging and Hospitals, 1962; Recreation in Gerontology, 1963. Contbr. articles to profl. jours. Home: 141 Wyckoff Pl Woodmere NY 11598 Office: Town Hall Hempstead NY 11550

LUCAS, CAROL LEE, mathematician; b. Aberdeen, S.D., Feb. 13, 1940; d. Howard Cleveland and Sarah Ivy (Easterby) Nogle; B.A., Dakota Wesleyan U., 1961; M.S., U. Ariz., 1967; Ph.D., U. N.C., 1973; m. Richard Albert Lucas, Feb. 26, 1961; children—Wendy Lee, Sean Richard. Tchr. Spanish, Mitchell (S.D.) High Sch., 1960-61; tchr. math, English, sci. U.S. Army, Furth, Ger., 1961-62; systems analyst Cargill Inc., Mpls., 1962-65; research asso. U. N.C., Chapel Hill, 1973-76, lectr., 1976-77, asst. prof. curriculum in biomed. engring. and math, 1977—. NIH trainee, 1968-73. Mem. Am. Heart Assn., N.C. Heart Assn., Biomed. Engring. Soc. Democrat. Methodist. Contbr. articles to profl. jours. Home: 2421 Sedgefield Dr Chapel Hill NC 27514 Office: Dept Surgery U NC Chapel Hill NC 27514

LUCAS, LINDA DIANNE, mfg. co. mgr.; b. Mpls., Nov. 1, 1942; d. Earl Winton and Shirley Grace (Holmgren) Skoog; B.S., Calif. Western U., 1981, M.B.A. candidate; m. Allen Joseph Lucas, Feb. 9, 1963; children—Teresa, Hollyanne, Scott (dec.), Jaime. Cons., Coppercraft Guild, Taunton, Mass., 1963-66; cons. Princess House, Inc., North Dighton, Mass., 1966-75, unit organizer, 1968-72, area dir., 1972-76; br. mgr. Leisure Home Parties, Inc., Racine, Wis., 1976-79, regional dir., 1976-79; dir. sales devel. Act II Jewelry, Inc., Bensenville, Ill., 1979-81; nat. mktg./sales mgr. Life Style Art, Inc., Kenyon, Minn., 1981—; profl. instr. adult edn., St. Louis Park, Minn. Mem. All the Good Old Girls (exec.), Nat. Assn. Female Execs., Am. Soc. Profl. and Exec. Women. Lutheran. Author various co. publs. Home: 4730 Barbara Dr Minnetonka MN 55343

LUCAS, SUZANNE, statistician; b. Baxter Springs, Kans., Jan. 16, 1939; d. Ralph Beaver and Marguerite (Sancocie) L.; B.A. in Math., Calif. State U., Fresno, 1967, M.A. in Ednl. Theory, 1969; M.S. in Stats., U. So. Calif., 1979; children—Patricia Sue Jennings, Neil Patric Jennings. Asst. to dir. NSF Inst., Calif. State U., Fresno, 1968; Tchr. secondary math. Fresno city schs., 1968-78; statistician corp. indsl. relations Hughes Aircraft Co., Los Angeles, 1979-80; personnel adminstr. Hughes Aircraft Co. Space and Communications Group, Los Angeles, 1981-82, mem. tech. staff in math., 1982—; lectr. in biostats. U. So. Calif., 1979. Kiwanis scholar, 1958. Mem. Soc. Women Engrs., Am. Statis. Assn., Am. Psychol. Assn., U. So. Calif. Alumni Assn. (life), Kappa Mu Epsilon. Home: 1026 E Imperial Ave Apt 2 El Segundo CA 90245 Office: Hughes Aircraft Co PO Box 92919 Bldg S61 Mail Sta T310 Los Angeles CA 90009

LUCCHI, SISTER, LUCIAN, social worker; b. Queens, N.Y., Aug. 4, 1938; d. Louis and Velma (Mazza) L.; B.S. in Edn., Brentwood Coll., 1964; M.S.W., Hunter Coll., 1976. Joined Sisters of St. Joseph, Roman Catholic Ch., 1957; tchr. Cath. Sch. System, Bklyn., 1957-72; social worker, operational mgr. Bushwick Human Services Center, Cath. Charities, Bklyn., 1972—. Sec., Bklyn. Community Bd. 4, 1976—; mem. Ridgewood-Bushwick Interagy. Council, 1976—, Bushwick Arson Task Force, 1976-78, Mayor's Council Intergroup Relations, 1978—. Mem. Nat. Assn. Social Workers, Nat. Conf. Cath. Charities. Office: 144 Bleecker St Brooklyn NY 11221

LUCE, CLARE BOOTHE, playwright, former congresswoman, former ambassador; b. N.Y.C.; d. William F. and Ann (Snyder) Boothe; ed. St. Mary's, Garden City, N.Y., 1915-17, The Castle, Tarrytown, N.Y., 1917-19; Litt.D. (hon.), Colby Coll., Fordham U., Mundelein Coll.; LL.D. (hon.), Temple U., Creighton U., Georgetown U., Mt. Holyoke Coll., Seton Hall Coll., Boston U., A.F.D., St. John's U., Westminster Coll.; m. George Tuttle Brokaw, Aug. 10, 1923 (div. 1929); m. 2d, Henry R. Luce, Nov. 23, 1935 (dec.). Asso. editor Vogue, 1930, Vanity Fair, 1931-32, mng. editor, 1933-34; newspaper columnist, 1934; playwright, 1935—; mem. 78th-79th congresses from 4th Conn. dist.; U.S. ambassador to Italy, 1953-57; mem. Pres.'s Fgn. Intelligence Adv. Bd.; cons., mem. bd. editors Ency. Brit.; cons. in Am. letters Library of Congress. Trustee Alfred E. Smith Meml. Fund, Am. Mus. Immigration, Honolulu Acad. Arts; nat. adv. bd. U.S. Capitol Hist. Soc. Recipient Dag Hammarskjold medal, Laeture medal, Am. Statesman medal, Fourth Estate award, Sylvanus Thayer award, Disting. Service to Congress award, Am. Eagle award, Woodruff award Assn. U.S. Army, Bob Hope 5-Star Civilian award, others. Mem. Acad. Polit. Sci., Nat. Fedn. Press Women, Internat. Platform Assn. Am. Inst. Fgn. Trade, U.S. Strategic Inst. (dir.), Aspen Inst. for Humanistic Studies. Republican. Roman Catholic. Club: Oversees Press. Author: Stuffed Shirts, 1933; Europe in the Spring, 1940; (plays) Abide with Me; The Women, 1937; Kiss the Boys Goodbye, 1938; Margin for Error, 1939; Child of the Morning, 1951; Slam the Door Softly, 1970. Contbr. articles and fiction to mags. Collector, editor Saints for Now, 1952. Home: 4559 Kahala Ave Honolulu HI 96816

LUCE, MARCIA RAE, educator, councilwoman; b. Sterling, Colo., July 25, 1944; d. Ray Charles and Marie Amanda (Welo) L.; A.A., Northeastern Jr. Coll., 1964; B.A., Adams State Coll., 1967, M.A., 1970; postgrad. Santa Clara U., U. No. Colo., Colo. State U. Resident advisor Clinton (Iowa) Job Corps, Gen. Learning Corp., 1968-69; tchr. Hagen Elem. Sch., Sterling, 1969-74: social scis. tchr., coach Sterling High Sch., 1974-77, asst. dean of students, tchr., 1977-80, asst. prin., 1980; asst. prin. Sterling Jr. High Sch., 1980—; mem. Sterling City Council, 1973—; project dir. Whistlewind Mag., Sterling, 1978—. Mem. Urban Renewal Authority, Sterling, 1979, ad hoc com. Northeastern Jr. Coll., 1979-80; bd. trustees Police and Fireman's Pension Bd., 1973—; chmn. bd. Northeastern Colo. Council Govts., 1978—; mem. Colo. Criminal Justice Commn., 1980-81; mem. Colo. Jail and Standards Commn.; mem. 4th Congl. Dist. Equal Rights Commn. Democratic Party, 1976. Named Outstanding Young Educator, Jaycees, 1976, recipient Disting. Service award, 1976. Mem. United Teaching Profession, Nat. Assn. Secondary Sch. Prins., Colo. Assn. Sch. Execs., Valley Assn. Sch. Execs., AAUW, Colo. Mcpl. League, Smithsonian Assos., Nat. Wildlife Fedn., Alpha Delta Kappa. Presbyterian. Club: Sterling Country. Home: 332 Platte St Sterling CO 80751 Office: 715 N 4th St Sterling CO 80751

LUCE, NANCY EBEY, univ. adminstr.; b. Ada, Okla., Jan. 22, 1932; d. Harmon and Monte (Jackson) Ebey; student U. Okla., Norman, 1950-52; B.A. in Sociology and Psychology with honors, East Central Okla. State U., Ada, 1968; M.S. in Sociology, Okla. State U., 1973; m. William G. Luce, Nov. 24, 1970; children—Harmon Ebey Ballard, Bowie Eugene Ballard. Child devel. worker Ada Guidance Center, 1968-69; instr. East Central Okla. State U., 1970-72, No. Okla. Coll., 1972-74; rep. Okla. State U., 1974-75, asst. dir., coordinator campus based programs, dept. fin. aids, 1975-82; assoc. dir. fin. aids Langston U., 1982—; cons. course material. Den mother Cub Scouts Am., 1960-62. Recipient Sociology award Chi Omega, 1968. Mem. Higher Edn. Alumni Council, Okla. Coll. Personnel Assn., Nat., S.W., Okla. assns. student financial aid adminstrs., D.A.R., Kappa Kappa Gamma Alumni Assn., Phi Kappa Phi, Alpha Kappa Delta. Methodist. Home: 2817 W 17th St Stillwater OK 74074 Office: Langston U PO Box 668 Langston OK 73053

LUCENTE, ROSEMARY DOLORES, ednl. adminstr.; b. Renton, Wash., Jan. 11, 1935; d. Joseph Anthony and Erminia Antoinette (Argano) Lucente; B.A., Mt. St. Mary's Coll., 1956, M.S., 1963. Tchr. pub. schs., Los Angeles, 1956-65, supr. tchr., 1958-65, asst. prin., 1965-69, prin. elem. sch., 1969—; nat. cons., lectr. Dr. William Glasser's Educator Tng. Center, 1968—; nat. workshop leader Nat. Acad. for Sch. Execs.-Am. Assn. Sch. Adminstrs., 1980. Recipient Golden Apple award Stanford Ave. Sch. PTA, Faculty and Community Adv. Council, 1976, resolution for outstanding service South Gate City Council, 1976. Mem. Nat. Assn. Elem. Sch. Prins., Los Angeles Elem. Prins. Orgn. (v.p. 1979-80), Assn. Calif. Adminstrs., Assn. Elem. Sch. Adminstrs. (vice-chmn. chpt. 1972-75, city-wide exec. bd., steering com. 1972-75, 79-80), Asso. Adminstrs. Los Angeles (charter), Pi Theta Mu, Kappa Delta Pi, Delta Kappa Gamma. Democrat. Roman Catholic. Home: 6501 Lindenhurst Ave Los Angeles CA 90048 Office: Encino Elementary Sch 16941 Addison St Encino CA 91316

LUCERO, ERMINDA, clin. social worker; b. Pueblo, Colo., Feb. 5, 1928; d. Ezekiel D. and Gladys Margaret (Crouch) Jaramillo; B.A., U. Calif., Berkeley, 1971, M.S.W., 1973; m. Cipriano Joseph Lucero, May 28, 1947; children—Jeanne Marie, Charles Joseph, Stephen William, Martha Anne. Clin. social worker Centro de Salud Mental, Oakland, Calif., 1973-79; pvt. practice clin. social work, Alameda, Fremont, Calif., 1979—. Chmn., East Oakland Citizens Adv. Health Com.; mem. Alameda County Citizens Adv. Revenue Sharing Rev. Bd.; chmn. Alameda County Mental Health Adv. Bd.; bd. dirs. Big Sisters; mem. adv. com. Casey Family Program. Mem. Nat. Assn. Social Workers, Soc. Clin. Social Work. Address: 1111 Fontana Dr Alameda CA 94501

LUCERO, MARCELA, educator; b. Alamosa, Colo.; b. Agapito and Rose (Torres) Lucero; B.A. in English and Edn., Denver U., 1959; M.A. in Spanish and Linguistics, U. Kans., Lawrence, 1968; Ph.D. in Spanish and Linguistics, U. Minn., 1981; 1 dau., Patricia. Instr., Center for Students from Abroad, U. Denver, 1968-69, dir. Mexican Am. edn. program, 1969-72; teaching asst. U. Colo. and U. Kans., 1965-68; asst. dir. Pinto project, Denver, 1972-73; instr. U. Minn., Mpls., 1973-80; asst. prof. Mankato State U., 1980-81; asso. prof., dir Chicano studies Adams State Coll., Alamosa, Colo., 1981—; chmn. Hispanic adv. com. Mpls. pub. schs., 1976-78. Trustee, Mpls. YWCA; bd. dirs. United Way, 1980; mem. Gov.'s Appts. Commn., 1979. Named hon. citizen, Pueblo, Colo., 1976; Tchr. of Yr., U. Colo. Denver Center, 1971; named to Denver Post Gallery of Fame, 1971. Mem. Am. Assn. Tchrs. Spanish and Portuguese, MLA, Colo. Assn. Chicano Researchers (editorial bd.), Centro Cultural Chicano (dir.), Internat. Platform Assn., Kappa Delta Pi, Phi Sigma Iota. Author articles, poems. Home: 114 Richardson St Alamosa CO 81102 Office: Adams State College Alamosa CO 81102

LUCK, TONI YVONNE, legal tax cons.; b. N.Y.C., Nov. 6, 1950; d. Benjamin Franklin and Anne Mae Luck; B.A. in Econs. magna cum laude, Fordham U., 1980; student Georgetown U. Law Sch., 1982—; 1 dau., Aushann Yvonne. Mgr. Holiday Magic Inc., San Rafael, Calif., 1969-71; v.p. sales and tng. Stephanie Jans, Inc., Bridgetown, Barbados, 1971-72; dir. circulation Encore Communications Inc., N.Y.C., 1972-75; pres. Ben Franklin Assos., N.Y.C., 1975-78; legal adminstr. Mobil Oil Corp., N.Y.C., 1978—; cons. Nat. Black Republic Council, 1974. Com. co-chmn. Scholarship Com. PACE awards, 1976; founder Future Bus. Leaders Program for Young Ams., 1971; co-dir. First Street Salon. Recipient Gold Cert. for service Holiday Magic, Inc., 1971. Mem. Am. Mgmt. Assn., Profl. Negro Woman's Orgns., Public Relations Assos., Phi Beta Kappa. Republican. Club: Order Eastern Star. Office: Mobil Oil Corp 3225 Gallows Rd Fairfax VA 22037

LUCKHARDT, ESTHER DOUGHTY, state legislator; b. Horicon, Wis.; d. Frederick August and Selma Augusta (Hanser) Schwertfeger; student Horicon schs.; m. Lyle E. Doughty, July 6, 1940 (dec.); children—Thomas Perry, Mary, Patricia; m. 2d, Howard L. Luckhardt, Mar. 3, 1967. Engaged in ins. and real estate, Horicon, 1945-71; mem. Wis. Ho. of Reps., 1962—; dir. Capitol Transam. Corp. Named Legislator of Year, Wis. Am. Legion, 1982. Republican. Lutheran. Office: 334N State Capitol Madison WI 53702

LUDLOW, JEAN WILHELMINA, ins. co. mgr.; b. Statesville, N.C., Apr. 16, 1935; d. John Hilton and Lucille Caroline (Pounds) Hodges; student Occidental Coll., 1953-55, Jacksonville U., 1970-72; m. Richard Scott Ludlow, July 13, 1955; children—Susan Elizabeth, Elizabeth Caroline. Columnist, Orange County (Calif.) Evening News, 1963-65, Ridgewood (N.J.) News, 1968-69; editor Prudential Ins. Co., Jacksonville, Fla., 1972-73, mgr. public relations, 1976—; mem. adv. bd. public relations council U. Fla., 1979-82. Pres. bd. Jacksonville Art Mus., 1980-82; bd. dirs. Fla. Endowment Humanities, 1981—. Named An Outstanding Public Relations Person Jacksonville, Public Relations Soc. Am., 1976. Mem. Public Relations Soc. Am. (accredited; pres. North Fla. chpt. 1978, S.E. dist. bd. treas. 1980, nat. co-chmn. social responsibilities com. 81, accreditation bd. 1983—), Fla. Public Relations Assn. (state accreditation com.). Republican. Home: 3246 Front Rd Jacksonville FL 32217 Office: 841 Prudential Dr Jacksonville FL 32207

LUDMER, TRINI CASASIN, sales and trading asso.; b. N.Y.C., June 5, 1949; d. Joaquin P. and Pilar M. (Frau) Casasin; B.A., N.Y. U., 1971; M.B.A., Fordham U., 1978; m. William M. Ludmer, Aug. 19, 1972. With Mut. of N.Y., 1971-74, tng. specialist, 1973-74; with Reuben H. Donnelley Corp., N.Y.C., 1974-78, corporate tng. mgr., 1977-78; asst. to divisional mdse. mgr. Accelerated MBA Exec. Devel. Group, Bloomingdale's, N.Y.C., 1978-79; account rep. Control Data Corp., N.Y.C., 1979-80; sales and tng. asso. The First Boston Corp., N.Y.C., 1980—; dir., sec. Apt. Corp. Roman Catholic. Club: Town Squash. Home: 600 West End Ave New York NY 10024 Office: 20 Exchange Pl New York NY 10005

LUDWIG, CHRISTA, mezzo soprano; b. Berlin, Mar. 16; d. Anton and Eugenie (Besalla) L; came to U.S., 1958; ed. German schs.; m. Walter Berry, Sept. 29, 1957 (div. 1970); 1 son, Wolfgang. m. 2d, Paul-Emile Deiber, Mar. 3, 1972. Appeared at Staedtische Buehnen, Frankfurt, W.Ger., 1946-52, Landestheater, Darmstadt, W. Ger., 1952-54, Landestheater, Hannover, W.Ger., 1954-55, Vienna (Austria) State Opera, 1955—, Avery Fisher Hall, N.Y.C., 1978; appearances in U.S., 1958—, including Met. Opera, N.Y.C., 1959, 66-71, 73-74, Carnegie Hall, N.Y.C., 1959, 69, 70, 71, 74, Lyric Opera, Chgo., 1959-60, 70-71, 73-74. Philharmonic Hall, N.Y.C., 1968, 69, 72, 74; guest artist London, Buenos Aires, Munich, Berlin, Tokyo, Salzburg Festival, Athens Festival, Saratoga Festival, Hunter Coll., Met. Mus., Scala Milano, Expo 67, Montreal, and others; rec. artist. Named Kammersaengerin, Govt. of Austria, 1962; recipient Mozart medal, Mahler medal, Hugo Wolf medal, Silver Rose, Vienna Philharm., Golden Ring, Vienna Staatsoper. Office: care Colbert Artists Mgmt Inc 111 W 57th St New York NY 10019

LUEBBERT, KAREN MERRITT, librarian; b. St. Louis, Oct. 3, 1942; d. Joseph Henry and Lorene Laura (Amrhine) Merritt; B.A., Webster Coll., 1964; M.S. in Library Sci., Case Western Res. U., 1967; m. Jack R. Luebbert, Jan. 27, 1968; 1 dau., Katharine Merritt. Acting dir. Webster Coll. Library, St. Louis, 1967-68, dir., 1968—, adminstrv. librarian Eden-Webster Library, 1969—; chmn. Learning Resources Council of Higher Edn. Center of St. Louis, 1973-75; bd. dirs. St. Louis Regional Library Network, 1979—, pres., 1982—; v.p. Mo. Library Network Bd., 1982—; lectr. Washington U., St. Louis, 1977-80. Mem. Ronald S. Beasley Sch. Bd., 1982—. Mem. ALA, Mo. Library Assn., Beta Phi Mu. Home: 7417 Huntington St Saint Louis MO 63121 Office: 470 E Lockwood St Saint Louis MO 63119

LUECKE, FREIDA BELLE, banker; b. Navarro County, Tex., Oct. 21, 1931; d. Ben F. and Vera (Davis) Shell; student Brevard Community Coll., 1967; m. Conrad John Luecke, Dec. 15, 1979; children by previous marriage—Ben M. Bristow, Belinda J. Bristow. Loan officer Sheppard AFB Credit Union (Tex.), 1956; mgr. Fed. Credit Union Kennedy Space Center, Fla., 1964-74; mortgage loan officer Commonwealth Corp., Cocoa, Fla., 1974-76; mortgage loan officer, head mortgage loan dept. Barnett Bank Brevard County, Cocoa, Fla., 1976—; instr. real estate lending Brevard Community Coll., 1978—. Bd. dirs. Performing Arts Council. Mem. Am. Inst. Banking, Beta Sigma Phi. Democrat. Baptist. Club: Order Eastern Star. Home: S Tropical Trail Merritt Island FL 32952 Office: 430 Brevard Ave Cocoa FL 32922

LUEDTKE, MELINDA CARTER, state ofcl.; b. Salisbury, Md., Jan. 16, 1946; d. William A. and Ann (Whitmore) Carter; B.A., U. Del., 1967; M. Public Adminstrn., U. So. Calif., 1978; m. Laurence L. Luedtke, Dec. 28, 1975; 1 son, William Laurence. With Del. Dept. Community Affairs and Econ. Devel., Dover, 1970-73; dep. dir. Office Bus. and Indsl. Devel., Calif. Dept. Econ. and Bus. Devel., Sacramento, 1978-80, dir. dept. econ. and bus. devel., 1980—. Mem. Nat. Assn. State Devel. Agencies (dir. 1980—), Nat. Council for Urban Econ. Devel. (dir. 1980-82), Indsl. Devel. and Research Council, Urban Land Inst. Democrat. Office: Dept Economic and Business Development 1030 13th St Suite 200 Sacramento CA 95814

LUEPKE, GRETCHEN, geologist; b. Tucson, Nov. 10, 1943; d. Gordon Maas and Janice (Campbell) Luepke; B.S., U. Ariz., 1965, M.S., 1967; U. Colo., summer, 1962. With U.S. Geol. Survey, Menlo Park, Calif., 1967—, geologist, Pacific-Arctice Br. of Marine Geology, 1976—. Registered geologist, Ore. Mem. Soc. Econ. Paleontologists and Mineralogists, Geol. Soc. Am., Ariz. Geol. Soc., Peninsula Geol. Soc., Bay Area Mineralogists (chmn. 1979-80), Sigma Xi. Contbr. articles on heavy-mineral analysis to profl. jours. Office: 345 Middlefield Rd Menlo Park CA 94025

LUGER, LOIS J., motion picture co. exec.; b. Manhattan, N.Y., Aug. 8, 1945; d. Bernard M. and Hilda (Fuerstein) Luger; B.A., Queens Coll., 1967, postgrad., 1968. Asst. v.p. Dreyfus Corp., N.Y.C., 1967-69; asso. dir. film acquisition Home Box Office, N.Y.C., 1975-77; v.p. t.v./non-theatrical sales New World Pictures, Los Angeles, 1977-80; v.p. TV Embassy Telecommunications, Los Angeles, 1980—; speaker, Film Expo 1980, Australia; program co-coordinator seminar UCLA Extension, 1981. Mem. Hollywood Radio and TV Soc., Acad. TV Arts and Scis., Women in Film, Women in Cable, Nat. Cable TV Assn., Nat. Assn. TV Program Execs. Address: 956 Seward St Los Angeles CA 90038

LUGO, DEANNA LEE, telephone co. ofcl.; b. Southgate, Calif., Apr. 11, 1942; d. Henry Weber and Geneva Julie (Jones) Gross; student San Bernardino Valley Coll., 1967-79; A.S., Victor Valley Coll., 1982; m. Claudio Lugo, Apr. 16, 1960; children—Orlando Renee, Claudio Kent, Vince Anthony. Mgr., Lake Drive-Inn Theatre, Big Bear Lake, Calif., 1969; adminstrv. asst. Big Bear Lake Fire Dept., 1969-75; adminstrv. sec. Big Bear Mcpl. Water Dist., 1975-79; service rep. Continental Telephone Co., Big Bear Lake, 1979-80, bus. office supr., Manteca, Calif., 1980-81, Victorville, Calif., 1981-82, adminstrv. sec. mktg. div., 1982—. Vice pres. Big Bear Lake Little League Assn., 1973-74; sec. Big Bear Lake PTO, 1975-77. Recipient commendation Big Bear Lake Fire Dept., 1978. Republican. Roman Catholic. Club: Big Bear Ski (sec. 1975-76). Home: 20511 Yucca Loma Rd Apple Valley CA 92307 Office: 16515 Mojave Dr Victorville CA 92392

LUKAS, ELLEN, author, editor; b. Shenandoah, Pa.; d. Alexander J. and Margaret (McGuire) L.; A.B. in History, Coll. New Rochelle; student Pa. State U., Fordham U. UN corr. Newsweek mag., 1961-65; UN bur. chief Hearst Newspapers, 1965-67; with Harper's Mag., 1969; UNICEF press cons., 1970; editor Orbis Books, 1971; press analyst to Sec. Gen. of UN, N.Y.C., 1977-81; editor, writer UN Dept. Info., 1982—. Mem. PEN, Authors Guild. Author: (with Mary Lukas) (biography) Teilhard de Chardin, 1977; contbr. Antiquity Mag., Cambridge U.

LUKIN, RHODA VOGEL, assn. exec.; d. Sol and Esta (Laster) Vogel; B.A. cum laude, Adelphi Coll., 1949; 1 dau., Melissa. Editor, Lebhar-Friedman Pubs., N.Y.C., 1950-62, Harcourt Brace, Jovanovich, N.Y.C., 1973-75, N.Y. Womensweek, 1975-77; dir. mgmt. devel. seminars N.Y. C. of C. and Industry, 1976—. Mem. Exec. Women Internat., Am. Soc. Tng. and Devel. Home: 39 Fifth Ave New York NY 10003 Office: 200 Madison Ave New York NY 10016

LUMADUE, JOYCE ANN, hobby co. exec.; b. New London, Conn., Oct. 21, 1941; d. James E. and Camilla (Romeo) Hayes; student U. Conn.; m. Donald Dean Lumadue, June 28, 1958; children—Dawnia Jean, Donald Dean, Robert Ryan, Ronald Jeffrey. Partner, Joydon's Coin Shop, New London, 1958—, House of Leisure, New London, 1967—, Hobby Crafts, New London, 1969—; v.p. New Eng. Internat. Inc., New London, 1969—, Lumadue Inc., New London, 1978—. Mem. Hobby Industry Assn. Am., Internat. Mgmt. Council, Nat. Assn. Female Execs., NOW. Methodist. Contbr. articles to profl. jours. Office: 78-88 Captains Walk New London CT 06320

LUMLEY, JUANITA LANGFORD, paper co. exec.; b. Uvalda, Ga., June 5, 1918; d. Walter Currie and Lexie Ora (Youmans) Langford; student Swainsboro Vocat. and Tech. Sch., 1971; m. Marvin Bernard Lumley, May 13, 1939; children—Mary Anne Lumley Pierce, Lexie Margaret Lumley Atkinson. Office clk. Swainsboro Laundry & Dry Cleaners (Ga.), 1941-49; with So. Laundry & Dry Cleaners, 1950-70; accountant, bookkeeper Allied Timber Co., Inc., Swainsboro, 1971-73, St. Regis Paper Co., 1973—. Mem. Swainsboro Bus. and Profl. Womens Club (pres. 1970-72). Baptist. Home: 217 W Church St Swainsboro GA 30401 Office: St Regis Paper Co Georgia Hwy 297 PO Box 768 Swainsboro GA 30401

LUMMUS, CAROL TRAVERS, artist, printmaker; b. Hyannis, Mass., Nov. 2, 1937; d. Frank and Doris (Brown) Travers; student Walnut Hill Sch. Performing Arts, Natick, Mass., 1952-55; A.A., Colby-Sawyer Coll., New London, N.H., 1957; student U. Geneva (Switzerland), 1960-62; m. Bertrand W. Lummus, Jan. 27, 1962; children—Sarah Travers, Jonathan Ames. Artist and printmaker; one-woman shows include Hammerquist, N.Y.C., 1979, La Galeria, San Mateo, Calif., 1980, Alice Bingham, Memphis, 1980, P.S. Gallery, Ogunquit, Maine, 1980; group shows include All New Eng. show, 1975-76, Currier Mus., Manchester, N.H., 1976, 80, Fitchburg (Mass.) Mus., 1975-76, Instituto Brasil-Estadios Unidos, Brazil, 1978, Hobe Sound (Fla.) Gallery, 1976—, Payson-Waldron, Portland, Maine, 1982; mem. art adv. panel N.H. Commn. on Arts. Recipient Rosmond de Kalb award Currier Mus., 1975, 1st prize Fitchburg Mus. Art, 1973; N.H. Commn. on Arts grantee, 1980. Mem. Cape Cod Performing Arts Assn. (dir.), Artists Equity, Silvermine Guild Arts, Conn. League N.H. Craftsmen. Episcopalian. Club: Barnstable (Mass.) Yacht. Home: Lang Rd Cornish NH 03781

LUMPE, SHEILA, state legislator; b. York, Pa., 1935; B.A., Ind. U., 1957; postgrad. Johns Hopkins U.; married; 4 children. Mem. Mo. Ho. of Reps. from 77th Dist., 1980—. Mem. University City (Mo.) Sch. Bd., 1973-81; mem. St. Louis Danforth Leadership Group, 1980-81; bd. dirs. English Sch., University City, Mo., 1981—. Mem. LWV, Am. Field Service, Women's Polit. Caucus, ACLU, Coalition for Environ., Univ. Heights Neighborhood Assn., Friends Univ. City Library. Democrat. Address: 6908 Amherst St University City MO 63130

LUMPKIN, DONNA GALE, educator; b. Hyannis, Mass., May 27, 1945; d. Claude W. and Gladys (Goodspeed) L.; B.A. magna cum laude and with distinction in major (Bixler scholar), Colby Coll., 1967; M.Ed., Bridgewater State Coll., 1976. Actuarial research asst. John Hancock Mut. Life Ins. Co., Boston, 1967-68; tchr. math. Nauset Regional Jr.-Sr. High Sch., Orleans, Mass., 1968-71, tchr. math. and reading Nauset Regional Middle Sch., 1971—. Mem. Nauset Edn. Assn., Mass. Tchrs. Assn., NEA, Phi Beta Kappa. Methodist. Home: 76 Hitching Post Rd Chatham MA 02633 Office: Route 28 Orleans MA 02653

LUMPKIN, PENNY PALMER, wholesale periodicals co. exec.; b. Topeka, Aug. 20; d. William H. and Vivian J. Palmer; student U. Ariz., 1957-59, U. Kans., 1959-60; m. Joseph Henry Lumpkin, Nov. 26, 1960; children—William Henry, Kelley Kathleen. Buyer, merchandiser City News & Gift Shop, Topeka, 1954-57; mgr., buyer Vivian's Gift Shop, Topeka, 1961-76; book buyer Palmer News, Inc., Topeka, 1976-79, book buyer, personnel dir., 1979-80, dir. retail ops., treas., 1980—, also dir.; dir. Ultra Fund-Security Benefit Life, Life Ins. Investors. Bd. dirs. Mulvane Art Center, Topeka, 1968-80, Seven Step Found., Topeka, 1969-72; bd. dirs., charter mem. Mulvane Women, Topeka, 1969; div. chmn. United Way, Topeka, 1969; chmn. King of Hills Pro/Celebrity Tennis Benefit, 1977-79; spl. events chmn. Shawnee County unit Am. Cancer Soc., Topeka, 1976-78, v.p. bd. dirs., 1977, pres. bd. dirs., 1979. Named an Outstanding Woman Am., Jr. League of Topeka, 1975; recipient Outstanding Service award Am. Cancer Soc., 1976, Kans. div., 1978. Mem. Central States Periodicals Distbrs. Assn., Am. Booksellers Assn., Mid-Am. Periodicals Distbrs. Assn., Ind. Periodicals Distbrs. Assn., Topeka Friends of Zoo, Am. Heritage Assn., Kappa Kappa

Gamma Alums. Republican. Episcopalian. Club: Jr. League (pres. Topeka 1971). Researcher, pub. fund-raising manual Assn. Jr. Leagues, 1974. Home: 3161 Shadow Ln Topeka KS 66604 Office: 1050 Republican Topeka KS 66604

LUMSDEN, CHARLIE HARRIS, mfg. co. buyer; b. Lynchburg, Va., Nov. 12, 1924; d. Charles Harris and Rosalie Collier (Jackson) L.; stenographic cert. Phillips Bus. Coll., 1943. Clk., Appalachian Power Co., Lynchburg, 1943-57; with naval nuclear fuel div. Babcock & Wilcox Co., Lynchburg, 1958—, sec., to 1968, buyer, 1969—. Mem. Jr. League Am. Episcopalian. Home: 28A Princeton Circle W Apts 64 Lynchburg VA 24503 Office: PO Box 785 Lynchburg VA 24505

LUMSDEN, LYNNE ANN, pub. co. exec.; b. Battlecreek, Mich., July 30, 1947; d. Arthur James and Ruth Julia (Pandy) L.; B.A., Sarah Lawrence Coll., 1969; postgrad. U. Paris, 1967-69, N.Y. U., 1970, CCNY, 1980-81. Editorial asst. Harcourt Brace Jovanovich, N.Y.C., 1969-70, copy editor, 1970; acquisitions editor Appleton-Century Crofts, N.Y.C., 1971-73; editor coll. div. Prentice-Hall, Englewood Cliffs, N.J., 1973, Spectrum Books, Prentice-Hall, 1974-77, sr. editor, 1977-80, asst. v.p., editor-in-chief gen. pub. div. Prentice Hall, 1981, v.p., editorial dir., 1982—; lectr. U.S., Europe, 1975—; pub. cons., 1979—. Mem. fund raising com. Retarded Infants Services, 1979—. Mem. Am. Assn. Pubs., Sarah Lawrence Alumnae Assn. (dir.). Democrat. Episcopalian. Clubs: St. Barts Community, Sandbar, Jr. League. Home: 333 E 79th St New York NY 10021 Office: Prentice Hall Inc Englewood Cliffs NJ 07632

LUND, BONNIE RAE, finance co. exec.; b. Beardstown, Ill., Dec. 1, 1940; d. Raymond George and Melba Maureen (Lobb) Brocksieck; grad. high sch.; 1 dau., Marsha Kay Cox; m. William G. Lund; 4 stepchildren. Cashier, bookkeeper Gen. Fin. Co., Springfield, Ill., 1960-62, Orlando, Fla., 1963-64; head cashier Beneficial Fin. Co., Orlando, 1962-63, 65-71; with Assos. Fin. Services, Orlando, 1971—, div. auditor, Atlanta, 1976—, auditor, 1978—, credit counselor in charge of woman's loan program, 1978—. Lic. real estate salesperson, Ga. Mem. Internat. Consumer Credit Assn. (credit edn. chmn., bd. dirs.), Credit Women Internat. (pres. Atlanta 1979-80, chmn. bd. 1980-81; Credit Woman of Year Atlanta 1980, also Ga. and Dist. 3 and 4), Vols. in Bus. Edn. DeKalb County, Soc. Cert. Consumer Credit Execs., Women's C. of C. Atlanta (bus. resource com.). Named Credit Woman of Yr., Fla. Credit Women Internat., 1974-75. Home: 1211 DeLeon Ct Clarkston GA 30021 Office: 3395 NE Expressway Suite 350 Atlanta GA 30341

LUND, SISTER, CANDIDA, coll. chancellor; b. Chgo.; d. Fred S. and Katharine (Murray) Lund Heck; B.A., Rosary Coll., River Forest, Ill., 1942; M.A., Cath. U. Am., 1954; Ph.D. (LaVerne Noyes scholar, AAUW fellow), U. Chgo., 1963; Litt.D., Lincoln (Ill.) Coll., 1968; LL.D. (hon.), John Marshall Law Sch., 1979; H.H.D. (hon.), Marymount Manhattan Coll., 1979. Pres., Rosary Coll., River Forest, Ill., 1964-81, chancellor, 1981—. Exec. com. Fedn. Ind. Ill. Colls. and Univs., 1972—; non-pub. adv. com. Ill. Bd. Higher Edn., 1974-80; commr. Ill. Commn. Status of Women, 1977—; trustee Carnegie Found. for Advancement Teaching, 1970-78, Clarke Coll., Dubuque, Iowa, 1981—. Recipient Profl. Achievement award U. Chgo. Alumni Assn., 1974. Fellow Royal Soc. Arts (London); mem. Thomas More Assn. (dir. 1975—), Am. Council Edn. (dir. 1977—), Am. Polit. Sci. Assn. Editor: Moments to Remember, 1980, The Days and the Nights, Prayers for Today's Woman; Nunsuch, 1982. Address: Rosary Coll 7900 Division St River Forest IL 60305

LUND, DOLORES MARIE, psychologist; b. Mpls., Apr. 20, 1923; d. Albert Casmir and Leona Clara (Langlais) Kacher; B.A. (scholar), U. Minn., 1944; postgrad. U. Fla., 1973-74, Antioch Coll., 1975; children—Tracy, Mark, Laurie, Annette. Mgr. All Service Placement, Mpls., 1969-71; job devel. specialist Opportunities Indsl. Center, Clearwater, Fla., 1972-73; Coordinator Mental Health Assn., St. Petersburg, Fla., 1973; dir. Wilson House, Lakeland Fla., 1974, Wayside House, Mpls., 1975, Abbott-Northwestern, Mpls., 1975-77; coordinator St. Luke's Hosp. Med. Center, Phoenix, 1977-78; with Dolores Lund Inst., Phoenix, 1978—, psychologist, 1979—. Mem. Orgn. Rehab. Centers, Bus. and Profl. Women, Assn. Profl. Alcohol Specialists (sec., treas.). treas.). Republican. Home: 3432 N 12th Pl Apt 18 Phoenix AZ 85014 Office: 6829 N 12th St Suite 37 Phoenix AZ 85014

LUNDBERG, ELLEN RAE WENDROW, med. technologist; b. N.Y.C., Aug. 11, 1942; d. Max and Martha (Miller) Wendrow; B.S., Fairleigh Dickinson U., 1964; children—Gregory, Andrew. Intern med. tech. Newark Presbyn. Hosp., 1963-64; med. technologist histology sect. Parke Davis & Co., Ann Arbor, Mich., 1964-65; supr. chemistry sect. pvt. lab., Ann Arbor, 1965-66; med. technologist pulmonary function and blood gas lab. VA Hosp., Ann Arbor, 1966-70; med. technologist pvt. labs., Durham, N.C., 1970-72; research technologist coagulation lab. Duke U. Med. Center, 1972-75, staff med. technologist blood bank, 1975-76, supr. nuclear medicine lab., 1976—, instr. Sch. Med. Tech., 1976—. Registered med. technologist. Asso. mem. Am. Soc. Clin. Pathologists; mem. Clin. Ligand Assay Soc. Home: 2813 McDowell St Durham NC 27705 Office: Duke U Med Center Box 3304 Durham NC 27710

LUNDGAARD, MARTHA JOHANNA BAKKE, cons. nurse anesthetist; b. Stockholm, Sweden, Oct. 18, 1909; d. O.M. and Johanna Bakke; came to U.S., 1910, naturalized, 1940; R.N., Luth. Deaconess Hosp., Mpls., 1930; postgrad. U. Hosp. Sch. for Nurse Anesthetists, 1933-34; B.A.S., Gen. Coll. U. Minn., 1975; m. Harold F. Lundgaard, Oct. 22, 1938. Private duty nurse, Mpls., 1931-32; operating room supr., anesthetist Iowa Luth. Hosp., Des Moines, 1934-36; operating room supr. and anesthetist San Joaquin Valley Hosp., Stockton, Calif., 1936, Luther Hosp., Watertown, S.D., 1936-37; surgery supr. and relief anesthetist Sioux Valley Hosp., Sioux Falls, S.D., 1937; night anesthetist Swedish Hosp., Mpls., 1937-38; free lance anesthetist St. Paul and Mpls. Hosps., 1938-40; nurse anesthetist Mpls. Gen. Hosp., 1940-51; instr. Nurse Anesthetists Sch., N.W. Hosp., Mpls., 1952; staff nurse anesthetist Eitel Hosp., Mpls., 1953-56; cons. nurse in anesthesia Minn. Dept. of Health, 1956-75; condr. statewide survey on anesthesia services, 1957-59, on emergency room services, Minn., 1968-70. Past sec. bd. Trustees Bethel Evang. Luth. Ch., sec., 1974-76, chmn. Martha's Women Circle, 1976-78; active ARC; vol. instr. cardiopulmonary resuscitation. Certified nurse anesthetist. Mem. Am. Assn. of Nurse Anesthetists (mem. exam. com. 1945-51), Am., Minn. pub. health assns., Am., Minn. respiratory therapy assns., Minn. Assn. Nurse Anesthetists, Am. Retirement Assn., Minn. Ret. State Employees Assn., Minn. Alumni Assn. Univ. Sch. Nurse Anesthetists (pres. 1970-73, exec. sec. 1975—). Republican. Contbr. articles to profl. jours. Home: 5922 Chicago Ave S Minneapolis MN 55417

LUNDIE, LOUISE MARIE, electric sign mfg. co. exec.; b. Meeme Twp., Wis., Mar. 2, 1940; d. Harry Joseph and Irene Theresa (Salm) Schwartz; A.A., Milw. Area Tech. Coll., 1978; B.S., Carroll Coll., 1982; m. Mel A. Lundie, Oct. 2, 1976; 1 dau. by previous marriage, Ann Louise Mathews. Sec. to gen. mgr. St. Regis Paper Co., Milw., 1961-65; asst. to pres. Wells Badger Corp., Milw., 1966-74; sec. to v.p. mktg. Everbrite Electric Signs, South Milwaukee, Wis., 1975, nat. sales adminstr., 1976-81, mgr. mktg. adminstrn., 1981, mgr. corp. planning, advt. and market research, 1981—. 4-H Club leader City of Cudahy (Wis.), 1977-82. Mem. Nat. Secs. Assn. (pres. Milw. chpt. 1971-73), Adminstrv. Mgmt. Soc. Home: 5938 S Pennsylvania Ave Cudahy WI 53110 Office: Everbrite Electric Signs 315 Marion Ave South Milwaukee WI 53172

LUNDQUIST, MYRTLE VERNICE, educator, author; b. Chgo.; d. Martin Luther and Anna Emily (Lorenz) Lundquist; B.A., U. Chgo., 1951, M.A., 1963. Editor, The Commentator, Fed. Res. Bank Chgo., 1942-60; tchr., Wheeling, Ill., 1960-65, Schaumburg, Ill., 1965—. Mem. Women in Communications, Internat. Assn. Bus. Communications, AAUW, NEA, Internat. Assn. Bus. Communicators Chgo., Thimble Guild, Thimble Collectors, Dorcas Thimblers. Author: The Book of a Thousand Thimbles, 1970; Thimble Treasury, 1975; Thimble Americana, 1981; contbr. articles to mags. Home: 630 Prairie Ave Wilmette IL 60091

LUNDQUIST, PATRICIA ANN, accountant; b. Chgo., Aug. 11, 1948; d. Paul B. and Viola A. Berberet; B.S., No. Ill. U., 1979; A.A., Waubonsee Community Coll., 1977; m. Roy Allen Lundquist, Jan. 4, 1980; children—Wesley Michael. Acct., Western Electric Co., Montgomery, Ill., 1979-81; acct. Nickels & Beilman, C.P.A., P.C., Aurora, Ill., 1981—. Treas., bd. dirs. Smith Sch. P.T.A. Aurora Found. scholar, 1977-79. C.P.A., Ill. Mem. Am. Inst. C.P.A.s, Ill. C.P.A. Soc., Phi Theta Kappa. Home: 1088 Cascade St Aurora IL 60506 Office: 13 S Broadway Aurora IL 60505

LUNDQUIST, VIOLET ELVIRA, agy. adminstr.; b. Bristol, Conn., Jan. 28, 1912; d. Otto Nimrod and Mabel Elvira (Lindeen) Ebb; diploma music Augustana Coll., Rock Island, Ill., 1932; postgrad. mgmt. systems U. Mo., 1969; m. Vernon Arthur Lundquist, May 14, 1935; children—Karen Ebb, Jane Christine. Tchr. music, public schs., Olds, Iowa, 1932-35; editor Warsaw (Mo.) Times, 1935-45, Anthon (Iowa) Herald, 1945-57; field dir. Iowa Heart Assn., Des Moines, 1957-66; exec. dir. S.E. Iowa Community Action Program, Burlington, 1966-74; adminstrn. dir. S.E. Ariz. Govts. Orgn. Community Services, Bisbee, Ariz., 1975-77; statewide advocate developmentally disabled adults, 1977—; adminstr. Arizona City Med. Center, part-time, 1979-80; adminstr. Dist. V Council on Developmental Disabilities, 1980—. Bd. dirs. Central Ariz. Health Systems Agy., 1979—; chmn. Arizona City Home and Property Owners Assn., 1979-82; mem. Ariz. Dist. V Human and Legal Rights Com. Recipient Carol Lane award Nat. Safety Council, 1956; USPHS scholar, Columbia U., summers 1963, 64; cert. vocat. rehab. adminstr. Mem. Nat. Soc. Community Action Program Dirs. (dir. 1966-75), Iowa Fedn. Press Women, Nat. Rehab. Assn. Lutheran. Clubs: Zonta (chmn. Casa Grande 1982—), Women of Moose. Recipient 1st place awards Nat. Fedn. Press Women, 1952, 53, 55, 57. Home: 609 W Cochise St Arizona City AZ 85223 Office: 313 Sunland Gin Rd Arizona City AZ 95223

LUNDSTROM, LINDA CESKY, banker; b. Balt., May 19, 1950; d. James William and Elaine M. (Taylor) Cesky; student Fa. So. Coll., Lakeland, 1968-69, A.A., Broward Community Coll., Ft. Lauderdale, 1980; grad. Fla. Sch. Banking, Gainesville, 1976; m. Richard Lundstrom, Oct. 19, 1980. Teller, Fla. Coast Bank of Lighthouse Point, Pompano Beach, 1969-71, auditor, 1971-72, asst. cashier, 1972-75, ops. officer, 1975-77, customer service officer, 1977-78; cashier Fla. Coast Bank of Palm Beach County, Boca Raton, 1978-79; v.p., br. ops. coordinator Fla. Coast Bank of Broward County, Pompano Beach, 1979-81; v.p. mktg. Fla. Coast Banks, Inc., Pompano Beach, 1981—. Named an Outstanding Young Woman of Am., Greater Pompano Beach C. of C., 1977. Mem. Bank Adminstrn. Inst. (dir. 1979-82), Fla. Bankers Assn. (com. 1979), Am. Inst. Banking (instr.), Greater Pompano Beach C. of C. (dir. 1979-82, treas. 1981-82), Boca Raton C. of C. (com. chmn. 1978-79). Methodist. Club: Soroptomist (pres. 1982-83). Home: 5100 Dupont Blvd Apt 10-2 Fort Lauderdale FL 33308 Office: 1101 E Atlantic Blvd Pompano Beach FL

LUNDSTROM, MILDRED KATHRYN MCGRAW, nurse; b. Gary, Ind., Dec. 4, 1928; d. James Phillips and Eunice Fern (Tanner) McGraw; diploma Meth. Hosp. Sch. of Nursing, 1950; m. Harold Lundstrom, Nov. 25, 1950; children—Susan, Stephen, Robert. Staff nurse Meth. Hosp., Gary, Ind., 1950-57; supr. Parramore Hosp., Crown Point, Ind., 1957-66, dir. of nurses, 1966-73; dir. of nurses Munster (Ind.) Med-Inn, 1973-77; staff nurse Luth. Home, Crown Point, 1978—, asst. dir. nursing service, 1979; mem. bd. Med. Personnel Pool. Registered nurse, Ind. Mem. Meth. Hosp. Alumnae Assn. Lutheran.

LUNDY, JANET CECILE, histotechnologist; b. Laverty, Okla., May 20, 1942; d. Cecil LeRoy and Grace (Arnold) Parish; student pub. schs., Chickasha, Okla.; m. J.W. Lundy, Oct. 20, 1963. Histology technician Presbyterian Hosp., Oklahoma City, 1960-68; supr. histotech. Okla. Health Scis. Center, Oklahoma City, 1968-71; supr. histotech. Hillcrest Osteo. Hosp., Oklahoma City, 1972-75; supr., histotechnologist Bapt. Med. Center Okla., Oklahoma City, 1975—; mem. adj. faculty Oscar Rose Jr. Coll., 1978—. Mem. steering com. Linwood Pl. Neighborhood Assn., 1980—. Mem. Okla. Soc. Histotechnologists, Nat. Soc. Histotech. Mem. Ch. Nazarene. Home: 3132 NW 22d St Oklahoma City OK 73107 Office: 3300 North West Expressway Oklahoma City OK 73112

LUNDY, KAREN LUCIENNE, media specialist; b. Albany, Ga., Feb. 19, 1950; d. Walter Hillyer and Antoinette France (Kniskern) Lundy; student St. Andrews Presbyn. Coll., 1968-71; B.A., U. S. Fla., 1973. Media specialist public affairs office, U.S. Marine Corps Logistics Base, Albany, Ga., 1974—. Publicity chmn. S.W. Ga. Mayors' Com. on Employment of Handicapped, 1974—; public relations chmn. Albany Jr. League, 1976-77, Fed. Women's Program Week, 1974—, Hire the Handicapped Week, 1975—; emcee Very Spl. Arts Festival, 1978; publicity chmn. Albany Charity Horse Show, 1980, Albany Symphony Guild, 1979-80; rec. sec., dir. Albany Community Concert Assn., 1979-81; active Albany Little Theatre, Albany Art Mus., Albany Community Chorus. Recipient outstanding performance award, Dept. Def., 1980-81; named Ga. Handicapped Worker of Yr., 1975; Albany Profl. Handicapped Woman 1981-82. Mem. Ga. Assn. Newscasters, Marine Corps Combat Corrs. Assn., Albany Communications Council. Republican. Episcopalian. Clubs: Debutante. Contbr. articles to profl. jours. Home: 1211 Hilltop Dr Albany GA 31707 Office: Public Affairs Office Marine Corps Logistics Base Albany GA 31704

LUNN, ELLEN SUE FELDMAN, market researcher; b. N.Y.C., Aug. 27, 1951; d. Morris N. and Dorothy (Silberman) F.; B.A. cum laude, Brandeis U., 1973; M.B.A, Dartmouth Coll., 1975; m. Randall Reidy Lunn, July 1, 1982. Asst. analyst research dept. Leo Burnett, Chgo., 1975-76, asst. account exec., 1976-77; account exec. Needham, Harper & Steers Advt., Chgo., 1977-79; account exec. Gen. Foods Corp., White Plains, N.Y., 1980-82, research supr., 1982—. Home: 8 Mitzi Rd Stamford CT 06905 Office: 250 North St White Plains NY 10625

LUNNER, SHARON MITCHELL, state ofcl.; b. Elmira, N.Y., Dec. 5, 1944; d. Earl A. and Mary E. (Whitney) Mitchell; student Corning Community Coll., 1964-66; Elmira Coll., 1968-70; m. Chet Lunner, Aug. 2, 1967; children—Kristina, Kimberly. Exec. dir. Elmira Aid, Inc., 1972-76; project coordinator Regional Housing Council, Elmira, 1976; exec. dir. York Cumberland Housing Devel. Corp., Gorham, Maine, 1976-78; v.p. Housing Resources Corp., Portland, Maine, 1978-80; chmn., dir. Maine Housing Authority, Augusta, 1980—. Mem. Nat. Assn. Rehab. Officers, Council State Housing Fin. Agys. Office: Maine Housing Authority 295 Water St Augusta ME 04330

LUNSFORD, N. JO, controller; b. Hackleburg, Ala., Apr. 8, 1934; d. Buford Curtis and Lou Ella (Vance) L.; student San Diego public schs.; children—Philip Marlon, Paul William, Michael Christopher Lindsten. Controller, treas. Consol. Air Conditioning, Inc., 1961-65; controller, dir. Cert. Air Conditioning, Inc., 1967-69; adminstrv. asst. APW/Evans Automotive, 1970-75; sec.-treas., controller Green Thumb Nurseries, Inc., 1975-80; owner, operator Acctg. and Fin. Devel., San Diego, Calif., 1980—; dir. Demko Drywall Co., Inc. Mem. acctg. adv. com. Southwestern Coll. Mem. Am. Soc. Women Accts., Soc. Calif. Accts., Nat. Assn. Female Execs., C.G. Jung Found. Analytical Psychology. Office: 6209 Pontiac St San Diego CA 92115

LUPU, JANICE, physician; b. Phila., May 22, 1952; d. Michael N. and Barbara (Morris) Lupu; B.S., U. Md., 1973; M.D., Thomas Jefferson Med. Coll., 1978; m. Lawrence J. Kohn, Aug. 31, 1980. Resident in internal medicine Evanston (Ill.) Hosp., 1978-81; staff physician Mercy Hosp. and Treatment Center, Chgo., 1981-82; med. dir. Med. Clinics, 1982—. Vol., United Way. Mem. ACP. Office: Mercy Hosp Stevenson Expressway and King Dr Chicago IL 60616

LURIA, ZELLA, psychologist; b. N.Y.C., Feb. 18, 1924; d. Hyman and Dora (Garbarsky) Hurwitz; B.A., Bklyn. Coll., 1944; M.A., Ind. U., 1948, Ph.D., 1951; m. Salvador Edward Luria, Apr. 18, 1945; 1 son, Daniel. Ford Found. fellow, U. Ill., Urbana, 1951-53, Russell Sage Found. fellow, 1953-56, asst. prof. psychology, 1956-58; asst. prof. to prof. Tufts U., Medford, Mass., 1958—; lectr. psychiatry Harvard U. Med. Sch., 1971-79. USPHS fellow, Paris, 1963-64; Mellon Found. faculty devel. fellow, 1978-79. Fellow Am. Psychol. Assn.; mem. Soc. for Research in Child Devel., AAUP. Author: The Psychology of Human Sexuality, 1979. Office: Dept Psychology Tufts U Medford MA 02155

LURIE, ALISON, educator, author; b. Chgo., Sept. 3, 1926; d. Harry and Bernice (Stewart) L.; A.B. magna cum laude, Radcliffe Coll., 1947; m. Jonathan Bishop, Sept. 10, 1948 (separated); children—John, Jeremy, Joshua. Mem. faculty Cornell U., 1969—, prof. English, 1979—; author: (fiction) Love and Friendship, 1962, The Nowhere City, 1965, Imaginary Friends, 1967, Real People, 1969, The War Between the Tates, 1974, Only Children, 1979; (non-fiction) The Language of Clothes, 1981; also 3 books for children; co-editor The Garland Library of Children's Classics, 1976. Recipient award in lit. Am. Acad. Arts and Letters, 1978; Fellow Guggenheim Found., 1965, Rockefeller Found., 1968; grantee N.Y. State Council Arts, 1972. Mem. PEN, Author's Guild, Children's Lit. Assn., MLA, AAUP. Address: English Dept Cornell U Ithaca NY 14853

LURIE, BONNIE, fin. co. exec.; b. Bronx, N.Y., June 28, 1949; d. Arthur and Estelle Lurie; B.A., Queen's Coll., 1970; M.A., Adelphi U., 1971; M.S., Northwestern U., 1972; postgrad. So. Ill. U., 1972-74. Mgmt. cons. Queens Mgmt. Assn., N.Y.C., 1975-78; dir. tng. and devel. dept. Union Dime Savs. Bank, N.Y.C., 1978-80; mgr.-dir. performance, tng. and devel. Citicorp/Citibank, N.Y.C., 1980—; asst. prof. Morris County (N.J.) Coll., 1978-80. Teaching fellow, So. Ill. U., Carbondale, 1973-75. Mem. Am. Soc. Tng. and Devel., Soc. Indsl. Psychologists. Democrat. Home: 1 Stuyvesant Oval New York NY 10009 Office: 399 Park Ave New York NY 10036

LURIE, MURIEL, psychiat. social worker; b. N.Y.C., June 16, 1915; d. Arthur and Celia (Nochimson) L.; B.A., SUNY, Albany, 1967, M.S.W., 1972; children—Daniel, Carolyn. Sec., fund raiser, fund-raising concerns, 1937-39; researcher/editor U.S. Senate Com. Investigating R.R.s, 1939-42; newswriter/editor OWI, London, 1942-45; mgr. advt. agy., N.Y.C., 1946-49; dir. social services depts. Childs Nursing Home and University Heights Health Center, Albany, 1972-79; legis./policy asso. N.Y. State chpt. Nat. Assn. Social Workers, 1979—; pvt. practice counseling and psychotherapy, Albany, 1978—; cons. area nursing homes, 1972—. Alt. del. White House Conf. on Aging, 1981; mem. Long-Term Care Task Force, Health Systems Agy. N.E. N.Y., 1976—, mem. Albany Sub-Area Council, 1980—. Mem. Nat. Assn. Social Workers, Long-Term Care Social Workers N.E. N.Y. (co-founder 1974), Acad. Cert. Social Workers, Urban League, LWV, Health Edn. and Welfare Club Albany (dir. 1978—). Home: 21 Park Ln S Menands NY 12204 Office: Nat Assn Social Workers 225 Lark St Albany NY 12210

LURIE, NANCY OESTREICH, anthropologist; b. Milw., Jan. 29, 1924; d. Carl Ralph and Rayline (Danielson) Oestreich; B.A., U. Wis., 1945; M.A., U. Chgo., 1947; Ph.D., Northwestern U., 1952; LL.D., Northland Coll., 1976; m. Edward Lurie, 1951 (div. 1963). Instr. U. Wis.-Milw., 1947-49, 51-53, asst. prof., 1961-63, prof., 1963-72, chmn. anthropology dept., 1967-70; curator anthropology Milw. Public Museum, 1972—; lectr. U. Mich., 1956-61, cons. expert witness for attys. representing tribal clients before U.S. Indian Claims Commn., 1957-64; Fulbright lectr. U. Aarhus, Denmark, 1965-66. Recipient (with co-editor) Anisfield-Wolf award for best scholarly book in intergroup relations, The American Indian Today, 1968. Fellow AAAS, Am. Anthrop. Assn. (exec. bd. 1977-80); mem. Am. Ethnol. Soc., Soc. Applied Anthropology, Central States Anthrop. Soc. (pres. 1967), Sigma Xi. Editor, translator: Mountain Wolf Woman, The Autobiography of a Winnebago Woman, 1961. Home: 3342 N Gordon Pl Milwaukee WI 53212

LURTH, SHARON ERICKSON, investment broker, tax specialist; b. Mpls., Nov. 14, 1938; d. Ivar Carl and Beatrice Josephine (Wiberg) Erickson; B.A. in Sociology and Psychology, Macalester Coll., St. Paul, 1961; postgrad. in bus. adminstrn., fin. U. Minn., N.Y.U.; separated; children—Kathleen Ann, Deborah Jean, Rebecca Joanne. Chief exec. officer Erickson Motor & Oil Co., Inc., Mpls., 1972—; pres., owner Kabobs, Inc., St. Paul and Edina, Minn., 1972-76; investment broker Bache, Halsey Stuart Shields, Inc., Mpls., 1977—; cons., seminar speaker in field. Founder Minn. chpt. Alliance Displaced Homemakers, also chmn., regional cons., 1974-77; nat. speaker, local officer, chmn. employment com. Mpls. chpt. NOW, 1972-76; founding mem., mem. steering com. Minn. Women's Polit. Caucus, 1971; Minn. rep. LWV, 1974-75; founder St. Croix Valley Human Rights Com., 1965. Mem. Internat. Soc. Registered Reps., Am. Mgmt. Assn., Minn. Women Investment Brokers Assn., AMEX Club. Lutheran. Clubs: Greenway Athletic, Blaisdell Women's. Home: 6566 France Ave S Edina MN 55435 Office: 2020 IDS Tower Minneapolis MN 55402

LUSCOMBE, WENDY, real estate cons.; b. Seend, Wilshire, Eng., Oct. 29, 1951; came to U.S., 1981; d. Norman Percival and Betty (Hall) Luscombe; diploma in estate mgmt., Oxford Sch. Architecture, 1972. Investment analyst Taylor Woodrow Property Co., World Trade Center, London, 1972; surveyor N. European Regional Group, Chase Manhattan N.A., London, 1973-77; head research div. Knight Frank & Rutley, intern. property cons., London, 1977-78; property mgr. Nat. Coal Bd. Pension Funds, also pres., dir. subs. Pan-Am. Properties, Inc., N.Y.C., 1978—; dir. Midas SA, First Intercontinental and Third Intercontinental Properties, Inc.; arbitrator London Small Claims Ct., 1976-79. Chartered surveyor; chartered arbitrator. Mem. Royal Instn. Chartered Surveyors (dep. chmn. eastern U.S. region), Chartered Inst. Arbitrators (U.K.). Contbr. articles in field to profl. jours. Office: 521 Fifth Ave Suite 1407 New York NY 10175

LUSK, JOAN EDITH, chemist, educator; b. Teaneck, N.J., July 29, 1942; B.A., Radcliffe Coll., 1964; Ph.D. in Biol. Chemistry, Harvard U., 1970. Nat. Cystic Fibrosis Research Found. fellow in biology M.I.T., 1970-71; NIH fellow in biology, 1971-72; asst. prof. chemistry Brown U., 1972-77, assoc. prof., 1977—. Prin. investigator NIH research grant, 1973; NSF grantee, 1974; NIH Career Devel. awardee, 1976. Mem. Am. Soc. Microbiology, AAAS. Office: Dept Chemistry Brown University Providence RI 02912 *

LUSKY, LOIS FREESE, pub. relations exec.; b. Wahpeton, N.D., Sept. 28, 1931; d. James and Edna Elizabeth (Eckes) Freese; student N.D. Sch. Sci., 1949-52, U. Denver, 1953-55; m. Sam Lusky, July 14, 1966; 1 stepson, Mark. Pub. relations asst. United Bank Denver, 1958-60, asst. pub. relations dir., 1960-63, dir. pub. relations, 1963-65; exec. v.p. Sam Lusky Assos., Inc., Denver, 1965-79; sr. v.p. Hill and Knowlton Inc., 1979—. Mem. pub. relations com. United Fund Agy., 1960-65; pub. relations counsel Boys Clubs Denver, 1963-65; mem. Gov.'s Com. Status of Women, 1969-71; bd. dirs. Auraria Community Center, 1958-62, Denver Partnership; co-chmn. media div. Mile High United Way; publicity/promotion chmn. Gov.'s and Mayor's Colo. Pro Sports Com.; bd. advisers Salvation Army; bd. dirs., v.p., mem. exec. com. Jr. Achievement Met. Denver, 1977—; bd. dirs. Colo. Celebration of Arts, 1978; mem. adv. bd., exec.-in-residence U. Denver Sch. Bus. Adminstrn. Mem. Pub. Relations Soc. Am. (state v.p. 1966), Colo. Indsl. Press Assn. (past dir.), Am. Assn. Advt. Agencies, 1st Advt. Agy. Network, Denver Advt. Fedn., Denver C. of C. (past dir., exec. com., vice chmn. membership and communications group). Home: 6340 E 6th Ave Denver CO 80220 Office: 909 17th St Suite 505 Denver CO 80202

LUSSI, ELSBETH, transl. co. exec.; b. Zurich, Switzerland, Mar. 26, 1949; came to U.S., 1971; d. Henri and Emmi (Suter) L.; degree in bus. and econs. Raeber's Handelsschule, Zurich, 1968. Sec. to tech. dir. Moevenpick-Zentralverwaltung, Zurich, 1968-69, asst. chief accountant, 1969-71; exec. asst. to owner and chmn. Wolfschmidt Ltd., N.Y.C. and London, 1971-72, mgr., London, 1972-74, mng. dir., officer, London, 1974-78; co-owner, exec. v.p. Translation Co. of Am. Inc., N.Y.C., 1978—; co-owner, pres. Eurasia Lang. Services, Ltd., N.Y.C., 1979—. Mem. Am. Mgmt. Assn., Swiss Soc. N.Y., Women's Nat. Republican Club. Home: 244 Asharoken Ave Northport NY 11768 Office: 500 Fifth Ave New York NY 10036

LUST, VIRGINIA, art gallery dir.; b. Chgo., July 23, 1930; d. Nathaniel K. and Helen (Dillmann) Wertheimer; B.A., Mundelein Coll., Chgo., 1952; m. Herbert C. Lust, Aug. 17, 1963. Freelance publicist, 1952-68; dir. Gallery Bernard, Chgo., 1968-73; owner, dir. Virginia Lust Gallery, N.Y.C., also Graphics Club, Ltd., N.Y.C., 1973—; dir. Delvaux Retrospective of Prints and Drawings, 1969, Bellmer Retrospective, 1970. Home: 54 Porchuck Rd Greenwich CT 06830 Office: 1356 Madison Ave New York NY 10028

LUSZKI, MARGARET BARRON, psychologist; b. Washington, Mar. 24, 1907; d. Charles Henry and Helena (Johnson) Butler; A.B., U. Mich., 1928; M.A., U. Md., 1930; postgrad. Cath. U. Am. Sch. Social Work, 1939-40, Washington Sch. Psychiatry, 1945-47, M.I.T., 1947-48; Ph.D., U. Mich., 1951; m. Walter A. Luszki, Mar. 15, 1950. Employee counselor Social Security Bd. and FSA, 1939-43; chief employee relations sect. HEW, 1943-50; lectr. U.S. Dept. Agr. Grad. Sch., 1945-47, Am. U., 1951; project coordinator work confs. in mental health research Nat. Tng. Labs., 1951-57; cons. student personal adjustment Paine Coll., Augusta, Ga., 1957-58; psychologist VA Hosp., Augusta, 1958-59; psychol. cons. Crippled Children's div. Ga. Dept. Health, 1958-59; study dir. Research Center for Group Dynamics, Inst. Social Research, U. Mich., 1960-61; clin. psychologist, vocat. counselor VA Hosp., Ann Arbor, Mich., 1961-66; research asso. Center Research on Utilization Sci. Knowledge, Inst. Social Research, U. Mich., 1961-66; clin. psychologist VA Hosp., Charleston, S.C., 1966-72; asso. psychiatry dept. psychiatry and behavioral scis. Med. U. S.C., Charleston, 1968—; cons. psychologist, Charleston, 1966—. Founder, exec. sec. Goodwill Industries of Lower S.C., Inc., 1975-79. Fellow Am. Psychol. Assn., Soc. Psychol. Study Social Issues, Am. Sociol. Assn. Unitarian. Author: Interdisciplinary Team Research: Methods and Problems, 1958; (with Fox and Schmuck) Diagnosing Classroom Learning Environments, 1966; (with Walter A. Luszki) How to Test Your Dog's IQ, 1980, How to Test Your Cat's IQ, 1982; contbr. articles to profl. jours. Home: 502 E Indian Ave Box 72 Folly Beach SC 29439 Office: 165 Maple St Charleston SC 29403

LUTHER, FLORENCE JOAN (MRS. CHARLES W. LUTHER), lawyer; b. N.Y.C. June 28, 1928; d. John Phillip and Catherine Elizabeth (Duffy) Thomas ; J.D. magna cum laude, U. Pacific, 1963; m. William J. Regan (dec.); children—Kevin P., Brian T.; m. 2d, Charles W. Luther, June 11, 1961. Admitted to Calif. bar; mem. firm Luther, Luther, O'Connor & Johnson, Sacramento, 1964—. Mem. faculty McGeorge Sch. Law, U. Pacific, Sacramento, 1966—, prof., 1968—. Judge Bank Am. Achievement awards, 1969-71. Bd. dirs. Sacramento Suicide Prevention League, 1969-70. Mem. Am., Calif., Sacramento County bar assns., AAUP, Womens Legal Groups, Am. Judicature Soc., Order of Coif, Iota Tau Tau. Mem. bd. advisors Community Property Jour., 1974—, state decision editor, 1974—. Home: 8455 Winding Way Fair Oaks CA 95628 Office: PO Box 2151 Fair Oaks CA 95628

LUTHER, GRACE ANN, psychologist; b. Dayton, Ohio, July 18, 1926; d. Aloysius B. and Viola Luther; B.S., U. Dayton, 1948; student L'Institut Catholique de Paris, France, 1950-52; M.A., Catholic U. Am., 1962; Ph.D., U. Ill., 1972. Tchr., Holy Angels Sch., Dayton, Ohio, 1948-49; novice Marianist Sisters, Sucy-en-Brie, France, 1949-52; tchr., prin. St. Joseph Sch., Devine, Tex., 1952-62; residence hall dir. U. Dayton, 1962-69; prof., grad. advisor dept. edn. St. Mary's U., San Antonio, 1972-76, chairperson dept. human services, 1976-81; supr. schs. Marianist Sisters, 1956-69, mem. provincial council, 1956-69. Mem., chairperson Bexar County (Tex.) Mental Health-Mental Retardation Adv. Bd., 1975-79; mem. state certification bd. Tex. Assn. Alcoholism Counselors, 1976-79; mem. regional alcoholism adv. council Alamo Area Council Govts., 1975-81. Mem. S. Tex. Personnel and Guidance Assn. (pres. 1977-78), Am. Psychol. Assn., Am. Personnel and Guidance Assn., Am. Assn. Marriage and Family Therapists, Am. Mental Health Counselors Assn., Tex. Assn. Counselor Edn. and Supervision (pres. 1980-81), Assn. for Counselor Edn. and Supervision, Tex. Assn. Alcoholism Counselors. Roman Catholic. Contbr. articles to profl. jours. Home: St Mary's U 1 Camino Santa Maria San Antonio TX 78284 Office: Dept Human Services St Mary's U 1 Camino Santa Maria San Antonio TX 78284

LUTMAN, MARLENE ELIZABETH, constrn. co. exec.; b. Newark, Dec. 1, 1933; d. Abraham and Shirley (Janow) Carnow; B.S. in Commerce and Fin., Bucknell U., 1955; m. Stanley Kramer, Aug. 7, 1955 (dec. 1967); children—Deborah Frances, Elizabeth Anne; m. 2d, Martin Lutman, Aug. 27, 1969 (dec. 1981). Asst. research dir. Modern Materials Handling Co., Boston, 1955-57; econ. analyst, project adminstr. United Research Inc., Cambridge, Mass., 1957-58; free lance tech. writer, econ. analyst, 1958-66; asst. mgr. survey planning and market research IBM, White Plains, N.Y., 1967-69; mgr. research services McKinsey & Co., Cleve., 1969-72; v.p., dir. Am. Custom Homes, Cleve., 1971—; sec., dir. S.W. Fla. Bldg. Corp., Cape Coral, 1979—; part owner, v.p., dir. Am. Custom Builders Inc., Cape Coral, Fla., 1978—; partner, dir. Star Realty Inc., Coral Gables, 1980—. Mem. Econ. and Indsl. Devel. Task Force, City of Cape Coral, 1979. Mem. Nat. Assn. Homebuilders, Nat. Bd. Realtors, Fla. Assn. Realtors, Bldg. Industry Assn., Constrn. Industry Assn. Home: 1624 Palaco Grande Pkwy Cape Coral FL 33904 Office: Am Custom Builders Inc 2706 Del Prado Blvd Cape Coral FL 33904

LUTTBEG, LINDA EISENSTATT, wholesale co. exec., civic worker; b. Omaha, Dec. 30, 1948; d. Leo and Aileen Phyliss (Feder) Eisenstatt; B.S. in Edn., U. Nebr., Omaha, 1970, M.S. in Social Scis., 1971; m. Steven M. Luttbeg, June 14, 1970; children—David, Lisa. Social studies tchr. Central High Sch., Omaha, 1970-75; exec. dir. Girls' Club Omaha, 1975-78, developer advocacy for girls campaign, San Diego, Calif., 1979-80; partner L&L Products, San Diego, 1981-82; pres. A Thing or Two, Inc., San Diego, 1982—. Mem. Mayor's Task Force on Police and Community Relations., 1973-74; active LWV, 1971-78, Clarkson Hosp. Service League, 1972-78, Mayor's Commn. Status of Women, 1976-77, CETA Planning Council, 1976-77, San Diego Juvenile Justice Commn., 1979-81; chairperson Girls Rehab. Facility inspection team, 1980; adv. bd. Girls' Club Pasadena, 1979—; bd. dirs. Western region Girls' Clubs Am., 1980—; bd. dirs. Jewish Community Center, chairperson presch. com., 1980-81; Named hon. citizen of Omaha, 1975, Women of Yr. in human services Nebr. Women's Polit. Caucus, 1977; recipient nat. award Girls' Clubs Am., 1978, Founder's Day award Girls' Club Omaha, 1979. Club: Jr. League (San Diego). Office: 438 Camino Del Rio S Suite B213 San Diego CA 92108

LUTZ, DEBORAH S., beverage mktg. exec.; b. Columbus, Ohio, Mar. 15, 1948; d. Robert E. and Carol M. Clark; B.S. in Journalism cum laude, Ohio U., 1969; m. Steven J. Lutz, May 25, 1975; children—Julie Anne, Jennifer Joyce. Pub. relations assoc. Clairol Corp., N.Y.C., 1968; fgn. currency teller Chase Manhattan Bank, Heidelberg, W.Ger., 1969-70; mdse. buyer F&R Lazarus, Columbus, 1971-74; product publicist, brand mgr. Borden, Inc., Columbus, 1974-77; co-owner C&L Real Estate Agy., Columbus, 1979—; market planning mgr. Beverage Mgmt., Inc., Columbus, 1977-81, v.p. mktg., 1981—; cons. in field, 1974—. Active Nat. Republican party, 1975—, Franklin County Rep. party, 1975—, Working Assn. of Columbus Zoo, 1980—, Pro Met, 1982—. Mem. Women in Communications, Dublin Bus. and Profl. Women. Home: 6164 Karrer Pl Dublin OH 43017 Office: Beverage Mgmt Inc 1001 Kingsmill Pkwy Columbus OH 43229

LUTZ, EDITH LEDFORD, state legislator; b. Lawndale, N.C., Oct. 20, 1914; d. Thomas Curtis and Annie (Hoyle) Ledford; grad. pub. schs.; m. M. Everett Lutz, Oct. 25, 1933; 1 son, E. Jacob. Farmer, fruit grower, Lawndale, N.C.; mem. N.C. Ho. Reps., 1976—; mem. various coms. Bd. dirs. Farm Bur. Cleveland County. Mem. Cleveland County Farm Bur., Upper Cleveland County C. of C. (bd. dirs.), N.C. Apple Grower's Assn., Sheltered Workshops of Rutherford County (bd. dirs.), Am. Assn. Bus. Women. Methodist (Sunday sch. tchr., treas. Woman's Orgn., counselor Youth Fellowship). Office: NC Ho Reps State Capitol Raleigh NC 27602 *

LUTZ, GAIL LAVERNE MCGRADY, univ. adminstr.; b. Jackson, Miss., Oct. 12, 1941; d. Henry C. and Maude W. Skinner; B.A., DePaul U.; 1 son, Steven. Office mgr. Quartet Mfg. Co., Lincolnwood, Ill., 1960-66; internat. banking specialist Am. Express Co., Mannheim, Germany, 1967-69; sr. acct. Bland Lincoln Mercury, Chgo., 1969-70; exec. adminstr., office of pres. Johnson Products Co., Inc., Chgo., 1970-81; dir. univ. relations Sangamon State U., Springfield, Ill., 1981—. Mem. allocation panel United Way. Recipient cert. of leadership YMCA of Met. Chgo., 1975; Beautiful Black People award Chgo. Urban League, 1976. Mem. People United to Save Humanity, Springfield Urban League (dir.), Public Relations Soc. Am. Roman Catholic. Office: Sangamon State U Shepherd Rd PAC-570 Springfield IL 62708

LUTZ, HELEN IRENE DRAKE (MRS. WILFORD RAY LUTZ), city ofcl.; b. Dayton, Ohio, Sept. 4, 1918; d. Charles Francis and Hattie May (Smith) Drake; grad. Miami-Jacobs Jr. Coll., 1937; student U. Dayton, 1938-40; grad. Ohio State U. mcpl. clks. career devel. program, 1980; m. Wilford Ray Lutz, June 26, 1948; children—Gary Ray, Lynnette Irene. Exec. sec. to advt. and sales promotion mgr. Frigidaire div. Gen. Motors Sales Corp., Dayton, 1937-40; adminstr. asst. statis. services div. USAF Hdqrs. Air Force Logistics Command, Wright-Patterson AFB, 1940-53; with City of Kettering (Ohio), 1956—, clk. city council, 1973—, council liaison Kettering Sister City Com., Kettering Citizen Award Com. asst. to exec. editor EUB Bd. Publ., 1965-68. Vice pres. Orville Wright Elem. Sch. PTA, Dayton, 1963-64; pres. fellowship class First Luth. Ch., Dayton, 1973-74, also chmn. public relations com. Named Kettering Woman of Yr., 1977; Kettering Citizen of Yr., 1981; cert. mcpl. clk. Mem. Internat., Ohio (pres.) mcpl. clks. assns., Kettering Hist. Soc., Aurean Lit. Soc. (pres. 1935-36), DAR, Children Am. Revolution (local pres. 1935-36, nat. registrar 1937-38, Ohio pres. 1936-38). Mem. Order Eastern Star. Home: 840 E David Rd Kettering OH 45429 Office: Kettering Govt Center 3600 Shroyer Rd Kettering OH 45429

LUTZ, SHIRLEY RIFE, mfg. co. ofcl.; b. Richlands, Va., Aug. 17, 1952; d. Mack and Clara (Sword) Rife; student Southwest Va. Community Coll., 1971-73; m. Oct. 28, 1972; 1 dau., Tracey Denise. With S&S Corp., Cedar Bluff, Va., 1971—, buyer maintenance-repairs-ops., 1977-79, sr. buyer, 1979—, dir. credit union, 1974—. Mem. Nat. Secs. Assn. (pres. Lonesome Pine chpt.), Secs. Guild Am., Hon. Order Ky. Cols., Nat. Assn. Female Execs. (network dir.). Republican. Home: 430 Fincastle Tazewell VA 24651 Office: Rt 3 Box 70 Cedar Bluff VA 24609

LUTZE, MARIETTA, psychotherapist, psychoanalyst; b. San Francisco, Mar. 17, 1919; d. Felix and Frederika C. (Durkes) L.; M.D. with honors, U. Berlin, 1943; m. Arthur Mitchell Sackler, 1949 (div. 1981); children—Arthur Felix Sackler, Denise Marika. Intern, Rockaway (L.I., N.Y.) Beach Hosp., 1946-47, Queens Gen. Hosp., Queens Village, N.Y., 1948-49; psychiatrist Creedmore State Hosp., Queens Village, 1953-54; coordinator videotape dept. of family therapy dept. Postgrad. Center Mental Health, N.Y.C., 1964-74, asso. dir. family therapy dept., 1974-75; pvt. practice individual and family therapy, N.Y.C., 1974—; owner, chmn. bd. Dr. Kade Pharmazeutische Fabrik, GmbH, Berlin and Konstanz, Germany, 1949—. Mem. internat. task force to assess future needs world med. health manpower WHO. Mem. adv. council dept. art history and archaeology Columbia U., N.Y.C., 1971, 75. Life fellow Met. Mus. Art, N.Y.C.; mem. Internat. (sec. gen. 1972-74), Am. assns. social psychiatry, AMA, Am. Group Psychotherapy Soc., Am. Med. Women's Assn., Eastern Group Therapy Assn., German Women's Mgrs. Assn.

LUTZKER, EDYTHE, historian, writer, researcher; b. Berlin, Germany, June 25, 1904; d. Solomon and Sophia (Katz) Levine; B.A., City Coll. N.Y., 1954; M.A., Columbia U., 1959; m. Philip Lutzker, June 14, 1924; children—Michael Arnold, Arthur Samuel, Paul William. Bookkeeper, sec., exec. for bus. cos., N.Y.C., 1922-49; research asst. to Prof. Edward Rosen, City Coll. N.Y., 1951-54; author: Women Gain a Place in Medicine, 1969; Edith Pechey-Phipson M.D., Story of England's Foremost Pioneering Woman Doctor, 1973. Pres. Child Care Center Parents Assn., 1943-51. Grantee Am. Philos. Soc., 1964, 65, Nat. Library of Medicine, 1966, 68-71, 72-74. Fellow Royal Soc. Medicine; mem. Am. Assn. History of Medicine, Am. Soc. for Microbiology, Soc. Internat. History Medicine, History of Sci. Soc., Am. Hist. Assn., Jewish Acad. Arts and Scis., Fawcett Soc. Democrat. Contbr. articles profl. publs., lectr. profl. orgns. Founder, v.p. Waldemar M. Haffkine Internat. Meml. Com. Home and Office: 201 W 89th St New York NY 10024

LUZURIAGA, ADEL, Realtor, investment counselor; b. Philippines, Oct. 31, 1949; came to U.S., 1969; d. Laurie Trinidad; student Maryknoll Coll., U. Madrid, Glendale Coll.; m. Apr. 1, 1970 (div.). With Kramer Wilson Co., 1971-74, Barnes Ins. Agy., 1974-75; salesperson PRO Realty, 1975-80; pres. Realty Benefit Systems Inc., 1980—. Mem. Nat. Assn. Realtors, Calif. Assn. Realtors, Glendale Bd. Realtors. Roman Catholic. Clubs: Toastmistress, Glendale Messengers. Office: 210 E Glenoaks Blvd Glendale CA 91207

LUZZATI, RUTH ELWOOD, state legislator; b. Omaha, Oct. 19, 1922; d. Harold Elwood and Pleasant Holyoke; student UCLA, 1940-43; divorced; 1 dau., Katharyn (Mrs. Reiser). Mem. Kans. Ho. Reps., 1972—. Mem. Nat. Womens Polit. Caucus, NAACP, YWCA (dir.), LWV, Alpha Chi Omega. Unitarian. Office: Kans Ho Reps State Capitol Topeka KS 66612

LYBARGER, ADRIENNE REYNOLDS (MRS. LEE FRANCIS LYBARGER, JR.), coll. adminstr.; b. Boston, Mar. 8, 1926; d. Joseph Anthony and Albertine Mouton (Drevet) Reynolds; B.A., Mills Coll., 1947; certificate Katharine Gibbs Sch., 1948; m. Lee Francis Lybarger, Jr., Sept. 15, 1955 (dec.); children—Linda, Lauretta, James (dec.), Lisa, Leslie (dec.), Jeffrey (dec.), Lucia, Lana. Asst. to dir. Mid-Century convocation M.I.T., Cambridge, 1949, asst. to dir. West Coast regional office Mid-Century devel. program, 1949-50, asst. dir. So. regional office, 1950-51; asst. to dir. convocation program Ithaca (N.Y.) Coll., 1951; asst. to dir., devel. program U. Buffalo (N.Y.), 1951-52; asst. to dir. Diamond Jubilee program Case Inst. Tech., Cleve., 1952-54; asst. dir., expansion and improvement program John D. Archbold Hosp., Thomasville, Ga., 1954-55; partner Lybarger Prodns., comml. films, N.Y.C., 1955-61; asst. dir., then dir. regional campaigns, Ohio, Boston, Mass., N.Y.C., also supr. all other nat. regional campaigns Mt. Holyoke Coll. Fund for Future, South Hadley, Mass., 1961-63; fund-raising cons. to capital programs, Vocation Service Center and Bronx-Westchester YMCA, YMCA Greater N.Y., 1963-65; dir. devel. and pub. relations Bank Street Coll. Edn., N.Y.C., 1965-79; cons. South Bronx Overall Econ. Devel. Corp., 1978-79; cons. Manhattan Community Coll., 1979—; v.p. for devel., dir. Capital Campaign, Wells Coll., Aurora, N.Y., 1979—; Realtor-asso. Century 21 Realtors, Clinton, N.J., 1979—. Mem. Council for Advancement and Support Edn., Deferred Giving Group of N.Y.; trustee, pres. Birch Island Corp., 1978-79. Author: (with L.F. Lybarger) Proven Guides to Effective Soliciting (slide film), 1950, rev., 1960, 81; exec. producer, script writer Now More Than Ever (film). Home: Kings Manor Pittstown NJ 08867 Office: Wells Coll Aurora NY 13026

LYERLY, VICKI ANN, social worker; b. El Paso, Tex., Nov. 17, 1945; d. Paul Junior and Mary Lucille (Ludwig) L.; B.A. with honors, U. Tex., Austin, 1968; M.A., Georgetown U., 1981. Tchr. public schs. Clark County, Nev., 1968; caseworker Monroe County (N.Y.) Dept. Social Services, 1968-79; pvt. practice social work, Washington, 1980—; cons., researcher Latin American social problems. Mem. Nat. Assn. Social Workers, Soc. Intercultural Edn., Tng. and Research. Contbr. articles in field to profl. publs. Home and Office: 310 N Street SW Washington DC 20024

LYLE, GLENDA WILHELMA SWANSON, planner; b. Knoxville, Tenn., Sept. 29, 1940; d. Richard James and Mary Elizabeth (Fudge) Swanson; B.A., U. Denver, 1964, M.A., 1973; m. Percy Howard Lyle, Jr., Aug. 25, 1962; children—Kipp Elise, Jennifer Beth, Anth. Swanson. Social worker Cath. Community Services, 1965; dir. Head Start Agy., Denver, 1967-70; instr., coordinator early childhood devel. Community Coll. of Denver, 1970-71, div. dir. community and personal services, 1971-73; program dir. United Way Info. and Referral Services, 1974-75; owner, pres. Planners, Etc., profl. planners, Denver, 1974—. Mem. Nat. Pub. Lands Adv. Council, 1980-81; bd. dirs. YWCA, 1980—, N.E. Women's Center, Denver; v.p. Found. for Urban and Neighborhood Devel., Denver; mem. adv. council SBA. Named Colo. Outstanding Profl. and Bus. Woman, 1981. Mem. Am. Planning Assn., Nat. Assn. Women in Planning, Women and Bus. Inc. (exec. com.), Colo. Black Women for Polit. Action, Am. Assn. Blacks in Energy, Black Women's Network, Black Econ. Forum. Home: 1619 Monaco Pkwy Denver CO 80220 Office: Planners Etc 1722 Lafayette St Denver CO 80218

LYLE, JEROLYN ROSS, economist: b. Meridian, Miss., Sept. 12, 1937; d. Fred A., Sr., and Everette B. Ross; B.A., So. Meth. U., 1958; M.A., U. Md., 1966, Ph.D., 1970; spl. studies in Spanish, Inst. Francisco Marroquin, Guatemala, 1975; m. Frank Allen Lyle, June 21, 1958; children—Kathryn E., James Jeffrey. Tchr., Dallas Public Schs., 1958-59, Arlington County County Schs., Arlington, Va., 1961-62, 63-64; tchr., curriculum specialist Houston Public Schs., 1959-61; office mgr. No. Va. Fair Housing Assn., 1965-67; economist, program specialist Office of Edn. and HEW, 1966-68; economist EEO Commn., 1968-71; mem. faculty econs. Am. U., 1971-75, Smith Coll., 1971; sr. economist Inter-Am. Devel. Bank, 1974-75; sr. economist Office Mgmt. and Budget, Exec. Office of the Pres., 1975-76; sr. economist Fed. Emergency Mgmt. Agy., Washington, 1976—; cons. Urban Inst., 1971-72, Office Statis. Policy, Office Mgmt. and Budget, 1972, Office of Edn. and HEW, 1974; research asso. 1963. Prin. investigator corp. affirmative action programs EEO, 1971-73; travel grantee to India and Brazil, Internat. Communications Agy., 1978-79. Mem. Am. Econ. Assn., Am. Statis. Assn., Soc. Govt. Economists (dir. 1979-80), Indsl. Relations Research Assn., Allied Social Sci. Assns. Methodist. Author: Women in Industry, 1973; The Dynamics of Recent Inflation in Latin America, 1975; (with E. Zabrowski) A Proposed Method for Estimating the Critical Characteristics of Stockpile Materials, 1979; Estimating the Employment Impact of Trade Deficits for Input-Output Sectors of the U.S. Economy, 1980; contbr. articles to profl. jours. Home: 5512 Center St Chevy Chase MD 20815 Office: Federal Emergency Management Agency Washington DC 20407

LYLE, MARGUERITE RICHARD, educator; b. Lafayette, La., Sept. 13, 1929; d. Clarence Phillip and Jacqueline (Weil) Richard; B.A., U. Southwestern La., 1950; M.A., Fla. State U., 1970; m. Michael Guy Lyle, Aug. 3, 1952; children—Melinda, Jacqueline, Michael Guy II, Elizabeth. Tchr., Lake Charles (La.) City Sch. System, 1951-52, Allen Parish Sch. System, 1952-64; asst. prof. speech communication U. Southwestern La., 1965—; communication cons. U.S. Office Personnel Mgmt.; cons. on listening skills profl. and civic groups. Mem. Lafayette Natural History Mus. and Planetarium Commn., chmn., 1971-74; mem. 100 mem. Task Force on Ednl. Accountability, La., chmn. pupil proficiency com., 1978-80; mem. La. Adv. Com. Exceptional Children, 1970-71; mem. Lafayette Sch. Bd. Recipient service award Lafayette Natural History Mus. and Planetarium, 1976, Future Bus. Leaders Am., 1976; named Lafayette Woman of Achievement, 1982. Mem. La. Speech Assn. (pres. 1980-81), So. Speech Communication Assn. (exec. council 1981-82), Speech Communication Assn. Am., Internat. Listening Assn. (charter), Speech Communication Assn., Greater Lafayette C. of C. (profl. lectr.), Future Farmers Am. (hon.), Phi Kappa Phi, Pi Kappa Delta. Democrat. Roman Catholic. Author: Design for Speaking, 1971; Effective Oral Communication, 1971. Office: Box 43650 University of Southwestern Louisiana Lafayette LA 70504

LYMAN, ELLYN ELIZABETH, personnel exec.; b. Albuquerque, Sept. 3, 1951; d. Robert Joseph and Mary Coletta (Burkhardt) L.; B.A., Purdue U., 1973; M.B.A., Keller Grad. Sch. Mgmt., Chgo., 1980. Research asst. Heidrick and Struggles, Chgo., 1974-75; with AT&T Long Lines, 1975-82, staff supr. nat. markets planning, Bedminster, N.J., 1980-82; mgr. employment and staffing AT&T, Jacksonville, Fla., 1982—. Pres., 525 Grove Condominium Assn., Evanston, Ill., 1979-80. Nat. Merit Scholar, 1970-73. Mem. Nat. Assn. Female Execs., Women in Communications, Purdue U. Alumni Assn., Assn. for Research and Enlightenment, Assn. M.B.A. Execs., AT&T Women's Network, Chgo. Women's Network. Clubs: The Sounding Board, AT&T Ski. Home: 2 Ash Ln Harding Green Morristown NJ 07960 Office: AT&T PO Box 2018 New Brunswick NJ 08903

LYMAN, HELEN HUGUENOR, librarian, educator, author; b. Hornell, N.Y., Mar. 16, 1910; s. Leon and Lora (Hamilton) Huguenor; B.A., SUNY, Buffalo, 1932, B.S. in Library Sci., 1940; postgrad. U. Chgo., 1955-56; m. Vreelandt B. Lyman, Jr., Apr. 29, 1939; m. 2d, Samray Smith, June 17, 1953. Circulation asst. Buffalo Public Library, 1932-35, co-head readers' bur., 1935-42, adminstrv. asst., 1942-43, head adult edn. dept., 1943-52; dir. adult edn. survey ALA, Chgo., 1952-53; adult services librarian Hild br. Chgo. Public Library, 1953-59; public library cons., specialist in adult services Wis. Free Library Commn., Madison, 1959-63; asso. librarian, dir. reference dept. Lockwood Library, 1964-65; public library specialist for adult services, library services br. Office of Edn., HEW, Washington, 1965-67; instr. U. Wis., Madison, 1966, asst. prof., 1967-73, asso. prof., 1973-76, prof., 1976-78, prof. emerita, 1978—, dir. and cons. Reading Guidance Inst., Library Sch., 1965; adj. prof. SUNY, Buffalo, 1982—; vis. prof. U. Denver, summer 1978, SUNY, Buffalo, spring 1980, summer 1982; cons. No. Ill. U., Literacy Vols. Am., Inc. and Nat. Endowment Humanities, numerous others; lectr., cons. Library Assn. Australia, 1979; lectr. Kuring-gai Coll. Advanced Edn., U. New South Wales, Ballarat Coll. Advanced Edn., Royal Melbourne Inst. Tech., Melbourne State Coll., Canberra Coll. Advanced Edn., Tasmanian Coll. Advanced Edn., S. Australia Inst. Tech., W. Australia Inst. Tech. (all Australia); mem. Chgo. Public Library Staff Assn., 1958-59, chmn. com. profl. devel., 1958-59; mem. D.C. Library Assn., 1966-67; mem. nat. adv. bd. Center for the Book, Library of Congress, 1978-82. Bd. dirs. Buffalo Council World Affairs, 1949-52, Great Books Found., Chgo., 1950-54; mem. Buffalo Council Adult Edn., 1950-52, Madison Adult Edn. Group, 1961-63; mem. Wis. Arts Found. and Council, 1959-63, bd. dirs., 1961-63; mem. Albright-Knox Art Gallery, Buffalo, 1964-67, 78—; treas. Adult Edn. Assn. Greater Washington, 1965-67; mem. Adult Edn. Assn. Wis., 1967-69; bd. dirs. Univ. Book Store, Madison, 1973-77, chmn. awards com., 1974-76, sec., 1976-77. Recipient Joseph W. Lippincott award for Disting. Librarianship, 1979. Mem. AAUP, Am. Assn. Adult and Continuing Edn., ALA (adult services div.: reading guide project promotion com. 1961, publs. com. 1962-63, chmn. nominating com. 1963; mem.-at-large council 1962-65, 68-70, v.p. adult services div. 1968-69, pres. div. 1969-1970, chmn. div. publs. adv. com. 1971-73, adv. to editors and contbr. Yearbook 1976—), N.Y. State Library Assn. (chmn. adult edn. com. 1947), Wis. Library Assn. (adult edn. com. 1961-63), Adult Edn. Assn. U.S. (com. social philosophy 1951-52). Democrat. Episcopalian. Author: Adult Education Activities in Public Libraries: A Report of the ALA Survey in Public Libraries and State Library Extension Agencies of the U.S., 1954; Library Materials in Service to the Adult New Reader, 1973, 74; Reading and the Adult New Reader, 1976; Literacy and the Nation's Libraries, 1977; MAC Checklist: Materials Analysis Criteria, 1979; Guide to the Use of the MAC Checklist: Materials Analysis Criteria, 1979; How to Use the Reading for an Age of Change Series: A Handbook for Libraries, 1963; others. Cons. editor Wis. Library Bull., 1961, 62, 63; editor Library Trends, 1971; contbr. articles to profl. jours. Address: S4528 Freeman Rd Orchard Park NY 14127

LYMAN, RUTH ANN, health services adminstr.; b. Nashville, Ark., Feb. 2, 1948; d. Oren Ernest and Frances Emeline (Urban) Frerking; B.S., U. Ala., Tuscaloosa, 1969, M.A. (Ala. Dept. Mental Health fellow), 1972, Ph.D., 1974. Counselor, Camp Ponderosa, summer program for emotionally disturbed children, Mentone, Ala., summers 1969, 70; staff psychologist Montgomery (Ala.) Area Mental Health Authority, summer 1971; cons. Lowndes County (Ala.) Sch. System, 1971; tng. group leader Tuscaloosa Community Crisis Center, 1972; instr. in psychology Psychol. Clinic, dept. psychology U. Ala., Tuscaloosa, 1971-72, psychometrist, summer 1972, clin. psychologist Univ. Health Service, Coll. Community Health Scis., 1973-75, now adj. asst. prof. dept. psychology; instr. div. spl. studies U. Ala., Birmingham, 1977—, adj. asst. prof. psychology, 1978—; instr., clin. psychology intern U. N.C., Chapel Hill, 1973; asso. Resource Design and Devel. Corp., University, Ala., also N.Y.C., 1973-77; profl. dir. Tuscaloosa Pregnancy Counseling Center and Rape Relief Service, Tuscaloosa, 1973-75, chmn. bd. dirs., 1974-75; cons. NW Ala. Mental Health Center, Hamilton, 1974-75; mem. exec. com. Southeastern Assn. Crisis Intervention Centers, 1974-77; dir. Western Mental Health Center, Jefferson County Dept. Health, Birmingham, 1975—; mem. group home adv. com. Jefferson-Blount-St. Clair Mental Health/Mental Retardation Authority, Birmingham, 1976—; community rep. Head Start Policy Council, Jefferson County Com. Econ. Opportunity, 1976-78; bd. dirs., sec., mem. exec. com. Alcohlism Recovery Center, Birmingham, 1977—; chmn. mental health com. Birmingham Regional Health Systems Agency, 1978. Recipient Martin S. Wallach award, dept. psychiatry U. N.C. Sch. Medicine, 1973, Outstanding Young Career Woman award Tuscaloosa Bus. and Profl. Women's Club, 1975; licensed psychologist, Ala. Mem. Am., Southeastern, Ala. psychol. assns., Nat. Register Health Service Providers, Ala. Council Mental Health/Mental Retardation Dirs., Ala. Acad. Neurology and Psychiatry, Am., Ala. pub. health assns., Assn. Advancement Psychology, Assn. Licensed Psychologists Ala., Chestnut Hill Assn., Highland Neighborhood Assn. Methodist. Club: Zonta Internat. Contbr. articles to profl. publs. Home: 3228 Highland Dr Birmingham AL 35205 Office: 1701 Ave D Ensley Birmingham AL 35218

LYNCH, BEATRICE B., educator; b. LeRoy, Mich., Sept. 23, 1917; d. Ora E. and Myrtle (Lockhart) Holmes; student Mich. State Coll., 1940, St. Mary's Coll., 1946, Rutgers U., 1964; B.S., M.A., Ed.S., Central Mich. U., 1962-70; m. Joseph C. Lynch, Sept. 14, 1940; children—Maura C., Daniel Odell. Research dir. asst. Impact 7, Reed City, Mich., 1968-70; regional dir. Mich. Lung Assn., Reed City, 1970-73; cons. devel. nursing edn. programs, Harrison, Mich., 1976-77; asso. prof. St. Mary's Coll., Notre Dame, Ind., 1977—; advisor to community and pvt. schs. in sch. health curriculum. Bd. dirs. Mich. div. Am. Lung Assn.; pres. Osceola Cancer Soc. Mem. Am. Public Health Assn., Nat. League Nursing Edn., Am. Sch. Health Assn., Am. Assn. Curriculum and Supervision Devel., Mich. Sch. Health Assn., Mich. Sch. Nurses Assn., Eta Sigma Gamma, Pi Lambda Theta. Roman Catholic. Clubs: Notre Dame University, Pentwater Yacht. Author: (with A. Levin) Human Sexuality in Family Life Education, 1977. Home: Glocca Morra Box 136 Reed City MI 49677 Office: Havican Hall 15-C Notre Dame IN 46556

LYNCH, BEVERLY ANNE, nurse anesthetist; b. Norfolk, Va., Oct. 8, 1937; d. Willis Vinson and Edna Lois (Holt) Beale; R.N., DePaul Sch. Nursing, 1960, student Sch. Anesthesia, 1974-75; div.; children—John Christopher Lynch, Suzanne Siobhan Lynch. Nurse anesthetist Chesapeake (Va.) Gen. Hosp., 1975, Hampton (Va.) Gen. Hosp., 1975-78, Bayside Hosp., Virginia Beach, Va., 1978-79, Bayside Anesthesia Assos., Ltd., Virginia Beach, 1979—. Mem. Am. Assn. Nurse Anesthetists, Va. Assn. Nurse Anesthetists, Tidewater Ednl. Dist. Assn. Nurse Anesthetists. Home: 4040 Windymille Dr Portsmouth VA 23703

LYNCH, CAROLINE HIRTH, cons.; b. Hartford, Conn., Feb. 15, 1935; d. Richard William and Emilie M. Hirth; student U. Conn., 1954-55, U. Hartford, 1953-54, 55-58; m. John Clement Lynch, June 1, 1957; children—Richard John, Allison Emilie. Nurse, med. asst., office mgr. various physicians, Tex., Conn., 1956-78; adminstrv. asst. Survey Research Scis., Dallas., 1970-73; cons. to med. and dental professions, Rockville, Conn., 1978-80, Joliet, Ill., 1980-82; exec. dir. Drs. Service Center, 1982—. Water safety instr. ARC, 1967-73; project coordinator Bicentennial Courier Project State Conn. for Youth for Understanding, 1976. Mem. Nat. Assn. Female Execs., U. Conn. Alumni Assn. Mem. Ch. of Jesus Christ of Latter-Day Saints. Office: 201 W Prospect Ave Mount Prospect IL 60056

LYNCH, LINDA DENSMORE, nurse; b. Toledo, Aug. 18, 1946; d. Melvin Howard and Sybil (House) Densmore; A.A. in Comml. Art, Middle Ga. Coll., Cochran, 1964-66; R.N. cum laude, Med. Center Central Ga., Macon, 1975; B.S. in Nursing, Med. Coll. Ga., Augusta, 1977; nurse practitioner, Emory U., 1980; m. Michael Handley Lynch, May 13, 1976; 1 dau., Jennifer Allison. Mem. nursing staff Med. Center Central Ga., 1975-79; nurse sr. Ga. Health Dept., Macon, 1979-80, Ob-Gyn nurse practitioner, 1980; Ob-Gyn coordinator and patient educator Coliseum Park Hosp., Macon, 1982—. Mem. Nurses Assn. Am. Coll. Ob-Gyn, Nat. Assn. Nurse Practitioners in Family Planning. Methodist. Home: PO Box 127-3256 S Lizella Rd Lizella GA 31052 Office: 350 Hospital Dr Macon GA

LYNCH, SISTER, MARY DENNIS, librarian; b. Phila., Apr. 23, 1920; d. J. Raymond and Ida A. (Teal) L.; A.B., Temple U., 1941; B.S. in L.S., Drexel U., 1942; M.S. in L.S., Catholic U., 1956; M.A., Villanova U., 1970, St. Charles Sem., 1980. Joined Soc. Holy Child Jesus, 1942; tchr., librarian Sch. Holy Child Jesus, Sharon Hill, Pa., 1942-45, 53-62, Summit, N.J., 1945-47; tchr. social studies West Phila. Cath. Girls High Sch., 1947-53; librarian Rosemont (Pa.) Coll., 1962—, lectr. methods of social studies, 1963-68, chmn. Am. studies com., 1970-73, lectr. polit. sci., 1973—; instr. library sci. dept. Villanova U., summers 1964-65; mem. ednl. adv. bd. St. Charles Borromeo Sem., 1968-76, 78—; bd. dirs. Tri-State Coll. Library Coop., 1967—, pres., 1980-81, exec. sec., 1967-70. Mem. Am., Cath. (nat. exec. council 1975—, pres. 1983—), Pa. (chairperson coll. and research sect. 1975-76, mem. Pa. bibliog. access study adv. com. 1977—, parliamentarian 1977—) library assns., OCLC Users Council (exec. com. 1982-83), Am. Acad. Polit. and Social Scis., Acad. Polit. Sci., Am. Studies Assn., Nat. Cath. Ednl. Assn., Nat. Council Social Studies, Beta Phi Mu. Address: Rosemont Coll Rosemont PA 19010

LYNCH, MARY MARGARET, businesswomen, real estate exec.; b. San Francisco, Sept. 8, 1920; d. Jeremiah John and Susan M. (McKean) Mahoney; student U. Calif., San Francisco, 1965-66; m. Joseph David Lynch, June 10, 1945; children—Suzanne M., Timothy Jeremiah. Clk., Mahoney Estate Co., San Francisco, 1945-50, sec., asst., 1950-61, prin. trustee Mahoney Corp., San Francisco, 1961-78, gen. prin., adminstr. Mahoney Estate Co., San Francisco, 1978-81, gen. owner, trustee, San Francisco, 1981—. Mem. San Francisco Bay Area Council, 1982—, Upper Noe Valley Improvement Assn., 1982—, San Francisco Planning & Urban Renewal Assn., 1982—, World Affairs Council No. Calif., 1982—, United Bay Area Crusade, 1982—, others; chairwoman Boys' Town of Italy. Mem. San Francisco C. of C., Apt. House Owners and Lessee Consol., Calif. Credit Consumers Assn., Calif. Hotel and Motel Assn., Calif. Bankers Assn., Visitors and Conv. Bur. Assn. Republican. Roman Catholic. Clubs: Palo Alto Hills Country, St. Francis Yacht, San Francisco Women's, Palo Alto Women's, Poinciana, Castilleja Women's, Women's Benefit Assn., others. Home: 501 Forest Ave Palo Alto CA 94301 Office: 519 Valley St San Francisco CA 94131

LYNCH, MARY SUE, controller; b. Annapolis, Md., Sept. 10, 1954; d. Walter Joseph and Gloria Phyllis (Bouthilette) Lynch; A.A., Anne Arundel Community Coll., 1974; B.S., U. Md., 1976; M.B.A., U. Balt., 1979. Clerical adminstr. Friendship Flying Service, Balt., 1973-76; retail sales mgr. Goodyear Tire & Rubber Co., Alexandria, Va., 1976-77; asst. to pres. D.P. Solutions Co., Balt., 1977-78; asst. controller Bowie (Md.) Coll., 1979—. Pvt. pilot. Mem. Am. Mktg. Assn., U. Md. Alumni Assn. Roman Catholic. Home: 412 F Starwood Dr Glen Burnie MD 21061 Office: Controller's Office Bowie State Coll Bowie MD 20715

LYND, NANCY HELLMAN, tech. writing co. exec.; b. Bklyn., Nov. 10, 1944; d. Al and Esther Deborah (Kleinspiec) Hellman; B.S., N.Y. U., 1965; M.A., Calif. State U., Northridge, 1973, postgrad., Fullerton, 1978-79, Dominguez Hills, 1977-78; m. William Lynd, July 3, 1973; children—Allyn David Herman-Lynd, Barry Howard Herman-Lynd. Secondary sch. tchr., N.Y., La., Calif., 1965-67; free lance ghost writer, 1968-72; tchr. Calif. State U., Northridge, 1972-73; programmer/tech. writer Logicon/Intercomp, Inc., Torrance, Calif., 1974-76; pres. Lynd Assos., Santa Ana, Calif., 1976-80; pres. Tech. Text, Inc., 1980—; asst. sec. Mfrs. Resources and Planning, Inc., Santa Ana, 1977-78; cons. Bauer's Mus., 1979—. Active Women for Polit. Action, Orange County Music Center, Inc., South Coast Repetorary Theater. Mem. NOW, Am. Bus. Women's Assn., Nat. Women's Network. Jewish. Office: 1232A S Village Way Santa Ana CA 92705

LYNDS-CHERRY, PATRICIA GAIL, psychologist; b. Woodlake, Calif., Feb. 7, 1950; d. Edgar David and Frances Jean (Eberle) L.; B.A., Calif. State U., Fresno, 1972; M.A., U. Nebr., Lincoln, 1975, Ph.D., 1977; postgrad. U. Calif., Davis, 1978—; m. Albert L. Cherry, Nov. 13, 1982. Project coordinator SOMPA II, U. Calif., Davis, 1979-80; psychologist Sacramento County Office of Edn., 1980-81, Kings County Supt. Schs., Hanford, Calif., 1981—. Chairperson, Kings County Child Abuse Com. Maude Hammond Fling fellow, 1973-74. Mem. Am. Psychol. Assn., Western Psychol. Assn., Calif. Assn. Sch. Psychologists and Psychometrists, Women in Neurosci. Democrat. Research on mechanism controlling aggression in house mice, 1972-78, assessment culturally diverse children, 1978—. Home: 460 W Deodar Dr Lemoore CA 93245 Office: Kings Govt Center Hanford CA 93230

LYNN, ELIZABETH MEAGHER, educator; b. Oshkosh, Wis.; d. Joseph E. and Gertrude J. (DeYoung) Meagher; B.A., Marygrove Coll., Detroit, 1960; M.A., Villanova U., 1962; M.Ed., Columbia U., 1971; Ph.D., Ind. U., 1974; m. Lowell A. Lynn (dec. 1981). Chem. sales corr. Westvaco, 1963-65; tchr. English, Phila. Bd. Edn., 1965-66; film production coordinator Marathon Internat. Productions, 1966; broadcast editor Nat. Assn. Broadcasters, Code Authority, 1966-67; writer CBS-TV's 21st Century, Nat. Citizens Com. Pub. Broadcasting, 1967-68; lectr. City Coll. N.Y., 1968-71; asso. instr. Ind. U., 1971-74; instr. Cuyahoga Community Coll., Cleve., 1974-75; sr. research asso. Case Western Res. U., Cleve., 1975-76; communications cons., profl. lectr., Cleve., 1976-77; staff asso.-tng. Standard Oil Co. (Ohio), Cleve., 1977-82; adj. asso. prof. Sch. Bus. Adminstrn. U. So. Calif., 1982—; speaker, cons. corps., univ. schs. mgmt., profl. assns.; speech writer, lectr.; editorial reviewer profl. manuscripts ERIC, Wadsworth and Addison-Wesley publishing orgns. Grantee, Nat. Inst. Edn., Ind. U., Pi Lambda Theta, Hunter Coll. (CUNY), Villanova U.; fellow Columbia U. Mem. Am. Arbitration Assn., Am. Soc. Tng. and Devel., Speech Communication Assn., Am. Bus. Communication Assn., Internat., Central States communication assns., Alpha Psi Omega (hon.), Lambda Iota Tau (hon.), Pi Lambda Theta (hon.). Author: Improving Classroom Communication, 1976; co-author U.S. govt. HEW report: The Role of the Professional Nurse in Primary Health Care. Contbr. articles to profl. jours., ERIC system. Office: Bus Communication Dept-BRI204 Sch Bus Adminstrn USO Calif Los Angeles CA 90089

LYNN, LORETTA WEBB, singer; b. Butcher Hollow, Ky., Apr. 14, 1935; d. Ted and Clara (Butcher) Webb; student pub. schs.; m. Oliver V. Lynn, Jr., Jan. 10, 1948; children—Betty Sue Lynn Markworth, Jack Benny, Clara Lynn Lyell, Ernest Ray, Peggy, Patsy. Country vocalist with MCA records, 1961—; numerous gold albums; sec.-treas. Loretta Lynn Enterprises; hon. chmn. bd. Loretta Lynn Western Stores. Hon. rep. United Giver's Fund, 1971. Named Country Music Assn. Female Vocalist of Year, 1967, 72, 73; Grammy award, 1971; Entertainer of the Year,, 1972; named Top Duet of 1972, 73, 74, 75; Am. Music award, 1978; named Entertainer of Decade, Acad. Country Music, 1980. Recorded 1st album to be certified gold by a country female vocalist. Author: Coal Miner's Daughter, 1976, released as motion picture, 1979. Office: care United Talent Inc PO Box 23470 Nashville TN 37202 *

LYNN, PATRICIA PIFER, educator; b. Winchester, Va., Oct. 24, 1954; d. William Earl and Edythe (Renner) Pifer; B.S. in Spl. Edn., James Madison U., Harrisonburg, Va., 1977; m. Thomas G. Lynn, Oct. 27, 1979; 1 son, Matthew Reese. Tchr. public schs., Stephens City, Va., 1977-80; tchr. learning disabled Berryville (Va.) Primary Sch., 1981—. Democrat. Methodist. Home: 120 Bellview Ave Winchester VA 22601 Office: Berryville Primary Sch Berryville VA 22611

LYNN, PAULINE JUDITH WARDLOW (MRS. ARTHUR D. LYNN, JR.), lawyer; b. Columbus, Ohio, Nov. 14, 1920; d. Charles and Helen P. (Christman) Wardlow; student Wellesley Coll., 1938-40; B.A., Ohio State U., 1942, J.D., 1948; m. Arthur D. Lynn, Jr., Dec. 29, 1943; children—Pamela Wardlow, Constance Karen, Deborah Joanne, Patricia Diane. Admitted to Ohio bar, 1948; practiced in Columbus, 1948-49. Troop leader Girl Scouts U.S.A., 1969-71. Mem. Columbus Bar Assn., Phi Beta Kappa, Kappa Kappa Gamma (mem. research com. Heritage mus.), Pi Sigma Alpha. Republican. Episcopalian. Club: Columbus Met. Home: 2679 Wexford Rd Columbus OH 43221

LYNN, SUE NELL, univ. adminstr.; b. Sheffield, Ala., Nov. 22, 1930; s. Turner Whitten and Mattie Elizabeth (Douthit) Scott; student public schs.; m. William Lyman Lynn, Mar. 27, 1949; children—William Scott Scott, Jack Bradford, Deborah Jo Lynn Long. Various secretarial, clerical and sales positions, 1952-54, 55-57, 59-64; with U. Ala., 1965—, now registrar and acad. adv. Sch. Social Work. Mem. So. Assn. Collegiate Registrars and Admissions Officers. Methodist. Clubs: Morayshire Community (pres. 1980-81), Soroptimist (pres. Tuscaloosa 1980-82), Registrar's No Name. Home: 1306 Montrose Dr Tuscaloosa AL 35405 Office: PO Box 1935 University AL 35486

LYON, BERENICE IOLA CLARK, civic worker; b. Westfield, Pa., June 4, 1920; d. Stephen Artemus and Ruth Gertrude (Tubbs) Clark; m. Robert Louis Lyon, May 28, 1944. Pres., Twin Tiers Geneal. Soc., N.Y. and Pa., 1976—, pub. jour. Gemini; Pa. state pres. Colonial Dames XVII Century, 1981—, state chmn. heraldry, 1977-79, organizer-pres. Tyoga Gateway chpt., 1973-75, Treaty Elm chpt., 1975-77, state yearbook-directory compiler, 1979-80; N.Y. state chmn. DAR, 1968-71, pres. N.Y. council of regents, 1968-71, regent Corning (N.Y.) chpt. 1965-68, Wellsboro (Pa.) chpt., 1977-80, Pa. state vice chmn., 1980—; N.Y. state chmn. Daus. Am. Colonists, 1968-76, Atlantic Coast chmn., 1970-79, organizer-regent Forbidden Trail chpt., 1967-76; condr. geneal. seminars; speaker to convs., meetings, TV, radio. Recipient medal of appreciation SAR, 1966. Mem. Ams. of Royal Descent, Descs. Knights of Garter, Magna Carta Dames, Old Plymouth Colony Descs., Order of Crown, Order of Washington, Plantagenet Soc., Mansfield Friends of Library (pres. 1980—). Clubs: Kiwanis Ladies, Clionian Circle (Corning); Mansfield (Pa.) Garden (pres. 1979-80), N.Y. Fedn. Garden Clubs (sect. chmn. 1969-73). Author series of articles on heraldry 17th Century Rev., 1978-79; subject of article DAR Mag. Home: Lowenhof 168A Bailey Creek Rd Millerton PA 16936

LYON, JEAN BURCHAM, beverage co. exec.; b. Tucson, Mar. 8, 1917; d. Gouley Neal and Irma Emilie (Rosenstern) Burcham; student U. Ariz., 1934; m. Lowman Weddle Lyon, Mar. 22, 1935; children—Lowman Burcham, Ann Lyon Jackson. With Santa Rita Bottling Co., Inc., Tucson, 1948—, sec., treas., dir., 1952—, pres., 1964—; dir. Casa Grande Mgmt., Casa Grande Enterprises, Tucson, 1971. Mem. Nat. Soft Drink Assn. Am., Ariz. Hist. Soc., Soft Drink Assn. Ariz., DAR. Democrat. Mem. Christian Ch. Clubs: Order Eastern Star, Temple of Music and Art. Contbr. children's stories various mags.

LYON, PATRICIA LOUISE, utility ofcl.; b. Clarksdale, Miss., Sept. 4, 1948; d. Richard Bailey and Mignonne Louise (Stanford) L.; A.B. with distinction, Mary Baldwin Coll., 1970; M.Computer Sci., U. Va., 1972. Instr., U. Va., Charlottesville, 1970-72; with Honeywell, 1972-82, regional mktg. mgr., Atlanta, 1979-80, nat. mktg. product mgr., computers, 1980-82; supr. mgmt. info services product evaluation and support Ga. Power Co., Atlanta, 1982—; cons. CII-Honeywell Bull, Honeywell French affiliate. Pres. Wieuca's Way single's program Wieuca Rd. Baptist Ch., Atlanta, 1981-82. Mem. Assn. Computing Machinery, Nat. Assn. Female Execs., Republican. Club: Beech Aero. Home: 1290 Roxboro Dr Atlanta GA 30324 Office: 333 Piedmont Ave Atlanta GA 30306

LYON, RUTH ALTA, editor; b. Moline, Ill., Nov. 23; d. Eugene Cassius and Hazel Ramona (Rouch) Lyon; B.A., Central Bible Coll., 1958. Sec., asst. bookkeeper First Nat. Bank, McCook, Nebr., 1930-36; supr. bus. office South Central Bible Inst., Fort Worth, 1940-41; asst. to evangelist, 1947-50; with Signal Corps, Washington, 1942; with Assemblies of God Ch., Springfield, Mo., 1950—, sec. to nat. rep. and tech. editor nat. Sunday Sch. dept., 1950-57, promotions editor, home missions div., 1958-78, editor/promotions coordinator, 1979—, also editor bi-monthly mag. Assemblies of God Home Missions. Mem. Mo. Writers Guild (sec.-treas. 1966). Home: 909 W Woodridge St Springfield MO 65803

LYON, WENDY JANE, educator; b. Bklyn., Oct. 29, 1946; d. Herbert Allan and Lucy (Zinberg) L.; B.S., Cornell U., 1967; M.Ed., Springfield (Mass.) Coll., 1978. Adv. planning and devel. monthly newspaper Dimensions for Weight Watchers, Inc., also lectr., 1968-72; editor Health Foods and Nutrition News, 1972-73; instr. yoga and women's fitness YM-YWCAs, community centers, also N.Y.C. Bd. Edn., 1972; yoga cons. YMCAs Greater N.Y., 1976-81; adj. lectr. City U. N.Y., 1978-80; supervising yoga instr. and women's conditioning program West Side YMCA, N.Y.C., 1979-81; developed Nat. YMCA Yoga Tchrs. Cert. Program, 1977-81; now specialist in stress reduction and fitness, Eugene, Oreg. Mem. AAHPER, Pres.'s Council Phys. Fitness and Sport, Omicro Nu. Author papers in field. Office: PO Box 1984 Eugene OR 97440

LYON-COOK, JONNETTA SUE, bus. exec., mgmt. cons., author; b. Custer, Ky., Apr. 28, 1935; d. Sparrel K. and Ava (Lockard) Lyon; student Blackburn Coll., 1953-57, U. West Fla., 1970-72; B.S., U. Md., 1975; Calif. State U., Northridge, 1978, U. So. Calif., 1979; M.B.A., Calif., Luth. Coll., 1979; M.Accountancy, U. Denver, 1982; m. Larry Lester Cook, Nov. 16, 1957; children—Larry Lee, Vicki Sue. Asst. to foundry div. supt. Nat. Steel & Shipbldg., San Diego, 1966-69; adminstrv. asst. faculty fin. and acctg. U. Fla., Pensacola, 1969-72; Okinawa br. adminstrv. mgr. Price Waterhouse & Co., 1972-75; corp. acct. Trust Co. of West, Los Angeles, 1975-76; controller Nuclear Medico Services, Inc., Van Nuys, Calif., 1976-79; officer Am. Nucleonics Corp., Westlake Village, Calif., 1980-81; partner Cooks' R.I.T.Y., Klamath, Calif., 1979-81; dir. fiscal services South Central Community Mental Health Center, Bloomington, Ind., 1982—. Committeewoman, Fla. Gulf Coast council Boy Scouts Am., 1970-72; active Reagan presdl. campaign. Cert. adminstrv. mgr. Mem. Mensa, Assn. M.B.A. Execs., Adminstrv. Mgmt. Soc. (sec. Los Angeles area chpt. 1979-80), Nat. Assn. Female Execs., Am. Mgmt. Assn., Soc. Advancement Mgmt., Women's Network So. Calif., Christian Businesswomen's Network (founder). Republican. Methodist. Home: PO Box 1848 Bloomington IN 47402 Office: 631 S Rogers St Bloomington IN 47401

LYON-RODMAN, SYLVIA, TV co. exec.; b. Santiago, Chile, June 25, 1946; came to U.S., 1971, naturalized, 1982; d. Arturo A. and Julie

(Valverde) Lyon; student UCLA, 1971-73; m. John S. Rodman, June 6, 1980; 1 dau., Lindsay Lyon. Copywriter Eastman Advt., Chile, 1968-70, J. Walter Thompson Advt., Brazil, 1970-71; receptionist KMEX-TV, 1974, public relations exec., 1974-75; dir. advt. and public relations Spanish Internat. Network, Inc., N.Y.C., 1977, asst. to pres., 1978, dir. programming Galavision, 1979—. Trustee Burden Center for the Aged, N.Y.C., 1981—. Mem. Women in Cable. Home: 19 E 72d St New York NY 10021 Office: 250 Park Ave New York NY 10177

LYONS, BETTE, hosp. adminstr.; b. N.Y.C., Jan. 26, 1935; d. Nathan and Helen (Kohn) Sroka; R.N., Mt. Sinai Hosp. Sch. Nursing, 1955; B.S., SUNY, 1973; M.S., L.I. U., 1977; m. Jerome Lyons, Feb. 8, 1959; children—Robyn, Nancy. Nursing care coordinator L.I. Jewish Med. Center, Hillside Div., Glen Oaks, N.Y., 1970-75; v.p., adminstrv. organizer Dist. 1199, Nat. Union of Hosp. and Health Care Employees, N.Y.C., 1976-79; dir. nurse recruitment-retention Cath. Med. Center of Bklyn. and Queens, Inc., Jamaica, N.Y., 1979—. Mem. Assn. Bklyn. and Queens Nurse Recruiters (chmn. 1981-83), Am. Nurses Assn., N.Y. State Nurses Assn., Nat. League for Nursing, Nat. Assn. Nurse Recruiters, NOW, ACLU. Home: 37 Sugar Maple Dr Roslyn NY 11576 Office: 88 25 153rd St Jamaica NY 11432

LYONS, MARCIA GREENBERG, designer; b. N.Y.C., Mar. 29; d. Harold and Ruth (Weiss) Greenberg; B.S., N.Y.U., 1963; m. Maurice Lyons, June 9, 1974; 1 son, Alexis. Buyer, Lord & Taylor, 1963-73; designer Micke Lyons Raingear, 1973-76; designer, pres. Premier Etage, Inc., 1976—. Mem. Fashion Group. Office: 64 W 36th St New York NY 10018

LYONS, MARGARET LEWIS, nurse, counselor; b. Orlando, Fla., Oct. 4, 1926; d. Herbert R. and Lyla Buck Lewis; A.A.S., Coll. Lake County, 1971; B.A., Northeastern Ill. U., 1975, M.A., 1978; m. David Lyons, Jan. 14, 1948 (dec.); children—Peggy Scholtes, Cathy Spear, Elizabeth, Dave, Jon Lyons. Nurses aide Highland Park (Ill.) Hosp., 1961-65, operating room technician, 1965-66, L.P.N., 1966-71, staff nurse, 1971-72, critical care, trauma nurse, 1972-74, night adminstr., 1975—, crisis counselor, 1975-80, coordinator chaplaincy, 1975-80, founder, dir. Hospice, 1979—; dir. counseling services, asst. dean student devel. King's Coll., Briarcliff Manor, N.Y., 1980—. Active Civil Def. Am. Cancer Soc. R.N., Ill. Mem. Audubon Soc., Nat. Hospice Assn., Assn. Christian Colls., Am. Nurses Assn., Christian Assn. Psychol. Studies, Assn. Personnel and Guidance. Democrat. Lutheran Brethren. Home and Office: King's Coll Briarcliff Manor NY 10510

LYONS, VIRGINIA MARY, ednl. psychologist; b. Bosco, La., June 20, 1940; d. John Sidney and Bernadette Bearb L.; B.S., U. Southwestern La., 1962; M.Ed., Nicholls State U., 1970; Ph.D., U. Minn., 1982. Elem. tchr. St. Pierre Elem. Sch., Carencro, La., 1964; phys. edn. tchr. St. Michael and Fatima High Schs., Lafayette, La., 1965-68; instr. phys. edn. Nicholls State U., Thibodaux, La., 1969; prin. St. Charles Borremeo High Sch., Destrahan, La., 1970; counselor Northside High Sch., Lafayette, La., 1971-78; lectr. U. Minn., Mpls., 1978-80, 81-82, coordinator coop. learning research project, 1980-81; adminstr. Opelousas (La.) Found. Counseling Center, 1982—. Mem. Internat. Reading Assn., Am. Ednl. Research Assn., Internat. Assn. Study Coop. Learning, Minn. Assn. Retarded Citizens, Phi Delta Kappa. Democrat. Roman Catholic. Home: Route 2 Box 648 Church Point LA 70525 Office: Opelousas Found 839 Creswell Ln Opelousas LA 70570

LYPECKYJ, CHRISTINA ROMANA, mezzo-soprano; b. Stanyslaviv, Ukraine, Feb. 20; d. Roman and Anna (Skochdopol) Semaniuk; came to U.S., 1957, naturalized, 1969; student Macomb County Community Coll., Warren, Mich., 1976, Boris Goldovsky's opera workshop Oglebay Inst.; pupil of Aurelia Peralta, Marilyn Cotlow, Avery Crew, Josef Blatt; m. Lubomyr Alexander Lypeckyj, July 9; children—Alexander Ihor, Natalia Christina. Debut, Mich. Opera Theatre, 1972, Opera Orgn. and Warren Symphony Orch., 1977; concert performances, recitals, U.S., Can., Italy; recording for symfonia. Recipient award Met. Opera Nat. Council, 1971. Mem. Met. Opera Guild. Greek Catholic. Home: 11219 Irene Dr Warren MI 48093 Office: PO Box 525 Warren MI 48090

LYSTAD, MARY HANEMANN (MRS. ROBERT LYSTAD), sociologist, author; b. New Orleans, Apr. 11, 1928; d. James and Mary (Douglass) Hanemann; A.B. cum laude, Newcomb Coll., 1949; M.A., Columbia, 1951; Ph.D., Tulane U., 1955; m. Robert Lystad, June 20, 1953; children—Lisa Douglass, Anne Hanemann, Mary Lunde, Robert Douglass, James Hanemann. Postdoctoral fellow social psychology S.E. La. Hosp., Mandeville, 1955-57; field research social psychology, Ghana, 1957-58, South Africa and Swaziland, 1968; chief sociologist Collaborative Child Devel. Project, Charity Hosp. La., New Orleans, 1958-61; feature writer African div. Voice Am., Washington, 1964-73; program analyst NIMH, Washington, 1968-78, asso. dir. for planning and coordination div. spl. mental health programs, 1978—; chief Nat. Center for Prevention and Control of Rape, 1980—; cons. on youth Nat. Goals Research Staff, White House, Washington, 1969-70. Author: Millicent the Monster, 1968; Social Aspects of Alienation, 1969; Jennifer Takes Over P.S. 94, 1972; James the Jaguar, 1972; As They See It: Changing Values of College Youth, 1972; That New Boy, 1973; Halloween Parade, 1973; Violence at Home, 1974; A Child's World As Seen in His Stories and Drawings, 1974; From Dr. Mather to Dr. Seuss: 200 Years of American Books for Children, 1980; At Home in America, 1981. Home: 4900 Scarsdale Rd Washington DC 20016 Office: 5600 Fishers Ln Rockville MD 20852

LYTLE, EVELYN POMROY, educator, author; b. Indiana, Pa., Dec. 5, 1920; d. Joseph Bertram and Sarah Emma (Kunkle) Lytle; B.S., Ind. U. of Pa., 1943; M.A., Princeton Theol. Sem., 1947; Brazilian Ministry Fgn. Affairs fellow Universidade de São Paulo (Brazil), 1953-54; Fulbright fellow Universidad de Valladolid, 1962; Ph.D., Tulane U., 1967. Ednl. missionary United Presbyterian Ch., Brazil, 1949-50; vis. prof. English, Pontificia Universidade Catolica de São Paulo, 1950-51; asst. prof. Spanish, Randolph-Macon Woman's Coll., Lynchburg, Va., 1965-67; instr. Spanish and Portuguese, U. New Orleans, 1958-65, asst. prof., 1967-71, asso. prof., 1971-79, prof., 1979—; mem. nat. adv. council on bilingual edn. Office Edn., 1974-77, chmn., 1976-77; cons. Consulate of Portugal, New Orleans, 1973—, Jud. Conf. U.S. Bicentennial Com., Washington, 1977, U.S. Dept. Agr., 1982, U.S. Dept. Interior, 1982. Ford Venture Fund grantee, 1975. Mem. Modern Lang. Assn. Am., Dante Soc. Am., Renaissance Soc. Am., S.-Central Modern Lang. Assn., Brazilian-Am. Cultural Inst. New Orleans. Episcopalian. Author: Os Novissimos do Homem de Rolim de Moura: um poema biblico da epica portuguesa, 1970; contbr. articles to profl. jours. Home: 6169 Paris Ave Apt 100 New Orleans LA 70122 Office: U New Orleans Dept Fgn Langs New Orleans LA 70122

MAASS, VERA SONJA, psychologist; b. Berlin, Ger., July 6, 1931; came to U.S., 1958, naturalized, 1970; d. Willy Ernst and Walli Elisabeth (Reinke) Keck; B.A., Monmouth Coll., 1971; M.A., Lehigh U., 1974; Ph.D., U. Mo., 1978. Teaching asst. Lehigh U., 1971-72; tutor in adult basic edn. Teaching Assistance Orgn., Kansas City, Mo., 1973-74; grad. research asst. U. Mo., Kansas City, 1974-76; intern U. Ky. Med. Sch., Lexington, 1975-76; psychologist-therapist Dunn Mental Health Center, Richmond, Ind., 1976-80, psychologist, br. dir., Winchester, Ind., 1980—; pres., clin. dir. Living Skills Inst., Inc.; v.p. Vitatronics, Inc., N.J., 1969—. Mem. Am. Psychol. Assn., Am. Personnel and Guidance Assn., Am. Assn. Sex Educators, Counselors and Therapists, Internat. Assn. Applied Psychology, Nat. Council Family Relations, Internat. Platform Assn. Contbr. in field. Home: 221 N Meridian St Winchester IN 47394 Office: 112 1/2 W Washington St Winchester IN 47394

MABE, EDNA LOUISE, educator; b. Avery, Tex., Aug. 16, 1930; d. Bennie Gus and Thelma Oteline (Harris) Runyan; A.A., Paris (Tex.) Jr. Coll., 1950; B.S., E. Tex. State U., 1951, M.Ed., 1960; m. Millard Dee Mabe, May 2, 1953. Tchr., coach Sulphur Springs (Tex.) High Sch., 1951-54, drill team dir., 1970-80, asst. prin., 1981—; coach Killeen (Tex.) High Sch., 1954-56; English tchr. South Franklin Sch. Dist., 1956-59; elem. tchr. Sulphur Springs Ind. Sch. Dist., 1959-65, girls' phys. edn. tchr., 1965-70, adminstrv. asst., 1980-81. Mem. NEA, Tex. State Tchrs. Assn., Classroom Tchrs., Dance and Drill Team Assn. Tex., Assn. for Supervision and Curriculum Devel., Bus. and Profl. Women. Democrat. Baptist. Home: PO Box 674 Sulphur Springs TX 75482 Office: 1200 Connally Sulphur Springs TX 75482

MABEE, JEAN FRANCES, nurse; b. Goshen, N.Y., Dec. 28, 1927; d. Alphonse and Frances (Spinelli) Bonauto; R.N., Lenox Hill Hosp. Sch. Nursing, 1948; m. Harry W. Mabee, June 26, 1949; children—Kathleen, William. Charge nurse emergency and operating room Towanda (Pa.) Hosp., 1962-66; head nurse ICU and CCU, Vassar Bros. Hosp., Poughkeepsie, N.Y., 1966-71; public health nurse Dutchess County Dept. Health, Poughkeepsie, 1971-76; med.-surg. clin. instr. Thompson Sch. for Practical Nurses, Brattleboro, Vt., 1976-78; area rev. nurse team leader Vt. PSRO, Brattleboro, 1978-79; dir. nursing Eden Park Nursing Home, Brattleboro, 1979—. Mem. health occupations adv. com. Brattleboro Union High Sch., 1978—; mem. adv. bd. Thompson Sch. for Practical Nurses, 1978—; bd. dirs. ARC, Windham County, 1979—. Recipient Pediatric Achievement award, Lenox Hill Hosp., 1948. Mem. Brattleboro Registered Nurses Assn., Vt. Long Term Care Com. Roman Catholic. Contbr. articles to profl. jours. Home: Rural Route 2 PO Box 63E West Brattleboro VT 05301 Office: Eden Park Nursing Home Pine Heights Brattleboro VT 05301

MABIE, RUTH MARIE, realtor; b. Pueblo, Colo., Feb. 7; d. Newton Everett and Florence Ellen (Porter) Allen; student San Diego State U., 1957-60, Grossmont Jr. Coll., 1970-71, U. Calif., San Diego, 1970, 72; m. Richard O. Mabie, Nov. 29, 1947; 1 son, Ward A. Mgr., LaMont Modeling Sch., San Diego, 1962; tchr. Am. Bus. Coll., San Diego, 1964-66; free-lance modeling, 1960-72; owner, broker Ruth Mabie Realty, San Diego, 1972—; asst. v.p. Skil-Bilt, Inc., 1976—; dir. Mabie & Mintz, Inc. Bd. dirs. Multiple Sclerosis Dr., 1971—. Mem. San Diego Bd. Realtors, Nat. Assn. Female Execs. Republican. Home: 4481 Palo Verde Terr San Diego CA 92115 Office: 6280 Riverdale St San Diego CA 92121

MACALEESE, JO FOLKMAN, city ofcl.; b. San Antonio, July 27, 1947; d. Richard Homer and Myrtle Elizabeth (Rose) F.; student U. Houston, 1965-66; m. Gregory B. MacAleese, 1975; 1 son, Jason Richard Folkman. Sales rep. Sta.-KOB, Albuquerque, 1973; sales mgr. Jason Bus. Systems, Albuquerque, 1974-77; mem. Albuquerque City Council, 1977—, v.p., 1979—, chmn. rules com.; mem. Urban Transp. Planning Bd.; mem. N.Mex. Criminal Justice Coordinating Council, 1978—, mem. council task force for policy planning, 1979—; co-founder Albuquerque Crime Stoppers Program, 1976, bd. dirs., 1976-78. Mem. John Connally Nat. Presdl. Com., 1980. Named Woman Most Likely to Succeed, Bellaire C. of C., 1965; recipient Law Enforcement award Optimist Internat., 1977. Mem. Middle Rio Grande Council Govts. (dir.), Women in Mcpl. Govt. (founder 1977, pres. 1977-79), N.Mex. Mcpl. League, Nat. League Cities (state dir. Women in Mcpl. Govt.), Beta Sigma Phi (city sponsor). Republican. Episcopalian. Office: PO Box 1293 Albuquerque NM 87103

MACARUSO, MARILYNN LOUISE, pipe mfg. co. exec.; b. Mpls., Dec. 28, 1932; d. Edward Dexter and Floy Adelaide (Abbs) Smith; student Frances Shimer Coll., 1949-50; m. Ralph B. Macaruso, Oct. 13, 1962; 1 son, Stephen David. Personnel mgr. Continental Can Co., Santa Ana, Calif., 1964-71; sec.-treas. Colby Plastic Converters, Inc., Anaheim, Calif., 1971—, Brenco Sales, Inc., Anaheim, 1975—, Bradley Specialties, Inc., Anaheim, 1979—; dir. Colby Plastic Converters, Inc., Brenco Sales, Inc. Republican. Episcopalian. Home: 18103 Yosemite Ct Fountain Valley CA 92708 Office: 1335 Allec St Anaheim CA 92805

MACAULAY, ALICE ITTNER, physician; b. Bklyn.; d. William and Anna (Holzman) Ittner; B.A. cum laude, Barnard Coll., postgrad., 1944-46; M.D., N.Y. Med. Coll., 1950; postgrad. N.Y. U., 1952-53; M.Sc., Mercy Coll., 1982; m. David Harvard Macaulay, July 10, 1936 (dec. 1971). Tchr. N.Y.C. high schs., until 1946; actress Columbia Lab. Players Summer Stock, Roxbury, Conn., 1932-34, Old Vic, London, 1934-35; intern and resident Grasslands Hosp., Valhalla, N.Y., 1951-56, hosp. practice internal medicine Grasslands Hosp., 1956-74, dir. outpatient services, 1956-74, asso. attending internal medicine, 1958-76, chmn. pharmacy and therapeutics com., 1967-74, mem. adminstrv. team, 1961-74; hon. attending in internal medicine Westchester County Med. Center, 1976—; liaison hosp. officer for devel. of Neighborhood Health Centers; chmn. med. adv. bd. Westchester County Public Health Nursing; med. cons., dir. med. affairs Westchester Community Coll.; cons. Office of Vocat. Rehab. and State Med. Programs; cons. hypertension, 1956—; med. adv. bd. Westchester Heart Assn., chmn. com. on hypertension, 1973-75; prof. medicine Pace U. Grad. Sch. Nursing, 1974-77; vocat. rehab. specialist, 1975—. Bd. dirs., med. cons. Donald Reed Speech Center, 1976—. Mem. Westchester Acad. Medicine, N.Y. State Med. Soc., Westchester, Am. heart assns., AAAS Cor et Manus, Contin, Am. Lung Assn., N.Y. Trudeau Soc., Alpha Epsilon Iota. Clubs: Soroptimists; Ardsley Country. Address: Hudson House Ardsley-on-Hudson NY 10503

MACBRIDE, MARY HUSSEY, state legislator; b. Blaine, Maine, May 11, 1916; d. Stetson Harlow and Gladys (Goodhue) Hussey; A.B., Wheaton Coll., Norton, Mass., 1939; m. M. Milton MacBride, July 10, 1942 (dec.); children—M. Milton, Barbara H. Tchr. high sch. English, 1939-42; mem. Maine Ho. of Reps., 1978—. Pres. Hosp. Aux., Pierian Club; bd. dirs. Am. Cancer Soc.; mem. corp. bd. Aroostook Med. Center; moderator, deaconess Presque Isle Congl. Ch.; mem. nursing adv. bd. U. Maine, Presque Isle; mem. adv. bd. No. Maine Vocat. Tech. Inst.; bd. dirs. Presque Isle Joint Adult Edn. Bd. Republican. Home: 63 Hillside St Presque Isle ME 04769 Office: State House Augusta ME 04333

MACCARRONE, RENEE BENNETT, pub. co. exec.; b. Alexandria, La., June 6, 1943; d. William James and Amy Armintha (Jackson) Bennett; B.S., La. Poly. Inst., 1964; postgrad. N.Y. U., 1966-76, Adelphi U., 1977-78; m. Anthony Maccarrone, Nov. 9, 1968; 1 son, Joseph Anthony. With Davis Publs., N.Y.C., 1964-68; with Scholastic Inc., N.Y.C., 1968—, editorial and advt. adminstr. publ. div., 1980—; cons. in field. Mem. Advt. Women N.Y., Women in Communications. Editor: Fashion Smarts, 1980; Co-ed's Guide to Getting Married, 1982. Office: 50 W 44th St New York NY 10036

MACCLARENCE, JANET COLLINS, social worker; b. Richmond, Va., Oct. 10, 1945; d. Murrel Becton and Cornelia (Bristow) Collins; A.B., Coll. William and Mary, 1970; M.S.W., Washington U., St. Louis, 1974; m. John William MacClarence, Aug. 15, 1964; children—John William, Harold Bryan. Social worker Hampton (Va.) Dept. Social Services, 1970-71; community organizer Joint Community Work Bd., St. Louis, 1972; staff therapist Centre for Creative Change, St. Louis, 1975; clin. social worker Creative Counseling Services, Inc., St. Louis, 1975—; adj. faculty U. Mo., St. Louis, 1976-80, Washington U., 1978-80. Cons., dir. Westminster Neighborhood Sch., St. Louis, 1971-73; vol., trainer Life Crisis Services, St. Louis. Mem. Nat. Assn. Social Workers, Assn. Women in Psychology, NOW, George Warren Brown Alumni Assn. Episcopalian. Home: 7574 Amherst St University City MO 63130 Office: 8631 Delmar St Suite 204 Saint Louis MO 63124

MAC CREADY, INGRID MARIA, instrument mfg. co. exec.; b. La Paz, Bolivia, Nov. 21, 1940; came to U.S., 1961, naturalized, 1963; d. Albert and Ilse S. (Wienmann) Samter; B.A., Am. Inst., La Paz, 1959; M.Langs., U. Munich (W. Ger.), 1961; divorced; children—Paul Barclay, Howard V. Export clk. Packard Internat. Co., Downers Grove, Ill., 1971-74; internat. ops. mgr. Portec Inc., Oakbrook, Ill., 1974-76, Sargent Welch Sci. Co., Skokie, Ill., 1976-78; mgr. internat. div. Continental Can Co., 1978—, also supr. internat. distbn. Exec. bd. Darien Youth Club. Mem. N.W. Internat. Trade Club (sec. Ill. 1979-80), Nat. Assn. Female Execs. Republican. Christian Scientist. Home: 7333-3 Winthrop Way Downers Grove IL 60515 Office: 1700 Harvester Rd West Chicago IL 60185

MACDONALD, ANNE ELIZABETH, arts adminstr.; b. Vancouver, B.C., Can., Mar. 18, 1930; d. Wilfrd Robinson and Jessie (Buckerfield) McDougall; B.A., U. B.C., 1952; m. Malcolm MacDonald, Dec. 12, 1953; children—Mary Elizabeth, Michael Alexander. Tchr. comml. studies, Vancouver, 1955-56; sec. Buckerfields Ltd., Vancouver, 1956-58; exec. sec., 1958-60; founder North Vancouver Arts Council, 1969, exec. dir., 1974-78; exec. dir. Vancouver Arts Council, 1978—; pres. Coordinare Cons. Services, Ltd., Vancouver, 1977—. Bd. govs. Canadian Conf. of Arts, 1976-80; senator U.B.C., 1981—; commr. Dist. Adv. Planning Commn., 1970-73; Recipient Queen Elizabeth medal, 1977. Mem. Bus. and Profl. Women's Club, Jr. League Vancouver. Anglican. Clubs: Hollyburn Country. Contbr. to New Life for Old Buildings, 1977. Office: 315 W Cordova St Vancouver BC V6B 1E5 Canada

MACDONALD, ELIZABETH HELEN, bassoonist, educator; b. Lancaster, Pa., July 5, 1942; d. Joseph Harold and Verna Elizabeth (Schaeffer) Bishop; B.Mus. in Music Edn., Eastman Sch. Music, Rochester, N.Y., 1964, M.Mus. in Music Lit. and Performance, 1966; m. William Dallas MacDonald, Aug. 17, 1968. Bassoonist, Music in Maine Woodwind Quintet, Bangor, 1966-67; dir. jr. high sch. band and elem. instrumental music, Brewer, Maine, 1967-69; instr. music history, woodwind class and bassoon No. Conservatory Music, Bangor, 1967-69; tchr. jr. high sch. gen. and instrumental music, Orono, Maine, 1969-72; tutor bassoon and oboe Colby Coll., Waterville, Maine, 1972-75; instr. bassoon, woodwind ensemble coach U. Maine, Orono, 1977—; prin. bassoonist Portland (Maine) Symphony Orch., 1967—; pvt. woodwind instr., 1972—; recitalist, soloist, music adjudicator, 1966—. Mem. Music Educators Nat. Conf., Internat. Double Reed Soc., Maine Music Educators Assn. Republican. Methodist. Home: 48 Dillingham St Bangor ME 04401 Office: Lord Hall U Maine Orono ME 04473

MACDONALD, FLORA ISABEL, Can. govt. ofcl.; b. North Sydney, N.S., Can., June 3, 1926; d. George Frederick and Mary Isabel (Royle) MacD.; attended Empire Bus. Coll.; grad. Nat. Def. Coll., 1972; D.H.L. (hon.), Mt. St. Vincent U., 1979. Formerly in various secretarial positions; with Progressive Conservative Party Hdqrs., Ottawa, Ont., Can., 1956-65, exec. dir., 1960-65; adminstrv. officer, tutor dept. polit. studies Queen's U., 1966-72, also cons. Student Vo. Bur.; mem. Can. Parliament for Kingston and the Islands, Ont., 1972—, Progressive Conservative spokesman for Indian Affairs and No. Devel., 1972, for Housing and Urban Devel., 1974, chmn. Progressive Conservative Caucus Com. on Fed.-Provincial Relations, 1976, minister of state for external affairs, from 1979. Vice pres. Kingston and Islands Progressive Conservative Assn., 1962-72; nat. sec. Progressive Conservative Assn. of Can., 1966-69; exec. dir. Com. for Ind. Can., 1971; pres. Elizabeth Fry Soc. of Kingston, 1968-70; mem. fin. com. Hotel Dieu Hosp., 1969-71; co-chmn. Kingston Waterfront Com., 1971. Mem. Can. Inst. Fgn. Affairs (dir. 1969-73), Can. Polit. Sci. Assn. (dir. 1972-75), Can. Inst. Internat. Affairs, Can. Civil Liberties Assn. Mem. United Ch. of Canada. Office: House of Commons Ottawa ON K1A 0A6 Canada *

MACDONALD, KATHLEEN VOUTÉ, coll. ofcl.; b. N.Y.C., Jan. 13, 1937; d. Arthur Jerome and Josephine (Rolleston) Vouté; cert. Japanese Lang. Sch., Kyoto, 1963; B.S., Columbia U., 1968, M.A., 1969; M.B.A., Golden Gate U., San Francisco, 1979; m. Daniel Stuart MacDonald, Jr., May 21, 1972; children—Daniel Stuart, Christine Rolleston. Maryknoll missionary sister, 1956-72; dir. Day Care Center, Marin, Calif., 1978-79; mem. faculty Coll. of New Rochelle, 1980; dir. continuing edn. Coll. of Mt. St. Vincent, Riverdale, N.Y., 1981—. Mem. Columbia U. Alumni Assn., Japan Internat. Women Group for Internat. Christian U., Nat. Assn. Profl. Women, Women in Mgmt. Assn.; Am. Soc. Profl. and Exec. Women, LWV, AAUW. Author, actress children's TV puppet show Let's Talk about God, NBC, 1959-61. Home: 316 Pondfield Rd Bronxville NY 10708 Office: College of Mount Saint Vincent Riverdale NY 10471

MACDONALD, MARIAN LOUISE, psychologist, educator; b. Jackson, Tenn., June 1, 1947; d. John Daniel and Dona Louise (Skinner) MacDonald; B.A., Auburn U., 1969; M.A., U. Ill., 1972, Ph.D., 1974. Clin. counselor, instr. U. Ill., Urbana-Champaign, 1973-74; asst. prof. SUNY, Stony Brook, 1974-78; vis. asso. prof. U. Hawaii, Manoa, 1978; asso. prof. dept. psychology U. Mass., Amherst, 1978—. USPHS tng. fellow, 1973-74; Stony Brook faculty fellow, 1977; NASA tng. grantee, 1969-72; Biomed. Scis. Support grantee, 1974-75; Nat. Inst. Aging research grantee, 1977-78; U. Mass. Research Found. grantee, 1979-80. Mem. Am. Psychol. Assn., AAAS, Midwestern Psychol. Assn., Assn. Women in Psychology, Assn. for Advancement of Behavior Therapy (dir.), Sigma Xi, Psi Chi. Author: Behavioral Approaches to Community Psychology, 1977; mem. editorial bds. various jours.; contbr. articles to profl. jours. Home: 28 Union St Northampton MA 01060 Office: Dept Psychology U Mass Amherst MA 01003

MACDONALD, PATRICIA LILLIG, public health ofcl.; b. Ridley Park, Pa., Apr. 29, 1941; d. John A. and Sethna Frances (Woods) Lillig; A.B., Immaculata (Pa.) Coll., 1963; M.A. in Communication, Wichita State U., 1979; m. Guy W. MacDonald, Aug. 7, 1965. Analytical chemist McNeil Labs., Inc., Ft. Washington, Pa., 1963-65; Peace Corps vol., tchr., Nepal, 1965-68; organic chemist Frinton Labs., Vineland, N.J., 1968-69; program cons. Lung Assn. So. N.J., Hammonton, 1969-72; program dir. Arthritis Found., Wichita, Kans., 1972-73; dir. health edn. Health Dept., Wichita, 1973—; mem. adj. faculty and interim faculty Wichita State U. Vol. worker ARC, 1973—; bd. dirs. Am. Cancer Soc., 1977—, Am. Heart Assn., 1980—. Mem. Public Relations Soc. Am. (pres. 1981), Nat. Fedn. Press Women, Kans. Public Health Assn. (dir. 1977—), Kans. Press Women, Wichita Press Women (pres. 1978), LWV, Kans. Women's Polit. Caucus. Republican. Roman Catholic. Home: 4701 N Hillcrest Ave Wichita KS 67220 Office: Health Dept 1900 E 9th St Wichita KS 67214

MACDONALD, VIRGINIA B., state legislator; b. El Paso, Tex.; student U. N.Mex.; m. Alan Hunter Macdonald; 1 son, 1 dau. Mem. Ill. Ho. Reps., sec. Ho. Republican Caucus in Gen. Assembly, 1972—, Democratic del. 6th Ill. Constl. Conv., 1970; asst. dir. EPA; pres. Ill. Fedn. Republican Women; chairwoman Cook County Republican Com., 1964-68; committeewoman Wheeling Twp. Rep. Com.; chmn. Statewide Women's div. Everett McKinley Dirksen's Campaign, 1968; mem. adv. council Community Counciling Center, Suburban Br. Salvation Army;

mem. citizens' adv. com. Northwest Suburban Mental Health Assn.; mem. Ill. Water Resources Commn.; vice-chmn. Ill. Sudden Infant Death Syndrome Commn. Mem. Northwestern U. Guild Club: Arlington Heights Women's. Office: Ill Ho Reps State Capitol Springfield IL 62706 *

MAC DOUGALL, AUDREY BALINSKY, social worker; b. Cleve., June 11, 1938; d. Theodore Thomas and Bernice Hedwig (Grys) Balinsky; A.B., Ohio U., 1960; M.S.S.A., Case Western Res. U., 1964; children—Jennifer Erin, Michael Sean. Caseworker, supr. Cuyahoga County (Ohio) Welfare Dept., Cleve., 1964-66; supr. casework services Cleve. Soc. Blind, 1966-70; asst. dir. dept. social services Fairview Gen. Hosp., Cleve., 1970-71; social work cons. Rome (N.Y.)-Parkway SNF, 1976-78; social worker Rome (N.Y.) Devel. Center, 1978-81, social work supr., admissions-placement coordinator, 1981—; field instr. social work Utica Coll. Mem. exec. bd. Meals-on-Wheels, Rome, N.Y., 1974-78, sec., 1975-78; sec. Ridge Mills Elem. Sch. Parent Tchr. Orgn., Rome, 1977-79. Mem. Nat. Assn. Social Workers, Acad. Cert. Social Workers, Bus. and Profl. Women's Club (chmn. publicity 1975-76, 80-81, pres. 1976-78, 2d v.p. 1982—). Home: 7796 Bel Air Dr Rome NY 13440 Office: PO Box 550 Rome NY 13440

MAC DOUGALL, GENEVIEVE ROCKWOOD, journalist, educator; b. Springfield, Ill., Nov. 29, 1914; d. Grover Cleveland and Flora Maurine (Fowler) Rockwood; B.S., Northwestern U., 1936, M.A., 1956, postgrad., 1963—; m. Curtis D. MacDougall, June 20, 1942; children—Priscilla Ruth, Bonnie MacDougall Cottrell. Reporter, Evanston (Ill.) Daily News Index, 1936-37; asso. editor Nat. Almanac & Yearbook, Chgo., 1937-38, News Map of Week, Chgo., 1938-39; editor Springfield (Ill.) Citizens' Tribune, also area supr. Ill. Writers Project, 1940-41; reporter Chgo. City News Bur., 1942; tchr. English-social studies Skokie Jr. High Sch., Winnetka, Ill., 1956-68, coordinator TV, 1964-68; tchr. English Washburne Sch., Winnetka, 1968-81; editor Winnetka Public Schs. Forum, Staff Newsletter, 1981—; dir. Winnetka Jr. High Archeology Field Sch., 1971—; cons., lectr. in field. Winnetka Tchrs. Centennial Fund scholar, 1964, 68. Named Tchr. of Year, Winnetka, 1976; Educator of Decade Northwestern U. and Found. Ill. Archeology, 1981. Mem. Winnetka Tchrs. Council (pres. 1971-72), NEA, Ill. Edn. Assn., Ill. Assn. Advancement Archeology, Women in Communications (pres. N. Shore alumni chpt. 1949-53), Pi Lambda Theta. Author: Grammar Book VII, 1963, 68; (with others) 7th Grade Language Usage, 1963, rev. 1968. Contbr. articles to profl. publs. Home: 537 Judson Ave Evanston IL 60202 Office: 515 Hibbard Rd Winnetka IL 60093

MACDUFFEE, BONITA LOIS, state ofcl.; b. Corning, Calif., Nov. 26, 1946; d. John Emerick and Nora Lee (Stedman) Jiles; A.A., Cosumnes River Coll., Sacramento, 1977; B.A., St. Mary's Coll., Moraga, Calif., 1978; m. Robert Joseph MacDuffee, Mar. 13, 1971; 1 son, Michael Vincent Boyd. Cashier, bookkeeper Doc Clearies Restaurant, Redding, Calif., 1967-69; sales clk. Woolworth's, Sacramento, 1969-72; from clk. typist to acctg. officer Calif. Dept. Corrections, 1972-78; acctg. officer Calif. Dept. Justice, 1978-80, asst. budget officer, 1980—; instr. Calif. Personnel Devel. Center. Bd. dirs. Sacramento Area Spl. Olympics, 1979-82, treas., 1980-82. Mem. Nat. Assn. Female Execs., Calif. State Women's Club. Democrat. Club: Aqua Knights Diving. Office: 1315 5th St Sacramento CA 95814

MACE, SHARON ELIZABETH, physician; b. Syracuse, N.Y., Oct. 30, 1949; d. James Henry and Leona Helen (Bednarski) M.; B.S., Syracuse U., 1971; M.D., SUNY, 1975. Intern and resident in pediatrics Case-Western Res. U. Hosps., Cleve., 1975-77, fellow in cardiology, 1977-79, instr. dept. emergency medicine, 1980—; research asso. div. investigative medicine Mt. Sinai Med. Center, Cleve., 1979-80, staff physician depts. emergency medicine and investigative medicine, 1980—, faculty emergency medicine residency program; dir. edn. dept. emergency medicine Cleve. Met. Gen. Hosp.; instr. Case Western Res. U. Sch. Medicine; helicopter flight physician; lectr. Lakeland Community Coll.; instr. Advanced Cardiac Life Support. Mem. Am. Coll. Emergency Physicians (edn. com. Ohio chpt.). Congregationalist. Contbr. articles to med. jours. Home: 8243 Merrie Ln Chesterland OH 44026 Office: 3395 Scranton Rd Cleveland OH 44109 also Mt Sinai Med Center 1800 E 105th St Cleveland OH 44106

MACELROY, CLAIRE MORRIS, communications co. ofcl.; b. Middlesex, Eng., Nov. 13, 1939; d. Daniel and Gladys Emma (Wilson) Morris; came to U.S., 1962; B.A., Stanford U., 1970; m. Robert D. Macelroy, Jan. 7, 1977; 1 dau., Sarah. Research sec. elec. engring. Stanford U., 1975-77; mktg. and contract adminstr. Interactive Applications, Palo Alto, Calif., 1978-79; cons. C. M. Assos., Palo Alto, 1979—. Mem. Soc. Tech. Communication. Unitarian. Office: 653 Forest Ave Palo Alto CA 94301

MACESICH, SUSANA SONIA, educator; b. Buenos Aires, Argentina, Oct. 29, 1933; came to U.S., 1946, naturalized, 1954; d. George and Radoslava Radmila (Simovijevich) Svorkovich; B.A., Fla. State U., 1967, M.A., 1969, Ph.D., Fla. State U. and U. Belgrade, Yugoslavia, 1972; m. George Macesich, Feb. 20, 1955; children—Maya, Milena, George. Research asso., lectr., student adviser Center for Yugoslav Am. Studies and Exchanges, Fla. State U.-U. Belgrade, summers 1969-76; asst. prof. history dept. Fla. A&M U., Tallahassee, 1973—; research asso. Fla. State U.; instr. bus. communications Tallahassee Community Coll. Nat. teaching fellow, 1973-76. Mem. LWV, Am. Hist. Assn., Am. Assn. for Advancement Slavic Studies, Civic Ballet Guild Tallahassee, LeMoyne Art Found., Delta Tau Kappa, Sigma Delta Pi. Mem. Serbian Orthodox Ch. Club: Univ. Women's. Contbr. papers, articles, revs. to profl. jours., socs. Home: 2401 Delgado Dr Tallahassee FL 32304

MAC FARLANE-JOHNSON, ANNETTE ROWANE, space and tech. co. exec.; b. Brigham City, Utah, Aug. 10, 1952; d. Ted D. and Lynette I. (Gardner) Macfarlane; B.A., Utah State U., 1974; m. Tracy L. Johnson, Nov. 19, 1971. Property mgr., bookkeeper Vill. Green Realty Co., Provo, Utah, 1973-74; accountant, property mgr. Fred Sands Realty Co., Los Angeles, 1974-76; bookkeeper for constrn. budgets and forecasting Southwick Realty Co., Tremonton, Utah, 1976-77; budget analyst space shuttle program fin. team Thiokol Corp., Promentory, Utah, 1977—. Vice chmn. Am. Party, Box Elder County, Utah; choreographer, bd. dirs. Heritage Theater, Brigham City; fund raising divisional dir. Ballet West, Ogden Guild. Mem. Bus. and Profl. Women (Young Careerist 1977, pres. local club 1978-79), Delta Delta Delta. Mormon. Home: PO Box 5 Tremonton UT 84337

MAC GILLIVRAY, MARYANN LEVERONE, mktg. cons.; b. Mpls., Oct. 18, 1947; d. Joseph Paul and Genevieve Gertrude (Ozark) Leverone; B.S., Coll. of St. Catherine, St. Paul, 1969; Med. Technologist, Hennepin County Gen. Hosp., 1970; M.B.A., Pepperdine U., 1976; m. Duncan MacGillivray, Apr. 28, 1973; 1 son, Duncan Michael. Med. technologist Mercy Hosp., San Diego, 1970-72; with Diagnostics div. Abbott Labs., S. Pasadena, Calif., 1972-79, tech. service rep., 1972-74, sr. tech. service rep., 1974-75, product coordinator, mktg., 1975-77, mktg. product mgr., 1977-79; clin. diagnostic mktg. cons., Sierra Madre, Calif., 1979—. Recipient Pres.'s award Abbott Diagnostics Div., 1975. Mem. Biomed. Mktg. Assn., Am. Assn. Clin. Chemistry, Am. Assn. Clin. Pathologists, Am. Soc. Med. Tech., Calif. Assn. Med. Lab. Technologists. Roman Catholic. Home: 608 Elm Ave Sierra Madre CA 91024

MACGOWAN, CAROL ANN, med. technologist; b. Gt. Falls, Mont., June 27, 1932; d. James A. and Lila J. (Davis) MacGowan; B.S. in Chemistry, Coll. of Gt. Falls, 1954; A.S.C.P.M.T., Columbus Sch. Med. Tech., 1955; children—Shannon, Timothy. Generalist/hematology Columbus Hosp. Lab., Gt. Falls, 1954-68, now sect. chief, mem. teaching staff; work dir. hematology Arabian Am. Oil Co., Dhahran, Saudi Arabia, 1960-62; adminstrv. technologist Seattle Gen. Hosp., 1962-64; sect. chief MacGregor Clinic Lab., Gt. Falls, 19 - , part-time staff Coll. of Gt. Falls. Mem. Am. Soc. Clin. Pathologists, Am. Soc. Med. Technologists. Address: 1509 3d Ave N Great Falls MT 59401

MACGRAW, ALI, actress; b. Pound Ridge, N.Y., 1939; ed. Wellesley Coll.; m. 2d, Robert Evans, 1970 (div.); m. 3d, Steve McQueen, 1973 (div.). Previous to film career was editorial asst. Harper's Bazaar Mag., asst. to photographer Melvin Sokolsky; actress films including Goodbye, Columbus, 1969, Love Story, 1971, The Getaway, 1973, Convoy, 1978, Players, 1979, Just Tell Me What You Want, 1979. Office: care William Morris Agy 151 El Camino Beverly Hills CA 90212 *

MACHACEK, PATRICIA LYNNE, architect; b. Berkeley, Calif., Feb. 8, 1947; d. Isaac Delmar and Meredith Lucille (Halstead) Crowder; B.S. (Univ. Mother's Club scholar 1965-66, tuition scholar 1966-68), U. Oreg., 1969; B.Arch. (tuition scholar 1974), U. Idaho, 1975; m. Gary Alan Machacek, May 18, 1974; 1 son, Jason Gary. Grad. asst. Community Devel. Center, U. Idaho, 1974-75; draftsman Boise Cascade Corp., Idaho, 1976; apprentice architect Bradford Paine Shaw, Boise, 1977; architect Keys, Olson and Ensley, Nampa, Idaho, 1978-81; vis. prof. Boise State U., 1981—; active hist. restoration bldg., Silver City, Idaho; coordinator land-use planning workshops, Moscow, Idaho, 1974, 75; mem. com. survey housing and bldg. standards, Sandpoint, Idaho, 1973-74; partner Machacek Investments, 1979—; archtl. works include recreation structures, housing, lodging, retail and office bldgs., schs.; condr. research alt. energy sources. Office: Dept Art Boise State U Boise ID 83725

MACHEMER, CHRISTINE ANNA, psychiatrist; b. Duesseldorf, W.Ger., May 24, 1933; came to U.S., 1966, naturalized, 1972; d. Arnold W. and Elisabeth Haller; Med. Diploma with high honors, U. Freiburg (W.Ger.), 1959; m. Robert Machemer, July 30, 1961; 1 dau., Ruth Elisabeth. Intern, U. Hosp., Dusseldorf, U. Hosp., Freiburg, W.Ger., 1960, 61; resident in psychiatry U. Miami (Fla.) Sch. Medicine, 1969-72; practice medicine specializing in psychiatry, Miami, 1973-78, Durham, N.C., 1979—; clin. instr. psychiatry Jackson Meml. Hosp., Miami, 1975-78; clin. asst. prof. dept. psychiatry Duke U., Durham, N.C., 1978—; mem. staff Duke Hosp. Diplomate Am. Bd. Psychiatry and Neurology. Mem. Am. Psychiat. Assn., N.C. Neuropsychiat. Assn., Am. Med. Women's Assn., So. Med. Assn., Durham-Chapel Hill Psychiat. Soc., Durham-Orange County Med. Soc. Home: 1532 Pinecrest Rd Durham NC 27705 Office: Box 3125 Duke Med Center Durham NC 27710

MACHNOWSKI, MARCELLA ANNE LAUZON, social worker; b. Providence, R.I., June 27, 1954; d. Theodore Ephrem and Gloria Margaret L.; B.A., Cath. U. Am., 1976. Social worker Georgetown U. Med. Center, Washington, 1977-80; med. social worker Holy Cross Hosp., Silver Spring, Md., 1980—. Lic. social worker, Md. Home: 8225 Adenlee Ave Fairfax VA 22031 Office: 1500 Forest Glen Rd Silver Spring MD 20910

MACHTIGER, HARRIET GORDON, psychoanalyst; b. N.Y.C., July 27, 1927; d. Michael J. and Miriam D. (Rand) Gordon; B.A., Bklyn. Coll., 1947; dipl. with distinction, U. London, 1966, Ph.D., 1974; m. Sidney Machtiger, Feb. 7, 1948; children—Avram Coleman, Marcia Gordon, Bennett Rand. Tchr., Phila. Public Schs., 1962-64; ednl. therapist Child Guidance Tng. Center, London, 1966-68; ednl. therapist Sch. Psychol. Service, Inner London Edn. Authority, 1968-70; therapist Paddington Day Hosp., London, 1970-71, London Centre for Psychotherapy, 1971-74, Staunton Clinic, U. Pitts., 1974-78; pvt. practice psychoanalysis, Pitts., 1976—; pres. C.G. Jung Center, Pitts., 1976-81; cons. in field. Mem. SW Pitts. Community Mental Health, 1976-78. Recipient award for Disting. Contributions to Advancement in Edn., Pa. Dept. Edn., 1962; Social Sci. Research Council award, 1973; cert. psychologist, Pa. Fellow Am. Orthopsychiat. Assn.; mem. Inter-Regional Soc. Jungian Analysts. (dir. Pitts. program 1975—), Am. Acad. Psychotherapists, Am. Psychol. Assn., N.Y. Assn. Analytical Psychologists, Internat. Assn. Group Psychotherapists, Pa. Psychol. Assn., Brit. Psychol. Soc., Brit. Assn. Psychotherapists, Assn. Child Psychology and Child Psychiatry, Western Pa. Group Psychotherapy Assn., Nat. Assn. for Advancement Psychoanalysis, Exec. Women's Council, NOW, Democrat. Jewish. Club: B'nai B'rith Women. Home: 207 Tennyson Ave Pittsburgh PA 15213 Office: 110 The Fairfax 4614 Fifth Ave Pittsburgh PA 15213

MACILWAINE, PAULA JEANNE, county ofcl.; b. Butler, Pa., Feb. 11, 1941; d. Gerald Beckwith and Sara Pauline (Sloan) Sanders; B.A., Ohio Wesleyan U., 1962; m. John Charles MacIlwaine, Feb. 10, 1962; children—Stacey Anne, Wendy Louise, John Hamilton. Dist. dir. Buckeye Trails Girl Scouts, 1962-65; pres. Montgomery County Commn., Dayton, Ohio, 1980—. Mem. bd. Community Improvement Corp., Dayton Opera, Dayton Art Inst., Mus. Natural History; mem. Community Adv. Council; mem. Miami Valley Regional Planning Commn.; chmn. Muscular Distrophy Telethon, 1978. Mem. Nat. Assn. County Ofcls. (chmn. jobs subcom.), Task Force on Regulatory Procedures, County Commrs. Assn. Ohio, Dayton Women's Network, League Women Voters (pres. 1974-76) C. of C. (bd. govs. 1978-80). Democrat. Presbyterian. Office: 451 W 3d St Dayton OH 45422

MACINNES, HELEN, writer; b. Glasgow, Scotland, Oct. 7, 1907; came to U.S., 1937, naturalized, 1951; d. Donald and Jessica (MacDiarmid) MacI.; M.A., Glasgow U., 1928; postgrad. U. Coll., London U., 1930-31; m. Gilbert Highet, Sept. 22, 1932 (dec. 1978); 1 son, Gilbert Keith MacInnes. Novels: Above Suspicion, 1941, Assignment in Brittany, 1942, While Still We Live, 1944, Horizon, 1946, Friends & Lovers, 1947, Rest and Be Thankful, 1949, Neither Five Nor Three, 1951, If My True Love, 1953, Pray For A Brave Heart, 1955, North From Rome, 1958, Decision at Delphi, 1960, The Venetian Affair, 1963, The Double Image, 1966, The Salzburg Connection, 1968, Message From Malaga, 1971, Snare of the Hunter, 1976, Agent in Place, 1976, Prelude to Terror, 1978, The Hidden Target, 1980; (play) Home is the Hunter, 1964. Recipient Wallace award, Am-Scottish Found., 1973. Presbyterian.

MACINTYRE, JEAN NATALIE, artist; b. Long Beach, Calif., Feb. 6, 1927; d. Ronald Everette and Natalie Floyd (Josselyn) Sype; A.A., Moorpark (Calif.) Community Coll., 1976; B.S., Calif. State U., Northridge, 1978; m. William Terrill MacIntyre, Feb. 2, 1946; children—Ronald William, Charles Ian, Daniel Carey, Wanda Mae, Cecilia Lynn. Practical nurse, 1955-68; domestics supr. Kresges K-Mart, 1968-71; owner Mac's Wicks, arts and crafts store, Ventura, Calif., 1971-72; propr. The Art Experience, multi-media art sch., Newbury Park, Calif., 1978—; tchr. painting and printmaking, organizer art shows, 1979—; treas. Westlake Village Art Guild, 1977-79, show organizer, 1980-82; ednl. chmn. Thousand Oaks Art Assn., 1979-82. Recipient awards in printmaking, photography. Mem. Artists Equity Assn., Westlake Village Art Guild, Thousand Oaks Art Assn., Buenaventura Art Assn., Internat. Fine Arts Guild, Nat. Fedn. Ind. Businessmen, Internat. Platform Assn. Republican. Presbyterian. Club: Soroptimist. Author: The Color Mixing Book, 1980.

MACIVER, PEGGE FARMER (MRS. DONALD GORDON MACIVER), monodramatist, educator; b. Colon, C.Z.; d. Alfred Gibson and Minnie (Cuckler) Farmer; B.A., Ohio U., 1935; B.L.L., Cin. Conservatory Music, 1938; M.A., George Washington U., 1964; m. Donald Gordon MacIver, June 7, 1957; 1 stepson, Neil. Monodramatist, lectr., writer touring U.S., Can. writing, performing own plays for one woman theatre presentations, 1938-67; speech therapist D.C. Public Schs., 1959-67, tchr. in-service tng. programs, program coordinator Ednl. Resources Center, 1967-70, asst. dir. dept. spl. edn., 1970-72, supervising dir. for staff devel. dept. spl. edn., 1972-78; ret., 1978; tchr. in-service tng. programs D.C. Tchrs. Coll. TV moderator, panelist Its Your World and World Headliner programs; mem. speakers burs. Dayton (Ohio) Council World Affairs, LWV, 1950-57. Mem. Nat. League Am. Pen Women, Am. Speech and Hearing Assn. (cert. of clin. competence in speech pathology), D.C. Speech and Hearing Assn., Assn. for Supervision and Curriculum Devel., Internat. Platform Assn., Phi Beta Kappa, Pi Beta Phi, Alpha Delta Kappa, Delta Kappa Gamma. Contbr. articles to profl. publs. Home: 8500 New Hampshire Ave Silver Spring MD 20903

MACK, BRENDA LEE, public relations cons. co. exec.; b. Peoria, Ill., Mar. 24, 1940; d. William James and Virginia Julia (Pickett) Palmer; A.A., Los Angeles City Coll., 1969; B.A. in Sociology, Calif. State U., Los Angeles, 1980; m. Rozene Mack, Jan. 13, 1960 (div.); 1 son, Kevin Anthony. Ct. clk. City of Blythe, Calif., 1962; partner Mack Trucking Co., Blythe, 1961-64; ombudsman, sec. bus facilities So. Calif. Rapid Transit Dist., Los Angeles, 1974-81; owner Brenda Mack Enterprises, Los Angeles, 1981—. Bd. dirs. Narcotic Symposium, Los Angeles, 1968. Served with U.S. WAC, 1960-61. Mem. Black Women's Forum, Women For, Nat. Council Negro Women, City Employees for Tax Reform, Hollywood C. of C., Calif. State U. Los Angeles Alumni. Home: 8749 Cattaraugus Ave Los Angeles CA 90034 Office: Brenda Mack Enterprises PO Box 5942 Los Angeles CA 90055

MACK, CAROLYN HOURIGAN, ret. pub. co. exec.; b. Wilkes-Barre, Pa., Feb. 2, 1907; d. John Aloysius and Caroline G. (Henderson) Hourigan; B.A., Manhattanville Coll., 1928; m. Thomas J. Mack, Sept. 20, 1956. Vice pres. Wilkes-Barre Pub. Co., 1945-78; treas., dir. Bertels Metal Ware Co., Inc., Kingston, Pa., 1951—; sec. dir. Mack Supply Co., Wilkes-Barre, 1956—. Mem. Wilkes-Barre City Planning Commn., 1971—. Bd. dirs., v.p. Legal Aid Soc., Wilkes-Barre, 1955-60; bd. dirs. Wyoming Valley Heart Assn.; bd. dirs., chmn. Cath. Youth Center, Wilkes-Barre; past trustee Misericordia Coll., Dallas, Pa. Republican. Roman Catholic. Club: Westmoreland (Wilkes-Barre). Home: 182 S Franklin St Wilkes-Barre PA 18701

MACK, PHYLLIS FRIEDMAN (MRS. DAVID MACK), interior designer, civic worker; b. N.Y.C., Apr. 15, 1941; d. Maurice and Anne (Price) Friedman; student Vassar Coll., 1958-60, Sorbonne, Paris, 1960; B.S., Columbia U., 1963; grad. N.Y. Sch. Interior Design; m. David Mack, Oct. 8, 1961; children—Alexander H., Nicholas R. Interior designer domestic interiors, N.Y.C., 1963—. Bd. dirs. Stanley Isaacs Community Center, 1965-67; bd. dirs. Children's Blood Found., 1978—, benefit chmn., 1980; chmn. Friends of Children's Blood Found., 1979-80; dance chmn. George Jr. Republic, also mem. jr. bd., 1966-69; bd. dirs. Yorkville Youth Council, 1974-77; mem. public relations com. Asso. YM-YWHA, N.Y.C. Mem. Allied Bd. Trade, Brearley Alumnae Assn. (reunion chmn.). Club: Bailiwick Tennis. Home: 100 Bedford Rd Greenwich CT 06830 also 800 Park Ave New York City NY 10021

MACK, SANDRA FAYE MILES, sch. adminstr.; b. Denton, Tex., Aug. 15, 1939; d. Monroe Benjamin and Wilma Delores (Bell) Miles; B.S., U. Wash., 1961; M.A. in Adminstrn. and Higher Edn., San Jose State U., 1972; Ed.D., U. LaVerne, 1981; m. Daniel Javah Mack, Sept. 27, 1958; children—Sherri, Ronald, Lori. Tchr., Seattle public schs., 1961-68, San Jose High Sch., 1968-75, San Jose State U., 1974-75; dean student activities Los Altos (Calif.) High Sch., 1975-79; coordinator continuing and adult edn. and emergency sch. aid act New Haven Unified Sch. Dist., Union City, Calif., 1979—; cons. human relations, meeting facilitator, exec. sec. Calif. Assn. Student Councils Summer Leadership Conf., 1979. Bd. dirs. Santa Clara County Girl Scouts Am., 1975-77. Mem. NAACP (life), Nat. Council Negro Women (v.p.), AAUW, Nat. Assn. Female Execs., Calif. Assn. Sch. Adminstrs., Calif. Coalition Black Sch. Bd. Members and Adminstrs., Delta Sigma Theta (chpt. pres. 1972-73). Democrat. Methodist. Home: 3434 Gila Dr San Jose CA 95148 Office: 34200 Alvarado-Niles Rd Union City CA 94587

MACKAIG, JANET BROWNLEE, artist, printmaker, educator; b. Santa Monica, Calif., July 16, 1931; d. Roy Edward and Lorna (Feckler) Murphy; A.A., Pasadena City Coll., 1964; B.A., Calif. State U., Los Angeles, 1969, M.A., 1971, postgrad., 1975; postgrad. UCLA, 1975; m. Richard Allaire Mackaig, Dec. 15, 1950; children—Janet (Mrs. William Chadwick), Steven Richard. Tchr., Creative Arts Group, Sierra Madre, Calif., 1965-75, Duarte (Calif.) Unified Sch. Dist., 1973-76; tchr. Otis Art Inst., Los Angeles, 1975-76, Saddleback Coll., Mission Viejo, Calif., 1976-78, Laguna Beach Sch. Art, 1980—; one-man shows: Upstairs Gallery, Claremont, Calif., 1969, U. Oreg., 1976, Fine Arts Gallery, Laguna Beach, Calif., 1981, Minot (N.D.) State Coll., 1981; group shows include: Colorprint U.S.A., Tex. Tech. U., 1975, U. Ala., 1975, Pioneer Press Traveling Print Show, Africa, 1975-76, Art-A Multi-Cultural Show, Calif. Mus. Sci. and Industry, 1978, Contemporary Korean Printmakers Assn. Print Show, 1978, Coos Art Mus., Coos Bay, Oreg., 1979, La Grange (Ga.) Coll., 1980, Trenton (N.J.) State Coll., 1980, Internat. Print Biennial, Miami, Fla., 1982; represented in permanent collections. Bd. dirs. Womanspace, 1974—. Recipient Calif. Purchase awards Santa Monica Coll., 1973, Calif. State U., Los Angeles, 1976, Calif. Poly. U., Pomona, 1979. Mem. Laguna Beach Art Assn., Calif. Soc. Printmakers, Los Angeles Printmaking Soc. (pres. 1977-78), Los Angeles Inst. Contemporary Art, Print Club Phila., Pasadena Artists Concern. Club: Pioneer Press. Home: 23821 Salvador Bay Laguna Niguel CA 92677

MAC KAY, AUDREY STOMBS, resort facilities adminstr., civic worker; b. St. Paul, Aug. 1, 1920; d. Daniel Colby and Myrtle May (Hoffstetter) Stombs; student Woodbury Bus. Coll., 1939; m. Alan Donald MacKay, July 1, 1939 (dec. 1955); children—Alta Diane, Alan Donald. Pvt. sec. Smiling Irishman Used Cars, Los Angeles, 1939-41; office mgr. Charles Marsalisi Used Cars, 1941; successively personnel mgr., pvt. sec., adminstrv. asst., adminstr. resort facilities Owners of Lake Arrowhead (Calif.), 1946—; now adminstr. New Lake Arrowhead Village; asst. sec. Lake Arrowhead Devel. Co., 1968-71. Pres., Women's Club, 1959; bd. dirs. Lake Arrowhead C. of C., 1974—; rec. sec. Soroptimists Internat. of Lake Arrowhead, 1978-80, pres., 1980-81; vice chmn. County Service Area 70D1, 1975-79, chmn. Dam Com., 1979—; mem. archtl. com. Arrowhead Woods, 1960-75; active Jr. Women's Club. Named hon. mayor Lake Arrowhead, 1958; Citizen of Yr., 1976. Mem. Lake Arrowhead Resorts C. of C. (v.p. 1981-82). Republican. Baptist. Home: PO Box 777 Lake Arrowhead CA 92352 Office: Lake Arrowhead Village Lake Arrowhead CA 92352

MACKAY, PATRICIA MCINTOSH, counselor; b. San Francisco, Sept. 12, 1922; d. William Carroll and Louise Edgerton (Keen) McIntosh; A.B. in Psychology, U. Calif., Berkeley, 1944, elem. teaching credential, 1951; M.A. in Psychology, John F. Kennedy U., Orinda, Calif., 1979; Ph.D. in Nutrition Donsbach U., Huntington Beach, Calif.; m. Alden Thorndike Mackay, Dec. 15, 1945; children—Patricia Louise, James McIntosh, Donald Sage. Elem. tchr. Mt. Diablo Unified Sch.

Dist., Concord, Calif., 1950-60; exec. supr. No. Calif. Welcome Wagon Internat., 1960-67; wedding cons. Mackay Creative Services, Walnut Creek, Calif., 1969-70; co-owner Courtesy Calls, Greeters and Concord Welcoming Services, Walnut Creek, 1971—; marriage, family and child counselor, nutrition cons., Pleasanton and Walnut Creek, 1979—; bd. dirs. New Directions Counseling Center, Inc., 1975—, founder, pres. aux., 1977—. Bd. dirs. Ministry in the Marketplace, Inc.; founder, dir. Turning Point Counseling. Recipient Individual award New Directions Counseling Center, 1978, awards Neo-Life Co. Am. Prestige Club, 1977, 78, 79, 80, 81. Mem. Christian Assn. Psychol. Studies, Calif. Assn. Marriage and Family Therapists, C. of C., Prytanean Alumnae, Delta Gamma. Republican. Presbyterian. Clubs: Soroptomist (dir. 1976) (Walnut Creek). Home: 1101 Scots Ln Walnut Creek CA 94596 Office: 1666 Oakland Blvd Walnut Creek CA 94596

MAC KAY, SANDRA JEAN, anthropologist, nurse; b. N.Y.C., Nov. 26, 1936; d. Kenneth Bernard and Gertrude Alice (Miller) Schon; B.S. Nursing, Cornell U., 1959; M.A., Columbia U., 1962; A.M., Dartmouth Coll., 1972; Ph.D. in Anthropology, Boston U., 1979; m. Donald Noyes MacKay, Sept. 11, 1959; children—Nancy, Susan, Sandra. Pub. health nurse at health centers, Port Chester, N.Y., Judson Health Center, N.Y.C., 1959-61; research asst. child psychology dept. Cornell U. Med. Sch., N.Y.C., 1963-64; remedial reading tchr. U.S. Army High Sch., Vicenza, Italy, 1965-66; instr. social sci. Mary Hitchcock Meml. Hosp., Hanover, N.H., 1967-70; pub. health nursing coordinator VA Hosp., White River Junction, Vt., 1970-72; instr. dept. community medicine Dartmouth Med. Sch., Hanover, N.H., 1977-78; coordinator clin. studies, nursing service VA Hosp., White River Junction, Vt., 1979-82, staff Research Service, 1982—; research asst. prof. dept. psychiatry Dartmouth Med. Sch., Hanover, N.H., 1980—. Nurse scientist fellow HEW, 1972; multidisciplinary univ.-wide fellow in health services research and policy Boston U., 1975-77. Mem. Am. Anthrop. Assn., Am. Nurses Assn., AAAS. Democrat. Home: 5 Dana Rd Hanover NH 03755

MACKENZIE, AMANDA FISK, tng. and devel. ofcl.; civic worker; b. Buffalo, Jan. 18, 1936; d. Bradley and Erma (Johnson) Fisk; B.A., Smith Coll., 1957; children—Bradley John, Alice Fisk, Douglas Bain. Editorial asst. N.E.A., Washington, 1957-58; research asst. to prof. polit. sci., Africa, 1958; sec. to pres. Charles Scribner's Sons, N.Y.C., 1959; writer, producer Washington Ednl. TV, 1961-64; pub. affairs coordinator Can. Performing Arts Festival, 1975; publ. coordinator The Pa. Co. Vol. co-ordinator Adams-Morgan Community Council, Washington, 1966-68; public liaison ethics adv. bd. HEW, 1979-80; public affairs asst. to dir. Select Panel on Child Health, Dept. Health and Human Services, 1980; tng. program and devel. dir. Nat. Center Clin. Infant Programs, 1981—; mem. Mayor's Inter-Agy. Com. on Beautification. Bd. dirs. Jr. League, Washington, 1969-70, Hillcrest Children's Center, 1972-74, Eagles Mere Assn., 1972-75, Woodley House, 1973-76, Inter/Met, 1973-75; trustee Washington Theater Club, 1969-72; trustee Opera Soc. Washington, 1969-76, exec. v.p., 1973-75; trustee Soc. for More Beautiful Nat. Capital, 1971-76, v.p., 1972-76; trustee Selma M. Levine Sch. Music, Lester Hereward Cooke Found., Greg Reynolds Dance Quintet. Democrat. Episcopalian. Clubs: Women's Nat. Democratic, Internat., Smith Coll. (pres. 1972-74) (Washington); Eagles Mere Yacht (sec.-treas. 1968-72). Home: 3501 Macomb St NW Washington DC 20016

MACKERY, BARBARA EUNICE, corporate sales rep.; b. Cedar Bluff, Va., Aug. 21, 1942; d. Robert Orville and Eunice Mae (Bluhm) Brown; student Bethany Bible Coll., 1962-63, U. No. Colo., 1963-64; m. Jimmie Lee Mackery, Mar. 31, 1972. Exec. sec. Sunset Internat. Petroleum, Beverly Hills, Calif., 1965-68; tchr. Sawyer Coll. Bus., Panorama City, Calif., 1968-69; personal sec. to pres. World Challenge, Inc., Lindale, Tex., 1969-81; corp. sales rep. Mackery Copier Systems, Inc., Dallas, 1982—; research and resource editor David Wilkerson Publs., Lindale, 1969-81; asst. to producer David Wilkerson Film Prodns., Dallas, 1971-80; tchr. Twin Oaks Leadership Acad., Lindale, 1977-78. Mem. Nat. Assn. Female Execs., Nat. Office Machine Dealers Assn. (Dallas chpt. sec. 1982-83). Republican Mem. Assembly of God Ch. Address: 625 Southwynd Dr Mesquite TX 75150

MACKEY, DIANNA DEE, nurse, educator; b. San Francisco, May 17, 1943; d. Louis Renaldo and Hazel Evelyn (Holten) DiLuzio; A.A., Coll. of Notre Dame, Belmont, Calif., 1963; A.S. in Nursing, Coll. San Mateo, 1965; student West Valley Coll., 1965-66, U. Calif., Berkeley, 1971-73; B.S. in Nursing Edn., Coll. of Holy Names, Oakland, Calif., 1973-74; postgrad. San Francisco State U., 1974-75, Mission Coll., 1979; M.A., Consortium of Calif. State Colls. and Univs., 1977; m. John Henry Mackey, June 25, 1966; children—John Louis, David Michael. Staff nurse Sequoia Hosp., Redwood City, Calif., 1965-66, Los Gatos (Calif.)-Saratoga Community Hosp., 1966-71; instr. health services edn. West Valley Joint Community Coll. Dist., West Valley Coll., Mission Coll., 1971—; asst. dir. vocat. nursing program Mission Coll., 1977-78, dir. allied health project, 1978; co-dir., partner Health Edn. Services, Menlo Park, Calif., 1979—. Chairperson spl. project com. Multiple Sclerosis Soc., 1981—. Mem. Nat. League Nursing, Calif. Vocat. Nurse Educators, Am. Soc. Allied Health Professions, Nat. Assn. Female Execs. Democrat. Roman Catholic. Club: Ind. Order Foresters Am. Home: 122 Belvale Dr Los Gatos CA 95030 Office: Mission Coll 3000 Mission College Blvd Santa Clara CA 95050 also Health Edn Services 200 Waverly Ave Menlo Park CA 94025

MACKEY, ELIZABETH JOCELYN, musicologist; b. Corbin, Ky., Oct. 30, 1927; d. Elbert Thomas and Flora (Bryant) M.; B.S., Peabody Coll., 1948; Mus.B., Greensboro Coll., 1953; Mus.M., U. Mich., 1956; Ph.D., U. Mich., 1968; Tchr. voice, public schs., N.C., 1948-52, Calif., 1953-55; instr. Indiana (Pa.) State Coll., 1956-58; asso. prof. Minot (N.D.) State Coll., 1964-67; asst. prof. music history and musicology Ball State U., Muncie, Ind., 1969-74, asso. prof., 1974-80, prof., 1980—. Fulbright scholar, Berlin, 1961-62; AAUW fellow, 1963-64. Mem. Pi Kappa Lambda, Sigma Alpha Iota (nat. program counselor 1968-78, pres. 1978—; Sword of Honor, Rose of Honor). Lutheran. Home: 1205 W Riverside Dr Muncie IN 47303 Office: Sch Music Ball State U Muncie IN 47306

MACKNIGHT, SHARON MAGNUS, med. technologist; b. Westerly, R.I., Nov. 13, 1942; d. George Robert and Helen (Magnus) MacK.; A.S., Colby Jr. Coll., New London, N.H., 1963, B.S., 1964; diploma Hartford (Conn.) Hosp. Sch. Med. Tech., 1964; M.S., U. Bridgeport (Conn.), 1980. Med. technologist Conn. and Calif. hosps., 1964-69; supr. hematology lab. Stamford (Conn.) Hosp., 1969—; bd. dirs. Stamford Hosp. Credit Union, 1979—, sec. credit com., 1982—. Am. Soc. Med. Tech. (P.A.C.E. Setter award 1978), Am. Soc. Clin. Pathologists (asso.), Suomi Soc., Finlandia Found. Home: 131-12 Courtland Ave Stamford CT 06902

MACLAINE, SHIRLEY, actress; b. Richmond, Va., Apr. 24, 1934; d. Ira O. and Kathlyn (MacLean) Beaty; ed. high sch.; m. Steve Parker, Sept. 17, 1954; 1 dau., Stephanie Sachiko. Broadway plays include Me and Juliet, 1953, Pajama Game, 1954; actress movies The Trouble With Harry, 1954, Artists and Models, 1954, Around the World in 80 Days, 1955-56, Hot Spell, 1957, The Matchmaker, 1957, The Sheepman, 1957, Some Came Running, 1958 (Fgn. Press award 1959), Ask Any Girl (Silver Bear award as best actress Internat. Berlin Film Festival), 1959, Career, 1959, Can-Can, 1959, The Apartment (Best Actress prize Venice Film Festival), 1959, Children's Hour, 1960, Two for the Seesaw, 1962, Irma La Douce, 1963, What A Way to Go and The Yellow Rolls Royce, 1964, John Goldfarb Please Come Home, 1965, Gambit and Woman Times Seven, 1967, The Bliss of Mrs. Blossom and Two Mules for Sister Sara, 1969, Desperate Characters, 1971, The Possession of Joel Delaney, 1972, The Turning Point, 1977, Being There, 1979, A Chang of Seasons, 1980, Loving Couples, 1980; TV shows include: Shirley's World, 1971-72, If They Could See Me Now, 1974, The Other Half of the Sky: A China Memoir, 1975, Gypsy in My Soul, 1976, Shirley MacLaine at the Lido, 1979, Shirley MacLaine...Every Little Movement, 1980. Author: Don't Fall Off the Mountain, 1970; The New Celebrity Cookbook, 1973; You Can Get There From Here, 1975; editor: McGovern: The Man and His Beliefs, 1972. Office: Chasin-Park-Citron Agy 9255 Sunset Blvd Suite 13 Los Angeles CA 90069 *

MAC LENNAN, BERYCE W., psychologist; b. Aberdeen, Scotland, Mar. 14, 1920; came to U.S., 1949, naturalized, 1965; d. William and Beatrice (MaCrae) Mellis; B.Sc. with honors, London Sch. Econs., 1947; Ph.D., London U., 1960; m. John Duncan MacLennan, Nov. 29, 1944. Group psychotherapist, youth specialist cons. N.Y.C. and Washington, 1949-63; dir. Center for Prevention Juvenile Delinquency and New Careers, Washington, 1963-66; sect. chief Mental Health Study Center, NIMH, Adelphi, Md., 1967-70, chief, 1971-74; regional adminstr. Mass. Dept. Mental Health, Springfield, 1974-75; sr. mental health adv. GAO, Washington, 1976—; prof. George Washington U., 1970—. Mem. tech. adv. com. Prince George's City Mental Health Assn., 1968—. Fellow Am. Psychol. Assn., Am. Orthopsychiat. Assn., Am. Group Psychotherapy Assn. Democrat. Club: So. Md. Sailing. Home: 6307 Crathie Ln Bethesda MD 20816 Office: General Accounting Office NIH Bldg 31 2B-11 Bethesda MD 20505

MAC MILLAN, VELMA JEANNE, educator; b. Chgo., 1926; d. Ernest Wilfred and Velma Jennie (Paramore) B.M., Coe Coll., 1948, 1949; M.S. in Music Edn., U. Ill., 1959; Ph.D. (NDEA Title IV fellow), U. Wis., 1969. Instr. vocal music Buffalo Center (Iowa) Consol. Schs., 1948-49; music supr. Manchester (Iowa) Pub. Sch., 1949-52; music instr. Kenosha (Wis.) Pub. Schs., 1952-67; critic tchr., 1963-66; asso. prof. ednl. adminstrn. U. Wis., Superior, 1969—, coordinator ednl. adminstrn. programs, 1978-82. Mem. pres.'s adv. council Coe Coll., 1980-83. Named Outstanding Educator, 1975. Mem. Gov.'s Commn. on Edn. Seminar, 1966; chmn. Regional Pub. Hearing Kellett Commn. Gov.'s Commn. on Edn., 1970. Mem. Assn. for Supervision and Curriculum Devel., Nat. (dir. 1965-67), Wis. fedns. bus. and profl. women's clubs (pres. 1965-67), Assn. Wis. Sch. Adminstrs., Assn. U. Wis. Faculty, Mu Phi Epsilon, Pi Kappa Lambda, Pi Lambda Theta, Phi Delta Kappa. Lutheran. Home: 2909 John Ave Superior WI 54880 Office: Coll Edn U Wis Superior WI 54880

MAC MULLAN, MARCIA WELLMAN, social worker; b. Columbus, Ohio, Jan. 27, 1925; d. Burton Singley and Blanche (Gardner) Wellman; A.B., U. Mich., 1947, M.S.W., 1967; m. Harry L. Fitch, May 7, 1948; children—Marcia L. Fitch Meyer, Sarah, Peter; m. 2d, Donald D. MacMullan, May 16, 1967. Intelligence analyst Dept. Def., 1947-49; artist, art tchr., Key West, Fla., 1958-63; caseworker Fla. Dept. Welfare, 1963-65; coordinator intake and community services Washtenaw County (Mich.) Juvenile Ct., 1967—; exec. sec. Center Occupational and Personalized Edn., Inc., Ann Arbor, Mich., 1980; v.p. Washtenaw County Coordinating Council Children at Risk, 1980; instr. U. Mich. Symposia, 1976-77, Eastern Mich. U., 1977-78; chmn. drug crime task force Ann Arbor Citizens Council, 1975-76; mem. children and youth com. Mich. League Human Services, 1976-77; project coordinator Peaceable Community Games, 1981-82. Mem. Nat. Assn. Social Workers (chmn. juvenile justice com. Mich. chpt. 1975-80; Social Worker of Year, Huron Valley chpt. 1975, Huron Valley unit 1980), ACLU, NOW, Law and Soc. Assn., Mich. Assn. Ednl. Options (legis. chmn. 1980), Phi Beta Kappa, Phi Kappa Phi, Delta Gamma. Author papers, reports in field. Home: 2020 Chalmers St Ann Arbor MI 48104 Office: 2270 Platt St Ann Arbor MI 48104

MACPHERSON, JANET TAYLOR WOLFENDEN, civic worker; b. Phila.; d. Edward Musker and Annette (Robertson) Wolfenden; B.S., M.A., U. Pa.; postgrad. Columbia U.; m. Herbert Grenfell MacPherson, June 5, 1937; children—Janet Lynne MacPherson O'Donel-Browne, Robert Duncan. Pres., Franklin Sch. PTA, Lakewood, Ohio, 1954-56; bd. dirs. Oak Ridge chpt. AAUW, 1957-59; pres. Oak Ridge LWV, 1961-63, LWV of Tenn., 1967-69, Friends of Oak Ridge Pub. Library, 1966-67; bd. dirs. Oak Ridge Civic Music Assn., 1963-66, pres. Women's guild, 1963-64; mem. Nat. Com. for Support Pub. Schs., 1967-70; mem. Com. of 100, Found. for Better Govt. for Tenn., 1967-70; mem. Tenn. com. 1970 White House Conf. on Children and Youth, 1969-70; mem. salary structure study com. Bd. Edn. Oak Ridge, 1969-71; chmn. Youth Com. Oak Ridge, 1969-70; mem. state planning com. Air Quality Project for Tenn., 1970-71; bd. dirs. Awareness House Oak Ridge, 1970-73; mem. Oak Ridge Charter Commn., 1972-74; bd. dirs. Anderson County (Tenn.) Health Council, 1974-83, CONTACT, telephone counseling service, Oak Ridge, 1975-79, Mental Health Assn. Oak Ridge Region, 1977-83, Planned Parenthood East Tenn., 1978-81; mem. mental health statewide planning adv. com. Tenn. Dept. Mental Health and Mental Retardation, 1981-83. Editor: This Is Oak Ridge, Tennessee, 1961. Home: 102 Orchard Circle Oak Ridge TN 37830

MACRAE, SHEILA STEPHENS, entertainer; b. London, Sept. 24; d. Louis and Winifred (Baker) Stephens; m. Gordon MacRae, May 21, 1941; children—Meredith, Heather, Gar, Robert Bruce; m. 2d, Ron Wayne. Formerly appeared in roles with summer theatre, Roslyn, N.Y., then disc jockey, also radio actress; writer material for husband on TV and in nightclubs, now mem. act; appeared in TV series Jackie Gleason Show, 1966-70, Sheila MacRae Show, 1971; rec. artist Capitol records. Bd. dirs., a founder Share, Inc. Address: care Talent Mgmt Internat 6380 Wilshire Blvd Suite 910 Los Angeles CA 90048 *

MACRORIE, CAROL ANN, mfg. co. ofcl.; b. Little Falls, N.Y., Feb. 14, 1946; d. Harold D. and Lena Irene (Grassel) MacR.; student Northeastern U., 1973-76, Holyoke Community Coll., 1977—; 1 adopted son, Francis Gulla. Inventory control clk. Salada Foods, Inc., Woburn, Mass., 1964-69; distbn. supr. Addison Wesley Publ. Co., Reading, Mass., 1969-73; with Digital Equipment Corp., Maynard, Mass., 1973—, inventory and prodn. control supr., Westfield, Mass., 1979-80, distibn. mgr., 1980—. Mem. Am. Mgmt. Assn., Delta Nu Alpha. Home: 1749 E Mountain Rd Westfield MA 01085 Office: 1111 Southampton Rd Westfield MA 01085

MACSISAK, PATRICIA DIANE, data processing adminstr.; b. San Antonio, Jan. 13, 1949; d. Robert Linday and Etna Joyce (Archer) Hicks; B.A., So. Meth. U., 1975, M.B.A., 1978; m. Stephen Foster Macsisak, Sept. 27, 1975. Standards and tng. adminstr. Central & South West Services, Dallas, 1978-80; supt. support services, 1980-81, mgr. info. services planning, 1981—. Mem. industry coop. com. Computer Sci. Tech. Sch., Tex. State Tech. Inst., 1981—. Mem. AAUW, M.B.A. Assn. So. Meth. U. (dir.), Friends of Sch. Libraries. Democrat. Episcopalian. Clubs: 500, Inc., Colophon (dir.). Author: (with Jody Potts) The Edwin L. Cox School of Business: A Historical Perspective, 1978. Home: 912 Melville Plano TX 75075 Office: 27001 Main Pl Dallas TX 75250

MACTAVISH, MARGARET ANNE SMITH, coll. adminstr.; b. Rural Retreat, Va., July 13, 1943; d. Lewis Wilson and Rita Gillis (Hall) Smith; B.A. in Bus. Adminstrn., Oakland U., 1965; M.B.A., Wayne State U., 1972; m. Neil Curtis MacTavish, July 29, 1966. Personnel interviewer William Beaumont Hosp., Royal Oak, Mich., 1965-69; systems and procedures coordinator Macomb Community Coll., Warren, Mich., 1969-73, registrar, 1973-75, asso. dean student and acad. services, 1975-80, asso. dir. employee relations, 1980—. Trustee Oakland Community Coll., 1980—. Mem. Coll. and Univ. Personnel Assn., Indsl. Relations Research Assn., Am. Assn. Women in Community and Jr. Colls. (treas.), Mich. Assn. Women Deans, Adminstrs. and Counselors, Am. Assn. Women Deans, Adminstrs. and Counselors. Office:14500 Twelve Mile Rd Warren MI 48093

MACY, JANET (THOMPSON), educator; b. Omaha, Nov. 9, 1935; d. Val and Marie (Letovsky) Kuska; B.S., U. Nebr., 1957; M.S., Kans. State U., 1961; M.Ed., S.D. State U., 1970; m. Duane Thompson, Jan. 2, 1982. With Fed. Extension Service, U.S. Dept. Agr., Washington, 1956, Kans. State U. Sta. KSAC, 1957-61, U. Nebr. Sta. KUON, 1961-62, Iowa State U. Sta. WOI-TV, 1962-67, S.D. State U. Sta. KESD-TV, 1967-71; mem. faculty U. Minn. Sta. KUOM, Mpls., 1971—, now asso. prof. dept. family Soc. Sci., with Meredith Pubs., Better Homes & Gardens, 1972-73; cons. U.S. Consumer Product Safety Commn., 1978-79. Recipient U. Nebr. Masters award, 1973; Minn. Edn. Assn. Sch. Bell award, 1980, 81, 82; Agrl. Communicators in Edn. Superior awards, 1966, 68, 79, 81; Am. Women in Radio and TV Communication Nutrition award, 1977. Mem. Agrl. Communicators in Edn., Am. Soc. Training and Devel., Minn. Intergovtl. Tng. Council, Minn. Edn. Assn., NEA, Epsilon Sigma Phi. Home: 1621 Orchard Springs Rd Minneapolis MN 55420 Office: 433 Coffey Hall Saint Paul MN 55108

MADDEN, IRENE RODWAY, lawyer; b. Birkenhead, Eng., July 16, 1944; d. George Allan and Caroline Jessica (Colwell) Rodway; B.S. in Edn., U. Maine, 1966; cert. in pub. adminstrn. U. Conn., 1968; LL.B., Loyola U., Los Angeles, 1974; m. William X. Madden, Oct. 11, 1969; children—Caroline, William X. III, Jane. Admitted to Calif. bar; ptnr. firm Madden & Madden, San Marino, Calif. Bd. dirs. Victims Assistance League, 1980-82. Recipient Service award Constitutional Rights Found. Mem. Calif. Women Lawyers (gov. 1980-82), Calif. Trial Lawyers, Am. Arbitration Assn. (service award), Los Angeles County Bar Assn., Pasadena Bar Assn., San Gabriel Valley Women (pres.), Los Angeles Women Lawyers, San Gabriel Trial Lawyers (pres.), Women in Bus. Republican. Roman Catholic. Office: 2600 Mission St Suite 202 San Marino CA 91108

MADDOX, GRACE BERYL, economist, former govt. ofcl.; b. Hayward, Wis.; d. McPherson C. and Grace (Bailey) Maddox; student U. So. Calif., 1926-27, U. Calif. at Los Angeles, 1927-28; A.B., Am. U., 1954, M.A. in Econs., 1958. With various U.S. govt. agys., 1937-67; staff of U.S. mem. Internat. Mil. Tribunal, Nuremberg, Germany, 1945-46; Near East polit. analyst CIA, Washington, 1947-51, East European economist, Washington, 1952-56; economist FTC, Washington, 1956-67; researcher in field industry and finance. Recipient Superior Service award FTC, 1961, 67. Mem. Am. Econ. Assn., D.A.R., Phi Delta Gamma. Contbr. articles to govt. publs. Home: 5796 Encina Rd Apt 5 Goleta CA 93117

MADDOX, NOVA CARTER, librarian; b. Columbus, Tex., Sept. 26; d. Earnest Carter and Daisy Sammie Carter; B.S., Tillotson Coll., 1948; M.Ed., Prairie View A&M U., 1953; M.L.S., Our Lady of the Lake U., 1978; m. Clemon Maddox, May 23, 1975. Librarian, Prairie View A&M U., 1957-60; librarian, Base Library, Randolph AFB, Tex., 1960-68; librarian aeromed. library Brooks AFB, Tex., 1968-74, base librarian, 1974-81; base librarian Randolph AFB, Tex., 1981—; librarian St. Philips Coll., part time 1968-74. Methodist. Mem. ALA, Tex. Library Assn., AAUP, Pan Hellenic Council, Huston-Tillotson Coll. Alumni Assn. (Practical Endeavor award 1976), NAACP, Zeta Phi Beta (pres. Alpha Pi Zeta chpt. 1974-76, treas. 1977, fin. sec. 1977—, charter mem. Epsilon Lambda Zeta chpt., Zeta of Yr. 1978). Club: Aerospace Toastmistress. Home: 6801 Neston Dr San Antonio TX 78239

MADDOX, ROTHA M., broadcasting co. exec.; b. Waltham, Mass., Mar. 30, 1946; d. Curtis A. and Rotha Maddox; B.S., Barnard Coll., 1967. Med. research asst. USPHS study, Bellevue Hosp., N.Y.C., 1967-69; media planner Grey Advt., N.Y.C., 1969-71, Wells, Rich, Greene Advt., N.Y.C., 1971-73; sales mktg. dir. ABC-FM, 1973-74; account exec. Sta. WPLJ-FM, N.Y.C., 1974-75, Sta. WINS-AM, N.Y.C., 1975-77; account exec. nat. sales CBS-FM, N.Y.C., 1977-78; sales mgr., Detroit, 1978-79; nat. sales mgr. Sta. WCBS-FM, N.Y.C., 1979-82; local sales mgr. WCAU-FM Radio, Phila., 1982—. Mem. Internat. Radio and TV Soc., N.Y. Market Radio Broadcasters, Adcraft Club Detroit, Nat. Assn. Female Execs. Democrat. Methodist. Office: WCAU-FM City Line and Monument Aves Philadelphia PA 19131

MADORE, BERNADETTE, coll. pres.; b. Barnston, Que., Can., Jan. 24, 1918; came to U.S., 1920, naturalized; d. Joseph George and Mina Marie (Fontaine) M.; A.B., U. Montreal, 1942, B.Ed., 1943; M.S., Cath. U. Am., 1949, Ph.D., 1951. Instr. math. and English, Marie Anne Coll., Montreal, Que., 1943-44; prof. biology, dean of coll. Anna Maria Coll., Paxton, Mass., 1952-76, v.p., 1975-77, pres., 1977—; fund-raising cons.; corporator Consumer Savs. Bank. Bd. dirs. Central Mass. chpt. ARC. Mem. AAAS, Am. Soc. Microbiology, Nat. Assn. Biology Tchrs., AAUW, Am. Assn. Higher Edn., Worcester C. of C. Roman Catholic. Club: Soroptimist. Home and office: Anna Maria College Sunset Ln Paxton MA 01612

MADORY, MARTICIA MOORE, writer, editor, public relations specialist; b. Kansas City, Mo., Oct 21, 1941; d. Albert Wilson Luce and Faith Marie (Coffman) Moore; B.Journalism, U. Mo., 1963; m. Edward Madory, June 15, 1968; children—Paul Edward, Douglas Carl. Coordinator communications Marist Coll., Poughkeepsie, N.Y., 1976-77; public relations regional asst. Civil Service Employees Assn., Fishkill, N.Y., 1977-78; interim dir. public relations Culinary Inst. Am., Hyde Park, N.Y., 1981; co-founder, creator Mid-Hudson Communicators, Poughkeepsie, 1980—, pres., 1981—; founder, dir. Madory & Assocs., 1982—. Mem. Women in Communications, Inc., Women's Nat. Book Assn., Publicity Club N.Y., Women's Press Club N.Y., Mid-Hudson Communicators. Unitarian. Home: 13 Greenbush Dr Poughkeepsie NY 12601

MADSEN, DOROTHY LOUISE (MEG), orgn. exec.; b. Rochester, N.Y.; d. Charles Robert and Louise Anna Agnes Meyer; B.A., Mundelein Coll., Chgo., 1968; m. Frederick George Madsen, Feb. 17, 1945. Public relations rep. Rochester Telephone Corp., 1941-42; feature writer Rochester Democrat & Chronicle, 1939-41; exec. dir. LaPorte (Ind.) chpt. ARC, 1964; dir. adminstrv. services Bank Mktg. Assn., Chgo., 1971-74; exec. dir. Eleanor Assn., Chgo., 1974—; women's career counselor; founder, editor Clearinghouse Internat. Newsletter; founder Eleanor Women's Forum, Clearinghouse Internat., Eleanor Intern Program Coll. Students and Returning Women. Served to lt. col. WAC, 1942-47, 67-70. Decorated Legion of Merit, Meritorious Service award. Mem. Internat. Orgn. Women Execs., Adminstrv. Mgmt. Soc., Women's Info. Services Network, Nat. Assn. Female Execs., Res. Officers Assn., Execs. Club Chgo., Chgo. Soc. Assn. Execs., Chgo. Assn. Commerce and Industry, Mundelein Alumnae Assn., Central Eleanor Club, Phi Sigma Tau (charter mem. Ill. Kappa chpt.). Home: 1030 N State St Chicago IL 60610 Office: 211 E Chicago Ave Suite 1010 Chicago IL 60611

MADSEN, JANE MARIE, educator; b. Rochester, N.Y., Mar. 9, 1929; d. Niels Gerhard and Nora Lee (Thompson) M.; A.B., Syracuse (N.Y.) U., 1950; M.Ed., Ariz. State U., 1967, Ed.D., 1969; m. Harold E. Mitzel,

Aug. 21, 1981; children by previous marriage—Rex, Marlene. Tchr. English, ednl. cons. Japanese Public High Sch., Beppu, 1955-56; tchr. English, French Public Boys Sch., Bois Colombes, France, 1960-62; remedial reading tchr., Minot, N.D., 1962-64; primary tchr., fgn. student cons. Am. Internat. Sch. Presch., New Delhi, 1964-65; field specialist for presch. primary minorities S.W. Coop Ednl. Lab., Albuquerque, 1968-69; supr. student tchrs. Ariz. State U., 1969; asso. prof. edn. Pa. State U., 1969—; cons., adv. in field. Chmn., Centre County adv. council Pa. Human Relations Commn., 1977-79. U.S. Office of Edn. grantee, 1969. Mem. Am. Ednl. Research Assn., Children's Lit. Assn., Council Anthropology and Edn., Internat. Bd. Books Young People, Internat. Reading Assn., NAACP (chmn. edn. chmn. 1976), Nat. Council Tchrs. English, Nat. Indian Edn. Assn., Oral History Assn., Pa. Assn. Tchr. Educators, Pa. Edn. Assn., Phi Delta Kappa. Author articles, kinescope and video tape prodns. Home: 530 Hillside Ave State College Park PA 16801 Office: 180 Chambers Bldg University Park PA 16802

MADSEN, LINDA GAIL, property mgmt. controller; b. Cleburne, Tex., Dec. 7, 1942; d. Raymond Woodrow and Georgialee (Stephens) M.; student Tex. Lutheran Coll., 1961-62, El Camino Coll., 1964-69. Jr. accountant Inglewood Wholesale Electric Co. (Calif.), 1962-66; office mgr. Christensen Orthopedic Co., Redondo Beach, Calif., 1966-71, Dryterior Inc., Lawndale, Calif., 1971-72; controller, corp. officer Patraco Inc., Gardena, Calif., 1973-74; chief fin. officer, dir. Head Shampoo, Inc., Carson, Calif., 1974-80; controller Cloverleaf Group Inc., 1980—. Mem. Christian Bus. and Profl. Women's Council (treas. 1978—), Nat. Assn. Female Execs., Nat. Notary Assn. Democrat. Lutheran. Home: 3724 Spencer St Apt 319 Torrace CA 90503 Office: 1801 Century Park E Suite 500 Los Angeles CA 90067

MADSON, LINDA JANENE, radio sta. exec.; b. Glasgow, Mont., Oct. 28, 1940; d. George Edward and Paladia T. (Diemert) Oderman; grad. Glasgow public schs.; m. David A. Madson, June 19, 1958. Copywriter, traffic dept. KLTZ Radio, Glasgow, 1958-60, talk show hostess, sales rep., 1962-73, gen. mgr., 1973—; announcer, sales rep. KPKW Radio, Pasco, Wash., 1960-62. Vice chmn. Developmental Disabilities Planning and Adv. Council, State of Mont.; trustee Frances Mahon Deaconess Hosp., Glasgow. Mem. Am. Women in Radio, Mont. Broadcasters Assn. (dir., sec.-treas.), Mont. Council for Developmentally Disabled (chairperson Region I). Republican. Lutheran. Club: Soroptimist (past pres.). Home: 1004 Wedum Dr Glasgow MT 59230 Office: 504 2d Ave S Glasgow MT 59230

MADURO, FLORENCE ROSE, chemist; b. St. Thomas, V.I., May 23, 1938; d. Maxwell K. and Amay (Fraser) M.; A.A.S., N.Y.C. Community Coll., 1964; B.A., City U. N.Y., 1971; M.S., L.I. U., 1974. Lab. asst. Goldwater Meml. Hosp., N.Y.C., 1962-64, lab. technician, 1964-68, sr. lab. technician, 1968-71, jr. chemist, 1973-75, clin. chemist, supr. clin. chemistry, 1976—; lab. technician Lenox Hill Hosp., N.Y.C., 1971-73; clin. bioanalyst N.Y. Hosp., N.Y.C., 1975; tchr. continuing edn. course in lab. instruments Manhattan Community Coll., 1969. Treas., v.p. Brit. V.I. Action Com., 1964-67. Cert. chemist Am. Soc. Clin. Pathologists. Mem. Am. Soc. Med. Technologists, Clin. Lab. Mgmt. Assn., Bklyn. Coll. Alumni Assn., Altar Guild. Episcopalian. Home: 111 Wadsworth Ave New York NY 10033 Office: Goldwater Meml Hosp Roosevelt Island New York NY 10044

MADUZIA, EDNA W., mgf. co. exec.; b. Oak Lawn, Ill., Feb. 19, 1950; d. Thaddeus Robert and Joan Ellen (Lewis) M.; A.B., Roosevelt U., 1973, B.S. in Bus. Adminstrn., 1975. Adminstrv. asst. Mayfair Mfg. Co., Chgo., 1975-76, dir. tng., 1976-78; purchasing agt. Lomax Corp., Chgo., 1978-79; asst. v.p. purchasing Werik Corp., Chgo., 1979-81, v.p. purchasing, 1981—. Vol. United Way, Chgo. Mem. Am. Assn. Purchasing Execs., Am. Mgmt. Assn., Internat. Platform Assn. Republican. Roman Catholic. Clubs: Quota, Toastmistress (Chgo.). Address: Werik Corp 24 N Wabash Ave Suite 823 Chicago IL 60602

MAGAFAN, ETHEL, artist; b. Chgo., Oct. 10, 1916; d. Peter J. and Julie (Bronick) Magafan; student Colorado Springs Fine Arts Center; m. Bruce Currie, June 30, 1946; 1 dau., Jenne Magafan. John Stacey scholar, 1947; Tiffany fellow, 1949; Fulbright grant recipient, 1951; painter of 8 murals including Social Security Bldg., Washington, Recorder of Deeds Bldg., Senate Chamber, South Denver Post Office, Fredericksburg (Va.) Nat. Mil. Park, 1978; paintings exhibited Carnegie Inst. Corcoran Gallery, Pa. Acad. Fine Arts, NAD, Met. Mus., Denver Art Mus., San Francisco Mus., N.Y. Exhbn., 1950-51, 53, 55, 56, 59, 61, 63, 66, 69, 70, 73, 79, 81, Art Gallery, SUNY, Albany, 1981; represented in permanent collections, including Springfield (Mo.) Art Mus., Provincetown Art Assn., Met. Mus. Art, Denver Art Mus., Del. Soc. Fine Arts, Des Moines Art Center, Norfolk Mus., Columbia Mus., Butler Inst. Art, others, also pvt. collections; guest artist in residence Syracuse U., 1976. Recipient Collectors Am. Art award, 1947, 48, Adele Hyde Morrison prize San Francisco Mus., 1950, hon. mention Am. Painting Today exhbn., Met Mus. Art, 1950, 1st Hallgarten prize NAD, 1951, Ida Wells Stroud award, Am. Watercolor Soc., 1955, purchase prize Nat. Exhbn. Contemporary Arts, 1956, Altman prize for landscape NAD, 1956, Hallmark Art award, 1952, Purchase award, Ball State Tchrs. Coll. Art Gallery, 1958, Columbia (S.C.) Mus., 1959, Portland (Maine) Mus., 1959, 1st award Albany Inst. Art, 1962, Benjamin Altman award NAD, 1964, 73, Andrew Carnegie prize, 1977, award Conn. Acad. Fine Arts, 1965, purchase award Watercolor U.S.A., Springfield Mus., 1966, Kirk Meml. award NAD, 1967, Berkshire Art Assn. award, 1966, 67, 68, 75, jurors prize Albany Inst. Art, 1969, Grumbacher award, 1970, 75, Hassam Fund purchase, 1970, Arches Paper award Am. Watercolor Soc., 1973, Zimmerman award Phila. Watercolor Soc., 1973; Pres.'s award Audubon Artists, 1974, Emily Lowe award, 1979, Stefan Hirsch Meml. award Audubon Artists Ann., 1976, award Rocky Mountain Nat. Watermedia Exhbn., 1976; Condec award Silvermine Guild Artists, 1978, award, 1979; Cooperstown Art Assn. award, 1978; drawing award Ball State U., 1981. Mem. NAD (2d v.p. 1975, Benjamin Altman award 1980). Office: Midtown Galleries 11 E 57th St New York NY 10022

MAGDOL-CONRAD, ALICE, exec. search exec.; b. N.Y.C., Aug. 30, 1939; d. Nathan H. and Beatrice (Grossman) Gates; B.A. cum laude, Brown U., 1961; postgrad. Ecole de Louvre, 1960, Sorbonne, 1960; m. Richard Conrad, Apr. 14, 1979; 1 son, David Gates Magdol. Exec. SSC & B Advt., 1971-72; sr. partner PGI Inc., 1972-76; v.p., account supr. new product devel. Foote Cone Belding, 1976-79; pres. Magdol & McCone; lectr. in field. Fundraiser, Parents Assn. St. David's Sch. Mem. Am. Mktg. Assn. Club: Brown. Office: 124 E 65th St New York NY 10021

MAGENTA, MURIEL, artist, educator; b. N.Y.C., Dec. 4, 1932; d. James E. and Sara (Wallman) Gellert; B.A., Queens Coll., 1953; M.A. in Art History, Ariz. State U., 1962, M.F.A. in Painting, 1965, Ph.D., 1970; m. Gerald Zimmerman; children—Jean, Eric Vermilion. One-woman shows: Ariz. State U., 1976, Phoenix Art Mus., 1977, U. So. Calif., 1978, Marian Locks Gallery, Phila., 1979, Rutgers U., 1981, Yares Gallery, Scottsdale, Ariz., 1981; group shows include: Los Angeles Inst. Contemporary Art, 1978, Rutgers U. at A.I.R. Gallery, N.Y.C., 1981, Ariz. State U. at Phoenix Art Mus.; represented in permanent collections: Ariz. State U., Valley Nat. Bank, Phoenix; prof. art Ariz. State U., 1969—; juror of exhbns. Phoenix Art Mus. grantee, 1975-77; Ariz. State U. grantee, 1981-82. Mem. Women's Caucus for Art (nat. pres. 1982—), Coll. Art Assn. Am., Mid-Am. Coll. Art Assn., NOW, Nat. Women's Polit. Caucus. Home: 8322 E Virginia St Scottsdale AZ 85257 Office: School of Art Ariz State U Tempe AZ 85281

MAGER, HELEN VICTORIA HRIBAR, nurse; b. Aliquippa, Pa., June 9, 1934; d. Victor Vincent and Helen Dolores (Abdis) Hribar; R.N., Washington Hosp. Sch. Nursing, 1955; student Case Western Res. U., 1974, Ohio State U., 1976-77; B.S. in Nursing and Sociology, Youngstown State U., 1977; m. Wilfred R. Mager, Jan. 1, 1955; children—Kevin, Darlene. Nurse, Washington Hosp., 1955-57, Brownsville (Pa.) Hosp., 1957, Uniontown Hosp., 1962; pub. health nurse Commonwealth of Pa., 1962-66; nursing dir. Diamondhead Extended Care Facility, Youngstown, Ohio, 1968-69; asst. head nurse Warren Gen. Hosp., Warren, Ohio, 1969-70, head nurse phys. therapy dept., 1970-72; nursing dir., family nurse practitioner Mahoning County Health Dept., Youngstown, 1972—. Chmn., Canfield Charter Rev. Commn.; mem. state adv. com. March of Dimes; chmn. Com. to Study Emergency Med. Care in Community, Canfield; active various polit. campaigns, Canfield. Mem. Am., Ohio pub. health assns., Am. (certified family nurse practitioner), Ohio (sec. pub. health sect.) nurses assns., N.E. Ohio Nurse Practitioners. Home: 51 Sleepy Hollow Dr Canfield OH 44406

MAGNER, MARJORIE ELENE, educator; b. Omaha, Jan. 21, 1921; d. John Lee and Mary Ethel (Gatchell) M.; B.S., U. Nebr., Omaha, 1943; profl. cert. Clarke Sch. for Deaf, 1944; M.A., Smith Coll., 1949, M.E.D., 1964; cert. in edn. of deaf (Fulbright scholar) U. Manchester (Eng.), 1955. Tchr., Nebr. Sch. for Deaf, 1939-43; tchr. Clarke Sch. for Deaf, Northampton, Mass., 1943-55, supervising tchr., 1956-68, 72—, coordinator speech program, 1968-72, coordinator curriculum, 1982—; instr. Smith Coll., Northampton, 1950—. Named Tchr. of Yr., Northampton C. of C., 1970, Women of Yr., Hampshire County Bus. and Profl. Women, 1967. Mem. Alexander Graham Bell Assn. (life), Am. Speech, Lang. and Hearing Assn., Am. Instrs. Deaf, Delta Kappa Gamma. Democrat. Mem. United Ch. of Christ. Club: Zonta (past pres.) (Northampton). Contbr. articles to profl. jours. Home: 88 Round Hill Rd Northhampton MA 01060 Office: Clarke Sch for Deaf Northhampton MA 01060

MAGNER, RACHEL HARRIS, banker; b. Lamar, S.C., Aug. 5, 1951; d. Garner Greer and Catherine Alice (Cloaninger) Harris; B.S. in Fin., U. S.C., 1972; postgrad. UCLA, 1974, Calif. State U., 1975; m. Fredric Michael Magner, May 14, 1972. Mgmt. trainee Union Bank, Los Angeles, 1972-75, comml. loan officer, 1975-77; asst. v.p. comml. fin. Crocker Bank, Los Angeles, 1978, asst. v.p., factoring account exec. subs. Crocker United Factors, Inc., 1978-81; v.p. comml. services div. Crocker Bank, 1981-82, v.p., sr. account mgr. bus. banking div., 1982—. Mem. Los Angeles Bank Creditmen's Assn., NOW, Wilshire Women's Bus. and Profl. Assn., Los Angeles Women's Profl. Bank Assn., Textile Profl. Assn. Home: 2200 Pine Ave Manhattan Beach CA 90266 Office: 2029 Century Park E Suite 3590 Los Angeles CA 90067

MAGNUS, LAVELLE GRABER, ret. sch. prin.; b. Ottumwa, Iowa, Jan. 3, 1920; d. Harold Wordworth and Opal (Funk) Graber; B.Ed., Chgo., Tchrs. Coll., 1942; M.A., Long Beach State U., 1956; m. Gordon Eugene Magnus, June 4, 1960 (dec.); 1 son, Larry Coffman; stepchildren—Joyce McQuade, Jack Magnus, Clark Magnus. Tchr. public schs., Chgo., 1942-44, Little Lake Sch. Dist., Norwalk, Calif., 1944-45; tchr. Lynwood (Calif.) Sch. Dist., 1947-65, elem. sch. prin. 1965-76. Mem. NEA (life), Nat. Assn. Elem. Sch. Prins. Assn. Calif. Sch. Adminstrs., AAUW, DAR (past dist. dir., state rec. sec.), Republican Women. Methodist. Clubs: Universe, Order Eastern Star (Past Matrons club), Gethsemane White Shrine. Home: 1221 Oakmont Rd 178-B Seal Beach CA 90740

MAGNUSON, NANCY LEE, ednl. adminstr.; b. Lincoln, Nebr., Aug. 16, 1948; d. Clifford Frank and Bonnie Lee (Price) M.; B.A., U. N.Mex., 1970, M.A., 1980. Tchr., Los Lunas (N.Mex.) Consol. Schs., 1970-73; alumni field rep. U. N.Mex., Albuquerque, 1973-76, spl. asst. to pres. for sch. relations, 1976-77, dir. sch. relations and prospective student services, 1977—, mem. pres.'s com. on excellence, adv. Mortar Bd., 1978-81, chmn. univ. combined fund dr., 1982-83. Mem. Council Advancement and Support of Edn., Nat. Assn. Women Deans, Adminstrs. and Counselors, Nat. Assn. Coll. Admission Counselors, Greater Albuquerque C. of C. (edn. com. 1977-82), Pi Alpha Alpha, Pi Beta Phi. Democrat. Home: 505 Hermosa NE Albuquerque NM 87108 Office: Univ N Mex Albuquerque NM 87131

MAGNUSSON, LINDA ANNE, data processing search firm exec.; b. Bklyn., Sept. 22, 1950; d. Sten Viking and Anne Irene (Kaarto) M.; B.F.A., Pratt Inst., 1972. Data processing search cons. Embark, N.Y.C., 1976-77; sr. mktg. rep. C. G. A. Computer Assos., Cranford, N.J., 1977-79; pres. Linda Magnusson Assos. Ltd., N.Y.C., 1979—. Mem. Nat. Assn. Female Execs. Office: 341 Madison Ave New York NY 10017

MAGUIRE, CHARLOTTE EDWARDS, physician; b. Richmond, Ind., Sept. 1, 1918; d. Joel Blaine and Lydia (Betscher) Edwards; student Stetson U., 1936-38, U. Wichita, 1938-39; B.S., Memphis Tchrs. Coll., 1940; M.D., U. Ark., 1944; m. Raymer Francis Maguire, Sept. 1, 1948 (dec.); children—Barbara, Thomas Clair II. Intern Orange Meml. Hosp., Orlando, Fla., 1944-46; resident Bellevue Hosp. and Med. Center, N.Y. U., N.Y.C., 1955; instr. nurses Orange Meml. Hosp., 1947-57, staff mem., 1946-48; staff mem. Fla. Sanatarium and Hosp., Orlando, 1946-56, Holiday House and Hosp., Orlando, 1950-62; mem. courtesy and cons. staff West Orange Meml. Hosp., Winter Garden, Fla., 1952-67; active staff, chief dept. pediatrics Mercy Hosp., Orlando, 1965-68; med. dir. med. services and basic care Fla. Dept. Health and Rehab. Services, 1975—; chief of staff of physicians and dentists Central Fla. div. Children's Home Soc. of Fla., 1947-56; dir. Orlando Child Health Clinic, 1949-58; engaged in pvt. practice, medicine, Orlando, 1946-68; asst. regional dir. HEW, 1970-72; pediatric cons. Fla. Crippled Children's Commn., 1952-70, dir., 1968-70; med. dir. Office Med. Services and Basic Care, Fla. Dept. Health and Rehab. Services; clin prof. dept. pediatrics U. Fla. Coll. Medicine, Gainesville, 1980—. Mem. profl. adv. com. Fla. Center for Clin. Services at U. Fla., 1952-60; del. to Mid-century White House Conf. on Children and Youth, 1950; U.S. del. from Nat. Soc. for Crippled Children to World Congress for Welfare of Cripples, Inc., London, Eng., 1957; pres. of corp. Eccleston-Callahan Hosp. for Colored Crippled Children, 1956-58; sec. Fla. chpt. Nat. Doctors' Com. for Improved Med. Services, 1951-52; med. adv. com. Gateway Sch. for Mentally Retarded, 1959-62; bd. dirs. Forest Park Sch. for Spl. Edn. Crippled Children, 1949-54, mem. med. adv. com., 1955-68, chmn. 1957—; mem. Fla. Adv. Council for Mentally Retarded, 1965-70; dir. central Fla. poison control Orange Meml. Hosp.; mem. orgn. com., chmn. com. for admission and selection policies Camp Challenge; participant 12th session Fed. Exec. Inst., 1971; del. White House Conf. on Aging, 1980. Mem. Nat. Rehab. Assn., Am. Congress Phys. Medicine and Rehab., Fla., Central Fla. (dir. 1949-58, pres. 1956-57) socs. crippled children and adults, Am. Assn. Cleft Palate, Fla. Soc. Crippled Children (trustee 1951-57, v.p. 1956-57, profl. adv. com. 1957-68), Mental Health Assn. Orange County (charter mem.; pres. 1949-50, dir. 1947-52, chmn. exec. com. 1950-52, dir. 1963-65), Fla. Orange County heart assns., AMA, Am. Med. Women's Assn., Am. Acad. Med. Dirs., So. Fla. (chmn. com. on mental retardation), Orange County med assns., Fla. Orlando pediatric socs., Fla. Cleft Palate Assn. (counselor-at-large, sec.). Home: 2013 E Randolph Circle Tallahassee FL 32312 Office: 1323 Winewood Blvd Tallahassee FL 32301

MAHADEVIAH, ERMA PINKSTON, med. technologist; b. Winston-Salem, N.C., Dec. 29, 1926; d. Julius Allen and Lelia Adele (Dwire) Pinkston; A.B., Catawba Coll., 1947; cert. med. tech. Bowman-Gray Sch. Med. Tech., 1948; M.S., U. Cin., 1960; m. Inally Mahadeviah, Nov. 23, 1960; children—Stuart, Eric, Ann. Staff med. technologist, asst. chief technologist, dir., coordinator Sch. Med. Tech., St. Elizabeth Hosp., Med. Center, Youngstown, Ohio, 1963-69, 73—; instr. in field. Mem. Am. Soc. Clin. Pathologists (affiliate mem.), Am. Soc. for Med. Tech., Am. Assn. Blood Banks, Ohio Soc. for Med. Tech. Episcopalian. Club: Quota Internat. Inc. Home: 38 N Cadillac Dr Youngstown OH 44512 Office: St Elizabeth Hosp Med Center 1044 Belmont Ave Youngstown OH 44501

MAHAFFEY, JOAN, nurse; b. Richmond, Utah, Feb. 7, 1926; d. Joseph Perry and Annie Marie (Christofferson) Peart; R.N., Meth. Hosp., Los Angeles, 1950; B.S. in Health Sci., Calif. State U., Northridge, 1971, M.P.H., 1976; m. J.B. Mahaffey, June 5, 1949 (div. Jan. 1967). Hosp. and office nurse, Calif., 1951-72; mem. staff Calif. Nurses Assn., 1972—, regional dir. epicenter region 3, Van Nuys, 1981—; cons., speaker in field. Mem. Nat. League Nursing, Am. Nurses Assn., Calif. Sch. Nurses Orgn., Valley Nursing Edn. Council. Democrat. Mormon. Clubs: Soroptimist, San Fernando Emblem. Home: 6620 Glade Ave Canoga Park CA 91303 Office: 7417 Van Nuys Blvd Suite O Van Nuys CA 91405

MAHAIRAS, EVELYN PHILLIPINE, clin. social worker, psychotherapist, educator, researcher; b. N.Y.C., Sept. 25, 1933; d. Otto and Henrietta (Dolman) Poestges; B.A. in Clin. Psychiatry, Queens Coll., 1954; tchr. cert. Eastern Nazarene Coll., 1972; M.S.W., Ohio State U., 1976; postgrad. Bryn Mawr Coll., 1979—; m. C. Gus Mahairas, June 27, 1954; children—Pamela Linda, Janet Susan, Karen Lee, Evelyn Jean. Psychiat. social worker N.Y. State Dept. Mental Hygiene, 1954-56; bus. rep. N.Y. Telephone Co., Jackson Heights, N.Y., 1956-57; substitute tchr. public schs., Mass., Conn., 1970-74; dir. social services Wives Self Help/City Police and Fire Counselling Service, Phila., 1976-81; research specialist social work service Coatesville (Pa.) V.A. Med. Center, 1981—. Sec., Social Action Com., 1968-70; coordinator Headstart, W. Springfield, Mass., 1968-70; mem. Lake Champlain Com., Vt., 1968—. Mem. Nat. Assn. Social Workers (dir. Pa. chpt., exec. com., fin. com., program chmn., v.p. 1979-81, exec. bd., pres. Brandywine div. 1978-79, co-chmn. continuing edn. 1978-80, mem. social action com., legis. com.), Acad. Cert. Social Workers, Nat. Register Clin. Social Workers, Mental Health Assn. of Southeastern Pa. Presbyterian (youth fellowship adv.). Co-editor: The Aging Veteran: Interorganizational Relations; contbr. articles to profl. jours. Home: 650 W Wind Dr Berwyn PA 19312 also Thompson's Point Charlotte VT 19312 Office: Coatesville VA Med Center Coatesville PA 19320

MAHAN, FRANCES JANE, educator; b. Manchester, N.H., Jan. 13, 1926; d. David Charles and Frances Jane (Dolan) O'Keeffe; B.S., Am. Internat. Coll., 1950, M.A., 1962; Ph.D., U. Conn., 1972; children—Jane, Carol. Sec., Mass. Mut. Life Ins. Co., Springfield, 1950-62; secondary sch. bus. tchr., Springfield, 1962-73; asso. prof. edn. dept. Bryant Coll., Smithfield, R.I., 1973—; mem. edn. subcom. Gov.'s Adv. Commn. on Women. Served with USN, 1944-46. Mem. Nat., New Eng., R.I. bus. edn. assns., Bus. and Profl. Women N. Providence, Mensa. Author: An Objective Determination and Statement of Robert M. Hutchins' Educational Theory, 1972; contbr. Webster's Legal Secretaries Handbook, 1981; contbr. articles to profl. jours. Office: Bryant Coll Smithfield RI 02917

MAHAN, GENEVIEVE ELLIS, sociologist; b. Canton, Ohio, Aug. 1, 1909; d. William and Lillian (Ellis) Mahan; A.B., Western Res. U., 1931, A.M., 1941; postgrad. (Ford Found. fellow) Yale U., 1952, Akademie für Politische Bildung, Tutzing, Germany, 1963. Tchr. high schs., Canton, 1937-52; research asst. dept. sociology Yale U., New Haven, 1953-55; lectr. dept. sociology Walsh Coll., Canton, 1970—. Del., Instns. Atlantic and European Cooperation, Coimbra, Portugal, 1970; participant 6th World Congress Sociology, Evian, France, 1966. Trustee, Stark County Psychiat. Found., 1961-68. Fellow Am. Sociol. Assn.; mem. Eastern Sociol. Soc., Am. Acad. Polit. and Social Sci., Nat., Ohio (exec. bd. 1962-69, pres. 1965-66) councils for social studies, Internat. Sociol. Assn., Ohio Acad. Sci., Ohio Soc. N.Y., AAUW, AAAS. Clubs: Canton College; Canton Woman's; Massillon Woman's. Research in polit. caricature, 1955—. Address: 804 5th St NW Canton OH 44703

MAHAN, NANCY ELLEN, legal asst.; b. Springfield, Ohio, Nov. 27, 1938; d. Gerald Eugene and Ethel Gladys (Pendleton) M.; paralegal cert. U. Md., 1980. Sec. to engring. staff White Motor Co., Springfield, 1956-58; sec. to project engr. Glidden Co., Glen Burnie, Md., 1958-60; legal sec. W. Russell Gorman, Atty., 1960-62; legal asst. Isidore H. Wachtel, Atty., 1962-66, firm Beatty & McNamee, Hyattsville, Md., 1956-80, Benjamin Michaelson, Jr., P.A., Annapolis, Md., 1980-82, firm Pullam & Pullam, P.A., Leesburg, Fla., 1982—. Coach little girls and young women's softball; counselor United Methodist Youth Fellowship; ch. clk., sec., ch. trustee 1st Baptist Ch. of Eastport. Mem. Nat. Assn. Female Execs., Nat. Capital Area Paralegal Assn. Clubs: Peninsula Athletic League, Hillsmere Shores Improvement Assn. Democrat. Methodist. Home: Route 2 Box 874-A6 Umatilla FL 32784 Office: PO Drawer 2160 Leesburg FL 32748

MAHARIS, MERCEDES, interior designer; b. Bedford, Ind., Aug. 20, 1942; d. Harry William and Edith Marie (Lindley) Pipher; B.A., Ind. U., 1966, M.A., 1967; M.S., U. Ariz., 1976. Tchr., Ariz., Pa. schs., 1967-72; interior designer, Santa Monica, Calif., 1976—; exhibited art work: Mercado Nacional de la Artesania, San Jose, Costa Rica, 1972, Phoenix Art Mus., 1974, Ariz. State Mus., 1970; interiors published in Designers West, Perfect Home, Home Mag., Kitchens and Baths, Los Angeles Jr. League News, Sunset Mag. Mem. Am. Soc. Interior Designers, Internat. Soc. Interior Designers. Address: PO Box 1678 Santa Monica CA 90406

MAHER, FRAN, advt. agy. exec.; b. Chgo., June 22, 1938; d. Edward Stephan and Virginia Rose (Harrington) M.; student (Univ. scholar) U. Minn., 1956-57; student Spectrum Inst., 1968-71; B.A. summa cum laude, Kean Coll. N.J., 1979; m. Anthony Peter Petrella, Sept. 17, 1957; children—Roland, Louis, Marcus. Office mgr. Lead Supplies, Inc., Mpls., 1957-59; free-lance artist and writer, Warren, N.J., 1968-72; prin. Visuals, Warren, N.J., 1974-79; pres. Fran Maher, Inc., Stirling, N.J., 1980—; dir. Parent Edn. Advocacy Tng. Center, Alexandria, Va., 1979—. Officer, Friends of Weigand Farm, Milton, N.J., 1977-80; founding mem. Flintlock Boys' Club. Recipient N.J. Art Dirs. Show award, 1978, 1st place award in graphics Watchung Art Center, 1980. Mem. Exec. Women N.J., Art Dirs. Club N.J., Printmaking Council N.J., Am. Women's Econ. Devel. Corp. Office: 1390 Valley Rd Stirling NJ 07980

MAHER, MARY-BARBARA, state legislator; b. N.Y.C., Apr. 30, 1933; m. Frederick J. Maher, Jr.; 4 sons, 1 dau. Chmn., South Burlington Planning Commn., 1971—; apptd. Vt. Jud. Council, 1973; apptd. Capitol Complex Commn., 1974; mem. South Burlington Democratic Com., Chittenden County Dem. Com.; mem. Vt. Ho. Reps., 1975—. Mem. Vt. Fedn. Dem. Women, Chittenden County Dem. Women's Club; pres. South Burlington Dem. Women's Club; mem. Council State Govts., 1977-80; mem. Joint Com. on Voters, Jud. Retention, 1979-80; mem. Spl. Legislative Com. to Investigate State Police, 1979-80; mem. Judicial Nominating Bd., 1980-81. Mem. LWV. Office: Vt Ho Reps State Ho Montpelier VT 05602 *

MAHLAND, JANET CAROL POLING, transp. co. exec.; b. N.Y.C., Jan. 15, 1936; d. Robert L. and Carol V. (Jacobsen) Poling; student

Syracuse (N.Y.) U., 1954-55; diploma Katherine Gibbs Sch., N.Y.C., 1955; cert. World Trade Inst., 1979; m. Robert H. Mahland, Apr. 22, 1960; children—June Carol, Jeanne Caron. With Am. Oil Co., N.Y.C., 1955-56, Sinclair Refining Co., N.Y.C., 1956-57; with Poling Transp. Corp., N.Y.C., 1958—, v.p., 1976-79, pres., dir., 1979—; pres., dir. other corps. Bd. dirs., v.p. alumni bd. Packer Collegiate Inst., 1980; a founder Staten Island Childrens' Mus. Mem. Am. Petroleum Inst., Assn. Energy Profls., N.Y. Oil Trades Assn., Maritime Assn. Port N.Y., S.I. C. of C., N.Y. Towboat and Harbor Carriers Assn. (dir.), S.I. Hist. Soc. Lutheran. Clubs: Downtown Athletic (N.Y.C.); Richmond County Country, S.I. Garden. Office: 1 Edgewater Plaza Staten Island NY 10305

MAHLE, LORRAINE MILDRED, mgmt. analyst; b. Huntington, W.Va., Apr. 25, 1939; d. Shelley W. and Glendora (McLauglin) Hill; B.S., Calif. State U., 1972, M.B.A., 1978; m. O. Joseph Mahle, Nov. 23, 1956; 1 dau., Cynthia Lee. Asst. buyer Gottschalk's Dept. Store, Fresno, Calif., 1972-73; ter. mgr. Burrough's Bus. Machines, Fresno, 1973-75; indsl. sales Container Corp. Am., Fresno, 1975-78; mgmt. analyst Nat. Econ. Devel. Assn., Fresno, 1978—. Recipient Bank of Am. Bus. Student award, 1969. Mem. NOW, Fresno Pvt. Industry Council, Alpha Gamma Sigma, Beta Gamma Sigma, Phi Kappa Phi. Office: 2006 N Fine St Suite 101 Fresno CA 93727

MAHLENDORF, PATRICIA ANN, shopping center exec.; b. Sheboygan, Wis., Jan. 6, 1938; d. Arthur Leander and Mildred Josephine (Guse) Braun; student public schs.; m. Melville Carl Mahlendorf, July 25, 1981; children by previous marriage—Quinn Michael, Christopher Jay. With Sheboygan Press, 1956-58; propr. fur tailoring and design bus., 1973-76; staff asst. for urban youth U. Wis. extension, 1973-76; mktg. dir. Plaza 8 Mall, Sheboygan, 1976—; cons. in field. Pres. Mother of Good council Immaculate Conception Roman Cath. Ch., Sheboygan, 1967; v.p. Deland Receiving Home, Sheboygan, 1981—; public relations chmn. Sheboygan Area United Way, 1980—; mem. Mayor Sheboygan Citizens Adv. Bd., 1969. Recipient CAROL award, 1969, Outstanding Young Woman award, 1968. Club: Sheboygan Jr. Woman's (v.p. 1975). Home: 803 Panther Ave Sheboygan WI 53081 Office: 832 A Plaza 8 Sheboygan WI 53081

MAHMOUDI, HOMA, clin. psychologist; b. Tehran, Iran, Apr. 24, 1941; came to U.S., 1959, naturalized, 1977; d. Jalil and Badri M.; grad. certificate Middle Eastern studies, U. Utah, 1967; Ph.D. in Clin. Psychology, 1970; 1 son, Jason. Tng. officer Peace Corps, 1962-68; dir. police selection research project County of Los Angeles, 1970-73, chief psychologist Occupational Health Service, 1977—; asst. clin. prof. med. psychology Sch. Medicine UCLA, 1973—. Mem. Am. Psychol. Assn., Western Psychol. Assn., Soc. for Intercultural Edn. Tng. and Research, Am. Soc. Tng. and Devel. Baha'i. Author: The Urban Policeman in Transition: A Psychological and Sociological Review, 1973; co-author: Persian Phrasebook & Dictionary, 1977; contbr. articles in field to publs. Home: 909 Stonehill Ln Los Angeles CA 90049 Office: 2615 S Grand Ave Los Angeles CA 90007

MAHNKE, SUSAN MARGARET, editor; b. Sheboygan, Wis., Feb. 28, 1947; d. Edward Anton and Margaret Emma (DeBack) M.; B.A., U. Wis., 1970; postgrad. U. Mass., 1976-77; Asso. editor Wis. Trails mag., Madison, 1970-74; asst. editor The Stephen Greene Press, Brattleboro, Vt., 1974-76; freelance editor and writer, 1976-77; sr. editor Yankee mag., 1977—, The Old Farmer's Almanac, 1977—. Town clk. Town of Nelson, N.H., 1981—. Author: Portrait of the Past (2 vols.), 1972-73; Looking Back: Images of New England 1860-1930, 1982; editor: Wisconsin, A State for All Seasons, 1972; contbr. articles in field. Home: Old Stoddard Rd Nelson NH 03457 Office: Dublin NH 03444

MAHON, EDITH GRACE, social worker; b. Galveston, Tex., Apr. 25, 1945; d. Rufus and Helen M. (Barkmer) Knotts; B.S., Tex. Woman's U., 1967; M.S.W., Boston U., 1975; postgrad. Universidad Interam., Mexico, summer, 1964; m. Calixto Garcia, Nov. 28, 1981; children by previous marriage—Gillian Thais Mahon, Micheline Isadora Mahon. Group worker Dallas Juvenile Detention Home, 1967; vocat. counselor div. employment security Skill Center, Lowell, Mass., 1969-70; case-worker Cath. Charitable Bur., Lowell, 1970-72; social worker Lawrence (Mass.) Detoxification and Rehab. Center, 1973-74, VA Outpatient Mental Hygiene Clinic, Lowell, 1974-75; psychiat. social worker Andover (Mass.) Jr. Coll., 1975-76; instr. (part-time) div. continuing edn. Merrimac Coll., North Andover, Mass., 1976-78; social worker (part-time) teen health service St. John's Hosp., Lowell, 1976-78; psychiat. social worker (part-time) Human Resource Inst., Lawrence, 1976—, Greater Lowell Regional Tech. High Sch., Tyngsboro, Mass., 1978—; youth dir. Christ Ch., Andover, Mass., 1980—; parent effectiveness and youth effectiveness tng. instr., 1976—. Lic. clin. social worker. Mem. Nat. Assn. Social Workers, Assn. Cert. Social Workers, Soc. for Family Therapy and Research. Episcopalian. Office: Greater Lowell Regional Vocational Sch Pawtucket Blvd Tyngsboro MA 01879

MAHON, MARGARET MARY, mfg. co. ofcl.; b. Crossmolina, Ireland, Nov. 19, 1928; came to U.S., 1951, naturalized, 1970; d. Patrick John and Mary Christina (McNamara) M.; B.S., Fordham U., 1974, M.B.A., 1977. Sec., NCR Corp., N.Y.C., 1951-54, 63-74, adminstrv. specialist, 1974-77, dist. sect. mgr., 1977-78, N.Y. dist. adminstrv. mgr., 1978—; mgr. family bus., 1954-63. Mem. Assn. M.B.A. Execs., Grad. Bus. Alumni Assn. Fordham U., N.Y. C. of C. and Industry. Democrat. Roman Catholic. Club: Lake Isle Country. Home: 12 Yonkers Ave Tuckahoe NY 10707 Office: 50 Rockefeller Plaza New York NY 10020

MAHONE, BARBARA JEAN, automobile co. exec.; b. Tuskegee, Ala., Apr. 19, 1946; d. Fred D. and Sarah Lou (Simpson) Mahone; B.S., Ohio State U., 1968; M.B.A., U. Mich., 1972; postgrad. Harvard U., 1980. Systems analyst Gen. Motors Corp., Detroit, 1968-71; staff assignment/sr. staff asst., 1973-75, mgr. career planning, 1975-77, exec.-in-tng., 1978, dir. personnel adminstrn., Rochester (N.Y.) Product Div., 1979-82, mgr. indsl. relations Packard Electric div., Warren, Ohio, 1982—. Bd. dirs. ARC, Rochester, 1979—, Urban League of Rochester, 1979—, Rochester Area Multiple Sclerosis, 1980—; mem. YMCA human resources com., 1979-82; mem. United Way allocation com., 1981-82. Named one of 10 outstanding women in Mich., Redbook Mag., 1978. Mem. Nat. Black M.B.A. Assn. (bd. dirs. 1975—, Outstanding M.B.A. of Yr. award 1981), Nat. Council Negro Women (exec. com., Mary McLeod Bethune award 1977). Home: 119 Manor Brook Chagrin Falls OH 44022 Office: Divisional Headquarters PO Box 431 Warren OH 44486

MAHONEY, SISTER, COLETTE, coll. pres., biologist; b. Jamaica, N.Y., July 19, 1926; d. Timothy and Lillian (Boylan) M.; B.S., Marymount Coll., 1949, LL.D. (hon.), 1973; M.S., Fordham U., 15952, Ph.D., 1961; H.H.D. (hon.), St. Francis de Sales, 1974. Joined Religious of Sacred Heart of Mary, 1945; tchr. biology Acad. Sacred Heart of Mary, N.Y.C., 1947-57, prin., 1965-67; instr. biology Marymount Coll., Arlington, Va., 1957-61, also chmn. sci. dept.; assoc. prof. biology Marymount Coll., Tarrytown, N.Y., 1961-65; pres., trustee Marymount Manhattan Coll., N.Y.C., 1967—; dir. Dollar Savs. Bank, Manhattan Life Ins. Co., Jack Lenor Larsen, Inc.; nominating com. Am. Stock Exchange. Mem. Pres.' Adv. Com. Econ. Role of Women, 1973-74; mem. Commn. Status of Women; commr. Middle States Assn., Women's Coll. Coalition; bd. advisors China Inst. Am., Inc.; bd. dirs. Inst. Mediation and Conflict Resolution, N.Y. Council Higher Edn., Council Higher Edn. N.Y.C., Marymount Secondary Sch. N.Y., Fordham Prep. Sch., Yorkville Civic Council, Council Career Planning, Inc.; pres. Women's Forum, 1979; trustee Coll. Boca Raton, Marymount Coll., Tarrytown, N.Y., Mt. St. Mary's Coll.; mem. David Rockefeller's N.Y.C. Partnership Task Force for Youth Employment, 1980—. Recipient Extraordinary Woman of Achievement award NCCJ, 1978, Brotherhood award NAACP, 1980, Pres.' award Malcolm-King Harlen Coll. Extension, 1980; decorated Cavaliere Order of Merit (Italy). Fellow AAUW; mem. Am. Assn. Higher Edn. (dir.), Am. Inst. Biol. Scis., N.Y. Acad. Scis., N.Y. Bus. and Profl. Women's Assn., N.Y. State Legis. Inst. Contbr. articles on biology to sci. publs. Office: Marymount Manhattan College New York NY 10021 *

MAHONEY, JOANNE GETCHELL, psychologist; b. Brockton, Mass., May 4, 1933; d. James Edward and Josephine Mary (Belmore) Getchell; B.S., Simmons Coll., 1954; M.Ed., Northeastern U., 1956, postgrad., 1956-59; m. Paul Lawrence Mahoney, June 30, 1956; children—Paula-Jo, James Emmett, Sean Michael. Tchr. Am. history and sci. Whitman (Mass.) Jr. High Sch., 1954-57; sch. psychologist Whitman public schs., 1957—; cons. psychologist to various sch. systems in S.E. Mass., 1959-77; cons. psychologist, counselor Marion (Mass.) Center for Human Services, 1979—; trustee Peoples Savs. Bank, Brockton, 1975—; mem. bd. investment, 1979—; cons. in field. Pres. Women's Guild of Brockton Hosp., 1970-72; trustee Brockton Hosp., 1970-72; bd. dirs. Old Colony Mental Health Assn., 1962-66, Brockton Hist. Soc., 1975—. Mem. NEA, Mass. Sch. Psychologists Assn., Mass. Tchrs. Assn., Plymouth County Tchrs. Assn. Roman Catholic. Clubs: Piney Point Beach (dir. 1965—), Beverly Yacht, Kittansett (Marion, Mass.). Home: 28 Landing Rd Marion MA 02738 Office: Sch Adminstrn Bldg Whitman Ave Whitman MA 02382

MAHONEY, MARGARET ANN, lawyer; b. Alliance, Nebr., Apr. 22, 1949; d. John Charles and Grace Margaret (Hoban) M.; B.A. (Nat. Merit scholar), Coll. of St. Catherine, 1971; J.D. cum laude, U. Minn., 1974; m. Peter B. Ogren, June 28, 1980. Admitted to Minn. bar, 1974, Fla. bar, 1975; shareholder firm Stringer, Courtney & Rohleder, Ltd., St. Paul, 1974—. Mem. adv. bd. dirs. St. Paul YWCA. Mem. Minn. Bar Assn., Ramsey County Bar Assn., Minn. Women Lawyers, Fla. Bar Assn., Phi Beta Kappa, Sigma Delta Pi. Republican. Clubs: Chrysalis, St. Paul Athletic. Office: Stringer Courntey and Rohleder Ltd 1200 Northwestern Nat Bank Bldg Saint Paul MN 55101

MAHONEY, MARGARET ELLERBE, found. exec.; b. Nashville, Oct. 24, 1924; d. Charles Hallam and Leslie Nelson (Savage) M.; B.A. magna cum laude, Vanderbilt U., 1946; L.H.D. (hon.), Meharry Med. Coll., 1977, U. Fla., 1980, Med. Coll. Pa., 1982. Fgn. affairs officer State Dept., Washington, 1946-53; exec. asso., asso. sec. Carnegie Corp., N.Y.C., 1953-72; v.p. Robert Wood Johnson Found., Princeton, N.J., 1972-80; pres. Commonwealth Fund, N.Y.C., 1980—. Mem. vis. com. Phila. Mus. Art, 1978; trustee Nat. Humanities Center, 1978—; vis. fellow Sch. Architecture and Urban Planning, Princeton U., 1973-80. Bd. dirs. NRC; trustee Found. Center. Mem. Inst. Medicine, AAAS, Council Fgn. Relations, Nat. Trust Hist. Preservation. Contbr. articles to profl. publs. Office: Commonwealth Fund 1 E 75th St New York NY 10021

MAHONEY, PATRICIA ANN NORDSTROM, personal services co. exec.; b. Hastings, Minn., Apr. 13, 1939; d. Harold Edward and Mary Patricia (Ahern) Nordstrom; B.S. cum laude, U. Minn., 1961; m. Edward James Mahoney, Feb. 17, 1962; children—Patrick Sean, Erin Mary. Tchr., head curriculum com. Hopkins (Minn.) Sr. High Sch., 1961-64; mgr. Bridal Services, Inc., Mpls., 1969-73; buyer, gen. mgr. Anderson's Wedding World Stores, Mpls., 1973-77; dir. fashion div. Nat. Bridal Service, Richmond, Va., 1975—, also dir.; mktg. and tng. specialist Minn. Dept. Edn., 1977-80; edn. cons. Mpls. Star & Tribune Newspapers, 1981—. Mem. Phi Beta Kappa. Home: 5604 Colfax Ave S Minneapolis MN 55419

MAIBENCO, HELEN CRAIG, educator; b. Scotland, June 9, 1917; came to U.S., 1946, naturalized, 1950; d. Benjamin C. and Mary (Brown) Craig; B.S., Wheaton (Ill.) Coll., 1948; M.S., DePaul U., Chgo., 1950; Ph.D., U. Ill., Chgo., 1956; m. Nichilas P. Maibenco, June 30, 1957 (dec.); children—Douglas Craig, Thomas Allan. Mem. faculty U. Ill. Coll. Medicine, Chgo., 1955-73, prof. anatomy 1973—; prof. anatomy Rush Med. Coll., Chgo., 1973—. Mem. AAAS, Endocrine Soc., Am. Assn. Anatomists, Am. Physiol. Assn., Am. Assn. Zoologists, Audubon Soc. Republican. Presbyterian. Home: 1324 S Main St Wheaton IL 60187 Office: 505A Acad Facility Rush Med Col 600 S Paulina St Chicago IL 60612

MAIDES, SHIRLEY ALLEN, psychologist; b. Roanoke Rapids, N.C., Sept. 16, 1951; d. John Thomas and Mary Shirley (Allen) Maides; B.A. with honors in Psychology, U. N.C., 1973; M.A., Vanderbilt U., 1975, Ph.D., 1978; m. John Thomas Keane, Nov. 8, 1980. Clin. psychology intern U. Calif. Med. Center, Davis, 1977-78; USPHS fellow U. Chgo. and Michael Reese Hosp., 1978-79; sr. supervising psychologist Incentives Inst., Des Plaines, Ill., 1980-81; pvt. practice psychology, Chgo., 1981—; account exec. N.P.D. Research, Rosemont, Ill., 1982—. USPHS clin. psychology fellow, 1974-77; USPHS Nat. Research Scientist, awardee, 1978-79. Mem. Am. Psychol. Assn., Am. Assn. Biofeedback Clinicians, Assn. Women in Psychology, Ill. Psychol. Assn. Democrat. Methodist. Contbr. articles to various publs. Office: Psychol Resources 20110 Governors Dr Suite 200 Olympia Fields IL 60461

MAIER, PAULINE, educator; b. St. Paul, Apr. 27, 1938; d. Irvin Louis and Charlotte (Winterer) Rubbelke; A.B., Radcliffe Coll., 1960; postgrad. London Sch. Econs., 1960-61; Ph.D. in History, Harvard U., 1968; m. Charles Steven Maier, June 17, 1961; children—Andrea Nicole, Nicholas Winterer, Jessica Elizabeth Heine. Asst. prof., then asso. prof. history U. Mass., Boston, 1968-77; Robinson-Edwards prof. history U. Wis., Madison, 1977-78; prof. history M.I.T., 1978—; mem. council Inst. Early Am. History, 1982-85. Recipient Douglass Adair award Claremont Grad. Sch.-Inst. Early Am. History, 1976, Kidger award New Eng. History Tchrs. Assn., 1981; fellow Nat. Endowment Humanities, 1974-75; Charles Warren fellow, 1974-75. Mem. Orgn. Am. Historians (exec. bd. 1978-82), Am. Hist. Assn., Soc. Am. Historians, Am. Antiquarian Soc., Colonial Soc. Mass. Author: From Resistance to Revolution: Colonial Radicals and the Development of American Opposition to Britain, 1765-1766, 1972; The Old Revolutionaries: Political Lives in the Age of Samuel Adams, 1980. Home: 60 Larchwood Dr Cambridge MA 02138 Office: MIT 14N-413 Cambridge MA 02139

MAIERHAUSER, FRAN ELIZABETH, home economist, journalist; b. Manfred Twp., Minn., Oct. 4, 1919; d. Joseph Lorenzo and Elizabeth (Maher) Dougherty; B.A., Sioux Falls Coll., 1940; B.S., S.D. State U., 1957; M.S., 1968; m., Dec. 28, 1950. Tchr. secondary schs. S.D. Sch. Systems, 1940-48; cashier No. States Power Co., Sioux Falls, S.D., 1948-50, home service adv., 1957-58; home econs. tchr. Irene (S.D.) Public Schs., 1952-57; home service adv. Sioux Valley Empire Assn., Colman, S.D., 1958-64; extension home econs. editor S.D. State U., Brookings, 1964-68; dir. consumer edn., women's editor Rural Kentuckian, Ky. Assn. Elec. Coops., Louisville, 1968—; guest lectr. and tchr. communications workshops, Ky. univs. Vice pres. women's activities Ky. Farm-City Council, 1972-73; publicity chmn. Ky. Safety Council, 1979-80. Recipient ALMA award Assn. Home Appliance Mfrs., 1972, 76, 78, 1st Pl. award Nat. Assn. Press Women, 1972, 2d Pl., 1975; Outstanding Service award Ky. Assn. Home Econs. Tchrs., 1979; HEIB Woman of Yr., 1982. Mem. Am. Home Econs. Assn., S.D. Home Econs. Assn. (pres. 1962-64), Ky. Home Econs. Assn. (pres. 1979-80), Louisville Home Econs. Assn. (pres. 1972-73), Ky. Home Economists in Bus. (pres. 1977-78), Women in Communications, Ky. Press Women (pres. 1976-77), Am. Women in Radio and TV (edn. chmn. 1978-79), Elec. Women's Round Table (charter chmn. Blue Grass chpt. 1968, chpt. chmn. 1978). Illuminating Engring. Soc. Democrat. Roman Catholic. Author: Let Mike Help You, 1967; First Aid for Appliances, 1970; series of tchr. and student handbooks on use and care of appliances, 1976-77. Home: 4432 Cordova Rd Louisville KY 40207 Office: PO Box 32170 Louisville KY 40232

MAIGRET, MAUREEN E., state legislator; b. Pawtucket, R.I., Feb. 11, 1944; R.N., Meml. Hosp., 1964; B.S., R.I. Coll., 1974; student M.P.A., U. R.I. Registered nurse-tchr.; mem. R.I. Ho. of Reps., 1974—, dep. majority leader, 1977-80, dep. speaker, from 1981, mem. Adv. Commn. on Women, 1977—. Bd. dirs. Kent County Vis. Nurses' Assn., 1978—; mem. R.I. Women's Polit. Caucus, 1979—. Recipient service award, R.I. Rape Crisis Center, 1979, legis. award, Citizens Against Child Abuse, 1979, legis. service award Assn. Home Health Agys., 1980, legis. award R.I. Council on Domestic Violence, 1980, Woman of Yr. award R.I. Women's Polit. Caucus, 1979. Democrat. Office: Rhode Island State House Providence RI 02903 *

MAIL, PATRICIA DAVISON, public health specialist; b. Kamloops, B.C., Can., Dec. 10, 1940; d. George Allen and Constance (Davison) M.; B.S., U. Ariz., 1963, M.A., 1970; M.S., Smith Coll., 1965; M.P.H., Yale U., 1967; postgrad. Seattle U., 1974. Commd. officer USPHS, 1970—, chief Health edn. br. Portland Indian Health Service, 1979—; mem. faculty Seattle U., 1974-78. Recipient Early Career award Public Health Edn. sect. Am. Public Health Assn., 1979; USPHS Service Plaque, 1979; USPHS trainee Yale U., 1965-67; NDEA grantee, 1968-70. Mem. Am. Public Health Assn., Soc. Public Health Edn., Med. Anthropology Soc., Soc. Applied Anthropology, Am. Sch. Health Assn., AAAS, AAHPER, Commd. Officers Assn. USPHS, Smith Coll. Alumnae Assn. Episcopalian. Club: Dorian Group. Author: (with D.R. McDonald) Tulapai to Tokay, 1980; editor SOPHE Sounds, 1976-82; contbr. articles to profl. jours. Home: 265 2500 S 370 St Federal Way WA 98003 Office: Fed Center S 4735 E Marginal Way S Seattle WA 98134

MAILLETT, LOUISE ELIZABETH, lawyer; b. Rumford, Maine, May 16, 1953; d. Noel C. and Lydia V.; B.A., Assumption Coll., 1975; J.D., U. Maine, 1978. Admitted to Maine bar, 1978, D.C. bar, 1981; asst. gen. counsel, designated ethics ofcl. Office Gen. Counsel Action, Washington, 1979—. Mem. Am. Bar Assn., D.C. Bar Assn., D.C. Women's Bar Assn., Maine Bar Assn. Office: 806 Connecticut Ave NW Washington DC 20525

MAINE, ARDIS LOUISE, property mgmt. co. exec.; b. Thief River Falls, Minn, July 21, 1940; d. Clarence O. and A. Louise (Hallameck) Engen; degree in Bus. Mgmt., Kinman Bus. U., 1959; m. Donald L. Maine, Apr. 25, 1959 (div. 1980); children—Mark Edward, April Leigh. Escrow officer, bookkeeper Panhandle Title Co., Coeur d'Alene, Idaho, 1964-68; escrow officer Transamerica Title Ins. Co., Seattle, 1968-69; escrow/comml. loan closer Firstbank Mortgage Corp., Seattle, 1969-71; sr. comml. loan closer, asst. sec. Securities-Intermountain, Inc., Seattle, 1972-78; sec., treas. Forest Investment Corp., Bellevue, Wash., 1978-82; with Continental Property Mgmt. Inc., Bellevue, 1982—. Mem. Nat. Assn. Profl. Mortgage Women, Nat. Assn. Female Execs. Roman Catholic. Clubs: Edmonds Yacht, Elks. Office: 11027 NE 4th St Bellevue WA 98004

MAIONE, DOROTHY MARIE, guidance counselor; b. Syracuse, N.Y., Aug. 22, 1927; d. Anthony S. and Caroline A. (Vincent) Maione; B.A. in Psychology, Seton Hill Coll., 1949, B.A. in Comparative Lit., 1949; M.S. in Edn., Syracuse U., 1965, M.A. in Guidance, 1967; postgrad. Manhattan Coll., 1981—. Social worker Guardian Angel Home, Troy, N.Y., 1949-52; dir. advt. Schenectady Union-Star, 1952-55; with N.Y. Telephone Co., Syracuse, 1955-60; tchr. Sacred Heart Sch., Syracuse, 1960-65; guidance counselor Bishop Ludden High Sch., Syracuse, 1965—, dir. guidance, 1973—. Mem. Bishop's Task Force Secondary Edn. in Onondaga County, 1970-74; chmn. public relations com. Bishop Ludden High Sch., 1969-74; mem. Middle State Evaluation com., 1975, 77, participant Congress of Women in the Ch., Washington, 1981; mem. exec. bd. Bishop Ludden Parent Tchrs. Guild, 1970—; faculty rep. Tchrs. Council, Onondaga County, N.Y., 1981-82, mem. exec. com., 1981-82; pres. Syracuse Diocesan Guidance Council, 1970. Recipient (spell out IFCA) Internat. Fedn. Cath. Alumnae Rose award, 1970; named Outstanding Cath. Alumna, 1969; N.Y. State Dept Edn. grantee, 1981-82 Mem. Seton Hill Coll. Syracuse Alumnae (pres. 1965—, past dir.), Internat. Fedn. Cath. Alumnae (pres. 1960-64), Am. Personnel and Guidance Assn., N.Y. State Personnel and Guidance Assn., Dirs. of Guidance Onondaga County, Nat. Cath. Edn. Assn., Nat. Cath. Guidance Conf., Onondaga County Counselors Assn. Roman Catholic. Editor, Luddenlife, 1971-77; spl. reviewer for text books in secondary schs. Feminist Press, 1977-81. Home: 206 Walberta Rd Syracuse NY 13219 Office: 815 Fay Rd Syracuse NY 13219

MAIORISI, CATHERINE THERESA, data processing cons. co. exec.; b. Hackensack, N.J., Mar. 23, 1938; d. George and Helen (Spagnuolo) M.; B.A., Douglass Coll., 1960; M.A., Fairleigh Dickenson U., 1966. Statis. analyst A. C. Nielsen Co., N.Y.C., 1960-63; programmer Home Ins. Co., N.Y.C., 1963-64; systems rep. Honeywell, Inc., N.Y.C., 1964-66; systems analyst, project leader Colgate-Palmolive, N.Y.C., 1966-70; asst. v.p. systems and programming Group Health, Inc., N.Y.C., 1970-76; mng. cons Data Architects, Inc., Waltham, Mass., 1976-79; owner, pres. Computer Concepts, Inc., N.Y.C., 1979—. Mem. Nat. Assn. Women Bus. Owners, Assn. Systems Mgmt., Networks Unltd., Inc., Soc. Mgmt. Info. Systems, Women in Info. Processing, Inc., NOW. Office: 928 Broadway New York NY 10010

MAJEED, SALIMAH, clin. social worker; b. St. Paul, Feb. 20, 1946; d. Charles Scott and Dorothy Olivia (Lee) Compton; B.A., Carleton Coll., Minn., 1968; M.S. in Social Services, Boston U., 1970; m. Nasif Rashad Majeed, Oct. 8, 1975; children—Akbar, Faheem Wafeeq. Group worker Boston Children's Services, 1970; social worker II, Guilford County (N.C.) Dept. Social Services, Greensboro, 1971-72; clin. med. social worker II, Cook County Hosp., Chgo., 1974-77; clin. social worker Alamance County (N.C.) Mental Health and Mental Retardation Center, Burlington, 1977-79, unit coordinator outpatient children's services, 1979-81; field instr. U. N.C. Sch. Social Work, 1978-81; lectr. dept. sociology, anthropology and social work U. N.C., Charlotte, 1981—. Bd. dirs. Sr. Day Care Center, Greensboro, 1980—, Youth Advocacy Assn., 1980—, PTA, 1980-81; mem. Afro-Am. Culture Center, Charlotte, 1981—; mem. Child Interest Com., Chgo., 1975. Mem. Acad. Cert. Social Workers, Nat. Assn. Social Workers, Triad Assn. Human Services, Nat. Assn. Black Social Workers, N.C. Black Women's Polit. Caucus. Mem. Am. Muslim Mission. Home: 1615 Bonnie Ln Charlotte NC 28213 Office: UNCC Station Dept Sociology Anthropology and Social Work Charlotte NC 28213

MAJEWSKI, JANICE, museum ofcl.; b. Springfield, Mass., Apr. 15, 1951; d. Henry Bruno and Dorothy Bernice (Bobrowski) M.; A.B., Conn. Coll., 1973; M.E.D. (Zonta Internat. fellow 1974), Smith Coll., 1975. Tchr. hearing impaired children Arlington County (Va.) public schs., 1975-78; coordinator spl. edn. Smithsonian Instn., 1978—, instl. liaison for 1981 Internat. Yr. Disabled Persons, guest editor mus. Roundtable Reports, 1981. vol. Nat. Very Spl. Arts Festival. Membership chmn. Young Democrats Arlington, 1977-78, sr. party rep., 1978-79; treas. Democratic Joint Campaign Com., 1977-78 bd. dirs. United Cerebral Palsy of Washington. Mem. Alexander Graham Bell

Assn. for Deaf, Mus. Edn. Roundtable, Nat. Assn. of Deaf, Council for Exceptional Children. Roman Catholic. Office: 900 Jefferson Dr Washington DC 20560

MAJORS, JUDITH SOLEY, writer, health educator; b. Portland, Oreg., June 17, 1946; d. Alford H. and Leora L. (Carpenter) Soley; B.A., Marylhurst Coll., 1980; A.A., Mt. Hood Community Coll., 1970; m. Jack B. Majors, Mar. 18, 1967; 1 dau., Carrie. Sr. editor Apple Press, Milwaukie, Oreg., 1978—; local TV personality; author; works include: Sugar Free—That's Me, 1978; Sugar Free—Kid's Cookery, 1979; Sugar Free—Microwavery, 1980; Diet Out—Oregon, 1981; Meatless Wonder, 1982. Bd. dirs. Oreg. Diabetes Assn.; adv. bd. North Clackamas Sch. Dist.; mem. Milwaukie Citizens Adv. Com.; bd. dirs. Milwaukie Festival Daze. Mem. Nat. Fedn. Presswomen, Women in Communications, Willamette Writers, Oreg. Community Edn. Assn. Democrat. Home and Office: 5536 SE Harlow St Milwaukie OR 97222

MAKAR, NADIA EISSA, educator; b. Cairo, Egypt, Oct. 7, 1938; d. Michel Issa and Yvonne Bitar; student Cairo U., 1958-59, 64-65; cert. Moscow U., 1964; B.A., St. Peter's Coll., 1969; Hon. Dr. Liberal Arts, Gt. China Arts Coll., 1973; m. Boshra Halim Makar, Jan. 1, 1960; children—Ralph, Roger. Tchr. chemistry Hudson Cath. High Sch., Jersey City, 1970-72, chmn. sci. dept., 1972-79; sci. specialist Union Hill High Sch., 1979—, sci. specialist convocation model project, 1979-81. Chmn. jr. poets Ann. Internat. Poetry Festival, 1973—. Bd. dirs. World Poets Resource Center, N.Y.C. Recipient Spl. award Poetry Soc. London, 1972; Regional award excellence in teaching chemistry Mfg. Chemists Assn., 1975; Leadership in Poetry crown 3d World Congress Poets, 1976; named outstanding secondary educator Am., 1973, Hudson County Woman of Achievement, 1975, Internat. Woman of Year, 1976. Mem. AAAS, Nat. (rep. edn. com. 1979—), N.J. sci. tchrs. assns., Nat., N.J. sci. suprs. assns., Poetry Soc. London (life), Assn. for Edn. Tchrs. in Sci., Am. Chem. Soc. (Nichols award N.Y. sect. 1977, Met. Regional award in high sch. chemistry teaching 1978), Hudson-Bergen Chem. Soc. (pres. 1982—), Centro Studi e Scambi Internaziolali (mem. internat. com. on sci. 1973—), United Poets Laureate Internat. (co-v.p. 1976-79), N.Y., N.J. acads. sci., Internat. Platform Assn., Bus. and Profl. Women (1st v.p. 1979-81, pres. 1982—, chmn.-elect 1982). Home: 410 Fairmount Ave Jersey City NJ 07306 Office: Union City Bd Edn Union City NJ 07087

MAKAROVA, NATALIA, ballerina; b. Leningrad, Russia, Nov. 21, 1940; grad. Kaganova Ballet Sch., Leningrad Choreographic Sch., 1959; m. Edward Karkar, 1976; 1 son, Andrei Michel. Formerly ballerina Leningrad Kirov Ballet; performed at Royal Opera House, Covent-Garden, London, 1961; toured U.S., 1961, 64; defected from Russia, 1970; danced with Rudolf Nureyev; roles include Giselle, Swan Lake, Chopiniana (Les Sylphides), Sleeping Beauty, Cinderella, Raymonda, Nikiya (La Bayadire), others; joined Am. Ballet Theatre, 1970-72; guest appearances U.S. and London, 1972—; formed dance co. Makarova & Co., 1980—. Recipient Gold medal 2d Internat. Ballet Competition, Varna, Bulgaria, 1965. Author: A Dance Autobiography, 1979. Home: London England Office: care Herbert Breslin Inc 119 W 57th St New York NY 10019 *

MAKINS, DICY OLIVIA, biologist; b. Kansas City, Kans., July 7, 1951; d. Clifford Lloyd and Edna Mae (Chisholm) M.; B.A., Claremont Coll., 1973; postgrad. Drexel U., 1979. Fellow spl. cancer virus group U. So. Calif., Los Angeles, 1972; adv. enrichment program for high sch. minority students interested in health professions U. So. Calif. Sch. Medicine, Los Angeles, 1973; bus. assoc. R. C. Med. Carrier, Phila., 1981—. Instr. elem. sch. children Presbyn. Ch., Pasadena. Meth. Found. grantee, 1971-81. Mem. Assn. Women in Sci., Nat. Assn. Female Execs. Methodist. Home: PO Box 2206 Philadelphia PA 19103

MAKK, EVA HOLUSA (MRS. AMERICO MAKK), painter; b. Ethiopia, Africa, Dec. 1, 1933; came to U.S., 1962, naturalized, 1967; d. Bertalan and Julie Elizabeth (Ribenyi) Holusa; Agrl. Engr.; student Acad. Fine Arts, Paris, France, 1946-50; m. Americo Makk, Oct. 18, 1950; 1 son, Americo B. Prof. painting Acad. Fine Arts, Sao Paulo, Brazil, 1950-62; ofcl. hist. painter for Brazilian Govt., 1956-62; chmn. Internat. Carnegie Exhibit, N.Y.C., 1966-67; exhibited internat. one-man and group shows, Rome, 1949, Sao Paulo, 1950, 56, 59, Rio de Janeiro, Brazil, 1956, 59, Monte Carlo, Monaco, 1968, Paris, 1969, N.Y.C., 1963-67, Miami, Fla., 1968-73, Munich, Germany, 1972, Lisbon, Spain, 1973, S.W. U.S., 1969-82; executed numerous murals in govt. palace, Pernambuco, Manaus, Brazil, various chs., basilicas; represented in permanent collections at Sao Paulo, Rio de Janeiro, Rome, Budapest, Monaco, others. Mem. UNICEF, Art for Heart, Honolulu, co-chmn., 1971. Recipient numerous awards, prizes, including internat. gold medals. Mem. Fifty Am. Artists Assn., Am.-Hungarian Art Assn. (dir.), World Fedn. Hungarian Artists, Am. Profl. Art League, Assn. Paulista De Imprensa Brazil, Arpad Acad. U.S. Address: 1515 Laukahi St Honolulu HI 96821

MAKLARY, MARY LAURON, pipe and steel products supply co. exec.; b. Detroit, Jan. 28, 1941; d. Angelo and Lenore (O'Rorke) Lauron; student Wayne State U., Detroit, 1958-59, Houston Community U., 1972-73; m. David Russell Whitney, May, 1980; children by previous marriage—Becky Ann, John Gerard. Sales staff J.L. Hudson Co., Detroit, 1957-60; with Terry White Metals, Inc., Houston, 1974-76; pres. Trinity Pipe & Steel Co., Inc., Houston, 1977—. Active 4-H Clubs, Boy Scouts Am. Recipient Humanitarian award Dale Carnegie Schs., 1976; Sponsorship award Little League Football, Alief, Tex., 1977-78; Two-Year Old Halter Stallion award, 1981. Mem. Am. Quarter Horse Assn., Tex. Quarter Horse Assn., Greater Houston Quarter Horse Assn. Roman Catholic. Office: PO Box 42024 Houston TX 77242

MAKO, MARY ELIZABETH, biochemist; b. Hammond, Ind., July 11, 1939; d. Steve and Helen (Lengyel) M.; B.S. in Zoology, Wheaton (Ill.) Coll., 1953; M.S., N.D. State U., Fargo, 1968. Research asst. Northwestern U., Chgo., 1968-69; research technologist U. Chgo., 1969-74, research assoc. dept. medicine, 1974-78, research assoc., instr., 1978-82, research assoc., asst. prof., 1982—. Mem. Am. Diabetes Assn., Am. Chem. Soc., Am. Fedn. Clin. Research, AAAS, Assn. Women in Sci., Lincoln Park Conservation Assn., Midnorth Assn. Mem. Ch. of Christ. Contbr. articles to profl. jours. Home: 2333 N Geneva Terr Chicago IL 60614 Office: Dept Medicine Box 435 U Chgo 950 E 59th St Chicago IL 60637

MAKUPSON, AMYRE PORTER, TV exec.; b. River Rouge, Mich., Sept. 30, 1947; d. Rudolph Hannibal and Amyre Ann (Porche) Porter; B.A., Fisk U., 1970; M.A., Am. U., Washington, 1970; m. Walter H. Makupson, Nov. 1, 1975; children—Rudolph Porter, Amyre Nisi. Asst. news dir. Sta. WGPR-TV, Detroit, 1975-76; public relations dir. Mich. Health Maintenance Orgn., Detroit, 1974-76, Kirwood Gen. Hosp., Detroit, 1976-77; news and pub. affairs mgr. Sta. WKBD-TV, Southfield, Mich., 1977—. Mem. adv. com. Mich. Arthritis Found.; bd. dirs. Barat House. Recipient numerous service awards, including: Arthritis Found. Mich., Mich. Mchts. Assn., DAV, Jr. Achievement, City of Detroit, Salvation Army. Mem. Pub. Relations Soc. Am., Am. Women in Radio and TV (Outstanding Achievement award 1981), Women in Communications, Detroit Press Club, Ad-Craft. Roman Catholic. Office: 26955 W 11 Mile Rd Southfield MI 48034

MALAS, CORNELIA, ret. bus. exec.; b. Cin.; d. John C. and Katherine (Farres) Malas; student U. Cin., 1940-42; bus. cert. Littleford Nelson Bus. Coll., 1943; student Schuster Martin Sch. Drama, 1943; cert. Patricia Stevens Modeling Sch., 1944; student Campbell Bus. Coll., 1956. Head central filing dept. Gruen Watch Co., Cin., 1945-50; expediter purchasing dept. MacGregor Sport Products, Cin., 1950-57; personnel adminstr. Eagle-Picher Industries, Inc., Cin., 1957-79, indsl. relations sec., 1979-82. Chmn., Rosie Reds Night at Crosley Field, Rooters Organized to Stimulate Interest and Enthusiasm in Cin. Reds Baseball Team, 1967, v.p., 1971, trustee, 1971-79, pres., 1975-76; mem. women's com. Nat. Gov.'s. Conf., 1968; mem. ticket com. Cin. Symphony Orch., 1968; publicity chmn. May Festival, 1969, mem. women's com., 1971-73; mem. Women's com. United Fine Arts, 1973-75; judge Jr. Achievement, 1965, 67; bd. dirs. Opera Guild, 1980—. Mem. Profl. Secs. Internat. (pres. Ohio div. 1969-70), Internat. Assn. for Personnel Women, Cin. Personnel Assn., Adminstrv. Mgmt. Soc., Internat. Platform Assn., Alpha Delta Pi. Clubs: Hyde Park Golf and Country, Wyoming (Ohio) Women's, Cincinnati, Internat. Toastmistress, Williams (pres. 1966-67). Home: 9303 Constitution Dr Cincinnati OH 45215

MALBROCK, JANE C., mathematician, computer scientist; b. N.J.; d. George and Camille (Sabie) Malbrock; B.A. summa cum laude, Montclair State Coll., 1964; M.A., Pa. State U., 1966, Ph.D. (NSF fellow), 1971; M.S. in Computer Sci., Fairleigh Dickinson U., 1982. Asst. prof. math. and computer sci. Kean Coll. of N.J., 1971-78, asso. prof., 1978—. Recipient Outstanding Math. Grad. award Montclair State Coll., 1964. Mem. Am. Math. Soc., Math. Assn. Am., Assn. Math. Tchrs. N.J., Assn. Computing Machinery. Research on approximation theory. Office: Dept Math and Computer Sci Kean Coll of NJ Union NJ 07083

MALCOM, SHIRLEY MAHALEY, sci. profl. assn. exec.; b. Birmingham, Sept. 6, 1946; d. Ben Lee and Lillie Mae (Funderburg) Mahaley; B.S. with distinction, U. Wash., 1967; M.A. in Zoology and Animal Behavior, U. Calif. 1968; Ph.D. in Ecology and Animal Behavior, Pa. State U., 1974; m. Horace Malcom, May 31, 1975; children—Kelly Alicia, Lindsey Ellen. Asst. prof. biology U. N.C., 1974-75; research asst., staff assoc., project dir. AAAS, Washington, 1975-77, program head Office of Opportunities in Sci., 1979—; program officer Directorate for Sci. Edn., NSF, 1977-79; commr. Sci. Manpower Commn.; mem. ad hoc com. sci. and engring. personnel Sci. Resources Studies, NSF. Regents fellow. Mem. AAAS, Fedn. Orgns. Profl. Women (dir.). Contbr. to profl. jours. Office: 1776 Massachusetts Ave NW Washington DC 20036

MALDEN, JOAN WILLIAMS, phys. therapist; b. Bayshore, N.Y., Apr. 14; d. Sidney S. and Myrtle L. (Williams) Siegel; B.S., N.Y. U., 1957; m. Alan A. Chasnov, Jan. 20, 1951; children—Marc, Robin, Debra and David (twins); m. 2d, Miroslav Mladenovic, Sept. 14, 1967; 1 dau., Kristine. Phys. therapist hosps. and orgns. in N.Y.C. area, 1956-57; phys. therapist Brunswick Hosp. Center, Amityville, N.Y., 1968-69; pvt. practice phys. therapy, Wantagh, N.Y., 1968—; licensure examiner, N.Y. State; cons., tchr. in field. Pres. internat. scholarships com. Massapequa chpt. Am. Field Service, 1962-64. Mem. Am. Acad. Cerebral Palsy, Am. Phys. Therapy Assn. (chmn. polit. action com. N.Y. chpt., chmn. L.I. dist.), AAUW (pres. Massapequa chpt. 1962-64), N.Y. State Soc. Continuing Edn. in Phys. Therapy, Airplane Owners and Pilots Assn., Ninety-Nines, Exptl. Aviation Assn., Farmingdale Flyers (officer). Democrat. Unitarian. Home: 35 S Bay Ave Massapequa NY 11758 Office: Wantagh Med Bldg 1228 Wantagh Ave Wantagh NY 11793

MALDONADO, ANA MARIA, cellist; b. El Paso, Tex., Feb. 23, 1949; d. Francisco E. and Berta (Medrano) Maldonado; B. Mus., Tex. Tech. U., 1971; M. Mus., U. So. Calif., 1975. With Bangkok (Thailand) String Quar., 1972-74; prof. Silapakorn U., Bangkok, 1972-74; with Heidelberg City Orch., 1975-77; prof. Wiesloch (Ger.) Music Sch., 1975-77; cello instr. U. Calif., Riverside, 1979-82; faculty Calif. Poly. Inst., 1978—. Rockefeller Found. grantee, 1972-74. Roman Catholic. Home: 1460 Indian Hill Claremont CA 91711 Office: Cal Poly 3801 W Temple Pomona CA 91768

MALDONADO-BEAR, RITA MARINITA, economist, educator; b. Vega Alta, P.R., June 14, 1938; d. Victor and Marina (Davila) Maldonado; B.A., Auburn U., 1960; Ph.D., N.Y.U., 1969; m. Larry Alan Bear, Mar. 29, 1975. With Min. Wage Bd. & Econ. Devel. Adminstrn., Govt. of P.R., 1960-64; asso. prof. fin. U. P.R., 1969-70; asst. prof. econs. Manhattan Coll., 1970-72; asso. prof. econs. Bklyn. Coll., 1972-75; vis. asso. prof. fin. Stanford (Calif.) Grad. Bus. Sch., 1973-74; asso. prof. fin. and econs. Grad. Sch. Bus. Adminstrn., N.Y.U., N.Y.C., 1975-81, prof., 1981—; cons. Morgan Guaranty Trust Co., N.Y.C., 1972-77, Bank of Am., N.Y.C., 1982—, Res. City Bankers, N.Y.C., 1978—. P.R. Econ. Devel. Adminstrn. fellow, 1960-65; Marcus Nadler fellow, N.Y.U., 1966-67, Phillip Lods Dissertation fellow, 1967-68. Mem. Am. Econs. Assn., Am. Fin. Assn., Metro. Econ. Assn. N.Y., Assn. for Social Econs. (2nd v.p.). Author: Role of the Financial Sector in the Economic Development of Puerto Rico, 1970; contbr. articles to profl. jours. Home: 315 W 70 St New York NY 10023 Office: 100 Trinity Pl New York NY 10006

MALEADY, ANTOINETTE KIRKPATRICK, author, publisher; b. Powell, Wyo., Dec. 9, 1918; d. Sherman S. and Beatrice E. (Chrisman) Kirkpatrick; B.S., W.Va. Wesleyan Coll., Buckhannon, 1940; M.L.S., U. Calif., Berkeley, 1968; m. Thomas J. Maleady, Sept. 21, 1954; 1 dau., Sarah Ann. Various clerical positions, 1940-44; asst. billet mgr. USAF, Tokyo, 1946-48; consular clk. Dept. State, 1948-54; pres. Chulainn Press, Inc., San Anselmo, Calif., 1975—. Served with USN, 1944-45. Mem. Am. Recorder Soc., Choral Dirs. Assn., Music Library Assn., Western Book Pubs. Assn., Assn. Recorded Sound Collections, Pvt. Libraries Assn., Calif. Press Women, Press Club San Francisco, World Affairs Council, Met. Opera Guild, San Francisco Opera Guild. Home: 1040 Butterfield Rd San Anselmo CA 94960 Office: PO Box 770 San Anselmo CA 94960

MALETZ, LORRAINE JONES, sch. adminstr.; b. New Brunswick, N.J.; d. Henry Seal and Muriel Regina (Rule) Jones; B.S., Southeastern U., 1972; M.Ed., Antioch Coll., 1974; 1 son, Richard Eric. Sec. to dir. research E.R. Squibb & Sons, New Brunswick, N.J., 1946-56; asst. comptroller Sandy Spring (Md.) Friends Sch., 1970-71, comptroller, 1971—. Mem. Am. Mgmt. Assn., AAUW, Eta Upsilon Gamma. Quaker. Author: Accounting for Small Private Schools, 1975. Office: Sandy Spring Friends School Sandy Spring MD 20860

MALFER, NANCY ROSE STEINBOCK, speech-lang. pathologist; b. Montclair, N.J., Feb. 24, 1950; d. Marvin Aaron and Elinor (Whittlesey) Steinbock; student Hendrix Coll., 1968-70, Sophie Newcomb Coll., 1970-71; B.A. in English, U. Ark., 1973; M.A. in Speech Pathology, Hunter Coll., 1977; postgrad. City U. N.Y., 1978—; m. Douglas Paul Malfer, Sept. 1, 1979. Grad. trainee fellow VA Hosp., N.Y.C., 1976; speech and hearing therapist Willowbrook Devel. Center, United Cerebral Palsy Assn. N.Y. State, S.I., 1977; clin. supr. Queens Coll. Speech and Hearing Clinic, Flushing, N.Y., 1979-81; adj. instr., clin. supr. C.W. Post Coll., Greenvale, L.I., N.Y., 1981—. HEW fellow, 1973-74; Rehab. Services Adminstrn. grantee, 1978-79. Mem. Am. Speech and Hearing Assn. (cert. clin. competence). Democrat. Episcopalian. Home: Old Bedford Rd Goldens Bridge NY 10526

MALFITANO, CATHERINE, opera singer; b. N.Y.C., Apr. 18, 1948; d. Joseph and Maria (Flynn) M.; B.A., Manhattan Sch. Music, 1971; m. Stephen Jon Holowid, Oct. 28, 1977. Debuts include: Falstaff, Central City, Colo., 1972, Le Nozze di Figaro, Holland Festival, 1973, La Boheme, N.Y.C. Opera, Los Angeles, 1973; appeared with Met. Opera, 1979. Mem. Am. Guild Mus. Artists. Office: care Columbia Artists Mgmt Inc 165 W 57th St New York NY 10019 *

MALINCHOK, MARTHA, nurse, educator; b. Ashland, Pa., May 15, 1932; d. John and Anna (Holowathy) Polansky; R.N., Ashland State Gen. Hosp., 1952; B.S. in Nursing, Villanova (Pa.) U., 1954; m. Paul Malinchok, Aug. 4, 1957; children—John, Michael. Instr. nursing Ashland State Gen. Hosp., summer 1954, clin. instr., dir. in-service edn., 1957-58; instr. nursing Fitzgerald Mercy Hosp. Sch. Nursing, Darby, Pa., 1954-55, Pottsville (Pa.) Hosp. Sch. Nursing, 1955-56; exec. dir. Easter Seal Soc., Schuylkill County, 1961-66; coordinator practical nursing Schuylkill County I.U. 29 Vocat.-Tech. Sch., Marlin, Pa., 1966—; v.p. bd. dirs. Mountain Manor Nursing Home Aux., 1972-74; bd. dirs. Schuylkill County Cancer Soc., 1978-80. Republican judge of election 1964-68. Mem. Am. Nurses Assn., Am. Vocat. Adminstrs. Assn., Nat. League Nursing, Pa. Nurses Assn. (dist. 2 dir.), Pa. Vocat. Adminstrs. Assn., Pa. Coordinators Practical Nursing Assn., Pa. Hospice Assn., Ashland State Gen. Hosp. Alumnae Assn. (pres. 1967-76). Mem. Russian Orthodox Ch. Club: Lady Elks (club v.p. 1961-63). Home: 326 N Nice St Frackville PA 17931 Office: Schuylkill County IU 29 Area Vocat-Tech Sch Marlin PA 17951

MALKIN, JAIN ROSENTHAL, interior designer; b. Chgo., Apr. 8, 1943; d. Murray and Ethel (Kritzberg) Rosenthal; B.A., U. Wis., 1963; B.A. in Environ. Design, San Diego State U., 1976. Pres., Jain Malkin, Inc., La Jolla, Calif., 1970—; cons. curricula San Diego City Schs., San Diego Community Coll. Dist.; instr. design U. Calif., San Diego, 1980—. Recipient Hexter award, 1973; Burlington Industry award, 1974. Mem. AIA, Ikebana Internat., Women in Design. Democrat. Author: The Design of Medical and Dental Facilities, 1981. Contbr. articles to design and med. mags. Work included in Women in Design Internat. Competition Compendium, 1982.

MALKNECHT, PAULINE GENEVA, educator; b. Dodd City, Ark., Jan. 2, 1919; d. Fred Ernest and Bessie Lenore (Morrow) Morrow; A.B. summa cum laude, N.W. Nazarene Coll. 1941; A.B., U. Mich., 1977; m. Arthur James Malknecht, Nov. 18, 1944 (div. 1980); children—Kay, Diane, Roland, Lenora, Steven. Tchr. public schs., Idaho, 1941-45; sec. Boeing Aircraft Co., Seattle, 1943; tchr., public schs., Flint, Mich., 1947-49, Gaines, Mich., 1949-51; tchr. bus. edn., public schs., Swartz Creek, Mich., 1966—; sponsor Future Bus. Leaders Am., 1966-72, Bus. Office Edn. Club, 1972-79. Mem. Mich. Bus. Edn. Assn. Clubs: DAV Aux. (jr. v.p. club 1971, sr. v.p. 1972, adjutant 1979-80), Am. Legion Aux. (sec. club 1976), VFW Aux. (conductress club 1972-73). Home: 10221 Corunna Rd Swartz Creek MI 48473 Office: 8320 Ingalls St Swartz Creek MI 48473

MALLARY, GERTRUDE ROBINSON (MRS. R. DEWITT MALLARY), civic worker; b. Springfield, Mass., Aug. 19, 1902; d. George Edward and Jennie (Slater) Robinson; student Bennett Coll., 1921-22, U. Conn., 1941-42; m. R. DeWitt Mallary, Sept. 15, 1923; children—R. DeWitt, Richard Walker. Co-owner, partner Mallary Farm, Bradford, Vt., 1936—; mem. Vt. Ho. of Reps., 1953-56, sec. agr. com., 1953, mem. appropriations com., 1955; mem. Vt. Senate, 1957-58, mem. appropriations com., clk. pub. health com., vice chmn. edn. com., mem. interim legis. com. for study nursing, 1958-59. Pres., Jr. League, Springfield, 1931-33; chmn. Springfield Council Social Agys., 1938-40; mem. Vt. Bd. Recreation, 1959-65; trustee Fairlee (Vt.) Public Library, 1953—, Asa Bloomer Found., 1963-71, Orange County 4-H Found., 1969-71; trustee Justin Smith Morrill Found., 1964-71, pres., 1968-71; pres. Vt. Holstein Club, 1951-53; mem. Vt. Gov.'s Commn. for Library Services, 1966; regional v.p. Nat. Beef Council, 1960-64; mem. adv. com. Swift Water council Girl Scouts U.S.A., 1971-74; Vt. chmn. Nat. Library Week, 1973; chmn. Fairlee Bicentennial Com., 1974-77; mem. Com. for New Eng. Bibliography, 1971—, vice chmn. for Vt., 1977; trustee Wesson Meml. Hosp., Springfield, 1935-38, chmn. nursing services, 1937; mem. planning com. Gov.'s Conf. Future of Vt.'s Heritage, 1982. Recipient Theresa R. Brungardt award, 1979. Mem. Vt. Library Trustees Assn. (pres. 1965-67), Vt. (trustee), Bradford (pres. 1965-69), Fairlee (program chmn. 1976—) hist. socs., Am. Antiquarian Soc. Editor New Eng. Holstein Bull., 1947-50. Address: Mallary Farm Bradford VT 05033

MALLERY, SYLVIA ELAINE, educator; b. Albany, N.Y., Mar. 10, 1934; d. Roger Henry and Margaret (Provost) M.; B.A., Syracuse U., 1955; Ed.M., Harvard U., 1957; profl. diploma Tchrs. Coll. Columbia U., 1967; Ed.D., Nova U., 1976. Prof. social sci. SUNY, Cobleskill, 1958—; instr. Tchrs. Coll., Columbia U., 1966. Bd. dirs. Mohawk Valley Symphony Cobleskill, 1978-81, pres., 1979-80. Mem. U.S. Nat. Com. for Early Childhood Edn., Kappa Delta Pi, Pi Lambda Theta. Republican. Methodist. Club: Schohaire County Women's Republican (past pres.). Home: 12 Washington Ave Cobleskill NY 12043

MALLET, LAURIE HELENE, apparel co. exec.; b. Tunisia, Apr. 13, 1948; d. Rene and Emmeline (Aidan) Belhassen; student Faculté de Sciences Economiques, Paris, 1968-72, Institut d'Etudes Politiques, Paris, 1968-71; m. Jacques R. Mallet, May 30, 1973; 1 dau., Clementine. Asst. designer, 1972-74; asst. desinger Ellen Tracy, 1974-75; owner, operator Laurie Mallet Inc., 1975-76; owner, pres. Williwear, Ltd., N.Y.C., 1976—. Mem. Fashion Group. Office: 209 W 39th St New York NY 10018

MALLINCKRODT, MARTHA GRAVES (MRS. CHARLES O. MALLINCKRODT), club woman; b. Louisville, Dec. 2, 1905; d. Allison and Ellen (Monks) Graves; student N.Y. Sch. Applied Design for Women, 1924, U. Louisville, 1924; m. Charles Olcott Mallinckrodt, Oct. 3, 1934; children—Charles Olcott, Ellen Louise. Active Jr. Service League, Summit, N.J., 1941-51, Girl Scouts U.S.A. and Boy Scouts Am., 1945-46, 49-55; dir. Hobby Show, Palos Verdes Woman's Club, 1953-54, asst. dir., 1954-55; dir. Sr. Assembly of Palos Verdes Estates, 1953-54; dir. Palos Verdes Community Arts Assn., 1957-59; founding mem. Palos Verdes Surf-Writers, 1957, treas., 1957, asst. v.p., program adviser, 1958, 59; hospitality chmn. Palos Verdes Peninsula chpt. Am. Assn. for UN, 1958-59; vol. staff Children's Hosp., Los Angeles, 1958—; mem. Los Angeles Mayor's Citizens Com., 1964. Mem. Jr. League Newport Harbor (Calif.) (sustainers' adv. bd.), Assistance League Laguna Beach, Old Treas. Antique Guild Laguna Hills, Orange County Antiques Soc., Leisure World Astronomy Club, Art Assn. Laguna Hills, Aux. IEEE, Town and Gown Soc. U. Calif. at Irvine; affiliate Laguna Beach Mus. Art. Clubs: Ebell (Laguna Hills), Old Treasures (chmn. treasure mart 1965). Home: 3193-A Buena Vista Laguna Hills CA 92653

MALLONE, SUSAN MARIE CHRISTNER, nursing adminstr.; b. Ashtabula, Ohio, Oct. 23, 1943; d. Ralph E. and V. Marion (Maki) Christner; diploma Fairview Park Hosp. Sch. Nursing, 1964; B.S. in Applied Sci., Youngstown State U., 1978. Charge nurse Fairview Park Hosp., Cleve., 1964-65; staff nurse Northeastern Ohio Gen. Hosp., Madison, 1965, asst. dir. nursing service, 1972-77, dir., 1977—; charge nurse George Washington U. Hosp., Washington, 1965-66; staff nurse Lake County Meml. Hosp., Painesville, Ohio, 1966-67; cons. Applied Nursing Consultation and Ednl. Resources. Mem. Am. Assn. Critical Care Nurses, Am. Heart Assn. (mem. council cardiovascular disease), Northeastern Ohio Heart Assn., Northeastern Ohio Hosp Assn., Nat. League Nursing, Ohio League Nursing. Republican. Lutheran. Contbr. articles on critical care nursing to profl. jours. Home: 125 S Ridge

Geneva OH 44041 Office: Northeastern Gen Ohio Hosp 2041 Hubbard Rd North Madison OH 44057

MALLORY-BARKLEY, BARBARA Z., psychologist; b. New Haven, May 25, 1936; d. Peter and Estelle (Serba) Zommer; B.S. cum laude, So. Conn. State Coll., 1968; M.S., U. Conn., 71; postgrad. Harvard U., 1973; children—Deborah L. Boudreau, George B. Boudreau, Scott P. Boudreau. Dir. research study Mass. Gen. Hosp. Child Devel. Lab., 1972-74; dir. edn. Beacon Sch., Boston, 1974-76; diagnostician Eagle Hill Clinic, Greenwich, Conn., 1976-78; dir. New Eng. office Ednl. Records Bur., Wellesley, Mass., 1978—; cons. nat. ind. schs.; lectr. Harvard U. Mem. Internat. Neuropsychology Assn., Am. Psychol. Assn., Phi Delta Kappa. Republican. Home: 411 Marret Rd Lexington MA 02173 Office: 37 Cameron St Wellesley MA 02181

MALM, RITA, brokerage house exec.; b. May 8, 1932; d. George Peter and Helen Marie (Woodward) Pellegrini; student Packard Jr. Coll., 1950-52, N.Y. Inst. Fin., 1954, Wagner Coll., 1955; m. Robert J. Malm, Apr. 19, 1969. Sales asst. Dean Witter & Co., N.Y.C., 1959-63, asst. v.p., compliance dir., 1969-74; v.p., dir. Securities Ind. Assocs., N.Y.C., 1969-72; resident br. mgr. Kelly Services, Inc., N.Y.C., 1974-78; br. mgr. Manpower Inc., N.Y.C., 1978-81; chief exec. officer Muriel Siebert & Co., Inc., N.Y.C., 1981—; art mktg. cons. Mem. Women's Bond Club N.Y. (dir., v.p., program chmn., pres. 1980-82), Am. Cancer Soc., Sales Execs. Club, Zonta Internat. Home: 3 Hanover Sq New York NY 10005 Office: 77 Water St New York NY 10005

MALOLA, MARY E., educator; b. Evansville, Ind., May 25, 1923; d. John M. and Irene Christine M. (Heinlin) Work; A.B., Ind. State U., 1945, M.A., 1959, 6th Yr. degree, 1968; m. John C. Tranbarger, Jan. 10, 1945 (dec. 1968); 1 dau., Ann Irene Phillips; m. 2d, Mousa Asaaf Malola, Nov. 24, 1976; 1 son, Hane M. Classified advt. supr. Tribune-Star Pub. Co., Terre Haute, Ind., 1945-58; tchr. English and journalism, public relations chmn. Gerstmeyer High Sch.. Terre Haute, 1959-72, Terre Haute N. Vigo High Sch., 1972-80, Terre Haute S. Vigo High Sch., 1980—; founder 1st chpt. Quill and Scroll in local public schs., 1959. Sunday sch. supt. St. George Orthodox Ch., 1979—, sec. parish council, 1978-79, pres. ladies soc., 1978-79. AAUW fellowship grant named in her honor, 1977. Mem. NEA, Ind. State Tchrs. Assn., Vigo County Tchrs. Assn., Assn. Tchr. Educators, Nat. Assn. Journalism Dirs., Ind. Council of Tchrs. English, Nat. Council Tchrs. English, Ind. High Sch. Press Assn., AAUW (dir. Terre Haute br. 1969-76, sec. 1969-70, 1st v.p. 1971-72, pres. 1973-74), Delta Kappa Gamma. Republican. Club: Ind. State U. Wives. Contbr. to poetry anthology, 1960—; newsletter editor Vigo County Sch. Corp.; 1961-65, ARC, 1961-66. Home: 4422 S 10th St Terre Haute IN 47802 Office: 3737 S 7th St Terre Haute IN 47802

MALONE, CLAUDINE BERKELEY, fin. and mgmt. cons.; b. Louisville, May 9, 1936; d. Claude McDowell and Mary Katharine (Smith) M.; B.A., Wellesley Coll., 1963; M.B.A., Harvard U., 1972. Systems engr. IBM Corp., Washington, 1964; sr. systems analyst Crane Co., Chgo., 1966; controller, mgr. data processing Raleigh Stores, Washington, 1967-70; asst. prof. Harvard U., 1972-76, asso. prof., 1977-81; fin. and mgmt. cons., Bethesda, Md., 1981—; dir. Scott Paper Co., Campbell Soup Co., Boston Co., Dart Drug Co., Ltd. Stores, Knapp King-Size, SCA Services, Supermarkets Gen. Corp.; trustee Penn Mut. Life Ins. Co. Chmn. Bus. for Reagan-Bush Com. Mass., 1980; trustee Wellesley Coll., 1982—. C.P.A., Md. Mem. Assn. Women C.P.A.s, Wellesley Coll. Alumnae Assn. Episcopalian. Club: Washington Wellesley. Home and Office: 7026 Oak Forest Ln Bethesda MD 20817

MALONE, JEAN ARDELL, retail exec.; b. Wisconsin Dells, Wis., Mar. 13, 1930; d. Hans Arnold and Isla Marie (Stafford) Kneubuhler; B.S., U. Wis., 1964; m. Francis William Malone, June 10, 1971; 1 dau., Tara. Tchr. home econs. Est Bend (Wis.) Sch. Dist., 1964-65; owner, pres. Elsie's Inc., women's wear, Burlington, Wis., 1965—; dir. Bank of Burlington. Bd. dirs. Burlington United Fund, 1975-81; bd. dirs. Human Resource Center, Burlington, 1975—, chmn., 1978; del. Gov.'s Small Bus. Conv., 1981. Mem. Burlington C. of C. (pres. 1973), Nat. Retail Mchts. Assn., Wis. Retail Mchts. Assn., Bus. and Profl. Women's Club. Congregationalist. Club: Order Eastern Star.

MALONE, JEAN HAMBIDGE, ednl. adminstr.; b. South Bend, Ind., Nov. 23, 1954; d. Craig Ellis and Dorothy Jane (Piechorowski) Hambidge; B.S. in Edn., Butler U., 1976, M.S. in Edn., 1977; m. James Kevill Malone, July 8, 1978. Tchr., Indpls. Public Schs., 1977-78; dir. student center and activities Butler U., Indspl., 1978—; Eisenhower Meml. scholarship trustee, 1977-80. Bd. dirs. Campfire of Central Ind., 1980—. Recipient Outstanding Faculty award, Butler U., 1980. Mem. Ind. Assn. Women Deans, Adminstrs. and Counselors, Ind. Assn. Coll. Personnel Adminstrs., Nat. Assn. Women Deans, Adminstrs. and Counselors, Kappa Delta Pi, Phi Kappa Phi, Alpha Lambda Delta (nat. liaison officer), Mortar Bd. (nat. liaison officer), Kappa Kappa Gamma (Mu house corp. bd. 1981—). Roman Catholic. Office: 4600 Sunset Ave Indianapolis IN 46208

MALONE, PERRILLAH (PAT) ATKINSON, state ofcl.; b. Montgomery, Ala., Mar. 17, 1922; d. Odolph Edgar and Myrtle (Fondren) Atkinson; B.S., Oglethorpe U., 1956; M.A.T., Emory U., 1962. Asst. editor-acting editor Emory U., 1958-64; asst. project officer Ga. Dept. Pub. Health, Atlanta, 1965-68; asst. project dir. Ga. Ednl. Improvement Council, 1968-69; asso. dir. Ga. Edn. Improvement Council, 1970-71; dir. career services State Scholarship Commn., Atlanta, 1971-74; rev. coordinator Div. Phys. Health, Ga. Dept. Human Resources, Atlanta, 1974-79; project dir. So. Regional Edn. Bd., 1979-81; planner Div. Family and Children Services, Atlanta, 1982—; mem. Gov.'s Commn. on Nursing Edn. and Nursing Practice, 1972-75; book reviewer Atlanta Jour.-Constn., 1962-79. Recipient Recognition award Ga. Nursing Assn., 1976, Alumni Honor award Emory U., 1964. Mem. Nat., Ga. (Korsell award 1974) leagues for nursing, Am., Ga. public health assns. Methodist. Club: Atlanta Press. Home: 1146 Oxford Rd NE Atlanta GA 30306 Office: 618 Ponce de Leon Ave Atlanta GA 30308

MALONE, ROWENA JAMES, editor; b. Hastings, Iowa, Aug. 6, 1915; d. Mearl Arthur and Ethelyn Leota (McKie) Gable; A.B., U. Iowa, 1937; M.S., Iowa State U., 1959; m. Gerald E. Malone, Aug. 14, 1975; 1 dau., Margaret E. James. Staff research asst., writer, sec. Des Moines Register and Tribune, 1949-52; writer, asst. producer WOI-TV, 1954-55; promotion mgr., asso. editor Iowa State U. Press, Ames, 1958-63, mng. editor, 1963-81, spl. projects editor, 1981—. Mem. PEO, Phi Delta Gamma, Delta Delta Delta. Episcopalian. Home: 1116 Kennedy St Ames IA 50010 Office: ISU Press S State St Ames IA 50010

MALONEY, ELIZABETH ANN, coll. pres.; b. Baldwin, N.Y., Dec. 12, 1925; d. Francis Xavier and Julia (Mueller) M.; A.B., Coll. St. Elizabeth, Convent Station, N.J., 1947; M.A., Fordham U., 1952; postgrad. U. Notre Dame, Yeshiva U. Joined Sisters of Charity, Roman Cath. Ch., 1947; tchr. math. high schs., N.J., 1949-60; mem. faculty Coll. St. Elizabeth, 1963—, asst. to pres., 1967-70, dean studies, 1970-71, pres., 1971—; sec. Ind. Coll. Fund N.J., 1978—; bd. mgrs. Morris County Savs. Bank, 1977—. Sec. bd. trustees Hosp. St. Elizabeth. Grantee NSF, summer 1968, 69, Inst. Ednl. Mgmt., summer 1971. Mem. Assn. Ind. Colls. and Univs. N.J. Address: Coll St Elizabeth Convent Station NJ 07961

MALONEY, FLORENCE CECELIA, ednl. adminstr.; b. N.Y.C., Apr. 23, 1926; d. David Christopher and Catherine Cecelia Maloney; B.B.A., Pace U., 1962; M.S. in Edn., Hunter Coll., 1965; Ed.D. in Adminstrn. and Supervision, St. John's U., 1978. Tchr., chmn. dept. bus. edn. Sachem Central Sch. Dist., Holbrook, N.Y., 1969-70, secondary supr., 1970-73, prin. elem. sch., 1973-75, supr. curriculum, 1975-78; asst. examiner N.Y.C. Bd. Examiners, 1978-80; asst. prof. Kingsborough Community Coll., 1980—; adj. asst. prof. secretarial sci. Pace U., 1962-70. Mem. Nat. Assn. Elem. Sch. Prins., N.Y. State Assn. Supervision and Curriculum Devel., Suprs. and Adminstrs. Assn. N.Y. State, Bus. Edn. Assn. N.Y. (past pres., exec. bd. 1981—, editor BEA Jour. 1982), Gregg Shorthand Tchrs. Assn. (past pres.), Cenacle Retreat League (pres. 1978—), Delta Pi Epsilon, Delta Kappa Gamma, Phi Delta Kappa. Co-author: Legal Dictation, Machine Transcription, and Typewriting Practice, 1982; contbr. articles to profl. jours. Home: 43-34 192d St Auburndale NY 11358 Office: Kingsborough Community Coll Oriental Blvd Manhattan Beach Brooklyn NY 11235

MALONEY, MARY CATHERINE, family ct. judge; b. Peterborough, Ont., Can., June 26, 1917; d. John Richard and Mary Gertrude (Somers) Corkery; student St. Joseph's Coll.; B.A., U. Toronto; grad. Osgoode Hall Law Sch., Toronto; m. James A. Maloney, Nov. 11, 1945; children—Catherine, Martin, Maureen, Margaret. Formerly assoc. firm John R. Corkery, Q.C.; now judge Family Ct., Province of Ont., Peterborough. Mem. Ont. Family Ct. Judges Assn., Cath. Women's League. Roman Catholic. Office: Provincial Court Court House Peterborough ON K9H 3M3 Canada

MALONEY, PATRICE F., chemist; b. Utica, N.Y.; d. Jack A. and Susan B. (Szot) M.; B.S., Utica Coll., Syracuse U., 1968; postgrad. SUNY, Binghamton, 1968-69. Metall. technician Gen. Electric Co., Utica, summers, 1967-69, specialist in metallography, 1969-73, specialist tech. assignment, 1973-75, specialist materials evaluation, Utica, 1975-81, supr. adminstrv. services and tng., 1981—; teaching asst. SUNY, Binghamton, 1968-69. Mem. Am. Soc. Quality Control (sec.), Assn. Gen. Electric Profl. Employees (sec.). Roman Catholic. Clubs: GE Ski, Utica Tennis Assn. Home: 91 Bedford Dr Whitesboro NY 13492 Office: Gen Electric Co French Rd MD 106 Utica NY 13503

MALONEY, THERESE ADELE, ins. co. exec.; b. Quincy, Mass., Sept. 15, 1929; d. James Henry and F. Adele (Powers) M.; B.A. in Econs., Coll. St. Elizabeth, Convent Station, N.J., 1951. With Liberty Mut. Ins. Co., Boston, 1951—, asst. v.p., asst. mgr. nat. risks, 1974-77, v.p., asst. mgr. nat. risks, 1977-79, v.p., mgr. nat. risks, 1979—, pres. subs. Liberty Mut. (Bermuda) Ltd., 1981—; mem. faculty Inst. Inst., Northeastern U., Boston, 1969-74; mem. adv. bd., risk mgmt. studies Ins. Inst. Am. C.P.C.U. Mem. Soc. C.P.C.U.s (past pres. Boston chpt.). Club: Univ. (Boston). Office: Liberty Mus Ins Co 175 Berkeley St Boston MA 02117

MALOOLY, MARY HILL (MRS. DONALD ALBERT MALOOLY), writer, civic worker; b. Austin, Tex., Feb. 10, 1928; d. Daniel Lafayette and Florence Chalfont (Peak) Hill; student U. Tex., El Paso, 1945-48; B.A., U. Ala., 1949, M.A., 1951; m. Donald A. Malooly, July 9, 1955; children—Donald Ellis, Mary Elizabeth, Mark Hill. Radio continuity writer Sta. KEPO, El Paso, 1949-50; mng. editor U. Ala. Alumni News, Tuscaloosa, 1950; script TV writer Sta. KTSM-TV, El Paso, 1951-55; freelance writer, El Paso, 1951—; vol. tutor in field. Bd. dirs. Vols. Pub. Schs., 1975-76; mem. bd. Potter-Randall County Med. Aux.; mem. Art Mus. Guild, Symphony Guild. Mem. El Paso County Hist. Soc., C. of C., U. Tex.-El Paso Women's Aux., El Paso County Med. Soc. Aux. (pres. 1977-78), Nat. Soc. Arts and Letters (v.p. 1953-55), AAUW (v.p. 1954-55), DAR, Delta Gamma (El Paso alumni pres. 1953-55, 75-77, sec. nat. scholarship com.), Theta Sigma Phi, Alpha Chi, Delta Sigma Phi. Roman Catholic. Author: TV scripts, newspaper articles in field. Research in med. history. Address: 3920 Kileen Amarillo TX 79109

MALOUF, ALICE ANN, radio sta. exec.; b. Lowell, Mass., Dec. 13, 1925; d. Abraham Elias and Zickie Mary (Hanna) M. Supply chief U.S. Marine Corps, Washington, 1949-58; crystal technician Epsco, Inc., Cambridge, Mass., 1958-63; traffic ops. mgr. Gateway Broadcasting, Inc., New Kensington, Pa., 1963—. Democrat. Roman Catholic. Home: PO Box 33 New Kensington PA 15068 Office: 810 5th Ave New Kensington PA 15068

MALSON, NANCY CARLEEN, educator; b. Jeffersonville, Ohio, Apr. 10, 1940; d. Carl Russell and Virginia Lois (Griffith) Allen; R.N., Riverside-White Cross Sch. Nursing, Columbus, Ohio, 1961; B.A. in Elem. Edn., Cedarville Coll., 1975; m. Donald W. Malson, Dec. 21, 1975; 1 dau., Karla Elise Johnson. Clin. instr. psychiat. nursing Columbus (Ohio) State Hosp., 1962-67; staff/sch. nurse Fayette County Health Dept., Washington Court House, Ohio, 1967-70; Title I remedial reading tchr. Miami Trace Local Sch. Dist., Washington Court House, 1970-73, elem. tchr., 1973-75; coordinator, instr. orientation to health occupations Morris County Vocat.-Tech Sch., Denville, N.J., 1978-79, coordinator, instr. practical nursing program, 1979-81, mem. self-evaluation steering com. and conf. planning com.; tchr. 6th grade Mt. Olive Twp. Sch. System, N.J., 1982—; free lance writer including curriculum notebook for practical nursing, Morris County Vocat.-Tech. Sch., 1980; co-author articles on internat. muzzle loading competition and hunting; contbr. articles to publs., 1976—; active profl. nurses assn., Ohio, 1965-75. Mem. Nat. Muzzle Loading Rifle Assn. Am., Ohio Gun Collectors Assn., U.S. Internat. Muzzle Loading Team (yearly silver medal for marksmanship, Madrid, 1978 fund raising chmn., gold medal, Bisley, Eng., 1977, silver and bronze medals, Bisley, 1979, officer, 1979-82). Republican. Presbyterian. Club: North Morris County Women's.

MALTBY, HAZEL FARROW, weaver; b. San Francisco, Dec. 26, 1917; d. Richard Harry and Effie Isabelle (Hardin) Johnstone; student San Francisco State Coll., 1935-36; m. Jack Allen Maltby, Nov. 11, 1974; children—Charlene Sue McAuley, Claudia Jane Polzl. Tchr.-lectr. weaving Foothill Community Coll., Los Altos, Calif., De Anza Coll., Cupertino, Calif., 1973-74, Nat. Conf. Handweavers, San Francisco, 1974; pvt. tchr., 1970—; one-woman exhbns. include Menlo Park Civic Center, libraries and banks in Palo Alto, Woodside, Los Altos, San Jose, Calif., 1972-75, also exhibited San Jose Fine Art Mus., Triton Mus., San Jose, Calif. Art Festival, Nat. Conf. Handweavers, No. Calif. Handweavers Conf., Bay Area Arts and Crafts, Internat. Weaving exhbn., others; author: Painting Warps, 1974; group exhbns. include Los Vegas Art League, 1971, Tex. Fine Arts League, 1974, Internat. Weaving Exhbn., Kouvola, Finland, 1977; 6 tapestries commd. by Epiphany Episc. Ch., San Carlos, Calif.; other commns. indsl. offices and pvt. collectors. Mem. Palo Alto Art Club (v.p.), Tramporus Weaving Guild (past pres.), Handweavers Guild Am., Bay Area Arts and Crafts Guild, Loom and Shuttle Weaving Guild, Calif. PTA (hon. life; past pres. San Carlos). Clubs: Order Eastern Star, Order Jobs Daus. Address: 118 Plazoleta St Los Gatos CA 95030

MALTHOUSE, NANCY SIBBLES, computer systems engr.; b. Mobile, Ala., Nov. 16, 1943; d. Grant B. and Elma Sibbles; student Fla. State U., 1962-65, U.S.C., 1965-66, Clemson U., 1966-68; B.S., U. Tenn., 1969, M.S., 1975; m. June 26, 1965. Research and lab. technician ORTEC, Inc., Oak Ridge, 1969-72; programmer Oak Ridge Nat. Lab., 1972-75; programmer Boeing Computer Services, McLean, Va., 1975-78; systems engr. The MITRE Corp., McLean, 1978—; pres. M-Squared Systems, Inc., Springfield, Va., 1982—; vice chmn. task force on edn. and tng. software profls. Commn. on Software Issues for 80's. Mem. Assn. Computing Machinery, IEEE, Women in Info. Processing, Nat. Council Career Women, Nat. Assn. Female Execs. Club: Toastmasters (past pres.). Home: 5918 Veranda Dr Springfield VA 22152 Office: 1820 Dolley Madison Dr McLean VA 22102

MALZ, GRACE CHARLENE, personnel adminstr.; b. Chgo., Jan. 6, 1930; d. Chester Richard and Ethel Leona (Young) Chaney; B.S. cum laude, U. Akron, 1964; m. Sam D. Malz, Dec. 31, 1966; children—John, Michael, Stephen. Long distance operator Star Telephone, Seville, Ohio, 1945-47; long distance supr. No. Ohio Telephone, Seville, 1947-48; sec. Western & So. Life, Wadsworth, Ohio, Cleve., 1948-50; policy typist Westfield Cos., Westfield Center, Ohio, 1953-58, sec. to v.p. personnel, 1958-63, personnel asst., 1963-72, personnel adminstr., 1972—; v.p. Pleasant Hill Mgmt., Seville, Ohio, 1969—; v.p. Gracelane, Inc., Seville, 1978—; sec. Country Manor Square, Seville, 1978—. Mem. Medina County Joint Vocat. Sch. Adv. Bds., 1974-81; trustee Village Seville Bd. Public Affairs, 1979-82; mem. Seville Village Planning and Zoning, Commn., 1979-80; chmn. World's Largest Yard Sale, Seville, 1981; program chmn. Capt. Bates Festival, Seville, 1982; mem. Cloverleaf High Sch. Adv. Bd., 1979-81; mem. Wayne Coll. Adv. Bd., Orrville, Ohio, 1978-81. Recipient Scholarship, U. Akron, 1961, 62, 63. Mem. Am. Soc. Personnel Adminstrn. (chpt. pres. 1976-77, nat. com. 1976-78; region 8 publicity and program coms.; chmn. Akron Merit award 1976—), AAUW, Landlords Council, Seville C. of C. (exec. com. 1979-82, pres.-elect 1983. Methodist. Clubs: Order Eastern Star (past matron), Order Rainbow (past mother adv.), Bus. Women's Investment (v.p.), White Shrine. Home: PO Box 175 109 Pleasant View Dr Seville OH 44273 Office: 1 Park Circle Westfield Center OH 44251

MAMALIS, TANYA JOY, bus. ofcl.; b. Salinas, Calif., Apr. 29, 1948; d. Solon and Joyce (Economou) M.; student Am. U. Beirut (Lebanon), 1967-70. Staff asst. Presdl. Personnel Office, White House, Washington, 1976-77; personnel mgr. Beveridge, Fairbanks & Diamond, Washington, 1977-78, Wheelabrator-Frye Inc., Hampton, N.H., 1978-79; secretarial supr., personnel adminstr., mgr. report prodn. McKinsey & Co., N.Y.C., 1979—. Mem. Internat. Assn. Women in Personnel, Am. Mgmt. Assn., Nat. Assn. for Female Execs. Republican. Greek Orthodox. Office: 55 E 52nd St New York NY 10022

MAMIN, ESTHA LEE GINSBERG (BEBE), real estate broker; b. Dallas; d. Jacob B. and Hinda (Bernstein) Ginsberg; B.A., U. Tex., 1945; student Lumbleau Sch. Real Estate, 1955-56; children—Cynthia Anne, Victoria Lynn, H. Jonathon, Marshall Timothy. Research asst. Cancer Lab., U. Tex. Med. Coll., Galveston; biochemist, pathology lab. James Walker Meml. Hosp., Wilmington, N.C., Tex. Children's Hosp., Dallas, 1946-47; research asst., pathology dept. Harvard Med. Coll., 1947-48; med. technologist, bus. mgr. doctor's office, Pasadena, Calif., 1948-56; real estate salesman H. H. Armistead Co., Pasadena, 1956-64, broker Mamin Co., Pasadena, 1964—. Mem. Women's Civic League. Mem. Pasadena Bd. Realtors (edn. com. 1966, mem. com. 1967, sec. womens council, 1967), Calif. Real Estate Assn., Nat. Assn. Real Estate Bds., World Affairs Council Los Angeles, Town Hall, LWV, AAUW. Clubs: Officers Wives, Curtain Raiser. Home and Office: 161 S Oak Knoll Ave Pasadena CA 91101

MAMON, DORIS ELAINE, mgmt. cons.; b. Chgo., Jan. 31, 1943; d. Julius S. and Helen M. Bonk; B.S., Mundelein Coll., 1976; M.B.A., Marquette U., 1981; M.T., St. Mary of Nazareth Sch. Med. Tech., 1964; children—Deborah, Vincent. Sect. head immunohematology Alexian Bros. Med. Center, Elk Grove Village, Ill., 1969-78; supr. implementation Medistat, Milw., 1978-80; supr. product analyst Tymshare Med. Systems, Brookfield, Wis., 1980-81; cons. The Kennedy Group, Menlo Park, Calif., 1981—. Mem. Am. Hosp. Assn., Am. Soc. Clin. Pathologists, Am. Assn. Blood Banks.

MANAGO, LINDA FANETTA, gas pipeline co. acct.; b. Charlotte, N.C., Feb. 6, 1954; d. Frank and Mildred Luetta (McIver) M.; B.S. in Commerce cum laude, N.C. Central U., 1976. Jr. analyst PCA Internat., Inc., Matthews, N.C., 1977-79; cost acct. Hosiery div. Hanes Corp., Winston-Salem, N.C., 1980; gas acct. SONAT, Inc., So. Natural Gas Co., Birmingham, Ala., 1980—. Recipient award for outstanding services to sr. class N.C. Central U., 1976. Mem. Nat. Assn. Female Execs., Nat. Assn. Black Accts. (founder Winston-Salem chpt. 1980, treas. chpt. 1979), N.C. Central U. Alumni Assn. (v.p. chpt. 1979), Alpha Kappa Alpha. Home: 1008 86th St N Birmingham AL 35206 Office: PO Box 2563 Birmingham AL 35282

MANCHEE, KATHERYN HAIT, historian, lectr.; b. Bklyn., Sept. 21, 1904; d. James Merritt and Belle (Silvey) Hait; student Parsons Sch. Art, 1923, Newark Sch. Art, 1924, Western Res. U., 1941-43; m. William F. Dorflinger, Apr. 1927 (dec. 1944); 1 dau., June (Mrs. John Alexander Hardy, Jr.); m. 2d, Arthur Leavens Manchee, Sept. 21, 1957; stepchildren—Mrs. R.W. Bachelder, Mrs. M.D. Brown, Mrs. Harry Wortman. Instr., lectr. Cleve. Mus. Art, 1941-44; lectr., historian Steuben Glass, N.Y.C., 1946-48; dir. advt. and publicity Midhurst Importing Corp., N.Y.C., 1952-54; dir. pub. relations and product promotion Fostoria Glass Co., N.Y.C., 1954-58. Mem. Jr. League Morristown (N.J.), 1930-39, 45-54, Jr. League Cleve., 1939-44; vice chmn. jr. council Cleve. Mus. Art, 1943-44; vol. Cleve. Orch. Woman's Com., 1942-44, ARC drives, Cleve., 1939-44; leader Girl Scouts U.S.A., Cleve., 1934-35. Fellow Met. Mus. Art (life); mem. Nat. Home Fashions League, Am. Women in Radio and TV, Nat. Soc. Colonial Dames, China Inst. Am., Asia Soc., Fgn. Policy Assn., English Speaking Union, Soc. Woman Geographers, Clubwomen's League Patriotic Services, Mus. Natural History, Newark Mus., Corning Mus. Glass, Drama League N.Y. Presbyterian. Clubs; Colony (N.Y.C.); Garden of Onteora. Contbr. articles profl. publs.

MANCHESTER, MELISSA TONI, singer, song writer; b. Bronx, N.Y., Feb. 15, 1951; d. David and Ruth Manchester; grad. High Sch. Performing Arts, N.Y.C., 1969; m. Larry Brezner, Feb. 13, 1971. Singer with Bette Midler, 1971-72; rec. artist Bell and Arista records; recordings include Home to Myself, Bright Eyes, Melissa (Gold Album award), Better Days and Happy Endings, 1975, Help Is On The Way, 1976; pres., owner Rumanian Pickleworks Music. Recipient Best New Female Vocalist of Year award Cashbox mag., 1974; New Female Vocalist of Year award Billboard mag., 1975; Wright award for Midnight Blue, Broadcast Music Inc., 1975. Mem. Broadcast Music Inc., AFTRA, Screen Actors Guild, Am. Fedn. Musicians. Address: 5451 Marathon St Los Angeles CA 90038 *

MANCINA-BATINICH, MARY ELLEN, sch. adminstr.; b. Eveleth, Minn.; d. James V. and Mary (Noldin) Mancina; B.S. in Music Edn., Northwestern U., 1946, M.A., 1958, Ph.D., 1963; M.A., DePaul U., 1980; m. Alex Batinich, Apr. 20, 1946. Tchr., Chgo. Public Schs., 1949-62, master tchr., 1962-65, adminstr., 1965-80; dir. Italians in Chicago Oral History Project, U. Ill., Chgo., 1979-82. Pres., Ill. State Reading Council, 1970-71. Mem. Joint Civic Com. Italian Americans (founder women's div. 1965, scholarship com. 1968), Am. Italian Hist. Assn. (founder, pres. Midwest chpt. 1974, editor newsletter 1977), Am. Italian War Veterans Aux. (founder, pres. Victor Arrigo Post 1974-78, scholarship com. 1972—, pres. Dept. Ill. 1978-79), Soc. History Edn., Internat. Reading Assn., Midwest Women's Center Ill. Agenda, Chgo. Hist. Soc., Range Hist. Soc., Inst. Plurality and Group Identity, Phi Delta Kappa. Author: Minnesota Souvenir Coloring Book for Children, 1965; Italian American Ethnic Studies Guide, 1972; Historic City, 1978;

Invest in the Future: A College Education, 1974; The Italian Immigrant Women in North America, 1980. Office: 228 N La Salle St Chicago IL 60601

MANCINI, JOANNE SICA, pharmacist; b. Phila., Dec. 3, 1949; d. Joseph James and Esther (Maggio) Sica; B.Sc., Phila. Coll. Pharmacy and Sci., 1972; postgrad. St. Joseph's U., 1980—; m. Anthony Joseph Mancini, Sept. 23, 1978. Pharmacist, Parkview Hosp., Phila., 1970-77; asst. dir. pharmacy Roxborough Meml. Hosp., Phila., 1977-81, dir. pharmacy, 1981—. Mem. Am. Soc. Hosp. Pharmacists, Am. Pharm. Assn., Pa. Pharm. Assn., Pa. Soc. Hosp. Pharmacists, Delaware Valley Soc. Hosp. Pharmacists, Delaware Valley Women in Pharmacy (pres.-elect 1982), Lambda Kappa Sigma. Democrat. Roman Catholic. Club: King of Prussia Racquetball. Office: Roxborough Meml Hosp 5800 Ridge Ave Philadelphia PA 19128

MANDEL, MRS., LEON (CAROLA PANERAI MANDEL), found. trustee; b. Havana, Cuba; d. Camilo and Elvira (Bertini) Panerai; ed. pvt. schs., Havana and Europe; m. Leon Mandel, Apr. 9, 1938. Mem. women's bd. Northwestern Meml. Hosp., Chgo. Trustee Carola and Leon Mandel Fund Loyola U., Chgo. Life mem. Chgo. Hist. Soc., Guild of Chgo. Hist. Soc., Smithsonian Assos., Nat. Skeet Shooting Assn. Frequently named among Ten Best Dressed Women in U.S.; chevalier Confrerie des Chevaliers du Tastevin. Capt. All-Am. Women's Skeet Team, 1952, 53, 54, 55, 56; only woman to win a men's nat. championship, 20 gauge, 1954, also high average in world over men, 1956, in 12 gauge with 99.4 per cent; European women's live bird shooting championship, Venice, Italy, 1957, Porto, Portugal, 1961; European woman's target championship, Torino, Italy, 1958; woman's world champion live-bird shooting, Sevilla, Spain, 1959. Named to Nat. Skeet Shooting Assn. Hall of Fame, 1970. Mem. Soc. Four Arts. Club: Everglades (Palm Beach, Fla.). Home: 324 Barton Ave Palm Beach FL 33480

MANDEL, MARJORIE COE, civic worker; b. Haverhill, Mass., Mar. 14, 1923; d. Erving Harding and Fannie Augusta (Noyes) Malcolm; student Haverhill public schs.; m. John Rhodes Mandel, Jan. 27, 1945; children—Lynn Rhodes, William Coe, James Burgess, Jonathan Chase. With Liberty Mut. Ins., Boston, 1942-43, Western Elec. Co., Haverhill, 1944. Bd. dirs. Haverhill Day Nursery, 1950-51, Haverhill Girl Scouts U.S.A. Council, 1956-58, Haverhill Girls Club, 1958; v.p. School St PTA, Haverhill, 1960-62, pres., 1962-64; corr. sec. Republican Conservative Action Club of Union County (N.J.), 1968-72; bd. dirs. Westfield Citizens Orgn., 1970-74; v.p. Westfield Women's Rep. Club, 1972-74; legis. com. Westfield Sch. Bd., 1973-74; corr. sec. Leadership Found. N.J., 1974-78; pres. Westfield Women's Rep. Club, 1975-79; bd. govs. N.J. Fedn. Rep. Women, 1976-80; bd. trustees Rep. Conservative Action Club Union County, 1979-80; campaign mgr. N.J. Assemblyman Chuck Hardwick, 1979. Mem. Sons and Daus. 1st Settlers of Newbury (Mass.). Baptist. Home: N Main St Wolfeboro NH 03894

MANDELBAUM, DOROTHY ROSENTHAL, psychologist; b. N.Y.C., May 18, 1935; d. Benjamin Daniel and Rachael (Osofsky) Rosenthal; A.B. cum laude, Hunter Coll., 1956; Ph.D., Bryn Mawr Coll., 1975; m. Seymour Jacob Mandelbaum, Aug. 19, 1956; children—David Gideon, Judah Michael, Betsy Daniella. Tchr., Valley Road Sch., Princeton, N.J., 1956-59; instr. ednl. psychology dept. Temple U., Phila., summer 1970; asst. prof. dept. edn. Rutgers, The State U., Camden, N.J., 1974-80, asso. prof., 1980—, dir. women's studies, 1981—. Chmn., Jr. Faculty Wives, Carnegie Inst. Tech., 1960-61; bd. dirs. LWV, 1961-64; capt. Pitts. Symphony fund dr., 1961-62. Recipient Claude Kleinfelter award, 1956; named Woman of Day, Sta. WRYT, 1964; AAUW predoctoral fellow, 1973-74. Mem. Am. Psychol. Assn., AAUP, Jean Piaget Soc., Soc. Psychol. Study of Social Issues, Soc. Research in Child Devel., Kappa Delta Pi (counselor 1975-77). Contbr. articles on psychology of women and med. edn. to profl. publs. Author: Work, Marriage, and Motherhood: The Career Persistence of Female Physicians, 1981. Home: 2290 N 53d St Philadelphia PA 19131 Office: Rutgers U Camden NJ 08102

MANDELL, ELAINE, clin. pathologist; b. N.Y.C., Nov. 11, 1952; d. Max and Ruth Adele (Spitzer) Mandell; B.S. in M.T., SUNY, Buffalo, 1973; postgrad. C.W. Post Coll., 1982—, M.P.H., 1981. Med. technologist N.Y. U. Med. Center, N.Y.C., 1973-79; tech. specialist diagnostic oncology N. Shore Univ. Hosp., Manhasset, N.Y., 1979-81; asst. scientist cytoanalytical systems Technicon Corp., Tarrytown, N.Y., 1981—; cons. Westchester County Med. Center, 1981—. Mem. Am. Soc. Clin. Pathologists, Am. Soc. Public Adminstrs., Pi Alpha Alpha. Contbr. articles to profl. jours. Home: 69 60 108 St Forest Hills NY 11375 Office: 511 Benedict Ave Tarrytown NY 10591

MANDELL, ELIZABETH ELLEN, psychologist; b. Cin., Jan. 31, 1936; d. Robert Webster and Florence May (McClure) Kehr; B.A., Reed Coll., 1957; M.A., U. Colo., 1959; Ph.D., U.S.C., 1969; m. Richard Donald Mandell, Dec. 28, 1957; children—Victoria, Eleanor, Maximillian, Isabelle. Statistician, Sch. of Public Health, U. Calif., Berkeley, 1960-61; asst. prof., U. S.C., Columbia, 1971-72, research asso., 1969—, dir. Title IX Sex Desegregation Tng. Inst., 1978-80; cons. S.C. Commn. on Aging, 1973-81; founder, chmn. bd. trustees Resource Assos., Inc., 1976—. Trustee, Palmetto Sch. Dist.; S.C. steering com. ERA, 1977—. Mem. Am. Psychol. Assn., Gerontol. Soc. Am., Assn. for Women in Psychology, S.C. Gerontol. Soc. (founding pres. 1978-80), S.C. Psychol. Assn., Capitol Bus. and Profl. Woman's Club. Democrat. Contbr. articles in field to profl. jours. Home: 814 Barnwell St Columbia SC 29201 Office: Senate Plaza USC Columbia SC 29208

MANDELL, FRAN GARE, writer, pub. co. exec.; b. Jersey City, Dec. 5, 1939; d. David A. and Henrietta (Rich) Rhein; B.A., Fairleigh Dickinson U., 1963, M.A., 1965; cert. N.Y. Sch. Interior Design, 1966; M.S., U. Bridgeport, 1980; Naturopathic Dr., Braintridge Forest Sch., Eng., 1977; m. Marshall Mandell, Oct. 21, 1979; children by previous marriage—David Gare, Marc Gare. Owner, Wynken, Blynken & Nod, Englewood, N.J., 1967-70; pres. Nutri-Plan, Inc., N.Y.C., 1975—; pres. MarFran Publs., Inc. (name now Gare Inc.), Basket Magic, Norwalk, Conn., 1979—. Mem. Assn. Food Technologists, Am. Soc. Journalists and Authors, N.Y. Acad. Scis. Jewish. Club: Atrium. Author: (with Atkins and Monica) Dr. Atkins Diet Revolution, 1972; (with Monica) Dr. Atkin's Diet Cook Book, 1974; (with Monica) The Super Energy Diet Cook Book, 1978; (with Bomser) Dr. Mandell's Allergy Cookbook, 1980; (with Alan Pressman) A Complete Guide to Chiropractic, 1981; The Nutrition Cookbook, 1982; (with Marshall Mandell) It's Not Your Fault You're Fat; contbr. articles to profl. jours. Home: 180 Steephill Rd Weston CT 06883 Office: 3A Brush St Norwalk CT 06850

MANDIBERG, MYRTLE, psychologist; b. N.Y.C., July 1, 1918; d. Samuel and Sadie (Friedman) M.; B.A., Bklyn. Coll., 1938; M.A., U. Pa., 1940. Intern Wayne County Gen. Hosp., Eloise, Mich., 1940-41, staff psychologist, 1941-42; tchr. nursery sch. Detroit Bd. Edn., 1942-44; staff psychologist Detroit Recorders Ct. Psychopathic Clinic, 1944-49; psychotherapist Devereux Ranch Sch., Santa Barbara, Calif., 1949-51; supr. Reiss-Davis Child Guidance Clinic, Los Angeles, 1959-62; cons., coordinator profl. services Los Angeles Child Devel. Center, 1979—, also pvt. practice child psychology, 1951—; assoc. in psychology UCLA, 1978—. Mem. Am. Psychol. Assn., Calif. State Psychol. Assn., Los Angeles County Psychol. Assn., Assn. Child Psychoanalysis. Home and Office: 1470 Glendon Ave Los Angeles CA 90024

MANDRELL, BARBARA ANN, entertainer; b. Houston, Dec. 25, 1948; d. Irby Matthew and Mary Ellen (McGill) M.; grad. high sch.; m. Kenneth Lee Dudney, May 28, 1967; children—Kenneth Matthew, Jaime Nicole. Country music singer and entertainer, 1959—; performed throughout U.S. and in various fgn. countries; mem. Grand Ole Opry, Nashville, 1972—; appeared in TV variety series The Barbara Mandrell Show, 1980-82. Named Miss Oceanside (Calif.), 1965; Most Promising Female Singer, Acad. Country Music, 1971, Female Vocalist of Year, 1979; Female Vocalist of Year, Music City News Cover awards, 1979, Country Music Assn., 1979, 81; entertainer of the Year Country Music Assn., 1980, 81. Mem. Musicians Union, Screen Actors Guild, AFTRA, Country Music Assn. (dir.), Assn. Country Entertainers. Mem. Order Eastern Star. Home: PO Box 332 Hendersonville TN 37075

MANFORD, BARBARA ANN, mezzo-soprano; b. St. Augustine, Fla., Nov. 13, 1929; d. William Floyd and Margaret (Kemper) Manford; Mus.B. in Voice, Fla. State U., 1951, Mus.M., 1970; studied with L. Palazzini, A. Strano, Japelli, E. Nikolaidi, E. Joseph. Appearances in Europe, performing major roles in 12 leading opera houses, 1951-68, with condrs. including Alfred Strano, Felice Cilario, Robert Shaw, Arnold Gamson, Guiseppe Patané, Ottavio Ziino, also numerous concerts and recitals in Paris and throughout Italy and Belgium; performed in world premiere Fugitives (C. Floyd), Fla. State U., Tallahassee, 1950; chosen by Gian Carlo Menotti for leading role in world premiere The Leper, Fla. State U., 1970; numerous radio, TV, and concert appearances, U.S., 1968—; artist-in-residence, asso. prof. voice Ball State U., Muncie. Ind., 1970—; numerous recs. Semi-finalist vocal contest, Parma, Italy, 1964; winner contest, Lonigo, Italy, 1965. Mem. Nat. Assn. Tchrs. Singing, Chgo. Artists Assn., Am. Tchrs. Nat. Assn., Sigma Alpha Iota, Pi Kappa Lambda. Christian Scientist. Home: 104 Colonial Crest Apts Muncie IN 47304 Office: Ball State Univ Muncie IN 47306

MANFREDO, MARY ANN, retail exec.; b. Tehachapi, Calif., Sept. 15, 1913; d. John and Pauline (Klaich) Krilanovich; grad. Fresno Tech. Sch., 1934; m. Al Manfredo, Dec. 17, 1938. Model, San Francisco, 1947-72; owner, mgr. Wicker Garden Gallery, Morro Bay, Calif.; owner Manfredo Sq. Shopping Center; decorator, artist. Mem. Morro Bay Art Assn. Roman Catholic. Club: Quota. Office: 3118 N Main St Morro Bay CA 93442

MANFREDONIA, NANCY DIEHL, environ. orgn. exec.; b. N.Y.C., Aug. 21, 1943; d. Norton Alphonsus and Dorothy Elizabeth (Miller) Diehl; student Ladycliff Coll., Highland Falls, N.Y., 1961-63; B.S. in Fgn. Service, Georgetown U., 1965; postgrad. Queens Coll., CCNY, 1968; m. Peter Manfredonia, June 26, 1965; children—Kathryn, Dorothy. Claims rep. Social Security Adminstrn., U.S. HEW, Patchogue, N.Y., 1965-70; legislative asst. County of Suffolk, Riverhead, N.Y., 1976-77; lectr., writer, Central Islip, N.Y., 1971—; exec. dir. L.I. Greenbelt Trail Conf., Inc., Central Islip, 1977—; bd. dirs. Fire Island Wilderness Area Com., 1979—; mem. Congressman Thomas Downey's Sci. and Energy Adv. Com., 1976-78; mem. adv. com. Save Our Farms, 1977—; mem. Suffolk County Council on Environ. Quality, 1980—; founder L.I. Greenbelt Trail, 1978. 2d v.p. Suffolk County Police Athletic League, 1975—; chmn. Citizens for a Clean Environment, 1975—; coordinator Islip Town Fair Housing Practices Com., 1977-79; founding mem. Suffolk Women's Polit. Caucus, 1971-74; committeewoman Democratic party, 1974—. Recipient Environ. award N.Y. State Council Environ. Advs., 1975; Regional Spl. award of merit EPA, 1979, L.I. Leadership award L.I. Assn. Commerce and Industry, 1979. Mem. L.I. Women's Network, Phi Beta Kappa, Pi Sigma Alpha. Home and Office: 23 Deer Path Rd Central Islip NY 11722

MANGANO, ROSEMARY, writer, advt. agy. exec.; b. N.Y.C., Nov. 11, 1947; d. Constantino Louis and Adele Rose (Dergentis) M.; student Lab. Inst., 1964-66, New Sch. Social Research, 1971-75, Center for N.Y.C. Affairs, 1973, N.Y. U., 1974, 80, Womanschool, 1975. Copywriter, Montgomery Ward & Co., N.Y.C., 1966-68, Allied Stores Corp., 1969-70; freelance writer and editor, N.Y.C., 1970-75; assoc. creative dir., partner Tatham-Laird & Kudner, N.Y.C., 1978—. Promotion and publicity dir. Francis Lewis Civic Assn., N.Y.C., 1969-73; judge Caples awards. Mem. Media Educators Assn., Direct Mktg. Creative Guild. Plays include: The Going-Away Present, 1971; Fame and Fortune, 1973; Bobby Fortune, 1975. Office: 605 3d Ave New York NY 10016

MANGE, JUDITH, phys. therapist, adminstr.; b. St. Louis, July 8, 1946; d. Willard Lesman and Bernice (Quicksilver) M.; student Ind. U., 1964-66; B.S., Washington U. Med. Sch., St. Louis, 1968; M.B.A. (grantee), U. Mo., St. Louis, 1980. Staff phys. therapist Jewish Hosp., St. Louis, 1968-71, supr. phys. therapy, 1971-78; housing coordinator Convenient House, St. Louis, 1980; dir. phys. therapy services Irene Walter Johnson Inst. Rehab., St. Louis, 1980-82; hospice cons., St. Louis, 1982—; mem. admissions com., phys. therapy program Washington U., 1979—, lectr., 1979—. Bd. dirs. Am. Cancer Soc. Mem. Mo. Hospice Orgn. (treas.), Nat. Hosp. Organ. (chmn. planning ann. meeting), Am. Phys. Therapy Assn. (treas. Mo., chmn. St. Louis), Mo. Phys. Therapy Assn., Gerontological Soc., Jewish.

MANGELS, GAIL NEILSON, retail buy; b. Talbot County, Md., May 30, 1949; d. Walter Bernard and Dorothy Harcourt (Noble) M.; student Dickinson Coll., Carlisle, Pa., 1967-68; m. David George McCulloch, May 21, 1977; 1 son, Brae Noble McCulloch. Mgr. car delivery center Chrysler Co. Mil. Sales, Bremen, W. Ger., 1971-75; apt. leasing agt. Lincoln Property, Houston, 1977; constrn. supt. Harris Devel. Corp., Houston, 1978-81; sales supr., apparel buyer Children's Collection, Houston, 1981—. Lic. real estate salesman, Tex. Mem. Nat. Assn. Women in Constrn. Home: 10167 Oakberry St Houston TX 77042 Office: 1717 Post Oak Blvd Houston TX 77056

MANGIN-ANIEBONA, JEAN LOUISE, clin. social worker, psychotherapist; b. S.I., N.Y., July 11, 1942; d. Leon Francis and Louise Bannaker (Chase) Mangin; B.S., N.Y. U., 1967; M.S.W., Smith Coll., Northampton, Mass., 1973. Caseworker, N.Y.C. Bur. Child Welfare, 1969-71; asst. psychiat. social worker Creedmoor State Psychiat. Hosp., 1971-72; psychiat. social worker Brookdale Hosp., Bklyn., 1973-75; fellow Postgrad. Center for Mental Health, N.Y.C., 1975-79, staff therapist, tchr., 1979—; pvt. practice psychoanalysis and psychotherapy, N.Y.C. Mem. Assn. Black Social Workers N.Y. Home: 46 Henry St New York NY 11201 Office: 210 E 15th St New York NY 10003

MANGUBAT, JUDITH RÉGNIER, customs insp.; b. Washington, Mar. 12, 1949; d. Cornelio and Ann Elizabeth (Price) M.; B.A., Mich. State U., 1971. Substitute tchr. Prince George's County Bd. Edn., Md., 1970-71; customs insp. trainee U.S. Customs Service, Phila., 1971-73, journeyman insp., 1973-77, sr. customs insp., 1977-80, supervisory customs insp., 1980-82, asst. chief insp., 1981, customs insp., 1982—, instr. treasury enforcement communications system Phila. dist., inspection and control field rep. customs effectiveness measurement program, Hispanic employment coordinator Phila. dist., 1973-80. Bd. dirs. Pa. SER/JOBS for Progress Inc., 1974-82; devel. council Mich. State U., 1975-79; bd. advs. Acción Puertorriqueña, 1975-82; task force on Hispanic concerns Fed. Regional Council; adv. bd. Nat. Ednl. Services Center, League of United Latin Am. Citizens, Phila., del. nat. conv., 1975-79; steering com. Society Hill Towers Condominium Buyers Assn.; life mem. Pearl S. Buck Found. Recipient Spl. Achievement award U.S. Dept. Treasury, 1976; named to Mich. State U. Kedzie Assos., 1976, 77, 78. Mem. Nat. Assn. Female Execs., Am. Mgmt. Assn., Nat. Treasury Employees Union, ACLU (life), Mich. State U. Alumni Assn. (life), NOW, Phila. Zool. Soc. (life), Mensa, Phi Beta Kappa. Lutheran. Clubs: Mich. State U. President's, Fraternal Order of Police. Home: 3514 55th Ave Hyattsville MD 20784 Office: US Customs Service Room 4417 1301 Constitution Ave NW Washington DC 20229

MANIATES, MARIA RIKA, musicologist, educator; b. Toronto, Ont., Can., Mar. 30, 1937; d. Euripides and Sophia (Samaras) M.; A.R.C.T., Royal Conservatory of Music, Toronto, 1958; B.A., U. Toronto, 1960; M.A., Columbia U., 1962, Ph.D., 1965. Reader music Columbia U., N.Y.C., 1962-63, vis. prof., 1976; lectr. U. Toronto, 1965-66, asst. prof., 1966-70, asso. prof., 1970-74, prof., 1974—, chmn. dept. music history and lit., 1973-78. Music fellow Victoria Coll., 1979-82; Connaught sr. fellow in the humanities, 1982-83; grantee in field. Mem. Internat. Musicol. Soc., Am. Musicol. Soc., Renaissance Soc. Am., Canadian Renaissance Soc., Toronto Renaissance and Reformation Colloquium (pres. 1969-70), Canadian U. Music Schs. Assn., Internat. Soc. History of Rhetoric. Author: Mannerism In Italian Music and Culture, 1530-1630, 1979; asso. editor: Current Musicology, 1963-65, Renaissance and Reformation, 1970-72. Office: Faculty of Music Toronto Toronto ON M5S 1A1 Canada

MANLEY, AUDREY FORBES, physician; b. Jackson, Miss., Mar. 25, 1934; d. Jesse Leonard and Iralee (Buckhalter) Forbes; A.B., Spelman Coll., 1955; M.D., Meharry Med. Coll., 1959; m. Albert Edward Manley, Apr. 3, 1970. Intern, St. Mary Mercy Hosp., Gary, Ind., 1959-60; resident Cook County Children's Hosp., Chgo., 1960-62, chief resident, 1962-63, asso. attending, 1963-69; NIH fellow, research asso. in newborn physiology, Sch. Medidine, U. Ill., Chgo., 1963-65; practice medicine specializing in pediatrics, Chgo., 1964-66; staff pediatrician N. Lawndale Neighborhood Health Center, Chgo., asso. in pediatrics, Chgo. Med. Sch., 1966-67; med. dir. Woodlawn Child Health Center, U. Chgo., 1967-69; asst. dir. pediatrics, asst. dir. ambulatory pediatrics, Mt. Zion Hosp. and Med. Center, San Francisco, 1969-70; med. cons. Spelman Coll., Atlanta, 1970-71, med. dir. Family Planning Program, chmn. Health Careers Adv. Com., 1972-76; med. dir., chief med. services Emory U./Grady Meml. Hosp., Altanta, 1972-76; commd. capt. USPHS, med. dir., chief Family Health and Preventive Services Group, Bur. Community Health Services, Health Services Adminstrn., Rockville, Md., 1976-77, dir. Sickle Cell Disease Program/Genetic Services, 1977-78, chief Genetic Diseases Br., Office for Maternal and Child Health, 1978-81; guest attending physician Inter-Inst. Genetics Clinic, NIH, 1981—; clin. asst. prof. dept. pediatrics Howard U. Sch. Medicine, 1981—; clin. instr. pediatrics U. Chgo. Med. Center, 1965-69, U. Calif. Med. Sch., San Francisco, 1969-70; asso. attending Nat. Naval Med. Center, 1981—; group leader med. team Operation Crossroads, Enugu Gen. Hosp., W. Africa, 1963; med. cons. public health programs W.I., 1973-76. Bd. dirs. Easter Seal Soc., Atlanta, 1972-75, Community Health Center, Atlanta U. Center, 1974-76, Atlanta Southside Comprehensive Neighborhood Health Center, 1974-76; mem. grants rev. com. NIH, 1972-75; chmn. service com. Atlanta Area Family Planning Council, 1971-74; mem. vis. faculty com. Harvard U. and Radcliffe Coll., 1974—; mem. com., commr., Atlanta Regional Commn., 1974-76; trustee Spelman Coll., 1966-70. Diplomate Am. Bd. Pediatrics. Fellow Am. Acad. Pediatrics; mem. Nat. Med. Assn., Am. Public Health Assn., AAUW, Inst. of Medicine of Nat. Acad. Scis., Cook County Children's Hosp. Alumni Assn. (v.p., 1973—). Baptist. Contbr. articles to profl. publs. Office: 5600 Fishers Ln Rockville MD 20857

MANLEY, JOAN ADELE DANIELS, publisher; b. San Luis Obispo, Calif., Sept. 23, 1932; d. Carl and Della (Weinmann) Daniels; B.A., U. Calif., Berkeley, 1954; D.B.A. (hon.), U. New Haven, 1974; LL.D. (hon.), Babson Coll., 1978; m. Jeremy C. Lanning, Mar. 17, 1956 (div. Sept. 1963); m. 2d, Donald H. Manley, Sept. 12, 1964. Sec., Doubleday & Co., Inc., N.Y.C., 1954-60; sales exec. Time Inc., 1960-66, v.p., 1971-75, group v.p., 1975—, dir., 1978—; circulation dir. Time-Life Books, 1966-68, dir. sales, then pub., 1968-76, chmn. bd., 1976—; supervising dir. Time-Life Internat. (Nederland) B.V.; mem. adv. bd. Center for the Book; vice chmn. Book-of-Month Club, Inc., N.Y.C.; chmn. bd. Pacifica Ltd., Tokyo; alt. dir. Organizacion Editorial Novaro S.A. (Mexico City); chmn. bd. N.Y. Graphic Soc., Alva Mus. Replicas, Inc.; dir. Little Brown & Co., Edits. Robert Laffont, Paris; advisory council Stanford U. Bus. Sch. Trustee, Babson Coll., Bennington Coll. Mem. Assn. Am. Pubs. (past chmn.), Direct Mail Mktg. Assn. (past dir.). Clubs: Pubs. Lunch, Hemisphere. Office: Time-Life Bldg Rockefeller Center New York NY 10020 also 777 Duke St Alexandria VA 22314

MANLY, CAROL ANN, speech-lang. pathologist; b. Canton, Ohio, Nov. 21, 1947; d. William George and Florence (Parrish) Manly; B.S. in Edn. (PTA scholar, 1965, Penhellenic scholar, 1965), Kent State U., 1969; M.A. (VA fellow), U. Cin., 1970; postgrad. N.Y.U. Instr., U. Cin. Med. Center, 1970-72; staff speech pathologist, N.Y.U. Med. Center, Goldwater Meml. Hosp., N.Y.C., 1972-75, sr. speech pathologist, 1975-78, supr., 1978-81, asst. dir., 1981—; cons. speech pathologist Mary Manning Walsh Nursing Home, 1974—; speaker profl. convs. Jr. asso. mem. Solomon R. Guggenheim Mus., 1976—. Mem. Am. Speech-Lang.-Hearing Assn., N.Y. State Speech-Lang.-Hearing Assn. (com. on communication problems of aging), N.Y.C. Speech-Lang.-Hearing Assn. Office: NYU Medical Center Goldwater Meml Hosp Roosevelt Island New York NY 10044

MANN, CAROL RUTH, literary agt.; b. Cambridge, Mass., July 23, 1949; d. Arthur and Sylvia (Blut) M.; B.A., Smith Coll., 1971; M.A. in Teaching, Columbia U., 1972. Tchr., Brearley Sch., N.Y.C., 1972-74; asst. dir. edn. dept., editorial dir. children's books Avon Books, 1974-76; pres. Carol Mann Lit. Agy., Bklyn., 1977; cons., lectr. in field. Mem. Ind. Lit. Agts. Assn. (council 1979-82). Address: 168 Pacific St Brooklyn NY 11201

MANN, GRACE CARROL, ballerina, choreographer; b. Berkeley, Calif, Nov. 30; d. Robert H. and Nell Jeanette (Curry) M.; B.A., U. Calif., Berkeley, 1941; student Theodore Kosloff. Dancer, San Francisco Ballet and Opera, 1940, 41, Kosloff Ballet, Hollywood, Calif., 1942-46, film Spectre of the Rose for Ben Hecht, 1945; prin. dancer original Ballet Russe of Col. de Basil including season Convent Garden, 1947-48; founder Studio of Dance Art, 1951; dir. Ballet Center, Oakland, Calif., 1971—; co-founder Ballet Valmann also choreography; instr. master classes; judge regional ballet auditions; choreography includes: Concerto in D (Poulenc), Concerto (Mendelssohn), Mikrocosmos (Bartok). Mem. Delta Epsilon. Home: 5960 Margarido Dr Oakland CA 94618 Office: 452 Santa Clara Ave Oakland CA 94610

MANN, HELENE DAVIS POWNER (MRS. CECIL W. MANN), psychologist; b. Greensburg, Ind., June 30, 1899; d. Charles Tracy and Olive (Davis) Powner; student U. Ariz., 1917-19; A.B., U. Calif., Berkeley, 1922; M.A., U. So. Calif., 1927; postgrad. U. So. Calif., Sorbonne, Paris, U. Madrid, 1927; pvt. study, France, U.S.A.; m. Cecil William Mann, Oct. 16, 1937; 1 dau., Jennifer O. Psychologist, tchr. gifted children Pasadena (Calif.) City Schs., 1926-29; chief psychol. examiner Los Angeles County Juvenile Hall Clinic, 1929-39; spl. lectr. U. Denver, 1939-41; psychologist Bur. Testing and Guidance, also Specialized Tng. and Reassignment Unit, U.S. Army, La. State U., 1943-45; dir. Tulane U. reading improvement program, 1953-57; editor Charles T. Powner Corp., Regan Pub. Co., Chgo., 1922-60; pvt. practice psychology, New Orleans, 1945-61; pvt. practice, research, Jackson County, N.C., 1961-74; psychol. cons. Western N.C. U. Mental Health Center, 1969-70, Dept. Interior Bur. Indian Affairs, Cherokee, N.C.,

1962-70; pvt. practice psychology, Henderson County, 1974-79. Mem. AAUW, LWV, Am., Southeastern, N.C. psychol. assns., Pi Beta Phi. Club: Book. Contbr. articles to profl. jours.; also children's stories. Address: 11 Quail Trail Hendersonville NC 28739

MANN, IRMA FISHER, hotel corp. exec.; b. Bklyn., Nov. 30, 1933; d. Martin Anthony and Marge Berg (Fields) Fisher; B.A. with honors, Emerson Coll., 1967; grad. Advanced Mgmt. Program, Harvard U., 1976; m. Allan Mann, Sept. 26, 1953; children—Robert Carl, Elizabeth Darcy. Dir. spl. projects Boston Sch. System, 1969-72; project coordinator Gov.'s Office, State of Mass., Boston, 1972-75; v.p., dir. mktg. Sonesta Internat. Hotel Corp., Boston, 1975—. Founder, exec. com. Job Placement Project for State of Mass., Boston; bd. dirs. Greater Boston Youth Symphony Orch., Center House; mem. adv. bd. Boston U. Hotel Sch., 1981; trustee Emerson Coll. Cert. hotel sales exec. Mem. Hotel Sales and Mgmt. Assn. (internat. dir. 1977—), Am. Soc. Travel Agts., Assn. Travel Mktg. Execs., Internat. Congress and Conv. Assn., Am. Mgmt. Assn., AAUW, Nat. C. of C. for Women (dir.), U.S. Eastern Amateur Ski Assn. Clubs: Univ., Charles River Tennis. Home: 26 Merrill Rd Newton MA 02159 Office: John Hancock Tower 200 Clarendon St Boston MA 02116

MANN, JEAN ADAH, potter, sculptor; b. Schenectady, June 27, 1927. Working primarily in porcelain, experimenting with high fire copper red and crystal glazes; one-man shows include New Haven Paint and Clay Club, New Haven, Conn., Silvermine Guild Artists, 1977, Stonington (Conn.) Gallery, 1977, Hammond Mus., North Salem, N.Y., 1975, 77, 82, The Galerie, Chester, Conn., 1981, 82; represented in permanent collections Nat. Mus. History and Tech. Smithsonian Instn.; tchr. Donald Mavros Studio, N.Y.C., 1964; tchr. The Kick Wheel, sculpture and pottery studio, Sandy Hook, Conn., 1964-70, New Fairfield, Conn., 1970—; tchr. Heritage Village, Southbury, Conn., 1965-75, Waterbury YWCA, 1966-69, Adult Edn. Programs, Newtown, New Fairfield and Sherman, Conn., 1966—Brookfield (Conn.) Craft Center, 1981, 82; co-instr. Phoenix Pottery, Goffstown, N.H., 1977. Recipient numerous art prizes and awards. Mem. Am. Crafts Council, Conn. Craftsmen, New Haven Paint and Clay Club, Brookfield Craft Center, Silvermine Guild Artists. Home and Studio: The Kick Wheel Route 39 RFD 1 Box 27 New Fairfield CT 06810

MANN, JEANNE CEZANNE (FIORETTO), cons., assn. exec., editor; b. Raleigh, N.C., Nov. 27, 1947; d. Julius and Risha (Goldberg) Grosberg; B.A., Mich. State U., 1968; 1 son, Robert; m. 2d, Stephen Mann. Dir. public relations United Cerebral Palsy of Wis., Madison, 1978; mgr. chpt. services Am. Soc. Tng. and Devel., Madison, 1978-79; editor The Wis. Architect of Wis. Soc. Architects, Madison, 1980; assn. exec. editor Calif. Mfrs. Assn., Sacramento, 1980—; founder Overspenders Anonymous, 1979; pub. Overspenders Anonymous Newsletter. Mem. Sacramento Soc. Assn. Execs., Am. Soc. for Tng. and Devel. Jewish. Club: Southland 6000 Racquetball. Home: 43 Quay Ct Sacramento CA 95831 Office: Calif Mfrs Assn 923 12th St Sacramento CA 95814

MANN, KAREN, state legislator; b. Fairbanks, Alaska, July 26, 1948; d. Karl and Beatrice Swanson; B.A., Dickinson State Coll., 1971; m. Randolph Mann, 1959; 1 dau. Employed pvt. sector, 1971—; now mem. Iowa Ho. of Reps. Active, Pleasant Ridge Community Ch. Office: Iowa State House Des Moines IA 50319 *

MANN, MARY ALICE, acct.; b. Somerset, Ky., Aug. 9, 1916; d. George Harrison and Lesta Etna (Nelson) Blankenship; student Ind. Central Coll., 1959-60; m. Oren Winfield Mann, Dec. 4, 1937 (dec.); children—Oren William, Karen Mann Johns; m. 2d, Allan Coulson, June 27, 1981. Acct., sec., treas. Mann Seed Farms Inc., Merom, Ind., 1969—; income tax practitioner, 1965-80; owner T-P Services, 1974-80; pvt. instr., registered profl. counselor parliamentary procedures, 1966—; author: Committee Cues, rev. edit., 1973. Mem. Marion County Sch. Reorgn. Com., 1959-65, Ind. Dept. Instrn. Reorgn. Com., 1970-72, Ind. Adv. Com. Day Care Services, 1969-73, Ind. Right-to-Read Com., 1970-74; del. White House Conf. Children; pres. Ind. PTA, 1969-71, Marion County PTA, 1958-60; bd. mgrs. Nat. PTA, 1969-71; v.p. Hoosier Capital council Girl Scouts U.S.A., 1965-68; regional legis. coordinator, 1966-74; sec. Southport Christian Ch., Indpls., 1967-68, fin. sec., 1965-67; founder Widowed Club, 1979. Hon. life mem. Ind. PTA. Mem. Nat., Ind. assns. registered parliamentarians, Prairie Homemakers. Club: Woman's (pres. 1977-78, 81-82) (Sullivan, Ind.). Address: RR 1 Box 117 Merom IN 47861

MANN, MARY LEE, civic worker, educator; b. Fernandina Beach, Fla., Apr. 25, 1941; d. John Campbell and Kossie Alberta (Goodbread) Ferguson; student Fla. State U., 1959-61; B.S., George Peabody Coll., Vanderbilt U., 1963; m. Franklin Balch Mann, June 1, 1961; children—Franklin Balch, Ian Ferguson. Sci. tchr. Cypress Lake Jr. High Sch., Ft. Myers, Fla., 1964; biology tchr. Ft. Myers High Sch., 1968-74, dean of girls, 1974-75; tchr. gifted children elem. sch., Lee County, Fla., 1976; dir. Latch Key Child Services, Inc., 1976-78, sec., 1978-81; dir. Christian edn. First Presbyn. Ch., Ft. Myers, 1979-81. Mem. Ft. Myers Community Relations Bd., 1975-77; campaign mgr. state rep. Frank Mann, 1978; dir. SW Fla. Dist. Mental Health Bd., 1978—; pres. Jr. Welfare League, Ft. Myers, 1978-79; trustee Jr. Mus. and Planetarium, 1979, pres., 1981—. Named Lee County Woman of Yr., 1978-79. Mem. SW Fla. Audubon Soc. (dir. 1976-81, sec., 1979-80), AAUW, Kappa Delta Alumnae Assn. (pres. 1978). Democrat. Presbyterian. Clubs: Rotary Ann, Women's Community (rec. sec. 1981-82), Dem. Women's. Home: 1415 Sandra Dr Fort Myers FL 33901

MANN, RUTH ANNE, computer system specialist; b. Framingham, Mass., June 24, 1939; d. Eugene Joseph and Ruth Agnes (Gordon) McCarthy; M.A., Lesley Coll., 1959; m. Robert Charles Mann, June 28, 1959; children—Kyle, Brent, Jonathan, Rebecca. Co-founder, Merikyle Co., Framingham, Mass., 1961-65, Orthotect Corp., Framingham, 1965-75; cons. Western Micro Systems, Cupertino, Calif., 1978—; v.p. McRam Info. Systems, Framingham, Mass., 1981—. Mem. Women in Word Processing, Women in Info. Processing, Framingham C. of C., Women West of Boston, Boston Assn. Women Bus. Owners, Women in Power, Northeast Women Adminstrs., Womens Rights and Polit. Issues. Democrat. Roman Catholic. Home: 14 Shaw Dr Wayland MA 01778 Office: 1071 Worcester Rd Framingham MA 01701

MANN, SHARON PRISCILLA, paper co. sales exec.; b. Newark, Feb. 3, 1956; d. Norman Clifford and Priscilla Louella (Stanley) M.; B.A., U. Iowa, 1976. Investigator, Essex County (N.J.) Probation Dept., 1976-80; coordinator youth program Hollow Day Care Center, Montclair, N.J., 1979; account exec. Seaman Patrick Paper Co., Detroit, 1980—. Mem. Essex County Dist. Bd. Elections, 1978-80. Cert. ind. life and health ins. agt., Mich. Mem. Nat. Assn. Female Execs., Nat. Assn. Profl. Saleswomen. Office: 2000 Howard Detroit MI 48226

MANNELLO, DEBORAH CRESPINO, speech and lang. pathologist; b. Kingston, N.Y., Mar. 5, 1949; d. Anthony Louis and Shirley June Crespino; B.S., SUNY, Geneseo, 1970; M.S., SUNY, Albany, 1976; m. Joseph J. Mannello, June 17, 1972. Speech therapist Newburgh (N.Y.) City Schs., 1970; speech and lang. pathologist Children's Rehab. Center, Kingston, N.Y., 1971—; pvt. practice speech and lang. pathology, Kingston, 1976—. Lic. and cert. speech pathologist, NY. Mem. Mid-Hudson Speech and Hearing Assn., Am. Speech and Hearing Assn., Ulster County Speech/Lang. Pathologists Assn., Jr. League Kingston, AAUW Address: 231 Clifton Ave Kingston NY 12401

MANNELLY, KATHY OLSON, mgmt. cons.; b. Lawrence, Mich., Jan. 24, 1945; d. Willie Edward and Marjorie Ellen (Holton) Olson; student Grand Rapids Sch. Cosmotology, 1963; A.B. in Behavioral Sci., Grand Rapids (Mich.) Jr. Coll., 1971; B.S. in Psychology, Grand Valley State Coll., Allendale, Mich., 1973; m. Patrick K. Mannelly, Apr. 9, 1980; stepchildren—Brian, Michael. Coordinator edn., coordinator Sunrise Program, Grand Rapids, 1974-75; trainer Dymaxion Corp., 1974-78; supr. Employee Assistance Resource, Grand Rapids, 1975-77; personnel and mktg. mgr. Project REHAB, Grand Rapids, 1977-78; sr. citizen and substance abuse specialist Mich. Dept. Mgmt. and Budget, 1978-80; mem. faculty Profl. Update, 1980-82; dir. coop. edn. Pacific Luth. U., Tacoma, 1981-82; faculty asso., cons. in field. Mem. Herpolsheimers Consumers Bd., Grand Rapids, 1970-71; pres. Faculty Wives Grand Rapids, 1970-71; active Switchboard Inc., Grand Rapids, 1971-74, Rape Crisis, Grand Rapids, 1975-76, Substance Abuse Bd., Lake Superior Street Coll., Mich., 1976-78, Tacoma Crisis Clinic, 1980-81; mem. adv. com. CompCare, 1977-78; mem. program com. ARC, 1975-77; mem. placement, site and legis. coms. Coop. Edn. Assn., 1981-82; mem. exec. com. N.W. Coop. Edn. Assn., 1980-81; mem. adv. bd. N.W. Coop. Edn. Tng. Center, 1981-82; mem. work study adv. bd. Wash. State Council for Post Secondary Edn., 1981-82. Recipient various service awards; lic. social worker, Mich. Mem. Nat. Assn. Female Execs., South Sound Womens Network. Author articles, manuals in field.

MANNING, CAROL ANN, ins. co. exec.; b. Chgo., Nov. 26, 1942; d. Gernon S. and Anne M.; B.S., Marquette U., 1964. Assigned risk supr. Zurich-Am. Ins. Co., Chgo., 1964-65, chief rate clk., 1965-66, large lines underwriter, 1966-69, processing supr., 1969-72, processing and services mgr., 1972-73, sr. devel. specialist, 1973-75, dir. product devel., 1975, prodn. mgr., Los Angeles, 1975—; sales mgr. Northbrook P. & C., Brea, Calif., 1980—. Asst. to campaign mgr. Jack Shaffer for Congress, 1976. Mem. AAUW. Home: 519 E F St Tehachapi CA 93561

MANNING, CATHERINE DEISHER, social worker; b. Camden, N.J., Jan. 3, 1948; d. George Reuben and Mabel Anna (Brown) Deisher; A.B., Muhlenberg Coll., 1969; M.S.W., Rutgers U., 1971; m. Howard Alvin Manning, III, Aug. 20, 1971; 1 dau., Jessica Anne. Caseworker, Berks County Children and Youth Services, Reading, Pa., 1969-70, supr., 1974-81; social work cons. Wyomissing Lodge, Reading, Pa., 1981—; supr. Lebanon County Children's Services, Lebanon, Pa., 1972-74. Mem. Nat. Assn. Social Workers, Acad. Cert. Social Workers. Democrat. Lutheran. Home: 80 Wedge Ln Reading PA 19607 Office: 6th St and Court St Reading PA 19601

MANNING, MARGUERITE, univ. dean, clergywoman; b. Phoenix; d. Walter Jerald and Elizabeth (Smith) Manning; A.B., Scarritt Coll., 1942; M.A., Boston, 1943; M.Div., Union Theol. Sem., 1957; M.A., Columbia Tchrs. Coll., 1966, Ed.D., 1975. Ordained to ministry Congregationalist Ch.; dir. student activities U. Tenn., 1943-46; ednl. asst. Riverside Ch., N.Y.C., 1947-55; parish worker East Harlem Protestant Parish, 1955-57; minister East Congl. Ch. and Waits River Meth. Ch., Vt., 1958-61; tchr. English and phys. edn. Baghdad (Iraq) High Sch., 1961-62; adminstrv. asst. dept. guidance and student personnel adminstrn. Columbia Tchrs. Coll., 1962-66; research asso. Bank St. Coll. Edn., N.Y.C., 1966-68; with Bur. Research, N.Y.C. Bd. Edn., 1968-69; sec. personnel United Bd. Christian Higher Edn. in Asia, 1969-71; dean student affairs Rutgers U., Newark, 1971—. Active Red Feather drive; social worker ARC, Camp Shanks, N.Y., World War II; moderator Grafton-Orange Assn. Congl. Chs.; mem. minister's assn. Vt. Congl. Conf., 1958; pres. Women of Grace Ch., Newark; bd. dirs. YWCA. Mem. Nat. Assn. Women Deans and Counselors, Am. Assn. Ednl. Research, Am. Personnel and Guidance Assn., NEA, Am. Assn. Higher Edn., Am. Assn. U. Adminstrs., Bus. and Profl. Women's Club, Pi Lambda Theta (pres. Alpha Epsilon chpt. 1966-68, treas., 1969-72, chmn. nat. nominating com. 1966-67), Kappa Delta Pi, Phi Delta Kappa. Home: 351 Broad St Apt 1009 Newark NJ 07104

MANNING, SHERRY FISCHER, coll. pres. emerita; b. Washington, Apr. 28, 1943; d. Fred W. and Eleanor A. (Mertz) Fischer; B.A., Western Md. Coll., 1965; M.A., William and Mary Coll., 1967; D.B.A., U. Colo. 1973; m. Charles W. Manning, Dec. 23, 1966; children—Shannon Marie, Charles Fischer. Mktg. rep., systems engr. IBM, 1967-71; staff assoc. Nat. Center for Higher Edn. Mgmt. Systems, 1971-72; exec. asst. to exec. dir. Nat. Commn. of the Financing of Postsecondary Edn., 1972-73; adj. prof. U. Colo., 1973-74; asst. prof. U. Kans., 1975-77; cons. to pres. for acad. planning Universidade Fed. de Ceara, 1976-77; exec. v.p. Colo. Women's Coll., 1977-78, pres., 1978-81, pres. emerita, 1981—; dir. United Bank Services Co. Trustee Adopt-A-School 1978-81, Denver Symphony 1978-81. Recipient DAR Outstanding Citizen award, 1961, Faculty Devel. award U. Kans., 1976, Soroptimists Women Helping Women award, 1980. Mem. Women's Forum, Zonta, Altrusa. Republican. Presbyterian. Club: Denver. Host: Community Affairs program Sta. KHOW 1979-80; contbr. articles in field.

MANNING, SYLVIA, educator; b. Montreal, Que., Can., Dec. 2, 1943; came to U.S., 1967; d. Bruno and Lea Bank; B.A., McGill U., 1963; M.A., Yale U., 1964, Ph.D. in English, 1967; m. Peter J. Manning, Aug. 20, 1967; children—Bruce David, Jason Maurice. Asst. prof. English Calif. State U., Hayward, 1967-71, asso. prof., 1971-75, asso. dean, 1972-75; asso. prof. U. So. Calif., 1975—, asso. dir. Center for the Humanities, 1975-77, chmn. freshman writing, 1977-80, chmn. dept. English, 1980—. Woodrow Wilson fellow, 1963-64, 66-67. Mem. MLA, Dickens Soc. Author: Dickens as Satirist, 1971; contbr. essays to mags. Office: Department of English University of Southern California Los Angeles CA 90089

MANNING, TONI RUTH, home economist; b. Greenfield, Mass., Oct. 17, 1946; d. Farley and Ruth (Koegel) M.; B.S., U. Mass., Amherst, 1971; M.B.A., U. Balt., 1980. Planning coordinator corp. tech. functions McCormick & Co., Inc., Balt., 1977-79, home economist corp. research and devel., 1971-79, asst. to v.p. sci. and tech., 1980—, mem. multiple mgmt. bd., 1973-78. Mem. Inst. Food Technologists (chmn. Md. sect. 1978-79), Am. Home Econs. Assn., Home Economists in Bus., Am. Mktg. Assn., Soc. Consumer Affairs Profls. Club: No. Chesapeake Bay Catalina. Office: 11350 McCormick Rd Hunt Valley MD 21031

MANNING-HINDS, BROOKE, advt. exec.; b. Balt., Nov. 11, 1945; d. Richard and Ellen Alford (Walton) Manning; student Bethany Coll., 1963-64, Bridgeport U., 1964-65; cert., Katharine Gibbs Sch., 1967; m. William Spencer Hinds, May 8, 1976. Sec., The Singer Co., N.Y.C., 1967-69; adminstrv. asst. to co-mgr. customer service Baldwin-Gegenheimer, Stamford, Conn., 1969-73; spl. assignment, White House, Washington, 1971; sr. sec. to advt. mgr. Barnes Engring. Co., Stamford, 1974-81; advt. mgr. Irtronics, Inc., Stamford, 1981-82; dir. devel. First Presbyn. Ch. of New Canaan, 1982; public relations cons. Xerox Internat. Hdqrs., Stamford, 1982; partner Spencer Brooke Shaklee Products, Ridgefield, Conn., 1977—; cons. in field. Bd. dirs. Person to Person, Darien, Conn., 1981—; campaign dir. New Canaan YMCA, 1982-83. Mem. Bus. Profl. Advt. Assn., Nat. Assn. Female Execs., Jr. League of Stamford/Norwalk. Presbyterian. Home: 284 Great Hill Rd Ridgefield CT 06877

MANNIX, BERNICE LENA, banker; b. Deer Lodge, Mont., June 23, 1922; d. Jens M. and Lena (Markelson) Hansen; B.A. in Bus. Adminstrn., U. Mont., 1944; m. William (Ted) Mannix, Apr. 3, 1945; children—Katherine M., Mary B., Margaret V., Teresa M. Teller Deer Lodge Bank & Trust Co., 1944-45, mem. acct. dept., 1967-69, installment loan sec., 1969-76, asst. cashier, 1976-78, asst. v.p., 1978—, real estate loan officer, trust officer, escrow officer, 1978—; bookkeeper Mannix Feed, Deer Lodge, 1948-63; bookkeeper Barmont Sales, Deer Lodge, 1966-67. Leader, 4-H, Deer Lodge, 1961-71, sec. Powell County council, 1965-68, pres., 1969-71; sec. Powell County (Mont.) Mus. & Arts, 1974-77, v.p., 1978-80; chpt. mother Future Homemakers Am., 1965-66, state chpt. mother 1965. Mem. Nat. Assn. Bank Women (chmn. Rocky Mountain group 1977). Republican. Roman Catholic. Clubs: Woman's (sec. 1957-58, pres. 1959), Am. Legion Aux., Deer Lodge Golf. Home: 708 Milwaukee Ave Deer Lodge MT 59722 Office: PO Box 599 Deer Lodge MT 59722

MANOR, FILOMENA ROBERTA, air force officer; b. Troy, N.Y., July 6, 1926; d. Gabriel Robert and Mary Carmina (Siciliano) Fusco; B.S. in Foods and Nutrition with high honors, Russell Sage Coll., Troy, 1948; M.S. in Hosp. Dietetics and Instn. Mgmt., Ohio State U., 1960. Dietetic intern Peter Bent Brigham Hosp., Boston, 1949; commd. 2d lt. USAF, 1950, advanced through grades to col., 1971; chief med. food service div., dir. dietetic internship Malcolm Grow USAF Med. Center, Andrews AFB, Washington, 1972—; assoc. chief dietetics/nutrition Biomed. Scis. Corps, Office Surgeon Gen., Hdqrs. USAF, 1972-82; mem. various govt. panels, cons. in field. Recipient Disting. Alumnus award Ohio State U., 1973. Mem. Am. Dietetic Assn., Assn. Mil. Surgeons U.S. (McLester award 1962), Aeromed. Assn., Air Force Assn., Council Ednl. Practice, Omicron Nu. Author papers in field. Home: 307 Yoakum Pkwy Apt 1104 Alexandria VA 22304 Office: Malcolm Grow USAF Med Center Andrews AFB DC 20331

MANOV, ELLY, civil engr.; b. Sofia, Bulgaria, Nov. 6; came to U.S., 1967; d. Velichko Genov and Dora Christov (Plelkov) Nedev; M.S. in Geology/Geochemistry, State U. Sofia, 1956; M.S.C.E., N.J. Inst. Tech., 1972; m. Val Manov, July 22, 1961; 1 dau., Eileen. Dept. mgr. State Enterprise for Indsl. Constrn., Sofia, 1959-64; cons. Bulgarian Cons. A/E Bur., Kabul, Aghanistan, 1964-67; sr. project engr. Storch Engrs., Inc., Florham Park, N.J., 1967-71; exec. dir. VEP Assos., Inc., West Caldwell, N.J., 1971—, chmn. bd., 1981—. Vice-pres. LWV, Livingston, N.J., 1981-83, bd. dirs., 1979-83; mem. Essex County Transp. Adv. Bd., 1982-83. Lic. profl. engr., N.J., Pa., Md., Conn. Mem. Nat. Soc. Profl. Engrs., ASCE, N.J. Soc. Profl. Engrs., Pa. Soc. Profl. Engrs. Club: Four Seasons Tennis Country. Office: 1140 Bloomfield Ave West Caldwell NJ 07006

MANSFIELD, ANNA ELIZABETH, social worker; b. Norristown, Pa., June 18, 1915; d. John Henry and Anna Lewis (Ourt) Mansfield; B.S. in Edn., U. Pa., 1937, M.A. in Sociology, 1942, M.S.W., 1956. Dir., Residence for Women, U. Pa., Phila., 1938-42; with peace sect. Am. Friends Service Com., 1942-53, dir. Internat. Work Camps, Mex., 1943-44, Ger., 1949; dir. social services Youth Service, Inc., Phila., 1957-62, 72-74, social service dir. Interch. Child Care Soc., Phila., 1962-66; editor-in-chief Child Welfare Mag., N.Y.C., 1967-69; adminstr. Children's Aid Soc. and Girls Town, Florence Crittenden/Barrett House, N.Y.C., 1969-72; sr. planning asso. Community Services Planning Council, Phila., 1974-80; developer Coordinating Council for Services to Families and Children in Sch. Dist. V, Comprehensive Services System for Families and Children in Phila.; cons., writer, lectr. in field. Mem. Acad. Cert. Social Workers, Nat. Assn. Social Workers, Internat. Conf. Social Welfare; Internat. Assn. Schs. Social Work, Otto Rank Assn., NAACP, Urban League, Workers Def. League, Martin Luther King Center, Mortar Bd., Union Concerned Scientists, Environ. Action, Com. for Effective Congress, Dickens Soc., Phila. Trail Club, Pi Lambda Theta. Editor, Child Welfare mag., 1967-69; contbr. articles to profl. jours. Address: 1420 Locust St 11D Philadelphia PA 19102

MANSFIELD, BARBARA LOUISE, ednl. adminstr.; b. Perryville, La., Oct. 9, 1927; d. Luther Glister and Lureatha Davison Mansfield; B.S., Grambling State U., 1957; M.Ed., Tuskegee (Ala.) Inst., 1964; children—Freddye Pettet, Anita Rubin, Quinton Harris, Gerry Mansfield. Tchr., Morehouse Parish Schs., Bastrop, La., 1957-64, guidance counselor, 1964-80, prin. South Side Elem. Sch., 1980—. Pres. Concerned Citizens for Community Affairs, Bastrop, 1981—; sec., mem. exec. bd. Bastrop Boys Club, 1976—. Recipient Woman of Yr. award, 1977. Mem. United Tchrs. Profession, La. Assn. Sch. Execs., Third Dist. Sch. Prins., Morehouse-Grambling Alumni Assn. (pres. 1977). Democrat. Baptist. Home: PO Box 72 Bastrop LA 71220 Office: 500 S Vine St Bastrop LA 71220

MANSFIELD, CARMELLA ELIZABETH, educator; b. Cleve., June 2, 1925; d. Peter and Antoinette Lucy (Minute) Nuccio; B.B.A., Cleve. State U., 1958; M.A., Ohio State U., 1961, Ph.D., 1965; m. Walter R. Mansfield, Jr., June 1, 1974; 1 stepson, Marc R. Sec., 1943-58; tchr. bus. edn., math. Wickliffe (Ohio) Public Schs., 1958-62; asst. instr. bus. edn. Ohio State U., 1962-64; asst. prof. bus. edn. U. Akron, 1964-66; prof. bus. edn. and office adminstrn. Ball State U., Muncie, Ind., 1966—. Dir. publs. St. Mary's Roman Cath. Ch., 1970—, pres. Legion Mary, 1970—. Mem. Am. Bus. Communication Assn., Nat. Bus. Edn. Assn., Assn. Tchr. Educators, Am. Council Consumer Interests, Ind. Bus. Edn. Assn., Delta Pi Epsilon. Author: (with others) Writing Business Letters and Reports, 1981; contbr. articles to profl. jours. Office: Sch Bus Ball State U Muncie IN 47306

MANSFIELD, JEAN ELIZABETH, credit union adminstr.; b. Hawthorne, Calif., Mar. 5, 1928; d. Chester Isdale and Gaynal Faye (Ramage) Sime; student Riverside City Coll.; children—William Robert, Donna Marie, James Chester. Sec., Charlotte High Sch., Rochester, N.Y., 1963-67; clk. County Treas.' Office, Canandaigua, N.Y., 1967-68; office mgr. Gigi Mfg. Co., Canandaigua, 1968-72; mgr. Rafe Fed. Credit Union, Riverside, Calif., 1972—. Mem. Riverside (Calif.) City Council, 1979—; bd. dirs. Riverside Vol. Center; bd. dirs., pres. Riverside Area Rape Crisis Center. Mem. Consumer Credit Counselors of Inland Empire (v.p.), Calif. Credit Union League (v.p. Tri-county chpt.), Internat. Consumer Credit Assn. (pres. chpt.), Mission Bell Bus. and Profl. Women, Credit Women Internat. of Riverside, So. Calif. Mgrs. Assn., Nat. Women's Polit. Caucus. Republican. Mem. Ch. of Christ. Club: Soroptimist Internat., Toastmasters. Home: 3427 Trinity Ct Riverside CA 92506 Office: 4422 Brockton Ave Riverside CA 92501

MANSFIELD, JOYCE COPELAND, mathematician, educator; b. Dallas, Apr. 23, 1926; d. James Robert and Hazel Marie Copeland; B.A., Baylor U., 1947, M.A. in Math., 1948; postgrad. U. Wash., 1952-53, 1978—; m. Barney Stiles Mansfield, June 28, 1953; children—Charles R., Steven B., John S. Instr. math., Baylor U., Waco, Tex., 1948-52, asst. dean women, 1951-52; dist. exec. Seattle-King County Girl Scouts, 1953-55; instr. math. San Antonio Coll., 1957-58, Everett (Wash.) Community Coll., 1962—. Membership chmn., newsletter editor Pilchuck Audubon Bd., 1977-80. Mem. AAUP, Nat. Council Tchrs. Math., Assn. Women in Math., Research Council for Diagnostic and Prescriptive Math., AAUW (chmn. Ednl. Found. Edmonds br., individual projects grantee, 1980), Baylor U. Alumni Assn. (dir. 1979-81), Kappa Kappa Gamma. Democrat. Baptist. Office: Everett Community Coll Math Dept 801 Wetmore St Everett WA 98201

MANSFIELD, NANCY, psychologist, business exec.; b. Milw.; d. John and Melanie Szeremeta; Ph.D., U. Chgo., 1971; children—Alison, John. Staff psychologist Vernon Psychol. Lab., Chgo., 1954-70; founder, prin. Hume Mansfield Silber, Chgo., 1970-77; founder, pres. Mansfield Human Resources, Chgo., 1977—; lectr., indsl./orgnl. cons.; cons. on test devel., assessment. Mem. Am. Psychol. Assn., Midwest Psychol. Assn., Ill. Psychol. Assn., Indsl. Orgn. Psychologists of Ill. (pres. 1976), Acad. Health Care Educators (adv. bd.), Nat. Orgn. Women Bus. Owners. Office: 520 N Michigan Suite 516 Chicago IL 60611 also 811 E Wisconsin Ave Suite 231 Milwaukee WI 53202

MANSFIELD, SHERRY DIANE, educator; b. Conway, Ark., Nov. 22, 1948; d. Edward Lee and Lorene Ann (Fleming) Shock; B.S.Ed., U. Central Ark., 1970, M.S.Ed., 1971; children—Jon Scott Mansfield, Amy Mansfield. Tchr., Anthony Schs., Little Rock, Ark., 1971-72; tchr. mentally retarded Pulaski County Schs., Little Rock, 1972-73; tchr. mentally retarded, learning disabilities North Little Rock (Ark.) schs., 1973-75; tchr. Cutter Morning Star, Hot Springs, Ark., 1977-78; edn. examiner pilot program for autistic children Hot Springs Public Schs., 1978-79; dir. Faulkner County Day Sch., Conway, Ark., 1979—. Mem. Ark. Assn. Adminstrs. Community Programs, Council Exceptional Children, Am. Assn. Mental Deficiencies, Delta Kappa Gamma, Kappa Kappa Iota. Baptist. Home: 12 Post Oak St Conway AR 72032 Office: 314 Elizabeth St Conway AR 72032

MANSON, JENNIFER JOY, state ofcl.; b. Naples, Italy, Jan. 10, 1953 (parents Am. citizens); d. Frank Albert and Orie Lee (Pickren) M.; B.A. in Speech, U. N.C., 1974. Adminstrv. asst. Electronic Industries Assn., Washington, 1974-75; adminstrv. asst. to dir. research President Ford Com., 1975-76; asst. to dep. spl. asst. to president The White House, 1976-77; dir. research Dalton Com., Richmond, Va., 1977; exec. asst. to gov. of Va., 1978—; chmn. staff adv. com. So. Governors Assn., 1979-80; mem. Youth Govt. Day Adv. Commn., 1979—. Mem. Va. Hist. Soc., U. N.C. Alumni Assn. Republican. Episcopalian. Office: State Capitol Richmond VA 23219

MANSOUR, AGNES MARY, coll. pres.; b. Detroit, Apr. 10, 1931; d. Said Thomas and Marie (Mabarak) M.; B.S., Mercy Coll., Detroit, 1953; M.S., Catholic U. Am., 1958; Ph.D., Georgetown U., 1964. Joined Sisters of Mercy, Roman Cath. Ch., 1953; Ednl. coordinator med. tech. program Mt. Carmel Mercy Hosp., Detroit, 1958-61, lectr. nurse anesthetist program, 1959-61; mem. faculty Mercy Coll., 1958—, chmn. med. assocs. div., 1960-61, chmn. dept. phys. sci. and math., 1964-70, pres., 1971—; dir. Mich. Bell Telephone Co., NBD Bancorp, Nat. Bank Detroit; cons. in field. Mem. Mich. Planning Com. for Advancement Women, 1977-80. Mem. Nat. Assn. Ind. Colls. and Univs. (vice chmn. 1982-83), Women's Econ. Club Detroit (dir. 1977-79), Am. Assn. Higher Edn., Am. Soc. Allied Health Professions, AAUW, Internat. Inst. Detroit, Econ. Club Detroit, Kappa Gamma Pi. Democrat. Club: Georgetown of Mich. Author articles in field. Office: 8200 W Outer Dr Detroit MI 48219

MANTELL, SUZANNE R., editor; b. West Orange, N.J., Nov. 26, 1944; d. Milton A. and Florence B. M.; B.F.A., Pratt Inst., 1967. Asso. editor Harper's Mag., N.Y.C., 1977-78, editor Harper's Bookletter, 1974-77, exec. editor mag., 1978-80; instr. mag. writing Stanford U., 1980-81, U. Calif. at Santa Cruz, 1981, Learning Mag., 1980-81; editor Phila. Mag., 1982—. Mem. P.E.N., Nat. Book Critics Circle. Home: 302 W 12th St New York NY 10014

MANTHORNE, JACKIE ANN, writer, adminstr.; b. Halifax, N.S., Can., Dec. 3, 1946; d. Ralph Eugene and Mildred Freda (Rhuland) M.; B.A., Dalhousie U., 1968, B.Ed., 1970. Teaching asst. Miriam Sch. for the Exceptional, Montreal, Que., Can., 1972-73; tchr. Peter Hall Sch. for the Exceptional, Montreal, 1973-75; info. officer Women's Info. and Referral Centre, Montreal, 1975-78, asst. dir., 1978—, adult edn. tchr. of women and fin. and women's discussion group, 1974—; editor-in-chief Les Editions Communiqu' Elles, 1981—. Mem. Feminist Party of Can., Internat. Women's Writing Guild, Women's Info. and Referral Centre, Federation des femmes du Quebec, Centre Investigative Journalism. Editor Communiqu' Elles. (French and English), 1975—, Montreal Women's Yellow Pages (French and English), 1977, 80, 82, Newcomer's Handbook (French, English, Greek, Portuguese, Hindi), 1979. Office: 3585 St-Urbain Montreal PQ H2X 2N6 Canada

MANTON, DEBORAH JEAN, mfg. engr.; b. Phila., Feb. 16, 1955; d. Russell Frederick and Lois Eileen (Lord) M.; B.A. Franklin and Marshall Coll., 1976; B.S., Phys. in Engring. Physics, Washington U. 1978; postgrad. Rochester Inst. Tech., 1981—. Devel. engr. Corning Glass Works, Erwin, N.Y., 1978-80; mfg. devel. engr. Xerox Corp., Webster, N.Y., 1980-82; project mgr. Schlegel Corp., Rochester, N.Y., 1982—. Chmn. Rochester area alumni admissions asst. program Franklin and Marshall Coll., 1981-82. NSF fellow, 1976. Mem. Soc. Women Engrs., Nat. Soc. Profl. Engrs. Democrat. Episcopalian. Home: 272 Linden St Rochester NY 14620 Office: 1555 Jefferson Rd Rochester NY 14692

MANTOVANI, JUANITA MARIE, univ. dean, educator; b. Chgo., Sept. 18, 1943; d. Norman Bert and Marie Frances (Byczkowski) Watson; A.B. summa cum laude, Marymount Coll., 1965; A.M., UCLA, 1966; Ph.D. in English, U. So. Calif., 1974; m. Robert Albert Mantovani, June 6, 1970. Acting chmn. freshman English program U. So. Calif., 1972-73, asst. dean student affairs, 1973-75, asst. dean humanities, 1975-81, chmn. ethnic studies program, 1980-81, mem. English faculty, 1966-75, mem. adj. faculty, program for study women and men in society, 1975-81; dean undergrad. studies, asso. prof. English, Calif. State U., Los Angeles, 1981—; mem. English faculty Long Beach City Coll., 1974-77, Pepperdine U. Liberal Studies Program, 1975-77; lectr., condr. workshops on profl. devel. for women, career devel. and liberal arts edn., images of women and ethnic minorities in lit. and media; panelist Nat. Endowment for Humanities Research Seminar on Feminism, 1979. Office: ADM 707 Calif State U 5151 State University Dr Los Angeles CA 90032

MANTZ, LINDA SUE, nurse, air force officer; b. Coudersport, Pa., July 4, 1951; d. Kenneth Adrian and Dorothy Helen (Boorum) M.; R.N., Millard Filmore Hosp., Buffalo, 1972. Nurses aide, L.P.N., Millard Filmore Hosp., 1970-72; staff nurse Olean (N.Y.) Gen. Hosp., 1972-78, asst. head nurse, 1974-78; commd. 1st lt., U.S. Air Force, 1978, advanced through grades to capt.; staff nurse ICU, Davis Monthan AFB, Ariz., 1978—. Republican. Methodist. Office: USAF Hospital Davis Monthan Air Force Base AZ 85707

MANUEL, BETTY LOUISE, car rental agt.; b. Phila., Oct. 20, 1928; d. William Gordon and Mary (May) Rennie; student pub. schs., Phila.; children—Loretta, Debra, Clinton. Beautician, Dobbins Vocat. Sch., 1941-45; owner Dual Control Driving Sch., 1965-79; receptionist Rohrer Chevrolet, 1955-56; owner Nat. Car Rental Agy., 1977-82; owner Manuel Investments and Rentals, Cherry Hill, N.J., 1972—; self-employed real estate investor, Cherry Hill, 1972—. Active United Fund, Multiple Sclerosis. Mem. C. of C. Roman Catholic. Office: 404 Saw Mill Village Cherry Hill NJ 08034

MANUEL, CAROLYN GAIL, air force officer; b. Carroll County, Va., June 4, 1947; d. Omar Wayne and Kathleen Nelson M.; B.S., Radford Coll., 1969; postgrad. U. Okla., 1976—. Commd. 2d lt. U.S. Air Force, 1969, advanced through grades to maj., 1973; intelligence officer 320 Bomb Wing, Sacramento, 1973-75; intelligence watch officer U.S. Forces, Japan, 1975-77; chief ops. intelligence inspection br. Hdqrs. Pacific Air Forces, 1977-79; intelligence planner 2d Airborne Command and Control Squadron, Offutt AFB, Nebr., 1979—. Decorated Bronze Star, Air Force Commendation medal with oak leaf cluster, Meritorious Service medal with oak leaf cluster. Mem. Air Force Assn., AAU. Mem. Reorganized Ch. Latter Day Saint. Office: 2d Airborne Command and Control Squadron Offutt Air Force Base NE 68113

MANUEL, VIVIAN, public relations co. exec.; b. Queens County, N.Y., May 6, 1941; d. George Thomas and Vivian Anderson M.; A.B., Wells Coll., Aurora, N.Y., 1963; M.S. in Polit. Sci., U. Wyo., Laramie, 1965. Mgmt. analyst Dept. of Navy, Washington, 1966-68; account supr. Gen. Electric News Bur., N.Y.C., 1968-72; bus. and fin. corp. rep. Gen. Electric Co., N.Y.C., 1972-76; corp. communications dir. Standard Brands Inc., N.Y.C., 1976-78, cons., 1978-81; pres. VM Communications, Inc., N.Y.C., 1981—. Recipient Sustained Superior Performance award Dept. of Navy, 1967, Mgmt. award Gen. Electric Co., 1972. Mem. Econ. Roundtable, Nat. Bus. Council for ERA, N.Y. Women Public Relations, Women Bus. Owners N.Y. Office: 370 Lexington Ave New York NY 10017

MANULKIN, DENA JEAN, editor; b. New Brunswick, N.J., Apr. 23, 1947; d. Herbert Spencer and Jean (Guth) Rogin; B.A., Temple U., 1968. Copy editor Fortress Press, Phila., 1968-69; test devel. editor Nat. Bd. Med. Examiners, Phila., 1969-72; mng. editor A.S. Barnes & Co., Inc., Cranbury, N.J., 1972-78; copy editor Aretê Pubs., Princeton, 1978-80; copy editor Med. Pub., Morganville, N.J., 1981—. Office: Med Pub 50 Route 9 Morganville NJ 07751

MANZ, BETTY ANN, nurse adminstr.; b. Paterson, N.J., Nov. 30, 1935; d. James Albert and Elsie (Basse) Brown; diploma Newark Beth Israel Hosp. Sch. Nursing, 1955; B.S.N., Seton Hall U., 1964; m. Richard C. Manz, Oct. 30, 1954; children—Laura, Richard, Garry. Staff nurse operating room Newark Beth Israel Hosp., 1955-56, recovery room head nurse, 1956-57, operating room head nurse, 1957-58, supr. operating room, 1958-60; substitute tchr. pub. schs. Harding Twp., 1966-70; charge nurse St. Barnabas Med. Center, Livingston, N.J., 1965-70, head nurse emergency room, 1970-72; operating room supr. St. Clares Hosp., Denville, N.J., 1972-77; asst. dir. for operating rooms and post anesthesia rooms Newark Beth Israel Med. Center, 1977-82; asst. dir. nursing operating room care program Thomas Jefferson U. Hosp., Phila., 1982—; faculty mem. postgrad. course in microsurgy for Am. Coll. Obstetricians and Gynecologists, Newark, 1982; profl. cons. operating room products, also health cons. Henry E. Wessel Assos., Moraga, Calif.; profl. tech. cons., lectr. Surgicot, Inc., Smithtown, N.Y. Dep. dir. Harding Twp. CD, 1967-75. Recipient Service award Essex County Med. Soc., 1979. Mem. Assn. Operating Room Nurses, Am. Soc. Post Anesthesia Nurses, Newark Beth Israel Hosp. Nursing Alumnae Assn., Seton Hall U. Alumnae Assn., Harding Twp. Civic Assn., Am. Field Service. Republican. Club: Mt. Kemble Lake Community. Editor operating room sect. SCORE mag. Home: 401 Cooper Landing Rd Unit 624 Cherry Hill NJ 08002 Office: 9th and Chestnut Sts Philadelphia PA

MAPES, EVELYN ADAMS, beautitian; b. Stanley County, N.C., Mar. 8, 1928; d. Lee Jerome and Carrie (Brooks) Walters; student Thomas Nelson Community Coll., Hampton, Va., 1978-79; m. Herbert C. Mapes, Nov. 11, 1979; 1 son, James Glenn Adams. Hairdresser, Charlotte, N.C., 1942-52; owner Grant's Beauty Salon, Newport News and Hampton, 1953—, Jan Mar of Norfolk and Williamsburg, Va., 1953—, Laines House of Beauty, Newport News, 1953—, Hayes Beauty, Inc., Newport News and Hayes, Va., 1953—; owner Jan Mar Beauty Acad., 1968—. Mem. Nat. Assn. Cosmetology Schs. (sec. 1974), Tchrs. Ednl. Council (pres. 1975-77), Am. Bus. Women's Assn., Nat. Hairdressers Assn., Va. Hairdressers Assn. Democrat. Jewish. Address: Tchrs Ednl Council 411 Jan Mar Dr Newport News VA 23606

MAPES, JUDITH ANN, mgmt. cons. co. exec.; b. Suffern, N.Y., Aug. 27, 1939; d. Charles Marvin and Mary Louise (Melvin) Mapes; B.A., in Econs., Conn. Coll. for Women, 1961; m. Frank A. Metz, Jr., July 21, 1979. Ops. asst. First Nat. City Bank, N.Y.C., 1965-66; asst. to dir. Animal Med. Center, N.Y.C., 1966-70; systems designer Keydata Corp., N.Y.C., 1970-74; dir. mktg. McCall Pattern Co. div. Norton Simon, Inc., N.Y.C., 1974-77; asso. Booz, Allen & Hamilton, N.Y.C., 1977-80; prin. Egon Zehnder Internat., N.Y.C., 1980—. Officer adminstrv. bd. of Soc., Meml. Sloan-Kettering Cancer Center, N.Y.C. Mem. N.J. Jr. League. Office: Olympic Tower 645 Fifth Ave New York NY 10022

MAPLE, MARILYN JEAN, coordinator ednl. media; b. Turtle Creek, Pa., Jan. 16, 1931; d. Harry Chester and Agnes (Dobbie) Kelley; B.A., U. Fla., 1972, M.A., 1975; 1 dau., Sandra Maple. Journalist various newspapers, including Mountain Eagle, Jasper, Ala., Boise (Idaho) Statesman, Daytona Beach (Fla.) Jour., Lorain (Ohio) Jour.; account exec. Frederides & Co., N.Y.C.; producer hist. films Fla. State Mus., Gainesville, 1967-69; writer, dir., producer med. and sci. films and TV prodns. for six medically related colls. U. Fla., Gainesville, 1969—; pres. Media Modes, Inc., Gainesville. Recipient Blakslee award, 1969, spl. award, 1979, Monsour Lectureship award, 1979. Mem. Health Edn. Media Assn. (dir., awards, 1977, 79), Phi Delta Kappa, Kappa Tau Alpha. Columnist: Health Care Edn. mag.; contbr. Fla. Hist. Quar. Home: 6722 SW 53d Ave Gainesville FL 32608 Office: University of Florida Box J-16 Gainesville FL 32610

MAPLES, TERRY, application analyst; b. Sacramento, Dec. 12, 1950; d. Clyde Alexander and Blanche (Crawford) M.; A.S. in Data Processing, Grossmont Jr. Coll., 1971; B.S.B.A., Towson State U., 1980. Sr. computer operator IRS, Fresno, Calif., 1972-73; programmer/operator AVCO Community Developers, La Jolla, Calif., 1974; computer cons. EDP Mgmt. Co., San Diego, 1974-75; computer operator McCormick & Schilling Co., Salinas, Calif., 1975-76, Balt., 1976-77; programmer McCormick & Co., Balt., 1977-80, chmn. Fall Festival, 1979; programmer analyst Md. Nat. Bank, Balt., 1980-82; application analyst, programmer team leader Fed. Res. Bank of San Francisco, 1982—. Active Perry Hall Baptist Ch. and Choir, Balt., Big Buddy Program, Monterey, Calif. Mem. Nat. Assn. Female Execs. Democrat. Home: 1617 Central Ave Alameda CA 94501 Office: Fed Res Bank of San Francisco San Francisco CA 94120

MAPP, RAMONA HARTLEY, coll. adminstr.; b. Hartleys Corners, Ala., Jan. 18; d. Smith Culp and Annie Bess (Owens) Hartley; student Ind. U., 1956-57, City Lit. Inst., London, 1959-61, Huntingdon Coll., 1961-62; B.A., Old Dominion U., 1965, M.A., 1966; Ed.D., Va. Poly. Inst. and State U., 1980; m. Malcolm Conner Hamby, June 26, 1949 (dec. Jan. 1967); children—Gregory Stuart, Geoffrey Alan; m. 2d, Alf Johnson Mapp, Jr., Aug. 1, 1971. Instr. English, Old Dominion U., Norfolk, Va., 1966-69, 70-71; instr. English, Tidewater Community Coll., Portsmouth, Va., 1971-73, English coordinator, 1973-74, chmn. div. humanities and social scis., 1974—; judge internat. essay contest Nat. Assn. Tchrs. of English, 1974; profl. devel. coordinator Southeastern Conf. English in Two-Year Coll., 1981, state rep., 1978-82. Mem. Portsmouth Public Library Bd., 1978—, chmn., 1978-80; bd. dirs. Tidewater Child Care Assn., 1974-81, pres., 1975-77; v.p. Tidewater Literacy Council, 1971-72; corr. sec. Poetry Soc. Va., 1975-76; bd. dirs. Va. Opera Guild, Met. Arts Congress, Tidewater Assembly Family Life. Recipient Nat. Service award Family Found. Am., 1980. Mem. Nat. Council Tchrs. of English, South Atlantic MLA (sec. two-yr. coll. sect. 1982, program chmn. 1983), Am. Assn. Colls. and Jr. Colls. (nat. com. internationalizing the curriculum 1976-80), AAUW, Phi Kappa Phi, Internat. Intercultural Consortium. Club: Internat. Assn. Torch Clubs. Home: Willow Oaks 2901 Tanbark Ln Portsmouth VA 23703 Office: Tidewater Community College Portsmouth VA 23703

MARABLE, DOROTHY GRASHAM, nurse; b. Rome, Ga., Apr. 15, 1939; d. Thomas Taft and Essie (Kinsey) Grasham; R.N., Tift Coll. and Ga. Bapt. Hosp. Sch. Nursing, 1960; registered nurse practitioner Emory U., 1972; student Floyd Jr. Coll., Rome, 1975-76; B.S.N., Med. Coll. Ga., 1977; postgrad. Columbia Pacific U.; m. Charles Edward Marable, Aug. 16, 1961; children—Shawna, Charles Edward, Misty. Charge nurse Floyd Med. Center, Rome, 1960-66, charge nurse emergency dept., 1966-67, med. supr., 1969-70, nursing office supr., 1970-72, asst. dir., 1972-78, asso. dir. nursing, 1978—; charge nurse nursing home, Cedartown, Ga., 1966; cons. in field; dir. The Womanless Wedding, Shotgun Style, 1975. Baptist. Home: 18 Crestwood Dr Rome GA 30161 Office: Turner McCall Blvd PO Box 233 Rome GA 30161

MARABLE, JUNE MOREHEAD, educator; b. Columbus, Ohio, June 8, 1924; d. J. W. and Minnie J. Morehead; B.S. in Secondary Edn., Central State U., Wilberforce, Ohio, 1948; M.S. in Guidance, U. Dayton (Ohio), 1965; Ph.D. in Edn. Adminstrn. and Reading, Miami U., Oxford, Ohio, 1975; m. James Palmer Marable; children—James Palmer, Manning, Madonna. Tchr. elem. sch. Dayton Bd. Edn., 1954-68, elem. reading supr., 1968-70; grad. asst. Miami U., 1970-72; asst. prof. edn. Wright State U., Dayton, 1972-77; Tchrs. Corps asso. vis. prof. Miami U., 1978-80; v.p. Black Research Assos., Inc.; state commr. Right to Read. Past pres. Dayton chpt. Jack and Jill of Am., Inc.; nat. coordinator Alpha Kappa Alpha Reading Program for Minorities; ednl. dir., co-owner Marable Early Childhood Edn. Center, Dayton. Mem. NEA, Internat. Reading Assn., Nat. Assn. Edn. Young Children, Assn. Elem. Tchrs. English, Assn. Childhood Edn. Internat., Central State U. Alumni Assn., Phi Delta Kappa, Delta Kappa Gamma, Alpha Kappa Alpha, Alpha Kappa Mu, Sen Mer Rek. Authored articles and audio media devel. materials. Specialist in reading. Home: 5145 Dayton Liberty Rd Dayton OH 45418

MARAKIS, ANN ANTICOL, psychiat. social worker; b. Chgo., Feb. 21, 1948; d. Irving and Edythe Ann (Friedman) Anticol; B.A. (Ill. State scholar 1964-68), U. Ill., 1968; M.A., U. Chgo., 1970; m. Yannis Marakis, Oct. 8, 1972; 1 son, Daniel Constantine. Caseworker, Ill. Dept. Children and Family Services, 1970-72; social worker, then case supr. Jewish Children's Bur., Chgo., 1972-79, intake coordinator, 1979—; field instr. Jane Addams Grad. Sch. Social Work, 1974-78, Loyola U. Grad. Sch. Social Work, 1975—. Recipient Helen Cody Baker award Welfare-Public Relations Forum, 1978. Mem. Nat. Assn. Social Workers, Acad. Cert. Social Workers. Home: 1652 Peartree Rd Deerfield IL 60015 Office: 1 S Franklin St Chicago IL 60606

MARAN, JANICE WENGERD, pharmacologist; b. Balt., June 30, 1942; d. Edgar Arthur and Mildred Ilease (Laughter) Wengerd; B.S., Juniata Coll., 1964; Ph.D. (NIH fellow 1969-71, Shafer fellow 1971-74), Stanford U., 1974. NATO postdoctoral fellow in sci. U. Bristol, Eng., 1974-75; NIH fellow Johns Hopkins Med. Sch., Balt., 1976-77; research asst. Stanford (Calif.) U., 1964-66, research asso., 1966-69; research scientist McNeil Labs., Fort Washington, Pa., 1977-78; sr. scientist McNeil Pharm., Spring House, Pa., 1978—, project mgr., 1980—. Mem. Internat. Platform Assn., Am. Physiol. Soc., AAAS, Biomed. Engring. Soc., Soc. for Neurosci., N.Y. Acad. Sci., Sigma Xi. Contbr. articles in field to profl. jours., books. Home: 106 Anton Rd Wynnewood PA 19096 Office: McNeil Pharmaceutical Spring House PA 19477

MARANO, LEONORA LICATA, librarian, cons.; b. Bklyn., May 31, 1949; d. Mario Charles and Frances Teresa (Palladino) Licata; B.A., Bklyn. Coll., 1972; M.L.S., Queens Coll., 1974; m. W.J. Marano, Jan. 21, 1978; 1 son, Mario Licata. Mem. staff Grad. Center Library, City U. N.Y., 1967-74, asst. librarian math. and sci. library, 1972-74; chief librarian Am. Paper Inst., N.Y.C., 1974-79; individual practice as cons. info. sci., 1979-81; trial preparation asst., librarian for Office of Prosecution, Spl. Narcotics Cts., N.Y.C., 1981—. Mem. Spl. Libraries Assn., Internat. Assn. for Human Relations. Republican. Episcopalian. Home: 77-15 113th St Forest Hills NY 11375 Office: 80 Centre St 6th Floor New York NY 10013

MARANTO, DONNA FAY, phys. edn. educator; b. Oakmont, Pa., Aug. 16, 1936; d. Anthony and Margaret (Beck) Maranto; B.S., Nyack Missionary Coll., 1960; M.S., Oneonta State U., 1964; cert. in phys. edn. Hunter Coll. and SUNY, 1964-70. Corr. sec. Eastern Freight Lines, 1954-56; tchr. elem. sch., Baltimore County, Md., 1960-61; tchr. Kindergarten, North Rockland County, N.Y., 1962-66; jr. high sch. phys. edn. tchr. Susquehanna Valley Central Sch., Conklin, N.Y., 1966—; coach hockey, 1970-75, softball, 1971-74, 76-78; asso. exec. sec. So. Tier Athletic Conf., 1973-79 league rep., 1962-64, sec., 1974-79. Mem., U.S. Field Hockey Assn., Susquehanna Valley Tchrs. Assn., North Rockland Tchrs. Assn., N.Y. AHPER. Methodist. Address: PO Box 44 Conklin NY 13748

MARCALI, JEAN GREGORY, chemist; b. Jermyn, Pa., May 29, 1926; d. John Robert and Anna Marie Gregory; student U. Pa., 1948-52, U. Del., 1971-72; m. Kalman Marcali, Oct. 6, 1956; children—Coleman, Frederick. Microanalyst E. I. du Pont de Nemours & Co., Deepwater, N.J., 1943-60, tech. info. analyst, Jackson Lab., Deepwater, N.J. also Wilmington, Del., 1960-67, sr. adviser tech. info., Wilmington, 1967-70, supr. tech. info., 1970—. Sec., Alfred I. DuPont Elem. PTA, 1971, pres., 1972; pres. PTA of Brandywine Sch. Dist., 1973; mem. Wilmington Dist. Republican Com., 1976—. Mem. Am. Chem. Soc., Am. Soc. Info. Sci., Nat. Assn. Female Execs. Lutheran. Clubs: Order Eastern Star, Du Pont Country, European Health. Home: 312 Waycross Rd Wilmington DE 19803 Office: E I du Pont de Nemours & Co Info Systems Dept 3211 Centre Rd Bldg Wilmington DE 19898

MARCH, JACQUELINE FRONT, chemist; b. Wheeling, W.Va., July 10, 1914; d. Jacques Johann and Antoinette (Orenstein) Front; B.S., Case Western Res. U., 1937, M.A., 1939; Wyeth fellow med. research U. Chgo., 1940-42; postgrad. U. Pitts., 1945, Ohio State U., 1967, Wright State U., 1970-76; M.B.A., U. Dayton, 1979; m. Abraham W. Marcovich, Oct. 7, 1945 (dec. 1969); children—Wayne Front, Gail Ann March Cohen. Chemist, Mt. Sinai Hosp., Cleve., 1934-40; med. research chemist U. Chgo., 1940-42; research analyst Koppers Co., also info. scientist Union Carbide Corp., Mellon Inst., Pitts., 1942-45; propr. March. Med. Research Lab., etiology of diabetes, Dayton, Ohio, 1950-70; guest scientist Kettering Found., Yellow Springs, Ohio, 1953; Dayton Found. fellow Miami Valley Hosp. Research Inst., 1956. mem. chemistry faculty U. Dayton, 1959-69, info. scientist Research Inst., 1968-79; prin. investigator Air Force Wright Aero. Labs., Wright-Patterson AFB Tech. Info. Center, 1970-79; tech. info. specialist, div. tech. services Nat. Inst. Occupational Safety and Health, Dept. Health and Human Services, Cin., 1979—; propr. JFM Info., 1980—; designer info. systems, speaker in field. Recipient Recognition cert. U. Dayton, 1980. Mem. Am. Soc. Info. Sci. (treas. South Ohio 1973-75), Am. Chem. Soc. (pres. Dayton 1977, Patterson-Crane award com.; nat. councilor 1982-85), Soc. Advancement Materials and Process Engring. (pres. Midwest chpt. 1977-78), Affiliated Tech. Socs. (Outstanding Scientist and Engr. award 1978), AAUP (exec. bd.), Sigma Xi (treas. Dayton 1976-79, Conrad P. Straub lectr. 1982). Club: Royal Oak Country (Cin.). Contbr. articles to profl. publs. Home: 154 Stillmeadow Dr Cincinnati OH 45245 Office: 4676 Columbia Pkwy Cincinnati OH 45226

MARCHAND, NANCY, actress; b. Buffalo, June 19, 1928; d. Raymond L. and Marjorie F. M.; B.F.A., Carnegie Inst. Tech., 1949; m. Paul Sparer, July 7, 1951; children—David, Kathryn, Rachel. Vol. actress Am. Theater Wing, N.Y.C.; TV appearances include: Studio One, Love of Life, The Edge of Night, Another World, Look Homeward Angel, After the Fall, A Touch of the Poet; series regular on Beacon Hill, Lou Grant, 1977-81; theater engagements at Circle in the Sq., N.Y.C., Los Angeles Music Center, Lincoln Center, N.Y.C., Am. Shakespeare Festival, Goodman Theater, Chgo., appeared on Broadway in Much Ado About Nothing, After the Rain, 40 Carats, And Miss Reardon Drinks a Little, Mornings at Seven, in Off Broadway plays Heartbreak House, Children. Recipient Obie award, 1960, Emmy award, 1978, 80. Office: care Arcara Bauman Hiller 9220 Sunset Blvd Los Angeles CA 90069

MARCHESANO, CAROLE VIRGINIA, advt. co. exec.; b. Des Moines, July 30, 1940; d. Samuel Thomas and Geneva Carol (Horner) Mazza; ed. Catholic U.; m. Martin R. Marchesano, Aug. 7, 1956 (div. July 1963); children—Michele, Richard. Office mgr. Kieffer Assos., Des Moines, 1963-65; comptroller W.A. Lemer Advt., Inc., Washington, 1966-69; owner Goldberg, Marchesano & Assos., Inc., Washington, 1970—, pres., 1978—; cons. advt. office systems. Media dir. Mayor Washington's campaign, 1974, also Congressman McClosky Presdl. Nomination Orgn. Mem. Met. Washington Bd. Trade, Advt. Club Met. Washington, League Advt. Agys., Nat. Acad. TV Arts and Scis. Home: 2139 N St NW Washington DC 20036 Office: 1910 Sunderland Pl Washington DC 20036

MARCINEK, JOYCE E., bus. services ofcl.; b. Nevada, Ohio, July 28, 1930; d. W. Frank and Bernice Marie McCallister; student Newark Coll. Engring., 1952-53, Sinclair Community Coll., 1968-69. With sales, service, public relations depts. Standard Oil Co., Canton and Akron, Ohio, 1957-63; with TRW Supermet, Dayton, Ohio, 1966-70, sales engr., 1972-75; acct. Texaco Inc., Atlanta, 1970-72; asst. to pres. Hot Sam div. Internat. Host, Troy, Mich., 1975-76; accounts rep. Kelly Services, Lexington, Ky., 1976-77, br. mgr., 1977-80; v.p. Career Mgmt., Inc., Lexington, 1980-82; dir. personnel EBS Inc., subs. Traveler's Ins. Co., Lexington, 1982—. Active Urban League, Todd Trease Teddy Bear Fund; bd. dirs. Jr. Achievement, program chmn., 1981-82, also contest judge; sponsor, coordinator secretarial scis. Explorer Troop, Bluegrass council Boy Scouts Am.; team capt. United Way, 1978-81; mem. Better Bus. Bur. Recipient Distributive Edn. award Lexington Edn.-Work Council, 1978. Mem. Sales Mktg. Execs. (dir., coordinator seminar 1979), Adminstrv. Mgmt. Assn. (dir.), Lexington C. of C. (dir., mem. President's Council). Club: Zonta (regional dir. public relations). Home: 546 Woodfire Dr Casselberry FL 32707 Office: EBS Inc 2701 Maitland Center Pkwy Maitland FL 32751

MARCINKEVICH, JUNE SELBERG, county ofcl.; b. Portland, June 1, 1923; d. John R. and Jennie (Vander Meulen) S.; student Oreg. State U., 1940-41, U. Wash., 1957-61, Seattle U., 1979; m. John Marcinkevich, Jan. 31, 1943. Staff acct. Benson & McLaughlin, Seattle, 1959-64; controller Nicholson Mfg. Co., Seattle, 1964-70; comptroller Sid Eland Inc., Seattle, 1970-78; pvt. practice acctg., Seattle, 1959-82; adminstrv. officer div. solid waste County of King, Wash., 1979-82. C.P.A., Wash. Mem. Am. Inst. C.P.A.s, Wash. Soc. C.P.A.s, Am. Woman's Soc. C.P.A.s, Mcpl. Fin. Officers Assn. Republican. Home: 2719 W Galer St Seattle WA 98199 Office: 601 FX McRory Bldg 419 Occidental S Seattle WA 98104

MARCOTTE, KAREN RUTH, energy specialist; b. Mpls., Nov. 16, 1953; d. Harold Robert and Gladys Marjorie (Wilson) M.; student in Resource Mgmt., U. Minn., 1971-74; B.S., U. Wyo., 1977. Engring. technician U.S. Forest Service, Encampment, Wyo., summers 1976, 77, 78, City of Laramie, Wyo., 1978-79; cartographer and environ. field technician Marish Assos., Laramie, 1979; research asso. Wyo. Geothermal Office, Laramie, 1979-81, program dir., 1981—; condr. workshops on renewable energy; participant Senate Sub-Com. hearings on energy issues. Mem. NOW, Albany County Pro-Choice Alliance, Wyo. Citizens Alliance, Albany County Friends of Library, Geothermal Resources Council. Contbr. articles and graphic arts projects to profl. lit. Office: Wyo Geothermal Office PO Box 4096 Univ Sta Laramie WY 82071

MARCOVICCI, ANDREA LOUISA, actress, singer; b. N.Y.C.; d. Eugene Ernst and Helen (Figura) M.; student Bennett Coll. Appeared on TV commls.; appeared regularly on TV series Love Is A Many Splendered Thing; TV guest appearances include Medical Center; TV movies: Cry Rape, Smile Jenny, You're Dead, 1975, also episodes of Kojak, Baretta and Mannix; appeared in motion picture The Front (Golden Globe nomination), 1976, The Hand, 1981; stage performances include Hamlet, Nefertiti, 1976. Recipient Jefferson award nomination for original musical Dance on a Country Grave. Mem. ASCAP, AFTRA, Screen Actors Guild, Actors Equity. Office: care STE Representation Ltd 211 S Beverly Dr Suite 201 Beverly Hills CA 90212 *

MARCOVICH, CAROL SUE., personnel cons.; b. St. Louis, June 10, 1942; d. Ralph and Nancy (Blumenfield) Bolozky; student Washington U., St. Louis, 1958-61; married. Office mgr. Goodman Dean Scott, Chgo., 1962-70; fashion stylist Huntington Industries, Chgo., 1970-73; v.p. Interviewing Dynamics, Chgo., 1973-78; pres. MKM Consultants, Inc., Chgo., 1978—. Mem. Nat. Assn. Women Bus. Owners, Women in Mgmt., Word Processing Mgmt. Assn., Internat. Word Processing Assn., Nat. Employment Assn., Chgo. Assn. Commerce and Industry, No. Ill. Indsl. Assn. Clubs: Whitehall, Michigan Avenue. Office: MKM Consultants Inc 625 N Michigan Ave Chicago IL 60611

MARCUCCI, SALLIE WHISTLER LIPPITT, painter; b. Atlanta, Mar. 11, 1940; d. Devereux Haigh and Betty (Gage) Lippitt; student Acad. Florence (Italy), Art Student's League, N.Y.C.; pupil of Oscar Kokoshka; m. Moreno Marcucci, Dec. 20, 1960; children—Carlo, Massimo. Stage designer, illustrator, fashion designer, corr. Dayton (Ohio) Daily News, 1964-65, Miami (Fla.) News, 1964, Atlanta Jour. Constn., 1964-65; one-woman exhbns. in Italy, France and U.S.; represented in permanent collection Ann Jacob Gallery, Atlanta; art dir. for Roloff Beny, photographer, 1976—. Home: Via Dandolo 24 00153 Rome Italy Office: Via San Calisto 7 00153 Rome Italy

MARCUM, DEANNA BOWLING, systems cons.; b. Salem, Ind., Aug. 5, 1946; d. Anderson and Ruby C. (Mobley) Bowling; student Ind. U., 1964-66; B.A., U. Ill., 1967, M.A., 1969; M.L.S., U. Ky., 1971; m. Thomas P. Marcum, June 13, 1974; 1 dau., Ursula. Intern, U. Ky. Libraries, Lexington, 1969-70, librarian, 1970-74; dir. research and devel., asst. dir. Vanderbilt U. Libraries, Nashville, 1974-77; tng. program specialist Assn. Research Libraries, Office of Mgmt. Studies, Washington, 1977-80, sr. cons. Info. Systems Cons., Inc., Washington, 1980-81; program officer Council on Library Resources, 1981—; instr. U. Ky., Cath. U. Am., U. Md. Recipient students to Dallas award, 1971. Mem. ALA, Am. Soc. Tng. and Devel., D.C. Library Assn., Beta Phi Mu. Democrat. Author: Resource Notebook on Staff Development, 1979; Catalog Options: On-line and COM, 1980; Automated Acquisitions Systems, 1981; bi-monthly columnist Wilson Library Bull. Home: 622 Ellsworth Dr Silver Spring MD 20910 Office: One Dupont Circle Suite 620 Washington DC 20036

MARCUM, OLIVE ERNESTINE, educator; b. Huntington, W.Va., Nov. 6, 1921; d. Ernest Jennings and Irene (Jarrell) Riggs; B.S., U. Dayton, 1954; M.A., Marshall U., 1968; R.N., Roanoke Meml. Hosp., 1944; m. William Wert Marcum, July 1, 1950: children—Andrew, Fred, James. Evening supr. St. Elizabeth Hosp., Indpls., 1948-49; emergency room supr. Kings Daus. Hosp., Ashland, Ky., 1949-51; hosp. supr. St. Elizabeth Hosp., Dayton, Ohio, 1952-54; dir. edn. Meml. Hosp., Huntington, 1954-60; staff D.C. Gen. Hosp., Washington, 1960-62; tchr. Wayne (W.Va.) Elem. Sch., 1962—. Treas., Prichard Vol. Fire Dept., 1975-77; chmn. Fair and Equitable Assessment of Taxes, 1980—. Served with Nurses Corps, U.S. Army, 1944-48. Recipient Spl. Recognition, U. Dayton, 1980; HEW fellow, 1960; Marshall U. fellow, 1966-68. Mem. W.Va. Nurses Assn. (sec. dist. 9, 1954-56), Nat. Assn. Female Execs., Early Am. Soc., Smithsonian Inst., Am. Legion, Needleworkers Guild, W.Va. Bd. Examiners for Registered Nurses, NOW (sec. 1977-78), Alpha Delta Kappa. Club: Homemakers (pres. 1962-64). Home: 4557 Riggs Br Rd Prichard WV 25555 Office: Wayne Elem Sch Wayne WV 25570

MARCUS, CAROL SILBER, radiobiologist, nuclear physician; b. N.Y.C., July 2, 1939; d. Max and Lillian (Fertik) Silber; B.S., Cornell U., 1960, M.S. (NIH fellow 1962-63; Teaching fellow 1960-62), 1961, Ph.D., 1963; M.D., U. So. Calif., 1977; m. Bruce David Marcus, Dec. 21, 1958; children—Craig Howard, Romy Elise. Intern Los Angeles County/U. So. Calif. Med. Center, Los Angeles, 1977-78; resident in internal medicine, 1978-80; resident in nuclear medicine VA Wadsworth Med. Center, Los Angeles, 1980-82; radiobiologist RVO-TNO, Rijswijk, The Netherlands, 1963-64, UCLA Lab. of Nuclear Medicine, 1964-66; instr. biology Santa Monica (Calif.) City Coll., 1966-69, Pierce Coll., Woodland Hills, Calif., 1967-69; assoc. prof. radiobiology/radiopharmacy, U. So. Calif., Los Angeles, 1969—; cons. in radiopharmacy to FDA, 1971-76, 1982—. NIH research grantee, 1962-79. Mem. Soc. Nuclear Medicine, AAAS, N.Y. Acad. Scis., ACP. Republican. Jewish. Patentee in field. Office: Dept of Radiopharmacy Stauffer Hall Univ So Calif Los Angeles CA 90033

MARCUS, HELEN, photographer; b. N.Y.C.; d. Joseph M. and Augusta (Hittleman) M.; B.A., Smith Coll., 1947. TV casting CBS, N.Y.C., 1951; in charge subs. rights, play dept. MCA Mgmt., N.Y.C., 1952-54; program coordinator Names the Same TV show, N.Y.C., 1955, Two for the Money, 1955-57; asso. producer Beat the Clock, N.Y.C., 1958-61, Number Please, N.Y.C., 1961; casting dir. To Tell The Truth, Goodson-Todman Prodns., N.Y.C., 1962-68, What's My Line, 1968-75; free-lance photographer, 1966—; exhibited photos Parents Mag. Gallery, Asia Soc., N.Y.C., N.Y. Public Library. Pres., Council of Phoenix Theatre, 1969-72; mem. adv. bd. Smith Coll. Theatre Dept., 1965-80. Mem. Am. Soc. Mag. Photographers (chpt. pres. 1981—). Home: 120 E 75th St New York City NY 10021

MARCUS, KAREN WESSEL, mag. editor; b. Bronxville, N.Y., Apr. 2, 1953; d. F. David and Patricia E. (Pieper) Wessel; B.A. cum laude, Mt. Holyoke Coll., 1975; M.A. in English, Hollins (Va.) Coll., 1976; m. Fraser Eliot Marcus, Oct. 18, 1980. Asst. editor Field & Stream mag., CBS Consumer Pub., div. CBS Inc., N.Y.C., 1978-79, production editor, 1979-80, sr. editor, 1980—, also asso. editor 4 mag. anns. Mem. Am. Soc. Mag. Editors, Women in Communications, Women in Production. Office: 1515 Broadway New York NY 10036

MARCUS, LYNNE, accountant; b. Bklyn., June 13, 1945; d. Samuel and Estelle F. (Diamond) M.; B.A. in Acctg., Queens Coll., 1970; postgrad. St. John's U. Acct., Price, Waterhouse & Co., C.P.A.s, 1970-71, Willkie, Farr & Gallagher, N.Y.C., 1971-74, Western Union Internat. Co., N.Y.C., 1975-77, N.Y.C. Bd. Edn., 1977-79, Citibank, N.Y.C., 1979—; adult edn. tchr., cons. in field. C.P.A., N.Y. Mem. Am. Inst. C.P.A.s, Am. Woman's Soc. C.P.A.s, Am. Mgmt. Assn., N.Y. State Soc. C.P.A.s, Omicron Delta Epsilon (life). Club: Hadassah. Home: 65-84 Booth St Rego Park NY 11374 Office: Citibank 153 E 53d St 15th Floor New York NY 10043

MARCUS, PEGGY SCHIFFMAN, educator; b. Oneonta, N.Y., 1951; d. Charles and Shirley (Bruder) Schiffman; B.S., Cornell U., 1947, M.S. in Family Studies, 1960. Tchr. Fallsburgh (N.Y.) Central Sch., 1947; grad. teaching asst. Cornell U., 1947-50, asst. prof. home econs., 1951-54; asst. prof. social studies SUNY at Oneonta, 1965-67, asst. prof. family studies, home econs. dept., 1967-82, pre-retirement seminar leader, 1982—; counselor; lectr. in field. Active Community Maternity Services, 1979-81, Stamford Village Improvement Assn., 1977-79; mem. Upper Catskill Council Arts; trustee Rural Supplementary Edn. Center, 1976-79; del. N.Y. State Conf. on Aging, 1981—, White House Conf. on Aging, 1981—; organizer Support Group for Relatives of Persons with Alzheimer's Disease, 1981—, Women's Consciousness Raising Group, 1981—. Mem. Am. Home Econs. Assn., Cornell U. Alumni Assn., Nat. Council Family Relations, Planned Parenthood Assn., Secondary Sch. Alumni Assn. of Cornell U., Sex Info. and Edn. Council U.S., Delta Kappa Gamma. Home: 13 Hobart Rd Stamford NY 12167 Office: Dept Home Econs 106 SUNY Oneonta NY 13820

MARCUS, RUTH BARCAN, philosopher, educator; d. Samuel and Rose (Post) Barcan; B.A., N.Y. U., 1941; M.A., Yale U., 1942, Ph.D., 1946; children—James Spencer, Peter Webb, Katherine Hollister, Elizabeth Post. AAUW fellow, 1947-48; vis. prof. Northwestern U., 1950-57, Guggenheim fellow, 1953-54; asst. prof., asso. prof. Roosevelt U., Chgo., 1957-60; NSF fellow, 1963-64; prof. philosophy U. Ill., Chgo. Circle, 1964-70, head philosophy dept., 1964-68, Center for Advanced Study, 1968-69; prof. philosophy Northwestern U., 1970-73; Halleck prof. philosophy Yale, 1973—; fellow Center Advanced Study Behavioral Scis., 1979. Fellow Am. Acad. Arts and Scis.; mem. Council Philos. Studies, Assn. Symbolic Logic (past exec. council, exec. com. 1973, v.p. 1980), Am. Philos. Assn. (past sec.-treas., nat. dir. 1967—, pres. 1982—, chmn. nat. bd. officers 1976—), Internat. Union History and Philosophy of Sci. (chmn. U.S. nat. com.), Institut International de Philosophie, Phi Beta Kappa. Editorial bd. The Monist, Jour. Philos. Logic, Philos. Studies, Jour. Symbolic Logic, others. Contbr. to books and profl. jours. Office: Dept Philosophy Yale U New Haven CT 06520

MARDIAN, SUSAN CHRISTINE, reporter, writer, artist; b. Phoenix, Aug. 10, 1947; d. Aram Stephen and Grace (Saksanian) M.; student Ind. U., 1967-68, Stanford U., 1967, 68; B.A., Ariz. State U., 1970; postgrad. U. Calif., 1977-78. Stringer, NBC, ABC Radio News, AP Radio, NBC-TV News Program Service, 1974; reporter, consumer action column, free lance reporter city desk Phoenix Gazette, 1971-72; reporter, newscaster, producer Sta. KTAR, KBBC and KTAR-TV, Phoenix, 1973-75; asst. editor public info. office, Washington, 1972; with U.S. Postal Service, San Diego, 1978—; staff researcher, writer: Call for Action, Sta. KGTV, San Diego, 1976-77; writer PAW Soc., San Diego Zoo; media task force NOW, San Diego; reader, page Ariz. Senate, 1973. Recipient Media Excellence award San Diego County Med. Soc., 1982. Mem. Am. Women in Radio and TV, Nat. Fedn. Press Women (nat. award 1974), Ariz. Press Club (award 1973), Ariz. Press Women (2 awards 1974), Phoenix Press Club, Calif. Press Women (state award 1982), Nat. Acad. TV Arts and Scis., Ind. U. Alumni Assn. (life), Soc. Profl. Journalists-Sigma Delta Chi. Mem. United Ch. of Christ. Radio documentaries: Alcohol Abuse (first pl. nat. competition 3M Corp.), 1974; Child Abuse (nat. award), 1974; contbr. articles to various publs. Home: 7223 Enders Ave San Diego CA 92122

MARECEK, JEANNE ANN, psychologist, educator; b. Berwyn, Ill., May 28, 1946; d. Frank J. and Josephine A. (Serio) Marecek; B.S., Loyola U., Chgo., 1968; M.S., Yale U., 1972, M.Phil., 1973, Ph.D., 1973. Asst. to asso. prof. psychology Swarthmore (Pa.) Coll., 1972—; cons. in field, 1972—. NSF fellow, 1968-70; NIMH fellow, 1971-72; Nat. Inst. Child Health and Human Devel. grantee, 1977-80; Nat. Heart, Lung and Blood Inst. grantee, 1976-78; Nat. Inst. Environ. Mental Health Scis. grantee, 1976-80. Mem. Am. Psychol. Assn., Assn. for Women in Psychology, Eastern Psychol. Assn., Women in Transition (bd. dirs. Phila. 1979—, Chmn. 1980-82). Contbr. articles to profl. jours. Office: Dept Psychology Swarthmore Coll Swarthmore PA 19081

MAREK, ANN ARMSTRONG, mktg. and public relations exec.; b. N.Y.C., Feb. 20, 1935; d. Andrew F.H. Armstrong and Florence Elizabeth (White) Bowen; A.A.S., N.Mex. State U., 1956; B.A., U. Tex., Arlington, 1975; postgrad. U. Dallas, 1977; m. Gabriel Robert Marek, July 28, 1956; children—Andrew Vincent, Elizabeth Ann, Melissa Jean. Sales rep. Parker Bros., Ft. Worth, 1979, George Farha Toy Distbr. Co., Oklahoma City, 1980; area mgr. retail merchandising Mattel Sales Corp., Dallas, 1980-81; dir. community affairs Family and Individual Services Assn., Ft. Worth, 1981—; lectr. U. Tex., Arlington, 1973—. Chmn., Tarrant County Study Commn. on Children and Youth, 1973; vice chmn. Ft. Worth Utility Bd., 1976; mem. task panel on the family Pres.'s Commn. on Mental Health, 1977. Recipient Newsmaker of Yr. award Ft. Worth Press Club, 1973, Child Advocacy award Ft. Worth Mayor's Council on Youth Opportunity. Mem. Network Exec. Women, Internat. Assn. Bus. Communicators, Forum Ft. Worth. Episcopalian. Author report: The Enhancement of Parenting Skills, 1977. Home: 2324 Edwin St Fort Worth TX 76110 Office: 716 W Magnolia St Fort Worth TX 76104

MARESCA, ROSALIA LORETTA, opera co. exec.; b. N.Y.C., Aug. 16, 1923; d. Salvatore and Elizabeth Maresca; hon. grad. Cin. Conservatory of Music, 1958; studied voice with Carmen du Belier and Mario Laurenti; 1 dau., Rena Laurenti. Operatic debut as Adalgisa in Norma, Acad. of Music, N.Y.C., 1944; performances with opera cos. throughout U.S. including those of Cin., Phila., Hartford, Chautauqua, New Orleans, Bklyn., Tampa, Rochester, Washington and Syracuse; appearances in theatres throughout U.S. and Europe; tchr. music Manhattan Sch. Music, 1967-73; mgr., dir. San Carlo Opera, Fla. Lyric Opera, Matinee Opera Theatre, Clearwater, Fla., 1973—. Mem. Am. Guild Mus. Artists, Am. Guild Radio and TV Artists. Home: 1055 Stephen Foster Dr Largo FL 33541 Office: PO Box 5162 Clearwater FL 33518

MARET, KATHRYN LOUISE, coll. ofcl.; b. Reading, Pa., Sept. 23, 1925; d. Harrison M. and Emma Louise (Zerbe) Fix; B.A. in Journalism, Pa. State U., 1946; M.S., U. Wyo., 1971; m. Darrell E. Maret; children—Marcia L. Smith, Michael D. News editor U. Wyo., 1955-61, publs. editor, 1968-71; free lance editorial cons./writer, 1971-76; adminstrv. asst. for public relations Adams County (Colo.) Sch. Dist., 1976-77; editor Credit mag. Nat. Consumer Fin. Assn., Washington, 1978-80; creator, editor SERVICES mag. Bldg. Service Contractors Assn. Internat., Vienna, Va., 1980-81; info. officer Extended Learning Inst., No. Va. Community Coll., Springfield, 1982—. Recipient 1st pl. awards (2) Colo. Press Women, 1975; 1st place awards (2) Wyo. Press Women, 1970, 1st place award, 1969, 2d place awards (2), 1970, 3d place award, 1969; 3d place award Nat. Fedn. Press Women, 1969. Republican. Office: Extended Learning Inst NVCC 8000 Forbes Pl Springfield VA 22151

MARGE, DOROTHY KUNSEVILCH, gerontologist; b. Long Branch, N.J., July 30, 1938; d. John and Helen (Hladke) Kunsevich; B.A. (Irvington PTA scholar, N.J. Bell Telephone Co. scholar), Montclair State Coll., 1960; M.A., Seton Hall U., 1964; M.P.A., Syracuse U., 1978, gerontology cert., 1978, postgrad., 1978—; m. Michael Marge, July 9, 1960. Speech pathologist Clifton (N.J.) Bd. Edn., 1960-61; cons. in speech pathology and audiology, Upper Montclair, N.J., 1961-64, Springfield, Va., 1968-74; adminstr. div. speech and hearing services Prince George's County Health Dept., Cheverly, Md., 1965-68; cons. in gerontology and health delivery services, Fayetteville, N.Y., 1978—; resource cons. Affirmative Action, 1971-74; cons. to consumer info. agys., Washington, 1971-74; rep. Conf. on Gifted Children, 1977. Account exec. United Way, Syracuse, N.Y., 1978; mem. census subcom. Demographic task force Jamesville-DeWitt Central Sch. Dist., 1977; patrol leader Girl Scouts U.S.A., DeWitt, N.Y., 1979-80, co-leader Cadette Girl Scouts, 1980-82; chmn. program com. Cub Scouts Am., DeWitt, 1980-82. Recipient God and Service award Nat. Ch. Commn. for Youth Serving Agys., 1981; lic. speech pathologist, Va. Mem. Am. Speech, Lang. and Hearing Assn. (cert. clin. competence, founder, chmn. women's caucus 1970-74, founder, editor Newscap newletter 1970-74, chmn. com. on women 1971-73), Am. Soc. Public Adminstrn., Am. Public Health Assn., Gerontol. Soc., N.Y. State Public Health Assn., N.Y. State Speech and Hearing Assn., Internat. Assn. Logopedics and Phoniatrics. Contbr. to Contemporary Readings in Articulation, 1979. Home and Office: 111 Clarmar Rd Fayetteville NY 13066

MARGOLIES, ALLISON, clin. psychologist; b. N.Y.C., Feb. 11, 1953; d. Sol and Bunny (Wertans) M.; M.A., Hofstra U., 1976, Ph.D., 1979. Psychologist, Bernard Fineson Developmental Ctr., Queens Village, N.Y., 1979-82; cons. psychologist Aurora Concept, Flushing, N.Y., 1981—; assoc. psychologist Queens Children's Psychiat. Hosp., Bellerose, N.Y., 1982—; pvt. practice clin. psychology, Lawrence, N.Y., 1982—. Lic. psychologist N.Y. State; cert. sch. psychologist N.Y. State. Mem. Am. Psychol. Assn., Nassau County Psychol. Assn., Phi Beta Kappa. Qualified expert witness, N.Y. Supreme Ct. Home: 611 Arbucke Ave Woodmere NY 11598 Office: 371 Central Ave Lawrence NY 11559

MARGOLIN, CYNTHIA RAE, psychologist, educator; b. Los Angeles, Aug. 19, 1941; d. Samuel Isaac and Pearl Victoria (Grody) Margolin; B.A., U. Calif. Berkeley, 1963; M.A., U. Minn., Ph.D. (NIMH fellow), 1966; children—Kevin Murray Gliner, Meegan Ilene Gliner. Research asso., instr. Inst. Child Devel., U. Minn., Mpls., 1966-68; asst. prof. psychology Stanford (Calif.) U., 1968-69; adminstrv. fellow Calif. State U., Hayward, 1981-82; prof. psychology and child devel. San Jose State U., Calif., 1969—. Mem. Soc. for Research in Child Devel. Am. Psychol. Assn., Western Psychol. Assn., NOW, Calif. Women in Higher Edn., Phi Beta Kappa. Contbr. articles in field to profl. jours. Office: Psychology Dept San Jose State U San Jose CA 95192

MARGOLIS, ESTHER LUTERMAN, adminstrv. asst.; b. Pitts., Jan. 12, 1939; d. Nathan and Belle (Fogel) Luterman; B.S., Ariz. State U., 1976, M.S., 1978; m. Herbert Marvin Margolis, Apr. 15, 1962; children—Ruth Lys, Judith Lyn. Statistician, court planners office Ariz. Supreme Ct., 1976-77; planner Ariz. Dept. Corrections, 1979; adminstrv. asst. planning and research bur. Phoenix Police Dept., 1979—; instr. Phoenix Community Coll., 1980-82. Mem. textbook selection com. Roosevelt Sch. Dist., Phoenix, 1975; chmn. bd. YMCA, South Mountain br., 1977-81; bd. mgrs. Phoenix and Valley of the Sun YMCA, 1978-81; pres. bd. dirs. Do it Now Found., 1978-80; bd. dirs. Boys' Clubs Phoenix, 1982—. Mem. Am. Soc. Public Adminstrn., Am. Soc. Criminology, Nat. Council Crime and Delinquency, Nat. Assn. Women in Criminal Justice, Profl. Women for Kennedy. Editor ann. report Phoenix Police Dept., 1979-81. Home: 9046 S 22d St Phoenix AZ 85040 Office: 620 W Washington St Phoenix AZ 85003

MARGOLIS, JAN RUTH, pharm. co. exec.; b. Rahway, N.J., Feb. 14, 1944; d. Tyrus William and Clara Belle (Gratcyk) Peck; B.S., Boston U., 1966, M.Ed., 1967; m. Fredrick H. Margolis, Mar. 14, 1969 (div.). Dir. credit union devel. low-income areas Bur. Fed. Credit Union, New Eng. region, 1967-68; asst. dir. Center for Vol. Soc., Washington, 1970-73; dir.

div. life devel. for women F.M. Assos., Ltd., subs. Middle West Service Corp., Washington, 1973-74; pres. Jan Margolis & Co., Washington, 1974-76; dir. human resource devel. Greater S.E. Community Hosp., Washington, 1976-78; dir. mgmt. edn. and orgn. devel. Bristol-Myers Co., N.Y.C., 1978-80, corp. dir. personnel devel., 1980—; founder Race Inst., Met. Ecumenical Tng. Center, Washington, 1969; vis. prof. Sch. Public Adminstrn., U. So. Calif., 1973-76; instr. U. Wis. Extension, 1973-76; vis. prof. Community Coll. Mgmt. Devel. Program, 1973-76; instr. Hosp. Ednl. and Research Found. Pa., 1973-76, Georgetown U. Sch. Summer and Continuing Edn. and Xavier U. Inst. Bus. and Community Devel., 1973-76, U. Md., Univ. Coll., 1973-76. Boston U. Grad. Sch. Edn. and Coll. Bus. Adminstrn., 1973-77; mem. adv. council Nat. Center Research in Vocat. Edn., 1980-81; mem. adv. bd. Ednl. Testing Service, Princeton, N.J., 1980-81; asso. Am. Center Quality Work Life, Washington, 1979-82; mem. Ind. U. Exec. Program Adv. Bd., 1979-83; dir. Russell Co., Ltd., U.K., 1981—. Mem. Internat. Fedn. Tng. and Devel. Orgns. (dir. 1979-81), Adult Edn. Assn. Am., NOW, Orgn. Devel. Network for NTL Inst., Am. Soc. Tng. and Devel. (nat. pres. 1979), Am. Assn. Humanistic Psychology, Human Resource Planning Soc., AAAS, World Future Soc., Pi Lambda Theta. Author: A Project Writer's Manual, 1968; Management Training for Nursing Home Supervisors, 1969; Politics of Training and Development, 1980; contbr. articles in field to profl. jours. Home: 181 Maple Ave Metuchen NJ 08840 Office: 345 Park Ave New York NY 10154

MARGOSIAN, LUCILLE K. MANOUGIAN (MRS. ERVIN M. MARGOSIAN), artist, educator; b. Highland Park, Mich.; d. George Krikor and Vera Varsenig (Jernukian) Manougian; B.F.A., Wayne State U., 1957, M.A., 1958; postgrad. Calif. State U., Fresno, 1959-60, U. Calif. at Berkeley, 1960-61; m. Ervin M. Margosian, Oct. 28, 1960; children—Rebecca L., Rachel L. One-man show at Jackson's Gallery, Berkeley, Calif., 1961; exhibited in group shows at Detroit Art Inst., 1958, Oakland (Calif.) Art Museum, 1961, Wayne State U. Community Arts Center, Detroit, 1965, San Francisco Ann. Art Festivals, 1967, 68, 69, Jack London Square Arts Festival, Oakland, 1969, 70, Judah L. Magnes Meml. Mus., Berkeley, 1970, Kaiser Center Gallery, Oakland, 1970, Oakland Mus. Changing Gallery, 1969, Olive Hyde Art Center, Fremont, 1971, 73, Richmond (Calif.) Art Center, 1972, Villa Montalvo Galleries at Phelan Estate, Saratoga, Calif., 1976, others; faculty Peralta Community Colls., Laney campus, Oakland, 1967—, prof. art, 1970—, chmn. dept., 1982— . Charter mem. univ. art mus. council U. Calif. at Berkeley, 1965—. Recipient Certificate of Distinguished Achievement, Am. Legion, 1950; Best of Show 1st prize 5th Ann. Textile Exhbn., Fremont, Calif., 1973; Merit award City of Fremont, 1973, Zellerbach Bldg. Gallery, San Francisco, 1975. Mem. Calif. Art Edn. Assn., Oakland Museum Assn., Richmond Art Center, Women of Wayne, Wayne State U. Alumni Assn., East Bay Watercolor Soc., Internat. Platform Assn., Am. Fedn. Tchrs., Peralta Fedn. Tchrs. Office: Laney Coll Art Dept 900 Fallon St Oakland CA 94607

MARGULIS, MARTHA SUSAN BOYER, artist; b. Jersey City, Jan. 5, 1928; d. Henry and Jeanette (Sams) Boyer; B.F.A., Syracuse U., 1949; postgrad. Columbia U., 1950-51; m. Melvin Margulis, Mar. 11, 1951; children—Caryn, Shari, Beth. One woman shows include: White Plains (N.Y.) Library, 1965, Brook Artists Gallery, 1966, Avanti Gallery, N.Y.C., 1970, Harvey Sch., Katonah, N.Y., 1974, Mamaroneck (N.Y.) Artists, 1977, Bell Gallery, Greenwich, Conn., 1977, 79, 80, Pindar Gallery, N.Y.C., 1978, 79, 81, Vered Internat. Gallery, Easthampton, N.Y., 1979, River Gallery, Irvington, N.Y., 1979, 80, Silvermine Guild Center for the Arts, 1981; exhibited in group shows Audubon Artists Ann., 1965-75, Nat. Arts Club, 1970, Nat. Soc. Painters in Casein and Acrylic, 1973, 74, N.Mex. Internat., 1976, Bklyn. Mus., 1975, Riverside Mus., N.Y.C., 1968, Hudson River Mus., Yonkers, N.Y., 1972, Bruce Mus., Greenwich, 1974, Marymount Coll., 1973, Southampton U., 1970, Stamford (Conn.) Mus., 1979, Butler Inst. Arts, Youngstown, Ohio, 1980, Nat. Assn. Women Artists Invitational, Israel, Egypt, 1981-82, Cayuga Mus., Auburn, N.Y., 1981, Nicolaysen Art Mus., Casper, Wyo., 1981, Jesse Besser Mus., Alpena, Mich., 1982, Charles and Emma Frye Mus., Seattle, 1982; represented in permanent collections Pepsico Inc., Syracuse U., Fed. Home Bank Bd., N.Y. State Coll. Optometry, Herbert F. Johnson Mus. Art, Cornell U., Everson Mus. Art, Syracuse, N.Y., Mobil Oil Corp., Hearst Corp., IBM Corp., Bankers Trust Co., Inc., Smith, Kline and French, Inc. Recipient 1st prizes in painting Westchester Arts Soc., 1975, Brook Artists Guild, 1970, Sindin Harris award, 1974, Jean Magid Leeman meml. prize New Eng. Exhbn. Painting, Drawing and Sculpture, 1979. Mem. Pindar Gallery, N.Y.C., Artists Equity N.Y., Nat. Assn. Women Artists (Jean Magid Leeman Meml. award 1979), Women in Arts, Mamaroneck Artists Guild (membership chmn., dir., 2d prize 1979), Hudson River Contemporary Artists. Home and Office: Valley Ridge Rd Harrison NY 10528

MARIANI, JEANNE MARIE, advt. co. exec.; b. N.Y.C., Dec. 19, 1950; d. Robert Richard and Mary Theresa (Palmeri) M.; B.A., Fordham U., 1972. Media buyer Carity-Hoffman Advt., N.Y.C., 1972-77; media dir. Sweet & Co. Advt., N.Y.C., 1977—. Mem. Nat. Assn. Female Execs. Office: 845 3d Ave New York NY 10022

MARIEL, photographer, former fabrication co. exec.; b. Pasadena, Calif., Aug. 5, 1938; d. Oscar Branche and Mary Lincoln (Hicks) Jackson; adopted dau. William Nathan Turner; m. Donald E. Coombes, June 13, 1957 (div. June 1972); children—William Cullen, Anna Maria, Joel Howard; 1 son by previous marriage, Scott Craig Goodwin. Co-incorporator, Mineral Harvestors Inc., Salem, Oreg., 1966-71, Ariz. Custom Mfg. Inc, Phoenix, 1971-81, bus. mgr., pres., 1972-81; pres. Ariz. Custom Steel, Phoenix, 1976-81, Eagle Erectors, Phoenix, 1979-81; now with Lazarus Enterprises; former co-owner WCS Constrn., Inc. Asst. dist.coordinator Oreg. Republican Party, 1964. Mem. Nat. Assn. Women Bus. Owners, Nat. Assn. Female Execs., Ariz. Network Profl. Women, Women Emerging, Internat. Platform Assn., Tolsum Farm Homeowners Assn., Ariz. Steel Fabricators Assn. (past pres.). Republican. Mem. Reorganized Ch. Jesus Christ of Latter-day Saints. Clubs: Intertel, Mensa. Home: PO Box 344825 Dallas TX 75234

MARIL, NADJA, writer, businesswoman; b. Balt., Mar. 24, 1954; d. Herman and Esta (Cook) M.; B.A. cum laude in Anthropology, U. Calif., Santa Barbara, 1975; m. Cyril J. Patrick, Aug. 26, 1978. Free lance newspaper feature writer, Santa Barbara, 1973-76; asst. mgr. J.C. Patrick Ltd., Provincetown, Mass., 1976—; mgr. Gryphon, Provincetown, 1977-80; co-owner Rare and Beautiful Things, 1980—; dir. Cottage Gallery, Provincetown, 1979—; author: Me, Molly Midnight: The Artist's Cat, 1977; Runaway, Molly Midnight: The Artists Cat, 1980. Sec., Provincetown Democratic Town Com., 1979. Mem. LWV (dir. lower Cape Cod chpt. 1978-79). Office: 210 Commercial St Provincetown MA 02657

MARIN, CAROL A., TV journalist; b. Evanston, Ill., Oct. 10, 1948; d. Knut H. and Bernice M. (Johnson) M.; B.A. in English, U. Ill., Urbana, 1970. Reporter, weekend anchor, asst. news dir. Sta. WBIR-TV, Knoxville, Tenn., 1972-76; reporter, anchor Sta. WSM-TV, Nashville, 1976-78, WMAQ-TV, Chgo., 1978—. Recipient Media award John Howard Assn., 1981; 5 Emmy's, Chgo. Acad. TV Arts and Scis. Address: Sta WMAQ-TV News Merchandise Mart Chicago IL 60654

MARIN, ROSA CELESTE, research cons., social work educator; b. Arecibo, P.R., June 1, 1912; d. Angel M. and Justa (Marin) Marin; B.S., U. P.R., 1933; M.S., U. Pitts., 1944, D.S.W., 1953. Social welfare officer, acting dist. dir., supr. Fed. Emergency Relief Adminstrn., 1933-36; social worker, gen. supr. in charge of research P.R. Reconstrn. Adminstrn., 1936-40; supr. spl. projects and head research sect. Div. of Pub. Welfare P.R., 1940-44; asst. prof. U. P.R. Sch. Social Work, 1944-59, dir. Grad. Sch. Social Work, 1967-74, dir. research unit, 1955-74, prof., 1967-74, prof. emeritus, 1980—; cons. on research to supr. ednl. council cons. VA, Dept. Services Against Addiction, Coll. Pharmacy, Municipal Govt. San Juan; chmn. Welfare Devel. Corp.; mem. Council Human Resources. Mem. Assn. Tchrs. P.R., Nat. Assn. Social Workers, Nat. Conf. on Social Welfare, Coll. Social Workers, Soc. Newspaperwomen, Am. Acad. Polit. and Social Scis., Am. Assn. Statisticians, Assn. Research Centers Adminstrn. Editor: Revista Servicio Social, 1949-50, 52-65. Author: Compilation of Adminstrative Cases: Study of dependent Multiproblem Families in Puerto Rico; co-author: Manpower Resources and Projections. Editor Jour. Humanidad. Contbr. articles to profl. jours. Home: PO Box 6679 Santurce PR 00914 Office: 2153 Teniente Lavergne St Santurce PR 00913

MARIN, VIRGINIA PARKER, data processor; b. Huntsville, Ala., Dec. 27, 1937; d. Lawrence Goldsmith and Hester W. Parker; A.A., West Valley Coll., Saratoga, Calif., 1976; m. Richard P. Marin, Jan. 26, 1974. Sr. sec. specialist IBM Corp., 1962-73; sr. sec. specialist, tech. writer Service Bur. Co., Campbell, Calif., 1973-74, installation specialist data processing, 1976—. Mem. Internat. Platform Assn., Nat. Assn. Female Execs. Republican. Club: Still Waters Golf and Country (Dadeville, Ala.). Home: 3131 Homestead Rd Santa Clara CA Office: 700 W Hamilton Ave Campbell CA 95008

MARINA, DORITA ROCA, clin. psychologist; b. Havana, Cuba, Jan. 15, 1929; came to U.S., 1942, naturalized, 1951; d. Luis and Dora (Rodriguez) Roca; Ph.D. in Psychology, U. Miami, 1975; children—Marc Robinson, Lili Forni. Instr., Fla. Atlantic U., Boca Raton, 1968-70; research asst. Center for Advanced Internat. Studies, U. Miami (Fla.), 1973-75; research asst. prof. Spanish Family Guidance Clinic, U. Miami, 1975-77; dir. Family and Children's Achievement Center of Dade County, Miami, 1977-80; dir. Miami Psychol. Services. Treas. Dade-Monroe Mental Health Bd., 1978-79, v.p., 1979-81; 2d v.p. Mental Health Assn. Dade County, 1978; bd. dirs. YWCA, Miami. Recipient award Mental Health Assn. Dade County, 1977, 78. Mem. Fla. Psychol. Assn. (exec. council 1979-81), Dade County Psychol. Assn. (exec. council), Nat. Hispanic Psychol. Assn., So. Fla. Hispanic Psychol. Assn. (exec. com. 1979—), Fedn. Hispanic Employees Met. Dade. Unitarian. Club: Cuban Women's. Home: 11880 Bird Rd Miami FL 33175

MARINAN, ONDRIA ROSE CARBONE, nursing home adminstr.; b. Bklyn., Jan. 14, 1942; d. Gennaro A. and Mary J. (Alessio) Carbone; student Brookdale Community Coll., 1973-74; m. John Joseph Marinan, 3d, May 27, 1962; children—John, Lynn, Gene. Mcpl. bond. sec. Halsey Stuart & Co., N.Y.C., 1960-63; exec. sec. Henry Strauss Prodns., N.Y.C., 1964-65; adminstrv. sec. Atlantic Highlands (N.J.) Nursing Home, 1972—. Democrat. Home: 13 Lakeside Dr Navesink NJ 07752 Office: Atlantic Highlands Nursing Home 8 Middletown Ave Atlantic Highlands NJ 07716

MARINER, MARION BRANUM, home economist; b. Loyston, Tenn., Feb. 18, 1925; d. Elvin and Gertrude (Coppock) Branum; B.A., Berea Coll., 1946; M.S., U. Tenn., 1968; m. George Thomas Mariner, Feb. 26, 1949; 1 son, George Thomas. With U. Tenn. Agrl. Extension Service, Campbell County, 1946-49, Claiborne and Roane counties, 1957-70; tchr. Anderson County, Union County and Campbell County schs., Tenn., 1949-57; asso. prof. home econs. Agrl. Extension Service, U. Tenn., Knoxville, 1970—. Mem. Norris Community Library Bd. Recipient Disting. Service award Nat. Assn. Extension Home Economists, 1965. Mem. Am. Home Econs. Assn., Tenn. Home Econs. Assn., Knoxville Area Home Econs. Assn., Tenn. Assn. Extension Home Economists, Nat. 4-H Agts. Assn., Nat. Council Family Relations, Southeastern Council Family Relations, Tenn. Council Family Relations, Nat. Assn. for the Young Child, Tenn. Assn. for the Young Child, Knoxville Assn. for the Young Child, Lake City Bus. and Profl. Women's Club (corr. sec.), Berea Coll. Alumni Assn., Delta Kappa Gamma (pres. Pi chpt. 1982—), Epsilon Sigma Phi, Gamma Sigma Delta. Republican. Methodist. Club: U.T. Century. Home: 49 Deer Ridge Rd Norris TN 37828 Office: 123 Morgan Hall PO Box 1071 Knoxville TN 37901

MARINO, KAREN LUCILLE, assn. exec.; b. Trenton, N.J., Dec. 2, 1953; d. Francesco Salvatore and Alvera (Settipane) M.; B.S., So. Conn. State Coll., 1975; M.B.A., U. New Haven, 1981. Adminstrv. control analyst Gen. Dynamics div. Electric Boat, Groton, Conn., 1976-78; maritime researcher, tech. editor Eclectech Assocs., North Stonington, Conn., 1978—. Mem. Assn. MBA Execs., Am. Mktg. Assn., Am. Mgmt. Assn. Office: North Stonington Profl Center Eclectech Assos North Stonington CT 06359

MARINO, PAULA VARSALONA, fashion designer; b. Kansas City, Mo., Nov. 10, 1949; d. Paul Lewis and Dorothy (Crockett) Varsalone; student Washington U., St. Louis; m. Joseph A. Marino, Aug. 19, 1978. Designer, Loungees Loungewear, N.Y.C., 1971, Profolio Technique, N.Y.C., 1971-72, Pandora Frocks, N.Y.C., 1972-75; designer, owner Paula Varsalona Ltd., N.Y.C., 1975—; cons., speaker in field. Mem. Fashion Group. Roman Catholic. Office: 499 7th Ave New York NY 10018 *

MARIS, LORRAINE, publisher; b. Nyssa, Oreg., Sept. 7, 1941; d. Robert H. Cooper I and Edna O. Thomsen; degree in acctg. U. Nebr., 1972; degree in journalism Peninsula Coll., Port Angeles, Wash., 1973; m. John Albert Maris, Oct. 11, 1980; children—Chris King, Alan King, Collin King. Owner, Forks Forum-Peninsula Herald, Olympic Peninsula, Wash., 1976—; pres. Forum-Herald Pub. Corp., Forks, 1978—; pub. Property Rights Review, Forks, Wash., 1980—; v.p. Berg Shake, Inc., Forks, 1967-78. Committeewoman Republican party; mem. Clallam County Mus. Bd.; pres. PTA; bd. dirs. Nat. Land Alliance; mem. Wash. Gov.'s Com. Rural Devel. Mem. Wash. Newspaper Pubs. Assn., West End Bus. and Profl. Assn., Clallan County Econ. Devel. Council. Republican. Club: Toastmistress. Home: PO Box 908 Forks WA 98331 Office: PO Box 300 Forks WA 98331

MARISKA, FLORENCE MAE, cons. b. Chgo., May 14, 1928; d. Henry Louis and Mae (Skach) M.; B.A. magna cum laude in Acctg., Calif. State U., Fullerton, 1975, M.B.A. in Internat. Bus., 1977; children—M. Christine, Gregory C. Acct., controller Gulf & Western Industries, Orange, Calif., 1966-73; controller Boehringer Mannheim, Fountain Valley, Calif., 1976; controller Mead Corp., Garden Grove, Calif., 1977-81; instr. Santa Ana Coll., UCLA, Cypress Coll.; pres. Mariska and Assocs., cons., 1981—. Mem. Nat. Assn. Accts., Internat. Platform Assn. (Woman of Yr. 1973), Beta Alpha Psi, Phi Kappa Phi. Home: 13761 Carlsbad Dr Santa Ana CA 92705 Office: PO Box 202 Tustin CA 92680 sculptress; b. Paris, May 22, 1930; ed. Ecole des Beaux-Arts, Paris, 1949, Art Students League, N.Y.C., 1950, New Sch. for Social Research, 1951-54, Hans Hofmann Sch., N.Y.C., 1951-54. Exhibited in one-man shows at Sidney Janis Gallery, N.Y.C., 1966, 67, 75, Hanover Gallery, London, 1967, Boymans-van Beuningen Mus., Rotterdam, Netherlands, 1968, Moore Coll. Art, Phila., 1970, Worcester (Mass.) Art Mus., 1971, N.Y. Cultural Center, 1973, Columbus (Ohio) Gallery of Fine Arts, 1974, numerous others; exhibited in group shows, including Painting of a Decade, Tate Gallery, London, 1964; New Realism, Municipal Mus., The Hague, 1964; Carnegie Internat., Pitts., 1964; Art of the U.S.A., 1670-1966, Whitney Mus. Am. Art, N.Y.C., 1966; American Sculpture of the Sixties, Mus. of Art, Los Angeles, 1967; Biennale, Venice, 1968; Art Inst. Chgo., 1968; Image of Man Today, Inst. Contemporary Arts, London, 1968; represented in permanent collections at Mus. Modern Art, N.Y.C., Whitney Mus. Am. Art, Albright-Knox Gallery, Buffalo, Hakone Open Air Mus., Tokyo, Nat. Portrait Gallery, Washington, Harry N. Abrams Collection, N.Y.C., Yale U. Art Gallery, numerous others. Mem. Am. Acad., Inst. Arts and Letters. Address: care Sidney Janis Gallery 6 W 57th St New York NY 10019 *

MARK, JONI LIPTON, psychiatric social worker; b. N.Y.C., Dec. 1, 1937; d. Daniel M. and Beatrice C. (Lazar) Lipton; B.S., N.Y. U., 1962, M.A., 1963; M.A., So. Conn. State Coll., 1969; M.S.W., U. Conn., 1973; m. Harry H. Mark, Feb. 3, 1963; children—Tami, Hayley. Pvt. practice psychotherapy Women's Counseling and Psychotherapy Center, New Haven, 1975—; staff Greater Bridgeport (Conn.) Community Mental Health Center, 1973-75, Conn. Mental Health Center, New Haven, 1975-77. Fellow Am. Orthopsychiat. Assn.; mem. Conn. Soc. for Clin. Social Work, Nat. Registry of Health Care Providers in Clin. Social Work, Acad. Cert. Social Workers, Nat. Assn. Social Workers. 34 Janet Dr North Haven CT 06473 Office: 210 Prospect St New Haven CT 06511

MARKHAM, JUDIE ANNE, personnel and tng. cons.; b. Roanoke, Va., May 5, 1944; d. Maxine B. Phelps; B.S. in Psychology, Coll. William and Mary, Williamsburg, Va., 1977; divorced; children—William Joseph, Kelly Marie. Mdse. buyer, store mgr. So. Dept. Stores, 1966-67; div. mgr., then regional personnel dir. and tng. mgr. Leggett Stores, Manannssas, Roanoke, Norfolk, Newport News and Hampton, Va., 1968-77; tng. specialist Thalhimers, Hampton, then regional personnel dir., Greensboro, N.C., 1978-81; owner, Profl. Devel. Resources, Greensboro, 1981—. Mem. Roanoke County Sch. Bd., 1973-74; co-chmn. Roanoke United Way, 1973-74; adv. Roanoke Adult Edn. Bd., 1972-74; mem. adv. bd. Thomas Nelson Coll., 1975-76, Roanoke Meml. Hosp., 1973-75. Recipient Employer of Yr. award Regional Distributive Edn. Roanoke County, 1974. Mem. Am. Soc. Tng. and Devel., Am. Soc. Personnel Adminstrs., Nat. Assn. Women Execs. Presbyterian. Author handbook. Home: 4608-D Mercury Dr Greensboro NC 27410 Office: PO Box 7894 Greensboro NC 27407

MARKHAM, MARY ELIZABETH THORNTON (MRS. REGINALD A. MARKHAM), state ofcl.; b. Haverhill, Mass.; d. John W. and Mary E. (Murphy) Thornton; B.A., Regis Coll., 1937; M.Ed., Salem State Coll., 1968; m. Reginald A. Markham, Feb. 26, 1954 (dec. 1981). With Mass. Div. Employment Security, 1937-81, prin. counselor N.E. area Mass., Lawrence, 1965-70, mgr. concentrated employment program, Lowell, 1970-71, supervising mgr., 1971-73, supervisory mgr., Lowell, 1973-75, Haverhill-Newburyport area, 1975-77, Lawrence, 1977-81. Bd. dirs. Merrimack River council Girl Scouts Am., 1965-73, chmn. personnel com., 1965-73, v.p., 1972-75; sec. Medford Ancillary Manpower Planning Bd., 1972-73; mem. steering com. project vol. power Malden Mayor's Com. for Employment of Handicapped, 1972-73; bd. dirs. No. Essex Regional Community Action Commn., Area Manpower Planning Bd.; mem. advisory bd. Whittier Regional Vocat. and Tech. Sch.; mem. Merrimack Valley Econ. and Devel. Com., Greater Lawrence, Haverhill coms. employment of handicapped, Greater Lawrence Community Service Assos. Address: 180 Water St Apt 503 Haverhill MA 01830

MARKIEWICZ, ROSEMARY ERRIGO PATRICK, Realtor; b. Los Angeles, Apr. 26, 1955; d. Harry and Rose (Ohayon) Errigo; cert. real estate acad.; m. Joseph S. Markiewicz, Aug. 13, 1982. Flight dispatcher flight sch., Van Nuys, Calif., 1971-74, Flying Tiger Line, Los Angeles, 1974-75; salesperson Brown Realtors, Thousand Oaks, Calif., 1975-79; sales mgr. Spring Realty, Westlake Village, Calif., 1979-81; br. mgr. Coldwell Banker, Westlake Village, 1981—. Mem. Calif. Republican Women's Club: publicity chairperson Conejo Valley Bd., 1978-80. Mem. Women's Council Realtors, Nat. Assn. Realtors, Calif. Assn. Realtors. Office: 650 Westlake Blvd Westlake Village CA 91362

MARKKULA, BEULAH PETERS, real estate broker, educator; b. Chgo., Sept. 25, 1917; d. George H. and Margaret G. (Schneider) Schumacher; cert. in Real Estate, Victor Valley Coll., 1973, A.S., 1979, Cert. in Escrow, 1980; m. Frank Lanser, Sept. 28, 1940 (dec. Aug. 1954); children—Vivian, Yvonne Fox, Valerie Deems, Frank G., Jack F., Jill Marie; m. William Peters, Dec. 16, 1961 (dec. Aug. 1972); m. Raymond F. Markkula, Sept. 26, 1975. Salesman, V.A. Cornish Realty, Victorville, Cal., 1965-69; broker, owner Tri-Valley Realty Co., Victorville, 1969—. Instr., Victor Valley Coll., 1970—, mem. real estate adv. com., 1970-72. Vice pres. bd. dirs. Victor Valley Meml. Park. Named Realtor of Year, 1973. Mem. Victor Valley Bd. Realtors (pres. 1972, edn. chmn. 1980), Calif. Real Estate Assn. (state dir.), Santa Maria (pres. 1952-53), Victor Valley (pres. 1971-72) bus. and profl. women's clubs, Victor Valley Altrusa Club (pres. 1975-76). Home: 15700 Rimrock Rd Apple Valley CA 92307 Office: 15647 Village Dr Victorville CA 92392

MARKLEY, BLANCH LUCIEL, interior designer; b. Lima, Ohio; d. Frank C. and Emma (Rouge) Frisbie; student Lima Bus. Coll., Northwestern U.; m. Merritt M. Markley. Interior designer; formerly builder homes; owner, interior designer Blanch L. Markley Shoppe, Lima, Ohio, 1953—; lectr. interior design; appraiser fine arts estates and Oriental rugs. Mem. Am. Soc. Interior Designers, Oriental Rug Retail Assn., Better Bus. Bur., Lima C. of C., Internat. Platform Assn., Armenian Rug Soc. Club: Shawnee Country. Home: 5210 S Dixie Lima OH 45806 Office: 4208 S Dixie Lima OH 45806

MARKLEY, KAROL JEAN, mfr., designer riding apparel, exec. constrn. co.; b. Los Angeles, Mar. 26, 1939; d. Ashby V. Pearce and Jean (Xuma) Pearce Himes; B.A. cum laude, UCLA, 1968; M.A. in Psychology, U. Calif., Riverside, 1971; m. Francis Edward Markley, July 20, 1957; children—Teal Len, Tawne Anne. Research asst. to psychologist Arthur Janov, Los Angeles, 1967-70; dir., officer Francis E. Markley Corp., Francis E. Markley & Co., Inc., Palm Springs, Calif., 1971—, pres., 1977—; exec. mgr. Markley Mgmt. Services, Palm Springs, 1971—; co-designer, builder Francis E. Markley Corp., constrn. co., Palm Springs, 1971—; designer, coordinator, mfr. riding apparel Karol Markley Enterprises, Palm Springs, 1975—; owner The Final Touch, Palm Springs, 1975—; guest speaker horsemanship clinics. Mem. Am. Horse Shows Assn. (stock seat equitation com. 1977—, vice chmn. 1982—), Internat. Arabian Horse Assn. (equitation com. 1971—). Address: 2966 Via Vaquero Palm Springs CA 92262

MARKMAN, EDITH HALADJOFF, violinist; b. Detroit, Nov. 4, 1950; d. Luben Jecheff and Ilona (Potye) Haladjoff; student New Eng. Conservatory of Music, 1968-70, Yale U. Sch. Music, 1973; m. Michael Markman, Nov. 21, 1974; 1 dau., Shayne Laurel. Concertmaster, Las Vegas Celebrity Show, 1974-79; various solo and chamber music appearances in the Southwest; 1st violin sect. Los Angeles Philharm., 1979; recs. for comml. TV and motion pictures, Hollywood, Calif. Home: 6420 Antigua Pl Canoga Park CA 91307

MARKOVICH, OLGA, mag. editor; b. Toronto, Ont., Can., Feb. 24, 1940; d. Bozidar Marinko and Milica (Trumich) Markovich; diploma in journalism Ryerson Poly. Inst., 1965, B. Applied Arts in Journalism, 1973. Asst. editor Shoe and Leather Jour., Southam Communications, Ltd., Don Mills, Ont., 1965-72, asso. editor, 1972; editor Southam Bldg. Guide, Don Mills, 1972—; mng. editor Can. Indsl. Equipment News, 1975-77, editor, 1977—. Recipient Thomas Turner Meml. award

Southam Communications Ltd., 1973, Mktg. award Southam Communications, 1977. Mem. Bus. Press Editors Assn., Am. Bus. Press, Soc. Serbian Writers and Artists Abroad (London), Serbian Nat. Shield Soc. Can., Serb Nat. Fedn. Progressive Conservative. Eastern Orthodox. Author: Serbs in Canada—Their Immigration and Settlements, 1965. Editor: Tributes to Mihailovich, 1966; Vinka Testimonial Book, 1977; Souvenir Book: 35th Anniversary of the Circle of Serbian Sisters, 1976; contbr. Am. Srbobran, Voice of Can. Serbs. Home: 254 Chine Dr Scarborough ON M1M 2L8 Canada Office: 1450 Don Mills Rd Don Mills ON M3B 2X7 Canada

MARKOVICH-TREECE, PATRICIA HELEN, economist; b. Oakland, Calif., Sept. 26, 1941; s. Patrick Joseph and Helen Emily (Prydz) Markovich; B.A. in Econs.; M.S. in Econs.; postgrad. (Lilly Found. grantee) Stanford U., (NSF grantee) Oreg. Grad. Research Center; children—Michael Sean, Bryan Jeffry, Tiffany Helene. Analyst, Dean Witter & Co.; with public relations dept. Pettler Advt., Inc.; pvt. practice polit. and econs. cons.; aide to majority whip Oreg. Ho. of Reps.; lectr., instr., various Calif. instns., Chemeketa (Oreg.) Coll., Portland (Oreg.) State U.; free lance urban and corp. planning cons.; mktg. and sales dir. Peritek Corp. Commr., City of Oakland (Calif.), 1970-74. Mem. Mensa.

MARKS, BARBARA DIANE, physician; b. Johnstown, Pa., June 22, 1938; d. Robert Herman and Vera Mae (Koontz) M.; B.S., Georgetown U., 1959; M.D., U. Miami, Coral Gables, Fla., 1965, Ph.D., 1972. Intern, St. Mary's Hosp., Grand Rapids, Mich., 1981-82; psychiat. resident Mich. State U./Pine Rest Christian Hosp., Grand Rapids, 1982—; mem. staff St. Mary's Hosp. Trustee Child Guidance Center, Kalamazoo, 1981-82. Served with USAF, 1968-70. Decorated Air Force Commendation medal, Legion of Merit. Mem. Am. Psychiat. Assn., Am. Psychol. Assn., Acad. Mgmt. Mich. Acad. Arts and Scis., S.W. Mich. Psychiat. Assn., Kalamazoo Acad. Medicine, AMA, Mich. Med. Soc., Phi Beta Kappa (pres. S.W. Mich. assn. 1980-82). Republican. Roman Catholic. Reviewer Am. Reference Books Ann., 1982; cons. reviewer Reference & Subscription Rev., 1981. Home: 2729 Mockingbird Dr Kalamazoo MI 49008 Office: St Mary's Hosp Grand Rapids MI 49503

MARKS, ELAINE, educator; b. N.Y.C., Nov. 13, 1930; d. Harry and Ruth (Elin) M.; A.B. magna cum laude, Bryn Mawr Coll., 1952; M.A., U. Pa., 1953; Ph.D., N.Y.U., 1958. Instr. French N.Y.U., 1957-60, asst. prof., 1960-62; assoc. prof. dept. French, U. Wis., Milw., 1963-65; prof. of French, U. Mass., Amherst, 1965-66, 72-73, vis. prof., 1971; prof. dept. French and Italian, U. Wis., Madison, 1966-68, 80—, dir. Women's Studies program, 1977—, lectr., 1977; manuscript reader several book pubs., 1980-82; mem. grad. record exams. com. Examiners for Advances Test in French, 1978-82; mem. Council of French Social and Cultural Affairs, N.Y.U., 1981—. Panelist, Nat. Endowment for the Humanities, 1973-77. Mem. MLA (exec. com. div. women's studies in lang. 1977-82), Midwest Modern Lang. Assn. (exec. com. 1978-81), Am. Assn. Tchrs. French, Nat. Women's Studies Assn. Author: Colette, 1960; Encounters with Death: An Essay on the Sensibility of Simone de Beauvoir, 1973; contbr. numerous articles and revs. on French lit. to profl. pubs.; editorial bd. Signs: Jour. of Women in Culture and Society, 1976—; co-editor Homosexualities and French Literature, 1979; New French Feminisms, 1980. Home: 2040 Field St Madison WI 53713 Office: 618 Van Hise Hall U Wis Madison WI 53706

MARKS, ESTELLE, ednl. adminstr.; b. N.Y.C., Nov. 28, 1924; d. Harry and Dora (Altman) Horowitz; B.S., N.Y. U., 1950; M.S., Columbia U., 1951, profl. diploma Tchrs. Coll., 1970; m. George Peabody Marks, III, Oct. 9, 1945; children—George Peabody, Hugh Zachary. Periodical checker periodicals div. N.Y. Public Library, 1948-50; serials cataloger cataloging dept. Columbia U. Library, 1950-51; librarian young adult, asst. br. Bklyn. Public Library, 1951-53; librarian Morris Hills Regional High Sch., Rockaway, N.J., 1954-55, Cranford (N.J.) High Sch., 1955-56; with Woodbridge Twp. Sch. Dist., Woodbridge, N.J., 1957—, supr. lang. arts and media, 1981—. Mem. bd. trustees Free Library of Woodbridge, 1974-82. Served with U.S. Army WAC, 1945. Mem. Am. Library Assn., Am. Assn. Sch. Librarians, N.J. Adminstrs. Assn. Unitarian-Universalist. Home: 260 A Main St Woodbridge NJ 07095 Office: PO Box 428 School St Woodbridge NJ 07095

MARKS, HELENA LIN, med. technologist; b. Peking, China, Oct. 6, 1935; came to U.S., 1955, naturalized, 1961; d. Kung and Shu-Fan (Lee) Lin; B.A. in Math. and Physics, Hunter Coll., N.Y.C., 1972; m. John S. Marks, Nov. 28, 1958 (dec. 1973); children—John Lin, Paul Lee; m. 2d J.B. Celleri 1977. Supr. chemistry lab. Tompkins County Hosp., Ithaca, N.Y., 1962-64; supr. labs. Calvary Hosp., Bronx, N.Y., 1964-67; med. technologist N. Central Hosp., Bronx, N.Y., 1977—; real estate saleswoman. Mem. Am. Soc. Clin. Pathologists, N.Y.C. Med. Lab. Suprs. Home: 4 Raleigh Dr New City NY 10956 Office: Blood Bank 3424 Kossuth Ave Bronx NY 10467

MARKS, JEAN COATE, state legislator; b. Forsyth, Mont., Mar. 6, 1934; d. Jesse Allen and Leah Alwayne (Tompkins) Coate; B.A. in Polit. Sci., Met. State Coll., 1973; m. Floyd Marks, Feb. 5, 1956; children—Vicki, David, Susan, Lynda, Daniel. Mem. Colo. Ho. of Reps. from 33d Dist., 1974-82. Bd. dirs. Community Corp., Women's Assistance Service. Democrat. Jewish. Club: Altrusa.

MARKS, JEANETTE, mktg. research agy. exec.; b. Bklyn., Nov. 4, 1929; d. Abraham and Sophie (Kessler) Fine; student Bklyn. Coll.; children—Rhonda, Craig, Alan. Nat. field dir. N.E. Field Facts, Natick, Mass., 1961-76; mktg. mgr. Market Research Agy., 1976—; mgr. The Opinion Center, Mesa, Ariz. Mem. Mktg. Research Assn., Am. Mktg. Assn. Jewish. Club: Jewish Bus. and Profl. Women. Home: 1216 E Vista Del Cerro Apt 2089 Tempe AZ 85281 Office: 1156 Fiesta Mall Mesa AZ 85202

MARKS, JUDITH ANGELA, educator; b. Milw., Aug. 11, 1949; d. Alois A. and Lucille M. Casper; B.S., U. Wis., Milw., 1972, M.A., 1976; m. James Arthur Marks, Aug. 18, 1972. Teaching asst., then lectr. interpersonal communications U. Wis., Milw., 1974-78; guest lectr. Marquette U. Sch. Nursing Office Continuing Edn., spring 1981; lectr. U. Wis., Whitewater, 1976-77, 78—; workshop leader, judge, cons. in field. Scholar AAUW, 1974. Mem. Speech Communication Assn., Central States Speech Assn. Home: W247 S7465 Scotland Dr Waukesha WI 53186 Office: Communication Dept U Wis Whitewater WI 53190

MARKS, LILLIAN SHAPIRO (MRS. JOSEPH MARKS), educator; b. Bklyn., Mar. 16, 1907; d. Hayman and Celia (Merowitz) Shapiro; B.S., N.Y. U., 1928; m. Joseph Marks, Feb. 21, 1932; children—Daniel, Sheila Blake, Jonathan. High sch. tchr., N.Y.C., 1929-30; tchr. Evalina de Rothschild Sch., Jerusalem, Palestine, 1930-31; social worker United Jewish Aid, Bklyn., 1931-32; tchr. Richmond Hill High Sch., 1932-40, Andrew Jackson High Sch., Cambria Heights, N.Y., 1940-71; mem. faculty New Sch. Social Research, N.Y.C., 1977—; staff Vassar Summer Inst., 1946. Mem. Am. Fedn. Tchrs., English-Speaking Union, Comml. Edn. Assn., Inst. Ret. Profls. Democrat. Jewish. Am. editor: Teeline, A System of Fast Writing, 1970; author: College Teeline, 1977; Shorthand Made Simple, 1983. Home and Office: 117-16 Park Lane S Kew Gardens NY 11418

MARKS, MARGUERITE MCBURNEY, univ. adminstr., educator; b. Binghamton, N.Y., Feb. 11, 1919; d. William Henry and Grace (Richardson) McBurney; B.S. in History, Portland State U., 1963, M.S.T. in History, 1965; Ph.D., U. Oreg., 1980; m. Kenneth Arthur Marks, Feb. 4, 1940; 1 dau., Diane M. Reader, dept. history Portland State U., 1962, grad. asst., 1963-65, dir. internat. student services, 1964-73, asst. prof. English as a Second Lang. Center, 1964—, mem. summer session faculty, 1967—, asst. prof. history, 1972-78, asst. prof. edn., 1977—, admissions officer internat. students, 1973—; cons. in field; producer Foreign Student Friends, Local Public Radio, 1965-75, mem. adv. council for community listening, 1967—; mem. com. for UN, City of Portland; mem. Portland Pan-Am. Com., 1965-74; adv. internat. relations com. Portland Jr. C. of C., 1968-70; evaluator Nat. Liaison Com. Fgn. Students. Recipient Leader commendation Campfire Girls, 1959, Pres.'s award Portland Jr. C. of C., 1971, 72. Mem. Oreg. Congress Parents and Tchrs. (legis. dir. 1961-64; life), Nat. Assn. Fgn. Student Affairs, Am. Assn. Collegiate Registrars and Admission Officers, Pacific Coast Assn. Collegiate Registrars and Admissions Officers, Am.-Mideast Ednl. and Tng. Services. Author: Handbook on the Placement of Foreign Graduate Students, 1979; contbr. numerous poems to children's publs., 1959—. Home: 3033 NE Hancock Portland OR 97212 Office: Admissions Office Portland State U PO Box 751 Portland OR 97207

MARKS, PHYLLIS EVANS, advt. splty. exec.; b. Montrose, Colo., Sept. 27, 1927; d. Dale Washington and Norma (Stebbins) Evans; student Mesa Jr. Coll., Grand Junction, Colo., 1945-46, Colo. State U., 1947-48, Springfield (Mass.) Coll., 1968, Millersville (Pa.) State U., 1971; m. Edmund Lawrence Marks, Aug. 21, 1949; children—Sharon Ann, David Michael. Substitute tchr. Springfield public schs., 1965-68; sales counselor John David Advt. Co., Lancaster, Pa., 1973-76; sales mgr. Impact Sales, Lancaster, 1976, owner, pres., 1976—. Leader Springfield Girl Scouts U.S.A., 1958-64; tour guide Amish Country, Lancaster County, 1970-73. Mem. Lancaster Advt. Club (treas. 1978-79), Sales and Mktg. Execs. Club Lancaster, Pa. Craftsmen Guild, Advt. Splty. Inst., Lancaster Assn. Commerce and Industry, Am. Bus. Women's Assn., Advancement Mgmt. Soc., Splty. Advt. Counselors of Delaware County. Mem. P.E.O. Sisterhood (state dir. Mass. 1968, past pres. Pa.). Author: Quill with Phyl, 1973. Home: 1042 Olde Hickory Rd Lancaster PA 17601 Office: 1116-R Manheim Pike Lancaster PA 17601

MARKSON, ELIZABETH WARREN, sociologist; b. Norfolk, Va., Nov. 27, 1934; d. Lloyd Earl and Ruby Lee (Barker) Warren; B.A., Bryn Mawr Coll., 1955; postgrad. U. Chgo., 1955-56; M.A. (George F. Kilborn scholar) Yale U., 1960, Ph.D. (Commonwealth U. fellow), 1966; m. Ralph Joseph Markson, Apr. 29, 1967; 1 dau., Alison Warren. Research analyst for Pa., Joint State Govt. Commn., 1957-63; instr. Dickinson Coll., Carlisle, Pa., 1957-59 research asso. Temple U., Phila., 1963-65; asst. dir. Bur. Social Research, N.Y. State Dept. Social Services, 1966-67; asso. research scientist Mental Health Research Unit, N.Y. State Dept. Mental Hygiene, 1967-71, dir. Mental Health Research Unit, 1971-74; dir. research and evaluation Mass. Dept. Mental Health, Boston, 1974-76; asso. prof. Wellesley (Mass.) Coll., 1976-79; asso. research prof. and research coordinator Gerontology Center, Boston U., 1979—; lectr. to adj. prof. SUNY, Albany, 1968-76; Mem. Am., Eastern Mass. (exec. council 1976-77, pres. 1977-78) sociol. assns., Soc. for Study Social Problems (chmn. div. youth, aging and life course 1975-77, exec. council 1978-81), Sociologists for Women in Soc. Author: (with Beth Hess) Aging and Old Age, 1980; (with Beth Hess and Peter Stern) Sociology, 1982; editor: (with David Allen) Trends in Mental Health Evaluation, 1976; (with Gretchen R. Batra) Public Policies For an Aging Population; Older Women: Issues and Prospects; guest editor Internat. Jour. Aging and Human Devel, 1975; cons. editor Sociol. Practice, 1976—; editorial bd. New Eng. Sociologist, 1978—. Contbr. articles and revs. to profl. jours. Home: 46 Kendal Common Rd Weston MA 02193 Office: Boston U Gerontology Center 730 Commonwealth Ave Boston MA 02115

MARKSON, HADASSAH BINDER, music adminstr.; b. N.Y.C., Aug. 9, 1927; d. Abraham W. and Anna (Freidman) Binder; B.A., Queens Coll., 1949; postgrad. Hunter Coll., 1976-80; m. Martin Markson, Feb. 6, 1949; children—Naomi Steinberger, Dina Markson. Dir., producer Lyrics and Lyricists series 92 St. Y Sch. Music, N.Y.C., 1969—; artistic dir., producer Jewish Opera at Y, N.Y.C., 1978—. Sec., then pres. Nat. Guild Community Schs. Arts; bus. mgr. Musica Judaica Jour., 1977—. Mem. Am. Soc. Jewish Music (sec.). Office: Sch Music 1395 Lexington Ave New York NY 10028

MARKSTAHLER, JOYCE BALLE BOLSTER, motion picture producer; b. Chgo., June 20, 1933; d. Einer Marinous and Florence Anna (Mueller) Balle; student Carthage (Ill.) Coll., 1950-51, Northwestern U., 1951-52, North Park Coll., Chgo., 1967; m. William Markstahler, July 7, 1956 (dec.); m. 2d, Richard H. Bolster, May 31, 1980. Copy girl Chgo. Tribune, 1949-52; film re-editor sta. WGN-TV, Chgo., 1952-54; negative cutter, asst. editor Kling Studios, Chgo., 1954-55; film editor, prodn. asst. Colmes Werrenrath Prodns. Co., Chgo. and Glenview, Ill., 1956-60; freelance asst. editor, asst. dir., 1960-61; editorial adminstrv. supr. Fred A. Niles Communications Centers, Chgo., 1961-63; asst. motion picture producer Sears, Roebuck & Co., Chgo., 1963-67, motion picture producer, 1968-74, exec. motion picture producer, dir. point-of-purchase programs, nat. advt. dept., 1974-81; pres., owner Mark Todd Prodns. Inc., 1971—; exec. v.p. mktg. Transmedia Systems Inc., Glenview, Ill., 1981—; dir. Chgo. Unlimited; founder, exec. v.p., exec. com. Our World-Underwater, 1970-78, scholarship coordinator, 1974-78. Named Scuba Diver of Yr., Chgo. Met. YMCA, 1969; Miss Ill. Scuba Diver of Yr., 1968, 69. Mem. Info. Film Producers Am. (nat. pres. 1980), Chgo. Film Council, Underwater Med. Soc. Office: 1200 Waukegan Rd Glenview IL 60025

MARKUM, ARLENE, banker; b. N.Y.C., June 15, 1942; d. John Thomas and Mary Louise McAllister; student Pace U., 1975—; m. Onzelo Markum, July 28, 1960; children—Onzelo III, Andrea Gail. Credit adminstrn. clk. Franklin Simon, N.Y.C., 1963; supr. Lord & Taylors, N.Y.C., 1963-68; with Citibank N.Y., N.Y.C., 1969—, asst. mgr., 1974-81, mgr., 1981—. Mem. Nat. Assn. Female Execs. Republican. Home: 8400 Shore Front Pkwy Rockaway Beach NY 11693

MARLATT, ABBY LINDSEY, nutritionist; b. Manhattan, Kans., Dec. 5, 1916; d. Frederick Albert and Annie Elsie (Lindsey) M.; B.S. in Dietetics, Kans. State U., 1938; cert. hosp. dietetics, U. Calif., Berkeley, 1940, Ph.D. in Animal Nutrition, 1947. Assoc. prof. food and nutrition Kans. State U., 1945-52, prof., 1952-56; dir. Sch. Home Econs., U. Ky., Lexington, 1956-63, prof. nutrition and food sci. 1963—, dir. grad. studies nutrition and food sci., 1975—; vis. prof. Beirut (Lebanon) Coll. Women, 1953-54; vis. research prof. Ky. State Coll., Frankfort, 1968-71; pres. Kans. Dietetic Assn., 1951-52; cons. in field. Bd. dirs. Community Action Lexington-Fayette County, 1967-71, 72—, sec., 1970-71, treas., 1974-78, vice chmn., 1979—; chmn. Bluegrass Community Services, 1976-80, vice chmn., 1981—; vice chmn. Emerson Center, Lexington, 1980—. Named Ky. Dietitian of Year, 1982. Fellow AAAS; mem. Ky. Dietetic Assn. (pres. 1958-59), Am. Dietetic Assn., Am. Home Econs. Assn., Soc. Nutrition Edn., Am. Sch. Health Assn., Gerontol. Soc., Ky. Nutrition Council, AAUP, AAUW, Sigma Xi, Omicron Nu, Phi Upsilon Omicron. Unitarian-Universalist. Author articles in field. Home: 256 Tahoma Rd Lexington KY 40503 Office: 212 Funkhouser Bldg U Ky Lexington KY 40506

MARLEK, MARILYN ANN, lawyer; b. Jackson Heights, N.Y., Feb. 7, 1953; d. Edward S. and Alfreda M.; A.B. cum laude, Harvard U., 1974; J.D., Georgetown U., 1977; m. John D. Logigian, Aug. 6, 1977; 1 son, Douglas Tate Logigian. Admitted to N.Y. State bar, 1978, U.S. Dist. Ct. bars, 1978; law clk. Council on Environ. Quality, Exec. Office of the Pres., Washington, 1975; law clk. to gen. counsel Dept. Commerce, Washington, 1975-76; asso. firm Shea & Gould, N.Y.C., 1977-80; litigation counsel Grumman Allied Industries, Inc., Melville, N.Y., 1980-82, Bethpage, N.Y., 1982—. Mem. Am. Bar Assn., N.Y. State Bar Assn., Suffolk County Bar Assn., Nassau County Bar Assn. Clubs: Harvard, Radcliffe (N.Y.C.); Harvard-Radcliffe of Long Island. Office: 1111 Stewart Ave Bethpage NY 11714

MARLER, LINDA SUSAN, clin. microbiologist; b. Bloomington, Ind., May 28, 1951; d. Lynne Lionel and Lucille Elizabeth (Widman) Merritt; B.S. in Med. Tech., Ind. U., 1973, M.S. in Allied Health Edn., 1978; m. David William Marler, May 21, 1977; children—Brian David, Brittney Lynne. Med. technologist, then sr. med. technologist Ind. U. Med. Center, Indpls., 1973-78, edn. coordinator dept. microbiology, 1974—, asst. prof. div. allied health Sch. Medicine, 1978—; speaker in field. Mem. Am. Soc. Microbiology, Am. Soc. Med. Tech., S.Central Assn. Clin. Microbiologists. Methodist. Office: Fesler 416 1120 South Dr Indianapolis IN 46223

MARLETT, JUDITH ANN, nutritionist; b. Toledo, June 20, 1943; d. Waldo Ison and Anna Gladys (Beaviers) M.; B.S., Miami U., Oxford, Ohio, 1965; Ph.D., U. Minn.-Mayo Grad. Sch. Medicine, 1972; postdoctoral research fellow, Harvard U. Sch. Public Health, 1973-75. Dietetic intern U. Minn. Hosps., Mpls., 1965-66; therapeutic and metabolic unit dietitian VA Hosps., Mpls., 1966-67; spl. instr. Simmons Coll., Boston, 1973-74; mem. faculty U. Wis., Madison, 1975—, assoc. prof. nutrition, 198—, acting dir. coordinated undergrad. program dietetics, 1977-78. Grantee NIH. Mem. Am. Inst. Nutrition, Am. Dietetic Assn., Soc. Nutrition Edn., Sigma Xi, Sigma Delta Epsilon. Author research papers in field. Office: Dept Nutritional Scis 1415 Linden Dr Madison WI 53706

MARLOW, AUDREY SWANSON, artist, designer; b. N.Y.C., Mar. 3, 1929; d. Sven and Rita (Porter) Swanson; student (scholarships) Art Students League, 1950-55; spl. courses SUNY (Stony Brook), L'Alliance Française m. Roy Marlow, Nov. 30, 1968. With Cohn-Hall-Marx Textile Studio, 1961-65, R.S. Assos. Textile Studio, 1965-73; freelance designer, illustrator Prince Matchabelli, Lester Harrison Agy., J. Walter Thompson Agy., 1957-78; portrait and fine artist, Wading River, N.Y., 1973—; instr. Phoenix Sch. Design (N.Y.C.). Trustee, Middle Island Public Library, 1972-76. Recipient John W. Alexander medal, 1976, award Council on Arts, 1978, award of excellence Cork Gallery, Lincoln Center, 1982. Mem. Pastel Soc. Am. (award 1977, 80), Am. Artists Profl. League (1st prize award), Hudson Valley Art Assn., Knickerbocker Artists, Catharine Lorillard Wolfe Art Club (award 1982), Salmagundi Club (5 awards), Nat. League Am. Pen Women (Gold award). Works represented at N.Y. U., pvt. collections; one-woman show Salmagundi Club, 1982. Home: 76 Northside Rd Wading River NY 11792

MARLOWE, MARION PAULINE, actress, singer; b. St. Louis, Mar. 7, 1929; d. George R. and Marion J. (Hofmeister) Townsend; student Sir Thomas Beecham Royal Acad. Dramatic Arts, London, 1947-48; Katherine Dunham Sch. Dance, London, 1947-48; Rosait Sch., 1951-64; Actors Studio, N.Y.C., 1955-60; D. Theatre Arts (hon.), Kensington U., 1978; m. Lawrence Puck, May 5, 1955 (dec.). Appeared in (Broadway plays) The Sound of Music, 1959-63, Man of La Mancha, 1967-68, Follies, 1971-72 (radio shows) Garry Moore Show, Steve Allen Show, Merv Griffin Show, Arthur Godfey Show, (TV shows) BBC, London, 1947-48, Virginia Graham Show, 1951, Jack Parr Show, 1951-55, Ed Sullivan Show (28 appearances), 1955-64, Perry Como Show, 1957, co-host Mike Douglas Show, 1966, A.M. N.Y., 1971, 72, 73, (musicals) Gypsy, My Fair Lady, Showboat, Oliver, Kiss Me Kate, The King and I, Music in the Air, Hello Dolly, French Revue; headliner at cafes and hotels including Copacabana, N.Y.C., Chez Paree, Chgo., Shamrock, Houston, Desert Inn, Las Vegas; guest soloist London Philharmonic Orch., 1946-47, Merembloom Symphony Orch., 1950, St. Louis Symphony Orch., 1953, Rochester Symphony Orch., 1954; command performance King George, London, 1947, 48; pres. Pukmar Corp., N.Y.C.; artist-in-residence U. Pensacola (Fla.). Mem. Nat. Acad. TV Arts and Scis., Assn. Understanding of Man, Defenders of Wildlife, Audubon Soc., Humane Soc., Fund for Animals, Animal Protection Inst., Friends of Animals, Soc. Animal Rights. Unitarian. Author (poetry): Make Known the Thoughts of your Heart, 1971.

MARONEY, JANE, Del. state rep.; b. Boston, July 29, 1923; d. John H. and Mary (Boland) Perkins; student Radcliffe Coll., 1940-41; m. John Walker Maroney, 1946; children—Jane, John Walker. Mem., Del. State Ho. of Reps., 12th Dist., 1979—, chmn. Health and Social Service Com., 1981—. Chmn. pediatrics com. Del. Hosp. Jr. Bd.; chmn., mem. exec. com. Holly Ball Found. Inc.; mem. adv. council Marka T. duPont Inst. Human Behavior; chmn. Del. Antique Show, 1979. Club: Jr. League Wilmington. Office: Del Ho of Reps State Capitol Dover DE 19901 *

MAROSCHER, BETTY JEAN, librarian; b. Ashland, Ky., Aug. 12, 1934; d. Raymond and Virginia Dell (Staten) Boggs; student Columbus Coll. (Ga.), 1963-64; B.S., Hardin-Simmons U., 1967; M.S. in L.S., Our Lady of Lake U., San Antonio, 1970; M.Ed., Trinity U., 1975; m. Albert G. Maroscher Mar. 21, 1955 (dec.). Tchr., McAllen (Tex.) Ind. Sch. Dist., 1967-68; tchr. Northside Ind. Sch. Dist., San Antonio, 1968-69, librarian, 1969-71; reference librarian ednl. media Trinity U., San Antonio, 1971-76; reference librarian St. Philip's Coll., San Antonio, 1976, audiovisual librarian, mgr. audiovisual dept., 1977—; lectr., cons. in field; chmn. subcom. programming and scheduling Univ. and Fine Arts Cable TV Com., 1980-81. Active ARC; sec., trustee Compañia de Arte Espanol, 1982—. Recipient Minter/Medal Hardin-Simmons U., 1965, 66. Mem. Tex., S.W., Bexar County, Catholic library assns., Tex. Jr. Coll. Tchrs. Assn., Tex. Assn. Chicanos in Higher Edn. (sec. St. Philip's chpt. 1982—), Audiovisual Instructional Media Services Group, Council Research and Acad. Libraries Coop. Circulation Group (sec.-treas. 1977-79), Pi Gamma Mu (sec. chpt. 1965-67), Alpha Chi (historian 1965-67), other orgns. Republican. Roman Catholic. Home: 5230 Galahad Dr San Antonio TX 78218 Office: 2111 Nevada St San Antonio TX 78203

MAROT, LOLA, buyer; b. Providence, Oct. 6, 1939; d. Frank and Iola (Lombardi) Ansuini; B.A. with distinction, U. R.I., 1973; M.B.A. candidate Bryant Coll. Bookkeeper, Diamond Paper Box Co., Providence, 1958-69; export sales adminstr. Brite Industries, Providence, 1973-77; property services asst. Met. Property and Liability Ins. Co., Warwick, R.I., 1977-79, buyer, 1979—. Mem. Univ. Soc. Providence (pres. 1978). Office: 700 Quaker Ln Warwick RI 02886

MARQUARDT, CHRISTEL ELISABETH, lawyer; b. Chgo.; d. Herman A. and Christine M. (Geringer) Trolenberg; B.S., Mo. Western Coll., St. Joseph, 1970; J.D. with honors (Mabee scholar), Washburn U., 1974; children—Eric, Philip, Andrew, Joel. Admitted to Kans. bar, 1974; partner firm Cosgrove, Webb & Oman, Topeka, 1970—. Bd. dirs. YWCA; mem. Topeka Mayor's Commn. on Status of Women; bd. dirs. Sheltered Living for Retarded Citizens, Topeka Lutheran Sch. Mem. Kans. Bar Assn. (chmn. sect. on corp., bus. and banking, sec.-treas. 1981-82), Topeka Bar Assn. (chmn. public relations com., chmn. continuing legal edn.), Am. Bar Assn., Am. Bus. Women's Assn., Kans. Women's Polit. Caucus, Topeka Women's Polit. Caucus. Exec. Women's Forum, Phi Kappa Phi, Phi Alpha Delta. Republican. Lutheran. Mng. editor Washburn Law Jour., 1973-74; contbr. articles to legal jours.

Home: 3121 Briarwood Circle Topeka KS 66611 Office: 1100 First Nat Bank Topeka KS 66603

MARQUART, ALISON LEE, nurse, naval officer; b. Summit, N.J., Oct. 8, 1949; d. Charles Stanley, Jr. and Elizabeth Bleaker (Henry) Williams; student Cazinonia Coll., 1967-68, U. Calif. Sch. Medicine, San Diego; R.N., Mercy Hosp., Denver, 1971; children—Tiffany Leigh, Grant Williams. Commd. lt. comdr., Nurse Corps, U.S. Navy, 1970—; stationed at Naval Regional Med. Center, Oakland, Calif., 1971-74; surg. intensive care staff, charge nurse recovery room Naval Regional Med. Center, San Diego, 1974-77; charge nurse emergency room Patuxent River Naval Hosp., Md., 1977-80, family nurse practitioner Family Practice Clinic, Naval Regional Med. Center, Camp Pendleton, Calif., 1981; tchr. nursing classes to LPN students. Decorated Nat. Def. medal, Vietnamese Humanitarian medal; cert. family nurse practitioner, in advanced cardiac life support. Mem. Emergency Dept. Nurses Assn., Am. Nurses Assn. Home: 171 Lejeune St Camp Pendleton CA 92055 Office: Naval Regional Med Center Camp Pendleton CA 92055

MARQUIS, GERALDINE MAE HILDRETH (MRS. FORREST W. MARQUIS), educator; b. Ankeny, Iowa, Aug. 8; d. Vernon Otto and Alma Leona (Woods) Hildreth; student U. No. Iowa; M.A., Drake U., 1972; m. Forrest William Marquis; 1 son, Robert William. Elementary tchr., Ankeny and Ft. Dodge, Iowa, 1944-49, 56—; organizer Ft. Dodge Coop. Nursery Sch. Mem. NEA, Iowa Ft. Dodge edn. assns., Assn. Childhood Edn. Internat. (Iowa pres. 1974-77), Nat. Assn. Edn. Young Children, Civic Music Assn., TTT Nat. Soc. (pres. chpt.), Delta Kappa Gamma (pres. Kappa chpt. 1974-78), World Orgn. Early Childhood Edn., Phi Sigma Alpha. Republican. Methodist. Home: 2602 Williams Dr Fort Dodge IA 50501 Office: 615 N 16th St Fort Dodge IA 50501

MARR, GAIL REBECCA, television news anchor; b. Hamilton, Ohio, Aug. 27, 1947; d. George Edward and Floreine Victoria M.; B.A., Trinity Coll., Washington, 1969; M.S., Boston U., 1976. Art editor Houghton Mifflin Co., Boston, 1969-70; graphics editor Ginn and Co., Lexington, Mass., 1970-74; producer, moderator weekly radio talk show Now, Cambridge, Mass., 1973-74, radio show Open Doors, Cambridge, 1974-76; TV news anchor/reporter Sta. WEHT-TV, Evansville, Ind., 1976-79; TV news anchor WSBT-TV, South Bend, Ind., 1979—. Mem. NOW (adminstrv. v.p. Boston 1975, producer, moderator radio programs Boston 1974-75), Women in Communications, Sigma Delta Chi. Roman Catholic. Club: River City Civitan. Office: 300 W Jefferson Blvd South Bend IN 46601

MARRINAN, ROCHELLE ANN, anthropologist; b. Beaver Dam, Wis., Aug. 17, 1944; d. Richard and Ruth Ardis (Salzman) M.; R.N., St. Vincent's Hosp., 1965; A.A., Polk Jr. Coll., 1969; B.A. with high honors, U. Fla., 1971, Ph.D., 1975; M.A., Tulane U., 1973. Nurse, St. Vincent's Hosp., Jacksonville, Fla., 1965-66, Winter Haven (Fla.) Hosp., 1966-69; asst. prof. Ga. So. Coll., Statesboro, 1976-79; adj. asst. prof. hist. archaeology and zooarchaeology Fla. State Mus., Gainesville, 1979-81; adj. lectr. dept. anthropology Fla. State U., Tallahassee, 1982—. Mem. task force Ga. Archeol. Research Design, 1976—. NSF grantee, 1979, Nat. Park Service grantee, 1982. Mem. Am. Anthrop. Assn., Soc. Am. Archaeology, Soc. Hist. Archaeology, Soc. Post-Medieval Archaeology. Democrat. Office: Florida State University Dept Anthropology Tallahassee FL 32304

MARRIOTT, ALICE SHEETS, hotel corp. exec.; b. Salt Lake City, Oct. 19, 1907; d. Edwin Spencer and Alice (Taylor) Sheets; B.A., U. Utah, 1927, D.H.L., 1974; D.H.L., Mt. Vernon Coll., 1980; m. John Willard Marriott, June 9, 1927; children—John Willard, Richad Edwin. Co-founder Marriott Corp., Washington, 1927—, v.p., 1927—. Committeewoman D.C. Republican Nat. Com., 1959-76, vice chmn., 1965-76; chmn. Pres.'s Adv. Commn. on Arts for John F. Kennedy Center, 1970-76; trustee J. F. Kennedy Center, also mem. exec. com., 1971—. Mem. Arthritis and Rheumatism Assn. Washington, Am. Newspaper Women's Assn., Phi Kappa Phi, Chi Omega. Republican. Mormon. Clubs: Capitol Hill, Washington, Capitol Speakers, F Street. Home: 4500 Garfield St NW Washington DC 20007 Office: 1 Marriott Dr Washington DC 20058

MARRIOTT, BARBARA, mgmt. cons.; b. Trenton, N.J., June 1, 1932; d. Salvator and Elvira (Esandrio) Barretta; B.A., Fairleigh Dickinson U., Rutherford, N.J., 1954; M.A., U. Okla., 1980; postgrad. Equal Opportunity Mgmt. Inst., 1981, Tavistock Inst., London, 1981; m. Michael Marriott, June 16, 1956; children—William P., Minette Ivy. Copy chief Hahne & Co., Newark, 1955-57; freelance copy and fashion coordinator, U.S. and France, 1960, 79; creative dir. Hubbard Duckett, Mason Dow, Jacksonville, Fla., 1978-79; copy chief Matthais & Redmond, Virginia Beach, Va., 1968-69, 70-72; cons. Marriott Mgmt. Corp., 1980-81; mgmt. cons., trainer, workshop designer, 1981—. Counselor, U.S. Navy Relief, 1965-74; vol. ARC Hosp., 1965-72. Winner Prix de Paris, 1954. Mem. Nat. Assn. Female Execs. Republican. Episcopalian. Clubs: Beaconsfield (Eng.), Am. Women's; Officers Wives (London); Ret. Navy Wives (chmn. 1980-81). Author, editor: What's New Jersey, Tour Guide, 1972; co-author: U.S. Navy Port Guides, 6 vols., 1978; creator, editor newspaper in Riveria, France, 1960-62. Address: Lodge Farm House Village Rd Dorney SL4 6QJ England UK

MARRIOTT, GLADYS, state legislator; b. Spearman, Tex., Jan. 3, 1922; student pub. schs., Kansas City; m. Lloyd H. Marriott, Sept. 28, 1941; 2 daus. Mem. Mo. Ho. of Reps., 1968—, sec. Democratic Caucus, 77th Gen. Assembly, chmn. Dem. Caucus, 78th Gen. Assembly. Mem. U.S. Task Force on Retirement and Pensions, 1965—; committeewoman 23d Ward, Kansas City; past vice chmn. Mo. 4th Congressional Dist.; past deaconess New Hope Ch.; past bd. dirs. Kansas City Council PTA. Mem. Nat. Order Women Legislators (past pres.), Chi Omega Alumnae, Am. Bus. Women's Assn. Club: Order of Eastern Star. Office: Mo State Ho of Reps Jefferson City MO 65101 *

MARRIOTT, JOANNE BLANCHE, sci. co. exec.; b. Trenton, N.J.; d. George Thomas and Riva Elizabeth (DaBronzo) Marriott; B.S., Rider Coll., 1962; postgrad. St. Francis Sch. Med. Tech., 1962; M.A., U. Central Mich., 1976. Bacteriologist, St. Francis Hosp., Trenton, 1962-64; bacteriologist and asst. chief lab. service Andrew Rader Army Clinic, Arlington, Va., 1964-67, chief lab. serivce, 1968-69; indsl. bacteriologist and asst. dir. quality control Burton, Parsons & Co., Inc. (became div. Alcon Labs. 1979), Washington, 1970-74, dir. quality control, 1974-79, dir. quality assurance, 1979—; cons. contact lens mfg. cos., 1974-75. Mem., vol. Fairfax Hosp. Aux. Mem. Am. Soc. Clin. Pathologists, Am. Soc. Microbiology, Soc. Indsl. Microbiology, Parenteral Drug Assn., Am. Soc. Quality Control (sec. Washington sect. 1982), Am. Mgmt. Assn. Democrat. Roman Catholic. Research in ophthalmic drugs. Office: 120 Westhampton Ave Washington DC 20027

MARSH, CARYL AMSTERDAM, psychologist, curator; b. N.Y.C., Mar. 9, 1923; d. Louis and Kitty (Weitz) Amsterdam; B.A., Bklyn. Coll., 1942; M.A. (CUNY grad. fellow), Columbia U., 1946; Ph.D. (scholar), George Washington U., 1978; m. Michael Marsh, Sept. 3, 1942; children—Susan, Anna. Asst. cultural attaché Am. Embassy, Paris, 1946-48; psychologist D.C. Recreation Dept., 1957-69; spl. asst. Smithsonian Instn., Washington, 1966-73; fellow Nat. Mus. Am. Art, Washington, 1975-77; curator exhbns. and research Nat. Archives, Washington, 1978—; cons. White House, Nat. Zoo, Meyer Found. Bd. dirs. Anacostia Neighborhood Mus., 1974—; mem. D.C. Commn. on Arts, 1968-72, sec., 1970-72; pres. presch. parents council D.C. Recreation Dept., 1956-57. NSF grantee, 1972-73, 75-76. Mem. Am. Psychol. Assn., D.C. Psychol. Assn., Am. Assn. Mus., Assn. State and Local History. Author: Encouraging the Expression of Curiosity, 1978; The American Image, 1979. Home: 3701 Grant Rd NW Washington DC 20016 Office: National Archives Washington DC 20408

MARSH, DOROTHY DENNIS, civic worker; b. Orange, N.J., Sept. 8, 1891; d. Samuel Shepherd and Eliza (Thomas) Dennis; ed. pvt. schs.; M.A. (hon.) Bowdoin Coll., 1964; m. Harold Newman Marsh, May 25, 1921 (dec. 1949); children—Richard Symmes Thomas, Harold Newman, Samuel Shepard Dennis, David Monroe. Treas. women's bd. House of Mercy, Washington, 1924-35; chmn. women's com. Kiwanis Internat. Conf., Washington, 1936; pres. Farmington Soc., Washington, 1937-39; pres. Women's Internat. League, Washington br., 1938-40, mem. finance and nat. exec. com. 1939-40; chmn. citizens adv. com. Emergency Homemaker Service, 1943-54; adv. com. pub. health nursing D.C. Health Dept., 1941-52; mem. fin. and nat. exec. com., 1939-40; chmn. women's membership com. Dewey-Bricker Club, 1944 (all Washington); mem. D.C. Commrs. bd. visitors to inspect Mcpl. Hosps., 1944-46; chmn. sr. hostess Stage Door Canteen, Washington, 1943-45; bd. mem. Vis. Nurse Assn., 1951-69, 3d v.p., 1955-60, pres., 1960-64; council mem. women's com. Nat. Symphony Orch., 1933-43, 52-53; bd. mem. Washington Planned Parenthood Assn., 1952-55; mem. D.C. exec. com. UNICEF, 1960-65; nat. sponsor Margaret Sanger Inst., 1967—; chmn. Washington Internat. Center vols., 1952-55, 61-70; mem. D.C. com. for Nat. Library Week, 1958-60; mem. com. on representation indigents Jud. Conf. D.C. Circuit, 1959; del. to Nat. Conf. Exchange of Persons, Inst. Internat. Edn., 1954, 56; mem. D.C. Commrs. Citizens Adv. Council, 1954-62, 1st vice chmn., 1961, chmn., 1962, mem. com. pub. welfare, 1962, com. to study alcoholic beverage control laws, 1962; 6th v.p. Washington League Rep. Women, 1953-55, chmn. pub. relations, 1955-57; bd. mem. Citizens for Eisenhower-Nixon, Washington, 1956-59; mem. Rep. State Com. for D.C., 1956-64. Mem. exec. bd. health sect. United Community Services, Washington, 1954-57; regional com. Health and Welfare Council, 1957-59; mem. bd. Homemaker Service of Nat. Capital Area, 1957-67, pres., 1959-60; chmn. membership com. Capitol area Assn. for UN, 1954-56, sec., 1956-58; mem. nat. sponsors' com. Theodore Roosevelt Centennial Observance, 1958; mem. adv. ednl. council Freedmen's Hosp. Sch. Nursing Washington, 1955-58; chmn. citizens conf. on nursing Washington League Nursing, 1957; del. to conf. Nat. League Nursing, Chgo., 1957; mem. adv. council Juvenile Ct., Washington, 1957. Chmn. council Washington Youth Gardens, 1962-68; trustee Miss Porter's Sch. Farmington, Conn., 1962-68, Meridian House Found., 1965-71; mem. religious resources project Washington Urban League, 1962-64; mem. bd. Met. Wash. Health Facilities Planning Council, 1962-66; mem. com. on study vol. services Health, Welfare Council, 1962-65; mem. nat. adv. council Soc. for a More Beautiful Capital, 1965—; mem. Nat. Council Homemaker Services, 1962-66; bd. Pastoral Inst., 1964-70. Served with YMCA, officer club work, overseas, 1917-19. Recipient John Benjamin Nichols award D.C. Med. Soc., 1958; citiation for community service D.C. LWV, 1961; Meritorious Pub. Service award, D.C. Govt., 1962; citation Nat. Recreation Assn., 1965, Washington Urban League, 1967; govtl. award for service to Internat. Center Program, tribute of appreciation Dept. State, 1970; certificate of cooperation AID, 1970; certificate of appreciation Meridian House Found., 1970; Alumnae Assn. award Miss Porter's Sch., 1970; cert. of appreciation Homemaker Health Aide Service of Nat. Capital Area, 1972; recognition for good will and understanding UN Assn. U.S.A., 1974; named hon. Washington youth gardener, 1971. Mem. Ki-Wives, Bowdoin Alumni Assn. (Washington v.p. 1955-58). Episcopalian. Club. Chevy Chase (Md.). Home: 2022 Columbia Rd Washington DC 20009

MARSH, ELLA JEAN, pediatrician; b. Chgo., Dec. 16, 1941; d. Charles and Eleanor (Canfield) M.; B.A., St. Mary of Woods (Ind.) Coll., 1963; D.O., Chgo. Coll. Osteo. Medicine, 1971. Intern, Doctor's Hosp., Columbus, Ohio, 1971-72; resident in pediatrics, then asst. prof. Chgo. Coll. Osteo. Medicine, 1972-78, asso. prof. pediatrics, 1978-82; asst. prof. W.Va. Coll. Osteo. Medicine, 1975-77; now dir. pediatric and newborn nursery, asso. dir. med. edn. Orlando (Fla.) Gen. Hosp.; pediatric cons. Nat. Bd. Osteo. Examiners; lectr., cons. in field. Donald Bucknar Moore scholar, 1963; diplomate Am. Coll. Osteo. Pediatricians (chmn. evaluating com. 1981—), Nat. Osteo. Bds. Mem. Am. Osteo. Assn., Fla. Osteo. Assn., AMA, Women's Med. Assn., Ill. Osteo. Assn. (chmn. com. health affairs 1981), Ill. Med. Assn., Ill. Assn. Osteo. Phys. and Surgeons, Chgo. Med. Soc., Chgo. Pediatric Soc., Chgo. Coll. Osteo. Medicine Alumni Assn., Delta Omega. Roman Catholic. Home: 8210 Imber St Orlando FL 32807 Office: 7824 Lake Underhill Rd Orlando FL

MARSH, JAYNE ELIZABETH, info. coordinator; b. Detroit, May 11, 1954; d. Guy Rendell and Jean Beulah (Render) M.; B.A., Mich. State U., 1976, M.A., 1978. Freelance public relations and communications work, East Lansing, Mich., 1974—; prodn. and research asst. Sta. WKAR-TV, East Lansing, 1974-75; legis. reporter Mich. Senate Info. Office, Lansing, 1975-76; comml. prodn. Sta. WCER-AM-FM, Charlotte, Mich., 1976-77; editorial asst. Mich. State U. Info. Services-4-H Youth, 1976-77, info. specialist, 1977-79, info. coordinator, 1979—. Mem. Nat. Assn. Ext. 4-H Agts. (public relations and promotional chmn. nat. conv. 1980), Nat. Agrl. Communicators in Edn. (steering com. chmn. nat. conv. for 1981), Women in Communications, Inc., (chpt. pres. 1979-81, nat. adv. task force for profl. chpt. affairs, chmn. Gt. Lakes regional meeting 1983), Women's Inst. for Freedom of the Press, Am. Women in Radio and TV, Public Relations Assn. Mich. Office: 10 Agriculture Hall Mich State U East Lansing MI 48824

MARSH, JEAN LYNDSEY TORREN, actress, writer; b. London, July 1, 1934; d. Henry Charles John and Emmeline Susannah Nightingale Poppy (Bexley) M.; student in dance, piano, voice and mime; D.H.L. (hon.), Marymount Coll.; m. Jon Devon Roland Pertwee, Apr. 2, 1955 (div. 1960). Photographers' model; with repertory cos.; Broadway debut in Much Ado About Nothing, 1959; other theatrical appearances include: Habeas Corpus, Broadway, 1975, Travesties, The Importance of Being Earnest, 1977, Too True to Be Good, 1977, My Fat Friend, Whose Life Is It Anyway?, 1979; movie appearances include: Where's Charley?, Tales of Hoffmann, The Horsemasters, Cleopatra, 1963, Frenzy, 1972, Dark Places, The Eagle Has Landed, 1977, The Limbo Line, 1969, The Changeling, 1980, also in Uncle Vanya, Twelfth Night, Fallen Angels, Blithe Spirit; artistic dir. Adelphi U. Theatre, 1981; co-creator, story cons. I.T.V. series Upstairs, Downstairs, also starred; TV appearances include: The Grover Monster/Jean Marsh Cartoon Spl., 1975, A State Dinner for Queen Elizabeth II, 1976, Mad About the Boy: Noel Coward—A Celebration, 1976; appears on TV series 9 to 5. Winner Emmy award, 1975; named Most Outstanding New Female Actress of 1972. Office: care The Pheasant Chinnor Hill Oxfordshire OX9 HBN England *

MARSH, JOSEPHINE PATRICIA, educator; b. Boston, Nov. 25, 1921; d. Ernest Joseph and Agnes Bridget (Morahan) Marsh; A.B., Emmanuel Coll., 1943; Ed.M., Harvard U., 1946; Ed.D., 1959; cert. Nottingham U., 1950. Dir. Appointment Bur., Emmanuel Coll., Boston, 1946-50; tchr., Boston Public Schs., 1950-59, adminstr. gifted edn., 1966-75, adminstr. staff devel., 1966—; lectr., prof., chmn. dept. edn. Newton (Mass.) Coll., 1954-63; asso. prof. dept. edn. Emmanuel Coll., Boston, 1963—; mem. Mass. State Team Nat. Leadership Tng. Inst., 1973; cons. schs., Mass. Inst. Internat. Edn. grantee, 1950. Mem. AAUW, Council Exceptional Children, Am. Ednl. Studies Assn., Internat. and Comparative Edn. Soc., Assn. Supervision and Curriculum Devel., Nat. Assn. Gifted, Emmanuel Coll. Alumnae Assn. Democrat. Roman Catholic. Contbr. articles in field to profl. jours. Office: 26 Court St Boston MA 02108 also 400 Fenway Boston MA 02115

MARSH, LINDA KESSLER, psychologist; b. N.Y.C., Aug. 15, 1943; d. Max and Anna (Straus) Kessler; B.A., Queens Coll., 1964; M.S., CCNY, 1966; Ph.D., N.Y. U., 1974; m. Kenneth Marsh (div.); 1 dau., Allison Andra. Sch. psychologist, bur. child guidance N.Y.C. Bd. Edn., 1968-70; staff psychologist, postdoctoral research fellow, clin. instr. psychiatry N.Y. U. Med. Center, N.Y.C., 1974—. NIMH fellow, 1974-76; Gralnick Found. grantee, 1977-80. Mem. Am. Psychol. Assn., Eastern Psychol. Assn., N.Y. State Psychol. Assn., Am. Orthopsychiat. Assn. Home: 2 E 67 St New York NY 10021 Office: 550 First Ave New York NY 10016

MARSH, LOIS LEIDAHL, biopsychologist, educator; b. Sioux Rapids, Iowa, Jan. 23, 1950; d. Gordon Authur and Florence Victoria (Burgeson) Leidahl; student Buena Vista Coll., 1968-70; B.A. cum laude, Coe Coll., 1972; M.S., U. Chgo., 1975, Ph.D., 1976; m. Robert H. Marsh, Aug. 19, 1976 (dec.). Trainee NIH, 1974-76; assoc. prof. Mundelein Coll.. Chgo., 1976—, chmn. psychology dept., 1978—. Mem. Am. Psychol. Assn., AAAS, Phi Beta Kappa, Phi Kappa Phi. Home: 2485 Scott St Des Plaines IL 60018 Office: 6363 N Sheridan Rd Mundelein Coll Chicago IL 60660

MARSH, MARY WARREN, ednl. adminstr.; b. Huron, S.D., July 16, 1918; d. Charles Parker and Angie Garfield (Pierce) Warren; student Huron Coll., 1935-37; A.B., U. Ill., Urbana, 1941; m. Richard R. Marsh, Dec. 25, 1941; children—Norma, William, Helen. Sec., S.D. Code Commn., Gov.'s Office, 1937-39; with St. Anthony Falls Hydraulic Lab., U. Minn., Mpls., 1947—, adminstr., 1975-81; supr. U.S. and Can. Office of Internat. Assn. Hydraulic Research. Cert. profl. sec. Mem. Am. Water Resources Assn. (asso. editor Water Resources Bull. 1970—, treas., bd. dirs., exec. com. 1976—; Pres.'s Outstanding Service award 1979), Soc. Research Adminstrs. Democrat. Unitarian. Club: Campus (U. Minn.). Home: 1315 Raymond Ave Saint Paul MN 55108 Office: St Anthony Falls Hydraulic Lab Mississippi River at 3d Ave SE Minneapolis MN 55414

MARSH, MICHELE MARIE, TV news corr.; b. Detroit, Mar. 9, 1954; d. Howard Charles and Gloria Joan (Gadd) M.; B.S. in Speech, Northwestern U., 1976. Reporter, news anchor sta. WABI-TV, Bangor, Maine, 1976-77, sta. KSAT-TV, San Antonio, 1977-79; week-end anchor, corr., sta. WCBS-TV, N.Y.C., 1979, 11 p.m. anchor, corr., from 1979, currently co-anchor, 5 PM News. Telethon hostess Easter Seals Soc., San Antonio, 1979. Mem. AFTRA. Episcopalian. Office: WCBS-TV 524 W 57th St New York NY 10019 *

MARSHAL, NELLIE JEAN, fin. exec., b. Pulaski, Tenn., Jan. 30, 1933; d. William Vernon and Elsie Beatrice (Glover) DeRamus; student Baxter Sem.; 1 son, Jerami A. Marshal. Owner, Trailestate Realty, Reno, 1957-60; v.p. Bank Mortgage Loan Co., Los Angeles, 1960-66; mgr. first trust deed dept. Union Home Loans, Los Angeles, 1966-69; owner Marshal Plan, Inc., Santa Monica, Calif., 1969—; chmn. bd. Golden State Holding Co., Inc., 1980—; speaker in field. Democrat. Office: 3101 Ocean Park Blvd Suite 101 Santa Monica CA 90405

MARSHALL, CLAUDIA ELLEN, banker; b. N.Y.C., Sept. 17, 1946; d. Rudolph Gerhart and Ellen Marie (Walsh) M.; B.A., Cedar Crest Coll., 1968; M.A., Mich. State U., 1971; M.B.A., N.Y. U., 1979; m. James Douglas Shelton, Oct. 20, 1973; children—Christopher John. Systems mktg. rep. IBM, N.Y.C., 1968-72; with Chase Manhattan Bank, N.Y.C., 1972—, asst. treas., 1973, 2d v.p., mgr. orgn. planning and devel., 1974-76, v.p., 1976-79, v.p., dir. mktg., 1979—; instr. communications Mich. State U., 1970-71. Bd. dirs. YMCA Metroclub, 1973; pres. Forum for Parents in the Bus. Community, 1980. Mich. State U. fellow, 1970-71. Mem. Am. Mktg. Assn. Clubs: Strathmore Bath, Strathmore Village Civic Assn. Women's. Office: 1 Chase Plaza New York NY 10015

MARSHALL, DORIS BINKLEY (MRS. FRED TAYLOR MARSHALL), ret. info. scientist; b. Troy, Ohio, June 27, 1918; d. Charles Gordon and Onda Marie (Quinn) Binkley; B.A. in Chemistry, Ohio State U., 1940; postgrad. U. Chgo., 1940-41; M.A. in Library and Info. Sci., U. Mo., 1975; m. Fred Taylor Marshall, Mar. 28, 1942; children—Karen Louise (Mrs. Stephen Paul Booth), Carol Anne (Mrs. Paul Edward Derrickson), Fred Gordon. Asst. tech. librarian Universal Oil Products Co., Chgo., 1940-41; tech. librarian Monsanto Co., Dayton, Ohio, 1941-44; librarian Am. Zinc, Lead & Smelting Co., Kirkwood, Mo., 1956-60; owner pvt. bus., Kirkwood, 1960-64; librarian mgmt. info. center Ralston Purina Co., St. Louis, 1966-72, info. scientist, 1972-81; pvt. cons., 1981—; trainer data base Nat. Agrl. Library Kansas State U., 1977; workshop leader in field. Mem. Spl. Libraries Assn. (pres. St. Louis chpt. 1972-73, mem. internat. adv. council 1971-73, mem. div. cabinet 1976-78, chpt. employment chmn. 1976-78, editor chpt. bull. 1968-70; mem. nominating com. documentation div. 1975; mem. nominating com. food and nutrition div. 1973, 81, nominating com. chmn. 1974, div. sec. 1975-76, chmn. 1977-78, internat. nominating com. 1974-75, internat. standards com. 1978-82), Greater St. Louis Library Club (nominating com. 1976), ALA, Inst. Info. Scientists (Eng.), Am. Soc. Info. Sci. (chmn. nominating com. Mo. chpt. 1974-75), St. Louis Online Users Group (1st hon. mem. 1981), Am. Chem. Soc., Nat. Geneal. Soc. Am., Soc. Mayflower Descs. (Mo. bd. assts. 1975—, corr. sec. Mo. chpt. 1976, chpt. membership chmn. 1977-80, chpt. edn. chmn. and jr. membership 1981—), Ch. Women United (chmn. nominating com. St. Louis area 1964, auditor 1965-68), Lutheran Ch. Women (del. nat. conv. 1970; Luth. Laymen's Movement). Lutheran. Contbr. articles to profl. jours. Home: 477 Burns Ave Kirkwood MO 63122

MARSHALL, ELLEN BROUGHTON, refrigeration and air-conditioning co. exec.; b. Reddick, Ill., Oct. 6, 1913; d. William Wheeler and Caroline Ora (Gould) Broughton; student Ill. State Normal U., 1932-34; m. Richard Douglas Marshall, Jan. 13, 1934; children—Janet, Jo Ellen, Douglas. Co-founder, sec., treas. R.D. Marshall & Co., Inc., Albany, N.Y., 1945-71, pres., 1971-80, chmn. bd., 1980—. Bd. dirs. Albany Girls Club, 1977-79; vol. Albany Tulip Festival, 1978-79. Mem. Nat. Assn. Wholesaling (trustee), Air-Conditioning, Refrigeration Wholesalers, Nat. Heating and Air-Conditioning Wholesalers, Refrigeration and Service Engrs. Soc., Albany Exec. Assn., Albany C. of C. Unitarian. Clubs: Univ., Soroptimist (dir. 1973-80)(Albany). Home: 6 Willow Dr Delmar NY 12054 Office: R D Marshall & Co Inc One Marshall Pl Albany NY 12210

MARSHALL, HOLLY R., data processing exec.; b. Chgo., Sept. 28, 1945; d. Welton E. and Ferne Louise (Templeton) Richburg; student Macalester Coll., 1965. Various positions, data processing and sales Hartford, Conn. and Chgo., 1965-75; regional v.p. sales Advanced Systems Inc., Elk Grove, Ill., 1975-77, v.p. mktg., 1977-78; pres. Merit Assos., Schaumburg, Ill., 1978-81; chief exec. officer Universal Bus. Computing, Schaumburg, 1981—; dir. Ken Garen Inc., Skokie, Ill. Regular chorister Lyric Opera Chgo., 1967-69; founding mem. Chicagoans Choir, 1970. Office: PO Box 95134 Schaumburg IL 60195

MARSHALL, JANET CASH, banker; b. Lexington, Va., Apr. 1, 1945; d. Russell O. and Vera E. (Seaman) Cash; m. Thomas A. Marshall, Apr. 6, 1963; 1 son, Russell H. With S.C. Nat. Bank, Columbia, 1966—, ops. officer, 1972-80, asst. v.p. customer acctg., 1981—. Mem. Nat. Assn. Bank Women (sec. 1980), Beta Sigma Phi (pres. Gamma Beta chpt.

1979). Club: Laurel Meadows Swim (sec. 1981, pres. 1982). Office: 101 Greystone St Columbia SC 29226

MARSHALL, JEANIE, tng. cons.; b. Cambridge, Mass., Jan. 21, 1944; d. Wilfred James and Mary (Cadwallader) Combellack; B.A. in Sociology, Boston U., 1966; m. Donald W. Marshall, Aug. 8, 1980. Owner, Marshall House, Inc., tng. cons., Ballston Lake, N.Y., 1971-80, pres., 1981—; human relations trainer continuing edn. program Sch. Social Welfare, SUNY, Albany, 1979-81; tchr. parliamentary procedures Schenectady County Community Coll., 1980; tchr. career devel., presentation techniques Union Coll., Schenectady, 1980-82. Mem. AAUW (pres. Schenectady br. 1977-78, grantee Ednl. Found. 1978-79), Am. Soc. Tng. and Devel., Am. Inst. Parliamentarians, Assn. Creative Change, Assn. Psychol. Type, Nat. Assn. Female Execs., Nat. Assn. Parliamentarians, Sagamore Inst., Hudson-Mohawk Soc. Tng. and Devel. Author articles, tng. manuals, modules. Home: 15 Ashley Dr Ballston Lake NY 12019 Office: Northway 10 Executive Park Ushers Rd Ballston Lake NY 12019

MARSHALL, JUDITH ANN, employee and labor relations counselor, psychotherapist; b. Saginaw, Mich., Nov. 15, 1946; d. Edward Thomas and Margaret Camille (French) Krug; A.A., Phoenix Coll., 1976; B.A., Grand Canyon Coll., 1977; postgrad. Loyola Marymouht Coll., 1981—; m. Lee A. Marshall, Oct. 18, 1980; children by previous marriage—Stephen, Eve. Correctional counselor Justice Planning Agy., 1975-77; activity therapist Camelback Psychiat. Hosp., Phoenix, 1975-76; cons. Honeywell Large Info. Systems Div. 1977-79, employee relations counselor, 1979-80; employee relations counselor Northrop Aircraft, Hawthorne, Calif., 1980—; condr. workshops in lifestyles and reality therapy. Served with USN, 1966-68; Vietnam. Recipient Key to City of Memphis, 1966; cert. reality therapist Inst. Reality Therapy. Mem. Bus. and Profl. Women, Am. Soc. Tng. and Devel., NCCJ, Navy League, Am. Fedn. Reform Zionists, Phi Theta Kappa, Gamma Phi Beta. Democrat. Jewish. Office: 1 Northrop Ave Hawthorne CA 90250

MARSHALL, MARY AYDELOTTE, state legislator; b. Cook County, Ill., June 14, 1921; d. John A. and Nell. A. Rice; B.A. with highest honors, Swarthmore Coll., 1942; m. Roger Duryea Marshall, Mar. 3, 1944; children—Nell Aydelotte, Jenny Winslow Marshall Davies, Alice Marie. Economist anti-trust div. Dept. Justice, Washington, 1942-46; mem. Va. Ho. of Dels., 1966-70, 72—, mem. privileges and elections com., rds. and internal nav. com., counties, cities and towns com., health, welfare and instns. com.; chmn. Legis. Study Commn. on Needs Elderly Virginians, 1973-78; mem. No. Va. Transp. Commn., 1974-80; mem. exec. com. State Fed. Assembly, Nat. Conf. State Legislators, 1981—; mem. Legis. (Bagley) Commn. on Mental Health and Mental Retardation, 1977-79; chmn. Task Force on Social Security for Women, Fed. Council on Aging, 1978-81; bd. dirs. Washington Met. Council Govts., 1978, 80. Pres., Va. Assn. Mental Health, 1970-73, Va. Fedn. Democratic Women's Clubs, 1971-72; bd. dirs. Nat. Assn. Mental Health, 1972-78; mem. Dem. Central Com. Va., 1976-78. Recipient Achievement award Va. Assn. Mental Health, No. Va. Assn. Mental Health, Va. Fedn. Bus. and Profl. Women's Clubs, Va. Assn. Ind. Retail Gasoline Dealers, No. Va. Altrusa, No. Va. Retarded Citizens Assn. Mem. AAUW, LWV. Congregationalist. Clubs: Bus. and Profl. Women's, Home Demonstration, No. Va. Dem., Downtown.

MARSHALL, MARY WILLIAMS, nutritionist, educator; b. Covington, Ga., Nov. 5, 1919; d. Charles R. and Alberta J. (Hendricks) Williams; A.B. magna cum laude, Clark Coll., 1939; M.S. (research fellow), Iowa State U., 1943; postgrad. Wayne State U., 1946, Howard U., 1963-64, U. Calif., Berkeley, 1978; Catholic U. Am., 1979; m. Lawrence M. Marshall, June 6, 1939 (dec. 1977); children—Lawrence M., Gwendolyn Marshall Whitfield, Judith E. Tchr. gen. sci. Merrill High Sch., Pine Bluff, Ark., 1943-44; prof., head dept. home econs. Morris Brown Coll., Atlanta, 1945-46; research asst. (part-time) Wayne U. Med. Sch., Detroit, 1946-47; tchr. and cafeteria mgr. Farrand Trade Sch., Detroit, 1947; public health nutritionist Detroit Dept. Public Health, 1947-48; tchr. nutrition ARC, 1947-48; nutrition specialist U.S. Dept. Agr., Beltsville, Md., 1950-56, supervisory nutrition specialist Exptl. Nutrition Lab., 1956-66, research nutritionist, 1966-70, research nutritionist Lipid Nutrition Lab., 1970—; asso. prof. (part-time) Howard U., Washington, 1975, asso. prof. (full time) Sch. of Human Ecology, 1976-77, prof., 1978—. Pres. St. Anthony High Sch. PTA, 1977-78; mem. adv. com. EEO, Beltsville area, Md., 1973-76. Recipient achievement award in home econs. Iowa State U. Alumni Assn., 1981. Mem. Soc. for Nutrition Edn., Nutrition Soc. Today, Animal Nutrition Research Council, Am. Oil Chemists Soc., Am. Inst. Nutrition, Am. Assn. for Lab. Animal Sci., Phi Kappa Phi, Sigma Delta Epsilon, Iota Sigma Pi, Omicron Nu. Democrat. Episcopalian. Contbr. articles on lipid metabolism and research in nutrition to sci. jours. Office: Human Nutrition Center Lipid Nutrition Lab US Dept of Agriculture Room 115 Bldg 308 Beltsville MD 20705

MARSHALL, MAXINE BESSER, editor; b. St. Louis, Mar. 14, 1926; d. Herbert and Ida (Rubenstein) Besser; B.S., Ariz. State U., 1976; m. Jonathan Marshall, Apr. 8, 1955; children—Lucinda, Laura, Robert Louis, Jonathan Herbert. Mem. staff Scottsdale (Ariz.) Progress, 1969—, sr. editor Scene, 1974—, editor Saturday mag., weekly supplement, 1979—. Chmn. adv. com. Area Agy. Aging, 1975-76; co-chmn. Ariz. Bicentennial Com., 1975-76. Recipient Editorial Excellence award Ariz. Newspapers Assn., 1979. Mem. Nat. Fedn. Press Women, Ariz. Press Women (various 1st pl. awards). Editor: The Shopping Cart Best Recipes, 1969. Office: PO Box 1150 Scottsdale AZ 85252

MARSHALL, MILDRED DELEVETT, ret. educator; b. Balt., Aug. 15, 1904; d. William Amoss and Lutie (Kemp) Delevett; grad. Balt. Tchrs. Tng. Sch., 1922; student Johns Hopkins, 1923-24, N.Y. U., 1927; m. William Harvey Marshall, Aug. 15, 1931 (dec.). Tchr. public schs., Balt., 1922-71; demonstration tchr.; mem. curriculum com. Balt. pub. schs.; mem. supt. com. ednl. tests and measurements. Supporting com. Walter's Art Gallery, Balt. Mus. Art; mem. women's com. Balt. Symphony Orch. Mem. Pub. Sch. Tchrs. Assn., Md. Tchrs. Assn., NEA, Alumnae Assn. Samuel Ready Sch., Daus. Colonial Wars, Harford County Assn. (sec. 1950-52), Bishop's Guild, Md. Hist. Soc., Hist. Annapolis Inc., Nat. Trust Historic Preservation, English Speaking Union, Balt. Civic Opera Guild, Soc. Preservation Md. Antiquities, Descs. Colonial Govs., DAR. Democrat. Episcopalian. Address: 3701 Edgewood Rd Baltimore MD 21215

MARSHALL, NATALIE JUNEMANN, coll. ofcl.; b. Milw., June 13, 1929; d. Harold E. and Myrtle B. (Findlay) Junemann; A.B., Vassar Coll., 1951; M.A., Columbia U., 1952, Ph.D., 1963; widow; children—Frederick S., Alison B. Mem. faculty Vassar Coll., Poughkeepsie, N.Y., 1952-54, 58-60, prof. econs. 1973—, dean studies, 1973-75, v.p. student affairs, 1975-80, v.p. adminstrv. and student services, 1980—; mem. faculty Wesleyan U., Middletown, Conn., 1955-56, SUNY, New Paltz, 1964-73, Bd. mgrs. Children's Home, Poughkeepsie, N.Y., 1968-71; trustee St. Francis Hosp., Poughkeepsie, 1979—, Dutchess Area Fund, 1983—. Mem. AAUW (chpt. pres. 1961-63, v.p. N.Y. State 1964-66), Am. Econ. Assn. Am. Assn. Higher Edn. Author: The History of Economic Thought, 1968; Keynes Updated or Outdated, 1970; Collective Bargaining, 1971. Home: 17 Thelberg Rd Poughkeepsie NY 12601 Office: Box 3 Vassar Coll Poughkeepsie NY 12601

MARSHALL, PATRICIA ANN, educator; b. Dallas, Dec. 21, 1941; d. Warren Vernon and Charlene (McCarley) Stafford; student Tex. Women's U., 1960-61; B.S., U. Houston, 1972, M.Ed., 1976; postgrad. Houston Bapt. U., 1981—; children—Robin Christine, Sherry Lynn. Sec., Tex. A.&M. Engring. Expt. Sta., Bryan, Tex., 1961-62; nurse aide obstetrics ward St. Joseph's Hosp., Bryan, 1962-63; dr.'s asst./sec. Eugene J. Goldman, M.D., Houston, 1964-69; tchr. Spring Br. Ind. Sch. Dist., Houston, 1973-76, ednl. diagnostician, 1976-81, asst. dir. appraisal services, 1981—, tchr. adult continuing edn., 1980—; tutor grade sch. children. Mem. Hou-Met Diagnosticians (cert.), Council for Exceptional Children, Tex. Assn. Ednl. Diagnosticians, Tex. Tchrs. Assn., NEA, Assn. for Children with Learning Disabilities, Spring Br. Edn. Assn., Assn. Retarded Children, Phi Kappa Phi. Clubs: Country Playhouse, Order of the Rainbow for Girls. Home: 5523 Maywood St Houston TX 77053 Office: 955 Campbell St Houston TX 77024

MARSH-CURTIS, ALVA DOROTHEA, artist; b. N.Y.C., June 15, 1911; d. Charles Johan and Elizabeth (Hagstrom) Berg; student Art Students League, N.Y.C., 1928-29, Grand Central Art Sch., 1934-36, N.Y. Sch. Fine Arts, 1930-31, Nat. Acad., N.Y.C., 1934-35, Columbia U., 1943-44, Yale U., 1969-70; m. Terrill Belknap Marsh, Nov. 3, 1932; children—Owen Thayer, Charles Ames, Ronald Belknap; m. 2d, Aug. 11, 1979. One woman shows: Scranton Meml. Library, Madison, Conn., 1969, Phippsburg (Maine) Library, 1964, Town and County Club, Hartford, Conn., 1976, Conn. Bank & Trust Co., Madison, 1977, 1st Fed. Savs. & Loan, Madison, 1977; group shows include: Smithsonian Inst., Washington, 1964, 66, Nat. Arts Club, N.Y.C., 1952, 53, 54, 57; 57, Internat. Maritime Art Award Show (Sculpture award), 1981, Nat. League Am. Penwomen Art Show (Sculpture award), Atlanta, 1982; represented in permanent collections: Swedish Club, Chgo., Conn. Bank & Trust Co., Windsor, Phippsburg Library, also pvt. collections; partner, art dir. Terrill Belknap Marsh, Assos., N.Y.C., 1934-69; lectr. in field. Pres. Madison (Conn.) Taxpayers Assn., 1975—; vice chmn. Madison Inland Wetlands Agy., 1974—. Mem. Am. Artists Profl. League, Nat. Arts Club, Nat. League Am. Penwomen (pres. 1978—, Greenwich br. 1958). Republican. Episcopalian. Clubs: Lyme Art Assn., Madison Winter, Garden Madison. Home: 12 Dogwood Ln Madison CT 06443

MARSICO, BEVERLEY BRINKERHOFF, banker; b. N.Y.C., Nov. 25, 1932; d. Charles Van Buskirk and Dorothea Marion (Smith) Brinkerhoff; student Fairleigh Dickinson U., 1963-67; m. Louis J. Marsico, Apr. 8, 1978; children—Adrian S. Roberts, Beverly A. Roberts, David B. Roberts. Clk., First Nat. Bank, Madison, N.J., 1950-53; bookkeeping machine operator Nat. Bank of Washington, 1953-54, 55-56; mgr. bookkeeping dept. Somerset Hills Nat. Bank, 1960-65, asst. cashier, 1965-69; asst. v.p. computer services, mktg. and personnel depts. Somerset Hills and County Nat. Bank, 1969-73; v.p. computer services, mktg. and personnel depts. First Nat. State Bank of West Jersey, 1973-75; dir. communications Nat. Computer Analysts, Inc., 1975-76; v.p. ops. and personnel Peapack-Gladstone Bank, Gladstone, N.J., 1976—; tchr. Am. Inst. Banking. Bd. dirs. Vis. Homemakers Assn., Somerset Hills Community Chest; bd. fin. advisers Somerset County Coll. Mem. Am. Inst. Banking (gov.), N.J. Bankers Assn. Republican. Presbyterian. Office: Peapack-Gladstone Bank Main St Gladstone NJ 08846

MARSTELLER, JULIE V., coll. adminstr.; b. Chgo., Aug. 17, 1943; d. William A. and Gloria (Crawford) Marsteller; A.B. with honors, Barnard Coll., 1969. Archivist, Barnard Coll., 1969-77, asst. to pres., 1978-79, dean for disabled students, asst. dean studies, 1979—; cons. accessibility and compliance Whitney Mus. Am. Art, R.I. Sch. Design, Columbia U. Tchrs. Coll., U.S. Rehab. Services Adminstrn. Bd. dirs. Untapped Resources, Inc. Recipient Ruth Kurzon Handicapped Children Humanitarian award, 1979; Handicapped Profl. Woman of Yr. award, 1981. Mem. Nat. Assn. Visually Handicapped, Assn. Handicapped Student Service Programs in Postsecondary Edn., Am. Coalition Citizens with Disabilities, Council Citizens with Low Vision, Nat. Rehab. Assn., Soc. Am. Archivists, Oral History Assn. Home: 15 Claremont Ave New York NY 10027 Office: Barnard Coll 606 W 120th St New York NY 10027

MARSTON-SCOTT, MARY VESTA, nurse, educator; b. St. Stephen, N.B., Can., Apr. 5, 1924; d. George Frank and Betsey Mildred (Babb) Marston; B.A., U. Maine, 1946; M.N., Yale U., 1951; M.P.H., Harvard U., 1957; M.A., Boston U., 1964, Ph.D., 1969; m. John Paul Scott, June 30, 1979. Research asst. Roscoe B. Jackson Meml. Lab., Bar Harbor, Maine, 1946-48; nurse, 1952-54; instr. Yale U. Sch. Nursing, 1955-56; nurse cons. Div. Nursing, Washington, 1957-62; asso. prof. Frances Payne Bolton Sch. Nursing, Case Western Res. U., Cleve., 1969-74; prof. grad. program Community health nursing Boston U., 1974—; cons. infield. Served with USPHS, 1957-62. Fellow Am. Acad. Nursing; mem. Am. Psychol. Assn., Am. Public Health Assn., Am. Nurses Assn., Sigma Theta Tau. Contbr. articles to profl. jours. Home: 3 Lois Ln Lexington MA 02173 Office: 635 Commonwealth Ave Boston MA 02215

MARTELL, ANTOINETTE DIANE, clin. social worker; b. Altadena, Calif., Nov. 12, 1945; d. John Edward and Josephine (Rodriguez) M.; B.A. in Psychology, San Francisco State U., 1972; M.A., Pepperdine U., 1976; doctoral candidate Profl. Sch. Humanistic Studies, 1982. Parish social worker Epiphany Parish, San Francisco, 1969-72; program dir. Bayside Settlement House, San Diego, 1972; dir. Grossmont Coll., Newman Center, El Cajon, Calif., 1972-74; interim dir. dept. social work services, Mercy Hosp., San Diego, 1979; supr. outpatient social work services Mercy Med. Center, San Diego, 1974—; mem. faculty Calif. Pacific U., San Diego, 1978; supr. social work interns San Diego State U., 1974—. Mem. U.S. Mexico Border Health Assn., 1975—; bd. dirs. Bayside Settlement House, Inc., 1980—. Mem. S.D. Ambulatory Care Social Workers Group (chmn.), Calif.-Baja Binat. Health Care Council, Nat. Assn. Social Workers, S.D. Big Sisters, AAUW, S.D. Career Women's Network. Democrat. Roman Catholic. Club: Pepperdine U. Century. Office: Mercy Hosp 4077 5th Ave San Diego CA 92103

MARTELL, SAUNDRA ADKINS, lawyer; b. Huntginton, W.Va., June 26, 1946; d. Edgar and Mildred (Harless) A.; B.A., Vanderbilt U., 1968; J.D., U. Va., 1971. Admitted to Va. bar, 1972, D.C. bar, 1972, Minn. bar, 1982; with Office of Gen. Counsel, Dept. Navy, Washington, 1971-78; atty. fraud sect., criminal div. U.S. Dept. Justice, Washington, 1978-80; assoc. firm John Murray and Assocs., Ltd., St. Paul, 1982—. Active Big Sisters D.C.; leader Girl Scouts U.S.A., Alexandria, Va. Mem. ABA, Nat. Assn. Women Judges, Exec. Women in Govt. Office: North Central Life Tower Suite 610 Saint Paul MN 55101

MARTEN, MARY ELIZABETH, sch. adminstr.; b. Jennings, La., Nov. 7, 1941; d. Earl Wilson and Florence Elizabeth (Peters) Horne; B.S., U. Southwestern La., 1963; M.Ed., Miami U., 1973, Ph.D., 1977; m. William Douglas Marten, Apr. 7, 1977; 1 dau. by previous marriage—Dawn Elizabeth Holt. Tchr., Lafayette (La.) Parish Sch., 1962-63, Palm Beach County Schs., West Palm Beach, Fla., 1963-66, Princeton City Schs., Cin., 1966-76; prin. Northwest Local Schs., Cin., 1976-79, curriculum supr., 1979—; adj. prof. Coll. Mt. St. Joseph, Cin., 1980-82; partner Edn. for Excellence, Cin., 1981—. Mem. N.W. Assn. Sch. Adminstrs. (treas. 1977-78), Ohio Valley Assn. Gifted and Talented, Ohio Assn. Gifted Children, Internat. Reading Assn., Phi Beta Kappa, Delta Kappa Gamma. Methodist. Author: Don't Teach! Let Me Learn! series; The Woods, 1980, The Zoo, 1980; Discovering Philosophy, 1980; A Middle Ages Pageant, 1981; Discovering Psychology, 1981; Creative Writing in Action, 1981; Guiding Young Authors to Write Fiction, 1981; Guiding Very Young Authors to Write Fiction, 1981; Discovering Geology, 1982. Home: 2117 Weron Ln Cincinnati OH 45225 Office: 3240 Banning Rd Cincinnati OH 45239

MARTENS, PATRICIA ANN, univ. adminstr.; b. Chadron, Nebr., July 18, 1952; d. Lloyd Ernest and Glendene (Wallingford) M.; B.S., Chadron State Coll., 1973, M.S., 1978. Phys. edn. tchr. Hot Springs (S.D.) High Sch., 1973-75, Sterling (Colo.) High Sch., 1975-76; state tng. mgr. Nebr. Head Start, Chadron, 1976-77; grad. asst. Chadron (Nebr.) State Coll., 1977-78; asso. dir. admissions Eastern N.Mex. U., Portales, 1978-79; admissions counselor N.Mex. State U., Las Cruces, 1979—, recruitment and publicity chmn., evening degree program com. chmn., 1980-82; sec. N.Mex. Coll. Day Com., 1979-81. Recipient Scholarships, Elks, 1970, Chadron State Coll., 1970, Chadron C. of C., 1970. Mem. Am. Assn. Collegiate Registrars and Admissions Ofcls., Rocky Mountain Assn. Counselors and Admissions Counselors, Rocky Mountain Assn. Collegiate Registrars and Admissions Ofcls., N.Mex. Assn. Collegiate Registrars and Admissions Ofcls. N.Mex. Sch. Counselors Assn. (secondary v.p. 1979-81), Am. Legion Aux., Am. Assn. Female Execs., Chadron State Coll. Alumni Assn., Phi Delta Kappa, Cardinal Key, Sigma Delta Nu, Kappa Mu Epsilon. Republican. Baptist. Club: Pentax Owners. Office: Box 3A N Mex State U Las Cruces NM 88003

MARTHALER, ANN ELIZABETH BERESWILL, nursing educator; b. Milw., Wis., June 21, 1936; d. Frederick J. Bereswill and Catherine A. (Grosspietsch) Bereswill Esser; B.S. in Nursing, Alverno Coll., 1960; postgrad. U.Wis., 1968; M. in Nursing, U. Washington, Seattle, 1969; postgrad. Ariz. State U., 1980, 81; m. Edward J. Marthaler, Aug. 23, 1969; children—Robert J., Peter J., Michael J., Daniel E., Thomas N. Staff nurse St. Mary's Hill Hosp., Milw., 1960-61; charge nurse, nurse anesthetist Waupun (Wis.) Meml. Hosp., 1962-68, St. Joseph's Hosp., Beaver Dam, Wis., 1968; staff nurse Children's Orthopedic Hosp., Seattle, Wash., 1969; instr. Coll. Nursing, U. Wis., Milw., 1969-70; instr., then asst. prof. Coll. Nursing, Alverno Coll., Milw., 1970-74; clin. dir. Family Hosp. New Life Center, Milw., 1974-75; staff nurse Western Med. Temporary Home Health and Counseling, Walnut Creek, Calif., 1976-77; asst. prof. Coll. Nursing, Ariz. State U., Tempe, 1977-82, asso. mem. dept. family studies, 1979—; instr. U. Phoenix and Glendale Community Coll., 1982—; cons. maternity nursing State Bd. Rev., Ariz., 1978—. Vol. Friends of Family, 1978-79; team mother Olympian Soccer Team, Scottsdale, Ariz., 1981—. Mem. Childbirth Edn. Assn., Am. Nurses Assn., Ariz. Nurses Assn., Nurses Assn. of Am. Coll. of Ob-Gyn., Sigma Theta Tau, Beta Upsilon (pres. 1982-84). Contbr. articles on nursing edn. to profl. jours.; coordinating editor: Maternity Nursing New Role for a New Age, in progress. Home: 11818 N 86th St Scottsdale AZ 85260 Office: Glendale Community Coll Dept Nursing Glendale AZ 85302

MARTHIS, MAUREEN BRAMLAGE, zoo ofcl.; b. Chgo., Mar. 28, 1938; d. Russell Anthony and Alice Alma (Wilkins) Bramlage; B.A., Xavier U., Cin., 1972, M.Ed., 1974; 1 dau. Creative dir. M. Bizzarri Advt., Cin., 1963-67; tchr. elem. and secondary schs. in Ohio, 1967-76; office mgr. Perfect Sound of Ohio, 1972-74; ednl. programs coordinator Cin. Zoo, 1977-78, devel. officer, 1978—. Mem. community affairs commn., parish council St. Robert Bellarmine Chapel, Xavier U. Mem. Am. Assn. Zool. Parks and Aquariums, Am. Assn. Museums, Ohio Museums Assn., Great Cin. Soc. Fund Raising Execs. Office: 3400 Vine St Cincinnati OH 45220

MARTIGNONI, JOANNE L., personnel cons.; b. N.Y.C., Sept. 28, 1940; d. Charles V. and Emily Martignoni; B.S., Fordham U., 1962. With Markite Corp., N.Y.C. and Ramsey, N.J., 1962-69; asst. v.p. Drexel Burnham Lambert, Inc., N.Y.C., 1969-76; exec. v.p. D.J. Hertz & Assos., Ltd., N.Y.C., 1976—. Mem. Assn. Personnel Consultants of N.Y. (treas. 1980-81, controller 1982-83), N.Y. Employment Council. Office: 475 Fifth Ave New York NY 10017

MARTIKAINEN, A(UNE) HELEN, former health edn. specialist; b. Harrison, Maine, May 11, 1916; d. Sylvester and Emma (Heikkinen) M.; A.B., Bates Coll., 1939, D.Sc. (hon.), 1957; M.P.H., Yale, 1941; D.Sc., Harvard U., 1964, Smith Coll., 1969. Health edn. sec. Hartford Tb and Public Health Assn., 1941-42; cons. USPHS, 1942-49; chief health edn. WHO, Geneva, 1949-74, now mem. expert adv. panel. Trustee, Bridgton Acad., North Bridgton, Maine; mem program adv. bd., also membership com. U.S. Assn. Club of Rome; mem. N.C. Citizens Council Public Health; bd. dirs. N.C. Center of Laws Affecting Women, Inc.; mem. Gov.'s Commn. N.C.-2000; mem. network N.C. Council on Status of Women. Recipient Delta Omega award Yale; Nat. Adminstrv. award Am. Acad. Phys. Edn.; Bates Key award; Internat. Service award, France, 1953; Prentiss medal, 1956; spl. medal, certificate for internat. health edn. service Nat. Acad. Medicine for France, 1959; profl. award Soc. Public Health Educators, 1963. Fellow Am. Public Health Assn. (chmn. health edn. sect., Excellence award 1969); mem. AAUW mem. state task force on membership, rep. to N.C. Council Social Legis.), U.S. Soc. Pub. Health Educators, Internat. Union Health Edn. (Parisot medal, tech. adviser), Acad. Phys. Edn. (asso.), Phi Beta Kappa. Episcopalian. Home: PO Box 3059 Chapel Hill NC 27514

MARTIN, AGNES BERNICE, painter; b. Maklin, Sask., Can., 1912; came to U.S., 1930, naturalized, 1949; d. Malcom Ian and Margaret (Kinnon) M.; ed. Western Wash. Coll., 1932, Columbia U., 1941-42, 51-52; B.F.A., U. N.Mex. Exhibited paintings in one-woman shows: Betty Parsons Gallery, N.Y.C., 1958-61, Robert Elkon Gallery, N.Y.C., 1962-70, Pace Gallery, N.Y.C., 1975-80; exhibited in one-woman retrospectives including: Inst. Contemporary Art, Phila., 1973, Mus. Modern Art, N.Y.C., 1973, Heyward Gallery, London, 1977, Stedjlick Mus., Amsterdam, Netherlands, 1977; represented in permanent collections; Mus. Modern Art, N.Y.C., Whitney Mus., N.Y.C., Guggenheim Mus., N.Y.C., many other mus., U.S. and Europe. Author: The Perfection Underlying Life; The Untroubled Mind. Office: care Pace Gallery 32 E 57th St New York NY 10022

MARTIN, ALICE LOUISE MCCLURE, purchasing exec.; b. Ottumwa, Iowa, Mar. 23, 1926; d. Floyd Edgar and Lena Olive (Shepherd) McClure; student Iowa State Coll., 1946-47; m. George Kenneth Martin, Oct. 19, 1947; 1 son, Douglas Bruce. Draftsman, engring. dept. Ottumwa Iron Works (Iowa), 1944-46; order receiver John Morrell & Co., Ottumwa, 1946-50; clk. production control Proto Tool div. Ingersoll-Rand Co., Portland, Oreg., 1970-72, steel inventory planner, 1972-77, steel buyer, 1978—. Mem. Clackamas County Election Bd., 1961-70; pres. women's assn. Oak Hills Presbyn. Ch., 1965-66. Mem. Nat. Assn. Female Execs., Inc., Sigma Kappa. Republican. Presbyterian. Home: 5332 SE El Centro Way Portland OR 97222 Office: 10330 SE 32d Ave Portland OR 97222

MARTIN, ALICE MCNULTY, accountant; b. Bklyn., Aug. 7, 1920; d. Raymond Peter and Alice Marie (Roche) McNulty; student Smith Coll., 1938-40, Katharine Gibbs Sch., N.Y., 1940-41, U. N.Mex., 1947-49, 79-80, U. Albuquerque, 1973; m. George Edward Martin, Apr. 27, 1946 (div. Dec. 1967); children—Margaret A., Roberta E., George E., Annette M., Raymond A. Sec., Christiansen Mil. Tailors, N.Y.C., 1941-42; office mgr., real estate broker George Martin Realty, Albuquerque, 1957-66; cashier U. N.Mex., 1966; chief bookkeeper County Treas. Office, Bernalillo County, N.Mex., 1966-74; acct. fin. dept. Bernalillo County, Albuquerque, 1974—. Vol., bd. dirs. Albuquerque Suicide Prevention and Crisis Center. Served to 1st lt. WAC, 1942-46. Mem. Nat. Assn. Accts. (sec. Albuquerque 1974). Republican. Roman

Catholic. Home: 1308 Kentucky St NE Albuquerque NM 87110 Office: 620 Lomas St NW Albuquerque NM 87102

MARTIN, ANGELIQUE, assn. exec.; b. N.Y.C., Nov. 24, 1946; d. Kenneth and Patricia (Ramos) McDuffy; B.S., John Jay Coll. Criminal Justice, 1975, M.A. in Mgmt. and Human Resources, 1977; 1 son, Michael Shawn Motta. Program coordinator Bronx Community Coll., 1972-74; program developer John Jay Coll. Criminal Justice, N.Y.C., 1976-77; asst. dir. admissions, dir. recruitment LaGuardia Community Coll., 1977-79; exec. dir. Mid-Manhattan br. NAACP, N.Y.C., 1979—, dir. Mid-Manhattan br. Project Rebound, 1979—; cons. Jobs for Youth. Mem. Am. Mgmt. Assn., Internat. Assn. Personnel Women, Nat. Alliance for Bus., Nat. Assn. Female Execs. Democrat. Roman Catholic. Office: 270 W 96th St New York NY 10025

MARTIN, ANITA ELLEN, nurse; b. Chgo., Aug. 5, 1925; d. Cornelius James and Sophie Ann (Bruczyk) M.; diploma DePaul Hosp. Coll. Nursing, St. Louis, 1949; B.S.N., Mt. St. Mary's Coll., Los Angeles, 1955; postgrad. UCLA, 1955-56, Rutgers U., 1969. Supr. pediatrics St. Mary's Hosp., Evansville, Ind., 1950-52; supr. medicine St. Vincent's Hosp., Los Angeles, 1952-56; supr. pediatrics Hotel Dieu Hosp., El Paso, 1956-60; head nurse Hanson's Disease, USPHS Hosp., Carville, La., 1960-62; head nurse, night supr. gen. surgery Hines (VA) Hosp., 1962-65, head nurse oncolgy, 1965-68, head nurse Restoration Center, 1968-72, community health nurse hosp.-based home care, 1972-74, coordinator hosp.-based health care, 1974—, counselor alcoholic treatment program Restoration Center, 1968-72, cons. palliative care com., 1979—; lectr. high schs., civic orgns. Mem. Am. Nurses Assn., Nat. Orgn. VA Nurses, Am. Assn. Rehab. Nurses, Ill. State Hospice Assn. (charter). Roman Catholic. Contbr. articles to profl. jours. Home: 29W Crossman Box 24 Hines IL 60141 Office: VA Hospital Hines IL 60141

MARTIN, ANN BODENHAMER, writer, broadcaster; b. El Dorado, Ark., Oct. 24, 1927; d. R.C. and Jewel (Little) Bodenhamer; student Lindenwood Coll., 1945-46, U. Ark., 1946-47; B.A., Southeastern U., 1974, also M.A. in Journalism, Ph.D. in Behavioral Sci.; children—Richard Clinton, Mark Andrew (Elliott). Radio/TV performer, freelance model, writer Sta. KELD, El Dorado, 1948-50, Sta. KSJB, Minot, N.D., 1950-52; public relations, prodn. writer Sta. WWEZ, New Orleans, 1952-56; performer Hospitality House, producer, performer New Orleans Bandstand, Sta. WJMR-TV, 1956-60; performer, producer Ann Elliott Show, Sta. WWL-TV, New Orleans, 1960-64; freelance model, public relations cons., 1964-66; performer, producer Sta. KTVE-TV, El Dorado, 1967-68; freelance tchr., writer, broadcaster, St. Petersburg and Ft. Lauderdale, Fla., 1968-76; freelancer, editorial asst AVCO's Money Tree mag., Newport Beach, Calif., 1976-78, sr. writer, asst. editor, 1978—; producer ednl., religious radio programs, 1972—. Mem. New Thought Alliance, 1972—, ordained minister, 1976; mem. World Fellowship of Religions, New Delhi, 1973—; founder Friends of Manava Bharati, 1974—; founder (with D.P. Pandey) Manava-Bharati Heritage Schs., 1978—. Recipient various broadcast awards. Author: Calico Families, 1974; Metabionics: Mystic Power of the Mind, 1980; Build A Better You-Starting Now, 1980. Home: 1433 Superior Ave Apt 353 Newport Beach CA 92663

MARTIN, BARBARA LENNOX, plastics broker; b. Eng., July 21, 1934; came to U.S., 1957, naturalized, 1970; d. Arthur and Emily (Wheelhouse) Lennox; bus. degree Millers Coll. for Girls, Nottingham, Eng. Pvt. sec. to chmn. Bennett's Automobiles, Nottingham, 1955-57; with M. Holland Co., Northbrook, Ill., 1957—, controller, 1968—, asst. corp. sec., 1969—, v.p., 1978—, treas., 1981—. Corr. sec. B'nai B'rith, Highland Park, Ill., 1972-78, bd. dirs., 1972—; bd. dirs. Beth El Sisterhood, 1980. Mem. Am. Jewish Com., Pioneer Women, Womens Am. ORT. Democrat. Club: Highland Park Racquet. Home: 625 Mulberry St Highland Park IL 60035 Office: PO Box 125 Northbrook IL 60062

MARTIN, BETTY CLEMENT, advt. exec.; b. Dallas, Sept. 17, 1938; d. Henry Grady and Annette (Clayton) King; B.A., So. Meth. U., 1961; m. John L. Clement, Dec. 20, 1967 (dec. Dec. 1969); m. 2d, Howard L. Martin, May 23, 1975. Public relations asst. Dallas C. of C., 1960-65; advt. copywriter Lone Star Gas Co., Dallas, 1965-68; public relations account exec. Rominger Advt. Agy., Dallas, 1968-69, advt. account exec., 1969-75, also v.p. recruitment advt. div., 1971-75, corp. sec., 1972-75; advt. mgr. Baker-Crow Co., Dallas, 1975-76; owner Betty Martin Advt. Services (Inc. 1980), 1975-80, pres., 1980—. Mem. Nat. Assn. Home Builders, Gamma Alpha Chi. Methodist. Home: Box 99 Grapevine TX 76051 Office: 5005 Royal Ln Suite 125 Irving TX 75063

MARTIN, CAROLANN FRANCES, educator, condr., cellist; b. Woodward, Okla., Nov. 20, 1935; d. John C. and Leah Mae (Heaston) Shilling; B.Mus.Edn., Oklahoma City U., 1957; M.A. (fellow), Ohio State U., 1964; D.M.A., U. Ariz., 1979. Tchr. music, public schs., Okla., 1957-58; asst. prof. Wilson br. Chgo. City Coll., 1964-67; asso. prof. Morningside Coll., Sioux City, Iowa, 1969-76; dir. opera theater, cellist Oklahoma City Symphony, 1957-58, 67-69, Norfolk Symphony, 1958-61, Columbus (Ohio) Symphony, 1961-64; prin. cellist Chgo. Chamber Orch., 1964-67, Chgo. Civic Orch., 1964-67; prin. cellist Sioux City Symphony; condr. Siouxland Youth Symphony; asst. prin. cellist Tucson Symphony and Ariz. Opera Co., 1976-77; condr. S.E. Kans. Symphony and Pittsburg State U. Opera Theater, also Mid-Am. Youth Symphony, 1977—; mem. faculty Pittsburg (Kans.) State U., 1977—. Served to 1st lt. USMCR, 1958-61. Winner Nat. Conducting Competition, 1980. Mem. Am. String Tchrs. Assn., Music Educators Nat. Conf., Nat. Sch. Orch. Assn., Am. String Tchrs. Assn., Condrs. Guild, Delta Zeta, Sigma Alpha Iota. Roman Catholic. Home: 107 E Carlton Pittsburg KS 66762 Office: Dept Music Pittsburg State U Pittsburg KS 66762

MARTIN, CAROLE MARY, mag. editor; b. Bronx, N.Y., Mar. 25, 1938; d. Harold and Ada Rita (Huhn) M.; A.B. in Journalism, U. Ky., 1960; M.A., Sarah Lawrence Coll., Bronxville, N.Y., 1977. With UPI, 1961-67; bus. writer, then edn. writer AP, N.Y.C., 1967-75; freelance writer, 1978; asso. editor Diversion mag., N.Y.C., 1979—, editor Diversion Vacation Planner, 1980—; sec. Columbia U. Seminar Women and Soc., 1976-77. Mem. Nat. Women's Polit. Caucus. Club: Deadline (v.p. 1974-75) (N.Y.C.). Contbg. editor: Get 'em and Go Travel Guide: Europe, 1979. Office: 60 E 42d St New York NY 10017

MARTIN, CECILIA ANN, educator; b. Broken Bow, Okla., Nov. 10, 1934; d. Cecil C. and Faye (Burks) Martin; B.S., Baylor U., 1955; M.Ed., North Tex. State U., 1962; Ed.D., U. No. Colo., 1975. Instr. phys. edn. Stripling Jr. High Sch., Ft. Worth, 1955-65; cons. in phys. edn. Ft. Worth Ind. Sch. Dist., 1965-74; dir. profl. preparation dept. phys. edn. Colo. State U., Fort Collins, 1974—, asst. dean Coll. Profl. Studies, 1979-80. Mem. Tex. Tchrs. Assn., Am., Tex. (asso. conv. mgr. 1970-71), Colo. (sec. elect) assns. health, phys. edn. and recreation, Nat., Central (membership chmn.) assns. phys. edn. in higher edn., Colo. Assn. Health, Phys. Edn., Recreation and Dance (sec., pres.), Phi Delta Kappa, Kappa Delta Pi, Delta Psi Kappa. Home: 1977 17th Ave Greeley CO 80631 Office: Moby Gymnasium Colo State Univ Fort Collins CO 80521

MARTIN, CHERYL LANE, govt. ofcl.; b. Pine Bluff, Ark., Dec. 27, 1945; d. James Roscoe and Willie Mae (Sites) Lane; student Golden Gate U., 1978, U. Albuquerque, 1979, U. N.Mex., 1980—; m. Kenneth Gerald Martin, May 3, 1969; children—Charles Lewis, Kristine Lyn. Key punch operator, 1967-70; tape dubbing technician, sales rep., bookkeeper, supply clk. Bitburg (Ger.) Audio Club, 1973-74; bookkeeper, cashier Edwards (Calif.) NCO Club, 1975; office mgr., mil. public health and bioenviron. engring. Edwards AFB, Calif., 1975-76; procurement specialist, 1976-78; contract specialist Bur. Indian Affairs, Albuquerque, 1979—. Vol., Red Cross, 1972-73, Family Services, 1972-73. Mem. Am. Mgmt. Assn., Federally Employed Women, Nat. Contract Mgmt. Assn., LWV. Republican. Office: 500 Gold St SW Albuquerque NM 87105

MARTIN, CLEO EILEEN, educator; b. Goldfield, Iowa, Aug. 5, 1925; d. Roy Bertram and Fannie Grace (Zinser) Martin; B.A., U. No. Iowa, 1946, M.A., 1954; postgrad. U. Iowa, 1961. Tchr. English, high schs., New Hampton and E. Waterloo, Iowa, 1946-53; teaching asst., instr., asst. prof., writing supr. freshman rhetoric program U. Iowa, Iowa City, 1954—; con. high sch. and coll. writing programs; dir. writing workshop five sessions SE Iowa Writing Project, Writing Workshop Iowa Inst. on Writing. Mem. Iowa Council of Tchrs. of English, Nat. Council of Tchrs. of English, Coll. Conf. on Composition and Communication. Democrat. Home: 405 Crestview Ave Iowa City IA 52240 Office: 72 English-Philosophy Bldg Iowa City IA 52242

MARTIN, DEBORAH LOUISE MORGAN (MRS. JOHN DICK MARTIN, JR.), realtor asso.; b. Goodview, Va., Oct. 21, 1917; d. Jimmie Jubal and Callie Maude (Wright) Morgan; grad. Nat. Bus. Coll., Roanoke, Va., 1937; postgrad. U. Va., 1960-68, St. Leo Coll., 1975; grad. numerous profl. courses; m. John Dick Martin, Jr., Oct. 8, 1939; 1 son, John Dick III (dec.). Housing mgr. Fed. Public Housing Authority, Morgan City, La., 1943-45, asst. housing mgr., Bearden, Ark., 1945-46; asst. to project mgr. erection of housing City of Roanoke, 1946-47; br. mgr. Peggy Newton Cosmetics, Vinton, Va., 1948-58; housing constrn. mgr. John D. Martin Co., Vinton, 1947-49; ind. contractor Powell & Morewitz Realty, Inc., Newport News, Va.; mktg. cons. Universal Equipment & Supply Co., 1980. Founder, Friendship Force Club Eastern Va., exchange dir. The Friendship Force, 1980—, Friendship ambassador to W. Berlin, 1978, Korea, 1979; mem. Nat. Republican Congressional Com., 1981; charter mem. Rep. Presdl. Task Force. Recipient Spl. Recognition award Sen. Howard Baker, 1980; cert. of recognition Nat. Congressional Com., 1981; medal of Merit, Rep. Presdl. Task Force, 1981; award Women's Clubs Va. Mem. Nat. Assn. Realtors, Women's Council Realtors, Va. Assn. Realtors, Va. Women's Council Realtors, Va. Peninsula Women's Council Realtors, Newport-Hampton Bd. Realtors, Realtors Found. Va., Realtor-Salesman Assn., Internat. Platform Assn., U.S. Hist. Soc. Methodist. Clubs: Shriners; Women's (Vinton). Home: 106 Booth Rd Hidenwood Newport News VA 23606

MARTIN, DONNA LEE, publishing exec.; b. Detroit, Aug. 7, 1935; d. David M. and Lillian Paul; B.A., Rice U., 1957; m. Rex Martin, June 5, 1956; children—Justin, Andrew. Mng. editor dept. trade Appleton-Century-Crofts, N.Y.C., 1961-62; dir. publs. Lycoming Coll., Williamsport, Pa., 1966-68; editor Univ. Press of Kans., Lawrence, 1970-74; mng. editor Andrews & McMeel, Inc., Fairway, Kans., 1974-80, v.p., editorial dir. 1980—; v.p. Universal Press Syndicate, Fairway, 1980—; panelist Avila Writers Conf. 1975—. Mem. Women in Communications, Phi Beta Kappa. Contbr. articles to profl. jours. Office: 4400 Johnson Dr Fairway KS 66205

MARTIN, EDITH KINGDON GOULD (MRS. GUY MARTIN), pianist, volunteer; b. N.Y.C., Aug. 20, 1920; d. Kingdon and Annunziata (Lucci) Gould; student Barnard Coll., N.Y.C., 1939-40; pvt. study piano; m. Guy Martin, Oct. 12, 1946; children—Isaiah Guyman III, Jason Gould, Christopher Kingdon, Edith Maria Theodosia Burr. Actress, Barter Theater, 1941, Summer Stock, Nyack, 1942, A Young American, 1946, Louis Bromfield's West of the Moon, 1946, Agatha Christie's Hidden Horizons, 1946; guest pianist Werner Lywen Quartet, 1965—. Bd. dirs. Paul VI Inst. for Arts, 1979—; trustee, past pres. Washington Opera. Served with USNR, 1942-46. Decorated Navy Expert Pistol medal. Clubs: City Tavern, Sulgrave (Washington). Author: Poems, 1934. Composer: Song Cycle on Poems of Lenau and Schiller, 1968. Home: 3300 O St NW Washington DC 20007

MARTIN, ELIZABETH MASON, lawyer, state legislator; b. Moneta, Va., Mar. 14, 1934; d. Alvin Archer and Dasye (Shelton) Mason; B.A., Mary Washington Coll., 1954; M.A., George Peabody Coll. Tchrs., 1955; J.D., W.Va. U., 1974; m. James Douglas Martin, June 22, 1956; children—James Douglas, Julia Elizabeth, Ann Louise. Tchr., Nashville Pub. Schs., 1955-59, Charlottesville (Va.) Public Schs., 1959-61; instr. W.Va. U., 1974-80; admitted to W.Va. bar, 1974, U.S. Dist. Ct. bar, 1974; individual practice law, Morgantown, W.Va., 1974—; mem. W.Va. Ho. Delegates, 1980—. Chmn. bd. dirs. Morgantown Day Sch., 1970-71; mem. state exec. com. Democratic Party, 1978—. Mem. W.Va. State Bar Assn., Monongalia County Bar Assn., Am. Trial Lawyers Assn., W.Va. Trial Lawyers Assn., W.Va. U. Alumni Assn. Lutheran. Clubs: Service League Morgantown, Morgantown Woman's Music, Zonta, Heart Fund. Home: Route 10 Box 392 Morgantown WV 26505 Office: 180 Chancery Row Morgantown WV 26505

MARTIN, FRANCES FRANKLIN (MRS. WAYNE S. MARTIN), educator, club woman; b. Gary, W.Va., May 3, 1915; d. John Thomas and Mabel (Marion) Franklin; student Concord Coll., 1935; A.B., Fairmont State Coll., 1942; M.A. in Psychology, Chapman Coll., 1963; m. Wayne S. Martin, Nov. 25, 1937; children—Carolyn Noel (Mrs. Maynard William Gurnsey, Jr.), Marilyn Curtis. Tchr. pub. schs., McDowell County, W.Va., 1935-39; exec. dir. Girl Scouts U.S.A., Fairmont, W.Va., 1954-59, Retarded Children's Council, Fairmont, 1960-61; psychol. and ednl. cons., Anaheim, Calif., 1962-63. Mem. Gov.'s Adv. Council on Children and Youth, 1975. First v.p. Fairmont Woman's Club, 1953-55; dist. dir. W.Va. Garden Club, 1959-61; pres. Fairmont Music Club, 1952-55, Marion County (W.Va.) Garden Council, 1954-56, Marion County council Girl Scouts U.S.A., 1952-54; mem. Nev. Tax Commn., 1972—. Named Woman of Year Beta Sigma Phi, 1955; recipient nat. certificate of recognition Assn. for Spl. Class Tchrs. of Handicapped, 1968, Distinguished Service award Washoe County Tchrs. Assn., 1971. Mem. NEA, Nat., Nev. assns. retarded children, Phi Delta Kappa. Republican. Presbyterian. Author: Current Trends in Elementary School Guidance Programs, 1963; Guidance Handbook for Teachers, 1964. Home: 1019 LaRue Ave Reno NV 89509 Office: Marvin Picollo Sch for Retarded Children Reno NV 89511

MARTIN, GRACE ANN, retail exec.; b. Shanghai, China, Jan. 9, 1939; came to U.S., 1961, naturalized, 1974; d. Chun-Lien and Yun-Chen (Wen) Sun; B.A. in Bus. Adminstrn., St. Mary-of-the-Woods (Ind.) Coll., 1965; M.S. in Bus. Edn., Ind. State U., 1966; m. Dean Martin, Sept. 29, 1973; 1 dau., Ellen Kirsten. Joined Sisters of Providence, St. Mary-of-the-Woods, 1961-70; instr. bus., chmn. dept., registrar Providence Coll., Taichung, Taiwan, 1966-69; tchr. bus., chmn. dept. Marywood High Sch., Evanston, Ill., 1969-70; from dir. edn. to mgr. personnel adminstrn. Borg Warner Acceptance Corp., Chgo., 1970-76; owner Chicago Ltd. Clothier, 1975-81; owner Chgo. Ltd. for Her, 1982—. Mem. Nat. Assn. Female Execs. Roman Catholic. Home: 440 Aldine Apt 2E Chicago IL 60657 Office: 2828 N Clark St Chicago IL 60657

MARTIN, GRACE BURKETT, psychologist; b. Sumter, S.C., Aug. 27, 1939; d. John Hazel and Grace Thomasine (Briggs) Burkett; B.A. magna cum laude, Armstrong State Coll., 1976; M.S., Fla. State U., 1979, Ph.D., 1980; m. H. Russell Martin, Jr., Oct. 9, 1957; children—H. Russell, Carolyne, Melinda. Hist. preservationist, 1962—; dir. Christian edn. St. Thomas Parish, Savannah, Ga., 1970-74; asst. prof. psychology Armstrong State Coll., Savannah, 1980—; organizational cons.; lectr.; radio and TV appearances. Bd. dirs. Coastal Empire YMCA, 1972-75; mem. Savannah Symphony Soc.; mem. commn. on mission Episcopal Diocese of Ga., 1972-74, mem. liturg. commn., 1972-74, also lic. lay reader; pres. Operation Return, 1972-76. Named Mrs. Ga., 1962. Mem. Am. Psychol. Assn., Southeastern Psychol. Assn., Ga. Ednl. Research Assn. Cons. editor Jour. Supplementary Abstract Service, 1980, 81. Home: 111 Herb River Dr Savannah GA 31406 Office: Armstrong State Coll Savannah GA 31406

MARTIN, GWENDOLYN ROSE, union ofcl.; b. Cleve., Dec. 12, 1926; d. Monroe and Rosa M. (Johnson) Fuller; student Ohio State U., Western Res. U.; m. Aaron Martin, Apr. 3, 1953; 1 son, Jeffrey. Service rep. comml. dept. Ohio Bell Telephone Co., 1967-72; mem. Communications Workers Am.-AFL-CIO, 1967—, dir. Ill. div., 1975-76, adminstrv. asst. to v.p., Elk Grove Village, Ill., 1976—; v.p. Ill. AFL-CIO, 1978—; mem. Coalition Labor Union Women; del. Chgo. Fedn. Labor. Vice pres. Ill. Democratic Women's Caucus, Leadership Council Met. Open Communities; bd. dirs. Ill. ERA; mem. labor com. Chgo. Crusade of Mercy; chmn. new applicants, mem. membership standards com. United Way Met. Chgo.; mem. labor com. Ill. Commn. Status Women; mem. Ill. Statewide Health Coordinating Council, 1977-78; del. Dem. Nat. Conv., 1976, 80; mem. Dem. Nat. Platform Com., 1976, 80; Presdl. elector Dem. Party Ill., 1976; mem. Dem. Commn. on Presdl. Nominations, 1981-82. Recipient Harriet Tubman award Coalition Black Trade Unionists, 1975, Sojourner Truth award Mich. Women Trial Lawyers Assn., 1974, Florence Criley award Coalition Labor Union Women, 1980. Office: 790 Busse Rd Elk Grove Village IL 60007

MARTIN, HELEN ELIZABETH, educator; b. West Chester, Pa., Feb. 19, 1945; d. Thomas Edwin and Elizabeth Temple (Walker) M.; B.A., King's Coll., Briarcliff Manor, N.Y., 1967; M.Ed., West Chester State Coll., 1970. Tchr. math. and sci. Unionville (Pa.) High Sch., 1967—. Mem. Republican State Com. Mem. AAAS, Am. Sci. Affiliation (chpt. treas.), Nat. Sci. Tchrs. Assn., Nat. Council Tchrs. Math., So. Chester County Rep. Women's Council (dir.), Red Clay Valley Assn., Brandywine Valley Assn. Clubs: Delaware Camera, Women's Rep. of Chester County. Home: Box 231 RD 2 West Grove PA 19390 Office: Unionville High Sch Unionville PA 19375

MARTIN, JOANNE, utility co. exec.; b. Akron, Ohio, Feb. 2, 1941; d. John and Ann M. (Capp) Martin; A.Secretarial Sci., U. Akron, 1968. Stenographer, Gen. Tire & Rubber Co., Akron, 1958-61; with Ohio Edison Co., Akron, 1961—, sec. to corp. sec., 1968-72, asst. corp. sec., 1972—. Active Goals for Greater Akron Area, 1979. Cert. profl. sec., 1972. Mem. LWV of Akron, Women's Network Akron, U. Akron Alumni Assn. Clubs: Bus. and Profl. Women's. Buchtelles. Home: 520 Meredith Ln Apt 305 Cuyahoga Falls OH 44223 Office: 76 S Main St Akron OH 44308

MARTIN, JULIA MAE, biochemist, educator; b. Snow Hill, Md., Nov. 9, 1924; d. Frank and Helen Christine (McKissick) Martin; B.S. (Carver Research Found. fellow), Tuskegee Inst., 1946, M.S. (Carver Research Found. fellow), 1948; Ph.D., Pa. State U., 1963. Asst. prof. chemistry Fla. A. and M. U., Tallahassee, 1949-63; asso. prof. chemistry Tuskegee (Ala.) Inst., 1963-66; prof. chemistry So. U., Baton Rouge, La., 1966—, acting dean grad. sch., 1974-76, dean Coll. Scis., 1978—; mem. council La. Univs. Marine Consortium for Research and Edn., 1979—. Union Carbide Research fellow, 1968, Hoffmann La Roche fellow, 1969. Mem. Am. Chem. Soc., Am. Inst. Chemists, AAAS, AAUP, Gamma Sigma Delta, Alpha Kappa Mu, Beta Kappa Chi, Iota Sigma Pi, Sigma Delta Epsilon. Home: 1564 78th Ave Baton Rouge LA 70807 Office: Box 9608 Southern U Baton Rouge LA 70813

MARTIN, JUNE JOHNSON CALDWELL, journalist; b. Toledo, Oct. 6; d. John Franklin and Eunice Imogene (Fish) Johnson; A.A., Phoenix Jr. Coll., 1939-41; B.A., U. Ariz., 1941-43, 53-59; student Ariz. State U., 1939, 40; m. Erskine Caldwell, Dec. 21, 1942 (div. Dec. 1955); 1 son, Jay Erskine; m. 2d, Keith Martin, May 5, 1966. Free-lance writer, 1944—; columnist Ariz. Daily Star, 1956-59; editor Ariz. Alumnus mag., Tucson, 1959-70; fashion editor, book editor, gen. feature writer Ariz. Daily Star, Tucson, 1970—; panelist, co-producer TV news show Tucson Press Club, 1954-55, pres., 1958. Mem. Tucson CD Com., 1961; vol. campaigns of Samuel Goddard, U.S. Rep. Morris Udall, U.S. ambassador and Ariz. gov. Raul Castro. Recipient award Nat. Headliners Club, 1959, Ariz. Press Club award, 1957-59, Am. Alumni Council, 1966, 70. Mem. Jr. League of Tucson, Tucson Urban League, Pi Beta Phi. Democrat. Methodist. Club: Tucson Press. Contbg. author: Rocky Mountain Cities, 1949; contbr. articles and stories to mags. Home: PO Box 2631 Tucson AZ 85702 Office: PO Box 26807 Tucson AZ 85726

MARTIN, KATHLEEN ANNE, librarian; b. Rochester, N.Y., Aug. 19, 1942; d. Edwin Wilkins and Hilda Ellen (Hartell) Martin; B.A., Marygrove Coll., Detroit, 1964; M.A. in L.S. (Josenhans scholar 1965), U. Mich., 1965; advanced online tng. cert. Nat. Library Medicine, 1979; m. Oliver Kalman Peterdy, Oct. 15, 1971 (div. 1981); children—Elizabeth, Matthew. Librarian, Detroit Public Library, 1964-66; bibliographer, then asst. tech. services librarian Edward G. Miner Med. Library, U. Rochester, 1969-72; librarian lab. indsl. medicine Eastman Kodak Co., Rochester, 1966-69, librarian health, safety and human factors lab., 1972-78, tech. info. analyst, 1978—. Mem. AAUW (treas. Rochester br. 1979-80), Spl. Libraries Assn., Med. Library Assn., Am. Chem. Soc. Home: 4 Belmont Rd Rochester NY 14612 Office: Eastman Kodak Co Kodak Park Div Bldg 320 Rochester NY 14650

MARTIN, KATHRYN WORLEY, educator; b. Nashville; d. Winfield Hansford and Alice (Meacham) M.; B.A., Vanderbilt U., M.A., 1943; student U. Madrid, 1956-59. Tchr., Litton High Sch., Nashville, 1943-46; instr. Coll. of Wooster, 1946-49; asst. prof. Maryville (Tenn.) Coll., 1950-56, 59—. Mem. Am. Assn. Tchrs. Spanish and Portuguese, MLA, AAUW (v.p. Maryville br. 1952-56, pres. Maryville br. 1971-73, 79-81, sec. Tenn. div. 1955-57, 2d v.p. 1973-74), AAUP (sec.-treas. chpt. 1973—), S. Atlantic MLA, Maryville Coll. Faculty Club (sec. treas. 1976—), Sigma Delta Pi (chpt. adviser), Phi Sigma Iota. Methodist. Home: 129 Stanley Ave Maryville TN 37801

MARTIN, LAURA PAEZ REED, clin. psychologist; b. Los Angeles, May 18, 1935; d. Howard Richard and Laura (Paez) Reed; B.A., UCLA, 1958; M.A. (NIMH fellow), U. So. Calif., 1974, Ph.D., 1974; m. Warren Leicester Martin, Aug. 24, 1957; children—Laura, Susan, Warren. Instr. psychology Los Angeles Community Coll. Dist., 1975-77; pres. Laura Martin, Ph.D., Inc., 1977—; psychotherapist Psychiat. Assocs. Med. Group, Covina, Calif., 1976—; chief psychologist (adolescence) Sierra Royale Hosp., Azusa, Calif., 1976—; hosp. cons. nursing edn.; lectr.; chmn. Hosp. Evaluation Research Project, 1981—. Mem. Flintridge Guild Children's Hosp.; sponsor Los Angeles County Art Mus. Mem. Am. Psychol. Assn., Calif. Psychol. Assn., Assn. Mex.-Am. Psychologists, Assn. Women in Sci. Republican. Roman Catholic. Club: U. So. Calif. Golden Circle, Flintridge Riding. Home: 4172 Forest Hill Dr La Cañada CA 91011 Office: Psychiat Assos Med Group 750 Terrado Plaza Suite 245 Covina CA 91723

MARTIN, LINDA REID, govt. ofcl.; b. Hollywood, Calif., July 1, 1940; d. Frederick Sherman and Kathryn Elizabeth (Jaynes) Reid; B.A., U. Calif., Berkeley, 1963; m. John S. C. Shields (dec. 1971); 1 dau., Kelley Rene; m. 2d, Howard T. Martin, Sept. 11, 1976. Tax auditor IRS, San Francisco, 1963-70, group mgr., 1970-73, mgmt. analyst, staff asst.,

1973-74, br. chief audit div., 1974-77, chief problem resolution staff, Washington, 1977—; legis. fellow, 1981. Recipient Superior Performance and spl. act awards IRS. Republican. Episcopalian. Home: 408 Watts Branch Pky Rockville MD 20854 Office: 1111 Constitution Ave NW Washington DC 20224

MARTIN, LUCY Z., public relations exec.; b. Alton, Ill., July 8, 1941; d. Fred M. and Lucille J. (Kirk) Zimmerman; B.A., Northwestern U., 1963; m. Gary J. Rood, Sept. 20, 1981; stepchildren—Debi, Randy, Tami. Adminstrv. asst., copywriter Batz-Hodgson-Neuwoehner, Inc., advt., St. Louis, 1963-64; news reporter, Midwest fashion editor Footwear News, St. Louis bur. Fairchild Publs., 1965-67; account exec. Millici Advt., Honolulu, 1967-68; editor, mem. communications staff Barnes Hosp., St. Louis, 1969-72; communications cons. Fleishman-Hillard Public Relations, St. Louis, 1972-74; owner Lucy Z. Martin & Assos., Portland, Oreg., 1974—; cons. mem. women's com. Reed Coll., Portland, 1967-79, chmn., 1977-79. Recipient Outstanding Profl. Achievement award Women in Communications, Inc., 1977; Rosey award Portland Advt. Fedn., 1980; Headliner award Daily Jour. Commerce, 1980; 2 nat. awards Soc. for Tech. Communicators, 1981, 3 awards Internat. Assn. Tech. Writers, 1981, Offbeat award Women in Communications, Inc., 1981; numerous writing, editing and design awards Internat. Assn. Bus. Communicators (6 awards Oreg./Cascade chpt. 1981, 5 awards 1982), Assn. Western Hosps., St. Louis Soc. Communicating Arts, Acad. Hosp. Public Relations, Club Corp. Am., Inc. Mem. Public Relations Soc. Am. (chpt. pres.-elect 1982 chpt. pres. 1983; accredited), Public Relations Roundtable (2d v.p. 1982), Am. Soc. Hosp. Public Relations, Oreg. Hosp. Public Relations Orgn. (pres. 1979). Address: 1881 SW Edgewood Rd Portland OR 97201

MARTIN, MARY, actress, singer; b. Weatherford, Tex., Dec. 1, 1913; d. Preston and Junita (Pressly) M.; ed. Ward-Belmont Sch., Nashville; m. Benjamin Hagman; 1 son, Larry; m. 2d, Richard Halliday, May 5, 1940 (dec. 1973); 1 dau., Mary Heller. Singer in mus. comedy Leave It to Me, N.Y.C., 1938; with Paramount Pictures, Inc., Hollywood, Calif., 1939-43; films include: The Great Victor Herbert, Rhythm On the River, Kiss the Boys Goodbye, Love Thy Neighbors, Birth of the Blues, Star Spangled Rhythm, Happy Go Lucky, True to Life; One Touch of Venus (stage), Night and Day (motion picture); Lute Song (stage); starred in Eng., 1946-47, Noel Coward's musical, Pacific 1860, 1947-48; star in tour of U.S. in musical Annie Get Your Gun, 1948, South Pacific (stage), N.Y. and London, 1949-52, Kind Sir, 1953-54, Peter Pan, 1954-55, The Skin of our Teeth (play), 1955, The Sound of Music, 1959-61, Jennie, 1963; on tour U.S., Japan, Vietnam, London, Hello Dolly, 1965; I Do, I Do, N.Y. stage and on tour, 1968-70; A Celebration of Richard Rogers, 1972; stage Do You Turn Somersaults, 1977; appeared in TV film Valentine, 1979; co-host Over Easy, PBS, 1981—. Recipient numerous awards including Tony, 1948, 55, 60, Emmy, 1955; winner N.Y. Drama Critics Poll, 1944, 49, 60. Episcopalian. Author: Needlepoint, 1969; (autobiography) My Heart Belongs, 1976. Address: care Mgr 9243 1/2 Doheny Rd Los Angeles CA 90069 *

MARTIN, MARY AGNES, state legislator; b. Balt.; d. John and Helen Marie Kukon; m. Howard W. Martin, Aug. 23, 1948 (dec.); children—John Thomas, Howard Wright, Kathleen Helen Martin Pollard. Rep., Groton (Conn.) Town Meeting, 1965-69; mem. Groton Bd. Selectmen, 1969-71, Conn. Ho. of Reps. from 65th Dist., 1971-73, Groton Town Council, 1973-74, Conn. Senate from 18th Dist., 1975—. Mem., past vice chmn. Groton Democratic Town Com.; active local Big Bros.-Big Sisters. Mem. Conn. Fedn. Dem. Women's Clubs. Roman Catholic. Home: 34 Pegasus Dr Groton CT 06340 Office: State Capitol Hartford CT 06115

MARTIN, MARY ANNE CHRISTMAS, dir., educator; b. Logtown, Miss., Oct. 28, 1941; d. Horace Lee and Ethel Fannie (Willis) Christmas; B.S., Alcorn A & M U., 1963; M.A., Azusa Pacific U., 1977; m. Samuel S. Martin, III, Aug. 1, 1964; 1 son, Kenneth Wayne. Typist Los Angeles Unified Sch. Dist., 1963; sec. Carver Community Center, Los Angeles 1964-65, Los Angeles Urban League, 1965-66; tchr. Fedn. Nursery Sch. Tchrs. Headstart, Los Angeles, 1966-68, Compton (Calif.) Unified Sch. Dist., 1968—; dir. EKO Multi Purpose Center, 1979—. Recipient Oratorical scholarship, 1959. Mem. NEA, Calif. Tchrs. Assn., Council Exceptional Children, Calif. Assn. Pvt. Spl. Edn. Sch., Delta Sigma Theta. Roman Catholic. Home: 1655 Cyrene Dr Carson CA 90746 Office: 403 S Santa Fe Compton CA 90224

MARTIN, MARY MARGARET KINKADE, civic worker; b. Columbus, Ohio, Sept. 11, 1908; d. John S. and Lillie D. (Crooks) Kinkade; student Ohio State U., 1925-27; m. William Andrew Martin, June 29, 1929; children—James Andrew, John William. Mem. staff Family Counseling and Crittenden Services, Columbus, 1971—; past pres. Indianola Jr. Child Conservation League, Ohio Child Conservation League, Salvation Army Women's Aux. of Columbus and Delaware Counties (Ohio), Salvation Army Unit 31; past chmn., past treas. Women's State Com. for Health, Edn. and Welfare, Ohio; past treas., pres. trustees, past pres. assisting bd. Florence Crittenden Services; past crew pres. cancer research edn. workers Am. Cancer Soc. Franklin County. Recipient Outstanding Service award Family Counseling and Crittenden Services, 1978, Outstanding Service award Columbus Civitan Club, 1965. Mem. Women in Communication, Ohio Hist. Soc., Gallia County Hist. Soc. Ohio, Alpha Sigma Alpha (past chpt. pres.). Methodist. Home: 338 E Dunedin Rd Columbus OH 43214

MARTIN, MELLIE CHANCEY, nurse; b. Bee Ridge, Fla., Oct. 9, 1924; d. Edmond Sylvester and Margaret Ann (Johns) Chancey; R.N., Fla. State Hosp. Sch. Nursing, 1946; A.A., Lake City (Fla.) Community Coll., 1970; m. William Thomas Martin, July 21, 1945 (dec. Jan. 1981); children—David George, Joseph Wesley. Nurse, Sunnyside Convalescent Home, Orlando, Fla., 1946, Orange Meml. Hosp., 1949-51, West Orange Meml. Hosp., 1953-59, Clermont (Fla.) Hosp., 1959, VA Hosp., Ft. Bayard, N.Mex., 1959-63, Lake City Hosp., 1963—; charter mem. Fla. Nurses Polit. Action Com. Bd. dirs. Community Concert Assn. Mem. Am. Nurses Assn., Fla. Nurses Assn., Dist. 16 Nurses Assn. Democrat. Mem. Ch. of Christ. Home: 812 Hickory Ln Lake City FL 32055

MARTIN, MYRA MAE, med. technologist; b. Sunnyside, Wash., Mar. 26, 1952; d. Richard Dallas Myers and Barbara (Lehman) Myers McDaniel; B.S. in Bacteriology and Pub. Health, Wash. State U., Pullman, 1974; cert. med. tech. St. Luke's Meml. Hosp., 1975; m. Timothy Lyle Martin, Sept. 1, 1973. Lab. aide, sec. U.S. Testing Co., Inc., Richland, Wash., 1973; med. technologist Sacred Heart Med. Center, Spokane, Wash., 1975-77; emergency med. technician Spokane's Mercy Ambulance, 1982—; med. technologist Deaconess Hosp., Spokane, 1977—; profl. model Char's Modeling Agy., Spokane, 1981—. Pres. 4-H, 1963; accompanist Men's Glee Club, 1970, mem. piano ensemble, 1970-71; vol. fireman Sta. 6, Dist. 9, Spokane County, 1982—; co-chairwoman YWCA expanded cabinet, 1971; parish shepherd Zion Lutheran Ch., Spokane, 1975; tchr. women's Bible Studies Foothills Community Ch., also choir mem. Mem. Am. Soc. for Med. Tech., Am. Soc. Clin. Pathology (affiliate mem., cert. med. technologist), Nat. Certification Agy. (cert. lab. scientist). Republican. Clubs: Christian Women's, Rainbow Girls. Home: Route 2 Box 186 Spokane WA 99207 Office: Char's Modeling Agy S 1414 Bernard Spokane WA 99204 also Deaconess Hosp W 800 Fifth Spokane WA 99204

MARTIN, PEGGY MUSTON, oil co. exec.; b. Palestine, Tex., Jan. 15, 1936; d. Aubra V. and Ora Mae (Lamberth) Muston; student Kilgore Jr. Coll., 1960, 76; tech. courses in petroleum tech., delay rentals and lease adminstrn.; m. Jan. 28, 1954 (dec.); children—Ronald, Lana K. Hutchison, Carey Alan, Tim Martin. With L.E. Myers Co., 1954-55, C&I Life Ins. Co., 1960-61, Alford Ins. Co., 1962-63; with Art Machin & Assos., Longview, Tex., 1963—, corp. sec., 1964—, treas., 1980—. Mem. Assn. Bus. Women Am. (Woman of Yr. 1980, pres. 1980-81), Desk and Derrick Club. Mem. Ch. of Christ. Club: Oak Forest Country. Home: 1600 Fowler St Longview TX 75603 Office: 1800 Judson Rd Longview TX 75601

MARTIN, ROSEMARY SCARBROUGH, librarian; b. Cumberland, Miss., Feb. 12, 1935; d. James Eurel and Jessie Estelle (Hood) Scarbrough; B.S., Miss. Women's U., 1961; M.S.L.S., U. Wis., Madison, 1973; m. Gary Frank Martin, Nov. 25, 1962; 1 dau., Caitlin. Mem. staff Memphis Public Library, 1961, 70-76, coordinator children's services, 1974-76; staff Shelby County (Tenn.) Public Library, 1965-67, Austin (Tex.) Public Library, 1967-68, Memphis Acad. Arts, 1968-70; zone mgr. Dallas Public Library, 1977-78; dir. Central Ark. Library System, Little Rock, 1978—; vis. lectr. Memphis State U., U. Ark., Little Rock. Mem. Ark. Gov.'s Com. Employment Handicapped, 1980, Downtown Transit Terminal Complex Steering/Adv. Com., 1980—. Staff Assn. scholarship Memphis Public Library, 1971, Trustees scholarship, 1972; teaching fellow U. Wis., 1972-78. Mem. ALA, Southwestern Library Assn., Ark. Library Assn. (chmn. polit. action com. 1983), Central High Sch. Neighborhood Assn., Beta Phi Mu. Democrat. Office: 700 Louisiana St Little Rock AR 72201

MARTIN, SALLY ANN, social worker; b. Montpelier, Wis., July 8, 1948; d. Harvey J. and Marcella Mary (Dart) Robertson; B.S., Cardinal Stritch Coll., 1970; M.S.W., U. Wis., 1973. Childcare worker Cedarcrest Girls Residence, Milw., 1970-72; psychiat. social worker Goodwill Industries, Milw., 1974-75, dir. counseling and social services, 1975-78, dir. med. related services, 1978-79, dir. personnel, 1980-82, dir. adminstrn., 1982—; pres. Datin-Mar Corp., 1982—; group dynamics instr. Drunk Driving Sch., Milw. Area Tech. Coll., 1973—; instr. mgmt. Cardinal Stritch Coll., Milw., 1982—; cons. in field. Mem. Acad. Cert. Social Workers, Nat. Assn. Social Workers, Wis. Assn. Alcoholism and Other Drug Abuse, Nat. Council on Alcoholism, NOW. Roman Catholic. Author: Juvenile Delinquency: Is the Family a Factor, 1970; Soft Whispers, 1974; Tender Moments, 1976; Warm Feelings, 1978; Just Memories, 1981; producer record album: Dew Drops and Dandelion Dust, 1969. Home: 6657 N Bourbon St Milwaukee WI 53224 Office: 6055 N 91st St Milwaukee WI 53225

MARTIN, SANDRA JEAN, speech pathologist; b. Phoenix, July 18, 1947; d. Claudie Lloyd and Beatrice (Greenrock) Martin; B.A., U. Ark., 1969, M.A., 1970. Speech therapist Jefferson County Easter Seal Soc., Lakewood, Colo., 1970-71, Samuel Gompers Rehab. Center, Inc., Phoenix, 1971-72; audiometrist Ariz. Dept. Health, Maternal and Child Health, Phoenix, 1973; instr./clinic supr. No. Ariz. U., Flagstaff, 1973-76; pvt. practice speech pathology, Farmington, N.Mex., 1976-79; speech pathologist Coop. Ednl. Services, Albuquerque, 1980—; asso. Dean Inst., 1980. Vice pres. Assn. for Retarded Citizens and Services for Physically Handicapped, 1977-79; co-founder Family Crisis Center, Inc., Farmington, 1979. HEW Bur. Handicapped Children fellow, 1969-70; named Faculty Woman of the Yr., No. Ariz. U. Assn. Women Students, 1974. Mem. Assn. for Autistic Children, Nat. Assn. Female Execs. Club: Pilot. Home: 818 Lamp Post Circle SE Albuquerque NM 87123 Office: 208 Carlisle NE Albuquerque NM 87110

MARTIN, SHIRLEY DORSEY, univ. adminstr.; b. St. Louis, Apr. 27, 1929; d. George Henry and Ellen Ada (Hall) Dorsey; B.Gen. Studies with high distinction, Wayne State U., 1981; m. Gordon Richard Martin, July 21, 1946; children—Shawn Renault, Michael Richard, Gail Ellen. Adminstrv. supr. Office of Dir., U. Mich. Hosps., 1958-64, supr. accounts payable dept., 1966-68; adminstr. for student affairs U. Mich. Med. Sch., 1968—. Corr. sec. Ann Arbor (Mich.) chpt. Jack & Jill Am., Inc., 1977-80, chairwoman fund-raiser Dr., 1979-80, treas., 1981-82; fin. sec., chairwoman arts com. Ann Arbor chpt. Links, Inc., 1981-82. Mem. Am. Assn. Collegiate Registrars and Admission Officers, Mich. Assn. Collegiate Registrars and Admission Officers, Nat. Assn. Acad. Affairs Adminstrs., Am. Assn. Med. Colls. (inter-assn. rep.), Nat. Assn. Coll. Deans, Registrars and Admissions Officers, Nat. Council Negro Women, Delta Sigma Theta, Golden Key. Lutheran. Office: 1301 Catherine Rd Arbor MI 48109

MARTIN, SHIRLEY WHITCHURCH, home economist; b. Centralia, Ill., Sept. 29, 1936; d. Harry Robert and Lula Ann (King) Whitchurch; A.A., Centralia Jr. Coll., 1956; B.S., So. Ill. U., 1958, M.S., 1969; m. Bob J. Martin, Oct. 29, 1977. Home adv. Randolph County Extension Service, Sparta, Ill., 1958-63; home adv. Franklin County Extension Service, Benton, Ill., 1963-65, area resource devel. adv., 1965-74; program specialist in home econs. U. Ill. State Staff, Benton, 1974—. Chmn., Sparta Beautification, 1962-68; tchr., music dir. Zion Hill Baptist Ch., 1954-76. Recipient Job Corps award, 1968, Rural Service award OEO, 1969; honored by Shirley Whitchurch Day, Sta. WHCO, Sparta, 1963. Nat. Assn. Extension Home Economists (conv. chmn. 1969), Am. Home Econs. Assn., Ill. Home Econs. Assn., Adult Edn. Assn., Epsilon Sigma Phi (sec.-treas., Disting. Service award 1972, Leadership award 1979), Gamma Sigma Delta. Home: 1605 E Main St Benton IL 62812 Office: 901 W Washington St Benton IL 62812

MARTIN, SUSAN, nurse; b. Dublin, Tex., Jan. 12, 1953; d. Howitt Gaston and Delma Jean (Howard) M.; R.N., Mary Meek Sch. Nursing, 1974. Staff nurse operating room and med.-surg. unit Hendrick Med. Center, Abilene, Tex., 1974-75, charge nurse, 1979; supr. ICU Deleon (Tex.) Hosp., 1975-79, supr. DeLeon Hosp., 1979-80, dir. nurses, 1980-81; nursing supr. W. Central Tex. Home Health Agy., Stephenville, 1981-82; ICU/CU unit mgr. DeLeon (Tex.) Hosp., 1982—. Mem. Am. Heart Assn., Erath County Hospice Assn., VFW Ladies Aux. Baptist. Home: 201 East Rd Stephenville TX 76401 Office: 407 S Texas St DeLeon TX 76444

MARTIN, SUSAN KATHERINE OROWAN, librarian; b. Cambridge, Eng., Nov. 14, 1942; d. Egon and Jolan (Schonfeld) Orowan; came to U.S., 1950, naturalized, 1961; A.B. cum laude, Tufts U., 1963; M.S., Simmons Coll., 1965; Ph.D., U. Calif., Berkeley, 1982; m. David S. Martin, June 30, 1962. Systems librarian Harvard U. Library, Cambridge, Mass., 1965-73, head Library Systems Office, Gen. Library, U. Calif. at Berkeley, 1973-79; dir. Johns Hopkins U. Library, Balt., 1979—; cons. Inforonics Inc., 1972, Info. Design Inc., 1972-73, Knowledge Industries, Inc., 1975, Informatics, Inc., 1977, Info. Access Corp., 1978, Calif. Library Services Bd., Faxon, Inc., 1979, Earlham Coll., 1981, Ziff-Davis Corp., 1982. Trustee Phila. Area Library Network; mem. bd. Universal Serials and Book Exchange, 1981-82. Council on Library Resources fellow, 1972-73. Recipient Disting. Alumni award Simmons Coll., 1977. Mem. ALA (instr. library and info. tech. assn. 1969-71, dir. div. 1972-75, pres. 1978-79), Am. Soc. Info. Sci. (chmn. tech. program ann. meeting 1976), Phi Beta Kappa. Author: Library Networks, 1976-77; Library Networks, 1978-79, 81-82; editor: Jour. Library Automation, 1973-77; co-editor: Library Automation—The State of the Art, 1975. Contbr. articles to profl. jours. Home: 3518 Garrett Ct Ellicott City MD 21043 Office: Johns Hopkins U Library Baltimore MD 21218

MARTIN, SUZANNE, nutritionist, educator; b. Grant Island, Nebr., Mar. 12, 1946; d. Frank Edward and Melva (Frable) Gallup; B.S., Va. Commonwealth U., 1969; M.S., U. Iowa, 1975, postgrad., 1975—; m. Stephen Russell Martin, Aug. 12, 1967; children—Stephen, Andre, Nicholas. With public relations dept. internat. foods dept. Safeway Stores, Inc., Richmond, Va., 1970-72; grad. teaching asst. nutrition U. Iowa, 1972-74; asst. prof. nutrition Sch. of Ozarks, Point Lookout, Mo., 1975—; cons. dietitian to nursing homes, Branson, Mo., 1977—. Mem. Am. Dietetic Assn. (registered), Am. Home Econs. Assn., Soc. Nutrition Edn., S.W. Mo. Dietetic Assn., P.E.O., Phi Lambda Theta, Omicron Nu. Republican. Presbyterian. Research on liquid protein diet with rats. Home: Star Route 1 Hollister MO 65672 Office: Sch of Ozarks Point Lookout MO 65726

MARTIN, VIOLA DORCINA, artist; b. Burtonsville, Alta., Can., Dec. 22, 1910; d. Cornelius and Marie Louise (Facette) Burton; student Alta. Coll., 1930-31; m. Raymond Murch Martin, July 29, 1935; children—Marlo Raymond, Marlene Helen. Exhibited oil paintings, watercolors, landscape sketches in shows in Spokane, Wash., Kellogg, Idaho, Regina, Sask., Can., Chgo., Sacramento, Lodi and Stockton, Calif., St. Petersburg, Clearwater, Dunedin, Ozona, Largo, Orlando, Fla.; pub. The Gaspe, sketches of Que., Can., 1972; tchr. oil painting to sr. citizens, Victoria, B.C., Can., and Clearwater, Fla.; organizer small dance bands, Sacramento, Dunedin, Fla., Victoria, B.C., Can., performer on banjo, mandolin, violin, harmonica, dulcimer; script writer, dir., producer, performer variety shows, Fla. and Calif. Active Sacramento City Coll. Faculty Wives, 1947-65, pres. 1956-57; program organizer Aerojet Art Soc., Sacramento, 1964; donor hist. paintings to Hist. Soc., Ft. Mac Murray, Alta., 1979, Multicultural Heritage Centre, Stony Plain, Alta., 1982. Mem. Fla. Watercolor Soc., Fla. Miniature Art Soc., Dunedin Art Guild (program organizer 1964-65). Democrat. Roman Catholic. Donor collection of paintings and hist. documents to Provincial Archives Alta., 1978. Home: 215 Windsor Mill Rd Hudson FL 33568

MARTIN, VIRGINIA LEE, med. technologist; b. St. Joseph, Mo., Sept. 16, 1926; d. Everett C. and Bertha Anna (Vey) Howard; A.A., St. Joseph Jr. Coll., 1946; A.B., Baker U., 1948. Med. technologist Sims & Holder, M.D.s, Kansas City, Kans., 1949-50, H. C. Senne, M.D., St. Joseph, Mo., 1950-57; med. technologist in charge spl. chemistry VA Hosp., Kansas City, Mo., 1957-68; lead med. technologist So. Nev. Meml. Hosp., Las Vegas, 1969—. Mem. Am. Soc. Clin. Pathologists (registered affiliate), Am. Bus. Womens Assn. Club: Order Eastern Star. Home: 4613 Baxter Pl Las Vegas NV 89107 Office: So Nev Meml Hosp 1700 W Charleston St Las Vegas NV 89102

MARTIN, WANDA, banker; b. Lake Charles, La., Oct. 10, 1931; d. Fred E. and Lula Belle (Dickens) Jackson; grad. Mathieu Bus. Coll., 1948-49, U. So. La., 1981; m. John Richard Martin, Jan. 18, 1951; d. John Michael, Kathy Ann, Keith Alan. Bookeeper, Calcasieu Marine Nat. Bank, Lake Charles, 1949-51; asst. cashier, tng. dir., proof and transit supr. Lakeside Nat. Bank, Lake Charles, 1981—. Mem. Nat. Assn. Bank Women, Am. Bus. Women Assn. Mem. Pentecostal Ch. Home: 145 W Lee St Sulphur LA 70663 Office: One Lakeside Plaza Lake Charles LA 70601

MARTIN, YOLANDA CRISTINA, writer; b. Havana, Cuba, Sept. 6, 1955; d. Colfax T. and Marta (Luque) M.; B.S., Syracuse U., 1976; M.A., Georgetown U., 1981. Cameraperson, studio technician Public Broadcasting System affiliate Sta. WGBY-TV, Springfield, Mass., 1974, ABC affiliate Sta. WHYN-TV, Springfield, Mass., 1974-76; newswriter asst. Wall Street Jour. and Barron's Fin. Weekly, Dow-Jones & Co., Chicopee, Mass., 1976-78; contbg. columnist The Georgetowner newsmag., Washington, 1980-81; researcher Woodrow Wilson Internat. Center for Scholars, Smithsonian Instn., Washington, 1980-81; editor, Georgetown Grad. Rev., 1980-81; scriptwriter Life and Writings of Mary Wollstonecraft, docudramas, 1981—; cons. Sydney Edelberg Public Relations Assos. Inc., Springfield, Mass., 1978-79; account exec. Doremus and Co., Inc., Washington, 1982—; audio-visual prodn. specialist Dept. Def., Washington, 1982—. Press sec. Rep. Richard Roche Campaign for State Senate Mass., 1979. Recipient Syracuse U. Scholarship award, 1975; Cintas Found. grantee 1981-82. Mem. Women in Communications, Am. Film Inst., Scriptwriters Assn. Internat. Inc., Alpha Epsilon Rho. Roman Catholic Address: 25 Valentine St Springfield MA 01108 also 2300 S 24th Rd Suite 935 Arlington VA 22206

MARTIN, YVONNE CONNOLLY, chemist; b. St. Paul, Sept. 13, 1936; d. Elvert Farrell and Irene Mildred (Aitken) Connolly; B.A., Carleton Coll., Northfield, Minn., 1958; Ph.D., Northwestern U., 1964; m. William Brady Martin, Dec. 14, 1963; children—Margaret Anne, Catherine Irene. With Abbott Labs., North Chicago, Ill., 1958—, assoc. research fellow, 1970-74, research fellow theoretical medicinal chemistry, 1974—. NSF predoctoral fellow, 1960-64. Mem. Am. Chem. Soc. (treas. medicinal div. 1980-81), AAAS, Phi Beta Kappa, Sigma Xi (chpt. pres. 1978-79). Author: Quantitative Drug Design, 1978; also articles, book revs. Home: 2415 N Jackson St Waukegan IL 60087 Office: Dept 466 Abbott Labs North Chicago IL 60064

MARTIN BRIGGS, PATRICIA ANN, accountant; b. Chgo., May 21, 1942; d. Timothy and June (McFadde) Coffey; B.A., Calif. State U., Northridge, 1965; m. Dennis M. Martin, Dec. 26, 1965 (div.); m. 2d, David M. Briggs, Dec. 19, 1981; 1 son, Dennis; stepchildren—John, Joseph. Computer programmer Systems Devel. Corp., Santa Monica, Calif., 1969-70; bookkeeper Mastate Acoustics, Van Nuys, Calif., 1971-74; staff acct., Sherman Oaks, Calif., 1975-76; controllor AutoLand Leasing Inc., Sherman Oaks, 1976-78; partner Briggs & Nartin, San Fernando, Calif., 1978—. C.P.A. Republican. Roman Catholic. Home: 17717 San Fernando Mission Blvd Granada Hills CA 91344 Office: 566 S Brand Blvd San Fernando CA 91340

MARTIN-BROOKS, DIANNE, univ. program adminstr.; b. Syracuse, N.Y., June 16, 1943; d. G. William and Alyce (O'Brien) Martin; B.S., Syracuse U., 1976, M.S.W., 1977; children—Timothy, Allyson. Counselor, program coordinator, mgr. family service dept. The Salvation Army, Syracuse, 1974-77; br. dir., adminstrv. asst. Huntington Family Centers, Inc., Syracuse, 1977-81; Eastern fin. asso., mng. editor The Fin. Rev., Syracuse, 1981—; program adminstr. profl. devel. Univ. Coll. Syracuse U., 1981—, mem. adj. faculty, 1978. Mem. Onondaga Citizens League, 1981—. Cert. social worker N.Y. State. Mem. Bus. and Profl. Women's Club, Assn. Continuing Higher Edn., N.Y. State Assn. Human Services, Phi Kappa Phi, Alpha Sigma Lambda. Home: 504 Bronson Rd Syracuse NY 13219 Office: University Coll Syracuse Univ Syracuse NY 13202

MARTINDELL, ANNE CLARK, ambassador; b. N.Y.C., July 18, 1914; d. William and Marjory Bruce (Blair) Clark; student Smith Coll., 1931-32, Sir George Williams Coll., Montreal, Que., Can., 1945-46; m. Jackson Martindell, Aug. 12, 1948; children—Marjory S. Luthes, George C. Scott, David C. Scott, Roger Martindell. Tchr., reading supr. Miss Mason's Sch., 1963-67; mem. N.J. Public Broadcasting Authority, 1970-73; mem. N.J. Senate, 1973-77, vice chmn., acting chmn. edn. com., chmn. joint state library com.; dir. Office Fgn. Disaster Assistance Aid, 1977-79; ambassador to N.Z., 1979—. Trustee North Country Sch., 1967-79, chmn. bd., 1969-72, trustee Mercer County Coll., 1972-76; chmn. N.J. delegation Democratic Conv., 1972, del., 1976. Office: US Embassy NZ FPO San Francisco CA 96690 *

MARTINEZ, ATILIA MARIA, pathologist; b. Tegucigalpa, Honduras, Oct. 27, 1935; d. Carlos E. and Enriqueta Martinez; A.A., John

Muir Jr. Coll., 1954; student UCLA, 1954-55; M.D., Women's Med. Coll. Pa., 1959; m. Gordon E. Stewart, June 20, 1959; children—Catherine, Susan, Carol. Resident in pathology Los Angeles County-U. So. Calif. Med. Center, 1964; practice medicine specializing in pathology, Orange County, Calif.; pathologist Costa Mesa Med. Center Hosp.; asso. clin. prof. U. Calif., Irvine. Fellow Am. Soc. Clin. Pathologists, Coll. Am. Pathologists, Am. Assn. Blood Banks, Orange County Soc. Pathologists (sec.-treas. 1969-71), Calif. Med. Assn., Orange County Med. Assn. Calif. Blood Bank System. Contbr. articles to profl. jours. Office: 275 Victoria St Suite 1A Costa Mesa CA 92627

MARTINEZ, CYNTHIA J., convalescent hosp. adminstr.; b. Alameda, Calif., Aug. 27, 1952; d. Joe Aquilar and Azucena (Ortega) M.; A.S. in Vocat. Nursing, Laney Jr. Coll., 1973. Charge nurse Homemakers-Upjohn, Oakland, Calif., 1973-74; charge nurse Lake Park Retirement Residence, Oakland, 1975-76, med. coordinator, 1976-78; asst. adminstr. Parkside Convalescent Hosp., Oakland, 1978-79; asst. adminstr. Belmont Convalescent Hosp., Belmont, Calif., 1979-81, adminstr., 1981—; staff nurse Orientation Center for the Blind, Albany, Calif., 1979—. Mem. East Bay Activity Dirs. Group. (dir.). Baptist. Office: 1041 Hill St Belmont CA 94002

MARTINEZ, DELIA E., state govt. ofcl.; b. Mexico City, Mex., Jan. 28, 1948; came to U.S., 1957, naturalized, 1968; d. Charles W. and Concepcion M. Coop; B.S. in Bus. Adminstrn., U. Nev., Reno, 1972, postgrad., 1966-72; Fiscal audit trainee Nev. State Legis. Counsel Bur., 1973; grad. research fellow U. Nev. System, Reno, 1971-73, budget and research analyst, EEO officer, 1973-77, sr. budget analyst, EEO officer, 1977-79; asst. dir. Nev. Equal Rights Commn., Reno, 1979-82, exec. dir., 1982—; bd. dirs. Hispanic Am. Cons. in Edn. and Research; cons. in field. Treas. Washoe County Democratic Party, 1980-82; mem. State Dem. Party exec. com., 1980-82, state central com., 1978-82; chmn. Washoe County Personnel Com., 1977-82; adv. bd. Centro de Informacion Latino Americano, 1977-79; bd. dirs. United Way, 1980-82, Nev. Humanities Com.; mem. Commn. on Status of Women, Reno, 1979—; nat. bd. dirs. Friends of the Library; chmn. Faculty Senate, 1974-76; mem. League United Latin Am. Citizens; mem. Fed. Jud. Merit Selection Adv. Commn.; Nev. del. to White House Conf. on Libraries, 1979, mem. gen. resolutions com.; chmn. White House Conf. on Libraries and Info. Systems Task Force, 1980-82. Mem. Am. Soc. Pub. Adminstrn. (chpt. pres. 1979-80), Nat. Assn. Coll. and Univ. Bus. Officers, Rocky Mountain Assn. for Instl. Research, Am. Bus. Women's Assn., AAUW, Coll. and Univ. Personnel Assn., U. Nev. Alumni Assn. (pres., treas. 1972-82). Roman Catholic. Clubs: University (pres. 1980), Faculty, Soroptimists of Reno (award 1982). Contbr. papers to profl. confs. and workshops. Home: 962 Count Wutzke St Las Vegas NV 89119 Office: 1515 E Tropicana Suite 590 Las Vegas NV 89158

MARTINEZ, ELENA, psychiat. social worker; b. Havana, Cuba, Jan. 4, 1947; came to U.S., 1961, naturalized, 1974; d. Jose and Manuela (Duarte) M.; B.A., Mundelein Coll., Chgo., 1969; M.S.W., U. Ill., Chgo. Circle, 1974. Team leader I, Catholic Charities Chgo., 1970-76; psychiat. social worker children's div. Katharine Wright Clinic, Chgo., 1976-79, part-time 1979—; dir., planner Evanston (Ill.) Latinam. Assn., 1979—; part-time psychiat. social worker St. Francis Hosp., Evanston, 1979; cons. in field, condr. workshops. Mem. Pres.'s Adv. Com. Women, 1980—; del. Democratic Nat. Conv., 1980. Cath. Charities Chgo. scholar, 1972. Mem. Acad. Cert. Social Workers, Nat. Assn. Social Workers (chpt. del.), Progressive Assn. Latino Americans (dir. 1976—), Nat. Coalition Cuban Americans (dir. 1978—), Mental Health Assn. Greater Chgo. (dir. edni. com. 1979—), Ill. Women's Polit. Caucus, Nat. Fedn. Dem. Women. Roman Catholic. Home: 3925 N Claremont Ave Chicago IL 60618 Office: 800 Custer St Suite 3 Evanston IL 60202

MARTINEZ, HERMINIA S., banker, economist; b. Havana, Cuba; came to U.S., 1961, naturalized, 1972; d. Carlos and Amelia (Santana) Martinez Sanchez; B.A. in Econs. cum laude, Am. U., 1965; M.S. in Fgn. Service (Univ. fellow), Georgetown U., 1967; postgrad. Nat. U. Mex. Instr. econs. George Mason Coll., U. Va., Fairfax, 1967-68; researcher World Bank, 1967-69, indsl. economist, industrialization div., 1969-71, loan officer, Central Am., 1971-79, loan officer, economist, Mex., 1973-74, Venezuela and Ecuador, 1973-77, sr. loan officer in charge of Panama and Dominican Republic, Washington, 1977-81, sr. loan officer, Middle East and North Africa, 1981—. Mem. Am. Econ. Assn., Soc. Internat. Devel., Brookings Inst. Latin Am. Study Group. Roman Catholic. Contbg. author: The Economic Growth of Colombia: Problems and Prospects, 1973. Home: 4734 Massachusetts Ave NW Washington DC 20016 Office: 1818 H St NW Washington DC 20037

MARTINEZ, SUSANNE, lawyer; b. San Francisco, Mar. 3, 1945; d. Floyd W. and Mary Katherine (Grier) Sitton; B.A., U. Calif., Davis, 1967; J.D., U. Calif., San Francisco, 1970; 1 dau., Jennifer Sue. Admitted to Calif. bar, 1971, U.S. Supreme Ct. bar, 1976; legal asst. San Francisco Neighborhood Legal Assistance Found., 1968-70; staff atty. Youth Law Center, 1970-77; counsel Subcom. on Child and Human Devel., Com. Labor and Human Resources, U.S. Senate, Washington, 1977-80; legis. asst. Senator Alan Cranston, 1980—. Mem. ACLU, San Francisco Bar Assn., Order of the Coif. Democrat. Office: Senate Office Bldg 229 Russell Washington DC 20510

MARTÍNEZ, YOLANDA R., social services adminstr.; b. San Bernardino, Calif., Feb. 11, 1936; d. Eduardo R. and Consuelo (Rincon) M.; A.A., San Bernardino Valley Coll., 1959; B.A., U. Wash., 1974; m. William Edward Hawkins, Mar. 27, 1963; children—Ricardo, Eduardo, William T. Tchr. public schs., Calif., 1958-59; parole adviser, project dir., counselor Active Mexicanos, Seattle, 1972-76; instr. Everett Community Coll., Everett, Wash., 1975-76; research, translator Wash. State Council Crime and Delinquency, Seattle, 1977; program asst., minority affairs Seattle Central Community Coll., cons. to community offenders programs 1977-81; sr. community service rep. Seattle Dept. Human Resources, 1981—; cons. Chicano mental health. Democratic precinct committeeman, 1968, 70; vol. worker various local and state polit. campaigns; chmn. Region 10 Chicano Task Force on Drug Abuse, 1977-79; mem. Seattle Women's Commn., 1977-81; v.p. Concilio for Spanish Speaking; state dir., mem. nat. exec. bd. League United Latin Am. Citizens, 1980-82; chmn. Hispanic adv. bd. Seattle Community Coll. Dist. 6, 1982—; chair Seattle/Mazatlan Sister City Assn., 1981—; bd. dirs. United Way of King County; dist. adv. com. group health Northgate Clinic; del. White House Conf. on Families, Los Angeles, 1980. Recipient Gov.'s citation, 1974. Mem. MUJER Hispanic Woman's Orgn. Author: Usted y La Ley, 1977. Home: 1602 NE 73d St Seattle WA 98115 Office: Dept Human Resources City of Seattle 400 Yesler Bldg Seattle WA 98104

MARTINI, ELLA JANE, twp. govt. ofcl.; b. Pinconning, Mich., July 22, 1928; d. Frank Steve and Ella Edna (Boetefuer) Michalski; student Delta Coll., Saginaw Valley (Mich.) State Coll., 1969-70; m. Frederick C. Martini, Oct. 6, 1951; children—Cynthia, James. Acct., Dow Chem. Co., Midland, Mich., 1948-53, Delta Coll., 1962-63, Essexville-Hampton Sch. Dist., 1964-68; office mgr. Bangor Twp. Sch. Dist., Bay City, Mich., 1968-69; twp. clk., dep. assessor Charter Twp. Hampton, Bay County, 1970—, twp. trustee, 1968-70; commr., mem. exec. bd. East Central Mich. Planning and Devel. Region, 1972-82; mem. Hampton Twp. Planning Commn., 1974-82. Bd. dirs. Bay County Library, 1964—, chmn., 1974-76, sec.-treas., 1978-82; vice chmn. Bay County Republican Party, 1979-81, sec., 1970-74. Mem. ALA, Mich. Twp. Assn., Mich. Assessors Assn., Bay County Twp. Assn. Republican. Lutheran. Home: 1277 W Cecelia Dr Essexville MI 48732 Office: 801 W Center Ave Rd Essexville MI 48432

MARTINSON, RUTH MARIE BRACKMAN, sales exec.; b. Blaine, Wash., Sept. 11, 1924; d. Theodore E. G. and Marie S. B. (Gieseke) Brackman; student Knapp Bus. Coll., Tacoma, Wash., 1942-43; m. Robert Delmar Martinson, Sept. 22, 1946; children—Steven Delmar, Kenneth Neil. Sec. Puyallup (Wash.) High Sch., 1943-46; grocery clk. Carrs' Food Center, Anchorage, 1955-56; dealer Tupperware Home Parties, Anchorage, 1957, unit mgr., 1958, distbr. for State of Alaska, 1959—. Pres., Alaska chpt. Lutheran Women's Missionary League, 1967-69. Recipient 100,000 Mile Club plaque, 1965. Republican. Home: 2815 E Tudor Rd Anchorage AK 99507 Office: 2801-2815 E Tudor Rd Anchorage AK 99507

MARTOCCIA, JOYCE SGRO, ednl. adminstr.; b. Cleve., Aug. 24, 1939; d. Santo M. and Johanna Mathilda (Lienerth) Sgro; B.A. in Bus. Edn., Baldwin-Wallace Coll., 1959; M.A. in Guidance and Counseling, Case Western Res. U., 1967; M.A., John Carroll U., 1974; m. William R. Martoccia, Mar. 28, 1968; 1 son, Marc William. Legal sec. Van Aken, Arnold, Bond and Withers, Cleve., 1959-62; bus. tchr. Cleve. Public Schs., 1963-66, guidance and placement counselor high schs., 1966-73; adminstr., asst. prin., unit prin. Audubon Jr. High Sch., Cleve., from 1973; now spl. projects counselor Damascus High Sch. and Sligo Intermediate Sch., Gaithersburg, Md.; mem. accrediting team N. Central Assn. High Schs. and Colls. Fine arts chmn. Cleve. Ballet, 1976—; co-chmn. vols. Shaker Lakes Regional Nature Center, 1975—; mem. Cleve. Opera Assn., Cleve. Mus. Art, Smithsonian Soc.; women's com. Cleve. Orch.; hon. v.p. Lincoln Jr. High Sch. PTA; adv. bd. John Carroll U.; vol. fundraising Am. Cancer Soc., Muscular Dystrophy Assn. Honored for best tutorial program in City of Cleve., 1975-78; honored as Outstanding Asst. Prin., 1978. Mem. Am., Ohio, NE Ohio (pres. 1976-77) personnel and guidance assns., Cleve. Council Adminstrs. and Suprs., Ohio, Nat. (commn. on profl. employment practices, co-author handbook 1977) assns. women deans, adminstrs. and counselors, Ohio Sch. Counselors Assn., Montgomery County Counselors Assn., Ohio Assn. Secondary Sch. Adminstrs., Indsl. Edn. Club of Cleve., Greater Cleve. Prins. Discussion Group (pres.), John Carroll U. Educators Alumni Assn. (pres., educators cons.), Delta Phi Alpha, Phi Delta Kappa, Alpha Delta Kappa. Republican. Roman Catholic. Home: 84 Pontiac Way Gaithersburg MD 20760 Office: 850 Hungerford Rd Gaithersburg MD 20760

MARTONE, JOANNE, acct.; b. Yonkers, N.Y., Mar. 3, 1951; d. August Jerome and Winnie (Rudolf) M.; B.A. in History, Centre Coll. Ky., 1973; postgrad. Ariz. State U., 1979-81. Tchr., basketball coach Junction City (Ky.) Elem. Sch., 1973-77; staff analyst Met. Life Ins. Co., 1975-77; tchr. Glendale Elem. Sch., 1977-78, Camelback Desert Sch., 1978-79; C.P.A., De Marcus & Assos. P.C., Phoenix, 1979-82; individual practice, 1982—; partner Investment Co. Acres, 1976—, The Lucky Leopard, 1977—; dir. Adaman Mutual Water Co., 1981- , sec. treas., 1981—. Cert. tchr., Ky., Ariz.; C.P.A., Ariz. Mem. Am. Inst. C.P.A.s, Ariz. Soc. C.P.A.s, Am. Woman's Soc. C.P.A.s, Nat. Assn. Female Execs., Mut. Assn. Profl. Services. Home: Route 1 Box 348 Litchfield Park AZ 85340 Office: 7112 N 55th Ave Glendale AZ 85302

MARTSOLF, EDITH LYON, state govt. ofcl.; b. Nashville, Mar. 3, 1927; A.B. in Psychology, Youngstown (Ohio) State U., 1968; M.Spl.Edn., Kent (Ohio) State U., 1972; divorced; children—Kenneth Wayne, Karen Elaine. Classroom tchr., prin., then home tng. cons. and asst. adminstr. Trainable Program Mentally Retarded, Columbiana County, Ohio, 1959-68; supt. Sch. Mentally Retarded, Columbiana County, 1968-72; chief protective services sect. Ohio Dept. Mental Retardation, 1978—. Mem. Council Exceptional Children (past officer), Am. Assn. Mental Deficiency, Profl. Assn. Mental Retardation, Nat. Assn. Female Execs., Delta Kappa Gamma. Club: Quota Internat. (pres. Salem, Ohio 1972-73, lt. gov. Ohio 1978, gov. Ohio 1979-80). Home: 664 Jasonway Ave Columbus OH 43214 Office: 30 E Broad St State Office Towers Room 1236 Columbus OH 43215

MARTZ, HELEN ELIZABETH, ret. govt. agy. adminstr.; b. Cin., Aug. 12, 1906; d. Hyman and Bertha (Robin) Rosin; B.A., U. Pa., 1938; M.S.W., Pa. Sch. of Social Work, 1939; Ph.D., Bryn Mawr Coll., 1946; m. Samuel E. Martz, Nov. 27, 1936; children—Peter, Maria (dec.). Research asst. Gov.'s Com. on Public Relief in Pa., 1935-36; caseworker Phila. County Bd. of Assistance, 1937-38; procedure analyst Pa. State Dept. Public Assistance, 1939-42; tech. adv. Office of Asst. Dir., Social Security Bd., Washington, 1943-44; analyst Bur. of Public Assistance, Social Security Adminstrn., Washington, 1945-47; tech. adv. Bur. Public Assistance, FSA, 1948-50, social adminstrn. adv., 1955-63; public welfare adv. Bur. of Public Assistance, Welfare Adminstrn., Washington, 1950-54; adj. prof. Am. U., Washington, 1960-70; lectr. Washington Internat. Center, 1958-61; program analyst Office of Asst. Sec. HEW, Washington, 1961-62, chief spl. reports sect. Bur. of Family Assistance, Welfare Adminstrn., 1963-67, staff asst. Adv. Council on Public Welfare, Office of Commr., Welfare Adminstrn., 1964-66, social adminstrn. adv. HEW Task Force on Orgn. of Social Services, 1967-68, health care program specialist Med. Services Adminstrn., Social and Rehab. Service, 1969-75, program analyst Med. Services Adminstrn., Social and Rehab. Service, 1975-77; med. care planning specialist Office of Child Health, Dept. Health and Human Services, Washington, 1977-81. Recipient Mary Switzer award, 1973; Woerischoffer fellow, 1941-42. Mem. Am. Public Welfare Assn., Acad. Cert. Social Workers, Nat. Assn. for Children and Adults with Learning Disabilities, Am. Assn. Social Workers, No. Va. Assn. Children and Adults with Learning Disabilities, Smithsonian Instn. Contbr. articles on med. care and public welfare adminstrn. to profl. publs. Home: 7304 Stafford Rd Alexandria VA 22307

MARTZ, MIRIAM LETHEA, data processing exec.; b. LaGrange, Ga., Dec. 5, 1938; d. Robert C. and Marie R. Cobb; diploma Marsh Bus. Coll., Atlanta, 1959; div.; 1 dau., Julie. Supr. computer ops. Equafax, Atlanta, 1959-70; mgr. data processing Crum & Forster Ins. Co., Atlanta, 1974-81; owner Accuracy Plus, word processing and data entry service, Alpharetta, Ga., 1981—. Mem. Nat. Assn. Female Execs. Mem. Unity Truth Ch. Home: 170 Crestwood Ct Alpharetta GA 30201 Office: 21 N Main St Alpharetta GA 30201

MARUMOTO, BARBARA CHIZUKO, state legislator; b. San Francisco, July 21, 1939; d. Takeo and Kathleen (Tsuchiya) Okamoto; B.A., U. Hawaii, 1971; student U. Calif., 1957-60, UCLA, 1957; children—Marshall, Jay, Wendy, Megan. Legis. aide, researcher, Honolulu, 1972-78; mem. Hawaii Ho. of Reps., 1978—, minority floor leader, 1981; elected del. to Constl. Conv., 1978; real estate agt., 1979—. Mem. exec. bd. Hist. Hawaii Found.; bd. dirs. Pacific council Girl Scouts U.S.A.; active Rep. Party, Common Cause, LWV, PTA, Ripon Soc. Clubs: Honolulu, Jr. League Honolulu. Contbr. various news columns to publs. Office: Capitol Room 322 Honolulu HI 96813

MARVIN, BARBARA METZ, fin. planner, educator; b. San Diego, Sept. 19, 1939; d. Hughes Clecknor and Edith Lenore (Monroe) Metz; student Antelope Valley Coll., 1957; B.S., U. So. Calif., 1961; teaching credential Los Angeles State Coll., 1963; m. Henry Burdette Marvin, June 10, 1961; 1 son, Henry H. Arts and crafts tchr., swimming tchr. Los Angeles County Parks, 1954-60; bus. clk. So. Calif. Edison, Lancaster, 1961-62; tchr. Lancaster Sch. Dist., 1963-71; substitute tchr. Westside Schs., Lancaster, 1975—; fin. planner, 1979—. Mem. Antelope Valley Assistance League, Children Am. Revolution (sr. pres.), Calif. Honor Soc., Va. Hist. Gen. Soc., DAR. Republican. Lutheran. Club: Order Eastern Star. Address: 2250 W Ave N Lancaster CA 93534

MARVIN, HELEN RHYNE, state senator; b. Gastonia, N.C., Nov. 30, 1917; d. Dane S. and Tessie (Hastings) Rhyne; B.A. magna cum laude, Furman U., 1938; M.A., La. State U., 1938; postgrad. Winthrop Coll., U. N.C., Chapel Hill, U. N.C., Charlotte, U. Colo., U. Vt., U. Oslo (Norway); m. Ned Marvin, Nov. 21, 1941; children—Kathryn Nisbet, Richard Morris, David Rhyne. Part-time instr. polit. sci. Gaston Coll.; pres. Gaston County Democratic Women, 1973-75; mem. Gaston County Dem. Exec. Com., 1973-76; mem. N.C. State Dem. Exec. Com., 1973-76; del. Nat. Dem. Conv., 1972; mem. N.C. Senate, 1975—, vice chairperson edn. com., 1979-82, vice-chairperson law enforcement and crime control com., 1981-82, appropriations com., 1981-82. Bd. dirs. Gaston County United Way, Gaston County Mental Health Assn., Gaston County Family Planning Council, Gaston County Council for Children with Spl. Needs; past mem., sec. So. Piedmont Health Services Agy.; mem. N.C. State Health Coordinating Council, N.C. State Textbook Commn.; past chairperson N.C. Council on Status of Women, N.C. State Social Services Commn., N.C. Day Care Adv. Council; mem. N.C. Commn. on Yr. 2000; mem. Gov.'s Advocacy Council on Children and Youth; mem. N.C. Apprenticeship Council; trustee Vagabond Sch. Drama, Flat Rock Playhouse. Mem. So. Polit. Sci. Assn., N.C. Polit. Sci. Assn., Delta Kappa Gamma. Club: Altrusa. Office: NC Senate State Capitol Raleigh NC 27602

MARVIN, KAREN ANN, health care services adminstr.; b. Buffalo, Feb. 7, 1947; d. Frances Robert and Phyllis (Townsend) Kirsch; B.S. in Nursing, D'Youville Coll., 1975; postgrad. SUNY, Buffalo, 1978-79; m. Matthew Glenn Marvin, Nov. 25, 1977; children—Ray D., Dean A.; stepchildren—Victor, Mary, Glenda, Rebecca. Nurses aide Mt. View Hosp., Lockport, N.Y., 1969-73; mem. nursing staff Newfane Health Facility, Lockport, 1976, asst. dir. nursing service, 1976-78, infection control nurse, 1976-78, dir. nursing service, 1978; dir. nursing service Erie County Home and Infirmary, Alden, N.Y., 1978-79; dir. health care services Manpower Inc., Buffalo, N.Y., 1979-81; dir. home care services Health Assn. of Niagara County Inc., Niagara Falls, N.Y., 1981-82; nursing cons., 1981—; mem. profl. adv. bd. Erie County Long Term Home Health Care, 1978-80; mem. citizens adv. bd. community mental health Niagara Falls Meml. Med. Center. Niagara Falls Quota Club scholar, 1973-75. Mem. Dirs. Nursing in Nursing Homes (sec. treas. 1977-79), Am. Assn. Critical Care Nurses, N.Y. State Nurses Assn., Council World Affairs. Republican. Presbyterian. Home: 26 Bob-O-Link Ln Lockport NY 14094

MARVIN, PATRICIA HARMON, librarian; b. Idabel, Okla., Sept. 21, 1927; d. Alton Ernest and Louise Ann (Park) Harmon; B.A., U. Denver, 1948, M.A., 1950; m. John Robert Marvin, Aug. 14, 1948 (div. 1976); children—Stephen Anthony, Timothy Andrew. Circulation librarian U. Nebr., Lincoln, 1950-51; reserves librarian U. Denver, 1952-53; cataloger Johns Hopkins U. Library, 1953-54; head circulation U. Notre Dame, 1960-61; supr. circulation Newton (Mass.) Free Library, 1967-79. Mem. Mass., New Eng. library assns. Poetry reviewer Library Jour., 1969-75; editor Newton Free Library Jour., 1973-79; copy editor Am. Inst. C.P.A.s, 1980—. Home: 780 Riverside Dr New York NY 10032

MARVIN, SHIRLEY GREEN, humanist, social scientist; b. Boston, July 2, 1922; d. Isadore and Marion (Walper) Green; B.A., Wellesley Coll., 1943; M.A., La. State U., 1971; m. Wilbur Marvin, Mar. 18, 1945 (div.); children—Michael, Ann Elizabeth Swanson, Richard. Founder, dir. Marvel Research Assos., Baton Rouge, 1972—; adminstrv. officer Office Spl. Ednl. Services, La. Dept. Edn., 1979—; spl. program coordinator div. continuing edn. La. State U., 1975-78. Co-chmn., Houston del. for La. Women's Conf. for Internat. Women's Year, 1977; pres. La. Orgns. for State Legislation, 1958-62; del., mem. Gov.'s Exec. Com. for White House Conf. Children and Youth, 1960; sec. La. Citizens Edn. Found. for Criminal Justice, 1972-76; co-founder La. Women's Polit. Caucus; state bd. La. League Women Voters, 1956-58. Recipient Outstanding Service award La. Mental Health Assn., 1980. Mem. Assn. Continuing Higher Edn., La. Assn. Sch. Execs., Council Exceptional Children, Nat. Assn. Dirs. of Spl. Edn., Mental Health Assn. Greater Baton Rouge (bd. dirs.), Nat. Alliance for Mentally Ill, Wellesley Coll. Center for Research on Women. Jewish. Home: 1127 Longwood Dr Baton Rouge LA 70806

MARX, GERTIE F(LORENTINE), anesthesiologist; b. Frankfurt/Main, Ger., Feb. 13, 1912; came to U.S., 1937, naturalized, 1943; d. Joseph and Elsa (Scheuer) M.; M.D., U. Bern (Switzerland), 1937; m. Eric P. Reiss, Sept. 26, 1940 (dec. 1968). Intern, then resident in anesthesiology Beth Israel Hosp., N.Y.C., adj., then asso. anesthesiologist, 1943-55; attending anesthesiologist Bronx (N.Y.) Mcpl. Hosp., 1955—; attending anesthesiologist Bronx VA Hosp., 1966-72, cons., 1972—; mem. faculty Albert Einstein Coll. Medicine, Bronx, 1955, prof. anesthesiology, 1970—, also attending anesthesiology coll. hosps. Recipient Gold medal Obstetric Anaesthetist Assn. Eng., 1980; diplomate Nat. Bd. Med. Examiners, Am. Bd. Anesthesiology. Fellow Am. Coll. Anesthesiology, Am. Coll. Ob-Gyn, N.Y. Acad. Medicine; mem. Am. Soc. Anesthesiologists, AMA, N.Y. State Soc. Anesthesiologists (chmn. anesthesia study com. 1967-69), N.Y. Acad. Scis., Bronx County Med. Soc., Soc. Obstet. Anesthesia and Perinatology. Co-author: Physiology of Obstetric Anesthesia, 1969. Asso. author Survey Anesthesiology, 1957—; editor: Parturition and Perinetology, 1973; Clinical Management of Mother and Newborn, 1979; Obstetrics Anesthesia Digest, 1981; co-editor: Obstetric Analgesia and Anesthesia, 1980. Contbr. articles profl. jours., chpts. in books. Home: 642-A Heritage Village Southbury CT 06488 Office: Dept Anesthesiology Albert Einstein Coll Medicine-J 1226 Bronx NY 10461

MARX, MARY ANN HALMI, automobile dealer; b. Cin., Apr. 23, 1929; d. Harold F. and Alice Marie (Dooley) Nolting; student Edgecliff Coll., 1948-49, U. Cin., 1949-50; m. Eugene N. Halmi, Jr., Aug. 5, 1950 (dec. 1974); children—Allyson, Melissa, Nickolas E.; m. 2d, W.T. Marx, Jr., Apr. 23, 1976. Owner, operator Queen City Chevrolet Co., Inc., Cin., 1973—; appeared on David Suskind TV show, 1979. Trustee, Greater Cin. Kidney Found., 1967—, Cin. Better Bus. Bur., 1976—; bd. dirs. Greater Cin. Internat. Airport, 1974—, Edgecliff Coll., 1976-77. Lic. pilot. Mem. Cin. Auto Dealers Assn. (officer). Roman Catholic. Club: Hyde Park Golf and Country. Participant Power Puff Derbies, 1969-71. Home: 5 Twin Hills Ridge Dr Cincinnati OH 45228 Office: 414 E Court St Cincinnati OH 45202

MASARANI, MARCELIA CRUZ, gemologist; b. Baliwag, Bulacan, Philippines, Aug. 30, 1949; came to U.S., 1973, naturalized, 1982; d. Lazaro Alamazar Cruz and Petronila Labao Jimenez Cruz; B.S. in Bus. Adminstrn., St. Theresa's Coll., Quezon City, 1972; postgrad. child psychology, Columbia U., 1973; diploma in gemology Gemological Inst. Am., 1974; m. Fathi Masarani, Nov. 22, 1979. Jewelry appraiser P.J. Cruz Pawnshop, Manila, 1969-71; loan processor, bookkeeper First Nat. City Bank, Makati, 1972-73; gemologist, saleswoman Rupperthal-Am., Ltd., N.Y.C., 1974-75; head colored stone and gem identification dept., diamond grader, lectr. Gemological Inst. Am., 1975-78; gemologist, saleswoman, diamond grader, buying cons. Diaco Internat., N.Y.C., 1978—; instr., cons. in field. Mem. Am. Gem Soc., Nat. Assn. Female Execs., Coalition Asian-Am. Pacific Women. Club: N.Y. Health and Racquet. Office: 1185 Ave Americas New York NY 10036

MASENG, MARI, writer; b. Chgo., Mar. 15, 1954; d. Leif Erick and Betty (Hagen) M.; B.A. in Journalism, U. S.C., 1975. Reporter, Charleston (S.C.) Eve. Post, 1976-78; polit. aide various Republican senatorial and presdl. campaigns, 1978-80; presdl. speechwriter, 1981—. Mem. U. S.C. Alumni Assn., Sigma Delta Chi, Chi Omega. Presbyterian. Office: The White House Washington DC 20500

MASHBURN, ENID RANEY, pianist, organist, educator; b. Frederick, Okla., Jan. 18, 1910; d. Alex Veron and Dolly Mae (McCurdy) McKinney; student pub. schs., Frederick; corr. student harmony and theory Sherwood Conservatory, Chgo.; student Wash. State U.; pupil pvt. music tchrs.; m. Cecil E. Mashburn, Apr. 30, 1927; children—Monroe, Bruce, Velma Mashburn Goodwin. Piano and organ tchr., Quincy, Wash., 1952—; piano and orch. performances. Mem. Nat. Guild Piano Tchrs. (chmn., organizer Eastern Wash. Centers, Hall of Fame 1968), Am. Coll. Musicians, Wash. Music Tchrs. Assn. Mem. Nazarene Ch. Address: Route 1 1500 RD 6 NW Quincy WA 98848

MASKALL, MARTHA JOSEPHINE, computer software systems engr.; b. Kearny, N.J., Mar. 30, 1945; d. Charles Edgar and Mathilda Comba M.; B.A. in Biology, Stanford U., 1966; M.A., Duke U., 1969; m. Edward C. Page, Apr. 4, 1981. Programmer-analyst Leasco Systems and Research, Bethesda, Md., 1969-70; systems analyst Mitre Corp., McLean, Va., 1970-71; data base adminstr. Armco Steel, Ashland, Ky., 1972-74; cons., project mgr. Rand Info. Systems, San Francisco, 1974-78; mgr. systems devel. fleet services div. Itel Corp., San Francisco, 1978-79; Datacom sales rep. ADR, San Francisco, 1980-81; systems engr. Four Phase Systems, Sacramento, 1981—; coordinator data base series info. sci. seminars Golden Gate U., 1979-80. Mem. citizens adv. com. on wastewater mgmt., 1977-78. NDEA fellow, 1966-68. Mem. Data Processing Mgmt. Assn. (program dir. 1980), Nat. Assn. Female Execs., Am. Mgmt. Assn., NOW. Democrat. Home: 8456 Hidden Valley Circle Fair Oaks CA 95628 Office: 800 Howe Ave Suite 100 San Francisco CA

MASKREY, JOYCE ELOISE, real estate co. exec.; b. Des Moines, Apr. 11, 1944; d. Earl Raymond and Bernice Elizabeth (Taylor) Wagner; B.A. in Journalism, Drake U., 1967; M.S.T., Drake U., 1970; m. Richard Maskrey, Apr. 11, 1970; children—Chris, Chad, Natalie Jo. Advt. copywriter Sta. KCBC, Des Moines, 1967-68; writer Iowa Credit Union League, Des Moines, 1968; tchr. Fed. Tchr. Corps Program, 1968-69; tng. officer, manpower coordinator, employee counselor Greater Opportunities, 1969-73; pharm. sales rep. Lederle Labs., Des Moines, 1973-75; pharm. saleswoman sales Rachelle Labs., Des Moines, 1975-81; pres., broker So. Realty, Des Moines, 1977—; owner, pres. R & J Enterprises, R & J Trucking, R & J Snow Removal, R & J Lawn Aid (all Des Moines). Active local PTA, Des Moines; Mem. Drug Travelers Assn., Homebuilders Assn., Iowa Assn. Realtors, South Des Moines C. of C. Home: 4310 SW 26th St Des Moines IA 50321 Office: 1135 SW Army Post Rd Des Moines IA 50315

MASLACH, CHRISTINA, educator; b. San Francisco, Jan. 21, 1946; d. George James and Doris Ann (Cuneo) Maslach; B.A. magna cum laude, Radcliffe Coll., 1967; Ph.D., Stanford U., 1971; m. Philip Zimbardo, Aug. 10, 1972; children—Zara, Tanya. Prof. psychology U. Calif., Berkeley, 1971—. Mem. Am. Psychol. Assn., AAAS, Soc. for Psychol. Study of Social Issues, Soc. for Clin. and Exptl. Hypnosis (Henry 1980). Author: Infuencing Attitudes and Changing Behavior, 1977; Experiencing Social Psychology, 1979; Burnout: The Cost of Caring, 1982. Office: U Calif Dept Psychology Berkeley CA 94720

MASLAR, SUSAN ANNE, govt. ofcl.; b. Latrobe, Pa., Sept. 18, 1948; d. Andrew George and Eleanor Irene (Allison) M.; student U. Pitts., 1966-68; B.S., Pa. State U., 1970; M.B.A., U. Md., 1978; m. William Grant Hamilton, Apr. 10, 1977; 1 dau., Terra Liana Maslar Hamilton. Asst. mdse. mgr. Richard's Dept. Store, Miami, Fla., 1971-72; passenger service rep. Amtrak, N.Y.C., 1972-73, budget and cost analyst, Washington, 1973-74; transp. industry analyst ICC, Washington, 1975—. Vol., Girl Scout Council Washington. Recipient Equal Opportunity Achievement award ICC, 1979. Mem. Womens Transp. Seminar (nat. v.p.), Transp. Research Forum. Home: 3581 University Dr Fairfax VA 22030 Office: ICC Bldg 12th St and Constitution Ave NW Washington DC 20423

MASON, AIMEE HUNNICUTT ROMBERGER, educator; b. Atlanta, Nov. 3, 1918; d. Edwin William and Aimee Greenleaf (Hunnicutt) Romberger; B.A., Conn. Coll., 1940; postgrad. Emory U., 1946-48; M.A., U. Fla., 1979, Ph.D., 1980; M.A., Stetson U., 1968; m. Samuel Venable Mason, Aug. 16, 1941; children—Olivia Elizabeth (Mrs. James Butcher), Christopher Leeds. Jr. exec., merchandising G. Fox & Co., Hartford, Conn., 1940-41; air traffic controller CAA, Atlanta, 1942; partner Coronado Concrete Products, New Smyrna Beach, Fla., 1953-81; adj. faculty Valencia Jr. Coll., Orlando, Fla., 1969; instr. philosophy and humanities Seminole Community Coll., Sanford, 1969—. Area cons. ARC, 1947-50; del. Nat. Red Cross, Washington, 1949; founding mem. St. Joseph Hosp. Aux., Atlanta, 1950-53; v.p., treas. New Smyrna Beach PTA 1955-60. Bd. dirs. Atlanta Symphony Orch., Fla. Symphony Orch., 1954-59. Served to lt. USCGR, 1943-46. Recipient award in graphics Nat. Assn. Women Artists, 1939, 41, Golden Hatter award Stetson U., 1973, 74. Mem. Am. Philos. Assn., AAUP, AAUW (founding mem. New Smyrna Beach), Fla. Philos. Assn. (exec. council 1978-79), Collegium Phenomenologicum, Soc. Existential and Phenomenological Philosophy, Soc. Phenomenology in Human Scis., Merleau-Ponty Circle, Fla. Assn. Community Colls. Home: 2103 Ocean Dr New Smyrna Beach FL 32069 Office: Seminole Community College Sanford FL 32771

MASON, BETTE ALBERTA, artist, educator; b. Tex., July 28, 1927; d. Thomas Jefferson and Alberta (Burris) Martin; student Trinity U., 1944-46, Syracuse U., 1966-68, Art Students League, 1970; B.A., Stephens Coll., 1976; postgrad. U. New Orleans, 1977-79; m. David E. Mason, July 2, 1964; children by previous marriage—Hobart Quentin Sibley, Jeffrey Joe Sibley, William Jack Sibley, Suzanne Sibley. Gallery dir. Asso. Artist, Syracuse, N.Y., 1967-69; pres. Westchester Art Soc., Tarrytown, N.Y., 1970-72; gallery dir. Todd Galleries, N.Y.C., 1972; art dir. Westchester Learning Center, Mt. Vernon, N.Y., 1970-72, owner/operator Studio Gallery, New Orleans, 1973-76; art cons. Delgado Coll., New Orleans, 1977-78, chmn. fine arts dept., 1978-80; one-woman shows: New Orleans Center for Performing Arts, 1981, Nat. Art Center, N.Y.C., 1980, Womenart, N.Y.C., 1980, St. Philip Gallery, New Orleans, 1974, New Orleans Fedn. Chs., 1975-79, Scarsdale Gallery Contemporary Art, 1972, Westchester Community Coll., Valhalla, N.Y., 1971, Christopher Gallery, N.Y.C., 1970; group shows include: Syracuse U., 1970, Nat. Assn. Women Artists, N.Y.C., 1971, Union Carbide, N.Y.C., 1972, Westchester Art Soc., 1971-72, New Orleans Art Assn., 1972-77; represented in numerous pvt. collections. Recipient award Chautauqua Art Festival, 1970, Jefferson Parish Sesquicentennial, 1976, Internat. Trade Mart, 1977, New Orleans Art Assn., 1973-76, Scarsdale Arts Soc., 1971, Federated Women's Club, 1971, Westchester Art Soc., 1972. Mem. Coll. Art Assn., Women in the Arts, Women's Caucus for Art, New Orleans Art Assn., New Orleans Opera Guild. Baptist. Home: 527 Saint Philip St New Orleans LA 70116

MASON, COLLEEN SUZANNE, med. technologist; b. San Diego, Mar. 8, 1952; d. Albert Michael and Pauline (Whitaker) Ross; student San Diego State U., 1970-72; B.S., Calif. Poly. Inst., 1975; M.S., U. Calif., Dominguez Hills, 1980; m. Alan James Mason, Apr. 8, 1972; children—Danielle Christine, Jennifer Suzanne. Med. technology trainee City of Hope Med. Center, Duarte, Calif., 1974-75; med. technologist U. Calif., Irvine, 1975-76, City of Hope Med. Center, Duarte, 1976-77; sr. med. technologist Victor Valley Hosp., Victorville, Calif., 1977—. Recipient Outstanding Student award Calif. Poly. Inst., 1974. Mem. Am. Soc. Clin. Pathologists, Calif. Soc. Med. Technologists, Am. Soc. Med. Technologists, Beta Beta Beta, Phi Kappa Phi. Office: 15248 11th St Victorville CA 92392

MASON, DOROTHY MARIE WISSBAUM, med. social worker; b. St. Paul, Nebr., Sept. 6, 1930; d. Ernest Andrew and Mary Wissbaum; B.A., Marymount Coll., Salina, Kans., 1965; M.S.W., U. Kans., Lawrence, 1971; m. Gene Mason, Feb. 19, 1977; 4 stepchildren. Tchr. elem. and high schs., Kans., 1952-67; music tchr., 1971-74; psychiat. social worker, Hastings, Nebr., 1971-74; coordinator Mental Health Center, Lexington, Nebr., 1974-79; dir. dept. social services Tri County Hosp., Lexington, 1979-81; pvt. practice social work, Lexington, 1979-80; dir. social services Westside Care Home, Lexington, 1980—; asst. prof. part time Kearney (Nebr.) State Coll., 1975-79; cons. to nursing homes; founder hospice program for care county-wide. Mem. Nat. Assn. Social Workers, Acad. Cert. Social Workers, Soc. for Hosp. Social Work Dirs., State Hospice Assn. Home: 1406 W 37th St Kearney NE 68847 Office: 13th and Erie St Lexington NE 68850

MASON, ELIZABETH JANE, ednl. adminstr., cons.; b. Uniontown, Pa., Aug. 22, 1935; d. William Sherman and Margaret Catherine (Luman) M.; B.S. in Nursing, U. Pitts., 1959; M.S., Wayne State U., 1962; Ph.D. (USPHS predoctoral nurse fellow 1970-72), U. Wis., Madison, 1972; Instr. med.-surg. nursing U. Pitts., 1962-66; asst. prof. med.-surg. nursing U. Wis., Madison, 1966-70; assoc. prof. med.-surg. nursing and ednl. planning and devel. Va. Commonwealth U., Richmond, 1972-76; asst. dir. undergrad. edn. Ohio State U., Columbus, 1976-80; program dir. grad. program in nursing adminstrn. edn. U. Pitts., 1980—; cons. nursing standards, evaluation of nursing care. Mem. Am. Nurses Assn., Council Nurse Researchers, Am. Ednl. Researchers Assn., Am. Psychol. Assn., Pi Lambda Theta, Sigma Theta Tau. Author: How to Write Meaningful Nursing Standards, 1978. Office: 3500 Victoria St Victoria Hall Rm 429 Pittsburgh PA 15261

MASON, HELEN RINGER, physician; b. Newberry, S.C., Apr. 13, 1937; d. Homer Lominick and Bessie Mozel (Nichols) Ringer; B.S. in Biology, U. S.C., 1959; M.D., Med. U. S.C., 1963; m. Claude A. Mason, May 17, 1964; children—William Brett, Kaye Marie. Intern, Emory VA Hosp., 1963-64; resident Med. U. S.C., 1964-65, dept. psychiatry Tulane Med. Sch., 1965-67; psychiat. dir. New Orleans Mental Health Center, 1970-80; practice medicine specializing in psychiatry, New Orleans, 1973—; instr., asst. prof. dept. psychiatry Tulane Med. Sch., 1965-73, clin. asso. prof. psychiatry, 1973—. Mem. AMA, Am., La. psychiat. assns., La. Med. Assn., Orleans Parish Med. Soc., Phi Beta Kappa, Alpha Omega Alpha. Lutheran. Home: 356 Fairfield Ave Gretna LA 70053 Office: 4450 General de Gualle Dr Suite 1112 New Orleans LA 70114

MASON, JANE ELIZABETH, confectionery mfg. co. exec.; b. Chgo., Oct. 21, 1924; d. Albert Eugene and Mary Ellen (Egan) Paque; student Ohio State U., 1942-43, Triton Coll., 1954-55; student exec. course U. Chgo., 1953; m. James Thomas Mason, Sept. 8, 1945 (dec.); 1 dau., Dale Anne. Editor, Elmwood Park (Ill.) Herald, 1943-45; sec. Standard Wire Draw, Chgo., 1945-46; owner, operator secretarial and ghostwriting service, Chgo., 1946-49; sec. Leaf Confectionery, Inc., Chgo., 1949-54, asst. sales mgr., 1955-59, dir. sales, 1960—, gen. mgr. U.S. Chewing Gum Co. subs. Leaf Confectionery, Inc., Chgo., 1981—; speaker to industry groups. Vol. for battered wives, 1970—, LaRibida Children's Hosp., Chgo., Spl. Olympics, Chgo.; election judge Democratic Party, Oak Park, Ill. Named Salesman of Yr., Hotel Corp. Am., 1963, Newsmaker of Yr., Billboard Pub. Co., 1959; recipient cert. Optimist Clubs, 1968. Mem. Nat. Bulk Vendors Assn. (Exec. Sec. award 1961, 64, 68, nat. pres. 1981—), Nat. Candy Wholesaler's Assn., Nat. Automatic Merchandising Assn. (asso.), Nat. Candy Brokers Assn. (asso.), Nat. Secs. Assn., Women's Share (Ill. Speakers Bur.). Roman Catholic. Club: Bus. and Profl. Women (Woman of Achievement award). Founder and dir. Tasters Club, children's consumer testing group Leaf Confectionery, Inc., 1980—. Office: 1155 N Cicero Ave Chicago IL 60651

MASON, MARGARET DWYER, nursing adminstr.; b. Boston, Sept. 13, 1931; d. William Embry and Allice Mae (Williams) Dwyer; R.N., Children's Med. Center, Boston, 1953; B.S., Coll. St. Francis, Joliet, Ill., 1978, postgrad. in hosp. adminstrn., 1982; m. G. William Mason, Oct. 9, 1954; children—Ingrid, Oren, Barry, Heidi, Gretchen. Staff nurse Children's Hosp., Boston, 1953-54; head nurse New Eng. Hosp., Boston, 1954-55; staff nurse, supr. Zion Benton Hosp., Zion, Ill., 1966-70; staff nurse emergency room Kenosha (Wis.) Meml. Hosp., 1970-73; staff nurse Porter Hosp., Valparaiso, Ind., 1973-74; staff nurse, primary nurse, supr. St. Anthony's Med. Center, Crown Point, Ind., 1974-75, 77-78; indsl. nurse, Continental Ins., Wheatfield, Ind., 1975-77; asso. dir. nursing service St. Anthony Med. Center, 1978—. Mem. Emergency Dept. Nurses Assn., Nat. League Nursing, Coll. St. Francis Alumni Assn. Mem. Reformed Ch. Am. (dir. sanctuary choir). Home: 1020 15th Ave NW Demotte IN 46310 Office: St Anthony's Med Center Main and Franciscan Sts Crown Point IN 46307

MASON, MARSHA, actress; b. St. Louis, Apr. 3, 1942; d. James and Jacqueline Mason; grad. Webster (Mo.) Coll.; m. Gary Campbell, 1964 (div.); m. 2d, Neil Simon, Oct. 25, 1973. Mem. Broadway and nat. tour cast Cactus Flower, 1968; other stage appearances include: The Deer Park, 1967, The Indian Wants the Bronx, 1968, Happy Birthday, Wanda June, 1970, Private Lives, 1971, Merchant of Venice, 1972, You Can't Take It With You, 1972, Cyrano de Bergerac, 1972, A Doll's House, 1972, The Crucible, 1972, The Good Doctor, 1973, King Richard III, 1974; film appearances include: Blume in Love, 1973, Cinderella Liberty, 1973, Audrey Rose, 1977, The Goodbye Girl, 1977, The Cheap Detective, 1978, Promises in the Dark, 1979, Chapter Two, 1979; TV appearances include: daytime series Love of Life, Cyrano de Bergerac, 1974, The Good Doctor, 1978. Recipient Golden Globe award for Cinderella Liberty, 1974, The Goodbye Girl, 1978. Address: c/o William Morris Agency 1350 Ave of the Americas New York NY 10019

MASON, MARTHA LIGHT, community relations mgr. b. West Collingswood, N.J., Mar. 27, 1930; d. Wesley William Light and Jessie Arelia (Fry) Light Folkins; student Drexel Inst. Tech., 1947-50; Real Estate Broker, Rutgers U., 1973; m. Roland Vanneman Mason, June 30, 1951; children—Linda, Sheryl, Douglas, Ronald, Barbara. Sales mgr. Harbour Bay Homes, Brigantine, N.J., 1970-72; exec. v.p. Mican Realty Co., Brigantine, 1972-76; exec. dir. Historic Gardner's Basin, Atlantic City, 1976-78; project coordinator SS Atlantic City Ltd., from 1978; project mgr. Atlantic City Devel. Corp.; now community relations mgr. Harrah's Marina Hotel Casino, Atlantic City; cons. community relations. Sec. bd. recreation City of Linwood, N.J., 1970, chmn. planning bd., 1978-80; bd. dirs. Found. Atlantic Community Coll., Atlantic County Red Cross, Atlantic Area Boy Scout Council, Historic Gardners Basin, Young Am. Soc.; trustee Shore Meml. Hosp. Mem. Atlantic City C. of C., Atlantic City Women's C. of C., N.J. Builders Assn. Republican. Lutheran. Home: Parkshore Plaza Apt 3-G Somers Point NJ 08244

MASON, PENELOPE EVELYN, art historian; b. Orange, N.J., July 15, 1935; d. Warren Perry and Evelyn Stuart (McNally) Mason; B.A., Swarthmore Coll., 1957; M.A., N.Y.U., 1963, Ph.D., 1970. Instr., Vassar Coll., Poughkeepsie, N.Y., 1968-69; asst. prof. art history N.Y.U., N.Y.C., 1969-75, Yale U. New Haven, 1975-78; asso. prof. Fla. State U., Tallahassee, 1978—. Recipient Jr. Humanist award Nat. Endowment Humanities, 1971; Japan Found. fellow, 1973, 78-79. Mem. Coll. Art Assn. Am., Assn. Asian Studies, Columbia U. Seminar on Modern Japan, Fla. Seminar on Japan. Author: A Reconstruction of the Hogen Heiji Monogatari Emaki, 1977; Japanese Literati Painters: The Third Generation, 1977; contbr. articles to profl. jours. Home: 2013 Trescott Dr Tallahassee FL 32312 Office: Dept Art History Fla State U Tallahassee FL 32306

MASON, SANDRA ATKINSON, govt. ofcl.; b. Newport News, Va., Oct. 18, 1951; d. George W. and Hula Grey (Bynum) Atkinson; B.A., Dillard U., New Orleans, 1973. Mgmt. auditor GAO, N.Y.C., 1973-75; auditor Dept. Energy, N.Y.C., Houston and Los Angeles, 1974-80; contract auditor Def. Contract Audit Agy., Los Angeles, 1980-82; contract price analyst Dept. Air Force, 1982—. Mem. Phi Gamma Nu, Delta Theta Phi. Democrat.

MASON, TWYLA, Okla. state rep.; b. Oct. 26, 1954; ed. Ariz. State U., U. Tulsa. Mem. Okla. State Ho. of Reps., 1981—. Office: Okla Ho of Reps State Capitol Oklahoma City OK 73105 *

MASSAD, CAROLYN EMRICK, ednl. psychologist; b. Cleve., Nov. 24, 1935; d. Steven George and Mary Elizabeth (Evans) Emrick; B.S. in Edn., Kent State U., 1957, M.Ed., 1963, Ph.D., 1967; 1 son, Mark. Tchr. English, Havana (Cuba) schs., 1955; tchr. Solon (Ohio) Bd. Edn., 1957-67; asso. examiner test devel. div., edn. dept. Ednl. Testing Service, Princeton, N.J., 1967-74, examiner devel. group of elem. and secondary sch. programs div., 1974-80; faculty Kent (Ohio) State U., 1964, Pa. State U., University Park, 1970, Trenton (N.J.) State Coll., 1979; cons. various sch. dists. including Bermuda Dept. Edn.; cons. various internat. profl. groups on research and pub.; lectr., condr. workshops in field. NDEA fellow, 1961, 64; Spencer Found. fellow, 1972-73. Mem. Am. Ednl. Research Assn., Am. Psychol. Assn., Internat. Reading Assn., Nat. Council on Measurement in Edn., Am. Council on Teaching of Fgn. Langs., Nat. Council Tchrs. of English, Assn. for Supervision and Curriculum Devel., Internat. and Comparative Edn. Soc., NEA, N.J. Edn. Assn., Kappa Delta Pi, Sigma Delta Pi, Phi Alpha Theta. Roman Catholic. Asst. bus. editor Comparative Edn. Rev., 1964-65; rev. editor Am. Ednl. Research Jour., 1973-75; editorial bd./adv. NCME Measurement News, 1977-78; contbr. articles to profl. jours.; author: Linguistics and the Student Taking the AEC Tests, 1970; Massad Mimicry Test I, II, and II Revised, 1971; (with E.G. Lewis) English as a Foreign Language in Ten Countries, 1975; Information for Assessment and Evaluation, 1978. Home: 303 Emmons Dr 5B Princeton NJ 08540 Office: ETS Rosedale Rd Princeton NJ 08540

MASSARI, LINDA THERESE, coll. adminstr.; b. Chgo., July 13, 1949; d. Romeo and Gloria C. (Rizzo) M.; B.A., Northeastern Ill. State Coll., 1971; M.S., George Williams Coll., 1972. Tchr., Proviso West High Sch., Hillside, Ill., 1972-73; asst. registrar Stritch Sch. Medicine, Loyola U., Chgo., 1974-76, supr. med. sch. admissions, 1976-77, adminstrv. asst. dept. medicine, 1977-80, adminstrv. dir. dept. medicine, 1980—. Mem. Nat. Assn. Female Execs., Adminstrs. of Internal Medicine. Office: 2160 S 1st Ave Maywood IL 60153

MASSE, MICHELINE, fin. analyst, investigation co. exec.; b. Montreal, Can., Dec. 17, 1938; d. Paul and Alice (Dcarie) M.; B.A., U. Montreal, 1958, B.Commerce, 1964; m. Joseph Bonneau, Dec. 20, 1958 (dec.); children—Paul, Danielle, Pierre. Legal researcher Masse & Masse; high sch. tchr. English and history; founder, pres. Stock Market Info. Service, Inc., Montreal, 1969—; fin. cons. Mem. Montreal C. of C., Montreal Soc. Profl. Investment Advisors, Adminstrn. Mgmt. Soc. Office: PO Box 120 Station K Montreal PQ H1N 3K9 Canada

MASSELLO, BARBARA CAROLYN, librarian, educator; b. Springfield, Mo., Sept. 27, 1944; d. Sidney Herbert and Elinor Mae (Boehm) Williams; B.A., S.W. Mo. State U., Springfield, 1966; M.S., U. Ill., 1967; m. James William Massello, Feb. 6, 1971. Asst. reference librarian Ozark Pioneer Library System, Springfield, 1967-72; reference librarian, instr. library sci. S.W. Mo. State U. Library, 1972—. Mem. Greene County Democratic Central Com., 1978—. Mem. Mo. Library Assn., Springfield Area Librarians Assn., Friends of Earth, Beta Phi Mu. Presbyterian. Home: 307 Cordova Ct Springfield MO 65802 Office: SW Mo State U Library Springfield MO 65804

MASSENGILL, ELLEN WEBB, librarian; b. Littlefield, Tex., Mar. 6, 1932; d. Lester L. and Bessie (Webb) M.; B.S., Tex. Tech. U., 1953, M.S., 1959; M.L.S., N. Tex. State U., 1969. Homemaking tchr., Floyd, N.Mex., 1953-55, Crane, Tex., 1955-56, Seminole, Tex., 1956-68, Littlefield, Tex., 1971-73; librarian Odessa (Tex.) High Sch., 1969-71, Littlefield Jr. High Sch., 1973—; dist., area, state adv. bd. mem. Future Homemakers Am., N.Mex., Tex., 1954-68, adv. mem. nat. exec. council, 1954-55; adv. Young Homemakers Tex., 1958-73; co-leader Girl Scouts U.S.A., 1948-49; del. Nat. Citizenship Council, 1954. Recipient Home Econs. Scholarship award Borden Co., 1953, Panhellenic award Lubbock (Tex.) Panhellenic Soc., 1953; Forum award Tex. Tech. U., 1953. Mem. AAUW (reporter, historian, sec., parliamentarian 1956-68), Sch. Library and Info. Sci. Assn., NEA, Am. Home Econs. Assn., Am. Vocat. Assn., PTA, Tex. State Tchrs. Assn. (life), Tex. Library Assn. (life), Tex. Classroom Tchrs. Assn., Vocat. Homemaking Tchrs. Assn. Tex., Tex. Home Econs. Assn., County Classroom Tchrs. Assn. (treas.), Phi Kappa Phi, Phi Upsilon Omicron, Alpha Lambda Delta, Alpha Chi, Alpha Lambda Sigma. Democrat. Baptist. Home: 510 E 6th St Littlefield TX 79339 Office: 105 N Lake Ave Littlefield TX 79339

MASSETTE, DOLORES CATANDO, advt. agy. exec.; b. Woodbury, N.J., July 4, 1934; d. Ralph A. and Anne Rita (Campellone) Catando; B.A., U. Pa., 1953; postgrad. Dickenson Coll., 1957-58; student Juilliard Sch. Music, 1946-54, Am. Acad. Fine Arts, 1949-52. Singer, Phila. Opera Co., 1946-54; appeared in Broadway theatrical prodns., 1952-56; with Eastern Airlines, 1960-65; with Parker Allen, Phila., 1965-70, Scanforms, Inc., 1970-76; mktg. cons. Advt. Specialization Inst., Trevose, Pa., 1976-78; v.p. direct response div. Smith-Langerman Agy., Phila., 1978-81; mktg. and sales promotion/advt. specialist RCA Service Co., Cherry Hill, N.J., 1981—; advt. dir. Nan Duskin Store, Phila. Pres. Our Lady of Lourdes Hosp. Aux., 1953-63. Recipient various awards for advt. campaigns. Mem. Direct Mail Mktg. Assn. (award), Nat. Assn. Female Execs., Phila. Direct Mail Club (award), Advt. Women, Nat. Retail Mchts. Assn., Greater Bay C. of C., AAA Advt. Assn., Postal Forum, Lambda Sigma Chi. Republican. Roman Catholic. Clubs: Oaklands Trenton Country. Home: 1215 Elm Ave West Collingswood NJ 08107 Office: RCA Service Co Route 38 Cherry Hill NJ 08358

MASSEY, ANITA LOUISE, nurse; b. Springfield, Ill., Aug. 23, 1954; d. William and Jeannette Ruth (Bradley) M.; B.S.N., U. Mo., Columbia, 1976. Staff and charge nurse DePaul Hosp., St. Louis, 1977-78; nurse surg. ICU, Johns Hopkins Hosp., Balt., 1978; nursing coordinator surg. unit Anne Arundel Hosp., Annapolis, Md., 1978-79; staff nurse, then head nurse/nursing supr. DePaul Hosp., St. Louis, 1979-80; asst. dir. nursing, dir. nursing St. Louis Eye Hosp., 1980—. Mem. Am. Soc. Ophthalmic Registered Nurses, Am. Nurses Assn. Lutheran. Home: PO Box 443 Saint Peters MO 63376 Office: 1027 Bellevue Saint Louis MO 63117

MASSEY, DOROTHY BUTLER (MRS. GUY M. MASSEY), accountant; b. LaFayette, Ga.; d. R. Maihue and Cora (Sisemore) Butler; student U. Chattanooga, 1949; LL.B., Atlanta Law Sch., 1957, LL.M., 1958; B.B.A., Ga. State Coll., 1966; m. Guy M. Massey, Feb. 21, 1953. Accountant Gulf Oil Corp., Chattanooga, 1944-53, Crawford and Porter, Atlanta, 1953-54; accountant Baker Audio Assos., 1955-70, sec.-treas., 1955-70, also dir.; accountant Glenkaron Assos., Inc., 1955-68, sec.-treas., 1957-68; pres. Massey Co., 1971—, also dir.; pres. Profl. Credit Bur., Inc., 1977—; real estate agt. Shotz Assos. Mem. Am. Soc. Women Accountants (dir.), Ga. Soc. C.P.A.'s, Notaries Pub. Assn., Bus. and Profl. Women, Kappa Delta. Home: 1534 Peachtree Battle Ave NW Atlanta GA 30327

MASSEY, JEFFIE JANETTE, lawyer; b. Corpus Christi, Feb. 2, 1954; d. Owen Quincy and Lucille (Stokes) M.; B.A., So. Meth. U., 1974, J.D., 1977. Admitted to Tex. bar, 1977; individual practice law, Dallas, 1977-80; with Office of Spl. Counsel, Dept. Energy, 1980—; asso. firm William T. Knox, Dallas, 1979. Mem. Tex. Criminal Def. Lawyers Assn., Dallas County Criminal Bar Assn., Tex. Young Lawyers Assn., Dallas Assn. Young Lawyers. Office: 1341 W Mockingbird Ln Dallas TX 75247

MASSEY, PAMELA RAND, phys. therapist; b. Augusta, Maine, Mar. 6, 1946; d. Ernest Glenwood and Virginia Laird (Taylor) Harris; B.S., Boston U., 1968; M.S., U. Pitts., 1977; m. Michael J. Massey, Oct. 13, 1979. Phys. therapist Knox County Gen. Hosp., Rockland, Maine, 1968-69; chief phys. therapy dept. Akron (Ohio) Gen. Med. Center, 1970-74; cons. phys. therapist South Hills Home Health Agy., Pitts., 1974; ednl. supr. Western Pa. Arthritis Project, Pitts., 1974-77; cons. phys. therapist Episcopal Ch. Nursing Home, Pitts., 1975—; dir. edn., dept. comprehensive medicine and rehab. St. Margaret Meml. Hosp., Pitts., 1977—. Bd. dirs. Concept Care Inc., 1978—. Arthritis Found. fellow, 1975-77. Mem. Am. Phys. Therapy Assn., Am. Hosp. Assn., Pa. Phys. Therapy Assn., Arthritis Found. Contbr. articles to profl. mags. Home: 5750 Kentucky Ave Pittsburgh PA 15232 Office: Dept Comprehensive Medicine and Rehabilitation 265 46th St Pittsburgh PA 15201

MASSEY, PHYLLIS STARR, home economist; b. Hawthorne, Calif., Nov. 5, 1946; d. Herschal Charleston and Anna Mae (Haskins) Starr; student U. Calif., Davis, 1964-66; B.A., Calif. State U., Long Beach, 1968; postgrad. in bus. adminstrn. U. So. Calif.; m. Christopher Patrick Massey, Apr. 22, 1967; children—Steven Thomas, Jeffrey David. Consumer affairs rep. Ralphs Grocery Co., Los Angeles, 1968-71; sales coordinator Waste King Universal, Los Angeles, 1972-74; divisional sales mgr. Frigidaire Sales Corp., Los Angeles, 1974-76; mgr. home econs. microwave oven mktg. Toshiba Am., Inc., Los Angeles, 1976-77, mgr. consumer mktg., Los Angeles, 1977-81, product mgr., 1982—; public speaker. Mem. Am. Home Econs. Assn., Home Economists in Bus., Soc. Consumer Affairs Profls., Elec. Women's Round Table. Republican. Author: Everyday Microwave Cooking for Everyday Cooks, 1978. Home: 10922 Bent Tree Santa Ana CA 92705 Office: 19500 S Vermont Ave Torrance CA 90502

MASSEY, W(ILMET) ANNETTE, nurse; b. Big Chimney, W.Va., June 30, 1920; d. Robert Lee and Twila Augusta (Pringle) M.; student Morris Harvey Coll., 1938-39; R.N., Phila. Gen. Hosp., 1943; B.S. in Edn., U. Pa., 1948; M.S. in Nursing, Yale U., 1959. Nurse cadet instr. U.S. Cadet Nurse Corps, Huntington (W.Va.) Meml. Hosp., 1943-45; nurse instr. St. Mary's Sch. Nursing, Huntington, 1948-51; WHO nurse cons. Govt. Ceylon, 1951-55; staff nurse instr. VA Hosp., Ft. Thomas, Ky., 1955-57; asst. prof. nursing Brigham Young U., Provo, Utah, 1959-61; asso. prof. nursing W.Va. U., Morgantown, 1961—, chmn. dept. psychiat. nursing, 1968-72; cons. Appalachian Regional Hosp., Beckley, W.Va., W.Va. Dept. Mental Health, Charleston, Valley Community Mental Health Center, Kingwood, W.Va.; group leader med.-nursing group to India, Expt. Internat. Living, Brattleboro, Vt., 1965. Mem. Appalachian Trail, Morgantown Hospice. NIMH grantee, 1964-75. Mem. Am. Nurses Assn., League Nursing, Am. Orthopsychiat. Assn., Internat. Transactional Analysis Assn., Am. Counseling Assn. (dir. 1981-82, v.p. 1982), Am. Soc. Profl. and Exec. Women, Tarrytown Group, Nat. Registry Psychiat. Nurse Specialists (edn. and resources com.), Internat. Acad. Cancer Counselors and Cons., Nat. Alliance Family Life, Inc. (founding), AAUP, Nat. Hist. Soc., Hastings Center, Nat. Wildlife Fedn., Smithsonian Assos., Phila. Gen. Hosp. Sch. Nursing Alumni, U. Pa., Yale U., W.Va. U. Sch. Nursing (hon.) alumni assns., Sigma Theta Tau. Republican. Methodist. Club: Alpine Lake Recreation Community (Terra Alta, W.Va.). Home: 432 Western Ave Morgantown WV 26505 Office: WVa U Sch Nursing Med Center Morgantown WV 26505

MASSINGILL, PENNY ANN, nurse; b. Waco, Tex., July 29, 1953; d. Walter Thomas and Imogene (Curry) Spencer; A.S., McLennan Community Coll., 1973; m. Lynn Massingill, Dec. 9, 1972; 1 son, Gavin Lynn. Nurse, Coryell Meml. Hosp., Gatesville, Tex., 1973-74, head nurse, 1974-76, critical care supr., 1976-79, infectious control nurse, 1979—, clin. coordinator, 1979, dir. quality assurance, 1979—. Mem. Tex. Hosp. Assn., Tex. Soc. Infection Control Practitioners, Soc. Quality Assurance Profls. Tex., Nat. Assn. Quality Assurance Profls. Mem. Ch. of Christ. Club: Gatesville Country. Home: Route 5 Box 498 Gatesville TX 76528 Office: PO Box 659 Gatesville TX 76528

MASTERS, MARGERY MAY, civic worker; b. Sheridan, Wyo., Nov. 6, 1909; d. Homer H. and Linnie A. (Alden) Loucks; m. Leonard E. Masters, June 29, 1932; children—Richard Thomas, Marcia Lynn. Tchr. elem. schs., Dayton, Wyo., 1929-35. Mem. Sheridan County (Wyo.) Republican Central Com., 1933—; pres. Sheridan County Meml. Hosp. Aux., 1964-47. Mem. D.A.R. (past regent Sheridan chpt., state regent 1979—). Methodist. Clubs: Wyo. State Cow-Belles (past pres.), Eastern Star (past pres.). Home: Box 107 Ranchester WY 82839

MASTERTON, NANCY NYE, state legislator; b. Newton, Mass., Nov. 28, 1930; d. Harold Edward and Mabel Evelyn (Roberts) Nye; B.A. in English Lit. and Lang., Boston U., 1952; postgrad. U. Maine, 1964-65; m. Robert R. Masterton, Jr., May 23, 1953; children—Peter R., Laurie. Engaged in retail advt. bus., 1952-53, 55-56; mem. Maine Ho. of Reps., 1976—, Maine Task Force on State Govt. Reorgn., 1967-69, Gov.'s Commn. on Senate Reapportionment, 1971; chmn. House Apportionment Commn., 1971. Bd. dirs. Portland (Maine) YWCA, 1963-71; pres. Portland area LWV, 1965-67, Maine LWV, 1971-73; mem. Cape Elizabeth (Maine) Planning Bd., 1973-76. Mem. LWV, Maine Audubon Soc., Natural Resources Council, Maine Hist. Soc. Republican. Author: How We Govern; The Law and the Land. Home: 36 Delano Park Cape Elizabeth ME 04107 Office: State House Augusta ME 04333

MASTRIA, MARIE ANTOINETTE, clin. psychologist; b. Jersey City, June 24, 1944; d. Ernest and Rose (Marmora) M.; B.A., Gonzaga U., 1966; M.S., Eastern Wash. U., 1968; Ph.D., U. So. Miss., 1975. Acting clin. dir. Alcoholism Rehab. Center, Eastern Miss. State Hosp., 1974-75; faculty Jackson (Miss.) State U., 1975-79; asst. prof., dir. behavioral medicine consultation service U. Miss., Med. Sch., Jackson, 1975-79; pvt. practice Behavior Therapy Assos., Jersey City, 1979—; cons. Miss. Rape Crisis Service, 1975-79; mem. nat. task force on rape NOW, 1975-76. Mem. Am. Psychol. Assn., Assn. Advancement of Behavior Therapy, Soc. Behavioral Medicine, N.J. Psychol. Assn., NOW. Roman Catholic. Author: (with Peter Miller) Alternatives to Alcohol Abuse, 1977; contbr. chpts. to books. Office: 627 Summit Ave Jersey City NJ 07306

MASZKIEWICZ, RUTH AGNES, nurse, univ. adminstr.; b. Pitts., July 24, 1928; d. Sylvester Patrick and Alvina Ann (Munch) Conlogue; nursing diploma Braddock Gen. Hosp., Pitts., 1950; B.S. in Nursing Edn., Duquesne U., 1954, M.Ed., 1969; Ph.D., U. Pitts., 1977; m. Steve J. Maszkiewicz, Feb. 2, 1954 (dec.); children—Stephen, Valli, Daniel, Mark, Suzanne, Amy. Staff nurse Braddock Gen. Hosp., Pitts., 1950; asst. head nurse Montefiore Hosp., Pitts., 1951, head nurse, 1952-54, supr. nursing, 1955; pvt. practice nursing, Pitts., 1956-66; instr. nursing I, Presbyn.-Univ. Hosp., Pitts., 1967, instr. II, 1968, instr. III, chmn. dept. nursing, 1968-72; instr. nursing U. Pitts., 1972-73, asst. prof. nursing, 1973-77, assoc. prof., dir. grad. program med.-surg. nursing, 1978—; field dir. Appalachian Health Team Project, Ky., 1975-76, mem. fundraising and med. supplies com., Pitts., 1977-78; educator com. long-range planning Gateway Sch. Dist., 1981-82; chmn. Commn. on Nursing, Pitts., 1974-75. Mem. Am. Assn. Critical Care Nurses, Am. Nurses Assn., Internat. History Nursing Soc., Nat. League Nursing, Pa. Nurses Assn., Carroll F. Reynolds Hist. Soc., Sigma Theta Tau (Leadership in Nursing Edn. award 1981), Alpha Tau Delta, Phi Delta Gamma. Democrat. Roman Catholic. Author: The Presbyterian Hospital of Pittsburgh: A Critical Analysis of its Early History, 1893-1927; The Continuing Heritage of a Hospital that Cares: Presbyterian-University Hospital of Pittsburgh, 1928 to the mid '70's. Office: Victoria Hall Rm 367 U Pitts Victoria Way Pittsburgh PA 15261

MATCHETTE, PHYLLIS LEE, editor; b. Dodge City, Kans., Dec. 24, 1921; d. James Edward and Rose Mae (McMillan) Collier; A.B. in Journalism, U. Kans., 1943; m. Robert Clarke Matchette, Dec. 4, 1943; children—Marta Susan, James Michael. Reporter, Dodge City Daily Globe, 1944; tchr. English, Dodge City Jr. High Sch., 1944-45; asst. instr. Coll. Liberal Arts, U. Kans., Lawrence, 1945-47; dir. Christian edn. Southminster United Presbyn. Ch., Prairie Village, Kans., 1963-65; editor publs., dir. communications, supr. in-plant printing Village United Presbyn. Ch., Prairie Village, 1965—. Hon. mem. Commn. of Ecumenical Mission and Relations, United Presbyn. Ch., U.S.A.; ordained elder Village United Presbyn. Ch., 1964. Mem. Women in Communications, Kans. U. Dames (pres. 1946), Kansas City Young Matrons, Alpha Chi Omega (pres. edn. found. Phi chpt. 1951). Republican. Club: Order of Eastern Star. Home: 7405 El Monte Rd Prairie Village KS 66208 Office: 6641 Mission Rd Prairie Village KS 66208

MATECHAK-BLACK, TESSIE, nursing adminstr., educator; b. Peckville, Pa., Mar. 19, 1926; d. Wasil and Anna (Horbal) Matechak; A.A. (scholarship), Keystone Jr. Coll., 1947; diploma nursing (scholarship) Sinai Hosp., Md., 1953; B.S. in Nursing, Johns Hopkins U., 1962; M.S. in Nursing, U. Md., 1970; m. James Franklin Black, Jan. 27, 1974. Staff nurse Sinai Hosp., Balt., 1953-54, instr. med.-surg. nursing, 1959-67, asst. dir. inservice edn., 1967-70; head nurse Johns Hopkins Hosp., Balt., 1954-59, asst. instr. emergency service, 1956-56; asso. dir. patient care services Balt. City Hosp., 1970-71; dir. nursing services Bon Secours Hosp., Balt., 1971-73; asso. prof. nursing U. Md., Balt., 1971-73; dir. nursing service Taylor Manor Hosp., Ellicott City, Md., 1974-75; asso. dir. nursing service King Faisal Specialist Hosp., Saudia Arabia, 1975, asst. adminstr. nursing, 1975-77; med. surg. clin. specialist Md. Gen. Hosp., Balt., 1977; asst. dir. nursing service Balt. City Hosps., 1978-79, dir. nursing services, 1981—; asst. prof. nursing Community Coll., Balt., 1981—. Sec., VFW Ladies Aux., 1947-48; fund raiser Jewish Charities, 1970-74. Recognition award King Faisal Hosp., 1977. Mem. Am. Nurses Assn., Md. Nurses Assn. (pres. dist. 2 1978-82), Cancer Soc. Md., Am. Bus. Women's Profl. Orgn., Johns Hopkins U. Alumni Assn., Sinai Nurses Alumni (pres. 1973-75), Keystone Jr. Coll. Alumni. Democrat. Greek Catholic. Home: 3619 Lochearn Dr Baltimore MD 21207 Office: Community College of Baltimore Baltimore MD 21215

MATES-BENTON, KATHIE ANN, nurse; b. Greensburg, Pa., July 27, 1952; d. John Andrew and Ruth Elizabeth (Shrader) Mates; B.S.N., U. Pitts., 1975; m. James G. Benton, Jr., Dec. 18, 1976; 1 son, Michael Thomas. Staff nurse Eye & Ear Hosp., Pitts., 1975-77; staff nurse Carson-Tahoe Hosp., Carson City, Nev., 1977, night supr., 1977-79, clin. coordinator surg. floor, 1979-80, charge nurse, 1980—. Recipient Award of Clin. Excellence, Surg. Floor Staff, Carson-Tahoe Hosp., 1979—. Mem. Carson-Tahoe Employees' Assn. Methodist. Club: United Meth. Young Adults. Home: PO Box 394 Dayton NV 89403 Office: 1201 N Mountain St 2nd E Carson City NV 89701

MATESICH, SISTER MARY ANDREW, coll. pres.; b. Zanesville, Ohio, May 5, 1939; d. Matthew M. and Margaret (Gonda) M.; B.A., Ohio Dominican Coll., 1962; M.S., U. Calif., Berkeley, 1963, Ph.D., 1966. Joined Dominican Sisters St. Mary of Springs, 1957; tchr. Pitts. Cath. Schs., 1961-62; mem. faculty, chmn. chemistry dept. Ohio Dominican Coll., Columbus, 1965-73, chmn. natural sci. div., 1967-73, exec. v.p., acad. dean, 1973-78, pres., 1978—; bd. mem. Higher Edn. Council Columbus, 1981—, sec.-treas., 1981—; mem. exec. com. Encouraging Responsible Citizenship, Columbus, 1978—; mem. undergrad. assessment program policy council Ednl. Testing Service, 1975-80, vice-chmn., 1976-78, chmn., 1978-80. Mem. YWCA Centennial Group, 1981—; hon. trustee Columbus Council World Affairs, 1981—. Woodrow Wilson fellow, 1962, NSF fellow, 1962-65. Mem. Nat. Assn. Ind. Colls. and Univs. (govt. relations adv. commn. 1982—), Council Ind. Colls. (commn. intercultural edn.), Assn. Cath. Colls. and Univs., Ohio Coll. Assn., Ohio Found. Ind. Colls., Assn. Ind. Colls. and Univs. Ohio, Ohio Acad. Sci. Club: Torch (Columbus). Contbr. articles to profl. jours. Office: 1216 Sunbury Rd Columbus OH 43219

MATHER, BETTY BANG, music educator; b. Emporia, Kans., Aug. 7, 1927; d. Read Robinson and Shirley (Smith) Bang; Mus.B., Oberlin Conservatory, 1949; M.A., Tchrs. Coll. Columbia U., 1951; m. Roger Mather, Aug. 3, 1973. Mem. faculty U. Iowa, Iowa City, 1952—, asso. prof. music, 1959-73, prof., 1973—. Harriet Hale Wooley grantee Fondation des Paris, 1958-59; Fulbright travel grantee, 1958-59; Old Gold fellow, summer 1965; faculty devel. fellow, 1975-76; sr. faculty fellow in humanities, 1982. Mem. Nat. Flute Assn. (dir.), Am. Recorder Soc. (editorial bd.), Nat. Assn. Coll. Wind and Percusion Instrs., AAUP. Author: Interpretation of French Music from 1675-1775, 1973; (with Lusocki) Free Ornametation in Woodwind Music, 1976, The Classical Woodwind Cadenza, 1978, The Art of Preluding, 1982; contbr. articles to profl. jours. Home: 308 4th Ave Iowa City IA 52240 Office: Sch Music U Iowa Iowa City IA 52242

MATHER, KATHARINE SELDON KNISKERN, geologist; b. Ithaca, N.Y., Oct. 21, 1916; d. Walter Hamlin and Katharine Emily (Seldon) Kniskern; A.B. in Geology, Bryn Mawr Coll., 1937; student Sch. Higher Studies Johns Hopkins, 1937-40; D.Sc. (hon.) Clarkson Coll., 1978; m. Bryant Mather, Mar. 27, 1940. Research asst. Johns Hopkins Univ., 1939; research asso. Field Mus. Natural History, Chgo., 1940-41; geologist Corps Engrs., U.S. Army, 1942—, assigned Waterways Expt. Sta., Vicksburg, Miss., 1946—, chief petrography and x-ray br., engring. scis. div., concrete lab., 1947-76, chief engring. scis. div., 1976-80; spl. tech. asst., 1980—; mem. Internat. Symposia Chemistry Cement, 1960, 68, 80, 4th Internat. Congress Non-Destructive Testing, 1963; mem., chmn. tech. coms. Transp. Research Bd. Nat. Acad. Scis.-NRC; mem. U.S. panel Tech. Coop. Program. Recipient Exceptional Service award Sec. Army, 1962; Fed. Woman's award, 1963; Disting. Civilian Service award Sec. Def., 1964. Fellow Mineral. Soc. Am., Am. Concrete Inst. (co-recipient Wason Research medal 1955; dir. 1968-71); Life mem. Mineral. Soc. London; mem. Soc. Mining Engrs., ASTM (Stanford E. Thompson award 1952; hon. mem.), Am. Ceramic Soc., Am. Crystallographic Assn., Geochem. Soc., Am. Geophy. Union, Soc. Econ. Paleontologists and Mineralogists, Clay Minerals Soc. (pres. 1973), Glay Sci. Soc. Japan, Alumnae Assn. Bryn Mawr Coll. (past dist. councillor), Sigma Xi. Co-author: (with Bryant Mather) Butterflies of Mississippi, 1958. Bd. dirs., editor Jour. Miss. Acad. Scis., 1960-66. Home: 213 Mt Salus Dr Clinton MS 39056

MATHER, MERRILIE, educator; b. Melrose, Mass., Mar. 28, 1921; d. Thomas Ray and Ruth Evelyn (Hutchins) Mather; A.B., Boston U., 1942, M.A., 1943, Ph.D., 1950. Teaching fellow, Sargent Coll., Boston U., 1943-44; children's room, Dorchester Br., Boston Pub. Library, 1946-47; instr., Morningside Coll., Sioux City, Iowa, 1947-51; prof. English and children's lit. Eastern Ill. U., Charleston, 1951—; speaker, teller children's stories, writer, reader poetry for children. Vol. children's school camp, Ont., Can. Mem. Phi Beta Kappa, Delta Kappa Gamma. Theistic Unitarian-Universalist. Office: English Dept Eastern Ill Univ Charleston IL 61920 *

MATHER, SUSAN HOWARD, physician; b. Salisbury, Md., Feb. 6, 1940; d. Dalton Bailey and Jenny Louise (Whaley) Howard; B.S. with honors, U. Md., 1961, M.D., 1965; M.P.H., Johns Hopkins U., 1978; m. John H. Mather, June 17, 1967; children—Stephen, Alexandra. Instr. ambulatory medicine/student health physician U. Md., 1971-75; dir. adult health and epidemiology Prince George's County, Md., 1975-79; program chief pulmonary and infectious diseases VA, Washington, 1979—. Pres., Am. Lung Assn. Md., 1978-80, Am. Lung Assn. So. Md., 1980-82. Mem. Am. Pub. Health Assn., Am. Thoracic Soc. Presbyterian. Home: 2234 Hindle Ln Bowie MD 20716 Office: VACO 610 Vermont Ave Washington DC 20420

MATHESON, LINDA, social worker; b. Martna, Estonia, Dec. 29, 1918; came to U.S., 1962, naturalized, 1969; d. Endrek and Leena Endrekson; Diploma, Inst. for Social Scis., Tallinn, Estonia, 1944; M.S., Columbia U., 1966, D.S.W., 1974; m. Charles McLaren Matheson, Feb. 5, 1955. Social work officer UN Rehab. and Resettlement Assn., Germany, 1946-48; social worker Victorian Mental Hygiene, Australia, 1955-62; research asst., social work project dir. Arthritis Midway Ho., N.Y.C., 1966-68; researcher Columbia Presbyn. Med. Center, N.Y.C., 1971-75, now social worker; field instr. Columbia U. Sch. Social Work, 1966-68. Family Found. fellow, 1966; NIMH grantee, 1969-72. Mem. Nat. Assn. Social Workers, Am. Security Council, Nat. Wildlife Fedn., Center for Study of Presidency, Smithsonian Assn., English Speaking Union, Alliance Francaise, Columbia U. Alumni Assn. Lutheran. Home: 30-95 29th St Astoria NY 11102

MATHESON, VELDRON ROBISON, musician, educator, writer; b. Montpelier, Idaho, Apr. 15, 1907; d. Robert Lewis and Ellen Ashley Robison; B.A., U. Utah, 1927; postgrad. Northwestern U., 1958; m. Leslie Royal Brown Matheson, Sept. 2, 1927; children—Joan Ellen Matheson Stevens, John Scott. Piano tchr., 1924-82; elem. sch. tchr., 1954-72; tchr. Chgo. Mus. Coll., 1951-54; tchr. Chgo. Mus. Coll., Roosevelt U., 1954-77; accompanist Chgo. Mormon Choir, Orchestra Hall, 1952, 64, 65, accompanist Handels Oratorio, 1949, 50, 52, 54, 68, 73. Sec. LWV, Skokie-Lincolnwood, Ill., 1979-80. Named Merit Mother of Ill., 1980; NDEA grantee 1965. Mem. NEA (del. conv. 1958), Ill. Fedn. Music Clubs (state sec. 1980-82, 1st dist. pres. 1955-57, recognized in club mag. for achievements 1980), Ill. Edn. Assn., DAR, Chgo. Club Women Organists (sec. 1954). Mormon. Author: The Matheson Clan 1974; The Illustrious Robisons 1976; The Brownes of Beccles 1978; Our Shakespearean Heritage, 1980; Our Neat-Nate Ancestral Lineage, 1980.

MATHEWS, ANN ODONNA, food co. exec.; b. Washington, July 6, 1950; d. Thomas Odon and Kathryn (Augustine) M.; B.S., U. Md., 1972, M.B.A., 1982. Asst. to v.p. consumer programs Giant Food, Washington, 1971, consumer specialist, 1972-74, product safety officer, 1974-75, coordinator consumer program, 1975-76, consumer advisor, 1977—; tchr. U. Md., 1976. Pres. Md. Citizens Consumer Council, 1979-81; bd. mem. Alumni Bd. Coll. Human Ecology, U. Md., 1978-80. Mem. Nat. Consumer League, Soc. Consumer Affairs Profls., AFTRA, Md. Citizens Consumer Council, South Prince George's Bus. and Profl. Women's Club (Young Careerist award 1979). Office: PO Box 1804 Washington DC 20013

MATHEWS, BARBARA EDITH, gynecologist; b. Santa Barbara, Calif., Oct. 5, 1946; d. Joseph Chesley and Pearl (Cieri) Mathews; A.B., U. Calif., 1969; M.D., Tufts U., 1972. Intern, Cottage Hosp., Santa Barbara, 1972-73, Santa Barbara Gen. Hosp., 1972-73; resident in ob-gyn Beth Israel Hosp., Boston, 1973-77; clin. fellow in ob-gyn Harvard U., 1973-76, instr., 1976-77; gynecologist Sansum Med. Clinic, Santa Barbara, 1977—. Bd. dirs. Meml. Rehab. Found., Santa Barbara, Channel City Women's Forum, Santa Barbara; mem. citizen's continuing edn. adv. council Santa Barbara Community Coll. Diplomate Am. Bd. Ob-Gyn. Fellow ACS, Am. Coll. Obstetricians and Gynecologists; mem. AMA, Am. Soc. Colposcopy and Cervical Pathology (dir. 1982—), Harvard U. Alumni Assn., Tri-counties Obstet. and Gynecol. Soc. (pres. 1981-82), Phi Beta Kappa. Clubs: Birnam Wood Golf, Coral Casino Beach and Cabana (Santa Barbara). Author: (with L. Burke) Colposcopy in Clinical Practice, 1977; contbg. author Manual of Ambulatory Surgery, 1982. Home: 2105 Anacapa St Santa Barbara CA 93105 Office: 317 W Pueblo St Santa Barbara CA 93102

MATHEWS, GEORGIE MARGARET MILSTEAD (MRS. GRANT ELSTON MATHEWS), former ednl. adminstr.; b. West Plains, Mo., Mar. 12, 1918; d. Albert and May (Henry) Milstead; student Park Coll., 1935-37; B.A., Lewis and Clark Coll., 1955; M.A., U. Oreg., 1962; m. Grant Elston Mathews, Aug. 28, 1937; 1 dau., Patricia Mae (Mrs. Patricia Walhood). Elementary tchr. Caldwell (Idaho) Pub. Schs., 1951-53, Portland (Oreg.) Sch. Dist. 1, 1953-65; clin. prof. Portland State U., 1965-68; elementary prin. Markham Annex Primary Sch., Portland, 1968-70; area adminstr. Portland Pub. Schs. Area III, 1970-79. Group leader, supr. student tchrs. Clin. Supervision Inst., Portland State U., summer sessions, 1965-70. Mem. Nat., Oreg. assns. for supervision and curriculum devel., Oreg. Elementary Sch. Prins. Assn., Assn. Area and Central Adminstrs., Delta Kappa Gamma. Presbyn. Democrat. Home: Rt 2 Box 412 R Otis OR 97368

MATHEWS, MARGARET CARRYL, accountant; b. Albuquerque, Sept. 14, 1954; d. James Joseph and Catherine Jane (Vogel) Carryl; student Mercer U., 1972-73; A.A., Fla. State U., 1974, student, 1974-75; B.B.A., U. N. Fla., 1976; m. Donald Galen Mathews, June 2, 1979. Jr. acct. Alexander Grant & Co., C.P.A.s, Orlando, Fla. and Tallahassee, 1976-78; internal auditor Barnett Bank of Jacksonville (Fla.), 1978-79; sr. internal auditor Seaboard Coast Line Industries (now CSX Corp.), Jacksonville, 1979-80; sr. acct. Arthur Andersen & Co., C.P.A.s, Jacksonville, 1980—. Dansforth award for excellence, 1972; C.P.A., Fla.; cert. internal auditor. Mem. Inst. Internal Auditors (chpt. bd. dirs. 1979-81), Acctg. Alumni Assn. of U. N. Fla. (sec. 1981-82), Am. Inst. C.P.A.s, Fla. Inst. C.P.A.s, Am. Woman's Soc. C.P.A.s, Beta Alpha Psi. Office: 1900 Independent Sq 1 Independent Dr Jacksonville FL 32202

MATHEWS, WILMA, public relations specialist; b. Danville, Va., Dec. 23, 1945; d. Clarence Blanchard and Tina Collins (Powell) Kendrick; A.A., Stratford Coll., 1966, B.A., 1970; student East Carolina U., 1966-67, U. Md., European div., 1967-68, Guilford Coll., 1978-80. Asst. editor The Commonwealth Mag., Richmond, Va., 1970-72; news editor The Commercial Appeal, Danville, Va., 1972-73; public relations mgr. Danville (Va.) C. of C., 1973-74; publs. officer Bowman Gray Bapt.

Hosp. Med. Center, Winston-Salem, N.C., 1974-78; sr. public relations specialist Western Electric, 1978-82; mgr. public relations AT&T Internat., Basking Ridge, N.J., 1982—; sr. public relations adv. N.C. Epilepsy Info. Service, 1979-80. Mem. Danville Bicentennial Commn., 1972-74; bd. dirs. Nat. Tobacco-Textile Mus., 1973-74; mem. Danville City Beautiful Com., 1973-74. Mem. Danville Hist. Soc. (dir. 1973-74), N.C. Zool. Soc., Smithsonian Instn., Internat. TV Assn. (sec. N.C. chpt. 1979-80), Nat. Assn. Female Execs., Internat. Assn. Bus. Communicators (dir. 1978-81, pres. N.C. chpt. 1977, 78), Stratford Coll. Alumni Assn. Democrat. Baptist. Club: Internat. Order Job's Daus. Home: 28 Colony Ct New Providence NJ 07974 Office: PO Box 7000 Basking Ridge NJ 07920

MATHEWS-ROTH, MICHELINE MARY, physician; b. Mineola, N.Y., July 26, 1934; d. John Francis and Micheline Genevieve (Doguereau) Mathews; B.S. magna cum laude, Coll. St. Elizabeth, Convent Station, N.J., 1956; M.D. with honors in microbiology (Borden award 1961), N.Y.U., 1961; m. Robert Steele Roth, May 13, 1966; 1 son, John Doguereau. Intern, fellow in pathology Boston City Hosp., 1962-63; mem. research staff Harvard U. Med. Sch., 1965—, prin. research assoc. in medicine, 1975—; asst. physician med. microbiology Boston City Hosp., 1973-74; jr. assoc. in medicine Peter Bent Brigham div. Brigham's Women's Hosps., Boston, 1977—. Bd. dirs. Peabody-Mason Music Found. NIH research grantee. Diplomate Nat. Bd. Med. Examiners. Mem. Am. Soc. Clin. Investigation, Am. Fedn. Clin. Research, Am. Soc. Microbiology, Am. Soc. Photobiology. Author numerous articles in field. Assoc. editor Photochemistry and Photobiology. Office: Channing Lab 180 Longwood Ave Boston MA 02115

MATHIAS, BETTY JANE, real estate investment co. exec., communications cons.; b. East Ely, Nev., Oct. 22, 1923; d. Royal F. and Dollie B. (Bowman) M.; student Merritt Bus. Sch., 1941, 42, San Francisco State U., 1941-42; 1 dau., Dona Bett. Asst. publicity dir. Oakland (Calif.) Area War Chest and Community Chest, 1943-46; various positions in public relations Am. Legion, Oakland, 1946-47; asst. to public relations dir. Central Bank of Oakland, 1947-49; public relations dir. East Bay chpt. of Nat. Safety Council, 1949-51; propr., mgr. Mathias Public Relations Agy., Oakland, 1951-60; gen. assignment reporter and teen news editor Daily Rev., Hayward, Calif., 1960-62; free lance public relations and writing, Oakland, 1962-66, 67-69; dir. corp. communications Systech Fin. Corp., Walnut Creek, Calif., 1969-71; v.p. corp. communications Consol. Capital companies, Oakland, 1972-79, v.p. community affairs, Emeryville, Calif., 1981—; v.p., dir. Consol. Capital Realty Services, Inc., Oakland, 1973-77; v.p., dir. Centennial Adv. Corp., Oakland, 1976-77; communications cons., 1979—; bd. dirs. Oakland YWCA, 1944-45, ARC, Oakland, So. Alameda County chpt., 1967-69, Family House, Children's Hosp. Med. Center No. Calif., 1982—; adult and publs. adv. Internat. Order of the Rainbow for Girls, 1953-78; communications arts adv. com. Ohlone (Calif.) Coll., 1979—, chmn., 1982; pres. San Francisco Bay Area chpt. Nat. Reyes Syndrome Found., 1981—. Recipient Grand Cross of Color award Internat. Order of Rainbow for Girls, 1955. Mem. Women in Communications (dir. 1979—), Nat. Assn. of Real Estate Editors, East Bay Press Club, East Bay Women's Press Club (pres. 1960-61). Club: Order Eastern Star (publicity chmn. Calif. state 1955). Editor East Bay Mag., 1966-67, Concepts, 1979—. Office: 1900 Powell St Suite 1000 Emeryville CA 94608

MATHIAS, KATHRYN MARIE ERB, former assn. exec.; b. Altoona, Pa., Jan. 23, 1954; d. John Daniel and Virginia Mae (Eagan) Erb; student Beckley (W.Va.) Jr. Coll., 1971-72; B.S.W., W.Va. U., 1975; m. Thomas P. Mathias. Field dir. Talus Rock council Girl Scouts U.S.A., Johnstown, Pa., 1975-81. Mem. Blair County Health and Welfare Council, rec. sec., 1978-79; bd. dirs. Blair County Mental Health Assn.; active Blair County Republican Party. Mem. Nat. Assn. Social Workers, W.Va. Alumni Assn., Hollidaysburg Area C. of C. Lutheran (Sunday sch. tchr.). Clubs: Blair County Soroptimists, Hollidaysburg Women's. Home: 1105 Allegheny St Hollidaysburg PA 16648 Office: Penn Alto Hotel Altoona PA 16602

MATHIESEN, ANNA PAULINE, social worker; b. Carroll, Iowa, Apr. 28, 1932; d. Matthew Raymond and Eileen Merceda (Murray) Murtogh; B.S., Creighton U., 1963; m. R.J. Mathiesen, Feb. 16, 1952; children—Roberta J. Mathiesen Behm, R.J., Raymond Joseph. Tchr., St. Peter's Sch., Omaha, 1964; with Douglas County Social Services, Omaha, 1966—, social services supr., 1970—, unit mgr. income maintenance, 1976—. Mem. Nat. Assn. Social Workers, Nebr. Welfare Assn. Roman Catholic. Home: 3564 Poppleton Ave Omaha NE 68105 Office: 1909 Burt St Omaha NE 68102

MATHIESON, MADELYN LOUISE, accountant; b. Alliance, Nebr., Sept. 22, 1913; d. Peter John and Anna Mary (McQuay) Long; student Helena Bus. Coll., 1932, Kinman Bus. U., 1938; m. William P. Mathieson, Apr. 10, 1948; children—Richard J., Janet Sharon. Personnel supr. Kaiser Co., Inc., Vancouver, Wash., 1940-45; accountant Jack Carr Flying Service, Anchorage, 1947-50; radio operator, asst. agent Alaska Airlines, Inc., Bethel, 1950-51; sec., treas., acct. Hohn Plumbing & Heating Co., Inc., Anchorage, 1951-63; acct. Glass, Sash & Door Supply Co., Inc., Anchorage, 1964-70; corporate sec., comptroller C.R. Lewis Co., Inc., Anchorage, 1970—. Mem. Nat. Assn. Women in Construction, Bus. and Profl. Womens Club. Republican. Club: Quota. Home: PO Box 511 Eagle River AK 99577 Office: C R Lewis Co Inc 1500 Post Rd Anchorage AK 99501

MATHIS, BEVERLY TAYLOR, lectr. service and tourist attraction mgmt. co. exec.; b. Pauls Valley, Okla., Apr. 2, 1920; d. Herbert John and Gloria Josephine (Forbrich) Taylor; B.S., Northwestern U., 1942; m. Allen Washington Mathis, Jr., Oct. 26, 1942; children—Caryl Lynn, Beverly Gayle, Allen Washington. Freelance radio-TV actress, model, 1942-49; dramatic programs and book reviews for corp., social and assn. meetings in U.S. and Europe, 1942—; speech coach profl. speakers, Montgomery, Ala., 1942—; dir., v.p., treas. Mathis & Mathis, Inc., lectr. service and operator DeSoto Caverns, Montgomery, 1975—. Sec., Young Life Com., Montgomery, 1971-72; sec., trustee Christian Workers Found., 1976. Mem. DAR, PEO (pres. chpt. 1973), Zeta Phi Eta, Kappa Alpha Theta. Presbyterian. Clubs: Jr. Thespians, Dogwood Garden. Address: 3577 Bankhead St Montgomery AL 36111

MATHIS, CAROLYN WILLIAMSON, N.C. state senator; b. N.C.; d. Horace Williamson; B.S., U. N.C., Greensboro, 1963; M.Ed., U. N.C., Chapel Hill, 1970; m. Alfred Ray Mathis; 1 dau., Carole Bentley. Spl. educator Charlotte-Mecklenburg Sch. System; mem. N.C. Ho. Reps., 1973-74, 75-76; mem. N.C. Senate, 1976-77, 78-79, 80-81, chmn. ins. com., vice-chmn. Base Budget and Alcohol Beverage Control. Mem. Legis. Research Commn., Commn. on Children with Spl. Needs; chmn. Council on Ednl. Services for Exceptional Children; mem. Sch. Health Edn. Adv. Com., So. Legis. Conf. Com. on Human Resources, Nat. Legis. Conf. Com. on Urban Affairs, Coop. Planning Consortium of Univ. Spl. Educators, New Generation Interagy. Com.; adv. bd. Charlotte Council on Alcoholism; nat. committeewoman N.C. Fedn. Young Republicans; bd. dirs. Goodwill Industries, Inc., Youth Homes, Inc. Mem. Charlotte Council Exceptional Children, Mecklenburg Assn. Retarded Citizens, Charlotte Classroom Tchrs. Assn., Assn. Children with Learning Disabilities, Assn. Community Educators, Exceptional Children's Advocacy Council, N.C. Assn. Educators (past legis. chmn. Charlotte), Charlotte Women's Caucus. Methodist. Office: NC Senate State Capitol Raleigh NC 27602 *

MATHIS, LAURA ANNE, psychologist; b. Oceanside, Calif., July 18, 1948; d. Karl John and Laura Carolyn (McCarty) Palmberg; B.A., Westmont Coll., 1970; M.A., So. Methodist U., 1972; M.A., Rosemead Sch. Psychology, 1974, Ph.D., 1977; M.A., Fuller Theol. Sem., 1979; m. Terry Richard Mathis, June 15, 1974. Psychol. intern Delannay Mental Health Center, Portland, Oreg., 1975-76; psychol. asst. Hacienda Psychol. Services, Hacienda Heights, Calif., 1977-78, staff psychologist, 1979-81; co-dir. Associated Psychologists of Diamond Bar (Calif.), 1981—; speaker on mental health. Lic. clin. psychologist, Calif. Mem. Calif. State Psychol. Assn., Am. Psychol. Assn., Christian Assn. Psychol. Studies, Nat. Register Health Service Providers in Psychology. Republican. Office: 23341 E Golden Springs Dr Suite 100 Diamond Bar CA 91765

MATHIS, MURIEL CANNON, city ofcl.; b. St. George, Utah, July 29, 1925; d. Raymond and Elizabeth Matilda (Truman) Cannon; student public schs., St. George; m. Dayne Andrus Mathis, Aug. 3, 1946; children—Christine Mathis Nielson, Robert Dayne, John G., Pauline Mathis Barney; 1 foster son, Harold Brown. Med. sec. D.A. McGregor Hosp., St. George, 1943-46; with U.S. Forest Service, part-time, 1962-63; sec. South Sevier High Sch., Monroe, Utah, 1963-69; mem. Monroe City Council, 1975—. Vice chmn. Sevier County Republican Com., 1971-77; mem. Utah Rep. Adv. com., 1973-75; sec. Sevier County Rep. Women, 1972-76; chmn. Monroe City Beautification Com., 1974-75; bd. dirs. Sevier County Farm Bur., 1974-76, Tri-County Health Found., 1979—; sec. Sevier Sch. Adv. Com., 1973-74; tchr. various leadership positions Ch. of Jesus Christ of Latter-day Saints. Recipient award for spl. service South Sevier High Sch., 1978. Club: Monroe Literose. Home: 187 E Center St Monroe UT 84754

MATHIS, THELMA ATWOOD, artist; b. Creal Springs, Ill.; d. Hubert L. and Mima (Hutchison) Atwood; B.S., So. Ill. U., 1955, M.F.A., 1957; student Art Students League, 1957-59; m. John A. Mathis, Sept. 1, 1928 (div. 1950); children—John Atwood, Shirley (Mrs. Frank Woosley), James Stevens. One-man shows So. Ill. U., 1957, 59, Sparta (Ill.) Pub. Library, 1960, Art Mart, Inc., St. Louis, 1961, St. Louis Artists Guild, 1962, Midwestern Coll. (Iowa), 1967; two-man show Madison Galleries, N.Y.C., 1963; juried N.Y.C. Center, 1958, 59, Madison Sq. Garden, N.Y.C., 1958, Nat. Old Testament, St. Louis, 1961, 62, Mo. Art Show, St. Louis City Art Mus., 1954, 55, Nat. Arts & Crafts, Wichita, Kans., 1953, 55; instr., asst. prof. art dept. Midwestern Coll., Denison, Iowa, 1965-70. Recipient Grand prize oil and drawing DuQuoin State Fair, 1955, 56, 58, 59. Mem. St. Louis Artists Guild, AAUW, Pi Lambda Theta. Baptist. Home: Box 13 Pinckneyville IL 62274

MATIN, DOROTHY HORWITZ (MRS. HARMON MATIN), pub. relations exec.; b. Chgo., July 29, 1920; d. Harry and Eva (Light) Horwitz; student Wright Jr. Coll., 1937-38, Northwestern U., 1938-41, U. Wash., 1946-48; m. Harmon Matin, May 30, 1942; 1 son, Lowell Reed. Pub. relations Hamrick Evergreen Theatres, Seattle, 1958-61, Nat. Gen. Theatres, Seattle, 1961-66, Sterling Recreation Orgn., Seattle, 1966-70; founder, owner Dorothy Matin Agy., Seattle, sold to Thunder Media, now cons. Active vol. work Brandeis U., Seattle; membership chmn. Seattle Conv. Bur., 1966—; mem. Hadassah, City of Hope; mem. Wash. Com. for Motion Picture Prodn. Mem. Nat. Assn. Press Women, Press Women Wash., Pub. Relations Soc. Am., Nat. Acad. TV Arts and Scis. (bd. govs.), Foremost Women Communications, Nat. Council Jewish Women, Seattle Symphony Women's Assn., Nat. Platform Assn. (com.), Am. Women in Radio and TV, Women in Communications, Variety Club Pacific Northwest. Club: Zonta. Home: 9711 Mercerwood Dr Mercer Island WA 98040 Office: 2148 Waverly Pl N Seattle WA 98109

MATIS, NANCY JOY, speech pathologist; b. Chgo., Sept. 20, 1954; d. Jacob David and Rosalie Bette (Metzger) Matis; B.A., Columbia U., 1976; M.S., Tchrs. Coll., Columbia U., 1978. Staff speech pathologist diagnosis, program planning, treatment of multiply handicapped pre-sch.-age children St. Agnes Hosp., White Plains, N.Y., 1978—. Mem. N.Y. Speech and Hearing Assn., Am. Speech and Hearing Assn. (cert. clin. competence), NE Communication Enhancement Group. Home: 25 Central Park W New York NY 10023 Office: 305-311 North St White Plains NY 10605

MATISTIC, JANICE PESOLA, ednl. adminstr.; b. Tampa, Fla., Sept. 9, 1938; d. Hugo Elmer and Cantzon Jean (Foster) Pesola; B.S., U. Tampa, 1960; M.A., U. South Fla., 1970; doctoral candidate Seton Hall U.; m. Robert Richard Matistic, June 2, 1959; children—Brenda Lee, Karen Sue. Tchr. biology Hillsborough County (Fla.) Pub. Schs., Tampa, 1960-67, guidance counselor, 1967-69, coordinator research and evaluation, 1969-73; dir. testing, program evaluation and planning Summit (N.J.) Pub. Schs., 1973-78; elem. prin. Summit (N.J.) Public Schs., 1978—. NSF scholar, 1962. Mem. Am. Ednl. Research Assn., Assn. Supervision and Curriculum Devel., Nat. Assn. Elem. Prins., Evaluation Research Soc., Am. Personnel and Guidance Assn., Kappa Delta Pi. Republican. Home: 1320 Rahway Rd Scotch Plains NJ 07076 Office: 110 Ashwood Ave Summit NJ 07901

MATLACK, ARDENA LAVONNE, state legislator; b. Carlton, Kans., Dec. 20, 1930; d. Walter D. and Bessie B. (Major) Williams; student Kans. Wesleyan U., 1948-49, Kans. State U., 1949-51, Washburn U., 1955; B.A. cum laude, Wichita State U., 1969; m. Don Matlack, June 10, 1951; children—Lucinda Dawn, Roxanne, Terry Clyde, Rex William, Timothy Alan. Tchr., Carlton Grade Sch., 1948-49; substitute tchr. Clearwater (Kans.) Schs., 1969-74; mem. Kans. Ho. of Reps., 1974—. Democratic precinct committeewoman, 1966-68; mem. Dem. State Com., 1974-78; pres. Kans. State Dem. Club, 1978; chmn. Clearwater March of Dimes, 1980, Clearwater Area United Fund, 1980; project leader 4-H, 1962-71. Recipient Gold Star Legis. award Assn. for legis. action by Rural Mayors, 1981. Mem. Clearwater United Methodist Women (hon. life; pres. 1972), Dist. United Meth. Women (hon. life, dist. coordinator social involvement 1975-76), Gold Key, Mu Phi Epsilon. Clubs: Clearwater Federated Women's Study (pres. 1966-67); Kans. Federated Women's Dem. (Disting. Achievement award 1977), Clearwater Bus. and Profl. Women's, West Side Dem. Home: 615 Elaine St Clearwater KS 67026 Office: State Capitol Bldg Topeka KS 66612

MATLAW, JANE RACHAEL, social worker; b. Hartford, Conn., Aug. 27, 1951; d. Bernard and Doris June (Siegel) M.; A.A., Lasell Jr. Coll., 1971; B.A., Boston U., 1973, M.S.W., 1975. Social worker older adult program United South End Settlements, Boston, 1975-78; social work coordinator positive aging services Mass. Mental Health Center, Boston, 1978-81; chief social worker for community liaison Beth Israel Hosp., Boston, 1981—; vol. counselor/staff Casa Myrna Vasquez, temp. shelter for battered women and their children, 1978-81; bd. dirs. Area II Home Care for Sr. Citizens, Inc., 1977—; guest lectr. Boston U. Sch. Social Work, 1976-80, field instr., 1977-80. Mem. Gerontol. Soc., Mass. Assn. of Older Ams., Boston Soc. for Gerontologic Psychiatry, Nat. Assn. Social Workers, Mass. Fair Share, NOW, Acad. Cert. Social Workers. Home: 44 Page Rd Newtonville MA 02160 Office: Beth Israel Hosp Dept Social Service 330 Brookline Ave Boston MA 02215

MATSA, LOULA ZACHAROULA, social services adminstr.; b. Piraeus, Greece, Apr. 16, 1935; came to U.S., 1952, naturalized 1962; d. Eleftherios Georgiou and Ourania E. (Fraguiskopoulou) Papoulias; student Pierce Coll., Athens, Greece, 1948-52; B.A., Rockford Coll., 1953; M.A., U. Chgo., 1955; m. Ilco S. Matsa, Nov. 27, 1953; 1 son, Aristotle Ricky. Marital counselor Family Soc. Cambridge, Mass., 1955-56; chief unit II, social service Queen's (N.Y.) Children's Psychiat. Center, 1961-74; dir. social services, supr.-coordinator family care program Hudson River Psychiat. Center, Poughkeepsie, N.Y., 1974—; field instr. Adelphi and Fordham univs., 1969—. Fulbright Exchange student, 1952-53; Talcott scholar, 1953-55. Mem. Internat. Platform Assn., Internat. Council on Social Welfare, Nat. Assn. Social Workers, Assn. Cert. Social Workers, Civil Service Employees Assn., Pierce Coll. Alumni Assn. Democrat. Greek Orthodox. Contbr. articles to profl. jours.; instrumental in state policy changes in treatment and court representation of emtionally disturbed and mentally ill. Home: 81-11 45th Ave Elmhurst NY 11373 Office: Hudson River Psychiat Center Branch B Poughkeepsie NY 12601

MATSON, FRANCES SHOBER, social worker; b. Cin., Mar. 21, 1921; d. Frank Lyford and Florence Leone (Bridgeford) Shober; student U. Cin., 1939-41, B.A., 1951, postgrad., 1951-52; M.S.W., U. Calif., 1956; m. John Alan Matson, Dec. 2, 1942 (dec.). Councillor, County of San Mateo, 1956-57; therapist, supr. Center for Treatment and Edn. on Alcoholism, Oakland, Calif., 1957-63; pvt. practice social worker, Berkeley, Calif., 1960-64; supr. dept. social service County of Marin, Calif., 1966; psychotherapist Marin Inst., 1966-70, Oaknoll Naval Hosp., 1969; public health social worker Dept. Health County of Contra Costa (Calif.), 1972; psychotherapist Day Care Center for Schizophrenics, Contra Costa County Med. Services, 1972-74; dir. Martinez Mental Health Clinic, Contra Costa County Med. Services, 1974-81; psychotherapist, coordinator adult outpatient services, edn., group therapy Contra Costa County Mental Health Center, 1982—. Lic. clin. social worker. Mem. Nat. Assn. Social Workers, Acad. Cert. Social Workers, Internat. Transactional Analysis Assn., Marin Assn. Mental Health. Home: Box 2073 Martinez CA 94553 Office: 2500 Alhambra St Martinez CA 94553

MATSON, JOANNE SANDRA, educator, social worker; b. St. Paul, July 23, 1940; d. Rosser Holloway and Jessie Louise (Baldwin) Matson; B.A. cum laude, U. Minn., 1962, M.S.W., 1967; student Lake Forest Coll., 1958-60. With disaster aid to mil. families ARC, Brooke Army Med. Center, San Antonio, also St. Paul chpt. ARC, also Ky. floods, 1962-65; social worker U. Minn. Hosps., 1965-67, State of Calif., Sacramento, 1967-70; tchr. pvt. schs., Miami, Fla., 1970-73, Lee County Schs., Riverdale, 1973, Riverdale High Sch., Ft. Myers, Fla., 1973-76, North Ft. Myers High Sch., 1976—; sales agt. Rosinus Realty, Cape Coral, Fla. Chmn. bd. Watersways Civic Assn., 1981—. Recipient spl. award DAR, 1958; lic. real estate asso., Fla.; rank II postgrad. teaching cert., Fla.; cert. jr. coll. math., social studies, sociology, vis. tchr. Mem. Fla. Bd. Realtors of Cape Coral and Ft. Myers, Cape Coral Bd. Realtors, U. Minn. Alumni Assn., VFW Aux., Internat. Platform Assn., DAR, Tchrs. Assn. Lee County, AAUW, Sigma Kappa, Nat. Assn. Social Workers. Clubs: Sunshine Singles (dir.), R-R Investment. Address: 1729 Inlet Dr Waterway Estates North Fort Myer FL 33903

MATSUMOTO, SHIGEMI, soprano, educator; b. Denver; d. Moriichi and Suki Matsumoto; B.A. in Mus. Performance, Calif. State U., Northridge; m. Martin J. Stark, Apr. 27, 1967. Performances with opera companies in Brussels, San Francisco, Phila., Portland, Oreg., Wolf Trap, Va., Kansas City, Mo., Tucson, San Antonio, Toledo/Dayton, Ohio, Augusta, Ga., Little Rock, Lake George, N.Y., also Spring Opera Theatre; with symphonies in Antwerp, Belgium, Lourdes, France, Mexico City, San Francisco, Mpls., Pitts., St. Louis, Houston, Denver, New Orleans, Memphis and Wichita, other cities; numerous internat. recitals including Tokyo, Washington, Chgo., Los Angeles, San Francisco, Houston, Vancouver, B.C., Kansas City, San Antonio, Milw.; lectr. demonstrations, master classes coll. campuses; guest artist, lectr. Can. Fedn. Music Tchrs.; guest soloist 25th Anniversary Celebration Founding UN, 1970. Recipient 1st prize Western Regional Met. Opera Auditions, 1967; grand winner San Francisco Nat. Opera Auditions, 1968; award winner Geneva Internat. Music Competitions, 1971; grantee Nat. Opera Inst., Internat. Inst. Edn., Los Angeles Bur. Music; named Japanese Woman of Year in So. Calif., Japanese-Am. Soc., 1969-70. Mem. Am. Guild Mus. Artists. Republican. Presbyterian. Home: 60 Riverside Dr Apt 1D New York NY 10024 also 18142 Arminta St Reseda CA 91335 Office: Care Miss Nelly Walter Columbia Artists Mgmt 165 W 57th St New York NY 10019

MATSUMURA, VERA YOSHI, pianist; b. Oakland, Calif.; d. Naojiro and Aguri Tanaka; B.A. in Piano Pedagogy, Coll. of Holy Names, Oakland, 1938; pvt. studies with F. Moss, M. Shapiro, L. Kreutzer, P. Jarrett; m. Jiro Matsumura, Aug. 8, 1942; 1 son, Kenneth N. Staff mem., pianist Radio Sta. KROW, Oakland, 1938-39; numerous concert performances in Far East (Japan, Thailand), 1940—; numerous teaching appointments, 1940—; dir. Internat. Music Council, Berkeley, Calif., 1969—. Named to Hall of Fame, Piano Guild, 1968. Mem. Music Tchrs. Nat. Assn., Music Tchrs. Assn. Calif., Internat. Platform Assn., Alpha Phi Mu. Methodist. Home: 2 Claremont Crescent Berkeley CA 94705

MATT, ANN MARIE CHRISTENE, med. diagnostic co. exec.; b. Pittston, Pa., May 25, 1953; d. Andrew Joseph and Sophie Theresa (Loncala) M.; B.A. in Biology, Johns Hopkins U., 1975, M.S. in Communicative Disorders, 1976; m. Willis C. Maddrey, Apr. 18, 1981; 1 son, Thomas Blake. Mem. pharm. sales staff E.R. Squibb & Sons, Princeton, N.J., 1975-78; mktg. specialist Ortho Diagnostics, Raritan, N.J., 1978-80; clin. specialist Boehringer Mannheim Diagnostics, Houston, 1981—; tchr. ednl. seminars for hosps. Bd. dirs. Balt. Women's Health Coalition; mem. Balt. Assn. Retarded Citizens. Mem. Am. Assn. Clin. Chemistry, Nat. Assn. Female Execs., NOW, Assn. Profl. and Exec. Women, Am. Bus. Assn., Woman's Med. Study Research Group. Roman Catholic.

MATTAUSCH, ELEANOR MAE, union ofcl., owner orchard; b. Chgo., May 9, 1931; d. Gary and Nellie (Lindemulder) M.; A.A. in Journalism, Chgo. City Jr. Coll., 1950; B.A. in Mass Communications, Ariz. State U., 1963; M.A. in Social Sci., U. N. Colo., 1976; m. Armand J. Mattausch, Sept. 20, 1951; children—Susan Mattausch Bleakmore, Gary, Laura Mattausch Bosseler. Newswriter, San Pedro Valley News-Sun, Benson, Ariz., 1963-65; newspaper editor, press chief U.S. Army, Ft. Huachuca, Ariz., 1966-72, tech. writer, 1972-80; co-owner Teran Pecan Orchards, Benson, 1972—; pres. Am. Fedn. Govt. Employees, Ft. Huachuca, 1977—; tchr. journalism; speaker on labor mgmt. Bd. dirs. San Pedro Valley (Ariz.) Hosp. Dist., Benson Hosp., 1964-74. Mem. Ariz. Press Women (dist. pres. 1980—), Southwestern Pecan Growers Assn. Democrat. Contbr. numerous articles to newspapers. Home: Rt 1 Box 42F Benson AZ 85602

MATTE, JEANINE LOUISE, lawyer; b. Ridgewood, N.J., Apr. 18, 1949; d. Lucien J. and Anne T. M.; B.S., Va. Poly. Inst., 1971; J.D., U. N.C., 1974. Admitted to N.C. bar, 1974, D.C. bar, 1978, U.S. Supreme Ct. bar, 1978; atty. U.S. Dept. Agr., Washington, 1975-80; sr. atty. U.S. Dept. Energy, Washington, 1980-82, U.S. Synthetic Fuels Corp., Washington, 1982—. Recipient Exceptional Service award U.S. Dept. Energy, 1982. Mem. Am. Bar Assn. (synthetic fuels com.), Fed. Bar Assn., D.C. Bar Assn., N.C. Bar Assn., Mortar Bd. Home: 4811 A-1 S 30th St Arlington VA 22206 Office: 2121 K St Washington DC 22206

MATTES, NADINA PALMER, nurse; b. Jersey City, Feb. 28, 1928; d. Irving John and Sarah Kathryn (Bradley) Palmer; student N.J. Coll. for Women, 1944-45; R.N. diploma Hosp. U. Pa., 1949, B.S. in Nursing Edn., U. Pa., 1952; M.A., Marywood Coll., 1973, cert. sch. psychology, 1978; m. Roger Mattes, May 27, 1950; children—Victoria, Philip,

Jonathan, Roger. Staff nurse Hosp. U. Pa., 1949-50; dir. inservice edn. Community Med. Center, Scranton, Pa., 1964-67; founder, coordinator practical nursing Scranton Sch. Dist., 1967-73, Lackawanna County Area Vocat. Tech. Sch., Scranton, 1973—; advisor Edn. Opportunities Consortium; adv. Northeastern Pa. League Lic. Practical Nurses. Committeewoman, Glenburn (Pa.) Democratic Com., 1953-61. Recipient Letitia White award Sch. Nursing, Hosp. U. Pa., 1949, cert. of appreciation Pres. U.S., 1974. Mem. Pa. Nurses Assn. (v.p. Dist. III 1968-69), Nat. Assn. Sch. Psychologists, N.E. Pa. Psychol. Assn., Nat. League Nursing, Nat. Assn. Practical Nursing Edn. and Service, Pa. Vocat. Assn., Vocat. Adminstrs. Pa., Psi Chi. Episcopalian. Clubs: Jr. League Scranton, Lackawanna Assn. Lawyers' Wives. Home: RD 3 Box 391 Dalton PA 19414 Office: 3201 Rockwell Ave Scranton PA 18508

MATTFELD, JACQUELYN PHILLIPS ANDERSON, coll. dean and ofcl.; b. Balt., Oct. 5, 1925; d. David Lindsay and Dorothy (Wheless) Anderson; diploma Peabody Conservatory Music, 1943-47; B.A. magna cum laude, Goucher Coll., 1948; Ph.D., Yale U., 1959; D.H.L., Kalamazoo Coll., 1979, Wagner Coll., 1976, Columbia U.,1976; M.A., Brown U., 1972; LL.D., U. Mass., 1972, Goucher Coll., 1972; m. Victor Henry Mattfeld, Aug. 28, 1949 (div. Aug. 1970); children—Stefanie, Felicity. Dir. fin. aid Radcliffe Coll., 1958-60, asso. dean instrn., also dean of East House, 1960-63; asso. dean student affairs M.I.T., 1963-65; dean Sarah Lawrence Coll., Bronxville, N.Y., 1965-69, prof. music history, 1965-71, provost, dean of faculty, 1969-71; assn. provost, dean faculty, dean acad. affairs, prof. music Brown U., Providence, 1971-76; pres. Barnard Coll., 1976-80; provost, dean faculty Coll. of Charleston (S.C.), 1982—; lectr. dept. music Harvard U., 1960-63; ednl. cons. Kenyon Coll., 1965; cons., assoc. Kirkland Coll., 1965-72; cons. on coedn. Princeton U., 1967-68; mem. project selection com. Nat. Endowment for Humanities, 1970-73, project panel, 1970-74, devel. grant panel, 1974-75, nat. bd. cons., 1976—; mem. New Eng. adv. com. Higher Edn. Resource Service to Women, 1972-76, Mid-Atlantic adv. com., 1976—; mem. Nat. Com. Cultural Resources, 1974-75, Coop. Assessment Exptl. Learning, 1973-76, Conf. Faculty Adminstrv. Mgmt. U. Mich., 1974—. Adv. bd. Assn. Mentally Ill Children of Westchester, 1967-71; ednl. bd. dirs. Coop. Coll. Center, State U. N.Y., 1967-68, 70-71; mem. corp. Cambridge Sch. of Weston, 1970-72; trustee Goucher Coll., 1972—; bd. dirs. Japan Internat. Christian Found., 1966-68, N.Y. Philharm., 1976-77; bd. dirs., pres. bd. trustees Exptl. Center for Visual Edn. Recipient Wilbur Lucius Cros medal Yale U., 1979; Rockefeller fellow Aspen Inst., 1978—. Mem. Am. Council Edn. (commn. leadership devel. 1974-75, commn. acad. affairs 1976—), Am. Conf. Acad. Deans, Eastern Assn. Coll. Deans and Advisers Students (exec. com. 1969-71), Am. Musicol. Soc., Am. Mgmt. Assn. (trustee 1977—), Renaissance Soc., AAUW, Yale U. Council (chmn. com. edn. women 1973—, mem. com. on music 1972—), Phi Beta Kappa. Address: College of Charleston Charleston SC *

MATTHEWS, ANNIE MAE, gas co. exec.; b. Boydell, Ark., Aug. 4, 1916; B.A., U. Ark., Monticello, 1942; m. James M. Matthews, July 10, 1944; children—James M., Jane Matthews Evans. Tchr. elem. sch., Dry Bayou Community, Ashley County, Ark., 1937-40; tchr. high sch. English, Portland, Ark., 1940-43, Dumas, Ark., 1943-44; founder, mgr. Matthews Hobby House, Dumas, 1964-74; with Matthews Inc., Dumas, 1954—, pres., from 1966. Chmn., City Beautification Com., 1981. Mem. Dumas C. of C. (dir. 1980-83). Democrat. Baptist. Club: Ark. Fedn. Garden (2d v.p. 1981—). Home: 930 E Waterman St Dumas AR 71639 Office: Junction Hwys 65 and 54 Dumas AR 71639

MATTHEWS, BARBARA ANN, telecommunications account exec.; b. Columbia, S.C., Oct. 16, 1951; d. William Nathan and Lilly Ruth (Harvey) M.; B.A., U. S.C., 1973, M.B.A., 1976. Public relations dir. United Way, Columbia, 1973-75; S.C. Med. Assn., Columbia, 1975-76; mng. dir. Pi Sigma Epsilon, N.Y.C., 1976-78; account exec. Pacific Telephone Co., Los Angeles 1979—. Mem. Los Angeles Transp. Club, Pi Sigma Epsilon, Delta Nu Alphs. Office: 2020 S Central Ave #260 Compton CA 90220

MATTHEWS, BURNITA SHELTON, judge; b. Burnell, Miss., Dec. 28, 1894; d. Burnell and Lora Drew (Barlow) Shelton; LL.B., George Washington U., (formerly Nat. U.), 1919, LL.M., 1920, LL.D. (hon.), 1950; LL.D. (hon.), Am. U., 1966; m. Percy Ashley Matthews, Apr. 28, 1917. Admitted to D.C., Miss., U.S. Supreme Ct. bars; practice in Washington, 1920; active in securing equal rights for women; formerly mem. faculty Washington Coll. Law; judge U.S. Dist. Ct., D.C., 1949-68, sr. judge, 1968—. Past mem. Com. Experts Women's Work ILO; formerly mem. research com. Inter-Am. Commn. Women; former mem. Nat. Woman's Party. Mem., past 1st v.p. nat. bd. Med. Coll. Pa. (formerly Woman's Med. Coll. Pa.); nat. devel. com. Am. U. Recipient Alumni Achievement award George Washington U., 1968; Distinguished Service award Bar Assn. D.C., 1968. Mem. Am. Bar Assn., Nat. Assn. Women Lawyers (past pres.). Drafted many laws sponsored by Nat. Woman's Party. Home: 5420 Connecticut Ave NW Washington DC 20015 Office: US Courthouse 3d and Constitution Ave NW Washington DC 20001

MATTHEWS, DORIS BOOZER (MRS. CHARLES L. MATTHEWS), educator; b. Lexington, S.C., Aug. 18, 1932; d. Otto Raymond and Ruth (Sox) Boozer; B.S., Newberry Coll., 1952; M.Ed., U. S.C., 1955, advanced cert., 1971, Ph.D., 1972; m. Charles L. Matthews, Aug. 20, 1952; children—Shirley Ruth, Charles Ray, Sylvia Ann. Tchr., Brennen Sch., Columbia, S.C., 1952-64; supr. counseling S.C. State Employment Service, Columbia, 1964-66; counseling supr. and basic edn. specialist S.C. Com. for Tech. Edn., Columbia, 1966-68; instr. elem. edn. U. S.C., Columbia, 1968-72; asst. prof. Coll. of S.C. State Coll., Orangeburg, 1972-75, asso. prof., 1975-79, prof., 1979—; profl. lectr. Chmn., Columbians Youth Com., 1968-72, treas., 1966-72; chmn. Cayce Neighborhood Center, 1967-70. Mem. S.C. Edn. Assn., Assn. Supervision and Curriculum Devel., Employment Counselors Assn., Am., S.C. (pres. 1976-77) vocat. guidance assns., Am., S.C. personnel and guidance assns., Am. Communications and Tech. Assn., AAUP (pres. chpt. 1976-79, pres. S.C. conf. 1981-83), Assn. Tchr. Educators, Assn. for Individually Guided Edn., Am. Vocat. Assn. Phi Delta Kappa (v.p. local chpt. 1978-79, pres. 1979-81). Lutheran (pres. ch. women 1971-74). Clubs: Cayce Womens (pres. 1965-67), Fashion Rose Garden (pres. 1962-64). Contbr. numerous articles to profl. jours. Home: 101 Deliesseline Rd Cayce SC 29033 Office: SC State Coll Orangeburg SC 29117

MATTHEWS, DOROTHEA ELIZABETH, lawyer; b. Englewood, N.J., June 12, 1947; d. John Clark and Dorothea (Kidd) Matthews; A.B., Smith Coll., 1969; J.D., Fordham U., 1974. Admitted to N.Y. State bar; assoc. Reid & Priest, N.Y.C., 1974-82, partner, 1983—. Vice pres. Met. Republican Club; N.Y. County Rep. committeewoman. Mem. ABA. Presbyterian. Club: Smith Coll. Contbr. articles to profl. jours. Office: 40 Wall St New York NY 10005

MATTHEWS, ELAINE LOUISE (MRS. ROBERT THOMAS MATTHEWS), antique dealer; b. East St. Louis, Ill., June 17, 1925; d. Joseph M. and Josephine L. (Quiros) Garcia; student So. Ill. U., 1955-57, St. Louis U., 1958-62; m. Robert Thomas Matthews, Aug. 4, 1945; 1 dau., Elaine Lila (Mrs. Robert J. Kern). Owner, Antiques by Elaine, Belleville, Ill., 1964—; antique show exhibitor, 1965—; tchr. pub. schs., Belleville, 1958-71; instr. Belleville Area Coll., Uptown Center Program for Older Persons. Bd. dirs. Belleville Girl Scouts, 1957-58, neighborhood chmn., 1958-59; bd. dirs. ARC, 1958-59, 1st aid instr., 1958-62. Recipient award NSF, 1963. Mem. Nat. Antique Dealers Assn. Club: Soroptimist (pres. Metro-East (Ill.) club 1972-73, dist. dir. South Central region). Home: Route 3 Box 381A Belleville IL 62221 Office: Antiques by Elaine 510 Freeburg Ave Belleville IL 62221

MATTHEWS, ELIZABETH WOODFIN (MRS. SIDNEY E. MATTHEWS), librarian, educator; b. Ashland, Va., July 30, 1927; d. Edwin Clifton and Elizabeth Frances (Luck) Woodfin; B.A., Randolph Macon Coll., 1948; M.S., U. Ill., 1952; Ph.D., So. Ill. U., 1972; m. Sidney E. Matthews, Dec. 20, 1947; 1 dau., Sarah Elizabeth. Cataloger and librarian Ohio State U., Columbus, 1952-56, 57-59; acting head catalog dept. Battelle Meml. Inst., Columbus, 1956; cataloger, instr. U. Ill., Urbana, 1962-63, vis. lectr., 1964; cataloger Va. Mil. Inst. Library, Lexington, 1963-64; cataloger, instr. So. Ill. U., Carbondale, 1964-67, classroom instr., 1967-70, cataloger-librarian, 1972—, asst. prof., 1972-79, asso. prof., 1979—. Mem. ALA, AAUW, Am. Assn. Law Libraries, Ill. library assns., Phi Kappa Phi, Beta Phi Mu. Contbr. articles to profl. jours., chpt. to book. Home: 811 Skyline Dr Carbondale IL 62901

MATTHEWS, ELSIE CATHERINE SPEARS, lawyer, editor, author; b. Chgo., Aug. 8, 1901; d. Byron Alexander and Catherine (Clark) Spears; A.B., Wheaton (Ill.) Coll., 1923; J.D., Northwestern U. 1926; m. Thomas A. Matthews, June 27, 1925; children—Thomas Alexander, Byron Stewart. Asst. editor, asst. compiler Codes of Ordinances for Ill. communities, 1927-70; asst. editor Current Mcpl. Problems, Callaghan & Co., Chgo., 1959-76, 78—; writer Comments for Dept. Agr., Bur. Land Mgmt. Washington County chmn. Keep Okla. Beautiful, 1970, co-chmn., 1971-72; pres. River Forest (Ill.) Ind. Republican Womens Club, 1940-42; spl. advisor to Congl. adv. com. Recipient cert. of merit Green Country, 1971, Bicentennial award Personalities of South, 1975-76, Golden Anniversary cert. Northwestern U. Law Alumni Assn., 1976; cert. of merit Congl. adv. com. Fellow Internat. Civic Service Soc., Internat. Biog. Soc. (Bronze medallion); mem. Bartlesville C. of C. (anti-litter chmn. 1968-74), Okla. (Johnny Horizon state chmn.), Osage Hills (press and publicity chmn., cert. of merit, chmn. Save the Selenite Crystal Collecting Area), Osage Hills gem and mineral. socs., Rocky Mountain Mineral. Soc. (chmn. conservation and multiple use of public lands), Am. Fedn. Mineral. Socs. (mem. public relations com.), Am. Fedn. Police (contbg.), Smithsonian Assos., Nat. Security Council (charter, nat. adv. bd.), Conservative Caucus, Northwestern U. Alumni Assn., World Peace Through Law Center, World Peace Through Strength, World Peace Through Amity, World Assn. Lawyers (founding), Am.'s Against Union Control of Govt., Nat., Internat. wildlife assns., Sierra Club, Am. Forests Assn., Automobile Club Okla., Washington Legal Found., Nature Conservancy, Gun Owners Am., Citizens Com. for Right to Bear and Keep Arms, Nat. Conservative Polit. Action Com., Ye Old Timers Mineral Club, Stella Woodall Poetry Soc. Internat. Intergalactic Petrology Club (founder, pres.). Presbyn. Clubs: River Forest women's (life mem.); Rolling Rock. Home: 926 Sandstone St Bartlesville OK 74003

MATTHEWS, GAIL THUNBERG, mktg. co. exec.; b. Hartford, Conn., July 29, 1938; d. Harold Einar and Mildred (Wentland) Thunberg; student Boston U., 1958-59; m. Glenn Holbrook Matthews, Aug. 9, 1959; children—Scott Holbrook, Brett Holbrook. Hostess show, copywriter Sta. WJDA, Boston, 1956-58; fashion coordinator Jordan Marsh, Boston, 1958-59, Miller & Rhoades, Richmond, Va., 1959-60, Sage Allen, Hartford, 1960-61; columnist Boston Globe, 1962-63, Hartford Times, 1961-63; free-lance writer, contbr. articles to New Englander mag., Christian Sci. Monitor, Yankee, 1961-65; v.p., treas. Coll. Mktg. Group, Inc., Winchester, Mass., 1968—; corporator Reading Savs. Bank; mem. adv. council Baybank Middlesex. Choral dir. Barrows Sch., Reading; pres. local PTA; chmn. Heart Fund Reading; founder, chmn. Reading chpt. Am. Cancer Soc. Recipient Service to Youth award Reader's Digest, 1962; CAP award 1965; Spl. award Am. Cancer Soc., 1981, 82; Citizenship award Reading Tchrs. Assn., 1980. Author: Hor'doeuvre Cooking, 1966; Gourmet Cooking, 1966; Birthday Fortune Book, 1967; (children's series) The Adventures of a Shihtzu, The Good Luck Puppy, 1980. Office: The Mill 1873 50 Cross St Winchester MA 01890

MATTHEWS, HARRIETT, sculptor, educator; b. Kansas City, Mo., June 21, 1940; d. Francis Holms and Virginia (Daniels) Matthews; B.F.A., U. Ga., 1962, M.F.A., 1964. Vis. instr. art U. Okla., 1964-65; instr. art Colby Coll., Waterville, Maine, 1966-70, asst. prof., 1970-76, asso. prof., 1976—; vis. critic grad. sculpture program U. Pa., 1976; one woman shows at Coll. of Atlantic, Bar Harbor, Maine, 1974, 75, Frost Gulley Gallery, Portland, Maine, 1975, Vanderbilt U., Nashville, 1974, U. Maine, 1977, Hebron (Maine) Acad., 1977, Unity (Maine) Coll., 1978, Treat Gallery, Bates Coll., Lewiston, Maine, 1979, U. So. Maine, Gorham, 1982. Mem. Maine Commn. for Arts and Humanities. Colby Humanities research grantee, 1968, 73, 74, travel grantee, 1971, 76, 78, 81; Colby Mellon grantee, 1981; Ingram Merrill Found. award, 1980-81. Mem. Coll. Art Assn., Women Caucus for Arts. Home: RFD 2 Hinckley Rd Clinton ME 04927 Office: Art Dept Colby Coll Waterville ME 04901

MATTHEWS, LAMOYNE MASON, fgn. service officer; b. Emporia, Va., Aug. 8, 1931; d. Edgar Dallas and Theresa Oliver Mason; A.B., Morgan State Coll., 1951; M.S.W., Howard U., 1961; Ph.D., U. Md., 1976; children—Derrick, Yvette, Kevin. Teaching fellow U. Md., 1973-74; mem. faculty Morgan State U., Balt., 1969-82 asst. dean continuing edn./community outreach, 1978-82; joined Fgn. Service, 1982. Mem. Balt. County Sch. Bd., 1979—. Mem. Nat. Assn. Social Workers, Council on Social Work Edn., Delta Sigma Theta. Home: 209 Suter Rd Catonsville MD 21228 Office: US Dept State Washington DC

MATTHEWS, LINDA LLEWELLYN FINK, profl. assn. adminstr.; b. LaPort, Ind., Oct. 29, 1950; d. Omar Ray and Marianne Denham (Smith) Fink, Jr.; student U. N.C., Greensboro, 1968-70; B.A., George Washington U., 1973; m. Daniel G. Matthews, Oct. 25, 1975; children—Strelka Jamila, Francesca Alina. Admnstrv. asst. African Bibliog. Center, Washington, 1974-75, adminstrv. editor, 1975-79, adminstrv. dir., 1979—; adminstrv. dir. African Devel. Info. Assn. U.S.A., 1981—; treas., bd. dirs. African Communications Liaison Services, Washington, 1978—. Asso. mem. Women's Inst. for Freedom of Press, Washington, 1977—; coordinator communications liaison com. Washington Task Force on African Affairs, 1975-78; cons. article on Rhodesia, Nat. Geog. Mag., 1975. Mem. African-Am. Women's Assn. Editorial bd. and reviewer A Current Bibliography on African Affairs, 1974—; editor AMA: Women in African & American Worlds, An Outlook, 1975-80, HABARI Special Reports, 1978—; asso. producer Film Leopold Sedar Senghor, 1975; cons., writer Changing Africa, NBC/WRC-TV, 1976; asst. editor Am-South African Relations: Bibliographic Essays, 1975; compiler, co-author: Burundi: A Selected Bibliography & Resource Guide, 1975. Mem. Am. Mgmt. Assn., Internat. Platform Assn., African Studies Assn. Home: PO Box 13096 Washington DC 20009 Office: 1346 Connecticut Ave NW Suite 901 Washington DC 20036

MATTHEWS, MARY EILEEN, foodservice scientist, educator; b. Rochester, N.Y., May 22, 1938; d. Henry Craven and Helen Mary (McCarthy) M.; B.S., Drexel U., 1960; M.S., Okla. State U., Stillwater, 1962; Ph.D., U. Wis., Madison, 1970. Intern, adminstrv. dietetic internship program Okla. State U., Stillwater, 1960-61; asst. nutritionist Nat. Diet-Heart Study, Johns Hopkins U. Hosp., Balt., 1963-65; asst. prof. foodservice adminstrn. dept. food sci. U. Wis., Madison, 1970-74, asso. prof., 1974-79, prof., 1979—. Mem. long range planning com. to assess needs of elderly in Dane County in the Year 2000, 1981; mem. fin. com. Tamarack Trails Community Services Assn., 1977-82, sec., 1981, vice chmn., 1982. Recipient Medallion award Am. Dietetic Assn., 1980, Mead Johnson award Am. Dietetic Assn., 1967-68; Am. Dietetic Assn., HEW grantee, 1972-73, Gen. Foods Fund fellow, 1961-62. Mem. Am. Dietetic Assn., Am. Sch. Food Service Assn., Am. Soc. Hosp. Food Service Adminstrs., Inst. Food Technologists, Internat. Microwave Power Inst., Nat. Restaurant Assn., Research and Devel. Assos. for Mil. Food and Packaging Systems, Inc., Foodservice Systems Mgmt. Ednl. Council, Wis. Assn. Milk and Food Sanitarians, Inc., Wis. Dietetic Assn., Wis. Sch. Food Service Assn., Madison Dist. Dietetic Assn., Phi Sigma, Phi Upsilon Omicron, Sigma Delta Epsilon. Mem. editorial bd. Sch. Food Service Research Review, 1977—, Jour. Microwave Power, 1979-82; jour. bd. Jour. Am. Dietetic Assn., 1971-74; chmn. jour. bd. Jour. Am. Dietetic Assn., 1971-74; contbr. articles to profl. jours. Home: 4 Bayberry Trail Madison WI 53717 Office: Dept Food Sci 103 Babcock Hall U Wis Madison WI 53706

MATTHEWS, VERNECIA NEELEY, life ins. co. exec.; b. Columbia, S.C., Aug. 23, 1924; d. Arthur Z. and Pinkoner (Harrington) Wilson; m. Philip Garland Matthews, May 16, 1942; children—Paula M. Kennedy, Steve A. Matthews. Exec. sec. S.C. State Bd. Cosmetic Art Examiners, Columbia, 1944-53; corp. sec., office adminstr. Francis Marion Life Ins. Co., Columbia, 1956-61; life underwriter Am. Sentinel Life Ins. Co., Columbia, 1961-63; v.p., asst. sec.-treas., 1963—. Recipient FLMI designation, 1973. Mem. Nat. Sec. Assn. (founding mem. Palmetto chpt. 1951). Mem. Ch. Christ. Home: 3138 Pine Belt Rd Columbia SC 29204 Office: 1200 Main St Columbia SC 29201

MATTHEWS-EVANS, DEBORAH YVETTE, clin. psychologist; b. Nashville, Aug. 25, 1952; d. Corinne Wilson Matthews; B.A., Fisk U., 1974; M.A., Fisk-Meharry, 1976; m. Arnold C. Evans, Apr. 16, 1978. Psychology intern Crownsville (Md.) Hosp. Center, 1976-77; psychologist II, Garfield Park Comprehensive Community Mental Health Center, Chgo., 1977-78; clin. asso. Inst. for Life Enrichment, Washington, 1979—; research asso. J.E.S. & Assos., Washington, 1979—; clin. psychologist D.C. Public Sch. System, Washington, 1980—; cons. Seat Pleasant Youth Crime Prevention Program, 1979—. Active various polit. campaigns. Mem. Am. Psychol. Assn., Assn. Black Psychologists, Assn. for Childhood Edn. Internat., Tenn. Assn. for Retarded Citizens, Davidson County Assn. for Retarded Citizens, Nat. Hook-Up Black Women, Fisk Alumni Assn. Office: 7852 16th St NW Washington DC 20012

MATTHYS, ELIZABETH KLEIN, distributive edn. educator, coordinator; b. Stamford, Conn., Sept. 10, 1927; d. Henry and Emily Catherine (Weir) Klein; B.S., Simmons Coll., 1949; M.A., Framingham State Coll., 1978; m. Leon T. Matthys, Aug. 29, 1949; children—Lynne, Donna, Beth. Asst. buyer Jordan Marsh Co., Boston, 1949-51; asst. sales mgr. Curity Nursery Products, 1951-52; dir. comml. continuity Gen. Electric Co., Radio Sta. WGY, Schenectady, 1952-53; fashion merchandising tchr., coordinator Henry O. Peabody Sch., Norwood, Mass., 1970—; adv. Tri-County Regional Vocat. Tech. Sch., 1975—. Leader, Girl Scouts Am., Walpole, Mass., 1951-52, Acton, Mass., Norfolk, Mass., 1960-70; chmn. study group LWV, Acton, Mass., 1962-68. Mem. NEA, Am. Vocat. Assn., Mass. Vocat. Assn., Norfolk City Tchrs. Assn., Nat. Assn. Distributive Edn. Tchrs., Distributive Edn. Clubs Am. Republican. Baptist. Home: 11 King Philip Trail Norfolk MA 02056 Office: HO Peabody Sch Peabody Rd Norwood MA 02062

MATTHYSSE, ANN GALE, biologist; b. Chgo., Oct. 25, 1939; d. George W. and Ann (Van Nice) Gale; A.B. in Biochem. Scis. magna cum laude, Radcliffe Coll., 1961; postgrad. Rockefeller U., N.Y.C., 1961-63; Ph.D. in Biology, Harvard U., 1967; m. Steven Matthysse, Aug. 25, 1962; 1 son, Michael. Postdoctoral fellow Calif. Inst. Tech., 1966-69, Harvard U. Med. Sch., 1969-70; lectr. biology Harvard U., 1970-71; asst. prof. microbiology Ind. U. Med. Sch., 1971-75; mem. faculty U. N.C., Chapel Hill, 1975—, assoc. prof. botany, mem. genetics curriculum, 1977—, assoc. prof. biology, 1982—; Allen lectr. phytobacteriology U. Wis., 1982. Treas. Orange County Assn. Retarded Citizens, 1976-78. Grantee NIH, 1972—, Dept. Agr., 1981—. Mem. Am. Soc. Microbiology, Am. Phytopathol. Soc., Am. Soc. Plant Physiologists, AAAS, Phi Beta Kappa. Quaker. Editorial bd. Jour. Bacteriology. Office: Coker Hall 010A U NC Chapel Hill NC 27514

MATTINGLY, CECELIA JEAN, elec. appliance mfg. co. ofcl.; b. Louisville, July 25, 1929; d. Edward Grove and Kathrine Elise (Winter) M.; B.S., Webster Coll. of St. Louis U., 1951. With Gen. Electric Co., Louisville, 1951—, beginning as layout artist product service, successively illustrator product service and appliance layouts, kitchen designer, supr. designers, specialist kitchen modernization, 1951-74, mgr. home modernization, 1974—; appeared on TV shows including Dinah Shore show; leader seminars on kitchen design; speaker civic and builder groups. Mem. Thorobreds of Ky. Derby Festival; former pres. Cath. Theater Guild; dir., choreographer, music dir. little theater groups. Recipient 100th ann. award Gen. Electric Co., 1978; Trouper award Cath. Theater Guild, 1964; 3 artistic achievement awards; cert. kitchen designer. Mem. Am. Inst. Kitchen Dealers, Nat. Assn. Home Builders, Nat. Assn. Remodeling Industry, Fedn. Ky. Women's Clubs, Ky. Cols. Republican. Roman Catholic. Club: Webster Alumni. Home: Louisville KY Office: Gen Electric Co Appliance Park Louisville KY 40225

MATTSON, ESTHER JOAN, chem. co. exec.; b. Worcester, Mass., Mar. 5, 1935; d. John Arthur and Mary Ann (Falcone) Santomenno; A.S., Becker Jr. Coll., Worcester, Mass., 1954; B.S., Pace U., 1977. Personnel programs adminstr. Crompton & Knowles, N.Y.C., 1969-70, mgr. employee benefits, 1970-73, mgr. benefits and compensation, 1973-78, dir. compensation, benefits and career planning, 1978—. Mem. Am. Soc. Personnel Adminstrn., Am. Soc. Tng. and Devel., N.Y. Personnel Mgmt. Assn., Am. Compensation Assn., Am. Arbitration Assn. Home: 301 E 63d St New York NY 10021 Office: 345 Park Ave New York NY 10154

MATTY, MARILYN LIEBE, chem. co. ofcl.; b. Detroit, Sept. 26, 1929; d. Benjamin and Gertrude (Wolgin) Hass; student Detroit public schs.; m. Michael Milan Matty, July 15, 1973; children by previous marriage—Glenn Singer, Deborah Brown, Tina Caplan, Barbara Von Tungeln. Sec., Hebrew Union Coll., Los Angeles, 1963-64, Bill Gallien & Assos., Los Angeles, 1964-66, Mike Stobin & Assos., Van Nuys, Calif., 1966-69; confidential sec., adminstrv. asst. Bio-Sci. Enterprises subs. Dow Chem. Co., Van Nuys, 1969—. Mem. Profl. Secs. Internat. (pres. Satellite chpt., Mem. of Yr. 1980). Jewish. Club: Patriotic Order of Does. Home: 5738 Wilhelmina Ave Woodland Hills CA 91367 Office: 7600 Tyrone Ave Van Nuys CA 91405

MATUJA, MARY, city ofcl.; b. Habbura, Czechoslovakia, Jan. 4, 1939; came to U.S., 1949, naturalized, 1949; d. Julian and Anne (Shafron) Bobak; student Macomb County Community Coll., 1958-60, Oakland U., 1978; m. Robert D. Matuja, Sept. 17, 1960; children—Leslie, Jennifer, Nicole. Councilwoman, City of Roseville (Mich.), 1975—, mayor pro tem, 1981, chmn. hobby shows, 1979-80. Chmn., Patton Sch. PTA, Roseville, 1969-70; exec. v.p. Women for United Found., Detroit, 1969, dir., 1970-76; bd. dirs. Mich. Cancer Found. Democrat. Presbyterian. Clubs: Detroit Women's Symphony Assn., St. Joseph Aux., Mich. Dem. Home: 19273 Shadowoods St Roseville MI 48066 Office: 29777 Gratiot St Roseville MI 48066

MATUNAS, MARIAN STARRETT (MRS. ANTHONY L. MATUNAS), psychoanalyst; b. Indpls.; d. Wendell Holmes and Evalyn Elizabeth (Haig) Starrett; Ph.D., N.Y. U., 1960; diploma in psychoanalysis Postgrad. Center for Mental Health, N.Y.C., 1970, diploma in child guidance and child psychiatry, 1971; m. Anthony L. Matunas, Nov. 7, 1956; 1 son, Anthony Laurence. Staff psychologist Kings County Hosp., Bklyn., 1960-64; dir. psychol. services Jewish Meml. Hosp., N.Y.C., 1964-67; supervising clin. psychologist Postgrad. Center for Mental Health, 1967-69, mem. faculty, supr., 1970—; pvt. practice psychoanalysis and psychotherapy, N.Y.C., 1965—; adj. prof. Union Grad. Sch. at Antioch, 1969-74. Mem. Am., N.Y. State psychol. assns., Soc. for Projective Techniques, Psi Chi, Pi Lambda Theta, Kappa Delta Pi. Home: 333 E 30th St Apt 3L New York NY 10016 Office: 11 E 68th St Suite 1B New York NY 10021

MATURIN, THERESA POIRIER, nurse; b. St. Martinville, La., Apr. 21, 1932; d. Leopold and Emilie (Poche) Poirier; Cosmetician, Lafayette (La.) Beauty Sch., 1963; diploma Teche Area Nursing Sch., New Iberia, La., 1975; m. Joseph Newby Maturin, Aug. 23, 1953; 1 son, Roland Joseph. Staff nurse Lafayette Gen. Hosp., 1974, Oakwood Village Nursing Care Center, Lafayette, 1975-80; pvt. duty nurse, Lafayette, 1980—. Pres. La. chpt. Nat. Fedn. Democratic Women, 1979-83; mem. La. Dem. Fin. Council, 1982; pres. St. Mary's Guild, Lafayette. Mem. Lafayette Town House, Am. Bus. Women's Assn. (chmn. local membership 1964), La. Hist. Soc., Smithsonian Assos., Nat. Trust Hist. Preservation, Right to Life, Attakapas Hist. Assn., Am. Security Council, U.S. Capitol Hist. Soc., Nat. Hist. Soc., L'Heure de Musique, France Amerique de la Louisiane (v.p. 1982-83), DAR, Soc. Dames Ct. of Honor, Lafayette Ballet Assn., Soc. Confederacy, Beta Sigma Phi. Roman Catholic. Clubs: Catholic Daus. Ams. (ct. regent 1975-79), UDC (corr. sec. chpt. 1982-83). Home: 2710 Pinhook Rd Lafayette LA 70508

MATUSAK, LARRAINE R., ednl. adminstr.; b. Chgo., July 22, 1930; d. Theodore and Rose (Kasper) M.; B.A., Coll. St. Benedict, 1962; M.S., U. Minn., 1966; Ph.D., Fielding Inst. Grad. Studies, 1972. Asso. prof., prof. extension div., coordinator for Alt. Baccalaureate degree, Gen. Coll., U. Minn., Mpls., 1967-74; dean Coll. of Alt. Programs, U. Evansville, Ind., 1974-79; pres. Thomas A. Edison State Coll., Trenton, N.J., 1979-82; program dir. in edn., dir. Kellogg Nat. Fellowship Program, W.K. Kellogg Found., Battle Creek, Mich., 1982—; bd. dirs. Coll. St. Benedict, 1981—; bd. trustees U. Mid-America, 1981—; chmn. N.J. Ednl. Computer Network, 1981—. Bd. dirs. Lenni Lenape Camp Fire Council, Mercer, Burlington, Bucks Counties, N.J., 1980. Named distinguished Am. educator, U. Ga. Med. Coll., 1976; recipient Evansville Civic Award, 1976. Mem. AAUP, AAAS, AAUW, Am. Council Edn.-Nat. Indentification Program (nat. panelist, nat. forum, 1980), Phi Delta Kappa, Delta Kappa Gamma. Roman Catholic. Club: Zonta. Internat. Contbr. to: What Next: New Directions for Experimental Learning, 1981; author handbooks; speaker various community groups.

MATZ, MARY JANE PHILLIPS, musicologist writer, lectr.; b. Lebanon, Ohio, Jan. 30, 1926; d. William Mason and Hazel Spencer Phillips; B.A., Smith Coll., 1947; M.A., Columbia U., 1951; postgrad. City U. N.Y., 1968-69; Litt.D. (hon.), Centre Coll., Danville, Ky., 1976; children—Mary Ann, Catherine Eleanor, Margaret Spencer, Clare Ann, Charles Albert III. Asst. editor Opera News, Met. Opera Guild, Inc., N.Y.C., 1950-56, contbg. editor, 1956-66, contbr., 1948—; lectr. City of Venice Ednl. Programs, 1969-71; asst. prof. U. Venice (Italy), 1970-72; lectr. continuing edn. programs Columbia U., N.Y.C., 1978—, dir. professions for women in arts program, 1978-80; writer TV scripts Live from the Met, 1978— adminstrv. dir. Clarion Concerts Cavalli Festival, 1979—. Founder, mem. exec. bd. Am. Inst. for Verdi Studies, N.Y.U.; bd. dirs. Regional Art Center, Danville, Ky. Martha Baird Rockefeller Fund for Music research grantee, 1978—; Ford Found. research grantee, 1979—. Mem. Am. Musicol. Soc., Essex Inst., Ohio Hist. Soc., Ky. Hist. Soc., Am. Inst. for Verdi Studies, DAR, Historic Salem, Am.-Italy Soc., Smith Coll. N.Y. Alumnae Assn., Amici di Verdi (Busseto, Italy). Quaker. Club: Smith Coll. (N.Y.). Author: Opera Stars, 1955; Opera Manual, 1956; The Many Lives of Otto Kahn, 1963; Opera; Grand and Not So Grand, 1966; editor The World of Opera jour., 1979—; contbr. articles on music and theatre and gen. history to various publs. Home: Box 66 Lebanon OH 45036

MATZEN, MARY MARGARET POSTILL, writer, editor; b. Rensselaer, Ind., Feb. 20, 1919; d. William H. and Cora (Simons) Postill; student Ind. Bus. Coll., Lafayette, 1936-37, Famous Writers Sch., Westport, Conn., 1967-69; m. Edwin H. Matzen, June 13, 1942; children—Martin W., Mary Marlene. Employee discount rep. Woodward & Lothrop, Chevy Chase, Md., 1960-62; sec. behavioral scis. dept. Naval Med. Research Inst., Bethesda, Md., 1963-69, writer-editor, 1969-82, with Environ. Stress Program Center, 1982; free lance writer, editor, 1982—. Mem. Am. Med. Writers Assn. (pres. Mid-Atlantic chpt. 1978-79; editor interchpt. newsletter 1979-80), Undersea Med. Soc. (asso.), Cousteau Soc., Sigma Phi Gamma. Republican. Methodist. Asst. editor Undersea Biomed. Research, 1974-76. Home: 7307 Durbin Terr Bethesda MD 20817 Office: Naval Medical Research Inst Bethesda MD 20814

MAUCH, RUTH ELLEN, engring. co. exec.; b. East Chicago, Ind., Sept. 17, 1952; d. Albert and Verna (Hamnik) Dray; B.A., Purdue U., 1974, postgrad., 1982—; m. Christopher Mauch; 1 dau., Elizabeth Tara. Editor Pub. Relations Ctr., Harza Engring Co., Chgo., 1974—; operator cake decorating service, Ind. and Ill., 1980—; instr. bus. etiquette and dressing for upward career mobility NW Ind. area; founder, pres. Tooth Fairy Express; cons. in field. Mem. Western Soc. Engrs., Nat. Fedn. Bus. and Profl. Women (chmn. state com., pres. Hammond, Ind.), Sigma Kappa, Alpha Lambda Delta. Address: 9031 Bunker Hill Dr Munster IN 46321

MAUGER, PATRICIA ANN, TV producer; b. Allentown, Pa., Dec. 21, 1937; d. Von Edgar and Ruth (Kreitz) Mauger; ed. Berkeley Sch. With NBC, 1964—, now producer religion unit Network News. Mem. Nat. Acad. TV Arts and Sci. Presbyterian. Office: NBC 30 Rockefeller Plaza New York NY 10020

MAULDIN, BONNIE MARDEN, nursing adminstr.; b. Marion, Ind., Sept. 29, 1948; d. Norman L. and Alice A. (Cloonen) Marden; diploma Parkview Meth. Sch. Nursing, 1969; 1 son, Jason B. Asst. head nurse emergency room Children's Hosp., Columbus, Ohio, 1969-71; evening supr. Brookline Manor Convalescent Home, Mifflintown, Pa., 1973-78; dir. nursing Lewisburg (Pa.) United Meth. Homes, 1978—; mem. adv. bd. Williamsport (Pa.) Emergency Med. Transfer Service, Inc., 1978—. Office: Lewisburg United Meth Homes Lewisburg PA 17837

MAULDIN, JEAN HUMPHRIES, aviation co. exec.; b. Gordonville, Tex., Aug. 16, 1923; d. James Wiley and Lena Leota (Noel-Carin) Humphries; B.S., Hardin Simmons U., 1943; M.S., U. So. Calif., 1961; postgrad. Westfield Coll., U. London, 1977-78, Warnborough Coll., Oxford, Eng., 1977-78; m. William Henry Mauldin, Feb. 28, 1942; children—Bruce Patrick, William Timothy III. Psychol. counselor social services 1st Baptist Ch., 1953-57; pres. Mauldin and Staff, public relations, Los Angeles, 1957-78; pres. Stardust Aviation, Inc., Santa Ana, Calif., 1962—. mem. Calif. Democratic Council, 1953-70; mem. exec. bd. Calif. Dem. Central com. exec. bd., 1957—, Orange County Dem. Central Com. exec. bd., 1960—; del. Dem. Nat. Conv., 1974, 78; Calif. State adv. U.S. Congressional Adv. Bd., 1982—; mem. U.S. Congressional Adv. Bd.; rep. 37th Senate Caucus; pres. Santa Ana Friends of Public Library, 1973-76, McFadden Friends of Library, Santa Ana, 1976-80; chmn. cancer crusade Am. Cancer Soc., Orange County, 1974; mem. exec. bd. Lisa Hist. Preservation Soc., 1970—; lay leader Protestant Episcopal Ch. Am., Trinity Ch., Tustin, Calif. Named Woman of Yr., Key Woman in Politics, Calif. Dem. Party, 1960-80. Am. Mgmt. Assn. (pres.'s club), Bus. and Profl. Women Am., Exptl. Aircraft and Pilots Assn., Nat. Women's Polit. Caucus, Dem. Coalition Central Coms., Calif. Friends of Library (life), Women's Missionary Soc. (chmn.), LWV, Nat. Fedn. Dem. Women, Calif. Fedn. County Central Com. Mems., Internat. Platform Assn., Nat. Women's Pilot. Caucus Club: U. So. Calif. Ski. Author: Cliff Winters, The Pilot, The Man, 1961; The consummate Barnstormer, 1962; The Daredevil Clown, 1965. Home: 1013 W Elliott Pl Santa Ana CA 92704 also 102 E 45th St Savannah GA 31405 Also 112 8th St Seal Beach Ca 90740 Office: 16542 Mount Kibby St Fountain Valley CA 92708

MAUNSBACH, KAY BENEDICTA, investment co. exec.; b. N.Y.C., Apr. 25, 1933; d. Eric and Katherine M.; B.A., Hunter Coll., 1961; postgrad. N.Y. U., 1961-64; C.L.U., Coll. Ins., 1977. Jr. security analyst fin. instns. Vilas & Hickey, N.Y.C., 1960-62; v.p. investment services Shearson Loeb, Rhoades & Co., Inc., N.Y.C., 1962-73; v.p., dir. corporate communications Manhattan Life Ins. Co., N.Y.C., 1974-80; pres. Atrium Group Ltd., 1980—; chmn. Co-Vest Mgmt., 1981—; gen. partner Prospero Properties, 1982—. Bd. dirs. Regis Camp Devel. Fellow Fin. Analysts Fedn.; mem. Life Advertisers Assn. (mem. exec. com.), Public Relations Soc. Am., Nat. Assn. Bus. Economists, Nat. Investor Relations Inst., Public Relations Council, Am. Council Life Ins., Internat. Assn. Bus. Communicators, Financial Communications Soc., Public Affairs Council, Women's Econ. Roundtable, Ins. Women N.Y., Life Ins. Council N.Y., N.Y. Soc. Security Analysts, C.L.U.s (mem. public relations liaison com. N.Y. chpt.), Life Underwriters Assn. N.Y. (mem. polit. action com.), N.Y. Bd. Realtors, Publicity Club N.Y., N.Y. Bus. Communicators, World Futurists Soc. Office: 16 W 16th St New York NY 10011 also Farm Ln East Hampton NY 11937

MAUPIN, CAROL GRINSTEAD, food cons.; b. Pawhuska, Okla., Jan. 31, 1936; d. Randolph Henry and Mildred Asilee (Pfaff) Grinstead; B.A., U. Okla., 1958. Asst. to food dir. Neiman Marcus, Dallas, 1958-62; asst. to food dir. So. Meth. U., Dallas, 1963-64; asso. dir. food ops. Mut. of Omaha, 1964-69; dir. tearoom, parties and spl. events Denver Dry Goods, 1970-74; dir. food and party services Jr. League of Houston, 1974-81; partner Jackson and Co., catering service; food cons. Mus. Food Arts; cooking instr. Batterie de Cuisine Cooking Sch., Foleys Gourmet Kitchens; food lectr.; food and party cons. protocol office City of Houston; food service cons., bd. dirs. Alley Theatre of Houston. Mem. Am. Home Econs. Assn., Nat. Assn. Cooking Schs., Houston Culinary Guild. Republican. Episcopalian. Home: 4319 Bettis St Houston TX 77027 Office: 1707 Stanford St Houston TX 77006

MAURER, JERALYN ANN, social worker; b. Syracuse, June 17, 1949; d. Kenneth W. and Geraldine (Curtis) Mace; student St. Lawrence U., 1967-69; B.A. summa cum laude, Harpur Coll., 1971; M.S.W., SUNY, Albany, 1973; m. Gary C. Maurer, Aug. 9, 1969. Med. social worker St. Mary's Hosp., Lewiston, Maine, 1973-79; oncology social worker, supr. Central Maine Med. Center, Lewiston, 1979—. Pres., Androscoggin unit Am. Cancer Soc., 1979—; treas. Mandala Hospice, 1979—. Mem. Social Work Oncology Group Maine, Nat. Assn. Social Workers (co-chmn. profl. standards com.), Acad. Cert. Social Workers, Phi Beta Kappa. Office: Central Maine Med Center Main St Lewiston ME 04240

MAURER, LUCILLE DARVIN, state legislator; b. N.Y.C., Nov. 21, 1922; d. Joseph Jay and Evelyn (Levine) Darvin; student U. N.C., Greensboro, 1938-40; B.A., U. N.C., Chapel Hill, 1942; M.A., Yale U., 1945; m. Ely Maurer, Apr. 29, 1945; children—Stephen Bennett, Russell Alexander, Edward Nestor. Economist, U.S. Tariff Commn., 1942-43; econ. and market research for pvt. firms, 1957-60; cons. Nat. Center for Ednl. Stats., 1969-70; mem. Md. House of Dels., 1969—, mem. ways and means com., 1971—; mem. intergovtl. adv. council U.S. Dept. Edn., 1980-82. Del., Md. Constl. Conv., 1967-68; mem. Montgomery County Bd. Edn., 1960-68; trustee Montgomery Community Coll., 1960-68; vice chmn. nat. planning com., advanced leadership program of seminars on edn. and ednl. policy for state legislators Edn. Commn. of States, 1979—; mem. exec. com. of edn. com. Nat. Conf. of State Legislatures, 1975—, chmn., 1978-79; mem. adv. com. Servicemen's Opportunity Colls., 1978—; mem. nat. adv. bd. Inst. for Ednl. Leadership, 1979-81; co-chmn. Md. Commn. on Intergovernmental Cooperation, 1976—; mem. Nat. Com. on Postsecondary Accreditation, 1974-1979; bd. dirs. Montgomery United Way, 1971-76. Recipient Legislator of Yr. award Md. Assn. for Retarded Children, 1972; John Dewey award Montgomery County Fedn. Tchrs., 1972; Hornbook award Montgomery County Edn. Assn., 1972. Mem. LWV (past dir. Montgomery County, past dir. Md.), AAUW (Internat. Women's Yr. award Silver Spring 1975), Bus. and Profl. Women's Club, NOW (Legis. Excellence award 1981), Women's Equity Action League, Women's Polit. Caucus, Montgomery County Hist. Soc., Order Women Legislators, Delta Kappa Gamma. Jewish. Office: 223C Lowe Ho of Dels Bldg Annapolis MD 21401

MAUS, BETTY JEAN, hosp. adminstr.; b. Balt., July 13, 1929; d. Howard Arrington and Edna May (Brown) Smith, Jr.; student Strayer's Bus. Coll., 1946-47; m. Bernard Harvey Maus, Sept. 24, 1950. Asst. cashier Sykesville State Bank, 1950-53; head teller Randallstown (Md.) State Bank, 1953-55; med. records staff Springfield Hosp. Center, Sykesville, 1955, prin clk. purchasing office, 1960-67, coordinator vol. services, 1967—. Bd. dirs. Vol. Action Carroll County, 1975-80, Vol. Action Central Md., 1977-79, v.p., 1980; mem. Ad Hoc. Com. for Health Systems Central Md.; sec. Westminster Recreational Council; leader 4-H; instl. rep. Boy Scouts; den mother Cub Scouts, treas. St. Paul's United Methodist Ch., also Sunday sch. tchr., counselor Meth. Youth Fellowship, chmn. council of ministries. Named Outstanding Woman of Carroll County, 1976; recipitn Rotary Internat. award, 1971; South Carroll Community award, 1980; numerous others. Mem. Am. Soc. Dirs. Vol. Services, Md. Council Dirs. Vol. Services, Assn. Vol. Action Scholars, Assn. Vol. Adminstrn., Carroll County Assn. Retarded Citizens, Washington County Mental Health Assn. Democrat. Clubs: Bonnette (Sykesville); Order Eastern Star; Soroptimist (pres. Westminster 1973-75, treas. 1975-77, v.p. 1977-78, pres. 1978-80). Home: 7344 Springfield Ave Sykesville MD 21784 Office: Springfield Hosp Center Sykesville MD 21784

MAVILLE, PAULINE BRIGGS, indsl. engr.; b. Lebanon, N.H., Jan. 29, 1924; d. Clifton Charles and Grace Francis (Lovering) Briggs; student U.S. Naval Aviation Tech. Tng. Sch., 1944; grad. Plus Sch. Bus., 1968; student Stonehill Coll., 1975-76, Massasoitt Community Coll., 1978-79; m. Feb. 24, 1945 (div.); 1 son, Thomas Briggs. Machinist, various cos., Lebanon, N.H. and Waltham, Mass., 1946-68; jr. indsl. engr. Compo Industries, Inc., Waltham, 1968-70; scheduling coordinator Heath Cons., Inc., Stoughton, Mass., 1971-72; cost estimator Metal Bellows Co., Sharon, Mass., 1972-75; sr. cost estimator Bird-Johnson Co., Walpole, Mass., 1975-79; sr. cost estimator MAPO div. Disney Prodns., Glendale, Calif., 1980-81, indsl. engr. WED div., Glendale, 1981—. Served with USN, 1944-47, Mem. Am. Inst. Indsl. Engrs., Am. Legion. Democrat. Club: Bus. and Profl. Women's. Home: 1231 N Verdugo Rd Glendale CA 91206 Office: 800 Sonora Ave Glendale CA 91201

MAVRONIKOLAS, RUTH THORP HARVEY, educator, real estate broker; b. Phila., July 3, 1931; d. Cyril Hingston and Ruth Sharpless (Thorp) Harvey; B.F.A. in Art Edn., Phila. Coll. Art, 1956; M.S. in Edn., U. Pa., 1964; m. Christopher George Mavronikolas, Nov. 27, 1958; children—Elia Ruth, George Christopher. Tchr., Baldwin Sch., Bryn Mawr, Pa., 1956-66, chmn. art dept., 1960-66; asso. prof. art edn. Phila. Coll. Art, 1966-74; tchr. Moorestown (N.J.) Friends Sch., 1974-76, chmn. art dept., 1974-76; tchr. Franklin Learning Center, Phila., 1976-82; salesperson Colonial Realty Co., Westmont, N.J., 1982—. T. Wistar Brown Fund Endl. grantee, 1952-64; Mary Jeannes Fund Ednl. grantee, 1952-53; Anne Townsend Fund grantee, 1952-53. Mem. Nat. Trust Hist. Preservation. Republican. Home: 208 West End Ave Haddonfield NJ 08033 Office: 142 Haddon Ave Westmont NJ 08108

MAWARDI, BETTY HOSMER, educator; b. Elkhart, Ind., Feb. 1, 1921; d. George Henry and DeLoscia Ruth (Longacher) Hosmer; A.B., Radcliffe Coll., 1943, cert. Mgmt. Tng. program, 1946, Ph.D., 1959; M.A., Wellesley Coll., 1952; m. Osman K. Mawardi, Nov. 23, 1950. Personnel clk. Allison div. Gen. Motors, Indpls., 1943-44; asst. registrar Bulter U., Indpls., 1944-45; placement counselor Wellesley (Mass.) Coll., 1946-52, asst. dir., acting dir. placement, 1953-54; asst. prof. med. edn. research Case Western Res. U., Cleve., 1960-65, asst. clin. prof. psychology, 1960-65, asso. prof. med. edn. research, 1965—, asso. clin. prof. psychology, 1965—; v.p. Collaborative Planners, Inc., Cleve., 1977—. Chmn., Northeastern Ohio div. Radcliffe Centennial Fund Dr., 1979-82. Nat. Endowment Humanities fellow, 1980; grantee in field. Mem. Assn. Am. Med. Colls., Assn. Study of Med. Edn., Soc. Health and Human Values, Women Faculty of Sch. Medicine, Am. Psychol. Assn., Soc. Psychol. Study of Social Issues, Eastern Psychol. Assn., Am. Sociol. Assn., Am. Ednl. Research Assn., AAAS, Internat. Platform Assn. Clubs: Harvard U. of Cleve., Print of Cleve., Wellesley of Cleve., Western Res. Hist. Soc., Play House of Cleve. Author: Physicians and Their Careers, 1979; contbr. chpts to books, articles in field to profl. jours. Home: 15 Mornington Ln Cleveland Heights OH 44106 Office: Div Research in Med Edn Sch Medicine Case Western Res U 2119 Abington St Cleveland OH 44106

MAXEY, LOIS BRUNSON, clin. social worker; b. DeKalb County, Ind., Jan. 6, 1929; d. Tom Bennett and Clara Lodell (Bash) Brunson; student Cin. Bible Sem., 1946-49; A.B., SW Christian Sem., Phoenix, 1951; postgrad. Phoenix Coll., 1953-54, Catherine Spalding Coll., Louisville, 1963-64; M.S.S.W., U. Louisville, 1966; m. Victor L. Maxey, Sept. 14, 1949; children—Thomas, Victor L., David. Oral proof reader Am. Printing House for the Blind, Louisville, 1959-63; group worker Neighborhood House, Louisville, 1963-64; social service dir. Headstart, 4 schs., Louisville, 1966; caseworker Family and Children's Agy., Louisville, 1966-68; clin. social worker Comprehensive Care Center No. Ky., Newport, 1968-72, 75-80, team leader 5 offices, 1972-75, coordinator children's services Catchment B, 1980—. Active No. Ky. Chpt. Mental Health Assn. Named Social Worker of Yr., No. Ky., 1978; lic. clin. social worker, adminstrn. and mgmt., Ky. Mem. Nat. Assn. Social Workers, Acad. Cert. Social Workers. Mem. Ch. of Christ. Home: 5119 Grossepointe Ln Cincinnati OH 45238 Office: 18 N Fort Thomas Ave Fort Thomas KY 41075

MAXFIELD, MALINDA RUTH, educator; b. Jackson, Miss., Dec. 22, 1936; d. Harry W. and Ruth (Porter) M.; B.A., Vanderbilt U., 1955, Ph.D., 1969. Asso. prof. English, Queens Coll., 1965-72, also chmn. dept.; prof., chmn. dept. English Elizabethtown Coll., 1972-76; asso. prof. English and humanities Converse Coll., Spartanburg, S.C., 1976—, also chmn. dept. humanities. NDEA fellow, 1959-62; Piedmont Center grantee, 1968. Mem. MLA, Philol. Assn. Carlinas, So. Humanities Conf., Phi Beta Kappa, Delta Phi Alpha, Phi Sigma Iota. Episcopalian. Editor: Images and Innovations: Update 70's, 1979; contbr. articles in field. Office: Converse Coll Spartanburg SC 29301

MAXIE, PEGGY JOAN, human resources cons.; b. Amarillo, Tex., Aug. 18, 1936; d. Cleveland and Rebecca H. (Jackson) M.; B.A. in Psychology, Seattle U., 1970; M.S.W., U. Wash., Seattle, 1972; LL.D. (hon.), St. Martin's Coll. Counselor, Seattle U.; exec. dir. Central Area Council Alcoholism; mem. Wash. Ho. of Reps. from 37th Legis. Dist., chmn. higher edn. com.; now pres. Peggy Maxie & Assos., Seattle; condr. seminars in field. Mem. Bus. and Profl. Women, LWV, Seattle Mcpl. League, NAACP, Wash. Hist. Soc., Nat. Assn. Social Workers, Nat. Data Library System Higher Edn., Delta Upsilon Omega. Democrat. Roman Catholic. Address: 1441 Madrona Dr Seattle WA 98122

MAXIMOV, JUDITH B., computer co. exec.; b. Chgo., Sept. 16, 1943; d. Marshall and Helaine (Friedlen) Salzman; B.A., North Park Coll., 1976; m. Michael J. Maximov, June 20, 1965; children—Justin, Marc, Hannah. Chairwoman, Ariz. ERA Coalition, 1976-80; owner, operator Judith's Computer Works, Tucson, 1978—. Bd. dirs. Temple Emanu-El, Tucson, 1982-83, Tucson Center for Women and Children, 1982-83; state bd. NOW, 1980-82; pres. Tucson sect. Nat. Council Jewish Women, 1982-84, bd. dirs., 1980-82; pres. Women in Tucson, 1982-83; v.p. Mt. Lemmon Homeowners Assn., 1981-82, pres., 1982-83. Address: 5602 E S Wilshire Dr Tucson AZ 85711

MAXSON, LINDA ELLEN, biologist; b. N.Y.C. Apr. 24, 1942; d. Albert and Ruth (Rosenfeld) Resnick; B.S., San Diego State U., 1964; M.A., 1966; Ph.D., U. Calif., Berkeley, 1973; m. Richard Dey Maxson, June 13, 1964; 1 son, Kevin. Instr. biology San Diego State U., 1966-68; gen. sci. tchr. San Diego Unified Sch. Dist., 1968-69; instr. biochemistry U. Calif., Berkeley, 1974; mem. faculty U. Ill., Urbana, 1974—, asso. prof. dept. genetics and devel., dept. ecology, ethology and evolution, 1979—, dir. biology programs, 1979—. Grantee NSF, 1976-78, 79-84, Smithsonian Instn., 1978-79, 80—. Mem. Soc. Study Evolution, Soc. Systematic Zoology, AAAS, Am. Soc. Ichthyologists and Herpetologists, Assn. Tropical Biology, Herpetologists League, Sigma Xi. Home: 612 W Washington St Urban IL 61801 Office: 515 Morrill Hall 505 S Goodwin St U Ill Urbana IL 61801

MAXWELL, FLORENCE HINSHAW (MRS. JOHN WILLIAMSON MAXWELL), civic worker; b. Nora, Ind., July 14, 1914; d. Asa Benton and Gertrude (Randall) Hinshaw; B.A. cum laude, Butler U., 1935; m. John Williamson Maxwell, June 5, 1936; children—Marilyn, William Douglas. Coordinator, Sight Conservation and Aid to Blind, 1962-73, nat. chmn., 1969-73, active various fund drives; chmn. jamboree, hostess coms. North Central High Sch., 1959, 64, Girl Scouts U.S.A., 1937-38, 54-56; mus. chmn. Sr. Girl Scout Regional Council, 1956-57; scorekeeper Little League, 1955-57; bd. dirs. Nora Sch. Parents' Club, 1958-59, Eastwood Jr. High Sch. Triangle Club, 1959-62; bd. dirs. women's com. Ind. State Symphony Soc., 1965-67, 76-79; vision screening Indpls. innercity public sch. kindergartens, pre-schs., 1962—; chmn. vision screening Head Start, 1967—, health adv. com., 1976—, assessment team of compliance steering com., 1978-79; asst. glaucoma screening clinics Gen. Hosp., Glendale Shopping Center, City County Bldg., Am. Legion Nat. Hdqrs., Ind. Health Assn. Conf., 1962—; chmn. sight conservation and aid to blind Nat. Delta Gamma Found., Indpls., Columbus, Ohio, 1969-73; mem. telethon team Butler Univ. Fund, 1964; Symphoguide hostess Internat. Conf. on Cities, 1971, Nat. League of Cities, 1972; Symphoguide chmn. Gray Line Symphony City Tours, 1976-79; bd. dirs. Ind. Soc. to Prevent Blindness, 1962—, exec. com., sec., 1971—; mem. women's com. Ind. State Symphony Soc. Recipient Key to City of Indpls., 1972; Those Spl. People award Women in Communications, 1980. Mem. Ind., Nat. (Sight-Saving award 1974) socs. to prevent blindness, People of Vision Aux. (founder 1981), Delta Gamma (Cable award 1969, Outstanding Alumna award 1973, chmn. communication and decades com. 50th anniv. celebration Alpha Tau chpt. 1975, treas. Alpha Tau House Corp., 1975-78, nat. chmn. survey and coordination parents clubs 1976-77; Service Recognition award 1977, Shield award 1981, scholarship named in her honor 1981). Republican. Address: 1502 E 80th St Indianapolis IN 46240

MAXWELL, GERTRUDE GLADYS, animal welfare orgn. exec.; b. Chgo., Apr. 17, 1911; d. Isadore and Sophia (Alpert) Zeplowitz; B.S., Northwestern U., 1940, M.A., 1952; M.S., Loyola U., Chgo., 1943; m. Mark T. Maxwell, Nov. 30, 1934; 1 dau., Nancy Beth Maxwell Bell. Adminstr. farm security WPA, Henderson, Ky., 1939; social worker Chgo. Relief Assn., 1935-38; parole officer, Evansville, Ind., 1940; sch. tchr. Bd. Edn., Chgo., 1941-71; founder, life time chmn. Save-A-Pet, Inc., Highland Park, Ill., 1972—; founder Save-A-Pet, Miami, Fla., 1975—; v.p. Fla. Soc. Prevention Cruelty to Animals; chmn. adv. bd. for animal regulation Palm Beach County. appeared on various radio and TV talk shows, 1972—. Fund raiser for animal welfare, 1972—; bd. dirs. George J. Goldman Home for Aged. Recipient Proclamation award for pioneer in humanitarian work, Highland Park, Highwood, Deerfield, Skokie, Lincolnwood, Northbrook and Wilmette, Ill., 1977, 78, 79, 80; award Women's Aux. Atlanta Humane Soc., 1977, other awards. Contbr. articles on animal welfare to newspapers and periodicals; Goldman-Maxwell Animal Sanctuary, Save-A-Pet Adoption Center, Palatine, co-named in her honor. Office: Save-A-Pet Inc PO Box 193 Highland Park IL 60035

MAXWELL, KATHERINE GANT, sch. psychologist, ednl. cons.; b. El Paso, Tex., Nov. 27, 1931; d. Leslie and Lillian (Beard) Gant; B.S., Abilene Christian U., 1955; M.S., Miss. State U., 1967, Ph.D., 1974; m. Fowden Gene Maxwell, July 14, 1955; children—Steve, Becky, Randy. Teaching asst. Miss. State U., Starkville, 1969-72, practicum in sch. psychology, 1973-74; adminstr. psychol. tests Starkville Pub. Schs., 1974-75; sch. psychologist Dixie & Gilchrist (Fla.) County Schs., 1977-79; instr. continuing edn. dept. U. LaVerne (Calif.), 1979—; sch. psychologist Bryan (Tex.) Ind. Sch. Dist., 1979-80; owner, dir. Reading Improvement Center, College Station, Tex., 1979-80; sch. psychologist, ednl. diagnostician Temple (Tex.) Ind. Sch. Dist., 1980-81; sch. psychologist Franklin (Tex.) Ind. Sch. Dist., 1981-82; ednl. cons., College Station, Tex., 1982—. Cub Scout leader Boy Scouts Am., Starkville, 1960; Brownie leader Girl Scouts U.S.A., Starkville, 1961-64; pres. Starkville Overstreet PTA, 1962; sec. Starkville Civic League, 1962-65; active Mental Health Assn. Alachua County (Fla.), 1976-77; treas. Citizens Com. for Mental Health in Bryan, 1979-80. Mem. Nat. Assn. Female Execs., Mid-South Ednl. Research Assn., Miss. Psychol. Assn., AAAS, Am. Psychol. Assn., Tex. Psychol. Assn., Brazos Valley Psychol. Assn., Council for Exceptional Children, AAUW (youth com. 1982—), Bryan-College Station C. of C., Opera and Performing Arts Soc., Arts Council Brazos Valley, Nat. Edn. Honor Soc., Phi Delta Kappa. Clubs: Sorosis (sec. 1962-65), Tex. A&M Faculty Wives, Tex. A&M Newcomers, Altrusa. Address: Redmond Terr Sta PO Box 10027 College Station TX 77840

MAXWELL, MARGARET FINLAYSON, librarian, educator; b. Schenectady, Sept. 9, 1927; d. Frank Emerson and Harriet Winnifred (Rallison) Finlayson; B.A. magna cum laude, Pomona Coll., 1948; B.L.S., U. Calif., Berkeley, 1950; M.A., George Washington U., 1953; Ph.D. U. Mich., 1971; m. W. LeGrand Maxwell, Apr. 7, 1954; children—Robert L., Brian J., Bruce A. Intern. descriptive cataloger Library of Congress, 1950-56; asso. librarian Upper Iowa U., Fayette, 1956-66; instr. Upper Iowa U., 1966-68; lectr. library sci. U. Mich., 1968-71; prof. Grad. Library Sch., U. Ariz., Tucson, 1971—. Genevieve McEnerney fellow in library sci. U. Calif., 1949-50; Higher Edn. Act fellow, 1968-71; U. Ariz. Found. grantee, 1976-77; recipient Creative Teaching award U. Ariz. Found., 1982. Mem. ALA, S.W. Library Assn., Ariz. Library Assn., Westerners Internat., Ariz. Hist. Soc., Am. Assn. Library Schs., Phi Beta Kappa. Democrat. Mem. Ch. Jesus Christ of Latter-day Saints. Author: Shaping a Library: William L. Clements as Collector, 1973; Voices from the Southwest, 1976; Hambook for Anglo-American Cataloguing Rules, 1980; A Passion for Freedom: The Life of Sharlot Hall, 1982. Home: 2733 E Elm St Tucson AZ 85716

MAXWELL, MARGARET LOUISE, librarian; b. Bklyn., Dec. 4, 1923; d. John Fred and Sarah Alker (Gaskell) M.; student Westminster Coll., 1942, Cedar Crest Coll. for Women, 1943-44; grad. Barmore Sch., N.Y.C., 1945. Engaged in communications, 1945—; owner Real New Books, pubs., N.Y.C., 1951, Panorama, 1969—, Knight's Prison Library Service, N.Y.C., 1971—. Lutheran. Author: 101 Office Short Cuts, 3d edit., 1962; others. Home: 753 9th Ave New York NY 10019 Office: PO Box 1037 GPO New York NY 10116

MAXWELL, NICOLE J. SULLIVAN, nurse, cons.; b. Tuscaloosa, Ala., Nov. 8, 1955; d. Edgar Lee and Sarah Joyce (Belcher) Sullivan; B.S.N., U. Ala., 1978; postgrad. Baylor U., 1980—; m. Alan J. Maxwell, Feb. 16, 1980; 1 dau., Alana. Staff nurse Druid City (Ala.) Hosp., 1978-79; med.-surg. staff nurse W. Ala. Gen. Hosp., 1979; intensive care unit, emergency room dir. nursing Forest Manor Nursing Home, Northport, Ala., 1979-80; CPR instr., Tuscaloosa, Ala., 1978—; cons. Waco McLennan County Legal Aid, Waco, Tex., 1981—; workshop leader Tex. State White House Conf. Aging, 1981. Chmn. McLennan County Med. Aux., Sr. Citizens Com., 1981-82. Recipient Arion award, 1973; Center of Aging grantee, 1978. Mem. Honn Soc., Alpha Kappa Delta. Contbr. articles to profl. jours. Home: 809 NW 38th St Oklahoma City OK 73118

MAXWELL, ROBERTA, actress; b. Toronto, Ont., Can., June 17, 1945; d. Robert Gilbert and Patricia Maher (MacGregor) M.; student pvt. schs., Toronto. Appeared in plays: The Prime of Miss Jean Brodie, 1967, Equus, Broadway, 1974, Ashes, N.Y.C., 1977, The Merchant, 1977; appeared at: Stratford (Ont., Can.) Festival, 1966-67, Tyrone Guthrie Theatre, Mpls., Long Wharf Theatre, New Haven, 1968-76, Stratford, Conn., 1969-74. Recipient Drama Desk award for Whistle in the Dark, 1969; Obie award for Slag, 1970; Obie award for Ashes, 1977. Mem. AFTRA, Actors Equity. Christian Scientist. Office: STE Representation Ltd 888 7th Ave New York NY 10019 *

MAXWELL, SARA ELIZABETH (SALLY), speech pathologist, sch. psychologist, educator; b. DuQuoin, Ill., Jan. 23, 1941; d. Jean Alice Patterson Green; B.S. (Perry County (Ill.) scholar 1959-64), So. Ill. U., 1964, M.S. (Gloria Credi Meml. scholar 1964, Office Vocat. Rehab. fellow 1964), 1965, specialist's cert., (fellow), 1966; postgrad. Emerson Coll., Boston, 1969; emergency med. technician cert., Northeastern U., 1979; M.Ed., Boston Coll., 1982, doctoral candidate, 1982—; m. David Lowell Maxwell, Dec. 27, 1960; children—Lisa Marina, David Scott. Grad. clin. supr. Clin. Center, So. Ill. U., Carbondale, 1964-65, grad. instr. spl. edn., 1965-66; speech, lang., hearing pathologist, counselor Westwood (Mass.) Public Schs., 1967—; grad. clin. instr., supr. dept. communication disorders Emerson Coll., Boston, 1979—, grad. lectr., 1979—; cons. Community Pre-Sch. Therapeutic Nursery, Mass. Mental Health, 1979-81, S. Shore Mental Health Project Optimus/Outreach, 1981—; grad. clin. supr. Robbins Speech/Hearing Center, Boston, 1979—; participant profl. workshops, nat. and internat. confs. Vol. emergency med. technician Westwood Athletic Dept.; mem. adv. com. Westwood Bd. Health, 1977-80. Participant, So. Ill. U. honors seminar, 1961; recipient honors day award So. Ill. U., 1965. Episcopalian. Contbr. articles to profl. jours., chpt. to textbook Home: 43 Greenacre Westwood MA 02090 Office: 168 Beacon St Boston MA 02116

MAXWELL, SHARON LEE REYNOLDS, govt. ofcl.; b. Taft, Calif., Mar. 2, 1939; d. Theodore Roosevelt and Adelaide Velma (Johnson) Reynolds; B.A., U. Ariz., 1966, M.A., 1969; children—Maurynne Ruth, Edward Stuart. Asst. cataloger Tucson Public Schs., 1966-68, tchr., 1968-72; with City of Tucson, 1972—, citizen participation adminstr., 1978—. Mem. Pima area adv. group Health Systems Agy. So. Ariz., 1978—. Mem. Internat. Reading Assn., NEA, Ariz. Edn. Assn., Am. Soc. Public Adminstrn., Am. Soc. Tng. and Devel., Nat. Assn. Female Execs., Pi Lambda Theta. Home: PO Box 13388 Tucson AZ 85732 Office: PO Box 27210 Tucson AZ 85726

MAXWELL, SHIRLEY ANN EUBANKS, editor, reporter, city ofcl.; b. Atkins, Ark., May 14, 1945; d. Steve Ray and Alta Laverne (Coffman) Morris; student public schs., Atkins; children—Jo Ann, Jason, Jenny. Community corr., copy editor Petit Jean Country Headlight, Perryville, Ark., 1969, editor, reporter, photographer, 1974—; clerk Mcpl. Ct. Perry County (Ark.), 1976—. Past v.p. Perryville PTA; past county publicity chmn. Am. Cancer Soc.; past publicity chmn. Arthritis Found., CD; past recorder City of Adona; past treas. Adona PTA; mem. nominating com. Perry County Farm Family of Yr.; mem. adv. com. Perry County Fair Assn., past chmn. entertainment com.; past mem. Dixie Cut-ups Bluegrass Band. Recipient award Am. Cancer Soc. Baptist. Office: PO Box 418 Perryville AR 72126

MAY, AVIVA, educator; b. Tel-Aviv; came to U.S., 1939, naturalized, 1958; d. Samuel and Paula (Gordon) Rabinowitz; B.A., in Piano Pedgogy, Northeastern Ill. U., 1979; m. Stanley Lee May, Aug. 20, 1950; children—Rochelle, Alan, Risa, Ellanna. Tchr., pianist, 1948—; tchr. adult B'nai Mitzva, 1973; tchr. music, dir. McCormich Health Centers, Chgo., 1978-79, Cove Sch. Perceptually Handicapped Children, Chgo., 1978-79; prof. Hebrew and Yiddish, Spertus Coll. Judaica, Chgo., 1980—; tchr. continuing edn. Northeastern Ill. U., 1978-80, also Jewish Community Centers. folksinger, guitarist, 1962—; composer classical music for piano, choral work, folk songs. Recipient Magen David Adom Public Service award, 1973; Ill. State grantee, 1975-79; Ill. State Congressman Woody Bowman grantee, 1978-79. Mem. Music Tchrs. Nat. Assn., North Shore Music Tchrs. Assn. (a founder, charter mem., sec.), Ill. Music Tchrs. Assn., Organ and Piano Tchrs. Assn., Am. Coll. Musicians, Ill. Assn. Learning Disabilities, Sherwood Sch. Music, Yivo Inst. Yiddish. Democrat. Contbr. articles to profl. jours. Address: 1239 Asbury Ave Evanston IL 60202

MAY, BARBARA CATHERINE, nurse; b. N.Y.C., July 20, 1937; d. Nathan and Thelma Ella Lucille (Kirkwood) Jones; R.N., Manhattan State Hosp. Sch. Nursing, 1957; B.S.N., N.Y. U., 1972; M.P.S., C.W. Post Coll., 1975; postgrad. Columbia Pacific U., 1982—; m. William Canty, Jr., Dec. 12, 1982; 1 dau. by previous marriage, Cynthia Joelle Webster. Mem. staff, Bronx Mcpl. Hosp. Center, 1961—, nursing supr. psychiatry, 1961—; cons. in field. Bd. visitors Bronx Children's Psychiat. Center, 1981—; co-leader Girl Scouts. Am., 1981—. Recipient Psychiat. Nurse award, Manhattan State Hosp. Sch. Nursing, 1957; NIMH grantee, 1971, others. Mem. C.W. Post Alumni Assn., Am. Indian Assn., Am. Nurses Assn., N.Y. State Nurses Assn., Caribbean Nurses Assn., N.Y. Zool. Soc. Democrat. Episcopalian. Co-author manuals in field; contbr. articles to profl. jours. Home: 100 10 Coop City Blvd Bronx NY 10475 Office: Pelham Pkwy S and Eastchester Rd Bronx NY 10461

MAY, CHRISTINE BECKER, direct mail advt. exec.; b. N.Y.C., June 17, 1941; d. Christian Frederick and Adele (Redavid) Becker; B.A., Cornell U., 1963; m. Lawrence Chester May, 1964 (div. 1977); children—Victoria Susan, Lawrence Chester, David Christian. Systems engr. data processing div. IBM Corp., 1964-67; cons., 1968-73; mktg. mgr. Mead Digital Systems div. Mead Corp., 1974-78; v.p. mktg. Jetson Direct Mail Services, Inc., Deer Park, N.Y., 1978—; seminar speaker, cons. ink-jet imaging tech. Recipient Graphic Arts award Printing Industry Assn., 1978. Mem. Direct Mail Mktg. Assn., Alpha Phi. Home: 36 Cottontail Rd Melville NY 11747 Office: 160 E Industry Ct Deer Park NY 11729

MAY, EDNA BREZIE, adminstr., writer; b. Pine Creek, Wis., Mar. 12; d. John P. and Anna (Collins) Brezinski; teaching cert., Winona State U., 1933; B.A., No. Ariz. U., 1941; m. Fred M. May, June, 1948 (dec.). Mgr. city ticket office Am. Airlines, Phoenix, 1942-47; women's news commentator, interview host, writer Sta. KAWT, Douglas, Ariz., 1947-50; state sales and public relations mgr. Frontier Airlines, Phoenix, 1950-60; Ariz. writer Drug News, Supermarket News, 1962-65; asst. adminstr. U. Minn. Law Sch. Fund, Mpls., 1968-77; columnist, free lance writer field of aging; newsletter editor Vols. Am., Sr. Citizen Centers of Greater Mpls., Inc., 1978—; mem. RSVP; news writer; hon. lectr. Am. Grad. Sch. Internat. Mgmt. Phoenix, 1959. Recipient award Brit. Overseas Airways, 1957. Mem. Press Women of Minn., Ariz. Press Women, Phoenix Press Club, Minn. Hist. Soc., Minn. Geneal. Soc., Wis. Geneal. Soc., NOW Clubs: Soroptimist, U.S.-China Peoples Friendship Assn., Audubon Soc. Home and Office: 1346 LaSalle Suite 505 Minneapolis MN 55403

MAY, ELAINE, entertainer; b. Phila., 1932; d. Jack Berlin; ed. high sch.; studied Stanislavsky method of acting with Marie Ouspenskaya; m. Marvin May (div.); 1 dau., Jeannie Berlin; m. 2d, Sheldon Harnick (div.). Stage and radio appearances as child actor; performed Playwright's Theatre, Chgo.; appeared in student performance Miss Julie, U. Chgo.; with Mike Nichols, others, appeared with improvisational theatre group in night club The Compass, Chgo., to 1957, with Mike Nichols appeared N.Y. supper clubs Village Vanguard, Blue Angel, also night clubs other cities; TV debut on Jack Paar Show, also appeared Steve Allen Show, Omnibus, 1958, Dinah Shore Show, Perry Como Show, TV specials; mem. panel Laugh Line, NBC, 1959; recording spoken comedy Improvisations to Music, Mercury Records; weekly appearance NBC radio show Nightline; appeared with Mike Nichols, N.Y. Town Hall, 1959, An Evening with Mike Nichols and Elaine May, Golden Theatre, N.Y.C., 1960-61; dir. films A New Leaf (also acted), 1972, The Heartbreak Kid, 1973, Mikey and Nicky, 1976; appeared in film Luv, 1967, California Suite, 1978; co-author screenplay Heaven Can Wait, 1978; author: (play) Better Part of Valor. Office: care Dirs Guild Am 110 W 57 St New York NY 10019 *

MAY, ESTELLE MATTHEWS, nurse; b. Athens, Ala., Oct. 31, 1917; d. Ira H. and Jo Anna (Montgomery) Matthews; student Wilson Jr. Coll., 1934-35; R.N., Freedman's Hosp., Washington, 1940; postgrad. U. Calif., San Francisco, 1949, U. Ill., 1963; B.S., Rockford (Ill.) Coll., 1972; m. Ellis J. May, Jr., June 30, 1946; children—Karen Wicker, Ellis J. III, Pamela Cole. Staff nurse VA Hosp., Tuskegee, Ala., Waco, Tex. and Kecohtan, Va., 1941-43; vis. nurse Vis. Nurses Assn., Rockford, 1943-46; camp nurse Camp Rotary, Rockford, summers 1944-46; public health nurse Chgo. Health Dept., 1946-47; staff nurse St. Anthony Hosp., Rockford, 1947-55, Rockford Meml. Hosp., 1955-56; dir. health Rockford Coll. Speech Center, summers 1956-59; pvt. duty nurse, winters 1956-59; sch. nurse Dist. 252, 1959-63; founder, dir. Central Day Nursery, 1963; psychiat. nurse Swedish Am. Hosp., Rockford, 1964-69; psychiat. nurse H.D. Singer Mental Health Center, Rockford, 1969—, dir. nursing services, 1979—. Bd. dirs. Booker Washington Center; pres. Nat. Council Negro Women, 1977-81. Mem. Am. Nurses Assn., Ill. Nurses Assn., 3d Dist. Nurses Assn. Baptist. Clubs: Soroptimist, Order Golden Circle. Home: 1824 Green St Rockford IL 61102

MAY, GITA, educator; b. Brussels, Belgium, Sept. 16, 1929; came to U.S., 1947, naturalized, 1950; d. Albert and Blima (Sieradska) Jochimek; B.A. magna cum laude, Hunter Coll., 1953; M.A., Columbia U., 1954, Ph.D., 1957; m. Irving May, Dec. 21, 1947. Instr., Columbia Coll., N.Y.C., 1956-58; asst. prof. Columbia U., N.Y.C., 1958-61, asso. prof., 1961-68, prof., dept. rep., 1968—. Guggenheim fellow, 1964; Fulbright grantee, 1965; Nat. Endowment Humanities fellow, 1971. Decorated chevalier dans l'Ordre des Palmes Académiques (France) 1968, officier, 1981; recipient Disting. Teaching award Columbia U., 1980. Mem. Am. Assn. Tchrs. of French, Am. Soc. French Acad. Palms, Société d'Etude du Dix-Huitème Siècle, MLA (del. from Northeastern region to Gen. Assembly 1973-75, com. on research activities 1975-78, exec. council 1980—, com. on amendments to constn. 1981, exec. com. of div. on European Lit. Relations 1981—), N.E. Am. Soc. for Eighteenth Century Studies (pres. 1981—, v.p. 1980-81, exec. bd. 1976-79), Am. Soc. for Eighteenth Century Studies, Phi Beta Kappa. Author: Diderot et Baudelaire, Critiques d'Art, 1957; De Jean-Jacques Rousseau à Madame Roland: Essai sur la Sensibilité Préromantique et Révolutionnaire, 1964; Madame Roland and the Age of Revolution (Van Amringe Disting. Book award 1971), 1970; Stendhal and the Age of Napoleon, 1977; editor: (with Otis Fellows) Diderot Studies III, 1961; critical edit. Essais sur la Peinture (Diderot), 1978; mem. editorial bd. Romanic Rev., 1959—, French Rev., 1975—, Eighteenth-Century Studies, 1975-78; contbr. numerous articles and essays in field to profl. jours. Home: 404 W 116th St New York NY 10027 Office: Columbia U 501 Philosophy Hall French Dept New York NY 10027

MAY, JANICE EVELYN CHRISTENSEN, educator; b. Mpls., May 29, 1923; d. Arnold Michael and Bernice Evelyn (Schauer) Christensen; B.A. summa cum laude, U. Minn., Mpls., 1944, M.A., 1946, Ph.D., 1952; m. Francis Barns May, June 9, 1956. Asst. instr. U. Minn., 1947-48; instr. U. Tex., 1948-53; instr., asst. prof. U. Okla., 1953-56; lectr. U. Tex., Austin, 1959, 64-65, instr., 1965-72, asst. prof., 1972-74, asso. prof. govt., 1974—; lectr. U. Minn., Mpls., 1960; researcher Office Gov., State Tex., 1966, Inst. Public Affairs, U. Tex., 1969, 71, Tex. Adv. Commn. Intergovtl. Relations, 1972, Inst. Urban Studies, U. Houston, 1974. Public mem. bd. dirs. State Bar Tex., 1979-82; mem. Austin Commn. Status of Women, 1975-80, vice-chmn., 1978-79; mem. Tex. Constl. Revision Commn., 1973-74, 67-68; mem. S.W. Regional Panel, Pres. Commn. White House Fellows, 1970; mem. Nat. Com. Rep. Govt., LWV, 1974-75. Mem. League Women Voters (mem. state bd. 1964-70), AAUW (award 1980, nat. legis. com. 1967-73), Am. Polit. Sci. Assn., Am. Acad. Polit. and Social Sci., Am. Judicature Soc., Nat. Mcpl. League, So. Polit. Sci. Assn., Southwestern Polit. Sci. Assn. (sec.-treas. 1980-84), Southwestern Social Sci. Assn., Women's Polit. Caucus, Austin World Affairs Council. Author: Amending the Texas Constitution, 1951-72, 1973; The Texas Constitutional Revision Experience in the 70's, 1975; (with Stuart A. MacCorkle and Dick Smith) Texas Government, 7th edit., 1974, 8th edit., 1980. Home: 6504 Auburnhill Dr Austin TX 78723 Office: Dept Govt U Tex Austin TX 78712

MAY, JOAN CHRISTINE, chemist; b. Buffalo, May 25, 1943; d. Frank John and Natalie Dolores May; B.S., Nazareth Coll., Rochester, N.Y., 1965; M.S., U. Wis., Madison, 1968; Ph.D., U. Notre Dame, 1971. Instr., research asst. U. Wis., 1965-68, U. Notre Dame, 1968-71; postdoctoral tng. Roswell Park Meml. Inst., Buffalo, 1971-72; presdl. intern analytical chemistry Nat. Bur. Standards, 1972-73, sr. chemist, then supervisory chemist analytical chemistry br., 1973-77; dir. analytical chemistry br. Bur. Biologists, FDA, 1977—. Recipient award merit FDA, 1977, Commendable Service award, 1978. Mem. Internat. Assn. Biol. Standardization, Am. Chem. Soc., Assn. Ofcl. Analytical Chemists, Sigma Xi, Sigma Delta Epsilon. Roman Catholic. Author articles in field. Office: 8800 Rockville Pike Bethesda MD 20205

MAY, JULIA MAYO, city ofcl., lawyer; b. Prestonsburg, Ky., Apr. 5, 1936; d. Robert V. and Emma Alice (Wells) May; A.B., Wellesley Coll., 1958; LL.B., U. Va., 1961; LL.M., Georgetown U., 1965. Admitted to Ky. bar, 1961; law clk. Ky. Supreme Ct., Frankfort, 1961-62, U.S. Tax Ct., Washington, 1963-67; mem. firm Chadbourne, Parke, Whiteside & Wolff, N.Y.C., 1968-69; tax atty. U.S. Dept. Justice, Washington, 1969-70; Exec. Dir. Prestonsburg (Ky.) Housing and Community Devel. Agy., 1973—; pres. May Mgmt. Co., Inc., Ky. Highland Highland Housing, Inc.; v.p. Chase Options, Inc. Trustee Floyd County (Ky.) Library Bd.; bd. dirs. Calico Corner Nursery, Inc. Recipient Am. Jurisprudence award, 1965. Mem. Ky. Housing and Redevel. Assn. (pres.), Ky. Women's Lawyers Assn., Nat. Assn. Housing and Redevel. Ofcls. Democrat. Episcopalian. Club: Kiwaniannes. Home: 38 Arnold Ave Prestonsburg KY 41653 Office: PO Box 230 Prestonsburg KY 41653

MAY, LINDA DIANNE, mktg. co. exec.; b. Missoula, Mont., Dec. 3, 1950; d. Doran Calvin May and Alice Margaret (Torgrimson) May Oates; B.S. with honors, Calif. Poly. State U., 1973; M.A., 1974; postgrad Sch. Law U. Pacific, 1980. Med. asst., various physicians' offices, San Luis Obispo, Calif., 1968-74; lectr. Calif. Poly. State U., San Luis Obispo, 1974-76; sales rep. Mut. Benefit Life Ins. Co., San Luis Obispo, 1976-78; profl. service rep. Schering Pharm. Co., Kenilworth, N.J., 1978-80; sr. account exec. Calif. Western Life Ins. Co., Sacramento, 1980; exec. dir. Community Care, Inc., Santa Ana, Calif., 1981—. Active Big Sisters of Orange County. Registered dietitian. Mem. Affiliated Networks of Exec. Women, Womens' Econ. and Career Advancement Network, Am. Dietetic Assn., Nat. Assn. Life Underwriters, Soc. Advancement Mgmt., AAUW, Nat. Orgn. Exec. Women, Phi Upsilon Omicron. Republican. Episcopalian. Club: Sierra. Office: PO Box 1044 Santa Ana CA 92702

MAY, MARGRETHE, allied health educator; b. Tucson, Oct. 6, 1943; d. Robert A. and Margrethe (Holm) M.; student in nursing U. Mich., 1961-65, B.S. in Human Biology, 1970. Mem. operating room staff Hartford (Conn.) Hosp., 1965-68, U. Mich. Hosp., Ann Arbor, 1968-70; asst. operating room supr. U. Ariz. Hosp., Tucson, 1971-72; coordinator operating room tech. Pima Community Coll., Tucson, 1971-76; coordinator surg. tech. program, asst. prof. Delta Coll., University Center, Mich., 1978—; cons. in surg. tech.; mem. Health Care Team Project; mem. Nat. Certifying Exam. Writing Com., 1974-76, 80—, chmn., 1981; co-chmn. Liaison Council on Certification, 1977, chmn., 1978, sec.-treas., 1979; mem. Visitation Team for Surg. Tech. Program Accreditation, 1974—; workshop presenter. Cert. surg. technologist, emergency med. technologist. Mem. Assn. Surg. Technologists, Am. Soc. Allied Health Professions. Home: 2616 Abbott Rd Apt I3 Midland MI 48640 Office: Delta College University Center MI 48710

MAY, PHYLLIS JEAN, adult foster care corp. exec.; b. Flint, Mich., May 31, 1932; d. Bert A. and Alice C. (Rushton) Irvine; grad. Dorsey Sch. Bus., 1957; cert. Internat. Corr. Schs., 1959, Nat. Tax Inst., 1978; M.B.A., Mich. U., 1970; m. John May, Apr. 24, 1971; children—Phillip, Perry, Paul. Office mgr. Comml. Constrn. Co., Flint, 1962-68; bus. mgr. new and used car dealership, Flint, 1968-70; controller 6 corps., Flint, 1970-75; fiscal dir. Rubicon Odyssey Inc., Detroit, 1976—; acad. cons. acctg. Detroit Inst. Commerce, 1980-81; pres. small bus. specializing in adminstrv. cons. and acctg., 1982—; notary public, 1968—. Pres. PTA Westwood Heights Schs., 1972; vol. Fedn. of Blind, 1974-76, Probate Ct., 1974-76. Recipient Meritorious Service award Genesee County for Youth, 1976, Excellent Performance and High Achievement award Odyssey Inc., 1981. Mem. Am. Bus. Women's Assn. (treas. 1981, rec. sec. 1982, v.p. 1982-83, Woman of Yr. 1982), Nat. Assn. Profl. Female Execs. Baptist. Home: 12050 Barlow St Detroit MI 48205 Office: Rubicon Odyssey Inc 7441 Brush St Detroit MI 48202

MAY, SHARON ELLEN, ednl. adminstr.; b. Birmingham, Ala., Oct. 13, 1942; d. John Edward and Annie Ruth (Daniels) M.; B.S., Wayne State U., 1973; M.A., U. Mich., 1976; Ed.D. candidate Wayne State U., 1982—. With Detroit Public Schs., 1960—, tchr., 1974-77, counselor, 1977-79, equal ednl. opportunity adminstr., 1980—. Mem. Women's Conf. of Concerns, 1979—; lay minister Tabernacle Missionary Baptist Ch. Mem. Women's Assn. U. Mich., New Profl. Women's Network, Am. Personnel and Guidance Assn., Guidance Assn. Met. Detroit, Detroit Inst. Arts, Phi Delta Kappa. Democrat. Office: 5057 Woodward Ave Room 1302 Detroit MI 48202

MAY, TAMARA IVA, social worker; b. Holdrege, Nebr., Dec. 14, 1948; d. Thomas Ludwig and Lois Elva (Beck) Swanson; B.S., Kearney (Nebr.) State Coll., 1974; m. Roger Stanley May, Sept. 25, 1976 (dec.); children—Thomas Mitchell, Pepper Lea. Activities dir. Methodist Homes, Holdrege, Nebr., 1974-75; social worker Bethphage Mission, Axtell, Nebr., 1976-77; social worker Walker Post Manor, Oxford, Nebr., 1976-80, Colonial Villa, Alma, Nebr., 1978—, Good Samaritan Nursing Center, Arapahoe, Nebr., 1978—; sponsor essay contest for sr. citizens in Nebr., 1980. Mem. Nat. Assn. Social Workers, Democrat. Presbyterian. Clubs: Holdrege Country, Eagles Aux. Home: Rural Route 3 Holdrege NE 68949

MAYBERRY, LILLIAN FAYE, biologist; b. Portland, Oreg., May 19, 1943; d. Wayne R. and Olive (Lynch) M.; A.A., San Jose City Coll., 1963; B.A., Calif. State U.-San Jose, 1967; M.S., U. Nev.-Reno, 1970; Ph.D., Colo. State U.-Ft. Collins, 1973; m. John R. Bristol, Aug. 22, 1975. Research assoc. dept. anatomy Colo. State U., 1973-74; postdoctoral research assoc. molecular, cellular and devel. biology dept. U. Colo., 1974-76; protozoologist Yugoslavian Internat. Biol. Program, Titograd, 1975-76; adj. asst. prof. N.Mex. State U., 1976-80, instr. biology U. Tex., El Paso, 1977, instr. nursing, 1977—, adj. assoc. prof., 1982—; physiology cons. HEW grantee, U. Tex., El Paso, 1979—; exchange scientist Am. Nat. Acad. Scis./Eastern European Acad. Scis., summer 1978. Mem. Am. Soc. Parasitologists, Soc. Protozoologists, AAAS, Helminthological Soc. Wash., Sigma Xi, Phi Beta Kappa, Phi Kappa Phi. Presbyterian. Research in physiology of host parasite relationships. Office: Dept Biology U Tex El Paso TX 79968

MAYBURY, MARY ELLEN, nursing adminstr.; b. Corbin, Ky., June 11, 1946; d. Henry N. and Sarah D. (Anderson) Campbell; diploma Miami (Ohio) Valley Hosp. Sch. Nursing, 1967; m. Charles R. Maybury, June 28, 1970; children—Charles Robert, Howard Neal. Staff nurse Miami Valley Hosp., Dayton, Ohio, 1967-69, head nurse, 1969-70; partner, mgr. Cottage Antiques and Auctioneering, Marshfield Hills, Mass., 1970-79; charge nurse Stetson Hall, Norwell, Mass., 1971-74; supr. South Shore Nursing Facility, Rockland, Mass., 1973-78; asst. dir. nursing Laughlin Meml. Hosp., Greeneville, Tenn., 1979—, co-instr. nursing mgmt. program, 1979—; participant Nat. Nurse Health Study, 1975—. Mem. com. Cub Scouts Am., 1981—. Recipient Cert. Appreciation, Cub Scouts Am., 1981. Mem. Tenn. Hosp. Assn. (pres. elect assos. div. 1981, pres. 1982-83). Baptist. Home: Route 1 States View Rd Mosheim TN 37818 Office: Laughlin Meml Hosp 215 N College St Greeneville TN 37743

MAYBURY-MCKIM, JOANNE CLARICE GANGE, historian; b. Pasadena, Calif., Feb. 9, 1939; d. John Ross and Ann Cecilia Westphalen Gange; B.A., U. Calif., Riverside, 1966; secondary teaching credential Calif. State U., Northridge, 1970; M.A., UCLA, 1971; m. Stanley E. Spangler, Jan. 31, 1958; 1 dau., Julia Watt; m. 2d, Bruce T. McKim, Aug. 25, 1965. Tchr. social scis. and lit. adult edn. Univ. High Sch., Los Angeles, 1968-71; mem. faculty history dept. Santa Ana (Calif.) Coll., 1971—, now prof., founder women's studies program, 1972, coordinator women's studies dept., 1972-77. Mem. Hollywood Arts Council. Mem. Holistic Edn. Network, Soc. Suggestive-Accelerative Learning and Teaching, Assn. Humanistic Psychology, Am. Fedn. Tchrs. (founder, acting pres. Santa Ana Coll. chpt.), Am. Film Inst., Filmex Soc., NOW, Nat. Women's Polit. Caucus, Nat. Women's Book Assn., Women in Mgmt., Nat. Women's Studies Assn., West Coast Women's Historians Assn. Democrat. Home: 2315 Kenilworth Ave Los Angeles CA 90039 Office: Dept History Santa Ana Coll Santa Ana CA 92706

MAYER, BEATRICE CUMMINGS, civic worker; b. Montreal, P.Q., Can., Aug. 15, 1921; came to U.S., 1939, naturalized, 1944; d. Nathan and Ruth (Kellert) Cummings; B.A. in Chemistry, U. N.C., 1943; postgrad. U. Chgo., 1946; m. Robert Bloom Mayer, Dec. 11, 1947 (dec.); children—Robert N., Mrs. Stephen P. Durchslag. Mem. vis. com. Sch. Social Service Admnstrn. U. Chgo., 1964—, dept. art, 1972; dir. women's bd., 1973—; governing life mem. Art Inst. Chgo., also mem. women's bd.; trustee Michael Reese Hosp. and Med. Center, Chgo., 1974—; trustee Kenyon Coll., Gambier, Ohio, 1976—; bd. fellows Brandeis U., Waltham, Mass., 1977—; mem. womens bd. Northwestern U., 1978—; trustee Anshe Emet Synagogue, Chgo., 1974—, v.p., 1978—; trustee Mus. Contemporary Art, Chgo., 1974—, v.p., 1978—; dir. Consol. Foods Corp., also chmn. public responsibility com. Recipient Brandeis U. Disting. Community Service award, 1972; Am. Jewish Com. Human Rights medallion, 1976; YMCA Leadership award, 1979; Woman of Year in Arts, YWCA Met. Chgo., 1979. Clubs: Tavern, Standard (Chgo.); Lake Shore Country (Glencoe, Ill.). Home: 175 E Delaware Pl Apt 7403 Chicago IL 60611

MAYER, CATHERINE ANNE, psychiatrist; b. Evanston, Ill., Oct. 10, 1945; d. George Andrew and Lorna (Lindsay) M.; B.A. cum laude, Stanford U., 1967; M.D., U. Wis., 1978. Intern, C. F. Menninger Meml. Hosp., Topeka, 1978-79, resident in psychiatry, 1979-82, staff psychiatrist, 1982—. Mem. A.M.A., AAAS, Am. Psychiat. Assn., Alpha Omega Alpha. Office: Box 829 Topeka KS 66601

MAYER, EDITH PEACOCK, state legislator; b. Cin., July 24, 1929; d. Howard William and Serene (Allan) Peacock; student Ind. U.; m. Charles D. Mayer, Apr. 24, 1959; children—Sandra, Charles D. Tchr. math. and English, Madison County, Ala., 1951-53; staff asst. toilet goods product research Procter & Gamble, Cin., 1956-59; mem. Ohio Ho. of Reps., 1977—; dir. Enterprise Fed. Savs. & Loan, Cin. Mem. Greenhills-Forest Park Bd. Edn., 1968-77, pres., 1969, 71, 73; parliamentarian Great Oaks JVS Bd. Edn., 1972-77; mem. Ohio PTA Bd. Mgrs., 1972-77. Recipient Outstanding Leadership awards Ohio Sch. Bds. Assn., 1976, Ohio Elem. Adminstrs., 1980, Ohio Twp. Trustees Assn., 1980, Humane Soc. U.S., 1981, Ohio Assn. Gifted and Talented, 1981. Mem. Nat. Assn. Women Legislators, Nat. Assn. Republican Legislators. Republican. Episcopalian. Home: 10120 Winstead Ln Cincinnati OH 45231 Office: State House Columbus OH 43215

MAYER, ELLEN DONNELLY, nursing service adminstr.; b. Ayrshire, Scotland, Nov. 14, 1919; came to U.S., 1923, naturalized, 1929; d. Alexander and Annie Brown (Finnie) Aitken; R.N., City Hosp. of Akron Nursing Sch., 1941; student Rutgers U., 1965, Ind. Grad. Sch. Bus., 1966, 69; m. Richard T. Mayer, Oct. 11, 1960. Head nurse Akron (Ohio) City Hosp., 1941; staff nurse McKeesport (Pa.) Hosp., 1942-46; nursing supr. Shore Meml. Hosp., Somers Point, N.J., 1958-62, dir. nursing, 1962-72, asst. adminstr., 1972—. Mem. adv. com. dept. nursing Atlantic Community Coll., 1973—; mem. coms. to rev., revise standards for hemodialysis units N.J. Dept. Health, Perinatal Coop., So. N.J., 1978—; del. U.S. Nursing Service Adminstrv. Leaders, People to People Travel Mission, 1980. Mem. Am. Soc. Nursing Service Adminstrs., N.J. Soc. Nursing Adminstrs., Am. Nurses Assn., Am. Hosp. Assn., N.J. Hosp. Assn., N.J. Nurses Assn., Nursing Adminstrs. Forum of N.J., City Hosp. of Akron Alumni Assn., ARC. Home: 500 16th St Ocean City NJ 08226 Office: Shore Meml Hosp New York Ave Somers Point NJ 08244

MAYER, SUSAN LEE, nurse; b. N.Y.C., Feb. 10, 1946; d. Hans and Frieda (Schein) Abramson; B.S.N., Hunter Coll., 1968; M.A., N.Y.U., 1974, postgrad., 1974; m. Steven Mayer, June 24, 1973; children—Jason, Stuart, Richard. Staff nurse ICU-CCU, Montefiore Hosp., Bronx, N.Y., 1968; organizer CCU, Jewish Meml. Hosp., N.Y.C., 1968; supr., adminstr. Morrisania City Hosp., N.Y.C., 1969-76; instr. Adelphi Univ., Garden City, N.Y., 1977-78; substitute nurse Great Neck (N.Y.) Public Schs., 1980—; tchr. CPR, 1972-80; lectr. PTA groups, 1981-82. Bd. dirs. Great Neck Synagogue, 1981—, v.p. Sisterhood, 1978-79, pres., 1979-81; bd. dirs. Russell Gardens Assn., 1976—; founder Work for Share, Zedek Hosp., 1977—. N.Y. State Regents scholar, 1963. Mem. Am. Nurses Assn., Nat. League Nursing, N.Y. Counties Registered Nurses Assn., N.Y. Heart Assn., Sigma Theta Tau. Democrat. Club: New York University. Home: 2 Dunster Rd Great Neck NY 11021

MAYER, VELIA ANN, lawyer; b. nr. Mt. Pleasant, Tex., Feb. 13, 1943; d. Velia John and Opal (Dale) Mayer; B.A. cum laude, U. Miss., 1965, J.D., 1968. Admitted to Miss. bar, 1968; practiced in Jackson, 1971—; law clk. for judge of Miss. Supreme Ct., Jackson, 1968-69; spl. asst. atty. gen. State of Miss., Jackson, 1969-71; assoc. firm Watkins and Eager, attys. at law, Jackson, 1971-75, partner, 1975-82. Mem. Am., Miss., Hinds County bar assns., Am. Judicature Soc. Home: 787 Arlington St Jackson MS 39202 Office: Box 650 Jackson MS 39205

MAYERS, TEENA, mgmt. cons.; b. Bklyn., Dec. 25, 1924; ed. public schs. Pres. cons. firm, Rome, 1960-75; mem. advisers and experts group SALT II delegation, Geneva; mgr. SALT Task Force ACDA, 1971-81; mgmt. cons., Washington, 1981-82; state rep. Peace Links Internat., 1982. Independent. Home: 3800 N Fairfax Dr Arlington VA 22203

MAYES, CAROLYN DELORIS, nurse; b. West Monroe, La., Feb. 1, 1953; d. Willie Henry and Freddie Mae (Wesley) M.; student Stanford U., 1971-73; B.S. in Nursing, Tex. Christian U., 1976; M.S.N., U. Calif., San Francisco, 1982. Supr., Salem Luth. Homes, Inc., Oakland, Calif., 1976-77; staff nurse II, Children's Hosp. Med. Center, Oakland, 1977-78, asst. unit. coordinator, pediatric intensive care, 1978-80, nurse supr., 1980-82, asso. coordinator med.-oncology unit, 1982—. Registered nurse, Calif., Tex. Mem. Calif. Nurses Assn., Sigma Theta Tau, Alpha Kappa Alpha. Democrat. Roman Catholic. Club: Supreme Court Racquetball. Home: 5059 Fairfax St Oakland CA 94601 Office: Children's Hosp Med Center 51st St and Grove St Oakland CA 94609

MAYESKI, FRAN ELIZABETH, ednl. adminstr.; b. Rolla, Mo., Nov. 6, 1941; d. Charles Emil and Katherine Dorothy (Parker) Gelven; B.S. in English, St. Louis U., 1964; postgrad. U. Wash., Seattle, 1974; M.B.A., City Coll., Seattle, 1980; m. John Kent Mayeski, May 21, 1966; 1 son, Mark Edward. Publs. asst. St. Louis U., 1965-66; tchr. St. Charles Schs., Spokane, Wash., 1967-68, Holmes Jr. High Sch., Colorado Springs, 1969, Sacred Heart Sch., Bellevue Wash., 1971-74, Interlake High Sch., Bellevue, 1974-76, area chairperson social studies, 1976-77; tchr., project leader Bellevue Public Schs., 1979-80; dir. staff devel. and spl. projects Ednl. Service Unit 10, Kearney, Nebr., 1980—; instr. Seattle Pacific U., Kearney State Coll. Pres. Sch. Bd. Holy Family Sch., Kirkland, Wash., 1976-77. Mem. Assn. Supervision and Curriculum Devel., Nebr. Assn. Supervision and Curriculum Devel., Women in Mgmt. Assn. Club: Kearney State Coll. Faculty Wives. Office: PO Box 2007 Kearney NE 68847

MAYHEW, FRANCES WHITAKER, educator; b. Bristol, Va., Mar. 15, 1941; d. Earle Edward and Marjorie Lin (McGhee) Whitaker; B.S., U. Del., 1963, M.S., 1974; postgrad. U. Md., 1980—; m. Eric Walter Mayhew, Dec. 21, 1962; children—Robin Margaret, Wendy Rebecca. Lectr. comml. design Brandywine Coll., Wilmington, Del., part-time, 1974-76; instr. U. Del., Newark, 1976-78, asst. prof. historic costume, textile conservation, basic garment constrn. and tailoring, 1979—; cons. in field. Vol., CONTACT Wilmington, 1977—. Recipient William H. Danforth award, 1962. Mem. Am. Home Econ. Assn. (adv. student mem. sect. 1978-81), Del. Home Econ. Assn. (treas. 1977-81), Assn. Coll. Profs. Textiles and Clothing, Assn. for Devel. Computer-Based Instructional Systems, SIG/Home Ec., Omicron Nu. Office: 317 Alison Hall Coll Human Resources Univ Del Newark DE 19711

MAYKUT, MADELAINE OLGA, clin. pharmacologist; b. Toronto, Ont., Can., July 8, 1925; d. Wasily and Mary (Kleban) M.; B.A., U. Toronto, 1948, M.A., 1950, Ph.D., 1957, M.D., 1964. Asst. cancer research U. Toronto Med. Sch., 1948-49; asst. biochemist Ford Hosp., Detroit, 1950-51; research local anesthesia, demonstrator pharmacol. lab. course Shouldice Surgery-U. Toronto Med. Sch., 1951-59, asst. in surgery, 1965-66; sr. pharmacologist Pitman-Moore Co. Research Center, Indpls., 1959-60; rotating intern Mt. Sinai Hosp., Toronto, 1964-65; asst. dir. clin. research William S. Merrell Co., Cin., 1966-67; asst. dir. clin. pharmacology Bristol Labs., Syracuse, N.Y., 1967-72; adviser medicine and pharmacology Food and Drug Directorate Can., Ottawa, 1972-73; chief biomed. research Non-Med. Use Drugs Directorate Can., Ottawa, 1973-78; chief biomed. research health protection br. Health and Welfare Can., Ottawa, 1978—. Author, editor in field. Office: Room 141 Health Protection Br Bldg Tunney's Pasture Ottawa ON K1A 0L2 Canada

MAYNARD, JANE HENDERSON, pub. relations cons.; b. Beverly, Mass., Mar. 30, 1936; d. Warwick and Elizabeth (Davidson) Henderson; student Newton (Mass.) Coll., 1954-57; m. Walter Maynard. Public relations dir. McCall Pub. Co., 1970-71, Allen-A Co., N.Y.C., 1971-72; pub. relations cons., N.Y.C., 1972—. Exec. com. Council of N.Y. Pub. Library; exec. com. N.Y. Com., U.S. Ski Team Fund; N.Y. affiliate Am. Fedn. Arts, 1977—; trustee Archives Am. Art, 1980—. Club: Cosmopolitan (N.Y.C.). Home: 19 E 72d St New York NY 10021

MAYNARD, VIRGINIA MADDEN, assn. ofcl.; b. New London, Conn., Jan. 29, 1924; d. Raymond and Edna Sarah (Madden) Maynard; B.S., U. Conn., 1945; postgrad. Am. Inst. Banking, 1964-66, Cornell U., 1975. With Nat. City Bank (now Citibank), N.Y.C., 1954-79, asst. cashier, 1965-69, asst. v.p., 1969-74, v.p. internat. banking group, 1974-76, comptroller's div., 1976-79; v.p. First Women's Bank, N.Y.C., 1979-80; Internat. Fedn. Univ. Women rep. UN, 1982—; cons. in field. Trustee fellowships endowment fund AAUW Ednl. Found., Washington, 1977-80, Va. Gildersleeve Internat. Fund Univ. Women, Inc. Mem. AAUW (fin. chmn. N.Y.C. br. 1976-79, bylaws chmn. 1979—, Woman of Achievement 1976). Republican. Congregationalist. Home: 601 E 20th St New York NY 10010

MAYNARD PRIGGE, ELIZABETH, pub. co. mgr.; b. Los Angeles, Jan. 5, 1952; d. Robert Graham and Emily Jeannette (Prouty) Maynard; student Regis Coll., U. Calif., Santa Barbara, 1970-75; m. Paul Joseph Prigge, May 1, 1982. Production asst. ABC-CLIO, Inc., Santa Barbara, Calif., 1971-75; sales asst. R. R. Donnelley, Palo Alto, Calif., 1975-76; asst. mfg. mgr. Addison-Wesley Pub. Co., Menlo Park, Calif., 1976-77; prodn. editor, prodn. mgr., editorial prodn. mgr. and mgr. editorial and graphic services, Info. Handling Services, Denver, 1977—; co-owner and editorial dir. Bookmakers Guild; mem. faculty Folio Face-to-Face Pub. Conf. Mem. Graphic Arts Production Club (Denver). Democrat. Home: 3052 E Peakview Circle Littleton CO 80121 Office: 15 Inverness Way E Englewood CO 80150

MAYNE, LUCILLE STRINGER, educator; b. Washington, June 6, 1924; d. Henry Edmond and Hattie Benham (Benson) Stringer; B.S., U. MD., 1946; M.B.A. (grad. scholar), Ohio State U., 1949; Ph.D. (fellow), Northwestern U., 1966; children—Patricia Anne, Christine Gail, Barbara Marie. Asst. to promotion mgr. NBC, Washington, 1946-48; instr. fin. Utica (N.Y.) Coll., 1949-50; analytical statistician Air Material Command, Dayton, Ohio, 1950-52; lectr. fin. Roosevelt U., Chgo., 1961-64; lectr. Pa. State U., State College, 1965-66, asst. prof., 1966-69, asso. prof., 1969-70; asso. prof. banking and fin. Case Western Res. U., Cleve., 1971-76, prof., 1976—, dean Sch. Grad. Studies, 1980—. Bd. dirs. Cleve. Citywide Devel. Corp., 1981—. Mem. Am. Fin. Assn., Midwest Fin. Assn., Fin. Mgmt. Assn. (dir. 1982-83), Phi Kappa Phi, Beta Gamma Sigma. Episcopalian. Asso. editor Jour. Money, Credit and Banking, 1980—, Bus. Econs., 1980—; contbr. articles to profl. jours. Office: Case Western Reserve U Weatherhead Sch Mgmt and Grad Studies University Circle Cleveland OH 44106

MAYO, ALICE L., economist; b. Va.; B.A., Ohio State U., 1969; M.A., Georgetown U., 1971. Economist, U.S. Dept. Transp., Washington, 1973-75, U.S. Fed. Preparedness Agy., Washington, 1975-76, Export-Import Bank of U.S., Washington, 1976—. Office: Export-Import Bank 811 Vermont Ave NW Washington DC 20571

MAYO, NORMA, sales cons.; b. Los Angeles, Sept. 22, 1926; d. Henry N. and Rina D. (Arcy) Amarillas; grad. Holiday Inn U., 1973; m. Jack D. Mayo, Sept. 22, 1946; children—Jack D., H. Gerard. Sales mgr. Holiday Inn Airport, El Paso, 1966-67; dir. sales Sheraton El Paso, 1967-70; dir. sales Holiday Inn Downtown, El Paso, 1970-73, mgr., 1973-82; sales cons., El Paso, 1982—. Vice chmn. El Paso Bd. Devel., 1976-77; mem. adv. council Tex. Film Commn. Named Sales Mgr. of Year, Holiday Inns, Inc., 1973, El Paso Innkeeper of Year, 1977. Mem. El Paso Innkeepers Assn. (life; pres. 1977), El Paso (dir. 1977—), West Tex. chambers commerce, Downtown Devel. Assn. (dir.), Am. Advt. Fedn., Hotel Sales Mgrs. Assn. (hon. life; organizer local chpt. 1972, pres. Tex. chpt. 1977), NCCJ, Tex. Soc. Assn. Execs. (hon.), Discover Tex. Assn., Tex. Tourist Council, Discover Am. Travel Orgn. (El Paso liaison Tex. div.), Nat. Assn. Tour Brokers, Tex. Hotel, Motel Assn., El Paso C. of C. (dir.), Tex. Assn. Bus. Republican. Roman Catholic. Research on tourism for City of El Paso, 1975. Home: 8339 Turrentine St El Paso TX 79925 Office: 8339 Turrentine El Paso TX 79925

MAYO, VERNA DEL MARIE JOINER, biologist; b. Hammond, La., Sept. 7, 1926; d. Charles Bozeman and Verna (Jones) Joiner; A.B. cum laude, Anderson (Ind.) Coll., 1947; M.S., Tulane U., 1950; Ph.D., Ind. U., 1958; m. Gradie L. Mayo, June 7, 1946; children—David LaNoyette, Lowell Dean. Mem. faculty Anderson Coll., 1950—, prof. biology, 1977—. Mem. AAAS, AAUW, Am. Soc. Cell Biology, Am. Inst. Biol. Scis., Devel. Biology Soc., Ind. Biology Tchrs. Assn., Ind. Acad. Sci., Sigma Xi, Sigma Delta Epsilon, Sigma Zeta. Republican. Mem. Ch. of God. Contbr. articles to profl. publs. Home: 1013 Imel Dr Anderson IN 46012 Office: Anderson Coll Anderson IN 46012

MAYOR, HEATHER DONALD, molecular biologist; b. Melbourne, Australia, July 6, 1930; came to U.S., 1956, naturalized, 1959; d. Joseph Arthur Lindsay and Elizabeth Emily (Boyd) Donald; B.S., U. Melbourne, 1950, D.Sc., 1971; Ph.D., U. London, 1954; m. Richard Blair Mayor, May 28, 1956; children—Diana B., Philip H. Research assoc. in virology Walter and Eliza Hall Inst. Med. Research, Melbourne, 1950-51; research assoc. in bacteriology and immunology Harvard U. Med. Sch., 1956-59; mem. faculty Baylor U. Coll. Medicine, Houston, 1960—, prof. virology, 1965-70, assoc. in microbiology and exptl. biology, 1971-75, prof. microbiology and immunology, 1975—; vis. prof. div. animal health Commonwealth Sci. and Indsl. Research Orgn., also dept. microbiology U. Melbourne, 1965; cons. in field. Recipient Disting. award Center Interaction-Man, Sci. and Culture, 1970; grantee Robert A. Welch Found., Damon Runyon Found., Nat. Cancer Inst., Cockrell Found. Mem. Am. Assn. Immunologists, Soc. Cell Biology, Biophys. Soc., Am. Soc. Microbiology, Am. Assn. Cancer Research, Sigma Xi. Episcopalian. Clubs: Doctors, Houstonian. Author articles in field. Home: 226 Pine Hollow Ln Houston TX 77056 Office: Dept Microbiology Baylor U Coll Medicine Houston TX 77030

MAYORGA, JANET MARIE, nurse; b. Ottawa, Ill., Aug. 8, 1937; d. Shirley Franklin Taggart and Edith Mae (Caplinger) Carr; diploma St. Joseph's Sch. Nursing, 1958; B.S. in Nursing, Purdue U., 1972; M.S.N., U. Tex., El Paso, 1979; postgrad. N.Mex. State U.; m. Alfredo Mayorga, June 20, 1959; children—Susan, Josefina, Kathleen, Maria, Janet. Staff nurse, Chgo., 1960-62; office nurse, Gary, Ind., 1963-71; instr. nursing Purdue U., Hammond, Ind., 1972-73; asst. prof. nursing U. Tex., El Paso, 1976—; pres. Lake County Med. Aux., 1968-69, El Paso County Med. Aux., 1975—. Served with Nurses Corps, U.S. Army, 1958-60. Mem. Am. Nurses Assn., Pan Am. Round Table, Phi Delta Kappa, Phi Kappa Phi. Roman Catholic. Office: 1101 Campbell St El Paso TX 79902

MAYS, GENEVA, govt. ofcl.; b. N.Y.C., Mar. 17; d. John and Clara (Lancaster) Wise; B.A., Bernard Baruch Sch. Bus. Adminstrn., N.Y.C., 1959; m. Paul Mays, Aug. 29, 1959; children—Paul Eric, Jon William. Various secretarial and adminstrv. asst. positions, 1957-71; EEO specialist, mgr. fed. women's program Dept. Transp., Washington, from 1971—, now spl. asst. to dir. minority and women's affairs. Recipient Meritorious Achievement Honor award Dept. Labor, 1966. Mem. Am. Soc. Public Adminstrn., Federally Employed Women, Urban League, Blacks in Govt., Black Women's Agenda, Suitland Civic Assn., Links, Jack and Jill Am. (founder, 1st pres. Prince George's County chpt. 1974). Home: 5010 Luci Ln Suitland MD 20023 Office: 2100 2d St SW Washington DC 20590

MAYS, RUBY WATKINS, ins. agy. adminstr.; b. Jackson, Miss., Sept. 14, 1928; d. Edward Franklin and Gertrude (Tatum) Watkins; student public schs., Jackson; m. William Edgar Mays, Feb. 28, 1947; children—William Edgar, Myra Evelyn, Richard Carroll, Cynthia Cain, Benjamin Ross. With Ashcraft Realty, 1946, Jackson Daily News, 1947; with McMurphy Ins. Agy., Jackson, 1964—, adminstrv. asst., 1980—. Den mother Cub Scouts. Cert. profl. ins. woman; cert. Ins. Inst. Am. Mem. Nat. Assn. Ins. Women (past regional dir., past nat. chmn., past editor), Am. Bus. Women's Assn. (pres. Jackson charter chpt.), Ins. Women Jackson (pres.). Methodist. Clubs: Order of Eastern Star (sec., past matron Northwood chpt. 370). Home: 2939-A University Dr Jackson MS 39216 Office: PO Box 4674 Jackson MS 39216

MAYWALT, GERALDINE MARGARET, nurse; b. Woodcliffe Lake, N.J., Sept. 19, 1941; d. Robert Emmet and Mary Agnes (Hartnett) Mitchell; R.N., St. Mary's Sch. Nursing, Rochester, N.Y., 1962; m. James Charles Maywalt, Sept. 7, 1963; children—Colleen, Susan, James. Staff nurse hosps. in N.Y. State, 1962-76; community mental health nurse Cayuga County Mental Health Center, Auburn, N.Y., 1976-77; coordinator in-patient psychiat. services Monmouth Med. Center, Long Branch, N.J., 1977-81, transitional services liaison and cons. edn. Pollak outpatient psychiat. services, 1981—; cons. in field. Fellow Nat. Council Alcoholism, 1979. Mem. N.J. Assn. Cons. and Edn., Psychiat./Mental Health R.N.s Monmouth County. Office: Outpatient Psychiatry Monmouth Med Center 3d Ave Long Branch NJ 07740

MAZER, GWEN VERNEA, image cons.; b. N.Y.C., May 23, 1937; d. Theodore Roosevelt and Edythe Belle (Winfrey) Goodman; student Hunter Coll., 1952-54, N.Y. U., 1954-57. Fashion dir. Advt. Images,

N.Y.C., 1961-68; fashion editor Harper's Bazaar, N.Y.C., 1968-73; founder Narcissa, boutique, N.Y.C., 1970-75; mktg. dir. Nazareno Gabrielli, fashion co., N.Y.C., 1976-78; creative dir. Espirt de Corp, San Francisco, 1978-80; prin. Gwen Mazer and Assos., San Francisco, 1980—; lectr. U. Calif., Berkeley, 1980-81; instr. Skyline Coll., 1981-82. Trustee Magic Theatre, Ft. Mason, San Francisco. Recipient Excellence award Communication Arts mag., 1979, Excellence cert. Am. Inst. Graphic Arts, 1979. Mem. Black Women's Roundtable, San Francisco C. of C. (small bus. exec. com.), San Francisco Conv. Bur., The Fashion Group. Address: 2210 Jones St San Francisco CA 94133

MAZUR, STELLA MARY, former orgn. exec.; b. Lowell, Mass.; d. Stanley and Katherine (Cichowicz) M.; B.S. in Edn., U. Lowell; student ARC Mgmt. Tng. Sch., 1962, Nat. Tng. Lab. for Applied Behavioral Sci., 1963. USO club dir., Windsor Locks, Conn., 1942; gen. field rep. ARC, 1944, exec. dir., Waltham, Mass., 1944-79. Spl. assignment State Dept. USIA Graphic Arts Cultural Exchange Program, Eastern Europe, Poland, 1965. Recipient Waltham Rotary Club spl. citation, 1952; Waltham Community 25 Year Service award, 1969; Recognition award Waltham chpt. ARC, 1971; Outstanding Woman, Waltham News Tribune, 1974; Woman of Today, Waltham Bus. and Profl. Women's Club, 1976; Outstanding Service award ARC New Eng., 1979; Disting. Alumni award U. Lowell, 1979. Mem. Internat. Platform Assn., ARC Retiree Assn., Am. Assn. Ret. Persons, Smithsonian Assos., U. Lowell Alumni Assn., Seton Guild Lowell, Lowell Hist. Soc., Lowell Mus. Corp. Clubs: Vesper Country (Tyngsboro, Mass.); Longmeadow Golf, Country (Lowell). Author, pub.: Roots and Heritage of Polish People in Lowell, 1976. Home: 170 Andover St Lowell MA 01852

MAZUY, CAROL ANN, info. systems co. exec.; b. Boston, Aug. 19, 1942; d. William Joseph and Beatrice L. (Rodde) Cox; B.S., Boston Coll., 1964; M.Ed., Fitchburg State Coll., 1972; Ed.D., Nova U., 1980; m. Jon Claude Mozuy, May 14, 1979; children—Kelly Marie Dolan, Sean William B. Dolan Tchr., Littleton (Mass.) public schs., 1964-73; dir., grad. advisor Elem. Master Program, Fitchburg State Coll., 1977-80, adj. faculty, 1975—; dir. Title III Tchr. Tng. and dir. Mentorship Gifted Title IVC Program, Lexington, Mass., 1979-80; dir. staff devel. Merrimack (Mass.) Edn. Center, 1978-80; cons., mgr. Honeywell Info. Systems, Waltham, Mass., 1980—; adj. faculty mem. U. Laverne (Calif.), 1976—. Mem. NEA, Am. Mgmt. Assn., Nat. Assn. Female Execs. Contbr. articles to profl. jours. Home: 77 Strawberry Hill Rd Acton MA 01720

MAZYCK, ANN MARIE, telephone co. exec.; b. Winston-Salem, N.C., Sept. 26, 1949; d. Edward Harleston and June (Carroll) M.; B.A., U. N.C., Greensboro, 1971; postgrad. Wake Forest U. Babcock Sch. Mgmt., 1973, Rutgers U., 1976. Tech. publs. editor Western Electric Co., Winston-Salem, 1971-75; mktg. asst. AT&T, Morristown, N.J., 1975-76, Basking Ridge, N.J., 1976-78, mktg. assoc., 1978-79, mgr. tng. So. Bell Telephone Co., Atlanta, 1979-82, staff mgr., 1982—. Vol. asst. Forsyth County (N.C.) Pub. Library, 1974; active LWV, 1980—, Cobb Women's Polit. Alliance, 1982—; choir pres. St. Luke's Episcopal Ch., 1982-83, mem. steering com. Ch. Fellowship Orgn., 1981—; dep. registrar Cobb County, 1982—; gubernatorial campaign vol., 1981-82. Democrat. Office: So Bell Telephone Co 675 W Peachtree St NE Atlanta GA 30375

MAZZO, KAY, ballet dancer; b. Evanston, Ill., Jan. 17, 1946; d. Frank Alfred and Catherine M. (Hengel) M.; student Sch. Am. Ballet, 1959-61. Joined Ballet's U.S.A., touring Europe with co., performing for Pres. Kennedy at White House, 1961; joined N.Y.C. Ballet, 1962—, soloist, 1965-69, prin. ballerina, 1969—; leading roles include Jewels, Movements for Piano and Orch., Afternoon of A Faun, Midsummer Night's Dream, La Valse, Nutcracker, La Sonnambula, Agon, Stravinsky Violin Concerto and Duo Concertant; appeared as guest artist with Boston Ballet, Washington Ballet, Berlin Ballet, Geneva Ballet; appeared on television in U.S., Can., Germany. Recipient Mademoiselle Merit award, 1970. Office: care Sharon Wagner Artists Service 150 West End Ave New York NY 10023 *

MC ADA, GAIL HATZENBUEHLER, civic worker; b. Dallas, June 5, 1940; d. Hollis Howard and Maurice Marie (Smith) Hatzenbuehler; student public schs., Dallas; m. James William McAda, July 23, 1959; children—Paul Jeffrey, Kelley Deanne, Karen Michelle, Kimberly Carol, James William. Mem. sales staff W.A. Green Dept. Store, Dallas, 1957-59; mem. customer service staff Howard Wolfe Inc., Dallas, 1969; sec., part-time bookkeeper McAda Electric Co., Richardson, Tex., 1971—. Leader, Girl Scouts U.S.A., 1966-70; Sunday sch. tchr., 1966-72; chmn. Mothers March of Dimes, 1969-74; pres. PTA, 1971-77, council pres., 1978-79, dist. chmn., 1979—; mem. ednl. com. Richardson C. of C., 1978—; chmn. Richardson YWCA, 1971-74; vol. Richardson Gen. Hosp., 1971. Mem. Nat. PTA (hon. life), Tex. PTA (life), Beta Sigma Phi (pres. 1966-67, 68-69, 71-72, state conv. co-chmn. 1971, Order of Rose, Girl of Yr. 1967, 69). Recipient Outstanding Educator award Richardson Jaycees, 1974. Republican. Baptist. Clubs: Canyon Creek Racquet, Richardson Woman's. Home: 204 Canyon Valley St Richardson TX 75080 Office: 506 N Central Expy Richardson TX 75080

MCADEN, MARY CATHERINE OVERFELT, educator; b. Franklin County, Va., Oct. 22, 1931; d. Walter Madison and Lizzie Oberson (Angel) Overfelt; A.A., Ferrum Coll., 1951; B.A., High Point Coll., 1953; postgrad. Scarritt Coll., 1956; M.A. (Phi Epsilon Omega grantee), U. Va., 1977; m. Robinson H. McAden, Aug. 21, 1954; children—Marcella, James, Ellen, John, Robert. Dir. Christian edn. Mt. Vernon Meth. Ch., Danville, Va., 1953-54, First Meth. Ch., Gainsville, Ga., 1955-56; ednl. missionary Meth. Ch., Bolivia, 1957-67; reading tchr. Callaway (Va.) Elem. Sch., 1974-76, Sandhills Youth Center, McCain, N.C., 1976-79; resource tchr. Samarkand Manor, Eagle Springs, N.C., 1979-81; learning disabilities resource tchr. Western Albemarle High Sch., Crozet, Va., 1981—. Bd. trustees Ferrum Coll., 1974-75. Named Outstanding Leader in Elem.-Secondary Edn., Callaway Elem. Sch., 1976. Mem. NEA, N.C. Assn. Educators, Assn. Classroom Tchrs. Methodist. Contbr. religious writings to mags., youth publs. Home: PO Box 504 Crozet VA 22932 Office: Western Albemarle High Sch Crozet VA 22932

MCAFEE, ROSE LUCILLE, writer; b. Senecaville, Ohio, Mar. 2, 1920; d. Michael and Anne (Wargo) Bailey; student Cambridge Bus. Coll., 1960, Ohio U., Zanesville, 1970-71; m. Herbert McAfee, June 6, 1937; children—Rose Arlene McAfee Stackhouse, Carol Ann McAfee Rodgers, Nancy Lou McAfee Gardner. Free-lance writer, 1954—; with People's Ins. Co., Cambridge, Ohio, 1963-64; with The Daily Jeffersonian, Cambridge, 1964—, successively women's and ch. editor, columnist, feature writer; lectr. in field. Bd. dirs. ARC, Cambridge; past officer Guernsey County Hist. Soc., Living Word Biblical Drama Bd. Named Outstanding Woman, AAUW, 1979; cited for spl. dedication Guernsey County Trustees and Clks. Assn., Cambridge Concert Assn. Mem. Cambridge Bus. and Profl. Womens Club, Cambridge Bus. and Profl. Girls Club, Ohio Press Women, Ohio Newspaper Women's Assn (dir.), Nat. Fedn. Press Women, Senecaville Alumni Assn., Beta Sigma Phi. Presbyterian. Clubs: Lioness, Valley Grange. Contbr. articles to mags. Home: 1211 Foster Ave Cambridge OH 43725 Office: 821 Wheeling Ave PO Box 10 Cambridge OH 43725

MCALISTER, FEROL CLOGSTON, electronics co. exec.; b. Eureka, Calif., Aug. 24, 1950; d. Carl Hawk and Eleanor (Nielson) Clogston; student Colo. Women's Coll. in Geneva (Switzerland), 1970-71; B.A., U. Oreg., 1972; M.B.A., Northeastern U., 1980; m. Kenneth Campbell McAlister, July 1, 1972; 1 dau., Cameron Hart. Policy analyst Sanders Assos., Inc., Nashua, N.H., 1973-76, fin. analyst, 1976-79, sr. program adminstr., 1979—. Mem. Northeastern U. M.B.A. Assn., Phi Beta Kappa, Beta Gamma Sigma. Home: 190 Farley Rd Hollis NH 03049 Office: Daniel Webster Hwy S Nashua NH 03061

MCALLISTER, DOROTHY ELSEY, psychologist, educator; b. Detroit, Nov. 18, 1923; d. Raymond Joseph and Edna Lydia (Neumann) Elsey; B.A., Mich. State U., 1948; M.A., U. Iowa, 1950, Ph.D., 1952; m. Wallace R. McAllister, Dec. 19, 1948; Research asso. U. Iowa, 1949-52, assoc. project supr., 1952-53; research asso., co-prin. investigator Syracuse U., 1954-70, lectr., 1956-66, 68-69; research asso., co-prin. investigator No. Ill. U., DeKalb, 1971-81, adj. prof., 1972—. NSF research grantee, 1954-56, 71-75; NIMH grantee, 1961-70, 76-81. Fellow Am. Psychol. Assn.; mem. Psychonomic Soc., Midwestern Psychol. Assn., Eastern Psychol. Assn., Sigma Xi. Asso. editor Animal Learning and Behavior, 1978-80; contbr. articles to profl. jours., chpts. to books. Office: Psychology Dept Northern Ill Univ DeKalb IL 60115

MC ANERNEY, LEE URIE, former state ofcl.; b. San Francisco, July 14, 1920; d. Sol J. and Hilma J. (Hihnala) Urie; student U. Wash.; children—Jane, Ann (dec.), Peter. Mem. Seward (Alaska) City Council, 1971-73, mayor, 1973-74; commnr. Alaska Dept. Community and Regional Affairs, Juneau, 1974-82. Past bd. dirs. Alaska Crippled Childrens Assn. Mem. Alaska Municipal League (past dir.), Pioneers Alaska Aux., Kappa Delta. Republican. Catholic. Home: 308 Bear Dr Seward AK 99664 Office: Pouch B Juneau AK 99811

MC ANULTY, MARY CATHERINE CRAMER (MRS. CHARLES GILBERT MCANULTY), ret. educator; b. Braddock, Pa., June 26, 1908; d. Albert R. and Sara (Kelly) Cramer; A.B., Fla. So. Coll., 1929; M.A., Tchrs. Coll. Columbia, 1937; postgrad. Fla. State U., 1946-50; m. Charles Gilbert McAnulty, Dec. 25, 1937. Elementary tchr. Lake Ann Sch., Lake Garfield, Fla., 1930-31, elem. prin., 1932-34; prin. South Winter Haven Elem. Sch., Winter Haven, Fla., 1935-55; adminstrv. asst. to supervising prin. Winter Haven Area Schs., 1956-60; prin. Fred Garner Elem. Sch., Winter Haven, 1961-68, Lake Alfred Elem. Sch., 1969-70. Asst. chmn. vols., asst. tng. chmn., local chpt. ARC, 1967-68, 2d v.p., also chmn. vols., 1969-70, bd. mem., chmn. service to mil. families, 1970-71, chmn. coll. youth, 1971-72; treas. Imperial Harbours Condominium, 1980-82; v.p. Beymer United Methodist Women, 1973, 74, 75, pres., 1976, 77; lay del. ann. conf. Meth. Ch., 1978, 79; pres. Lake Region Extension Homemaker's Club, 1974, 75. Mem. Am. Assn. Supervision and Curriculum Devel., Internat. Reading Assn. (Polk County chmn.), NEA, Fla. Edn. Assn. (dir. dept. elem. sch. prins. 1965-67), Polk County Elem. Prins. Assn. (sec.), LWV (local dir. 1962), AAUW (local br. chmn. status women com. 1963), DAR (chpt. treas. 1967-68, historian 1969-70, regent 1970-72, state chmn. jr. Am. citizens 1972—, dir. dist. VI 1973-74), Fla. So. Coll. Alumni Assn. (sec.), Internat. Platform Assn., P.E.O. (chpt. treas. 1970-74, 80—, chaplain 1976, 77, chpt. pres. 1978-79), Ch. Women United (v.p. 1977—, chmn. adv. bd. 1980-81), Pi Gamma Mu, Delta Kappa Gamma (State Achievement award 1964, Fla. pres. 1962-63, chpt. parliamentarian 1968-73, pres., v.p., treas.). Methodist (choir mem., chmn. commn. edn. 1959-60, supt. study program 1969-70, organist 1970-77, pres. Wesley fellowship class 1972-73, chmn. adminstrv. bd. 1980, 81, trustee 1983). Clubs: Pilot (charter, pres. 1954-55, 61-62), Poinsettia Garden (sec.), Winter Haven Woman's (edn. chmn. 1967-68). Home: 333 W Lake Howard Dr Apt 104D Winter Haven FL 33880

MCARDLE, BETTY ANN, nurse; b. Chgo., Jan. 27, 1941; d. Merwin and Jeanette (McAtic) Kuykendall; student U. Ill., 1959-63; A.D.N., Coll. of DuPage, 1973; B.S.N., U. Ill. Coll. Nursing, 1978; m. James Francis McArdle, Jan. 26, 1963; children—James Patrick, Michael Brendan, Lawrence Emmett Sean. Staff nurse obstetrics and gynecology Presbyn.-St. Luke's Med. Center, Chgo., 1973; charge nurse high risk obstetrics Rush-Presbyn.-St. Luke's Med. Center, Chgo., 1974-75; adminstrv. nurse gynecology U. Ill. Med. Center, Chgo., 1975-80, clin. nurse II, 1980-81, adminstrv. nurse III med. oncology, 1981—. Recipient citation for excellence in practice in ob-gyn and neonatal nursing Am. Nurses Assn. and Nurses Assn. Am. Coll. Obstetricians and Gynecologists, 1976-81; hon. nursing practice award Am. Nurses Assn., 1980. Mem. Am., Ill. (human rights commn. 1977-81, econ. and gen. welfare commn. 1977-81, div. women and newborns, v.p. 1981-83, chairperson platform/priorities com. 1982), Chgo. Dist. nurses assns., Nurses Assn. Am. Coll. Obstetricians and Gynecologists. Democrat. Roman Catholic. Home: OS 729 Grant St Winfield IL 60190 Office: 840 S Wood St Chicago IL 60612

MCARDLE, GLORIA N., newspaper publisher; b. N.Y.C., Feb. 28, 1927; d. Rudolph and Pauline P. (Feist) Harms; grad. Washington Sch. of Bus., children—Kathleen McArdle Mace, Terence George, Thomas Michael. Asst. editor Queens (N.Y.) Ledger, 1960—; publisher, 1965—, editor, 1965—; pres. Conglor Publishing Co., Inc., C M C Ventures, Inc. Founding pres. Ridgewood, Glendale, Middle Village Little League Aux., 1959; pres. Mothers Club Public Sch. 91, 1962; sec. to bd. dirs. Queens Bot. Gardens Soc., 1977—; crusade chmn., sec. Queens div. Am. Cancer Soc., 1979—, nat. bd. dirs., 1982—; bd. dirs. ARC, 1979—; mem. adv. council Salvation Army, 1977—; bd. dirs. Queens Outreach Council, 1980-81. Recipient awards including Am. Legion Post 104, Glendale, 1962, Ridgewood Glendale Middle Village Little League, 1968, Parents and Taxpayers, 1966, Queens County Cath. War Vets., 1979, U.S. Army Recruiting, 1975, VFW John V. Daniels Post, 1978, Queens County, 1973, Girl Scout U.S.A. Glenville Dist., 1975, Laurel Dist., 1974, USMC, 1976, Am. Cancer Soc. of Queens, 1979, St. Adalbert's Drum Corps, 1977, Boy Scouts Am., 1978, Maspeth Lions Club, 1981, nat. award Am. Cancer Soc., 1980, Social Security Adminstrn., 1981, Salvation Army, 1981, BVD Softball League, 1979, Am. Legion Press Assn., 1980; named woman of year Queens' County VFW Womens Aux., 1980. Mem. N.Y. State Press Assn., Queensborough C. of C., Maspeth C. of C. (pres., 1978, 79, award, 1980), Glendale C. of C. Office: 67-17nGrand Ave Maspeth NY 11378

MCARTHUR, BARBARA JEAN, epidemiologist; b. Dubuque, Iowa, July 7; d. James Laurence and Ada Virginia (Boone) Martin; B.S. in Nursing, DePaul U., Chgo., 1957, M.S. (nurse trainee 1957-58), 1958; M.S. (nurse trainee 1969-75, Sigma Theta Tau grantee 1974), U. Wash., Seattle, 1971, Ph.D., 1976; m. William H. McArthur, Aug. 24, 1957 (div.); children—Michele Jean, William Michael. Asst. prof. biology Knoxville (Tenn.) Coll., 1958-69; prof., dir. grad. program instl. epidemiology Wayne State U., Detroit, 1976—; dir. Total Health Care Detroit, Inc.; cons. in field. Mem. Assn. Practitioners in Infection Control (mem. cert. bd.), Am. Acad. Nursing, Am. Public Health Assn., Mich. Soc. Infection Control, Phylon Soc., Sigma Theta Tau, Delta Sigma Theta. Author articles in field. Co-editor: Nursing Clinics of North America: Prevention of Infections for the Staff Nurse, 1980; editorial adv. bd. Infection Control; rev. bd. Nursing Research. Home: 26500 Summersale Dr Southfield MI 48034 Office: Coll Nursing Wayne State U 5557 Cass Ave Detroit MI 48202

MCARTHUR, JANET WARD, physician; b. Bellingham, Wash., June 25, 1914; d. Hyland Donald and Alice Maria (Frost) McA.; B.A. magna cum laude, U. Wash., 1935, M.S., 1937; M.B., Northwestern U., 1941, M.D., 1942; Sc.D. (hon.), Mt. Holyoke Coll., 1962. H. P. Walcott fellow clin. medicine Harvard Med. Sch., Boston, 1945-47, research fellow, 1948-50, instr., 1950-57, clin. assoc., 1957-60, asst. clin. prof., 1960-71, assoc. prof., 1971-73, prof. obstetrics and gynecology, 1973—; mem. Ctr. for Population Studies, Harvard Sch. Pub. Health, Boston, 1970—; adj. prof. Sargent Coll. Allied Health Professions, Boston U., 1982—; gynecologist Mass. Gen. Hosp., Boston, 1977—; mem. med. adv. com. Med. Research Inst. Worcester; med cons. The Pathfind Fund. Fellow ACP, Boston Obstet. Soc. (assoc.); mem. Endocrine Soc. (council 1973-76), Am. Fertility Soc., Mass. Med. Soc. Republican. Anglican. Clubs: Aescolarian; Pre-Journal. Author: (with N. B. Talbot) Functional Endocrinology From Birth Through Adolescence, 1952. Editor: (with T. Colton) Statistics in Endocrinology, 1970. Contbr. articles to profl. jours. Home: 19 Brimmer St Boston MA 02108 Office: Mass Gen Hosp 32 Fruit St Boston MA 02114

MCARTHUR, JOSEPHINE, cosmetic corp. exec.; b. Aragona, Italy, Oct. 12, 1920; came to U.S., 1926, natrualized, 1926; d. Raymond and Antonina (Salamone) Fanara; B.S. in Edn., Bridgewater State Coll., 1944; M.Ed. cum laude, Fla. Atlantic U., 1967; m. John H. Kill, Mar. 10, 1973. Tchr. elem. schs., Mass., 1945-46, Calif., 1948-49, R.I., 1950-56, Fla., 1956-66; tchr. Hallandale (Fla.) Elem. Sch., 1967-68; instr. Hallandale Jr. High Sch., Nova Complex Research and Devel. Facility, Ft. Lauderdale, Fla., 1968-80; dir. Prim-al, Inc., Hallandale. Recipient Ralston Purina award, 1975. Mem. Nat. Assn. Ret. Tchrs., Nat. Council Social Studies, Bridgwater Alumni Assn., Fla. Atlantic Alumni Assn., Am. Security Council (charter), Cousteau Soc., Hallandale Cultural Arts, Nat. Assn. Female Execs., Linus Pauling Inst. Sci. and Medicine, Young Am. Found. Club: Does. Author: Multisensory Geographic Models for Exceptional Children: A Manual for Teachers, 1974; Minutes - A - Day Smoothe Lines Away, 1981; developed formula for non-cortisone lotion for problem skin.

MC ATHIE, MARYLOU, nursing cons.; b. Huron, S.D., July 9, 1927; d. John and Agnes Virginia (Mangan) McA.; diploma Oak Park Hosp. unit Loyola U., Chgo., 1948; B.S. in Nursing, DePaul U., 1954, M.S. in Nursing, 1956; Ed.D., U. San Francisco, 1980. Cons. Calif. State Dept. Health, 1961-68; dir. nursing San Joaquin Gen. Hosp., Stockton, Calif., 1960-68; regional nursing cons., spl. asst. Pacific Basin affairs USPHS, HEW, San Francisco, 1968—; ex officio mem. exec. com. Western Council on Higher Edn. for Nursing. Mem. scholarship com. San Joaquin March of Dimes, 1964-68. Recipient award HEW Region IX, 1974, commendation March of Dimes, 1968, citizen's commendation San Joaquin County, 1967, cert. of merit UCLA, 1972, cert. in leadership tng. Western Council on Higher Edn. in Nursing, U. Calif., San Francisco, 1962, cert. in pub. health nursing Calif. Dept. Pub. Health, U. San Francisco, 1964. Mem. Am., Calif. (conv. del. 1972) nurses assns., Nat., Western (chmn. com. nursing service adminstrs.) leagues for nursing, AAUW, Am. Pub. Health Assn., Western Soc. Research in Nursing, Nat. Assn. Fed. Suprs., Fed. Exec. Women's Assn., Council on Grad. Edn. in Nursing Service Adminstrn., Sigma Thetas Tau. Speaker, convs., confs.; contbr. to audio and TV tapes, articles to profl. publs. Home: 8109 Arroyo Way Stockton CA 95209 Office: 50 United Nations Plaza San Francisco CA 94102

MCBATH, AUDREY MARTINA, civil engr.; b. Cleve., Aug. 4, 1954; d. Harry Martin and Lelia (Smith) McB.; B.S. in Engring. (Nat. Achievement scholar 1972), Duke U., 1976. Engrs. aid Woodruff, Inc., Beachwood, Ohio, 1975; cost engr. Arthur G. McKee & Co., Cleve., 1976; constrn. project engr. Gt. Lakes Constrn. Co., Cleve., 1976-77; environ. engr. EPA, Durham, N.C., 1977-79, Cin., 1979—, program mgr. fed. women's program, Cin., 1981—. Mem. Nat. Tech. Assn. (v.p. Cleve. chpt. 1977, Cin. chpt. 1981), Blacks in Govt. (del. 1982), Federally Employed Women, Soc. Women Engrs., ASCE, MENSA. Mem. United Ch. Christ. Home: 4201 Victory Pkwy Cincinnati OH 45229 Office: 26 W St Clair St Cincinnati OH 45268

MCBEE, SUSAN GURLEY, state legislator; b. Dec. 9, 1946; B.A., Tex. A&M U. Mem. Tex. Ho. of Reps., 1975—, chmn. calendars com., mem. agrl. and livestock com., elections com. Democrat. Office: Tex Ho of Reps Rm G14-A1 Austin TX 78711 *

MCBEE, SUSANNA BARNES, journalist; b. Santa Fe, Mar. 28, 1935; d. Jess Stephen and Sybil Elizabeth (Barnes) McBee; A.B., U. So. Calif., 1956; M.A., U. Chgo., 1962. Staff writer Washington Post, 1957-65, 73-74, 77-79, asst. nat. editor, 1974-77; asst. sec. for public affairs HEW, 1979; articles editor Washingtonian mag., 1980-81; asso. editor U.S. News & World Report, 1981—; Washington corr. Life mag., 1965-69; Washington editor McCall's mag., 1970-72. Recipient Penney-Missouri mag. award, 1969. Mem. Washington Press Club, Sigma Delta Chi (Public Service award 1969). Club: Internat. (Washington). Home: 3834 T St NW Washington DC 20007 Office: 1828 L NW Washington DC 20036

MCBRIDE, JOYCE BROWNING, accountant; b. Ga., May 28, 1927; d. Eph and Zula (Harden) Browning; grad. So. Bus. U., 1947; married; children—Jan Burge, Gary McBride, Kandie McBride. Asst. controller Hampton Court Knits, Los Angeles, 1967-78; owner, mgr. McBride & Assos. Bookkeeping Service, Sepulveda, Calif., 1978—.

MCBRIDE, KATHLEEN, state legislator; b. San Gabriel, Calif., July 17, 1952; B.S. with distinction, U. Redlands, 1974; M.S., U. Mont., 1977; m. John R. McBride, 1977. Mem. Mont. Ho. of Reps. 1979—. Named Outstanding Young Women of Yr., Mont. 1979. Office: Mont Ho of Reps Capitol Sta Helena MT 59620

MCBRIDE, MARY FLETCHER, educator; b. Kosciusko, Miss., Aug. 31, 1927; d. Clarence Ashley and Cassie Ruth (Taylor) Fletcher; B.A., Miss. Coll., 1949; M.A., U. Miss., 1962, Ph.D., 1968; m. L.J. McBride, Jr., June 5, 1972. Tchr. English high schs., Miss. and Ark., 1949-61; instr. English, U. Miss., 1963-67; prof. Delta State U., Cleveland, Miss., 1967-72; prof. Tex. Tech. U., Lubbock, 1972—. NDEA fellow, 1961-64. Mem. MLA, Nat. Council Tchrs. English, South Central MLA, Coll. English Assn., Am. Soc. 18th Century Studies. Baptist. Author: Folklore of Dryden's England: Gleanings From the Plays of MacFlecknoe; contbr. articles in field to profl. jours. Office: Dept English Tex Tech U Lubbock TX 79409

MCBRIDE, PATRICIA, ballerina; b. Teaneck, N.J., Aug. 23, 1942; m. Jean-Pierre Bonnefous. Made profl. debut as mem. Andre Eglevsky's Petit Ballet Co., 1957; apprentice N.Y. City Ballet, 1958, mem. corps de ballet, 1959—, now prin. dancer; danced leads in ballets, including Concerto Barocco, Ivesiana, Liebeslieder Walzer, Divertimento No. 15; roles in many ballets, including Figure in the Carpet, 1960, Swan Lake, Fantasy, The Cage, Dim Lustre, Harlequinade, A Midsummer Night's Dream, Raymonda Variations, Nutcracker, Brahms-Schoenberg Quartet, 1966, Jewels, 1967, Who Cares?, 1970, Goldberg Variations, 1971, Divertimento from Le Baiser de la Fée, 1972, Coppelia, 1974, Dybbuk Variations, 1974, The Steadfast Tin Soldier, 1975, Pavane pour une Infante défunte, 1975; many concert and TV appearances, including Coppelia, 1978. Office: care Sharon Wagner Artists Service 150 West End Ave New York NY 10023 *

MCBRIDE, ROBIN MCGLEW, advt. agy. exec.; b. Dallas, Oct. 30, 1952; d. Robert Thomas and Jackie (Daley) McGlew; B.F.A., Tex. Tech. U., 1975; m. Lawrence C. McBride, IV, May 12, 1979. Designer, Omnigraphix Advt., Dallas, 1975-77; dir. advt. Planergy, Inc., Austin, Tex., 1977-78, Merrill Lynch Realty, Paula Stringer, Inc., Dallas, 1978-79; creative dir., prin. McBride & Brown Advt., Dallas, 1979—; prin. McBride & Brown Pub., Inc. Mem. North Dallas C. of C., Women in Communications, Dallas Advt. League, Dallas Soc. Visual Arts. Republican. Home: 9401 Viewside St Dallas TX 75231 Office: 8350 Meadow Rd Suite 254 Dallas TX 75231

MCCABE, ANITA KYRIAKOS, health services co. exec.; b. Clarksville, Tenn., Jan. 12, 1953; d. Peter Leon and Juanita (Dunn) Kyriakos; student Austin Peay State U., 1971-74; B.S. Bus. Adminstrn., U. Tenn., Knoxville, 1976; m. Thomas J. McCabe, Dec. 29, 1979. Sales staff IBM, Knoxville, 1976-78, Stimtech div. Johnson & Johnson Co., Houston, 1978-79; territory mgr. Electro-Biology, Inc., Dallas, 1980—, nat. sales trainer, 1981—. Mem. Dallas Symphony Orch. League, Chi Omega. Republican. Baptist.

MCCABE, ANN ELIZABETH, psychologist, educator; b. Green Bay, Wis., Feb. 13, 1942; d. Paul Edward and Elizabeth Jane (Jacobs) Miskella; B.S., St. Norbert Coll., 1964; M.S., Iowa State U., 1966; Ph.D., U. Wis., Madison, 1973; m. Bernard Oliver McCabe, Nov. 26, 1966; 1 son, Brian. Asst. prof. Trinity Coll., Dublin U., 1967-69; asst. prof. U. Windsor (Ont., Can.), 1973-77, asso. prof. devel. psychology, 1977—; vis. asso. prof. U. Toronto, 1979-81. Bd. dirs. Childrens Achievement Centre. Recipient grant Royal Commn. Study Violence in Communications Industry, 1976. Mem. Am. Psychol. Assn., Soc. Research in Child Devel., Can. Psychol. Assn. Clubs: U. Windsor Faculty, U. Windsor Faculty Women's. Asso. editor Can. Jour. Early Childhood Edn.; contbr. articles to profl. jours. Home: 7 Elderfield Crescent Etobicoke ON M9C 3K6 Canada Office: Dept Psychology Univ Windsor Windsor ON N9B 3P4 Canada

MCCABE, CAROL JOAN, lawyer; b. N.Y.C., Feb. 10, 1944; d. Patrick Joseph and Margaret Irene (McDonald) McC.; B.A., CCNY, 1966; J.D., Georgetown U., 1975; m. Simeon S. Booker, Aug. 4, 1973. Admitted to D.C. bar, 1975, Md. bar, 1976, U.S. Supreme Ct., 1982; atty. Corp. Public Broadcasting, Washington, 1976-77, asst. gen. counsel, 1978-79; dep. gen. counsel Nat. Public Radio, Washington, 1977-78; gen. counsel Neighborhood Reinvestment Corp., Washington, 1979—. Mem. Phi Delta Phi. Club: Washington Press. Co-author: The Navajo Nation: An American Colony, 1975; editor: Equal Opportunity in Suburbia, 1974.

MC CABE, ELIZABETH GAILEY, bank ofcl.; b. Troy, N.Y., Nov. 5, 1928; d. William and Jean (McKay) Gailey; grad. Rochester (N.Y.) Inst. Tech., 1949; m. Raymond J. McCabe, Sept. 30, 1960. Club teller Troy Savs. Bank, 1951-53, paying and receiving teller, 1953-58, gen. ledger bookkeeper, 1958-62, acct., 1962-66, asst. auditor, 1966-67, auditor, 1967—, v.p., 1982—. Cert. internal auditor Inst. Internal Auditors. Mem. Savs. Bank Auditors and Controllers of N.Y. State, Eastern N.Y. chpt. Bank Adminstrs. Inst., Nat. Assn. Bank Women, Am. Inst. Banking (life), Nat. Assn. Mut. Savs. Banks. Office: 2d and State Sts Troy NY 12180

MCCAFFREY, MARTHA MCMAHON, ins. co. exec.; b. Beverly, Mass., July 19, 1932; d. William G. and Edna C. (Morton) McMahon; B.A., Albertus Magnus Coll., 1954; Ed.M., Harvard U., 1960; Ph.D., Fordham U., 1976; m. John P. McCaffrey, Sept. 15, 1970. Mem. tchr. Congregation of Dominican Sisters, Columbus, Ohio, 1954-69; v.p. Equitable Life Assurance Soc. U.S., N.Y.C., 1969-82; pres., chief exec. officer Monumental Nat. Life Ins. Co. N.Y., Buffalo, 1982—; tchr. Grad. Sch. Bus., Fordham U. Shell Merit fellow Cornell U., 1963; NSF grantee, 1959-60. Mem. Buffalo Life Underwriters Assn., Com. of 200. Office: 709 Westchester Ave White Plains NY

MCCAHAN, JOAN HELEN, hosp. adminstr.; b. Balt., June 12, 1951; d. Anthony Joseph and Frances Helen (Waclawski) Bartynski; A.A. in Mental Health and Human Services, Anne Arundel Community Coll., 1973; B.A. in Edn., Music, Fine Arts, U. Md., 1977; postgrad. in bus. U. Balt., 1980—; conservatory diploma Peabody Inst. of Peabody Conservatory, 1969; 1 dau., Valerie Kay. Instr. music Stringer Music Center, Balt., 1969-73; musician, pianist, organist, Balt., 1975-77; instr. music Acad. Music, Glen Burnie, Md., 1973-77; acctg. clk. Johns Hopkins Hosp., Balt., 1979-80, cash mgr., 1980—. Mem. Hosp. Fin. Mgmt. Assn., Nat. Assn. Accts., Inst. Mgmt. Acctg., Mid-Atlantic Cash Mgmt. Assn. Office: 601 N Broadway Baltimore MD 21205

MCCAHON, MARY ELIZABETH, banker; b. Bklyn., Oct. 12, 1925; d. Daniel K. and Ellen K. (Gault) McC.; B.S. in Bus. Adminstrn., N.Y.U., 1962, postgrad. Grad. Sch. Bus. With Green Point Savs. Bank, Bklyn., 1942—, v.p., corp. sec., 1979—. Mem. Savs. Bank Women, Nat. Assn. Bank Women, Investment Officers Assn. Savs. Bank N.Y. State, Beta Gamma Sigma, Phi Chi Theta. Congregationalist. Home: 214-03 46th Rd Bayside NY 11361 Office: 807 Manhattan Ave Brooklyn NY 11222

MCCAIN, BETTY LANDON RAY (MRS. JOHN LEWIS MCCAIN), polit. party ofcl.; b. Faison, N.C., Feb. 23, 1931; d. Horace Truman and Mary Howell (Perrett) Ray; student St. Marys Jr. Coll., 1948-50; A.B. in Music, U. N.C., Chapel Hill, 1952; M.A., Columbia U., 1953; m. John Lewis McCain, Nov. 19, 1955; children—Paul Pressly, III, Mary Eloise. Courier, European tour guide Ednl. Travel Assos., Plainfield, N.J., 1952-54; asst. dir. YWCA, U. N.C., Chapel Hill, 1953-55; chmn. N.C. Democratic Exec. Com., 1976-79; mem. Dem. Nat. Com., 1976-79, 80—, mem. com. on Presdl. nominations, 1981-82; mem. Winograd Commn., 1977-78; pres. Dem. Women of N.C., 1972—, dist. dir., 1969-72; pres. Wilson County Dem. Women, 1966-67; precinct chmn., 1972-76; del. Dem. Nat. Conv., 1972. Sunday sch. tchr. First Presbyn. Ch., Wilson, 1970-71; mem. Council on State Goals and Policy, 1970-72, Gov.'s Task Force on Child Advocacy, 1969-71, Wilson Human Relations Commn., 1975-78; charter mem. Wilson Edn. Devel. Council; active Arts Council of Wilson, Inc., N.C. Art Soc., N.C. Lit. and Hist. Assn.; regional v.p., bd. dirs. N.C. Mental Health Assn.; bd. dirs., legis. chmn. Wilson County Mental Health Assn.; bd. dirs. Friends of U. N.C.-TV, Country Doctor Mus., Wilson United Fund; bd. govs., sec. personnel and tenure com. U. N.C.; bd. regents Barium Springs Home for Children; bd. dirs., pres. N.C. Mus. History Assos., 1982-83; co-chmn. Com. to Re-elect Jim Hunt Gov., 1976, 80; bd. visitors Peace Coll.; bd. visitors Wake Forest U. Sch. Law. Recipient state awards N.C. Heart Assn., 1967, Easter Seal Soc., 1967, Community Service award Downtown Bus. Assos., 1977, Order of Old Well and Valkyries, U. N.C., 1952; named Dem. Woman of Yr., N.C., 1976. Mem. St. Marys Alumni Assn. (regional v.p.), AMA Aux. (dir., nat. vol. health services chmn., aux. liaison rep. Council on Mental Health, aux. rep. Council on Vol. Health Orgns.), N.C. (pres., dir., parliamentarian) med. auxs., UDC (historian John W. Dunham chpt.), DAR, N.C. Soc. Internal Medicine Aux. (pres.), Pi Beta Phi. Contbg. editor History of N.C. Med. Soc. Clubs: Book (pres.); Little Book; Wilson Country. Home: 1134 Woodland Dr Wilson NC 27893

MCCAIN, ELIZABETH VIRGINIA REYNOLDS, newspaper editor; b. Starkville, Miss., Sept. 30, 1910; d. Archibald William and Charlie Elise (Harrison) R.; B.A., Miss. U. for Women, 1931; m. Dewey Marven McCain, June 8, 1933; children—Jane Douglas, Charles M., William H., Susan B. Women's editor Starkville (Miss.) News, weekly, 1931-46, Starkville Daily News, 1959—; mem. faculty Miss. State U., 1941-44. Mem. Miss. Press Women, Nat. Fedn. Press Women, Am. Guild Organists, D.A.R. (regent chpt. 1968-71), Chi Omega. Episcopalian. Office: 316 University Dr Starkville MS 39759

MCCAIN, SARAH SULLIVAN, bank exec.; b. Reading, Pa., July 1, 1938; d. Robert J. and Caroline H. (Horst) S.; B.A., Vassar Coll., 1960; children—Anna Tobin, Robert Sullivan. Programmer/analyst Bankers Trust Co., N.Y.C., 1960-65; v.p. Morgan Guaranty Trust Co. N.Y., N.Y.C., 1974—, mgr. Morgan Info. Center, 1982—. Home: 40 E 10th St New York NY 10003 Office: 23 Wall St New York NY 10015

MCCALL, CAROLYN SUE WILSON, club woman; b. Bullard, Tex., Jan. 14, 1937; d. Otis Wilford and Mary Elizabeth (Barnes) Wilson; grad. Brackenridge Hosp. Sch. of Nursing, Austin, Tex., 1958; A.A., Blinn Coll., 1958; student Biola Coll., 1959, E.Tex. State U., 1979; m. Thomas Screven McCall, Aug. 2, 1958; children—Thomas Kevin, Carol Kathleen. Charge nurse Shriner's Hosp. for Crippled Children, Los Angeles, 1959; nurse, nursery dept. Presbyn. Hosp., Whittier, Calif., 1959-60, Midway Hosp., Los Angeles, 1961-62, Baylor Hosp., Dallas, 1962-63; nurse Presbyn. Hosp., Dallas, 1968-74. Nat. def. chmn. James Campbell chpt. DAR, 1976-78, rec. sec., 1978-80, corr. sec., 1980-82; 3d v.p. Dallas chpt. 6, UDC, 1970-80, 3d v.p. Tex. div., 1976-78, pres. Dallas chpt. 6, 1980-82; mem. Dallas Area chpt. Freedoms Found. at Valley Forge. Recipient Jefferson Davis medal U.D.C., 1978. Mem. Soc. Mayflower Descs., Nat. Soc. Magna Charta Dames, Daus. Am. Colonists, Dallas So. Meml. Assn., Friday Forum, Dallas Symphony Orch. League. Republican. Baptist. Clubs: Brookhaven Country, Order of Eastern Star, Marianne Scruggs Jr. Garden. Home: 6516 Aberdeen St Dallas TX 75230

MCCALLA, SANDRA ANN, high sch. prin.; b. Shreveport, La., Nov. 6, 1939; d. Earl Gray and Dorothy Edna (Adams) McC.; B.S., Northwestern La. State U., 1960; M.S., U. No. Colo., 1968. With Caddo Parish Sch. Bd., Shreveport, 1960—, asst. prin. Capt. Shreve High Sch., 1977-79, prin., 1979—; instr. math La. State U., evenings 1979-81. Danforth fellow, 1982; recipient Educator of Yr. award Shreveport Times-Caddo Tchrs. Assn., 1966. Mem. Nat. Assn. Secondary Sch. Prins., La. Assn. Prins., NEA, La. Assn. Educators, Caddo Assn. Educators, Phi Delta Kappa. Democrat. Club: Altrusa.

MC CALLEN, PEGGY, retail store exec.; b. Terre Haute, Ind., Jan. 6, 1929; d. Bernard Theodore and Jessie Rose (Connett) Van Borssum; student Ind. State U., 1946-47, Eastern Ill. U., 1947-48; m. Robert Ray McCallen, Jr., June 20, 1948; children—Peggy, Page, Bryan, Paula, Robert III. Asst. to exec. sec. Meth. Bd. Edn., Bloomington, Ind., 1953-56; owner-retailer The Village Annex, Wabash, Ind., 1976-82; pres. Maid-In-Wabash, Inc., 1979—; pres. Antiques Anonymous; chmn. Wabash County Roush for Congress Com., 1962; mem. Wabash County Centennial Com., 1966; newsletter editor Friendly Nursing Homes, 1968-70; aux. sec., newsletter editor Wabash County Hosp. Aux., 1971-77. Pres. bd. trustees Wabash City Sch. Bd., 1979; mem. City Parks Bd., 1978-80; precinct committeewoman Democratic Party, 1980. Lic. real estate broker. Mem. Nat. Fedn. Ind. Bus. Democrat. Presbyterian. Home: PO Box 546 Crestwood Dr Wabash IN 46992 Office: 1209 N Cass St Wabash IN 46992

MCCALLUM, PATRICIA ANN, pub. relations specialist; b. Cleve., Apr. 25, 1944; d. Jacob and Ruth (Eckert) Palomaki; B.S.J., Northwestern U., 1966, postgrad., 1966; m. James S. McCallum, July 2, 1966; children—Julie Lynn, David James. Reporter, New Brunswick (N.J.) Daily Home News, 1966-68; mng. editor Central Post, Kendall Park, N.J., 1969-70; govt. reporter Stewart Citizen, Walden, N.Y., 1972-75; editor Army Community Services Bull., Schweinfort, Ger., 1976; pub. info. officer No. Va. Community Coll., Woodbridge campus, 1978-81; pub. affairs specialist Directorate of Personnel and Community Activities, Ft. Sill, Okla., 1981—. Bd. dirs. summer enrichment program, 1977, v.p. nursery bd., 1977-78, sec. PTA, 1977-78 (all Schweinfurt); v.p. PTA, New Windsor, N.Y., 1974-75; bd. dirs. Greentree Village Homeowners Assn., 1981. Recipient 1st place award govt. news feature N.J. Press Assn., 1970; Community Achievement award Schweinfurt Mil. Community, 1976, 77, others. Mem. Women in Communications. Home: 521 Lauman Ave Fort Sill OK 73503

MC CAMBRIDGE, MERCEDES, actress; b. Joliet, Ill., Mar. 17, 1918; d. John Patrick and Marie (Mahaffry) McC.; A.B., Mundelein Coll., 1937; Litt.D. (hon.), St. Scholastica U., 1973; 1 son, John Markle. Appeared on stage in Hope for the Best, 1945, Place of Our Own, Twilight Bar, Woman Bites Dog, The Young and Fair; films include: Lightning Strikes Twice, All the King's Men (Acad. award Best Supporting Actress 1950), Inside Straight, The Scarf, Johnny Guitar, Giant (Acad. award nomination 1956), A Farewell to Arms, Suddenly Last Summer, Cimarron, Angel Baby, 1961, Last Generation, Jigsaw, 1965, 99 Women, 1969, Thieves, 1977, The Concorde-Airport '79, 1979; voice used in film The Exorcist; artist-in-residence Cath. U., Washington, 1973. Mem. adv. council Nat. Inst. Alcohol Abuse and Alcoholism, Washington. Recipient Drama award Mundelein Coll., 1937; AP Poll, Look award, 1950; Fgn. Corr. award for Best Newcomer and Best Supporting Actress, 1950; nominated for Tony award, 1972; recipient Gold Key award Nat. Council Alcoholism. Author: The Two of Us, 1960. Address: care Contemporary-Korman Artists Ltd 132 Lasky Dr Beverly Hills CA 90212 *

MC CANDLESS, ANNA LOOMIS, club woman; b. Aspinwall, Pa., July 21, 1897; d. George Wilberforce and Estella (Loomis) McC.; B.S., Carnegie-Mellon U., 1919. Pres., Vis. Nurses Assn. of Allegheny County, 1955-57; mem. vis. com. Margaret Morrison Carnegie Coll., 1962-66; v.p. Alumni Fedn. Carnegie Inst. Tech., 1963-66. Trustee Carnegie-Mellon U., 1966—. Mem. AAUW. Clubs: Coll., Univ., Twentieth Century (pres. 1956-58) (Pitts.); Appalachian Mountain. Home: Park Plaza Apts Craig St Pittsburgh PA 15213

MCCANDLESS, BARBARA J., home econs. cons.; b. Cottonwood Falls, Kans., Oct. 25, 1931; d. Arch G. and Grace (Kittle) McCandless; B.S., Kans. State U., 1953; M.S., Cornell U., 1959; postgrad. U. Minn., 1962-66, U. Calif., Berkeley, 1971-72; m. Allyn O. Lockner, 1969. Home demonstration agt. Kans. State U., 1953-57; teaching asst. Cornell U., 1957-58, asst. extension home economist in marketing, 1958-59; consumer mktg. specialist, asst. prof. Oreg. State U., 1959-62; instr. home econs. U. Minn., 1962-63, research asst. agrl. econs., 1963-66; asst. prof. U. R.I., 1966-67; asso. prof. family econs., mgmt., housing, equipment dept. head S.D. State U., 1967-73; asst. to sec. Dept. Commerce and Consumer Affairs, S.D., 1973-79; now cons. Mem. Nat. Council Occupational Licensing, dir., 1973-75, v.p., 1975-79. Mem. Am. Mktg. Assn., Am. Agrl. Econs. Assn., Am. Home Econs. Assn., Nat. Council on Family Relations, Am. Council Consumer Interests, LWV, Kans. State U. Alumni Assn., S.D. Consumers League, Pi Gamma Mu. Club: Brookings (S.D.) Country. Research on profl. and occupational licensing bds. Address: 2114 Potomac Dr Topeka KS 66611

MCCANN, EILEEN M., state legislator; b. St. Louis, Sept. 22, 1952; B.S. in Nursing, St. Louis U. Mem. Mo. Ho. of Reps., 1980—. Bd. dirs. Mo. Epilepsy Fedn. R.N., Mo. Mem. Am. Nurses Assn., Mo. Nurses Assn., Third Dist. Nurses Democrat. Office: Mo State Ho of Reps Jefferson City MO 65101 *

MC CANN, JOAN MARILYN, sch. adminstr.; b. Malden, Mass., Jan. 23, 1936; d. Vincent Jacob and Helen Lorraine (Pontone) Celia; A.B. cum laude, Tufts U., 1957; M.A., U. Mich., 1968; postgrad. Fordham U.; m. William J. McCann, Aug. 23, 1958; children—Susan, Peter. Tchr. 1st grade Gleason Sch., Medford, Mass., 1957-58, Hutchinson Sch., Pelham, N.Y., 1958-61; tchr. 1st grade Siwanoy Sch., Pelham, 1968-69, reading cons., 1969-71, prin., 1971-75; prin. Fox Meadow Sch., Scarsdale, N.Y., 1975—; mem. adminstrv. adv. com. internship St. John's U., 1973—. Mem. Pelham Bicentennial Com., 1974—, sch. cons. Between the Lines publ., 1975; mem. adv. bd. Scarsdale Hist. Soc., 1975—; chmn. Pelham Bicentennial Ball, 1976. Recipient award in appreciation for cooperation Pelham Manor Fire Dept., 1974; IDEA fellow Charles Kettering Found., 1976, 77. Mem. Internat. Reading Assn., N.Y. State Adminstrs. Assn., Nat. Assn. Elementary Sch. Prins., Jackson Coll. Alumnae Assn., U. Mich. Alumni Assn., Phi Delta Kappa, Chi Omega. Club: Internat. Garden. Home: 242 Eastland Ave Pelham NY 10803 Office: Fox Meadow Sch Brewster Rd Scarsdale NY 10583

MCCANN, MARIE ELIZABETH, child therapist; b. New Castle, Pa., Sept. 6, 1921; d. Martin Patrick and Ann Mercedes (Travers) McC.; B.S. in Edn., Duquesne U., Pitts., 1942; M.S. in Social Adminstrn., Case-Western Res. U., Cleve., 1949; child analyst cert. Cleve. Center for Research in Child Devel., 1963. Caseworker, supr. Youth Services of Cleve., 1949-56; therapist, supr. Children's Aid Soc., Cleve., 1956-65, 70-75; therapist, supr. Cath. Counseling Center, Cleve., 1965-70, dir. profl. services, 1968-70; child therapist Univ. Hosps., Cleve., 1975-77; asst. prof. child therapy Case Western Res. U., Cleve., 1975-77; coordinator individual and family therapy adolescent treatment program Dorothea Dix Hosp., Raliegh, N.C., 1977—. Mem. Nat. Assn. Social Workers, Am. Assn. Child Psychoanalysis, Cleve. Psychoanalytic Soc., N.C. Psychoanalytic Assn., N.C. Assn. Clin. Social Workers. Democrat. Roman Catholic. Contbr. articles to profl. publs. Home: 1401 Arboretum Dr Chapel Hill NC 27514 Office: Ashby Bldg Dorothea Dix Hosp Raleigh NC 27611

MC CANN, MARY COLLEEN, dietitian; b. Johnstown, Pa., Oct. 8, 1934; d. Patrick Joseph and Hilda Marie (Ott) McC.; B.S., Seton Hill Coll., 1956; M.P.H., U. Pitts., 1964. Dietitian, Lawrence F. Flick State Hosp., 1957-63; dir. dietetic internship Pa. State U., University Park, 1964-67, dir. instn. food research and services program, asst. prof. Inst. Human Devel., 1967-77; dir. Bur. Food Service Mgmt., Dept. Gen. Services Pa., Harrisburg, 1977-80; pres. FooDynamics, Harrisburg, 1980—; cons. Maria Manor Nursing Home, Drexel U. Mem. Citizens Council on Status of Women in Pa., 1967-70. Mem. Am. Dietetic Assn., Pa. Dietetic Assn., Central Pa. Dietetic Assn., Am. Mgmt. Assn., Am. Public Health Assn., Pa. PUblic Health Assn., Am. Home Econs. Assn., Kappa Omicron Phi. Roman Catholic. Club: Altrusa. Home and Office: PO Box 1931 Harrisburg PA 17104

MCCANTS, CHARLENE G., govt. ofcl.; b. Oct. 28, 1946; B.S., U. S.C., 1968; M.B.A., The Citadel, 1977; m. Roger Heyward McCants; 1 son, Darren. Asst. to controller and budget dir. Med. U. S.C., 1968-75, asst. to hosp. fin. dir., 1975-76, budget dir., 1976-77, instr. acctg., 1973-78; adj. asst. prof. pharm. adminstrn., 1978-81; treas., trustee Health Scis. Found., 1980-81; assoc. adminstr. external affairs Health Care Financing Adminstrn., Dept. Health & Human Services, Washington, 1981—. Mem. Nat. Assn. Accts., Hosp. Fin. Mgmt. Assn. Republican. Methodist. Office: Health Care Fin Adminstrn 330 C St SW Washington DC 20201

MC CARDEL, JANET, psychologist; b. Aurora, Ill., Aug. 21, 1938; d. Forrest Lee and Irma (Nigil) Brackett; A.A., Miami-Dade Jr. Coll., 1965; B.A. in Psychology, U. Miami, Fla., 1967, M.S. in Clin. Psychology, 1970, Ph.D. in Clin. Psychology, 1972; m. Ben W. McCardel, Mar. 4, 1966; children—Melanie, Jerry H. Ticket agt. Eastern Airlines, Miami, Fla., 1957-58; policewoman Detective Bur., Dade County Public Safety Dept., Miami, Fla., 1958-67; asst. to dir. clin. psychology U. Miami, Fla., 1968-70; staff psychologist U. Miami Guidance Center, Coral Gables, Fla., 1969-71; psychology intern VA Hosp., Miami, 1970-71; staff psychologist Kendall Children's Home, Miami, 1972; supr. Women's Detention Center, Dade County (Fla.) Corrections and Rehab. Dept., 1972-76; regional dir. region IV, Fla. Dept. Corrections, Miami, 1976-79; adj. instr. social psychology U. Miami (Fla.), 1974; adj. instr. Pepperdine U., various locations in U.S. and Japan, 1975-77; cons. exec. devel. and human relations tng., Jerome Barnum Asso., White Plains, N.Y., 1977—; psychologist Psychiat. Assos., Dade County, Fla.; mem. Fla. Council on Criminal Justice, 1979—. Mem. Gov.'s Met. Planning Council, State of Fla., 1972-79; mem. City of Miami, Fla. Substance Abuse Com., 1973-78. Mem. Am. Psychol. Assn., Am. Correctional Assn., Fla. Council of Criminal Justice, Fla. Internat. U. Women's Studies Inst., Women in Criminal Justice (co-founder 1972). Home: 16540 SW 77th Ave Miami FL 33157 Office: 16540 SW 77th Ave Miami FL 33157

MCCARDLE, ELLEN STEELE, social services adminstr.; b. Washington, Pa., July 19, 1924; d. Donald Alexander and Martha Flora (Booth) Steele; B.A. with honors in Music, Wilson Coll., Chambersburg, Pa., 1946; M.S.W., U. Pitts., 1966, postgrad., 1974; postgrad. Oxford (Eng.) U., summer 1974; divorced; children—Martha Ellen, Earl, Susan Valentine, Donald Steele. Social worker Pa. Dept. Public Welfare, Washington, 1966-68; sr. social worker Western Psychiat. Inst., Pitts., 1968-73; supr., asst. dir. Child Welfare Services, Waynesburg, Pa., 1974-76; exec. dir. South Hills Community Council Older Adults, Pitts., 1976-81. Mem. Nat. Assn. Social Workers, Acad. Cert. Social Workers, Wilson Coll. Alumnae Assn. Presbyterian. Author: Nonverbal Communication, 1974. Home: 1037 Magnolia Dr Washington PA 15301

MCCARLEY, CAROLYN JOSEPHINE SPENCE, shoe store exec.; b. Emporium, Pa., Oct. 16, 1919; d. Charles Burnell and Marguerite (Schoenbohm) Spence; student West Tex. State U., 1938-40; B.A., Tex. Arts and Industries, U., 1942; postgrad. U. Guadalajara, 1944; m. Clint Weldon McCarley, June 8, 1945; children—Clint Weldon, Philip Allen, Charles Aubra, Kelvyn Joe. Tchr., Kingsville, Tex., 1942-43, Falfurrias, Tex., 1943-44, Gregory, Tex., 1944-45, Clarkwood, Tex., 1948-49, Harlingen, Tex., 1952-53; co-owner Carolyn's Shoe Store, Harlingen, 1954—, McAllen, Tex., 1973—. Vice pres. Stephen F. Austin Sch. PTA, Harlingen, 1964-65; sec. St. Paul's Luth. Sch. PTA, 1966-68; chmn. Project Goodwill, 1966-68; ruling elder Treasure Hills Presbyn. Ch., 1977-81, chmn. Christian edn. com.; bd. dirs. Rio Grande Valley Mus., 1976—, sec., 1977—; bd. dirs. Family Emergency Assistance, 1975—, sec., 1980-81. Recipient citation State Fine Arts Commn., 1966-67, cert. community service City of Harlingen, 1981. Mem. South Tex. Dist. (pub. affairs dept. chmn. 1968-70, pres. 1970-72, chmn. edn. dept. 1975-76), Rio Grande Valley (conv. coordinator 1969-71, hospitality chmn. 1971-77, chmn. cultural affairs 1975-77), Outstanding Fedn. Clubwoman 1975), Tex. (internat. hostess chmn. 1972-74, sec. scholarship fund com. 1973-76, chmn. gerontology div., chmn. scholarship fund com., sec. 1980-82) fedns. women's clubs, Lower Rio Grande Valley Hist. Mus. Assn. (pres. 1973-75). Clubs: Zonta (pres. 1968-70, service chmn. 1971-72), Afflatus (sec. 1969-70, pres. 1970-72, v.p. 1975-76), City Federation Past Presidents (sec. 1969, pres. 1975-77) (all Harlingen). Home: 102 Wildwood St Harlingen TX 78550 Office: 705 Coronado Village Harlingen TX 78550

MCCARTER, KATHERINE SAUTER, assn. exec.; b. Nyack, N.Y., Nov. 12, 1942; d. William Charles and Josephine Rosina (Schoenle) Sauter; B.A. in Biology, Cedar Crest Coll., Allentown, Pa., 1964; M.H.S. (EPA trainee), Johns Hopkins U., 1973; m. Robert James McCarter, Dec. 6, 1969; 1 dau., Emily Katherine. Chmn. sci. dept. Arundel (Md.) Jr. High Sch., 1964-68; program asso. career devel. program Am. Lung Assn., N.Y.C., 1968; air conservation cons. Mass. Lung Assn., 1968-69; exec. dir. Met. Boston Citizen's Coalition Clean Air, 1968-69; community health educator Environ. Health Adminstrn., Md. Dept. Health, 1971-76; dir. govt. relations Am. Public Health Assn., Washington, 1976-80, asst. exec. dir., 1980—; bd. dirs. Nat. Coalition Health and

Environ., 1980—; mem. nat. air pollution manpower devel. adv. com. EPA, 1973-76. Mem. Nat. Environ. Health Assn., Am. Public Health Assn., Am. Soc. Assn. Execs., Health on Wednesday. Office: 1015 15th St NW Washington DC 20005

MCCARTER, RENATE BOHNE, magazine publisher; b. Berlin, Feb. 9, 1939; came to U.S., 1957, naturalized, 1963; d. Wilhelm and Regina (von Boyens) Bohne; B.A., in Philosophy, U. Americas, Mexico City, 1963; m. Thomas McCarter, June 22, 1976. Lit. agt., N.Y.C., 1976—; pub. UN Plaza mag., N.Y.C., 1979—, UN Weekly Report, 1982—; del. to UN, Internat. Fedn. Bus. and Profl. Women. Mem. Nat. Council Women. Clubs: Mid Atlantic; River (N.Y.C.); Meadow (South Hampton, N.Y.). Address: 823 Park Ave New York NY 10021

MCCARTHY, GRACE MARY, provincial govt. ofcl.; b. Vancouver, B.C., Can., Oct. 14, 1927; d. George and Allrieta (McCloy) Winterbottom; m. Raymond McCarthy, June 23, 1948; children—Mary, Calvin. Pres., Grayce Florists, Victoria, B.C.; minister without portfolio B.C. Legislature, 1966-72, dep. premier, minister recreation and travel industry, provincial sec., 1975-76, dep. premier, provincial sec., minister travel industry, 1976-78, dep. premier, minister human resources, 1978—. Commr. Bd. Parks and Recreation, 1961-66; bd. govs. Vancouver Aquarium Assn.; adv. bd. Salvation Army; dir. Can. Assn. Christians and Jews. Mem. Florists Telegraph Delivery Assn. (past dist. rep.), Victoria C. of C. Mem. Social Credit Party. Anglican. Club: Vancouver Credit Women's Bus. (past pres.). Office: Rm 248 Parliament Bldgs Victoria BC V8V 1X4 Canada

MCCARTHY, HELEN FRANCES, nurse; b. Shreveport, La., Mar. 23, 1938; d. James Bernhart and Martha Elizabeth (Whitten) McC.; B.S., Northwestern State Coll., 1959; cert. U. Colo., 1963. Staff nurse Shumpert Hosp., Willis Knighton Hosp., Shreveport, La., 1959-63; head nurse Cook County Hosp., Chgo., 1963-64; cardiovascular nurse specialist Meth. Hosp., Houston, 1964-76; nurse specialist Quality Control Team, ARA Services, Houston, 1976-79, dir. quality control, 1979—; instr. CPR; cons. Am. Cancer Soc. Precinct del. Tex. State Republican Conv., 1974. Mem. Am. Cancer Soc., Am. Heart Assn., Nat. League Nursing, Am. Critical Care Assn. Republican. Roman Catholic. Clubs: Zonta, Chancellors Racquet. Home: 6019 Bankside St Houston TX 77096 Office: 777 Post Oak Rd Houston TX 77056

MCCARTHY, JEAN CATHERINE, city parks, playgrounds and forestry ofcl.; b. Fitchburg, Mass., Jan. 3, 1925; d. Charles H. and Catherine I. (Beer) McC.; grad. mgmt. course U. Mass. Inst. Govtl. Services, 1980. Clk. typist Fitchburg Park-Recreation-Forestry Dept., 1948-53, prin. clk., 1953-70, adminstrv. asst., 1970-76, supt. parks and playgrounds, city forester, 1976-82. Founder, 1st pres. Montachusett unit Am. Cancer Soc., 1970-71, chmn. public info., 1976-77, mem. cancer crusade com., 1981—, bd. dirs., 1970-82, chmn. Montachusett Unit Cancer Prevention Study II, 1982—; bd. dirs. Micah Housing Rehab. Program, 1974-76; mem. adv. com. for adult and occupational edn. Fitchburg Public Sch. System, 1979-82; U.S. Nat. Council Catholic Laity rep. World-Wide Consultation of Cath. Laity, Rome, 1975; bd. dirs. founding assembly Nat. Council Cath. Laity, 1971-82, sec. exec. bd., 1974-78; bd. dirs. U.S. Cath. Mission Council, 1980-82; mem. Worcester Diocesan Council, Worcester, Mass., 1966-76, pres., 1968-74; mem. Worcester Diocesan Pastoral Council, 1972-74; internat. conv. clk. Daus. of Isabella, 1970, 74, sec. Mass. Circle, 1961-62, regent Jeanne d'Arc Circle, 1959-60, trustee Jeanne d'Arc Circle, 1979-82, chmn. liturgy Jeanne d'Arc Circle, 1979-82; Mem. Worcester Diocesan Cursillo Secretariat and Leaders' Sch., mem. Team for Women's Weekends, editor diocesan newsletter Cursillo Movement. Recipient State award Am. Cancer Soc., 1972, 77, state cert. appreciation, 1976; cert. for advancement public service in Commonwealth Mass., U. Mass. Inst. Govtl. Services, 1980; cert. appreciation United Neighbors of Cleghorn Inc., 1980, Brain Injured Children Softball Marathon Com., 1980. Home: 294 Madison St Fitchburg MA 01420 Office: Park and Recreation-Forestry Dept City Hall 718 Main St Fitchburg MA 01420

MCCARTHY, KATHRYN AGNES, physicist; b. Lawrence, Mass., Aug. 7, 1924; d. Joseph A. and Catherine A. (Barrett) McC.; A.B., Tufts U., 1945, M.S., 1946; Ph.D., Radcliffe Coll., 1957; D.Sc. (hon.), Coll. Holy Cross, Worcester, Mass., 1978; L.H.D. (hon.), Merrimack Coll., North Andover, Mass., 1981. Mem. faculty Tufts U., 1946—, prof. physics, 1962—, dean Grad. Sch., 1969-74, provost, sr. v.p., 1973-79; dir. Mass. Electric Co., Mass. State Mut. Assurance Co. Trustee Merrimack Coll., 1974-83; trustee Coll. Holy Cross, 1980; bd. dirs. Lawrence Meml. Hosp., Medford, Mass., 1975—. Recipient Radcliffe medal, 1975. Fellow Am. Phys. Soc., Am. Optical Soc. (dir.-at-large 1982—); mem. Soc. Women Engrs., Phi Beta Kappa, Sigma Xi. Author articles in field. Home: 1580 Massachusetts Ave Cambridge MA 02138 Office: Robinson Hall Dept Physics Tufts U Medford MA 02155

MCCARTHY, MARY ELIZABETH, psychologist, social service adminstr.; b. N.Y.C., Feb. 22, 1937; d. Timothy and Beatrice T. (Hester) McC.; B.A., Hunter Coll., 1964; M.S. (N.Y. State scholar), 1965; M.A., U. Santo Tomas, Philippines, 1971, Ph.D., 1970. Wage and salary analyst Sperry Rand Corp., N.Y.C., 1960-63; legal investigator firm David D. Bays; Esq., Jackson Heights, N.Y., 1964-65; group therapist St. Vincent's Home for Boys, Bklyn., 1965-66; tchr. and dir. guidance Notre Dame Acad., N.Y.C., 1965-66; career placement counselor Bklyn. Coll., 1966-68; asst. prof. dept. edn. Ateneo de Manila U., Quezon City, Philippines, 1968-71; professorial lectr. psychology Grad. Sch., U. Santo Tomas, Manila, 1969-71; spl. lectr. theology and psychology Assumption Coll., Philippines, 1970-71; lectr. U. Ife (Nigeria), 1972-73; dir. Epoch House, Friends Med. Sci. Research Center, Inc., Balt., 1971-72; participant archaeology excavation, Guatemala, summer 1974; asso. prof. psychology Coll. of V.I., St. Thomas, 1973-80, chmn. social sci. div., 1977-79; prof. (part-time) psychology Caribbean Center for Advanced Studies, P.R., 1975-76; dir. (part-time) Pastoral Guidance Center, St. Thomas, 1975-79; planner and evalulator Office of Evaluation, Dept. Health and Rehab. Services, State of Fla., 1980-81; program dir. Santa Rosa Geriatric Residential Center, Milton, Fla., 1981—; psychologist (part-time) Fla. State Hosp., summer 1980; clin. cons. Parole and Probation Bd., Balt., 1971, Golden Grove Correctional Facility, St. Croix, V.I., 1977; cons. to govt. agys., human service orgns. and ednl. workshops, 1968—. Mem. adv. council for community drug edn. Dept. Edn., St. Thomas, 1974-75; bd. dirs. St. Dunstan's Episcopal Sch., St. Croix, 1976-78, Antilles Sch., St. Thomas, 1979; bd. dirs. V.I. Council on Alcoholism, 1975-79, v.p., 1976-78. Recipient Cert. of Appreciation, Philippine Guidance and Personnel Assn., 1968, Philippine Mental Health Assn., 1971; USPHS fellow, 1979-80; NDEA grantee, 1967, V.I. Commn. on Aging grantee, 1978; lic. tchr. and counselor, N.Y.; lic. sch. psychologist, N.Y. State. Mem. Am. Personnel and Guidance Assn. (field rep. 1977), Am. Psychol. Assn., Nat. Council Family Relations, Am. Assn. Marriage and Family Therapy, Acad. of Psychologists in Marital, Sex and Family Therapy, Alliance Française (sec. Fla. 1980-81). Contbr. numerous articles on guidance and counseling to profl. jours. U.S. and abroad. Address: 502 Rocklyn Ave Pikesville MO 21208

MCCARTHY, RHODA ANN, nurse; b. N.D., Apr. 6, 1928; d. Roy Leavitt and Emma (Norby) Hall; R.N., Sisters of St. Joseph Sch. Nursing, Fargo, N.D., 1949; B.C.S., Valley City (N.D.) State Coll., 1981; m. James McCarthy, Oct. 1, 1949; children—Kathryn, Margaret, Shirley, John, Patrick. Staff nurse Jamestown and Trinity hosps., Jamestown, 1949-62; dir. nurses Trinity Hosp., 1962-66; staff nurse Hibbing (Minn.) Gen. Hosp., 1966-69; Waukegan (Ill.) Meml. Hosp., 1969-72; mem. nursing staff N.D. State Hosp., Jamestown, 1972—, staff nurse forensic unit, 1975-80, asst. dir. nurses forensic unit, 1980—. Mem. Am. Nurses Assn., N.D. Public Employees Assn. (state pres., chpt. pres. 1982). Mem. Tabernacle Soc. Club: Eagles Aux. (past pres.). Address: 1506 4th Ave NE Jamestown ND 58401

MCCARTHY, SANDRA GIFFORD, stockbroker; b. Decatur, Ala., July 16, 1946; d. William and Elizabeth (Cox) Long; student Lurleen B. Wallace Jr. Coll., 1964-66, Tallahassee Jr. Coll., 1968-69, Personnel Sch., Am. Banking Inst., 1973, Merrill Lynch Extended Study, 1980; m. James M. McCarthy, Aug. 15, 1980; 1 dau., Lori Lynn. Asst. v.p., asst. personnel dir. First Nat. Bank Mobile (Ala.), 1973-75; property mgr. Bryson Realty, Tallahassee, 1975-76; sales mgr. NASCO, Inc., Springfield, Tenn., 1976-79, personnel recruiter cons., 1980—; stockbroker Merrill Lynch, Nashville, 1980—. Fund raising chmn. Robertson County (Tenn.) Republican Party, 1981. Named Top Salesman NASCO, Inc., 1977, Top Rookie in Sales, 1977; recipient Exceeding Sales Quota award 1978. Mem. SEC Brokers. Baptist. Club: Key to City (chmn. arts fund raising 1981) (Hendersonville, Tenn.). Home: 106 Surrey Hill Point Hendersonville TN 37075

MCCARTHY, SHARON KAY, credit corp. exec.; b. Buchanan, Mich., Mar. 2, 1946; d. Galen A. and Dorothy J. (Harroff) Weaver; A.A., Lake Mich. Coll., 1965; student Marywood Coll., 1978—. Personnel adminstr. Clark Equipment Co., Buchanan, 1974, personnel rep., 1975; employee relations supr. Clark Equipment Credit Corp., Buchanan, 1976-79, employee relations mgr., 1979—, v.p., human resources mgr., 1980—. Bd. dirs., treas., chmn. fin. com. Unity Hosp. Named Woman of Year, YWCA, 1981. Mem. Internat. Assn. Bus. Communicators, Am. Soc. Personnel Adminstrn., Adminstrv. Mgmt. Soc. Office: 128 E Front St Buchanan MI 49107

MCCARTY, VIRGINIA DILL, lawyer; b. Plainfield, Ind., Dec. 15, 1924; d. E. Millard and Martha Gertrude (Paddack) Dill; A.B., Ind. U., 1946; LL.B., 1950; m. Mendel O. McCarty, Apr. 26, 1946 (dec. 1973); children—Michael Brent, Janet Martha. Admitted to Ind. bar, 1950; with Wasson's Dept. Store, Indpls., 1950; legal staff OPS, Indpls., 1950-52; final title examiner Union Title Co., Indpls., 1952-53; dep. atty. gen. State of Ind., 1965-66, asst. atty. gen., 1966-69; partner firm Dillon, Kelley, McCarty, Hardamon & Cohen, Indpls., 1969-77; pres. Dill-Fields Implement Co., Inc., Greenfield, Ind., 1967-77; U.S. atty. for So. Ind., Indpls., 1977-81; mem. firm Landman & Beatty, Indpls., 1981—; sec. treas., v.p. Ind. Bd. Law Examiners, 1971-76. Mem. Indpls. Mayor's Task Force Women, 1972-76, chmn. legal status com., 1974-75; pres. Greater Indpls. Women's Polit. Caucus, 1971-73, Ind. Women's Polit. Caucus, 1972-73, precinct vice committeeman, 1966-69, chairperson orgn. com. Nat. Women's Polit. Caucus, 1973-75, adv., com., 1975-77; v.p. Hoosiers for Equal Rights Amendment, 1973-74, mem. steering com., 1976-77; mem. Ind. Gov.'s Commn. Privacy, 1976-77; mem. U.S. atty.'s adv. com. to atty. gen., 1977-80; mem. Fed. Adv. Corr. Council, 1978-80; chmn. Greater Capital Fund Dr. Indpls. Girls' Clubs, 1981-82; mem. Internat. Women's Year Com., 1977; Dem. candidate for Ind. Atty. Gen., 1976; bd. dirs. Concord Center, 1974, Info., Inc., 1974-75, Greater Indpls. County Girls' Club, 1979. Mem. Ind. Bar Assn. Indpls. Bar Assn. (legis. chmn. 1972), Fed. Bar Assn. (pres. 1982-83), Order of Coif, Phi Beta Kappa. Clubs: Stansfield Circle, Economic (dir.) (Indpls.). Home: 5809 Washington Blvd Indianapolis IN 46220 Office: Room 400 45 N Pennsylvania St Indianapolis IN 46204

MCCAUGHRIN, WENDY BORDOFF, educator; b. Windsor, Ont., Can., Nov. 24, 1944; d. Jack and Tillie (Starker) Bordoff; B.A., Wayne State U.; B.A. with honors, U. Windsor, 1974; M.A., Merrill Palmer Inst., 1977; M.S., U. Ill., 1981, now postgrad; m. Scott Jame McCaughrin, July 1, 1972. Guidance counselor, instr. high sch., Chatham, Ont., 1967-70; reading therapist, instr., Windsor, Ont., 1971-77; reading and lang. therapist The Reading Group Program, Urbana, Ill., 1980-81; now educator, cons. learning disabilities program Mercy Hosp., Urbana. Mem. Cousteau Soc., Am. Speech and Hearing Assn., Orton Soc., Internat. Reading Assn. Jewish. Author reading and writing tests. Home: 401 1/2 E Michigan Ave Urbana IL 61801 Office: Mercy Hosp 1400 N Park Ave Urbana IL 61801

MCCAULEY, MARY ANN JACKSON, communications co. exec.; b. Moline, Ill., Feb. 20, 1947; d. Alvin Southern and Helen Ruth (Reamy) Jackson; B.J., U. Mo., 1969; m. Gary W. McCauley, Nov. 2, 1973. Reporter, editor Mason City (Iowa) Globe Gazette, 1969-71; editor Hallmark, Cards, Inc., Kansas City, Mo., 1971-72; asso. editor Am. Nurses Assn., Kansas City, Mo., 1972-76; pres., editor Galena Sentinel-Times, Kans., 1976-78; cons. Bi-State Region ARC BloodCenter, 1978; mgr. public relations First Union Bancorp./First Nat. Bank in St. Louis, 1978-81, Gen. Dynamics Communications Co., St. Louis, 1981—. Mem. grant proposal com. Galena Congregate Meals Program/Meals-on-Wheels. Mem. Public Relations Soc. Am., Internat. Assn. Bus. Communications (dir.), Women in Communications, Galena Merchants Assn. Office: 12101 Woodcrest Exec Dr St Louis MO 63141

MCCAULEY, PATRICIA ANN, health care adminstr.; b. Harrisonburg, Va., June 30, 1946; d. Auston Garfield and Rose Ann (Wood) McC.; R.N., Roosevelt Hosp. Sch. Nursing, 1967; student (Alumni scholar) Columbia U., 1968-71; B.A., U. So. Calif., 1972; M.B.A., Pepperdine U., 1980. Staff nurse Columbia-Presbyn. Med. Center, 1967-71; charge nurse of adolescents UCLA, 1971-72, supr. Neuropsychiat. Inst., 1972-73; nursing adminstr. Central City Community Mental Health Center, Los Angeles, 1973-75; staff nurse in neurology Los Angeles County Med. Center, 1976; staff nurse, nursing coordinator Cedars-Sinai Med. Center, Los Angeles, 1976-80, asst. dir. nursing, 1980—; cons. practical aspects nursing, Los Angeles, 1974—.

MC CHESNEY, KATHRYN MARIE (MRS. THOMAS DAVID MCCHESNEY), educator; b. Curwensville, Pa., Jan. 14, 1936; d. Orland William and Lillian Irene (Morrison) Spencer; B.A., U. Akron, 1962; M.L.S., Kent State U., 1965, postgrad., 1971—; m. Thomas David McChesney, June 12, 1954; 1 son, Eric Spencer. Tchr. English, Springfield Local High Sch., Akron, Ohio, 1962-63, librarian, 1963-64, head librarian, 1965-68; asst. to dean, instr. Kent (Ohio) State U. Sch. Library Sci., 1968-69, asst. dean, asst. prof., 1969-77, asst. prof. on leave, 1977-78, asst. prof., 1978—. Rep., Uniontown Community Council, 1964-66. Mem. Am., Ohio (chmn. Library Edn. Roundtable 1971-72, exec. council Div. VI Library Edn. 1972—) library assns., Am. Assn. Univ. Profs., Am., Ohio assns. sch. librarians, Beta Phi Mu, Phi Sigma Alpha, Phi Alpha Theta, Sigma Phi Epsilon. Club: Uniontown Jr. Woman's (pres. 1965-66). Contbr. articles, book revs. to profl. periodicals. Home: 3611 Edison St NW Uniontown OH 44685 Office: Kent State U Kent OH 44242

MC CLAIN, ALICE, library adminstr.; b. Telluride, Colo., Apr. 20, 1918; d. Henry Griffiths and Rebecca Sophia (Kesner) McClain; student U. Mont., 1935-37, State U. Iowa, 1938-39; A.B., U. Denver, 1940; M.A., Western State Coll., Colo., 1942. Asst. librarian Western State Coll., Gunnison, Colo., 1940-43; army librarian U.S. Armed Services, Hill Field, Utah, 1943-45, Am. Army, Germany, 1945-47; circulation asst. Seattle Public Library, 1948-51; reference librarian Idaho State U., Pocatello, 1952, asso. librarian, 1953-66; asso. dir. Mont. State U. Library, Bozeman, 1966-69, dir. libraries, 1970-80, emeritus, 1981—. Great Decisions chmn., Pocatello, 1962; UN Day coordinator for Pocatello, 1956. Grad. fellow Western State Coll., 1940-42. Mem. ALA, Pacific Northwest (pres. 1966-67), Mont. (ALA council 1973-77) library assns., AAUW, AAUP, PEO Sisterhood, Delta Kappa Gamma. Home: 710 S 16th Ave Bozeman MT 59715

MC CLAIN, CHARLENE FERTIG, real estate broker; b. Indpls., Mar. 22, 1930; d. Dayton Deland and Ida (Murphy) Fertig; student Ind. U., 1947-49; m. Lewis H. McClain, June 26, 1949 (div. 1965); children—William Dayton, Barbara Harper, Karen, Janet McClain Curry, Louise. Real estate salesperson Blake & Young Co., 1966-70, AHM Graves Realtors, Indpls., 1970—. Mem. adminstrv. bd. Meridian St. United Meth. Ch., 1970-73; mem. Jr. Symphony Bd., 1960. Mem. Nat. Assn. Realtors, Women's Council Realtors (bd. 1970, 72, 78, 79, sec. 1977), Met. Indpls. Bd. Realtors (sec.), Oriental Art Soc., Indpls. Mus. Art, Pi Beta Phi. Republican. Clubs: SCORE, Million Dollar. Home: 578 Hunters Dr Carmel IN 46032 Office: 1119 Keystone Way 46032

MCCLAIN, ELSIE TALLEY, diversified co. exec.; b. Bascom, Fla., Oct. 6, 1927; d. William Russell and Hattie Mae (Benton) Talley; student Jacksonville U., Harvard Bus. Coll., 1975-76, U. N. Fla., 1978-79; children—Elizabeth McClain Jenkins, Leslie Wayne. Sec., USDA, 1945-47; sec., bookkeeper Duval County Sch. Bd., 1959-60; with Patterson Enterprises, Jacksonville, Fla., 1960—, exec. sec., adminstrv. asst., 1971-73, controller, 1973—. Mem. Jacksonville Equal Opportunity Council; bd. dirs. USO Internat.; auctioneer Public TV, 1973-79; tchr. Sunday sch. Presbyterian Ch., ruling elder, 1980-83. Mem. Exec. Women Internat., Women in Constrn., NCR Computer Users Group, Nat. Users Constrn. Group, Adminstrv. Mgmt. Soc., Am. Soc. Personnel Adminstrn. Winner 1st place cooking contest Jacksonville Jour., 1979, 80, 81. Home: 1018 Lamboll Ave Jacksonville FL 32205 Office: PO Drawer 2699 Jacksonville FL 32203

MCCLAIN, SHIRLA ROBINSON, educator; b. Akron, Ohio, Feb. 4, 1935; d. Dumas Defoe and Marcella Carolyn (Macbeth) Robinson; B.S. in Edn. with distinction, U. Akron, 1956, M.S. in Edn., 1970, Ph.D. in Edn., 1975; m. Henry Lee McClain, Apr. 6, 1957; children—Kelli Jesselyn, Scott Jay. Tchr. Akron Pub. Schs., 1956-65, remedial tchr., 1966-71, ednl. specialist, 1971-76; asst. prof. edn. Kent (Ohio) State Univ., 1976-81, asso. prof. edn., 1981—; multicultural edn. cons. Gt. Rivers council Girl Scout U.S.A., 1981-82; mem. State of Ohio Library Bd., 1979—; bd. dirs. Summit County Hist. Soc., 1981—, 2d v.p., 1982—; mem. City of Akron Human Relation Commn., 1982—; bd. trustees Akron Urban League, 1980—; mem. WAKR Community Relations Bd., 1976-81. Recipient Black Applause award for outstanding achievement in edn., Phi Beta Sigma, 1980; Achievement award Akron Urban League, 1975. Mem. Nat. Council Social Studies, Am. Ednl. Research Assn., Delta Kappa Gamma, Pi Lambda Theta. Episcopalian. Home: 865 Packard Dr Akron OH 44320 Office: 404 White Hall College of Edn Kent State Univ Kent OH 44242

MCCLANAN, REBA SALYERS, civic leader; b. Martin, Ky., Oct. 25, 1937; d. Hudson and Golda (Martin) Salyers; B.S., Berea Coll., 1959; student Merrill Palmer Inst., Detroit, 1958; M.S., Va. Poly. Inst. and State U., 1979; m. Glenn B. McClanan, Aug. 5, 1962; children—Martin Whitehurst, Anne Laura, Glenn B. Home demonstration ext. agt. U. Ky. Extension Service, 1960-62; tchr. Waynesboro (Va.) public schs., 1963-64; tchr. Virginia Beach (Va.) public schs., 1964-66, 67-68; pres. Virginia Beach Council Civic Orgns., Inc., 1976-78; pres. Virginia Beach Council Garden Clubs, 1973-75; pres. Plaza Elem. PTA, 1975-76; mem. Virginia Beach City Clean Communities Task Force, 1978-79; mem. Virginia Beach Beautification Commn. Adv. Council, 1974—; mem. Virginia Beach Tomorrow Com. of 100, 1976; mem. Virginia Beach City Council-Princess Anne Borough rep., 1980; hon. crusade chmn. Virginia Beach unit Am. Cancer Soc., 1981. Mem. Va. Home Econs. Assn., Am. Home Econs. Assn., Plaza Civic League, Princess Anne Hist. Soc., Home Economists in Homemaking. Methodist. Address: 3224 Burnt Mill Rd Virginia Beach VA 23452

MCCLAY, MERI JANE, med. technologist; b. Colorado Springs, Colo., May 9, 1944; d. Charles David and Alice (Livengood) McC.; B.A., U. Oreg., 1966. Med. technologist Sacred Heart Hosp., Eugene, Oreg., 1966-67, Highland Alameda County Hosp., Oakland, Calif., 1967-68; chief technologist Arlington (Tex.) Community Hosp., 1968-72, chief technologist Fannin County Hosp., Bonham, Tex., 1972—. Mem. Am. Soc. Clin. Pathologists (registered, affiliate). Presbyterian. Home: PO Box 273 Bonham TX 75418 Office: 504 Lipscomb St Bonham TX 75418

MCCLEAN, LENORA JAMES, dean, nursing educator; b. Jesup, Ga., Apr. 22, 1937; d. Ealey and Mary (Howard) Hayes; diploma St. Vincent's Hosp. Sch. Nursing, Jacksonville, Fla., 1958; B.S., Fla. State U., 1961; M.A., Tchrs. Coll., Columbia U., 1963, Ed.D., 1972; m. Robert William McClean, July 13, 1963; children—Anne-Marie St. John, Sharman Danielle, Tara Lauren, Marshall Hayes. Asst. prof. nursing Fla. State U., Tallahassee, 1963, Tchrs. Coll., Columbia U., N.Y.C., 1964-73; clinician Bronx Psychiat. Center, 1966-73; prof. SUNY, Stony Brook, 1973-81, dean Sch. Nursing, 1981—; cons. intervention in self-destructive behavior. Vis. fellow Sturt Coll. Advanced Edn., Bedford Park, South Australia, 1981-82; grantee. Mem. N.Y. State Nurses Assn. (v.p. 1980-82), Am. Nurses Assn. Democrat. Episcopalian. Author: (with Dorothy Anderson) Indentifying Suicide Potential, 1976; contbg. author: Comprehensive Psychiatric Nursing, 1979, 2d edit., 1982; also articles. Office: SUNY Stony Brook NY 11794

MC CLEARY, BERYL NOWLIN, civic worker, travel agency exec.; b. Fort Worth, Feb. 22, 1929; d. Henry Bryant and Phyllis (Tenney) Nowlin; B.S. in Zoology, Tex. Tech U., 1950; m. Henry Glenn McCleary, May 29, 1950; children—Laura Gail, Glenn Nowlin, Neil Ray, Paul Tenney. Treas., Kappa Alpha Theta Ednl. Found., Tex. Christian U., Ft. Worth, 1958-61; pres. study club Jr. Woman's Club, Ft. Worth, 1959-60; pres. Symphony League, Ft. Worth, 1961-62; v.p., dir. Ft. Worth Symphony Orch. Assn., Inc., 1961; treas. Jr. Pro-Am Tarrant County, 1961-62; corr. sec. Ft. Worth Children's Mus. Guild, 1961; sec. Tarrant County (Tex.) Democratic Exec. Com., 1956-62; pres. guild, bd. dirs. Maadi Community Ch., Cairo, 1964-66; mem. women's bd. Lincoln Park Zool. Soc., Chgo., 1976—; mem. Episcopal Ch. Women's Diocesan Bd., Chgo., 1976-79; pres., charter mem. Rainbow Investment Club, London, 1970-71; owner, mgr. Beryl McCleary Travels, Chgo., from 1975. 1975, Denver, 1981—; travel dir. Over the Hill Gang Ski Team Internat., Denver, 1982—. Mem. AAAS, DAR, Geol. Geophys. Aux., Service Club Chgo., Jr. League Chgo., Alpha Epsilon Delta, Kappa Alpha Theta (charter mem. Gamma Phi chpt. 1953). Address: 275 S Eudora St Denver CO 80222

MCCLEARY, CAROL MAY, air force officer; b. Salem, Oreg., Mar. 12, 1932; d. Elgin Levi and Edna Marion (Abbott) McC.; R.N., Good Samaritan Hosp., 1955; B.S., U. Oreg., 1958; M.N., U. Wash., 1967; diploma Air War Coll., 1971, Indsl. Coll. Armed Forces, 1973. Instr. Good Samaritan Hosp., Portland, 1958-61; commd. capt. U.S. Air Force, 1962, advanced through grades to col., 1972; mem. faculty USAF Sch. Health Care Scis., 1968-72; asst. chmn. dept. nursing, Elmendorf AFB, Alaska, 1972-74, chmn. dept. nursing USAF Med. Center, Scott AFB, Ill., 1974-76; div. chief nursing Wilford Hall USAF Med. Center, Lackland AFB, Tex., 1976-81; command nurse Hdqrs. U.S. Air Forces Europe, 1981—; cons. to surgeon gen.; adj. asst. prof. Webster Coll. Bd. dirs. Lackland Fed. Credit Union, 1978-79, 80-81. Decorated Air Force Commendation medal (2), Legion of Merit, Air Force Meritorious Service medal. Mem. Am. Nurses Assn., Assn. Mil. Surgeons U.S., Air Force Assn., Aerospace Med. Assn. (v.p. 1979-81), Sigma Theta Tau,

Delta Gamma. Republican. Episcopalian. Contbr. articles to profl. jours. Home: 6330 Mary Jamison Dr San Antonio TX 78238 Office: HQ USAFE/SGN APO New York NY 09012

MCCLEARY, IVA DENE, educator; b. Beaver, Okla., Nov. 12, 1936; d. Arthur L. and Thelma L. (Eden) Carter; B.S., Emporia (Kans.) State U., 1960; M.Ed., U. Ill., 1969; Ph.D., U. Utah, 1976, postgrad. (fellow), 1977-79; m. Lloyd E. McCleary, June 13, 1971; 1 dau., Victoria. Tchr. kindergarten Anthony (Kans.) schs., 1956-58, Harper (Kans.) schs., 1958-59, Shawnee (Kans.) schs., 1960-62; dir. Pre-sch. Pilot Project for Multiple Handicapped, State of Mo., 1965-68; dir. Region IV Inst. Materials Center, U. Ill., 1969-71; curriculum specialist dept. spl. edn. U. Utah, 1971-73, asst. prof., dir. community affairs, 1978—; v.p. ILM Publisher, Inc., Salt Lake City, 1973—. Mem. Council Exceptional Children, Assn. Children with Learning Disabilities, Nat. Assn. Edn. Young Children, Phi Kappa Phi, Kappa delta Pi. Contbr. in field. Home: 1470 Wilton Way Salt Lake City UT 84108 Office: 213 MBH University of Utah Salt Lake City UT 84112

MCCLEARY, MARY LOUISE, clin. med. technologist; b. Detroit, Mar. 3, 1954; d. Richard Roy and Rita Mae (Tenbusch) Gohl; B.S., Marycrest Coll., 1975; med. tech. degree Quad Cities Hosps. Sch. Med. Tech., Davenport, Iowa, 1976; m. Tim Lee McCleary, May 23, 1975; 1 dau., Angela Lynn. Asst. mgr. So-Fro Fabrics, Davenport, part-time 1971-74, diamond sales agt. Helzberg Jewelers of Davenport, part-time 1974-75; sr. technologist Drs. Clinic, P.C., Davenport, 1977—; cons. technologist for affiliate clin. labs., 1979—. Mem. Am. Soc. Med. Tech., Iowa Soc. Med. Tech., Am. Soc. Clin. Pathologists (asso.), Am. Bus. Women's Assn., Palamino Horse Assn. Am. Clubs: Moose, Walcott Buying. Office: Drs Clinic PG 3618 N Division St Davenport IA 52726

MC CLELLAN, CAROLE KEETON, mayor; b. Austin, Sept. 13, 1939; d. W. Page and Madge Anna (Sewart) Keeton; B.A. in Govt. with honors, U. Tex., 1961; m. Barr McClellan, Oct. 14, 1960; children—Mark Barr, Bradley Dean and Dudley Page (twins), Scott Keeton. Tchr. civics and history, coach girls tennis McCallum High Sch., 1961, 63; trustee Austin Ind. Sch. Dist., 1972-77, v.p., 1974-76, pres., 1976-77; founding mem., trustee Austin Community Coll., pres. bd. trustees, 1976-77; mayor City of Austin, 1977—; mem. adv. bd. U.S. Conf. Mayors, mem. mayors adv. bd. urban health care financing program, mem. community devel., housing and econ. devel. com.; mem. Gov.'s Adv. Com.; mem. nat. community edn. adv. council HEW; vice chmn. Austin Parks and Recreation Bd.; mem. Criminal Justice Planning Unit. Trustee, United Fund, Austin; adv. bd. John F. Kennedy Sch. Govt.; bd. dirs. Austin Symphony, Big Bros. Austin, Austin Mental Health Assn., United Cerebral Palsy of Capital Area, Austin. Named an Outstanding Woman of Austin, Am.-Statesman, 1970; a Woman of Year, Austin Citizen, 1976; 1 of Austin's 6 Valiant Women, Ch. Women United, 1976; Outstanding Woman in Govt., AAUW, 1978; 1 of Austin's 5 Outstanding Women, Women in Communications, 1976; 1 of 50 Faces for Am.'s Future, Time mag., 1979; recipient Pendant award Austin Assn. Children with Learning Disabilities, 1976; Capital Eye Public Service award, 1978. Mem. Nat. League Cities (vice-chmn. environ. com.), LWV, Austin Women's Polit. Caucus, Tex. Mcpl. League (dir., 1st v.p.), Tex. Arts Alliance, Jr. League Austin, Austin Women's Tennis Assn. (past pres.), Capital Area Tennis Assn., Chi Omega Alumnae, Delta Kappa Gamma. Methodist. Clubs: Jr. Austin Women's, Austin Mothers of Twins (past pres.). Office: City of Austin PO Box 1088 Austin TX 78767 *

MCCLELLAND, GLADYS SCOTT, farmer; b. Lee County, Ga., Feb. 18, 1923; d. Emmett Alonzo and Annie Belle (Page) Scott; student Albany Vocat. Sch., 1959, Patterson Bus. Sch., 1945; m. Carlton Dwight McClelland, Feb. 18, 1951 (dec. 1970); children—Linda Carla, Vicki Anne. Sales staff, S.H. Kress Co., Americus, Ga., 1940-42; head record dept. Souther Field Primary Tng. Sch., nights 1942-45; hostess Paramount Supper Club, Albany, Ga., 1945-50; sec. treas., head bookkeeper Harveys Peanut Co., Leary, Ga., 1959—; owner, mgr. McClelland Farms, Morgan, Ga., 1970—. Sec., Sunday Sch., asst. treas., treas. Morgan Bapt. Ch. Democrat. Home: PO Box 167 Morgan GA 31766 Office: PO Box 368 Leary GA 31762

MCCLELLAND, MARY ALICE, fgn. service officer; b. Brownwood, Tex., July 6, 1924; d. Roswell DeWitt and Eva Ione (Blinn) McC.; B.A. in Bus. Adminstrn., U. Tex., El Paso, 1944. With Fgn. Service, Dept. State, 1944—, service in Cd. Juarez, Mex., Asuncion, Paraguay, Vienna, Austria, Canberra, Australia, Tel-Aviv, Israel, Athens, Greece, Seoul, Korea, Saigon, Laos, Cambodia, Bangkok, Thailand, exec. sec. Bur. Refugee Programs, Dept. State. 1979—. Recipient Vietnam award for civilian service, 1969, 70. Mem. Nat. Assn. Female Execs., Am. Fgn. Service Assn., Delta Delta Delta. Home: 5300 Holmes Run Pkwy Alexandria VA 22304 Office: Bur Refugee Programs Dept State Washington DC 20520

MC CLELLAND, MARY REGIS, nurse; b. Pomeroy, Ohio, June 12, 1940; d. George V. and Catherine (Tracy) Angeletti; A.S., Cuyahoga Community Coll., 1966; B.A., Baldwin Wallace Coll., 1972; M.A., Kent State U., 1974; m. Howard J. McClelland, Nov. 28, 1959; children—Danette, Deborah, David. Staff nurse Parma Community Gen. Hosp. (Ohio), 1966-69, staff nurse coronary care unit, 1969-74, nursing supr., 1974-76, dir. nursing, 1976—; lectr. Cleve. State U., 1974-76. Chmn., Am. Heart Assn., 1966-81, chairperson nursing edn. com., 1978-81; leader Girl Scouts, 1972-74. Recipient cert. of appreciation Am. Heart Assn., 1979. Mem. Am. Assn. Critical Care Nurses, Nat. League Nursing, Am. Soc. Nursing Service Adminstrs., Ohio Soc. Nursing Service Adminstrs., Am. Hosp. Assn., Ohio Hosp. Assn., Parma, Kent State, Baldwin-Wallace alumni assns., Early American Soc., Psi Chi, Kappa Delta Pi, Eta Sigma Gamma. Roman Catholic. Club: Baldwin Wallace Women's. Editorial bd. Topics in Clin. Nursing, 1979—; contbr. to profl. jours. Home: 11930 Kader Dr Parma OH 44130 Office: 7007 Powers Blvd Parma OH 44129

MCCLENAHAN, ANN CATHERINE, psychologist; b. Sioux City, Iowa, Apr. 17, 1932; d. Harold L. and Beatrice A. (Wilbur) McClenahan; B.A., U. S.D., 1953, Ed.D., 1974; M.Ed., S.D. State U., 1969. Tchr. public schs., Sioux Falls, S.D., 1955-60; counselor/psychometrist Brandon Valley Schs., Brandon, S.D., 1969-71; asst. prof. edn., psychology Dakota Wesleyan U., Mitchell, S.D., 1974-75; child psychologist Intercommunity Human Service Center, Mitchell, 1975; child psychologist Area Edn. Agy., Sioux Center, Iowa, 1976—; pvt. practice psychology, Sioux Falls, part-time, 1977—. Mem. Am. Psychol. Assn., Iowa Assn. Sch. Psychologists, S.D. Psychol. Assn., Pi Beta Phi. Home: 2202 Pendar Ln Sioux Falls SD 57105 Office: 102 S Main St Sioux Center IA 51250 also Burnside Plaza 801 N Elmwood Sioux Falls SD 57104

MC CLENDON, MAXINE, artist; b. Leesville, La., Oct. 21, 1931; d. Alfred Harry and Clara (Jackson) McMillan; student Tex. U., 1948-50, Tex. Woman's U., 1950-51, Pan Am. U., 1963-64; m. Edward Edson Nichols, Mar. 28, 1967; children—Patricia Ann, Joan Terri, Christopher. One-man shows include: Art Mus. S. Tex., Corpus Christi, 1971, McAllen (Tex.) Internat. Mus., 1976, Amarillo (Tex.) Art Center, 1982 group shows in Wichita, Kans., 1972, Marietta, Ohio, 1975, Dallas, 1977; represented in permanent collections: Mus. Internat. Folk Art, Santa Fe, Ark. Mus. Fine Art, Little Rock, McAllen Internat. Mus., Lauren Rogers Mus., Laurel, Miss.; commns. include: Caterpillar Corp., Peoria, Ill., Union Bank Switzerland, N.Y.C., Crocker Bank, Los Angeles, Tarleton U., Tex., Hyatt Regency, Ft. Worth Forbes Inc., San Francisco, First Savs. & Loan, Shreveport, La., Continental Plaza Hotel, Ft. Worth. curator Mexican folk art McAllen Internat. s., 1974-80. Recipient judges award 4th Nat. Marietta, 1975, numerous others. Mem. World Crafts Council, Am. Crafts Council (Tex. rep. 1976-80), Tex. Designer/Craftsmen (pres. 1973-74). Christian Scientist. Home and Studio: 2018 Sharyland St Mission TX 78572

MC CLENDON, SARAH NEWCOMB, journalist; b. Tyler, Tex., July 8, 1910; d. Sidney Smith and Annie Rebecca (Bonner) McC.; B.J., U. Mo.; divorced; 1 dau., Sally O'Brien MacDonald. With Tyler and Beaumont, Tex. papers, 1931-42; propr. McClendon News Service, Washington, 1946—, Washington corr., 1944—; nat. columnist Inter-Continental Press. Mem. nat. council Nat. Woman's Party; adv. bd. Nat. Assn. Concerned Vets.; chmn. 25th ann. celebration, mem. def. adv. com. Women in Service. Served to 1st lt. WAC, World War II. Named Nat. Headliner, Women in Communications, 1972. Mem. Am. Newspaper Women's Club (past pres.), White House Corrs. Assn., Sigma Delta Chi. Democrat. Roman Catholic. Clubs: Nat. Press (past v.p.), Capitol Hill First Friday (past pres.) (Washington); Tex. Breakfast (historian). Author: My Eight Presidents, 1978. Address: 2933 28th St NW Washington DC 20008

MC CLENNEY, CHERYL ILENE, arts adminstr.; b. Chgo., July 18, 1948; d. Samuel James and Gwendolyn (Carter) McC.; B.F.A., Sch. Art Inst. Chgo./U. Chgo., 1969. Instr., Raymund Fund, Art Inst. Chgo., 1968; instr. art history Sch. Art Inst. Chgo., 1968-69; tchr. Benjamin Franklin High Sch., N.Y.C., 1969-70; curatorial coordinator Solomon R. Guggenheim Mus., N.Y.C., 1970-74; asst. program dir. Museums Collaborative, N.Y.C., 1974-76; asst. commr. N.Y.C. Dept. Cultural Affairs, 1976-78; dir. museums and hist. orgns. humanities projects Nat. Endowment for Humanities, Washington, 1978—; Scholastic Art Mag. scholar, 1965; Internat. Council Museums/N.Y. State Council on Arts travel grantee, 1974. Mem. Am. Assn. Museums, Am. Assn. for State and Local History, African Am. Museums Assn. Office: 806 15th St NW Washington DC 20506

MC CLINTOCK, BARBARA, scientist; b. Hartford, Conn., June 16, 1902; B.S., Cornell U., 1923, M.A., 1925, Ph.D. in Botany, 1927; Sc.D. (hon.), U. Rochester, 1947, Western Coll., 1949, Smith Coll., 1958, U. Mo., 1968, Williams Coll., 1972. Asst. in botany Cornell U., Ithaca, N.Y., 1924-27, instr., 1927-31; asst. in plant breeding, 1934-36, Andrew D. White prof.-at-large, 1965; NRC fellow Calif. Inst. Tech., 1931-33; Guggenheim fellow Bot. Inst. U. Freiburg, 1933-34; asst. prof. botany U. Mo., 1936-41; staff mem. Carnegie Inst., Washington, 1941-67, Disting. Service mem., 1967—. Recipient Kimber Genetics award, 1967; Nat. Medal Sci., 1970; Rosenstiel award, 1978. Mem. Nat. Acad. Sci., Am. Soc. Naturalists, Am. Philos. Soc., Bot. Soc. Am., Genetics Soc. Am. (v.p. 1939, pres. 1945). Research in cytogenetics of maize. Office: Cold Spring Harbor Lab Cold Spring Harbor NY 11724 *

MCCLINTOCK, EVA KARIN, cosmetics co. exec.; b. Lithuania, Mar. 23, 1938; naturalized U.S. citizen, 1962; d. Franz and Lydia (Petrat) Slawinski; student bus. sch., W.Ger., 1953-57; m. Ronald James McClintock, Feb. 8, 1957; 3 children. Dist. mgr. Avon Products, Pasadena, Calif., 1966-76; div. sales mgr. Luzier Cosmetics, Kansas City, Kans., 1976-77; dir. sales tng. Pola USA, Inc., Carson, Calif., 1977-79; with Concept Now Cosmetics Co., Santa Fe Springs, Calif., 1979—, dir. mktg., v.p. sales, 1981-82, corp. v.p., 1982—. Den mother, Cub Scouts Am., 1966-68, 72. Mem. Am. Bus. Women Assn., Nat. Assn. Female Execs., We Can Women's Network. Democrat. Lutheran. Home: 5183 Melbourne Dr Cypress CA 90630 Office: 14000 S Anson Ave Santa Fe Springs CA 90670

MCCLINTOCK, MARIAN STYLES, orgn. exec.; b. Spartanburg County, S.C., May 12, 1935; d. Woodrow and Elizabeth (Payden) Styles; B.S., U. R.I., 1973; M.A., Wayne State U., Detroit, 1974; Ph.D., Grad. Sch. Union, Cin., 1980; div.; children—Cynthia G., Kenneth M. Project cons. Nat. Bd. YWCA, N.Y.C. and Greensboro, N.C., 1974-80, program dir., N.Y.C., 1980—; asso. African Am. Cultural Found. Westchester, 1981—; tutor Literacy Vols. Am., 1981—. Chmn. econ. devel. com. White Plains (N.Y.) br. NAACP, 1981, 1st v.p. Providence br., 1970-75; mem. Task Force to Study Overcrowded Jails, Westchester County, 1981; chmn. supportive community United Meth. Women, Trinity United Meth. Ch., White Plains, 1981—. Recipient Community Service award Providence br. NAACP, 1973. Mem. Nat. Assn. Female Execs., Rural Am. Women, Black Women's Polit. Caucus, Assn. Black Social Workers. Address: 150 Fisher Ave White Plains NY 10606

MCCLINTOCK, SHIRLEY SPRAGUE, govt. ofcl.; b. Flushing, N.Y., Jan. 3, 1928; d. George Wilkie and Mary Dorothea (O'Rourke) Sprague; student Cornell U., 1949-51; m. John William McClintock, Sept. 22, 1951; children—Barton, Charles, Scott. Personnel adminstr. Gen. Motors Co., 1952-54, analyst, overseas ops., N.Y.C., 1965-68; mem. U.S. Govt. Transition Com., 1968-69; housing adminstr. HUD, Buffalo, 1969-82, N.Y.C., 1982—. Bd. dirs. Soc. Prevention Cruelty to Children Mass., 1962-64; sec. LWV, N.Y.C., 1960-62. Recipient Cert. Superior Service, HUD, 1975. Mem. Cornell Club Greater Buffalo (pres. 1981—), Cornell U. Alumni Assn. Club: Cornell (N.Y.C.). Home: 541 E 20th St New York NY 10010 Office: 26 Federal Plaza New York NY 10278

MCCLOSKEY, DORIS JEAN, ch. orgn. exec.; b. Searcy, Ark., Mar. 6, 1945; d. Emory Norris and Emma Imogene (Prince) Dye; student UCLA, 1973, U. Md., 1979; m. Guy Corbett McCloskey, Aug. 1, 1971; children—Brian, Vincent, Mary. Regional, then nat. youth exec. Nichiren Shoshu Buddhist Orgn., 1967-72, Southeastern regional terr. exec., Cheverly, Md., 1978—; condr. seminars on Buddhism, 1968—; market devel. and researcher Teleflora, El Segundo, Calif., 1970-72; land developer Joseph M. Girard, Westwood, Calif., 1972-76; real estate marketer William H. Riley, Beverly Hills, Calif., 1976-78, Barrington Butts, Washington, 1978—; devel. officer Town and Country Day Schs., Silver Spring, Md., 1980-81; dir. J.M. Girard Found., Nev. Land and Water Co. Recipient awards Soka Gakkai Internat. Buddhist Orgn. Mem. Nichiren Shoshu Am., Washington Bd. Realtors. Address: 3015 Lake Ave Cheverly MD 20785

MC CLOSKEY, EUNICE L. (EUNICE LONCOSKE), author, artist; b. Ridgway, Pa., May 25, 1904; d. Fred William and Ada Amelia (Nelson) Loncoske; student Columbia, 1930-31; m. Lewis Frank McCloskey, Jan. 9, 1932; 1 dau., Mimi Marie. Sec., Olson & Larson, Inc., 1926-38; author and illustrator books: Coal Dust and Crystals, 1938; Strange Alchemy, 1940; The Heart Knows This (prize Driftwind Press), 1944; This Is the Hour, 1949; The Golden Hill, 1952; These Rugged Hills, 1954; This is My Art, Vol. 1, 1956, Vol. 2, 1957, Vol. 3, 1958, Vol. 4, 1962; So Dear to My Heart, Vol. I (biography), 1964; Potpourri (biography), 1966; Songs and Paintings for The Heart, 1969; Symbols of My Life, 1970; O Shana, Shana, 1972; The Last Furrow, 1975; O, Thessaly Beloved, 1977; The Last Furrow, 1977; Secret Wisdom, 1978; The End of the Road for Me, 1979; There Should Have Been Music, 1979; Light, Love and Sorrow, 1980; contbr. poetry, articles, essays and short stories to mags. U.S. and Can., including Ladies Home Jour., McCall's, Good Housekeeping, Household. Water colors and etchings exhibited at Carnegie Inst., Pitts., Nat. Mus., Washington, Nelson Art Gallery, Kansas City, Creative Art Gallery, Hammer Gallery (both N.Y.C.), Edwin Forrest Gallery, Everyman's Gallery, Phila., Pitts. Plan for Art Gallery, Upstairs Gallery, Raymond Duncan Galleries, Paris, Ligoa Duncan Gallery; paintings at Galerie Paula Insel, N.Y.C., Women's City Club, Phila., Philbrook Art Center, Tulsa; one-man show art, Chautauqua, N.Y., 1957, Theil Coll., 1960, Langenheim Gallery, Greenville, Pa., Indiana (Pa.) State Coll., 1960, Upstairs Gallery Asso. Artists, Pitts., 1961, 72; art show Lioga Duncan Gallery, 1967, Carnegie Gallery, Raymond Duncan Gallery, Paris, 1970, 71, other mus.'s; one-artist show Lynn Kottler Galleries, N.Y.C., 1974; represented in permanent collections: William Penn Mus., Harrisburg, Am. Folk Art Mus., N.Y.C., Pa. State U., Thiel Coll., Indiana (Pa.) U. Publicity dir. Jr. Women's Club, Girl Scouts, Art Club (Ridgway, Pa.); dir. Pitts. Assn. Artists; chmn. edn. V.I.A.; chmn. ann. Clothesline Exhibit, Ridgway; poetry chmn. for Elk County. Recipient prizes for poems, articles and short stories Pa. Fedn. Women's Clubs, 1st prize for interior decoration Good Housekeeping, 1941, 1st prize for art Nat. League Am. Penwomen, Asso. Artists prize for watercolor Carnegie Mus., 1950, 53, Henry Posner prize for watercolor Carnegie Mus., 1950, Aimee Jackson Short prize for art, Phila. for watercolor chosen as best watercolor to rep. Pa. and sent to Nat. Mus., Washington; poetry prizes, Ted Malone, Am. Lit. Assn., award Pa. State Legislature, 1976, 81; elected Woman of the Yr., Ridgway, 1958-59; 1st prize for watercolor Bryn Mawr State Show, 1959, honorable mention for watercolor Carnegie, 1959, Nat. 1st prize for lyric Nat. League Am. Pen Women, 1954; elected to Hall of Fame, 1966; rooms named in her honor Thiel Coll., Greenville, Pa., Indiana (Pa.) U., DuBois, Pa., William Penn Mus., Harrisburg Fellow Internat. Inst. Arts and Letters; mem. Phila. Art Alliance, Nat. League Am. Pen Women (v.p. Oil City br.; nat. poetry editor 1950-52, poetry prizes; 1st prize nat. 1953; asst. art chmn., nat. editor Sonnets 1958-60, short story editor 1972), Pa. Fedn. Women's Clubs (fine arts chmn.), Pitts. Assn. Artists, Mark Twain Soc., Am. Lit. Assn., Centro Studi, Scampi Internationale, Delta Kappa Gamma. Home: 403 Oak St Ridgeway PA 15853

MCCLUNG, SISTER ROSE ANNELLE, univ. dean; b. Oklahoma City, Dec. 16, 1925; d. Guy Lamont and Gladys T. (Noret) McClung; B.S. in Bus. Adminstrn., Our Lady of Lake Coll., 1946; M.A. in Econs., Cath. U. Am., 1965. Tchr. bus. St. Francis Xavier High Sch., Alexandria, La., 1948-49, Providence Central High Sch., Alexandria, 1949-56, Providence High Sch., San Antonio, 1956-62; chmn. dept. bus. adminstrn., Our Lady of Lake U., San Antonio, 1962-74, dir. div. bus. studies, 1974-80, dean Sch. Bus. and Public Adminstrn., 1980—. Recipient Outstanding Alumna in Profession award, Our Lady of Lake U., 1979; named Coll. Bus. Tchr. of Yr. Tex. Bus. Edn. Assn., 1979. Mem. AAUP, Am. Acctg. Assn., Am. Econ. Assn., Nat. Assn. Female Execs., Data Processing Mgmt. Assn., Freedom Found., Univ. Aviation Assn., Soc. Logistics Engrs., World Future Soc., Nat. Bus. Edn. Assn., Nat. Assn. Bus. Tchr. Edn. Am. Soc. Tng. and Devel. Roman Catholic. Home and Office: 411 SW 24th St San Antonio TX 78285

MCCLURE, ELAINE LOUISE MUNRO, real estate tax cons.; b. Kansas City, Mo., Mar. 7, 1943; d. Robert DeBolt and Adrienne (Sprotte) Munro; B.A. in Edn., Eastern Wash. State Coll., 1969; postgrad. U. Wis., 1973; children—Mark Robert, Caryn Louise. Tchr. elem. schs., Kans. and Minn.; art tchr., Spring, Tex., 1969-80; co-owner, founder Discover Houston, tours, 1980-81; supr. ind. research firm Tarrance & Assos., Houston, 1980-81; real estate tax cons. land devel. dept. Gibraltar Savs. Assn., Houston, 1981—; vol. career devel. Leader Brownies, Cub Scouts.; mem. exec. bd. Parent-Tchr. Orgn.; docent Mus. Fine Arts; social dir. local homeowners' assn.; tchr. Sunday Sch.; pres. Welcome Wagon Internat. Mem. Greater Houston Conv. and Visitors Council, Delta Delta Delta Alumni. Club: Jr. League (Houston). Home: 6815 Farnaby Ct Spring TX 77373 Office: PO Box 73404 Houston TX 77090

MC CLURE, LUCILLE WILMA, mktg. researcher; b. Salem, Ill., Feb. 26, 1932; d. Leland G. and Nina Agnes (Branson) Brown; B.S., Fla. So. Coll., 1972; M.B.A., Rollins Coll., 1974; m. Theodore Eugene McClure, Dec. 21, 1948; children—Larry Ray, Theodora Eugena, Gwendolyn Lucille, Emma Jane, Michael Glen. Info. specialist Martin Marietta Aerospace, Orlando, Fla., 1957-78, mktg. specialist, 1978—; adj. prof. mktg. Fla. So. Coll., Orlando, 1977—. Mem. AIAA (adv. council central Fla. sect. 1974—), Central Fla. Astron. Soc. (pres. 1966-68), Am. Mktg. Assn., Am. Def. Preparedness Assn. Democrat. Lutheran. Clubs: Martin Marietta Mgmt. (historian 1977—, spl. recognition award 1981), Martin Marietta Astronomy (pres. 1966, 78). Contbr. over 200 research bibliographies to profl. publs. Home: 5620 Minaret Ct Orlando FL 32809 Office: PO Box 5837 MP 457 Orlando FL 32855

MCCLURE, M. MALINDA, educator; b. Pana, Ill., Nov. 9, 1937; d. Samuel Brantner and Ethel May (Long) McClure; B.S., Ill. State U., 1959; postgrad. (NSF workshop), U. Ill., 1967. Tchr., Erie (Ill.) High Sch., 1959-66, Kempton (Ill.)-Cabery High Sch., 1966-73, TriPoint Schs., Kempton, 1966-73; extension advisor home econs. Coop. Extension Service, U. Ill., Vandalia, Ill., 1974—; mem. Ill. White House conf. on Children, 1981. Bd. dirs. Comprehensive Health Planning in So. Ill., 1976—, exec. com., 1977-81; mem. South Central Health Council, chmn. plan devel. com., 1979-81, v.p., 1979-81; mem. family life com. Presbyn. Ch., 1975-76; Bd. dirs. Am. Cancer Soc., Fayco Enterprises, Central 4-H Camp Bd. NSF fellow, 1967-68. Mem. NEA, Ill. Edn. Assn., Ill. Assn. Extension Home Economists, Nat. Assn. Extension Home Economists (chmn. region 9, 1980-81). Presbyterian. Clubs: Friends of the Old Capital (v.p. 1976, exec. bd. 1977-78), Soroptimist (dir. 1976, pres. 1977, 78, bd. dirs. 1979), Cumberland Trails Camera (sec. 1981—). Office: 118 N 6 St Vandalia IL 62471

MCCLURE, MARILYN EUNICE, social worker; b. Embudo, N.Mex., Jan. 11, 1943; d. Eloy G. and Evangeline (Garcia) Vigil; B.A., Macalester Coll., 1964; M.A., U. Chgo., 1969; m. Michael A. McClure, Aug. 21, 1964; 1 dau., Miquela Nicole. Sch. social worker St. Paul (Minn.) Pub. Schs., 1970-76; clin. social worker Latino program Ramsey County Mental Health Dept., St. Paul, 1976-78; instr., coordinator U. Minn. Sch. Social Work, Mpls., 1978-79; commr. Minn. Dept. Human Rights, St. Paul, 1979—; cons. Human Resource Assocs., 1972-75. Vice-chmn. Minn. Spanish Speaking Affairs Council, 1978; bd. dirs. Family Service Greater St. Paul, People, Inc., 1981—. Mem. Nat. Assn. Social Workers (dir. Minn. chpt. 1982), Acad. Cert. Social Workers, Minn. Chicano Fedn. (chmn.), Minn. Spanish Speaking Affairs Council (vice-chmn. 1978). Democrat. Presbyterian. Office: Minn Dept Human Rights 500 Bremer Tower 7th Pl and Minnesota St Saint Paul MN 55101

MC CLURE, MARY ANNE, state senator; b. Milbank, S.D., Apr. 21, 1939; d. Charles Cornelius and Mary Lucille (Whittom) Burges; B.A. magna cum laude, U. S.D., 1961; postgrad. U. Manchester (Eng.), 1961-62; M.P.A., Syracuse U., 1981; m. D.J. McClure, Nov. 17, 1963; 1 dau., Kelly Joanne. Mem. staff U.S. Senator Francis Case, 1959-61; sec. to Lt. Gov. Nils Boe, 1963; exec. sec. to Lewis Dymond, pres. Frontier Airlines, 1963-64; tchr. public schs., Pierre, S.D., 1965-66, Redfield, S.D., 1968-70; mem. S.D. Senate, 1975—, pres. pro tem, 1979-82. Mem. Phi Beta Kappa. Republican. Congregationalist.

MCCLUSKEY, DOROTHY SOEST, state legislator; b. Middletown, Conn., June 28, 1928; d. Hugo Conrad and Dorothy (Hazen) Soest; B.A., Wheaton Coll., 1949; postgrad. (Fulbright grantee) U. Oslo, 1953-54; M.F.S., Yale U., 1973; m. Donald Shepard McCluskey; children—Peter Conrad, Martha Timmons, Christine Ann. Project mgr. Conn. Inland Wetlands Project, Ford Found. Pilot Program, Middletown, 1973-74; mem. North Branford Conservation Commn., 1966-70, chmn., 1967-70; dir. Conn. Assn. Conservation Commns., 1969-71; mem. North Branford Planning and Zoning Commn., 1970-75, sec., 1972-74, chmn., 1974; mem. Conn. Conn. Ho. of Reps., 1975-82; dir. Conn. Environ.

Mediation Ctr., 1982—. Active Nat. Order Women Legislators, Nature Conservancy, LWV, Friends of the Earth, North Branford Democratic Women's Club. Recipient public service award LWV, North Branford, 1972. Author: Conservation Plan for North Branford, 1970; co-author: Implementation Aids for Inland Wetland Agencies, 1973, Evaluation of Inland Wetland and Water Course Functions, 1974, Conn. Inland Wetlands Project. Episcopalian. Office: Environ Mediation Center Hartford CT 06102

MCCOACH, PAMELA SUE, Realtor; b. Abington, Pa., June 9, 1945; d. George E. and Hildagarde McCoach; grad. Peirce Sch. Bus. Adminstrn., 1964. Sec., FBI, Phila., also Alexandria, Va., 1964-70; legis. asst. U.S. Ho. Reps., Washington, 1970-75: Realtor, Town & Country Properties, Inc., Springfield, Va., 1975—. Chmn., Va. Commn. on Status of Women, 1979—; mem. Va. State Crime Commn.'s Spl. Adv. Task Force on Criminal Sexual Assault, 1977—; mem., chmn. Fairfax County Commn. for Women, 1974-78. Mem. No. Va. Bd. Realtors (chmn. govtl. affairs com. 1979—, dir. 1981-82), Va. Assn. Realtors (mem. legis. com. 1980—). Episcopalian. Clubs: Fairfax County Bus. and Profl. Women's (pres. 1979—, named woman of year 1975), Monticello Republican Women's (pres. 1972). Columnist, The Status of Women, Springfield Independent, 1974-76. Office: 7221 Keene Mill Rd Springfield VA 22150

MC COLLOUGH, LUCILLE HANNA (MRS. CLARENCE LINDSAY MCCOLLOUGH), state legislator; b. Huron County, Mich., Dec. 30, 1905; d. William and Stella (Stover) Hanna; grad. Western Mich. U., 1923; m. Clarence Lindsay McCollough, June 16, 1925; children—Clarence, Marilyn (Mrs. Edwards), Patrick. Past tchr., sec., stenographer; mem. Mich. Ho. of Reps., 1955—. Active Dearborn Fedn. Civic Assns., N. Am. Benefit Assn., Citizens Traffic Safety Council, YWCA. Mem. Aviation Property Owners Assn., McDonald Sch. Mothers' Club, Navy Mothers' Club, Ladies Aux. VFW, League of Women Voters, Nat. Order Women Legislators, Hist. Soc., Nat. Fedn. Bus. and Profl. Women. Recipient Sr. Auto Worker award U.A.W. Ret. Workers, 1964, citation for service Nat. Ret. Tchrs. Assn. and Am. Assn. Ret. Persons, 1965, certificate of appreciation Vets. World War I, 1966, citation VFW Mich., U.S., citation Allied Vets. Council, Dearborn, 1966, Outstanding Health Service award Mich. Med. Soc., 1969; named Bus. Woman of the Year, Mich. Fedn. Bus. and Profl. Women, 1965, 68. Democrat. Presbyn. Mem. Women of Moose. Listed in Guinness World Book of Records for 100 percent attendance record in Mich. Legislature. Home: 7517 Kentucky Ave Dearborn MI 48126 Office: Mich State Capitol Ho of Reps Lansing MI 48901

MC COLLUM, PEGGY KENNEDY, assn. and conv. exec.; b. Chattanooga, June 21, 1930; d. Robert Louis and Margaret Jo (Mathews) Kennedy; student U. Ga., U. South Fla.; children—Margaret Teresa McCollum Lyons, Deborah McCollum Cheshire. Dir. adminstrn. Fla. Assn. Ins. Agts., Tampa, 1959-71, meetings dir., Tallahassee, 1971-75; owner McCollum Mgmt. and Meetings, Tallahassee, 1975—. Past bd. dirs. LWV, Albany, Ga., also Tampa. Mem. Fla. (exec. v.p.), Am. (membership chmn.) socs. assn. execs., Meeting Planners Internat., Fla. Public Relations Assn., U.S. C. of C., Fla. Vol. Health Assn. (exec. dir.), Fla. Aviation Trades Assn. (exec. dir.), Fla. Wall and Ceiling Contractors Assn. (exec. v.p.). Home: 423 E Virginia Tallahassee FL 32301 Office: PO Box 703 Tallahassee FL 32302

MCCOMBS, BARBARA (LEHERISSEY), ednl. psychologist; b. Galesburg, Ill., Nov. 30, 1942; d. Raymond Louis and Emily Marie (Schulz) Adolf; B.S., Fla. State U., 1968, M.S. (U.S. Office Edn. fellow 1968-69), Ph.D., 1971; divorced; children—Heather Rae, Ryan William. Research asso. Computer Assisted Instrn. Center, Fla. State U., 1969-71; unit chief human factors McDonnell Douglas Corp., 1971-82; sr. research psychologist Denver Research Inst., 1982—. Grantee, Def. Advanced Research Projects Agy., 1977-81, Navy Personnel Research and Devel. Center, 1980-84, Air Force Human Resources Lab., 1982-83, Army Research Inst., 1982-84. Mem. Am. Psychol. Assn., Am. Ednl. Research Assn., Human Factors Soc., Assn. Devel. Computer-Based Instructional Systems. Author book chpts., articles, papers, reports in field. Home: 1050 S Monaco Pkwy Unit 66 Denver CO 80224 Office: SSRE Division 2135 E Wesley St Denver CO 80208

MCCOMBS, HARRIET GWENDOLYN, psychologist; b. Columbia, S.C., Nov. 9, 1954; d. William Franklin, Jr. and Harriet Louise (Coleman) McC.; B.S., U. S.C., 1974; M.A., U. Nebr., Lincoln, 1976, Ph.D., 1978. Research asst. U. S.C., 1971, grad. teaching asst. U. Nebr., 1974-78; congressional intern U.S. Ho. of Reps., Washington, 1976; asst. prof. psychology Wayne State U., Detroit, 1978—; dir. Social Policy Evaluation and Research Services, Detroit, 1980-82. Recipient Herbert Lehman Ednl. Fund award, 1971-74. Mem. Am. Psychol. Assn. (Minority fellow 1975-78), Evaluation Research Soc., Sigma Xi, Sigma Gamma Rho. Mem. A.M.E. Ch. Founder, editor Sojourner: A Third World Women's Research Newsletter. Home: 98 W Hancock St Detroit MI 48201 Office: Dept Psychology Wayne State Univ Detroit MI 48202

MCCONAHEY, PATRICIA JANE, immunologist; b. Dover, Ohio, June 9, 1936; d. Wallace Veigh and Edith Elizabeth McConahey; B.S., Waynesburg Coll., 1958. Sr. technician dept. pathology U. Pitts., 1958-61; research asst. dept. immunopathology Scripps Clinic & Research Found., LaJolla, Calif., 1961-63, research asso., 1964-74, asst. mem. dept. immunology, 1974—. Mem. Am. Assn. Immunologists. Contbr. articles in field to profl. jours. Home: 8882 Caminito Primavera LaJolla CA 92137 Office: Scripps Clinic and Research Foundation 10666 N Torrey Pines Rd LaJolla CA 92037

MC CONNELL, ALMA EASTWOOD, educator, artist; b. Charleston, W.Va.; d. John Watson and Lula (Martin) Eastwood; student Harvard U., 1929-30; B.A., Marshall U., 1930; M.Ed., Central Wash. U., 1959; m. Robert E. McConnell, July 3, 1929; children—Robert E., Douglas E. Asst. prof. art San Francisco State Coll., 1959-69, prof. emeritus, 1969—; exhibited in one-woman and group shows of paintings and jewelry, Yakima, Wash., Concord, Walnut Creek and Carmel, Calif., art faculty shows San Francisco. Vol., Bay Area Community Chest, 1963-64, ARC, Ellensburg, Wash., 1936-46; vol. philanthropic orgns. Mem. PEO, Alpha Psi Omega, Kappa Delta Pi, Kappa Pi, Sigma Sigma Sigma. Presbyterian. Contbr. articles to popular mags. Address: 8545 Carmel Valley Rd Carmel CA 93923

MC CONNELL, DONNA JUNE, fin. co. exec.; b. Morgan County, Ohio, Oct. 28, 1932; d. Louis Stanley and Elsie Leota (Ribble) Lindimore; student acctg. and fin., Walsh Coll., Canton, Ohio; m. Ben R. McConnell, Sept. 2, 1949; children—Carol Anne, Edward R. Sec.-bookkeeper Ferrell Constrn. Co., Canton, 1957-59; from bookkeeper to treas. Boyd G. Heminger, Inc., Canton, 1959-69; controller Williams Asphalt Paving Co., Canton, 1969-73; mgr. acctg. Fiscal Assos., Inc., Canton, 1973—, gen. mgr., 1980—; pres. Women in Constrn., 1965-66, 70-71. Named Woman of Yr. in Constrn., Nat. Assn. Women in Constrn., 1970. Mem. Nat. Assn. Accts. (dir. 1966-71, sec. 1971-73, Mem. of Yr. award 1974), Nat. Assn. Female Execs. Baptist. Clubs: Meadowlake Country, Order Eastern Star. Home: 3609 Vicary Sq NE Canton OH 44714 Office: 1700 Gateway Blvd SE Canton OH 44707

MCCONNELL, JANE LINDSAY WALKER, med. services co. exec.; b. Steubenville, Ohio, Apr. 19, 1936; d. Clifford R. and Hazel Elizabeth (Shepherd) Walker; student Ohio U., 1954-55, Hunter Coll., 1956-58, UCLA, 1967-68; B.A. magna cum laude, Bethany Coll., 1981; m. D. Verne McConnell, June 17, 1955; children—Matthew D., Kathleen C., Sarah S., William W. Sec., Gen. Features Corp., 1955-56; dept. sec. Columbia U. Sch. Public Health and Adminstrn. Medicine, 1956-59; elem. sch. tchr., Balt., 1959-60; sec. dept. surgery Vanderbilt U., 1960-63; conf. sec., editor UCLA Forum in Med. Scis., 1964-66; sec.-treas. Plastic Surgery, Inc., Wheeling, W.Va., 1973—; sec.-treas. Cosmesis, Inc., Wheeling, 1981—. Bd. dirs. Altenheim; co-chmn. Centre Market Celebration, Wheeling, W.Va., Friends of Wheeling. Mem. Plastic Surgery Adminstrv. Assn., Med. Execs. Soc., Ohio County Med. Aux., Toronto Arts Council. Republican. Presbyterian. Clubs: Fort Henry; Princeton (N.Y.C.). Home: 1315 National Rd Wheeling WV 26003 Office: 1300 Chapline St Wheeling WV 26003

MC CONNELL, MARGARET MAHLER (MRS. J.H. TYLER MCCONNELL), civic worker; b. Wilmington, Del., July 3, 1944; d. John Anthony and Maggie Naomi (Davis) Mahler; A.A., Marjorie Webster Coll., 1964; m. James Hoge Tyler McConnell, Apr. 25, 1973. Sec., CIA, Washington, 1964-65, Hercules, Inc., Wilmington, 1965-66; with Delaware Trust Co., Wilmington, 1966-73, asst. corp. sec., 1969-72, asst. v.p., 1972-73. Bd. dirs., corp. sec. Del. Mus. Natural History, Wilmington, 1969-79; asst. sec., treas. Cecil County (Md.) Breeders' Fair, 1969-75; sec., mem. exec. com. Fair Hill (Md.) Races, 1969-75; bd. dirs. Wilmington Vis. Nurse Assn., 1974—, sec., 1982—; bd. dirs. Brandywine YMCA, Wilmington, 1977-82. Mem. Nat., Del. assns. bank women, Nat. Steeplechase & Hunt Assn., Del. Soc. Fine Arts. Democrat. Episcopalian. Clubs: Wilmington Country, Greenville Country, Vicmead Hunt, Rehoboth Beach Country, River. Home: 805 Snuff Mill Rd Wilmington DE 19807 also 400 S Ocean Blvd Palm Beach FL 33480 Office: 101 Delaware Trust Bldg Wilmington DE 19899

MCCORD, CAROL MCCRACKEN, personnel co. exec.; b. Pitts., June 26, 1949; d. Ellis Ray and Ruth (Thomas) McCracken; A.A., So. Sem., 1969; postgrad. Elon & Albright Coll.; m. Thomas McCord, Sept. 4, 1970; 1 son, Jeffrey. Loan asst. Franklin State Bank, Princeton, N.J., 1974-76; cons. Associated Personnel, Humble, Tex., 1978-80; owner Kingwood (Tex.) Personnel, 1980—. Active, Kingwood Community Theater. Mem. Women in Action (dir.), Houston Area Assn. Personnel Cons., Better Bus. Bur., Humble C. of C. Republican. Presbyterian. Home: 2919 Laurel Fork Kingwood TX 77339

MCCORD, JULIA ANN, internal auditor; b. Waurika, Okla., May 22, 1924; d. William Solon and Eurah Pearl (Watson) Osteen; B.S., Okla. Coll. Liberal Arts, 1968; M.B.A., U. Tampa, 1980; m. Elmer C. McCord, Jr., June 10, 1943 (div. 1974); children—Perry Houston, Linda Ann. Bookkeeper, Dyer & Watkins Ins. Agy., Durant, Okla., 1947-50, Thornton Ins. Agy., Oklahoma City, 1950-51, Gene Strauss Ins. Agy., Kansas City, Mo., 1951-52; controller Fla. Div., Am. Cancer Soc., Tampa, 1968-71; supr. auditing Sch. Bd. Hillsborough County, Tampa, 1973—; tchr. acctg., adult edn. Mem. Inst. Internal Auditors (chpt. bd. govs. 1978-81), Nat. Assn. Accts. (chpt. sec. 1977), Fla. Assn. Sch. Bus. Adminstrs. (v.p. 1982—), LWV, AAUW (ednl. founds. chmn. 1981-82). Methodist. Club: The Commerce. Home: 4209 W Sevilla St Tampa FL 33609 Office: 901 E Kennedy St Tampa FL 33601

MCCORDIC, ROSALIE ANN, advt. exec.; b. Los Angeles, Mar. 11, 1954; d. Robert Lee and Jessie Magnolia McC.; B.A., Calif. State U., Northridge, 1976; postgrad. UCLA, 1980-82. Sales staff Simi Valley Enterprises (Calif.), 1976-78; advt. sales rep. Los Angeles Times, 1978-80, display account exec., 1980, account exec. fast foods and restaurants, 1980-81; account exec. advt. Los Angeles Mag., 1981—. Calif. State scholar, 1976; recipient Sales Achievement award Los Angeles Times, 1979. Mem. Advt. Club Los Angeles, Mag. Reps. Home: 5446 Colfax Ave North Hollywood CA 91601 Office: 1888 Century Park E Suite 920 Los Angeles CA 90067

MCCORKLE, LINDA ANN, lawyer; b. Raymond, Wash., Nov. 13, 1947; d. Marcus Eugene and MaryLynn (Lamping) McC.; B.A. with distinction in Polit. Sci., U. Wash., 1969; M.P.A., Syracuse U., 1970; J.D., Georgetown U., 1974. Admitted to Wash. bar, 1974, D.C. bar, 1977, U.S. Supreme Ct. bar, 1979; program analyst Office for Civil Rights, HEW, Washington, 1971-72; law clk. Zuckert, Scoutt & Rasenberger, Washington, 1972-73; staff counsel Com. on Commerce, U.S. Senate, Washington, 1973-77; individual practice law, Washington, 1977-78; asso. firm Blum & Nash, Washington, 1977-79; counsel ITT Rayonier Inc., Seattle, 1980—; vol. atty. Women's Legal Def. Fund. Active, Nat. Women's Polit. Caucus. Mem. Fed. Bar Assn., Washington Women Lawyers, Mortar Board. Episcopalian. Address: 1717 16th Ave #18 Seattle WA 98122

MC CORMACK, ELIZABETH JANE, found. exec.; b. N.Y.C., Mar. 7, 1922; d. George H. and Natalie J. (Duffy) McC.; B.A., Manhattanville Coll., 1944; M.A., Providence Coll., 1957; Ph.D., Fordham U., 1966; LL.D., Brandeis U., 1972, Princeton U., 1974; m. Jerome I. Aron, 1976. Asst. to pres., acad. dean Manhattanville Coll., 1958-66, prof. philosophy, pres., 1966-74; asso. Rockefeller Family and Assos., N.Y.C., 1974—; dir. Gen. Foods Corp., Champion Internat. Corp., Stamford, Conn.; trustee Am. Savs. Bank, N.Y.C. Mem. Faculty Fellowship program United Negro Coll. Fund; trustee Spelman Coll., Atlanta, Hamilton Coll., Clinton, N.Y., N.Y.C. Police Found.; bd. dirs. Am. Ditchley Found.; bd. mgrs. Swarthmore (Pa.) Coll., 1980—; bd. overseers and mgrs. Meml. Sloan-Kettering Cancer Center, N.Y.C. Mem. Council on Fgn. Relations. Home: 201 E 62d St New York NY 10021 Office: 30 Rockefeller Plaza New York NY 10112

MCCORMACK, JUDITH GAIL, med. technologist; b. Chgo., Oct. 4, 1939; d. Milton and Marie Hedwig (Schroeder) Srail; B.S., Roosevelt U., Chgo., 1960; Med. technologist, Mt. Sinai Hosp., Chgo., 1960; m. Robert George McCormack, Sept. 17, 1960. Med. technologist Mt. Sinai Hosp., 1962-65; serology supr. Meml. Hosp. DuPage County, Elmhurst, Ill., 1965-69, immunology supr., 1982—; immunovirology supr. Lutheran Gen. Hosp., Park Ridge, Ill., 1969-82; v.p. Bion Enterprises, Ltd.; dir. Advance Designs Cons., Inc. Mem. Am. Soc. Clin. Pathologists, Am. Soc. Microbiology, South Central Assn. Clin. Microbiology, Ill. Soc. Microbiology. Mem. Ind. Fundamental Chs. Am. Home: 5 Oak Brook Club Dr Oak Brook IL 60521 Office: 200 Berteau Ave Elmhurst IL 60126

MC CORMACK, SHIRLEY MARIE, govt. auditor; b. Arcadia, Kans., Mar. 21, 1930; d. Frank Lee Wheeler and Stella Marie (Garrett) Brinkle; B.S. in Bus. Edn., Kans. State U., Pittsburg, 1957, M.S. in Bus. Edn., 1970; postgrad. Washburn U., 1964-65, U. Okla., 1973-74; M.A. in Bus., Central Mich. U., 1979; m. Joseph Marion McCormack, Apr. 29, 1949 (dec.); children—Johnny Joe, Joseph Marion. Tchr. public high schs., Kans., 1957-65, 66-72; clk. Emporia (Kans.) Bd. Edn., 1965-66; instr. Dakota State Coll., 1972-73, Southwestern State Coll., 1973-74, Coffeyville Community Jr. Coll., 1974-75; auditor Region VII, HUD, 1975—. Recipient spl. award HUD Disaster Field Office, 1979, letter of commendation HUD, 1979; C.P.A., Mo.; cert. internal auditor. Mem. Am. Women's Soc. C.P.A.s, Inst. Mgmt. Accts., Internat. Platform Assn., Delta Epsilon, Delta Pi Epsilon. Democrat. Methodist. Home: 2910 S 51st Terr Kansas City KS 66106 Office: HUD Office Insp Gen 13th Floor 1103 Grand Kansas City MO 64106

MCCORMICK, ALMA HEFLIN, writer, ret. educator, psychologist; b. Winona, Mo., Sept. 2, 1910; d. Irvin Elgin and Nora Edith (Kelley) Heflin; B.A., E. Wash. Coll., 1936, Ed.M., 1949; Ph.D., Clayton U., 1977; m. Archie Thomas Edward McCormick, July 14, 1942; children—Thomas James, Kelly Jean. Press relations E. Wash. Coll., Cheney, 1948-49; instr. Wash. State U., Pullman, 1952-53; instr. E. Los Angeles Coll., Monterey Park, Calif., 1972-73; originator dept. severely mentally retarded Tri-City Public Schs., Richland, Wash., 1953, Parkland, Wash., 1955; co-founder, dir. Adastra Sch. for Gifted Children, Seattle, 1957-64; writings include: Adventure Was The Compass, 1942, Merry Makes a Choice, 1950; contbr. articles to various publs., 1937—. Mem. Am. Psychol. Assn., Kappa Delta Pi. Republican. Episcopalian. Clubs: Women's Internat. Bowling Congress, Citrus Belt Women Bowlers. Editor: Club/Flyer. First Am. woman test pilot, 1942. Home and Office: Apple Valley CA 92307

MCCORMICK, JUDITH ANN, engr.; b. Providence, July 11, 1952; d. John and Marjorie (Tuener) McC.; B.S., Union Coll., 1974. Sr. lab. technologist Block Drug Co., Jersey City, 1974-76; program planner Knolls Atomic Power Lab., West Milton, N.Y., 1976-78; engr. Stone and Webster Engring. Corp., Boston, 1978-81, lead planning engr., 1981—. Mem. Am. Nuclear Soc. Episcopalian. Office: 245 Summer St Boston MA 02107

MCCORMICK, MARJORIE, horticulture co. exec.; b. Baker, Oreg., Nov. 10, 1928; d. William Everett and Hulda Alice (Scantlin) Price; student Met. Bus. Coll., Seattle, 1952, Yakima Bus. Coll., 1955; m. Charles W. McCormick, Nov. 6, 1958; children—Stephen, Victoria, Cheryl. owner, v.p., sec., Sec., mgr., partner Antles & Price, Yakima, Washington, 1954-58; Callahan Nursery, Inc., Yakima, Wash., 1976—; owner, mgr. McCormick Fruit Tree Co., Inc., Yakima, Wash., 1958—, pres., sec. 1982—; owner, broker McCormick Realty, Yakima, 1961—; cons. in field. Sec.-treas. Naches Pass Tunnel Hwy. Assn., Miracle Mile Assn.; dir., founder Spring Acres Group Home for Retarded, 1969-76; v.p. Young Republican Club, 1957. Recipient Top Nat. Salesman award Stark Bros. Nurseries, 1962, 64, award Zonta Women's Club, 1959. Mem. Nat. Peach Council, Wash. State Hort. Assn. (life), Yakima Bd. Realtors, Yakima C. of C. (chmn. agr. com.). Republican. Presbyterian. Club: Altrusa Internat. (recording sec. 1963-65). Author: The Golden Pollen, 1960, 73; patentee on Silverspur red delicious, 1977, Firmgold delicious apple, 1977, Rose Red delicious apple, 1972. Office: 6111-A Englewood Blvd Yakima WA 98908

MCCORMICK, SHIRLEY ANNE, energy mgmt. and bldg. automation systems co. exec.; b. Timberville, Va., Mar. 17, 1936; d. Stanley William and Lottie Catherine (Higgs) Messick; B.A., Madison Coll., 1957; B.B.A., Old Dominion U., 1974; M.B.A., 19 ; m. Robert L. McCormick, Sr., Aug. 18, 1979; 1 dau., Peggy Ruth. Sec., R. J. Clower Ins. Co., Harrisonburg, Va., part-time, 1953-57; sec. residential office S. L. Nusbaum Co., Norfolk, Va., 1958-60; br. sec., office mgr. acctg. dept. Va. Tractor Co., Inc., Norfolk, 1960-73; acct., field auditor Christian Broadcasting Network, Virginia Beach, Va., 1973-75; with Johnson Controls, Inc., Norfolk, Va., 1976—, office adminstr., 1980—. Vol. Chesapeake Gen. Hosp., 1979—. Mem. Am. Bus. Women's Assn. (v.p. 1974-76), Beta Sigma Phi (chpt. pres. 1979-81). Republican. Baptist. Home: 353 Hurdle Dr Chesapeake VA 23320 Office: 953 Norfolk Square Norfolk VA 23502

MC COTTER, MARGARET ROSEMOND PALMER (MRS. BURNEY RICHARD MCCOTTER), former librarian; b. Thomasville, N.C., Nov. 7, 1921; d. Jacob Alexander and Etna (Little) Palmer; A.B., Catawba Coll., 1942; M.L.S., U. N.C., 1944; m. Burney Richard McCotter, June 21, 1946; children—Richard Palmer, Karen Ellen. Librarian, Southern Pines (N.C.) Sch. System, 1944-47; post librarian Fort Story (Va.), 1950-51; librarian LeRoy Martin Jr. High Sch., Raleigh, N.C., 1959-62, 65-81; library cons. N.C. Dept. Public Instrn., Raleigh, 1963-65. Mem. NEA, UDC, N.C. Library Assn., N.C. Assn. Educators, Historic Preservation Soc. N.C., DAR, Delta Kappa Gamma, Beta Phi Mu, Sigma Pi Alpha. Democrat. Presbyn. Clubs: Capital City, Carolina Country (Raleigh). Joint author AV Cataloging and Processing Simplified, 1971. Editor: Reference Materials for School Libraries, 1965. Home: 332 Buncombe St Raleigh NC 27609

MC COY, DORIS LEE, psychotherapist, educator, TV producer; b. Pitts., Apr. 16, 1929; d. Bernard Lenard and Alvena Elizabeth (Meyer) Raymond; B.A., Muskingum Coll., 1951; M.A., Stanford U., 1953, Ph.D., Claremont U., 1973; children—Jeffrey, Rhonda Lee, Mark. Faculty, Nat. U., LaJolla, Calif., 1973—; pvt. practice psychotherapy, La Jolla, 1973—; moderator, producer TV spls. on marriage and the family, also celebrity interviews, 1973—. Trustee, Mexican and Am. Found., 1978-80; bd. dirs. YWCA, 1953-55; mem. state bd. LWV Mo., 1962-65; v.p. Chgo., UNICEF, 1966-68; a founder Johnston Coll., U. Redlands (Calif.). Mem. Nat. Acad. TV Arts and Scis., League Am. Pen Women (pres. Charterloo). Presbyterian. Author: They Took the Challenge: 12 Traits of Successful People. Home: 5758 Beaumont Ave La Jolla CA 92037 Office: 7755 Fay Ave Suite G La Jolla CA 92037

MCCOY, ELEANOR LOUISE RICE, communications co. exec.; b. Wichita, Kans., May 29, 1928; d. Claude R. and Gwen Laura (Palmer) Rice; student Wichita State U., 1946-48, 60, Kans. U., 1978, 80—; m. Dale Wesley McCoy, Aug. 10, 1948; children—Cathi Lynn McCoy Robillard, Michael Wesley, Marc Alan, Timothy John, Dale Wesley III. Womens dir. Sta. KKOY, Chanute, Kans., 1970—, Sta. KQSM-FM, Chanute, 1970—. Docent, Wichita Art Mus., 1964-68, bd. dirs. 1967-68, chmn. art auction, 1966; cofounder Chanute Art Gallery, 1973, chmn., 1973—; docent Wichita Hist. Mus., 1967-68; chmn. Cancer Crusade, Neosho County, Kans., 1969-75; pres. Martin Johnson Safari Mus., Chanute, 1976; mem. vestry Grace Episcopal Ch., Chanute, 1976-79; mem. Supreme Ct. nominating commn. State of Kans., 1975, 78—; bd. dirs. Kans. Childrens Service League; pres. Four County bd. Tri-Valley Devel. Center, 1979—. Republican. Clubs: Art and Lit. (pres. 1976), St. Cecelia Music. Author: Ellys Cookbook, 1977. Home: 9 Windsor Rd Chanute KS 66720 Office: PO Box 788 Chanute KS 66720

MCCOY, FRIEDA ANN, mgmt. cons.; b. Casper, Wyo., July 15, 1945; d. William B. and Helen C. (Brattis) Noell; A.A., Casper Coll., 1965; B.S., U. Wyo., 1967; M.L.S., U. Denver, 1968; M.B.A., U. Utah, 1975; m. Gerald E. McCoy, Oct. 12, 1968. Social sci. librarian U. Utah Marriott Library, Salt Lake City, 1968-71, govt. documents dept. head, 1971-75; document control supr. Alyeska Pipeline Co., Fairbanks, 1975-77; document control supr. N.W. Alaskan Pipeline Co., Salt Lake City, 1977-78, records and data mgmt. mgr., 1978-80, records and methods dir., 1980-82; owner, pres. CRM, cons., Salt Lake City, 1982—; instr. mgmt. U. Utah Coll. Bus., 1973-75; mgmt. cons., 1972-75. Mem. Am. Mgmt. Assn., Alaska Pipeline Builders Assn. (v.p. 1982—), Assn. M.B.A. Execs., Assn. Records Mgrs. and Adminstrs., Nat. Micrographics Assn., Porject Mgmt. Inst. Contbr. articles to profl. jours. Home: 1192 S 9th St E Salt Lake City UT 84105 Office: 1192 S 9th E Salt Lake City UT 84105

MCCOY, JANICE MAXINE, nurse; b. Bremerton, Wash., Oct. 11, 1945; d. Conrad Clark and Mae Maxine (Yeakle) Kaiser; R.N., St. Luke's Methodist Hosp., Cedar Rapids, Iowa, 1966; postgrad. Coll. St. Francis, Joliet, Ill., 1981—; m. David Loren McCoy, Aug. 27, 1966; children—Marsha Lynn, Mark David. Office nurse, 1966-67; staff nurse U. Iowa Hosps., Iowa City, 1969-70, pvt. duty nurse, office nurse relief, ambulance call nurse, 1971-74; staff nurse St. Francis Hosp. Med. Center, Peoria, Ill., 1975-78; supr. ob-gyn Proctor Community Hosp., Peoria, 1978-80, v.p. nursing services, 1980—. Co-chmn. Christmas Tree Lane Bazaar, First United Meth. Ch., Peoria, 1976-77, co-chmn. Vietnamese Refugee Family Relocation program, 1975. Cert. ob-gyn nurse, Ill. Mem. Nurses Assn. of Am. Coll. Ob-Gyn, Ill. Soc. Nurse Adminstrs., Am. Soc. Nurse Adminstrs., Internat. Villa Vacations. Club: Newcomer's (pres. Mendota, Ill. 1973). Office: 5409 N Knoxville Ave Peoria IL 61614

MC COY, KATHLEEN LYNNE, writer; b. Dayton, Ohio, Apr. 25, 1945; d. James Lyons and Ethel Elizabeth (Curtis) McC.; B.S. in Journalism, Northwestern U., 1967, M.S. in Mag. Journalism, 1968; m. Robert Miles Stover, May 28, 1977. Free lance writer, 1965—; contbr. to Glamour, Mademoiselle, Woman's Day, TV Guide, Readers Digest, Families, Bride's, Seventeen; feature editor 'TEEN Mag., Los Angeles, 1968-77; frequent guest various TV, radio talk shows. Mem. Screen Actors Guild, AGVA, AFTRA, NOW, Women in Communications, Soc. Profl. Journalists. Author: Discover Yourself, 1976; Discover Yourself II, 1978; The Teenage Body Book, 1979; Your Guide to Planning Your Future, 1979; The Teenage Survival Guide, Coping with Teenage Depression: A Parents Guide, 1982; The Teenage Body Book Guide to Sexuality, 1983; The Teenage Body Book Guide to Dating and Love, 1983. Home: 25665 Rancho Adobe Rd Valencia CA 91355

MCCOY, LINDA LEE, personnel exec.; b. Balt., Mar. 1, 1949; d. Martin Burnette and Emma (Kucherer) McC.; cert. legal sec., Columbus Bus. U., 1974; children—Tonya Lynn, Christopher Laurence, Dawn Renee. Clerk-steno HEW, Social Security Adminstrn., Arlington, Va., Columbus, Ohio, 1969-74, Dept. Army, Security Br., Fort Ord, Calif., 1975-77; purchasing mgr. Quality Inns Internat., Inc., Silver Spring, Md., 1978-81; personnel coordinator Martin Marietta Aluminum, Inc., Bethesda, Md., 1981—; bd. dirs. Purchasing Mgmt. Assn. Washington, 1975-81. Mem. Nat. Assn. Female Execs. (network dir.), Am. Legion Women's Aux. Home: 5400 Manorfield Rd Rockville MD 20853 Office: 6801 Rockledge Dr Bethesda MD 20817

MCCOY, LOIS CLARK, county ofcl.; b. New Haven, Oct. 1, 1920; d. William Patrick and Lois (Dailey) Clark; B.S., Skidmore Coll., 1942; student Nat. Search and Rescue Sch., 1974; m. Herbert I. McCoy, Oct. 17, 1943; children—Whitney, Kevin, Marianne, Tori, Debra Jill, Sally Gay., Daniel. Asst. buyer R.H. Macy & Co., N.Y.C., 1942-44, assoc. buyer, 1944-48; instr. mountain medicine and survival U. Calif., San Diego., 1973-74; cons. editor Search and Rescue mag., 1975; coordinator San Diego Mountain Rescue Team, LaJolla, 1975-80; disaster officer, San Diego County, 1980—; editor-in-chief Response mag., 1981—. Chmn. search and rescue com. Calif. Seismic Safety Commn., 1982—; pres. San Diego com. Los Angeles Philarm. Orch., 1978-79; chmn. search and resuce com. Gov.'s Task Force on Earthquakes, 1981-82. Recipient Hal Foss award, 1982. Mem. Nat. Assn. Search and Resucue (dir. 1980—), Am. Astron. Soc., AIAA, Council Survival Edn., Mountain Rescue Assn., Nat. Jeep Search and Rescue Assn., IEEE, Am. Soc. Indsl. Security. Episcopalian. Author handbooks in field. Office: 5201-Q Ruffin Rd San Diego CA 92123

MCCOY, MARY ANN, state ofcl.; b. Duluth, Minn., Oct. 13, 1924; d. Homer Burke and Avis (Woodworth) Hursh; B.A., Grinnell Coll., 1946; postgrad. Laval U., 1946, Mankato State U., 1964-65, U. Minn., 1970-73; m. Charles Ramon McCoy, June 11, 1949; children—Jeffrey, Mary, Jeremy. Exec. trainee Younkers, Inc., Des Moines, 1946; advt. copywriter Des Moines Register & Tribune, 1947; field dir. Duluth (Minn.) Girl Scout Council, 1947-49; with merchandising dept. Dayton's, Inc., Mpls., 1966-75; dir. election and legis. manual div. Office of Sec. of State of Minn., St. Paul, 1975-81; exec. dir. Minn. State Ethical Practices Bd., St. Paul, 1981—. Mem. exec. council Minn. Hist. Soc., 1972-81; mem. Minn. Supreme Ct. Bd. for Continuing Legal Edn., 1981—; sec. State Rev. Bd. for Nominations to Nat. Register, 1976—. Mem. Am. Judicature Soc., Women Historians of Midwest, Am. Assn. State and Local History. Editor, Minn. Legis. Manual, 1975-81. Office: Ethical Practices Bd 41 State Office Bldg St Paul MN 55155

MCCOY, MARY JO, mgmt. analyst; b. Boise, Idaho, July 6, 1938; d. Charles Herbert and Evelyn (Horgan) Buckel; student U. Oreg., 1957, Alaska Meth. U., 1967, Cochise Coll., 1973-75; M.A., U. No. Colo., 1978; m. Joseph G. McCoy, June 13, 1978; children—David, Susan, Joseph. With U.S. Army, Fort Huahuca, Ariz., 1972—, program analyst, communication command, 1979—; family counselor Cath. Social Services, Sierra Vista, Ariz., 1978-81; counselor Cochise County Conciliation Ct., 1980-81; instr. Cochise Coll., part time, 1981—; mem. Oblate Order St. Benedict, 1971—; founder Community of the Holy Trinity, 1964. Mem. Anchorage Council Chs., 1966-70; bd. dirs. Cath. Charities Anchorage, 1966-70. Mem. Am. Soc. Mil. Comptrollers. Republican. Club: Jobs Daughters. Home: 501 Chantilly Dr Sierra Vista AZ 85635

MC COY, PATRICIA ALICE, deaf interpreter; b. Cheverly, Md., Feb. 18, 1952; d. George Dudley and Louise Adeline (Waterholter) McC.; student Prince Georges Community Coll., 1973—, Gallaudet Coll., 1973. Cashier, G. C. Murphy Co., Hyattsville, Md., 1969-73; sec., George's Radio and TV, Washington, 1973-77; sec., interpreter Gallaudet Coll., Washington, 1978—; chmn. consultancy com. Deaf Media Council, 1974-77. Recipient cert. of appreciation Nat. ARC, 1976. Mem. Registry Interpreters for Deaf (Potomac bd. mem.), Nat. Assn. Deaf, Md. Assn. Deaf, Washington Met. Deaf Alliance (v.p.), Met. Washington Assn. for Deaf, Internat. Platform Assn., World Poetry Soc., Telecommunicators for Deaf, Inc., Nat. Geog. Soc., Am. Biog. Research Assn., Deaf Awareness. Home: care I Hear Your Hand PO Box 26 6025 Springhill Dr Greenbelt MD 20770 Office: Gallaudet Coll Office of Admissions and Records 800 Florida Ave NE Washington DC 20002

MCCOY, SONDRA JO VAN METER, historian; b. San Francisco, Dec. 27, 1934; d. Elliott Lee and Bertha Dorothy (Sjoholm) Bachman; B.A., Wichita U., 1958, M.A. in History, 1962; m. George W. Van Meter, Aug. 18, 1957 (div. 1978); children—Alan, Don, Clare; m. 2d, Donald R. McCoy, June 29, 1980. Tchr., Valley Center (Kans.) Jr. High Sch., 1958-59; lectr., instr. Wichita State U., 1966-70, 73-78; writer Marion County Hist. Soc., 1970-72; writer Almanac Researchers, 1974; historian, researcher C.E., U.S. Army, 1975; historian, writer Wichita Bd. Edn., 1976-77; tchr. Derby (Kans.) Sr. High Sch., 1978-79; historian, writer United Telecommunications, Kansas City, Kans., 1979-80; freelance writer, 1980—. Mem. Kans. State Hist. Soc., Am. Assn. State and Local History (commendation 1974), Nat. Fedn. Press Women, Kans. Fedn. Press Women (1st pl. award non-fiction 1978). Author: Marion County, Kansas, Past and Present, 1973; Our Common School Heritage, A History of the Wichita Public Schools, 1977; contbr. articles to profl. jours. Home: 3213 Saddlehorn Lawrence KS 66044

MC CRACKEN, ALICE IRENE, psychotherapist; b. Indpls., May 4, 1942; d. Neal and Falma Dorothy (Rice) McC.; B.A. with honors, Mills Coll., Oakland, Calif., 1963; M.A., U. Calif., Davis, 1965; Ph.D., Tulane U., 1968; M.Counseling, Ariz. State U., 1975; 1 dau., Tammy Maru. Library asst., head current periodicals service Ariz. State U. Library, 1968-70; community program specialist City of Scottsdale, Ariz., 1971-72; women's editor Scottsdale Daily Progress, 1972-74; activities therapist Camelback Hosp., Phoenix, 1972-74, dir. public relations, psychotherapist, 1975-78; psychotherapist Family Service Agy., Tempe, Ariz., 1978-81; pvt. practice psychotherapy, Scottsdale, Ariz., 1981—. Served with USAR, 1976-78. Recipient Ariz. Press Women editing and writing awards, 1972-75; Ariz. Bus. Communicators editing award, 1975. Mem. Am. Group Psychotherapy Assn., Phoenix Psychoanalytic Study Group, Ariz. Group Psychotherapy Soc., Am. Personnel and Guidance Assn., Am. Mental Health Counselors Assn. Office: Dynamic Counseling Assos 6730 E McDowell Rd Suite 115 Scottsdale AZ 85257

MC CRACKEN, SHIRLEY ANN, ednl. cons.; b. Rochester, N.Y., Aug. 15, 1937; d. Bernard Anthony Ross and Marian Elizabeth Heimann; B.A., Nazareth Coll., 1959; B.S. in Math., Marquette U., 1968; Ph.D. in Human Behavior, LaJolla U., 1980; m. Paul A. McCracken, June 25, 1971; children— Donna Ann, Glenn. Tchr. math. Mt. Carmel High Sch., Auburn, N.Y., 1959-68; asst. workshop tng. supr. Jewish Vocat. Service, Milw., 1968; counselor Curative Workshop, Milw., 1968-69; tchr. Anaheim (Calif.) Union High Sch. Dist., 1969-72; pvt. ednl. cons., workshop leader, Anaheim, 1972—; mgr. law office, 1980. Rep. to Ednl. Congress of Calif., 1976-77; rep. for Edn. of Calif. State Div., 1976-77, coordinator group effectiveness tng. team, 1978-79. Nazareth Coll. scholar, 1954-59; NSF Inst. participant, 1963, 64, 66-67; recipient Woman of Yr. award Anaheim C. of C., 1978. Mem. AAUW (exec. council 1977-80, br. pres. 1974-76), Internat. Fedn. Univ. Women, Nazareth Acad. Alumnae Assn., Marquette U. Alumni Assn., Nazareth Coll. Alumni Assn., Anaheim Hist. Mus. Assn., Orange County Music Center Assn., Broadmoor Northridge Community Assn. Clubs: Ebell (sec. 1977-78, 4th v.p. 1978-79), Am. Fedn. Women's Clubs, TOPS, Keep Off Pounds Sensibly. Author: Creative Leadership, 1980. Home: 6553 E Calle del Norte Anaheim CA 92807 Office: 1502 E Katelle St Anaheim CA 92805

MCCRARY, EUGENIA LESTER (EUGENIA CAMPBELL LESTER), civic worker, writer; b. Annapolis, Md., Mar. 23, 1929; d. John Campbell and Eugenia (Potts) Lester; A.B. cum laude, Radcliffe Coll., 1950; M.A., Johns Hopkins U., 1952; postgrad. Harvard U., spring 1953, Pa. State U., 1953-54, Drew U., 1957-58, Inst. Study of USSR, Munich, W.Ger., 1964; m. John Campbell Howard, July 15, 1955 (dec. Sept. 1965); m. 2d, Dennis Daughtry McCrary, June 28, 1969; 1 son, Dennis Campbell. Grad. asst. dept. Romance langs. Pa. State U., 1953-54; tchr. dept. math. The Brearley Sch., N.Y.C., 1954-57; dir. Sch. Langs., Inc., Summit, N.J., 1958-69, trustee, 1960-69. Dist. dir. Eastern Pa. and N.J. auditions Met. Opera Nat. Council, N.Y.C., 1960-66, dist. dir. publicity, 1966-67, nat. vice chmn. publicity, 1967-71, nat. chmn. public relations, 1972-75, hon. nat. chmn. public relations, 1976—. Mem. Nat. Soc. Colonial Dames, Playhouse Assn. Summit, Met. Opera Nat. Council, Mayflower Soc., Soc. Daus. of Holland Dames. Republican. Episcopalian. Club: Colony. Home: 24 Central Park S New York NY 10019

MCCRARY, KATHERINE ELENE, paper tube mfg. ofcl.; b. Carbon Hill, Ala., June 15, 1926; d. Grady Franklin and Ophelia Ann (Terrell) Files; student Oglethorpe U., 1956-57, Kennesaw Coll., 1978-79; m. Thomas Nathan McCrary, June 15, 1963; children by previous marriage —Darla, Terrell. Successively sec., bookkeeper, asst. treas., asst. to pres., asst. sec.-treas. Star Paper Tube Co., Inc., Austell, Ga., 1960—; speaker. Active ARC, United Way; treas. Congregational Methodist Ch. Served with WAVES, USNR, 1942-44. CPS (cert. profl. sec.). Mem. Nat. Secs. Assn. (editor bull. 1978-80), Internat., Am. Bus. Women's Assn. Republican. Club: Eastern Star. Contbr. to co. quar. newsletter. Home: Rt 7 Box 61 Dallas GA 30132 Office: PO Box 8 Austell GA 30001

MC CRAVEY, MARY ALVARETTA, bus. exec.; b. Blairsville, Ga., Jan. 3, 1921; d. Ernest Leroy and Elsie (Owensby) McC.; A.B., U. Ga., 1948, J.D. summa cum laude, 1948. Admitted to Ga. bar, 1947; with Ga.-Pacific Corp., Atlanta, 1948—, asst. sec., 1951-56, sec., 1956—, v.p., 1981—; sec., dir. Ga.-Pacific Investment Co., Ga.-Pacific Internat. Corp., Ga.-Pacific Found. Mem. Am., Ga. bar assns., Am. Soc. Corp. Secs., Phi Beta Kappa, Phi Kappa Phi. Office: 133 Peachtree St NE Atlanta GA 30303

MCCREA, JOAN MARIE, educator; b. Chgo., Jan. 24, 1922; d. Alexander Charles and Sophia Veronica (Hagan) Ryan; B.A. in French, Ind. U., 1942; M.A. in Econs., UCLA, 1957, Ph.D. in Econs., 1965; m. James Aloysius McCrea, Jan. 26, 1947. Metall. observer Republic Steel, Chgo., 1942-45; orgn. and methods examiner U.S. Air Force, 1946-55; instr. U. Calif., Riverside, 1959-61; asst. prof. econs. Hollins Coll., 1961-66; prof. econs. U. Tex., Arlington, 1966—. Ford Found. fellow, 1962; Econ. in Action fellow, 1965. Mem. Am. Econ. Assn., So. Econ. Assn., Western Econ. Assn., History of Econs. Soc., AAUW, World Social Prospects Study Assn., Mensa. Contbr. in field. Office: Dept Econs PO Box 19479 U Tex Arlington TX 76019

MC CRENSKY, MARY GORDON, dietitian, health systems co. exec.; b. Cambridge, Mass., Apr. 4, 1919; d. Bannie and Pessie (Hirsch) Gordon; B.S., Simmons Coll., 1939; postgrad. in health systems mgmt. Harvard Bus. Sch., 1972; m. Harold A. McCrensky, Aug. 19, 1942; children—Paula, Susan, Jay, Andrea. Intern, Montefiore Hosp., N.Y.C., 1940; clin. nutritionist dept. outpatient Mt. Sinai Hosp., Phila., 1940-42; dir. dietetics Babies Hosp., Phila., 1942-44; instr. nutrition Burbank Hosp., Fitchburg, Mass., 1950-55; cons. nutrition, health systems mgmt. Harold A. McCrensky & Assos., Boston, 1965-70, v.p., dir. health systems, 1970—; pres. Forward Services, Inc., Boston, 1978—; cons. Mass. Dept. Mental Health, Mass. Dept. Public Health, Mass. Dept. Edn. Trustee, Belmont (Mass.) Public Library, 1971—; mem. clin. counseling com. Family Service Assn. Greater Boston. Recipient Key to City of Cin., 1976. Mem. Am. Dietetic Assn. (del. 1968-71), Mass. Dietetic Assn. (pres. 1969), Mass. Public Health Assn., Simmons Coll. Alumni Assn. (pres. 1966-68). Office: Harold A McCrensky Assos Park Square Bldg Boston MA 02116

MCCRICKARD, RUBY ASHWELL, nursing adminstr.; b. Huddleston, Va., Apr. 19, 1931; d. Harry Odell and Nellie (Cundiff) Ashwell; diploma Riverside Hosp. Sch. Nursing, 1953; cert. health care adminstrn. U. So. Calif., 1976; B.A., Goddard Coll., 1975; M.S., Med. Coll. Ga., 1977; m. George T. McCrickard, Aug. 9, 1952; 1 son, George T. Operating room staff nurse, head nurse med. unit Riverside Hosp., Newport News, Va., 1953-55; asst. operating room supr., operating room staff nurse, acting operating room supr., Kecoughtan Vets. Hosp., Hampton, Va., 1955-60; intensive care and central supply supr. Lynchburg (Va.) Gen.-Marshall Lodge Hosps., 1962-66, asst. dir. nursing services, 1966-69, dir. nursing services, 1969-78, dir. nursing service, asst. adminstr., 1978—; mem. Va. Bd. Health, 1981-85; mem. Lynchburg Coll. Nursing Edn. Adv. Council, 1979-80; mem. adv. com. respiratory therapy Central Va. Community Coll., 1978—; mem. Central Va. Health Planning Emergency Med. Adv. Council, 1975-77; mem. primary care com. S.W. Va. Health Systems Agy., Inc. Recipient Ella T. Whitten award Registered Nurses Associated Alumnae Assn. Lynchburg, Va., 1966. Mem. Am. Nurses Assn. (past mem. membership and by-laws coms.), Nat. League Nursing, Nat. Forum Adminstrn. Nursing Services, Am. Soc. Hosp. Nursing Service Adminstrn. (pres. Va. chpt. 1981, dir. Va. chpt. 1982, candidate, program for excellence in nursing adminstrn. 1980), Nat. Soc. Lit. and Arts, AAUW, Va. Nurses Assn. (chmn. profl. nursing practice com.), Va. League Nursing (past mem. nominating com.), Va. Hosp. Assn. (com. on nursing, com. emergency med. services), Piedmont Heart Assn. (past dir., chmn. nursing com.), Riverside Hosp. Sch. Nursing Alumnae (pres. 1959-60), Sigma Theta Tau. Baptist. Clubs: Order Eastern Star, Scottish Rite Women's Nobletts. Home: Route 1 Box 483 Rustburg VA 24588 Office: Tate Springs Rd Lynchburg VA 24506

MC CRORY, JANET CLAIRE, fgn. service officer; b. Kansas City, Mo., Mar. 18, 1928; d. William Neal and Florence Matilda (Griess) McC.; A.B., U. Nebr., 1949. With U.S. Army, The Hague, Netherlands and Washington, 1951-62; with U.S. Fgn. Service, 1962—, budget and fiscal officer Am. embassies in Djakarta, Indonesia, Tel Aviv, Buenos Aires, Argentina, Bucharest, Romania, Peking, China, budget and mgmt. officer, Vienna, Austria, 1976-80, Santo Domingo, Dominican Republic, 1980-82, Jidda, Saudi Arabia, 1982—. Mem. Am. Fgn. Service Assn. Home: 1311 Nebraska St Mound City MO 64470 Office: Am Embassy APO New York NY 09697

MCCROSSEN, MARY ELLEN, mfg. co. exec.; b. Rochester, N.Y., Sept. 28, 1948; d. Fred C. and Katherine (Lapham) McC.; B.A., Cornell U., 1970; M.B.A., Rochester Inst. Tech., 1976. With Xerox Corp., 1976—, fin. project leader reprographic mfg. group, Rochester, 1979-81, plant controller Washington Centralized Refurbishing Center, Springfield, Va., 1981-82, engring. fin. planning and analysis mgr. Printing Systems div., El Segundo, Calif., 1982—. Democrat. Office: 555 S Aviation Blvd El Segundo CA 90245

MC CRYSTAL, CARLANNE LOUISE, pharm. co. exec.; b. Harrodsburg, Ky., Nov. 1, 1949; d. Carl Matthew and Ethel Louise (Pulliam) McC.; B.Gen. Studies, Chaminade U., Honolulu, 1976; 1 dau., Charline. Accountant, Har-lyn Constrn. Co., Honolulu, 1973-76; sales rep. domestic apparel div. Internat. Playtex, Hawaii, 1976-78; sales rep., food service specialist Foremost Dairies Hawaii, Ltd., Honolulu, 1978-79; asso. realtor Barbara Odor Realty, 1979—; sales rep. Parke-Davis Co., Hawaii, 1979—. Mem. Network Mktg. Women, Nat. Assn. Female Execs., NOW, Women's Polit. Caucus, Honolulu Bd. Realtors, Hawaii Assn. Realtors, Nat. Assn. Realtors. Office: PO Box 172 Kailua HI 96734

MCCUE, DONNA CAPRARI, advt. and public relations cons., agy. exec.; b. Scranton, Pa.; d. Samuel R. and Teresa M. Caprari; B.A., Rosemont Coll., 1974; m. Timothy P. McCue. Program dir. hypertension screening Am. Heart Assn., Binghamton, N.Y., 1974-75; owner, pres. McCue Advt. & Pub. Relations, Inc., Binghamton, 1975—. Bd. dirs. Am. Heart Assn., Binghamton, 1982. Mem. Pub. Relations Soc. So. Tier (v.p. and sec.), Broome County C. of C., NOW. Office: 407 Press Bldg 19 Chenango St Binghamton NY 13901

MCCULLOCH, JUNE MARIE WILLIAMS, govt. ofcl.; b. Knoxville, Tenn., June 20, 1930; d. Fred Thomas Dewey and Trula Caldonia (Lewis) Williams; student U. Va., 1968-69, George Washington U., 1970, U.S. Dept. Agr. Grad. Sch., 1979; m. Robert L. McCulloch, June 27, 1975; children by previous marriage—Ralph Edward Turner, Jr., Ann Marie Turner Alderson, David Wayne, Amy June. Partner, Turner Constrn. Co., Knoxville, Tenn., 1953-60; clk.-typist Dept. State, 1962-63; adminstrv. asst. AID, Washington, 1963-68, office mgr., 1968-69, adminstrv. officer, 1969-70; applications officer Overseas Private Investment Corp., Washington, 1971-76; asst. to dir. nursing Anne Arundel Gen. Hosp., Annapolis, Md., 1976-77; br. chief SEC, Washington, 1977-81; spl. asst. to dir. OARS, 1981-82, securities industry consumer affairs specialist, 1982—. Active Cub Scouts, 1968-70; tchr. Baptist Sunday Sch. Recipient longevity service award NASA, 1977. Mem. Nat. Assn. Female Execs. Club: Order of Eastern Star (past matron). Home: 529 Bayview Point Dr Edgewater MD 21037 Office: SEC 450 5th St NW Washington DC 20549

MCCULLOH, WANDA, real estate broker; b. Hanna, Okla., Dec. 22, 1936; d. Clifton Cleva and Vera Frances (Hubbard) Ketchum; degree in edn. Humboldt State Coll., 1961; children—Lori, Lanna, Melanie. Instr. bus. edn. Humboldt State Coll., Santa Rosa Jr. Coll., 1961-63, Empire Coll., Santa Rosa, Calif., 1962-63, Burbank (Calif.) Bus. Coll., 1963-64; cons. Met. Life Ins., Santa Rosa, 1965-68; owner, real estate broker, developer Plaza Brokerages, Inc., Rohnert Park, Calif., 1970—; mem. Realtors Arbitration Bd., 1975-76; treas. Brokers Council, Electronic Realty Assos., 1975—. Mem. Nat. Assn. Realtors, Soc. Indsl. Realtors, Sonoma County Bd. Realtors, Rohnert Park C. of C. (pres. 1978). Republican. Presbyterian. Clubs: Wikiup Tennis, Million Dollar. Office: 5810 Commerce Blvd Rohnert Park CA 94928

MCCULLOUGH, CHERYL LEE, nursing adminstr.; b. Denver, Oct. 15, 1943; d. Leland W. and Helen (Gilmore) Keller; B.S. in Nursing, Seton Sch. Nursing, 1964; m. John Harold McCullough, June 6, 1964; children—Thomas John, Cheryl Lu. Supr. evening shift Rogers Meml. Hosp., Rogers, Ark., 1968-74, head nurse med. intensive care unit, 1974-77; dir. nursing service Medi-Home of Rogers (Ark.), 1977—. Mem. Am. Nurses Assn., Ark. League for Nursing. Republican. Roman Catholic. Home: 820 Chateau Dr Rogers AR 72756 Office: 1603 W Walnut St Rogers AR 72756

MCCULLOUGH, LEE BOATRIGHT, med. microbiologist; b. Kansas City, Mo., Mar. 2, 1929; d. Ernest Grover and Lola Pearl (Hand) Boatright; student Ward Belmont Prep. Sch., 1946; B.A., William Jewell Coll., 1949; M.A., U. Kans. Med. Center, 1961; postgrad. Rutgers U., 1976—, Fairleigh Dickinson U., 1981—; m. William N. McCullough, July 20, 1958; children—Jock N., Kip L., Anna Delaine. Med. technologist Dr. Harry Underwood, Kansas City, Mo., 1951-52, part-time, 1952-55; cytotechnologist, part owner Kansas City Cytological Screening Center, 1954-59; chief histologist Research Hosp. and Med. Center, Kansas City, 1952-53, chief microbiologist, ednl. coordinator, 1954-58; cytotechnologist U. Okla. Med. Center, Oklahoma City, 1958; lab. supr., chief microbiologist Bapt. Meml. Hosp., Oklahoma City, 1959-60; chief microbiologist, chief cytotechnologist Upsher Labs., Kansas City, Mo., 1961-63; chief microbiologist, teaching supr. Bapt. Hosp. S.E. Beaumont, Tex., 1963-65; microbiologist, teaching supr. G. I. Lab. Tng. Program, Walson Army Hosp., Fort Dix, N.J., 1965-66; cytotechnologist, cons. microbiologist part-time R. L. Breckenridge Med. Lab., Collingswood, N.J., 1966-78; lab. supr. Leland Brown Med. Labs., Upper Derby, Pa., 1966-68; microbiologist Burlington County Meml. Hosp., Mt. Holly, N.J., 1968-69; chief microbiologist Pathologists Labs., Inc., Phila., 1969-71; cytotechnologist part-time Phila. Med. Lab., Inc., 1971-73; mgr. microbiology Roche Clin. Labs., Raritan, N.J., 1973—. Leader, Camp Fire Girls, 1959; denleader Cub Scouts Am., 1968. Mem. N.J. Soc. Med. Tech. (pres. 1978-80, dir. 1978—; pres. Central N.J. chpt. 1977-78), Theobad Smith Soc. (chmn. clin. div. 1978-79), Am. Soc. Med. Tech. (exec. council region II 1977-81), Am. Soc. Microbiologists, Am. Soc. Cytology, Am. Soc. Clin. Pathologists, Med. Mycol. Soc. Am., N.Y. Acad. Scis., Alpha Mu Tau. Republican. Episcopalian. Home: 8-9 Cardinal Lane Somerville NJ 08876 Office: RCL 5 Johnson Dr Raritan NJ 08869

MC CULLOUGH, MABELLE G., educator; b. Mt. Pleasant, Iowa, Feb. 27, 1914; d. Thomas E. and Martha (Cone) McCullough; B.A. summa cum laude, Ia. Wesleyan Coll., 1943; M.A. in Religious Edn., Yale, 1945; postgrad. U. Minn., 1949-54; Ed.D. in Guidance and Student Personnel Adminstrn., Columbia, 1956; wards—Maryam Ali Abadi, Elaheh Ali Abadi, Hossein Ali Abadi, Bardia Kamrad, Shahab Kamrad, Rab Kamrad. Asso. dir. Wesley Found., St. Paul campus U. Minn., 1945-49; dir. student housing bur., office dean of students U. Minn., Mpls., 1949-66, office v.p. for student affairs, 1969—, asst. prof. edn., 1956-66, asst. dean students, asso. prof. edn., 1966—, spl. cons. to v.p. student affairs, 1978—; certified cons. psychologist, Minn., 1962-74. Mem. Gov.'s Commn. Status of Women, 1963-67, also chmn. edn. com.; mem. Nat. Adv. Council on Health Professions Ednl. Assistance, 1970-71. Mem. Women's Adv. Council Civil Def., State Minn., 1961-62; St. Paul alumni rep. Iowa Wesleyan Coll.; adv. bd. Univ. YWCA, 1943-46, 62-65, treas., 1963-64, adv. bd. chmn., 1964-66, 70-75; bd. dirs. Mpls. YWCA, 1968-74, chmn. personnel com., 1969-73; bd. dirs., chmn. program com., mem. exec. com. Wesley Found., U. Minn., 1960-64. Mem. Shoreview Village Planning Commn., 1968-71, chmn., 1971-77; mem. Shoreview Council, 1978—. Mem. AAUW (status of women chmn. Mpls. and St. Paul br. 1958-80, dir. Mpls. br. 1968-69; Minn. div. bd. status of women chmn. 1960-62, roster chmn. 1962-64, chmn. com. study financing pub. edn. 1961-63, producer 2 TV programs on pub. sch. financing, bd. mem. representing corp. mems. 1978-80, mem. nat. com. on standards in higher edn. 1967-73, chmn. 1969-73, bd. dirs. Edn. Found. 1969-73, internat. fellowships com. 1973-75, named fellowship endowment 1978—), Am. Assn. Higher Edn., Nat. Assn. Women Deans and Counselors (mem. bylaws com. 1968-70), Nat. (chmn. status of women com. 1974-76), Minn. Met. (mem. bd. 1977—) councils adminstrv. women in edn., Am. Personnel and Guidance Assn., Am. Coll. Personnel Assn., Assn. Coll. and Univ. Housing Officers (institutional rep., co-chmn. 5th nat. conf., chmn. off-campus housing com., mem. internat. com.), St. Andrews Soc. of Minn. (sec., charter mem., dir. 1976—). Methodist. Club: Columbia University Alumni of Minnesota (dir., sec.). Author publs. in fields of student housing, internat. edn., and status of women. Home: 5883 Carlson St Shoreview MN 55112 Office: 10 Morrill Hall 100 Church St SE U Minn Minneapolis MN 55455

MCCULLOUGH, PHYLLIS, mfg. co. exec.; b. Indpls., Aug. 8, 1944; d. Charles Ray and Vera Louise (Cope) Arthur; student public schs., Indpls.; m. Jerry W. McCullough, Nov. 1, 1963; children—Julia Lynn, Elizabeth Anne. Exec. sec. Rough Notes, Printing Co., Indpls., 1962-65, Ind. Bankers Assn., Indpls., 1965-68, Alcoa Aluminium Corp., Indpls., 1968-69; exec. sec. Cook, Inc., Bloomington, Ind., 1972, office mgr., 1972-76, customer service mgr., 1976-77, exec. asst., 1977-78, v.p. ops., 1978—; v.p. Cook Group, Inc., 1982—; dir. Data Solutions, Inc., Bloomington. Advisor, Bd. Industry and Edn., Bloomington High Schs. North and South, 1980-82; mem. Bloomington Community Progress Council, 1981-82. Mem. Greater Bloomington C. of C., Nat. Assn. Accts., South Central Ind. Personnel Assn., Am. Mgmt. Assn., Psi Iota Xi. Office: 925 S Curry Pike Bloomington IN 47402

MCCULLOUGH, PHYLLIS (HOGOBOOM), mfg. co. exec.; b. St. Louis, Aug. 6, 1936; d. Lester Robert and Gladys Helen (Sollar) Hogoboom; grad. Hickey's Bus. Sch., St. Louis, 1955; children—Maureen, Megan, Sean. Exec. sec., adminstrv. asst. Gardner Advt., St. Louis, 1955-60, adminstrv. asst. internat. div., art buyer, prodn. mgr., acct. exec., 1964-78; corp. advt. mgr. Huffy Corp., Dayton, Ohio, 1978—. Mem. Am. Mgmt. Assn., Nat. Assn. Exec. Womens, Am. Soc. Profl. and Exec. Women, Internat. Assn. Bus. Communicators, Oreg. Hist. Soc., Dayton Advt. Club, Bicycle Fedn., Ohio Bicycle Fedn., League Am. Wheelmen, Bike Centennial. Republican. Club: Dayton Cycling. Home: 236 Green St Dayton OH 45402 Office: PO Box 1204 Dayton OH 45401

MCCULLOUGH, ROSE VERNIE, writer, editor; b. Charleston, S.C., Oct. 9; d. David Augustus and Rose Eunice (Paille) Rodgers; student parochial schs., Charleston; m. John Hudson McCullough (dec. 1974); 1 son, Alan David. Editorial asst. Rough Notes Co., Inc., Indpls., 1955-65, asst. editor, 1965-79, asso. editor, 1979—; editor Bulls. on Effective Agy. Mgmt., Indpls., 1975—. Mem. Adminstrv. Mgmt. Soc. (dir. publs., public relations, adminstrv. services), Nat. Assn. Ins. Women, Indpls. Assn. Ins. Women (past dir.), Ins. Co. Edn. Dirs. Soc., Soc. Ins. Research, Women in Communications, Assn. Female Execs., Indpls. Opera Guild, North Group, Indpls. Symphony, People of Vision. Democrat. Presbyterian. Author: ABCs of Agency Evaluation, Acquisition, and Merger, 1982. Editor: Insights for the Profl. Ins. Woman, monthly, 1979-81; Agy. Mgmt. Briefs, newsletter, 1981—; Stairsteps to Professionalism, 1981—. Home: 5263 Crestview St Indianapolis IN 46220 Office: 1200 N Meridian St Indianapolis IN 46204

MC CUNE, MARY ELIZABETH BACKENSTOSE, psychotherapist; b. Hershey, Pa., Oct. 29, 1943; d. Daniel Lee and Elizabeth Dorothy (Hyland) Backenstose; A.A., Hershey Jr. Coll., 1963; B.S. in Nursing, Cornell U., 1966; M.S. in Psychiat. Nursing, U. Md., 1971; postgrad. Georgetown U., 1972-73, 79-80; m. Richard Barry McCune, Feb. 2, 1973. Gen. staff nurse Cornell U.-N.Y. Hosp., N.Y.C., 1966-67; gen. staff nurse Harrisburg (Pa.) Hosp., 1967, clin. nurse specialist in psychiatry, 1971-78; nursing supr. Polyclinic Med. Center, Harrisburg, 1967-68; instr. psychiat. nursing Harrisburg Hosp. Sch. of Nursing, 1968-71; co-dir., therapist Inst. for Family Care, Inc., Hershey, Pa., 1974—; adj. faculty, instr. nursing courses Pa. State U., Hershey, 1973-76; clin. faculty mem., psychiat. nursing Bloomsburg (Pa.) State Coll., 1977-78; vis. asst. prof. nursing U. Va., Charlottesville, 1979—; cons. Mem. Am. Family Therapy Assn. (charter), Group for Advancement of Family Systems (sec.-treas.), Am. Nurses Assn., Cornell U.-N.Y. Hosp. Sch. of Nursing Alumnae Assn., U. Md. Sch. Nursing Alumnae Assn., Am. Assn. Sex Educators, Counselor and Therapists, AAUW, Sigma Theta Tau. Republican. Club: Quentin Riding. Home: Box 175 Sheep Hill Rd Schaefferstown PA 17088 Office: Inst for Family Care Inc 1135 E Chocolate Ave Room 201 Hershey PA 17033

MC CURDY, DEBORAH LAMB, social worker; b. Evanston, Ill., Jan. 10, 1939; d. Theodore Warren and Deborah Fessenden (Bent) Lamb; student Earlham Coll., 1958-59; B.A., Wellesley Coll., 1960; postgrad. Smith Coll. Sch. Social Work, 1963-64; M.S.W., Boston U., 1966; m. Michael Charles McCurdy, Sept. 7, 1968; children—Heather, Mark. Caseworker, Mt. Auburn Hosp., Cambridge, Mass., 1968-69; adoption caseworker Commonwealth Mass. Div. Child Guardianship, 1970-71; co-founder, adoption supr. My Friends' House Adoption Program, Newton, Mass., 1974-75; co-founder, supr. social work Internat. Adoptions, Newton, 1975-78; supr. social work World Adoption Services, Newton, 1978-79; co-founder, co-dir. Adoption Listing, Internat. Concerns Com. for Children, Lincoln, Mass., 1979-81; cons. intercountry adoptions, 1970—. Mem. Nat. Assn. Social Workers, Acad. Cert. Social Workers, Open Door Soc. Mass. Democrat. Mem. United Ch. of Christ. Office: RD 2 Box 145 Great Barrington MA 01230

MCCURDY, MARY JACQUELINE, lawyer; b. Balt., Dec. 1, 1933; d. Robert Davis and Lillian J. (Schmidt) McC.; B.A., Hood Coll., 1955; J.D., U. Md., 1958. Admitted to Md. bar, 1958; asst. state's atty. Baltimore County, 1962-63, asst. county solicitor, 1967-68; mem. Md. Ho. of Dels., 1963-66; asso. gen. counsel Distilled Spirits Council U.S., 1969-76; v.p., regulatory counsel Joseph E. Seagram & Sons, Inc., N.Y.C., 1979—; vice-chmn. DISCUS, 1979—. Treas., Democratic Congressional Campaign Com.; bd. dirs. YWCA N.Y., Assn. Hood Coll.; bd. visitors Towson State U.; trustee Social Security Fund Distillery Wine and Allied Workers Internat. Union AFL-CIO. Mem. Md. State Bar Assn., N.Y. Bar Assn., Baltimore County Bar Assn., Nat. Assn. Alcoholic Beverage Importers (dir.), Women's Assn. Allied Beverage Industries (dir.). Democrat. Episcopalian. Club: Cricket. Office: 375 Park Ave New York NY 10152

MCCUSKER, SISTER, MARY LAURETTA, nun, educator; b. Sillery, Que., Can., Jan. 18, 1919; came to U.S., 1931, naturalized, 1942; d. Albert J. and Laura (Cleary) McC.; B.A., Western Md. Coll., 1944; M.S. in Library Sci., Columbia U., 1952, D.Library Sci., 1963. Joined Order of Preachers, Roman Catholic Ch., 1961; asst. prof. Iowa State Tchrs. Coll., Cedar Falls, 1948-59; faculty Rosary Coll., River Forest, Ill., 1967—, prof. library sci. since 1963—, dean Grad. Sch. Library and Info. Sci. 1967—. Mem. ALA (Council 1980—), Cath. Library Assn. (chmn. Library Edn. div. 1980-81), Assn. Am. Library Schs. (chmn. Council of Deans and Dirs. 1980-81). Club: Zonta.

MCDANIEL, CONNIE DAVENPORT, home economist; b. Kent, Iowa, Dec. 15, 1943; d. John Nelson and Marjorie Gwendolen (Chandler) Davenport; B.S., Iowa State U., 1965, M.S., 1970; postgrad. U. Tenn., Knoxville; m. Gary L. McDaniel, July 31, 1966; 1 dau., Kerstin Ann. Tchr. home econs., Iowa, Kans. and Tenn., 1965-78; extension agt. Colo. State U., Ft. Collins, 1978—. Mem. NEA, Nat. Assn. Extension Home Economists, Nat. Home Econs. Assn., Nat. Assn. Female Execs., Bus. and Profl. Women. Republican. Methodist. Clubs: Atlantic Golf and Country, Ft. Morgan Country, Order Eastern Star. Author curriculum guides, textbook and instrn. manuals, articles. Home: Box 745 Montrose CO 81402 Office: 1001 N 2d St Friendship Hall Montrose CO 81401

MC DANIEL, FRANCES JENICE, city ofcl.; b. Leigh, Tex., Mar. 9, 1914; d. Lee Abner and Ruby (Barber) Johnson; A.A., Cooke County Coll., 1962; m. William Anderson McDaniel, July 6, 1936; 1 son, Jan Lee. Sec., Nocona (Tex.) Public Schs., 1944-45, Nocona Truck & Tractor Co., 1946-57; exec. dir., mgr. low-rent housing City of Nocona, 1959—. Baptist. Home: 518 Montague Nocona TX 76255 Office: 400 Hobson Nocona TX 76255

MC DANIEL, JEANNE ADELE, sch. adminstr.; b. Battle Creek, Mich., Aug. 26, 1914; d. Arnold Herman and Viola May (Rice) Kambly; R.N., Michael Reese Hosp. Sch. Nursing, Chgo., 1935; m. Lloyd G. McDaniel, Feb. 6, 1937; children—Lloyd Kambly, Stephanie McDaniel Wirt, Patricia McDaniel Paddock. Asst. to dir. Lanham Fund Day Care Centers, Battle Creek Pub. Schs., 1945-46; dir., pres. bd. dirs. Kambly Sch. Retarded Children, Battle Creek, 1959—. Bd. dirs. Woodlawn Nursery; sponsor troop Boy Scouts Am. Mem. Michael Reese Nurses Alumnae Assn., D.A.R., Council Exceptional Children, Calhoun County Assn. Retarded Children, Beta Sigma Phi. Republican. Presbyn. Home: 115 Irving Park Dr Battle Creek MI 49017 Office: 1003 North Ave Battle Creek MI 49017

MCDANIEL, LORETTA MARIE, ednl. adminstr.; b. LaGrande, Oreg., Dec. 21, 1938; d. Wilfred J. and Margaret F. (Briggs) Lyon; B.S., Eastern Oreg. State Coll., 1978; m. Gale E. McDaniel, July 28, 1956; children—Larry B., Peggy S., Kevin K. Dep. county clk. Union County, LaGrande, 1964-77; juvenile ct. counselor Union County, 1977-79; dir. student services Modern Bus. Coll., Kennewick, Wash., 1980, dir., 1980—. Mem. Sch. Bd., Cove Sch. Dist., 1974-76; mem. Union County Republican Central com., 1974. Mem. Union County Legal Secs. Assn. (v.p. 1968), Nat. Assn. Female Execs., Pacific N.W. Personnel Mgrs. Assn., Am. Soc. Personnel Adminstrn., Am. Soc. Tng. and Devel. (exec. bd. Columbia Basin chpt.). Republican. Home: 1601 S Nelson St Kennewick WA 99336 Office: 127 W Kennewick Ave Kennewick WA 99336

MCDANIEL, (MARJORIE) WYVONNE, librarian, real estate broker; b. Sulphur Springs, Tex., Aug. 25, 1933; d. Earl Hamilton and Willie Juanita (Martin) Clapp; student Wayland Bapt. Coll., 1950, Frank Phillips Coll., 1952; B.B.A., Tex. Tech. U., 1954; postgrad. West Tex. State U., 1958-60, North Tex. State U., 1971; M.Ed., East Tex. State U., 1975; m. Charles Raymond McDaniel, Jan. 14, 1955; children—Shannon Kaye, Sharron Lee, Shawn Michael. With gas measurement dept. Phillips Petroleum Co., 1954-58, Natural Gas Pipeline Co. Am., 1959-61; tchr. bus. Frank Phillips Coll., 1955-58; librarian, media dir. Canadian (Tex.) High Sch., 1970—; owner McDaniel Realty Co., Inc., 1981—. Sunday Sch. tchr. Baptist Ch. Lic. real estate salesman, real estate broker, Tex. Mem. Daus. Rep. of Tex. (treas.), DAR, Colonial Dames XVII Century (chpt. pres.), Children Am. Revolution (sr. pres.), ALA, Assn. Ednl. Communications and Tech., Delta Kappa Gamma. Home: 413 Panhandle St Canadian TX 79014 Office: 400 5th St Canadian TX 79014

MCDANIEL, MONICE WILLIAMS, ednl. counselor; b. Memphis, Aug. 15, 1936; d. J.D. and Bernice Margaret (Pinkston) Williams; B.A., Fisk U., 1958; M.Ed., U. Ill., 1959; Ed.D. (Grad. fellow 1975-79), Fordham U., 1979; m. James A. McDaniel, June 1, 1958; 1 dau., Kyla Lynn. Employment interviewer Ill. Employment Service, Chgo., 1960-63; dir. work-study program Wilson Jr. Coll., 1963-66; dir. curriculum program Manhattan Community Coll., 1966-68; counselor Bklyn. Coll., 1968—; participant profl. insts. and programs; cons. in field; Tchr.'s Scholarship grantee, West Africa, 1971; Fellowship Leave award Profl. Staff Congress, 1978. Mem. Am. Assn. Higher Edn., Am. Personnel and Guidance Assn., Am. Coll. Personnel Assn., Am. Non-White Concerns Assn., Univ. Council Ednl. Adminstrn., NAACP, Hemlock Farms Assn., Washington Sq. Village S.E. Apts. Assn., Nat. Urban League, Phi Delta Kappa (award 1978). Mem. Liberal Party. Presbyterian.

MCDARGH-ELVINS, EILEEN, communications cons.; b. Denver, Sept. 5, 1948; d. H. J. and Mary S. (Reineberg) McDargh III; B.A. in Speech Communications, U. Fla., 1969; postgrad. U. Calif., Irvine, 1978—; m. W. T. Elvins, May 18, 1980; children by previous marriage—Todd, Holly, Heather. Public relations, mktg. dir. Amelia Island Plantation, Amelia Island, Fla., 1973-78; corp. communications exec. Comprehensive Care Corp., Newport Beach, Calif., 1978-79; sr. account exec. Gloria Zigner & Assos., Newport Beach, 1979-80; pres. McDargh Communications, Laguna Niguel, Calif., 1980—; lectr. U. Calif., Irvine, 1980—, Orange Coast Community Coll., Costa Mesa, Calif., 1980—. Reading tutor South Coast Literacy Council, Laguna Niguel, Calif., 1981—. Recipient Outstanding Tchr. award Nassau County, 1972. Mem. Women in Communications (dir. Orange County chpt. 1979), Assn. Profl. Cons. (founding mem. 1980, dir. 1980-82), Calif. Press Women, Public Relations Soc. Am. Contbr. articles in field to profl. publs. Home and Office: 23731 Montego Bay Laguna Niguel CA 92677

MC DERMID, ALICE MARGUERITE CONNELL (MRS. RALPH MANEWAL MCDERMID), civic and polit. worker, lectr.; b. Sterling, Ill., May 25, 1910; d. William Hayes and Margaret (Durr) Connell; A.B., U. Ill., 1931; m. Ralph Manewal McDermid, Nov. 28, 1931; children—Ralph Manewal, Jane Dillon (Mrs. Anders Wiberg), Michael Metcalf, John Fairbanks. Bd. dirs. Scarsdale (N.Y.) Womans Exchange, 1953-60; mem. social service bd. N.Y. Infirmary, 1960-76, vice chmn., 1964-76; trustees team United Hosp. Fund, 1965-75; case policy bd. Spence-Chapin Adoption Service, 1960—; fund raising Vis. Nurse Assn., 1960-64, Greer Sch., 1958-73; co-chmn. UN Program, Westchester County; bd. dirs. Charles Hosmer Morse Found., 1980—; mem. adv. council Morse Gallery of Art, Winter Park, Fla., 1974—; sec. exec. com. Morse Gallery Art Assos., 1977-78, v.p., 1978-80, pres., 1980—; bd. dirs. Council Arts and Scis. Central Fla., 1975—, v.p., 1976-78; bd. dirs. Charles Hosmer Morse Found. Sec., Young Republicans Ill., 1930-31, mem. bd. Scarsdale (N.Y.) Womens Rep. Club, 1961-67, pres., 1965-67, legis. chmn., 1981—; del. Washington Conf. Nat. Fed. Rep. Women, 1965-72; mem. council Fedn. Womens Rep. Clubs N.Y. State, 1967-76; Rep. dist. leader, 1967-75; del. Rep. Jud. Conv., 1969-71; vice chmn. Rep. Town Com., 1969-75, mem. Rep. Presidents Club, Scarsdale; mem. N.Y. State Rep. Com., 1970-72; adv. council for srs. and handicapped Rep. Inaugural Com., 1981; N.Y. Rep. committee woman 90th Assembly Dist., 1970-72; mem. adv. council Presdl. Inaugural Com. for Srs. and Handicapped. Recipient Rep. Woman of Yr. award, Scarsdale, 1974, other awards. Mem. Women's Rep. Federated Club of Winter Park (pres. 1978-80), Lock Haven Art Center, Friends of Winter Park Library, Orlando Opera Guild, Winter Park Hist. Soc., English Speaking Union U.S., Alpha Xi Delta. Episcopalian. Clubs: Scarsdale Womens, Scarsdale Golf; Capitol Hill (Washington); Ladies Harvard (N.Y.C.); Women's of Winter Park (dir. 1977-79), Racquet (Winter Park). Home: 1445 Granville Dr Winter Park FL 32789

MCDERMOTT, HELENA E., state legislator; b. Bklyn., June 9, 1911, ed. Johnson and Wales. Mem. R.I. Ho. of Reps., 1976—, mem. HEW com., others. Vice chmn. Commn. to Study Homes for Sheltered Care of Adults., mem. Permanent Adv. Commn. on Women; active R.I Women's Polit. Caucus, St. Citizens' Transp., Inc., Gov.'s Com. on Mental Health and Retardation, Kent County Assn. for Retarded; pres. Meadowbrook Terr. Tenants Assn.; mem. Warwick Waterfront and Park Devel. Commn. Democrat. Office: RI State House Providence RI 02903 *

MCDERMOTT, PAMELA MCCLURE, educator; b. Buffalo, Nov. 20, 1938; d. Charles Henry and Esther Cecilia (Butler) Balme; student U. Md., 1965-67; B.A., Jacksonville State U., 1971; M.Ed., U.S. Ala., 1978; postgrad. Fla. State U., 1978—; m. Charles L. McDermott, Mar. 18, 1962; children—Monica, Alison, Charles David. Editor, This Week on Okinawa, Isle Tell, Okinawa, 1965; tchr. Calhoun County/Anniston (Ala.) public schs., 1967; free lance flight instr., 1967-71; ground instr. Am. Air Service, Gadsden, Ala., 1972; instr. Accelerated Ground Schs., Atlanta, 1973; dir. flight program U. S. Ala., Mobile, 1974—; FAA accident prevention counselor. Served with U.S. Army, 1960-62. Mem. Am. Soc. Aerospace Edn., AIAA, Aviation-Space Writers Assn., Univ. Aviation Assn. Roman Catholic. Club: Zonta. Office: 2001 Brookley USA Mobile AL 36688

MCDERMOTT, PATRICIA LOUISE, lawyer, state legislator; b. Washington, Feb. 19, 1938; d. Peter A. and Emily L. (Wolfe) McDermott; student Creighton U., 1955-56; B.A., Idaho State U., 1958; J.D., George Washington U., 1961; LL.M., Georgetown U., 1964. Admitted to D.C. bar, 1961, U.S. Ct. Appeals bar for D.C., 1961, U.S. Supreme Ct. bar, 1965, Idaho bar, 1966; mem. staff U.S. Senator Frank Church, Washington, 1958-61; atty. solicitor's office U.S. Labor Dept., Washington, 1961-64, cons. Office Manpower, 1966; house counsel United Planning Orgn., Washington, 1964-65; partner firm McDermott & McDermott, Pocatello, Idaho, 1966—; mem. Idaho Ho. of Reps., 1968—, minority house leader, 1975-81; instr. communications law Idaho State U., 1973-76; speaker to bus., civic assns., schs., polit. groups. Del. Idaho Democratic Conv. 1966-80; pres. Bannock County Young Dems., 1966-68; regional v.p. Idaho Young Dems., 1966-68; alt. del. Dem. Nat. Conv., 1972, 76; mem. adv. com. Idaho Alcohol Safety Action Project; mem. Bannock County Bicentennial Commn., 1973-76; mem. Idaho Commn. on Women, 1969-72; bd. dirs. State Legis. Leaders Found. Recipient Martin Luther King award NAACP, 1970; certificate of appreciation Assn. Idaho Cities, 1974, Asso. Students Idaho State U., 1975. Mem. Am., Idaho trial lawyers assns., Am., Fed., 6th Dist. (sec.-treas. 1966), Idaho bar assns., Nat. (law and criminal justice com. 1973—), Western (law and criminal justice com. 1973—) confs. state legislators, St. Anthony's Council Catholic Women, Zonta Internat., Idaho State U. Alumni Assn. (dir. 1972-78, pres. 1976). Roman Catholic. Home: 218 N 10th St Pocatello ID 83201 Office: PO Box 3 Pocatello ID 83201

MC DERMOTT, SUSAN JEAN, newspaper sales rep.; b. Queens, N.Y., Mar. 1, 1953; d. Walter George and Jean Louise (Krivicich) Cassi; A.A., Nassau Community Coll., 1973; B.A., SUNY, Oneonta, 1975; postgrad. Hofstra U., 1977; m. Michael I. McDermott, Apr. 13, 1980. Classified advt. telephone ad-taker N.Y. Daily News, 1975-77, telephone solicitor, 1977-78, circulation sales rep. in home delivery, 1978-79, street sales, 1980-81, Nassau home delivery, 1981—. Mem. Nat. Assn. Female Execs., Eastern Seaboard Communication Assn. Roman Catholic. Home: 342 Hilda St East Meadow NY 11554 Office: 220 E 42d St New York NY 10017

MCDEVITT, SUSAN COROMINAS, psychologist; b. Montreal, Que., Can., May 25, 1951; came to U.S., 1968; d. Juan and Ida (Warszawska) Corominas; B.A., U. San Francisco, 1972; M.A., Temple U., 1974, cert. sch. psychology, 1979; m. Sean Conway McDevitt, Aug. 18, 1974. Psychologist, Elwyn Inst., Elwyn, Pa., 1974-79; counseling psychologist B'nai B'rith Career and Counseling Services, Phila., 1978-79; sch. psychologist Phoenix Elem. Sch. Dist. 1, 1980—; cons. psychologist Isaac Elem. Sch. Dist. 5. Cert. sch. psychologist, Ariz., Pa.; lic. psychologist, Pa. Mem. Am. Psychol. Assn., Ariz. Assn. Sch. Psychologists. Home: 4030 E Charter Oak Rd Phoenix AZ 85032 Office: 125 E Lincoln St Phoenix AZ 85022

MCDIARMID, DOROTHY SHOEMAKER, state legisltor; b. Waco, Tex.; B.S., Swarthmore Coll.; m. N. Hugh McDiarmid; children—Mary S., Robert C. Ptnr., McDiarmid Assocs. and McDiarmid Realty, Vienna, Va.; mem. Va. Ho. of Reps., 1960-62, 64-70, 72—. Mem. spl. edn. adv. bd. George Mason U.; mem. adv. council in dietetics Va. Poly. Inst. and State U.; mem. adv. bd. Fairfax County YWCA; mem. Va. Juvenile Justice and Delinquency Prevention Adv. Council; pres. Fairfax County Council PTAs; mem. Va. Council on Health and Med. Care, Task Force on Deinstitutionalization of Mentally Retarded Patients; chmn. Va. Found. for Humanities and Pub. Policy; mem. Va. Rhodes Scholarship Selection Com., Fairfax County Human Rights Commn.; Fairfax-Falls Church Mental Health-Mental Retardation Services Bd. Mem. LWV, Internat. Platform Assn., No. Va. Mental Health Assn. Office: Va Ho of Dels State Capitol Richmond VA 23219 *

MCDIVITT, THELMA SUE, bus. services co. exec.; b. Riverside, Calif., June 5, 1952; d. Gerald R. and Jewelene S. (West) Snyder; 1 son, Justin E. Mgr. Colony Kitchens, Sunnyvale, Calif., 1971-79; mgr. deferred compensation and health dept. Dawson & Co., Anchorage, 1974-78; owner, mgr. ABC Bus. Services, Las Cruces, N.Mex., 1978—. Mem. N.Mex. Mobile Housing Commn., Las Cruces, 1981-82. Mem. Las Cruces Bus. Assn. (pres. 1980-82), Franklin Mint Collectors Soc., Goebel Collectors Club. Clubs: Parents without Partners, Women's Internat. Bowling Congress. Home: Las Cruces NM 88001 Office: 1700 N Main St Las Cruces NM 88001

MCDONALD, ALICE COIG, state govt. ofcl.; b. New Orleans, Sept. 26, 1940; d. Olas Casimere and Genevieve Louise (Heck) C.; B.Ed., Loyola U., New Orleans, 1962; M.Ed., 1965; m. Glenn McDonald, July 16, 1967; 1 dau., Michel. Dir., Neighborhood Devel. Office, Louisville, 1977-78; chief exec. asst. to mayor of Louisville (Ky.), 1978-80; dep. supt. public instrn. Ky. State Dept. Edn., 1980-81, asst. supt. fed. programs, 1981—. Mem. Pres.'s adv. com. for women, 1978—; mem. Democratic Nat. Com., 1975—, mem. exec. com., 1976—; mem. Pres.'s Nat. Council Edn. Research, Nat. Inst. Edn., 1981; bd. dirs., mem. exec. com. Louisville Fund for the Arts, 1978-79; bd. dirs., mem. exec. com. McCauley Theatre, 1978-79. Mem. NEA, Ky. Edn. Assn., Am. Soc. Public Adminstrs., Democrat. Roman Catholic. Home: 6501 Gunpowder Ln Prospect KY 40059 Office: 930 Capital Plaza Tower Frankfort KY 40601

MC DONALD, BARBARA ANN, psychotherapist; b. Mpls., July 15, 1932; d. John and Georgia Elizabeth (Baker) Rubenzer; B.A., U. Minn., 1954; M.S.W., U. Denver, 1977; m. Lawrence R. McDonald, July 27, 1957; adopted children—John, Mary Elizabeth. Day care cons. Minn. Dept. Public Welfare, St. Paul, 1954-59; social worker Community Info. Center, Mpls., 1959-60; exec. dir. Social Synergistics Co., Littleton, Colo., 1970—; cons. to community orgns., Indian tribes. Family therapist Listen Found., Denver, 1978—, Am. Inst. Public Service, Washington, 1979—. Named 1 of 8 Women of Yr. and featured on TV spl. Ladies Home Jour., 1974; Clairol scholar, 1974; Am. Bus. Women's Assn. scholar, 1974; Alpha Gamma Delta scholar, 1974; lic. psychotherapist, Colo. Mem. Minn. Pre-Sch. Edn. Assn. (hon. life), Internat.

Council Exceptional Children (hon.), Nat. Assn. Social Workers, Am. Bus. Women's Assn. (exec. bd. chpt.), Alpha Gamma Delta (Disting. Citizen award 1975). Club: Altrusa (hon.). Author: Selected References on the Group Day Care of Pre-School Children, 1956. Office: 6897 S Elizabeth St Littleton CO 80122

MCDONALD, BETTY HESSERT, purchasing co. exec.; b. Lakewood, Ohio, Feb. 11, 1920; d. Louis and Jennie (Reimer) Hessert; student Cleve. Sch. Art, 1938-39, Cleve. Coll., 1938-40, John Huntington Inst. Tech., 1940-44, U. Detroit, 1959-60; m. Owen McDonald, Aug. 11, 1942 (dec.); children—Kathleen, Michael. Sales supr., buyer Lakewood (Ohio) Bakeries, 1938-43; auditor navy contracts GAO, 1945-47; treas., pres. City Asbestos Co., 1950-55; with contracting div. Owens-Corning Fiberglas Corp., 1955—, area purchasing and service supr., 1976-78, regional purchasing and service supr., 1978-80, purchasing mgr., 1980—; speaker in field. Recipient Homer Hauger award, 1979; Nat. Insolation Contractors Assn. Disting. Service award, 1982. Mem. Purchasing Mgmt. Detroit, Nat. Assn. Purchasing Mgmt. Republican. Roman Catholic. Contbr. articles to profl. jours.

MC DONALD, GAIL FABER, musician, educator; b. Jersey City, Oct. 24, 1917; d. Samuel and Jennie (Weiss) Faber; diploma Mannes Music Sch., N.Y.C., 1938; B.A., U. Md., 1962; Mus.M., Cath. U., 1968; D.Mus. Arts, U. Md., 1977; m. Angus McDonald, Nov. 10, 1946; children—Lora McDonald Ferguson, Charles, Henry. Legis. asst. Capitol Hill, 1943-46; pvt. tchr. piano and music theory, Washington and Md., 1950—; piano soloist Nat. Gallery Art, 1977. Mem. D.C., Md. (pres. 1977—) music tchrs. assns., D.C. Fedn. Music Clubs, Nat. Guild Piano Tchrs. (adjudicator 1972—), Friday Morning Music Club. Author: Muzio Clementi and the Gradus Ad Parnassum, 1968. Address: 6807 Farmer Dr Fort Washington MD 20744

MCDONALD, GLORIA DRAKE, town councilwoman; b. Buffalo, Dec. 7, 1928; d. Harold and Vera Katherine (Seitz) Drake; B.S. in Commerce, D'Youville Coll., Buffalo, 1949; m. Thomas C. McDonald, Oct. 2, 1954 (dec. 1979); children—Paul H., Mary Kay. Various secretarial positions, 1949-55; dist. congressional asst., 1965-74; legal asst. to husband, 1956-79; councilwoman Town of Tonawanda (N.Y.), 1976—; bd. dirs. Tonawanda Devel. Corp., Tonawanda Housing Authority. Past pres. Green Acres Republican Women's Club; mem. women's aux. Salvation Army. Named Woman of Yr. Green Acres Rep. Women's Club, 1977. Mem. Western N.Y. Paralegal Assn. (asso.), N.Y. State Fedn. Women's Club (dist. dir., treas. elect 1982-84), Buffalo Fedn. Women's Clubs (dir.), Honorarians (2d v.p. 1982-84, past treas.). Roman Catholic. Club: Kenmore Zonta (chmn. status women com. 1980-82). Home: 350 Grayton Rd Tonawanda NY 14150 Office: 2919 Delaware Ave Kenmore NY 14217

MC DONALD, M. KILEY JOYCE, psychologist; b. Boston, Dec. 20, 1939; B.S. in Edn., Boston State Coll., 1961; M.Ed. (NDEA fellow 1967), R.I. Coll., 1967; M.A. (NDEA fellow 1967-68), Mich. State U., 1968; doctoral candidate No. Ill. U., 1982; m. Edward McDonald, Aug. 24, 1960 (div. Mar. 77); children—Catherine, Maureen, Edward. Tchr. schs. in Mass. and R.I., 1962-66; guidance counselor Grand Ledge (Mich.) schs., 1966-67; diagnostician Eaton County Intermediate Sch. Dist., Charlotte, Mich., 1968-69; psychometrist, Hammond, Ind., 1969-70; coordinator programs emotionally disturbed and learning disabled, sch. psychometrist N.W. Ind. Spl. Edn. Coop., Highland 1970-72; instr. Ind. U., Northwest campus, Gary, 1970-72; program dir. Trade Winds Rehab. Center, Gary, Ind., 1972-73; supervising sch. psychologist Thornton Fractional Twp. High Sch. 215, Calumet City, Ill., 1973—. Vice pres. Wilbur Wright Middle Sch. PTA, Munster, Ind., 1975-76; mem. planning bd. Lake Area United Way, 1973—; 1st v.p. Greater Hammond Community Council, 1974-76. Recipient award Hammond Community Council, 1974, 75, 76, Community Service award Greater Hammond Community Council, 1975. Mem. Nat. Assn. Sch. Psychologists, Council Exceptional Children, Am. Fedn. Tchrs., Ill. Psychol. Assn., Ill. Sch. Psychol. Assn., Assn. Supervision and Curriculum Devel., Phi Delta Kappa. Office: 1601 Wentworth Ave Calumet City IL 60409

MCDONALD, MARIANNE, classicist; b. Chgo., Jan. 2, 1937; d. Eugene Francis and Inez (Riddle) McD.; B.A. magna cum laude, Bryn Mawr Coll., 1958; M.A., U. Chgo., 1960; Ph.D., U. Calif., Irvine, 1975; m. Torajiro Mori, Aug. 12, 1978; children—Eugene, Conrad, Bryan, Bridget, Kirstie, Hiroshi. Teaching asst. classics U. Calif., Irvine, 1972-74, instr. Greek, Latin and English, mythology, modern cinema, 1975-79, researcher Thesaurus Linguae Graecae Project, 1979—; dir. Centrum. Bd. dirs. Am. Coll. of Greece, 1981—, Scripps Hosp., 1981—, LaJolla Country Day Sch., 1971-73; nat. bd. advisors Am. Biog. Inst., 1982—. Mem. Am. Philol. Assn., Am. Classical League, Philol. Assn. Pacific Coast, MLA, Am. Comparative Lit. Assn., Modern and Classical Lang. Assn. So. Calif., AAUP, Hellenic Soc., Calif. Fgn. Lang. Tchrs. Assn., Internat. Platform Assn. Republican. Buddhist; Greek Orthodox. Clubs: KPBS Producers, Hellenic Univ. (dir.). Author: Terms for Happiness in Euripides, 1978; Semilemmatized Concordances to Euripides' Alcestis, 1977; Cyclops, Andromache, Medea, 1978; Heraclidae, Hippolytus, 1979; Hecuba, 1982; Euripides in Cinema: The Heart Made Visible, 1983; contbr. numerous articles to profl. jours. Home: Box 929 Rancho Santa Fe CA 92067 Office: Thesaurus Linguae Gracae Project U Calif Irvine CA 92717

MCDONALD, MARIE LOUISE, elevator co. exec.; b. Seattle, Oct. 21, 1927; d. Sherman A. and Josephine (O'Neill) Camp; student San Francisco City Coll., 1946, Golden Gate Coll., 1955-60; m. John R. McDonald, Oct. 4, 1969; children—Kimara Enos, Marquette Lustig, Lori Lustig, Adam Lustig. With various acctg. and constrn. firms, Calif., 1946-54; office mgr. Dwan Elevator Co., San Francisco, 1955-62, asst. to pres., 1963-68, sales mgr., 1968-76; pres. McDonald Elevator Co., San Francisco, 1976—; incline elevator cons., 1970—, handicapped elevator cons. Bd. dirs. Ind. Living Project of San Francisco, 1977—. Lic. elevator contractor, Calif. Mem. Nat. Assn. Women in Constrn. (co-founder, chpt. pres.), Nat. Assn. Elevator Contractors (chmn. spl. lifts com. 1974-76), Nat. Assn. Elevator Safety Authorities (bd. advisors 1976—), Women Entrepreneurs, Calif. Assn. Physically Handicapped, No. Calif. Elevator Industry Group (pres. 1981). Home: 1259 15th Ave San Francisco CA 94122 Office: 260 Dore St San Francisco CA 94103

MCDONALD, OUIDA STONESTREET (MRS. R.T. MCDONALD), ret. educator, editor; b. Morgantown, W.Va., May 18, 1910; d. Washington Waters and Ola Summit Trauty (Draudé) Stonestreet; A.B., W.Va. U., 1932, M.A., 1934, postgrad., 1957-75; m. Romeo Tell McDonald, Mar. 2, 1935; children—Romeo Michael, James Patrick, Candace McDonald Springer. Tchr., Monongalia County Public Schs., 1933-35; prin. Stumptown Sch., Morgantown, 1935-38; founder W.Va. DAR News, 1951, editor, 1980—; tchr., librarian Mannington High Sch., 1957; tchr. French and English, Fairmont Jr. High Sch., 1958-61; tchr. journalism and English, East Fairmont High Sch., 1961-75. Mem. Nat. Press Women, NEA, W.Va. Edn. Assn., Marion County Classroom Tchrs., DAR. Democrat. Presbyterian. Clubs: Theater Guild, Fairmont Field Club, YWCA. Home: 231 Locust Ave Fairmont WV 26554

MCDONALD, RITA THERESE, clin. psychologist, educator; b. Milw., Sept. 3, 1929; d. Peter Matthew and Elizabeth Lucille (Gonia) Kluczny; B.A. magna cum laude, Alverno Coll., 1962; M.S., Marquette U., 1969; Ph.D. Loyola U., Chgo., 1971; m. James Charles McDonald, Jan. 18, 1970. Tchr. pvt. schs., Milw. and Green Bay, Wis., 1950-65; chief psychologist Curative Rehab. Center, Milw., 1970-72; dir. Marquette U. Honors Program, Milw., 1975-78, asst. prof., 1972-75, 78-80, asso. prof., 1981—; cons. Milw. Public Schs.; mem. adv. bd. St. Camillus Health Center, Milw.; chmn. subcom. on health needs United Way of Greater Milw., 1980-81, subcom. on allocations, 1981-82. Mem. Goals for Milw. 2000, 1981—. Mem. Am. Psychol. Assn., Wis. Psychol. Assn., Milw. Area Psychol. Assn., Forum for Death Edn. and Counseling. Contbr. articles to profl. jours. Home: 1229 N Jackson St Milwaukee WI 53202 Office: Psychology Dept Marquette U Milwaukee WI 53233

MCDONALD, ROSE MARIE, real estate exec.; b. Oak Park, Ill., Mar. 28, 1926; d. Robert Charles and Irene (O'Leary) Carey; B.A., Rosary Coll., 1947; M.A. in Library Adminstrn. (Ill. state scholar), 1970; m. Richard McDonald, May 1, 1948; children—Richard, Maureen, Dennis, Kevin, Kathleen, Teresa, Terrence, Marguerite, Virginia. Head adminstrv. librarian, Prospect Heights, Ill., 1975; tng. dir. Starck Real Estate, Palatine, Ill., 1980; pres., owner Inst. for Devel. of Sales Potential, Inc. (real estate sch.), Palatine, 1982—; cons. ERA regional, No. Ill., 1979. Sec. Women's Polit. Caucus, Ill.; mem. president's circle ERA, Behrens-Zaun-Palatine. Mem. AAUW, Nat. Assn. Realtors, NW Suburban Bd. Realtors, Real Estate Educators Assn. Roman Catholic. Club: St. James Women's Council.

MC DONALD, RUTH DUNCAN, pianist, educator; b. St. Joseph, Mo., May 26, 1921; d. Harry E. and Muriel G. (Hockett) Duncan; B.Mus., Kansas City (Mo.) Conservatory Music, 1942; grad. diploma Juilliard Sch. Music, 1946; m. Patrick Sandys, Aug. 11, 1948; children—Patricia, Karen, Michael; m. 2d, Charles McDonald, Feb. 19, 1966. Concert tours, 1950-55; jazz pianist, Montgomery, Ala., 1956-57, Roosevelt Hotel, Jacksonville, Fla., 1957-60, DeSoto Hotel, Savannah, Ga., 1960-64, Dinkler Hotel, Atlanta, 1964, Hilton Inn, Atlanta, 1965; mem. faculty Ga. State U., Atlanta, 1966—, asst. prof. piano, 1971-77, asso. prof. piano, 1977—; performed at Keele U., U. Sussex (Eng.), 1978, Internat. Piano Workshop, Honolulu, 1981, Innsbruck, Austria, 1982. Mem. Nat. Fedn. Music Clubs (state student adviser, audition chmn.), AAUP (Internat. Women's Year award in performing arts 1975), Music Educators Nat. Conf., Mu Phi Epsilon. Author articles; pianist tapes for blind students; performed N.Y. premier of Meyer Kupferman Sonata, 1976; performed Am. music Wigmore Hall, London, 1977. Home: 751 Briar Park Ct Atlanta GA 30306 Office: Ga State Univ Univ Plaza Atlanta GA 30302

MC DONALD, SHIRLEY PETERSON, social worker; b. Indpls., July 7, 1934; d. Harry and Marcella Iona (Kober) Peterson; B.A., Denison U., 1956; teaching credentials Chgo. State U., Nat. Coll. Edn., Prairie State U.; M.S.W., U. Ill., 1976; m. Stanford Laurel McDonald, Apr. 26, 1964; children—Stacia Elizabeth Virginia, Jeffrey Jared Stern, Kathleen Shirley, Patricia Marie. Tchr., Chgo. Public Schs., 1962-64, Flossmoor, Ill., 1972-74; communication devel. program social worker S. Met. Assn., Harvey, Ill., 1976-79; sch. social worker S.W. Cook County Coop. Spl. Edn., Oak Forest, Ill., 1979—; community prof. Governor's State U., 1982—; pvt. practice Athenia Park Psychol. Assos., Olympia Fields, Ill., 1980—. Religious edn. dir. All Souls Unitarian Ch., 1968-71; religious edn. dir. Unitarian Community Ch., Park Forest, 1975-79, also bd. dirs., 1978-81, chmn. ch. bldg. com., 1981-82. Mem. Acad. Cert. Social Workers, Nat. Assn. Social Workers, Ill. Assn. Sch. Social Workers (area rep.; mem. com. consultation service, mem. com. to rev. Sunset legislation), Kappa Kappa Gamma, Women's Internat. League Peace and Freedom (past chpt. pres.), Pi Sigma Alpha. Home: 255 Rich Rd Park Forest IL 60466

MCDONALD, SYLVIA CORNELIA, educator; b. St. Louis, July 10, 1921; d. James Elmer and Mary Darline (Wilhoit) Williams; student Stowe Jr. Coll., 1939-41; B.S., Lincoln U. of Mo., 1944; M.Ed., St. Louis U., 1960, postgrad. 1971-73, So. Ill. U., summer 1971, Purdue U., 1966; m. Bruce McDonald July 21, 1955 (dec.). Tchr., Lincoln Elem. Sch., Collinsville, Ill., 1946-58; remedial reading tchr. Coll. Community Unit 10, Collinsville, 1958-65; tchr. Collinsville (Ill.) Bd. Edn., 1965-81, ret., 1981. Leader, council Girl Scouts Am., Collinsville, 1950-51; mem. phys. improvement com. YWCA, 1981-82. Mem. Nat. Ret. Tchrs. Assn., Ill. Ret. Tchrs. Assn., Delta Sigma Theta. Baptist. Club: American Woodmen. Home: 4400 Lindell 17L Saint Louis MO 63108

MCDONALD, TERESA CARTER, home economist; b. Lawrence County, Ala., Apr. 15, 1953; d. James Wesley and Dorothy Mae (Austin) Carter; B.S. (Outstanding Female Student award), Ala. A&M U., 1975, M.Ed. in Home Econs. Edn., 1980; m. Curtis Lee McDonald, May 24, 1975. Claims clk. Ala. Dept. Indsl. Relations, Sheffield, 1975-76; extension home economist 4-H, Colbert County (Ala.) Extension Service, Ala. Coop. Extension Service, Tuscumbia, 1976—. Named Outstanding Young Women Am., U.S. Jaycees, 1978. Mem. Ala. Assn. Extension Home Economists, Ala. Home Econs. Assn., Muscle Shoals Area Home Econs. Assn., Ala. Coop. Extension Service Employees Orgn., Ala. 4-H Agts. Assn., Young Matrons Assn. (v.p.), Kappa Delta Pi, Delta Sigma Theta (sgt.-at-arms Muscle Shoals area 1977-79). Home: PO Box 240 Leighton AL 35646 Office: PO Box 648 Tuscumbia AL 35674

MC DONNELL, HELEN MARGARET, educator; b. Bogata, N.J., July 31, 1923; d. Maurice Martin and Helen (Vollmer) McD.; B.A., Monmouth Coll., 1958; M.A., Seton Hall U., 1959; postgrad. Oxford (Eng.) U., summer 1964; Ph.D., (Woodrow Wilson fellow) Rutgers U., 1970. Civil service employee, Ft. Monmouth, N.J., 1942-58; tchr. English, Asbury Park (N.J.) High Sch., 1958-59; chmn. English dept., tchr. English, Wall High Sch., Wall Twp., N.J., 1959-64; chmn. English dept., tchr. English Ocean Twp. High Sch., Oakhurst, N.J., 1965—. Lectr. English, Monmouth Coll., part-time, 1960-62. Recipient Ford Found. grant summer study, 1959. Mem. N.J., Monmouth County edn. assns., N.J. Secondary Sch. Tchrs. Assn., Assn. Secondary Sch. Dept. Heads N.J., N.J. Assn. Tchrs. English, Nat. Council Tchrs. English (mem. com. on comparative and world lit. 1966—, asso. chmn. 1970-74, chmn. 1975-77, mem. commn. on lit. 1979—). Author: Nobel Parade, 1975. Co-author: (anthology series) Man in Literature, 1970; England in Literature, 1972, rev. edit., 1979; Literature and Life, 1979. Address: 2927 Bangs Ave Neptune NJ 07753

MC DONNELL, LORETTA WADE, educator; b. San Francisco, May 31, 1940; d. John H. and Helen M. (Tinney) Wade; B.A., San Francisco Coll. for Women, 1962; M.A., Stanford U., 1963; grad. Coro Pub. Affairs Tng. Program for Women, 1976; m. John L. McDonnell, Jr., Apr. 27, 1963 (div.); children—Elizabeth, John L. III, Thomas. High sch. tchr. East Side Union High Sch. Dist., San Jose, Calif., 1962-63; project coordinator Inter Agency Collaboration Effort, Oakland, Calif., 1977—; legal asst. Pacific Gas and Electric Co., 1980—. Bd. dirs. Carden Redwood Sch., 1975-77, St. Paul's Sch., 1974-75; budget panelist United Way of Bay Area, 1975-77; community v.p. Jr. League, 1976-77, nat. conv. del., 1976; bd. dirs. Alameda County Vol. Bur., 1973-74; chmn. speakers panel Focus on Am. Women, 1973-74. Mem. Jr. League of Oakland-East Bay, Inc., Stanford Alumni. Democrat. Roman Catholic. Club: Stanford East Bay Metro. Asso. editor The Antiphon, 1971-74.

MC DONNELL, VIRGINIA BLEECKER, author; b. Short Hills, N.J.; d. J. Barclay and Helen Borden (Farley) Bleecker; R.N., Samaritan Hosp. Sch. Nursing, Troy, N.Y., 1941; student Russell Sage Coll., 1942; m. John Henry McDonnell, Feb. 13, 1954; 1 son, Gordon. Night supr. male surg. ward N.Y. Post Grad. Med. Sch. and Hosp., N.Y.C., 1942-43; co-dir. Gore Mountain Ski Sch., North Creek, N.Y., 1947-55; mem. N.Y. State Winter Sports Council, 1950-60; asst. to exec. dir. pubs. and pub. relations Grand Lodge, Free and Accepted Masons, N.Y.C., 1958; reporter, feature writer Macy Westchester Rockland Newspapers, Westchester County, N.Y., 1959-61, editor, 1961-63; free lance author, 1963—; asso. writer TV daytime serial The Guiding Light, 1977—. Recipient citation Leukemia Soc., 1959, City of Hope, 1959. Mem. Authors' Guild and League, Mystery Writers of Am., Romance Writers Am., Writers Guild Am. East, Nat. Acad. TV Arts and Scis., N.Y. Bot. Soc. Author: Your Future in Nursing, 1963; Aerospace Nurse, 1966; The Irish Helped Build America, 1969; Careers in Hotel Management, 1971; Miscalculated Risk, 1972; Silent Partner, 1972; The Deep Six, 1973; The Long Shot, 1974, others; (pen name Virginia Barclay) Emergency, 1981; High Risk, 1981; Trauma, 1981; Crisis, 1982; Life Support, 1982; Double Face, 1982. Author numerous short stories and articles. Address: care Richard Curtis Assos Inc 340 E 66th St New York NY 10021

MCDONOUGH, LEAH BROOKS, psychologist; b. N.Y.C., Apr. 24, 1924; d. Nicholas and Leah (Griffin) Brooks; A.B., Coll. of New Rochelle, 1944; M.A., Fordham U., 1946; Ph.D., Mich. State U., 1958; m. Joseph Manning, McDonough, July 3, 1949; 1 dau., Susan Mar. Research and clin. psychologist N.Y., State Psychiat. Inst., N.Y.C., 1948-49; clin. psychologist VA Hosp., Coral Gables, Fla., 1958-61, San Mateo (Calif.) County Mental Health Services, 1961-67; chief Cts. and Corrections Unit, Redwood City, Calif., 1967-79, forensic psychologist, 1980—. Mem. Am. Psychol. Assn., San Mateo County Psychol. Assn., Am. Psychology-Law Soc., Amnesty Internat., ACLU, Nat. Hist. Trust, Oceanic Soc., NOW. Office: 500 Allerton St Redwood City CA 94063

MCDOUGAL, BARBARA JEANNE, educator; b. Greenville, Tenn., Jan. 20, 1932; d. Homer Roy (dec.) and Alice Odessa (Mason) B.S., Carson Newman Coll., 1954; M.S., U. Tenn., 1955, Ed.D., 1980; m. Samuel F. McDougal, Dec. 20, 1955; children—Karen, Jeanne. Tchr. Nebo High Sch., Marion, N.C., 1954; instr. U. Ga., Athens, 1955-56; assoc. prof. home econs. Carson Newman Coll., 1963-80, asst. dean students, 1980—. Speaker for civic clubs, 1960-82. Delta Kappa Gamma scholar, 1977, Spl. State scholar, 1980. Mem. Alpha Lambda Delta, Kappa Omicron Phi, Omicron Nu, Delta Kappa Gamma, Pi Lambda Theta. Republican. Baptist. Club: Faculty Women's. Home: Laurel Hills Route 1 Jefferson City TN 37760 Office: Carson Newman Coll Jefferson City TN 37760

MC DOUGALL, ANN JEAN SOSSAMON, chem. co. exec.; b. Cabarrus County, N.C., Sept. 15, 1931; d. John Carl and Blanche Sarah Ann (Barringer) S.; m. Duane Donald McDougall, Mar. 7, 1951; children—DeAnn Marie, Steven Duane. Sec., Eielson AFB, Alaska, 1953-55; sec. to v.p. Charlotte Aircraft (N.C.), 1957-62; with Quaker Chem. Corp., Charlotte, 1963-81, mgr. Quaker Chem. Warehouse, to 1981; sales engr. Glosson Enterprises, Inc., Lexington, N.C., 1981—. Mem. Greater Charlotte C. of C., N.C. Traffic League (gov.), Charlotte Women's Traffic Club (past pres.), Charlotte Traffic and Transp. Club. Democrat. Home: Route 1 Box 38 Mount Pleasant NC 28124 Office: Route 15 Box 55 Lexington NC 27292

MCDOW, HOLLY ANNE, oil recycling consultant; b. Portsmouth, Va., Oct. 28, 1953; d. Louis Anthony and Joanne Marie (Fox) Socorso; A.A., Seminole Jr. Coll., 1973; student Fla. Tech. U., 1974, Hinds Jr. Coll., 1976; B.S., Middle Tenn. State U., 1979; m. B. David McDow, Dec. 28, 1977. Chief chemist Tenn. Oil & Refining, Portland, 1979-80; tech. rep. Recra Environ. & Health Scis., Nashville, 1980-81; ind. cons. oil re-refining, Nashville, 1981; mgr. mktg. Gulf Coast ops., Canonie Environ. Services, Houston, 1981-82; prin. H.A. Assos., Houston, 1982—. Mem. Houston C. of C., ASTM (vice chmn. P-VI and P III of tech. div. 1979-82), Am. Petroleum Inst., Sales and Mktg. Execs. Houston, Nat. Assn. Female Execs., Beta Beta Beta. Republican. Contbr. articles to profl. jours. Office: 6363 San Felipe Suite 151 Houston TX 77057

MCDOWELL, AMELIA KAYE, med. technologist; b. Shawnee, Okla., Nov. 24, 1952; d. Kelsey Lawrence and Nada Joline (Stamps) Garman; B.A., U. Ark., 1974, B.S., 1976, postgrad., 1979; m. David Thomas McDowell, Aug. 13, 1971; children—Cynthia Lynne, Catherine Anne, Christopher Thomas. Med. technologist microbiology Bapt. Med. Center, Little Rock, 1976-79; asst. epidemiologist Bapt. Med. Center, Little Rock, 1979-80; med. technologist St. Vincent Infirmary, Little Rock, 1980—. Mem. Am. Soc. Microbiology, Ark. Soc. Clin. Microbiology, Phi Beta Kappa. Office: Markham and University Ave Little Rock AR 72205

MC DOWELL, JENNIFER (MRS. MILTON LOVENTHAL), editor, sociologist, composer; b. Albuquerque, May 19, 1936; d. Willard A. and Margaret Frances (Garrison) McDowell; B.A., U. Calif., 1957; M.A. in English, San Diego State U., 1958; M.L.S., U. Calif., Berkeley, 1963; Ph.D. (fellow) in Sociology, U. Oreg., 1973; m. Milton Loventhal, July 2, 1973. Tchr. English, Abraham Lincoln High Sch., San Jose, Calif., 1960-61; free lance editor in Soviet field, 1961-63; research asst. dept. sociology U. Oreg., Eugene, 1964-66; reader for the Jour. for Sci. Study of Religion, 1974-75, 79—; co-producer radio shows for Sta. KALX, 1971-72; tchr. numerous workshops in writing, 1969-73; research cons., 1973—; editor and publisher Merlin Press, San Jose, 1973—; music pub. Lipstick & Toy Balloons Pub. Co., 1978—; composer for Paramount Pictures, 1982—. Calif. Arts Council grantee, 1976-77. Mem. Am. Sociol. Assn., Soc. for Sci. Study of Religion, Soc. for Study of Religion and Communism, Phi Beta Kappa, Sigma Alpha Iota, Beta Phi Mu, Kappa Kappa Gamma. Democrat. Author: Black Politics, 1971; Contemporary Women Poets, an Anthology, 1977; contbr. poems, essays and short stories to lit. mags., articles to profl. jours.; composer songs Money Makes a Woman Free, 1976, My Love Is Stronger than Life Itself, 1979; composer music for play Simple Gifts, 1980. Office: PO Box 5602 San Jose CA 95150

MC DOWELL, MARY JUANITA, educator; b. Smithfield, Pa., July 4, 1918; d. Samuel W. and Mary H. McD.; B.Sc., Calif. State Coll., 1944. Relief investigator Dept. Public Assistance, Harrisburg, Pa., 1939-40; tchr. Fayette County Schs., Uniontown, Pa., 1940-53; tchr., prin. Dept. Def. Dependent Schs., Camp Wood, Kumumotto, Japan, 1953-54; tchr. Fayette County Schs., Uniontown, Pa., 1954-55, Dept. Def. Dependent Schs., Ramstein Air Base, Germany, 1955-57; tchr. Sch. Dist. Abington, Montgomery County, Phila., 1957-59; tchr. Sch. Dist. Mt. Lebanon, Allegheny County, Pitts., 1959—, dir. student activities, 1961-71; cons. Harcourt, Brace & Jovanovich, 1971. Mem. NEA, Pa. Congress Parents and Tchrs. (hon. life), Pa. Edn. Assn., Mt. Lebanon Edn. Assn. Clubs: Order White Shrine Jerusalem, Order Eastern Star.

MCDOWELL, NANCY ANN, anthropologist, educator; b. Woodstock, Ill., Sept. 4, 1947; d. Robert Warfield and Leone Margaret (Stading) McD.; B.A., U. Ill., Urbana, 1969; M.A., Cornell U., 1972, Ph.D., 1975. Vis. instr. Franklin and Marshall Coll., Lancaster, Pa., 1974-75, asst. prof., 1975-81, asso. prof., 1981—; project dir. Papua (New Guinea) Inst. Applied Social and Econ. Research, 1981. Chmn., Lancaster Women's Liberation, 1976, exec. bd., 1975-77. NIMH fellow, 1972-73; NSF grantee, 1982-83. Mem. Am. Anthrop. Assn., Northeastern Anthrop. Assn., Am. Ethnol. Soc. Assn. Social Anthropology in Oceania, South Pacific Social Sci. Assn., Polynesian Soc. Democrat. Contbr. articles to profl. jours. Office: Dept Anthropology Franklin and Marshall Coll Lancaster PA 17604

MCDOWELL, PAT LEWIS, entrepreneur; b. Bronaugh, Mo., July 7, 1933; d. Clarence L. and Mary Bell (Pitts) Lewis; student public schs., Shreveport; La.; m. E. A. McDowell, June 4, 1954; children—David Albert. Adminstrv. asst. Cities Service Oil Co., Shreveport, 1950-54; with Riley-Beaird, Inc., Shreveport, 1956-58, Pitney & Bowes, Inc., Shreveport, 1958-70; owner Pat McDowell & Assos., Inc., Shreveport, 1979—; partner Stoner Co., Shreveport, 1975-80; The Gordian Knot, Shreveport, 1979—; owner Tapes 'n Thoughts, Inc., Shreveport, 1982—; v.p. public relations Accu-Med Corp., Shreveport, 1982—; lectr. in field. Pres. bd. dirs. La. Assn. for Blind, Shreveport, 1978-80, 79-80, chmn. bd., 1980-81; adv. bd. Nat. Industries for the Blind, Bloomfield, N.J., 1977-82, bd. dirs. Community Action for Corrections in La., 1975, Youth Advocates, Inc., 1976. Recipient J. Cheshire Peyton award; numerous awards Success Motivation Inst. Mem. Sales and Mktg. Execs., Am. Soc. for Training & Devel. Episcopalian. Clubs: Positive Mental Attitude Breakfast (bd. dirs., founding mem.), Toastmasters Hi-Noon. Home: 427 Pennsylvania St Shreveport LA 71105 Office: 1700 Centenary Blvd Shreveport LA 71101

MC DUFFIE, DEBORAH JEANNE, composer; b. N.Y.C., Aug. 8, 1950; d. Thomas Elliott and Nan Ruth (Woods) McD.; B.A., Western Coll. Women; 1 child, Kijana Babatu. Music producer, composer McCann-Erickson Advt., Inc., N.Y.C., 1971-81; pres. Jana Prodns, Inc., N.Y.C., 1977—; profl. singer, jingle composer, arranger, producer. Recipient numerous advt. awards. Mem. Nat. Assn. Female Execs. Vocal arranger: I'd Like to Teach the World to Sing, 1972; composer producer Miller High Life campaigns, 1980-83; album: I Am an Illusion, 1981. Office: 485 Lexington Ave 26th Floor New York NY 10017 *

MC EACHERN, BETTE WHITEHURST, club woman; b. Jesup, Ga., July 13, 1925; d. James Albert and Lois Louise (Thomas) Whitehurst; student U. S.C., 1962-63; m. Don Robert McEachern, Jan. 1, 1948; children—Beverly McEacherm Werner, Barbara Lorraine, Bonnie McEachern Korycki, Don Robert. Garden club vol., 1964—; pres. Rachel Jackson Garden Club, 1966, 71, Davidson County Hort. Soc., 1977-78; dist. dir. Tenn. Fedn. Garden Clubs, 1973-75, chmn. study com., 1979-80, life mem.; mem. Davidson County Hort. Bd., 1971—, Cheekwood Garden Bd., 1975—; chmn. Deep S. Regional Bd., 1977—; master judge flower shows, 1969—; chmn. conservation com. Stone River's Woman's Club, 1979; bd. dirs. Donelson YMCA, 1974; life mem. Nat. Council Federated Garden Clubs. Recipient numerous awards for flower arrangements, hort. work. Mem. Camellia Soc., Daffodil Soc., Ikebana Internat. (treas. chpt. 1976, 77. Republican. Presbyterian. Club: Cedar Creek. Address: 3220 Knobview Dr Nashville TN 37214

MC ELFRESH, PATRICIA JEAN SEITTERS, journalist; b. Akron, Ohio, July 27, 1933; d. Lamoine B. and Elizabeth H. (Myers) Seitters; B.A. in Journalism, U. Akron, 1955; postgrad. (fellow) Medill Sch. of Journalism, Northwestern U., 1955; m. Gerald R. McElfresh, Apr. 16, 1955; children—Stephen, Philip, Suzanne. Part-time reporter Akron bur. Cleve. Plain Dealer, 1952-62, Chagrin Valley Herald, 1960-62; free-lance journalist Mesa (Ariz.) Tribune, 1962-64, edn. writer, religion editor, columnist, 1964-72, Lifestyle editor, 1979—; publicist Mesa Community Coll., 1969-71; faculty asso. Ariz. State U., 1974-77; stringer Time mag., 1978-79; sect. editor, columnist Scottsdale (Ariz.) Daily Progress, 1972-79; producer Voice of Jazz, Sta.-KMCR, 1979—. Recipient service to edn. award Phi Delta Kappa, 1968; best writing awards Ariz. Edn. Assn., 1967-71; best entry winner Ariz. Newspaper Assn., 1974, 79; numerous state awards. Mem. Nat. Fedn. Press Women (.9 nat. awards), Ariz. Press Women (pres. 1970-71), Mortar Bd. Alumnae Assn., Jazz in Ariz. Inc., Z Club of Ariz., Alpha Gamma Delta. Office: 120 W 1st Ave Mesa AZ 85202

MCELHANNON, ANNETTE NEELY, govt. ofcl.; b. Atlanta, May 26, 1934; d. Amos Hiram and Nina Mae (Barrett) Neely; A.A., DeKalb Coll., 1976; student Ga. State U., 1977; children—Timothy Sean, Stephen King. Sec., 3d Army Hdqrs., Fort McPherson, Ga., 1951-57, 62-67; sec. Nat. Centers for Disease Control, Atlanta, 1967-71, public health technician, 1971-75, mgr. fed. women's program, 1975—. Mem. North Atlanta Federally Employed Women (v.p. 1979-81), centers for Disease Control Mgmt. Forum (sec. 1981). Republican. Home: 6803 Park Ave NE Atlanta GA 30342 Office: Centers for Disease Control Room 1-2405 1600 Clifton Rd NE Atlanta GA 30333

MCELMURRY, JUDITH ANN, educator; b. Phoenix, July 18, 1944; d. Jacob Milford and Annie (Brown) Cunningham; A.A., Christian Coll., 1964; B.A., Central Mo. State U., 1966; M.Ed. (fellow 1966-68), U. Hawaii, 1968; m. Gary Wilson McElmurry, June 22, 1968. Tchr., Hawaii Assn. Retarded Children, 1966-68, Honolulu Public Schs., 1967-68, Columbia (Mo.) Public Schs., 1968-70; dir. spl. edn. instructional materials center U. Mo., Columbia, 1970-80, instr. spl. edn., 1970—, dir. Mo. Spl. Edn. Dissemination Center, 1980—; mem. Mo. Adv. Council Spl. Edn. Personnel Devel. and Inservice Edn.; mem. adv. bd. Mo. Facilitator Center. Mem. adminstrv. com. 1st Christian Ch., chmn. edn. com., refugee families. Mem. Columbia Coll. Alumni Assn. (nat. bd. dirs.), Central Mo. Pastoral Care Assn., Council Exceptional Children, Mo. Assn. Children with Learning Disabilities, Assn. Spl. Edn. Technology, Pi Lambda Theta, PEO. Club: King's Daughters. Editor, Mo. SEDC Newsletter, 1970—; contbr. articles to profl. jours. Home: Rt 13 Cedar Grove Columbia MO 65201 Office: Dept Spl Edn U Mo Columbia MO 65211

MCELWAIN, JUANITA MURIEL, educator; b. Geneva, Ohio, Jan. 17, 1928; d. George Myron and Muriel Maude (Randolph) Stilwell; B.M.E., Fla. State U., 1958, M.M.E., 1959, M.Mus., 1974, Ph.D., 1978; m. O.D. McElwain, Aug. 21, 1948; 1 son, Thomas George. Tchr., Jennings (Fla.) Public Sch., 1961-62; tchr. piano, organ Monterey Bay Acad., Watsonville, Calif., 1962-67; tchr. organ, piano Antillian Union Coll., Mayàguez, P.R., 1967-69; music therapist Sunland Tng. Center, Marianna, Fla., 1978-80; asst. prof., dir. music therapy Sch. Music, N.Mex. U., Portales, 1980—; condr. workshops on music in spl. edn. Mem. profl. adv. com. Community Services Portales, 1981—; bd. dirs. Campfire Girls, Portales, 1982—. Mem. Nat. Assn. Music Therapy, Pi Kappa Lambda. Adventist. Home: 1621 S Main Ave Portales NM 88130 Office: School Music Eastern New Mexico Portales NM 88130

MC ENROE, PATRICIA SOLON, assn. exec.; b. Algona, Iowa, Nov. 19, 1922; d. John Edward and Kathryn Leone (Solon) McE.; student (scholar) Briar Cliff Coll., Sioux City, Iowa, 1942-44; B.Mus.Edn., Northwestern U., 1946, Mus.M., 1948; postgrad. Am. Conservatory of Music, Chgo. With Iowa Sch. for Braille and Sight Saving, Vinton, 1948-51; various positions Chgo. Bd. Edn., 1952-54, 56-57, 65-70; tchr. jr. high sch., Dover, Minn., 1954-55; music tchr. Ft. Carson, Fountain, Colo., 1955-56; v.p., program chmn. AAUW, Algona, 1976—. Founder, Kossuth County Democratic Women's Club, Algona, 1958; recreation leader ARC, Evanston, Ill., 1951; rep. Archdiocese Chgo. in pub. schs., Chgo., 1965-70. Mem. NOW, LWV, Iowa Women's Polit. Caucus, Internat. Platform Assn., Delphion Soc., Nat. Historic Preservation. Home and Office: 408 N Thorington Algona IA 50511

MCENTEGART, EILEEN FRANCES, oil co. exec.; b. N.Y.C., July 1, 1929; d. Thomas Emmet and Mary Amelia (Dewhurst) McE.; B.A. in Math., Coll. New Rochelle, 1951; M.B.A. in Fin., N.Y.U., 1980. Jr. engr., math. asst., programmer M.W. Kellogg Co., N.Y.C., 1951-62; programmer, analyst, supr. sci. applications Mobil Corp., N.Y.C., 1962-69, mgr. systems support, mgr. computer services dept., 1969-75, sr. industry analyst, supr. planning assos. corp. planning, 1975-81, controller payroll and personnel systems, Dallas, 1981—. Trustee Manhattan Coll., N.Y., 1980—; mem. Pres.' adv. bd. Coll. New Rochelle, 1975-79. Mem. Am. Mgmt. Assn., Mobil Polit. Action Com. (vice chairperson 1978—). Roman Catholic. Club: Lancers. Office: 1201 Elm St Dallas TX 75270

MC ENTIRE, HELEN LOUISE STARLEY, architect; b. Salt Lake City, Apr. 14, 1936; d. Rulon Faye and Hettie Luella (Teeples) Starley; B.F.A. in Architecture, U. Utah, Salt Lake City, 1959. Owner, Helen S. McEntire, Design Cons. to Architects, Utah, 1961-73, Helen S. McEntire, Architect, Ogden, Utah, 1973-78; co-owner, pres. Design Consultants, Inc., Interior Design, Ogden, 1971—; owner McEntire Assn., Salt Lake City and Ogden, 1978—; asso. prof. U. Hawaii, 1982—; founder, dir. Heritage Bank and Trust, Salt Lake City; archtl. works include: Entrance Gate, Weber State Coll., Ogden, 1978, Heritage Bank & Trust, Salt Lake City, 1978, Weber County Nutrition Center, Ogden, 1979, Hi-Rise Condominium, Salt Lake City, 1980. Recipient certs. in value engring., comml. and indsl. lighting, solar design; lic. architect, Utah, Nev. Mem. AIA (nat. task force for women, nat. com. on design, mem. past pres. Utah soc., chmn. ann. conv. 1978), Am. Soc. Interior Designers, Illuminating Engring. (asso.). Clubs: Soroptomist Internat., Ogden Golf and Country, Weber. Address: 411 Hobron Ln #3603 Honolulu HI 96815

MCENTYRE, ELIZABETH MAYFIELD, accountant; b. Cleveland, Tenn., Mar. 18, 1947; d. Charles Stanwix and Mary Ellen (Freeman) Mayfield; B.S. in Bus. Adminstrn. with honors, U. Tenn., Knoxville, 1969; cert. Goethe Inst., Berlin, 1974; m. John Culbreth McEntyre, Sept. 18, 1977; 1 dau., Dawn Nicole. Staff acct. Hickman, Pugh & Co., Knoxville, 1971; auditor/tax acct. J. K. Lasser & Co., C.P.A.s, Boston, 1971-74, tax acct., Wellesley, Mass., 1977; auditor M.I.T., 1975-76; chief acct. Galaxy Carpet Mills, Inc., Chatsworth, Ga., 1977; tax acct. Magic Chef, Inc., Cleveland, Tenn., 1978; prin. Elizabeth Mayfield McEntyre, C.P.A.s, Cleveland, 1979—. Adv., Jr. Achievement, Cleveland, 1978; pres. Cleveland Civitan Club; bd. dirs. United Way of Bradley County (Tenn.). C.P.A., Tenn., Mass. Mem. Am. Inst. C.P.A.s, Tenn. Soc. C.P.A.s, Phi Kappa Phi, Beta Gamma Sigma, Beta Alpha Psi. Club: Cleveland-Athens Cotillion. Home: Route 1 Riverbend Rd Ocoee TN 37361 Office: 2043 Ocoee St NW Cleveland TN 37311-9990

MCEVOY, PAMELA THOMPSON, therapist; b. Forest Hills, N.Y., Mar. 8, 1937; d. Reynolds Thomas and Pamela Shipley (Sweeny) McE.; B.A., U. La Verne, 1978, M.S., 1980; Ph.D., U.S. Internat. U., 1982; children—Michael B. Anderson, Jeffery A. Thomas, Candy L. Anderson Nott, Kenneth L. Anderson. Data processing coordinator Ernest Righetti High Sch., Santa Maria, Calif., 1974-78; instr. psychology-sociology Allan Hancock Coll., Santa Maria, 1977-78; mental health asst. Santa Barbara City Alcoholism Dept., 1977-78; gen. mgr. Profl. Suites, San Diego, 1978-81; therapist Chula Vista Community Counseling Center, San Diego, 1978—; research asst. U.S. Internat. U., 1979—. Bd. dirs. San Diego County Mental Health Assn., 1978-80; pres. Chula Vista (Calif.) Counseling Center, 1978; mem. Delinquency Prevention Commn., 1978. State fellow, 1979, 80, 81, 82, Calif. State scholar, 1976-77. Mem. Am. Personnel and Guidance Assn., Am. Bus. Women's Assn., Christian Assn. Psychol. Counselors, Calif. Assn. Marriage and Family Therapists. Republican. Roman Catholic. Home: 17452 Ashburton Rd San Diego CA 92128 Office: 17452 Ashburton Rd San Diego CA 92128

MCFADDEN, ALMA, lab. adminstr.; b. El Paso, Tex., Apr. 21, 1928; d. Salvador and Aurelia (Reyes) Saenz; grad. high sch.; m. Herchel McFadden, Dec. 16, 1952; children—Philip Neal, Diane McFadden Urrutia. Legal sec. Wm. A. Cocke, El Paso, 1945-48; exec. sec. El Paso Nat. Bank, 1948-52, State Nat. Bank, El Paso, 1969-74; adminstrv. asst. PathLab P.A., El Paso, 1974—, also personnel dir., dir. client services; asst. corporate sec. Bus. Cons. Inc.; pres. MFS, Inc. Chmn. sect. El Paso United Way, 1983. Mem. El Paso C. of C. Am. Soc. Personnel Adminstrn., El Paso Exec. Women's Council. Republican. Roman Catholic. Author monthly newsletter: Profiles. Home: 3445 Greenock El Paso TX 79925 Office: 1501 Arizona Plaza Bldg Suite B-21 El Paso TX 79902

MC FADDEN, BETTY MAXINE, marketing exec.; b. Portland, Ind., Feb. 6, 1922; d. Claude A. and Treva M. (Heston) Brubaker; B.S., Ohio State U., 1943; m. Edward J. McFadden, Apr. 7, 1946; children—Melinda Anne. Mdse. trainee to asst. buyer F & R Lazarus, Columbus, Ohio, 1943-45; clk. accounting dept. Jewel Home Shopping Service, Barrington, Ill., 1946-50, buyer, 1950-64, wearing apparel mdse. mgr., 1964-66, gen. mdse. mgr., 1966-67, v.p. merchandising and advt., 1967-74, group v.p. mktg., 1974-76, pres. direct mktg. div. Jewel Cos., Inc., Barrington, 1976-81; chmn. bd., chief exec. officer IHSS Inc., Barrington, 1981—; dir. Cluett, Peabody & Co., Inc., G.R.I. Corp., Ball Corp. Mem. adv. council Bus. Sch., Ohio State U., 1974-76, also mem. alumni adv. group, 1978-79; treas. Partners Ohio State U., 1975-76. Mem. Mail Order Assn. Am. (dir. 1976-78), NAM (dir. 1978-80), Chgo. Assn. Commerce and Industry (dir. 1980), Chgo. Network (dir.), Northwestern U. Assos. Club: Economic (Chgo.). Office: Jewel Park Barrington IL 60010

MCFADDEN, MARY, lawyer; b. Bethlehem, Pa., Nov. 7, 1950; d. Joseph B. and Catherine M. McFadden; B.A. magna cum laude, Boston U., 1972; J.D. cum laude, Suffolk U., 1978; m. Lawrence T.P. Stifler, Nov. 25, 1977. Research asso. Med. Found., Inc., Boston, 1973-78; admitted to Mass. bar, 1978; trial atty. for Child Welfare Unit, Mass. Dept. Public Welfare, Boston, 1978-80, Mass. Dept. Social Services, 1980-82; exec. sec. Mass. Commn. on Jud. Conduct, Boston, 1982—. Mem. Am. Bar Assn., Mass. Bar, Mass. Bar Assn., Boston Bar Assn., Women's Bar Assn., Phi Beta Kappa, Psi Chi, Phi Delta Phi. Co-author articles on alcohol use; editorial referee Jour. Studies on Alcohol. Home: 150 Mountfort St Brookline MA 02146 Office: 14 Beacon St Suite 102 Boston MA 02108

MC FADDEN, MARY JOSEPHINE, fashion designer; b. N.Y.C., Oct. 1, 1938; d. Alexander Bloomfield and Mary Josephine (Cutting) McFadden; student Columbia, New Sch. Social Research, Traphagen Sch. Design; 1 dau., Justine Emma Harari. Pub. relations dir. Christian Dior, N.Y.C., 1962-64; merchandising editor Vogue mag. in S. Africa, 1964; polit. and travel columnist Rand (S. Africa) Daily Mail, 1965-68; founder, dir. Vukutu, sculptural workshop for African artists, Inyanga Province, Rhodesia, 1968-70; spl. project editor Vogue mag., N.Y.C., 1970-73; designer of dresses, jewelry, fabric, accessories, stationary and home furnishings, 1973—; pres., owner Mary McFadden, Inc., N.Y.C., 1976—; pres. Mary McFadden Jewels, 1978—; curator Lannan Mus., Palm Beach, Fla., 1970—. Trustee, Lannan Found. Recipient Fashion Hall of Fame award, 1977; Coty award, 1979; President's award R.I. Sch. Design, 1979. Office: 264 W 35th St New York NY 10001

MC FADDEN, SYBILL MARTIN, mus. curator; b. Pitts., Mar. 22, 1918; d. Alfred Nicholas and Rachel (Church) Martin; B.A. in Journalism, Pa. State U., 1941; m. William Patrick McFadden, Aug. 19, 1942; children—Suzanne Sybill, William Patrick, Gary J. Public relations dir. advt. ARC, Eastern Area Hdqrs., Alexandria, Va., 1941-46; owner, curator Mus. Antique Dolls and Toys, Lakewood, N.Y., 1960—; artist, one-woman shows, N.Y. and Fla.; writer, photographer nat. doll and toy mags., antiques mag.; writer, columnist Hobbies Mag. Mem. United Fedn. Doll Clubs, Inc., Western N.Y. Doll Club, Fla. West Coast Doll Collectors, Doll Study Club Jamestown (founder). Author: Famous People in Miniature. Home and Office: 96 W Summit Ave Lakewood NY 14750

MCFADDEN, VELMA ONEIDA, social worker; b. Haddock, Ga., Nov. 27, 1933; d. Bennie and Ada (Tatum) Drewery; B.A., Bellevue (Nebr.) Coll., 1972; M.A., Calif. Christian U., Los Angeles, 1975; m. Edward McFadden, Aug. 13, 1950; children—Patricia Ann, Edward, Karen Denese, Kenneth Michael. Dir. day care Sembach AFB, W.Ger., 1967-69; social worker Douglas County (Nebr.) Social Service, 1970-73; exec. dir. Bryant Center Community House, Omaha, 1973-75; owner Ms. Boutique, ladies apparel, Bellevue, Nebr., 1975-78; area dir. Big Bros.-Big Sisters, Omaha, 1978—; tchr. sociology Buena Vista Coll., Storm Lake, Iowa, 1980-81; bd. dirs. Salvation Army Booth Meml. Hosp., Omaha, 1976-77. Sec.-treas. Bellevue Housing Authority, 1979-80, chmn., 1980-81. Served with USAF, 1951-53. Child Welfare fellow U. Nebr., Omaha, 1980; named Vol. of Yr., Grand Fork (N.D.) ARC, 1960, Citizen of Week, Sta. KOWH, Omaha, 1975. Mem. Nat. Assn. Black Social Workers, Jack and Jill Am., Urban League Guild, Am. Bus. Women's Assn., Nebr. Social Workers Assn., Alpha Kappa Alpha. Democrat. Mem. AME Ch. Club: Order Eastern Star. Home: 1408 Willow Ave Bellevue NE 68005 Office: 2211 Paul St Omaha NE 68102

MC FADDEN, WILMOT CURNOW HAMM, chief librarian; b. Lead, S.D., Oct. 3, 1919; d. William and Ingeborg (Christianson) Curnow; student S.D. State Coll., 1938-41; m. Kenneth G. Hamm, Jan. 8, 1944 (div. 1963); 1 dau., Wilmot Christine; m. 2d, John Stinson McFadden, Mar. 1965. Asst. librarian Rock Springs (Wyo.) Pub. Library, 1947-48, head librarian, 1953—; exec. dir. Wyo., Nat. Library Week, 1969; mem. Wyo. Adv. Council for Libraries, 1977. State committeewoman Democratic Party, 1952—, also state vice chmn. Mem. adv. bd. Fed. Commn. Civil Rights, 1963—; treas. Dist. 4 Sch. Bd., 1966-78, clk. dist. 1, 1969—; adv. bd. Western Wyo. Community Coll. Bd. dirs. State Library Archives and Hist. Bd., 1959-64, 66-71, 77—, mem., 1967—. Recipient Grolier Nat. Library Week award 1969; award for outstanding service to Sweetwater County, 1975. Mem. Federated Woman's Club, Am. Legion Aux., Mountain Plains (Wyo. rep. 1967-68, v.p. 1972, pres. 1972-73), Am., Wyo. (chmn. conf. 1966, v.p. 1972, pres. 1972-73, Librarian of Yr. award 1977, Georgia Shovlain spl. projects award 1980) library assns., Am. Library Trustees Assn., Wyo. Sch. Bds. Assn. (hon., commendation 1979), Alpha Delta Kappa. Author: Handbook Wyoming Library Trustees. Home: 28 Cedar St Rock Springs WY 82901 Office: 400 C St Rock Springs WY 82901

MCFALL, ELIZABETH, microbiologist; b. San Diego, Oct. 28, 1928; d. Clifford Ellsworth and Teresa (Moore) McF.; B.S., San Diego State Coll., 1950; M.A. in Econs., U. Calif., Berkeley, 1954, Ph.D. in Biochemistry, 1957; m. Andrew Leslie Floyd, Dec. 19, 1980. Research fellow Harvard U., 1957-60; research assoc. M.I.T., 1960-61, 62-63; NIH spl. research fellow Nat. Inst. Med. Research, London, 1961-62; mem. faculty N.Y.U. Med. Sch., 1963—, prof. microbiology, 1963—; mem. microbial genetics study sect. NIH, 1977-81. Recipient Career Devel. award NIH, 1964-74. Mem. Am. Soc. Microbiology, Am. Soc. Biol. Chemistry, AAAS. Democrat. Editor Jour. Bacteriology, 1975—. Address: Dept Microbiology NYU Med Sch New York NY 10016

MCFANN, MARGUERITE (VIRGINIA), real estate broker; b. Va., Nov. 8, 1926; d. Ernest Harold French and Leila Ellen Bishop Roberts; B.A., Miami Jacobs Bus. Coll., Dayton, Ohio, 1952; postgrad. Antelope Valley Coll.; m. Virgil Lewis McFann, Sept. 8, 1946; children—Wayne, Judith, Linda K. Sec., NASA, 1961; owner, dir. modeling Schs., 1961-65; dir. Teen Screen Modeling Agy., 1962-65; owner, broker West Side Real Estate, Lancaster, Calif., 1971—. Recipient various service awards. Mem. Exec. Female Assn. (dir. Calif.). Republican. Clubs: Quarts Hill Woman's, Christian Woman's, Rebeccas, Royal Neighbors Am. Address: 4332 W Ave L Lancaster CA 93534

MCFARLAND, CLAUDETTE, real estate exec., lawyer, sociologist, minister; b. St. Louis, Dec. 8, 1935; B.A., Roosevelt U., Chgo., 1958; LL.B., N.C. Central U., 1965, J.D., 1970; M.S.W., U. Ill., 1971, M.A. in Bus. Adminstrn., 1973, Ph.D. in Sociology, 1977; D.D.; m. Vernon A. Winstead, 1964; children—Claudette, Vernon A. Automobile saleswoman, 1956; social worker, 1957; real estate broker, 1959; probation officer Cook County Juvenile Ct., Chgo., 1961; pres. McFarland Enterprises, Inc., real estate mgmt. and investments, Chgo., 1962—; v.p. V.A.W. Industries, Inc., indsl. maintenance, manpower and investment cons., Chgo., 1971—; pres. Multi-Medi Services, Inc., public relations cons. and advt.; Chgo.; co-founder, dir. South Shore Sr. Citizens Center; co-founder, co-pastor Holy Family United in God First Soc., Inc.; ordained minister Universal Life Ch., 1978; cons. Dept. Housing, City of Chgo., 1980—. Sponsor, participant youth and sr. citizens programs, 1975—; mem. consumer adv. bd. Chgo. Defender, newspaper; exec. bd. dirs. Girl Scouts U.S.A., Chgo. Beautiful Com., Friends of Park, Chgo. South Shore Commn.; trustee Du Sable Mus. African Am. History; mem. women's aux. bd. Provident Hosp., Chgo.; ofcl. observer, Ill. travel coordinator ERA Nat. Women's Conv., Houston; mem. community adv. bd. South Shore Bank; exec. sec. 5th ward Citizens For Democrats, 1982-83; pres. 5th ward Regular Dem. Orgn., 1982. Recipient numerous awards and citations for civic work, including Outstanding Pub. Service award Sta. WAIT. Mem. Nat. Bar Assn., Am. Assn. Cath. Women, Ch. Women United, Nat. Assn. U. Women, LWV (past pub. relations dir., exec. bd.), AAUW, Chgo., Ill. assns. commerce and industry, N.C. Central U. Alumni Assn. (treas.), League Black Women, Ill. Women's Soc., Jack and Jill Am. (chmn. Chgo.), Nat. Council Jewish Women (life), Nat. Council Negro Women (an Outstanding Woman of Yr. 1972-74), Nat. Links, Inc., Women's Internat. League for Peace and Freedom, Women In Community Service Assn., Chgo. Council Fgn. Relations, South Shore Ministerial Assn. (corr. sec.), Culver Mil. Acad. Mother's Club, Nat. Council Negro Women (life), Nat. Assn. Women in Ministry (v.p. 1979-82), U. Chgo. Lab. Schs. Parents Assn., NOW, Lyric Opera Citizens of Greater Chgo. Council, Tau Gamma Delta (life), Alpha Kappa Alpha (life), Wive's Aux. of Alpha Phi Alpha. Address: 7433 S Constance Ave Chicago IL 60649

MC FARLAND, DORIS BARBARA HEBNER, metal products co. exec.; b. Snoqualmie, Falls, Wash., May 6, 1922; d. George H. and Ethel M. (Provan) Hebner; student Wash. State U., 1940-41, U. Wash., 1943, Shoreline Community Coll., 1975; m. Earl D. McFarland, Feb. 16, 1943; children—Annette, Constance, Candy, Graham, Marilyn. Acct., N.W. Hosiery Co., Seattle, 1941-46, D.K. McDonald Ins. Co., Seattle, 1958-60, Universal Furnace Co., Seattle, 1960-62, Seacrest Marina, Seattle, 1962-63; propr. variety store, Seattle, 1956-58; acct. Nelson Iron Works, Inc., Seattle, 1963-69, treas., 1969—; treas. G.C.N., Inc., 1980—. Leader 4-H Horse Club. Mem. Nat. Assn. Credit Mgmt., Seattle Credit Women (past pres.), Women's Bus. Exchange, Seattle C. of C. Home: 16010 124th St NE Woodinville WA 98072 Office: 3423 13th Ave SW PO Box 80816 Seattle WA 98108

MCFARLAND, J. RUTH, state senator, biologist; b. Zita, Okla., June 10, 1925; d. Albert and Dorotha Anne (Patterson) McF.; B.S., U. Okla., 1954; B.A., Central Wash. State U., 1960; M.S., U. Oreg., 1966, Ph.D., 1970; children—Linda J. Blanchard, Nancy R. Logan, Janice L. Kunz. Tchr., Wash. and Oreg. public schs., 1961-67; instr. biol. scis. Mt. Hood Community Coll., Salem, Oreg., 1970—; mem. Oreg. Senate from 12th Dist., 1981—. Mem. Multnomah County Econ. Devel. Commn., 1976—; pres. E. Multnomah County chpt. LWV, 1975. Mem. AAUW, Bus. and Profl. Women, Oreg. Women's Polit. Caucus (Mary Rieke award 1978). Democrat. Club: Order Eastern Star. Office: Box 68 Salem OR 97308

MCFARLAND, KAY ELEANOR, state justice; b. Coffeyville, Kans., July 20, 1935; d. Kenneth W. and Margaret E. (Thrall) McF.; B.A. magna cum laude, Washburn U., Topeka, 1957, J.D., 1964. Admitted to Kans. bar, 1964; pvt. practice, Topeka, 1964-71; probate and juvenile judge Shawnee County, Topeka, 1971-73; dist. judge, Topeka, 1973-77; justice Kans. Supreme Ct., 1977—; owner, operator Quilts by Kay McFarland, Topeka, 1961-64. Mem. Am., Kans., Topeka bar assns., Dist. Judges Assn., Nat. Assn. Juvenile Judges, Nat. Assn. Probate Judges. Office: Supreme Ct Kansas State House Topeka KS 66612 *

MCFARREN, ANN ELISABETH, health care exec.; b. Detroit, July 6, 1937; d. Paul Stevens and Grace (Lister) Bigby; B.S. in Nursing, U. Mich., 1959; divorced; children—Stanley William Larmee, Jr., Kimberly Ann Larmee. Profl. figure skater, 1957-64; office nurse, Ann Arbor, Mich., 1959-61; asst. Washtenaw County League Planned Parenthood, Ann Arbor, 1959-62; exec. dir. Planned Parenthood Assn. N.W. Ind., Merrillville, 1965—; project developer Planned Parenthood N.Y., 1967-68; cons. in field. Bd. dirs. N.W. Ind. Symphony Soc. Mem. Am. Assn. Sex Educators, Counselors and Therapists, Am. Public Health Assn., ACLU. Club: Columbia (Indpls.). Office: 8645 Connecticut St Merrillville IN 46410

MC FATE, PATRICIA ANN, found. adminstr., educator; b. Detroit, Mar. 19, 1936; d. John Earle and Mary Louise (Bliss) McF.; B.A. (Alumni Scholar), Mich. State U., 1954; M.A., Northwestern U., 1956, Ph.D., 1965; M.A. (hon.), U. Pa., 1977. Asso. prof. English, asst. dean liberal arts and scis. U. Ill., Chgo., 1967-74, asso. prof. English, asso. vice chancellor for acad. affairs, 1974-75; asso. prof. folklore Faculty of Arts and Scis., U. Pa., Phila., 1975-81, prof. tech. and soc. Coll. Engring. and Applied Sci., 1975-81, vice provost, 1975-78; dep. chmn. Nat. Endowment for Humanities, Washington, 1978-81; exec. v.p. Am. Scandinavian Found., N.Y.C., 1981-82, pres., 1982—; vis. asso. prof. dept. medicine Rush U., Chgo., 1970—; dir. Associated Dry Goods Corp., Phila. Nat. Corp. Bd. dirs. Inst. for Cancer Research, Bishop Anderson House Found. U. Ill. Grad. Coll. faculty fellow, 1968. Fellow N.Y. Acad. Scis.; mem. Acad. Scis. Phila. (founding mem., corr. sec. 1977-79), AAAS, Am. Com. on Irish Studies, Can. Assn. for Irish Studies, Internat. Assn. for Anglo-Irish Studies, MLA, Theta Alpha Phi, Omega Beta Pi. Club: Cosmopolitan (Phila.). Author: The Writings of James Stephens, 1979; contbr. articles to various jours.

MCGAFFIGAN, PEGGY WEEKS, govt. ofcl.; b. Houlton, Maine, June 27, 1952; d. Francis P. and Ruth Conrad (Steeves) Weeks; B.A., U. Maine, Orono, 1974; M.A., Tufts U., 1975; m. Edward McGaffigan, Jr., July 3, 1982. Analyst div. nat. security and internat. affairs Congl. Budget Office, Washington, 1975-79; legis. asst. to Senator William S. Cohen, Washington, 1979—. Mem. Phi Beta Kappa. Home: 4818 N 37th St Arlington VA 22207 Office: 1251 Dirksen Senate Office Bldg Washington DC 20510

MC GANN, GERALDINE, govt. ofcl.; b. Bklyn., Dec. 21, 1937; d. Daniel and Geraldine (LeGrande) Essex; B.A. with honors, Hofstra U., 1974; M.Profl. Studies in Health Care Adminstrn. with honors, C.W. Post Coll., L.I. U., 1978; m. Edward J. McGann, Apr. 7, 1956; children—Daniel, Kevin, Kerrie, Jacqueline. Tchr., Hempstead and East Rockaway Schs., 1974; coordinator sr. citizen services Town of Hempstead, N.Y., 1974-78, dep. commr. dept. services for aging, 1978-81; spl. asst. to regional adminstr. HUD, N.Y.C., 1981—. Chairperson Island Park (N.Y.) Housing Authority, 1975-81; mem. Republican Nat. Com. Mem. Am. Soc. Public Adminstrn., Assn. Pub. Adminstrn. and Health Care Profls., Pi Alpha Alpha. Republican. Home: 42 Roosevelt Pl Island Park NY 11558 Office: 26 Federal Plaza New York NY 10278

MC GAURAN, MADELEINE R., social worker; b. Providence; d. Michael J. and Mary (Flanagan) McGauran; B.S., U. R.I., 1938; postgrad. Boston Coll., 1943-46; M.S., Boston U., 1949. Social worker Providence Dept. Public Welfare, 1939-41, asst. dist. supr., 1941-42, dist. supr., 1942-43; casework supr. R.I. Div. Public Assistance, Providence, 1943-48; field supr. sch. social work Boston Coll., 1946-48, Boston U., 1947-48; area supr. div. public assistance R.I. Dept. Social Welfare Div., 1949-64, chief med. assistance for aging, 1964-68, chief of field ops., 1968-71; chief casework supr., chief field ops., div. mgmt. services and assistance payments R.I. Dept. Social and Rehab. Services, Granston, 1971-76, asst. adminstr., 1976-78. Mem. Newport Council Social Agys., 1950-58, Warwick Council Community Services, 1958-60, R.I. Council Community Services, 1962-64. Mem. Nat. Assn. Social Workers, Acad. Cert. Social Workers, Pinewoods Inst., Am. Pub. Welfare Assn., Nat. Conf. Social Work. Home: 73 Mount View Dr Cranston RI 02920 Office: 600 New London Ave Cranston RI 02920

MC GAW, JESSIE BREWER, author, educator; b. Clarksville, Tenn., Oct. 17, 1913; d. Lewis Vernon and Birdie (Basford) Brewer; A.B., Duke U., 1935; M.A., Peabody Coll., 1940; postgrad. Columbia U., 1948-50, (Fulbright scholar) Am. Acad. Rome, 1959; m. Howard Franklin McGaw, Dec. 28, 1939 (div. 1958); children—Miriam Katherine, Vernon Howard; m. 2d, Harold L. Geis, Aug. 1964 (div. 1972). Tchr. Latin, Ward Belmont Sch., Nashville, 1938-40; tchr. Lausanne Sch., Memphis, 1940-42; asso. prof. English and Latin, U. Houston, 1952—. Bd. dirs. YWCA, 1957-59, Day Care Assn., 1956-61, Houston Civic Music Assn., 1958-60, Houston Council Human Relations. Recipient Cokesburg Juvenile award; Theta Sigma Phi lit. award. Fulbright grantee Am. Acad. in Rome, 1959; research grantee, 1964, 72; Delta Kappa Gamma ednl. grantee, China, 1981. Mem. Tex. Folklore Soc., South Central Modern Lang. Assn., Houston Council, Tchrs. Fgn. Lang. (treas.), League Women Voters, AAUW, Tex. Inst. Letters, U. Houston Women's Assn. (pres. 1967-68), Mus. Fine Arts (asso.), Delta Kappa Gamma, Kappa Kappa Gamma. Democrat. Methodist. Club: University Houston Woman's (pres. 1954-55, 67-68). Author: How Medicine Man Cured Paleface Women, 1956; History of Houston YWCA, 1957; Painted Pony Runs Away, 1958; Little Elk Hunts Buffalo, 1961; Chief Red Horse Tells About Custer, 1981. Translator: Heptaphus (Pico delia Mirandola), 1977. Home: 2405 Dickey Pl Houston TX 77019

MC GEE, ALETHA KENDRICK, club woman; b. Page County, Iowa, May 12, 1910; d. Miles Thornton and Ora Orieanna (Orme) Kendrick; student pub. schs., Page County and Villisca, Iowa; m. Lester M. Christensen, Apr. 15, 1934; 1 dau., Janet Lee; m. 2d, Harry F. McGee, Dec. 14, 1947. With May Seed & Nursery, Shenandoah, Iowa, 1927-29; advt. mgr., editor Tyler Echoes, Tyler Bros., Villisca, Iowa, 1929-30; office mgr., bookkeeper Beatrice Foods Co., Villisca, 1930-35; asst. to head voucher dept. Carpenter Paper Co., Omaha, 1940-42; office mgr., cashier bookkeeper Tyler Coca-Cola Co., Villisca, 1942-47; sch. bd. sec. Villisca Community Sch. Dist., 1952-58; statis. typist, asst. to auditor Robert R. Wade, C.P.A., Omaha, 1959-62; sec., bookkeeper Van Horne Investments, Inc., Omaha, 1963-75. Sec. Omaha Republican Woman's Club, 1966-68; precinct chmn. Rep. Party, 1968-72; regent Maj. Isaac Sadler chpt. DAR, 1975-78, chaplain, 1980-82, state chmn. motion picture-TV com., 1976-78, state chmn. Americanism and DAR manuals for citizenship com., 1978-80, state chmn. insignia com., 1980-82, nat. vice chmn. motion picture-TV com. N.W. Central div. 1977-80; mem. Freedoms Found. Valley Forge, Am. Security Council. Methodist. Home: 9103 Susan Circle Omaha NE 68124

MCGEE, CAROLYN BOGAN, computer services co. exec.; b. Pottstown, Pa., Jan. 8, 1947; d. John Joseph and Beverley Valeria McGee; B.S., Carnegie Mellon U., 1968, M.S., 1970; Ph.D., U. Ala., 1971; m. Denis J. Bogan, June 7, 1969; children—Kathleen Bogan, John Bogan. Mem. faculty Kans. State U., Manhattan, 1972-74; v.p. Am. Mgmt. Systems, Arlington, Va., 1974—. Recipient Cert. of Merit, GAO, 1979. Mem. AAUW. Contbr. articles to profl. jours. Home: 5110 Althea Dr Annandale VA 22003 Office: 1777 N Kent St Arlington VA 22209

MC GEE, DOROTHY HORTON, author, historian; b. West Point, N.Y., Nov. 30, 1913; d. Hugh Henry and Dorothy (Brown) McGee; ed. Sch. of St. Mary, 1920-21, Green Vale Sch., 1921-28, Brearley Sch., 1928-29, Fermata Sch., 1929-31. Asst. historian Inc. Village of Roslyn, N.Y., 1950-58; historian Inc. Vilage of Matinecock, 1966—. Author: Skipper Sandra, 1950; Sally Townsend, Patriot, 1952; The Boarding School Mystery, 1953; Famous Signers of the Declaration, 1955; Alexander Hamilton—New Yorker, 1957; Herbert Hoover: Engineer, Humanitarian, Statesman, 1959, rev. edit., 1965; The Pearl Pendant Mystery, 1960; Framers of the Constitution, 1968; author booklets, articles hist. and sailing subjects. Chmn., Oyster Bay Am. Bicentennial Revolution Commn., 1971—; mem. Nassau County Am. Revolution Bicentennial Commn. Dir., The Friends of Raynham Hall, Inc.; treas. Family Welfare Assn. Nassau County, Inc., 1956-58; dir. Family Service Assn. Nassau County, 1958-69. Recipient Cert. of award for outstanding contbn. children's lit. N.Y. State Assn. Elem. Sch. Prins., 1959; award Nat. Soc. Children of Am. Revolution, 1960; award N.Y. Assn. Supervision and Curriculum Devel., 1961; hist. award Town of Oyster Bay, 1963; Cert. Theodore Roosevelt Assn., 1976. Fellow Soc. Am. Historians; mem. Soc. Preservation L.I. Antiquities (dir.), N.Y. Geneal. and Biol. Soc. Oyster Bay Hist. Soc. (pres. 1971-75, chmn. 1975-79, trustee), Theodore Roosevelt Assn. (trustee), Townsend Soc. Am. (trustee), Nat. Trust Historic Preservation, others. Republican. Address: Box 142 Locust Valley NY 11560

MCGEE, PATRICIA ANN, computer mgmt. cons.; b. N.Y.C., July 22, 1939; d. Patrick James and Bridget Mary (O'Leary) Brennan; B.A., CCNY, 1961; 1 dau., Ayn Maureen. Sr. cons., analyst Western Ops., Inc., San Francisco, 1968-71; data processing mgr. R. H. Lapin & Co., San Francisco, 1971-73; project leader, systems analyst Transmaerica Corp., San Francisco, 1973-74; systems analyst United Vintners, Inc., San Francisco, 1974-75; systems planner Fiberboard Corp., 1975-76; customer rep. Computer Scis. Corp., 1976-78; project mgr. Crocker Nat. Bank, 1978-80; cons. Bechtel Co., 1980, Mason-McDuffie & Co., 1980, Pacific Telephone Co., 1980-81; partner The Profls., San Francisco, 1981—. Mem. Am. Mgmt. Assn., Republican Women San Francisco, Women Entrepreneurs, World Affairs Trade Council, Profl. Women's Network, Assn. System Mgrs. Republican. Roman Catholic. Clubs: Commonwealth of California; San Francisco Bay. Home: 430-10th Ave San Francisco CA 94118 Office: 249 Front St San Francisco CA 94111

MCGIBBON, PAULINE MILLS (MRS. DONALD WALKER MCGIBBON), former lt. gov. Ont.; b. Sarnia, Ont., Can., Oct. 20, 1910; d. Alfred William and Ethel (French) Mills; B.A., U. Toronto, 1933, LL.D., 1975; LL.D., U. Alta., 1967, U. Western Ont., 1974, Queen's U., 1974, McMaster U., 1981, Carleton U., 1981; B.A.A. in Theatre, Ryerson Poly. Inst., 1974; Dr. Univ., U. Ottawa, 1972, U. Laval, 1976; D.Hum.L. (hon.), St. Lawrence U., Canton, N.Y., 1977; D.Litt.S. (hon.), Victoria U., Toronto, 1979; m. Donald Walker McGibbon, Jan. 26, 1935. Dir. IBM, Canada, 1972-74; chancellor U. Toronto, 1971-74, mem. senate, 1952-61; lt. gov. Province of Ont., 1974-80; chancellor U. Guelph, 1977—; past dir. IBM Can. Ltd., IMASCO Ltd. Pres. Dominion Drama Festival, 1957-59; mem. Can. Council, 1968-71; pres. Can. Conf. Arts, 1972-73; v.p. Massey Hall, 1973-74, bd. dirs., 1980—; Bd. dirs. du Maurier Council for Performing Arts, 1973—, Nat. Theatre Sch. Can., 1966-69; chmn. bd. dirs. Women's Coll. Hosp., 1970-74; gov. Upper Can. Coll., 1971-74. Decorated officer and companion Order of Can., grand prior Order St. Lazarus Jerusalem, Dame Grand Cross; recipient Can. drama award, 1957; civic award of merit City of Toronto, 1967; Centennial medal, 1967; named hon. col. 25th Toronto Service Bn., 1975; award of merit Canadian Public Relations Soc., 1972; Silver Jubilee medal, 1977; Paul Harris fellow Rotary Club, 1970; B'nai Brith Humanitarian award, 1980, others. Fellow Royal Coll. Physicians and Surgeons Can. (hon.); mem. U. Toronto Alumni Assn. (past pres.), Victoria Coll. Alumnae Assn. (past pres.), Royal Canadian Legion, Heraldry Soc. Can., Imperial Order Daus. Empire (nat. pres. 1963-65). Clubs: Univ. Women's, Toronto Ladies (Toronto); Heliconian, Can.

MCGILL, KATHLEEN ANN, human resources specialist; b. Columbus, Ohio, Oct. 16, 1952; d. James Dawn and Madolin Rose (Gardner) McG.; B.Sc. in Biology-Chemistry, Bowling Green State U., 1974; postgrad. Western State Coll., 1974-75, U. Colo., 1977-79, Capital U., Columbus 1981—. Tutor biology Bowling Green State U. 1971-74; grad. teaching asst. Western State Coll. 1974-75; sales agt., office mgr. Heritage Mt. Homes, Inc., Woodland Park, Colo. 1976-80; mgr. human resources United McGill Corp., Inc., Columbus, Ohio, 1980—. Docent Columbus Zoo, 1982—. Lic. real estate salesperson, Colo. Mem. Am. Soc. Personnel Adminstrs., Central Ohio Personnel Assn., Midwest Coll. Placement Council, Colo. Assn. Cert. Closers, Am. Compensation Assn., Tri-Beta, Delta Phi Alpha. Republican. Clubs: Alaskan Malamute Am., Southwestern Ohio Alaskan Malamute Fanciers Assn., Nat. Audubon Soc., Columbus Audubon Soc. Office: 1 Mission Park PO Box 7 Groveport OH 43125

MCGILLEY, SISTER, MARY JANET, coll. pres.; b. Kansas City, Mo., Dec. 4, 1924; d. James P. and Peg (Ryan) McG.; B.A., St. Mary Coll., 1945; M.A., Boston Coll., 1951; Ph.D., Fordham U., 1956; postgrad. U. Notre Dame, 1960, Columbia U., 1964. Social worker, Kansas City, 1945-46; joined Sisters of Charity of Leavenworth, Roman Catholic Ch., 1946; tchr. English, Hayden High Sch., Topeka, 1948-50, Billings (Mont.) Central High Sch., 1951-53; faculty dept. English, St. Mary Coll., Leavenworth, Kans., 1956-64, pres. coll., 1964—; mem. Commn. on Instns. Higher Edn., North Central Assn. Colls. and Schs., 1980—; Roman Cath. rep. Nat. Congress on Ch.-Related Colls. and Univs., 1979. Bd. dirs. Kans. Ind. Colls. Assn., Kansas City Regional Council for Higher Edn., United Leavenworth Way, 1965-80; trustee at large Ind. Coll. Funds Am., 1975-76, exec. com., 1974-77; bd. dirs. Kans. Ind. Coll. Fund, pres., 1972-74, 77-78; mem. Leavenworth Planning Commn., 1977-78; mem. Commn. on Women in Higher Edn., Am. Council on Edn., 1980—. Recipient Alumnae award St. Mary Coll., 1969. Mem. Nat. Assn. Ind. Colls. and Univs. (dir. 1982—), Nat. Council Tchrs. English, Am. Assn. Higher Edn., Leavenworth C. of C. (hon. dir.), Assn. Am. Colls. (commn. liberal edn. 1970-73, com. curriculum and faculty devel. 1979—), St. Mary Alumnae Assn. (hon. pres.), Delta Epsilon Sigma. Democrat. Contbr. articles, fiction, poetry to various jours. Address: St Mary Coll Leavenworth KS 66048

MCGILVRAY, JOAN BAILEY, stockbroker; b. Monrovia, Calif., Nov. 4, 1926; d. William James and Helen Jane (Davis) Bailey; student Stanford U., 1944-47; divorced; children—Alexander Crane, Jr., Mark Rankin, Lynn. Asso. v.p. Dean Witter & Co., Pasadena, Calif., 1966-76; 1st v.p. Bateman Eichler Hill Richards, Los Angeles, 1976—. Mem. Nat. Options Soc. (founding dir.), So. Calif. Options Soc. (pres. 1978). Republican. Club: Live Oak Tennis. Office: 700 S Flower St Suite 2700 Los Angeles CA 90017

MCGINNIS, CYNTHIA WOLF, microbiologist; b. Lancaster, Pa., Jan. 17, 1949; d. H. LeMar and Rosemary A. (Snyder) Wolf; student Millersville Coll., 1979—. Staff technician St. Joseph Hosp., Lancaster, 1966-67; staff technician Lancaster Osteo. Hosp., 1968-72, microbiology supr., 1972—, mem. infection control com., 1973—; mem. adv. panel Med. Lab. Observer, 1979-81. Mem. Am. Med. Technologists, Am. Soc. Microbiology, Central Pa. Microbiology Assn., Pa. Soc. Med. Technologists, N.Y. Acad. Scis., Nat. Cert. Agy. Med. Lab. Personnel. Roman Catholic. Office: 1175 Clark St Lancaster PA 17604

MC GINNIS, NANCY SULLIVAN, communication cons. agy. exec.; b. Balt., Oct. 5, 1930; d. Leo Aloysius and Angeline (Stelmach) Sullivan; student U. Mo., Columbia, 1949, U. Minn., Mpls., 1949-51, U. Wash., 1982—; m. William H. McGinnis, Dec. 26, 1955 (dec. Nov. 1977); children—Shannon, Mary-Erin, Heather, Megan. Bus. editor Dayton's Mpls., 1951-55, Occidental Life Ins. Co., Los Angeles, 1956-57; sole propr. Killarney Cons., Creve Coeur, Mo., 1966—; lectr. in communications II, Washington U., St. Louis, 1973; lectr. in feature writing U. Mo., St. Louis, 1979, also various writers' workshops, Mem. Women in Communications, Internat. Assn. Bus. Communicators (accredited), Public Relations Soc. Am., Mensa. Home and office: 9934 NE 144th Ln #106 Bothell WA 98011

MCGINNISS, MARY HARRELL, research biologist; b. Washington, May 14, 1925; d. Cornelius Gay and Catherine Esther (Cowles) Harrell; A.B., Trinity Coll., 1947; m. W. Robert McGinniss, June 21, 1947; children—Patricia Ann, W. Robert, Mary Catherine. Research biologist Clin. Center Blood Bank, NIH, Bethesda, Md., 1956—; mem. grad. sch. faculty NIH. Mem. Commn. on Hereditary Diseases, State of Md., 1973-76; grounds com. chmn. Bethesda Ct. Condominium, 1979—. Recipient NIH Dir.'s award, 1977. Mem. Internat. Soc. Blood Transfusion, Am. Assn. Blood Banks (recipient Ivor Dunsford Meml. award 1977), Am. Soc. Clin. Pathologists, Mid-Atlantic Assn. Blood Banks. Democrat. Roman Catholic. Contbr. articles on immunohematology to profl. jours. Home: 10262 Arizona Circle Bethesda MD 20817 Office: Nat Inst Health Bethesda MD 20205

MCGINTY, DORIS EVANS, musicologist; b. Washington, Aug. 2, 1925; d. Charles and Vallean Judith (Richardson) Evans; B.Mus.Edn., Howard U., 1945, B.A., 1946; M.A., Radcliffe Coll., 1947; D.Phil., Lady Margaret Hall, Oxford (Eng.) U., 1954; m. Milton Oliver McGinty, Sept. 6, 1956; children—Derek Gordon, Dana Winston, Lisa Megan. Music librarian D.C. Public Library, 1943-46; mem. faculty Howard U., 1947—, prof. music, 1970—, chmn. dept., 1975—; mem. commn. and mgmt. bd. Howard U. Press, 1980—; trustee Sta. WETA-AM-TV, 1980—, D.C. Youth Chorale, 1970—; mem. edn. and community outreach com. Nat. Symphony Orch., 1978-81. Fulbright fellow, 1950-51, 51-52; fellow Caribbean-Am. Scholars Exchange, 1974. Mem. Am. Musicol. Soc. (past chpt. sec.), Assn. Study Afro-Am. Life and History, Delta Sigma Theta. Author articles in field; book rev. editor Black Perspective in Music, 1975—. Office: Howard U Music Dept 6th and Fairmont Sts NW Washington DC 20059

MCGINTY, JEAN LADELLE EPPERSON, educator, historian; b. Houston, Jan. 12, 1927; d. Thomas Marvin and Marguerite LaDelle (Mitchell) Epperson; B.S., U. Houston, 1957, M.Ed., 1973; m. Billy Baten McGinty, Jan. 20, 1947; children—Desiree LaDelle, Mia Colleen, Marla Marie. X-ray technician to pvt. physician, Houston, 1949-51; mem. staff Spectrographic Lab., Dickinson Gun Plant, Galena Park, Tex., 1951-53; tchr. Channelview (Tex.) Sch. Dist., 1960-62, tchr., ednl. psychologist Goose Creek Sch. Dist., Baytown, Tex., 1963—; pres. Texana Heritage Services, Dayton, Tex., 1982—. Mem. Tex. Ret. Tchrs. Assn., Chambers County Heritage Soc. (pres. 1976-82), Liberty County Hist. Commn., Houston Archeol. Soc. (sec.-treas. 1979-80), Tex. Archeol. Soc. Democrat. Unitarian. Contbr. articles on history to profl. jours.

MCGINTY, KATHY, social worker, counseling agy. dir.; b. Seattle, Jan. 31, 1946; d. Coy Wayne and Catherine (Sander) McG.; B.A. in Social Sci., Seattle U., 1968; M.S.W., St. Louis U., 1972. Joined Congregation of Sisters St. Joseph of Peace, Roman Cath. Ch., 1964; caseworker Cath. Children's Services, Seattle, 1968-70; counselor, grantwriter Cath. Community Services, Ketchikan, Alaska, 1972-77; dir. Cath. Community Resources, Fairbanks, Alaska, 1977-81, Fairbanks Counseling and Adoption Services, 1977—; mem. governing bd. Ketchikan Gen. Hosp. and Island View Nursing Home, Ketchikan Children's Home; mem. gov.'s adv. bd. Alaska Medicaid Program and chmn. early periodic screening diagnosis and treatment program for children; cons. to social service dept. Ketchikan Gen. Hosp. and Nursing Home, 1974-77; cons. and grantwriter S.E. Alaska Nutrition Program for Elderly, 1972-73, Ketchikan Alcoholism Program, 1973-74, Title III Program, 1972-74. S.E. Alaska Health Systems Agy., 1973-74, Community Edn. Programs Alaska Humanities Forum, 1974. Chmn. Fairbanks United Way Mem. Agys., 1982. Recipient United Way award, 1981. Mem. Nat. Assn. Social Workers (chmn. com. of inquiry Alaska chpt.), Nat. Assn. Clin. Social Workers, Acad. Cert. Social Workers. Home: Rosie Creek Rd PO Box 1544 Fairbanks AK 99707 Office: 1019 College Rd PO Box 1544 Fairbanks AK 99707

MCGIVERN, MARY ELIZABETH, chem. engr.; b. Parkersburg, W.Va., Jan. 28, 1954; d. William Edward and Glenda Louise (Bowers) McGivern; B.Chem.Engring., W. Va. U., 1975; M.B.A., U. Houston, 1982; m. James R. McKinley, Feb. 29, 1980. Process engr. Gulf Oil Chem. Co., Baytown, Tex., 1975-76, ops. specialist, 1976-79, zone supr., 1979-80, bus. analyst, Houston, 1980—. Vol. advisor Jr. Achievement, 1975-78. Recipient Woman of the Yr. award, YWCA, Houston, 1980. Mem. Houston Bus. Forum, Am. Inst. Chem. Engrs. Republican. Roman Catholic. Address: 5611 Arenas Timbers Humble TX 77346

MC GLASSON, CHRISTINE LOUISE, communications cons.; b. Glendale, Calif., Nov. 13, 1944; d. Howard Allen and Christine (Fee) McGlasson; B.A. in Radio and TV, Fla. State U., 1966; M.A. in Communications, Calif. State U., 1980; student Am. Acad. of Dramatic Arts, 1964. Asst. dir. of news program Sta. WFSU-TV, Fla. State U., Tallahassee, 1965-66, radio announcer Sta. WFSU-FM, 1964-66; copywriter and programming asst. Sta. WSB-AM-FM, Atlanta, Ga., 1966; continuity dir., announcer and promotion dir. Sta. KCTC, Sacramento, Calif., 1968-76; copy supr. and account exec. Brown, Clark & Elkus Co., Sacramento, 1972-73; writer and combl. producer for Sta. KCRA-TV, Sacramento, 1974-75; propr., creative dir. Chris McGlasson & Assos., Communications Cons., Sacramento, 1973—; mktg. dir. Rancho Murieta Properties, Inc., near Sacramento, 1976-80, also gen. mgr. Rancho Murieta Country Club, 1977-78; v.p. Miller, McGlasson & Baker, Inc., 1980—; guest lectr. on communications and broadcasting to local secondary schs. and jr. colls., 1972—; mgmt. cons. to various clubs and tng. seminars in Calif., 1977—; dir. Sacramento Better Bus. Bur., 1975-76. Broadcast chmn. Sacramento Red Cross, 1970-73; publicity chmn. Soc. for the Prevention of Cruelty to Animals, 1976-77; music festival chmn. Sacramento Symphony Assn., 1977—, bd. dirs., 1979—; mem. publicity com. Sacramento Opera Guild, 1977-79. Served to capt. USAF, 1966-70; maj. with Calif. State Info. Office Air NG, 1972—. Recipient Sacramento C. of C. award, 1970, Nat. Retail Advt. award, 1972, Am. Radio/TV Commls. awards (Clios), 1972-73, Am. Advt. Fedn. award, 1973, Calif. Assn. Realtors award (3), 1978, Superior Calif. Builders Assn. awards (4), 1978, 79; Cable Car awards San Francisco Ad Club, 1979; mktg. Dir. of Yr. award Superior Calif. Bldg. Industries, 1979; Appreciation awards for public service by various community and civic orgns., 1973-77; named Sacramento Advt. Person of Yr., 1974. Mem. Am. Acad. of Advt., Sacramento Advt. Club (past pres.; 60

awards for creativity 1971-80), Sacramento Women in Media, Sacramento Women in Advt., Women in Communications, Internat. Communications Assn., Sacramento Press Club, Nat. Guard Assn. Episcopalian. Contbr. feature articles to local publs. Home: 2805 Adirondack Way Sacramento CA 95827 Office: Chris McGlasson & Assos 9309 La Riviea Dr Suite C Sacramento CA 95826

MCGLAUN, RITHIA ANNA, educator; b. Webster County, Ga., Dec. 24, 1940; d. Charles Eugene and Anna (Pickett) McG.; B.A., Mercer U., 1962; postgrad. U. Leeds (Eng.), 1962-63; M.A., U. N.C. at Greensboro, 1965; postgrad. Emory U., 1969-71. Grad. asst. in English, U. N.C. at Greensboro, 1963-64; asst. prof. langs. dept. lang. and humanities Columbus (Ga.) Coll., 1966—; guest artist Musemont Fine Arts Camp, Jekyll Island, Ga., 1972. Marshall scholar, 1962. Mem. S. Atlantic MLA, Intercontinental Biog. Assn. (life), Nat. Trust Hist. Preservation, Am. Mus. Natural History, World Wildlife Fund. Baptist. Author: A Bright Compulsion—Poems, 1972. Home: 2120 Rosemont Dr Columbus GA 31904

MCGOLDRICK, BONNIE ANNETTE, word processing co. exec.; b. Bellingham, Wash., Apr. 28, 1943; d. Bert Alphonoso and Ella Ruth (Palmer) Tuor; student Western Wash. State U., 1961-62; m. John Mark McGoldrick, Dec. 26, 1964; 1 son, Mark Patrick. Supr. dishonored check sect. European Exchange System, Nuremberg, Ger., 1965-66; sec. The Boeing Co., Seattle, 1962-64, 66-68; self-employed sec., 1968-76; owner Secretarial Assistants, Seattle, 1976—, Tng. Sch., Seattle, 1982—. Mem. Secretarial Services Assn. (pres.), Women Bus. Owners, Seattle C. of C., Puget Sound Advt. Fedn. Roman Catholic. Clubs: Magnolia Community (sec.), Magnolia Comml., Rainbow Girls. Office: 2424 Bank of California Center Seattle WA 98164 also 3214A W McGraw St Seattle WA 98199

MCGOUGH, ALICE MARIE, chem. co. purchasing agt.; b. Tarentum, Pa., June 25, 1937; d. Edward Albert and Frances Amelia (Gross) Gase; B.A. magna cum laude, Carlow Coll., Pitts., 1957; postgrad. U. Pitts., 1958-59; children—Mary Gase, Paul Aidan, Daniel John. Research asst. in biophysics U. Pitts., 1957-59; lab. technician GAF Corp., Wayne, N.J., 1973, chems. buyer, 1973-76; buyer organic chems. div. Am. Cyanamid Co., Bound Brook, N.J., 1976-78, purchasing agt. materials planning and procurement div., 1978-81, purchasing agt. chems. group, 1981—. mem. exec. bd. LWV of Wayne Twp., N.J., 1969-72; vol. Paterson (N.J.) Task Force, Day Care Center, 1972. Mem. Smithsonian Assos. Democrat. Roman Catholic. Club: Sierra. Office: One Cyanamid Plaza Wayne NJ 07470

MCGOVERN, LAUREN MARYANNE, psychologist, electric co. exec.; b. Mpls., July 5, 1940; d. Earl Joseph and Luverne Marion (Ramgren) McG.; student Coll. of St. Catherine, 1958-60; B.S., U. Minn., 1962, M.A., 1968, Ph.D., 1974. Intern clin. psychology Hennepin County Med. Center, Mpls., 1974-75; sch. psychologist Mpls. Public Schs., 1975; pres. McGovern Assos., Mpls., 1975-78; corp. human resource cons. Westinghouse Electric Corp., Pitts., 1978—. Del., White House Conf. on Families, 1979-80. Lic. psychologist. Mem. Am. Psychol. Assn., Pa. Psychol. Assn., Minn. Psychol. Assn. Roman Catholic. Office: 11 Stanwix St Pittsburgh PA 15222

MCGOVERN, MAUREEN THERESE, singer, actress; b. Youngstown, Ohio, July 27, 1949; d. James T. and Mary Rita (Welsh) McG.; diploma Boardman (Ohio) High Sch., 1967. Recorded The Morning After, 1973, Can You Read My Mind, 1979, Different Worlds, 1979; cameo appearance in movie The Towering Inferno; appeared as singing nun in movie Airplane, 1979, as Mabel in stage play The Pirates of Penzance, N.Y.C., 1981—. Mem. Com. to Ratify ERA, Com. of Performing Artists for Nuclear Disarmament, Celebrity Com. of UNICEF. Recipient Grand prize Tokyo Music Festival, 1975. Mem. Actors Equity Assn., Screen Actors Guild, Am. Fedn. Musicians, AFTRA, Am. Soc. Composers and Performers. Composer (with lyricist Judy Barron) You Love Me Too Late, 1978, Thief In the Night, 1978, Don't Stop Now, 1979, (children's album) I Want to Learn to Fly, 1981. Office: 216 Chatsworth Dr San Fernando CA 91340

MCGOVERN, SHARON ANNE ANDERSON, aerospace exec.; b. San Angelo, Tex., Dec. 14, 1942; d. Harold Monroe and Helen Kathryn (Kirby) Anderson; B.S., E. Tex. State U., 1965, M.S., 1970; Ph.D., Ind. U., 1976; children—James Kirby. Univ. and public sch. tchr., 1965-74; process and nondestructive testing engr. Vought Corp., Dallas, 1974-77, tech. project mgr., advanced composites, 1977-80; mgr. advanced composite material and process engring. Northrop Corp., Hawthorne, Calif., 1980—. Ind. U. fellow, 1970-72, Nat. Inst. Neurol. Diseases and Stroke grantee, 1971-72. Mem. Soc. Advancement Materials and Process Engring., Soc. Women Engrs., LWV (treas. Rockwall, Tex. chpt. 1977-79). Office: 1 Northrop Ave Hawthorne CA 90250

MCGOVERN-HEHMAN, PATRICIA ELLEN, fin. writer, editor; b. N.Y.C., May 2, 1947; d. Albert Michael and Mary Francis (Broderick) McGovern; B.S., U. Dayton, 1970, M.A., 1973; m. Thomas W. Hehman, May 17, 1980; 1 dau., Marisa McGovern. Teaching asst. U. Dayton; instr. English schs. V.I., Jamaica, 1970-75; adminstrv. asst. Standard Security Life Ins. Co., 1976-77; research asst., fin. editor E.F. Hutton & Co., Inc., 1977-80; sr. fin. writer, editor Smith Barney, Harris Upham & Co., N.Y.C., 1980—; cons. E.F. Hutton & Co. Mem. AAUP, Nat. Assn. Female Execs. Republican. Roman Catholic. Contbr. articles to Portfolio Letter. Home: 301 E 78th St New York NY 10021 Office: 1345 Ave of Americas 47th Floor New York NY 10105

MCGOWAN, DIANNE ALICE, public relations specialist; b. Medford, Mass., Oct. 3, 1933; d. Clifton Otis and Esther Kathleen (Morang) Dyer; B.S., Boston U., 1955; m. Richard J. McGowan, 1957 (div. 1968); children—Michael Kevin, Matthew Richard. Asst. editor J. Walter Thompson, N.Y.C., 1955-57; editorial asst. St. Regis Paper Co., N.Y.C., 1957-58; co. publs. editor Acacia Mut. Life Ins. Co., 1962-69; promotion specialist U.S. Savs. Bond div. U.S. Dept. Treasury, 1969-74; mgr. women's activities Hwy. Users Fedn. Safety and Mobility, 1974-76; exec. dir. Md. Assn. Hwy. Safety Leaders, 1977-79; pres. McGowan Assos. Public Relations, 1977—. Mem. Md. Transp. Fedn. (sec.), Internat. Assn. Bus. Communicators, Washington Soc. Assn. Execs., Nat. Assn. Women Bus. Owners, Nat. Restaurant Assn., Nat. Safety Council, Md. Assn. Hwy. Safety Leaders (pres.; state rep. Nat. Assn.). Club: Soroptomist Internat. Home: Ocean Pines Box 2891 Berlin MD 21811

MCGOWAN, ELISSA MARGARET, mfg. co. exec.; b. N.Y.C., Aug. 25, 1939; d. Francis Joseph and Mildred Carmel (Gisondi) McG.; student N.Y. U., 1958-60. Fashion model, 1959-63; law sec., 1964-70; corp. sec. Basic Resources Corp., N.Y.C., 1970—; dir. Phila. Printing Properties, Inc., 1977—. Mem. Am. Soc. Corp. Secs. Home: 401 E 80th St New York NY 10021 Office: 595 Madison Ave New York NY 10022

MCGOWAN, JAN CAROL, nurse; b. Evansville, Ind., Oct. 20, 1953; d. Robert Eugene and Mary Edith (Nicholson) McG.; B.S. in Nursing, U. Evansville, 1975, M.S., 1978. With St. Mary's Hosp., Rochester, Minn., 1975-76; with CCU, Welborn Hosp., Evansville, Ind., 1976-78; instr. emergency room, emergency med. technician Deaconess Hosp. Sch. Nursing, Evansville, Ind., 1978—; instr. CPR. Cert. advanced cardiac life support. Mem. Emergency Dept. Nurses Assn., Tri-State Emergency Med. Technician Assn., Phi Mu, Alpha Tau Delta. Home: 2135 Mahrendale Evansville IN 47714 Office: 600 Edgar St Evansville IN 47710

MCGOWAN, KATHLEEN KEER, artist; b. Newark, Mar. 8, 1918; d. Theodore F. and Florence (MacRae) Keer; B.A., Smith Coll., 1940; postgrad. Columbia U., 1943, N.J. Tchrs. Coll., 1946-49; m. B.C. Breeden, June 29, 1940 (div. 1943); 1 dau., Kathy; m. 2d, Harold F. Allenby, July 28, 1949 (div. 1977); m. 3d, John Francis McGowan, Apr. 24, 1981. Kindergarten tchr. Kimberly Sch., Montclair, N.J., 1946-49; tchr. art to handicapped Kessler Inst. Rehab., West Orange, N.J., 1961-77. Exhibited one-man shows Woman's Club Montclair, 1st Savs. & Loan Bank, Cedar Grove, N.J., Music Sch., Cedar Grove, Piggins Art Gallery, Montclair, N.J., all 1972; 2-man show 1st Nat. Bank of Palm Beach, 1978; exhibited in group shows N.J. State Fedn. Women's Clubs, Art Center of Oranges. Leader, Girl Scouts U.S.A., Little Falls, N.J., 1955-56; social dir. PTA, Great Notch, N.J., 1955-56. Recipient art awards Upper Montclair Women's Club; cert. of merit in art N.J. Fedn. Women's Clubs, 1st pl. essay award, 1973. Mem. Art Center Oranges, West Essex Art Assn., N.J. State Fedn. Women's Clubs (7th dist. art chmn. 1973-74), West Palm Beach Coin Club (sec. 1978-81). Clubs: Glen Ridge Country (N.J., handicap chmn. 1970, past publicity chmn. women's golf group); Upper Montclair Women's (dir. art dept. 1971-72, garden chmn. 1976-77); Little Falls Women's (treas. 1959-61); Beach (Palm Beach); Smith of the Palm Beaches (treas. 1976-77); Palm Beach Yacht; Indian Springs Golf (Jupiter, Fla.). Home: Apt 303 The Waterford 603 South US Hwy 1 Juno Beach FL 33408

MCGOWAN-SASS, BRENDA KATHLEEN (MRS. ROBERT CARL SASS), neuropsychologist; b. Winchester, Mass., May 23, 1939; d. Thomas Patrick and Katharine Louise (Regan) McGowan; B.A., Northeastern U., 1962; M.S., U. Mass., 1965, Ph.D., 1967; postgrad. U. Geneva, 1964; m. Robert Carl Sass, Oct. 18, 1969; children—Taryn Elizabeth, Kira Anne. Research psychologist Stanley Cobb Labs., Mass. Gen. Hosp., Boston, 1964-65; research fellow in psychiatry Harvard Med. Sch., Boston, 1966-68; research asso. div. neurobiology Barrow Neurol. Inst., Phoenix, 1968-70; research asso. dept. physiology, anatomy U. Calif. at Berkeley, 1971-75, cons. to program in Med. Health Scis.; cons. Miramonte Mental Health Center, Palo Alto, Calif., 1976-77, Blossom Hill Mental Health Center, San Jose, Calif., 1977; clin. psychologist Santa Clara County Mental Health, San Jose, 1978—; pvt. practice clin. psychology, San Jose and Morgan Hill, Calif., 1979—. Bd. dirs. The Bridge Counseling Center, 1980—. Recipient Abram Aaron Levy award, 1962. Mem. Am., Western psychol. assns. Contbr. articles on neurobiology to sci. jours. Home: 13900 Sheila Ave Morgan Hill CA 95037

MC GOWEN, CAROLYN LEWIS, oil and gas exploration co. exec.; b. Nashville, Dec. 27, 1940; d. Thurman DeLois and Juanita Mills Manley; student U. Houston, 1976; m. Bill S. McGowen, Nov. 24, 1962; children—Robert William, Thurman Payton, Joseph Kenton, Melissa Carol. Lic. vocat. nurse Sadler Clinic, Conroe, Tex., 1975-78; co-owner, exec. adminstrv. asst. McGowen Exploration Co., Houston, 1978—; exec. v.p. McGowen Oil & Gas Co., Houston, 1976—; v.p. BSMI, Inc., Houston, 1980—. Mem. Lic. Vocat. Nurse Nursing Assn. Republican. Club: Houstonian.

MCGRADY, ANN LORRAINE, child devel. adminstr.; b. New Haven, May 16, 1947; d. John and Lena Abbate; B.Ed., Radford Coll., 1972, M.S., 1975; student Va. Poly. Inst. and State U., 1976—; m. Joseph H. McGrady, Jan. 1969; children—Jonathan, Chadwick. Tchr., Ft. Lauderdale (Fla.) Research Lab. for Mentally Retarded Children, 1965-67; tchr. Little Flower Montessori Sch., Orange, Conn., 1967-68; master tchr. Carroll County Head Start Center, 1972-73; kindergarten tchr. Hillsville Elem. Sch., 1973-75; kindergarten cons., mem. task force for Kindergarten for Carroll County, Va., 1972-76; tchr. Hillsville (Va.) Elem. Sch., 1976-77; dir. Carroll-Grayson-Galax Early Childhood Devel. Program, Inc., Hillsville, Va., 1977-81; child devel. specialist, sr. social worker Carroll County Dept. Social Services, Hillsville, 1981—. Chmn., Carroll County Human Services Advocate Adv. Com., 1976—; bd. dirs. Planning Dist. 3 Subarea Health Council Southwest Va. Health Systems Agy. Inc., 1969-71; leader Blue Ridge council Girl Scouts Am., 1969-71; neighborhood chmn. Mother's March, March of Dimes, Knoxville, Tenn., 1967—. Recipient awards for outstanding leadership. Mem. Va. Edn. Assn., NEA, Carroll Edn. Assn., Am. Assn. Elem., Kindergarten and Nursery Sch. Educators, So. Assn. for Children Under Six, Va. Assn. Early Childhood Edn., Delta Kappa Gamma. Christian. Home: Route 2 Box 15 Hillsville VA 24343 Office: Carroll-Grayson-Galax Early Childhood Devel Program Inc PO Box 68 Hillsville VA 24343

MCGRATH, CORA ELISIA, educator; b. Mora, N.Mex., Apr. 29, 1922; d. Tom and Guadalupe McG.; student Hunter Coll., summer 1943, Okla. A&M U., 1943, N.Mex. Highlands U., 1940-43, 62-80, B.A., 1964, M.A., 1967; postgrad. U. N.Mex., 1969-70; m. George O. Maloof, Dec. 23, 1943; children—Wardie J. Hennessy, George O., Zian H. Swanson. Tchr., Guadalupe County, N.Mex., 1942-43; tchr. West Las Vegas Schs., 1964-69, 70-79, 80-82, dir. spl. edn., 1979-80; tchr. Albuquerque City Schs., 1969-70; ret., 1982. Democratic precinct chairwoman; presiding election judge; mem. San Miguel County Central Com.; commd. dep. sheriff; mem. E. Romero Hose and Fire Dept. Aux.; leader 4-H, Girl Scouts; den mother Boy Scouts Am.; dist. rep. PTA. Roman Catholic. Club: Order of Does. Composer songs. Served with USNR, World War II. Mem. Council for Exceptional Children, Retarded Children Assn., Internat. Reading Assn., NEA, Am. Legion, Nat. League Am. Pen Women, DAV.

MCGRATH, LUCILLE MARIE, mfg. co. exec.; b. Milbank, S.D., Feb. 10, 1951; d. Victor Frank and Irene Clara (Reiffenberger) Stolpman; B.A., U. Minn. (scholar), 1973; postgrad. U. Calif., Santa Barbara, 1973-76. Buyer, mech., also integrated mfg. systems adminstr. Raytheon Electromagnetic Systems Div., Goleta, Calif., 1976; buyer ITT Barton Instruments, City of Industry, Calif., 1976-79; sr. buyer electronics Perkin-Elmer Memory Products Div., Garden Grove, Calif., 1979-80; sr. purchasing agt. electronics BASF Video Corp., Fountain Valley, Calif., 1980; commodity purchasing mgr. Def. and Space Systems Group, TRW, Redondo Beach, Calif., 1980—. Mem. Nat. Assn. Purchasing Mgrs. (dir. Santa Barbara 1975-76). Democrat. Home: 323 E 68th St Long Beach CA 90805 Office: One Space Park Redondo Beach CA 90278

MCGRATH, SAREPTA ROYAN, med. supplies co. exec.; b. Oklahoma City, May 28, 1957; d. William R. and Royetta R. McG.; student Tex. Tech U., 1981. Adminstrv. sec. U. Tex. Health Sci. Center, Dallas, 1977-79; tech. sales rep. Cardiovascular Systems Inc., San Antonio, 1979-81; owner, operator Cardiovascular Spltys., Inc., Lubbock, Tex., 1981—. Mem. Am. Bus. Women's Assn. Republican. Episcopalian. Office: PO Box 64906 Lubbock TX 79464

MCGRATH, SYLVIA FREEMAN WALLACE, educator; b. Montpelier, Vt., Feb. 27, 1937; d. George John and Martha Eloise (Cooper) Wallace; B.A., Mich. State U., 1959; M.A., Radcliffe Coll., 1960; Ph.D., U. Wis., 1966; m. W. Thomas McGrath, June 11, 1966; children—Sandra Jean, Charles George. Tchr., Falmouth (Mass.) Public Schs., 1960-61, Marin County Day Sch., Courte Madera, Calif., 1961-62; with U. Wis., 1962-66; asst. prof. history Stephen F. Austin State U., 1968-73, asso. prof., 1973—. Bd. elders Westminister Presbyn. Ch., Nacogdoches, 1975-80. Grantee in field. Mem. Orgn. Am. Historians, So. Hist. Assn., History Sci. Soc., State Hist. Soc. Wis., So. Assn. Women Historians, Tex. Assn. Coll. Tchrs., Women in Tech. History. Author: Charles Kenneth Leith, 1971; contbr. articles to profl. jours. Home: 216 N Mound St Nacogdoches TX 75961 Office: PO Box 13013 Stephen Austin U Nacogdoches TX 75962

MCGRAW, MARY HOLLAND, educator; b. Ardmore, Okla., May 12, 1920; d. Ray T. and Ida E. (Duston) Holland; student E. Central U., 1938-40; B.A. in English, U. Okla., 1947, M.A. in English, 1956; Ph.D. in English, Okla. State U., 1979; m. DeLoss McGraw, Apr. 12, 1944 (div., 1947); 1 son, DeLoss Holland. Tchr. English and speech, Okemah (Okla.) High Sch., 1947-64; faculty English dept. E. Central U., Ada, Okla., 1964—, asso. prof., 1980—. Participant Women's Mental Health Conf., 1982; active Christian Sci. Ch. Served with USN, 1941-44. Mem. S. Central MLA, Delta Kappa Gamma (pres., 1980, 82, grantee, 1975), Sigma Tau Delta, Phi Delta Kappa. Democrat. Clubs: Am. Legion, Order Amaranth (historian, 1979-81). Home: 1100 E 18th St Ada OK 74820 Office: E Central Univ Ada OK 74820

MCGREAL, MARIANNE KELLY, banker; b. Chgo., Feb. 24, 1935; d. Frank J. and Esther M. (O'Keefe) Kelly; 1 dau., Denise McGreal Sheston. With Heritage Standard Bank, 1958-65, Heritage Pullman Bank, 1965-66; with Heritage County Bank and Trust Co., Blue Island, Ill., 1966—, public relations officer, sec. to pres., 1971-77, personnel officer, 1977—. Asst. to chmn. Radio Free Europe, Chgo., 1967-68; asst. to chmn. Crusade of Mercy, 1967-72. Mem. Ill. Bank Women. Office: 12015 S Western Ave Blue Island IL 60406

MCGREEVY, SUSAN BROWN, mus. dir.; b. Chgo., Jan. 28, 1934; d. Irving Leslie and Edna (Joselit) Colby; student Mt. Holyoke Coll., 1951-53; B.A. with honors, Roosevelt U., 1969; M.A., Northwestern U., 1971; m. Thomas J. Mc Greevy, June 16, 1973; children by previous marriage—Patricia Leigh Brown, Lori Alyn Brown, Cynthia Diane Brown. Curator, N. Am. ethnology Kansas City Mus. History & Sci., 1975-77; curator of collections Wheelwright Mus. Am. Indian, Santa Fe, 1978, mus. dir., 1978—. Fellow Am. Anthrop. Assn., Soc. Applied Anthropology; mem. Am. Assn. Mus., N.Mex. Mus. Assn., Am. Soc. for Ethnohistory, Council for Mus. Anthropology. Office: Wheelwright Museum PO Box 5153 704 Camino Lejo Santa Fe NM 87502

MCGREGOR, AUDREY ANN, mfg. co. exec.; b. Guttenberg, Iowa, Mar. 11; d. Reuben and Evelyn (Baldwin) Kuempel; student U. Minn.; m. Donald William McGregor, June 21, 1945; children—Carolyn McGregor McMahon, Mary Jean. Pres., owner Kuempel Chime Clock Works, Inc., Excelsior, Minn., 1970—. Pres. Mpls. Women's Christian Assn., 1977-79; pres. trustees Hennepin Ave. United Methodist Ch., Mpls., 1981-82. Republican. Club: Mpls. Women's (dir. 1982-83). Home: 19940 Lakeview Ave Excelsior MN 55331 Office: 21195 Minnetonka Blvd Excelsior MN 55331

MCGREGOR, GEORGETTE FOSTER, educator, mgmt. cons.; b. Lincoln, Nebr., June 27, 1917; d. George Nimmons and Esther Mosher (Burritt) Foster; A.B., UCLA, 1938, Ed.D., 1949; M.S., Syracuse U., 1940; m. John Porter McGregor, July 25, 1942. Head dept. fine arts prodns. and public lectures UCLA, 1951-58, prof. effective speech, 1949-69; cons. mgmt. Bank of Am., San Francisco, 1959—; star tng. film Applause, 1977. Bd. dirs. San Diego Symphony, 1970-74, San Diego Opera, 1975—. Mem. Theta Sigma Phi, Pi Lambda Theta. Republican. Author: (with Joseph A. Robinson) The Communication Matrix (Ways of Winning with Words), 1981; also booklets in field. Address: 17323 Campillo Dr San Diego CA 92128

MCGRIFF, ERLINE PERKINS, educator; b. Petersburg, Va., Feb. 18, 1924; d. Thomas Dunlop and Bessie May (Webb) Perkins; B.S. in Nursing Edn. Catholic U. Am., 1950, M.S. in Nursing Edn., 1953; Ed.D., Tchrs. Coll. Columbia U., 1967; m. Vern Holt McGriff, Sept. 22, 1965. Staff nurse Sibley Meml. Hosp., Washington, 1945-50, head nurse, 1950-51, supr., 1951-56, clin. instr., 1951-56; asso. dir. nursing services Med. Coll. Va., Richmond, 1956-63, asst. prof. nursing, 1956-63; profl. staff asst. Am. Nurses Assn., N.Y.C., 1965-67; lectr. Tchrs. Coll. Columbia U., 1967-69; asst. prof. nurse edn. N.Y. U., 1969-71, asso. prof., 1971-73; prof. Trenton State Coll., 1973-75, also asso. dean; prof., head div. nursing N.Y. U., 1975-82. Commr. N.Y.C. Tchr. Coll., Bklyn., 1979—. McLeod-Smith fellow, 1963-64, Isabel Hampton Robb fellow, 1965; HEW-USPHS grantee, 1971-74, 77-80. Fellow Am. Acad. Nursing, Am. Nurses Assn.; mem. Nat. League Nursing, AAUP, AAUW, Soc. Advancement Nursing, Inc., Nursing Edn. Alumni Assn. Tchrs. Coll. Columbia U. (pres. 1974-76), N.Y. State Nurses Assn., Sigma Theta Tau, Pi Lambda Theta, Kappa Delta Pi. Democrat. Contbr. articles in field to profl. jours. Office: 429 Shimkin Hall New York University Washington Square New York NY 10003

MCGRORY, M. KATHLEEN, edнl. adminstr.; b. N.Y.C.; d. Patrick Joseph and Mary K. (Gilvary) McG.; student Coll. of White Plains, 1951-56; B.A., Pace U., 1957; M.A., U. Notre Dame, 1962; Ph.D., Columbia U., 1969; L.H.D. (hon.), Albertus Magnus Coll., 1981. Asst. registrar Coll. of White Plains, N.Y., 1958-62, asso. prof. English, 1958-69; prof. English, Western Conn. State Coll., Danbury, 1969-78; dean of arts and scis. Eastern Conn. State U., Willimantic, 1978-81, v.p. acad. affairs, 1981—; ednl. cons., communications, 1972—; mem. commn. on instns. of higher edn. New Eng. Assn. Schs. and Colls., 1979—; chmn. Conn. Humanities Council, 1982—. Community adv. council Windham Public Schs./Tchr. Corps, 1979—; bd. dirs. Northeastern Conn. Rape Crisis Center, 1980—, Sr. Job Placement Center, 1981—. Samuel Fels Found. fellow, 1966-67; Ludwig Vogelstein Found. grantee, 1973; N.Y. State Regents Doctoral fellow, 1963-67. Mem. MLA, Medieval Acad. Am., James Joyce Found., AAUW (pres. Danbury chpt. 1975-77), N.E. MLA, Assn. for Advancement of Humanities, Acad. Affairs Adminstrs. Dir., gen. editor James Joyce Cassette Series, 1978—; asso. editor Am. Orthopedic Assn. Jour. of Sports Medicine, 1974-76; author: Yeats, Joyce and Beckett, 1975; contbr. articles to Ency. of Modern Biography, scholarly articles to publs. Office: 83 Windham St Willimantic CT 06226

MCGRORY, MARY, newspaperwoman; b. Boston, 1918; d. Edward Patrick and Mary (Jacobs) McG.; A.B., Emmanuel Coll. Reporter, Boston Herald Traveler, 1942-47; book reviewer Washington Star, 1947-54, feature writer for nat. staff, 1954-81; syndicated columnist. Recipient George Polk Meml. award; Pulitzer prize for commentary, 1975. Office: UPI 220 E 42d St New York NY 10017 *

MCGUINNESS, ADELAIDE HELEN, mgmt. cons.; b. Yonkers, N.Y., Mar. 19, 1932; d. James John and Adeline Isabelle (Kern) Kavanaugh; ed. Pa. State U.; div.; children—Kevin, Darcy. Sales coordinator Coppercraft Guild subsidiary Armor Bronze & Silver, Taunton, Mass., 1960-62; co-originator, sales mgr. Princess House, North Dighton, Mass., 1962-64, nat. v.p. sales, 1964-78; mgmt. cons., 1981—; dir. G.A. Rogers Inc., North Dighton, Baybank United, Taunton, Mass., 1978, 79. Mem. Internat. Platform Assn. Home: 501 Fletcher Rd North Kingstown RI 02852

MCGUIRE, CATHERINE, lawyer; b. Patuxant River, Md., Nov. 24, 1948; d. Walter John, Jr. and Helen Elizabeth (Suiter) McG.; A.B., U. Mich., 1970; J.D., U. Kans., 1973. Admitted to Kans. bar, 1973; with SEC, 1973—, asst. dir. div. market regulation, 1979-82, legal asst. to commr., 1982—. Office: 500 N Capitol St Washington DC 20549

MCGUIRE, GERTRUDE MYNEAR, ednl. adminstr.; b. Nicholas County, Ky., May 12, 1939; d. John Cecil and Mary Keller (Sanders) Mynear; B.A., Union Coll., 1961; A.A., Midway Coll., 1959; M.A.,

Eastern Ky. U., 1967; Ed.D., U. Tenn., 1970; postgrad. in higher edn. adminstrn. Bryn Mawr Coll., 1980; m. Robert Frank McGuire, June 16, 1962. Sec., Fountain City United Meth. Ch., Knoxville; Tenn., 1961-63; instr. office adminstrn. Eastern Ky. U., Richmond, 1964-67; grad. teaching asst. U. Tenn., Knoxville, 1967-70, coordinator student teaching, 1969-70; asso. prof. bus. Knoxville Coll., 1970-71; asso. prof. bus. U. Montevallo (Ala.), 1971-79, prof., 1979-80, asst. to pres. for faculty-staff relations, prof. bus., 1980—, Univ. scholar, 1978-79; state coordinator Am. Council Edn.'s Nat. Identification Program for Women in Higher Edn. Adminstrn. Pres., Montevallo United Meth. Women, 1975, exec. bd., 1973-75, 1977-78, 1982; mem. First United Meth. Ch. Adminstrv. Bd., 1971—. Mem. Nat. Bus. Edn., So. Bus. Edn. Assn., Ala. Bus. Edn. Assn. (treas. 1982—), Am. Bus. Communication Assn., Ala. Bus. Communication Assn., AAUW (pres. Montevallo br., 1980-82, Ala. div. nominating com., 1982-83, standing rules chmn., 1982), Ala. Assn. Women Deans, Adminstrs. and Counselors, Union Coll. Alumni Assn. (dir. 1977-81), Delta Pi Epsilon, Phi Chi Theta, Sigma Alpha Sigma. Clubs: Civitan, Ala. Conservancy. Home: 224 Sequoia Montevallo AL 35115 Office: Station 143 U Montevallo Montevallo AL 35115

MCGUIRE, JENNIE RAE, ct. reporter; b. Chgo., Apr. 2, 1953; d. William D. and Marilyn R. McGuire; A.A., MacCormac Jr. Coll., Chgo., 1973. Ct. reporter Hartnett & Catellani Co., Chgo., 1973-75; founder, pres., co-owner Morrissy & McGuire Ct. Reporting Services, Chgo., 1975-77; pres., owner McGuire, Inc., 1977—; sole owner McGuire's Reporting Service div. McGuire, Inc. Mem. Nat. Shorthand Reporters Assn., Chgo. Exchange Reporters Assn., Original Reporters Assn. Democrat. Roman Catholic. Home: 745 S East Ave Oak Park IL 60304 Home: 400 E Randolph Chicago IL 60601 Office: 189 W Madison Chicago IL 60602

MCGUIRE, MARGARET JEANNE, mktg. mgr.; b. Pittsburg, Kans., Oct. 15, 1950; d. Edward and Margaret (Matthews) Schuberger; B.S., Pittsburg State U., 1971; m. William F. McGuire, Nov. 27, 1968 (div. Aug. 1976); 1 dau., Shelly Anne. Loan processor Regional Investment Co., Kansas City, Mo., 1971-73; asst. v.p., br. mgr. Amortibanc, Inc. Kansas City, Mo., 1973-75; dir. corporate services Eugene D. Brown Co., Kansas City, Mo., 1975-77; Western region mgr. homesearch div. Executrans, Inc., 1977-79; mktg. mgr. NJR Corp. Mountain View, Calif., 1979-82; mktg. mgr. PULNIX Am., Inc., Mountain View, 1982—; dir. Seeker Security Systems, Inc., 1980—; partner T.J. Schuberger Assos., Sunnyvale, Calif. 1980—. Sec. bd. dirs. Home Owners Assn., 1978-79, pres., 1980. Mem. Am. Soc. Indsl. Security, Nat. Assn. Female Execs. Office: 453-F Ravendale Dr Mountain View CA 94043

MCGUIRE, SANDRA LYNN, educator; b. Flint, Mich., Jan. 28, 1947; d. Donald Armstrong and Mary Lue (Harvey) Johnson; B.S.N., U. Mich., 1969, M.P.H., 1973; m. Joseph L. McGuire, Mar. 6, 1976; children—Matthew, Kelly, Kerry. Staff nurse Univ. Hosp., Ann Arbor, Mich., 1969; public health nurse Wayne County Health Dept., Eloise, Mich., 1969-72; instr. Madonna Coll., Livonia, Mich., 1973; public health coordinator Plymouth Center for Human Devel., Northville, Mich., 1974-75; asst. prof. community health nursing Sch. Nursing, U. Mich., Ann Arbor, 1975—; resource person Gov.'s Com. Unification of Mental Health Services in Mich.; speaker profl. assns. and workshops. USPHS fellow, 1972-73. Mem. Nat., Mich. leagues nursing, Am., Mich. (chmn. mental health sect. 1976) public health assns., Nat., Mich. (dir., co-chmn. residential services com. 1976-79, chmn. health services 1979-82), Plymouth (chmn. residential services com. 1975-77) assns. retarded citizens, Sigma Theta Tau. Author: (with S. Clemen. and D. Eigsti) Comprehensive Family and Community Health Nursing, 1981. Home: 9347 Silver Maple Whitmore Lake MI 48189 Office: 400 N Ingalls Ann Arbor MI 48109

MCGUIRE-RASKIN, LINDA SPEER, clin. psychologist; b. Spokane, Wash., Feb. 12, 1944; d. Austin N. and Virginia M. (Mohrmann) Speer; B.A. magna cum laude, U. Wash., Seattle, 1965, M.S., 1967, Ph.D., 1973; m. David E. Raskin, Sept. 25, 1978; children—Ramona, Aaron. Instr. dept. Ob-Gyn, Sch. Medicine, U. Wash., Seattle, 1973-74, asst. prof., 1974-79, now asso. clin. prof., asst. prof. dept. psychiatry, 1974-79; pvt. practice clin. psychology, Seattle; cons. Title VII, Garfield High Sch., Sexual Assault Center, Wash. State Heart Assn.; research cons. to depts. urology and infectious disease, U. Wash.; expert witness women's health care issues. Rockefeller Found. postdoctoral research grantee. Mem. Am. Assn. Sex Educators, Counselors and Therapists (pres. Wash. chpt.), Wash. State Psychol. Assn. (exec. bd., 1977-79), AAUP, Phi Beta Kappa. Contbr. articles in field to profl. publs. Home: 1649 Federal Ave E Seattle WA 98102 Office: 914 2nd Ave Seattle WA 98102

MCGUIRI, MARLENE DANA, lawyer, educator, librarian; b. Hammond, Ind., Mar. 22, 1938; d. Daniel David and Helen Elizabeth (Baludis) Callis; A.B., Ind. U., 1956; J.D., DePaul U., 1963; M.A. in Library Sci., Rosary Coll., 1965; LL.M., George Washington U., 1978; m. James Franklin McGuirl, Apr. 24, 1965. Law library asst. DePaul Coll. Law Library, 1961-62, asst. law librarian, 1962-65; admitted to Ill. bar, 1963, Ind. bar, 1964, D.C. bar, 1972; reference law librarian Boston Coll. Sch. Law Library, 1965-66; law librarian D.C. Bar Library, 1966-70; library cons. Nat. Clearinghouse on Poverty Law, OEO, 1967-69, Northwestern U. Nat. Inst. for Edn. in Law and Poverty, 1969, D.C. Office Corp. Counsel, 1969-70; instr. legal librarianship Grad. Sch., Dept. Agr., 1968; lectr. legal lit., law for librarians, advanced legal lit. grad. dept. library sci., Cath. U., 1972-73, adj. asst. prof., 1973—; asst. chief Am.-Brit. law div. Library Congress Law Library, Washington, 1970, div. chief, 1970—; instr. Ph.D. program in Am. civilization George Washington U., 1976, 79, lectr. environ. law, 1979—; pres. Hamburger Heaven, Inc., Palm Beach, Fla., 1981—. Mem. Georgetown Citizens Assn.; del. Ind. Democratic Conv., 1964; trustee D.C. Law Students in Ct. Recipient Meritorious Service cash award Library Congress, 1974. Mem. Am. (facilities of Law Library of Congress com. 1976-81), Fed. (mem. council Capitol Hill chpt. 1972-76), Ill., D.C. (inter-Am. bar relations com. 1968-70, memls. com. 1969-70), Women's (treas. 1970-72, pres. 1972-73, exec. bd. 73-77, parliamentarian 1975, chmn. constn. and by-laws com. 1975-76) bar assns., D.C. Bar (election bd. 1973-75, specialization com. 1975-76), Am. Bar Found. (library service com. 1969-72), Nat. Assn. Women Lawyers (co-chmn. legis. com. 1976-77), Internat. (program chmn. 1974), Am. (co-chmn. stats. com. 1970-72, chmn. legis. and legal devels. 1972-73, exec. bd. 1973-77, chmn. indexing periodical lit. com. 1979-82) assns. law libraries, Law Librarians Soc. Washington (pres. 1971-73), Brit. and Irish Assn. Law Librarians, Assn. Am. Library Schs. (prison libraries com. 1975-76), Exec. Women in Govt. Clubs: Nat. Lawyers, Zonta. Contbr. articles to profl. jours. Home: 3416 P St NW Washington DC 20007 Office: Law Library Am-Brit Law Div Library Congress Washington DC 20540

MCHALE, MAGDA CORDELL, educator; b. June 24, 1921; widow. Mem. staff Center Integrative Studies, SUNY, Binghamton, Center Integrative Studies, U. Houston 1977-79; mem. staff Center Integrative Studies, SUNY, Buffalo, 1980—, dir. Sch. Architecture and Environ. Design; artist and designer. Grantee UNESCO, Center Econ. and Social Studies of 3d World, Population Reference Bur., Aspen Inst., Hubert H. Humphrey Inst. Public Affairs. Fellow Royal Soc. Arts; mem. N.Y. Acad. Scis., World Future Studies Fedn. (v.p.), Futuribles Assn. Internat. (dir.), World Future Soc. Author articles, papers, reports in field. Editorial bd. profl. publs. Office: 108 Hayes Hall SUNY Buffalo NY 14214

MC HUGH, ARONA LIPMAN, author; b. Boston, Aug. 8, 1924; d. Nathaniel and Miriam (Bahn) Lipman; B.A., U. Iowa, 1950; M.S., Columbia U., 1951, M.A., 1953; m. Warren McHugh, Dec. 27, 1950; children—Michael Warren, Jonathan Adam. First asst. research and reference librarian New Sch. Social Research, 1951-53; children's librarian N.Y. Pub. Library, 1954-56; mem. staff Georgetown U. Writer's Conf., 1972, Wesleyan U. Writers Conf., 1981; lectr. on creative writing Boston U., 1980; author: (novels) A Banner with a Strange Device, 1964, The Seacoast of Bohemia, 1965, The Van Meers: A Tradition, 1969, The Calling of the Mercenaries, 1973; A Novel of the Sea; also essays. Served with WAC, 1944-48. Bernard de Voto fellow in fiction writing, 1967; MacDowell Colony fellow, 1969; Edward Albee Found. fellow, 1972. Mem. PEN, Authors Guild. Office: care Paul Reynolds Lit Agy 12 E 41st St New York NY 10019

MCHUGH, CAROL MORGAN, consumer products co. mgr.; b. Bryn Mawr, Pa., Dec. 24, 1953; d. George Hussey and Katherine (Jennings) Morgan; B.A. magna cum laude in Mktg., Glassboro State Coll., 1976; m. Thomas Peter McHugh, Oct. 13, 1979. Ter. mgr. for central N.J., McNeil Consumer Products Co., Elizabeth, 1976-78, ter. mgr., sales trainer for met. dist., Allentown, Pa., 1979-80, sales mgr. Phila. unit, 1980, dist. sales mgr., Ft. Washington, Pa., 1981-82, mgr. sales tng., 1982, dist. mgr. N.Y. dist., 1982—. Recipient 1st pl. Ring Club award McNeil Consumer Products Co., 1977, 78. Mem. Am. Mgmt. Assn., Nat. Assn. Female Execs. Roman Catholic. Office: McNeil Consumer Products Co Camp Hill Rd Fort Washington PA 19034

MCHUGH, HELEN FRANCES, economist, univ. dean; b. Tucson, Aug. 19, 1931; d. James Patrick and Mary Catherine (Hochstatter) McHugh; B.S. with distinction, U. Mo., Columbia, 1958, M.S., 1959; Ph.D., Iowa State U., 1965. Instr., U. Tex., Austin, 1961-63, asst. prof., 1963-66, asso. prof., 1966-67; asso. prof. Ind. State U., Terre Haute, 1967-69; asso. prof., dept. head Oreg. State U., Corvallis, 1969-73; prof., dean Coll. Home Econs., U. Del., Newark, 1973-75; prof. consumer econs., dean Coll. Home Econs., asso. dir. Colo. Experiment Sta., Colo. State U., Ft. Collins, 1976—; cons. in field. Recipient Disting. Service award U. Mo. Alumni Assn., 1975. Mem. Am. Econ. Assn., Am. Agrl. Econs. Assn., Am. Home Econs. Assn. (bd. dirs. 1973-75), Assn. Adminstrs. Home Econs. (pres. 1978-79), Sigma Xi, Gamma Sigma Delta, Phi Kappa Phi. Roman Catholic. Chmn. policy bd. Jour. Consumer Research, 1978-80. Office: 104 Gifford Bldg Colo State U Fort Collins CO 80523

MC HUGH, MARGARET ANN GLOE, therapist; b. Salt Lake City, Nov. 8, 1920; d. Harold Henry and Olive (Warenski) Gloe; B.A., U. Utah, 1942; M.A. in Counseling and Guidance, Idaho State U., 1964; Ph.D. in Counseling Psychology, U. Oreg., 1970; m. William T. McHugh, Oct. 1, 1943; children—Mary Margaret McHugh Shuford, William Michael, Michelle. Tchr. kindergarten, Idaho Falls, Idaho, 1951-62, tchr. high sch. English, 1962-63; counselor Counseling Center, Idaho State U., Pocatello, 1964-67; instr. U. Oreg., Eugene, 1967-70; asst. prof. U. Victoria (B.C., Can.), 1970-76; therapist Peninsula Counseling Center, Port Angeles and Sequim, Wash., 1976-81, McHugh & Assos. Counseling Center, 1981—. Served with WAVES, 1944-45. Mem. Am. Psychol. Assn., Am. Personnel and Guidance Assn., Western Psychol. Assn. Research on women in relationships, also depression and women. Home: 249 F Cameron Rd Sequim WA 98382

MCHUGH-SHUFORD, MARY MARGARET, educator, real estate broker; b. Salt Lake City, Dec. 15, 1944; d. William Thomas and Margaret Ann (Gloe) McHugh; B.A., Idaho State U., 1966, M.Ed. in Exceptional Child, 1969; diploma N.Y. Sch. Interior Design, 1975; m. Walter Julius Shuford, Sept. 28, 1968; children—Michael Troy, Trenton Charles. Tchr., Pocatello (Idaho) Sch. Dist., 1967-70, Groton (Conn.) Sch. Dist., 1970—; chief negotiator for tchrs., 1975-76; real estate asso., 1977. Vol. fund raiser, Ledyard Campaign chmn. Planned Parenthood Assn., Am. Heart Assn.; dir. early family dinner and variety show St. David's Episcopal Ch., 1972; chmn. Fathoms of Fun Variety Show, Port Orchard, Wash., 1978. Named Million Dollars Salesperson, 1978, 79. Idaho State scholar, 1968. Mem. Nat. (del. 1976), Conn. (del. 1975-76), Groton edn. assns., Kitsap Bd. Realtors. Home: 9505 Caulfield Ln SW Port Orchard WA 98366 Office: Naval Regional Med Center Puget Sound Naval Shipyard Bremerton WA 98314 also South Kitsep High Sch Port Orchard WA 98366

MC INNIS, MARTHA ANN, assn. exec.; b. Montgomery, Ala., July 28, 1937; d. Miles and Rose Mills (Stoner) McI.; student Huntingdon Coll., 1955-57; B.S., U. Ala., 1959, M.S., 1962. Fabric designer Avondale Mills, Inc., Sylacauga, Ala., 1959-62; lectr. Judson Coll., Marion, Ala., 1961-62; instr. U. Miami, Coral Gables, Fla., 1962-63; adult edn. cons. McCall Corp., N.Y.C., 1963-64, asst. prof. Ariz. State U., Tempe, 1964-67; program devel. dir. Ala. Farm Bur. Fedn., Montgomery, 1967-72; exec. v.p. Ala. Environ. Quality Assn., Montgomery, 1972—; pres. Enivro South, Inc., Montgomery, 1975—, editor Enviro South mag., 1976—; dir. Birmingham br. Fed. Res. Bank of Atlanta; mem. nat. adv. council environ. edn. HEW, 1975-78; nat. weather modification bd. U.S. Dept. Commerce, 1977-78; agribus. and rural affairs com. U.S. C. of C., 1971-73; vice chmn. adv. council Auburn U. Sch. Home Econs., 1971-72; chmn. Bartram Trail Conf., 1976-81. Bd. dirs. Dixie Zool. Soc., 1975-80; mem. exec. com. Ala. Democratic Com., 1979—. Mem. AAAS, Am. Soc. Assn. Execs., Southeastern Outdoor Press Assn., Ala. Soc. Assn. Execs., Am. Home Econs. Assn., Ala. Home Econs. Assn., Public Relations Council Ala., Ala. Acad. Sci. Methodist. Office: 3815 Interstate Ct Suite 202 Montgomery AL 36109

MC INNIS, MARY, govt. ofcl.; b. Newton, N.J., June 30, 1950; d. Norman Kenneth and Sara (Bollinger) McI.; B.A., U. Wash., Seattle, 1972, J.D., 1975. Admitted to Wash. State bar, 1975; counsel com. commerce U.S. Senate, 1975-77; asst. dir. domestic policy staff White House, 1977-79; gen. counsel CAB, Washington, 1979—. Mem. Wash. State Bar Assn., D.C. Bar Assn. Office: Room 1006 CAB 1825 Connecticut Ave NW Washington DC 20428

MCINTOSH, MICHAELE D., group controller; b. Warsaw, Ind., Mar. 12, 1946; d. Paul E. and Dorothy E. (Seiffert) Hodges; B.B.A., U. Miami (Fla.), 1968; cert. in acctg. UCLA, 1976; m. J.W. McIntosh, Apr. 8, 1972; 1 son, James Kyle. Asst. dist. credit mgr. W.T. Grant Co., Los Angeles, 1969-70; v.p., treas. R & B Enterprises, Los Angeles, 1970-80; pres., exec. dir. L.I.F.E. Inc., Warsaw, Ind., 1981; recreational vehicles group controller Coachmen Industries, Middlebury, Ind., 1981—; mgmt. cons. City of Warsaw; real estate broker, Ind. Trustee, Kosciusko Leadership Acad.; mem. Madison Sch. Parent-Tchr. Orgn. Mem. Nat. Bd. Realtors, Ind. Bd. Realtors, Kosciusko County Bd. Realtors, Chi Omega. Club: Women of Moose.

MCINTOSH, POLLY BOGGS, edn. programs specialist; b. Petersburg, Va.; d. Clarence E. and Evelyn (Gresham) Boggs; B.A., Clark Coll., 1952; Cert. Edn., Northwestern U., 1960; M.Ed., U. Miami, 1970; m. Mel. L. Davis, Nov. 23, 1979; children—Marsha A Scott, Marshall B. Arnold, Jr. Sr. program officer Edn. and Community Services, U.S. Office of Edn., Atlanta, 1973-74, asst. regional commr. for planning and spl. programs, 1974-77, dep. regional commr. of edn., 1977-78, chief intergovtl. and spl. services, 1978—; cons. South Fla. Desegregation Center, U. Miami. Mem. Leadership Atlanta, 1980—; mem. City of Atlanta Youth Employment Council, 1980—; chmn. subcom. on minority bus. devel. Minority Bus. Opportunity Commn., Atlanta, 1980; mem. adv. council Sch. Edn., U. Miami, 1971—; steward United Methodist Ch. Mem. NEA, Atlanta Urban League, Nat. Assn. Female Execs., Nat. Alliance of Black Educators, Delta Sigma Theta. Office: 101 Marietta Tower Suite 2221 Atlanta GA 30323

MCINTYRE, CHRISTINE SWANK, speech and lang. pathologist; b. Sharon, Pa., Mar. 16, 1917; d. John Neilson and Lucy (Swank) McI.; B.S. Ed., State Coll., California, Pa., 1939; M.Ed., Pa. State U., 1954. Instr. math., high sch., Confluence, Pa., 1941-42; instr. math., jr.-sr. high sch., North Fayette Twp., Pa., 1942-44, high sch. Latrobe, Pa., 1944-45; statis. clk. Carnegie Illinois Steel Corp., Pitts., 1945-48; instr. math., high sch., Rockwood, Pa., 1948-53; speech and lang. pathologist, Carlisle (Pa.) public schs., 1953-78; pvt. practice speech and lang. pathology Carlisle. Tchr. Sunday Sch., Grace United Meth. Ch., 1967-77. Recipient Good Samaritan award Holy Land Christian Mission, 1973. Mem. Am. Speech, Lang. and Hearing Assn., Pa. Speech and Hearing Assn., Council for Exceptional Children. Address: 140 Dorwood Dr Carlisle PA 17013

MC INTYRE, MARY ARNETTA, computer programmer; b. Canon City, Colo., May 16, 1938; d. David Taggart and Mary Arnetta (Forney) McIntyre; A.S., Chemeketa Community Coll., Salem, Oreg., 1971, A.A., 1974; postgrad. Oreg. State U., 1974-77. Prototype assembly technician Nortronics Co., Hawthorne, Calif., 1961-63; elec., electronic and mech. assembly technician C.T. Engring. Corp., Lawndale, Calif., 1963-64, engring. technician, 1964-67, quality control technician, 1963-67; bookkeeper, accountant, tax preparer Valley Bookkeeping Service, Dallas, Oreg., 1971-75; scale house operator Stayton Canning Co., Dayton, Oreg., 1968-79; computer programmer Oreg. Dept. Employment, Salem, 1979—; dir. Inform-Facts, Amity, Oreg., 1975—; acctg. clk., computer operator City of McMinnville, Oreg., 1978. Served with USMC, 1956-60. Democrat. Baptist. Author: Mailorder Handbook, 1978. Home: Route 1 Box 187 McMinnville OR 97128 Office: PO Box 285 Amity OR 97101

MC INTYRE, RAE MORSE, ins. asso., corp. exec., fin. planner; b. Lowell, Mass., May 26, 1945; d. Walter Silas and Regina Marie (Trudel) Morse; student Coll. Fin. Planning, 1980—; m. Robert Lawrence McIntyre, Jr., Mar. 30, 1978; children—Eugene, Regina. Sales asso. Paul Revere Cos., Miami, Fla., 1978—; owner, pres. R/R Discovery, Inc., Miami, 1979—; participant seminars on fin. mgmt. Recipient various ins. sales awards, 1979; certified Fin. Planners Inst. Mem. Nat. Assn. Female Execs., Nat. Assn. Security Dealers. Pub. Newsletter for Profl. Women - State of Fla. Home: 6128 Schooner Way Tampa FL 33615

MCIVER, SUSAN BERTHA, educator; b. Hutchinson, Kans., Nov. 6, 1940; d. Ernest Dale and Thelma Faye (McCrory) McIver; B.A., U. Calif., Riverside, 1962; M.S., Wash. State U., 1964, Ph.D., 1967. Asst. prof. dept. parasitology U. Toronto (Ont.), 1967-72, assoc. prof., 1972-81, prof. dept. zoology, 1981—; cons., surgeon gen., U.S. Army, 1977-82. Recipient C. Gordon Hewitt award Entomol. Soc. Can., 1978; Vis. Scientist award Med. Research Council Can., 1978; InterAm. Fellow in tropical medicine NIH, 1973. Mem. Entomol. Soc. Ont. (pres. 1981), Entomol. Soc. Can. (dir. 1975-78), Entomol. Soc. Am. (chmn. sect. 1982), Canadian Soc. Zoologists, Am. Soc. Parasitologists, Micros. Soc. Can. Presbyterian. Contbr. articles to various publs.

MC KAIG, DIANNE L., lawyer, soft drink co. exec.; b. Massillon, Ohio, Nov. 17, 1930; d. Sherman J. and Kathryn (Shaidnagle) McKaig; B.A., U. Ky., 1952, J.D., 1954; LL.M., Harvard U., 1955. Admitted to Ky. bar, 1954, Mass. bar, 1956; law clk. Ky. Ct. Appeals, Frankfort, 1954; atty. firm Palmer, Dodge, Gardner & Bradford, Boston, 1955-56; practice law, Boston, 1956-58; atty.-adviser Office of Solicitor, U.S. Dept. Labor, Washington, 1958-62, regional dir. Women's Bur., Atlanta, 1963-66, chief div. legislation and standards, Women's Bur., Washington, 1966-68; spl. asst. to sec. (consumer interests) HEW, Washington, 1968, dir. Office Consumer Services, 1968-69; exec. dir. Mich. Consumers Council, 1969-72; asst. v.p. consumer affairs Coca-Cola Co., Atlanta, 1972-74, v.p., 1976—; v.p. Coca-Cola U.S.A., 1974-76; mem. Major Appliance Consumer Action Panel, 1970-72; dir. Fleet Fin. Group Inc.; spl. lectr. Coll. Indsl. Mgmt., Ga. Inst. Tech., 1975. Bd. dirs. Nat. Council for Family Fin. Edn., 1970-72, Nat. Council Better Bus. Burs., 1971-72, Girl Scouts U.S., Met. chpt. ARC; chmn. pub. affairs com. Food Safety Council, 1977-79; trustee Pace Acad., Atlanta, 1979—; mem. vis. com. U. Ky. Law Sch., 1978—. Mem. Ky., Fed., Mass. bar assns., Soc. Consumer Affairs Profls. (dir. 1973-77, pres. 1975-76), Grocery Mfrs. Am. (consumer rep. task force 1978-80), U.S. C. of C. (consumer affairs com. 1978-80), U. Ky. Alumni Assn. (pres. Washington 1962), Bus. and Profl. Women's Clubs, Order of Coif, Mortar Bd., Alpha Delta Pi (chpt. outstanding alumna 1965), Eta Sigma Phi, Phi Beta. Asso. editor Ky. Law Jour., 1953. Home: 4 Mooregate Sq NW Atlanta GA 30327 Office: Coca-Cola Co 310 North Ave Atlanta GA 30313

MCKAIN, F. JOAN, data processing educator; b. May 28; d. Frank Frederick and Esther Mae Iwan; B.B.A., Woodbury U., 1965; postgrad. UCLA. Sucessively writer and editor tech. and non-tech. texts, tchr. data processing and personal/bus. communication skills Xerox Corp., Los Angeles, 1971—; cons.; guest lectr. Office: 5310 Beethoven St Los Angeles CA 90066

MCKAIN, REBECCA DIANE, real estate mgmt. co. exec.; b. Los Angeles, May 17, 1951; d. Jack Edmund and Rebecca Jean McK.; student Calif. State U., Fullerton, 1969-71, Los Angeles Valley Coll., 1977-81, Calif. State U., Northridge, 1981—. Bookkeeper, Creative Litho Printing, Whittier, Calif., 1966-70; clk., note teller Bank of Am., Los Angeles, 1971-75; asst. v.p., mgr. Coldwell Banker Mgmt. Corp., Los Angeles, 1975—. Lic. real estate broker, Calif. Democrat. Office: 533 S Fremont St Los Angeles CA 90071

MC KAY, CONSTANCE GADOW, hotel exec.; b. Aurora, Ill., Mar. 7, 1928; d. William H. and Esther E. (Olson) Gadow; student U. Ill., U. Wis.-Madison, U. Wis.-Milw.; widow; children—Richard A., Scott A., Mark G. Dir. catering Arlington Park (Ill.) Race Track, 1966-68, Arlington Park Hilton Hotel, Arlington Heights, Ill., 1969—. Commr., Arlington Heights Bd. Local Improvements, 1979—, Arlington Heights Relocation of Post Office Com., 1958-59, Arlington Heights Zoning Bd., 1959-60; commr. Youth Commn., 1981—. Named Outstanding Bus. Woman, Paddock Publs., Arlington Heights, 1977. Mem. Catering Execs. Club Am. Republican. Home: 604 S Waterman Ave Arlington Heights IL 60004 Office: Arlington Park Hilton Hotel Euclid Ave and Rohlwing Rd Arlington Heights IL 60006

MC KAY, EMILY GANTZ, civil rights orgn. exec. b. Columbus, Ohio, Mar. 13, 1945; d. Harry S. and Edwina (Bookwalter) Gantz; B.A., Stanford U., 1966, M.A., 1967; m. Jack Alexander McKay, July 3, 1965. Public info. specialist Community Action, Pitts., 1967-68, exec. asst. to manpower dir., 1968-69, research asso., 1969-70; freelance cons., 1969-70; public relations and materials specialist Met. Cleve. JOBS Council, 1971-72; research and mgmt. cons. BLK Group, Inc., Washington, 1970-73; dir. tech. products Am. Tech. Assistance Corp., McLean, Va., 1973-74; research and mgmt. cons. CONSAD Research Corp., Pitts., 1974-76, v.p., 1976-78; spl. asst. to Pres. for planning and evaluation Nat. Council La Raza, Washington, 1978-81, v.p. research, advocacy and legislation, 1980—; guest lectr. Union Grad. Sch.; cons. City of Cleve., Nat. Assn. Community Devel.; mem. exec com. Citizens Adv. Com. D.C. Bar; co-chmn., bd. govs. Citizens Commn. on Adminstrn. of Justice, Washington; mem Mayor's Commn. on Coop. Econ. Devel.; mem. adv. com. D.C. office Immigration and Naturalization Service; exec. com. Coalition on Block Grants and Human Needs. Ford Found. nat. honors fellow, 1966-67. Mem. Women in Communications, Am. Mgmt. Assn., NAACP, Phi Beta Kappa. Democrat. Home: 3200 19th St NW Washington DC 20010 Office: 1725 Eye St NW Suite 200 Washington DC 20006

MC KAY, JOY H., real estate exec.; b. Warrenville, N.J., June 14, 1914; d. Arthur and Helen (Milius) Hofheimer; grad. Dalton Sch., N.Y.C., 1932, Sarah Lawrence Coll., 1934; m. Joseph J. Siccardi, Sept. 5, 1934 (div. 1952); children—Helene Gay, Carol Ann (Mrs. William Williams Wyman), Arthur J., Marilyn Jill (Mrs. Thomas Iuliucci, Jr.); m. 2d, Raymond Roth, Aug. 25, 1955 (dec.); m. 3d, Samuel J. McKay, Dec. 1970. Mem. Bd. Edn. Warren Twp., N.J., 1940-47, pres., 1947; chmn. Warren Twp. ARC, v.p. Mental Hygiene Soc. Union County, N.J., 1946-49, pres., 1949-51; bd. mgrs. N.J. Neuropsychiat. Inst., Princeton, N.J., 1951-55, v.p., 1953-54; pres. N.J. Assn. for Mental Health, 1951-56, mem. bd., 1951-64, exec. com. 1951-63, chmn. planning com., 1958-62; chmn. com. orgn. Nat. Assn. Mental Health, 1953-57, dir., 1951-62, mem. exec. com., 1953-62, chmn. planning com. 1959-61, mem. program com., 1961-63, chmn. direct services com., 1961-63; exec. dir. Somerset County Assn. for Mental Health, 1965-67; dir. div. services N.J. Heart Assn., 1967-70; supr. Heart Sunday Broward County (Fla.) Heart Assn., 1970-71, dir. fund raising, 1971-72; assoc. J.G. Realty, Deerfield, Fla., 1972-73; assoc. Gold Palm Realty, Boca Raton, Fla., 1973—, v.p., 1976—; v.p. Robert Kerber Realty Inc., 1976-77; sec. Ratner Assocs., Inc., 1977-78, Boca Real Estators Inc., 1978-81; pres. Ocean Plaza Realty Inc., 1981-82; dir. Alan Bush Realty Inc. Trustee Nathan Hofheimer Found., 1945-70. Mem. Fla. Assn. Realtors (dir. 1981-82, profl. standards com. 1981-82, membership com. 1982), Boca Raton Bd. Realtors (membership com. 1976, chmn. 1979, mem. grievance com. 1977-79, treas. 1980-81, chmn. budget and fin. com. 1980-81, Realtor of Yr. award 1981, pres.-elect 1982), Women's Council Realtors (sec. Boca Raton chpt. 1975—, v.p. 1976-77). Home: 750 NE Spanish River Blvd Boca Raton FL 33431

MC KAY, RENEE, artist; b. Montreal, Que., Can.; came to U.S., 1946, naturalized, 1954; d. Frederick Garvin and Mildred Gladys (Higgins) Smith; B.A., McGill U., 1941; m. Kenneth Gardiner McKay, July 25, 1941; children—Margaret Craig, Kenneth Gardiner. Tchr. art Peck Sch., Morristown, N.J., 1955-56; one woman shows: Pen and Brush Club, N.Y.C., 1957, Cosmopolitan Club, N.Y.C., 1958; group shows include: Weyhe Gallery, N.Y.C., 1978, Newark Mus., 1955, 59, Montclair (N.J.) Mus., 1955-58, Nat. Assn. Women Artists, Nat. Acad. Galleries, 1954-78, N.Y. World's Fair, 1964-65, Audubon Artists, N.Y.C., 1955-62, 74-79, N.Y. Soc. Women Artists, 1979-80, Provincetown (Mass.) Art Assn. and Mus., 1975-79; traveling shows in France, Belgium, Italy, Scotland, Can., Japan; represented in permanet collections: Slater Meml. Mus., Norwich, Conn., Norfolk (Va.) Mus., Butler Inst. Am. Art, Youngstown, Ohio, Lydia Drake Library, Pembroke, Mass., many pvt. collections. Recipient Jane Peterson prize in oils Nat. Assn. Women Artists, 1954, Famous Artists Sch. prize in watercolor, 1959, Grumbacher Artists Watercolor award, 1970; Solo award Pen and Brush, 1957; Sadie-Max Tesser award in watercolor Audubon Artists, 1975, Peterson prize in oils, 1980. Mem. Nat. Assn. Women Artists (2d v.p. 1969-70, adv. bd. 1974-76), Audubon Artists (pres. 1979), Artist Equity (dir. 1977-79, v.p. 1979-81), N.Y. Soc. Women Artists, Asso. Artists of N.J., Pen and Brush, Nat. Soc. Painters in Casein and Acrylic, Nat. Arts Club, Provincetown Art Assn. and Mus. Club: Cosmopolitan. Address: 200 E 66 St New York NY 10021

MCKAY, RUTH CAPERS, former educator, adminstr.; b. Ridgewood, N.J., Mar. 24, 1902; d. William Worth, Jr. and Grace Lefferts (Stephens) Capers; A.B., Wheaton Coll. (Mass.), 1923, D.Litt. (hon.), 1973; A.M., U. Pa., 1924, Ph.D. (Bennett fellow and scholar, 1924-27), 1927; m. Donald C. McKay, June 16, 1930; children—Anne, Ferguson, Donald C. Asst. prof. Wheaton Coll., Mass., 1927-30; tutor, instr. in English, Radcliffe Coll., 1938-41, Harvard U., 1944-49; lectr. acad. dept. New Eng. Conservatory of Music, 1949-55, dean grad. sch., 1962-68, dean, founder New Eng. Conservatory Summer Sch., Castle Hill, Ipswich, Mass., 1965, 66, 67, 68; lectr. English and gen. lit. Smith Coll., 1955-61; exec. dir. Opera Co. of Boston, 1968-72; apptd. asso. commr. parks and recreation, City of Boston, 1982—; chmn. Common Com., Friends of Public Garden and Common, Boston, 1976—. Trustee Wheaton Coll., 1947-79, vice chmn., 1976-79, mem. Woodrow Wilson regional scholarship com., 1959-63; active Schlesinger Library, Radcliffe Coll.; bd. advisers Arrowhead. Mem. Arnold Arboretum, Berkshire Hist. Soc. (Pittsfield, Mass.), Garden Club Am. (Zone 1 rep., publs. and program coms., 1979—), Beacon Hill Garden Club (pres., 1976-78), Phi Beta Kappa. Democrat. Episcopalian. Clubs: Harvard Faculty, Cosmopolitan (N.Y.C.), Boston Athenaeum. Author: George Gissing and his Critic Frank Swinnerton, 1932; editor: Hidden Gardens of Beacon Hill, 1972; contbr. articles on lit. and hort. to publs. Home: 5 Chestnut St Boston MA 02108

MC KEAN-SMITH, VICKI, artist; b. Douglas, Wyo., June 10, 1913; d. Arthur Eaton and Florence (Leonard) Eaton; student U. Nebr., 1930-31, 42-43; postgrad. U. Per Stranieri, Perugia, Italy; m. Edward P. McKean-Smith, May 10, 1960; children—Walter, Roland (dec.), Cheryl. One-woman exhbns. in Coquille, Coos Bay, Bend, Brookings, Port Orford, Tillamook, Astoria, The Dalles, Portland (all Oreg.); group exhbns. in DeLake, Salem, Burns (Oreg.), Lincoln, Nebr.; tchr. art Coquille Valley Art Center, 1950—; supr. art dept. Coos County Fair, 1960-65; mem. Gov. Oreg. Com. Arts and Humanities, 1962-75; bd. dirs. Arts in Oreg. Council, 1972-78, Creative Arts Assn., Everett, Wash., 1966-67; pres., art dir. Sawdust Theatre, 1970-78. Recipient 1st place awards Coos and Curry county fairs, Nebr. State Fair; Best of Show award, Marysville, Wash., 1966; named Coos Bay Zontian of Year, 1966. Mem. League Oreg. Artists (past pres.), Coquille Valley Art Assn. (founder, past pres.), Little Theatre on the Bay (life). Clubs: Zonta (past dist. sec., past pres. Coos Bay area), Toastmistresses (past chpt. pres.), Soroptimist (sec.), Royal Neighbors. Address: 587 N Elliott St Coquille OR 97423

MCKEE, ANITA LEA SHERAR, nurse; b. Spokane, Wash., Dec. 3, 1927; d. Archie P. and Helen C. (Sargeant) Sherar; diploma Providence Sch. of Nursing, 1950; B.A., Ft. Wright Coll., 1977; m. Richard M. McKee (dec.); children—William, David, Stuart. Gen. duty/operating room nurse Sacred Heart Hosp., Spokane, 1950-55, VA Hosp., Spokane, 1957-66; operating room nurse Deaconess Hosp., Spokane, 1966-69; supr. operating room, recovery room, central service Spokane Valley Gen. Hosp., Spokane, 1969-77; adminstrv. supr. operating room, recovery room St. Lukes Hosp., Duluth, Minn., 1977-80; dir. operating room, services Providence Med. Center, Seattle, 1980—; chmn. adv. council for operating room technicians Spokane Community Coll., 1975-77; mem. adv. bd. operating room technicians Anoka Vocat. Tech. Inst., Anoka, Minn., 1979-80. Mem. Assn. Operating Room Nurses (pres. Inland Empire chpt. 1974), Nat. Assn. Female Execs., Internat. Graphoanalysis Soc. Club: Elks. Home: 8900 NE 191st Pl Bothell WA 98011 Office: Providence Med Center 500 17th Ave Seattle WA 98124

MCKEE, EDITH MERRITT, geologist; b. Oak Park, Ill., Oct. 9, 1918; d. Eustis Ewart and Edith (Frame) McK.; B.S., Northwestern U., 1946. Geologist, U.S. Geol. Survey, 1943-45, Shell Oil Co., 1947-49, Arabian Am. Oil Co., 1949-54, Underground Gas Storage Co. Ill., 1956-58; ind. cons. geologist, Winnetka, Ill., 1958—; mem. environ. adv. com. Fed. Energy Adminstrn., 1974; mem. Nat. Adv. Com. Oceans and Atmosphere, 1975; speaker, cons. in field. Commr., Winnetka Park Bd., 1976-79. Fellow Marine Tech. Soc., Geol. Soc. Am.; mem. Am. Geol. Inst., Am. Inst. Profl. Geologists (cert., charter), Assn. Engring. Geologists, Ill. Geol. Soc., Am. Oceanic Orgn. Research on shore erosion, mapping of Gt. Lakes basins and deep ocean basins. Address: 416 Maple St Winnetka IL 60093

MCKEE, ELAINE COOPER, found. exec.; b. Dewey, Okla., Sept. 26, 1937; d. Peter Milton and Lucile Evelyn (Bostic) Cooper Webber; student public schs.; 1 son, J. Duane Parton. With Avacare Co., and predecessor, 1972, 77-82, div. mgr. U.S. and Can., area coordinator, Dallas, 1981-82; regional mgr. Sarah Coventry Co., 1968-77; dir. public relations Internat. Biotechnology Found., 1982—; motivational and sales tng. cons.; v.p. mktg. Leadership Dynamics. Mem. Nat. Assn. Female Execs., Christian Women's Self Devel. Republican. Baptist. Address: 2921 Southern Cross Dr Garland TX 75042

MC KEE, FRAN, naval officer; b. Florence, Ala., Sept. 13, 1926; d. Thomas W. and Geneva (Lumpkins) McKee; B.S., U. Ala., 1950; M.S. in Internat. Affairs, George Washington U., 1970; D.Public Adminstrn. (hon.), Mass. Maritime Acad., 1978. Commd. ensign U.S. Navy, 1950, advanced through grades to rear adm., 1976; comdr. Naval Security Group Activity, Fort George G. Meade, Md., 1973-76; dir. naval ednl. devel. Naval Edn. and Tng. Command, Pensacola, Fla., 1976-78; asst. chief naval personnel for human resource mgmt. Bur. Naval Personnel, Washington, 1978; dir. human resource mgmt. div. Office Chief of Naval Ops., Washington, 1978-81; ret., 1981. Decorated Legion of Merit with gold star, Meritorious Service medal; named to Ala. Acad. Honor, 1979. Episcopalian. Home: 7420 Adams Park Ct Annandale VA 22003

MC KEE, MARGARET JEAN, govt. relations exec.; b. New Haven, June 20, 1929; d. Waldo McCutcheon and Elizabeth (Thayer) McKee; A.B., Vassar Coll., 1951. Staff asst. United Republican Fin. Com., N.Y.C., 1952; staff asst. N.Y. Rep. State Com., N.Y.C., 1953-55; staff asst. Crusade for Freedom (name later changed to Radio Free Europe Fund), N.Y.C., 1955-57; researcher Stricker & Henning Research Asso., Inc., N.Y.C., 1957-59; exec. sec. New Yorkers for Nixon (name later changed to N.Y. State Ind. Citizens for Nixon Lodge), N.Y.C., 1959-60; asst. to Raymond Moley, polit. columnist, N.Y.C., 1961; asst. campaign com. Louis J. Lefkowitz for Mayor, N.Y.C., 1961; research programmer, treas. Consensus, Inc., N.Y.C., 1962-67; spl. asst. to U.S. Senator Jacob K. Javits, N.Y., 1967-73, adminstrv. asst., 1973-75; dep. adminstr. Am. Revolution Bicentennial Adminstrn., 1976, acting adminstr., 1976-77; chief of staff Perry B. Duryea (minority leader) N.Y. State Assembly, 1978; public affairs cons., 1979-80; dir. govt. relations Gen. Mills Restaurant Group, Inc., 1980—; dir. Interam. Life Ins. Co. Mem. N.Y. State Bingo Control Commn., 1965-72, U.S. Adv. Commn. on Public Diplomacy, 1979-82; pres. Bklyn. Heights Slope Young Republican Club, 1955-56; co-chmn. Bklyn. Citizens for Eisenhower-Nixon, 1956; chmn. 2d Jud. Dist. Assn. N.Y. State Young Rep. Clubs, Inc., 1957-58, vice-chmn., mem. bd. govs., 1958-60, v.p., 1960-62; pres., 1962-64; mem. exec. com. Fedn. Women's Rep. Clubs N.Y. State, Inc., 1960-64, mem. council, 1964-70; mem. exec. com. N.Y. Rep. State Com. 1962-64; co-chmn. spl. assts. Rockefeller for Pres. Nat. Campaign com., N.Y.C., 1964; co-dir. N.Y. Rep. State Campaign Com., 1964; asst. campaign mgr. Kenneth B. Keating for Judge Ct. Appeals, N.Y., 1965; dir. scheduling Gov. Rockefeller campaign, 1966, Sen. Charles E. Goodell campaign, 1970; dir. scheduling and speakers' bur. N.Y. Com. to Re-elect the Pres., 1972. Mem. bd. govs. Women's Nat. Rep. Club, N.Y.C., 1963-66. Mem. Jr. League of Bklyn. (past (dir.), Exec. Women in Govt., Nat. Women's Edn. Fund (mem. bd.), Am. Newspaper Women's Club, Nat. Soc. Colonial Dames Am. Episcopalian. Club: Vassar (past dir.) (Bklyn.). Home: 3001 Veazey Terr NW Washington DC 20008 also 785 Park Ave New York NY 10021

MCKEE, NANCY ANN, fgn. service officer; b. Tulsa, Mar. 12, 1933; d. Charles and Estelle Marie (Larrieu) McK.; student U. Tulsa, 1950-52. Sec., Jones & Laughlin Supply Div., Tulsa, 1952-63; sec. Am. Embassy, Bonn, W.Ger., 1963-66, Lagos, Nigeria, 1963-68, Dept. State, Washington, 1968-70, 71-72, Am. Embassy, Nicosia, Cyprus, 1970-71; commd. fgn. service officer Dept. State, 1972; consular officer Am. Embassy, Manila, 1972-74, Mexico City, 1975-79, Nairobi, Kenya, 1979-82; supr. visa sect., dept. prin. officer Am. Consulate Gen., Juarez, Mex., 1982—. Republican. Roman Catholic.

MCKEE, MRS. WALDO (ELIZABETH BROOKS THAYER MCKEE), club woman; b. Bklyn; d. John Van Buren and Elizabeth B. (Chatfield) Thayer; grad. Bklyn. Heights Sem., 1914; m. Waldo McCutcheon McKee, Oct. 3, 1925; children—Elizabeth Brooks (Mrs. J. Eugene Lewis), M. Jean. Hon. dir. Orphan Asylum, Bklyn.; past chmn. social service com. Cumberland Hosp., Bklyn.; past treas. Bklyn. com. Met. Opera; past mem. N.Y. Philharm. Com.; mem. Cheshire Bicentennial 1980 Com.; past polit. edn. chmn. Woman's Republican Club, Cheshire; mem. Cheshire com. Am. Revolution Bicentennial, 1976. Mem. Bklyn. Jr. League (past pres.), Nat. Soc. Colonial Dames (past v.p. N.Y.), New Haven, Colony hist. socs., Conn. Antiquarian and Landmarks Soc. Cheshire Historic Dist. Com. Clubs: Civitas (past v.p.), Mrs. Fields Literary (past v.p.). Home: 532 S Brooksvale Rd Cheshire CT 06410

MCKEEVER, JANICE MARY, ednl. adminstr.; b. Los Angeles, July 28, 1929; s. Louis C. and Lela E. (Lewis) Schildwachter; B.A., Occidental Coll., 1948; M.A., Calif. State U., Dominguez Hills, 1974; postgrad. U. So. Calif., 1975-76; m. Kirk LeRoy McKeever, July 2, 1948 (dec. 1977); children—Kevin Miles, Wendelyn. Reading specialist Los Angeles Unified Sch. Dist., 1969-73, tchr., 1948-69; coordinator early childhood edn. Gulf Ave. Sch., Wilmington, Calif., 1974-78; prin. 15th St. Sch., Los Angeles, 1978-79; coordinating asst. prin. 102d St. Magnet Fundamental Acad., Los Angeles, 1979—; asst. prin. Wadsworth Year Round Elementary Sch., Los Angeles; parent edn. instr. Los Angeles Adult Schs., 1975-79; instr. UCLA, 1972-73; instr. Calif. State U., Dominguez, 1980—. Recipient Hon. Service award Avalon Council PTA, 1973; cert. reading specialist, Calif. Mem. Harbor Reading Council (pres. 1975-76), Nat. Year Round Sch. Assn., Town Hall of Calif., World Affairs Council of Los Angeles, Phi Delta Kappa, Delta Kappa Gamma (pres. 1978-80), Kappa Kappa Iota. Republican. Episcopalian. Author: The Orange County Appetizers Cookbook, 1980. Office: Los Angeles City Unified School Dist Area 2 PO Box 3307 Los Angeles CA 90051

MCKEEVER, MABEL JEAN, youth orgn. exec.; b. Spokane, Wash., Dec. 29, 1924; d. Harry and Maude Olina (MacComber) O'Connor; student Wash. State Coll., 1957; m. Charles Lee McKeever, Aug. 15, 1943; children—Patrick Lee, Barbara Ann, Nancy Jo. Adminstrv. asst. Community Action Com., Richland, Wash., 1965-67; office mgr. Chinook council Camp Fire, Inc., Richland, 1967-75, exec. dir., 1975—. Mem. Richland C. of C., Camp Fire Assn. Profls. Episcopalian. Club: Job's Daus. (past guardian). Home: 924 Empire Dr Pasco WA 99301 Office: Route 4 Box 9533 Richland WA 99352

MC KELL, MARION ELIZABETH TERWILLIGER, artist; b. Dayton, Wash., Mar. 8, 1919; d. Lloyd Ranson and Florence Marion (Harper) Terwilliger; student Chouinard Sch. Art, Los Angeles, 1936-37; B.A., Scripps Coll., 1941; postgrad. Claremont U. Grad. Sch., 1941, Pa. Acad. Fine Arts, Phila., 1941-42; m. James Cook McKell, III, Dec. 2, 1942; children—Marion Lloyd McKell Fogler, Lynn Gaylord McKell Gazjuk, James Forrest. Staff, Alexander Film Co., Colorado Springs, 1943-44; painter portraits on commns., 1946-55; pvt. tchr. art, 1965-68; instr. youth classes in art Chester County (Pa.) Art Assn., 1968-72; one-person shows: Lancaster County (Pa.) Art Assn. Center, 1959, Chester County Art Assn. Center, 1960, 76, West Chester (Pa.) State Coll., 1964, Strawbridge & Clothier, Springfield, Pa., 1975, S.E. Nat. Bank, West Chester, Pa., 1978; group shows include: Los Angeles Art Mus., 1941, Chester County Assn. Retarded Citizens Anns., 1965-77, Pa. Acad. Fine Arts, Yellow Springs, 1977, others; represented in permanent collections; lectr. in field. Exec. bd. Chester County Council on Addictive Disease, 1964-71; founding com., adv. bd. Vitae House Inc., 1969—; active Women's div. Del. Valley Council on Alcoholism; bd. dirs. Del. Valley Main Line Council on Alcohol and Drug Abuse. Recipient awards Chester County Art Assn., 1965, Nat. League Am. Pen Women State Bienniels, 1972-80. Mem. Nat. League Am. Pen Women (pres. Chester County br. 1974-76), Chester County Art Assn., (v.p. bd. dirs., dir. public relations 1979), Internat. Platform Assn., Scripps Coll. Alumnae Assn. Republican. Mem. Christian Ch. Home: Box E Dayton WA 99328 also 1133 W Street Rd Box 177 Pocopson PA 19366

MCKELVEY, JEANNE WOLFORD, oil co. exec.; b. Johnstown, Pa., Feb. 10, 1947; d. Donald Ralph and Wilma Miller Wolford; B.S. in Med. Tech., U. Pitts., 1967; M.S. in Biochemistry, Indiana U. of Pa., 1976; postgrad. Dickinson Sch. Law, 1980—; m. William Graham McKelvey, Sept. 29, 1979. Chief technologist Conemaugh Valley Meml. Hosp., 1967-72, Johnstown Regional Blood Center, 1972-73; instr. med. tech. Johnstown Vocat.-Tech. Sch., 1973-76; asst. dir. public affairs U. Pitts. at Johnstown, 1976-78; v.p. McKelvey Oil Co., Inc., Harrisonville, Pa., 1978—, McKelvey Petroleum, Inc., Somerset, Pa., 1978—; dir. Summit Bank. Bd. dirs. Windber (Pa.) Hosp., Cumberland Valley Humane Soc. Mem. Am. Soc. Clin. Pathologists, Lawyer-Pilot's Bar Assn., Pa. Student Bar Assn., Mensa. Republican. Presbyterian. Home: Tall Timbers Farm McConnellsburg PA 17233 Office: Box 105 SR 3 Harrisonville PA 17228

MC KELVEY, JUDITH GRANT, lawyer, educator; b. Milw., July 19, 1935; d. Lionel Alexander and Bernadine R. (Verdun) Grant; B.S. in Philosophy, U. Wis., 1957, J.D., 1959. Admitted to Wis. bar, 1959, Calif. bar, 1968; atty. adviser FCC, Washington, 1959-62; adj. prof. U. Md. (Europe), 1965; prof. law Golden Gate U. Sch. Law, San Francisco, 1968-74, 81—, dean Sch. Law, 1974-81. Bd. dirs. San Francisco Neighborhood Legal Assistance Found. Fellow Am. Bar Found.; mem. ABA, Wis., Calif., San Francisco (dir. 1975-77, chmn. legis. com. 1977, pres.-elect 1983) bar assns., Calif. Women Lawyers (1st pres.), Law in a Free Soc. (exec. com.), Continuing Edn. of Bar (chmn. real estate subcom., mem. joint adv. com.). Democrat. Contbr. to Damages Book, 1975, 77. Office: Golden Gate U Sch Law 536 Mission St San Francisco CA 94105

MC KENNA, CHERYL SOBOCINSKI, social worker; b. Detroit, Dec. 12, 1954; d. Edmund Leonard and Edith Mary (Sarasin) Sobocinski; B.S.W., Western Mich. U., 1977; m. William Gerard McKenna, Sept. 2, 1978. Foster care worker Lula Belle Stewart Center, Detroit, 1977—. Mem. Nat. Assn. Social Workers. Roman Catholic.

MCKENNA, CYNTHIA HAMMES, social worker; b. Racine, Wis., Oct. 18, 1947; d. Quinten Arthur and Lois Jean (Newman) Hammes; B.B.A., U. Wis.-Milw., 1970; M.S.W., Columbia U., 1975. Social worker Sheltering Arms Childrens Service, N.Y.C., 1974-76; exec. dir. Casey Family Program East, Bridgeport, Conn., 1976-82, Hartford, Conn., 1982—. Mem. exec. com. Hartcom Inc., Stamford, Conn., 1981—, bd. dirs., 1980—; bd. dirs. YWCA of Greater Bridgeport, 1978—, pres., 1980-81; bd. dirs. Nat. Black Child Devel. Inst., Washington, 1980—; mem. State Task Force on Foster Care, 1979-81; mem. regional adv. com. Conn. Dept. Children and Youth Services. Recipient Vol. Recognition award United Way, 1976. Mem. NOW, ACLU, NAACP, Nat. Assn. Social Workers, Acad. Cert. Social Workers, Concerned Women Colleagues. Home: 1 Woodbury Ln West Hartford Ct Office: 60 Lorraine St Hartford CT 06105

MCKENNA, MARY CATHERINE, biochemist; b. Bethesda, Md., Dec. 17, 1945; d. John Reilly and Mary Cusack (McManus) McK.; B.A., U. Md., 1968, Ph.D., 1979; m. Alan Mink, Dec. 18, 1974. Stewardess, Overseas Nat. Airways, N.Y.C., 1969-72; grad. teaching and research asst., dept. chemistry U. Md., 1973-78, research asst. prof. dept. pediatrics Sch. Medicine, Balt., 1982—; staff fellow, nutritional biochemistry sect. Lab. of Nutrition and Endocrinology, Nat. Inst. Arthritis, Diabetes, Digestive and Kidney Disease, NIH, Bethesda, Md., 1979-82. Sigma Xi Research Excellence awardee and research grantee, 1977. Mem. Am. Inst. Nutrition (asso.), Am. Chem. Soc., Am. Oil Chemists Soc., N.Y. Acad. Scis., AAAS, Assn. for Women in Sci., Am. Forestry Assn. Home: 13088 Williamfield Dr Ellicott City MD 21043 Office: Div Pediatric Research Dept Pediatrics U Md Sch Medicine Baltimore MD 21201

MCKENZIE, FLORETTA DUKES, supt. schs.; b. Lakeland, Fla.; d. Ruth Jeter Dukes; B.S. in History, D.C. Tchrs. Coll., 1956, postgrad., 1967-69; M.A. (grad. sch. fellow 1957), Howard U., 1957; postgrad. George Washington U., Am. U., Catholic U. Am., Union Grad. Sch., Balt.; children—Kevin Donald, Dona Ruth. Tchr., Balt. and Washington Schs., 1957-67; from asst. supt. charge secondary schs. to dep. supt. ednl. programs and services D.C. public schs., 1969-74; area asst. supt. Montgomery County (Md.) public schs., 1974-77, dep. supt. schs., 1978-79; asst. dep. supt. schs. State of Md., 1977-78; with U.S. Dept. Edn., 1979-81, dep. asst. sec. Office Sch. Improvement, 1980-81; edn. cons. Ford Found., 1981; supt. D.C. public schs., 1981—; adv. com. Washington office Coll. Entrance Exam. Bd., 1970—; trustee Ednl. Products Info. Exchange, 1970; cons., speaker in field. Recipient various service awards; hon. life mem. Md. PTA. Mem. Am. Assn. Sch. Adminstrs., Urban League, Gamma Theta Upsilon, Phi Alpha Theta, Phi Delta Kappa. Baptist. Address: Presdl Bldg 415 12th St NW Washington DC 20004

MCKENZIE, PATRICIA PATTERSON, city ofcl.; b. New Orleans, Dec. 5, 1917; d. Harry Howard and Alexandra Grace (de Palkowsko) Patterson; student Sweetbriar Coll., 1936-37, U. Ala., 1937-39; m. John Albert McKenzie, May 2, 1965; children—Celine Lambert, Emilie Mims Clarice Horton. Social worker ARC, Mobile County, Ala., World War II; pres. Atmore (Ala.) Realty Co., with mineral leasing Atmore Realty Co., Patterson Oil; mayor City of Atmore, 1976—; bd. S.Ala. Regional Planning Commn.; mem. planning and adv. bd. CETA Mobile Consortium. Chmn. March of Dimes, Atmore, 1970; pres. United Fund of Atmore, 1976-77; Atmore City council mem., 1971-76; dir. First Nat. Bank of Atmore. Mem. Ala. League Municipalities (exec. and legis. com.), Nat League of Cities (community and econ. devel. policy com.), Women in Mcpl. Govt., Atmore C. of C. (bd mem., named outstanding citizen of year, 1979), Kappa Kappa Gamma. Democrat. Episcopalian. Clubs: Jr. League of Mobile, Atmore Jr. Service League (advisory mem.), Atmore Pilot Internat. (hon. mem.). Home: 108 Alexandra Dr Atmore AL 36502 Office: PO Drawer G Atmore AL 36504

MCKENZIE, SALLY FREEMAN, civic worker; b. Paris, Tex., Sept. 16, 1928; d. Samuel Horace and Pearl (Humphries) Freeman; A.A., Hockaday Jr. Coll., 1947; B.A., U. Tex., Austin, 1949; m. William A. McKenzie, July 17, 1954; children—Martha, Peter. Pres. Paris Properties (Tex.), 1949-52; saleswoman Sabena Airlines, Dallas, 1953-56; adv. dir. Prestonwood Nat. Bank, Dallas. Co-founder Dallas Civic Opera Guild, 1957; chmn. Dallas Civic Opera Women's Bd., 1973; pres. Jr. League Dallas, 1967-68; bd. dirs., sec. Assn. Jr. Leagues Am., 1968-72; Western regional dir. Pres.'s Adv. Com. on Arts of Kennedy Ctr.,

1970-76; bd. dirs., mem. exec. com. Vol. Ctr. Dallas County (Tex.), 1973-79; sec. bd. trustees Dallas County Mental Health/Mental Retardation Ctr., 1975-77; pres. Community Council Greater Dallas, 1978-79; bd. dirs. Dallas United Way, 1978—, Met. Dallas YMCA, 1978—; mem. Tex. Gov.'s Task Force on Equal Opportunities for Women and Minorities, 1981—; co-chmn. Tex. Vol. Conf., 1982; chmn. community relations com. Nat. Fedn. Republican Women, 1974-76; co-chmn. George Bush for Pres., Tex., 1979-80; del. Rep. Nat. Conv., 1980; chmn. Rep. Precinct, Dallas; v.p. Friends of Dallas Pub. Library; mem. Tex. Gov.'s Task Force on Pvt. Sector Initiatives, 1982—; chmn. 1981 Pi Beta Phi Frat. Nat. Conv. Designated 78 in 78 by D mag., 1977; recipient Service award Zonta, 1979, Community Service award Pi Beta Phi, 1981. Presbyterian. Home: 4517 Beverly Dallas TX 75205

MCKEON, JANE F., nurse, health mgmt. cons.; b. Cleve., Sept. 11, 1941; d. John Thomas and Mary Jane (Werwage) McK.; R.N., Good Samaritan Hosp. Sch. Nursing, Dayton, Ohio, 1969; B.S., Mt. St. Joseph Coll., 1971; M.Ed., Loyola U., Chgo., 1975; Instr., Wesley/Passavant Sch. Nursing, Chgo., 1971-75; asst. dir. nursing Franklin Blvd. Hosp., Chgo., 1975-76; dir. nursing, staff devel. and quality assurance Children's Meml. Hosp., Chgo., 1976-77; mgr. A. T. Kearney Inc., Health Services Cons., Chgo., 1977—. Mem. Speakers Bur., Chgo. Heart Assn., 1978—; patron Lyric Opera of Chgo., 1981-82. Mem. Women in Mgmt. Inc., Am. Nurses Assn., ACLU, Jazz Inst. Chgo. Home: 175 E Delaware Pl Chicago IL 60611 Office: 222 S Riverside Plaza Chicago IL 60606

MCKEON, PATRICIA PASSMORE, mgmt. cons.; b. Bryn Mawr, Pa., Oct. 4, 1950; d. Lincoln Alan and Helen (Vrooman) Passmore; B.A., Skidmore Coll., 1972; M.B.A., Golden Gate U., 1977; m. Thomas Christopher McKeon, Mar. 31, 1973. Research asst. Bur. Econ. Geology, Austin, Tex., 1972-73; cons. human relations Gilroy Foods, Inc. (Calif.), 1976; operational bus. planner Gen. Electric Co., Burlington, Vt., 1977-79; mgr. mktg. planning and adminstrn. Simmonds Precision Products, Inc., Vergennes, Vt., 1979-80; mem. faculty dept. bus. and econs. Trinity Coll., Burlington, Vt., 1980-82; pres. McKeon Mgmt. Assocs., Williston, Vt., 1981-82; ptnr. Applied Leadership Systems, Burlington, 1982—. Chmn., task force on edn. women Trinity Coll., 1980—; trustee Vt. Symphony Orch., 1980; mem. long range planning com. George Bishop Lane Series, 1979-81. Recipient cert. of disting. acad. achievement Golden Gate U., 1977. Mem. Skidmore Coll. Alumni Assn. (dir. 1980—), Am. Mgmt. Assn., Nat. Assn. Female Execs., Am. Soc. Profl. and Exec. Women, AAUW. Address: PO Box 76 Route 1 Partridge Hill Williston VT 05495

MCKEOWN, HELEN GAIL, lab. adminstr.; b. Hartford, Ky., June 11, 1947; d. Ivan Dennie and Ovelia (Pillow) Allen; B.S., Western Ky. U., 1973; m. Earl Glenn McKeown, June 25, 1966; children—Cary Reid, Adam Kyle. Med. technologist Sacred Heart Hosp., Idaho Falls, Idaho, 1968, Cytomed. Lab., Norwich, Conn., 1969-71, Med. Lab., Bowling Green, Ky., 1971-72, Western Ky. U., Bowling Green, 1972-74, Newell & Assos., Chattanooga, 1976-80; lab. supr. Red Bank (Tenn.) Community Hosp., 1980—; instr. microbiology rev. Chattanooga State Community Coll. Pres. Chattanooga PTA Council, 1979-81; historian Hixson Elem. Sch. PTA, 1977-79. Recipient cert. of appreciation City of Idaho Falls, 1968. Mem. Am. Soc. Clin. Pathologists, Assn. for Practitioners in Infection Control, Chattanooga Edn. in Music Arts Assn., Inc., Children's Internat. Summer Village, Sister City Assn. of Chattanooga, Inc. Democrat. Methodist. Home: 6515 Grubb Rd Hixson TN 37343 Office: Morrison Springs Rd Red Bank TN 37415

MC KEOWN, MARY ELIZABETH, educator; d. Raymond Edmund and Alice (Fitzgerald) McNamara; B.S., U. Chgo., 1946; M.S., DePaul U., 1953; m. James Edward McKeown, Aug. 6, 1955. Supr. high sch. dept. Am. Sch., 1948-68, prin., 1968—, trustee, 1975—, v.p., 1979—. Mem. Nat. Assn. Secondary Sch. Prins., Central States Assn. Sci. and Math Tchrs. Nat. Council Tchrs. Math., Assn. for Supervision and Curriculum Devel., LWV, Adult Edn. Assn. Home: 1469 N Sheridan Rd Kenosha WI 53140

MCKEOWN, PATRICIA LUCAS, public radio news dir.; b. N.Y.C., Jan. 8, 1939; d. Gordon Maskell and Ruth (Lounsbery) Lucas; B.A., Moravian Coll., 1963; postgrad. Lehigh U., 1964; children—Matthew, Adam, Joshua. Library asst. Moravian Coll., 1961-63; acct. Durkee Foods div. Glidden Co., 1958-61; tchr. Bethlehem (Pa.) Schs., 1963-67; news corr. Bethlehem Globe-Times, 1973-74; reporter Park Newspapers, St. Lawrence, N.Y., 1975-77; editor Massena (N.Y.) Observer, 1977-82; news and public affairs dir. North Country Public Radio, Canton, N.Y., 1982—; lectr. sch. dists. Liaison Tchrs. Union, 1966-67; treas., fin. chmn. LWV, 1969-72; bd. dirs. Moravian Coll. Alumni, 1968, Renewal House; active NOW; chmn. Mayor's Task Force on Drug Abuse, 1979-80; bd. dirs. North Country Women's Shelter, Inc., 1977-79; bd. dirs. Massena Salvation Army; mem. program on gifted children N.Y. Bd. Coop. Edn. Services. Mem. Massena C. of C. (dir.), Nat. Women's Polit. Caucus. Club: Moravian Coll. Alumni (pres. 1966-67). Home: RD 3 339 Massena NY 13662 Office: Payson Hall Saint Lawrence U Canton NY

MC KERNAN, JANIS LEIGH, nurse, union ofcl.; b. New London, Conn., June 17, 1949; d. Joseph Bernard and Shirley Mae (Kenyon) McK.; R.N., Hartford (Conn.) Hosp., 1972; student R.I. Coll., 1978, Salva Regina Coll., 1977—. Nurse hosps. in R.I., 1972—; charge nurse, supr. registered nurses Inst. Mental Health, Cranston, 1974-77, supr. registered nurse rehab. unit, 1977-80; nat. v.p. Nat. Assn. Nurses, Nat. Health Care Union, 1980—. Served with Nurse Corps, U.S. Army, 1975; capt. Res. Mem. Am. Nurses Assn., R.I. State Nurses Assn., Am. Soc. Law and Medicine Res. Officers Assn., Assn. U.S. Army, Nat. Assn. Govt. Employees (pres. unit collective bargaining 1976-81). Home: 81 Killey Ave Warwick RI 02889

MCKIBBIN, ELISE PERRY, advt. agy. exec.; b. N.Y.C. Apr. 7, 1922; d. Herbert H. and Freda (Schroth) Perry; B.A., Hunter Coll., 1944; postgrad. Columbia U., 1947-49; m. James M. McKibbin, Nov. 24, 1962; m. 2d, Robert E. Hall, Feb. 16, 1980. Technologist, Columbia Presbyn. Hosp., N.Y.C., 1944-48, research asso., 1948-52; med. lit. analyst Lederle Labs., N.Y.C., 1954-61; v.p., copywriter James M. McKibbin, Inc., N.Y.C., 1961-66, pres., 1966-68; sr. v.p., account supr. Dean L. Burdick Assos., N.Y.C., 1968-75; prin. Hall Decker McKibbin & Singer, Inc., N.Y.C., 1975—. Mem. Spl. Libraries Assn. Club: Pharm. Advt. Address: 1041 3d Ave New York NY 10021

MCKILLIP, MARY ELIZABETH, publishing co. exec.; b. Gary, Ind., July 3, 1950; d. Milton G. and Mary Louise (McEnery) Thomas; B.A., Coll. St. Teresa, Winona, Minn., 1971; m. Michael R. McKillip, Aug. 15, 1970. Adminstrv. coordinator U. Chgo. Med. Center, 1971-80; mgr. adminstrv. services Am. Hosp. Pub., Inc., Chgo., 1980—. Campaign dir. Crusade of Mercy, Chgo., 1979—. Mem. Nat. Assn. Female Execs., Nat. Assn. Women Bus. Owners, Women in Mgmt. Home: 915 Lakeside Pl Chicago IL 60640 Office: 211 E Chicago Ave Suite 700 Chicago IL 60611

MC KILLOP, LUCILLE MARY, coll. pres., nun; b. Chgo., Sept. 28, 1924; d. Daniel and Catherine (Hamill) McK.; B.A., St. Xavier Coll., 1951; M.S., U. Notre Dame, 1959; Ph.D., U. Wis., 1965. Joined Religious Sisters of Mercy; tchr. schs., Chgo. and Ottawa, Ill., 1946-58; instr. Edgewood Coll., Madison, Wis., 1961-62; vis. prof. Ill. Inst. Tech., Chgo., 1969; faculty St. Xavier Coll., Chgo., 1958-59, 63-73; pres. Salve Regina Coll., Newport, R.I., 1973—; mem.-at-large bd. dirs. Nat. Assn. Ind. Colls. and Univs.; mem. accreditation team New Eng. Assn. Schs. and Colls.; mem. R.I. Gov.'s Adv. Commn. on Ednl. TV, 1977—; bd. dirs. Council for Advancement Small Colls. Mem. Nat. Cath. Edn. Assn. (exec. com. of coll. and univ. dept. 1977—).

MCKINLEY, CONSTANCE GOERDES, pub. co. exec.; b. Orange, N.J., Feb. 23; d. Frederick and RoseMarie (Desch) Goerdes; B.A., Edison State Coll., 1978; M.A., William Paterson Coll., 1980; children—Chip, Nancy, David, Marcy, John. Info. specialist U.S. Govt., Western Europe, 1946-48; advt. mgr. Ehlenberger Co. div. Seymour Packing, N.Y.C., 1949-52; sales mgr. UK/Scandinavia, Electronic Design div. Hayden Publs., Rochelle Park, N.J., 1973—; contbg. writer Trends, Butler, N.J., 1965-73, Wayne (N.J.) Today, 1965-73, Herald News, Passaic, N.J., 1956-59. Chmn. voters service LWV, Wayne, 1956-60. Mem. Am. Bus. Press (internat. com.), Catholic Writers Guild. Roman Catholic. Editor: Know Your Town, 1955, Dedication—Immaculate Heart of Mary, 1960. Home: 195 Hillcrest Dr Wayne NJ 07470 Office: Hayden Pub Co 50 Essex St Rochelle Park NJ 07662

MCKINLEY, GERALDINE GAIL, banker; b. Franklin County, Va., Aug. 30, 1936; d. James T. and Ruth A. (Law) Williams; student U. Miami (Fla.); m. Arthur R. McKinley, Jan. 5, 1960; children—Joseph Michael, Lee Frank, Patrick Dennis. With North Shore Bank of Miami Beach (Fla.), 1958-60; with First Peninsula Bank Trust, Hampton, Va., 1960—, asst. v.p., 1978-79, v.p., cashier, 1979—. Active local Little League, Thorobred Baseball League. Mem. Am. Inst. Banking, Nat. Assn. Bank Women, Bank Adminstrn. Inst., Olde Hampton Assn. Republican. Home: 715 Pelham Dr Newport News VA 23602 Office: 1 S Armistead Ave Hampton VA 23669

MCKINLEY, RUTH JOANN, psychotherapist; b. Los Angeles, Sept. 24, 1933; d. Ward Ivan and Lilah May (Conger) Hallin; B.A., Calif. State U., Northridge, 1966; M.S.W., U. So. Calif., 1972; Ph.D. cum laude, Am. Western U., 1981; m. John Clyde McKinley, Nov. 19, 1954 (dec. 1972); children—Terance Phillip Green, Mark Stuart. Adminstr., Pacoima (Calif.) br. San Fernando Valley Child Guidance Clinic, 1965-68; dependency supr. placement services Los Angeles County Juvenile Ct., Van Nuys, Calif., 1968-72; psychotherapist Simi Valley and Conejo Mental Health, Ventura County Mental Health Services, Thousand Oaks, Calif., 1972—; pvt. practice psychotherapy Capper Psychiat. Med. Group, Camarillo, Calif., 1979—; cons., tng. cons. Hospice of the Conejo, Conejo Community Hotline. Dir., Lifeline, Westlake Village, Calif., 1972-75; mem. White Ho. Conf. on Children and Youth, 1970; mem. Ventura County Coalition Against Household Violence, 1980. Children's Bur. Fed. grantee, 1970-72. Mem. Acad. Cert. Social Workers, Soc. Clin. Social Work, Internat. Transactional Analysis, Los Angeles Group Psychotherapy Assn. Office: 1459 Thousand Oaks Blvd Thousand Oaks CA 91361

MCKINNEY, BETTY JO, publisher; b. Maryville, Mo., July 16; d. Joseph Glenn and Virginia Joy (Schubert) Thomas; student N.W. Mo. State U., 1959, Tarkio (Mo.) Coll., 1960-62, Colo. State U., 1967-69; m. George Wendell McKinney, Jan. 29, 1966. Asst. dir. office public relations, Tarkio Coll., 1963-65; publ. specialist office univ. communications, Colo. State U., Ft. Collins, 1966-81; founder, pres., partner Alpine Publs., Loveland, Colo., 1975-80, pub., 1980—. Mem. Dog Writers Assn. Am., Am. Kennel Club. Am. Shetland Sheepdog Club, Com. Small Mag. Editors and Pubs., Nat. Writers Club. Baptist. Author: Sheltie Talk, 1976; Beardie Basics, 1978. Address: 1901 S Garfield St Loveland CO 80537

MC KINNEY, LOLA UTTERBACK, health care cons. co. mgr.; b. Corpus Christi, Tex., Nov. 18, 1934; d. Clifford Rogers and LaJuana (Knowles) Utterback; student public schs., Corpus Christi. Sec., Gt. A&P Tea Co., Dallas, 1953-62; exec. secretarial asst. Baylor U. Med. Center, Dallas, 1962-79; office mgr., exec. sec. to v.p. Hamilton Assos., Inc., Dallas, 1979—; mem. adv. com. Exec. Secretarial Sch.; mem. secretarial careers adv. com. Richland Jr. Coll. Mem. com. on adminstrn. Central Br., YWCA, Dallas, 1976—, chmn., 1977. Mem. Nat. Secs. Assn. (Big D Chpt. Sec of Yr. 1972). Republican. Baptist. Office: 4633 N Central Expy #315 Dallas TX 75205

MCKINNEY, NORMA GAYLE, librarian; b. Troy, Ala., Sept. 7, 1939; d. Robert Foster and Eunice Inez (Price) McKinney; B.S., Auburn (Ala.) U., 1960; M.S. (Library Sch. fellow), Fla. State U., 1962; postgrad. Emory U., 1962-64. Reference librarian Montgomery (Ala.) Pub. Library, summer 1961; Russian cataloger, reference librarian Emory U., Atlanta, 1962-64, reference librarian in charge interlibrary loans, 1964-66; gen. services librarian Ga. Inst. Tech., Atlanta, 1966-70; asst. head reference dept. Ga. State U., Atlanta, 1970-79, computer searching coordinator, 1979—. Librarian, Library U.S.A., N.Y. World's Fair, 1965. Mem. Ga. (mem. publicity com. 1970-71, handbook com. 1971—, chmn. handbook com. 1975—, treas. 1981-83, sec. coll. and univ. div. 1979-81), Southeastern (chmn. handbook com. 1980-82), Met. Atlanta (sec. 1974-75) library assns., AAUP (mem. com. Ga. State U. chpt. 1974-75, mem. at large exec. com. 1978—), Sigma Tau Delta, Phi Kappa Phi, Beta Phi Mu. Office: Pullen Library Ga State Univ 100 Decatur St SE Atlanta GA 30303

MC KINNEY, TATIANA LADYGINA, artist; b. Smolensk, Russia; came to U.S., 1944, naturalized, 1944; d. Sergei Mironovich and Antonina Vladimirovna (Belskaya) Ladygin; student Escola Nacional de Belas Artes, Rio de Janeiro, Brazil, 1950-53; cert. New Coll., Fine Arts Inst., Sarasota, Fla., 1967; m. Samuel H. McKinney, Sept. 12, 1928; children—George Clagett, Frederick Henry, Tatiana McKinney O'Connor. One woman shows at Dartmouth Coll., Hanover, N.H., 1963, Buyways Gallery, Sarasota, 1971-73, 75, 77, 80, Via Gambaro, Washington, 1977, Inst. for Arts, Washington, 1978, 80, 82, Interchurch Center, N.Y.C., 1979; exhibited in group shows at Ringling Mus., Sarasota, 1965, four Arts Plaza, West Palm Beach, Fla., 1966, Lowe Gallery, Miami, Fla., 1968; represented in permanent collections Dartmouth Coll., Van Wezel Performing Arts Hall, Sarasota, Fla.; executed mural hangings St. Marks Episcopal Ch., Venice, Fla., St. Raphaels Ch., Englewood, Fla., Apostolic Del.'s Residence, Washington, St. Francis de Sales Sem. Chapel, Milw., The Vatican; instr. Venice (Fla.) Art League, 1968—. Recipient Merit award Nat. Salon, Rio de Janeiro, 1955, 1st prize Arts Council S.W. Fla., 1970, Fine Arts Commn., Brussels, Belgium, 1973. Mem. Allied Arts Council Sarasota (dir. 1967-72), Venice Area Art League (dir. 1964-71, v.p. 1967-70), Artists Equity, Fla. Artists Group, Nat. Soc. Pen Women. Russian Orthodox. U.S. Info. Service solo exhibits, Rio de Janeiro, 1955, Athens, 1961-62. Home: 409 Darling Dr Venice FL 33595

MCKINNEY, VIOLET HELEN MARINES, public relations rep.; b. Crosby, Wyo.; d. George Chris and Edna Ester (Ekis) Marines; student Casper Coll.; m. Charles Edward McKinney; children—Richard Lars (dec.), Marvin Wayne. Dir. public relations First Wyo. Bank, Casper, 1969-78; public relations rep. First Internat. Bank of Casper, 1979—. Bd. dirs. Blue Envelope Health Fund, Sr. Citizen Projects, Salvation Army. Mem. Am. Inst. Banking, Wyo. Press Women's Assn., Casper Area C. of C. (dir. 1972-75). Lutheran. Clubs: Zonta, Daus. of Nile. Home: 2551 Belmont St Casper WY 82601 Office: Box 40 Casper WY 82602

MCKINNIE, GERTHA DUKE, ry. ofcl.; b. Selma, Ala., Apr. 10, 1943; d. John H. and Carolyn Duke; student Triton Coll., 1970-73; B.A. in Psychology, U. Ill., Chgo., 1975; m. William McKinnie, Dec. 24, 1966; children—Martel Denise, Derek Justin. Employment coordinator Minority Info. Referral Center, Des Plaines, Ill., 1975-76; employment rep. Central Telephone Co., Des Plaines, 1976-78, wage and salary asso., 1978-79, sales rep., 1979-80; asst. mgr. staffing and planning Milw. Rd., Chgo., 1981, mgr. EEO and affirmative action plans, 1981—. Recipient Black Achiever award, 1978. Mem. Nat. Assn. Female Execs., Charisma, U. Ill. Chgo. Circle Alumni Assn., Chgo. Area Assn. Affirmative Action, Ill. Affirmative Action Officers Assn., Assn. Am. R.R.s, Black Women's Forum. Lutheran. Club: Chgo. Health. Home: Maywood IL Office: 516 W Jackson Blvd Chicago IL 60606

MCKINNON, DOROTHY ELAINE, automobile assn. exec.; b. Oakland, Nebr., Sept. 20, 1946; d. Charles Clarke and Dorothy Margaret (Corbin) Jewell; student Prince George Community Coll., 1964-65, U. Md., 1971-72, N. Va. Community Coll., 1975-76; 1 dau., Rebecca Long. With FBI, Washington, 1965-66; prodn. analyst Am. Automobile Assn., Falls Church, Va., 1966-71, club cons., 1971-74, mgmt. analyst, 1974-78, mgr. spl. projects, 1978-79, mgr. credit card ops., 1979-81, mng. dir. adminstrv. services, Madison, Wis., 1981-82; v.p., asst. gen. mgr. Auto Club, Rochester, N.Y., 1983—; treas. bd. dirs. Wisconsin Safety Patrols, 1981—. 4-H instr., 1977; v.p. bd. dirs. Loudoun County (Va.) Citizens Assn., 1975-79; mem. Va. Taxpayers Assn., 1977-79; chmn. bd. dirs. Loudoun County Taxpayers Assn., 1978-79; adv. budget com. Loudoun County Bd. Suprs., 1979. Mem. Nat. Assn. Female Execs., Am. Soc. Profl. and Exec. Women, Data Processing Mgmt. Assn., Women in Communications, Profl. Bus. Women's Assn. Home: 254 Culver Rd Rochester NY 14607 Office: 777 Clinton Ave S Rochester NY 14620

MC KINNON, MARGUERITE F., ednl. adminstr.; b. Brundidge, Ala., Aug. 22, 1922; d. Merton O. and Inez (Turner) Fleming; B.S., U. Ala., 1944; M.S., Troy State U., 1977; m. Dan L. McKinnon (dec.). Tchr. home econs. Barbour County Schs., 1944-46; supr. Farmer's Home Adminstrn., Greensboro, Ala., 1946-47, home supr., 1948-53; home economist Ala. Power Co., 1947-48; rehab. supr., area home tchr. State Dept. Edn., Central, Ala., 1953-55, dist. supr., 1955-72, rehab. supr. I, 1972-75, adminstr. blind and deaf services, 1975-79, state supr., spl. services, 1970—; mem. Adv. Council Libraries for Blind and Handicapped. Mem. Ala. Rehab. Assn. (pres. 1975), Nat. Rehab. Assn. (regional pres. 1977-78), Ala. Assn. Workers for the Blind, Ala. State Employees' Assn., Ala. Fed. Blind, Am. Council for the Blind, Montgomery Bus. and Profl. Womens' Club. Presbyterian. Home: Route 1 Box 133 Prattville AL 36067 Office: 2129 E South Blvd Montgomery AL 36198

MC KINSTER, IRENE GLADYS, bank exec.; b. Sulphur, Okla., Mar. 14, 1922; d. Matthew W. and Nola Mae (Holbrook) Smith; student Kiowa County Jr. Coll., 1941, courses in fin. and banking Amarillo Coll., 1968-72; m. Jack W. McKinster, Nov. 7, 1943; 1 dau., Virginia Sue. Salesperson, buyer Bowers Fashion Shop, El Reno, Okla., 1941-46; proof reader, reporter Okla. Livestock Newspaper, 1950-53; interior decorator Ozzie's Carpets and Draperies, North Platte, Nebr., 1962-66; receptionist Hereford State Bank (Tex.), 1967-74, dir. mktg., adv. spl. organizational services, 1972—; speaker in field. Bd. dirs. Opportunity Plan, Hereford div. W. Tex. State U.; chmn. Vocat. Office Edn. Program; chmn. Hereford Hustlers, 1977; chmn. tour com. and beautification com., 1969; mem., chmn. Am. Cancer Soc.; bd. dirs. Sr. Citizens, 1976; deacon Presbyn. Ch., 1973-77, Sunday sch. tchr., 1959—, trustee; active United Way, Heart Fund, March of Dimes; bd. dirs. Guiding Star council Girl Scouts U.S.A., 1958-63, troop leader, 1953-58. Mem. Nat. Assn. Female Execs., Deaf Smith County C. of C. (pres. women's div. 1970, parliamentarian, Torch Light award 1977, dir. 1970). Democrat. Clubs: Newcomers (founder), Tex. Cowbelles (charter), Community Concert, Whiteface Booster, Elkette. Home: 303 Westhaven St Hereford TX 79045 Office: 3d and Sampson St Hereford TX 79045

MCKINSTRY, DORIS NAOMI, clin. pharmacologist; b. McVeytown, Pa., Sept. 8, 1936; d. Cecil Joseph and Elva (Marshman) McK.; B.S. in Biology with honors, Pa. State U., 1958; Ph.D. in Pharmacology, U. Pa., 1965. Research assoc. Merck Sharpe & Dohme, West Point, Pa., 1958-61, sr. toxicologist, 1969-70; sr. scientist McNeil Labs., Ft. Washington, Pa., 1966-69; sr. research investigator The Squibb Inst. for Med. Research, Princeton, N.J., 1971-75, assoc. clin. pharmacology dir., 1975-79, dir. clin. pharmacology, 1979—. Mem. Am. Soc. Clin. Pharmacology and Therapeutics, Am. Coll. Clin. Pharmacology, Am. Soc. Pharmacology and Exptl. Therapeutics, AAAS, N.Y. Acad. Scis., Physiol. Soc. Phila. Contbr. articles to profl. jours. Home: 8 Weidel Dr Pennington NJ 08534 Office: PO Box 4000 Princeton NJ 08540

MC KIRCHY, KAREN ANNE, mgmt. cons.; b. Ames, Iowa, Aug. 21, 1949; d. D.J. and S.R. (Lewis) McK.; B.A. in English, U. Iowa, 1971. Communications rep. Mercy Hosp., Iowa City, 1969-71; office mgr. to Gary F. Hodson, architect, Rock Island, Ill., 1973-75; profl. employment counselor Snelling & Snelling, Davenport, Iowa, 1975-76; personnel and mgmt. cons., propr. McKirchy & Co., Bettendorf, Iowa, 1976—. Mem. personnel com. Neighborhood Housing Services, 1979-80. Cert. personnel cons. Mem. Am. Mgmt. Assn., Data Processing Mgmt. Assn., Nat. Assn. Personnel Cons., Am. Soc. Personnel Adminstrn., Soc. Women Engrs., Quad City Engring. and Sci. Council, Am. Inst. Indsl. Engrs. Roman Catholic. Office: Suite B Georgian Sq 1035 Lincoln Rd Bettendorf IA 52722

MC KNIGHT, ALICE LORRAINE POLLAKOFF (MRS. ROBERT VICTOR MCKNIGHT), business exec.; b. El Paso, Tex.; d. Phillip Lipman and Josephine (Gardner) Pollakoff; student U. Tex. at El Paso, 1949-52; m. Robert Victor McKnight, Aug. 12, 1950. With Popular Dry Goods Co., El Paso, 1947-69, asst. buyer jr. and infants wear, 1947-69, buyer cosmetics, 1955-70; dir. sales Yves St. Laurent and Lanvin Parfums, N.Y.C., 1969-72; v.p. Leni Inc., 1972—; pres. Alice McKnight Merchandising, Ltd., N.Y.C., 1973—; pres. McKnight & Kirksey; exec. v.p., gen. mgr. Calvin Klein Cosmetic Corp., N.Y.C., 1980—; cons. distributive edn. Recipient Achievement award City of Hope. Mem. Cosmetic Career Women, Foragers of Am. (bd. govs.). Home: Ridgefield CT Office: 9 W 57th St New York NY 10019

MCLAFFERTY, DEE HARTMANN, tchr. learning disabled; d. Henry J. and Ottilie (Truebenbach) Hartmann; B.Sc., U. Nebr.; postgrad. Western Ky. U.; m. Charles Lowry McLafferty; children—Ardith McLafferty Zander, Karen Dee McLafferty Foust, Charles Lowry, Kevin Paul. Sci. tchr. Franklin-Simpson High Sch., Franklin, Ky., 1949-50; sec. A.B. Dick Co., Niles, Ill., 1950-51; tchr. chemistry A.G. Parrish High Sch., Selma, Ala., 1967-68; tchr. learning disabled children, Orangeburg, S.C., 1975—. Mem. Dogwood Garden Club, Orangeburg, 1974—, pres. 1976-77; mem. Orangeburg Garden Council, 1976—, 2d v.p., 1977-79, pres., 1979-80; bd. dirs. Orangeburg Festival of Arts, 1976—; mem. Orangeburg Music Club, 1974—, pres., 1977-78; mem., bd. dirs. Orangeburg Attention Home, 1974—; mem. Maude Schiffley chpt. SPCA, Orangeburg, 1976—, treas., 1977-82; bd. dirs. Jubilee, Corinth, Miss., 1973; mem. Charity League Selma, 1963—, follies chmn., 1964; mem. Nat. Head Injury Found., 1980—. Named hon. Ala. adm., 1964, hon. Ala. col., 1968. Mem. Orton Soc. Lutheran. Clubs: Orangeburg Country, Tarantella, Dinner-Dance. Address: 1587 Tolly Ganly Circle Orangeburg SC 29115

MCLAIN, LOIS MAE, banker; b. San Francisco, Apr. 11, 1928; d. Oliver Clifton and Libby (Handelsman) McLain; A.A., City Coll. San Francisco, 1966; B.S. in Bus. Adminstrn., U. San Francisco, 1977. With Bank of Am. N.T. & S.A., San Francisco, 1951—, asst. trust officer, 1964-70, trust officer, 1971-75, adminstr. trusts, 1976—. Mem. Marin County Status of Women Commn., 1974-76; del. Calif. Legis. Roundtable, 1969-72; pres. Marin Community Roundtable, 1973-75; mem. Atty.

Gen.'s Voluntary Adv. Council, 1972-75. Served with USNR, 1950-80. Recipient Woman of the Yr. award, Bus. and Profl. Women, Marin County, 1972, San Francisco County, 1978; Women Helping Women award, Soroptomist Regional, 1980. Mem. Am. Inst. Banking (bd. govs. San Francisco chpt. 1972-74), Calif. Parliamentarians Assn., Nat. Parliamentarians Assn., Nat. Fedn. of Bus. and Profl. Womens Clubs. (Calif. state pres. 1971-72, state parliamentarian 1975-80, nat. parliamentarian 1981-82). Republican. Roman Catholic. Club: Sierra. Home: 317 Knight Dr San Rafael CA 94901 Office: 180 Montgomery St San Francisco CA 94137

MCLAIN, SYLVIA ESTELLA, data processing exec.; b. Arlington, Calif., Apr. 8, 1932; d. Arthur Lee and Mabel Ella (Waughtel) Turner; student Grant Tech. Coll., 1948, Western Bible Inst., 1957-58, U. Calif., Sacramento, 1966; m. Harley Arden McLain, Jan. 4, 1953; children—Doris Elizabeth McLain Warren, Harley Arden, Kirsten Lynne, Kimberly Star. Data processor State of Calif., Sacramento, 1949-58; data processing supr. IBM Corp., Sacramento, 1958-60; data processing conversion coordinator N.Am. Waste, Sacramento, 1960-61; bus. mgr. Pacific Coast Bldg. Maintenance, Inc., Sacramento, 1961-69; data processing mgr. CTC Computer Corp., Sacramento, 1969-71; gen. mgr. Optimum Data Systems, Inc., Sacramento, 1972—, also corp. sec. Mem. Christian Bus. Women's Assn., Republican Women's Assn., Internat. Platform Assn., Data Processing Mgmt. Assn. Mem. Assembly of God. Office: 10378 Rockingham Dr Sacramento CA 95827

MCLANE, JEAN, state legislator; b. Laurel, Mont., Oct. 27, 1926; d. Frank L. and Doris (Sanderson) Baird; student schs. Laurel, Mont.; m. Harry H. McLane, June 10, 1951; children—Norman, Shannon C. Sales staff various retail stores, 1945-49; legal sec., Laurel, Mont., 1949-52; now mem. Mont. Ho. of Reps. Pres., Laurel Republican Women; chmn. Yellowstone County Rep. Central Com., 1970; active Stillwater County Rep. Women. Methodist. Clubs: Daus. of Nile, Order Eastern Star (worthy matron 1962-63), Mont. Optometric Aux., Am. Legion Aux. (pres. 1962), Mont. Stockman, Cowbelles, Mont. Woolgrowers.

MCLANE, WILHELMINA, pianist, educator; b. Franklin, Ohio, Sept. 30, 1910; d. George and Margaret (Brannon) McLane; B.M., Coll. Conservatory of Music Cin., 1932, M.M., 1934; student of Nadia Boulanger in France, 1963; student Am. Conservatory of Music, Chgo.; m. Edwin Sidney Vinnell, Jan. 22, 1957. Tchr. piano, Middletown, Ohio, 1950—; organist United Meth. Ch., Franklin, 1968—; asso. tchr., adjudicator Am. Scholarship Assn.; adjudicator Nat. Guild Piano Tchrs. Recipient Springer Gold Merit award, George Ward Nichols award. Mem. Am. Guild Piano Tchrs., Nat. Music Tchrs. Assn., Dayton Music, Am. Matthey Assn. (workshop mem.). Club. Home and studio: 1618 Gage Dr Middletown OH 45042

MCLAREN, MARILYN PATRICIA, packaging corp. mgr., aviator; b. Jamaica, N.Y., July 5, 1942; d. Raymond Lionel and Katherine Marie (Doepp) Cowan; student public schs., also various aviation schs.; m. Richard Edward McLaren, July 17, 1976; 1 son, Paul William Hibner. Exec. sec. to chief design Wiedersum Assos., architects and engrs., Valley Stream, N.Y., 1960-61; officer mgr., interior designer Keith I. Hibner, architect, Hicksville and Garden City, N.Y., 1961-73; owner, pres. Hibner Atelier, Ltd., interior design and gen. constrn., Garden City, 1968-75; office mgr. Ward Assos./Planning Assos., architects and engrs., Bohemia, N.Y., 1975-76; flight/ground aviation instr. Islip Aviation, Ltd. (N.Y.), 1974-77; asst. to pres. Arkay Packaging Corp., Hauppauge, N.Y., 1977—, in-house constrn. mgr., 1980-82; ind. aviation flight/ground instr. airplane and instrument, 1977—; safety counselor FAA, 1974—; past bd. dirs., officer Aviation Council L.I.; founder Seminar on Air Travel for Everyone (S.A.F.E.), 1975, Fly-C-Cure/We Air Condition People, 1979. Mem. Ninety-Nines (past chmn. L.I. chpt., founding internat. chmn. safety edn., Amelia Earhart Bronze medal 1975), Aircraft Owners and Pilots Assn., Nat. Aero Assn., Nat. Assn. Flight Instrs., L.I. Early Fliers Club, Profl. Secs. Internat. Author articles in field, also seminar syllabus. Home: 3 Park St Lake Grove NY 11755 Office: 22 Arkay Dr Hauppauge NY 11787

MCLAUGHLIN, ANN DORE, govt. ofcl.; b. Newark, Nov. 16, 1941; d. Edward Joseph and Marie (Koellhoffer) Lauenstein; B.A., Marymount Coll., Tarrytown, N.Y., 1963; m. John Joseph McLaughlin, Aug. 23, 1975. Supr. network comml. schedule ABC, N.Y.C., 1963-66; dir. alumnae relations Marymount Coll., 1966-69; account exec. Meyers-Infoplan Internat., Inc., N.Y.C., 1969-71; dir. communications Presdl. Election Com., 1971-72; asst. to chmn., press sec. Presdl. Inaugural Com., 1972-73; dir. Office Pub. Affairs, EPA, 1973-74; with govt. relations dept., asst. dir. communications dept. Union Carbide Corp., Washington, N.Y.C., 1974-77; propr. McLaughlin & Co., pub. affairs, 1977-81; asst. sec. pub. affairs Treasury Dept., 1981—; dir. Nat. Savs. & Trust Co., Washington, 1977-78. Mem. Nat. Fedn. Republican Women (adv. com.). Clubs: Nat. Press, Fed. City (Washington). Office: Treasury Dept Room 3124 15th and Pennsylvania Ave NW Washington DC 20220

MCLAUGHLIN, BLANDINE LAFLAMME, educator; b. Fairfield, Maine, Dec. 4, 1929; d. Eugene and Leda (Pouliot) Laflamme; B.A., Colby Coll., 1960; M.A., Middlebury Coll., 1961; Docteur de l'Université, U. Paris, Sorbonne, 1966; m. Albert Lawrence McLaughlin, July 16, 1955 (dec.). Instr., Mary Washington Coll., Fredericksburg, Va., 1962-63; asst. prof. Smith Coll., Northampton, Mass., 1966-72; asso. prof. French U. Ala., 1974-78, prof., 1978—, acting chmn. fgn. lang. dept., 1982—. Fulbright scholar, 1960-62; Parapsychology Found. N.Y. grantee, 1964-66. Mem. Southeastern Am. Soc. 18th Century Studies, Am. Soc. 18th Century Studies, Société Internationale d'Etudes du 18ème Siècle, MLA, S. Atlantic MLA, Ala. Assn. Tchrs. French. Author: Diderot et l'Amitie, 1973; contbr. articles in field to profl. jours. Home: 3109 Carlisle Rd Birmingham AL 35213 Office: Dept Fgn Langs Bldg 3 407C U Ala Birmingham AL 35294

MCLAUGHLIN, ELSA MAE, nurse; b. Cin., Dec. 17, 1943; d. Richard R. and Elvie L. (King) Weaver; L.P.N., Indpls. Sch. Practical Nursing, 1969; A.S. in Nursing, Marian Coll. Indpls., 1978; m. James Edgar McLaughlin, July 18, 1964; children—James Edgar, Suzzanna Kai. Charge nurse Northside Health Care Center, Indpls., 1975-77; in-service coordinator Greenview Manor Nursing Home, Indpls., 1979-80; head nurse Fountainview Nursing Home, Indpls., 1980-81; asst. dir. nurses Colonial Crest Convalescent Center, Indpls., 1981—. Democrat. Mem. Christian Ch. Clubs: Internat. Assn. Jim Beam Bottle and Splty., Crossroads Jim Beam Bottle and Splty. Home: 3316 Tansel Rd Clermont IN 46234

MC LAUGHLIN, EMILY LYNN, cosmetic co. exec.; b. Fairmont, W.Va., Feb. 17, 1939; d. Albert Lynn and Martha Edith (Jenkins) Springston; B.A. in Elem. Edn., Fairmont State Coll., 1961; m. John Richard McLaughlin, June 17, 1961; children—Randy, Timothy, Steven. Elem. and nursery sch. tchr., 1961-63, 67-68; with Mary Kay Cosmetics Inc., 1971—, unit sales dir., Somerville, N.J., 1972-78, nat. sales dir., 1979—. Recipient numerous sales awards. Republican. Methodist. Address: 111 Flanders Dr Somerville NJ 08876

MCLAUGHLIN, MARGUERITE PEARL, state legislator; b. Matchwood, Mich., Oct. 15, 1928; d. Harvey Martin and Luella Margaret Livingston Miller; student public schs.; m. George Bruce McLaughlin; 1947; children—Pamela McLaughlin Clift, George Bruce, Cynthia McLaughlin Francisco. Mem. Idaho Ho. of Reps., 1978—. Trustee, Joint Sch. Dist. 171, 1976—; precinct committeewoman Clearwater County (Idaho), 1976-78; pres. Orofino Celebrations. Named Woman of Yr. in Clearwater County, Beta Sigma Phi, 1972. Mem. Idaho Council Cath. Women (deanery pres.), VFW Aux. (treas.). Roman Catholic. Office: Idaho Ho of Reps Boise ID 83720 *

MC LAUGHLIN, MEGAN ELAINE, found. exec.; b. Jamaica, W.I., Feb. 22, 1938; came to U.S., 1962, naturalized, 1979; d. Cecil Washington and Casserene Roselma (Allen) McL.; B.A., Howard U., 1962, M.S.W., 1968; postgrad. City U., 1970-72; D.S.W., Columbia U., 1981; 1 dau. Afiya McLaughlin White. Research asst. Bur. Social Sci. Research, Washington, 1966; psychiat. social worker dept. psychiatry Harlem Hosp. Center, 1968-70; lectr.-counselor City U. N.Y., 1970-72; social planner Nat. Planning Agy., Office Prime Minister, Jamaica, 1972-74; cons. Alternative to Detention, Hamilton Madison House, N.Y.C., 1974-75; lectr. Columbia U. Sch. Social Work, 1975-78; program officer N.Y. Community Trust, N.Y.C., 1980—. Mem. N.Y.C. Youth Bd.; mem. bd. Edwin Sould Found. Recipient Inabel Lindsay award Edwin Gould Found., 1967-68; Whitney M. Young acad. and intern fellow, 1978-79. Mem. Nat. Assn. Black Social Workers, Nat. Assn. Social Workers, Jamaica Progressive League. Editor: (with George Brager) Training Social Welfare Managers, 1978. Home: 380 Riverside Dr New York NY 10025 Office: 415 Madison Ave New York NY 10017

MC LAY, JANET FRANCIS, nurse; b. Ossining, N.Y., Oct. 12, 1946; d. James Henry and Irene (Brown) Francis; R.N. (Hosp. Scholar), Vassar Bros. Hosp. Sch. Nursing, 1966; student U. Ariz., 1969-70; m. Apr. 19, 1969. Staff nurse Vassar Hosp., Poughkeepsie, N.Y., 1966-67; 3-11 charge nurse, surg. recovery room Tucson Med. Center, 1967-71; weekend charge relief nurse, emergency room and maternity ward Putnam Community Hosp., Carmel, N.Y., 1972-73; part-time nurse, constrn. site Wedco Corp. div. Westinghouse Co., Buchanan, N.Y., 1971-73; supr. nuclear med. services Indian Point Sta., Consol. Edison of N.Y., Buchanan, 1973—. Cert., Indsl. Hygiene Found., Audiology Assos.; ECG cert. Am. Assn. Indsl. Nurses. Republican. Roman Catholic. Home: 113 Requa St Peekskill NY 10566 Office: Med Bur Consol Edison of NY Buchanan Service Center Buchanan NY 10511

MC LEAN, EVELYN LOUISE, social worker; b. Rantoul, Kans., Mar. 4, 1920; d. John Theron and Esther E. (Welton) Mercer; A.B., Baker U., Baldwin, Kans., 1942; M.A., Scarritt Coll., Nashville, 1946; S.T.M., Boston U., 1962, M.S.S.S., 1965; m. Robert C. McLean, Sept. 27, 1965. Missionary, Methodist Ch., Fukien, China, 1947-51; social service worker, adult edn. and community devel., Malaysia, 1952-61; psychiat. social worker, Boston, 1965-70; mental health program developer and adminstr. Lindeman Center, Boston, 1971-76; asso. area dir. mental health program Franklin and Hampshire Counties, Northampton, Mass., 1976-81; dir. research and devel. Incentive Community Enterprises, Greenfield, Mass., 1981—; field supr. Simmons Coll., 1967-70, Boston Coll., 1973-74; vis. asso. Harvard U. Lab. Community Psychology, Sch. Public Health, 1968-74. Mem. Nat. Assn. Social Workers, Acad. Cert. Social Workers, Mass. Acad. Psychiat. Social Work (charter mem.), Nat. Registry Health Care Providers in Clin. Social Work. Democrat. Home: Box 270 Main Poland Rd Conway MA 01341

MCLEAN, MARGARET STONER (MRS. MALCOLM DALLAS MCLEAN), researcher; b. Victoria, Tex., June 5, 1915; d. Thomas Royal and Mame Victoria (Stoner) Stoner; A.A., Victoria Jr. Coll., 1936; B.S., U. Tex., 1939; m. Malcolm Dallas McLean, Feb. 11, 1939; 1 son, John Robertson. Receptionist, postmaster San Jacinto Mus. History, Houston, 1939-41; microfilm camera operator Library of Congress, Washington, 1942; bibliog. researcher, 1947-53; tchr. elem. sch., Fayetteville, Ark., 1954-55; elem. tchr. Am. Sch., Tegucigalpa, Honduras, 1957-58; tchr. English, U.S. Binat. Center and Am. High Sch., Guayaquil, Ecuador, 1959-61; newspaper microfilm archivist Amon Carter Mus. Western Art, Ft. Worth, 1963-73; microfilm research specialist Spanish Tex. Microfilm Center, Presidio La Bahia, Goliad, Tex., 1973-74; researcher, editorial asst. Papers Concerning Robertson's Colony in Tex., Ft. Worth, 1975—; bibliog. researcher Jenkins Garrett Library, U. Tex., Arlington, 1981—. Clubs: U. Tex. at Arlington Woman's; Texas Christian U. Woman's (Ft. Worth). Contbr. articles to profl. jours. Address: 409 Baylor Dr Arlington TX 76010

MCLEAN, MARQUITA SHEILA MCLARTY, univ. ofcl.; b. Richmond, Va., Aug. 5, 1933; d. William Charles and Daisey (Dabney) McLarty; B.A. with distinction, Va. State Coll., 1953; M.A., Ohio State U., 1956; postgrad. U. Cin., 1957-69; m. Cecil P. McLean, July 25, 1958. Tchr. girls' sch., Delaware, Ohio, 1954-57, Robert A. Taft High Sch., Cin., 1957-62; counselor Sawyer Jr. High Sch., Cin., 1962-65, Withrow High Sch., Cin., 1965-67; asso. Guidance Services div. Cin. Public Schs., 1968-73; dir. Office Univ. Commitment to Human Resources, U. Cin., 1973-77, asso. sr. v.p. Univ. Personnel Services, 1978—. Mem. Columbus adv. council Region V, SBA, 1980-82; bd. dirs. Cin. Minority Contractors Assistance Corp., 1982-83, Minority Bus. Devel. Coalition, 1980, Hamilton County chpt. Am. Cancer Soc., 1980-83, 1980 Mental Health Levy Campaign; trustee Camp Joy, 1979-80, Travelers Aid-Internat. Inst. Cin., 1978-80, Sch. Found. Greater Cin., 1978-80; mem. Leadership Cin., 1978; campaign sec. sch. tax levy campaign Cincinnatians Active To Save Edn., Cin. Public Schs., 1980; active Community; past trustee Cin. Tech. Coll. Guidance Task Force, 1970—, City of Cin. Manpower Commn., 1970-71; mem. alumni adv. council Ohio State U., 1971-74. Mem. Ohio Edn. Assn., Am. Personnel and Guidance Assn., Cin. Personnel and Guidance Assn. (pres. 1967-68), Am. Sch. Counselor Assn. (nat. task force counselor negotiations 1969-71, v.p. middle sch., 1970-71), Ohio Sch. Counselor Assn. (Southwestern rep. 1969), Assn. Counselor Edn. and Supervision (co-chmn. commn. non-white concerns), Nat. Assn. Sch. Counselors (nat. dep. chmn., v.p. 1972), Cin. Personnel Assn. (dir. 1980), Delta Sigma Theta (pres. 1963). Club: Ohio State Alumni (Greater Cin. scholarship chmn. 1969-72). Home: 5324 Kenwood Rd Cincinnati OH 45227 Office: Univ Personnel Services U Cin Mail Location 631-A Cincinnati OH 45231

MC LEAN, MILDRED MURRAY (MRS. JOHN MC LEAN), advt. exec.; b. Summit, N.J.; d. Edward Everett and Lilliam (Williams) Murray; grad. Coleman Bus. Coll., 1929; m. John McLean, Oct. 9, 1935. Office mgr., accountant William C. Siebert, Summit, N.J., 1929-39; controller Overlook Hosp., 1940-46; personnel dir., gen. supr., sec. bd. dirs. Martindale-Hubbell, Inc., 1946-55; advt. prodn. dir. Silver Burdett Co., Morristown, N.J., 1955-75; advt. prodn. cons., 1975—. Co-chmn. Seminar on Status of Women, Fairleigh Dickinson U., 1963; chmn. advt. production seminar Drew U., 1975; mem. N.J. State Commn. Women, 1970-72, charter chmn., 1971-72. Bd. dirs. Tri-County Children's Center, Morristown, N.J.; trustee, nat. support gifts chmn., YWCA, Summit, N.J., 1975-78, mem. adv. bd., 1978-81; pres. bd. trustees Oakes Meml. United Meth. Ch., 1975-77. Recipient Industry award State of N.J., 1971; named hon. col. Rgmt. of Militia State of N.J., 1976. Mem. Bus. and Profl. Women's Club Summit (charter mem., pres. 1958-60, Woman of Achievement award 1972), N.J. Fedn. Bus. and Profl. Women's Clubs (career advancement chmn. 1960-62, 3d v.p. 1962-64, 2d v.p. 1964-66, 1st v.p. 1966-67, pres. elect. 1967-68, pres. 1968-69, bicentennial chmn. 1975-77), Nat. Fedn. Bus. and Profl. Women's Clubs (nat. bd. 1968-69, resolutions chmn. nat. conv. 1970), Nat. Assn. Parliamentarians, N.J. Assn. Parliamentarians (newsletter editor 1979-81, publicity chmn. 1981—, v.p. Cranford unit 1981-82, pres. 1982—). Club: Zonta (charter mem., dir. 1956-59, pres. 1959-61), Zonta Golden Z (adv. chmn. Fairleigh Dickinson U. 1964-66); Summit Area Women's Republican (Parliamentarian 1981—), Fortnightly (Summit). Home and Office: 13 Ridgedale Ave Summit NJ 07901

MCLEAN, SHEILA AVRIN, lawyer; b. Phila., Nov. 1, 1941; d. Alexander A. and Pauline (Cross) Avrin; A.B. magna cum laude, Smith Coll., 1963; LL.B., Yale U., 1966; m. David Lyle McLean, Apr. 27, 1968; children—Alexandra Andrews, David Benjamin Avrin. Admitted to N.Y. bar, 1968; asso. Cravath, Swaine & Moore, N.Y.C., 1966-70; cons. Ford Found., N.Y.C., 1970-71, asst. gen. counsel, 1971-75, asso. gen. counsel, officer, 1975-79; gen. counsel Internat. Devel. Cooperation Agy., 1979-80; partner McLean, Pfeifer, Bklyn., 1980—. Bd. dirs. Assn. Bar City N.Y. Fund, Inc., 1971-75; bd. counselors Smith Coll., 1976-80, Center for Effective Philanthropy, 1980—. Mem. Council Fgn. Relations, Assn. Bar City N.Y. (exec. com. 1971-75), Am. Bar Assn. Office: 848 Carroll St Brooklyn NY 11215

MCLEAN-BARDWELL, CLAIR JEAN, banker; b. South Weymouth, Mass., Aug. 4, 1947; d. Cecil Leo and Jimmie Beatrice (Collins) McL.; student Harbor Jr. Coll., 1965-68; grad. Am. Inst. Banking, 1971-73; student N.Y. Sch. Interior Design, 1979-80, Long Beach City Coll., 1979-80, El Camino Coll., Torrance, Calif., 1981—. With May Co. of Calif., Redondo Beach, 1966-67; agy. accountant Transamerica Ins. Co., Los Angeles, 1968; teller First Fed. Savs. & Loan Assn. of Long Beach (Calif.), 1969-71; loan credit clk. Bank of Calif., Long Beach, 1971-72, gen. ledger clk., 1972, loan clk., 1972-73, bookkeeper, San Francisco, 1973-74; Master Charge clk., loan clk. Calif. Can. Bank, San Francisco, 1974-75; acting installment loan officer Calif. Canadian Bank, Los Angeles, 1975-76; br. mgr. sec. Imperial Bank, Los Angeles, 1976-77; adminstrv. asst. Mfrs. Bank, Los Angeles, 1977-78, asst. cashier 1978-79; prin. br. retail lender Crocker Nat. Bank, Los Angeles, 1979-80, retail banking officer and unit mgr. Bankcard products, Walnut Creek, Calif., 1980-81; tchr. asst. Los Angeles Unified Sch. Dist., 1981—. Active Spl. Olympics, Long Beach, 1977-80. Mem. Beta Sigma Phi. Democrat. Baptist. Club: Order Eastern Star.

MCLEAVEY, CAROLYN ANNE, nurse; b. Chelsea, Mass., Apr. 13, 1944; d. James Francis and Bernice Marie McLeavey; diploma Mass. Gen. Hosp. Sch. Nursing, 1965; postgrad. St. Joseph's Coll., 1980—. Charge nurse Mass. Gen. Hosp., Boston, 1969-72; head nurse U. Miss. Med. Center, Jackson, 1972-74, research nurse, 1974-77; head nurse U. Miami/Jackson Meml. Med. Center (Fla.), 1977-80, coordinator clin. edn., 1980—. Served with U.S. Army, Nurse Corps, 1966-68. Recipient Cert. of Appreciation Miss. Heart Assn., 1977. Mem. Am. Assn. Critical Care Nurses (pres. Greater Jackson chpt. 1975-76), Nat. Inst. Critical Care, Soc. Critical Care Medicine. Contbr. articles in field to profl. publs. Home: 13974-C SW 46th Terr Miami FL 33175 Office: Surgical Services Hosp Center Univ Miami/Jackson Meml Med Center 1611 NW 12th Ave Miami FL 33136

MCLELLAN, MYRA ANN, sci. assn. exec.; b. Lexington, N.C., June 17, 1947; d. Charles Reid and Vivian (Venable) Sechrest; B.A., Catawba Coll., 1969; m. Joseph A. McLellan, Jan. 16, 1971. Copywriter, Jewel Box Stores Corp., Greensboro, N.C., 1969-70; telephone analyst Nat. Geog. Soc., Washington, 1971-74, asst. prodn. coordinator Nat. Geog. mag. and publs., 1974-79, exec. asst. to exec. v.p., 1979—. Home: 527 Bradford Dr Rockville MD 20850 Office: 11555 Darnestown Rd Gaithersburg MD 20878

MC LELLAND, ERNESTINE BELL, civic worker; b. Mexico City; d. Ernest Anderson and Mary King (Nixon) Ord-Bell; student U. Madrid, 1957, U. Barcelona (Spain), 1958, U. Vienna (Austria), 1959, U. Aix-Marseilles (France), 1960; student N.Y.U., 1964-72, M.A. in History, 1977, postgrad., 1977—; m. Claude McLelland; 1 son, James Middleton. Tchr., Central Cupey, Oriente, Cuba, 1927-29, Dominican Republic Sch. of Am. Children, 1929-40, McLelland Sch., Dominican Republic, 1940-45; hostess Bergdorf Goodman, N.Y.C., 1945-59; sec. Sex Info. and Edn. Council U.S., N.Y.C., 1959-69, Better Bus. Bur. Met. N.Y.; asst. to sec. Lulu Thorley Home for Crippled Children, Claverack, N.Y., 1945-55. Mem. Contract Bridge League Am., McLeod Soc. Am., English-Speaking Union, Soc. Desc. of Signers of Declaration of Independence, Art Students League. Episcopalian. Clubs: N.Y. U., Yale (N.Y.C.) Home: 301 E 62d St New York NY 10021

MCLEMORE, JACQUELINE RUTH, educator; b. Columbus, Ga., Apr. 13, 1939; d. Oscar and Clyde Ruthelle (Spinks) Smith; B.A., Winthrop Coll, 1961; M.S.W., Fla. State U., 1963; m. William Pearman McLemore, Dec. 14, 1963; children—Mary Kathryn, Billy, Christopher-Michael. Caseworker I, Alexandria (Va.) Dept. Public Welfare, 1963-65; math. instr. Levy County Bd. Edn., Cedar Key, Fla., 1965-66; caseworker Fla. Dept. Public Welfare, Chiefland, 1966-67, Wayne County Found. Exceptional Children, Jesup, Ga., 1971-73; instr. dept. sociology Auburn (Ala.) U, 1974-76, instr. dept. family and child devel., 1978—; cons. Central Ala. Home Health Service, 1977-80; reader Dickenson Pub. Co., 1975-76; cons. social services Wayne Meml. Hosp., 1972-73, E. Ala. Services for Elderly, 1974. Mem. LWV (dir. 1978-80), Acad. Cert. Social Workers, Am. Assn. Marriage and Family Therapy (asso.), Nat. Assn. Social Workers, Nat. Council Family Relations. Democrat. Episcopalian. Home: 1 Church Dr Auburn AL 36830 Office: Auburn U Auburn AL 36830

MCLEOD, DEBORAH JACKSON, mus. ofcl.; b. Little Compton, R.I., Aug. 20, 1915; d. Eugene Bailey and Caroline Wilbour (Patten) Jackson; grad. pvt. schs.; m. Harry McIntosh McLeod, June 19, 1934 (dec.); 1 dau., Penelope McLeod Beekman; m. 2d, Wilfred A. Dunderdale, May 19, 1980. With dept. reprodns. Met. Mus., N.Y.C., 1962-63; adminstrv. asst. U.S. Com. for UNICEF, 1955-59; mem. exec. com. Bklyn. Mus., 1974-77, gov., 1975-77; mem. exec. com. council of friends Inst. Fine Arts, N.Y. U. Pierpont Morgan Library fellow, 1975. Mem. Am. Assn. Museums (asso.), Internat. Council Museums, Friends of Asia Soc., Albert Gallatin Assos. Presbyterian. Club: Colony (N.Y.C.).

MCLEOD, MARILYNN HAYES, ednl. adminstr.; b. Lake View, S.C., Jan. 2, 1924; d. Cary Victor and Benna (Price) Hayes; B.A., Furman U.; M.Ed., U. S.C., 1952, postgrad., 1975; m. Charles Edward McLeod, Aug. 24, 1947; children—Cary Franklin, Mary Marilynn. Tchr., Hamer-Kentyre Sch., Hamer, S.C., 1944-45, Bennettsville (S.C.) City Schs., 1946-59, Clio (S.C.) Elem. Sch., 1960-63; asst. prof. elem. edn. St. Andrews Presbyn. Coll., Laurinburg, N.C., 1964-67; instr. U. S.C., Florence, 1971; reading supr. Marlboro County Sch. Dist., Bennettsville, S.C. 1967—. Chmn. adminstrv. bd. Trinity United Meth. Ch., 1982—, chmn. pastor-parish relations com., 1979—. Mem. NEA, Internat. Reading Assn., S.C. Edn. Assn., S.C. Internat. Reading Assn., Marlboro County Edn. Assn., Pee Dee Internat. Reading Assn., Delta Kappa Gamma. Democrat. Methodist. Home: PO Box 38 S Main St Clio SC 29525 Office: 122 Broad St Bennettsville SC 29512

MCLEOD, NANCY JANE, city adminstr.; b. St. Louis, June 19, 1946; d. Kenneth Leroy and Velma Jane (Muchmore) McL.; B.A., U. Ariz., 1967, M.B.A., 1970; postgrad. Ariz. State U., 1981—. Adminstrv. aide LEAP dept. City of Phoenix, 1972-73, planning asst., 1973-74, chief program planner, 1974-75, planning coordinator dept. human resources, 1975—. Mem. Bus. and Profl. Women's Club of Phoenix (1st v.p. 1978-80, pres. 1980—), Soc. Advancement of Mgmt. (dir. 1977-81), Am. Mgmt. Assn., Am. Soc. Pub. Adminstrn., Am. Planning Assn., Acad. Polit. Sci. Club: Toastmasters. Home: 3753 E Bloomfield Rd Phoenix AZ 85032 Office: 302 W Washington St Phoenix AZ 85003

MC LOUGHLIN, ELLEN V(ERONICA), ret. editor; b. Utica, N.Y.; d. James Henry and Mary Frances (Riley) McLoughlin; student Utica Free Acad.; A.B., Smith Coll., 1915; postgrad. Radcliffe Coll., 1921-22; L.H.D., Lincoln Coll., 1949. Asst. editor woman's page Country Gentleman, 1915-17; circulation promoter Crowell Pub. Co., 1922-24; asst. advt. mgr. Grolier Soc., 1924-34, advt. mgr., 1934-41, editorial dir., 1947-59, v.p., 1956-64; mng. editor Book of Knowledge, Children's Ency., 1936-42, editor Book of Knowledge Annuals, 1940-53, Book of Knowledge, 1942-60, Story of Our Time, 1947-53, L'Encyclopedie de la Jeunesse, 1948-60, Le Livre de l'Annee, 1950-60, La Science Pour Tous, 1960-64. Pres. bd. trustees Cragsmoor (N.Y.) Library, 1967-70. Roman Catholic. Author: The Murder of Doctor Casenova (with Lucile Rathbun, Anetia McLoughlin), 1934. Contbr. verse to mags., articles to encys. Home: 500 Osceola Ave Apt 202 Winter Park FL 32789

MC LURE, GAIL THOMAS, ednl. administr.; b. Cullman, Ala., Sept. 1, 1935; d. Omer Eugene and Cora Agnes Thomas; B.A., U. Ala., 1957; student Kans. State U., 1958-59; M.Ed., U. Ill., 1965; Ph.D., U. Iowa, 1973; cert. mgmt. of lifelong edn. Harvard U., 1981; m. John William McLure, June 3, 1956; children—David Paul, John Rankin. English tchr. Rantoul and Champaign (Ill.) Schs., 1959-67, Iowa City (Iowa) Schs., 1969-72; instr. Kirkwood Community Coll., 1969-70; teaching, research asst. U. Iowa, 1971-73, instr., 1972-73; research asso., research psychologist Am. Coll. Testing Program, 1973-76; planning coordinator Iowa Higher Edn. Facilities Commn., Iowa City, 1976-77; interinstnl. program coordinator Iowa Regents' Univs., Iowa City, 1976—. Co-dir. grants NSF to ACT Program, 1975-76. Mem. Am. Assn. Higher Edn., Nat. Univ. Continuing Edn. Assn. (bd. dirs. 1982—), NEA, Unitarian Universalist Soc. Iowa City (pres. 1979-81), Phi Beta Kappa, Phi Delta Kappa. Democrat. Unitarian Universalist. Contbr. numerous articles to profl. jours. Home: Route 6 River Heights Iowa City IA 52240 Office: W316 Seashore Hall U Iowa Iowa City IA 52242

MCMAHON, HELEN GRIFFIN, writer; b. Carlinville, Ill., Apr. 11, 1911; d. John and Catherine Theresa (McSherry) Griffin; student Blackburn Jr. Coll., Washington U. Extension Sch., St. Louis, St. Louis U., Fontbonneand Coll., Webster Coll.; also student bus. coll.; m. Edward McMahon, May 7, 1966. Held various secretarial and supervisory positions with ins. cos.; reporter Bank-Trust News, 1950-54; editor Reliable Round Robin, Reliable Life Ins. Co., 1961-67; free-lance writer mag. articles, editorial cons.; Recipient awards, including 1st Pl. Graphic award for bicentennial calendar, 1976. Mem. St. Louis Writer's Guild (sec. 1970-72), Internat. Assn. Bus. Communicators, Women in Communication, Am. Assn. Ret. Persons, Legion of Mary (officer, designer ann. pamphlets), Theta Sigma Phi. Republican. Roman Catholic. Clubs: St. Louis Press, St. Michael's Ch. Plus 50. Author: Portals to Protection, 1972; Shrewsbury of All Places, 1978; Rhyme of My Life (poetry), 1980; author religious and profl. orgns., books, pamphlets; contbr. to anthology 'Neath the Oaks. Home: 7511 Weil St Shrewsbury MO 63119

MCMAHON, JUDITH WANTLAND, clin. psychologist, educator; b. Seminole, Okla., May 19, 1940; d. William Lindsay and Edna Louise (Yost) Wantland; B.A. magna cum laude, U. Mo., 1968; Ph.D. in Clin. Psychology (NDEA fellow), Washington U., 1972; m. Frank B. McMahon, June 15, 1967; children—Russell Lindsay, Charles Gregory. Vis. lectr. Washington U., St. Louis, 1971-79, So. Ill. U., Edwardsville, 1970-81; asst. prof. psychology dept. The Lindenwood Colls., St. Charles, Mo., 1981—; pvt. practice clin. psychology, St. Louis, 1972-74; cons., clin. psychologist, Profl. Counseling Center, New Haven, Mo., 1975-76; reviewer psychology textbooks Prentice-Hall, Inc., 1973-77; cons. Holt, Rinehart and Winston, 1977-78. Mem. Am. Psychol. Assn., Mo. Psychol. Assn. (cert. clin. psychologist 1974). Lic. clin. psychologist, Mo. Author: Instructor's Manual for Abnormal Psychology, 1976; (with Frank B. McMahon) Psychology: The Hybrid Science, 1982; Abnormal Behavior: Psychology's View, 1983. Home: 132 Ridgecrest Dr Chesterfield MO 63017 Office: Roemer Hall 203 The Lindenwood Colls St Charles MO 63301

MCMAHON, LINDA RUTH, coll. dean; b. Cleve., Feb. 5, 1942; d. Harold John and Ordell Emily (Paul) McM.; B.A., Marymount Coll., 1963; M.A., Oberlin Coll., 1964; Ph.D., George Washington U., 1980; postgrad. Am. U., U. Menendez (Spain), Harvard U. Inst. Ednl. Mgmt. Tchr. history and polit. sci. Marymount Coll. Va., Arlington, 1965-72, dean student services, prof. social scis., 1972—; asst. prof., recruiter Head Start; project dir. Project Educare. Mem. Arlington County Citizens Com. Alcohol and Drug Abuse. Mem. Brent Soc., Am. Assn. Higher Edn., Am. Personnel and Guidance Assn., Nat. Assn. Women Deans and Adminstrs., Delta Epsilon Sigma, Pi Sigma Alpha. Author: Independent College Interest Groups' Influence on State Policy, 1981. Home: 6800 Fleetwood Rd McLean VA 22101 Office: 2807 N Glebe Rd Arlington VA 22207

MCMAHON, MARY FRANCES, state legislator, lawyer; b. Providence, Apr. 2, 1955; d. Paul Bernard and Mary Patrica (Schuette) McM.; B.A., St. Mary's Coll., 1977; J.D., Suffock U., Boston, 1980. Admitted to R.I. bar, 1980; asso. firm McMahon, Hendel & Mc Mahon, Pawtucket, R.I., 1980—; mem. R.I. Ho. of Reps., 1981—. Mem. Adv. Bd. Library Commrs., 1981—; mem. energy com. Nat. Conf. State Legislatures, 1981—. Mem. R.I. Bar Assn., Mass. Bar Assn. Democrat. Roman Catholic. Office: 200 Main St Pawtucket RI 02860

MCMAHON, POLLY PAUL, psychologist; b. Saginaw, Mich., Feb. 15, 1949; d. Raymond Jacob and Christine (Chappell) Paul; B.A., Emory U., 1970; M.A., Morehead State U., 1971; Ph.D. (grantee), Calif. Sch. Profl. Psychology, 1975; m. Terry McMahon, Sept. 28, 1973. Intern, Community Mental Health Center, Maysville, Ky., 1970-71; program coordinator in patient unit Metro Atlanta Central State Hosp., 1971-72; intern, Salesian Manor, San Francisco, 1972-75; clin. dir. psychology Children's Hosp., Macon, Ga., 1975-82; pvt. practice, Macon, 1976—; instr. Ga. Coll., part time, 1976—; mem. adv. bd. Cerebral Palsy Center, 1976—. Mem. Ga. Psychol. Assn. (treas. sec. dir. lic. psychologists 1976-78), Am. Psychol. Assn., Southeastern Psychol. Assn., Macon Assn. Retarded Citizens, Nat. Assn. Autistic Citizens, Am. Acad. Psychotherapists. Home: Macon GA Office: 544 Mulberry St Suite 420 Macon GA 31202

MC MANUS, ARLEEN FRANCES, banker; b. Scottsburg, Ind., Jan. 5, 1948; d. John Robert and Iva Frances (Price) Martin; student U. Evansville, 1966-70, Delta Coll., 1974-77; B.A. in Speech and English, Saginaw Valley State Coll., 1981; m. Richard Kent McManus, Sept. 2, 1972. Bookkeeper, Ind. State Hwy. Commn., Indpls., 1970-72; clk. 2d Nat. Bank of Saginaw (Mich.), 1972-74, installment loan interviewer, 1974-76, mgmt. trainee, 1976-77, br. mgr., 1980—; instr. Am. Inst. Banking; loaned exec. Nat. Alliance Bus., 1978-79. Chmn. Bus. and Industry Council of Saginaw; mem. Manpower Devel. Planning Council, 1978-79. Mem. Nat. Assn. Bank Women (chmn. Mich. state group). Methodist. Club: Saginaw Twp. Republican. Office: 101 N Washington Saginaw MI 48607

MC MANUS, MAUREEN ELEANOR, publicity exec.; b. N.Y.C.; d. Terence J. and Mary Eleanor (Lynn) McM.; student pvt. schs. In charge recruitment blood donors ARC Blood Bank, Bklyn., 1941-45; publicity dir. G.P. Putnam's Sons, N.Y.C., 1945-48, Henry Holt & Co., (now Holt, Rinehart & Winston, Inc.), N.Y.C., 1948-52, 54-68, Cowles Book Co., 1968-71; publicity dir. Stephen Greene Press, Brattleboro, Vt., 1971-73; free-lance publicity dir., 1974—; publicity, researcher Readers Digest, Pleasantville, N.Y., 1952-54; instr. creative writing Vt. Community Coll., 1978— ; advocate for the elderly. Lectr., Radcliffe Coll., Georgetown U. Mem. Nat. Book Awards Com., 1948-72. Mem. Women's Nat. Book Assn., Pubs. Publicity Assn. Home: 5 Tyler St Brattleboro VT 05301

MCMEANS, LORRETTA JUNE EVANS, recreational vehicles sales ofcl.; b. Indpls., June 28, 1945; d. Clayton L. and Florence J. (Bunce) Evans; student Ind. Sch. Real Estate, 1965; m. H. Eugene McMeans, July 10, 1965 (div., 1976); children—Lisa R., Melissa D., Traci L. Cashier, Credithrift/Am. Security Finance, 1963, head cashier, 1964-65; with Bob Peak Realty, 1965-70; sales staff recreational vehicles Fun Vehicles, Indpls., 1976-78; recreational vehicles sales staff Holiday of Orlando (Fla.), Inc., 1978—, public relations dir., 1979—; producer, sponsor, participant camping, sales, safety seminars, clinics for clubs and campgrounds. Blue Bird leader, Dist. V. Campfire Girls Assn., 1973-76, sec. Dist. V. 1975-76; sponsor Muscular Dystrophy Carnival, 1976; sec. adv. bd. Palmetto Elem. Sch., 1978-79. Mem. Million Dollar Club, Holiday of Orlando, top sales producer, 1979-81. Mem. Nat. Assn. Female Execs., Women's Info. Network, Fla. State Campground Owners' Assn. (rep.), Osceola County Campground Assn., Osceola C. of C. (rep.), Nat. Campers and Hikers Assn. (speaker), Good Sam Club (Fla. state speaker). Club: Silva Mind Control Grads. Home: 11221 Aries Dr Orlando FL 32809 Office: 5001 Sand Lake Rd Orlando FL 32809

MCMEEKIN, DOROTHY, educator; b. Boston, Feb. 24, 1932; d. Thomas L. and Vera (Crockatt) McM.; B.A., Wilson Coll., Chambersburg, Pa., 1953; M.A., Wellesley Coll., 1955; Ph.D., Cornell U., 1959. Asst. prof. biology Upsala Coll., East Orange, N.J., 1959-64, Bowling Green (Ohio) State U., 1964-66; prof. natural sci. Mich. State U., East Lansing, 1966—. Mem. Mycological Soc. Am., Bot. Soc. Am., Am. Phytopathol. Soc., AAAS, Am. Inst. Biol. Scis., Mich. Acad. Sci., Arts and Letters, Mich. Bot. Club. Office: Dept Natural Sci 335 N Kedzie Mich State U East Lansing MI 48824

MC MENIMEN, KATHLEEN BRENNAN, educator; b. Cambridge, Mass., June 15, 1944; d. John Joseph and Catherine (Healy) Brennan; B.S. in Edn., Boston Coll., 1966, M.Ed., 1974; m. Joseph Paul McMenimen, Aug. 22, 1970; children—Meghan, Joseph Paul. Tchr., Boston public schs., 1966—, Operation Head Start, Charlestown, Mass., summers, 1966, 67, 68; ednl. dir. John F. Kennedy Family Service Center, Charleston, 1969; seminar leader Worcester (Mass.) State Coll., 1974. Mem. Waltham (Mass.) City Council, 1976-78; bd. dirs. John F. Kennedy Family Service Center, 1970-71; mem. Waltham Democratic City Com., 1975—; mem. Waltham Housing Authority, 1981—. Recipient Commendation for community service Waltham City Council, 1978; Disting. Service award Waltham Jaycees, 1978. Mem. Boston Coll. Alumni Assn. (dir. 1972-74), Boston Tchrs. Union, Met.-Beaverbrook Mental Health Assn. Democrat. Author: A Curriculum Guide for Operation Head Start, 1970. Home: 147 Trapelo Rd Waltham MA 02154 Office: 63 Prince St Boston MA 02113

MCMILLAN, ANN ENDICOTT, composer; b. N.Y.C., Mar. 23, 1923; d. Andrew and Dorothy York (Wadhams) McMillan; B.A., Bennington Coll.; student French horn Joseph Singer, N.Y.C., 1940's, composition Otto Luening, 1940's, Eddard Varese, 1952-55. Rec. and copu holder Talking Books Studio, Am. Found. for the Blind, N.Y.C., 1947, 49, 54, 55; music editor Masterworks LPs of Columbia Records, N.Y.C., 1949, Red Seal LPs RCA Victor Rec. Co., N.Y.C., 1949-55; program dir. French Broadcasting (RTF), N.Y.C., 1958-62; music dir. WBAI, N.Y.C., Pacifica Radio, 1964-68; freelance radio essays Can. Broadcasting Corp. in French and Eng., 1959-71; works include: Gong Song, 1969, April-Episode for harpsichord and tape, 1978, Strings, 1980, A Little Cosmic Dust, 1982, Whales I & II, 1973-82, Solar Wind, 1982, Gateway Summer Sound; recs. Folkways and Opus I labels; freelance cons. Mus. Contemporary Crafts for Sound Show, 1968, 69; lectr. presentations N.Y.U., Columbia U., Bennington Coll., Met. Mus. Art, 1974, 78, Maison Française, N.Y.U., 1982. Fulbright grantee, 1955-57; Guggenheim fellow, 1972; Creative Artists Public Service grantee, 1972; Rockefeller Found. grantee, 1979-80. Mem. MacDowell Colony Corp. (mem.-at-large), Am. Composers Alliance, Am. Music Center, Broadcast Music In. (composer mem.). Office: American Composers Alliance 170 W 74th St New York NY 10023

MC MILLAN, MADELYN RINGUS, health underwriter, ins. exec.; b. Des Moines, Oct. 1, 1944; d. Tony J. and Gertrude (Zanios) Ringus; student Drake U., 1963-64; A.A., Jones Coll., 1965; children—Cassandra Lee, Anthony Malcolm, Suzanna Lynn. Sales rep. Prudential Ins. Co., San Diego, 1970; owner, mgr. Fla. Fin. Planners, Tarpon Springs, 1972-77; sales rep. Paul Revere Companies, Tampa, 1978-80, brokerage supr., 1981—. Pres., PTA, 1972, v.p., 1973-74, state rep., 1972; fin. chmn. Tarpon Springs Police Aux., 1974-75; chmn. Sch. Adv. Com., 1974, 78. Mem. Resident Home Assn. (dir.), Am. Businesswomen's Assn. (v.p. 1972), Nat. Assn. Life Underwriters (sec. speakers bur.), Fla. Assn. Life Underwriters, Tampa Assn. Life Underwriters (chmn. health ins. com. 1982—), Women Life Underwriters Conf. (state co-chmn. Fla. 1979-82, state chmn. 1982-83), Nat. Assn. Health Underwriters (registered), Network of Exec. Women. (audit com. Tampa Bay area 1982), Nat. Assn. Female Execs. Republican. Greek Orthodox. Clubs: Toastmistresses (v.p. 1971), Ins. Women West Pasco County. Contbr. to profl. publs. Office: 5511 Executive Dr Suite 247 Tampa FL 33609

MC MILLAN, MARGARET LANGSTAFF, librarian; b. Eaglegrove, Iowa; d. Harry C. and Elizabeth Louise (Tryon) McM.; B.S., Central Mo. State U., 1921; M.S., U. Mo., 1923; postgrad. U. Neuchatel (Switzerland), 1947. Dir. library Columbia (Mo.) Coll., 1926-59; librarian Mo. State Hist. Soc. Library, Columbia, 1959-60; reference librarian Mid Continent Library Service, Independence, Mo., 1961-76; faculty summer sessions Central Mo. State U., Warrensburg, Northwest Mo. State Coll., Maryville, U. Mo., Columbia; speaker various local groups. Bd. dirs. Med. Center Aux., Independence. Mem. AAUW, State Hist. Soc., Jackson County Hist. Soc., Pi Lambda Theta, Delta Kappa Gamma. Republican. Methodist. Clubs: Women's City (Kansas City); Mary Paxton Study. Home: 2525 Lees Summit Rd Independence MO 64055

MC MILLAN, MARIE ELIZABETH (MRS. JAMES BATES MCMILLAN), casino exec., aviation dir.; b. Exeter, Calif., Aug. 1, 1926; d. James Martin and Eva Marie (Cash) Stever; student Calif. Sch. Fine Arts, 1943, U. Calif., 1944-45, San Jose State U., 1956; U. Nev., 1966, 75-76; m. James Bates McMillan, June 20, 1964; children—Michelle (dec.), John, Jeffrey. Sec., U. Calif. Radiation Lab., 1956-60; adminstrv. sec. AEC, Las Vegas, Nev., 1960-65; employment interviewer State of Nev. Employment Security, Las Vegas, 1965-67; mgr. McMillan Ranches, Reedley, Calif., also aviation lectr. and ferry pilot, 1974-80; v.p., aviation dir. Presdl. Casino, Port Harcourt, Nigeria, 1980—. Recipient Amelia Earhart medals, 1974, 76; named Woman Pilot of Yr., 1976-77, S.W. sect. 99's, Las Vegas chpt., 1973-76. Mem. The Ninety-Nines, Nat. Aero. Assn., All Woman Transcontinental Air Race Assn., Soaring Soc. Am., Aircraft Owners and Pilots Assn., CAP, Nev. Safety Council (aviation com.). Democrat. Holder world and U.S. nat. records for speed over recognized course between Fresno and Las Vegas, 1978, for time to climb 3,000 meters, 1979, holder 28 additional world and U.S. nat. aviation speed records from Las Vegas to Hermosillo, Mazatlán, Puerto Vallarta, Guadalajara, Mexico City, Acapulco (all Mexico) and return to Las Vegas, 1981. Home: 705 Twin Lakes Dr Las Vegas NV 89107 Office: Presidential Casino PMB 5141 Port Harcourt Nigeria

MCMILLAN, MINNIE, educator; b. Sunderland, Eng., Nov. 13, 1941; came to U.S., 1969; d. William Forster and Williamina Dunnet (Dinwoodie) McM.; B.A. with honours, Oxford U., 1964, B.Sc., 1965, D.Phil., 1967; m. John Hall Richards, June 21, 1975. Tutorial fellow U. York, 1966-69; vis. scientist Ctr. of Radiobiology and Molecular Biology, Bucharest, summer 1968; research fellow Calif. Inst. Tech., 1969-73, sr. Gosney fellow, 1975-77, sr. research fellow, 1975-81; postgrad. research chemist UCLA, 1974-75; asst. prof. microbiology U. So. Calif. Sch. Medicine, Los Angeles, 1982—; vis. assoc. Calif. Inst. Tech., 1982—. Nuffield Exhbn. at Somerville Coll., Oxford, 1960-64; Sr. Lievre fellow Calif. div. Am. Cancer Soc., 1978-79. Mem. Royal Soc. Chemistry (London), Brit. Soc. Immunology, Brit. Transplantation Soc., Am. Assn. Immunologists. Home: 677 Deodar Ln Bradbury CA 91010 Office: Dept Microbiology U So Calif Med Sch 2025 Zonal Ave Los Angeles CA 90033

MC MILLEN, PATRICIA LOUISE, pharmacist; b. Sewickley, Pa., Jan. 16, 1951; d. Lyle Trump and Eleanor Louise (Perrott) McM.; B.S., W.Va. U., 1974. Pharmacist, Porter's Pharmacy, Coraopolis, Pa., 1974-75; staff pharmacist Ft. Myers (Fla.) Community Hosp., 1975—. Recipient Boss of Yr. award Am. Bus. Women's Assn., 1978. Mem. W.Va. U. Alumni Assn., Am. Pharm. Assn., Fla. Pharm. Assn., Pa. Pharm. Assn., Fla. Soc. Hosp. Pharmacists, So. Gulf Soc. Hosp. Pharmacists, Lambda Kappa Sigma. Democrat. Presbyterian. Club: Park Meadows Racquet. Home: 1722-1 Park Meadows Dr Fort Myers FL 33907 Office: 3785 Evans Ave Fort Myers FL 33907

MCMILLIN-WOOD, JEANIE BYRD, educator, scientist; b. Spartanburg, S.C., Sept. 26, 1939; d. Walter Louis and Frances Elizabeth (Austell) McMillin; B.A., Converse Coll., 1961; Ph.D. in Biochemistry, U. N.C., 1967; children—Elizabeth, David Emerson. Research assoc., instr. U. N.C., Chapel Hill, N.C., 1967-68; research assoc. Cornell Med. Coll., N.Y.C., 1968-69; instr. Baylor Coll. Medicine, Houston, 1969-72, asst. prof., 1972-80, assoc. prof. medicine, biochemistry and pediatrics, 1980—; cons. NIH, 1979—, mem. cardiovascular pulmonary study sect., 1982-86; mem. central research rev. com. Am. Heart Assn., 1981—. Fulbright fellow in chemistry, 1961-62; NASA fellow, 1962-66; USPHS fellow, 1966-67; grantee Am. Heart Assn., 1978-81, Muscular Dystrophy Assn., 1980—, NIH, 1977—. Mem. Internat. Study Group for Research in Cardiac Metabolism, Biophys. Soc., Am. Soc. Biol. Chemists, Am. Physiol. Soc., N.Y. Acad. Scis., Bioenergetics Club. Democrat. Editorial bd. Am. Jour. Physiology, 1980—; contbr. articles to various publs. Home: 2600 Bellefontaine C28 Houston TX 77025 Office: Dept Medicine Section Cardiovascular Scis Baylor Coll Houston TX 77030

MC MILLION, RUTH CAROL HARVEY, newspaper columnist; b. Cheney, Kans., Sept. 21, 1909; d. George P. and Ivy May (Conner) Harvey; student Kans. State Tchrs. Coll., 1928, Kans. U., Lawrence; m. Raymond G. McMillion, Sept. 23, 1928; 1 dau., Monica McMillion Wilkinson. Area editor Kans. Farmer mag., Topeka, 1939-61; feature writer Tex. Cattleman, Ft. Worth, 1951-53; with Clark County Clipper, Ashland, Kans., 1956—, columnist, weekly news and feature, 1956—; exhibited one-woman art shows: Dodge City (Kans.) Library, 1970, Rock Springs (Kans.) 4-H Bldg.; exhibited group shows: Artland Gallery, Ashland, S.W. Art Assn., Dodge City, Kans. State Fair (prize), others; represented in collection Kans. Heritage House, Johnson, Rock Springs Gallery. Hostess, Gov.'s Mansion, Topeka, 1952; mem. Bearcreek unit Clark County Extension. Named One of Outstanding Kans. Presswomen, 1954. Mem. Kans. Press Women (dir. SW dist.) Nat. Press Women, Clark County Hist. Soc., Ashland Art Assn., Kans. Native Sons and Daus. (life), DAR. Mem. Christian Ch. (past clk. ch. bd., past ch. clk.). Pub., Knights of the Range booklet, 1975. Home: Box 115 Ashland KS 67831 Office: Clark County Clipper Ashland KS 67831

MC MONIGLE, PATRICE ANN, corp. psychologist; b. Pitts., Sept. 27, 1949; d. Bernard and Anita (Bromberg) McM.; B.A. in Psychology, Radford Coll., 1971, M.A., 1972; Ph.D. in Indsl.-Organizational Psychology (fellow), Rice U., 1975; m. John Vaillant Gaudreau, May 19, 1973. Cons. psychologist Lifson, Wilson, Ferguson & Winick, Houston, 1975-78, Reid, Merrill, Brunson & Assos., Denver, 1979-80; corp. psychologist Rohrer, Hibler and Replogle, Inc., Denver, 1980—; tchr. Denver U., Colo. Women's Coll., Loretto Heights Coll. Mem. Am. Psychol. Assn., Colo. Indsl.-Organizational Psychol. Assn., Phi Kappa Phi, Denver C. of C., Colo. Whitewater Assn. Contbr. articles to profl. jours. Home: 6551 Elaine Rd Evergreen CO 80439 Office: 441 Wadsworth St Suite 200 Denver CO 80226

MCMORRIS, GRACE ELIZABETH, bank exec.; b. Malden, Mass., Feb. 6, 1922; d. John Edward and Selma Florence (Swanson) O'Brien; B.A., Boston U., 1944; postgrad. Ariz. State U., 1962; m. William Michael McMorris, May 14, 1944 (dec.); children—Sheila Elizabeth McMorris Christenson, Michael, James, John. Clk., Parlin Meml. Library, Everett, Mass., part-time, 1938-40; clk. student post office Boston U., 1941-42; supr. classified advt. desk The Boston Post, 1942-44; substitute tchr. public schs., Randolph, Mass., 1956-57; with Valley Nat. Bank Ariz., Phoenix, 1960—, trust adminstr., 1969-73; trust officer, 1973-75, asst. v.p., 1975-78, v.p., 1978—, corp. trust mgr., 1977—. Active PTA, Little League. Mem. Nat. Assn. Bank Women (sec. 1974-75, dir. 1973-75), North Central Ariz. Group, Western Stock Transfer Assn., Stock Transfer Assn. N.Y., Am. Soc. Corp. Secs., Valbanqueras. Roman Catholic. Office: 241 N Central Ave Phoenix AZ 85004

MCMULLEN, RUTH ANNE, univ. ofcl.; b. Edwardsville, Ill., Feb. 21, 1948; d. Tillmon and Doris (McMurray) Gordy; B.S. in Social Scis., So. Ill. U., 1982; m. William T. McMullen, Nov. 12, 1963 (div.); children—Thomas, Rodney. Community aide Madison County (Ill.), 1969-70; family services specialist Econ. Opportunity Commn. Madison County, 1970-71, dir. youth devel. program, 1971-73; staff asst. So. Ill. U., Edwardsville, 1981—. Recipient Scholastic award Soc. Ethnic and Social Studies, 1981. Mem. Am. Affirmative Action Assn., Ill. Affirmative Action Officers Assn., NAACP, Urban League, St. Louis EEO Group, Edwardsville Bus. and Profl. Women's Club. Home: PO Box 624 Edwardsville IL 62025 Office: So Ill U Campus Box 25-A Edwardsville IL 62026

MCMULLIN, MARY JO, nurse; b. Sedalia, Mo., July 8, 1933; d. Robert Henry and Rose Mary (Alt) Welliver; R.N., St. Mary's Hosp., Kansas City, Mo., 1954; m. Jesse Francis McMullin, Nov. 26, 1955; children—James, Tom, Rose, Jane. Staff nurse St. Mary's Hosp., 1954-55; mem. nursing staff Bothwell Hosp., Sedalia, Mo., 1955-58, head nurse, 1958-70, asst. dir. nursing, 1970—; tchr. stoma care, 1976—. 4-H Club leader, 1975—; pres. Pettis County Extension Council, 1982. Mem. Am. Nursing Assn., Mo. Nursing Assn., 10th Dist. Nursing Assn. (v.p. 1982), Profl. Nurses Assn. Bothwell Hosp. Roman Catholic. Home: Route 2 La Monte MO 65337 Office: PO Box 1706 Sedalia MO 65301

MCMURRAY, CAROLINE DOLBER, social worker; b. Marilla, N.Y., July 31, 1948; d. Clinton Charles and Frances Ann (Gilmore) Dolber; B.A., SUNY, Binghamton, 1970; M.S.W., Va. Commonwealth U., 1977; m. James Michael McMurray, Oct. 21, 1972. Foster care caseworker Warren County Children Services, Lake George, N.Y., 1973-75; social planner Va. Commn. Children and Youth, 1975-76, Henrico County Planning Office, Henrico, Va., 1976-77; social worker Crisis program Chesterfield (Va.) Mental Health Center, 1977-79; dir. Vol. Emergency Foster Care Va., Richmond, 1979-80; regional tng.

coordinator Va. Baptist Children's Home Regional Centers, Richmond, 1980—. Organizer, past pres., bd. dirs. Richmond Domestic Violence Project, Inc., 1977-79. Mem. Fan Dist. Assn., NOW, Nat. Assn. Social Workers, Va. Assn. Vols. in Criminal Justice, Va. Council Social Welfare. Home: 1915 Floyd Ave Richmond VA 23220 Office: 700 E Belt Blvd Richmond VA 23224

MCMURRIN, TRUDY ANN, editor; b. Los Angeles, May 28, 1944; d. Sterling Moss and Natalie (Cotterel) McMurrin; B.A. in History and Philosophy, U. Utah, 1981; m. William M. Howard, Mar. 9, 1963 (div. 1967); m. 2d. Robert Bruce Evans, Sept. 24, 1969 (div. 1971); m. 3d, Mick McAllister, June 16, 1982; children— Natalie Roberta, Howard. Editor U. Utah Press, Salt Lake City, 1967-74, asst. dir., 1974-80, editor-in-chief, 1980—; cons., lectr. for pvt. groups, 1967—; art dir., co-designer award winning books, 1972—. Mem. Coalition to Save Our Sch. Libraries, 1981—; mem. adv. bd. Children's Mus. Utah, 1979-81; mem. Com. for Rowland Hall-St. Mark's Sch. Centennial Symposium Quality in Pre-Coll. Edn., 1980-81. Nat. Endowment Humanities fellow, Am. Assn. State and Local History fellow, 1977; Inst. Am. West fellow, 1981, 82. Mem. Assn. Utah Pubs. (pres. 1978—), Assn. Am. Univ. Presses, Western Univ. Presses, Soc. Scholary Pub., Western Book Pubs. Assn., Western Lit. Assn., Utah Library Assn., Medieval Acad. Am., Utah State Hist. Soc., Utah Opera Assn., Utah Cinema Council. Home: 1456 Lincoln St Salt Lake City UT 84105 Office: U Utah Press Univ Services Bldg Salt Lake City UT 84112

MCMURRY, GWENDOLYN WEATHERBY, home economist; b. Lubbock, Tex., June 10, 1947; d. Lee Methvin and Mildred Madge (Moore) Weatherby; B.S. in Home Econs. Edn., Tex. Tech. U., 1969; M.Ed., Sul Ross State U., Alpine, Tex., 1979. Tchr. vocat. homemaking high schs. in Tex., 1971-75; home econs. extension agt. Dimmit County, Carrizo Springs, Tex., 1976—. Pres. United Methodist Women, Carrizo Springs, 1977. Mem. Nat. Assn. Extension Home Economists, Tex. Assn. Extension Home Economists, Dimmit County Livestock Show Assn., Am. Home Econs. Assn., Tex. Home Econs. Assn. Office: PO Box 157 Carrizo Springs TX 78834

MCNAB, SUSAN ELIZABETH, bldg. materials co. personnel exec.; b. Chgo., Nov. 4, 1949; d. James Orville and Betty Edith (Westlake) McN.; B.A., Purdue U., 1971; M.A., U. Md., 1977. Asso. buyer Procter & Gamble Co., Cin., 1971-72; personnel cons. Girl Scouts U.S.A., Chgo. and San Francisco, 1973-76; personnel and safety supt. Monsanto Co., Seattle, 1976-80, mgr. personnel World Hdqrs., St. Louis, 1980-82; dir. personnel Lanoga Corp., Seattle, 1982—. Mem. Profl. Secs. Internat. Exec. Adv. Bd. Bd. dirs. Seattle SEAFAIR Orgn., 1978-80; mem. Seattle Mayoral Com. on Energy, 1978-80; ofcl. recreation commn. City of Foster City, Calif., 1975-76. Mem. Am. Soc. Personnel Adminstrn. (mem. nat. com. on employee and labor relations 1981-82), NOW (v.p. Va. Minor chpt. 1982), Womens Commerce Assn., Indsl. Relations Assn., Women's Info. Network, Sigma Kappa Alumni Assn. Home: 10203 47th Ave SW Seattle WA 98146

MC NABB, COLETA PEOPLES, clinic adminstr.; b. Marquez, Tex.; d. James Harmon and Ida Maude (McDaniel) Peoples; student Sam Houston U. (scholar), U. Houston, 1962-65; m. Marvin J. McNabb; children—Jimanne McNabb Durkee, Michael James; m. 2d, Samuel V. Smith, Aug. 11, 1973 (div. 1977). With Gulf Oil Corp., Houston, 1950-53, Hermann Hosp., Houston, 1956-58, Tellepsen Petrochemical Corp., Houston, 1958-60; exec. sec. Goodwin, Dannenbaum, Littman & Wingfield, Inc., Houston, 1960-62; with Med. Clinic Houston, 1962—, asst. mgr., 1968, adminstr., 1968—. Reader, Taping for the Blind, 1968-70; mem. Mus. Fine Arts, Houston; mem. Republican Nat. Com. Recipient awards for creative writing Theta Sigma Phi. Mem. Med. Group Mgmt. Assn., Am. Group Practice Assn., Med. Adminstrs. Tex., Nat. Assn. Female Execs., So. Mgmt. Assn., Jr. League Houston (patron). Republican. Asso. editor: Harvest, 1964; editor newsletter Houston Heart Assn., 1971-72. Recipient Short Story Excellence achievement award Storymag., 1962, Short Story award Harvest mag., 1962. Office: 1707 Sunset St Houston TX 77005

MC NABB, (MARTHA) SUE, assn. exec.; b. Howard County, Mo., Mar. 18, 1936; d. Cecil Milton and Sue Ann (Forbes) Williams; student Kirksville State Tchrs. Coll., 1953-54, N.E. Mo. State Tchrs. Coll., 1962-64; B.S.E., U. Calif., Berkeley, 1965; m. Marion Marshall, June 4, 1954; children—M. Ronald Marshall, Deborah Sue Marshall. Tchr., Dudgeon Sch., rural schs., Fayette, Mo., 1965-75; employment specialist Dept. Labor, Washington, 1977; older Ams. supr. Mo. Green Thumb, Buffalo, 1978; manpower dir. N.E. Mo. Community Action Agy., CETA, Kirksville, Mo., 1979-80; distbr. Lord Jim's Parlour Restaurants, 1978-82; exec. dir. March of Dimes Chariton Valley chpt., Kirksville, Mo., 1982—; mem. adv. bd. Regional Manpower Adv. Council; asst. tchr. Dale Carnegie. Recipient cert. appreciation and commendation Disadvantage/Handicapped N.E. Mo., 1978. Mem. Nat. Assn. Female Execs., Nat. Ret. Tchrs. Assn., Internat. Entrepreneus Assn., Mo. Assn. Community Action, NOW (task-master Nat. Action Center 1975-76), Nat. Fedn. Bus. and Profl. Women (regional dir. 1971). Democrat. Adventist. Author: The Basic Aspects and Concepts of Play Therapy, 1965; Culture and Personality, 1966; Treatment of Seasons; Climing the Crystal Stairs, 1981; The Pheromone Phenomenon; Praimeri Kaer, 1982; contbr. articles to profl. jours. Home: Rd M Route 3 Green City MO 63545 Office: 207 W Harrison Kirksville MO 63501

MCNAIR, LOIS I., speech therapist; b. New Brunswick, Can.; d. George W. and Mary (McColl) McN.; B.Sc., Emerson Coll., 1967; M.Ed., Boston State Coll., 1969, postgrad., 1969-70; postgrad. Boston U., 1975-76; Ph.D., Heed U., Fla., 1982; Radiologic technician Can. Dept. Vets. Affairs, 1947-62, 67-68; tchr. speech and hearing Boston Sch. System, 1969; radiographer Radiologic Group Greater Boston, 1970-71; counselor, tchr. speech and hearing Manchester (N.H.) Sch. System, 1970-71; tchr. speech therapy Houlton (Maine) Sch. System, 1972—. Cert. tchr., Maine, Mass., N.H. Mem. Can. Med. Radiation Technologists, Royal Soc. Health, Nat. Council Family Relations, NEA, Am. Personnel and Guidance Assn., Maine Personnel and Guidance Assn., Maine Speech and Hearing Assn., Am. Public Health Assn., AAAS, Speech Communication Assn. Home: PO Box 393 Houlton ME 04730

MC NAMARA, MARY ELLEN, mktg. adminstr.; b. Long Branch, N.J., May 26, 1942; d. Edward Ward and Alice Marie (Reynolds) McN.; B.A., Glassboro State U., 1965; M.B.A., N.Y.U., 1975, Advanced Profl. Cert., 1980. Tech. asst. Bell Labs., Holmdel, N.J., 1965-66, sr. tech. asst., 1966-68; programming writer, analyst IBM, N.Y.C., 1968-71, systems programmer, 1971-72, bus. planner, 1972-74, industry planning adminstrn., Princeton, N.J., 1974-77, industry mktg. adminstr., 1977-81, product mktg. adminstr., White Plains, N.Y., 1981—. Mem. IEEE (treas. computer soc. N.J. 1977-79, chmn. 1982, treas. N.J. sect. 1980-81, sec. 1982 AAAS, Assn. Computing Machinery, AAUW, Assn. Women in Computing, Nat. Council Women U.S.A., Women's Econ. Roundtable, Exec. Women of Palm Beaches, N.Y. Acad. Sci., N.Y. U. Alumni Assn., Glassboro State U. Alumni Assn. Republican. Roman Catholic. Office: 1133 Westchester Ave White Plains NY 10604

MC NAMARA, MAUREEN ANN, ednl. adminstr.; b. Burlington, Vt., June 11, 1923; d. Joseph Augustine and Mary Patricia (Magner) McNamara; B.S., Regis Coll., 1945; postgrad. St. Michael's Coll., 1965, 70. Coll. recorder, asst. registrar St. Michael's Coll., Winooski, Vt., 1960-67, coordinator extension services and grad. program, 1967-69, registrar, 1969—; mem. bd. corporators Burlington Savs. Bank, 1973-75; dir. Chittenden Trust Co. Mem. Adv. Council U.S. Cath. Bishops, 1969-74; mem. Vt. Diocesan Ecumenical Commn., 1971-78, 79—; trustee Vt. Ecumenical Council, 1975-82; pres. Vt. Council Cath. Women, 1963-67; mem. Gov.'s Commn. on Status Women, 1965-69; mem. Burlington Democratic City Com., 1973—, Chittenden County Dem. Com., 1973—, Dem. Nat. Com., 1978—; mem. Burlington Zoning Bd., 1968—; mem. Vt. Ednl. TV Broadcast Council, 1977-79; mem. Vt. Dem. Com., 1976—, sec., 1977; trustee Vt. State Colls., 1973-79, sec., 1976-79. Mem. New Eng. Assn. Registrars and Adminstrv. Officers (treas. 1971—), Vt. LWV (v.p. 1969-73), Burlington Bus. and Profl. Womens Club (v.p. 1967-68), Vt. Cath. Press Assn. (dir. 1969—, sec. 1975—), Am. Assn. Collegiate Registrars and Admissions Officers (registration techniques com. 1976-79, placement com. 1980—), Delta Epsilon Sigma. Home: 14 Summit St Burlington VT 05401 Office: St Michaels College Winooski VT 05404

MCNAMEE, CAROLE SCHWIMER, govt. ofcl.; b. N.Y.C., Dec. 12, 1941; d. Sam and Lillian Elizabeth (Feldman) Schwimer; B.S. in Home Econs., U. Md., 1963; m. Frederick M. McNamee, Sept. 2, 1973. Personnel mgmt. specialist Dept. Navy, 1974-76, Internat. Trade Commn., 1976-77; personel mgmt. specialist Nat. Endowment Arts, 1977-80, chief program br., personnel div., 1980—. Publicity chmn. Pinecrest Heights Homeowner's Assn., 1978-79. Mem. Internat. Personnel Mgmt. Assn. (chpt. v.p., conf. publicty com. 1982). Office: 2401 E St NW Washington DC 20506

MCNAMEE, CATHERINE T., nun, coll. adminstr.; b. Troy, N.Y., Nov. 13, 1931; d. Thomas Ignatius and Kathryn Elizabeth (Quinn) McN.; B.A., Coll. of St. Rose, 1953, D.H.L., 1975; M.Ed., Boston Coll., 1955, M.A., 1958; Ph.D., U. Madrid, 1967. Joined Sisters of St. Joseph of Carondelet, Roman Catholic Ch., 1957; tchr. Spanish and Latin, Gilbertsville (N.Y.) Central Sch., 1953-54; asst. registrar Boston Coll. Grad. Sch., Chestnut Hill, Mass., 1955-57; tchr. Spanish and history McCloskey Meml. High Sch., Albany, N.Y., 1960-61; instr. Spanish, acad. dean Coll. of St. Rose, Albany, 1961-75; dir. liberal arts Thomas Edison State Coll., Trenton, N.J., 1975-76; pres. Trinity Coll., Burlington, Vt., 1976-79, Coll. St. Catherine, St. Paul, 1979—; dir. First Nat. Bank of St. Paul, Minn. Mut. Ins. Co. Bd. dirs. Minn. Mus. Art, 1979-82, Minn. Orchestral Assn., 1979, St. Joseph's Hosp., 1979, St. Mary's Jr. Coll., 1979. Mem. Am. Assn. Higher Edn., Assn. Cath. Colls. and Univs. (chmn. 1982—), Internat. Fedn. Cath. Univs. (v.p. 1980—), AAUW. Clubs: Town and Country, Zonta. Office: College of St Catherine 2004 Randolph Ave Saint Paul MN 55105

MC NARY, JEANNE CECILE, tire distbr.; b. Norwich, Conn., Dec. 30, 1943; d. Georges Joseph and Aldea (Bellerose) Desrosiers; B.S. in Secretarial Scis., Bryant Coll., 1964; m. David Glenn McNary, Feb. 18, 1965; children—Dawn Lesley, David Jean. Sec., Naval Submarine Med. Research Lab., Groton, Conn., 1964—; propr. Discount Tire and Nat. Discount Tires, Groton, Saybrook, Southington, Elmwood, Enfield, East Lyme, and West Hartford, Conn., 1977—; v.p. Intrastate Tire, Inc., Groton; dir. Am. Tire Co., East Hampton, Conn. Rec. sec. Ledyard Community Council, 1971-73, rep., 1971-72; chmn. civilian welfare and recreation Navy Submarine Base, Groton, 1978-80, 82—. Mem. Federally Employed Women (rec. sec. 1980, pres. Dolphin chpt. 1981-82, New Eng. regional mgr. 1982—), Bus. and Profl. Women. Democrat. Roman Catholic. Home: Grassy Hill Rd Route 3 Lyme CT 06371

MCNEAL, MARY ANN, realtor; b. Miami, Fla., Oct. 8, 1942; d. Sidney Earl and Mary Marcella (Feldkamp) McNeal; student U. Cin., 1960-64, Cin. Art Acad., 1962-64. Art dir. Ralph Jones Advt., Cin., 1964-66, Integon Corp., Winston-Salem, N.C., 1966-68, Coalition Advt., Fayetteville, N.C., 1970-72; realtor Plessinger & Co., Denver, 1973-74, Mary Rae & Assos., Denver, 1974-76; pres., realtor Vintage Properties Ltd., Denver, 1976—. Mem. bd. dirs. Civic Centre E., Denver, 1980—, N. Capitol Hill Devel. Corp., Denver, 1981—; mem. bd. realtors City Govt. Com., Denver, 1980—. Mem. Denver Bd. Realtors (1st pl. Denver Inner Elegance award 1980), Hist. Denver, Denver C. of C., Contbr. articles to profl. publs. Office: 811 E 17th Ave Denver CO 80218

MC NEAL, THEDA MAXINE TOLLIVER, state ofcl.; b. Pine Bluff, Ark., June 4, 1941; d. Forest and Lena Mae (Barker) Tolliver; B.S., Calif. State U., Hayward, 1969; M.A. in Employment Studies, San Francisco State U., 1977; m. Luther McNeal, Jr., June 21, 1969 (div.); 1 dau., Thelena Celeste. With State of Calif., 1964—, program supr. service center program, 1977-79, coordination specialist employment devel. dept., Bay Area Region, 1979-81, mgr. Richmond (Calif.) Manpower Services office, 1981—; mem. Berkeley Workreaction Council, 1977-80; counselor in field. Recipient Sustained Superior Accomplishment award State of Calif., 1979. Mem. Internat. Assn. Personnel in Employment Security, Black Advisors in State Service, Bus. and Profl. Women's Aux. Oakland (pres.), Calif. Personnel and Guidance Assn. Baptist. Home: 1527 Ashby Ave Apt 4 Berkeley CA 94703 Office: 330 25th St Richmond CA 94804

MCNEELY, ANN LOUISE, univ. adminstr.; b. Alexandria, La., Aug. 27, 1916; d. George Charles and Kathrine O. (Clements) Wilson; B.A., Northwestern State U., La., 1937; m. Ludlow N. McNeely, Apr. 1, 1939; children—Charles LeRoy, Ludlow N. Tchr., Rapides Parish Sch. Bd., 1937-41, Natchitoches Parish Sch. Bd., 1941-42; account clk. Northwestern State U., Natchitoches, 1957-63, clk., 1963-66, asst. supr. loans and grants, 1966-70, asst. dir. student fin. aid, 1971-73, dir. bur. research, 1973-74, dir. student fin. aid, 1974—. Mem. Service League Natchitoches, 1951—, pres., 1955-56; mem. Assn. Preservation Hist. Natchitoches, 1974-82. Mem. La. Assn. Student Fin. Aid Adminstrs., Southwestern Assn. Student Fin. Aid Adminstrs., Sigma Sigma Sigma. Roman Catholic. Home: PO Box 246 Natchitoches LA 71457 Office: Caldwell Hall Northwestern State University Natchitoches LA 71457

MCNEER, ELIZABETH JANE, librarian, adminstr.; b. Radford, Va., Dec. 27, 1946; d. Rembert Durbin and Lottie Grey (Frazier) McNeer; B.A., Randolph-Macon Woman's Coll., 1968; M.L.N., Emory U., 1969; Ph.D., Ohio State U., 1981. Asst. curator spl. collections U. Houston Libraries, 1969-71; undergrad. librarian Ohio State U., Columbus, 1972-78; coordinator Columbus Extension Program, Kent (Ohio) State U. Sch. Library Sci., 1980-81; dir. library No. State Coll., Aberdeen, S.D., 1982—. Recipient Ruth Weimer Mount award Ohio State U., 1974, 77. Mem. ALA, Nat. Assn. Women Deans, Adminstrs., and Counselors, Phi Delta Kappa, Beta Phi Mu. Author: The Role of Mentoring in the Career Development of Women Administrators in Higher Education, 1981. Office: Library 14th and Washington Sts Aberdeen SD 57401

MC NEESE, BETTY ALLISON, sch. adminstr.; b. Shreveport, La., Jan. 26, 1927; d. John Richard Preston and Leora (Byram) Allison; B.A., Northwestern State U., 1947; M.Ed., U. Miss., 1965, Ed.D. (teaching fellow), 1968; m. Robert L. McNeese, June 10, 1951 (div.); children—Sara Allison, Robert Hilliard. Tchr. English, Rodessa High Sch., 1947-50, Ida High Sch., 1950-51, Fair Park High Sch., Shreveport, 1957-66; guidance counselor Oak Terr. Jr. High Sch., Shreveport, 1967-68; parish supr. English and social studies Central Staff, Caddo Parish Sch. System, Shreveport, 1968-71, dir. secondary edn., 1971-79, asst. supt. curriculum and instrn., 1979—. Trustee, exec. com. La. Council Econ. Edn.; trustee CUP adv. bd. La. Tech. U.; edn. com. La. Div. Arts; minuteman youth task force Bicentennial Com., 1976. Recipient award Phi Alpha Theta, 1944. Mem. La. Council for Social Studies (exec. bd., pres.), La. Council Econ. Edn. (exec. com., bd. trustees), Caddo Adminstrs. Club, La. Assn. Educators, Nat. Assn. Educators, La. Assn. Sch. Suprs., PTA. Democrat. Baptist. Author: Factors Influencing College Choice of University of Mississippi Freshmen, 1968; The Story of American History, 1969; History of the Fifty States, 1970; Elementary Story Starters, 1971; Advanced Story Starters, 1971. Home: 233 Pierremont Rd Shreveport LA 71105 Office: Box 37000 Shreveport LA 71130

MCNEESE, CYNTHIA, network design engr.; b. Seattle, June 23, 1946; d. William Joseph and Velma Lucille (Miller) McN.; student Foothill Jr. Coll., 1972, Deanza Jr. Coll., 1975-76. Operator, clk. Pacific N.W. Bell Telephone Co., Seattle, 1964-68; engr. AT&T, San Francisco, 1968-70, supr. overseas ops., 1970-71, employment supr., 1971-72; employment supr. Pacific Telephone Co., Los Angeles, 1978-79, engr. ETN design, 1979—. Mem. Women in Mgmt., Nat. Assn. Female Execs., Career Planning Center, Inc., San Gabriel Assn. Physically Handicapped. Republican. Methodist. Home: 911 N Greenpark St Covina CA 91724 Office: 1010 Wilshire Blvd Los Angeles CA 90017

MC NEESE, WILMA WALLACE, social worker; b. Chgo., Apr. 30, 1946; d. Nettie Fletcher Wallace; student Wilson City Coll., 1964-66; B.A., So. Ill. U., 1969; M.S.W., Loyola U., Chgo., 1976; m. Mose D. McNeese, Dec. 27, 1969; children—Derrick, Christina. Program coordinator Intensive Tng. and Employment Program, East St. Louis, Ill., 1970-71; methods and procedures adviser Ill. Dept. Pub. Aid, Chgo., 1972-73; social work intern Robbins (Ill.) Presch. Center, 1974; with U.S. Probation Office, Chgo., 1975; officer U.S. Pretrial Services Agy., Chgo., 1976—; undergrad. field work instr. dept. corrections Aurora (Ill.) Coll., 1981, Chgo. State U., 1981—. Recipient Community Service award Village of Robbins, 1975; advanced tng. cert. Fed. Jud. Center.; cert. social worker, Ill. Mem. Nat. Assn. Social Workers, Acad. Cert. Social Workers, Fedn. Probation Officer's Assn. Baptist. Home: 209 Todd St Park Forest IL 60466 Office: 219 S Dearborn St Room 1100 Chicago IL 60604

MCNEILL, ALICE JEANETTE, athletic trainer, educator; b. Caribou, Maine, July 17, 1958; d. Robert Eugene and Melba Fern (Davis) McN.; B.Edn., Ohio U., 1980; M.S., W.Va. U., 1981. Grad. asst. athletic trainer W.Va. U., 1980-81; head women's athletic trainer Iowa State U., Ames, 1981—. Recipient Al Hart Scholarship award, 1979-80. Mem. Nat. Athletic Trainers Assn., Iowa Athletic Trainers Assn. Methodist. Home: 4329 Lincoln Swing Apt 27 Ames IA 50010 Office: 111 Phys Edn Bldg Iowa State U Ames IA 50011

MCNEILL, M(ARY) JANET, univ. adminstr.; b. Austin, Tex., Nov. 9, 1945; d. Robert B. and Jeanne Lancaster McN.; B.A., Oberlin Coll., 1967; postgrad. Columbia U., 1968. Asst. to artist mgr. Baldwin Piano & Organ Co., N.Y.C., 1970-71; performer Minn. Opera Co., 1973-75; dir. pub. relations St. Paul Chamber Orch., 1973-76, Eastman Sch., Music, Rochester, N.Y., 1978-79; dir. pub. info. and publs. U. Redlands (Calif.), 1980-82; dir. publs. Stanford U., 1983—; cons., editor, writer, designer various promotional materials for colls. and univs. Nat. Merit Corp. scholar, 1963-67; Am. Field Service scholar, 1962; NSF scholar, 1961. Mem. Council for Advancement and Support of Edn. (2 Grand awards for publ. excellence 1982), Coll. and Univ. Designers Assn., Am. Symphony Orch. League. Office: Publs Stanford U Press Courtyard Santa Teresa St Stanford CA 94305

MCNEILL, RUTH ETTA, cytotechnologist; b. Balt., July 1, 1935; d. William Edward and Arrie Blanche (Cox) Hayes; B.S. Morgan State U., 1977; cert. in cytotechnology Johns Hopkins Sch. Cytotechnology, 1962; children—Craig V., Rhonda Michelle. Cytotechnologist, USPHS Hosp., Balt., 1962-66, supr., 1966-81; cytotechnologist, Sinai Hosp., Balt., part-time, 1977-80; supr. cytotechnologist Wyman Park Health Systems Inc., Balt., 1982—; faculty USPHS Hosp. Sch. Med. Tech., 1973-81. Treas., Cordelia-Cuthbert Hayward Neighborhood Assn., 1979; mem. zoning com. Northwestern Neighborhood Assn., 1981. USPHS fellow, 1961. Mem. Md. Assn. Cytotechnologists, Am. Soc. Cytology, Am. Soc. Clin. Pathology. Contbr. articles to profl. jours. Home: 5368 Cordelia Ave Baltimore MD 21215 Office: 3100 Wyman Park Dr Baltimore MD 21211

MC NEILL, SUSAN HUNTER, real estate exec.; b. Prescott, Ariz., Feb. 26, 1936; d. Glenn Samuel and Alma (Johnson) Hunter; B.A., U. Ariz., 1957; postgrad. Academe de Beaux Artes, Paris, 1959-60, Immaculate Heart Coll., 1973; m. Kenneth Ian McNeill, Nov. 23, 1971; children—Kathleen Dawn Bryant, Robert, John. Freelance artist and writer, 1960-70; with Sunset Mag., Menlo Park, Calif., 1970-72, Haagen Devel. Co., Los Angeles, 1973-75; owner, mgr. Susan McNeill & Assos., Palos Verdes, Calif., 1975-78; real estate syndicator, investment counselor Seaview Properties, Rolling Hills Estates, Calif., 1978—. Bd. dirs. Palos Verdes Community Arts Assn., 1979-80; pres. Rembrandt Crew, 1977-79. Democrat. Episcopalian. Home: 4511 Sugarhill Dr Rolling Hills Estates CA 90274 Office: Seaview Properties 908 Silver Spur Rd Rolling Hills Estates CA 90274

MC NETT, HAZEL CHARLOTTE, nursing adminstr.; b. Norwood, Ohio, Feb. 24, 1920; d. James Benjamin and Anna Margaret (Schmidt) Standley; R.N., Deaconess Sch. Nursing, 1941; student U. Cin., 1949-54; A.A., Cuesta Coll., 1969; B.S., Calif. Poly. State U., 1973; 1 dau., Ann Louisa Hall. Supr., Deaconess Hosp., Cin., 1948-54; head nurse Drake Meml. Hosp., Cin., 1954-59; asst. dir. nursing services San Luis Obispo (Calif.) Gen. Hosp., 1959—, in-service dir., 1959-67. Served with Nurses Corps, U.S. Army, 1942-46. Mem. Am. Nurses Assn., Am. Heart Assn., Am. Cancer Soc., Assn. Practitioners in Infection Control, Calif. Nurses Assn., Marine Corp. League Aux., Am. Assn. Ret. Persons, San Luis Obispo Bus. and Profl. Women's Club, San Luis Obispo Hist. Soc. Republican. Presbyterian. Club: Soroptomist, Women's Internat. Bowling Congress. Home: 2019 Sierra Way San Luis Obispo CA 93401 Office: 2180 Johnson Ave San Luis Obispo CA 93401

MC NITT, MIRIAM ELIZABETH, craft artist; b. Syracuse, Kans., Feb. 13, 1916; d. Frank Dunham and Nina (Kirkpatrick) Davis; student Coll. of Sequoias, 1952—; m. William O'Neal McNitt, June 30, 1934; children—Nela (Mrs. David J. Dunaway), Nancy (Mrs. Bernard K. Knoll). Accountant, office mgr. Delta Mosquito Abatement Dist., Visalia, Calif., 1951-56; office mgr. Hathaway Nursery, Visalia, 1956-58; office mgr. Anchor of Calif., Fresno, 1958-62; personal studio craft artist, Fresno, 1962-68, 75—; adminstrv. asst. Yosemite Nat. Park, Calif., 1968-72, Merced Coll., 1972-75; exhibited Elders Gallery, Fresno, 1980, Ansel Adams Studio, Yosemite Nat. Park, 1976, 81, Le Entrepreneur Gallery, Fresno, Bank of Calif., Modesto, 1982, Farmers & Mchts Bank, Modesto, 1982; exhibited juried shows ACC S.W. Crafts Fair, San Francisco, Presdl. Mus., Odessa, Tex., The Art Pl., Pen Women's Art Show, Modesto, Gallo Winery, Modesto, Yosemite Nat. Park, Fresno Arts Center, McHenry Mus., Modesto, Calif., Profl. Artists Show, Fresno, Needlework Show, Woodlawn Plantation, Mt. Vernon, Va., No. Calif. Artists Show, Crocker Mus., Sacramento; commd. work Yosemite Nat. Park. Vol. mem. Area 4 Neighborhood Council, Fresno, 1979—; Christmas Seal sale chmn. Tulare Kings Counties Tb Assn., 1956-57, sec.-treas., 1954-58; v.p. Fresno County Epilepsy Soc., 1965-68; active Camp Fire Girls, Reseda, Calif., Van Nuys and North Hollywood (Calif.) Girl Scouts, Visalia and El Portal (Calif.) 4-H Clubs. Mem. Calif. Congress Parents and Tchrs. (life), Visalia Bus. and Profl. Women (radio TV chmn. 1956-58), Am. Craftsmans Council N.Y., Central Calif. Art League, Modesto Symphony Assn., Turlock (Calif.) Regional Arts Council, Benicia (Calif.) Community Arts. San Joaquin Valley Town Hall, Yosemite Natural History Assn. Republican. Club: Calif. Fedn.

Women's Clubs (art chmn. 1965-67). Address: 1141 Cambridge Ct Modesto CA 95350

MCNULTY, FRANCES HELEN, TV sta. exec.; b. Thompsonville, Conn., Oct. 25, 1940; d. Hugo Bonefacio and Delia Katherine (Pieczarka) Marinaccio; B.A., Am. Internat. Coll., Springfield, Mass., 1964; m. Peter J. McNulty, June 20, 1964 (separated); children—Peter J., Sara Jane. Secondary sch. English tchr. in Mass., 1964-69; citizen advocacy coordinator Assn. Retarded Citizens, 1977-79; alumni dir. Am. Internat. Coll., Springfield, Mass., 1979-80; dir. public info. Sta. WGBY-TV (PBS), Springfield, 1980—; corporator Florence Savs. Bank (Mass.), 1973—, trustee, 1976—; mem. consumer adv. council Mass. Electric Co., 1976-77; past trustee U. Mass.; city councilor, Northampton, Mass., 1974-79; v.p., sec. Citizen Adv. Com., Northampton, 1971-73; bd. dirs. Hampshire County and Mass. div. Am. Cancer Soc., 1973-81; bd. dirs., co-chmn. Hampshire Community United Way, 1979—, vice chmn., 1980—, exec. com., 1980—. Recipient Outstanding Leadership award Hampshire Community United Way, 1979. Democrat. Home: 61 Crescent St Apt 6 Northampton MA 01060 Office: Sta WGBY-TV 44 Hampden St Springfield MA 01103

MCNULTY, MARIAN STEVER, educator; b. Quakertown, Pa., Sept. 24, 1929; d. J. Alvin and Grace (Daily) Stever; B.A., Goucher Coll., 1951; M.A., Vanderbilt U., 1953; Ph.D., Cornell U., 1962; children—Michael, Gregory, Clare. Instr., Hobart and William Smith Coll., Geneva, N.Y., 1957-61; asst. prof. N.Y. State Coll., Cortland, 1961-63; asso. prof. Sch. Bus., Seton Hall U., South Orange, N.J., 1970-80, asso. dean, 1977-79; dean profl. studies Stockton State Coll., Pomona, N.J., 1980-82; asso. dean, asso. prof. mgmt. Sch. Bus., U. Ark., Little Rock, 1982—; cons. in field, 1975—. Mem. acad. council Thomas A. Edison Coll., Trenton, N.J., 1976-82; mem. South Orange Adv. Com. to Planning Bd., 1978-79. Mem. Acad. Mgmt., Assn. Social Econs., AAUW (Stockton rep. 1980-82), Phi Beta Kappa, Phi Kappa Phi. Lutheran. Home: 2218 Breckenridge Rd Little Rock AR 72207 Office: Coll Bus Adminstr U Ark Little Rock AR

MCNULTY, MARY ELIZABETH, assn. adminstr.; b. Teaneck, N.J., May 4, 1930; d. Daniel Joseph and Margaret Henry McN.; B.A., Hunter Coll., 1968; postgrad. Fordham Grad. Sch. Bus., 1979-81. Ednl. tng. asst. U.S. Steel Corp., 1950-56; asso. producer Rountree Productions, 1957-61; dir. communications Am. Textbook Pubs. Inst., N.Y.C., 1961-70; staff asst. Assn. of Am. Pubs., N.Y.C., 1970-75, dir. public relations, 1975-79, dir. sch. div. and direct mktg. book club div., 1979—; bd. dirs. Literacy Vols. of Am. Pres. parish council St. John the Evangelist Ch., 1979. Mem. Advt. Club N.Y., Public Relations Soc. Am., Edn. Writers Assn., EdPress Assn., Internat. Reading Assn., Assn. Supervision and Curriculum Devel., N.Y. State Communicators. Republican. Roman Catholic. Office: 1 Park Ave New York NY 10016

MCNUTT, ALICE HITE, state legislator; b. Henderson, Ky., June 22, 1917; d. Leslie Peyton and Mary Gladys (Flaherty) Hite; student Paducah Community Coll., 1934-36, Am. Acad. Dramatic Art, 1936-37; m. S. H. McNutt, Feb. 25, 1941. Pres., Royal Crown-Nehi Bottling Co., 1942-73; city commr., Paducah, Ky., 1968-70; mayor, City of Paducah, 1973-76; mem. Ky. Ho. of Reps., 1976—; exec. dir. Paducah Tourist Commn., 1980—; dir Paducah Bank & Trust Co. Chmn., McCracken County Red Cross; mem. Civic Beautification Bd.; active McCracken County Tb Assn., McCracken County Mental Health Assn. Recipient Mrs. Lyndon B. Johnson Community Service award Keep Am. Beautiful, 1980, Clyde W. Ware Leadership award Hands Found., 1981. Democrat. Roman Catholic. Office: 417 Washington St Paducah KY 42001

MC PARTLAND, MARIAN, pianist, composer; b. Slough, Eng., Mar. 20, 1920; d. Frank and Janet Payne Turner; attended Guildhall Sch. Music, London; m. Jimmy McPartland, Feb. 3, 1945 (div.). Toured English vaudeville theaters as pianist with Milly Mayerl, 1941; toured with Brit. ENSA in Europe, 1943, with USO camp shows, France, 1944; came to U.S., 1946; formed group with husband, played with Billie Holiday; formed own group, 1951; toured U.S. nightclubs; played Hickory House, N.Y.C., 1952-60; performed with Benny Goodman, 1963; now leads group in nightclub and sch. appearances; founded Halcyon Records, 1969; toured S. Am. with Earl Hines and Teddy Wilson, 1974; composer Twilight World, Ambience; albums include: Ambience, Fine Romance, Now's the Time, Solo Concert at Haverford. Address: Halcyon Records 302 Clinton St Bellmore NY 11710 *

MCPHERSON, MARY PATTERSON, coll. pres.; b. Abington, Pa., May 14, 1935; d. John B. and Marjorie Hoffman (Higgins) McP.; A.B., Smith Coll., 1957, LL.D. (hon.), 1981; M.A., U. Del., 1960; Ph.D., Bryn Mawr Coll., 1969; LL.D. (hon.), Juniata Coll., 1975; Litt.D. (hon.), Haverford Coll., 1981. Instr. philosophy U. Del., 1959-61; asst., fellow and lectr. dept. philosophy Bryn Mawr Coll., 1961-63, asst. dean, 1964-69, asso. dean, 1969-70, dean Undergrad. Coll., 1970-78, asso. prof., 1970—, acting pres., 1976-77, pres., 1978—; bd. dirs. Agnes Irwin Sch., 1971—, Shipley Sch., 1972—, Phillips Exeter Acad., 1973-76, Wilson Coll., 1976-79, Greater Phila. Movement, 1973-77, Internat. House of Phila., 1974-76, Josiah Macy, Jr. Found., 1977—, Carnegie Found. for Advancement Teaching, 1978—, Univ. Museum, Phila., 1977-79, Univ. City Sci. Center, Phila., 1979—, Am. Council on Edn., 1979—; dir. Provident Nat. Bank of Phila., Provident Nat. Corp., Bell Telephone Co. Pa. Mem. Soc. for Ancient Greek Philosophy. Clubs: Fullerton, Cosmopolitan. Address: Taylor Hall Bryn Mawr College Merion Ave Bryn Mawr PA 19010 *

MCQUADE, KAREN MARIE, plant biologist; b. Cleve., Sept. 10, 1952; d. Lawrence Edward and Colette Marie (Lynch) McQ.; B.S., U. Dayton (Ohio), 1974; M.S., Northwestern U., 1975. Research asst. Northwestern U., 1974-75; tech. rep. Meistergram, Inc., Cleve., 1975-76; tchr. sci. Magnificat High Sch., Rocky River, Ohio, 1976-77; dir. quality control Bonne Bell Co., Lakewood, Ohio, 1977-79; project asso. plant biochemistry/genetic engrng. research and devel. Standard Oil of Ohio, Cleve., 1979—; judge high sch. sci. fairs, 1981—. Asst. Nat. Spl. Olympics Danceathon, 1981; fitness cons., aerobic dance instr. Grantee Huntington Fund, 1970-72. Mem. AAAS, Plant Molecular Biology Assn., Tissue Culture Assn., Nat. Assn. Female Execs. Democrat. Roman Catholic. Clubs: Ski West Ski (activities chmn. 1976-77), Fagowees Internat. Ski, North Coast Volleyball Assn. (sec.), U.S. Volleyball Assn. Home: 22954 Mastick Rd 202 Fairview Park OH 44126 Office: 3092 Broadway Ave Cleveland OH 44115

MC QUADE, MARGARET ANN, publishing group exec.; b. Newark, Apr. 28, 1931; d. Francis Andrew and Lucy Mary (Ford) McQ.; B.A. magna cum laude in Chemistry and Math., Ladycliff Coll., 1959; M.A. in Gen. Profl. Edn., Seton Hall U., 1966. Instr., chmn. dept. chemistry Ladycliff Coll., 1960-62; elem. sch. tchr., adminstrv. intern North Rockland Sch. Dist., 1963-73; pres. Human Resources Devel., Inc., 1973-79; sr. project mgr. Xerox Learning Systems, Xerox Pub. Group, Greenwich, Conn., 1979—; adj. asst. prof. psychology Pace U. Recipient Bausch & Lomb sci. award, 1959, Outstanding Tchr. award St. Thomas Aquinas Coll., 1965; permanently cert. sch. supt. and adminstr., N.Y. Mem. Am. Soc. Tng. and Devel., Sales and Mktg. Execs. Internat., Exec. Woman, NOW, AAUW. Contbr. articles to Working Wives Mag., interviews to Newark News. Home: 103 Gedney St Nyack NY 10960 Office: 1600 Summer St Stamford CT 06904

MCQUEARY, CHERYL LEE BATH, telecommunications exec.; b. Long Beach, Calif., July 31, 1944; d. Philip Raymond and Rosa Lee (Barnett) Bath; B.A., Drew U., 1978; M.P.A., Fairleigh Dickinson U., 1980; m. Charles Everette McQueary, July 8, 1972. Pricing analyst McDonnell Douglas Astronautics Corp., Santa Monica, Calif., 1966-70; teaching asst. Drew U., Madison, N.J., 1977-78; staff mgr. AT&T, Basking Ridge, N.J., 1980—. Mem. exec. com., bd. dirs. Regional Health Planning Council. Mem. Am. Health Planning Assn. (bd. dirs.), Am. Pub. Health Assn., Am. Soc. Pub. Adminstrs., Beta Beta Beta. Republican. Presbyterian. Club: N.J. Shakespeare Festival. Office: 1 Speedwell Ave Morristown NJ 07960

MC QUIDDY, MARIAN ELIZABETH, newspaper pub.; b. Los Angeles, Mar. 21, 1952; d. Arthur Robert and Aleen Frampton (Hinkle) McQuiddy; B.J., Purdue U., 1974; postgrad. press photography Northwestern U., 1973, Webster Coll., 1981. Summer editorial intern Chgo. Daily News, 1973; news dir. KSVP, Artesia, N.Mex., 1974; police reporter, polit. editor Roswell (N.Mex.) Daily Record, 1974-77; UPI night editor, sports and feature editor, Des Moines, 1977-79; editor Mt. Vernon (Iowa) Democrat, 1979; news editor Cadillac (Mich.) Evening News, 1979-80; tchr. adult edn. Pine River High Sch., LeRoy, Mich., 1979-80; editor Portage (Wis.) Daily Register, 1980-81; pub. Las Lunas (N.Mex.) Village Voice, 1981—. Bd. dirs. Cadillac Area Arts Council, Community Theater. Recipient journalism award N.Mex. Press Assn., Wis. Press Assn., N.Mex. Farm Bur., service awards Roswell Library, Optimists, Boy Scouts Am. Mem. Nat. Fedn. Press Women, Women in Communications, Jr. League, Sigma Delta Chi. Methodist. Home and Office: PO Box 1090 Las Lunas NM 87021 Office: 309 DeWitt St Portage WI 53901

MCQUILLAN, FRANCES CARROLL, artist; b. Chgo.; d. Thomas William and Jane Ellen (Connors) Carroll; B.A., Caldwell Coll., 1975; postgrad. Parsons Sch. Design, 1932; m. Edward J. McQuillan, Apr. 23, 1941; children—Thomas, Kathleen. Fashion artist, N.Y. and Chgo. papers, 1933-35; freelance window display, N.Y. and N.J., 1936-38; instr. art Yard Art Sch., 1967-69, Montclair Art Mus. Sch. Art (N.J.), 1950—; one person shows Argent Galleries, N.Y.C., Seton Hall U., Newark; exhibited in group shows Nat. Arts Club, N.Y.C., Dayton Art Inst., Conn. Acad. Fine Arts, Seton Hall U., Paris, Exposition Continental, Monaco and Dieppe, France, Mus. Fine Arts, Springfield, Mass. Mem. Am. Artists Profl. League, N.J. Watercolor Soc., Montclair Art Mus., Art Centre N.J. Home: 3 Godfrey Rd Upper Montclair NJ 07043 Office: South Mountain Ave Montclair Mus Montclair NJ 07042

MCQUILLAN, JOAN ANNE, educator; b. Springfield, Ill., Jan. 3, 1950; d. Edgar William and Wanda Lou (Gagnon) Miller; B.S.Ed., Ill. State U., 1972; M.A. in Ednl. Adminstrn., Sangamon State U., 1981. Spl. edn. tchr., educationally handicapped Sch. Dist. 117, Jacksonville, Ill., 1972-74, behaviorally disordered, 1975-82, elem. tchr., 1982—; adj. prof. learning disabilities, social and emotional disorders MacMurray Coll., 1981. Cert. spl. edn., kindergarten through 12th grades, elem. tchr., gen. adminstr. kindergarten through 12th grades, Ill. Mem. NEA, Ill. Edn. Assn., Jacksonville Edn. Assn., Ill. Reading Council. Office: Franklin Elem Sch 352 E Franklin St Jacksonville IL 62650

MC QUILLAN, MARGARET MARY, publishing co. exec.; b. N.Y.C.; d. John A. and Margaret (Higgins) McQ.; A.B., Coll. New Rochelle, 1945; M.A. Columbia U., 1948. With Harcourt Brace Jovanovich, Inc. (formerly Harcourt, Brace & World), N.Y.C., 1949—; asst. sec., 1960-70, sec., 1971—, v.p. 1975-78, adminstrv. v.p., 1978-80, sr. v.p., 1980—. Home: 125 Crestwood Ave Tuckahoe NY 10707 Office: 757 3d Ave New York NY 10017

MCQUILLAN, ROSEMARIE BIAGI, educator; b. Boston, July 8, 1954; d. Mario Louis and Frances Eleanor (Bottini) Biagi; B.A. magna cum laude, Boston Coll., 1976, M.Ed., 1977; m. John Joseph McQuillan, Jr., June 12, 1977; 1 son, Jordan Ross. Co-dir. Sunlight-Fernald Project, Boston, 1975-77; tchr. Lynchburg Tng. Sch. and Hosp., Madison Heights, Va., 1976; tchr. deaf-blind Como Spl. Programs, St. Paul Sch. System, 1977—. Mem. Assn. for Severely and Profoundly Handicapped. Home: 14240 11th Ave S Burnsville MN 55337 Office: Como Spl Programs 780 W Wheelock Pkwy Saint Paul MN 55119

MC QUOWN, JUDITH HERSHKOWITZ, publ. cons., author; b. N.Y.C., Apr. 8, 1941; d. Frederick Ephraim and Pearl (Rosenberg) Hershkowitz; A.B., Hunter Coll., 1963; postgrad. N.Y. Inst. Fin., 1965-67. Portfolio analyst Walston; chief underwriting Div. Municipal Securities City of N.Y., 1972-73; pres. Judith H. McQuown & Co. Inc., publ. cons., N.Y.C., 1973—; pub. McQuown's Designer Markdowns newsletter, 1982—. Mem. Am. Soc. Journalists and Authors. Author: Inc Yourself: How to Profit by Setting Up Your Own Corporation, 1977, 79, 81, 82; Tax Shelters that Work for Everyone, 1979; The Fashion Survival Manual, 1981; Playing the Takeover Market: How to Profit from Mergers, Tender Offers, Spinoffs and Liquidations, 1982; contbg. editor Boardroom Reports Mag., 1978-79. Home: 333 E 80th St New York NY 10021 Office: 127 E 59th St New York NY 10022

MCQUOWN, PATRICIA GRACE, broadcasting co. exec.; b. Shreveport, La., May 26, 1921; d. Wirt Owen and Grace Isabel (Simms) Taylor; grad. public schs., Detroit Lakes, Minn.; m. Edmund James McQuown, Oct. 29, 1939; children—Michael, Kathleen, Colleen. Continuity dir. Sta. KRGI, Grand Island, Nebr., 1953-59; producer, continuity dir. Sta. KMMJ, Grand Island, 1959-61; continuity dir., public service dir., asst. mgr. Sta. KTAN, Tucson, 1961-67; asst. for radio, program mgr. Sta. KUAT-AM, Tucson, 1967-79, asst. gen. mgr., dir. programming and prodn., 1980—. Bd. dirs. Nat. Public Radio, 1976-77, Rocky Mountain Public Radio, 1976—; pres. So. Ariz. Arthritis Found., 1975-77, dir., 1978—; bd. dirs. Young Audiences of So. Ariz., 1973—. Republican. Episcopalian. Club: Order of Eastern Star. Home: 7433 Princeton Dr Tucson AZ 85710 Office: Station KUAT-AM/FM University of Arizona Tucson AZ 85721

MCRAE, ANNIE MOORE, educator; b. Edgemoor, S.C., Oct. 29, 1936; d. Johnnie Star and Mary Anderson Moore; B.A., S.C. State U., 1958; M.A., U. No. Colo., 1977; postgrad. Rutgers U., So. U. La., Fla. A&M U., Fla. Internat. U. Tchr. Greenville County (S.C.) Public Schs., 1958-60; instr. Miami-Dade (Fla.) Community Coll., 1974-76; tchr. Dade County Public Schs., 1961-80, now guidance counselor. Committeewoman State Democratic Com., Miami, 1975-78; v.p. Greater Miami sect. Nat. Council Negro Women, 1979—; mem. bd. govs. Culmer Youth Outreach Program, Miami, 1981-82, Nat. Ch. of Christ, N.Y.C., 1979—. Merril fellow, Atlanta U., 1960-61. Mem. NAACP, United Tchrs. of Dade County, Dade County Personnel and Guidance Assn., Am. Fedn. Tchrs., Nat. Assn. Female Execs., Delta Sigma Theta. Mem. African Meth. Episcopal Zion Ch. (dist. dir. Christian edn., dist. supt. bds. 1977—). Club: Internat. Toastmistress. Editor: Finley High Voice, 1953-54, The Share Cropper, 1979-80, Newsletter Cue Cue, 1981. Home: 2031 NW 93d St Miami FL 33147

MCRAE, BERNEESE DISON, farmer; b. Talladega, Ala., Aug. 19, 1920; d. Miles Pierce and Letha (Phillips) Dison; B.S., U. Montevallo, 1942; m. James H. McRae, June 12, 1942 (dec. 1969); children—James D., Thomas G.; m. Ted Campbell, 1973 (div. 1981). Tchr. vocat. home econs. Washington County High Sch., 1942-44, sc., Lamar County High Sch., 1944; mgr. dairy farm and milk distributorship McRae Dairy Farm, Hamilton, Ala., 1958-72, plant hybridizer, 1976—, partner, 1982—. Editor, publisher Bexar Bugal, 1959-64. Mem. Farm Bur. (chmn. womens div. county, state bd. sec., del. state legislature, nat. congress). Mem. Am. Day Lily Soc., Ala. Environ. Quality, Keep Am. Beautiful, U. Montevallo Alumni, Ala. Farm Bur. Democrat. Methodist. Address: Route 5 Box 65 Hamilton AL 35570

MC RAE, CARMEN, singer; b. Apr. 8, 1922. Solo vocalist, 1954—; music festival appearances include Monterey, Newport, Concord, Brussels; albums include: I Am Music, Great American Song Book, Sound of Silence, Just a Little Lovin', Portrait of Carmen, For Once in My Life, It Takes a Whole Lot of Human Feelings, Ms. Jazz, Carmen, Carmen McRae, Carmen's Gold, Live and Doin' It, Alive!, In Person, I Want You. Address: care Pattack Productions Inc 314 Huntley Dr Los Angeles CA 90048 *

MCRAE, DEE (DOROTHY SUE), writer, editor; b. Huntsville, Ala., May 29, 1939; d. Alan and Dorothy Adel (Heffernan) McR., Jr.; student Florence (Ala.) State Coll., 1957-59; B.J., U. Mo., Columbia, 1961; m. Paul W. Chesser, May 29, 1973; 1 son, Timothy Paul. With Florence Herald, 1962-63; newsroom writer-editor USIA, Washington, 1963-64, editor, writer Am. Illustrated mag., 1964-67, picture editor Topic mag., 1967-69, mem. pamphlets staff, editor, writer, 1969-72; free lance writer, editor, picture editor, 1972-74; asst. editor Smithsonian Mag., Washington, 1974-77, asso. editor, 1977-81; freelance writer/editor, 1981—. Mem. NOW. Home: Dragonlair Saint George Island MD 20674

MC REE, JANICE LORENE ROWLAND, home economist; b. Athens, Tenn., Mar. 14, 1942; d. Calvin Frank and Nora Ethel (Scarbrough) Rowland; B.S. in Home Econs., U. Tenn., Knoxville, 1963; M.S. in Home Econs. Edn., Fla. State U., 1974; m. John Thomas McRee; children—Ann Michelle, Jonathan Damon. Asst. home demonstration agt. U. Tenn., Dickson, 1963-67; social worker Dept. Public Welfare, Clarksville, Tenn., 1968-70; extension home economist, program leader U. Fla., Live Oak, 1970-75; coordinator expanded food and nutrition edn. program, asst. prof. home econs. Clemson (S.C.) U., 1975—. Mem. Am. Home Econs. Assn., Nat. Assn. Extension Home Economist Agts., S.C. Home Econs. Assn., Epsilon Sigma Phi (scholarship 1974). Episcopalian. Clubs: Clemson U. Women's, Gourmet, Clemson Area Home Economists, Episc. Women's Guild, Order Eastern Star. Home: 316 Lancelot Dr Clemson SC 29631 Office: 108 Barre Hall Clemson U Clemson SC 29631

MCROY, RUTH GAIL, social worker, educator; b. Vicksburg, Miss., Oct. 6, 1947; d. Horace David and Lucille A. (McKinney) Murdock; B.A. in Sociology and Psychology, U. Kans., 1968; M.S.W., 1970; Ph.D. in Social Work (Danforth Found. fellow 1980-81, Black Analysis, Inc. fellow 1980-81), U. Tex., Austin, 1981; m. June 5, 1968 (div.); children—Myra Louise, Melissa Lynn. Marriage counselor Family Consultation Service, Wichita, Kans., 1970-71; adoption specialist Kans. Children's Service League, Wichita, 1971-73; asst. prof. social work U. Kans., Lawrence, 1973-77; asst. prof. sociology and social work Prairie View A&M U., 1977-78; tech. asst. specialist Region VI Adoption Resource Center, Austin, 1979-81; asst. prof. social work U. Tex., Austin, 1981—; guest speaker in field; cons. adoptions; instr. in continuing edn.; pres. bd. dirs. Black Adoption Program and Services, Kansas City, Kans., 1976-77. Mem. Nat. Assn. Social Workers, Council Social Work Edn., Phi Delta Kappa, Phi Kappa Phi. Episcopalian. Author: Black Homes for Black Children, 1974; Instructor's Guide to Accompany Human Responses to Social Problems, 1981. Office: 2609 University Ave Austin TX 78712

MCROY-MORGAN, AGNES DEJOYCE, univ. adminstr.; b. Syracuse, N.Y., Oct. 21, 1951; d. Fletcher and Agnes Kennebrew (Young) McRoy; A.A., Brevard Community Coll., 1971; B.S., Tuskegee Inst., 1973; M.A., Fla. State U., 1976; postgrad. Fla. A&M U., 1976—; m. Warren W. Morgan, May 31, 1980. Part-time instr. Cocoa Correctional Center-Brevard Community Coll., 1974-75; supr., counselor Brevard County Mental Health Center, Rockledge, Fla., 1973-75; asst. dir. Seminole youth program Fla. State U., 1975, sec. III, Office of Orientation, 1975; adminstrv. asst. legis. affairs Office of Gov. Fla., Tallahassee, 1975-76; project coordinator Fla. Drug Abuse Prevention and Edn. Trust, Tallahassee, 1972-79; exec. dir. Fla. A&M U. Industry Cluster Program, coordinator corp. relations, 1979—. Mem. Am. Bus. Women's Assn. (pres. Silver Dome chpt. 1980-81, Outstanding Woman of Yr. 1980-81), Nat. Hookup of Black Women Inc. (sec.-treas. 1979-81), Nat. Council Negro Women, NAACP, Nat. Urban League, Fla. Econs. Club, Fla. A&M U. Alumni Assn. Democrat. Methodist. Home: 1572 Jack's Dr Tallahassee FL 32301 Office: Fla A&M Univ NAB Room 416 Tallahassee FL 32307

MC SHERRY, ENID FORD JONES, assn. adminstr.; b. New Haven, Apr. 23, 1940; d. William Ford and Elinor (MacBrayne) Jones; A.A., Briarcliff (N.Y.) Coll., 1960; student N.Y. Sch. Interior Design, 1961, Silvermine Coll. Art, 1961-62; m. John Anthony McSherry, Jan. 21, 1967. Asst. to dir. devel. Met. Mus. Art, N.Y.C., 1965-70; dir. alumnae affairs, editor alumnae publs. Finch Coll., N.Y.C., 1970-75; fund raising ofcl. Jackson for Pres. Com., N.Y.C., 1975-76; adminstr. Delta Psi, N.Y.C., 1979—. Aux. police officer mounted div. N.Y.C. Police Dept. Mem. Am. Alumni Council, Alumnae Adv. Center. Home: 130 E 94th St New York NY 10028 also Box 23 Sea Island GA 31561 Office: 16 E 64th St New York NY 10021

MC SPADDEN, CAROL FRANCES, psychologist; b. Knoxville, Tenn., June 17, 1935; d. James Tilley and Carrie Frances (Egbert) McS.; B.S., U. Tenn., Knoxville, 1957, M.S., 1970, Ed.D., 1972. Elem. tchr. Alcoa (Tenn.) City Schs., 1957-69; area lead psychologist Charlotte-Mecklenburg Schs. (N.C.), 1972—. Mem. Nat. Assn. Sch. Psychologists, Am. Psychol. Assn., N.C. Sch. Psychology Assn., NEA, N.C. Assn. Educators, Pi Lambda Theta, Alpha Delta Kappa, Phi Kappa Phi, AAUW, Delta Zeta. Democrat. Baptist. Home: 164 Shady Oak Trail Charlotte NC 28210 Office: 1501 Euclid Ave Charlotte NC 28203

MCSWAIN, BYRDIE ENGLE, clin. lab. scientist, immunohematologist; b. Ethel, Ark., Oct. 13, 1939; d. James Marvin and Katherine Engle (Martin) McSwain; B.S., U. Ark., 1968; B.S. in Med. Tech., U. Ark. Sch. Medicine, 1969; M.S., U. Central Ark., 1973; Specialist in Blood Banking, U. Ark. Med. Scis., 1976. Med. technologist, Supr. blood bank, Univ. Ark. Med. Scis., Little Rock, 1970-77, clin. instr., 1977—; dir. tech. services and product mgmt. ARC Blood Services, Little Rock, 1977—. Recipient Grad. scholarship, Am. Soc. Med. Tech., 1975; named Med. Technologist of Yr. Ark. Soc. Med. Tech., 1981. Mem. Ark. Soc. Med. Tech. (chmn. com.), Am. Assn. Blood Banks, South Central Assn. Blood Banks (dir., chmn. membership com. 1980—), Am. Soc. Med. Tech., Central Ark. Assn. Lab. Scientists, Little Rock Antibody Club, Lab. Mgrs. and Suprs. Assn., Am. Soc. Clin. Pathologists, Phi Theta Kappa. Home: 2800 Vancouver Dr Little Rock AR 72204 Office: 401 S Monroe St Little Rock AR 72205

MCSWEENEY, FRANCES KAYE, psychologist, educator; b. Rochester, N.Y., Feb. 6, 1948; d. Edward William and Elsie Winifred (Kingston) McSweeney; B.A., Smith Coll., 1969; M.A., Harvard U., 1972, Ph.D., 1974. Lectr., McMaster U., Hamilton, Ont., Can., 1973-74; asst. prof. Wash. State U., Pullman, 1974-79, assoc. prof., 1979—. Mem. Environ. Quality Commn., Pullman, 1975-79. Woodrow Wilson fellow, 1969; NSF fellow, 1969-73; NIMH fellow, 1972-73. Mem. Am. Psychol. Assn., Western Psychol. Assn., Assn. for Behavior Analysis, Psychonomic Soc., Phi Beta Kappa, Sigma Xi. Contbr. articles in field to profl.

jours. Home: NW90 Thomas-D Pullman WA 99163 Office: Wash State U Dept Psychology Pullman WA 99164

MC TAGGART, MARJORIE JANE ROGERS, vocat. counselor; b. Mercer County, Mo., July 2; d. Don C. and Nannie (Duncan) Rogers; M.A., Roosevelt U., 1965; postgrad U. Callodolid (Spain), 1967, Colo. State U., 1971-73, U. Colo., 1969, Chgo. Tchrs. Coll., 1961-62; 1 son, Phillip Duncan. Passenger agt. Eastern and Delta airlines, 1945-50; primary tchr. Colegio Roosevelt, Lima, Peru, 1950-53; stylist, fashion cons. Formfit and Maidenform Bra Co., Chgo., N.Y.C., 1953-57; substitute tchr. Spanish, Chgo. Public Schs., 1961-65; instr. Spanish, Colo. State U., Fort Collins, 1965-70; sr. technician, Larimer County Dept. Social Services, Fort Collins, 1971-75; employment counselor Colo. Div. Employment and Tng., Fort Collins, 1975—. Pres. bd. dirs. Elizabeth Stone Resource Center, 1977-81. Recipient Fulbright award, 1967, Gov. Colo. Employee of Month award, 1978, NDEA awards, 1962, 64. Mem. Colo. Counselors Assn., CETA Pvt. Industry Council (vice chmn. 1979-80), Colo. Personnel and Guidance Assn., AAUW. Clubs: Toastmistress (council officer; chmn. internat. com. 1979), Ports of Call Travel. Home: 3417 Dixon Cove Dr Fort Collins CO 80526 Office: 1501 Blue Spruce Dr Fort Collins CO 80524

MC TAGGART, PENELOPE SHANE, publisher; b. Winnipeg, Man., Can., Mar. 4, 1947; came to U.S., 1952, naturalized, 1960; d. Daniel and Tana Maureen Shane; B.A. in English Lit., U. Wash., 1969; postgrad., 1970. Writer, Seattle Community Coll., 1969-71; public relations asst. Embassy of Japan, San Francisco, 1972-73; asso. public relations dir. San Francisco Ballet, 1973-74, dir. public relations, 1975-76; asso. pub. Arts and Leisure Publs., San Francisco, 1976—. Named Kabl San Francisco Citizen of the Day, 1976. Mem. Assn. Theatrical Press Agts. and Mgrs., San Francisco Press Club. Home: 1843 Pine St San Francisco CA 94109 Office: 950 Battery St San Francisco CA 94111

MC TEER, MAUREEN ANNE, lawyer; b. Cumberland, Ont., Can., Feb. 27, 1952; d. John J. and Beatrice E. (Griffith) McT.; B.A., U. Ottawa (Ont.), 1973, LL.B., 1977; m. Charles Joseph Clark, June 30, 1973; 1 dau., Catherine Jane. Called to Ont. bar, 1980. Bd. govs. U. Ottawa, 1980—. Named Woman of Future, Ladies Home Jour., 1979. Mem. Nat. Council Women of Can. (hon. pres.), Nat. Assn. Women and Law, Nat. Action Com. on Status of Women. Progressive Conservative. Roman Catholic.

MCVAY, JACQUELINE BRAYER, assn. exec.; b. Phoenix, Dec. 19, 1949; d. I. W. and Gay Elizabeth (Marks) Brayer; B.S., Ariz. State U., 1972; m. James Douglas McVay, July 25, 1970; children—Victoria, Matthew Michael, Ian Patrick. Co producer, host talk show KPHO, Phoenix, 1975-76; dir. consumer affairs Retail Grocers Assn. Ariz., Phoenix, 1976—; cons. foods and appliance companies. Mgr. public relations and communications Ariz. Rep. Peter Dunn. Mem. Ariz. Home Econs. Assn. Ariz. Press Women, Am. Home Economists Assn. Republican. Episcopalian. Club: Jr. League Phoenix, Phoenix Zoo Aux. Office: PO Box 3541 Phoenix AZ 85030

MCVEY, LEZA SULLIVAN, ceramic sculptor, potter, weaver; b. Cleve., May 1, 1907; d. Alexander and Ruth (McDaniel) Sullivan; grad. Cleve. Inst. Art, 1929-32; student Cranbrook Art Acad., 1949; m. William Mozart McVey, Mar. 31, 1932. One-woman shows include: Univ. Gallery, Mpls., 1951, Akron Art Inst., 1954, Art Colony Gallery, Cleve., 1955, Syracuse U., 1955, Woman's City Club, Cleve., 1957, Albright Knox Gallery, Buffalo, 1962; group shows include: Cleve. Mus. Art, Syracuse Mus. Art, Detroit Inst. Art, Smithsonian Instn., Pa. Acad. Fine Art, Bklyn. Mus., Am. Fedn. Art traveling exhbn., Scripps Coll., Univ. Galleries, Mpls., Wis., Nebr., Ill., Syracuse, Pomona, J. Blumenfeld Gallery, N.Y.C., Intown Gallery, Cleve., Disting. Alumni Show Cleve. Inst. Art, 1965; fgn. exhbns. include: 2d Internat. Congress Contemporary Ceramics, Ostend, Belgium, Internat. Cultural Exchange Exhbn., Geneva; works represented permanent collections: Mus. Art Cleve., Syracuse Mus. Fine Arts, Butler Mus., Gen. Motors Corp., Detroit, Cleve. Art Assn.; instr. museums Houston, 1936, San Antonio, 1943, Cranbrook Art Inst., 1956; executed ceramic mural Coll. and Cultural Center, Flint, Mich., 60 stoneware panels Rice U., Houston, stoneware Caduceus for Riverside Med. Bldg., Cleve., others. Recipient prizes and awards Syracuse Mus. Fine Art, 1950, 51, Mich. Arts and Crafts, 1951, Cleve. Mus. Art, 1953-57, 60-61, Butler Mus., 1956. Contbr. articles to House Beautiful, Ceramic Monthly, Everyday Art Quar. Home: 18 Pepper Ridge Rd Cleveland OH 44124

MCVEY, LOLA WINIFRED CLAAR, speech pathologist; b. Lakin, Kans., Feb. 21, 1923; d. Leonard Thomas and Anna Katrina (Kieft) Claar; B.A., Wichita State U., 1964; m. Raymond Ernest McVey, June 1, 1947 (dec. Feb. 1981); children—Marlyn Roann, Lyndon Eugene, Raymond Lee. Tchr. public schs., Seward and Reno Counties, Kans., 1943-48; speech pathologist Great Bend (Kans.) Public Schs., 1964-66, Kismet (Kans.) Plains Unified Sch. Dist., 1966-79; cons. in speech pathology, Kismet, 1979—; reporter Southwest Daily Times, Liberal, Kans., 1979; lang. devel. tchr. Public Schs. Liberal, 1980—. Mem. Kans. Speech and Hearing Assn. (sec.), Am. Speech and Hearing Assn. (cert.), NEA, Kans. Edn. Assn., Kans. High Plains Spl. Educators Assn. United Methodist. Home: 813 Main St Box 315 Kismet KS 67859

MCWHINNEY, MADELINE H. (MRS. JOHN DENNY DALE), economist, banker; b. Denver, Mar. 11, 1922; d. Leroy and Alice (Houston) McW.; B.A., Smith Coll., 1943; M.B.A., N.Y.U., 1947; m. John D. Dale, June 23, 1961; 1 son, Thomas Denny. Economist, Fed. Res. Bank N.Y., 1943-73, chief fin. and trade statis. div., 1955-59, mgr. market stats. dept., 1960-65, asst. v.p., 1965-73; pres. First Women's Bank, N.Y.C., 1974-76; trustee Retirement System Fed. Res. Bank, 1955-58; vis. lectr. N.Y.U. Grad. Sch. Bus., 1976-77; pres. Dale, Elliott & Co., Inc., N.Y.C., 1977-82; mem. N.J. Casino Control Commn., 1980-82; bd. govs. Am. Stock Exchange, 1977-81. Trustee, Carnegie Corp. N.Y., 1974-82, Central Savs. Bank of N.Y., 1980-82, Charles F. Kettering Found., 1975—, Inst. Internat. Edn., 1975—, Investor Responsibility Research Center, Inc., 1974-81; mem. adv. bd. Banking Law Jour., Grad. Sch. Bus., N.Y.U., Grad. Sch. Bus., Denver U. Recipient Smith Coll. medal, 1971, Alumni Achievement award N.Y.U. Grad. Sch. Bus. Adminstrn. Alumni Assn., 1971; N.Y.U. Crystal award, 1982. Mem. Am. Fin. Assn. (past dir.), Money Marketeers (v.p. 1960, pres. 1961-62), Nat. Assn. Bank Women, Alumni Assn. Grad. Sch. Bus. Admin. N.Y.U. (dir. 1951-63, pres. 1957-59), Am. Econ. Assn., Soc. Meml. Center, Phi Beta Kappa Assos. (v.p. 1979—). Home: 24 Blossom Cove Rd Red Bank NJ 07701 Office: PO Box 458 Red Bank NJ 07701

MCWILLIAMS, CLAIRE JESSIE, town ofcl.; b. Wareham, Mass., Jan. 21, 1928; d. James H. and Jean L. (Collins) Coville; student N.E. Sch. of Art, 1946-47; student Assessors Sch., U. Mass., 1965-73; m. Francis H. McWilliams, Jr., Oct. 8, 1948. Chief assessing clk. Wareham Bd. Assessors, 1951-70, mem. Bd. Assessors, 1970-73, mem. local govt. adv. com., 1975-76, mem. Bd. of Selectmen, 1970-82, chmn. Cemetery Commn., 1972-82, mem. Wareham Hist. Dist. Commn. Mem. Plymouth County (Mass.) Adv. Bd., 1974-77, mem. various town coms., Town of Wareham; mem. exec. bd. March of Dimes, 1974-79; trustee Tobey Hosp., Wareham, 1971—. Named hon. dep. sheriff Plymouth County. Mem. Mass. Selectmen's Assn. (life mem., sec. 1975-76, exec. bd. 1974-78), Mass. Mcpl. Assn., Plymouth County Selectmen's Assn. (pres. 1974-75), Wareham Bus. and Profl. Women's Club. Roman Catholic. Home: 138 Hathaway St PO Box 21 Wareham MA 02571 Office: Town Hall Wareham MA 02571

MCWILLIAMS, CONNIE OPAL, ins. co. exec.; b. Magnolia, Iowa, June 28, 1947; d. Thomas E. and Ila M. (Vore) Chatburn; m. Dale Roy McWilliams, Sept. 29, 1973. Sec. Kovar Agy., Inc., Missouri Valley, Iowa, 1965-76; owner McWilliams Enterprises, Missouri Valley, 1976—. Chairperson, Harrison County (Iowa) March of Dimes, 1970-73; commr. Iowa Jud. Qualifications Commn., 1981—. Mem. Assn. Life Underwriters, (past pres. chpt.), Toppers Club of Farmers Ins. Group, Lifemasters Club, Comml. Masters Club. Democrat. Mormon. Club: Community Band and Chorus (dir. 1981). Home: Rural Route 2 Box 172 Logan IA 51546 Office: 301 E Erie St Missouri Valley IA 51555

MCWILLIAMS, MARGARET ANN EDGAR, educator; b. Osage, Iowa, May 26, 1929; d. Alvin Randall and Mildred Irene Edgar; B.S., Iowa State U., 1951, M.S., 1953; Ph.D., Oreg. State U., 1968; children—Roger, Kathleen. Mem. faculty Calif. State Univ., Los Angeles, 1961—, chmn. home econs. dept., 1968-76, coordinator health related programs, prof. food and nutrition, 1981—. Registered dietitian. Mem. Am. Dietetic Assn., Am. Home Econs. Assn., Inst. Food Technologists, Soc. Nutrition Edn., Calif. Nutrition Council. Author: Food Fundamentals, 1979; Nutrition for the Growing Years, 1980; Living Nutrition, 1981; Fundamentals of Meal Management, 1978; Illustrated Guide to Food Preparations, 1982; Experimental Foods Laboratory Manual, 1981; Modern Food Preservation, 1977; Understanding Food, 1969; Food For You, 1976; World of Nutrition, 1983. Home: PO Box 220 Redondo Beach CA 90277 Office: Calif State U Los Angeles CA 90032

MEAD, ANN, personnel agy. exec.; b. Charleston, W.Va., Jan. 10, 1943; d. Lester G. and Eleanor Segerman; B.B.A., U. Cin., 1966. Adminstrv. asst. Appalachian Regional Commn., Washington, 1966-69; personnel counselor personnel agys., Washington, 1969-74; pres. A. Job Bank Ltd., Alexandria, Va., 1974—, J.B. Temps Inc., 1978-82. Mem. corp. bd. Alexandria Hosp., 1967—. Mem. Alexandria C. of C., Va. Assn. Personnel Services, Nat. Assn. Female Execs., Am. Bus. Women's Assn., Nat. Assn. Ind. Businesses. Home: 6003 Liberty Bell Ct Burke VA 22015 also Sundance Newmarket VA Office: 716 Church St Alexandria VA 22314

MEAD, CATHERINE SMITH, librarian; b. Sharon Springs, N.Y., July 11, 1924; d. Elmer Charles and Marguerite (Brady) Smith; B.A. in English, N.Y. State Coll. Tchrs., Albany, 1944, B.S. in L.S., 1947; m. John Mead, Feb. 6, 1947; 1 son, Gregory. Post librarian Camp Drake, Japan, 1953-55; cataloger post library Fort Hood, Tex., 1955-63, Pa. State Library, Harrisburg, 1964-65; asst. state librarian info. resources State Library Ohio, Columbus, 1971—. Mem. ALA, Ohio Library Assn., Ohio Assn. Archivists. Office: 65 S Front St Columbus OH 43215

MEAD, EILEEN (WANDA), newspaper reporter and photographer; b. Golva, N.D., Feb. 23, 1929; d. David Morton and Edna Adelia (Johnson) Howie; student U. Alaska, 1947-51; m. John E. Mead, May 19, 1951; children—Barbara, John E. III, Gregory, Mark, Shawn, Kathleen, Maureen. Reporter, Eastside Jour., Kirkland, Wash., 1967-68, Potomac News, Woodbridge, Va., 1969-79, on leave with Port Townsend (Wash.) Leader, 1973-74; stringer UPI, Richmond, Va., and Washington, 1975-79. Recipient 40 writing and photography awards, Va., U.S., Wash. Mem. Va. Press Women (regional dir. 1978-79), Nat. Fedn. Press Women, Washington Press Women, Hist. Dumfries. Lutheran. Club: Quantico Toastmistress. Home: 6001 140th Ave NE Apt 699 Redmond WA 98052

MEAD, MARJORIE ELAINE, educator; b. Braymer, Mo., Oct. 29, 1927; d. Bernard Franklin and Myra George (Post) M.; B.S., Iowa State U., 1949, M.S., 1957. Tchr. home econs., Bedford, Iowa, 1949-51; extension agt. Lewis County, Mo., 1951-53; tchr. home econs., Fergus Falls, Minn., 1953-56; extension specialist textiles and clothing U. Ill., Champaign-Urbana, 1958-81, head dept. textiles and interior design, prof., 1981—. Mem. Am. Home Econs. Assn., Ill. Home Econs. Assn., PEO, Omicron Nu, Gamma Sigma Delta, Epsilon Sigma Phi. Author leaflets, circulars. Office: 233 Bevier 905 S Goodwin St Urbana IL 61801

MEAD, MILDRED LOUISE, fashion writer, public relations cons.; b. Valliant, Okla., Feb. 13, 1913; s. Oliver N. and Cleo (Lick) Bridges; m. William H. Mead; children—Frances Mead-Messinger, Melinda Louise. Founder, chmn. Mildred Mead, Fashion Services, Newport Beach, Calif., 1970—; chmn. The Fashionables support group Chapman Coll., 1971-80, exec. dir., 1980—; writer weekly fashion column Coast Media News Group, Newport Harbor, Calif., 1977—. Vice pres. women's activities Orange County Philharm. Soc., 1960-64; sustaining mem. Angelitos de Oro; mem. Assistance League So. Calif., 1949-78. Mem. Fashion Group, Calif. Press Women, Nat. Press Women. Republican. Episcopalian. Clubs: Balboa Bay, Newport Beach, Newport Harbor Yacht, Balboa. Home: 736 Via Lido Nord Newport Beach CA 92663 Office: PO Box 1666 Newport Beach CA 92663

MEADE, MELINDA SUE, geographer, educator; b. N.Y.C., Nov. 2, 1945; d. Melville J. and Katherine (Ditmas) M.; B.A., Hofstra U., 1966; M.A., Mich. State U., 1968; Ph.D., U. Hawaii, 1974; Vol., Peace Corps, 1966-68; research asso. Internat. Center for Med. Research, Kuala Lumpur, 1972-74; acting asst. prof. UCLA, 1974-76; asst. prof. U. Ga., 1976-78; asst. prof. U. N.C., Chapel Hill, 1978-80, asso. prof., 1980—. NSF trainee, 1968-70; East-West Center grantee, 1970-72; Internat. Research Asso. program fellow, 1972-74; Mem. Assn. Asian Studies (regional councillor 1981—), Southeastern Conf. Assn. Am. Geographers (sec.; edit. bd.), Assn. Am. Geographers (chmn. med. geography splty. group 1974-80), AAAS, Population Assn. Am., Geo-chemical Environ. and Health Soc., Common Cause, Amnesty Internat. Unitarian. Contbg. editor Conceptual and Methodological Issues in Medical Geography, 1980; contbr. articles to profl. jours. Office: Dept Geography U NC Chapel Hill NC 27514

MEADOR, FANNIE MURIEL, legal asst.; b. Greenville, Tex., Dec. 6, 1951; d. Fannon and Deora (McMillan) Garrett; Asso. Sci., Henderson County Jr. Coll., 1972; postgrad. E. Tex. State U., 1972-76; B.A., U. Tex., Dallas, 1977; paralegal cert. Okla. City U., 1977; postgrad. (scholar) So. Meth. U., 1979—; children—LaFeyshia, KaVayshia, Fannon. Legal sec. Worsham, Forsythe & Sampels, Dallas, 1978; legal asst. Hughes & Hill, Dallas, 1978-80, Strasburger & Price, Dallas, 1980—; organizer, presenter Strasburger & Price Seminars for legal assts. and secs., 1980. Named Miss Rains County, 1966. Mem. Dallas Legal Assts. (pres. 1977-80), Dallas Legal Secs. Assn., NAACP, Nat. Assn. Legal Assts., Alpha Kappa Alpha. Democrat. Baptist. Author articles. Office: 1200 One Main Pl Dallas TX 75250

MEADOWS, PHYLLIS ADKISSON, corp. communications cons.; b. Ft. Sill, Okla., Nov. 28, 1948; d. Glenn William and Phyllis (Trax) Adkisson; B.A., Hunter Coll., CUNY, 1976; postgrad. Loyola U. Law Sch. With Litton Industries, Washington, 1971-72, Continental Corp., N.Y.C., 1972-76, Stoorza Co., San Diego, 1977-79, Meadows Co., Los Angeles, 1979—. Mem. Am. Bar Assn. Public Relations Soc. Am. (accredited), Internat. Assn. Bus. Communicators, Am. Mktg. Assn., San Diego Investor Relations Group, San Diego Stock and Bond Club. Office: 925 Gayley Ave Los Angeles CA 90024

MEADS, PATRICIA JEAN, mkgt. co. ofcl.; b. Fargo, N.D., Apr. 10, 1950; d. Raymond Byron and Isabel Edith (Barrett) Whiting; student So. Meth. U., 1968-69; B.A., U. Minn., 1971. Advt. coordinator Sun Newspapers, also mng. editor Zenith Express, 1973-74; dir. consumer communications A.S. Industries, Mpls., 1974-76; sales promotion coordinator Carlson Mktg. Group div. Carlson Cos., Mpls., 1976-79, dir. mktg. services, 1979—. Mem. Women in Communications, Minnetonka Chorale. Contbr. to Pro-Con Mag. Home: 18900 Shady Ln S Minnetonka MN 55343 Office: 12755 Hwy 55 Minneapolis MN 55441

MEALEY, CATHERINE ELIZABETH, lawyer, librarian, educator; b. Ames, Iowa, Apr. 4, 1928; d. Lloyd Vernon and Katherine Jane (Parry) Crum; B.A., U. Iowa, 1950, M.A., 1951, J.D. with distinction, 1957; M.Law Librarianship, U. Wash., 1962; m. Michael C. Mealey, Aug. 8, 1947; (div. 1954); children—Karen Kay, Gwen. Admitted to Ariz. bar; practiced in Flagstaff, Ariz., 1958-60; law librarian U. Wyo., Laramie, 1962—, asst. prof. law, assoc. prof., now prof. Bd. dirs. Laramie Sr. Center, Inc. Mem. Am. Assn. Law Libraries, Wyo. Bar Assn. Home: 121 Ivinson Laramie WY 82070 Office: U Wyo Coll Law Laramie WY 82071

MEANA, SANDRA JEAN, nursing adminstr.; b. Marquette, Mich., Mar. 7; d. Eugene Carl and Evelyn Genevieve (Bongartz) Weiger; R.N., Michael Reese Hosp., 1968; B.S., Coll. St. Francis, 1979; m. Fernando Meana, July 27, 1968; children—Timothy Charles, Melissa Ann. Scrub nurse, office nurse, Chgo., 1968-69; office nurse, radium therapist, Breed Radium Inst., Chgo., 1969-70; recovery room staff nurse, Northlake Community Hosp., Northlake, Ill., 1970, head nurse surg. unit, 1970-71, nursing supr., 1971-72, asso. dir. nursing, 1972-74, dir. nursing service, 1974-76; nursing adminstrv. supr., Northwest Community Hosp., Arlington Heights, Ill., 1976-77, nursing coordinator quality assurance, 1977-79, staffing supr., 1979-80, dir. nursing staff services, 1980—; clin. faculty Joint Commn. on Accreditation of Hosps.-Outcome Audit. Mem. Am., Ill. nurses assns., Am. Critical Care Nurses Assn., Nat. Assn. Nurse Recruiters, Chgo. Area Nurse Recruiters. Republican. Lutheran. Home: 78 King Arthur Ct Sherwood Oaks Elgin IL 60120 Office: Northwest Community Hosp 800 W Central Rd Arlington Heights IL 60005

MEANS, SUSAN IRENE, psychologist; b. Richland, Oreg., Jan. 7, 1933; d. Winston Elmer and Elizabeth Jane (Cundiff) Saunders; B.S., U. Oreg., 1969, M.S., 1971, Ph.D., 1975; m. Howard L. Means, Nov. 10, 1973; children—Danee Sue Kramer, Ted Winston Kramer. Counselor, Div. Vocat. Rehab., Salem, Oreg., 1971-73; dean students Good Samaritan Nursing Sch., Portland, Oreg., 1974-76; psychologist dept. workers' compensation William A. Callahan Center, Wilsonville, Oreg., 1976—; tchr. mid-life crisis, stress mgmt., type A behavior workshops. Treas., Lane County (Oreg.) Democratic Women, 1974-75. Mem. Am. Psychol. Assn., Western Psychol. Assn., Oreg. Psychol. Assn., Inst. Managerial and Profl. Women. Democrat. Methodist. Club: Toastmasters (Lake Oswego, Oreg.). Home: 6380 SW Washington Ct Lake Oswego OR 97034 Office: William A Callahan Center 29500 SW Grahams Ferry Rd Wilsonville OR 97070

MEANS-BRATSCH, JACQUELINE ALLENE, priest; b. Peoria, Ill., Aug. 26, 1936; d. Theodore R. and Minnett M. Ehringer; student Ind. U., Cath. Sem. Found., Ind. Central U., Christian Theol. Sem., 1981; m. David H. Bratsch, June 16, 1980; children—David R. Means, Patrick L. Means, Deborah A. Means, Delton L. Means. With Vis. Nurse Assn., 1969-73; ordained priest Episcopal Ch., 1977; asst. chaplain St. John's Ch. and Indsl. Ministry, Indpls., 1981; asst. St. John's Ch., instl. chaplain Diocese Indpls., 1982—; mem. standing com. Commn. on Aging, 1976-78; v.p. Episcopal Urban Ministries, Human Equality Commn., 1980-81; chmn. Diocesan Commn. on Justice and Corrections, integrity chpt., 1977-78. Bd. dirs. Ind. Juvenile Justice Task Force; mem. adv. com. Marion County Juvenile Center. Named Woman of Yr. YWCA, 1977. Office: St John's Episcopal Ch 5625 W 30th St Indianapolis IN 46224

MEARA, ANNE, actress; b. Bklyn.; d. Edward Joseph and Mary (Dempsey) Meara; student Herbert Berghoff Studio, 1953-54; m. Gerald Stiller, Sept. 14, 1954; children—Amy, Benjamin. Apprentice in summer stock, Southold, L.I. and Woodstock, N.Y., 1950-53; off-Broadway appearances include Ulysses in Nighttown, 1958, Maedchen in Uniform (Show Bus. Off-Broadway award), 1955, A Month in the Country, 1954, The House of Blue Leaves, 1970; mem. Shakespeare Co., Central Park, N.Y.C., 1957; film appearances include The Out-of-Towners, 1968, Lovers and Other Strangers, 1969, Nasty Habits, 1976, The Boys From Brazil, 1978, Fame, 1979; comedy act (with husband Jerry Stiller), 1963—, syndicated TV series Take Five With Stiller and Meara, 1977-78; appearances include Happy Medium and Medium Rare, Chgo., 1960-61, Village Gate, Phase Two and Blue Angel, N.Y.C., 1963, The Establishment, London, 1963; numerous appearances on TV game and talk shows, also spls. and variety shows; rec. numerous commls. for TV and radio; star TV series Kate McShane, 1975, Archie Bunker's Place, 1979. Co-recipient Voice of Imagery award Radio Advt. Bur., 1975. Address: care Internat Creative Mgmt 8899 Beverly Blvd Los Angeles CA 90048 *

MEARA, HANNAH LOUISE, sociologist; b. Flint, Mich., Nov. 23, 1939; d. Louis D. and Helen G. Meara; student Willamette U., 1957-59; B.S., U. Calif., Berkeley, 1961; M.A. in Sociology, Northwestern U., 1966, Ph.D. in Sociology, 1970; children—John Louis and Alexander Wade Marshall. Research asst. Orthogenic Sch., U. Chgo., 1961-63; grad. asst., instr. Northwestern U., 1963-67; asst. prof., asst. dept. chmn. No. Ill. U., DeKalb, 1968-73; asst. prof. U. Ill. Med. Center, Chgo., 1973-77; sr. asso. Center for New Schs., Chgo., 1977-78; dir. research Planned Parenthood, Chgo., 1978-80; founder, dir., pres. Chgo. Assos. for Social Research, 1978—; cons., program evaluator health and ednl. orgns., instns. Chgo. area. Grantee VA, Nat. Inst. Child Health and Human Devel., Nat. Inst. Edn., W. K. Kellogg Found. Mem. Am. Sociol. Assn., Soc. Study of Social Problems, Sociologists for Women in Soc., Am. Public Health Assn., Evaluation Research Soc. Unitarian. Asso. editor Social Problems, 1977-80; contbr. articles to profl. jours. Home: 5521 S Cornell Ave Chicago IL 60637 Office: 410 S Michigan Ave Chicago IL 60605

MEARS, DARLENE WANDA HIND (MRS. DAVID EDMUND MEARS), lawyer; b. Oceanside, N.Y., July 19, 1946; d. Ira Flint and Wanda Mary (Terry) Hind; student El Camino Jr. Coll., 1965; B.A., Valparaiso U., 1968, J.D., 1971; m. David Edmund Mears, Jan. 25, 1969. Admitted to Ind. bar, 1971; nat. examining and closing atty. Chgo. Title & Trust Co., 1971-72; pvt. practice law, Hammond, Ind., 1971-76; dep. prosecutor Lake County Ind. Juvenile Div., Hammond, 1972-76; referee Juvenile div. Lake Superior Ct., 1976-78, sr. judge, 1978—. First v.p. Calumet Area Humane Soc., Inc., Hammond, 1971—, atty., 1971-74, pres., 1977-78; bd. dirs. Hammond YWCA, v.p., 1977-78; v.p. Christ Lutheran Ch. Women, Hammond, 1976. Recipient Distinguished Alumni award Lutheran High Sch. Assn. So. Calif., 1975; Lake County Outstanding Woman award, 1978. Mem. Am. Bar Assn., Ind. Bar Assn. (treas. family and juvenile law sect., chmn. 1976-77, dir. 1977-78), Hammond Bar Assn., Nat. Council Family and Juvenile Ct. Judges, Ind. Council Family and Juvenile Ct. Judges (treas. 1979—), Am. Judges Assn., Ind. Judges Assn., Valparaiso U. Sch. Law Alumni Assn. (treas. 1973-74, v.p. 1974-75, pres. 1975-76, dir.), Phi Alpha Delta, Kappa Tau Zeta (sec. alumni 1972, treas. 1975-76). Home: 7303 88th Pl Crown Point IN 46307 Office: 400 Broadway Gary IN

MECHANIC, JANET LOVE (MRS. MELVIN OLIVER ARONSON), optometrist; b. Cambridge, Mass., June 30, 1921; d. Leon and Clarice Olga (Hameson) Mechanic; Dr. Optometry, New Eng. Coll. Optometry, 1942; postgrad., U. Maine, 1942-43, Frankfort Arsenal,

1943-44; m. Melvin Oliver Aronson, Oct. 25, 1953; children—Leanne Ruth, Joyce Merle. Chief optical insp. Boston Ordnance Dept., 1942-45; editor sci. optical material M.I.T., Cambridge, 1945-46; pvt. practice optometry, Brookline, Mass., 1947—; head optometrist New Eng. Hosp., 1949-70; cons. indsl. optometrics, 1949-70; optometrist for various rehab. instns. Cert. in gen. and ocular pharmacology, Mass. Trustee New Eng. Tech. Inst., 1980-82. Mem. Mass. (contact lens com.), Boston socs. optometrists, Am. Optometric Assn., New Eng. Coll. Optometry Alumni Assn. (class agt. 1967-69), Epsilon Omicron Sigma. Contbr. articles to profl. jours. Home: 105 Gardner Rd Brookline MA 02146 Office: 1146 Beacon St Brookline MA 02146

MECHEM, VERNA LIPS, sales exec., museum adminstr.; b. New Orleans, Sept. 6, 1932; d. Henry Julius and Verna Marie (Bourg) Lips; student Tulane U., 1948-49, Soule Bus. Sch., 1949-50; m. Dec. 26, 1956 (div.); children—Craig, Adrienne, Daryl, Madelynne, Roderick. Legal sec. Wisdom & Stone, New Orleans, 1951-54, Phelps, Dunbar, Marks, Claverie & Sims, New Orleans, 1954-58; owner, pro shop buyer, instr. Sangre de Cristo Racquet Club, Santa Fe, 1968-81; exec. sec. Wheelwright Mus. of Am. Indian, Santa Fe, 1981—; dir. sales El Gancho Tennis Club, Santa Fe, 1982—. Mem. U.S. Tennis Assn. Republican. Address: 2172 Chamisos Ct Santa Fe NM 87501

MECHTENBERG, DOROTHY MARGARET, fin. planner; b. Council Bluffs, Iowa, Mar. 15, 1943; d. Charles and Tresse Agnes (McIntosh) Botos; student Coll. Fin. Planning; m. William L. Mechtenberg, June 27, 1964; 1 dau., Patricia Anne. With Dean Witter & Co., Omaha, 1965—, financial planner, 1972—. Mem. Omaha Life Underwriters Assn., Internat. Assn. Fin. Planners. Lutheran. Home: 1416 N 120th Plaza Omaha NE 68154 Office: 14927 Industrial Rd Omaha NE 68144

MECKFESSEL, IRMA SOPHIA, banker; b. O'Fallon, Ill., Oct. 21, 1901; d. Christian and Sophia (Luchsinger) Schacher; B.S. in Elem. Edn., McKendree Coll., 1920; student Hailman Secretarial Sch., 1923, Am. Inst. Banking, 1923-25; m. Albert H. Meckfessel, Oct. 12, 1940. With First Nat. Bank, Fallon, Ill., 1922—, sec. to pres., 1922-40, asst. cashier, 1940-53, asst. trust officer, 1953-69, asst. v.p., 1953-65, v.p., trust officer, 1969-81, v.p., dir. sec. bd., mem. trust com., 1980—. Treas. ARC, 1920-45, March of Dimes, 1930-50. Recipient leadership award O'Fallon C. of C., 1980. Mem. Nat. Assn. Bank Women (Ill. group), Am. Inst. Banking. Mem. Ch. of Christ. Clubs: St. Clair County Republican; O'Fallon Women's. Home: 204 Marilyn Dr O'Fallon IL 62269 Office: 200 S Lincoln Ave O'Fallon IL 62269

MEDEIROS, VIVIAN ANN, neuro-histopathology technician; b. Fall River, Mass., Aug. 18, 1948; d. Manuel Soares, Jr. and Mary Olivera (Pavao) M.; cert. histology technician, Truesdale Hosp., Fall River, Mass., 1970; A.S., Suffolk (N.Y.) Community Coll., 1977. Histology technician Truesdale Hosp., 1969-71; histopathology technician VA Med. Center, Northport, N.Y., 1972-74, neurohistopathology technician, 1974—; chmn. med. lab. assisting cons. com. Lewis A. Wilson Tech. Center, Dix Hills, N.Y., 1978. Mem. Am. Soc. Clin. Pathologists, Nat. Soc. Histotech., N.Y. State Histotech. Soc. (chmn. nomination com. 1980). Author papers in field. Office: Bldg 200 Room CO-45 VA Med Center Northport NY 11768

MEDELOFF, SUSAN MERLE, personnel counselor; b. N.Y.C., June 1, 1941; d. Max and Pearl Winegar; B.A., Rider Coll., Trenton, N.J., 1963; m. Samuel Medeloff, Apr. 30, 1972. Registrar, acad. sec. N.Y. U. Grad. Sch. Art History and Archelogy, 1964; v.p. Winmar Temp. Service Inc., N.Y.C., 1980—; pres. Winmar Personnel Agy. Inc., N.Y.C., 1977—. Home: 13 Thorne Ave North Massapequa NY 11758 Office: 535 Fifth Ave New York NY 10017

MEDLIN, MARSHA FAYE, temp. services co. exec.; b. Washington, July 7, 1937; d. Hazel William and Pansy Greene (Fortner) Cashion; student Central Piedmont Community Coll., 1978-79; m. Ronald Jones Medlin, June 9, 1956; children—Rhonda Faye, Sheridan Adair. Payroll clk., cost acct. asst. Pneumafil Corp., Charlotte, N.C., 1959-67; mgr. Hazel Keller Cosmetics, Charlotte, 1967-73; acctg. mgr., controller Manpower of Charlotte, Inc., 1974—. Mem. Exec. Women Internat. (treas. 1980-81, chmn. publicity com. 1979-80). Home: 532 Carole Ln Charlotte NC 28214 Office: 916 S Kings Dr Charlotte NC 28204

MEDWAY, JOAN GINSBERG, social worker; b. Middletown, Conn., June 24, 1940; d. Isidore and Elsie (Kaufman) Ginsberg; B.A. in Edn., Bklyn. Coll., 1962; M.Ed., U. Md., 1973; M.S.W., Cath. U. Am., 1976; m. Lawrence E. Medway, Jan. 29, 1961; children—Robert W., Richard A. Tchr. elem. sch. N.Y.C. Bd. Edn., 1962-65; psychiat. social worker Spring Grove Hosp. Center, Catonsville, Md., 1976-79; social worker D.C. Psychiat. Inst., 1979-81; chief social worker Psychiat. Inst. Montgomery County (Md.), Rockville, 1981; psychotherapist Gaithersburg Guidance and Eval. Services, Inc., 1981—; chmn. community adv. bd. Prince George's County Family Service Aftercare. Lic. cert. social worker, Md. Mem. Am. Acad. Cert. Social Workers, Am. Group Psychotherapy Assn. Jewish. Lectr., participant workshops in field; author, co-author articles in profl. jours. Home: 10008 Colebrook Ave Potomac MD 20854 Office: 14901 Broschart Rd Rockville MD 20850

MEDZIE, DEENA MICKELBERG, librarian; b. Phila., Mar. 16, 1946; d. Rubin and Miriam F. Mickelberg; A.B., Temple U., 1967; M.L.S., U. Pitts., 1968; M.B.A., Widener U., Phila., 1976; m. Kenneth S. Medzie, Aug. 17, 1974. Civilian army librarian U.S. Army Office Spl. Services, Hawaii, 1968-71; reference librarian Edinboro (Pa.) State Coll., 1972; bus.-econs. reference librarian, acquisitions librarian Widener U., 1973—; cons. in field. Mem. Assn. Coll. and Research Libraries, AAUP, ALA, AAUP (chpt. sec.-treas. 1980—), Pa. Library Assn. Home: 307 Hastings Ave Wallingford PA 19086 Office: Wolfgram Meml Library Widener U Chester PA 19013

MEEDER, DONNIS LEA, accountant, constrn. co. exec.; b. Stockton, Kans., May 20, 1929; d. Floyd Harold and Mable Louise (Harsh) Kenworthy; student San Bernardino Valley Coll., 1962-67; m. Allison W. Meeder, Aug. 13, 1949 (div., 1971); children—Lizbeth Louise (Mrs. Paul Stone), Andrew William, Kurt Allison. Purebred dairy goat breeder Grade A Dairy, San Bernardino, 1952-62; bookkeeper Rialto Corp. (Calif.), 1961-62, Triangle Constrn. Co., Inc., San Bernardino, Calif., 1962-70; v.p. A-J Constrn. Co., Inc., San Bernardino, 1970—, also dir.; dir. Triangle Equipment Co., Triangle Constrn. Co., Inc. Mem. Nat. Assn. Women in Constrn. (chpt. v.p. San Bernardino-Riverside chpt. 1972-73, pres. 1973-74, nat. dir. 1978-79). Democrat. Presbyterian. Office: PO Box 2247 San Bernardino CA 92406

MEEHAN, LYNNE A., dietitian; b. Jersey City, Oct. 23, 1948; d. Oliver H. and Mildred A. (Knapp) Paris; B.A. in Home Econs., Montclair State Coll., Upper Montclair, N.J., 1970; postgrad. Rutgers U.; m. Lance D. Meehan, June 26, 1971; children—David, Alison, Kathleen. Sr. dietitian N.J. Hosp. Chest Diseases, Glen Gardner, 1972-74; supervising dietitian N.J. Dept. Human Services, Trenton, 1974-78; instr. Ocean County Coll., Toms River, N.J., 1978-80; food service dir. Whelan Food Service, Phila., 1981—; tchr. Monmouth County Vocat. Sch. Dist. Mem. Nat. Assn. Female Execs. Home: 13 Holly Rd Breton Woods Bricktown NJ 08723 Office: 2923 Cheltenham Ave Philadelphia PA 19150

MEEHAN, PAULA KENT, cosmetic co. exec.; b. West Los Angeles, Calif., Aug. 9, 1931; d. Richard Moorehead and Lois Evelyn (Martin) Bear; extension student UCLA; m. John Edwin Meehan, Apr. 20, 1973; children—Michael D. Miller, Chris Meehan, Matthew Meehan. Founder, 1960, since pres., chmn. bd. Redken Labs. Inc., Canoga Park, Calif.; dir. Union Bank, Los Angeles. Bd. regents Loyola U., Los Angeles; mem., chmn. regulatory com. Econ. Devel. Commn. Calif. Mem. Cosmetic Toiletry Fragrance Assn. Republican. Address: 6625 Variel Ave Canoga Park CA 91303

MEEK, SAUNDRA JUDITH, univ. dean; b. Wheeler, Tex., July 23, 1942; d. Jack Edward and Evelyn Bennie Meek; B.S., W.Tex. State U., Canyon, 1963, M.Ed., 1968. Tchr. public schs., N.Mex. and Tex., 1963-67; asst. dean women, then asso. dean student affairs W.Tex. State U., 1968-77, dean student affairs, 1977—. Mem. Randall County Cancer Bd. Mem. Nat. Assn. Women Deans, Counselors and Adminstrs., Am. Personnel and Guidance Assn., So. Assn. Coll. Student Affairs, Southwestern Assn. Coll. and Univ. Housing Officers (Disting. Service award 1978), Tex. Assn. Women Deans, Counselors and Adminstrs. Home: 3203 Conner St Canyon TX 79015 Office: WT Box 779 Canyon TX 79015

MEEKS, CONSTANCE MARIE, bank exec.; b. Ft. Wayne, Ind., May 10, 1929; d. Harold Ray and Viola Margaret (Mason) Wells; student Internat. Bus. Coll., 1947-49, Grad. Sch. Banking U. Wis., 1976-78; m. Ronald Lawrence Meeks, Aug. 28, 1948; children—Cynthia Kay, Rhonda Sue Meeks Gulley, Brian Keith, Kevin Scott. Sec., Radio Equipment Co., Ft. Wayne, 1948-51; exec. sec. Anthony Wayne Bank, Ft. Wayne, 1965-72, adminstrv. asst., 1972-74, asst. cashier, 1974, asst. v.p., 1974-78, v.p. adminstrn. and ops., 1978-79, v.p. ops., personnel dir., 1979—. Active, Big Bros./Big Sisters, Ft. Wayne; treas., bd. dirs. YWCA of Ft. Wayne. Mem. Ft. Wayne C. of C., Ft. Wayne Women's Bur., Ind. Bankers Assn., Nat. Assn. Bank Women, Am. Inst. Banking, Am. Bus. Women's Assn., Nat. Assn. Female Execs., Am. Soc. Personnel Adminstrn., Toastmasters. Republican. Methodist. Clubs: Pine Valley Country, Scottish Rite Ladies, Mizpah Shrine Ladies. Home: 6824 Kanata Ct Fort Wayne IN 46815 Office: 203 E Berry St Fort Wayne IN 46802

MEEKS, FRANCES WHITT, utility co. customer services advisor; b. Blanche, Tenn., Mar. 25, 1920; d. Wilburn Woody and Margaret (O'Neal) Whitt; B.S. in Vocat. Home Econs., U. Montevallo (Ala.), 1942; M.S. in Adminstrn. and Supervision, Auburn U., 1967; m. William Frederick Meeks, Sept. 30, 1948 (dec., 1973). Tchr. home econs. Cullman County (Ala.) Bd. Edn., 1942-44, Winston County Bd. Edn., Haleyville, Ala., 1944-46; dir. sch. food service Montgomery County (Ala.) Bd. Edn., Montgomery, 1946-70; supr. sch. food service state dept. edn., Montgomery, 1970-76; nutrition specialist regional office HEW, Atlanta, 1976-77; residential energy services advisor Ala. Power Co., Haleyville, 1978—; tchr. workshops for sch. food service personnel State of Ala., summers, 1947-76. Bd. dirs. Montgomery Retarded Children's Assn., 1962-70, sch. treas., 1962-70; mem. rev. panels, budget panels United Appeal, Montgomery, 1960-74; tchr. Sunday Sch. Bapt. chs., 1942—. Named Businesswoman of Yr., Montgomery, 1963. Mem. Am. Bus. Women's Assn., Montgomery Bus. Women's Assn., Am. Home Econs. Assn., Ala. Home Econs. Assn., Nat. Mgmt. Assn., Home Economists in Bus. Assn., Nat. Ret. Teachers Assn., Ala. Ret. Teachers Assn., Delta Kappa Gamma. Democrat. Home: Route 1 Box 245 Haleyville AL 35565 Office: PO Box 790 Haleyville AL 35565

MEFFERT, MARCY, radio producer; b. Milw., June 10, 1934; d. John George and Margaret (Stankiewicz) Czarnecki; student Marquette U., 1952-53; m. Roland M. Meffert, June 12, 1954; children—Jeffrey, Lisa, Sarah, Gregory, Douglas. Writer humor column Cactus Garden, Citizen News, San Antonio, 1974-76; editor N.W. Citizen, San Antonio, 1975-76; staff writer San Antonio Light, 1976-82, Living Today sect., 1978-82, columnist Finds, Sunday women's mag., 1981-82, Eye on S.A., 1981-82; producer Morning Mag. and Allan Dale shows WOAI radio, San Antonio; freelance writer various mags. and newspapers. Mem. adv. bd. St. Mary's U., Focus Women's Programs, 1981; co-chmn. Archdiocesan Women's Conv., San Antonio, 1968; pres. Women in Parish Service, St. Vincent de Paul Cath. Ch., 1967-68; leader Girl Scouts U.S.A., Wiesbaden, Ger., 1969-72. Mem. Women in Communications, Tex. Press Women (chmn. high sch. press workshop 1981), San Antonio Press Club, Sigma Delta Chi (adv. bd. 1980-81). Roman Catholic. Clubs: Lackland Officers Wives, others. Home: 6532 Adair Dr San Antonio TX 78238 Office: WOAI 6222 NW IH1O San Antonio TX 78201

MEGGERS, BETTY J., anthropologist; b. Washington, Dec. 5, 1921; d. William Frederick and Edith Marie (Raddant) M.; A.B., U. Pa., 1943; M.A., U. Mich., 1945; Ph.D., Columbia U., 1952; m. Clifford Evans, Sept. 13, 1946. Instr. anthropology Am. U., Washington, 1950-51; exec. sec. Am. Anthrop. Assn., Washington, 1959-61; research asso. Smithsonian Instn., 1954—, expert, 1981—; mem. com. research and exploration Nat. Geog. Soc. Decorated Order Merit (Ecuador), 1966; recipient award sci. achievement Washington Acad. Scis., 1956, Gold medal Internat. Congress Americanists, 1966. Mem. AAAS, Am. Anthrop. Assn., Soc. Am. Archeology, Assn. Tropical Biology. Author: Ecuador, 1966; Amazonia, 1971; Prehistoric America, 1972. Translator: The Civilization Process, 1968; Peoples and Cultures of Ancient Peru, 1974; others. Home: 1227 30th St NW Washington DC 20007 Office: Mail Stop NHB-112 Smithsonian Instn Washington DC 20560

MEHERIN, MARGARET WILSON, acct.; b. Mobile, Ala., Jan. 5, 1955; d. Joseph Henry and Rose Patricia (McNamara) Wilson; B.S.C., Spring Hill Coll., 1975; m. Dennis Peter Meherin, May 31, 1975; 1 dau., Bridget Claire. Staff acct. L.E. Nicholas & Co., Mobile, 1975, Morrison & Smith, C.P.A., Mobile, 1975-77; pvt. practice public acctg., Mobile, 1977-80; pvt. practice C.P.A., Mobile, 1980—; sec.-treas. Wilson Electric Co., Inc., Mobile, 1980—, Gulf Coast Electronics, Inc., Mobile, 1980-81. Sec.-treas., Med. Clinic Bd. Second City of Mobile, 1980-82. C.P.A., Ala. Mem. Am. Inst. C.P.A.s, Am. Soc. Women Accts., Am. Women's Soc. C.P.A.s, Ala. Soc. C.P.A.s. Roman Catholic. Home and Office: 5228 S Maudelayne Dr Mobile AL 36609

MEHRA, NIRMAL, educator; b. India, Sept. 12, 1934; d. Bhagat Ram and Vidya Wati (Malik) Chandhoke; B.A., Punjab U., 1950; B.Ed., U. Delhi, 1952; M.A. in History, Punjab U., 1955; M.A. in Ednl. Adminstrn., U. Calif., Berkeley, 1961, Ed.D., 1967; m. Krishen L. Mehra, Oct. 9, 1956; 3 children. Tchr. sr. high sch., India, 1952-55; prin. Higher Secondary Sch., Directorate of Edn., Delhi, India, 1955-58; sr. research asst. Sch. Edn., U. Calif., Berkeley, 1959-62; research dir., Office of Instnl. Research and Planning, U. Alta., Edmonton, Can., 1969—. Recipient several citations and awards for contbns. as educator and champion Women's rights. Mem. Indo-Can. Soc. Alta. (exec. mem. 1974-76), Alta. Council India Socs., Assn. Instnl. Research, Can. Soc. Study of Higher Edn., Delta Kappa Gamma. Hindu. Contbr. articles to profl. jours. Home: 39 Westbrook Dr Edmonton AB T6J 2C8 Canada Office: 1-16 University Hall Univ of Alberta Edmonton AB T6G 2J9 Canada

MEHRMANN, CRAIGANN, health care facility adminstr.; b. Hershey, Pa., Jan. 6, 1953; d. Charles Craig and Martha Arlene (Shepler) M.; B.S., Bloomsburg State Coll., 1974; A.A. in Nursing, Harrisburg Area Community Coll., 1979. Substitute tchr., Derry Twp., Central Dauphin, and Middletown Area sch. dists., 1974-77; nursing asst. Milton Hershey Med. Center, 1978; staff nurse Holy Spirit Hosp., Camp Hill, Pa., 1979, Milton Hershey Med. Center, Hershey, Pa., 1979-80; clin. coordinator Hillcrest Clinic and Counseling Services, Harrisburg, Pa., 1980—. Vol., Am. Cancer Soc., ARC. Mem. Nat. Assn. Female Execs., Inc., Am. Nurses Assn., Am. Coll. Obstetricians and Gynecologists (Nurses Assn.), Pa. Nurses Assn. (treas. dist.), Harrisburg Area Community Coll. Alumni Assn., Am. Bus. Women's Assn. (rec. sec.), Bloomsburg State Coll. Alumni Assn. Methodist. Home: 426 W Granada Ave Hershey PA 17033 Office: 2709 N Front St Harrisburg PA 17110

MEIER, KAREN LORENE, educator; b. Davenport, Iowa, Aug. 17, 1942; d. Charles Frank and Minnie Louise (Arp) Meier; B.A., U. Iowa, 1963, M.A., 1974. Tchr., librarian Plano (Ill.) High Sch., 1963-67; tchr. social studies Moline (Ill.) High Sch., 1967—; coordinator Moline Secondary Social Studies, 1978—. Bd. dirs. Quad-City World Affairs Council; active LWV. Mem. Nat., Iowa, Ill. (sec. 1973-74, v.p. 1974-75) councils social studies, NEA, Ill. (sec.-treas. regional council 1975-79, legis. chmn. 1980-81), Moline (pres. 1977-78) edn. assns., Social Studies Suprs. Assn., Assn. for Supervision and Curriculum Devel., Am. Soc. Profl. and Exec. Women, AAUW, Alpha Delta Kappa. Home: 2230 1/2 Ripley Davenport IA 52803 Office: 3600 23d Ave Moline IL 61265

MEIER, PARALEE BINGHAM, publishing co. exec.; b. Ericson, Nebr., May 31, 1931; d. William David and Violet Geniece (Benson) Bingham; A.B., Calif. State U., Chico, 1965, M.A., 1966; divorced; children—Kathryn, John, James. Secondary sch. Reading and English tchr., Chico, 1969-72; asst. prof. Calif. State U., Chico, 1966-72; dir. cons. services Random House Pubs., 1972-79; sales rep. Bowmar/Nobles Pubs., 1979; regional sales mgr. Raintree Pubs. Group, 1979-80, regional mktg. mgr., Altadena, Calif., 1980—. Named Outstanding Tchr. of English in Calif., 1970. Mem. Women in Mgmt., Nat. Assn. Female Execs., Calif. Mgrs. Assn. (past exec. com.). Address: 2006 N Grand Oaks St Altadena CA 91001

MEIERS, BEATRICE DOMINGUEZ, personnel psychologist; b. Albuquerque, Nov. 7, 1946; d. Ben F. and Emma Jean (Chavez) Dominguez; B.B.A. cum laude, Coll. Santa Fe, 1975, cert. in teaching, 1975; M.A.P.A., M.B.A., U. N.Mex., 1977; m. Jerald Lynn Meiers, June 24, 1978; children— James Dennis, Steven Joseph. Grad. asst. U. N.Mex. Law Sch., Albuquerque, 1975-77; personnel research asst. State of N.Mex., Santa Fe, 1977-79, personnel research psychologist, 1979—; instr. No. N.Mex. Jr. Coll., Santa Fe, 1977—; guest lectr. Western N.Mex. U., 1980. Mem. Gov.'s Career Devel. Conf. for Women in State Govt., 1979, 80, 81. Mem. Internat. Personnel Mgmt. Assn., Nat. Assn. Female Execs., AAUW, AAUP, Am. Soc. Public Adminstrn., Am. Soc. Personnel Adminstrs., Am. Mktg. Assn., Assn. MBA Execs., N.Mex. Women in Criminal Justice, Nelle's Girls Service Orgn. (sec., v.p.), Delta Sigma Pi, Pi Gamma Mu, Pi Alpha Alpha, Phi Delta Kappa, Beta Sigma Pi. Democrat. Roman Catholic. Home: 8513 Cherry Hills Rd NE Albuquerque NM 87109 Office: New Mexico State Personnel 130 S Capitol Santa Fe NM 87503

MEIERS, RUTH LENORE, state legislator; b. Parshall, N.D., Nov. 6, 1925; d. Axel and Grace Mary (Williams) Olson; B.S., U. N.D., 1946; m. Glenn E. Meiers, June 28, 1950; children—David, Michael, Monte, Scott. Mem. Mountrail County Welfare Bd., 1947-71; mem. N.D. Ho. of Reps., 1975—; mem. Disciplinary Bd., N.D. Supreme Ct., 1978—. Bd. dirs. Upper Mo. Dist. Health Unit, 1958—. Mem. Order Women Legislators, N.D. Public Health Assn. Democrat. Lutheran. Club: Sew and So Homemakers.

MEIJER-HIRSCHLAND, JOAN ELLEN, writer, lectr.; b. N.Y.C., May 19, 1939; d. Richard Simon and Bonnie (Prudden) Hirschland; B.A. in History, U. Vt., 1961; student Emergency Care Inst., Beekman Downtown Hosp., 1978; m. Hans Meijer, Apr. 6, 1964; children—Peter Jan, Richard Simon, Jacqueline Cristina. Emergency med. technician, paramedic, N.Y., 1975-82; instr. ARC, Woodstock, Vt., 1976—, Vt. affiliate Am. Heart Assn., 1976—; founder, pres. Nat. Emergency Care Adv. Council, Barnard, Vt., 1977—; cons. emergency care nat. TV, 1977—. Mem. Vt. Democratic State Com., 1972-74. Mem. Nat. Assn. Female Execs., N.Y.C. Assn. Paramedics, Nat. Registry Emergency Med. Technicians. Author: Student Workbook of Cardiopulmonary Resuscitation, 1983; Disaster Jones Children's Stories, 1982. Home: The North Rd Barnard VT 05031 Office: Box 98 Barnard VT 05031

MEIKLEJOHN, (LORRAINE) MINDY JUNE, polit. organizer; b. Staunton, Colo., June 9, 1929; d. Edward H. and Erna E. (Schwabe) Mindrup; student Ill. Bus. Coll., 1948, Red Rocks Community Coll., 1980-81; m. Alvin J. Meiklejohn, Apr. 25, 1953; children—Pamela, Shelley, Bruce, Scott. Pvt. sec. Ill. Liquor Commn., 1948-51, David M. Wilson, Ill. Sec. of State's Office, 1951-52; flight attendant Continental Airlines, 1952-53, pvt. sec. to mgr. flight ops. office, 1953-54; organizational dir. Colo. Republican Party, Denver, 1972—; active campaigns; del., alt. to various, county, state, dist. and nat. assemblies and convs. Mem. Jefferson County (Colo.) Hist. Commn. 1974-82, pres., 1979; vol. Jefferson County Legal Aid Soc., 1970-74; vice chmn. Jefferson County Rep. Party, 1977-81; vice chmn. Colo. State Rep. Party, 1981—; mem. adv. council U.S. Peace Corps, 1982—; sect. chmn. Jefferson County (Colo.) United Way Fund Dr.; mem. exec. bd. Colo. Fedn. Rep. Women. Lutheran. Club: Jefferson County Women's Rep. Home: 7540 Kline Dr Arvada CO 80005 Office: 1275 Tremont Pl Denver CO 80204

MEILI, JACQUELINE WISHNACK, public relations exec.; b. Paterson, N.J., Feb. 7, 1929; d. Jack and Marie F. Wishnack; A.B., Wellesley Coll., 1949; divorced; children—Paige Andrea, Robin Cheryl, Brett Randall. Account exec. McDonald, Davis & Assos., Milw., 1970-74; v.p. Bishea, Meili & Assos., Inc., Milw., 1975—; guest lectr. U. Wis., Milw.; instr. public relations U. Wis. extension. Bd. dirs. Channel 10/36 Friends Public TV, 1971-80, pres., 1977-79, chmn. nominating com., 1980—; bd. dirs., chmn. public relations DePaul Sertoma Industries, vocat. rehab. alcohol and drug abuse, 1979-80; v.p. bd. Friends Art, Milw. Art Center, 1974—; bd. dirs. Milw. Council on Alcoholism. Mem. Public Relations Soc. Am. (v.p. Wis. chpt.), Ind. Businessmans Assn. Wis., Women in Communications (pres., program v.p., dir. S.E. Wis. chpt.), TEMPO, Nat. Soc. Fund Raising Execs. Republican. Home: 9141 N Briarwood Court Milwaukee WI 53217 Office: 312 E Wisconsin Ave Milwaukee WI 53202

MEIS, PATTIE MORELAND, advt. co. exec.; b. Oklahoma City, Feb. 24, 1933; d. Harold Lewis and Ezekeiel Alta-Alice (Herndon) Moreland; B.B.A. in Mktg., U. Okla., 1954; children—Craig, Chris, Cameron, Meis. Adminstrv. asst. U.S. Air Forces Europe/DCS Personnel, Weisbaden, W.Ger., 1954-56; media dir. Lowe Runkle Co., Oklahoma City, 1957-64; v.p., media dir., mem. bd. Lowe Runkle Co., Oklahoma City, 1964-79; v.p., media dir., prin., med. bd. Strong/Hill/Meis Advt. Agy., Oklahoma City, 1979-82; exec. v.p., mktg. media dir., prin., mem. bd. Strong/Hill/Meis/Rozier Advt. Agy., Oklahoma City, 1982—. Named Oklahoma City Advt. Woman of Yr. Oklahoma City Advt. Club, 1972. Mem. Am. Women Radio and TV (dir.), Sales and Mktg. Execs. Internat. (v.p., dir.), Oklahoma City Advt. Council, Alpha Delta Pi. Home: 6313 N Warren St Oklahoma City OK 73112 Office: 1300 City National Bank Tower Oklahoma City OK 73102

MEISLER, BARBARA ALTMAN, speech pathologist; b. Wilkes-Barre, Pa., Oct. 5, 1943; d. Julius and Ann (Garber) Altman; B.A. in Speech Correction, George Washington U., 1965, M.A., 1967; m. Jules Murray Meisler, July 4, 1965; children—Marc Alan, Jan David. Speech clinician and lectr. George Washington U., Washington, 1967-68; tchr. Silver Spring (Md.) Nursery Learning Center, 1973-75, speech-lang. pathologist, 1972-79; speech pathologist Silver Spring Speech and Lang. Center, 1974-77; pvt. practice speech pathology, 1977—; cons. Learning

Diagnostics, Inc., Silver Spring, 1976-79; guest lectr. Montgomery County public schs., 1979; v.p. Speech and Hearing Discussion Group, 1971-73. Liaison to bd. dirs. Silver Spring Jewish Center, 1975-79, sisterhood pres. 1975-79; bd. dirs., v.p. Silver Spring Hebrew Day Inst., Rockville, Md., 1979—, pres. day sch., 1982—; bd. dirs. Sisterhood Young Israel Shamrei Emunah, Silver Spring; mem. women's div. United Jewish Appeal Fedn., recipient award of merit, 1980, 81. Recipient Service award Silver Spring Jewish Center, 1978. Mem. Am. Speech and Hearing Assn., Md. Speech and Hearing Assn., D.C. Speech and Hearing Assn., Alexander Graham Bell Assn., Sigma Alpha Eta (pres. 1964-65, hon. mem. award 1965), Am. Mizrachi Women. Jewish. Home: 11411 Monticello Ave Silver Spring MD 20902 Office: in care SSHDI 4511 Bestor Dr Rockville MD 20853

MEISNER, MARY JOAN, newspaper editor; b. Chgo., Dec. 24, 1951; d. Robert J. and Mary Elizabeth (Casey) M.; B.A. in Journalism, U. Ill., Champaign-Urbana, 1974, M.A., 1976; m. Martin G. Gradel, Jan. 8, 1977. Copy editor, then bus. reporter Wilmington (Del.) News-Jour., 1975-78; labor and gen. assignment reporter Phila. Daily News, 1979, city editor, 1979—. Mem. Pa. Soc. Newspaper Editors, Sigma Delta Chi. Office: 400 N Broad St Philadelphia PA 19101

MEISSNER, CONNIE KLINE, flutist; b. Cleve., Oct. 5, 1940; d. Edward Mahon and Muriel (Mace) Kline; B.M.E., Northwestern U., 1962, M.M.E., 1963; m. Ronald R. Meissner, May 5, 1973; children—Belinda, Rebecca. First flutist Lyric Opera Orch., Chgo., 1963—, Fla. Symphony, 1963, N.C. Symphony, 1964, Fish Creek Music Festival, 1965; soloist Chgo. Chamber Orch., U. Wis. Band, Parkside, Glenbrook North Symphony Orch.; tchr. high sch. students. Address: 1755 Carol Ct Deerfield IL 60015

MEITZLER, DANALEE CAROLINE, educator; b. Marcellus, Mich., Jan. 8, 1934; d. Clarence Elliott and Eva Belle (Beach) M.; B.S., Ball State U., 1958, M.A., 1965, lic. in adminstrn., 1974. Tchr. schs. in Ind. and Calif., 1958—; tchr. homebound, Elkhart, Ind., 1972—; county coordinator nutrition for elderly, Elkhart, 1979—. Pres. Elkhart Symphony Aux., 1976-77; mem. Elkhart Symphony Chorus, 1969—. Mem. NEA, Elkhart County Tchrs. Assn. (sec. 1963). Methodist. Home: 1119 Columbian Ave Elkhart IN 46514

MEIXNER, MARY LOUISE, educator; b. Milw., Dec. 7, 1916; d. Ernest and Wilhemina (Heinz) Meixner; B.A., Downer Coll., Milw., 1938; M.A., State U. Iowa, 1945; student Art Students League, 1947, 66, U. Minn., Duluth, 1953, 56, Fontainebleau, France, 1961, Carpenter Center, Harvard U., 1966. Faculty, Downer Coll., 1947-52, Eastern Ky. U., 1952-53; faculty Iowa State U., Ames, 1953—, prof. art, design, 1959, Mary B. Welch Disting. prof., 1975—. Recipient Faculty Teaching citation Iowa State U., 1972. Mem. Coll. Art Assn. Am., AAUP, Intersoc. Color Council, Nat. League Am. Penwomen Arts and Letters, Am. Home Econs. Assn., Phi Kappa Phi. Contbr. poetry to Lyrical Iowa Poetry, 1962—, articles in field to various publs.; dir. 4 films on light and color. Office: 162 Coll of Design Iowa State U Ames IA 50011

MEJIA, JEANETTE, social worker; b. Santurce, P.R., May 29, 1952; d. Rafael and Carmen (Medina) M.; B.A., Oral Roberts U., Tulsa, 1975; M.S.W., U. P.R., 1977. Social work trainee VA Hosp., San Juan, 1977; counselor Catholic Social Service, El Monte, Calif., 1977-78; med. social worker, quality assurance worker Tulsa Rehab. Ctr., 1979-80; adj. instr., practicum supr. Oral Roberts U., 1980-82. Lic. pvt. pilot. Mem. Nat. Assn. Social Workers. Methodist. Address: 7734D S Victor St Tulsa OK 74136

MEJIA, MARIA TERESA, pediatrician; b. San Salvador, El Salvador, Nov. 23, 1932; d. Marco Tulio and Maria Teresa (Escobar) Payes; M.D., U. El Salvador, 1964; m. Alfonso Mejia, Oct. 19, 1962; children—Alfonso, Alberto. Intern, Mercy Hosp., Chgo., then resident in pediatrics; practice medicine specializing in pediatrics, Blue Island, Ill. Mem. AMA, Ill. Med. Soc., Chgo. Med. Soc. Roman Catholic. Office: 2320 High St Blue Island IL 60406

MELDAU, ELIZABETH UZZLE, agrl. extension service adminstr.; b. Wilson's Mills, N.C., Nov. 9, 1935; d. James Thomas and Olive Herberta (Stuckey) Uzzle; B.S., U. N.C., Greensboro, 1958, M.S., 1970; Ed.D., N.C. State U., 1981; 1 dau., Elizabeth Sharpe. Asst. home econs. ext. agt. Durham County, N.C. Agrl. Ext. Service, 1958-65; home econs. ext. agt. Orange County, 1965-67; dist. home econs. ext. agt. East Central, Northwestern dists., 1967-75, dist. ext. chmn. Northwestern dist., 1975—. Mem. Am. Home Econs. Assn., N.C. Home Econs. Assn. (co-chmn. ann. meeting registration com. 1973), East Central Region Home Econs. Assn. (1st v.p. 1973), Durham-Orange Home Econs. Assn. (sec.-treas. 1963-64), N.C. Assn. Ext. Specialists, N.C. 4-H Agts. Assn., N.C. Assn. Ext. Home Economists, N.C. Adult Edn. Assn., Am. Business Women's Assn. (pres. 1966-67), U. N.C., Greensboro Alumni Assn. Office: Ricks Hall NC State U PO Box 5066 Raleigh NC 27650

MELDON, GERI MICHELLE, jewelry designer; b. Cleve., Feb. 4, 1944; d. Paul E. and Rhoda (Goldberg) M.; student Stephens Coll., 1962-63, Parsons Sch. Design, 1963-64; 4 yr. diploma in PEN silversmithing Cleve. Inst. Art, 1968; Grad. Gemologist-in-residence diploma Gemological Inst. Am., Santa Monica, Calif., 1969; Calif. lifetime teaching credentials in adult edn. UCLA, 1972; B.A., Calif. State U., 1974. Tchr. jewelry and design Los Angeles Dept. Recreation and Parks, 1970-76; retail sales staff May Co. Fine Jewelry, Los Angeles, 1974-75, Tiffany and Co., Beverly Hills, Calif., 1975-77, Slavicks Jewelers, Los Angeles, 1977; instr. jewelry retailing and Am. Gem. Soc. selling and merchandising program Gemological Inst. Am., 1977-78; free-lance jewelry designer, 1970—. Sec. ch. guild, art editor newsletter Ventura County Ch. of Religious Science, Ventura, Calif., 1980-81. Recipient 2d Pl. award Oxnard (Calif.) Cake Decoration Competition, 1980, 1st pl. and 2d pl. for most original, 1981, 1st pl. and Best in Show, 1982. Mem. Nat. Assn. Jewelry Appraisers, Internat. PEN Friends, Calif. Jewelers Assn. Office: 107 W Oak St Ojai CA 93023

MELDRUM, ARLENE ELIZABETH, vol. orgn. exec.; b. Edmonton, Alta., Can., Oct. 13, 1929; d. Richard Evan and Ada Elizabeth (Richards) Jones; B.A., U. Alta., 1951; m. John Andrew Meldrum, Sept. 13, 1952; children—Elizabeth Leigh, Wendy Anne, Karen Dee. Tchr., dir. tchrs. Figure Skating Program, Edmonton Fedn. Community Leagues, 1958—, figure skating chmn., 1964-68, pres. Edmonton Fedn. Community Leagues, 1974-76; mem. Edmonton Parks and Recreation Adv. Bd., 1976-78, Edmonton Mayor's Com. on Citizen Participation, 1974-78; chmn. City of Edmonton Com. on Remuneration of Mayor and Council, 1981-82; mem. adv. com. on vol. mgmt. program Grant McEwan Community Coll., 1981-82. Recipient City award Edmonton Parks and Recreation Adv. Bd., 1970; Outstanding Vol. Service to Community awards Edmonton Fedn. Community Leagues, 1966, 77; Citizen of Yr. award Edmonton Jaycees, 1979. Mem. Alta. Recreational Skating Assn. (program chmn.). Author: A.R.S.A. Power Skating Manual, 1969. Home: 13319-110A Ave Edmonton AB T5M 2M6 Canada

MELDRUM, BARBARA RUTH HOWARD, educator; b. Albany, Oreg., Apr. 13, 1934; d. Hal H. and Vera Louise (Bond) Howard; student Oreg. State U., 1953-54; B.A., Westmont Coll., 1956; M.A., Claremont Grad. Sch., 1957, Ph.D., 1964; m. Ronald M. Meldrum, 1960; children—Deirdre Ruth, Cynthia Leigh (twins). Instr., English U. Redlands (Calif.), 1959-62; asst. prof. English Ariz. State U., Tempe, 1962-65; vis. prof. Alaska Meth. U., Anchorage, 1967; asst. prof. English U. Idaho, Moscow, 1965-67, asso. prof., 1967-73, prof., 1973—, dir. grad. studies, vice chmn. dept., 1968-71; cons. Nat. Endowment for Humanities, 1977—; invited participant in symposiums. Mem. AAUP (pres. Idaho state conf. 1975-78, pres. U. Idaho chpt. 1973-75), Western Lit. Assn. (exec. council 1972-75, 79-82), MLA (del. assembly 1977-79), Pacific N.W. Am. Studies Assn. (pres. 1974-76), Am. Studies Assn., Melville Soc., Soc. Study of Midwestern Lit. Contbr. articles profl. jours., chpts. in books. Mem. editorial adv. bd. Western Am. Lit. Office: Dept of English University of Idaho Moscow ID 83843

MELGEORGE, MARCIA ANN, alt. energy products mfg. exec.; b. St. Paul, Sept. 18, 1933; d. Robert Wesley and Myrtle Emily Meyers; B.A., Macalester Coll., St. Paul, 1955; m. Edward L. Melgeorge, Sept. 19, 1959; children—Robert Frank, Mark Edward. Tchr., Hastings and Virginia, Minn., 1955-58; dist. dir., camp dir. St. Paul council Camp Fire Girls, 1958-68; underwriter All Nation Ins. Co., 1969; co-owner Wynne Lake Assos., Inc., 1969-72; sec.-treas. ELM Industries, Inc., The Furnace Works, Watertown, S.D., 1975—. Mem. Women in Mgmt., Watertown Area C. of C., Wood Heating Alliance, Can. Wood Energy Inst. Home: Route 3 Box 168 Watertown SD 57201 Office: ELM Industries Inc 724 14th St SW Box PO 773 Watertown SD 57201

MELIA, ETHEL (JINX), editor, cons.; b. Chevy Chase, Md., Dec. 29, 1936; d. Malcolm Parker and Euphrasia Jeanne (Raffo) Hanson; B.A., Trinity Coll., Burlington, Vt., 1959; M.Ed., George Mason U., 1975; m. Peter T. Melia, Nov. 15, 1969; children—Christopher, Brendan. Founder, exec. dir., pres. Martha Movement, Arlington, Va., 1976-79; sr. editor Am. Mother mag., 1979—; cons. women's issues, Rockville, Md. Mem. Am. Soc. Trainers and Developers, Nat. Assn. Women Bus. Owners. Home: 608 Blandford St Rockville MD 20850

MELLERT, LUCIE ANNE, writer; b. Charleston, W.Va., June 6, 1932; d. Wilbur Conant and Grace Martin (Taylor) Frame; student Mason Coll. Music and Fine Arts, Charleston, W.Va. U.; m. William J. Mellert, Mar. 15, 1957; 1 son, James F. Kelly, III. Public relations exec., asst. treas., office mgr. J.H. Milam, Inc., Dunbar, W.Va., 1959-71; public relations exec., office mgr. Hallcraft, Inc., Dunbar, 1972-74, Kanawha Stone Co., Inc., Nitro, W.Va., 1975-78; freelance writer, public relations cons., Dunbar, 1978—. Beautification commr. City of Dunbar, 1969-72; activity coordinator, program dir. Dunbar Bicentennial Com., 1971; coordinator Dunbar City Wide Beautification and Improvement Com., 1969-72. Mem. Nat. Fedn. Press Women. Clubs: Pioneer Women's (past pres.), Women of Moose. Address: 1017 W Virginia Ave Dunbar WV 25064

MELLON, ELEANOR MARY, sculptor; b. Narberth, Pa., Aug. 18, 1894; d. Charles Henry and Loraine W. (Roberts) M.; studied with Victor Salvatore, A.A. Weinman, Robert Aiken at Art Students League, N.Y.C., Harriet Frishmuth, Edward McCartan, Charles Grafly. Exhibited since 1921 with Nat. Sculpture Soc., N.Y. and San Francisco, NAD, N.Y.C., Pa. Acad. Fine Arts, Phila., Allied Artists Am., Soc. Washington Artists, Nat. Assn. Women Artists, N.Y.C., N.Y. World's Fair, Art Inst. Chgo., Bklyn. Mus., Nat. Arts Club, N.Y.C., North Shore Art Assn., Gloucester, Mass., Archtl. League, N.Y.C., Artists for Victory Exhbn. at Met. Mus., N.Y.C., 1942. Recipient Helen Foster Barnet prize NAD, 1927, Bronze medal Soc. Washington Artists, 1931, hon. mention Nat. Assn. Women Painters and Sculptors, 1932, Profl. prize N.Y. Jr. League, 1942; 2d Silver medal Am. Artists Profl. League, 1944, Gold medal N.Y. chpt., 1958; cash prize Pen and Brush Club, 1947, Silver medal, 1963; cash prize Brick Store Mus., Kennebunk, Maine, 1947; Bishop's Cross, Bishop, N.Y., 1969. Benjamin Franklin fellow Royal Soc. Arts Eng. Fellow Nat. Sculpture Soc. (sec. 1936-40, 45); mem. Brookgreen Gardens (trustee), NAD (academician, asst. treas. 1965-69), Pen and Brush, Am. Artists, Profl. League (dir. 1959—), Allied Artists. Republican. Episcopalian. Clubs: Colony, Cosmopolitan; Acorn (Phila.). Office: 440 W 22d St New York NY 10011 *

MELONE, MARGIE RUTH, health care co. exec.; b. Shawnee, Okla., Oct. 9, 1933; d. Jonah H. and Barbara Nancy (Krause) Haze; vocat. nurse diploma Fairmont Hosp., San Leandro, Calif., 1965; postgrad. Chabot Coll., U. Calif.; m. Victor P. Melone, Apr. 26, 1952; children—Victor P., Terri R. Vocat. nurse Barrett Convalescent Hosp., Hayward, Calif., 1965-68; v.p. La-Mar Co., Hayward, 1968—, Hunt-Malone Enterprises, Hayward, 1968-78; v.p. True Care, Inc., Hayward, 1970-77, Embassy House, Walnut Creek, Calif., 1970-81; pres., adminstr. Barrett Convalescent Hosp., Inc., 1968-78, owner, pres., 1978—, adminstrv. cons., 1980—; trustee Barret Rest Home, Inc.; co-chmn. Adv. Bd. Mentally Ill and Retarded, 1973. Cert. care developmentally disabled. Mem. So. Alameda County Commn. Aging, Am. Health Care Assn., Alameda County Mentally Retarded Assn., Calif. Assn. Health Facilities. Clubs: Met. Yacht, Order Eastern Star. Author articles, short story, poetry. Home: 1535 Denton Ave Hayward CA 94545 Office: 1625 Denton Ave Hayward CA 94545

MELOY, SYBIL PISKUR, lawyer; b. Chgo., Dec. 1, 1939; d. Michael M. and Laura (Stevenson) P.; B.S., U. Ill., 1961; J.D., Chgo.-Kent Coll. Law, 1965; m. Paul W. Meloy, June 29, 1963 (div. 1979), children—William, Bradley. Admitted to Ill. bar, 1965, U.S. Supreme Ct. bar, 1972; patent chemist G.D. Searle & Co., Skokie, Ill., 1961-65, patent atty., 1965-69, sr. patent atty., 1969-71, dir. internat. legal affairs, 1971-72; regional counsel Pacific and Far East, Abbott Labs., North Chicago, Ill., 1972-78; pvt. practice, Arlington Heights, Ill., 1978-79; asst. gen. counsel Alberto-Culver Co., Melrose Park, Ill., 1979—; of counsel Palmer, Blackman, Mancini & Rieband, Park Ridge, Ill., 1980—. Mem. Am. Chem. Soc., Am., Chgo. bar assns., Am. Patent Law Assn., Women's Bar Assn. Ill., N.W. Suburban Bar Assn., Licensing Execs. Soc., Phi Beta Kappa, Phi Kappa Phi, Iota Sigma Pi, Kappa Beta Pi, Sigma Kappa. Home: 431 N Northwest Hwy Park Ridge IL 60068 Office: 2525 Armitage St Melrose Park IL 60160 also 950 N Northwest Hwy Park Ridge IL

MELROY, LUELLA ELIZABETH, ins. agy. exec.; b. Churchs Ferry, N.D., May 22, 1920; d. Roy Arthur and Grace Alma (Dingman) Noltimier; student Dakota Bus. Coll., 1938-39; m. Richard Melroy, May 25, 1957. With various ins. offices, Fargo, N.D., 1939-51, Mpls. and St. Paul, 1951-53, Toledo, 1953-61; with Manhattan Ins. Service, Inc., Toledo, 1961—, pres., owner, 1971—. Bd. dirs. Toledo YWCA, 1963-76, pres., 1973-75; bd. dirs., treas. Girls Club of Toledo, 1981-82; chmn. Community Planning Council Com. on Battered Women; bd. dirs., treas. Rescue-Crisis Bd., 1979-81. Named Woman of Yr., Toledo chpt. Nat. Mgmt. Assn., 1975; Bus. Woman of Yr., Dist. 2 Bus. and Profl. Women, 1978; Ins. Woman of Yr., Toledo Assn. Ind. Ins. Agts., 1967. Mem. Ohio Assn. Profl. Ins. Agts. (dir. 1980—, membership chmn. 1981—), Toledo Assn. Ind. Ins. Agts. (pres. 1980-81, dir. 1973-82), Nat. Assn. Ins. Women (v.p. 1978-79, regional dir. 1976-77), Women Bus. Owners, Nat. Mgmt. Assn. (nat. dir. 1982—), Women Involved in Toledo. Republican. Office: 709 Madison Ave Toledo OH 43624

MELTON, PAMELA JEAN, sales exec.; b. Fullerton, Calif., Nov. 25, 1952; d. Douglas Neal and Jean (Kahl) French; student U. No. Colo., 1970-72; B.S., Ariz. State U., 1974; m. Dennis Patrick Melton, June 22, 1974. Vice pres., sec. Westunited Realty Corp., Phoenix, 1974-76; home economist Nat. Brands Inc., Phoenix, 1976-77; home economist Noble Distbrs., Inc., Phoenix, 1977-78, ter. sales rep., home economist, 1977-80; wholesale rep. for major appliances Nat. Brands Inc., Phoenix, 1980—; mem. faculty microwave cooking Rio Salado Community Coll., 1978—. Active Chicano Awareness activities thru Barrio Youth Project, 1979—. Named Salesperson of Yr., Gibson Mfg. Co., 1979, others. Mem. Am. Home Econ. Assn., Am. Home Econ. Central Div. (sec. 1978), Home Economists in Bus. (sec. 1979, chmn. 1981-82), Nat. Assn. Underwater Instrs., Ariz. State U. Alumni Assn., Alpha Phi. Republican. Club: Ariz. Real Estate. Home: 1537 W Tuckey Ln Phoenix AZ 85015 Office: 4633 W Polk St Phoenix AZ 85043

MELUM, MARA MINERVA, former assn. exec.; b. Mpls., June 21, 1951; d. Dan and Phyllis (Mondshein) Minerva; B.A., Princeton U., 1973; M.P.A., Syracuse U., 1974; m. Eric Melum, June 12, 1971. Adminstrv. resident Blue Cross/Blue Shield of Central N.Y., Syracuse, 1973; asst. dir. Health Services Assn., Syracuse, 1973-74; cons., policy analyst InterStudy, Mpls., 1974-75; v.p. Minn. Hosp. Assn., Mpls., 1975-82; preceptor U. Minn. Sch. Hosp. and Health Care Adminstrn.; preceptor dept. health adminstrn. U. N.C.; tchr. health facilities mgmt. program St. Mary's Coll.; cons. Region VI Center for Health Planning, HEW. Recipient DeWitt Clinton Poole Meml. prize Princeton U., 1973. Goldman Health Care Delivery scholar, 1973-74. Mem. Am. Hosp. Assn. (adv. panels on planning and on privacy and confidentiality of med. records), Am. Health Planning Assn., Soc. for Hosp. Planning (past pres.). Author: Assessing the Need for Hospital Beds: A Review of Current Criteria, 1975; Model to be Used to Determin Optimal Premium Rates for HMOs, 1975; An Analysis of the Claims Processing and Payment System Employed by the Central State SE and SW Areas Health and Welfare Fund, 1975; Criteria for Plan Evaluation, 1978; The Hospital Industry in Transition: New Roles and Service Diversification, 1980; The Changing Role of the Hospital: Options for the Future, 1980. Home: 5124 Xerxes Ave S Minneapolis MN 55410 Office: 900 S 8th St Minneapolis MN 55404

MELVIN, DIANE IRENE, educator; b. Ann Arbor, Mich., Aug. 15, 1946; d. Clinton A. and Marjorie E. (Delaforce) M.; B.S. in Phys. Edn., Eastern Mich. U., 1968, M.S., 1969, Ed.S., 1976; postgrad. U. Mich., 1975—. Tchr. phys. edn. Taylor (Mich.) Sch. Dist., 1968—, cheerleading coach, 1968-73, pep club adv., 1969-74, girl's athletic assn. sponsor, 1969-75, girl's varsity volleyball coach, 1974-77, girl's varsity club adv., 1975—, phys. edn. dept. chmn. John F. Kennedy High Sch., 1973—; meet dir. Mich. Girl's Gymnastics State Finals, 1976. Mem. AAHPER, NEA, Mich. Assn. Health, Phys. Edn. and Recreation, Mich. Fedn. Tchrs., Am. Fedn. Tchrs., Taylor Fedn. Tchrs., Nat. Bus. and Profl. Women, Mich. Bus. and Profl. Women, Belleville Bus. and Profl. Women, Delta Psi Kappa. Home: 12910 Lake Point Pass Belleville MI 48111 Office: 13505 Kennedy Dr Taylor MI 48180

MELVIN, DOROTHY MAE, parasitologist; b. Fayetteville, N.C., Jan. 27, 1923; d. Willie J. and Lillie M. (Bain) M.; B.A., U. N.C., Greensboro, 1942; M.S., U. N.C., Chapel Hill, 1945; Ph.D., Rice U., Houston, 1951. Parasitologist, Center Disease Control, Atlanta, 1945—, chief parasitology tng. br., 1963—; asst. prof. Emory U. Med. Sch. Mem. Am. Soc. Parasitologists, Am. Soc. Tropical Medicine and Hygiene, Sigma Xi. Author manuals in field, chpts. in books. Home: 2418 Kingscliff Dr NE Atlanta GA 30345 Office: Center Disease Control Atlanta GA 30333

MELVIN, KATHERINE MARIE, mfg. co. ofcl.; b. Carrollton, Ill., Dec. 22, 1947; d. Gary Leland and Mary Rita (Naber) M.; B.S. in Home Econs. Edn., Ill. State U., Normal, 1970, postgrad. in art edn., 1973. Instr., Ill. State U., 1972-73; tchr. Maxwell (N.Mex.) Mcpl. Schs., 1973-75; office mgr. Colo. chpt. Associated Builders & Contractors, Inc., Denver, 1975-76; food service specialist Groussman Brokerage, Ltd., Denver, 1976-78; regional sales mgr. West central region Ore-Ida Foods, food service div. H. J. Heinz, Inc., Pitts., 1978-79; ter. mgr. Rocky Mountain region Chicopee Mfg. subs. Johnson & Johnson, Denver, 1979—, corp. sales trainer, 1980—. Chmn. script Night In Old Denver, Hist. Denver, 1975, 76. Winner Indsl. Sales Achievement Contest, Chicopee Mfg., 1980, Sales award, 1981. Mem. Nat. Assn. Female Execs., NOW. Home and Office: 1935 S Columbine Denver CO 80210

MELVIN, MARCELLA BARBARA, ret. village clerk; b. Chgo., July 22, 1918; d. Nicholas J. and Julia M. (Stoll) Schneider; certification municipal clk., Syracuse U., 1971; student U. Ill., Champaign, 1966-67, Roosevelt U., Chgo., 1968-69; m. Lawrence S. Melvin, Oct. 26, 1940; children—Julia Ann Melvin Wood, Lawrence S. Sec., Fairbanks, Morse & Co., Chgo., 1936-44; supr. typists Harris Kerr Forrester Co., Chgo., 1950-52; accountant S. Fred Jarrow & Co., Chgo., 1952-58; village collector Matteson, Ill., 1953—, village clk., 1956-77, ret., 1977; tchr. seminar class, Syracuse U., 1973-74, seminar class for municipal clks. U. Ill., 1969, 75. Disaster rep. ARC, 1966—, blood drive vol., also chmn. south region personnel devel.; officer Family Service and Mental Health Center S. Cook County, 1965-71; organizer, leader 4-H Club, 1951-62; life mem. Matteson Elementary Sch. PTA (pres. 1955); dir. United Way-Crusade for Mercy, Matteson, 1960—; vol. Rich Twp. Sr. Services. Recipient Clerk of the Week award by resolution Ill. State Legis., 1975, Good Govt. award Matteson Bicentennial Commn., 1976; Ill. Municipal Clks. Assn. (past state dir., chmn. filing indexing manual), Municipal Clerks of South and West Suburbs of Cook County (past pres.), South Suburban Geneal. and Hist. Soc. (pres.), Matteson Hist. Soc. Roman Catholic. Clubs: St. Lawrence O'Toole Women's. Contbr. to Manual for Municipal Clerks of Illinois (1st place award Internat. Municipal Cks. Conv., 1975). Home: 3849 W 217th St Matteson IL 60443

MELVIN, RUTH WERTENBERGER, environ. cons.; b. Wayne County, Ohio, Aug. 5, 1909; d. Orlow Henry and Sarah (Good) Wertenberger; B.A., Ohio Wesleyan U., 1932; d. John H. Melvin, June 13, 1933 (dec.); children—John L., Judith Noel, Linda Graham, Jane Diedrick, Michael, Patricia Porteous. Caseworker, ARC and Fed. Relief Agency, 1933-34; exec. dir. Delaware County (Ohio) Council Social Agys., 1954-57; dist. adv. Allegheny County (Pa.) council Girl Scouts USA, 1960-61; dist. adv. Seal of Ohio Girl Scout Councils, 1960-64, program services dir., 1965-66; asst. to exec. officer Ohio Acad. Sci., Columbus, 1968-75; instr. geology The Nat. Audubon Camp of Wis., 1967-72, 78; lectr. geology Capital U., Columbus, 1968-69; pvt. practice cons. in environ. edn., Delaware, Ohio, 1981—. Pres. Delaware High Sch. PTA, 1957-58, Mt. Lebanon High Sch. PTA, 1957-58; chmn. Ohio Natural Areas Council, 1977—; mem. Ohio Dept. Natural Resources Recreation and Resources Commn., 1982; bd. dirs. Ohio chpt. Nature Conservancy. Mem. Ohio Conservation and Outdoor Edn. Assn. (past pres.); Am. Nature Study Assn. (past pres.), Nat. Audubon Soc., Columbus Natural History Soc., Ohio Acad. Sci., Ohio Alliance Environ. Edn. (past pres.), Ohio Environ. Council, Ohio Wesleyan U. Alumni Assn. (dir.). Republican. Mem. Ch. of Christ. (sec. Commn. for Outdoor Ministries, Ohio Conf.) Clubs: Fortnightly, Philomath. Author: A Guide to Ohio Outdoor Education Areas, 1971, rev., 1975; A Guide to the Literature of Ohio's Natural Areas, 1973. Home and Office: 122 Downing St S Delaware OH 43015

MEMORY, CATHERINE ANN, psychologist; b. Boston, Sept. 8, 1939; d. Roger and Mary (Loftus) Keane; A.B. magna cum laude, Regis Coll., 1960; Ed.M., Harvard U., 1961; postgrad. Boston U., 1964-69; m. Robert Edward Memory, Oct. 12, 1969; 1 son, Robert James. Tchr. public schs., Stoneham, Mass., 1961-63, sch. counselor, 1963-68; sch. counselor, Brookline, Mass., 1968-70; psychologist, public schs., Attleboro, Mass., 1970—; cons. Bridgewater State Coll. spl. edn. workshop, 1974; instr. Bristol Community Coll., Fall River, Mass., 1972-73; guest panelist Boston Catholic Family Life program, 1970—; lectr. Project Interserv Tchr. and Parent Tng. Program, 1975—; presenter Project

IMPACT Parent Edn. Program, 1978-79. Mem. City of Attleboro Social Services Com., 1970-74; South Attleboro residential chmn. Attleboro United Fund, 1973; com. pack mem. Cub Scouts Am., 1981—. NDEA grantee, San Diego State Coll., 1965; recipient Stoneham Jaycees Outstanding Young Educator award, 1967. Mem. Am. Psychol. Assn., Mass. Psychol. Assn., Mass. Sch. Psychologists Assn., Delta Epsilon Sigma. Club: Regis Coll. Alumnae Assn. Researcher with hyperkinetic children; contbr. paper on subject to profl. confs. Home: 145 Park Circle South Attleboro MA 02703

MENARD, JOAN MARIE, state legislator; b. N.Y.C., Sept. 6, 1935; d. John T. and Mary F. (Quintin) Hickey; B.S., Bridgewater State Coll., 1967, M.A., 1971; postgrad. Boston U.; m. Charles Menard, Jr., July 28, 1954; children—Jody Marie, Jennifer J. Tchr., Sacred Hearts Acad., Fall River, Mass.; dir. spl. edn. Somerset (Mass.) Public Schs.; now mem. Mass. Ho. of Reps., mem. house com. on edn., house com. on health care; trustee Fall River Five Cents Savs. Bank. Active, Salvation Army Building Drive; mem. adv. bd. Fall River Community Service; mem. Gov.'s Task Force on Spl. Edn., Mass.; mem. Somerset Democratic Town Com.; del. to Democratic Mid-term Conf., 1974; vice chmn. Fall River (Mass.) Sub-area Health Council. Mem. LWV of Greater Fall River (pres.), Mass. Tchrs. Assn. (cons. spl. edn.), Greater Fall River Bus. and Profl. Women. Roman Catholic. Club: Somerset Cath. Women's. Home: 4059 Riverside Ave Somerset MA 02726 Office: Room 473-G State House Boston MA 02133

MENDEL, LOUISE A., interior design co. exec.; b. New Orleans, Nov. 3, 1896; d. Jacob and Stella (Bloom) Abraham; m. Walter Scott Mendel, Aug. 2, 1916; children—Louise Stella, Charles. With The Strassel Co., Louisville, 1929—, pres., 1946-79, chmn. bd. dirs., 1979—. Mem. Am. Soc. Interior Decorators Nat. Antique and Art Dealers Asso.of AM., Inc. Republican. Home: 6114 Longview Ln Louisville KY 40222 Office: 1000 Hamilton Ave Louisville KY 40204

MENDELBERG, HAVA EVA, clin. psychologist; b. Cordoba, Argentina, Dec. 26, 1942; came to U.S., 1975, naturalized, 1977; d. Israel and Celia (Rubin) Gleser; B.A., Hebrew U. Jerusalem, 1969; M.S., U. Wis., Madison, 1977, Ph.D., 1981; M.A., U. Madrid, 1971; m. Uri Mendelberg, May 25, 1963; children—Tali, Gabi. Tchr., Kibbutz, Israel, 1964-69; tchr. Inst. Leaders from Abroad, Israel, 1969, 71-72; tchr., research asst. U. Madrid, 1970-71; psychologist Psychol. Services, Jerusalem, 1971-75; psychologist, counselor Ministry of Edn., Israel, 1974-75; project asst. U. Wis., Madison, 1975-76; sch. psychologist, Madison, Oregon and Racine, Wis., 1976-79; clin. psychologist Psychoanalytic Psychology Assos., Milw., 1979-81; lectr. Midwest Desegregation Center, Ill. and Wis., 1979-80; cons. U.S. Office of Edn., 1979-80; psychologist Mt. Sinai Med. Center, Milw., 1980-81; prof. psychology dept. U. Wis., 1981-82; psychologist Family Service of Milw., 1981-82; clin. psychologist Psychoanalytic Psychology Assos., Milw., 1981—. Mem. Am. Psychol. Assn., Wis. Psychol. Assn., Wis. Sch. Psychologists Assn., Psychol. Assn. Israel, Psychol. Assn. Spain. Home: 3611 N Morris Blvd Shorewood WI 53211 Office: 2040 W Wisconsin Ave Suite 515 Milwaukee WI 53233

MENDELOWITZ, MARY JANE, hosp. adminstr.; b. Denver, Mar. 7, 1921; d. Louis Gerson and Jennie (Cohen) Keinon; B.A., U. Denver, 1943; m. Monroe Richard Mendelowitz, May 5, 1943 (dec. Apr. 1977); children—Andrea Jo, David. Exec. sec. conv. dept. Lions Internat., Chgo., 1960-65; conv. coordinator AMA, Chgo., 1965-71; asst. exec. v.p. Am. Soc. Plastic and Reconstructive Surgeons, Chgo., 1971-79; pres. JWS Service Corp., N.Y.C., 1979-80; projects coordinator Northwestern Meml. Hosp., Chgo., 1980—. Active Chgo. Community Theater, 1956-73. Mem. Profl. Conv. Mgmt. Assn., Am. Assn. Med. Soc. Execs., Conf. Med. Soc. Execs. Greater Chgo. Democrat. Jewish. Home: 260 E Chestnut Apt 1104 Chicago IL 60611 Office: 333 E Superior St Chicago IL 60611

MENDELSON, AVA GARDNER, home economist, educator; b. Miami, Fla., Dec. 11, 1949; d. Alvin Frederick and Esther (Shochet) G.; B.S. with honors and distinction, U. Conn., 1971; Ed.M., Rutgers U., 1973; m. Philip L. Mendelson, Aug. 8, 1976. Tchr. home econs. Herbert Hoover Jr. High Sch., Edison, N.J., 1971-73; tchr. North Bethesda (Md.) Jr. High Sch., 1973-78, chmn. dept. home econs., 1973-78; chmn. dept. home econs. Ridgeview (Md.) Jr. High Sch., 1978—. Mem. Am. Home Econs. Assn., Md. Home Econs. Assn., NEA, Md. Tchrs. Assn., Montgomery County Edn. Assn., U. Conn. Alumni Assn., Parent Tchr. Student Assn. North Bethesda Jr. High Sch., Mortar Bd., Phi Sigma Sigma, Phi Upsilon Omicron, Omicron Nu, Kappa Delta Pi. Author: Creative Clothing Supplement, 1975; Craft Corner, 1975; MCPS Junior High Home Economics Program of Studies, 1977; Clothing and Textiles Middle/Jr. High School, 1978; Crafts/Leisure Time Activities, 1978; Who We Are and How We Grow, 1979; Home Economics for Special Needs Students, 1980; Food Services Curriculum, 1981, 82. Home: 19213 Bonmark Ct Germantown MD 20874

MENDELSON, MARY ADELAIDA JONES, assn. exec.; b. Grand Rapids, Mich., Aug. 13, 1917; d. Paul Walton and Florence (Diamond) Jones; A.B., Radcliffe Coll., 1939; M.A., U. Mich., 1940; tchrs. degree Fenn Coll., 1959; L.H.D. (hon.), Cleve. State U., 1981; m. Ralph Richard Mendelson, Feb. 22, 1941; children—Walton Lewis, Philip Heath. Caseworker Children's Aid Soc., Detroit, 1940; caseworker ARC, Cleve., 1941, asst. home service dir., Grand Rapids, Mich., 1942-46; high sch. history tchr. Laurel Sch., Shaker Heights, Ohio, 1959-63; polit. sci. instr. Cuyahoga County Community Coll., 1963-64; nursing home cons. Fedn. Community Planning, Cleve., 1964-73; lectr., 1974-76; exec. dir. Nursing Home Adv. and Research Council, Inc., Cleve., 1976—, mem. subcom. met. health planning, 1977-78; mem. com. on older persons Fed. Community Planning, 1978—; mem. adv. com. gerentology Ohio Bd. Regents, 1978—. Bd. dirs. Citizens League Cleve. Recipient George Polk Meml. award L.I. U. Dept. Journalism, 1974, Francis Payne Bolton award Jr. League Cleve., 1975, Alumnae award Radcliffe Coll., 1977, Woman of Yr. award YWCA, 1978. Mem. LWV (dir. Ohio 1958), Cleve. Coll. Women's Assn. (dir.). Clubs: Women's City, Jr. League (Cleve.); Radcliffe Harvard. Author: Tender Loving Greed, 1974; The Screwing of the Average Man - Where it all Ends, 1974; The Political Economy of Nursing Homes, 1974; Beating the High Cost of Funerals, 1975; Position Papers - Patient Abuse, 1967—; monthly columnist Insight on Medicare, Medicaid Nursing Home Problems, 1977—. Home and Office: 3137 Fairmont Blvd Cleveland Heights OH 44118

MENDHEIM, GAIL YVONNE, psychiat. social worker; b. Newark, Aug. 12, 1936; d. George E. and Gertrude S. (Rogers) M.; B.A., Rutgers U., 1966, M.S.W., 1969. Caseworker, County Welfare Bd., 1966-68, supr., 1969-70, field instr. grad. social work students, 1970-75; dir., consultation and edn. Mt. Carmel Guild Community Mental Health Center, Newark, 1975-77, dir. outpatient services, 1977-78, asso. dir. youth consultation service, 1978-81; dir. Essex County Guidance Center, 1981—. Com. mem. Rutgers Adv. Council; media chmn. Common Cause, 1973-75. Served with USAF, 1957-60. Decorated Am. Spirit of Honor medal. Mem. Nat. Assn. Social Workers, Acad. Certified Social Workers, Am. Public Health Assn., Register Clin. Social Workers. Democrat. Unitarian. Club: Soroptimist. Home: 42 Fairmount Terr East Orange NJ 07018

MENDILLO, PRISCILLA, gen. contractor; b. Providence, June 8, 1945; d. George and Lillian (Paquette) Mullins; A.A., Bryant Coll., 1962; student R.I. Sch. Design, 1963-64; m. Anthony Mendillo, Oct. 15, 1966; 1 son, Anthony. Founder, pres. Priscilla Enterprises, Inc., East Greenwich, R.I., 1971—. Mem. R.I. Podiatry Aux. (pres. 1973-78). Address: 75 Falcon Circle East Greenwich RI 02818

MENDIZABAL, MARITZA SALUD, ins. co. exec.; b. Mexico City, Mexico, Sept. 14, 1942; came to U.S., 1960, naturalized, 1965; d. Rafael and Brigida (Hernandez) Jauregui; B.A., Calif. State U., Los Angeles, 1968; postgrad. Mexico City U., 1970; m. Manuel E. Mendizabal, Feb. 10, 1978; children—Marytza J., Myra L. Dir. public relations Girl Scouts U.S.A., Los Angeles, 1965-68; coordinator community affairs Blue Cross of So. Calif., Los Angeles, 1968-73, dir. community affairs, 1973—; producer programs on community issues for radio and TV stas., Los Angeles area, 1975—. Vice pres. Mexican Civic Com., 1966—; bd. dirs. ARC, 1980—, Am. Lung Assn., 1966—, Mexican Am. Legal Defense and Edn. Fund, 1968—; bd. dirs. Mexican Am. Opportunity Found., 1975—, chmn., 1968-80. Recipient Human Relations award City of Los Angeles, 1980; Community Human Relations award Women's Mexican C. of C., 1979; Coro fellow, 1979-80. Mem. Nat. Assn. of Latin Elected Ofcls., Women in Communications, Calif. Women in Govt., Calif. Assn. of Latins in Broadcasting, Radio-TV News Assn. of So. Calif., Los Angeles C. of C., Peruvian C. of C., Am. Translators Assn., Publicity Club of Los Angeles, Hispanic Cultural Soc., World Affairs Council. Home: 19109 Derwent Pl Northridge CA 91326 Office: PO Box 70000 Van Nuys CA 91470

MENDLOVITZ, SARAH MCLAUGHLIN, psychologist; b. White Plains, N.Y., May 15, 1932; d. Richard Meredith and Dorothy Whitmore McL.; student SUNY, Purchase, 1969-70; B.A. with honors, Manhattanville, 1972; Ph.D. in Clin. Psychology (Danforth fellow, NIMH trainee), CUNY, 1976; m. W.H. Bittner, Apr. 18, 1953 (div.); children—Christopher Clarke, Richard Williamson, Elizabeth Marie, Jeffrey Whitmore; m. 2d, Al A. Mendlovitz, May 22, 1981. Trainee, Time/Life, N.Y.C., 1950-51; with Westchester County Recreation Commn., 1951-53; psychol. aide Bd. Coop. Ednl. Services 1, Carmel, N.Y., 1968-69; trainee NIMH, 1972-76; psychology intern Jewish Child Care Assn., N.Y.C., 1975-76, staff psychologist psychiat. clinic, 1978-80; staff psychologist Pleasantville (N.Y.) Diagnostic Center, Jewish Child Care Assn., 1976-78; psychologist Winston-Salem (N.C.) Child Guidance Clinic, 1980-81; pvt. practice psychol. counseling, 1981—. Bd. dirs. Welfare Rights Orgn., Westchester County, 1968-72, Westchester Community Service Council, 1972-76; pres. Yorktown (N.Y.) Community Players, 1960-62; bd. dirs. Assn. Couples for Marriage Enrichment, 1982; edn. chmn. Beth Jacob Synagogue, 1982. Recipient Bernard Ackerman award Grad. Psychology Dept., CCNY, 1973; lic. psychologist, N.Y. State, N.C. Fellow Soc. for Values in High Edn.; mem. Am. Psychol. Assn., Manhattanville Alumni Assn. (dir. 1976-78). Home and office: 647 Hawthorne Rd S Winston-Salem NC 27103

MENDOZA, LOURDES ROSARIO REFORMA, architect; b. Santa Cruz, Marinduque, Philippines, Oct. 21, 1947; came to U.S., 1967, naturalized, 1980; d. Mayolo Recella and Rosario Ricafort (Reforma) M.; B.S. in Architecture, U. Santo Tomas, Manila, 1966; postgrad. Am. U., Washington, 1974-75. Draftsman, Airways Engring., Corp., Manila, 1966-67, designer, Washington, 1967-69; architect Bechtel Corp., Gaithersburg, Md., 1969-72, Marriott Corp., Washington, 1972-74, Am. Hosp. Bldg. Corp., Silver Spring, Md., 1974-75; cost estimator Atlas Machine & Ironworks, Gainesville, Va., 1975-77; sr. cost engr. Ralph M. Parsons Co., Washington, 1977—. Home: 7528 Republic Ct Alexandria VA 22306 Office: 1201 Connecticut Ave NW Washington DC 20036

MENENDEZ-BOTET, CELIA JULIANA, chemist; b. Havana, Cuba, July 27, 1943; came to U.S., 1960, naturalized, 1966; d. Carlos M. and Celia A. (Martinez) Menendez; B.S. in Chemistry (H. and T. Griffith scholar 1963, Inst. Internat. Edn. scholar 1960, Gardner Whitecar award 1964), Phila. Coll. Pharmacy and Sci., 1964; M.S. in Chemistry Fordham U., 1968, Ph.D. in Chemistry, 1969; m. Jose Botet, Nov. 24, 1971; children—Celia Alexandra, Patricia Georgina. Postdoctoral trainee biol. scis. Columbia U., 1969-71; research asso. biochemistry Cornell U. Med. Sch., 1971-73; asso. attending biochemist Meml. Sloan Kettering Cancer Center, N.Y.C., 1973—, acting dir. clin. chemistry lab., 1974. Mem. Am. Chem. Soc., Am. Assn. Clin. Chemists, N.Y. Acad. Scis., AAAS, Meml. Sloan Kettering Cancer Center Assn. Profl. Women, Assn. Clin. Scientists, Sigma XI, Lambda Kappa Sigma, Iota Sigma Pi. Roman Catholic. Club: N.Y. Athletic. Contbr. articles to profl. jours. Home: 2 Woodland Terr Orangeburg NY 10962 Office: 1275 York Ave New York NY 10021

MENES, PAULINE HERSKOWITZ, state legislator; b. N.Y.C., July 16, 1924; d. Arthur B. and Hannah Herskowitz; B.A. in Bus. Econs. and Geography, Hunter Coll., 1945; m. Melvin Menes, Sept. 1, 1946; children—Sandra J., Robin J., Bambi L. Economist, Office of Quartermaster Gen., 1945-47; geographer U.S. Army Map Service, 1949-50; chief clk. Prince George's County (Md.) Bd. Elections, 1963; substitute tchr. Prince George's County Public Schs., 1965-66; mem. Md. Ho. of Dels., 1966—. Bd. dirs. Jewish Social Services Agy., 1975—. Recipient Ann London Scott Meml. award for legis. excellence Md. Nat. Orgn. Women, 1976; Woman of the Year award, Md. Bus. and Profl. Women's Club, 1978. Mem. Nat. Order Women Legislators (pres. 1979-80), Nat. conf. State Legislatures (chairperson women's network 1978-79), Md. Assn. Elected Women (dir. 1979—). Democrat. Jewish.

MENKE, JOANNE FAY, med. technologist; b. Mendon, Ill., Feb. 13, 1939; d. Kenneth Alton and Nora Jane (McCormick) Haistings; diploma in med. tech., Blessing Hosp., Quincy, Ill., 1960; B.S. in Med. Tech., Culver Stockton Coll., Canton, Mo., 1963; m. John Bernard Menke, Oct. 1, 1960; children—Jeffrey Bernard, Jeann Marie. Med. technologist Blessing Hosp., 1960-61, instr. Sch. Med. Tech., 1960-61; technologist, then chief med. technologist St. Mary Hosp., Quincy, 1961-70, instr., lectr. Sch. Med. Tech., 1961-70; chief adminstrv. med. technologist Levering Hosp., Hannibal, Mo., 1971—; past instr., microbiology Hannibal-LaGrange Coll.; adv. com. Hannibal Area Vocat. Tech. Sch.; bd. dirs. Marion County chpt. ARC; chmn. Marion County Blood Com. Mem. Am. Soc. Med. Technologists, Mo. Soc. Med. Technologists, Culver Stockton Coll. Alumni Assn. (bd. dirs.); assoc. mem. Am. Soc. Clin. Pathologists. Home: 3618 Tilden Ave Hannibal MO 63401 Office: 1734 Market St Hannibal MO 63401

MENKEN, DONNA JEAN, newspaper editor; b. Creston, Iowa, Apr. 30, 1941; d. Donald Albert and Doris Irene (Devol) Butler; student U. No. Iowa, Cedar Falls, 1959-61; divorced; children—Deanne Lynn, Dennis Jon. Physician's receptionist, 1971-72; med. librarian-lab. technician Central Community Hosp., Elkader, Iowa, 1972-73; with Clayton County Register, Elkader, 1973—, society editor, advt. saleswoman, 1974-78, editor, advt. mgr., 1978—. Mem. Nat. Fedn. Press Women, Iowa Press Women, Elkader C. of C. (exec. sec. 1975—). Republican. Lutheran. Office: 106 Cedar St NW Elkader IA 52043

MENKING, SUSAN MARGUERITE, psychologist; b. Blair, Nebr., Oct. 1, 1934; d. Bennard and Teresa (Foley) Reeh; B.A., Nebr. State Tchrs. Coll., 1955; M.S., So. Conn. State Coll., 1967; M.A., Tex. Woman's U., 1977, Ph.D., 1980; m. George D. Menking, Sept. 1, 1954; children—Angela M., Ellen S., Mark D., Lisa A., Keith J. Instr. stats. U. Nebr., Omaha, 1969; cons. Lewisville (Tex.) Schs., 1978-81; prof. psychology Pace U., N.Y.C., 1981-82; co-founder Bereaved Parents Group, Lewisville. Mem. St. Gerald's Parish Sch. Bd., Ralston, Nebr., 1967-69, Denton County (Tex.) Child Welfare Bd., 1980-81. So. Conn. Coll. fellow, 1966-67. Cert. psychologist, Tex. Mem. Am. Psychol. Assn., Westchester County Psychol. Assn., Phi Delta Gamma. Roman Catholic. Office: 7000 Blvd E Suite 141D Guttenberg NJ 07093 also 2429 Camino de Vida Santa Fe NM 87501

MENNELL, CONSTANCE JACKSON, mfg. co. advt. and mktg. exec.; b. Boston, July 26, 1940; d. Frederick M. and Josephine P. Jackson; B.A. in Psychology, Skidmore Coll., 1962; m. Michael A. Mennell, Oct. 26, 1968 (div.). Advt. mgr. Lake Tahoe Assos., San Francisco, 1967-68; account exec. in land devel. Don Frank & Assos., Los Angeles, 1968-69; media dir., account exec. Wilton, Coombs and Colnett, Inc., Los Angeles, 1969-71; media dir., account service exec. Meyers & Muldoon Advt., San Francisco, 1972-74; free-lance account exec., San Francisco, 1975-76; advt./mktg. mgr. Geyser Peak Winery subs. Joseph Schlitz, San Rafael, Calif., 1976-80; advt./mktg. dir. Buck Stove West, Inc., Benicia, Calif., 1980—. Home: 72 Corte Real Greenbrae CA 94904

MENSCH, MARLENE MARJORIE, mktg. exec.; b. Chgo., Sept. 25, 1932; d. Louis J. and Elvira (Bostrum) M.; student public schs., Chgo.; children—Kathleen Marie, Mark David. Various gen. office positions Wheeler Overall Service, Chgo., 1949-58; paymaster Hurletron Co., Wheaton, Ill., 1959-65; buyer Wilcox Internat. Inc., Chgo., 1965—. Tchr. Sunday sch. Trinity Episcopal Ch., Wheaton, 1963-66; dir. women's program Belmont YMCA, Chgo., 1954-56. Mem. Inst. Prodn. and Inventory Control, Nat. Assn. Female Execs., Wheaton Drama Club. Office: 564 W Randolph Chicago IL 60606

MENYUK, PAULA, educator; b. N.Y.C., Oct. 2, 1929; d. Louis and Helen (Weissman) Nichols; B.S., N.Y.U., 1951; M.Ed., Boston U., 1954; D.Ed., 1961; m. Norman Menyuk, Mar. 5, 1950; children—Curtis R., Diane E., Eric D. Chief lang. clinic Mass. Gen. Hosp., Boston, 1952-54; lectr., teaching fellow Boston U., 1955-58, predoctoral fellow, 1958-61; postgrad. fellow M.I.T., 1961-64, mem. research staff, 1964-72; mem. faculty Boston U., 1972—, prof. psycholinguistics, 1973—, dir. reading and lang. devel. div., 1982—; cons. in field. Fulbright fellow, 1971; NIMH fellow, 1958-64. Fellow Am. Speech, Lang. and Hearing Assn.; mem. Soc. Research Child Devel., Linguistic Soc. Am., Internat. Soc. Study Behavioral Devel., Internat. Soc. Phonetic Scis., Internat. Child Lang. Assn., AAAS. Author: Sentences Children Use, 1969; Acquisition and Development of Language, 1971; Language and Maturation, 1977; also monographs. Office: 605 Commonwealth Ave Boston MA 02215

MENZIES, JEAN STORKE (MRS. ERNEST F. MENZIES), ret. newspaperwoman; b. Santa Barbara, Calif., Dec. 30, 1904; d. Thomas More and Elsie (Smith) Storke; B.A., Vassar Coll., 1927; M.A. in Physics, Stanford, 1931; m. Ernest F. Menzies, Oct. 20, 1937; children—Jean Storke (Mrs. Dennis Wayne Vaughan), Thomas More. Teaching asst. dept. physics Stanford, 1927-29; instr. of physics Vassar Coll., 1929-30; tchr. math., chemistry, gen. sci. Sarah Dix Hamlin Sch., San Francisco, 1931-34; sec. to Dr. and Mrs. Samuel T. Orton, N.Y.C., 1935-36; press reporter, spl. writer Santa Barbara News-Press, 1954-63. Rec. sec. nat. YWCA, India, Burma and Ceylon, 1941-42; rec. sec., Calcutta YWCA, 1942-47, v.p., 1949-51; sec. Tri-County adv. council Children's Home Soc., Santa Barbara, 1952-54; founding dir., sec. corp. Santa Barbara Film Soc., Inc., 1960-66. Bd. dirs. Santa Barbara County chpt. Am. Assn. UN, 1954-59, Friends U. Calif. at Santa Barbara Library, 1970-74, Small Wilderness Area Preservation, 1971-79; sec. bd. trustees Crane Country Day Sch., 1955-57; trustee Mental Hygiene Clinic of Santa Barbara, 1956-60, U. Calif. Santa Barbara Found., 1974-80, Santa Barbara Mus. Natural History, 1977-81; adv. council Santa Barbara Citizens Adult Edn., 1958-62, v.p., 1960-62; bd. dirs. Internat. Social Sci. Inst., sec., 1963-68, mem. adv. bd., 1969; bd. dirs. Planned Parenthood Santa Barbara County, Inc., 1964-65, adv. council, 1966-67; trustee Santa Barbara Botanic Garden, 1967-81, hon. trustee, 1981—; trustee. Santa Barbara Trust for Historic Preservation, 1967-68, 72-77; mem. affiliates bd. dirs. U. Calif. at Santa Barbara, 1960-61, 67-70, 72-77; sec. Santa Barbara Mission Archive-Library, 1967—; mem. Santa Barbara Found., 1977-81. Mem. Santa Barbara Hist. Soc. (dir. 1957-62, founding mem. women's projects bd. 1959-63, sec. 1961-62), Channel City Women's Forum (v.p. 1969-73, bd. dirs. 1973—), Phi Beta Kappa, Sigma Xi. Club: Vassar of Santa Barbara and the Tri-Counties (1st v.p., founding com. 1956-57, 2d v.p. 1959-61, chmn. publicity com. 1961-73). Home: 2298 Featherhill Rd Santa Barbara CA 93108

MEO, YVONNE COLE, artist, printmaker, educator; b. Seattle, Wash., June 5; d. Thomas A. and Lorenza (Jordan) Cole; B.A., UCLA, 1948; M.A., Calif. State U., Los Angeles, 1960; Ph.D., Union Grad. Sch., Ohio, 1977; Arts D. (hon.), Gt. China Arts Coll., Hong Kong, 1973; student of Glenn Lukens, Los Angeles, 1952, Maestro José Gutiérrez, Mexico City, 1952, Guy MacCoy, Los Angeles, 1962, 65, 68; 1 son, Byron Meo. Instr. ceramics, interior design, painting and drawing Fisk U., Nashville, Tenn., 1948-50; tchr. stage design, ceramics and crafts secondary schs. of Los Angeles Unified Sch. Dist., 1951-67; mem. faculty art dept. Pasadena (Calif.) City Coll., 1969-70; prof. lectr. art Calif. State U., Northridge, 1969-70; instr. design, painting and art history Van Nuys (Calif.) High Sch., 1964-79; vis. prof. painting and drawing Calif. State U., Los Angeles, 1972; instr. dept. art East Los Angeles Coll., 1975-76; U.S. del. Internat. Black and African Festival of Arts and Culture, Nigeria, 1977; mem. curriculum com. Calif. State U. System, 1970; guest artist Space Symposium Brit. Interplanetary Soc., 1976; one-women shows of sculpture, paintings, prints various galleries, mus., and univs. in Calif., 1965—, group shows include: Los Angeles County Art Mus., Ankrum Gallery, Taft Mus., Cin., Oakland (Calif.) Mus. Archives, also Mishima (Japan), Leipzig (Germany), Moscow, Nigeria and Mexico, 1977—; represented in permanent collections: Mus. African and African Am. Art, Buffalo, Mary McLeod Bethune Br. Library, U. So.Calif., Calif. State U., Fullerton, Oakland Mus. Archives. Recipient Arc of Achievers award Calif. Inst. Tech., 1967, numerous other art awards. Mem. Pasadena Soc. Artists, Nat. Conf. Artists, AAUW, Artists Equity Assn., League Allied Arts (Bicentennial award 1981), Delta Kappa Gamma, Delta Sigma Theta.

MÉRAS, PHYLLIS LESLIE, journalist; b. Bklyn., May 10, 1931; d. Edmond Albert and Leslie Trousdale (Ross) M.; B.A., Wellesley Coll., 1955; M.S. in Journalism, Columbia U., 1954; Swiss Govt. Exchange fellow, Inst. Higher Internat. Studies, Geneva, 1957; m. Thomas H. Cocroft, Nov. 3, 1968. Reporter, copy editor Providence Jour., 1954-57, 59-61; feature writer Ladies Home Jour. mag., 1957-58; editor Weekly Tribune, Geneva (Switzerland), 1961-62; copyeditor, travel sect. N.Y. Times, 1962-68; mng. editor Vinyard Gazette, Edgartown, Mass., 1970-74, contbg. editor, 1974—; asso. editor Rhode Islander, Providence, 1970-76; travel editor Providence Jour., 1976—; editor Wellesley Alumnae mag., 1979—; assoc. in journalism U. R.I., 1974-75; adj. instr. Columbia U. Sch. Journalism, 1975-76; author: First Spring: A Martha's Vineyard Journal, 1972; A Yankee Way With Wood, 1975; Miniatures: How to Make Them, Use Them, Sell Them, 1976; Vacation Crafts, 1978; The Mermaids of Chenonceaux and 828 Other Tales: An Anecdotal Guide to Europe, 1982; co-author: Christmas Angels, 1979; Carry-out Cuisine, 1982; Pulitzer fellow in critical writing, 1967. Mem. Soc. Am. Travel Writers. Home: Sunnyside Ave Vineyard Haven MA 02568 Office: Providence Jour Providence RI 02902

MERCADO, LINDA ISMAEL DICKEN, elec. designer; b. San Francisco, June 13, 1955; d. Daniel I. and Mary F. Ismael; student public schs., Los Angeles, Clark County Community Coll.; m. Robert Dicken, Aug. 6, 1978; 1 son, Daniel; m. 2d, Jesuito Mercado, Dec. 19, 1981; 1

dau., Linda Ismael; Asst. mgr. Clancy Muldoon, Santa Monica, Calif., 1972-73; instr. math. and sci. Clover Elem. Sch., Los Angeles, 1974; accounts receivable supr. Advance Indsl. Fin. Co., Beverly Hills, Calif., 1974-77; asst. controller Nev. Beauty and Barber Supply Co., 1977-78; elec. designer James Glover Cons. Engrs., Las Vegas, Nev., 1978-80; owner L&R Services, Las Vegas, 1980—; owner Little Dickens Child Care, 1981—; notary public. Mem. at large bd. dirs. Girl Scouts U.S.A. Recipient Excellence in Music award C. of C., 1969. Mem. Am. Soc. Profl. and Exec. Women, Clark County Child Care Assn., (rec. sec.-treas.), Nev. State Child Care Providers Assn., Nat. Assn. Deaf, Nat. Com. Prevention Child Abuse, Clark County Child Services Guild, Nat. Assn. Female Execs., Nat. Notary Assn. Republican. Mem. Christian Ch.

MERCE, ANNE MARIE, reinsurance underwriter; b. Denison, Ohio, Nov. 5, 1947; d. Russel and Leona (Berry) M.; student Alderson Broaddus Coll., 1967-68; B.Mus. Edn., Westminster Choir Coll., 1972. Cons., tchr. Nat. Keyboard Arts Assos., Princeton, N.J., 1972-73; homeowners underwriting clk. Walter B. Howe, Inc., Ins., Princeton, 1973; adminstrv. asst. E.D. Sayer, Inc., Princeton, 1974-79, asst. v.p., underwriter, 1979—. Mem. Nat. Assn. Female Execs., Soc. Profl. and Exec. Women, Assn. Profl. Ins. Women. Republican. Baptist. Home: 189 Princeton Arms N Cranbury NJ 08512 Office: PO Box 3112 Princeton NJ 08540

MERCER, SHARON LYNNE, tax preparation franchise owner; b. Aurora, Ill., July 11, 1948; d. Robert Salisbury and Arlene May (Fredres) Brewer; student Sauk Valley Jr. Coll., 1975-76; m. Tedd A. Mercer, Nov. 26, 1976; children by previous marriage—Dennis Jeffrey, Amy. Tax preparer, H & R Block Co., Sycamore, Ill., part-time, 1970, tax preparer, Waterman, Ill., full time, 1971, franchise owner, office mgr., Princeton, Ill., 1972—, Mendota, Ill., 1981—, mem. satellite adv. council, 1978-79; instr. Basic Tax Sch., Princeton, Ill., 1972—, Advanced Tax Sch., Dixon, Ill., 1973-74. Project coordinator Econ. Devel. Adminstrn., U.S. Dept. Commerce for Arlington, Ill., 1977-78, Putnam County, Ill., 1978, City of Princeton, 1978, mem. Bureau County (Ill.) overall econ. devel. plan com., 1978—; mem. community devel. staff, HUD grant-project coordinator City of Princeton, 1978—; mem. Satellite Adv. Council, 1979-82; program dir. Princeton Elderly Housing Project, 1979, Bureau County Gateway Center Project, 1979—, Princeton Downtown Redevel. Plan, 1979—. Recipient H & R Block Inc. Nat. Award of Recognition for Public Relations Excellence, 1977. Mem. Princeton C. of C., Mendota C. of C. Lutheran. Home: 230 N Mercer St Princeton IL 61356 Office: 405 S Main St Princeton IL 61356

MERCHANT, VASANT V., educator; b. Bombay, India, Sept. 11, 1933; came to U.S., 1957; d. Vallabhdas P. and Ratanbai Merchant; B.A. with honors U. Bombay, 1955, M.A., 1957, LL.B., 1957; M.A., U. Minn., 1960; Ph.D., U. So. Calif., 1966. Researcher, counselor U. Minn., Mpls., 1957-63, U. So. Calif., Los Angeles, 1963-66; asst. prof. humanities No. Ariz. U., Flagstaff, 1966-68, asso. prof., 1968—; lectr.; ednl. cons. Fellow Internat. Council Psychologists; mem. Pilot Internat. Assn., Nat. Assn. for Humanities Edn. (pres. 1982—), Assn. for Asian Studies, Ariz. Humanities Assn. (pres. 1980—), Phi Kappa Phi. Author: Religion and World Peace; contbr. articles to profl. jours. Home: 1436 N Evergreen Flagstaff AZ 86001 Office: Box 6031 Humanities Northern Arizona University Box 6031 Flagstaff AZ 86011

MERCINCAVAGE, JANET ELAINE, accountant, educator; b. Wilkes-Barre, Pa., July 19, 1954; d. George Michael and Anne Margaret (Chescavage) M.; B.S. in Bus. Adminstrn. and Spanish, Juniata Coll., 1976; postgrad. Temple U. Public acct. Reading (Pa.) office Ernst & Whinney, 1976-78; acct., asst. to treas. Reading Alloys, Inc., Robesonia, Pa., 1978-80; mem. evening acctg. faculty Alvernia Coll., Reading, 1977-80; mem. faculty King's Coll., Wilkes Barre, Pa., 1980—. Active Found. of Ind. Colls. campaigns, 1978, 79. C.P.A., Pa. Mem. Am. Inst. C.P.A.s, Pa. Inst. C.P.A.s Roman Catholic. Home: 85 N Thomas Ave Kingston PA 18704 Office: King's Coll Wilkes Barre PA 18711

MEREWETHER, ADELINE MARJORIE, social worker, psychotherapist; b. Lancaster, N.Y., Oct. 29, 1919; d. Adam Edward and Florence Emily (Notley) Snyder; B.A., Wayne State U., 1964, M.A., 1975, specialist cert. in Aging, 1975; M.S.W., U. Mich., 1980; m. John Armstrong Merewether, Sept. 9, 1943; children—Bruce Arnold, Jean Ann Merewether Coverdill. Social worker supr. Homemaker Service of Met. Detroit, 1965-78; tchr. Sr. Adult Programs, Wayne County Community Coll., Detroit, Redford, Mich., 1978—; tchr. Adult Edn. Program, Highland Park (Mich.) Community Coll., 1975-78; social worker hemodialysis unit Henry Ford Hosp., Troy, Mich., 1978-79; med. social worker Met. Home Health Care, Dearborn, Mich., 1978—; clin. social work psychotherapist Montgomery and Assos. Outpatient Clinic and Personal Growth Center, Birmingham, Mich., 1979—. Sponsor, Parent's Anonymous Group, 1980—. Cert. social worker, Mich.; cert. specialist in Gerontology, Mich. Mem. Nat. Assn. Social Workers, Mich. Interprofl. Assn. on Marriage, Divorce and Family. Office: 690 E Maple Birmingham MI 48011

MERGENOVICH, AGATHA FRANKLIN, govt. ofcl.; b. Gilmer, W.Va., June 9, 1925; d. Rosen and Audra Leola (Brown) Franklin; student Am. U., 1962; m. Peter Mergenovich, July 10, 1943 (div.); 1 dau., Janice Mergenovich Shamsi. Clk., adminstr. Dept. Navy, VA and Dept. Justice, 1957; with ICC, Washington, 1957—, beginning as mgmt. intern, successively chief paperwork mgmt. br., chief mgmt. br., chief sect. adminstrv. services, asst. to mng. dir., 1957-79, sec. of Commn., 1979—. Recipient Fed. Paperwork Mgmt. award, 1978. Mem. Nat. Assn. Female Execs. Home: 5303 41st Ave Hyattsville MD 20781 Office: Room 2215 ICC Washington DC 20423

MERIDITH, EVA EDMOND WALKER, water well contractor; b. Orlando, Fla., Aug. 8, 1926; d. Bruckner H. and Frances Lottie (Turner) Walker; student Orlando schs.; m. Emery Noah Meridith, Dec. 8, 1942; children—Danny N., Larry G., Debra S. With Meridith Corp., Orlando, 1948—, sec.-treas., 1958—. Past pres. various sch. PTAs; pres. W. Orange Service League, 1965-66. Mem. Nat. Water Well Assn. (dir. ladies div. 1973-78), Fla. Water Well Assn. (organizer, pres. ladies div. 1972), PEO. Democrat. Methodist. Home: 500 Lake Butler Blvd Windermere FL 32786 Office: 2911 W Washington St Orlando FL 32805

MERINGOFF, LAURENE KRASNY, media researcher; b. N.Y.C., Dec. 16, 1945; d. Morris L. Krasny and Helen (Meyer) Brauner; B.S., Cornell U., 1966; M.A. with honors, Tchrs. Coll., 1967; Ed.D., Harvard U., 1978. Tchr. headstart, Bronx, N.Y., 1965; researcher Fed. Evaluation Headstart, Boston U., 1967-68; staff psychologist Cape Cod (Mass.) Child Guidance Center, 1968-71; sr. research asso. G. R. G. (consumer research with children), Darien, Conn., 1972-74; NSF grantee, 1975-76; expert witness FTC, 1978-79, cons.; research asso. Harvard U., Cambridge, Mass., 1978-82. Markle Found. grantee, 1978-82. Mem. Am. Psychol. Assn., Soc. for Research in Child Devel. Co-author: The Effects of TV Advertising on Children, 1980; contbr. articles in field to profl. jours. Home: South Rd Gay Head MA 02535 Office: Harvard Project Zero Longfellow Appian Way Cambridge MA 02138

MERINO, ROSE ELLIS, physician; b. El Paso, Tex., 1924; d. Frederick and Elizabeth Ellis; M.D., N.Y. Med. Coll., 1949; m. Francsico Merino, Feb. 1953; children—Rosa, Margaret, Frances, Frank. Intern, St. Vincent's Hosp., N.Y.C., 1949-50, resident, 1951-52; resident Willard Parker Hosp., N.Y.C., 1950; pediatrician N.Y.C. Dept. Health, 1952-53; clin. asst. pediatrician Meml. Hosp., N.Y.C., 1967-73, med. dir. Health Center, 1982—; cons. Bur. Child Welfare; adj. attending physician Meml. Sloan-Kettering Cancer Center, 1974—. Diplomate Am. Bd. Pediatrics, Am. Bd. Family Practice. Fellow Am. Acad. Family Physicians, AMA, N.Y.C. Med. Soc. Roman Catholic. Home: 444 E 57th St New York NY 10022 Office: 1285 Ave of the Americas New York NY 10019

MERKLE, LINDA L., legal adminstr.; b. Washington, Apr. 6, 1947; d. Robert Clifton, Shreeves II and Esther A. (Harrison) Cumming; lic. real estate, Prince Georges Community Coll., Largo, Md., 1972; children—Christina L., Regina L. Various secretarial positions, 1964-65, 67-72; real estate saleswoman, 1973-74; div. sec. Prince Georges Community Coll., 1974-75; real estate saleswoman Harvest Realty Inc., Clinton, Md., 1974-75; legal adminstr., property mgr., investment mgr. firm Tucker, Flyer, Sanger, Reider & Lewis P.C., Washington, 1975—; dir. Md. Corp.; pres. Lawtabs Inc. Del. Corp.; cons., speaker Mem. Assn. Legal Adminstrs., Am. Bar Assn. (asso.). Home: 8715 Baskerville Pl Upper Marlboro MD 20772 Office: 1730 Massachusetts Ave NW Washington DC 20036

MERLE, NANCY MCCLURG, real estate exec.; b. Pico Rivera, Calif., Aug. 2, 1934; d. Mervin John and Rahma Louise (Westover) McClurg; student Fresno State Coll., 1951-52, Vallejo Jr. Coll., 1954-55, Hancock Coll., 1958, Sierra Coll., 1960-61, U. N.Mex., 1962, Columbia U. N.Y. Sch. Social Work, 1962-63; m. William E. Merle, Nov. 4, 1966; children—Valerie, Vicki, Michael, Jeffrey. Owner, operator Am. Engring. Co., Vallejo, Calif., 1954-59; asst. supt. hwys. State of Calif., San Luis Obispo County, 1959-62; owner, pub., editor Mother Lode Press, Auburn, Calif., 1963; owner, operator Merle & Assos., Auburn, 1964—. Candidate for state senate Calif. Republican Party, 1963; chmn. Placer County (Calif.) Young Republicans, 1966-76; mem. Calif. Rep. Central Com., 1964-68; mem. Nat. Conservative Action Com. Episcopalian. Home: 555 Conifer Lane Auburn CA 95603 Office: 560 Wall St Suite L Auburn CA 95603

MERMAN, ETHEL, singer, actress; b. Astoria, N.Y., Jan. 16, 1909; d. Edward and Agnes Zimmerman; student pub. schs. Long Island City, N.Y.; m. William B. Smith, Nov. 16, 1940 (div. Oct. 1941); m. 2d, Robert D. Levitt (div.); m. 3d, Robert F. Six (div. 1961); m. 4th, Ernest Borgnine, July 1964 (div.). Sec. to pres. B.K. Vacuum Booster-Brake Co.; night club singer, also singing with Jimmy Durante, Clayton and Jackson; made Broadway debut in Girl Crazy, 1930; other theatre appearances include: George White's Scandals, 1931-32; Take a Chance, 1932; Anything Goes, 1934; Red, Hot and Blue, 1936; Stars in Your Eyes, 1939; Dubarry Was a Lady, 1939; Panama Hattie, 1940; Something for the Boys, 1943; Annie Get Your Gun, 1946; Call Me Madam, 1950; Happy Hunting, 1956; Gypsy, 1959; Hello, Dolly!, 1970; radio program. Rhythm at Eight, 1935; appearances in motion pictures include: We're Not Dressing, Kid Millions, 1934; The Big Broadcast, 1935; Strike Me Pink, 1936; Anything Goes, 1936; Happy Landing, 1938; Alexander's Ragtime Band, Straight, Place and Show, Stage Door Canteen, 1943; Call Me Madam, 1953; No Business Like Show Business, 1954; Gypsy, It's a Mad, Mad, Mad, Mad World, 1963; Won Ton Ton, 1976; numerous TV appearances, including Merv Griffin's Salute to Irving Berlin, 1976. Winner N.Y. Drama Critics award, 1943, 46, 59; Donaldson award, 1947; Tony award, 1951, 72; Barter Theatre of Va. award, 1957; Drama Desk award, 1969-70. Author: Merman, An Autobiography, 1978. Address: care Gus Schirmer 1403 N Orange Grove Ave Los Angeles CA 90046 *

MERMELSTEIN, PAULA, TV exec.; b. N.Y.C., Nov. 8, 1947; d. Robert and Dorothy (Asch) Mermelstein; B.A. in Speech and Theater cum laude, Bklyn. Coll., 1968; m. Francis W. James, Jr., Nov. 23, 1975. Writer/producer On-Air promotion NBC, N.Y.C., 1970-78, supervising writer/producer, 1978-79, dir., 1979, v.p., 1979—. Recipient First Place News award U.S. TV Commls. Festival for NBC Profile, David Brinkley, 1977. Mem. Writers Guild Am. Author protest column, Glamour Mag., 1970. Office: NBC 30 Rockefeller Plaza New York NY 10020

MEROCA, MARY LOUISE FRANCES, physician; b. N.Y.C., Oct. 9, 1950; d. John A. and Mary T. (Guidera) M; B.S. in Biology, St. John's U., Jamaica, N.Y., 1972; M.D., U. Bologna (Italy), 1979. Resident in family practice Community Hosp., Glen Cove, N.Y., 1979-82, asst. dir. family practice residency program, 1982—. Mem. Am. Assn. Family Practitioners, AMA, Am. Med. Women's Assn., N.Y. Acad. Scis., Nassau Acad. Medicine. Office: Community Hosp St Andrews Ln Glen Cove NY 11542

MEROLA, EMMA M. VARVARO, physician; b. N.Y.C., Jan. 1, 1908; d. Ettore and Anna (Borghini) Varvaro; B.S., Douglass Coll., 1930; student Woman's Med. Coll., 1930-33; M.D., Middlesex Coll., 1936; m. Joseph F. Merola, Nov. 30, 1939; children—Frank, Joseph, Henry, Anthony, Marianne. Intern Glens Falls (N.Y.) Hosp., 1936-37; X-ray, lab. work Victory Meml. Hosp., Bklyn., 1937-39; practice, Waltham, Mass., 1939—; staff Waltham Hosp. Tchr. elementary sch., 1964-65; instr. in Teaching English as Fgn. Lang. program, 1968-69. Leader Girl Scouts and Boy Scouts. Mem. adv. bd. Salvation Army of Waltham, 1961-65; mem. Am. Med. Polit. Action Com. Mem. AMA, Mass. Med. Soc., Middlesex Aux. Mass. Med. Soc., Am. Med. Women's Assn. (pres. 1960), Douglass Boston Alumnae Club (pres. 1959), League Women Voters, Grapho-Analyst Study Group, Charles River Med. Soc., Charles River Aux., Am. Soc. Family Physicians, Internat. Platform Assn., St. Luke's Guild Mass. Cath. Physicians, Am. Police Acad. Club: College. Home: 114 Church St Waltham MA 02154 Office: 117 Summer St Waltham MA 02154

MEROW, FLORENCE LOMBARDI, mayor; b. Detroit; d. Giuseppe Dominic and Louise (Amati) Lombardi; cert. Steubenville (Ohio) Bus. Coll., 1941; B.S., W.Va. U., 1946, postgrad. in drama and directing, 1967-68; postgrad. in writing Johns Hopkins U., 1948-49; cert. Am. Lung Assn. Tng. Inst., 1976; m. William Wayne Merow, Feb. 5, 1944; children—William Wayne, Robert Christopher. Tchr. high schs., Howard County, Md., 1946-50; disability determination examiner Rehab. Center, Ohio Bd. Edn., Columbus, 1958-59; substitute high sch. tchr. Whitehall Yearling High Sch., Ohio, 1959-60, Worthington, Ohio, 1962-65; instr. Monongalia County (W.Va.) Cultural Arts Program, 1966-67; instr. prep. drama U. W.Va., 1967-68; mem. City Council, Morgantown, W.Va., 1971-80; dep. mayor City of Morgantown, 1979-80, mayor, 1980—; mem. housing and community devel. com., standing com. for arts U.S. Conf. Mayors, 1980—; chmn. Region VI Planning and Devel. Council; pres. W.Va. Mcpl. League, 1982-83; steering com. Nat. League Cities, 1982-84. Pres., Grafton (W.Va.) Hosp. Aux., 1955-57; chmn. Community Achievement Council, Grafton, 1957-58; sec. PTA, Worthington, 1964-65; pres. Monongalia County Republican Women, 1976-78; mem. adv. council Fairmont (W.Va.) State Coll. Respiratory Therapy Tech. Program, 1976-79; mem. adv. council Ret. Citizen's Vol. Program, 1978—; W.Va. del. White House Conf. for Handicapped Individuals, 1977; chmn. Religious Arts Festival, Morgantown, 1975-77; chmn. Rep. Exec. Com., Monongalia County, 1979—; bd. dirs. Town and Country Players, Morgantown, 1965-68, v.p., 1967-68, play dir., 1966-69; founder, dir. Univ. Chancel Players, Morgantown, 1968-71; bd. dirs. Monongalia County Respiratory Disease Assn., 1971-73; adv. council Ret. Citizens Vol. Program, Monongalia County, 1977—; bd. dirs. Monongalia County Youth Services Home, 1978—. Recipient Vol. Service award Kennedy Youth Center, 1971, 1st Woman award Nat. Fedn. Women's Clubs, 1975, Outstanding Working Woman award Sta. WCLG, Morgantown, 1980, Disting. West Virginian award, 1980. Mem. Monongalia County Dental Aux. (pres., 1971-72), W.Va. Lung Assn. (program dir. 1975-79, founder Mountain Breathers, 1977), W.Va. Dental Assn. Women's Aux. (pres., 1977-78), AAUW (pres. Morgantown br., 1979-80), Nat. Assn. Parliamentarians, Alpha Psi Omega. Club: Zonta Internat. (dist. chmn. constn. and legis. com. 1977-79). Author: Point of Intersection (drama), 1976, Kick the Habit (manual), 1978. Home: 669 Colonial Dr Morgantown WV 26505

MERRELL, ANITA KATHLEEN, clin. social worker; b. Seattle, July 30, 1941; d. Creighton Irvin and Georgia Esta (McDonald) Merrell; A.B. cum laude, Whitman Coll., 1963; M.S.W., U. Calif., Berkeley, 1967; m. William C. Cristy, Apr. 9, 1977; stepchildren—Gail, Marc, Linda. Med. social worker Contra Costa County Med. Services, Martinez, Calif., 1967-69; clin. social worker, planner, program evaluator Contra Costa County Mental Health Services, Martinez, 1969-79; social work supr., dir. tng. and edn. Regional Center of East Bay, Oakland, Calif., 1979—; part-time clin. practice with Center for Psycho-Spiritual Integration, Alameda County Child Abuse Council, 1979—. Lic. clin. social worker, Calif. Mem. Acad. Cert. Social Workers, Nat. Assn. Social Workers, Am. Assn. Mental Deficiency, Calif. Com. on Sexuality of Developmentally Disabled. Club: Berkeley Ski (2d v.p. 1972-73, treas. 1971-72). Home: 85 Valley Ave Martinez CA 94553 Office: 2201 Broadway Oakland CA 94612

MERRIAM, MARY-LINDA SORBER, coll. adminstr.; b. Jeannette, Pa., May 31, 1943; d. Everett S.C. and Madeleine (Case) Sorber; B.A., Pa. State U., 1965, M.A., 1967, Ph.D., 1970. Spl. asst. to pres. Emerson Coll., Boston, 1977-78, asst. prof. speech and communication, 1972-79, v.p. adminstrn., 1978-79; asst. to pres. Boston U., 1979-81; pres. Wilson Coll., Chambersburg, Pa., 1981—; cons. in field. Bd. dirs. Boston/New England Nat. Acad. TV Arts and Scis., 1980-81; bd. dirs. Public Broadcasting Council South Central Pa., 1981—. Am. Council Edn. fellow, 1977-78. Mem. AAUW, Speech Communication Assn., Am. Assn. Higher Edn., Phi Kappa Phi, Rho Tau Sigma, Pi Kappa Delta. Presbyterian. Office: Wilson College Chambersburg PA 17201

MERRICK, EUNICE PEACOCK (MRS. GEORGE E. MERRICK), civic worker; b. Coconut Grove, Fla.; d. Alfred and Lillian (Frow) Peacock; student pvt. and pub. schs.; m. George Edgar Merrick, Feb. 5, 1916. Treas., George E. Merrick, Inc., real estate, 1934-42, pres., 1942-45. Active in establishing Dade County Schs., Coral Gables, 1922-25. Recipient Book of Golden Deeds, Exchange Club Coral Gables, 1957, Headliner award Women in Communications, 1976. Mem. Hist. Soc. So. Fla., Fla. Hist. Soc., Fairchild Tropical Garden, Nat. League Am. Pen Women (patroness), Coral Gables C. of C. (hon.), Sigma Alpha Iota (patroness). Christian Scientist. Clubs: Coral Gables Woman's (charter mem., dir.), Coral Gables Music (hon. active), Coral Gables Garden (past pres.), George E. Merrick, the original owner, founder Coral Gables, Fla. Home: 1015 Coral Way Coral Gables FL 33134

MERRIFIELD, SHIRLEY ANNE, mgmt. cons.; b. Phoenix, Nov. 8, 1948; d. Rae Allen and Mary Margaret (Smith) Echols; B.S. in Mgmt. and Info. Sci., Golden Gate U., San Francisco, 1979; m. Francis Carl Merrifield, July 14, 1978; 1 dau., Jennifer Anne. Engring. asst. Gen. Electric Co., 1969-74; engr., then engring. supr. Bechtel Inc., 1974-76; mgmt. cons. Nat. Mgmt. Inst., 1976-77; analyst, team leader Rand Info. Systems Co., 1977-78; founder, 1978, since partner Merrifield Cons. Services, Rohnert Park, Calif.; pub. Merrifield Directory of Women in Bus.; dir. Datafield Co., Los Angeles; v.p. Pacific Assn. Gen. Electric Scientists and Engrs., 1973. Lobbyist, Nat. Women's Polit. Caucus, 1973. Mem. Data Processing Mgmt. Assn. (pres. N. Bay Counties chpt.), Nat. Speakers Assn., Women Entrepreneurs, Nat. Assn. Female Execs. Democrat. Address: Merrifield Cons Services C of C Bldg 6050 Commerce Blvd Suite E Rohnert Park CA 94928

MERRILL, DINA (MRS. CLIFF ROBERTSON), actress; b. N.Y.C.; d. E.F. Hutton and Marjorie Merriweather Post; ed. Mt. Vernon Sem.; student George Washington U., Am. Acad. Dramatic Arts, Am. Mus. and Dramatic Acad.; m. Stanley M. Rumbough, Jr., Mar. 23, 1946 (div. Dec. 1966); children—Stanley M. David, Nina; m. 2d, Cliff Robertson, Dec. 21, 1966; 1 dau., Heather. Broadway debut in The Mermaids Singing, 1945; star Angel Street, 1976; appeared off-Broadway plays My Sister Eileen, George Washington Slept Here, 1945; motion picture debut in Desk Set, 1957, other films include: Don't Give Up the Ship, 1958, Operation Petticoat, 1959, The Sundowners, 1960, Butterfield 8, 1961, Courtship of Eddie's Father, 1963, I'll Take Sweden, 1964, Walking Major, 1970, Throw Out the Anchor, 1972, Run Wild, 1973, The Meal, 1975, The Greatest, 1976, A Wedding, 1978, Just Tell Me What You Want, 1980; appeared in play The V.I.P.s, 1981; Shakespeare debut with Helen Hayes Equity Group in Twelfth Night, Othello, 1960; summer theatre tours in Voice of the Turtle, 1961, Write Me a Murder, 1963, Shaw Festival Repertory, Major Barbara, Misalliance, 1965; guest star over 100 TV shows; dir. E.F. Hutton & Co., Contel. Pres., N.Y.C. Mission Soc.; bd. dirs. N.Y. Com. Olympic Ski Team, Juvenile Diabetes Found., Joslin Diabetes Found. Office: care Hesseltine Baker & Assos 119 W 57 St New York NY 10019

MERRILL, HELEN, lit. agt.; b. Cologne, Germany, May 11, 1918 (parents Am. citizens); d. Theodore Edwin and Gertrude (Ahn) M.; student schs. Hamburg, Germany; m. Niels Groen, May 8, 1944 (div.). Photographer, N.Y.C., 1940-65; lit. agt., owner Helen Merrill Agy., N.Y.C., 1970—. Bd. dirs. Chelsea Theatre Center, 1963-77. Mem. Soc. Authors Reps. (officer).

MERRILL, SHARON FITZ PATRICK, investor relations cons.; b. Marblehead, Mass., Dec. 6, 1948; d. James Joseph and Conner Marie (Mardis) F.; A.S., Colby-Sawyer Coll., 1968; M.B.A., Simmons Coll., 1979. Mem. customer service dept. State St. Bank, Boston, 1968-70; research asst. State St. Research & Mgmt. Co., Boston, 1970-73; investment officer Boston Co. Investment Research & Tech., Inc., 1974-78; research officer Temple, Barker & Sloane, Boston, 1979; sr. account exec. Newsome & Co., Boston, 1979—; lectr. Simmons Coll. Grad. Sch. Communications. Mem. Nat. Assn. Female Execs., Nat. Assn. M.B.A. Execs., Nat. Investor Relations Inst., Public Relations Soc. Am., Mus. Fine Arts, Inst. Contemporary Art.

MERRIS, DONNA ROSE, orchestral condr.; educator; b. Bluffs, Ill., Nov. 25, 1939; d. Donald Doyle and Helen Louise (Frohwitter) Merris; B.S. in Edn., Ill. State U., 1961; M.M., Northwestern U., 1965; postgrad. (scholar) Mannes Coll. Music, 1974-77. Dir. bands Lanark (Ill.) Public schs., 1961-64; music dir. Winchester (Ill.) High Sch., 1965-66; dir. Div. Music, Malden (Mass.) Public Sch., 1966-74; faculty Mannes Coll., N.Y.C., 1974—; exec. dir. Bklyn. Music Sch., 1977—; asst. to Lukas Foss, Bklyn. Philharmonia, 1975-77. Mem. Boerum Hill Assn., Bklyn., 1978-82, Nat. Congressional Arts Caucus, 1982—. Ill. State scholar, 1957-61. Mem. NOW, Nat. Guild Community Schs. of Arts, Kappa Delta Epsilon, Kappa Epsilon. Democrat. Office 126 St Felix St Brooklyn NY 11217

MERRITT, ANNA JOHANNA, editor; b. N.Y.C., Sept. 4, 1934; d. Alexander and Johanna (Roeser) Gode-von Aesch; B.A., Smith Coll., 1956; m. Richard L. Merritt, Aug. 9, 1958; children—Christopher, Geoffrey, Theodore. Freelance editor and translator, 1957—; editor, staff asso. Inst. Govt. and Public Affairs, U. Ill., Urbana, 1978—. Mem.

Urbana Bd. Edn., 1979—. Mem. Am. Translators Assn. Democrat. Author: (with R.L. Merritt) Politics, Economics and Society in the Two Germanies 1945-75, 1978, Public Opinion in Semi-Sovereign Germany, 1980. Home: 715 W Indiana Ave Urbana IL 61801 Office: U Ill Inst Govt and Public Affairs 1201 W Nevada St Urbana IL 61801

MERRITT, DORIS HONIG, pediatrician, univ. dean; b. N.Y.C., July 16, 1923; d. Aaron and Lillian (Kunstlich) Honig; B.A., City U. N.Y., 1944; M.D., George Washington U., 1952; children—Kenneth Arthur, Christopher Ralph. Pediatric intern Duke Hosp., 1952-53; teaching and research fellow pediatrics George Washington U., 1953-54; pediatric asst. resident Duke U. Hosp., 1954-55, cardiovascular fellow pediatrics, 1955-56, instr. pediatrics, dir. pediatric cardiorenal clinic, 1956-57; exec. sec. cardiovascular study sect., gen. medicine study sect. div. research grants NIH, 1957-60; dir. med. research grants and contracts Ind. U. Sch. Medicine, 1961-62, asst. prof. pediatrics, 1961-68, asst. dean med. research, 1962-65, asst. dir. med. research, aerospace research application center, 1963-65, asso. dir. med. research, 1965-68, asst. dean for research, office v.p. research and dean advanced studies, 1965-67, dir. sponsored programs, asst. to provost, 1965-68, asso. dean for research and advanced studies, office v.p. and dean for research and advanced studies, 1967-71, asso. prof. pediatrics, 1968-73, prof., 1973-80; spl. asst. to dir. NIH, 1978—, research tng. and research resource officer, 1980—; cons. USPHS, NIH div. research grants, Div. Health Research Facilities and Resources, Nat. Heart Inst., 1963-78, Am. Heart Assn., 1963-67, Ind. Med. Assn. Commn. Vol. Health Orgns., 1964-67, Bur. Health Manpower, Health Profession's Constrn. Program, 1965-71, Nat. Library Medicine, Health Center Library Constrn. Program, 1966-72; dir. office sponsored programs Ind. U.-Purdue U. Indpls. Office Chancellor, 1968-71, dean research and sponsored programs, 1971-79; mem. Nat. Library Medicine biomed. communications rev. com., 1970-74. Chmn. Indpls. Consortium for Urban Edn., 1971-75; v.p. Greater Indpls. Progress Com., 1974-79; mem. Community Service Council, 1969-75; bd. dirs. Bd. for Fundamental Edn., 1973-77, Ind. Sci. Edn. Found., 1977-78, Community Addiction Services Agy., Inc., 1972-74; trustee Marian Coll., 1977-78; exec. com. Nat. Council U. Research Adminstrs., 1977-78; bd. regents Nat. Library Medicine, 1976-80; chmn. adv. screening com. for life scis. Council Internat. Exchange of Scholars, 1978-81. Served to lt. (j.g.), USNR. Diplomate Nat. Bd. Med. Examiners, Am. Bd. Pediatrics. Fellow Am. Acad. Pediatrics; mem. AAAS, George Washington U., Duke U. med. alumni assns., Phi Beta Kappa, Alpha Omega Alpha. Contbr. articles to profl. jours. Office: Bldg 1 Room 118 NIH Bethesda MD 20014

MERRITT, DOROTHY (DEE) ELIZABETH, former travel agy. exec.; b. Detroit, Sept. 23, 1926; d. Charles Arthur and Gladys Martha (Stevens) Cooper; student public schs. Model, Detroit, 1944-57; broadcaster stas. WHOA, WELI, San Juan, P.R., 1957-62; vol. social worker N.Y.C. Youth Bd., 1963-64; freelance broadcaster, Sydney, Australia, 1964-69; broadcaster WNAB, Bridgeport, Conn., 1971-72, KNEW, Oakland, Calif., 1972-74, KLOK, San Jose, Calif., 1974-76; owner Dee Merritts Small World Travel Agy., Mill Valley, Calif., 1975-81; treas., bd. dirs. Bay Area Travel Assn. Recipient Outstanding Achievement awards Am. Airlines, 1977, 78, 79, United Airlines, 1977, 79, TWA, 1976, 77. Mem. Am. Soc. Travel Agts., Asso. Marin Travel Agts., Bay Area Travel Assn.

MERRITT, MARY ELIZABETH, fin. planner; b. Warren, Pa., Nov. 26, 1924; d. Francis Hilding and Wilma Mary (Burkett) Nelson; student Westmar Coll., 1950-52, Coll. of Desert, 1962-63, Mira Costa Coll., 1964, Cypress Coll., 1965-67; cert. fin. planner Coll. Fin. Planning, 1979; m. Milton Merritt, Aug. 9, 1947; children—Susan, Judith, Milt, Betsy. Instructional aide, Ocean View Sch. Dist., Huntington Beach, Calif., 1968; owner, mgr. Merritt Book Shoppe, Twentynine Palms, Calif., 1970-72; fin. planner Am. Pacific Securities Co., San Diego, 1972—. Mem. Internat. Assn. Fin. Planners, Inst. Cert. Fin. Planners. Methodist. Clubs: Soroptimists, Eastern Star. Office: 6150 Mission Gorge Suite 208 San Diego CA 92120

MERRITT, PATRICIA ANNE, data processing exec.; b. Rochester, N.Y., Jan. 12, 1945; d. Richard Henry and Florence Elizabeth (Adams) M.; student Long Beach (Calif.) City Coll., 1972-74, Foothill Jr. Coll., 1974-77; grad. Bryman Paramed. Sch., San Jose, Calif., 1977; m. Steve Verderber. Data processing clk. Lincoln Rochester Trust Co., Rochester, N.Y., 1965-67; keypunch operator Eastman Kodak, Rochester, 1967-70; keypunch and verify operator Reliance Steel Co., Los Angeles, 1971; keypunch operator Automatic Data Processing, Long Beach, 1971, Fed. Civil Service, Los Alamitos, Calif., 1971-73, Varian Assos., Palo Alto, Calif., 1973-78; tech. typist, word processor lead-operator Watkins Johnson, Palo Alto, 1978-79, 79-81; supr. office systems Smith Kline Instruments, Sunnyvale, Calif., 1981—; word processor sr. operator Palo Alto Unified Sch. Dist., 1979. Leader, Monroe County council Girl Scouts U.S.A., Rochester, 1969-70, Santa Clara County council, Mountain View, Calif., 1978—. Mem. Beta Sigma Phi. Office: 485 Potrero Ave Sunnyvale CA 94086

MERRITT, ROSE BILLINGSLEY, accountant; b. Pitts., May 10, 1936; d. Harold James and Rose Stephanie (Sladack) Billingsley; student Mt. Mercy Coll., Pitts., 1952-53, Coll. Notre Dame, San Mateo, Calif., 1968, Met. Coll., Denver, 1972-74; B.A. in Acctg., Golden Gate U., San Francisco, 1978; 1 son, William Paul. Treas., mgr. Burke Rubber Fed. Credit Union, San Jose, Calif., 1962-64; office mgr. Cal-ida Mfg. Corp., Oakland, Calif., 1965-69, Acme Door Mfg. Co., Inc., Englewood, Colo., 1972-74; owner, operator Southway Lodge, Grand Lake, Colo., 1969-72; controller CBISF, San Francisco, 1974-79; controller U.S. group Chem. Bank, N.Y.C., 1979-82; in bus. devel. Chem. Bank, Chgo., 1982—. speaker at colls. and univs., profl. groups. Choral dir. various secular and religious groups, 1960-75; a founder, coordinator vol. classroom and assistance program, Grand County, Colo., 1970-71; sec. Calif. Assn. Neurologically Handicapped Children, 1968-69; pres. Colo. Assn. Children With Learning Disabilities, 1972. Mem. Am. Bankers Assn., Fin. Womens Club San Francisco, Fin. Women's Assn. N.Y. Editor: (with L. Anderson and others) Helping the Adolescent With The Hidden Handicap, 1969. Home: 1540 N State Pkwy 4C Chicago IL 60610 Office: 3 First Nat Plaza 70 W Madison St Chicago IL 60603

MERSHART, EILEEN DEGRAND, city ofcl., sociologist, educator; b. Evanston, Ill., Dec. 16, 1944; d. Alexander Joseph and Mary Ellen DeG.; B.A., U. Ill., 1967; M.S.W., U. Minn., 1976; m. Ronald V. Mershart, Sept. 4, 1965; children—Marielle, Paul. Social worker Douglas County Dept. Social Services, Superior, Wis., 1968-70; crew leader in census Dept. Commerce, Superior, 1970; alderman, pres. Superior City Council, 1977—; asst. prof. dept. sociology and social work Coll. of St. Scholastica, Duluth, Minn., 1979—, dir. adult edn., 1982—. Commr. Interstate Port Authority, 1976; mem. Wis. Coastal Mgmt. Council, 1975-78, Fed. Coastal Zone Mgmt. Adv. Com., 1979-83; vice chmn. Wis. Environ. Adv. Council, 1975-77; del. White House Conf. on Balanced Growth and Econ. Devel., 1978; mem. Democratic Nat. Com., 1976-80; del. to Dem. Nat. Nominating Conv., 1976, 80; mem. Fed. Jud. Nominating Commn. for U.S. Dist. Ct., Western Dist. Wis., 1979-83. Mem. citizens adv. com. KBJR. Named Outstanding Young Woman in Wis., 1976, 77. Mem. League of Municipalities (v.p. 25th Dist.), LWV, Daus. of Potato Famine, Wilderness Soc., Nat. Conf. Social Welfare, Council Advancement of Experiential Learning. Roman Catholic. Home: 2421 Hughitt Ave Superior WI 54880 Office: Coll St Scholastica Duluth MN 55811

MESEK, JEANIE MAY, therapist; b. Omaha, May 18, 1926; d. Archie Mason and Lela May (Lanning) Schreiber; B.S., George Williams Coll., 1976; postgrad. No. Bapt. Theol. Sem., 1976; M.S. in Social Work, U. Louisville, 1978; m. Fred Mesek, Nov. 18, 1944; children—Fred, Randelyn, Gary. Advocate, Ill. Status Offenders Services, DuPage County, 1975-77; social worker Riveredge Hosp., Forest Park, Ill., 1978; child care worker Fox Hill Home for Girls, Batavia, Ill., 1979; clin. therapist Guardian Angel Home, Joliet, Ill., 1979—; dir. social service Westmont (Ill.) Health Centre, 1978-81; prin. May Cons. Service, Downers Grove, Ill., 1978-80. Vol. Hinsdale Hosp., 1965-72; v.p. Clyde Estates Property Owners, 1967. Cert. tchr., Ill.; cert. social worker, Ill. Mem. Nat. Assn. Social Workers, Acad. Cert. Social Workers.

MESHEKOW, BARBARA MAE, paper products co. exec.; b. Bklyn., May 3, 1935; d. William J. and Charlotte (Rosenberg) Bienstock; A.A., Pierce Coll., 1969; student Calif. State U., Northridge, 1969-71; m. Henry Meshekow, Feb. 19, 1954 (div. 1976); children—Rachel, Vicki, Joseph. Acct., Lou Greenwood Acctg. Services, North Hollywood, Calif., 1969-71; office mgr. J. Schulman & Assos., Fin. Cons., 1971-74; controller, v.p. fin. Ovation Cosmetics, Northridge, 1974-79; controller Marfred Paper Co., Pacoima, Calif., 1979—. Mem. Nat. Notary Assn. Democrat. Jewish. Home: 6911 Tampa Ave Reseda CA 91335 Office: 12154 Montague St Pacoima CA 91331

MESICK, JUDITH ESTHER, fund raising corp. ofcl.; b. Paw Paw, Mich., June 12, 1948; d. Morris James and Jean Evelyn (Holm) M.; student Mich. State U., 1966-68; B.S. in Elem. Edn., U. Tex., El Paso, 1972, M.Ed., 1976. Tchr., Ysleta Ind. Sch. Dist., El Paso, 1973-78; Tex. dist. mgr., outside sales rep. Nationwide Fund Raisers, Inc., of Tucker, Ga., 1978—, recruiter, mgr. confs., cons. Mary Kay Cosmetics, 1982—. Active Robert Kennedy campaign, 1967. Served with U.S. Army, 1968-70. Mem. Nat. Assn. Female Execs. Republican. Baptist. Office: 2649 Mountain Ind Blvd Tucker GA 30084

MESKE, EUNICE BOARDMAN, educator; b. Cordova, Ill., Jan. 27, 1926; B.M., Cornell Coll., Mt. Vernon, Iowa, 1947; M.M.E., Tchrs. Coll. Columbia U., 1951; Ed.D., U. Ill., 1963; m. Delmar Meske. Elem. music specialist, high sch. choral dir. Iowa Public Schs., 1947-56; instr. music edn. No. Ill. U., 1956-57; prof. music edn. Wichita State U., 1957-72; vis. prof. Ill. State U., Normal, 1972-74, Chgo. Mus. Coll. Roosevelt U., 1974-75; prof. music edn. U. Wis., Madison, 1975-80, dir. Sch. Music, 19—. Grantee in field. Mem. Music Educators Nat. Conf., Ill. Music Educators, AAUP, NEA, Assn. Suprs. Student Tchrs., Coll. Music Soc., Mu Phi Epsilon, Phi Kappa Lambda. Home: 314 Lake Shore Dr Lake Mills WI 53551 Office: 455 N Park St Madison WI 53706

MESKELL, UNA, nurse, educator; b. N.Y.C., Mar. 9, 1947; d. Stephen Joseph and Una (Malanaphy) M.; R.N., St. Clares Hosp., 1968, B.A., Marymount Manhattan Coll., 1976; M.S., Hunter Coll., 1981. Staff nurse Bronx (N.Y.) Mcpl. Hosp. Center, 1968-69, head nurse psychotherapeutic nursing, 1969-72, nursing supr. evenings, 1972-76, nursing supr. day psychiatry, 1976-80; mental health nurse specialist Hebrew Hosp. for Chronic Sick, Bronx, 1980—; clin. instr. Med. Aid Tng. Sch., Bronx, 1982—. Mem. community bd. Bronx Mcpl. Hosp. Center, 1978-80. Mem. N.Y. State Nurses Assn. (grievance chmn. Bronx Mcpl. Hosp. Center unit 1975-80), Nat. League for Nursing, Marymount Manhattan Coll. Alumni Assn., St. Clare's Hosp. Nursing Sch. Alumni Assn., Community Health Edn. Alumni Assn. Democrat. Roman Catholic. Home: 3235 Grand Concourse Bronx NY 10468 Office: Hebrew Hosp Chronic Sick 2200 Givan Ave Bronx NY 10475

MESNEY, DOROTHY TAYLOR, mezzo-soprano, pianist, composer, educator; b. Bklyn., Sept. 15, 1916; d. Franklin and Kathryn Munro Taylor; diploma Berkeley Inst., 1934; B.A., Sarah Lawrence Coll., 1938; postgrad. Columbia U., 1938-41, Juilliard Sch. of Music, 1963-71, Manhattan Sch. Music, 1971-73; m. Peter Michael Mesney, Oct. 15, 1942; children—Douglas, Kathryn, Barbara. Mezzo-soprano, operetta, mus. comedy, concert and oratorio; ch. soloist, N.Y.C., 1956—; debuts include: N.Y. Cultural Center, 1971, Carnegie Recital Hall, 1974; leading roles with local opera and Gilbert and Sullivan groups; rec. artist Folkways Records; founder American Experience ensemble, also An Elizabethan Encounter, also Musicanza records for children; tchr. piano and singing, Douglaston, N.Y., 1958—, also tchr. introduction music classes; founder children's series Concerts for Children; innovator Introduction to Music for preschoolers; performer Am. music for mus., hist. socs., schs., colls.; performer N.Y. State Renaissance Festival, 5 yrs.; rec. artist for Folkways; authority on Am. and Renaissance music. Com. chmn. PTA, Douglaston, 1952-55; den mother Greater N.Y. council Cub Scouts Am., 1953-56; Brownie leader Greater N.Y. council Girl Scouts U.S.A.; bd. dirs. Community Concerts Assn. of Great Neck, N.Y. Mem. Nat. Piano Tchrs. Guild, Nat. Fedn. Music Clubs (N.Y. chpt.), Met. Opera Guild, Tuesday Morning Music Club (pres. 1979-81). Democrat. Congregationalist. Composer hymns, songs and ballades including Spread Your Wings and Fly, 1960, Walk Into the Promised Land, 1964, Song of Creation, 1974, Zion's Hill, 1975; also songs for children, instrumental quartets and trios.

MESSAC, MAGALI ERNESTINE JOSEPHINE, ballerina; b. Toulon, France, Nov. 10; came to U.S., 1978; d. Robert Leopold Joseph and Georgette Marie Simone (D'Esmenard) M.; grad. Taneeff Ballet Sch., Toulon, 1968; m. Lars G.O. Súderstrúm, July 29, 1978. Apprentice, Hamburg (W. Ger.) State Opera Ballet, 1969-70, from group dancer to prin. dancer, 1970-78; prin. dancer Phila. Ballet, 1978-80, Am. Ballet Theatre, N.Y.C., 1980—; tours throughout Europe, U.S. and Israel. Recipient Oberdúrfer Culture award City of Hamburg, 1971. Office: Am Ballet Theatre 890 Broadway New York NY 10003

MESSALL, SANDRA KAY, marine corps officer; b. St. Louis, July 2, 1943; d. Richard Dudley and Onieda Barbara (Haberberger) Messall; student various mil. schs. Revenue coordinator Am. Airlines Co., N.Y.C., 1962-65; enlisted USMC, 1966, commd. warrant officer, 1975, chief warrant officer, 1977, advanced through grades to 1st lt., 1981, air traffic controller, supr. instr. Marine Corps Air Sta., Kaneohe, Hawaii, 1969-72, air traffic controller, facility operator, instr., Cherry Point, N.C., 1972-75, asst. fiscal officer Marine Corps Base, Camp Lejeune, N.C., 1975-77, asst. budget officer, 1977, fiscal acctg. officer 4th Marine Aircraft Wing, New Orleans, 1977-78, fiscal officer Consol. Acctg. Office, 1978-80; acctg. officer Camp H.M. Smith, Hawaii, 1980-82; acctg. officer Marine Corps Air Sta., Kaneohe Bay, Hawaii, 1982—. Mem. Soc. Mil. Controllers (chpt. sec. 1976-77, 78-79, reporter, staff asst. New Orleans chpt. newsletter), Women's Mil. Assn. Roman Catholic. Office: CFAO Marine Corps Air Sta Kaneohe Bay HI 96863

MESSER, EVELYN CATTON, social services adminstr.; b. Weehawken, N.J., Mar. 23, 1931; d. William Frederick and Caroline Marie Catton; student U. Bristol (Eng.), 1951-52; B.A., Antioch Coll., 1953; M.S. in Social Work, Columbia U., 1956; m. Alfred Ames Messer, Dec. 31, 1954; children—Adam Catton, David Alexander. Social worker Devel. Evaluation Clinic for Children, Decatur, Ga., 1967-68, sr. social worker, 1968-72; dir. social work, Ga. Retardation Center, Atlanta, 1972-74, dir. program services, 1974—; pres. Internat. Found. for Scholarly Exchange, 1981. Bd. dirs. Atlanta Florence Crittenton Services, 1970-73, Child Service and Family Counseling, Atlanta, 1973-79. Nat. Found. Infantile Paralysis fellow, 1955. Mem. Am. Assn. Mental Deficiency, Am. Orthopsychiat. Assn., Nat. Assn. Social Workers (pres. N. Ga. chpt. 1974-75, named Ga. Social Worker of Yr. 1978). Home: 801 Douglas Rd NE Atlanta GA 30342 Office: Ga Retardation Center 4770 N Peachtree Rd Atlanta GA 30338

MESSICK, BARBARA GRAHAM, psychologist; b. Teaneck, N.J., Jan. 10, 1936; d. George Cecil and Elsie May (Bayliss) Graham; student Endicott Jr. Coll., 1953-54; B.A. in Psychology, U. Del., 1957; M.Ed., Rutgers U., 1964, Ed.D., 1968; m. Robert Lee Messick, Apr. 13, 1957 (div. 1972); children—Scott Robert, Graham Robert. With N.W. Ayer & Son, advt. agy., Phila., 1957-63, Collingswood (N.J.) Public Schs., 1964-69, Camden County Child Guidance Clinic, Collingswood, 1964-69, Temple U., Phila., 1968, Bancroft Sch., Haddonfield, N.J., 1969-71; sch. psychologist Haddonfield Public Schs., 1971—; cons. N.J. Commn. for Blind, 1967—; pvt. practice psychology, Haddonfield, 1967—. Lic. psychologist, N.J.; cert. sch. psychologist, N.J. Mem. Am. Psychol. Assn., Nat. Assn. Sch. Psychologists, N.J. Assn. Sch. Psychologists, Camden County Psychol. Assn. Democrat. Home: 111 E Park Ave Haddonfield NJ 08033 Office: Haddonfield Public Schs HMHS Kings Hwy Haddonfield NJ 08033

MESSICK, DALE, cartoonist; b. South Bend, Ind., 1906; d. Cephas and Bertha M.; student Art Inst. Chgo.; m. Oscar Strom (div. 1975, dec. 1980); 1 dau. by previous marriage, Starr. Designer greeting cards, Chgo. firm; creator comic strip Brenda Starr, Reporter, appearing Sunday newspapers Chgo. Tribune-N.Y. News Syndicate, 1940—, daily feature, 1945—. Address: Chicago-Tribune NY News Syndicate 220 42d St New York NY 10017 *

MESSIN, MARLENE ANN, mfg. co. exec.; b. St. Paul, Oct. 6, 1935; d. Edgar Leonard and Luella Johanna (Rahn) Johnson; m. Frank Messin; children—Rick, Debora, Ronald, Lori, Carlson. Bookkeeper Jeans Implement Co., Forest Lake, Minn., 1952-53, part-time bookkeeper, 1953-57; bookkeeper Great Plains Supply, St. Paul, 1960-62; bookkeeper Plastic Products Co., Inc., Lindstrom, Minn., 1962-75, pres., major owner, 1975-81. Bookkeeper, Trinity Lutheran Ch., Lindstrom, 1976—. Mem. Nat. Assn. Women Bus. Owners, Soc. Plastic Engrs. (chmn. membership com.), Swedish Inst. Home: 28940 Olinda Trail Lindstrom MN 55045 Office: 30355 Akerson St Lindstrom MN 55045

MESSNER, KATHRYN HERTZOG, civic worker; b. Glendale, Calif., May 27, 1915; d. Walter Sylvester and Sadie (Dinger) Hertzog; B.A., UCLA, 1936, M.A., 1951; m. Ernest Lincoln, Jan. 1, 1942; children—Ernest Lincoln, Martha Allison. Tchr. social studies Los Angeles schs., 1937-46, 58-73; mem. Los Angeles County Grand Jury, 1961. Mem. alumni council UCLA, 1942-46; mem. exec. bd. Los Angeles Family Service, 1959-62; mem. Dist. Atty.'s Adv. Com., 1965—, chmn. San Marino chpt. Am. Cancer Soc.; bd. dirs. Pasadena Rep. Women's Club, 1960-62, San Marino dist. council Girl Scouts U.S.A., 1959-68; pres. San Marino High Sch. PTA, 1964-65; bd. dirs. Pasadena Vol. Placement Bur., 1962-68, Los Angeles Women's Philharmonic Com., 1973-82; mem. adv. bd. Univ. YWCA, 1956—, bd. dirs., 1960—; co-chmn. Dist. Atty.'s adv. bd. Young Citizens Council, 1968—; mem. San Marino Red Cross Council, 1966—, chmn., 1969-71, vice chmn., 1972-73; mem. San Marino bd. Am. Field Service, 1971—; bd. dirs. Reachout com. Los Angeles Music Center, 1975—; trustee Pacificulture Art Mus., 1973-79; mem. Atty. Gen.'s Vol. Adv. Council, 1972-78; mem. adv. bd. Beverly Hills-West Los Angeles YWCA, 1973—, Los Angeles Met. YWCA, 1975—; mem. San Marino Community Council, 1964-73; hon. bd. Pasadena chpt. ARC, 1978-82, vice chmn., 1980—; bd. dirs. Vol. Action Center, West Los Angeles, 1980—, Pasadena Philharm. Com., 1980—, Stevens House, 1980—, San Marino Hist. Soc., 1977—. Recipient spl. commendation Am. Cancer Soc., 1961, 73, Community Service award UCLA, 1981. Mem. DAR, Pasadena Philharmonic, Los Angeles Lawyers' Wives (dir. 1973—), Las Floristas, Huntington Meml. Clinic Aux., Nat. Charity League, Law Wives of Los Angeles (mem. bd. 1976—), Pasadena Dispensary Aux., Gold Shield (co-founder), Pi Lambda Theta, Pi Gamma Mu, Mortar Bd., Prytanean Soc. Home: 1786 Kelton Ave Los Angeles CA 91108

MESTEK, PATRICIA RUTH DILLON, civic worker; b. Hibbing, Minn., Jan. 23, 1927; d. Gerald A. and Hope E. (Lind) Dillon; student Hibbing Jr. Coll., 1945, Mesaba Community Coll., 1978, Hibbing Community Coll., 1979-80; m. John Paul Mestek, Aug. 31, 1946; 1 dau., Teressa Ruthann. Area chmn. consolidation of rural sch. dist.; rural sch. vol., 1961-69; chmn. Hibbing Local History Com., 1974; founder Hibbing Hist. Soc., pres., 1974-76; curator First Settlers Mus., 1974—; dir., bd. govs. Hibbing Hist. Soc.; mem. Hibbing Tourism Com.; sec., recorder Northland chpt. ARC, 1979; v.p. First Settlers' Assn.; mem. Hibbing Bicentennial Com.; mem. Hibbing Humanities Commn., 1977; mem. Hibbing Local Hist. Preservation Com. Mem. Women Historians of Midwest, Nat. Trust Hist. Preservation, Minn. Hist. Soc., St. Louis Hist. Soc., Mesaba Concert Assn., Smithsonian Nat. Assos. Roman Catholic. Club: Hibbing Bird Watchers. Home: Star Rt 4 Box 195 Hibbing MN 55746 Office: Hibbing Hist Soc City Hall 21st St and 4th Ave E Hibbing MN 55746

MESZAROS, PEGGY JEAN SISK, coll. dean; b. Hopkinsville, Ky., Apr. 3, 1938; d. Eugene Lee and Geneva Evelyn (Thomason) Sisk; B.S., Austin Peay State U., 1960-63; M.S., U. Ky., 1972; Ph.D., U. Md., 1977; m. Alexander L. Meszaros, Feb. 6, 1967; children—Lisa Kimberly Meszaros Kriss, Elizabeth Meszaros Villarreal, Louis T. Tchr., Hopkinsville Public Schs., 1963-67, Omaha Public Schs., 1972-73; chmn. dept. home econs. Hood Coll., Frederick, Md., 1973-77; state supt. home econs. Md. Dept. Edn., Balt., 1977-79; asso. dean Coll. Home Econs. Okla. State U. Stillwater, 1979—. Mem. Am. Home Econs. Assn. (dir. 1980-82), Future Homemakers Am. (dir. 1977-78), Stillwater C. of C., AAUW, Okla. Home Econs. Assn., Phi Delta Kappa. Democrat. Episcopalian. Author: Developing Learning Centers in Home Economics, 1978; editor: Maryland Survival Skills, 1979; contbr. articles to profl. jours. Home: 1111 Woodcrest Dr Stillwater OK 74074 Office: Coll Home Econs Okla State U Stillwater OK 74078

METAYER, ELIZABETH NENER, state legislator; b. Boston, Aug. 21, 1911; d. John Willoughby and Lucy Helena (Philips) Nener; student Harvard U., 1931-32; m. Edward Achille Metayer, Apr. 27, 1947; children—Richard Edward, Gael Elizabeth. Spl. sales. rep. Postal Telegraph Cable Co., 1930-35, br. mgr., Boston, 1935-38; owner, operator Elizabeth N. Mahoney Secretarial Service, Boston, 1946-48; mem. Mass. Ho. of Reps., 1974—; mem. Mass. Caucus Women Legislators, 1974—. Mem. Braintree (Mass.) Town Meeting, 1956-77; founding mem., 1st pres. Braintree LWV, 1961-64; mem. Braintree Democratic Town Com., 1974—. Mem. Mass. Legislators Assn., Mass. State Fedn. Women's Clubs (pres. 2d dist., chmn. state). Clubs: Sacred Heart Mothers, Braintree Point Woman's, Philergians. Columnist, Cabbages and Kings weekly column Braintree Star, until 1974, Lady of the House, 1974—. Office: State House Boston MA 02133

METCALF, JUNE ANN, hosp. adminstr.; b. Redmon, Ill., June 24, 1930; d. Sandford Douglas and Hazel Mary (Whittington) M.; grad. Am. Laundry and Linen Coll., 1979. With Bargain Leader, Anderson, Ind., 1949-59; store mgr. Army Surplus Store, Anderson, 1959-62; with Anderson Community Hosp., 1962—, instl. services coordinator, 1974—; ednl. dir. Am. Laundry and Linen Coll., 1979—. Bd. dirs. Madison County Mental Health Assn., 1981—, v.p., 1982—. Named Laundry Mgr. of Yr. in Ind., Ind. Assn. Instl. Laundry Mgrs., 1968, 75; cert. laundry mgr.; registered laundry and linen dir., 1979. Mem. Nat. Assn. Instl. Laundry Mgrs. (nat. treas. 1975-79), Ind. Assn. Instl. Laundry Mgrs. (pres. 1975-79, 81—), Am. Bus. Women's Assn., Am. Laundry and Linen Coll. Democrat. Christian Ch. Club: Grandview Golf. Office: 1515 N Madison Ave Anderson IN 46012

METCALF, MARGARET LOUISE, church adminstr.; b. Washington, Jan. 1, 1943; d. Marshall Lee and Martha Noreen (Mogan) Faber; B.A. in Math. (Centennial scholar), U. Denver, 1966; J.D., South Tex. Coll. Law, 1974; m. George Taft Metcalf, June 1, 1968. Draftsman, Denver Research Inst., 1961-65; mathematician Falcon Research & Devel., Denver, 1965-67; programmer Space Div., Chrysler Corp., New Orleans, 1967-68; with Philco Ford, Houston, 1968-69; programmer analyst Lockheed Co., 1969-71; system analyst Celanese Chem. Co., Bayport, Tex.; adminstr. Ch. of Redeemer, Houston, also dir. Altar Guild; corp. sec., dir. bus.; mem. Overseas Div. Bd. Missions, Episcopal Diocese Tex.; corp. sec. Eastwood Ltd. Inc.; trustee St. James' House, 1980-82. Mem. IEEE, Soc. Women Engrs., Assn. Computing Machinery (chpt. treas. 1969). Episcopalian. Club: South Tex. Coll. Law Alumni. Designer liturgical vestments. Office: 4411 Dallas St Houston TX 77023

METCALFE, ELOISE LOPEZ, educator; b. Los Angeles, Oct. 1, 1942; d. Santiago and Clothilde (Arranaga) Lopez; B.A., UCLA, 1964, tchr. cert., 1966, postgrad., 1982—; m. Michael Stohlman, June 24, 1967; children—Michael Brady, Marisol Susana, Morgan Wesley. Tchr., Los Angeles Unified Sch. Dist., 1965-69; tchr. Beverly Hills (Calif.) Unified Sch. Dist., 1969—, coordinator sch. improvement program, 1980-82. Supr. Shaklee Corp., Los Angeles, 1977—. Del. Democratic Nat. Conv., 1980; mem. founding com. Los Angeles Hist. Park, 1982. Mem. NEA, Calif. Tchrs. Assn., Beverly Hills Edn. Assn., Ams. for Dem. Action, Nat. Assn. Latino Elected and Apptd. Ofcls. Roman Catholic. Home: 1421 Pandora Ave Los Angeles CA 90024 Office: 605 Whittier Dr Beverly Hills CA 90210

METHENITIS, NANCY LEE, social worker; b. Fredericksburg, Iowa, Oct. 17, 1932; d. Champ Clark and Leola Anna (Drape) Gross; student William Woods Coll., 1950-51; B.A. summa cum laude, Calif. State U., 1975, M.S.W., 1976; m. Louis T. Methenitis, Nov. 24, 1951; children—Timothy, Melanie, Darcy Ann, Clark. Therapist, out-patient service Mental Health Services for Madera County, Kings View Corp., Madera, Calif., 1976, chief day-treatment service, 1976-79, program mgr. day-treatment and continuing-care services, 1979-80, chief continuing-care service, 1980; chief of service II, Chowchilla Outreach Clinic, 1980-81; founder, dir. Tranquillity Unltd., cons., Chowchilla, Calif., 1981—; pvt. practice adult, adolescent, marriage and family counseling, Madera, Calif., 1979—. Lic. clin. social worker, Calif. Mem. Nat. Assn. Social Workers (Register of Clin. Social Workers), Phi Kappa Phi. Home: 2205 W 4th St Madera CA 93637 Office: Madera CA 93637 also Chowchilla CA 93610

METTEE-MCCUTCHON, ILA, army officer; b. Mobile, May 1, 1945; d. John Martin and Anna Ruth (Cleveland) Mettee; B.S., Auburn (Ala.) U., 1967, M.S., 1969; grad. various army schs.; m. John Robert McCutchon, Oct. 13, 1974; 1 dau., Erin Tempest. Research psychologist VA Hosp., Tuskegee, Ala., 1967-69; clin. psychologist U. Ala. Med. Center, Birmingham, 1969-71; commd. 1st lt. U.S. Army, 1971, advanced through grades to maj., 1981; OIC, Alcohol and Drug Abuse Rehab. Center, Presidio, San Francisco, 1971-73; strategic intelligence officer 8th Psychol. Bn., 1973-75; tactical mil. intelligence officer, ops. officer, co. comdr. 525th MI Group CEWI (Airborne), Ft. Bragg, N.C., 1976-79; project officer Command, Control, Communications and Intelligence Directorate, Combined Arms Combat Devel. Activity, Ft. Leavenworth, Kans., 1979-82; instr. U.S. Mil. Acad., 1975; student Command and Gen. Staff Coll., 1982-83. Decorated Army Commendation medal, Meritorious Service medal, Army Achievement award. Mem. Assn. U.S. Army. Home: 1723 Michael St Leavenworth KS 66048 Office: Comdr Combined Arms Center Attn CGSC STU DET Fort Leavenworth KS 66027

METTLER, MARY A., business exec.; b. Akron, Ohio, Oct. 9, 1937; d. William M. and Margaret E. (Young) M.; B.A. with distinction in Econs., Stanford U., 1959; postgrad. program in bus. adminstrn. Harvard U.-Radcliffe Coll., 1960; M.B.A., Am. U., 1962. Dir. research Ferris & Co., Washington, 1960-63; systems engr. IBM, San Francisco, 1964-68; pres. Western Ops., Inc., San Francisco, 1968-74; dir. fin. United Vintners, San Francisco, 1975-79; sr. v.p., chief fin. officer Lawrence Systems Inc., San Francisco, 1979—; dir. Lawrence Venture Capital Co. Recipient Elijah Watt Sells award, 1974. Club: Commonwealth of Calif. Home: 4462 24th St San Francisco CA 94114 Office: 340 Market St San Francisco CA 94111

METZ, MARY SEAWELL, coll. pres., educator; b. Rockhill, S.C., May 7, 1937; d. Columbus Jackson and Mary (Dunlap) Seawell; B.A. summa cum laude in French and English, Furman U., 1958; postgrad. Institut Phonetique, Paris, 1962-63, Sorbonne, Paris, 1962-63; Ph.D. magna cum laude in French, La. State U., 1966; m. F. Eugene Metz, Dec. 21, 1957; 1 dau., Mary Eugena. Instr. French, La. State U., 1965-66, asst. prof., 1966-67, 68-72, asso. prof., 1972-76, dir. elem. and intermediate French programs, 1966-74, spl. asst. to chancellor, 1974-75, asst. to chancellor, 1975-76; prof. French, Hood Coll., 1976-81, provost, dean acad. affairs, 1976-81; pres. Mills Coll., Oakland, Calif., 1981—; vis. asst. prof. U. Calif., Berkeley, 1967-68; lectr. NDEA fellow, 1960-62, 63-64; Fulbright fellow, 1962-63; Am. Council Edn. fellow, 1974-75. Mem. Western Coll. Assn. (v.p. 1982—), Assn. Ind. Calif. Colls. and Univs. (exec. com. 1982—), So. Conf. Lang. Teaching (dir. 1975-78, vice chmn. 1975-76, chmn. 1976-77), Bus.-Higher End. Forum, Women's Forum West, Phi Kappa Phi, Phi Beta Kappa. Author: Reflets du monde français, 1971, 78, Cahier d'exercices: Reflets du monde français, 1972, 78; (with Helstrom) Le Français à découvrir, 1972, 78; Cahier d'exercices: Le Français à découvrir, 1972, 78; Le Français à vivre, 1972, 78; Cahier d'exercices: Le Français à vivre, 1972, 78; author standardized tests. Office: Mills College Oakland CA 94613

METZ, NANCY HERRON, med. technologist; b. Guthrie County, Iowa, Nov. 8, 1940; d. Raymond E. and Lillian M. Herron; B.S., Wheaton Coll., 1962; cert. in med. tech. U. Kans., 1964; m. William Mason Metz, Aug. 14, 1966; children—Steven James, Gail Leanne, Marcia Jane. Staff technologist Blood Bank Lab., U. Kans. Med. Center, Kansas City, 1964-70; staff technologist lab. and x-ray Lookout Meml. Hosp., Spearfish, S.D., 1971—. Mem. Am. Soc. Clin. Pathologists. Home: 821 10th St Spearfish SD 57783

METZ, SHARON KAY, state legislator; b. Omro, Wis.; d. Henry Berthold and Elfrieda Schmude W.; ed. U. Wis., Green Bay; m. Thomas O. Metz, 1952; children—Michael Lee, Mark Lane, Mitchell Lin, Matthew Laird. Adminstrv. asst. action program U. Wis., Green Bay, 1972-74; welfare commr., Green Bay, Wis., 1973-75; mem. Wis. Ho. of Reps., 1975—. Bd. dirs. United Way; vol. Commn. Human Rights. Lutheran. Club: Woman's (Green Bay). Office: Wis Gen Assembly Madison WI 53702 *

METZLER, MARY, handwriting and document examiner; b. Pitts., Sept. 3, 1923; d. Mark and Mary (Cop) Katich; student schs., Pitts.; m. Donald Francis Metzler, Jr., Sept. 7, 1947; children—Judith Kay, Richard Michael, Susan Marie. Psychology and sales instr. Duff's Bus. Inst., Pitts., 1967-70; handwriting analyst and expert Attitude Dynamics Co., Pitts., 1970-80; handwriting and document examiner, owner Analytical Handwriting Experts, Pitts., 1980—; cons. legal, bus., ednl. and profl. orgns.; lectr., condr. seminars; ct. qualified; motivation lectr. schs., civic orgns., 1973-80. Master cert. graphoanalyst, 1962; recipient award Community Leaders and Noteworthy Americans, 1975-76, chief attitude engr. award USNR, McKeesport, Pa., 1969. Mem. Internat. Graphoanalysis Soc. (service awards 1970-76, master cert. graphoanalyst), Ind. Assn. Questioned Document Examiners, World Assn. Document Examiners, Nat. Assn. Document Examiners. Democrat. Roman Catholic. Club: Internat. Entrepreneurs. Author: Anonymous Letters O Classification of Types and Authors, 1979; Letters of the Alphabet Analyzed, 1981; Margins, 1981; also articles. Home: RD 2 Box 394 Oakdale PA 15071 Office: 4120 Jenkins Arcade Pittsburgh PA 15071

METZLER, YVONNE LEETE, travel agt.; b. Bishop, Calif., Jan. 25, 1930; d. Ben Ford and Gladys Edna (Johnson) Leete; student U. Calif., Berkeley, 1949; m. Richard Harvey Metzler, June 2, 1950; children—David Grant, Regan M., Erin E. Vocat. instr. Ukiah (Calif.) Jr. Acad., 1962-63; bookkeeper Sid Beamer Volkswagen, Ukiah, 1963-64; acct. Ukiah Convalescent Hosp., 1964, Walter Woodard P.A., Ukiah, 1964-66; asso. dir. Fashion Two Twenty, Ukiah, 1966-67, dir., Santa Rosa, Calif., 1967-71; acct. P.K. Marsh, M.D., Ukiah, 1971-72, Walter Woodard P.A. and Clarence White C.P.A., Ukiah, 1972-74; partner, travel agt. Redwood Travel Agy., Ukiah, 1973-76; owner, mgr. A-1 Travel Planners, Ukiah, 1976—; owner A-1 Travel Planners of Willits (Calif.), 1979—. Commr., Ukiah City Planning Commn., 1979—, vice chmn., 1981, chmn., 1981-83; mem. Republican County Central Com., 1978-80. Mem. Ukiah C. of C. (1st v.p. 1980, pres. 1981-83), Internat. Platform Assn. Clubs: Soroptimist (pres. 1977-78), Bus. and Profl. Women (treas. 1977-78). Office: 505 E Perkins St Ukiah CA 95482

MEUSE, ANN TERRELL, ins. co. ofcl.; b. Massillon, Ohio, Jan. 16, 1943; d. Douglass Fuqua and Jane (Chidester) Terrell; B.A. magna cum laude, Coll. White Plains (N.Y.), 1974; diploma paralegal edn. N.Y. U., 1975; m. Lewis Andrew Meuse, Apr. 16, 1960; children—Ann W., Laura A. Corp. sec., compliance dir. Gerber Life Ins. Co., White Plains, 1974-78; dir. legis. and policy research services Colonial Penn Group, Inc., Phila., 1978-82; dir. product devel. and market research Montgomery Ward Life Ins. Co., Chgo., 1982—. Mem. Chgo. Women's Direct Response Group. Sigma Delta Chi. Office: 140 S State St Chicago IL 60603

MEYER, ALICE VIRGINIA, state legislator; b. N.Y.C.; d. Martin G. and Marguerite Helene (Houze) Kliemand; B.A., Barnard Coll.; M.A., Columbia U.; m. Theodore H. Meyer, June 28, 1947; children—Robert, John. Formerly tchr. high sch.; mem. Conn. Ho. of Reps., 1976—. Vice chmn. Easton (Conn.) Republican Town Com.; mem. Commn. on Local Govt., Conn. Adv. Bd. on Career and Vocat. Edn.; bd. dirs. Southwestern Conn. Library Council; mem. profl. devel. council Conn. Dept. Edn.; trustee Mus. Art, Industry and Sci.; v.p. regional council Sacred Heart U.; mem. Small Cities Policy Adv. Com.; former mem. Conn. Edn. Council, Conn. Humanities Council. Mem. AAUW (grantee), Order Women Legislators (v.p. Conn.), LWV. Congregationalist. Office: Room 111 State Capitol Hartford CT 06115

MEYER, ANNE, psychologist; b. Balt., Nov. 19, 1947; d. Eugene, III and Mary (Bradley) M.; B.A. magna cum laude, Radcliffe Coll., 1969; M.Ed., Harvard U., 1975, doctoral candidate; m. Conrad Lee Willeman, June 11, 1977; 1 dau., Sarah Bradley. Tutor, classroom tchr., supr. tutors Landmark Sch., Prides Crossing, Mass., 1970-74; clin. supr. masters level courses diagnosis and treatment learning disorders Harvard U. Grad. Sch. Edn., 1975-76; reading specialist Children's Hosp. Med. Center, Boston, 1975; research asst. Harvard U. Grad. Sch. Edn., 1977-78, clin. fellow psychology Med. Sch., 1977-79; psycho-ednl. diagnostician N. Shore Children's Hosp., Salem, Mass., 1979—; cons. Hillel Acad., Swampscott, Mass., 1980—. Mem. Am. Psychol. Assn., Internat. Reading Assn., Soc. Research Child Devel., Orton Dyslexia Soc., Mass. Psychol. Assn. Office: 248 Bay Rd Hamilton MA 01936

MEYER, BETTY ANNE (MRS. JOHN R. BASKIN), lawyer; b. Cleve.; d. William Henry and Monica (McSherry) Meyer; student Denison U., 1941-43; A.B., Flora Stone Mather Coll., Western Res. U., 1946, LL.B., 1947; m. John R. Baskin, 1967. Admitted to Ohio bar, 1947; asst. to dean Adelbert Coll., Western Res. U., 1948-49; asso. Kiefer, Hunter, Knecht & Williams, Cleve., from 1965; now mem. firm Knecht, Rees, Meyer, Mekedis & Shumaker. Mem. Alpha Phi. Home: 2679 Ashley Rd Shaker Heights OH 44122 Office: Terminal Tower Cleveland OH 44113

MEYER, BETTY JANE, librarian; b. Indpls., July 20, 1918; d. Herbert and Gertrude (Sanders) M.; B.A., Ball State Tchrs. Coll., 1940; B.S. in L.S., Western Res. U., 1945. Student asst. Muncie Public Library (Ind.), 1936-40; library asst. Ohio State U. Library, Columbus, 1940-42, cataloger, 1945-46, asst. circulation librarian, 1946-51, acting circulation librarian, 1951-52, adminstrv. asst. to dir. libraries, 1952-57, acting asso. reference librarian, 1957-58, cataloger in charge serials, 1958-65, head serial div. catalog dept., 1965-68, head acquisition dept., 1968-71, asst. dir. libraries, tech. services, 1971-76, acting dir. libraries, tech. services, 1976-77, asst. dir. libraries, tech. services, 1977—, instr. library adminstrn., 1958-63, asst. prof., 1963-67, asso. prof., 1967-75, prof., 1975—; library asst. Grandview Heights Public Library, Columbus, 1942-44; student asst. Case Inst. Tech., Cleve., 1944-45; mem. Ohio Coll. Library Center Adv. Com. on Cataloging, 1971-76, mem. adv. com. on serials, 1971-76, mem. adv. com. on tech. processes, 1971-76; mem. Inter-Univ. Library Council, Tech. Services Group, 1971—; mem. bd. trustees Columbus Area Library and Info. Council Ohio, 1980-83. Ohio State U. grantee, 1975-76. Mem. ALA, Assn. Coll. and Research Libraries, AAUP, Ohio Library Assn. (nominating com. 1978-81), Ohioana Library Assn., Ohio Valley Group Tech. Services Librarians, No. Ohio Tech. Services Librarians, Franklin County Library Assn., Acad. Library Assn. Ohio, PEO, Beta Phi Mu, Delta Kappa Gamma. Club: Ohio State U. Faculty Women's. Home: 970 High St Unit H2 Worthington OH 43085 Office: Ohio State U Libraries 1858 Neil Ave Mall Columbus OH 43210

MEYER, CAROLYN ANNE, direct sales co. communications exec.; b. Abilene, Kans., Jan. 30, 1945; d. Bernard Francis and Mary Edith (Carroll) M.; student Marymount Coll., 1963-65; B.A., Wichita State U., 1969. Copywriter, Crown Drug Co., Kansas City, Mo., 1969-71; traffic supr., copywriter Ray Advt. Agy., Kansas City, Mo., 1971-74; advt. mgr. Adler's, Kansas City, Mo., 1974-77; advt. and promotion mgr. Lily div. Owens-Ill. Inc., Toledo, 1977-79; communications coordinator Fuller Brush Co. subs. Consol. Foods Corp., North Kansas City, Mo., 1979—. Mem. Advt. Club Toledo (recipient Silver award 1978, Gold award 1979, Bronze award 1979), Am. Advt. Fedn., Womens Advt. Club Toledo (dir. 1978-80), Direct Sell Assn. (mem. adv. council, human resources com.), Women in Communications, Public Relations Soc. Am. Democrat. Roman Catholic. Home: 2031 NE Russell Rd Apt 15 Kansas City MO 64116 Office: 2800 Rockcreek Pkwy Suite 400 North Kansas City MO 64117

MEYER, CHARLOTTE LOIS, clin. social worker; b. Chelsea, Mass., June 15, 1932; d. James and Anne (Berson) Sampson; B.S., Simmons Coll., 1952, M.S. in Social Welfare, 1954; m. Irving Meyer, June 7, 1953; children—Fredric B., Marc H., James S. Social worker Jewish Nursing Home of Western Mass., Longmeadow, 1972-73, dir. social services, 1973—; cons., lectr. on geriatric social work. Mem. Nat. Assn. Social Workers, Acad. Cert. Social Workers, Mass. Acad. Psychiat. Social Work, Boston Soc. for Gerontol. Psychiatry, Gerontol. Soc. Am. Office: 770 Converse St Longmeadow MA 01106

MEYER, CHERRILL LYNN, mktg. communications exec.; b. Los Angeles, Nov. 22, 1948; d. Leonard August and Theresa Verette (Rawlinson-Cruse) M.; A.A., Santa Monica Coll., 1970; B.A. in Journalism, Calif. State U., Long Beach, 1972. Asst. news bur. dir. Loyola-Marymount U., Los Angeles, 1968-70; spl. events and publicity dir. Inglewood (Calif.) C. of C., 1970-75; internal communications editor Security Pacific Bank Corp., Los Angeles, 1975-76; mgr. publs. dept. Centinela Hosp. Med. Center, Inglewood, 1976-78; asso. dir. mktg. communications Northrop Corp., Hawthorne, Calif., 1978-80, sr. proposal engr., publs. specialist, mktg. communications specialist, 1980—. Recipient Excellence award Am. Assn. C. of C. Execs., 1973, 74. Mem. Long Beach C. of C., Internat. Assn. Bus. Communicators, Nat. Assn. Female Execs., Long Beach-Toyota Grand Prix Com. of 300. Office: One Northrop Ave Hawthorne CA 90250

MEYER, DOROTHY DIEHL, addiction counselor; b. Cheyenne, Wyo., Jan. 31, 1943; d. Edwin Showalter and Marguerite (Wilding) Diehl; diploma Sch. Alcohol Abuse and Alcoholism, U. Utah, 1977, Sch. Alcohol Studies, U. Nebr., 1978; children—Donald Michael, Gregory Carl. Drug and alcohol addiction counselor Alcohol Receiving Center S.E. Wyo. Mental Health Center, Cheyenne, 1976-77; cons. Gov. Wyo. Office Hwy. Safety, 1979—; dir. Laramie County Alcohol Traffic Safety Program, Cheyenne, 1977—; mem. Wyo. Addiction Specialists Cert. Bd.; adv. bd. Project Hope, Cheyenne Halfway House, Alcohol Receiving Center; cons. in field. Mem. Nat. Assn. Alcoholism Counselors, Wyo. Assn. Addiction Specialists, Laramie County Citizens Mental Health. Clubs: Toastmistress, Order Eastern Star. Home: 3615 Duff St Cheyenne WY 82001 Office: 1604 D East Lincolnway Cheyenne WY 82001

MEYER, GRACE BERNSTEIN, social worker; b. Chgo., Sept. 19, 1926; d. Louis and Elizabeth (Heilbrun) Bernstein; B.A. summa cum laude, Barry Coll., 1970, M.S.W., 1972; m. Joseph Meyer, July 28, 1945; children—Richard Paul, Hollis Jill Meyer Barnett. Adminstrv. asst., Childrens Psychiat. Center, Inc., Miami, 1963-68; case worker Family Service Agy., Fort Lauderdale, 1972-76, supr. program services, 1976—, acting exec. dir., 1977-78; clin. faculty Barry Coll. Sch. Social Work, 1973-78; pvt. practice individual and family counseling, North Miami Beach, Fla., 1978—; v.p. charge community affairs Dade chpt. Assn. for Advancement Mentally Handicapped. Mem. Nat. Assn. Social Workers, Acad. Cert. Social Workers, Am. Assn. Marriage and Family Therapy (clin. mem.), Fla. Assn. Marriage and Family Therapy, Dade County Assn. Marriage and Family Therapy, Lambda Sigma, Kappa Gamma Pi. Home and Office: 1180 176th St NE North Miami Beach FL 33162

MEYER, IVAH GENE, social worker; b. Decatur, Ill., Nov. 18, 1935; d. Anthony and Nona Alice (Gamble) Viccone; A.A. with distinction, Phoenix Coll., 1964; B.S. with distinction, Ariz. State U., 1966, M.S.W., 1969; postgrad. U.S. Internat. U.; m. Richard Anthony Meyer, Feb. 7, 1954; children—Steven Anthony, Stuart Allen, Scott Arthur. Social worker Florence Crittendon Home, Phoenix, 1969-70; social worker Family Service of Phoenix, 1970-73; faculty asso. Ariz. State U., 1973; field supr. Pitzer Coll., Claremont, Calif., 1977—; social worker Family Service of Pomona Valley, Pomona, Calif., 1975—; field supr. Grad. Sch. Social Services, U. So. Calif., 1978—; pvt. practice Chino (Calif.) Counseling Center. Lic. clin. social worker, Calif. Mem. Nat. Assn. Social Workers, Acad. Cert. Social Workers. Republican. Roman Catholic. Home: 778 Via Montevideo Claremont CA 91711 Office: 12632 Central Ave Chino CA 91710

MEYER, KAREN ANN GRITZAN, speech/lang. pathologist; b. Bronx, Nov. 7, 1947; d. Stephan and Pauline Theresa (Linkiewicz) Gritzan; B.A., Herbert H. Lehman Coll., 1969; M.A. (fellow), Northwestern U., 1971; m. Charles J. Meyer, Oct. 17, 1970; children—Matthew, Thomas. Speech and lang. pathologist Mt. St. Ursula Speech Center, Bronx, 1971; speech and lang. pathologist Westchester Assn. Retarded Children (N.Y.), 1971-72; clin. communicologist, instr. rehab. medicine Mental Retardation Inst., N.Y. Med. Coll. and Flower Fifth Ave. Hosp., N.Y.C., 1972-75; pvt. practice speech and lang. pathology for children, Brewster, N.Y., 1980—; adj. lectr., clin. supr. Hunter Coll. Center for Communication Disorders, 1980-83, asst. to coordinator Inst. Lang. and Learning Disabilities, 1981. Mem. Am. Speech Lang. and Hearing Assn. (moderator 2 sessions 1981 conf.), N.Y. State Speech Lang. and Hearing Assn., Westchester Speech Lang. and Hearing Assn., Phi Beta Kappa. Roman Catholic. Home: 506 Village Dr Brewster NY 10509

MEYER, LINN, assn. exec.; b. Oak Park, Ill., May 21, 1947; d. Leo A. and Virginia M. (Larkins) Perczak; B.A., Bradley U., 1969; m. Michael A. Meyer, Feb. 15, 1969. Editorial asst., sec. Nuclear News Mag., Am. Nuclear Soc., Hinsdale, Ill., 1969-70; editor Allied Med. Edn. Newsletter, AMA, Chgo., 1970-71; asst. editor Hosp. Med. Staff mag. Am. Hosp. Assn., Chgo., 1971-75, staff editor Hosps. Jour. Am. Hosp. Assn., 1975-76, asso. mng. editor Hosps., 1976-82, asst. mgr. editorial dept., 1980-82; mgr. public info. A.C.S., 1982—. Mem. Nat. Assn. Female Execs. Contbr. articles to Am. Hosps. Assn. publs. Home: 709 S Spring St La Grange IL 60525 Office: Suite 700 211 E Chicago Ave Chicago IL 60611

MEYER, M. KATHERINE, sociologist; b. Balt., Apr. 4, 1943; d. Walter Francis and Winifred Marie (Kenney) M.; A.B., Trinity Coll., Washington, 1964; M.A., U. N.C., Chapel Hill, 1971, Ph.D., 1974; m. John Seidler, June 25, 1978; children—Anne Meyer Seidler, Elizabeth Meyer Seidler. Tchr. jr. high sch., Balt., 1964-67, Hyattsville, Md., 1967-68; assoc. prof. sociology Ohio State U., 1974—. NIMH trainee, 1969-73, fellow, 1979; Johns Hopkins Deans fellow, 1979; NSF grantee, 1970-74; Ohio State U. grantee, 1977. Mem. Am. Sociol. Assn., N. Central Sociol. Assn., So. Sociol. Assn. Democrat. Roman Catholic. Contbr. articles to profl. jours. Home: 653 Glenmont Ave Columbus OH 43214 Office: Dept Sociology Ohio State U Columbus OH 43210

MEYER, NANCY J., investment banker; b. Iowa; d. Frank Jacob and Marjorie Estelle (Duhme) M.; B.A., Barnard Coll., 1969; m. Charles Linzner, Nov. 14, 1970. With Krambo Corp., N.Y.C., 1969-76, San Francisco, 1976-77, v.p. and treas., 1973-77, also dir.; 2d v.p., sr. budget officer Chase Manhattan Corp., N.Y.C., 1977. Chartered fin. analyst, 1976; Nat. Merit scholar, 1965-69. Fellow Fin. Analysts Fedn.; mem. Inst. Chartered Fin. Analysts, N.Y. Soc. Security Analysts, mem. Barnard Coll. Alumnae Assn. Home: 45 Ave George V Paris France 75008

MEYER, PATRICIA HANES, psychiat. social worker; b. Champaign, Ill., Feb. 10, 1947; d. Walter Ernest and Mary Kathryn (Kemp) Hanes; B.A., Carroll Coll., Waukesha, Wis., 1969; M.S.W., Cath. U. Am., 1976; m. Scott Kimbrough Meyer, June 15, 1969; children—Jennifer Suzanne, Claire Catherine. Dir. family therapy program Fairfax County Juvenile Ct., Fairfax, Va., 1970-77; clin. instr. Georgetown U. Med. Sch., Washington, 1976—; pvt. practice family psychiatry, 1976—. Mem. Am. Orthopsychiat. Assn., Am. Family Therapy Assn., Nat. Assn. Social Workers. Adv. editor The Family, 1977—. Home: 3419 Tilton Valley Dr Fairfax VA 22033 Office: 4380 MacArthur Blvd NW Washington DC 20007

MEYER, PEARL, mgmt. cons.; b. N.Y.C.; d. Allen Charles and Rose (Goldberg) Weissman; B.A. cum laude N.Y. U., also postgrad.; m. Ira A. Meyer. Statis. specialist Exec. Compensation div. Gen. Goods Corp., White Plains, N.Y.; now exec. v.p., exec. cons. Handy Assocs., Inc.,

N.Y.C.; speaker in field. Mem. Am. Mgmt. Assn., Am. Compensation Assn., Am. Soc. Personnel Accreditation, Women's Econ. Roundtable, Personnel Accreditation Inst., Phi Beta Kappa, Beta Gamma Sigma, Pi Mu Epsilon, Kappa Pi Sigma. Clubs: Sedgewood, The Boardroom, Women's Forum, The Atrium. Contbr. articles to mags. Office: 245 Park Ave New York NY 10167 also Carmel NY 10512

MEYER, PHYLLIS BARBARA, travel agt.; b. Atlanta, Sept. 12, 1942; d. Henry Wall and Martha Kate (Bledsoe) Bland; A.A., Gulf Park Coll., Gulf Port, Miss., 1962; postgrad. U. Nebr., Omaha; m. Charles M. Meyer, Sept. 9, 1962; 1 son, Michael B. Civilian mgr. Eielson AFB Aero Club, Fairbanks, 1969-71; sales mgr. Nebr. Clothing Co., Bellevue, 1973-75; exec. v.p. TV Travel, Inc., Omaha, 1975-82; pres. Travel Etcera Inc., Omaha, 1979—; owner, pres. TV Travel/Bellevue Inc., 1982—; dir. A Growing Concern, Inc; cons. in field. Co-chmn. EXPO, Bellevue, 1982—; steering com. Inst. Career Advancement Needs, 1972-83. Mem. Am. Soc. Travel Agts., Nat. Assn. Female Execs., Bellevue C. of C. (v.p., dir.). Club: Altrusa. Home: 3409 Leawood Dr Omaha NE 68123 Office: 1500 JF Kennedy Plaza Bellevue NE 68005

MEYER, SANDRA W., communications, fin. and travel services co. exec.; b. N.J., Aug. 20, 1937; student U. Mich.; B.A. cum laude, Syracuse (N.Y.) U., 1957; postgrad. London Sch. Econs., 1958; divorced; children—Jenifer Anne Schweitzer, Samantha Boughton Schweitzer. Advt. account exec. London Press Exchange, 1959-63; product mgr. Beecham Products Inc., Clifton, N.J., 1963-66; with Gen. Foods Co., White Plains, N.J., 1966-76, mktg. mgr. coffee div., dir. corp. mktg. planning, 1975-76; with Am. Express Co., N.Y.C., 1976—, pres. communications div., 1980—; dir. A.D.R. Inc., Warner/Amex Cable Communications Co. Trustee Met. Opera Guild, Phoenix Theatre, N.Y. Urban Coalition. Office: American Express 125 Broad St New York NY 10004

MEYER, SHEREL LYNNE, mfg. co. exec.; b. Covington, Ky., Sept. 24, 1945; d. William P. and Viola Meyer; A.S., U. Cin., 1965. With Xerox Corp., 1966—, br. mktg. support mgr., 1976, sales mgr., 1976-78, Cin. region supply products mktg. mgr., 1978-79, regional low vol. sales ops. mgr., Washington, 1980, program mktg. mgr. office products div., Dallas, 1980—. Named Citizen of Day, Sta. WLW, 1969. Home: 1105 Whispering Oaks Ln Richardson TX 75081 Office: 1341 W Mockingbird Ln Dallas TX 75247

MEYER, URSULA, librarian; b. Free City of Danzig, Nov. 6, 1927; came to U.S., 1941, naturalized, 1949; d. Herman S. and Gertrude (Rosenfeld) M.; B.A., UCLA, 1949; M.L.S., U. So. Calif., 1953; postgrad. U. Wis., Madison. County librarian Butte County (Calif.) Library, 1961-68; asst. div. library devel. N.Y. State Library, Albany, 1969-72; coordinator Mountain Valley Coop. System, Sacramento, 1972-73; dir. library services Stockton (Calif.)-San Joaquin County Public Library, 1974—. Higher Edn. Title II fellow, 1968-69. Mem. ALA (council 1979-83, chmn. nominating com. 1982-83), Am. Assn. Public Adminstrs., Freedom to Read Found., Calif. Library Assn. (pres. 1978, council 1974-79), AAUW, LWV, Common Cause, NOW. Club: Soroptimist. Office: 605 N El Dorado St Stockton CA 95202

MEYERS, ANNA BRENNER, lawyer; b. Lodz, Poland, Dec. 18, 1896; d. Joseph and Edith (Gutman) Brenner; came to U.S., 1900, naturalized, 1925; R.N., Bklyn. Jewish Hosp. Nurses Tng. Sch. 1918; student Tchrs. Coll., Columbia, 1920-22, N.Y. Sch. Social Work, 1923-24; LL.B., Bklyn. Law Sch., 1928; LL.D., Bethune-Cookman Coll., 1964, U. Miami, 1972; m. Benjamin Meyers, May 18, 1939 (dec. 1974). Tchr. elementary sch., Stepney, Conn., 1913-14; vis. nurse Henry Street Settlement, 1919-20; dir. social service Maimonides Hosp., Bklyn., 1924-26; nat. dir. farm and rural dept. Nat. Council Jewish Women, 1926-29; social worker Crime Prevention Bur., N.Y.C. Police Dept., 1929-31; dist. office adminstr. N.Y.C. Emergency Home Relief Bur., 1931-33; admitted to N.Y. State bar, 1934, Fla. bar, 1936, U.S. Supreme Ct. bar, 1941, ICC bar, 1942; practiced in N.Y.C., 1934-35, Miami, Fla., 1936—; social worker Fed. Emergency Relief Adminstrn., Miami, 1935; sec., dir. Miami Bottled Gas, Inc., 1936-60. Past mem. budget com. Community Chest of Dade County, Fla., United Fund; pres. Jewish Family and Children's Service, Miami; nat. v.p. Am. Jewish Congress, 1958; mem. Dade County Sch. Bd., 1953-71; founder Miami-Dade Jr. Coll.; founder Miami pub. TV channel; founding mem. Miami Jewish Hosp. and Home for Aged; mem. Miami Beach Devel. Commn., 1965-67, Miami Beach Rent Control Commn., 1973; del. White House Conf. on Children, 1970, World Zionist Congress, Zurich, Switzerland, 1937. Trustee, Mt. Sinai Hosp., Miami Beach, 1973—, Miami Beach Pub. Library, 1961-75; former mem. bd. dirs. Greater Miami Philharmonic Orch.; past trustee Cedars of Lebanon Hosp.; past chmn. bd. trustees Miami Beach Art Center; trustee, sec. bd. Greater Miami Jewish Fedn.; mem. bd. Welfare Planning Council. Recipient Outstanding Citizen of Dade County award, 1957; State of Israel medallion, Eleanor Roosevelt-Israel Humanitarian award, 1964, Tower of David award, Jerusalem Liberation award; Man of Year award U. Miami chpt. Delta Kappa, 1969, Abess Human Relations award Anti-Defamation League, 1971; Sch. Bell award Dade County Classroom Tchrs. Assn., 1971; award Greater Miami Jewish Fedn.; others. Mem. Internat. (past v.p., treas.), Nat. (past treas.) Fla. (organizer, 1st pres.) assns. women lawyers, Fla. Fedn. Bus. and Profl. Women's Clubs (past state legislation chmn.), Am. Judicature Soc., Phi Theta Kappa. Democrat. Jewish. Miami-Dade Community Coll. Med. Center dedicated as Anna Brenner Meyers Hall, 1977; Anna Brenner Meyers Ednl. Telecommunication Center bldg. named in her honor by Dade County Sch. Bd., 1979. Home: 5055 Collins Ave Miami Beach FL 33140 Office: PO Box 431157 South Miami FL 33143

MEYERS, CAROL LYONS, educator, archeologist; b. Wilkes Barre, Pa., Nov. 26, 1942; d. Harry J. and Irene (Winkler) Lyons; A.B., Wellesley Coll., 1964; postgrad. Hebrew Union Coll., Jerusalem, 1965, Hebrew U., Jerusalem, 1964-65; M.A., Brandeis U., 1966, Ph.D., 1975; m. Eric M. Meyers, June 25, 1964; children—Julie Kaete, Dina Elise. Asst. prof. dept. religion Duke U., Durham, N.C., 1976—; instr. Bible, Acad. Jewish Studies Without Walls, N.Y.C., 1974-78; vis. asst. prof. U. N.C., Chapel Hill, 1975, 76-77; asso. dir. Meiron Excavation project, Israel, 1978—; v.p., trustee Albright Inst. Archaeol. Research, 1982—. Thayer fellow Albright Inst. Archeol. Research, Jerusalem, 1975-76; Duke U. Research Council grantee, 1981, 82; Nat. Endowment Humanities research fellow, 1982-83; recipient Hadassah Myrtle Wreath, 1981. Mem. Am. Acad. Religion, Am. Schs. Oriental Research (trustee 1976-78; corp. rep. 1980—), Archeol. Inst. Am. (v.p. N.C. 1976), Assn. Jewish Studies, Brit. Sch. Archeology in Jerusalem, Cath. Bibl. Assn., Israel Exploration Soc., Palestine Exploration Soc., Soc. Bibl. Lit., Soc. Values in Higher Edn. Author: The Tabernacle Menorah, 1976; Excavation of Ancient Meiron, 1981; mem. editorial bd. Bibl. Archaeologist; contbr. articles to profl. jours. Home: 3202 Waterbury Dr Durham NC 27707 Office: PO Box 4735 Duke U Durham NC 27706

MEYERS, DOROTHY, gerontologist; b. Chgo., Jan. 9, 1927; d. Gilbert and Harriet (Levitt) King; B.A., U. Chgo., 1945, M.A., 1961, also postgrad.; postgrad. Columbia U., New Sch. Social Research, Northwestern U.; m. William J. Meyers, Oct. 9, 1947; children—Steven, Lynn, Jeanne. Instr. sr. adults, Chgo. Bd. and City Colls. Chgo., 1961-78; coordinator pub. affairs forum and health maintenance program City Colls. Chgo.-Jewish Community Centers, Chgo., 1975-78. Chmn. legislation PTA; chmn. civic assembly Citizens Sch. Com.; v.p. community relations Womens Fedn. and Jewish United Fund; discussion leader League Women Voters; program chmn. Jewish Community Centers, 1966-67, also mem. sr. adult com.; bd. dirs. council Jewish Elderly, Open U.; mem. art and edn. com. Chgo. Mayor's Com. for Sr. Citizens and Handicapped; mem. com. on media Met. Council on Aging. Mem. Am. Sociol. Assn., Gerontol. Assn., Nat. Council Aging, Chgo. Met. Sr. Forum (media com.), Council Women Chgo. Real Estate Bd., Chgo. Real Estate Bd., Nat. Assn. Real Estate Bds., Art Inst. Chgo., Mus. Contemporary Art, Soc. Contemporary Art. Contbr. articles to profl. jours. Office: 77 Washington St W Chicago IL 60602

MEYERS, JUDITH ANN, hosp. adminstr.; b. Cedar Rapids, Iowa, May 5, 1934; d. Amos A. and Helen Meyers; B.S., Mt. Mercy Coll., 1960; M.S. in Hosp. Adminstrn., St. Louis U., 1966. Entered Order Sisters of Mercy, Roman Catholic Ch., 1953; tchr. various schs., 1955-60; adminstrv. resident St. Francis Hosp., Topeka, Kans., 1965-66; asst. adminstr. Mercy Hosp., Cedar Rapids, Iowa, 1966-77, assoc. adminstr. ops., 1977-82, trustee, 1969—; v.p. Marian Health Ctr., Sioux City, Iowa, 1982—; hosp. supr. Sisters of Mercy, Cedar Rapids, Iowa, 1967-69. Mem. budget rev. panel United Way Services, 1981; mem. Citizens Com. for the Jail, Linn County Bd. Suprs., 1981; mem. Linn County Mental Health Assn. Bd., 1967-69. Trustee, Mercy Hosp., Oelwein, Iowa, 1969-74; Kalispell (Mont.) Gen. Hosp., 1969-72. Mem. Am. Bus. Women's Assn., Iowa Hosp. Assn., Am. Coll. Hosp. Adminstrs. Home: 2931 Nebraska St Sioux City IA 51104

MEYERS, MARLENE HOPE, cable TV adminstr.; b. N.Y.C., Nov. 25, 1935; d. Albert and May (Masef) M.; B.A., Vassar Coll., 1956. Cancer research Bellevue Hosp., N.Y.C., 1956-70; new products research BASF Chem. Co., 1963-70; with Madison Sq. Garden, 1970—, dir. personnel and benefits, now, dir. cable affiliate relations. Mem. Exec. Women Internat., Women in Cable. Club. B'nai Brith. Office: Madison Sq Garden 4 Penn Plaza New York NY 10001 *

MEYERS, PATRICIA ANN, newspaper mgr.; b. Forreston, Ill., Nov. 20, 1932; d. Elmer Wilbur and Marie Leona (Abels) Brockmeier; student No. Ill. U., 1950-51; m. Richard Meyers, Mar. 17, 1956; children—Joey, Stuart, William, Robert. Acct., Micro Switch, Freeport, Ill., 1951-57; office asst. Forreston Jour., 1974-80, mgr., news dir., 1980—. Methodist. Home: RR 2 Box 218 Forreston IL 61030 Office: Box 237 Forreston IL 61030

MEYERS, VIRGINIA NICHOLS, employment agy. exec.; b. Austin, Tex., June 3, 1932; d. Taylor and Fannie Irene (Jones) Nichols; B.S. in Edn., U. Tex., 1953; m. E. Stuart Meyers, Apr. 16, 1966; children—Bill, Virginia Leigh, David McCord. Secondary sch. tchr., 1953-61; public relations exec. Maury Foladare & Assos., Los Angeles, 1963-66; public relations exec., fund raiser White Oaks Theatre, Carmel Valley, Calif., 1966-67; editor Carte Blanche mag., 1967-68; freelance publicist, 1969-72; founder, 1973, since pres., owner Bright Futures Agy., Los Angeles. Co-founder, officer North Hollywood High Sch. Boosters Club, 1972; bd. dirs. Pride House, 1976; co-founder Toluca Lake-Studio City Sr. Little League, 1968. Mem. Calif. Assn. Personnel Cons. (pres., dir. 1981-82), Bus. and Profl. Women, Nat. Assn. Personnel Cons., Los Angeles C. of C., Greater Los Angeles Conv. and Visitors Bur., Chi Omega. Democrat. Methodist. Club: Braemar Country. Author articles in field. Office: 3600 Wilshire Blvd Los Angeles CA 90010

MEYERSON, MARGY ELLIN, urbanist; b. Washington, Feb. 25, 1923; d. Arthur Lazarus and Frieda (Langer) Lazarus; B.A., U. Chgo., 1943; postgrad. Harvard U., 1947-48, U. Pa., 1953-56; M.A., Bryn Mawr Coll., 1953; m. Martin Meyerson, Dec. 31, 1945; children—Adam, Laura, Matthew. Field investigator Bur. Labor Statistics, 1944; asst. to counsel Pa. Postwar Planning Commn., 1944-45; asso. Phila. Housing Assn. and Citizens Council on City Planning, 1945; mgmt. staff Chgo. Housing Authority, 1946; cons. Ill. Postwar Planning Commn., 1948; asso. Com. on Nat. Policy, Yale U., 1948-49; lectr. social scis. Drexel U., 1956-57; bd. dirs., exec. com. Phila. Housing Assn., 1952-57; v.p., treas. Community Devel. Co., Inc., 1957-63; lectr. city and regional planning U. Calif., Berkeley, 1965-66; trustee Oakland Mus., 1965-66; bd. dirs., exec. com. Niagara Frontier Housing Devel. Corp., 1967-70; co-chmn. Cathedral Park Devel., Buffalo, 1968-70; v.p. Care-Medico Greater Phila., 1971-75; commr. Phila. City Planning Commn., 1972—; dir. Girard Bank and Girard Co., Phila., 1976—. Bd. trustees Rosenbach Found., Rosenbach Mus. and Library, 1975—, chmn., 1979—; trustee Lewis Stevens Community Trust, 1977—, v.p., 1979—; mem. Phila. Tricentennial Com., 1979; mem. Pa. Humanities Council, 1981—; mem. adv. council Hampshire Coll., 1981—. Mem. Nat. Assn. Housing and Redevel. Ofcls., Phila. Art Alliance. Recipient Susan B. Anthony Prize, Bryn Mawr Coll., 1953; named Disting. Dau. of Pa., 1982. Clubs: Harvard, Cosmopolitan (Phila.). Co-editor: Urban Housing, 1966, Japanese translation 1975; co-editor abstracts sect. Jour. Am. Inst. Planners, 1952-60. Address: 2016 Spruce St Philadelphia PA 19103

MEYNER, HELEN STEVENSON, former congresswoman, co. dir.; b. N.Y.C., Mar. 5, 1929; d. William Edward and Eleanor (Bumstead) Stevenson; B.A. in History, Colo. Coll., 1950, LL.D. (hon.), 1973; m. Robert B. Meyner, Jan. 19, 1957. With ARC, Korea, 1950's; later with UN, N.Y.C. then consumer adv. TWA; staff Adlai E. Stevenson; columnist Newark Star Ledger, 1962-69; hostess TV interview program, 1965-68; mem. 94th and 95th Congresses from 13th N.J. Dist.; dir. Prudential Ins. Co., 1979—, Allied Co., 1979. Opened N.J. gov.'s mansion Morven to public; mem. N.J. Rehab. Commn., 1961-75. Bd. dirs. Newark Mus. Mem. N.J. Democratic Policy Council; congressional candidate from 13th N.J. Dist., 1972. Mem. UN Assn. Home: 16 Olden Ln Princeton NJ 08540

MEYNINGER, RITA, civil engr.; b. Newark; B.S. in Civil Engring., Newark Coll. Engring., 1958; M.S. in Civil Engring., N.Y.U., 1973; postgrad. engring. sci. in civil engring. N.J. Inst. Tech. With Clinton Bogert & Assos., Ft. Lee, N.J., 1970-74; v.p., gen. mgr. Resource Planning div. Hydrosci., Inc., Emerson, N.J., 1974-78; regional dir., region II, Fed. Emergency Mgmt. Agy., N.Y.C., 1979-81; fed. coordinating officer in emergency declaration at Love Canal, N.Y. State, 1980; fed. coordinating officer in drought emergency declaration in N.J., 1980. Recipient Alumni Honor Roll award N.J. Inst. Tech., 1980. Mem. ASCE, Am. Water Works Assn., Water Pollution Control Fedn. Home: 300 Winston Dr Cliffside Park NJ 07010

MICCICHE, PAULINE F., librarian; b. Scranton, Pa., Feb. 5, 1939; d. Salvator A. and Mary Sadie (Occulto) M.; B.S., U. Buffalo, 1961; M.S., Canisius Coll., Buffalo, 1963; M.S. in L.S., Western Res. U., Cleve., 1964. Asst. serials librarian U. Wash., Seattle, 1964-66; head periodicals dept. Fresno (Calif.) State Coll., 1966-68; automation asso. SUNY, Stony Brook, 1969-76; systems analyst OCLC, Inc., Columbus, Ohio, 1976-78, dept. mgr., 1978-81, bid coordinator, 1982—. Mem. ALA, Am. Soc. Info. Sci., Assn. Computing Machinery, Mensa. Office: 6565 Franz Rd Dublin OH 43017

MICCIO, KRISTIAN MARIA, polit. scientist, feminist educator; b. N.Y.C., Dec. 14, 1951; d. Guy Joseph and Lucille (D'Andrea) M.; B.A. in Politics and Philosophy magna cum laude, Marymount Coll., Tarrytown, N.Y., 1973; postgrad. Loyola U., Rome, 1971-72; M.A. in Public Policy, SUNY, Albany, 1975. Research asso. Inst. Public Policy Alternatives, 1974-75; dir. returning adult program Hudson Valley Community Coll., Troy, N.Y., 1975-76; dir. women's programs Albany (N.Y.) YWCA, 1976-79; dir. community relations and devel. Family Planning Advocates N.Y. State, Albany, 1979; mem. faculty SUNY, Albany, bd. advs. women's studies program; prof. women's studies SUNY, New Paltz, 1980—; founder, chmn. Women's Action Alliance, 1977-79; adv. bd. Inst. Women and Access to Edn., 1980; mem. steering com. Albany Women's Forum. Recipient award Albany YWCA, 1979; grantee SUNY, Albany, 1975. Mem. N.Y. State Women's Studies Assn. Coordinating Council, Nat. Women's Studies Assn., Union Radical Polit. Economists. Office: SUNY New Paltz NY 12561

MICHAEL, CAROL JEAN MUSSELMAN, home economist; b. Dayton, Ohio, July 20, 1949; d. Orville Glen and Evelyn Charlotte Musselman; student Manchester Coll., 1967-69; B.S., Ohio State U., 1971, M.S. in Home Econs., 1973, Post Master Degree Coursework, 1979—; m. James L. Michael, Sept. 16, 1972. Food service inst. Bur. Vocat. Rehab. program, Montgomery County Joint Vocat. Sch., Trotwood, Ohio, summer 1973; substitute tchr. Hamilton (Ohio) City Schs., 1973; instr. dept. home econs. Miami U., Oxford, Ohio, 1974-78, asst. prof. dept. home econs. and consumer scis., 1978—; speaker on energy conservation in food service ops. Chmn. World Hunger Task Force So. Ohio Ch. of the Brethren, 1976, 77, speaker on subject, 1977—. Mem. Am. Home Econs. Assn., Ohio Home Econs. Assn. (dist. officer), Coll. Educators in Home Equipment, U.S. Metric Assn., Phi Upsilon Omicron, Omicron Nu. Editor College Educators in Home Equipment Newsline; contbr. articles to publs. in field. Home: 409 E Chestnut St Oxford OH 45056 Office: 191 McGuffey Hall Miami University Oxford OH 45056

MICHAEL, COLETTE VERGER, educator; b. Marseille, France, May 3, 1937; d. Raymond Marc and Fanny (Kindler) Verger; B. Philosophy, U. Wash., Seattle, 1969, M.A. in Roman Langs., 1970; M.S. in History of Sci., U. Wis., 1975, Ph.D. in French, 1973; m. Ernest A. Michael, Aug. 26, 1956; children—Alan, David, Gerard. Tchr. French, U. Wis., 1973-75, Shimer Coll., Mt. Carroll, Ill., 1976; prof. French, No. Ill. U., DeKalb, 1977. Fellow Ford Found., 1970-73, Nat. Endowment Humanities, summer 1977. Mem. Am. Assn. Tchrs. French, Fedn. Internat. Professeurs Francais, Am. Philos. Assn., 18th Century Studies Assn., Aircraft Owners and Pilot Assn. Author: Choderlos de Laclos: The Man, His Work and His Critics, 1982; Intemperies (poetry), 1982. Home: 5 Moraine Terr DeKalb IL 60115 Office: 315 Weston Hall No Ill U DeKalb IL 60115

MICHAEL, DIANN DEE, psychologist; b. Charleston, W.Va., July 19, 1947; d. E. John and Asma (Radwan) M.; B.A. in Psychology and Philosophy, W.Va. State Coll., 1969; M.A. in Psychology, U. Akron, 1971, Ph.D. in Psychology, 1978. Grad. asst., instr. psychology dept. U. Akron (Ohio), 1972-78; psychologist Eastern Mental Health Center, Struthers, Ohio, 1972-74; dir., 1974-77; pvt. practice psychology, Youngstown, Ohio, 1975-81, Tampa, Fla., 1981—; clin. psychologist U. South Fla., Fla. Mental Health Inst., Tampa, 1981—; instr. psychology dept. Youngstown State U., 1975-80. Kferian Reunion Scholar, 1964-66. Mem. Am. Psychol. Assn., Fla. Psychol. Assn., Ohio Psychol. Assn., Ohio Acad. Neuropsychology, Internat. Neuropsychology Soc., Nat. Acad. Neuropsychology, NOW, LWV, Psi Chi. Clubs: Youngstown, Poland Swim. Home: 418 Danube Ave Tampa FL 33606 Office: FMHI-U South Fla 13301 N 30th St Tampa FL 33612

MICHAEL, JULIA GOBLEA, mech. engr., mfg. co. exec.; b. Bucharest, Romania, Feb. 6, 1939; came to U.S., 1969, naturalized, 1975; d. Ladislau and Rozalia (Schmelko) Assael; M.S. in Mech. Engring., State Poly. Inst., Bucharest, 1960; B.S., Columbia U., 1970; grad. Program Mgmt. Devel., Harvard U., 1978; m. Alan J. Michael, July 16, 1980. Engaged in engring. and mgmt., Romania, 1960-70; environ. designer Metcalf & Eddy, N.Y.C., 1970-72; with Pope, Evans & Robbins, cons. engrs., N.Y.C., 1972-77, mgr. environ. dept., 1975-77; mgr. environ. dept. Ford Motor Co., Dearborn, Mich., 1977-79, mgr. plant engring. and environ. and energy dept., casting div., 1979—. Registered profl. engr., N.Y. Sr. mem. Soc. Women Engrs.; mem. ASME, Detroit Engring. Soc. Office: Casting Div Ford Motor Co 3001 Miller Rd Room 2439 Dearborn MI 48121

MICHAEL, MARY JO, health dept. adminstr.; b. Monongalia County, W.Va., Nov. 8, 1924; d. William Washington and Gaye Ruth (Tennant) White; student Elliott's Sch. Bus., Wheeling, W.Va., 1940-41; m. Edsel G. Michael, June 1, 1946; children—Gregory G., Jane Ann Michael Reynolds. Stenographer, Monongahela Power Co., Fairmont, W.Va., 1943-46; sec. Hutchinson Coal Co., Fairmont, 1946-47; stenographer Marion County Health Dept., Fairmont, 1944-50, supr., 1958—. Mem. exec. bd. Central United Methodist Ch., 1976-77, 78, 80, 81; v.p. Women's Soc. Christian Service, 1978—; mem. Gov.'s Interagy. Council Child Devel. Services, 1977; chmn. Civic League Dept. Woman's Club Fairmont, 1978-80; bd. dirs. W.Va. Easter Seal Soc. Crippled Children and Adults, 1968-69, 70, 82; pres. Marion County Easter Seal Soc. Crippled Children and Adults, 1977-81. Recipient Disting. Service to Physically Handicapped award W.Va. Eastern Seal Soc., 1977. Mem. W.Va. Public Health Assn. (pres. award 1977, mem. exec. council, awards chmn. 1979-80, chmn. clerical and vital stats. sect. 1965, 74-75). Republican. Methodist. Clubs: Woman's, Lioness (Fairmont). Home: 1176 Sands Dr Fairmont WV 26554 Office: PO Box 649 300 2d St Fairmont WV 26554

MICHAEL, PHYLLIS CALLENDER, hymnwriter; b. nr. Berwick, Pa., Dec. 24, 1908; d. Bruce Miles and Emma (Harvey) Callender; grad. Bloomsburg Coll., 1928; B. Mus., U. Extension Conservatory, Chgo., 1953; m. Arthur L. Michael, Aug. 21, 1933; children—Robert Bruce, Keith Winton. Elem. tchr. Berwick Schs., 1928-33; substitute tchr. Shickshinny and Northwest Area, Pa., 1954-66; tchr. Northwest Area High Sch., 1966-71; gen. tchr. piano, organ, theory and voice, 1943—; hymnwriter, poet, author, composer, 1943—. Recipient first place in Nat. Favorite Hymns contest for Take Thou My Hand, 1953, Cert. of Merit for disting. service to composition outstanding hymns, 1967, and others. Adv. mem. MBLS. Mem. Nat. Ret. Tchrs. Assn., Internat. Platform Assn., Nat. Soc. Lit. and the Arts, Hymn Soc. Am. Author: Poems for Mothers, 1963; Poems From My Heart, 1964; Beside Still Waters, 1970; Fun to Do Showers, 1971; Bridal Shower Ideas, 1972; Is my Head on Straight, 1976; contbr. songs, articles, poems to books, hymn-books, booklets, mags. Address: Oak Haven RFD 3 Shickshinny PA 18655

MICHAELS, CATHERINE MARIE, museum dir., artist; b. Newport Beach, Calif., Mar. 13, 1953; d. Donn Owen and Marian Marie (Melandri) M.; B.F.A., U. Calif., Irvine, 1975. With retail sales and display dept. J. C. Penney Co., Newport Beach, 1972-77; retail display asst. mgr. Neiman-Marcus, Newport Beach, 1978-79; graphics cons. Mus. N. Orange County, Fullerton, Calif., 1977-79; dir. La Habra (Calif.) Children's Mus., 1979—. Mem. Mus. Educators So. Calif., Orange County Arts Alliance, Calif. Confedn. of Arts, La Habra Cultural Arts Council, Am. Assn. Mus. Office: 301 S Euclid La Habra CA 90631

MICHAELS, JOANNE, editor; b. N.Y.C., Dec. 30, 1950; d. Lawrence William and Renee M.; B.A., U. Conn., Storrs, 1972; m. Stuart A. Ober, Sept. 20, 1981. Asst. editor Viking Press, N.Y.C., 1972-74; editor David McKay Co., N.Y.C., 1974-76, St. Martin's Press, N.Y.C., 1977-78; v.p. mktg. and dir. Beckman Pub., Woodstock, N.Y., 1978-82; editor-in-chief Hudson Valley mag., Woodstock, 1982—; instr. Union Coll., Schenectady, 1982-83; hostess Speak Out Show, Sta. HV-TV, Port Ewen, N.Y., 1982-83. Mem. Woodstock C. of C., Ulster County C. of C., Ulster County Coalition for Free Choice, Catskill Alliance for Peace. Author:

Living Contradictions: The Women of the Baby Boom Come of Age, 1982. Home: PO Box 888 Woodstock NY 12498 Office: PO Box 425 Woodstock NY 12498

MICHAELS, MARY T., sr. citizen center exec.; b. Dunkirk, N.Y., Jan. 24, 1914; d. Robert James and Helen (Dillenkoffer) Dotterweich; student public schs., Dunkirk; m. Joseph Nicholas Michaels, Apr. 9, 1948; children—Joseph Robert, James William. Clk., Samalson's Dress Shop, Dunkirk, 1936, Fusco Jewelry, Dunkirk, 1940-47, Darling's Jewelry, Dunkirk, 1947-48, Leeds Jewelry, Dunkirk, 1948-53; mgr. Hexagon Wholesale House, Dunkirk, Present Co. Wholesale House, Dunkirk, 1953-56; sec. bd. dirs. Sr. Citizen Center of Dunkirk, Inc., 1977—. Mem. Republican Election Bd., 1977-80. Mem. Am. Assn. Ret. Persons (past pres.), Am. Legion. Roman Catholic. Clubs: Dunkirk-Fredonia Grandmothers (pres.); Knights of St. John (dep. organizer ladies' aux., pres. aux.). Home: 743 Deer St Dunkirk NY 14048

MICHAK, HELEN BARBARA, educator, nurse; b. Cleve., July 31; d. Andrew and Mary (Patrick) Michak; Diploma Cleve. City Hosp. Sch. Nursing, 1947; B.A., Miami U., Oxford, Ohio, 1951; M.A., Case Western Res. U., 1960. Staff nurse Cleve. City Hosp., 1947-48; pub. health nurse Cleve. Div. Health, 1951-52; instr. Cleve. City Hosp. Sch. Nursing, 1952-56; supr. nursing Cuyahoga County Hosp., Cleve., 1956-58; pub. information dir. N.E. Ohio Am. Heart Assn., Cleve., 1960-64; dir. spl. events Higbee Co., Cleve., 1964-66; exec. dir. Cleve. Area League for Nursing, 1966-72; dir. continuing edn. nurses, adj. asso. prof. Cleve. State U., 1972—. Trustee N.E. Ohio Regional Med. Program, 1970-73; mem. adv. com. Dept. Nursing Cuyahoga Community Coll., 1967—; mem. long term care com. Met. Health Planning Corp., 1974-76, plan devel. com. 1977—; mem. policy bd. Center Health Data N.E. Ohio, 1972-73; mem. Rep. Assembly and Health Planning and Devel. Commn., Welfare Fedn. Cleve., 1967-72; mem. Cleve. Community Health Network, 1972-73; mem. United Appeal Films and Speakers Bur., 1967-73; mem. adv. com. Ohio Fedn. Licensed Practical Nurses, 1970-73; mem. tech. adv. com. TB and Respiratory Disease Assn. Cuyahoga County, 1967-74; mem. Ohio Commn. on Nursing, 1971-74; mem. Citizens com. nursing homes Fedn. Community Planning, 1973-77; mem. com. on home health services Met. Health Planning Corp., 1973-75. Mem. Nat. League Nursing (mem. com. 1970-72), Am. Nurses Assn. (accreditation visitor 1977-81), Ohio (com. continuing edn. 1974—), Greater Cleve. (joint practice com. 1973-74, trustee 1975-76) nurses assns., Cleve. Area Citizens League for Nursing (trustee 1976-79, nominating com. 1982—), Zeta Tau Alpha. Home: 4686 Oakridge Dr North Royalton OH 44133 Office: Cleve State Univ 2344 Euclid Av Cleveland OH 44115

MICHALS, LEE MARIE, travel agy. exec.; b. Chgo., June 6, 1939; d. Harry Joseph and Anna Marie (Monaco) Perzan; B.A., Wright Coll., 1959; children—Debora Ann, Dana Lee, Jami. Internat. travel sec. E.F. MacDonald Travel, Palo Alto, Calif., 1963-69; owner, mgr. Travel Experience, Santa Clara, Calif., 1973—. Mem. Am. Soc. Travel Agts., Inst. Cert. Travel Agts., Bay Area Travel Assn., Pacific Area Travel Agts. Office: Travel Experience 3255 7F Scott Blvd Santa Clara CA 95051

MICHEL, GERTRUDE COHEN, artist, sculptor; b. Roanoke, Va., Mar. 21, 1915; d. Hyman and Ann (Goldman) Cohen; student of Hans Hoffman; mem. Morris Louis Seminar Group, Washington, Roanoke Coll., 1933, Johns Hopkins U., 1937, Md. Inst. Towson Coll., 1975; m. Leopold S. Michel, Aug. 23, 1936; children—Alan, Roger. Painter; various one-man shows U.S.; exhibited group shows Balt. Mus. Art and Peale Mus.; Flagler Mus., Norton Gallery, Palm Beach, Fla., 1976-77; represented in traveling show, 1969-70; instr. of painting Md.; represented in permanent collection Towson U. Recipient prize Balt. Mus. Art, 1961; awards Peale Mus. and Goucher Coll. Mem. Artists Guild Palm Beach, Artist Equity, Nat. League Pen Women (profl.). Jewish. Home: 31 Caveswood Ln Owings Mills MD 21117

MICHEL, MARY ANN KEDZUF, coll. adminstr.; b. Evergreen Park, Ill., June 1, 1939; d. John Roman and Mary (Bassar) Kedzuf; diploma in nursing Little Company of Mary Hosp., Evergreen Park, 1960; B.S. in Nursing, Loyola U., Chgo., 1964; M.S., No. Ill. U., 1968, Ed.D., 1971; m. Jean Paul Michel, 1974. Staff nurse Little Co. of Mary Hosp., 1960-64, instr. sch. nursing, 1964-67; instr. No. Ill. U., DeKalb, 1968-69, asst. prof., 1969-71; chmn. dept. nursing U. Nev., Las Vegas, 1971-73, dean Coll. Allied Health Professions, 1973—, prof. nursing, 1975—; mem. So. Nev. Health Manpower Task Force, 1975; mem. plan devel. commn., manpower com. Clark County (Nev.) Health System Agy., 1977-79, bd. govs., 1981—; mem. bd. advs. So. Nev. Vocat. Tech. Center, 1976—; mem. Health Fair Adv. Bd.; 1980-81; bd. dirs. Nathan Adelson Hospice, 1981; sec.-treas. Pools by J.P. Inc.; pres. PERC, Inc.; dir. FIER, Inc. Trustee, Desert Springs Hosp., Las Vegas, 1976—; chmn. Nev. Commn. on Nursing Edn., 1972-73, Nursing Articulation Com., 1972-73, Year of Nurse Com., 1978; NIMH fellow, 1967-68. Mem. Am., Ill., Nev. (dir. 1975-77, treas. 1977-79, conv. chmn. 1978) nurses assns., AAUP, Assn. Sch. Allied Health Professions (moderator internat. conf. on continuing edn. 1978), Nat. League for Nursing, Nev. Heart Assn., Local Honor Soc. Nursing, Phi Kappa Phi (chpt. sec. 1981—), Alpha Beta Gamma (hon.) Club: Slovak Catholic Sokols. Contbr. articles to profl. jours. Office: 4505 Maryland Pkwy Las Vegas NV 89154

MICHELFELDER, PHYLLIS DEVENEAU, rehab. counselor and adminstr.; b. Chgo., Dec. 30, 1921; d. George A. and Gertrude (Proctor) Deveneau; B.A. (Cogswell scholar), U. N.H., 1943; M.S., Nova U., 1978; m. William F. Michefelder, May 1, 1948. Asst. dir. public relations U. N.H., Durham, 1944-47; dir. public relations N.J. Coll. for Women (name now Douglass Coll.), New Brunswick, 1947-51, Barnard Coll., N.Y.C., 1951-59; assoc. dir. Ind. Coll. Funds Am., N.Y.C., 1959-61; dir. coll. relations Columbia U., N.Y.C., 1961-64; fund raising cons. Bennington (Vt.) Coll., 1964-69; dir. devel. Finch Coll., N.Y.C., 1969-71, Marymount Coll., Boca Raton, Fla., 1971-72; co-founder, rehab. specialist, exec. dir. Wayside House, Delray Beach, Fla., 1974—; vice chmn. Alcoholism Edn. Council, West Palm Beach Fla., 1977-79; dir. Fla. Alcohol and Drug Abuse Assn. Mem. Fla. Task Force on Women and Alcohol and Drug Problems (co-chmn.), Women Execs. in Public Relations, Womens Div. of Alcohol and Drug Problems Assn. N.Am., NOW, Common Cause. Home: 3851 N Ocean Blvd Delray Beach FL 33444 Office: 378 NE 6th Ave Delray Beach FL 33444

MICHELSEN, JANICE, editor; b. Chgo., June 5, 1955; d. William Andrew and Lilian Elsie M.; B.S. summa cum laude, Bradley U., 1977. Asst. dir. admissions Bradley U., Peoria, Ill., 1977-78, univ. editor, 1978—, instr. calligraphy, 1980—; owner, operator Ink Spot, 1979—; freelance communications cons., 1979—. Mem. Nat. Orientation Dirs. Assn., Nat. Assn. Coll. Admissions Counselors, Am. Assn. Higher Edn., Ill. Assn. Coll. Admissions Counselors, Ill. Writers Assn., Council Advancement and Support Edn., Soc. Calligraphy, Soc. Italic Handwriting, Mensa, Mortar Bd., Sigma Delta Chi, Phi Kappa Phi, Omicron Delta Kappa, Pi Lambda Theta. Contbr. articles to profl. jours.

MICHELSON, CAROLE COLEMAN, ednl. writer; b. Myrtle Beach, S.C., Apr. 6, 1944; d. Willson Bohl and Margaret Luebbe Coleman; B.F.A., Kent State U., 1966; m. Seth Michelson, Mar. 12, 1978. Copywriter, Compton Advt., San Francisco, 1969-70; freelance ednl. media writer, Los Angeles, 1971-76; writer, producer filmstrips Cousteau Soc., Los Angeles, 1976-79; writer, and producer filmstrips, multi-image films, Los Angeles, 1979—; cons. in field. Liturgy coordinator, chmn. St. Paul the Apostle Parish, Westwood, Calif., 1976-78; co-chmn. Los Angeles Jewish-Cath. Women's Dialogue, 1980, NCCJ Dialogues. Recipient Gold Cindy award Info. Film Producers of Am., 1977, Silver Cindy award, 1977. Mem. Nat. Geog. Soc., Smithsonian Inst., Women's Ordination Conf. Home: 9057 1/2 Carson St Culver City CA 90230

MICHELSON, MARLENE GHERRA, newspaper editor; b. Tacoma, Jan. 19, 1938; d. William Lucien and Trudy Louise (Bellman) Gherra; student U. Calif., Berkeley, 1955-58; B.A. in Journalism, San Francisco State U., 1963; children—Molly Leah, Charles Matthew. Copy girl, women's page reporter, teen editor Oakland (Calif.) Tribune, 1962-66; women's page reporter Akron (Ohio) Beacon Jour., 1966-67; gen. assignment reporter, feature writer Hayward (Calif.) Daily Rev., 1972-76; gen. assignment reporter, editorial page editor, spl. sects. editor Contra Costa Times, Walnut Creek, Calif., 1977-80, real estate editor, 1981—; editor Concord (Calif.) Transcript, 1980-81; vis. instr. journalism Holy Names Coll., Oakland. Recipient hon. mention for feature story Suburban Newspaper Assn., 1978. Clubs: Contra Costa Press (awards) East Bay Press (awards), East Bay Women's Press. Home: 5916 Sherwood Dr Oakland CA 94611 Office: 2640 Shadelands Dr Walnut Creek CA 94598

MICKEY, BARBARA HARRIS, univ. adminstr.; b. Michigan City, Ind., Nov. 7, 1925; d. Willard M. and Elsie Irene (McAlpine) Harris; B.A. in English and Philosophy, Ind. U., 1950, M.A. in Anthropology, 1953, Ph.D. in Anthropology and Folklore, 1958; m. John R. Mickey, Aug. 14, 1953, 1 son, Jeffry Alan. Teaching asst. Ind. U., 1951-52, asst. to editor Jour. Am. Folklore, 1952-55; vis. instr. U. Colo., 1958-62; mem. faculty dept. anthropology U. No. Colo., Greeley, 1963—, prof., 1973—, asst. v.p. for acad. affairs, 1971-73, asso. v.p., dean of acad. programs, 1973-75, asso. v.p. for acad. devel. and evaluation, 1975-77, v.p. for acad. devel. and evaluation, 1977-80; cons.-evaluator N. Central Assn. of Colls. and Schs., 1973—, mem. commn. on instns. of higher edn., 1979—. Named Colo. Woman of Achievement, Am. Council on Edn., 1979; Wenner-Gren Found. research fellow, 1955-56. Mem. Am. Anthropol. Assn., Council on Anthropology and Edn., Sigma Xi. Democrat. Office: U No Colo Greeley CO 80639

MICKINS, ANDEL WATKINS, ret. sch. adminstr.; b. Central, S.C., Oct. 28, 1924; d. Ernest Samuel and Estelle Charlotte (Jamison) Watkins; B.S., Tuskegee Inst., 1946; M.A., Columbia, 1962; postgrad. Iowa State Coll., 1948, U. Miami, m. Isaac C. Mickins, July 11, 1952; 1 son, Isaac Clarence, II. Head home econs. dept. Anderson County Tng. Sr. High Sch., Pendleton, S.C., 1946-52; classroom tchr. Holmes Elem. Sch., Miami, Fla., 1952-62; asst. prin. for curriculum Liberty City Elem. Sch., Miami, 1962-67; prin. R.R. Moton Elem. Sch., Miami, 1967-71, Rainbow Park Elem. Sch., Miami, 1971-81; supervising tchr. U. Miami, summer 1965. Pres., Friendship Garden and Civic Club, 1969-75; 1st v.p. Bapt. Women's Council, 1966—; pres. Ministers Wives Council Greater Miami. Recipient Sarah Blocker award Fla. Meml. Coll., 1966; plaques Liberty City Elem. Sch., 1967, Rainbow Park Elem. Sch., 1974, Friendship Garden and Civic Club, 1969, Mt. Olivette Bapt. Ch., 1965. Mem. NEA (life), Dade County Admintrs. Assn., Nat. Assn. Elem. Sch. Prins., Alpha Kappa Alpha, Phi Delta Kappa, Kappa Delta Pi, Pi Delta Kappa. Democrat. Clubs: Jack and Jill of Am., Order of Eastern Star. Home: 16300 NW 44th Ct Miami FL 33054

MIDDLEBROOK, PATRICIA NILES, educator, social psychologist, author; b. Magnolia, Md., Jan. 9, 1936; d. Norman Edward and Anne (Howell) Niles; Ph.D., Yale U., 1964. Asso. prof. Central Conn. State Coll., Avon, 1964-76, adj. prof., 1976—. Mem. Am. Psychol. Assn., Phi Beta Kappa, Sigma Xi. Club: Pequabuck Golf. Author: Social Psychology and Modern Life, 1980. Home and Office: 21 Guernsey Ln Avon CT 06001

MIDDLETON, PAULETTE BAUER, environ. scientist; b. Beeville, Tex., Dec. 8, 1946; d. Paul Wylie and Lillian Grace (Schoppe) Bauer; B.A., U. Tex., Austin, 1968, M.A., 1971, Ph.D., 1973; m. John William Middleton, July 12, 1970; 1 dau., Mären Katherine. Research asst., then instr. chemistry U. Tex., 1968-73, research asso. chem. engring., 1973-75; postdoctoral fellow Nat. Center Atmospheric Research, Boulder, Colo., 1975-76, sci. visitor, 1977-79, spl. project scientist, 1979, staff scientist, 1979—; research asso. Atmospheric Scis. Research Center, SUNY, Albany, 1976-77; lectr., seminar leader in field. Grantee EPA, 1982. Mem. Air Pollution Control Assn., AAAS. Author papers. Home: 1345 Elder St Boulder CO 80302 Office: Box 3000 Boulder CO 80307

MIDDLETON, RANDA CHRISTINE, aerospace co. exec.; b. Carlsbad, N.Mex., July 2, 1952; d. William Randolph and Porter Kate (May) Middleton; B.S., U. Tulsa, 1974; M.B.A., U. Denver, 1976. Fin. analyst Guaranty Nat. Bank, Tulsa, 1976-77; cost mgmt. supr., cost account mgr. Martin Marietta Aerospace Co., Denver, 1977-81; mgr. fin. planning Martin Marietta Corp., Bethesda, Md., 1981—. Mem. Nat. Assn. Female Execs., Nat. Assn. M.B.A. Execs., U. Tulsa Alumni Assn., Nat. Wildlife Assn., Internat. Fund Animal Welare, Beta Gamma Sigma. Home: 20011 Hobb Hill Way Gaithersburg MD 20879 Office: 6801 Rockledge Dr Bethesda MD 20817

MIDDLETON, ROSE NIXON, social worker; b. Gum Tree, Pa., June 3, 1932; d. Havard Downing and Margaret Beatrice (Black) Nixon; B.A., U. Pa., 1950; M.S.S., Bryn Mawr Coll., 1958; m. C.T.H. Middleton, Jr., Mar. 12, 1955; children—Karen Ann, Tanya Hope Nixon. Psychiat. social worker Embreeville State Hosp., 1958-60; child welfare worker Chester County Child Care Service, 1960-62; sr. psychiat. social worker Child Study Center, Inst. of Pa. Hosp., Phila., 1962-66; diagnostic cons., 1968-75, dir. preschool program for the handicapped, 1975—. Sec. Chester County Local Child Team, 1980-81; dir. Chester County ARC. Mem. Nat. Assn. Social Workers, Nat. Assn. Early Childhood Edn., Acad. Cert. Social Workers. Republican. Presbyterian. Home: Skyview Box 242A RD 1 Coatesville PA 19320

MIDEA, NORA JULIEN, public relations, mgmt. firm exec.; b. Mount Vernon, Ohio, July 7, 1939; d. Alfred Edson and Mary Elizabeth (Beck) Julien; student Mt. Vernon Bus. Coll., 1956-57, Georgetown U., 1957-58; m. Matthew John Midea, Aug. 2, 1958; children—Mary Amelia, Jane Elizabeth, Matthew John, Daniel Julien. Stenographer, FBI, Washington, 1957-58; exec. sec. John M. Ramsey, Cons. Engr., Columbus, Ohio, 1959-60; asst. credit mgr. Roberts Fin. Orgns., Wheeling, W.Va., 1971-72; comptroller Carvern Prodns., Inc., Washington, Pa., 1973—. Past pres. Democratic Women's Club Knox County (Ohio); jr. bd. dirs. YMCA, 1959-61; mem. organizational group Head Start Program Central Ohio. Mem. Bus. and Profl. Women's Club, Child Conservation League. Roman Catholic. Office: 347 Locust Ave Washington PA 15301

MIDLARSKY, ELIZABETH RUTH, psychologist; b. N.Y.C., Apr. 29, 1941; d. Abraham Allan and Francis Lucille (Wiener) Steckel; B.A. magna cum laude, Bklyn. Coll., City U. N.Y., 1961; M.A., Northwestern U., 1966, Ph.D., 1968; m. Manus Issachar Midlarsky, June 25, 1961; children—Susan Rachel, Miriam Joyce, Michael George. Lectr., Northwestern U., Evanston, Ill., 1965-67; asst. prof. U. Denver, 1968-73; dir. research and evaluation, cons. clinician Malcolm X Mental Health Center, Denver, 1973-76; asso. prof., dir. psychiat. services Met. State Coll., Denver, 1975-77; asso. prof. psychology U. Detroit, 1977—; chmn. Center for the Study of Human Devel. and Aging, 1978-81, dir., 1981—; pvt. practice clin. psychology; v.p., sec. Summit Human Resources; mem. crime and deliquency commn. NIMH. Mem. Am. Psychol. Assn. (task force on prins. and procedures Psychology of Women div. 1980-81), Midwestern Psychol. Assn., Mich. Psychol. Assn. (exec. council), Gerontol. Soc. Am., Soc. for Psychol. Study of Social Issues, Phi Beta Kappa, Psi Chi. Contbr. numerous articles in field to profl. jours.; mem. adv. bd. Acad. Psychol. Bull., 1981-82, editor, 1982—. Home: 13158 Nadine St Huntington Woods MI 48070 Office: Center for the Study of Human Devel and Aging U Detroit Detroit MI 48221

MIDLER, BETTE, singer, actress, entertainer; b. Honolulu, 1945; student U. Hawaii, 1 year. Debut as actress film Hawaii, 1965; mem. cast Fiddler on the Roof, N.Y.C., 1966-69, Salvation, N.Y.C., 1970, Tommy, Seattle Opera Co., 1971; nightclub concert performer on tour U.S., 1972-73; appearance Palace Theatre, N.Y.C., 1973; TV appearances include David Frost Show, Tonight Show; appeared revue Clams on The Half-Shell Revue, N.Y.C., 1975; rec. The Divine Miss M, 1972; Bette Midler, 1973; Broken Blossom, 1977. Recipient After Dark Ruby award, 1973, Grammy award, 1973, spl. Tony award, 1973, Tony award for One Woman Show on Broadway, 1974, Emmy award, 1978, Grammy award, 1981, Golden Globe awards (2), 1980. Author: A View from Abroad, 1979. Address: care Miss M Prodns Inc 4000 Warner Blvd Burbank CA 91505 *

MIEDEMA, SYLVIA ANN, savs. and loan exec.; b. Chgo., June 19, 1904; d. Celestin and Julia (Kropacek) Serp; student pub. schs.; m. Charles L. Klima, Jr., June 28, 1924 (dec. Sept. 1951); children—Carol L. (Mrs. Thomas J. Martin). Charles L. III; m. 2d, Jacob A. Miedema, Oct. 24, 1953 (dec. Oct. 1966). Dir., asst. sec. Clyde Savs. & Loan Assn., North Riverside, Ill., 1927-33, co-mgr., 1933-51, mgr., pres., dir., 1951—, chmn. bd., 1974—; dir. Clyde Service Corp., North Riverside, 1971—; chartering dir., cashier, dir. Bank for Savs. & Loan Assns., Chgo., 1968—; chartering dir. Darien Bank (Ill.), 1972—; dir. Home Loan Assocs.; chmn. adv. com. to bd. dirs. Ill. Savs. and Loan League, 1971-73, bd. dirs., mem. exec. com., 1975-76, mem. polit. liaison com., legis. sect. league com. 1976—; mem. com. internal ops. U.S. Savs. and Loan League, 1973, mgmt. com., 1974-75; mem. com. on industry devel. Ill. savs. and loan commr., 1974; mem. legis. com. U.S. League of Savs. Assns., 1979; mem. Ill. Savs. and Loan Bd., 1982—. Founder, past pres. Burnham PTA; past pres. Cicero Edn. Council; bd. govs. Cicero Community Chest, 1970-75; bd. sponsors Evang. Hosp. Assn., Oak Brook, Ill., 1977—; bd. dirs. Central Suburban unit Ill. div. Am. Cancer Soc., 1972-75, Berwyn-Cicero Council on Aging, 1977—; adv. bd. South Suburban Home Health Service, Inc., North Riverside, 1975—; mem. Ill. Gov.'s Gannons/Proctor Commn., 1982—. Recipient Spike Club designation Nat. Home Builders, 1956; recipient citation U.S. Treasury Dept., 1943. Mem. U.S. League of Savs. Assns. (legis. com. 1982—), Ill. Fedn. Bus. and Profl. Womens Clubs (Woman of Achievement award Dist. 1, 1970), Nat. Home Builders, Lyric Opera Guild. Clubs: Ill. Fedn. Women's, West Suburban exec. Breakfast Cicero Woman's (life mem., past pres.); Berwyn Women's Civic (Berwyn, Ill.). Office: 7222 W Cermak Rd North Riverside IL 60546

MIELKE, THELMA JANE, librarian; b. Rochester, N.Y., Dec. 14, 1916; d. Charles Frederick and Sophia Louise (Gottschalk) Mielke; A.B., Elmhurst Coll., 1937; M.A., U. Rochester, 1939; postgrad. Union Theol. Sem., Columbia, 1941-45, N.Y.U., 1954-60; M.S., Columbia, 1961. Asst. dept. philosophy U. Rochester, 1937-39; group worker Baden St. Settlement House, 1939-41; resident Ch. of All Nations, N.Y.C., 1942-43; librarian Harlem Boys Club, 1943-45; UN corr. Revista, P.R., 1945-50; observer UN, 1945-50, OAS, Commn. of Dependent Territories, Havana, Cuba, 1949; pub. relations Hill & Knowlton, N.Y.C., 1952-54; reference asst. to sr. reference librarian, N.Y. U., 1954-63; reference librarian L.I. U., Bklyn., 1963-78, head reference services, 1978—, asst. prof., 1963-65, asso. prof. 1965-76, prof., 1976—, v.p. faculty fedn., 1979—. Exec. sec. Eastern States Hist. Clearing House, 1965-78. Mem. A.L.A., United Fedn. Coll. Tchrs. (sec., exec. bd. 1972-74, v.p. 1976-78), NOW, Nat. Women's Polit. Caucus, Am. Mus. Natural History, Salalm. Editor: Library Leaves, 1964—. Home: 175 W 12th St New York NY 10011 Office: LI U Plaza Brooklyn NY 11201

MIELKE-AMARAL, MARY ELLEN, telecommunications co. exec.; b. Kenosha, Wis., Aug. 5, 1946; d. Nestor Johnson and Mary Louise (Parker) Thompson; B.A. in Journalism, U. Mich., 1968; J.D., U. Denver, 1973; M.S. in Advanced Mgmt., Pace U., 1979; m. Charles Patrick Amaral; 1 dau., Maura Patricia. Staff adminstr. Mountain States Tel. and Tel., Denver, 1970-76; admitted to Colo. bar, 1974; supr. regulatory matters AT&T, N.Y.C., 1976-79, dist. mgr. regulatory planning, 1980—; Conf. Bd. congressional asst. U. S. Senate Banking Com., Washington, 1980. Active U. Denver fundraising campaign, 1979; mem. Bethlehem Luth. Ch. Parish Edn. Bd., 1974-76, chmn. youth com.; vol. Beth Israel; active United Fund. Mem. Colo. Bar Assn., Am. Bar Assn., Denver Bar Assn., Denver Law Forum (asso. editor 1973, sr. editor 1971-72, asst. editor 1971), Nat. Bus. and Profl. Women's Assn., Lawyers for Colo. Women, Kappa Beta Pi (treas. 1974-75, internat. conv. del. 1973). Republican. Lutheran. Club: Gotham Bus. and Profl. Women's (legis. chmn. 1977-79, dist. nominating com. 1977, club nominating chmn. 1978, 79, dist. legis. chmn. 1979, state conv. del. 1978, nat. conv. alt. 1978), Zonta of N.Y. (mem. nominating com. 1979, 82, corr. sec. 1977-79). Home: 292 Main St Staten Island NY 10307 Office: 195 Broadway New York NY 10007

MIGALA, LUCYNA, radio sta. exec.; b. Krakow, Poland, May 22, 1944; d. Joseph and Estelle (Suwala) M.; came to U.S., 1947, naturalized, 1955; student Loyola U., Chgo., 1962-63, Chgo. Conservatory of Music, 1963-70; B.S. in Journalism, Northwestern U., 1966; m. Kazimierz Wieclaw, Nov. 27, 1971 (div. Jan. 1978). Radio announcer, producer sta. WOPA, Oak Park, Ill., 1963-66; writer, reporter, producer NBC news, Chgo., 1966-69, 1969-71, producer NBC local news, Washington, 1969; producer, coordinator NBC network news, Cleve., 1971-78, field producer, Chgo., 1978-79; v.p. Migala Communications Corp., 1979—; program dir., on-air personality Sta. WCEV, Cicero, Ill., 1979— ; lectr. Chgo. City Colls., 1981. Soloist, mgr. Lira Singers, Chgo., 1965—; mem., chmn. various cultural coms. Polish Am. Congress, 1970—; v.p., bd. dirs. Cicero-Berwyn Fine Arts Council, 1980—. bd. dirs. Nationalities Services Center, Cleve., 1973-78. Washington Journalism Center fellow, spring 1969. Office: Sta WCEV 5356 W Belmont Ave Chicago IL 60641

MIGDOL, SHARON GRACE, personnel exec.; b. Yazoo City, Miss., Oct. 8, 1948; d. Jake and Sylvia Miron; student Okla. U., 1966-67, U. Houston, 1967-68, Memphis State U., 1968-69; m. Marvin J. Migdol, Dec. 26, 1970; children—Michael Alan, Susan Renee. With Marvin J. Migdol, Inc., Dallas, 1970—, treas., 1971-73, v.p., 1973—; dir. Nationwide Franchise Mktg. Services, Internat. Distbrs., A Roommate 4-U. Recipient Top Twenty award Snelling & Snelling, Inc., 1970. Mem. Dallas Pvt. Employment Assn., Dallas C. of C., Nat. Council Jewish Women. Jewish. Asst. editor The Migdol Manual, 1972. Home: 7853 La Cosa Dr Dallas TX 75248 Office: 12800 Hillcrest Suite 112 Dallas TX 75230

MIKA, MARY JANE, physician; b. Chgo., Mar. 8, 1943; d. John and Mary (Milas) M.; student U. Ill., 1960-62; B.S. (scholar), Roosevelt U., 1965, M.S. 1970; Ph.D., U. Ill. Med. Center, Chgo., 1973; M.D., Universidad Autonoma de Ciudad Juarez (Mexico) Escuela de Medicina, 1978. Reviewer current gas chromatography lit. Preston Tech. Abstracts Co., Evanston, Ill., 1968-73; contbg. editor Internat. Jour. Pharm. Abstracts, Am. Soc. Hosp. Pharmacists, Washington, 1972-73; asst. in chemistry U. Ill. Coll. Pharmacy, Chgo., 1970-73; biochem. researcher

VA Hosp., North Chicago, Ill., 1975-76; intern in internal medicine Cook County Hosp., Chgo., 1978-79, fellow in gastroenterology, 1981—; resident in internal medicine St. Francis Hosp., Evanston, 1979-81. Mem. ACP. Research in gaso-chromatography in flavor volatiles, mass spectrometric analysis of aromatic amines.

MIKLAS, PAULINE ROBINSON (MRS. MICHAEL J. MIKLAS), clubwoman, writer; b. Balt., Nov. 15, 1913; d. Emmanuel Ellinger and Mary Alice (Dunn) Robinson; grad. Inst. de Notre Dame; m. Michael J. Miklas, Dec. 23, 1946; children—Patricia (Mrs. Rudolph Henning), Joanne P. Free-lance advt. and public relations, Balt., Miami Beach, Fla., Tampa, Fla.; dir. public relations Miami Beach Pub. Co., 1946-49, Coppertone, Inc., Coconut Grove, Fla., 1947-48. Chmn. TV and communications Mother's March of Dimes, 1955-58; pres. Women of Gallery, Tampa Art Inst., 1956-58; cons. Clearwater (Fla.) Symphony League, 1957-60; pres. Tampa Philharmonic Women's League, 1957-60, United Cerebral Palsy Assn., Tampa, 1958, Sunstate Opera Guild, Tampa, 1965-69; Eastern U.S. chmn. Am. Art Week, Am. Artists Profl. League, 1965. Bd. dirs. Tampa Gen. Hosp. Women's Aux., 1955-58, Tampa Philharmonic Assn., 1952-63, Multiple Sclerosis Assn., 1962-64, Religious Arts Theatre, Tampa, 1964-66. Named Outstanding Woman of Fla., 1960. Mem. Nat. League Am. Pen Women (pres. Davis Island br. 1960-64, Fla. pres. 1970-72, nat. biennial chmn. 1972-74, pres., founder Tallahassee br. 1978-80, Disting. award for service), Internat. Platform Assn., UDC (chpt. v.p. 1968-70, 78-79, pres. Winnie Davis chpt. 1979-82, chmn. Fla. div. 1981; Disting. award for service), Fla. Fedn. Music Clubs (dir. 1955-62, Tampa C. of C. (chmn. edn. Davis Island 1958), LWV (dir. 1960-64), Hillsborough County Fedn. Women's Clubs (chmn. 1962-66), Friday Morning Musicale (artistic dir. 1962-66). Clubs: Tampa Women's (certificate of recognition 1976), Davis Island Garden (Tampa); May Oaks Garden (pres. 1980—). Editor Crescendo mag., 1963-65. Home: 2555 Marston Rd Tallahassee FL 33303

MIKOLS, PATRICIA ELAINE, counseling psychologist; b. Balt., May 7, 1946; d. Christopher David and Aldona Brooks M.; B.A., Hollins Coll., 1968; M.A., Temple U., 1973; Ph.D., U. Pa., 1981. Research asst. Friends of Psychiat. Research, 1968-70; instr. psychology Bucks County Community Coll., 1972-73; dir. adult evening program Thomas Jefferson U. Community Mental Health Center, 1973-75; founding mem., psychotherapist Phila. Feminist Therapy Collective, Inc., 1973-79; counseling psychologist Community Coll. Phila., 1975-77; staff psychologist Univ. Counseling Service, U. Pa., Phila., 1977—; pvt. practice psychol. counseling, Phila., 1979—. Mem. Am. Psychol. Assn., Assn. for Women in Psychology, Nat. Feminist Therapist Assn. Home: 4631 Pine St Philadelphia PA 19143

MIKULSKI, BARBARA ANN, Congresswoman; b. Balt., July 20, 1936; d. William and Christina Eleanor (Kutz) Mikulski; B.A., Mt. St. Agnes Coll., 1958; M.S.W., U. Md., 1965; LL.D., Goucher Coll., 1973, Hood Coll., 1978. Tchr., Mt. Saint Agnes Coll., 1969, Community Coll. Balt., 1970-71, VISTA Tng. Center, 1965-70; with Balt. Dept. Social Services, 1961-63, 66-70, York Family Agy., 1964, Asso. Cath. Charities, 1958-61; former city councilwoman 1st dist. Balt.; mem. 96-97th Congresses from 3d Md. Dist.; mem. interstate and fgn. commerce com., mcht. marine and fisheries com.; mem. Congressional Steel Caucus, Congresswomen's Caucus, Democratic Study Group, Environ. Study Conf., Mems. Congress for Peace Through Law; cons. orgns. including Nat. Center Urban Ethnic Affairs. Mem. Polish Women's Alliance, Polish Am. Congress, Citizen Planning and Housing Assn., S.E. Community Orgn.; chmn. commn. community devel. Archiocesan Urban Commn. Mem. Nat. Women's Polit. Caucus; mem. nat. com. Muskie for Pres., 1971-72; chairperson commn. del. selection and party structure Dem. Nat. Com.; Dem. nominee U.S. Senate, 1974, Ho. of Reps., 1976; mem. Dem. Nat. Strategy Council; nat. bd. dirs. Urban Coalition; bd. dirs. Valley House. Named One of Outstanding Young Women in Am.; Md. Outstanding Young Women of Year, 1968; recipient hon. degrees Hood Coll., Goucher Coll., Pratt Inst. Mem. Am. Fedn. Tchrs., Nat. Assn. Social Workers, LWV. Contbr. articles to N.Y. Times, U.S. Steelworker Jour., Red Book and others. Home: Fell's Point Baltimore MD 21231 Office: 1414 Federal Bldg Baltimore MD 21201 also 407 Cannon House Office Bldg Washington DC 20515

MIKUS, ELEANORE ANN, artist; b. Detroit, July 25, 1927; d. Joseph J. and Bertha M. (Englot) M.; student Sch. of Arts and Crafts, Detroit, 1946-47, Art Students League, N.Y.C., 1958-59; B.F.A., U. Denver, 1967, M.A., 1967; children by previous marriage—Richard, Hillary, Gabrielle Burns. Asst. prof. art Monmouth Coll., West Long Branch, N.J., 1966-70; vis. lectr. painting Cooper Union for Advancement Sci. and Art, N.Y.C., 1970-72, Harrow (Eng.) Coll. Tech. and Art, 1975-76; vis. tutor painting Kensington Inst., London, 1974-77; vis. lectr. painting Central Sch. Art and Design, London, 1973-77; prof. art Cornell U., Ithaca, N.Y., 1979—; one-woman shows: Pietrantonio Gallery, N.Y.C., 1960, Pace Gallery, Boston, 1963, N.Y.C., 1964, 65, Loeb Center, N.Y. U., N.Y.C., 1965, OK Harris Gallery, N.Y.C., 1970, 71, 72, 73, 74, Webb-Parsons Gallery, Bedford Village, N.Y., 1973, Wells Coll., Aurora, N.Y.; numerous group shows, latest being: U. Utah, 1972, Columbus (Ohio) Mus., 1972, Finch Mus., N.Y.C., 1972, Aldrich Mus., Ridgefield, Conn., 1972, Newark Mus., 1973, Akron (Ohio) Art Inst., 1973, Whitney Mus., N.Y.C., 1974, Mus. Modern Art, N.Y.C., 1974, Richmond (Va.) Mus., 1977, Weatherspoon Art Gallery, Greensboro, N.C., 1977, Upstairs Gallery, Ithaca, 1980, Johnson Mus., 1979, 80, 81; represented in permanent collections: Library of Congress, Washington, Mus. Modern Art, N.Y.C., Whitney Mus., N.Y.C., U. Denver, Aldrich Mus., Ridgefield, Conn., Cornell U., Indpls. Mus. Art, Victoria and Albert Mus., London, U. N.C., Chapel Hill, Akron Art Inst., N.Y. Public Library, UCLA, Los Angeles County Mus., numerous others. Guggenheim fellow, 1966-67; Tammarind fellow, 1968; McDowell fellow, 1969. Mem. AAUP. Studio: 645 1st Ave New York NY 10016

MILAM, EVELYN LOUISE, coll. pres.; b. Memphis, Tex., Feb. 12, 1921; d. John K. and Bessie Lee (Harper) M.; B.A., W. Tex. State U., 1942; M.A., Tex. Tech. U., 1951; Ph.D., U. Wyo., 1968. With U.S. Civil Service Censorship, San Antonio, 1942-43; high sch. tchr. Hereford (Tex.) Ind. Sch. Dist., 1943-46, Perryton (Tex.) Ind. Sch. Dist., 1946-47; registrar, counselor, coordinator guidance Pampa (Tex.) Ind. Sch. Dist., 1947-62; admissions counselor, dir. admissions and fin. aid Austin Coll., Sherman, Tex., 1962-68, asso. prof. edn. and psychology 1968-74, prof., 1974; pres. Cottey Coll., Nevada, Mo., 1974—. Recipient Disting. Alumnus award W. Tex. State U., 1980, U. Wyo., 1981. Mem. Nat. Assn. Ind. Colls. and Univs., NOW, Am. Psychol. Assn., Am. Personnel and Guidance Assn., AAUW, Delta Kappa Gamma (M. Margaret Stroh internat. scholar 1967-68), Phi Kappa Phi. Office: Cottey College Nevada MO 64772

MILAM, JUNE MATTHEWS, ins. agt.; b. Preston, Ga., Mar. 27, 1931; d. Curtis Jackson and Mary Lee (Doster) Matthews; student Queens Coll., 1948-49; B.A., La. State U., 1952; m. Walker H. Milam, Jr., June 15, 1957; children—James L., Melinda K, Lisa W., Matthew W. Part-time sec. to sheriff Jefferson Parish, La., 1964-66; ins. agt. N.Y. Life Ins. Co., New Orleans, 1966—; lectr. in field; mem. La. Ins. Commr.'s Adv. Com., 1978—. Active various fund raising orgns.; bd. dirs. YWCA, New Orleans, 1979—, Harahan Booster's Club, 1979-81, adv. bd. Battered Women's Program, New Orleans, 1979—; mem. Bd. Aldermen, City of Harahan, 1980—. Named Woman of Yr., New Orleans Assn. Life Underwriters, 1975, La. Assn. Life Underwriters, 1976; named Boss of Yr., Am. Bus. Women's Assn., 1976; Nat. Quality awards, 1969-81. Mem. New Orleans Life Underwriters Assn., La. Assn. Life Underwriters, Nat. Assn. Life Underwriters, Women Life Underwriters Conf., Million Dollar Round Table, Harahan Civic and Improvement Assn. Presbyterian. Contbr. articles to profl. jours. Office: 1421 N Causeway Blvd Metairie LA 70001

MILANO, PAMELA CREESE, systems and software co. exec.; b. Ensenada, P.R., Sept. 28, 1947; d. Philip Guy and Jean Craig (Cooper) Creese; exec. sec. degree, Bixby Bus. Coll., 1965; student St. Petersburg Jr. Coll., 1965-72, Tampa Coll., 1976-78; spl. courses; m. Richard Nicholas Milano, May 26, 1973; children—Saria Pattan, Richard Creese. Platform sec. Barnett Bank, St. Petersburg, Fla., 1967-73; asst. cashier Ellis N.E. Nat. Bank, St. Petersburg, 1967-73; corp. officer Cheezem Devel. Corp., St. Petersburg, 1973-74; legal sec. Marlow, Shofi, Ortmayer, Smith & Spangler, Tampa, Fla., 1974-76; office mgr./acct. SHS Assos., Inc., St. Petersburg, 1977-81; group v.p. loans and v.p., dir. mortgage loans Fla. Software Services, Inc., Orlando, 1979-82; dir. edn. services Digital Systems, Inc., Pensacola, Fla., 1982—; condr. banking seminars for students; cons. seminars on lending instruments. Formerly active League to Aid Retarded Children, Young Republicans. Lic. real estate asso., Fla.; cert. profl. sec. Mem. Am. Inst. Banking, Am. Bus. Women's Assn., Nat. Assn. Female Execs., Fla. Soc. Cert. Profl. Secs. , Pensacola Arts Council, North Hills Preservation Dist. Episcopalian. Home: 110 W Strong St Pensacola FL 32501 Office: 114 E Gregory St Pensacola FL 32501

MILANT, JACQUELINE, educator; b. Milw., June 23, 1948; d. Jacques Jean Robert and Virginia Anita (Zeller) M.; student Wis. State U., LaCrosse, 1966-67; B.S. magna cum laude, Wis. State U., Whitewater, 1970; student Pepperdine U., 1972-75, LaVerne U., 1971-72. With Pomona (Calif.) Unified Sch. Dist., 1970—, Neil Armstrong Elem. Sch., 1970-79, Hamilton Elem. Sch., 1979-80, Roy G. Decker Elem. Sch., 1980—; tchr. Cirrus Gallery, Los Angeles, 1979-82. Mem. Asso. Pomona Tchrs., Calif. Tchrs. Assn., NEA. Republican. Address: 3070 E Frontera St Apt 145 Anaheim CA 92806

MILBURN, DOLORES LOUISE, telephone co. exec.; b. Balt., June 11, 1943; d. William W. Bernard and Louise (Johnson) Perrin; student pub. schs.; m. Donald Harold Milburn, Oct. 7, 1961; 1 son, Dwayne Steven. Data processing clk. C&P Telephone Co., Silver Spring, Md., 1963-66, unit supr. data processing, 1966-68, programmer/analyst, 1969-73, staff mgr., 1973-78, dist. staff mgr. data systems, 1978—. Dept. coordinator United Way campaign, 1980.

MILES, ELIZABETH NESTOR, speech and lang. pathologist; b. Medford, Mass., Nov. 10, 1923; d. James Francis and Agnes Agatha Nestor; B.S., Salem State Coll.; M.Ed., Boston U., 1951, CAGS in Speech Pathology, 1960; m. E. Robert Miles, May 29, 1955; 1 dau., Lisa Marie. Speech and hearing cons. West Hartford (Conn.) schs., 1952-55; speech pathologist Lexington (Mass.) Sch. Dept., 1966-67; speech and hearing specialist Medford Sch. Dept., 1967-73, supr. instrn. and related services, 1973-76, dir. Title I, ESEA, 1976—; lectr. speech pathology Boston U., 1962-63, supr. clin. practicum, 1962-67. Recipient award Tri-City Council for Children, 1976. Mem. Am. Speech and Hearing Assn. (cert. clin. competence, mem. legis. council 1974-76), Am. Assn. Clin. Counselors, Mass. Speech and Hearing Assn. (sec. 1970-74, exec. bd. 1970-76, award 1975), Council Adminstrs. of Compensatory Edn., Boston U. Osgood Hill Alumni (exec. bd.). Pi Lambda Theta. Roman Catholic. Home: 32 Catherine Rd Reading MA 01867 Office: 215 Harvard St Medford MA 02155

MILES, JANET KAYE (NIEBRUEGGE), real estate salesperson; b. Nebraska City, Nebr., July 3, 1944; d. Melvin H. and Erleen A. (Haase) Niebruegge; student Midland Lutheran Coll., 1962-64; B.A. in Tech. Journalism, Colo. State U., 1966; m. Zane S. Miles, Oct. 27, 1967; children—Mark McDill, Melissa Margaret. Staff reporter, Ft. Collins Coloradoan, 1966-68; reporter Ely (Nev.) Daily Times, 1969; asso. editor-pub. Carson City (Nev.) Rev. and Advertiser, 1970-72; co-owner, office mgr. Miles & Miles Communication Services, Carson City, 1972-74; ct. planning and coordinating officer Nev. Supreme Ct., 1974-76, 77; real estate sales-person Fred C. Worline & Assos., Elko, Nev., 1977—; adminstrv. asst. Nev. Home Health Services, Inc., Elko, 1977—. Rural Elko County coordinator Heart Fund, 1978-80; publicity chmn. Elko chpt. Am. Cancer Soc., 1978-79, sec., 1980; alt. organist, Christian edn. com. St. Paul's Episcopal Ch., Elko. Mem. AAUW (state editor Sage Hen newsletter 1979-80, treas. Elko unit 1979-80), Elko County Bd. Realtors (legis. chmn., polit. affairs chmn. 1981-82). Republican. Home: 907 Hillside Dr Elko NV 89801 Office: 501 Oak St Elko NV 89801

MILES, JOSEPHINE, educator, poet; b. Chgo., June 11, 1911; d. Reginald Odber and Josephine (Lackner) Miles; B.A., UCLA, 1932; M.A., U. Calif., Berkeley, 1934, Ph.D., 1938; D.Litt. (hon.), Mills Coll., 1965. Mem. faculty dept. English, U. Calif., Berkeley, 1940—, prof. English, 1952—, Univ. prof., 1973—. Recipient Shelley Meml. award for poetry, 1935; Nat. Inst. Arts and Letters award for poetry, 1956; award for poetry Nat. Commn. Arts, 1966; MLA Lowell award for lit. scholarship, 1974; Phelan fellow, 1937-38; AAUW fellow, 1939-40; Guggenheim fellow, 1948-49; Am. Council Learned Socs. fellow, 1965; Nat. Endowment for Arts fellow, 1980. Mem. MLA, Poetry Soc. Am., Acad. Am. Poets, Am. Acad. Arts and Scis., Am. Soc. Aesthetics, Am. Acad. and Inst. Arts and Letters, Phi Beta Kappa, Chi Delta Phi. Author: Lines at Intersection, 1939; Poems on Several Occasions, 1941; Local Measures, 1946; The Vocabulary of Poetry (3 studies), 1946; The Continuity of English Poetic Language, 1951; Prefabrications, 1955; Eras and Modes in English Poetry, 1957, rev. edit., 1964; Renaissance, Eighteenth Century and Modern Language in Poetry, 1960; Poems 1930-60, 1960; House and Home (verse play), 1961; Emerson, 1964; Style and Proportion, 1967; Kinds of Affection, 1967; Civil Poems, 1966; Fields of Learning Poems, 1968; To All Appearances: Poems New and Selected, 1974; Poetry and Change, 1974; Coming to Terms, 1979; Working Out Ideas, 1980; co-editor anthology: Criticism, Foundations of Modern Judgment, 1948; Idea and Experiment, 1950-54; editor: The Poem, 1959; The Ways of the Poem, rev. edit., 1972; Classic Essays in English, rev. edit., 1965; contbr. to Fifteen Modern American Poets, 1956; Poets' Choice, 1963; Modern Hindi Poetry, 1965; Voyages, 1968; Norton Anthology of Modern Poetry, 1975; The State of the Language, 1980; Epoch, 1982; also cassette; contbr. articles, poems to critical revs. Recs: 12 Contemporary Poets, 1966, Todays Poets, vol. II, 1967.

MILES, LIZZIE FLOYD, govt. EEO ofcl.; b. Laurens, S.C., Apr. 2, 1940; d. Willie James and Clariander (Ferguson) Floyd; B.S., Allen U., 1961; M.A.T., U. S.C., 1977; M.A., U. Okla., 1979; m. Arthur Miles, Jr., June 11, 1973; children—Robert, Rhayda, Rhadshun. Tchr., coach girls athletics S.C. public schs., 1961-72; dir. youth activities Shaw AFB, S.C., 1972-74; sports specialist Ft. Jackson, S.C., 1974-76, edn. specialist, 1976-78; adminstrv. officer Ft. Clayton, Panama, 1978-80; EEO officer Charleston (S.C.) Naval shipyard, 1980—; tutor, advisor for Upward Bound program Coll. of Charleston, 1981—. Mem. Community Counsel for Improvement, 1980—; vol. March of Dimes, 1980—; mem. VIP com. Middleton High Sch., 1980—; mem. PTA, Orange Grove Elem. Sch., 1980—. Named Tchr. of Yr., Crayton Middle Sch., 1971; recipient Outstanding Performance awards U.S. Govt., 1975, 76, 77, 79. Mem. Nat. Assn. Female Execs., Am. Personnel and Guidance Assn., Mil. Educators and Counselors Assn., Zeta Phi Beta. Baptist. Home: 1404 Lenevar Dr Charleston SC 29407 Office: Chas Naval Shipyard EEO Office Code 108.2 Charleston SC 29408

MILES, YVONNE ZEIGLER, bus. owner; b. Bklyn., June 6, 1948; d. George Balnton and Rebecca (Moore) Zeigler; student Northwestern Okla. U., 1966-67, Temple U., 1967-69; m. Anthony C. Miles, Feb. 17, 1968; children—Yvonne Adrienne, Anthony. Account mgr. Dun & Bradstreet, N.Y.C., 1969-74; owner, mgr. Buddha's Delicatessen & Catering, Copiague, N.Y., 1974—. Sec., North Amityville Fire Co. Ladies Aux, 1981—. Emergency med. technician, N.Y. Mem. Nat. Fedn. Ind. Businessmen. Liberal Democrat. Roman Catholic. Office: 3296 Great Neck Rd Copiague NY 11726 *

MILGRAM, GAIL GLEASON, educator; b. S. Amboy, N.J., June 14, 1942; d. John Thomas and Evelyn Patricia (Lynch) Gleason; B.S., Georgian Ct. Coll., 1963; M.Ed., Rutgers U., 1965, Ed.D., 1969; m. William Howard Milgram, Aug. 6, 1966; children—Lynn Patricia, Anne Melissa. Tchr., New Sayreville (N.J.) Sch. System, 1963-69; asso. prof. Rutgers State U., New Brunswick, N.J., 1971—, dir. edn. Center of Alcohol Studies, 1976—; cons. N.J. Div. Alcoholism, Johnson & Johnson, Prudential Ins. Co. Am., Vision Assos. Mem. Author's Guild, Am. Sch. Health Assn. (com. on drugs). Author: Coping With Alcohol, 1980; Your Career in Education, 1976; The Teen-ager and Sex, 1974; Alcohol Education Resource Unit (with Paul Weber), 1973; The Teen-Ager and Smoking, 1972; (with Albert Ayars) The Teen-ager and Alcohol, 1970; contbr. articles in field to profl. jours. Office: Center of Alcohol Studies Rutgers State U New Brunswick NJ 08903

MILKMAN, BEVERLY LYFORD, govt. ofcl.; b. Ft. Pierce, Fla., Jan. 9, 1945; d. Robert George and Annette (Leatherwood) Lyford; student Centenary Coll., La., 1963-65; B.A. magna cum laude, U. Ariz., 1967; M.L.A. with honors, Johns Hopkins U., 1972; M.A., George Washington U., 1981; m. Raymond Henry Milkman, Feb. 27, 1972; 1 dau., Katherine Lyford. Research asso., tech. editor Peat Marwick, Mitchell & Co., Washington, 1967-69; program analyst, eval. div. Econ. Devel. Adminstrn., Dept. Commerce, Washington, 1970-72, spl. asst. to Dep. Asst. Sec. for Econ. Devel., 1972-74, spl. asst. to Asst. Sec. for Econ. Devel., 1974-80, dir. Office Tech. Assistance, 1980-81, dir. Office Planning, Tech. Assistance, Research and Evaluation, 1981—. Recipient Spl. Achievement award Dept. Commerce, 1971, 73, 76, 79. Mem. NOW, Nat. Women's Polit. Caucus, Common Cause, Nat. Abortion Rights Action League, ACLU, Phi Beta Kappa, Phi Kappa Phi, Theta Sigma Phi. Author: Alleviating Economic Distress: Evaluating a Federal Effort, 1972. Office: Dept Commerce Washington DC 20230

MILLAN, ELLEN ANN DAGON (MRS. LYLE JORDAN MILLAN IV), physician; b. Balt., Feb. 3, 1936; d. Emmett Paul and Annie (Sollers) Dagon; A.B., George Washington U., 1959; M.D., U. Md., 1964; postgrad. Johns Hopkins U., 1965-68; m. Lyle Jordan Millan IV, Dec. 21, 1963; children—Lyle Jordan V, Elizabeth Lyle, Ann Sheridan Worthington. Intern, Union Meml. Hosp., Balt., 1964-65; resident anesthesiology Johns Hopkins Hosp., Balt., 1965-68, fellow in surgery, 1965-68; practice medicine specializing in anesthesiology, Balt., 1968—; attending staff Union Meml. Hosp., Church Home and Hosp., Franklin Sq. Hosp., Children's Hosp., James Lawrence Kernan Hosp. (all Balt.); faculty Church Home and Hosp., Balt., 1969—, affiliate cons. emergency room, 1969—, mem. med. audit and utilizations com., 1970-72, mem. emergency and ambulatory care com., 1973-74, chief emergency dept., 1973-74; cons. anesthesiologist Md. State Penitentiary, 1971; fellow in critical care medicine Md. Inst. Emergency Medicine, 1975-76; mem. infection control com. U. Md. Hosp., 1975—; instr. anesthesiology U. Md. Sch. Medicine, 1975—; staff anesthesiologist Mercy Hosp., 1978—, audit com., 1979-80, 82. Mem. AMA, Am. Coll. Emergency Physicians, Met. Emergency Dept. Heads, Am., Md. socs. anaesthesiologists, Balt. City Med. and Chiurgical Soc., Internat. Congress Anaesthesiologists, Internat. Anaesthesia Research Soc., Am., Md. horse shows assns. Magotha River Sailing Assn., U.S. Yacht Racing Union, Chesapeake Bay Yacht Racing Assn. Episcopalian. Address: PO Box 76 Brooklandville MD 21022

MILLAR, JEAN ROY, psychotherapist; b. Berkeley, Calif., June 2, 1930; d. Roy and Jean (Roy) Cunningham; B.E., U. Miami, 1953; M.S.W., Smith Coll., 1962; postgrad. Center for Mental Health, N.Y.C., 1964-68. Program adv. edn. div. Girl Scouts U.S.A., N.Y.C., 1954-58; program dir. N.Y.C. YWCA, 1958-59; clin. social worker Patterson House, N.Y.C., 1962-63; dir. Williamsburg Greenpoint Mental Health Clinic, Bklyn., 1964-65; pvt. practice psychotherapy, N.Y.C., 1968—; cons. and tchr. Met. Mental Health Center, N.Y.C., 1977—. Mem. 12th St. Block Assn. Fed. Mental Health grantee. Mem. NOW, Am. Acad. Psychotherapists, N.Y. State Soc. Clin. Social Work Psychotherapists, Nat. Assn. Socil Workers. Home and Office: 129 W 12 St New York NY 10011

MILLARD, LAVERGNE HARRIET, free-lance artist; b. Chgo., July 8, 1925; d. Lewis and Julia (Smolk) Bassmire; student Chgo. Art Inst., 1937-39; m. Samuel Costales, Jan. 31, 1943 (div. 1957); m. 2d, Bailey Millard, Mar. 9, 1958 (div.); children—Bryan Lewis Costales, Julie Crump, Candace Lynn Millard. Cocktail waitress Verdis, Grant Street, Concord, Calif., 1955-61; mgr. used book shop Joyce Book Shop, Concord, 1964-79, seller art works, prints created by her; free-lance artist, 1979—. Recipient ribbons local fairs, art shows. Republican. Copyright holder for pastel art work. Home: 1500 Ellis St Apt 39 Concord CA 94520

MILLBERRY, KIMBERLEE WHITNEY, geol. scientist, educator; b. N. Adams, Mass., Apr. 3, 1959; d. Donald Robert and Joan (Whitney) Millberry; B.A. in Geology with highest honors; Williams Coll., 1981; postgrad. U. Tex., Austin, 1981—. Summer research asst. to govtl. sponsored study of the coastal erosion of Saco Bay, Maine, 1979; tutor, teaching asst. geology Williams Coll., 1977-81; assoc. instr. Ind. U., Bloomington, 1981; teaching asst. U. Tex., Austin, 1981—, tutor for geology/petroleum engring. students. Active Big Bros. and Big Sisters, 1978-81. Williams Coll. grantee, 1977-81; Nat. Assn. Geology Tchrs. and Amax Corp. scholar, 1980; Bronfman Sci. research grantee, 1980-81. Mem. Nat. Assn. Women in Sci. Found., Internat. Assn. Sedimentologists, Soc. Econ. Paleontologists and Mineralogists, Am. Assn. Petroleum Geologists, Geol. Soc. Am., Phi Beta Kappa. Episcopalian. Contbr. articles to profl. jours. Home: 3405 Grooms St Austin TX 78705 Office: Dept Geol Scis Univ Tex Austin TX 78712

MILLEDGE, SARAH FRANKLIN (MRS. STANLEY MILLEDGE), civic worker; b. Melrose, Mass., July 8, 1906; d. Albert Barnes and Edith (Bradbury) Franklin; B.A., Wellesley Coll., 1927; m. Stanley Milledge, Sept. 1, 1928 (dec. Oct. 1965); children—Allan Francis, Sarah (Mrs. Harold S. Nelson), Eleanor (Mrs. Barry Decker). Dir. community service Sta. WCKT-TV, Miami, Fla., 1962-76; dir. Sunbeam TV Co., Miami, 1954-70. Mem. nat. bd. Girl Scouts U.S.A., 1952-66; chmn. Fla. Com. Children and Youth, 1968-70; pres. Miami YWCA, 1969-73; bd. dirs. Fla. Mental Health Assn.; pres. Council Continuing Edn. of Women, 1971-72; co-chmn. womens div. Fla. chpt. NCCJ, 1966-72. Mem. Soc. Mayflower Descs., Women in Communications, Conglist. Clubs: Miami Wellesley (pres. 1979). Home: 1600 S Bay Shore Ln Miami FL 33133

MILLER, ADELE ENGELBRECHT, ednl. adminstr.; b. Jersey City, July 31, 1946; d. John Fred and Dorathea Kathryn (Kamm) Engelbrecht; B.S. in Bus. Edn., Fairleigh Dickinson U., 1968, M.B.A. magna cum laude, 1974; cert. in public sch. adminstrn. and supervision, Jersey City State Coll., 1976; m. William A. Miller, Jr., Dec. 1981. Bus. tchr. Jersey City Bd. Edn., 1967—, coordinator coop. office edn. programs, 1973—; adj. instr. St. Peter's Coll.; curriculum cons. Cittone Bus. Sch.;

chmn. adv. council Dickinson High Sch., 1978-80, organizer, bd. dirs. Frances Nadel and Cooke-Connolly-Coffey-Witt Faculty Meml. Scholarships. Mem. Citizens Adv. Council to Mayor of Jersey City, 1968-71; mem. juvenile conf. com. Hudson County Juvenile Ct., 1978—; active annual telethon Stevens Inst. Tech., 1978-80; trustee Jersey City Coll.-Community Orch., 1979—. Mem. NEA, N.J. Edn. Assn. (dir., treas.), Jersey City Edn. Assn., N.J. Bus. Edn. Assn., N.J. Coop. Office Edn. Coordinators Assn. Republican. Mem. Ref. Ch. of Am. Clubs: Jersey City Woman's (scholarship chmn.), AAUW, Jersey City Coll. (pres.). Author coop. office edn. study course Jersey City Public Schs., 1980. Home: 91 Sherman Pl Jersey City NJ 07307 Office: Dickinson High School 2 Palisade Ave Jersey City NJ 07306

MILLER, ADELIA DUHON, nurse, educator; b. Conroe, Tex., Jan. 20, 1936; d. Lawrence Bradford and Angel Emilanne (Gigout) Duhon; R.N., Lamar U., 1956; B.S.N., U. Tex., Tyler, 1978, M.S., 1982; m. Robert Lloyd Miller, Aug. 19, 1956; children—Kurt Bradford, Eve Marie, Karl William. Staff nurse Mother Frances Hosp., Tyler, Tex., 1966-70, dir. nursing service, 1970-75; office nurse, Shreveport, La., 1957-59; instr. nursing Tyler Jr. Coll., 1978-79, chmn. dept. vocat. nursing, 1979—. Mem. Am. Nurses Assn., Tex. Nurses Assn., Tex. Assn. Vocat. Nurse Educators. Methodist.

MILLER, ALFREDA REED, educator; b. Monticello, Iowa, Mar. 6, 1907; d. Ervin E. and Gwendolen (Doxsee) Reed; B.A., Cornell Coll., Mt. Vernon, Iowa, 1927; M.A., U. Iowa, 1932; m. Nathan A. Miller, July 5, 1949; children—Gwenna Leu, Thomas Reed. Tchr. pub. schs., Toledo, Iowa, 1927-28, Shenandoah, Iowa, 1928-31, U. Iowa Demonstration Sch., 1931-32, Knoxville, 1933-37, Wapello, 1937-38, Dade County, Fla., 1938-72, Ada Merritt Jr. High Sch., 1941-54, Hialeah High Sch., 1954-72. Mem. Women in Communicatons (chmn. scholarship com. 1957-77), P.E.O. (pres. 1976-79). Baptist. Home: 570 Hunting Lodge Dr Miami Springs FL 33166

MILLER, ANITA ELAINE, owner day care center; b. Terre Haute, Ind., Oct. 12, 1946; d. Melvin Doris and Beneta Gladys (Cooper) McConchie; B.S., Ind. State U., 1968; postgrad. Lincoln Trail Jr. Coll., 1976—; m. Arthur Delbert Miller, June 3, 1967; 1 dau., Jennifer Jo. Tchr., Oblong Community Consolidated Grad Sch., Oblong, Ill., 1968-70, Mother Goose Nursery Sch., Robinson, Ill., 1974-77; owner, dir. Humpty Dumpty Child Care Center, Inc., Robinson, 1977—; tchr. piano, 1964-74; substitute tchr. Blue Bird leader, Robinson, 1978-80; pres. Camp Fire Girls, 1975-79, v.p. 1980-83; bd. dirs. March of Dimes, 1978-80, chmn. mother's march and reading olympics, 1978-80, chmn. Super Walk, 1982; mem. Republican Federated Women, 1978—; treas. Crawford County, 1981—; v.p. Crawford County Young Reps., 1979—. Mem. AAUW (pres. 1973-75, v.p. 1971-72, treas. 1977-80), Sigma Alpha Iota. Club: Bus. and Profl. Women's. Home: Star Route Robinson IL 62454 Office: 907 W Mefford St Robinson IL 62454

MILLER, ANN (LUCILLE ANN COLLIER), actress, dancer, singer; b. Houston, Apr. 12; d. John Alfred and Clara Emma (Birdwell) Collier; student Lawlors Profl. Sch., Los Angeles, 1937. Appeared in numerous motion pictures, including: You Can't Take It With You, 1939, Room Service, 1939, Easter Parade, 1949, Kiss Me Kate, 1956, On the Town, 1950, Hit the Deck, 1952, That's Entertainment, Part I, 1976, Part 2, 1977, Won Ton Ton, 1976; star stage show Mame on Broadway, 1969-70, also in Los Angeles, Fla., Ohio, Ga., 1970-71; star Broadway show Sugar Babies (Tony nomination 1980), 1979-81; appeared TV shows including: Perry Como, 1961, Magic of Christmas, 1968, Bob Hope Show, 1961, Jonathan Winters Show, 1969, Ed Sullivan Show, 1958, 59, 4 Palace Shows, 1966-68, also Heinz Soup Comml., 1971; appeared in Hello Dolly in Ohio and Indpls., 1971; tour with Anything Goes, Cactus Flower, 1978-79; TV spl. Dames at Sea, 1971, Can Can, 1972; appearances on all talk shows; semi-regular on Merv Griffin Show. Created dame Knights of Malta; recipient Israeli Cultural award, 1980; Woman of Yr. award Anti Defamation League, 1980. Author: Miller High Life, 1972; Tops in Taps, 1981. Office: care Contemporary Korman Agy 132 Lasky Dr Beverly Hills CA 90212

MILLER, ANNA MAE, mfg. co. exec.; b. Chgo., May 13, 1935; d. John and Therese (Adams) Ziak; grad. Mt. St. Mary Coll., 1955, Dun & Bradstreet Bus. Sch., 1966, Elgin (Ill.) Community Coll., 1980; m. Marvin Miller, May 25, 1957; children—Kevin, Linda. Various secretarial positions, 1957-70; asst. to pres. Suburban Plastics Co., Elgin, 1970-74, corp. sec., 1974—. Active local Camp Fire Girls, Cub Scouts. Recipient various service awards. Mem. Bus. and Profl. Women (Charter award Schaumburg chpt. 1974), Elgin C. of C., Elgin Women's Council, Elgin Personnel Assn., Catholic Women's Orgn. Bartlett (Ill.) (past pres.). Clubs: St. Ansgar Bowling League, St. Peter Bowling League, Ladies Aux. KC. Office: 340 Renner Dr Elgin IL 60120

MILLER, ANNE GILBERT, pub. relations cons.; b. Peterborough, N.H., May 4, 1943; d. Horace D. and Katharine (DePierrefeu) Gilbert; student Nathaniel Hawthorne Coll., 1963, Alliance Française, Paris, 1963, Boise State U., 1976; m. James R. Miller, III, May 1, 1965 (div.); children—Elizabeth, Katharine Anne, Alain Geoffrey Sargent. Account exec. Wood River Jour., Hailey, Idaho, 1973-74; reporter Ketchum (Idaho) Tomorrow newspaper, 1974; editorial asst. Sun Valley (Idaho) Mag., 1974-76; project dir. Idaho Park Found., Boise, 1976; with Jour. Commerce, Boise, 1976-77; sales asso. Personal Mgmt. Assos., Boise, 1977-78; owner, founder AM-PR, Public Relations, Boise, 1978—. Chmn. Boise City Arts Commn., 1979-81. Mem. Public Relations Soc. Am., Idaho Public Relations Roundtable, Media Club Boise, Nat. Writer's Club, Publicity Club N.Y. Democrat. Author: Hitting Your Target with PR, 1980. Home: 3620 N 36th St Boise ID 83703 Office: 205 N 10th St Boise ID 83702

MILLER, ARLENE, social worker; b. Phila., Oct. 10, 1943; d. Nathan S. and Bella S. (Schuman) Miller; B.A., U. Miami, 1965; M.S.W., U. Md. Sch. Social Work and Community Planning, 1971. Social worker HUD, Dade County, Fla., 1965-71; dir. sr. adults program Jewish Community Center So. Fla., Miami, 1971-76; project dir. Sr. Aides Program Dade County, Miami, 1977—; vol. cons. variety sr. citizen projects. Charter mem. Miami/Dade Jr. Coll. Alumni Assn. Planning Bd., 1981. NIMH fellow, 1969-71; recipient Community Service award Met. Dade County, 1981; cert. of appreciation City of Miami, 1981. Mem. Dade County Mental Health Assn., Nat. Assn. Social Workers, Nat. Council Sr. Citizens. Office: 1407 NW 7th St Miami FL 33125

MILLER, ARLENE LOUISE GEIBE, hotel exec.; b. Lancaster County, Pa., July 23, 1923; d. Lewis Rose and Etta Mae (Hilbert) Geibe; student Salem Coll., 1943-45, Franklin and Marshall Coll., 1966-68, Lancaster Theol. Sem., 1967-69, Crozier Theol. Sem., 1967; children—Marvine E., Jr., Lorrie Louise. Interior display and fashion coordinator Garvin's Dept. Store, Lancaster, Pa., 1956-58; interior designer, merchandiser Watt & Shand and Washaw Design, Lancaster, 1958-67; motel supr. Holiday Inns, Roanoke, Va., 1970-77; mktg. dir. Sherwood Knoll Inn Ltd., Lancaster, 1977-79; gen. mgr. Sherwood Knoll Quality Inn, Lancaster, 1979—; regional chmn. Quality Inns Internat., 1981-82. Mem. com. Pa. Dutch Tourist Bur., 1977-79; bd. dirs. Lancaster chpt. Multiple Sclerosis Soc.; trustee Camp Hope, 1966-69, camp dir., 1956-66; ch. sch. tchr.; active state legis. polit. campaigns, 1967-79. Cert. hotel adminstr. Mem. Hotel Sales and Mktg. Assn. Internat., Internat. Operators Council (bd. dirs. 1981-82), Am. Bus. Assn., Nat. Tour Brokers Assn., Am. Hotel Mgmt. Assn., Sales and Mktg. Execs. (bd. dirs. 1981-82), Nat. Soc. Interior Designers, LWV, Nat. Assn. Female Execs., Lancaster Assn. Commerce and Industry, Columbia C. of C., Procrastinators Club Am. Republican. Mem. Moravian Ch. Clubs: Indian Springs Racquet, Woodrige Swim (charter), Hemlock Archers, Chiques Archery. Home: 501 Valley Rd Lancaster PA 17601 Office: Sherwood Knoll Quality Inn 500 Centerville Rd Lancaster PA 17601

MILLER, ARLYN HOCHBERG, psychologist; b. N.Y.C., Dec. 2, 1925; d. Nathaniel and Marie (Weinstein) Hochberg; B.S., CCNY, 1946; M.S. in Psychology, 1946; Ed.D. in Psychology, Temple U., 1965; children—David, Eve. Tchr. elem. schs., N.Y.C., 1946-48, tch. spl. edn., 1948-52; dir. spl. classes Gloversville, N.Y., 1953-58; sch. psychologist Fulton County, N.Y., 1953-58, Cherry Hill (N.J.) Public Schs., 1958-63; staff psychologist Children's Hosp., Phila., 1963-64; sr. psychologist Community Child Guidance, Camden, N.J., 1964-69; mem. adj. faculty Drexel U., Rutgers U., 1969-70, Temple U., 1975; pvt. practice psychology (child and adolescent), 1964—; cons., mem. adv. bd. Robins Nest for Delinquent Girls. Mem. Am. Psychol. Assn., N.J. Psychol. Assn., Camden County Psychol. Assn., Am. Acad. Psychotherapists, Del. Valley Group Psychotherapy Assn., Am. Soc. Sex Educators, Counselors and Therapists, Internat. Council Psychology, N.Y. State Assn. for Help of Retarded Children (past dir.), Camden County Mental Health Assn. (adv. bd., dir.), N.J. Sch. Psychologists Assn., N.J. Assn. for Learning Disabilities (cons.). Contbr. articles in field to profl. jours. Home: 1420 Locust St Apt 31 D Philadelphia PA 19102 Office: 75 Haddon Ave Haddonfield NJ 08033

MILLER, BARBARA ELLEN, phys. therapist; b. Lakewood, N.J., Dec. 31, 1954; d. Robert and Carolyn (Seiden) M.; B.S.P.T., Washington U., 1977; m. Harry N. Friedman, Dec. 5, 1982. Staff therapist, then sr. therapist Nassau Hosp., Mineola, N.Y., 1977-82; phys. therapist Jewish Inst. Geriatric Care-Geriatric Community Health Center, Mineola, 1977—; pvt. practice, Mineola, 1977—; guest lectr.; cons. Coma Recovery Assn., Internat. Coma Recovery Inst. Mem. Am. Phys. Therapy Assn. Office: 222 Station Plaza N Mineola NY 11501

MILLER, BARBARA STALLCUP, univ. ofcl.; b. Mayten, Calif., Sept. 4, 1919; d. Joseph Nathaniel and Maybelle (Needham) Stallcup; B.A., U. Oreg., 1942; m. Leland Frank Miller, May 16, 1946; children—Paula, Susan, Daniel, Alison. Women's editor Eugene (Oreg.) Daily News, 1941-43; law clk. J. Everett Barr, atty., Yreka, Calif., 1943-45; mgr. Yreka C. of C., 1945-46; dir. public relations Columbia River Girl council Scouts U.S.A., Portland, Oreg., 1962-67; dir. public relations and info. U. Portland, 1967-78; dir. devel. U. Portland, 1978-79, exec. dir. devel., 1979—. Public relations cons. Portland Jr. Civic Theatre, 1964-71, Women for Agr., 1970-71. Bd. dirs., mem. edn. com. Portland Civic Theatre, 1964-71; bd. dirs., public relations chmn. Portland Columbia River council Girl Scouts U.S.A., 1960-62, leader, 1954-72; public relations cons. Vols. Am. of Oreg., 1968-71, pres. bd. dirs., 1980—; bd. dirs. Oreg. Black History Project, Providence Child Care Center, 1980-82. Recipient Rose award Alpha Xi Delta, Presdl. Citation, Oreg. Editors and Communicators, Miltner award U. Portland, 1977; named Woman of Dedication, Portland Fedn. Women's Clubs, 1978. Mem. Women in Communications Inc. (N.W. regional v.p. 1973-75, Matrix award 1976, 80), Public Relations Soc. Am. (accredited, accreditation chmn. Columbia River chpt. 1981—), Oreg. Assn. Editors and Communicators (dir. 1975-76), Oreg. Press Women (dist. v.p. 1977-79), Oreg. Fedn. Women's Clubs (public relations chmn. 1978-80), Alpha Xi Delta. Clubs: Portland Zenith (pres. 1975-76, 81-82), City of Portland. Home: 5930 SW Meadows Rd Lake Oswego OR 97034 Office: 5000 N Willamette Blvd Portland OR 97203

MILLER, BARBARA STOLER, linguist, educator; b. N.Y.C., Aug. 8, 1940; d. Louis O. and Sara (Cracken) Stoler; A.B. magna cum laude, Barnard Coll., 1962; M.A. in Sanskrit Philology, Columbia U.; Ph.D. with distinction, U. Pa., 1966. Asst. prof. Oriental studies Barnard Coll., Columbia U., N.Y.C., 1968-72, asso. prof., 1972-77, prof., 1977—, chairperson dept. Oriental Studies, 1979-81, faculty rep. to bd. trustees, 1977-79; mem. Joint Com. on South Asia, Am. Council Learned Socs.-Social Sci. Research Com., 1982—. Guggenheim Meml. fellow, 1974-75, Mellon fellow, 1976; Smithsonian grantee, 1980. Mem. Am. Oriental Soc. (dir. 1982), Phi Beta Kappa. Author: Phantasies of a Love-Thief, 1971; (with Leonard Gordon) A Syllabus of Indian Civilization, 1973; Love Song of the Dark Lord: Jayadeva's Gitagovinda, 1977; The Hermit and the Love-Thief, 1978; translator: Bhartrihari: Poems, 1967. Office: Oriental Studies Barnard College Columbia Univ New York NY 10027

MILLER, (BENTE) BIRGITTE, clin. psychologist; b. Elsinore, Denmark, July 13, 1951; came to U.S., 1959, naturalized, 1965; d. Ochthave Ulrich and Rita (Christiansen) Blidt; B.S. in Psychology, U. Wash., 1973; M.A. in Clin. Psychology, U. S.D., 1975, Ph.D., 1977; m. Theodore Robert Miller, Aug. 21, 1976; 1 dau., Jennifer Kristen. Sr. clinician Northwestern Mental Health Center, Front Royal, Va., 1977-79; adult outpatient clin. psychology Grant-Blackford Mental Health, Inc., Marion, Ind., 1979—. Cert. psychologist, Ind. Mem. Am. Psychol. Assn. Lutheran. Home: RR 1 Box 442C Alexandria IN 46001 Office: 505 Wabash Ave Marion IN 46952

MILLER, BERNADETTE JANE, ins. co. exec.; b. Dayton, Ohio, Nov. 30, 1947; d. Carl Burdette and Betty Jane Miller; student Wright State U., Dayton, 1966. With Am. Bankers Life Ins. Co., 1976-81, regional career cons., 1980-81; dir. women's mktg. Universal Guaranty Life Ins. Co., Columbus, Ohio, 1981-82; pres. Money Concepts Internat. of Miami Valley, Dayton, Ohio, 1982—; mem. Industry Task Force Women and Minorities in Ins., 1981—; seminar instr. in field. Recipient various sales awards; mem. Millionaires Club, 1976-80; named Internat. Woman of Yr., Am. Bankers Life, 1977, 79. Mem. Am. Bus. Women's Assn. (chpt. pres. 1979, 81, nat. del. 1978), Nat. Assn. Life Underwriters, Women in Ins., Ohio Assn. Life Underwriters, Dayton Assn. Life Underwriters (chmn. 1981), Columbus Assn. Life Underwriters, Ohio Forestry Assn. Republican. Lutheran. Clubs: Zonta, Order Eastern Star. Office: 7940 N Main St Dayton OH 45415

MILLER, BETH, educator, critic; b. Chgo., Jan. 13, 1941; d. Bert and Anita (Lome) Kurti; B.S. summa cum laude, Northwestern U., 1962; M.A., U. Calif., Berkeley, 1965, Ph.D., 1973; student U. Mex., 1959, U. Madrid, 1960-61, U. Padua, summer 1961. Instr. Spanish, San Francisco State U., 1967-68; asst. prof. Spanish and French, State U. Coll. N.Y., New Paltz, 1968-69; instr., asst. prof. Rutgers U., New Brunswick, N.J., 1969-76; assoc. prof. U. So. Calif., Los Angeles, 1976—, chmn. dept. Spanish and Portuguese, 1977-78. Recipient grants Rutgers U., 1972-75, Ford Found., 1974-75, U. So. Calif., 1976-79, Del Amo Found., 1976-77, Am. Council Learned Socs., 1979; Fulbright fellow, 1981. Mem. Am. Assn. Tchrs. Spanish and Portuguese, AAUP, Latin Am. Studies Assn., Pacific Coast Council Latin Am. Studies (bd. govs.), Modern Lang. Assn., Women's Coalition Latin Americanists, Philol. Assn. Pacific Coast. Author: La poesía constructiva de Jaime Torres Bodet, 1974; Mujeres en la Literatura, 1978; 26 Autoras del Mexico de hoy, 1978; editor: Ensayos contemporáneos sobre Jaime Torres Bodet, 1976; trans., intro. Siete poetas norteamericanas, 1977; Women in Hispanic Literature: Icons and Fallen Idols, 1982; contbr. articles to profl. jours.; asso. editor: MELUS, 1977; editorial bd. Caribe, Fem., Latin Am. Lit. Rev. Home: 4102 Harter Ave Culver City CA 90230 Office: Dept Spanish U So Calif Los Angeles CA 90089

MILLER, BETTE HOKANSON, mortgage co. exec.; b. Winthrop, Minn., July 16, 1930; d. Horace Raymond and Irene Mae (Johnson) Hokanson; student Minn. Sch. Bus., 1948-49, U. Wis., 1970-73, U. Minn., 1974; m. Robert H. Miller, June 14, 1952 (dec. 1960); children—Hokan Charles, Roberta Mae, Win Raymond, Jacquelyn Louise. Mortgage loan closer Mobilhome Corp., Bloomington, Minn., 1949-52, First Nat. Bank of Mpls., 1952; accountant, corporate sec.-treas. Sick Optik Elektronik, Inc., Stillwater, Minn., 1972-80; mortgage loan officer Miller Mortgage Co., Mpls., 1981—. Mem. Nat. Assn. Accountants. Republican. Congregationalist. Home: 507 N 6th St Bayport MN 55003 Office: 1000 Carrie Ave Minneapolis MN 55403

MILLER, BETTY BROWN, writer; b. Altus, Ark., Dec. 21, 1926; d. Carlos William and Arlie Gertrude (Sublett) Brown; B.S., Okla. State U., 1949; M.S., U. Tulsa, 1953; student Am. U., 1966-68; m. Robert Wiley Miller, Nov. 15, 1953; children—Janet Ruth, Stephen Wiley. Tchr., LeFlore (Okla.) High Sch., 1947-48, Osage Indian Reservation High Sch., Hominy, Okla., 1948-50, Jenks (Okla.) High Sch., 1950-51; instr. Sch. Bus., U. Tulsa, 1950-51; tchr. Tulsa public schs., 1951-54; instr. Burdette Coll., Boston, 1954-55; reporter Bethesda-Chevy Chase Tribune, Montgomery County, Md., 1970-73; freelance writer, contbr. newspapers and mags., 1973—. Vice-pres. Kenwood Park (Md.) Citizens Assn., 1960; mem. Ft. Sumner Citizens Assn., editor newsletter, 1969; mem. Md. State PTA, editorial coordinator leadership conf., 1973-74; chmn. Montgomery County Forum for Edn., 1970-75. Mem. Nat. Soc. Arts and Letters (past editor mag., dir. public relations), Nat. League Am. Pen Women (budget chmn.), PEO Montgomery County Press Assn., Internat. Platform Assn., Capital Speakers Club of Washington (past pres.), Adventures Unltd., U.D.C., Soc. Descs. of Washington's Army at Valley Forge, DAR, Huguenot Soc. Republican. Clubs: Washington; Sedgeley (Phila.). Address: PO Box 573 Valley Forge PA 19481

MILLER, BETTY LOUISE LEE, nurse; b. Kansas City, Kans., Aug. 9, 1929; d. Gerald Wesley and Elizabeth Louise (Miller) Lee; R.N., Research Hosp. Sch. Nursing, Kansas City, Mo., 1950; student Emporia U., 1978-79; B.A., Ottawa U., 1980; m. Marvin Dale Miller, Oct. 30, 1950; children—Dale Wesley, Cathy Louise, Christine Ann, Lee Marvin. Emergency room nurse, various hosps., Kansas City, Mo., intermittently, 1950-64; public health nurse Kansas City-Wyandotte County (Kans.) Health Dept., 1969-73; nurse Sch. Dist. #500, Kansas City, Kans., 1973—; tchr., cons. in field. Sec., PTA, Welborn Sch., Kansas City, Kans., 1956-58, chaplain, 1957-59, mem. exec. bd., 1973-75; active Boy Scouts Am., 1956-66, Girl Scouts U.S.A., 1957-68. Recipient Den Mothers Tng. award Boy Scouts Am., 1961, Den Mother Nat. Key award, 1963; R.N., Mo., Kans. Mem. Public Health Assn., Bus. and Profl. Women, Research Hosp. Alumni, NEA, Kans. Edn. Assn., Democrat. Lutheran. Clubs: Order Eastern Star, Shriners. Home: 5312 Yecker Kansas City KS 66104 Office: 625 Minnesota Kansas City KS 66101

MILLER, BEVERLY WHITE, coll. pres.; b. Willoughby, Ohio, Dec. 29, 1923; d. Joseph Martin and Marguerite Sarah (Storer) White; A.B., Western Res. U., 1945; M.A., Mich. State U., 1957; Ph.D., U. Toledo, 1957; L.H.D. (hon.), Coll. St. Benedict, 1979; m. Lynn Martin Miller, Oct. 11, 1945; children—Michaela Ann, Craig Martin, Todd Daniel, Cass Timothy, Simone Agnes. Chemistry and biology researcher, 1945-57; tchr. schs. Mich., Mercy Sch. Nursing, St. Lawrence Hosp., Lansing, Mich., 1957-58; mem. chemistry and biology faculty Mary Manse Coll., Toledo, 1958-71, dean grad. div., 1968-71, adminstrv. v.p., 1968-71; acad. dean Salve Regina Coll., Newport, R.I., 1971-74; pres. Coll. St. Benedict, 1974-79, Western New Eng. Coll., Springfield, Mass., 1980—; cons. U.S. Office Edn., 1980. Recipient Pres. Citation, St. John's U., 1979. Mem. Am. Assn. Higher Edn., AAAS, Assn. Cath. Colls. and Univs. (exec. bd.), Internat. Assn. Sci. Edn., Nat. Assn. Biology Tchrs., Nat. Assn. Research Sci. Tchrs., Springfield C. of C. (dir.), Delta Kappa Gamma, Sigma Delta Epsilon. Office: 1215 Wilbraham Rd Springfield MA 01119

MILLER, BLANCHE ESTHER, cytologist; b. Georgetown, N.Y., July 28, 1915; adopted d. Ralph Raymond and Mary Margaret (Hetrick) M.; A.B., Fairleigh Dickinson U., 1976. Cytotechnologist, Roosevelt Hosp., N.Y.C., 1953-55, screener cytotechnologist, 1955-56; with R.I. Hosp., Providence, 1956; mem. staff Newark City Hosp., 1957-68, chief cytology lab., 1960-66, co-dir. cancer detection center, 1966-68; sect. head cytology lab. N.J. Coll. Medicine and Dentistry, 1968-75; supr. continuing edn. in cytology Gyn Cytology and Pathology Assos., Leonia, N.J., 1975-78; teaching supr. cytology dept. Metpath, Teterboro, N.J., 1979—. Mem. Am. Soc. Cytology, Am. Soc. Clin. Pathologists (cert. technologist, med. technologist), Pan Am. Cancer Cytology Soc., N.Y. Assn. Cytology (founder mem., sec.-treas., mem. exec. bd., service award). Methodist. Home: 18 Engle St Apt 10-D Tenafly NJ 07670 Office: Metpath 1 Malcolm Ave Teterboro NJ 07608

MILLER, BONNIE MAE, ins. co. exec.; b. Oto, Iowa, Sept. 6, 1925; d. Fred George and Olive Lorraine (Stratton) Burgess; grad. public schs.; m. William Harry Miller, July 6, 1945; children—Dennis W., Ellen Lorraine Miller Garoutte. Br. sec., asst. office mgr. Midwest Region, Pa. Life Ins. Co., Sioux City, Iowa, 1966-71; agy. sec. Equitable of Iowa, Sioux City, 1971-76; agy. sec. Bankers Life Ins. Co., Sioux City, 1976-79, mktg. asst., 1979—. Recipient DAR award, 1944. Mem. Am. Bus. Women's Assn. (pres. 1976, named Woman of Yr., Iowana chpt. 1982). Republican. Lutheran. Clubs: Women's Internat. Bowling Congress, Citizens Band Radio Assn. Home: 4441 Fillmore St Sioux City IA 51108 Office: 508 Frances Bldg Sioux City IA 51101

MILLER, CARLA, lawyer; b. Phila., Jan. 15, 1951; d. Carl Kenneth and Dorothy Ruth M.; B.A., Fla. State U., 1972; J.D., U. Fla., 1979. Nat. coordinator Narconon Drug Abuse Program, 1972-74; coordinator alcohol and drug abuse services Whitehaven Mental Health Center, Memphis, 1974-75; crime prevention specialist Office of Mayor, Jacksonville, Fla., 1975-77; prosecutor intern Office of State's Atty., Jacksonville, 1979; admitted to Fla. bar, 1980; asst. public defender 5th Dist. Ct. Appeals, Daytona Beach, 1980; asst. U.S. atty., Jacksonville, 1980—; cons., lectr. in field; dep. comdr. Jacksonville Sheriff's Community Crime Prevention Possee, 1977. Bd. dirs. Fla. chpt. ACLU, 1971-72; coordinator Jacksonville Citizens Dispute Settlement Program, 1977; pres. Young Democrats, Tallahassee, Fla., 1971. Recipient Internat. Disting. Service award for crime prevention, 1977; Community Service award Jacksonville, 1977. Mem. Am. Bar Assn., LWV, NOW, Women's Polit. Caucus, Phi Delta Phi, Lambda Alpha Epsilon, Delta Zeta. Roman Catholic. Author manuals, papers in field.

MILLER, CAROL ANN, interior designer; b. Bronx, N.Y., Dec. 21, 1949; d. Anthony Joseph and Marie Rita (Montesarchio) Mayo; grad. Katharine Gibbs Sch., 1968; m. Larry Michael Miller, May 11, 1979; 1 dau., Tara Marie; 1 stepdau., Darcy Robin. Exec. sec. Conde Nast Publs., N.Y.C., 1968-69, Kelly Girls Temporary, Phoenix, 1969-70, Builders Resources Corp., Middletown, N.J., 1972-74; sec./treas. D.C. Reilly Assos., Middletown, N.J., 1975-78; v.p. Miller Design, Inc., comml. and resdl. interior design, Davie, Fla., 1979—; profl. club singer, N.J., 1972-74; notary public, Fla., 1979—. Leader Monmouth County council Girl Scouts U.S.A., 1976-77. Recipient Loyalty award Prin. Mater Dei High Sch., New Monmouth, N.J., 1967. Mem. Nat. Assn. Female Execs., Am. Bus. Women's Assn. Office: 6559 Stirling Rd Davie FL 33314

MILLER, CECELIA ELEANOR LOTKO (MRS. GEORGE E. CHAMBERS), physician; b. Chgo., Oct. 24, 1917; d. Joseph S. and Zofia

H. (Baizer) Lotko; student Northwestern U., 1945-47; B.S., U. Ill., 1949, M.D., 1951; m. James R. Miller, Sept. 3, 1938 (dec. 1958); 1 dau., Josephine Ann (Mrs. John E. Mitchell); m. 2d, George E. Chambers, Dec. 5, 1970; stepchildren—Ronald, Lawrence, Leon, Marilyn (Mrs. John Raglione). Intern, Cook County Hosp., Chgo., 1951-53; resident Hines (Ill.) VA Hosp., 1953-54; practice medicine, specializing in phys. therapy, Hammond, Ind., 1955, Chgo., 1956-77, 82—; med. adviser Argonaut Ins. Co., Chgo., 1976—. Mem. Field Mus. Natural History, Art Chgo., Chgo. Zool. Soc. Chgo. Fellow Am. Coll. Anesthesiologists (ret.); mem. AMA (ret.), Am. Med. Women's Assn., Ill., Chgo. med. socs., Am., Ill., Chgo. socs. anesthesiologists, Hines Surg. Soc., Cook County Hosp. Interns and Residents Alumni Assn., U. Ill. Alumni Assn., Dean's Club U. Ill. Coll. Medicine (charter), Alpha Epsilon Iota, Alpha Sigma Lambda. Home: 3464 Golfview Dr Hazel Crest IL 60429 Office: 10522 S Cicero Ave Oak Lawn IL 60453

MILLER, CLAIRE GLASS, media producer; b. N.Y.C., Apr. 29; d. Morris and Dorothy (Aborn) Glassburg; B.A., Hunter Coll., 1937; M.A., Columbia U., 1939; m. Seymour W. Miller, Dec. 25, 1951; children—John Stevenson, Thomas Jeremy. Instr., pub. relations mgr. Hunter Coll., N.Y.C., 1937-42; mag. editor, promotion and pub. relations dir. Hillman periodicals, Parents' Enterprises, N.Y.C., 1942-60; co-founder Miller-Brody Prodns., Inc., N.Y.C., exec. v.p.; pres. Newbery Award Records, Inc. div. Miller-Brody Prodns., 1964-79; del. Conn. Gov.'s Conf. on Library and Info. Services, 1978, alt. del. White House Conf., 1979. Trustee, Town Hall Found., Central Synagogue; bd. overseers N.Y. Sch., Hebrew Union Coll.-Jewish Inst. Religion. Named to Hall of Fame, Hunter Coll. Mem. Assn. Library Service to Children (legis com.), ALA, Hunter Coll. Alumni Assn. (dir.), Phi Beta Kappa. Author: What Boys Want to Know about Girls, 1962.

MILLER, DEANE GUYNES, beauty, cosmetic co. exec.; b. El Paso, Tex., Jan. 12, 1927; d. James Tillman and Margaret Anne (Brady) G.; student U. Tex., El Paso, 1944-47, Austin, 1951; m. Richard G. Miller, Apr. 12, 1947; children—Jay Michael, Marcia Deane. Pres., owner The Velvet Door, Inc., El Paso, 1967—; pres., owner Merle Norman Cosmetic Studios, El Paso, 1975—; dir., Mountain Bell Tel. Co. Bd. dirs. El Paso Mus. Art, El Paso Internat. Airport, Fgn. Trade Zone, Pan Am. Roundtable; pres. YWCA, 1958-59; v.p. Sun Carnival Assn., 1965-66. Republican. Episcopalian. Club: Junior League of El Paso. Address: 1 Silent Crest El Paso TX 79902

MILLER, DEBORAH, assn. exec.; b. Chgo., Mar. 3, 1938; d. Maurice and Anabel (Goldberg) Kabb; B.A. in English, U. Ill., 1975; m. Robert A. Miller, Dec. 26, 1957; children—Andrew, Tracy. Bd. dirs., pres. North Suburban Library System, Wheeling, Ill., 1974-80; bd. dirs. Schaumburg Twp. (Ill.) Public Library, 1971—; dir. govt. services Ill. Library Assn., Chgo., 1980—. Mem. ALA, Am. Library Trustees Assn. (chmn. legis. com. 1979—), Ill. Library Assn. (treas. 1977, chmn. Legis.-Library devel. com. 1978-80), Ill. Library Trustees Assn. (pres. elect 1980). Home and office: 840 Rosedale Ln Hoffman Estates IL 60195

MILLER, DIANA HORTON, banker; b. Southampton, N.Y., June 3, 1948; d. William Chester and Audrey Avery Horton; A.B. with honors, Palmer Coll., 1970; B.S., U. S.C., 1982; grad. S.C. Bankers Sch., S.C. Supervisory Sch.; m. Jerome Miller, Dec. 23, 1966. Sec., acctg. dept. Army and Air Force Exchange Service, Columbia, S.C., 1968-72; adminstrv. asst., vice-chmn. C & S Bank, Columbia, 1972-75, methods analyst, 1975-77, asst. ops. officer, 1977-81, ops. officer, 1981-82, compliance officer, 1982—. Mem. S.C. Bankers Assn. (mem. edn. com., exec. com.), Nat. Assn. Bank Women (chmn. arrangements com., chmn. edn. and tng. com., chmn. state conf. 1982), Am. Inst. Banking (instr., edn. com., dir.), Aiken County Dog Fanciers Assn. Methodist. Club: Civitan. Home: 122 Pebble Brook Dr West Columbia SC 29169 Office: PO Box 727 Columbia SC 29222

MILLER, DORIS PARSONS, artist; b. Bangor, Pa., Aug. 6, 1927; d. Alfred H. and Evelyn May P.; student Baum Sch. Art, Allentown, Pa., 1955-58; pvt. studies in art; m. Lewis E. Miller, June 10, 1946; 1 son, Alex Lewis. Portrait artist, 1955-63; pvt. studio artist, Wyomissing, Pa., 1977—; works represented in pvt. and permanent collections in U.S.; one-woman shows include: Nat. Bank of Boyertown, Jacksonwald, Reading, Pa., 1981; group shows: Berks Art Alliance, 1978-80, Nat. Portrait Seminar, N.Y.C., 1979, Catherine Lorillard Wolfe Art Club, N.Y.C., 1980. Sec. women's com. Reading Symphony Orch., 1972-77. Mem. Berks Art Alliance, Berks Art Council (1st prize 1980), Portrait Club Am., Catherine Lorillard Wolfe Art Club (asso.), DAR (Nat. award of excellence 1982), Daus. Am. Colonists (chpt. librarian 1982—). Episcopalian. Home: 19 Birchwood Rd Wyomissing PA 19610

MILLER, DOROTHY, banker; b. Mineola, N.Y., Apr. 15, 1928; d. James and Grace (Backer) M.; basic cert. Am. Inst. Banking, 1976, standard cert., 1976. Asst. mgr. Nat. Bank of N.Am., East Hills, N.Y., 1959-68, mgr., 1968—, asst. v.p., 1973—. Treas. Nassau council Girl Scouts U.S.A., Garden City, N.Y., 1974-75. Mem. Am. Inst. Banking (pres. 1981-82), Nat. Assn. Bank Women (chmn. L.I.-Nassau group 1979-80). Office: 1 Old Westbury Rd East Hills NY 11577

MILLER, DOROTHY ANNE SMITH, geneticist; b. N.Y.C., Oct. 20, 1931; d. John Philip and Anna Elizabeth (Hellberg) Smith; B.A., Wilson Coll., 1952; Ph.D., Yale U., 1957; m. Orlando J. Miller, July 10, 1954; children—Richard L., Cynthia K., Karen A. Research asst. ob-gyn Columbia Univ., N.Y.C., 1963-71, research asso., 1971-74, asst. prof., 1974-81, sr. research asso. dept. human genetics and devel., 1981—. Mem. Am. Soc. Human Genetics, Genetics Soc. Am., Sigma Xi. Presbyterian. Contbr. articles to sci. jours. Home: 145 Pinewood Pl Teaneck NJ 07666 Office: 701 W 168th St New York NY 10032

MILLER, DOROTHY BARBARA, nurse; b. Mascoutah, Ill., Mar. 22, 1927; d. Earl Arthur and Mabel (Gustman) Roehrig; Asso. Sci., Belleville Area Coll., 1969, postgrad., 1970-71; m. Rowland W. Miller, Nov. 23, 1947 (dec. May 1978); children—Barbara Ann, Mary Lynne. Nurses aide Meml. Convalesent Center, Belleville, Ill., 1966-69, registered nurse supr., 1969-73; asst. dir. nurses Castle Haven Nursing Center, Belleville, 1973—, health service supr., 1973—, dir. nurses, 1979; coordinator inter-facility quality assurance Mgmt. Alts. Corp., 1979-81; staff nurse Meml. Hosp. Belleville, 1981; dir. nurses Notre Dame Hills Convalescent Center, Belleville, 1981—. Cert. geriatric nurse, rehab. nurse. Mem. Assn. Rehab. Nurses, Am. Nurses Assn. (council nursing home nurses), Ill. Nurses Assn., Nat. League Nurses, Mid Am. Congress on Aging, Am. Legion Aux. Clubs: Grange, Fraternal Order Patrons of Husbandry. Home: 407 W Oak St Mascoutah IL 62258

MILLER, ELEANOR CARROLL, broadcasting co. exec.; b. Asheboro, N.C., June 7, 1949; d. Garnet Edward and Willie Berte (Upchurch) M.; B.A., Duke U., 1971; postgrad. Université de Bordeaux, 1972-73. Translator, Algerian Embassy, Washington, 1973-74; public affairs projects coordinator Corp. for Public Broadcasting, 1974-76, asst. to publs. mgr., 1976-78, publs. mgr., 1981—; editor Public Telecommunications Letter, Nat. Assn. Ednl. Broadcasters, 1978-79, Public Telecommunications Review, 1980-81. Mem. Am. Women in Radio and TV, Women in Communications, Broadcast Promotion Assn., Phi Beta Kappa. Club: Nat. Press. Office: Corp for Public Broadcasting 1111 16th St NW Washington DC 20036

MILLER, ELIZABETH CAVERT, oncologist, educator; b. Mpls., May 2, 1920; B.S., U. Minn., 1941; M.S., U. Wis., 1943, Ph.D. in Biochemistry, 1945. Finney-Howell Found. med. research fellow in oncology Med. Center, U. Wis., Madison, 1945-47, instr. to asso. prof., 1947-69, prof. oncology, 1969-80, WARF prof., 1980—. Co-recipient Teplitz-Langer award Ann Langer Cancer Research Found., 1963, Lucy Wortham James award James Ewing Soc., 1965, Papanicolaou Research award Papanicolaou Cancer Research Inst., 1975, Lewis S. Rosenstiel award Brandeis U., 1976, nat. award basic sci. Am. Cancer Soc., 1977; Bertner award in cancer research M.D. Anderson Hosp. and Tumor Inst., 1971, Wis. Nat. Div. award Am. Cancer Soc., 1973, Founders award Chem. Industry Inst. Toxicology, 1978, Bristol-Myers award Cancer Research, 1978, internat. ann. award Gairdner Found., 1978, Griffuel prize, 1978, Lewis and Bert Freedman award in biochemistry N.Y. Acad. Sci., 1979, Mott award Gen. Motors Found., 1980. Mem. Nat. Acad. Sci., Am. Soc. Biol. Chemists, Am. Assn. Cancer Research. Researcher exptl. chem. carcinogenesis. Office: McArdle Lab University of Wisconsin 450 N Randall Ave Madison WI 53706

MILLER, ELIZABETH LOUISE, hypnotist, bus. cons.; b. Chattanooga, May 12, 1930; d. Cecil C. and Carolyn Windom (Mayton) Noecker; student Mich. State U., 1948; grad. Williams Inst. Hypnological Sci. and Research, 1969; m. Robert Andrew Miller, July 1949 (dec.); 1 dau., Pamela Kay Miller Painschab. Owner, operator Mondoric Theatre (Wis.), 1949-69; woman's editor Eau Claire (Wis.) Leader, 1965-66, La Crosse (Wis.) Tribune, 1966-69; exec. editor Skyway News, Mpls., 1970-71; promotional mgr. Barberio Corp., Mpls., 1972-73; assoc. Culler & Assos., Mpls., 1975—; pres. Hypnotism Inst. Inc., Onalaska, Wis., 1974—, Mpls., 1978—; tchr., lectr., cons. in field. Active Republican Party. Recipient Showmanship citation Allied Theatre Owners, 1964, citation Biafran Govt., 1967, award USAF, 1967. Mem. Assn. Advancement Ethical Hypnosis, Bus. and Profl. Women, Wis. Regional Writers Assn. Methodist. Author: Just People of the Friendly Valley, 1965; I Am the Mississippi, 1975. Home: 9101 Cedar Ave S Penthouse 405 Minneapolis MN 55420

MILLER, ELSIE THOMAS, home economist; b. Headland, Ala., Mar. 6, 1942; d. M. Howard and Fannie (Harrell) Thomas; B.S. with honors, Fla. State U., 1975, M.S., 1976; m. Roger Wilson Miller, July 22, 1960; children—Derek, Chad. Teaching asst. home econs. Fla. State U., 1975-76; home econs. agt. Fla. Coop. Extension Service, 1976-79; nutrition/edn. cons. Dept. Edn., State of Fla., Tallahassee, 1979—. Recipient Etta Joe award, Fla. State U., 1974, Singer Industry award, 1979. Mem. Am. Home Econs. Assn., Fla. Home Econs. Assn. (dist. chmn. 1980-81, state public relations chmn. 1980-82), Fla. Extension Assn. Home Econs. Agts. (Florence Hall award 1979), Phi Delta Kappa, Omicron Nu (chpt. pres. 1975-77, nat. conclave del. 1976-78, nat. sec. 1978-80, nat. v.p. 1980-82), Phi Kappa Phi. Democrat. Baptist. Home: 394 Ridgeland Ct Tallahassee FL 32312

MILLER, ESTELLE BINN, psychotherapist; b. Bklyn., May 27, 1936; d. Murray and Rose (Fels) Binn; B.A., Bklyn. Coll., 1958; M.S.W., Yeshiva U., 1970; grad. Inst. Mental Health Edn., Englewood, N.J., 1980; postgrad. Union Coll., Cin.; m. David Miller, May 19, 1957; children—Mitchell Paul, Lauren, Malaine. Social investigator N.Y.C. Dept. Welfare, 1958; social worker N.J. Div. Youth and Family Services, Hackensack, 1965-68; psychotherapist, Teaneck, N.J., 1972—; founder Am. Anorexia Nervosa Assn., Inc., Teaneck, 1978, exec. dir., 1980—. Mem. Nat. Assn. Social Workers (cert.), Acad. Cert. Social Workers. Home: 1477 Jefferson St Teaneck NJ 07666 Office: 133 Cedar Ln Teaneck NJ 07666

MILLER, EVELYN LOUISE, banker; b. Conception Junction, Mo.; d. Charles E. and Lucy Jane (Stackhouse) Martin; B.A., Tarkio Coll., 1941; m. John R. DeVore, Apr. 22, 1943; 1 son, Ted R.; m. Robert M. Miller, Nov. 22, 1956. Head commerce dept. Watson (Mo.) High Sch., 1945-51; editor Watson Ind., 1951-52; exec. sec. S. Riekes & Sons, Omaha, 1952-54; editor Bellevue (Nebr.) Press, 1954-55; with Peoples State Bank, Ellinwood, Kans., 1955—, v.p., cashier, 1976-80, sr. v.p., cashier, 1980—, sec. bd., 1955—, dir., 1981—. Chmn., Centennial Com., 1972; co-chmn. Bicentennial Com., 1976; bd. mem. Salvation Army, 1956—; pres. Library Bd., 1979—. Recipient Disting. Servant award Ellinwood Rotary Internat., 1979. Mem. Bank Adminstrn. Inst. (pres. Golden Belt chpt.), Am. Inst. Banking, Nat. Assn. Bank Women, Kans. Bankers Assn. Republican. Methodist. Clubs: Modern Literature (pres. 1971, 75, 82); Great Bend Petroleum. Home: 200 W 5th St Ellinwood KS 67526 Office: 13 N Main St Ellinwood KS 67526

MILLER, GLORIA M., county govt. ofcl.; b. Mercer County, Pa., Oct. 24, 1940; d. Cecil F. and Edith H. (Bittler) Gill; B.S. in Bus. Adminstrn., Youngstown (Ohio) State U., 1966; divorced; 1 son, Mark William. Sr. acct. Mort-Bohn Assos., C.P.A.s, Sharon, Pa., 1963-67; asst. controller Hynes Steel Products Co., Youngstown, 1967-70; exec. dir. Crawford County Community Action Agy., Meadville, Pa., 1970-73; planning and devel. dir. Multi-County Human Resources Corp., Meadville, 1973-76; adminstr., chief exec. officer Mercer County Consortium Services, Inc., Clark, Pa., 1976—; bd. dirs., regional rep. Nat. Assn. County Employment and Tng. Adminstrn., 1978-81; bd. dirs., sec. Mercer County Area Agy. Aging, 1976-82; v.p. Mid-Atlantic Manpower Profl. Assn., 1979-80; gen. adv. com. Mercer County Area Vocat. Tech. Sch., Mercer, 1979-82, Venango County Area Vocat. Tech. Sch., Oil City, Pa., 1981-82. Recipient various certs. appreciation. Mem. Am. Mgmt. Assn., Am. Soc. Tng. and Devel. Democrat. Presbyterian. Home: PO Box 171 12 N Main St Greenville PA 16125 Office: PO Box 462 3665 Valley View Rd Clark PA 16113

MILLER, HELEN CARTER, zoologist, educator; b. Indpls., Dec. 7, 1925; d. George William and Lucy (Niehoff) Carter; A.B., Butler U., 1948; M.S., Cornell U., 1952; Ph.D., 1961; m. Rudolph J. Miller, Mar. 2, 1957; children—Mark Carter, Michel James, Leslie Ann. Tchr., high sch., Indpls., 1947-50; instr. Okla. State U., Stillwater, part-time 1963-74, asst. prof., 1974-79, asso. prof. zoology, 1979—. Pres., bd. dirs. Payne County Audubon Soc. Recipient Outstanding Tchr. award Okla. State U., 1979. Research in ecology Okla. birds, sunfish behavior. Home: 2616 Black Oak Dr Stillwater OK 74074 Office: Dept Zoology Okla State U Stillwater OK 74074

MILLER, HELEN MARIE DILLEN (MRS. J. CARTER MILLER), bus. exec.; b. Sedalia, Mo.; d. John Barney and Lulu (Blume) Dillen; student Central Coll., 1936-37; m. J. Carter Miller, Dec. 3, 1941; 1 son, J. Carter. Sec.-treas. Midwest Supply Co., Lansing, Ill., 1946—, Midwest Supply Co. of Can., 1946—; sec.-treas. Carter Controls, Inc., Lansing, also Livonia, Mich., 1952—, v.p., 1956—; v.p. Carter Controls Internat., Windsor, Can., Antwerp, Belgium, 1960—; sec.-treas. Carter Controls U.K. Ltd., Sheffield, Eng., Carter Controls, GmbH, Busingen, Germany, Carter Controls., A.G., Schaffhausen, Switzerland. Social worker ARC, Hammond, Ind., 1942-44. Mem. Principia Patrons No. Ind. (pres. 1963-65), Chgo. Symphony, Sarah Siddons Soc., Chgo. Art Inst. Christian Scientist. Clubs: Principia Mothers (dir. Chgo. 1962-64); Fortnightly, Woman's Athletic (Chgo.); Woodmar Country (Hammond); Everglades (Palm Beach, Fla.). Home: 1731 Wilson Ave Munster IN 46321 also Ibis Isle Rd Palm Beach FL Office: 2800 Bernice Rd Lansing IL 60438

MILLER, JACQUELINE WINSLOW, library dir.; b. N.Y.C., Apr. 15, 1935; d. Lynward Roosevelt and Sarah Ellen (Grevious) Winslow; B.A. in English, Morgan State Coll., 1957; M.L.S., Pratt Inst., N.Y.C., 1960; m. Percy St. Clair Miller, June 29, 1968; 1 son, Percy Scott. Young teen librarian trainee Bklyn. Public Library, 1957-59, reading improvement instr., 1959-60, young teen specialist, 1960-63, br. librarian, 1963-64; dir. young teen services, 1964-68; head extension services New Rochelle (N.Y.) Public Library, 1969-70; br. adminstr. Yonkers (N.Y.) Public Library, 1970-75, dir. library, 1975—; mem. Commr.'s Com. on State-Wide Library Devel., 1980; resource person N.Y. State task force on fed. depository library service, 1982. Mem. Colonial Heights Assn. Taxpayers, Yonkers Employment Service for Srs., Inc.; mem. adv. com. Work Opportunity Referrals for Kids; mem. Westchester adv. council Pratt Inst., pres., 1978-81; mem. budget crisis subcom. METRO, 1976; mem. adv. bd. Sta. WEBS, 1980—; mem. Westchester Ednl. Brokering Service, Citizens Library Council N.Y. State. Honored Citizen of Yonkers, Ch. of Our Saviour, 1980; recipient Ann. award Westchester County club Nat. Assn. Negro Bus. and Profl. Women's Clubs, 1981; Community Service award Women's Civic Club of Nepperhan, 1982. Mem. ALA (chpt. pubs. relations com. 1969-70; dir. public library assn. div. 1976-80, div. nominating com. 1980-81, div. planning com. 1980-82), N.Y. Library Assn. (2d v.p. 1980—, dir. 1967-68, scholarship and grants com. 1982-84, legis. com. 1978), Public Library Dirs. Assn. (exec. bd. 1976-80), Westchester Library Assn. (v.p. 1978, pres. 1979), N.Y. Library Club (council 1969-70, chmn. publicity com. 1977-78, council 1979-82). Home: 219 Grandview Blvd Yonkers NY 10710 Office: 7 Main St Yonkers NY 10701

MILLER, JANEL HOWELL, psychologist; b. Boone, N.C., May 18, 1947; d. John Estle and Grace Louise (Hemberger) Howell; B.A., DePauw U., 1969; postgrad. Rice U., 1969; M.A., U. Houston, 1972; Ph.D., Tex. A&M U., 1979; m. C. Rick Miller, Nov. 24, 1968; children—Kimberly, Brian, Audrey, Rachel. Asso. sch. psychologist Houston Ind. Sch. Dist., 1971-74; research psychologist VA Hosp., Houston, 1972; asso. sch. psychologist Clear Creek Ind. Sch. Dist., Tex., 1974-76; instr. psychology, counseling psychology intern Tex. A. and M. U., 1976-77; clin. psychology intern VA Hosp., Houston, 1977-78; coordinator psychol. services Clear Creek Ind. Sch. Dist., 1978-81, assoc. dir. psychol. services, 1981-82; pvt. practice, Houston, 1982—; cons. in field. DePauw U. Alumni scholar, 1965-69; NIMH fellow U. Houston, 1970-71; lic. psychologist, sch. psychologist; lic. social psychotherapist, Tex. Mem. Am. Psychol. Assn., Tex. Psychol. Assn., Houston Psychol. Assn., Am. Assn. Marriage and Family Therapists, Tex. Assn. Marriage and Family Therapists, Houston Assn. Marriage and Family Therapists, Tex. Psychotherapy Assn., Tex. Sch. Psychol. Affiliates, Houston Behavior Therapy Assn. Home: 806 Walbrook Dr Houston TX 77062 Office: Southpoint Psychol Services 11550 Fugua St Suite 450 Houston TX 77034

MILLER, JANICE MARGARET, research veterinarian; b. McPherson, Kans., Nov. 11, 1938; d. Charles Harris and Margaret Irene (Tolle) Lilly; B.S., Kans. State U., 1960, D.V.M., 1962, M.S., 1963; Ph.D., U. Wis., 1969; m. Lyle Devon Miller, Apr. 18, 1962; children—Donald Devon, Brenda Joanne. Research asso. M.I.T., Cambridge, Mass., 1964-65; postdoctoral fellow U. Wis., Madison, 1969-72; vet. med. officer U.S. Dept. Agr. Nat. Animal Disease Center, Ames, Iowa, 1972—. Recipient Spl. fellowship, Leukemia Soc. Am., 1970; named Woman Veterinarian of Yr. Women's Vet. Med. Assn., 1977. Mem. AVMA, Nat. Assn. Fed. Veterinarians, Am. Coll. Vet. Pathologists, Conf. Research Workers Animal Disease, U.S. Animal Health Assn. Methodist. Contbr. articles to sci. jours. Home: 2803 Northwood Dr Ames IA 50010 Office: National Animal Disease Center Box 70 Ames IA 50010

MILLER, JEANNE-MARIE ANDERSON (MRS. NATHAN JOHN MILLER), educator; b. Washington, Feb. 18, 1937; d. William and Agnes Catherine (Johns) Anderson; B.A., Howard U., 1959, M.A., 1963, Ph.D., 1976; m. Nathan John Miller, Oct. 2, 1960. Instr. dept. English Howard U., Washington, 1963-76, also asst. dir. Inst. for Arts and Humanities, 1973-75, asst. prof. English, 1976-79, asso. prof., 1979—, asst. to v.p. acad. affairs, 1976—, grad. asst. prof., 1977-79, grad. asso. prof., 1979—; cons. Am. Studies Assn., 1972-75; cons. several ednl. book pub. cos. Mem. Washington Performing Arts Soc., 1971—, Friends of WETA-TV, 1971—, Mus. African Art, 1971—, Arena Stage Assos., 1972—; chmn. theatre and poetry com. D.C. Public Library for Arts, 1976-79. Ford Found. fellow, 1970-72, So. Fellowships Fund fellow, 1972-74; Am. Council Learned Socs. grantee, 1978-79; Nat. Endowment for Humanities grantee, 1981-84. Mem. Nat. Council Tchrs. of English, Coll. English Assn., Am. Studies Assn., Am. Theatre Assn. (editor Black Theatre Bull. 1977—), AAUP, AAUW, LWV, ACLU, Am. Acad. Polit. and Social Sci., Nat. Assn. Women Deans, Adminstrs. and Counselors, Coll. Lang. Assn., MLA, Nat. Assn. Advancement Humanities, Am. Assn. Higher Edn., Asso. Writers Guild Am., Friends Kennedy Center for Performing Arts. Democrat. Episcopalian. Contbr. articles to profl. jours. Home: 1100 6th St SW Washington DC 20024

MILLER, JO ANN, educator; b. Reed, Okla., Aug. 24, 1935; d. Claude Edgar and Dicy Mae (Sanders) Pruitt; B.S., Easter N. Mex. U., 1972; postgrad. Hardon Simmons U., 1979-81; m. Alford James Miller, May 15, 1953; children—Abe Eddie, Dovie Mae, Mary Jo, Danny James, Darla Sue. Tchr. grade sch., 1972-76; tchr. remedial reading, Maple, Tex., 1977; spl. edn. tchr. Old Glory (Tex.) Elem. Sch., 1978, Hawley, Tex., 1978—. Mem. Tex. State Tchrs. Assn., Nat. Edn. Assn. Democrat. Baptist. Club: Garden. Home: Box 465 Hawley TX 79525

MILLER, JOAN MARY, educator; b. Braddock, Pa., Sept. 10, 1941; d. Roy William and Hedwig J. (Sakowicz) Miller; B.A. in Math. and Philosophy (Coll. scholar), Carlow Coll., 1963; Ph.L. cum laude, Institut Catholique de Paris, 1967; Graduate in Religious Studies, U. Louvain (Belgium), 1969, postgrad. in philosophy, 1968-70, 73-78; intern developmental psychology École Pratique des Hautes Études, Paris, 1969-70. Tchr. math. St. Elizabeth High Sch., Pitts., 1962-64, Pensionnat des Ursulines, Tildonk, Belgium, 1968-70; asso. prof. philosophy Villa Maria Coll., Erie, Pa., 1970-73, 78—, coordinator freshman year studies program, 1972-73; translator Center for Socio-Religious Research, Louvain, 1973-77; translator, mem. research team Prospective, Internat. Center for Research and Communication, Brussels, 1974-78; lectr. European div., U. Md., 1975. Mem. AAUP, Am. Cath. Philos. Assn. (sec.-treas. N.W. N.Y. region 1971-73), Am. Humanist Assn., Am. Philos. Assn., Am. Translators Assn., Internat. Phenomenological Soc., Soc. for Philosophy and Psychology, Soc. Women in Philosophy, LWV. Author: French Structuralism: A Multidisciplinary Bibliography, 1981; contbg. author New Cath. Ency. Home: 1418 Pearce Park Apt 5 Erie PA 16502 Office: Dept Humanities Villa Maria Coll 2551 W Lake Rd Erie PA 16505

MILLER, JOELLEN, edn. counselor; b. Buffalo, July 6, 1942; d. Edward Charles and Audrey Isobel (Bowes) Schwartz; B.A. in Sociology/Social Work, Grove City Coll., 1964; M.A. in Guidance and Counseling, No. Mich. U., 1975; m. William Wallace Miller, III, Dec. 22, 1962; children—William David, James Andrew, Mark Edward, John Michael. Staff counselor, office supr. Cradle Beach Camp, Angola, N.Y., 1960-62; peer group counselor, leader No. Mich. U. Women's Center, Marquette, 1975-77; mil. and dependent counselor, social actions office K.I. Sawyer AFB, Mich., 1976; coordinator Universal Coll. Program at McClellan AFB for Azusa Pacific Coll., 1977-80; registrar Embry-Riddle Aero. U., Sacramento, 1980, univ. dir., 1980—; spl. program adv. Chapman Coll., Sacramento, 1980—. Tchr., Sunday Sch., Air Force Chapel, 1973-77, Winding Way Community Ch., 1978-80; office asst. Air Force Family Services, 1967-77, coordinator, 1970; pharmacy asst.

ARC, 1969-71, blood bank worker, 1973; den mother Cub Scouts Am., 1973-76, awards chmn., 1976-77; active Elem. and Middle Sch. Ednl. Goals Com., 1975, Elem. Sch. Library Aid, 1975-77; mem. Bell Choir, Christ Community Ch., 1980—. Named Family Services Vol. of Yr., K.I. Sawyer AFB, 1969, Outstanding Young Woman Am., 1970, 76. Mem. Am. Personnel and Guidance Assn., Phi Kappa Phi. Clubs: Air Force Officer's Wives (mem. mag. staff 1970, 75, mem. bd. 1972-73, sec. 1973-74), Mather AFB Officers Wives; Mather AFB Protestant Women of Chapel (2d v.p., program chmn. 1977—). Author: (with Linda Teeple) Expanding With Christ, 1976. Home: 6984 Ellsworth Circle Fair Oaks CA 95628 Office: Embry-Riddle Aero U Ednl Services Bldg 2015 2852 ABG/DPE McClellan Air Force Base CA 95652

MILLER, JOYCE DANNEN, labor union ofcl.; b. Chgo., June 19, 1928; d. Reuben L. and Lillian (Rosenson) Dannen; B.Ph., U. Chgo., 1950, M.A., 1951; children—Joshua, Adam, Rebecca. With Amalgamated Clothing Workers Am., 1962—, adminstr. asst., dir. social services, 1966-72, edn. dir., 1962-66, exec. asst. to gen. officers and dir. social services, 1972—; v.p., dir. social services Amalgamated Clothing and Textile Workers Union, AFL-CIO, N.Y.C., 1976—; nat. pres. Coalition of Labor Union Women, 1977—; exec. dir. Sidney Hillman Found. Mem. U.S. Metric Bd.; trustee German Marshall Fund of U.S., George Meany Center for Labor Studies, Amalgamated Social Benefits Assn., Amalgated Chgo. Group Employees Pension Plan; mem. Nat. Commn. on Working Women, U.S. Nat. Women's Com., AFL-CIO Standing Com. on Civil Rights; mem. exec. bd. Girls Clubs Am.; mem. N.Y. State Manpower Services Council, N.Y. State Internat. Women's Year Com.; mem. exec. bd. Am. Fedn. for Blind; mem. adv. com. Com. for a Nat. Health Service; mem. exec. bd. Jewish Labor Com., Nat. Trade Union Council for Human Rights, Nat. Commn. on Social Security, President's Export Council. Mem. ACLU, Adult Edn. Assn., Indsl. Relations Research Assn., Internat. Press Assn., NAACP, Nat. Council on Aging, Nat. Women's Polit. Caucus, NOW. Office: 15 Union Sq New York NY 10003 *

MILLER, JUDITH ANN SHRUM, ch. adminstr.; b. Chgo., Sept. 8, 1941; d. Frank George and Kathryn Marie (Stocklin) Bell; student Ind. Central Coll., 1960-61, DePauw U., 1963-64; m. William L. Miller, Jr., Nov. 28, 1976; children by previous marriage—Steven William Shrum, Vickie Lynn White, Lisa Ann Shrum, Mark Allen Shrum, Brian David Shrum. Asst. treas. Missions Bldg. Fed. Credit Union, Christian Ch. (Disciples of Christ), Indpls., 1970-72, asst. treas. Bd. Higher Edn., 1972-73, treas., asst. sec. corp., 1973-77, exec. dir. ednl. personnel Bd. Higher Edn., St. Louis, 1973-77, chmn. outreach workshop Capital area, 1979—; adminstrv. asst. Nat. City Christian Ch. (Disciples of Christ), Washington, 1977—, Interfaith Forum on Religion, Art and Architecture, Washington, 1979—; mem. steering com. Project on Aging, Washington, 1979—; mem. exec. com. Emmaus Fellowship Project on Aging, 1979—; county council rep. Fairfax County Schs., 1979—; youth sponsor Nat. City Christian Ch., 1979—. Mem. citizens adv. council Parkway Sch. Dist., St. Louis, 1976-77; mem. exec. com., vol. chmn. St. Louis Children's Home, 1976-78. Mem. P.E.O. Sisterhood. Democrat. Asst. editor Nat. City Christian, 1977; mng. editor Faith and Form, 1979—. Home: 8623 Langport Dr Springfield VA 22152 Office: 1777 Church St NW Washington DC 20036

MILLER, JUDITH KAY, floor covering co. exec.; b. Flint, Mich., Jan. 21, 1939; d. William Samual and Amelia Jenny (Videan) Thorp; student Flint Jr. Coll., 1956-57; m. Louis Jerome Grobe, Aug. 11, 1957; m. 2d, Walter Ralph Miller, Aug. 13, 1977; stepchildren—Sharon Miller Rakoczy, Walter Elliott Miller, Katherine Miller Eschenbach, Dawn Miller. Bookkeeper, Genesee Radio, Buffalo, 1973; office mgr. Del. Audio Visual, Inc., Buffalo, 1973-76, Fireplace Distbg., Inc., Buffalo, 1976-79; gen. mgr. Miller Floor Covering, Tonawanda, N.Y., 1979—. Former bd. dirs. YWCA; formerly active Girl Scouts U.S.A., Big Sisters Am.; treas. North Tonawanda mayor's election campaign, 1979. Mem. Am. Bridge League, Chords, Wives of Ismailia Shrine Chanters, Daus. of Nile (Athor Temple 19), Tonawanda Council on Arts. Republican. Lutheran. Home: 849 Park Ave North Tonawanda NY 14120 Office: 8 Longs Ave Tonawanda NY 14150

MILLER, JUDITH SKLAR, psychologist; b. Phila., June 18, 1942; d. Henry Ross Sklar and Dorothy G. Kort; B.S. in Edn., Temple U., 1964, M.Ed. in Counseling Psychology, 1974, Ph.D. in Counseling Psychology, 1979; m. L. Martin Miller, Jan. 21, 1962; children—Philip Roger, Marjorie Lynn. Tchr., Kinsey Elem. Sch., Phila., 1964-67; counselor Holmesburg Prison, Phila., 1972-73; therapist, supr. Horizon House, Phila., 1973-78; asso. dir. community counseling clinic Temple U., Phila., 1978-79, teaching asso., 1978-79, adj. asst. prof. dept. counseling psychology, 1980—; tng. project dir. Matrix Research Inst., Phila., 1980; pvt. practice therapy, Haverford, Pa., 1980—; bd. dirs. Transitional Rehab. Ind. Services, Stratford, N.J.; cons. Vol. guide Phila. Mus. Art, 1970-74. Recipient cert. of appreciation Phila. Prisons, 1975; cert. in family therapy Phila. Child Guidance Clinic and Office of Mental Health; lic. psychologist, Pa.; cert. rehab. counselor, Pa. Mem. Am. Psychol. Assn., Am. Rehab. Counseling Assn., Internat. Assn. Psycho-Social Rehab. Services, Pa. Psychol. Assn., Phila. Soc. Clin. Psychologists Internat. Assn. for Near-Death Studies. Contbr. to profl. publs. Home: 204 Dove Ln Haverford PA 19041

MILLER, JUDY ANN FRANCES, county ofcl.; b. Cleve., Sept. 16, 1940; d. Frank Albert Jagoda and Antoinette (Serba) Parise; B.S. in Public Adminstrn., U. Ariz., 1963. Supr. social services dept. Contra Costa County, Calif., 1969-72, dir. allied services/projects adminstrn., 1972-76, dir. community services adminstrn., 1976-77, dir. dept. manpower programs, 1977—. Mem. exec. com. Combined Assn. Prime Sponsor Adminstrs. Recipient for services integration Nat. Assn. Counties, 1974; award for job placements Dept. Labor, 1978. Mem. Am. Mgmt. Assn., Am. Soc. Public Adminstrs., Nat. Assn. Employment and Tng. Adminstrs. (v.p. 1980-81), Phi Chi Theta. Roman Catholic. Home: PO Box 623 Pinole CA 94564 Office: 2425 Bisso Ln Suite 100 Concord CA 94520

MILLER, KAREN BAREDZIAK, chem. co. exec.; b. Chgo., Feb. 12, 1951; d. Joseph Henry and Alice Ann (Tatosian) Baredziak; B.A., Ill. State U., 1973; m. Craig Stephen Miller, Nov. 24, 1973. With Velsicol Chem. Corp., Chgo., 1973—, internat. acctg. clk., 1973-76, asst. credit mgr., 1976-78, corp. credit mgr., 1978—, vice-chmn. Agri Export Credit Group, 1981—. Mem. VFW Aux. (treas.), Nat. Assn. Credit Mgrs., Nat. Chem. Credit Assn. (div. sec.-treas. 1982-83), Internat. Credit Execs., Fgn. Credit Interchange Bur., Agri Export Credit Group. Office: 341 E Ohio St Chicago IL 60611

MILLER, KATHRYN PAIGE, software co. ofcl.; b. Clifton Forge, Va., Feb. 1, 1952; d. Everett Lynn and Kathryn (Smith) M.; B.A., Marshall U., 1974; M.S. in Journalism, W.Va. U., 1976; m. Steven P. Gulkus, Sept. 4, 1976. Research asso. Research and Tng. Center, W.Va. U., 1974-76; devel. asst. Grad. Hosp., Phila., 1976-78; dir. devel. Friends Select Sch., Phila., 1978; product mgr. SEI Corp., Valley Forge, Pa., 1978—. Mem. Kappa Tau Alpha.

MILLER, LAVERNE GERTRUDE, nurse; b. Monroe, Wis., May 4, 1922; d. Frederick Helmuth and Ida Marie (Brand) Flueckiger; R.N., Presbyn.-St. Luke's Hosp., Chgo., 1966; B.S. in Health Arts, Coll. St. Francis, postgrad. in health service adminstrn.; m. Edward J. Miller, Jr., Nov. 16, 1946; 1 son, Gary E. Charge nurse surg. unit Presbyn.-St. Luke's Hosp., 1966-69; head nurse supr. Oak Park (Ill.) Hosp., 1969-77; nurse West Suburban Hosp. Recipient Presbyn.-St. Luke's Med. Staff award for outstanding patient care, citizenship and scholastic achievement. Fellow Am. Biog. Inst. (life); mem. Nat. League Nursing, Am. Assn. Critical Care Nurses, Chgo. Council Cath. Nurses Assn. (dir.), Am. Nurses Assn., Women's Tabernacle Guild, Oak Park Hosp. Women's Aux., Fenwick High Sch. Mother's Club (life), Swiss Benevolent Soc., Swiss Ladies Benefit Soc., Internat. Platform Assn. Republican. Roman Catholic. Home: 525 W Jackson Blvd Oak Park IL 60304

MILLER, LILLIAN RUTH, offshore oil and gas technologist, tech. writer; b. Des Moines, Dec. 5, 1948; d. Charles N. and Marjorie R. (Hammons) Miller; A.A. in Petroleum Tech., Nichols State U., Thibodaux, La., 1977. Galley hand Offshore Foods & Service Co., Houma, La., 1973-74; with Ocean Drilling & Exploration Co., New Orleans, 1974—, jr. gauger, 1975-77, gauger, 1977-79, lead gauger, 1979-82, project coordinator offshore field tng. com., 1979-82; pres. SPEC Internat., Inc., 1982—. Publicity chmn. 1st Bapt. Ch.; capt. Daniel Little, Inc.; publicity dir. Friends of Library, Thibodeux, La.; publicity coordinator Martha Sowell Utley Meml. Library and Cultural Center. Mem. Nichols State U. Alumni Assn., DAR (chmn. conservation com.), Soc. Mayflower Descs., Friends of Library, Terrebonne Writers Guild. Republican. Research on oil field history and offshore devel. Home: 1414 W Main St Houma LA 70360 Office: PO Box 956 Gray LA 70359

MILLER, LINDA LOUISE, annuity co. exec.; b. Bay City, Mich., Aug. 14, 1945; d. Victor Hugo and Dolores Juanita (Martin) Floyt; B.A. in Communication Arts, Mich. State U., 1967; m. Arthur R. Newberger, Feb. 14, 1981. Speech tchr. Southfield (Mich.) Bd. Edn., 1967-68; sales rep. Revlon, Inc., N.Y.C., 1971-76; sales rep. Security First Group, Inc., Los Angeles, 1976-77, regional sales dir., Marina Del Rey, Calif., 1977—. Recipient Glen A. Holden Mgr. of Yr. award Security First Group, 1980. Mem. Nat. Assn. Female Execs. Lutheran. Home: 18067 Karen Dr Encino CA 91316 Office: 4640 Admiralty Way Suite 219 Marina Del Rey CA 90027

MILLER, LOIS GOLDBERG, glass co. exec.; b. Salem, Mass.; d. Saul and Ruth (Chandler) Goldberg; A.A., Lasell Jr. Coll., 1955; B.A., Boston U., 1957; m. Kenneth Miller, Mar. 31, 1957; children—Robin, Laurence, James. Office clk. Salem Glass Co., 1960-70, office mgr., 1970-74, v.p., 1974-78, pres., 1978—. Mem. Salem C. of C., Mass. Glass Dealers Assn., Flat Glass Mktg. Assn. Jewish. Address: 75 Canal St PO Box 3024 Salem MA 01970

MILLER, LYNN FIELDMAN, librarian; b. Newark, Oct. 9, 1938; d. George Martin and Helen Golda (Friedman) Fieldman; B.A., Barnard Coll., 1959; M.L.S., Rutgers U., 1971, M.A., 1977; m. Arthur Harold Miller, Aug. 24, 1958; children—Jennifer Lyn, Jonathan Daniel. Asst., Mid-Century Book Soc., 1959-61; pub. asst. Stein and Day, 1961-62; reference librarian Douglass Coll. Library, New Brunswick, N.J., 1971-79; media services librarian Rutgers U., 1979—, curator Women Artists Series, 1971-79, mem. series adv. bd., 1979—. Bd. dirs. Women Helping Women, Metuchen, N.J., 1979-81. N.J. State Council Arts grantee, 1974-75, N.J. Com. for Humanities grantee, 1974-76. Mem. ALA, N.J. Library Assn. (mem. exec. bd. 1978-81), Assn. Coll. and Research Libraries (exec. bd. N.J. chpt. 1980-81, v.p./pres.-elect 1981-82, pres. 1982-83), NOW. Democrat. Jewish. Author: (with M.E. Comtois) Contemporary American Theater Critics: A Directory and Anthology of their Works, 1977; (with S. S. Swenson) Lives and Works: Talks with Women Artists, 1981; bibliog. editor Women and Literature, 1978, 79; compiler: Slide Registry of N.J. Women Artists; Guide to N.J. Women Artists. contbr. articles to theatre and library service jours. Office: Alexander Library Rm 420 Rutgers University New Brunswick NJ 08903

MILLER, LYNNE CATHY, parasitologist; b. Washington, Dec. 25, 1951; d. Albert and Lorraine Shirley (Sweet) M.; B.S. in Pharmacy, U. R.I., 1974; M.S., U. Tex., El Paso, 1977; Ph.D., N.Mex. State U., 1980. Registered pharmacist Meml. Gen. Hosp., Las Cruces, N.Mex., 1979; postdoctoral research asso. dept. entomology and plant pathology N.Mex. State U., Las Cruces, 1980-81; asst. prof. biology and allied health Bloomsburg (Pa.) State Coll., 1981—; parasitology and pub. health field worker, Mexico, El Paso, Tex. Sponsor, Creature-Feature program, 1982. Bloomsburg State Coll. faculty research grantee, 1982. Mem. AAAS, Rocky Mountain Conf. Parasitologists, Sigma Xi, Beta Beta Beta, Phi Kappa Phi. Contbr. sci. articles to profl. jours. Office: Biology and Allied Health Bloomsburg State Coll Bloomsburg PA 17815

MILLER, MABRY BATSON, educator; b. Birmingham, Ala.; d. Ezra Orestes and Mabry Ward (Arnold) Batson; B.A., Athens (Ala.) Coll., 1937; grad. North Ala. Coll. Commerce, 1958; M.B.A., Ala. A&M U., 1974; Ph.D. (Anna M. Dice fellow), Ohio State U., 1981; m. Harry Edward Miller, Oct. 10, 1937; children—Harry Edward, Mabry Miller O'Donnell. Instr. French, Athens Coll., 1938; tchr. music, high sch. choral dir., pub. schs., South Pittsburg, Tenn., 1942-43; staff asst. dept. engrng., missile div. Chrysler Corp., Huntsville, Ala., 1958-61; grad. asst. Coll. Adminstrv. Sci., Ohio State U., 1977-80; asst. prof. mgmt. Drake U., 1980—; cons., lectr., condr. workshops in field. Recipient Virginia Hammill Simms award Community Ballet Assn., Huntsville, 1971, cert. for patriotic civilian service Dept. Army, 1972; citation of merit City of Huntsville, 1972, County of Madison (Ala.), 1972. Mem. Acad. Mgmt., AAUW, Nat. Fedn. Music Clubs (life; dist. pres.), Phi Theta Kappa. Home: 1235 66th St Apt 36 Des Moines IA 50311 Office: PO Box 9A Drake U Des Moines IA 50311

MILLER, MADELINE LESLIE, nat. franchising co. exec.; b. Balt., July 30, 1944; d. Charles John and Marie Frances (Deca) Lutz; B.A. in Econs. and Acctg., Jersey City State Coll., 1975; M.B.A. in Mgmt. Sci., Rutgers U., 1978; 1 son, Adrian K. Managerial acct. Nelson Resource Corp., Secaucus, N.J., 1971-76; fin. acct. analyst Am. Standard, Inc., N.Y.C., 1976-79; planning dir. Adorence Co., Inc., N.Y.C., 1979-80; corp. controller Manow Internat. Corp., N.Y.C., 1980-81; v.p., corp. controller Lee Myles Corp., Englewood Cliffs, N.J., 1981—. Named Career Woman of Yr., Bus. and Profl. Women's Assn., 1972. C.P.A., N.J. Mem. Planning Execs. Inst., N. Am. Soc. Corp. Planning. Home: 752 County Ave Secaucus NJ 07094 Office: 325 Sylvan Ave Englewood Cliffs NJ 07632

MILLER, MADELYN SUE, advt. exec.; b. Chgo., Mar. 4, 1947; d. Seymour and Estelle (Klotwogg) Jensky; student N.Y. U., 1966-67; B.A. in Journalism, U. Mich., 1968; m. Howard Brian Miller, May 26, 1968; children—Mallorie Ann, Gregory Scott. Copywriter, Young & Rubicam, Detroit, 1968-69, Yaffe Stone August, Huntington Woods, Mich., 1969-70, Dancer Fitzgerald Sample, N.Y.C., 1970-71, Neiman-Marcus, Dallas, 1975-76; sr. copywriter Tracy, Dallas, 1976-81; pres. Madelyn Miller, Inc., Dallas, 1982—. Recipient Clio award, 1981; Matrix award Outstanding Dallas Woman in Advt., 1981; Effie award, 1980; Addy award (2), 1980; cert. of merit Dallas Soc. Visual Communications, 1979, Dallas Ad League, 1979; Bronze medal Dallas Soc. Visual Communications, also Bronze award, 1979; Bravo award (4) Detroit Art Dirs. Club, 1981; numerous others. Mem. Dallas Soc. Visual Communications, Women in Communications (student pres. 1968), Am. Women in Radio and TV. Jewish. Club: Hadassah Nat. Fedn. Jewish Women. Home: 9619 Rocky Branch Dallas TX 75243 Office: 3100 Carlisle Plaza Suite 124 Dallas TX 75204

MILLER, MARGARET ANN, ins. agt.; b. Warren, Ohio, Mar. 1, 1939; d. Arthur Morgan and Harriet Elizabeth (Burrows) Duff; student U. Ariz., 1957-59; 1 son, Mark Russell. Inland marine underwriter Home Ins. Co., Phoenix, 1959; underwriter Messimer Ins. Agy., Williams, Ariz., 1959-62; admitting clk. Williams (Ariz.) Hosp., 1966-67; claims clk. Blue Cross/Blue Shield, Phoenix, 1967; personal lines underwriter/comml. lines underwriter, comml. agt. Beal & Assocs., Ins., Phoenix, 1967—. Mem. Exec. bd., Jr. Achievement, 1977-80; mem. Women's Com. of Fiesta Bowl, 1971-80. Named Midtowners Bus. and Profl. Women's Club Woman of Achievement, 1980-81, Woman of the Yr., 1981—. Mem. Nat. Fed. Bus. and Profl. Women's Clubs (chpt. pres. 1981-82, Ariz. membership chmn. 1981-82, Ariz. rec. sec. 1982-83), Phoenix C. of C., Alpha Chi Omega. Republican. Presbyterian. Home: 5562 N 10th St Phoenix AZ 85014 Office: 5635 E Thomas Rd Phoenix AZ 85018

MILLER, MARIAN HAYES, govt. ofcl.; b. Kuling, China, July 21, 1919 (parents Am. citizens); d. Egbert and Eva (Morris) Hayes; student Syracuse U., 1938-39; A.B., Wellesley Coll., 1940; M.A., U. Chgo., 1942; m. Francis Miller, May 6, 1944; children—Leonard James, Janet Clare. Employed with pvt. and public social service agys., Chgo., Syracuse, N.Y. and San Diego, 1942-49; with San Diego County Dept. Public Welfare, 1957-68; mem. faculty Sch. Social Work, Calif. State U., San Diego, 1967-68; head San Diego component Calif. project on aging Am. Public Welfare Assn., 1964-67; with Adminstrn. on Aging, 1968—, acting dir. tng. div., Washington, 1972-74, regional program dir. Region V, Chgo., 1974—; bd. dirs. Met. Chgo. Coalition on Aging, 1978—, mem. exec. com., 1979-80; lectr. on miniature Chinese porcelains. Mem. ch. council, chmn. social ministry com., 1971-74; mem. ch. council, 1977—, chmn. stewardship com., 1979—. Recipient Spl. Achievement award Adminstrn. on Aging, 1971, Region V Affirmative Action award, 1976, Outstanding Performance award, 1978. Mem. Nat. Conf. Social Welfare, Gerontol. Soc., Nat. Assn. Social Workers, Acad. Cert. Social Workers, Am. Public Welfare Assn. Lutheran. Clubs: Chgo. Wellesley; San Diego Wellesley (pres. 1956-57). Author: (with others) Toward a Brighter Future for the Elderly, 1970. Office: Adminstrn on Aging 300 S Wacker Dr 15th Floor Chicago IL 60606

MILLER, MARIE BELLANTI, nurse; b. Granville, France, Mar. 13, 1946; came to U. S., 1948, naturalized, 1965; d. Thomas Peter Bellanti and Suzanne M. Thevenot Dodd; grad. S.C. Bapt. Sch. Radiol. Tech., 1965; R.N., S.C. Bapt. Sch. Nursing, 1968; postgrad. U. S.C., 1972; m. Franklin Brooke Miller, Apr. 30, 1977. Health nurse, med. adminstrv. reviewer Prudential Ins. Co., Atlanta, 1978-80; counselor Ga. Bapt. Med. Center, Atlanta, 1980-81; human rights coordinator Ga. Regional Hosp., Decatur, 1981—. Mem. exec. bd. Am. Cancer Soc. Mem. S.C. Soc. Radiol. Tech. (pres., v.p., sec., treas. 1965-68), S.C. Bd. Nursing, Ga. Bd. Nursing. Roman Catholic. Home: 1115 Palisades Dr Ellenwood GA 30049

MILLER, MARION HELEN, ins. agy. exec.; b. Chgo., Aug. 8, 1940; d. Chester Albert and Dorothy Marcella (Chaneske) M.; student DePaul U., Chgo., also various ins. courses. With Amalgamated Ins. Agy. Services, Inc., Chgo., 1960—, claims mgr. dental/vision depts., 1968-73, claims dir. accident, health, dental, vision and prescription claims, 1973—; spl. cons. subsidiary Meridian Agy., Fed. Computer Systems Inc. Sec., bd. dirs. Lakeside Condominium D Assn., 1978-79, 81-82, v.p., 1982—, author newsletter, 1979—. Ill. State scholar, 1958; Mayor Daley Youth Found. grantee, 1958. Mem. Nat. Assn. Female Execs.

MILLER, MARJORIE CAVINS LEEPER (MIDGE), educator, state legislator; b. Morgantown, W.Va., June 8, 1922; d. Lorimer V. and Neva (Adams) Cavins; student Spokane Jr. Coll., 1939-40, Morris Harvey Coll., 1940-41; B.A., U. Mich., 1944; M.S., U. Wis., 1962; m. Harry Dean Leeper, Nov. 5, 1944 (dec. 1954); children—Steven Lloyd, David Dean, Linda Jean, Kenneth Chandran; m. 2d, Edward Ernst Miller, May 12, 1963; stepchildren—Mark, Sterling, Jeffrey, Nancy, Randy. Teen-age program dir. Ann Arbor YWCA, 1944-45; married women's program dir. New Haven YWCA, 1945-46; teaching asst. U. Wis., Madison, 1957-60, asst. dean letters and sci., 1960-66, coordinator univ. religious activities, 1966-68; mem. Wis. Assembly, 1970—, chmn. commerce and consumer affairs com., 1977—, state affairs com., 1975-76; co-chmn. law revision com.; vice chmn. Dane County Democratic Com., 1967-68; mem. Dem. Nat. Com., 1975—; mem. nat. adv. bd. Interchange Resource Center, Nat. Council Alternative Work Patterns. Mem. Madison Inst., Nat. Orgn. Women Legislators, Nat. Women's Polit. Caucus (nat. adv. com.). Methodist.

MILLER, MARJORIE LOIS, business adminstr.; b. Mineola, N.Y., Aug. 14, 1937; d. J. Kenneth and Margaret (Campbell) M.; B.A. magna cum laude, Muskingum Coll., New Concord, Ohio, 1959; M.Litt., U. Pitts., 1960; M.A., Princeton Theol. Sem., 1965. Tchr., Jericho (N.Y.) High Sch., 1960-63; area rep. United Presbyn. Ch., Kansas City, Mo., 1965-68; exec. Am. Bible Soc., 1968-72; fellowship program dir. United Bd. Christian Higher Edn. in Asia, 1973-76; evening sch. dir. Katharine Gibbs Sch., N.Y.C., 1977-80; bus. adminstr. Miller Secretarial Services, 1980—. Mem. Fifth Ave. Presbyterian Ch., N.Y.C. Republican. Home: 170 West End Ave New York NY 10023

MILLER, MARY, educator; b. Lebanon, Ind., July 15, 1900; d. George T. and Lydia Ann (Etchison) Miller; student MacMurray Coll., 1918-20; A.B., U. Ill., 1923, M.A., 1924; postgrad. Denver U., Mich. State U., U. Mich., Butler U. Tchr. English, head English dept., 1926-62, dir. dramatics Danville (Ill.) High Sch., 1926-61, asst. dir. Danville Jr. Coll., 1946-48, exec. dean, 1948-66, pres., 1966-72, pres. emerita, 1972—; coordinator English, Jr. and Sr. High Schs., 1961-62. Pres., Danville Jr. Coll.-Community Symphony, 1973-76. Named Danville Woman of Year, 1965; Boss of Year, Danville br. Nat. Secs. Assn., 1970; recipient Communication and Leadership award Dist. 54, Toastmasters Internat., 1975. Mem. Ill. Assn. Tchrs. English (pres. 1941), Danville Assn. Secondary Edn. (pres. 1949), Nat. Council Tchrs. English (com. mem.), Nat., Ill., Danville edn. assns., AAUW, Ill. Assn. Jr. Colls. (sec.-treas. 1965-66), Vermilion County Mus. Soc., Danville Jr. Coll. Found. (exec. sec. 1972—), Delta Kappa Gamma, Alpha Psi Omega, Delta Delta Delta, Psi Iota Xi, Red Mask, Thespians. Club: Altrusa. Author plays: S'No Haven, 1954, Murder Walks Among Us, 1956, Remember the Mayne; A Chance for All, History of Danville Junior College, 1981. Contbr. articles to profl. jours. Home: 1618 N Vermilion St Danville IL 61832

MILLER, MARY JEANNETTE, cons.; b. Washington, Sept. 24, 1912; d. John William and David Evangeline (Hill) Sims; student Howard U., 1929-30, U. Ill., 1940-42; real estate cert. LaSalle U., 1969; student U. Md., 1975, 77, Dept. Agr. Grad. Sch., 1958-59; m. Cecil Miller, June 17, 1934; children—Sylvenia Delores, Ferdi Agusto, Cecil. Chief mail clk., records supr. AID, records mgmt. cons., mail clk. Dept. Interior, 1943-57; records supr. AID, Washington, 1957-71, records mgmt. cons., 1971—; real estate sales assoc. Hugh T. Peck Co., Wheaton, Md., 1976-78; office mgr. Bechtel Assocs., Washington, 1976-78; tchr. ESL, Ministry Edn., Seoul, Korea, 1959-60; cons. AID, Liberia, 1980-81. Bd. dirs. U.S. Embassy Seoul, Korea, 1959-60. Mem. Soc. Am. Archivists, Records Mgmt. Assn., Am. Mgmt. Assn., Am. Fgn. Service Assn., Montgomery Bd. Realtors, Zeta Phi Beta. Roman Catholic. Author: Secretaries Handbook, 1972; Records Management Handbook, 1974; Principles and Practices of Records Management and Paperwork Control, 1974; Index for Alpha-Numeric Filing System and Records Disposal Manual, 1974; Manual of Instructions for Official Bio-data

Card, 1973; Secretarial Handbook USAID/Liberia, 1981; editor-in-chief Club 8953 Employee's Newsletter, 1977-78. Home: 700 7th St SW Washington DC 20024

MILLER, MELANIE LEE, legal assn. adminstr.; b. Denver, Aug. 14, 1952; d. Neal Clark and Jacquelie Jean (Westbrook) Yorker; B.S. in Home Econs. Communications, U. Wyo., 1974, M.S. in Agrl. Extension, 1977; m. Samuel M. Miller, Sept. 20, 1981; 1 dau. by previous marriage, Jacqueline Alicia. Instr. U. Idaho Coop. Extension Service, Ft. Hall Indian Reservation, 1977-81; asst. prof., 4-H agt. Oreg. State U. Coop. Extension Service, Pendleton, 1981; adminstrv. asst. to dir. Fed. Bar Assn., Washington, 1981— adv. cooks for tribal law, also elderly nutrition program; mem. Elderly Nutrition Council, 1977-80. Mem. Am. Home Econs. Assn., Nat. Extension Home Economists Assn. (rep.), Nat. Assn. Extension 4-H Agts. Assn., Idaho Home Econs. Assn., Idaho Assn. Extension Home Economists, Idaho Assn. Extension 4-H Agts. (dist. dir. 1979-80, state sec. 1980-81). Home: 5302 Knole Ct Apt 141 Alexandria VA 22311 Office: 1815 H St NW Suite 408 Washington DC 20006

MILLER, MERLE GENE, nurse; b. Vernon, Tex., May 15, 1932; d. Herman Carl and Trudy Vera (Ford) Gfeller; diploma nursing Dallas Meth. Hosp., 1952; m. Jake Miller, Feb. 14, 1953; 1 dau., Judy. Supr., Vernon Clinic Hosp., 1952-53; pvt. duty nurse, Vernon, 1953-60; sch. nurse Wilbarger County Schs., 1960-63; dir. vocat. nursing sch. Wilbarger Gen. Hosp., Vernon, 1967-70, asst. dir. nursing service, dir. inservice, 1972—. Democrat. Lutheran. Home: Route 3 Vernon TX 76384 Office: 920 Hillcrest Dr Vernon TX 76384

MILLER, MERSHON BROWNLEE, packaging engr.; b. Fortress Monroe, Va., June 13, 1940; d. Laurance Hilliard and Mary Mershon (Kessler) Brownlee; student U. Ariz., 1957-59, Coll. of San Mateo, 1961-67, Coll. Notre Dame, 1967-69; m. Patrick Bernard Miller, Mar. 18, 1967. Prodn. artist Fortune House Pub., San Francisco, 1959; theatre costume design instr. Nat. Music Camp, Interlochen, Mich., 1959; display artist Halle Bros., Cleve., 1959-60; asst. buyer Sterling Lindner Davis, Cleve., 1960-61; with Maurice Roberts Jewelry, Cleve., 1961, Joseph Magnin, San Francisco, 1961-63; with Carlisle Litho div. Litton Industries, San Francisco, 1963-66, Western Family Foods, Inc., San Francisco, 1966-69; prodn. mgr. Albert Frank Guenther Law Advt., San Francisco, 1969-73; with Fortune House Pub., San Francisco, 1973; prodn. mgr. David W. Evans Advt., San Francisco, 1974-76; purchasing agt. Raychem Corp., Menlo Park, Calif., 1976-79, packaging engr., purchasing agt., 1979-82, packaging engr., purchasing sect. mgr. graphics/packaging, 1982—; lectr. in field. Performing mem. Claypipers Melodrama Theatre, Drytown, Calif., 1968—, asst. play dir., 1979; mem. adv. bd. Food Adv. Service/Gallery Faire, Brisbane, Calif., 1978—. Mem. Soc. Litho and Printing House Craftsmen, In-Plant Printing Mgmt. Assn., Peninsula Women in Advt., Soc. Packaging and Handling Engrs., Prodn. Women's Club (past pres.). Author: Fast But Fancy Secrets to Gourmet Entertaining, 1976. Office: 300 Constitution Dr Menlo Park CA 94025

MILLER, MILDRED IONEY, social worker; b. N.Y.C.; d. Thomas A. and Elma L. (King) Jones; B.S., Wilberforce U., 1944; M.S.W. Fordham U., 1964; 1 son by previous marriage, Robert V. Asst. tchr. Eissman Day Nursery, 1944-45; case aide Cath. Charities, Diocese of Bklyn., 1945-49; probation officer Domestic Relations Ct., Bklyn., 1949-62, Bklyn. Children's Ct., 1960-62; supervising probation officer N.Y.C. Dept. Probation, 1964—; dir. Queens Probation Reading Clinic, 1972—; field supr. Sch. Social Service, Fordham U., 1965—, Sch. Social Work, Columbia U., N.Y.C., 1975, 78-79, N.Y. U. Sch. Social Work, N.Y.C., 1977-79, Adelphi U. Sch. Social Work, 1979—. Sec., Holly Civic Assn., 1959-61; sr. usher Bd. of Macedonia A.M.E. Ch., 1977—. Mem. Nat. Assn. Social Workers, Acad. Cert. Social Workers, United Probation and Parole Officers Assn., Delta Sigma Theta. Democrat. Club: Hansel and Gretel. Home: 58-03 Calloway St Apt 5J Corona NY 11368 Office: 153-30 89th Ave Jamaica NY 11432

MILLER, NAN LOUISE, jewelry co. exec.; b. Atlanta, Aug. 6, 1948; d. William Mitchell and Harriet Irene (Wilkie) Schotanus; B.S., Kans. State U., 1970; postgrad. UCLA, 1979-80, Media Communications, 1981, Weist Barron Sch. TV, 1982; m. Robert W. Miller Jr., Oct. 31, 1981. Buyer, Jones Store Co., Kansas City, Mo., 1971-75, Harzfeld's, Kansas City, 1975-76; exec. sales rep. Monet, Los Angeles, 1976-80; mgr. corp. buying offices Trifari, N.Y.C., 1980—, field mktg. coordinator and media pub. relations rep., 1981—; TV comml. actress; media/pub. relations cons. Willowbrook Devel. Corp. Mem. Nat. Assn. Female Execs., Fashion Group of N.Y., Am. Mgmt. Assn., Chi Omega. Presbyterian. Home: PO Box 3832 Kingsport TN 37660 Office: Trifari 16 E 40th St New York NY 10016

MILLER, NANCY ELIZABETH, librarian; b. Campbellsville, Ky., Sept. 17, 1916; d. Isaiah K. and Mallie (Davis Graham) M.; student S.D. State Coll., 1934-36; A.B., U. Ky., 1938; B.S. in Library Sci., U. Ill., 1942, M.S., 1947; M.A., Western Res. U., 1960. Librarian, Campbellsville (Ky.) High Sch., 1938-40; librarian, sect. reviser dept. library sci. U. Ky., 1940-43; head reference dept. Canton (Ohio) Public Library, 1943-49; asso. prof. library sci. Kent State U. (Ohio), 1949-55; head Chamberlain br. Akron Public Library, 1955-56, head extension dept., 1956-59; asst. dir. Law Library Ohio State U., Columbus, 1959—, instr. cataloging, 1955-74. Mem. Ohio Regional Assn. Law Librarians (pres. 1964-65), Am. Assn. Law Librarians (chmn. cataloging and classification com. 1962-64, 67-68, 71-72), Beta Phi Mu. Democrat. Methodist. Club: Pilot (pres. 1971-72). Home: 1995 Tewksbury Rd Columbus OH 43221 Office: 1659 N High St Columbus OH 43210

MILLER, NAOMI, art historian; b. N.Y.C., Feb. 28, 1928; d. Nathan and Hannah Miller; B.A., CCNY, 1948; M.A., Columbia U., 1950; M.A., N.Y.U., 1960, Ph.D., 1966. Asst. prof. art history R.I. Sch. Design, 1963-64; asst. prof., then asso. prof. U. Calif., Berkeley, 1969-70; mem. faculty Boston U., 1964—, prof. art history, 1981—. Jr. fellow Nat. Endowment Humanities, 1972-73; sr. fellow Dumbarton Oaks, 1976-77. Mem. Coll. Art Assn., Soc. Archtl. Historians, Renaissance Soc. Author: French Renaissance Fountains, 1977; Heavenly Caves, 1982; also articles, catalogues; book rev. editor Jour. Soc. Archtl. Historians, 1974-80, editor 1980—. Office: 725 Commonwealth Ave Boston MA 02215

MILLER, NORMA JEAN, banker; b. Cashton, Wis., July 8, 1936; d. Bernard J. and Nora C. (Schmitz) Brueggen; grad. Grad. Sch. Banking, U. Wis., 1978; m. Levi Miller, Sept. 7, 1959; 1 foster child, Iris McAloney. With Bank of Cashton, 1955—, cashier, dir., 1976—. Chairperson, treas. Cashton Centennial; treas. Monroe County Bicentennial. Mem. Nat. Assn. Bank Women, Monroe County Hist. Soc., Bank Adminstrn. Inst., Bankers Installment Loan Assn. Office: PO Box 98 Cashton WI 54619

MILLER, PAMELA GUNDERSEN, broadcasting exec., city ofcl.; b. Cambridge, Mass., Sept. 7, 1938; d. Sven M. and Harriet Adams Gundersen; A.B. magna cum laude, Smith Coll., 1960; m. Ralph E. Miller, July 7, 1962; children—Alexander, Erik, Karen. Feature writer Congressional Quar., Washington, 1962-65; dir. cable TV franchizing Storer Broadcasting Co., Louisville, Bowling Green, Lexington, and Covington, Ky., 1978-80, 81-82; mem. 4th Dist. Lexington, Fayette County Urban Council, 1973-77, councilwoman-at-large, 1982—; dep. commr. Ky. Dept. for Local Govt., Frankfort, 1980-81. Mem. Fayette County Bd. Health, 1975-77, Downtown Devel. Commn., 1975-77; alt. del. Dem. Nat. Conv., 1976; bd. dirs. YMCA, Lexington, 1975-77, Council of Arts, 1978-80, Sister Cities, 1978-80. Mem. LWV (dir. 1970-73), Profl. Women's Forum, NOW, ACLU, Land and Nature Trust of the Bluegrass. Home: 140 Cherokee Park Lexington KY 40503 Office: Mcpl Bldg 136 Walnut St Lexington KY 40507

MILLER, PATRICIA CROUGH, physician; b. Cleve., Feb. 8, 1925; d. Thomas Anthony and Hilda May (Sampier) Crough; student Syracuse U., 1952-53, B.A. cum laude, 1961; student U. Wis., Madison, 1955-56; M.D., SUNY Upstate Med. Center, Syracuse, N.Y., 1964; m. George H. Miller, 1947 (div. 1962); children—Bruce Douglas (dec.), Brian Scott, Jeffrey Burke; m. 2d, Paul F. Swarthout, Feb. 9, 1967. Med. sec. to Arthur D. Ecker, M.D., Syracuse, N.Y., 1946-50; intern SUNY, Upstate Med. Center, Syracuse, N.Y., 1964-65; house physician Community Gen. Hosp., Syracuse, N.Y., 1965-67; pvt. practice medicine specializing in family practice, Manlius, N.Y., 1967—; mem. staff Community Gen. Hosp., Crouse Irving Meml. Hosp. Mem. med. adv. bd. Planned Parenthood, Syracuse, 1977—; bd. dirs. Rape Crisis Center, 1982—. Diplomate Am. Bd. Family Practice. Mem. Onondaga County Med. Soc., AMA (Physician's Recognition award 1979-82, 82-85), Am. Med. Women's Assn., NOW, SUNY Alumni Assn. (dir. 1973-80, sec. bd. 1974-76). Office: Fairgrounds Dr Manlius NY 13104

MILLER, PATRICIA DAWN ROBERTSON, union ofcl.; b. Westminster, Md., Oct. 18, 1941; d. Ralph Luther and Anna Elizabeth (Frock) Robertson; student pub. schs., New Windsor; m. Roy Douglas Miller, May 5, 1979. Profl. photographer Englar Studios, Westminster, 1959; airline reservationist Eastern Airlines, Washington, 1960-62; passenger service agt. Piedmont Aviations, Inc., Washington, 1962-65, flight attendant, Wilmington, N.C., Roanoke, Va., 1965-74, Washington, 1979—; v.p. Assn. Flight Attendants, Washington, 1975, nat. pres., 1976-79, also regional v.p., chmn. Master Exec. Council, safety rep., chmn. negotiations com., mem. System Bd. Adjustment; condr. tng. seminars George Meany Center for Labor Studies; lectr. various profl. assns. Mem. Assn. Flight Attendants, Ariz. Indsl. Relations Assn., Aero Club Washington, Nat. Aviation Club, Nat. Aero. Assn., Internat. Flight Attendants Assn., Coalition Labor Union Women, Washington Union Women, Womens Transp. Seminar. Mem. United Ch. of Christ. Home: 2314 Old New Windsor Pike New Windsor MD 21776 Office: 1625 Massachusetts Ave NW Washington DC 20036

MILLER, PATRICIA ELIZABETH CLEARY, educator, civic worker; b. Kansas City, Mo., May 2, 1939; d. John M. and Helen Elizabeth (Kelton) Cleary; B.A., Radcliffe Coll., 1961; M.A. in English, U. Mo., 1970; Ph.D., U. Kans., 1979; m. James Ludlow Miller, July 8, 1961; children—Jo Zach James, Honour Helena, Marika Elizabeth. Docent and docent trainer Nelson Art Gallery, Kansas City, 1962-72; vis. lectr. English lit. U. Mo., 1975, 77; asst. instr. English composition and lit. U. Kans., 1974-76; lectr. English dept. U. Mo., Kansas City, 1979—; founding mem., poetry editor Helicon 9, Women's Jour. Arts and Letters, 1977-78, mem. adv. bd., 1978—; juror Carruth poetry contest U. Kans., 1981; juror EPA poetry contest, 1981; founder St. Augustine's Marlborough Neighborhood Orgn., Kansas City, Mo., 1976, chmn. bd., 1976—; art cons. to Conception Abbey, 1977; fund raising cons. to Jr. League, Contemporary Art Soc., Marlborough Neighbors Assn., 1977. Vol., United Way, 1962-77; treas. St. Paul's PTA, 1969-70; vice chmn., trustee Harvard/Radcliffe Fund of Kansas City (Mo.), 1977—; hon. bd. dirs. Rockhurst Coll.; bd. dirs. Kansas City Mus. Regional History, Friends of Library, U. Mo., 1974, Vis. Nurse Assn., 1980—, Westport Tomorrow Inc., 1980—; bd. regents Conception Sem. Coll., 1979—. Mem. MLA, Soc. of Fellows and Friends of Art of Nelson Art Gallery, Contemporary Art Soc., Notre Dame de Sion, U. Mo., Radcliffe alumni assns. Democrat. Roman Catholic. Clubs: Kansas City Country, Kansas City Athletic, Harvard-Radcliffe of Kansas City (pres. 1979-81, founding trustee, vice chmn. endowment fund 1977—, mem. schs. com. 1962—, founder membership com. 1979 Rockhill Tennis, University. Mem. adv. bd. Chouteau Rev., 1978-80. Home: 708 E 47th St Kansas City MO 64110

MILLER, PATRICIA LYNN, clin. psychologist; b. Chgo., Jan. 27, 1938; d. Joseph L. and Gertrude R. Lynn; student Carleton Coll., 1955-56; A.B., U. Chgo., 1958; M.S., Ill. Inst. Tech., 1971, Ph.D. in Psychology, 1979; m. Eric E. Miller, Feb. 27, 1960; children—Kurt, Nathan, Peter. Pub. relations dir. Chgo. Area council Camp Fire Girls, 1958-68, asst. exec. dir., 1966-68; task force tchr., mem. assessment team for 45-15 yr. 'round sch. plan Valley View Sch. Dist., Romeoville, Ill., 1968-70; sch. psychologist Lockport (Ill.) Area Spl. Edn. Coop., 1971-80; pvt. practice psychology, Joliet, Ill., part-time 1977-80; pvt. practice psychology, diagnostics and treatment of children and women, Joliet, 1980—; cons. sch. psychology program Ill. Inst. Tech., Chgo., 1975-77, instr. dept. psychology, 1975; condr. tng. seminars to crisis line vols. and staff residential children's sch. Cath. Charities, 1980—; field supr. Chgo. Sch. Profl. Psychology, 1981-82. Mem. Tribune Charities Youth Com., Chgo., 1958-60; former mem. Com. To Repeal Ill. Personal Property Tax, Citizen's Com. for Wider Use of Schs., Mayor Daley's Youth Commn.; former mem. Women's Network for ERA. State of Ill. grad. fellow. Mem. Am. Psychol. Assn., Ill. Psychol. Assn. (health services adv. bd.), Internat. Neuropsychol. Soc., Nat. Sch. Psychologists Assn., Ill. Sch. Psychologists Assn., Sigma Xi. Club: Zonta (charter) (Joliet). Co-developer Psy-Dx, electronic Halstead neuropsychol. test battery. Home: 3510 Bankview Ln Joliet IL 60435 Office: 310 N Hammes Ave Joliet IL 60435

MILLER, PAULINE MONZ, librarian, biologist; b. Harrisburg, Pa., Apr. 2, 1931; d. Henry and Susanne (Fisher) Monz; B.A., Pa. State U., 1952; Ph.D. (univ. scholar 1954-55, AAUW fellow 1955-56), U. Pa., 1956; M.L.S., Syracuse (N.Y.) U., 1976; m. John H. Miller, Dec. 28, 1954 (div. Sept. 1981). Instr. biology Wheaton (Mass.) Coll., 1956-57, Conn. Coll., 1957-61; research asso. Yale U., 1961-62; research asso. Syracuse U., 1963-74, adj. asso. prof. biology, 1974—, life scis. bibliographer, 1976—, head sci. and tech. libraries, 1978—. Mem. ALA, Spl. Libraries Assn., AAUW, Sigma Xi, Beta Phi Mu. Author, co-author articles in field. Home: 117 Euclid Terr Syracuse NY 13210 Office: Sci and Tech Library Syracuse U Syracuse NY 13210

MILLER, PHYLLIS FOREMAN, nurse, nursing adminstr.; b. Pitts., Aug. 1, 1929; d. William Arthur and Ruthadel (Rollier) Foreman; diploma Hosp. of U. Pa., 1950; B.S. Millersville State Coll., 1963, M.Ed., 1968; m. Edwin Garvin Miller, Aug. 26, 1950; children—Edwin Randall, Geoffrey Blair. Staff nurse St. Joseph Hosp., Lancaster, Pa., 1950; office nurse, Lancaster, 1950; indsl. nurse RCA, Lancaster, 1955-56; pediatric staff nurse Lancaster Gen. Hosp., 1960, pediatric head nurse, 1960-61, supr., 1961-62; sch. nurse Manheim Twp. Sch. Dist., 1962-73; asst. dir. nursing, staffing and staff devel. Ephrata (Pa.) Community Hosp., 1974-76; asst. dir. nursing, staff devel. Hershey Med. Center, 1976-77, asso. hosp. dir., dir. nursing Milton S. Hershey Med. Center, Hershey, Pa., 1979—; cons. Mem. Pa. Nurses Assn., Am. Nurses Assn., Nat. League Nursing, Pa. League for Nursing, Am. Nurses Found., Pa. Soc. Nursing Service Adminstrs., Hosp. Assn. Pa., Am. Heart Assn. Republican. Methodist. Office: 500 University Dr Hershey PA 19033

MILLER, RHOETA BETH, nurse; b. Plainfield, N.J., Aug. 14, 1927; d. Reginald Bazil and Ruth Naugle; B.R.E., Arlington Bapt. Coll., 1971; A.D. in Nursing, El Centro Coll., 1974; postgrad. Northwestern State U., 1981, La. Inst. Tech.; m. Harold Stanley Miller, Oct. 31, 1980; children—Dawn H. Butler, W. David Butler, Paul D. Butler, Clay D. Butler, Dwight A. Broach, Gregg M. Miller. Staff nurse Brookhaven Hosp., Dallas, 1974-75; charge nurse Bossier Med. Center, Bossier City, La., 1975-77; public health nurse Shreveport, La., 1977-79; dir. nursing Midway Manor Nursing Home, Shreveport, 1979-80; sch. nurse Caddo Parish Sch. Bd., Shreveport, 1980—. Vol., ARC, 1974—; mem. Substance Abuse Team for Prevention by Edn., 1981-82; active PTA, 1953-82. Sue Armstrong Nursing scholar, 1972, 73, 74; recipient Service award, B.T. Washington High Sch., Shreveport, 1981. Mem. Am. Nurses Assn., La. Sch. Nurses Assn., Nat. Sch. Nurses Assn. Democrat. Baptist. Contbr. articles to profl. jours. Home: 1810 Pollyanna St Bossier City LA 71112 Office: 7600 Cornelius Ln Shreveport LA 71109

MILLER, RIMA, family therapy, mgmt. cons.; b. Phila., Oct. 7, 1945; d. Joseph and Eleanor Miller; A.B. in Theatre Arts and Edn., Goddard Coll., 1970; Ed.M. in Curriculum and Instrn., Temple U., Phila., 1974-75; Ed.D. in Orgnl. Devel. and Adminstrn., U. Mass., 1978. Tchr. English and world cultures, then prin. Columbia Sch., Phila., 1970-75; instr. tchr. devel. U. Mass., 1975-76, program dir. leadership devel. for women Inst. Govtl. Services, 1976-77, staff asso. at inst., 1977-78; dir. partial hospitalization, intramural program Phila. Child Guidance Clinic, 1978-80; program dir. Abraxas Found., Pitts., 1980-82; family therapy, mgmt. cons., 1982—; eval. cons. access to power: program of leadership edn. Mass. State grantee, 1973-75. Mem. Am. Ednl. Research Assn., Assn. Supervision and Curriculum, Council Adminstrs. Spl. Edn., Council Exceptional Children, Am. Assn. Sch. Adminstrs., Am. Assn. Psychiat. Services for Children, Assn. Partial Hosps., NOW. Author: Teachers in Transition: New Directions, New Meanings, 1977; A Systems Approach to Acute Care Partial Hospitalization Within a Family Therapy Oriented Setting . . . . . Diffusing the Myths, also papers. Home: 1913 Delancey St Philadelphia PA 19103

MILLER, ROSALIND SCHNITZER, social worker; b. Allentown, Pa., July 12, 1923; d. Jacob and Gertrude H. (Price) Schnitzer; A.B., Pa. State Coll., 1944; A.M., Columbia U., 1945; M.S., Simmons Coll., 1954; m. Edwin Haviland Miller, June 25, 1946; 1 dau., Pamela Miller Ness. Psychiat. social worker child psychiatry Mass. Mental Health Center, Boston, 1952-61; asst. dir. social work edn. Presbyn. Hosp., N.Y.C., 1961-62; asso. prof. social work Columbia U., N.Y.C., 1962—; project dir. NIMH, 1978—; cons. hosp. depts. social work. Mem. Nat. Assn. Social Workers, Council Social Work Edn., Nat. Conf. Social Welfare, Am. Public Health Assn. Contbr. articles to profl. jours., chpts. in books. Home: 4642 Waldo Ave Riverdale NY 10471 Office: 622 W 113th St New York NY 10025

MILLER, ROSEMARY ELLISTINE REED, retailer; b. Delaware County, Pa., June 22, 1939; d. Byron Fabaraux and Eloise (Scott) Reed; student Clark U., 1957-58; A.B., Temple U., 1961; m. Paul E. Miller, Jan. 7, 1965 (dec.); children—Sabrina Eloise, Paul Dennis. Journalist, columnist, Jamaica, West Indies, columnist Amsterdam News-West Indian Report, 1963-64; with community relations Urban League, Washington, 1965; info. specialist Consumer Marketing Service, U.S. Dept. Agr., Washington, 1965-67; founder Toast and Strawberries, Washington, 1967—; seminar leader SBA Inst., Howard U., 1979. Bd. dirs. Interracial Council for Bus. Opportunities, 1969; mem. presdl. task force on edn. and tng. for minority bus. enterprises, 1973-74; del. White House Conf. on Small Bus., 1980; mem. White House Conf. on Small Bus., 1981. Named Businesswoman of Yr., Nat. Council for Small Bus. Devel., Eastern Region, 1974; recipient service award Washington Black Econ. Devel. Corp., 1973; bus. award Nat. Assn. Negro Bus. and Profl. Women, 1973; Small Bus. Person of Yr. award SBA, 1981; honoree Alpha Kappa Alpha, 1975, Iota Phi Lambda, 1976. Mem. Assn. Women Bus. Owners, Howard U. Faculty Wives (pres., 1973-75). Clubs: Jack and Jill of Am., Pierians. Contbr. feature articles to newspapers including N.Y. Herald, Miami Times, Gleaner (Jamaica), Washington Post, Washington Star. Home: 1300 Geranium St NW Washington DC 20012 Office: 2009 R St NW Washington DC 20009

MILLER, ROSEMARY MARGARET, accountant; b. Jersey City, Jan. 3, 1935; d. Joseph John and Marguerite (Delatush) Corbin; student Barnard Coll., 1953-54, Rutgers U., Newark, 1954-56, Howard U., 1962-63, No. Va. Community Coll., 1976—; A.A., Thomas A. Edison State Coll., 1981; cert. H & R Block, 1981; m. Julian Allen Miller, Oct. 14, 1978; children—Alexandria Lynn Orton Pollard, Jennifer Ann Orton. Bookkeeper, Cunningham Paint Co., Bethesda, Md., 1969-70, Gretchen Cole Dress Shop, Bethesda, 1970, Gen. Electronics, Inc., Washington, 1970-73; cost acct. Radiation Systems, Inc., Sterling, Va., 1973-80; acct. Bilsom Internat., Inc., Reston, Va., 1980—; owner, prin. RCOM Cons., acctg., bookeeping, Manassas, Va. Mem. Accreditation Council for Accountancy (accredited 1981), Nat. Soc. Public Accts., Accts. Soc. Va. Democrat. Lutheran. Home: 7554 Alleghany Rd Manassas VA 22111 Office: 11800 Sunrise Valley Dr Reston VA 22091

MILLER, RUTH, educator; b. Chgo., Apr. 5, 1921; d. Michael and Sarah (Niemsky) Miller; M.A., U. Chgo., 1945; Ph.D., N.Y.U., 1965; m. Irving Kriesberg, 1945; children—Hadea, Matthias. Faculty, SUNY, Stony Brook, 1962—, prof. English, 1972—; prof. Am. lit. Ben Gurion U. of the Negev, Israel, 1981—; asst. acad. v.p. SUNY, Stony Brook, 1974-80. Recipient Melville Cane award, Poetry Soc. Am., 1968; Fulbright Hays award to India, 1965-66, Russia, 1978. Author: The Poetry of Emily Dickinson, 1968; Black American Literature 1760 to present, 1971; Poetry: An Introduction, 1981. Office: Dept English SUNY Stony Brook NY 11794

MILLER, RUTH LOUISE, found. adminstr.; b. Akron, July 11, 1915; d. Arthur W. and Elizabeth (Pfeiffer) M.; B.S., U. Akron, 1939; M.S. in Religious Edn., Hartford (Conn.) Sem., 1942. Sec., Girls Mission work United Brethren Ch., Dayton, Ohio, 1942-46; coordinator non-Western dels. to World Conf. of Christian Youth, Oslo, 1947; adminstrv. sec. Japan Internat. Christian U. Found., N.Y.C., 1948-62, exec. dir., 1963—. Recipient citation Internat. Christian U., Tokyo, 1973, named hon. councillor, 1980. Mem. Japan Soc., Religious Public Relations Council, Inc. Presbyterian (elder). Home: 180 West End Ave New York NY 10023 Office: 475 Riverside Dr New York NY 10115

MILLER, RUTH RATNER, urban cons., educator; b. Cleve., Dec. 1, 1925; d. Leonard and Lillian B. (Bernstein) Ratner; student U. Wis., 1944; B.S., Case Western Res. U., 1969, Ph.D., 1972; m. Samuel H. Miller, Aug. 10, 1946; children—Aaron, Richard, Gabrielle, Abraham. Cons., Ednl. Devel. Center, Berea, Ohio, 1969-70; grad. asst. dept. edn. Case Western Res. U., 1971-73, lectr., counselor, 1973; dir. dept. pub. health and welfare City of Cleve., 1974-76; dir. community devel. City of Cleve., 1976-77; adj. prof. Cleve. State U., 1978—; urban cons., 1978—; dir. Greater Cleve. Growth Corp., Nat. Housing Conf.; news analyst WBBG Radio, 1978—. Mem. Gov.'s Manpower Commn.; bd. dirs. Cuyahoga Women's Polit. Caucus, Womanspace; pres. Greater Cleve. Safety Council, 1979; candidate from 22d Cong. Dist. of Ohio. Recipient Distinguished Citizens award Brandeis U., 1978. Mem. Am. Humanist Assn., Am. Personnel and Guidance Assn., Am. Soc. Adlerian Psychology, NOW, Phi Delta Kappa. Home: 17220 Aldersyde Dr Shaker Heights OH 44120

MILLER, SHARON MONAHAN, med. technologist, educator; b. Oak Park, Ill., Jan. 1, 1942; d. Douglas and Elaine Iva (Markuson) Monahan; B.A., Northwestern U., 1963, M.S., 1965; Ph.D., U. Calif., Santa Cruz, 1972; postgrad. Stanford U., 1968; diploma Sch. Med. Tech., Silver Cross Hosp., Joliet, Ill., 1975; m. Thomas Raymond Miller, May 29, 1965. Asst. prof. med. tech., dir. allied health programs Coll. St.

Francis, Joliet, 1969-75; edn. coordinator med. tech. program Northwestern U. Med. Center, 1975; asso. prof., coordinator med. tech. program Sch. Allied Health Professions, No. Ill. U., DeKalb, 1975—; mem. bd. Comprehensive Health Planning N.W. Ill., 1980-82; CPR instr. ARC, 1980-82; bd. dirs. Adv. Bd. Vocat. and Career Edn., Regional Office Edn., Boone-Winnebago Counties, 1978—. NSF fellow, 1965-66, 68-69; Arctic Inst. N. Am. grantee, 1971-73; Peace Corps tng. grantee, 1982. Mem. Am. Soc. Med. Tech. (trustee edn. and research fund 1980-83, chmn. scholarship com. 1981-82, regional chmn. biochemistry sci. assembly 1981-83), AAAS, Am. Assn. Clin. Chemists, Am. Soc. Clin. Pathologists (affiliate), Am. Soc. Allied Health Professions, Ill. Med. Tech. Assn. (chmn. coms. 1979-82, pres. Rockford br. 1981-82), Ill. Acad. Sci., Naval Res. Assn., Forest City Dog Tng. Club, Pine Tree Pistol Club, Phi Beta Kappa, Omicron Sigma, Beta Beta Beta. Republican. Episcopalian. Club: Order Eastern Star. Author, editor in field. Home: 1604 Homewood Dr Rockford IL 61108 Office: Williston Hall Room 217 No Ill U DeKalb IL 60115

MILLER, STEPHANIE MATTERSDORF, psychotherapist, mental health agency exec.; b. N.Y.C., June 5, 1933; d. Leo and Jeanne S. Mattersdorf; A.B., Barnard Coll., 1968; M.S.W., N.Y. U., 1972; children—Nancy Susan, Daniel Harold, David Spencer. Mem. psychiat. social work staff Community Center for Mental Health, Dumont, N.J., 1972-74, sr. pyschiat. social worker, 1974-75, program dir., coordinator deinstitutionalization program Project Link-Up, 1975-77, acting exec. dir., 1977; founder, coordinator Women's Counseling and Psychotherapy Service, Bergen County, N.J., 1973—; dir. Women's Counseling and Psychotherapy Service, Wayne, N.J., 1977—; pvt. practice psychotherapy, N.Y.C., 1975—; mem. Teaneck Mental Health Profl. Adv. Bd., 1975-77; asst. adj. prof. Jersey City State Coll., 1976; exec. dir. Wall St. Counseling Center, N.Y.C., 1982—; cons. Mem. vestry Christ and St. Stephen's Episcopal Ch., 1981. Cert. social worker, N.Y.; lic. marriage counselor, N.J. Mem. Acad. Cert. Social Workers, Nat. Assn. Social Workers (treas., dir. Bergen-Passaic chpt. 1975—), Am. Group Psychotherapy Assn., NOW. Contbr. articles to profl. jours. Home: 225 Central Park W Apt 601 New York NY 10024 Office: 1625 Anderson Ave Fort Lee NJ 07024

MILLER, SUZANNE MELANIE, psychologist, educator; b. Montreal, Que., Can., May 28, 1951; came to U.S., 1977; d. Gerald and Joanne Miller; B.S. (Univ. scholar), McGill U., Can., 1972; Ph.D., Inst. Psychiatry, U. London, 1976. Asst. prof. dept. psychology U. Western Ont. (Can.), 1976-77; research fellow div. family studies dept. psychiatry U. Pa., Phila., 1977-79; vis. scholar dept. psychology Stanford (Calif.) U., 1978-79; asst. prof. dept. psychology Temple U., 1979—. Recipient Scientist award Brit. Psychophysiol. Soc., 1975; Nat. Research Council of Can. grantee, 1976; Temple U. biomed. grantee, 1979-83; Robert Wood Johnson Found. scholar, 1982—. Mem. Am. Psychol. Assn., Assn. of Behavior Therapists, Assn. for the Advancement of Behavior Therapy, Soc. of Psychophysiol. Research, AAAS. Mem. editorial bd. Cognitive Research and Therapy; contbr. numerous articles on behavior therapy, stress and depression to profl. jours. Home: 120 Broadmead St Princeton NJ 08540 Office: Dept Psychology Temple Univ Weiss Hall Philadelphia PA 19122

MILLER, TRUDI CLAIRE, found. exec.; b. Kingston, N.Y., Feb. 4, 1941; d. Paul Anton and Alice (Heutchi) M.; B.A., Cornell U., 1962; Ph.D., U. N.C., 1969; Asst. prof. polit. sci. SUNY, Buffalo, 1969-72; program mgr. for applied social sci. NSF, Washington, 1972-81, program dir. decision and mgmt. sci., 1982—. Mem. Am. Polit. Sci. Assn. (Franklin L. Burdette Pi Sigma Alpha award 1980), Am. Soc. Public Adminstrn., Inst. Mgmt. Scis., Assn. Public Policy Analysis and Mgmt. Contbr. articles to profl. jours. Office: National Science Foundation Washington DC 20550

MILLER, VESTA HELENE, city ofcl.; b. Stockton, Kans., Oct. 23, 1928; d. George William and Emma May (Sander) Colburn; B.S. in Home Econs. and Edn., Kans. State U., 1949; postgrad. U. Colo., Denver, 1966, Regis Coll., 1973; m. George Stanley Miller, Aug. 31, 1947; children—Judy, Cindy, Shelley, Gregory. Home econs. tchr. Dodge City (Kans.) Jr. High Sch., 1950-54; substitute tchr. Jefferson County Schs., 1966-75; councilwoman City of Arvada (Colo.), 1973—, mayor pro tem, 1975-79, mayor, 1979-81; chmn. Denver Regional Council Govts., 1980-81, chmn. Gov.'s Goals Task Force, 1971-72, mem. planning commn., 1973, mem. citizens adv. group, 1972-73. Treas., Arvada Hist. Soc., 1972; leader Girl Scouts U.S.A., 1964-66; bd. mem. Denver Metro Ministries, United Methodist Ch.; active Arvada Center Found. for Arts and Humanities. Recipient Arvada Image award Arvada C. of C., 1975, Disting. Service award Denver Regional Council Govts., 1977, 79, Met. Denver Fed. Exec. Bd. Mem. Nat. Assn. Regional Councils (bd. mem.), Nat. League Cities, Colo. Mcpl. League, Jefferson County Govts., Jefferson County Coalition Cities. Republican. Methodist. Mem. editorial rev. com. HUD Capacity Bldg. Project, 1976. Office: 8101 Ralston Rd Arvada CO 80002

MILLER, VIRGINIA IRENE, fine art galleries exec.; b. Tampa, Fla., May 29, 1943; d. Chester Howard and Marie Miller; student Miami-Dade Community Coll., 1962-70; B.A., U. Miami, 1973; m. William Robert DuPriest, June 16, 1974. Art cons., organizer, dir. numerous art exhbns. for leading charities, fin. instns., Dade County, Fla., 1969-73; owner, dir. Virginia Miller Galleries, Inc., Coconut Grove, Fla., 1974—; owner, dir. ArtSpace, Coral Gables, Fla., 1981—; pres. MACH I, Met. Mus. and Art Centers, Coral Gables, also mem. community relations com., dir. Panelist, New Sch., N.Y.C., 1978; del. Gov.'s Conf. on Small Bus., 1981; community relations com., dir. Met. Mus. and Art Centers, 1979-80; mem. loan com. Fla. Feminist Credit Union, Miami, 1978-80. Mem. Coral Gables C. of C. (chmn. cultural affairs com. 1979-81), Coconut Grove C. of C. (dir., chmn. tourism com. 1979-81), Art Dealers Assn. South Fla. (treas. 1978-79), Phi Kappa Phi, Psi Chi. Address: ArtSpace 169 Madeira Ave Coral Gables FL 33134

MILLER, ZOYA DICKINS (MRS. HILLIARD EVE MILLER, JR.), civic worker; b. Washington, July 15, 1923; d. Randolph and Zoya Pavlovna (Klementinovska) Dickins; grad. Stuart Sch. Costume Design, Washington, 1942; student Sophie Newcomb Coll., 1944, New Eng. Conservatory Music, 1946; grad. Internat. Sch. Reading, 1969; m. Hilliard Eve Miller, Jr., Dec. 6, 1943; children—Jeffrey Arnot, Hilliard Eve. Fashion coordinator, cons. Mademoiselle mag., 1942-43; instr. Stuart Summer Sch. Costume Design, Washington, 1942; fashion coordinator Julius Garfinckel, Washington, 1942-43; star TV show Cowbelle Kitchen, 1957-58, Flair for Living, 1958-59; model mags. and comml. films, also nat. comml. recs., 1956—; dir. program devel. Webb-Waring Lung Inst., Denver, 1973—. Mem. exec. com., bd. dirs. El Paso County chpt. Am. Lung Assn., 1954-63; bd. dirs., mem. exec. com. Colo. chpt., 1955—, chmn. radio and TV council, 1963-68, mem. med. affairs com., 1965-72, pres., 1965-66, procurer found. funds, 1965-72; developer nat. radio ednl. prodns. for internat. use Nat. Tb and Respiratory Disease Assn., 1963-68, coordinator statewide screening programs Colo., other states, 1965-72; chmn. benefit fund raising El Paso County Cancer Soc., 1963; founder, coordinator Colorado Springs Debutante Ball, 1967—; coordinator Nat. Gov.'s Conf. Ball, 1969; mem. exec. com. Colo. Gov.'s Comprehensive Health Planning Council, 1967-76, chmn., 1973-75; chmn. Colo. Chronic Care Com., 1969-72, chmn. fund raising, 1970-72, chmn. spl. com. congressional studies on nat. health bills, 1971-72; mem. Colo.-Wyo. Regional Med. Program Adv. Council, 1969-74; mem. Colo. Med. Found. Consumers Adv. Council, 1972-78; mem. decorative arts com. Colorado Springs Fine Arts Center, 1971-74; nat. founder, coordinator benefit fund raising Nov. Noel, 1973—. Recipient James J. Waring award Colo. Conf. on Respiratory Disease Workers, 1963; Zoya Dickins Miller award established Am. Lung Assn. of Colo., 1978; Nat. Public Relations award Am. Lung Assn., 1979, Gold Double Bar Cross award, 1980. Lic. pvt. pilot. Mem. Nat. (chmn. nat. father of year contest 1956-57), Colo., El Paso County (pres. 1954, TV chmn. 1954-59) cowbelle assns. Club: Broadmoor Garden (ways and means chmn. 1967-69, civic chmn. 1970-71, publicity chmn. 1972)(Colorado Springs, Colo.). Contbr. articles, lectures on health care systems. Home: 74 W Cheyenne Mountain Blvd Colorado Springs CO 80906

MILLER-CHILLCOTT, DOLORES MARIE, real estate devel. co. exec.; b. Pitts., Mar. 3, 1937; d. Joseph Anthony and Irene Clara (Blausen) M.; student San Diego State U., 1975-76, Mesa Community Coll., 1976-77, Nat. U., 1982—; m. George Edward Chillcott, July 19, 1968 (dec. Aug. 1981). Asst. v.p. Trans-State Title Co., Los Angeles, 1967-70; controller Pacific Scene, Inc. and subs., San Diego, 1971-73; treas. Bruce Farley Corp., also v.p. Four Farley Corp. subs., San Diego, 1973-74; controller Tschantz Devel. Co., San Diego, 1975-76; treas., acting pres. Duluth Scientific, Inc., San Diego, 1976-79; controller Patrick Devel. Co., San Diego, 1979—. Bd. dirs., pres. Meadow Villas Assn., 1979—. Mem. Nat. Assn. Accts., Nat. Assn. Female Execs. Republican. Roman Catholic. Home: 2858 Luciernaga St Rancho La Costa Carlsbad CA 92008 Office: 2643 4th Ave San Diego CA 92103

MILLET, NAOMI CASSELL, mathematician; b. Washington, Nov. 15, 1923; d. Smith Maxwell and Eva (Hill) Cassell; B.S., Howard U., 1945; m. James Joseph Millet, Apr. 5, 1948; children—James Joseph, Andre Anthony, Michael Gregory, John Adler, Philip Avery. Mathematician, Dept. Def., 1951-63, mathematician/systems analyst, 1963-73; mathematician, analyst Dept. Agr., Kansas City, Mo., 1973—. Home: 115 W 99th Terr Apt 105 Kansas City MO 64114 Office: 8930 Ward Pkwy Kansas City MO 64114

MILLETT, KATHERINE MURRAY (KATE), feminist leader, author; b. St. Paul, Sept. 14, 1934; B.A. magna cum laude, U. Minn., 1956; postgrad. St. Hilda's Coll. Oxford (Eng.), 1956-58; Ph.D., Columbia, 1970; m. Fumio Yoshimura, 1965. Instr. English, U. N.C. at Chapel Hill, 1958; sculptor, Tokyo, 1961-63; file clk., N.Y.C., then kindergarten tchr. N.Y.C.; tchr. Barnard Coll., 1964-68; formerly tchr. English Bryn Mawr (Pa.) Coll.; distinguished vis. prof. Sacramento (Cal.) State Coll., 1973—; co-producer, co-dir. film Their Lives, 1970; one-woman shows of sculpture: Minami Gallery, Tokyo, Judson Gallery, Greenwich Village, 1967, Noho Gallery, N.Y.C., 1976, 78, 80, Levitan Gallery Soho, N.Y.C., 1978. Mem. Congress Racial Equality, 1965—; chmn. edn. com. N.O.W., 1966; active supporter women's liberation groups. Mem. Phi Beta Kappa. Author: Sexual Politics, 1970; The Prostitution Papers, 1973; Flying, 1974; Sita, 1977; The Basement, 1979; Going to Iran, 1981. Address: care Coward Mc Cann & Geoghegan Inc 200 Madison Ave New York NY 10016 *

MILLIGAN, EVA JANE, retail co. exec.; b. Carbondale, Ill., Nov. 16, 1919; d. James W. and Alma E. (Cruse) M.; B.Ed. magna cum laude, So. Ill. U., 1941. High sch. tchr., Benton, Ill., 1941-44; mng. partner Town & Country, Benton, 1944-52; with Marshall Field & Co., Chgo., 1952—, mgr. induction and systems tng., 1952-55, tng. dir., 1955-74, v.p., gen. personnel mgr., 1974-78, sr. v.p., gen. personnel mgr., 1978—; dir. First Fed. of Chgo., Ill. Power Co. Chmn. adv. council Sch. Bus., U. Ill.; adv. council NCCJ, Double E; bd. dirs. Jr. Achievement; trustee Fourth Presbyn. Ch. Recipient leadership award for outstanding achievement in bus. YWCA, 1979. Mem. Indsl. Relations Assn., Chgo. Network. Club: Women's Athletic. Office: 111 N State St Chicago IL 60690

MILLIKEN, SUSAN JOHNSTONE, mathematician, educator, govt. ofcl.; b. Woodstock, Conn.; d. Francis U. and Violet Floyd (Ward) Johnstone; A.B., Vassar Coll.; M.A., Columbia U., m. Peter H. Milliken, Dec. 15, 1950; children—Peter H. III, Frances U. Johnstone Balsam. Chief statistician, research analyst E. W. Axe & Co., investment counsel, N.Y.C., 1940-42, 48-52; economist War Prodn. Bd., Washington, 1943-44; chief economist for sugar and allied products OPA, 1945-46; head sugar price control in U.S. and its possessions U.S. Dept. Agr., 1947; profl. genealogist, 1953—; tutor in stats., math., French, econs. Columbia, 1962—; instr. math. N.Y. Bd. Edn., 1966—. Life mem. Gov. William Bradford Compact, editor bull., 1963-69. Mem. Colonial Dames Am. (docent, co-chmn., house com. museum), Soc. Daus. Holland Dames, N.Y. Geneal. and Biog. Soc. Episcopalian. Author articles in field. Home: 423 W 120th St New York NY 10027 Office: 110 Livingston St New York NY 11201

MILLIS, PATRICIA ANN, cardiac diagnostic co. exec.; b. Honolulu, Feb. 29, 1952; d. Billy John and Bette Jo (White) M.; student Eastern Ill. U., 1970-72, Tex. A4M U., 1973-74. Researcher, Stanford and VA Hosps., Palo Alto, Calif., 1976; founder Cardiotrac Labs., 1977-79; pres. Americscan, Inc., San Jose, Calif., 1979-80; owner, operator Echo Tech., Cupertino, Calif., 1981—. Republican. Office: PO Box 1631 Cupertino CA 95015

MILLOT, ROSEMARY, interior designer; b. St. Johns, Nfld., Can., June 3, 1953; d. John George and Lottie Lucille (Webster) Kotch; B.S., Fla. State U., 1975; m. Ray H. Millot, July 23, 1977. Interior designer Thomas W. Ruff Co., Maitland, Fla., 1975-77, Meehan Stationery Co. Inc., Melbourne, Fla., 1977—. Mem. Inst. Bus. Designers (chpt. treas. 1980-82). Home: 4909 Fauna Dr Melbourne FL 32935 Office: 907 E Strawbridge Ave Melbourne FL 32901

MILLS, ANNE PARKER, economist; b. Roanoke, Va., Oct. 28, 1944; d. Victor Moore Mills and Marian Parker Sedgwick; B.A. in Econs., Swarthmore Coll., 1966; postgrad. London Sch. Econs., 1966-67, Columbia U., 1969-73. With Irving Trust Co., N.Y.C., 1967—, asst. sec., internat. economist, 1973-74, asst. v.p., internat. economist, 1974-77, v.p., internat. economist, 1977—. Mem. Am. Econ. Assn., Nat. Assn. Bus. Economists, Downtown Internat. Economists Luncheon Group, Nat. Fgn. Trade Council, Fin. Women's Assn., Met. Mus. Art, Mus. Modern Art. Republican. Episcopalian. Contbr. articles to bus. econ. periodicals. Office: Irving Trust Co 1 Wall St New York NY 10021 *

MILLS, BARBARA NASH, psychotherapist; b. Emporia, Kans., Dec. 7, 1929; d. Bert and Ruth (Bushong) Nash; B.S., U. Kans., 1951; M.A., Ohio State U., 1952; Ed.D., UCLA, 1973; m. Stephen Mills, Nov. 3, 1951; children—Stuart Allen, Creighton David, Kevin Stephen, Tobin Andrew. Counselor, Sch. Edn. UCLA, 1962-65; lectr. Calif. State U., Northridge, 1967-69; psychologist John Tracy Clinic, 1973-80; core faculty Antioch Coll.-West, 1979-81; dir. mental health services for deaf people, 1979—; pvt. practice, 1979—; cons. childrens programming NBC-TV, 1979—. Bd. dirs. San Fernando Valley Youth Found. Fulbright scholar, 1951. Mem. Am. Assn. Marriage and Family Therapy, Calif. State Psychol. Assn., Am. Soc. Clin. Hypnosis, Bell Assn. for Deaf. Home: 316 S Lapeer Beverly Hills CA 90211

MILLS, CAROL MARGARET, trucking co. exec.; b. Salt Lake City, Aug. 31, 1943; d. Samuel Lawrence and Beth (Neilson) M.; B.S. magna cum laude, U. Utah, 1965. With W.S. Hatch Co., Woods Cross, Utah, 1965—, corp. sec., 1970—, traffic mgr., 1969—, dir. publicity, 1974—; dir. Hatch Service Corp., Nat. Tank Truck Carriers, Inc., Washington; chmn. bd. dirs. Intermountain Tariff Bur. Inc. Fund raiser March of Dimes, Am. Cancer Soc., Am. Heart Assn.; active senatorial campaign, 1976. Mem. Nat. Tank Truck Carriers, Utah Motor Transport Assn. (dir. 1982—), Transp. Club Salt Lake City, Am. Trucking Assn. (public relations council), Beta Gamma Sigma, Phi Kappa Phi, Phi Chi Theta. Home: 77 Edgecombe Dr Salt Lake City UT 84103 Office: 643 S 800 W Woods Cross UT 84087

MILLS, DALE DOUGLAS (MRS. WILLIAM RUSSELL MILLS), writer; b. Seattle, Oct. 4, 1930; d. Donald Emery and Antoinette (Kinleyside) Douglas; B.A., U. Wash., 1952; m. William Russell Mills, Aug. 13, 1955; children—Lida Susan, William Russell, Peter Donald, Jane Douglas. Reporter, Seattle Times, 1954-55, 1975—; asst. librarian Harvard U., 1955-56; free-lance journalist, 1967-75; editor Puget Soundings mag., 1968-70. Mem. com. sign control Seattle City Council, 1970-72; research dir. Bruce Chapman City Council campaign, 1971; bd. mgrs. King County Juvenile Ct.; trustee Allied Arts Seattle. Recipient awards for excellence in reporting Wash. Press Women, 1972-82; award Nat. Fedn. Press Women, 1978; 2d pl. C.B. Blethen Meml. award for disting. investigative reporting, 1981; Excellence award Pacific N.W. chpt. Sigma Delta Chi, 1981. Mem. Kappa Kappa Gamma.

MILLS, FRANCES JONES, state ofcl.; b. Gray, Ky.; d. William Harrison and Bertie (Steely) Jones; student Union Coll., Barbourville, Ky., Eastern Ky. U., Richmond; grad. Cumberland Coll., Williamsburg, Ky.; m. Gene Mills, 1949. Mem. Ky. Ho. of Reps., 1961-62, asst. to speaker, 1963-65; dir. womens activities Ky. CD, 1965-72; clk. Ky. Ct. of Appeals, 1972-76; treas. Commonwealth of Ky., Frankfort, 1976-80, now sec. state; mem. Personal Service Contract Rev. Commn., 1976-80, Ky. Tchrs. Retirement Bd., 1976-80; del. Democratic Nat. Convs., 1964, 68, 76, 80, alt. del., 1972. Named Woman of Achievement, Bus. and Profl. Women's Club, 1976; Outstanding Alumna, Cumberland Coll., 1978; Outstanding Woman of Yr. in Ky., 1973. Mem. Nat. Assn. State Treas. (v.p., So. region chairperson 1976-78), Nat. Conf. Appellate Ct. Clks. (pres. 1975-76), Nat. Assn. State Auditors, Comptrollers and Treasurers, AMA Aux., Whitley County Med. Aux. Baptist. Clubs: Williamsburg Order Eastern Star (Williamsburg); Bus. and Profl. Womens. Author CD booklet, What Would You Do?. Office: Capitol Bldg Frankfort KY 40601

MILLS, HELEN SLABY, educator; b. Cleve., Apr. 8, 1923; d. Ollie F. and Nettie J. (Hejl) Slaby; B.A. magna cum laude, Western Res. U., 1944; M.A., Calif. State U., Sacramento, 1965; m. LeRoy Kenneth Mills, June 12, 1948; children—Marilyn Antoinette, David Ellsworth. Women's editor Cleve. Citizen, 1945-48; tchr. (part-time) Western Res. U., Cleve., 1945-48; sec. to dir. Cleve. Inst. Art, 1948-50; x-ray technician and office mgr. dr.'s office, Sacramento, 1957-65; prof. English, Am. River Coll., Sacramento, 1965—; instr. U. Calif. Extension, Davis, 1972; instr. various workshops for tchrs., 1972—; book reviewer Harper & Row Publishers, 1972, Foresman & Co., 1974—, Holt, Rinehart and Winston Co., 1975. Mem. Nat. Council Tchrs. English (com. coll. composition 1966—), Calif. Assn. Tchrs. English, Capitol Council Tchrs. English, Calif. State U. Alumni Assn., Kappa Delta Pi. Author: Commanding Communication, 1972; Commanding Sentences, 1974, 3d edit., 1983; Commanding Paragraphs, 1977, 2d edit., 1981; Commanding Essays, 1978, 2d edit., 1982; Commanding Composition, 1980; Connecting and Combining in Sentence and Paragraph Writing, 1982; contbr. articles on learning to profl. jours.; editorial bd. Jour. Personalized Instruction, 1974-81. Home: 3157 Oak Cliff Circle Carmichael CA 95608 Office: American River College 4700 College Oak Dr Sacramento CA 95841

MILLS, JANET TRAFTON, lawyer; b. Farmington, Maine, Dec. 30, 1947; d. Sumner Peter and Katherine Louise (Coffin) M.; B.A., U. Mass., 1970; J.D., U. Maine, 1976. Admitted to Maine bar, 1976; asst. atty. gen. criminal div. Maine Dept. Atty. Gen., 1976-80; dist. atty. for Androscoggin, Franklin and Oxford counties (Maine), 1980—; adv. com. Maine Rules Profl. Responsibility, 1981—. Bd. dirs. Maine Civil Liberties Union, 1978-80, Western Regional Council Alcoholism, 1981—; sec. platform com. Maine Democratic Party, 1981—; del. Dem. Nat. Conv., 1980, Nat. Women's Conf., 1977. Mem. Maine Prosecutors Assn. (dir.), Maine Trial Lawyers Assn., AAUW, LWV, Maine Women's Lobby, Bus. and Profl. Women. Editor legal publs. Home: 26 High St Farmington ME 04938 Office: 2 Turner St Auburn ME 02410

MILLS, MARGARET MARY HOWARD, assn. exec.; b. Levenshulme, Eng., Dec. 16, 1921; came to U.S., 1953, naturalized, 1973; d. Leonard and Katharine (Howard) M.; student U. London, 1939-42, Colegio Superior de Vicosa, Minas Gerais, Brazil, 1943-45. Translator, writer O Observador Economico, Rio de Janeiro, 1945-47; researcher Brazilian embassy, London, 1948-53; asst. dir. purchasing commn. Brazilian Treasury del., N.Y.C., 1954-64; asst. Cheryl Crawford Prodns., 1965-67; asst. to dir. Am. Acad. Arts and Letters, N.Y.C., 1968-73, exec. dir., 1973—; adv. com. Am. Art Directory, 1978. Bd. advisers Community Environments, N.Y.C., 1978. Recipient various certs. merit. Democrat. Office: 633 W 155th St New York NY 10032 *

MILLS, MARY LENORA, audiologist; b. Muscatine, Iowa, Sept. 16, 1938; d. Jesse Jeremiah and Josephine Frances (Lord) Korte; B.A., U. Iowa, 1960, M.A., 1969; m. Harley E. Mills, Feb. 2, 1962; children—Larry, Barry. Speech clinician Muscatine-Scott County Sch. System, 1962-67; audiologist Mississippi Bend Area Edn. Agy., Muscatine, 1967—; clin. assoc. dept. speech pathology and audiology U. Iowa.; chmn. Iowa Bd. Examiners for Hearing Aid Dealers, 1978—; cons. on hearing impaired United Way Muscatine, 1977—. Mem. Cablevision adv. commn. City of Muscatine, 1982. Mem. Muscatine Assn. Hearing Impaired, Iowa Speech, Lang. and Hearing Assn., Am. Speech, Lang. and Hearing Assn. (cert. of appreciation 1973, mem. speech and hearing in schs. com. 1978-81), Profl. Staff Orgn. (chmn. legis. com. 1982). Republican. Roman Catholic. Club: Geneva Golf and Country. Home: 1901 Hammann Ave Muscatine IA 52761 Office: 1422 Houser St Muscatine IA 52761

MILLS, REBECCA ANN, advt. exec.; b. Storm Lake, Iowa, May 11, 1950; d. Omer H. and Awanda Lucille (Mathison) Roth; B.A. with honors in Journalism, Drake U., 1972; m. Timothy Lemar Mills, Dec. 22, 1973; 2 daus., Sarah Rebecca, Abby Elizabeth. Editor, The Spirit, Des Moines Register & Tribune, 1972-73; coordinator Iowa Credit Union League Mktg. Services, 1973-74; account exec. The Prescott Co., 1974-75; pres. The Mills Agy., Storm Lake, 1975—; guest lectr. Buena Vista Coll.; conf. speaker. Mem. Women in Communications, Am. Soc. Exec. and Profl. Women, Internat. Platform Assn., Am. Fedn. Ind. Bus., Ad Club Sioux Cities, Internat. Soc. Bus. Communicators, Iowa Soc. Bus. Communicators, Storm Lake C. of C. (dir. 1980-82), DAR (regent 1981-82). Republican. Presbyterian. Clubs: Keystone (v.p.), Eastern Star (past officer). Home: 131 N Emerald Dr Storm Lake IA 50588 Office: PO Box 28 Storm Lake IA 50588

MILLS, ROBERTA VILVEN, nurse; b. Alma, Kans., Mar. 18, 1938; d. Edward Eugene and Regina Julia (Schmitt) Vilven; B.S.N., St. Thomas U., 1960; M.S.N., St. Louis U., 1963; m. Dan C. Mills, June 19, 1970. In-service edn. coordinator St. Mary's Hosp., St. Louis, 1963-65; asst. dir. nursing Methodist Hosp., Memphis, 1965-67, asso. dir. nursing, 1967-77; asso. dir. nursing City of Memphis Hosp., 1977-80; asst. prof., adj. faculty U. Tenn. Coll. Nursing, Memphis, 1978-82; asso. dir. nursing Baptist Meml. Hosp., Memphis, 1980—. Mem. Am. Nurses Assn. (council of nursing adminstrn.), Nat. League Nursing, Tenn. Hosp. Assn., Soc. Nursing Service Dirs., Frat. of Air N.G. Nurses.,

Sigma Theta Tau. Republican. Roman Catholic. Home: 4715 Normandy Rd Memphis TN 38117 Office: 899 Madison Ave Memphis TN 38146

MILLS, ROBIN KATE, law librarian; b. Chgo., Jan. 10, 1947; d. Dumont Cromwell and Virginia Anne (Nordeng) M.; A.B., Ind. U., 1969, M.L.S., 1970; J.D., U. S.C., 1976. Circulation/reference librarian Ind. U. Sch. Law, Bloomington, 1970-73; asst. law librarian U. S.C. Sch. Law, Columbia, 1973-76, asst. prof. law and law librarian, 1976-81, asso. prof. law and law librarian, 1981—. Mem. Am. Assn. Law Libraries (chpt. pres. 1980-82), Am. Bar Assn., S.C. Bar Assn., S.C. Library Assn. Author: South Carolina Legal Research Handbook, 1976. Office: Coleman Karesh Law Library U SC Law Center Columbia SC 29208

MILMAN, DORIS HOPE, physician; b. N.Y.C., Nov. 17, 1917; d. Barnet S. and Rose (Smokeroff) M.; B.A., Barnard Coll., 1938; M.D., N.Y.U., 1942; m. Nathan Kreeger, June 15, 1941; 1 dau., Elizabeth Kreeger Goldman. Intern, resident in pediatrics Jewish Hosp. Bklyn., 1942-46, fellow in neonatology research, 1946-47; extern in child psychiatry Bellevue Hosp., 1948-51; practice medicine specializing in child and adolescent psychiatry, Bklyn., 1950—; mem. faculty Downstate Med. Center, SUNY, Bklyn., 1956—, prof. pediatrics, 1973—, acting chmn. dept., 1973-75, 81-82; cons. in field. Fellow Am. Acad. Pediatrics, Am. Psychiat. Assn.; mem. Am. Assn. Social Psychiatry, Am. Orthopsychiat. Assn., N.Y. Pediatric Soc., Bklyn. Pediatric Soc., Bklyn. Psychiat. Assn., Phi Beta Kappa, Alpha Omega Alpha. Author articles in field. Home: 126 Westminster Rd Brooklyn NY 11218 Office: 450 Clarkson Ave Box 49 Brooklyn NY 11203

MILNER, PATRICIA PARSONESE, land devel. and real estate investment co. exec.; b. Washington, Mar. 8, 1947; d. Peter Paul and Mary Elizabeth (McBride) Parsonese; B.A., U. N.Mex., 1971; grad. N.Mex. Tech. and Vocat. Inst., 1976; lic. real estate Broker, N.Mex. Real Estate Inst., 1979; postgrad. Webster Coll., 1981—; 1 dau. Lisa Michelle. Exec. legal asst. N.Mex. Supreme Ct., Santa Fe, 1973-75; legal asst. S & F Corp., Albuquerque, 1975-76; v.p. Parco Industries, Albuquerque, 1977-79; owner Pat Milner & Assos., Albuquerque, 1977—. Leader, troop organizer Chaparral council Girl Scouts U.S.A. Mem. Nat. Assn. Realtors, N.Mex. Bd. Realtors, Albuquerque Bd. Realtors. Democrat. Roman Catholic. Home: 7442 Prairie Rd NE Albuquerque NM 87109 Office: 7442 Prairie Rd NE Albuquerque NM 87109

MILONA, MARGARET CALLIOPE, psychologist; b. Lexington, Va., July 8, 1944; d. Arthur Victor and Clara Virginia (Ashburne) M.; A.B., Coll. William and Mary, 1967; M.S. Radford Coll., 1972. Tchr., Prince William County (Va.) Schs., 1967-70, Roanoke County (Va.) Schs. 1970-71; sch. psychologist Norfolk (Va.) City Schs., 1972-74, Roanoke County-Salem City Schs., 1974—. Mem. Am. Psychol. Assn., Nat. Assn. Sch. Psychologists, Va. Assn. Sch. Psychologists, Assn. Roanoke County Sch. Adminstrs., Phi Kappa Phi. Methodist. Office: 526 College Ave Salem VA 24153

MILONE, JERALDINE MAE, nursing adminstr.; b. Blair, Nebr., July 19, 1928; d. Phillip Roland and Isabel Louise (Pruess) Salisbury; R.N., Nebr. Methodist Hosp., 1949; B.S. in Nursing, U. Omaha, 1951; M.S., U. Nebr., Omaha, 1981; m. Jesse Milone, July 7, 1951; children—Mark, Joseph, Lyssa, Denise, Sandra. Nurse, Nebr. Meth. Hosp., Omaha, 1949-51; vis. nurse, Omaha, 1951-52; nurse St. Joe's Hosp., Omaha, 1952-54; instr. County Hosp., Omaha, 1954-57; staff nurse Nebr. Meth. Hosp., 1967-72, Bergen Mercy Hosp., Omaha, 1972-73, Drs. Hosp., Omaha, 1973-76, Midlands Community Hosp., Papillion, Nebr., 1976-77, night supr., 1977-78, staff devel. coordinator, 1979-81, dir. edn. and tng., 1981—. Mem. Am. Soc. Health Manpower Edn. and Tng. (sec. Omaha conf. group). Republican. Roman Catholic. Home: 1646 Pine Rd Omaha NE 68144 Office: 1111 S 84th St Papillion NE 68046

MILTON, KATHLEEN BAILEY BURTS (MRS. JOHN DEAN MILTON), civic worker, club woman; b. Hurtsboro, Ala.; d. Willard Newton and Lucy Josephine (Evenson) Bailey; student Brenau Conservatory of Music, Wesleyan Coll. Conservatory of Music, Macon, Ga.; m. Luther Ransom Burts, Sept. 8, 1928 (dec.); children—Martha Elizabeth (Mrs. Robert H. Smith, Jr.), Luther Ransom; m. 2d, John Dean Milton, June 12, 1969 (dec.). Ga. chmn. jr. com. Atlanta chpt. DAR, organizing regent Cherokee chpt., 1948, hon. regent, Ga. state treas., 1956-57, regent Mayaimi chpt., 1968-70, treas. Fla. Soc., 1972-74, vice-regent, 1974-76, state regent, 1976-78, state officers club pres., 1979, mem. fin. com. Kate Duncan Smith Sch., trustee Tamassee Sch., 1976; hon. state regent, gov. Sons and Daus. of Pilgrims, 1977-80, curator Gen. Dames of Ct., 1980-82, corr. sec. gen., 1980-83; curator Gen. Dames of Ct. of Honor, 1979-81, pres. gen. nat. soc., 1981-83; trustee Third Century U.S.A. Bicentennial Orgn. Dade County, Fla., 1974-76; mem. Women's Aux. to Doctors Hosp.; mem. Women's Aux. to Internat. Coll. Surgeons; mem. Met. Mus. and Art Center, Daus. of Founders and Patriots Mem. Nat. Assn. Parliamentarians, Americans of Royal Descent, Colonial Dames Am., Magna Charta Dames, Huguenot Soc., Dames of Ct. of Honor (parliamentarian Fla. soc. 1980-82), So. Dames Am. (state pres. 1974-76, nat. v.p. 1976-78), U. Miami Women's Guild, Women's Cancer Assn. of U. Miami (Granada chpt.), Nat. Gavel Soc. United Methodist. Clubs: Miami Music, Riviera Country, Country Club of Coral Gables. Address: 3916 Palmarito St Coral Gables FL 33134

MILTON, PATRICIA ANN, journalist; b. Rockville Centre, N.Y., Mar. 14, 1948; d. Arthur G. and Marie F. (Landis) Milton; B.A. in History/Polit. Sci., C.W. Post Coll., 1970; M.Pub.Adminstrn., L.I. U., 1973; postgrad. St. John's U., 1971; m. Charles Roy Steinfort, June 28, 1980. Reporter gen. news The AP, N.Y.C., 1971-76, corres., L.I. Bur. chief, 1976—. Democratic leader Village of Westbury, L.I., 1971-73. James Gordon Bennett scholar, 1967-70. Mem. Women in Communications, Sigma Delta Chi. Roman Catholic. Clubs: Deadline, Overseas Press. Author: For Mercy Sake (booklet), 1966; contbr. articles to profl. jours. Home: 40 Eureka Terr Stamford CT 06902 Office: AP State Supreme Ct Mineola NY 11501

MIMS, NANCY ELLEN, educator; b. Chgo., Mar. 11, 1941; d. Walter Thomas and Mary Elizabeth (Lax) Griffin; A.A., Palm Beach Jr. Coll., 1961; student Fla. Atlantic U., 1965, B.A. in English, 1979, M.Ed. in English, 1981, postgrad., 1982—; m. Kenneth Lee Mims, May 5, 1962; children—Erron Scott, Garrett Todd, Holly Lynne. Tchr. Boca Raton (Fla.) High Sch., 1963-64, St. Joseph's Day Sch., Boynton Beach, Fla., 1964-69, Atlantic High Sch., Delray Beach, Fla., 1975-77; tchr. Am. lit., Cardinal Newman High Sch., West Palm Beach, Fla., 1977-81; chmn. English dept. Pope John Paul II High Sch., Boca Raton, Fla., 1981—; adj. instr. Palm Beach Jr. Coll. Vice pres. Exchangettes, 1965-68; organizing pres. Children Am. Revolution, 1966; active Delray Beach Hist. Soc., 1970-75, Lake Ida Property Home Owners, 1976-79, pres., 1976; leader Palm Glades council Girl Scouts U.S.A., 1963-68, trainer, 1969-70, neighborhood chmn., 1972-73; active Seminole council Boy Scouts Am., 1976-82, United Fund, 1968-82. Mem. So. Assn. for Children Under Six, Children's Home Soc., Home and Sch. Assn., Fla. Atlantic U. Alumni Assn., Nat. Council Tchrs. English (speaker nat. conv. Cin. 1980), Internat. Reading Assn., Fla. Council Tchrs. English, South Fla. Poetry Symposium (speaker 1981), Nat. Cath. Educators Assn. Democrat. Roman Catholic. Clubs: Order Rainbow Girls (mother advisor, 1967-69), Order Eastern Star (worthy matron, 1968-69), D.A.R. (state outstanding jr. mem. 1970, 75, state chmn. jr. mems. 1976-77, 2d. vice regent, 1969, vice regent, 1971, regent, 1973-75), Beta Sigma Phi (pres. 1973, advisor 1974-79, girl of the year 1973, 74, Valentine Queen 1974). Home: 1104 NW 4th Ave Delray Beach FL 33444 Office: Military Trail Boca Raton FL 33432

MINARIK, ELSE HOLMELUND (BIGART), author; b. Aarhus, Denmark, Sept. 13, 1920; d. Kaj Marius and Helga Holmelund; B.A., Queens Coll., 1940; m. Walter Minarik, July 14, 1940 (dec.); 1 dau., Brooke Ellen; m. 2d Homer Bigart, Oct. 3, 1970. Tchr. 1st grade, art, pub. schs., Commack, N.Y., 1950-54; author children's books: Little Bear, 1957; Father Bear Comes Home, 1959; Little Bear's Friend, 1960; Little Bear's Visit, 1961; No Fighting, No Biting, 1958; Cat and Dog, 1960; The Winds That Come From Far Away, 1960; The Little Giant Girl and the Elf Boy, 1963; A Kiss for Little Bear, 1968. Mem. PEN Club. Home: Rural Delivery Barrington NH 03825 Office: care Harper & Row Inc 10 E 53d St New York NY 10022

MINCEY, ANN JEANETTE, lab. exec.; b. Wauseon, Ohio, Jan. 30, 1947; d. Wesley K. and Pauline M. (Bearinger) Poole; B.S., Bethany Nazarene Coll., 1969. Asst. promotion dir. Griffin TV, Inc., Oklahoma City, 1969-72; advt. dir. London House Models, Inc., Kansas City, Mo., 1972-73, Designers' Loft, Inc., Dayton, Ohio, 1973-75; internat. sales lectr./trainer Redken Labs., Inc., Canoga Park, Calif., 1975—. Mem. Nat. Speakers Assn., Internat. Platform Assn., Am. Film Inst., Nat. Assn. Female Execs. Republican. Author: (with Johnny Bench) All Stars in Your Crown, 1982. Office: 6625 Variel Ave Canoga Park CA 91303

MINDEY, MARLENE STEPHANIE, nurse; b. Chgo., July 18, 1950; d. Victoria Mindey; R.N., St. Mary of Nazareth Hosp., Chgo., 1971. Nurse asso. of physician, Oak Park, Ill., 1972-79; organ transplant coordinator Rush-Presbyn.-St. Luke's Med. Center, Chgo., 1979-82; nurse neonatal intensive care Children's Meml. Hosp., Chgo., 1982—. R.N., Calif., Ill.; cert. rehab. nurse, IV therapist. Mem. Nat. Assn. Transplant Coordinators, Nat. Assn. Female Execs., Am. Assn. Critical Care Nurses, Ill. Transplant Soc. (v.p. coordinators council 1982). Jewish. Club: Lake Shore Centre. Patentee inflatable heel protector. 2728 N Hampden Ct Apt 1505 Chicago IL 60614 Office: 676 Saint Clair St Suite 1745 Chicago IL 60611

MINER, CAROL SPALDING, educator; b. Louisville, Jan. 6, 1950; d. Wallace H. and Martha Lee (Ratterree) S.; B. in Internat. Studies, U. Louisville, 1972; M.A. in Human Resource Mgmt., Pepperdine U., 1976; m. John Boyd Miner, Oct. 2, 1971. Instr., Fla. Jr. Coll. at Jacksonville, 1972—, coordinator/counselor offender assistance program, 1975-77; asso. dir. Jacksonville Community Council, 1977—. Mem. United Way rev. com., 1977-78; pres. Spring Homeowners Assn.; chmn. state public affairs com. Jr. League; host Politics is Your Business, LWV and Leadership Jacksonville; v.p. Goodwill Industries; bd. dirs. Tree Hill. Mem. Am. Soc. Public Adminstrn. (dir.), Am. Planning Assn., Jacksonville Women's Network. Home: 2487 Cypress Springs Rd Orange Park FL 32073 Office: Florida Junior College 101 W State St Jacksonville FL 32202

MINER, DORIS, state senator; b. Dallas, S.D., Mar. 13, 1936; student pub. schs., Tripp and Gregory, S.D.; m. Kenneth Miner, Oct. 14, 1953; 4 children. Former med. sec.; mem. S.D. Ho. of Reps., 1977-78, S.D. Senate, 1979—. Past mem. sch. bd.; leader 4-H Club; county leader Extension Assn.; chmn. Farmers Union; mem. S.D. bd. nat. chpt. Multiple Sclerosis Soc., state chmn. S.D. chpt., mem. Nat. Council on Health Planning. Mem. Altar Soc. Democrat. Roman Catholic. Office: South Dakota Senate Pierre SD 57501 *

MINER, JACQUELINE, polit. cons.; b. Mt. Vernon, N.Y., Dec. 10, 1936; d. Ralph E. and Agnes (McGee) Mariani; B.A., Coll. St. Rose, 1971, M.A., 1974; m. Roger J. Miner, Aug. 11, 1975; children—Laurence, Ronald Carmichael, Ralph Carmichael, Mark. Ind. polit. cons., Hudson, N.Y.; instr. history and polit. sci. SUNY, Hudson, 1974-79. Republican county committeewoman, 1958-76; vice chmn. N.Y. State Ronald Reagan campaign, 1980; candidate for Rep. nomination for U.S. Senate, 1982; chmn. Coll. Consortium for Internat. Studies. Mem. Nat. Commn. on Am. Fgn. Policy, U.S. Sup. Ct. Hist. Soc., P.E.O. Address: Route 2 Hudson NY 12534

MINETOLA, ALLENE CATHERINE, nurse, educator; b. Camden, N.J., Dec. 1, 1948; d. Allen H. and Emma Elizabeth (Carr) Budinger; R.N., Frankford Hosp., Phila., 1970; B.S. in Nursing Edn., LaSalle Coll., 1974; m. Leonard Minetola, Sept. 25, 1970; children—Todd M., Michelle L., Jaimee F., Nicholas C., Jillian M. Staff R.N., Nazareth Hosp., Phila., 1970; nurse clinician Friend's Hosp., Phila., 1970-75; staff R.N., nursery coordinator, prenatal edn. coordinator Thomas Jefferson Univ. Hosp., Phila., 1975—, childbirth edn. asso. instr., 1974—. Mem. Nurses Assn. Am. Coll. Ob-Gyn, Childbirth Edn. Assn. (profl. adv. bd.). Office: Thomas Jefferson Univ Hosp Room 5600 BNH 11th and Walnut Sts Philadelphia PA 19107

MINI, LOUISE ANN, psychotherapist; b. Bklyn., Apr. 28, 1949; d. Enrico H. and Anna Marie (Ventrice) M.; B.A. in Psychology, Bklyn. Coll., 1971, M.S. in Edn., 1973, profl. diploma in sch. psychology, 1973; M.A. in Psychology, Hofstra U., Hempstead, N.Y., 1977, Ph.D. in Philosophy, 1979. Ednl. cons. Follow-Through program N.Y.C. Bd. Edn., 1972; research asst., adj. lectr. Bklyn. Coll., 1972-73, instr., 1973, adj. lectr., 1973-75; sch. psychologist Bklyn. Center Psychotherapy, 1973-79; psychologist-in-tng., then psychologist N.Y.C. Bur. Child Guidance, 1973-76; instr. N.Y. Inst. Tech., 1976-77; teaching asst. Hofstra U., 1977, adj. lectr., 1978-79; doctoral intern Southeast Nassau Guidance Center, 1977-78; cons. sch. psychologist New Hyde Park Sch. Dist., 1979-80; psychologist St. Christopher's Residential Treatment Center, Sea Cliff, N.Y., 1977-80; coordinator childhood unit, chief psychologist Shield Inst. Developmentally Disabled and Mentally Retarded, Queens, N.Y., 1980-81; cons. psychologist group homes for mentally retarded, 1981—; pvt. practice psychotherapy Hewlett (N.Y.) Consultation Center, 1981—. Cert. psychologist, N.Y. Mem. Am. Psychol. Assn. (divs. of sch. psychology, mental retardation, psychology and the law), Nassau County Psychol. Assn., Bklyn. Psychol. Assn. (dir.). Author papers in field. Office: 1200 W Broadway Hewlett NY 11557

MINICK, PHYLLIS BRIDGE, editor; b. Los Angeles, Jan. 15, 1929; d. Louis A. and Gertrude E. Bridge; B.A., U. Calif., Los Angeles, 1952; m. Stanley R. Minick, Jan. 25, 1951; children—Lloyd Scott, Ricky Patrice. Freelance editor, writer, 1967—; contbr. articles to Dive Mag., Skin Diver, Genie, San Diego Mag, Aquarius, Atlante; oceanographic statis. researcher, scuba diver Fathoms Plus, Inc., 1967-70; sci. writer Health Communications, Inc., 1973-74; sr. house editor Scripps Clinic and Research Found., La Jolla, Calif., 1974—; instr. extension div. U. Calif., San Diego; lectr. tech. English. Mem. Soc. Tech. Communications (past chmn. San Diego chpt.), Am. Med. Writers Assn., Council Biology Editors. Home: 5860 Cactus Way La Jolla CA 92037 Office: 10666 N Torrey Pines Rd La Jolla CA 92037

MINK, MARJORIE LEE, interior designer; b. Los Angeles, Apr. 20, 1944; d. DeWitt and Marjorie Vernon (West) McIver; student Willamette U., Salem, Oreg., 1964, Calif. State U., San Jose, 1966; m. Douglas Hamilton Barr, Oct. 24, 1981; children by previous marriage—Jason C., Marne Anne. Textile cons. J.H. Thorpe Co., Los Angeles, 1967-68; designer Sally Sirkin Interior Design, Beverly Hills, Calif., 1968-71; pres. Lee Mink & Assocs., interior design and planning, Beverly Hills, 1971—; propr. Lee Mink Sch. Interior Design, Laguna Hills, Calif.; author weekly newspaper column Ask Lee; prin. works include corp. hdqrs. Occidental Petroleum Co. Active local Young Life, Cystic Fibrosis drives. Recipient Community Service award LaSertoma Club Internat., 1962; named Cook of Year, 17 mag., 1958. Mem. Alpha Chi Omega. Democrat. Presbyterian. Home: 1900 Ganter Rd LaHabra Heights CA 90631 Office: 9350 Wilshire Blvd Beverly Hills CA 90212

MINK, MAXINE MOCK, pub. relations exec.; b. Lakeland, Fla., Jan. 17, 1938; d. Idus Frank and Elizabeth (Warren) Mock; student Fla. So. Coll.; children—Lance Granger, Justin Chandler. With Union Fin. Co., Lakeland, Fla., 1956-62; partner/owner S & S Ent. & Arrow Lake Mobile Home Pk., Lakeland, Fla., 1957-66; head bookkeeper Seaboard Fin., Lakeland, 1964-68; partner Custom Chem., Inc., Lakeland, 1968-75; partner Don Emilio Perfumers, Newport Beach, Calif., 1978-79; owner Maxine Mink Public Relations, Newport Beach, 1978—. Bd. dirs. Guild of Lakeland Symphony Orch., 1972-75; mem. Lakeland Gen. Hosp. Aux., 1974-76. Mem. Newport Beach C. of C., Anaheim Visitors and Conv. Bur., Hoag Hosp. Aux., NOW, Nat. Assn. Female Execs., Orange County Music Center Guild. Republican. Clubs: Lido Isle Woman's, Lido Players, Balboa Bay, Lido Isle Yacht. Home: 115 Via Undine Newport Beach CA 92663 Office: PO Box 8042 Newport Beach CA 92660

MINK, PATSY TAKEMOTO, city ofcl., former congresswoman, lawyer; b. Paia, Maui, Hawaii, Dec. 6, 1927; d. Suematsu and Mitama (Tateyama) Takemoto; student Wilson Coll., 1946, also recipient hon. degree; student U. Nebr., 1947; B.A., U. Hawaii, 1948; LL.D., U. Chgo., 1951; hon. degrees Lindenwood (Mo.) Coll., Duff's Inst., Pa.; D.H.L., Chaminade Coll., 1975, Syracuse U., 1976, Whitman Coll., 1981; m. John Francis Mink, Jan. 27, 1951; 1 dau., Gwendolyn. Admitted to Hawaii bar; practiced in Honolulu, 1953-65; lectr. U. Hawaii, 1952-56, 59-62, 79-80, 81; atty. Territorial Ho. of Reps., 1955; mem. Ter. Hawaii Ho. of Reps., 1956-58; mem. Ter. Hawaii Senate, 1958-59, State Hawaii Senate, 1962-64; mem. 89th-94th congresses from 2d Dist. Hawaii, mem. edn. and labor com., interior com., budget com.; mem. City Council, 1982—; asst. sec. for oceans, internat. environ. and sci. Dept. State, 1977-78; mem. U.S. del. to UN Law of Sea, 1975-76, Internat. Womans Yr., 1975, UN Environment Program, 1977, Internat. Whaling Commn., 1977. Charter pres. Young Democratic Club Oahu, 1954-56, Ter. Hawaii Young Dems., 1956-58; del. Dem. Nat. Conv., 1960, 72; nat. v.p. Young Dem. Clubs Am., 1957-59; v.p. Ams. for Dem. Action, 1974-76, nat. pres., 1978-81; mem. nat. adv. com. White House Conf. on Families, 1979-80; mem. nat. adv. council Federally Employed Women, Adv. Com. for Campaign for UN Reform; v.p. Women USA; nat. bd. dirs. Planned Parenthood; bd. dirs. Hawaii ACLU, Nat. Women's Law Center, Public Citizen; past bd. dirs. Hawaii Assn. Help Retarded Children, UNA-Hawaii, Hawaii NAACP, Rural Oahu YMCA, Honolulu Symphony. Recipient Leadership for Freedom award Roosevelt Coll., Chgo., 1968; Alii award 4-H Clubs Hawaii, 1969; Nisei of Biennium award; Freedom award Honolulu chpt. NAACP, 1971; Disting. Humanitarian award YWCA, St. Louis, 1972; Creative Leadership in Women's Rights award NEA; 1977; Human Rights award Am. Fedn. Tchrs., 1975. Mem. Bus. and Profl. Womens Club.

MINKLEY, SUZANNE SAWYER, educator; b. Middletown, Ohio, May 15, 1915; d. Clifford Louis and Harriett May (Logan) Sawyer; A.B., John B. Stetson U., 1937, M.A., 1942; B.L.S., George Peabody Coll. of Vanderbilt U., 1940; postgrad. Manatee Jr. Coll., 1960, Fla. So. Coll., 1966, U. South Fla., 1966-67; m. Carl Henry Minkley, Apr. 3, 1943; children—Elizabeth Suzanne Jarrard, Philip Carl. Tchr., librarian Mt. Dora High Sch., 1937-41, Leesburg High Sch., 1941-43, Delray Beach High Sch., 1943-45, Samsula Elem. Sch., 1955-56, Sarasota High Sch., 1956-57; reading specialist Bayshore Jr. High Sch., 1963-74, chmn. lang. arts dept. Bayshore Middle Sch., 1967-74; tchr. social studies Bradenton Middle Sch., 1974—; cons. tchr. tng. program Edn. Professions Devel. Act of U.S. Dept. Edn., 1970-71; parliamentarian Manatee County Edn. Assn., 1968-72; mem. Volusia County Continuing Council on Edn., 1954-56; parliamentarian Bradenton Middle Sch. PTA, 1976—. Chmn. bd. Deland (Fla.) Children's Mus., 1954-56; state bd. dirs. Am. Cancer Soc., 1954-61. Recipient citation Am. Cancer Soc., 1952-55; cert. of profl. acceptance NEA, 1966-67. Mem. Volusia County Fedn. Women's Clubs (legis. chmn. 1952-54), Fla. Fedn. Women's Clubs (chmn. radio and TV 1962-66), DAR, NEA, Nat. Council Tchrs. of English, AAUW (chmn. edn. com. Deland br. 1943-45, Sarasota br. 1960-62), Am. Inst. Parliamentarians, Nat. Assn. Parliamentarians (pres. Sarasota unit 1973-77, 79-82, parliamentarian 1982—, edn. chmn. Bradenton unit 1980-82), Fla. Assn. Parliamentarians, Gen. Fedn. Women's Clubs, Leonardy Gaveliers (pres. 1972-73), Mu Omega Xi, Sigma Kappa. Democrat. So. Baptist. Clubs: Primrose Garden (pres., founder 1953-55), Orange Blossom Garden (pres. 1962-63), DeLand Women's (pres. 1951-53), Woman's of Sarasota (pres. 1960-61), Fla. Fedn. Women's Clubs (dist. dir. 1960-63, parliamentarian dist. 1963-65). Coordinator Have Gavel, Will Travel panels for civic and social orgns., 1959-65. Home: 2540 Hibiscus St Sarasota FL 33579

MINNE, LONA, state legislator; ed. Hibbing Community Coll.; m. Jon Minne; children—Heather, Wendy, Jon. Former clk. Town of Stuntz (Minn.); mem. Minn. Ho. of Reps., 1978—, mem. coms.: gen. legis. and vets. affairs, labor mgmt. relations, reapportionment and elections, taxes. Vice pres. Range Assn. Municipalities and Schs., Hibbing; mem. Hibbing Ednl. Adv. Council. Mem. Minn. Clks. and Fin. Officers Assn. Office: 239 State Office Bldg Saint Paul MN 55155 *

MINNELLI, LIZA, singer, actress; b. Los Angeles, Mar. 12, 1946; d. Vincente and Judy (Garland) M.; m. Peter Allen, 1967 (div. 1972); m. 2d, Jack Haley, Sept. 15, 1974 (div.); m. 3d, Mark Gero, Dec. 4, 1979. Appeared in Off Broadway revival of Best Foot Forward, 1963; recorded You Are for Loving, 1963; appeared with mother at London Palladium, 1964; appeared in Flora, The Red Menace, 1965 (Tony award), The Act, 1977 (Tony award); nightclub debut at Shoreham Hotel, Washington, 1965; appeared in numerous films including Charlie Bubbles, 1967, The Sterile Cuckoo, 1969, Tell Me That You Love Me, Junie Moon, 1970, Cabaret, 1972 (Oscar award), Lucky Lady, 1975, A Matter of Time, 1976, New York, New York, 1977, Arthur, 1981; appeared on TV in own spl. Liza With a Z, 1972. Address: care Creative Mgmt Assos 40 W 57th St New York NY 10022 *

MINNER, SISTER, JEANNE FRANCIS, educator; b. Colusa, Calif., Mar. 30, 1917; d. Oscar Lee and Minnie (Postlethwaite) Minner; student San Antonio Jr. Coll., 1935-37; B.S., Our Lady of Lake Coll., 1939; M.A., Catholic U. Am., 1949; Ph.D., U. Tex., 1965. Tchr., St. Vincent's Coll. and Acad., Shreveport, La., 1939-41; tchr. Incarnate Word Acad., Corpus Christi, Tex., 1941-46, tchr. biology, head sci. dept., 1948-63; tchr. Villa Maria High Sch., Brownsville, Tex., 1946-48; dean, head div. natural sci. and math. Christopher Coll., 1963-66, dir. Piper Meml. Lab. 1965-68, pres., 1966-68; chmn. dept. edn. Coll. Santa Fe, 1968-70; chmn. dept. St. Mary's U., San Antonio, 1970-80; prof. biology Our Lady of Lake U., San Antonio, 1980—; adj. prof. Morningside Manor, San Antonio, 1982. Fellow Tex. Acad. Sci.; mem. AAAS (life), Nat. Assn. Biology Tchrs. (Tex. chmn. pvt. schs. 1963-68), Nat. Sci. Tchrs. Assn. (life), Sci. Tchrs. Assn. Tex. (v.p. 1964, adv. bd. 1963, pres. elect 1965, pres. 1966, editor 1967-68, hon. life mem.), Tex. Tchrs. Assn. (life), Am. Inst. Biol. Scis. (life), Ex-Students Assn. U. Tex. (life), Am. Radio Relay League (life), NEA (life), Corpus Christi Interracial Council, AAUP, Nat. Wildlife Fedn., Pilot Internat., Nat. Audubon Soc., M.B.L.S. Club: Corpus Christi Outdoor. Contbr. articles to profl. jours. Home: PO Box 28475 San Antonio TX 78228

MINNICH, SHERRY GORDON, bank exec.; b. London, Jan. 4, 1945; d. Arthur and Pamela (McGuire) Gordon; came to U.S., naturalized, 1948; student U. N.C., 1962-64, Sch. Bank Mktg., 1976-77, La. State U., 1979-82; m. William R. Minnich, May 27, 1972. Mgr. employee incentive program 1st Nat. Bank Atlanta, 1969-70, adminstrv. asst., 1970-71, mgr. newcomer dept., 1971-75, mgr. sales and mktg. Honest Face check verification system, 1975-76, asst. v.p., 1975-79, dir. consumer affairs, 1975-78, adminstrv. mgr. market planning div., 1976-78, mktg. coordinator trust dept. and mgr. trust investment service, 1978-79, v.p., mgr. trust dept., nat. employee benefit sales, 1979—; speaker in field. Bd. dirs. Atlanta Humane Soc., 1976—, Atlanta Ballet, 1980—; sec. consumer adv. council Peachtree-Parkwood Mental Health Hosps., Atlanta, 1976—. Mem. Soc. Consumer Affairs Profls. (v.p. Atlanta chpt. 1976), Atlanta Mental Health Assn., Nat. Assn. Bank Women, Ga. Bankers Assn., Am. Inst. Banking. Democrat. Episcopalian. Club: Piedmont Driving. Contbr. articles to profl. and popular mags. Office: First Nat Bank of Atlanta 2 Peachtree St NW Atlanta GA 30303

MINNICH, VIRGINIA, hematologist, educator; b. Zanesville, Ohio, January 24, 1910; d. Rufus Humphrey and Ollie (Burley) Minnich; B.S. in Home Econs., Ohio State U., 1937; M.S. in Nutrition, Ia. State Coll., 1938; D.Sc., William Woods Coll., 1972. Research asst. dept. medicine div. hematology Washington U. Sch. Medicine, St. Louis, 1939-54, research asso., 1954-58, research asst. prof., 1958-67, research asso. prof., 1967-74, prof., 1974-78, prof. emeritus, lectr., 1978—. Named St. Louis Woman of Achievement, Group Action Council, 1947; recipient Distinguished Service award Ohio State U. Home Econs. Alumni Assn., 1975. Fulbrigh-Hays research award, Turkey, 1964. Mem. Am. Fedn. for Clin. Research, Soc. for Exptl. Biology and Medicine, Internat. Soc. Hematology, Am. Soc. Hematology, Turkish Soc. Hematology (hon.), Sigma Xi, Omicron Nu, Phi Upsilon Omicron. Contbr. numerous articles to profl. jours. Address: Dept Medicine School of Medicine Washington Univ Lindell and Skinner Blvd Saint Louis MO 63130

MINOT, ANNA SEDGWICK (MRS. JOSEPH WARREN), actress; b. Boston; d. Wayland Manning and Anna (Shaughnessy) M.; B.A., Vassar Coll.; m. Arthur S. Franz, Oct. 25, 1942 (div. 1947); 1 son, Michael Minot; m. 2d., Joseph Warren, June 7, 1953. Debut as actress in The Strings, My Lord, Are False, N.Y.C., 1942; appeared in Broadway prodns. including The Russian People, 1943, The Visitor, 1944, The Iceman Cometh, 1946, An Enemy of the People, 1951, The Love of Four Colonels, 1953, The Trip to Bountiful, 1953, The Tunnel of Love, 1957, Ivanov, 1966, also Off-Broadway in Getting Out, 1978, 79; TV appearances include Bachelor Party, 1953, The Edge of Night, 1958-59, As The World Turns, 1966-70, A World Apart, 1970-71, Somerset, 1973, The Best of Families, 1977; stage mgr. Broadway prodn. Ivanov, 1966; staff playreader, copywriter Play of the Month Guild, 1957-67. Reader, Rec. for the Blind, Inc., 1968—; performer Plays for Living, Family Service Assn. Am., 1965—. Mem. Urban League Greater N.Y., Actors' Fund, Phi Beta Kappa. Democrat. Home: 226 W 10th St New York NY 10014 Office: care Actors Equity Assn 165 W 46th St New York NY 10036

MINOT, JACYNTH PATRICIA, arts adminstr; b. London; d. Giuseppe and Betty Elaine Diana (Moore) de Lellis; B.A. summa cum laude in Music Theory and Composition, U. N.H., 1970; children—Diana Joan, Peter Hamilton, Judith Anne, Benjamin Nathaniel. Pianist, instr. music, 1971-76; lectr. U. N.H., Durham, 1971-76; staff asst. Am. Symphony Orch. League, Vienna, Va., 1976; artist rep. Columbia Artists Mgmt., Inc., N.Y.C., 1976-77; gen. mgr. Johnstown (Pa.) Symphony Orch., 1977-80; exec. dir. Center for Chamber Music, East Sullivan, N.H., 1980-82; arts mgmt. cons., 1978—. Mem. Am. Council for the Arts, Am. Symphony Orch. League, Chamber Music Am., Assn. Coll., Univ. and Community Arts Adminstrs., Kappa Phi Kappa. Democrat. Unitarian. Office: Center for Chamber Music at Apple Hill East Sullivan NH 03445

MINTER, JIMMIE RUTH, med. adminstr.; b. Greenville, S.C., Sept. 28, 1941; d. James C. and Lois (Williams) Jannino; B.S. Acctg., U. S.C., 1962; m. Charles H. Minter, Nov. 3, 1972; 1 dau., Regina M. Asst. controller Package Supply & Equipment Co., Greenville, 1964-70, Olympia Knitting Mills, Spartanburg, S.C., 1970-72; controller Diacou Knitting Mills, Spartanburg, 1972-74; adminstr. Atlanta Med. Specialists, P.C., Riverdale, Ga., 1974-79; adminstr., corp. sec. David L. Cooper, M.D. P.C., Riverdale, 1979—. Program chmn. 4th of July Celebration and Beauty Pageant, City of Riverdale; active local and state election campaign fund raising. Mem. Am. Bus. Women's Assn. (chpt. Bus. Woman of Yr. 1969), Nat. Assn. Female Execs. Home: 1674 Adrian Dr Riverdale GA 30296 Office: 150 Med Way Suite C-2 Riverdale GA 30274

MINTER, NIKI GENE, film dir., producer, writer; b. Austin, Tex., July 5, 1941; d. Gordon Eugene and Ellouise Elizabeth (Mitchell) M.; student UCLA, 1964; postgrad. Northwestern U.; m. Frederick Porter Moore, Dec. 17, 1976. Casting dir. John Urie Prodns., Los Angeles, 1967; producer Cascade Pictures Co., FilmFair, also Wakeford Orloff Prodns., 1968-72; exec. producer, gen. mgr. Wylde Films Co., Los Angeles, 1972-74; producer for various advt. agys., 1974-76; dir. Coast Prodns. Co., Los Angeles, 1976—; author: (screenplay) The Long Way Home, 1979. Mem. Dirs. Guild Am. Democrat. Quaker. Home: 7330 Pyramid Dr Los Angeles CA 90046 Office: 1001 N Poinsettia Pl Los Angeles CA 90046

MINTER, VALERIE ANN, former sch. adminstr.; b. Harrow, Eng., Mar. 10, 1938; came to U.S., 1963, naturalized, 1970; d. Thomas James and Elsie Catherine Beatrice (Knevett) Spicer; diploma St. James's Secretarial Coll., 1956; B.A., Hofstra U., 1975; m. William Arthur Minter, Aug. 21, 1976. Exec. sec. Humphreys & Glasgow, Ltd., London, 1957-60; adminstrv. asst. to chmn. Thomas De La Rue & Co., Ltd., London, 1960-65; tchr. Assn. for Help of Retarded Children, Brookville, N.Y., 1965-70; adminstrv. asst., dir. social services Good Samaritan Hosp., West Islip, N.Y., 1971-73; dir. Bauer Industries, Inc., Hempstead, N.Y., 1973-75; adminstrv. asst. to pres. Purolator Services, Inc., New Hyde Park, N.Y., 1975-77; asst. to chmn. Hazeltine Corp., Greenlawn, N.Y., 1977-78; asst. to pres., dir. personnel and adminstrn. Stone Sch., New Haven, 1979-81; lectr. career devel., 1979. Chmn. bd. A Better Chance, Inc., Guilford, Conn., 1979—. Mem. Kappa Delta Phi. Democrat. Home: 645 Durham Rd Guilford CT 06437

MINTZ, BEATRICE, biologist; b. N.Y.C., Jan. 24, 1921; d. Samuel and Janie (Stein) M.; A.B. magna cum laude, Hunter Coll., 1941; postgrad. N.Y.U., 1941-42; M.S., U. Iowa, 1944, Ph.D., 1946; D.Sc. (hon.), N.Y. Med. Coll., 1980, Med. Coll. Pa., 1980, Northwestern U., 1982. Successively instr. biol. scis., asst. prof., assoc. prof., U. Chgo., 1946-60; assoc. mem. Inst. for Cancer Research, Phila., 1960-65, sr. mem., 1965—; Fulbright research scholar U. Paris, U. Strasbourg (France), 1951. Recipient Bertner Found. award in fundamental cancer research U. Tex. M.D. Anderson Hosp. and Tumor Inst., 1977; NIH lectureship and citation, 1978; award in biol. and med. scis. N.Y. Acad. Scis., 1979; Papanicolaou award for sci. achievement Papanicolaou Cancer Research Inst., 1979; Lewis S. Rosenstiel award in basic med. research Brandeis U., 1980; Lalor Found. fellow, 1954, 55. Fellow AAAS, Am. Acad. Arts and Scis., Am. Ob-Gyn Soc. (hon.); mem. Nat. Acad. Scis., Am. Philos. Soc., Genetics Soc. Am. (first recipient medal 1981), Soc. Study Developmental Biology, Internat. Soc. Developmental Biology, Am. Soc. Zoologists, Am. Inst. Biol. Scis., Phi Beta Kappa, Sigma Xi. Office: 7701 Burholme Ave Philadelphia PA 19111

MINTZ, FLORENCE SHIRLEY, educator; b. Paterson, N.J., Sept. 4, 1923; d. Harry and Louise (Gallay) Eichman; B.A., Montclair State Coll., 1944, M.A., 1969; Ed.D., Rutgers U., 1976; m. Murray Mintz, Oct. 2, 1943; children—Beth Mintz Woolf, Adin. Auditor, office fiscal dir. U.S. Govt., Newark, 1944; tchr. Paulsboro (N.J.) High Sch., 1945-46, 64-70; office mgr. Charles W. Carvin Co., N.Y.C., 1948-50; research asst., mem. adj. faculty Rutgers U., 1970-76, curriculum specialist, 1977—; career edn. coordinator N.J. Dept. Higher Edn., Trenton, 1976-77; condr. workshops on women, elimination of sex bias and stereotyping, behavioral objectives for vocat. educators; cons. curriculum devel. Mem. Nat., Eastern bus. edn. assns., Assn. Supervision and Curriculum Devel., Am. Vocat. Assn., N.J. Vocat. Edn. Assn., Am. Vocat. Edn. Research Assn., Phi Delta Kappa, Kappa Delta Pi, Epsilon Pi Tau, Delta Pi Epsilon. Jewish. Office: NJ Dept Edn Bur Basic Skills 225 W State St Trenton NJ 08625

MINTZ, GILDA YOLLES, public relations co. exec.; b. N.Y.C.; d. Naftali and Sarah Pearl (Langner) Yolles; B.A., Hunter Coll., 1956; m. David A. Mintz, Apr. 21, 1963; children—Louis Neil, Stephen Matthew. With Ruder Finn & Rotman Inc., N.Y.C., 1960—, account supr., 1970—, sr. v.p., 1978—. Chmn. public relations adv. bd. Twp. of Teaneck (N.J.). Mem. Public Relations Soc. Am. (Silver Anvil 1978), Nat. Home Fashions League (v.p., past dir.), Am. Soc. Interior Designers. Office: 110 E 59th St New York NY 10022

MINTZER, DORIAN, psychotherapist; b. Pitts., Feb. 19, 1946; d. Oscar A. and Minna (Giffen) M.; B.A. in Social Scis., U. Calif., Berkeley, 1968; M.S.W. with honors, U. Pitts., 1970; Ph.D., Smith Coll., 1979. Group worker Assn. Retarded Citizens Allegheny County, Pitts., 1970-72; chief social worker devel. clinic Children's Hosp., Pitts., 1972-75; research asso. child devel. unit Children's Hosp. Med. Center, Boston, 1977-78; clin. cons. Learning Therapies, Inc., Newtonville, Mass., 1977-81; research asso. social work and child psychiatry Beth Israel Hosp., Boston, 1980—, also pvt. practice psychotherapy, Boston and Newton Centre, Mass., 1977—; lectr. Allegheny Community Coll., 1971-75; instr. U. Pitts., 1970-75. Cert. Nat. Registry Health Care Providers in Clin. Social Work; lic. clin. social worker, lic. clin. psychologist, Mass. Mem. Nat. Assn. Social Workers, Am. Assn. Mental Deficiency, Am. Orthopsychiat. Assn., Soc. Research in Child Devel. Home: 43 W Boulevard Rd Newton Centre MA 02159 Office: 82 Marlborough St Boston MA 02116

MINUDRI, REGINA URSULA, librarian; b. San Francisco, May 9, 1937; d. John Camillo and Molly (Halter) M.; B.A., San Francisco Coll. for Women, 1958; M.L.S., U. Calif., Berkeley, 1959. Reference librarian Menlo Park (Calif.) Public Library, 1959-62; regional librarian Santa Clara County Library, San Jose, Calif., 1962-67; coordinator Fed. Young Adult Library Project, Mountain View, Calif., 1967-71; asst. county librarian Alameda County Library, Hayward, Calif., 1972-77; dir. Berkeley Public Library, 1977—; lectr. U. Calif., Berkeley Library Sch., 1977—. Mem. Calif. Library Assn. (pres. 1981, council 1969-72, 75-79, 80-82), ALA (exec. bd. 1981—, council 1980—; Grolier award 1975), Women Library Workers, Bay Area Young Adult Librarians, LWV (dir. Berkeley 1980-81). Club: Soroptimists (Berkeley). Author: Getting It Together, 1970; also articles. Office: 2090 Kittredge St Berkeley CA 94704

MINUS, BERTHA DUNLAP, speech pathologist, educator; b. Washington, Nov. 11, 1951; d. James Allen and Nina Mae (Gilliam) Dunlap; B.A., George Washington U., 1973; M.S., U. Pacific, 1974; m. Reginald C. Minus, May 20, 1978. Speech pathologist, Washington, 1974—; instr. speech dept. D.C. Tchrs. Coll., 1974-78; asst. prof. dept. communications scis., field supr. student tchrs. U. D.C., 1978—, instr. sign lang. Career Edn. Inst., 1979—; clin. supr. D.C. Public Schs., U. D.C. Speech and Hearing Clinic, Archdiocese of D.C., 1978—. Mem. Nat. Council Negro Women, Am. Speech and Hearing Assn., D.C. Speech and Hearing Assn., AAUP, Ki Wives of Silver Spring, Zeta Phi Beta. Democrat. Baptist. Home: 5905 Southgate Dr Temple Hills MD 20748 Office: 724 9th St NW Washington DC 20002

MINUZZO, ANTOINETTE, educator; b. Lake Forest, Ill., Nov. 20, 1938; d. Frank and Maria Minuzzo; B.A., Lake Forest Coll., 1960; M.A., Northwestern U., 1967. Tchr., Oak Terrace Sch., Highwood, Ill., 1960—; cons. Xerox Ednl. Publs., My Weekly Reader. Local and state edn. lobbyist; chairperson Ill. Polit. Action Com. for Edn., 1974-80. Recipient Those Who Excel award, 1974. Mem. NEA, Ill. Edn. Assn. (dir. 1972-80), Highwood-Highland Park Edn. Assn., Nat. Assn. Female Execs., Phi Delta Kappa, Delta Kappa Gamma (pres. Alpha Nu chpt. 1982—). Home: 569 Oakwood Ave Lake Forest IL 60045

MIRABELLA, GRACE, mag. editor; b. Maplewood, N.J., June 10, 1930; d. Anthony and Florence (Bellofatto) M.; B.A., Skidmore Coll., 1950; m. William G. Cahan, Nov. 24, 1974. Mem. exec. tng. program Macy's, N.Y.C., 1950-51; mem. fashion dept. Saks Fith Ave., N.Y.C., 1951-52; with Vogue mag., N.Y.C., 1952-54, 56—, assoc. editor, 1965-71, editor-in-chief, 1971—; mem. public relations staff Simonetta & Fabiani, Rome, 1954-56; lectr. New Sch. Social Research, 1980, 81, 82. Hon. bd. dirs. Catalyst; adv. bd. Columbia Grad. Sch. Journalism. Recipient Outstanding Grad. Achievement award Skidmore Coll., 1972. Mem. Women's Forum N.Y. Office: Vogue 350 Madison Ave New York NY 10017

MIRANDA, JACQUELINE FRY, mgmt. cons. co. exec.; b. St. Anthony, Idaho, Nov. 3, 1953; d. Jack P. and Noreen (Daugherty) Fry; A.A., Cottey Coll., 1974; A.B., U. Calif., Berkeley, 1975; m. Daniel F. Miranda, Dec. 28, 1975; 1 son, David F. Research asso. Paul R. Ray & Co., N.Y.C., 1975-79; cons. Bartholdi & Co., Chgo., 1979-80; v.p. Houze, Shourds & Montgomery, Chgo., 1980—. Office: 3 1st National Plaza Suite 4488 Chicago IL 60602

MIRANTI, PAMELA GAYLE, educator; b. Pryor, Okla., June 16, 1951; d. Robert Lee and Alberta M. (Green) Nutting; B.A. magna cum laude, William Woods Coll., 1973; Ed.M., Drury Coll., 1976; m. Joseph Peter Miranti Jr., May 5, 1973; children—Pamela Gayle, Joseph Peter III. Tchr., English and journalism Cherokee Jr. High Sch., Springfield, Mo., 1973—. Recipient Robert Greef award Mo. Assn. Tchrs. English; Award of Distinction, AAUW. Mem. NEA, Nat. Council Tchrs. English, MLA, Mo. Tchrs. Assn., Springfield Edn. Assn., Phi Beta, Alpha Chi, Alpha Mu Gamma, Sigma Tau Delta. Democrat. Mem. Christian Ch. Home: RR 2 Box 198C Nixa MO 65714 Office: Cherokee School 420 E Plainview Rd Springfield MO 65807

MIRCI, SELMA ERK, clin. psychologist; b. Turkey, Mar. 15, 1944; came to U.S., 1969; d. Kamil and Faika Erk; B.S., Middle East Tech. U., 1965; M.A., Hacettepe U., Turkey, 1968; Ph.D., U.S. Internat. U., 1976. Instr. psychology Hacettepe U., 1966-69; psychol. intern Orange County Mental Health, 1974-75; pvt. practice clin. psychology, Irvine, Calif., 1975—; cons. to women's groups. Mem. Am. Psychol. Assn., Calif. Psychol. Assn., Orange County Psychol. Assn., AAUW, NOW. Office: 2070 Business Center Dr Irvine CA 92715

MIRELL, SANDEE LYNN, librarian; b. New Haven, May 31, 1942; d. J. R. and Ruth B. White; A.B., Chapman Coll., 1964; postgrad. Calif. State U., Fullerton, 1965; m. Michael A. Mirell, Apr. 7, 1973; 1 dau., Hope. Tchr. English, Villa Park High Sch., Orange, Calif., 1965-67; adminstrv. asst. World Campus Afloat, Orange, 1968; law librarian City Atty. Law Library, Los Angeles, 1971—. Mem. ALA. Democrat. Mem. Christian Ch. (Disciples of Christ). Office: City Hall East Room 1700 Los Angeles CA 90012

MIRON, RHODA PASCO, club woman; b. Cornwall, Eng., Feb. 16, 1902; brought to U.S., 1904, naturalized, 1940; d. William and Jane (Dymond) Pasco; student pub. schs., Hancock, Mich.; m. William E. Miron, June 19, 1926 (Dec. Jan. 1962); children—William E., John, Mary Miron Cota. Dep. sheriff, Escanaba, Mich., 1933-57; pres. House and Senate Club, Lansing, Mich., 1961-62; historian, chaplain Am. Legion Aux., Escanaba, Mich.; guide Daus. of Isabella, Escanaba; mem. Mich. Democratic Central Com.; mem. St. Francis Hosp. Aux. Club: Women's (Escanaba, Mich.). Home: 518 8th St Escanaba MI 49829

MIRZA, LEONA LOUSIN, educator; b. Chgo., July 1, 1944; d. Max B. and Opal Lousin; B.A. in Math., North Park Coll., Chgo., 1965; M.A. in Edn., Western Mich. U., Kalamazoo, 1967, Ed.D. in Edn., 1972; m. David B. Mirza; children— Sara Anush, Elizabeth Ann. Tchr. Kalamazoo Pub. Schs., 1965-69; asso. prof. edn. North Park Coll., 1969—, also dept. chmn. Chmn. adv. com. on edn. in Ill., 1975—. Mem. Nat., Ill. assns. supervision and curriculum devel., Ill. Assn. Colls. of Tchr. Edn., Ill. Assn. Tchrs. Edn. in Pvt. Colls. (officer, 1974—). Contbr. articles to profl. jours. Specialist in elem. curriculum and adminstrn. Home: 795 Lincoln Ave Winnetka IL 60093 Office: 5125 N Spaulding Ave Chicago IL 60625

MISCHAKOFF, ANNE, musician; b. N.Y.C., May 12, 1942; d. Mischakoff and Hortense (Moritz) M.; A.B. magna cum laude, Smith Coll., 1964; M.A., U. Iowa, 1965; D.M.A., U. Ill., 1975. Prin. violist Evansville Philharm. Orch. and Quartet, 1965-66, Am. Chamber Symphony, 1981—; violist Contemporary Chamber Players and Lexington String Quartet, Chgo., 1966-68, Detroit Symphony, Mischakoff Quartet, Cranbrook Music Festival, 1968-72; asst. prof. music U. Pacific, Stockton, Calif., 1975-80; violist Sierra String Quartet, 1975-80, Sacramento Symphony, 1975-80, Sinfonia Musicale, Chgo., 1981—; asso. prof. viola Northwestern U., Evanston, Ill., 1980—; soloist Detroit Symphony Chamber Orch., various univ. and community orchs.; recitalist, Ann Arbor, Mich., Chgo., Los Angeles, Milw., 1982; tchr. master classes Internat. String Tchrs. Assn. Workshop, Innsbruck, Austria, 1982. Bd. dirs. Stockton Friends of Chamber Music, 1978—. Rockefeller player fellow, 1966-67; Tanglewood Player fellow, 1966; Internat. Research and Exchanges fellow, 1974-75. Mem. Am. String Tchrs. (pres. Calif. chpt. 1977-80), Am. Viola Soc., Am. Musicol. Assn., Music Educators Nat. Council, Phi Beta Kappa, Phi Kappa Lambda, Mu Phi Epsilon. Home: 47 Williamsburg Evanston IL 60203 Office: Sch Music Northwestern U Evanston IL 60202

MISCHIARA, PAMELA LEE, assn. exec.; b. Passaic, N.J., Apr. 23, 1945; d. Ernest Robert and Jeanne de la Montaigne Betz; master cosmetologist Jos. Paterno Coll. Beauty, 1973; postgrad. Pasco-Hernando Community Coll., 1979-82, Nova U., 1982—; m. Richard Mischiara, May 19, 1965; 1 son, Timothy. Pvt. practice cosmetology, Andover, N.J., 1973, Holiday, Fla., 1974-79; office mgr. Forguson Real Estate, New Port Richey, Fla., 1979-81, Ednl. Service Bur., New Port Richey, 1979-81; exec. dir. Nat. Assn. Ednl. Negotiators, Brooksville, Fla., 1980—. Sec., Shady Hills Little League Assn., Brooksville, 1979, v.p., 1980-82. Mem. Nat. Assn. Female Execs., Fla. Soc. Assn. Execs., Fla. Ednl. Negotiators, NOW, LWV, Phi Theta Kappa (charter sec. 1979-80). Home and Office: 225 Shirla Rae Dr Brooksville FL 33512

MISCHKE, NYLA JEANNE, advt. mgr.; b. Junction City, Kans., Mar. 18, 1956; d. James Nels and Lorraine Adell (Gleason) Aspelin; B.S. in Journalism and Mass Communications, Kans. State U., 1977; postgrad. U. Mo., 1978; m. Karl Reynolds Mischke, Nov. 24, 1978. Chief copywriter Burstein-Applebee Co., Kansas City, Mo., 1978-80; advt. coordinator Clinic Masters, Inc., Independence, Mo., 1980-81; mgr. advt. Am. White Goods Co., Kansas City, 1981—. Mem. Direct Marketing Club Kansas City, Advt. Club Kansas City. Club: German Shepherd Dog (Kansas City). Editor: The Schaferhunde News, 1982. Home: 5438 Northeast Carmel Rd Kansas City MO 64119

MISER, MARTHA ARDEN, social worker; b. Fort Worth, Apr. 14, 1935; d. Tarleton Alonzo and Nedra Irene (Cooper) Jenkins; student Rice U., 1953-54; B.A., U. Tex., 1956; postgrad. Calif. State U., 1964-65; M.S.W., U. So. Calif., 1969; m. Frank Donald Miser, Sr., July 4, 1970; children—Sara Dyck, Susan Jeffreys. Social worker Los Angeles County, Compton, Calif., 1964-65, child welfare worker, Compton, 1968, Long Beach, Calif., 1969-70; med. social worker Kaiser Permanente Med. Group, Bellflower, Calif., 1972-75; social caseworker Concept 7 Group Homes, Fullerton, Calif., 1978—; mem. Orange County Coalition Against Domestic Violence. Mem. AAUW, Acad. Cert. Social Workers, Nat. Assn. Social Workers. Republican. Methodist. Office: 1524 W Commonwealth St Fullerton CA 92803

MISHNE, JUDITH MARKS, educator; b. Cleve., Feb. 21, 1932; d. Moses Isaac and Lillian (Kemelman) Marks; B.S., U. Wis., 1953; M.S.W., Case Western Res. U., 1955; Ph.D., Sch. Social Work, Hunter Coll., 1981; grad. child therapy program Chgo. Inst. Psychoanalysis, 1974; 1 son, Jonathan Michael. Clin. social worker, social work educator various child service agys., faculty Sch. Social Work U. Chgo., 1966-77; faculty Sch. Social Work, Columbia U., N.Y.C., 1977-79; asso. prof. Sch. Social Work, N.Y.U., N.Y.C., 1979—; part time pvt. practice psychotherapist and cons.; summer faculty Smith Coll. Sch. Social Work. Mem. Council Social Work Edn., Nat. Assn. Social Workers, Assn. Child and Adolescent Psychotherapy (Chgo.). Author: Education for the Practice of Clinical Social Work at the Masters Level, 1978; Psychotherapy and Training in Clinical Social Work, 1980; Clinical Work with Children, 1983; co-editor: Ego and Self Psychology (Jason Aronson), 1983. Home: 255 W 88th St Apt 4E New York NY 10024 Office: 2 Washington Sq N New York NY 10003

MISISCHIA, KATHLEEN MARIE, travel agt., civic worker; b. Joliet, Ill., Apr. 23, 1942; d. Arthur Robert and Hazel Cecelia (Hartnett) Holden; spl. courses travel tng.; m. Cosmo Alfred Misischia, Feb. 22, 1964; children—Matthew William, Jason Hayes. Pres., dir., founder The Travel Bag, Ltd., Manhattan, Ill., 1978—. Bd. dirs. Will County Easter Seals, 1974, pres., dir., 1975-77, Humanitarian award, 1978; founder Manhattan Jr. Women's Club, 1975, pres., 1976, life mem., 1979; founder Manhattan C. of C., 1978, pres., 1980; mem. Will County Republican Central Com. Mem. Am. Soc. Travel Agts. (ltd.), New Lenox C. of C. Roman Catholic. Club: Lincolnway Bus. and Profl. Women's. Home: Rural Route 2 Manhattan IL 60442 Office: 1005 Laraway Rd #250 New Lenox IL 60451

MISSEL, ESTHER BARBARA, artist; b. Hartford, Conn., Apr. 4, 1926; d. Gasper and Lucy (Melandrillo) Lissandrello; A.A., Bay Path Coll., 1949; student in gen. studies Columbia U., 1949-52; m. Frederick F. Missel, July 16, 1949; children—Deborah, Gillian, Frederick Allen. Exhibited paintings in one-woman shows: Framer's Gallery, Moorestown, N.J., 1973, Perkins Center for Arts, 1979, also numerous pub. bldgs.; group shows include: Burlington County (N.J.) Art Guild, 1974, South Jersey All-Profl. Art Show, Cape May, 1973, Rider Coll., 1973, Nat. League Am. Pen Women Club House, Washington, 1977, N.J. Center for Performing Arts, 1974, Haddon Fortnightly, Haddonfield, N.J., 1970, Am. Artists Profl. League, Princeton, N.J., 1981, Perkins Center for Arts, Moorestown, N.J., 1982; represented in public collections: 1st. Presbyn. Ch., Moorestown, Squibb Co., Princeton, N.J., also pvt. collections, U.S., abroad. Recipient awards, including 1st Pl. in oils

Burlington County Art Guild, 1970, 2d Pl., 1972, 1st in oils Haddonfield Fortnightly, 1973, Popular Vote award Cape May Art League Nat. Summer Art Show, 1969. Mem. Nat. League Am. Pen Women, Inc. (Women in the Arts), Am. Artists Profl. League, Inc. Presbyterian. Home and Office: 264 E Main St Moorestown NJ 08057

MITCHAM, KAREN JO, plastic products retail exec.; b. Erie, Pa., Nov. 12, 1946; d. Chrstian Niels and Marguerite Lucille (Shaffer) Blumensaadt; B.F.A., Mercyhurst Coll., 1969; m. John B. Stoeckley, Nov. 14, 1981; 1 son, Clark Shaffer; children by previous marriage, Aaron Urie, M. Denton; 1 stepson, Reed B. Owner, The Crow's Nest, retail store, Oil City, Pa., 1973-77; pres. Karen Mitcham Assos., mfrs. rep., Monroeville, Pa., 1974-78; mktg. dir., culinary cons. Cousances div. Schiller & Asmus, Inc., Chgo., 1978-80; exec. adminstr. Ingrid At Home, direct selling, North Chicago, Ill., 1980—. Vice pres. Assn. Promotion Oil City, 1976; bd. dirs. Greater Pitts. Mdse. Mart, 1977. Mem. Direct Selling Assn., Bus. and Profl. Women's Club. Democrat. Episcopalian. Home: 34 Kyle Ct Clarendon Hills IL 60514 Office: 3601 N Skokie Hwy North Chicago IL 60064

MITCHELL, ARLENE LEE HUBBARD, bus. cons., accountant; b. Sheridan, Wyo., Jan. 17, 1936; d. Cecil H. and May E. (Whapples) M.; B.A. in Edn., UCLA, 1956; M. Acctg., Eastern Wash. State U., 1972; M.B.A., Va. Commonwealth U., 1974; m. Moyer Hubbard, Feb. 2, 1957; children—Janine Marie, Stephanie V., Moyer V., Linley R. Acct., Froehling & Robertson, Inc., Richmond, Va., 1973-74; acct., office mgr. North State Hulling Coop., Inc., Chico, Calif., 1974-76; pres. Bus. Services & Assos., Inc., Reno and Chico-Orland, Calif., 1977—; public speaker; leader workshops on bus. and fin. planning. Mem. Nat. Assn. Female Execs., Network Female Execs. Republican. Clubs: Chico Bus. and Profl. Women's (past pres.), Toastmistress (past regional pres.). Office: PO Box 929 Orland CA 95963

MITCHELL, BARBARA JEAN ELLIS DONEGAN, elementary sch. prin.; b. Chgo., Mar. 22, 1933; d. C.B. and Hilda (Davis) Ellis; B.E., Chgo. Tchrs. Coll., 1952; M.A., Roosevelt U., 1955; postgrad. U. Chgo., 1955, Chgo. State U., 1959, 68-69; m. Leon A. Donegan, Nov. 25, 1960 (div. 1963); 1 son, Leon Ellis; m. 2d, Ivory D. Mitchell, Apr. 16, 1966 (div. 1969); 1 son, Brian DeWitt. Tchr., Betsy Ross Sch., Chgo., 1952-57, Andrew Carnegie Sch., Chgo., 1957-62; tchr. 61st and University Sch., Chgo., 1962-63, asst. prin., 1963-68; asst. prin. Robert A. Black Mini-Magnet Sch., Chgo., 1968-71; prin. Charles S. Brownell Sch., Chgo., 1971-77; prin. Henry Clay Sch., Chgo., 1977-80, Edward Dunne Sch., Chgo., 1980—; adult edn. tchr., 1964-66; adjustment counselor, 1964-68; sch. librarian, 1964-68; curriculum coordinator, 1970. Recipient merit certificate Carnegie Sch. PTA, 1959, Distinguished Service recognition Ill. Congress Parents and Tchrs., 1961, recognition award for outstanding community service, Park Manor Neighbors Community Council, 1975. Mem. Chgo. Prins. Assn., Nat. Council Adminstrv. Women, Phi Delta Kappa. Episcopalian. Author: A Comparative Study of Faculty Meeting Procedures, 1955. Home: 2231 E 67th St Chicago IL 60649 Office: 10845 S Union Ave Chicago IL 60628

MITCHELL, BARBARAANN, govt. ofcl.; b. Balt.; d. Herbert George and Marion Mildred Welburne; div. ed. Morgan State Coll., U. Md., Balt., Community Coll. Balt.; B.A., Antioch Coll.; cert. U.S. Dept. Agr. Grad. Sch. Contract compliance officer Dept. Def., Ft. Holabird, Balt., 1974-76; equal opportunity specialist Bur. Hearings and Appeals EEOC, 1976-79; with Health Care Financing Administrn., Balt., 1979-80; mgr. Fed. Women's Program, 1982—. Recipient Community Action Agy. award; Outstanding Service award. Mem. Urban League, Am. Bus. Women's Assn., Federally Employed Women, Nat. Assn. Female Execs, LaGrande Dames. Home: 717 Sturgis Pl Baltimore MD 21208 Office: Room 601 6325 Security Blvd Baltimore MD 21235

MITCHELL, BETTY JO, library adminstr.; b. Coin, Iowa, May 2, 1931; d. Edith Darrah McWilliams; B.A., S.W. Mo. State U., Springfield; M.S.L.S., U. So. Calif. Asst. acquisitions librarian Calif. State U., Northridge, 1967-69, librarian for personnel and fin., 1969-71, acting asso. library dir., 1971-72, asso. dir. univ. libraries, 1972-81; cons. Western Interstate Commn. for Higher Edn. USOE Inst. for Tng. in Staff Devel. Problem Solving; participant workshops in field. Bd. dirs. San Fernando Valley council Girl Scouts U.S.A., 1974-77, employed personnel com., 1979—; bd. dirs. Bear Valley Springs Condominium Owners Assn., 1978, Empyrean Found., 1978—. Mem. ALA (mem., chmn. various coms.), Nat. Library Assn., Calif. Library Assn., Assn. Calif. State U. Profs. (sec., exec. com., 1971-72), AAUP, Pi Beta Chi, Alpha Mu Gamma. Co-author: Cost Analysis of Library Functions: A Total System Approach, 1978; author: ALMS: A Budget Based Library Management System, 1982; co-author: How to See the U.S. on $12 a Day; speaker profl. confs.; contbr. writings to profl. publs.; editor Staff Development column in Special Libraries, 1975-76. Home: Star Route 3 Box 5G Tehachopi CA 93561 Office: California State University 18111 Nordhoff St Northridge CA 91330

MITCHELL, BEVERLY ANNE, lab. asst.; b. Altus, Okla., May 26, 1946; d. Clarence Willard and Velma Ruth (Dorsey) Garrison; Cert. lab. asst. St. Anthony's Hosp., 1965; student Tex. Tech. U., 1968, Ariz. Western Coll., 1981—; m. Donald M. Mitchell, Aug. 19, 1966; children—Robin Page, Valerie Ruth. Lab. technician St. Anthony's Hosp., Amarillo, Tex., 1965-66, West Tex. Hosp., 1966-69, Riley Hosp., Meridian, Miss., 1970, Med. Arts Clinic, Lab., Lubbock, Tex., 1973-74; sec./receptionist Frontier Realty, Yuma, Ariz., 1980; lab. technician Younglove Lab., Yuma, 1980-81. Mem. Am. Soc. Clin. Pathologists, Beta Sigma Phi, Phi Theta Kappa. Democrat. Baptist. Clubs: Marine Officers Wives, Marine Air Weapons and Tactics Squadron-1 Officers Wives. Address: 1758 Camino Cerro Yuma AZ 85364

MITCHELL, CAROL ACKERMANN, social worker; b. Takoma Park, Md., Apr. 14, 1947; d. Rolland Fredrick and Helen Louise (Donaldson) Ackermann; B.A., Wheaton Coll., 1969; M.S.W., Smith Coll., 1975; m. Roy G. Mitchell, Jr., May 30, 1969; children—Alison Browning and Rebecca Donaldson (twins). Child welfare specialist adoption placement unit Mass. Dept. Public Welfare, Boston, 1970-74, homefinding coordinator, 1975-76; social work student intern Framingham (Mass.) Youth Guidance Center, 1974-75, psychiat. social worker, part-time, 1975-78; clin. asso. Walker Home and Sch., Needham, Mass., 1976-81; group leader Resolve Inc., 1981-82; workshop leader U. Conn. Sch. Social Work, West Hartford, 1979, New Eng. Child Care Assn., 1979-80; pvt. practice social work, Sherborn, Mass., 1982—. Mem. Acad. Cert. Social Workers, Nat. Assn. Social Workers, Children's Group Therapy Assn. Contbr. articles to profl. jours. Home: 121 Coolidge St Sherborn MA 01770

MITCHELL, EDNA STEINER, educator; b. Sacramento, June 29, 1931; d. Howard F. and Thelma (Johnson) Steiner; B.A., William Jewell Coll., Liberty, Mo., 1952; M.A., Kansas City U., 1956; Ph.D., U. Mo., Kansas City, 1971; children—Debra, Tom, Kris. Tchr. elem. schs., Independence, Mo., 1953-55; from instr. to prof. dept. edn. William Jewell Coll., 1955-71; asst. prof. Smith Coll., Northampton, Mass., 1969-73; prof., head dept. edn. Mills. Coll., Oakland, Calif., 1973—; research asso. MidContinent Regional Ednl. Lab., Kansas City, Mo., 1967; spl. asst. to Congressman Tom Lantos, 1981-82. Congressional Sci. fellow, 1980-81; NSF grantee, 1978-80, Spencer Found. grantee, 1981, AEI grantee, 1982. Mem. Soc. Research in Child Devel., Assn. Supervision and Curriculum Devel., Calif. Council Edn. Tchrs., Am. Edn. Research Assn., Phi Delta Kappa. Democrat. Contbr. articles in field. Office: Mills College Oakland CA 94613

MITCHELL, ELIZABETH FERGUSON, nurse; b. Bklyn., Feb. 1; d. Wilbur Paul and Alice (Wilson) Ferguson; R.N., Methodist Hosp., Bklyn., 1948; student N.Y. U.; m. Donald P. Mitchell, Oct. 3, 1953; children—Brett, Todd. Staff nurse, supr. hosps. in N.Y., Oreg. and N.J., 1948-53; occupational health nurse Freightliner Corp., 1974; coordinator occupational health program St. Vincent Hosp., Portland, Oreg., 1980-82; hosp. loss prevention rep. St. Paul Fire & Marine Ins. Co., Portland, 1982—. Pres., Maplewood (N.J.) Sch. PTA, 1966; v.p. Women's Soc., United Methodist Ch., Maplewood, 1967. Mem. Columbia River Assn. Occupational Health Nurses (pres. 1982—). Republican. Presbyterian. Home: 6730 SW 89th Pl Portland OR 97223 Office: 825 NE Multnomah Portland OR 97232

MITCHELL, GAIL ELLEN, utility co. exec.; b. N.Y.C., Sept. 23, 1951; d. Howard Bernard and Veronica Thelva (LeDoux) M.; B.A., Boston U., 1973; M.U.P., N.Y. U., 1975. Transp. planner Office Upper Manhattan Planning and Devel., 1974-75; sr. planner N.J. Dept. Community Affairs, 1975-78; sales rep. Xerox Corp., N.Y.C., 1978; market adminstr. N.Y. Tel., N.Y.C., 1978—. Recipient various awards N.Y. Tel.; grantee Boston U., N.Y. U. Mem. Nat. Council Negro Women, NAACP, Nat. Urban League, Delta Sigma Theta. Office: One Astor Plaza Floor 43 New York NY 10036

MITCHELL, GRACE LOUISE (MRS. DONALD BATES MITCHELL), ednl. adminstr., author; b. Natick, Mass., Jan. 10, 1909; d. Aubrey A. and Ruperta M. (Woodward) Forster; B.S., Tufts U., 1954; M.Ed., Harvard U., 1962; Ph.D., Union Grad. Sch.; m. Donald Bates Mitchell, Aug. 26, 1948; children by previous marriage—F. Lee Bailey, Nancy C. Archipretе, William E. Bailey. Dir. Green Acres Day Sch., Waltham, Mass., 1933-76; ednl. dir., v.p. Living and Learning Centres, 1970-80; v.p. Child Care Mgmt., Inc., 1980—; cons. in field; coordinator early childhood edn. program Quinsigamond Community Coll., Worcester, Mass., 1968-71. Pres. Waltham Family Service, 1953; corporate mem. Waltham Hosp., 1970—. Bd. dirs. Jr. Achievement, Boston. Mem. Assn. Childhood Edn., Nat. Assn. Edn. Young Children (dir. 1974—), Waltham C. of C. (dir. 1944), Am. Camping Assn. (pres. New Eng. sect. 1966-67). Author: Fundamentals of Day Camping, 2d edit., 1981; I Am, I Can, 1977; The Day Care Book, 1979. Home: Eden Rd Rockport MA 01966 Office: 609 Hunnewell St Needham MA 02194

MITCHELL, JO BENNETT, educator, civic worker; b. Laredo, Tex., Jan. 14, 1928; d. Hilary Joseph and Inez Bell (Drake) Bennett; B.A., N.Mex. State U., 1949; postgrad. Hartford Sem. Found., 1951-52, U. Wash., 1973; M.A., Pacific Oaks Coll., 1981; m. Robert Curtis Mitchell, Aug. 30, 1949; children—Drake Curtis, John Douglas, Mary Cecilia. Day care tchr. Seattle Day Nursery, 1949-50, University Heights Sch., 1950-51; nursery sch. and kindergarten tchr. Campus Sch., N.Mex. State U., 1961-65; child care cons. HELP, Albuquerque, 1965; teaching assoc. Central Wash. U., Ellensburg, 1970-82; dir. Alaska/N.W. Extension Center, San Francisco Theol. Sem., Seattle, 1982—. Mem. policy bd. Kittitas County Head Start, 1967-70; trustee Westminster Found. United Presbyterian Ch. Synod Alaska N.W., 1979-82; bd. dirs. United Ministries in Higher Edn., Central Wash. U., 1975-82. Mem. AAUW, NOW, LWV, Coalition on Women and Religion, Fellowship of Reconciliation, Wash. Assn. Educators of Personnel for Early Childhood Programs (v.p.), Adminstrv. Women in Edn., AAUP, Nat. Assn. Edn. of Young Children, Assn. Childhood Edn. Internat., Organisation Mondiale pour l'Education Prescolaire, Phi Delta Kappa. Office: Alaska Northwest Extension Center San Francisco Theological Seminary 720 Seneca St Seattle WA 98101

MITCHELL, JOAN, artist; b. Chgo., 1926; d. James Herbert and Marion (Strobel) M.; student Smith Coll., 1942-44; M.F.A., Art Inst. Chgo., 1947; hon. degrees Western Coll. Ohio, 1972, Miami U., Oxford, Ohio, 1971. One-person shows: Galerie Fournier, Paris, 1967-80, Everson Museum, Syracuse, N.Y., 1972, Whitney Mus. Am. Art, N.Y.C., 1974, Arts Club, Chgo., 1974, Carnegie Mus., Pitts., 1974, Corcoran Gallery Art, Washington, 1975, Xavier Fouurcade Inc., N.Y.C., 1976-80; group shows include: M.I.T., 1962, Pa. Acad. Fine Arts, 1966, Mus. Modern Art, N.Y.C., Japan, India and Australia, 1967, U. Ill., 1967, Mus. Modern Art, N.Y.C., 1971, N.Y. State Mus., Albany, 1977, Albright-Knox Art Gallery, Buffalo, 1978, Hirshhorn Mus. and Sculpture Garden, Washington, 1980; represented in permanent collections: Basel (Switzerland) Mus., Albright-Knox Art Gallery, Art Inst. Chgo., Mus. Modern Art, Phillips Collection, Washington, Corcoran Gallery Art. Recipient Premio Lissone, Milan, Italy, 1961, Brandeis award, 1974; Art Inst. Chgo. travel fellow, 1947. Office: care Xavier Fourcade Inc 26 E 75th St New York NY 10021 *

MITCHELL, JONI, singer, songwriter; b. Ft. MacCleod, Alta., Can., Nov. 7, 1943; d. William A. and Myrtle M. (McKee) Anderson; student Alta. Coll. Art. Chuck Mitchell, 1965 (div.). Albums include Clouds; For the Roses; Blue; Miles of Aisles; Court & Spark; Joni Mitchell; Hissing of Summer Lawns; Hejira; Ladies of the Canyon; Don Juan's Reckless Daughter; Mingus (Jazz Album of the Year and Rock-Blues Album of the Year, Downbeat Mag., 1979); Shadows and Light; compositions include Both Sides Now, Michael from Mountains, Urge for Going, Circle Game. Recipient Grammy award for best folk artist, 1971, 75; Playboy award for best female artist, 1974; 1st Ann. Rocky award for best female vocalist, 1975. Address: care Lookout Mgmt Co 9120 Sunset Blvd Hollywood CA 90069 *

MITCHELL, JOSEPHINE GRAY, musician; b. Bonham, Tex.; d. Moses Vashti and Bertie (Hoy) Gray; B.S., Tex. Woman's U., 1926, M.A., 1971; m. T.A. Mitchell, Mar. 21, 1929; children—Richard Gray, Thomas Albert. Pianist in profl. concerts in Tex., Okla., and Colo., 1927—; tchr. music Port Arthur (Tex.) High Sch., 1928-29; lectr. on Tex. music and composers; established Southwestern Folk Music Archive in Ft. Worth Library; chmn. in establishment of Tex. Composers Manuscript Archives in Dallas Public Library; mem. bd. Tex. Girls' Choir Youth Orch. Greater Ft. Worth; chmn., adv. Tex. Composers Commn. Fund, 1978—, founder, chmn., 1980-82; mem. contest Van Cliburn Piano Quadrennial Contest, 1976-82; bd. dirs. Fine Arts Soc. Tex., 1980—, S.W. Ballet Assn.; presented hist. ballet with commd. composers and choreographers Tex. Women's U., 1980; established Modern Dance-Ballet Archive, Lyndon Baines Johnson Library, Austin, Tex., 1980; bd. dirs. S.W. Ballet Center. Recipient various citations; named 1st Lady of Music in Ft. Worth, 1967. Mem. Am. Coll. Musicians, Ft. Worth League Composers (founder 1958, pres. 1958-76), Fine Arts Guild, Nat. Fedn. Music Clubs (folk music archivist 1963-65, research chmn. 1958-68), Tex. Fedn. Music Clubs (dist. pres. 1964-65), Tex. Composers Guild (pres. 1952-76, adv. 1978-82), Tex. Woman's U. Alumnae Assn. (past pres.), Ft. Worth Ballet Assn. (charter), Symphony League (charter), Ft. Worth Opera Guild (charter), Fine Arts Soc. Tex. (charter dir.), Tex. Hist. Assn., Tarrant County Hist. Soc., Nat. Guild Piano Tchrs. (nat. adjudicator), Sigma Alpha Iota (pres. 1961-62). Episcopalian. Clubs: Ft. Worth Piano Forum, Ft. Worth Women's, Euterpean Music (pres. 1952-54), E. Clyde Whitlock Music (charter, past pres.). Editor: Texas Composers Handbooks, 2d edit., 1974; author: Creative Music of Texas, 1976; Column editor Tex. Composers News, 1978—.

MITCHELL, KATHLEEN LAURA, writer, pub.; b. Detroit, July 21, 1953; d. Donald Harrison and Helen (Shifter) M.; student Chapman Coll., 1971, Ariz. State U., 1972, U. Hawaii, 1972-74; children—Miandra Field, Elonka Dawn. Editor, Noncom News, Honolulu, 1975; reporter Sandpoint (Idaho) Daily Bee, 1979; editor Priest River (Idaho) Times, 1980, Catalog Shopper, Scottsdale, Ariz., 1980; editor, pub. The Exchange, Phoenix, 1981—; cons. small publs., 1970—. Bd. dirs. Ariz. Girls Ranch. Recipient award Lions Club, 1979. Club: Soroptimist Internat. of Scottsdale. Home: 4233 N 47th Dr Phoenix AZ 85031

MITCHELL, MARGARETTA KUHLTHAU, photographer, author; b. Bklyn., May 27, 1935; d. Conrad William, Jr. and Margaretta (Rice) Kuhlthau; B.A. magna cum laude, Smith Coll., 1957; m. Frederick Cleveland Mitchell, May 23, 1959; children—Margaretta Anne, Catharine Francesca, Julia Warren. Research asst. to pres. Polaroid Corp., Cambridge, Mass., 1957-59; tchr. photography U. Calif. extension, 1976-78, City Coll. San Francisco, 1980, Walnut Creek (Calif.) Civic Arts Program, 1980-82, Calif. Arts Council artist in the community Berkeley Art Center, 1981-82; guest curator Internat. Center Photography, 1977-79; exhbns. include group shows: Friends of Photography, 1968, Focus Gallery, San Francisco, 1969, 71-74, San Francisco Mus. Modern Art, 1978, Internat. Center Photography, 1979, Yuen Lui Gallery, Seattle, 1980, Marcuse Pfeifer Gallery, N.Y.C., 1981, Douglas Elliott Gallery, San Francisco, 1982; author: Gift of Place, 1969; Recollections; Ten Women of Photography, 1979; introduction to After Ninety (Imogen Cunningham), 1977; co-author: To A Cabin, 1973. Grantee, Levi-Strauss Found., 1978-79, Internat. Center Photography, 1979, Calif. Council Humanities, 1980, L.J. and Mary C. Skagga Found., 1981, Calif. Arts Council, 1981-82. Mem. Am. Soc. Mag. Photographers, San Francisco Women Artists, Inst. Hist. Study, Soc. Photog. Edn. Address: 280 Hillcrest Rd Berkeley CA 94705

MITCHELL, MARION MIRANDA MCWILLIAMS (MRS. WILLIAM HENRY MITCHELL), former social work adminstr.; b. Elgin, Ill., Nov. 14, 1914; d. Henry Edgar and Ada (Young) McWilliams; B.A., U. Chgo., 1936, M.A., 1959; m. William Henry Mitchell, Jan. 11, 1941. Caseworker, Chgo. Relief Adminstrn., 1938-41; library asst. Chgo. Public Library, 1941-42; caseworker Chgo. Orphan Asylum, 1943-44, caseworker spl. day care project, 1947-50; probation officer Juvenile Ct. of Cook County (Ill.), 1945-47; caseworker Chgo. Child Care Soc., 1950-54, supr. child placement and adoptions, 1954-74. Chmn. Chgo. chpt. Nat. Council on Illegitimacy, 1966-70; del. to Ill. Commn. on Children, 1970, mem. state cooperating orgns. com., 1970—, mem. adoptions com., 1972-73, com. on rights of minors, 1975-77; mem. adv. com. Subsidies for Black Adoptions, 1972-74; dir. foster care and adoption Chgo. Child Care Soc., 1974-78; ret., 1978; chmn. Adoption Info. Service Assn., 1974-77; mem. Com. Youth and the Law Ill. Commn. Children, 1977—; mem. adoptions adv. com. Ill. Dept. Children and Family Services, 1979-81; mem. statewide com. Ill. White House Conf. on Children, 1979-80; bd. dirs. Midwest Adoption Facilitating Service, 1971-77, treas., 1974-77; bd. dirs. Council on Unplanned Pregnancy, 1971-73. Mem. Ill. Welfare Assn. (mem. study course com. 1965—, dir. 1972—, 3d v.p. 1975-77), Nat. Assn. Social Workers, Nat. Conf. Social Welfare, Child Care Assn. Ill., Acad. Cert. Social Workers. Home: 7552 S Wabash Ave Chicago IL 60619

MITCHELL, MARY, retail store advt. exec.; b. Cheery Ridge, La., July 25, 1934; d. W. C. and Ora Mae (Henderson) Webb; student St. Louis Bus. Coll., 1961; m. Bill H. Mitchell, May 15, 1966. Womens' dir., noontime hostess KTHV-TV, Little Rock, 1964-73; v.p. Holland & Assos., Little Rock, 1973-76; nat. merchandise mgr. Jimmy Dean Foods, 1973-76; mdse. mgr. Ole South Foods, Little Rock, 1974-76; corp. broadcast advt. dir. Dillard Dept. Stores, Inc., Little Rock, 1976—. Active Christmas program Salvation Army, United Fund, ARC and Am. Cancer Soc. local units. Mem. Ark. Advt. Fedn., S.W. Regional Advt. Sales and Mktg. Execs. Assn. Office: 900 W Capitol St Little Rock AR 72203

MITCHELL, MARY HAMILTON, artist; b. Clovis, N.Mex., July 7, 1918; d. Carl and Margueriete Mildred (Morrison) Hamilton; student Amarillo Coll., 1937-38; m. John Zinn Mitchell, Feb. 24, 1940; 1 dau., Kayla Jo Mitchell Palmer. With Bur. of Reclamation, Amarillo, Tex., 1962-65; founder, exec. officer Artists Studio, Inc., Amarillo, 1965—; co-owner The Gallery, 1969-75; one man shows: Gallery III, Dogwood Gallery, Ruidoso, N.Mex., XIT Mus., Dalhart, Tex., Lee Babb Gallery, Tulsa, 1965, House of Pictures, Lubbock, Tex., 1966-69, No-Mans Land Hist. Mus., Panhandle State Coll., Goodwell, Okla., 1978; group shows include: Finley Cultural Center, Sherman, Tex., Hill County Found. Center, Ingram, Tex., St. MAary's Univ. Center, San Antonio, U. Corpus Christi (Tex.), U. Tex., Dallas, McMurray Coll., Ryan Fine Arts Center, Abilene; represented in permanent collections: St. Anthonys Hosp., High Plains Baptist Hosp., Amarillo Psychiat. Hosp., Whitlow Lee Bldg., Happy, Tex., Union County News, Clayton, N.Mex. Mem. Internat. Soc. Artists, Internat. Platform Assn., Nat. League Am. Pen Women, Tex. Fine Arts Assn., Panhandle Art Assn., Epsilon Sigma Alpha. Democrat. Baptist. Author: Pens & Brushes II, 1982. Home and Office: 1813 Mustang St Amarillo TX 79102

MITCHELL, MAXINE VENITA, real estate and public policy planning co. exec.; b. Martinsville, Va., May 13, 1949; d. Matthew and Evelyn (Redd) M.; B.A., Northwestern U., 1971; M.C.P., M.I.T., 1973; m. Arthur Barry Wicklund, Aug. 16, 1974. Asst. v.p. Real Estate Research Corp., Chgo., 1973-81; sr. v.p. Comprehensive Mktg. Systems, Chgo., 1981—; lectr. Loyola U., Chgo. Organizer Chgo. chpt. A Better Chance, 1981. HUD fellow, 1971-73. Mem. Am. Planning Assn., Chgo. Women in Housing. Contbr. articles in field to profl. jours. Office: 343 S Dearborn St Suite 1704 Chicago IL 60604

MITCHELL, MILDRED ANN, businesswoman; b. Mayo, Fla., May 26, 1935; d. James Martin and Hazel (Folsom) Williams; widowed, 1972; m. James Kenneth Puckett, Nov. 29, 1978. Co-owner, Waldron Furniture Mfg. Co. (Ark.), 1968-72; owner Waldron Jour. newspaper, 1975-77; co-owner, operator Willis Shaw Express, Elm Springs, Ark., 1978—. Coordinator chmn. fund-raising Sodie Davidson Park, Waldron, Ark., 1968-69; coordinator Scott County Dale Bumpers for Gov., 1969-70, Dale Bumpers for Senator, 1975-76. Recipient Liberty award Congress of Freedom, 1976. Mem. Waldron Bus. and Profl. Women's Club (pres. 1976-77), Nat. Press Women, Ark. Press Women, Waldron C. of C. (fund raising chmn. 1974-76), Ark. Sheriffs Assn., Am. Furniture Dealers Assn., Nat. Fedn. Bus. and Profl. Women. Democrat. Methodist.

MITCHELL, NANCY BROWN, psychologist; b. Chgo., Mar. 7, 1931; d. Edward Berrien and Jeannette (Landes) B.; B.A., Montevallo U., 1967; M.S., U. Ga., 1974, Ph.D., 1976; m. James Evans Mitchell, Jr., July 29, 1951 (dec.); children—James Evans, Thomas Edward, Janet Lucille. Tchr., Coosa County Bd. Edn., Goodwater, Ala., 1967-71; research asst., grant coordinator U. Ga., 1971-75; asst. to head spl. projects So. Regional Edn. Bd., Atlanta, 1977; psychologist Ala. Dept. Youth Services, Birmingham, 1977; mem. tech. adv. team U.S. Army Inf. Sch., Ft. Benning, Ga., 1977-80; psychologist Army Research Inst. Advanced Simulation Tech., Alexandria, Va., 1980—. Mem. Am. Psychol. Assn., Women in Sci. and Engring., Human Factors Soc., Sigma Xi, Psi Chi, Kappa Delta Pi. Office: Army Research Inst PERI-SF 5001 Eisenhower Ave Alexandria VA 22333

MITCHELL, RIE ROGERS, psychologist, ednl. adminstr.; b. Tucson, Feb. 1, 1940; d. Martin Smith and Lavaun (Peterson) Rogers; student Mills Coll., 1958-59; B.S., U. Utah, 1962, M.S., 1963; postgrad. San

Diego State U., 1965-66; M.A., UCLA, 1969, Ph.D., 1969; m. Rex C. Mitchell, Mar. 16, 1961; 1 son, Scott Rogers. Tchr., Coronado (Calif.) Unified Sch. Dist., 1964-65; sch. psychologist Glendale (Calif.) Unified Sch. Dist., 1968-70; psychologist Glendale Guidance Clinic, 1970-77; asst. prof. ednl. psychology Calif. State U., Northridge, 1970-74, asso. prof., 1974-78, prof., 1978—, chmn. dept. ednl. psychology, 1976-80, acting exec. asst. to pres., 1981-82; acting exec. asst. to pres. Calif. State U., Dominguez Hills, 1978-79; cons. to various Calif. sch. dists.; pvt. practice psychology, Tarzana, Calif. Mem. planning com. for San Fernando Valley, Consensus 2000, 1982—. Recipient Outstanding Educator award Maharishi Soc., 1978, Woman of Yr. award U. Utah, 1962. Mem. Calif. Assn. Counselor Edn., Supervision and Adminstrn. (dir. 1976-77), Western Assn. Counselor Edn. and Supervision (officer 1978-82, pres. 1980-81), Assn. Counselor Edn. and Supervision (dir. 1980-81, program chmn. 1981-82, treas. 1983—), UCLA Doctoral Alumni Assn. (pres. 1974-76), Am. Psychol. Assn., Am. Ednl. Research Assn., Am. Assn. Higher Edn., Calif. Women in Higher Edn. (pres. chpt. 1977-78), Pi Lambda Theta (pres. chpt. 1970-71, chairwoman nat. resolutions 1971-73), Psi Chi, Mu Phi Epsilon, Pi Sigma Alpha. Contbr. numerous articles on group process, juvenile delinquency, adminstrn., counselor edn. to profl. jours. Home: 22945 Paul Revere Dr Calabasas CA 91302 Office: Calif State U Northridge CA 91330

MITCHELL, RUTH ANN, accountant; b. Memphis, Sept. 16, 1928; d. Emanuel and Lorain (Gore) Harper; student Bethume Cookman Coll., 1948; grad. Am. Nursing Adminstrs., 1972; divorced; children—Loretta DeCarol, Georita DeVal, Anastasia Marie. Mortgage bookkeeper Sack Realty Co., 1967-72; resident mgr. Wedgewood Towers Hotel, 1949-60; adminstr. Albany Gardens Nursing Home, 1972-75; adminstrv. sec. to Muhammad Ali, 1975-79; acct., bookkeeper Rainey's Security Agy., Inc., Chgo., 1979—. Active Catholic Charities. Mem. Internat. Accts. Soc., Am. Assn. Nursing Home Adminstrs. Club: Original Towne and Country Social and Civic. Home: 6942 S Paxton Ave Chicago IL 60649 Office: 435 E 35th St Suite 5 Chicago IL 60616

MITCHELL, RUTH HARRIET BRYANT, community devel. co. exec.; b. Birmingham, Ala., June 28, 1943; d. Harrison Armstead and Ora Ardell (Knight) B.; student Hunter Coll., 1959-63; m. Ronald Joseph Mitchell, Dec. 3, 1966; 1 child, Sydney Adele. Asst. librarian City Hosp., Queens, N.Y., 1964-65; asst. librarian Chem. Construction Corp., N.Y.C., 1965-68; asst. librarian St. Vincents Hosp., N.Y.C., 1968-69; asst. researcher, graphics mgr. Ford Found., N.Y.C., 1969-71; dir. pub. info. Bedford-Stuyvesant Restoration Corp., Bklyn., 1971-79, asst. to pres., 1980; exec. dir. Magnolia Tree Earth Center of Bedford Stuyvesant, Inc., 1980—; chmn. Early Childhood Devel. Center. Named Hon. Citizen City of Louisville, 1977; recipient N.Y. Recorder Citizens award, 1975; certificate for Outstanding Brotherhood NCCJ. Mem. Jaycees, Jr. League. Author articles, speaker on community devel. Home: 4 Herkimer Ct Brooklyn NY 11216 Office: 1512 Fulton St Brooklyn NY 11216

MITCHELL, SHARON RUTH, univ. dean; b. Muncie, Ind., Oct. 9, 1945; d. Ira T. and Martha Ann (Osgood) Buffin; B.S., Ball State U., Muncie, 1969; M.Ed., Xavier U., 1973; m. Sidney E. Mitchell, June 4, 1967; children—Sebastian Paul, Samuel Alexander. Music specialist Ohio public schs., 1969-71; instr. music edn., appeals officer Coll. Conservatory Music, U. Cin., 1971-77; asst. dean student life U. N.C., Chapel Hill, 1978—; guest lectr. Miami U., Oxford, Ohio; lectr., workshop dir., cons. in field. Recipient Katherine Kennedy Carmichael award for contbns. to women students, 1982. Mem. Zeta Tau Alpha (co-chmn. nat. scholarship). Club: Order of Valkyries. Author articles, revs. in field. Office: 11 Steele Bldg 050 U NC Chapel Hill NC 27514

MITCHELL, SUSAN MILLER, state ofcl.; b. Appleton, Wis., Apr. 13, 1945; d. James Frederick and Bernice Eileen (Bleick) Miller; B.A. magna cum laude, Lawrence U., Appleton, 1967; M.A. in Journalism, U. Wis., 1970; m. George Allen Mitchell, Oct. 28, 1973; children—Margaret Kim, Mary Eleanor. Tchr., Wakefield (Mass.) Elem. Schs., 1967-68; reporter Wall St. Jour., Chgo., 1970-72, San Francisco Examiner, 1972-73, Riverside (Calif.) Press Enterprise, 1973; exec. asst. Wis. Dept. Regulation and Licensing, 1975-78, sec., 1978-79; commr. ins. State of Wis., 1979—; mem. U.S. Supplement Health Ins. Panel. Recipient award Center Public Representation, Madison, 1981. Office: 123 W Washington Ave Madison WI 53702

MITCHELL, SUSAN WEAMAH EMMA, mental retardation specialist; b. Stamford, Conn., Sept. 27, 1953; d. John Payne and Esther Arvilla (Harrison) M.; B.A., Fisk U., 1982. Workshop supr. South Middlesex Assn. for Retarded Citizens, Framingham, Mass., 1976-77; mental retardation specialist Wrentham (Mass.) State Sch., 1977—. Mem. Nat. Assn. Female Execs., Alpha Kappa Alpha. Home: 65 E Washington St Apt 2203 North Attleboro MA 02760 Office: Wrentham State Sch Box 144 Wrentham MA 02093

MITCHELL-JACKSON, ANNA, clin. psychologist; b. Wetumpka, Ala.; B.A., Bowling Green State U., 1959; M.A., U. Denver, 1960; Ph.D., Colo. State U., 1967; children—Sean William, Stevan Mitchell. Psychologist, State Home and Tng. Sch., Lapeer, Mich., 1960-61; chief psychologist State Home and Tng. Sch., Wheatridge, Colo., 1962-68; acting dir. clin. child psychology sect. dept. psychiatry U. Colo. Sch. Medicine, Denver, 1978, dir. Children's Diagnostic Center, 1973-79, dir. student adv. officer, 1979-81; interim dir. Minority Student Affairs Office, U. Colo. Health Scis. Center, 1979-80, instr. psychiatry, 1968-70, asst. prof., 1970-73, asso. prof., 1973—; adj. prof. Sch. Profl. Psychology, U. Denver, 1976; vis. lectr. Afro-Am. Studies Dept. Met. State Coll., Denver, 1971-72; lectr. U. Colo., Boulder, 1970; cons. health center, hosps.; adv. bd. Sch. Community and Human Services, Met. State Coll.; alumni adv. bd. Coll. of Natural Scis., Colo. State U., Ft. Collins. Bd. dirs. Colo. Christian Home, Denver. Lic. clin. psychologist, Colo.; diplomate Am. Bd. Profl. Psychology. Mem. Assn. Black Psychologists (recipient Outstanding Service award Rocky Mountain chpt. 1981), Am. Psychol. Assn., Rocky Mountain Psychol. Assn., Soc. for Psychotherapy Research. Contbr. numerous articles in field to profl. jours. Office: 4200 E 9th Ave PO Box C258 Denver CO 80262

MITELMAN, BONNIE COSSMAN, writer, lectr.; b. Flint, Mich., Feb. 15, 1941; d. Maurice B. and Frieda H. (Ragir) Cossman; student U. Mich., 1958-61; B.A., Northwestern U., 1969; M.A., Manhattanville Coll., 1977; m. Alan N. Mitelman, July 23, 1972; children—Joanne, Stephen, Geoffrey. Copywriter trainee Dancer-Fitzgerald-Sample, Inc., Chgo., 1956-60; advt. copywriter Spiegel, Inc., Chgo., 1961-63; free lance advt. and public relations writer, Chgo., N.Y., 1963—; co-founder Mitelman & Assos., Briarcliff Manor, N.Y., 1972—; adj. lectr. dept. history Mercy Coll., Dobbs Ferry, N.Y., 1979—; contbr. articles to N.Y. Times, Reform Judaism, 1977—. Mem. Am. Hist. Assn., Conf. Group on Women's History, Women in Communications, Nat. Women's Studies Assn. Mem. editorial bd. Reform Judaism, 1977—. Home: 639 Pleasantville Rd Briarcliff Manor NY 10510

MITFORD, JESSICA, author; b. Batsford Mansion, Eng., Sept. 11, 1917; d. Lord and Lady Redesdale; m. Esmond Romilly, June 1937; 1 dau., Constancia; m. 2d, Robert Treuhaft, June 21, 1943; 1 son, Benjamin. Author: (autobiography) Daughters and Rebels, 1960; The American Way of Death, 1963; The Trial of Dr. Spock, 1969; Kind and Usual Punishment-The Prison Business, 1973; A Fine Old Conflict, 1977; Poison Penmanship: The Gentle Art of Muckraking, 1979. Address: 6411 Regent St Oakland CA 94618 *

MITTELSTAEDT, JOAN NAOMI, educator, cons.; b. Fond du Lac, Wis., Feb. 9, 1950; d. H. Arthur and Naomi Genevieve (Maltby) Steiner; B.S. in Edn., U. Wis., Stevens Point, 1972, M.S. in Edn., 1978; 1 son, Robert John. Tchr., Menasha (Wis.) High Sch., 1972—, also owner Fox Valley Bus. Cons., Neenah, Wis., 1978—; tchr. English, facilitator Wis. Dept. Edn.; tchr. positive mental attitude classes for bus. people; leader sales tng. seminars; curriculum and sales tng. system developer; public speaker on free enterprise, entrepreneurship and assertiveness, 1978—. Cert. tchr. English and speech, Wis.; cert. Amway Gold Direct Distbr. Mem. Republican Presdl. Task Force, 1982. Mem. Nat. Council Tchrs. of English, Wis. Council Tchrs. of English, Wis. Regional Writers, Worldwide Diamond Assn., Nat. Assn. Female Execs. (network dir.), Am. Mgmt. Assn., Citizens Choice, Am. Fedn. Tchrs. (local sec. 1974-76), Delta Zeta, Delta Kappa Gamma. Episcopalian. Research on imagists influence on contemporary poets. Home: 304 Quarry Ln Neenah WI 54956

MITTS, KATHRYN IRENE, physician; b. Los Angeles, Sept. 5, 1949; d. John and Elizabeth Ann (Garabedian) Musich; B.A. in Biology and German, Loma Linda U., LaSierra Campus, 1971, B.S. in Med. Tech., Loma Linda Campus, 1972, M.D., 1977. Flexible intern Harbor Gen. Hosp., 1977-78, resident in surgery, 1978; staff physician, emergency medicine Harbor City (Calif.) Kaiser Found., 1979—, now edn. dir. Recipient Young Careerist award Bus. and Profl. Women, 1982. Mem. Am. Diabetes Assn., Am. Heart Assn., Cancer Soc., Los Angeles County Med. Women's Assn., Am. Med. Women's Assn. (Glasgow Med. Scholastics Achievement award), Alpha Omega Alpha, Phi Sigma. Republican. Mem. Christian Ch. (Disciples of Christ). Club: DAR. Office: 1050 Pacific Coast Hwy Harbor City CA

MITZ, BEULAH, med. center adminstr.; b. Milw., Oct. 14, 1925; d. Frederick Lewis and Edna (Firestone) Grombacher; B.S., U. Wis., 1943, M.S., 1970; m. Morris Mitz, Sept. 19, 1945; children—Frederick Lewis, Robin Lee. Prin. investigator, project dir. Social Welfare Manpower Research Project, Milw., 1970; psychiat. social worker St. Mary's Hill Hosp., Milw., 1970-72; dir. dept. social service Mt. Sinai Med. Center, Milw., 1972-76; rehab. counselor Jewish Vocat. Service, Milw., 1977-78; exec. dir. Arthritis Center of Southeastern Wis., Med. Coll. Wis., Milw., 1979—, asst. instr., 1979—. Mem. Southeastern Wis. Health Systems Agy., 1979—, Women's Aux. Med. Coll. Wis., 1960—; v.p. Jewish Family and Childrens Services Aux., 1970—. Mem. U. Wis. Alumni Assn., NOW, ACLU, People for the Am. Way, Amnesty Internat., Assn. Cert. Social Workers, Nat. Assn. Social Workers, Wis. Arthritis Found., Nat. Arthritis Found., Arthritis Health Profl. Assn. (exec. com.). Home: 609 E Lexington Blvd Milwaukee WI 53217 Office: 8700 W Wisconsin Ave Milwaukee WI 53127

MIX, ESTHER, U.S. magistrate; b. Warner, Okla., Dec. 21, 1920; d. Burk and Bertie (Hawkins) Markham; student U. Okla., 1937-39; LL.B., McGeorge Coll. Law, 1948; children—Sarah Jane, Richard, Jr. Pvt. practice law, 1951-71; U.S. magistrate, Sacramento, 1971—. Mem. Am. Bar Assn., Nat. Council Fed. Magistrates, Calif. Bar Assn., Women Lawyers Sacramento. Office: US Courthouse Rm 1034 650 Capitol Mall Sacramento CA 95814

MIXON, ROSALIE WARD, social work cons.; b. Maysville, Mo., Feb. 17, 1908; d. Luther Thomas and Mary (Bray) Ward; A.B., Park Coll., 1929; postgrad. (Univ. scholar 1929-30, 32-35), U. Chgo., 1929-34; M.S.W., U. So. Calif., 1944; postgrad. UCLA, 1965, Riverside, 1970, San Diego, 1975-76; m. John Lewis Mixon, Dec. 20, 1929; children—Rosemary Mixon Snow, John Lindley, David Lewis, Robert Nelson. Dir. med. social service Children's Meml. Hosp., Chgo., 1951-52; researcher in religious demography, 1952-58; instr. social work La Verne (Calif.) Coll., 1958-59; with Calif. Dept. Mental Hygiene, San Bernardino and Pomona, 1959-66, 69-74; Fulbright lectr., cons. psychiat. and med. social work Med. Sch., Pahlavi U., Shiraz, Iran, 1966-67; lectr. Sch. Social Work, Teheran, Iran, 1966-67; social researcher Meth. Bd. World Missions, Lima, Peru, 1968-69; pvt. practice psychiat. social work cons., Redlands, Calif., 1974—; vis. prof. Alaska Pacific U., Anchorage, 1978-79. Active Chgo. Community Fund Adv. Com., 1951, Claremont Community Services Com., 1960-75, Redlands A.B.L.E. Com., 1975—. Lic. clin. social worker, Calif. Mem. Nat. Assn. Social Workers, Nat. Acad. Cert. Social Workers, Register Clin. Social Workers, Soc. Internat. Devel. Club: Browser's Book. Author: The Methodist Churches of Arizona, 1966; The Barriadas of Lima, Peru, 1969; contbr. chpt. to Choice and Change, 1966.

MIXSON, ELIZABETH ANN, spl. educator; b. Archer, Fla., Sept. 7, 1926; d. Loretta Porter White; B.S. in Elementary Edn., Fla. State U., Tallahassee, 1951; M.Ed. in Spl. Edn., Stetson U., DeLand, Fla., 1974; m. James K. Mixson. Tchr., Levy County, Williston, Fla., 1948-55, City of Charleston (S.C.) Sch. Bd., 1956-61, Volusia County Sch. Bd., Enterprise, Fla., 1961-65, Sch. Bd. Volusia County, Woodward Avenue Elem. Sch., 1966—. Mem. NEA, Volusia Edn. Assn., Fla. Teaching Profession, Volusia County Assn. for Children with Learning Disability, Council for Exceptional Children, AAUW, Delta Kappa Gamma. Home: Rt 2 Box 185 402 Garden Ct Deland FL 32720

MIYASAKI, ELLEN KAZUKO, telecommunications cons.; b. Kalopa, Hawaii, June 10, 1930; d. Uichi and Tsuyako (Yamada) M.; student U. Hawaii, 1948-49; cert. Sawyer Sch. Bus., Los Angeles, 1950. Med. sec. U.S. Dept. Army, Dept. Air Force, Japan, Okinawa, Germany, Morocco, 1951-57; med. sec. dept. psychiatry Jackson Meml. Hosp., Miami, 1958-62; med. asst. Jim S. Jewett, Internist, 1963-66; med. research asst. Dome Labs., N.Y.C., 1966-67; field office asst. ARC, Japan, Korea, Okinawa, 1967-69; adminstr. MCA Engring. Corp., Rockville, Md., 1969-73; with The Mktg. Programs and Services Group, Inc., Gaithersburg, Md., 1973—, corp. sec., 1975, corp. v.p., 1976—, also dir. Notary public, Md. Mem. Nat. Fedn. Bus. and Profl. Women's Club, Nat. Assn. Female Execs., Nat. Registry Med. Secs. Home: 9145 Centerway Rd Gaithersburg MD 20879 Office: 656 Quince Orchard Rd Suite 411 Gaithersburg MD 20760

MIZE, PATRICIA JONES, librarian, educator; b. McLean County, Ky., Nov. 10, 1941; d. Richard Louis and Helen (Hancock) Jones; student Murray State U., 1959-60; B.A., Ky. Wesleyan Coll., 1962; M.A., Western Ky. U., 1974, postgrad., 1977-82; M.S.L.S., U. Ky., 1982; m. Jerry Mize, Mar. 19, 1960; children from previous marriage—Martin Paul, Elizabeth Lynn. Librarian elem. sch. Public Schs. Daviess County (Ky.), 1963-70; media specialist Public Schs. McLean County, 1970-78; mem. adj. faculty Western Ky. U., 1977-78; head public services, asst. prof. library sci. Ky. Wesleyan Coll., 1978—. Adv., Kentuckiana council Girl Scouts U.S.A., 1980-83; vol. ARC. Recipient Silver Cardinal award Girl Scouts U.S.A., 1979; Nat. Endowment Humanities/Assn. Coll. and Research Libraries workshop grantee, 1982. Mem. ALA, Am. Assn. Sch. Librarians (del. Affiliate Assembly 1981), Southeastern Library Assn., AAUW (chmn. Ednl. Found. 1981-83), AAUP, Ky. Library Assn. (dir. 1980-81, pres. Library Instrn. Roundtable 1982-83), Ky. Sch. Media Assn. (dir. 1973-82, pres. 1980-81), Ky. Assn. Communications and Tech. (dir. 1980-81). Democrat. Baptist. Home: Route 1 Calhoun KY 42327 Office: Ky Wesleyan Coll 3000 Frederica St Owensboro KY 42301

MLAY, MARIAN, govt. ofcl.; b. Pitts., Sept. 11, 1935; d. John and Sonia M.; A.B., U. Pitts., 1957; postgrad. (Univ. fellow) Princeton U., 1969-70; J.D., Am. U., 1977. Mgmt. positions HEW, Washington, 1961-70, dep. dir. Chgo. region, 1971-72, dir. div. consol. funding, 1972-73, dep. dir. office policy devel. and planning USPHS, Washington, 1973-77; dir. program evaluation EPA, Washington, 1978-79, dep. dir. office of drinking water, 1979—. Bd. dirs. D.C. United Fund, 1979-80. Recipient Career Edn. award Nat. Inst. Public Affairs, 1969. Mem. Am. Bar Assn., D.C. Bar, Exec. Women in Govt., D.C. Women's Bar, Nat. Cathedral Choral Soc. Eastern Orthodox. Author articles in field. Home: 3747 1/2 Kanawha St NW Washington DC 20015 Office: 401 M St SW Washington DC 20460

MLYNEK, JUDITH KENDALL, mfg. co. exec.; b. Duluth, Minn., Mar. 30, 1938; d. Gustav Adolf and Marjorie Mildred (Kendall) Nordin; B.S. in Mgmt., Pepperdine U., Los Angeles, 1979; divorced; children—Marjorie Dawn, Marie Heather. Teller, U.S. Nat. Bank, Pasadena, Calif., 1965-67; sr. acctg. clk., then asso. adminstr. Xerox Corp., Pasadena, 1967-78, fin. adminstr., 1979-81, sr. fin. adminstr.; 1981—; income tax cons., 1975—. Mem. Nat. Mgmt. Assn., Exec. Female, Career Guild. Club: Xerox Ski. Home: 50 W Floral Ave Arcadia CA 91006 Office: 300 N Halstead Ave Pasadena CA 91107

MOATTS, FRANCES SUSAN, nurse; b. Clanton, Ala., Aug. 31, 1937; d. Ray and Marjorie Lee (Price) Mizell; R.N., Sylacauga Sch. Nursing, 1959; postgrad. U. Ala., 1979; m. Thomas Raymond Moatts, July 9, 1965; 1 son, Michael Thomas. Staff nurse Chilton County Hosp., Clanton, Ala., 1959-65, 65—, asst. dir. nursing, 1978—; staff nurse Jackson Hosp., Montgomery, Ala., 1965. Vol. ARC Blood Program, 1959—. Recipient Good Citizenship award, 1953; Kiwanis scholar, 1956. Republican. Baptist. Club: Progressive Woman's Orgn. Home: Route 5 PO Box 157 Clanton AL 35045 Office: Laydam Rd Clanton AL 35045

MOCK-MORGAN, MAVERA ELIZABETH, artist, art educator; b. McClellan, Fla., May 14, 1926; d. Arthur Charles and Mary Esther (Jones) Mock; student J.B. Stetson U.; B.A. in Fine Arts, Am. U., 1965, M.A. in Art Edn., 1968; Ph.D. in Art Edn., U. Md., 1976; m. Joseph Mulford Morgan, Nov. 2, 1950; children—Arthur Chester, David Mulford. Asst. to gen. counsel Nat. Capitol Planning Commn., Washington, 1955-58; mem. faculty U. Hawaii, 1959-60; adj. faculty Chulalorghorn U., Bangkok, 1958-61; instr. art D.C. Tchrs. Coll., Washington, 1967-70, U. Md., College Park, 1970-71; asst., then asso. prof. art, chmn. div. fine arts D.C. Tchrs. Coll., Washington, 1971-77; prof. U. D.C., 1978—; chmn. div. fine arts U. D.C., Harvard-Ga. Campus, Washington, 1977-78; cons. NRC, Ford Found.; lectr. Queen's U., Kingston, Ont., Can., 1979-80; painter, sculptor; works exhibited: Bangkok, 1960, Washington Art Club, 1974, Am. Art League, 1974, 75, 76, 78; cons., lectr. in art U. Md., 1971-79; mem. Washington Com. on Fine Arts, 1976-78. Nat. Arts and Humanities Inst. fellow to Fla. State U. and HEW, 1968. Mem. Nat. Art Edn. Assn., Internat. Soc. Edn. through Art, U.S. Soc. Edn. through Art (former nat. conv. chmn., editor conf. proc. 1978), Miniature Artists Am., Am. Art League, Md. Art Edn. Assn., Asia Soc., Assn. for Asian Studies, Thai Com. (bd. dirs.), Am. Nepal Soc., Emerald Schillelagh Marching and Chowder Soc., Phi Delta Gamma (past chpt. pres.). Presbyterian. Club: Washington-Bangkok Women's (pres. 1965, bd. dirs. 1966-74). Author: (with others) UDC Graphics Manual, 1977, Self-Study Manual UDC, 1977; The Theories and Methods of Arthur Wesley Dow on Art Education, 1976. Home: 3 Carvel Circle Westmoreland Hills Bethesda MD 20816 Office: Univ DC Art Dept Van Ness Campus Washington DC 20005

MOELHMAN, AMY JO, social worker; b. Lafayette, Ind., Mar. 18, 1954; d. Charles Richard and Marian Gertrude (Young) M.; B.S., Ball State U., 1976; M.S.W., U. Denver, 1979. Tng. specialist, Tippecanoe County Dept. Career Devel., Lafayette, 1976-78; social worker Adams County Dept. Social Services, Commerce City, Colo., 1979-81; counselor Pleasant Run Children's Home, Indpls., 1981—. Vol. program chmn. Muncie (Ind.) Boys Club, 1973-76; vol. coordinator Tippecanoe County Youth Services Bur., 1975. Mem. Nat. Assn. Social Workers, Alpha Sigma Alpha. Democrat. Methodist. Office: 1404 S State St Indianapolis IN

MOELLER, BEVERLEY BOWEN, agrl. co. exec.; b. Long Beach, Calif., Oct. 12, 1925; d. George Walter and Agnes Ruth (Coffey) Bowen; B.A., Whittier Coll., 1956; M.A., UCLA, 1965, Ph.D., 1968; m. Roger David Moeller, Dec. 11, 1955; children—Claire Agnes, Barbara Bowen, Thomas David. Writer, Valley News and Green Sheet, Van Nuys, Calif., 1961-64; scholar-tchr. Valley Coll., Los Angeles, 1968-69, UCLA, 1970; instr. Petroeos Brasileiros, Salvador, Bahia, Brazil, 1972-73; pres. Nova Pioneira Agroindustrial Ltda., Belém Pará, Brazil, 1982—; dir. Associcão Cultural Brasil-Estados Unidos, 1972-73. Mem. Calif. Regional Water Quality Control Commn., 1970-71. Mem. IEEE (history com., chmn. region 2 com. on profl. opportunities for women), Soc. for History of Tech., Inter-Am. Soc., Internat. Soc. Tropical Foresters. Republican. Author: Phil Swing and Boulder Dam, 1971. Home: 1590 Forest Villa Ln McLean VA 22101

MOEN, LORETTO CAMPBELL, town ofcl.; b. Middlesex, N.J., May 3, 1917; d. John J. and Loretto B. (Englesbe) Campbell; student pvt. schs.; m. James Lyman Moen, Apr. 11, 1944; children—Loretto, Audrey, Barbara, J. Kevin, Mark, David. Selectman, Town of Groton (Mass.), 1975—. Mem. Mass. Mcpl. Assn., Mass. Selectmen's Assn., Middlesex County Selectmen's Assn., Women Elected Mcpl. Ofcls., Mass. Fedn. Women's Clubs. Roman Catholic. Club: Groton Women's (pres. 1978-80). Home: 428 Chicopee Row Groton MA 01450 Office: Town Hall Main St Groton MA 01450

MOERSCH, DEWEENTA CONRAD (MRS. HERMAN J. MOERSCH), former banker, club woman; b. Omaha; d. James Harvey and Lila (Weeks) Conrad; student pvt. schs., Wellesley, Mass.; m. Howard Kramer Gray, Sept. 2, 1925 (dec. 1955); children—Howard Kramer, DeWeenta Russell (Mrs. Walter Bones, Jr.); m. 2d, Herman J. Moersch, Jan. 3, 1973 (dec. 1981). Women's rep. first Nat. Bank, Rochester, Minn., 1956-64. Vice pres. YWCA, Rochester, 1933-36, bd. dirs., 1930-36; pres. U.S.O., Rochester, 1942-45; bd. dirs. Art Center, Rochester, 1956-64, v.p., 1959-61; sec., bd. dirs. YMCA, Rochester, 1957-60; mem. women's exec. com. Minn. Statehood Centennial, 1958; mem. Minn. hospitality com. WHO Internat. Meeting, Mpls.; sustaining mem. Jr. League Omaha Bd. dirs. Rochester Community Chest, 1962-64, Christmas Anonymous, Rochester, 1956-64, Ability Bdlg. Center, Rochester, 1957-64. Trustee St. Mary's Hosp., Rochester, 1968-76, Tyrone Guthrie Theatre Found., Mpls., 1962-68. Recipient Service to Mankind award Sertoma Internat., 1965. Mem. Nat. Assn. Bank Women (chmn. regional meeting Rochester 1961), UN Assn., U.S.A. (Minn. bd. dirs. 1958-62, Rochester chpt. bd. dirs. 1959-62, pres. 1960-62), League Women Voters (dir., pres. Rochester 1948-49), Minn. Hist. Soc. (women's bd. dirs. 1952-55, chmn. 1954-55, exec. council 1955-57), Bus. and Profl. Women's Club (Bus. Woman of Yr. Rochester 1961), Rochester C. of C. (priorities com. 1966). Methodist. Clubs: Woman's (Mpls.); Country; Rochester Golf and Country. Home: 2221 Hillside Ln SW Rochester MN 55901

MOFFATT, JOYCE A., performing arts exec.; b. Grand Rapids, Mich., Jan. 3, 1936; d. John Barnard and Ruth Lillian (Pellow) M.; B.A. in Lit., U. Mich., 1957, M.A. in Theatre, 1960. Stage mgr., lighting designer Off-Broadway plays, costume, lighting and set designer, stage mgr. stock cos., 1954-62; nat. subscription mgr. Theatre Guild/Am. Theatre Soc., N.Y.C., 1965-67; subscription mgr. Theatre, Inc.-Phoenix Theatre, N.Y.C., 1963-67, also cons.; subscription mgr. N.Y.C. Ballet and N.Y.C. Opera, 1967-70; asst. house mgr. N.Y. State Theater, 1970-72; dir. ticket sales City Center of Music and Drama, Inc., N.Y.C., 1970-72; prodn. mgr. San Antonio Symphony/Opera, 1973-75, gen. mgr., 1975-76; gen. mgr. 55th St. Dance Theater Found., Inc., N.Y.C., 1976-77; gen. mgr. Ballet Theatre Found., Inc./Am. Ballet Theatre, N.Y.C., 1977—; cons. Ford Found., N.Y. State Council on Arts, Kennedy Center for Performing Arts. Mem. Assn. Theatrical Press Agts. and Mgrs., Actors Equity Assn., United Scenic Artists Local 350. Club: Argyle (San Antonio). Office: American Ballet Theatre 890 Broadway Ave New York NY 10003 *

MOFFETT, LORETTA DELOIS, businesswoman; b. Mars Hills, N.C., Oct. 19, 1938; d. George Allen and Cora B. (Rice) Curtis; student in acctg. and bus. mgmt. Seattle Community Coll., 1962-63, 70, 80, U. Wash., 1977; m. Robert Lee Moffett, June 20, 1970. Purchasing and office mgr. Image Control Systems, Seattle, 1969-72; adminstrv. asst. Leckenby Co., Seattle, 1972-75; treas., office mgr. Buckner-Weatherby Co., Inc., Seattle, 1975-78; controller, credit mgr. Aptex, Inc., Seattle, 1978-81; partner R & L Rentals, 1975-81; bus. adminstr. T&T Gen. Contractors, 1980-81; office mgr. Rembold Corp., Seattle, 1981—. Dist. area chmn. Republican party. Mem. Westward Shippers Assn. (treas., bd. dirs. 1976-78), Adminstrv. Mgmt. Soc. (dir. 1981-82), Nat. Assn. Credit Mgmt.-Credit Women of Seattle (pres. 1978-79, dir. 1975-79), Nat. Assn. Female Execs., West Seattle C. of C., Seattle Urban League, LWV, Seattle Working Women, Asso. Republican Women, Women's Profl. Network, Genessee Hill Community Council. Club: 34th Dist. Republican (dir.). Home: 4523 53d SW Seattle WA 98116 Office: 2301 Alaskan Way 101 Seattle WA 98121

MOFFETT, LORRAINE LOIS, resort, health center exec.; b. Tacoma, June 17, 1921; d. Franklin Walter and Lois Fern (Foster) Justman; student U. Puget Sound, 1940-41; m. Robert J. Moffett, Dec. 30, 1941 (dec. Dec. 1977); children—Donald Robert, Stanley George, Norman Alan. In various retail positions, Tacoma, 1937-42, Watsonville, Calif., 1942-43; Wash. state foods editor Wash. Health News, Tacoma, 1958-60; v.p. Wash. State Natural Food Assos., Tacoma, 1962-75, dir. Good Health To You tours, 1967-72; v.p. Metabiotics Inc., Tacoma, 1971-74, pres., 1974—; sales dir. Resort of the Mountains, Norton, Wash., 1972-79, gen. mgr., 1972—, editor newsgram, 1974—; nat. dir. Natural Food Assos., 1975—, nat. v.p., 1978-79, 82—; co-originator, reporter Good Health To You radioshows, throughout U.S.; instr., lectr. on nutrition. Vice pres. bd. trustees Children's Chiropractic Center, Tacoma, 1957-69; pres. exec. council Women's Health League, Tacoma, 1957-67; dir. city-wide pageant Horizon council Camp Fire Girls Am., 1962. Recipient first cert. merit Palmer Chiropractic Coll., 1957. Club: Tacoma Writer's (Article Contest 1st pl. 1964). Co-author Triangle of Health column Pep Talk, 1965-71. Home: 1130 Morton Rd Rainbow's End Rainbow Ct W Morton WA 98356 Office: 1130 Morton Rd Morton WA 98356

MOFFO, ANNA, opera singer; b. Wayne, Pa.; d. Nicholas and Regina (Cinti) M.; grad. with honors Curtis Inst.; m. Robert Sarnoff, Nov. 14, 1974. Appeared TV opera Madame Butterfly, Italy; singer opera houses, Paris, London, Salzburg, Vienna, Milan, numerous others abroad; Am. debut Lyric Opera Co., Chgo., 1957, Met. Opera Co., N.Y.C., 1959; appeared Voice of Firestone telecast, 1957; operatic roles (soprano) include Norma, La Boheme, Mignon, Rigoletto, Falstaff, Madame Butterfly, Barber of Seville, La Traviata, Thais, Daughter of Regiment, Stiffelio, Tosca, Hansel & Gretel, Faust, Don Pasquale, Romeo & Juliette, Magic Flute, Turandot, La Juive, Marriage of Figaro, Othello, Trovatore, Luisa Miller, La Belle Helene, Czardasfurstin; recital tours U.S.; appeared film versions Adriana LeCouvreur, La Traviata, Lucia, also films The Adventurers, A Love Story, Menage Italian Style, The Divorcee, A Girl Named Jules, Napoleon at Austerlitz, Concerto; numerous TV appearances U.S. and Italy; numerous recordings Emi, Ariola, Angel, Columbia, RCA Victor. Decorated comdr. Order of Merit (Italy); recipient Young Artists award Phila. Orch.; Fulbright award for study in Europe; Silver Griffo award for film Love Story; Liebe Augustin award; Michelangelo award. Address: care John Meelan Carl Byoir & Assos 380 Madison Ave New York NY 10022

MOFFORD, ROSE, state ofcl.; b. Globe, Ariz., June 10, 1922; attended public schs. Sec. to Joe Hunt, Ariz. State Treas., 1941-43, Ariz. State Tax Commr., 1943-54, to Wesley Bolin, Ariz. Sec. of State, 1954-55; asst. sec. of state of Ariz., Phoenix, 1955-79, sec. of state, 1979—. Democrat. Office: Office of Sec of State West Wing State Capitol Phoenix AZ 85007 *

MOGGE, HARRIET MORGAN, ednl. assn. exec.; b. Cleve., Jan. 2, 1928; d. Russell VanDyke and Grace (Wells) Morgan; B.M.E., Northwestern U., 1959; postgrad. Ill. State U., 1969; m. Robert Arthur Mogge, Aug. 17, 1948 (div. 1977); 1 dau., Linda Jean. Instr. piano, Evanston, Ill., 1954-58; instr. elem. music public schs., Evanston, 1959; editorial asst., archivist Summy-Birchard Co., Evanston, 1964-66, asst. to editor-in-chief, 1966-67, cons., 1968-69, ednl. dir., 1969-74, also historian, 1973-74; asst. dir. profl. programs Music Educators Nat. Conf., Reston, Va., 1974—; supr. vocal music jr. high sch., Watseka, Ill., 1967-68. Active various community drives. Mem. Music Educators Nat. Conf., Am. Choral Dirs. Assn., In and About Chgo. Music Educators Assn. (dir.), Suzuki Assn. Ams. (exec. sec. 1972-74), Mu Phi Epsilon, Kappa Delta (province pres. 1960-66, 72-76, regional chpt. dir. 1976-78, nat. dir. scholarship 1981—). Republican. Presbyterian. Clubs: Business and Professional Women's (dir. Watseka 1968-70); Antique Automobile Club, Model T Ford Internat. (v.p. 1971-72, 76-77, nat. pres. 1981, dir. 1971—). Mng. editor Am. Suzuki Jour., 1972-74; display advt. mgr. Model T Times, 1971—. Home: 1554 Northgate Sq Apt 21B Reston VA 22090 Office: 1902 Association Dr Reston VA 22091

MOHAMED, DONITA LEE, nurse, counselor; b. Wendell, Idaho, May 31, 1941; d. Frank B. and Billie L. (Parkinson) Burton; A.A. in Liberal Arts, St. Mary's Coll., 1962; R.N., St. Benedict's Sch. Nursing, Ogden, Utah, 1964; B.A. in Psychology, Antioch Coll., 1974, M.A. in Psychology, 1976; m. Rezk Mohamed II, Mar. 24, 1979; children by previous marriage—Heidi Garriss, Jill Garriss, Eric Garriss. Staff nurse So. Baptist Meml. Hosp., Jacksonville, Fla., 1967; head nurse Cape Fear Hosp., Wilmington, N.C., 1964-65, St. Lukes Hosp., Boise, Idaho, 1969-71; supt. pre-sch. St. Francis De Sale, Las Vegas, 1970; v.p. Deer Creek Inst., Boulder, Utah, 1974-77; pres. Curalogos Corp., Las Vegas, 1977-79; mgr. women's programs EG&G Idaho, Inc., Idaho Falls, 1979—. Bd. dirs. Idaho Falls YMCA, 1981—, Eastern Idaho Vocat. Sch. Mem. Idaho Falls C. of C., Idaho Assn. Affirmative Action, Am. Assn. Affirmative Action, Am. Psychol. Assn., Am. Nurses Assn., AAUW (chpt. dir.), LWV, NOW, Am. Bus. Women's Assn., UN Assn. Club: Soroptimists (chpt. dir., recipient Women Helping Women award). Contbr. articles in field to profl. publs. Home: 11250 Bellerive Dr Idaho Falls ID 83401 Office: EG&G Idaho Inc PO Box 1625 Idaho Falls ID 83415

MOHR, DEBORAH CURRIE, stockbroker; b. Bryn Mawr, Pa., Apr. 23, 1952; d. George Frederick and Sarah (Jamison) M.; B.A., Lafayette Coll., 1975; student Pa. State U., 1970-72; m. Gary Arthur Geffken, Sept. 29, 1979. Specialist clk. Ragnar Options, Phila., 1975; specialist and phone clk. Butcher & Singer, 1975-76; options floor broker Wallace Securities, 1976-77; options floor broker, mgr. floor brokerage operation D.H. Wallach, 1977-79; mgr. floor brokerage ops., v.p., option specialist in waste mgmt., asst. specialist in cities service Casella Securites, Inc., Phila., 1979—. Registered options trader Phila. Stock Exchange. Mem. Narberth Civic Assn., Phila. Stock Exchange, Investment Traders Assn., Pa. Hort. Soc., Ducks Unltd. Clubs: Cosmopolitan, Cynwyd, Jr. League (council sec. 1981-82). Office: 1904-10 Arch St Philadelphia PA 19103

MOHR, PATRICIA PRUDEN, educator, social worker; b. Johannesburg, S. Africa; came to U.S., 1947, naturalized, 1955; d. John Thomas and Alice (Dickinson) Pruden; R.N., A.A., Sacramento Jr. Coll. Sch. Nursing, 1956; M.A., Pacific Oaks Coll., 1974; postgrad. Claremont Grad. Sch., 1967-68, U. Calif., San Diego, 1973; married July 6, 1958 (div. 1973); children—Donald Edmond, Hilary Day, Andrew Dickinson, Stacey Stafford. Nurse Los Angeles County Head Start, 1966-68; dir./tchr. pilot parent edn. program Ontario-Montclair Sch. Dist., 1970-72; instr. Mt. San Antonio Community Coll., 1968-72; teaching fellow Pacific Oaks Coll., 1973-74; asso. prof., dir. student health and child devel. programs Chaffey Community Coll., 1976-82; adminstr. child devel. programs Hacienda-LaPuente Unified Sch. Dist., Calif., 1982—; cons. in field. Bd. dirs. Channel of Love, Los Angeles, 1966-70; bd. dirs., pres. Claremont Civic Assn., 1972-73; active Wheeler Park Neighbors, Claremont, 1970-72; mem. Community Coll. Chancellor's Task Force on Early Childhood, 1976-78; grants writer San Bernardino County Schs.; San Bernardino Title XX grantee, 1980-81. Mem. Assn. Community Coll. Adminstrs., Calif. Child Devel. Adminstrs. Assn. (cert. of merit 1972, bd. dirs., pres.), Nat. Assn. Edn. Young Children, So. Calif. Assn. for Edn. Young Children. Mem. Am. Friends Soc. Editor: Broadcasting for Children, 1979-81. Office: Hacienda La Puenta Sch Dist 1110 Fickewirth Ave La Puente CA 91744

MOIR, BETTY SCOTT, heavy equipment, leasing and constrn. co. exec.; b. Columbus, Kans., July 14, 1934; d. William Howard and Esther Laura (Mitchell) Scott; R.N., St. Luke's Hosp., 1955; m. James Sterling Moir, Aug. 31, 1957; children—James Sterling, John Thomas, Heather Logan. Partner, B & T Equipment Co., Honolulu, 1958-61; partner Moir Ranch & Constrn. Co., Eugene, Oreg., 1971-80; sole proprietor Brown Bear Constrn. Co., Eugene, 1980—. Vol. docent U. Oreg. Art Mus., 1974-81. Republican. Clubs: Eugene Country, Town and Country Garden. Address: 86510 Pine Grove Rd Eugene OR 97402

MOKROS, KAREN LEE, nurse; b. Duluth, Minn., Sept. 2, 1941; d. Marvin Albin and Irma Irene (Kangas) Larson; B.S. in Nursing, U. Minn., Mpls., 1964, M.S., 1975, Ph.D., 1976; M.A., U. Minn., Duluth, 1972; m. Norbert W.W. Mokros, Nov. 14, 1964; children—Andrea Margarita Marie, Peter Marcus Bernhardt. Staff nurse U. Minn. Hosps., Mpls., 1964, St. Luke's Hosp., Duluth, 1964; instr. U. Minn., Duluth, 1964-66; instr., then coordinator St. Luke's Hosp. Sch. Nursing, 1968-73; asst. prof. nursing, chmn. dept. Coll. St. Scholastica, Duluth, 1976-81; cons. KLM Enterprises, Duluth, 1981—. Bd. dirs. Arrowhead Epilepsy League, 1978-79; bd. dirs. St. Francis Home, Superior, Wis., 1979—, v.p., 1982; exec. com. Health Systems Agy. Western Lake Superior, 1976-78. Mem. Am. Nurses Assn., Nat. League Nursing (site visitor), AAUW, Minn. Assn. Colls. Nursing (pres. 1980-81), Jr. League Duluth, Assn. Jr. Leagues. Address: 114 Chester Pkwy Duluth MN 55805

MOLAGHAN, MARY, dancing schs. co. exec.; b. Fitchburg, Mass., Feb. 4, 1920; d. Joseph Bernard and Marguirite (Mahoney) M.; student Lasalle Jr. Coll., Auburndale, Mass., 1938-40, Leland Powers Sch. Theatre, Boston, 1940-42. Coordinator, Katherine Dunham Sch. Cultural Arts, N.Y.C., 1943-48; dir. Fred Astaire Dance Studio, Ridgewood, N.J., 1952-67; treas. Nat. Dance Assn., 1966-71; chmn. Am. Ballroom Co., Miami, Fla., 1970-82; pres. World of Travel, Dance Tours; lectr., speaker in field. Recipient Outstanding Contbr. award Nat. Dance Assn., 1968, Woman of Yr. award Imperial Soc. Tchrs. Dance, 1972, Chmn.'s Merit award Nat. Council Dance Tchrs., 1979. Democrat. Home: 260 Bridies Path Southampton NY 11968 Office: 1660 Jewel Box Ave Naples FL 33942

MOLANO, CELIA, health care adminstr.; b. Maiquetia, Venezuela, Oct. 9, 1935; d. Felipe and Isabel de Molano (Cardenas) M.; B.S., U. Panama, 1957, postgrad., 1959-61; masters degree U. P.R., 1976; 1 child, Otilda I. Pinilla. Med. technologist Gorgas Meml. Lab., Panama, 1957-62; asst. prof. natural scis. and Pharmacy Sch., U. Panama, 1960-61, asst. prof. microbiology Med. Scis. Sch., 1960-62, asst. prof. microbiology Med. Tech. Sch., 1961-62; microbiologist FDA, Panama, 1961-62; dir. Pavia Hosp. Lab., P.R., 1962-68; owner, dir. San Martin Hosp. Lab., Rio Piedras, P.R., 1968—; asst. adminstr. San Martin Hosp., 1975-80, personnel dir., 1977—; pres. Lab. Services Group, Hato Rey, P.R., 1980—, Celia Molano & Assos., Rio Piedras, 1982—. Trustee I. Gonzalez Martinez Oncological Hosp., 1970—. Recipient Pres.'s award Health Service Adminstrn., 1976, 77, 78; various recognition awards. Mem. P.R. Hosp. Adminstrs. Assn. (pres. 1981), Hosp. Fin. Mgmt. Assn., P.R. Hosps. Assn., Am. Soc. Clin. Pathologists, Am. Soc. Med. Technologists, P.R. Coll. Med. Technologists, P.R. Labs. Owners Assn. (pres. 1982—), P.R. Profls. Assn. Roman Catholic. Office: PO Box 29689/65 Inf Sta Rio Piedras PR 00929

MOLBERG, ANDREA, psychologist, educator; b. Mpls., Jan. 3, 1951; d. Allen Luther and Phillis Ann Molberg; B.A. summa cum laude, Ariz. State U., 1971; Ph.D. in Indsl. Orgn. and Counseling Psychology, U. Minn., 1976; m. Jeffrey Rogers Basford, Feb. 27, 1982. Teaching asst., teaching asso., instr. Gen. Coll., U. Minn., 1972-75, instr. dept. psychology, 1974, asst. prof. extended programs, 1976-77; instr. dept. psychology Coll. St. Thomas, St. Paul, 1974-77, asst. prof. counseling psychology, 1977-81, adj. prof., 1981—; pvt. practice cons. psychology, St. Paul, 1976—. Mem. Am. Psychol. Assn., Am. Personnel and Guidance Assn. Contbr. in field. Home and Office: 465 Brimhall St Saint Paul MN 55105

MOLER, ELIZABETH ANNE, lawyer; b. Salt Lake City, Jan. 24, 1949; d. Murray McClure and Eleanor Lorraine (Barry) M.; B.A., Am. U., 1971; postgrad. Johns Hopkins U., 1971, 72; J.D., George Washington U., 1977; m. Thomas Blake Williams, Oct. 19, 1979. Admitted to D.C. bar, 1978; staff asst. Hon. Laurence J. Burton, 1967-69, Senator Mike Gravel, 1971-72; chief legislative asst. Senator Floyd K. Haskell, 1973-75; law clk. Sharon, Pierson, Semmes, Crolius & Finey, Washington, 1975-76; profl. staff mem. Com. Energy and Natural Resources, U.S. Senate, Washington, 1976-77, counsel, 1977—. Mem. Am. Bar Assn., D.C. Bar Assn. Democrat. Author: (with James T. Bruce) Mexico: The Promise and Problems of Petroleum, 1979. Office: Com Energy and Natural Resources US Senate 3208 Dirksen Office Bldg Washington DC 20510

MOLHOLT, PAT A., librarian; b. Fond du Lac, Wis., Oct. 19, 1943; d. Elmore Harrison and Leona Ann (Reschke) Leu; B.S., U. Wis., 1966, M.L.S., 1970, specialist degree, 1978; m. Garrett Molholt, May 21, 1967; children—Becca, Stephanie. Librarian, Woodman Astron. Library, U. Wis.-Madison, 1970-73, librarian physics library, 1973-77; asst. prof., dir. Sci. and Tech. Library, U. Wyo., Laramie, 1977-78; asso. dir. libraries Rensselaer Poly. Inst., Troy, N.Y., 1978—; lectr. Sch. Library and Info. Sci., SUNY, Albany; sr. fellow UCLA Grad. Sch. Library and Info. Sci., Mem. Spl. Libraries Assn. (pres.-elect), Internat. Fedn. Library Assn. (sec. sci. and tech. libraries sect., fin. officer spl. libraries div.). Office: Folsom Library Rensselaer Polytechnic Inst Troy NY 12181

MOLINA, MARIA ELBA, bank exec.; b. Cananea, Sonora, Mex., Mar. 17, 1944; came to U.S., 1949, naturalized, 1969; d. Ramon and Victoria Acostaa de Leon; student U. Ariz., 1964—, Pima Community Coll., 1979—; m. Bill Molina, Oct. 3, 1975. Bilingual sec. So. Ariz. Bank, Tucson, 1964-71; asst. v.p., security officer Southwestern Bank, Tucson, 1971-74; v.p. community relations and bus. devel. officer Home Fed. Savs., Tucson, 1974—. Bd. dirs. Ariz. Office Econ. Planning and Devel., 1981; chmn. bd. trustees El Dorado Hosp.; Ariz. rep. U.S. Commn. on Civil Rights. Recipient award Adolf Coors Decade of the Hispanic Outstanding Woman; Outstanding Citizen award League United Latin-Am. Citizens, 1975. Mem. Tucson Airport Authority, Better Bus. Bur. (dir.), Exec. Women's Council So. Ariz., Exec. Women Internat. Club: Soroptomists. Home: PO Box 7156 Tucson AZ 85725 Office: PO Box 2871 Tucson AZ 85702

MOLITOR, SISTER, MARGARET ANNE, coll. pres.; b. Milford, Ohio, Sept. 19, 1920; d. George Jacob and Mary Amelia (Lockwood) Molitor; B.A., Our Lady of Cin. Coll., 1942; M.Ed., Xavier U., 1950, LL.D. (hon.); M.A., Cath. U. Am., 1963, Ph.D., 1967. Joined Sisters of Mercy, 1943; tchr. elem. schs., Cin., 1946-50, secondary schs., Cin. and Piqua, Ohio, 1951-60; faculty Edgecliff Coll., Cin., 1962-73, pres., 1973-80; Research cons. various religious communities. Bd. dirs. Citizens Com. on Youth; trustee Chatfield Coll.; mem. Area Council Planning Task Force; mem. Cin. Commmunity Devel. Adv. Council. Recipient Woman of Yr. award Cin. Enquirer, 1977. Mem. Greater Cin. Consortium Colls. and Univs. (pres. 1980). Address: 2335 Grandview Ave Cincinnati OH 45206

MOLLER, HELLA, ret. child psychologist; b. Frankfurt, Germany, June 26, 1912; came to U.S., 1936, naturalized, 1942; d. Gustav and Jenny (Berger) Morgenthau; B.S., Boston U., 1951, M.Ed., 1952, Ed.D., 1960; m. Herbert Moller, May 8, 1939. Dir., Cambridge Art Center for Children, 1942-45; dir. Nursery Sch., Community Center, Lynn, Mass., 1947-48; psychol. cons. Quincy (Mass.) Public Schs., 1952-55, Lesley Dearborn Sch., Cambridge, Mass., 1955-56; psychol. counselor Arlington (Mass.) Public Schs., 1955-67; field work supr. doctoral sch. psychology program Boston U., 1962-67, doctoral counseling program Harvard U., Cambridge, Mass., 1963-65; child psychologist dir. Head Start, City of Boston, 1967-68; cons. OEO, Volt Tech. Corp., N.Y.C., 1968-70; asso. Powell Assos., Cambridge, 1968-70; pvt. practice psychology, Lexington, Mass., 1969-77; instr. Boston Coll., 1973-77; psychol. cons. Coop. Kindergartens, Chelmsford, Mass., 1973-75; psychol. cons., second evaluator Lexington Public Schs., 1975-77; psychol. evaluator Regional Diagnostic Center, Sarasota, Fla., 1977-79; cons. McClellan Park Sch., 1978-80. Mem. Am. Psychol. Assn., Am. Orthopsychiat. Assn., Fla. Psychol. Assn., Boston U. Alumni Assn., Bank St Alumni Assn., Pi Lambda Theta. Contbr. articles to profl. jours. Address: 6808 Woodwind Dr Sarasota FL 33581

MOLLICA, MARIE THERESE, acctg. co. exec.; b. N.Y.C., Jan. 6, 1929; d. Dominick and Ripalda (Sulla) M.; student public sch., also various specialized coll. courses. Asst. to bookkeeper Douglas T. Johnston & Co., investment counselors, N.Y.C., 1946-47; office mgr., adminstrv. mgr. Rogers & Butler, architects, N.Y.C., 1947-57; exec. asst. to treas. All State Properties, Inc., Floral Park, N.Y., 1957-61; exec. asst. to bus. mgr. Careers Inc., publishers, N.Y.C., 1961; exec. asst., sec. to prin. partner Hertz, Herson & Co., C.P.A.s, N.Y.C., 1962-69; adminstrv. mgr. tax compliance dept. J.K. Lasser & Co., C.P.A.s, N.Y.C., 1969-74; exec. asst. to adminstrv. partner Eichler, Tannebaum & Co., C.P.A.s, N.Y.C., 1974-76; office mgr., adminstrv. mgr. Glenn, Ingram & Co., C.P.A.s, N.Y.C., 1976-79; fin. adminstr., adminstrv. mgr. Mitchell/Titus & Co., C.P.A.s, N.Y.C., 1979—. Mem. Am. Mgmt. Soc., Nat. Assn. Female Execs., Nat. Secs. Assn.

MOLOFF, PAULA FAITH BEIDES, pub. health adminstr.; b. N.Y.C., Apr. 4, 1944; d. Isidore and Molly (Percik) Beides; B.A., CUNY, 1965; M.S.W., U. Nebr., 1974; M.B.A., U. No. Colo., 1982; m. Paul Moloff, 1965; children—Andrew R., Lisa Francesca. Dir. dept. social service Baptist Home of Nebr., Omaha, 1972-74; health and social work resource cons. Pima Health Systems, Tucson, 1975; case mgr. Child Protective Services, Tucson, 1976; social work discharge planner Kino Community Hosp., Tucson, 1976-78; pvt. practice individual and group therapy, Tucson, 1976-78; group therapist Pime County (Ariz.) Juvenile Ct., Tucson, 1976-78; div. dir. Child and Youth project Dept. Health County of Pima, 1978-80; dir. dept. health Pascua-Yaqui Tribe, Tucson, 1980-82; health program mgr. Ariz. Health Care Cost Containment System, Ariz. Dept. Health Services, 1982—; practicum instr. U. Nebr., 1974, Ariz. State U., 1977—; vice-chmn. foster care rev. bd. Ariz. Supreme Ct. Recipient Cert. of Recognition, World Muslim Community, Tucson, 1979. Mem. Nat. Assn. Social Workers, Acad. Cert. Social workers, Am. Public Health Assn., Vis. Nurses Assn. (dir. 1977-80). Democrat. Home: 7126 N 19th Ave Suite 122 Phoenix AZ 85021 Office: 1200 W Washington St Phoenix AZ

MOLTENI, BETTY PHILLIPS, painter; b. Norfolk, Va., Dec. 15, 1913; d. William Henry and Margaret (Brownley) Phillips; A.B., Coll. William and Mary, 1938; student art U. Nev., Reno, 1966-71; m. Peter G. Molteni, Jr., July 22, 1939; children—Peter G. III, Margaret Elizabeth, Christopher Phillips, Marianne Stephanie. Founder, chmn. Armed Forces Art Show Hawaii, 1962; one-woman shows Artist Coop., Reno, 1978, 81, Mother Lode Nat. Art Exhbn., Sonora, Calif., 1977, 79, Delta Art Assn. Show, Antioch, Calif., 1978, Lodi (Calif.) 19th Ann. Art Exhbn., Acampo, Calif., 1979; two-person shows Artist Coop., Reno, 1966-79, 82; exhibited group shows Nev. Women Art Show Las Vegas, 1976, Nat. League Am. Pen Women, Salt Lake City, 1973, Sacramento, 1978, Nev. State Exhibit (Best of Show award), 1971, Lake Tahoe Ehrman Art Festival, 1980, 81; represented in pvt. collections. Bd. dirs. Nev. Art Gallery, 1975-78; del. Sierra Arts Assembly, 1977-82. Mem. Nat. League Am. Pen Women (v.p. 1973, pres. Reno chpt. 1980-82, pres. Nev. 1982-84), Soc. Western Artists, Latimer Art Club (pres. 1974, art scholarship chmn. 1978, treas. 1978), Carson City Alliance (charter mem.), Nev. Artists Assn., Nev. Art Gallery, Sierra Nev. Mus. Art Aux., Sierra Arts Assembly, Artist Co-op. (charter). Republican. Roman Catholic. Home: 1130 Alpine Circle Reno NV 89509

MOMIYAMA, NANAE, artist; b. Tokyo; came to U.S., 1954; d. Tokutaro and Kimie (Ito) M.; B.F.A., Banka Gakain Coll., Tokyo; M.F.A., Tokyo Women's Coll.; postgrad. Art Students League N.Y., 1954-56; children—Haniwa, Anne Kesa, Richard. One-women shows: Ligoa Duncan Gallery, N.Y.C., 1975, Galerie Raymond Duncan, Paris, 1975, 78, Seibu Galeries, Tokyo, 1974, 77, 79, 82, group shows include: Nat. Mus. Modern Arts, Tokyo, 1953, Nat. Acad., N.Y.C., 1968, 69, 70, Salon Internat. di Pittura, Rome, 1973, Grand Prix Humanitaire de France, Paris, 1975, Union Carbide, N.Y.C., Liver House, N.Y.C., 1976, 81, Lincoln Center, N.Y.C., 1981, 82; represented in permanent collections; illustrator for Columbia U. Press, Oxford U. Press, London Rev. of Paris. Recipient Silver medal Grand Prix Humanitaire de France, 1975, Gold medal Acad. Italy, 1979. Mem. Art Equity Assn. N.Y., Nat. Assn. Women Artists, Japanese Artists Assn. N.Y., Modern Art Assn. Japan. Author: Sami-e an Introduction to Ink Painting. Home: PO Box 44 Glenville Gleenwich CT 06830 Office: 155 Bank St New York NY 10014

MONACO, GRACE POWERS, lawyer; b. Union City, N.J., Sept. 3, 1938; d. Rea John and Grace (FitzGibbons) Powers; B.A. summa cum laude, Coll. of Misericordia, 1960, L.H.D. (hon.), 1979; J.D., Georgetown U., 1963; m. Lawrence A. Monaco, Jr., Aug. 10, 1963; children—Kathleen Rea (dec.), David Gordon, Stephen Michael, Peter Joseph. Admitted to D.C. bar, 1964, Supreme Ct. U.S. bar, 1975; with honor grad. program, natural resource div. Dept. Justice, Washington, 1963-64; pvt. practice law, Va., 1965-66; asso. firm Wheatley & Miller,

Washington, 1967-78; partner firm Fairman, Frisk & Monaco, Washington, 1978-82; asso. firm White, Fine & Verville, Washington, 1982—. Founder, pres. Candlelighters Found., 1976—; vice-chmn. bd. Washington Hosp. Health Systems, Inc.; bd. dirs. St. Francis Center; chmn. bd. dirs. Capitol Hill Hosp., Washington, Coll. of Misericordia, Women's Bar Found. Recipient Ann. Nat. award Am. Cancer Soc., 1978. Mem. D.C., U.S. Supreme Ct., Am., Fed., Women's bar assns., Capitol Hill Restoration Soc., Fed. Energy Regulatory Bar Assn., Kappa Delta Pi. Democrat. Roman Catholic. Home: 123 C St SE Washington DC 20003 Office: 302 Marshall B Coyne Bldg 1156 15th St NW Washington DC 20005

MONAHAN, JEANETTE, hosp. adminstr., organizational devel. cons.; b. Dallas, May 9, 1949; d. John I. and Julia M. (Galloway) Welsh; B.A. in English, U. Tex., Austin, 1971; M.P.A., U. Colo., 1975; diploma Internat. Inst. Study of Systems Renewal, Seattle, 1981; m. Terence F. Meany, Mar. 17, 1977; 1 dau., Theresa K. Monahan. Intern, City of Boulder (Colo.), summer 1975, Colo. Dept. Regulatory Agys., Denver, summer 1976; tng. specialist Municipality of Met. Seattle, 1977-78; mgr. employee tng. and devel. U. Wash. Hosps., Seattle, 1978-82; dir. mgmt. devel. Virginia Mason Med. Center, Seattle, 1982—. Recipient Suggestion award Municipality of Met. Seattle, 1978. Mem. Am. Soc. Tng. and Devel. (Outstanding Contbr. award 1977, 78; region VIII conf. planning com. 1983), Am. Soc. Healthcare Edn. and Tng. (nat. program planning com. 1982, 83). Democrat. Roman Catholic. Club: Toastmasters (Seattle). Contbr. articles on organizational devel. to profl. jours. Office: PO Box 1930 Seattle WA 98111

MONAHAN, VIRGINIA, public relations counsel; b. N.Y.C., Apr. 13, 1928; d. Thomas Louis and Mary Margaret (Glynn) Smith; children—Maureen, Cathleen, Sharon, Elizabeth. Dist. rep. Congressman Richard Ottinger of N.Y., 1964-70; exec. asst. Builders Inst. of Westchester/Putnam Counties, 1971-73; dir. Westchester Found., White Plains, 1973-81; adminstr. Constrn. Industry Employee Assistance Program, White Plains, 1977—. Editor: Impact, 1979—; editor Builders Inst. ann. yearbook, 1978—.

MONALOY, GAIL ELAINE, speech/lang. pathologist; b. Paterson, N.J., May 16, 1943; d. Morris Aaron and Florence (Perlman) M.; B.S. cum laude, Pa. State U., 1964; M.A. (Vocat. Rehab. Adminstrn. grantee 1964-66), Stanford U., 1966. Speech pathologist Goldwater Meml. Hosp., N.Y.C., 1966-70, Montgomery County Public Schs., Rockville, Md., 1970-74, Montclair (N.J.) Bd. Edn., 1974-75; speech and hearing therapist Ramsey (N.J.) Bd. Edn., 1975-76; pvt. practice speech and lang. pathology, Passaic, N.J., 1976—; lectr. Acad. Gen. Dentistry, N.J. Coll. Medicine and Dentistry; cons. in field. Lic. speech pathologist, N.Y.; cert. elem. sch. tchr., N.J.; cert. speech correctionist, N.J.; cert. speech therapist, Md. Mem. Am. Speech and Hearing Assn. (cert. of clin. competence in speech pathology), N.J. Speech and Hearing Assn., N.Y. State Speech and Hearing Assn. Clubs: Princeton, Stanford. Address: 414 Passaic Ave Passaic NJ 07055

MONCRIEF, CAROL YVONNE, systems engr.; b. Coulee Dam, Wash., Apr. 19, 1950; d. Lawrence Edward and Mary Elizabeth (Haile) M.; B.S. in Systems Engring., Boston U., 1972; postgrad. Marist Coll. 1973; postgrad. in bus. adminstrn. George Mason U., 1976-80. Jr. programmer IBM, Poughkeepsie, N.Y., 1972-74; asso. systems engr., Manassas, Va., 1974-78; systems engr. MITRE Corp., McLean, Va., 1978-80; staff systems test engr. Satellite Bus. Systems, McLean, 1980—. Chmn. sect. membership Nat. Council Negro Women, Washington, 1978-80; bd. dirs. Tanner's Cluster, Reston, Va., 1982. Recipient Community Action Program Inst. for Urban Affairs and Research award Howard U., 1979. Mem. Soc. Women Engrs., Black Ski, Alpha Kappa Alpha (treas. chpt. 1976-78, parliamentarian chpt. 1982-83). Democrat. Baptist. Home: 11987 Barrel Cooper Ct Reston VA 22091 Office: 8003 Westpark Dr McLean VA 22102

MONCURE, JANE BELK, author, cons. childhood edn.; b. Orlando, Fla., Dec. 16, 1926; d. John B. and Jennie W. Belk; B.S., Va. Commonwealth U., 1952; M.A., Columbia U., 1954; m. James Ashby Moncure, June 14, 1952; 1 son. Tchr., Woodward Sch., N.Y.C., 1952-53; guest instr. Adelphi Coll., Garden City, N.Y., 1953; dir. First Presbyn. Ch. nursery-Kindergarten, N.Y.C., 1953-54, Southside Day Nursery, Richmond, Va., 1954-56, Town and Garden Nursery Sch., Richmond, 1957-64; tchr. Jr. Primary program Richmond City Schs., 1964-66; instr. dept. edn. Va. Commonwealth U., Richmond, 1966-71; mem. staff Va. Union U., Richmond, 1972-73; instr. dept. edn. Westhampton Coll., U. Richmond, 1973-74; tchr. kindergarten Burlington (N.C.) Day Sch., 1974-78; author over 50 books for young children, 1954—, including books on arts and crafts, sci. and social sci. lang. arts, creative dramatics, alphabet books, rhyme books and primary grade readers; cons. in childhood edn. Active, Elon Coll. Community Ch. of Christ, 1974—. Recipient Outstanding Service award Va. Assn. for Early Childhood Edn., 1979. Mem. Nat. Assn. for the Edn. of Young Children, Delta Kappa Gamma. Home: 1046 Briarcliff Rd Burlington NC 27215

MONDAY, JANET TALLEY, med. lab. technician; b. Hopewell, Va., Jan. 31, 1953; d. John Harrison and Marie (LaForce) Talley; student Petersburg Gen. Hosp. Cert. Lab. Asst. Sch., 1972-73; m. William Gregory Monday, Aug. 17, 1974. Gen. bench technician John Randolph Hosp. Lab., Hopewell, Va., 1973-74; gen. lab. technician Lee Med. Lab., Inc., Richmond, Va., 1974-77; med. lab. technician Temporary Lab. Services, Richmond, 1981—; 3-11 lab. shift supr. John Randolph Hosp. Lab., Hopewell, Va., 1978—. Active Hopewell-Prince George chpt. ARC. Mem. Am. Soc. Clin. Pathologists, Internat. Soc. Clin. Lab. Tech., Clin. Lab. Mgmt. Assn. Methodist. Home: 3611 Settlers Ln Hopewell VA 23860 Office: 700 N 4th Ave Hopewell VA 23860

MONDY, NELL IRENE, educator; b. Pocahontas, Ark., Oct. 27, 1921; d. D. Daley and F. Ethel (Carroll) M.; B.A. in Chemistry summa cum laude, Ouachita U., 1943, B.S. in Chemistry summa cum laude, 1943; M.A. in Biochemistry, U. Tex., 1945; Ph.D. in Biochemistry (Sigma Xi fellow), Cornell U., 1953. Asst. prof. chemistry Ouachita U., 1943-44; research asst. biochem. inst. U. Tex., 1944-45; research assoc. in biochemistry and nutrition Cornell U., Ithaca, N.Y., 1945-46, instr. food and nutrition, 1948-51, asst. prof., assoc. prof., prof. food and nutrition and nutritional scis., 1953—; instr. chemistry Asso. Colls. of Upper N.Y., 1946-47, asst. prof. chemistry, 1947-48; supervisory food specialist human nutrition research div. Food Quality Lab., U.S. Dept. Agr., Beltsville, Md., 1960-61; food cons. R.T. French, 1966-67; prof. food and nutrition Fla. State U., 1969-70; food cons. Holmen Brenderi - Gjovik, Norway, 1972-73; cons. S & B Shokuhim Co., Ltd., Tokyo, 1978-79, Nihon Kaken Co., Ltd., Tokyo, 1978-79, EPA, Washington, 1979-80; Birkett-Williams lectr., Ouachita, 1980—; participant confs., seminar, congresses in field, France, Poland, Switzerland, Scotland, Eng.; mem. N.Y. State Potato Adv. Council. Fund raiser United Way; active Cornell Centennial Campaign, Cornell Tower Club; vice chmn. Ouachita Baptist U. Campaign, Historic Ithaca. Recipient Danforth award, 1954, 58. Fellow AAAS, Am. Inst. of Chemists; mem. AAUP (exec. com. 1980—), Am. Chem. Soc., Inst. Food Technologists, N.Y. Acad. Scis., Am. Home Econs. Assn., European Assn. for Potato Research, Potato Assn. Am. (charter mem. physiology com. 1974—, chmn. site selection com. N.Am. and S.Am. 1973—), Soc. for Cryobiology, Am. Dietetics Assn., N.Y. State Hort. Soc., Empire State Potato Assn., Am. Soc. Plant Physiologists, Internat. Platform Assn., Washington Women's Network, Grad. Women in Sci. (v.p. nat. orgn. 1981—, nat. historian 1978—, gen. coordinator nat. awards 1974-75), Sigma Xi, Iota Sigma Pi, Sigma Delta Epsilon, Phi Kappa Phi, Omicron Nu, Pi Lambda Theta, Phi Tau Sigma. Democrat. Baptist. Clubs: Cornell Campus, Cayuga Trails (exec. bd.). Author: Experimental Food Chemistry, 1980; contbr. papers to profl. confs. in field in U.S., France, Japan, Korea, India, Poland; contbr. writings to publs. U.S., France, Japan. Office: Div Nutritional Scis Cornell Univ N204 MVR Ithaca NY 14853

MONGAN, MARY ANNE, library media specialist; b. Winston-Salem, N.C., Jan. 29, 1934; d. William Curtis and Martha Jackson Logan; B.A., Westhampton Coll., U. Richmond, 1955; M.S., Radford U., 1976; div.; children—Brenton Lee, William Quinn, Martha Anne. Tchr., Washington Heights Sch., Roanoke, Va., 1955-59; tchr. South Salem Sch., Salem, Va., 1964-65, 70-71; library media specialist Glen Cove Elem. Sch., Roanoke, 1971—. Mem. Va. Ednl. Media Assn. (dir. 1977-79, treas. 1980-82), Roanoke County Librarians Assn. (pres. 1979—), ALA, Va. Library Assn., Am. Assn. Sch. Librarians, Assn. Ednl. Communication and Tech., Va. Reading Assn., NEA, Va. Edn. Assn., Roanoke County Edn. Assn., Salem Hist. Soc., Phi Delta Kappa, Delta Kappa Gamma, Kappa Delta Pi, Phi Kappa Phi. Methodist. Club: Salem Novel Book. Home: 211 Taylor Ave Salem VA 24153 Office: 5901 Cove Rd Roanoke VA 24019

MONGERSON, SUSAN CLAY, art gallery exec.; b. Indpls., Jan. 30, 1942; d. Sherman Paul and Virginia Jean Clay; ed. Colby Jr. Coll., 1962; m. Mel A. Mongerson, Feb. 6, 1965; children—Christina, Lindsey, Tyler. Owner, mgr. Mongerson Gallery, Chgo. Clubs: Racquet, Arts (Chgo.). Home: 1199 Edgewood Rd Lake Forest IL 60045 Office: Mongerson Gallery 620 N Michigan Ave Chicago IL 60611

MONGNO, ADELE GRACE, fin. cons.; b. Bklyn., Feb. 28, 1947; d. Biagio Alfred and Maria Grace (Caputo) Scala; student Suffolk Community Houstonic Coll., 1970-72; 1 dau., Michelle Suzanne. Vice pres. S.L. Scala Leasing, Inc., Commack, N.Y., 1976—, Nat. Fiscal Cons., Commack, 1979—, Am. Fiscal Cons., Commack, 1979—, Nat.-Am. Fiscal Cons., 1982—; mgr. Lipton, Deitler & Gelfand, Fairfield, Conn., 1972-78; controller E.M. Graves, Southport, Conn., 1978-79; Mem. Am. Collectors Assn., Comml. Law League, Am. Mgmt. Assn., NOW, Kings Park C. of C. Home: 1 Fireplace Dr Kings Park NY 11754 Office: 21 E Northport Rd Kings Park NY 11754

MONK, LORRAINE, photography curator; B.A., McGill U., Montreal, Que., Can., 1944, M.A., 1946; D.Letters, York U., 1982; 4 children. Writer Nat. Film Bd. Can., Ottawa, 1957-60, dir. still photography div., 1960-80; hon. chmn. bd. Photo Ecology Found. Am. Decorated Order Can., 1973; recipient Excellence of Service award Federation Internationale de l'Art photographique, 1966; Centennial medal Can. Govt., 1967; hon. fellow Ont. Coll. Art, Toronto, 1980; dir. Can. Mus. Photography, Toronto. Producer books, including: Canada A Year of the Land (numerous awards), 1967; Stones of History-Canada's Houses of Parliament, 1967; Call Them Canadians (numerous awards), 1968; Canada (Best Designed Book in Can. award, Silver medal Most Beautiful Book in World Competition), 1973; The Female Eye, 1975; Between Friends/Entre Amis (numerous awards including Internat. Gallery Superb Printing Best Printed Book award, Internat. Leipzig Book Fair Gold medal), 1976; Robert Bourdeau Monograph, 1980; Canada with Love/Canada avec Amour, 1982. Office: Can Mus Photography 176 Balmoral Ave Toronto ON M4V 1J6 Canada

MONK, MEREDITH JANE, composer, choreographer, dir., singer, dancer; b. Lima, Peru, Nov. 20, 1942; came to U.S., naturalized, 1942; d. Theodore Glenn and Audrey Lois (Zellman) M.; B.A., Sarah Lawrence Coll., 1964. Artistic dir., composer, choreographer, dir. Meredith Monk/The House, N.Y.C., 1968—; artistic dir. The House Found. for Arts, Meredith Monk Vocal Ensemble; mem. faculty N.Y.U., 1971, 72, 74, 78, Goddard Coll., 1971, 75, Sarah Lawrence Coll., 1975, Naropa Inst., 1975, 76, 78; mem. bd. advs. Jewish Theatre Found. Recipient Obie award Village Voice, 1972, 76, Creative Arts award Brandeis U., 1974; Guggenheim fellow, 1972, 82; Creative Artists Public Service fellow, 1976, 81, 82; Nat. Endowment for Arts grantee, 1970-82; N.Y. State Council grantee, 1970-81. Mem. ASCAP. Compositions include: Our Lady of Late, 1972; Tablet 1977; Dolmen Music, 1979, Turtle Dreams, 1981; large theater works include: Vessel, 1971; Quarry, 1976; Recent Ruins (Villager award for outstanding prodn. 1979-80), 1979; Specimen Days, 1981.

MONKS, RUTH ELLEN, tax service exec.; b. Kilgore, Tex., Feb. 5, 1935; d. John Herbert and Gladys Mary (Coats) Brock; student acctg. and mgmt. Houston Community Coll., 1979-80; student computer sci. U. Houston, 1982; m. Gerald Paul Monks, Feb. 26, 1955; children—John Michael, Gerald Patrick, Robert Stephen, Ruth Annette, Lawrence Paul. Dir. Confraternity Christian Doctrine, St. Vincent de Paul Ch., Houston, 1974-76; sec. Marian High Sch. Fin. Bd., Houston, 1975-78; gen. mgr. Jerry Monks-Mr. Insurance, Houston, 1968—; pres. Tax Service, Inc., Houston, 1973—. Mem. Profl. Ins. Agts., Tex. Restaurant Assn., Houston Apt. Assn., Nat. Assn. Female Execs., Internat. Graphoanalysis Soc. Republican. Roman Catholic. Home: 3730 Tartan Ln Houston TX 77025 Office: 4189 Bellaire Blvd Suite 2422 Houston TX 77025

MONOHAN, GERALDINE LEA, child care supr.; b. Los Angeles, Sept. 24, 1955; d. Clyde Kenneth and Geraldine Elsie (Kuschell) Mawhinney; B.S.W., Calif. State U., Long Beach, 1977. Child-care worker Maryvale, residential treatment center for girls, Rosemead, Calif., 1977-79, evening supr., 1979—. Cert. trainer mgmt. assaultive behavior, Calif. Mem. Nat. Assn. Social Workers. Roman Catholic. Home: 13720 E Valley Blvd Apt 16 La Puente CA 91746 Office: 7600 E Graves Ave Rosemead CA 91770

MONOHON, CAROL A., state legislator; b. Raymond, Wash., July 15, 1945; d. Adrian W. and Marjorie M. (Madden) Hull; student Grays Harbor Coll., 1973; B.A. with honors in Polit. Sci., U. Puget Sound, 1975, postgrad. Sch. of Law; m. Robert I. Monohon, June 9, 1962; children—Bryon David, Sharron Aileen. Mem. Wash. State Ho. of Reps., 1976, 78—, Wash. State Senate, 1977. Mem. Precinct Democratic Com., Wash., 1972—, Wash. State Dem. Com., 1972-78, Wash. State Dem. Exec. Bd., 1974-76, Pacific County Dem. Central Com., Grays Harbor County Dem. Central Com. Office: care Washington Ho Reps State Capitol Olympia WA 98504 *

MONROE, DONNA CHAMBERS, public relations exec.; b. Cin., Jan. 2, 1948; d. Russell James and Rita Marie (Fuson) Chambers; B.A. magna cum laude, Newcomb Coll. of Tulane U., 1970; m. Gary Alan Monroe, Feb. 17, 1973. Editor, Southwestern Gen. Life Ins. Co., Dallas, 1970-73, Southwestern Life Ins. Co., Dallas, 1973-76; community relations dir. St. Paul Hosp., Dallas, 1976; dir. pub. relations Southwestern Gen. Life Ins. Co., Dallas, 1977-79, asst. v.p., dir. pub. relations, 1979—. Bd. dirs. People's Goals for Plano (Tex.), 1978. Recipient Matrix award for bus. communications Women in Communications, 1980. Fellow Life Mgmt. Inst.; mem. AAUW (br. pres. 1980—), Internat. Assn. Bus. Communicators, Life Ins. Advertisers Assn., Phi Beta Kappa, Kappa Alpha Theta.

MONROE, MARIAN LOUISE, educator; b. Wichita, Kans., Dec. 2, 1934; d. Everett C. and Opal Lois (Stover) Badgley; B.S. in Home Econs., U. Ark., 1955; M.S. in Child Devel., U. Ala., 1957; m. Gregory T. Monroe, Oct. 11, 1959; children—Stacey Terence, Tracey Lawrence, Patricia Lynn. Home economist agrl. extension service U. Ark., 1955-56; grad. asst. U. Ala., 1956-57; home economist agrl. extension service U. Ariz., 1957-59, Tex. A. and M. U., 1960-63; nursery sch. tchr. U. Houston, 1965-66; home mgmt. supr. Family and Children's Service, Houston, 1966-67, Harris County Community Action Assn., Houston, 1967-68; edn. dir. Head Start, Houston, 1968-70; contract mgr./program specialist Tex. Dept. Human Resources, Austin, 1970-80, child devel. dir., 1980—. Mem. Nat. Assn. Edn. Young Children, So. Assn. Children Under Six, Assn. Childhood Edn. Internat., Tex. Public Employees Assn., Tex. Assn. Young Children, Phi Upsilon Omicron, Kappa Delta Pi, Phi Kappa Phi. Methodist. Author articles in field. Mng. editor Tex. Child Care Quar., 1981—. Home: 6708 Notre Dame Dr Austin TX 78723 Office: 523-A TDHR PO Box 2960 Austin TX 78769

MONROE, MARY ROBERTA, state ofcl.; b. Culver, Oreg., Oct. 8, 1921; d. Mason Ray and Bessie Annettia (Robinson) Grant; m. Herman S. Monroe, Oct. 27, 1940; children—Frederic LeRoy, John Edward, James David, Carol Suzanne, Ronald Melvin. Clk., buyer Thrifty Drug, Madras, Oreg., 1962, 69; clk., buyer Erickson's Dept. Store, Madras, 1969-71; statis. enumerator Crop & Livestock Reporting Service, U.S. Dept. Agr., Redmond, Oreg., 1970-75; supr. Nat. Assn. State Depts. Agr., Redmond, 1975-81. Sec., v.p., pres. Christian Women's Council, Culver and Redmond, Oreg., 1950-80. Recipient cert. U.S. Dept. Agr., 1975. Mem. Oreg. PTA, Jefferson County 4H Leaders Assn., DAR (def. chmn. 1978-80, state librarian 1980-81, chpt. regent 1982-83), Democrat. Clubs: Olla Podrida Study (pres. 1978-79), Green Thumb Garden (pres.), Pleasant Valley Garden. Home: 4395 SW Reservoir Dr Redmond OR 97756

MONROE, URSULA, educator; b. Berlin, June 28, 1919; d. Johannes and Gertrud Rohrbeck; M.A., Colo. Coll., 1953; Ph.D., Free U. Berlin Tenn. Christian U., 1974; m. Clifford C. Monroe, Feb. 2, 1950 (dec. 1972). Mem. faculty dept. English and German, Colo. Coll., Colorado Springs, 1960-68; instr. humanities Pikes Peak Community Coll., Colorado Springs, 1969—. Nat. Endowment Humanities grantee, 1976-77. Mem. NEA, Colo. Edn. Assn., Theosophical Soc. Am., Anthroposophical Soc. Am. Lutheran. Research on arts of pre-Columbian Indians of Ams. Home: 3 Stratton Ave Colorado Springs CO 80906 Office: 5675 S Academy Blvd Colorado Springs CO 80906

MONSON, LUDMILLA SEIDL, coll. adminstr.; b. Solen, N.D., May 5, 1918; d. Frank Joseph and Ludmilla (Broxmeyer) Seidl; B.A. in Sociology, Marylhurst (Oreg.) Coll., 1939; M.A., U. Oreg., 1971; m. Robert B. Monson, Dec. 28, 1941; children—Robert Joseph, Anthony Frederick (dec.), David Bruce, Sharon Marie, Mary Ann. Admissions counselor, asst. to pres. Marylhurst Coll., 1949-51; med. office mgr., 1953-73; instr. sociology, women's programs Linn-Benton Community Coll., Albany, Oreg., 1971-73; coordinator inter-agy. pilot program Home Start for Head Start Mothers, Sweet Home, 1972-73; coordinator community edn. Sweet Home for Linn-Benton Community Coll., 1971-74; v.p. acad. affairs Marylhurst Coll., 1974—; mem. steering com. Oreg. Council Advancement Exptl. Learning, 1978-79; bd. regents Marylhurst Coll., 1954-68, trustee, 1968-74; chmn. bd. govs. Oreg. Sch. Study Council, 1966-68; mem. bd. Sch. Dist. 55, Sweet Home, 1962-68, chmn., 1964-65, 67-68. Bd. dirs. Nat. Council Catholic Laity, 1971—; pres. Oreg. Archdiocesan Council Cath. Women, 1966-68; pres. women's aux. Linn County Med. Assn., 1967-68; regional v.p. women's aux. Oreg. Med. Assn., 1967-68; mem. Linn. County Juvenile Adv. Com., 1958-60; bd. dirs. Linn County Mental Health Assn., 1972-74; steering com. Oreg. Women's Conf., 1978. Recipient Pro Ecclesia Papal award, 1961, Benemerenti Papal award, 1969; named Linn County Edn. Citizen of Year, 1964, Sweet Home Woman of Yr., 1958. Mem. AAUW (pres. Oreg. div. 1973-75), Adult Edn. Assn., Am. Assn. Higher Edn., Nat. Assn. Parliamentarians. Democrat. Roman Catholic. Office: PO Box 124 Marylhurst OR 97036

MONTAGUE, RUTH DUBARRY (CRIQUETTE), artist, writer, lectr., educator; b. Paris; d. Roland Beauvais and Maria Violette (DuBarry) M.; student Ecole des Beaux Arts, pvt. ateliers, Paris, U. Nev., Lumis Art Acad., Prickett Sch. Painting, Ecole Marsan, Vernon, France. Dir. Prickett-Montague Studios of Painting, U.S.A., 1955-61; owner, dir. Montague Studio of Painting, New Orleans, 1962-63, Washington, 1964-69; asso. Ecole Marsan, 1970-72, Field Studio, Otter Rock, Oreg., 1974-76, Blue Ridge Mountains, Sterling, Va., 1976—; freelance writer, 1955—; tchr. oil painting, 1955—, color cons., 1955—. Recipient Lumis Art award, 1955. Life fellow Internat. Inst. Arts and Letters (Switzerland); hon. mem. Int. Com. Centro Studi e Scambi Internat. (Rome), Internat. Acad. Leonardo da Vinci (Rome), Internat. Arts Guild (Monaco). Author: 100 monographs in oil painting, 1961—; author-illustrator travel chronicle Bahamian Ah-h-h, 1969, Prose Poems, Sunburst Anthology, 1972, Internat. Bouquet of Poems, 1972. Home: Blue Ridge Studio PO Box 344 Sterling VA 22170

MONTEFERRANTE, JUDITH CATHERINE, cardiologist; b. N.Y.C., Jan. 27, 1949; d. Stanley Paul and Monica Maryann (Vinckus) Sosaris; B.S. cum laude (Young and Rubican, Inc. scholar), Adelphi U., 1970; M.S. in Adult Health, SUNY, Buffalo, 1973, postgrad. Sch. Medicine, 1974-76; M.D., Mt. Sinai Sch. Medicine, 1978; m. Ronald Joseph Monteferrante, June 28, 1970; 1 son, Jason Paul. CCU staff nurse Millard Fillmore Hosp., Buffalo, 1970-71; acute care clin. nurse specialist, research asst. Buffalo Gen. Hosp., 1972-75, coordinator intensive care inservice, 1974-75; clin. assoc. prof. adult health SUNY Sch. Grad. Edn. in Nursing, Buffalo, 1973-76; resident in internal medicine St. Vincent's Hosp. and Med. Center, N.Y.C., 1978-81; fellow in cardiology Westchester County Med. Center, Valhalla, N.Y., 1981-83; free-lance writer Cardiology Product News. Diplomate Am. Bd. Internal Medicine, Nat. Bd. Med. Examiners. Mem. Soc. Critical Care Medicine, Am. Coll. Cardiology, ACP, AMA, Am. Heart Assn., Sigma Theta Tau. Contbr. articles to profl. jours.; research on cardiac electrophysiology, nuclear probe analysis, burn care, mitral stenosis. Office: Dept Cardiology Westchester County Med Center Valhalla NY 10595

MONTEFUSCO, CHERYL MARIE, cardiovascular physiologist; b. New Kensington, Pa., May 14, 1948; d. Benjamin Bosco and Edith (Costanzo) Bongiovanni; B.S., St. Francis Coll., 1970; Ph.D., Coll. Medicine and Dentistry N.J., 1975. Surgery research asso. Newark Beth Israel Med. Center, 1975-76; tech. rep. W. L. Gore Assos., Newark, 1976-77; asst. prof. surgery Albert Einstein Coll. Medicine, N.Y.C., 1977—; coordinator lung transplantation Montefiore Hosp., N.Y.C., 1977—; pres. Contemporary Weight Control Systems, Ltd., N.Y.C., 1981—; guest lector cardiovascular physiology U. Utrecht, 1976. Fellow Am. Coll. Angiology, Internat. Coll. Angiology; mem. Am. Physiol. Soc., AAAS, N.Y. Transplant Soc., N.Y. Acad. Scis. Republican. Roman Catholic. Office: 111 E 210th St New York NY 10467

MONTEMAYOR, GRACIELA DURAN-TROISE, biomed. cons., cancer research scientist; b. Buenos Aires, Argentina, Sept. 14, 1943; d. Eduardo and Melida Ethel (Troise) Duran; M.S., U. Buenos Aires, 1969, Ph.D., 1973; m. Ernest A. Montemayor, May 24, 1974; 1 son, Diego. Fellow U. Buenos Aires, Argentina, 1969-70, Argentinian League for Fight Against Cancer, Buenos Aires, 1970-71; WHO fellow Curie Found. and Gustave Roussy Inst., Paris, France, 1971-73; postdoctoral fellow Nat. Cancer Inst., NIH, Bethesda, Md., 1973-76, vis. asso., 1976-78; sr. research scientist Meloy Labs., Rockville, Md., 1979-80; dir. DTM Cons., Bethesda, Md., 1981—. Bd. dirs. Hispanic Orgn. Profls. and Execs., 1981—; mem. Argentine Woman's Commn. Charity, 1978—. Mem. Am. Soc. Microbiology, AAUW, Tissue Culture Assn., AAAS, Assn. Women in Sci., Argentine Genetic Soc., Am. Transalators

Assn., N.Y. Acad. Scis., San Martin Soc. Washington. Contbr. numerous articles to various publs. Home: 3353 East-West Hwy Chevy Chase MD 20815 Office: 4405 East-West Hwy Bethesda MD 20814

MONTGOMERY, BETTY JUNE, civic worker; b. Fairfax, Okla., Oct. 1, 1939; d. Benjamin Franklin and Dorthey Mazie (Mallonnee) Cameron; m. Carl Montgomery, June 8, 1956; children—Walter, Carla, Alan. Program coordinator 1st United Meth. Ch., Miami, Okla., 1976; pres. Wilson PTA, 1972-73, Miami PTA Council, 1973-75; public relations chmn. Okla. PTA, 1975-76; bus. mgr. Girl Scout Day Camp, 1972-74, mem. Girl Scout council, 1975—; dir. Cub Scout Day Camp, 1975-76, 80; mem. exec. bd. Boy Scouts Am., 1978—; pres. United Fund, Miami, 1979-80; dist. vice chmn. Cub Scouts, 1975—. Recipient Silver Beaver award Boy Scouts Am. Mem. Fellowship of Adults in Youth Ministry, Christian Educators Fellowship. Methodist. Home: 716 N Northwest Miami OK 74354

MONTGOMERY, CAROLYN WILLIAMS, educator, actress; b. Houston, Nov. 12, 1940; d. Paul Girard and Nina Jewell (Anderson) Williams; B.A., Baylor U., 1962; student U. Houston; div. Tchr. history and English, Houston, 1962—, tchr. Westbury Sr. High Sch. profl. actress, 1975—. Mem. Houston Tchrs. Assn., Tex. Sch. Tchrs. Assn., NEA, Nat. Council Social Studies. Baptist. Office: 11544 S Gessner St Houston TX 77071

MONTGOMERY, ELEANOR MOORE (MRS. A. MOORE MONTGOMERY), author, editor, poet, artist; b. Chgo.; d. Herbert Joseph and Edith (Olson) Scully; B.A., U. Chgo., 1930; m. A. Moore Montgomery, 1942 (dec. Nov. 1965). Asso. fashion editor Vogue mag., N.Y.C., 1935-51; one-man show Galeries Raymond Duncan, Paris; exhibited in group shows Festival Internat., de Peinture et d'Art Graphico-Plastique de St. Germain des Pres, 1974, 75, Salon des Surindependants, Salon de Thouet, Thouars, France, Parrish Art Mus., Southampton, N.Y., pub. poetry Eng., U.S., India. Pres., Found. for World Edn., Sri Aurobindo Internat. Center. Decorated dame of Grace, Order Knights Hospitaller of St. John Jerusalem, Las Palmas de Oro al Mérito Belgo-Hispanico, medaille d'Argent, Grand Prix Humanitaire de France, diploma Mertisimos de Academia de Ciencias Humanisticas y Relaciones (Dominican Republic); recipient Humanitarian award Becton Soc., Fairleigh Dickinson U. Mem. Mortar Board (pres. 1929-30). Clubs: Regency Whist (N.Y.C.); Meadow, Southampton (Southampton, L.I.). Author: Tantra Today. Home: 875 Fifth Ave New York NY 10021

MONTGOMERY, ELIZABETH FLANAGAN (MRS. STEWART MAGRUDER MONTGOMERY), ch. and civic worker; b. Cary, Miss., July 25, 1898; d. Robert Edward Lee and Annie May (Purdy) Flanagan; grad. Northwestern Sch. Speech, 1918; A.B., Miss. State Coll. for Women, 1924; summer study Peabody Coll., U. Cal., Columbia; m. Stewart Magruder Montgomery, Jan. 5, 1935. Instr. elementary grades, high sch. English and dramatics, Cary, Miss., 1924-51. Mem. King's Daus. and Sons, state pres. 1949-51, 55-56, dir. Indian work, speaker internat. conv.; state pres. Miss. Women's Cabinet, 1954-55; mem. adv. council Miss. Children's Code Commn.; edn. com. Miss. Assn. Mental Health, 1958—, dir., exec. com., nominating com., 1963-66, dir., 1966—, sec., 1973—; chmn. Miss. Mental Health Conv., 1964; county commr. Fifth Region Mental Health Center, 1967—; del. Nat. Mental Health Conv., 1963, meeting, N.Y.C.; dir. State Mental Health Bd.; sec. Miss. Mental Health Assn., 1971-73; county campaign chmn. A.R.C., 1962. Mem. pub. relations com. Miss. Women's Cabinet, 1961—, now also recreation chmn.; mem. Gov.'s Ladies Staff, Miss., 1960-64; sec. Miss. Mental Health, 1969—; mem. Sharkey County Mental Health Commn., 1967—. Trustee King's Daus. Home, Natchez, Miss., 1948-52, pres. gov.'s bd., 1956—, gov.'s bd. trustees, 1965—. Recipient Woman of Achievement award Rolling Fork Bus. and Profl. Women, 1965; named Outstanding Civic leader Am., 1967; Community Leader award Hist. Preservation Am., 1979-80. Mem. Miss. King's Daus. and Sons (historian 1969—, parliamentarian), Internat. Platform Assn., Daus. Am. Colonists, Order of Washington, Daus. of 1812, Colonial Dames of XVII Century (chpt. pres. 1971-73, state 1st v.p. 1971-73, state pres. 1973—), Dames of Court Honor, Daus. Confederacy, Soc. Magna Charta Dames, Ams. Royal Descent, Zeta Phi Eta. Episcopalian (state pres., women's orgn., 1952-55; pres. IV province Episcopal Ch. 1957-60). Clubs: Highland (pres. aux. 1963-64), Delta Debutante (patron 1961—).

MONTGOMERY, EVANGELINE JULIET, exhibits and mus. specialist, artist; b. N.Y.C., May 2, 1933; d. Oliver Paul and Carmelite Thompson; student Calif. State U., Los Angeles, 1958-62, U. Calif., Berkeley, 1969-70; A.A., Los Angeles City Coll., 1958; B.F.A., Calif. Coll. Arts and Crafts, 1969. Ethnic art cons. Oakland (Calif.) Mus., 1968-74; free-lance art and hist. exhibits and mus. specialist, Calif. and Washington, 1968—; exhibits and workshops coordinator Am. Assn. for State and Local History, Nashville, 1979; dir. community affairs WHMM-TV, Washington, 1980; v.p. bd. dirs. Ark Urban Systems Inc., 1973-77; exhibited in one man shows including: Bowie State Coll., 1973, Hampton Inst. Mus., 1974, Taylor Gallery, 1974, De Paul U. Gallery, 1974, Seattle World Expo Black Pavilion, 1974; group shows include: travelling exhibit Mills Coll. Art Gallery, 1971-73; Oakland (Calif.) Mus., 1974; Berkeley Arts Center, 1975; Brook Meml. Gallery, Memphis, 1979; represented in permanent collections including: Los Angeles Bd. Edn., Oakland Mus., So. Ill. U., Normal, Mus. Afro-Am. Artists, Roxbury, Mass.; mem. San Francisco Art Commn., 1976-79, chmn. visual arts com., 1976-79. Smithsonian fellow, 1973; Nat. Endowment for Arts grantee, 1973; Third World Fund grantee, 1974. Mem. Am. Assn. Mus., Nat. Conf. Artists (nat. coordinator regions 1973-79), Am. Assn. for State and Local History, Am. Craftsmen Council, Nat. Assn. for Negro Bus. and Profl. Women (nat. fine arts dir. 1976-79), Metal Arts Guild Calif. (pres. 1972-74). Baptist. Home: 259 W Radcliffe Dr Claremont CA 91711

MONTGOMERY, JEAN CAMPBELL, librarian; b. Cleveland, Feb. 19, 1923; d. Lesslie Gordon and Emma Marie (Aubel) Campbell; B.S. in Edn., Ohio State U., 1947; M.A. in Edn., Case Western Reserve U., 1954; postgrad. Ind. U., 1967-69, Coll. William and Mary, 1969, U. Va., 1976—; m. Paul Lewis Montgomery, Dec. 2, 1950; children—John Alan, Sue Ann. Tchr., Solon (Ohio) Elem. Sch., 1951-55, Ft. Wayne (Ind.) Community Schs., 1967-68, Crewe (Va.) Elem. Sch., 1968-69; tchr., librarian Green Valley Elem. Sch., Roanoke, Va., 1969-72; librarian Penn Forest Elem. Sch., Roanoke, 1972—. Tchr. Sunday sch., elder Disciples of Christ Ch., Roanoke. Recipient Schoolmen award Freedoms Found., 1977. Mem. PTA (hon. life), NEA, Va. Edn. Assn., Roanoke County Edn. Assn., Va. Ednl. Media Assn., Roanoke County Librarians Assn., Kappa Delta Pi. Home: 1940 Bridle Ln SW Roanoke VA 24018 Office: 6328 Merriman Rd SW Roanoke VA 24018

MONTGOMERY, JEAN OLIVE, antique dealer; b. Springerville, Ariz., June 1, 1919; d. Henry T. and Cordelia Carol (Shideler) Miller; B.A. with honors, U. Pacific, Stockton, Calif., 1939; M.S. with honors, Simmons Coll., Boston, 1940; m. George W. Montgomery, Jr., Feb. 21, 1942. Owner, mgr. Montgomery Antiques, Los Gatos, Calif., 1948—, Opera House Antiques, Los Gatos, 1964—; appraiser mem. Los Gatos Heritage Preservation Adv. Commn., 1974—. Mem. Calif. Republican Central Com., 1962-64; officer, mem. bd. Los Gatos-Saratoga Rep. Assembly, 1950-68; founding mem. bd. Calif. Rep. League, 1960-73. Mem. Antique Dealers Assn. Calif., Antique Dealers Orgn. No. Calif., U. Pacific Alumni Assn. Club: Wiscasset Yacht. Home: 262 E Main St Los Gatos CA 95030 also Middle St Wiscasset ME 04578 Office: 140 W Main St Los Gatos CA 95030

MONTGOMERY, MARY BETH HARSHBARGER, social worker; b. Elkins, W.Va., Oct. 5, 1950; d. Rankin Wesley and Anne Lee (Parsons) Harshbarger; B.A. in Psychology (Presdl. scholar 1971), W.Va. U., 1971, M.S.W., 1973; doctoral student U. Calif. at Berkeley; m. James Robert Montgomery, July 6, 1976. Clin. social worker Community Mental Health Center Escambia County, Pensacola, Fla., 1973-76; adj. prof., field instr. U. W.Fla., Pensacola, 1973-76; clin. social worker Stanford Lathrop Home, Sacramento, 1976-78; lectr. Sch. Social Work, Calif. State U., Sacramento, 1977—; pvt. practice social work, 1978—; cons. in field. Lic. clin. social worker. Mem. Nat. Assn. Social Workers (past unit ptes.), Acad. Cert. Social Workers, Assn. Rational Thinkers, Council Social Work Edn., AAUW, Faculty Women's Assn., Sacramento Area Mental Health Assn., DAR, Daus. of Confederacy, Phi Alpha Theta, Psi Chi, Delta Gamma. Democrat. Roman Catholic. Clubs: Lawyers Wives, Law Partners. Author: (cookbook) Judicious Dishes, 1978. Home: 5994 Lake Crest Way Apt 2 Sacramento CA 95822 Office: Sch Social Work 6000 J St Sacramento CA 95816

MONTGOMERY, NANCY JEAN, nurse; b. Twin Falls, Idaho, Sept. 26, 1940; d. Orville D. and Ruth L. (DeMoss) Sackett; R.N., St. Alphonsus Sch. Nursing, 1961; m. Paul W. Montgomery, Sept. 16, 1961; children—Kevin James, Jeffrey Paul. Night supr. St. Alphonsus Hosp., Boise, Idaho, 1961; staff nurse, clin. instr. LPNs, Magic Valley Meml. Hosp., Twin Falls, 1961-65; staff nurse Sacred Heart Hosp., Idaho Falls, Idaho, 1965-66, Drs. Hosp., Santa Ana, Calif., 1966-69; emergency room staff float nurse St. John's Hosp., Oxnard, Calif., 1969-70; pvt. duty/staff nurse Dr.'s Hosp., Santa Ana, Calif., 1970-71, relief staff, 1972; intensive care nurse Anaheim (Calif.) Gen. Hosp., 1970-72; staff nurse InterValley Community Hosp., Saugus, Calif., 1972-73; supr., asst. dir. nursing, St. Francis Convalescent Pavilion, Daly City, Calif., 1973-74; staff nurse, inservice coordinator Twin Falls Clinic, 1974—; part-time instr. health professions Coll. of So. Idaho, Twin Falls, 1978—. Mem. Idaho Nurses Assn. (bd. dirs. 1980-83), Am. Heart Assn., Am. Arthritis Found. Republican. Roman Catholic. Club: Ladies of the Elks. Home: 376 Meadows Ln Twin Falls ID 83301 Office: 666 Shoshone St E Twin Falls ID 83301

MONTGOMERY, OLIVE (OLIVE SCHMAUSS), writer, actress, musician, advt. exec.; b. West Hartford, Conn., Oct. 29, 1909; d. M. Goode and Katharine (Slayback) Wolfe; student piano Aurelio Giorni, Rome and N.Y.C., Bruce Simonds, New Haven; student (scholar) Smith Coll., 1932; m. Carl John Schmauss, May 14, 1960 (dec.); children—Joan Elise, Mary Ann, Daniel, John. Actress in summer stock, radio and films; last appeared in Man on the Swing, 1973; concert pianist, 1927-42; writer radio drama, serials, drama and commls.; founder Montgomery Agency, N.Y.C., 1942, now pres.; founder, dir., tchr. drama and music Silvermine Music and Drama Center, 1960—; a founder Am. Shakespeare Theatre (Stratford, Conn.), Lincoln Center for Performing Arts, N.Y.C., Norwalk (Conn.) Symphony Orch.; bd. dirs. New Haven Symphony Orch., 1932-42. Mem. Nat. League Am. Pen Women (pres. Greenwich br. 1972-77, treas. br. 1978—), Jr. League Stamford-Norwalk, Inc., DAR, Colonial Dames XVII Century, Wilton, Norwalk, Westport hist. socs. Republican. Congregationalist. Club: Silver Spring Country (Ridgefield, Conn.). Home: 185 Perry Ave Silvermine Norwalk CT 06850 also 1114 2d Ave S Tierra Verde FL 33715 Office: 41 1 E 42d St New York NY 10017

MONTI, NANCY, social work adminstr.; b. N.Y.; d. Antonio and Kate (Liga) Malvagna; B.A., St. Joseph's Coll., 1952; M.S.W., Fordham U., 1954, Ph.D., 1977; m. Peter Monti, May 28, 1955; children—Helen, Peter, Barbara. Dir., Community Mental Health Center, Mt. Carmel Guild, Newark, N.J., 1972-75; dir. community mental health center St. Mary's Hosp., Hoboken, N.J., 1975-78, adminstrv. dir. ambulatory care, 1977-78; Essex County dir. Catholic Community Services, Archdiocese of Newark, 1980—, exec. dir., 1980—; mem. adv. council N.Y. U., 1979-80; adj. prof. Rutgers U., 1980-81. Mem. Essex County Profl. Adv. Bd., 1973-74; mem. Essex County Hosp. County Hosp. Planning Council, 1974-75; mem. Hudson County Mental Health Profl. Adv. Bd., 1968-69, 75-78, v.p., 1976; mem. Marion Towers Adv. Bd., 1977-79; mem. Newark Mayor's Employment and Tng. Adv. Council, 1978—; div. chairperson Newark United Way, 1980—. Mem. Nat. Assn. Social Workers, Acad. Accredited Social Workers, Am. Orthopsychiat. Assn., Nat. Conf. Cath. Charities, Assn. Mental Health Adminstrs. Roman Catholic (adv. mem. N.J. Catholic Conf.). Office: 1 Summer Ave Newark NJ 07102

MONTIEL, ALEXANDRA, cosmetic chemist; b. Canary Island, Spain, Aug. 24, 1930; d. Bartolomé and Margaret (Leon) Cordero; Cosmetologist, Dr.Pharmacy, Havana U.; children—Gema, Cordero. Pres., Alfandra Enterprises, Inc., Bklyn., 1973—; host Ci Belleza? TV show, N.Y., Miami, also syndicated nationally and in C. Am. Mem. planning bd. #4, Cuban Newspaper Writers Union; mem. Pres. Reagan's Task Force; mem. Republican Chmn.'s Com. Named to Hall of Fame, Hispanic Caucus of Bushwick. Mem. Soc. Cosmetic Chemists, Cosmetologists Assn. Patentee, Insta-Lash. Home: 2 Stanwick St Brooklyn NY 11206 Office: 639 Bushwick Ave Brooklyn NY 11206

MONTORI, SUSANA EUGENIA, social worker; b. Havana, Cuba, Sept. 15, 1934; came to U.S., 1961, naturalized, 1970; d. Arturo Rene Montori and Petronila Sara Valdes-Gilbert de Montori; grad. in piano Laura Rayneri Conservatory, 1951; J.D., U. Havana (Cuba), 1956; M.S.W., Barry Coll., 1969. Public defender Ct. of Justice, Havana, 1956-60; with Fla. State Dept. Health & Rehab. Services, Miami, 1962-69; caseworker, counselor United Family and Children's Services, Miami, 1969—; activities coordinator Arturo Montori Sch., Miami, 1970-76. Recipient José A. González Lanuza nat. award Cuba, 1957; award Cuban lawyers program U. Miami, 1961; recognition plaque Project Follow Through, City of Miami, 1972, 73, 74; others. Mem. Nat. Assn. Social Workers (accredited), Havana Bar Assn., Nat. Assn. Cuban Lawyers, Nat. Ballet Assn. Cuba. Roman Catholic. Club: Profl. Contbr. articles to profl. jours. Office: 9370 Sunset Dr Miami FL 33174

MOODY, BARBARA GAREY, nursing adminstr.; b. Medford, Mass., June 23, 1931; d. DeMelle and Mildred (Holman) Garey; B.A., William Jewell Coll., Liberty, Mo., 1953; M.Ed., Northeastern U., Boston, 1964; M.B.M., Leslie Coll., Boston, 1983; m. Richard H. Moody, May 15, 1954; children—Meredith, Heather, Richard B., Janice. Dir. personnel P.W. Moody Co., Andover, Mass., 1954-70; guidance counselor Lawrence (Mass.) Gen. Hosp. Sch. Nursing, 1971-77, asst. dir. nursing, 1980-81; adminstrv. asst. in nursing New Eng. Deaconess Hosp., Boston, 1977-80, adminstrv. asst., 1981—; asso. dir. Lawrence Coop. Bank, 1976—. Dir., sec. Gale Systems, 1972-74; dir. Coulter Fibers, Inc., 1968-77. Pres. Andover Vis. Nurse Assn., 1964-74. Mem. Andover Sch. Com., 1963-66. Bd. dirs. Andover council Girl Scouts, 1956-60, Andover YMCA, 1968-73; bd. dirs. Greater Lawrence Family Service, 1972-77, v.p., 1971-78. Mem. Nat. Assn. Women Deans, Adminstrs. and Counselors, LWV, Mass. Assn. Hosp. Fin. Mgrs., Nat. League Nursing, Am. Personnel and Guidance Assn., Pi Kappa Delta. Mem. United Ch. Christ (clk., past mem. bd. Christian edn.). Club: Andover Tennis. Home: 12 Suncrest Rd Andover MA 01810 Office: New Eng Deaconess Hosp Boston MA 02215

MOODY, EVELYN WILIE, cons. geologist; b. Waco, Tex.; d. William Braden and Enid Eva (Holt) Wilie; student Baylor U., 1934-35; B.A. with honors in geology and edn. U. Tex., 1938, M.A. with honors in geology, 1940; children—John D., Melissa L., Jennifer A. Geologist Ark. Fuel Oil Co., Shreveport, La., New Orleans and Houston, 1942-45; teaching asst. Colo. Sch. Mines, Golden, 1946-47; exploration cons. geologist Gen. Crude Oil Co., Houston, 1975-77; ind. cons. geologist, Houston, 1977—; exploration cons. geologist Shell Oil Co., Houston, 1979-81; faculty dept. continuing edn. Rice U., Houston, 1978. profl. geologist. Cert. Mem. Am. Assn. Petroleum Geologists, Soc. Ind. Profl. Earth Scientists (sec. 1978-79, vice chmn. 1979-80, chpt. chmn. 1980-81, nat. dir. 1982-85), Geol. Soc. Am., Watercolor Soc. Houston, Manhasset (N.Y.C.) Art Assn., Am. Inst. Profl. Geologists, Houston Geol. Soc., Pi Beta Phi (nat. officer 1958-60, 66-68). Republican. Presbyterian. Contbr. articles to profl. jours.; author: How (To Try) To Find An Oil Field, 1981. Office: 956 The Main Bldg 1212 Main St Houston TX 77002

MOODY, FLORENCE ELIZABETH, educator, coll. dean; b. Penn Yan, N.Y., Sept. 29, 1932; d. James William Southby and Rebecca (Worrall) M.; B.S., SUNY, Geneseo, 1954; M.S., Syracuse (N.Y.) U., 1961; Ed.D. (NDEA fellow), U. Rochester (N.Y.)., 1969. Elem. sch. tchr., N.Y. State, 1954-64, 66-68; coordinator profl. devel. Eastern Regional Inst. Edn., Syracuse, 1969-71; mem. faculty SUNY, Oswego, 1971—, prof. elem. edn., 1978—, asso. dean profl. studies Coll. Arts and Scis., 1981—. Nat. sec. Nat. Women's Party, 1974-76; bd. dirs. Oswego County Extension Service, 1974-76. Danforth asso., 1978—. Mem. Am. Assn. Colls. Tchr. Edn. (pres. elect N.Y. State chpt.), Assn. Tchr. Educators, Assn. Supervision and Curriculum Devel., Am. Ednl. Research Assn., N.Y. State Assn. Tchr. Educators (sec., exec. bd. 1976-78), Kappa Delta Pi, Pi Lambda Theta, Phi Delta Kappa, Delta Kappa Gamma. Presbyterian. Club: Order Eastern Star. Author reports, curriculum materials in field. Home: 5143 Franklin Ave Oswego NY 13126 Office: 611 Culkin Hall State Univ Coll Oswego NY 13126

MOODY, LIZABETH ANN, lawyer; b. Johnson City, Tenn., July 11, 1934; d. Robert Alexander and Clara Pauline (Fine) M.; A.B., Columbia U., 1956; LL.B., Yale U., 1959; m. Alan P. Buchmann, Sept. 5, 1959. Admitted to Ohio bar, 1960, Conn. bar, 1959; asso. firms in Cleve., 1960-66; partner firm Metzenbaum, Gaines, Finley & Stern, Cleve., 1967-71; mem. faculty Cleve. State U. Law Sch., 1970—, prof. law, 1973—; vis. prof. U. Toledo Law Sch., 1976-77, George Washington U. Law Sch., 1981-82; dir. Allied Steel & Tractor Co.; mem. Ohio Public Defender Commn., 1976—; mem. Reviewing Authority Civil Rights HEW, 1974-79; pres. Women's Law Fund, 1972-76, trustee, 1972—. Adv. council Ohio Bur. Employment Services, 1970-74; trustee Gt. Lakes Shakespeare Assn., 1972—; exec. com. Cuyahoga County Republican Orgn., 1980—; mem. vestry St. Paul's Episcopal Ch. Cleveland Heights, 1979-82. Recipient award Ams. for Democratic Action, 1976. Mem. Am. Bar Assn., Assn. Am. Law Schs. (exec. com. 1976-79), Nat. Assn. Women Lawyers, AAUP, Greater Cleve. Bar Assn. (Meritorious Service award 1973), Delta Theta Phi (hon.). Author: Smith's Review of Estates, Trusts and Administration, 3d edit., 1982; Smith's Review of Corporations, 1976; also articles. Home: 17210 Parkland Dr Shaker Heights OH 44120 Office: Cleve State U Cleveland OH 44115

MOODY, RHEA PHENON, fin. exec.; b. Portland, Ind., Oct. 6, 1930; d. George D.C. and Mollie F. Moody; B.S. in Acctg., Ind. U., 1959; div. Chief clk. First Nat. Bank, East Chicago, Ind., 1959-65; credit officer LaSalle Nat. Bank, Chgo., 1966-73; asst. v.p. State Nat. Bank, Evanston, Ind., 1973-77; v.p. Lakeview Trust & Savs. Bank, Chgo., 1977-82; v.p. loan adminstrn. W.N. Lane Interfin., Northbrook, Ill., 1982—. Served with WAC, 1952-55. Mem. Nat. Assn. Bank Women, Robert Morris Assos. (pres. Chgo. chpt. 1980-81), Chgo. Fin. Exchange. Republican. Office: 1200 Shermer Rd One Lane Center Northbrook IL 60062

MOODY-YANIGA, SHERRY MYRA, assn. exec.; b. Bridgeport, Conn., Oct. 10, 1947; d. Charles A. and Maria R. Moody; B.A., Sacred Heart U., 1969; M.A., Fairfield U., 1973, postgrad., 1974-76. Tchr., Shelton Sch. System (Conn.), 1969-76; nat. membership specialist Student NEA, Washington, 1976-77; UniServ field rep. Tchrs. Assn. Anne Arundel County, Md., Annapolis, 1977—. Active Young Democrats of Anne Arundel County; bd. dirs. Sheltered Workshop of Anne Arundel County; chmn. spl. events com. City of Annapolis; sec. Annapolis Transp. Policy Adv. Com. Mem. NEA, Urban Dirs. Assn., Nat. Assn. Female Execs., Annapolis Jaycees/Annapolis Jr. Citizens (pres. 1981-82, Jaycee of Yr. 1980-81). Roman Catholic. Home: 163 Acton Rd Annapolis MD 21403 Office: 2521 Riva Rd Annapolis MD 21401

MOOK, SARAH, chemist; b. Bklyn., Oct. 29, 1929; d. Wong and Lie Won (Woo) M.; B.A., Hunter Coll., 1952; postgrad. Columbia U., 1954-57, 62-65, U. Hartford, 1958-59. Cartographic aide U.S. Geol. Survey, Dept. of Interior, Washington, 1952-54; research asst. Mineral Beneficiation Lab., Columbia U., N.Y.C., 1954-57; analytical chemist nuclear div. Combustion Engring., Inc., Windsor, Conn., 1957-59; research scientist Radiation Applications Inc., Long Island City, N.Y., 1959-62; chemist Marks Polarized Corp., Whitestone, N.Y., 1962-64; sr. chemist NRA Ins. subs. Nuclear Research Assos., Inc., New Hyde Park, N.Y., 1964-75; clin. chemist Coney Island Hosp., Bklyn., 1974—, mem. community bd., 1978—; mem. Adv. Com. to State Assemblyman, State of N.Y., 1970-72; trustee Park Avenue Christian Ch., 1973—, sec., 1973-80, vice chmn., 1980-81, chmn. bd. trustees, 1981-82, mem. ofcl. bd., 1962—, vice chmn., 1974-76, pres. Christian Women's Fellowship, 1962-65. Mem. Am. Chem. Soc., Am. Acad. Polit. and Social Sci., AAAS. Republican. Contbr. articles on inorganic chemistry to profl. publs. Home: 2042 E 14th St Brooklyn NY 11229 Office: 2601 Ocean Parkway Brooklyn NY 11235

MOON, JANINE ANNETTE, telephone co. exec.; b. Toledo, Nov. 2, 1948; d. Menard R. and Edith E. (David) Mossing; B.Sc., Bowling Green State U., 1970; M.A., Ohio State U., 1977; m. Burnell Thomas Moon, June 27, 1970; 1 child, Lara Nicholle. Instr., Bishop Luers High Sch., Ft. Wayne, Ind., 1970-72; instr. Mt. Mercy Acad., Grand Rapids, Mich., 1973; instr., drama-sports dir. Forest Hills No. High Sch., Grand Rapids, 1973-76; instr. N. Central Tech. Coll., Mansfield, Ohio, 1976-79; program dir. Ohio Program in Humanities, YWCA, Mansfield, 1977-78; devel. edn. coordinator N. Central Tech. Coll., Mansfield, 1978-79; curriculum specialist United Telephone Co. of Ohio, Mansfield, 1979-81, tng. and devel. cons., 1981—; communications and women's concerns cons.; lectr. in field. Bd. dirs. YWCA, Mansfield, 1976—, pres., 1979-80; coordinator/organizer, chmn. task force for women's resource center, Mansfield, 1978-79. Mem. Am. Soc. for Tng. and Devel. (regional rep. Women's Network), Am. Soc. Profl. Cons., Nat. Assn. Female Execs., AAUW, LWV, NOW, Ohio State U. Alumni Assn. Office: 240 W Cook Rd Mansfield OH 44907

MOON, MARJORIE RUTH, state treas. Idaho; b. Pocatello, Idaho, June 16, 1926; d. Clark Blakeley and Ruth Eleanor (Gerhart) M.; student Pacific U., Forest Grove, Oreg., 1944-46; A.B. cum laude in Journalism, U. Wash., Seattle, 1948. Reporter, Pocatello (Idaho) Tribune, 1944, Caldwell (Idaho) News-Tribune, 1948-50; bur. chief Boise, Deseret News, Salt Lake City, 1950-52; owner Idaho Pioneer Statewide weekly newspaper, Boise, 1952-55; founder, pub. Garden City (Idaho) Gazette, 1954-68; partner Sawtooth Lodge, Grandjean, Idaho, 1958-60; partner Modern Press, Boise, Idaho, 1958-61; treas. State of Idaho, Boise, 1963—. Del. nat. nominating com. Idaho Democratic Com., 1972, 76, 80; chmn. Idaho Commn. on Women's Programs, 1971-74. Mem. Nat. Assn. State Treasurers (sec.-treas. 1976-78, regional v.p. 1978-79), Nat. Fedn. Press Women, Idaho Press Women (past pres.). Congregationalist. Club: Soroptimist (past pres. Boise Club). Office: 102 Statehouse Boise ID 83720

MOON, SHARON BARGDILL, therapist; b. Westboro, Ohio, July 11, 1944; d. Robert L. and Hazel F. Bargdill; A.B., Wilmington (Ohio) Coll., 1967; M.S.W., Ohio State U., 1971; s. Lewis Oscar Moon, Jan. 8, 1966; children—Brendon Oscar, Jeremy Lewis. Program dir. YWCA, Cin., 1966-67; social worker Children's Services, Cin., 1967-73; outpatient therapist Comprehensive Care No. Ky., Covington, 1973-75; dir. Children's Service Agy., Ross County, Ohio, 1975-76; dir. children's mental health services Region II Community Mental Health Center, Huntington W.Va., 1977-81; pvt. practice therapy, Elkins, W.Va., 1977—; cons. in field. Mem. Acad. Cert. Social Workers, Nat. Assn. Social Workers. Episcopalian. Home: 20 Locust St Elkins WV 26241

MOONEY, KATHLEEN HARDIN, nurse, educator; b. Pasadena, Calif., Aug. 9, 1950; d. Ralph Albert and Elizabeth (Brainard) Hardin; B.S. in Nursing, U. San Francisco, 1972; M.N., U. Wash., 1976; postgrad. Coll. Health, U. Utah, 1980—; m. George F. Mooney, Mar. 20, 1982. Charge nurse children's oncology program Children's Hosp., Stanford U., 1973-75; staff nurse bone marrow transplant unit Fred Hutchinson Cancer Research Center, Seattle, 1975-76; dir. patient family services Hospice Salt Lake, Salt Lake City, 1977—, bd. dirs., 1977-78, chairperson profl. adv. council, 1977-79, interim exec. dir., 1980-81, also co-founder, 1977; instr. U. Utah, 1976-80, asst. prof. nursing, 1980—, asst. dean for continuing edn., 1982—; bd. dirs., mem. profl. edn. com., chairperson nurse subcom. Utah div. Am. Cancer Soc., 1980—; speaker to profl., pub. groups on hospice, needs of terminally ill, needs of families facing chronic-terminal illness, 1978—; cons. in field. Recipient cert. appreciation Salt Lake Jaycees, 1979, Utah div. Am. Cancer Soc., 1980. Mem. Assn. Pediatric Oncology Nurses, Am. Nurses' Assn., Utah Nurses' Assn., Sigma Theta Tau (Gamma Rho chpt. Clin. Excellence award 1980). Contbr. articles to profl. jours. and books. Office: U Utah Coll Nursing 25 S Medical Dr Salt Lake City UT 84112

MOONEY, YVETTE MIGDALIA, nurse; b. Santurce, P.R., Nov. 7, 1944; d. Jose and Olga Iris (Lopez) Octavio; B.S. in Nursing, Hunter Coll., City U. N.Y., 1965; M.S., L.I. U., 1977; m. Michael Mooney; children—Yvette Christina, Marissa Gabrielle, Kelly Aileen. Asst. dir. II, Albert Einstein Coll. Hosp., Bronx, N.Y., 1970-77; asso. dir. nursing So. Nassau Communities Hosp., Oceanside, N.Y., 1977-81, dir. nursing, 1982—. Mem. Nat. Assn. Female Execs., Res. Officers Assn., Nat. League Nursing, Assn. Mil. Surgeons U.S., N.Y. Nurses Assn. Roman Catholic. Club: Island Scribes. Office: 2445 Oceanside Rd Oceanside NY 11572

MOONEYHAN, ESTHER LOUISE, nurse, educator; b. Wabash, Ind., Oct. 2, 1920; d. Edward Lamont and Ina Louretta (Adams) Smithee; diploma (scholar 1940-43), Meth. Hosp. Sch. Nursing, Indpls., 1943; student (scholar 1938-39), Marion (Ind.) Coll., 1938-40; B.S. in Gen. Nursing, Ind. U., 1964, M.S. in Nursing Edn., 1965, Ed.D. (fellow 1965, 70), 1973; children—William Cecil, Mary Kathleen, Stephen Alan. Staff nurse Putnam County (Ind.) Hosp., 1943-44, Meth. Hosp., Indpls., 1951; pvt. duty nurse Ind. U. Med. Center, Indpls., 1953-60; staff nurse, asso. supr., ednl. dir. Bur. Public Health Nursing, Indpls. and Marion County, Ind., 1960-67; nurse advisor U.S. AID, Haile Selassie I U. Coll. Public Health, Ethiopia, 1967-69; asst. prof. nursing Tex. Woman's U., Denton, 1972-73; asso. prof. nursing Fla. Internat. U., Miami, 1973-79, chairperson, 1974-76; prof., dir. Sch. Nursing, Ind. U., South Bend, 1979—. Am. Nurses Assn., Nat. League for Nursing, Am. Public Health Assn., Internat. Health Soc. (bd. dirs.), Am. Assn. for Higher Edn., Am. Acad. Polit. and Social Sci., Inter-Am. Soc., Midwest Nursing Research Soc., Nursing Research Consortium N.Central Ind., Pi Lambda Theta, Sigma Theta Tau. Baptist. Contbr. articles to profl. jours.; speaker state workshops. Home: 1135 E Bronson St South Bend IN 44615 Office: 1700 Mishawaka Ave PO Box 7111 South Bend IN 46634

MOONIE, LIANA MARIA, artist; b. Trieste, Italy, Mar. 22, 1922; came to U.S., 1947, naturalized, 1950; d. Angelo and Maria (Canciani) Gabrielli; B.A., U. Trieste, 1940; student Robert Brachman, Art Students League, also Edgar Whitney, Franklin Jones, 1972-77; m. Clyde W. Moonie, June 18, 1949; children—Gregory J., Barbara M. Tchr. schs., Italy, 1941-44; artist, Scarsdale, N.Y., 1960—; exhibited one-woman shows: Scarsdale Nat. Bank, Westchester Fed. Savs. Bank, White Plains Women's Club, Bronxville Women's Club, MAG Gallery, Larchmont, N.Y.; exhibited group shows: Bruce Mus., Greenwich, Conn., Union Carbide, N.Y., Lincoln Center Cork Gallery, N.Y., Silvermine Artists Guild, Conn., Mus. Gallery, NAD, Allied Artists Am., N.Y.C., Audubon Artists, N.Y.C., Nicolaysen Art Mus., Casper, Wyo., Jesse Besser Mus., Alpena, Mich., U. Wyo., Laramie, Western Ill. U., Macomb, White Plains, N.Y., others; judge art shows; Slide presentation Internat. Festival Women Artists, Carlsberg Glyptotek Mus., Copenhagen. Recipient 1st prizes numerous juried exhbns., including Beaux Arts Shows in Westchester, Scarsdale Art Assn., Westchester Art Soc., others. Mem. Nat. Assn. Women Artists (spl. award exhbn. 1980), Artists Equity Assn. N.Y.C., Silvermine Artists Guild, Hudson River Contemporary Artists, Mamaroneck Artists Guild Inc. (past pres.). Clubs: Salmagundi, Candlewood Lake. Contbr., editor Beaux Arts Mag., 1974-77. Address: 40 Taunton Rd Scarsdale NY 10583

MOOR, DINA MAVIS, advt. exec.; b. Phoenix, Aug. 23, 1943; d. Isaac Lowery and Anna Mavis (Stinson) M.; student State U. Iowa, 1961-62; B.A., So. Meth. U., 1967; M.B.A., U. Dallas, 1976; 1 son, Aaron Michael. Free-lance model, 1965-71; sec. to academic dean U. Dallas, 1971-72, asst. to dean, 1972-74, dir. affiliated programs, 1974-76; dir. Mgmt. Labs. Am., Exec. Edn. Inst., Center for Publishing, 1974-76; owner Moor and Assos., Inc., Dallas, 1976—; owner Standby Club, Highlands Trading Co.; dir. Lynn Weiss & Assos.; bd. dirs. Screen Actors Guild and AFTRA, 1967-70. Recipient Wall St. Jour. award, 1976. Mem. Savs. Instns. Mktg. Soc. Am., Sales and Mktg. Execs. Dallas, Women in Communications, Inc., N. Dallas C. of C., Grad. Sch. Mgmt. Alumni Assn. (past pres.), Sigma Iota Epsilon. Episcopalian. Clubs: Slipper, 500 Inc. (past dir.). Office: 2851 Maydelle Ln Dallas TX 75234

MOOR, JOAN THORNTON ROTHWELL, biochemist; b. Lynn, Mass., Feb. 19, 1921; d. Paul Taylor and Adeline (Magrane) Rothwell; A.B., Vassar Coll., 1942; S.M., M.I.T., 1945; m. Edgar Jacques Moor, Aug. 5, 1950. Instr., Vassar Coll., Poughkeepsie, N.Y., 1946; research asst. Children's Hosp., Boston, 1947-48; research asst. New Eng. Deaconess Hosp., Boston, 1949-51; staff div. sponsored research M.I.T., Cambridge, 1952-77. Treas., dir. Multinational Bus. Assos., Inc., Cambridge, 1967-77; cons., author, 1978—. Fellow Internat. Acad. Law and Sci.; mem. Am. Chem. Soc., AAAS, Boston Council Fgn. Relations, Pan Am. Soc. New Eng., World Affairs Council (mem. com. Diplomats Off the Record), AAUW, New Eng. Council Latin Am. Studies, Sigma Xi. Republican. Roman Catholic. Contbr. articles to profl. jours. Home: Taborknoll Lincoln MA 01773

MOORE, AIMEE NOTT, dietitian, educator; b. Conway, S.C., Nov. 8, 1918; d. DeSaussure Parker and Cornelia (Trezevant) M.; B.S., U. N.C., Greensboro, 1939; M.A., Tchrs. Coll. Columbia U., 1947; Ph.D., Mich. State U., 1959. Instr. to asso. prof. Coll. Human Ecology, Cornell U., Ithaca, N.Y., 1947-61; dir. nutrition and dietetics U. Mo. Med. Center, Columbia, 1961-80, dir. dietetic edn., prof. food systems mgmt., 1981—; cons. Hacceteppe U., Ankara, Turkey 1967, Ramatibodi Hosp., Bangkok, Thailand 1968, Pan Am Health Orgn., 1975, Govt. V.I., 1979. Served with AUS, 1943-45. Recipient Faculty/Alumni award U. Mo., Columbia, 1979. Mem. Am. Dietetic Assn. (past dir., Mary S. Rose fellow 1956-58), Am. Home Econs. Assn., Am. Mgmt. Assn., Assn. Schs. Allied Health Professions, Food Service Systems Mgmt. Ednl. Council. Democrat. Episcopalian. Computer Assisted Food Management Systems, 1971, 82; contbr. articles to profl. jours. Office: Dept Dietetic Edn Health Scis Center Mo Columbia MO 65212

MOORE, ALDERINE BERNICE JENNINGS (MRS. JAMES F. MOORE), club woman; b. Sacramento, Apr. 17, 1915; d. James Joseph and Elise (Thomas) Jennings; A.B., U. Wash., 1941; m. James Francis Moore, Aug. 14, 1945. Sec. to div. Plant supr. Pacific Tel. & Tel. Co., Sacramento, 1937-39; exec. sec. Sacramento Community Chest Fund Raising Dr., 1941; sec. USAAF, Mather Field, Sacramento, 1942; statistician Calif. Western States Life Ins. Co., 1943; treas. Women's Aux. Stranger's Hosp., Rio de Janeiro, Brazil, 1964-65. Vice pres. Douglaston (N.Y.) Women's Club, 1955; mem. Douglaston Garden Club, 1951-55; pres. Nina Opland chpt. Women's Cancer Assn. U. Miami, 1960-61; corr. sec. Coral Gables (Fla.) Garden Club, 1960-62; pres. Miami Alumnae Club of Pi Beta Phi, 1961-62; mem. Putnam Hill chpt. D.A.R., Greenwich Conn., 1967-75, Palm Beach chpt., 1978—; mem. Woman's Club, Greenwich, Conn., 1967-75; mem. Women's Panhellenic Assn., Miami, 1961-62; internat. treas. Ikebana Internat., Tokyo, Japan, 1966-67, parliamentarian Tokyo chpt., 1966-67, N.Y. chpt., 1968-69; mem. Coll. Women Assn. Japan, 1965-66; mem. Tchrs. Assn. Sogetsu Sch. Japanese Flower Arranging, 1966—. Served to lt. USNR, 1943-45. Mem. Internat. Platform Assn., AAUW, Pi Beta Phi (local v.p. alumnae club 1969-71). Baptist. Club: Steamboat Investment (pres. 1972-73). Home: 316 Fairway Ct Atlantis FL 33462

MOORE, ANNE GOODALE, hosp. adminstr.; b. Detroit, Oct. 15, 1922; d. John Chester and Jeannette (Armstrong) Goodale; student U. N.Mex., 1940-41; B.A., U. Wis., 1944; m. John Darsey Moore, June 18, 1949; children—Martha A., Darsey J. Asst. advt. mgr. Brills, Milw., 1944-48, Stuarts, Milw., 1948-49; columnist Delray Beach (Fla.) Jour., 1950-51; woman's page editor Delray Beach News, 1951-52; vol. public relations dir. Bethesda Meml. Hosp., Boynton Beach, Fla., 1957-70, dir. public relations, 1970—. Chmn. publicity S. Palm Beach County Republican Com., 1956; sec. Bethesda Hosp. Assn., Inc., 1957-61, dir., 1957-72, active benefit ball com., 1958—; co-chmn. Mothers March on Polio, Delray Beach, 1956. Recipient certificate of commendation Public Relations Council of Fla. Hosp. Assn., 1974, The Bethesda Hosp. Assn., Inc., 1972, The Southeastern Palm Beach County Hosp. Dist. Commn., 1972, 80, Heart Assn. of Palm Beach County, 1973. Mem. Am. Soc. Hosp. Public Relations, Public Relations Council Fla. Hosp. Assn., U. Wis. Alumni Assn., AAUW, Women in Communications. Republican. Episcopalian. Clubs: Delray Beach Poinciana Garden, Seacrest Assn. Univ. Women, Aux. of Bethesda Meml. Hosp., Delray Dunes Women's Golf Assn. Home: 1409 Lake Dr Delray Beach FL 33444

MOORE, BARBARA JO, interior designer; b. Bowie, Tex., July 20, 1948; d. Robert L. and Mary M. M.; student Okla. State U., 1966-67; B.A. in Interior Design, Okla. U., 1970. Head design dept. Southwestern Stationers, 1971-76; pres. Imprimis Designs, Oklahoma City, 1976—; v.p. i.e. Constrn., Oklahoma City, 1982—. Bd. dirs. Grover Cleveland Arts Inst., Oklahoma City chpt. UN Assn. Mem. Am. Soc. Interior Design (chmn. Western sect.; sec. Okla. chpt.; Outstanding Service award), Inst. Bus. Designers, Gamma Gamma, Chi Omega. Office: Imprimis Designs Inc 6478 Avondale Dr Oklahoma City OK 73115

MOORE, BERNICE MILBURN (MRS. HARRY E. MOORE), mental health adminstr., author; b. San Antonio, June 17, 1904; d. Ted Hatton and Carrie (Coley) Milburn; B.J., U. Tex., 1924; M.A., 1932; Ph.D., U. N.C., 1937; m. Harry Estill Moore, Nov. 27, 1924 (dec. July 1966). Reporter, Austin Am. and Statesman, 1924-26; dir. Child Welfare Survey of Tex., Tex. Relief Commn., 1933-34; asst. Inst. for Research in Social Sci., U. N.C., 1934-37; asst. dir. Austin (Tex.) Regional Office, Profl. Projects, WPA, 1938-41; cons. Hogg Found. for Mental Hygiene (name now Hogg Found. for Mental Health), U. Tex., 1941-55, asst. to dir. community and profl. edn., 1955-72, exec. asso., 1972—, now spl. cons., exec. asso. emeritus; asso. dir. Philanthropy in Southwest, 1964-71; cons. Home and Family Edn. div. Tex. Edn. Agy., 1941-64, past chmn. state adv. com., innovation and assessment in edn.; chmn. state adv. com. med. and dental edn. Coordinating Bd. Tex. State Coll. and U. System, 1972-74; spl. cons. Clin. Facilities div. Research Utilization br. Nat. Inst. Mental Health 1963-65; mem. program adv. com., cons. social devel. curriculum S.W. Ednl. Devel. Lab.; cons. Gov.'s Task Force on Child Devel.; mem. Task Force on Youth, Joint Commn. on Mental Health Children; coordinator Tex. Coop Youth Study and profl. edn., adviser seminars for chaplains in marriage and family counseling, USAF, sponsored by Hogg Found. for Mental Health, 1956-66. Mem. chancellor's council U. Tex. Recipient Nat. Headliner award Women in Communications, Theta Sigma Phi, 1956; Spl. Service award, Tex. Soc. for Mental Health, also Ft. Worth-Tarrant County Soc. for Mental Health; award of merit Am. Vocational Assn., 1963; Moore-Bowman award of excellence Tex. Council on Family Relations; Bernice Milburn Moore scholarship for continuing edn. for women established by Ex-Students Assn., U. Tex.; Distinguished Alumnae award Ex-Students Assn. U. Tex., 1974. Fellow Am. Assn. Marriage and Family Counselors (hon.), Am. Sociol. Assn.; mem. Nat. Assn. for Mental Health, Am. Home Econs. Assn., Southwestern Social Sci. Assn., Tex. Soc. for Mental Health, Tex. Council on Mental Health Research (past pres.), Philos. Soc. Tex., Future Homemakers of Am. (nat. hon. mem.), Women in Communications, Alpha Kappa Delta, Delta Kappa Gamma, Phi Upsilon Omicron, Omicron Delta Kappa (hon.). Democrat. Mem. Disciples of Christ Ch. Author: (with Harry Estill Moore) Through Your Own Front Door, 1945; (With Dorothy M. Leahy) You and Your Family, 1948, rev. 1954; (with Robert L. Sutherland) Family, Community and Mental Health, 1950; Juvenile Delinquency, Research, Theory, Comment, 1959; (with Wayne H. Holtzman) Tomorrow's Parents, 1965; pamphlets and study guides on mental health and the family. Contbr. to ednl. yearbooks, profl. jours. Home: 1215 W 22 1/2 St Austin TX 78705 Office: Hogg Found for Mental Health U Tex Austin TX 78712

MOORE, BETTY ANN MITCHUM, mfg. co. exec.; b. Roanoke, Ala., Dec. 2, 1934; d. James Henry and Avris (Sherrer) Mitchum; student Mercer U., Macon, Ga.; diploma Draughns Bus. Coll., Savannah, Ga., 1953; m. Jimmie Lamar Moore, June 13, 1953; children—James Larry, Douglas Eugene, Stacy Ann. Various clerical and bookkeeping positions, 1953-80; office mgr. Interlocking Wood Products Co., Roanoke, 1976-80; sec., treas., dir. JLM Co., Inc., Roanoke, 1976—. Mem. West Central Ga. Geneal. Soc. (charter), Roanoke Jaycettes (charter). Methodist. Clubs: Lowell Study; Roanoke Country (charter). Home: Lafayette Hwy Roanoke AL 36274 Office: PO Box 208 Roanoke AL 36274

MOORE, CAROLE ELIZABETH, educator; b. San Diego, Apr. 14, 1945; d. Melvin Eugene and Eula LaDere M.; B.A., U. Calif., Santa Barbara, 1967, M.A., 1969, Ph.D., 1973. Teaching asst. U. Calif., Santa Barbara, 1970-72; asst. prof. history U. Notre Dame (Ind.), 1972-77; lectr., instr. Emory U., Atlanta, 1977-79; asst. dean students, adj. prof. history Ga. Inst. Tech., Atlanta, 1980—. Mem. Am. Hist. Assn., AAUP, Ga. Coll. Personnel Assn., Phi Alpha Theta. Address: 21 Delmont Dr NE Apt 3 Atlanta GA 30305

MOORE, CATHRYN CALLAWAY, educator; b. Smithville, Tex., Sept. 25, 1912; d. Roy Olan and Bertha Estelle (Powell) Callaway; B.S., Tex. State Coll. Women, 1933; M.S., U. Tex., 1955; Counselor Cert., Trinity U., 1963; m. Carver Yates Moore, Nov. 27, 1952; 1 dau., Susan Cathryn Moore Farrimond. Exec. sec. Tex. Sheep and Goat Raisers, San Angelo, 1934; tchr. various high schs., 1935-62; counselor Sam Houston High Sch., 1962-65; chmn. dept. reading and edn. San Antonio Coll., 1965-77, coordinator devel. studies, 1977—; reading cons. Mem. AAUP, AAUW, Women Deans and Counselors, Nat. Reading Assn., Women in Communications, Alpha Delta Kappa. Republican. Methodist. Club: Philomathic (sec. 1979-80, pres. 1980—). Home: 208 Sutton St San Antonio TX 78228

MOORE, CHARLENE DANIEL, chem. co. sales rep.; b. Blairsville, Ga., Apr. 4, 1935; d. Roy Lee and Michael Lee (England) Daniel; student Young Harris Coll., 1952-53, Evans Coll. Commerce, 1957-59, Gaston Coll., 1968-69; m. William H. Moore, Oct. 10, 1970; children—Earlene, James, Adam, Joey. Saleswoman, John Bagwell Realty, Spartanburg, S.C., 1973-75, Westgate Realty, Spartanburg, 1975-77; sales rep. Guardian Chem. Co., Spartanburg, 1978—. Vice chmn. S.C. Fedn. Republican Women, 1978-81; vice chmn. S.C. Rep. Party, 1980-82, 4th Dist. Rep. Party, 1980-82. Mem. Spartanburg County Exec. Women, Nat. Assn. Profl. Women Club: Spartanburg County Rep. Women's (pres. 1975-77). Home: 106 Wakerobin Circle Spartanburg SC 29301

MOORE, CLARA EVELYN MITCHELL, sch. counselor; b. Newark, Aug. 20; d. James Hugo and Pattie Evelyn (Booker) Mitchell; student Clark U., 1952-54; A.B., Boston U., 1956; M.A., Columbia, 1957; postgrad. John Carroll U., summers 1966, 69; Ph.D., Case Western Res. U., 1973; children—Tanya Monique, Lance Randall. Tchr. English, Cleve. Bd. Edn., 1957-66, coordinator Schsl. Neighborhood Youth Corps Program, 1966-68, instr.-counselor adult edn. div. Work-Study Program, 1968-71, counselor adult edn. div., 1973—; tutor-counselor Case Western Res. U., 1971-73; faculty dept. ednl. specialists Cleve. State U., 1975—. Recipient Meyer H. Sarkin award, 1981. Mem. NEA, Ohio, Cleve. edn. assns., Am., Ohio personnel and guidance assns., NE Ohio Tchrs. Assn., NE Ohio Personnel and Guidance Assn., Ohio Sch. Counselors Assn. Home: 8907 Columbia Ave Cleveland OH 44108 Office: 4966 Woodland Ave Cleveland OH 44104

MOORE, DOROTHY DAVIS, civic leader; b. LaGrange, Ga., June 13, 1931; d. Dewey Edward and Myrtice (Heard) Davis; A.B., U. Montevallo (Ala.), 1952; m. Joseph M. Moore, Jr., May 30, 1954 (dec. 1970); children—Marjorie, Russell, Laura, Will. Pres., LWV, 1970; chmn. dist. chpt. Common Cause, 1972; charter officer Urban League, 1970; mem. Montgomery County (Ala.) Election Commn., 1979; chmn. Democratic County Exec. Com., 1978—; chmn. Ala. del. Dem. Nat. Conv., 1978, 2d Congl. del., 1978. Presbyterian.

MOORE, DOROTHY MARIE, conglomerate-diversified co. exec.; b. Turnersville, Tex., Apr. 8, 1928; d. Alexander Bethel and Effie (Huskerson) Hawkins; student Baylor U., 1945-47, So. Meth. U., 1951-68; m. Charles Marshall Moore, Jan. 1, 1954 (div.); children—Marsha, Dennis, Melinda, Melanie. Exec. sec., office mgr. Kilgore & Kilgore, Dallas, 1950-57; adminstrv. asst., exec. sec. Ira G. Corn, Jr., Dallas, 1960-68; corp. sec., dir. stockholder relations Mich. Gen. Corp., Dallas, 1968-73, dir., 1973—, v.p., 1978—; v.p., dir. Aces Internat., Inc., Community Water Service, Dallas, 1964—. Mem. Nat. Investor Relations Inst. (pres. chpt. 1977-78), Am. Soc. Corp. Secs., Dallas C. of C. (free enterprise com.), Am. Contract Bridge League (life master). Presbyterian. Clubs: Cipango, Exec. Women (Dallas); Catalyst (N.Y.C.). Represented U.S. women's pair World Bridge Olympiad, 1978, dep. capt. U.S. women's team, Holland, 1980. Office: 4505 LB Johnson Freeway Dallas TX 75234

MOORE, ELAINE, ins. co. ofcl.; b. Jersey City, Nov. 18, 1947; d. Gerald and Lula (Thompson) M.; student Drake's Secretarial Coll., 1965; B.S. in Mgmt., Rutgers U., 1979. Ins. checker Home Ins. Co., N.Y.C., 1966-72; research clk. Model Cities Employment Center, Jersey City, 1972-73; asst. to underwriter Hartford Ins. Group, N.Y.C., 1973-80; systems analyst Continental Ins. Cos., Piscataway, N.J., 1980—. Exec. bd., consumer protection chairperson Jersey City NAACP, 1978-81; founder, fin. sec. Concerned Community Women, 1978, edn. award, 1979; human resource editor LWV; v.p. Virginia Avenue Block Assn. Mem. Alumni Assn. Rutgers U., Nat. Fedn. Colored Women's Clubs, Phi Chi Theta, Alpha Omega. Baptist. Club: Univ. Coll. Home: 112 Virginia Ave Jersey City NJ 07304 Office: 2 Corporate Pl S Piscataway NJ 08854

MOORE, ELENA DANNETTE, businesswoman; b. Long Beach, Calif., Mar. 9, 1951; d. Edward Arthur and Hazel Belle (Springman) Gardner; student Jamestown (N.D.) Coll., 1970-72; B.S. in Commerce and Acctg., Cumberland Coll., 1974; postgrad. Eastern Ky. U., 1974-76, U. Ky., 1976-78; m. Mar. 29, 1980; children—Amber Lynne, Micah Joseph. Office mgr., bookkeeper Archlace, Inc., Hawthorne, Calif., 1964-70; asst. chief acct. Lester, Ryons & Sons, Ltd., Los Angeles, 1969-70; sr. acct. NCR Corp., systemedia div., Corbin, Ky., 1974-76; corp. treas./comptroller Central Rock Co., Lexington (Ky.), Concrete Products, Inc., 1976-80; co-owner Re-designs, Lexington. Vol., Campaign for Human Devel.; staff mem., columnist The Collegiate. Mem. Nat. Assn. Exec. Women, Smithsonian Instn., Nat. Geographic Soc. Republican. Roman Catholic. Club: Newman. Home: 1924 Cottonwood Dr Lexington KY 40503 Office: 402 Stone Rd Lexington KY 40503

MOORE, ELIZABETH BENNING, chem. process engr.; b. Thomasville, Ga., Oct. 30, 1945; d. Edward Benning and Juanita (Minchew) M.; B.Chem.Engring., Ga. Inst. Tech., 1974. Devel. engr. UOP Inc., Des Plaines, Ill., 1974-75; process engr. Fluor Corp., Irvine, Calif., 1975-77; mgr. engring. J.C. Schumacher Co., Oceanside, Calif., 1977-81; sr. process engr. Holmes & Narver, Inc., Orange, Calif., 1981—; semiconductor materials processing cons., 1978—. Mem. Pacific Energy Assn., Am. Inst. Chem. Engrs. Office: 999 Town and Country Rd Orange CA 92668

MOORE, ELIZABETH DUPREE, librarian; b. nr. McIntyre, Ga., Jan. 27, 1922; d. John Thomas and Effie Pearl (Douglas) DuPree; B.S., Ga. State Coll. for Women, 1942; M.L.S., Emory U., 1953, postgrad., 1966; m. William Walker Moore, Apr. 9, 1944 (div. Oct. 1952); children—Walker Dupree, George Harold, Melanie. Tchr., librarian Gordon High Sch., (Ga.), 1942-46; tchr. Emanuel County Inst., Twin City, Ga., 1948-49; reference librarian Middle Ga. Regional Library, Macon, 1954-56; dir. Oconee Regional Library, Dublin, 1957—; tchr. extension library courses U. Ga., 1968-70. Mem. Am., Southeastern, Ga. library assns., Order of the Blarney Stone. Baptist. Clubs: Parnassus, Pilot (both Dublin, Ga.). Home: 207 Coney St Dublin GA 31021 Office: Oconee Regional Library 801 Bellevue Ave Dublin GA 31021

MOORE, FAYE EMILY, educator; b. Barberton, Ohio, Apr. 22, 1934; d. Frank Knapp and Flora Etta (Allred) McCraw; B.A., Bethany Nazarene Coll., 1955; M.Ed., Northeastern Ill. U., 1973; Ed.D., No. Ill. U., 1976; m. J. Wesley Moore, Aug. 12, 1955; children—Janet K., Duane W., Clint S. Tchr., Luther Burbank Elem. Sch., Oklahoma City, 1955-56, Pinkerton Elem. Sch., Kansas City, Mo., 1957-58; kindergarten tchr. St. Michael and All Angels Sch., Shawnee Mission, Kans., 1961-63; tchr. St. Paul's Episcopal Day Sch., Kansas City, Mo., 1965-66; instr. William R. Harper Coll., Palatine, Ill., 1973-74; dir. Child Devel. Center, Seminole Community Coll., Sanford, Fla., 1976-79; adj. instr. Rollins Coll., Winter Park, Fla., 1976-79; asst. prof. edn. William Jewell Coll., Liberty, Mo., 1979—. Mem. Fla. State Adv. Com. Child Care Licensing, 1978-79; mem. Mayor's Adv. Commn. on Human Relations, Kansas City, Mo.,

1969-70, Orlando, Fla., 1976-79. Recipient Annual award Community Coordinated Child Care Central Fla., 1977. Mem. Nat. Assn. Edn. Young Children, Assn. Childhood Edn. Internat., Pi Lambda Theta. Author: Instructional Modules for the CDA, Books I-V, 1979. Home: 4000 NE 57th Pl Kansas City MO 64119 Office: Dept Edn William Jewell Coll Liberty MO 64068

MOORE, GWEN, state legislator; d. Willis and Edna Osborne; B.A., Calif. State Coll.; teaching credential U. Calif., 1970; postgrad. U. So. Calif.; m. Ron Dobson; 1 son, Ron. Asst. coordinator Manpower Devel. div. Los Angeles County Probation Dept., 1963-69; cons. Social Action Research Center, 1970-72; dir. personnel Greater Los Angeles Community Action Agy., 1969-76; cons. Inner-City Info. System, 1976-77; mem. Calif. Assembly, 1978—, chmn. subcom. on cable TV, pub. broadcasting and telecommunications Utilities and Energy Com., 1981; mem. coms. including Utilities and Energy, Transp., Pub. Employees and Retirement, Revenue and Taxation, Criminal Justice, Human Services; pres. Moore and Assocs., Los Angeles; instr. Compton Jr. Coll.; mem. Legis. Joint Com. on Legal Equality, Calif. Senate Select Com. on Children and Youth, Calif. Legis. Joint Com. on Revision of Calif. Election Code. Trustee Los Angeles Community Coll., 1975; chmn. Operation Womanpower; mem. Democratic Party State Central Com., Council on Radio and TV, Loyola-Marymount U. Inst. for Intergroup and Religions, Am. Jewish Com., 1974-75, Regional Adult and Vocat. Edn. Council, Los Angeles Mayor's Manpower Council. Recipient pub. affairs award Calif. Regional Med. Programs, service award Women for Good Govt., 1976, outstanding citizen award Assemblyman Julian Dixon, 1976; named Women of Image, U. So. Calif. Black History Week Com., 1976. Mem. Calif. Sch. Bds. Assn. (del.), Community Coll. Urban Dist. Assn. (exec. bd.), Black Probation Officers Assn., Nat. Assn. Market Devel., Calif. Parole, Probation and Correction Assn., Pub. Indsl. Relations Assn. (governing bd. univ. and colls.), Assn. Community Coll. Trustees, Calif. Community Coll. Trustees Assn. (bd. dirs.), Community Coll. Urban Dist. Assn. (v.p.). Nat. Women's Polit. Caucus, Los Angeles Urban League, NAACP, Alpha Kappa Alpha. Office: 3731 Stocker St Suite 106 Los Angeles CA 90008 also Room 4121 State Capitol Sacramento CA 95814

MOORE, JACQUELYN CORNELIA, labor union ofcl., editor; b. Balt., Dec. 25, 1929; d. James C. and Harriette I. (Conaway) Thomas; m. Clarence Carbin Moore, Jan. 19, 1947 (dec. Feb. 1970); children—Clarence Joseph, Janet Elizabeth Moore Oliver. Mail clk. U.S. P.O., Phila., 1966—; editor Local 509 Newsletter, Nat. Alliance of Postal and Fed. Employees, Washington, 1969-74, editorial newsletter chmn., 1969-74, sec. Dist. 5, 1972-74, nat. editor Nat. Alliance, 1974—, mem. exec. bd., 1974—, union photographer, 1974—, dir. 202 Housing for Elderly Corp. bds., Chattanooga, New Orleans, 1981—, sec. supervisory com. Nat. Fed. Credit Union, 1977-82. Vol. D.C. Voting Rights Corp., Washington, 1979—; sustaining mem. Democratic Nat. Com., 1977—. Mem. Coalition of Labor Union Women. Democrat. Roman Catholic. Clubs: Capitol Press, Nat. Bus. and Profl. Women's, Nat. Press. Home: 4040 B 8th St NW Washington DC 20011 Office: 1644 11th St NW Washington DC 20001

MOORE, JANE ROSS, librarian; b. Phila., Apr. 24, 1929; d. John William and Mary (McClure) Ross; A.B., Smith Coll., 1951; M.S. in L.S., Drexel U., 1952; postgrad. Columbia U.; M.B.A. (with distinction), N.Y.U., 1965; Ph.D., Case Western Res. U., 1974; m. Cyril Howard Moore, Jr., June 1, 1956 (div. Mar. 1967). Cataloguer Yale U. Library, 1952-54; chief tech. processes librarian Lederle Labs., Am. Cyanamid Co., Pearl River, N.Y., 1954-58; chief serials catalog librarian Bklyn. Coll. Library, 1958-65, asst. prof., chief catalog div., 1965-70, asso. prof., chief catalog div., 1971-73, asso. prof., asso. librarian adminstrv. services, 1973-76; prof., chief librarian Grad. Sch. and Univ. Center, City U. N.Y., 1976—; lectr. Syracuse U. Grad. Sch. Library Sci., summer 1967, 69; lectr. Queens Coll. Grad. Dept. Library Sci., 1967-69, adj. asso. prof., 1974-76, adj. prof., 1977—. HEW Title IIB fellow Case Western Res. U. Sch. Library Sci., 1970-72. Mem. N.Y. Library Assn. (pres. 1979-80, pres. resources and tech. services sect. 1966-67, councilor 1966-67, 75-76, 1978-81, sec.-treas. acad. and spl. libraries sect. 1973-75), ALA (membership com. 1967-71; chmn. council of regional groups, resources and tech. services div. 1968-69, dir. div. 1968-70, 75-76, chmn. div. cataloging and classification sect. 1975-76), N.Y. Tech. Services Librarians (pres. 1963-64, award 1976), AAUP, AAUW, Am. Soc. for Info. Sci., Archons of Colophon, Spl. Libraries Assn., N.Y.U. Grad. Sch. Bus. Adminstrn. Alumni Assn. (rec. sec. 1967-69, dir. 1969-70, 75-79), Library Club (sec. 1964-66, council 1966-70, 73-77, 1979—, pres. 1980-81), Phi Beta Phi. Presbyterian (elder). Clubs: Smith College (pres. Bklyn. 1966-67, 67-68, class treas. 1976-81), Civitas (Bklyn.). Home: 35 Schermerhorn St Brooklyn NY 11201 Office: Library Grad Sch and Univ Center City U NY 33 W 42d St New York NY 10036

MOORE, JANET MARIE, state ofcl.; b. Butler, Pa., Mar. 13, 1947; d. Jesse Robert and Katherine Mae (Pisor) Moore; Asso. in Specialized Bus., New Castle Bus. Coll., 1972. Cost accountant Package Products Inc., Pitts., 1967-68; audit clk. Liberty Mut. Ins. Co., New Castle, Pa., 1968-71; acct. S.R. Snodgrass & Co., C.P.A.s, New Castle, 1971-74; clerical supr. Pa. vital statistics Pa. Dept. Health, New Castle, 1974—; pvt. practice acctg., Volant, Pa., 1974—. Mem. Owner Handler Assn. Democrat. Presbyterian. Club: New Castle Kennel (sec. 1978, dir. 1977-81, v.p. 1979-81). Home: RD 3 Box 101 Volant PA 16156 Office: PO Box 1528 New Castle PA 16103

MOORE, JOYCE HENDEE, psychologist; b. Pinckney, Mich., July 21, 1940; d. Cecil Leroy and Alvina Marie (Larson) Hendee; B.A., Mich. State U., 1961, M.A., 1964, Ph.D., 1967; m. Philip R. Spinelli, Nov. 26, 1974; children by previous marriage—Matthew Moore, Angela Moore. Tchr. English, Lansing (Mich.) public schs., 1961-64; instr. edn. Mich. State U., 1964-67; asst. prof., staff psychologist Colo. State U., 1967-74; psychologist Family Counseling Center, Salt Lake City, 1974-77; psychologist in pvt. practice, Salt Lake City, 1977—. Bd. dirs. LWV, Fort Collins, 1967-73, Rape Crisis Center, Salt Lake City, 1976-79. Mem. Utah Psychol. Assn., Rocky Mountain Psychol. Assn., Am. Psychol. Assn., NOW. Home: 4216 Durch Draw Circle Salt Lake City UT 84119 Office: 545 E 4500 S E-100 Salt Lake City UT 84107

MOORE, JUDITH MARIE, nurse; b. Evanston, Ill., June 2, 1947; d. Herbert Potter and Irene Ellen (Wagner) M.; B.S., Loma Linda (Calif.) U., 1970. Mem. staff White Meml. Med. Center, Los Angeles, 1970-80, coordinator edn. tng. MacPherson Applied Physiology Lab., 1979-80; critical care nurse Critical Care Services, Inc., Los Angeles 1980; coordinator health edn. and rehab. tng. program St. Helena Hosp. and Health Center, Deer Park, Calif., 1981—; bd. dirs. Napa County chpt. Am. Heart Assn., 1980—; speaker in field. Mem. Am. Assn. Critical Care Nurses (CCRN), Nat. Critical Care Inst., Am. Heart Assn., Calif. Soc. Cardiac Rehab. Seventh-day Adventist. Home: PO Box 154 Deer Park CA 94576 Office: HEART Program St Helene Hosp and Health Center Deer Park CA 94576

MOORE, JUDY LYNN, oil co. exec.; b. Nashville, Jan. 27, 1955; d. Harold William and Mary Ann (Cooper) M.; B.S., U. Tenn., 1977. With Cities Service Co., Tulsa, 1977-80, internat. distbn. mgr. Plastic div. Lake Charles, La., 1980-82; mgr. distbn. analysis Petrochems. div. Internat. Supply and Distbn. dept. Mobil Chem. Co., Houston, 1982—. Mem. Delta Nu Alpha, Traffic Club. Republican. Methodist. Home: 6124 Lake St Houston TX 77005 Office: One Greenway Plaza E Suite 1100 Houston TX 77046

MOORE, KATHRIN SCHAPER, urban designer, architect; b. Duisburg, Germany, Mar. 26, 1942; d. Werner and Hanna (Dupin) Schaper; came to U.S., 1968, naturalized, 1977; B.Arch., Technische Universität Hannover (Germany), 1965; Grad. Degree (Studienstiftung des Deutschen Volkes), Technische Universität Berlin, 1968; M.Arch. (Univ. scholar), Yale U., 1970. Carpenter's apprentice Simon Strate, Bad Salzuflen, Germany, 1963; draftsman, model builder Gerhardt Laage, Architect, Technische Universität Hannover, 1963-66; architect/designer, draftsman Robert S. McMillan, Inc., New Haven, 1969-70; architect/designer, planner Robert J. Ferguson, Abingdon, Va., 1970-71; architect/designer Werthheim & Van Der Ploeg, San Francisco, 1971; architect/engr. Bechtel Corp., San Francisco, 1971-72; urban designer and planner Skidmore, Owings & Merrill, San Francisco, 1972—, assoc., 1980—. Participating recipient Progressive Architecture award San Antonio River Corridor Study, 1974, Jondi Shahpour Newtown, 1979, Yanbu New Community, Saudi Arabia. Mem. Am. Inst. Planners, Am. Soc. Planning Ofcls., Am. Planning Assn. (dir. No. Calif. chpt.), San Francisco Mus. Modern Art, Yale Alumni Assn. Clubs: Golden Gateway Tennis, Yale of San Francisco. Home: 1230 Clay St San Francisco CA 94108 Office: Skidmore Owings & Merrill 1 Maritime Plaza San Francisco CA 94111

MOORE, LAURA LEE, nurse, health facility adminstr.; b. Elgin AFB, Fla., July 29, 1953; d. Laurence Gerald and Dorris Brett (Hammond) McMullen; A.A. in Social Welfare magna cum laude, Gulf Coast Community Coll., 1973, A.S., R.N. diploma cum laude, 1976; student U. Louisville, 1980—; m. Terry Randal Moore, July 28, 1979. Pediatric charge nurse Bay Meml. Med. Center, Panama City, Fla., 1976-77; intravenous therapist City County Hosp., Bowling Green, Ky., 1977-78, shift house dir., 1978-79; shift supr. Mallory Taylor Hosp., La Grange, Ky., 1979; nurse IV, Ky. State Reformatory, La Grange, 1979; asst. dir. nursing Summerfield Intermediate Care Facility, Louisville, 1979-81; dir. nursing Jefferson Manor Intermediate Care Facility, Louisville, 1981—; bd. dirs. dept. health careers Pleasure Ridge Park Vocat. Sch. Salome Johnson Acad. scholar, 1974-76. Mem. Ky. Assn. Health Care Facilities (sec.-treas.), Greater Louisville Assn. Nursing Dirs., Am. Heart Assn. Democrat. Baptist. Home: 1120 Heatherbourne Dr La Grange KY 40031 Office: Jefferson Manor 1801 Lynn Way Louisville KY 40222

MOORE, LILLIAN S., assn. exec., clubwoman; b. Chgo., Oct. 26, 1911; d. Charles and Mary (Burgess) Schlagel; A.A., Los Angeles City Coll., 1934; B.A., UCLA, 1936; M.A. in French, U. So. Calif., 1937; postgrad. N.J. Coll., 1964-73. Tchr., Antelope Valley Joint Union High Sch., Lancaster, Calif., 1937-42; tchr. English and French, Meml. High Sch., Cedar Grove, N.J., 1963-76; editor state div. bull. Colo. div. AAUW, 1978-80, 81—, area rep. internat. relations, 1979-81, mem. travel team, 1979-82, pres. Grand Junction (Colo.) br., 1981—. Active Grandteacher Program, Delhi, Iowa, 1979—; Grand Junction coordinator African Educators, 1981—. UN grantee, 1978. Unitarian. Address: 2855 Brittany Dr Grand Junction CO 81501

MOORE, LINDA GRACE, orch. mgr.; b. Monroe, Mich., May 18, 1948; d. Emmett R. and Mary E. (Scott) M.; B.Mus., Western Mich. U., 1971; M.Mus., Ball State U., 1973, D.A., 1976. Teaching fellow Ball State U., 1972-75; asst. prin. cellist Fort Wayne Philharmonic, 1975-79, adminstrv. asst., 1977-79; gen. mgr. Lexington (Ky.) Philharmonic Soc., 1979—; mem. performing arts review panel Ky. Arts Council, 1982; chmn. mem. com. Lexington Council Arts, 1979—. Recipient Future Scientist Am. award Ford Found., 1965; Carnegie Found. fellow Ball State U., 1975. Mem. Am. Symphony Orch. League, Met. Orch. Mgrs. Assn., AAUP, Music Educators Nat. Conf., S.E. Regional and Met. Orch. Mgrs. Office: 412 Rose St Lexington KY 40508

MOORE, LORETTA WESTBROOK, banker; b. Cameron, Tex., Jan. 2, 1938; d. Merrill H. and Gladys E. (Strelsky) Westbrook; student public schs.; m. Joe Moore, Jr., Sept. 22, 1956; children—Terri Lynn, J. Gregg. With Planters Mchts. State Bank, Hearne, Tex., 1956—, cashier, 1975—, v.p., 1980—, also dir. Mem. Nat. Assn. Bank Women (1st vice chmn. Heart of Tex. group 1979-80, chmn. 1980-81 Bank Adminstrn. Inst. (dir. Brazos Valley chpt. 1977—, treas. 1981-82). Club: Order Eastern State (past officer). Address: Planters Merchants State Bank 122 Box 273 4th St Hearne TX 77859

MOORE, LYNN, business cons. co. ofcl.; b. East Chicago Heights, Ill., Sept. 13, 1957; d. Clyde J. Moore and Irene S. (Dalian) Moore Kojder; student Princeton U., 1977-78, So. Ill. U., 1973-74; B.S., B.A. in Mktg./Advt., Loyola U., 1981. Project office mgr. Dart Industries, Joliet, Ill., 1976-77; mktg. orgn. coordinator Western Electric, Lisle, Ill., 1977-79; founder, pres. Moore Efficiency, Chgo.; assoc. Stedman and Assos., Inc., 1981—, Dombrowski and Holmes, Inc., 1981—; tchr. voice, piano, guitar, 1971-78; freelance singer, 1971-80; actress as Mary Magdalene in Jesus Christ Superstar, 1974; cast mem. Godspell, 1975. Mem. staff Reagan for Pres. Campaign, 1976. Recipient nat. writing awards. Mem. Internat. Orgn. Women Execs., Nat. Assn. Women Bus. Owners, Midwest Parts and Service Assn., Indsl. Waste Water and Sewage Group, Word Processing Assn. Chgo., Am. Biog. Inst., Internat. Word Processing Assn., Ill. Am., Writers Guild. Contbr. to various publs. Home: 123 Acacia Dr Apt 611 Indian Head Park IL 60525 Office: 5051 S Western Blvd Chicago IL 60609

MOORE, MARGARET ANN, rehab. services co. exec.; b. Bayonne, N.J., Sept. 6, 1942; d. Andrew F.X. and Virginia Milton; A.A., Fullerton Coll., 1962; B.A., Calif. State U., Fullerton, 1965; 1 son, Brian Andrew. Claims adjustor State Compensation Ins. Fund, Santa Ana, Calif., 1965-73; sr. claims rep. Firemans Fund, Santa Ana, 1975-77; rehab. supr. Comprehensive Rehab. Services, Arcadia, Calif., 1977, dist. mgr., Brea, Calif., Phila., and Southfield, Mich., 1977—. Cert. rehab. counselor. Mem. Nat. Rehab. Assn., Nat. Rehab. Counselors Assn., Nat. Assn. Female Execs., Nat. Assn. Rehab. Profls. in Pvt. Sector, Pa. Assn. Pvt. Rehab. Profls. (dir. 1980, sec. 1981, 82, standards and ethics com. 1981, 82), Nat. Rehab. Adminstrs. Assn., Pa. Rehab. Counselors Assn., Pa. Rehab. Assn., Mich. Rehab. Assn., Mich. Rehab. Counselors Assn. Republican. Roman Catholic. Home: 1801 Briarwood Madison Heights MI 48071

MOORE, (MARGARET) ELEANOR MARCHMAN, ret. librarian; b. Pinckard, Ala., Nov. 6, 1913; d. Robert Lee and Eleanor Rowena (Paris) Marchman; A.B., Fla. State Coll. for Women, 1936; B.S. in L.S., George Peabody Coll. for Tchrs., 1947, M.A. in Library Sci., 1962; m. James William Moore, Feb. 22, 1934 (div. 1940); 1 son, John Robert. Tchr. Alva (Fla.) High Sch., 1938-40, Wacissa (Fla.) Jr. High Sch., 1940-43; librarian Bartow (Fla.) Sr. High Sch., 1943-45, 48-67, Bartow Pub. Library, 1945-48; cataloger Roux Library, Fla. So. Coll., Lakeland, 1967-70, reference librarian, 1970-75; co-sponsor Polk County Student Library Assn., 1957-59; intern tchr. Fla. State U.; former mem. evaluating team So. Assn. Secondary Schs. and Colls. Recipient Polk County Career Increment award, 1961. Mem. NEA, Beta Phi Mu, Delta Kappa Gamma. Democrat. Baptist. Address: 411 Sonny St Apt B-210 Lafayette LA 70501

MOORE, MARGARET RUMBERGER, author; b. DuBois, Pa.; d. George F. and Mary E. (Means) Rumberger; B.S. in L.S., Syracuse U., 1926; m. John Travers Moore, June 16, 1928. Children's librarian Dayton (Ohio) Public Library, 1926-41; freelance writer, 1942—; asst. library dir., asst. prof. Xavier U., Cin., 1947-68; cons., 1969-71. Mem. Pi Lambda Sigma, Zeta Tau Alpha. Author: They Saw Him Fly, 1966; Pretty Kitty, 1966; (with John Travers Moore): Sing Along Sary, 1951; Little Saints, 1953; Big Saints, 1954; The Three Tripps, 1959; On Cherry Tree Hill, 1960; The Little Band and the Inaugural Parade, 1968; Pepito's Speech at the United Nations 1970 (Japanese trans.); Certainly, Carrie, Cut the Cake, 1972. Contbr. articles (fiction) to profl. jours., children's mags.; naturalist series appearing in N.C. Wildlife. Home: 827 Justice St Apt 6 Hendersonville NC 28739

MOORE, MARJORIE S., social worker; b. Dallas, Dec. 5, 1927; d. Fredrick G. and Vivian M. (Lyons) Smith; B.A., Tex. State Coll. Women, 1948; Asso. Social Work, Our Lady of Lake Coll., 1949; M.S.W., Tulane U., 1951; m. Robert H. Moore, Sept. 6, 1952 (div. Apr. 1972); children—Vivian, Barbara, Robert. Social worker Child and Family Services, Austin, Tex., 1950-52; psychiat. social workers VA Hosp., Houston, 1953-54; social worker Dept. Public Welfare, Houston, 1954-57; child placement supr. Dept. Human Resources, Greenville, Tex., 1971—; social work cons. Citizen's Gen. Hosp., Greenville, 1979—; sec.-treas. Moore's Toys and Hobbies; VPV Corp. Sec. Community Health Services, Inc.; pres. E. Tex. State U. Advisory Council Social Work. Sec. adv. bd. Salvation Army. Mem. Nat. Assn. Social Workers, Tex. Assn. Services to Children, Acad. Cert. Social Workers, Bus. and Profl. Women, Altrusa (v.p.). Democrat. Methodist. Home: 2214 King Greenville TX 75401

MOORE, MARTHA ANNELL, furniture co. exec.; d. James Edwin and Mattie Ardeen (Rice) Moore; student Draughn's Bus. Coll., 1935-36. With Firestone Tire & Rubber Co., Akron, Ohio, 1940-43; bookkeeper, office mgr. Fortner Furniture Co., Inc., Memphis, 1943-64, sec., 1964-74, sec.-treas., v.p., treas., 1981—. Methodist (chmn. Ch. Sch. edn. 1968—). Home: 4088 Walnut Grove Rd Memphis TN 38117 Office: 3400 Summer Ave Memphis TN 38122

MOORE, MARTHA BECK, interior designer; n. Jackson, Miss., Nov. 24, 1928; d. Earl Crafton and Lorraine (Harrington) Beck; B.A., Duke U., 1949; cert. bus. adminstrn., Harvard U.-Radcliffe Coll. Grad. Bus. Sch., 1961; cert. N.Y. Sch. Interior Design, 1972; m. Edward S. Moore, III, May 11, 1962 (dec.); children—Diana, John Donelson. Various clerical and secretarial positions, 1949-60; investment research analyst Tri-Continental Corp., also Union Service Funds, N.Y.C., 1961-64; fin. asso. corp. fin. Smith, Barney & Co., Inc., investment bankers, 1972-73; interior designer Village Residential Design, Lost Tree Village, Fla., 1975-79; designer, prin. Martha Smith, Inc., Palm Beach, Fla., 1979—; vol. restoration worker. Mem. Am. Soc. Interior Designers (asso.), Phi Beta Kappa. Republican. Episcopalian. Office: 308 Peruvian Ave Palm Beach FL 33480

MOORE, MARTHA LU, ednl. adminstr.; b. Kellogg, Idaho, June 22, 1929; d. Earnest Alfred and Ruth Eloise (Thwing) Layton; B.A., Point Loma Coll., 1950, M.A., 1975; postgrad. Pepperdine U., 1976-77; m. Marvin Richard Carlson, Dec. 16, 1950 (div. 1979); children—Cynthia Lu, Julie Ann, Wendy May, Chris Marvin; m. 2d, Robert Dean Moore, Oct. 25, 1981. Tchr., Pasadena (Calif.) City Schs., 1950-51, 54-58, Washington Public Schs., 1951-54; asst. dir. Friendship House, Washington, summer, 1952; tchr. Pasadena (Calif.) City Schs., 1973-78, adminstr., 1978—; bicentennial lectr.; curriculum specialist; recreation dir. Pasadena, summer 1950, Washington, summer 1951. Mem. Pasadena Bicentennial Commn., 1976-77. Recipient Jr. Am. Citizens citation Nat. DAR, 1976, 79; Valley Forge Tchrs. medal, 1977. Mem. NEA, Calif. Tchrs. Assn., Pasadena Edn. Assn., Magna Charta Dames, Colonial Order of Crown, Pasadena Jr. Chamber Wives (pres. 1963), Point Loma Coll. Alumni Edn. Assn., Arcadia Assn. AAUW, DAR, Order of Washington, Nat. Soc. New Eng. Women, Phi Delta Kappa (charter). Republican. Presbyterian. Club: Pilot. Author: Fundamental School Curriculum Manual K-6, 1977. Address: 750 Norumbega Monrovia CA 91016

MOORE, MARY CHARLOTTE, ins. co. exec.; b. Washington, Iowa, Nov. 22, 1945; d. F. Burdette and Martha E. (Caldwell) M.; B.B.A. in Acctg., U. Iowa, 1968. From mem. audit staff to audit mgr. Arthur Andersen & Co., C.P.A.s, Chgo. and Milw., 1968-80; dir. acctg. Blue Cross/Blue Shield, Chgo., 1980-81, v.p. fin. ops., 1981—. C.P.A., Ill., Wis. Mem. Am. Inst. C.P.A.s, Am. Soc. Women C.P.A.s, Ill. Soc. C.P.A.s, Chgo. Soc. Women C.P.A.s (dir.), Chgo. Fin. Exchange, Women's Forum. Presbyterian. Office: 233 N Michigan Ave Chicago IL 60601

MOORE, MARY FRENCH, potter, county ofcl.; b. N.Y.C., Feb. 25, 1938; d. John and Rhoda (Teagle) Walker French; B.A. cum laude, Colo. U., 1964; m. Alan Baird Minier, Oct. 9, 1982; children—Jonathan Corbet, Jennifer Corbet, Michael Corbet. Potter, Wilson, Wyo., 1969—; commr. County of Teton (Wyo.), 1976—, chmn., 1981, mem. dept. pub. assistance and social service, 1976—, mem. recreation bd., 1978-80, water quality adv. bd., 1976—. Bd. dirs. Teton Sci. Sch., 1968, vice chmn., 1979-81, chmn., 1982—; bd. dirs. Jackson Hole Art Assn., vice chmn., 1981, chmn., 1982; bd. dirs. Teton Energy Council, 1978-80; mem. water quality adv. bd. Wyo. Dept. Environ. Quality, 1979—; Democratic precinct committeewoman, 1978-81; mem. Wyo. Dem. Central Com., 1981—, platform chmn. state conv., 1982; mem. Gov.'s Steering Com. on Troubled Youth, 1982—. Mem. Nat. Assn. County Ofcls., Wyo. County Commrs. Assn. (dir. 1977—, co-chmn. legis. com.), Jackson Hole Bus. and Profl. Women (Woman of Yr. award 1981), Pi Sigma Alpha. Home: PO Box 161 Wilson WY 83014 Office: PO Box 1727 Jackson WY 83001

MOORE, MARY TYLER, actress; b. Bklyn., Dec. 29, 1937. Appeared TV series Richard Diamond, Private Eyes, 1957-59, Dick Van Dyke Show, 1961-66, Mary Tyler Moore Show, 1970-77, Mary, 1978, Mary Tyler Moore Hour, 1979, TV movies Love Am. Style, 1969, Run a Crooked Mile, 1970, First You Cry, 1978; numerous other TV appearances; motion pictures include: X-15, 1961, Thoroughly Modern Millie, 1967, Don't Just Stand There, 1968, What's So Bad About Feeling Good?, 1968, Change of Habit, 1969, Ordinary People (Acad. Award nominee for best actress 1981), 1980; TV spl. How to Survive the Seventies, 1978; chmn. bd. MTM Enterprises, Inc., Studio City, Calif. Recipient Emmy award Nat. Acad. TV Arts and Scis., 1964, 65, 73, 74, 76, Golden Globe award, 1965, 81. Address: care Agy Performing Arts 9000 Sunset Blvd Suite 315 Los Angeles CA 90069

MOORE, MELBA, actress, singer; b. N.Y.C., Oct. 29, 1945; d. Teddy and Melba (Smith) Hill; B.A., Montclair (N.J.) State Tchrs. Coll.; m. George Brewington (div.). Made Broadway debut in Hair; appeared Broadway musical Purlie; nightclub performer; appeared film Cotton Comes to Harlem, 1970, Hair, 1979; TV appearances include Comedy Is King, Ed Sullivan Show, Johnny Carson Show. Recipient Tony award for Best Supporting Actress in a Musical for Purlie. Address: care William Morris Agency 1350 Ave of the Americas New York NY 10018 *

MOORE, MELISSA LAIRD, public relations co. exec.; b. Watertown, N.Y., Aug. 3, 1939; d. Alton Wilson and Marie Alice (Beardsley) Laird; B.A., Vassar Coll., 1961; m. Theodore Wayne Moore, Oct. 16, 1971. Asst. photo researcher Western Printing Co., N.Y.C., 1961-63; asst. to photo lab. mgr. Saturday Evening Post, N.Y.C., 1963-65; freelance photojournalist, N.Y.C., 1965-68; owner, mgr. Melissa Laird Public Relations, Phoenix, 1970-71; v.p., account supr. Joanne Ralston & Assos., Inc., Phoenix, 1971-81; pres. Moore Public Relations, Inc., Phoenix, 1981—. Mem. Internat. Assn. Bus. Communicators, Public Relations Soc. Am., Public Relations Soc. Am. Counselors Acad.

Republican. Home: 10403 N 38th St Phoenix AZ 85028 Office: 2024 N 7th St Suite 200 Phoenix AZ 85006

MOORE, NELDA ELAINE, export co. exec.; b. Dallas, June 9, 1932; d. Joe Lorenzo and Tommie Edgar Pierce; student U. Houston, 1978; m. Alger Moore, Jr., Aug. 28, 1948; children—Alger, Cynthia Dianne, Susan Elaine. Cost acct. Recognition Equipment, Dallas, 1966-67; direct distbr. Amway Corp., Ada, Mich., 1967-70; acct. Central Crest Realty & Mgmt., Houston, 1970-71; owner, broker Nelda Moore Real Estate, Houston, 1971—; owner Triple M Delivery, Inc., Houston, 1976—; owner Worldwide Export Mgmt. Co., Houston. Mem. Houston Bd. Realtors, Women's Council, Nat. Assn. Women Bus. Owners. Baptist. Club: Moose. Office: 6035 Townsan St Houston TX 77205

MOORE, OLA C., govt. ofcl.; b. Smith County, Tex., Jan. 19, 1939; d. Luther J. and Lottie M. Clark; B.S., Tex. Coll., 1961; M.S., N. Tex. State U., 1971. Extension agt. Tex. Agrl. Extension Service, Paris, 1961-69; asst. to dir. Adminstrn. of Aging, HEW, Dallas, 1970-71; with U.S. Dept. Agr., Dallas, 1971—, mgr., civil rights dir. food and nutrition service, 1975—; dir. Smith's First Nat. Mortgage Corp., Dallas. Mem. adv. com. Tyler (Tex.) Nat. Security Bank, 1978—. Mem. Nat. Assn. Human Rights, Am. Home Econs. Assn., Urban League, NAACP. Baptist. Home: PO Box 222169 Dallas TX 75222 Office: US Dept Agriculture Food and Nutrition Service 1100 Commerce St Room 5A16 Dallas TX 75242

MOORE, PEARL B., nurse; b. Pitts., Aug. 25, 1936; d. Hyman and Ethel (Antis) Friedman; diploma Liliane S. Kaufmann Sch. Nursing, 1956; B.S. in Nursing, U. Pitts., 1968, M. Nursing, 1974; 1 dau., Cheryl. Staff nurse Allegheny Gen. Hosp., Pitts., 1957-60; instr. Liliane S. Kaufman Sch. Nursing, Pitts., 1960-70, asst. dir., 1970, dir., 1970-72; cancer nurse specialist Montefiore Hosp., Pitts., 1974-75; coordinator Brain Tumor Study Group, Pitts., 1975—; adj. instr. U. Pitts., 1974—. Mem. Am. Nurses Assn., Oncology Nurses Soc., Am. Soc. Clin. Onoclogy, Assn. Brain Tumor Research, Nurses Alumnae U. Pitts., Sigma Theta Tau. Contbr. articles in field to profl. publs. Home: 4221 Winterburn Ave Pittsburgh PA 15207 Office: 3459 5th Ave Pittsburgh PA 15213

MOORE, PEARL PRECIOUS, mfg. co. exec.; b. Boston, May 27, 1949; d. Ernest and Alzater (Gaines) Moore; B.S., Boston Coll., 1977. Salesperson, Jordan Marsh Co., Boston, 1967-68; policy inspector John Hancock Mut. Life Ins. Co., Boston, 1968-73; promotion coordinator Gillette Co., Boston, 1977—. Democrat. Roman Catholic. Office: Gillette Co Prudential Tower Bldg Boston MA 02199

MOORE, PEGGY LEE, lawyer, investment counselling co. exec.; b. Chgo., Oct. 30, 1941; d. Leland C. and Margaret H. (Bauer) Oliver; B.S. in Edn., Pa. State U., 1963; J.D., Western State U., 1978; children—Erik S., Christopher S. Admitted to Calif. bar, 1980; tchr. home econs., math. William Tennet High Sch., Warminster, Pa., 1963-65; office mgr. Oliver Sprinkler Co., Gladwyne, Pa., 1965-68; law clk. R. Carter Sanders, San Diego, 1975-78; pvt. practice law, San Diego, 1980—; pres. Oliver-Moore Co., investment counselors, San Diego, 1980—; 1979—. Mem. bd. Loma Portal Sch. PTA, San Diego, 1979-81; bd. dirs. Little League. Recipient Am. Jurisprudence Contracts Law Sch. award Bancroft Whitney Co., 1977. Mem. Am. Bar Assn., Calif. Bar Assn., San Diego County Bar Assn., Bd. Realtors. Republican. Clubs: San Diego City. Home: 3022 Voltaire St San Diego CA 92106 Office: 2254 Moore St Suite 101 San Diego CA 92110

MOORE, RITA JOANN, wholesale distbn. exec.; b. Green Bay, Wis., June 14, 1948; d. Ignatius John and Jean Mildred (Zadlo) Galikowski; diploma N.E. Wis. Vocat. Sch., 1967; spl. courses Dale Carnegie, Am. Mgmt. Assn.; m. Patrick J. Moore, Apr. 8, 1972; 1 stepdau., Dionne Marie; 1 son, Shannon Patrick. Purchasing agt. Imperial, Inc., Green Bay, 1967-70, exec. sec., 1970-71, telephone mktg. mgr., 1972-80, v.p. mktg., 1980—; br. mgr. Crown Fasteners, St. Paul, 1971-72. Recipient Citizenship award United Way of Brown County, 1979. Mem. Nat. Assn. Female Execs. Roman Catholic. Office: PO Box 97 789 Packer Dr Green Bay WI 54305

MOORE, ROSLYN HOLLIDAY, speech pathologist; b. N.Y.C., Jan. 20, 1954; d. Royal A. and Patricia (Clark) Holliday; B.A., Queens Coll., 1975; M.S., Tchrs. Coll. Columbia, 1977; m. Aug. 22, 1976; 1 son, Christopher Lawrence. Speech pathologist Suffolk Rehab. Center, United Cerebral Palsy N.Y. State, Commack, 1977—. Mem. Am. Speech and Lang. Assn. Office: 159 Indian Head Rd Commack NY 11725

MOORE, SONIA, author, theatre dir., drama coach; b. Gomel, Russia; d. Evser and Sophie (Pasherstnik) Shatzov; student U. Kiev, U. Moscow, 1918-20, Drama Studio Solovzov Theatre, Kiev, 1919-20, Studio of Moscow Art Theatre, 1920-23; diploma, Alliance Francaise, Paris, 1927, Istituto Interuniversitario Italiano, Rome, 1938, Reale Conservatorio de Musica Santa Cecilia, 1938, R. Accademia Filarmonica, Rome, 1939; m. Leon Moore, May 11, 1926 (dec. Mar. 1957); 1 dau., Irene (Mrs. Jack Jaglom). Came to U.S., 1940, naturalized, 1946. Appeared at Russian Theatre in Germany, 1923-26; Off Broadway dir., co-producer The Painted Days, 1961; dir. Sharon's Grave prodn. Irish Players, 1961; dir. Sonia Moore Studio of Theatre, N.Y.C., 1961—; founder, pres. Am. Center for Stanislavski Theatre Art, Inc., 1964, artistic dir. Am. Stanislavski Theatre, 1970—, prodns. include The Cherry Orchard, Desire Under the Elms, The Man With the Flower in his Mouth, The Stronger, The Crucible, A Streetcar Named Desire, others; lectr. series on Stanislavski System, Library and Museum of the Performing Arts at Lincoln Center, 1967-68; lectr. on WNYC-FM, 1968-69, 73; supr. Stanislavski System Workshop under auspices Recreation and Cultural Affairs Adminstrn. City N.Y., seminar Stanislavski Canadian Govt., 1969, 73; toured Can. and U.S. colls. with lecture, workshops, seminars and prodn. Long Day's Journey into Night, 1979; also various univs. and workshops, 1980. Author: The Stanislavski Method, 1960, rev. as The Stanislavski System, 1965, rev. edit., 1974; Training an Actor; The Stanislavski System in Class, 2d edit., 1979; translator, editor: Stanislavski Today, 1973; The Logic of Speech on Stage, 1976. Contbr. articles to profl. jours.; article on Stanislavski to Ency. Brit.

MOORE, VIRGINIA FAYE DIXON, ret. educator; b. Big Springs, Mo., July 23, 1919; d. William Marcellus and Cassie Mae (Walker) Dixon; A.A., Hannibal-LaGrange Coll., 1946; B.A., N.E. La. State Coll., 1956; M.Ed., Southwestern La. U., 1959; postgrad. U. Mo., 1948, U. Hawaii, 1952, 53, So. Ill. U., 1960-64, degree cert. of specialist So. Ill. U., 1969; m. A. E. Prince, Aug. 7, 1949 (dec. Sept. 1980); m. 2d, Edwin F. Moore, June 5, 1982. Sec. to pres. Hannibal-LaGrange Coll., 1946-48; tchr. pub. schs., Center, Mo., 1947-48, Honolulu, 1952-54, Monroe, La., 1954-56, Jennings Mo. 1958-82, ret., 1982; dietitian Hannibal-LaGrange Coll., 1948-50; sec. to pastor Auckland (New Zealand) Bapt. Tabernacle, 1951-52. Mem. Assn. Childhood Edn., NEA, Mo. Tchrs. Assn., DAR, Am. Bell Assn., Alpha Delta Kappa, Kappa Delta Pi. Address: 8932 Berkay St Louis MO 63136

MOORE, WANDA KATHERYNE, service assn. personnel exec.; b. Chgo., May 7, 1926; d. William Howard and Mary (Matthew) Williams; cert. in personnel N.Y. U., 19 ; m. Frank Moore, June 6, 1948; children—Ronald, Donald, Jill. Teletype operator N.Y. Telephone Co., N.Y.C., 1947-48; parent educator Moblzn. For Youth, N.Y.C., 1963-64; dir. personnel Planned Parenthood, N.Y.C., 1974—. Bd. dirs. N.E. Comprehensive Health Center, N.Y.C., 1968—, chmn. bd., 1972-79. Recipient Public Service award Nema Health Council, 1978. Mem. Am. Mgmt. Assn., Personnel Mgmt. Office: 380 2d Ave New York NY 10010

MOORHEAD, LUCY GALPIN, author; b. N.Y.C., Jan. 24, 1926; d. Perrin Comstock and Stephanie Kellogg (English) Galpin; B.A., Vassar Coll., 1946; m. William S. Moorhead, Dec. 23, 1946; children—William S., III, Perrin G., Stephen G., James B. Pres., Pitts. Vassar Club, 1958-60; founding mem. womens com. Carnegie Mus. Art, 1954; trustee Washington Gallery Modern Art. Democrat. Episcopalian. Club: Cosmopolitan (N.Y.C.). Author: Entertaining in Washington, 1978.

MOORHEAD, ROLANDE ANNETTE REVERDY, artist; b. Périgueux, France, Sept. 24, 1937; d. RémyJean and Andrée Marcelle (Lavollée) Reverdy; liberal arts degree Coll. Technique, Nice, France, 1954; m. Elliott Swift Moorhead, III, Sept. 30, 1960; children—Edward Marc, Roland Elliott, Rémy Bruce. Bi-lingual sec., France, 1957-58, French Embassy, 1959-60, 1968-70; chmn. exhibit com. Lauderdale-By-The-Sea Art Guild, Ft. Lauderdale, Fla., 1972-75, v.p., 1972-74; charter mem. Gold Coast Water Color Soc., Ft. Lauderdale, 1976; mem. exhibit com. Broward Art Guild, Ft. Lauderdale, 1976; treas., dir. Alliance Française, Miami, Fla., 1973-75; one-man shows include: numerous banks Ft. Lauderdale area, 1971—, Ocean Club Art Gallery, Ft. Lauderdale, 1971-74, Pier 66 Gallery, Ft. Lauderdale, 1973, 75, 76, Ft. Lauderdale City Hall, 1974, 77, 78, 81, St. Basil Orthodox Ch., North Miami Beach, 1977, Galerie Vallombreuse, Biarritz, France, 1977, Galerie du Palais des Fêtes, Périgueux, 1978, Le Club Internationale, Ft. Lauderdale, 1979; exhibited in group shows: Broward Art Guild, Ft. Lauderdale, 1971, 73, 74, Point of Am. Gallery, Ft. Lauderdale, 1971, 73, Internat. Festival, Miami, 1976, Internat. Salon, Biarritz, 1977, Internat. Summer Salon, Paris, 1977, Fine Art Gallery Show and Competition, Long Galleries, Ft. Lauderdale, 1979, Pembroke Pines (Fla.) City Hall, 1982, Hollywood (Fla.) City Library, 1982, also area banks, chs. and libraries, numerous local art festivals; represented in permanent collections: Ft. Lauderdale City Hall, DAV Hdqrs., Washington, Associated Aircraft Co., March of Dimes Bldg. (both Ft. Lauderdale), U.S. Air Force Mus., Ohio, Main Line Fleets, Inc., Palm Beach, Fla., Creditre form, Dusseldorf, W.Ger., St. Front Cathedral, Périgueux, St. Sacerdoce Cathedral, Sarlat, France, also numerous pvt. collections, U.S. and Europe. Recipient Best in Show award Internat. Salon, Biarritz, 1977. Mem. Lauderdale-By-The Sea Art Guild, Broward Art Guild, Boca Raton Center for Arts, Gold Coast Water Color Soc., Del Ray Beach Art Guild, Fla. League of Arts, Artists Equity, Everglades Artists, Çercle Français of Ft. Lauderdale, Alliance Française of Dade County, Internat. Platform Assn., Union des Français de l'Etranger. Office: PO Box 8692 Fort Lauderdale FL 33310

MOORING, PAULINE BISHOP, businesswoman; b. Summerfield, La., Nov. 27, 1928; d. Albert Gilespie and Martha Etta (Manning) Bishop; student Bossier Parish Community Coll., 1971-72, Parker Research Found., 1972-73, Palmer Coll. Chiropractic, 1970-71, Tex. Coll. Chiropractic, 1976-77; m. Sept. 18, 1969; 1 dau., Kathryn Delane Watkins. Mgr., Turner's Variety Stores, La., 1955-59; office mgr. Mooring Chiropractic Clinic, Shreveport, La., 1964-76; office mgr. Atlas Builders, Inc., Shreveport, 1977-80; Realtor-asso. Helen Moore & Assos., Inc., Shreveport, 1979—; pres. Polly & Partners, Inc., 1979—; part-time bookkeeper Foster Mobile Home Sales, 1980—; co-owner Champ Publs.; minister Assemblies of God Ch., 1949-67; bookkeeper McCrary's Jewelers, Shreveport, 1980—. Mem. Women's Council Realtors, Chiropractic Assn. La. Aux., Am. Bus. Women's Assn. (v.p. Bayou Rose chpt. 1979-80, pres. 1980-81, chpt. Woman of Yr. 1978-79). Democrat. Mem. Assembly of God Ch. Co-author, pub. Collections-24 Uncommon Recipes, 1979; Collections-Soup to Nuts, 1980; Collections-Christmas Memories, 1980. Home: 147 Pomeroy Dr Shreveport LA 71115 Office: 1255 Shreve City Shreveport LA 71105

MOOSE, MARY KAY, educator, realtor; b. Dansville, N.Y., Mar. 28, 1949; d. Cletus George and Anita Virginia (Wirth) Fries; B.S., SUNY, Geneseo, 1970; M.S., SUNY, Albany, 1971; student U. Va., part-time 1974-80; m. James Irving Moose, June 20, 1970; 1 son, Robert James. Residence hall dir. SUNY Coll., Plattsburgh, 1970-71, area coordinator of residences, 1971-73; tchr. Rappahannock County (Va.) Schs., 1973-75; tchr. Warren County (Va.) Schs., 1975—; real estate salesman Scott Reid Realty, Front Royal, Va., 1975—. Named N.Y. State Jr. Miss, 1967. Mem. NEA, Va. Edn. Assn., Warren County Edn. Assn., Va. Bd. Realtors, Blue Ridge Bd. Realtors, Beta Sigma Phi (pledge of yr. 1977, girl of yr. 1979, pres. 1978-79, corr. sec. 1979-80). Republican. Roman Catholic. Home: Route 1 Box 575 Front Royal VA 22630 Office: Leslie Fox Keyser Primary Sch 1015 Stonewall Dr Front Royal VA 22630

MOQUIN, SHERRY LYNN (GARNER), accountant; b. Honolulu, Feb. 11, 1950; d. Richard Lemuel and Martha Marjorie (Melvin) Garner; cert. acctg. Harford Community Coll., 1978, A.A., 1979; student in acctg. U. Balt., 19—; m. Daniel Dredonne Moquin, May 11, 1969; children—Crystal Renee (dec.), Seth Eric. Clk. typist Dow Chem. Co. at Kennedy Space Center, 1968-69; stenographer Bendix Corp. at Kennedy Space Center, 1969; sec. Fla. Parlor Car Tours, Inc. subs Greyhound, Inc., at Kennedy Space Center, 1970-72; exec. sec. Computer Scis. Corp., Falls Church, Va., 1973-74; dir. acctg. EMC Controls, Inc., Hunt Valley, Md., 1974—; cons. in field. Mem. NOW. Methodist. Office: PO Box 242 Cockeysville MD 21030

MORA, JUDITH STEVENS, fin. instns. cons.; b. Oakland, Calif., Dec. 5, 1946; d. Russell Norman and Lorraine C. Stevens; B.A., U. Hawaii, 1969; M.A. in Mgmt., U. Redlands, 1980; m. Gilbert Mora, Feb. 26, 1977. Acting editor ofcl. publ. Navy C.E. and Seabees, Pearl Harbor, Hawaii, 1967-70; mgr. public relations and advt. Bishop Trust Co. Ltd., Honolulu, 1970-73; mgr. mktg. and promotions Ala Moana Center (Dillingham Corp.), Honolulu, 1973-75; museum cons., Hilo, Hawaii, 1975-76; cons. Edward Carpenter & Assos., Los Angeles, 1976-79; pres., cons. J. Mora & Assos., Inc., cons. to fin. industry, Garden Grove, Calif., 1979—. Mem. spl. gifts and public relations coms. Am. Cancer Soc., 1973-76. Mem. Women in Communications (past chpt. pres.), Bank Adminstrn. Inst. (asso.), Am. Heart Assn. Contbr. to Hawaii Ency., 1977. Office: 12459 Lewis St Suite 202 Garden Grove CA 92641

MORADIANS, TANYA JOY ENCHEFF, clin. social worker; b. Chgo., Apr. 18, 1936; B.A., U. Calif., Berkeley, 1958; M.S.W., U. So. Calif., 1971; Ph.D., Inst. Clin. Social Work, 1981. Clin. social worker Olive View Children's Psychiat. Service, Sylmar, Calif., 1974-77, Olive View Psychiat. Emergency Service, 1970-75, Olive View Adult Psychiat. Outpatient Clinic, 1970-81; pvt. practice psychotherapy, Sherman Oaks, Calif., 1971—. Cert. group psychotherapist. Mem. Social Work Treatment Service (dir.; outstanding service award), Acad. Cert. Social Workers, Soc. Clin. Social Work (dir.), Los Angeles Group Psychotherapy Soc. (dir.), Nat. Assn. Social Workers. Office: 15422 Ventura Blvd Suite 204 Sherman Oaks CA 91403

MORAES, CLELIA DE TOLEDO LEITE, bus. exec.; b. Sao Paulo, Brazil; d. Joao de Almeida Leite and Leticia de Toledo Leite. Exec. sec. Brazilian Portland Cement Assn., Railroad Material of Brazil Co., Willys-Overland do Brasil, 1939-52; asst. account exec. Orion Advt. and Pub. Relations, Sao Paulo, Brazil, 1952-55; owner, dir. Am. Secretarial Service, Sao Paulo, 1955-60; adminstrv. officer, office mgr. Internat. Basic Economy Corp., Sao Paulo, 1955-60; with Internat. Basic Economy Corp., N.Y.C., 1960-79, asst. corp. sec., 1972-79, dir. public relations, 1975-79; internat. officer Banco Mercantil de São Paulo, N.Y.C., 1979-80; gen. mgr. Brazilian-Am. C. of C., 1980—; owner, dir. Clelia Moraes Assos., N.Y.C., 1962—. Bd. dirs. Brazilian Cultural Found., N.Y.C., 1978—. Roman Catholic. Clubs: Publicity, Altrusa (dir.). Office: 22 W 48th St New York NY 10036

MORAHAN-MARTIN, JANET MAY, psychologist; b. N.Y.C., Jan. 13, 1944; d. William Timothy and May Rosalind (Tarangelo) Morahan; A.B. in Psychology, Rosemont Coll., 1965; M.Ed. in Spl. Edn., Tufts U., 1968; Ph.D. in Counseling Psychology, Boston Coll., 1978; m. Curtis Harmon Martin, June 2, 1979; 1 dau., Gwendolyn May. Market research analyst Compton Advt., N.Y.C., 1965-6, Ogilvy & Mather, advt., N.Y.C., 1966-67; ednl. research coordinator Tufts U. Med. Sch., 1968-69; counseling dir., instr. psychology Bentley Coll., Waltham, Mass., 1971-72; mem. faculty Bryant Coll., Smithfield, R.I., 1972—, asso. prof. psychology, 1981—, counseling dir., 1972-76; bd. dirs. Multi-Service Center, Newton, Mass., 1980—, Adolescent Crisis Center, Newton, 1980—. Grantee U.S. Office Edn., 1980, NSF, 1975-76; NIMH fellow, 1967-68. Mem. Am. Psychol. Assn., World Population Soc., W. Surburban Council Children, Brewster (Mass.) Hist. Soc., Cape Cod Preservation Council. Office: Bryant Coll Smithfield RI 02917

MORAIN, MARY STONE DEWING, assn. exec.; b. Boston, Mar. 18, 1911; d. Arthur S. and Frances (Hall Rousmaniere) Dewing; student Radcliffe Coll., 1930-33; B.S., Simmons Sch. Social Work, 1934; M.A., U. Chgo., 1937; cert. social work U. So. Calif., 1941; m. Lloyd L. Morain, July 6, 1946. Social worker, Calif., N.Y.C., 1941-45; tchr. social scis. Keuka Coll., N.Y., 1945-46; v.p. LWV, Boston, 1946-53; bd. dirs., v.p. Planned Parenthood League Mass., 1948-52; bd. dirs., pres. Planned Parenthood Assn. San Francisco, 1953-60; bd. dirs. Internat. Humanist and Ethical Union, 1953-65; bd. dirs., v.p. Assn. Vol. Sterilization, 1963-77, 79—, UNESCO Assn. U.S.A., 1977—, Monterey YWCA, 1975-80, UN Assn. San Francisco, 1961-69; pres. Internat. Soc. Gen. Semantics, 1976—. Fellow World Acad. Art and Sci.; mem. Am. Assn. Social Workers. Club: Altrusa. Author: (with Lloyd Morain) Humanism as the Next Step, 1954; contbr. articles to profl. jours. Editor: Teaching General Semantics, 1969; Classroom Exercises in General Semantics, 1980. Home: PO Box 7190 Carmel CA 93921 Office: PO Box 2469 San Francisco CA 94126

MORALES, MARIA EUDELIA, educator; b. Taft, Tex., Aug. 9, 1930; d. Candelario and Brijida (Villarreal) Martinez; B.S., Tex. Woman's U., Denton, 1960; M.S., Tex. A&I U., 1964; Ph.D., U. Tex., Austin, 1980; m. Guadalupe Yarrito Morales, Aug. 6, 1966; children—Cynthia Ann, David Steven. Reading and lang. arts specialist, Edinburg, Tex., 1965-69; tchr. schs. in Tex., 1960-70; asst. prof. edn. Tex. A&I U., 1971—, dir. bilingual edn. baccalaurate program, 1979—; cons. in field. Recipient Leader award Camp Fire Girls, 1980. Mem. Nat. Assn. Bilingual Edn., Tex. Assn. Bilingual Edn. (award 1975), Tex. Assn. Coll. Tchrs., Assn. Tchrs. Speakers Other Langs., Legion of Mary, Phi Delta Kappa. Roman Catholic. Office: 176 Rhode Hall Tex A&I Univ Kingsville TX 78363

MORAN, JULIETTE M., chem. co. exec.; b. N.Y.C., June 12, 1917; d. James Joseph and Louise Moran; B.S., Columbia U., 1939; M.S., N.Y.U., 1948. Research asst., Columbia, 1941; jr. engr. Signal Corps. Lab. AUS, 1942-43; with GAF Corp. (formerly Gen. Aniline & Film Corp.), N.Y.C., 1943—, successively jr. chemist process devel. dept., tech. asst. to N.Y. process devel. dept., tech. asst. to dir. Central Research Lab., tech. asst. to dir. comml. devel. 1953-55, supr. tech. service, comml. devel. dept., 1955-59, sr. devel. specialist, 1959-60, mgr. planning, 1961, asst. to pres., 1962-67, v.p., 1967-71, sr. v.p., 1971-74, exec. v.p., 1974-78, vice chmn., 1980—, also dir.; dir. GAF Corp. and various subs.; trustee Am. Savs. Bank. Bd. dirs. N.Y. State Sci. and Tech. Found. Fellow AAAS, Am. Inst. Chemists; mem. Am. Chem. Soc., Comml. Devel. Assn. Clubs: Econ. of N.Y., Hemisphere. Office: GAF Corp 140 W 51st St New York NY 10020

MORAN, LINDA SUE, rehab. counselor; b. Welch, W.Va., July 22, 1943; d. Walter Thomas and Mattie Pauline (Richardson) M.; B.A., W.Va. Wesleyan Coll., 1965; M.S., W.Va. U., 1967. Contbr. relations dir. Goodwill Industries Kanawha Valley (W.Va.), 1965-66; vocat. rehab. counselor med. unit W.Va. Rehab. Center and Institute, 1968-76; asst. chief staff devel. W.Va. Div. Vocat. Rehab., 1976-81, vocat. rehab. field counselor, 1981—. Mem. Nat. Rehab. Assn. (life), W.Va. Rehab. Assn., Nat. Rehab. Counseling Assn., W.Va. Rehab. Counseling Assn. (pres. 1971-72), Nat. Rehab. Adminstrv. Assn., W.Va. Rehab. Adminstrv. Assn., Nat. Spinal Cord Injury Assn. Republican. Methodist. Clubs: Pilot (pres. St. Albans, W.Va. 1978-79; internat. trustee 1981—). Home: 2304 Myers Ave Dunbar WV 25064 Office: 1212 Lewis St Charleston WV 25301

MORAN, PATRICIA EI ZABETH, software engr.; b. Trenton, N.J., Dec. 4, 1947; d. William Patrick and Ruth (Harrison) M.; B.S., Albertus Magnus Coll., 1969; postgrad. New Sch. Social Research, 1970-72. Statistician, Am. Cancer Soc., N.Y.C., 1970-74; mgr. customer service, field programming Keydata Corp., N.Y.C., 1974-80; software engr. Shear Devel. Corp. (name now changed to Nat. Computer Systems), Boston, 1980—. Mem. Nat. Com. Small Press Pubs., NOW. Editor, Tree Shrew Press, 1978, The Serpentine Mews, 1978-80. Office: 75 Federal St Suite 619 Boston MA 02110

MORAN, THERESA ANN KUCKUCK, health care exec.; b. Phila., June 13, 1945; d. Alan McCollough and Theresa Ann (Healy) Kuckuck; A.S., Gwynedd-Mercy Coll., Gwynedd Valley, Pa., 1965; student Va. Commonwealth U., 1970, Sangamon State U., Springfield, Ill., 1976-78; m. Timothy F. Moran, Jr., June 18, 1966; children—Kerry, Tracey (dec.), Jennifer, Stephanie, Monica, Kristen, Lindsay, Timothy F. III, Patrick. Med. sec., 1965-66; bus. mgr. Moran Eye Center, Springfield, 1972—; pres. bd. dirs. Care Center, Springfield, 1979-80, outreach dir., 1981-82, treas., fin. chmn., 1982-83. Pres. Springfield Right-to-Life Com., 1976-79, legis. chmn., 1979-81; sec. Springfield Roman Catholic Diocesan Pastoral Council, 1977-78. Mem. Sangamon County Med. Wives Aux. (chmn. mental health com. 1976), Jr. League Springfield (co-chmn. impact com. 1977), Springfield Art Assn. Contbr. articles to profl. jours. Office: 1020 W Lawrence Springfield IL 62704

MORANCY, ELIZABETH, state legislator, pastoral minister; b. Fall River, Mass., May 12, 1941; d. Clarence Edward and Catherine Mary (Clark) M.; B.A. in History, Salve Regina Coll., 1964; M.A. in Polit. Sci., U. R.I., 1972. Joined Religious Sisters of Mercy, Roman Catholic Church; high sch. history tchr., 1964-71, 72-73; instr. polit. sci., 1974-75; social justice coordinator, 1973-74, 75-77; social service outreach worker, Providence, 1977—; now mem. R.I. Ho. of Reps., judiciary com., 1978—. Active, Elmwood Neighborhood Housing Services, Nat. Women's Polit. Caucus, R.I. Women's Polit. Caucus, R.I. LWV. Named one of 50 Faces for the Future, Time mag., 1979. Mem. Nat. Women's Ordination Conf., Cath. Com. on Urban Ministry, Sisters of Mercy Social Action Com. Democrat. Office: 239 Oxford St Providence RI 02905

MORATH, INGE, photographer; b. Graz, Austria, May 27, 1923; d. Edgar Eugen and Mathilde (Wiesler) M.; B.A., U. Berlin; m. Arthur Miller, Feb. 1962; 1 dau., Rebecca Augusta. Formerly translator and editor ISB Feature Sect., Salzburg and Vienna, Austria, later editor lit. monthly Der Optmist, Vienna and Austrian editor Heute Mag.; former free-lance writer for mags. and Red White Red Radio Network; with Magnum Photos, Paris and N.Y.C., 1952—, mem., 1953—; exhibited photographs one-woman shows: Wuehrle Gallery, Vienna, 1956, Leitz Gallery, N.Y.C., 1958, N.Y. Overseas Press Club, 1959, Chgo. Art Inst., 1964, Oliver Woolcott Meml. Library, Litchfield, Conn., 1969, Art Mus., Andover, Mass., 1971, U. Miami, 1972, U. Mich., 1973, Carlton Gallery, N.Y.C., 1976, Neikrug Galleries, N.Y.C., 1976, 79, Grand Rapids (Mich.) Art Mus., 1979, Mus. Modern Art, Vienna, 1980, Kunsthaus, Zurich, Switzerland, 1980; numerous group shows include: Photokina, Cologne, Ger. and World's Fair, Montreal, Que., Can.; represented in permanent collections: Met. Mus. Art, Boston Mus. Art, Art Inst. Chgo., Bibliothèque Nationale, Paris, Kunsthaus, Zurich, Prague (Czechoslovakia) Art Mus.; photographer for books: Guerre à la Tristesse (Dominique Aubier), 1956, Venice Observed (Mary McCarthy), 1956, (with Yul Brynner) Bring Forth the Children (Yul Brynner), 1960, From Persia to Iran (Edouard Sablier), 1961, Tunisia (Claude Roy, Paul Sebag), 1961, Le Masque (drawings by Saul Steinberg), 1967, In Russia (Arthur Miller), 1969, East West Exercises (Ruth Bluestone Simon), 1973, Boris Pasternak: My Sister Life (O. Carlisle, editor), 1976, In The Country (Arthur Miller), 1977, Chinese Encounters (Arthur Miller), 1979, Images of Vienna (Barbara Frischmuth, Pavel Kohout, Andre Heller, Arthur Miller), 1981; editor, co-photographer Paris/Magnum, Aperture Inc.; biography: Grosse Photographen unserer Zeit, 1975; contbr. numerous photographs to European, U.S., S. Am., Japanese mags., and to numerous anthologies including Life series on photography and photographic yearbooks; tchr. photography course Cooper Union, 2 years; lectr. at various univs. including U. Miami, U. Mich. Recipient various citations for shows. Mem. Am. Soc. Mag. Photographers. Home: Tophet Rd Roxbury CT 06783 Office: Magnum Photos 251 Park Ave S New York NY 10010

MORAWETZ, CATHLEEN SYNGE, mathematician; b. Toronto, Ont., Can., May 5, 1923; came to U.S., 1946, naturalized, 1951; d. John Lighton and Elizabeth Eleanor (Mabel) Synge; B.A., U. Toronto, 1945; S.M., M.I.T., 1946; Ph.D., N.Y.U., 1951; m. Herbert Morawetz, Oct. 28, 1945; children—Pegeen Ann, John Synge, Lida Joan, Nancy Babette. Research asso. M.I.T., 1950-51; research asso. Courant Inst. Math. Scis., N.Y.U., 1952-57, mem. faculty, 1957—, prof. math., 1965—, chmn. dept., 1971—, dep. inst. dir., 1981—; dir. NCR Corp., 1978—. Bd. trustees Alfred P. Sloan Found., 1980—; bd. trustees Princeton U., 1974-78. Guggenheim fellow, 1967, 79; grantee Office Naval Research. Mem. Am. Math. Soc. (trustee), Soc. Indsl. and Applied Math. Author papers in field. Home: 246 W 12th St New York NY 10014 Office: 251 Mercer St New York NY 10012

MOREHEAD, LOIS KATHRYN, educator; b. Columbus, Ohio, Jan. 4, 1944; d. Elwood and Kathryn Collines; ed. Chico State U.; m. John Franklin Morehead, June 28, 1963; chidren—Michael, Michele, Mindy, Matt. Sec., Track & Field News, Los Altos, Calif., 1959-60; sec. Sch. Planning Lab., Stanford U., 1961-62; tchr., Rosedale Elem. Sch., 1965-66, Chico Unified Sch. Dist., 1966-67; tchr. Citrus Sch., Chico, 1967—; Amway Corp. distbr. Recipient awards for civic activities. Mem. NEA, Calif. United Tchrs. Assn., Omega Nu. Clubs: Chico Racquet, Sports Medicine. Home: Route 2 Box 141 2200 Oak Park Ave Chico CA 95926 Office: Citus Sch 1350 Citrus Chico CA 95926

MOREHOUSE, DOROTHY VAN WINKLE, mus. dir.; b. Paterson, N.J., Oct. 1, 1928; d. John Shaw and Verna Kuett VanWinkle; B.A., Cornell U., 1949; m. Curtis Bradley Morehouse, Oct. 8, 1950; children—Susan B., Charles Schuyler, Elizabeth Curtis. Docent, Cin. Art Mus., 1961-63; trustee Monmouth Mus., Lincroft, N.J., 1964-67, 70-78, dir., 1978—; ednl. coordinator Stanford (Calif.) U. Art Mus., 1967-70; reader Inst. Mus., 1980, 81. Mem. bd. edn. Rumson Sch. Dist., 1979-83, pres., 1981-83. Mem. Monmouth County Hist. Assn., N.J. Mus. Council. Club: Jr. League Monmouth County. Editor: New Jersey, A Heritage for Now and Tomorrow, 1976. Office: Monmouth Mus Lincroft NJ 07738

MOREIRA, MARTHA CECILIA, engring. co. exec.; b. Guayaquil, Ecuador, June 7, 1951; came to U.S., 1962; d. Luis Manuel and Aurora (Rodriguez) M.; student Latin Am. Inst., N.Y.C., 1970-71; With Gibbs & Hill, Inc., N.Y.C., 1971—, adminstrv. support supr., 1978—. Mem. Internat. Word Processing Assn., Am. Mgmt. Assn., Nat. Assn. Female Execs. Office: 393 7th Ave New York NY 10001

MORELLA, CONSTANCE A., state legislator; b. Somerville, Mass., Feb. 12, 1931; A.A., Boston U., 1950, A.B., 1954; M.A., Am. U., 1967; married; 3 children, 6 wards. Formerly English prof.; mem. Md. Ho. of Dels., 1979—; cons. Nat. Center for Alcohol Edn. Adv. commn. C&O Canal Nat. Hist. Park, U.S. Dept. Interior, 1976—; trustee Capitol Inst. Tech., 1977—; coordinating com. Md. State Internat. Women's Yr., 1977; mem. Congressional Service Acad. Rev. Bds., 1973-77, Citizens Adv. Com. on Career and Vocat. Edn., 1973-77; mem. Montgomery County Commn. for Women, 1972-75, pres., 1973-74; mem. Montgomery County LWV, Md. Citizens Consumer Council. Mem. AAUW, AAUP, Md. State Tchrs. Assn. Contbr. article to Alcoholism Digest. Office: 220 Lowe Bldg Annapolis MD 21401 *

MORELLI, JOYCE ANDERS NELSON, nurse; b. Montgomery County, Md., Oct. 5, 1942; d. Paul Franklin and Ruby Frances (Giles) Anders; R.N., Johnston-Willis Hosp. Sch. Nursing, 1964; m. Armand Joseph Morelli, May 4, 1979; children by previous marriage—William Wingfield Nelson, Paige Marie Nelson. Part-time staff nurse, supr. Retreat Hosp., Richmond, Va. and supr. Forest Hill Manor, Richmond, 1970-75; part-time R.N., Chippenham Hosp., Richmond, also engaged in claims revue Aetna Life Ins. Co., Richmond, 1976-79; supr. utilization rev. Chippenham Hosp., Richmond, 1979-80; dir. home health care UpJohn Health Care Services, Bon Air, Va., 1980-81, dir. profl. services, Norfolk, Va., 1980-81; evening supr. adolescent psychiatry Tidewater Psychiat. Inst., Virginia Beach, Va., 1981—. Leader, Girl Scouts U.S.A., 1976, 77; mem. com. Southampton-Bon Air Athletic Assn., 1975-78; v.p. Crestwood Elem. Sch. PTA, 1977-78; mem. worship com. Crestwood Presbyn. Ch., 1978; asst. poll judge Crestwood Precinct, Bon Air, 1975-80; bd. dirs. Southam Civic Assn., 1968-72; precinct poll ofcl. Virginia Beach, 1980-81. Recipient cert. Richmond Met. Blood Service, 1979, Recognition cert. Nat. Republican Congressional Com., 1981; cert. in stress mgmt. Fla. Health Inst. Mem. Am. Nurses Assn., Va. Nurses Assn., Nat. Assn. Utilization Rev. Coordinators, Assertiveness for Nurses, Johnston-Willis Alumnae Nurses Assn. (v.p. 1969, 70). Republican. Clubs: Garden (Chelsea); Green Hill Farm, Mogul Ski, Westwood Racquet. Lynnhaven Yacht. Editor newsletter Chelsea-Green Hill Farms Garden Club, also Crestwood Presbyn. Ch., 1977-78. Home: 1795 Upper Chelsea Reach Virginia Beach VA 23454

MORELLI, THERESA ROSEMARIE, bibliog. retrieval services co. ofcl.; b. Albany, N.Y., Feb. 22, 1944; d. Anthony and Marie (Almendo) M.; ed. Fredonia State Coll., 1962-64, Russell Sage Coll., 1965-66; EDP cert. Cybernetics, 1965. Keypunch operator Research Found., Albany, 1968, programmer trainee, 1968; programmer, 1968, sr. programmer, 1969, asst. dir. data processing, 1970-77; dir. computer services Bibliographic Retrieval Services, Latham, N.Y., 1977-82, contract mgr., 1982—; cons. Active Performing Arts Center, Saratoga, N.Y., 1972-82. Mem. Data Processing Mgmt. Assn. (dir., chmn. membership, sec. regional confs.). Roman Catholic. Office: 1200 Route 7 Latham NY 12110

MORESKY, LANA, orgn. exec.; b. Youngstown, Ohio, Feb. 23, 1946; d. Edward S. and Rose (Gelfand) Zatell; B.S., Pa. State U., 1967; m. Marc Moresky, July 30, 1967; children—Rachel, Joanna. Mem. NOW, 1970—, pres. Ohio chpt., 1974-75, mem. nat. bd. dirs., 1976-77, pres. Cleve. East chpt., 1980-81, cons., 1981—; mem. Ohio Atty. Gen. ERA Implementation Task Force Sexism in Edn., 1975, Ohio Internat. Women's Year Coordinating Com., 1977; mem. Cuyahoga County steering com. White House Conf. Families, 1979. Mem. platform com., del. Democratic Nat. Conv., 1980; mem. Cuyahoga County Dem. Exec. Com., 1978; chmn. 22d Congl. Dist. Caucus, 1980; bd. dirs. Cleve. chpt. Ams. for Democratic Action, 1982. Recipient Susan B. Anthony award NOW, 1975; named Woman of Yr., Coalition Labor Union Women, 1980. Jewish. Address: 1918 Washington Blvd Cleveland OH 44118

MORETTO, JANE ANN, nurse; b. Belgium, Ill., Apr. 9, 1934; d. Bernard James and Mildred Bertha (Sutton) Moretto; R.N., Mercy Hosp. Sch. Nursing, Urbana, Ill., 1955; B.S. in Nursing, St. Joseph Coll., Emmitsburg, Md., 1969. Relief head nurse, staff nurse Mercy Hosp., Urbana, Ill., 1955-57; staff nurse in psychiatry VA Hosp., Danville, Ill., 1957-59; staff nurse pulmonary disease VA Hosp., Long Beach, Calif., 1959-60, staff nurse surg. unit, Los Angeles, 1960-61, staff nurse operating room, 1961-64; staff nurse USPHS Hosp., Galveston, Tex., 1964-66, staff nurse tumor ICU, Balt., 1967, asst. operating room supr., New Orleans, 1969-71, operating room supr., Brighton, Mass., 1971-78, dep. dir. nursing, dir. inservice edn. Carville, La., 1978-80, dir. nurses Nat. Hansen's Disease Center, 1980—; cons. in field; lectr. in field. Commd. lt. comdr., USPHS, 1969, advanced through grades to capt., 1975—. Recipient Superior Performance award, USPHS Hosp., Galveston, 1966. Mem. Am. Nurses Assn., La. Nurses Assn., La. Hosp. Assn., La. Soc. Nursing Service Adminstrs., Nat. Assn. for Uniformed Services, Assn. Mil. Surgeons of U.S., Assn. Operating Room Nurses, Alumnae Assn. of Schlarman High Sch., Alumnae Assn. of St. Joseph Coll., Commd. Officers Assn. USPHS. Roman Catholic. Home: 303 Bridgett St Westville IL 61883 Office: Nat Hansen's Disease Center Carville LA 70721

MORGAN, ALICE SWITZER, educator; b. Grand Bay, Ala., Apr. 14, 1936; d. Charles Henry and Rosa Lee (Merriwether) Switzer; B.S., U. So. Miss., Hattiesburg, 1960; M.A., U. Ala., 1968; Ed.D. (Delta Kappa Gamma grantee), Auburn (Ala.) U., 1974; m. John Vernon Morgan, Sept. 28, 1954; 1 son, Joey. High sch. tchr., 1957-70; research asso. Auburn U., 1970-75, asst. prof., chmn. bus. edn., 1975—, chmn. state course bus. edn., 1979-80; mem. Ala. Adv. Bd. Consumer Affairs, 1975-78; cons. in field. Mem. NEA, Nat. Bus. Edn. Assn., Nat. Assn. Tchrs. Educators Bus. and Office Edn., Am. Vocat. Assn., AAUW, Am. Vocat. Edn. Research Assn., So. Bus. Edn. Assn., Mid-South Edn. Research Assn., Ala. Vocat. Assn. (pres. 1971), Ala. Edn. Assn., Ala. Bus. Edn. Assn., Delta Kappa Gamma, Phi Delta Kappa (pres. 1980). Democrat. Baptist. Clubs: University, Auburn Cotillion, Saugahatchee Country. Author papers in field. Home: 807 E University Dr Auburn AL 36830 Office: 5018 Haley Center Auburn Univ Auburn AL 36830

MORGAN, ANNE LEE, social worker; b. Castor, La., Jan. 7, 1933; d. Ernie James and Bessie (Johnson) Yocum; B.A., Northwestern U., 1975; M.S.W., La. State U., 1977; m. William H. Morgan, Aug. 4, 1951 (div. 1976); children—William D., James S. Outpatient therapist South Ark. Regional Health, Eldorado, 1977-79; dir. family therapy F. Edward Herbert Hosp., New Orleans, 1980—, clin. dir. chem. dependency unit, 1982—; pvt. practice social work, part-time 1981—; field work supr. Holy Cross Coll., New Orleans. Vol., ARC, 1964-71; lectr. to groups, family systems. Mem. Nat. Assn. Social Workers, Acad. Cert. Social Workers, La. Bd. Cert. Social Workers, Phi Kappa Phi. Democrat. Methodist. Home: 1554 Kings Rd Harvey LA 70058 Office: One Sanctuary Dr New Orleans LA 70114

MORGAN, ANNETTE NOBLE, state legislature; b. Kennett, Mo., Aug. 31, 1938; d. John Willis and Alletha (Bradley) Noble; B.A., U. Mo., 1960, M.A., 1978; m. William B. Morgan, June 3, 1961; children—John Allen, Katherine Anne. Staff, Library of Congress, 1961; with Delta Area Econ. Opportunity Corp., Kennett, Mo., 1965-68; tchr. Independence (Mo.) Public Schs., 1969-72; instr. continuing edn. dept. Avila Coll., 1979-80; mem. Mo. Ho. of Reps., 1980—. Bd. dirs. Mo. Heritage Trust. Mem. Internat. Transactional Analysis Assn., Order Women Legislators, Adult Edn. Assn., NOW, LWV, ACLU. Democrat. Presbyterian. Office: Missouri Ho of Reps Jefferson City MO 65101

MORGAN, ANTONIA BELL (MRS. WILLIAM J. MORGAN), psychologist; b. London, Eng., Oct. 5, 1914 (came to U.S. 1946, naturalized 1948); d. James Young and Jean (Macnair) Bell; B.A., U. Oxford, 1936, M.A., 1945; tchrs. diploma U. London, 1938; m. William James Morgan, Nov. 2, 1944; children—William James, Jean Elizabeth, Robert Macnair. Chmn. dept. classical studies St. Albans Sch., Hertfordshire, Eng., 1938-41; Walter Hines Page scholar, lectr. English Speaking Union, 1941-42; lectr. Brit. Ministry of Info., 1942-43, asst. prin., India Office, 1943-45; sec. Aptitude Assos., Inc., 1946-49, asso. dir., 1949—; lectr. Nat. Mental Health Assn.; sec. No. Va. Mental Health Assn., 1955-56, v.p., 1958-59; cons. to Ch. Sch. of the Diocese of Va., Pain Clinic Nat. Orthopedic Hosp. Trustee Schefer Schs., 1970—. Licensed clin. psychologist, Va. Mem. Am. Psychol. Assn., AAAS, Am. Personnel and Guidance Assn., Nat. Assn. Sch. Psychologists. Episcopalian. Author psychol. tests, articles on edn. of gifted children, and psychol. testing. Address: 1322 Vincent Place McLean VA 22101

MORGAN, CINDY LYNN, editor; b. Pitts., Oct. 18, 1951; d. Elizabeth C. Morgan; student U. Pitts., 1969-72; B.A. in Journalism, N.Y. U., 1974. Reporter, Fairchild Publs., N.Y.C., 1972-73; asst. editor McFadden-Bartell Co., N.Y.C., 1974-75; free-lance writer, N.Y.C., 1975-76; asst. to pres. St. Regis Publs., N.Y.C., 1976-79, corr., a founding editor of ACE Internat., hi-fi bus. publ., Brussels, 1977—; editor C & S Trade News Daily, 1977-79, asso. editor High Fidelity Trade News, 1978-79. Home: 321 W 21st St Apt 3B New York NY 10011 Office: St Regis Publications 6 E 43d St New York NY 10017 also care Ace Internat Av des Ormeaux 26 Brussels 1180 Belgium

MORGAN, DORIS WHITTEN, graphic artist; b. Atlanta, Apr. 19, 1933; d. John Lovic and Cornelia Catherine (Slater) Whitten; student High Mus. Sch. Art, 1949-50; m. David Lewis Cofer, Sept. 3, 1951; children—Debra Jean, Dutch Whitten; m. 2d, John J. Morgan, Aug. 6, 1971. Founder, owner, mgr. Doris Morgans Quality Graphics, Atlanta, 1977—. Recipient excellence award for graphic communications Beckett Paper Co., 1981. Mem. Nat. Assn. Profl. Women Am. Home: 525 Kenbrook Dr NW Atlanta GA 30327 Office: 2379 John Glenn Dr Suite 103 Atlanta GA 30341

MORGAN, GISELA, computer mfg. co. exec.; b. Germany, Mar. 20, 1931; d. Leo Rudolph and Martha Elise (von Sydow) Stanke; came to Can., 1951, naturalized, 1961; M.B.A., U. Kiel (Germany), 1950; postgrad. U. Upsala (Sweden), 1950-51; m. Frank Edgar, Sept. 2, 1950; children—William-Tyrone, Karen-Gisela, Marie-Anne, Freya-Victoria, Charles-Richard, Francisca-May. Acctg. mgr. W. H. Smith & Son, Can., 1958-62; investment officer Gt.-Divide-U.S.A., 1962-64; asst. comptroller, office mgr. dir. responsible for internat. div. Howmark of Can., Toronto, Ont., 1964-69; comptroller Nightingale Industries Ltd., Toronto, 1969-74; v.p. fin. Parmor Devels. Inc., U.S.A., Toronto and Charlotte, N.C., 1974-77, also dir.; v.p. fin. Digital Video Systems Co., Toronto, 1977—; fin. cons.; dir. Otam of Can. Mem. Franklin Mint Collectors Soc. Conservative. Clubs: Sun'n Lake Golf and Racquet, Maple Flying. Home: 39 Derrydown Rd Downsview ON M3J 1R2 Canada

MORGAN, HAZEL NOHAVEC, musician, educator; b. Missouri Valley, Iowa; d. David A. and Ida M. (Matherly) Beckwith; B.F.A., U. Neb., 1924; A.B., Nebr. State Tchrs. Coll., 1927; A.M., Claremont (Calif.) Colls., 1929; Mus.D., MacPhail Sch. Music, 1937; Ph.D., U. Minn., 1942; student in voice with Gabriel Lapierre, Paris, 1931; m. Fred R. Nohavec, 1921 (dec. 1940); m. 2d, Russell V. Morgan, 1945 (dec. 1952). Former tchr. history and English in grade schs., Nebr., Wyo.; asst. prof. fine arts U. Nebr., 1917-28; supr. elementary sch. music, Lincoln, Nebr.; supr. music pub. schs., Claremont, Calif.; asst. prof. Coll. Edn., U. Minn., 1937-45; guest summer lectr. Claremont Colls. Grad. Sch., 1941, 60, Northwestern U., 1945, U. Nebr., 1946, U. Hawaii, 1948; extension lectr. Kent State U., 1952; mem. faculty Am. Inst. Music Edn., Boston, summers 1946-52, U. Calif., Los Angeles, summers 1954, 55; prof. music edn., grad. adviser Northwestern U., 1954-61; prof. music edn. Claremont Grad. Sch. and Univ. Center, 1961-63; rep. Nat. Fedn. Music Clubs 2d Nat. Conf UNESCO; speaker research meeting Internat. Soc. Music Edn., 1961. Trustee Fund for Advancement of Music Edn., 1978. Named Distinguished Dau., Phi Mu Centennial award, 1952; recipient research award U.S. Govt., 1966, Distinguished Service award Nebr. State Coll., 1973, Distinguished Alumna Service award Claremont Grad. Sch., 1974. Mem. Nat. League Am. Pen Women, Music Tchrs. Nat. Assn., Nat. Fed. Music Clubs, Music Educators Nat. Conf. (past pres. North Central div., mem. exec. bd.), Pi Lambda Theta, Mu Phi Epsilon, Delta Kappa Gamma, Phi Mu, Pi Kappa Lambda. Author, co-author books on music; author syndicated crossword puzzles; editorial bd. Music Clubs mag.; editorial bd. Young Am. Films; collaborator Coronet Films. Home: 931 W Bonita Ave Claremont CA 91711

MORGAN, INGA BORGSTROM, educator, pianist; b. Amarillo, Tex.; d. August and Charlotte (Jonsson) Borgstrom; grad. Amarillo Jr. Coll., 1938; Mus.B., Eastman Sch. Music, 1940, Mus.M., 1944, performer cert., 1942; postgrad. Sommer Akademie, Mozarteum, Salzburg, Austria, 1969, 71; student Friederich Wuhrer, Lilly Larsen, Esther Jonsson, Radie Britain; m. Edwin Phillip Morgan, Aug. 23, 1942; 1 son, Kent August. Mem. faculty, dept. music Coll. Fine Arts, U. Tex., Austin, 1942-43, N. Tex. State U., Denton, 1944-45; mem. faculty Sch. Music, U. N.C., Greensboro, 1946—, now asso. prof. music, piano; cons.; concert pianist (harpsichordist), lecture-recitalist, accompanist. Mem. Am. Liszt Soc., Coll. Music Soc., Music Tchrs. Nat. Assn., N.C. Music Tchrs. Assn., Greensboro Music Tchrs. Assn., Am.-Scandanavian Found. (officer Vasa Carolina Viking lodge), Pi Kappa Lambda, (past officer), Mu Phi Epsilon. Presbyterian. Club: Euterpe Music. Home: 1005 Guilford Ave Greensboro NC 27401 Office: 209 Music Bldg U NC Greensboro NC 27412

MORGAN, JANE DIANE, mayor; b. Gordon, Nebr., Apr. 23, 1941; d. Harold E. and Evelyn M. (Baker) Thompson; student Hastings (Nebr.) Coll., 1959-62; m. Marvin D. Morgan, July 1, 1962; children—Marchelle, Melanie, Meri Dee. Officer mgr. auto dealership, 1967-82; mem. Gordon City Council, 1974-75; mayor City of Gordon, 1975-82. Elder, Presbyterian Ch., 1982—. Mem. Nebr. League Municipalities (smaller cities rep.). Democrat. Home and Office: PO Box 94 325 Elm St Gordon NE 69343

MORGAN, JANE HALE, library adminstr.; b. Dines, Wyo., May 11, 1926; d. Arthur Hale and Billie (Wood) Hale; B.A., Howard U., 1947; M.A., U. Denver, 1954; m. Joseph Charles Morgan, Aug. 12, 1955; children—Joseph Hale, Jane Frances, Ann Michele. Mem. staff Detroit Pub. Library, 1954—, exec. asst. dir., 1973-75, dep. dir., 1975-78, dir., 1978—. Mem. Mich. Library Consortium Bd., exec. bd. Southeastern Mich. Regional Film Library; mem. Mich. State Library Advisory Council. Trustee New Detroit, Inc.; v.p. United Found.; pres. Univ.-Cultural Center Assn.; bd. dirs. Rehab. Inst., YWCA. Mem. ALA, Mich. Library Assn., Women's Nat. Book Assn., Assn. Municipal Profl. Women, NAACP, Alpha Kappa Alpha. Democrat. Episcopalian. Club: Women's Econ. Office: Detroit Public Library 5201 Woodward Ave Detroit MI 48202

MORGAN, JUDITH CLAIRE, educator; b. Leesville, La., Dec. 22, 1937; d. Richard T. and Mary Elaine (Tipton) M.; B.A. in Elem. Edn., Northwestern State U., 1958, M.A., 1962, Ed.D., 1971; postgrad. Lamar U., 1967, La. State U., 1967, U. Southwestern La., 1968, U. Tex., 1968. Tchr. Acadia (La.) Parish Schs., 1958-61, Calcasieu (La.) Parish Schs., 1961-63; tch. Lafayette (La.) Parish Schs., 1963-66, reading supr., 1966-67; lang. arts supr. St. Martin (La.) Parish Sch., 1967-69; grad. asst. Northwestern State U., 1969-71; asst. prof. dept. adminstrn. and supervision McNeese State U., 1971-74, asst. prof., 1974-78, prof., head dept., 1978-80, dean Grad. Sch., 1980—. Phi Delta Kappa grantee, 1970-71; U.S. Office of Edn. Right to Read grantee, 1974-76. Mem. NEA, La. Assn. Educators, Internat. Reading Assn., Assn. Supervision and Curriculum Devel., La. Assn. Supervision and Curriculum Devel., La. Coll. Reading Tchrs., Calcasieu Parish Reading Council, La. Coll. Profs. Ednl. Adminstrn., La. Reading Assn., Delta Kappa Gamma. Democrat. Roman Catholic. Contbr. in field. Home: 504 Scarlett St Lake Charles LA 70605 Office: Ryan St Lake Charles LA 70609

MORGAN, KATHLEEN ETHEL (GERARD), aerospace co. adminstr.; b. Dillonvale, Ohio, May 6, 1923; d. Hector Benjamin and Ethel Marie (Anderson) Gerard; grad. Elliott Sch. Bus., 1941; m. Leonard Carey Morgan, Apr. 18, 1944 (div. Aug. 1966, dec. Feb. 1976); children—Jacquelyn Morgan Goodman, Joann K., Janis K. Stenographer, Hazel Atlas Glass Co., Wheeling, W.Va., 1941-44; stenographer/relief telephone operator Henry Walke Co., Norfolk, Va., 1944-45; stenographer, adminstrv. aide, field Vought Corp., White Sands Missile Range, N.Mex., 1966-79, adminstrv. asst., field office, 1979—. Leader various councils Girl Scouts, Japan, Tex., S.C., Germany, 1952-58, 67-70. Mem. Nat. Assn. Female Execs. Methodist. Home: 1957 Peri Ann Dr Las Cruces NM 88001 Office: PO Box 57 White Sands Missile Range NM 88002

MORGAN, LILLIE GUINELL, orgn. devel. cons.; b. Winona, Miss., Sept. 24, 1951; d. Leslie Herman and Shirley Irene (Miller) M.; B.A. in Psychology (Gen. Motors scholar), Wilberforce U., Ohio, 1973; M. Labor and Indsl. Relations (Gen. Motors fellow), U. Ill., Urbana, 1974. Indsl. engr. Central Foundry div. Gen. Motors Corp., Defiance, Ohio, 1974, supr. edn. and tng., 1974-77, supr. tng. program, Pontiac, Mich., 1977-79, orgn. devel. cons. Packard Elec. div., Warren, Ohio, 1979—; cons. organizational and group devel. Active LWV, Jr. Achievement; co-chair Defiance Mayor's Commn. Human Relations; bd. dirs. Warren-Trumbull Urban League; v.p. Warren-Trumbull Community Vol. Council. Recipient award of excellence for community service, Gen. Motors Corp., 1976. Mem. Nat. Assn. Female Execs., Nat. Assn. Bus. and Profl. Women, Am. Foundrymen's Soc., Midwest Coop. Edn. Assn., Nat. Assn. Suggestion Systems. Baptist. Home: 8426 Old Farm Trail NE Warren OH 44484 Office: PO Box 431 Warren OH 44486

MORGAN, M. JANE, govt. ofcl.; b. Washington, July 21, 1945; d. Edmond John and Roberta (Livingstone) Dolphin; student U. Md., 1963-66, Montgomery Coll., 1966-70, SUNY, 1978-81; 1 dau., Sheena Anne. With HUD, Washington, 1965—, computer specialist, 1978—. Mem. Fed. Automatic Data Processing Users Group, Am. Mgmt. Assns. Democrat. Club: Order Eastern Star. Office: HUD 451 7th St SW Washington DC 20410

MORGAN, MARCIA CHILDS, educator; b. Bklyn., Feb. 21, 1913; d. Edward Delano and Marcia Hazelton (Tribou) Childs; B.A., Moravian

Coll., 1936; M.S.E., So. Conn. State Coll., 1972; m. Edward C. Morgan, Oct. 20, 1936; children—Marcia, Edward Childs, Kingsley, Sarah, Margaret. Correspondent Bridgeport (Conn.) Post, 1950-62; tchr. Stratford (Conn.) schs., 1962-63, Unquowa Sch., Fairfield, Conn., 1965-68, Shelton (Conn.) schs., 1970—. Mem. Trumbull (Conn.) Zoning Commn., 1953-58; mem. Trumbull Civil Service Bd., 1959-61; bd. dirs. Fairfield County Extension Service, 1967-80. Mem. TESOL, Moravian Coll. Alumni Assn., So. Conn. State Coll. Alumni Assn. Democrat. Episcopalian. Home: 1681 Huntington Turnpike Trumbull CT 06611 Office: 41 Church St Shelton CT 06484

MORGAN, MARITZA LESKOVAR, painter; b. Zagreb, Yugoslavia, Nov. 20, 1920; came to U.S., 1929, naturalized, 1930; d. Josef and Paula Mihailovic (Yunkovic) Leskovar; M.A., Cornell U., 1944; m. Norman Charles Morgan, May 10, 1941; children—Vincent, Penelope, Jonathan, Christopher, Catherine. Music editor Chautauquan Dailey, Chautaugua, N.Y., 1969—; one woman shows: Central Cathedral, N.Y.C., 1982, Downtown Cathedral, Rochester, N.Y., 1982, Bryn Mawr (Pa.) Presbyn. Ch., 1982; represented in permanent collections Hurlbut Ch., Chautaugua, All Souls Unitarian Ch., Tulsa, Downtown Presbyn. Ch., Rochester, Presbyn. Ch., Warren, Pa., St. Joseph Ch., Erie, Pa. Home: 10 Forest Ave Chautaugua NY 14722

MORGAN, MARTHA TRUITT, cons. engring. firm exec.; b. Nevada, Mo., Oct. 2, 1955; d. Arthur Leonard and Dorothy Velma Truitt; B.S., U. Kans., 1979. Chem. engr. power div. Black & Veatch, Kansas City, Mo., 1979—. Mem. Am. Inst. Chem. Engrs. Home: Apt 2-A 10346 Conser St Overland Park KS 66212 Office: Black & Veatch PO Box 8405 Kansas City MO 64114

MORGAN, MARY ELISE, nurse; b. Middletown, N.Y., Oct. 1, 1935; d. Edward B. and Mary Elizabeth M.; diploma in nursing, White Plains (N.Y.) Hosp., 1956; A.A., Peralta Jr. Coll., Oakland, Calif., 1968; B.S. in Nursing, U. Calif., San Francisco, 1975, M.S. in Nursing, 1978. Staff nurse hosps. in Calif., 1959-69; evening supr., relief nurse San Leandro (Calif.) Hosp., 1969; evening charge nurse Herrick Hosp., Berkeley, Calif., 1969-75; in-service educator Brookside Hosp., San Pablo, Calif., 1975-77; dir. in-service edn. Oakland (Calif.) Hosp., 1977-79; dir. operating rm. services Presbyn. Hosp., Albuquerque, 1979-82; asst. adminstr. nursing service Meth. Hosp., Sacramento, 1982—. Mem. Assn. Operating Rm. Nurses (nat. sec. 1966-69), Nat. League Nursing, Am. Nurses Assn., Calif. Nurses Assn. (sec. nursing council 1973-75), N.Mex. Nurses Assn., Sigma Theta Tau. Roman Catholic. Contbr. articles to profl. jours. Address: 9809 Alta Mesa Rd Wilton CA 95693

MORGAN, PATRICIA KATHRYN, consulting firm. exec.; b. Kittanning, Pa., Oct. 2, 1946; d. Charles Francis Nestler and Caroline (Mangiantini) Seitz; adopted d. Guido and Petrina Mangiantini; B.S. in Bus. Adminstrn. summa cum laude, Clarion State Coll., 1981; m. Don L. Morgan, Oct. 5, 1981; 1 son by previous marriage, Jeffrey Scott Thomas. Office mgr. E.C. Dean Contractor, Inc., New Bethlehem, Pa., 1964-67; sec. Jefferson County (Pa.) Bd. Edn., 1967-70; supr. student loans Clarion (Pa.) State Coll., 1970-78, fiscal asst. accounts payable and accounts receivable, 1978-81; pres., cons. Morgan Assos., Clarion, 1981—; dir. Interpersonal Dynamics; cons. Performax Systems Internat., Prime Time Assos., Pa. Dept. Edn. Chmn. supervisory com. Fed. Credit Union, 1971-77, asst. treas., mgr., 1977-79; active Humane Soc., United Way, campus planning commn.; victim advocate Rape Crisis Center. Certified cons. Mem. Tri-City Internat. Mgmt. Council, Pa. Accounting Assn., Clarion County Endl. Secs. (pres. 1976-80), Pa. Assn. Ednl. Secs. Am. Fedn. State, County and Mcpl. Employees (pres. local 2326, 1979-80, local union tng. instr.), Phi Beta Alpha, Omicron Delta Epsilon. Club: Bus. Women's Assn. :Home and Office: 1213 Chestnut St Clarion PA 16214

MORGAN, ROBIN, author, editor; b. Lake Worth, Fla., Jan. 29, 1941; d. Faith Berkeley Morgan; student Columbia U.; m. Kenneth Pitchford, Sept. 19, 1962; 1 son, Blake Ariel Morgan-Pitchford. Author: (poetry) Monster, 1972, Lady of the Beasts, 1976; Depth Perception, 1982; (prose) Going Too Far: The Personal Chronicle of a Feminist, 1977; The Anatomy of Freedom, 1982; compiler, editor (feminist anthology) Sisterhood is Powerful, 1970; co-editor: The New Women, 1971; contbg. editor Ms. mag., 1977—; speaker on feminist issues, poetry reader univs.; prof. feminist studies New Coll., Sarasota, Fla., 1971; bd. dirs. Women's Law Center, Feminist Self-Health Clinics, Battered Women's Refuge, Women's Inst. Freedom Press, Nat. Alliance of Rape Crisis Centers; founding mem. N.Y. Radical Women, Women's Internat. Terrorist Conspiracy from Hell, Women Against Pornography, Feminist Writers Guild. Mem. Authors Guild, ASCAP, Poetry Soc. Am., Nat. Women's Polit. Caucus. Office: care Ms Mag 119 W 40th St New York NY 10018

MORGAN, SHERLI JO, religious educator; b. Guymon, Okla., Mar. 13, 1953; d. James Leslie and Zola Loyce (Fike) M.; student Panhandle State U., 1971, Amarillo Coll., 1972; B.S., Southwestern Assemblies of God Coll., 1977; M.B.A., Belmont Coll., 1979. Dir. computer data J.C. Penney Co., Dallas, 1975-77; dir. pub. relations Your Place Inc., Nashville, 1978-79; asst. dir. artists relations and sales IBC Records Inc., Nashville, 1979-80; dir. music and Christian edn. First Assembly of God Ch., Lakewood, Calif., 1980—; pvt. instr. voice and piano. Pres., Young Republicans, 1972, 73; vol., Rep. campaigns, 1980. Mem. Country Music Assn., Gospel Music Assn., Female Execs. Club, Ch. Music Dirs. Assn., Women So. Calif. Coll. Mem. Assembly of God. Club: Hope of our Heritage. Home: 4591 Orange Ave Apt 207 Long Beach CA 90807 Office: 6022 E Candlewood St Lakewood CA 90713

MORGAN, SUZANNE, interior designer; b. Geneva, Sept. 3, 1932; came to U.S., 1932, naturalized, 1932; d. John and Miriam Elizabeth (Nelly) Reinhardt; A.A., Santa Monica City Coll., 1952; interior designer UCLA, 1979; children—Nancy Elizabeth Greene, Jonathan Danford Greene. Designer, Dorothy Ball Showroom, Los Angeles, 1964-65, Twentieth Century Fox Film Corp., Los Angeles, 1966, Suzanne Morgan Interiors, Santa Monica, Calif., 1966-76, Liberty House Dept. Stores, Inc., Honolulu, 1980—, Ansteth Ltd. Showroom, Honolulu, 1981—; educator Interior Designers Guild Coll., Encino, Calif., 1982—. Mem. Am. Soc. Interior Designers, Internat. Soc. Interior Designers. Republican. Office: 16311 Ventura Blvd Suite 1010 Encino CA 91436

MORGAN, VICKI ANNE, illustrator's rep.; b. N.Y.C., Oct. 16, 1945; d. Robert Edward and Margot Susan (Blum) Lederer; student Syracuse U., 1963-65; cert. fine art Cooper Union, 1969; m. Robert Grossman; 1 dau., Anna Grossman. Art researcher J. Walker Thompson Advt. Agy., N.Y.C., 1968-69; photographer, artists' rep. Darwin M. Bahm Inc., N.Y.C., 1970-74; owner, operator Vicki Morgan Satisfies, N.Y.C., 1974—; guest speaker at art schs.; participant panel discussion on illustration as a bus. Mem. Soc. Photographers' and Artists' Reps. (dir. 1977), Graphic Artists Guild, N.Y. Assn. Women Bus. Owners. Home and Office: 194 3d Ave New York NY 10003

MORGAN (FERRY), CHRISTINE ADELE, pharm. co. researcher; b. Los Angeles, Dec. 8, 1952; d. Thomas Henry and Evelyn (Schmidt) M.; B.A., La Verne Coll., 1974, M.A. in Edn., 1976; m. Michael Corbett Ferry, June 28, 1981; children—James, Sara (twins). Tchr., Corona-Norco Sch. Dist., Corona, Calif., 1974-76; mktg. rep. Dun. & Bradstreet, Santa Ana, Calif., 1976-77; pharm. rep. Sandoz Pharms., East Hanover, N.J., 1977-78; hosp. research assoc. Miles Pharms., Dominguez Hills, Calif., 1978—, sales trainer, 1981—. Zonta Club scholar, 1970-71; La Verne Coll. scholar, 1970-71. Mem. Ins. Women of Inland Empire, Los Angeles County Pharm. Reps. Assn. Democrat.

MORGANROTH, JANICE MARILYN COHN, lawyer; b. Detroit, Mar. 14, 1940; d. Sidney Lewis and Beverly Monica (Shapero) Cohn; student U. Colo., 1958-59; B.A., Mich. State U., 1961; J.D., Wayne State U., 1964; m. Fred Morganroth, June 23, 1963; children—Greg Scot, Candi Lyn, Erik Jon. Admitted to Mich. bar, 1964; partner firm Morganroth & Morganroth, Southfield, 1963—. Coordinator community edn. Birmingham Bd. Edn., 1977-78; chmn. women's com. Met. Opera, 1975-79, co-chmn. advt., 1976-77, chmn., 1977-78; leader Jr. Gt. Books; community chmn. United Found.; resource rep. Oakland County Cultural Arts Council. Mem. State Bar Mich., World Wide Sportsman Club, Music Study Club, 99ers Woman's Pilots Assn., Nat. Council Jewish Women, Chaine des Routisseurs, Founders Soc. Detroit Inst. Arts, Aircraft Owners and Pilots Assn., Mich. Poetry Soc., Mich. Poetry Resource Center, Alpha Epsilon Phi. Clubs: Detroit Tennis, Danish-Am., Lady Adms., Braniff Council, Pan Am. Contbr. articles and poetry to mags. Home: 30920 Woodcrest Ct Franklin MI 48025 Office: 4000 Town Center Suite 555 Southfield MI 48075

MORGENSTERN, ELLEN ANN, communications exec.; b. Bklyn., Oct. 7, 1949; d. Irving and Evelyn (Goodman) Morgenstern; B.A., SUNY, 1971; postgrad. George Washington U., 1971-72. Legis. aide Congresswoman Bella S. Abzug, 1971-72; legis. asst. Congressman James C. Corman, 1974-78; pub., editor Potomac Jour., Washington, 1978-79; dir. public relations AAUP, Washington, 1979-81; dir. communications Alliance to Save Energy, Washington, 1981—. Founder, Capitol Hill Women's Polit. Caucus, 1971; bd. dirs. Nat. Council to Control Hand Guns, 1974-76, Ams. for Dem. Action, 1975-77; mem. Arlington Complete Count Com., 1980 Mem. Washington Women in Public Relations. Democrat. Jewish. Home: 4623 S 31st Rd Arlington VA 22206 Office: 1925 K St Washington DC 20006

MORGENTHAU, JOAN ELIZABETH, physician; b. N.Y.C., Oct. 9, 1923; d. Henry and Elinor M.; A.B., Vassar Coll., 1945; M.D., Columbia U., 1949; m. Fred Hirschhorn, Jr., Oct. 6, 1957; children—Elizabeth, Joan, Elinor. Intern, Maimonides Hosp., Bklyn., 1949-50; resident N.Y. Hosp., 1950-54; dir. adolescent health center Mt. Sinai Hosp., N.Y.C., 1968-81, prof. clin. pediatrics, 1975-81; dir. health service Smith Coll., Northampton, Mass., 1981—, adj. prof. psychology, 1981—; professorial lectr. Mt. Sinai Sch. Medicine, City U. N.Y., 1982—. Trustee, Henry J. Kaiser Family Found., Vassar Coll. Mem. Am. Acad. Pediatrics, Am. Public Health Assn., Soc. Adolescent Medicine, Ambulatory Pediatrics Assn. Club: Cosmopolitan (N.Y.C.). Contbr. articles to profl. jours. Home: 55 Binney Ln Old Greenwich CT 06870 Office: 69 Paradise Rd Northampton MA 01060

MORIARTY, FLORENCE JARMAN (MRS. VINCENT P. MORIARTY), editor; b. Flushing, N.Y.; d. George W. L. and Sarah (Tuite) Jarman; A.B., N.Y. U., 1936; m. Robert Austin Schetty, Jan. 22, 1938 (div.); m. 2d, Vincent Paul Moriarty, June 16, 1961. Coll. textbook editor Prentice-Hall, Inc., N.Y.C., 1936-38; schoolbook editor Truquois Pub. Co., Syracuse, N.Y., 1938-40; asso. editor Modern Romances, Dell Pub. Co., 1940-43; mng. editor Personal Romances, Ideal Pub. Corp., 1943-48, editor Intimate Romances, 1948-53; editor, originator of title True Life Stories, Pines Publs., 1953-54; editor-in-chief True Confessions, N.Y.C., 1954—. Mem. Theta Upsilon. Club: N.Y. University (bd. govs.). Office: 215 Lexington Ave New York NY 10017 *

MORISSEAU, DOLORES SCHANNÉ, psychologist, govt. agy. ofcl.; b. N.Y.C., Dec. 1, 1936; d. Lawrence Charles and Anne Lucy (Jelincic) Schanné; B.A. summa cum laude, George Mason U., 1978, M.A. in Psychology, 1980; M. Kenneth Clay Morisseau, May 3, 1958; children—Anne Lavita, Kenneth Clay. Stewardship editor Luth. Woman's Quarterly, St. Louis, 1969-75; mng. editor patient newsletter Georgetown U. Center for Continuing Health Edn., Washington, 1975, faculty moderator, 1974-75; instr. activated patient skills Nat. Public Broadcasting, 1975; fed. intern, personnel psychologist, U.S. Office Personnel Mgmt., Washington, 1979; lectr. psychology No. Va. Community Coll., Loudoun, 1981—; tng. and assessment specialist U.S. Nuclear Regulatory Commn., Washington, 1981—. Mem. Fairfax (Va.) Hosp., Aux., 1969-78, coordinator library service for patients, publicity dir., 1974-76. Mem. Am. Psychol. Assn., Human Factors Soc., AAUW, Alpha Chi, Psi Chi. Contbr. articles in field to profl. jours. Home: 11800 Breton Ct 32B Reston VA 22091

MORISSETTE, DOROTHY ELLEN, social worker; b. Portland, Oreg., Apr. 25, 1916; d. William Henry and Eva Mable (Morriss) Adams; B.A., U. Oreg., 1938; B.S., Simmons Coll., 1939, M.S.W., 1940; m. Russell A. Morissette, Aug. 4, 1943; children—Claire, Elizabeth, Russell A. Med. social work cons. Div. Child Health, Maine Dept. Human Services, 1962-66; founder, part-time social worker Lewiston-Auburn Occupational Tng. Center, 1964-65; organizer, dir. social work dept. St. Mary's Gen. Hosp., Lewiston, Maine, 1966—. Founder, pres. Day Care Center for Handicapped Children, 1966-69; co-pres. Occupational Tng. Center, 1973-75; bd. dirs. Am. Cancer Soc., 1976-78, ARC, 1979-81. Mem. Nat. Assn. Social Workers, Acad. Cert. Social Workers, Soc. Hosp. Social Work Dirs. (organizer, pres. Maine chpt. 1978-80), Woman's Aux. Androscoggin Med. Soc., Woman's Aux. AMA, Am. Hosp. Assn. Republican. Baptist. Home: 69 Western Promenade Auburn ME 04210 Office: St Mary's Gen Hosp Golden St Lewiston ME 04210

MORLEY, BERDA FISHER, ethnic clothing cons.; b. Phila., Dec. 22, 1933; d. Israel and Sarah (Norvick) Fisher; student Temple U., 1951-55; m. Harry J. Morley, Jr., July 26, 1966; 1 son, Ivan Charles. Social caseworker Phila. Dept. Welfare, 1958-60; self-employed designer, mfr. and sales fashion mdse., 1960-71; ethnic fashion cons. Ethnic Fashions Cons. & Sales, Betty Bottom Showroom, Los Angeles, 1973—; cons. to designers and importers. Active Alliance for Survival, Union Concerned Scientists, Cousteau Soc., Am. Friends Service Com. Mem. Fashion Alliance Los Angeles. Jewish. Office: 110 E 9th St Los Angeles CA 90015

MORLEY, PATRICIA ANN, educator and writer; b. Toronto, Ont., Can., May 25, 1929; d. Frederick Charles and Mabel Olive (Winsland) Marlow; B.A. with honors, Trinity Coll., U. Toronto, 1951; M.A., Carleton U., 1967; Ph.D. in English, U. Ottawa, 1970; m. Lawrence W. Morley, June 17, 1950; children—Lawrence, Patricia, Christopher, David. Freelance writer, 1970; lectr. U. Ottawa, 1971-72; asst. prof. Sir George William U., 1972-75; asso. prof. Concordia U., 1975-80, prof. English and Canadian Studies, 1980—. Grantee in field. Mem. Assn. Canadian Univ. Tchrs. English, The Writers Union of Can., MLA, Assn. Canadian and Que. Literatures, Commonwealth Lang. and Lit. Studies, PEN. Anglican. Author: The Mystery of Unity: Theme and Technique in the Novels of Patrick White, 1972; The Immoral Moralists, 1972; Robertson Davies, 1976; The Comedians, 1977; Morley Callaghan, 1978; Margaret Laurence, 1981; contbr. books revs. to newspapers, articles to acad. jours. Home: PO Box 137 Manotick ON K0A 2N0 Canada Office: Sir George Williams Campus Concordia U 1455 de Maisonneuve Blvd W Montreal PQ H3G 1M8 Canada

MORNER, AIMEE LACOMBE, writer; b. N.Y.C.; d. Gustav Hampus and Florence (Lacombe) M.; B.A., Mt. Holyoke Coll., 1966. Ins. underwriter Chubb & Son, N.Y.C., 1966-67; asst. fin. analyst Smith, Barney & Co., N.Y.C., 1968-71; writer, asso. editor Fortune Mag., N.Y.C., 1971—. Republican. Episcopalian. Club: Rockaway Hunting (Cedarhurst, N.Y.). Office: Time & Life Bldg Rockefeller Center New York NY 10020

MORPHOS, DIANE BELOGIANIS (MRS. PANOS PAUL MORPHOS), civic worker; b. Chgo.; d. Demetrios and Alice (Rousseas) Belogianis; B.S., U. Chgo., 1937, M.A., 1938; m. Panos Paul Morphos, Dec. 11, 1948; children—Evangeline, Paul. Mem. faculty U. Chgo. Orthogenic Sch., 1938-45, U. Chgo. Remedial Reading Clinics, 1945-48; vis. lectr. Tulane U., 1947. Bd. dirs. S.E. La. council Girl Scouts U.S.A., New Orleans, 1959-65, v.p., 1965-68, pres., 1968—; bd. dirs. AAUW, New Orleans, 1969, v.p., 1970-75, pres., 1975-80; Republican candidate for La. 2d Congl. Dist., 1974. Mem. Athenee Louisianais, France-Amerique. Mem. Greek Orthodox Ch. Home: 1404 Audubon St New Orleans LA 70118

MORRILL, JOYCE MARIE, social worker, cons. firm exec.; b. Rockland, Maine, Dec. 27, 1939; d. Henry Higgins and Julia Ellen (Philbrook) Thompson; B.A., U. Hartford, 1964; M.S.W., Hunter Coll., 1972; m. Edward Morrill, Sept. 7, 1972; 1 son, Gregory Hodgman. Co-host Today in Conn. Program, Sta. WHNB-TV, Hartford, 1964-65; clin. social worker, field instr. Rehab. Inst., N.Y., 1972-78; dir., founder Wellness Services, Jamaica Estates, N.Y., 1979—, Stress Mgrs., 1981—; mem. faculty New Sch. for Social Research, Coll. of New Rochelle. Mem. Nat. Assn. Social Workers, N.Y. Assn. Women Bus. Owners (fin. com.). Home and Office: 181-38 Midland Pkwy Jamaica Estates NY 11432

MORRILL, NANCY PORTER, mgmt. cons. co. exec.; g. Natick, Mass., Apr. 14, 1939; d. Rupert Felch and Vera (Richardson) Porter; A.B. in Polit. Sci., Bryn Mawr (Pa.) Coll., 1960; m. William A. Morrill. Sr. report specialist McKinsey & Co., San Francisco, 1960-61; personal sec. to Hon. Edward W. Brooke, Mass. State Atty. Gen.'s Office and U.S. Senate, 1962-69; personal asst. to chmn. The Diebold Group, N.Y.C., 1969-70; staff asst. Am. Revolution Bicentennial Commn., Washington, 1970-71; Washington rep. Girl Scouts U.S.A., 1971-73; spl. asst. to Sec. U.S. Dept. HEW, Washington, 1973-77; owner, pres. New Perceptions, Newtown, Pa., 1977—. Nat. bd. dirs. Girl Scouts U.S.A., 1974-78, also chmn. evaluation and planning com.; bd. dirs., 2d v.p. Friends of the Nat. Zoo, Washington, 1972-78, chmn. vol. and edn. services com.; nat. bd. dirs., v.p. Epilepsy Found. Am.; del. Women's Nat. Conf., Houston, 1977, White House Conf. on Family, Balt., 1980; bd. dirs. Planned Parenthood Bucks County (Pa.), 1981—; trustee Wilson Coll., Chambersburg, Pa., 1981—; vice chmn. citizens adv. com. Bucks County Community Devel. Bd., 1980—; mem. subcom. on human service issues, govt. relations com. United Way, 1981—. Mem. AAUW, World Assn. Girl Guides and Girl Scouts (del. Internat. Women's Yr. conf. Mexico City 1975). Republican. Club: Bryn Mawr (Phila.). Home and office: PO Box 536 Newtown PA 18940

MORRIN, VIRGINIA WHITE, educator; b. Escondido, Calif., May 16, 1913; d. Harry Parmalee and Ethel Norine (Nutting) Rising; B.S., Oreg. State Coll., 1952; M.Ed., Oreg. State U., 1957; m. Raymond Bennett White, 1933 (dec. 1953); children—Katherine Anne, Marjorie Virginia, William Raymond; m. 2d, Laurence Morrin, 1959 (dec. 1972). Social caseworker Los Angeles County, Los Angeles, 1934-40, 61-64; acctg. clk. War Dept., Ft. MacArthur, Calif., 1940-42; prin. clk. USAAF, Las Vegas, Nev., 1942-44; high sch. tchr., North Bend-Coos Bay, Oreg., 1952-56, Mojave, Calif., 1957-60; instr. Antelope Valley Coll., Lancaster, Calif., 1961-73; ret., 1974. Treas., Humane Soc. Antelope Valley, Inc., 1968—. Mem. Nat. Aeros. Assn. Office: PO Box 570 Lancaster CA 93534

MORRIS, CAROLINE JANE MCMASTERS STEWART (MRS. FRANCIS J. MORRIS), librarian; b. Ridley Park, Pa., Sept. 14, 1923; d. James Sterrett and Mildred M. (McCloskey) Stewart; B.S. in Commerce, Drexel U., 1950, M.S. in L.S., 1964; m. Francis Joseph Morris, Feb. 3, 1950; 1 son, Edward James Stewart. Adminstrv. trainee John Wanamaker, Phila., 1946-50; serials librarian Penn Morton Colls., Chester, Pa., 1964-65; dir. libraries Pa. Hosp., Phila., 1965-75, librarian, archivist, 1975—; instr., leader several library workshops Am. Hosp. Assn., Cath. Hosp. Assn., Med. Library Assn. Mem. Emergency Aid Pa., 1960—. Served with WAVES, 1943-45. Mem. Nat. Med. Library Assn. (sect. chmn. 1970 pres. local chpt. 1978—), ALA, Spl. Libraries Assn., Med. (local chpt. pres. 1969-70), Prospect Park library assns., AAUP, D. of R. (pres. Pa. 1947—), Victorian Soc. Am., Soc. Am. Archivists, Manuscript Soc., Delaware County Hist. Soc., Historic Delaware County, Valley Forge Hist. Soc., Geneol. Soc. Pa., Hort. Soc. Pa., Dames Loyal Legion (state pres. 1966-68), Phila. Mus. Art, Am. Assn. Records Mgrs., Am. Soc. Profl. and Exec. Women, Inst. Contemporary Art, Drexel U. Alumni Assn. (pres. 1969-71). Club: Art Alliance (Phila). Home: 555 13th Ave Prospect Park PA 19076 Office: 8th and Spruce Sts Philadelphia PA 19107

MORRIS, CELITA LAMAR, educator; b. Miami, Fla., Aug. 21, 1939; d. Carlos Pérez and Celia María (Fernández) Lamar; B.A., U. Miami, 1960, M.A., 1967, M.B.A., 1983; postgrad. (Woodrow Wilson fellow), U. Calif., Berkeley, 1960-61; m. James H. Morris, June 4, 1960; children—Linda Lamar, Kathleen Elizabeth. Instr. French, U. Miami, 1966-73, asst. prof., 1973—; coordinator Fla. Task Force on Fgn. and Bibl. Langs., 1972-82. Mem. policy bd. Fla. Statewide Course Numbering System. Mem. AAUP (pres. Fla. conf. 1974-75, 77-79), MLA, South Atlantic MLA, Am. Assn. Tchrs. French, Am. Assn. Tchrs. Spanish and Portuguese, Asociación de Literatura Femenina Hispánica, ACLU, Mus. Sci., NOW, Viscayans. Democrat. Roman Catholic. Contbr. articles to profl. jours. Home: 520 Castania Ave Coral Gables FL 33146 Office: Dept Fgn Langs POB 248093 U Miami Coral Gables FL 33124

MORRIS, CHRISTINE DEHARTE, med. lab. exec.; b. Danville, Va., Apr. 30, 1929; d. John Isam and Sarah Ellen (Burnette) DeHarte; B.S., Marywood Coll., Scranton, Pa., 1983; m. Charles Fillmore Morris, Nov. 26, 1949; children—Stephanie Gail, Dianne Elise. With Kenrose Mfg. Co., Roanoke, Va., 1947-48, William H. Branch & Co., Richmond, Va., 1948-49; acct. Arlington County (Va.) public schs., 1950-60, fed. fiscal clk., 1968-69; adminstrv. asst., office mgr. Metal Products, Inc., Cheverly, Md., 1964-66, Pell Mar Properties, Inc., Springfield, Va., 1966-68; acctg. office mgr. Log-Etronics, Inc., Springfield, 1969-79; supr. ins. and collections Am. Med. Labs., Inc., Fairfax, Va., 1979—; cons. in field. Mem. Selective Service Bd. 38, Vernon-Lee dist. Fairfax County, 1981—; receptionist Goodwin House, 1968—. Notary pub. Mem. Nat. Fed. Bus. and Profl. Women's Club, Nat. Assn. Female Execs., Am. Bus. Women's Assn. (chpt. pres.; Woman of Year award 1979). Methodist. Home: 5000 Talbois Pl Alexandria VA 22310 Office: 11091 Main St Fairfax VA 22030

MORRIS, EARLEEN, nurse; b. Jackson, Tenn., Oct. 31, 1932; d. Raymond N. and Lucille (Hurt) Golden; B.S. in Nursing, St. Louis U., 1958; m. Leonard Morris, Jan. 31, 1959; 1 son, Maurice. Mem. nursing staff St. Louis State Hosp. Complex, 1958—, asst. dir. nursing, 1977-80, dir. nursing, 1981—. Mem. Am. Hosp. Assn., Mo. Nurses Assn. Office: 5400 Arsenal St St Louis MO 63139

MORRIS, EDNA BROKAW, civic worker; b. N.Y.C., Nov. 13, 1908; d. Howard Crosby and Edna (Loew) Brokaw; m. John A. Morris, May 27, 1942; children—John A., Alfred H. Vice pres. Girl Scout Council Greater N.Y., 1970—, chmn. Gold Book com. and mem. exec. com., pres. Council Mus. of City of N.Y. Mem. Huguenot Soc., Colonial

Dames Am. Republican. Episcopalian. Club: Colony. Home: 4 E 72d St New York NY 10021

MORRIS, HELEN WINTER, state govt. ofcl.; b. Newark, Mar. 25, 1926; d. Georg Richard and Helene Wilhelmina (Wittke) Winter; student Centralia Community Coll., Olympia, Wash.; m. Earl Morris, Jr., Aug. 15, 1947; children—Earl George, Kathy Lynn. Dental asst., 1943-44; billing clk., 1944-47; with State of Wash., Olympia, 1965—, supr. corps. Office Sec. State, 1969—. Mem. Nat. Assn. Corp. Adminstrs. (sec.). Lutheran. Office: care Office Sec State Legis Bldg Olympia WA 98504

MORRIS, JUNE ELLEN, publishing co. exec.; b. Louisville, Sept. 26, 1934; d. E. Louis and Evelyn (Gilbert) M.; B.S., U. Louisville, 1956, M.A., 1960. Market research analysist Reynolds Metals Co., Louisville, 1957-58; statistician, unit supr. U.S. Dept. Commerce, Jeffersonville, Ind., 1958-59; various positions Dept. Ednl. Research, Am. Printing House for the Blind, Louisville, 1959-77, dir., 1977—. Mem. Am. Assn. of Workers for Blind, Am. Ednl. Research Assn., Am. Psychol. Assn., Assn. for Edn. of Visually Handicapped, Council for Exceptional Children. Republican. Baptist. Clubs: Collie Club of Am., Louisville Kennel, Collie Club of Ky. Contbr. numerous ednl. research articles to profl. publs. Home: 2203 Edgehill Rd Louisville KY 40205 Office: PO Box 6085 Louisville KY 40206

MORRIS, KAY WETZEL, psychotherapist; social worker; b. Salt Lake City, July 9, 1939; d. Nevin Frank Wetzel and Jane Rawlins Deakin; student U. Utah, 1957-59; B.A. with highest honors, U. Calif., San Jose, 1961; M.S.W. summa cum laude, Ohio State U., 1963; m. Richard L. Morris, July 9, 1966 (div.); 1 son, Michael David; m. 2d, John Chiplinsky, Aug. 14, 1980; stepsons—Adam, Ivan. Psychiat. social worker children's service Napa (Calif.) State Hosp., 1963-66; pupil personnel dir. Trinity County Supt. of Schs. Office, 1967-70; founder, social worker Trinity County Mental Health Services, 1970-76; pvt. practice psychotherapy and consultation, Redding, Calif., 1967—, Aptos, Calif., 1982—; dir. Victor Residential Center, Inc. (Stepping Stones), 1976-80, now cons. to bd. dirs.; rural services com., cons. children's service com. Calif. Conf. Local Mental Health Dirs., 1972-77; mental health cons. plan devel. com. No. Calif. Health Systems Agy., 1976-81; cons. Task Force for Handicapped Children, Shasta County Supt. of Schs., 1971-74; cons. to Meml. Hosp., Redding, 1980—; Seattle Childrens Home, 1982—; lectr. Women's Career Network, Seattle, 1981; developer Trinity County Mental Health Service, 1970; mem. com. on integration and coordination services to children and families Calif. Dept. Mental Health. Trustee, Redding Elem. Sch. Dist., 1977-82; vol. KIXE Public Broadcasting System; Trinity County chmn. McGovern for Pres., 1972; v.p. Redding Elem. Sch. Bd., 1979-81; bd. mem. Group Home Assn. Calif. NIMH fellow, 1961-62. Mem. Nat. Assn. Social Workers, AAUW, Psi Chi. Office: 2301 Park Marina Dr Suite 21 Redding CA 96001

MORRIS, LILLIE PEARL, real estate broker, civic worker; b. Little Elm, Tex., June 2, 1924; d. Herschel Lenora and Belva Bettie (Byrom) Walker; ed. Denton (Tex.) Public Schs., real estate course Tex. A&M U.; m. Alvie Edwin Morris, Oct. 15, 1949; 1 dau., Nikki Pearl. Jr. acct. Sears Roebuck & Co., Dallas, 1941-42; mem. acctg. dept. Equitable Life Assurance Soc. U.S., Dallas, 1942-44, Firestone Tire & Rubber Co., Dallas, 1944-46; bookkeeper, sec. Darvers Babyland and Children's Shop, Dallas, 1946-56; exec. sec., bookkeeper Chapman Constrn. Co., Inc., Carrollton, Tex., 1957-73; owner, operator L. Pearl Morris Real Estate, Frisco, Tex., 1973—. Former drive chmn. ARC; pres. Frisco PTA, 1954-56; sec. Dist. II, Tex. Congress Parents and Tchrs., 1962-64, life mem., 1956; pres. Frisco C. of C., 1978-79, bd. dirs., 1977-80. Mem. Am. Assn. Ret. Persons, Tex. PTA. Democrat. Mem. Ch. of Christ. Home: PO Box 403 North County Rd Route 2 Frisco TX 75034 Office: 1213 E Main St Frisco TX 75034

MORRIS, LINDA JOYCE, educator; b. Meeker, Okla., Nov. 28, 1949; d. Herschel Eugene and Grace (Wakole) Wallace; B.S. in Bus. Edn., U. Okla., 1971, M.S., 1973; postgrad. in ednl. adminstrn. U. Idaho, 1979-83; M.B.A., Central State U., Edmond, Okla., 1983; m. John Stephen Morris, Sept. 1, 1973. Instr. bus. LSI Draughon's Sch. Bus., Oklahoma City, 1971-72; coordinator Title IV Project, Coll. Edn., U. Idaho, 1973, coordinator BIA math. project, 1976-78, instr. Learning Skills Center, 1976—; instr. math. high sch. equivalency program Wash. State U., Pullman, 1973-74; cons. ednl. projects for minorities and women. Bur. Indian Affairs grantee, 1976-78; U. Idaho Faculty Devel. Program grantee, 1982-83. Mem. Idaho Edn. Assn., Nat. Indian Edn. Assn., Nat. Indian Counsellors Assn., Phi Delta Kappa. Home: 1402 Hall Rd Viola ID 83872 Office: Coll of Business U Idaho Moscow ID 83843

MORRIS, LUMMIE DENE, mgmt. co. exec.; b. Elbert, Tex., Sept. 4, 1931; d. Conley Clarence and Lora Alma (Fulton) Smith; student St. Marys U., 1968-70; m. Edwin J. Morris, Sept. 15, 1955 (dec.); children—Robin Dee, Tracy Lee Morris Hair. Instr. interior design St. Marys U., San Antonio, evenings, 1970-71; asst. dir. Faye Neri Modeling Studio, San Antonio, 1970-72; interior designer, San Antonio, 1972-77; v.p. Communications Services, Inc., San Antonio, 1977-79; gen. mgr. Nat. Electric Corp., San Antonio, 1979—; mgr. trucking div. Agribusiness Services, Inc., San Antonio, 1981—; lectr. San Antonio high schs. Coordinator family services program USAF, Zweibruecken, W. Ger., 1968. Mem. Internat. Guild Accredited Interior Designers, Beta Sigma Phi. Republican. Mem. Ch. of Christ. Home: 12200 Montgomery NE Apt F-101 Albuquerque NM 87111 Office: 11411 Rendezvous San Antonio TX 78216

MORRIS, MARGUERITE MARY, educator, psychotherapist; b. N.Y.C., Sept. 24, 1947; d. William L. and Elizabeth Jane (Boyle) M.; B.A., Fairleigh Dickenson U., 1969; M.A., Montclair State Coll., 1976. Tchr., Cresskill (N.J.) High Sch., 1970—; staff psychotherapist N.J. Center for Counseling and Psychotherapy, Fort Lee, 1976—. Mem. Am. Psychol. Assn., Am. Personnel and Guidance Assn., N.J. Edn. Assn., NEA, Bergen County Edn. Assn. Roman Catholic. Office: Cresskill High Sch Lincoln Dr Cresskill NJ 07626 and North Jersey Center For Counseling And Psychotherapy 444 Main St Fort Lee NJ 07024

MORRIS, MARIE B., legislative atty.; b. Arlington, Va.; d. Peter M. and Emma Lou (Hurst) Bosco; A.B., Coll. William and Mary, 1973; J.D., Georgetown U., 1976; LL.M., George Washington U.; m. Roy R. Morris, Aug. 18, 1973. Admitted to Va. bar, 1976, D.C. bar, 1977, Supreme Ct. bar, 1980; legis. atty. Am. Law div. Congressional Research Service, Library of Congress, Washington. Mem. ABA, Fed. Bar Assn. Office: Rm 230 James Madison Bldg 101 Independence Ave SE Washington DC 20559 *

MORRIS, MARILYN ANN, psychiat. social worker; b. Chgo., Feb. 18, 1945; d. Jack Sidney and Melba Lea (Hakan) M.; B.A. in Sociology, Roosevelt U., Chgo., 1967; M.A. in Social Work, U. Chgo., 1969. Psychotherapist, Ill. Dept. Mental Health, Chgo., 1968-74; coordinator intake Roscoe House, Chgo., 1974-75; psychiat. social worker Chgo.-Read Mental Health Center, 1976—; pvt. practice psychotherapy, Chgo., 1973—; field work instr. Jane Addams Sch. Social Work, 1970-74. Certified social worker, Ill. Mem. Nat. Assn. Social Workers, Acad. Certified Social Workers. Home: 1240 Park Ave W Highland Park IL 60035

MORRIS, MARJORIE HALE, retail exec., appraiser; b. Chattanooga, Aug. 4, 1940; d. Laurie Everett and Marjorie (Hunt) Hale; student El Camino Jr. Coll., 1958-60; 1 dau., 2 sons. Stewardess, Am. Airlines, 1960-62, mem. staff nat. advt. and publicity, 1961-62; mgr. Viking Ski Shop, Pacific Palisades, Calif., 1963-64; promotional adviser East Sierra Land Devel. Co., 1963-66; Pepsi Cola Corp. rep. to Republican Nat. Conv., 1964; co-owner, mgr. Ready Room Restaurant, Los Angeles, 1967; architects adv., restaurant devel. and design, Honolulu, Dallas, Atlanta, Los Angeles, 1967-73; mgr., buyer Great Things, Honolulu, 1972-74; mgr. Braille Inst. Thrift Shop, Los Angeles, 1975-78, dir., 1978—, devel. officer, 1980—; partner Arrasmith & Morris, appraisers; freelance writer and photographer, 1974—; designer floats Pacific Palisades Parade, 1965, TransPac Race Com., Honolulu, 1972. Team mother Pacific Palisades Little League, 1974-76. Mem. Beverly Hills C. of C. (Outstanding Service to Community awards 1976, 77). Originator, dir. Christmas Tree Project, Beverly Hills; cover editor Calif. Yacht Club Mag., 1976; founder, editor Waterlines, newsletter of Flotilla 12-7, USCG Aux., 1979—. Mem. Am. Soc. Appraisers. Home: PO Box 71 Pacific Palisades CA 90272 Office: 125 N Western Ave Los Angeles CA 90004

MORRIS, MARY LOUISE, student services adminstr.; b. Birmingham, Ala., Oct. 14, 1947; d. Martin Azelle and Mary Elizabeth (Doolittle) M.; B.S., U. Montevallo, 1969, M.Ed., 1972; student U. Ida., 1979-82. Tchr., Birmingham (Ala.) High Sch. System, 1969-71; program dir. Birmingham Girls Club, 1971-72; dispatcher, officer in tng., patrol officer Boise (Idaho) Police Dept., 1973-77; prodn. line worker Skyline Corp., Boise, 1978; dir. spl. services U. Idaho, 1980—. Mem. N.W. Women's Studies Assn., N.W. Assn. Spl. Programs (parliamentarian), Nat. Assn. Acad. Affairs Adminstrs. Home: RFD 01 Box 21 Desmet ID 83824 Office: U Ida FOCW 301 Moscow ID 83843

MORRIS, PATRICIA KUCZYNSKI, social worker; b. Binghamton, N.Y., Sept. 9, 1949; d. Anthony Joseph and Helen June (Hudak) Kuczynski; B.S. in Law Enforcement and Corrections, Pa. State U., 1971; M.S.W., Syracuse (N.Y.) U., 1976; m. Jeffrey K. Morris, Nov. 6, 1971; 1 dau., Megan K. Child care worker Susquehanna Valley Home, Binghamton, N.Y., 1971; houseparent N.Y. State Div. Youth, 1972-74; vol. family counselor, youth assist coordinator, 1974-75; intake supr., sr. social worker Elmcrest (N.Y.) Children's Center, 1976-77; rep. N.Y. State Bd. Social Welfare, 1977; asst. dir. Auburn Spl. Residential Center, N.Y. State Div. Youth, 1977-81, dir., 1981—; field instr. Syracuse U. Sch. Social Work; foster parent N.Y. State Div. Youth. Mem. Acad. Cert. Social Workers, Nat. Assn. Social Workers. Home: 1376 Route 49 North Bay NY 13123 Office: RD 4 Pine Ridge Rd Auburn NY 13021

MORRIS, RITA SOLOW, state ofcl.; b. Newark, Apr. 10, 1922; d. Alexander Saul and Sarah (Koch) S.; diploma, Sinai Hosp. Sch. Nursing, Balt., 1947; B.S., U. Md., 1958; M.S. in Nursing Edn., Ind. U., 1964; m. Vernon M. Morris. Head nurse Sinai Hosp., Balt., 1947-53; instr. Franklin Sq. Hosp. Sch. Nursing, Balt., 1953-58, Luth. Hosp. Sch. Nursing, Balt., 1958-63; instr., asst. prof. nursing Georgetown U., 1964-68; asso. exec. dir. Md. Bd. Examiners Nurses, Balt., 1968-74, exec. dir., 1975-79; commr. for nursing Md. Nurses Assn. 1972-79; mem. adv. bd. Montgomery Coll. Program Nursing, Frederick Community Coll. Program Nursing, until 1979, Dept. Health and Mental Hygiene Sch. Practical Nursing, until 1976; mem. adv. bd. Catonsville Community Coll. Program Nursing, 1977-79; mem. Nurses Cadre for Office of Mayor of Balt., 1977-79. Recipient certificate of high scholastic achievement Ind. U., 1964. Mem. Am. Nurses Assn., Nat. Council State Bds. Nursing, Nat. League for Nursing, Pi Lambda Theta, Sigma Theta Tau, Delta Phi Epsilon. Democrat. Jewish. Home: 8380 W Baker Ave Lakewood CO 80227

MORRIS, RUTH FALLS (MRS. VESTAL L. MORRIS), educator; b. Gastonia, N.C., Jan. 23, 1913; d. Charles Newton and Bryte (Stroupe) Falls; B.S., East Carolina Coll., 1951; M.A., Tchrs. Coll. Columbia U., 1958; M.S., LaVerne Coll., 1975; m. Vestal L. Morris, Oct. 22, 1943. Tchr. Lucia Sch., Mt. Holly, N.C., 1935-40; typist U.S. Army Engr. Corps., Am. Consulate, Colon, Panama, 1943-45; tchr. Gatun Sch., Gatun, C.Z., 1946-54; tchr. primary, intermediate educable mentally handicapped children Margarita Sch., Margarita, C.Z., 1958-66; staff mem. Ft. Gulick Elem. Sch., 1967-70, tchr. acad. enhancement, 1970-72; ednl. prescriptionist, vis. tchr. spl. classes Atlantic and Pacific dists. Panama Canal Schs. Div., 1973-75; owner-dir. Morris Tutoring Service, 1975—. Patron Tallahassee Symphony Orch., Tallahassee Little Theatre. Named Outstanding Tchr. Panama Canal Zone Schs. Div., 1967, 73, 75; recipient Outstanding Service cert. Spl. Edn. Assn. C.Z., 1975. Mem. AAUW, Atlantic Tchrs. Guild (v.p. 1952, treas. 1953), Am. Assn. Mental Deficiency, Caribbean Assn. Edn. Young Children, C.Z. Med. Wives Soc., Council Exceptional Children, Internat. Platform Assn., Assn. Exceptional Children, Internat. Reading Assn. (v.p. 1975-76, pres. 1976-77), Nat. League Am. Pen Women (Caribbean br. at Panama Canal), Isthmian Anthropology Soc., Sierra Club, Common Cause, NOW, Federally Employed Women (Atlantic area coordinator), Friends of Library, Lemoyne Art Found., Tallahassee Jr. Mus., Beta Sigma Phi (life mem., v.p. 1956), Phi Delta Kappa (Isthmus of Panama chpt.). Presbyterian. Clubs: Cristobal Woman's (life), Caribbean Coll. (life mem., charter pres. 1952), Soroptimist (pres. 1960, vice gov. Costa Rica and Panama 1965-69) (Colon, Panama); Inter-Am. Women's (life mem., charter, Colon unit); Republican Women's of Leon County. Contbr. articles to profl. jours. Home: 2419 Castletowers Ln Tallahassee FL 32301

MORRIS, SUSAN ELIZABETH, systems specialist; b. Louisville, Jan. 10, 1952; d. Adam and Agnes Bertha (Huber) M.; B.S. in Commerce, U. Louisville, 1978. Paralegal law firm Wyatt, Grafton & Sloss, Louisville, 1973-79; systems installer HBO & Co., Inc., San Mateo, Calif., 1979-81; systems specialist Whittaker Medicus, Evanston, Ill., 1981—. Active Third Century, Louisville, 1978-79. Mem. Bus. and Profl. Women's Assn., NOW, Ky. Hist. Soc., U. Louisville Alumni Assn., U.S. Capital Hist. Soc., Greenpeace, Internat. Platform Assn. Democrat. Roman Catholic. Clubs: Filson, Louisville Preservation Alliance. Home: 357 Half Moon Ln Apt 4 Daly City CA 94015 Office: 990 Grove St Evanston IL 60201

MORRIS, SUSAN MARIE, govt. ofcl.; b. Newark, Sept. 3, 1944; d. Michael and Helen Krawchuk; A.A., Middlesex County Coll., 1972; B.A., Rutgers Coll., 1974; postgrad. New Sch. for Social Research, N.Y.C., 1977—. Adminstr. mgmt. devel. CETA, New Brunswick, N.J., 1974-77; pres. Pvt. Employment Agy., Metuchen, N.J., 1977-78; asst. to pres. Franco Mfg. Co., N.Y.C., 1978-79; pres. Susan Products, New Brunswick, N.J., 1979—; dep. regional dir. U.S. Dept. Interior World Trade Center, N.Y.C., 1979—. Mem. Nat. Assn. Female Execs., Central N.J. Profl. Women's Network, NOW. Club: World Trade Center. Office: 6 World Trade Center Suite 612 New York NY 10048

MORRIS, SUSAN MCDONALD, event planning service exec.; b. Orange, Calif., Mar. 1, 1946; d. Coalson Clyde and Jesse Jean (Crawford) Morris; B.A., U. So. Calif., 1968. Press sec. Orozco for Congress, 1968; coordinator field services U. So. Calif., Los Angeles, 1969; dir. donor relations U. So. Calif., 1971, dir. event planning from 1976; pres., owner Susan McDonald Morris & Assocs., Inc., Los Angeles, 1981—. Mem. Nat. Assn. Female Execs., Los Angeles World Affairs Council. Republican. Presbyterian. Clubs: Los Angeles Athletic, Town Hall of Calif. Office: PO Box 54123 Los Angeles CA 90054

MORRIS, VIOLA MCKAY, retail sales exec.; b. Baytown, Tex.; d. Larkin and Laura Minnie (Sowell) McKay; B.S., U. Houston, 1958; cert. radiography tech. San Jacinto Meth. Sch. Radiol. Technologists, 1958; B.S., U. Houston, 1958; m. George F. Morris, Apr. 29, 1970; children from previous marriage—Shem L. Davis, Michael W. Davis. Registered radiography technologist San Jacinto Meth. Hosp., Baytown, 1958-67; field dir. ARC, Ft. Leonard Wood, Mo., Vietnam and Chanute AFB, Rantoul, Ill., 1967-70; social worker Salvation Army Facilities for Children, Honolulu, 1970-72; store mgr. Waldenbook Co., Lubbock, Tex., 1972-74, dist. mgr., Houston, 1974-76 regional mgr., Houston, 1976-81, nat. mgr. spl. sales, Stamford, Conn., 1981—; tchr. med. ethics, med. terminology and anatomy to radiography technologists, 1965-67; cons. book display in libraries, 1982. Vol. ARC, 1970. Mem. Am. Registry of Radiol. Technologists, Am. Assn. Med. Assts., Phi Kappa Phi. Home: 2309 W Settler's Way The Woodlands TX 77380

MORRISON, AGNES KIRKLAND, fin. exec.; b. Graceville, Fla., Aug. 3, 1911; d. Jeremiah Monroe and Alyce Laura (Casey) Kirkland; student Columbia U., 1935-37; m. Ralph L. Morrison, July 18, 1950; stepchildren—Betty Jane Church, Ralph L. Sec. to v.p. Charles H. Tompkins Co., Washington, 1955, sec. to sr. partner, 1956-68; v.p., asst. sec. Johnston, Lemon & Co., Inc., Washington, 1978—, trustee profit sharing plan and stock option plan, 1977-82; adminstr. James M. Johnston Charitable and Ednl. Trust, 1982—. Service with WASP, 1943-44. Mem. Women's Syndicate Assn. Presbyterian. Clubs: Bus. and Profl. Women's, Coral Beach and Tennis, Order Eastern Star (trustee, 1978—). Home: 3133 Connecticut Ave NW Washington DC 20008 Office: 1101 Vermont Ave NW Washington DC 20005

MORRISON, ALEXIA, lawyer; b. Los Angeles, Apr. 9, 1948; d. Alexander and Edith (Blayney) M.; B.A., Rutgers U., 1969; J.D., George Washington U., 1972; m. Robert A. Shuker, Feb. 11, 1978; 1 dau., Amanda Meighan. Legal asst. Office Drug Abuse Law Enforcement, U.S. Dept. Justice, 1972-73; admitted to D.C. bar, 1973, D.C. Circuit bar, 1975, Supreme Ct., 1981; asst. U.S. atty., Washington, 1973-81, chief grand jury sect. Superior Ct., 1977-78, chief felony trial div., 1979-81; chief litigation counsel Div. Enforcement, SEC, Washington, 1981—; mem. faculty Nat. Inst. Trial Advocacy, 1976-81. Recipient Dirs. award U.S. Dept. Justice, 1980. Republican.

MORRISON, CAROL SCHAEFER, office automation specialist; b. Edwardsville, Ill., Apr. 12, 1936; d. Elmer Henry and Elvira Bernadine (Feldman) Schaefer; student Elmhurst (Ill.) Coll., 1956-58; divorced; children—Louise Elizabeth Marton, John Charles Marton. Adminstrv. asst., then mgr. word processing Abbott Labs., North Chicago, 1969-76; word processing cons. Meredith Assos., Westport, Conn., 1976-78; mgr. written communications and word processing cons. Kellwood Co., St. Louis, 1978-80; mgr. advanced office tech. Ralston Purina Co., St. Louis, 1980—; instr. St. Louis Community Coll., Parkway Central High Sch., St. Louis; cons. Jefferson Coll., Hillsboro, Mo., So. Ill. U. Mem. Internat. Word Processing Assn. (past v.p., now dir. St. Louis chpt.), Word Processing Soc. Republican. Office: Ralston Purina Co Checkerboard Sq St Louis MO

MORRISON, CHLOE ANTHONY (TONI MORRISON), novelist; b. Lorain, Ohio, Feb. 18, 1931; d. George and Ella Ramah (Willis) Wofford; B.A., Howard U., 1953; M.A., Cornell U., 1955; children—Harold Ford, Slade Kevin. Tchr. English and humanities Tex. So. U., 1955-57, Howard U., 1957-64, Yale U., 1976-78, Bard Coll., 1979-80; editor Random House, N.Y.C., 1965—; author: The Bluest Eye, 1969; Sula, 1973; Song of Solomon, 1977. Mem. council Nat. Endowment for Arts. Recipient Inst. award Am. Acad. and Inst. Arts and Letters Acad., 1978, Nat. Book Critics Circle award, 1977; Cleve. Arts prize; Barnard medal of distinction. Mem. N.Y. State Council on Humanities, Center for Study So. Culture, Author's Guild (council). Office: care Random House Inc 201 E 50th St New York City NY 10022

MORRISON, CLAIRE ENID, lawyer; b. Pitts., Feb. 27, 1911; d. William Carleton and Catherine Elizabeth (Buchanan) M.; LL.B., Detroit Coll. Law, 1947. Admitted to Mich. bar, 1948; sec. U.S. Immigration and Naturalization Service, Detroit, 1931-43; sec. Ford Motor Co., Dearborn, Mich., 1951-67; sec. Matheson, Bieneman, Veale & Parr, Detroit, 1968-73; recorder-sec. Comprehensive Health Planning Council S.E. Mich., Detroit, 1974—. Dir. women's div. former 15th Congl. Dist., Detroit Democratic Com. Mem. Nat. Assn. Women Lawyers (pres. 1982—), Am. Bar Assn., Am. Acad. Polit. and Social Sci., Women Lawyers Assn. Mich., Mich. Bar Assn., Detroit Bar Assn. Methodist. Home and office: 1415 Parker St Detroit MI 48214

MORRISON, EILENE M(AY), ret. librarian, educator; b. Bellingham, Wash., Nov. 19, 1912; d. John Reid and Lillian (Cramer) Morrison; B.A., Western Wash. Coll. Edn., 1935; M.A., Columbia U., 1947, postgrad., 1947-48, 61; B.A. in Librarianship, U. Wash., 1950. Tchr., Wash. pub. schs., 1935-46; instr. demonstration sch. San Francisco State Coll., 1948-49; library supr., high sch. librarian Aberdeen (Wash.) pub. schs., 1950-54; asst. prof. library sci., asst. reference librarian Mont. State Coll., Bozeman, 1954-60; dist. librarian Bremerton (Wash.) Sch. Dist., 1961-73; vis. asst. prof. library sci. U. Oreg., summer 1960; asst. prof. extension sch. librarianship U. Wash., Seattle, winter 1963; vis. asst. in edn. Pacific Lutheran U., Parkland, Wash., summer 1963-64; asst. dir. Nat. Def. Edn. Act Sch. Library Inst., U. Okla., summer 1966. Mem. Am. (dir. 1965-67), Wash. (treas. 1963-65, chmn. region 2 1966-67, v.p. 1967-68, pres. 1968-69, editor Library Leads 1973-74) assns. sch. librarians, Wash. Assn. Ednl. Communications and Tech., Am., Pacific Northwest. Wash., library assns., N.E.A., Wash., Bremerton edn. assns., AAUW, Nat., Wash., Kitsap County ret. tchrs. assns., Delta Kappa Gamma (treas. Alpha Sigma chpt. 1972-74), Pi Lambda Theta, Kappa Delta Pi. Clubs: Kitsap County Golf and Country, Soroptimist, Order Eastern Star, Order of Amaranth. Contbr. to profl. jours. Home: Sea-Brim Condominium #23 1602 Naval Ave Bremerton WA 98310

MORRISON, GRACE BLANCH SIMPSON, acct., govt. ofcl.; b. Waterloo, Iowa, Dec. 18, 1933; d. Lyle Meredith and Grace Luella Blanch Simpson; B.S., So. Meth. U., 1956; M.Ed., U. Houston, 1973; m. Glenn Harry Murphree, July 2, 1955 (dec.); children—Gregory Alan, Gina Grace; m. 2d, Henry Joseph Morrison, Jr., July 23, 1974. Tchr. math., Mesquite (Tex.) Ind. Sch. Dist., 1957-58, Clear Creek Ind. Sch. Dist., Seabrook, Tex., 1967-73, Richardson (Tex.) Ind. Sch. Dist., 1973-74; equal opportunity asst. Office for Civil Rights, HEW, Dallas, 1974-75; govt. relations specialist, consumer affairs officer Region VI, Dept. Energy, Dallas, 1975-81; audit acctg. aide IRS, Dallas, 1981-82, revenue agt., 1982—. Mem. Mensa, Am. Amateur Press Assn., Commerce Bus. and Profl. Women's Club, Nat. Assn. Parliamentarians, Federally Employed Women, Tex. Assn. Parliamentarians, North Tex. Registered Parliamentarians. Unitarian. Home: Route 2 Box 178A Commerce TX 75428 Office: IRS 434 1100 Commerce St Dallas TX 75242

MORRISON, HALLEINE SHARP, ednl. adminstr.; b. Centralia, Wash., Aug. 12, 1928; d. Edwin and Lillian (Waters) Sharp; B.A., U. Calif., Berkeley, 1949; M.A., San Jose State U., 1976; m. Robert A. Morrison, June 23, 1951; children—David, Janet. Tchr., Richmond, Calif., 1950-51, Cranbury, N.J., 1951-54, Fremont, Calif., 1964-73, cons. early childhood edn., 1973-78; prin. Niles and Hacienda Elem. Schs., Fremont, 1978—; cons. Calif. Dept. Edn. Bd. dirs. Fremont-Newark Philharm. Soc., 1975-77; auditor PTA Council, 1979-80; cons. Niles Library Com., 1980; mem. Young Life Com., 1974-77, 79-82, Young Life

Mothers, Philharm. Guild, Centerian Choir; elder Presbyn. Ch. Named Outstanding Elem. Tchr., 1975. Mem. Fremont Sch. Adminstrs. Assn. (profl. relations com.), Assn. Calif. Sch. Adminstrs., AAUW, U. Calif. Alumni (dir., scholarship com. Washington Twp. chpt.), Delta Kappa Gamma, Alpha Delta Chi. Initiated early childhood edn. program Fremont Unified Sch. Dist., 1973. Home: 642 Marigold Ct Fremont CA 94539 Office: 37141 2d St Fremont CA 94536

MORRISON, JEANNE LUNSFORD, lawyer; b. Huntington, W.Va., Feb. 20, 1952; d. Harold D. and Dorothy Jones Lunsford; B.S., W.Va. U., 1974; J.D., Oklahoma City U., 1977; m. Bernard L. Morrison, Sept. 23, 1978. Admitted to W.Va. bar, 1977, Tex. bar, 1979; legal intern firm Lampkin, Wolfe, McCaffrey & Norman, Oklahoma City, 1977; staff atty. inheritance tax div. W.Va. Tax Dept., 1977-78; atty. El Paso Exploration Co. (Tex.), 1978—. Mem. Am. Bar Assn., Am. Judicature Soc., W.Va. Bar Assn., Tex. Bar Assn., El Paso Women's Bar Assn. (pres. 1981), El Paso Women's Polit. Caucus, El Paso Panhellenic, Delta Delta Delta. Republican. Methodist. Staff mem. The Verdict, Oklahoma City U. Office: PO Box 1492 El Paso TX 79978

MORRISON, LUCILE PHILLIPS, psychologist, author; b. Los Angeles, Sept. 8, 1896; d. Lee A. and Catherine (Coffin) Phillips; A.B., Vassar Coll., 1918; M.A. in Psychology, George Pepperdine Coll., 1958; Litt.D. (hon.), Calif. Sch. Profl. Psychology, 1978; m. Wayland Augustus Morrison, Dec. 27, 1917; children—Wayland Lee, Richard Holt, Lee Allen, Keith Norman; 1 adopted dau., Patricia Lee. Dir., Lee A. Phillips, Inc., 1930-49, v.p., 1938-42, pres., 1942-49; intern Am. Inst. Family Relations, Los Angeles, 1952-53, asso. counselor 1954-55, counselor, 1955-64, also v.p. bd. dirs., until 1964. Pres., founder mem. Duarte (Calif.) Community Service Council, 1946-48, editor newsletter, 1946-48, v.p., 1948-50, health chmn., 1951-54; bd. trustees Westminster Gardens Presbyn. Ch. U.S.A., 1953-66, hon. life trustee, 1966; dir., mem. Duarte Community Center Bd., 1949-57; dir. Children's Hosp., Los Angeles, 1921-44; trustee, mem. coms. Scripps Coll., 1930—, trustee emeritus, 1972—, chmn. ednl. policy com., 1965-70, Ellen Browning Scripps Assos. award, 1976; constituent mem. bd. fellows Claremont (Calif.) U. Center, 1967-70, mem. grad. sch. com., 1968-70, mem. adv. bd. Inst. Antiquity and Christianity, Claremont Grad. Sch., 1968—, mem. bldg. and grounds com.; v.p., dir., mem. staff Psychol. Guidance Center, Anaheim, Calif., 1960-63; trustee Calif. Sch. Profl. Psychology, 1972-78, hon. life trustee, 1978—, exec. council, 1973-74, mem. acad. commr., 1974-78; dir. Psychol. Publs., Inc., Los Angeles, 1966—. Active mus., hist., archeol. socs., So. Calif. Symphony Assn., Founders, Music Center For Performing Arts, Calif. Hist. Soc., Hist. Soc. So. Calif. Named Woman of Yr., Marlborough Sch. Class of 1914, 1979; lic. psychologist, lic. marriage, family and child counselor, cert. psychologist, State of Calif. Mem. N.Y. Acad. Scis., Child Study Assn. Am., AAUW, Am. (asso.), Calif., Western psychol. assns., DAR, Am., Calif., So. Calif. assns. marriage and family therapists, Calif. State Marriage Counseling Assn., Am. Assn. Humanistic Psychology, Inst. Achievement Human Potential, Phi Beta Kappa, Delta Kappa Gamma, Psi Chi. Club: Women's University (Los Angeles). Author: Mystery Gate, 1928; The Attic Child, 1929; Blue Bandits, 1930; The Lost Queen of Egypt (Nat. Pen Women's award for fiction), 1938; (with Robert M. Taylor) Taylor-Johnson Temperament Analysis; Research and Development of Test and Manual, 1963-67; also articles. Editor: Doll Dreams (4 vols.), 1927-32; The World of Books (for Scripps Coll.), 1934. Home: 1134 Rancho Rd Arcadia CA 91006

MORRISON, MARILYN GILTNER, lawyer; b. Ottumwa, Iowa, Mar. 31, 1940; d. Max A. and Helen (Gobble) G.; student U. Iowa, 1959-62, LL.B., 1965; children—Joel Paul, Helen Giltner. Admitted to Iowa bar, 1965, U.S. Supreme Ct., 1973, U.S. Ct. Customs and Patent Appeals, 1972; staff atty. IRS, 1965-71, U.S. Customs Service, Washington, 1971-78; chief comml. fraud and negligence br. U.S. Treasury Dept., 1978-80, dep. dir. entry procedures and penalties div., 1980-81, dir. carriers, drawback and bonds div., 1981—. Recipient letter of appreciation, Inst. Internat. Trade, Loredo State U., 1979, B.C. Ministry Econ. Devel. and Fed. Dept. Industry, 1979. Mem. Fed. Bar Assn., Iowa Bar Assn. Office: 1301 Constitution Ave NW Washington DC 20229

MORRISON, NANCY ELIZABETH, lawyer; b. Estevan, Sask., Can., May 20, 1937; d. William Harold and Jessie (Christopher) Morrison; B.A., U. B.C., 1958; LL.B., Osgoode Law Sch., Toronto, Ont., Can., 1961. Ptnr., LaMarsh & LaMarsh, Niagara Falls, Ont., 1963-66; ptnr. Morrison, MacDonald & Harrison, Sask.; asst. city prosecutor, Vancouver, B.C., 1970; provincial ct. judge, B.C., 1972-73, 1976-81; mem. Labour Relations Bd. B.C., 1973-76; pvt. practice, Vancouver, 198—; lectr. U. B.C., 1980, 81. Mem. Fedn. Women Tchrs. Assn. Ont., Can. Inst. Public Affairs. Address: 123 Main St Vancouver BC V6A 2S5 Canada

MORRISON, PATRICIA GAYLE, child care exec.; b. Oklahoma City, Aug. 23, 1944; d. Silas Marvin and Sue Martha (Boren) Vawter; B.S. in Elem. and Spl. Edn. (Duke award 1977), Southwestern Okla. State U., 1977, M.Ed. in Counseling and Guidance, 1979; children—Jay Thomas, Dena Marie, Bradley Thomas. Legal sec., 1975-77; coordinator Child Service Clinic, Weatherford, Okla., 1978—; co-dir. S.W. Area Spl. Olympics, 1978-79; music dir. spl. edn. camps, 1977-78. Mem. bd. Council of Arts, Weatherford, 1979-80. Mem. AAUW, Council Exceptional Children, Okla. Assn. Children with Learning Disabilities, Nat. Assn. State Dirs. Spl. Edn., Okla. Assn. Children Under Six, So. Assn. Children Under Six, Am. Personnel and Guidance Assn., Weatherford Community Theatre, Beta Sigma Phi (pres. 1968). Democrat. Mem. Ch. of Christ. Home: 513 N 1st St Weatherford OK 73096 Office: Child Service Clinic SWOSU Box 374 Weatherford OK 73096

MORRISON, WINIFRED ELAINE HAAS, social services adminstr., educator; b. Buffalo, Aug. 31; d. Edward Albert and Elaine Magdalene (McNamara) Haas; B.S. in Edn., SUNY, Buffalo, M.S. in Edn. magna cum laude, 1964; M.L.S., SUNY, Geneseo, 1969; postgrad. SUNY, Buffalo, Harvard U., UCLA; m. Robert Charles Morrison; children—Robert Edward, James Richard. Instr., Genesee Community Coll., 1972-78, 80, also asst. prof. SUNY, Buffalo, 1973-77; corr. course instr. Empire State Coll., Saratoga Springs, N.Y., 1975-78; dir. early edn. div. Park Sch., Buffalo, 1960-74, dir. lower sch., 1974-78; lectr. Coll. H, SUNY, Buffalo, also coordinator child care adv. service Early Childhood Research Center, SUNY, Buffalo, Amherst campus, 1978-80; dir. children's services Erie County Assn. for Retarded Children, 1980—; chairperson early childhood com. Nat. Office Gifted and Talented, HEW, 1976; panelist symposium Chautauqua Inst., 1974. Pres. bd. dirs. Day Care Council Western N.Y., 1971-72; adv. com. parenthood edn. project Buffalo and Erie County council Girl Scouts U.S.A., 1972-76; child adv. com. child/adult edn. project Western N.Y. div. Salvation Army, 1977-82; TV and reading com. WNED-TV Public Broadcasting, 1977-79; chmn. community com. Erie Community Coll., 1971-72. Recipient Outstanding Service award Villa Maria Coll. Child Devel. Adv. Council, 1979. Mem. AAUW, Nat. Assn. Edn. of Young Children, Council Exceptional Children, World Orgn. Presch. Edn., Assn. Childhood Edn. Internat., Center Women in Mgmt., Assn. Children with Learning Disabilities, ALA, Nat. Assn. Supervision and Curriculum Devel., Nat. Assn. Elem. Sch. Prins., Day Care and Child Devel. Assn. Am., N.Y. State Council for Children, Western N.Y. Edn. Communications Council, Pi Lambda Theta. Club: Zonta. Author: This Book Is About Your School, Early Education Unit, 1976, Primary Unit, 1977; You Are Your Child's First Teacher, 1974; (with Carol Woodard) You Can Help Your Baby Learn, 1979; (with Betty Jenkins) Kiddy Kards (screening materials), 1982. Home: 13 Karen Dr Tonawanda NY 14150 Office: Heritage Edn Program 1 Nagel Dr Cheektowaga NY 14225

MORROW, CAROLINE DONOVAN, social worker; b. Houston, Dec. 11, 1937; d. Ira and Verda Ree Donovan; B.A., Wiley Coll., 1960; M.S.W., Atlanta U., 1962; m. June 17, 1967; children—Emery Donovan, April Antoinette. Group worker, counselor Golden Age Center, Cleve., 1962-67; vol. social worker Rhein Main AFB, Frankfurg, W.Ger., 1968-69; counselor-adminstr. Job Corps extension program YWCA, Denver, 1970-75; med. social worker Rose Med. Center, Denver, 1976—. Recipient Outstanding Social Worker award YWCA, 1973; lic. psychotherapist, Colo. Mem. Nat. Assn. Social Workers. Episcopalian. Home: 1358 S Oswego Ct Aurora CO 80012

MORROW, MARY RUTH, bus. rep.; b. Eutaw, Ala., Dec. 17, 1941; d. Pearlie and Maggie Lee (Lavender) M.; student Los Angeles Met. Coll., 1961, Bryant & Stratton Bus. Inst., 1963; B.A., SUNY, 1980, cert. in materials mgmt., 1980, postgrad. in communications, 1980; With Buffalo Bisons Baseball Promotional, 1963-64, Hengerers' Dept. Store, Buffalo, 1964-65; clk.-typist Buffalo Distbg. Co., 1963-64; telephone operator N.Y. Telephone, Buffalo, 1964-65, jr. service asst., 1965-67, service asst., 1967-72, instr. tng. long distance operators, acting asst. mgr. operator services, customer service bur., 1972-73, rep. bus. service and sales, 1979—; chmn. Western Area Telephone Comml. Union, 1981; chmn. local 213, Telephone Comml. Union, also mem. raiding and edn. coms.; personnel interviewer S.M. Flickinger Co., 1974. Loan officer credit union St. John Baptist Ch., 1974-75, mem. youth adv. bd., 1970-75; tchr. Sunday sch., 1966-73; vol. Children's Hosp. Variety Club Telethon, 1981. Recipient Buffalo Bd. of Dirs. PUSH award, 1978; Black Achievers' award, 1979. Mem. Am. Bus. Women's Assn. (mem. hospitality com. and edn. com. 1974), Nat. Assn. Female Execs., Women in Communication, Buffalo Urban League (sec. guild 1976, co-chmn. golf com., entertainment chmn. 1981), NAACP (hon. chmn. 1978-80, dir.), PUSH Excel (dir.), PUSH (dir.), Delta Sigma Gamma, Alpha Kappa Alpha. Democrat. Baptist. Clubs: SUNY Buffalo Alumni, Golden Tee Golf (v.p. 1981-82), United Voices of St. John Booster. Home: 10 Hertel Ave Apt 804 Buffalo NY 14207 Office: 5th Floor Erie County Savings Bank Bldg Buffalo NY 14202

MORROW, SANDRA LEE, counselor; b. Toledo, Dec. 26, 1947; d. Virgil E. and Betty J. (Lake) M.; B.A., Mt. Union Coll., Alliance, Ohio, 1969; M.A., Seton Hall U., 1971; postgrad. Fordham U.; 1 son, Glen Morrow Pezzuti. Tchr., Dwight-Englewood Sch., Englewood, N.J., 1969-70; psychometrician, counselor Union Coll., 1971-72; counselor St. Peter's Coll., Jersey City, 1972-75; psychotherapist Psychiat. Center Central Jersey, Westfield, N.J., 1976-80; pvt. practice counseling, Westfield, 1980—. Mem. Am. Psychol. Assn., Am. Personnel and Guidance Assn. Methodist. Author: (with L. Malnig) What Can I Do With A Major In?, 1975. Office: 2277 South Ave Westfield NJ

MORROW, SARAH TAYLOR, state ofcl.; b. Charlotte, N.C., July 27, 1921; d. Frank Victor and Lois Eunice (McKeown) Taylor; student Queens Coll., 1938-40; B.S., U. N.C., Chapel Hill, 1942, M.D., 1960, M.P.H.; B.S. in Medicine, U. Md., 1944; m. Thomas Lacy Morrow, Jr., Oct. 26, 1946 (dec.); children—Sarah Lois Thompson, E. Lynne Perrin, Thomas Lacy III, Frank Paul, Alice Ann, John Howard. Practice medicine; now sec. human resources State of N.C., Raleigh. Recipient Sidney S. Chipman award U. N.C. Sch. Public Health, 1973; Disting. Service award U. N.C. Sch. Medicine, 1974; Disting. Alumnae award Queens Coll., 1977. Mem. AMA, N.C. Med. Soc., Guilford County Med. Soc., N.C. Public Health Assn., Am. Public Health Assn. Presbyterian. Office: Dept Human Resources Albemarle Bldg 325 N Salisbury St Raleigh NC 27611 *

MORSE, DIANA LOUISE, ct. reporter; b. Copperos Cove, Tex., Aug. 13, 1925; d. Joseph Robert and Cecile Rae (Carpenter) M.; grad. Nixon-Clay Comml. Coll., Austin, Tex., 1943. Hearings reporter Tex. Water Rights Commn., 1959-64; ofcl. ct. reporter 201st Jud. Dist. Ct., Travis County, Austin, Tex., 1964-75; owner freelance ct. reporting firm Louise Morse & Assos., Austin, 1975—; mem. Tex. Ct. Reporters Com. Mem. Travis County Ct. Reporters Assn., Tex. Ct. Reporters Assn., Nat. Ct. Reporters Assn. Republican. Methodist. Home: 1403 Red Bud Trail Austin TX 78746 Office: 707 Blanco St Austin TX 78703

MORSE, ELEANOR MEREDITH, art dealer; b. Bklyn., June 2, 1926; d. Daniel and Salley Beatrice Hershey; B.B.A., CCNY, 1947; m. Mitchell Ian Morse, Dec. 24, 1947; children—Jeffrey Aslan, Andrea Urdang. Vice pres. Art Gallery on Wheels, Floral Park, N.Y., 1953-54; product designer, v.p. Wall Decorating, Inc., Cedarhurst, and Lawrence, N.Y., 1954-70; free-lance window designer, 1955-61; interior designer, 1961-68; sec./treas. Mann-Morse Graphics, N.Y.C., 1968-69, Morse-Sun Art Assos., Inc., N.Y.C., 1972-75; v.p., Mitch Morse Gallery, Inc., N.Y.C., 1966—, Art Spectrum, 1979—, Yogre Bldg. Assos., Lawrence, 1964—; sec. China Spectrum, Inc., N.Y.C., 1981—; watercolorist. Office: 305 E 63d St New York NY 10021

MORSE, EUGENIA MAUDE, architect, educator; b. Houston, Feb. 23, 1920; d. Robert Emmett and Eugenia Elizabeth (Maddox) Morse Fry; B.A. in Architecture, Rice U., 1941, B.S. in Architecture, 1942. Practicing architect, 1949—; asso. prof. U. S.W. La., 1954-59; prof. architecture Tex. Tech. U., Lubbock, 1959—. Pres. bd. dirs. Storm Def. Club, 1970-73. Mem. West Tex. Watercolor Assn. (treas., dir. 1971-72), Nat. Geog. Soc., Museum Natural History, Am. Forestry Assn., Smithsonian Instn. Prin. works include Seitter Photography Bldg., Corpus Christi, Tex., Miles Ramagosa Clinic, Lafayette, La., also residences. Home: 2621 33d St Lubbock TX 79410

MORSE, GRETCHEN B., state legislator; b. Hyannis, Mass., Nov. 17, 1943; A.A., Colby-Sawyer Coll., 1963; B.S., U. Vt., 1975; m. James L. Morse. Formerly with Mus. Sci., Boston, Polaroid Corp., Cambridge, Mass.; mem. Vt. Ho. of Reps., 1977-78, 79-80, 81—. Mem. Gov.'s Commn. on Status of Women, Chittenden County Republican Com., Chittenden County Council on Families and Children, Charlotte Republican Com., Eastern Regional Conf. Human Resource Com., Council State Govts., Gov.'s Com. on Children and Youth, Juvenile Justice and Delinquency Prevention Adv. Group to Vt. Justice Commn. Office: Vt Ho of Reps State House Montpelier VT 05602 *

MORSE, MARCIA, artist; b. Detroit, Mar. 14, 1944; d. Joyce Odney and Gertrud Hermina (Kuenzel) Roberts; B.A. cum laude, Radcliffe Coll., 1966; M.F.A., Stanford U., 1974; 1 son, Daniel. One-woman shows: Galeria Artes, Quito, Ecuador, 1968, 71, 74, Gima's Art Gallery, Honolulu, 1969, 71, 75, 77, Mary Porter Sesnon Art Gallery, U. Calif., Santa Cruz, 1971, Contemporary Arts Center, Hawaii, 1978; group shows include: Artists of Hawaii, Honolulu Acad. Arts, 1964, 74, 75, 76, 77, 81, Bienal de Grabados, Santiago, Chile, 1968, U. Calif., Santa Cruz, 1970, 71, Esther Bear Gallery, Santa Barbara, Calif., 1973, 75, 9th Dulin Nat. Print and Drawing Competition, Knoxville, Tenn., 1975, Honolulu Printmakers, 1976, 77; represented in permanent collections: State of Hawaii, Honolulu Acad. Arts, Contemporary Arts Center Hawaii, Madison (Wis.) Art Center, U. Calif., Santa Cruz, Am. Embassy, Ecuador; owner, dir., master printer Printworks, Honolulu, 1975—; lectr. printmaking and drawing U. Hawaii, 1979—; art critic Honolulu Star Bull., 1979—. Hawaii Found. Culture and Arts grantee, 1977-78; Craftmen's fellow Nat. Endowment Arts, 1981-82. Mem. Nat. League Am. Pen Women (v.p. 1976-77), Am. Crafts Council, Hawaii Craftsmen, Honolulu Printmakers (pres. 1978-79), Honolulu Acad. Arts. Home: 4723 Moa St Honolulu HI 96816

MORSE, MARLENE TALBERT, coll. adminstr.; b. Roselle Park, N.J., Oct. 14, 1932; d. Peter John and Augusta Caroline (Mielke) Zimmer; student Internat. Corr. Schs., 1951; diploma Spanish, Berlitz Sch. Langs., 1958; divorced; children—Bonnie Melissa Talbert Rawls, Roderick Lloyd Talbert, Brandon Balfour Talbert. Rodeo trick rider, also film actress, 1948-51; social dir. El San Juan (R.R.) Hotel, 1962-63; officer adminstr. for periodontist, N.Y.C., 1966-73; dir. admissions Skadron Coll. Bus., San Bernardino, Calif., 1973—; coordinator employment task force San Bernardino County Commn. Status Women, 1977—, commr. 5th dist., 1981—. Pres. Los Padrinos Youth Service Orgn., San Bernardino, 1976-77; mem. personnel com. San Gorgonio Girl Scout Council, 1979-80. Recipient various service awards, certs. appreciation. Mem. San Bernardino Exec. Assn. (bd. govs. 1977-80), San Bernardino Bus. and Profl. Women (past pres.; named Woman of Achievement 1980), San Bernardino C. of C. (pres. women's div. 1980-81). Republican. Seventh-day Adventist. Club: San Bernardino Zonta (pres. 1979-80). Author: Culinary Capers, 1976. Home: 6084 Arden Ave San Bernardino CA 92404 Office: 798 W 4th St San Bernardino CA 92410

MORT, VIRGINIA ANN, aerospace co. exec.; b. Steubenville, Ohio, Oct. 25, 1938; d. Frank L. and Mary C. (Lucas) Petrola; B.S. in English, Calif. State U., Long Beach, 1970; M.S. in Mgmt. and Adminstrn., Pepperdine U., Los Angeles, 1975; divorced; children—Robert M., Susan A. Tchr., then counselor Anaheim (Calif.) Union High Sch. Dist., 1970-79; human resources adminstr. Northrop Corp., Anaheim, 1980, mgr. tng. and communications, 1981—; lectr., cons. in field. Mem. AAUW (chpt. v.p. 1975-77), Northrop Mgmt. Club (v.p. 1981), Am. Soc. Tng. and Devel., Orgn. Devel. Network, Nat. Assn. Female Execs., Calif. State U. Long Beach Alumni Assn., Phi Beta Kappa, Phi Kappa Phi, Alpha Mu Gamma. Home: 9681 Random Dr Anaheim CA 92804 Office: 500 E Orangethorpe St Anaheim CA 92801

MORTHLAND, CONSTANCE AMELIA GRANT (MRS. ANDREW MORTHLAND), civic worker; b. Eng., Mar. 31, 1915 (came to U.S. 1919, naturalized 1940); d. Douglas Gordon and Maud (Smith) Grant; ; A.B. summa cum laude, Stanford, 1936; m. Andrew Morthland, Aug. 8, 1937; children—Joan (Mrs. Warren C. Hutchins), Patricia (Mrs. James F. Draper). Research asst. RKO Studios, 1936-39; story dept. analyst Paramount Studios, 1941-46; free lance writer, 1955-60; cons. overseas program Stanford U. Pres. Friends of Claremont Colls., 1976-78; mem. Friends of Radcliffe Coll., 1962-70; chmn. finance com. Episcopal Ch. Women, 1959-60; mem. exec. bd. Assistance League, 1968-69; staff mem. Laguna-Moulton Community Playhouse, 1961-69, editor Callboard, 1955—; community adviser Jr. League, 1973-75. Trustee Pitzer Coll., Claremont, Calif.; bd. overseers Claremont Coll., 1965-73; bd. dirs. Lyric Opera Assn. Orange County, 1973—, Continuing Edn. at Claremont Coll., 1973-77; trustee South Coast Med. Center, 1978—; exec. bd. Assocs. of House Ear Inst., 1982—. Recipient Journalism award Sigma Delta Chi, 1936, Calif. Internat. Woman award 1971. Mem. Soc. Preservation Rural Eng. (hon.), Daus. Brit. Empire (regent 1972-73), Aircraft Owners and Pilots Assn., Ninety-Nines. Clubs: Stanford (Orange County sec.); Stanford Profl. Women's; Women's University (London); Newport Harbor Yacht; El Miguel Country; N.Y. Yacht. Home: 165 Moss Point Laguna Beach CA 92651

MORTIER, MARY PRESSLY LITZELMAN, mfg. co. exec.; b. Long Branch, N.J., Feb. 10, 1947; d. Karl Burns and Marjorie Watt (Pressly) Litzelman; B.A., Pratt Inst., 1970; m. Alain Daniel Mortier, Dec. 23, 1972. Knitwear stylist, coordinator Damon Creations, N.Y.C., 1970-78; mdse. mgr. knitwear H.I.S. Sportswear, N.Y.C., 1978-80; mdse. mgr. menswear Am. Argo Corp., N.Y.C., 1980-81, gen. mdse. mgr., 1981—. Home: 236 Washington Ave Brooklyn NY 11205 Office: Am Argo Corp 350 5th Ave Suite 1400 New York NY 10118

MORTIMER, ARMINE KOTIN, educator; b. Detroit, May 13, 1943; d. Arra Steve and Georgia Victoria (Keosaian) Avakian; B.A. magna cum laude, Radcliffe Coll., 1964; M.A., UCLA, 1970; M.Phil., Yale U., 1973, Ph.D., 1974; m. Rudolf G. Mortimer, Aug. 18, 1980; children—Daniel Kotin, Ilana Kotin. Asst. prof. French, U. Ill., Urbana, 1974-80, asso. prof., 1980—, asso. prof. humanities, 1981—. Fellow Center Advanced Study, U. Ill., fall 1977. Mem. MLA, Soc. Values in Higher Edn., Assn. Internationale des Etudes Françaises. Author: The Narrative Imagination: Comic Tales by Philippe de Vigneulles, 1977; contbr. articles to profl. jours. Home: 3 Florida Ct Urbana IL 61801 Office: 707 S Mathews Ave Urbana IL 61801

MORTIMER, DELORES MINERVA, govt. ofcl.; b. N.Y.C., July 23, 1949; d. Nathaniel Granville and Lenora (McKinney) M.; student Macalester Coll., 1969-70; B.A. (grantee), Howard U., 1971; M. Profl. Studies (fellow 1971-72), Cornell U., 1973; 1 dau., Dominique Filostrat. Freelance publs. cons., 1967—; research coordinator/project supr. African Bibliog. Center, Washington, 1972-75; adminstr. Phelps Stokes Fund, Washington, 1974-75; broadcaster/tech. resource person HABARI Info. Service, Washington, 1973—; social sci. analyst Smithsonian Instn., Washington, 1975-79; social sci. analyst U.S. Commn. on Civil Rights, Washington, 1979-81; acad. exchange officer USIA, Washington, 1981—. Mem. women's council Smithsonian Instn., 1976-79. Sponsors for Ednl. Opportunity grantee, 1970. Mem. Nat. Assn. Female Execs., Internat. Program Human Resource Devel., African Studies Assn., Latin Am. Studies Assn., Black Analysis. Co founder, editor AMA Women in African and Am. Worlds jours., 1976; contbr. articles to profl. jours. Office: USIA 1776 Pennsylvania Ave NW Washington DC 20547

MORTON, BERNICE ALICE FINLEY, nurse; b. Detroit, Aug. 29, 1923; d. Virgil and Minnie Alice (Batchelor) Finley; B.S.N., Wayne State U., 1954, M.S.N., 1961; Ph.D., U. Mich., 1980; m. Donald Allen Morton, Oct. 1, 1949; children—Donna Jean, Mildred Ellen. Staff nurse Grace Hosp., Detroit, 1948; public health nurse Detroit Dept. Health, 1948-58; instr. Deaconess Sch. Nurses, Detroit, 1960-62; instr. med. terminology Highland Park (Mich.) Community Coll., 1962; asst. dir. Met. Hosp., Detroit, 1962-63; mem. faculty Wayne State U., 1963—, asso. prof. nursing, chmn. community health nursing, 1973—; dir. nursing service Model Neighborhood Comprehensive Health Care Center, 1969-72; mem. Mayor Detroit Adv. Com. Health, 1970-72; cons., reviewer in field. Horace Rachkam fellow, 1975; grantee USPHS, 1959. Mem. AAUP, Am. Nurses Assn., Nat. League Nursing, Am. Public Health Assn., Detroit Dist. Nurses Assn., Wayne State U. Alumni Assn., Smithsonian Assos., Sigma Theta Tau, Delta Sigma Theta, Chi Eta Phi. Author papers in field. Address: 3790 Sturtevant Ave Detroit MI 48206

MORTON, ELIZABETH WILLIAMS, realtor; b. Chgo.; d. Charles Albert and Alice Mae (Ellsworth) Williams; student U. Ill., 1925-26; B.S., Conn. Coll. for Women, 1929; S.S.A., U. Chgo., 1930; m. Arthur M. Moody, Jr., Jan. 23, 1933 (div. Apr. 1945); 1 son, Arthur M. III; m. 2d, William B. Morton, Sept. 9, 1950 (div. Feb. 1975). Sr. caseworker Cook County Dept. Pub. Welfare, Chgo., 1929-30; social worker Chgo. Mcpl. Ct. System, 1930-32; asst. supr. Queens Emergency Relief Bd., N.Y.C., 1935; home service worker, dir. ARC, Providence, East Greenwich, R.I., Norwalk, Greenwich and Bridgeport, Conn., N.Y.C., 1941-52; real estate saleswoman Vick Realty Co., Stamford, Conn., 1953-54; broker, partner Morton Realty Co., New Canaan, Conn., 1954-63; broker, owner E. W. Morton Realty Co. (now William Pitt,

Inc.), New Canaan 1963-66, broker, mgr. br., 1966-69; self-employed as realtor, from 1970; ret. Dir. Norwalk Community Chest, 1945, Norwalk Council, 1946, chmn. health div. 1944; adminstrv. dir. New Canaan Community Council, 1962, real estate bd. del., 1963-64; chmn. Civic Study Forum, 1970; bd. dirs. Pub. Health Nursing Service, Southbury and Roxbury, Waterbury chpt. ARC, 1978-80. Mem. New Canaan Bd. Realtors (dir., sec. 1960-64), Heritage Village Civic Assn. (dir. 1972), Waterbury Bd. Realtors, Conn. Assn. Real Estate Bds. (sec. 1963), Nat. Assn. Real Estate Bds. (exec. officers council 1960-64), C. of C., LWV, Southbury Hist. Soc., Alpha Xi Delta Alumnae (pres. 1960, Order of Rose 1976). Republican. Clubs: Heritage Village Condominium 22 (dir. 1976, sec. 1975) (Southbury, Conn.); Conn. College Alumna. Address: 898B Heritage Village Southbury CT 06488

MORTON, FLORENCE HORTENSE BRASHEAR, high sch. dean; b. Cleburne, Tex., Apr. 18, 1926; d. Alpheus Webb and Eula Hortense (Burnett) Brashear; B.A., Fisk U., 1947; M.A., Murray State U., 1971; m. Andrew White Morton, Dec. 29. 1946; children—Lucia Diane Morton Moorman, Clifford Harrison, Tchr. lang. arts and social studies Paducah (Ky.) Public Schs., 1956-64; tchr. adult basic. edn., 1964-79; tchr. exceptional children Paducah Tilghman High Sch., 1965-74; dean students, 1974—; tchr., counselor Project Upward Bound, Murray State U., 1965-71. Mem. Paducah Mayor's Bi-Centennial Commn., 1975-76; counselor Bear Creek and West Ky. councils Girl Scouts U.S.A., 1959-62. Mem. NEA, Paducah Edn. Assn., First Dist. Edn. Assn., Ky. Edn. Assn., Ky. Dental Assn. Aux., Western Ky. Dental Assn. Aux., Nat. Dental Assn. Aux., Alpha Kappa Alpha, Phi Delta Kappa, Delta Kappa Gamma. Club: Order Eastern Star. Home: 1329 Rudy Ave Paducah KY 42001 Office: 2400 Washington St Paducah KY 42001

MORTON, MALVIN, public relations cons.; b. Teneha, Tex., June 24, 1906; d. Charles Newton and Bessie Howell (Warner) M.; A.B., Tex. Woman's Coll., 1933; M.S.S.A., U. Pitts., 1945. Caseworker, Ft. Worth Relief Commn., 1933-35; program dir. YWCA, Greensboro, N.C., 1935-40; program dir. teen members YWCA, Indpls., 1940-43; social work cons. dept. public relations Welfare Fedn., Pitts., 1945-47; public relations dir. United Charities of Chgo., 1947-52; exec. dir. Chgo. Fedn. Settlements & Neighborhood Centers, 1952-61; editor publs. Am. Public Welfare Assn., Chgo., 1961-71; public relations cons. Florence Crittenton Assn. of Am., Chgo., 1972-75; pvt. practice public relations cons., Chgo., 1975—; del. White House Conf. on Children, Washington, 1950, 60. Pres., United Meth. Women, Chgo. Temple, First United Meth. Ch., 1979, 80, life mem. adminstrv. bd., 1981—; bd. dirs. Contact Chgo. Buhl fellow, 1943-45; recipient Merit award Tex. Wesleyan Coll., 1978; Good Neighbor award Chgo. Fedn. Settlement and Neighborhood Centers, 1978; citizenship medal DAR, 1982. Mem. Nat. Assn. Social Workers, Nat. Conf. Social Welfare, Am. Med. Writers Assn., Friends of Lit., Internat. Settlement Conf. (del. Berlin 1956, Rome 1960). Methodist. Editor: Can Public Welfare Keep Pace?, 1969; editor Public Welfare, 1962-71. Home: 1130 N Dearborn St Chicago IL 60610

MORTON, MARGARET KIRCHER, advt. co. exec.; b. Chgo., Jan. 19, 1924; d. Albert and Mame Elizabeth (Murray) Kircher; B.S., Drake U., 1946, M.A., 1947; postgrad. Northwestern U., 1949; m. Richard G. Morton, Nov. 27, 1947; children—Margaret, Richard G. Pres., M.K. Morton C., advt., 1962—. Trustee, Lake Forest Acad., Ferry Hall, 1964—; sec.-treas. bd. dirs. Am. Hearing Research Found., 1963—, pres. women's bd., 1975—; bd. dirs., sec. Evang. Hosp. Assn., 1980-82, chmn. 75th anniversary com., 1981; founding dir. Nat. Hearing Assn., 1977; v.p. Door County Property Owners Assn.; bd. dirs. Christ Hosp., Oak Lawn, Ill., Good Samaritan Hosp., Downers Grove, Ill.; trustee First Congregational Ch., Western Springs, Ill., 1972-76. Mem. Nat. League Am. Pen Women, Kappa Kappa Gamma Alumnae Assn. Republican. Clubs: Woman's Athletic of Chgo., Rotary Women; Allied Arts (LaGrange, Ill.). Home: Locust Point Farm Box 263 Downers Grove IL 60515

MORTON, MIRIAM, author, anthologist, translator; b. Kishinev, Russia, June 14, 1916; came to U.S., 1921, naturalized, 1926; d. Efim and Sarah Rielberg; B.S., N.Y.U., 1939; m. Lewis Morton, Apr. 24, 1937. Co-op. nursery sch. tchr., 1940-42; social worker Dept. Pub. Welfare, N.Y.C., 1942-45, Bd. Child Welfare, N.Y.C., 1945-46; vis. tchr. Dept. Edn., N.Y.C., 1947-49; manuscript editor U. Chgo. Press, U. Calif. Press, 1958-60; vis. lectr. U.S. and Can. univs.; author: The Arts and the Soviet Child, 1972, Pleasures and Palaces, 1973, Said the Little Racoon to the Moon, 1973, The Making of Champions, 1974, Paths to Peace, 1978; Growing Up in the Soviet Union: From Cradle to Career, 1982; translator, selector anthologies including A Harvest of Russian Children's Literature, 1967, Twenty-Two Tales for Young Children by Leo Tolstoy, 1969; Voices from France (stories by French Nobel prize winners in lit.), 1969, The Moon is Like a Silver Sickle (poetry of Soviet children), 1972; translator, editor From Two to Five (Kornei Chukovsky), 1963, Fierce and Gentle Warriors (Mikhail Sholokhov), 1967, Shadows and Light (Anton Chekhov), 1968, The House of the Four Winds (Colette Vivier), 1969, Fifteen Stories by Maupassant, 1972; A Sampling of Russian Children's Plays, 1977, Where to, Turelu? (play, transl. from French), 1978, Through the Magic Curtain (essays on children's theatre in USSR), 1979; contbr. 25 articles to various jours. Active in war relief, World War II; tchr. English to fgn. students UCLA, 1971-72. Recipient spl. recognition citation Am. Theatre Assn., also Gorky prize for translation. Mem. Am. Children's Theatre Assn., Internat. Theatre Assn. for Children and Youth, Authors Guild, Women's Internat. League for Peace and Freedom.

MOSBY, CAROLYN BROWN, state legislator; b. Nashville, May 10, 1932; d. Alvin Thomas and Mary Elizabeth (Snelling) Brown; m. William Edward Jordan, Jr., 1950; 1 son, William Edward; m. 2d, John Oliver Mosby, Feb. 5, 1966; 1 dau., Carolyn Elizabeth. Adminstrv. asst. dept. econs. U. Chgo., 1961-80; mem. Ind. Ho. of Reps., 1979—; pres. Carolyn Mosby Enterprises, Inc., Gary, 1980—. Mem. platform accountability commn. Democratic Nat. Com. Recipient Women's Agenda for Action award, 1981; Omega Psi Phi Outstanding Citizen award, 1981. Mem. Gary C. of C. (dir. 1981-82), Nat. Assn. Minority Women in Bus. Baptist. Clubs: Toastmistress, Jack and Jill Am. Mem. editorial bd. AIM mag., 1980-82. Office: 465 Broadway Gary IN 46402

MOSELEY, LAURICE CULP, music mcht.; b. Chilton County, Ala., Feb. 15, 1927; d. John Curtis and Alma Roma (Hand) Foshee; student Air U. Extension Course Inst., 1951-57; m. Charles W. Culp, Oct. 23, 1958; children—Randall D., Robert C.; m. 2d Ernest B. Moseley, Jr. May 21, 1966. Auditor, personnel clk. fed. govt., 1949-55; owner, pres., treas. Culp Piano Co. (doing bus. as Fairview Piano Co., Inc., Electronics Organ Service Co., Moseley Piano Co., Crown Gems Internat., Culp Internat. Inc.), Montgomery, Ala., 1955—, also dir.; dir. Dimensions Inc., Montgomery. Mem. Nat. Assn. Music Mchts., Am. Music Conf. Republican. Club: Soroptimist. Author: (with A.T. Thomas) 6 Lessons Toward Keyboard Mastery, 1978. Home: 2543 Wildwood Dr Montgomery AL 36111 Office: 634 E Patton Ave Montgomery AL 36111

MOSELEY BRAUM, CAROL ELIZABETH, state legislator; b. Chgo., Aug. 16, 1947; d. Joseph John and Edna (Davie) Moseley; B.A., U. Ill., 1969; J.D., U. Chgo., 1972; m. Michael Allen Braum, Aug. 16, 1974; 1 son, Matthew John. Admitted to Ill. bar, 1973; asso. firm Davis, Miner & Barnhill, Chgo., 1972-73; asst. U.S. atty. No. Dist. Ill., Chgo., 1974-77; of counsel firm Feiwell, Galper & Lasky, Ltd., Chgo., 1977—; mem. Ill. Ho. Reps., 1977—. Bd. dirs. Hyde Park-Kenwood Health Center, Chgo. Recipient Atty. Gen.'s Spl. Achievement award U.S. Dept. Justice, 1977; Outstanding Service award Blackmen of the Roundtable, 1979; Chgo. Tchrs. Union award, 1980; Ill. Public Action Council award, 1980; Allbrand Youth Key Found. award, 1980; Best Legislator award Independent Voters Ill. 1980. Mem. Ill. State Bar Assn., Cook County Bar Assn., Chgo. Council Lawyers, Am. Judicature Soc. Office: 7124 S Jeffery St Chicago IL 60649

MOSER, ROSEMARIE SCOLARO, psychologist; b. Hackensack, N.J., June 16, 1954; d. Giovanni Natale and Mary (Bellaera) Scolaro; B.A. magna cum laude in Psychology, U. Pa., 1976, M.S. in Psychol. Services, 1977, Ph.D. in Counseling Psychology, 1981; m. Robert Lawrence Moser, June 4, 1978; 1 dau., Rachel Ann. Psychol. counselor Phila. Interdisciplinary Health and Edn. Program, 1976-77; counselor intern Intercommunity Action Mental Health/Mental Retardation Center, Phila., 1977; psychologist, cons. intern Cath. Home for Girls, Phila., 1977-78; sch. psychologist intern New Castle County, Newark, Del., 1978-79; intern Towson (Md.) State U. Counseling Center, 1979-80; counselor Sch. Nursing U. Md., Balt., 1980—; cons. Towson State U. Day Care Center, 1979-80; coordinator Jr. year minority student retention project Sch. Nursing, U. Md., 1980—; vol. Children's Hosp. of Phila., 1974, Hahnemann Hosp., Phila., 1975. Cert. sch. psychologist, Md. Mem. AAAS, Am. Psychol. Assn., Am. Personnel and Guidance Assn., Eastern Psychol. Assn., Phi Delta Kappa, Pi Lambda Theta. Office: U Md Sch Nursing 655 W Lombard St Baltimore MD 21201

MOSES, BETTE J., artist; b. Blackwell, Okla.; d. Walter W. and Mary Jane (Kirkpatrick) Swingle; B.A., Northwestern State U., Alva, Okla., 1946; m. Edward R. Moses, June 9, 1966; children—Kirk Rodgers, Joell Ireland. Tchr. English and speech pub. high sch., Washington, Okla., 1947-48; kindergarten tchr., Oklahoma City, 1948-60, Oklahoma City and Gt. Bend, Kans., 1960-66; owner Bette Moses Art Gallery, Gt. Bend; one woman shows: Gt. Bend Pub. Library, 1976, Hutchinson (Kans.) Pub. Library, 1976, Ft. Hays State U., Hays, Kans., 1977, Wichita (Kans.) Pub. Library, 1978, 1st Nat. Bank, Hutchinson, 1978; group shows include: Barton County Community Coll., Gt. Bend, 1970-79, Kans. State U., Manhattan, 1970, Ft. Hays State U., 1976, Hays Pub. Library, 1979, Wichita Art Mus., 1979, Kans. Watercolor Soc., 1980; represented in permanent collections: Nelson Sales Gallery, Kansas City, Mo., Wichita (Kans.) Art Mus., Galleria de Siles, Manzanillo, Mex., Bette Moses Gallery, numerous others. Founder, Art, Inc., Barton County Community Coll., 1970, mem. bd. advisers, 1972—. Mem. Kans. Watercolor Soc., Kans. Profl. Painters Assn. Republican. Mem. Christian Ch. Home: 3901 19th St Great Bend KS 67530 Office: Bette Moses Art Gallery 2110 10th St Great Bend KS 67530

MOSGROVE, ELSIE LOUISE, rehab. counselor; b. Walpole, Mass., Jan. 11, 1932; d. Werner Henry and Amy Irene (Lawson) Meyer; A.B. cum laude, Eastern Nazarene Coll., Wollaston, Mass., 1953; cert. Radcliff Secretarial Sch., Cambridge, Mass., 1953; postgrad. U. Va., Golden Gate U., San Francisco, United Bible Coll. and Sem.; m. Ralph Walter Mosgrove, June 5, 1954; 1 son, Reed Wesley. Various clerical and secretarial positions, 1953-60; tchr. schs. in Va. and Fla., 1961-66, 70; asst. Jacksonville (Fla.) Public Library, 1971; social worker, counselor, coordinator Fla. Dept. Health and Rehab. Services, St. Petersburg, 1975—; v.p. Gifted Assn. Pinellas County (Fla.), 1972-74; cons. in juvenile detention. Trustee, Lake Seminole (Fla.) Christian Sch., 1973; treas., Christian life dir., v.p. missions soc., mem. choir, tng. dir., also mem. ch. bd. Lealman Ch. of Nazarene, St. Petersburg, 1975—. Mem. Nat. Assn. Social Workers, Fla. Assn. Health and Social Services, Am. Assn. Christian Counselors, Nat. Assn. Christians in Social Work, Christian Bus. and Profl. Women's Council, Meadowlawn Civic Assn., PTA, Internat. Platform Assn., Ministerial Wives Assn. Office: 1100 Cleveland St Clearwater FL 33515

MOSHER, ELIZABETH ANNE, singer; b. San Francisco, Aug. 7, 1935; d. Austin Wilton and Dorothy Olive (Hall) M.; student Pomona Coll., 1953-55; B.M., U. So. Calif., 1957, M.M. cum laude (Fulbright scholar), 1958; postgrad. Hamburg Hochschule fur Musik, 1958-60; m. Herbert Kraus, July 26, 1962 (div.); 1 son, Zachary Stefan. Soprano, Biel-Solothurn Swiss Opera, 1961-63; freelance opera and concert singer in U.S., appearing with San Francisco Opera, Phila., N.Y. and Houston, 1963-70; asso. prof. voice U. Mich., v Ann Arbor, 1970-78; prof. voice U. Ariz., 1978—; concert singer; tchr. master classes. Rockefeller grantee, 1964, 66; winner Walter Naumburg award, 1964, Am. Opera auditions, 1966. Mem. Nat. Assn. Tchrs. of Singing (pres.) Tucson chapter; Music Tchrs. Nat. Assn., Mu Phi Epsilon, Pi Kappa Lambda. Office: College of Fine Arts School of Music 205 University of Arizona Tucson AZ 85721

MOSHER, JOAN BARR, educator; b. West Frankfort, Ill., June 17, 1935; d. Joseph John and Mary Ann (Pearson) M.; B.A., So. Ill. U., 1956; M.A., Ohio State U., 1958; M.A., U. Conn., 1970, Ph.D., 1974; m. Donald L. Mosher, Mar. 22, 1958 (div. 1977); children—Michelle L., Matthew B. Clin. psychologist Juvenile Diagnostic Center, Columbus, Ohio, 1958-60, Ohio State U. Counseling Center, Columbus, 1960-61; ednl. cons. Mansfield (Conn.) Sch. System, 1972-74; asst. prof. human devel. U. Conn., Storrs, 1974-75; family relations specialist Coop. Extension, U. R.I., Kingston, 1975—. Mem. Nat. Conf. Family Relations. Home: RFD 3 Willimantic CT 06226 Office: 23 Woodward Hall U RI Kingston RI 02881

MOSHER, KATHRYN SUZANNE, govt. ednl. adminstr.; b. Moline, Ill., Dec. 19, 1943; d. Raymond Bartel and Lucile (Zwicker) Nightingale; B.Music Edn., Augustana Coll., Rock Island, Ill., 1965; M.A., U. Iowa, 1980. Tchr. music, Public Schs., Aberdeen, Md., 1965, 3d grade, East Moline, Ill., 1966, 1st grade, Orion, Ill., 1967, 3d grade, East Moline, 1968; tchr. music Public Schs., East Moline, 1969-76; program coordinator Title VII, U.S. Office Edn., 1977-78, project dir. integration, 1978-79, dir. fed./state programs Title programs, East Moline, 1979—. Recipient awards Scouts of Am., 4-H, PTA. Mem. East Moline Edn. Assn. (pres. 1971-80), Ill. Edn. Assn. (dir. 1979—), East Moline Exec. Women's (pres.), Music Educators Nat. Council, NEA, Am. Adminstrs. Assn., Phi Delta Kappa, Sigma Alpha Iota. Lutheran. Home: 11314 176th Ave Orion IL 61273 Office: 836 17th Ave East Moline IL 61244

MOSHER, TENA LEE, title co. exec.; b. Atlanta, July 11, 1954; d. Herbert Cecil and Barbara Dolores (Taylor) Dodd; student public schs.; m. William Paul Mosher, June 12, 1976. Head bookkeeper K-Mart Ladies Apparell, 1975-76; with Stewart Title of Palm Beach County, 1976—, br. mgr., West Palm Beach, Fla., 1978-81, Tequesta, Fla., 1980—. Mem. Mortgage Bankers Assn. (chpt. sec.-treas. 1980), Women's Council Realtors (sec.-treas. 1981, chmn. publicity com. 1982), Jupiter/Tequesta/Hobe Sound Bd. Real Estate (Appreciation 1981), Nat. Assn. Female Execs. Office: 19626 US Hwy 1 Tequesta FL 33458

MOSKAL, LILYB, profl. speaker, author, Realtor; b. Biloxi, Miss., Sept. 26, 1929; d. Louis A. and Lillian Durward (Taylor) Staehling; B.A., U. Southwestern La., 1951; postgrad. in Spl. Edn. (Nat. Assn. Retarded Children scholar) Tulane U., 1962-64, in Real Estate Ft. Lauderdale U., 1974, Fla. Atlantic U., 1977; m. Thomas George Moskal, Dec. 20, 1970; children by previous marriage—Paul, Quentin, Danon, Chere. Supr. girls' sports New Orleans Recreation Dept., 1947; fashion model, coll. cons. D. H. Holmes Co., Ltd., dept. store, New Orleans, 1948-50; exec. sec. New Orleans Pub. Service, Inc., 1951; tchr. spl. edn. Lakeside Sch. for Spl. Children, Jefferson Parish (La.) Sch. Bd., 1961-64; real estate broker, pres. Medallion Gallery Homes, Inc., Metairie, La., 1965-70; host daily TV show Sta. WWOM-TV, New Orleans, 1968-69; dir. mktg., sales Taylor Hay Realtor, Louisville, 1973-74; pvt. practice Success Seminars, speaking-lecturing for sales tng., mgmt. workshops, 1975—. Pres. local PTA, 1960; reader for blind, Louisville Assn. Blind, 1971. Named Toastmistress of Year Jefferson Toastmistress Club, 1964, Exec. Woman of Year Women's Exec. Club, New Orleans, 1970. Mem. Nat. Speakers Assn. (bd. dirs. 1977-80), Fla. Speakers Assn. (charter pres.), Nat. Assn. Realtors, Women's Council Realtors, Fla. Assn. Realtors, Fla. Assn. Real Estate Educators, Phi Kappa Phi, Alpha Sigma Alpha. Republican. Presbyterian. Club: Women's Exec. (charter pres. La. club 1970, Fla. club 1976). Home and Office: Island Club 777 S Federal Hwy 107-0 Pampano Beach FL 33062

MOSKEWICZ, LORRAINE SHOSTACK, psychologist; b. Dayton, Ohio, Sept. 14, 1946; d. Walter and Goldie Grace Shostack; B.S., U. Dayton, 1968; M.A., Am. U., 1974, Ph.D., 1976; m. Michael Anthony Moskewicz, Aug. 16, 1969; children—Aron Anthony, Matthew Walter. Clin. psychology intern Eastern Shore Hosp. Center, Cambridge, Md., 1975-76; dir. Dorchester County Youth Counseling Center, Cambridge, 1976-78; clin. psychologist Caroline County Mental Health Clinic, Denton, Md., 1979—; adj. faculty Wor-Wic Tech. Community Coll., Salisbury, Md., 1980—. Cert. psychologist, Md. Mem. Am. Psychol. Assn., Dorchester County Mental Health Assn. Club: Bay Country Racquet. Home: Route 1 Box 7A Cambridge MD 21613 Office: 503 Byrn St Cambridge MD 21613

MOSKOWITZ, LISA JOYCE, psychotherapist; b. N.Y.C., Oct. 9, 1948; d. Abraham and Helen (Shulman) Moskowitz; B.A., CUNY, 1970; M.A., New Sch. for Social Research, 1973. Psychoanalytic psychotherapist in pvt. practice, N.Y.C., 1971—; co-dir./co-founder Univ. House, a therapeutic residence for schizophrenics, N.Y.C., 1973-76; sr. staff, acute psychiat. ward Lincoln Hosp., N.Y.C., 1972-73; lectr. Old Westbury campus SUNY, 1977. Mem. coordinating com. Feminist Therapy Collective, 1972-79; trustee Melia Found., 1975-77. Cert. psychotherapist, N.Y. State. Fellow Am. Inst. Psychotherapy and Psychoanalysis; mem. N.Y. State Assn. Practicing Psychotherapists (chairperson membership com.), Am. Psychol. Assn. (asso.), Feminist Therapy Collective. Contbr. articles to profl. jours. Address: 215 W 90 St New York NY 10024

MOSKOWITZ, RANDI ZUCKER, nurse; b. N.Y.C., Oct. 19, 1948; d. Seymour and Gertrude (Levy) Zucker; R.N., Jewish Hosp. & Med. Center Sch. Nursing, 1969; B.A., Marymount Manhattan Coll., 1975; M.S., Hunter Coll., 1979; m. Marc N. Moskowitz, July 11, 1976. Gen. staff nurse neurosurgery unit, N.Y. Hosp., N.Y.C., 1969-71, sr. staff nurse Recovery Room, 1971-76, nurse coordinator utilization rev., 1976-79; health educator Office of Cancer Communications, Meml. Sloan-Kettering Cancer Center, 1979-81; adminstrv. nurse oncologist Bklyn. Community Hosp. Oncology Program, Meth. Hosp., 1981—; instr. Div. Gen. Studies, Community Health and Health Adminstrn., St. Joseph's Coll., 1979—. Mem. Am. Public Health Assn., Oncology Nursing Soc., Soc. for Public Health Edn., Nat. Hospice Orgn., City-Wide Adv. Council on Sch. Health, Patient Edn. Consortium, Am. Cancer Soc. Home: 222 E 80th St New York NY 10021 Office: 506 6th St Brooklyn NY 11215

MOSKOWITZ, RITA JOYCE, Realtor; b. Little Rock, Aug. 31, 1928; d. Sam and Celia (Granoff) Schlesinger; X-ray technologist, radiation therapist, U. Ark., 1947; m. Frank David Moskowitz, Oct. 28, 1951; children—Marcy Ann, Mitchell Ben, Shelley Rae. X-ray technologist, radiation therapist Mo. Pacific Hosp., St. Louis, 1947-48; radiation therapist Jewish Hosp., St. Louis, 1948-49; X-ray technologist for pvt. physician, Kansas City, Mo., 1949-50, Mt. Sinai Hosp., Miami Beach, Fla., 1950-51; sec.-treas. Moskowitz Realty Co., Tulsa, 1963—; freelance writer, researcher, cons. Chairperson Okla. Real Estate Commn. 1973-76; mem. Okla. State Personnel Bd.; bd. dirs. Nursing Service Inc., Fenster Art Gallery. Mem. NCCJ, Am. Jewish Com., Nat. Council Jewish Women (life), Met. Tulsa Bd. Realtors, Nat. Assn. Realtors, Okla. Assn. Realtors (dir.), Real Estate Securities and Syndication Inst., Internat. Real Estate Fedn., Nat. Assn. Real Estate License Law Ofcls., Okla. Writers Fedn. Jewish. Office: 3530 E 31st St Suite 100 PO Box 2875 Tulsa OK 74101

MOSLEY, MAUREEN CECILIA, indsl. hygienist; b. Chgo., Nov. 28, 1953; d. Hubert Johnathan and Lucille (Daylie) M.; B.S., Western Ill. U., 1977; M.S., U. Iowa, 1980. Environ. health asst. U. Iowa, 1977-78; indsl. hygienist E. I. Du Pont & Co., Clinton, Iowa, 1980, occupational health coordinator, Circleville, Ohio, 1980—. Recipient Nat. Inst. Occupational Safety and Health tng. scholarship, 1979-80. Mem. Am. Indsl. Hygiene Assn., Nat. Tech. Assn. (treas. 1981-82). Roman Catholic. Office: EI DuPont Co PO Box 89 Du Pont Rd Circleville OH 43113

MOSLEY, RUTH MAE, clergywoman; b. Olive Branch, Miss., Mar. 10, 1930; d. Myles and Versie Mae (Davis) Newborn; student Highland Park (Mich.) Jr. Coll., 1962-64, U. Detroit, 1973-78, Wayne County Community Coll., Detroit, 1981; divorced; children—Richard, William James, Pearl Scott. Ordained to ministry Unity Ch., 1966; founder, pastor West Side Unity Ch., Detroit, 1964; pres. Gt. Lake Unity Conf., 1974; trustee Assn. Unity Chs., Unity Village, Mo., 1976—, v.p., 1980-81, pres., 1981-82; chaplain Rosa L. Gragg Civic Club; speaker weekly radio program. Trustee Western Wayne County Bd., 1980—. Recipient numerous certs. of appreciation, service awards, commendation and recognition awards. Mem. Internat. New Thought Alliance, Women Conf. of Concern, Assn. Study Afro-Am. Life and History. Author booklet, also cassette tapes. Home: 15157 Warwick St Detroit MI 48223 Office: 4727 Joy Rd Detroit MI 48204

MOSS, ANNA MARIE, textile co. exec.; b. Vienna, Austria, Apr. 20, 1904; came to U.S., 1922, naturalized, 1928; d. Wentzel and Maria (Rossler) Prevost; grad. Cleve. Sch. Art, 1930; student Max Reinhardt Sch. Acting, Austria, 1931; m. Theron Victor Moss, July 3, 1939; children—Theron Charles, Judith Ann. Artist-designer Lighting-Railley Corp., Cleve., 1933-39; plant. supr. South Eastern Cordage Co., Cleve., 1959-72, Cleveland, Tenn., 1972-80; exec. textile supr., SECO Industries, Inc., Cleveland, 1980—. Republican. Mem. Ch. of God. Club: Cleveland Country. Home: Holiday Inn Hilltop Interstate Cleveland TN 37311 Office: PO Box 234 Old Michigan Ave Rd Cleveland TN 37311

MOSS, BERNADINE YOCHELSON, artist, educator, art therapist; b. Chgo., July 13, 1932; d. Albert G. and Beatrice J. Yochelson; student U. Chgo., 1963-69; B.F.A., Art. Inst. Chgo., 1967, M.F.A., 1972; teaching cert. Lake Forest (Ill.) Coll., 1970; m. Edward A. Moss, Dec. 4, 1950; children—Gwen Moss Brush, Henry Dee. Art tchr. New Trier High Sch., Northfield, Ill., 1968-73; commd. muralist Phillips Bros. Ins., Chgo., 1973-74; adviser grad. program art therapy ind. study Lindenwood Coll., St. Charles, Mo., 1974-75; condr. short term art therapy groups to teach modality of art therapy to profls., 1976—; cons. art therapists, 1981-82; art therapist; pvt. painting tchr.; works included in many group competitive shows, gallery and mus. showings, pvt. collections. Recipient Blue Ribbon for painting, Hyde Park Art Center, 1976. Mem. Art Therapy Assn., Coll. Art Assn., Alumni Assn. Art Inst. Chgo. Home: 323 Glendale Winnetka IL 60093 Studio: 546 W Washington Blvd Chicago IL 60606

MOSS, JEANNETTE BEVERLY, life ins. co. exec.; b. Haverhill, Mass., Apr. 26, 1941; d. William Henry and Theresa Louise (Gill) Howard; grad. N.H. Coll., 1981; postgrad. Am. Internat. Coll.,

Springfield, Mass., 1983—; m. William F. Moss, July 17, 1970; 1 dau., Theresa L. Instr. English conversation Tenja Corp., Tukuoka, Japan, 1964-66; electronic data processing sec. Boston Herald Am. Corp., 1967-71; sr. key punch operator Raytheon Corp., Lowell, Mass., 1971-72; electronic data processing sec. Culverwell & Co., Inc., Springfield, 1972-74; trainer Conn. Gen. Life Ins. Co., Hartford, 1974-79; sr. personnel devel. specialist Mass. Mut. Life Ins. Co., Springfield, 1979—; pres. J/B Resource, Ltd., human resource devel. cons. Clk. bd. dirs. Urban League Springfield, Inc., 1979-82; pres. Springfield Urban League Guild, 1981-82. Mem. Am. Soc. Devel. and Tng., Organizational Devel. Network, Pioneer Valley Women's Network. Baptist. Office: 1295 State St Springfield MA 01111

MOSS, JUDITH, mayor, acad. adminstr.; b. Long Branch, N.J., July 11, 1924; d. Louis John and Bryna (Finegold) M.; B.A., Vassar Coll., 1944; M.A., Columbia U., 1947; M.S. (NSF fellow), Stanford U., 1971. Statistician, Statis. Research Group, Div. War Research, 1944-45; research asst. Nat. Bur. Econ. Research, 1945-48; econ. analyst Port of N.Y. Authority, 1948-55, electronics research analyst, 1955-56; electronics research specialist Revlon, Inc., 1956-58; chief Integrated data processing City of Phila., 1958-62; sr. system analyst Gen. Electric Computer Dept., 1962-64, cons. systems specialist, N.Y.C., 1964-66; sr. ops. research specialist, spl. projects ops. Lockheed Missiles & Space Co., Sunnyvale, Calif., 1966-72; staff cons. Govt. Info. Systems; research dir. San Francisco Community Coll. Dist., 1972—; mayor City of Mountain View (Calif.), 1975—. Mem. Mountain View City Council, 1972-80; mem. adv. com. on mgmt. info. systems, chancellor's office Calif. Community Coll.; chmn. research and devel. commn. Calif. Community and Jr. Coll. Assn.; mem. exec. bd. Health Systems Agy.; active Jewish Welfare Fedn., Am. Jewish Com.; pres. S. Peninsula Jewish Community Center. Mem. Inst. Mgmt. Sci. (nat. council 1975), Ops. Research Soc., Am. Soc. Public Adminstrn., Assn. Calif. Community Coll. Adminstrs., League Calif. Cities, Assn. Bay Area Govts. Office: 33 Gough St San Francisco CA 94103

MOSS, KAREN MANDLEBAUM, law librarian; b. Detroit, Mar. 11, 1938; d. Daniel and Naomi (Kranson) Mandlebaum; B.A. in Edn., Wayne State U., Detroit, 1959, M.S.L.S., 1971; children—Lauren Rachel, Jonathan David. Elem. sch. tchr., 1959-61; mem. tech. services staff Oakland County (Mich.) Law Library, 1972-75; tech. services librarian Adams-Pratt Oakland County Law Library, 1975-76; librarian U.S. Dist. Ct. Mich. East, 1977-79; circuit librarian U.S. Ct. Appeals 1st Circuit, Boston, 1979—. Mem. Am. Assn. Law Libraries, Law Librarians New Eng., Assn. Boston Law Librarians, Mich. Assn. Law Libraries, Ohio Regional Assn. Law Libraries, Fed. Ct. Librarians (user com.), Boston Group Govt. Librarians. Deocrat. Author articles in field. Home: Lincoln MA Office: 1208 McCormack Post Office and Courthouse Boston MA 02109

MOSS, MARTHA CALLICUTT, accountant; b. Union County, Miss., Feb. 10, 1945; d. King Avery and Mary Madella (Kerr) Callicutt; B.S., U. South Ala., 1976; m. J. L. Prather, Dec. 20, 1963; children—Robert Kerr Prather, William Allen Prather; m. 2d, Terry Edwin Moss, Feb. 12, 1977. Acct., R. M. Frellsen Acctg., Pascagoula, Miss., 1966-69; pvt. practice acctg., Pascagoula, 1969—. Active United Way, 1979, Dixie Youth, 1979. C.P.A., Miss. Mem. Am. Inst. C.P.A.s Am. Women's Soc. C.P.A.s, Miss. Soc. C.P.A.s. Club: Zonta (treas. 1981). Home: 3800 Quinn Pascagoula MS 39567 Office: 3623-B Lee St Pascagoula MS 39567

MOSS, SHIRLEY ANN, chemist; b. Wilmington, N.C., Nov. 28, 1943; d. Lucas Jackson and Hazel Elizabeth (Holmes) Howard; B.S. in Chemistry, Hampton (Va.) Inst., 1964; postgrad. St. Mary's U., San Antonio, Tex., 1967, San Jose State U., 1974-75; m. Luther Phillip Moss, Apr. 16, 1966 (div. 1975); 1 dau., Janis Nicole. Biochem. research asst. Pa. Hosp., Phila., 1964-66; research chemist Sch. Aerospace Medicine Brooks AFB, San Antonio, 1966-69; asso. engr. Gen. Electric, San Jose, 1973-78, chemist, 1978—. Mem. Am. Chem. Soc., Soc. Women Engrs., Delta Sigma Theta. Democrat. Episcopalian. Home: 2118 Canoas Carden # 27 San Jose CA 95125 Office: 175 Curtner Ave San Jose CA 95125

MOSS, THELMA GRACE CROMWELL, business exec., ednl. adminstr.; b. Boston, May 19, 1939; d. Anthony John and Archebell (McCarter) Cromwell; B.A.S., Met. Coll., Boston U., 1974; M.Ed., Antioch Inst. Open Edn., 1975; postgrad. Union Coll.; children—Willie James, Marwan Jonathan, Namala Thelma. Exec. dir. Innovative Sch. System Commonwealth of Mass., 1974-76; adj. faculty Inst. Open Edn. in Adminstrn., Boston, 1976—; dean continuing edn. and community services Berkshire Community Coll., Pittsfield, Mass., 1980—; mem. minority bus. opportunity com. Boston Fed. Exec. Bd.; pres. AA Glassmobile Inc. Exec. com., drug com., area bd. Boston State Hosp.; apptd. by Gov., State Mental Health and Mental Retardation Bd., 1978—, v.p., 1978-79; mem. Boston planning com. Internat. Women's Year, 1977; founder Roxbury YWCA, ASWALOS House, 1968-71; mem. NAACP; bd. dirs. Boston Pvt. Industry Council, Small Bus. Assn. New Eng., Black Corp. Pres. New Eng.; pres. Coalition of Women in Nat. and Internat. Bus.; mem. Gov.'s Council on Mass. Bus. Devel. Mem. Orgn. Ednl. Devel. (pres.), Black Corp. Pres.'s New Eng., Nat. Assn. Black Mfrs., Contractors Assn. Boston (pres.). Address: PO Box 950 Roxbury MA 02119

MOSTACCI, SUZANNE, home economist; b. N.Y.C., Sept. 7; d. Carmine Thomas and Johanna Mostacci; A.A., Queensborough Community Coll., 1974; B.A., Queens Coll., 1976. Home service dir. Macfadden Women's Group, N.Y.C., 1980—. Mem. legis. adv. com. N.Y. State Assembly, 1976—; mem. U.S. Consumer Adv. Panel, 1977—. Mem. Am. Home Econs. Assn., Home Economists in Bus., Phi Upsilon Omicron. Democrat. Roman Catholic. Office: 215 Lexington Ave New York NY 10016

MOSTEL, KATHRYN HARKIN, actress, writer; b. Phila., Oct. 8, 1918; d. High John and Anna (McCaffery) Harkin; grad. high sch.; m. Zero Mostel, July 1, 1944 (dec.); children—Joshua, Tobias. Dancer, Vaudeville act, 1926-30; mem. Littlefield Ballet Co., Phila., 1935-39; mem. Rockettes, N.Y.C., 1941-43; actress Broadway shows Bird Cage, 1950, Ladies of the Corridor, 1954, Ulysses in Night Town, 1958, One Night Stand, 1981; also appeared summer stock, Cambridge, Mass. Co-author (with Madeline and Jack Gilford and Zero Mostel): 170 Years of Show Business, 1978. Office: care David W Katz 21 E 40th St New York NY 10016

MOSTELLER, BETTE VAUGHAN, librarian; b. Amelia County, Va.; d. Lawson Paul and Rosa Vaughan (Mottley) M.; B.A., Longwood Coll., 1958; M.A. in L.S. (Va. State Library fellow), George Peabody Coll., 1959; postgrad. Coll. William and Mary, 1973—. Cataloger, Va. State Library, 1959-62; head librarian Christopher Newport Coll., Newport News, Va., 1962-67, library dir., 1967—; mem. library adv. com. Va. Council Higher Edn., 1971—; mem. Task Force Va. Plan for Libraries, 1975-76, Task Force State-Wide Library Storage Facility, 1977; vice chmn. Tidewater Consortium Library Dirs. Com., 1976—; chmn. Tidewater interlibrary loan subcom. library space guidelines State Council Higher Edn., 1981—. Mem. Eastern Va. Bicentennial Com., 1970-81. Mem. ALA (library equipment com. 1981—), Southeastern Library Assn., Va. Library Assn. (exec. asst. Va. Nat. Library Week com. 1969-71, mem. awards com. 1982—). Home: 163 Yeardley Dr Newport News VA 23601 Office: 50 Shoe Ln Newport News VA 23606

MOTE, WINNIFRED KATHLEEN, pharmacist; b. Des Moines, Oct. 13, 1918; d. Frederick Garfield and Mary Rebecca (Trevillyan) Mote; B.S., Drake U., 1942. Dir. pharmacy Broadlawns Polk County Hosp., Des Moines, 1942-62, instr. student nurses, 1946-58, acting dir. pharmacy service, 1962-64, dir., 1969—; instr. Drake U. at Broadlawns, 1949—. Mem. bd. YWCA, 1962-63; spl. projects chmn. S.S. Hope, 1964-66; nominating chmn. Broadlawns Guild, 1968-69, mem., 1946—; sec. Pharmacy and Therapeutic Com., 1973—; mem. Infectious Control Com. Recipient Good Citizenship award, 1963. Fellow Royal Soc. Health; mem. Des Moines Bus. and Profl. Women's Club, Drake U. Alumnae Assn., AAUW, Am. (ho. of dels. 1973—), Iowa (pres. 1948-49, v.p. 1966, 67, dir. 1973—, sec.-treas. 1974-78) socs. hosp. pharmacists, Am., Iowa (hosp. liaison com. 1967-68, com. on instnl. practice 1969-71, ho. of dels. 1972-78), Polk County pharm. assns., Lambda Kappa Sigma (internat. resolution chmn.). Clubs: Order Eastern Star (worthy matron 1963, grand rep. Ia. to Mass. 1975-76), Zonta (pres. 1953-54, 66-67, 75-77, chmn. 1964-65, dir. 1968-70, 73-78, service chmn. 1970-71, v.p. 1973-74, Amelia Earhart chmn. 1973-74, del. to internat. com., Ger.), White Shrine Jerusalem, Order of Job's Dau. (Bethel guardian 1978-81), Amaranth, Daus. Nile. Home: 3512 S Union St Des Moines IA 50315 Office: 18th and Hickman Rd Des Moines IA 50314

MOTHERSHEAD, ALICE BONZI (MRS. MORRIS WARNER MOTHERSHEAD), coll. program adminstr.; b. Milan, Italy, Dec. 25, 1914; came to U.S. 1920, naturalized 1925; d. Ercole and Alice (Spalding) Bonzi; pvt. pupil music and art; student Pasadena City Coll., 1958-60; m. Morris Warner Mothershead, Sept. 15, 1935; children—Warner Bonzi, Maria (Mrs. Andrei Rogers). Partner Floal Toy Co., Pasadena, Calif., 1942-44; community adv. Fgn. Student Program, Pasadena City Coll., 1952—, now dir. Community Liaison Center. Chmn., Am. Field Service Internat. Scholarships, Pasadena, 1953-55; mem. West Coast adv. com. Inst. Internat. Edn., San Francisco, 1957-70. Vice pres. San Rafael Sch. PTA, Pasadena, 1945-46; active Community Chest, ARC, Pasadena; chmn. Greater Los Angeles Com. Internat. Student and Visitor Services, 1962; mem. Woman's Civic League Pasadena, 1972. Decorated knight Govt. of Italy, 1975. Mem. Nat. Assn. Fgn. Student Affairs (chmn. community sect. and v.p. 1964-65, chmn. U.S. study abroad com. 1969-70), Am. Assn. UN (chpt. 2d v.p. 1964), Am. Friends Middle East, Omicron Mu Delta. Club: International (Pasadena). Author: Social Customs and Manners in the United States, 1957; Dining Customs Around the World, 1982; co-author: 15 Years of the Foreign Student Program at Pasadena City College, 1965. Editor: Students to People to Future, 1971. Home: 675 Burleigh Dr Pasadena CA 91105 Office: Pasadena City Coll 1570 E Colorado Blvd Pasadena CA 91106

MOTT, MELANIE MADGE, mfg. industry cons.; b. Houston, Oct. 12, 1951; d. Manning Marshall and Leonia Dolores (Grant) M.; B.A., Smith Coll., 1973. Production control analyst Gen. Electric Co., 1973-75, supr. prodn. planning and inventory control, 1975-76, subcontract adminstr., 1976-77; intern cons. I, Rath & Strong, Inc., 1977; sales rep. Gen. Electric Info. Services Co., 1977-78, account rep., 1978-79; intern cons. II Rath & Strong, Inc., Lexington, Mass., 1979, asso. cons. 1980-82, cons., 1982—. Mem. Inst. Mgmt. Cons., Am. Prodn. and Inventory Control Soc., NOW. Home: 23 Cortes St Boston MA 02116 Office: 21 Worthen Rd Lexington MA 02173

MOTZ, JANET KAY, social worker; b. Palisade, Colo., Oct 24, 1945; d. Merle Douglas and Joan Marilyn (Leeper) M.; B.A., U. Colo., 1968; M.S.W. (Social Services stipend 1972-74), U. Kans., 1974. Social worker Mesa County Dept. Social Services, Grand Junction, Colo., 1968-75; social services supr. Jefferson County Dept. Social Services, Lakewood, Colo., 1975-76, Adams County Dept. Social Services, Commerce City, Colo., 1976-79; protective services program supr. Colo. Dept. Social Services, Denver, 1979-81; human services coordinator Wirth Assos. Inc., Denver, 1981—. Bd. dirs. Mesa County Mental Health Assn., 1968-75, Nat. Council Alcoholism, 1972, Colo. Juvenile Council, 1976-78, Met. Child Protection Council, 1979—; bd. dirs., exec. com. Attention Youth, Inc., 1970-72; mem. Mesa County Task Force Drug Edn., 1970-72. Names Grand Junction Career Woman of Yr., 1971. Author papers in field. Home: 800 Pennsylvania St Apt 1112 Denver CO 80203 Office: 1009 Grant St Suite 304 Denver CO 80203

MOUCHKA, SUSAN ANNE (FOSSUM), govt. health planning ofcl.; b. Peoria, Ill., Nov. 18, 1941; d. Joseph L. and Bernadette Marie (O'Hearn) Hecht; B.S., Ind. U., 1964; M.S. in Clin. Psychology, San Francisco State U., 1974; postgrad. Fielding Inst., Santa Barbara, 1981—; m. G. Mouchka (div.); children—Catherine, Margaret; m. 2d Jim Fossum, May 18, 1980. Cons. on psychology of developmental disabilities Center for Edn. and Therapy, Sacramento, 1970—; clin. dir., Calif. Dept. Developmental Services, Sonoma State Hosp., 1977-78, cons. in program evaluation, 1979-80; coordinator Calif. Public Forums on Long Term Care and Aging, Calif. Health and Welfare Agy., Sacramento, 1981-82; project dir. NIMH grant Calif. Dept. Mental Health, Sacramento, 1982—. Lic. nursing home adminstr., lic. marriage, family, child counselor. Mem. Am. Psychol. Assn., AAAS, Assn. for Mental Health Affiliation with Israel. Contbr. papers and report to publs. in field. Home: 3400 Northrop Ave Sacramento CA 95825 Office: 1600 9th St Sacramento CA 95814

MOUCHLY-WEISS, HARRIET, public relations exec.; b. Bronx, N.Y., Aug. 12, 1940; d. Robert and Anita (Shawmut) Berg; B.A., Muhlenberg Coll., 1960; M.A., Hebrew U., Jerusalem, 1964; m. Charles Weiss, Sept. 13, 1975; children—Noa Weiss Temko, Joey. Clin. psychologist Hadassah Hosp., 1962-65; account exec. Ruder & Finn, Inc., N.Y.C., 1965-67; pres. Ruder & Finn Israel, 1968-80; chmn. Ruder & Finn Internat. Partners, Ltd., N.Y.C. and Washington, 1980—; sr. v.p. plans Ruder Finn & Rotman, Inc., Washington, 1981—; dir. Sterling Internat., London. Bd. dirs. Am. Acad. Rome. Mem. Public Relations Soc. Am., Internat. Public Relations Assn., Greater Washington Bd. Trade. Home: 8605 Long Acre Ct Bethesda MD 20817 Office: 110 E 59th St New York NY 10022 also 1225 19th St NW Suite 270 Washington DC 20036

MOULD, LILIAN JESSIE, clin. psychologist; b. Locust Valley, N.Y., June 26, 1914; d. Jesse Hayes and Lillia Weir (Cook) Mould; B.A., Barnard Coll., 1935; M.A., Columbia U., 1943; Ph.D., N.Y.U., 1957. Tchr. public schs. Hartsdale, N.Y., 1939-51; clin. psychologist N.Y. State Child Guidance Clinic, Binghamton, N.Y., 1953-57; child psychologist Hartley-Salmon Child Guidance Clinic, Hartford, Conn., 1957-63; staff psychologist Silver Hill Found., New Canaan, Conn., 1963-69; chief psychologist Mid-Fairfield Child Guidance Center, Norwalk, Conn., 1970—; vis. lectr. Grad. Sch. U. Conn., 1960-62; cons. Norwalk Headstart, 1971-74. Mem. Am. Psychol. Assn., N.Y. State Psychol. Assn., Conn. Psychol. Assn. Club: Barnard Coll. of Fairfield County. Home: 33 Cross Hwy Westport CT 06880

MOULTON, BARBARA EMILIE, nurse; b. Medford, Mass., Aug. 3, 1921; d. Chester Howard and Dorothea Louisa (Turner) M.; R.N., Mass. Gen. Hosp., Boston, 1943; B.S., Simmons Coll., Boston, 1946; M.S. in Nursing, Boston U., 1951, M.A., 1963. Staff nurse hosps. in N.Y. and Md., 1943-49; guest instr. U. N.C., summer 1957; mem. faculty Boston U. Sch. Nursing, 1950-82, prof. nursing, 1976-82; cons., workshop dir. in field. Mem. Photog. Soc. Am. Episcopalian. Address: 902 The Hollows 4900 E 5th St Tucson AZ 85711

MOULTON, GRACE CHARBONNET, physicist; b. New Orleans, Nov. 1, 1923; d. Wilfred James and Louise Antoionett (Hellmers) C.; B.A., Tulane U., 1944; M.S., U. Ill., 1948; Ph.D., U. Ala., 1962; m. William G. Moulton, June 1, 1947; children—Paul Charbonnet, Nancy Gates. Asst. prof. physics U. Ala., Tuscaloosa, 1962-65; asst. prof. physics Fla. State U., Tallahassee, 1965-74, asso. prof. physics, 1974-80, prof. physics, 1980—; cons. NIH, 1976. NIH grantee, 1963-66, 69-71; AEC grantee, 1965-70. Fellow AAAS; mem. Am. Phys. Soc., Assn. Women in Sci., Fedn. Am. Scientists, Sigma Xi. Contbr. articles to profl. jours. Home: 2305 Don Andres Ave Tallahassee FL 32304 Office: Dept of Physics FLorida State U Tallahassee FL 32306

MOUNT, SALLY ANNE, univ. ofcl.; b. Oregon City, Oreg., June 17, 1929; d. Guy and Gertrude Louise M.; B.A., U. Wash., 1951; cert. med. record adminstrn. program Providence Hosp., Seattle, 1957; M.Ed., Prairie View A&M U., 1975. Dir. dept. med. records Tacoma Gen. Hosp., 1958-62; asst. dir. dept. med. records U. Tex., Galveston, 1962-63, dir. dept. med. records, 1963-75, asso. prof., chmn. dept. med. record adminstrn., 1968-75; asso. prof., dir. med. record services Oreg. Health Scis. U., Portland, 1976—. Mem. Wash. Med. Record Assn. (pres. 1961-62), Tex. (pres. 1968-69, Disting. Mem. award 1974), Am. Med. Record Assn. (pres. 1972-73, dir. exec. bd. 1968-71, 73-74), Oreg. Med. Record Assn. (exec. bd. 1981-82, Disting. Mem. award 1982), Am. Hosp. Assn., Assn. Records Mgrs. and Adminstrs. Republican. Office: 3181 Sam Jackson Park Rd SW OPC Room 1235-A (OP17A) Portland OR 97201

MOUSER, MARCELLA, educator; b. Frontenac, Kans., Jan. 16, 1926; d. Frank and Lillie (Arkle) M.; B.S. in Edn., Pittsburg State U., 1947, M.S. in Edn., 1952; Ed.D. in Secondary Edn., U. Nebr., Lincoln, 1969. Tchr. bus. Louisburg (Kans.) High Sch., 1947-49, Yates Center (Kans.) High Sch., 1951-59; asst. prof. bus. and bus. edn. Emporia State U., 1959-69, asso. prof., 1969-73, prof., 1973—; bd. dirs. nat. Future Bus. Leaders Am./Phi Beta Lambda, Inc.; asst. chairperson Kans. Future Bus. Leaders Am. Capt., United Way, Sch. Applied Arts and Scis., Emporia State U., 1982. Emporia State U. Faculty Research and Creativity grantee, 1976, 82. Mem. NEA, Kans. Edn. Assn., Kans. Bus. Edn. Assn. (exec. bd.), Nat. Bus. Edn. Assn. (exec. bd.), AAUP, AAUW, Mountain-Plains Bus. Edn. Assn. (exec. bd.), Am. Bus. Women's Assn., Pi Omega Pi, Delta Pi Epsilon, Kappa Kappa Iota. Roman Catholic. Club: Am. Legion Aux. Advt. mgr. Kans. Bus. Tchr., 1976-82. Home: 1219 Merchant Emporia KS 66801 Office: 1200 Commercial Emporia KS 66801

MOUTON, WANDA CAROL, editor; b. Nacogdoches, Tex., Sept. 15, 1952; d. T.M. and Juanita (Peterson) Greer Peterson; B.A., Stephen F. Austin State U., 1974; m. Earl Bruce Mouton, Oct. 12, 1974. Lifestyle reporter Daily Sentinel, Nacogdoches, 1974-77; editor Scene mag., Dallas, 1978-79; communication specialist Southland Life Ins. Co., Dallas, 1979-82; lifestyle editor Midland (Tex.) Reporter Telegram, 1979—. Contbr. articles to profl. jours. Office: 201 E Illinois St Midland TX 79701

MOVITCH, ROSE EVELYN DIERNFELD, educator; b. Denver, Aug. 4, 1920; d. Samuel and Gertrude (Frank) Diernfeld; B.S., Temple U., 1942; M.S.W., Rutgers U., 1959; m. James Movitch, Aug. 2, 1942; 1 dau., Susan. Dir. older adult dept. Jewish Community Center, Trenton, N.J., 1953-68, bd. dirs., 1969—; asst. prof. group work dept. Rutgers, The State U., Grad. Sch. Social Work, New Brunswick, N.J., 1969-71, mem. adj. faculty Inst. on Aging, 1972—; cons., trainer City of Trenton Aging Office, 1973-78; cons., trainer outreach Mercer County (N.J.) Community Action Program, 1975-77; v.p. Sr. Citizen Housing Corp., 1978—. Mem. Nat. Assn. Social Workers (task force on aging, chmn. legis. com. 1976-78), Gerontol. Soc. N.J. (charter mem., trustee 1971-79), Jewish Fedn. of Greater Trenton (bd. dirs. 1971—, v.p. 1974-79, pres. 1979—), Assn. Jewish Center Workers (exec. dir. 1974-76), Nat. Council on Aging. Jewish. Home: 647 W State St Trenton NJ 08618 Office: Rutgers Grad School of Social Work New Brunswick NJ 08903

MOW, ANNA BEAHM (MRS. BAXTER MERRILL MOW), educator; b. Daleville, Va., July 31, 1893; d. Isaac N.H. and Mary (Bucher) Beahm; B.A., Manchester Coll., 1918, D.D., 1976; B.D., Bethany Theol. Sem., 1921, M.R.E., 1941, M.Th., 1943; D.D., 1959; Litt.D., Elizabethtown Coll., 1975; m. Baxter Merrill Mow, Mar. 30, 1921; children—Lois (Mrs. J. Ernest Snavely), Joseph, Merrill. Missionary to India, 1923-40; prof. Christian edn. Bethany Theol. Sem., 1942-58. Mem. gen. bd. Ch. of Brethren, 1967-75. Recipient alumni award Manchester (Ind.) Coll., 1963; named Va. State Mother of Year, 1973. Author: Say 'Yes' to Life, 1961; Your Child, 1963; Going Steady with God, 1965; Your Teenager and You, 1967; Who's Afraid of Birthdays, 1969; The Secret of Married Love, 1970; Your Experience and the Bible, 1973; Sensitivity to What, 1975; Find Your Own Faith, 1977; Springs of Love, 1979. Address: 1318 Varnell Ave NE Roanoke VA 24012

MOWRER, LILIAN T., author; b. London, Eng.; d. Octavius Leopold and Eliza Jane (Green) Thomson; student Liverpool U., 1911-13, Sorbonne, Paris, 1907, Sapienza, Rome, 1920-21; m. Edgar Ansel Mowrer, Feb. 8, 1916; 1 dau., Diana (Mrs. Jean Béllard). Author: Journalist's Wife, 1937; Arrest and Exile, 1940; Riptide of Aggression, 1942; Concerning France, 1944; The U.S. and World Relations, 1950; John Scott of L.I., 1960; I've Seen It Happen Twice, 1969; (with Edgar A. Mowrer) UMANO and The Price of Lasting Peace, 1973. D.C. chmn. Women's Action Com. for Lasting Peace, 1943-49; pres. emeritus Umano Found., 1979. Decorated for meritorious work with Red Cross (Italy). Mem. Am. News Women's Club, Women in Communications. Home: Wonalancet NH 03897

MOYER, BARBARA A., mag. editor; b. Pitts., July 18, 1953; d. Eugene R. and Sadie Marie (Kessler) Palowitch; B.A. with distinction, Pa. State U., 1975; postgrad. U. Oxford (Eng.), 1974; Parsons Sch. Design; m. Stephen B. Moyer, Oct. 10, 1981. Editorial/prodn. coordinator SAE Handbook and Specifications, both of Soc. Automotive Engrs., Warrendale, Pa., 1975-76; asst. editor Iron and Steel Engr. mag. Assn. Iron and Steel Engrs., Pitts., 1976-77; prodn. editor Modern Photography, ABC Pub., N.Y.C., 1977-78, mng. editor, 1978—; freelance writer, editor. Home: 329 E 92d St New York NY 10028 Office: 825 Seventh Ave New York NY 10019

MOYNEHAN, BARBARA MARIA, writer; b. Johnstown, N.Y., Dec. 18, 1948; d. John Dennis and Catherine Moynehan; B.A. in English, Nazareth Coll. of Rochester, 1971; student in journalism, N.Y.U., 1970; postgrad. in urban planning, SUNY Coll., Brockport, 1972-73. Staff writer, Rochester (N.Y.) Dioseas's Courier Jour., 1971-73; editor Rochester Mag., 1974-76; mng. editor N.Y.-Pa. Collector, 1976-77; asst. editor Time Life Books Series Collectibles, N.Y.C., 1977; copy editor Family Circle Mag., N.Y.C., 1978-80; editorial asst. Philip Morris Inc., N.Y.C., 1980—; freelance writer on art antiques Americana, on history for MS Mag., contbr. to Village Voice; researcher, writer for Gannet Newspapers, 1972; art reviewer for Italian art mags. Sergo, Flash Art; pub. collection of works by world wide artists, 1982. Mem. Women in Communications, Internat. Assn. Bus. Communicators, Sigma Delta Chi. Democrat. Home: 212 E 29th St New York NY 10016 Office: 100 Park Ave New York NY 10017

MOZAFFAR, THERESA ANNE FUESS, physicist; b. Houston, Nov. 8, 1953; d. Lawrence Joseph and Margaret Anne (Hayden) Fuess; B.S.,

Columbia U., 1981; postgrad. M.I.T., 1981—; m. Shakeel Mozaffar, Mar. 16, 1974. Jr. engr. IBM, Fishkill, N.Y., 1980; instr. math. and physics, also instr. Physics Lab., Columbia U., N.Y.C., 1980-81; research asst. M.I.T., Cambridge, 1981—. Mem. Am. Phys. Soc., Tau Beta Pi. Home: 60 Wadsworth St Apt 27B Cambridge MA 02142 Office: 575 Technology Square Room 408 Cambridge MA 02139

MOZAK, CAROL ANN, mktg. analyst; b. Celina, Ohio, Sept. 30, 1954; d. Edward E. and Lavon M. (Marhanka) M.; B.S. in Edn., Bowling Green State U., 1976; M.B.A., George Washington U., 1978. Conf. registrar Jr. Achievement, Inc., Stamford, Conn., 1975-76; intern U.S. Dept. Commerce, Washington, 1977; teaching asst. George Washington U., Washington, 1977-78; mgmt. cons. Mark Battle Assos., Washington, 1978; corporate trainee Stanley Works, New Britain, Conn., 1978, corporate market analyst, 1979—. Choir mem. Western Presbyn. Ch. Choir, 1976—; U.S. rep. Liege, Belgium Internat. Trade Fair, 1978. Wolcott fellow, 1977-78. Mem. Phi Delta Gamma, Alpha Kappa Psi, Mortar Bd., Pi Delta Phi, Alpha Lambda Delta. Contbr. articles in field to profl. jours. Home: 65 High Gate Rd Apt A-2 Newington CT 06111

MOZER, DORIS ANN, writer; b. July 10, 1929; d. Charles Ross and Mary Margaret (Redmiles) Werner; B.A., N.Mex. State U., 1963, M.A. in English, 1970; postgrad. in English, U. Md., 1982; div.; children—Stephen, Judith, Mary Catherine, Laura, John. Grad. asst. N.Mex. State U., 1963-65, instr., 1969-75; free-lance editor, 1969—; editor Sibyl-Child, women's arts and cultural jour., 1976—; grad. asst. U. Md., College Park, 1976-78, dir. Writing Center, 1978-80, acad. adviser, internship coordinator, 1980-82; tech. writer Environ. Satellite Data, Inc., Suitland, Md., 1982—. Vice pres., publicity chmn. Las Cruces (N.Mex.) Children's Theatre, 1968; pres., publicity chmn. Las Cruces Theater Guild, 1969. Folger Shakespearean Inst. fellow, 1979. Mem. MLA, S. Atlantic Modern Lang. Assn., Phi Kappa Phi. Democrat. Unitarian. Home: 13015 Marquette Ln Bowie MD 20715 Office: Environ Satellite Data Inc 5200 Auth Rd Suitland MD 20746

MOZLEY, ANITA VENTURA, curator; b. Washington, Aug. 29, 1928; d. Mario and Juanita Magruder (Lewis) Ventura; B.A., Northwestern U., 1950; m. Robert F. Mozley, June 23, 1967. Designer, contbg. editor Arts Mag., N.Y.C., 1953-59, mng. editor, 1959-60; curatorial asst. Guggenheim Mus., N.Y.C., 1961-62; asst. curator, editor Sea Letter, San Francisco Maritime Mus., 1963-68; curator of photography Stanford (Calif.) U. Mus. Art, 1971—. Mem. Friends of Photography, Phi Beta Kappa. Author: (exhbn. catalogue) Eadweard Muybridge: The Stanford Years, 1972; Mrs. Cameron's Photographs from the Life, 1974; American Photography: Past into Present, 1976; Thomas Annan's Old Closes and Streets of Glasgow, 1977; Eadweard Muybridge's Animal Locomotion, 1980; The Fault Zone, 1981; also revs. and hist. and critical essays. Office: Stanford University Museum of Art Stanford CA 94305

MOZZICATO, LINDA CLAIRE, bank exec.; b. Riverside, Calif., July 27, 1956; d. John Joseph and Joyce Carolyn (Lewis) M.; B.B.A. in Mgmt. and Fin., Washburn U., 1978. Ops. analyst Commerce Bank, Kansas City, Mo., 1978, asst. mgr. dept. lock box, 1979-80, comml. banking officer dept. cash mgmt., 1980—. Adviser Jr. Achievement, Kansas City; corp. vol. United Way, Kansas City; mem. Folly Council, Kansas City; active campaign for atty. gen. in Kans. Mem. Nat. Assn. Bank Women, Nat. Assn. Female Execs., Am. Inst. Banking, Delta Gamma Alumnae Assn. Republican. Roman Catholic. Home: 6140 W 51st St Apt 2 Mission KS 66202 Office: PO Box 248 Kansas City MO 64141

MRKONICH, DOROTHY EVANSON, educator; b. Echo, Minn., July 10, 1938; d. August Alfred and Tilda (Sollom) Evanson; B.S.N., St. Olaf Coll., 1960; M.Ed., U. Minn., 1961, Ph.D., 1982; m. Thomas Mrkonich, Aug. 15, 1959; children—Jana Kaye, Kirsten DeAnn, Jon Thomas. Mem. faculty dept. nursing Coll. of St. Catherine, St. Paul, 1961-62; mem. faculty dept. nursing St. Olaf Coll., Northfield, Minn., 1970—, assoc. prof., 1980—, chmn. dept. nursing, 1979—; mem. Minn. Bd. Nursing, 1981—. Mem. Am. Nurses Assn., Minn. Nurses Assn., Sigma Theta Tau, Pi Lambda Theta. Republican. Lutheran. Office: St Olaf Coll Northfield MN 55436

MUCCI, DRUSILLA MARY, bus. cons.; b. N.Y.C., June 15, 1941; d. Giulio Ernest and Madeline Clare (Mormile) M.; B.S. in Econs., Fordham U., 1966. Systems analyst, ops. IT&T Corp., N.Y.C., 1969-75; asst. commr. drug prevention City of N.Y., 1975-78; v.p. research Lee-Roche Internat. Group, N.Y.C., 1978—. Mem. Fordham U. Alumni. Democrat. Roman Catholic.

MUCCIOLI, ANNA MARIA, artist; b. Detroit, Apr. 23, 1922; d. Anthony and Josephine (Coccardi) De Pascale; student Coll. Art and Design, 1970-75; student of Sarkis Sarkision, Detroit, 1962-66, Charles Culver, Detroit, 1963-67; m. Joseph E. Muccioli, Dec. 26, 1942; children—Ronald, Nathan, Edward, James. One-woman shows of sculpture and/or paintings include: Verve Gallery, 1965, Left Bank Gallery, Flint, Mich., 1969; group shows include: Ford Motor Co. Art Exhbn. (17 awards), 1961-65, 68, 69, 74, 76, 77, 78, 79, Birmingham (Mich.) Art Festival, 1966, Oakland Community Coll., 1967, Mich. Watercolor Soc. (honorable mention), 1968-71, Mich. State Fair, 1968, 69, 71, 73, 76, 78, Am. Watercolor Soc., N.Y.C., 1971, Nat. Art Club, N.Y.C., 1971, Ala. Water Color Soc., 1972, Detroit Inst. Arts Rental Gallery. Recipient numerous art awards, including Water Color award Oakland Community Coll. Mem. Founders Soc. Detroit Inst. Arts, Friends of Modern Art, Women's Caucus of Art, Mich. Watercolor Soc., Soc. Arts and Crafts. Home: 16194 Sprenger East Detroit MI 48021 Studio: 511 Beaubien Detroit MI 48226

MUCHOW, CHARLOTTE IRENE, engr.; b. Sioux Falls, S.D., Nov. 14, 1943; d. George W.F. and Irene Anna (Matthies) M.; B.S. in Engring. Physics, S.D. State U., 1965; postgrad. U. Ariz., 1970; M.S. in Geography, U. Calif., Riverside, 1980. Asso. engr. Westinghouse Research Labs., Pitts., 1965-67; engring. programmer Bell Telephone Labs., Whippany, N.J., 1967-69; sci. programmer Lockheed Aircraft Service, Ontario, Calif., 1971; physicist-mathematician for Bionetics at Jet Propulsion Lab., Pasadena, 1972-73; data analyst for Technicolor Graphics at EROS Data Center, Sioux Falls, 1974-76; tech. staff specialist Aerojet Electro-Systems, Azusa, Calif., 1980-81; systems engr. Measuronics, Gt. Falls, Mont., 1981—. Vol., Big Sisters, Gt. Falls. Mem. Soc. Women Engrs., IEEE, Am. soc. Photogrammetry, Nat. Assn. Female Execs., AAUW. Lutheran. Home: PO Box 1375 Great Falls MT 59403 Office: 4241 2d Ave N Great Falls MT 59401

MUCK, RUTH EVELYN SLACER (MRS. GORDON E. MUCK), educator; b. Buffalo, July 17, 1910; d. Robert A. and Hattie E. (Sheridan) Slacer; B.S., State U. Coll. at Buffalo, 1938, M.S., 1952; Ed.D., State U. N.Y. at Buffalo, 1966; m. Gordon E. Muck, Dec. 27, 1934; 1 dau., Linda Mae McGuire. Tchr. pub. schs., Lockport, N.Y., 1931-42; tchr. primary level campus sch. State U. Coll., Buffalo, 1942-66, prof. edn. div. elementary edn., from 1966, now emeritus; cons. tchr. edn. workshops, Minn., Fla. Dir. youth edn. Methodist Ch., 1960-69; pres. United Meth. Women, Grand Island, N.Y. Mem. Assn. Tchr. Educators (state pres. 1972-73), Internat. Reading Assn. (chmn. 1969-71), Delta Kappa Gamma, Pi Lambda Theta. Home: 1091 Stony Point Rd Grand Island NY 14072

MUCKLE, MARY KATHRYN, newspaper reporter, editor; b. Lansing, Mich., Oct. 3, 1953; d. Charles Alton and Leola Claire (MacAdoo) M.; B.S., Ball State U., 1976. Reporter, Huntington (Ind.) Herald-Press, 1976-77; reporter Warsaw (Ind.) Times-Union, 1977—, asso. editor, 1978—. Mem. Warsaw Bus. and Profl. Women's Club (past 1st v.p., past treas.), Nat. Fedn. Bus. and Profl. Women, Ind. Press Women's Club, Nat. Fedn. Press Women Inc., Sigma Delta Chi. Methodist. Home: 317 N Lake St Apt 2 Warsaw IN 46580 Office: Times-Union PO Box 1448 Warsaw IN 46580

MUCKLER, JULIE ROBINSON, educator; b. Mpls., Jan. 4, 1951; d. William Joseph and Martha (Snider) Robinson; B.S., Iowa State U., 1973, M.S., 1978; m. Richard D. Muckler, June 1, 1974. Personnel rep. John Deere, Des Moines, 1975-77; dir. recruitment and selection Social Services, Des Moines, 1978-79, asst. dir. field ops., 1979-80; co-owner, prin. Applied Mgmt. Assos., 1980—; instr. mgmt., dir. placement Iowa State U., Ames, 1980—. Mem. Am. Soc. Tng. and Devel., Am. Soc. Personnel Adminstrn., Midwest Coll. Placement Assn. Republican. Methodist. Office: Iowa State University 131 MacKay Hall Ames IA 50011

MUELLER, BETTY JEANNE, educator; b. Wichita, Kans., July 7, 1935; d. Bert C. and Clara A. (Pelton) Judkins; M.S.S.W., U. Wis., Madison, 1964, Ph.D. (E.B. Fred fellow, Nat. Inst. Child Health and Human Devel. fellow), 1969; children—Michael J., Madelynn J. Asst. prof. U. Wis., Madison, 1969-71; vis. asso. prof. Bryn Mawr (Pa.) Coll., 1971-72; asso. prof., dir. social work Cornell U., Ithaca, N.Y., 1972-78, prof. human services studies, 1978—; nat. cons. Head Start, Follow Through, Appalachian Regional Commn., N.Y. State Office Planning Services, N.Y. State Dept. Social Services, N.Y. State Div. Mental Hygiene, Nat. Congress PTA. HEW grantee, 1974-76, 79-80; N.Y. State grantee, 1975-82. Mem. Am. Sociol. Assn., Nat. Conf. Social Welfare, Nat. Assn. Social Workers, Council Social Work Edn., Groves Family Conf., Chi Omega. Democrat. Unitarian. Author: (with H. Morgan) Social Services in Early Education, 1974; contbr. articles to profl. jours. Home: 11 Forest Ln Ithaca NY 14850 Office: Human Services Studies N135 MVR Hall Cornell U Ithaca NY 14853

MUELLER, DORIS (LAND), educator; b. Lebanon, Mo., d. Joseph Leslie and Myrtle (Seay) Land; A.E., Hannibal La-Grange Coll., 1948; B.S., Washington U., St. Louis, 1952, M.A., 1963, Ph.D., 1971; postgrad. U. Colo., St Louis U., Bank St. Coll., U. Mo., St. Louis Community Coll.; m. John Fred Mueller, July 8, 1967; 1 foster son, James Edward Noack. Tchr. elem. schs., St. Louis area, 1948-60, reading specialist, 1960-64, research asst., 1965-67, supr. research, 1967-69; supr. research Harris-Stowe State Coll. (formerly Harris Tchrs. Coll.), St. Louis, 1969-77, asst. to pres., 1978-80, dean of students, 1977-78, chmn. edn./psychology div., asso. prof., 1980—; accreditation coordinator Nat. Council for Accreditation of Tchr. Edn., 1982; cons. St. Louis Public Schs. Supt. Ch. sch., mem. Christian com. United Ch. of Christ, also mem. statewide ednl. com. Mem. Am. Ednl. Research Assn., Assn. Tchr. Educators, Internat. Reading Assn., Coll. Reading Assn., Delta Kappa Gamma, Pi Lambda Theta, Kappa Delta Pi. Mem. editorial bd. Reading World, 1982—; contbr. articles in field to profl. jours. Home: 1921 Shardell St St Louis MO 63168 Office: Harris-Stowe Coll 3026 Laclede St St Louis MO 63103

MUELLER, LINDA KING, journalist; b. Indpls., June 17, 1952; d. William Z. and Sherry LaVon (McDowell) King; B.A. in Journalism, Radio-TV, Purdue U., West Lafayette, Ind., 1974; m. William Paul Mueller, Sept. 6, 1975; 1 dau., Melinda Kay. Public info. specialist Ind. Dept. Pub. Instrn. No. Regional Service Center, South Bend, Ind., 1974-75; free-lance writer, contbr. articles to Ind. Dept. Pub. Instrn. and Portage Press (Ind.), 1975-76; asst. editor Portage Press Newspaper, 1976-77, editor, columnist The Laughter Side of Linda, 1977-79; pub. relations coordinator Portage Twp. Schs., 1977-81; freelance writer, public relations specialist Gary (Ind.) Post Tribune, 1981—. Campaign press release writer Porter County (Ind.) United Way, 1977; chmn. energy edn. com. Portage PRIDE, 1977-78; mem. citizens adv. com. Portage Twp. Schs., 1978—; mem. exec. bd. Portage ADAPT Com., 1979-80. Named Outstanding Young Careerist, Portage Bus. and Profl. Women's Club, 1979. Mem. Nat. Sch. Pub. Relations Assn., Women in Communications (treas. N.W. Ind. chpt.), Communicators N.W. Ind., South Haven Jayshees (pres., support v.p., publicity chmn. Outstanding 1st yr. Jayshee 1977-78), Gold Peppers, Sigma Delta Chi, Alpha Delta Pi. Club: Job's Daus. Home: 6351 Venus Ave Portage IN 46368 Office: 5962 Central Ave Portage IN 46368

MUELLER, LOIS M., psychologist; b. Milw., Nov. 30, 1943; d. Herman Gregor and Ora Emma (Dettmann) M.; B.S., U. Wis.-Milw., 1965; M.A., U. Tex., 1966, Ph.D., 1969. Postdoctoral intern VA Hosp., Wood, Wis., 1969-71; counselor, asst. prof. So. Ill. U. Counseling Center and dept. psychology, Carbondale, 1970-72, coordinator personal counseling, asst. prof., 1972-74, counselor, asst. prof., 1974-76; individual practice clin. psychology, Carbondale, 1972-76, Clearwater, Fla., 1977—; owner, dir. Adult and Child Psychology Clinic, Clearwater, 1978—; staff mem. Horizon (Psychiat.) Hosp., Clearwater, 1979, Med. Center Hosp., Largo, Fla., 1979; mem. profl. adv. com. Mental Health Assn. Pinellas County, 1978, Alt. Human Services, 1979-80; cons. Face Learning Center, Hotline Crisis Phone Service, 1977—; public speaker local TV and radio stas., 1978, 79; talk show host WPLP Radio Sta., Clearwater. Campaign worker for Sen. George McGovern presdl. race, 1972. Lic. psychologist, Ill., Fla. Mem. Am., Fla., Ill., Pinellas (founder, pres. 1978) psychol. assns., Assn. Advancement Psychology, Bus. and Profl. Women of Clearwater, Assn. Women in Psychology, NOW. Contbr. articles to profl. jours. Home: 7 Elgin Pl Apt 705 Dunedin FL 33528 Office: 2520 Countryside Blvd Suite 201 Clearwater FL 33515

MUELLER, MARGARET REID, social worker; b. Cleve., Aug. 20, 1929; d. James Sims and Felice (Crowl) Reid; B.A., Smith Coll., 1951; M.A., Case Western Res. U., 1969, M.S.W., 1973; m. Werner D. Mueller, Sept. 6, 1952; children—Fred, John, Lydia, Felice, Omar. Social worker Cleve. Soc. for the Blind, 1969-71; social worker Childrens Services, Cleve., 1973-75; social worker Cuyahoga County Juvenile Ct., Cleve., 1975—, supr. probation dept., 1975—. Mem. Acad. Certified Social Workers, Nat. Assn. Social Workers. Republican. Presbyterian. Clubs: Kirtland Country, Womenspace, Jr. League. Home: 8848 Music St Novelty OH 44072

MUELLER, MARY ELSIE, med. technologist; b. Buffalo, Nov. 10, 1939; d. Thomas Michael and Elsie Mary (Kienke) Rusch; B.A., diploma med. tech., U. Buffalo and Buffalo Gen. Hosp. Sch. Med. Tech., 1961; m. Peter M. Mueller, Mar. 21, 1964; 1 son, Thomas P. Microbiology technologist, then microbiology supr. Buffalo Gen. Hosp., 1961-71, microbiology teaching supr., 1971—; clin. instr. area colls. and univs. Mem. Am. Soc. Clin. Pathologists, Nat. Cert. Agy. Med. Lab. Personnel. Lutheran. Home: 301 Forbes St Tonawanda NY 14150 Office: 100 High St Buffalo NY 14203

MUELLER, RUTH ANNEMARIE, food broker; b. Mannheim, Ger., Jan. 21, 1917; d. Paul and Marie (Halfen) Mueller; B.A., Fordham U., 1979. Sec., Francois L. Schwartz, Inc., 1943-45; corporate sec., dir., 1946-60; owner, chmn. bd., pres. ARFOR Inc., 1960-81; pres. Mueller Realty Inc.; corporate sec., treas. Chopard Watch Corp. Bd. dirs. Met. Mus.; fellow Frick Mus. Roman Catholic. Club: Knollwood Country. Home: 500 Fifth Ave New York NY 10036

MUELLER-ENGHOLM, MARY KORSTAD, art edn. cons., author; b. Seattle, May 7, 1918; d. Martin and Mary Emily (Greene) Korstad; B.E., UCLA, 1940; M.Ed., St. Lawrence U., 1949; postgrad. Syracuse U., 1950-52; m. Walter Weigel, Dec. 22, 1949 (div. 1967); 1 dau., Erica K. Elliott; m. 2d, Paul G. Mueller, Nov. 9, 1968 (dec. 1976); m. 3d, Glenn S. Engholm, Aug. 6, 1982. Tchr. art Riverside (Calif.) City Schs., 1944-46; art supr. Canton (N.Y.) Sch. Dist., 1946-48; asst. prof. art SUNY, Potsdam, 1948-58; art supr. Watertown (N.Y.) City Sch. Dist., 1962-67; cons., lectr. U. Nebr., Lincoln, summer 1966; art supr. Bakersfield (Calif.) City Sch. Dist., 1967-78; instr. art, continuing edn. Calif. State Coll., Bakersfield, 1971-74, 76; free-lance art cons., Bakersfield, 1978—. Trustee Kern County Arts Council, 1976—, Bakersfield Sister City Com., 1978—, H. Weil Child Guidance Clinic, 1980—, Kern County Mus. Alliance, 1978—; pres. Kern County chpt. Young Audiences of Am., 1978—; pres. bd. dirs. H. Weill Meml. Child Guidance Clinic, 1982—; community adv. Jr. League Bakersfield, 1980—; bd. dirs. Lori Brock Jr. Mus., 1975-78. Mem. Nat. Art Edn. Assn., Calif. Art Edn. Assn. (trustee 1979—), Kern County Art Edn. Assn., AAUW, Calif. Tchrs. Assn., Delta Kappa Gamma. Republican. Lutheran. Author: (with Thomas and Wells) Elementary Art, 1967; Murals: Creating an Environment, 1979; contbr. articles to profl. jours.

MUESSEN, JOAN LILLIAN, publishing co. exec.; b. Cranford, N.J., Nov. 5, 1932; d. Henry J. and Pauline N. Muessen; B.A. in English, Skidmore Coll., 1954. With McGraw Hill Inc., N.Y.C., 1960—, personnel adminstr., 1975-78, v.p. career planning, 1978-80, v.p. personnel relations adminstrn., 1981—; trustee Coalition of Pubs. for Employment. Mem. Am. Soc. Personnel Adminstrn., N.Y. Personnel Mgmt. Assn., Internat. Assn. Personnel Women. Home: 333 E 49th St Apt 11-0 New York NY 10017 Office: 1221 Ave of the Americas New York NY 10020

MUFF, JANET, nurse; b. Bombay, India, May 26, 1947 (parents Am. citizens); d. James Bertram and Fette K. (Britt) M.; R.N., St. Vincent's Coll. Nursing, Los Angeles, 1968; B.S. in Nursing, Columbia, 1976, M.S., 1977; m. James D. Boyce, July 26, 1975. Clin., teaching and adminstrv. positions, Los Angeles and N.Y.C., 1968-79; nurse psychotherapist, cons., South Pasadena, Calif., 1979—. Recipient Sigma Theta Tau award, 1976. Mem. Am. Nurses Assn., Calif. Nurses Assn., Sigma Theta Tau. Author/editor: Socialization, Sexism and Stereotyping: Women's Issues in Nursing, 1982. Address: 202 Oaklawn Ave South Pasadena CA 91030

MUGGLI, CLARA BARBARA, civic worker; b. Hebron, N.D., Nov. 10, 1927; d. Matt and Mary (Schneider) Maershbecker; student Dickinson State Coll.; m. Ewald Muggli, Sept. 27, 1948; children—Allen, Linda, Joyce, Carol, Gary, Holly. Tchr. rural schs., 1945-48; county chmn. establishment Bookmobile, 1960, bd. dirs., 1960—; bd. dirs., librarian Glen Ullin (N.D.) Public Library, 1956—; social services home health aide, 1972-76; co-owner, mgr. Rock Mus., Glen Ullin, 1970—, also instr. rocks and minerals, 1970—; sec. Glen Ullin Hist. Soc., 1978—; tchr. Sacred Heart Ch., 1969—, dir. religious edn., 1982—; weekly columnist Glen Ullin Times, 1977—. Recipient State Homemakers award for Cultural Arts, 1975; K. C. Religious Edn. award, 1979; Best of Show award Dakota Gem and Mineral Show, 1979. Mem. Morton County Hist. Soc., Central Dakota Gem and Mineral Assn., Badlands and Knife River Rock Clubs, Art Assn., Am. Legion Aux. Club: Homemakers. Home: 701 Oak Ave Glen Ullin ND 58631

MUHLER, MARIE S., state legislator; b. Bronx, N.Y., July 19, 1937; ed. Marymount Coll., Arlington, Va.; m. Hans Nuhler, 1959; children—Hans, Erika, Brenda, Patrick. Mem. N.J. Assembly, 1975—, dep. minority whip, 1978, 79, minority whip, 1980, 81, mem. edn. com., com. on public schs., Mobile Home Study Commn., mem. regional com. on energy Council State Govts.'s. Charter mem. Marlboro Republican Club; mem. Young Republicans; bd. dirs. Monmouth County Fedn. Rep. Women; mem. Marlboro Bd. Edn., 1972-74, Freehold Regional Bd. Edn., 1975-77; sec. Com. to Save Burnt Fly Bog; mem. Marlboro Bd. Adjustment, 1971-75; bd. dirs. Battleground Arts Center; adv. bd. Women's Resource and Survival Center; bd. dirs. Monmouth Council Boy Scouts Am.; trustee Monmouth County chpt. Nat. Council on Alcoholism; active NCCJ, Monmouth Ocean Devel. Council. Named Rep. Woman of Yr., N.J. Fedn. Rep. Women, 1977; Legislator of Yr., State Young Reps., 1980; Outstanding Legislator of Yr. Nat. Rep. Legislators Assn., 1981. Mem. Nat. Order Women Legislators, N.J. Order Women Legislators, Nat. Conf. State Legislators, Monmouth Coll. Pres.'s Council. Office: New Jersey Assembly Trenton NJ 08625 *

MUHN, JUDY ANN, microbiologist; b. Detroit, Dec. 29, 1952; d. Wilbur William and Dolores Eleanor (Sutinen) Nimer; B.S., Mich. State U., 1975; m. Dennis James Muhn, June 6, 1975. Research asst. Mich. State U., 1972-76; microbiologist Sacramento Med. Preventics Clinic, 1976-77; advt. mgr. J.C. Penney, Plattsburgh, N.Y., 1977-80; promoter Pepsi-Cola Bottling Co., Keeseville, N.Y., 1980; legal sec., 1980-81; legis. aide to Calif. state senator, 1982—. Bd. dirs., chmn. pub. affairs com. Planned Parenthood Clinton County (N.Y.), 1980-81; bd. dirs. Family Planning Advocates, Albany, N.Y., 1981, Planned Parenthood Assn. of Sacramento Valley, 1982—, mem. Sacramento Pro-choice Coalition, 1982—; adv. com. Lake Champlain (N.Y.) Com., 1981; founder Women's Roundtable, Plattsburgh, 1981. Mem. Am. Soc. Microbiology, Downtown Capitol Bus. and Profl. Women's Club (v.p., legis. chmn. 1982—, pub. relations vice chmn. 1982—), Nat. Writers Club, NOW, Sierra Club, Nat. Wildlife Fedn., Nat. Abortion Rights Action League, Common Cause. Home: 3752 Pullman Dr Sacramento CA 95827 Office: State Capitol Room 4040 Sacramento CA 95814

MUIR, DOROTHY LUELLA, constrn. co. exec.; b. Parkersburg, Iowa, July 15, 1916; d. Axel William and Gertrude Mae (Hersey) Jochumsen; student Gates Bus. Coll., Waterloo, Iowa; m. Harry Rex Muir, Sept. 26, 1937. Bookkeeper, Hughes Dry Goods Co., Cedar Falls, Iowa, 1937-43; office mgr., bookkeeper Cedar Crest Hatchery, Cedar Falls, 1943-68; asst. sec., acct. Wendell Lockard Constrn., Inc., Waterloo, 1968—. Pres., Waterloo-Cedar Falls women's aux. Shriners Crippled Children's Hosp., 1972. Mem. Nat. Assn. Women in Constrn. (treas. chpt. 1972-74, 75-76), Nat. Assn. Accts., Nat. Notary Assn. Republican. Methodist. Clubs: Eastern Star, White Shrine, Daus. of Nile. Home: 1804 Birch St PO Box 23 Cedar Falls IA 50613 Office: 901 Black Hawk Rd PO Box 2220 Waterloo IA 50704

MUIR, HELEN, journalist, author; b. Yonkers, N.Y., Feb. 9, 1911; d. Emmet A. and Helen T. (Flaherty) Lennehan; student public schs.; m. William Whalley Muir, Jan. 23, 1936; children—Mary (Mrs. Frederick W. Burrell), William Torbert. With Yonkers Herald Statesman, 1929-30, 31-33, N.Y. Evening Post, 1930-31, N.Y. Evening Jour., 1933-34, Carl Byoir & Assos., N.Y.C., and Miami, Fla., 1934-35; syndicated columnist Universal Service, Miami, 1935-38; columnist Miami Herald, 1941-42; children's book editor, 1949-56; woman's editor Miami Daily News, 1943-44; freelance mag. writer, numerous nat. mags., 1944—; drama critic Miami News, 1960-65. Trustee, Coconut Grove Library Assn., Friends U. Miami Library, Friends Miami-Dade Public Library; vis. com. U. Miami Libraries; bd. dirs. Miami-Dade County Public Library System; mem. State Library Adv. Council, 1979—, now chmn. Recipient award Delta Kappa Gamma, 1960; Fla. Library Assn. Trustees and Friends award, 1973. Mem. Women in Communications (Community Headliner award 1973), Soc. Women Geographers. Clubs: Florida Women's Press (award 1963); Cosmopolitan (N.Y.C.). Author: Miami, U.S.A., 1953. Home: 3855 Stewart Ave Miami FL 33133

MUIR, MARY SHARON, educator; b. Ft. Wayne, Ind., Sept. 19, 1942; d. Jack A. and Helen (Meurer) Pray; B.A., Graceland Coll., 1964;

M.A.Ed., U. No. Iowa, 1968; Ph.D., U. Nebr., 1976. Tchr. public schs., Wichita, Kans., 1964-68, Omaha, 1969-74; asst. to supr. schs. Boys Town, Nebr., 1975-76; asst. prof. early childhood and elem. edn. U. Nebr., Omaha, 1976-78; asso. prof. curriculum and instrn. Okla. State U., Stillwater, 1978—; cons., sch. dists.; mem. tchr. competence rev. panel Nebr. Profl. Practices Commn., 1974-75. Mem. edn. com. Mayor's Commn. on Status of Women, Omaha; bd. dirs. Open Elem. Schs., Omaha. Recipient Tchr.'s medal Freedoms Found., 1973; Outstanding Tchr. award Okla. State U. Alumni Assn., 1980. Mem. Am. Ednl. Research Assn., Nat. Council Social Studies (exec. com., coll. and univ. faculty assembly, Dissertation award 1977), Okla. Council Social Studies (dir.), Phi Delta Kappa. Democrat. Mem. St. Cecelia's Musical Soc., Contbr. articles to profl. jours. Home: 2517 N Star Dr Stillwater OK 74074 Office: 306 Gundersen Okla State U Stillwater OK 74078

MUKOYAMA, HELEN KIYOKO, social worker; b. Paia, Maui, Hawaii, Nov. 13, 1914; d. Ginichi and Shio (Takahashi) Takehara; B.A., Simpson Coll., 1937; postgrad. U. Denver, 1936; M.A., U. Chgo., 1943; m. Teruo Mukoyama, June 11, 1936 (div. 1956); children—Marshall H., Howard T., Wesley K. Caseworker, Chgo. Welfare Adminstrn., 1938-41, Cook County Dept. Welfare, Chgo., 1945-46; cons. to Japanese Ams. relocating to Chgo., Ill. Public Aid Commn., 1945-46, welfare adminstrv. aide supr., 1949-69; caseworker Travelers Aid Soc.-Immigrants Service, Chgo., 1951-65; intake worker Homemaker Service, Salvation Army Family Service, Chgo., 1957-65; social work supr. intake Ill. Dept. Children and Family Services, 1965-67; caseworker III, Salvation Army Family Service, Chgo., 1967-72; casework supr. Jewish Family and Community Services, Chgo., 1972-73; supr. intake Council for Jewish Elderly, Chgo., 1973-77, supr. community aides and welfare adminstrv. coordinator, 1977-79; coordinator elderly housing Japanese Am. Service Com and mgr. Heiwa Ter. Japanese Am. Elderly Housing, Chgo, 1980—; mem. Japanese Am. Housing Bd. Mem. Council of Ministries, Welfare Div. United Meth. Ch., 1963-69. Recipient award Japanese Am. Service com., 1963. Mem. Acad. Cert. Social Workers, Nat. Assn. Social Workers, Ill. Cert. Social Workers, Chgo. Human Relations Commn., Japanese-Am. Citizens League, Japanese-Am. Soc., Art Inst. Chgo., Epsilon Sigma, Pi Gamma Mu. Methodist. Contbr. articles to profl. jours. Home: 912 S Mason Ave Chicago IL 60644 Office: 920 W Lawrence St Chicago IL 60640

MULALLY, JAN COLLEEN, nuclear med. technologist; b. Princeton, Ill., July 27, 1948; d. Marvin Earl and Tillie Lillian (Patroff) M.; grad. Meth. Hosp. Central Ill. Sch. Radiologic Tech., 1968, Nuclear Medicine Inst., Cleve., 1973. Staff nuclear medicine technologist Meth. Med. Center Ill., Peoria, 1971-74, chief nuclear medicine technologist, 1974-79, adminstrv. dir. dept. nuclear medicine, 1979—; radiation safety coordinator, bd. dirs. Meth. Med. Center of Ill. Credit Union. Cert., Nuclear Medicine Tech. Cert. Bd. Mem. Soc. Nuclear Medicine, Central Ill. Assos. and Tech. Affiliates, Am. Hosp. Radiology Adminstrs., Ill. Soc. Radiologic Technologists. Democrat. Methodist. Office: Dept Nuclear Medicine Meth Med Center of Ill 221 NE Glen Oak Ave Peoria IL 61636

MULCAHY, LOIS ANN, nursing home adminstr.; b. Trenton, Dec. 11, 1931; d. Kenneth S. and Verna Louise (Hart) Applegate; R.N., Fitkin Meml. Hosp., 1952; student Seton Hall U., 1952-53, Columbia U., 1960-61, Rutgers U., 1969-70, Trenton State U., 1971-72, Stockton State U., 1973-74; m. David M. Mulcahy, Nov. 9, 1957; children—Karen Lee, David Michael. Head nurse VA Hosp., Chgo., 1955; sr. nurse Trenton Vis. Nurse Assn., 1955-58; supervising rehab. nurse Donnelly Meml. Hosp., Trenton, 1960-68; nursing dir., asst. adminstr. Mercerville (N.J.) Nursing Center, 1968-70, adminstr., 1970—; mem. N.J. Lic. Bd. Nursing Home Adminstrs., 1980—; mem. utilization rev. bd. Vis. Nurse Assn., 1974—. Fellow Am. Coll. Nursing Home Adminstrs. (treas. N.J. chpt. 1979-81); mem. Am. Health Care Assn., N.J. Assn. Health Care Facilities (peer rev. and edn. com. 1972—). Episcopalian. Office: 2240 Whitehorse Mercervile Rd Mercerville NJ 08619

MULDROW, TRESSIE WRIGHT, psychologist; b. Marietta, Ga., Feb. 1, 1941; d. Festus Blanton and Louise Wright Williams Summers; B.A., Bennett Coll., 1962; M.S., Howard U., 1965, Ph.D., 1976; 1 dau., DeJuan Denise. Research asst. W.C. Allen Corp., Washington, 1966-68; personnel research psychologist Dept. Navy, Washington, 1968-73, Office Personnel Mgmt., Civil Service Commn., 1973-79; chief, adv. council on alternative selection procedures Office Personnel Mgmt., Washington, 1979—; lectr. Howard U., 1979. Mem. Washington Inter-Alumni council United Negro Coll. Fund, 1970—. Named Alumnae of Yr., United Negro Coll. Fund, 1971, Outstanding Alumnae Morehouse Coll., 1978. Mem. Bennett Coll. Alumnae Assn. (pres. nat. 1978—), Am. Psychol. Assn., Nat. Assn. Black Psychologists, D.C. Assn. Black Psychologists, Info. Center Handicapped Individuals, Delta Sigma Theta. Presbyterian. Contbrs. articles to profl. publs. Office: 1900 E St NW Washington DC 20415

MULHAUSER, KAREN, orgn. exec.; b. Burlington, Vt., Nov. 5, 1942; d. Harold H. and Leta H. Webber; B.A. in Biology, Antioch Coll., 1965; m., Aug. 18, 1968; 1 son, Christopher. Research asso. Albert Einstein Coll. of Medicine, Bronx, N.Y., 1965-67; sci. tchr. Cambridge Sch., Weston, Mass., 1967-70; trainer/educator HEW Region X, Seattle, 1970-73; lobbyist Nat. Abortion Rights Action League, Washington, 1973-75, exec. dir., 1975-81; polit. cons., 1981-82; exec. dir. Citizens Against Nuclear War, Washington, 1982—; dir. Ind. Action; mem. adv. bd. Democratic Congl. Campaign Com.; mem. Antioch U. Alumni Bd. Mem. Planned Parenthood Met. Washington (dir.), Center for Population Options (dir.), Friends of Family Planning (exec. com.). Democrat. Office: 1201 16th St NW Washington DC 20036

MULHAUSER, LYNDA CAHAN, clin. social worker; b. Phila., July 29, 1947; d. Jules Leonard and Shirley R. (Lit) Cahan; B.A., U. Pitts., 1970; M.S.W. (HEW grantee), Cath. U. Am., 1976; m. Joel Carl Mulhauser, Apr. 11, 1970; children—Scott Howard, Dana Ann. Clin. social worker Presbyn. U. Hosp., Pitts., 1970-71, George Washington U. Med. Center, Washington, 1971-74, supr., 1976-78; cons. Spina Bifida Clinic, Children's Hosp. Nat. Med. Center, Washington, 1978—; cons. genetics dept., 1979—, Christ Ch. Infant Program, 1978-79; mem. profl. adv. com. Nat. Found., March of Dimes, 1982—. Bd. dirs. Tifereth Israel Synagogue, 1980—. Lic. clin. social worker, Md. Mem. Acad. Cert. Social Workers, Nat. Assn. Social Workers, Spina Bifida Assn. Am. (dir. 1980—), Mortar Bd. (pres. 1969-70), Pi Gamma Mu. Club: Women's Nat. Democratic. Office: 111 Michigan Ave NW Washington DC 20010

MULHERN, EILEEN M., Mfg. co. ofcl.; b. Queens, N.Y., Oct. 15, 1953; d. Patrick Joseph and Joan Francis (Cassidy) M.; B.A., Coll. New Rochelle (N.Y.), 1975; M.B.A., U. Notre Dame, 1977. Asst. met. banking div. Chem. Bank, N.Y.C., 1977-79; asst. to pres. First Nat. Bank, Houma, La., 1979, First Nat. Bank Colorado Springs (Colo.), 1980-81; sr. fin. supr. Colo. Telecommunications div. Hewlett-Packard, Colorado Springs, 1981—. Mem. Am. Soc. Profl. and Exec. Women, Nat. Assn. Female Execs., Kappa Gamma Pi. Home: 1045 Gatehouse Circle S Colorado Springs CO 80904 Office: PO Box 7050 Colorado Springs CO 80933

MULLAUGH, CAROL CUSHING, stockbroker; b. Pitts., Oct. 30, 1937; d. George Byron and Margaret Elizabeth (Smith) Cushing; B.S., Simmons Coll., 1959; cert. Securities Industry Assn. Inst., Wharton Sch., U. Pa., 1980; m. Michael Joseph Mullaugh, Jan. 21, 1967 (div. Feb. 1979); 1 dau., Elizabeth Preston; m. 2d, James Crossan Chaplin IV, Apr. 12, 1980. Mem. mdse. exec. staff Macy's, N.Y.C., 1959-63, 64-66; buyer Levy Bros., Elizabeth, N.J., 1963-64; dir. basic stock program Kaufmanns, Pitts., 1966-67; stockbroker Parker/Hunter, Inc., Pitts., 1968-82, v.p., 1978-82, dir., 1980-81; pres. Chaplin Mullaugh, Inc., 1982—; instr. Chatham Coll. community programs, 1975—; instr. W.Va. Sch. Banking, 1977—; instr. Carlow Coll., 1980-81, past mem. bus. adv. bd. Bd. dirs. Womens Assn. Pitts. Symphony Soc.; trustee Winchester-Thurston Sch., 1980—, co-chmn. fin. com., 1982—; trustee Securities Industry Assn. Inst., Wharton Sch., 1981—; bd. dirs. Vocat. Rehab. Center Allegheny County, 1981—. Mem. Securities Industry Assn. (econ. edn. com. 1979—), Exec. Women's Council Pitts. (dir. 1981). Club: Allegheny Country (Sewickley, Pa.). Home: RD 5 Camp Meeting Rd Sewickley PA 15143 Office: 435 Beaver St PO Box 567 Sewickley PA 15143

MULLEN, FRANCES ANDREWS, cons. psychologist; b. Chgo., Nov. 27, 1902; d. Edmund Lathrop and Ethel (Baker) Andrews; Ph.B. in Math., U. Chgo., 1923, M.A. in Edn., 1929, Ph.D. in Ednl. Psychology, 1939; m. Urban Joseph Mullen, Oct. 12, 1929, (div. 1945); children—Urban Edmund, Mary Ann, William, Ethel Alice. Tchr. high sch. Chgo. Public Sch. System. 1925-39, sch., psychologist, 1939-47, prin. elem. sch., 1947-49, dir. Bur. Mentally Handicapped Children, 1949-53, asst. supt. schs. for spl. edn., 1953-66; pvt. practice psychol. cons., Chgo. and Los Angeles, 1966-75; pres. Internat. Council Psychologists, Inc., 1977, sec.-gen., 1977-79, emeritus, 1979—; pvt. practice psychology, Sherman Oaks, Calif., 1975—; instr. Calif. State U., Northridge, 1978-80, dir. Inst. for Juvenile Research, Chgo.; mem. psychology adv. panel Office of Vocat. Rehab., HEW, 1961-63. Bd. dirs. Ill. Soc. for Crippled Children and Adults, United Cerebral Palsy of Chgo., Retarded Children's Aid, Girl Scouts U.S.A. of Chgo. Diplomate Am. Bd. Examiners in Profl. Psychology. Fellow Am. Psychol. Assn. (pres. div. sch. psychologists 1951-53); mem. Am. Orthpsychiat. Assn., Am. Assn. on Mental Deficiency, Council for Exceptional Children (life mem.), Internat. Council of Psychologists, Inc. Democrat. Presbyterian. Clubs: Am. Alpine, Can. Alpine, Sierra. Editor Internat. Psychologist, 1966-72; contbr. numerous articles to profl. jours. Home and Office: 4014 Cody Rd Sherman Oaks CA 91403

MULLER, CHARLOTTE FELDMAN, economist; b. N.Y.C., Feb. 19, 1921; d. Louis and Lillian (Drogin) Feldman; A.B., Vassar Coll., 1941; A.M., Columbia U., 1942, Ph.D. in Econs., 1946; m. Carl Schoenberg; children—Jeremy Lewis Muller, Sara Linda Muller. Instr. econs. Bklyn. Coll., 1943; lectr. Barnard Coll., 1943-46; asst. prof. Occidental Coll., 1947; asst. study dir. Survey Research Center, U. Mich., 1948; research asso. U. Calif., Berkeley, 1948-50; lectr. Yale U. Sch. Public Health, 1952-53; asst. prof. Columbia U. Sch. Public Health, 1957-67; assoc. dir. Center for Social Research, CUNY, 1967—, prof. econs., 1978—, prof. urban studies, 1967-78; prof. dept. community medicine Mt. Sinai Sch. Medicine, 1981—; Disting. Alumna speaker Vassar Centennial, 1971; mem. N.Y.C. Mayor's Com. on Prescription Drug Abuse, 1970-73; bd. dirs. Alan Guttmacher Inst., 1972-82; v.p. Med. and Health Research Assn. N.Y.C.; mem. health care tech. study sect. Nat. Center Health Services Research, 1976-79; mem. nat. commn. on urban policy Am. Jewish Congress. Ford/Rockefeller Founds. grantee, 1972-73, 75-76. Mem. Am. Econ. Assn., Am. Public Health Assn., NOW. Jewish. Editorial bd. Am. Jour. Public Health, Inquiry, Research on Aging, Women, and Health; contbr. numerous articles on health econs. to profl. publs. Office: CUNY 33 W 42d St Room 625 New York NY 10036

MULLER, DOROTHEA ROSALIE, educator; b. Bklyn., Oct. 29, 1924; d. William Thomas and Anna (Zataracz) Muller; B.A. cum laude, Hunter Coll., 1946; M.A. (scholar 1946-47), U. Wis., 1948; Ph.D. (fellow 1951-53), N.Y. U., 1956. Temporary tutor Hunter Coll., N.Y.C., 1948-50, 56; tchr. N.Y.C. Public Schs., 1950-53, White Plains (N.Y.) High Sch., 1953-54; mem. faculty C. W. Post Coll. of L.I. U., Greenvale, N.Y., 1957—, asst. prof., 1957-62, asso. prof., 1962-71, prof. history, 1971—. Recipient Founders Day award N.Y. U., 1956; AAUW fellow, 1964-65. Mem., Am. Hist. Assn., Orgn. Am. Historians, Am. Studies Assn., Western History Assn., Am. Soc. Church History, Wyo. State Hist. Soc., Nat. Council Women U.S., AAUW, AAUP, Nat. Trust Historic Preservations, Am. Teilhard Assn. for Future of Man. Contbr. articles to profl. jours. Office: Dept of History CW Post Coll Greenvale NY 11548

MULLER, ELSIE FERRAR, psychotherapist, psychiat. social worker; b. Worcester, Mass., Apr. 7, 1913; d. Frederic and Anne (Binns) Bonnet; B.S., Alfred U., 1934; M.S.W., U. Mo., Columbia, 1969; postgrad. U. Mo., Kansas City, 1962-63; m. Frederick Wentworth Muller, Oct. 10, 1936 (div. 1961); 1 dau., Jean Ferrar Muller Mackimmie. Art. instr. Alfred U., 1935-36; art therapist Gillis Home, Kansas City, Mo., 1958-70; psychotherapist Ozanam Home, Kansas City, Mo., 1970—; art therapy cons. Jackson County, Kansas City, Mo., 1975-78; Wyandotte County Sch. Social Workers, Kansas City, Kans., 1978—. Mem. Nat. Assn. Social Workers, Acad. Social Workers, Am. Art Therapy Assn. (hon. life). Episcopalian. Home: 9801 Lee Blvd Leawood KS 66206 Office: 421 E 137th St Kansas City MO 64145

MULLER, EMMA FLEER, ret. educator; b. Brillion, Wis., July 11, 1896; d. E. John and Emma (Collatz) Fleer; Mus.B., Marquette U., 1918; B.S. (honor entrance scholar, Marie Mergeler scholar), U. Chgo., 1923, postgrad., 1924-32, 50-53; m. Frederick H. Muller, Aug. 2, 1930 (dec. Nov. 1954); 1 son, Carl. H. Instr. music Maruqette U., 1915-21; organist, choir dir. Milw. and Chgo.; research asst. dept. physiology U. Chgo., 1924, 25; tchr. sci. Chgo. Tchrs. Coll., 1924-28, dean, 1928-38, dir. personnel, 1938-61, ret.; dean of women Woodrow Wilson Jr. Coll., 1934-37. Vol. worker Chgo. Wesley Meml. Hosp. (name changed to Northwestern Meml. Hosp. 1972), 1961—. Recipient citation Marquette U., 1965. Mem. Nat. Assn. Women Deans and Counselors (citation 1961), Ill. Assn. Women Deans and Counselors (citation 1953), Ill. Assn. Deans of Women (pres. 1940-42), Am. Personnel and Guidance Assn., Ill. Guidance and Personnel Assn., Student Personnel Assn. for Tchr. Edn., Am. Assn. Collegiate Registrars and Admissions Officers, Ill. Assn. Collegiate Registrars and Admissions Officers, Chgo. Conf. Collegiate Registrars and Admissions Officers (pres. 1953-54), NEA, Ill. Edn. Assn., Am. Assn. Sch. Adminstrs., Art Inst. Chgo., Field Mus. of Natural History, Lyric Opera Guild, Chgo. Symphony Soc., Chgo. Public TV Assn., Sigma Xi, Phi Beta Delta, Pi Lambda Theta, Delta Kappa Gamma (chpt. pres. 1953-54), Sigma Delta Epsilon (nat. treas. 1926-27, pres. chpt. 1929-30). Clubs: Woman's Univ., Chgo. Woman's. Contbr. articles to profl. jours.

MULLER, MARGIE H., banker; b. Los Angeles, Nov. 30, 1927; d. S. Jack and Marjorie Hellman; B.A., UCLA, 1949; m. Steven Muller, June 19, 1951; children—Julie, Elizabeth. Sales promotion asst. Joyce (Calif.) Ltd., London, 1950-51; copywriter Hamrick Advt., Ithaca, N.Y., 1951-54; sr. asso. Conant & Co., Public Relations Counsel, N.Y.C., 1954-57; advt. and public relations mgr. Theodore Presser Co., Bryn Mawr, Pa., 1957-58; account exec. Laux Advt., Ithaca, 1959-60; asst. v.p. Tompkins Co. Trust Co., Ithaca, 1960-71; v.p. Md. Nat. Bank, Balt., 1971-77; head mktg. div., v.p. Union Trust Co. of Md., Balt., 1977-82, sr. v.p. corp. affairs, 1982—; sr. v.p. Union Trust Bancorp, 1982—. Mem. adv. commn. Md. Dept. Community and Econ. Devel., 1973—; pres. Balt. Promotion Council, 1974-75, Balt. Public Realtions Council, 1974-75; mem. Health and Welfare Council Central Md., 1974—, v.p., 1979-80, pres., 1982—; trustee McDonogh Sch., mem. exec. com., 1980—. Mem. Bank Mktg. Assn. (dir. 1974-78, mem. exec. com. 1977-78, nat. conv. chmn. 1977), Balt. Exec. Women's Council. Home: 1405 Harper House Baltimore MD 21210 Office: PO Box 1077 Baltimore MD 21203

MULLET, DARLENE MARILYN, rehab. tchr.; b. Butte, Mont., Oct. 16, 1935; d. Ernest John Onnela and Iva Eleanor Onnela Sullivan; B.S., Western Mich. U., 1960; m. Stanley Mullet, Feb. 24, 1961 (dec. 1973); 1 son, Kevin. Rehab. tchr. Ohio Commn. for Blind, Columbus, 1960-61, 62-63; occupational therapist Goodwill Industries, Denver, 1966-70; rehab. tchr. for adults Tex. Commn. for Blind, Galveston, 1973—. Recipient service pin and cert. Tex. Commn. for Blind, 1978. Mem. Am. Assn. Workers for Blind, Tex. Assn. Workers for Blind. Devised, conducted functional testing program for disability determination for social security, 1966-70. Office: 2001 Ball St Galveston TX 77550

MULLIGAN, BARBARA E., coll. adminstr.; b. Grand Rapids, Mich., June 25, 1927; d. Raymond Christopher and Gertrude (Moran) M.; B.A., Marquette U., 1962, M.A., 1964. Instr. polit. sci., asst. dir. continuing edn. Alverno Coll., Milw., 1966-68, dir. continuing edn., 1968-71, asst. dean, 1971-72, co-dir. Research Center on Women, 1970-72; asst. dir. Div. Continuing Edn., Marquette U., 1972-74, assoc. dir. Div. Continuing Edn. and Summer Sessions, 1974—. Mem. Gov.'s Commn. on Status of Women, 1967-71; mem. Wis. Ednl. Approval Bd., 1968-71; 1st vice chmn. Wis. Women's Republican Club, 1964-68; bd. dirs. Greater Milw. chpt. ARC, 1973-74. Mem. Adult Edn. Assn. Wis. (dir. 1969-71, 75-77), Wis. Polit. Sci. Assn. (treas. 1970-72), Milw. Council Adult Learning, Wis. Soc. Health and Tng., Nat. Univ. Extension Assn., Marquette U. Alumni Assn., AAUW, Am. Assn. Univ. Adminstrs. (dir. Delta chpt. 1975-76), Am. Assn. Higher Edn., Smithsonian Assocs., Adult Edn. Assn., Council on Continuing Edn., Nat. Council Adminstrv. Women in Edn. Home: 2703 N Hackett Ave Milwaukee WI 53211

MULLIGAN, DOROTHY EDNA, editor; b. Topeka, Feb. 14, 1925; d. Charles Vernon and Faith (Hamaker) Cochran; B.S. in Journalism, Kans. State U., 1946; m. Eugene Worth Mulligan, Sept. 13, 1952; children—Greg, Laura, Mark, Cathy. Editor, Manhattan (Kans.) Tribune-News, 1946-48; public info. officer FAO, 1948-53; newsletter editor, vol. coordinator Alexandria (Va.) Public Schs., 1973-77; tutor learning disabled students Kingsbury Center, Washington, 1972-77; dir. editorial services Nat. Sch. Vol. Program, Alexandria, 1976-80; sr. project analyst, editor, writer Applied Mgmt. Scis., Silver Spring, Md., 1981—. Pres. MacArthur Elem. Sch. PTA, Alexandria, 1971; bd. dirs. Alexandria Mental Health Assn., Alexandria LWV. Recipient Dist. award Parent Coop. Pre-schs. Internat., 1970. Mem. Council Exceptional Children, Assn. Children with Learning Disabilities, Edn. Writers Assn., Washington Ind. Writers. Unitarian. Office: 962 Wayne Ave Silver Spring MD 20910

MULLIGAN, ELINOR PATTERSON, lawyer; b. Bay City, Mich., Apr. 20, 1929; d. Frank Clark and Agnes (Murphy) Patterson; A.B., U. Mich., 1950; J.D., Seton Hall U., 1970; m. John C. O'Connor, Oct. 28, 1950; children—Christine, Valerie, Amy, Christopher Criffan; m. 2d, William G. Mulligan, Dec. 6, 1975. Editorial asst. Silver Burdett Pub. Co. subs. Time, Inc., Morristown, N.J., 1964-65; asst. publicity mgr. Worthington Corp., 1965-67; dir. devel. and public relations Children's Aid and Adoption Soc. N.J., 1967-68; admitted to N.J. bar, 1970; practiced in Newark, 1970, Morristown, 1971, Springfield, 1972, Hackettstown, 1972—; partner firm Mulligan & Jacobson, N.Y.C., 1973—, Mulligan & Mulligan, Hackettstown, 1976—; atty. Hackettstown Planning Bd., 1973—, Blairstown Twp (N.J.) Zoning Bd., 1973—; mem. N.J. Supreme Ct. Spl. Com. Atty. Disciplinary Structure, 1981—. Sec. Warren County Ethics Com., 1976-78; sec. Dist. X Fee Arbitration Com., 1979—. Mem. Am., Warren County, Morris County bar assns., Assn. Bar City N.Y., Mensa, Kappa Alpha Theta. Republican. Clubs: Panther Valley Country, Baltusrol (Springfield); Union League, Harvard (N.Y.C.). Home: Panther Valley Hackettstown NJ 07840 also 35 Park Ave New York NY 10016 Office: 480 Hwy 517 Hackettstown NJ 07840

MULLIN, SHERON SIMMERMAN, educator; b. Washington, Nov. 3, 1949; d. George Mitchell and Dorothye (Hickman) Simmerman; B.S., Miss. Coll., 1970; M.A., U. South Ala., 1974, postgrad., 1981—; m. Leo Edward Mullin, III, Aug. 12, 1978; 1 dau., Laurin Dorothye. Tchr., Council Elem. Sch., Mobile, Ala., 1971-73, Shaw High Sch., Mobile, 1973-79; tchr. English, speech and drama Baker High Sch., Mobile, 1979—; dramatic and oratorical competition coach, 1973—. Sch. panel mem. Bi-Racial Com., 1972. Named Ala. Speech Tchr. of Yr., 1976, Tchr. of Yr., 1979, 82, Mobile Speech Tchr. of Yr., 1976. Mem. Mobile County Edn. Assn. (sec.), Ala. Edn. Assn. (sch. rep.), NEA, Classroom Tchrs. Assn. (pres.), Alpha Delta Kappa (sec., v.p.). Republican. Presbyterian. Home: 2363 Leroy Stevens Rd Mobile AL 36609 Office: Baker High School Route 5 Box 87 Mobile AL 36609

MULLINS, BARBARA JEANNE, petroleum mktg. exec.; b. Day, Fla., Aug. 29, 1938; d. James Eli and Bessie Geraldine (Johnson) Grantham; cert. in acctg. Longview Community Coll., Mo., 1977; m. Mikel Burton Mullins, Dec. 20, 1956; children—Ronald Lee, Richard Bryan, Mikel Duane. Fin. asst. J. M. Fields, Melbourne, Fla., 1962-63; acctg. clk. Radiation, Inc., Melbourne, 1963-64; bookkeeper/sec. Sam Hammonds, C.P.A., Oklahoma City, 1964-65; with Bride Co., Leawood, Kans., 1970—, bookkeeper, 1970-74, chief acct., 1974-75, controller, 1975-80, v.p. adminstrn., 1980—, corp. sec., 1973—, registered agt., 1973-80; corp. sec. Data Freight, Inc., 1980—, also dir. Recipient 1st Pl. award Distributive Edn. Clubs Am. Mo. Competition, 1976. Mem. Am. Petroleum Inst., Nat. Assn. Accts. (dir. Kansas City chpt. 1978—; treas. Heartland regional council 1981-82, mem.-at-large exec. com. Heartland council 1982-83). Democrat. Baptist. Home: 24303 W 86th Terr Olathe KS 66061 Office: 4701 College Blvd Suite 202 Leawood KS 66211

MULLINS, OBERA, microbiologist; b. Egypt, Miss., Feb. 15, 1927; d. Willie Ree and Maggie Sue (Orr) Gunn; B.S., Chgo. State U., 1974; M.S. in Health Sci. Edn., Governors State U., 1981; m. Charles Leroy Mullins, Nov. 2, 1952; children—Mary Artavia, Arthur Curtis, Charles Leroy, Charlester Teresa, William Hellman. Med. technician, microbiologist Chgo. Health Dept., Chgo., 1976—. Mem. AAUW, Am. Soc. Clin. Pathologists (cert. med. lab. technician). Roman Catholic. Home: 9325 S Marquette St Chicago IL 60617 Office: 3026 S California Ave Chicago IL 60623

MULLINS, RUTH GLADYS, pediatric nurse; b. Can., Aug. 25, 1943; naturalized 1954; d. William G. and Gladys (Page) Henderson; B.S., Calif. State U., Long Beach, 1966; M.Nursing, UCLA, 1973; m. Leonard E. Mullins, Jr., Aug. 27, 1963; children—Deborah, Catherine, Leonard E. III. Nurse, Los Angeles County Health Dept., 1967-68, Meml. Hosp. Med. Center, Long Beach, 1968-73; mem. faculty Calif. State U., Los Angeles, 1973—; mem. faculty Calif. State U., Long Beach, 1973—, asst. prof., 1974-80, asso. prof., 1980—, program dir. pediatric nurse practitioner program, 1975—, chmn. grad. div. level, 1978—, coordinator health services credential, 1979—; mem. Calif. Maternal, Child, Adolescent Health Bd., 1977—. Fellow Nat. Assn. Pediatric Nurse Practitoners/Assos.; mem. Am. Pub. Health Assn., AAUP. Democrat. Methodist. Author: (with Bobbie Nelms) Growth and Development: A Primary Health Care Approach, 1982; contbr. articles to profl. jours., chpts. to textbooks. Home: 6382 Heil Ave Huntington Beach CA 92647 Office: 1250 Bellflower Blvd Dept Nursing Long Beach CA 90840

MULLINS, SUE BEVERS, state legislator; b. Denver, June 18, 1936; d. Laurence Calvin and Helen Mae (Bevers) Blunt; B.S., Iowa State U.,

1967; m. James Aaron Mullins, Aug. 26, 1956; children—Michael John, Daniel Laurence, Jennifer Lynn. Free lance writer for state and nat. farm publs., 1960-73; mem. Iowa Ho. of Reps., 1978—; partner Prairie Flat Farms, Corwith, 1965—. Mem. Nat. Conf. State Legislators. Republican. Methodist. Office: Iowa House of Representatives State Capitol Des Moines IA 50319

MULLIN-TRAYNOR, VI ANNE, computer scientist; b. St. Paul, July 2, 1944; d. Vi Anne Sattre Christensen; B.S., Mankato (Minn.) State U., 1967; M.A., Old Dominion U., Richmond, Va., 1971; M.S. in Mgmt. (Sloan fellow), M.I.T., 1981; m. George F. Traynor, June 31, 1979; 1 son, Mark. Tchr. English, Norfolk (Va.) schs., 1968-70; instr. English, Old Dominion U., 1970-72; with Control Data Corp., Mpls., 1973—, market developer acad. edn., computer-bases edn., 1978-79, mgr. mktg. programs U.S. mktg. and sales, 1979-81, mgr. market research and strategic planning and new bus. devel., 1981—. Bush Leadership fellow, 1979. Mem. Soc. Applied Learning Tech., Assn. Devel. Computer-Bases Instn. Systems, Internat. Reading Assn., Common Cause, World Future Soc., Am. Mktg. Assn. Democrat. Lutheran. Home: 1489 Fairmount Ave Saint Paul MN 55105 Office: 8100 24th Ave S Bloomington MN 55440

MULQUEEN, ELLEN, ednl. adminstr.; b. Bklyn., Jan. 11, 1941; d. James C. and Jane E. (Jaenike) M.; A.B. in English, Pace U., 1962; M.A. in English, N.Y. U., 1967. Personnel clk. Book-of-the-Month Club, N.Y.C., 1962; activities sec. Pace U., N.Y.C., 1963; adminstrv. asst. Loeb Student Center, N.Y. U., N.Y.C., 1963-65; asst. dean students State U. N.Y., Geneseo, 1965-67; asst. dean students R.I. Coll., Providence, 1967-70; asst. dir. campus center Trinity Coll., Hartford, Conn., 1970-71, asst. dean student services, 1971-72, asso. dean for student services, 1972-74, dean student services, 1974-76; dean student affairs Post Coll., Waterbury, Conn., 1976-80, also adj. instr. English; asso. dean students Rider Coll., Lawrenceville, N.J., 1980—; mem. accrediting team New Eng. Assn. Colls. and Schs. Bd. dirs. Planned Parenthood Assn. Mercer Area, 1981—; bd. dirs. Planned Parenthood of Greater Waterbury, 1978-80, sec. bd., 1980; bd. dirs. LWV of Ewing Twp., 1981—, 1st v.p., 1981—. Recipient Trustees' award Pace U., 1962. Mem. Nat. Assn. Student Personnel Adminstrs., Nat. Assn. Women Deans, Adminstrs. and Counselors, Am. Assn. Univ. Adminstrs., Nat. Assn. Coll. Aux. Services, Am. Assn. for Higher Edn. Club: Soroptomist Internat. Contbr. papers to publs., also nat., regional confs. profl. orgns. in field. Home: 811 Scenic Dr Delaware Heights West Trenton NJ 08628 Office: Rider Coll PO Box 6400 Lawrenceville NJ 08648

MULVANEY, MARY JEAN, educator; b. Omaha, Jan. 6, 1927; d. Marion Fowler and Blanche (McKee) M.; B.S., U. Nebr., 1948; M.S., Wellesley Coll., 1951. Instr. phys. edn. Kans. State U., 1948-50; instr., then asst. prof. U. Nebr., 1951-62; asst. prof. U. Kans., 1962-66; mem. faculty U. Chgo., 1966—, prof. phys. edn. and athletics, 1976—, chmn. dept., 1976—; mem. coms. div. III, Nat. Collegiate Athletic Assn. Mem. Internat. Assn. Phys. Edn. and Sport for Girls and Women, AAHPER, Nat. Assn. Collegiate Dirs. Athletics, Nat. Assn. Phys. Edn. in Higher Edn., AAUP, Mortar Bd., Pi Lambda Theta, Alpha Chi Omega. Home: 5801 S Dorchester Ave Chicago IL 60637 Office: 5640 S University Ave Chicago IL 60637

MULVIHILL, MARY MARGARET, city ofcl.; b. Louisville, Dec. 15, 1942; d. Joseph Raymond and Flora Katherine (Uehlein) Mullaney; B.S., U. Louisville, 1969; postgrad. U. Louisville, 1980; m. Eamon Mulvihill, Sept. 21, 1963; children—Tom, Patrick. Tchr. parochial schs., Louisville, 1963-67; adminstrv. asst. to mayor Louisville, Ky., 1973-74; alderman City of Louisville, 1975—; exec. com. Louisville and Jefferson County. Bd. dirs. Health Care. Mem. Nat. League Cities, Women's Polit. Caucus. Democrat. Roman Catholic. Office: 601 W Jefferson St Louisville KY 40202

MUMFORD, EMILY HAMILTON, med. sociologist; b. Cape Girardeau, Mo., Dec. 19, 1922; d. Barney A. and Dola (Stolzer) Hamilton; A.B., U. Tulsa, 1941; M.A., Columbia U., 1958, Ph.D., 1963. Research asst. Bur. Applied Social Research, Columbia U., N.Y.C., 1958-59; instr., maj. adv. Hunter Coll., N.Y.C., 1960-64; vis. prof. behavioral and social scis. New Coll., Sarasota, Fla., 1965-66; asst. prof. sociology in psychiatry Mt. Sinai Sch. Medicine, N.Y.C., 1966-68, assoc. prof., 1968-73, cons. dept. psychiatry, 1969-71; assoc. prof. sociology Grad. Center, City U. N.Y., N.Y.C., 1968-73, prof. sociology grad. program in med. sociology Lehman Coll., 1973-74; prof. psychiatry Downstate Med. Center, SUNY, Bklyn., 1974-77, spl. asst. to dean, 1976-77, cons. nat. survey renal patients, 1972, cons. med. edn., 1977, cons. edn. in ethics, 1978; prof. psychiatry and preventive medicine U. Colo. Health Scis. Center, Denver, 1977—, mem. admissions com., 1978—; assoc. cons. in sociology to sci. adv. staff St. Luke's Hosp., N.Y.C., 1961; task force on studies devel. United Hosp. Fund N.Y., 1969-71; cons. Inst. for Study of Health and Soc., Georgetown, Md., 1972; co-chmn. panel, conf. on cancer rehab. Nat. Cancer Inst., Washington, 1972; mem. colloquium Am. Assn. Med. Colls., Washington, 1974; cons. on evaluation, dept. medicine Montefiore Hosp., N.Y.C., 1977; cons. Random House, 1978; cons., site visitor psychiat. edn. br. NIMH, 1978, mem. adv. council, 1979—; chmn. search com. for dir. Davis Inst. for Care and Study of Aging; mem. regent's monitoring bd. U. Riyadh, U. Colo. Travel grantee Milbank Meml. Fund, 1969; grantee Commonwealth Fund, 1968-70, NIMH, 1975-76, 77, project dir. HEW, 1978. Fellow Am. Public Health Assn., Am. Sociol. Assn. (med. sociology sect.), Am. Psychiat. Assn. (hon.); mem. Sigma Xi. Author: Interns: From Students to Physicians, 1970; (with J. Skipper, Jr.) Sociology in Hospital Care, 1967; editor Academic Guide, 1976-77; assoc. editor Jour. Health and Social Behavior, 1976—; mem. editorial bd. Jour. Med. Edn. cons. TV health series, 1976; contbr. invited book reviews to profl. publs.; reviewer manuscripts for pubs.; contbr. articles to profl. publs. Home: 6925 E Exposition St Denver CO 80224 Office: 4200 E 9th Ave Box C268 Denver CO 80262

MUNCASTER, BARBARA JEAN, educator; b. San Francisco, Dec. 22, 1943; d. Floyd Christopher and Era Mae (Peterson) Felkins; B.S. in Bus. Edn., Okla. State U., 1967, M.S., 1973; m. John Randolph Muncaster, III, Mar. 25, 1967; 1 son, Scott Christopher. Physician's sec., 1960-67; pianist First Baptist Ch., Stillwater, Okla., 1963-67; accounts payable clk. Borg-Warner Corp., Memphis, summer 1968; tchr. bus. edn. dept. chmn. high schs. in Tenn. and Okla., 1968-78; instr. bus. edn. Oscar Rose Jr. Coll., Midwest City, Okla., 1975-77, 78—. Adv. bd. Trinity Episcopal Sch., Oklahoma City, 1977-80; chmn. bd. dirs. Okla. Alliance Children, 1980-81. Consumer econs. scholar, 1971. Mem. Nat. Bus. Edn. Assn., Internat. Word Processing Assn., The Forum, Delta Pi Epsilon. Episcopalian. Home: 1707 Windsor Pl Oklahoma City OK 73116 Office: 6420 SE 15th St Midwest City OK 73110

MUNCY, DOROTHY KATHRYN, nurse; b. Knoxville, Tenn., July 4, 1924; d. Robert Ernest and Ethel Margaret (McDonald) Davis; diploma Knoxville Gen. Hosp., 1945; student Carson-Newman Coll., 1956-58, U. Tenn., 1968—; cert. in Acute Coronary Care, St. Mary's Hosp., Knoxville, 1977; m. Estle Pershing Muncy, Dec. 31, 1946 (div. Apr. 1981); children—Robert Hilton, Teresa Ann, Estle Pershing, Dorothy Jean, James William. Surg. nurse Oak Ridge (Tenn.) Hosp., 1946-47, Dallas Methodist Hosp., 1947-48; med. records librarian Milligan Clinic, Jefferson City, Tenn., 1965-70; head nurse med. unit Jefferson Meml. Hosp., Jefferson City, 1976-79, quality assurance coordinator, 1979-82, supr. evening shift, 1980—. Mem. adv. bd. Jefferson City Library, 1970-77, Jefferson County Dept. Human Services, 1971-74; mem. Jefferson County Heart Council; hon. pink lady, 1979-82. Recipient Cert. of Recognition, E. Tenn. Heart Assn., 1977. Mem. Am., Tenn., Dist. 18 nurses assns., Am. Assn. Critical Care Nurses, LWV, Smoky Mountain Hist. Soc. Republican. Episcopalian. Club: Jefferson City Friday Luncheon. Home: 7273 Cresthill Dr Apt F9 Knoxville TN 37919 Office: PO Box 577 Jefferson City TN 37760

MUNCY, KAREN EVELYN (YATES), editor; b. Ft. Worth, Feb. 13, 1952; d. Gordon Clayton and Vera Kathryn (Winningham) Yates; B.A. in Journalism and Polit. Sci., North Tex. State U., 1974; m. Steve A. Muncy, Apr. 26, 1975. Staff writer regional news Denton (Tex.) Record-Chronicle, 1974-75, staff writer Lifestyle sect., 1975-76, amusements editor, 1976-78, copy editor, 1977-78; mng. editor Dallas-Fort Worth Home/Garden Mag., 1978—. Recipient 1st Pl. Class A Women's Div. award AP Mng. Editors Assn. Tex. competition, 1976. Mem. Women in Communications. Home: 931 Huntington Dr Lewisville TX 75067 Office: 2930 Turtle Creek Plaza Suite 114 Dallas TX 75219

MUNDAY, LOIS REED, journalist; b. Bend, Oreg., Dec. 15, 1950; d. Ernest David and Ellouise (Chastain) Reed; B.A., Tex. Christian U., 1973. Copy chief Fort Worth Star-Telegram, 1972-74, 1974-77; news editor Amarillo (Tex.) Globe News, 1974; copy editor, nat. editor, asst. night met. editor Dallas Times Herald, 1977-78; asst. editor bus. and fin., editor Washington bus. Washington Post, 1978—; cons. in field. Sigma Delta Chi scholar, 1972-73, Walter Humphrey scholar, 1971-72, Wilbur Kidd Meml. scholar, 1970, Brown Meml. scholar, 1969; recipient AP Mng. Editors award, 1975. Mem. Women in Communications, Inc., Soc. Profl. Journalists-Sigma Delta Chi, Kappa Delta. Club: Washington Press. Office: 1150 15th St NW Washington DC 20071

MUNHALL, RUTH BEATRICE, banker; b. Mendon, Mass., Feb. 8, 1929; d. Lawrence B. and Elsie B. (Gaskill) M.; grad. Salvation Army Officers Coll., Bronx, N.Y., 1951; M.B.A., Calif. Western U., 1980, Ph.D., D.B.A., 1981. Civilian supr. U.S. Army and VA Hosp., Framingham, Mass., 1946-50; ordained clergywoman; officer Salvation Army centers in Mass., N.Y. and N.J., 1951-64; owner, operator acctg. and real estate firm, N.Y.C., 1964-68; supr. fiduciary and individual taxation Bank of N.Y., N.Y.C., 1968—; founder R.M. Scholarship Info. Services, Ark., N.Y., Mass. and Israel, 1981—; cons. in field. Recipient 5 Yr. Civil Def. award Gov. N.Y. State. Mem. DAR, Alumni Assn. Calif. Western U. Republican.

MUÑIZ DE OLMOS, SYLVIA, librarian; b. Anasco, P.R., Oct. 28, 1932; d. Pedro and Maria (Miranda) Muniz; B.A., Interamerican U. P.R., 1957; M.L.S., Tex. Woman's U., 1960; postgrad. Rutgers U., 1963-64; m. Osvaldo Olmos, June 3, 1960; children—Osvaldo, Myrna, Sylvia. Librarian Coll. Agr. and Mech. Arts, P.R., 1957-61; head cataloger, tchr. librarianship Humacao (P.R.) Regional Coll., 1964-67; dir. Library Sch. Architecture, U. P.R., Rio Piedras, 1967—, mem. acad. senate, 1980—. Cons., Coll. Engrs., Architects and Surveyors, 1965-66; Mem. ALA, Sociedad de Bibliotecarios de P.R. (sec. 1968). Presbyterian. Home: 2073 Hercules St Guaynabo PR 00657

MUNN, BEVERLY ANN, urban affairs specialist; b. Boston, July 11, 1943; d. Allen Roosevelt and Thelma Elizabeth (Gibson) M.; student Northeastern U., Burdett Coll. With Asso. Day Care Services, Boston; with Boston Gas Co., 1965—, now urban affairs specialist. Bd. dirs. Ellis Meml. Center; adv. bd. Groton (Mass.) Center for the Arts; bd. dirs. Family Day Care Program, Women's Neer City Resources Services. Mem. Urban League Guild Eastern Mass., Negro Bus. and Profl. Women's Club. Office: One Beacon St Boston MA 02108 *

MUNNELL, ALICIA HAYDOCK, economist; b. N.Y.C., Dec. 6, 1942; d. Walter H. and Alicia (Wildman) Haydock; B.A. in Econs., Wellesley Coll., 1964; M.A. in Econs., Boston U., 1966; Ph.D. in Econs., Harvard U., 1973; m. Henry Scanlon Healy, Feb. 2, 1980; children by previous marriage—Thomas Clark Munnell, Jr., Hamilton Haydock Munnell. Teaching fellow dept. econs. Boston U., 1965-66; research asst. to dir. econs. studies div. Brookings Instn., Washington, 1966-68, mem. associated staff, 1975; teaching fellow dept. econs. Harvard U., Cambridge, Mass., 1971-73; economist Fed. Res. Bank of Boston, 1973—, asst. v.p., 1976-78, v.p., 1979—; asst. prof. econs. Wellesley (Mass.) Coll., 1974; mem. Gov.'s Task Force on Unemployment Compensation, Mass., 1975; mem. funding adv. commn. on Mass. pensions, 1976; mem. Mass. Retirement Law Commn., 1976—; chmn. adv. com. New Eng. Retirement Law Council, 1977-79; staff dir. joint com. on public pensions Nat. Planning Assn., 1978; mem. pension research council Wharton Sch. of Fin. and Commerce, U. Pa., Phila., 1979—. Mem. Am. Econ. Assn. Author: The Impact of Social Security on Personal Saving, 1974; The Future of Social Security, 1977; Pensions for Public Employees, 1979; The Economics of Private Pensions, 1982; contbr. numerous articles on social security to profl. jours. Office: 600 Atlantic Ave Boston MA 02106

MUNRO, ALICE, author; b. Wingham, Ont., Can., July 10, 1931; d. Robert Eric and Anne Clarke (Chamney) Laidlaw; student U. Western Ont., 1949-51; m. James Armstrong Munro, 1951 (div. 1976); children—Sheila, Jenny, Andrea; m. 2d, Gerald Fremlin, 1976. Author: (short stories) Dance of the Happy Shades (Gov.-Gen.'s Lit. award 1969), 1968; Lives of Girls and Women (Can. Booksellers award), 1971; (short stories) Something I've Been Meaning To Tell You, 1974, Who Do You Think You Are, 1978; Stories of Flo and Rose (Gov. Gen.'s Lit. award 1979), 1979. Office: care Macmillan Co of Can Ltd 70 Bond St Toronto ON M5B 1X3 Canada

MUNRO, ELEANOR CARROLL, art critic, writer; b. Bklyn., Mar. 28, 1928; d. Thomas and Lucile (Nadler) M.; B.A., Smith Coll., 1949; M.A., Columbia U., 1966; m. E.J. Kahn, Jr., June 30, 1969; children—David T.M. Frankfurter, Alexander M. Frankfurter. With Am. Fedn. Arts, Washington, 1951; staff writer-editor Art News mag., 1952-59, asso. editor, 1954-59; mng. editor Art News Ann., 1954-59; freelance writer, critic, lectr., 1959—. Mem. Internat. Assn. Art Critics, Am. Assn. Art Critics, PEN, Authors' Guild. Author: Encyclopedia of Art, 1961, Through the Vermilian Gates, 1971, Originals: American Women Artists, 1979; also fiction, poetry, articles. Address: 1095 Park Ave New York NY 10028

MUNRO, JUNE EDITH, librarian; b. Echo Bay, Ont., Can., June 20, 1921; d. Neil and Agnes (MacLeod) M.; B.J., Carleton U., 1961; B.L.S., U. Toronto, 1962, M.L.S., 1972. Head children's library services Sault Ste. Marie (Ont., Can.) Public Library, 1941-51; children's librarian London (Ont.) Public Library, 1951-53; head children's library services Leaside Public Library, 1953-56; asst. to exec. dir., publs. prodn. editor Canadian Library Assn., 1956-61; supr. extension service, editor Ont. Library Rev., Ont. Provincial Library Service, 1961-70; book acquisition adv. Coll. Bibliocentre, Toronto, Ont., 1970-72; chief public relations div. Nat. Library Can., Ottawa, Ont., 1972-73; dir. library services St. Catharines (Ont., Can.) Public Library, 1973—. Past chmn. bd. dirs. Carousel Players, St. Catharines, Ont. Recipient Librarian of Year award Ont. Library Trustees Assn., 1971. Mem. ALA, Can. Library Assn., Council Adminstrs. Large Urban Public Libraries, Ont. Library Assn., Chief Exec. Officers Large Public Libraries Ont. Clubs: Golf and Country, Univ. Women's (St. Catharines). Editor Ont. Library Rev., 1961-70. Office: 54 Church St Saint Catharines ON L2R 7K2 Canada

MUNRO, MARY ELIZABETH, journalist; b. Salem, Mass., Feb. 18, 1924; d. Dennis Hartney and Anna Cecelia (Hildreth) Burns; student Boston U.; m. John E. Munro, Mar. 17. 1946 (dec.); children—John Burns, Anne Elizabeth. Reporter, Salem Evening News, 1951-54, 65—. Recipient AP New Eng. Press awards. Mem. New Eng. Women's Press Assn. (judge). Club: North Shore Press. Home: 8 Cornell Rd Danvers MA 01923 Office: 155 Washington St Salem MA 01970

MUNROE, MARY LOU SCHWARZ (MRS. ROBERT E. MUNROE), ednl. adminstr.; b. Denver, Nov. 18, 1927; d. John Anthony and Lutie A. (Benefiel) Schwarz; B.A. (Estelle Hunter scholar), U. Denver, 1949, M.A. in Guidance, 1970, Doctorate in Instructional Specialist, 1973; m. Robert E. Munroe, Nov. 20, 1948; children—Robert M., Carol E., John E. Dir., Jr. and Collegiate Great Books Program, Archdiocese of Denver, 1961-71, leader tng. staff, 1963-71, archdiocesan dir. grade and high sch., 1966-71; undergrad. counselor Sch. Edn. U. Denver, 1971-74; adminstrv. dir., ednl. coordinator adolescent unit Mt. Airy Psychiat. Center, Denver, 1975—; feature writer Register, Denver, 1963-71; lectr., workshop dir. Loretto Heights Coll., 1966, regional tng. centers for religion tchrs., 1967—. Mem. steering com. Cinema Critique Series of Denver, 1967; mem.-at-large Bd. Cath. Edn. of Denver Met. Area, 1969—, pres., 1974-75; mem. Denver Met. Adv. Com. Cath. Edn., 1968-69, Juvenile Ct. Task Force, 1979. Named Woman of Yr., Archdiocese of Denver Edn. Assn., 1971; named to Denver Post Gallery of Fame, 1975; recipient papal medal Pro Ecclesia et Pontifice, 1975. Mem. Cath. Edn. Guild, Mortar Bd., Ednl. Forum Colo. (charter), Phi Beta Kappa, Kappa Delta Pi, Delta Kappa Gamma, Phi Delta Kappa, Delta Gamma. Author: Counseling the Parishioner, 1967. Home: 3131 E Alameda Ave Apt 802 Denver CO 80209

MUNROE, SHIRLEY ANN, hosp. assn. exec.; b. Mpls., Mar. 31, 1924; d. Laurence John and Esther (Tuttle) M.; pre-nursing certificate La Sierra Coll., Arlington, Calif., 1943; R.N., Glendale Sanitarium and Hosp. Sch. Nursing, 1946; postgrad. U. Calif. at Los Angeles Extension, 1953-55, Los Angeles City Coll., 1948-51; certificate U. Calif. at Santa Cruz extension, 1971; m. Stanley G. Fjeistrom, Dec. 26, 1954 (div. June 1957). Chief nurse, office mgr. for Roger W. Barnes, R. Theodore Berman, Los Angeles, 1946-51; bus. mgr. Bolander Clinic and Emergency Hosp., Van Nuys, Calif., 1951-56, Mendocino Med. Center, Ukiah, Calif., 1956; adminstr. Hillside Community Hosp., Ukiah, 1956-78, sec., 1956-78; dir. Center for Small or Rural Hosps., Am. Hosp. Assn., Chgo., 1978-79, dir. constituency programs, 1979—; mem. adv. and eval. com. Ukiah Dist. Sch. Vocational Nursing, 1965-78; faculty U. Calif. extension at Berkeley, Basic Adminstrn. Hosp. Adminstrs. Program, 1966-70. Asst. dir. pub. relations alumni postgrad. assembly Loma Linda U., Los Angeles, 1949-55; dir. pub. relations world meeting Aerospace Med. Assn., Los Angeles, 1953; chmn. re-edn. nursing com. Cal. Dept. Employment, 1962; cons. lectr. nurse aide edn., adult education Willits, Ukiah high schs., 1962; chmn. Career Project for Sr. High Sch. Girls, 1962-64; mem. Mendocino-Lake adv. com. Regional Med. Program, 1969-73; mem. vocat. edn. adv. com. Ukiah Unified Sch. Dist., 1970-73. Dir., sec. Observatory Investment Co., Ukiah, 1957-67. Soloist, Presbyn. Ch., Ukiah, 1956-69, Ukiah Oratorio Soc., 1958-65. Co-chmn. edn. com. Mendocino County br. Am. Cancer Soc., 1961-62, bd. dirs., 1961-76, pres., 1963-65; mem. Ukiah Nursery Sch. Planning Com., 1961-62; mem. steering com. Am. Heart Assn., Mendocino County br. Calif. Heart Assn. Chmn. trustees Tri-County Pre-Payment Medi-Cal Pilot Project, State of Calif., 1969-71; trustee Nor Coa Health, 1967-76, 1st v.p. 1969-71, pres., 1971-72, chmn. South Planning council, 1972-74; mem. Mendocino-Lake counties council, 1966-76; bd. dirs. Mendocino County chpt. ARC, 1968-70; bd. dirs. Blue Cross No. Calif., 1971-78, exec. bd., 1973-78, hosp. provider rep., 1970-78; delegation leader People to People Internat. U.S. Citizen Ambassador Program, 1981. Recipient certificate of commendation Calif. Bd. Nurse Examiners, 1946; Civic Participation award, named Outstanding Women in Professions, Calif. Fedn. Bus. and Profl. Women's Clubs, 1965; Woman of Achievement award Soroptimist Club of Ukiah, 1965; Outstanding Service award Mendocino-Lake br. Am. Cancer Soc., 1963, 64, 65, Notable Service award, 1968; Walker fellow, 1973. Mem. Am. Hosp. Assn., (ho. of dels. 1974-78, regional adv. bd. 1974-78, rural resource com. 1976-78), Calif. Hosp. Assn. (membership com. 1960-61; legislative liaison 1960, panel hosp. peer rev. adminstrs. 1968-78; mem. ins. com. 1971-78), Redwood Empire Hosp. Conf. (ins. com. 1957-59, exec. com. 1968-71, 1st v.p 1968, pres. 1969), Hosp. Council No. Calif. (bd. dirs. 1968-77, pres. 1975-76, chmn. com. on program and edn. 1968-70), Assn. Western Hosps. (edn. research found. council 1963-65), Glendale Sanitarium and Hosp. Sch. Nursing Alumni Assn. (pres. Glendale 1947-48), Bus. and Profl. Women's Club (exec. bd. 1957-61, pres. 1959-60, 3d v.p. 1960-61, career advancement com. 1961-62, chmn. personal devel. com. 1962-64, music chmn. Redwood Empire dist. 1960-61), Bus. and Profl. Women's Club (mem. bd. 1962-65). Republican. Mem. Seventh-day Adventist Ch. (soloist, supt. children's edn. 1961-64, supt. youth div. 1964-65, dir. public relations 1967-78, chmn. finance com. 1967-78). Clubs: Cultus Women's (pres. Ukiah 1960-61, 2d v.p. 1961-62), Soroptimist (pres. Ukiah 1971-72, music chmn. 1962-63, service com. 1961-78, editor bull. 1965-66, dir. 1970-73). Home: 233 N Garfield St Hinsdale IL 60521 Office: 840 N Lake Shore Dr Chicago IL 60611

MUNSCHAUER, CAROL ANN, psychologist; b. Buffalo, Apr. 17, 1948; d. Frederick Eugene and Harriet (Swenson) M.; B.A. magna cum laude, Mt. Holyoke Coll., 1969; Ph.D., SUNY, Buffalo, 1976. Psychology intern Mass. Mental Health Center, Boston, 1973-74; research fellow McLean Hosp., Belmont, Mass., 1975-76; psychologist Wellesley (Mass.) Coll. Student Counselling Service, 1977-79; instr. in psychology dept. psychiatry Harvard U. Sch. Medicine, 1977—; cons. div. adolescent medicine Children's Hosp. Med. Center, Boston, 1977—. Mem. Am. Psychol. Assn., Mass. Psychol. Assn., Am. Soc. Adolescent Psychiatry (asso. mem.), Phi Beta Kappa. Home: 1 Longfellow Pl #1221 Boston MA 02114 Office: 300 Longwood Ave Boston MA 02115

MUNSCHY, DOROTHY GENEVIEVE, mfg. co. exec.; b. Manteca, Calif., Dec. 3, 1922; d. Manuel A. and Mary E. (Silva) Lopes; student Bakersfield Community Coll., 1975, Calif. State U., Bakersfield; m. Roy Charles Munschy, Jan. 31, 1942; children—Charleyne Dianne Branson, Michelle Marie O'Neal. Office mgr. Valley Wide Service Center, Bakersfield, Calif., 1966-78; real estate salesperson, Bakersfield, 1967-77; pres. Etta-Kit Enterprises, Bakersfield, 1971-82, owner, 1982—, also chmn. bd.; cons. new product devel. Mem. Nat. Assn. Female Execs., Bakersfield C. of C., Bus. and Profl. Women's Club (coordinator bicentennial project 1976). Patentee in field. Office: 217 Mount Vernon Ave 3 Bakersfield CA 93307

MUNSELL, ELSIE LOUISE, lawyer; b. N.Y.C., Feb. 15, 1939; d. Elmer Stanley and Eleanor Harriet (Dickinson) M.; A.B., Marietta Coll., 1960; J.D., Coll. William and Mary, 1972; m. George P. Williams, July 14, 1979. Admitted to Va. bar, 1972, U.S. Supreme Ct., 1980; asst. atty. Commonwealth of Va., Alexandria, 1927-74, asst. U.S. atty. Eastern Dist. Va., 1974-79, U.S. magistrate, 1979-81, U.S. atty., 1981—. Bd. visitors Coll. William and Mary, 1972-76. Mem. Am. Bar Assn., Nat. Assn. Women Judges, Alexandria Bar Assn., Va. Women's Attys. Assn. Republican. Episcopalian. Office: 701 Prince St Alexandria VA 22314

MUNSEY, SANDRA GOSS, state ofcl.; b. Portsmouth, N.H., July 8, 1937; d. Robert Bennett and Frances Lawrence (Drake) Goss; B.A. in Govt., U. N.H., 1959; M.P.A., Northeastern U., 1976; m. Donald Tucker Munsey, Jr., Sept. 12, 1959; children—Suzanne Gail, Carol Elizabeth. Intern, N.H. State Planning Office, 1959; adminstrv. asst. Town of Rye, N.H., 1957-59; social studies tchr. Md. and Mass., 1966-69; revenue officer IRS, 1969-71; budget examiner Mass. Budget

Bur., 1971; personnel mgmt. specialist, grant adminstrn. New Eng. region U.S. Civil Service Commn., Boston, 1972-77; project mgr. Mass. Exec. Office for Adminstrn. and Fin., Medfield, 1977—; lectr. Suffolk U., mem. public mgmt. adv. council, 1980-83. Selectman, mem. charter commn., planning bd., growth policy com. Town of Medfield, 1969-80; mem. Norfolk County Adv. Bd., 1977-80; treas. Norfolk County 4-H Leaders' Assn., 1975—. Recipient Norfolk County 4-H Alumni award, 1971. Mem. Nat. Council for Social Studies, Norfolk County Selectman's Assn., Internat. Personnel Mgmt. Assn., Am. Soc. Public Adminstrn. (Mass. chpt. pres., sect. on intergovtl. adminstrn. and mgmt., exec. council sect. on profl devel., nat. council, membership chmn. 1981-83), Sigma Pi Epsilon. Clubs: Medfield Music Boosters, Narragansett Bay Quilter's Assn., New Eng. Quilter's Assn. Club: Order Eastern Star. Contbr. articles in field to publs.; first woman as elected mem. Medfield chief exec. bd. Home and Office: 8 Clark Rd Medfield MA 02052

MUNSON, LUCILLE MARGUERITE (MRS. ARTHUR E. MUNSON), real estate broker; b. Norwood, Ohio, Mar. 26, 1914; d. Frank and Fairy (Wicks) Wirick; R.N., Lafayette (Ind.) Home Hosp., 1937; A.B., San Diego State U., 1963; student Purdue U., Kans. Wesleyan U.; m. Arthur E. Munson, Dec. 24, 1937; children—Barbara (Mrs. Charles Papke), Judith (Mrs. Judith Andrews), Edmund Arthur. Staff and pvt. nurse Lafayette Home Hosp., 1937-41; indsl. nurse Lakey Foundry & Machine Co., Muskegon, Mich., 1950-51, Continental Motors Corp., Muskegon, 1951-52; nurse Girl Scout Camp, Grand Haven, Mich., 1948-49; owner Munson Realty, San Diego, 1964—. Mem. San Diego County Grand Jury, 1975-76, 80-81. Mem. San Diego Bd. Realtors. Presbyterian. Home: 3538 Esterlina Dr Fallbrook CA 92028 Office: 2999 Mission Blvd #102 San Diego CA 92109

MUNSON, NORMA FRANCES, biologist, educator; b. Stockport, Iowa, Sept. 22, 1923; d. Glenn Edwards and Frances Emma (Wilson) M.; B.A., Concordia Coll., 1946; M.A., U. Mo., 1955; Ph.D. (NSF fellow 1957-58, Chgo. Heart Assn. fellow 1959), Pa. State U., 1962; postgrad. Ind. U., 1957, Western Mich. U., 1967, Lake Forest Coll., 1971, 72, 78; student various fgn. univs., 1964-71. Tchr., Aitkin (Minn.) High Sch., 1946-48, Detroit Lakes (Minn.) High Sch., 1948-54, Libertyville (Ill.) High Sch., 1955-79; researcher in nutrition, Libertyville, 1950—. Ruling elder First Presbyn. Ch., Libertyville, 1971-77; pres. Lake County Audubon Soc., 1975-82, Libertyville Edn. Assn., 1964-67; active Rep. Party of Ill., Citizens to Save Butler Lake, Citizens Choice, The Defenders. Recipient Hilda Mahling award, 1967, C. of C. award, 1971, Ill. Best Teacher's award, 1974; NSF fellow, 1970-71. Mem. Nat. Biology Tchrs. Assn. (award 1971), AAAS, Am. Inst. Biol. Sci., NEA, Ill. Edn. Assn., Ill. Environ. Council, Ill. Audubon Council, Nat. Health Fedn., Nat. Wildlife Fedn., Delta Kappa Gamma. Contbr. research articles to publs. Home and Office: 206 W Maple Ave Libertyville IL 60048

MUNTS, MARY LOU, state legislator; b. Chgo., Aug. 21, 1924; d. T. Hunton and Elizabeth (Vinsonhaler) Rogers; student Swarthmore Coll.; M.A., U. Chgo., 1947; J.D., U. Wis., 1976; m. Raymond Munts, July 19, 1947; children—Lisa Munts Redburn, Polly, Andy. Research asst. U.S. Dept. Treasury, 1947-48; instr. Sch. Bus. Wilkes Coll., Wilkes Barre, Pa., 1949-50; asst. to congressman, Washington, 1960; econ. research assoc. Robert R. Nathan Assocs., Bethesda, Md., 1964-66; admissions sec. Center for Devel., U. Wis., Madison, 1967-72; mem. Wis. Ho. of Reps., 1972—; chmn. nat. resources and environ. com. of Nat. Conf. of State Legislatures, 1980-81; mem. Nat. Sea Grant Rev. Panel, 1978-81, Dept. Energy Environ. Adv. Com., 1980—. Bd. dirs. Portal Foster Center, Madison; sec. Dane County (Wis.) Democratic Party. Recipient Dane County Assn. Retarded Children ann. recognition award, 1973, 74, 81; Wis. Assn. Mental Health Citizen of Yr. award, 1975; Public Service award Center for Public Representation, 1976; Disting. Service award Dane County Alliance for Mentally Ill, 1979; Legislator of Yr. award Wis. Wildlife Fedn., 1981; Wis. Assn. Marriage and Family Therapy ann. award, 1982. Office: 125 W State Capitol Madison WI 53702

MURAJDA, HELEN JEAN, psychologist; b. De Lancey, Pa., Mar. 5, 1936; d. Charles G. and Helen (Prehoda) M.; B.A., Mercyhurst Coll., 1965; postgrad. (NSF grantee), Northeastern U., 1966, Notre Dame U., 1967, (NDEA grantee) Genesco State U., 1968; M.Ed., Edinboro State Coll., 1971. Tchr., Erie (Pa.) Diocesan Schs., 1955-70; prin. St. Catherine Sch., DuBois, Pa., 1969-71; psychologist Clarion Manor Intermediate Unit, Shippenville, Pa., 1972—; mem. Adrian Housing Corp. Bd. dirs. Clearfield-Jefferson Community Mental Health Center, 1980—, sec., 1981—. Mem. AAUW, Nat. Assn. Sch. Psychologists, Pa. Psychologists Assn., Am. Psychol. Assn., Clarion Manor Edn. Assn. (pres. 1975-77), Pa. Edn. Assn. (pres. sch. psychology sect. 1979—, mem. spl. edn. com. 1978—). NEA, Clarion Manor Edn. Assn. (exec. com. 1981—). Roman Catholic. Home: Box 163 Anita PA 15711

MURAKAMI, MOMOKO, librarian; b. Los Angeles, Mar. 12, 1931; d. Edward Noboru and June Kisa (Kaimura) M.; B.A., U. Wash., 1953, M.L. in Librarianship, 1954; postgrad. Loyola Law Sch., 1982—. Librarian I, reference in br. libraries cataloging Chgo. Pub. Library, 1954-57; cataloger, acquisitions librarian U. Calif. Sch. Law Library, Los Angeles, 1957-69, head tech. processes, 1969-82, bibliographer, 1979-82. Mem. Calif. Library Assn. (treas. tech. services chpt. 1978), Am. Assn. Law Libraries, So. Calif. Assn. Law Libraries, So. Calif. Tech. Processes Group (program com. 1979-80). Home: 3429 Hillcrest Dr Los Angeles CA 90016 Office: 405 Hilgard Ave Los Angeles CA 90024

MURDEN, CARMELLA, educator; b. Pinewood, S.C., May 11, 1944; d. John H. and Janie (Cantey) White; B.A., Bklyn. Coll., 1974; M.S. 1978, postgrad., 1981—; m. Ernest C. Murden, Sept. 8. 1963; children—Ernest C., Anthony M. Personnel clk. U.S. Post Office, N.Y.C., 1964-70; tchr. math Jr. High Sch. 275, Bklyn., 1974—. Active, Lincoln Civic Block Assn., Ind. Voters of Crown Heights. Mem. Assn. Tchrs. Math N.Y.C., Nat. Assn. Tchrs. Math., Assn. Black Educators of N.Y., Bklyn. Coll. Student Assn. Ednl. Adminstrn. and Supervision (sec. 1982-83). Mem. African Methodist Episcopal Ch. Home: 947 St Johns Pl Brooklyn NY 11213

MURDOCH-KITT, NORMA HOOD, clin. psychologist; b. Clinton, S.C., May 16, 1947; d. Bernard Constantine and Martha Grace (Hood) Murdoch; B.A. (Most Outstanding Student award 1968-69), Wake Forest U., 1969; M.S., U. Pitts., 1971, Ph.D. (USPHS fellow 1969-72), 1975; m. Jonathan Michael Murdoch-Kitt, Mar. 23, 1974; children—Kelly Michelle, Mark Jason. Psychology intern Eastern Pa. Psychiat. Inst., 1972-73; asst. prof., therapist campus counseling center Coll. William and Mary, Williamsburg, Va., 1973-74; staff psychologist child psychiatry dept. Med. Coll. Va., 1974-75; pvt. practice individual psychotherapy and family and marital therapy, Richmond, Va., 1975—. Mem. Richmond Democratic Com., 1976-79, 82—; pres. Richmond Dem. Women's Club, 1979-81; chmn. govtl. relations com. Ginter Park Civic Assn., 1977-82; mem. Richmond Human Relations Adv. Commn., 1976-80; 1st state chmn. ratification polit. action com. ERA, 1977-78. Mem. Am. Psychol. Assn., Va. Psychol. Assn. (state legis. lobbyist 1978-79 (chmn. legis. com. 1981—), Va. Acad. Clin. Psychologists (chmn. legis. com. 1981—), Richmond Area Psychol. Assn., LWV, ACLU, NOW. Presbyterian. Club: Richmond First (chmn. edn. com. 1979-80, dir. 1980-81). Home: 3408 Moss Side Ave Richmond VA 23222 Office: 1805 Monument Ave Richmond VA 23220

MURDOCK, BEATRICE KNAPP, state legislator, realtor; b. Bristol, Conn., Oct. 14, 1932; d. Howard Monroe and Esther Sadie (Hanson) Knapp; B.A. in Econs. and Sociology, Mt. Holyoke Coll., 1954; m. James Milne Murdock, June 19, 1954; children—Alison, Pamela, Dorothy. Research analyst N.Y. Life Ins. Co., 1954-56; tchr. Pine Grove Nursery Sch., 1966-77; realtor assoc. Beres & Murdock Real Estate, Avon, Conn., 1977—; mem. Conn. Gen. Assembly, 1980—. Chmn. Avon ARC, 1963, Pine Grove Nursery Sch., 1963-65, Farmington Valley Assn. for Retarded and Handicapped, 1966-69, Avon Republican Women's Club, 1970-73; mem. Avon Bd. Selectmen, 1973-80, 1st selectman, 1975-80. Republican. Congregationalist. Home: 563 W Avon Rd Avon CT 06001 Office: State Capitol Hartford CT 06115

MURDOCK, ELEANOR ECKHART (MRS. KENNETH BALLARD MURDOCK), author; b. Chgo., June 13, 1904; d. Percy Bernard and Charlotte Briggs (Capen) Eckhart; B.A., Vassar Coll., 1924; M.A., Radcliffe Coll., 1935, Ph.D., 1960; m. Donald Hamilton McLaughlin, Sept. 12, 1925 (div. Aug. 1941); children—Donald Hamilton, Charles Capen; m. 2d, Kenneth Ballard Murdock, Jan. 1, 1942 (dec. Nov. 1975). Scout, Reynal & Hitchcock, pubs., Scandinavia, 1946; editorial reading Houghton Mifflin, 1943—, Little Brown, 1943-49. Vice chmn. Civil Liberties Union of Mass., 1946-49, adv. com., 1949-52; mem. coms. for scholarships for Longy Sch. Music, Cambridge, Mass., Boston Center Adult Edn.; asso. trustee New Eng. Conservatory Music; mem. steering com. Council of Villa I Tatti. Mem. Dante Soc. Am. Episcopalian. Clubs: Cosmopolitan, Chilton. Contbr. articles, revs. to lit. jours. Home: 301 Berkeley St Boston MA 02116

MURLOWSKI, MARILYN ANN SEVERIN, fashion exec.; b. Leigh, Nebr., Sept. 27, 1942; d. John G. and Libbie A. (Sedlacek) Severin; B.S., U. Nebr., 1964; m. Richard L. Murlowski, Sept. 27, 1975. Asst. buyer Miller & Paine, Lincoln, Nebr., 1964-65; sales mgr., asst. buyer Daytons, Mpls., 1965-70, buyer lingerie, 1973-76, group mgr., St. Paul, 1977-81; v.p. retail stores Gokeys, St. Paul, 1981—; buyer lingerie-hosiery Powers Dry Goods, Mpls., 1970-73; mem. adv. com. Asso. Mdsg. Corp., 1974-75. Mem. Mpls. Downtown Council, 1973; mem. adv. bd., community relations com. St. Paul YMCA, 1981. Named Boss of Year, Mpls. Bus. Women's Assn., 1975. Mem. Am. Home Econs. Assn., Home Econs. in Bus. Assn. (mem. exec. bd.), Mpls.-St. Paul Fashion Group. Home: 1535 Long Lake Blvd Long Lake MN 55356 Office: 84 S Wabasha Saint Paul MN 55107

MURNAN-SMITH, BETTY, educator; b. Indpls., Sept. 11, 1921; d. Carl J. and Helene Alice (Stephens) Murnan; B.A. in English cum laude, Butler U., Indpls., 1944; M.A. in Am. Lit., U. Iowa, 1950; m. Richard Norman Smith, Oct. 21, 1951; children—Allegra Louise Smith Jrolf, Timothy Dwight and Michael Murnan (twins). High sch. tchr., Mich. and Ind., 1944-48; instr. English, Ely (Minn.) Jr. Coll., 1950-51, U. Wis., Milw., 1961-66; mem. faculty U. Wis. Center, Waukesha, 1970—, asso. prof. English, 1981—, mem. U. Wis. Center System Faculty Senate, 1980-81; lectr. in field. Vice pres. Randall Sch. PTA, 1960's; program chmn. Waukesha County Human Relations Council, 1962; bd. dirs. Waukesha Symphony, 1969-72; bd. dirs., sec. Waukesha Civic Theatre, 1973-74; sec. Waukesha EEO Commn., 1970-73; ruling elder 1st Presbyterian Ch., Waukesha, 1980—; asst. to dir. Par-Cay Children's Theatre and Penny Players, 1960's. Recipient 1st place award for short story Butler U., 1944, Waukesha Community Service award, 1980. Mem. AAUP, Nat. Council Tchrs. English, AAUP (past chpt. pres.), MLA, Midwest MLA, NOW, Sigma Tau Delta, Kappa Delta Pi. Democrat. Author poetry, articles in field. Home: 1128 Oxford Rd Waukesha WI 53186 Office: 1500 University Dr Waukesha WI 53186

MURPHY, AMANDA LUCKETT, psychologist; b. Huntsville, Ala., Feb. 27, 1936; d. Erise and Willie Beatrice (Glover) Daniel; B.S. in Nursing, Washington U., St. Louis, 1969; M.A., St. Louis U., 1971, Ph.D., 1973; diploma in nursing Homer G. Phillips Hosp., 1955; m. George Earl Murphy, Mar. 24, 1976; 1 son, Marc Andrew Luckett. Nurse, VA Research Hosp., Chgo., 1959-61, Michael Reese Hosp., Chgo., 1961-62, Jewish Hosp., St. Louis, 1962-64; head nurse Barnes Hosp., St. Louis, 1964-70; coordination Mental Health Center, St. Clair County, East St. Louis, Ill., 1971-76, adminstrv. asst. clin. services, 1976-77; adminstr. Yeatman Union Sarah Mental Health Center, 1977-80, project dir., 1980—; pvt. practice psychology, St. Louis; cons. to various community orgns. and agys. Recipient community services award Top Ladies of Distinction Inc., 1976. Mem. Am. Psychol. Assn., Nat. Assn. Black Psychologists, Internat. Transactional Analysis Assn., NAACP, Phi Lambda Theta, Iota Phi Lambda. Home: 6211 McPherson St Saint Louis MO 63130 Office: Yeatman Union Sarah Mental Health Center 4731 Delmar Saint Louis MO 63108 and Counseling and Tng Assos 7349 Delmar St Saint Louis MO 63117

MURPHY, BARBARA MARIE, nurse; b. N.Y.C., Sept. 12, 1952; d. Thomas Patrick and Marie Dorothy (Cleary) M.; R.N., Beth Israel Sch. Nursing, 1973; B.A., Marymount Manhattan Coll., 1979. Head nurse emergency dept. Beth Israel Med. Ctr., N.Y.C., 1973-76; head nurse emergency dept. Cabrini Med. Ctr., N.Y.C., 1976-79; dir. edn. Emergency Care Inst., Beekman Downtown Hosp., N.Y.C., 1980-81; edn. dir. Inst. Emergency Care St. Vincent's Med. Center, N.Y.C., 1981; clin. specialist emergency dept. L.I. Coll. Hosp., N.Y.C., 1981—; cons. regional Emergency Med. Services Council, N.Y.C., 1980—, Profl. Exam. Service, 1981—. N.Y. Regents scholar, 1970-73. Cert. emergency nurse. Mem. N.Y. State Nurses Assn., Emergency Dept. Nurses Assn. Psi Chi

MURPHY, CAROLE DIANE, software mktg. co. exec.; b. Sacramento, Jan. 21, 1942; d. Carl G. and Mary T. (Domich) M.; student U. Calif., Berkeley, 1960, Am. Mgmt. Assn. Seminars, 1963, 69; m. Harris A. Herman, Oct. 5, 1973; children—Terri, Jami, Andria, Nick. Exec. sec. Mut. of New York, Sacramento, 1959-62, R. F. Brown & Assos., Sacramento, 1963-68; adminstrv. office mgr. Informatics Inc., Sacramento, 1968-72; v.p. Software Module Mktg. Co., Sacramento, 1974—, also dir. Mem. Software Industry Assn., Nat. Assn. Ins. Women, Am. Soc. Profl. and Exec. Women, Nat. Small Bus. Assn., Am. Mgmt. Assn. Democrat. Roman Catholic. Home: 2706 American River Dr Sacramento CA 95825 Office: 1007 7th St Penthouse Sacramento CA 95814

MURPHY, CATHERINE, artist; b. Cambridge, Mass., Jan. 22, 1946; B.F.A., Pratt Inst.; student Skowhegan Sch. of Painting and Sculpture. Exhibited in one-person shows including: Xavier Fourcase Inc., N.Y.C., 1975, 79, Inst. Contemporary Art, Boston, 1976, First Street Gallery, N.Y.C., 1975, 79, Inst. Contemporary Art, Boston, 1976, First Street Gallery, N.Y.C., 1972; exhibited in group shows including: Am. Fedn. Arts travelling exhbn., 1972-73, Whitney Mus., N.Y.C., 1973, Storm King Arts Center, N.Y.C., 1973, Indpls. Mus., 1974, Phila. Mus. Art, Smithsonian Inst. travelling exhbn., 1974-76, Mus. Contemporary Art, Chgo., 1977, Am. Acad. and Inst. of Arts and Letters, N.Y.C., 1979; represented in permanent collections including: Whitney Mus., N.Y.C., N.J. Art Mus., Newark Mus., Hirshhorn Mus., Washington. Office: care Xavier Fourcade Inc 36 E 75th St New York NY 10021 •

MURPHY, CHRISTINA MARIE, accountant; b. Malden, Mass., Dec. 22, 1950; d. Nicholas Joseph and Anna Maria (DiPirro) Del Torto; B.A., Regis Coll., 1972; postgrad. Bentley Coll., 1975-78, Nat. Grad. U., 1976, 78; m. Paul Thomas Murphy, July 1, 1973. Research acct. New Eng. Med. Center, Boston, 1974-78; research acct., adminstr. Lahey Clinic Found., Inc., Boston, 1978—; fin. cons. Kimberly Sales, Newton, Mass., 1979—. Mem. Nat. Council Univ. Research Adminstrs., Soc. Research Adminstrs., Research Adminstrs. Discussion Group. Office: 41 Mall Rd Burlington MA 01805

MURPHY, CLAIRE LOUISE, psychophysicist; b. Beverly, Mass., July 7, 1948; d. Philip David and Claire Priscilla (McGlynn) M.; B.S. magna cum laude, Loyola U., Chgo., 1971; M.S., U. Mass., Amherst, 1974, Ph.D., 1976; postdoctoral fellow Yale U. Med. Sch., 1975-77; m. Jack Stuart Madowitz, May 7, 1978; 1 son, Michael David. Vis. asst. fellow John B. Pierce Found., New Haven, 1975-77; Nat. Acad. Scis./NRC vis. scientist U.S. Army Natick (Mass.) Research and Devel. Command, 1977-79; asst. research psychologist UCLA, 1979-80; staff scientist Monell Chem. Senses Center, U. Pa., Phila., 1980—. Mem. AAAS, Am. Psychol. Assn., Eastern Psychol. Assn., Assn. Chemoreception Scis., Soc. Neurosci. Contbr. articles to profl. jours. Home: 56 E Levering Mill Rd Bala-Cynwyd PA 19004 Office: 209 Monell Chem Senses Center 3500 Market St Philadelphia PA 19104

MURPHY, DIANA E., fed. judge; b. Faribault, Minn., Jan. 4, 1934; d. Albert W. and Adleyne (Heiker) Kuske; B.A. magna cum laude, U. Minn., 1954, J.D. magna cum laude, 1974, postgrad., 1955-58; postgrad. Gutenberg U., Mainz, Germany, 1954-55; m. Joseph E. Murphy, July 24, 1958; children—Michael, John. Admitted to Minn. bar, 1974; asso. firm Lindquist and Vennum, Mpls., 1974-76; mcpl. judge Hennepin County (Minn.), 1976-78; dist. judge Minn., 1978-80; judge U.S. Dist. Ct. Minn., 1980—; instr. U.S. Dept. Justice Advocacy Inst., U. Minn. Law Sch., 1977. Bd. regents St. John's U., 1978—; chmn. Mpls. Charter Commn., 1974-76; mem., chmn. bill of rights com. Minn. Constl. Study Commn., 1971-73; bd. dirs. Hennepin County Bar Found.; bd. dirs. Bush Found., Spring Hill Conf. Center. Fulbright scholar, 1954-55. Fellow Am. Bar Found.; mem. Fed. Judges Assn. (dir. 1982—), Minn. Bar Assn. (bd. govs. 1976-81), U. Minn. Alumni Assn. (pres. 1981-82, dir. 1975—), Am. Judicature Soc. (dir. 1982—), 8th Circuit Dist. Judges Assn., Nat. Assn. Women Judges, Am. Bar Assn., Minn. State Bar Assn., Hennepin County Bar Assn., Minn. Women Lawyers, Order of Coif, Phi Beta Kappa. Editor Minn. Law Rev., 1954-55. Office: 609 US Courthouse 110 S 4th St Minneapolis MN 55401

MURPHY, DONALDA JEAN, aerospace mfg. co. exec.; b. Troy, N.Y., Feb. 16, 1952; d. Donald Edward and Grace Lorna (Betton) M.; student Kent State U., 1970-72; A.A., Miami Dade Community Coll., 1976; student Fla. Internat. U., 1976-77. Asst. mgr. Isaly's Grocery Chain, Warren, Ohio, 1970-71; exec. sec. Robco Enterprises, Niles, Ohio, 1971-72; cost control clk. Am. Hosp. Supply Corp., Miami, Fla., 1972-74, jr. inventory analyst, 1974-76, sr. inventory analyst/planner, 1976-78; systems mfg. planner Info. Internat. Inc., Culver City, Calif., 1978—, prodn. control supr., planning supr., 1980-81; prodn. control supr. Maiman div. Aeroquip Aerospace, Los Angeles, 1981—. Mem. Nat. Assn. Female Execs., Am. Prodn. and Inventory Control Soc., Archeol. Inst. Am. Office: 11214 Exposition Blvd Los Angeles CA 90064

MURPHY, DONNA JEANNE, educator; b. Columbus, Ind., Nov. 27, 1954; d. George Calvin and Jacqueline (Drake) M.; B. Music Edn., Ind. Univ. Sch. Music, 1980. Asst. recreation supr. Res-Care, Inc.-Atterbury Job Corps, Edinburgh, Ind., 1979-80; mgr. Nkenge's Nightclub, Houston, 1980-81; tchr. band Houston Ind. Sch., 1980—; pvt. tchr. music, 1970—; supr. Herbalife Nutrition Co. Active Neighborhood Civic Club. Recipient Sword of Honor, Sigma Alpha Iota, 1978. Mem. Houston Tchrs. Assn., Tex. State Tchrs. Assn., NEA, Tex. Music Educators Assn., Music Educators Nat. Conf., Nat. Assn. Female Execs. Methodist. Home: 11518 Sagegrove Ln Houston TX 77089 Office: 1711 Westover St Houston TX 77087

MURPHY, DORIS JEAN, fin. co. exec.; b. Monona, Iowa, Sept. 27, 1925; d. Louis Edward and Winnifred E. (Dull) Wagner; student Am. Inst. of Commerce, Davenport, Iowa, 1942-43; cert. property mgr. Inst. Real Estate Mgmt., Chgo., 1978; children—Patricia, William, James, Mary. Sec. to pres. Ventfabrics, Inc., Chgo., 1962-64; office mgr. Galiant Products, West Branch, Mich., 1964-65; office mgr., corporate sec. Asher N. Tilchin & Assos., Southfield, Mich., 1965-68; office mgr. for State of Mich., Robert F. Kennedy campaign, 1968; partner Sylvan Mgmt. Co., Southfield, 1968-77; pres. Four Seasons Mgmt. Inc., Troy, Mich., 1978—. Chmn. 18th dist. Oakland County Republican Com., 1980. Mem. Apt. Assn. of Mich., Exec Com., Apt. Owners and Mgrs. Assn., Inst. Real Estate Mgmt. (legis. com. 1977-80, treas. 1980), South Oakland County Bd. Realtors, Pearson Yacht Owners' Assn. (vice commodore 1976-79, commodore 1980). Clubs: Albatross Yacht, Detroit Yacht, Zonta Internat. Home: 123 Phillips Pl Royal Oak MI 48067 Office: Suite 2110 755 W Big Beaver St Troy MI 48084

MURPHY, ELEANOR ECKFORD, librarian; b. Greenville, Ga., May 13, 1919; d. Charles Gates and Nell (Hunnicutt) Eckford; A.B., U. Ga., 1940; 5th Yr. L.S., Emory U., 1941; m. James LeRoy Murphy, Jr., Jan. 9, 1944; children—James LeRoy, Gates Eckford. Circulation and cataloging asst. Atlanta Public Library, 1941-42; periodicals librarian Ga. Inst. Tech., 1942-43; head catalog dept. Middle Ga. Regional Library, 1950-52; asst. dir. Huntsville (Ala.)-Madison County Public Library, 1960-77, dir., 1977-81; library cons. U. Ala., Huntsville, 1960. Community adv. com. to Marshall Space Flight Center, NASA, United Givers Fund membership com.; bd. dirs. Huntsville Lit. Assn.; mem. Huntsville Symphony Orch. Guild, Huntsville Mus. of Art Guild. Mem. ALA, Ala. Library Assn., Mortar Bd., Phi Beta Kappa, Phi Kappa Phi. Democrat. Presbyterian. Eleanor E. Murphy Br. Library of Huntsville-Madison County Public Library named for her, 1981; contbr. book reviews to newspapers, articles to publs. in field. Home: 2206 Lytle St Huntsville AL 35801

MURPHY, ELISABETH ANNE, educator; b. Jacksonville, Ill., Dec. 23, 1950; d. Paul and Mary (Henderson) Hogan; B.A., MacMurray Coll., 1973; m. Donald Edward Murphy, Nov. 29, 1975; children—Megan Elizabeth, Metthew Edward. Instr. sign lang. John A. Logan Coll., Carterville, Ill., 1976-79; instr. sign lang. div. continuing edn. So. Ill. U., 1979—; tchr. primary deaf students Williamson County Spl. Edn. Coop., 1973—. Cert. Council Edn. Deaf, cert. tchr., Ill. Mem. Marion Edn. Assn., Ill. Edn. Assn., NEA, Ill. Tchrs. Hearing Impaired, Telecommunictors of Central Ill., Telecommunications ofr Deaf So. Ill. Interpretors of Deaf, Little Egypt Assn. Deaf. Roman Catholic. Home: 1104 W White St Marion IL 62959 Office: 700 E Blvd Marion IL 62959

MURPHY, EVRA SMITH, educator; b. Hayti, Mo., July 17, 1929; d. Tom J. and Annie Thomas Smith; L.P.N., Roosevelt U., 1970; M.S.W., U. Ill., Chgo., 1973; m. Carl Murphy, Nov. 22, 1954; children—Jerry, David, Yvonne, Margaret, Theeda. Lic. practical nurse Rush Presbyn.-St. Luke's Hosp., Chgo., 1965-69; med. social worker Dept. Children and Family Services-Protective Services, Cook County Hosp., 1970-74; asst. prof. U. Ark., Pine Bluff, 1977—. Mem. Midwest Community Council Chgo., 1962-74; mem. adv. council Garfield Community Service Center, 1962-73. Mem. Nat. Assn. Social Workers, Nat. Black Social Workers Assn., Ark. Human Service Providers. Home: 1815 Laurel St Pine Bluff AR 71601 Office: University Dr Pine Bluff AR 71601

MURPHY, GRETA W., coll. adminstr.; b. Milw., Aug. 24, 1910; d. Oscar and Johanna (Seelhorst) Werwath; ed. Ohio State U., 1943-45; m. John Heery Murphy, Sept. 18, 1941. With Milw. Sch. Engring., 1928—, head admissions dept., 1931-42, dir. pub. relations, 1945-66, v.p. pub. relations and devel., 1966-77, v.p., cons., 1978—, also regent. Mem. Milw. County Planning Commn., 1966—, vice chmn., 1974-75, chmn., 1976-77. Mem. Pub. Relations Soc. Am. (founder, past pres. Wis. chpt.), Am. Coll. Pub. Relations Assn. (past dir., sec., trustee), Women's Advt.

Club Milw. (past pres.). Republican. Lutheran. Clubs: Zonta (past pres. Milw., past internat. dir.), Woman's of Wis.

MURPHY, HELEN MARIE, psychologist; b. Cleve., June 6, 1943; d. John Francis and Helen Marie (Herbert) Murphy; B.S., Notre Dame Coll., 1965; M.S., John Carroll U., 1967; Ph.D. (NSF fellow), Ill. Inst. Tech., 1969. Grad. asst. dept. biology John Carroll U., Cleve., 1965-67, asst. prof. psychology, 1969-74, asso. prof., 1974-79, prof., 1979—; research asso. Michael Reese Hosp., Chgo., 1968-69; psychol. cons. Cleve. Cath. Diocese Marriage Tribunal. Recipient Disting. Faculty award, 1980. Mem. AAAS, Soc. for Neurosci., Ohio Acad. Sci., Kappa Gamma Pi. Republican. Roman Catholic. Contbr. articles to profl. jours. Home: 19376 Malvern Ave Rocky River OH 44116 Office: Dept Psychology John Carroll U Cleveland OH 44118

MURPHY, HELEN MARTHA, nurse; b. Pitts., Nov. 6, 1935; d. Matthew A. and Dorothy K. Murphy; B.S. Nursing, Mercy Coll. Detroit, 1956; M.S. Nursing, Wayne State U., 1968; M.P.H., U. Mich., 1975. Clin. nurse, 1956—; nursing educator, 1963—; faculty U. N.C. Sch. Nursing, Chapel Hill, 1975—, asso. prof. nursing, dept. chmn. core curriculum, 1977—; nursing edn. cons. various nursing orgns. for continuing edn. and curriculum devel., 1975—. Active interfaith council Newman Cath. Student Center, Chapel Hill, 1975-82, social justice com., 1975-82. Fed. Nursing trainee, 1967-68, USPHS award, 1974. Mem. Am. Nurses Assn., N.C. Nurses Assn. (legis. com. Dist. II 1976), Mich. Nurses Assn., Am. Public Health Assn. (subcom. maternal and child health 1975-82), Orange/Chatham Mental Health Assn., Nat. Assn. Public Health Policy, Nat. Wildlife Assn., Audubon Soc. Contbr. articles to profl. jours. Office: Sch Nursing U NC at Chapel Hill Carrington Hall 214H Chapel Hill NC 27514

MURPHY, KATHRYN MARGUERITE, archivist; b. Brockton, Mass.; d. Thomas Francis and Helena (Fortier) M.; A.B. in History, George Washington U., 1935, M.A., 1939; M.L.S., Cath. U., 1950; postgrad. Am. U., 1961. With Nat. Archives and Records Service, Washington, 1940—, supervisory archivist Central Research br., 1958-62, archivist, 1962—, mem. fed. women's com. Nat. Archives, 1974, rep. to fed. women's com. GSA, 1975; lectr. colls., socs. in U.S., 1950—; lectr. Am. ethnic history, 1978-79. Founder, pres. Nat. Archives lodge Am. Fedn. Govt. Employees, 1965—, del. conv., 1976, 78, 80, recipient award for outstanding achievement in archives, 1980. Recipient commendation Okla. Civil War Centennial Commn., 1965; named hon. citizen Oklahoma City, Mayor, 1963. Mem. ALA, Soc. Am. Archivists (joint com. hosp. libraries 1965-70), Nat. League Am. Pen Women (corr. sec. Washington 1975-78, pres. chpt. 1978-80), Phi Alpha Theta (hon.). Contbr. articles on Am. ethnic history to profl. publs. Home: 1500 Massachusetts Ave NW Washington DC 20005 Office: Nat Archives and Records Service 7th and Pennsylvania Aves NW Washington DC 20408

MURPHY, LINDA LEE, psychologist; b. San Angelo, Aug. 5, 1939; d. James William and Enona Bess (Folwell) M.; B.A., U. Tex., Austin, 1961; M.A., Tex. Tech. U., 1968, Ph.D., 1973. Employment counselor Youth Opportunity Center, 1965-66; psychologist Vocat. Guidance Service, Houston, 1967-69: instr. edn. Pa. State U., State College, 1972-73; dir. Christian Counseling Services, Inc., Fort Lauderdale, Fla., 1974—; prof. Fla. Bible Coll., Hollywood, 1975-79. Bd. dirs. Fair Haven Alcoholic Rehab. Center, Project Learn, Inc., 1980—. Mem. Am. Psychol. Assn., Christian Assn. for Psychol. Studies, Psi Chi. Home: 3100 Riverside Dr 110 Coral Springs FL 33065 Office: 660 W Oakland Park Blvd Fort Lauderdale FL 33311

MURPHY, LORRAINE MARGARET, educator; b. Egan, S.D., June 27, 1923; d. Charles F. and Elsie Agnes Penney; B.A., Augustana Coll., Sioux Falls, S.D., 1946; postgrad. U. Minn., 1947, U. Calif., 1949, U. Ind., 1961; M.A., Miami U., 1962; m. Harry C. Murphy, July 28, 1947; children—Kevin C., Patricia Ann, Thomas F., Steven J. Tchr., U. Minn. Curriculum Sch., 1947-48; editor Pflaum Pub. Co., Dayton, Ohio, 1950-52; asso. prof. English, dir. freshman English, U. Dayton, Ohio, 1953—. Mem. Coll. Composition and Communications (exec. com.), Nat. Council Tchrs. English, Ohio Tchrs. English, Midwest Modern Lang. Assn. Roman Catholic. Contbr. articles to profl. jours. Home: 1101 Independence St Dayton OH 45429 Office: English Dept U Dayton Dayton OH 45469

MURPHY, MARGARET ALDRIDGE (PEG), real estate broker; b. Huntington, W.Va., July 13, 1942; d. George Thompson and Margaret Jane (Bias) Aldridge; student Tex. Tech. U., 1960-61, U. Tenn., Nashville, 1966-67, Bluefield State Coll., 1975-76; children—Margaret Reagan, Shannon Elizabeth. Asst., D.H. Byrd Enterprises, Dallas, 1961-63; office mgr. State Fair of W.Va., Lewisburg, 1963-66; real estate agt. Lew Cook Realtors, Murfreesboro, Tenn., 1966-67; sec., asst. to dist. attys. W.Va. Dept. Hwys., Lewisburg, 1968-76; real estate cons. D. K. Hammond & Assos., Lewisburg, 1974-78; v.p. Emerald Isle Enterprises, Ltd., Lewisburg, 1976—; real estate broker, owner Path Finders Realtors, 1978—; tech. adv., cons. Wards, Washington; mem. adv. council re real estate tng. W.Va. Dept. Edn. Mem. Nat. Rifle Assn., Nat. Assn. Realtors, W.Va. Assn. Realtors (dir. 1979—, mem. steering com. of legis. com., chmn. edn. com. 1980-82), Greenbrier County Bd. Realtors (pres. 1979-81, dir. 1981—, chmn. public relations com. 1981—), Grad. Realtors Inst., Cousteau Soc. Kerr Family Assn. (chpt. treas. 1979-81). Presbyterian. Clubs: Greenbrier Civic League, Weimaraner Club Am. Office: 213 E Washington St Lewisburg WV 24901

MURPHY, MARGARET ANN HENRY, educator; b. Guntersville, Ala., Dec. 27, 1938; d. Marshall Cochran and Ruth Judson (Parnell) Henry; student Judson Coll., 1956-57; B.S. with honors, Auburn U., 1960; M.Ed., Livingston U., 1968; Ed.D., U. So. Miss., 1980; m. Cecil L. Murphy, Aug. 22, 1957; children—Lee Ann Murphy Wasden, Sherry Lynn Murphy Gregson, Tammy Cecile, Cecil L., Margaret Ann. Instr. English, Livingston U., 1968-70, William Carey Coll., 1970-71; chmn. lang. and fine arts div. So. Union State Jr. Coll., 1972-74; chmn. lang. and fine arts div., instr. English, Patrick Henry State Jr. Coll., Monroeville, Ala., 1974—; instr. English, Troy State U., part-time, 1975-81. Mem. steering com., mem. exec. com. Com. of 100; chmn. Sumter County Cancer Crusade, 1970. Mem. Nat. Council Tchrs. English (life), Southeastern Conf. English in the Two-Yr. Colls., NEA, Ala. Edn. Assn., Ala. Coll. English Tchrs. Assn., Phi Kappa Phi, Lambda Iota Tau. Democrat. Baptist. Home: PO Box 8 Peterman AL 36471 Office: PO Box 646 Monroeville AL 36461

MURPHY, MARGARET H., state legislator; b. Balt.; B.S., Coppin State Coll., 1952, postgrad. Morgan State U. Formerly ednl. assoc. Office of Reading, Balt. City Pub. Schs.; mem. Balt. City Democratic State Central Com., 1978—; mem. Md. Ho. of Dels., 1978—, mem. constl. and adminstrv. law com. Bd. dirs. Vanguard Polit. Orgn. Inc.; mem. Ethland Ave. Neighborhood Assn., Forest Park Golf Course Neighborhood Assn., bd. dirs. Threshold Inc.; sec. Md. Legis. Black Caucus. Mem. Public Sch. Tchrs. Assn., NEA, ARC, NAACP, Women Legislators of Md. (treas.), Delta Sigma Theta. Clubs: Ten Plus Social, Joyettes Social. Office: 319 Lowe Bldg Annapolis MD 21401 *

MURPHY, MARGARETTE CELESTINE EVANS, educator, writer; b. Chgo., June 25, 1926; d. Crawford and Ethel Hazel (Cartman) Evans; Ph.B., U. Chgo., 1945, M.A., 1949, postgrad., 1950-79, Ph.D., Colo. Christian Coll., 1972; m. Robert H. Murphy, Sept. 25, 1949; children—Linda, Michelle. Tchr., English, Spanish and French, Willard Elem. Sch., 1950-52, McKinley High Sch., 1952-60, chmn. fgn. langs. dept. Crane High Sch., 1960-64, Harlan High Sch., Chgo., 1965—; tchr. TESL, Chgo. City Jr. Colls., 1976—. Mem. Women's Share in Public Service, Brazilian Soc. Chgo., Am. Security Council (nat. adv. bd.), U. Chgo. Alumni Assn., AAUW, Alpha Kappa Alpha. Republican. Roman Catholic. Club: 1200 of Chgo. Author: Note on Martínez Zuviría, Argentinian Novelist, 1949. Home: 8214 S Evans Ave Chicago IL 60619 Office: care Mrs Eva Martin 907 Polk Ave Memphis TN 38104

MURPHY, MARY C., state legislator; B.A., Coll. St. Scholastica. Former tchr.; mem. Minn. Ho. of Reps., 1976—, vice-chmn. govtl. ops., mem. commerce and econ. devel. com., mem. labor-mgmt. relations com., chmn. negotiations and gen. labor legislation subcom. Office: 262 State Office Bldg Saint Paul MN 55155 *

MURPHY, MARY KATHLEEN CONNORS (MRS. MICHAEL C. MURPHY), ednl. adminstr., writer; b. Pueblo, Colo.; d. Joseph Charles and Eileen E. (McDermott) Connors; A.B., Loretto Heights Coll., 1960; M.Ed., Emory U., 1968; Ph.D., Ga. State U., 1980; m. Michael C. Murphy, June 6, 1959; children—Holly Ann, Emily Louise, Patricia Marie. Tchr. English pub. schs., Moultrie, Ga., 1959, Sacramento, 1960, Marietta, Ga., 1960-65, DeKalb County, Ga., 1966; tech. writer Ga. Dept. Edn., 1966-69; editorial asst. So. Regional Edn. Bd., Atlanta, 1969-71; dir. alumni affairs The Lovett Sch., Atlanta, 1972-75, dir. publs. and info. services, 1975-77; coordinator summer series in aging Ga. State U., 1979; dir. found. relations Ga. Inst. Tech., 1980—; free-lance edn. writer, 1968—; contbr. and contbg. editor numerous articles on teaching and secondary edn. to profl. publs.; columnist Daily Jour., Marietta, 1963-67, The Atlanta Constn., 1963-68. Bd. advisors Bridge Family Counseling Center, 1981—, Northside Sch. Arts, 1981—, Atlanta Women's Network, Sch. Religion, Cathedral of Christ the King, 1979—. NDEA fellow, 1965-66, Adminstrn. of Aging fellow, 1977-79. Mem. Council for Advancement and Support of Edn. (publs. com., dist. III bd. 1981—), Nat. Assn. Ind. Schs. (publs. com.), Edn. Writers Assn., Am. Vocat. Assn., Phi Delta Kappa, Kappa Delta Pi (pres. 1980-81). Co-author: Fitting in as a New Service Wife, 1966. Home: 2892 Castlewood Dr NW Atlanta GA 30327

MURPHY, MARY KATHRYN, indsl. hygienist; b. Kansas City, Mo., Apr. 16, 1941; d. Arthur Charles and Mary Agnes (Fitzgerald) Wahlstedt; B.A., Avila Coll., Kansas City, 1962; M.S., Central Mo. State U., 1975; m. Thomas E. Murphy, Jr., Aug. 26, 1963; children—Thomas E., III, David W. Indsl. hygienist Kansas City area office Occupational Safety and Health Adminstrn., 1975-78, regional indsl. hygienist, 1979—; asst. dir. safety office U. Kans. Med. Center, 1978-79. Summer talent fellow Kaw Valley Heart Assn., 1961; cert. in comprehensive practice indsl. hygiene. Mem. Am. Indsl. Hygiene Assn. (sec.-treas. Mid-Am. sect. 1978-79), Am. Chem. Soc., Am. Conf. Govt. Indsl. Hygienists (threshold limit value com. chem. agts.), Am. Coll. Toxicology (asso.), Am. Acad. Indsl. Hygiene. Home: 1019 E 109th Terr Kansas City MO 64131 Office: 911 Walnut St Suite 406 Kansas City MO 64106

MURPHY, MAUREEN MARY, coll. dean; b. Newark, Feb. 1, 1938; d. William Joseph and Elizabeth (Flanagan) M.; B.S. in Edn., Seton Hall U., South Orange, N.J., 1966; M.A., Cath. U. Am., 1968, Ph.D., 1973; m. Joseph A. LaBarge, May 30, 1970; children—Joseph W., Michelle A., William M. Elementary sch. tchr., 1957-66; lectr., then grad. teaching asst. religion and religious edn. Cath. U. Am., 1967-70; mem. faculty Bucknell U., Lewisburg, Pa., 1970—, asst. dean Coll. Arts and Scis., 1973-80, asso. dean, 1980—, adj. asso. prof. religion, 1981—; mem. commn. religion in higher edn. Assn. Am. Colls., 1975-78. Mem. Am. Conf. Acad. Deans, Conf. Pa. Acad. Deans. Roman Catholic. Club: Buffalo Valley Equestrian 4-H (leader). Office: Bucknell U Lewisburg PA 17837

MURPHY, MURIEL J., nurse; b. Oshkosh, Wis., Aug. 9, 1928; d. Neal B. and Louise A. (Baier) Mitchell; diploma nursing St. Therese Sch. Nursing, 1949; B.S., Marquette U., 1952; m. William H. Murphy, June 5, 1954; children—Karen, Cynthia, William H. Indsl. nurse Evinrude Motors, Milw., 1949; pvt. duty nurse, Milw., 1950-52; staff nurse Doctors Clinic, Milw., 1952-53; public health staff nurse, Colorado Springs, Colo., 1953; emergency room staff nurse Miami Valley Hosp., Dayton, Ohio, 1953-54, personnel health supr., 1954-55; med. staff nurse Dee Meml. Hosp., Ogden, Utah, 1958-59, Stormont Vail Hosp., Topeka, 1963-64; ICU-CCU staff nurse Penrose Hosp., Colorado Springs, 1968-69; coordinator practical nurse program Seton Sch. Nursing, Penrose Hosp., 1969-70, El Paso Community Coll., Colorado Springs, 1970-73; charge nurse Sunset Manor, Brush, Colo., 1979; asst. dir. nursing Lower Valley Hosp. and Nursing Home, Fruita, Colo., 1979-80; dir. nursing, Fruita, 1980-81; pvt. duty nurse, personnel med. pool, staff nurse Sunnyrest Sanitorium, Colorado Springs, 1981—. Sec.-treas., Southwestern Teller County Hosp. Dist., Cripple Creek, Colo., 1974-79. Seventh-day Adventist. Home: 2618 W Serendipity Circle 125 Colorado Springs CO 80917

MURPHY, PATRICIA, speech pathologist, lang. learning disorders specialist; b. N.Y.C., Mar. 6, 1941; d. Michael and Nora (Dennehy) M.; B.A. in Speech Pathology and Audiology, Hunter Coll., N.Y.C., 1968, M.A. in Communication Scis. (Vocat. Rehab. Adminstrn. fellow), 1970; M.A. in Learning Disabilities/Reading, N.Y.U., 1977. Speech pathologist Goldwater Meml. Hosp., N.Y.U. Med. Center, 1970-78; lang. learning disorders specialist Met. Hosp., N.Y.C., 1980—; cons. Mary Manning Walsh Nursing Home, 1974—. Mem. Am. Speech and Hearing Assn., Orton Soc., Internat. Reading Assn., N.Y.U. Alumni Assn. Club: Appalachian Mountain. Address: 161 E 96th St New York NY 10028

MURPHY, PATRICIA ANN, ednl. adminstr.; b. Corning, N.Y., May 5, 1946; d. Thomas James and Bereniece Evangeline (La Fever) Murphy; B.S. in Edn., State U. N.Y., Geneseo, 1968; M.S. in Edn., State U. N.Y., Albany, 1969. Grad. intern Monroe Community Coll., Rochester, N.Y., 1969; coordinator Residence Living Program and Services Pa. State U., Middletown, 1969—; production mgr. Players Repertory Theatre, Harrisburg, Pa., 1974-75. Presdl. campaign worker Democratic party, 1975-76. N.Y. State Regents scholar, 1964-68. Mem. Nat. Assn. Student Personnel Adminstrs., NOW, Pa. Assn. of Coll. Personnel Adminstrs., ACLU, Mensa. Home: 835 Nelson Dr Middletown PA 17057 Office: Residential Life Program Office 946A Kirtland Ave Middletown PA 17057

MURPHY, RUBY SIMMS, nursing adminstr.; b. Tucker, Ark., Apr. 10, 1940; d. Lasto and Augusta (Wilkins) Simms; R.N., Fordham Sch. Nursing, 1960; student Wayne State U., 1967-69; m. Oliver Murphy, May 24, 1969; children—Connie, Oliver III. Staff nurse Fordham Hosp., Bronx, N.Y., 1960-61, Providence Hosp., Detroit, 1962, VA Hosp., 1963-66, Vis. Nurses Assn., Detroit, 1963-69; nursing supr. Kirwood Hosp., Detroit, 1969-75; afternoon nursing supr. Grace Northwest Hosp., Detroit, 1975—; mem. Conduct-Utilization Research in Nursing Team. Served to 1st lt. USAF, 1961-63. Recipient Best Bedside Nursing award Fordham Hosp., 1960. Mem. Am. Assn. Evening and Night Suprs. Democrat. Baptist.

MURPHY, SARAJANE LEONARD, printing and mailing co. exec.; b. St. Petersburg, Fla., Sept. 19, 1924; d. John Lawson and Mabel Lillian (Houser) Leonard; student Jones Coll., 1941-42; m. Stanley W. Murphy, Sept. 26, 1946; children—Cynthia Louise, Amy Elizabeth, Peggy Leonard, Stanley W., William Stone, Patrick Francis. Copy writer Convention Press, 1960-65, Inland Waterway Guide, 1964-65; v.p. Stan Murphy Co., Jacksonville, Fla., 1955—. Past pres., v.p., dir. local and dist. bd. United Methodist Ch.; sec. local unit Am. Cancer Soc.; dir., mem. exec. com. State Cancer Sos.; dir., bd. mem. Theatre Jacksonville. Clubs: Belle Meade Hunt (Ga.); Garden of Jacksonville. Office: 705 American Heritage Life Bldg Jacksonville FL 32202

MURPHY, SHARON MARGARET, educator; b. Milw., Aug. 2, 1940; d. Adolph Leonard and Margaret Ann (Hirtz) Feyen; B.A., Marquette U., 1965; M.A., U. Iowa, 1970, Ph.D., 1973; m. James E. Murphy, June 28, 1969; children—Shannon Lynn, Erin Ann. Tchr. public and parochial schs., Wis., 1959-69; tchr., publs. coordinator Kirkwood Community Coll., Cedar Rapids, Iowa, 1970-71; reporter Milw. Sentinel, 1967; editor Worldwide mag., 1965-68; asst. prof. mass communication U. Wis., Milw., 1973-79; asso. prof. journalism So. Ill. U., 1979—, dir. journalism grad. studies. Fulbright fellow, 1977-78. Mem. Women in Communications, Inc., Internat. Communication Assn., Assn. Edn. Journalism, NOW. Author: (with Don Wigal) Screen Experience: An Approach to Film, 1969; Other Voices: Black, Chicano and American Indian Press, 1974; (with James Murphy) Let My People Know: American Indian Journalism 1828-1978, 1981; (with Atwood and Bullion) International Perspectives on News, 1982; (with Madelon Schilep) Great Women of the Press, 1983. Home: Route 1 Box 329 Carbondale IL 62901 Office: School of Journalism S Ill U Carbondale IL 62901

MURRAY, ALICE JEAN HOWARD, law librarian; b. Wichita, Kans., Mar. 8, 1924; d. James Monroe and Mabel Jean (Laurie) Howard; student Am. River Coll., 1970-73; m. E. E. Callaway, 1945 (div. 1963); children—Michael A., Kathleen Margaret Callaway Troglia; m. 2d, Gerald Wesley Murray, June 24, 1967. Analyst, Calif. Dept. Justice, Sacramento, 1960-61; asst. librarian Sacramento County Law Library, 1961-63; asst. librarian U. Pacific-McGeorge Sch. of Law, Sacramento, 1963-69, dir., 1970—; instr. legal bibliography and research. Mem. Golden State Mobile Home Owners League, Inc., pres. chpt., 1980-81; past pres. Jr. Women's Club, Norwalk, Calif. Served with WAVES, USN, 1944-46. Mem. Am. Assn. Law Libraries (chmn. pub. relations com. 1980-81), Sacramento Ex-WAVES Assn., Am. Legion (past comdr. Capitol City Women's Post 389). Clubs: Zonta Internat. (corr. sec. 1981-82), Daus. of Scotia (past trustee Sacramento lodge). Contbr. articles to Law Library Jour. Office: 3282 Fifth Ave Sacramento CA 95817

MURRAY, ANNE, singer; b. Springhill, Nova Scotia, Can., June 20, 1945; d. Carson and Marion (Burke) M.; B.Phys. Edn., U. N.B. (Can.), 1966; m. William Langstroth, June 20, 1975; children—William Stewart, Dawn Joanne. Country and pop singer, 1970—; appearances on stage and TV; rec. artist; songs rec. include: Love Song (Grammy award for Best Country Vocalist 1974), You Needed Me (Grammy award for Best Pop Vocalist 1979), Could I Have This Dance (Grammy award for Best Country Vocalist 1980). Decorated officer Order Can.; recipient numerous Juno awards Can. Acad. Rec. Arts and Scis., 1970-80; named to Nashville Country Music Hall of Fame, 1974; star in Hollywood Walkway of Stars, 1980. Office: care Balmur Ltd 4881 Yonge St Suite 412 Toronto ON M2N 5X3 Canada

MURRAY, BARBARA OLIVIA, psychologist; b. Summit, N.J., July 8, 1947; d. Archibald and Anna Cutler (Mattison) M.; student Inst. d'Etudes Francaises Pour Etrangers, France, 1965, Universite de Grenoble, France, 1968; B.A. in Psychology, Lake Erie Coll., 1969; M.A. in Clin. Psychology, Cleve. State U., 1971; postgrad. Gestalt Inst. Cleve., 1971-73; Ph.D. in Clin. Psychology, Calif. Sch. Profl. Psychology, Fresno, 1976. Mental health worker Cleve. Clinic Hosp., 1970-71, asso. psychologist, 1971-73; psychiat. intake worker Cleve. Free Clinic, 1971, group leader, 1972; cons. St. John's Coll., Cleve., 1972-73; psychology intern Fresno County Dept. Health, 1973-75, student profl. worker, 1974; mem. faculty Calif. Sch. Profl. Psychology, Fresno, 1974; psychology intern Calif. State U., Fresno, 1975, lectr., 1976-77; treatment program dir. E. Ross Clark Home for Children, Inc., Modesto, Calif., 1976-77; clin. psychologist Santa Cruz County (Calif.) Community Mental Health Services, 1977-79, dir. psychol. services, 1979—; pvt. practice psychotherapy, Soquel, Calif., 1979—; cons. NOW, 1973-76, Community Hosp., Fresno, 1974. Mem. Women's Studies Adv. Bd., Fresno, 1975-76. Recipient Disting. Psychologist award Calif. State Psychol. Assn., 1982. Hill scholar, 1968, Smith scholar, 1969, Fritz Perls scholar, 1970; lic. psychologist, Calif. Mem. Am. Psychol. Assn., Western Assn. Women Psychologists, Western Psychol. Assn., Calif. State Psychol. Assn. (bd. dirs. Observer 1981-82), Mid-Coast Psychol. Assn. (pres. 1981), Santa Cruz Psychology Group, Laurel Soc., Psi Chi (v.p. 1968-69), Kappa Alpha Sigma. Club: Cotuit Mosquito Yacht. Contbr. articles to jours. in psychology. Home: 4595 Fairway Dr Soquel CA 95073 Office: 1040 Emeline Santa Cruz CA 95060

MURRAY, CHERRY ROBERTS, artist; b. Colfax, La., Jan. 3, 1921; d. John Bunyon and Mary (Procter) Roberts; student U. N.Mex., 1940-41; B.F.A., U. Tex., 1942; student Nagayama Studio, Tokyo, 1955; studied under numerous profl. artists, including Ward Lockwood, Best-Mougourd, Maynard Dixon, Peter Hurd, Georgia O'Keefe, Vincent Farrell; m. John Lewis Murray, May 2, 1942; children—John Roberts, James Procter, Cherry Ann, Nancy Lee. Tchr. painting, U.S., 1939-54, 70—, Japan, 1954-56, 60-64, Pakistan, 1957-60, Korea, 1965-68, Indonesia, 1968-70; instr. fine arts Pima Coll. East, Tucson, 1979—; exhbns. include: Baluche Regiment, Cherat, West Pakistan, 1965-68, Am. Embassy Residence, Seoul, Korea, 1965-68, Djarkarta, Indonesia, 1968-70, Abba Gallery, 1978-80, Kay Bonfoey Gallery, 1980, Rentschler Gallery, 1980, Casa Grande Art Gallery, Tucson, 1980; represented in permanent and pvt. collections: U. Tex., U. N.Mex., Nagayama Studio, Tokyo, Ayub Kahn, Baluche Regiment, West Pakistan, Mitha Collection, Lahore, Pakistan, Sir Ian McKensie, Brit. Isles, H. Allen Loomes, Australia, Ambassador Yehuda Horam, Israel, Chote-Kholgvista, Thailand, Kopper, Indonesia, Galbraith, Washington, USIS, Indonesia, Am. Embassy, Djarkarta, Am. Embassy, Seoul, Lathrum, Hicks, Woods, Elliott collections (all Washington), Valley Nat. Bank, City of Douglas, Old Adobe Patio Gallery, others. Recipient 45 awards, 1975-80, including: Creative Artist of Yr. award, 1976; 1st pl. award So. Ariz. Watercolor Guild, 1978; Merit award Watercolor Southwest III, Houston, 1978; Best of Show award Nat. League Am. Pen Women, 1978. Mem. U. Tex. Art Assn. (1st pres.), So. Ariz. Watercolor Guild, Tubac Center of the Arts, Santa Cruz Valley Art Assn., Sierra Vista Art Assn., Ariz. Watercolor Soc., Archeol. and Hist. Soc., Nat. Soc. Arts and Letters, Southwestern League Fine Arts, Gem and Mineral Soc., Nat. League Am. Pen Women, AAUW, Pilot Internat. Democrat. Presbyterian. Home: Route 8 Box 78 Tucson AZ 85710 Office: Pima Coll E Tucson AZ 85710

MURRAY, CONSTANCE SHATTUCK, assn. exec.; b. Bronxville, N.Y., Aug. 23, 1953; d. Harold Morgan and Jacqueline Cantine (Burnett) Shattuck; A.S. in Edn., Endicott Coll., Beverly, Mass., 1973; diploma Shepard Gill Sch. of Mass. Gen. Hosp., 1974. Staff nurse New Eng. Med. Center, Tufts U., Boston, 1974-75; sr. legal sec. Keystone Custodian Funds, Inc., Boston, 1976-77; adminstrv. asst. to chmn. bd. Provandie & Chirurg Advt., Boston, 1977-78; adminstrv. asst. to dir. ops. United Christian Evangelistic Assn., Boston, 1978, now office adminstr.; ind. cons. Mary Kay Cosmetics, Inc. Office: 910 Commonwealth Ave Boston MA 02215

MURRAY, ELIZABETH DAVIS REID, writer, lectr.; b. Wadesboro, N.C., June 10, 1925; d. James Matheson and Mary Kennedy (Little)

Davis; A.B. cum laude, Meredith Coll., Raleigh, N.C., 1946; postgrad. N.C. State U., 1957-58, 74-75; m. James William Reid, Feb. 7, 1948 (dec. June 1972); children—Michael Ernest, Nancy Kennedy, James William; m. 2d, Raymond L. Murray, May 12, 1979; stepchildren—Stephen, Ilah Garton, Marshall. Continuity writer Sta. WPTF, Raleigh, 1946-47; program mgr., women's commentator Sta. WADE, Wadesboro, 1947-48; dir. news bur. Meredith Coll., 1948-51; state woman's news editor, columnist Raleigh News and Observer, 1951-52; exec. sec. Gov.'s Coordinating Com. on Aging, 1959-61; research asst. to Dr. Clarence Poe, Raleigh, 1963-64; contbg. editor Raleigh Mag., 1969-72; local history corr. Raleigh Times, News and Observer Spectator of Raleigh; lectr. art and local history; tchr. local history courses Wake Tech. Coll.; research cons. Wake County Pub. Libraries, Mordecai Historic Park, State Visitor Center, Exec. Mansion; dir. Capital County Pub. Co.; writer; books include: From Raleigh's Past (cert. of commendation Am. Assn. State and Local History), 1965; editor, compiler: North Carolina's Older Population: Opportunities and Challenges, 1960; editor, contbr. Wake County Hist. Soc. newsletter, 1965-69; History of Raleigh Fire Dept., 1970; guest editor Raleigh Mag. Wake County Bicentennial Issue, 1971; author, photographer filmstrip for Wake Pub. Schs., 1971; author sect. Windows of the Way, 1964; Am. arts slide lectures for pub. library; author instructional materials State Exec. Mansion and Mordecai Hist. Park docents; author monthly history page Raleigh Mag., 1969-72; lectr., tour leader local history series N.C. Mus. of History Assos., 1980; contbr. to newspapers and mags. Mem. Raleigh City Council, 1973; pres. Jr. Woman's Club, 1956-57; organizing pres. Arts Council Raleigh, 1965; exec. com. N.C. Humanities Found., 1974-76; dir., officer North Carolinians for Better Libraries, 1965-69; mem. Meredith Bd. Assos., 1976—; trustee Pub. Libraries, 1956-67, Meredith Coll., 1966-69; pres. Wake Meml. Hosp. Aux., 1962-63; mem. Raleigh Hist. Sites Commn., 1969-73; trustee Pullen Meml. Bapt. Ch., 1975-78, chmn., 1977-78, also deacon; chmn. Mayor's Com. to Preserve Hist. Objects, 1965—; mem. Tryon Palace Commn., 1967-78; adv. council WUNC-FM, 1976-80; bd. dirs. Raleigh-Wake Symphony Orch. Devel. Assn., Inc., 1979—, Estey Hall Found., Inc., 1980—, Friends of Meredith Coll. Library, 1980—; docent, lectr. State Capitol, Exec. Mansion, Mordecai Hist. Park, N.C. Mus. Art, pres. docents N.C. Mus. Art, 1980-81. Recipient Outstanding Community Service award, 1952, best all-round Jr. Woman's Club mem., 1955, Disting. Alumna award Meredith Coll., 1970, recognition for service award Raleigh Hist. Sites Commn., 1973, Raleigh City Council, 1973; citation for disting. service in visual arts in N.C., 1979; named hon. patron N.C. Mus. of History Assos., 1980. Mem. N.C. Soc. County and Local Historians (life), N.C. Lit. and Hist. Assn., N.C. Art Soc. (adv. council 1980-81), Friends of N.C. State U. Library, Friends of Carlyle Campbell Library (charter, life), Kappa Nu Sigma. Democrat. Clubs: Carolina Country, Capital City (charter mem.). Home: Strickland Rd Raleigh NC 27612

MURRAY, FLORENCE KERINS (MRS. PAUL F. MURRAY), justice Supreme Ct. R.I.; b. Newport, R.I., Oct. 21, 1916; d. John X. and Florence (MacDonald) Kerins; A.B., Syracuse U., 1938; LL.B., Boston U., 1942; student R.I. Coll. Edn., 1942, Ed.D. (hon.), 1956; LL.D., Bryant Coll., 1956, U. R.I., 1963, Mt. St. Joseph Coll., 1972, Providence Coll., 1974, Johnson-Wales Coll., 1977, Salve Regina Coll., 1977, Suffolk U.; m. Paul F. Murray, Oct. 21, 1943; 1 son, Paul F. Admitted to Mass., R.I. bars, U.S. Supreme Ct. bar; pvt. law practice with husband, under name Murray & Murray, Newport, R.I., 1947; mem. R.I. Senate, 1948-56; asso. justice R.I. Superior Ct., 1956-78, presiding justice, 1978-79; justice R.I. Supreme Ct., 1979—; first woman judge State of R.I.; chmn. Nat. Jud. Coll., 1980—; staff, faculty adviser Nat. Coll. State Judiciary, 1971-72. Mem. Gov.'s Jud. Council, R.I. Alcohol Adv. Council Com., Adv. Council on Mental Health, Nat. Adv. Com. on Women in Service; mem. civil and polit. rights com. Pres.'s Commn. Status of Women, 1960-63; chmn. Newport Sch. Com.; bd. dirs., mem., sec. R.I. Physicians Service; sec. R.I. Commn. on Jud. Discipline and Tenure; dir., sec. R.I. Blue Shield; chmn. R.I. Nat. Endowment Humanities com., 1972; bd. dirs. YMCA, Newport, Nat. Coll. Judiciary, Reno, 1975—, Inst. Ct. Mgmt., Denver, 1977; trustee Syracuse U., 1974—, Bryant Coll.; bd. visitors Boston U. Law Sch. Served as lt. col., WAC, World War II, now hon. Res. Recipient Legion of Merit, Army Commendation Ribbon, Arents Alumni award Syracuse U., 1956, Carroll award R.I. Inst. Instrn., 1956; Regina medal Salve Regina Coll., 1962; Alumni award Boston U., 1965; named to R.I. Heritage Hall of Fame, 1980. Fellow Inst. Jud. Adminstrn.; mem. Am. Bar Assn. (jud. adminstrn. div. council), Am. Judicature Soc. (dir. 1976-80), Am. Legion (judge adv. post 7, mem. nat. exec. com.), AAUW (chmn. state edn. com., 1954-56), Bus. and Profl. Woman's Club (past state v.p., past pres. Newport, past pres. nat. legis. com.), Alpha Chi Omega, Kappa Beta Pi. Club: Quota (past gov. internat., past pres. Newport). Home: 2 Kay St Newport RI 02840 Office: Court House Providence RI 02903

MURRAY, HELEN HOLLOWAY, state tng. supr.; b. Monroe, N.C., Nov. 5, 1945; d. Claude Robert, Jr., and Rose (Purdy) Holloway; B.A. in Psychology, Winthrop Coll., Rock Hill, S.C., 1967; postgrad. in counseling U. S.C., Columbia, 1970-72; m. Emery G. Murray, July 21, 1979. Tchr., Morningside Elementary Sch., Charleston, S.C., 1967-70, Wallace Primary Sch., S.C., 1970-71; employment counselor, office supr. S.C. Employment Security Commn., Kingstree, 1971-73, job bank supr., Florence, 1973-74, state tng. supr., Columbia, 1974—. Certified instr. ARC; vol. Contact Help. Gen. Elec. Found. Guidance fellow, 1972; recipient state award for student research S.C. Psychol. Assn., 1966. Mem. Am., Carolina socs. tng. and devel., Internat. Assn. Personnel in Employment Security (exec. bd. S.C. chpt.), S.C. State Employers Assn. Club: Columbia Altrusa (2d v.p.). Home: Route 4 Box 158 Chapin SC 29036 Office: 1550 Gadsden St PO Box 995 Columbia SC 29202

MURRAY, JUDY FLACHSLAND, psychiat. social worker; b. Syracuse, N.Y., Aug. 27, 1946; d. William Charles and Thelma Emma (Middleton) Flachsland; B.A., Thiel Coll., 1968; M.S.W., Syracuse U., 1970. Psychiat. social worker Rome (N.Y.) Devel. Center, N.Y. State Dept. Mental Hygiene, 1968-72; psychiat. social work supr. Hutchings Psychiat. Center, N.Y. State Office Mental Health, Syracuse, 1972—; part-time instr. social work Mohawk Valley Community Coll., 1972—; part-time instr. human services Onondaga Community Coll., Syracuse, 1981—. Bd. mgrs., sec. Village Green Cond. II, 1977—. Cert. social worker, N.Y. State. Mem. Nat. Assn. Social Workers, Acad. Cert. Social Workers, Irish Wolfhound Club Am., Irish Wolfhound Club Ireland, Irish Wolfhound Club Central N.Y., Onondaga Kennel Assn., Alpha Gamma Delta. Office: Box 27 University Station Syracuse NY 13210

MURRAY, JULIA KAORU (MRS. JOSEPH EDWARD MURRAY), occupational therapist; b. Wahiawa, Oahu, Hawaii, 1934; d. Gijun and Edna Tsuruko (Taba) Funakoshi; B.A., U. Hawaii, 1956; cert. occupational therapy U. Puget Sound, 1958; m. Joseph Edward Murray, 1961; children—Michael, Susan, Leslie. Therapist, Inst. Logopedics, Wichita, Kans., 1958; sr. therapist Hawaii State Hosp., Kaneohe, 1959; part-time therapist Centre County Center for Crippled Children and Adults, State College, Pa., 1963; vice chmn. adv. bd. Hosp. Improvement Program, East Oreg. State Hosp., Pendleton, 1974; v.p. Independent Living, Inc., 1976-79; also job search instr.; mem. adv. com. Oreg. Ednl. Coordinating Commn., 1979-82; mem. Oreg. Bd. Engring. Examiners, 1979—. Rep. from Umatilla County Commrs. to Blue Mountain Econ. Devel. Council, 1976-78; bd. dirs. Ashland LWV, 1967-71, v.p., 1970; mem. Ashland Park and Recreation Bd., 1972-73; vice chmn. adv. bd. LINC, 1978; mem. exec. bd. Liberty-Boone Neighborhood Assn., 1979—. Mem. Am., Oreg., Hawaii (sec. 1960) occupational therapy assns., LWV (dir. Pendleton 1974, 77-78, pres. 1975-77; dir. Oreg. 1979-81). Address: 760 Ironwood Dr SE Salem OR 97306

MURRAY, KATHLEEN ELLEN, editor; b. Chgo., Feb. 23, 1946; d. John Joseph and Marie (Stoltzman) M.; A.A. in Bus., Am. River Coll., 1968; B.A. in Journalism, Calif. State U., 1973. File clk. Allstate Ins. Co., Sacramento, 1964-66; clk. typist Calif. Hwy. Patrol, Sacramento, 1968-69; copy editor Sacramento Bee, 1971—; tchr. Calif. State U., 1975-76; tutor Calif. Youth Authority Camp. Mem. Mystery Writers Am., Sacramento Press Club. Democrat. Home: PO Box 606 Nevada City CA 95959 Office: PO Box 15779 Sacramento CA 95813

MURRAY, KATHLEEN VIRGINIA, editor; b. Charleroi, Pa., Nov. 7, 1939; d. William Albert and Virginia (Behanna Carney) Clark; B.A. cum laude in Communications, Mundelein Coll., 1980; m. David Lee Murray, Dec. 29, 1961; children—Clark David, Timothy Lee. Div. sales mgr. Port-A-Bookstore, Palatine, Ill., 1973-74; editor Murray Communications, Evanston, Ill., 1975-81; asso. editor The Guarantor, Chgo. Title & Trust Co., 1981—. Mem. Internat. Assn. Bus. Communicators, Women in Communications, North Shore Choral Soc. (dir.), Kappa Gamma Pi. Editor: You, Your Children and Divorce, New Decision, 1981; mng. editor PACE, 1980. Home: 2517 Asbury Ave Evanston IL 60201 Office: 111 W Washington St Chicago IL 60602

MURRAY, KAY, librarian, educator, tax researcher; b. Connersville, Ind., Sept. 25, 1932; d. Rex and Goldie (Johnson) M.; B.A. (Spl. Merit scholar 1950-52), Ind. U., 1953; M.L.S., Rutgers U., 1968, Ph.D., 1972; m. Ray Kersey, Dec. 30, 1978; children by previous marriage—Michael, Murray, Matthew. Dept. head Roanoke (Va.) Public Library, 1953-55; cataloger Drew U., Madison, N.H., 1957-60; mem. co-adj. faculty Rutgers U., 1969-71, asst. prof. library sci., 1972-77; asst. prof. Fairleigh Dickinson U., Teaneck, N.J., 1971-72; asso. prof. library sci. U. N.C., Chapel Hill, 1977-82; dir. research, gen. mgr. Tax Analysts, Arlington, Va., 1982—. Ind. Library Assn. scholar, 1953; Title II-B fellow, 1969-72; grantee N.J. Bd. Edn., 1974-75, U. N.C., Chapel Hill, 1981-82. Mem. ALA, Assn. Am. Library Schs. (sec.-treas. 1982—), N.C. Library Assn. (dir. 1982—), PEO. Methodist. Author articles in field. Editor: Personnel Development in Libraries, 1976. Home: 7360 Montcalm Dr McLean VA 22102 Office: 6830 N Fairfax Dr Arlington VA 22213

MURRAY, LOIS A. HEIL, lawyer; b. Marshfield, Wis., June 3, 1953; d. Frank N. and Bertha J. (Hafenbreadl) Heil; B.A., B.S. in Acctg., U. Wis., River Falls, 1974; J.D. cum laude, U. Minn., 1978; m. Alan E. Murray, Aug. 18, 1973. Tax examiner Minn. Dept. Revenue, 1974-75; admitted to Wis. bar, 1978, Minn. bar, 1978, U.S. Dist. Ct. bar, 1978; law clk. firm Ralph Senn, River Falls, 1976; research asst. to prof. law and asso. dean Sch. Law, U. Minn., Mpls., 1976-78; law clk. Honeywell, Inc., Mpls., 1977; asso. firm Heywood, Cari & Murray and predecessor, Hudson, Wis., 1978-80, partner, 1980—; mem. faculty Wis. Indianhead Tech. Inst., Hudson Community Edn. Mem. State Bar Assn. Wis., State Bar Assn. Minn., Am. Bar Assn., St. Croix Valley Bar Assn., AAUW, LWV, Hudson Area C. of C. Roman Catholic. Home: 600 7th St Hudson WI 54016 Office: Micklesen Bldg 204 Locust St Hudson WI 54016

MURRAY, SAUNDRA RICE, psychologist; b. Atlanta, Jan. 6, 1947; d. George Halbert and Edna Louise (Lewis) Rice; A.B., Howard U., 1967, M.S., 1974, Ph.D., 1976; M.S., U. Ill., 1968; m. Donald G. Murray, Jr., Mar. 14, 1970; children—Kali Nicole and Alana Denise (twins). Info. systems research analyst Library of Congress, 1969-70; librarian Howard U., 1970-72; co-prin. investigator Sickle Cell Trait Project, Washington, 1977-78; asst. prof. African Am. studies, psychology U. Md., 1976-78, research asso., 1976-77; sr. research scientist Am. Inst. Research, Washington, 1978—; cons. in field. Title IIB Higher Edn. Act fellow, 1968-69; Woodrow Wilson fellow, 1975-76. Mem. Am. Psychol. Assn. (chairperson com. on Black women's concerns 1976-77), Phi Beta Kappa, Beta Phi Mu. Baptist. Contbr. articles to profl. jours. Office: 1055 Thomas Jefferson St NW Washington DC 20007

MURRAY-HICKS, MARGO, mgmt. cons.; b. Thornfield, Mo., Jan. 24, 1935; d. Marcus Hanna and Luvena Elvina (Howerton) Murray; A.A., Am. River Coll., 1957; B.S., Sacramento State Coll., 1963; M.B.A., John F. Kennedy U., 1977; 1 son, David Kemit Fox. Clk., supr., budget analyst USAF, McClellan AFB, Calif., 1953-61; demonstrator, seller Fox Camper Sales, Sacramento, 1961-63; mgr. Pacific Telephone Co., Sacramento, San Francisco and Oakland, Calif., 1963-74; prin., pres. Margo Murray-Hicks & Assos., Oakland, 1974—; asso. Mager Assos., Inc.; adj. faculty bachelors degree com. Antioch West U. Tutor, Involvement Corps Internat. assisting Barrios Youth in Oakland, 1972-74; fund raising vol. Alameda County Heart Assn., 1977. Mem. Nat. Soc. for Performance and Instrn. (Pres.'s citation 1973, 75, 77, 78, 79, nat. v.p. 1972-73, gen. mgr. Conf. 1978, Outstanding Mem. award 1979), Internat. Transactional Analysis Assn. Republican. Club: Internat. Toastmistress (v.p. bd. dirs. 1974-76). Author: Using Time Workshop, 1979; Effectiveness-My Competence & Communication, 1981; Feedback Principles and Techniques, 1981; Performance Appraisal, 1982; contbr. articles to profl. jours. Home: 2317 Mastlands Dr Oakland CA 94611 Office: 2317 Mastlands Dr Suite A Oakland CA 94611

MURYS, PATTI DARLENE, nurse; b. Connersville, Ind., Dec. 6, 1934; d. Frederick Jacob and Pattie Bernece (Perry) Quenzer; R.N. (scholar), St. Vincent's Hosp. Sch. Nursing, 1956; R.T., St. John's Hosp. Sch. Radiol. Tech., 1963; B.S.N., Purdue U., 1972; M.A. (grantee), U. Iowa, 1973; m. Donald Frank Murys, Aug. 19, 1973. Staff nurse St. Vincent's Hosp., Indpls., 1956-58; radiol. technologist, head nurse St. John's Hosp., Springfield, Ill., 1963-64; instr. St. Margaret's Hosp. Sch. Nursing, Hammond, Ind., 1965, St. Catherine's Hosp. Sch. Radiol. Tech., 1965; nurse ICU, St. Margaret's Hosp., Hammond, 1965-69; inservice instr. St. Catherines Hosp., East Chicago, Ind., 1969-71, supr., 1971-72; instr. Jackson Meml. Hosp., Miami, Fla., 1973; nurse clinician Parkway Gen. Hosp., Miami, 1974-79; inservice instr., acting dir. ednl. services Southeastern Med. Center, Miami, 1979—. Instr., CPR Am. Heart Assn., East Chicago, Ind., Miami; active Girl Scouts U.S.A. Mem. Am. Bus. Woman's Assn., Nat. League Nurses, Nat. Wildlife Fedn., Am. Soc. for Health Care Edn. and Tng., South Fla. Emergency Med. Assn. Office: Southeastern Med Center 1750 NE 167th St Miami FL 33162

MUSANTE, CATHERINE ANTOINETTE (SISTER MARY OF THE TRINITY), nun, writer, translator; b. San Francisco, Mar. 24, 1911; d. Attilio Stephen and Antoinette Veronica (Draghicevich) M.; B.A., Stanford U., 1931, M.A., 1932; tchr. French, Palo Alto, Calif., 1932-33, Flintridge Sch. for Girls, Pasadena, 1933-35; instr. Spanish San Francisco City Coll., 1935-42; joined Dominican Order, Roman Catholic Ch., 1942; dir. novices Corpus Christi Monastery, Menlo Park, Calif., 1952-63, procuratrix, 1963-65, subprioress, 1966-70, prioress, 1970-79, 1982—, novice mistress, 1979-82; del. Roman Commn. Revising Nuns' Constns., 1970, Roman Commn. Finalizing Nuns' Constns., 1982, Roman Liturgical Commn., 1976. Cert. tchr., Calif. Mem. Conf. of Nuns of the Order of Preachers (sec. 1978—). Translator: Recollection, Kinships, Rectitude, Spirituality (Sertillanges), 1954; Trinity Whom I Adore, Pledge of Glory (Eugene Vandeur), 1953, 57; Grace (Garrigou-LaGrange), 1952; Treatise on the Spiritual Life (St. Vincent Ferrer), 1957; Jesus (Sertillanges), 1976; Newman and the Holy Spirit (Pierre Masson), 1982; contbr. articles in field to religious jours. Home and office: 215 Oak Grove Ave Menlo Park CA 94025

MUSE, JUDITH ELAINE PAYNE, educator; b. Mountain View, Okla., Oct. 7, 1938; d. Frank E. and Alma L. (Lunsford) Payne; B.S. in Acctg. and Bus. Edn., Bethany (Okla.) Nazarene Coll., 1960; M.B.A. (NDEA fellow 1960-63), La. State U., 1962, Ph.D. in Acctg., 1964; m. W. J. Muse, May 17, 1972; children—Phillip, Dawna, Judith, Stephen, Paula. Asst. prof. bus. Bethany Nazarene Coll., 1963-67; acct. First Ch. Nazarene, Bethany, 1964-67; asso. prof. bus., then acting bus. mgr., controller Trevecca Nazarene Coll., Nashville, 1967-70; part-time instr. acctg. U. Tenn., Nashville, 1967-68, 69-70; prof. bus. Bethany Nazarene Coll., 1970-71, part-time prof., 1975-76; part-time prof. acctg. Central State Coll., Edmond, Okla., 1970-71, full-time prof., 1971—. Treas., Mustang (Okla.) Nazarene Ch., 1980—. C.P.A., Okla. Mem. Am. Inst. C.P.A.s, Am. Acctg. Assn., Okla. Soc. C.P.A.s (dir.-at-large 1979-81), Okla. Higher Edn. Alumni Council, Beta Alpha Psi, Phi Delta Lambda. Author manual. Home: 8004 NW 15th St Oklahoma City OK 73127 Office: Central State U Edmond OK 73034

MUSE, MARTHA TWITCHELL, found. exec.; b. Dallas, Sept. 1, 1926; d. John Blackburn and Kathryn (Poole) Muse; B.A., Barnard Coll., 1948; M.A., Columbia U., 1955. Personnel staff Ted Bates Advt. Agy., N.Y.C., 1954-58; asst. dir. personnel Young & Rubicam Advt. Agy., N.Y.C., 1959-64; exec. dir. Tinker Found., N.Y.C., 1965-68, pres., 1968—, chmn. bd., 1975—; dir. ACF Industries, Irving Bank Corp., Irving Trust Co., Associated Dry Goods Corp., Sterling Drug Inc. Vice chmn. bd. trustees Columbia U., N.Y.C.; bd. dirs. Americas Soc. Inc., Center for Inter-Am. Relations, Spanish Inst., Americas Found., Internat. Univ. Found.; mem. advisory com. U.S. Internat. Council, mem. adv. com. Center for Strategic and Internat. Studies, Georgetown U.; bd. visitors Edmund A. Walsh Sch. Fgn. Service, Georgetown U.; mem. advt. council-public policy com., council mem. Internat. Exec. Service Corps; mem. Wilson council Woodrow Wilson Internat. Center for Scholars; former mem. bd. fgn. scholarships Fulbright Commn., State Dept.; past mem. regional panel for selection White House Fellows, Greater Washington Ednl. Telecommunications Assn. Decorated comdr. Order St. John of Jerusalem (Gt. Britain), Lazlo de Dama de la Orden del Merito Civil (Spain). Mem. Nat. Soc. Colonial Dames, Huguenot Soc., N.Y. Council Fgn. Relations. Clubs: Colony, Metropolitan, Church (N.Y.C.); Internat. (Washington). Office: The Tinker Found 645 Madison Ave New York NY 10022

MUSE, PATRICIA ALICE, writer, educator; b. South Bend, Ind., Nov. 27, 1923; d. Walter L. and Enid (Cockerham) Ashdown; student Columbia U., 1946; B.A., Principia Coll., 1947; postgrad. Seminole Community Coll., 1977, U. Central Fla., 1978, 79, 80, 81, 82; m. Kenneth F. Muse, Dec. 2, 1950; children—Patience Eleanor, Walter Scott. Substitute tchr. public schs., Key West, Fla., also Brunswick, Ga., 1962-68; free lance writer, Casselberry, Fla., 1968—; novels: Sound of Rain, 1971, The Belle Claudine, 1971, paperback, 1973, Eight Candles Glowing, 1976; creative writing instr., Valencia Community Coll., 1974-75; instr. various writers confs. Community resource vol. Orange County (Fla.) Sch. Bd. (cert. of appreciation 1975, 76, 77). Mem. Mysteries Writers Am., Council Arts and Scis. Central Fla. Clubs: Naval Tng. Equipment Wives.

MUSGRAVE, THEA, composer, conductor; b. Edinburgh, Scotland; ed. Edinburgh U., Paris Conservatory; Mus.B.; hon. doctorate Smith Coll., Old Dominion U.; m. Peter Mark, 1971. Composer: (opera) The Decision (first performed by New Opera Co. at Sadler's Wells, 1967), The Voice of Ariadne (first performed Aldeburgh Festival 1973; U.S. premiere N.Y.C. Opera 1977), Mary Queen of Scots (first performed Scottish Opera 1977), A Christmas Carol (first performed Va. Opera Assn., 1979); (ballet) Beauty and the Beast, 1969; The Phoenix and the Turtle and The Five Ages of Man for choir and orch.; Triptych for tenor and orch.; clarinet, horn and viola concertos; Night Music for chamber orch.; chamber concertos 1, 2 and 3; other vocal, chamber and orchestral works. Recipient Koussevitzky award; Guggenheim fellow. Address: care Novello & Co Ltd 1-3 Upper James St London W1 England

MUSGROVE, BARBARA JEANNE, psychologist, cons. co. exec.; b. New Orleans, Mar. 24, 1946; d. Robert Earl and Lois Henrietta (Neale) Penn; B.A. (Univ. scholar), Howard U., 1968; M.A. (fellow), U. Pa., 1969; Ph.D. (fellow), Columbia U., 1974; m. Spain Musgrove, July 28, 1979; 1 dau., Vera Rose; 1 son by previous marriage, Adeyemi K. Stembridge. Lectr., counselor edn. dept. Queens (N.Y.) Coll., 1972-73; asst. prof. psychology Kean Coll. N.J., Union, 1973-75; psychologist Youth Services Agy., Newark, 1974-75; sr. research asso., mem. grad. faculty urban affairs program Howard U., Washington, 1975-78; pres., chmn. bd. Christian Workshops, Inc., Washington, 1978—; dir. program planning and evaluation div. Mark Battle Assos., Inc., Washington, 1979-81, dir. research, 1981—; pvt. practice psychology, 1981—; cons. various sch. systems, 1974—; adj. faculty U. D.C., 1977—. Mem. Christian edn. commn. Zion Bapt. Ch., 1977—; bd. dirs. Zion Bapt. Enterprises, Inc., 1978—. Recipient faculty research award Howard U., 1977. Mem. Am. Psychol. Assn., Am. Soc. for Tng. and Devel., Internat. Transactional Analysis Assn., Phi Beta Kappa, Delta Sigma Theta. Club: Soroptimist Internat. Contbr. to profl. publs. Home: 7300 Lois Ln Lanham MD 20706 Office: 1019 19th St NW Suite 300 Washington DC 20036

MUSICK, JUDITH SMITH, developmental psychologist; b. Chgo., Nov. 24, 1937; d. Walter Harvard and Janice May (Gottlieb) Smith; student Stephens Coll., 1955-56; B.A. in Psychology, Mundelein Coll., 1972; Ph.D. in Psychology (Univ. fellow), Northwestern U., 1976; m. Stuart Musick, Oct. 5, 1958; chilren—Margaret D., Hugh R. Profl. ballet and modern dancer, 1959-65; dir. research dance edn. programs Urban Gateways, Chgo., 1967-74; asst. prof. child devel. Northwestern U., Evanston, Ill., 1974-78, postdoctoral trainee in clin. developmental psychology Med. Sch., Chgo., 1977-78; dir. NIMH pilot project Mothers' Project, Thresholds, Chgo., 1978-82; exec. dir. Ounce of Prevention Fund, Chgo., 1982—; mem. faculty Erikson Inst.; co-founder Chgo. Com. on Toddlers and Infants, 1976; cons., lectr. in field, 1974—; host-moderator NBC-TV Series on Family, 1978. Mem. Am. Psychol. Assn., Soc. Research in Child Devel., Nat. Assn. Edn. Young Children, Am. Orthopsychiat. Assn. Jewish. Author, editor 2 books on infancy; contbr. articles to profl. jours. Home: 444 Sheridan Rd Highland Park IL 60035 Office: 160 N LaSalle St Chicago IL 60601

MUSKELLY, ANNA MARIE, editor; b. N.Y.C., May 31, 1947; d. Jay Perry and Anna Marie (Coleman) Muskelly; B.A. in English Lit., Hunter Coll., 1969; A.A.S. in Advt. and Communications, Fashion Inst. Tech., 1973; postgrad. N.Y.U. Interviewer, Nat. Opinion Research Center, N.Y.C., 1965-69; editorial trainee House Beautiful mag., N.Y.C., 1969-71; editorial asst. Random House, Inc., N.Y.C., 1971-73, editor, 1973—. Mem. Black Women in Pub. (pres.), Women in Communications, (v.p. for students), Women's Nat. Book Assn. (dir.), Nat. Assn. Female Execs., Networks Unltd. Office: 201 E 50th St New York NY 10022

MUSSO, DONNA ANN, editor; b. Bridgeton, N.J., Apr. 8, 1950; d. Harry Lore and Marylou Keller; student Cumberland County (N.J.) Coll., 1968-69; Glassboro State Coll., 1975; m. Gustavus Smith Musso, July 16, 1970; 1 dau., Kelle Rochelle. Sales clk., dept. head Rovner's, Bridgeton, 1968-69; with Bridgeton Evening News, 1969—, social and food editor, 1972—. Sec. Greenwich (N.J.) Recreation Com., 1976-78. Mem. Cumberland County News Media Assn. Nat. Fedn. Press Women, N.J. Fedn. Press Women. Clubs: Bridgeton Jr. Women's, Cumberland

County Hist. Soc. Home: PO Box 128 Ye Greate St Greenwich NJ 08323 Office: 100 E Commerce St Bridgeton NJ 08302

MUSTONE, AMELIA P., state senator; b. Salem, Mass., July 16, 1928; d. Udo A. and Alberta A. (Durand) Poppey; B.S., Goddard Coll., 1977; m. John J. Mustone, Oct. 8, 1950; children—John, Lisa, Paul, Mary Ellen, Anastasia, Jessica. Substitute tchr., Meriden, Conn., 1965-75; mem. Conn. Senate, 1978—, asst. chmn. edn. com. Gen. Assembly, 1978—, chmn. vocat. tech. subcom., 1979—, mem. labor com., 1978—, ins. and real estate com., 1978—; advisory dir. Colonial Bank, Meriden; corporator Central Bank, Meriden. Pres. Meriden Bd. Edn., 1974-78; bd. dirs. Conn. Student Loan Found.; pres. LWV, 1963-65; bd. dirs. YWCA; active NAACP, Meriden Dem. Women's Club, Meriden Humane Soc. Recipient Citizen of Year award Civitan Club, 1978. Mem. AAUW. Roman Catholic. Club: Soroptomist. Contbg. editor N.Y. Times, Dec. 10, 1979. Office: State Capitol Hartford CT 06511

MUTCHLER, JANE FRANCES, acct.; b. Janesville, Wis., Feb. 26, 1941; d. Frederick Gerald and Anne Marie (Healy) M.; B.A. in Edn., U. S. Fla., 1973, B.A. in Acctg., 1976, M.Acctg., 1977; Ph.D., U. Ill., 1983; children—Tami Jeanne, Susan Marie (Parr). Tchr., United Day Care Center, Tampa, Fla., 1971-73; instr. U. South Fla., Tampa, 1976-78; adminstrv. asst. intermediate acctg. program Arthur Andersen & Co., Champaign, Ill., summers 1979-81; grad. research asst., grad. teaching asst. U. Ill., Champaign, 1978-82; asst. prof. acctg. Ohio State U., fall 1983; mgmt. cons., 1977—. Am. Soc. Women Accts. Margaret Keldie scholar, 1979-80; Am. Inst. C.P.A.s fellow, 1982. C.P.A., Fla. Mem. Am. Acctg. Assn., Am. Inst. C.P.A.s, Fla. Inst. C.P.A.s. Office: Faculty of Acctg Ohio State Univ 408 Hagerty Hall 1775 College Rd Columbus OH 43210

MUTNIK, GAIL ELLEN, assn. exec.; b. Bronx, N.Y., Apr. 9, 1953; d. Marvin and Phyllis Beatrice (Appelbaum) M.; B.A., Am. U., 1975, M.P.A., 1982. Adminstrv. asst. Am. Soc. Public Adminstrn., Washington, 1975-77; conv. dir. Am. Women in Radio and TV, Washington, 1977-79; now adminstr. Group Health Assn. Am., Washington. Mem. Am., Washington socs. assn. execs., Meeting Planners Internat. Home: 8715 1st Ave Apt 1028C Silver Spring MD 20910 Office: Group Health Assn Am 624 9th St NW Suite 700 Washington DC 20001

MUTO, SUSAN ANNETTE, educator; b. Pitts., Dec. 11, 1942; d. Frank and Helen (Scardamalia) M.; B.A. in Journalism and English, Duquesne U., 1964; M.A., U. Pitts., 1967, Ph.D. in English Lit., 1970. Asst. dir. Inst. of Formative Spirituality, Duquesne U., Pitts., 1965-80, dir., 1980—, faculty coordinator grad. programs in foundational formation, 1979—, prof., 1981—; guest lectr. formative reading various colls. and community orgns., 1970—. Mem. Edith Stein Guild, Domus Dei Corp., Phi Kappa Phi. Author: Approaching the Sacred: An Introduction to Spiritual Reading, 1973; Steps Along the Way, 1975; A Practical Guide to Spiritual Reading, 1976; The Journey Homeward: On the Road of Spiritual Reading, 1977; (with Adrian van Kaam) The Emergent Self 1968, The Participant Self, 1969; Tell Me Who I Am, 1977; Celebrating the Single Life, 1982; Blessings That Make Us Be, 1982; contbr. articles on spiritual reading to religious and secular publs. Home: 229 Grandview Ave Pittsburgh PA 15211 Office: Institute of Formative Spirituality Duquesne U Pittsburgh PA 15282

MUZYKA, KATHERINE MARY FRAGALA, programmer analyst; b. Bklyn., Nov. 6, 1946; d. Augustine M. and Catherine A. (Campisi) Fragala; A.A.S. summa cum laude, No. Va. Community Coll., 1978; m. Joseph C. Muzyka, Jr., June 20, 1970; 1 son, Christopher. Programmer analyst Am. Automobile Assn., Falls Church, Va., 1978—, now mgr. production control, systems support. Bd. dirs. North Springfield Little League. Mem. Nat. Assn. Female Execs., Am. Soc. Profl. and Exec. Women, Phi Theta Kappa. Roman Catholic. Office: Am Automobile Assn 8111 Gatehouse Rd Falls Church VA 22047

MYERS, BERNICE, practical nurse; b. Ogden, Utah, Mar. 14, 1947; d. Benjamin and Goldie (Roskelley) M.; L.P.N., Weber State Coll. Nursing, 1971. Supply technician Dee Hosp., Ogden, 1965-68; charge nurse night shift Golden Manor Nursing Home, Ogden, 1972; afternoon charge nurse detoxification unit St. Benedict's Hosp., Ogden, 1973; charge nurse Parkview Nursing Home, Ogden, 1974-75, charge nurse Weber County Alcohol and Drugs Detoxification Unit, also Weber County Jail, Ogden, 1975—. CPR nurse, mem. organizing bd. Weber County Fire Dept. Aux.; instr. CPR, Heimlich maneuver. Democrat. Mormon. Home: 2050 Liberty St Ogden UT 84401 Office: 600 Exchange Rd Ogden UT 84401

MYERS, CLAUDIA BOLES, social worker; b. Nashville, Aug. 15, 1952; d. Claude C. and Marilyn (Davis) Boles; B.S.W., U. Kan., 1974, M.S.W., 1975; m. Richard Jay Myers, May 25, 1974; children—Megan Coleen, Lauren Mary. Sch. social worker Shawnee Mission (Kans.) Schs., 1974-76, Jefferson County Schs., Lakewood, Colo., 1976-77; tchr. parenting groups, improving self-concept groups, woman's awareness groups, social adjustment groups, 1974-77; organizer, dir. Mother's Day Out program. Mem. student panel that addressed Legis. Wive's Orgn., Topeka. Mem. Nat. Assn. Social Workers, Jr. League, Gamma Phi Beta. Presbyn. Home: 6911 E Costilla Pl Englewood CO 80112

MYERS, CONNIE LYCANS, ednl. adminstr.; b. Huntington, W. Va., May 18, 1950; d. Billy and Loretta Bea (Bentley) Lycans; B.S., Marshall U., 1972; cert. Cabell Huntington Hosp. Sch. Med. Tech., 1972; m. Terry Lee Myers, June 15, 1971. Med. technologist St. Mary's Hosp., Huntington, 1972, supr. microbiology, 1974-79; dept. supr. Halifax Med. Center, Daytona Beach, Fla., 1973-74; clin. instr. Marshall U., Huntington, 1975-79; clin. lab. supr./edn. coordinator Sch. Med. Tech., Decatur (Ill.) Meml. Hosp., 1979-81, lab. mgr., program dir., 1981—; clin. instr. Western Ill. U., Macomb, 1980—, Eastern Ill. U., Charleston, 1980—, Millikin U., Decatur, 1980—, Ill. State U., Normal, 1980—. Chmn., Decatur Meml. Hosp. Red Cross Blood Drive, 1979-80; solicitor United Way, 1979-82, Am. Cancer Soc., 1982. Mem. Am. Soc. Clin. Pathologists, Accreditation and Inspection Team, Vol. Hosp. Am., Inc. (lab. com.), Midwest Assn. Edn. Resource Sharing in Clin. Med. Tech. Home: 1375 W Sunset St Decatur IL 62522 Office: 2300 N Edward St Decatur IL 62526

MYERS, CONSTANCE ASHTON, historian; b. N.Y.C., Aug. 9, 1936; d. Frank Wilbur and Rachael (Ashton) Smith; B.A., Calif. State U., 1961; M.A., Claremont Grad. Sch., 1967; Ph.D. (U.S. Office Edn. grantee), U. S.C., 1974; m. Cecil Arthur Myers, June 11, 1954; children—Cecily, Russell, Carolyn, Rachael. Instr., Mt. San Antonio Coll., Walnut, Calif., 1964-65, Calif. State U., Sacramento, 1965-67; asst. prof. history Univ. System of Ga., Augusta, 1967-70, cons. oral history, 1974-77; prof. U. S.C., Aiken, 1977—; vis. asst. prof. Ariz. State U., 1978-79, summer 1980; fellow Smithsonian Instn., 1980-81, Woodrow Wilson Center, Washington, 1982; U.S.C. faculty exchange program prof. Shanxi U., T'ai Yuen, China, 1982-83; spl. lectr. Converse Coll., 1975, Stonehill Coll., 1975, Paine Coll., 1976. Del., Aiken County Democratic Conv., 1972, 74, 76, 78, S.C. State Dem. Conv., 1972; bd. dirs. Aiken County Arts Council, 1978—. U. S.C. Pres.'s Office grantee. 1974-75; Nat. Endowment for Humanities grantee, 1976, 77, 79; Newberry Library grantee, 1978. Mem. Am. Hist. Assn., Oral History Assn., Orgn. Am. Historians (membership chairperson for S.C.), Coordinating Com. for Women in Hist. Profession (charter), So. Women Historians (pres. 1972-74), Univ. South Caroliniana Soc. (life). Unitarian. Author: The Prophet's Army: Trotskyists in America, 1928-1941, 1977; contbr. articles, revs. to profl. publs. Home: 909 Holliday Dr North Augusta SC 29841 Office: U SC Div Social Sci C-12 171 University Pkwy Aiken SC 29801

MYERS, DONNA MARIE, med. technologist; b. Great Falls, Mont., Mar. 6, 1951; d. Thomas Roy and Agnes Angeline (Woods) Kuglin; B.S. in Chemistry and Biology, Coll. Great Falls, 1973; postgrad. Columbus Hosp., 1974; m. John Edward Myers, June 22, 1974; 1 son, Benjamin Harold. Med. technologist Physician's Lab. Service, Bozeman, Mont., 1974-77; med. technologist Great Falls (Mont.) Clinic, 1977—, supr. chemistry dept., 1978—. Mem. Am. Soc. Clin. Pathologists, Am. Assn. Clin. Chemists, AAUW, Coll. Great Falls Alumni Assn. Home: 709 25th St S Great Falls MT 59405 Office: 1220 Central Ave Great Falls MT 59401

MYERS, ELIZABETH ANN, phys. therapist; b. Cin., June 5, 1934; d. Edward J. and Emma E. (Burns) M.; B.S. in Phys. Therapy, St. Louis U., 1956. From staff mem. to supr. phys. therapy dept. Orthopedic Hosp., Los Angeles, 1956-65; asst. to dir. Christ Hosp., Cin., 1957; dir. phys. therapy Crystal Springs Rehab. Clinic, San Mateo, Calif., 1965-67; owner, operator Phys. Therapy Center Palo Alto (Calif.), 1967—; lectr., speaker, cons., workshop leader in field. Mem. Am. Phys. Therapy Assn. (chmn. Calif. council 1970-72, sec. 1980-82, nat. del. 1969, 73-81). Office: 3525 Alma St Palo Alto CA 94306

MYERS, ELLEN HOWELL, educator; b. Bryan, Tex., Feb. 16, 1941; d. Douglas Wister and Ann Olive (Emory) Howell; student Mt. Vernon Jr. Coll., 1959-61, U. Madrid, 1961-62; B.A., Sophie Newcomb Coll. of Tulane U., 1963; M.A., U. Va., 1965, Ph.D., 1970; m. William Allen Myers, Dec. 23, 1967; 1 son, William Webb. Lectr. U. Houston, 1966-67; instr. Okla. State U., Stillwater, 1967-70; asst. prof. San Antonio Coll., 1970-73, assoc. prof., 1973-77, prof. history, 1977—. S.W. Conf. Commn. on Higher Edn. and Campus Ministry Meth. Ch., 1978-81; bd. dirs. Family Services Assn., 1978—, San Antonio Area Red Cross, 1979—; bd. dirs. Laurel Heights Weekday Sch., 1980—, chmn., 1982-83. Mem. Tex. Jr. Coll. Tchrs. Assn., SW Conf. on Latin Am. Studies (exec. com., 1974-75), AAUP (exec. com. San Antonio Coll., 1973-74), Conf. on Latin Am. History, Phi Alpha Theta. Democrat. Methodist. Clubs: Jr. League of San Antonio (bd. dirs., 1977-79), Kappa Alpha Theta. Author student's rev. manuals for The American Nation (J. Garraty), 1975, 77, 79, 83, instrs. manuals, 1977, 79, 81, 83; contbr. articles to publs. in field. Home: 307 Arcadia Pl San Antonio TX 78209 Office: 1300 San Pedro San Antonio TX 78284

MYERS, GWEN MCHANEY, nurse, polit. worker; b. Dierks, Ark., May 15, 1925; d. Murray and Hattie M. (Ganno) McHaney; B.S. in Psychology, U. Ark., 1945; postgrad. Tenn. Sch. Nursing, 1958; Nursing Home Adminstr., Vanderbilt U., 1971; m. Ralph M. Myers, Jan. 27, 1973; children—Jimmy Webster, Patti Vance, Vicki Loree. Dir. of nursing Bristol (Tenn.) Nursing Home, 1960-69; adminstr. Smiths Nursing Home, Johnson City, Tenn., 1971-78; office mgr. Jim Cooper, Morristown, Tenn., 1982—. Cons. various polit. campaigns, 1979—; mem. Democratic State Resolution Com., Nashville, 1982—; del. Dem. Nat. Conv., 1980. Recipient Nurse of Yr. award Tenn. Nurses Assn., 1962. Mem. Nursing Home Assn., Tenn. Nursing Assn. Baptist. Clubs: DAR, Geneal. Soc., Garden. Columnist: Citizen-Tribune, Morristown; composer numerous songs, 1948—. Home: Route 5 Box 324F Morristown TN 37814

MYERS, JANET IRENE, fabric mfg. co. exec.; b. Gladwin, Mich., Nov. 9, 1948; d. Ralph E. and Eleanor E. (Roth) Myers; B.S., Mich. State U., 1970. Buyer, Goldwater's, Phoenix, 1970-75; product mgr. Olga Co., Van Nuys, Calif., 1975-78, mdse. mgr., 1978-80, dir. mktg. services, 1980-82; v.p. mktg. Saratoga Knitting Mill, Inc., N.Y.C., 1982—. Mem. Nat. Assn. Female Execs., Fashion Group, Underfashions Club. Republican. Episcopalian. Office: 350 Fifth Ave New York NY 10118

MYERS, MARIA ELENA MORRONE, weather service co. exec.; b. Phila., Sept. 9, 1943; d. Frank J. and Lena Ann Morrone; degree in med. tech. Hahnemann Med. Sch., 1964; postgrad. Pa. State U., 1975—; m. Joel Myers, Sept. 12, 1977; 1 dau., Erika; children by previous marriage—Brad Mason, Adrienne Mason. Mem. med. tech. staff Hahnemann Med. Sch., Phila., until 1964; head technologist, clin. lab. Pa. State U., 1964-66; hematology researcher Lawrence Meml. Hosp., New London, Conn., 1966-67; with Accu-Weather Inc., State College, Pa., 1974—, exec. mgmt. asst., office mgr., tech. supr., corp. sec., 1976—. Mem. Am. Mgmt. Assn. Republican. Office: Accu-Weather Inc 619 W College Ave State College PA 16801

MYERS, MARLINE MILDRED, heating and air conditioning co. exec.; b. Ayr, Nebr., Aug. 29, 1925; d. Ludwig Otto and Amelia (Flessner) Muhleissen; student public schs.; m. Bob J. Myers, Mar. 22, 1944 (dec. 1978); children—Karen Kay, Steven Ray, Susan Rene, Michael Jay. Owner, operator Blue Hill Cleaners (Nebr.), 1949-61, Meyers Heating and Air Conditioning, Inc., Grand Island, Nebr., 1961—, pres., 1979—. Mem. Grand Island C. of C. Lutheran. Home: 104 E 22d St Grand Island NE 68801 Office: 318 E Capital Grand Island NE 68801

MYERS, NORMA JANE MCKAY, psychologist; b. Springfield, Mass., Aug. 27, 1928; d. Claude Carson and Norma Alice (Scott) McKay; student Heidelberg Coll., 1945-47; student Bliss Bus. Coll., 1947-48; B.S., Bowling Green State U., 1960, M.S., 1963; postgrad. Internat. Grad. Sch., St. Louis.; m. W. Howard Myers, Sept. 15, 1947 (div. 1969); children—Virginia (Mrs. Jerry Stidham), Carl. Tchr. elem. schs. Port Clinton, Ohio, 1955-63; reading specialist Elyria (Ohio) City Schs., 1964-65; intern sch. psychologist Tiffin (Ohio) City Schs., 1965-66; sch. psychologist Fremont (Ohio) City Schs., 1966—. Tchr. in child devel. and psychology Michael J. Owens Tech. Coll., Perrysburg, Ohio, 1972—; cons. to sch. systems in reading and psychology. Bd. dir. Sandusky County Mental Health Assn., 1972-76. Mem. NOW, Fremont Bus. and Prof. Women (v.p. 1972-73), Maumee Valley Sch. Psychologist Assn. (pres. 1970-71), Nat. Assn. Sch. Psychologists, Ohio Sch. Psychologists Assn., Delta Kappa Gamma. Home: 1139 N Byrneal Dr Port Clinton OH 43452 Office: 211 S Park Ave Fremont OH 43420

MYERS, SALLY ANN, assn. exec.; b. New Castle, Pa., July 6, 1926; d. Howard Charles and Freida Elizabeth (Seh) Rodgers; student Va. Intermont Coll., 1943-45; m. Kermit Whitney Myers, Nov. 2, 1957; children—Howard Rodgers, Mary Whitney. Sr. program dir., Sumner G. Rahr, Chgo., 1974-79; devel. officer Community Renewal Soc., Chgo., 1980—; speaker, cons. in field. Active United Charities Legal Aid, 1965-67, Ecumenical Inst., 1966-72, Inst. of Cultural Affairs, 1972—. Mem. Chgo. Chpt. Nat. Soc. Fund Raising Execs., Landmarks Preservation Council. Home: 1125 Forest Ave Wilmette IL 60091 Office: 111 N Wabash Chicago IL 60602

MYERS, THERESE ELEANOR, office automation and software exec.; b. Pitts., July 1, 1944; d. Harold John and Eleanor Margaret (Schmitt) M.; B.A., Newton Coll. Sacred Heart, 1966; M.S.I.A., Carnegie-Mellon U., 1968. Mgmt. cons. Arthur Young & Co., N.Y.C., 1968-70; Asst. v.p. Citicorp Leasing, Citicorp, N.Y.C., 1970-72, dir. ops., transaction tech., Los Angeles, 1972-74; v.p. product mgmt. Lexar, 1974-79; v.p., product mgr. Lexar Bus. Communications/Axxa, Citicorp, Los Angeles, 1979-81; pres. Quarterdeck Office Systems, Los Angeles, 1981—; dir. Phys. Systems, Edgeprint Systems. Asst. chmn. provisional com. ednl. TV project Jr. League Los Angeles, 1981-82; pres. Hollywood Bowl Jrs., 1978. C.P.A., N.Y. Roman Catholic. Patentee integrated office system for execs. and profls. Home: 1 Quarterdeck St Marina del Rey CA 90291 Office: 2210 Wilshire Blvd Suite 117 Santa Monica CA 90403

MYERS, URSULA SENNEWALD, social services adminstr.; b. Rochester, N.Y., July 5, 1928; d. Arthur George and Luise (Moeller) Sennewald; student U. Rochester, 1946-48; B.S. in Indsl. and Labor Relations, Cornell U., 1950; M.S.W., U. Wis., Madison, 1970; m. Richard R. Myers, June 12, 1951; children—Lisa, Robin (dec.), Theodore, Bruce. Social worker Rock County Social Services, Janesville, Wis., 1965-70, supr. I, 1970-79, acting dir., 1979, dir., 1979—; instr. U. Wis., Whitewater, 1978-79. Mem. Acad. Cert. Social Workers, Nat. Assn. Social Workers. Unitarian. Contbg. author: Introduction to Social Welfare Institutions.

MYERS-BORDINI, LINDA LEE, steel co. ofcl.; b. Monongahela, Pa., May 21, 1942; d. Walter and Lucille F. (Archbold) Warren; B.S., California (Pa.) State Coll., 1976, postgrad., 1977—; m. Jack L. Myers, Jan. 8, 1960; children—Dana M., Jacqueline L., Kimberly A.; m. 2d, Primo Bordini, Apr. 28, 1978. Process analyst environ. health services dept. U.S. Steel Co., Clairton, Pa., 1978—. Mem. Bot. Soc. Am., Pa. Acad. Sci., Sierra Club, Nat. Audubon Soc., Bot. Soc. Westmorland County, Grad. Student Assn., Beta Beta Beta, Chi Gamma Psi. Democrat. Methodist. Home: 609 Hancock St Monongahela PA 15063 Office: US Steel Co Environmental Health Services Dept Clairton PA 15025

MYERSON, BESS, columnist, consumer cons.; b. N.Y.C., July 16, 1924; d. Louis and Bella Myerson; B.A., Hunter Coll., 1945, LL.D., 1973; D.Pub. Service, Seton Hall U., 1972; L.H.D., L.I. U., 1972; LL.D., Keuka Coll., 1973; 1 dau., Barra Grant. Piano soloist Carnegie Hall, N.Y.C., 1946; with Sta. WOR-TV, N.Y.C., 1947-51; mistress of ceremonies The Big Payoff, CBS-TV, 1951-59; comml. hostess Philco Playhouse, NBC-TV, 1954-55; TV commentator Miss Am. Pageant, ABC, 1964-68; co-commentator Tournament of Roses, 1960-68; panelist I've Got a Secret, CBS, 1958-68; news staff CBS Broadcasting Co., 1961-62; commr. consumer affairs City of N.Y., 1969-74; columnist N.Y. Daily News-Chgo. Tribune Syndicate, 1974—; broadcaster NBC Radio; vis. prof. Hunter Coll., 1974; mem. Commn. on Critical Choices, 1975; chmn. Consumer Credit Counseling Service; pres. Women United for N.Y.; exec. dir. Fashion Capital of World; hostess Women of Year, 1974, In the Public Interest, 1975. Chmn. Hunter Coll. Centennial Fund, N.Y.C., 1965-70; Greater N.Y. chmn. Bonds for Israel, 1965-72, hon. chmn., 1972—; mem. commn. on public health N.Y. Acad. Medicine; mem. Pres. Carter's Commn. on Mental Health, Pres. Carter's Commn. on World Hunger; mem. Nat. Alliance to Save Energy; bd. dirs. Freedom House, Pub. Broadcasting Service, Citizens Union, Anti-Defamation League, Another Mother for Peace, League Sch. for Seriously Disturbed Children, Am.-Israel Cultural Found., Pub. Devel. Corp., Com. to Advance Goal Higher Edn. for Disabled in City U. N.Y., Met. Opera, others. Recipient Outstanding Achievement award Hunter Coll., 1955; Presdl. medal, 1970; named Woman of Year, Anti-Defamation League, 1965; Clarion award Women in Communications. Author: The Complete Consumer Book, 1979. Home: 3 E 71st St New York NY 10021 *

MYERSON, JEANNE ROBIN, mcpl. econ. devel. adminstr.; b. Evanston, Ill., Apr. 9, 1953; d. Paul E. and Marilyn (Lapp) M.; B.A., Grinnell Coll., 1975; M.C.R.P., Harvard U., 1978. Research analyst, interviewer employment project Iowa Commn. on Status of Women, Des Moines, 1975-76; field survey and program evaluation Westat, Inc., Rockville, Md., 1976; mktg. asst. community affairs and mktg. dept. Mass. Bay Transit Authority, Boston, 1977-78; asst. dir. resource devel. Office of Communities & Devel., Commonwealth of Mass., Boston, 1978-80; econ. devel. dir. Riverside-Cambridgeport Community Corp., Cambridge, Mass., 1980—; dir. Cybermation, Inc. Bd. dirs. Boston Neighborhood Network, 1980—, Pvt. Industry Council, Cambridge, 1981—, Neighborhood Devel. Corp. of Jamaica Plain (Mass.), 1982—; mem. Democratic Ward Com., 1981—; Del. Mass. Dem. Issues Conv., 1981, Dem. Nominating Conv., 1982. Mem. Nat. Audubon Soc., Phi Beta Kappa. Democrat. Author articles on community devel. policy. Home: 42 Peter Parley Rd Jamaica Plain MA 02130

MYETT, MARILYN PHYLLIS, newspaper exec.; b. Gloucester, Mass., July 23, 1926; d. John Joseph, Jr. and Rozalinda (Safrino) Silveira; student Boston U., 1948-49; m. A. Arthur Myett, Sept. 13, 1958 (dec.); children—Michael Thomas, Susan Marie, John Patrick. Successively clerical worker, news photographer, women's editor Gloucester Daily Times, 1949-60, circulation mgr., 1975—; freelance writer and photographer Essex County Newspapers, Gloucester, 1960-75, circulation dir., 1975—. Publicity dir. Cape Ann Festival of Arts, 1963; publicity dir., bd. dirs. North Shore chpt. St. Jude's Children's Research Hosp., 1973-75; mem. parent adv. council Gloucester High Sch., 1976-78. Mem. Internat. Circulation Mgrs. Assn., New Eng. Assn. Circulation Execs., Nat. Wildlife Fedn., New Eng. Antivivisection Soc., Cape Ann Animal Aid. Author: History of the Gloucester Fishing Industry, 1973. Home: 6 Gerring Rd Gloucester MA 01930 Office: Whittemore St Gloucester MA 01930

MYHILL, (LEONA) SUSIE, secretarial service co. exec.; b. Lynwood, Calif., Jan. 6, 1951; d. Jack Gilbert and (Ozella) Joy (Lucas) Smith; B.A., So. Calif. Coll., 1972; postgrad. Calif. State U., Fullerton, 1975-76, Orange Coast Coll., 1973-75, Coastline Community Coll., 1980-82; m. Loren Lee Myhill, June 9, 1972. Office mgr., sec., bookkeeper Household Fin. Corp., Orange, Calif., 1969-72; legal sec. Heinly, Lindley & Thrasher, Santa Ana, Calif., 1972-77; owner, operator Myhill Profl. Services, Newport Beach, Calif., 1977—; wedding coordinator. Supt. Sunday sch., children's ch. leader, Bible study tchr. Mem. Nat. Assn. Female Execs., Christian Bus. and Profl. Women's Club. Republican. Club: After 5 (chmn. 1981-82). Home: 1059 Santa Cruz Circle Costa Mesa CA 92626

MYKYTA, MARY ANN, lab. exec.; b. Dover, Del., Aug. 5, 1937; d. Roland and Anna Elizabeth (King) Walls; R.N., Meml. Hosp., Wilmington, Del., 1958; m. Lubomyr Mykyta, June 20, 1959; children—Maria Lydia, Natalie Vera, John Lubomyr, Laryssa Ann. Med.-surg. charge nurse Meml. Hosp., Wilmington, 1958-60; partner, v.p., sales mgr. Delaware Valley Indsl. X-Ray Co., Springfield, Pa., 1960-65; realtor asso. Gordon A. Weinberg Real Estate, Harrisburg, Pa., 1968-72; partner, v.p., rental properties gen. mgr. Commonwealth Trading & Mortgage Corp., Harrisburg, 1970-72; sales rep. Astrotech, Inc., Harrisburg, 1972-74, sales dir., 1974-75, v.p., gen. mgr., 1975, v.p., dir. regional real estate ops. and investments, 1976—; dir. Cert. Testing Labs., Inc. Registered nurse, Del., Pa.; notary public. Mem. Nat. Assn. Female Execs., Am. Mgmt. Assn., Harrisburg Builders Exchange, Am. Assn. Notaries, Pa. Assn. Notaries, Meml. Hosp. Alumni Assn., Sanford Alumni Assn. Republican. Byzantine Catholic. Club: Penn-Garden Civic. Home: 5912 Colwyn Dr Harrisburg PA 17109 Office: PO Box 6159 7801 Allentown Blvd Harrisburg PA 17112

MYLES, ANN ETHEL, fin. exec.; b. Pennsauken, N.J., July 30, 1927; d. William Joseph and Ethel (Schaffer) M.; student St. Elizabeth's Coll., Acad. Advanced Traffic, St. Joseph's Coll. Indsl. Relations. Asst. mgr., credit rep. Farm Credit Service, Moorestown, N.J., 1963-72, aquatic loan officer, asst. gen. mgr., 1963-76, gen. mgr., 1976-81; pres. Farmers Prodn. Credit Assn., Moorestown, also Fed. Land Bank Assn.,

Moorestown, 1981—; lectr., workshop coordinator agrl. fin. confs. Mem. N.J. Marine Fishery Council, 1980—. Mem. N.J. Agrl. Soc., N.J. Farm Bur. Roman Catholic. Home: 15 Ambler Rd Cherry Hill NJ 08002 Office: Route 38 and South Church St Moorestown NJ 08057

MYLES, DOROTHY DUBOSE, shipbldg. co. personnel ofcl.; b. Shubuta, Miss., Feb. 8, 1947; d. Belovet DuBose and Edna Mae (Haynes) Gladney; B.S. in Bus. Admintrn., Jackson (Miss.) State U., 1970; m. Charlie Myles, Aug. 23, 1969; 1 dau., Shayla Michelle. Sec. to pres. Jackson State U., 1970-71; engring. asst., then tech. writer Ingalls Shipbldg. Co., Pascagoula, Miss., 1972-76, EEO specialist, 1976—; mem. youth motivation task force Nat. Alliance Bus., 1980—. Vice chmn. Jackson County Democratic Exec. Com., 1980-84; mem. Moss Point (Miss.) Sch. Bd., 1981—; sec. citizens adv. com. Jackson County Youth Ct., 1981-82; bd. dirs. Jackson County Arts Council, 1980—, Jackson County United Way; mem. adv. com. Region V CETA, 1981—. Recipient various outstanding service awards. Mem. Ingalls Mgmt. Assn., Miss. Sch. Bd. Assn., Gulf Coast Sch. Bd. Assn., Nat. Council Negro Women (pres. Jackson County sect. 1978-82), Zeta Phi Beta (v.p. 1979-80, parliamentarian 1980-82). Methodist. Home: 4101 Charles St Moss Point MS 39563 Office: PO Box 149 Mail Stop 1020-06 Pascagoula MS 39567

MYLES, JUNE BRILL, mktg. and data processing cons.; b. Louisville, June 8, 1943; d. George Anderson and Virginia (Rexrode) Myles; cert. Sorbonne U., 1962; B.A., Hollins Coll., 1964; m. States W. Coyle, Sept. 27, 1969 (div.). Sr. programmer Am. Tel. & Tel. Co., N.Y.C., 1964-66; project mgr. data processing and communications services Am. Airlines, N.Y.C., 1966-74, mgr. mktg. performance reports, 1974-77, mgr. mktg. info. systems, 1977-79; prin. June B. Myles Assos., N.Y.C., 1980—. NSF grantee, 1964. Club: N.Y. Road Runners. Office: 112 E 37th St New York NY 10016

MYRICK, BERTHA GRACE, nurse; b. Mt. Olive, N.C., June 12, 1943; d. Mable Louise (Gatling) M.; R.N., Kate Bitting Reynolds Meml. Hosp. Sch. Nursing, Winston-Salem, N.C., 1964; B.S. in Nursing, N.C. Central U., 1970; M.S. in Nursing, Wayne State U., 1971. Acting dir. nursing service Kirwood Gen. Hosp., Detroit, 1972; chief nursing service trainee VA Hosp., Miami, Fla., 1972-74; chief nursing service VA Center, Wichita, Kans., 1974-76, VA West Side Med. Center, Chgo., 1976-79, VA Med. and Regional Office Center, Wilmington, Del., 1979—; asst. prof. nursing Wichita State U., 1976, U. Ill., 1977-79. Bd. dirs. Kans. Heart Assn.; mem. Sedgwick County (Kans.) Cancer Soc., ARC. Served to maj. USAR, 1974—. Named Outstanding Young Woman of Kans., 1975. Mem. Am. Nurses Assn., Nat. League Nursing, Nat. Forum Adminstrs. Nursing Services, Nat. Black Nurses Assn., Am. Soc. Nursing Service Adminstrs., Assn. Mil. Surgeons U.S., AAUP, Res. Officers Assn. U.S., Nat. Assn. Female Execs., Chi Eta Phi, Delta Sigma Theta (plaque for community service Wichita chpt. 1976). Baptist. Home: 2726 N Robino Dr Wilmington DE 19808 Office: VA Medical and Regional Office Center (118) 1601 Kirkwood Hwy Wilmington DE 19805

MYRICK, SUELLEN, advt. co. exec.; b. Tiffin, Ohio, Aug. 1, 1941; d. William Henry and Margaret Ellen (Roby) Wilkins; student Heidelberg Coll., 1959-60; m. James E. Forest, May 5, 1962; children—Gregory Allyn, Daniel James; m. 2d, W. Edward Myrick, Jr., Sept. 11, 1977. Exec. sec. to mayor and city mgr. City of Alliance (Ohio), 1962-63; dir. br. office Stark County Ct. of Juvenile and Domestic Relations, Alliance, 1963-65; account supr., dir. mktg., media, research Ed Myrick, Inc., Charlotte, N.C., 1971—, also sec.-treas.; pres. Mktg. Designs, Inc., Charlotte, 1980—, To Market, Inc., Charlotte, 1981—. Mem. adv. bd. Children's Theatre, Charlotte, 1981—; adv. bd. Substance Abuse Council, Mental Health Authority, Charlotte; communications chmn. Charlotte Clean City Com.; chmn. public relations Republican Party, Charlotte. Recipient Woman of Yr. award Harrisonburg, Va., 1968. Mem. LWV, Women's Polit. Caucus, Nat. Assn. Women Execs., C. of C. Republican. Methodist. Club: Rep. Women's. Home: 310 W 8th St Charlotte NC 28202 Office: 505 N Poplar St Charlotte NC 28202

NACHBAR, CHARLOTTE BRESNICK, speech pathologist; b. Manchester, N.H., May 4, 1938; d. Abraham and Sarah Fanny (Lipinsky) Bresnick; B.S., Boston U., 1960; M.Ed., Rivier Coll., 1968; m. Robert Nachbar, July 5, 1970; children—Barbara Jane, Marjorie Robin. Pvt. practice speech pathology, Manchester, 1960-75; speech pathologist Crotched Mountain Rehab. Center, Greenfield, N.H., 1964-66; dir. speech pathology, supr. Union #40, Milford, N.H., 1967-69; tchr. Bakersville Sch., Manchester, 1970-71, Franklin Sch., Manchester, 1972-74; speech and lang. pathologist Manchester Public Schs., 1974—; asst. prof. Vocat. Tech. Coll., Manchester, 1979—. Coordinator, N.H. Kennedy Primary Campaign, 1979-80. Mem. Am. Speech and Hearing Assn., NEA, N.H. Speech and Hearing Assn., N.H. Edn. Assn., Manchester Edn. Assn., Alpha Delta Kappa. Democrat. Jewish. Author: Solomon and Sassy, 1977; Robert and His Frisbee, 1978; Louis and Lucy, 1978; Sheriff McNash and the Shoot-Out, 1979; The Chilling Chant, 1978; The Thundering Thud, 1979; also articles. Home: 161 Ray St Manchester NH 03104 Office: 88 Lowell St Manchester NH 03104

NACHISON, JOSEPHINE MARINO, personnel exec.; b. N.Y.C., Nov. 19, 1944; d. Paul Vincent and Kathryn Marino; B.A., Queens Coll., 1967; postgrad. U. Mo.; m. Jerold Speiser Nachison, Feb. 26, 1971; children—David Paul, Ida Rebecca. Vol., Peace Corps, Colombia, 1967-69; caseworker Catholic Guardian Soc., N.Y.C., 1969-70; group leader Experiment in Internat. Living, Mex., 1970; community analyst City Demonstration Agy., Office of Mayor Wilmington (Del.), 1972-74, dep. charge planning and evaluation, 1974-75; dir. recruitment and placement Internat. Vol. Services, Inc., Washington, 1977-79; exec. dir. Jodie Nachison Career Service, Washington, 1980—; community conflict mediator Citizens' Complaint Center, Washington, 1979—. Mem. Am. Soc. Tng. and Devel., Am. Personnel and Guidance Assn., Nat. Vocat. Guidance Assn., Assn. Non-White Concerns in Personnel and Guidance. Democrat. Address: 3235 McKinley St NW Washington DC 20015

NACHMAN, FRAN, indsl. cleaning service exec.; b. Phila., Feb. 17, 1951; d. Harold and Rose Lee (Gold) N.; B.A., Pa. State U., 1972; M.B.A., Temple U., 1982. Gen. mgr. Film Makers Phila., 1972-79; v.p. AAA Indsl. Cleaning Service, Inc., Flourtown, Pa., 1979—. Mem. AAUW, Nat. Assn. Female Execs., Am. Soc. Profl. and Exec. Women, Soc. Am. Baseball Research, NOW. Home: 2017 Spruce St Philadelphia PA 19103 Office: 1456 Bethlehem Pike Flourtown PA 19031

NACHTIGALL, LILA EHRENSTEIN, physician; b. N.Y.C., Feb. 23, 1934; d. Irving and Adele Pearl (Holzer) Ehrenstein; A.B., Bklyn. Coll., 1955; M.D., N.Y. Med. Coll., 1960; m. Richard Henry Nachtigall, Dec. 24, 1957; children—Margaret, Lisa, Ellen. Intern Bellevue Hosp., N.Y.C., 1960-60, resident 1961-64; instr. medicine N.Y. U. Med. Center, 1964-66, asst. prof. obstetrics and gynecology, 1966-74, asso. prof., 1974—, dir. endocrinology Goldwater div., 1966—, dir. gynecology-endocrinology out patient dept., 1973—; vis. lectr. Booth Meml. Hosp., Lenox Hill Hosp. Chmn. fund-raising Bank St. Coll. Sch. Children, 1969-74. Recipient Karl Harpuder award in phys. medicine N.Y. Med. Coll., 1960. Mem. AMA, Am. Med. Women's Assn., Soc. Study Reprodn., Am. Fertility Soc., Endocrine Soc. Research developed test for estriol determination in human plasma. Home: 355 Riverside Dr New York NY 10025 Office: 530 1st Ave New York NY 10016

NACOL, BARBARA LEIGH, health care exec.; b. Charleston, S.C., Feb. 2, 1948; d. Edheworth Blythe and Amelia (Neil) Hunt; B.A., U. Houston, 1973; M.A., Ph.D.; ed. Med. U. Houston, Tex. A&M U., Edison Coll. Mem. Tchr. Corps, Houston, 1973-75; tchr. Magnet program Houston Ind. Sch. Dist., 1975-77; adminstr. Law Office Mae Nacol and Assos., Houston, 1977-79, exec. dir. Hyperbaric Oxygen Med. Center, Houston, 1979—. Dep. constable precinct 1 Harris County, 1980. Mem. Undersea Med. Soc., Am. Judicature Soc., Environ. Edn. Assn. (charter). Presbyterian. Author papers in field. Office: 5220 Travis St Houston TX 77002

NACOL, MAE, lawyer; b. Beaumont, Tex., June 15, 1944; d. William Samuel and Ethel (Bowman) Nacol; B.A. in Behavioral Scis., Rice U., 1965; LL.B., South Tex. Coll. Law, 1969; children—Shawn Alexander, Catherine Regina. Admitted to Tex. Bar, 1969, since practiced in Houston. Diamond cons. for jewelry stores and ins. cos., 1961—. Pres. 240 basic police course Tex. A&M System; chmn. bd. HBO Med. Center Houston. Recipient Mayor's Recognition award, Houston, 1972. Ford Found. fellow, 1965. Mem. Am., Tex., Internat., Fed., Houston (chmn. candidates com. 1970, chmn. membership com. 1971, chmn. lawyer's referral com. 1972), bar assns., Tex. Trial Lawyers Assn., Houston Trial Lawyers Assn., Nat. Assn. Women Lawyers, Am. Judicature Soc. Home: 6012 Memorial Dr Houston TX 77007 Office: 1616 W Loop S Houston TX 77027

NADEL, CHARLOTTE, physician; b. Bucharest, Romania, Jan. 1, 1924; d. Solomon and Mathilda (Friedman) Iosef; came to U.S., 1964, naturalized, 1969; M.D., Faculty Medicine Bucharest, 1949; m. Ignat Nadel, Mar. 24, 1945. Intern, Columbus Hosp., N.Y.C., 1965; resident psychiatry Kings County Hosp., Downstate Med. Center, 1966-69; attending physician dept. psychiatry Kings County Hosp. Center, 1971—; fellow liaison service, Downstate Med. Center, 1969-71, instr. psychiatry, 1969-71, clin. asst. prof. psychiatry, 1972-77, asst. prof. psychiatry, 19 - , clin. asso. prof., 19 . Diplomate Am. Bd. Psychiatry and Neurology. Mem. Am. Psychiat. Assn., Am. Psychosomatic Soc., N.Y. Acad. Scis. Home: 681 Clarkson Ave Brooklyn NY 11203 Office: 195 Argyle Rd Brooklyn NY 11218

NADELMAN, LORRAINE, psychologist, educator; b. N.Y.C., May 12, 1924; d. William and Sally Nadelman; B.A., N.Y.U., 1945, Ph.D., 1953; m. Sidney Warschausky, June 20, 1953; children—Seth Andrew, Judith Sue, Carl William. Asst. tchr. Flatbush Day Nursery, Bklyn., 1945; teaching asst., then instr. psychology N.Y.U., 1945-51; asst. prof. Mt. Holyoke Coll., 1951-57; lectr. psychology U. Mich., Ann Arbor, 1962-69, asso. prof., 1969—; cons. in field. Vice pres., trustee Ann Arbor Hands-on-Mus., 1980—; bd. dirs. Ann Arbor Child and Family Service, 1969-72; adv. bd. Found House Children's Center, Ann Arbor, 1976-79. NSF sci. faculty fellow, 1965-66; Rackham faculty research grantee, 1975-76; faculty devel. awardee Center for Research on Learning and Teaching, 1978-79; Lit.-Sci.-Arts faculty devel. research grantee, 1979-80, 82-83. Mem. Am. Psychol. Assn., Soc. Research in Child Devel., Internat. Soc. Research Behavioral Devel., Midwestern Psychol. Assn., Phi Beta Kappa. Author: Research Manual in Child Development, 1982; also articles. Office: Mason Hall U Mich Ann Arbor MI 48109

NADELSON, CAROL COOPERMAN, physician; b. Bklyn., N.Y., Oct. 13, 1936; d. Hyman and Diana (Newman) Cooperman; B.A. magna cum laude, Bklyn. Coll., 1957; M.D. with honors, U. Rochester, 1961; m. Theodore Nadelson, July 16, 1965; children—Robert, Jennifer. Intern in medicine U. Rochester, N.Y.C., 1961-62; resident in psychiatry Mass. Mental Health Center, 1962-64, Beth Israel Hosp., Boston, 1964-66; teaching fellow in psychiatry Harvard Med. Sch., Boston, 1962-65, research fellow, 1965-66; practice medicine specializing in psychiatry, Boston, 1966—; clin. instr. psychiatry Harvard Med. Sch., 1969-72, asst. prof. psychiatry, 1973-76; asso. psychiatry Beth Israel Hosp., Boston, 1970-72, asst. psychiatrist, 1972-73, asso. psychiatrist, 1973-77; asst. in psychiatry Children's Hosp. Med. Center, Boston, 1973-79, instr. pediatrics, 1973-74; prof. psychiatry Tufts U. Sch. Medicine, Boston, 1979—; dir. tng. and edn. dept. psychiatry New Eng. Med. Center, Boston, 1979—; guest lectr. Harvard U. Summer Sch., 1975; vis. prof. U. Vt. Med. Sch., 1976, U. Pitts., 1977, SUNY, N.Y.C., 1978, U. Mo., Columbia, 1979; cons. NIMH, 1974, St. Paul's Sch., Concord, N.H., 1974, Groton (Mass.) Sch., 1974; Milton (Mass.) Acad., 1979. Recipient Gold Medal Mt. Airy Psychiat. Center, Denver, 1981; diplomate Am. Bd. Psychiatry and Neurology. Fellow Am. Psychiat. Assn. (mem. task force on women 1974—, v.p. 1981—), Am. Coll. Psychiatry; mem. Am. Med. Women's Assn., Soc. for Sex Therapy and Research (v.p. 1979-80), Am. Assn. Dirs. Psychiat. Residency Tng., Am. Orthopsychiat. Assn., Mass. Med. Soc., Assn. for Acad. Psychiatry (pres. 1982—), AMA, Assn. Women in Sci., Am. Psychopath. Assn., Group for Advancement of Psychiatry (mem. com. on family 1973—), Harvard Med. Women's Assn., Phi Beta Kappa, Alpha Omega Alpha. Contbr. numerous articles on psychiatry and sex therapy to profl. jours.; editor The Woman Patient, 1978; editorial bd. Jour. Hosp. and Community Psychiatry, 1980—, Jour. Marital and Family Therapy, 1981—.

NADER, HELEN, educator; b. Miami, Ariz., Apr. 29, 1936; d. Wade Nicholas and Heleneh (Hawie) N.; B.A., U. Ariz., 1958; M.A., Smith Coll., 1959; Ph.D., U. Calif., Berkeley, 1972. Asst. prof. history U. Hawaii, Honolulu, 1971-75; asst. prof. history Stanford (Calif.) U., 1975-76, vis. scholar Food Research Inst., 1978; asst. prof. history Ind. U., Bloomington, 1976-79, asso. prof., 1979—. Am. Council Learned Socs. research fellow, 1974-75; Tinker Found. fellow, 1978-79; Nat. Endowment for Humanities research fellow, 1982-83. Mem. Hispanic Soc. Am. (corr.), Renaissance Soc. Am. (nat. council 1982—), Am. Hist. Assn., Soc. for Spanish and Portuguese Hist. Studies. Author: The Mendoza Family in the Spanish Renaissance, 1350-1550, 1979; editor: Bull. of Soc. for Spanish and Portuguese Hist. Studies, 1977-80; asso. editor Am. Hist. Rev., 1982—. Home: 509 S Highland St Bloomington IN 47401 Office: Ind U Dept History BH 742 Bloomington IN 47405

NADLER, ANNETTA BARRON, psychologist; b. Balt., Mar. 28, 1940; d. Irving Israel and Sadie J. (Fraidin) Barron; student St. John's Coll., Md., 1957-60; M.A. Hunter Coll., 1970; Ph.D., City U. N.Y., 1973; postgrad. Am. Inst. Psychotherapy and Psychoanalysis, 1974-77; m. Henry Nadler, Mar. 28, 1961; children—Courtney Barron Natasha Barron. Research asso. Hunter Coll., N.Y.C., 1969, asst. prof. psychology, 1970-72; asst. prof. psychology John Jay Coll., N.Y.C., 1971-74; asst. prof. Lincoln Center campus Fordham U., 1972-74; supr. master and doctoral candidates City U. N.Y., 1973-76; pvt. practice clin. psychology specializing in child and adult psychoanalysis, N.Y.C.; cons., lectr. in field. NSF fellow 1970; Md. State scholar, 1957-60. Mem. Am. Psychol. Assn., AAAS. Address: 440 E 79th St New York NY 10021

NADLER, JANICE HOROWITZ, psychologist; b. Mpls., July 14, 1943; d. George E. and Edith L. Nadler; B.A., U. Mich., 1965; M.A., Calif. State U., Northridge, 1973; Ph.D., Calif. Sch. Profl. Psychology, 1976; m. Richard E. Horowitz, June 30, 1968. Counselor, Suicide Prevention Center, Los Angeles, 1973-74; staff counselor Las Palmas Sch. for Girls, Commerce, Calif., 1974-75; psychology intern Thalians Community Mental Health Center, Cedars Sinai Med. Center, Los Angeles, 1976-78; staff psychologist, 1978—; psychologist in pvt. practice, Beverly Hills, Calif., 1978—; dir. research Stepfamily Found. Calif., 1978—. Mem. Am. Psychol. Counselors, Calif. Psychol. Assn., Calif. Assn. Marriage and Family Counselors. Home: 9050 Briarcrest Ln Beverly Hills CA 90210 Office: 450 N Bedford Dr Beverly Hills CA 90210

NADLER, MYRA, librarian; b. N.Y.C., Nov. 10, 1945; d. Seymour and Julia (Odem) Liptzen; B.A., City U.N.Y., 1966; M.L.S., Rutgers U., 1967; m. Spencer Nadler, Sept. 1, 1968. Asst. to coordinator adult services Free Public Library, Woodbridge, N.J., 1967-68; area reference librarian Clifton (N.J.) Public Library, 1968-69; br. librarian Palos Verdes (Calif.) Library Dist., 1969-70, asst. supr. reference, 1970, supr. audio visual, 1970-77; dir. Civic Center Library, Torrance (Calif.) Public Library, 1977-79; asso. dir. Long Beach (Calif.) Library, 1979-81; account exec. Bateman Eichler, Hill Richards, Torrance, 1982—; bd. dirs. Edn. Film Library Assn., Film Library Info. Council. Bd. dirs. Peninsula Symphony Assn., Palos Verdes, Torrance Coordinating Council. Mem. ALA (chmn. Public Library Assn. audio visual com.), Calif. Library Assn., Calif. Soc. Librarians (pres.), Long Beach C. of C. (dir.), Beta Phi Mu. Author: How to Start an Audiovisual Collection, 1978; columnist Wilson Library Bull., 1974-75; asst. editor N.J. Libraries, 1966-68; editor Recommendations for AV Materials & Services for Small and Medium Sized Public Libraries, 1975, Guidelines for Audiovisual Materials and Services for Large Public Libraries, 1975. Office: 21515 Hawthorne Blvd Torrance CA 90503

NADLLER, BEVEALY, nutrition cons., health counselor, lectr.; b. N.Y.C., June 4, 1940; d. Jack and Miriam (Gordon) Beer; A.A., Fashion Inst. Tech., 1954; student Queens Coll., 1956-58; profl. tng., 1966—; m. Phill Nadller, Mar. 19, 1964; children—Karyn, Lauren, Denise. Asst. fashion designer, N.Y.C., 1954-56; auditing asst. A.P., N.Y.C., 1958-61; chiropractic asst. to Dr. Nadller, N.Y.C., 1964-69; cert. instr. concept therapy, N.Y.C., 1969-76; profl. singer, 1972-76; nutrition cons., 1974—; holistic health counselor, 1978—; lectr. Parker Chiropractic Research Found., 1972—; lectr. on natural health and nutrition to profl. and consumer groups, 1974—; also radio and TV guest; subject of diet and health mag. interviews. Recipient Papal blessing, 1973; Merit award Concept Therapy Inst., 1974, 75, 78; Merit award Parker Chiropractic Research Found., 1976, also Journalism award, 1980. Mem. Nutritional Counselors of Am., Internat. Health Inst. (cert. metabolic technician), Eastern Holistic Health Assn., Internat. Transactional Analysis Assn., Assn. for Research and Enlightment, Nat. Health Fedn., N.Y. Acad. Scis., Nat. Speakers Assn. Author: Taking Charge; (with others) Positive Power People; columnist Health & Diet Times Jewish. Contbr. articles on nutrition, subconscious mind and holistic health to profl. publs. Office: Holistic Health Services 150-10 79th Ave Flushing NY 11367

NADOR, SALLY JO, clin. social worker; b. Dubuque, Iowa, July 5, 1947; d. Ronald Everett and Geneveive May (Wilson) Northcraft; B.A., U. Ill., Champaign-Urbana, 1969; M.S.W., U. Ill., Chgo., 1972; m. Frank Nador, Dec. 11, 1970; children—Rachel Johanna, Michael Peter. Unit coordinator LaRabida Children's Hosp. and Research Center, Chgo., 1972-74; pvt. practice social work, Chgo., 1972—; mem. Psychotherapy Study Group, 1973-77. Mem. Nat. Assn. Social Workers. Home: 2514 Laurel Ln Wilmette IL 60091 Office: 612 N Michigan Ave Chicago IL 60611

NADRICH, MARION HOLMES, designer, mktg. cons.; b. N.Y.C., May 11, 1949; d. Tolbert and Carrie (Knights) Homes; cert. fine arts Cooper Union, 1970; m. Richard Nadrich, Sept. 16, 1979; 1 son, Garret Richard. Stylist, Van Heusen Shirts, N.Y.C., 1970-74; mdse. mgr. Mann Mfg., Inc. (now Hortex), El Paso, Tex., 1975-76; gen. mdse. mgr. Metro/Pants Co., N.Y.C., 1976-81; pres. Marion Holmes Enterprises Co., N.Y.C., 1981—; career counselor. Mem. Mensa, St. Paulia Soc. (Eng.). Patentee in field. Office: Marion Holmes Enterprises 303 Fifth Ave New York NY 10016

NADZICK, JUDITH ANN, accountant; b. Paterson, N.J., Mar. 6, 1948; d. John and Ethel (McDonald) N.; B.B.A. in Acctg., U. Miami (Fla.), 1971. Staff accountant, mgr. Ernst & Whinney, C.P.A.s, N.Y.C., 1971-78; asst. treas. Gulf & Western Industries, Inc., N.Y.C., 1979—, asst. v.p., 1980—. C.P.A., N.J. Mem. Am. Inst. C.P.A.s, Nat. Assn. Accts., N.Y. State Soc. C.P.A.s, U. Miami Alumni Assn., Delta Delta Delta. Roman Catholic. Home: 280 Lincoln Ave Elmwood Park NJ 07407 Office: 1 Gulf & Western Plaza New York NY 10023

NAGEL, MARY JANE, record/tape retail co. exec.; b. New Rochelle, N.Y., July 15, 1952; d. Lawrence William, Jr. and Frances Theresa (Meehan) N.; student public schs., New Rochelle. Mail order div. mgr. Citadel Record Club, Larchmont, N.Y., 1968-71; record store mgr. Longines Symphonette Stereo, Larchmont, 1971-74; divisional mgr. Sam Goody, Inc., Maspeth, N.Y., 1974-78, record/tape buyer, 1978-81, softgoods adminstrn. mgr., Edison, N.J., 1981—. Mem. Nat. Assn. Female Execs. Roman Catholic. Office: Sam Goody Inc 96 Executive Ave Edison NJ 08817

NAGEL SMITH, TONI ALEKSANDRA SZAMSKI, clin. social worker; b. Balt., Oct. 9, 1946; d. Edward Joseph and Edith Helen (Yankoski) Szamski; B.A., Muhlenberg Coll., 1968; M.S.W., Adelphi U., 1972; m. Thomas J. Smith; children—Jeffrey Roger Nagel, Christopher Glynn Smith. Grad. teaching fellow Adelphi U., 1968-76; clin. social worker, supr. pediatric project Bellevue Hosp., N.Y.C., 1974—; social worker Bedford (N.Y.) Central Sch. Dist., 1974—, Westchester Community Coll., Valhalla, N.Y., 1977-78; pvt. practice clin. social worker, 1975—; adj. prof. Westchester Community Coll.; guest speaker Adv. bd. Dept. Social Services, Mt. Kisco, BOCES Pre-Sch. Programs, Yorktown Heights, N.Y.; mem. Vista (N.Y.) Civic Assn. Mem. Nat. Assn. Social Workers, Acad. Cert. Social Workers, N.Y. State Sch. Social Workers Assn. Home: West Road Box 101 Pound Ridge NY 10576 Office: Bedford Central School District PO Box 180 Mount Kisco NY 10549

NAGLE, JEAN SUE, sociologist, psychologist; b. Detroit; d. Peter and Hedy (Grusczynski) Karabacz; student U. Chgo., 1953-55; M.A., N.Mex. Highlands U., 1960, M.S., 1967; Ph.D., Union Grad. Sch., 1977; postgrad. Bryn Mawr Inst. Women in Higher Edn. Adminstrn., 1981, U. Chgo.; m. Robert D. Nagle, Nov. 20, 1956; children—Carl A., Sonya L., Paula E. Diagnostic technician Vocat. Counseling Inst., Detroit, 1952; research technician United Auto Workers-CIO, Detroit, 1958; clin. psychology intern N.Mex. State Hosp., Las Vegas, 1962-63; clin. psychology trainee VA Hosp., Omaha and Lincoln, Nebr., 1963-64; instr. sociology N.W. Mo. State U., Maryville, 1966-70, asst. prof. sociology and psychology, 1971—. Bd. dirs. Inst. Discourse. N.W. Mo. State U. grantee, 1981, 82. Mem. Am. Psychol. Assn., Am. Sociol. Assn., Midwest Sociol. Soc., Psychology/Sociology Club, World Federalists, Psi Chi, Pi Gamma Mu. Home: 510 W 1st St Maryville MO 64468 Office: Dept Psychology/Sociology NW Mo State U Maryville MO 64468

NAGLE, JOANNE HARRIETT, telephone co. exec.; b. Detroit, Mar. 13, 1946; d. Harry Charles and Margaret Chelton (Harig) N.; B.A., U. N. Ala., 1968; M.B.A., U. Miss., 1970. Jr. acct., Deloitte, Haskins & Sells, N.Y.C., 1970-73; staff auditor GAF Corp., N.Y.C., 1973-74; sr. staff auditor RCA Corp., N.Y.C., 1974-75, Cherry Hill, N.J., 1975-77; mktg. fin. analyst Bell Tel. Co. Pa., Phila., 1977—. C.P.A., N.Y. Mem. Am. Inst. C.P.A.s, N.Y. State Soc. C.P.A.s, N.J. Soc. C.P.A.s, Pa. Inst. C.P.A.s, Nat. Assn. F nale Execs., Am. Soc. Profl. and Exec. Women, Nat. Assn. Accts. Roman Catholic. Home: 50 Georgetowne Rd Lindenwold NJ 08021 Office: 1617 JFK Blvd 13th Floor Philadelphia PA 19103

NAGLE, JUSTINE TERESA, advt. exec.; b. N.Y.C., Feb. 3, 1939; d. Nicholas J. and Marguerite P. (Battle) Nagle; student Pace Coll., 1955-59, Cornell Labor Coll., 1972—, New Sch. for Social Research, 1981—; m. Edward Dillon, Sept. 14, 1957 (div. May 1964); children—

Justine, Stacy. Asst. prod. Geyer Advt., 1957-58, coordinator Rose Marie Reid Bathing Suits, 1958-59; advt. dir. Temas Mag., N.Y.C., 1959-63; with Commerce Advt., N.Y.C., 1963—, v.p., account exec., 1969—; owner, pres. Elgan Communications, N.Y.C., J. Nagles Assocs., 1969—; owner Kibbe Cab Co., 1979—. Vol. worker The Shelter. Mem. Advt. Womens Club, Conservative Club, Met. Opera Guild, Mus. Natural History, Mus. Art. Republican. Clubs: Belle Harbor Yacht, N.Y. Athletic (asso.), Gaslight, Atrium. Home: 301 E 47th St New York NY 10017 also 537 Beach 130 St Belle Harbor NY 11694 Office: 8 W 40th St New York NY 10018

NAGLEY, MADOLYN SUE, menswear co. exec.; b. Columbus, Ohio, July 24, 1952; d. Kenneth Frye and Virginia (McDowell) N.; B.S., Adrian Coll., 1974; guest student Fashion Inst. Tech., 1973. Asst. buyer Abraham & Straus, Bklyn., 1974-75, Lord & Taylor, N.Y.C., 1975-80; merchandising analyst Asso. Merchandising Corp. Co., N.Y.C., 198 -82; v.p. sales Jonathan Bennett Neckwear, Inc., N.Y.C., 1982—. Vol. Bill Green for Congress. Mem. Women's Network of Fifth Ave. (pres.), Women's Assn. Fifth Ave., Phi Gamma Nu, Chi Omega. Republican. Presbyterian. Office: 50 W 34th St New York NY 10001

NAGOT, JOAN YVONNE, mfg. co. acctg. mgr.; b. Fitchburg, Mass., Aug. 12, 1932; d. Joseph and Yvonne (Fortin) Rheaume; student Fairfield U., 1952, 53, Merrills Sch. Bus., 1970; 1 dau., Debora. Accounting clk. Remington Rand, Norwalk, Conn., 1961-65; mgr., owner Hi-Ho Restaurant, Norwalk, 1957-61; gen. acctg. staff Baldwin Gegenheimer, Stamford, Conn., 1966-69; acctg. mgr. Firing Circuits, Norwalk, Conn., 1969—, now asst. treas., asst. sec. Recipient awards Am. Mgmt. Assn., Wharton Sch., N.E. Utilities, SBA. Mem. Nat. Assn. Female Execs., Nat. Assn. Accts., Nat. Assn. Credit Mgrs. Home: 77 E Rocks Rd Norwalk CT 06851 Office: Muller Ave PO Box 2007 Norwalk CT 06852

NAGY, JOAN BARBARA, publishing exec.; b. N.J., Dec. 4, 1943; d. Arthur Joseph and Paula Jean (Rosenburg) N.; B.A., U. N.H., 1965. Prodn. editor Harper & Row, N.Y.C., 1965-68; mng. editor Pitman Pub. Co., 1968-72; mng. editor Hawthorn Books Co., N.Y.C., 1972-76, v.p., 1976—. Home: 155 W 68th St New York City NY 10023 Office: 260 Madison Ave New York City NY 10016 *

NAGY, RUTH THEODORA, acct., tax cons.; b. Freeport, N.Y., Feb. 7, 1924; d. John Daniel and Isabel Anna (Kiss) Kormendy; student U. S.C., 1975; m. Gustave Joseph Nagy, May 6, 1945; children—Robert John, Patricia Jean, Gerald Joseph. With J.D. Kormendy, Acct., Freeport, N.Y., 1938-54; jr. acct. Am. Bus. Credit Corp., N.Y.C., 1941-50; payroll cost acct. C.E. Morris Co., Columbus, Ohio, 1964-65; tax cons., public acct., owner and mgr. Accu-Trol Tax Service, Cayce, S.C., 1967—; enrolled agt. IRS, 1979. Mem. Nat. Assn. Accts., S.C. Tax Council, Nat. Fedn. Ind. Bus. Republican. Baptist. Clubs: Edenwood Garden, Columbia Gem-Mineral Soc. Home: 513 Shady Ln Cayce SC 29033 Office: 924 Axtell Dr Cayce SC 29033

NAHEMOW, LUCILLE DAVIS, psychologist; b. N.Y.C., July 7, 1933; d. William and Flora (Fisher) Davis; B.S. in Psychology, Bklyn. Coll., 1955, M.A., 1957; Ph.D. in Social Psychology (Univ. fellow, NIMH fellow), Columbia U., 1963; m. Martin David Nahemow, 1952 (div. 1966); children—Katharine, Barbara; m. 2d, Stanley Fisher (div.). Teaching fellow, then grad. instr. Bklyn. Coll., 1955-64; research asso. Ednl. Clinic, Hunter Coll., N.Y.C., 1958-59; sr. scientist biometrics research N.Y. State Dept. Mental Hygiene, 1959-66; dir. research Lincoln Hosp.-Albert Einstein Coll. Medicine, 1967-68; research asso., mem. doctoral faculty environ. psychology program City U. N.Y., 1968-71; sr. scientist Phila. Geriatric Center, 1971-76; project dir. N.Y. State Health Dept., 1973-76, HEW, 1975-76; mem. grad. faculty Pratt Inst., 1967-68, CUNY Grad. Center, 1968-71, Sarah Lawrence Coll., 1971-72; dir. div. gerontology; psychologist Lincoln Inst. Psychotherapy, 1976-81; clin. psychologist Bellevue Hosp., 1980-81. N.Y.U. Med. Center 1978-81; dir. Gerontology Ctr., W.Va. U., 1981—. Mem. Am. Psychol. Assn., Eastern Psychol. Assn., Gerontol. Soc., N.Y. State Assn. Gerontol. Educators (pres. 1976), Soc. Psychol. Study Social Issues, AAAS, Piagetian Soc., Nat. Caucus Black Aged, Gray Panthers, Sigma Xi, Psi Chi, Alpha Kappa Delta. Author: (with Pousada) Geriatric Diagnostics, 1983. Editor: Methodology for the Evaluation of Residential Environments for the Functionally Handicapped, 1975; (with others) Establishing Geriatric Teaching Programs, 1983. Contbr. articles profl. jours. Address: Gerontology Ctr WVA U Morgantown WV 26506

NAKACHE, MARGARET ANN, artist; b. Hartford, Conn., Dec. 17, 1932; d. Joseph Charles and Alice Mable (Coyle) Lynch; B.F.A., R.I. Sch. Design, 1954; French cert. L'Ecole Nationale Superieure Des Beaux-Arts, Paris, 1954-56; m. Fernand Robert Nakache, Aug. 17, 1957; children—Catherine, Patricia. Artist, Universal Films, N.Y.C., 1956-57; designer Girl Scouts U.S.A., N.Y.C., 1959-62; one woman shows: Retrospective, Palos Verdes (Calif.) Gallery, 1971, La Gallerie du Meridien, Paris, 1975, 77, 79, Prince Royal Gallery, Alexandria, Va., 1978, Hunter House, Vienna, Va., 1982; group shows include: Art Barn, Washington, 1978, Cape Cod Art Assn., West Barnstable, Mass., 1979, Colvin Mill Run, Va., 1980; represented in permanent collections L'Ambassade du Liban, Paris, Clinique Adda, Creteil, France, Prince Royal Gallery. Mem. Nat. League Am. Pen Women, Vienna Arts Soc., New Eng. Gallery. Roman Catholic. Home: 1448 Woodacre McLean VA 22101

NAKRIN, SYLVIA ROSE, social worker; b. N.Y.C., Mar. 28, 1924; d. Abraham and Gussie (Gordon) Rose; B.A., Bklyn. Coll., 1944; M.S., Columbia U., 1947; m. Jerome Nakrin, Dec. 29, 1946; 1 son, Jeffrey David. Med. social worker N.Y. Postgrad. Hosp., 1943-45, King's County Hosp., 1945-46; cons. personal service dept. N.Y. Fedn. Jewish Philanthropies, N.Y.C., 1946-49; med. social cons. N.Y. State Dept. Public Welfare, 1947; field rep. Ohio Div. Aid Aged, Columbus, 1949-56; chmn. day camps and youth services Columbus Jewish Community Center, 1963-70; v.p. programs Columbus Jewish Center, 1970-72; chmn. youth activities and UAHC camps Temple Israel, Columbus, 1971-77, officer, 1977—; co-recipient Man of Yr. award, 1980; v.p. edn. ORT, 1961-63; v.p. edn. women's div. Columbus Jewish Fedn., 1970-71. Pres. Port Clinton (Ohio) Playmakers, 1953-55. Recipient Continuous dedication award Columbus Jewish Center, 1980. Mem. Nat. Assn. Social Workers, Acad. Cert. Social Workers, Brandeis Univ. Women, Nat. Council Jewish Women, Hadassah. Democrat. Clubs: B'nai B'rith Women, Order Eastern Star.

NALL, ANGIE MARTHA, learning disability specialist, educator; b. Beaumont, Tex., May 25, 1908; d. Ernest L. and Lola (Rachford) Nall; student Lamar U., 1928-29; B.E., Nat. Coll. Edn., Evanston, Ill., 1933; M.A., Peabody Coll., 1938. Tchr. pub. sch. kindergarten, Oak Park, Ill., 1933-35; tchr. pub. schs., Greenville, Miss., 1934-41; primary supr. Tchrs. Coll., Cape Girardeau, Mo., summer 1938; tchr. demonstration nursery sch. in home econs. dept. Beaumont High Sch., 1935-37; dir. Nursery Sch., West Tex. U., summers 1938-41; established Merry Day Sch., nursery sch., 1942-52; dir. Beaumont Remedial Center, 1950-67; dir., mgr. Angie Nall Hosp. for Learning Disabilities, Beaumont, 1967—. Mem. AAUW (dir.), Mental Health Assn. (dir.), Internat. (profl. bd.), Tex. (dir.) assns. for children with learning disabilities. Clubs: Altrusa, Beaumont Bus. and Profl. Author: Step by Step, 1952; also pamphlets, articles in profl. jours. Home: 75 Minor St Beaumont TX 77702 Office: 525 Buford St PO Box 3545 Beaumont TX 77701

NALLS, BONNIE GERMAN, educator; b. Tuscaloosa, Ala., Jan. 27, 1954; d. Fred Bee and Bessie Elizabeth (Hinton) German; student Tenn. State U., 1972-74; B.A., U. Ala., 1977, M.A., 1979; m. William F. Nalls, Jr. Kindergarten tchr. Tuscaloosa City Bd. Edn., 1977—. Mem. NEA, Ala. Edn. Assn., Profl. Educators of Tuscaloosa, Delta Sigma Theta. Democrat. Roman Catholic. Home: 3027 7th St Tuscaloosa AL 35401 Office: 3824 21st St Tuscaloosa AL 35401

NAMM, SUSAN HAMMEL, banker; b. Bklyn., June 28, 1939; d. William J. and Mildred (Henigson) Hammel; B.S., Emerson Coll., 1961; children—Adam Edward, Leslie Ellen. Vice pres., mktg. dir. Westchester Community Health Plan, White Plains, N.Y., 1976-78; v.p., exec. dir. So. Conn. Community Health Plan, Stamford, 1978-80; asst. to v.p. devel. Emerson Coll., 1966-76; dir. public relations Burke Rehab. Center, 1968-69; v.p. Citibank, N.Y.C., 1980—; tchr. Am. Mgmt. Assn., 1977. Active YWCA; tchr. swimming So. Conn. Bus. Assn., 1978-80; founder Westchester Assn. for Gifted and Talented Children, 1974; chmn. Programs of Cultural Enrichment for Children, Richmond, Va., 1967. Recipient award City of Richmond, 1968. Home: 11 Whitewood Rd White Plains NY 10605 Office: 33 Vanderbilt Ave New York NY 10017

NANCE, CECILE ABSTON, dept. store exec.; b. Richland, Wash., Mar. 26, 1945; d. John T. and Jean H. (Hall) Abston; B.S. in Home Econs. Edn., N. Tex. State U., Denton, M.S. in Guidance Counseling. With Neiman Marcus Co., 1967—, personnel mgr., Ft. Worth, then Houston, 1975—. Mem. Retail Mchts. Assn. Houston, Personnel Group Houston (co-chmn.). Republican. Baptist. Address: care Nieman Marcus Co 2600 Post Oak Blvd Houston TX 77056

NANCE, ELEANOR GLENN HANOVER (MRS. JOSEPH MILTON NANCE), artist, librarian; b. McGregor, Tex., Mar. 18, 1920; d. Hiram Howard and Edith Glenn (Crain) Hanover; B.A., Mary Hardin-Baylor Coll., 1941; m. Joseph Milton Nance, Mar. 19, 1944; children—Jeremiah Milton, Joseph Hanover, James Clifton. Arts and crafts counselor summer camps, 1941, 42; art. tchr. elem., high schs., Tex., 1941-43; prodn. illustrator Consol.-Vultee Aircraft Corp., Ft. Worth, 1943-44; draftsman, instrument repair specialist USAAF, Bryan, Tex., 1944-46; pvt. art tchr., substitute tchr. Bryan and College Station Public Schs., 1952-65; book illustrator, 1955—; librarian Tex. A&M U., 1965—. Tchr. kindergarten St. Thomas Episcopal Ch., College Station, Tex., 1951-56; organizer, dir. Brazos Valley Mus., Bryan, Tex., 1960-62, bd. dirs., 1969—, sec., 1970—; v.p. Crockett Elem. Sch. PTA, 1959-60; organizer, dir. College Station Summer Recreational Arts and Crafts Program, 1949, 50; art counselor Arrowmoon (Tex.) dist. Boy Scouts Am., 1958—; mem. Brazos County Hist. Survey Com., 1968—, sec., 1969—; dir. arts and crafts Camp Olympia, Trinity, Tex., 1971-75; sec.-treas. Friends of Tex. A&M U. Library, 1971—; fine arts council Tex. A&M U., 1974—; mem. Brazos County Bicentennial Com., 1976. Mem. D.A.R. (chpt. librarian 1968—, vice regent 1977-80, regent 1980—), Daus. Republic Tex. (chpt. pres. 1963-65), United Daus. of 1812 (v.p. 1976—), Daus. Am. Colonists (v.p. 1977—), Nat. League Am. Pen Women (treas. Brazos Valley br., pres. 1977—), AAUW, UDC (pres. 1968-71), Kappa Pi, Pi Gamma Mu, Sigma Tau Delta. Episcopalian (pres. women's group 1959, 74). Clubs: Art (pres. 1952), Poetry Soc. (pres. 1959-60, v.p. 1980-82) (Bryan-College Station): Women's Social (reporter 1962) (Tex. A&M U.) Contbr. poems, articles, stories, illustrations to mags., books. Illustrator: Becoming Physically Educated in the Elementary Schools, 1969. Home: 1403 Post Oak Circle College Station TX 77840 Office: Tex A and M U Library College Station TX 77843

NANCE, MARY DURHAM, hardware co. exec.; b. Danville, Va., Jan. 8, 1914; d. James Ambrose and Ambrose (Hill) Durham; student public schs.; m. John Francis Nance, May 12, 1940; 1 son, John Francis. Various secretarial positions, 1933-52; sec.-treas. Pittsylvania Hardware Co., Inc., Danville, Va., 1952—. Mem. Danville C. of C. (dir.), Bus. and Profl. Women's Club, Danville Mus. Fine Arts and History. Mem. Christian Ch. (Disciples of Christ). Home: 144 Fairmont Circle Danville VA 24541 Office: 816 Monument St Danville VA 24541

NANOVIC, CATHY LYNN, data processing cons. co. exec.; b. Schenectady, Nov. 12, 1949; d. William Ralph and Janice Ruth (Harries) Bradt; B.S., SUNY, Albany, 1971; m. Robert Thomas Nanovic, Apr. 2, 1977; children—Olivia Anne, Francesca Nicole. Programmer trainee Mergenthaler Linotype Co., Plainview, N.Y., 1973-75; programmer analyst Info. Concepts, Inc., N.Y.C., 1975-76; sr. systems analyst MacKay-Shields Fin. Corp., N.Y.C., 1976-77; asst. mgr. info. services Goldman Sachs & Co., N.Y.C., 1977-78; v.p. data processing Applied Computer Enterprises, Inc., N.Y.C., 1978-81; pres. Nanovic Assocs., N.Y.C., 1981—; registered rep. N.Y. Stock Exchange. Address: 30 Waterside Plaza New York NY 10010

NAPOLI, DALE SKYDANEK, Realtor; b. Richmond, Va., Sept. 8, 1945; d. Bernard and Jean (Clarke) Skydanek; student Coll. William and Mary, 1963-65; m. John Paul Napoli, Jan. 8, 1965 (div.); children—Andrea Louise, Paul Bernard. Project mgr. Davis Devel. Inc., Manassas, Va., 1970-72; asso. realtor Sudley Realty Inc., Manassas, 1972-73; broker, sales mgr. Century 21 Old Dominion Properties, Manassas, 1973-75; asso. broker Long & Foster Realtors, Manassas, 1975-82; sales mgr. Manassas office Mt. Vernon Realty, 1982—. County del., Va. Republican Conv., 1973. Mem. Prince William Bd. Realtors (1st v.p. 1980; salesperson of yr. 1978, realtor of yr. 1980), Nat. Assn. Realtors, Va. Assn. Realtors, No. Va. Bd. Realtors (top producer 1978, 79, 81), Women's Council Realtors (Va. pres. 1982), Nat. Mktg. Inst. (cert. residential specialist), Omega Tau Rho. Mem. Order Eastern Star. Home: 9644 Park St Manassas VA 22110 Office: 7820 Sudley Rd Manassas VA 22110

NAPOLI, DONNA JO, linguist; b. Miami, Feb. 28, 1948; B.A., Radcliffe Coll., 1970; Ph.D., Harvard U., 1973; m. Barry Ray Furrow, Dec. 29, 1968; children—Elena, Michael Enzo, Nicholas Umberto, Eva. Mem. faculty Smith Coll., Northampton, Mass., 1973-74, U. N.C., Chapel Hill, 1974-75, Georgetown U., Washington, 1975-80; mem. faculty U. Mich., Ann Arbor, 1980—, asso. prof. linguistics, 1982—. Nat. Endowment Humanities fellow, 1979; NSF grantee, 1981-83. Mem. Linguistic Soc. Am. Author: (with Emily Rando) Syntactic Argumentation, 1979; contbg. editor The Linguistic Muse, 1980; editor: Elements of Tone, Stress and Intonation, 1978, (with W. Cressey) Linguistic Symposium on Romance Languages: 9, 1981; contbr. articles to profl. jours. Home: 1809 Hill St Ann Arbor MI 48109 Office: Dept Linguistics U Mich Ann Arbor MI 48104

NARCINI, DEBORAH ANTOINETTE, ednl. adminstr.; b. Trenton, Apr. 20, 1953; d. Richard Raymond and Antoinette Lillian (DiMemmo) N.; B.A. summa cum laude, Trenton State Coll., 1975; M.T.S., Harvard U., 1975-77; M.A., Yale U., 1979, M.Phil., 1980, postgrad., 1981—. Research librarian Donald E. Gastwirth, lawyer, New Haven, Conn., 1980-81; teaching fellow Yale U., New Haven, 1980-81; legis. analyst N.J. Sch. Bds. Assn., Trenton, 1982—. Mem. Internat. Musicological Soc., Am. Musicological Soc., Am. Assn. Advancement Humanities, Mediaeval Acad. Am. Home: 57 Main Blvd Trenton NJ 08618 Office: New Jersey School Boards Association 315 W State St Trenton NJ 08605

NARDI, THEODORA PATRICIA, state legislator; b. Warwick, R.I., Aug. 28, 1922; d. Alfred Freeman and Carlotta Manente (Golini) McAlpine; student Manhattanville Coll. Sacred Heart, 1940-43; m. Bernard V. Nardi, June 7, 1943; children—Carlotta, Vincent, Bernard V., Josephine. Asst. to supt. of Roman Cath. Schs., Diocese of Manchester, 1960-71; mem. N.H. Ho. of Reps., 1971-82, chmn. appropriations subcom. on health and welfare, 1979-82, vice chmn. Manchester legis. del., 1975-78, chmn., 1979-82. Chmn., Merrimack Valley Regional Conf. on Edn., 1964; mem. Mayor's Com. on Econ. Opportunity, 1966-69; founder Manchester SMILE (serving Manchester's Ill, Lonely and Elderly); mem. adv. bd. Manchester Vocat.-Tech. Coll., 1974-80; chmn. Gov.'s Commn. for Handicapped, 1979—; mem. N.H. Council for Better Schs.; bd. dirs. Pine Haven Boys Center; pres. N.H. Public Broadcasting Council, 1973-75; mem. policy com. White House Conf. Aging, 1980; mem. adv. bd. Manchester Community Corrections Center; mem. adv. council Nat. Cath. Conf. Bishops, 1974-77; alt. del Democratic Nat. Conv., 1968; chmn. Hillsborough County Dem. Com., 1977-79. Recipient Hon. Citizens award City of Manchester, 1970; Outstanding Service award Manchester Mental Health Center, 1979; Outstanding Service award N.H. Assn. Mental Health, 1978; Disting. Alumni award Manhattanville Coll., 1979; Bancroft award N.H. Psychiat. Soc., 1980; Legislator of Yr. award N.H. Assn. Retarded Citizens, 1981. Mem. Order Women Legislators (past sec., v.p., pres. 1979—), Manhattanville Alumnae Assn. (dir.). Home: 776 Chestnut St Manchester NH 03104

NARDINI, MARY LOIS, educator; b. Evansville, Ind., Oct. 10, 1931; d. Franklin Walter and Grace Melone (Thompson) Richwine; B.S., Ind. Tchrs. Coll., 1952; M.S., Ind. State Coll., 1965; Ph.D., So. Ill. U., Carbondale, 1973; m. William Nardini, Aug. 5, 1978; children—Lynn Probio, Jane Bradshaw. Tchr., Evansville (Ind.) Vanderburgh Sch. Corp., 1952-53, Vigo County Sch. Corp., Terre Haute, 1953-54; prof. edn. Ind. State U., Terre Haute, 1965—. Mem. Republican Precinct Com., 1970-78; bd. dirs., mem. sanctuary choir Prairieton (Ind.) United Meth. Ch., 1970-72; leader Girl Scouts Am.; ward chmn. Am. Heart Assn.; canvasser, publicity Multiple Sclerosis Soc. Mem. Assn. Ind. Media Educators, Assn. Ednl. Communications and Tech., Ind. Film Council, Ind. Ednl. Research Assn., Mortar Bd., Delta Kappa Gamma, Kappa Delta Pi, Alpha Phi Gamma, Gamma Phi Beta. Author: (with Patricia Quinett) Fundamentals of Bulletin Board Designs, 1979; editor: Ind. Assn. Ednl. Communications and Technology Newsletter, 1973-76; contbr. articles to profl. jours. Home: RR 21 Box 65 Terre Haute IN 47802 Office: Sch Edn Ind State U Terre Haute IN 47808

NARISI, STELLA MARIA, heavy equipment mfg. co. exec.; b. Fort Smith, Ark., Oct. 24, 1950; d. Vincent J. and Norma J. Narisi; B.B.A., U. Tex., 1972, J.D., 1975. Admitted to Tex. bar, 1975; staff atty. enforcement div. Tex. State Securities Bd., Houston, 1975-79; corp. sec., in-house counsel Marathon Mfg. Co., Houston, 1979—. Mem. Am. Bar Assn., Tex. Bar Assn., Houston Bar Assn. Club: Houston Sailing. Office: 1900 Marathon Bldg 600 Jefferson Houston TX 77002

NARLOCK, VIRGINIA ROSE, med. technologist, educator; b. Ladysmith, Wis., Oct. 3, 1940; d. Joseph and Stephanie Rosalie (Majerski) Mikula; B.S. in Med. Tech., U. Wis., 1962, M.S. in Edn. for Profl. Devel., 1982; m. Donald Gene Narlock, Sept. 21, 1963; 1 son, Tyrone Eugene. Blood bank technologist St. Joseph's Hosp., Marshfield, Wis., 1962-64, blood bank supr., 1964-75, edn. coordinator med. tech. program, 1970—; program dir. lab. edn. programs Joint Venture Lab. of St. Joseph's Hosp. and Marshfield Clinic. Chairperson community ARC blood drives. Mem. Am. Soc. Med. Technologists, Wis. Assn. for Med. Technologists, Wis. Assn. Blood Banks, Am. Soc. Clin. Pathologists, Clin. Lab. Mgmt. Assn., Delta Kappa Gamma. Roman Catholic. Home: Box 48 Route 5 Marshfield WI 54449 Office: 1000 N Oak Ave Marshfield WI 54449

NARON, NANCY KLASTORIN (MRS. MICHAEL KATIMS), educator; b. N.Y.C., Apr. 30, 1949; d. Louis and Edwyna (Wachtel) Klastorin; B.A., Northwestern U., 1971, M.A., 1972, Ph.D., 1976. Instr., Northwestern U., 1974-75, Fall, 1977-78; cons. Dept. Research and Evaluation, Chgo. Bd. Edn., 1975-77, project coordinator Chgo. EARLY Project, 1977-78, curriculum devel. specialist dept. spl. edn., 1978-80, early childhood curriculum specialist dept. curriculum, 1980—. Mem. adv. bd. dept. spl. edn. Northeastern Ill. U. 1979—. Mem. AAAS, Assn. Children with Learning Disabilities, Am. Ednl. Research Assn., Am. Psychol. Assn., Nat. Assn. Edn. Young Children, Phi Delta Kappa. Contbr. articles to profl. jours. Home: 1314 Main St Evanston IL 60202 Office: 228 N LaSalle St Room 822 Chicago IL 60601

NAROV, FRUMA, structural engr.; b. Germany, Oct. 25, 1947; d. Abraham and Paula Arieli; B.S., Technion, Israel Inst. Tech., 1968; m. David Narov, Jan. 25, 1970; children—Hilla, Yoav. Structural engr. Lev Zetlin Assocs., Inc., N.Y.C., 1970-72, sr. structural engr., 1972-76, assoc., 1978—; project engr. Cannon Design Inc., Buffalo, 1977-78. Served to lt. Israeli Def. Forces, 1968-70. Registered profl. engr., N.Y. Mem. ASCE. Jewish. Office: Lev Zetlin Assocs Inc 95 Madison Ave New York NY 10016

NARUSIS, REGINA GYTÉ FIRANT, lawyer; b. Kaunas, Lithuania, Oct. 12, 1936; d. Victor and Eugenia S. (Cesnavicius) Firant; brought to U.S., 1949, naturalized, 1955; B.A., U. Ill., 1957, J.D., 1959; m. Bernard V. Narusis, June 19, 1959; children—Victor John, Ellen Marie, Susan Marie. Admitted to Ill. bar, 1960; partner firm Narusis & Narusis, Cary, Ill., 1961—; city atty. City of McHenry (Ill.), 1973—; village atty. Fox River Grove, Ill., 1967-73; asst. state's atty., McHenry County, Ill., 1968-75, head juvenile div., 1968-75. Mem. McHenry County Bd. Health, Woodstock, Ill., 1964-75; mem., pres. Dist. 46 Sch. Bd., McHenry County, 1964-79; mem. McHenry County Welfare Services Com., 1968-75; mem. Mem. adv. com. Bert H. Boerner Meml. Trust, Woodstock, 1972—; mem. adminstrv. council, mem. exec. bd. Marian Central Cath. High Sch., 1981—, v.p. council adminstrn., exec. bd., 1982—. Mem. Ill. Bar Assn., McHenry County Bar Assn., Women's Bar Assn., Am. Judicature Soc., Nat. Dist. Attys. Assn., Kappa Beta Pi. Address: 213 W Lake Shore Dr Cary IL 60013

NASH, EDNA MAY, counseling psychologist; b. Parksville, B.C., Can., Nov. 2, 1922; d. William and Harriet Ann (Plummer) McDermid; B.Ed., U. B.C., 1963, M.Ed., 1970; m. Arthur Bernard Nash, Dec. 27, 1943; children—Sylvia, Rosemary, Barbara, Gregory. Tchr., Pioneer Mine, B.C., 1942-43, Kitsilano High Sch., Vancouver, B.C., 1943-44; counselor, tchr. Vancouver Schs., 1956-69; head counseling dept. Britannia Tupper Templeton Secondary Schs., Vancouver, 1969-73; area counselor Vancouver Public Schs., 1973-80; vis. lectr. U. B.C., 1976—; pvt. practice counseling psychologist, Vancouver, 1977—; cons. various sch. dists. B.C., 1973—. Bd. dirs. Internat. Com. for Adlerian Summer Schs. and Insts., 1973—. Mem. N.Am. Soc. Adlerian Psychology (exec. com. 1974-82, pres. 1979-80), Can. Guidance and Counseling Assn., B.C. Psychol. Assn., Adlerian Psychology Assn. B.C., B.C. Sch. Counselors Assn. New Democrat. Roman Catholic. Home: 302-2020 Bellevue Ave West Vancouver BC V7V 1B8 Canada

NASH, ELIZABETH IVES, securities co. exec.; b. West Chazy, N.Y., Aug. 5, 1909; d. Alfred Peabody and Eleanor Collista (Stoughton) Ives; student bus. colls.; m. Maynard Nash, Dec. 7, 1929; 1 son, Paul Ives. Sec., treas., dir. Maynard Nash, Inc., contractor, Stamford, Conn., 1950-68; asst. v.p. Hardy, Hardy & Assos., Sarasota, Fla., 1961-76; stock broker, fin. planning exec. Raymond, James & Assos., Inc., mem. N.Y. Stock Exchange, Sarasota, 1976—. Mem. N.Y., Phila., Balt., Washington stock exchanges. Bd. dirs. First Step. Mem. Mut. Fund Council, Internat. Fin. Planners. Club: Field (Sarasota). Home: 1601 Pelican

Point Dr H215 Sarasota FL 33581 Office: 1718 Main St Sarasota FL 33577

NASH, HELEN ELIZABETH, pediatrician; b. Atlanta, Aug. 8, 1921; d. Homer Erwin and Marie (Graves) N.; B.A., Spelman Coll., 1942; M.D., Meharry Med. Coll., 1945; m. James B. Abernathy, Aug. 1, 1964. Intern, resident Homer Phillips Hosp., St. Louis, 1945-49; asso. prof. clin. pediatrics Washington U., St. Louis, 1949—; practice medicine specializing in pediatrics, St. Louis, 1949—; pediatric supr. H.G. Phillips Hosp., 1949-64; mem. staff St. Louis Children's Hosp., St. Luke's Hosp., Jewish Hosp. of St. Louis, St. Louis Maternity Hosp.; mem. Mo. Welfare Commn., 1969-73. Diplomate Am. Bd. Pediatrics. Mem. St. Louis Med. Soc. (Hon. life), Mo. Med. Soc., AMA, Am. Acad. Pediatrics, St. Louis Pediatric Soc. Home: 5783 Lindell Blvd St Louis MO 63112 Office: 1441 N Grand St Saint Louis MO 63106

NASH, MARIAN LLOYD (MRS. HAROLD H. LEICH), lawyer, editor; b. La., Jan. 31, 1924; d. Richard Melville and Annie Margaret (Lloyd) Nash; B.A. with honors, Sophie Newcomb Meml. Coll., 1942; LL.B., Loyola U. South, New Orleans, 1946; LL.M., Georgetown U., 1969; m. Harold H. Leich, July 19 (dec.). Admitted to La. bar, D.C. bar; with Dept. State, 1952—, with Fgn. Service, 1952-64, with Office of Legal Adviser, 1961—. Mem. La. Bar Assn., D.C. Bar Assn., Am. Soc. Internat. Law, Law Librarians Soc. D.C., Colonial Dames of 17th Century, DAR. Editor, Digest of U.S. Practice in Internat. Law. Home: The Westchester 4000 Cathedral Ave NW Washington DC 20016 Office: Office of Legal Adviser Dept State Washington DC 20520

NASH, MARILYN JEAN, editor, author; b. Houston, Oct. 17, 1950; d. Alfred Leroy and Doris Jean (Anderson) Lewis; B.B.A., U. Houston, 1975; m. Shannon T. Nash, Apr. 11, 1980; 1 dau. by previous marriage, Angela Christine Rittel. Acctg. clk. Gulf Oil Corp., Houston, 1971-75; mktg. rep. AM Internat., Houston, 1976-80; self-employed copywriter, 1980—; cons. in field; staff Houston Area Women's Ctr. Mem. Nat. Assn. Female Execs., Phi Gamma Nu Alumni. Republican. Club: Zonta. Contbr. articles, short stories to various publs.

NASH, MYRTLE CORLISS, psychologist; b. Long Island City, N.Y., Mar. 7, 1915; d. Augustin Pride and Hazel Keene Corliss; A.B., Swarthmore Coll., 1937; M.A., Bryn Mawr Coll., 1938, Ph.D., 1950; postgrad. NSF Inst., Beloit Coll., 1968; m. Thomas Nash, July 17, 1943; 1 son, Patrick Corliss. Asst. prof. Drake U., Des Moines, 1952-54; asso. prof. Southwestern U., Memphis, 1954-62, Converse Coll., Spartanburg, S.C., 1962-67; prof. psychology Keuka Coll., Keuka Park, N.Y., 1967-71; clin. psychologist Spartanburg Area Mental Health Center, 1971—, program evaluator, 1974—. Fellow in psychology Bryn Mawr U., 1938-39, 48-49. Mem. Am. Psychol. Assn., Southeastern Psychol. Assn., Soc. for Psychol. Study of Social Issues. Democrat. Unitarian. Contbr. articles in field to profl. publs. Home: 134A Oakwood Ave Spartanburg SC 29302 Office: 149 East Wood St Spartanburg SC 29303

NASH, RUTH COWAN (MRS. BRADLEY D. NASH), journalist; b. Salt Lake City, Utah; d. William Henry and Ida (Baldwin) Cowan; A.B., U. Tex., 1923; m. Bradley D. Nash, June 30, 1956. Tchr. pub. high sch., San Antonio, 1924-27; reporter San Antonio Evening News, 1928, United Press, 1929; corr. AP, Chgo., 1929-40, Washington, 1940-43, 45-56, war corr., North Africa, Gt. Britain, Europe, 1943-45, retired, 1956; free lance journalist, 1956—; asst. to undersec. of health edn. and welfare, 1958-61; pres. Travelers Service, Inc., Charles Town, W.Va. Cons., pub. relations dir. women's div., Republican Nat. Com., Washington; mem. Def. Adv. Com. on Women in the Services, 1958-61. Clubs: Washington Press (pres. 1947-48), Overseas Press, Am. Newspaper Women's; Writer and Press (London). Home: High Acres Farm Box 122 Route 3 Harpers Ferry WV 25425

NASH-MORGAN, LEONORA ELIZABETH, surgeon; b. Holyoke, Mass., Aug. 13, 1910; d. George Harlan and Edna Doris (Snell) Nash; B.A., Mt. Holyoke Coll., 1932, M.A., 1933; fellow Harvard U., 1933-34; M.D. (W.K. Kellogg grantee), U. Mich., 1939; m. John Dickinson Morgan, Aug. 27, 1947; children—John Dickinson, Leonora Elizabeth, Harlan Kellogg, Elizabeth Emily. Intern, resident in surgery U. Mich., 1938-39; physician Iowa State Coll., Cedar Falls, 1939-40; pvt. practice medicine and surgery, Erie, Ill., 1941-54, Moline, Ill., 1954—; chmn. utilization rev. com. Oak Glen Nursing Home, Coal Valley, Ill.; lectr. medicine, childhood, adolescence, marriage; mem. staff Lutheran, Moline Public hosps. Mem. Moline Youth Commn., 1964-68; physician Rock Island County Free Venereal Disease Clinic, 1975-77; mem. Center Study of the Presidency, 1976—, nat. adv. council, N.Y.C., 1979—. Recipient article of recognition Moline Dispatch, 1982. Fellow Am. Acad. Family Physicians; mem. Ill. Acad. Family Physicians (past pres., past dir., past del. Rock Island chpt.), Rock Island County Med. Soc., Ill. Med. Soc., Am. Assn. Physicians and Surgeons, AMA, Internat. Soc. Advanced Edn., Alpha Epsilon Iota. Republican. Episcopalian. Clubs: Harvard (Chgo.); Sanderling (Sarasota, Fla.). Research on permeability of capillaries, lymphatic system, tetanus; inventor specialized humidifier, 1975. Office: 1630 5th Ave Moline IL 61265

NASON, DORIS ELNORA, emeritus educator; b. North Girard, Pa., Apr. 25, 1913; d. Roy B. and Emma (Dean) Nason; student Edinboro (Pa.) State Coll., 1930-32; B.S. in Edn., Boston U., 1947, M.Ed., 1948, Ed.D., 1951. Elementary tchr. Union Twp., Pa., 1932-35, Union City, Pa., 1935-42, Millcreek Twp., Pa., 1942-43, 45-47; Link Trainer instr. USN, Sanford, Fla., 1943-45; teaching fellow elementary edn. Boston U., 1948-50, lectr. edn., summers 1948-50; asst. prof. edn. U. Conn., 1950-61, asso. prof. edn., 1961-70, prof., 1970-75, acting dir. reading-study center, 1969-72, dir., 1972-75, dir. Reading Resources Network Center in Conn., 1970-75, prof. emeritus, 1975—; adj. prof. Stetson U., 1978—; cons., lectr. in reading field; cons. for reading diagnosis in-service audio cassette program Scholastic Mags., 1975. Mem. Conn. Assn. Reading Research, Nat. Conf. Research English, Internat., New Eng. (mem. exec. bd., 1964-68, pres. 1966-67, pres. Eastern Conn. council 1974-75) reading assns., Fla. State Reading Council (disabled reader group), AAUW (pres. Daytona Beach br. 1979-81), NOW, Internat. Platform Assn., Pi Lambda Theta (adviser Beta Sigma chpt., life mem., faculty sponsor), Phi Delta Kappa. Democrat. Mem. United Ch. of Christ. Author (with Robert Norris, Herbert Tag and Richard Neville) Foundations for Elementary School Teaching, 1963; contbg. author: Educational Innovation, 1975. Editor: Teacher Education Quar., 1957-58; mem. editorial bd. 1952-66. Contbr. articles to profl. jours. Home: 95 Seminole Ave Ormond Beach FL 32074

NAST, CAROL ANN, diagnostic co. exec.; b. Champaign, Ill., Nov. 8, 1945; d. Christian Anthony and Lelia Mae (Glover) Nast; B.S., M.S., Tex. Christian U. Med. technologist Harris Hosp., Ft. Worth, 1967-72; chief med. technologist Presbyn. Hosp., Dallas, 1972-73; mfg. dir. Nuclear Med. Labs., Dallas, 1973—; adv. bd. Women in Sci. Program U. Tex., Arlington. Mem. Am. Prodn. and Inventory Control Soc., Am. Soc. Clin. Pathologists (asso. mem., cert. med. technologist), Sierra Club, Mensa. Clubs: Dallas Cross Country, Aerobics Center. Home: 2709 Belmeade Carrollton TX 75006 Office: 8700 Stemmons Freeway Dallas TX 75245

NATHAN, EDITH, artist; b. Leipzig, Germany, June 2, 1910; s. Josef and Johanna Schwartz; student Acad. Art Leipzig, Acad. Art Copenhagen, N.Y. U., Art Students League N.Y.C., with Carl Schmitz, Chaim Gross; m. Leo Nathan, Apr. 21, 1929; children—Ruth, Henry. One woman shows Fla. Atlantic U., 1975, Hollywood Art Mus., 1971, Neiman Marcus, Miami Beach, Fla., 1974, Staudt Gallery, Boca Raton, Fla., Lighthouse Gallery, Tequesta, 1980, Nova U., 1982; exhibited in group shows Bacardi Gallery, Miami, 1969-70, Bay Harbor Gallery, Miami, 1970, Palm Beach Gallery, 1975, 76, Harmon Gallery, Naples, Fla., 1978, 79 Coral Springs (Fla.) Artists Guild, 1975, 78, 79, 81, Patricia Judith Gallery, Boca Raton, 1982, others; instr. painting and sculpture Boca Raton Ctr. for Arts, 1974—, also Coral Springs Artists Guild; also restoration painting. Recipient awards Am. League Pen Women, Allied Art of North Miami, Broward Art Guild, also Hall of Fame award Nova U. Mem. Nat. League Am. Penwomen, Coral Springs Artists Guild and Cultural Soc.

NATHAN, GRACE JUNE, sales promotion co. exec.; b. Chgo., June 1, 1919; d. Joel Charles and Mary Frances (Majewska) Benjamin; 2 yr. diploma Wright Coll., 1938; B.S., U. Chgo., 1940; M.S., U. Ill., 1942; postgrad. U. Tex., 1948-49, Cornell U., 1956-57; m. Edward Reub Nathan, Apr. 5, 1975. Instr., Wright Coll., Chgo., 1943; bacteriologist Chgo. Health Dept., 1944-45; asst. sci. editor World Book Ency., Chgo., 1946-47; chief geology librarian U. Tex., Austin, 1948-49; instr. Texarkana (Tex.) Coll., 1950-52; editor Instrumentation Mag., 1953-55; acct. exec. Fulton Morrissey Advt. Agy., Chgo., 1958-61; v.p. Product Exposure, Inc., Chgo., 1961-73, pres., 1973—; cons. to various marketing firms. Mem. Am. Inst. Econ. Research, Am. Friends Austria, Council Fgn. Relations, Art Inst. Chgo., Premium Advt. Assn. Am., Assn. TV Merchandisers. Home: 3200 N Lake Shore Dr Chicago IL 60657 Office: 11 E Hubbard St Chicago IL 60611

NATHAN, ILSE BRILL, clin. counselor, psychotherapist; b. Montevideo, Uruguay, Dec. 28, 1937; came to U.S., 1956; d. Otto and Lotte (Kutzen) N.; B.A., Queens Coll., 1966; M.A., Hunter Coll., 1972; cert. Postgrad. Center for Mental Health, N.Y.C., 1972; m. Jay Mannes Brill, Feb. 2, 1969; children—Andra N., Eric Arden. Dir. individual, marital, personal, adolescent child treatment staff L.I. Consultation Center, N.Y.C., 1975—; pvt. practice psychotherapy, N.Y.C., 1974—; cons.-counselor to pvt. schs., 1974—; faculty staff Postgrad. Center for Mental Health, N.Y.C., 1980-81. Lic. high sch. tchr., N.Y., N.J.; lic. nurse, N.Y., N.J.; cert. clin. counselor. Mem. Am. Mental Health Counselors Assn., N.J. Mental Health Counselors Assn. (pres. 1980-81), Am. Personnel and Guidance Assn., N.J. Personnel and Guidance Assn., Nat. Assn. Social Workers, Tenafly C. of C. Home: 14 Homestead Rd Tenafly NJ 07670 Office: 150 E 74th St New York NY 10021

NATHAN, LESLEY JILL, television news producer, dir.; b. Waterbury, Conn., Apr. 17, 1950; s. Gustave and Sylvia (Crystal) N.; student Art Students League N.Y., 1968-70. Mem. staff Lewron TV, broadcast videotape co., N.Y.C., 1971-74; dir. studio and remote ops. Nat. Video Center, N.Y.C., 1975-78; freelance producer and dir. videotapes, including numerous commercials, specials, and series, N.Y.C., 1978-81; prodn. supr. net-work news CBS-TV, 1981—. Recipient Outstanding Service award Art Dirs. Club. Mem. Videotape Producers Assn., Nat. Acad. TV Arts and Scis.

NATHAN, PATRICIA ARLENE, health planner, demographer; b. Antigua, W.Indies, Aug. 1, 1952; came to U.S., 1961, naturalized, 1967; d. Patrick Anthony and Victoria Venita (Peters) N.; B.A. in Sociology, Lincoln U., Pa., 1975; M.A. in Demography (univ. fellow), Brown U., 1980. Research asst. Inst. Policy Research and Evaluation, Lincoln U., 1974-75; demographic cons. Brown U., 1975-76; planning asso. V.I. Planning Office, 1977; health plan developer V.I. Health Planning Agy., 1977-79, acting dir., sr. health planner, 1979—; mem. Gov. V.I. Alien Impact Com., 1977-78, V.I. Census Planning Com., 1978-79; mem. interagy. planning com. V.I. Planning Office, chairperson population impact subcom.; chairperson space utilization task com. V.I. Health Dept. Bd. dirs. Operation Sisters United, V.I., The Girls Center, St. Thomas. Mem. V.I. Public Health Assn., Bus and Profl. Women's Club (St. Thomas), St. Thomas Women's League, Alpha Kappa Alpha (founder, sec. Mu Gamma Omega chpt. 1980, v.p. chpt. 1982). Methodist. Home: Redhook Center Box 62 Saint Thomas VI 00801 Office: 1 Regjerings Gade Saint Thomas VI 00801

NATHANS, ELIZABETH STUDLEY, coll. dean; b. Springfield, Mass., Oct. 29, 1940; d. Robert Anson and Katherine Crossley (Sweet) Studley; A.B., Vassar Coll., 1962; M.A., Johns Hopkins U., 1964, Ph.D. (Social Sci. Research Council research tng. fellow 1964-65), 1966; m. Sydney Harold Nathans, Aug. 13, 1966; children—Heather Shawn, Stephen Frederick. Instr. history Towson (Md.) State Coll., 1965-66; lectr., then asst. prof. U. N.C., Chapel Hill, 1966-71; asst. dean instrn. Woman's Coll., Duke U., Durham, N.C., 1971-72, asst. dean for freshmen Trinity Coll., 1972-80, asst. dean Trinity Coll., dir. Pre-Maj. Advising Center, Duke U., 1980—; cons. in field. Unitarian. Author: Losing The Peace: Georgia Republicans and Reconstruction, 1968; also articles, papers. Office: Pre-Maj Advising Center Duke U Durham NC 27706

NATHANSON, SUSAN DEE DIAMOND, speech pathologist; b. N.Y.C., Mar. 4, 1942; d. Charles Herbert and Hana (Mackler) Diamond; B.A., Adelphi U., 1963, postgrad., 1977; M.A., Bklyn. Coll., 1966; postgrad. U. Ky., 1966-67, N.Y. U., 1978; m. Barry Frank Nathanson, Aug. 21, 1966; children—Richard Andrew, Laurie Jill. Speech improvement tchr., N.Y.C. public schs., 1963-66; speech pathologist United Cerebral Palsy, Lexington, Ky., 1966-67; clin. supr. Speech Center, U. Ky., Lexington, 1966-67; speech pathologist Orthopedically Handicapped unit Bur. for Speech Improvement, N.Y.C. Bd. Edn., 1967-70; pvt. practice, N.Y.C., 1970-74; tchr. lang. arts orthopedic unit, N.Y.C., 1974-75; tchr. deaf, speech pathologist Herricks public schs., New Hyde Park, N.Y., 1975—; pvt. practice, 1980—, Berrent Reading and Learning Center, Manhasset, N.Y., 1981—. Mem. Am. Speech and Hearing Assn., N.Y. State Speech and Hearing Assn. Office: Herricks Public Schs New Hyde Park NY 11540

NATILSON, NANCY LEE, internat. banker; b. Buffalo, July 1, 1952; d. Arnold Issac and Kane (Klein) Natilson; B.A., U. Pa., 1973; M.B.A., N.Y.U., 1979. Ednl. therapist Altro Health & Rehab., N.Y.C., 1975-77; internat. banking officer Crocker Nat. Bank, San Francisco, 1979-81, asst. rep., Caracas, Venezuela, 1981—. Mem. Venezuelan-Am. C. of C., Assn. Reps. Fgn. Banks in Venezuela. Club: Altamiro Tennis. Home: Los Tulipanes II B-9 6th Transversal Los Palos Gardens Caracas Venezuela Office: Crocker Nat Bank Apartado 61754 Caracas 1060 Venezuela

NATYSON, FRANCES, psychologist, educator; b. New Haven, Nov. 20, 1923; d. John Harry and Rozalia Natyson; R.N., Yale-New Haven Hosp. Sch. Nursing, 1946; B.A. in Psychology, Hunter Coll., 1969; M.A., New Sch. for Social Research, 1972; Ed.D., Columbia U., 1982. Various nursing positions at hosps. in N.Y.C., including Bellevue Hosp., Presbyn. Hosp., Roosevelt Hosp. and Hosp. For Cancer and Allied Diseases, 1946—; alcoholism counselor Cabrini Med. Center, N.Y.C., 1972—; pvt. practice counseling and psychotherapy. Mem. Mayor's com. on alcohol problems in schs., 1973. Mem. Am. Psychol. Assn., Soc. Behavioral Medicine, Am. Nurses Assn., N.Y. State Nurses Assn., Soc. for Public Health Edn., Inst. of Society, Ethics and Life Scis., N.Y. Fedn. of Alcoholism Counselors, Union Concerned Scientists, Kappa Delta Pi. Contbr. articles in field to profl. jours. Home: 562 West End Ave New York NY 10024

NAUD, PATRICIA ANN, tax practitioner; b. Washington, July 26, 1936; d. George W. and Beatrice (Hopkins) Ryan; enrolled to practice before IRS, 1973; children—Terree Naud King, Lorri, Jeannine. Self-employed tax practitioner, 1965—; organizer ann. practical tax seminar, San Diego County, Calif., 1976. Recipient Pub. Service award Alpine (Calif.) Fire Protection Dist., 1974. Mem. Am. Soc. Women Accountants, Nat. Assn. Enrolled Agts. (dir., pres. San Diego chpt.), Calif. Soc. Enrolled Agts. (pres.), Alpine C. of C.; life mem. Alpine Youth Center, Alpine Library Friends Assn. Office: PO Box 652 Alpine CA 92001

NAUGHTON, JODIE-KAY MARIE, mfg. co. exec.; b. Chgo., Sept. 9, 1951; d. Joseph Martin and Evelyn Marie (Milne) N.; A.B.A., Wright City Coll., 1979; student Lakeland Coll., 1980—; m. Robert Anthony Memmel, Jr., Nov. 17, 1979. With Western Electric Co., various locations, 1969—, customer service rep., 1979-80, payroll and acctg. specialist, Milw., 1980—. Bd. dirs. Future Pioneers, 1979, Concerner Consumers League Inc., Milw.; adviser Jr. Achievement, 1974, 75; v.p. Wright Newman Ctr., 1977; creator Weco Wackos, clown troupe, 1978; asst. adminstr. Midwest Region Hunger Project, 1980. Mem. Nat. Abortion Rights Action League. Home: 8032 N 45th St Brown Deer WI 53223 Office: 4353 N Richards St Western Electric Co Milwaukee WI 53212

NAUGHTON, MARIE ANN, speech-lang. pathologist; b. Boston, Feb. 19, 1954; d. Robert J. and Beatrice T. (McDonald) N.; B.S. in Speech magna cum laude, Emerson Coll., 1976; M.A., Ind. U., 1977. Speech-lang. pathologist Dedham (Mass.) public schs., 1977-79; speech-lang. pathologist Mass. Gen. Hosp., Boston, 1979-81; speech pathologist Mt. Auburn Hosp., Cambridge, Mass., 1982—. Mem. Am. Speech, Lang. and Hearing Assn. (cert. clin. competence), Mass. Speech and Hearing Assn., Boston Area Clin. Aphasiology Group, Zeta Phi Eta. Author: A Coarticulation Manuel for the Remediation of /S/, 1979. Home: 77 Circuit Rd Dedham MA 02026 Office: Speech Pathology Dept Clark Bldg Mt Auburn Hosp 330 Mt Auburn St Cambridge MA 02138

NAUGLE, CHARLOTTE JUNE, educator; b. Long Beach, Calif., June 1, 1938; d. Robert F. and Florence A. (Smith) Ballenger; A.A., San Bernardino Valley Coll., 1959; B.A., Calif. State U., 1966, M.A., 1978; m. John R. Naugle, Jr., June 26, 1965; children—Roberta Lynn, Marina Rae. Tchr., Barstow (Calif.) Sch. Dist., 1966, U.S. Dependent Sch., Kenitra, Morocco, 1967-69; tchr., bilingual coordinator, state demonstration tchr. Colton (Calif.) Sch. Dist., 1970—, Title I project dir., 1981—; ednl. cons.; extension instr. Calif. State U., San Bernardino, 1975-77. Public edn. chmn. San Bernardino-Riverside Counties, Am. Cancer Soc., 1979-81. Recipient Competent Toastmasters award, 1981; Outstanding Tchr. of Writing, Inland Area Writing Project, U. Calif., Riverside, 1980. Mem. Nat. Assn. Exec. Women, Assn. Supervision and Curriculum Devel., NEA, Calif. Reading Assn., Internat. Reading Assn., Phi Delta Kappa. Republican. Clubs: Order Eastern Star, Writers Circle, Toastmasters (internat. pres. 1980, div. ednl. v.p. 1981). Home: 17358 El Molino St Bloomington CA 92316 Office: 10009 Spruce St Bloomington CA 92316

NAUGLE, HELEN HARROLD, educator; b. West Point, Miss., Aug. 11, 1920; d. Judson N. and Helen (Weddle) Harrold; A.B., Miss. U. for Women, 1942; M.A., U. Miss., 1950; Ph.D., U. Ala., 1962; m. Jefferson B. Naugle, June 1, 1942; children—Helen Elizabeth Naugle Deibler. Tchr., elem. sch., West Point, Miss., 1943; asst. prof. English, U. Miss., Oxford, 1951-52; tchr., asst. dir. U.S. Armed Forces Inst., Mariannas Islands, 1952-53; prof. English, Ga. Inst. Tech., Atlanta, 1962—; grader advanced placement Ednl. Testing Service, 1974—. Nat. Endowment Humanities grantee, 1956-58; recipient Outstanding Tchr. award Alcoa, 1978. Mem. AAUW, Am. Soc. 18th Centuray Studies, Johnsonian Soc., Mortar Bd., Phi Kappa Phi. Methodist. Author: A Concordance to the Poems of Samuel Johnson, 1972. Home: 3929 Wieuca Rd Atlanta GA 30342 Office: Dept English Ga Inst Tech Atlanta GA 30332

NAURECKAS, KATHLEEN KEARNEY, newspaper exec.; b. Mt. Pleasant, Pa., Oct. 12, 1936; d. Christopher James and Adeline Regina (Murtha) Kearney; B.S. in Journalism, Northwestern U., 1958; m. Edward M. Naureckas, Sept. 20, 1958; children—Karen, Edward, James, Barbara. Editorial asst. Maclean-Hunter Pub. Corp., Chgo., 1958-59; successively reporter, women's editor, news editor, mng. editor Paddock Circle Newspapers, Mundelein, Ill., 1970-77; successively copy editor, asst. picture desk editor, graphics coordinator Chgo. Tribune, 1977—. Mem. Chgo. Press Club, Sigma Delta Chi. Home: 31482 N S O'Plaine Rd Gurnee IL 60031 Office: 435 N Michigan Ave Chicago IL 60611

NAVARRO, JOAQUINA, educator; b. Madrid, Sept. 1, 1916; d. Tomas and Dolores Guirao N.; B.A., Instituto Escuela, Madria, 1934; M.A., Columbia U., 1942, Ph.D., 1954. Instr., Smith Coll., Northampton, Mass., from 1943, prof., from 1963, now prof. emeritus. Social Sci. Research Council fellow, 1960-61. Mem. Am. Assn. Tchrs. Spanish and Portuguese, MLA, Instituto Internat. de Literatura Iberoamericans. Author: La Novela Realista Mexicana; contbr. articles to profl. jours. Home: 24 Hastings Heights Northampton MA 01060

NAVRATILOVA, MARTINA, profl. tennis player; b. Prague, Czechoslovakia, Oct. 18, 1956; came to U.S. 1975, naturalized, 1981; d. Miroslav Navratil and Jana Navratilova; student schs. in Czechoslovakia. Profl. tennis player, 1975—. Winner Czechoslovak Nat. Singles, 1972-74, U.S. Indoor Singles, 1975, Va. Slims Tournament, 1978, Wimbledon Singles Championship, 1978, 79, 82, French Open Singles, 1982, Wimbledon Doubles, 1982, Family Circle Cup, 1982, Fedn. Cup, 1982. Named hon. citizen Dallas Mem. Women's Tennis Assn. (dir. exec. com.). Office: care US Tennis Assn 51 E 42d St New York NY 10017 *

NAY, FLORENCE MORGAN, food processing equipment exec; b. Erie, Pa., Nov. 1, 1930; d. Earl Sears and Hazel M. (Perdue) Morgan; B.S., George Washington U., 1952; m. David S. Nay, May 26, 1962; children—Maria Anne, Anthony Mark. Ct. reporter, 1952-56; partner Columbus Arts & Crafts Supplies (Ohio), 1966-70; pres. Food Processing Ingredients, Worthington, Ohio, 1979-80; pres. Food Processing Supplies, Inc., also Seasonings Etcetera, Columbus, 1980—; chmn. bd. Barb Hall Studio. Chmn. profl. adv. com. Dominican Sisters of Sick and Poor, 19 ; mem. fin. com. St. Timothy Roman Cath. Ch., Columbus, 1978-79; sec. Twin Rivers Assn. Chs., 1976-78; pres. Elizabethan Guild, 1970-71; active local Democratic campaigns. Mem. Young Guard Soc. of Food Processing Industry, Ohio Meat Industries Assn., Ohio Food Processors Assn., Psi Iota Xi. Home: 5951 Tulip Hill Rd Box 294 Worthington OH 43085 Office: 407 N Grant Ave Columbus OH 43215

NAYLOR, CARLENE ANN, ednl. adminstr.; b. Canton, Ohio, Aug. 5, 1949; d. Carl William and Evelyn Vera (Friesel) Noretto; B.A., San Jose (Calif.) State U., 1976, teaching credential, 1979, M.B.A., 1981. Accountant, Kay Jewelers, Burlingame, Calif., 1971-72; asst. purchasing agt., accountant Am. Housing Guild, San Jose, 1972-74; bus. mgr. Franklin-McKinley Sch. Dist., San Jose, 1974-78; dir. bus. services/fin. dept. Santa Clara County Office Edn., San Jose 1978—; cons., lectr. in field. Mem. Am. Mgmt. Assn., Nat. Assn. Female Execs., Calif. Assn. Sch. Bus. Ofcls. Home: 863 Kevenaire Dr Milpitas CA 95035 Office: 100 Skyport Dr San Jose CA 95115

NEAL, CAROLYN ELIZABETH, advt. agy. owner; b. New Brunswick, N.J., Dec. 1, 1947; d. Charles William and Gertrude Helene (Wasilewski) Arnold; B.A. in Fine Arts, Calif. State U., Long Beach,

1971; m. James Edward Neal, Mar. 30, 1970; children—Victoria Elizabeth, Christopher Charles. Various secretarial and bookkeeping positions, 1967-75; pres., owner Kay Barr Fashions, Garden Grove, Calif., 1978-81; gen. partner BDN Bookkeeping and Tax Service, Westminster, Calif., 1982—; bus. mgr. Neyman Co. Advt., 1982—; sec., chief fin. officer WFN Corp., 1978—; corp. sec. Westminster Trading Inc., 1979—. Vice pres. Assistance League Garden Grove, 1978. Mem. Calif. State U. Long Beach Alumni Assn. (pres. 1979). Democrat. Roman Catholic. Office: 12095 Brookhurst St Garden Grove CA 92640

NEAL, FLORA MYRTLE, pub. co. exec.; b. Bridgeport, Conn., Sept. 15, 1934; d. Charles Nelson and Florence Eleanor (Bevans) Nichols; student LaSalle Extension U., 1968-69; m. Charles Orville Neal, Sept. 26, 1953 (div. 1980); children—Donna Lee, Linda Susan. With Billboard Pubs., 1967-78, bus. mgr., 1976-78; bus. mgr. F & W Pub., Cin., 1978—, also book club dir.; book club cons. Elder, chmn. parish life com. West Chester Presbyn. Ch. Club: Ohio Valley Direct Mktg. (treas.). Office: 9933 Alliance Rd Cincinnati OH 45242

NEAL, KATHY, city ofcl.; b. Los Angeles, Aug. 9, 1949; d. Elvin Vernon and Doris Eva (Golden) N.; student U. So. Calif., 1974-75; B.A., Calif. State U., Los Angeles, 1975; postgrad. U. San Francisco, 1980—; cert. in Spanish, U. Salamanca, 1967. Dir., Little Playmates Childrens Center, Los Angeles, 1971-74; legis. analyst Los Angeles City Council, 1975—; fund raising cons.; dir. Builders Mut. Surety Co. Bd. govs. Calif. Community Colls., also chmn. legis. and adminstrv. com., 1981—; mem. Calif. Democratic Central Com., 1979—; sponsor, adv. Black Womens Forum, 1979—; bd. dirs. Miss Watts Summer Pageant, 1976—; chmn. politics com. Coordinating com. Internat. Womens Yr. State Conf., 1977; asst. coordinator telethon United High Blood Pressure Found., 1978; Mem. Am. Soc. Public Adminstrs., Alpha Kappa Alpha. Office: 200 N Spring St Suite 255 Los Angeles CA 90012

NEAL, LAVON WITHAM, utility co. exec.; b. Ponca City, Okla., Jan. 26, 1932; d. Francis O. and Myrtle A. Witham; B.B.A., U. Okla., 1954. Stanolind Oil & Gas Co., Oklahoma City, 1954-56, with Continental Oil Co., Houston, 1956-57; with Okla. Natural Gas Co., Tulsa, 1957—, exec. asst. to chief exec. officer, asst. treas. and asst. sec., 1974-76, v.p., 1976—. Bd. dirs. Family and Children's Services, Inc., Tulsa, Better Bus. Bur., Tulsa, Mental Health Assn., Tulsa. Mem. Tulsa C. of C., Am. Gas Assn., Nat. Investor Relations Inst., Women in Energy, Pi Beta Phi. Republican. Presbyterian. Office: PO Box 871 Tulsa OK 74102

NEAL, LINDA NEEDHAM, personnel exec.; b. Oak Ridge, Tenn., Aug. 25, 1947; d. William Kenneth and Beatrice Diane (Dezube) Needham; B.S., U. Tenn., 1969; M.B.A., U. Tenn., 1976. Indsl. relations rep. Union Carbide Corp., Nuclear Div., Oak Ridge, Tenn., 1970-74, supr. job analysis, 1974-75; compensation adminstr. Sverdrup Tech., Inc., Tullahoma and Arnold AFS, Tenn., 1975-81, adminstr. compensation and benefits, 1981—. Bd. dirs. Coffee County Mental Health Assn./Multi-County Comprehensive Mental Health Center, 1980—, v.p., 1981—. Mem. Am. Compensation Assn., Nat. Assn. Female Execs., Am. Soc. Personnel Adminstrn., Internat. Assn. Personnel Women, Nat. Mgmt. Assn. (pres. bd. 1980-81), Highland Rim Personnel Assn. (v.p. 1978-79, pres. 1979-80). Home: PO Box 1227 Tullahoma TN 37388 Office: PO Box 884 101 W Lincoln St Tullahoma TN 37388

NEAL, MARGARET (MRS. PETER S. PATRIQUIN), editor; b. Springfield, Mass., Aug. 21, 1933; d. Robert Miller and Helen (Smith) N.; ed. Stephens Coll., U. Wis., U. Mo., Tulsa U.; Levintritt fellow in chamber music; student Yale U. Summer Music Sch.; children—Dorcas Alicia, Judith Elaine, Keith Lowell Neal. Profl. musician, 1945-62; advt. copywriter, group head Grey Advt. Inc., 1962-66; freelance advt. copywriter, 1966—, freelance copy editor, 1966-73; asst. v.p. editorial Bur. Bus. Practice div. Prentice-Hall, Waterford, Conn., 1973—; mng. editor Fair Employment Practices Guidelines, Exec. Action Series. Past pres. West River Village, Guilford, Conn., 1976-77; past mem. public relations com. Hammonassett Sch. Author: Management and the Metric System, 1975; Executives Desk Guide to Key Legal Problems, 1979, others. Home: 7 Mather Trail Old Lyme CT 06371 Office: 24 Rope Ferry Rd Waterford CT 06386

NEAL, MARIANA LUISA, med. technologist; b. Biloxi, Miss., Nov. 5, 1953; d. James Walter and Maria Luisa (Benitez) Neal; B.S. in M.T., Mich. State U., 1975; M.S., U. Mich., 1980. Med. tech. internship William Beaumont Hosp., Royal Oak, Mich., 1975-76, bench technologist, 1976-79; hematology supr. Crittenton Hosp., Rochester, Mich., 1979—; adj. instr. hematology Ferris State U., Big Rapids, Mich., 1979—; instr. Mercy Coll. Detroit, 1980. Mem. Oakland Soc. Med. Technologists (pres.), Am. Soc. Clin. Pathology, Am. Soc. Med. Tech., Mich. Soc. Med. Tech., Am. Soc. Allied Health Profls. Roman Catholic. Contbr. articles to profl. jours. Home: 1677 Bloomfield Pl Apt 518B Bloomfield Hills MI 48013

NEAL, MARIE AUGUSTA, sociologist; b. Brighton, Mass., June 22, 1921; d. Thomas Francis and Helen Agnes (Taylor) N.; A.B., Emmanuel Coll., Boston, 1942; M.A., Boston Coll., 1953; Ph.D., Harvard U., 1963. Joined Sisters of Notre Dame de Namur, Roman Cath. Ch., 1943; high sch. tchr., Mass., 1946-53; mem. faculty Emmanuel Coll., 1953—, prof. sociology, 1963—; vis. prof. U. Calif., Berkeley, 1969, Harvard U. Div. Sch., 1973-75; dir. Nat. Sisters Survey, 1966-74, 80-82; dir. S. African Cath. Edn. Study, 1981-82; research asso. in women's studies in religion program Harvard Div. Sch., 1982-83; vis. scholar Harvard U. Div. Sch., 1982-83; Furfey lectr., 1981; Selwyn lectr., 1981. Mem. Gov. Mass. Commn. Status Women, 1964-67; adv. com. Mass. Civil Liberties Union, 1972-74. Ford Found. grantee 1974-76. Mem. Am. Sociol. Assn., Soc. Sci. Study Religion (pres. 1982-84), Assn. Sociology in Religion (pres. 1971-72), Internat. Sociology Assn. Democrat. Author: Values and Interests in Social Change, 1965; A Sociotheology of Letting Go, 1977; Sisters Survey, 2d edit., 1980. Home: 4 Murdock Terr Brighton MA 02135 Office: Dept Sociology Emmanuel Coll Boston MA 02115

NEAL, SARAH LEE, state legislator; b.; b. Kanawha County, W.Va., Feb. 24, 1924; d. Joseph Ruffner and Frankie B. (Kelley) Parcell; student Greenbrier County Schs.; m. Clifton P. Neal.; children—Cynthia P., Clifton P., C. Patrick. Real estate broker; mem. W.Va. Ho. of Dels. from 4th Dist., 1972-74, 20th Dist., 1974—. Bd. dirs. Potomac House Nursing Home; pres. bd. dirs. Rainelle (W.Va.) Mcpl. Public Library; mem. Greenbrier Valley Hist. Soc.; bd. dirs. Greenbrier Retirement Village; mem. Rainelle Med. Center Black Lung Council, Pearl Buck Birthplace Found., Inc., Nat. Order Women Legislators, W.Va. Hwy. Safety Leaders, Southeastern Forest Protection Assn. Recipient W.Va. Wildlife Fedn. award, 1973-76. Mem. Bus. and Profl. Women's Club, Alpha Kappa Gamma. Democrat. Methodist. Clubs: Order Eastern Star, Order of Rainbow for Girls (mother advisor), Rainelle Woman's. Office: West Virginia House of Dels Charleston WV 25305 *

NEALE, BETTY IRENE, state legislator; b. Hiawatha, Kans., May 20, 1933; children—Dory Alan, Steve, Scott. Asst. treas., office mgr., pub. relations officer telephone supply co.; mem. staff Colo. Ho. of Reps., 1969-71; asst. to adminstr. fed. grants Office of Auditor, Denver, 1971-74; now mem. Colo. Ho. of Reps., vice-chmn. appropriations com., mem. interim health, environ., welfare and instns. com. Mem. Commn. on Children and Their Families; chmn. Correctional Industries Adv. Com. Mem. English-Speaking Union. Republican. Presbyterian. Office: Colo Ho of Reps State Capitol Denver CO 80203 *

NEASE, JUDITH ALLGOOD, marriage and family therapist; b. Arlington, Mass., Nov. 15, 1930; d. Dwight Maurice Allgood and Sophie (Wolf) Allgood Morris; student Rockford Coll., 1949-50; B.A., N.Y.U., 1953, M.A., 1954; M.S., Columbia U. Sch. Social Work, 1956; m. Theron Stanford Nease, Sept. 1, 1962; children—Susan Elizabeth, Alison Allgood. Social worker Bellevue Psychiat. Hosp., N.Y.C., 1956-59; psychiat. social worker St. Luke's Hosp., N.Y.C., 1959-62; asst. psychiat. social worker supr. N.J. Neuropsychiat. Inst., Princeton, 1962-64; marriage and family therapist Druid Hills Pastoral Counseling Service, Atlanta, 1973—, asst. dir. social work supr., co-leader group, 1973—; asst. dir., co-leader Pastoral Counseling Service, Columbia Theol. Sem., 1973—; marriage and family therapist Catholic Social Services, Atlanta, 1978—; pvt. practice marriage and family therapy. Mem. Nat. Assn. Social Workers, Acad. Cert. Social Workers, Am. Assn. Marriage and Family Therapy, MLA, Am. Group Psychotherapy Assn., Eastern Group Psychotherapy Assn., Southeastern Group Psychotherapy Assn., Atlanta Group Psychotherapy Assn. Republican. Episcopalian. Home: 310 Missionary Dr Decatur GA 30030 Office: 680 W Peachtree St NW Atlanta GA 30308 also 310 Missionary Dr Decatur GA 30030

NEASE, MARIAN PEARLMAN, lawyer; b. N.Y.C., May 20, 1940; B.A., Cornell U., 1961; LL.B., U. Pa., 1964. Admitted to N.Y. bar, 1965, D.C. bar, 1970, U.S. Supreme Ct. bar, 1969, also Fla. bar; atty., adv. U.S. Dept. Interior, Washington, 1966-68; legal adv. Four Corners Regional Commn., Farmington, N.Mex., 1968-69; asso. firm Strock & Stroock & Lavan, Washington, 1969-71; nat. treas. McGovern Presdl. Campaign, Washington, 1971-73; legal dir. Office Commonwealth of P.R., Washington, 1973-74; spl. counsel United Mine Workers Am. Health and Retirement Funds, Washington, 1974-78; asso. firm Holland & Knight, Ft. Lauderdale, Fla., 1978-81; commr. Fed. Mine Safety and Health Rev. Commn., Washington. Mem. Am. Bar Assn., D.C. Bar Assn., Fla. Bar.

NEBIL, CORINNE ELIZABETH, artist; b. Varmland, Sweden, Apr. 30, 1918; came to U.S., 1920, naturalized, 1942; d. Eric and Elisabet (Tillstrom) Erickson; student NAD, 1954, Traphagen Sch. Fashion, 1955-56, Art Students League, N.Y.C., 1949-52, Whitney Sch. Art, 1948, U. Bridgeport, 1955; 1 dau., Ninette. Co-owner The Little Gallery, Bridgeport, Conn., 1954-60; art dir. Kid Stuff mag., 1964; free lance fashion illustrator, 1976-81; one-woman shows: Westport Country Playhouse, 1955, Chappalier Gallery, N.Y.C., 1958, Radio City Music Hall, N.Y.C., 1955, others; group shows: Art-U.S.A., Madison Sq. Garden, N.Y.C., 1948, Pastel Soc. Am., N.Y.C., 1982, Smithsonian Instn., Washington, 1965, others; represented in numerous pvt. collections; instr. art Famous Artists Schs. Internat., Westport, Conn., 1975-76, Central Fla. Jr. Coll., 1981—, Silvermine Sch. Art, Norwalk, Conn., 1980, Bridgeport Art League and Conn. Classic Arts Workshop, 1981-82. Mem. Nat. League Am. Penwomen, Conn. Classic Arts, Pastel Soc. Am. Designer, painter ceiling mural St. Joseph's Ch., Bridgeport, Conn., 1958. Home: 104 Edward St Fairfield CT 06430 also 853 NE 10th Ave Ocala FL 32670

NEDDE, JOYCE FERRIS, lawyer; b. Cin., May 7, 1937; d. Ladell H. and Ruth (Clark) Ferris; B.A., Northwestern U., 1958; postgrad. Harvard U. Law Sch., 1958-59; J.D., U. Louisville, 1961; m. Norman Robert Nedde, Aug. 26, 1961; children—Crystal, Susan-Marie. Admitted to Ky. bar, 1961, U.S. Supreme Ct. bar, 1966, Calif. bar, 1967; atty. Corps Engrs., Louisville, 1961-62; atty. Ky. Dept. Hwys., Frankfort, 1963-64; asst. atty. gen., Frankfort, 1964-66; dep. atty. gen., San Francisco, 1966-72; dep. dist. atty., Monterey County (Calif.), 1972-74, Santa Clara County (Calif.), San Jose, 1974—. Mem. Ky. Gov.'s Commn. on Status Women, 1965-66. Mem. Santa Clara County Bar Assn. (trustee), Santa Clara County Women Lawyers (pres. 1977), Queen's Bench (pres. 1971-72), AAUW, Zeta Tau Alpha. Home: 15996 Grandview Ave Monte Sereno CA 95030 Office: 70 W Hedding St Suite 5W San Jose CA 95110

NEE, LINDA ELIZABETH, social worker; b. Boston, Dec. 29, 1938; d. Thomas Markham and Ellen Thomas (Jamieson) Nee; B.A., Russell Sage Coll., 1961; M.S. in Social Work, Va. Commonwealth U., 1968. Social worker, social service dept., N.Y. Neurol. Inst., Columbia Presbyn. Med. Center, N.Y.C., 1961-66; med. social worker Tb San., Med. Coll. Va., Richmond, summer 1967; clin. social worker social work dept. Clin. Center, NIH, Bethesda, Md., 1968-74, clin. research social worker sect. exptl. therapeutics, lab. clin. sci., NIMH, Bethesda, 1974—; mem. ethics com. Md. State Bd. Social Work Examiners, 1979—. Adv., organizer, bd. dirs. Met. D.C. chpt. Alzheimer's and Related Diseases Assn., 1979—. Mem. Nat. Assn. Social Workers (chmn. ethics and grievances 1977-79; pres. Met. Washington 1975-77). Editor: Jour. Social Work Met. Washington, 1975-77; columnist: The Bulletin newsletter Nat. Assn. Social Workers, 1975-77; contbr. articles to profl. jours. Office: Clin Center NIMH Bethesda MD 20205

NEE, M. COLEMAN, coll. pres.; b. Taylor, Pa., Nov. 14, 1917; d. Coleman James and Nora Ann (Hopkins) N.; A.B., Marywood Coll., Scranton, Pa., 1939, M.A., 1943; M.S., U. Notre Dame, 1959. Joined Sisters of Immaculate Heart of Mary, Roman Cath. Ch., 1941; high sch. tchr. Scranton Public Schs., 1939-41, Marywood Sem., Scranton, 1943-55; asso. prof. math. Marywood Coll., Scranton, 1959-68, pres., 1970—. Adv. bd. Scranton YWCA, 1978—, Jr. League of Scranton, 1981—. Named Outstanding Pennsylvanian, 1980. Mem. Pa. Assn. Colls. and Univs. (exec. com.), Commn. Ind. Colls., Am. Assn. Colls., Nat. Assn. Ind. Colls., Assn. Cath. Colls. Address: Marywood Coll Scranton PA 18509

NEEDELMAN, BARBARA, research health scientist; b. Phila., July 23, 1943; d. Alec and Margaret Grace (Pollina) N.; B.A., Beaver Coll., 1965; postgrad. Temple U., 1965-66. With dept. pediatrics Southwestern Med. Sch., Dallas, 1968-71; research technician dept. human genetics U. Pa., Phila., 1971-75; supervisory research health sci. specialist VA Hosp., Phila., 1975—; partner Danielle Hair & Makeup Salon, 1979—. Co-founder Women Organized Against Rape, mem. steering com., sec., 1972-75. Mem. Soc. Research Adminstrs. Home: 721-A South St Philadelphia PA 19147 Office: 151E VA Hosp 39th and Woodland Ave Philadelphia PA 19104

NEEDLE, SUSAN JUDITH, image cons.; b. Newark, June 18, 1941; d. Joseph J. and Betty (Levinson) N.; B.Ed., U. Miami (Fla.), 1962; M.A. in Human Resources and Psychology, U. Houston, 1980. Tchr. public schs., Fla., 1963-72, Houston, 1973-77; part-time profl. model, 1974-79; sales mgr. ADF Services, Houston, 1975-80; event mgr. Summit Arena, Houston, 1980—; pres. Colorific, Inc., Houston, 1976—. Named Outstanding Educator in Fla., 1968. Mem. Nat. Assn. Female Execs. (dir.), Exec. Link, Am. Inst. Esthetics, Hotel Sales Mgmt. Assn., Performax, Alpha Epsilon Phi, Alpha Kappa Alpha. Democrat. Jewish. Address: 15302 Pleasant Valley Rd Houston TX 77062

NEESE, GERTRUDE ELIZABETH FLESH KENNEDY, realty co. exec.; b. N.Y.C., Mar. 9, 1925; d. Bernard William and Dorothy Katherine (Reimund) Flesh; B.A., U. Havana (Cuba), 1944; m. Alonzo Aldrich Neese, Nov. 10, 1978 (dec. Aug. 1981); children—Christopher H. Bohner, Stephen Edward Bohner, Karen Elizabeth Bohner. Stewardess-purser Pan Am. World Airways, 1945-47; pvt. investments, Rio de Janeiro, Brazil, Coral Gables, Fla. and N.Y.C., 1947-57; pres. Lockhart Realty, Inc., Sewall's Point, Jensen Beach, Fla., 1957—, also dir.; pres., dir. Sewall's Point Estates, Inc., Jensen Beach, Lockhart Sales, Inc., Jensen Beach, Lockhart Devel., Inc., Sewall's Point, v.p., dir. Dunes Club, Hutchinson Island, Stuart, Fla.; chmn. Sewall's Point Code Enforcement Bd. Pres. United Fund of Sewall's Point, 1958-70, bd. dirs., 1958—; trustee Martin County (Fla.) Library, Martin County Hist. Soc.; bd. dirs. Am. Cancer Soc. Mem. Nat. Inst. Real Estate Brokers, Am. Inst. Real Estate Appraisers, NAREB, World Wings Internat., Fla. Assn. Realtors. Clubs: Bay Harbor, Yacht and Country (dir.) (Stuart); Sakonnet Golf (Little Compton, R.I.). Home and Office: 2 N Sewall's Point Rd Stuart FL 33494

NEFF, FRANCINE IRVING, corp. dir., former U.S. treas.; b. Albuquerque, Dec. 6, 1925; d. Edward Hackett and Georga (Henderson) Irving; B.A., U. N.Mex., 1948; D.H.L. (hon.), Mt. St. Mary's Coll., Newburgh, N.Y., 1974; LL.D. (hon.), Am. Internat. Coll., Springfield, Mass., 1975, N.Mex. State U., Las Cruces, 1976; m. Edward John Neff, June 7, 1948; children—Sindle Neff Tomforde, Edward Vann. Thirty Fifth Treas. of U.S. Treasury Dept., 1974-77, also nat. dir. U.S. Savs. Bonds div., 1974-77; v.p. Rio Grande Valley Bank, Albuquerque, 1977-82; dir. Hershey Foods Corp., 1978—, E-Systems, Inc., Dallas, 1978—. Active Republican Party, 1966—; pres. Albuquerque Rep. Federated Women's Club, 1977, Rep. Women's Fed. Forum, 1975; chmn. N.Mex. Women for Nixon Campaign Com., 1968; del. Rep. Nat. Conv., 1968, 72; mem. exec. com. Rep. Nat. Com., 1972-74, nat. committeewoman for N.Mex., 1970-74. Mem. nat. bd. Camp Fire Girls, 1976-78; campaign chmn. profl. div. United Way Greater Albuquerque, 1977, bd. dirs., 1977-79; bd. advs. Lovelace Med. Center, 1979-82; mem. def. adv. com. Women in the Services, 1981—; bd. trustees Cottey Coll., 1982—; bd. dirs. Horatio Alger Assn. Disting. Ams., 1981—. Recipient Disting. Alumnae citation Cottey Coll., Nevada, Mo., 1975, Horatio Alger award Am. Schs. and Colls. Assn., 1996, Exceptional Service award Treasury Dept., 1976. Mem. Am. Bankers Assn. (banking adv. 1979-81), Nat. Assn. Banking Women, Nat. Assn. Bus. and Profl. Women, PEO (past chpt. pres.), Mortar Board (past chpt. pres.), Phi Theta Kappa (Outstanding Alumni award 1976), Alpha Delta Pi (chpt. Outstanding Alumna award 1975, past chpt. pres.), Sigma Alpha Iota, Pi Lambda Theta. Episcopalian.

NEGLEY, JULIE CARITHERS, mus. dir.; b. Atlanta, May 18, 1960; d. Edward Ernest and Mary Howard (Watkins) Carithers; B.A., Agnes Scott Coll., 1982; m. Joseph Leslie Negley, Aug. 22, 1981. Research intern Atlanta Hist. Soc., summer 1980, research asst., 1980; archtl. survey project assoc. Atlanta Preservation Center, Atlanta Urban Design Commn., 1981; research cons. Soil Systems, Inc., Marietta, Ga., 1981; rare books asst. U. Ga. Libraries, Athens, 1981-82; mus. dir. Washington-Wilkes Hist. Mus., Washington, Ga., 1982—. Mem. Atlanta Hist. Soc., Ga. Trust for Historic Preservation, Washington-Wilkes Found., Agnes Scott Coll. Alumni Assn. Presbyn. Office: Washington-Wilkes Hist Mus 308 E Robert Toombs Ave Washington GA 30673

NEGLEY, SHIRLEY ANNE, educator; b. Pitts., May 4, 1937; d. Ronald Dickson and Helen (King) N.; B.S.N., U. Pitts., 1960, M.N.Ed., 1966. Staff nurse Allegheny Gen. Hosp., Pitts., 1960, head nurse, 1960-61, mem. faculty Sch. Nursing, 1961-64; instr. obstetric nursing Pa. State U. Sch. Nursing, Pitts., 1966-67; mem. faculty U. Pitts. Sch. Nursing, 1967—, assoc. prof., program dir. adult primary health care nursing, 1979—; cons. Pa. Bd. Nurse Examiners, 1981-82. Mem. Am. Nurses Assn., Nat. League Nursing, Sigma Theta Tau. Home: 5 Coral Dr Pittsburgh PA 15238 Office: 426 Victoria Hall Pittsburgh PA 15261

NEIDITCH, STEPHANIE LOUISE, structural and interior designer; b. Los Angeles, Apr. 12, 1941; d. Ozzie and Libby Faye (Gilner) Wolfberg; student Am. Sch. Religion, 1964; m. Dennis Jeffery Neiditch, Sept. 22, 1974; children—Jova St. Ives Geller, Kabrel Geller, Kiara Geller, Timon Neiditch, Judah Neiditch, Tobiah Neiditch. Structural and interior designer Rainbow Devel. Co., 1976—. Pres., Christians of Tijunga Sunland, 1973-74; tchr. Women's Aglow Fellowship, 1975. Mem. Bldg. Industries Assn. Republican. Pentecostal Christian. Home: 24421 Timon Ln Newhall CA 91321 Office: 23030 Lyons Ave PO Box 490 Newhall CA 91322

NEIFERT-BERTHOUEX, CLARA WINONA, advt. agy. exec.; b. Laurel, Md., Oct. 2, 1936; d. Martin Samuel and Dorothy Hildreth (Bowman) Ulsaker; student public schs., France; m. Merle Neifert, Aug. 16, 1957; children—Julie Brett Neifert Ridlon, Kriston Shane; m. 2d, Albert Keith Berthoux, May 11, 1980. With Jacksonville (Ark.) Daily News, 1968-73, Sta. WHBQ-TV, Memphis, 1973-76; owner, officer Cit Neifert & Assocs., Memphis, 1978—. Bd. dirs. Big Bros. Pulaski County, 1971-73. Mem. Mid-S. Advt. Agy. Assn. (pres. 1982—), Am. Women in Radio and TV (pres. 1973-74, 74-75), Ark. Newspaper Execs. Assn. (v.p. 1971-73), Jacksonville C. of C. Mem. Ch. of Jesus Christ of Latter Day Saints. Office: 1555C Lynfield St Memphis TN 38119

NEIL, JESSIE PRUITT, civic worker; b. Pasadena, Calif., Oct 20, 1927; d. Cecil D. and Jessie (Parsons) Pruitt; B.A., U. So. Calif., 1950; m. Edmund R. Neil, Mar. 24, 1956; children—Edmund R. II, Jessica R., Richard William. Dir. design Leland Gardens Bldg. Corp., 1950-56; sales dir. Washington Sq. Bldg. Corp., 1950-1952; pres. Barrett Devel. Corp., 1951-72; sec. Reliance Bldg. Corp., 1951-68; self-employed home designer, 1953; sec. So. Counties Escrow, 1956-76; pres. Futuramic Homes, Inc., 1956-68. Founder Cardiac League Guild of Huntington Meml. Hosp., 1963, pres., 1966, 67, pres. Women's Council, 1967; v.p. San Marino League, 1968-72; v.p. docent council Pasadena Mus. Modern Art, 1969, pres. docent council, 1971-72, mem. membership council, ex-officio trustee, 1971-72; mem. Assistance League. Asso. U. So. Calif.; mem. women's council KCET/28; patron Pasadena Art. Mus.; hon. life mem. Arcadia Meth. Hosp.; mem. costume council Los Angeles County Mus.; founder Los Angeles Music Center, also mem. blue ribbon 400. Recipient graphics award Pasadena Arts Council, 1968. Mem. Docent League So. Calif., Nine O'Clock Players, AIM (asso.), Opera Assos. of Met. Opera, World Affairs Council, Internat. Platform Assn. Delta Zeta. Home: 301 Hermosa St South Pasadena CA 91030

NEILL, REGINA ISABEL, oil co. exec.; b. Denver, Mar. 11, 1928; d. William Morgan and Elfrida (Lowenberg) Calhoun; B.S., U. Tex. at Arlington, 1949; m. Robert M. Neill, June 3, 1949. Bookkeeper, Forrest Lumber Co., Lubbock, Tex., 1949-51; acctg. positions, 1951-55; receptionist, sec. to pres. Carl J. Westland Drilling Co., Midland, Tex., 1955-62; sec. to dir. mgr. Rowan Drilling Co., Midland, 1963-64; receptionist Tom Brown, Inc., 1963—, now asst. sec. to corp. v.p. Republican. Presbyterian. Club: Bus. and Profl. Women's. Home: 2805 Stutz Dr Midland TX 79701 Office: 508 W Wall Empire Plaza Bldg Midland TX 79701

NELKIN, DOROTHY, educator; b. Boston, July 30, 1933; A.B. in Philosophy, Cornell U., 1954; m. Mark S. Nelkin. Research asst., history of sci., Cornell U., Ithaca, N.Y., 1954-55, research assoc. Sch. Indsl. and Labor Relations, 1963-69, sr. research assoc. program on sci., tech., society, 1970-72, assoc. prof. program on sci., tech., society and dept. of city and regional planning, 1973-76, prof. sociology, 1977—, also grad. fields of planning, pub. policy, sociology; vis. assoc. in polit. sci. M.I.T., 1975-76; maitre de conference associé U. Paris XII, 1975-76; vis. assoc. resources for future, Washington; maitre de recherche Ecole Polytechnique, Paris, 1980-81; also lectr. U. Edinburgh, Louvain U., Amsterdam, Energy Campaign, Council for Sci. and Soc., London, Paris; cons. OECD, Paris, 1973-74, 75-76, Edнl. Devel. Center, Cambridge, Mass., 1973-74, Einstein-Montefiore Med. Center, Bronx, 1974-75, Coll. of Sci. in Society, Wesleyan U., 1975, U. Wis., 1977-78, 1978, Inst. for Environ., Berlin, 1978-79, NSF, 1978-79, pub. TV Sta. KCTS, 1981, ACLU, 1981;

panel mem. Nat. Acad. Scis., 1976-78, del. to Internat. Union of History of Philosophy of Sci., 1977. Grantee NSF, 1971-73, 75-77, 76-78, 79-80, German Marshall Fund, 1978-80. Fellow Hastings Inst. of Soc., Ethics and Life Scis.; mem. AAAS (various coms.), Internat. Council for Sci. Policy Studies (conf. organizer, 1978), Soc. for History of Tech. (adv. council 1977-81), Soc. for Social Studies of Sci. (exec. council 1976-78, pres. 1978-79), Nat. Council on Health Tech., Medicine in Pub. Interest (dir. 1980—), Council for Advancement of Sci. Writers (dir. 1980—). Author: On the Season: Aspects of the Migrant Labor System, 1970; (with William H. Friedland) Migrant: Farm Workers in America's Northwest, 1971; Nuclear Power and its Critics, The Cayuga Lake Controversy, 1971; The Politics of Housing Innovation: The Fate of the Civilian Industrial Technology Program, 1971; The University and Military Research: Moral Politics at M.I.T., 1972; Methadone Maintenance—A Technological Fix, 1973; Jetport: The Boston Airport Controversy, 1975; Science Textbook Controversies: The Politics of Equal Time, 1977; Technological Decisions and Democracy: European Experiments in Public Participation, 1977; Controversy: Politics of Technical Decisions, 1979; The Atom Besieged: Extra-Parliamentary Dissent in France and Germany, 1981; The Creation Controversy, 1982; contbr. articles, book revs. to profl. publs.; editorial advisor to Social Studies of Sci., 1974—; mem. adv. bds. Sci., Tech. and Human Values, 1976—, Chgo. U. Press book series Science and Its Conceptual Foundations, 1980—; mem. adv. bd. of editors Zeit-schrift für umwelt politik, 1978; mem. editorial bds. Knowledge: Creation, Diffusion Utilization, 1978—, Govt. under Rev., 1980—; contbr. invited papers to profl. confs. U.S., Can., France, Scotland, Germany, Yugoslavia, Netherlands, Sweden, Norway. Home: 119 Heights Ct Ithaca NY 14850 Office: 632 Clark Hall Cornell Univ Ithaca NY 14853

NELMS, DOROTHY EDWARDS, orgn. exec.; b. Jersey City, N.J., Aug. 27, 1927; d. John Hallaman and Sarah Belle (Young) Edwards; B.S., Howard U., 1949; J.D., George Washington U. Law Sch., 1981; children—Adrienne S. Bruce, Kevin V. Bruce. With HEW, Washington, 1956-71, HUD, Washington, 1971-78; nat. pres. Federally Employed Women, Washington, 1978-80; mgmt. cons. Mem. Federally Employed Women, Bus. and Profl. Women's Club. Club: Internat. Toastmistress. Home and Office: 2435 Wagner St SE Washington DC 20020

NELSEN, BETTY JO, state legislator; b. Boston, Oct. 11, 1935; B.S., Mass. State Coll., 1957; married; 3 children. Mem. Wis. Ho. of Reps., 1979—. Mem. Citizens' Govtl. Research Bur.; former pres. Jr. League Milw.; bd. dirs. Milw. Mgmt. Support Orgn.; mem. North Shore Republican Club; trustee Shorewood Civic Improvement Found.; bd. dirs. United Way of Greater Milw.; mem. Goals for Milw. 2000. Office: Wis Ho of Reps Room 310 W State Capitol Madison WI 53702 *

NELSEN, LILLIAN LOUISE, nursing adminstr.; b. Victor, Idaho, May 5, 1924; d. Paul Levere and Lillian Sarah (Kearsley) Woolstenhulme; R.N., Good Samaritan Tng. Sch. for Nurses, 1946; B.S. i,n Nursing, U. San Diego Coll. for Women, 1964; B.B.A., Nat. U., San Diego, 1976; m. Feb. 2, 1946; children—Jack, Lilly, Linda, June, Sally, Esther, Mary, Richard. Electrician helper, 1942; nurse Good Samaritan Hosp., 1947; clk.-typist, Guam, 1948; nurse St. Mary's Hosp., Long Beach, Calif., 1947-49; obstet. nurse, night supr. Sharp Hosp., San Diego, 1955-73; supr., instr. Mission Bay and Centre City Hosp., San Diego, 1973-77; adminstrv. supr. Pomarado Hosp., San Diego, 1977-82. Pres. PTA, 1954-55. Cert. CPR instr. Mem. Am. Mgmt. Assn., Nat. Assn. Female Execs., Am. Security Council, Am. Soc. Profl. and Exec. Women. Home: 15625 Paymogo St San Diego CA 92129 Office: Centre City Hosp 120 Elm St San Diego CA 92101

NELSON, AGNES MAE, writer; b. Denver; d. Carl Oscar and Lillian Emma (Kepner) Lovestedt; student U. Nev., 1954-58; div.; children—Robert Kepner Bryant, Clifford Henri Warnken. Part-time staff mem. Reno newspapers, 1955-59; public relations sec. Riviera Hotel, Las Vegas, Nev., 1960-61; attache Nev. State Legislature, 1959-75; sec. Nev. Dept. Vocat. Edn., 1964-65, Union Fed. Savs. & Loan Assn., Reno, 1965-66, Bank of Calif., San Francisco, 1948-49, State of Nev. Mental Health Clinic, 1971-75; mem. girls singing trio The Sparkaleers, 1955-56; appearances in mus. prodns., 1964, 66; singer Reno Civic Chorus, 1967-68, Reno Women's Chorus, 1964, Meth. Ch. choir, 1968-73; author feature articles for bicentennial publs., contbr. articles to numerous mags. and Sunday newspapers, 1956—. Winner 2d pl. in feature writing Nat. Assn. Press Women, 1980. Mem. Nat. League Am. Pen Women (1st prize feature article Reno br. 1965, others), Nev. Press Women (41 awards 1971-81), Nev. Poetry Soc., Calif. Writers Club, Nat. Writers Club, No. Nev. Bluegrass Assn., Friends of Sierra Arts Found. Mem. Ch. Religious Sci. Address: 520A Howard Dr Sparks NV 89431

NELSON, BARBARA ANN BOLTON, orgn. exec.; b. Olean, N.Y., Mar. 2, 1935; d. Carl Newton and Evelyn Marguerite (Eliason) Bolton; R.N., Millard Fillmore Sch. Nursing, 1956; m. Ross W. Nelson, Aug. 5, 1961 (dec.); children—Kimberly, Karl, Kerri. Operating room nurse Millard Fillmore Hosp., 1956-59; emergency room nurse Bradford Hosp., 1959-63; pediatric office nurse, Canandaigua, N.Y., 1964-68; nurse 4-H Camp, Canandaigua, 1969-72; chmn. canteen and disaster ARC, Canandaigua, 1972-76, sec., 1976, exec. dir. West Ontario County chpt., 1977—. Dog obedience coordinator Ontario County 4-H Clubs, 1966—, obedience judge N.Y. State Fair, Syracuse, 1980, 81; bd. dirs. Am. Field Service, 1971-75; bd. dirs. Canandaigua Family YMCA, 1975—, chmn. Ann. Y Auction, 1975; mem. Canandaigua Safety Council, 1979; chmn. Lengths for Lives, Am. Cancer Soc., 1974-77; mem. Canandaigua Ambulance Squad, 1977—; pres. Canandaigua Emergency Squad, 1980-81. Cert. advanced first aid instr. Recipient recognition awards from various orgns. including: ARC, 1972, West Ontario County chpt. ARC, 1974, Bus. and Profl. Women's Orgn., 1970; Outstanding Vol. award Vol. Action Center, 1972; 4-H Gold Clover award, 1979; registered nurse, N.Y. State; registered emergency med. technician, N.Y. State; cert. cardio-pulmonary resuscitation instr. Baptist. Clubs: Elks, Kanadasaga Kennel (dir. 1977-79, show trophy chmn. 1976—). Home: 29 Dorset Dr Canandaigua NY 14424 Office: West Ontario County Chpt ARC 47 Phelps St Canandaigua NY 14424

NELSON, CATHERINE, educator; b. N.Y.C., Aug. 2, 1952; d. John Quincy and Virginia (Gatling) Clark; B.A. in Spanish, Colby Coll., 1974; M.A. in Spanish Edn., Columbia U. Tchrs. Coll., 1976; student Universidad de los Andes, Bogotá, Columbia, 1973, Universidad del Valle, Guatemala City, 1972; m. Keith W. Nelson, Sept. 1, 1979; 1 son, Darren Virgil. Bilingual tchr. Warren Snyder Elem. Sch., Bristol, Pa., 1976; English as 2d lang. instr. SUNY Ednl. Opportunity Center, N.Y.C., 1976—, N.Y.C. Tech. Coll., Bklyn., 1977—; instr. Coll. of New Rochelle Harlem extension. Mem. MLA, Nat. Assn. Female Execs. Democrat. Baptist. Office: 300 Jay St Brooklyn NY 11201

NELSON, CATHERINE ELEANOR, mfg. co. mgr.; b. Washington, Aug. 18, 1938; d. Willie James and Eleanor C. (Tucker) N.; student Southeastern U., Washington, 1970-73, Toledo U., 1978, Mercy Coll., 1979, Pace U., 1980. With Potomac Electric Power Co., Washington, 1957-66; with IBM, 1966—, field audit mgr., Armonk, N.Y., 1977-79, area audit mgr., 1979—. Active Big Sister Program, Washington, 1966-67; vol. VA Hosp., Washington, 1977-78; bd. dirs. Peekskill (N.Y.) YWCA; pres. Helping Hand Club; active Mt. Olivet Baptist Ch. Cert. data processing auditor. Mem. Nat. Assn. Female Execs., Am. Mgmt. Assn., Inst. Internal Auditors. Democrat. Author internal IBM publs. Home: 21 Winding Ct Mohegan Lake NY 10547 Office: 3000 Westchester Ave White Plains NY 10604

NELSON, DIANA, state legislator; b. Berlin, Wis., Oct. 15, 1941; d. Llewellyn James and Virginia Laurel (Shaver) Walker; B.S., U. Wis., 1963; m. Thomas David Nelson, Aug. 22, 1964; children—Stephanie, Brian. Mem. Ill. Ho. of Reps., 1981—. Republican. Congregationalist. Home: 5025 Woodland Ave Western Springs IL 60558 Office: 901 W Hillgrove Ave LaGrange IL 60525

NELSON, DONIE ALBERTA, TV and cable prodn. co. exec.; b. Los Angeles, June 13, 1942; d. Raymond Oscar and Corinne (Valdez) N.; A.A., Santa Monica City Coll., 1972; student U. Calif., Berkeley, 1960-61, UCLA, 1971; m. Foster George Phelps, May 30, 1981; 1 dau., Molly Corinne. Asst. story editor MGM Films, Culver City, Calif., 1972-75, story editor, 1975-77; dir. creative affairs Christiana Prodns., Los Angeles, 1977-79; freelance creative cons., story editor, ind. producer for TV, 1979-82; freelance mag. writer, pub. cons., book editor, Los Angeles, 1979-82; feature writer, asst. to editor Showcase mag., Encino, Calif., 1981-82; dir. devel. feature film, TV and cable Solofilm Co., Los Angeles, 1982; dir. devel. TV and cable Sherwood Prodns. Inc., Culver City, 1982—; guest speaker Los Angeles Career Planning Center, 1979, U. So. Calif. Film Sch., 1980. Vol., Hollygrove Home for Children, 1975-77; sec. Culver City Employees Assn., 1970, Culver City Parks and Recreation Commn., 1969-70. Recipient Service award Los Angeles chpt. Women in Communications, Inc., 1978; Outstanding Journalism Student of Year award Warren High Sch., Downey, Calif., 1960. Mem. Acad. TV Arts and Scis., Women in Communications (past Los Angeles chpt. pres.), Women in Film, NOW, Am. Film Inst. Asso. producer Like Normal People, 1979. Office: 3964 Overland Ave Suite 208 Culver City CA 90230

NELSON, DOROTHY GENE, banker; b. Fort Wayne, Ind., Feb. 15, 1923; d. James Harvey and Vera Virginia (Ferneau) Davis; student public schs., Metz, Ind., m. Lawrence S. Nelson, Oct. 14, 1972. With Fort Wayne Nat. Bank, 1961—, asst. cashier, mgr. depositor services, 1970-80, asst. v.p., 1980—, also mgr. savs. personnel and savs. programs. Adviser, Jr. Achievement, recipient citation. Mem. Am. Bus. Womens Assn. (recipient Nat. Achievement citation 1963), Fort Wayne C. of C., Am. Inst. Banking, Nat. Assn. Bank Women, Am. Legion Aux. Methodist. Home: 2204 Lakeland Ln Fort Wayne IN 46815 Office: 110 W Berry St Fort Wayne IN 46802

NELSON, DOROTHY WRIGHT (MRS. JAMES F. NELSON), judge; b. San Pedro, Calif., Sept. 30, 1928; d. Harry Earl and Lorna Amy Wright; B.A., UCLA, 1950, J.D., 1953; LL.M., U. So. Calif., 1956; m. James Frank Nelson, Dec. 27, 1950; children—Franklin Wright, Lorna Jean. Admitted to Calif. bar, 1954; pvt. practice law, Los Angeles, from 1954; research asso. fellow U. So. Calif., 1953-56; instr., 1957-58, asst. prof., 1958-61, asso. prof., 1961-67, prof., 1967, asso. dean., 1965-67, dean, 1967-80; judge U.S. Ct. Appeals 9th Circuit, Los Angeles, 1980—; cons. Project STAR, Law Enforcement Assistance Adminstrn.; adv. com. Nat. Jud. Edn. Program to Promote Equality for Women and Men in Cts., 1982—; dir. Farmers Ins. Co. Co-chmn. Confronting Myths in Edn. for Pres. Nixon's White House Conf. on Children. Bd. dirs. Council on Legal Edn. for Profl. Responsibility, 1971—, Constnl. Right Found., 1971—, Los Angeles County Bar Found., 1982—, Am. Nat. Inst. for Social Advancement; adv. bd. Nat. Center for State Cts., 1971-73; co-chair UN Day Calif., 1982. Named Alumnus of Yr., UCLA, 1967, recipient Profl. Achievement award, 1969; named Times Woman of Yr., 1968; recipient U. Judaism Humanitarian award, 1973; AWARE Internat. award, 1970; Ernestine Stalhut Outstanding Woman Lawyer award, 1972; Pax Orbis ex Jure Medallion award World Peace Through Law Center, 1975; Lustman fellow Yale U., 1977; CORO Found. Public Service award, 1978. Fellow Am. Bar Found.; mem. Am. Law Inst., Bar Calif. (bd. dirs. continuing edn. bar commn. 1967-74), Am. Judicature Soc. (exec. com. 1976—, dir. 1972-75, 76—, research adv. com. 1974—, editorial adv. bd. Judicature 1974—, v.p. 1977-79, chmn. bd. 1979-81), Am. Bar Assn. (sect. on jud. adminstrn.; chmn. com. on edn. in jud. adminstrn. 1972-79), Los Angeles World Affairs Council, Town Hall, Phi Beta Kappa, Phi Kappa Phi, Order of Coif (nat. v.p. 1974-76). Baha'i. Author: Judicial Administration and The Administration of Justice, 1975. Contbr. articles to profl. jours. Office: US Court House 312 N Spring St Los Angeles CA 90012

NELSON, EDINA CATHERINE, social services coordinator; b. Alameda, Calif., May 16, 1929; d. David Henry and Edina Caroline (Kaas) Heagerty; B.A., U. Calif., Berkeley, 1951, ceredential adult edn., 1976; m. Aldo Hadden Nelson, Aug. 19, 1950; children—Dea, Jack, Christian, John, James. Recreation leader City of Oakland (Calif.), 1947-53, sr. citizen leader, 1950-53, 62-63, sr. citizens coordinator, 1966—; adult edn. tchr., 1981—; group worker St. Jarlath Sr. Activity Center, 1981—. Pres., Grass Valley Sch. PTA, Oakland, 1974-75. Recipient Hon. Service award, named life mem. PTA. Mem. Nat. Council Sr. Citizens, Calif. Legis. Council Older Americans, Oakland Com. Aging, Chabot Park Women's Lit. Soc., Chi Kappa Rho. Democrat. Roman Catholic. Office: 1520 Lakeside Dr Oakland CA 94612

NELSON, ELINOR S., educator; b. Bklyn., Mar. 12, 1953; d. Aaron A. and Ruth (Goldstein) Nelson; B.A. magna cum laude, Marshall U., 1974; M.A. (fellow) U. Minn., 1976, Ph.D., 1980. Tchr., coach Cabell County Schs., Huntington, W.Va., 1974; res. tchr. Mpls. Public Schs., 1974-75; adminstr. Office Admissions and Records, U. Minn., St. Paul, 1975-78, researcher dept. ednl. adminstrn., 1978-80; asst. prin. Dist. 742 Community Schs., St. Cloud, Minn., 1980-81; asst. prof. edn. div. ednl. leadership St. Louis U., 1981—; co-developer workshop on tchr. evaluation, 1975; instr. speech communications Marshall U., 1973-74. Mem. Nat. Assn. Secondary Sch. Prins., Minn. Assn. Secondary Sch. Prins., Mo. Assn. Secondary Sch. Prins., Minn. Assn. Sch. Personnel Adminstrs., Adminstrv. Women in Edn., Nat. Assn. Women Deans, Adminstrs. and Counselors, Assn. Supervision and Curriculum Devel., Citizens League Minn., U. Minn. Ednl. Adminstrs. Alumni Assn. AAUP, Phi Delta Kappa. Jewish. Office: Dept Edn St Louis U 221 N Grand Blvd Saint Louis MO 63103

NELSON, ELIZABETH, educator; b. Birmingham, Ala.; d. John and Mary (Dunigan) Nelson; B.S., Ala. State Tchrs. Coll., 1939; M.S., Wayne State U., 1948; postgrad. N.Y. U., U. Heidelberg, Mich. State U., U. Md., U. Paris, U. Neuchatel (Switzerland), La Verne Coll., 1975. Tchr., Jefferson County (Ala.) Public Schs., 1939-45; tchr. George Washington Carver Sch., Ferndale, Mich., 1945-55, prin., 1955-58, curriculum coordinator, 1959; tchr. Bad Kreuznach (Germany) Elementary Sch., U.S. Army, 1962; tchr. Vassincourt (France) Am. Elementary Sch. Overseas Dependents Schs., Dept. Def., U.S. Army, 1963-65, Verdun (France) Am. Elementary Sch., 1966; tchr. SHAPE Internat. Elementary Sch., NATO SHAPE Support Groups Sect., SHAPE, Belgium, 1967—, minority studies coordinator Am. sect., 1975—, 1981 & 82. 3d grade chmn. Am. sect., 1978-79. Recipient award for contbns. to edn. and people of Mich., Gov. Mich., 1955. Mem. Nat., Overseas edn. assns., NAACP, League Women Voters, Zeta Phi Beta. Address: SHAPE American Elementary School APO NY 09088

NELSON, ETHELYN BARNETT, civic worker; b. Bessemer, Ala., Jan. 16, 1925; d. Laurence McBride and Ethel Victoria Fortesque (King) Barnett; student Huntingdon Coll., 1943, U. Ala., 1948, George Washington U., 1948-49, 74; m. Stuart David Nelson, May 6, 1949; children—Terryl Lynn, Cynthia Dianne, Jacqueline Margo. Sec., U.S. Air Force, Montgomery, Ala. and Panama Canal Zone, 1944-49; sec. to dep. undersec. U.S. Dept. State, Washington, 1951-53, U.S. Ho. of Reps. and U.S. Senate, 1959-60; adminstrv. asst. editorial div. Nat. Geog. Soc., Washington, 1962-65; rec. sec. Dist. IV, Nat. Capital Area Fedn. Garden Clubs, Inc., Washington, 1981—. Mem. Women's Com. Nat. Symphony Orch. Mem. Salvation Army Aux., Suburban Hosp. Assn. Republican. Clubs: Women's of Chevy Chase (Md.); Landon Woods Garden (pres. 1978-80), Internat., Congressional Country; Capital Speakers (Washington). Patentee. Home: 6410 Maiden Ln Bethesda MD 20817

NELSON, FRIEDA PATRACIA HUCKFELDT, nurse; b. Fort Pierre, S.D., June 12, 1921; d. Otto and Ina Inez (Conant) Huckfeldt; student No. State Coll., Aberdeen, S.D., 1942-43; A.A. in Nursing, Everett Community Coll., 1974; m. Rex Durwood Nelson, Jan. 9, 1945; children—Marvin Arthur, Russell Rex. William Otto, Merrial Ellen. Tchr., Pierce Sch., Fort Pierre, S.D., 1943-47, Iron Nation Sch., Kennebec, S.D., 1950-53; Fort Pierre (S.D.) Sch., 1953-56, Kennebec Sch. (S.D.), 1956-57, Fircrest Sch., Seattle, 1959; nurse's aide, ward clk. Children's Orthopedic Hosp., 1959-62, 63-65; substitute tchr. Edmond's Sch. Dist., Lynnwood, Wash., 1959-61, 62-73; staff nurse N.W. Villa Care, 1974-75; head nurse Merryhaven Nursing Home, Snohomish, Wash., 1975-76; night nurse Madeleine Villa Convalescent Center, Marysville, Wash., 1976-77; night nurse Anderson House, 1977; in-service dir. Lake Vue Gardens Convalescent Center, Kirkland, Wash., 1977-79; staff nurse So. Hills Gen. Hosp., 1979—. Republican. Presbyterian. Club: Order Eastern Star. Home: Box 664 Martin SD 57551

NELSON, GLADYS GRETHE FINSTAD, reporter; b. Steintkjer, Norway, Sept. 14, 1914; came to U.S., 1922, naturalized, 1943; d. Albert Flynn and Julie Marianne (Finstad) O'Keefe; m. Charles F. Nelson, Dec. 12, 1941 (dec.); 1 son, Richard Charles. Freelance writer, 1943-63; staff reporter home fashions Seattle Times, 1963—. Mem. Seattle Art Mus., Pacific N.W. Writers Conf. (past pres.; trustee), Nat. League Am. Pen Women, Seattle Free Lances, Sigma Delta Chi. Congregationalist. Home: 4909 Whitman Ave N Seattle WA 98103

NELSON, HAZEL FOWLER (MRS. BOWEN CRESTON NELSON), writer; b. Mulhall, Okla., May 16, 1905; d. Oscar Frederick and Belle Virginia (Lowe) Fowler; B.A., U. Okla., 1927; postgrad. U. Wis., 1928; m. Bowen Creston Nelson Oct. 26, 1941; 1 dau., Creston Annette. Tchr. journalism, English, sponsor publs. Chickasha (Okla.) High Sch., 1927-30; reporter Norman (Okla.) Transcript, 1930-37; feature writer Oklahoma City Times, 1937-41; mil. editor Miami (Fla.) Herald, 1942-45; officer Nelson Mortgage Co., Inc., Miami, 1941-69, sec., dir., 1942-69; now free-lance writer. Mem. bd. Children's Service Bur., Miami, 1952; v.p. Franklin Bush chpt. U. Miami Women's Cancer Assn., 1961, pres., 1970. Recipient silver award Miami's Fgn. War Brides for assistance through newspaper series, 1946. Mem. Soc. So. Families, Fla. Hist. Assn., Internat. Platform Assn., Women in Communications (pres. U. Okla. chpt. 1927, Miami chpt. 1952-53). Democrat. Mem. Christian Ch. (pres. women's fellowship 1963-64). Home: 10255 SW 53d Ave Miami FL 33156

NELSON, JANIE MAE, psychologist; b. Clarks, La., Nov. 23, 1935; d. Ermon and Helen (Stewart) N.; B.Ed., Chgo. Tchrs. Coll., 1956; M.A., Roosevelt U., 1968, 77; Ph.D., Kent State U., 1981. Tchr. elem. sch., psychologist Chgo. Public Schs., 1956—. Pres., v.p. Holy Angel's Blessed Sacrament Soc., 1975-77; bd. dirs. Nat. Alliance Black Feminists, 1979-81; co-founder; bd. dirs. WOMAN (Woman's Orgn. Minority Affairs and Needs), 1980—. Mem. Operation PUSH, Am. Psychol. Assn., NOW, Phi Delta Kappa. Home: 7659 S Normal Blvd Chicago IL 60620

NELSON, JULIE, psychologist; b. Coushatta, La., Feb. 13, 1952; d. Gordon H. and Evelyn (Hunter) Nelson; B.A., La. State U., 1973, M.A., 1976, Ph.D., 1980; m. Michael N. Dooley, Feb. 4, 1978; children—Cassandra Nelson-Dooley, Kate Nelson-Dooley. Intern The Psychology Group, Baton Rouge, 1977-79; instr. La. State U., Baton Rouge, 1978-79; intern Ariz. State Hosp., Phoenix, 1979-80, Women's Psychology Center, Tempe, Ariz., 1980; psychologist, mgr. orgnl. devel. Honeywell Large Info. Systems, Phoenix, 1980—. NIMH fellow, 1974-78; recipient Commendation, La. Psychol. Assn., 1976; T. Harry Williams scholar, 1970. Mem. NOW, Am. Psychol. Assn., Ariz. Psychol. Assn. Club: Bus. and Profl. Women's. Office: 13430 N Black Canyon Hwy Phoenix AZ 85005

NELSON, LINDA KATHERINE SUTTON, theatrical lighting cons.; b. Kankakee, Ill., Nov. 8, 1951; d. Milford E. and Dorothea A. Sutton; B.A., U. Md., 1974; m. John Morgan Nelson, Apr. 9, 1977; 1 son, Damon John. Lighting design cons. Alaska Stagecraft, Inc., Anchorage, 1976—, corp. v.p., 1979—; bus. agt. Internat. Alliance of Theatrical Stage Employees and Moving Picture Machine Operators of U.S. and Can., Local 770, Anchorage, 1978—; master electrician Anchorage Civic Opera, 1978-80, lighting designer, 1980-81; resident lighting designer Anchorage Community Theatre, 1980—; partner SRO Productions, Anchorage, 1981—. Vol. lighting designer Theatre Guild, Inc., Anchorage, 1976-81, technical instr., 1976-81. Mem. Nat. Assn. Female Execs., Am. Mgmt. Assn., Am. Rental Assn., Central Labor Council, Coalition of Labor Union Women. Democrat. Episcopalian. Office: PO Box 4637 Anchorage AK 99509

NELSON, MAC J., food processing co. exec.; b. Helmer, Ind., Aug. 8, 1927; d. Cyrus Robert and Georgia Mariam (Emrick) Hills; grad. Sawyer Sch. Bus., 1965-67; m. Robert G. Nelson, Oct. 10, 1968; children—Michael, Mark, Matthew, Kristi, Carol, Brian, Christopher. Spares and provisioning analyst Philco-Ford Aeronutronics Co., Newport Beach, Calif., 1967-69; with J.R. Simplot Co., Caldwell, Idaho, 1969—, benefits coordinator, 1974-76, benefits supr., 1976-78, benefits and office supr., 1978-79, personnel mgr., 1979-82, adminstrv. mgr., 1982—. Sec., Caldwell Mayor's Commn. for Handicapped, 1972-74, chmn., 1974-79; mem. steering com. Idaho White House Conf. on Employment Handicapped, 1976; bd. dirs. Western Idaho Tng. Co., 1978, v.p., 1979-80, pres., 1980—. Mem. Am. Soc. Personnel Adminstrs., Nat. Assn. Female Execs., Internat. Soc. Preretirement Planners (chmn. 1978-79, dir. 1980—), Western Gerontol. Soc.

NELSON, MARGARET FAYE, educator; b. Claremore, Okla., Aug. 16, 1922; d. Samuel and Bonnie Marie (Runnels) Dawson; B.A., Northwestern State U. (Okla.), 1969; M.A., Okla. State U., 1971, Ph.D., 1979; postgrad. Ind. U., 1972, 73; m. William Ellis Nelson, Aug. 1, 1942; children—John Ellis, Diana L. Nelson Fiorello, Mary L. Nelson Wyman, William H., Bette F. Instr. English, Okla. State U., Stillwater, 1970-80, asst. prof., 1980—, Mem. MLA, Am. Folklore Soc., Coll. English Assn., Okla. Edn. Assn., NEA, Nat. Indian Edn. Assn., Okla. Indian Edn. Assn., Ozark States Folklore Soc., N. Am. Indian Women's Assn., Okla. Fedn. Indian Women, Sigma Tau Delta, Kappa Delta Pi. Republican. Mem. Disciples of Christ Ch. Club: Order Eastern Star. Contbr. articles to profl. jours. Home: 1523 Wildwood St Stillwater OK 74074 Office: Dept English Okla State U Stillwater OK 74078

NELSON, MARILYN CARLSON, bank holding co. exec.; b. Mpls., Aug. 19, 1939; d. Curtis Leroy and Arleen Emily (Martin) Carlson; B.S. cum laude, Smith Coll., 1961; student Geneva Grad. Sch. Econs. and Polit. Sci., 1960; m. Glen Nelson; children—Diana, Curt, Juliet, Wendy. Owner, chmn. Citizens State Bank, Waterville, 1971—; pres. Minn. Bank Holding Co., Mpls., 1980—; asst. sec. Camel Bank, Phoenix, 1982—; dir. Carlson Cos., Inc., First Bank System, Mpls., First Trust Co., St. Paul, 1974—, Northwestern Bell Telephone Co. Bd. dirs. U. Minn. Sch. Mgmt., 1981—, Minn. Opera Co., Minn. Econ. Assn. Bd., Guthrie

Theatre, 1974—, Minn. Opera Co., Minn. Orchestral Assn., United Way Mpls.; chairperson Scandinavia Today-Minn.; trustee Macalester Coll. Methodist. Clubs: Minneapolis, Woodhill Country. Office: First Bank System Inc 1400 First Nat Bank Bldg Minneapolis MN 55480

NELSON, MARITA LEE, anatomist; b. Torrance, Calif., Aug. 8, 1934; d. Lee George and Marie Blanche (Waples) N.; B.S., UCLA, 1957, M.S., 1959; Ph.D. in Anatomy (Univ. fellow), U. Calif., Berkeley, 1968. Instr., Ill. State U., 1960-64; asso. U. Calif., Berkeley, 1965-68, instr., 1968-69, acting asst. prof., 1969, asst. prof., 1972-74; asst. prof. Georgetown U. Schs. Medicine-Dentistry, 1969-72; asso. prof. anatomy and reproductive biology John A. Burns Sch. Medicine, U. Hawaii, 1974-82, prof., 1982—. Recipient Teaching award Kaiser Found., 1977, Golden Pineapple award John A. Burns Sch. Medicine, 1979. Mem. Am. Assn. Anatomists, Soc. Study Reprodn., Endocrine Soc., AAAS, AAUP, Assn. Women in Sci., Hawaiian Assn. Women in Sci., Hawaiian Acad. Sci., Sigma Xi, Pi Lambda Theta. Research on environ. endocrinology and initiation of puberty, effects of high altitude on seasonal changes on maturation and pituitary function. Office: 1960 East-West Rd Honolulu HI 96822

NELSON, MARY JEAN, real estate broker; b. Hungary, Mar. 5; came to U.S., 1921, naturalized, 1939; d. Alexander and Mary (Cseh) Bartok; ed. public schs.; m. Julius C. Nelson, Oct. 24, 1938; children—Judith Ann, Robert J. Buyer, Edelman Bros. Dept. Store, Lindenhurst, N.Y., 1932-43, Hillman's Shoppe, Bayshore, N.Y., 1943-45; now pres. M.J. Nelson Realty Inc., Active Girls Scouts U.S.A. Recipient Dist. Service award South Shore Suffolk chpt. L.I. Bd. Realtors, 1976, 78. Mem. L.I. Bd. Realtors. Home: 37 Willow Ln Lindenhurst NY 11957 Office: 111 W Sunrise Hwy Lindenhurst NY 11757

NELSON, NANCY ELEANOR, pediatrician, educator; b. El Paso, Apr. 4, 1933; d. Harry Hamilton and Helen Maude (Murphy) Nelson; B.A. magna cum laude, U. Colo., 1955, M.D., 1959. Intern Case Western Res. U. Hosp., 1959-60, resident, 1960-63; practice medicine specializing in pediatrics, Denver, 1963-70; asso. clin. prof. U. Colo. Sch. Medicine, Denver, 1977—. Mem. Am. Acad. Pediatrics, AMA. Home: 1265 Elizabeth St Denver CO 80206 Office: 4200 E 9th Ave Denver CO 80262

NELSON, PAMELA LEIGH, pub. co. exec.; b. Des Moines, Oct. 18, 1947; d. Clare S. and Eleanor (Greef) Orth; B.S., U. N.Mex., 1969; M.S., U. Kans., 1975. Tchr., Albuquerque Public Schs., 1969-72, Shawnee Mission (Kans.) Public Schs., 1972-76; cons. Macmillan Pub. Co., Kansas City, 1976-79; dir. mktg. services Am. Book Co., N.Y.C., 1979-81; product mgr. D. C. Heath & Co., Lexington, Mass., 1981-82, Allyn and Bacon Inc., Newton, Mass., 1982—. Mem. Assn. Am. Pubs., Internat. Reading Assn., Nat. Council Social Studies, Nat. Council Tchrs. English, Phi Mu Alumni Assn., Kans. U. Alumni Assn., U. N.Mex. Alumni Assn. AAUW, PEO. Republican. Presbyterian. Home: 255 Massachusetts Ave Boston MA 02115 Office: 125 Spring St Lexington MA 02173

NELSON, REBECCA SUE, educator; b. Rochester, Ind., July 19, 1944; d. Everett William and Pauline (Ault) Russell; B.S., Ball State U., 1965, M.A., 1967; Ed.D., Ind. U. 1972; 1 son by previous marriage—Timothy Scott. Tchr., Yorktown (Ind.) Elem. Sch., 1967-69; asso. instr. Ind. U., Bloomington, 1969-71; mem. faculty Ball State U., Muncie, Ind., 1971—, asso. prof., 1975-79, prof., 1979—; cons. elem. math, Ind. schs. Mem. Recipient Outstanding Young Faculty award Ball State U., 1974. Mem. Nat. Council Tchrs. Math (Central Region rep. 1979-82), Ind. Council Tchrs. Math (nat. del. 1973-78, pres. 1977, adv. council 1978—), Nat. Assn. Suprs. Math, Mich. Council Tchrs. Math, Pi Lambda Theta. Author: Pattern Block Games, 1982; contbr. articles to profl. jours. Home: Route 11 Box 74 Muncie IN 47302 Office: Dept Math Ball State U Muncie IN 47306

NELSON, ROJEAN EVELYN, civic worker; b. Wilcox, Nebr., Oct. 20, 1927; d. August and Anna Angelina (Adam) Jesse; student Kearney (Nebr.) State Tchrs. Coll., 1946; m. Ward Stanley Nelson, Aug. 13, 1950; children—Kevin Ward, Kirk August. Public sch. tchr., 1946-54; substitute tchr., 1960-76; sec.-bookkeeper Wilcox Corp., 1972-76; sec. Jim Reiss Ins. Agy., Wilcox, 1977—. Sec., Holdrege (Nebr.) Women's Bowling Assn., 1966—; bd. dirs. Nebr. Women's Bowling Assn., 1970-77, sgt.-at-arms, 1977—; pres. Phelps County Democratic Women, 1975-79; sec. Phelps County Dem. Central Com., 1972-76; mem. Nebr. Dem. Central Com., 1978—; Sunday Sch. tchr. Fridhem Luth. Ch., Funk, Nebr., 1962-81, sec. ch. council, 1976-79; post pres. Am. Legion Aux., 1979—. Home: Route 1 Box 149 Wilcox NE 69882 Office: Jim Reiss Agy Wilcox NE 68982

NELSON, ROSETTA PEARSON, fin. exec.; b. Greenville, Miss., Sept. 14, 1948; d. Benny and Doll (Hemphill) Pearson; B.B.A., Fla. Internat. U., 1975; M.Human Resources, Biscayne Coll., 1980; m. Arthur V. Nelson, Dec. 31, 1967; children—Arthur V., Thomas Lee. Customer contract clk. Sears, Roebuck & Co., Miami, Fla., 1968-69; substitute tchr. Dade County (Fla.) Sch. Bd., 1970-72; acctg. fuel price analyst Fla. Power & Light Co., Miami, 1972-80, personnel trainer, 1980—. Supt., Sunday sch. Gibbs Chapel AME Ch., 1974—. Notary pub., Fla.; recipient award Eta Phi Beta, 1976, Gibbs Chapel AME Ch., 1979. Mem. Eta Phi Beta (rec. sec. 1975-77, fin. sec. 1977-79). Home: 2280 NW 187 St Opa Locka FL 33055 Office: 9250 W Flagler St Miami FL 33174

NELSON, RUBY EVERTON, banker; b. Logan, Utah, Feb. 18, 1923; d. John Elva and Lucy (Waldron) Everton; student Utah State Agrl. Coll.; m. Caril G. Nelson, Jan. 1, 1965; children—Sharilyn, Judy, Vicki; stepchildren—Alan, James. Cost acct. Wickes Engring. & Constrn. Co., Logan, Utah, 1943-45; with A.B. Robbs Trust Co., Phoenix, 1950-64, sec.-treas., 1955-64, mgr. mortgage servicing, 1960-64; with Continental Bank, Phoenix, 1964—, asst. v.p., comptroller, 1966-70, v.p., comptroller, 1970-76, sr. v.p., comptroller, 1976—, supr. mortgage servicing dept., 1960—; dir. Continental Service Corp. Mem. Nat. Assn. Bank Women, Ariz. Bankers Assn. Republican. Mormon. Clubs: Kiva, Moon Valley Country. Office: Continental Bank 4000 N Central Ave Phoenix AZ 85012

NELSON, SALLY ANN, mfg. co. exec.; b. Valentine, Nebr., June 17, 1933; d. Edward Monroe and Gladys May (Phillips) Hudson; diploma Henagers Bus. Coll., Salt Lake City, 1954; postgrad. U. Utah Extension; m. Carl G. Nelson, July 6, 1956; children—Deborah May Nelson Willard, Michael Edward, Janice Ann Nelson Trujillo. Sec., Henager Bus. Coll., 1954-56; with IBM, 1956—, adminstrv. ops. mgr. office products div., Salt Lake City, 1977-79, mktg. adminstrn. mgr., 1979-80, sr. ops. analyst, 1980—; v.p., chairwoman bd. Harmony Homes, Inc., gen. contractors, 1980—. Mem. Am. Affirmative Action Assn. Democrat. Episcopalian. Club: Order Eastern Star (past matron). Home: 4331 West 5255 South Kearns UT 84118 Office: 420 East South Temple Salt Lake City UT 84111

NELSON, SHIRLEY ELAINE, energy co. ofcl.; b. Terre Haute, Ind., Sept. 15, 1946; d. Mervil Ray and Sarah Kathryn (Tucker) White; student Coll. DuPage, 1977—; m. Stanley Richard Nelson, Aug. 4, 1979; children by previous marriage—Richard Alan, Gary Michael. Sec. to v.p. fin. Cence Inc., Oak Brook, Ill., 1972-75, adminstrv. asst. to group pres., 1975-76, adminstrv. asst. to pres., chmn., 1976-77, personnel mgr., 1977-80; asst. to pres. Warren & Sommer Inc., Denver, 1980-81; asst. corp. sec. Acadia Petroleum Corp., Denver, 1981—. Mem. Am. Soc. Personnel Adminstrs., DuPage Personnel Assn. (sec. 1979), Nat. Assn. Female Execs., Exec. Women Internat., Indsl. Relations Assn. Chgo., Am. Mgmt. Assn. Lutheran. Club: Desk and Derrick (Denver). Home: 11040 W 65th Way Arvada CO 80004 Office: 1616 Glenarm Pl Suite 2270 Denver CO 80202

NELSON, VERA JOYCE, author, poet; b. Dayton, Wash.; d. I. N. and Nina E. (Butler) Newkirk; student Behnke-Walker Bus. Coll., 1923-24; B.S. in Humanities, Portland State Coll., 1957; also various postgrad. studies; m. C. A. Nelson, May 31, 1925; 1 dau., Betty Nelson Schuld. Sec., Pacific Trading Co., Portland, Oreg., 1923-24, Phil Grossmayer Ins. Co., Portland, 1924-26, Fred Lockley Books, Portland, 1942-43, R. W. Mulhausen, Portland, 1943-46; out-of-town corr. Oreg. Jour., Portland, 1927-37; author books of poetry: Webs From An Old Loom, 1952; Moccasin Prints West, 1955, The Scent of Water, 1973, Swish of the Ski, 1975; author biography: David Douglas on the Columbia, 1978; contbr. to poetry publs. Mem. Poetry Soc. Am., Poets and Writers, World Poetry Soc., Wing Family Am., Nat. Audubon Soc., Mazamas (editor Mazama Monthly 1956-61). Clubs: Cascade Ski, Order Eastern Star. Poetry collection established at U. Oreg. Library, 1971. Home: 5558 SE Aldercrest Ln Milwaukie OR 97222

NELSON-HERBER, JOAN, educator; b. Bklyn., May 28, 1930; d. William Law and Camille Marie (Morgan) Baumann; B.A., Coll. William and Mary, 1962; M.Ed., U. Pitts., 1966, Ph.D., 1970; m. Harold L. Herber, July 3, 1974; children—Joanne Nelson, Craig Nelson, Mark Nelson. Tchr., Hampton (Va.) Pub. Schs., 1962-65; asst. prof. U. Pitts., 1970-71, dir. reading clinic, 1970-73, asso. prof., 1971-75, dept. chmn., 1972-74; asso. prof. SUNY, Binghamton, 1975-78, prof., 1978—, dir. profl. edn., 1979-81; pres. TRICA Cons., Inc., 1978—; cons. in edn. Bd. dirs. Cortland Repertory Theatre, 1980-81; asso. dir. Network of Secondary Sch. Demonstration Centers for Teaching Reading in Content Areas, 1980—. Mem. Internat. Reading Assn. (chmn. publs. com.), Am. Ednl. Research Assn., Nat. Council Tchrs. English, Nat. Reading Council, N.Y. Reading Assn., Pi Lambda Theta, Kappa Delta Pi. Republican. Club: Cortland Country. Author: Changing Views, 1980; Meeting Challenges, 1980; (with Harold Herber) Reading Across the Curriculum, 1977); contbr. articles to profl. jours. Home: 15 Braeside Dr Homer NY 13077 Office: Div Profl Edn SUNY Binghamton NY 13901

NELSON-UNTHANK, TESSA, author, educator; b. Yorkshire, Eng.; came to U.S., 1959; M.A. (AAUW fellow), U. N.C., 1965; Ph.D. (AAUW fellow), U. Liverpool (Eng.), 1973; m. Kenneth Nelson Brown (dec.); m. 2d, Cecil H. Unthank, 1963 (dec. 1979). Head dept. English, Walsall, Eng., 1956-58; dir. English studies Windsor Coll., Buenos Aires, Argentina, 1958-59; prof. English lit. Cumberland Coll., Williamsburg, Ky., 1964—; mem. Bread Loaf Writers' Conf., Middlebury, Vt., 1978. Fulbright fellow, 1955-56; Danforth award, 1964; recipient Short Story prize, U.K., 1975; Julia Cairns Silver Trophy, U.K., 1978, Best Actress award, 1962, 79; Mellon Found. grantee, China, 1981. Mem. AAUW, Mensa, Soc. Women Writers and Journalists U.K., Soc. Authors U.K., Nat. Council Tchrs. English, Nat. League Am. Pen Women, Laurel County Humane Soc., Vegetarian Soc. U.K. Author children's stories, mag. articles; columnist British Alive!, 1973—; contbr. poetry to Outposts, Confrontations. Home: York Cottage Route 2 Box 173 Williamsburg KY 40769 Office: Dept English Cumberland College Williamsburg KY 40769

NEMETH, CHARLAN JEANNE, psychologist; b. St. Louis, Dec. 29, 1941; d. Joseph Frank and Loretto Julia (Linkul) N.; A.B., Washington U., St. Louis, 1963; M.A., U. Wis., 1965; postgrad. Oxford (Eng.) U., 1965-66; Ph.D., Cornell U., 1968; m. Gibbs Walter Brown, June 23, 1979. Asst. prof. dept. psychology U. Chgo., 1968-73; asso. prof. U. Va., 1973-75; asso. prof. U. B.C., 1975-77; prof. dept. psychology U. Calif., Berkeley, 1977—; vis. prof. U. Bristol (Eng.), 1969, Ecole Pratique des Hautes Etudes, Paris, 1970, U. Mannheim, summer 1971; fellow Battelle Seattle Research Center, 1974-75; cons. psychology and law. NIMH research grantee, 1971-81. Fellow Am. Psychol. Assn.; mem. Internat. Assn. Applied Psychology, Am. Psychology and Law Soc. Democrat. Roman Catholic. Mem. editorial bd. Social Psychology Quar., 1977-81; mem. internat. adv. bd. Brit. Jour. Social Psychology, 1980—; contbr. articles to profl. jours. Home: 14 Sky Terr Danville CA 94526 Office: Dept Psychology U Calif Berkeley CA 94720

NEMETH, P(ATRICIA) LYNN BANNER, lab. adminstr.; b. Chattanooga, Mar. 11, 1954; d. Don Lawrence and Mary Josephine (Buttram) Banner; B.S. magna cum laude in Med. Tech., Tenn. Wesleyan Coll. and Baroness Erlanger Sch. Med. Tech., 1976; M.A. in Health Care Adminstrn., Central Mich. U., 1983; m. John Paul Nemeth, Aug. 3, 1974; Med. technologist microbiology Morristown (N.J.) Meml. Hosp., 1976-77, immunology, 1977-78, sect. chief microbiology and immunology labs., 1978-82, adminstrv. dir. lab., 1982—; adj. asst. prof. County Coll. of Morris, 1981. Mem. Am. Soc. Clin. Pathologists (affiliate mem., cert. med. technologist), Am. Soc. for Microbiology, Clin. Lab. Mgmt. Assn. Democrat. Home: 20 Zeller Rd Long Valley NJ 07853 Office: 100 Madison Ave Morristown NJ 07960

NEMETH, PATTI MARIE, biomed. research scientist, educator; b. Tulsa, Nov. 8, 1946; d. Eugene M. and Juanita V. Cox; B.S., U. Ariz., 1969; Ph.D. (USPHS fellow 1972-77), UCLA, 1977; Alexander von Humboldt fellow in biomed. research U. Konstanz (W.Ger.), 1977-80, postdoctoral fellow in biomed. research Univ. Coll., London, 1978; asst. prof. neurology, neurosurgery, anatomy, and neurobiology Washington U., St. Louis, 1980—. Mem. Biophys. Soc. Am., Soc. Neurosci., Fedn. European Biochem. Socs. Contbr. articles in field to profl. jours. Office: Washington U Sch Medicine Dept Neurology St Louis MO 63110

NEMHOUSER, MOLLY BEATRICE, security co. exec.; b. Bklyn., July 4, 1947; d. Bernard Phillip and Gertride (Rothman) N.; student Baruch Coll. Systems analyst, programmer Olivetti Corp. Am., 1972-74; systems engr. Four Phase Systems, Inc., 1974-76; sr. systems analyst, then project coordinator Bradford Securities Processings Services, N.Y.C., 1976-79; sr. systems analyst Mocatta Metals Corp., N.Y.C., 1979-81, mgr. bus. systems quality assurance, 1981—. Mem. Assn. Computing Machinery. Office: 4 World Trade Center New York NY 10048

NEMIRO, BEVERLY MIRIUM ANDERSON, writer, educator; b. St. Paul, May 29, 1925; d. Martin and Anna Mae (Oshanyk) Anderson; student Reed Coll., 1943-44; B.A., U. Colo., 1947; postgrad. U. Denver; m. Jerome Morton Nemiro, Feb 10, 1951 (div. May 1975); children—Guy Samuel, Lee Anna, Dee Martin. Tchr., Seattle pub. schs., 1945-46; fashion coordinator, dir. Denver Dry Goods Co., 1948-51; free lance fashion model, 1951-58, 78—; fashion dir. Denver Market Week Assn., 1952-53; moderator TV program Your Preschool Child, Denver, 1955-56; free lance writer gen. articles and nonfiction books, 1958—; dir. public relations Fairmont Hotel, Denver, 1979-80; instr. writing and communications U. Colo., Denver Center, 1970—, U. Calif., 1976-78. Active Denver Art Mus., Colo. Opera Guild, Denver Symphony Group, Achievement Rewards for Coll. Scientists, Children's Hosp. Assn.; pres. Denver Jr. Symphony Guild, 1959-60. Recipient Top Hand award Colo. Authors' League, 1969, 72, 79, 80, 81, 82, 100 Best Books of Yr. award N.Y. Times, 1969, 71; named One of Colo.'s Women of Yr., Denver Post, 1964. Mem. Public Relations Soc. Am., Am. Soc. Journalists and Authors, Nat. Writers Club, Colo. Authors League (dir. 1969—), Authors Guild, Authors League Am., U. Denver Woman's Library Assn., Colo. Women's Coll. Library Assn., Sigma Delta Chi, Kappa Alpha Theta. Author: The Complete Book of High Altitude Baking, 1961; Colorado a la Carte, 1963; The Lunch Box Cookbook, 1965; Colorado a la Carte, Series II, 1966; Where to Eat in Colorado, 1967; The High Altitude Cookbook, 1969; The Busy People's Cookbook (Better Homes and Gardens Book Club selection 1971), 1971; Single After Fifty, 1978 (paperback edit. 1980); The New High Altitude Cookbook, 1980; contbr. articles to periodicals and newspapers. Home: 420 S Marion Pkwy Apt 1003 Denver CO 80209

NEMITZ, NANCY LEE, bank exec.; b. Chamberlain, S.D., Nov. 1, 1949; d. Gerrit and Irene Theresa (Buettner) Brink; student Augustana Coll., 1968-70, Mankato State U., 1970-74, Coll. Gt. Falls, 1977-79, Mundelein Coll., 1981—; m. Floyd Brian Nemitz, Sept. 27, 1975; stepchildren—Todd, Robyn, Jeff, Chris, Rodney, Wendy; 1 fosterchild, Christine Russell. Aide firm Churchill, Sauer, Manolis & Hoyt, 1968; transit clk. First Nat. Bank, Sioux Falls, S.D., 1969-70; ops. staff First Nat. Bank, Owatonna, Minn., 1971-74; regional examiner First Bank System, Inc., Mpls., 1974-76, regional audit officer, 1976-77; auditor First Nat. Bank of Gt. Falls, Mont., 1977-78, ops. officer, 1978-79; corp. compliance officer First Bank System, Inc., Mpls., 1979-80, asst. v.p. compliance, 1980-81, asst. v.p., dir. product mgmt., 1981—; lectr. on consumer laws in bank industry; condr. compliance seminars; instr. Am. Inst. Banking, Bank Adminstrn. Inst.; faculty Am. Bankers Assn. schs. Lobbyist for foster care reform, Mont., 1979; treas. Gt. Falls Foster Parent Assn., 1979. Named Outstanding Young Career Women, Mont. Bus. and Profl. Women, 1978. Mem. Nat. Assn. Bank Women (Minn. state council, chmn. state conf., regional dir.). Home: 9601 Utica Rd Bloomington MN 55437 Office: PO Box 522 Minneapolis MN 55402

NEMSER, CINDY, writer; b. Bklyn., Mar. 26, 1937; d. William Isador and Helen (Nelson) Heller; B.A., Bklyn. Coll., 1958, M.A. in English Lit., 1964; M.A., Inst. Fine Arts N.Y.U., 1966; m. Charles Nemser, Dec. 16, 1956; 1 dau., Cathy. Tchr. elem. sch., N.Y.C., 1958-64; curatorial intern Mus. Modern Art, N.Y.C., 1966; contbg. editor Arts Mag., 1972-75; editor, pub. The Feminist Art Jour., 1972-77; books: Art Talk: Conversations with 12 Women Artists, 1975; Eve's Delight, 1982. Bd. dirs. Women's Caucus for Art, N.Y.C., 1975-78. Am. Fedn. Arts grantee, 1967; NEA Art Critics fellow, 1975. Mem. Internat. Assn. Art Critics, Authors Guild, Poets and Writers Assn., the Feminist Writers Guild, Women's Nat. Book Assn. Home: 41 Montgomery Pl Brooklyn NY 11215

NEMZOFF, RUTH ESTHER, state legislator; b. Boston, Dec. 10, 1940; d. Samuel Alexander and Sophia H. (Marcovitz) N.; B.A., Barnard Coll., 1962; M.A., Columbia U., 1964; Ed.D., Harvard U., 1979; m. Harris A. Berman, May 31, 1964; children—Kim Deborah, Seth Philip, Rebecca Abigail. Tchr., Sharon (Mass.) Public Schs., 1962-63, 64-65; counselor Am. Internat. Sch., New Delhi, 1966-67; dir. spl. services Mt. Hope. Sch., Nashua, N.H., 1971-74; mem. N.H. Ho. of Reps., 1979—, asst. minority leader, 1981—. Mem. NOW, Am. Personnel and Guidance Assn. Democrat. Jewish. Office: State House Minority Office Concord NH 03301

NENNER, VICTORIA ANNA, nurse; b. Marshall, Tex., Jan. 17, 1945; d. Bernard Paul and Mary DeLayne (Bowen) Corich; B.S. in Nursing (Regents scholar, Krost-Freeman scholar, Mary Gobbs Jones Nursing scholar), Tex. Women's U., 1966; cert. U. Paris, summer 1966; m. Paul Edwin Nenner, Aug. 12, 1970. Mem. nursing staff St. Thomas Hosp., London, 1966-67, Parkland Meml. Hosp., Dallas, 1967-68; coordinator nursing continuing edn. Scripps Meml. Hosp., La Jolla, Calif., 1974—; mem. part-time faculty U. Calif., San Diego; mem. vis. faculty U. B.C.; mem. Inservice Council San Diego and Imperial Counties, 1974—, pres., 1976-77; mem. San Diego Community Colls. Health Edn. Adv. Bd., 1976—. Served to capt. Nurse Corps, USAF, 1968-73. Named Tex. Student Nurse of Year, 1966. Mem. Am. Soc. Health Edn. and Tng., Nat. League Nursing, Am. Nurses Assn., Nat. Assn. Female Execs., Sigma Theta Tau. Author articles in field; producer oncology nursing ednl. videotapes. Home: 3937 Southview Dr San Diego CA 92117 Office: Scripps Meml Hosp 9888 Genesee Ave La Jolla CA 92038

NESBIT, PHYLLIS SCHNEIDER (MRS. PETER N. NESBIT), dist. judge; b. New Kirk, Okla., Sept. 21, 1919; d. Vernon Lee and Irma Mae (Biddle) Schneider; B.S. in Chemistry, U. Ala., 1948, LL.B., 1958; m. Peter N. Nesbit, Sept. 14, 1939. Draftsman, Drydock & Shipbldg. Co., Mobile, Ala., 1942-45; tech. sec. B. F. Goodrich Co., Tuscaloosa, Ala., 1949-55; sec. Ala. Bus. Research Council, University, 1955-58; admitted to Ala. bar, 1958; partner firm Brantley & Nesbit, and predecessor firm, Robertsdale, Ala., 1958-76; judge Mcpl. Ct., Daphne, Ala., 1964-76, Silverhill, Ala., 1969-76; city atty. City of Loxley (Ala.), 1974-76; dist. judge Baldwin County (Ala.), 1977—. Sec., Daphne Civic Assn., 1962—; treas. Joint Legis. Council Ala., 1972-73. Mem. Ala. State Bar, Baldwin County Bar Assn. (pres. 1967-68), Nat. Assn. Women Lawyers, Ala. Women Lawyers Assn. (pres. 1966-67), Ala. Mcpl. Judges Assn. (pres. 1970-73), Ala. Council Judges of Juvenile Ct. (treas. 1979-81), Ala. Assn. Dist. Judges, Am. Judicature Soc., Bus. and Profl. Women's Club (pres. 1974-75), Gamma Sigma Epsilon. Mem. Order Eastern Star (worthy matron 1963-64). Home: 302 Creek Dr Fairhope AL 36532 Office: 1138 Bay Minette AL 36507

NESBITT, MARGOT LORD (MRS. CHARLES R. NESBITT), fine arts appraiser; b. Tonbridge, Kent, Eng., Feb. 13, 1927; d. Douglas G.R. and Octave (Waghorne) Lord; came to U.S., 1930, naturalized, 1937; B.A. in English Lit., U. Okla., 1950, B.F.A. in Art History, 1970, M.A., 1975; m. Charles R. Nesbitt, June 6, 1948; children—Nancy Margot, Douglas Charles, Carolyn Jane. Appraiser fine arts, Oklahoma City, 1968—; treas. Apollo Oil Corp., 1974—. Mem. Okla. Arts and Humanities Council, 1971-76; mem. women's com. Oklahoma City Symphony, 1964—; life mem. Okla. Art Center, women's bd., 1962-63; chmn. art collection State of Okla., 1975-76; bd. dirs. Okla. Found. for Disabled, 1972-75; bd. advisers Nat. Trust Historic Preservation, 1976-81. Mem. English Speaking Union, Okla. Hist. Soc. (dir. 1975—), Hist. Preservation Oklahoma City (treas. 1977-80), Am. Soc. Appraisers (sr. mem.; pres. Okla. chpt. 1978-79), Appraisers' Assn. Am., Kappa Alpha Theta (pres. alumni chpt. 1962-64, Okla. chmn. Theta Link 1965-66, treas. corp. bd. 1976-77). Democrat. Episcopalian (treas. assemblies 1971-72, mem. women's bd. 1971-72, treas. altar guild 1972-73, treas. cathedral 1976-78, mem. vestry 1978—, jr. warden 1978-82). Clubs: Connoisseur (pres. 1956-57); Early American Glass (treas. 1973-75). Address: 1703 N Hudson St Oklahoma City OK 73103

NESBITT, NANCY ANNE, public utility ofcl.; b. Fort Worth, Aug. 19, 1937; d. Charles Keith and Naomi Lucille Nesbitt; student N. Tex. State U., 1957. Clk. invoice processing Gulf States Utilities, Beaumont, Tex., 1958-78, gen. clk. invoice processing, 1978-79, sect. head invoice processing and materials mgmt., 1979-81, supr. procurement control-materials mgmt., 1981—. Youth dir. Pine Burr Bapt. Ch. Mem. Nat. Assn. Female Execs., Am. Mgmt. Assn., Research Inst. Am., N. Tex. State U. Alumni Assn., Sabine Neches Purchasing Assn., Beaumont Assn. for Mental Health. Baptist. Clubs: Emeral Century, Order Eastern Star, Live Wires, Bus. and Profl. Men's.

NESBITT, RUTH, social worker, psychotherapist; b. Johnson City, N.Y., Sept. 18, 1936; d. James Roland and Mary Elizabeth (Ward) Flaherty; B.S. in Pharmacy magna cum laude, St. John's U., 1962; postgrad., N.Y.U., 1968-71; m. John W. Nesbitt, Dec. 6, 1974; stepchildren—Mary Terese, Patrick. Dept. dir. pharmacy and outpatient services DePaul Hosp., Norfolk, Va., 1962-68, instr. Sch. Nursing, bd. dirs., 1962-68; supr. childrens services Bklyn. Bur. Community Services,

1971-73; dir. social services Wyoming Conf. Childrens Home, Binghamton, N.Y., 1973-75; psychotherapist Broome Devel. Service, Binghamton, 1976—. Active human devel. service in parish church. Recipient Bristol award, St. John's U., 1962. Lic. psychotherapist, cert. social worker, N.Y. Mem. Nat. Assn. Social Workers, Acad. Cert. Social Workers, Va. Soc. Hosp. Pharmacists (pres. 1965-67). Home: 15 Boland Rd Apalachin NY 13732 Office: Arch St Johnson City NY 13790

NESCOT, MARCIA L. MALIN, radio sta. exec.; b. Rochester, N.H., Dec. 28, 1921; d. Samuel and Anna (Birnbaum) Belinsky; B.A., U. Wis., 1943; student U. N.H., 1942; m. William T. Nescot, Mar. 30, 1973; children—Robert J. Malin, James N. Malin. Economist, U.S. Dept. Labor, Washington, 1945; treas., pres., dir. Strafford Broadcasting Corp., Rochester, N.H., 1968—; dir. Community TV Corp., Laconia, N.H., 1953-68. Pres., Strafford County Prenatal and Family Planning, 1977-79, v.p., 1976-77, bd. dirs., 1973-76; bd. dirs. Strafford County Human Services Council, 1977—, v.p., 1979-80; mem. exec. com. Frisbie Meml. Hosp., Rochester, 1975-79, trustee, 1974; chmn. historic preservation com. Rochester Urban Revitilization Task Force, 1980—; bd. dirs. Arts Rochester, 1982—; mem. adv. bd. Salvation Army, Rochester; dir. Strafford County Homemakers Home Health Aide, 1981—. Office: WWNH AM-FM Rochester NH 03867

NESS, ANITA KAY, nurse, educator; b. Lexington, Nebr., Aug. 31, 1945; d. Robert Van and Dorothy Louise Whitson; B.S. in Natural Sci., Nebr. Wesleyan U., 1966; R.N., Bryan Meml. Hosp., Lincoln, Nebr., 1966; M.N., Wichita State U., 1981; m. Gary Dale Ness, Nov. 27, 1975; 1 son, Jason Robert. Instr. nursing, acting dir. nursing Butler County Community Coll., El Dorado, Kans., 1969-72; instr. nursing Wichita State U., 1972-75, Ft. Hayes State U., Hayes, Kans., 1975-80; home dialysis supr. clients, Ellis County, Kans., 1978-80; dir. nursing edn. Dodge City (Kans.) Community Coll., 1980—; bd. dirs., dir. vols. Hospice Orgn., Dodge City, 1980—. Mem. Am. Nurses Assn., Am. Heart Assn., Kans. Nurses Assn. Republican. Club: Soroptomists. Home: 2208 4th St Dodge City KS 67801 Office: Dodge City Community Coll Hwy 50 Bypass and 14th St Dodge City KS 67801

NESTER, THEOA GENEVA, broadcasting co. exec.; b. Carroll County, Va., May 15, 1935; d. Carbin Posey and Violett Marie (Lewis) Vass; student Wytheville Community Coll., 1976; m. Elmo Nester, June 2, 1950; children—Ronald Carlin, Faithe Yvonne Webb. Sales clk., Guynn Dept. Store, 1964, Towel Town Co., Hillsville, Va., 1971, Guynn Dept. Store, 1971-77; sales mgr. WHHV AM, Hillsville, 1977—. Mem. Beta Sigma Phi. Baptist. Home: PO Box 774 Hillsville VA 24343 Office: PO Box 648 Hillsville VA 24343

NETSCH, DAWN CLARK, state legislator; b. Cin., 1926; d. William Keith and Hazel Dawn (Harrison) Clark; B.A., Northwestern U., 1948, J.D., magna cum laude, 1952; m. Walter A. Netsch, Oct. 19, 1963. Mem. staff League Women Voters Cook County, Ill., 1949; admitted to D.C. bar, 1952, Ill. bar, 1953; pvt. practice, Washington, 1952-54; law clk. to fed. judge U.S. Dist. Ct. No. Dist. Ill., 1954-56; pvt. practice, Chgo., 1957-61; adminstrv. and legal aide to gov. Ill., 1961-65; mem. faculty Northwestern U. Law Sch., 1965—, prof. law; formerly mem. Ill. Senate, 13th Dist., from 1971, now mem. Ill. Senate, 4th Dist. Del., chmn. com. revenue and fin. Ill. Constl. Conv., 1970; mem. Ill. Intergovtl. Relations Commn., 1962-65, Commn. State Govt. Ill., 1965-67, Constn. Study Commn., 1967; active numerous local Democratic campaigns. Recipient Ethel Parker award Ind. Voters Ill., 1973, 75, 77; Best Legislator award Ill. Edn. Assn., 1973; Golden award environ. legislator Ill. League Conservation Voters, 1973; Environ. Legislators award Ill. Environ. Council, 1975, 77. Mem. Am., Ill. Chgo. bar assns., ACLU (dir. Ill. div.), Leadership Council Met. Open Communities (dir.), Nat. Program Ednl. Leadership (adv. bd.), Com. Ill. Govt. (dir.). Co-author: State and Local Government in a Federal System. *

NETTLESHIP, PATRICIA SHARYN, gen. contractor; b. Calif.; A.A., Stephens Coll.; A.B., U. Mo.; A.M.P., Harvard U.; children—Stephen, Lisa, Gunnar. Co-founder, sec.-treas. North Pacific Constrn. Co., Yakima, Wash., 1969-72, chmn., pres., chief exec. officer, 1973—; dir. Western Bank Commerce, Sacramento de la plata; chmn. Competitive Enterprise Found. Mem. tax policy subcom. Econ. Council, Republican Nat. Com. Mem. Young Pres. Orgn. Episcopalian. Clubs: Seattle Yacht, Wash. Athletic. Home: 7 Crest Circle Yakima WA 98902 Office: PO Box 2535 Yakima WA 98907

NETTLETON, LOIS, actress; b. Oak Park, Ill.; d. Edward L. and Virginia (Schaffer) N.; student Goodman Theater Sch., Actors Studio, 1951. Actress stage plays, films, television; film appearances include Period of Adjustment, 1962, Come Fly With Me, 1963, Mail Order Bride, 1964, Valley of Mystery, Bamboo Saucer, The Good Guys and the Bad Guys, Dirty Dingus Magee, The Sidelong Glances of a Pigeon Kicker, The Honkers, Echoes of a Summer; TV appearances include Medical Center, Barnaby Jones, Hawaii Five-O, Route 66, Gunsmoke, The Nurses, Alfred Hitchcock Show, Twilight Zone, Dupont Show, Eleventh Hour, Armstrong Circle Theatre, Naked City, Doctor Kildare, Portriat of Emily Dickinson, Emanuel, Duet for Two Hands, The Hidden River, The Women in White, The Light That Failed, Incident of Love, No Hiding Place; made Broadway debut in The Biggest Thief in Town; stage appearances include Darkness At Noon, The Rainmaker, God and Kate Murphy, Silent Night, Lonely Night, The Merchant of Venus, Much Ado About Nothing, Elektra, Cat on a Hot Tin Roof, The Wayward Stork, A Streetcar Named Desire. Recipient Clarence Derwent award, 1959, Laurel award, 1963. Mem. AFTRA, Screen Actors Guild, Address: care William Morris Agy 1350 Ave of Americas New York NY 10019 *

NEU, IRENE DOROTHY, historian, educator; b. Cin.; d. Frederick Francis and Mary Clara (Holterman) N.; B.A., Marietta Coll., 1944; M.A., Cornell U., 1945, Ph.D., 1950; m. Robert Leslie Jones, Nov. 25, 1976. Fellow, Research Center Entrepreneurial History, Harvard U., 1950-51; instr. Rockford (Ill.) Coll., 1951-52, Conn. Coll., New London, 1953-54; asso. prof. S.E. Mo. State Coll., Cape Girardeau, Mo., 1956-62, prof., 1962-64; asso. prof. Ind. U., Bloomington, 1964-70, prof. history, 1970—. Fulbright fellow Italy, 1954-55; Social Sci. Research Council faculty fellow, 1960-61; Eleutherian Mills Hist. Library sr. fellow, 1970. Mem. Am. Hist. Assn., Orgn. Am. Historians, Econ. History Assn., Bus. History Conf., AAUP, Ind. Hist. Soc., Phi Beta Kappa. Author: Erastus Corning, Merchant and Financier, 1794-1872, 1960; co-author: The American Railroad Network, 1861-1890, 1956; contbr. articles in field to profl. jours. Office: Dept History Ind U Bloomington IN 47405

NEUBERGER, CARMEN GUEVARA, univ. adminstr.; b. Manila, Philippines, Jan. 5, 1935; came to U.S., 1949, naturalized, 1952; d. Santiago Garcia and Carmen (Fernandez) Guevara; B.S., U. Md., 1955; M.Ed., Am. U., 1973, Ed.D., 1977; m. Jack Adams Neuberger, June 11, 1955; children—Catherine Adams, Cynthia Ann, Carmen Lea, Christine Jane, Mary Jo. Tchr. pub. schs., Washington, 1969-73; acting asst. dir. Internat. Student Ctr., Am. U., Washington, 1974, asst. to dir. acad. adminstrn., 1974-76, asst. to v.p. student life, 1976-77, dean students, 1977—; coordinator for D.C., Am. Council on Edn., Nat. Identification program for Women in Higher Edn. Adminstrn., 1980-82. Mem. Archdiocese of Washington Bd. Edn., 1976-79. Am. U. fellow, 1972-73; recipient St. Ann's medal, Girl Scouts U.S.A., 1974. Mem. Council for Advancement of Standards in Student Devel./Student Personnel, So. Regional Accreditation Assn. (vis. team 1981), Nat. Cath. Edn. Assn. (nat. forum for Cath. parent orgns. 1979-82), Nat. Assn. Women Deans, Adminstrs. and Counselors (nat. treas. 1979-81, nat. pres. 1983-84), Nat. Assn. Student Personnel Adminstrs. (dir. 1979-82, Mortar Bd. Cap and Gown chpt. citation 1982), Phi Kappa Phi, Omicron Nu. Democrat. Roman Catholic. Club: Welcome to Wash. Internat. Contbr. articles to profl. jours. Office: Div Student Life MGC 200 The Am Univ Washington DC 20016

NEUER, JUDITH ANN, mfg. co. ofcl.; b. Rochester, N.Y., Dec. 4, 1943; d. Edward George and Elizabeth Grace (Specht) N.; B.S. in Biology, Alfred U., 1965. Research assoc. U. Rochester Med. Sch., 1965-68; computer systems analyst Rochester Inst. Tech., 1968-70, now lectr.; systems cons. Sybron Corp., 1970-72, mgr. order processing, 1973-75, distbn. and customer service mgr., 1975-76; mgr. stores and receiving Xerox Corp., Webster, N.Y., 1976-77, mgr. systems and ops. planning, 1977-79, mgr. mfg. ops., 1980—. Program cons. women in bus. and career devel. Rochester YMCA; founding mem. steering com., bd. dirs. Women's Career Center of Rochester; bd. mgrs. Lost Mountain Manor Condominium Complex. Mem. Am. Prodn. and Inventory Control Soc., AAUW. Republican. Presbyterian. Home: 4 Lost Mountain Rochester NY 14625 Office: Xerox Corp 800 Phillips Rd Webster NY 14580

NEUFELD, ELIZABETH FONDAL, biochemist, govt. ofcl.; b. Paris, Sept. 27, 1928; U.S. citizen; m. 1951; Ph.D., U. Calif., 1956; D.H.C. (hon.), U. Rene Descartes, Paris, 1978; D.Sc. (hon.), Russell Sage Coll., Troy, N.Y., 1981. Asst. research biochemist Nat. Inst. Arthritis, Metabolism and Digestive Diseases, Bethesda, Md., 1963-73, research biochemist, 1973-79, chief sect. human biochem. genetics, 1979—, chief genetics and biochem. br., 1980—. USPHS fellow U. Calif., Berkeley, 1957-63, asst. biochemist, 1963—. Recipient Dickson prize U. Pitts., 1974, Hillebrand award, 1975, Gardner Found. award. Mem. Nat. Acad. Sci., Am. Acad. Arts and Sci., Am. Soc. Human Genetics, Am. Chem. Soc., Am. Soc. Biol. Chemists. Office: National Institute of Arthritis Diabetes Digestive and Kidney Diseases Bldg 10 GNZ 38 Bethesda MD 20205 *

NEUFELD, MARGARET LYNNE, info. scientist; b. Edmonton, Alta., Can., Sept. 3, 1939; came to U.S., 1964, naturalized, 1977; d. Benjamin O. and Catherine McNaughton (Arbuckle) Farnham; B.S. in Chemistry, U. Alta., 1959; M.S. in Info. Sci., Drexel U., 1972; m. Gordon Ross Neufeld, June 18, 1959; children—Katherine, David. Research officer coal sect. Research Council of Can., 1959-63; research asso. Johnson Labs., U. Pa., Phila., 1964-65; info. scientist Franklin Inst., Phila., 1970-71; group mgr. Inst. for Sci. Info., Phila., 1971-73, dir. library ops., 1973-74; sr. cons. info. storage and retrieval group Auerbach Assos., Phila., 1974-78, dep. group mgr., 1978-79; exec. dir. Nat. Fedn. of Abstracting and Info. Services, Phila., 1979—. Mem. adv. bd. Performing Arts Sch., Phila. Coll. Performing Arts, 1980—. Recipient spl. citation U.S. Consumer Product Safety Commn., 1976; Auerbach Outstanding Performance award, 1975, 76, 78. Mem. Spl. Libraries Assn., Am. Soc. Info. Sci. (mem. edn. com. 1976-78, mktg. com. 1978-80, co-editor local chpt. newsletter 1973-76), Am. Nat. Standards Inst. (mem. exec. council 1980—), Am. Computer Soc., AAAS. Home: 425 W Mermaid Ln Philadelphia PA 19118 Office: 112 S 16th St Philadelphia PA 19102

NEUHAUSER, CHARLOTTE LARRAINE, educator; b. Ft. Wayne, Ind., Jan. 27, 1936; d. Kenneth M. and Kathryn A. Hyman; B.A., DePauw U., 1958; M.Ed., Wayne State U., 1966, Ph.D., 1971; m. Robert W. Neuhauser, Aug. 23, 1958; children—Jane Ann, David Wayne. Tchr., project dir. Farmington (Mich.) Public Schs., 1962-67; research asst. Wayne State U., 1967-70, successively systems analyst, research asso., asst. project dir., 1970-75; chmn. dept. bus. adminstrn. and econs. Madonna Coll., Livonia, Mich., 1975—; cons. U. Mich., Mich. and Ind. Depts. Edn., Weber State Coll., U. S.D., Ill. State U.; systems cons. orgns. and assns. Mem. Farmington Community Bd.; bd. dirs. arts and crafts show PTA; rep. Farmington Arts Council. Name grant awardee AAUW, 1972. Mem. Am. Ednl. Research Assn., Am. Inst. Decision Scis., Am. Ednl. Data Systems, World Future Soc., Am. Soc. Personnel Adminstrs., Am. Soc. Tng. and Devel. (Outstanding Devel. award 1979), Am. Audubon Soc., Mich. Assn. Computer Users in Learning, Phi Delta Kappa, Delta Pi Epsilon, Delta Zeta. Presbyterian. Research on new bus. and office learnings systems competency-based edn., bus. leanings for high ability students; contbr. articles profl. jours. Office: 36600 Schoolcraft Rd Livonia MI 48150

NEULS-BATES, CAROL, businesswoman, musicologist; b. Bklyn., Dec. 1, 1939; d. Frederick Carl and Edith Tindall Neuls; B.A. cum laude, Wellesley Coll., 1961; Ph.D., Yale U., 1970; postgrad. N.Y.U. Sch. Bus. Adminstrn., 1979; m. William Boulton Bates, Jr., Sept. 1, 1962; 1 dau., Julia Barstow. Mng. editor RILM: Abstracts of Music Lit., Grad. Center City U. N.Y., 1972-75, project dir., co-prin. investigator Women in Am. Music, 1976-79; adj. asst. prof. music Hunter Coll., City U. N.Y., 1973-75; asst. to curator Lincoln Center Library Performing Arts, 1975-76; asst. editor Coll. Music Symposium, 1975-78; asst. prof. music Bklyn. Coll. City U. N.Y., 1978-82; account exec. John O'Donnell Co., N.Y.C., 1982—. Yale U. fellow, 1962-67; Radcliffe Inst. grantee, 1968-70; research grantee Nat. Endowment Humanities, 1976-79, Ford Found., 1977-79, Nat. Fedn. Music Clubs, 1978. Mem. Coll. Music Soc. (council 1975-78), Am. Musicol. Soc., Sonneck Soc., Nat. Women's Studies Assn., Nat. Soc. Fund Raising Execs., NOW. Author: Women in Music: An Anthology of Source Readings from the Middle Ages to the Present, 1982; Women in American Music: A Bibliography of Music and Literature, 1979; contbr. articles in field to music jours. Home: 145 E 16th St New York NY 10003

NEUMAN, NANCY ADAMS MOSSHAMMER (MRS. MARK DONALD NEUMAN), civic leader; b. Greenwich, Conn., July 24, 1936; d. Alden Smith and Margaret (Mevis) Mosshammer; B.A., Pomona Coll., 1957; M.A., U. Calif. at Berkeley, 1961; m. Mark Donald Neuman, Dec. 23, 1958; children—Deborah Adams, Jennifer Fuller, Jeffrey Abbott. Pres., Lewisburg (Pa.) area League Women Voters, 1967-70; bd. dirs. LWV Pa., 1970-77, pres., 1975-77; bd. dirs. LWV U.S., 1977—, 2d v.p., 1978-80, 1st v.p., 1982—; mem. Pa. Gov.'s Commn. on Mortgage and Interest Rates, 1973, Pa. Commonwealth Child Devel. Com., 1974-75; bd. dirs. Housing Assistance Council, Inc., Washington, 1974—, pres., 1978-80; bd. dirs. Nat. Council on Agrl. Life and Labor, 1974-79, Nat. Rural Housing Coalition, 1975—, Pa. Housing Fin. Agy., 1975-80; Disciplinary Bd. Supreme Ct. Pa., 1980—; mem. Pa. Gov.'s Task Force on Voter Registration, 1975-76, Nat. Task Force for Implementation Equal Rights Amendment, 1975-77; mem. adv. com. Pa. Gov.'s Interdepartmental Council on Seasonal Farmworkers, 1975-77; mem. Appellate Ct. Nominating Commn. Pa., 1976-79; chmn. Fed. Jud. Nominating Commn. Pa., 1977—; mem. Pa. Gov.'s Study Commn. on Pub. Employee Relations, 1976-78; del. Internat. Women's Yr. Conf., 1977; bd. dirs. ERAmerica, Inc., 1st v.p., 1977-79, Nat. Low Income Housing Coalition, 1979-82; Rural Am., 1979-81, Fed. Home Loan Bank Pitts., 1979—; mem. Nat. Adv. Com. for Women, 1978-79; mem. nat. adv. com. Pa. Neighborhood Preservation Support System, 1976-77. Recipient Disting. Alumna award MacDuffie Sch. for Girls. Home: 132 Verna Rd Lewisburg PA 17837

NEUMAN, STEPHANIE SELLORS, clin. psychologist; b. Pueblo, Colo., Dec. 14, 1945; d. John and Catherine (Swing) Sellors; B.A., Miami U., 1967; M.A., Case Western Res. U., 1974, Ph.D., 1976. Social worker, spl. edn. tchr., 1967-72; clin. psychologist, research dir. Mental Devel. Center, Cleve., 1973-77; psychology cons. Cuyahoga County Bd. Mental Retardation, Cleve., 1974-77; research coordinator State of Ohio Dept. Mental Health and Mental Retardation, Cleve., 1977-81; staff psychologist Cleve. Met. Gen. Hosp., 1978-80; asst. clin. prof. dept. psychiatry Sch. Medicine Case Western Res. U., Cleve., 1978—, asst. clin. prof. dept. pediatrics, 1980—; cons. psychologist United Meth. Children's Home, Berea, Ohio, 1977-81; pvt. practice psychology, 1981—; host Dr. Stephanie Neuman Show, Sta. WERE, 1981—; staff psychologist Sta. WEWS-TV, 1982—; cons. Hanna Perkins Sch., Lake Ridge Acad., Council Econ. Opportunities, Cleve., 1974-77, Lake County Mental Health Center, 1981—. Mem. Am. Psychol. Assn., Am. Orthopsychiat. Assn., Ohio Psychol. Assn., Cleve. Psychol. Assn., Nat. Registry Health Service Providers in Psychology. Home: 15515 Van Aken Blvd Shaker Heights OH 44120 Office: 26900 Cedar Rd Beachwood OH 44122

NEUMANN, DEBORAH, ins. co. exec.; b. Glens Falls, N.Y., Feb. 15, 1951; d. John Herman and Florence Mary (LaMarque) N.; student Albany State U., 1969-71. Accounts receivable clk. Continental Ins. Co., Glens Falls, N.Y., 1971-74; claims adjuster trainee Underwriters Adjustment Co., Malden, Mass., 1974-77, property claims specialist, Boston, 1977-78; property examiner Mass. Fair Plan, Boston, 1978-79, sr. property claims examiner, 1979-80, supr. property claims, 1980—. Mem. Mass. Assn. Ins. Women, Adjusters Roundtable, Internat. Assn. Arson Investigators, Nat. Assn. Underwater Instrs. Mormon. Clubs: Aquawoman, N.E. Aquarium Dive, Blue Goose (hon. Mem. Boston chpt.). Office: 3 Center Plaza Boston MA 02108

NEUMANN, EDITH, microbiologist; b. Vienna, Austria, May 26, 1902; came to U.S., 1948, naturalized, 1954; d. Alfred and Hermine Spitzer; Ph.D., U. Vienna, 1927; m. Frederick Neumann, Oct. 3, 1927. Tchr., Sr. High Sch. for Boys, Haifa, Palestine, 1945-46; technician Brit. Mil. Hosp., Haifa, 1946-47; med. lab. dir. PIC Oil Refineries, Haifa, 1947-48; asst. microbiologist Jewish Hosp. Bklyn., 1948-57; microbiologist Maimonides Hosp. of Bklyn., 1957-69; lab. dir. Jetti Katz Clin. Lab., N.Y.C., 1969-82; mem. faculty St. Francis Coll., Bklyn., 1961. Fellow AAAS; mem. N.Y. Soc. Microbiology, N.Y. Soc. Tropical Medicine, Am. Soc. Microbiology, Am. Soc. Tropical Medicine. Democrat. Presbyterian. Editor: Writings of Frederick Neumann, 1971; Ueber das Lachen, 1972; God's Fifth Columnist and Other Essays, 1972; Where do We Stand?, Vol. I, Law and Revelation, 1978, Vol. II, Faith and Realty in History, 1978, Vol. III, Escape from Futility, 1979; contbr. articles to profl. jours. Home: 138 E 78th St New York NY 10021

NEUMANN, PEGGY-ANN, coll. adminstr.; b. Balt., Sept. 13, 1927; d. Walter Edward and Wanda (Monath) N.; B.A. magna cum laude, N.Y. U., 1966, M.A., 1968. Asst. to dir. Va. Polytech. Inst., Danville, 1952-59; area supv. census bur. Dept. Commerce, Danville, 1960; project dir. for exec. dean arts and scis., N.Y. U., N.Y.C., 1962-64; asst. to dean Washington Sq. Coll., N.Y. U., 1970-72, isntr. English, 1970-72; dir. career counseling Hollins Coll., Roanoke, Va., 1972—; lectr., cons. in field. Bd. dirs., chmn. membership drive Danville Concert Assn., 1956-62; sec. ch. council Lutheran Ch. of Ascension, Danville, Va., also mem. choir, ch. visitors com., Sunday sch. tchr., chmn. edn. com., 1952-62; Recipient Lena Kastle award, 1966. Mem. Coll. Placement Assn., So., Va., Middle Atlantic coll. placement assns., Assn. Sch. Coll. and Univ. Staffing, Middle Atlantic Assn. Sch., Coll. and Univ. Staffing, Women Deans, Adminstrs. and Counselors, Am. Soc. Tng. and Devel., Catalyst, Roanoke Valley Bus.-Educators Consortium, Working Women on Their Own (founder, 1st pres.), Roanoke Network Profl. and Managerial Women (founder, 1st pres.). Contbr. articles to profl. jours. Home: PO Box 9565 Roanoke VA 24020 Office: Career Counseling Center Hollins Coll Roanoke VA 24020

NEUMEISTER, JULIA THERESA, data processing mgr.; b. Newark, June 17, 1954; d. Norman Francis and Marie Estell (Beach) Smith; degree in computer programming Chubb Inst. Computer Tech., 1976; 1 son, Brad Joseph. Ins. clk. Chubb & Son, Inc., Short Hills, N.J., 1972-74, policy rater, 1974-75, computer programmer, 1976-79, programmer analyst, 1979-80, sr. programmer, 1980--81, data processing project mgr., 1981—. Mem. Nat. Assn. Female Execs., Women's Internat. Bowling Congress (state champion N.J. 1978-79). Office: 51 JFK Pkwy Short Hills NJ 07078

NEUMILLER, ROSE MARIE, health care exec.; b. Wolf Point, Mont., Apr. 26, 1949; d. Jacob and Elizabeth Ann (Heser) N.; student Mont. State U., 1967-68. Med. records clk., then med. records dir. Trinity Hosp., Wolf Point, 1968-76; cons. med. record mgmt., 1974—, rev. coordinator Mont. Found. Med. Care, Helena, 1976—; mem. subarea council Health Systems Agy., 1980-82; organizer, pres. Wolf Point Diabetes Assn., 1982. Chmn. Roosevelt County nursing and health program ARC, 1982-83. Accredited records technician. Mem. Mont. Med. Record Assn. (chmn. public relations and recruitment 1981-83). Home: 427 Fallon St Box 505 Wolf Point MT 59201 Office: Trinity Hosp Knapp St Wolf Point MT 59201

NEUNDORFER, MARTHA LU, mfg. co. exec.; b. Cleve., Sept. 15, 1945; d. William and Evelyn Marie (Rodhe) N.; M.S. in Math., Allegheny Coll., 1966; postgrad. Cleve. State U., 1969-70, U. Houston, 1981—; m. Willard T. Dean, Apr. 18, 1970 (div. 1978). Info. retrieval tech. Univ. Hosp. Cleve., 1966-67; ALC programmer NCCS, Cleve., 1967-69; systems programmer Cleve. State U., 1970-71; systems analyst, project leader Celanese Piping Systems, Columbus, 1972-75; mktg. rep. Advanced Systems, Inc., Atlanta, 1975-78; market analyst ASI, Chgo., 1978-79; v.p., sec., dir. Nat. Air Vibrator Co., Houston, 1979—, trustee pension and profit sharing plans, 1979—; dir. Blanton Insulation Products. Cert. data processor. Mem. Am. Mgmt. Assn., Data Processing Mgmt. Assn., Ind. Computer Cons. Assn., Nat. Assn. Women Bus. Owners, Women in Data Processing, Am. Youth Hostels, Sierra Club, Nature Conservancy, Earthwatch. Roman Catholic. Home: 10220 Memorial Dr Houston TX 77024 Office: PO Box 42809 No 590 Houston TX 77042

NEVELS, ELIZABETH MARION, nutrition cons.; b. Hartford, Conn., Oct. 19, 1912; d. Anthony Louis and Jane Ovilla (Dunning) N.; cert. Pratt Inst., 1939; B.S., Columbia U., 1942, 1952; M.A., U. Denver, 1962. Dietitian, Gen. Electric Co., Bridgeport, Conn., 1942-44; intern Brooke U.S. Army Hosp., 1944-45; commd. officer U.S. Army, 1945, advanced through grades to maj., 1962; chief dietitian metabolic div. Army Nutrition Research Lab., 1957-62; dir. food service Colo. State Home and Tng. Sch., Wheatridge, 1962-66; med. care facilities nutritionist Colo. Health Dept., 1966-79; nutrition cons., Denver, 1979—; asst. prof. U.S. Army Med. Service Sch., Baylor U., 1952-54; mem. faculty U. Md., 1950-51; cons. vocat. schs., 1966-79. Mem. Colo. Commn. on Aging, 1980—. Mem. Am. Dietetic Assn., Colo. Dietetic Assn., Nat. Assn. Parliamentarians, Inst. Food Technologists, Colo. Public Health Assn., Colo. Realtors Assn. Republican. Presbyterian. Club: Mt. Vernon Country. Home: 537 Iola St Aurora CO 80010

NEVELSON, LOUISE, sculptor; b. Russia; d. Isaac and Minna Sadie (Smolerank) Berliaswky; ed. Rockland Maine, Europe, Mexico; studied with Hans Hoffman, Germany, 1931; hon. degrees Hamlin U., Mpls., Sch. Art and Design, Bowdoin Coll., Hobart and William Smith Coll.; husband dec.; 1 son, Myron Nevelson. One-woman shows Janis Gallery, The Bienniel, Venice, Italy, 1963, also in Germany, London, Paris, Documenta III, 1964, Pace galleries, N.Y.C., Columbus, 1969, 71, Museo Civico de Torino, 1969, Gal. Jeanne Bucher, Paris, 1969, Kroller-Muller Mus., Holland, 1969, Akron Art Inst., 1969, Museum Fine Arts, Houston, 1969, U. Tex., 1970; one-woman retrospective exhbn. Whitney Mus. Am. Art, 1970; represented permanent collections Julliard Sch., Princeton, Whitney Mus. Am. Art, Bklyn. Mus., Neward Mus., Carnegie Inst., Sara Robi Found., Brandeis U., Birmingham Mus., Houston Mus., Riverside Mus., Mus. Modern Art, Met. Mus. Art, N.Y. U. Mus., Nebr. Mus.; also numerous pvt. collections. Recipient 1st award United Soc. Artists, 1959; award Chgo. Inst., 1959; Ford Found. gift for Tamarind Workshop, Norfolk Mus., 1963; Brandeis U. Creative Arts award sculpture; Skowhegan medal sculpture. Mem. Am. Acad. and Inst. Arts and Letters Fedn. Modern Painters and Sculptors (v.p.), Artists Equity (past pres.), Am. Abstract Artists, Sculptors Guild (exec. bd.). Address: 29 Spring St New York NY 10012

NEVILLE, BONNIE JEAN, ednl. adminstr.; b. San Francisco, Feb. 2, 1955; d. Malcolm M. and Jean (Chesley) Jacobs; B.A., Calif. State U.; m. Oct. 2, 1982. Founder Kindercourt PreSchs., 1979—, now dir. owner 3 schs. Mem. congl. com. Republican party. Roman Catholic. Home: 36 Cove Ln Redwood City CA 94070 Office: 1225 Greenwood Dr San Carlos CA 94070

NEVILLE, JANICE NELSON, nutritionist; b. Schenectady, Dec. 1, 1930; d. William Anthony and Margaret (Adams) Nelson; B.S., Carnegie Inst. Tech., 1952; M.S. (research fellow 1953), U. Ala., 1953, M.P.H., 1962; D.Sc., U. Pitts., 1964; divorced; children—James Gleeson, Lynn Marie. Clinic dietitian, instr. Univ. Hosps., Birmingham, Ala., 1954, research dietitian alcoholism, obesity, serum lipids and diet Grad. Sch. Public Health, 1956-64, asst. research prof. nutrition, 1965; mem. faculty Case Western Res. U., 1965—, prof. nutrition, 1977—, chmn. dept., 1974-82; chmn. nutrition adv. com. N.E. Ohio chpt. Am. Heart Assn., 1969-73, trustee, 1975-84; chmn. nat. adv. com. Dial-a-Dietitian, 1975-78; adv. com. FDA, 1977-78; mem. grant and contract rev. com. USPHS, NIH. Recipient Meritorious Service medal N.E. Ohio affiliate Am. Heart Assn. Mem. Am. Dietetic Assn. (area coordinator 1978-81, speaker-elect 1982), AAAS, Am. Public Health Assn., Soc. Nutrition Edn., Am. Home Econs. Assn., Am. Coll. Nutrition, Dietetic Practice Groups, N.Y. Acad. Scis., Ohio Dietetic Assn. (pres. 1973-75; Pres.'s award 1981), Cleve. Dietetic Assn., Sigma Xi. Author articles in field, chpts. in books. Office: Dept Nutrition Case Western Res U Cleveland OH 44106

NEVILLE, MARGARET CHRISTA, communications co. mgr.; b. Finsterwalde, Ger., Aug. 30, 1941; came to U.S., 1952, naturalized, 1964; d. Eberhard Richard Hans and Wally Emma (Wunderlich) Dorfler; student N.W. Community Coll., 1970-81; m. Keith Jennings NeVille, Oct. 30, 1981; children by previous marriage—Rocky Lee Lehman, Ronald Lyle Lehman. Sec., Farm Bur. Ins., Worland, Wyo., 1969-71; officer mgr. Cody (Wyo.) Enterprise, 1972-73, salesperson, 1973-75; salesperson Shoshone Communications, Cody, 1975-76, sales mgr., 1976—; cons. Welsh Co., 1976-82. DECA adv. bd. Cody High Sch.; mem. Stampede Parade Com., Cody, 1974-79; patron Buffalo Bill Hist. Center, publicity dir. Ann. Buffalo Bill Birthday Ball. Recipient award for best comml. of yr. Wyo. Assn. Broadcasters, 1981. Mem. Cody County C. of C. (retail com. 1975—), Wyo. Assn. Broadcasters, Powell Valley C. of C. Republican. Methodist. Club: Soroptimist. Contbr. articles to profl. jours. Home: 2207 11th St Cody WY 82414 Office: 2001 Mountain View St Cody WY 82414

NEVINS, SHEILA, TV dir. and producer; b. N.Y.C.; d. Benjamin and Stella N.; B.A., Barnard Coll., 1960; M.F.A. (Three Arts fellow), Yale U., 1963; m. Sidney Koch; 1 son, David Andrew. TV producer Great Am. Dream Machine, NET, 1970-72, The Reasoner Report, ABC, 1973, Feeling Good, Children's TV Workshop, 1975-76, Who's Who, CBS, 1977-78; dir. documentary programming Home Box Office, N.Y.C., 1978—. Mem. Writers Guild Am., Women in Film.

NEW, DORRIS REGENEL, state ofcl.; b. Dade City, Fla., Mar. 20, 1930; d. Thomas Bennett and Beulah Marie (Lee) Sanders; A.S. in Secretarial Adminstrn., Va. Commonwealth U., Richmond, 1975; m. Alvin Richard New, Mar. 16, 1957; children—Thomas Bennett, Alvin Richard. Saleslady, Efird's Dept. Store, Rocky Mount, N.C., 1951-53; sec. to buyers Va. Dept. Purchases and Supply, 1958-64; sec. to dean Sch. Bus., Va. Commonwealth U., 1964-80; logistical service supr. Va. Dept. Personnel and Tng., Richmond, 1980—; adv. bd. secretarial dept. J. Sargent Reynolds Community Coll., Richmond, 1978—; condr. seminars, speaker in field. Chmn. adminstrv. bd. Corinth United Meth. Ch., Sandston, Va., 1980-81, supt. children's div., 1964-66, pres. ch. women, 1965-69; Richmond dist. officer United Meth. Women, 1980-81; chmn. troop com. local Boy Scouts Am., 1973-74; mem. Va. Selective Service Bd. Named Sec. of Yr., Old Dominion chpt. Nat. Secs. Assn., 1976; cert. profl. sec., 1975. Mem. Chesapeake, Potomac, Shenandoah Cert. Profl. Secs. Assn., Profl. Secs. Internat. (pres. Old Dominion chpt. 1978-80, 82-83), Phi Beta Lambda (chpt. hon. life mem.). Democrat. Home: 7 Clayman Rd Sandston VA 23150 Office: 12th Floor James Monroe Bldg 101 N 145th St Richmond VA 23219

NEWBERG, DOROTHY BECK (MRS. WILLIAM C. NEWBERG), portrait artist; b. Detroit, May 30, 1919; d. Charles William and Mary (Labedz) Beck; student Detroit Conservatory Music, 1938; m. William C. Newberg, Nov. 3, 1939; children—Judith Anne (Mrs. John Robert Bookwalter), Robert Charles, James William, William Charles. Mem. Thomas Hart Benton Assos., Kansas City Art Inst., 1975—. Trustee Detroit Adventure, 1967-71, originator A Drop in Bucket Program for talented inner-city children. Trustee, Franklin-Wright Settlements, 1971-74, Meadowbrook Gallery, Oakland U., 1972-74; bd. dirs. Your Heritage House, 1972-75. Recipient Heart of Gold award, 1969; Mich. vol. leadership award, 1969. Mem. Birmingham Soc. Women Painters, Birmingham-Bloomfield Art Assn. (dir. 1960-62, trustee 1965-67), Sierra Arts Found. Presbyterian. Home: 2000 Dant Blvd Reno NV 89509

NEWBORG, BARBARA CAROL, physician, med. educator; b. N.Y.C., Apr. 14, 1921; d. Sidney and Agnes N.; A.B., Swarthmore Coll., 1941; postgrad. Med. Sch. U. N.C., 1945-47; M.D., Johns Hopkins U., 1949. Intern, Duke U. Med. Center, Durham, N.C., 1949-50, resident in medicine, 1950-52, instr., 1952-55, asso. in medicine, 1955-71, asst. prof. medicine, 1971-80, asso. prof., 1980—. Mem. AMA, N.C. Med. Soc., Durham Orange County Med. Soc. Contbr. articles to profl. jours. Office: Box 3385 Duke U Med Center Durham NC 27710

NEWBORG, MARGARET NEWMAN, human resources cons.; b. N.Y.C.; d. Martin Henry and Caryl F. Newman; B.A., U. Wis., 1964; M.S.W., Fordham U., 1970; m. Kenneth D. Newborg, Dec. 20, 1964; 1 dau., Julie Elizabeth. Psychiat. social worker Mt. Sinai Med. Center, N.Y.C., 1970-81; outplacement cons. staff relations Citibank, N.Y.C., 1981—; founder, pres. Career Scope, Inc., corp. relocation cons., N.Y.C., 1976—; instr. Center Lifelong Learning, Hunter Coll. Bd. dirs. Midtown YM-YWHA, N.Y.C. Cert. social worker, N.Y. State. Mem. Fin. Women's Assn., Am. Soc. Tng. and Devel., Women's Econ. Round Table.

NEWBY, DOROTHY JANE, elec. mfg. co. exec.; b. Waco, Tex., July 23, 1932; d. Everett and Zella Mae (Parrigin) Barton; student bus. U. Houston, 1951; m. Bobby Jerome Newby, Nov. 16, 1974; children by previous marriage—Charmaine Rene Hebert, Marvin Reed Hebert. Sec., Farnsworth & Chambers, Inc., Houston, 1959-60; exec. sec. Butler Drilling Co., Houston, 1960-65, S.I.P., Inc., Houston, 1965-69; adminstrv. mgr. Mensor Corp., Houston, 1969-78; v.p. adminstrn. F.F. Smith & Assos., Inc., Houston, 1979—, dir., 19 —; dir. Mensor Corp., Castleberry Services, Inc. Mem. Am. Mgmt. Assn., Nat. Assn. Female Execs. Baptist. Clubs: Sweet Adelines, Inc., Antique Auto. of Am., Willys Overland Jeepster, Slavonic Benevolent Order Tex. Home: 1622 Tannehill St Houston TX 77008 Office: 5873 W 34th St Houston TX 77092

NEWCOMB, GLORIA JEAN (KING), printing co. exec.; b. Memphis, Aug. 26, 1942; d. Le Roy and Mary Ann (Campbell) King; student public schs., Barlow, Ky.; m. John B. Newcomb, Feb. 14, 1962; children—John Kelly, Paige Lynnette. Copywriter, traffic mgr. Sta. WDXR, Paducah, Ky., 1960-62; copywriter Sta. WOC-TV, Davenport, Iowa, 1962; research asso. Indsl. Research Inc., Beverly Shores, Ind., 1963-67, promotion mgr., 1967-70; originator and hostess daily and weekly talk shows Sta. WIMS, Michigan City, Ind., 1970-71; promotion dir., nat. conf. dir. Dun-Donnelley Pub. Corp., Chgo., 1971-73; v.p. sales Foster Printing Inc., Michigan City, Ind., 1973-76; founder, pres. Newcomb Printing Services, Inc., Michigan City, 1976—. Publicity chmn. Michigan City United Way, 1979; bd. dirs. Michigan City Heart Fund, 1979-82, Jr. Achievement, 1981-82; mem. Mich. City Summer Festival Com., 1982; co-chmn. fund raising Michigan City Tower Restoration Com., 1979-80; bd. dirs. Jr. Achievement, 1980-82. Recipient award of Excellence, Artists Guild of Chgo. Design Show, 1978, cert. of craftsmanship Weyerhaeuser Paper Co., 1978, Champion Papers award Champion Internat. Corp., 1978, cert. of excellence Strathmore Paper Co., 1978. Mem. Michiana Advt. Club (co-founder; dir. 1974-82, pres. 1976, Disting. Service award 1976), Chgo. Assn. Direct Mkgt., Chgo. Club Printing House Craftsmen, Michiana Craftsman's Club, LaPorte Purchasing Assn., Chgo. Assn. Bus. Pubs., Michigan City Area C. of C. (entertainment chmn. Home and Sports Show 1976). Home: 2027 E Coolspring Michigan City IN 46360 Office: PO Box 452 605 E Ninth St Michigan City IN 46360

NEWCOMB, MARY JANE, educator; b. Kansas City, Mo., July 10, 1916; d. Daniel Andrew and Lola Gladys (Kennedy) O'Connell; D.C., Cleve. Chiropractic Coll., 1946; B.S. in Edn., U. Kans., 1963, Ph.D., 1970; M.A. in English, Kans. State U., 1964; m. Byron D. Newcomb, June 4, 1960; children—Virginia Newcomb Harlan, David Vern. Pvt. practice chiropractic, Kansas City, Mo., 1947-60; instr. anatomy and chemistry Cleve. Chiropractic Coll., 1952-54, 61-62, dean student affairs, 1974-81, dean acad. affairs, 1981—; asst. instr. English, Kans. State U., 1963-64; asst. instr. U. Kans., 1964-66; instr. tech. writing Kans. U. Extension, 1966-67; asst. prof. English, Central Mo. State U. Residence Center, Independence, 1966-74; lectr. dept. English, U. Mo., Kansas City, 1974-76; layout dir. Interplay Mag., 1968-74, Moods Mag., 1976-77; poetry editor Fine Arts Discovery Mag., 1968-74. Mem. Internat. Com. on Sci. and Technology, Theosophical Research Inst., MLA, U. Kans. Alumni Assn., Am. Chiropractic Assn., Internat. Chiropractors Assn., Cleve. Chiropractic Coll. Alumni Assn. (editor newsletter 1975—), Theosophical Soc. (pres. Midwest fedn. 1980—, nat. dir. 1981—). Roman Catholic. Author: Sundry Songs of a Suburbanite, 1977; editor: (with Anna Boothe) Solitary Singers: An Anthology of New Poets, 1969. Home: 8504 Booth St Raytown MO 64138 Office: 6401 Rockhill Rd Kansas City MO 64131

NEWELL, GAIL WILLIAMS, geriatric services supr.; b. Polk County, Fla., Sept. 26, 1941; d. Joe Gary and Norma Kathryn (Bevis) Williams; student Centre Coll. Ky., 1959-61; B.S. in Social Work, Fla. State U., 1964; spl. postgrad. courses; m. Pete J.F. Newell, 1964 (div. 1981). Social worker Fla. Dept. Public Welfare, Winter Haven, 1964-69; family and children's supr. Fla. Div. Family Services, Winter Haven, 1969-74; area aging specialist Fla. Div. of Aging, Community Services Bur., Lakeland, Fla., 1974-75, area aging program coordinator, 1975-76; aging program specialist Dist. VIII, Fla. Dept. Health and Rehab. Services, Ft. Myers, 1976-81, geriatric direct services supr. Dist. VIII-A, Lakeland, 1981—; bd. dirs. Heartland Manpower Consortium, 1976-77. Sec. Polk County Community Service Council, 1976; mem. Area Health Planning Council, 1975-76; pres. Winter Haven City Council, 1976-77. Recipient service award Manpower Consortium, 1977. Mem. So. Gerentol. Soc., Fla. Council on Aging, Phi Alpha, Beta Sigma Phi. Baptist. Home: 259 Kilmer Ln SE Winter Haven FL 33880 Office: 1430 Lakeland Hills Blvd Suite 455 Lakeland FL 33801

NEWELL, GLADYS ELIZABETH, former educator, civic worker; b. Ticonderoga, N.Y., Aug. 31, 1908; d. Charles R. and Elizabeth (Ives) N.; A.B., SUNY, Albany, 1930, M.A., 1935. Tchr., Corinth (N.Y.) High Sch., 1930-33, Bethlehem Central High Sch., Delmar, N.Y., 1933-45; supr. social studies Bethlehem Central Schs., Delmar, 1946-71; mem. N.Y. State Regents Com. on Exams., 1950-53, N.Y. Social Studies Council Curriculum Com., 1961-63, N.Y. State Mental Health Planning Commn., 1963-64. Bd. dirs., v.p. SUNY, Albany Benevolent Assn.; adv. com. N.Y. delegation White House Conf., 1955. Recipient Bus. and Profl. Women Outstanding Citizen award Tri-Village area, 1953; State Coll. Alumni Bertha E. Brimmer award for outstanding teaching, 1955; Citizenship Conf. Outstanding Tchr. award Syracuse U., 1962; Distinguished Alumnus award State U. at Albany, 1969. Mem. N.Y. State Tchrs. Assn. (dir. 1950-69, pres. 1966-67), Eastern Zone Bethlehem Central (a founder, past pres.), Albany Supervisory Dist. (past pres.) tchrs. assns., NEA (life mem., rep. of N.Y. State Tchrs. Assn. at tchr. edn. and profl. standards meetings), N.Y. State (past pres.), Capital Dist. (past pres.), Nat. councils social studies, LWV (past pres. Albany County), UN Assn. U.S.A. (past chpt. dir.), World Affairs Council (past dir. Albany), AAUW (2d v.p. Essex County br.), Fort Carillon Bus. and Profl. Women's Club, N.Y. State Ret. Tchrs. Assn. (del. to Gov.'s Conf. Libraries 1978), N.Y. Ret. Tchrs. Assn., Delta Kappa Gamma, Pi Gamma Mu. Methodist. Club: New Horizons. Contbr. articles to profl. jours. Home: 17 John St Ticonderoga NY 12883

NEWELL, MARY ANN, personnel exec.; b. Alexandria, Va., Mar. 31, 1942; d. James W. and Margaret E. (Lyles) Forgie; student No. Va. Community Coll., 1967, George Washington U., 1973-74, Prince George's Community Coll., 1974; m. Thomas R. Newell, Dec. 9, 1960; children—Teresa A., Cynthia M. Typist, U.S. Dept. Agr., Washington, 1959-62; sec./bookkeeper U.S. Hosp. Supply Corp., Arlington, Va., 1964-67; sec. Teledyne/Earth Scis. Co., Alexandria, Va., 1967-68; adminstrv. asst. Analytical Systems div. Comtel Corp., Springfield, Va., 1968-69; personnel mgr. ENSCO, Inc., Springfield, 1969—, mem. retirement fund adminstrv. com., 1979—, chmn. retirement fund adminstrv. com., 1981—. Mem. IEEE, Adminstrv. Mgmt. Soc., Nat. Assn. Female Execs. Roman Catholic. Club: Lodge Creek Yacht. Office: 5400 Port Royal Rd Springfield VA 22151

NEWELL, REBECCA G., nurse; b. Savannah, Ga., July 4, 1953; d. Henry Morgan and Julia (Rogers) Grimes; A.A., Armstrong State Coll., 1973, B.S. in Nursing, 1980; postgrad. Sch. Grad. Nursing, Med. Coll. Ga., 1980; m. E. Andrew Newell, June 14, 1980. With Broad Oaks Hosp., Savannah, Ga., 1973—, coordinator utilization rev. and staff devel., 1975-80, asst. dir. nursing, 1980—; mental health counselor, 1977—; hosp. cons. Savannah Area Edn. Consortium, 1978—; profl. staff exchange cons. Recipient Leadership award Vocat. Indsl. Clubs Am., 1971. Mem. Hist. Savannah Found., Am. Nurses Assn., Ga. Nurses Assn., Am. Bus. Womens Assn., Ga. Hosp. Assn. Soc. Nursing Service Adminstrs., Ga. Hosp. Assn. Soc. Utilization Rev. Coordinators, Ga. Heart Assn. Baptist. Home: 11407 Willis Dr Savannah GA 31406

NEWELL, SALLY OTTAWAY, veterinarian; b. Ypsilanti, Mich., July 2, 1936; d. Henry Jackson and Ruth Marie (Montgomery) Ottaway; B.S., E. Carolina U., 1958; D.V.M., U. Ga., 1970; m. John Richard Newell, June 28, 1958; children—Deonne Marie, Mary Jo, Penni Sue. Research asst. N.C. State U., Raleigh, 1958-60; research asso. U. Ga., 1970-73; gen. practice vet. medicine, Elberton, Hartwell, and Athens, Ga., 1973-74; coordinator U. Ga. Lab. Animal Care, Athens, 1974—. Mem. Am. Assn. Lab. Animal Sci. (pres. 1982), AVMA, Am. Soc. Primatologists, Am. Soc. Lab. Animal Practitioners, Sigma Xi. Episcopalian. Author articles in field. Home: 305 Stoneland Dr Athens GA 30606 Office: Office of the Vice Pres for Research U Ga Athens GA 30602

NEWHOOK, HAZEL, Can. provincial minister; Minister of consumer affairs and the environ., Province of Nfld., 1979-81, minister of mcpl. affairs, 1981—. Conservative. Office: Confederation Bldg Saint John's NF A1C 5T7 Canada *

NEWHOUSE, KATHRYN LYNN AYERS, accountant; b. Panama Canal Zone, June 30, 1954; d. Thomas Dudley and Janice Marie (Belote) Ayers; B.B.A. in Acctg. cum laude, U. Tex., 1975; m. Charles Stephen Newhouse, May 25, 1975; children—Kelly Mae, Travis Stephen. Staff accountant Groesbeeck & Co., Austin, Tex., 1976-77, partner, 1978-79; controller H.L. Chapman Pipeline Constrn. Co., Austin, 1979-80; pvt. practice acctg., Austin, 1980—. C.P.A. Mem. Am. Soc. Women Accts. (pres. 1980-81), Am. Inst. C.P.A.s, Tex. Soc. C.P.A.s. Home and Office: 8208 Cliffview Austin TX 78759

NEWLIN, JANINE JORDAN, interior designer, Kitchen and bath cons.; b. N.Y.C., Oct. 12, 1932; d. Frank Bertram and Barbara (Schwinn) Jordan; student Columbia U., 1953-54; B.A., Chatham Coll., 1955; student Frank Reilly, 1949, Henry Koerner, 1951-52, Pompeo DeSantis, 1953-54, Amy Jones, 1964, Anthony Toney, 1964-65; cert. Boarman Sch. Kitchen Design Techniques, 1977; cert. Am. Inst. Kitchen Dealers, 1980, diploma, 1982; m. Christopher Roger Williams, May 28, 1956 (div. 1965); children—Jennifer Anne, Pamela Nan, Ian Clifford; m. 2d, George Christian Newlin, Dec. 23, 1967; 1 son, Nicholas C.C., Fashion and illustrator model, 1935-58; copy chief's asst. J. Walter Thompson, 1955-56; founder, pres., agt. Internat. Editorial Arts, N.Y.C., 1957-64; pvt. practice interior designing, Chappaqua, N.Y., and N.Y.C., 1965-74; pvt. practice kitchen and bath designing, Chappaqua, N.Y., 1975—; speaker in field; v.p. Braintree Mgmt. Ltd., also dir. Chmn. at large Trick or Treat com. UNICEF, No. Westchester County, N.Y., 1964-73; founder, co-chmn. Friends of Friends com. to raise Funds for Preservation of Chappaqua Meeting House, 1977; active Republican Party. Recipient Soc. Illust. Children's Art Show Water Color award, 1945; cert. appreciation Community Center of New Castle, 1980. Mem. Allied Bd. Trade, Am. Inst. Kitchen Dealers, Soc. Cert. Kitchen Designers, Jr. League, Internat. Soc. Interior Designers, AIA, Quaker. Designs featured in numerous publis. including House Beautiful, Family Circle, Woman's Day, newspapers, TV commls. Office: 42 Whippoorwill Rd Chappaqua NY 10514

NEWMAN, ANNETTE GOERLICH, shopping center mgr.; b. Fresno, Calif., Jan. 19, 1940; d. David August and Mary Eloise (Simpson) Goerlich; Pharm.D., U. Calif., San Francisco, 1963; children—Anne Kristen, Mark David, Gregory Hartley. Pharmacist, Village Drug, 1963-69; relief pharmacist, 1969-72; store mgr. The Drug Store of Fig Garden Village, 1972-77; mgr. Fig Garden Village Shopping Center, Fresno, 1977—; dir. Fig Garden Mcht. Assn., R.B. Bailey, Inc.; sec. bd. dirs. Sundown, Inc., Fig Garden Village, Inc. Active, Fresno Community Analysis Citizens Com., Littlest Angel chpt. Children's Home Soc., Ladies Aid to Retarded Children, Women's Symphony League; bd. dirs. Fresno Arts Center. Nominee, Rosalie M. Stern award, 1971, 72; registered pharmacist, Calif. Mem. Fresno-Madera Pharm. Assn., Pharm. Alumni Assn. U. Calif., Nat. Assn. Female Execs., Jr. League of Fresno, AAUW, Alpha Phi. Club: Soroptimists. Home: 3909 W Fir Ave Fresno CA 93711 Office: 5082 N Palm Ave Suite A Fresno CA 93704

NEWMAN, BARBARA MILLER, psychologist, educator; b. Chgo., Sept. 6, 1944; d. Irving George and Florence (Levy) Miller; student Bryn Mawr Coll.; A.B. with honors in Psychology, U. Mich., 1966, Ph.D. in Devel. Psychology, 1971; m. Philip R. Newman, June 12, 1966; children—Samuel Asher, Abraham Levy, Rachel Florence. Undergrad. research asst. in psychology U. Mich., 1963-64, research asst. in psychology, 1964-69, teaching fellow, 1965-71, asst. project dir. Inst. for Social Research, 1971-72, univ. lectr. in psychology and research assoc., 1971-72; asst. prof. psychology Russell Sage Coll., 1972-76, assoc. prof., 1977-78; assoc. prof. dept. family relations and human devel., chairperson dept. family relations and human devel. Ohio State U., 1978—. Mem. Eastern Psychol. Assn., Soc. Research in Child Devel., AAAS, Am. Psychol. Assn., Nat. Council Family Relations, Groves Conf. on Marriage and Family, N.Y. Acad. Scis., Midwestern Psychol. Assn., Western Psychol. Assn., Am. Home Econs. Assn. Author books including: (with P. Newman) Living: The Process of Adjustment, 1981; contbr. chpts., articles to profl. publs. Office: Dept Family Relations and Human Devel 1787 Neil Ave Room 315 Columbus OH 43210

NEWMAN, BLANCHE MARIE, brewing co. exec.; b. Mebane, N.C., July 2, 1947; d. Monty General and Nevada Lee (Tally) N.; A.S., Wingate Coll., 1967; student N.C. State U., 1967-68. Community worker Alamance County Community Action Program, Burlington, N.C., 1968-69; asst. mgr. Towel Town, Burlington, 1969-70; shift supr. E.I. DuPont, Wilmington, N.C., 1970-78; supr. packaging Miller Brewing Co., Eden, N.C., 1978-80, supr. inventory systems, 1980-82, prodn. planner, 1982—. Mem. Nat. Assn. Female Execs., Am. Mgmt. Assn. Democrat. Baptist. Home: 2955G Cottage Pl Greensboro NC 27405 Office: PO Box 3327 Eden NC 27288

NEWMAN, CLAIRE POE, business exec.; b. Jacksonville, Fla., Dec. 12, 1926; d. Leslie Ralph and Gertrude (Criswell) Poe; student Fla. State Coll. for Women, 1944-45, Tulane U., 1971-73; m. Robert Jacob Newman, July 3, 1948; children—Leslie Claire, Robert, Christopher David. Co-owner Vineyards in Burgundy, France; v.p., dir. Carrollton Realty Co. of New Orleans, 1956—. Mem. various coms. New Orleans Mus. Art. Mem. Women's com. New Orleans Philharmonic Symphony Assn., 1961—, chmn. orch. relations com., 1961-63; chmn. New Orleans Easter Seal Drive, 1963; La. trustee Nat. Soc. Crippled Children and Adults, 1963-65. Mem. Women's Aux. C. of C., New Orleans Soc. Archeol. Inst. Am. (v.p. 1972-74), Confrérie des Chevaliers du Tastevin, Sigma Kappa. Club: Metairie Country, Kitzbuehel (Austria) Golf, Golden Skibook (Kitzbuehel), Pass Christian (Miss.) Yacht; Ski (Arlberg). Home: 1111 Falcon Rd Metairie LA 70005 Also Tiemberg Kitzbuehel Austria

NEWMAN, COLLEEN ALEXANDER, utility co. exec.; b. Georgetown, Guyana, Feb. 11, 1942; came to U.S., 1969, naturalized, 1977; d. J.A. and Marian (Griffith) Alexander; B.A., U. West Indies/U. London, 1964; m. Alan Newman, Feb. 7, 1970. UN del., diplomat Govt. of Guyana in Chile and Venezuela, 1966-69; editorial services supr. AT & T, 1969-72; tech. news mgr. Consol. Edison Co. N.Y., Inc., 1972-77, asst. to v.p., 1977-79, asst. v.p., 1979-80, v.p. corp. communications, 1980—; chmn. N.Y. Power Pool Public Relations Com., 1978-80; lectr. tech. writing L.I. U., 1977; lectr. Black Execs. Exchange Program, 1977-81. Adv. bd. Boys Choir of Harlem, 1979-82; mem. Coalition of 100 Black Women. Recipient Black Achievers in Industry award, 1977. Mem. Edison Engring. Soc. (pres. 1980-81), Am. Assn. Blacks in Energy. Office: 4 Irving Pl New York NY 10003

NEWMAN, ELAINE ANN, social worker; b. Santa Monica, Calif., Feb. 3, 1938; d. George and Sarah Jennie (Davidson) N.; B.A., UCLA,

1960; M.S.W., U. So. Calif., 1968; m. Charles C. Pace, Oct. 1, 1980. Psychotherapist in pvt. practice, Beverly Hills, Calif., 1968-71; staff devel. specialist in mgmt. Los Angeles County Dept. Public Social Services, 1960-76; exec. dir. Big Sister League, Colleague Infant Care Center, Los Angeles, 1976-78; exec. dir. Children's Village U.S.A., Beaumont, Calif., 1978-79; exec. cons. social service/child abuse program and adminstrn., resdl. homes for children, Los Angeles, 1979—. Bd. dirs. Los Angeles Free Clinic, 1973-76, 80—; founder Lan Jordan Inst. Counseling and Psychotherapy, Beverly Hills, 1967; mem. steering com., council execs. Los Angeles United Way, 1976-78. U. So. Calif. scholar, 1966-68. Mem. Nat. Assn. Social Workers, Acad. Cert. Social Workers, Calif. Women in Govt., Am. Soc. Psychical Research (research bd. So. Calif.). Home: 421 S Van Ness Ave Apt 31 Los Angeles CA 90020

NEWMAN, ELLA TYRAS, fin. cons.; b. Hof, W.Ger., Jan. 2, 1948; came to U.S., 1950, naturalized, 1955; d. Leo and Olga (Agatstein) Tyras; B.A. in Econs., CCNY, 1968; M.B.A. Baruch Coll., 1973; m. Ian Frederick Newman, Sept. 7, 1969; children—Jamie Tyras, David Andrew. With Bankers Trust Co., N.Y.C., 1968-78, investment officer personal trust investment dept., 1973-78; ind. fin. cons., 1979-82; exec. recruiter acctg., fin. and banking Westfield Personnel, White Plains, N.Y., 1981-82; adj. prof. Pace U., 1980—; lectr. Coll. New Rochelle (N.Y.), 1979, 80, 83, Dutchess Community Coll., 1978; tchr. Am. Inst. Banking, 1978-79. Bd. dirs. Chappaqua (N.Y.) New Neighbors, 1980-82. Mem. Nat. Assn. Accountants, AAUW, Am. Soc. Acctg. Women.

NEWMAN, ELLEN MAGNIN, cons.; b. San Francisco, Apr. 19, 1928; d. Cyril Isaac and Anna Smithline Magnin; student Stanford U., 1945-48; m. Walter Simon Newman, Sr., Oct. 15, 1950; children—Walter Simon, Robert Magnin (dec.), John Donald. With Joseph Magnin Co., San Francisco, 1948-69, women's apparel buyer, 1948-54, developer sales tng., 1954-60, dir. product devel., 1960-64, dir. new products and new brs., 1964-69; spl. asst. to pres. Joseph Magnin, San Francisco, 1969-72; in house cons. consumer affairs Amfac, Honolulu, 1972-74; pres. Ellen Newman Assos., San Francisco, 1974—; dir. Wells Fargo & Co., Wells Fargo Bank, San Francisco, Kaiser Aluminum & Chem. Corp., Oakland, Calif. Mem. Econ. Devel. Adv. Council, State Calif.; mem. Mayor's Fiscal Adv. Com. City San Francisco; v.p. bd. govs. San Francisco Symphony; council mem. SRI Internat. Mem. Com. 200, Women's Forum West. Club: Metropolitan. Office: 323 Geary St Suite 507 San Francisco CA 94102

NEWMAN, FRANCES MAE, real estate mgmt. co. exec. b. Elm Grove, Ohio, Dec. 15, 1938; d. Earl E. and Phena (Dunn) Whitworth; student Ohio U., 1960—; asso. degree in acctg. Internat. Accts. Soc., 1969; m. Carson Newman, July 13, 1958; children—Brad, Carmen. Office mgr., credit mgr. Clarence Valley Sons, Inc., Waverly, Ohio, 1956-74; v.p. RMS Mgmt. Corp., Chillicothe, Ohio, 1974—; sec. to bd. RMS Properties, 1980—; owner, operator Clothes Corral, men and women's apparel, Waverly, 1981—; instr. cert. apt. mgr. tng. courses. Mem. Waverly Jaycettes (pres. 1970), Chillicothe Bus. and Profl. Womens Club, Nat. Assn. Female Execs. Home: 90 Prosperity Rd Waverly OH 45690 Office: Foulke Block Bldg S Paint St Chilliocthe OH 45601

NEWMAN, LUCILE FANNING, anthropologist, educator; b. N.Y.C., Jan. 13, 1930; d. Raymond Samuel and Lucile (Pettibone) Fanning; A.B., Brown U., 1951; M.A., Columbia U., 1957; Ph.D. in Anthropology, U. Calif., Berkeley, 1965; m. Frank Newman, Oct. 13, 1951; children—Kenneth, James, Michael. Lectr., Mills Coll., Oakland, Calif., 1965-68; asst. prof. U. Calif., San Francisco, 1969-74; asst. prof. anthropology Brown U., Providence, 1975-79, assoc. prof., 1979—; cons. Population Council. Bd. dirs. New World Found., Planned Parenthood R.I.; trustee Women and Infants Hosp. R.I. Fellow AAAS; mem. Am. Anthrop. Assn., Assn. Behavioral Sci. and Med. Edn., Internat. Soc. Psychosomatic Ob-Gyn, Am. Public Health Assn. Author: (with W. B. Miller) The First Child and Family Formation, 1978; assoc. editor Human Orgn., 1981—. Office: Brown U Providence RI 02912

NEWMAN, MARGARET ANN, nurse; b. Memphis, Oct. 10, 1933; d. Ivo Mathias and Mamie Love (Donald) N.; B.S.H.E., Baylor U., 1954; B.S.N., U. Tenn., Memphis, 1962; M.S., U. Calif., San Francisco, 1964; Ph.D., N.Y.U., 1971. Dir. nursing, asst. prof. nursing Clin. Research Center, U. Tenn., 1964-67; asst. prof. N.Y.U., 1971-75, asso. prof., 1975-77; prof. in charge grad. program and research dept. nursing Pa. State U., 1977-80, prof. nursing, 1977—; cons. to surgeon gen. U.S. Army; mem. research adv. bd. Am. Nurses Found.; mem. nurse theorist task force Nat. Conf. Classification of Nursing Diagnosis. Recipient Outstanding Alumnus award U. Tenn. Coll. Nursing, 1975; Am. Jour. Nursing Scholar, 1979-80. Fellow Am. Acad. Nursing; mem. Am. Nurses Assn. (exec. com. council nurse researchers). Author: Theory Development in Nursing, 1979; editor: (with others) Source Book of Nursing Research, 1973, 2d edit., 1977. Research on movement, time perception and consciousness as indices of health. Home: 792 W Aaron Dr State College PA 16801 Office: 201 Human Development East Pa State U University Park PA 16902

NEWMAN, MARY-ANNE, psychotherapist; b. Berlin, Mar. 23, 1926; d. Max Friedrich and Elly (von Rohmann) von Camnitzer; came to U.S., 1947, naturalized, 1952; B.S., Blue Coat Sch. Women, London, Eng., 1946; M.S., L.I. U., 1975; Ph.D., Union Grad. Sch., Yellow Springs, Ohio, 1976; m. Ralph Newman, Dec. 23, 1951; 1 son, Richard Mark. Asst. dir., then dir. med. dept. Workmen's Circle, N.Y.C., 1947-56; dir. N.Y. Sch., N.Y.C., 1970-76; adj. asst. prof. counseling/health edn. C.W. Post Center, L.I. U., 1975—, also coordinator spl. program human sexuality; dir. conf. planning Creedmoor Psychiat. Center, N.Y. State Dept. Mental Hygiene, 1979—; vis. prof. N.Y. Inst. Tech., 1977—; pvt. prdctice psychotherapy, 1975—. Certified sex educator, sex therapist. Mem. Am. Psychol. Assn., Am. Personnel and Guidance Assn., Am. Assn. Sex Educators, Counselors and Therapists, Royal Soc. Health. Contbr. articles to profl. publns. Address: 144-15 41st Ave Flushing NY 11355

NEWMAN, MAXINE PLACKER, ins. cons.; b. Haslem, Tex., Nov. 21, 1922; d. L. H. and Beatrice Rosetta (Stuart) Placker: B.S., Stephen F. Austin State U., 1943; m. Robert Wayne Newman, May 23, 1975; 1 son, Stephen Randall Hillin (by previous marriage). Acct., Lamar U., Beaumont, Tex., 1956-58; office mgr. Williamson Ins. Agy., Beaumont, 1958-72; v.p. Alexander & Alexander, Dallas, 1972-79; cons. Bellefonte Ins. Co., Cin., 1979—; office mgr., treas. Ralph K. Kemp & Assocs., Inc., Dallas. Mem. Am. Bus. Women Assn. (Woman of Yr. 1979), Nat. Assn. Ins. Women, Dallas Assn. Ins. Women, Beta Sigma Phi (Woman of Yr. 1966). Republican. Baptist. Clubs: Trophy, Women's, Trophy Ladies Golf Assn. Address: 114 Carnoustie Dr Roanoke TX 76262

NEWMAN, MELVA JEWELL COLLINS, social worker, educator; b. Shreveport, La., Mar. 3, 1932; d. William and Minnie Lee (Burton) Collins; A.B., U. Calif. at Los Angeles, 1953; M.S.W., U. So. Calif., 1957; m. Joseph Newman, June 25, 1957; children—Sheri, Toni, Colette. Social worker La Case de San Gabriel, 1957-58; probation officer Los Palmas Sch. for Girls, 1958-60; social group work specialist Neighborhood Youth Assn., 1962-72, Pasadena (Calif.) YWCA, 1969-70; chief social service Central City Community Mental Health Center, Los Angeles, 1969-70; dir. counseling service Foot Hill Free Clinic, asst. prof. dept. sociology Calif. State U., Los Angeles, 1970-77; lectr. child welfare Calif. State Poly. U., 1977—; co-founder, organizer Foothill Free Clinic; cons. Head Start Infant Day Care Center, Emergency Sch. Aid Act, Community Housing Services; co-founder, organizer Mother-Child Devel. Project, Pasadena YWCA. Mem. Advisory Council on Child Abuse Prevention. Recipient Aro of Achievers award Pasadena Soc. Study Negro History, 1968. Mem. Nat. Assn. Social Workers, Assn. Black Social Workers, Calif. Profs. Early Childhood Edn., So. Calif. Group Psychotherapy Assn., Alpha Kappa Alpha, Gamma Phi Delta, Democrat. Home: 524 E Loma Alta Dr Altadena CA 90001 Office: Family Actualization 524 E Loma Alta Dr Altadena CA 91001

NEWMAN, NANCY MARILYN, ophthalmologist; b. San Francisco, Mar. 16, 1941; d. Fred and Marion (Solomon) N.; B.A. magna cum laude, Stanford U., 1962, M.D., 1967. Intern, Mount Auburn Hosp., Cambridge, Mass., 1967-68; NIH trainee neuro-ophthalmology Washington U. Sch. Medicine, St. Louis, 1968-71, jr. asst. resident, 1968-69, sr. asst. resident, 1969-70, asso. resident ophthalmology, 1970-71; Internat. Eye Found. fellow, San Salvador, El Salvador, 1971; fellow neurol. surgery and ophthalmology U. Calif. Sch. Medicine, San Francisco, 1971-72; fellow Smith-Kettlewell Inst. Visual Scis., Pacific Med. Center, San Francisco, 1971-72; practice medicine specializing in neuro-ophthalmology San Frncisco, 1972—; clin. asst. prof. ophthalmology U. Calif. Sch. Medicine, San Francisco, 1972, cons. nerve fiber contract, Nat. Eye Inst., 1973-75; cons. neuro-ophthalmology San Francisco Gen. Hosp., 1972-78, VA Hosp., San Francisco, 1972-74, St. Mary's Hosp., San Francisco, 1972-74; asst. prof. ophthalmology Pacific Med. Ctr., San Francisco, 1972-73, asso. prof., 1973—, chief div. neuro-ophthalmology, 1973—; prof. dept. spl. edn. Calif. State U., San Francisco, 1974-79; vis. prof. Centre Nat. D'Ophtalmologie des Quinze-Vingts, Paris, France, 1980; physician, cons. dept. neurology U. Calif. Sch. Medicine, VA Med. Center, Martinez, Calif., 1978—; guest lectr. various hosps. and univs. in U.S., Eng., Australia and Can., 1972—. Recipient Cert. of award Internat. Eye Found., 1971; diplomate Am. Bd. Ophthalmology (asso. examiner 1974—). Fellow A.C.S., Am. Acad. Ophthalmology; mem. Am. Acad. of Ophthalmology and Otolaryngology, Internat. Soc. of Neuro-Ophthalmology (founding mem.), Pacific Coast Oto-Ophthalmology Soc., Am. Soc. of Ophthalmic Ultrasound, Orbital Soc., Pan Am. Assn. of Ophthalmology, Assn. for Research in Vision, Soc. of Heed Fellows, Cordes Soc., No. Calif. Soc. for Prevention of Blindness (dir. 1980—), Lane Med. Soc. (v.p. 1975-76), San Francisco Med. Soc., Calif. Med. Assn. (del. 1979), Societas Internationalis Pro Diagnostica Ultrasonica in Ophthalmologia. Contbr. articles on neuro-ophthalmology to profl. jours.; editorial bd. Jour. Clin. Neuro-Ophthalmology, 1981—. Office: 2340 Clay St San Francisco CA 94115

NEWMAN, SARAH ANN COUGHENOUR CASEY (MRS. WARD C. NEWMAN, JR.), journalist; b. Pitts., July 7, 1946; d. Jesse William and Mary Ellen (Wilt) Coughenour; B.J., U. Mo., 1968; m. Ward C. Newman, Jr., June 6, 1982. Asst. fashion editor, feature writer Phila. Inquirer, 1968-72, columnist, feature writer, copy editor, 1972-73; freelance fashion stylist, writer, copy editor Phila. Bull., 1973-75, food editor, 1975-82; copy editor, writer Omaha World-Herald, 1982—. Ballet dancer Phila. Civic Ballet, Phila., 1973-76. Mem. Women in Communications, Phila. Zool. Soc. (docent council), Henry Doorly Zoo Docents, Omaha Ballet Guild, DAR, Omaha Ballet Guild, Futures for Children. Methodist. Home: 1795 Kent Circle Papillion NE 68128 Office: Omaha World Herald World-Herald Sq Omaha NE 68102

NEWMAN, SOPHIE, artist, educator; b. Bklyn., Mar. 4, 1925; d. Benjamin and Mary (Margolis) Stein; student (plastics scholar), Bklyn. Mus. Art Sch., 1969-72, 79, Kreloff Art Sch., Bklyn., 1966-69, also specialized art courses; m. Morris Newman, July 6, 1946; 1 son, Scott. One-woman shows: Ward Nasse Gallery, N.Y.C., 1976, Valsamis Gallery, Bklyn., 1978, State of Arts Gallery, N.Y.C., 1979-80, Cincinelli Gallery, N.Y.C., 1980, 81; group shows include: Ward Nasse Gallery, 1973, Larry Aldrich Mus., Ridgefield, Conn., 1974, U. Tenn., Chattanooga, 1974, Bklyn. Mus., 1975, Women in Arts Gallery, N.Y.C., 1976, Randolph Macon Women's Coll., Binghamton Coll., Va. Poly., Lehigh U., Chatam Coll., Manhattan Community Coll., 1976-77, Bklyn. Coll., 1977, 82, Hudson River Mus., Yonkers, N.Y., 1980, Cincinelli Gallery, 1980, Les Armis Gallery, Lawrence, L.I., N.Y., 1980, Downtown Cultural Center, 1982, Queens Mus., 1982; travelling slide show Hudson River Mus.; lectr., cons. Bklyn. Mus., 1982—; tchr. in field; designer theatrical masks and costumes, also jewelry; works reproduced in various publs.; art educator, lectr., 1975—. Krevorkian grantee. Mem. Arts for All, Queens, Recipient 1st prize oils Nat. Pen Women's Assn., 1974. Mem. Women's Caucus for Arts, Creative Women's Collective (a founder, dir., v.p. 1973—), Women in Arts, Artists League Bklyn. (v.p. 1973), Nat. Art Workers Coalition. Address: 2680 E 29th St Brooklyn NY 11235

NEWMARK, EILEEN EVANS, lawyer; b. Bklyn., Nov. 19, 1932; d. John J. and Mollie Dugan; student Bklyn. Coll., 1949-51; LL.B., Bklyn. Law Sch., 1954; m. Gerald H. Evans, Oct. 19, 1952; 1 son, Bradley; m. 2d, Lawrence Newmark, May 1, 1966. Admitted to N.Y. bar, 1955, Fed. bar, 1956, U.S. Supreme Ct. bar, 1957; legal editor Baker Voohries, 1954-56; claims examiner Allstate Ins. Co., 1956-59; trial atty. for juveniles Family Ct. State of N.Y., Legal Aid Soc., 1959-61; trial atty. Hartford Ins. Co., 1961-63, Ins. Co. N.Am., 1963-66; individual practice law, East Northport, N.Y., 1966—. Bd. dirs. Huntington Mental Health Clinic, 1975—, v.p., 1976-78; bd. dirs. Townwide Fund of Huntington, 1980—; mem. art citizens adv. bd. Suffolk County Office Cultural Affairs, 1979—; trustee pension fund Piederson Krug Clinic, 1975-80; committeeman Republican party, Huntington, 1971-78; citizen's adv. council to county legislator LaBua. Mem. Suffolk County, Nassau-Suffolk Women's bar assns., Suffolk County Criminal Bar, Huntington C. of C. (dir., state legis. com.), Bus. and Profl. Women's Orgn. (sec. 1977-78), NOW, Huntington Hist. Soc. (life), Early Trades and Crafts Soc., Early Am. Industries Assn., Internat. Fedn. Women Lawyers, Profl. Women's Network, Club: Soroptimists. Home: 15 Alma Ln East Northport NY 11731 Office: 206 Laurel Rd East Northport NY 11731

NEWMARK, MARILYN (MRS. LEONARD J. MEISELMAN), sculptor; b. N.Y.C., July 20, 1928; d. Edward Ellis and Mabel (Davies) Newmark; student Adelphi Coll., 1945-47, Alfred U., 1949; m. Leonard J. Meiselman, Mar. 15, 1952. Sculptor, specializing in horses, equestrian figures, dogs in sporting scenes; exhibited in group shows: sculpture exhbn. NAD, Nat. Arts Club, Nat. Art Mus. of Sport (all N.Y.C.), James Ford Bell Mus., Wis., Smithsonian Instn., Washington, Pa. Acad. Natural Scis.; represented in permanent collections at Harvey Firestone (Ohio), Whitney Stone (Va.), Ogden Phipps (N.Y.), A.B. Hancock Jr. (Ky.), Charles Scribner (N.J.), Peggy Agustus (Va.), Morgan Firestone (Can.), A. Werk Cook (Mass.). Recipient Anna Hyatt Huntington award, 1970, 71, 72, 75, 78, 80, 81, 82, gold medal, 1973; award Council Am. Artists Socs., 1972, 73, 79, 80; Hudson Valley John Newington award, 1973, 77, gold medal, 1979; NAD Ellin P. Speyer award, 1974, Artist Fund award, 1982. Fellow Nat. Sculpture Soc. (council 1973-75, rec. sec. 1976, sec. 1977-79, council 1981-83), Am. Artists Profl. League (Gold medal 1974, 77); mem. Allied Artists Am. (gold medal 1981), Pen and Brush Club (gold medal 1977, Solo award 1974, 78, 80), Soc. Animal Artists (jury of admissions 1972-75), Nat. Acad. Equine Artists (founding mem.), Nassau Suffolk Horsemans Assn. (dir., corr. sec.). Clubs: Catherine Lorillard Wolfe Art (jury of admissions N.Y.C. 1972-74); Smithtown Hunt, Nat. Steeplechase and Hunt Assn., Past Meadowbrook Hunt (L.I., N.Y.). Address: Woodhollow Rd East Hills NY 11577

NEWSOM, DOUGLAS ANN JOHNSON, journalist, educator; b. Dallas, Jan. 16, 1934; d. J. Douglas and R. Grace (Dickson) Johnson; B.J. cum laude, U. Tex., 1954, B.F.A. summa cum laude, 1955, M.J., 1956, Ph.D., 1978; m. Mack Newsom, Jr., Oct. 27, 1956 (div. 1980); children—Michael Douglas, Kevin Jackson, Nancy Elizabeth, William Macklemore. Gen. publicity State Fair Tex., 1955; advt. and promotion Newsom's Women's Wear, 1956-57; publicity Auto Market Show, 1961; lab. instr. radio-tv news-writing course U. Tex., 1961-62; local publicist Tex. Boys Choir, 1964-69, nat. publicist, 1967-69; asso. prof. journalism Tex. Christian U., 1969-—, chmn. journalism dept., 1979—; public relations dir. ann. Gt. S.W. Boat Show, 1966-72; public relations cons., writer, 1965-—; public relations Horace Ainsworth Co., Dallas, 1971-75; dir. ONEOK, energy co. Trustee, Public Relations Found. Tex. Mem. Mortar Bd. Alumnae, Women in Communications (nat. public relations dir. 1969-71, rep. to World Press Freedom Com.), Public Relations Soc. Am. (accredited, chmn. nat. edn. com.), Am. Women in Radio and TV, Assn. for Edn. in Journalism (past pres. public relations div.), Tex. Public Relations Assn. (dir.), Accrediting Council for Edn. in Journalism and Mass Communications (nat. chmn. accrediting com.), Tex. Journalism Edn. Council (pres. 1981), Delta Delta Delta. Baptist. Author: This Is PR, 1976, 2d edit., 1980. Writing in Public Relations Practice: Forms and Style, 1980. Home: 4237 Shannon Dr Fort Worth TX 76116 Office: Dept Journalism Tex Christian U Fort Worth TX 76129

NEWSOM, LILA ROGERS, psychol. examiner; b. Pittsboro, Ind., Sept. 14, 1937; d. Alfred O. and Willa Mae (Giffin) Rogers; B.A., Abilene Christian Coll., 1959; M.A. (NDEA fellow), U. Hawaii, 1961; m. Bobby G. Newsom, Sept. 15, 1960; children—Robert Michael, James Eric, Dana Marie, Daniel Edward. Psychol. examiner Bristol Mental Health Clinic, Bristol Tenn.-Va., 1961-65; instr. psychology U. Tenn., Chattanooga, 1973-78; cons., psychol. examiner Hamilton County Juvenile Ct., Chattanooga, 1975-78; psychol. examiner Chattanooga Testing and Counseling, 1978—; cons. psychol. examiner Hamilton County Sch. System, Chattanooga, 1982—; cons. psychol. examiner Regional Psychol. Center. Mem. Am. Psychol. Assn. Republican. Mem. Ch. of Christ. Home: 1312 Scout Rd Hixson TN 37343 Office: 744 Mc Callie Ave Chattanooga TN 37402

NEWTON, ANETA SUE, mfg. co. exec.; b. Shawnee, Okla., May 17, 1946; d. John David and Oleta Margaret (Chambless) Newton; B.S., U. Okla., 1968, M.S., 1981. Pilot project lab. technician Corning (N.Y.) Glass Wks., 1969-70; with Allen Bradley Co., Magnetics Div., Shawnee, Okla., 1973—, now quality control supr.; instr. quality control Oscar Rose Jr. Coll., Oklahoma City, 1980—. Mem. Am. Soc. for Quality Control (sect. officer), Women Geoscientists Com., Gamma Theta Upsilon, Tau Beta Pi, Alphi Pi Mu. Republican. Club: Rebekah (presiding officer 1970).

NEWTON, CAROLYN SCANLON, orch. mgr.; b. Columbus, Miss., July 15, 1931; d. Leo Joseph and Mary Belton (Ezell) Scanlon; B.S., Miss. Coll. Women, 1952; divorced; children—Anne Newton McGuire, Donald W., Jeffrey Scott; m. 2d, Martin R. McLendon. Reporter, Clarion-Ledger, Jackson, Miss., 1952-54; account exec., co-owner Newton Advt. Agy., 1954-71; mng. editor Miss. Libraries, 1956-81; exec. dir. Mississippians Ednl. TV, 1971-77; pres. Miss. Tours, Inc., 1976—; gen. mgr. Jackson (Miss.) Symphony Orch., 1977—. Bd. dirs. Jackson Symphony League, 1959-77, Miss. Ballet Theatre; bd. govs. Jackson Symphony Orch. Assn.; pres. women's group St. James Episcopal Ch., Jackson, 1970. Recipient award for advt. Nat. Press Assn.; citation AP. Mem. Met. Orch. Mgrs. Assn. (regional sec.), Am. Symphony Orch. League, Miss. Library Assn. Club: Jackson Yacht. Author: Outdoor Mississippi, 1975; co-author: Meet Mississippi. Office: 201 E Pascagoula St Jackson MS 39205

NEWTON, DOROTHY RUTH ARMSTRONG, ednl. adminstr.; b. Dallas, Sept. 8, 1923; d. Albert Frederick and Mayme B. (Miller) Armstrong; B.A., U. Tex., Arlington, 1967, M.A., 1973; adminstr.'s cert. North Tex. State U., 1980; m. James L. Newton, Mar. 27, 1942; children—Diana Jay, Rena Kathleen, Carole Ruth. Sec., Reconstrn. Fin. Corp., CSC, Washington, 1941-42; tchr. Jefferson Middle Sch., Grand Prairie, Tex., 1968-69; tchr. Grand Prairie High Sch., 1969-81, asst. prin., 1981—. Served with Women's Res., USMC, 1943-45. Cert. tchr. for life, cert. sch. adminstr., Tex. Mem. Assn. Supervision and Curriculum Devel., Tex. Assn. Secondary Schs. Adminstrs., Grand Prarie Prins. Assn., Assn. Tex. Profl. Educators (local treas. 1980-81), Phi Delta Kappa. Republican. Mem. Christian Ch. (Disciples of Christ). Club: Roadrunners. Office: 101 High School Dr Grand Prairie TX 75050

NEWTON, ELISABETH GUERRY, geologist; b. Bennettsville, S.C., June 5, 1933; d. Walter Monroe and Annie Elisabeth (Guerry) N.; student Randolph-Macon Woman's Coll., 1951-54; B.S., U. S.C., 1956; postgrad. George Washington U., 1962-66. Researcher geol. div. U.S. Geol. Survey, Washington, 1956-73, environ. cons. conservation div., Reston, Va. and Menlo Park, Calif., 1973-76, programs officer conservation div., Washington, 1976-80, chief conveyances and sales solid minerals mgmt. Minerals Mgmt. Service, Reston, 1980—; mem. women geoscientists com. Am. Geol. Inst., 1980—. Recipient commendation Dept. Interior Alaska Oil Pipeline Program, 1974. Mem. Geol. Soc. Am., Assn. Engrng. Geologists, Internat. Assn. Engrng. Geologists, Am. Assn. Petroleum Geologists, Am. Inst. Profl. Geologists, Am. Inst. Mining Engrs. Research, publs. on terrain analysis and geohazards, 1968-73. Office: Nat Center MS650 Reston VA 22092

NEWTON, LILLIAN HINSON, writer; b. Templeman, Va., Apr. 17, 1921; d. George Washington and Mary Marks Hinson; student Am. U., 1960-63, Charles County Community Coll., 1968-71, Rappahanock Community Coll., 1979-80; m. John Norton Newton, Jan. 31, 1943 (dec.); children—Norton Byrd, Wanda Newton. Computer system analyst Naval Surface Weapons Center, Dahlgren, Va., 1946-76, EEO counselor and fed. woman's program coordinator; mgr. Profl. Mgmt. Services, Fredericksburg, Va., 1976-77; tech. writer, head quality control group Sperry Univac, Dahlgren, 1977—; tech. documentation cons. Past vice chmn. King George Planning Commn.; past pres. mission groups Potomac and Oakland Baptist Chs.; past pres. Potomac and King George PTA's; chmn. King George Med. Services; chmn. King George Bd. of Zoning Appeals. Mem. Am. Assn. Ret. Persons (pres. King George), King George C. of C. Club: Dahlgren Toastmistress (past pres.), Dahlgren Garden, Dahlgren Home Demonstration.

NEY, JUDY LARSON, business ofcl.; b. St. Louis, Mar. 4, 1951; d. Robert and Annette (Palan) Larson; B.A. (scholar), Bradley U., 1973; M.A., U. Mo., St. Louis, 1975; J.D., South Tex. Coll. Law, 1982; m. Leo Edwin Ney, Jr., May 25, 1975; 1 son, Leo Edwin IV. Teaching asst., lectr. Bradley U., Peoria, Ill., 1972-73; grad. teaching and research asst. U. Mo., St. Louis, 1973-74; sr. scheduler/supr. Brown & Root Inc., Houston, 1974—. Mem. ABA, Project Mgmt. Inst., Internat. Assn. Profl. Planners and Schedulers (dir.), Am. Nuclear Soc., Alumni Assn. South Tex. Coll. Law, Bradley U. Alumni Assn. (Tex. rep.), Chimes, Phi Alpha Delta. Jewish. Home: 12242 Brookvalley Houston TX 77071 Office: Brown & Root Inc PO Box 3 Houston TX 77001

NEYLAND, TONI ELIZABETH, nurse; b. San Francisco, Mar. 7, 1951; d. Frank Saverio and Rosalind Elizabeth (Zeilman) Crudo; B.S.N. St. Louis U., 1973; m. Bruce Harman Neyland, Sept. 20, 1975. Commd. 1st lt., Nurses Corps, U.S. Army, 1973, advanced through grades to capt., 1975; resigned, 1976; staff nurse Bexar County Hosp., San Antonio, 1976; charge nurse cardiac catheterization lab. Santa Rosa Med. Center, San Antonio, 1976-77; head nurse cardiology service S.W. Tex. Meth. Hosp., San Antonio, 1977; clin. nurse specialist Becton

Dickinson Med. Systems, Sharon, Mass., 1977-81; nursing instr. critical care Bapt. Meml. Hosp. System, San Antonio, 1981—. Mem. Am. Assn. Critical Care Nurses, Tex. Nurse's Assn., Nurse Cons. Assn. (charter mem.), Assn. for Advancement Med. Instrumentation (tech. com. on EKG devices). Roman Catholic. Home: Route 2 Box 294-E San Antonio TX 78229 Office: 111 Dallas St San Antonio TX 78286

NEZELEK, ANNETTE EVELYN (MRS. EDWARD NEZELEK), condominium mgr.; b. Chgo., Feb. 16, 1921; d. Frank and Susan (Linstra) Van Howe; B.A. in History magna cum laude, Hofstra U., 1952; M.A. in Am. History, State U. N.Y. at Binghamton, 1966; m. Edward L. Nezelek, Apr. 3, 1961. Editorial asst. Salute Mag., N.Y.C., 1946-48; asso. editor Med. Econs., Oradell, N.J., 1952-56; nat. mag. publicist Nat. Mental Health Assn., N.Y.C., 1956-60; exec. dir. Diabetes Assn. So. Calif., Los Angeles, 1960-61; corporate sec., v.p., editor, public relations dir. Edward L. Nezelek, Inc., Johnson City, N.Y., 1961-82; mgr. condominium, Fort Lauderdale, Fla., 1982—; substitute tchr. high schs., Binghamton, N.Y., 1961-63. Bd. dirs. Broome County Mental Health Assn., 1961-65, Fine Arts Soc., Roberson Center for Arts and Scis., 1968-70, Found. Wilson Meml. Hosp., Johnson City, 1972-81, Found. SUNY, Binghamton; trustee Broome Community Coll., 1973-78; mem. Broward County Commn. on Status of Women, 1982—. Mem. AAUW, Am. Med. Writers Assn., LWV (dir. Broome County 1969-70), Alumni Assn. SUNY Binghamton (dir. 1970-73), Am. Acad. Polit. and Social Sci., Nat. Assn. Female Execs., Am. Heritage Soc., Nature Conservancy, Nat. Hist. Soc., Alpha Theta Beta, Phi Alpha Theta, Phi Gamma Mu. Clubs: Binghamton Garden, Binghamton Monday Afternoon, Acacia Garden (pres.). Editor newsletter Mental Health Assn., 1965-68, newsletter Unitarian-Universalist Ch., weekly 1967-71, History of Broome County Meml. Arena, 1972. Home: 2100 S Ocean Dr Fort Lauderdale FL 33316 Office: 1650 S Ocean Ln Fort Lauderdale FL 33361

NICCOLINI, DIANORA, photographer; b. Florence, Italy, Oct. 3, 1936; d. George and Elaine (Augsbury) Niccolini; came to U.S., 1945, naturalized, 1960; student Hunter Coll., 1955-62, Art Students League, 1960, Germain Sch. Photography, 1962. Med. photographer Manhattan Eye, Ear and Throat Hosp., 1963-65; organizer med. photography dept., 1st chief med. photographer Lenox Hill Hosp., 1965-67; organizer, head dept. med. and audio visual edn. St. Clare's Hosp., N.Y.C., 1967-76; mem. Third Eye Gallery, N.Y.C., 1974-76; owner Dianora Niccolini Creations, 1976—; instr. photography Camera Club N.Y., 1978-79, Germaine Sch. Photography, 1978-79, N.Y. Inst. Photography, 1981—; one woman shows 209 Photo Gallery, Top of the Stairs Gallery, Third Eye Gallery, 1974, 75, 77, West Broadway Gallery, N.Y.C., 1981, Camera Club N.Y., 1982, Photographics Unltd. Gallery, N.Y.C., 1981; project dir. Photography over 65, N.Y.C., 1978; pub. portfolios. Mem. Women Photographers N.Y. (founder 1974), Biol. Photog. Assn., Assn. Ind. Video and Filmmakers, Internat. Center Photography, Am. Soc. Mag. Photographers, Am. Soc. Picture Profls., Profl. Women Photographers (coordinator), Internat. Kirlian Research Assn., Integral Yoga Inst., Unity Center Practical Christianity. Author: Women of Vision, 1982; editor: P.W.P. Times, 1981-82; contbr. to photog. books, 1979, 80; contbg. editor Functional Photography, 1979-80, N.Y. Photo Dist. News, 1980. Home: 356 E 78th St New York NY 10021 Office: Dianora Niccolini Creations 356 E 78th St New York NY 10021

NICHOL, BETTY JANE, pharmacist; b. Columbus, Ohio, July 31, 1926; d. Joseph Edward and Frances Dorothy (Nussbaum) Steinberg; B.Sc. in Pharmacy, Ohio State U., 1948; m. Joseph Nichol, Dec. 28, 1947; children—Allen, Steven Elliott. Pharmacist, co-owner Eastmoor Pharmacy, Inc., Columbus, 1971—; v.p. Ohio Bd. Pharmacy, 1977-78, adv. council continuing edn., 1978—. Mem. Am. Pharm. Assn., Acad. Pharmacy Practice, Ohio Pharm. Assn., Acad. Pharmacy Central Ohio, Nat. Assn. Bds. of Pharmacy, Kappa Epsilon, Rho Chi. Jewish.

NICHOLAS, COLOMBE MARGARET, fashion licensing exec.; b. Larchmont, N.Y., Nov. 6, 1944; d. Dimitri Paul and Colombe Irene Nicholas; student Coll. de Montreaux (Switzerland), 1960; B.A., U. Dayton, 1964; J.D., U. Cin., 1968; m. Leonard Rosenberg. Buyer Macy's N.Y.C., 1970-75; buyer, divisional mdse. mgr. Bloomingdale's, 1975-78; v.p., mdse. mgr. Bonwit Teller, 1978-80; pres. Christian Dior N.Y., Inc., N.Y.C., 1980—. Mem. Young Pres.'s Orgn. Office: 104 N 40th St New York NY 10018

NICHOLAS, MAY THERESA, string instrument co. exec.; b. Phila., Aug. 8, 1944; d. Charles B. and Irene L. N.; B.S. in Applied Music (scholar), Temple U., 1966; cert. Internazionale Sommerakademie des Mozarteums, Salzburg, Austria, 1965; diploma Orff-Institut, Salzburg, 1965. With House of Primavera, Phila., 1964-79, sec.-treas., 1968-79, dir., 1968-79; sec.-treas. Phila. Sales Co. Inc., div., 1971-79, dir., 1971-79; gen. mgr. RW Service and Supplies div. Italo-Am. String Instrument Co., Inc., Cherry Hill, N.J., 1979—, also dir.; violin maker. Recipient Vira I. Heinz award, 1965; N.J. State scholar, 1962-65. Mem. Violin Soc. Am. (charter), Nat. Assn. Music Mchts., Phila. Direct Mktg. Club. Democrat. Presbyterian. Home: 6338 Irving Ave Pennsauken NJ 08109 Office: PO Box 1301 Cherry Hill NJ 08034

NICHOLAS, NICKIE LEE, indsl. hygienist; b. Lake Charles, La., Jan. 19, 1938; d. Clyde Lee and Jessie Mae (Lyons) N.; B.S., U. Houston, 1960, M.S., 1966. Tchr. sci. Pasadena (Tex.) Ind. Sch. Dist., 1960-61; chemist FDA, Dallas, 1961-62, VA Hosp., Houston, 1962-66; chief biochemist Baylor U. Coll. Medicine, 1966-68; chemist NASA, Johnson Spacecraft Center, 1968-73; analytical chemist TVA, Muscle Shoals, Ala., 1973-75; indsl. hygienist, compliance officer Occupational Safety and Health Adminstrn., Dept. Labor, Houston, 1975-79, area dir., Tulsa, 1979-82, mgr., Austin, 1982—; ; mem. faculty VA Sch. Med. Tech., Houston, 1963-66. Recipient award for outstanding achievement German embassy, 1958, Suggestion award VA, 1963, Group Achievement award Skylab Med. Team, NASA, 1974. Mem. Am. Chem. Soc. (dir. analytical group Southeastern Tex. and Brazosport sects. 1971, chmn. elect 1973), Am. Assn. Clin. Chemists, Am. Harp Soc., Kappa Epsilon. Home: 1305 Shannon Oaks Austin TX 78746 Office: 611 E 6th St Austin TX 78701

NICHOLAS-WOLOSUK, WANDA ELMIRA, social work cons.; b. Genesee County, Mich., Jan. 25, 1936; d. Thomas Nelson and Viola Jane (Hippensteel) Brandon; student Mott Community Coll., 1966-70; B.A., U. Mich., 1973, M.S.W., 1975; m. Stanley James Wolosuk, Feb. 28, 1976; children by previous marriage—Robert H. Nicholas, David A. Nicholas, Theodore S. Nicholas, Stephen R. Nicholas. Caseworker, Genesee County Probate Ct., Flint, Mich., 1973-75; cons. Lakeville Sch. Dist., Otisville, Mich., 1975; exec. dir. Consortium on Child Abuse/Neglect, Flint, 1975-78; project dir. emergency parent demonstration and evaluation project, protective services Mich. Dept. Social Services, Lansing, 1978-80; social work cons., 1978—; dir. Child Receiving Home, Saginaw; mem. faculty Mott Community Coll.; past pres. bd. dirs. Mich. Com. for Prevention of Child Abuse. Cert. and lic., Mich. Mem. Nat. Assn. Social Workers (former dir. Flint area unit), Acad. Certified Social Workers, Mich. Assn. Children's Agys., Eval. Network. Home and Office: 12188 N Linden Rd Clio MI 48420

NICHOLS, ALLEAN BRIERS, educator, florist; b. Montgomery, Ala., Oct. 7, 1934; d. Fred James and Nellie Ophelia (Thomas) Briers; B.S. in Elementary Edn., Ala. State U., 1955; M.Elementary Edn., Troy State U., 1977; 1 son, Sean Patrick. Elementary tchr. Laurel High Sch., Alexandria City, Ala., 1955-63, North Highland Elementary Sch., Prattville, Ala., 1963-70, Union Springs (Ala.) Elementary Sch., 1970-73, Grandview Elementary Sch., Dothan, Ala., 1973-76, Vaughn Rd. Elementary Sch., Montgomery, Ala., 1976—; florist, Montgomery, 1978—; elementary choir dir., 1955-70; music workshop cons., 1976; guest soloist numerous orgns., 1951—. Fin. sec. Stars Social and Civic Club, 1977-80; chmn. of edn. HEER Project, Continental Socs. Inc., 1978-80; fin. sec. Jack & Jill of Am. Inc., 1975-77, pres., 1977-79; parish council Roman Cath. Ch. Mem. NEA, Ala. Edn. Assn., Montgomery County Edn. Assn., Assn. Classroom Tchrs. Democrat. Club: Four Seasons (founder), Delta Sigma Theta (Outstanding Delta, 1978, chmn. scholarship benefit 1978), Guest soloist Montgomery Mus. Fine Arts, 1979, St. Judes Parish Council Summer Musicale, 1978. Home: 1437 Cleveland Ave Montgomery AL 36108 Office: 1508 Cleveland Ave Montgomery AL 36108

NICHOLS, IRENE ANN, ednl. psychologist; b. Cambridge, Mass., Oct. 7, 1929; d. Philip and Jessie Ann (Ross) N.; B.S. in Edn., Boston State Coll., 1952; Ed.M., Harvard U., 1954, Ed.D., 1968. Tchr., Boston public schs., 1952-56; research psychologist Children's Hosp., Boston, 1961-63; asso. prof. ednl. psychology Northeastern U., Boston, 1963—; vis. scholar U. London, 1971. Grantee, Nat. Inst. Edn., 1979-82. Mem. Am. Psychol. Assn., Am. Ednl. Research Assn., Soc. Research Child Devel., AAUP, ACLU, Women's Equity Action League, Nat. Infact, Boston Area Faculty Group Polit. Issues. Author articles in field. Mng. editor Early Childhood Rev., 1981—. Home: 1622 Massachusetts Ave Cambridge MA 02138 Office: 102 The Fenway Boston MA 02115

NICHOLS, JACQUELINE BRUCE, archeologist; b. Harlan, Ky., Oct. 14, 1941; d. Jack Corum and Martha Jayne (Miracle) Bruce; B.A., Wellesley Coll., 1963; M.A., SUNY, Albany, 1977; m. David Edward Nichols, Mar. 4, 1963; children—Corinna Elizabeth, David Andrew, Patrick Edward. Tchr., Bedford (Eng.) Schs., 1963-64; dir. Archeol. Field Labs., SUNY, Albany, 1976-77, Cath. U., 1978; v.p. Gt. Basin Found. for Archeol. Research, 1979; pres. Atechiston, Inc., Albuquerque, 1980—; co-founder, editor Flintknappers Exchange, 1977; founder, pub. Contract Abstracts & CRM Archeology, 1980—. Wallace Stegner fellow, 1963-64. Mem. AAAS, Soc. Am. Archaeology, Nat. Assn. Women Bus. Owners, Soc. Archeol. Sci., Found. for Desert Archaeology (dir. 1980—). Republican. Home: 5313 Briley Pl Bethesda MD 20816 Office: 4426 Constitution NE Albuquerque NM 87110

NICHOLS, JANET ELLEN, educator; b. Rockville Centre, N.Y., Apr. 7, 1950; d. John B. and Virginia Florence (Raupp) Greenhouse; B.A., Adelphi U., 1971; M.S., Lehigh U., 1973; postgrad., Colo. State U., 1973-76; m. John G. Nichols, June 9, 1973. Teaching asst. Lehigh U., Bethlehem, Pa., 1971-73, Colo. State U., Fort Collins, 1973-76; instr. math. U. So. Colo., Pueblo, 1977-79, asst. prof., 1979—. NDEA Title IV fellow, 1971-73. Mem. Am. Math. Soc., Sigma Xi, Pi Mu Epsilon, Delta Tau Alpha, Delta Phi Alpha. Home: PO Box 214 Canon City CO 81212 Office: University of Southern Colorado Dept Mathematics Pueblo CO 81001

NICHOLS, JEANNETTIE DOORNHEIN, painter, educator; b. Holland, Mich., July 27, 1906; d. Jacob Lenard and Caroline (Hauk) Doornhein; B.A.E., Art Inst. Chgo., 1934; m. Charles Martin Nichols, Apr. 21, 1941; 1 dau., Jean Lawson. Art supr. Belvidere Pub. Schs., 1929-31; tchr. comml. art Crane Evening Sch., Chgo., 1933-36; tchr. art Chgo. pub. schs., 1933-71, art dept. head 1948-71. Exhibited Pa. Nat. Acad., Phila., Chgo. Asso. Galleries, Mandels Art Gallery, Conrad Hilton Hotel, 1952, Ind. State Fair, 1954, Artists Equity, Gary Artists League, Internat. Artists Exhibit, N.Y.C., 1959, Phoenix, 1959, W.A.A. Mpls. Art Gallery, 1964, 65, Occoquan (Va.) Art Fair, 1975-77, Art Works, Woodbridge, Va., 1976, and others; one-man shows Waukazoo, Holland, Mich., 1952, Cottage Studios, Chgo., 1953, Gary (Ind.) Hotel, 1957, Crespi Gallery, N.Y.C., 1959, Kriegart Art Gallery, Lombard, Ill., 1967, Gary Gallery, 1971-74; group shows Sherman Hotel Art Gallery, Chgo., 1960, Gary 1971-74; exhibited in juried shows at 57th St. Art Artists League, Gary Gallery; exhibited Gary Music and Arts Am., Chesterton (Ind.) Art Fair, 1961-74, Weatherspoon Gallery, U. N.C., 1969; represented permanent collections Albrecht Art Mus., St. Joseph, Mo., U. Ind., Smithsonian Instn., pub. schs., Portage, Ind., Chgo., Prince William, Va., others. Recipient 1st prize enamel on copper Gary Craftsman Guild, 1955; 2d prize mixed-medium Chesterton Ann., 1955; 3d prize water color Gary Artists League, 1955; 1st, 2d, 3d Purchase awards South Bend Art Center, 1956, Tri Kappa award, 1967, 1st award Ellis County Art Assn., 1978, other prizes. Fellow Internat. Inst. Arts and Letters (life); mem. Art Educators Chgo. (pres. 1961, bd. mem.), Artist Equity, Gary Artists League (past pres., 1st v.p. 1963), Woodbridge Art Guild (v.p. 1975, dir. 1976), Art Inst. Alumni Assn. (life), NEA, Nat. Art Edn. Assn., Porter County Arts and Crafts Assn. (pres. 1963), Ellis County Artists, Dallas Artists Equity. Author article profl. mag. Home and studio: Route 1 Buttonwood Village Waxahachie TX 75165

NICHOLS, LOUISE BENSON, computer systems analyst; b. Atlanta, Sept. 11, 1927; d. Carville Dickinson and Miriam (Connet) Benson; B.S. in Chemistry, George Washington U., 1948; postgrad. Am. U., 1964-66; m. Donald Raymond Nichols, June 11, 1948; children—Diane Louise, Lawrence Scott, Gregory Alan, Sharon Jean. Computer programmer U.S. Coast Guard, Washington, 1966-67; computer programmer U.S. Geol. Survey, Menlo Park, Calif., 1967-75, computer systems analyst, Reston, Va., 1975-79, computer systems analyst, Denver, 1979—. Cert. in data processing, 1971. Mem. Soc. Certified Data Processors, Assn. for Computing Machinery. Office: MS 801 PO Box 25046 Denver CO 80225

NICHOLS, SHARON DICKENSHEETS, assn. exec., editor; b. Laramie, Wyo., Oct. 4, 1936; d. Kenneth Bradfield and Catherine Ila (Linford) Dickensheets; student Casper Coll., 1955; B.A., U. Wyo., 1977; m. Ted. M. Nichols, June 14, 1957; children—Jon Scott, Lynne M'Liss, Lorri Kay. Reporter Casper (Wyo.) Star Tribune, 1954-56; tchr. pub. schs., Mountain View, Wyo., also Sunrise, Wyo., 1957-59; adminstrv. asst., editor Wyoming Trucker, Wyo. Trucking Assn. Sec. Wyo. Women for Hwy. Safety, 1970-75; bd. dirs. United Way; mem. Zoning Bd. of Adjustment, Casper, 1973-78; vice-chmn. Citizen's Com. on Optional 1% Sales Tax, 1974; pres. Friends of Library; chmn. Natrona County Library Bd.; sec. Bd. Public Utilities. Mem. Casper C. of C. Democrat. Mormon. Club: Wyo. Press Women. Home: 2405 E 8th St Casper WY 82609 Office: Box 1909 Casper WY 82602

NICHOLS, SUSAN WILMA, clothing mfg. co. exec.; b. Winthrop, Mass., July 19, 1948; d. Stephen Otis and Pauline Emily (Roberts) N.; A.A.S., Fashion Inst. Tech., 1968; student SUNY, Buffalo, summer 1967. Asst. fashion promotion dir., then retail fashion coordinator Ameritex Fabrics div. U.M.&M., N.Y.C., 1968-70; asst. fabrics editor Seventeen Mag., N.Y.C., 1970; asst. fashion dir. Milliken & Co., N.Y.C., 1971-73; sales exec. Burlington Industries, Inc., N.Y.C., 1973-78; creative dir., dir. sales and mktg. Fashion World Career Apparel, Inc., N.Y.C., 1978-82; exec. v.p., designer Starflite Uniforms, Inc., N.Y.C., 1982—; adj. instr. Fashion Inst. Tech., spring 1979. Mem. Nat. Assn. Female Execs., Women's Nat. Republican Club (exec. com. 1979-80), Fashion Inst. Tech. Alumnae Assn. (life mem.). Presbyterian. Designer first flight attendant uniforms for Republic Airlines. Home: 110 E 84th St New York NY 10028 Office: 29 W 30th St New York NY 10001

NICHOLS, VIRGINIA V., accountant; b. Monroe County, Mo., Oct. 26, 1928; d. Elmer W. and Frances L. (McKinney) N.; student Belleville (Ill.) Jr. Coll., 1959-60, Rockhurst Coll., 1964-65, Avila Coll., Kansas City, Mo., 1981-82. Sec., Panhandle Eastern Pipeline Co., Kansas City, Mo., 1964-65, St. Louis County Dept. Revenue, 1965-69, Forest Park Community Coll., 1969-71, Nooney Co., St. Louis, 1971-77, J. A. Baer Enterprises, St. Louis, 1979; acct. Panhandle Eastern Pipe Line Co., Kansas City, Mo., 1979—. Vol., ARC, 1965—. Mem. Profl. Secs. Internat. (Sec. of Year 1969, sec. Mo. div. 1975-76), Jr. Women's C. of C. (Girl of Year 1975, pres. 1974-75). Republican. Episcopalian. Home: PO Box 5832 Kansas City MO 64111 Office: 3444 Broadway Kansas City MO 64111

NICHOLSON, EDNA ELIZABETH, ret. pub. health ofcl.; b. Redwood Falls, Minn., Dec. 23, 1907; d. Ernest Crawford and Alma (Bordeaux) N.; A.B., U. Mich., 1930, M.S. in Pub. Health, 1931, certificate in social work, 1931. Nat. Tb Assn. fellow in social research, 1930-31; med. social work ARC, U.S. Naval Hosp., Great Lakes, Ill., 1931-33; asst. dir. med. relief service Cook County Bur. Public Welfare, Chgo., 1933-35; instr. social aspects of nursing Cook County Sch. Nursing and asst. dir. social service Cook County Hosp., Chgo., 1935-37; dir. med. relief service Chgo. Relief Adminstrn., 1938-42; vis. lectr. Sch. Hygiene and Pub. Health, U. Mich., 1939; cons. on med. assistance, bur. pub. assistance Fed. Security Agency, 1942-44; dir. Central Service for Chronically Ill, Inst. Medicine, Chgo., 1944-54; exec. dir. Inst. Medicine of Chgo., 1955-64; supr., med. assistance specialist Med. Services Adminstrn., HEW, 1964-71; spl. lectr. program in hosp. adminstrn. Northwestern U., 1945-60; tech. adviser Commn. on Chronic Illness, 1949-56. Recipient Cancer Care award Nat. Cancer Found., 1955. Mem. Am. Public Health Assn., Phi Beta Kappa, Delta Omega, Sigma Kappa. Author: Terminal Care for Cancer Patients, 1950; Surveying Community Needs and Resources for Care of the Chronically Ill, 1950; The Nurse and Chronic Illness: Planning New Institutional Facilities for Longterm Care, 1956; A Comprehensive Community Plan for Meeting the Problems of Chronic Illness, 1959. Contbr. to profl. jours. Home: 107 Brewster Ln La Grange Park IL 60525

NICHOLSON, ELAINE RUTHE, psychologist; b. Orange, N.J., June 7, 1934; d. Ernest Arthur and Ruthe C. (Stickel) Carlson; B.A., U. Ariz., 1955; M.A., U. Ariz., 1968, Ph.D., 1978; m. Everett V. Nicholson, Mar. 31, 1956; children—Lynda Ruthe, Julie Ann. Child welfare social worker, Tucson, 1955-58; dir. Girls Living Centers, Tucson, 1960-62; spl. edn. tchr. Tucson Public Schs., 1962-63; adminstr., tchr. Schweitzer Sch. Gifted Children, Tucson, 1964-65; research asso. U. Ariz. Coll. Edn., 1969-75; cons. Head Start, Ariz., 1974—; pediatric behavioral psychologist Thomas-Davis Med. Clinic, Tucson, 1972—; founder, dir. Physicians Family Counseling Services, Tucson, 1972—; psychologist Tucson Clinic, 1979—; adj. prof. U. Ariz., 1980-82; pres. Assos. in Psychol. Practice, P.C., 1980—. Mem. adv. bd. United Parents Against Child Stealing, Tucson, 1979-81. Mem. Am. Psychol. Assn., Ariz. Psychol. Assn., Nat. Assn. Sch. Psychologists, Soc. Pediatric Psychology, Assn. Advanced Behavior Therapy, Soc. Behavioral Medicine. Baptist. Home: 5950 San Remo Tucson AZ 85715 Office: Thomas Davis Clinic 5th and Alvernon Tucson AZ 85711

NICHOLSON, JOAN MARTIN, UN program rep.; b. Pontiac, Mich., Mar. 3, 1940; d. John Holden and Louise Elaine (Moysey) Martin; B.A., Allegheny Coll., Meadville, Pa., 1962; student J.F.K. Sr. Mgrs. Program, Harvard U., 1980; m. James C.L. Brown, Feb. 17, 1979; children—Wendy, Tim. Founder, pres. Bolton Inst., environ. issues, Washington, 1971-75; cons. Office Environ. Edn., HEW, Washington, 1970-71; sr. coordinator public interest relations Am. Petroleum Inst., Washington, 1975-77; dir. Office Public Awareness, EPA, 1977-81, spl. asst. to adminstr. consumer affairs, 1980-81; Washington rep. UN Environment Programme, 1981—. Bd. dirs. Chevy Chase (Md.) Citizens Found., 1979, Bolton Inst.; worldwide chmn. Concern, Inc.; adv. Earthscan, Women's Inst., Am. U. Mem. Nat. Assn. Female Execs., Fed. Exec. Women's Assn., U.S. Assn. Club of Rome (membership com.). Kappa Kappa Gamma. Episcopalian. Club: Nat. Press (Washington). Author papers in field. Office: Suite 209 2101 L St NW Washington DC 20037

NICHOLSON, ROSEMARY, govt. ofcl.; b. Meridian, Miss., Feb. 10, 1941; d. Roosevelt Ted and Mary Adeline (Burt) Thomas; student Ga. State U., Atlanta, Edison Community Coll., Ft. Myers, Fla.; m. Bobby Lee Nicholson, Aug. 9, 1959; children—Keith Wade, Sheila Kay, Glenn Alan. With Social Security Adminstrn., 1965—, asst. dist. mgr., Lakeland, Fla., 1979-80, dist. mgr., Ft. Myers Fla., 1980—. Bd. dirs. Community Coordinating Council Lee County, 1982-83. Recipient various HEW awards. Mem. Am. Bus. Women's Assn. (chpt. pres. 1977, 79, v.p. 1981-82; chpt. Women of Yr. award 1978), Fla. Assn. Health and Social Services (v.p. S.E. chpt. 1981-82), Nat. Assn. Female Execs., Am. Soc. Profl. and Exec. Women, Atlanta Regional Mgmt. Assn., Ft. Myers Network. Democrat. Baptist. Club: Zonta Internat. (Ft. Myers). Office: 3090 Evans Ave PO Box 06259 Fort Myers FL 33906

NICKELS, NANCY LOVE, energy cons.; b. Columbia, La., Aug. 15, 1953; d. Howard Allen and Claudine (Gregory) Love; student La. Tech. U., 1971-73; B.S. with honors, Northeast La. U., 1975; m. Michael Frank Nickels, Jan. 19, 1974; 1 son, Curtis Michael. Office mgr., firm McKeithen, Burns & Lewellyan, Columbia, 1975, C.A. Frey, Architect, Engrs., Shreveport, La., 1976-77; electric living cons. Southwestern Electric Power Co., Shreveport, 1977, residential cons., 1978, staff adv. consumer services, 1979-81; comml. cons., free lance home economist, 1981—. Judge, Adv. Council La. Coop. Extension, 1977-79. Recipient award Am. Legion, 1971. Mem. Am. Home Econs. Assn., Home Econs. in Bus., Alerting Women About Resources and Energy, La. Troopers Womens Assn., Sigma Kappa, Kappa Omicron Phi. Democrat. Methodist. Office: PO Box 21106 Shreveport LA 77156

NICKERSON, EILEEN TRESSLER, psychologist; b. Chgo., Oct. 1, 1927; d. Maurice Shearer and Sybil (Voss) Tressler; B.A. with honors, U. Ill., 1949; M.A., U. Minn., 1952; Ph.D., Columbia U., 1961; m. Richard Gorham Nickerson, June 7, 1957; children—Holly, Wendy, Susan. Counselor, Comstock Hall and Jr. Coll. Counseling Office, U. Minn., Mpls., 1949-51; research asst. Sociologiska Instituionen, Uppsala (Sweden) U., 1952-53; mental health cons. Minn. Dept. Public Health, Mpls., 1953-54; research asst. Bd. Higher Edn., N.Y.C., 1954-55; psychology intern VA Hosps., N.Y.C., 1954-57; staff psychologist Boston U. Counseling Center, 1957-59; instr., research asso. Harvard Grad. Sch. Edn., Social Relations Dept., 1958-63, psychologist family relations unit project, 1963-65; cons. psychologist Nordli, Wilson Assos., Worcester, Mass., 1964-71; lectr. psychology Grad. Sch. Edn. and Univ. Coll., Northeastern U., Boston, 1964-71; sr. research asso. Research Inst. for Ednl. Problems, Cambridge, Mass., 1970-71; cons. psychologist Krebs Sch. for Learning Disabilities, Lexington, Mass., 1970-71; supervising project dir. Sch. Consultation Project, Boston U., 1971-74, prof. counseling psychology Sch. Edn., 1971—, acting chmn. dept. counseling psychology, 1977-79, dir. specialization in counseling women, 1979—, dir. confs. for women's devel., 1981—; cons. to various groups; mem. exec. bd. Gifford Sch., Weston, Mass., 1976-78. Recipient award Nordli-Wilson Assos., 1969; Milton Fund research award Harvard U., 1961. Fellow Mass. Psychol. Assn. (exec. bd. 1976-78); mem. Am. Assn. Counselor Edn. and Suprs. (mem. exec. council 1977-78), Am. Personnel and Guidance Assn., Am. Psychol. Assn., Eastern Psychol. Assn., Greater Boston Personnel and Guidance Assn., Mass. Personnel and Guidance Assn. (pres. 1974-76), Nat. Assn. Sch. Psychologists, Nat. Assn. Psychol. Cons. to Mgmt., New Eng. Personnel and Guidance Conf. (exec. bd. 1976-79), New Eng. Psychol. Assn., North Atlantic Counselor Educators Assn. (pres. 1977-78), Inter Am. Soc. Psychology, LWV (dir. 1960-67). Author: Helping Children, 1974; Women Today! Tomorrow, 1975; Intervention Strategies for Modifying

Sex Stereotypes, 1975; Helping Women, 1978; Action Therapies, 1978; Mothering and Fathering, 1979; contbr. numerous articles to various publs. Home: 1 Colonial Way Weston MA 02193 Office: 765 Commonwealth St Boston MA 02215

NICKERSON, JENNIE RUTH, sculptor; b. Appleton, Wis., Nov. 23, 1905; d. Robert Wellington and Kate Mary (Ellis) N.; student Detroit Sch. Applied Art, 1924-27, NAD, 1928-32; pupil Ahron Ben-Shmuel; m. Edmund Greacen, Jr., Dec. 30, 1935; children—Elizabeth Ruth, Barbara Eleanor. Sculptor, 1932—; represented in permanent collections at Eden (N.C.) Post Office, New Brunswick (N.J.) Post Office, Cedar Rapids Art Assn., Newark Mus., Montclair Mus., Interchurch Center, N.Y.C., also pvt. collections; tchr. Roerich Mus., N.Y.C., 1933-34, Westchester Art Workshop, 1947-68, Nat. Acad. Sch. Fine Arts, 1979-81. Charter mem. White Plains Civic Art Commn. 1948-60. Recipient Saltus Gold medal, 1935; Am. Artists Profl. League medal, 1936; Montclair Art Mus. medal, 1936. Guggenheim fellow, 1946-47. Fellow Nat. Sculpture Soc. (council 1982—); mem. NAD (council 1978-81), Audubon Artists N.Y.C., Hudson Valley Art Assn. Republican. Home: 106 Woodcrest Ave White Plains NY 10604

NICKERSON, MARY CARTER, ednl. adminstr.; b. Washington, Mar 18, 1945; d. Marshall Sylvester and Preot (Nichols) Carter; B.A., Stanford U., 1968; M.A. in Guidance and Counseling, U. Colo., 1982; children—Erik Carter, Kitren Carter. Tchr. English, Public Schs. Palo Alto (Calif.), 1969-71; farmer, horse trainer, riding tchr., Starkville, Miss., 1971-77; dir. women's athletics. asst. dir. admissions Fountain Valley Sch., Colorado Springs, 1977-78, dir. admissions and fin. aid, 1978-81; dir. Ednl. Counseling Offices, Colorado Springs, 1981—; mem. long range planning com. Secondary Schs. Admissions Test Bd., 1979-82. Bd. dirs. A Better Chance (minority recruitment and scholarship), Denver, 1980—. Cert. secondary tchr., Calif. Mem. Ind. Ednl. Counselors Assn., Nat. Assn. Coll. Admissions Counselors, Rocky Mountain Assn. Coll. Admissions Counselors, Colo.-Wyo. Assn. Women Adminstrs. and Counselors, Northend Homeowners Assn., Stanford Alumni Assn. Episcopalian. Club: Whitworth Hunt (dir. 1975-77). Office: 2003 N Nevada Ave Colorado Springs CO 80907

NICKOLS, MARCIA ANNE, psychologist; b. Rahway, N.J., Nov. 29, 1932; d. George J. and Emma (Michels) Ceremsak; B.A., Antioch Coll., 1954; M.A., Cornell U., 1957; postgrad. Case Western Res. U., 1958, U. Ky., 1960, U. Md., 1962-74; children—Kurt Allan, Liese Elaine. Psychologist, Lexington Child Guidance Clinic, 1960-62; with Peace Corps, 1962; psychologist Arlington County (Va.) Schs., 1962-64, Montgomery County (Md.) Schs., 1964-71; cons. Curber Assos. Washington, 1969-73; sr. edn. cons. Aries Corp., McLean, Va., 1972-73; fed. women's program mgr. Alcohol, Drug Abuse and Mental Health Adminstrn., HEW, Rockville, Md., 1973-77, EEO officer, 1977-79; fed. women's program mgr. NASA, Washington, 1979—; pvt. practice psychology; forensic cons. Named Outstanding Profl. in Human Services, Am. Acad. Human Services, 1974. Mem. Am. Psychol. Assn., Va. Psychol. Assn., D.C. Psychol. Assn., Washington Women's Network, Va. Acad. Clin. Psychologists, N. Va. Soc. Clin. Psychologists, ACLU, NOW. Unitarian. Home: 1736 N Albemarle St McLean VA 22101 Office: NASA Code U Room 6115 Washington DC 20546

NICKOLS, SHARON YVONNE, home economist; b. Topeka, Kans., Nov. 10, 1942; d. Harold Taft and Letha (McClain) Reser; B.S., Kans. State U., 1965; M.A., Tchrs. Coll., Columbia U., 1967; Ph.D. (Gregory fellow), U. Mo., 1976; m. Samuel A. Nickols, Sept. 19, 1964; children—Douglas, Russell, Sharon Michelle, Matthew. Instr., Culver Stockton Coll., Canton, Mo., 1967-70; dir. family-to-family program Christian Ch. Mo., Columbia, 1971-73; asso. prof. home econs. Okla. State U., Stillwater, 1976—, also dir. Family Study Center. Del., White House Conf. Families, 1980; mem. Gov.'s Adv. Com. on Children, Youth and Families, 1981—. Mem. Am. Home Econs. Assn., Nat. Council Family Relations, Am. Council Consumer Interests, Okla. Demographics Group. Democrat. Mem. Christian Ch. Disciples of Christ. Co-editor Challenges of the 80's: Families Face the Future, 1980; contbr. articles to profl. jours. Office: Coll Home Econs Okla State U Stillwater OK 74078

NICKS, STEVIE, singer, songwriter; b. Calif., May 26, 1948; m. Lindsey Buckingham (div.). Singer, songwriter with Lindsey Buckingham; recorded album Buckingham and Nicks, 1975; solo album Bella Donna, 1982; joined group Fleetwood Mac, 1975; composer song Rhiannon. Co-winner, Billboard award for Album of Year, Group of Year, 1977. Office: care Penguin Promotions 1410 N Beachwood Hollywood CA 90028 *

NICOLAS-PONCE, MINERVA MALLARI, internist; b. Manila, May 17, 1943; d. Jose Osorio and Rosario Castro (Mallari) Nicolas; came to U.S., 1965; A.A., U. Santo Tomas, Manila, 1960, M.D. cum laude, 1965; m. Mario Valero Ponce, Dec. 2, 1967; children—Mario Jose, Martin Joseph. Intern, Mt. Sinai Hosp., Hartford, Conn., 1966; resident in internal medicine Hartford Hosp., 1967, Coney Island Hosp., Bklyn., 1968-70; attending physician outpatient services Coney Island Hosp., 1970-73, Neillsville (Wis.) Hosp., 1973; practice medicine specializing in internal medicine, Wisconsin Rapids, Wis., 1973—; mem. staff Doctor's Clinic; attending staff physician Riverview Hosp., Wisconsin Rapids. Diplomate Am. Bd. Internal Medicine. Mem. A.C.P., Am., Wis. socs. internal medicine, Wood County (Wis.), Wis. med. socs., AMA. Home: 520 Bruce Ln Wisconsin Rapids WI 54494 Office: 1041 Hill St Wisconsin Rapids WI 54494

NICOLL, ELIZABETH ANN, mfg. co. exec.; b. Troy, N.Y., June 22, 1939; d. Francis and Elizabeth (Pazzo) Gaunay; A.A.S. in Bus. Adminstrn., Hudson Valley Community Coll., 1973; postgrad. St. Rose Coll., 1981—; children—Theresa, Donald J., Steven F. Programmer analyst Bendix Corp., Troy, 1963-72, Huyck Felt, Rensselaer, N.Y., 1973-75, systems analyst, 1975-79, mgr. info. systems, 1979—. Mem. Data Processing Mgmt. Assn., Albany Women's Forum, Nat. Assn. Female Execs. Home: 1 Tillinghast Ave Menands NY 12204 Office: Huyck Felt Co Washington St Rensselaer NY 12144

NICOLOSI, DOROTHY EMILY, non-profit orgn. exec.; b. N.Y.C., July 15, 1931; d. Thomas and Aurora (Scoppa) Nicolosi; B.S. in Edn., Fordham U., 1963, cert. Introductory Mgmt. Devel., 1967, cert. Advanced Mgmt. Devel., 1968; M. Public Adminstrn., N.Y. U., 1979. Exec. sec. Arabol Mfg. Co., N.Y.C., 1950-55; research asst. Smith Richardson Found., N.Y.C., 1955-60; cons. Robert A. Taft Meml. Found., Washington, 1960-61; asst. sec., office mgr. United Student Aid Fund, Inc., N.Y.C., 1961-63; sec., treas., exec. adminstr. Nat. Strategy Info. Center, Inc., N.Y.C., 1963—, dir., 1978—. Mem. Am. Acad. Polit. and Social Sci., Am. Soc. Public Adminstrn., Acad. Polit. Sci. Republican. Roman Catholic. Home: 3103 Fairfield Ave Riverdale NY 10463 Office: 111 E 58th St New York NY 10022

NIDETCH, JEAN, health service exec.; b. Bklyn., Oct. 12, 1923; d. David and May (Rodin) Slutsky; children—David, Richard. Founding pres. Weight Watchers Internat., Inc., Manhasset, L.I. Cons., N.Y. State Assembly Mental Hygiene Com. 1968; adviser Joint Legis. Com. on Child Care Needs, Legislature N.Y. Pres., Weight Watchers Found. Named Mktg. Woman of Yr.; hon. adm. Gt. Navy Nebr. Woman of Yr., Forest Hills Youth Assn.; recipient Woman of Achievement award, Speakers award Sales Promotion Execs. Assn. Mem. Washington Sq. Bus. and Profl. Womens Club, AFTRA. Author: Jean Nidetch: Weight Watchers Cookbook, 1966; The Story of Weight Watchers, 1970; Program Cookbook. Office: care NAL Publishers 1633 Broadway New York NY 10019 *

NIEBAUER, RUBY RUTH DAY (MRS. THOMAS B. EARLE), film producer; b. Ontario, Wis., Dec. 11, 1910; d. Calvin B. and Mary (Haney) Day; B.S., U. Wis., 1946, M.S., 1947, postgrad., 1960-61; postgrad. U. Calif., 1953-55; m. H.J. Niebauer, June 24, 1936 (dec. Aug. 1940); children—Ruth Ann, Mary Jo; m. Thomas B. Earle, July 8, 1976. Elem. classroom tchr., prin., Westmont, Ill., 1930-32; tchr. art pub. schs., Madison, Wis., also supr. student tchrs. U. Wis., 1934-46; head art dept. U. Wis. at Menominie, 1947-49; asst. prof. edn., supr. art Calif. State U., San Diego, 1949-55; asst. prof. home econs. Mich. State U., 1955-58; producer ednl. films The Creative Craft series, CBS and Ency. Brit. Films, 1953—, also films for Visual Edn. Cons., Madison, Encore Visual Edn., Burbank, Calif.; asst. prof. art U. Mich., Ann Arbor, 1960; researcher dept. edn. U. Wis., Madison, 1960-61; asst. prof. edn., researcher, cons. U. Wis., Milw., 1962-64; asst. prof. home econs. So. Ill. U., 1964-65; assoc. prof. home econs. Western Ky. U., 1965-68; chmn. textiles and design, prof. Sch. Home Econs., U. Ky., 1968-70. Recipient internat. awards for films, Venice (Italy) Internat. Film Festival, 1955, Edinburg, Scotland, Eng., 1955, several nat. film awards, 1955-57. Fellow Internat. Inst. Arts, Letters and Scis.; mem. Nat. Soc. Interior Design, Internat. Platform Assn., Nat. Art Assn., AAUW, NEA, Nat. Home Econs. Assn., Nat. Edn. Communications and Tech., AAUP, Phi Delta Gamma, Pi Lambda Theta, Phi Upsilon Omicron. Home: 1770 Dennison Rd East Lansing MI 48823

NIED, BARBARA BURKE, journalist; b. Upper Darby, Pa., May 30, 1943; d. Joseph Anthony and Teresa Gertrude (Smart) Burke; A.B., Wheeling Coll., 1965; m. Joseph T. Nied, June 12, 1965 (div. Feb. 1977); children—Joseph Burke Nied, Laura Ann Nied, Michele Marie Nied. Asst. editor Jones & Laughlin Steel Corp., Pitts., 1965-66; reporter/photographer Democrat Messenger, Waynesburg, Pa., 1976-77; corr. McGraw-Hill & World News Pubs., N.Y.C., 1976—; writer Pitts. Bus. Times, 1981—. Public relations dir. Boy Scouts Am., Greene County, Pa., 1977—; editor, pub. Democrat Messenger, 1976. Mem. AAUW. Democrat. Roman Catholic. Asst. editor Men and Steel mag., 1965-66; editor Pa. chpts. Pan American's U.S.A. Guide Book, 1979, 80. Home: RD 1 Box 234A Clarksville PA 15322 Office: 100 Wood St Pittsburgh PA 15222

NIEDERHAUSER, MARY CHARLOTTE, hosp. adminstr.; b. Bucyrus, Ohio, Aug. 1, 1943; d. Richard Wayne and Mary Maxine (Cammarn) N.; grad. Ohio Valley Hosp. Sch. Nursing, 1964; B.A., Barat Coll., 1978; M.B.A., U. Chgo., 1981. Staff nurse L.A. Weiss Meml. Hosp., Chgo., 1965-68, nursing supr., 1968-76; critical care supr. Skokie Valley Community Hosp., Skokie, Ill., 1976-77; dir. nursing Forkosh Meml. Hosp., Chgo., 1977-79, v.p. patient care services, 1979—; guest speaker on critical care nursing mgmt., Kansas City, Apr. 1977, Atlanta, May 1977, Chgo., Oct. 1977, cons. adolescent alcoholism treatment programs, stress mgmt. for women. Mem. Chgo. Health Execs. Forum, Am. Coll. Hosp. Adminstrs., Lincoln Sq. C. of C., No. Bus. and Industry Council of Chgo., U. Chgo. Women's Bus. Club, Exec. Program Club of U. Chgo. Grad. Sch. Bus., Am. Heart Assn., Ill. Soc. Nurse Adminstrs., U. Chgo. Hosp. Adminstrn. Alumni Assn., Chgo. Area Health Planning Assn., Delta Epsilon Sigma. Home: 2634 W Berwyn St Chicago IL 60625 Office: 2544 W Montrose Ave Chicago IL 60618

NIEDERMEIER, CHRISTINE MARIE, lawyer, state legislator; b. Bridgeport, Conn., Oct. 21, 1951; d. Jerome J. and Marie Perkins N.; A.B. in Govt., Georgetown U., 1973, J.D., 1977. Legis. analyst in housing and urban affairs Library of Congress, Washington, 1973-74; legal and legis. asst. to Gov. of Conn., Hartford, 1975; legis. asst. Congressman Christopher J. Dodd of Conn., Washington, 1975-77; asso. firm Day, Berry and Howard, Hartford, Conn., summer 1976; schedule and advance aide Nat. Presdl. Campaign of Gov. Edmund G. Brown, Jr., 1976; admitted to Conn. bar, 1977, U.S. Dist. Ct. bar, 1977, D.C. bar, 1979; asso. firm Trager and Trager, Fairfield, Conn., 1977-81, Winthrop, Stimson, Putnam and Roberts, Stamford, Conn., 1982—; mem. Conn. Ho. of Reps., 1979—, chmn. subcom. regulation and protection of com. transp.; mem. arts and the states com. Nat. Conf. State Legislators. Lawyers com. rep. United Way Campaign, 1977-79; mem. Fairfield Rep. Town Meeting, 1977-79; mem. Democratic Town Com., Fairfield; bd. dirs. YWCA Greater Bridgeport, Conn. Audubon Soc.; mem. U. Bridgeport Law Sch. Fund Com., also bd. assos.; mem. Fairfield Parking Authority Adv. Com.; mem. Parents and Friends of Retarded Citizens, Inc.; vice chmn. president's council Sacred Heart U. Recipient Disting. Service award Georgetown U., 1973. Mem. Am. Bar Assn., Conn. Bar Assn., D.C. Bar Assn., Greater Bridgeport Bar Assn., Conn. Audubon Soc. (dir.), Fairfield LWV, Judeo-Christian Women of Fairfield County. Office: State Capitol Hartford CT 06115

NIEDLING, HOPE HOTCHKISS, dietitian; b. Meriden, Ill., Feb. 14, 1922; d. Bert and Myrle Glenn (Vaughn) Hotchkiss; student North Central Coll., 1939-40; B.S., U. Ill., 1943; M.S. in Food Sci. and Nutrition, U. Wis. 1974; m. Ivan Martin Niedling, June 26, 1948. Teaching dietitian Univ. Hosp., Balt., 1944; dietitian public sch. cafeterias, Balt., 1944-48; dir. admisions Thomas Sch. Retailing, Phila., 1954-55; instr. foods U. Wis., Stevens Point, 1967-68; food service supr., instr. Mid-State, N.Central and Fox Valley Tech. Insts., Wis., 1973-75; cons. dietitian nursing homes in Wis., 1973—. Chmn., Village of Plover Cancer Fund Drive, 1977-78; bd. dirs. Stout Found., U. Wis., 1977—. Recipient Loyalty award U. Ill., 1978, award of merit U. Ill. Home Econs. Assn., 1979. Mem. Am. Wis. dietetic assns., No. Wis. Dietetic Assn. (pres. 1971-73), Soc. for Nutrition Edn., Nutrition Today Soc., Nutritionists in Bus., Wis. Assn. Registered Parliamentarians (state corr. sec. 1978-80), Wis. Fedn. Women's Clubs (1st v.p. 1978-80), U. Ill. Home Econs. Alumni Assn. (bd. dirs. 1972-78), Colonia Dames XVII Century, Daus. Am. Colonists, Nat. Assn. Registered Parliamentarians, Wis. Public Health Assn. (mem. aging com. 1974-78), Portage County Humane Soc. (sec. 1973—), Wis. Fedn. Women's Clubs (pres. 1980—), Gen. Fedn. Women's Clubs (sec.-treas. region 1982—, chmn. internat. aid div. 1982—), Colonial Dames XVII Century (1st v.p. Wis. 1981-83, pres. 1983—), DAR (Sec. 1977-80, 1st vice regent 1980—, chpt. regent 1972-77, chpt. registrar 1977—, pres. Wis. state officers club 1976-77), AAUW (pres. br. 1968-72, state corr. sec. 1970-72), U. Ill. Alumni Assn. (dir. 1973), NCCJ (disting. merit citation 1976, vice chmn. Wis.), Wis. Fedn. Republican. Women (dist. chmn. 1969-74), Gamma Sigma Delta, Epsilon Sigma Omicron. Methodist. Clubs: Order Eastern Star, Order of Amaranth, Order White Shrine of Jerusalem, Stevens Point Area Woman's (pres. 1972-74, 76-78). Address: 1008 3rd St Stevens Point WI 54481

NIEHOFF, MARILEE SCHULTZ, indsl. psychologist; b. Horicon, Wis.; d. Carl J. and Myra (Mellenthien) Schultz; B.S. with honors in Elem. Edn. (fellow in econ. edn.), Ill. State U., 1972, M.S. in Psychology, 1973, Ph.D. in Ednl. Adminstrn., 1976; m. Carl Niehoff, Jr.; children—Nan Miller, K.C. Eynatten, Janet, Sally, Carl III. Asst. prof. elem. edn. Ill. State U., Normal, 1976-77; vis. asst. prof. psychology Kent State U., 1977-78; tng. coordinator Firestone Tire & Rubber Co., Akron, Ohio, 1978-80; practice as M.S. Niehoff and Assos., mgmt. and ednl. cons., 1981—; asst. prof. psychology Kent State U., also cons. bus. communications; condr. indsl. and tng. seminars. Mem. Am. Psychol. Assn., Am. Personnel and Guidance Assn., Assn. Specialists in Group Work, Am. Assn. Higher Edn., AAUP, Ill. State U. Adminstrs. Club, Am. Soc. Tng. and Devel., Assn. Humanistic Psychology, NOW. Unitarian. Co-author textbook series in career edn.; contbr. articles to jours. and periodicals. Home: 7702 Diagonal Rd Kent OH 44240 Office: Kent State U Kent OH 44242

NIELSEN, EVELYN ROSE, nurse; b. Minot, N.D., Apr. 16, 1926; d. Ernest R. and Tilda L. (Mostad) Smith; diploma Trinity Hosp. Sch. Nursing, 1946; children—Mary Smith, Gary, Jeffrey. Nurse med. floor Trinity Med. Center, Minot, 1947-49, supr. nursing service, 1965-81, dir. nursing service, 1981—. Mem. Am. Nurses Assn., N.D. Nurses Assn., Trinity Nurses Alumni Assn., Nat. League Nursing. Democrat. Lutheran. Clubs: Elks, Eagles Aux. Address: 1116 6th Ave NW Minot ND 58701

NIELSEN, LISA TAGE, opinion research co. exec.; b. Glen Ridge, N.J., June 8, 1946; d. Axel Tage and Winifred Phyllis (Eisenhart) N.; student Skidmore Coll., 1964-65; B.A., U. Miami, 1968, M.B.A., 1973; m. Jeffrey J. Gaydos, Apr. 21, 1978. Circulation trainee Miami Herald Pub. Co. (Fla.), 1972-74, research mgr., 1974-76; research mgr. Gannett Rochester Newspapers (N.Y.), 1976-77; sr. media analyst Market Opinion Research, Detroit, 1977-78, mgr. media div., 1978-81, v.p. media research, 1981—. Vol., Grosse Pointe (Mich.) Tree Com., 1981—. Mem. Women in Communications (v.p. Detroit chpt. 1981-82), Internat. Newspaper Promotion Assn., Am. Assn. Public Opinion Research. Presbyterian. Clubs: Economic of Detroit. Home: 19961 Norton Ct Grosse Pointe Woods MI 48236 Office: Market Opinion Research 550 Washington Blvd Detroit MI 48226

NIELSEN, NANCY ANNE, data processing specialist; b. Salem, Mass., Sept. 12, 1934; d. Frank Ellwood and Myrtle Annie (Peterson) Root; B.A. in Math., U. N.H., 1957; m. Glenn Foster Nielsen, Nov. 27, 1959; children—Peder Root, Edward Stapleford. Programmer Rand Corp., Hanscom Field, Lexington, Mass., Topsham AFB, Maine, 1957-58; sr. programmer analyst System Devel. Corp., Santa Monica, Calif., 1958-60, 1960-62; engrng. programmer Litton, Canoga Park, Calif., 1964; programming cons. Am. Inst. for Research, West Los Angeles, 1963-64; sr. programmer analyst System Devel. Corp., Santa Monica, 1965-69, sect. head, 1969-79, computer systems specialist, 1979—; tech. cons. U.S. Air Force. Den leader, troop com. sec. Boy Scouts Am., 1971-75; vestry mem. St. Martin-in-the Fields Episcopal Ch., 1972-74. Mem. System Devel. Corp. Mgmt. Assn. Club: Canoga Park Jr. Women's. (safety chmn., treas. 1963-65). Home: 25472 Via Novia Valencia CA 91355 Office: 2500 Colorado Blvd Santa Monica CA 90406

NIEMANN, JEAN HALL, civic worker; b. Kansas City, Kans., Mar. 2, 1918; d. Howard Fillingham and Vida (Biancy) Turner; student Upsala Coll., 1935-36, St. Mary's Sch. of Nursing, 1936-37; m. Harold Herman Niemann, Aug. 9, 1937; 1 son, Gary Hall. Pres. St. Elizabeth's Hosp. Aux., Hutchinson, Kans., 1961-62; bd. dirs. Grace Hosp. Aux., Hutchinson, 1962-63; regent Uvedale chpt. D.A.R., Hutchinson, 1968-69, Kans. state chmn. jr. membership, 1971-74; sr. soc. pres. Jesse Lee Reno chpt. Children Am. Revolution, 1977—; bd. Central States Synod, Luth. Ch. Women, 1977—; vol. service chmn. Hutchinson Hosp. Corp., 1979—. Dem. precinct committee woman, mem. Reno County Dem. Com.; mem. choir, Luth. Ch. Women Emanuel Luth. Ch., Hutchinson. Clubs: Prairie Dunes Country (Hutchinson), Golf. Home: 113 Carlton Rd Hutchinson KS 67501

NIEMANTSVERDRIET, GERALDINE (JERRY), nurse; b. Logansport, Ind., July 27, 1926; d. John and Anna Marie (Vitello) DeRosa; diploma St. Elizabeth Sch. of Nursing, Lafayette Ind., 1947; postgrad. external degree program Coll. of St. Francis, Joliet, Ill., 1976-79; m. Francis W. Niemantsverdriet, Dec. 27, 1947; children—K. Philip, Mary Jo, David John. Staff nurse Home Hosp., Lafayette, Ind., 1963-71, head nurse emergency, 1971-73, dir. emergency and out-patient depts., 1973-81; Red Cross vol., 1958—; mem. Task Force for Emergency Nurse Course, 1974-75; community coordinating com. for Drug Abuse Programs, 1974-75. Area chmn. Tippecanoe County Heart Assn. Fund Drive, 1975, 76; campaign worker Lafayette area Cath. Schs. Found., 1976. Mem. Am. Nurses Assn., Ind. State Nurses Assn. (convention del. 1973, 75), Ind. Joint Practice Commn. of Nurses and Physicians, Home Hosp. Assn., Lafayette Council of Cath. Nurses, St. Elizabeth Alumnae Assn., Lafayette Fire Fighters Aux., Tippecanoe Right to Life Orgn., Sagamore Bus. and Profl. Women's Club Roman Catholic. Home: 320 S 26th St Lafayette IN 47904

NIEMEYER, MAXINE BREWER, ins. exec.; b. Detroit, Jan. 14, 1920; d. Daniel Frederick and Ella (Case) Niemeyer; student Detroit Coll. Bus., 1938-39, Exec. Sec. Asso. (hon.), 1960; grad. Dale Carnegie course, 1946; student Wayne U., 1958, Wayne State and U. Mich. Extension Schs., 1961-64, 65—. Gen. office clk. Hart Sewing Machine Supplies Co., Detroit, 1938-39; cashier, sec. N.Am. Life Assurance Co., Detroit, 1939-41, office mgr., 1942-43; office mgr. L.A. Walden & Co., Detroit, 1943-46; asst. office mgr. Dr. Ralph H. Pino, Ophthalmologist, Detroit, 1946-48; registrar Leadership Tng., Inc., Detroit, 1948-50; sec. to mgr. market analysis and dealer orgn dept. Sales div. Chevrolet Motor Co., Detroit, 1950-56; office mgr., sec. to Walter R. Cavanaugh, C.L.U., 1956—, corp. sec. 1958—, mgr. policyholders service and sales promotion, 1966; staff mgr. Phoenix Mut. Life, also owner and pres. M.B. Niemeyer CLU & Assos., 1966—; advanced underwriting cons., agt., surplus lines mgr. Phoenix Cos.; registered rep. Phoenix Equity Planning Corp. Named Detroit Sec. of Yr. Detroit chpt. Nat. Secs. Assn. Internat., 1960, One of Top Ten Working Women Central Bus. Dist. Assn., Detroit, 1965; C.L.U.; lic. life ins. counselor. Mem. Nat. Secs. Assn. (pres. Detroit chpt. 1962-64), Detroit Assn. Life Underwriters (pres. 1974-75), Am. Soc. C.L.U.s (past regional dir.; pres. Detroit chpt. 1973-74), Am. Coll. C.L.U.s (trustee), Million Dollar Round Table, Fin. and Estate Planning Council Detroit, Life Ins. Leaders Mich., Mich. Assn. Life Ins. Counselors, Internat. Assn. Fin. Planners, Alpha Iota Internat. (chpt. pres. 1944). Presbyterian. Club: Soroptimist (pres. 1972—) (Grosse Pointe, Mich.). Home: 1792 Vernier Rd Grosse Pointe Woods MI 48236 Office: 3000 Town Center Suite 202 Southfield MI 48075

NIEMIRA, CAROLINE MARIE, direct mktg. co. exec.; b. Chgo., Nov. 22, 1947; d. Thaddeus Felix and Regina (Penkala) Niemira; B.A. with highest honors and distinction in Linguistics, U. Mich., 1969; M. Mgmt., Northwestern U., 1976. Editorial asst. Edmund A. Smason Public Relations, Chgo., 1969-72; sr. account supr. Jack E. Schlegal Advt., Chgo., 1972-75; gen. corr. Nielsen Communication Team, Dublin, Ireland, 1976; account exec. Communique Public Relations, Dublin, Ireland, 1977-78; account exec., prodn. mgmt. Exec. Mktg. Services, Houston, 1979, asst. nat. accounts mgr., 1981; freelance bus. communicator, Houston, 1980; owner Niemira Direct Communications, Houston, 1982—; Chgo. corr. Women's Almanac, 1975; corr. Writers' Internat., 1971. Advt., public relations mgr. Alderman Dick Simpson, Chgo., 1972-75. Recipient Matrix award Women in Communications, Inc., 1981; Award of Merit Internat. Assn. Bus. Communicators, Soc. Tech. Communication award, 1980; Leadership award Direct Mail Mktg. Assn., 1981. Mem. Direct Mktg. Creative Guild, Inc., Women in Communications, Inc., Internat. Assn. Bus. Communicators, U.S. Volleyball Assn., Iota Sigma Epsilon, Phi Chi Theta, Sigma Kappa. Creator, editor The Executive, 1979-82. Office: PO Box 92174 Houston TX 77206

NIEVES, PRISCILLA, commodities trading co. exec.; b. San Juan, P.R., Dec. 14, 1950; d. Benito and Benita (Nieves-Jimenez) Nieves-Baez; B.A. (Alice Baldwin scholar), Duke U., 1972; M.B.A., U. N.C., 1977;

m. Andrew E. Cardwell, July 2, 1981. Part-owner Waste Paper & Equipment, Durham, N.C., 1976-79; asst. brand mgr. Legg's Products div. Hanes Hosiery, Winston-Salem, N.C., 1977-79; asst. brand mgr. Miller Brewing Co., Milw., 1979; brand mgr. Wine Spectrum, Coca-Cola, Atlanta, 1979-82; partner Cardwell Nieves Inc., Atlanta, 1982—. Mem. High Mus. Art, Found. of Truth. Roman Catholic. Address: 400 Riverwood Ln Suite A Roswell GA 30076

NIGAGLIONI, CRUZ-JIMÉNEZ OLGA (MRS. JOSE E. NIGAGLIONI), lawyer, former state legislator; b. Rio Piedras, P.R., July 31, 1933; d. Manuel Cruz Horta and Dolores Jimenez; B.Social Sci., U. P.R., 1954, LL.B. cum laude, 1957; m. Jose E. Nigaglioni, Sept. 11, 1971; 1 dau., Olga Isabel. Admitted to P.R. bar, 1957; legal counsel Pub. Works Dept. San Juan, P.R., 1957-58, P.R. Housing Corp., San Juan, 1957-58; dist. judge at large, San Juan, 1958-60; spl. dist. atty., San Juan, 1960-62; spl. dist. atty. P.R. Justice Dept., San Juan, 1963-64; pvt. practice, 1964-68; mem. P.R. Ho. of Reps., 1968-76, majority alternate floor leader, chmn. judiciary com., 1972-76; prof. InterAm. U., 1977-82. Recipient award for polit. achievement Exchangettes, 1969; award of achievement Nu Sigma Beta, 1969; Most Outstanding Young Women of Year award Jr. C. of C., 1972. Mem. Am., P.R. (Achievement award 1969, award for betterment and devel. P.R. law 1976), bar assns., Am. Judicature Soc., Bus. and Profl. Women's Club, U. P.R. Alumni Assn., Kappa Beta Pi. Club: Zonta. Home: 313 Navarra St Rio Piedras PR 00923 Office: Capitol San Juan PR 00902

NIGHTINGALE, ELENA OTTOLENGHI, physician, geneticist; b. Leghorn, Italy, Nov. 1, 1932; came to U.S., 1939, naturalized, 1948; d. Mario L. and Elisa V. (Levi) Ottolenghi; A.B. summa cum laude, Barnard Coll., 1954; Ph.D. in Microbial Genetics (Grad. U. fellow), Rockefeller, U., N.Y.C., 1961; M.D. (Am. Cancer Soc. postdoctoral fellow), N.Y.U., 1964; m. Stuart L. Nightingale, July 1, 1965; children—Elizabeth, Marisa. Instr. medicine N.Y.U. Med. Sch., 1964-65; asst. prof. microbiology Cornell U. Med. Coll. and Grad. Sch. Med. Scis., 1965-70; asst. prof. Johns Hopkins U. Med. Sch., 1970-73; sr. staff officer Nat. Acad. Scis./NRC, 1975-76; mem. faculty Georgetown, U. Med. Sch., 1975—, clin. asst. prof. pediatrics, 1980—; mem. staff Inst. Medicine, Nat. Acad. Scis., 1976-82, sr. program officer, 1979-82, sr. scholar in residence, 1982—; vis. asso. prof. social medicine and health policy Harvard U. Med. Sch., 1980—. Fellow Nat. Acad. Scis./Sloan Found., 1974-75. Fellow N.Y. Acad. Scis.; mem. AAAS, Harvey Soc., Genetics Soc. Am., Am. Soc. Microbiology, Am. Soc. Human Genetics. Author numerous articles in field of genetics and health policy. Home: 6004 Osceola Rd Bethesda MD 20016 Office: 2101 Constitution Ave NW Washington DC 20418

NIHILL, KAREN BAILEY, nursing home exec.; b. Erie, Pa., Mar. 15, 1947; d. William C. and Eleanor (Danielson) Bailey; R.N., Hamot Med. Center, Erie, 1968; postgrad. U. Pa., 1974—; 1 son, Liam H. Critical care nurse Hamot Med. Center, 1968-71, VA Hosp., Phila., 1974-77; dir. nursing Chapel Manor and Nursing Home, Phila., 1977—, also Phila. Protestant Home and Elmira Jeffries Nursing Home. Active Lutheran Ch. Women's Orgn. Served to lt. Nurse Corps, U.S. Navy, 1971-73. VA grantee, 1974. Mem. Am. Assn. Critical Care Nurses, Pa. Nurses Assn. Republican. Home: 6131 N Mascher St Philadelphia PA 19120 Office: 1500 N 15th St Philadelphia PA 19121

NIKLAUSKI, MARIANNE NANCY, cytotechnologist; b. Phila., Aug. 19, 1942; d. Edward S. and Pauline S. (Polner) Bay; student Pa. State U., 1960-63; degree in cytotech. U. Pa., 1964; m. Leonard Niklauski, Oct. 27, 1977. Cytotechnologist, Lower Bucks County Hosp., Bristol, Pa., 1964-65; supr. cytology, clin. lab. Walter G. Sawchak, Trenton, N.J., 1965-80; cytotechnologist MDS Labs., Cherry Hill, N.J., 1980-81; supr. cytology Torresdale div. Frankford Hosp., Phila., 1981—. Am. Cancer Soc. grantee, 1963. Mem. Am. Soc. Clin. Pathologists, Del. Valley Soc. Cytotechnologists. Home: 211 Cleveland Ave Edgewater Park NJ 08010 Office: Frankford Hosp Red Lion and Knights Rd Philadelphia PA 19114

NILES, ANITA GALE, state legislator; b. Reading, Kans., Aug. 3, 1919; d. David Arthur and Sadie Catherine (Whittington) Thomas; B.S., Emporia State U., 1961, M.S., 1968; m. Herbert T. Niles, June 15, 1941; children—Sherrill, Douglas, Jana, Clair, Rebecca. Mem. Kans. Ho. of Reps., Topeka, 1974—. Democrat. Methodist. Office: State Capital Topeka KS 66612

NILSEN, BARBARA YVONNE, water utility exec.; b. Glendale, Calif., Oct. 23, 1941; d. Allen Blair and Ina Lee (Stewart) Scott; A.A., San Jose City Coll., 1972; B.S. in Bus., San Jose State U., 1974; postgrad. in law Lincoln U., 1978-82; m. William Nilsen, May 15, 1976; children—Tina, Valerie, Jamie Ng, Michael Ng. Dir. personnel, asst. sec. San Jose (Calif.) Water Works, 1964—. Chmn. allocations panel Santa Clara County United Way, 1982; bd. dirs. Central chpt., 1982; 1st v.p. League of Friends on Commn. Status of Women, 1982; pres. Seven Trees Village Homeowners Assn., 1974. Named Disting. Citizen of Yr., City of San Jose, 1981. Mem. Am. Water Works Assn. (sec. Calif./Nev. chpt. 1980, dir. 1982). Democrat. Roman Catholic. Clubs: Fairway Glen Women's Golf, San Jose Quota (pres. 1978-79). Office: 374 W Santa Clara St San Jose CA 95196

NILSON, PATRICIA JANE, psychologist; b. Boulder, Colo., Oct. 22, 1929; d. James and Vera (Peacock) Broxon; B.A., U. Colo., 1968; M.A., L.I. U., 1972, Ph.D., 1973; m. Eric Walter Nilson, Dec. 23, 1950; children—Stephen Daniel, Eric Jon, Christopher Lawrence. Staff phys. therapist Maryview Hosp., Portsmouth, Va., 1952-53; intern Mt. Sinai Hosp., Elmhurst, N.Y., 1972-73; staff psychologist Suffolk County Consultation Services Center, Hauppaga, N.Y., 1972—; adj. asst. prof. L.I. U., 1975—; pvt. practice psychology, Commack, N.Y., 1973—; cons. Wayside Sch. for Girls. Mem. Am. Psychol. Assn., Eastern Psychol. Assn., N.Y. State Psychol. Assn., Suffolk County Psychol. Assn., Nassau County Psychol. Assn., N.Y. Soc. Clin. Psychologists, Assn. Advancement of Behavior Therapy, Assn. Advancement of Psychology. Contbr. articles to profl. jours., books. Office: Suffolk County Consultation Services Center Hauppauge NY 11787

NILSSON, BEVERLY SWENSON, nurse; b. St. Paul, May 11, 1931; d. Clifford and Arenza Marian (Crist) Swenson; B.S. with high distinction in Nursing, U. Minn., 1967, M.S., 1973, now postgrad.; m. Harry Willard Nilsson; children—Thomas Richard, Steven Alain, Kaara Christine. Instr. nursing Fairview Hosp. Sch. Nursing, Mpls., 1967-71; asst. prof. psychiat. nursing S.D. State U. Coll. Nursing, 1973-77; asso. prof. nursing Augsburg Coll., Mpls., 1977-, chmn. dept., since 1978—; chmn. utilization rev. com. People Incorporated Epilepsy Program, 1981—; mem. community edn. adv. com. ARC; mem. speakers bur. Am. Cancer Soc. Mem. Am. Nurses Assn., Nat. League Nursing, Hastings Center, Inst. Soc., Ethics and Life Services, Am. Swedish Inst., NOW, Sigma Theta Tau. Democrat. Lutheran. Co-developer client goals theory in nursing. Office: 731 21st Ave S Minneapolis MN 55404

NILSSON, BIRGIT, soprano; b. Karup, Sweden; d. Nils P. and Justina (Paulsson) Svensson; student Royal Musical Acad., Stockholm; Mus.D. (hon.), Amherst (Mass.) U., Andover U.; m. Bertil Niklasson, Sept. 10, 1948. Appeared opera and concert houses in Europe, N.Am., S.Am., Japan and Australia; most famous roles include Bruennhilde, Isolde, Salome, Elektra, Turandot, Tosca, Lady Macbeth, Fidelio. Decorated 1st comdr. Order of Vasa (Sweden); Austrian and Bavarian Kammersaengerin; named Swedish Royal Court Singer. Hon. mem. Royal Acad. Music London, Royal Acad. Music Stockholm, Vienna State Opera. Address: Care Eric Lemon Assos Inc 111 W 57th St New York NY 10019

NIMS, JACQUELINE FAIN, photography co. exec.; b. Tampa, Fla., Mar. 26, 1945; d. John Mills and Barbara Hancock Fain; Mus.B., Fla. State U., 1967; m. Jerry Curtis Nims, Apr. 12, 1968; children—Jacqueline Barbara Ruth, Jerridean Elizabeth, John Curtis. Spl. rep. Campus Crusade for Christ Internat., 1967-76; corp. sec., dir. Nimslo Tech., Inc., Atlanta, 1971—. Bd. dirs., sec. Found. Researching Internat. Devel.; v.p. membership, publicity chmn. Atlanta Women's div. Freedoms Found. at Valley Forge, 1976-77; sec. for steering com. London Service League, 1979; nature guide, mem. prayer breakfast com. Jr. League of Atlanta, 1979-82. Recipient George Washington Honor medal Freedoms Found. at Valley Forge, 1976. Mem. DAR, Kappa Alpha Theta, Pi Kappa Lambda. Baptist. Club: North Side Jr. Woman's. Office: Nimslo Corp 1 Nimslo Park Atlanta GA 30338

NIPPER, MARY DON, oil and gas co. exec.; b. Amarillo, Tex., Feb. 3, 1940; d. Don H. and Mary Frances (Miller) Wood; student Amarillo Coll., 1958-60; m. Fred Don Nipper, June 23, 1958; children—Larry Don, Nancy Ann. Sec. land dept. Humble Oil & Refining Co., Amarillo, 1962-65; adminstrv. asst. land dept. J.M. Huber Corp., Amarillo, 1967-70; corp. sec. Tom F. Marsh, Inc., Amarillo, 1972-78, v.p., land, 1978—. Mem. Panhandle Natural Gas Soc. (sec.), Am. Assn. Petroleum Landmen, Desk and Derrick. Republican. Methodist. Home: 3420 Amherst Amarillo TX 79109 Office: 430 First Nat Bank Bldg Amarillo TX 79105

NISKA, MARALIN, opera singer; b. San Pedro, Calif.; d. William Albert and Vera Zoe (Stott) Dice; B.A., UCLA, postgrad., 1959-60; postgrad. Music Acad. of West, 1958-60, U. So. Calif., 1958-59, Long Beach State U.; m. William P. Mullen, May 23, 1970. Debut as Manon in Manon, Ebell Theatre, Los Angeles, 1959; with Met. Nat. Co., 1965-67, N.Y.C. Opera, 1967—, Met. Opera, 1972—; debuts include: Los Angeles Opera, 1959, Opera Co. of Boston, Tulsa Opera, San Diego Opera, 1965, Santa Fe Opera, 1968, Miami Opera, Phila. Opera. Mem. Am. Guild Mus. Artists (gov. 1977-79), Screen Actors Guild. Democrat. Office: care Tony Hartman 250 W 57th St Suite 1128A New York NY 10019

NISSMAN, BLOSSOM SNOYER, sch. adminstr.; b. Yonkers, N.Y., Feb. 23, 1928; d. Arthur Richard and Rose (Strauss) Snoyer; B.S. in Elem. Edn., Temple U., 1951; M.A. in Student Personnel Services, Trenton (N.J.) State Coll., 1969; Ed.D. in Social Philosophy Founds., Rutgers U., 1975; divorced; children—Debra Beth, David Arthur. Tchr. schs. in N.J. and Pa., 1951-70; counseling, learning cons., N.J., 1970-71; sch. adminstr. Burlington (N.J.) Region, 1972; regional coordinator 10-sch. consortium for spl. edn. Central Burlington County Region, 1974—; mem. part-time faculty Rider Coll., Trenton State Coll., U. Pa., Temple U. Named Woman of Yr., Orgn. Rehab. Therapists, 1980. Mem. Nat. Assn. Sch. Adminstrs. (rep. exec. council), Nat. Assn. Coll. Educators and Suprs., AAUP, Delta Kappa Gamma (scholarship 1974). Author: New Dimensions in Elementary Guidance, 1975; Improving Middle School Guidance, 1981; also booklets. Home: Box 106 Rancocas NJ 08073 Office: Westampton Sch Mt Holly NJ 08060

NISTLER, LORETTA, transp. co. exec.; b. Oakland City, Ind., Mar. 25, 1941; d. Gilbert and Velada Volkman; grad. high sch., Ind.; m. Paul B. Nistler, Dec. 2, 1961. Reporter, asst. to women's editor Evansville (Ind.) Sunday Courier and Press, 1958-61; women's editor Fairbanks (Alaska) Daily News-Miner, 1961; driver, office mgr., personnel mgr., bookkeeper, then partner Alaska Motor Coaches, Inc., also Nistler Enterprises, Delta Junction, Alaska, 1963—, v.p., 1979—; editor, pub. Delta Paper, 1976—; pres. TriDelta, Inc., 1978—. Mem. Delta C. of C. (past pres., dir.), Nat. Sch. Transp. Assn., Alaska Sch. Transp. Assn., Alaska Press Women, Nat. Press Women. Home: Mile 1 Nistler Rd Delta Junction AK 99737 Office: PO Box 952 Delta Junction AK 99737

NISWONGER, JEANNE DUCHATEAU (MRS. JOSEPH K. NISWONGER), wildlife biologist, writer; b. Indpls.; d. Simon Nicholas and Portia (Reeves) Du Chateau; A.B., Miami U., Oxford, Ohio; postgrad. Washington Sch. Psychiatry; M.A., Ph.D., Calif. Western U.; m. Joseph K. Niswonger; children—Kenneth Arnold, Laura Elaine, Nancy Jo. Research assoc. HEW and W.Va. Dept. Health, Charleston; research biologist Bio-Research Inst. Fla. So. Coll., Lakeland, 1958-61; writer Tampa (Fla.) Tribune, 1960-70. Bd. dirs. Polk Pub. Mus.; dir. pub. relations Polk County Council Parents and Tchrs.; pres. Fla. chpt. Nature Conservancy. Mem. Fla. Audubon Soc. (mem. adv. bd. 1960-72), Lake Region Audubon Soc. (bd. dirs. 1959—, pres. 1960-65), AAUW (br. sec. 1962-64), Wildlife Soc., Wilderness Soc., Am. Soc. Mammalogists, Am. Assn. Zool. Parks and Aquariums, Izaak Walton League, Fla. Wildlife Fedn. (dir. 1974—), Nat. Wildlife Fedn., Am. Mus. Natural History, Fla. Zool. Soc., Defenders of Wildlife, Nat. Parks and Conservation Assn., Womans Aux. Fla. Med. Assn. (chmn. pub. relations), United Fedn. Doll Clubs (gov.), Ginny (pres. 1973—), Tampa (pres. 1974-76), Tropical (pres. 1976-79) doll study clubs. Author: That Doll Ginny; editor Fla. Medaux, 1963-65; editor Lake Region Naturalist, 1959-69; asst. editor Fla. Naturalist, 1964-70; editor Fla. Wilderness Calendar, 1964-67. Home: 305 W Beacon Rd Lakeland FL 33803

NIX, BARBARA LOIS, real estate exec.; b. Yakima, Wash., Sept. 25, 1929; d. Martin Clayton and Norma (Gunter) Westfield; A.A., Sierra Coll., 1978; m. B.H. Nix, July 12, 1968; children—William Martin Dahl, Theresa Irene Dahl; step-children—Dennis Leon, Denise Lynn. Bookkeeper, office mgr. Lakeport (Calif.) Tire Service, 1966-69, Dr. K.J. Absher, Grass Valley, Calif., 1972-75; real estate sales and office mgr. Rough and Ready Land Co., Penn Valley, Calif., 1976-77, co-owner, v.p., sec., 1978—, also of Wildwood West Real Estate and Lake of the Pines Sales. Youth and welfare chmn. Yakima Federated Jr. Women's Club, 1957; den mother Cub Scouts, 1959-60; leader Girl Scouts, 1961-62. Recipient Pres.'s award Sierra Coll., 1973; others. Mem. Penn Valley C. of C., Nevada County Bd. Realtors, Nat. Assn. Realtors, Nat. Assn. Female Execs., Antique Soc. Penn Valley (founder, pres. 1978), St. Mary's Coll. Aux., Sierra Nevada Meml. Hosp. Aux., Nevada County Arts Council. Democrat. Roman Catholic. Clubs: Job's Daus. (life), Lady Elks. Home: 18321 Jayhawk Dr Penn Valley CA 95946 Office: PO Box 191 Rough and Ready CA 95975

NIX, JUDY CAROL, hosp. exec.; b. Kansas City, Mo., June 17, 1947; d. DeArmond and Virginia (Beauchamp) Gregory; student Boise State U., 1965-67; m. Franklin D. Kerns, May 16, 1966 (dec. 1975); 1 son, Michael David; m. 2d, Robert W. Nix, Sept. 4, 1977. Sec., Boise Cascade Corp. (Idaho), 1966-71, exec. sec., 1971-74, adminstrv. asst. Manufactured Housing div., 1974-79; personnel dir. Public Hosp. Dist. 1 Pend Oreille County, Newport, Wash., 1979—. Den mother, pack sec. Cub Scouts, 1977-78; sec. St. Anthony's Altar Soc., 1979; chmn. Jr. Miss Pageant, 1980-81. Panhellenic scholar, 1965-66. Roman Catholic. Mem. Personal Dynamics Assn., Idaho Women in Timber. Clubs: Lioness (dir.), Soroptimist, PEO. Home: Route 1 Box 93 Newport WA 99156 Office: PO Box 669 Newport WA 99156

NIXON, AGNES ECKHARDT, TV writer, producer; b. Chgo., Dec. 10, 1927; d. Harry Joseph and Agnes Patricia (Dalton) Eckhardt; B.S. in Speech, Northwestern U., 1948; m. Robert Henry Adolphus Nixon, Apr. 6, 1951; children—Catherine Agnes, Mary Frances, Robert Henry, Emily Anne. Writer TV programs Studio One, 1950, Hallmark, 1952-53, Robert Montgomery Presents, 1952-54; co-creator with Irna Phillips daytime serial As The World Turns, 1957-59; head writer The Guiding Light, 1959-65, Another World, 1965-67; creator, producer One Life to Live, ABC, 1967—, All My Children, 1970—. Trustee, TV Conf. Found. Inst. Recipient numerous citations for outstanding contbn. to daytime television and public service. Mem. Internat. Radio and TV Soc., Nat. Acad. TV Arts and Scis. (editorial bd. Jour., Trustees award). Roman Catholic. Guest columnist arts and leisure sect. New York Times.

NIXON, LILLIAN CONNOR, engring. analyst; b. Long Branch, N.J., Jan. 26, 1937; d. Timothy Joseph and Lillian Louise (MacIntosh) Connor; student Monmouth Coll., 1954-55, Ayers Bus. Coll., 1966-68; cert. legal asst., La. State U., Shreveport, 1977; children—Stephanie Nixon Timmons, Hilary Lisa. Exec. sec. Tenneco Oil Co., Shreveport, 1968-71; tech. asst. Crystal Oil Co., Shreveport, 1971-78, sr. engring. analyst, 1978—. Mem. Shreveport Women's Symphony Guild, Shreveport Symphony, Shreveport Art Guild, Civic Opera Assn. Women's Guild. Mem. Desk and Derrick Club (pres. 1979, 1st v.p. 1978), Beta Sigma Phi. Republican. Presbyterian. Clubs: Cotillion, Centenary Coll. Women's. Address: Box 21101 Shreveport LA 71120

NIXON, ROSEMARY C., utility co. ofcl.; b. Albany, N.Y., Sept. 19, 1942; d. Catherine R. Chase; student DeKalb Community Coll., 1972, Oglethorpe U.; postgrad. Ga. State U., 1978—; m. Ray Nixon, Jr., Oct. 4, 1975; 1 son, Christopher Regan Mashburn. Teller, Atlanta Fed. Savs. & Loan Assn., 1964, head teller, 1965-66; clk. Ga. Power Co., Atlanta, 1967, stenographer, 1969, sec., 1973, coordinator clerical devel., 1977-82, adminstrv. asst., 1982—. Mem. Am. Soc. Tng. and Devel., Atlanta Personnel Mgmt. Assn. Republican. Roman Catholic. Club: Feingold Assn. of Ga. Home: 320 Forest Hills Dr Atlanta GA 30342 Office: 333 Piedmont Ave Atlanta GA 30308

NOBEL, JEAN ANNE, cytotechnologist, histologist; b. N.Y.C., Feb. 28, 1934; d. Robert and Irene May (McCullough) Ritchie; Cert. lab. tech., St. Francis Hosp., Jersey City, 1956; cert. histology East Orange Gen. Hosp., 1960; cert. cytology Presbyterian Hosp., Newark, 1971; m. James L. Nobel, Oct. 30, 1954; 1 dau., Donna Jean Nobel Marsula. Supr. histology Paul Kimball Hosp., Lakewood, N.J., 1965-73, supr. histology and cytology, 1982—; supr. cytology Walson Army Hosp., Ft. Dix., N.J., 1973-75; cytotechnologist Obstet. Assocs., Bricktown, N.J., 1975-82. Leader Monmouth County and Ocean County councils Girl Scouts U.S.A., 1964-70; instr. Spl. Olympics Swimming, Ft. Dix, 1973-75. Mem. Greater N.Y. Assn. Cytotechnologists, N.J. Assn. Cytotechnologists, N.J. Histology Soc. Home: 22 Field St Toms River NJ 08753 Office: Paul Kimball Hospital Lakewood NJ 08701

NOBLE, BARBARA ANNETTE, lawyer, rehab. counselor for deaf; b. Crownpoint, N.Mex., May 13, 1943; d. Charles Edmund and Annette (King) N.; B.A. in English and Psychology, UCLA, 1965; postgrad. Calif. State U., Los Angeles, 1967-68; cert. in counseling for the deaf, U. Tenn., 1971; J.D., Northrop U., 1977. Disability analyst State of Calif., Los Angeles, 1965-68, rehab. counselor, 1968, rehab. counselor for the deaf and hard of hearing, 1968-78, sr. rehab. counselor for the deaf and hard of hearing, 1976-78; admitted to Calif. bar, 1977; vol. staff atty. So. Calif. Center Law and the Deaf, 1978; dep. atty. gen. State of Calif., 1978—; cons. U.S. Postal Service, 1970-78; cons. Silent Industries. Mem. com. for handicapped Los Angeles City Council. Certified rehab. counselor. Mem. Nat. Rehab. Assn., Nat. Rehab. Counseling Assn., Greater Los Angeles Council on Deafness, Profl. Rehab. Workers with Adult Deaf, El Camino Coll. Deaf Advisory Com., Calif. Bar, Women Lawyers Assn. Los Angeles, Los Angeles County Bar Assn., Northrop U., Alumni Assn., UCLA Alumni Assn. Office: 3580 Wilshire Blvd Suite 800 Los Angeles CA 90010

NOBLE, CLAUDIA JEANNE, playwright; b. Balt., Oct. 16, 1948; d. Hans and Ilse Dina (Lobenburg) Juergensen; B.A., U. S. Fla., 1970; M.A., Fla. State U., 1974, M.F.A., 1977; m. James W. Noble, Dec. 12, 1969; 1 son, Andrew Miles; m. 2d, Hector Perez, July 31, 1982. Social worker State of Fla., 1971-73; health educator Neighborhood Health Clinic, Tallahassee, 1977-78; seminars cons. Leon County Adult Edn., Tallahassee, 1978-79, tchr., 1977-79; advt.-copywriter Gayfers Dept. Store, 1981—; cons./poet Leon County Artists in Schs., Tallahassee, 1974—; Theatre critic Flambeau newspaper; author: The Net Synapse, The Real Truth About Oatmeal, Blood, The Mental Health of Henry O'Neill; Alma, Schwartz and Lipsey, Dry Spell. Bd. dirs. Foster Grandparents Tallahassee, 1979-80. Artist fellow Fla. Fine Arts Council, 1980. Mem. Phi Kappa Phi. Democrat. Jewish.

NOBLE, ELLENETTA BEACHLEY, physician; b. Pitts., Nov. 3, 1913; d. Vernon Smith and Ellen Catherine (Neikirk) Beachley; A.B., Allegheny Coll., 1933; M.D., U. Pa., 1938; m. 3d., George J. Melvin, Oct. 23, 1976; children—Susan, Vernon. Intern, Western Pa. Hosp., Pitts., 1938-39; psychiat. and med. staff Torrance (Pa.) State Hosp., 1939-45; gen. practice medicine, Washington, Pa., 1945—; mem. hosp. staffs. Pres., Southwestern Pa. Heart Assn., 1954-56. Recipient Disting. Service award Am. Heart Assn., 1955. Mem. AMA, Pa. County Med. Soc., Washington Med. Soc., Am. Med. Women's Assn., Bus. and Profl. Women (named Woman of Yr., Washington, Pa. br. 1973), AAUW, Pa. Gun Collectors Assn., Phi Beta Kappa. Republican. Clubs: Monday Music, Current Events, Order Eastern Star, Order Amaranth, Order White Shrine of Jerusalem.

NOBLE, ESTELLE BROCKINGTON, banker; b. N.Y.C., Dec. 28, 1925; d. William and Anna (Bell) Brockington; A.A.S., Baruch Sch., 1954. With Chase Manhattan Bank-Internat., N.Y.C., 1951-72, internat. mktg. rep. Middle East/Africa div. Chase Pvt. Banking Internat., 1972—. Mem. N.Y. Assembly, 1965-77; adviser White House Conf. Civil Rights, N.Y. State Commn. Small Bus. Recipient numerous awards. Mem. Am. Assn. UN. Democrat. Baptist. Address: 156-20 Riverside Dr W New York NY 10032

NOBLE, FRANCES ELIZABETH, educator, author; b. Chgo., Sept. 3, 1903; d. George William and Clara Louise (Lane) N.; B.A. cum laude, Northwestern U., 1924, M.A., 1926, Ph.D., 1945. Mem. faculty Western Mich. U., Kalamazoo, 1931—, prof. French, head dept., 1955-73, prof. emerita, 1973—; French tchr. Fort Lauderdale (Fla.) Public Library, 1978—. Pres., Crippled Children's Guild of Broward County. Decorated palmes academiques, 1945. Mem. Alliance Française (past pres.), Am. Assn. Tchrs. of French, Phi Beta Kappa. Republican. Author: (novel) Destiny's Daughter, 1980; The Political Ideas of Alfred de Musset, 1945; also articles. Home: 2915 NE Center Ave Fort Lauderdale FL 33308

NOBLE, JOYCE GAFKE, advt. agy. exec.; b. Wis., Dec. 2, 1922; d. John W. and Helen B. Gafke; B.A., U. Wis., 1944; m. Francis Sill Wickware, 1945 (dec.); children—Roxanne Wickware Tree, Jared G.; m. 2d, William L. Noble, 1957 (dec.); children—Margaret H., Richard E. With N.W. Ayer, Chgo. and N.Y.C., 1951-55; copywriter J. Walter Thompson Co., 1956-70, Grey Advt., 1971-74; v.p., creative dir. William Esty Co., N.Y.C., 1974—. Presbyterian. Home: 1240 Park Ave New York Ny 10028 Office: 100 E 42d St New York NY 10017

NOBLE, LUCINDA ANN, educator; b. Batavia, N.Y., July 16, 1931; d. Kenneth M. and Ethel L. (Brodie) N.; B.S., Cornell U., 1954; M.S., U. Wis., 1959; Ph.D., U. N.C., 1969. Home demonstration agt. Genesee County, N.Y., 1954-56; asst. state leader home demonstration agts. Coop. Extension N.Y. State Coll. Human Ecology, 1956-68, assoc. dir.,

1968-71, 74-78, dir., 1978—, also prof. dept. community service edn., assoc. dean pub. service and continuing edn., 1969-74. Mem. Am. Home Econs. Assn., N.Y. State Home Econs. Assn., Nat. Assn. Extension Home Economists, N.Y. State Assn. Extension Home Economists, Adult Edn. Assn. U.S.A., N.Y. State Assn. Continuing Edn., Nat. Assn. State Univs. and Land-Grand Colls. (sec. 1982), Epsilon Sigma Phi (cert. recognition 1977). Office: 103 Roberts Hall Cornell University Ithaca NY 14853

NOBLE, MARY PENNY, state govt. ofcl.; b. Rochester, N.Y., Oct. 29, 1942; d. Mason and Mary P. Noble; B.B.A., U. Toledo, 1967; M.B.A., Golden Gate U., San Francisco, 1973. From staff auditor to resource devel. officer GAO, 1967-79; asst. auditor gen. Calif. Auditor Gen.'s Office, 1980—. Recipient Meritorious Service award GAO, 1979. Mem. Am. Soc. Public Adminstrn. Address: Auditor Gen 660 I St Suite 300 Sacramento CA 95814

NOBLE, VIKKI LOU, univ. adminstr.; b. Troy, Ohio, Aug. 19, 1951; d. Cornelius and Nancy Louise (Petry) Rabada; B.A., Wright State U., 1973; M.S. in L.S., U. Ky., 1980; m. David Noble, Dec. 26, 1971; 1 dau., Emma Louise. Children's librarian Wichita Falls (Tex.) Public Sch. System, 1973-74; dir. blood donor resources Red River Regional Red Cross Blood Center, Wichita Falls, 1974-76, cons., Frankfort (Ky.) br., 1976-78; info. specialist Fin. Aid Office, Ky. State U., 1979-82; tchr. English Upward Bound. Bd. dirs. United Way, Frankfort, 1977—, Big Bros. Big Sisters, 1980—, ARC, 1982-83. Recipient Red Cross Cert. of Appreciation for Disaster Assistance, 1978. Mem. Ky. Assn. Fin. Aid Adminstrs., AAUW, Alpha Xi Delta. Clubs: Frankfort Younger Womens, Hiram Lodge, Order Eastern Star. Contbg. author: The Red Roses. Home: 800 Colonial Trace Frankfort KY 40601

NOCHMAN, LOIS WOOD KIVI (MRS. MARVIN NOCHMAN), educator; b. Detroit, Nov. 5, 1924; d. Peter K. and Annetta Lois (Wood) Kivi; A.B., U. Mich., 1946, A.M., 1949; m. Harold I. Pitchford, Sept. 6, 1944 (div. May 1949); children—Jean Pitchford Horiszny, Joyce Lynn Pitchford McGinnis; m. 2d, Marvin A. Nochman, Aug. 15, 1953; 1 son, Joseph Asa. Tchr. adult edn., Honolulu, 1947, Ypsilanti (Mich.) High Sch., 1951-52; spl. instr. English, Wayne State U., Detroit, 1953, 54; tchr. Highland Park (Mich.) Coll., 1950-51, instr. English, 1954—. Mem. exec. bd. Highland Park Fedn. Tchrs., 1963, 64, 65, 66, 71, 72, mem. 1st bargaining team, 1965-66, 73, del. to Nat. Conv., 1964, 71, 72, 73, 74, rep. higher edn. to Mich. Fedn. Tchrs. Exec. Com., 1972, 73, 74, 75, 76; mem. faculty adv. com. Gov.'s Commn. on Higher Edn., 1973—. Tchr. Baha'i schs., Davison, Mich., 1954, 55, 58, 59, 63, 64, 65, 66, Beaulac, Que., Can., 1960, Greenacre, Maine, 1965; sec. local spiritual assembly Baha'is, Ann Arbor, 1953, sec., Detroit, 1954, chmn., 1955; mem. nat. com. Baha'i U.S., 1955-68; sec. Davison Bahai Sch. Com. and Council, 1956, 58, 63, 64, 65, 66, 67, 68; Baha'i lectr. Mem. Modern Lang. Assn., Nat. Council Tchrs. English, Mich. Coll. English Assn., Am. Fedn. Tchrs., Nat. Soc. Lit. and Arts, Women's Equity and Action League (sec. Mich. chpt. 1975-79), Alpha Lambda Delta, Alpha Gamma Delta. Contbr. poems to mags. Home: 25227 Parkwood Huntington Woods MI 48070 Office: Highland Park Coll Highland Park MI 48203

NOCITA, DIANE MARY, mfg. co. exec.; b. Green Bay, Wis., Dec. 31, 1952; d. Edward Peter and Katherine Bertha (Vander Heiden) Hendricks; student U. Wis., Stevens Point, 1971-72, Pepperdine U.; cert. purchasing and materials mgmt., UCLA, 1979; m. Frank Edward Nocita, Dec. 24, 1978. Customer service rep. Hamilton Electro Sales Co., Culver City, Calif., 1976, Wyle Electronics Co., El Segundo, Calif., 1976-77; purchasing mgr. BGW Systems Co., Hawthore, Calif., 1977-79, Anaconda Ericsson, Chatsworth, Calif., 1979—; cons. in field. Cert. purchasing mgr. Mem. Women in Mgmt., Women in Electronics, Nat. Assn. Purchasing Mgmt., Purchasing Mgmt. Assn. Los Angeles (1st v.p. 1979—, past bd. dirs.). Democrat. Roman Catholic. Clubs: Magic Castle, Holiday Spa Health. Author articles in field. Home: 6736 Hillpark Dr Apt 203 Hollywood CA 90068 Office: 20660 Nordhoff St Chatsworth CA 91311

NODA, PHYLLIS ANN, ednl. adminstr.; b. Detroit, Apr. 27, 1945; d. Philip William and Norma Elizabeth (Berry) Clemens; B.A., Mercy Coll., 1966; M.Ed. in Ethno-Urban Cultures (scholar), Marygrove Coll., 1972; children—Pilar Alicia, Peter Anthony. Adj. asst. prof. edn., art criticism and studio art, supr. tchr. interns Mercy Coll., Detroit, 1970-80, also creator and implementr Children's Arts Complex, practicum coordinator for inservice instrs. in bilingual edn. Oakland U., Rochester (Mich.) 1976-77; bilingual program coordinator Detroit Public Schs., 1978—; cons. Detroit Archdiocese Schs.; workshop dir. for art in elementary sch.; cons. multi-ethnic workshops, 1975-76; cons. Mich. Ethnic Heritage Studies Program, 1973—; media relations coordinator Pontiac (Mich.) Schs., 1976-78; community relations cons. to bilingual edn. office Mich. Dept. Edn.; coordinator for multicultural curriculum guidelines, in-service tng. adminstrs. and tchrs. for multicultural edn. Detroit Pub. Schs. Adviser, Troy (Mich.) Am.-Ethnic Festival, 1975-76; adviser resource Pontiac Peoples' Progress Pavilion, 1975-76. Mem. Mich. Assn. for Tchr. Edn., Nat. Assn. for Bilingual Edn., Competency-based Tchr. Edn. Consortium, AAUP, Mich. Assn. for Sch. Pub. Relations, Arts Council Triangle, New Detroit Inc., Kappa Delta Pi. Designer, illustrator for Multi-Media Classroom Presentations, Let's Learn About Spanish-Speaking Americans, 1975, Alberto and the Missing Sock. Home: 1805 Woodgate St Troy MI 48084

NOE, ELNORA (ELLIE), chem. co. exec.; b. Evansville, Ind., Aug. 23, 1928; d. Thomas and Evelyn (West) Noe; student Ind. U.-Purdue U., Indpls. Sec., Pitman Moore Co., Indpls., 1946; with Dow Chem. Co., Indpls., 1960—, public relations asst. then mgr. employee communications, 1970—. Mem. public relations com. ARC, Indpls., Mem. Am. Bus. Women Assn. (woman of yr. 1965; past pres.), Ind. Bus. Communicators Assn. (communicator of yr. 1977), Women in Communications, Nat. Fedn. Press Women, Women's Press Club Ind. (3d v.p.), Club: Zonta Internat. (dist. public relations chmn. 1978-80, area dir. 1980-82, pres. Indpls. 1977-79). Office: PO Box 68511 Indianapolis IN 46268

NOELL, HELEN LOUISE MCCOLLOUGH, marine retail co. exec.; b. Sour Lake, Tex., Mar. 9, 1929; d. Emory Bland and Cora Lee (Frederick) Smith; B.A., Southwestern Bus. Coll., 1952; m. Apr. 30, 1967; children—Harold Wayne Stockdale, Charlotte Elizabeth Stockdale, Thomas Waters McCollough; m. 2d, Jack D. Noell, July 10, 1982. Clk.-steno Humble Oil Refinery, Tomball, Tex., 1956-58; prodn. clk. Superior Oil Co., Conroe, Tex., 1958-63; bus. driver Conroe Ind. Sch. Dist., 1967—; owner Conroe Marine Inc., 1967—, owner, pres., 1977—; agt. Tex. Parks and Wildlife, 1974—. Mem. Tex. Tchrs. Assn., Conroe Tchrs. Assn., Bus. and Profl. Club, Marine Retailers Assn. Am., Am. Soc. Profl. and Exec. Women, Boating Trades Assn. Tex., Boating Traders Assn. Met. Houston, Nat. Fedn. Ind. Bus., Am. Soc. Notaries, Internat. CB Radio Operators Assn. Baptist. Home: 413 Oak Hill Dr Conroe TX 77304 Office: 1100 Wilson Rd Conroe TX 77301

NOERR, JUDY ANNE, cons.; b. Dallas, Feb. 14, 1941; d. Arch Roy and Winnie Lucille (Robertson) Ballou; B.A., So. Meth. U., 1966. Tchr., Shockeyes Pvt. Sch., Dallas, 1963-64; dance tchr. Nebr., Mass. and Dallas, 1966-68; owner, dir. Judy Noerr Sch. Dance, Highland, Calif., 1972—; producer, dir. Peter Rabbit and Tales of Beatrix Potter, Calif. Theatre Performing Arts, San Bernardino, 1976-79, Nutcracker Ballet, 1978-79. Mem. Ceccheti Council Am., Arrowhead Allied Arts (past pres.), Kappa Alpha Theta. Home and office: 10 Captain's Landing Tiburon CA 94920

NOKES, JACKIE, ednl. services co. exec.; b. Salt Lake City, Feb. 9, 1929; d. James Owen and Edna Amelia (Hansen) White; student UCLA, 1946-49, U. Utah, 1949-50; m. Andrew Grey Nokes (div.); children—Patricia Nokes Kerbs, Laurence Paul, Beau James, Anthony Grey. Romper room tchr. KSL-TV, Salt Lake City, 1957-59, hostess, producer Midday TV program, 1961-74; now asst. to pres. for ednl. services KSL-AM-TV, Salt Lake City. Mem. Gov.'s Com. for Employment of Handicapped, 1972—; bd. dirs., mem. exec. com. Utah Soc. for Prevention of Blindness, 1977—, United Way, Salt Lake City, 1978; mem. adv. bd. Bus., Industry, Community Edn. Program, 1977-78.; mem. at large bd. dirs. Utah Council Girl Scouts U.S.A. Recipient Shield award Delta Gamma, 1973, award for patriotic programs Freedoms Found., 1969, Carnation Community Service award Vol. Action Center, Salt Lake City, 1978; Hon. Alumna award Utah State U., 1979; Person of Vision award, 1980. Mem. Am. Women in Radio and TV (nat. v.p. 1968-69). Home: 2075 Lincoln Ln Salt Lake City UT 84117 Office: 145 Social Hall Ave Salt Lake City UT 84111

NOLAN, AGNES FOLK (MRS. RICHARD NOLAN), real estate co. exec.; b. N.Y.C., 1931; d. William J. and Agnes (Sikora) Gilligan; B.A., Trinity Coll., 1952; LL.B., Columbia U., 1955; m. Richard E. Nolan, Jan. 31, 1959; children—Anthony R.G., Christopher W.P., Timothy R.W., Mariana, Katherine. Admitted to N.Y. bar, 1957, U.S. Supreme Ct. bar; mem. legal staff Cadwalader, Wickersham & Taft, N.Y.C., 1955-60; asst. gen. counsel Kayser-Roth Corp., N.Y.C., 1960-62; pres. Whitbread-Nolan, Inc., N.Y.C., 1962—; pres. Windham Properties, Ltd. Bd. dirs., pres. Am. Friends of Westminster Cathedral. Home: 271 Central Park W New York NY 10024 also Bolton Landing Lake George NY Officce: 600 Madison Ave New York NY 10022

NOLAN, AGNES PETERS, author; b. Salem, Va., June 24, 1908; d. James Sidney and Sara Lee (Robertson) Peters; student Randolph-Macon Woman's Coll., 1925-26; B.A., U. Richmond, 1929; postgrad. U. Va., summer 1932, Temple U., summer 1950, Columbia U., 1945-46; M.A., U. Del., 1957; m. Robert Wilson Nolan, Mar. 2, 1936; 1 son, Gordon Churchill. Tchr. pub. schs., Va., 1929-35; mem. faculty Young Harris (Ga.) Coll., 1935-36; chemist Newport News Shipbldg. Co. (Va.), 1943-44; instr. Langley AFB Sch., 1945-48; writer musico-dramatic radio programs Sta. WTAR, Va., 1947-48, Sta. WGH, 1949-50, others; contbr. numerous articles to various mags. including: Nat. Parent Tchr. mag., Jack and Jill, Del. Today, In and Around Wilmington; producer opera adaptations Sta. WHYY-TV, 1963-65; writer plays for various schs. chs. and clubs, 1932-69; writer, producer, lectr. recitals Cokesbury Village, 1981, Wilmington Opera Soc. editor: Historic Landmarks of Delaware (B. Macdonald), 1976; The Hospital for Mentally Retarded Story, 1967. Bd. dirs. Del. Ednl. TV Assn., 1955-72; chmn. tng. com. Supporters of Stockley (retarded), 1981-82. Recipient script awards Phila. Writers, 1953, 57, 67; 1st pl. children's radio nat. competition Billboard mag., 1948. Mem. Nat. League Am. Pen Women (officer Diamond State br. 1964-74, 80-82, co-chmn. Tristate Creativity Symposium 1981, nat., 3d place TV scripts 1974), Hist. Soc. Del., DAR, Daus. Am. Colonists (officer Del. chpt. 1965-68, 79-81), Jamestowne Soc., Del. Art Museum, AAUW (mass media chmn. Del. div. 1958), Wilmington Opera Soc. Unitarian. Club: Du Pont Country. Co-editor: Patchwork Made from Hidden Laughter. Home: 69 Cokesbury Village Hockessin DE 19707

NOLAN, ANNE MARIE (REA), advt. agy. exec.; b. Montclair, N.J., Apr. 17, 1952; d. Frank William and Anne (Gannon) N.; B.A., Manhattanville Coll., 1974. Sales staff Equitable Assurance Soc., New Haven, 1974-75; advt. writer, account exec. McDonough Communications, Mountain View, Calif., 1975-78; advt. mgr. Wabash Tape Corp., Des Plaines, Ill., 1978-79; pres., partner The Ad Agy., Inc., Des Plaines, 1979—. Mem. Am. Mgmt. Assn., Women's Advt. Club Chgo., NOW. Office: 2300 E Devon Ave Des Plaines IL 60018

NOLAN, LONE KIRSTEN, real estate investment counselor; b. Copenhagen, Oct. 9, 1938; d. Johannes and Elizabeth (Zachariassen) Jansen; came to U.S., 1957, naturalized, 1964; m. Gene Nolan, Mar. 19, 1973; children—Glenn Muller, Erik Muller. Adminstrv. asst. Am. Nat. Bank and Trust, Morristown, N.J., 1967-72; asst. cashier First Nat. Iron Bank, 1972; comptroller and ops. officer Panama City Nat. Bank, 1973-74; asst. v.p. Lee County Bank, Ft. Myers, Fla., 1974-76; customer and IRA investments exec. Priscilla Murphy Realty, Sanibel, Fla., 1976-77; pres. Century 21 Nolan Realty, Ft. Myers, 1977-80; pres. AAIM Realty Group, Ft. Myers, 1980-81; real estate investment counselor Merrill Lynch, Boca Raton, Fla., 1982—. Mem. Internat. Real Estate Fedn., Nat. Assn. Realtors, Realtors Nat. Mktg. Inst., Fla. Real Estate Exchangors. Home: 2707 N Ocean Blvd Apt D704 Boca Raton FL 33432 Office: 2301 W Glades Rd Boca Raton FL 33432

NOLAN, LOUISE MARY, serigrapher, educator; b. Boston, Sept. 28, 1947; d. John Joseph and Helen (Spiers) Nolan; B.A., Regis Coll., 1969; M.Ed., Boston U., 1971 postgrad., 1981-82; postgrad Fitchburg State Coll., 1972-74, Boston Coll., 1973—, Salem State Coll., 1977-79. Counselor, Camp Thoreau, Inc., Concord, Mass., 1964-68; tchr., chmn. sci. dept. John F. Kennedy Meml. Jr. High Sch., Woburn, Mass., 1969—; co-owner Ruth and Louise Silkscreening, Lexington, Mass., Fancypants, Carlisle, Mass.; dir. ecology program Curry Coll., Milton, Mass., summer 1977. Sec. Mass. Sci. Fair Com. NSF grantee, 1972-73, 77-79, 81-82. Mem. Mass. Tchrs. Assn., NEA, AAAS, Nat. Assn. Sci. Tchrs., Mass. Assn. Sci. Tchrs., Nat. Assn. Biology Tchrs., Nat. Assn. Research in Sci. Teaching, Middlesex County Tchrs. Assn., Woburn Tchrs. Assn., Beta Beta Beta, Pi Lambda Theta. Democrat. Roman Catholic. Clubs: Museum Fine Arts, Lit. Guild, Concord Art Assn., Mus. of Sci., Theatre Guild. Author: Y.E.S.—A Comprehensive Guide to Students Educating Youth in Environmental Sciences; Bioluminescence—An Experimental Guide; Marine Plankton; (tchr.'s edt.) Health Physical Science. Home: 9 Stevens Rd Lexington MA 02173 Office: John F Kennedy Jr High Sch Middle St Woburn MA 01801

NOLAN, MARY REGINA GILL, hosp. adminstr.; b. Tionesta, Pa., May 3, 1930; d. Bernard Mathias and Nora Veronica Gill; diploma in nursing St. Vincent's Hosp. Tng. Sch., Erie, Pa., 1951; B.S.N. summa cum laude, Calif. State U., Long Beach, 1972; M.N. with distinction, UCLA, 1974; m. Kenneth L. Nolan, June 4, 1958. Clin. nurse Warren (Pa.) Gen. Hosp., 1951-52, Queen of Angels Hosp., Los Angeles, 1952-54; head neurol. nurse Columbia Presbyn. Med. Center, N.Y.C., 1955-57; clin. nurse operating room St. Luke's Hosp., Spokane, Wash., 1958, Roswell Park Meml. Inst., Buffalo, 1958; vol., instr., emergency/disaster com. ARC, Madrid, 1958-61; clin. nurse ICU and operating room Sunmount VA Hosp., Tupper Lake, N.Y., 1961-63; clin. nurse, clin. instr. operating room St. Joseph's Hosp./Sch. Nursing, Phoenix, 1963-64; clin. nurse, charge nurse Daniel Freeman Hosp., Inglewood, Calif., 1965-74, mem. faculty dept. edn., 1974-78, clin. nursing specialist (pioneered perioperative splty.), 1974-77, clin. nursing supr. surg. units, 1977-78; asst. clin. prof. nursing UCLA Sch. Nursing, 1975-79, mem. faculty Western Center Continuing Edn., UCLA Extension, 1971-73; dir. nursing/surgery-PAR, Meml. Hosp. Med. Center, Long Beach, 1982, v.p. patient care services, 1982—. Mem. parish liturgy team Am. Martyrs Ch., Manhattan Beach, Calif. Recipient Scholarship awards Johnson & Johnson, 1970, Edith D. Hall, 1972; Fed. Nurse Traineeship grantee, 1972-74. Mem. Assn. Operating Room Nurses (DePuy Excellence in Journalism award; nat. operating room nursing research com. 1973-75, chmn. 1975-77; chpt. charter mem.; v.p. chpt. 1978-80, dir. 1976-78, chmn. nominating com. 1972-75, editor newsletter 1975-76), Am. Nurses Assn., Calif. Nurses Assn., Am. Soc. Nursing Service Adminstrs., Alpha Gamma Sigma, Pi Lambda Theta, Phi Kappa Phi, Sigma Theta Tau. Republican. Roman Catholic. Contbg. author: Operating Room Techniques for the Surgical Team, 1979; Alexander's Care of the Patient in Surgery, 6th edit., 1978; contbr. articles to profl. jours. Office: 2801 Atlantic Blvd Long Beach CA 90801

NOLAND, PATRICIA HAMPTON, editor, writer; b. New Orleans, Dec. 24, 1924; d. Leon Maxwell and Clara Hampton (Whittle) Noland; B.A., U. Houston, 1981; Dr. Leadership in Poetry (hon.), Internat. Acad. Leadership, Philippines, 1969; D.L.H. (hon.) Free U. Asia, 1973; Diploma of Merit in Lit., U. Arts, Salsomaggiore Terme, Italy, 1982. Vol., VA Hosp., Houston, 1950, St. Luke's Tex. Children's Hosp., 1969, Mental Health Center, St. Joseph's Hosp., Houston, 1970-71; founder, pres., editor monthly newsletter Internat. Poetry Inst., Houston, 1969—. Named Hon. Internat. Poet Laureate, United Poets Laureate Internat., Manila, 1969. Mem. Am. Hort. Soc., Mus. Fin Arts Houston, Met. Opera Guild, Am. Film Inst., Smithsonian Instn., Planetary Soc. Democrat. Christian Scientist. Author: Poems, 1960; editor: Whoever Heard a Birdie Cry?, 1970. Home: 2400 Westheimer Rd Apt 215W Houston TX 77098 Office: PO Box 53087 Houston TX 77052

NOLAND, PEGGY, lawyer; b. Arnegard, N.D., May 8, 1931; d. Floyd and Evelyn Grace (Calkins) Van Allen; B.S., Van Norman U., 1964, J.D., 1966; children—Winifred (Mrs. Paul Edmonds), Roberta, Warren Wagner, David Noland; adopted children—Thomas Russell, John Patrick, Jerre Kolin. Admitted to Calif. bar, 1967; county pub. defender, Inyo County, 1967-68; individual practice of law, Beverly Hills, Calif., 1967, Lone Pine, Calif., 1968—. Speaker various women's groups So. Calif. Served to capt. USAF. Mem. Women Lawyers Assn., Aircraft Owners and Pilots Assn., Calif. Bar Assn., Inyo County Bar Assn., Lawyer-Pilots Bar Assn., Lone Pine C. of C. (dir. 1968), Bus. and Profl. Women's Club, Mensa. Club: Mount Whitney Golf (Lone Pine). Office: 101 N Main St Lone Pine CA 93545

NOLE, ANGELA D., city ofcl.; b. Utica, N.Y., June 28, 1931; d. Nicholas and Angela (Graziadei) N.; grad. high sch.; m. James A. DeBella, Sept. 23, 1963; children—Bonnie, Elizabeth, Judiann, Jamie. Sec., Oneida County Dept. Social Services, 1950-63, Gen. Electric Co., 1956-59; admitting clk. St. Elizabeth Hosp., 1968-72; exec. sec. N.Y. State Teamsters, 1972-76; asst. budget dir. City of Utica, from 1978, now office mgr. Active local Democratic politics; bd. dirs. Notre Dame High Sch. Parents Orgn. Mem. Bus. and Profl. Women's Club, Nat. Assn. Bus. and Profl. Women. Roman Catholic. Home: 448 Elmhurst Rd Utica NY 13502 Office: 1 Kennedy Plaza Utica NY 13502

NOLIN, MARTA VICTORIA, coll. ofcl.; b. Eastchester, N.Y., May 23, 1952; d. Joseph H. and Victoria B. (Toteff) N.; B.A. magna cum laude, Boston U., 1974; M.A., Assumption Coll., 1977. Residence hall dir. Boston U., 1974-75; head of residence U. Mass., Amherst, 1977-78, sr. head of residence, 1978-79; asst. dean for student life Ohio Wesleyan U., Delaware, 1979—. Mem. Nat. Assn. Student Personnel Adminstrs., Nat. Assn. Women Deans, Adminstrs. and Counselors, Am. Coll. Personnel Assn., Am. Personnel and Guidance Assn. Democrat. Office: Memorial Union Bldg Ohio Wesleyan University Delaware OH 43015

NOMBERG, BEVERLY REDNER, social worker; b. Springfield, Mo., Dec. 12, 1942; d. Frederic Schofield and Agnes Lucille (Cunningham) Redner; student S.W. Mo. State U., 1960-62; B.A. in History, U. Mo., 1964; M.S.W., Adelphi U., 1968; m. Clifford I. Nomberg, Nov. 16, 1969; 1 dau., Ilana. Social worker I, Family Service League, Inc., Huntington, N.Y., 1968-70; social worker II, L.I. Jewish Med. Center, New Hyde Park, N.Y., 1970-72; psychotherapist Albuquerque Center Psychotherapy, 1980—; social worker N.Mex. Artificial Kidney Center, Albuquerque, 1977—; social worker Albuquerque Kidney Center, 1981—; agy. field instr. dept. social work, Coll. Santa Fe, 1977—; mem. Network VI, Social Work Task Force, 1980—, network coordinating com., 1982—, patients rights com., 1982—, Med. Rev. Bd. Rehab. Task Force, 1982—. Recipient Social Worker of Yr. award N.Mex. Nat. Assn. Social Workers, 1981; NIMH fellow, 1966-68. Mem. Acad. Cert. Social Workers, Nat. Assn. Social Workers (state treas. 1979—), Sierra Club. Democrat. Chavurat Hamidbar. Home: 2717 Darlene Pl SW Albuquerque NM 87105 Office: 400 Walter St NE Albuquerque NM 87102

NONKEN, JUNE MARIE AMSDEN (MRS. HARRY NONKEN), psychologist; b. Ogdensburg, N.Y., Aug. 16, 1920; d. Percy A. and Kathryn (Darmody) Amsden; A.B., Columbia U., 1942; M.A., Tulsa U., 1956; Ph.D., George Peabody Coll., 1965; m. Donald B. Good, June 12, 1943, (dec. Feb. 1953); 1 dau., Deborah B. (Mrs. Joe D. Johnson); m. 2d, Harry Nonken, Nov. 23, 1968; 1 stepson, Norman L. Psychometrist, psychologist Tulsa Pub. Schs., 1954-59; teaching asst. staff psychologist Child Guidance Center, George Peabody Coll., 1959-61; clin. psychology intern U. Tex. Med. Sch., Galveston, 1961-62; instr. dept. psychiatry U. Tex. Med. Sch., 1963-64, chief psychologist div. child psychiatry, 1965-66; chief psychologist Community Guidance Center of Bexar County, San Antonio, 1966-71; asso. prof., dir. clin. tng. Trinity U., 1968-69, asso. prof. ednl. psychology, 1971—; asst. clin. prof. U. Tex. Med. Sch., San Antonio, 1967-72; sec. bd. Nonkens, Inc., San Antonio, 1969—. Ednl. cons. Comal Ind. Sch. Dist., Comal County, New Braunfels, Tex., Judson Ind. Sch. Dist., Children's Center San Antonio, San Marcos (Tex.) Consol. Ind. Sch. Dist., 1978—, others. Bd. dirs. Tulsa chpt. Mental Health Assn., 1954-59, San Antonio Assn. Retarded Children, 1968-69, Friends Sch., San Antonio, Community Guidance Center Bexar County, San Antonio, 1977—; pres. adv. bd. Carmelite Day Care Center, San Antonio, 1975—. Mem. Am., Tex., Southwestern psychol. assns., Am. Orthopsychiat. Assn., Psi Chi. Republican. Presbyterian. Home: PO Box 8046 Horseshoe Bay Marble Falls TX 78654 Office: 715 Stadium Dr San Antonio TX 78284

NOONAN, PATRICIA SAULNIER, editor, writer; b. Lynn, Mass., Jan. 29, 1945; d. Paul Hypolite and Bernadette Florida (Dion) Saulnier; student Merrimack Coll., 1962-63, Siena Coll., 1970; m. Frank R. Noonan, Aug. 22, 1964; children—Kathleen, Kelly, Kristin. Free-lance writer, reporter Beacon Pub., Acton, Mass., 1978; writer, reporter, clipboard editor Voice Newspapers, Louisville, Ky., 1979, Ky. Bus. Ledger, Louisville, 1979; bus. editor Voice Newspapers, Scripps-Howard Co., Louisville, 1979, exec. editor, 1980-81; copy editor and part-time reporter Guy Gannett Newspapers, Portland, Maine, 1981—. Vol. editor mag. and dir. Speakers' Bur., Celebration 350, Portland, 1982—; dir. publicity Showhouse '82, Portland Symphony Orch., also editor Sounds of Symphony newspaper, 1982—. Mem. Sigma Delta Chi. Republican. Roman Catholic. Home: 10 Ship Channel Rd South Portland ME 04106 Office: Guy Gannett Newspapers 390 Congress St Portland ME 04101

NORBACK, DIANE HAGEMAN, pathologist; b. Comfrey, Minn., Mar. 22, 1946; d. Evan Herman and Emma Alvina (Meier) Hageman; B.A., Luther Coll., 1966; M.A.T., Northwestern U., 1967; Ph.D., U. Wis., 1973, M.D., 1974; m. John Palmer Norback, Aug. 20, 1966; children—Christopher James, Nathaniel Charles. Asst. prof. dept. pathology U. Wis., Madison, 1975-81, assoc. prof., 1981—, dir. hematology lab. Clin. Sci. Center, 1982—; chief electron microscopy VA Hosp., Madison, 1977-82. Am. Cancer Soc. Jr. Faculty fellow, 1977-80. Mem. Am. Assn. Pathologists, Soc. Toxicology, Internat. Acad. Pathology, Electron Microscopic Soc. Am., Wis. Soc. Pathologists. Home:

2622 Van Hise Ave Madison WI 53705 Office: Dept of Pathology Univ Wisconsin Madison WI 53706

NORBY, ALICE SIMONS, educator; b. Mogollon, N.Mex., July 19, 1914; d. John James and Delfina (Salcida) Simons; A.B. in Edn., U. Sacramento, 1955, A.B. in Social Scis., 1955. Tchr., Hennessy Elem. Sch., Grass Valley, Calif., 1947-52, Nevada Union Jr. High Sch., Grass Valley, 1952-55; tchr. Nevada Union High Sch., 1955-81, tchr. reading lab., 1968-79. Dist. pres. Capital Dist. Bus. and Profl. Clubs, 1972-73; adv. Future Tchrs. Am.; vol. tchr.'s aide, others. Recipient award Sacramento Diocese for Outstanding Youth, 1955, Trophy award Future Tchrs. Am. Club, 1969; certified tchr., Calif. Mem. NEA (life), Calif. (life), Nevada Union tchrs. assns., Grass Valley Bus. and Profl. Club (pres. 1964-65, Woman of Yr. award 1980). Home: 128 High St Grass Valley CA 95945

NORCROSS, LOIS MANLEY, profl. communicator; b. Orange, Conn.; d. Roy Ellis and Viola Agnes (Ericson) N.; A.A., Centenary Coll. for Women; B.S., Quinnipiac Coll.; M.A., Fairfield U. Dir. public relations Greater New Haven C. of C., 1966-68; acting dir. Better Bus. Bur. Greater New Haven, 1968-69; communications specialist Olin Corp., New Haven, 1969-74; editor employee newsletters, cons. editor employee communications Olin chem. plants in U.S., 1974-78; employee services coordinator Communications Office, Dept. Adminstrv. Services, State of Conn., 1978—, editor State Scene, 1979—. Cons. publicity adv. bd. Conn. Public TV, 1981-82. Recipient Outstanding Service award Conn. chpt. Internat. Assn. Bus. Communicators, 1980. Mem. Internat. Assn. Bus. Communicators (chpt. pres.), Conn. State Women in Mgmt. (dir. 1981—). Congregationalist. Club: Appalachian Mountain. Office: State Office Bldg 165 Capitol Ave Hartford CT 06106

NORDALE, MARY ANITA, lawyer; b. Fairbanks, Alaska, Apr. 8, 1934; d. Alton Gerald and Katherine (Driscoll) Nordale; B.A., Gonzaga U., 1957; J.D., George Washington U., 1966. Admitted to D.C. bar, 1967, Alaska bar, 1969; mem. staff U.S. Senator E.L. Bartlett, Washington, 1960-68; asst. U.S. atty., Fairbanks, 1968-69, asst. dist. atty., 1969-70; br. counsel SBA, Fairbanks, 1970-72; individual practice law, Fairbanks, 1972—. Mem. Central Dist. Dem. Com., Fairbanks, 1973; bd. dirs. Fairbanks Rehab. Assn., Inc., 1970-77, pres., 1971-73; bd. dirs. Compas, Fairbanks, 1971-77, Fairbanks chpt. Alaska Retarded Children's Assn., 1973—. Mem. Fed., Am., D.C., Alaska, Tanana Valley bar assns., Am. Judicature Soc. Office: 1919 Lathrop St Dr 33 Fairbanks AK 99701

NORDEEN, PEGGY ANN, advt. exec.; b. Muscatine, Iowa, July 27, 1946; d. Gene E. and Marylou Nordeen; B.A. in Journalism and English, U. Iowa, 1968. Gen. assignment news reporter Davenport (Iowa) Times-Democrat, 1966-69; with Sperry-Boom Inc., Chgo., 1970-78, v.p., dir. 1976-78; pres. Starmark, Inc., Chgo., 1978—. Mem. Viking Ship Restoration Com., Chgo., 1979; Iowa Realtors Assn. scholar, 1964. Mem. Am. Mktg. Assn. (v.p. communications Chgo. chpt. 1974), Publicity Club Chgo. (sec., dir. 1973-74), Gamma Phi Beta. Mem. Christian Ch. (Disciples of Christ). Office: Starmark Bldg 706 N Dearborn St Chicago IL 60610

NORDHAGEN, HALLIE HUERTH, nursing home adminstr.; b. Sarona, Wis., Apr. 2, 1914; d. Mathias James and Ethel Elizabeth (Fann) Huerth; B.Ed., U. Wis., Superior, 1938, M.A., 1949; m. Carl E. Nordhagen, May 24, 1947; children—Bruce Carl, Brian Keith. Prin., tchr. Wis. Public Schs., 1932-46; supervising tchr. Wis. Community Coll., 1946-48; psychiat. adminstr. Trempealeau County Health Care Center, psychiat. nursing home, Whitehall, Wis., 1959—; mem. Wis. Nursing Home Adminstrs. Examining Bd.; fellow Menninger Clinic, Topeka, 1979-81. Recipient Disting. Service award in edn. and hosp. adminstrn., London, 1967, award for services to human services programs Wis. Assn. Human Services, 1972, award for outstanding services to exceptional children Assn. Retarded Children, 1978, award for accomplishments in human resources Trempealeau County Conservation Service, 1981. Mem. Wis. Assn. County Homes, Wis. Edn. Assn., Wis. Assn. Human Services Programs, Am. Lutheran Ch. Women. Clubs: Whitehall Country, Women's. Author: Wisconsin Indians, 1966. Home: 2220 Claire St Whitehall WI 54773

NORDSTROM, SUSAN ELLEN, advt. agy. exec.; b. Tampa, Fla., Nov. 19, 1952; d. Ralph Samuel and Evelyn Seymour (Eynon) Hardman; B.A., Keuka Coll., Keuka Park, N.Y., 1974; m. Thomas J. Nordstrom, June 1, 1974. Br. rep. Household Fin. Corp., Edison, N.J., 1974-75; patient service rep. Rutgers Mental Health Center, Piscataway, N.J., 1975-76; asst. planner Conahay & Lyon Advt., N.Y.C., 1976-79; sr. media planner Foote Cone & Belding Advt., N.Y.C., 1979-82; asso. group head Weels Rich Greene Advt., N.Y.C. 1982—. Mem. Nat. Assn. Female Execs. Office: 767 Fifth Ave New York NY 10153

NORFORD, LAVENIA ALDRIDGE, educator, artist; b. Danville, Va.; d. Willie James and Anne Susan (Underwood) Aldridge; B.A., Bridgewater Coll., 1970; m. Lee Albert Norford, Aug. 15, 1970; children—Aaron Wesley, Thomas Marshall. Tchr., Rockingham County (Va.) Schs., 1970-77; pres. bd. dirs. Bridgewater Pre-School, 1979—; fiber artist, Bridgewater, Va., 1978—. Bd. dirs. Bridgewater Coll. Centennial Com., 1978—; sec. Bridgewater United Methodist Ch., 1982. Mem. Va. Edn. Assn. (rep. to conv., 1977), Nat. Edn. Assn. Club: Bridgewater Women's (pres. 1978-79; shop chmn. 1981—). Home: 123 W College St Bridgewater VA 22812

NORKIN, CYNTHIA CLAIR, phys. therapist; b. Boston, May 6, 1932; d. Miles Nelson and Carolyn (Green) Clair; B.S. in Edn., Tufts U., 1954; cert. phys. therapy Bouve Boston Coll., 1954; M.S., Boston U., 1973; m. Stanislav A. Norkin, Feb. 19, 1955 (dec. 1970); 1 dau., Alexandra. Instr., Bouve-Boston Coll., 1954-55; staff phys. therapist New Eng. Med. Center, Boston, 1954-55; staff phys. therapist Abington Meml. Hosp., Abington, Pa., 1965-70, Eastern Montgomery County Vis. Nurse Assn., 1970-72; asst. prof. phys. therapy Sargent Coll., Boston U., 1973—; cons. Boston Center Ind. Living, Cambridge Vis. Nurse Assn., Mass. Medicaid Cost Effectiveness Project, 1978; sec. Health Planning Council Greater Boston, 1976-78. Trustee Brimmer and May Sch., 1980. Mem. Am., Mass. (chmn. Mass. quality assurance com. 1980—) phys. therapy assns., Am. Public Health Assn., AAAS, Mass. Assn. Mental Health. Episcopalian. Author: (with others) Joint Structure and Function: A Comprehensive Analysis, 1983. Home: 92 Sunset Rd Weston MA 02193 Office: 1 University Rd Boston MA 02215

NORMAN, IRIS WELCH, educator; b. High Point, N.C., Oct. 12, 1914; d. Charles Banner and Cora (Swaim) Welch; B.A., High Point Coll., 1937, B.S. in Music, 1937; M.Music Edn., U. Hartford, 1966; m. Chester Gregory, Apr. 8, 1944 (dec. 1965); children—Richard Henry, William Worth, Charles Swaim; m. 2d, Richard Leonard Norman, Apr. 20, 1968. Tchr. music Pilot Mountain (N.C.) Public Schs., 1937-38, Sumter (S.C.) Public Schs., 1938-44, Norwich (Conn.) Public Schs., 1955-57; dir. instrumental music, 1957-65, supr. music, 1965-77, music coordinator, 1977—; mem. state adv. com. on music edn. Conn. Dept. Edn. Mem. Music Educators Nat. Conf., Conn. Music Educators Assn., Eastern Conn. Music Tchrs. Assn. (past pres.), NEA, Conn. Edn. Assn., Alpha Delta Kappa. Home: 56 Case St Norwich CT 06360 Office: Kelly Jr High Sch Mahan Dr Norwich CT 06360

NORMAN, LAURA GAIL, reflexologist; b. L.I., N.Y., Apr. 17, 1950; d. Steven S. and Irene Mazur; B.S. with distinction, Boston U., 1972; M.S., Adelphi U., 1976; postgrad. Internat. Inst. Reflexology, 1976, Swedish Inst. Med. Massage Therapy, 1981. Tchr., relaxation therapist, reflexologist Maimonides Inst., Far Rockaway, N.Y., 1974-79; pvt. practice reflexology, N.Y.C., 1972—; dir. Laura Norman & Assocs. Mem. Internat. Inst. Reflexology, Med. Massage Therapists Alliance, Am. Massage and Therapy Assn., Inc., Nat. Health Fedn., Am. Fedn. Tchrs. (pres. 1968), Nat. Assn. Female Execs. Club: B'nai B'rith (pres. 1968). Office: 80 Fifth Ave Suite 1504 New York NY 10011

NORMAN, MARGIE IRENE, counselor; b. Nixon, Tex., Jan. 24, 1930; d. Alexander Edmund and Alta Patricia (Childress) Hall; B.A., Mary Hardin-Baylor Coll., 1949; M.Ed., Our Lady of Lake Coll., San Antonio, 1970; m. Gene Franklin Norman, Aug. 31, 1951; children—Dale Alan, James Thomas, Stephen Wayne. Elementary sch. tchr., Tex. and N.C., 1949-51, 55-70; spl. edn. counselor, then media specialist Fenwick/Lamar Elem. Schs., San Antonio, 1970-75; spl. edn. counselor Austin Elem. Opportunity Sch., San Antonio, 1975—; dir. Project Prime, San Antonio Sch. Dist., 1971-72; cons. in field. Mem. Am. Personnel and Guidance Assn. (award 1977), Tex. Personnel and Guidance Assn. (Research award 1977), S. Tex. Personnel and Guidance Assn. (newsletter editor sect.; bd. dirs.), Am. Sch. Counselors Assn., Tex. Sch. Counselors Assn., San Antonio Dist. Sch. Counselors Assn. (pres. 1977-78), Tex. Psychol. Assn., Bexar County Psychol. Assn., Council Exceptional Children, San Antonio Assn. for Children with Learning Disabilities, NEA, Tex. Tchrs. Assn. (life), San Antonio Adminstrs. and Suprs. Assn., San Antonio Women Deans and Counselors, Hist. Phila. Soc. (sgt. at arms 1948-49) Delta Kappa Gamma (treas. 1974-78), Kappa Pi, Sigma Tau Delta. Mng. editor Tex. Personnel and Guidance Jour., 1977-79; editor TPGA Jour., 1979—; editor Guide-Write Newsletter; contbr. articles profl. jours. Office: 621 W Euclid St San Antonio TX 78212

NORMAN, MARY MARSHALL, ednl. adminstr.; b. Auburn, N.Y., Jan. 10, 1937; d. Anthony John and Zita Norman; B.S. cum laude, LeMoyne Coll., 1958; M.A., Marquette, U., 1960; Ed.D., Pa. State U., 1971. Tchr., St. Cecilia's Elem. Sch., Theinsville, Wis., 1959-60; vocat. counselor Marquette U., Milw., 1959-60; dir. testing and counseling U. Rochester (N.Y.), 1960-62; dir. testing and counseling, dean women, asso. dean coll., asst. dean students, dir. student activities, asst. prof. psychology Corning (N.Y.) Community Coll., 1962-68; research asst. Center for Study Higher Edn., Pa. State U., University Park, 1969-71; dean faculty South Campus, Community Coll. Allegheny County, West Mifflin, Pa., 1971-72, exec. dean, coll. v.p., 1972-82; pres. Orange County Community Coll., 1982—; cons. Boricua Coll., N.Y.C., 1976-77; reader NSF, 1977-78; mem. govtl. commn. com. Am. Assn. Community and Jr. Colls., 1976-79, bd. dirs., 1982—; mem. and chmn. various middle state accreditation teams. Mem. Am. Assn. Higher Edn., Nat. Assn. Women Deans Counselors, Am. Assn. Women in Community and Jr. Colls. (charter, Woman of Yr. 1981), Pa. Assn. Two-Yr. Colls., Pa. Assn. Acad. Deans, Pitts. Council Women Execs. (charter), Am. Council on Edn. (Pa. rep. identification women for adminstrn. 1978—), Pa. Council on Higher Edn., Gamma Pi Epsilon. Contbr. articles to profl. jours. Home: 17 Skylark Rd Bloomingburg NY 12721 Office: 115 South St Middletown NY 10940

NORMAN, TRUDY, data processing exec.; b. Carlinville, Ill., Mar. 12, 1936; d. Ralph Earl and Gladys Mae (Shade) Challans; student James Millikin U., 1968-70; children—Carol Lischalk, James Norman, Cheryl Spencer. Mgr. client services Central Computing Corp., Decatur, Ill., 1968-71; sr. systems analyst STAT:TAB Corp., Chgo., 1971-74; project mgr. Chgo. Bd. Edn., 1974-78; mgr. data services Central Telephone, Chgo., 1978-80; dir. system services, mgr. human resources Advanced System Applications, Inc., Bloomingdale, Ill., 1980—; cons. in field. Active Lakeview Citizens Council, 1979—, Riverview Neighbors, 1981—, Addams Center, 1975-82. Mem. Am. Mgmt. Assn., Fin. Mgrs. Soc., Data Processing Mgmt. Assn. Club: BMW Owners Club. Contbr. articles to profl. jours. Home: 3320 N Hamilton Ave Chicago IL 60618

NORRIE, SHARON FAYE ELY, equipment mfg. co. exec.; b. Enterprise, Oreg., Jan. 20, 1941; d. Jesse J. and Ada Faye (McCoy) Schaures; student Kinman Bus. U., 1959-60; m. Jack J. Norrie, Apr. 16, 1976. With Manito Golf and Country Club, Spokane, Wash., 1960-61; mktg. research analyst Thompson Pipe & Steel Co., Denver, 1961-62; bookkeeper, sec. Continental Advt., Denver, 1962; acctg./spare parts mgr. Western Constrn. Equipment Co., Gardena, Calif., 1962-63; with Tylan Corp., Torrance, Calif., 1964-74, dist. sales mgr., McAfee, N.J., 1975-79, nat. product mgr., McAfee, 1980—. Mem. Nat. Assn. Female Execs. Republican. Home: RD No 1 Box 65 Lafayette NJ 07848 Office: PO Box J McAfee NJ 07428

NORRIS, BARBARA THERESA, nurse, hosp. adminstr.; b. Bklyn., Nov. 20, 1948; d. William Valentine and Stella (Laskowski) N.; diploma, L.I. Coll. Hosp. Sch. Nursing, 1968; B.S. magna cum laude, City U. N.Y., 1982. Charge nurse medicine/surgery L.I. Coll. Hosp., Bklyn., 1968-69, asst. head nurse labor/delivery unit, 1969-72, asst. dir. nursing, 1972-74, staff devel. instr., 1974-79, staff cons. materials mgmt. and nursing recruitment, 1979-80, staff cons. materials mgmt., 1980—; pres. Barbara Norris, Inc. Recipient N.Y. State Regents Incentive award, 1966; Nursing Sch. scholar Women's Floral Assn., 1968; lic. nurse, N.Y. Mem. L.I. Coll. Hosp. Sch. Nursing Alumnae Assn., Am. Assn. Critical Care Nurses, N.Y. Heart Assn., Smithsonian Assos., Arline Shahmanesh Hodgkins Research Orgn. Editor Nursing Communications, 1976-79.

NORRIS, ELIZABETH DOWNE, librarian; b. White Plains, N.Y., Apr. 25, 1914; d. Albro Farwell and Alice Elizabeth (Morse) Downe; B.A., Smith Coll., 1936; M.Div., Yale U., 1939; M.L.S., Columbia U., 1955; 1 son, Donald E. Norris. Asst. residence dir. New Haven YWCA, 1940-42; religious edn. librarian Union Theol. Sem., N.Y.C., 1953-57; librarian NCCJ, N.Y.C., 1957-63; head librarian Nat. Bd. YWCA, N.Y.C., 1963—, dir. Nat. Bd. Archives Project, 1976—. Recipient Henry Foote Lewis prize in religion, 1934. Mem. Spl. Libraries Assn., Women Library Workers, Ednl. Film Library Assn. Mem. United Ch. Christ. Editor: Feminine Figures: Selected Facts about American Women and Girls, 1968-72; Trends, 1975—; Subject Headings on Women, 1973; Recent Trends in Professionalism, 1973; The YWCA Advances Women's Rights, 1855-1978, 1978; contbg. librarian Mental Health Book Rev. Index, 1961-72; editor, mem. adv. com. Books for Brotherhood, ann. 1957-76; contbr. articles to jours. Home: 505 La Guardia Pl New York City NY 10012 Office: 135 W 50th St New York NY 10020

NORRIS, FRANCES, histotechnologist; b. Bay Springs, Miss., Jan. 12, 1943; d. Roy and Dorothy Louise (Spell) N.; grad. Mt. Sinai Sch. Histotech., Chgo., 1963; student U. Ill., Chgo., 1982—. Chief research histotechnologist dept. medicine and pathology U. Chgo., 1964-73; project dir., conf. coordinator Am. Soc. Clin. Pathologists, Chgo., 1973—; part-time sr. research histotechnologist dept. pathology U. Ill., 1979—; cons., instr. in field. Mem. Am. Soc. Clin. Pathologists, Nat. Soc. Histotech., Ill. Soc. Histotech., Midwest Assn. Sickle Cell Anemia, Chgo. Urban League. Democrat. Methodist. Club: Ebonettes Social. Office: 2100 W Harrison St Chicago IL 60612

NORRIS, MARGOT CHRISTA, educator; b. Baden Vienna, Austria, Dec. 23, 1944; d. Josef Hofstaetter and Helga (Hochberger) Barisits; B.A., U. Fla., 1967; Ph.D., SUNY, Buffalo, 1972; 1 son by previous marriage—Anthony Josef. Asst. prof. English, U. Tulsa, 1972-76; asst. prof. U. Mich., Ann Arbor, 1976-78, asso. prof., 1978—, dir. women's studies program, 1979-80. Publicity coordinator Common Cause, Tulsa, 1974-76. Woodrow Wilson fellow, 1967; Am. Council Learned Socs. grantee U. Heidelberg, 1977-78. Mem. MLA, Phi Beta Kappa, Phi Kappa Phi. Democrat. Author: The Decentered Universe of Finnegans Wake, 1976. Office: Dept English U Mich Ann Arbor MI 48109

NORRIS, MARY JANE OVECKA, broadcasting co. exec.; b. Phila., July 21, 1952; d. Rudolph Joseph and Caroline E. (Churay) Ovecka; B.A., Pa. State U., 1974; postgrad. Temple U., 1975, Drexel U., 1976-77. Music instr. Tredyffrin/Easttown Sch. Dist., Paoli, Pa., 1975; ops. dir. Sta WMGK-FM, Greater Media Radio, Phila., 1976-78; promotions and music dir. Sta. WMMR-FM, Metromedia Radio, Phila., 1978-80; promotion and mktg. dir. Sta. WCOZ-FM, Blair Radio, Boston, 1980—; radio promotion and media cons., 1980—. Media coordinator spl. events for non-profit orgns. Mem. New Eng. Broadcasting Assn. (Best of Broadcasting 1st Pl. award 1980), Broadcasters Promotion Assn. (Silver award 1981), Nat. Assn. Broadcasting, Smithsonian Instn. Republican. Roman Catholic. Club: Advt. Greater Boston (Francis W. Hatch award 1981). Contbg. author: Broadcast Advt. and Promotion, 1982; program producer: Dateline Boston; Live at the Paradise, 1981; album producer: Breakout Album, 1979, Best of the Boston Beat, vol. II, 1980. Home: 157 W Canton St Boston MA 02118 Office: Sta WCOZ 441 Stuart St Boston MA 02116

NORRIS, NANCY NASBITT, acct.; b. Morganfield, Ky., Nov. 9, 1951; d. George Riley and Margaret Elizabeth (Holland) Nasbitt; A.S., Henderson Community Coll., 1971; B.S. in Acctg., U. Ky., 1973; m. Seton William Norris, III, Aug. 6, 1971. Instr., Henderson (Ky.) Community Coll., 1975-78; staff acct. Collins, Logan & Campbell, C.P.A.s, Henderson, 1973—. C.P.A., Ky. Mem. Ky. Soc. C.P.A.s. Baptist. Home: Route 6 Box 580 Henderson KY 42420 Office: 500 Ohio Valley Bank Bldg Henderson KY 42420

NORRIS, PATRICIA KILMER, public relations exec.; b. New Rochelle, N.Y., Feb. 7, 1933; d. Hugh and Patricia (Polk) Kilmer; student Sweet Briar Coll., 1951-52, Westchester Comml. Sch., 1953-54; m. James Alexander Norris, Feb. 16, 1957; children—Melissa Polk, Benjamin White II. Asst. beauty editor Glamour mag., N.Y.C., 1954-55; sr. exec. sec. McCann-Erickson Inc., N.Y.C., 1955-59; sec. to pres., office mgr. Thomson-Leeds Co., Inc., N.Y.C., 1959-62; dir. pub. relations Glenview (Ill.) Park Dist., 1975-78; freelance writer/pub. relations, Glenview, 1978—. Rec. sec. Glenview Aux., 1968-70, pres., 1970-72, v.p. pres.'s council of all auxs. Skokie Valley Hosp., 1972-73, pres., 1973-74; active Glenview Bi-Centennial Commn., 1976, recipient Merit cert., 1977; active Northfield Twp. Republican Women's Club, 1974—, publicity chmn., 1977-79, active 10th Dist. Rep. Women's Club, 1974—; publicity chmn. Glenbrook So. High Sch. Instrumental League, 1978-79, Glenview Area Hist. Soc. Coach House/Library, 1978-79; pres. Grove Heritage Assn., 1979—. Episcopalian. Club: North Shore Public Relations. Home: 4121 Kennicott Ln Glenview IL 60025

NORRISS, NORMA G., clin. psychologist, psychotherapist; b. Bronx, N.Y.; d. Harry and Ethel Isabelle (Aaronson) Ruskin; A.A. summa cum laude, Trenton Jr. Coll., 1956; B.A. with highest honors, Rutgers Coll., 1959; A.M., Temple U., 1960, Ph.D. (fellow), 1963; m. A. Harold Norriss, Apr. 18, 1943; 1 dau., Sharon Lee Norriss White. Psychology intern Johnstone Tng. and Research Center, Bordentown, N.J., 1961-62, Drenk Meml. Guidance Center, Mount Holly, N.J., 1962, Norristown (Pa.) State Hosp., 1962-63; staff psychologist Terrell (Tex.) State Hosp., 1963-64, Los Angeles County Gen. Hosp., 1964-66; research psychologist Adolescent Suicide Attempters Project, 1966-67; cons. Loma Linda (Calif.) U. Med. Sch., 1967-69, South Bay Child Guidance Clinic, Redondo Beach, Calif., 1968-70; community mental health psychologist South Bay Mental Health Service, 1968-69; asso. clin. prof. psychiatry Loma Linda U. Med. Center, 1969-77, dir. child psychology services, 1969-77; prof. psychology Calif. State U., Los Angeles, 1966-74; pvt. practice psychotherapy, 1977—; cons. Riverside Gen. Hosp., 1970-80, various sch. dists. in Calif., 1968—; guest lectr. mental health various schs. and community orgns., 1969—; pres. adv. bd. Youth Services Center, 1975-77. Lic. psychologist, Calif.; cert. psychologist Tex. Mem. Am. Psychol. Assn., Western Psychol. Assn., Soc. for Pediatric Psychology, Los Angeles Psychol. Assn. (exec. bd. 1970-72), Psychologists in Public Service (founding pres. 1966-68). Contbr. articles on pediatric psychology to profl. publs. Home: 20560 Rancho Los Cerritos Covina CA 91724 Office: 2086 South E St Suite 103 San Bernardino CA 92410

NORRY, PATRICIA GOODWIN, govt. exec.; b. Cin.; d. Robert Clifford and Marion Schmadel Goodwin; A.B., Seton Hill Coll., 1958; postgrad. George Washington U., 1958-61, (Nat. Inst. Pub. Affairs fellow) Stanford U., 1968-69; m. Leonard J. Norry, Dec., 1969; 1 son, Douglas. Staff asst. to chmn. AEC, Washington, 1961-68; spl. asst. to dir. research Nuclear Regulatory Commn., Washington, 1970-78, dep. dir. adminstrn., 1979-82, dir. adminstrn., 1982—. Pres., Bradley Elem. Sch. PTA, 1981-82; bd. dirs. Energy Fed. Credit Union, 1980-82. Mem. Am. Soc. Public Adminstrn. Home: 8216 Kerry Rd Chevy Chase MD 20815 Office: US Nuclear Regulatory Commn Washington NC 20555

NORTH, HELEN FLORENCE, educator; b. Utica, N.Y.; d. James H. and Catherine (Debbold) North; A.B., Cornell U., 1942, M.A., 1943, Ph.D., 1945. Instr. classical lang. Rosary Coll., River Forest, Ill., 1946-48; mem. faculty Swarthmore (Pa.) Coll., 1948—, prof. classics, 1961—, chmn. dept., 1959—, Centennial prof. classics, 1966-73, Kenan prof., 1973—; vis. asst. prof. Cornell U., 1952—; vis. asso. prof. Barnard Coll., 1954-55; vis. prof. LaSalle Coll., Phila., 1965, Am. Sch. Classical Studies, Athens, 1975; Blegen disting. vis. research prof. Vassar Coll., 1979. Bd. dirs. Am. Council Learned Socs., 1977—; trustee King's Coll., LaSalle Coll., Am. Acad. in Rome. Recipient Harbison prize Danforth Found., 1969; grantee Am. Council Learned Socs., 1943-45, 73, fellow, 1971-72; Mary Isabel Sibley fellow Phi Beta Kappa Found., 1945-46; Ford Fund Advancement Edn. fellow, also Fulbright fellow, Rome, 1953-54, Guggenheim fellow, 1958-59; grantee Danforth Found., 1962, Lindbach Found., 1966; fellow AAUW, 1963-64; sr. fellow Nat. Endowment for Humanities, 1967-68; Martin classical lectr. Oberlin Coll., 1972; Guggenheim fellow, 1975-76. Mem. Am. Philol. Assn. (dir. 1968—, pres. 1976, Charles J. Goodwin award of merit 1969), Classical Assn. Atlantic States, Catholic Commn. Intellectual and Cultural Affairs (chmn. 1968-69), Am. Acad. Arts and Scis., Soc. Religion Higher Edn., Phi Beta Kappa (mem. bd. vis. scholars 1975-76), Phi Kappa Phi. Author: Sophrosyne: Self-Knowledge and Self-Restraint in Greek Literature, 1966; From Myth to Icon: Reflections of Greek Ethical Doctrine in Literature and Art, 1979. Translator: John Milton's Second Defense of the English People, 1966. Editor: Interpretations of Plato: A Swarthmore Symposium, 1977; co-editor: of Eloquence, 1970; editor Jour. History of Ideas; mem. editorial bd. Catalogus Translationum et Commentariorum, 1979—. Home: 604 Ogden Ave Swarthmore PA 19081

NORTH, KATHRYN E. KEESEY (MRS. EUGENE C. NORTH), ret. educator; b. Columbia, Pa., Jan. 25, 1916; d. Isaac and Elizabeth (French) Keesey; B.S., Ithaca Coll., 1938; M.A., N.Y. U., 1950; m. Eugene C. North, Aug. 18, 1938. Dir. music Cairo (N.Y.) Central Sch. Dist., 1938; music edn. cons. Argyle (N.Y.) Central Sch. Dist., 1939; dir. gen. music curriculum Hartford (N.Y.) Central Sch. Dist., 1939; mem. staff Del. Dept. Pub. Instrn., Dover, 1943; dir. music edn. Herricks (N.Y.) Pub. Schs., 1944-71; ret., 1971. Vis. lectr. Ithaca Coll., summers 1959, 60, 62-65, Fairleigh-Dickinson U., Rutherford, N.J., summer 1966,

Albertus Magnus Coll., New Haven, summer 1968; instr. Adelphi Coll., 1954-55, Sch. Edn., N.Y.U., 1964-65. Mem. Music Educators Nat. Conf., N.E.A., N.Y. State Sch. Music Assn., N.Y. State Tchrs. Assn., Nassau Music Educators Assn. (exec. bd. 1947-58), N.Y. State Council Adminstrs. Music Edn. (chpt. v.p. 1967-68), Herricks Tchrs. Assn. (pres. 1948), Sigma Alpha Iota. Mem. Order Eastern Star. Home: 1645 Calle Camille La Jolla CA 92037

NORTHCUTT, HELENE LOUISE BERKING (MRS. CHARLES PHILLIP NORTHCUTT), artist, educator; b. Hannibal, Mo., July 6, 1916; d. Robert Stanley and Alice Lee (Adkisson) Berking; student Christian Coll., Columbia, Mo., 1932-33; B.S., U. Mo., 1939, A.M., 1940, Ed.D., 1959; m. Charles Phillip Northcutt, June 4, 1938 (dec.); children—John Berking, Francois Lee Northcutt Hedeen. Art tchr., supr. Oakwood High Sch. and Elem. Sch., 1937-39; tchr. jr. high sch. U. Mo. Lab. Sch., 1939-40; tchr. elem. art, Memphis, Mo., 1941; county fine arts supr., Ralls County, Mo., 1941-42; tchr. art high sch., Columbia, 1943-44; tchr. art jr. high sch., Hannibal, Mo., 1951-54; supr. art Ralls County Reorganized Sch. Dist. VI, New London, 1954-56; vis. prof. U. Upper Iowa, 1956; instr. U. Mo., 1956-57; prof. art Eastern Mont. Coll. unit U. Mont., Billings, from 1957, now prof. emeritus, mem. grad. faculty; vis. prof. art U. B.C., Vancouver, 1965. Cons. in curriculum in art edn.; cons. environ. edn., cons. on Indian edn., early childhood; exhibits fibers and paintings; state dir. Am. Art Week, Am. Artists Profl. League, 1963-65; exhibit chmn. E.M.C. Gallery Fine Arts; program chmn. Becky Thatcher council Girl Scouts U.S.A., 1946-48; bd. dirs., treas. United Christian Campus Ministry. Recipient scholarship Delta Kappa Gamma, 1956-57; Nat. Press award Gen. Fedn. Women's Clubs, 1951; named Outstanding Honor Grad. U. Mo., 1968; citations for service Eastern Mont. Coll. Mem. Nat. Soc. Coll. Profs., AAUP, Mont. Edn. Assn. (past pres. Eastern Faculty unit; v.p. dept. higher edn. 1966-68, dept. pres. 1968-70) Nat., Mont. (sec. 1967-69) art edn. assns., AAUW (past chpt. pres.), Mont. Early Childhood Edn. Assn., Gen. Fedn. Women's Clubs (local past pres.), Delta Kappa Gamma (past chpt. pres., chmn. com., chmn. state world fellowship), Delta Phi Delta, Kappa Delta Epsilon. Methodist (mem. commn. higher edn. ministries, trustee Yellowstone Conf.). Club: Eastern Montana College Faculty (Billings, Mont.). Author: Creative Expression, 1964; Competency base Module-Methods and Materials, 1974; contbr. to publs. in field; reviewer, editor manuscripts on art and art edn. Home: 4505 Rimrock Rd Billings MT 59106

NORTHEY, LOIS M., nursing home adminstr.; b. Mahanoy City, Pa., June 22, 1925; d. George H. and Della M. (Birch) N.; R.N., Episcopal Hosp., Phila., 1945. Dir. patient care service Negley House, Pitts., 1971-74, exec. dir., 1973-78; cons. Wightman Health Center, Pitts., 1979—; adminstr. Oakmont Residence, 1980—. Mem. Assn. Rehab. Nurses, Am. Acad. Med. Adminstrs., Nat. League Nursing, Am. Coll. Nursing Home Adminstrs., Health Care Facilities Assn. Pa. Republican. Roman Catholic. Address: 11 Kinzua Rd Pittsburgh PA 15239

NORTON, BARBARA GUTH, internat. economist; b. Washington, Sept. 20, 1951; d. Herbert J. and Florence Margaret Ellen (Foster) Guth; A.B. in English, Brown U., 1973; M.A. in Econs., George Washington U., 1978; m. Arthur Easton Norton, June 14, 1980. Summer employee Dept. State, Washington, 1970-73; clk. typist, 1973-74; internat. economist Office of Econs., U.S. Internat. Trade Commn., Washington, 1974—, adv. com. Fed. Women's Program, 1980—, chmn., 1981—. Recipient merit award U.S. Internat. Trade Commn., 1977, 80; Managerial Devel. Program selectee, 1981. Mem. Washington Women Economists. Presbyterian. Club: Ski (Washington). Office: USITC 701 E St NW Washington DC 20436

NORTON, CARMEL CORINNE, ednl. adminstr.; b. Orange, Tex., Apr. 9, 1922; d. Arthur Louis and Mathilde (Hotard) Boudreaux; B.S., Sam Houston State U., 1944; M.Ed., U. Houston, 1947; postgrad. Tex. Tech. U.; m. William Stancil Norton, Dec. 17, 1949; children—Therese, Michael, Alexine. Health and phys. edn. tchr., dir. Lee Brigadiers Drum and Bugle Corps, Robert E. Lee High Sch., Goose Creek Consol. Ind. Sch. Dist., Baytown, Tex., 1944-53, 61-65, phys. edn. tchr. Horace Mann Jr. High Sch., 1956-58, phys. edn. tchr. Ross Sterling High Sch., 1965, coordinator health and phys. edn. for girls, 1967-77, coordinator health and phys. edn., 1977—; mem. schs. and colls. com. Am. Cancer Soc., 1974—; mem. vis. coms. So. Assn. Colls. and Schs. Mem. AAHPERD (alliance rep.), NEA (conv. del. 1970), Tex. Found. Intercollegiate Athletics for Women (bd. govs. 1975—, exec. treas. 1979—), Tex. Assn. Health, Phys. Edn. and Recreation (honor award 1976, pres. 1974-75, chmn. honor award com. 1978-82, transition and future directions coms. 1982—), Am. Heart Assn. (task force chmn. Tex. affiliate 1983), Tex. State Tchrs. Assn. (mem. dist. ho. of dels.), Baytown Edn. Assn. (1st v.p. 1970-71), Delta Kappa Gamma. Roman Catholic. Club: Goose Creek Country. Home: 5004 Fairway Dr Baytown TX 77521 Office: Goose Creek Consol Ind Sch Dist PO Box 30 Baytown TX 77520

NORTON, COLLEEN KREBS, cardiovascular clin. specialist; b. Floral Park, N.Y., Jan. 3, 1946; d. Ernest C. and Dolores A. (Hendel) Krebs; B.S. in Nursing, Coll. Misericordia, 1967; M.S. in Nursing, Cath. U. Am., 1980; m. Robert F. Norton, Mar. 29, 1970; children—Justin Matthew, Heather Anne. Head nurse CCU, Good Samaritan Hosp., West Islip, N.Y., 1967-70, evening supr. (part-time) intensive care, coronary care, and emergency room, 1974-78, cardio-pulmonary instr., 1977-78 nurse specialist in cardiology Millard Fillmore Hosp., Buffalo, 1970-71, inservice coordinator ICU, 1972-74; critical care nurse educator Shady Grove Adventist Hosp., Rockville, Md., 1980—; health care cons. Resource Applications, 1982—; continuing cert. cardiopulmonary instr., 1977—. Mem. Am. Assn. Critical Care Nurses, Am. Heart Assn. (Outstanding Service award 1977), Sigma Theta Tau. Roman Catholic. Home: 20 Red Kiln Ct Gaithersburg MD 20878

NORTON, DONNA ELITHE, educator; b. Durand, Wis., Oct. 15, 1934; d. Earl William and Elithe Bernice (Longsdorf) Proue; B.S. (Elem. Edn. honors scholar), U. Wis., River Falls, 1956; M.S. in Curriculum and Instrn., U. Wis., Madison, 1973, Ph.D. in Curriculum and Instrn., 1976; m. Verland Wilson Norton, Aug. 9, 1958; children—Bradley Wilson, Saundra Elithe. Tchr., River Falls, 1956-59, Madison, 1959-63; remedial reading tchr., Madison, 1969-72, Title I reading cons., 1974-76; lectr. U. Wis., Madison, 1974-76; asst. prof. ednl. curriculum and instrn. Tex. A&M U., College Station, 1976-80, asso. prof., 1980—, dir. reading lab., 1977-80; cons.; conf. presenter. Treas., PTA, 1970-71, program chmn., 1971-72. Recipient Outstanding Univ. Teaching award Tex. A&M U., 1977, Disting. Achievement award, 1982; Tex. A&M U. research grantee, 1976, 80; Conoco grantee, 1982; cert. elem. tchr., reading tchr., reading specialist, Wis. Mem. Internat. Reading Assn., Nat. Council Tchrs. of English, Coll. Reading Assn., AAUW, Phi Delta Kappa, Alpha Delta Kappa. Methodist. Author: The Effective Teaching of Language Arts, 1980; Language Arts Activities for Children, 1980; Through the Eyes of Children: An Introduction to Children's Literature, 1983; contbr. articles and revs. to profl. jours. Home: 125 Lee Ave College Station TX 77840 Office: Dept of EDCI Texas A&M University College Station TX 77843

NORTON, ELEANOR HOLMES, chmn. Equal Employment Opportunity Commn.; b. Washington, June 13, 1937; B.A., Antioch Coll., 1960; M.A. in Am. Studies, Yale U., 1963, LL.B., 1964. Law clk. to Fed. Dist. Ct. Judge A. Leon Higginbotham, 1964-65; asst. legal dir. ACLU, 1965-70; mem., chmn. N.Y. Commn. on Human Rights, 1970-77; exec. asst. to mayor of N.Y.C., 1971-74; chmn. Equal Employment Opportunity Commn., 1977—. Recipient Louise Waterman Wise award. Democrat. Author: Sex Discrimination and the Law. Contbr. articles to jours. Office: 2401 E St Washington DC 20506 *

NORTON, KATHLEEN MUELLER, med. technologist, educator; b. Detroit, Feb. 24, 1947; d. Elmer Joseph and Jane Claire (Mulvaney) Mueller; B.S. in M.T., U. Cin., 1968; M.A., Central Mich. U., 1981; postgrad. U. Cin., 1982—; m. Robert Vincent Norton, Jr., Nov. 21, 1969. Med. technologist Hamilton County Diagnostic Clinic for Retarded Children, Cin., 1968-69, Christ Hosp. Dept. Lab. Medicine, Cin., 1969-70; program dir. Christ Hosp. Sch. Med. Tech., 1970-80, med. technologist, 1981-82; clin. instr. pathology U. Cin., 1978-80; condr. workshops, seminars in field. Vol. inpatient facility of Hospice, 1981—; mem. Hospice Speakers Bur. Recipient Ohio Soc. Med. Tech. Dist. 8 Mem. of the Yr. award, 1982. Mem. Am. Soc. Med. Technologists (sec. Cin. com. med. tech. edn. 1971-78), Cin. Soc. Med. Tech. (pres. 1981-82), Hematology Continuing Edn. Club of Cin. (founder, chmn. 1975-77), Am. Soc. Clin. Pathologists, Ohio Soc. Med. Tech. Roman Catholic. Clubs: Cin. Ski, Telemark Ski. Address: 3836 Broadview Dr Cincinnati OH 45208

NORTON, MARY BETH, historian, educator; b. Ann Arbor, Mich., Mar. 25, 1943; d. Clark Frederic and Mary Elizabeth (Lunny) Norton; B.A., U. Mich., 1964; M.A. (Woodrow Wilson fellow, Harvard Prize fellow), Harvard U., 1965, Ph.D., 1969. Asst. prof. U. Conn., 1969-71; asst. prof. history Cornell U., Ithaca, N.Y., 1971-74, asso. prof., 1975-81, prof., 1981—; fellow Charles Warren Center, Harvard U., 1974-75, Shelby Cullom Davis Center, Princeton U., 1977-78. Mem. Nat. Council on Humanities, 1978-84, chmn. research div. com., 1979-81, chmn. edn. div. com., 1982—. Nat. Endowment for Humanities fellow, 1974-75. Mem. Am. Hist. Assn., Orgn. Am. Historians, Soc. Am. Historians (Allan Nevins prize 1969), Am. Antiquarian Soc., Coordinating Com. of Women in Hist. Profession, Conf. Group on Women's History, Berkshire Conf. of Women Historians (book prize 1981), Upstate N.Y. Women's History Conf. Democrat. Methodist. Author: The British-Americans: The Loyalist Exiles in England, 1774-1789, 1972; Liberty's Daughters: The Revolutionary Experience of American Women, 1750-1800, 1980; co-author: A People and a Nation, 1982; editor: (with Carol Berkin) Women of America: A History, 1979. Office: History Dept McGraw Hall Cornell U Ithaca NY 14853

NORTON, VIRGINIA SKEEN (MRS. JOHN H. NORTON, JR.), civic worker; b. Atlanta, June 1, 1907; d. Lola Percy and Rebecca (Baldwin) Skeen; A.B., Agnes Scott Coll., 1928; student Columbia U., 1934-35; m. John Hughes Norton, Jr., Dec. 16, 1938; children—Virginia Skeen (Mrs. John K. Kraft), John Hughes III. With personnel dept. Retail Credit Co., Atlanta, 1929-31, sec. to v.p., gen. mgr. Davison-Paxon Co., Atlanta, 1931-34; with Aluminium Ltd., N.Y.C., 1935-41, sec. to pres., 1937-41; sec. to pres. Colonial Williamsburg, Inc., N.Y.C., 1943-44. Bd. dirs. North Shore Assos. Chgo. Commons, 1951-54, Infant Welfare Soc. Chgo., 1953-54, Catherine Morrill Day Nursery, Portland, Maine, 1956-59. Mem. Winter Park Meml. Hosp. Aux., Morse Art Gallery Assos. (exec. com.), Nat. Soc. Colonial Dames Am. Episcopalian. Address: 700 Melrose Ave Apt A-22 Winter Park FL 32792

NORWOOD, CAROLYN VIRGINIA, educator; b. Florence, S.C.; d. James H. and Mildred (Jones) Norwood; B.S. cum laude, N.C. A. and T. State U., 1956; M.A., Columbia U., 1958; grad. Seton Hall U., 1973; grad. student (EDPA fellow 1977-78), Temple U., 1976—. Sec. to exec. officer Office of Doctoral Studies, Tchrs. Coll. Columbia, 1956-59; instr. bus. edn. Gibbs Jr. Coll., St. Petersburg, Fla., 1959-60; instr. Fayetteville (N.C.) State U., 1960-65; asst. prof. Community Coll. Phila., 1965-68; prof. Essex County Coll., Newark, 1968—, chairwoman dept. sec. studies and bus. edn., 1968-78, also adviser Phi Beta Lambda chpt. Mem. Am., N.J. vocat. edn. assns., Am. Bus. Communication Assn., Eastern Bus. Edn. Assn. (membership dir., exec. bd., community coll. rep. 1976-81), N.J. Bus. Edn. Assn., Bus. and Profl. Women's Club, AAUP, Nat. Bus. Edn. Assn. (exec. bd.), NEA, Urban League Essex County, Am. Vocat. Assn., Adminstrv. Mgmt. Soc., Internat. Word Processing Assn., N.J. Word Processing Info. Exchange, Am. Assn. Women in Community and Jr. Colls., NAACP, Nat. Council Negro Women, Delta Pi Epsilon, Alpha Kappa Alpha, Phi Delta Kappa. Democrat. Baptist. Home: 635 Purce St Hillside NJ 07205 Office: Essex County Coll 303 University Ave Newark NJ 07102

NORWOOD, JANET LIPPE, economist, govt. ofcl.; b. Newark, Dec. 11, 1923; d. M. Turner and Thelma (Levinson) Lippe; B.A., N.J. Coll. Women, 1945; M.A., Fletcher Sch. Law and Diplomacy, 1946, Ph.D., 1949; LL.D. (hon.), Fla. Internat. U., 1979; m. Bernard Norwood, June 25, 1943; children—Stephen Harlan, Peter Carlton. Instr., Wellesley Coll., 1948-49; economist William L. Clayton Center, Fletcher Sch. Law and Diplomacy, 1953-58; with Bur. Labor Stats., Dept. Labor, Washington, 1963—, dep. commr. data analysis, 1973-75, dep. commr. bur., 1975-78, acting commr. bur., 1978-79, commr. labor stats., 1979—; mem. bd. overseers, vis. com., stats. dept. Harvard U., 1976-81. Recipient Disting. Achievement award, Sec. Labor, 1972, spl. commendation, 1977; Philip Arnow award Dept. Labor, 1979. Fellow Am. Stats. Assn.; mem. Douglass Soc., Am. Econ. Assn., Nat. Economists Club, Indsl. Relations Research Assn., Nat. Assn. Bus. Economists, Women's Caucus in Stats., Nat. Acad. Public Adminstrn., Internat. Statis. Assn. Author: (monograph) Labor Law and Practice in the Union of Burma, 1963; collaborator: International Trade Policy Issues, 1963; contbr. articles to profl. publs. Office: 441 G St NW Washington DC 20212

NOTEBOOM, PATRICIA JEAN, social worker; b. Corsica, S.D., May 3, 1933; d. Gerrit M. and Helen Cornelia N.; B.S., Sioux Falls (S.D.) Coll., 1962; M.S.W., U. Wis., 1970. Nat. bd. dirs. YWCA; asst. dir. USO Club, Columbia, S.C., 1962-63, program dir., Memphis, 1963-64, exec. dir., Lincoln, Nebr., 1964-65, program dir., Trenton, 1965-66, asso. dir., Seoul, Korea, 1966-68; family counselor Family Service, Milw., 1969-76; dir. staff devel. and tng. Family Counseling Center, Des Moines, 1976—. Mem. Nat. Assn. Social Workers, Acad. Cert. Social Workers, Am. Assn. Marriage and Family Therapy. Office: 1321 Walnut St Suite 200 Des Moines IA 50309

NOTTINGHAM, CARMEN EILEEN, utility exec.; b. Santurce, P.R., Oct. 27, 1948; d. Frederick and Carmen Imra (Nazario) Krause; student Cath. U. P.R., 1969; B.A., Calif. State U., San Diego, 1978, M.S., 1981; m. Donald James Nottingham, June 26, 1971. Home economist San Diego Gas & Electric, 1973-79, energy adv. services supr., 1979-80, sr. conservation coordinator, 1980-81, consumer program planner, 1981—, 2d v.p., 1982—. Mem. Energy Producers Service Assn., Am. Home Econs. Assn., Calif. Home Econs. Assn. (pres. dist.), Home Economists in Bus. Republican. Roman Catholic. Office: 101 Ash St PO Box 1831 San Diego CA 92112 *

NOTTINGHAM, JOANNE ELEANORA, airlines ofcl.; b. Bklyn., May 14, 1949; d. James Edward and Martha Eleanora (Eversley) N.; B.S., So. Conn. State Coll., 1972. Tchr. emotionally disturbed children Southside Comprehensive Health Center, Atlanta, 1972-73; flight attendant Delta Air Lines, Inc., Boston, Chgo., Miami, 1973-77, reservations agt., N.Y.C., 1977-79, mktg. rep., N.Y.C., 1979—. Office: Park West Office Center Bldg Two Pittsburgh PA 15275

NOTTKE, NANCY JANE, educator; b. Lakewood, Ohio, Mar. 30, 1948; d. Clark DeWitt and Frances (Watterson) Fiscus; B.S. with honors in Elementary Edn., Ohio U., Athens, 1969, M.Ed., 1977; M. Bruce Douglas Nottke; children—Sara Elizabeth, Nathan Douglas. Intern tchr. The Children's House, Pearl City, Hawaii, 1970-71; tchr. sci. St. Anthony's Schs., Kailua, Hawaii, 1971-72; tchr. Holy Family Sch., Honolulu, 1972-73; tchr. kindergarten Trimble Local Schs., Glouster, Ohio, 1973-77, tchr. 2d grade, 1977—. Martha Holden Jennings scholar, 1976-77. Mem. NEA, Trimble Local Tchrs. Assn. (pres. 1976-77), Southeastern Ohio Tchrs. Assn., AAUW (chmn. newsletter 1974-76, rec. sec. 1978-79, edn. founds. 1979-81, legis. chmn. 1981-83), Delta Kappa Gamma. Club: Eastern Star. Cert., Ohio. Home: RD 6 32 Chapel Ln Athens OH 45701 Office: Route 3 Box 447 Trimble Elementary Sch Glouster OH 45732

NOVAK, ALINA SIDNEY, life ins. co. exec.; b. London, Jan. 12, 1947; came to U.S., 1952, naturalized, 1963; d. Jan and Marta (Wendlandt) Nowosielski; B.A., CCNY, 1969. Research analyst Nat. Econs. Research Assos., Inc., N.Y.C., 1969-70, Royal Globe Ins. Co., N.Y.C., 1970-71, Analytical Methods and Applications, Inc., Washington, 1971-72, Scholarship, Edn. and Def. Fund Racial Equality, Inc., N.Y.C., 1972-74; fin. analyst Equitable Life Assurance Soc. U.S., N.Y.C., 1974—; founder Networks, 1976; pres. Networks Unltd., Inc. Recipient Big Apple award N.Y.C. Jr. C. of C., 1980. Mem. Am. Econs. Assn., Fortune 500 Bus. and Profl. Women's Club, NOW, Women in Info. Processing, Women in Communications, Women in Ins. Club: Toastmasters. Contbr. articles to books on networking. Home: 337 44th St Apt 6 Brooklyn NY 11220 Office: 1285 Ave Americas New York NY 10019

NOVAK, CAROLE ANN, educator; b. N.Y.C., July 20, 1941; d. John Michael and Dorothy (Britz) N.; B.S. in Spanish and French, Indiana U. of Pa., 1963; M.A., U. Mass., 1970, Ph.D. in Spanish, 1975. Tchr. French, Freeport (Pa.) Area Schs., 1963-64; tchr. French and Spanish, Franklin Area Schs., Murrysville, Pa., 1964-65; assoc. prof. Spanish, S.D. State U., 1970-78; instr. English as 2d lang. St. Vincent Coll., Latrobe, Pa., 1979-80, asst. dir. English Lang. Inst., 1979-80; asst. prof. Spanish and English as 2d lang. Tenn. Technol. U., 1980—, acad. coordinator English Lang. Inst., 1980—; cons. in field. Mem. Am. Assn. Tchrs. Spanish and Portuguese, MLA, Tchr. English to Speakers of Others Langs., South Atlantic Modern Lang. Assn., Tenn. Philol. Assn., Tenn. Fgn. Lang. Teaching Assn., AAUP, Mid-South Morgan Horse Assn., Am. Horse Show Assn., Am. Morgan Horse Assn., Middle Tenn. Quarter Horse Assn. Lutheran. Club: Middle Tenn. Horseback Riders. Contbr. in field. Home: 512 Jere Whitson Rd Cookeville TN 38501

NOVAK, CATHERINE ANN, nurse; b. Washington, Oct. 14, 1952; d. Joel Warren and Jeane Charlotte (Runge) N.; R.N., Johns Hopkins Hosp., 1973; B.S. in Nursing with honors, U. Va., 1975; M.S.N., U. Md., 1982. Staff nurse U. Va. Hosp., 1973-74, spl. assignment nurse implementation of problem oriented record system, 1974-75; staff nurse employment health unit Indsl. Health Services, Inc., McLean, Va., 1973-75; head nurse, nurse mgr. arthritis and connective tissues clinics Johns Hopkins Hosp., 1975-79; nurse specialist in rheumatology George Washington U. Med. Center, 1979-82; now with The Emmes Corp., Potomac, Md. Recipient Anna D. Wolfe award Johns Hopkins Hosp. Sch. Nursing, 1973, award of appreciation for vol. service Met. Washington Arthritis Found., 1980; USPHS trainee, 1974-75. Mem. Am. Nurses Assn., Johns Hopkins Nursing Alumni Assn. (sec. 1978-79), Arthritis Health Professions Assn. (chmn. publs. com. 1980-82), Sigma Theta Tau, Phi Kappa Phi. Editor mag., newsletters in field. Home: 4300 Old Dominion Dr Apt 804 Arlington VA 22207 Office: The Emmes Corp 11325 Seven Locks Rd Suite 214 Potomac MD 20854

NOVAK, DIANE MARIE, nurse; b. Chgo., June 7, 1951; d. William Charles and Bertha Marie (Rich) N.; R.N., Augustana Hosp., Chgo., 1971; postgrad. Loop Coll., Chgo., Northeastern Ill. U. Mem. nursing staff Augustana Hosp., 1971-73, 74—, asst. coordinator med.-surg. unit, 1976-80, staff nurse dept. pediatrics, 1980—; staff nurse surg. and burn unit Evanston (Ill.) Hosp., 1973-74; in-service instr., CPR tchr. Office: 411 W Dickens St Chicago IL 60614

NOVAK, JO-ANN STOUT, chem. engr.; b. Glen Ridge, N.J., June 25, 1956; d. Herbert Austin and Anna (Messina) Stout; B.Chem. Engring., Ga. Inst. Tech., 1977; postgrad., Oakland U., 1982—; m. John Robert Novak Jr., Oct. 30, 1976. Trainee AC Spark Plug div. Gen. Motors Corp., Flint, Mich., 1977-78, chemist, 1978-79, exptl. chemist, 1979-81, mfg. engr., 1981—. Cert. engr.-in-tng., Ga. Mem. Am. Electroplaters Soc. (dir. Saginaw Valley br.), Am. Inst. Chem. Engrs., Soc. Mfg. Engrs. Office: AC Spark Plug Div Gen Motors Corp 1300 N Dort Hwy Flint MI 48556

NOVAK, MARY MARGUERITE, home accessories designer; b. Potrerillos, Chile, July 20, 1953; came to U.S., naturalized, 1965; d. Joseph Francis and Marguerite Mary (Seiller) N.; student Stonehill Coll., 1970-71; B.S. in Home Econs., Housing and Design, Colo. State U., 1974. Kitchen designer Home and Kitchen Interiors, Sacramento, 1974-75, St. Charles of So. Calif., La Jolla, 1975-76; mech. draftsman Kennedy Engrs., San Francisco, 1977-78; partner, kitchen and bath designer Novak & Novak, Stockton, Calif., 1978-80; partner, designer Mostly Drapes, Stockton, 1980—. Mem. Western Merchandise Mart Assn., C. of C. (econ. devel. progress com.). Home: 3722 W Benjamin Holt Dr Stockton CA 95207 Office: 6385 Pacific Ave Stockton CA 95207

NOVAK, RUTH FRANCES VINCENT (MRS. NICHOLAS NOVAK), educator, psychologist; b. Los Angeles, Mar. 23, 1909; d. Fred Ezekiel and Almira (Smith) Vincent; A.A., Los Angeles Jr. Coll., 1934; B.A., UCLA, 1937, M.A., 1938; postgrad. Claremont Grad. Sch., 1942-43, 61-62, U. So. Calif., 1946-49, San Diego State Coll., 1961, Colo. State Coll., 1964, Calif. State Coll. at Los Angeles, 1963, 65, Mich. State U., 1966-68; m. Nicholas Novak, June 30, 1950 (dec. Mar. 1965). Field sec. Camp Fire Girls, Los Angeles, 1931-37; asst. clin. psychologist Childrens Hosp., Los Angeles, 1938; tchr. Ontario (Calif.) City Schs., 1939-41, Conora (Calif.) City Schs., 1941-43; tchr., counselor Glendale (Calif.) City Schs., 1947-50; instr. Imperial Valley Coll., El Centro, Calif., 1957-60; coordinator counseling, student activities Imperial Valley Coll., Imperial, 1961-63, dean counseling, 1963-72; adminstrv. cons. Maharishi Internat. U., 1972-76; research and ednl. cons., 1976—. Bd. dirs. Camp Fire Girls, Imperial County, Calif., 1951-57, Nat. Council Camp Fire Girls, 1954-56, A.R.C., 1953-55. Served to capt. WACS, 1943-47. Mem. Imperial Valley Guidance Council (pres. 1963), Calif. Jr. Coll. Assn. (sect. dir., sec. 1961-64), Calif. Counseling and Guidance Assn., Nat. Personnel and Guidance Assn., Nat. Vocational Guidance Assn., Imperial-San Diego Counties Jr. Coll. Counselors Assn. (sec. 1966-68), Calif. Community Coll. Counselors Assn. (sec. 1969-70), Nat., Calif. assns. women deans and counselors, Calif. Tchrs. Assn., NEA, AAUW, Calif. Cal. Personnel and Guidance Assn. (mem. senate 1969-70), Tau Alpha Epsilon, Psi Chi, Pi Gamma Mu, Pi Lambda Theta, Delta Kappa Gamma (chpt. pres. 1966-68), Delta Zeta, Theta Upsilon. Presbyterian. Clubs: Order Eastern Star (worthy matron 1960), Soroptimist. Address: Ventura Marina Park #179 1215 Anchors Way Dr Ventura CA 93003

NOVAK, VICKIE LYNN, librarian; b. Chgo., Feb. 17, 1952; d. Albert Henry and Elsie Marie (Bortolami) N.; B.A., Quincy Coll., 1973; M.S.L.S., U. Ky., 1974. Adminstrv. librarian Acorn Public Library Dist., Oak Forest, Ill., 1974—, joint cons. bldg., 1975-80; mem. adv. bd. Learning Exchange's Spl. Library Project, 1979-80; mem. Ill. White House Conf. on Library and Info. Services, 1978. Ill. State Library scholar, 1972-73, 73-74; named Outstanding Modern Lang. Student,

Quincy Coll., 1974. Mem. ALA (architecture for public libraries com. bldgs. and equipment sect. adminstrn. and mgmt. div. 1981-83), Ill. Library Assn. (mem.-at-large dist. library round table 1982), Library Adminstrs. Conf. No. Ill., South Suburban Library Assn. (pres. 1979-80), Oak Forest C. of C., Abu Arabian Horse Club, U. Ky. Alumni Club, Friends of Library, Arabian Horse Assnn. (Dressage com.), Am. Horse Shows Assn., U.S. Dressage Fedn., Ill. Dressage Assn., Beta Phi Mu. Roman Catholic. Office: 15624 S Central Ave Oak Forest IL 60452

NOVEY, RIVA, psychiatrist, psychoanalyst; b. Selma, Ala., Jan. 25, 1915; d. Meyer Simon and Julia (Isaacs) London; A.B., Goucher Coll., 1935; M.S.S., Smith Coll., 1938; M.D., U. Md., 1954; m. Samuel Novey, 1939 (dec. 1967); m. 2d, Jacob Glushakow, Dec. 31, 1975. Psychiat. social worker, 1938-49; chief social worker, U. Md. Psychiat. Inst., 1945-49; intern Union Meml. Hosp., Balt., 1954-55; psychiat. resident Sheppard and Enoch Pratt Hosp., Towson, Md., 1955-57, Springfield Hosp., Sykesville, Md., 1957-59; candidate Washington Psychoanalytic Inst., 1957-62, tng. and supervising analyst, 1967—; pvt. practice medicine, specializing in psychiatry and psychoanalysis, Balt., 1962—; cons. Johns Hopkins U. Counselling and Psychiat. Services; asst. prof. psychiatry Johns Hopkins U. Sch. Medicine, 1967—, asst. prof. psychology Homewood campus, 1975—. Diplomate Am. Bd. Psychiatry and Neurology. Fellow Am. Psychiat. Assn., Am. Orthopsychiat. Assn. (life); mem. Am., Internat. psychoanalytic assns., Phi Beta Kappa. Democrat. Editor: The Second Look, the Reconstruction of Personal History in Psychiatry and Psychoanalysis (Samuel Novey), 1968. Contbr. articles to med. and psychoanalytic jours. Home: 1920 South Rd Baltimore MD 21209 Office: Northway Apts #103 3700 N Charles St Baltimore MD 21218

NOVIASKY, ATSUKO, physician; b. Tokyo, Oct. 24, 1932; d. Hirotake and Chiyoko (Sasagawa) Arai; M.D., Nihon U., 1960; postgrad. N.Y. Polyclinic Med. Sch., 1963, St. Joseph's Hosp., Ft. Wayne, Ind., 1963-66; m. Joseph E. Noviasky, May 28, 1961; children—John A., Jacqueline A. Resident, Rochester Gen. Hosp., 1967-70; asso. pathologist, asst. dir. Genessee County Lab., Batavia, N.Y., 1970-73; asst. dir., asst. pathologist Utica Psychiat. Lab., 1973-76; dir., pathologist Utica-Marcy Psychiat. Center Lab., 1976—; cons. in field. Served with USAR, 1978—. Recipient Continuing Edn. award Oneida County Med. Assn., AMA award. Mem. Coll. Am. Pathologists (fellow), Med. Soc. State N.Y., Med. Soc. County of Oneida. Home: 1 Bradford Ln Whitesboro NY 13492 Office: 1213 Court St Utica NY 13502

NOVICKI, MARGARET ANN, editor; b. New Haven, May 15, 1955; d. Thaddeus Joseph and Martha Antoinette (Rafalowski) N.; B.S. in Fgn. Service, Georgetown U., 1977; M.A. in Internat. Affairs, Columbia U., 1979; m. Nobumasa Arakawa, Sept. 6, 1980. Dir., Africa Policy Info. Center, 1979—; asso. editor African Update sect. Africa Report mag., 1979—, editorial asst., 1979-80; asst. editor Africa Report, dir. Africa Policy Info. Center, African-Am. Inst., N.Y.C., 1980—. Bd. dirs. UN Assn. N.Y., 1979. Contbr. articles to Ency. Americana Ann., New Book of Knowledge, English Jour., Africa Report. Home: 40 E 21st St 8th Floor New York NY 10010 Office: 833 United Nations Plaza New York NY 10017

NOVINA, TRUDI (MRS. CHARLES E. COAKLEY), fibers and plastics co. ofcl.; b. Bklyn., Dec. 8; d. Isidor and Lilian (Greenberg) Novina; B.A., Bklyn. Coll., 1950; M.B.A., Fordham U., 1981; m. Leo H. Papazian, June 24, 1956 (dec. 1964); children—Lyssa D., Gregory M.; m. 2d, Charles E. Coakley, Apr. 27, 1968. Reporter, N.Y. World Telegram & Sun, N.Y.C., 1950-54, asst. woman's editor, 1954-57, home furnishings editor, 1957-60; free-lance writer, 1960-64; account exec., dir. home fashions publicity Donald Degnan Assos., N.Y.C., 1964-69; mgr. publicity Allied Fibers & Plastics Co., Allied Corp., N.Y.C., 1969—. Mem. Am. Inst. Interior Designers, Nat. Home Fashions League (chpt. v.p. 1972-73), Fashion Group. Club: Overseas Press (N.Y.C.). Editor: House and Garden Decorating Book, 1965. Contbr. articles to various mags. Home: 34 W 89th St New York NY 10024 Office: 1411 Broadway New York NY 10018

NOVITCH, CLARA MARGARET, acct.; b. New Haven, Mar. 30, 1937; d. Albert Walter and Helen M. (Torquato) Gaudette; student Felt & Tarrant Bus. Sch., 1955, IBM Computer Sch., 1956, Asbury Park Bus. Coll., 1969; m. Leonard Novitch, Apr. 2, 1975; children—Henry Chelston, Steven Chelston, Richard Chelston, Daniel Chelston, John Chelston, Joseph Chelston. With Schiffenhaus Bros., Newark, 1955-56, Cheque Real Estate, Freehold, N.J., 1966, Central Real Estate, Howell, N.J., 1966, Jay Kaplan Real Estate, Lakewood, N.J., 1966-72, McDonald Realty, Toms River, N.J., 1978—, Law Firm Russo & Courtney, Toms River, N.J., 1972-73; legis. aide State Sen. John F. Russo, 1973-74; with Novitronics Data Inc., Point Pleasant, N.J., 1974—; acct., partner L. Novitch & Co., Pt. Pleasant, 1973—. Exec. bd. mem. Emma Havens Young Sch., Brick Town (N.J.) PTA, 1977—, treas. for Williamsburg com., 1979—; Dem. committeewoman Dist. 8, Brick Town, 1977—. Lic. real estate agt., N.J., 1966—: lic. pub. acct., N.J. Mem. Nat. Assn. Pub. Accts., N.J. Assn. Pub. Accts., Nat. Assn. Women Accts., N.J. Assn. Women Accts., Nat. Assn. Female Execs. Roman Catholic. Club: Network (dir. 1979—). State editor, Tastic mag., 1977. Home: 64 Havens Dr Brick Town NJ 08723 Office: 600 Arnold Ave Point Pleasant Beach NJ 08742

NOWAK, EMMY, engring. co. exec.; b. Hamburg, Germany, Nov. 15, 1923; d. Erwin and Elfriede (Muller) Stamm; grad. Bridgeport (Conn.) Hosp. Sch. Nursing, 1945; m. Bernard Nowak, Feb. 12, 1966; 1 son, Richard. Asst. head nurse Bridgeport Hosp., 1945-55; gen. mgr., pres. Alloy Engring. Co., Inc., Bridgeport, Conn., 1958—. Mem. Bridgeport C. of C. (dir.) Club: Brooklawn Country. Home: 32 Palmer Pl Easton CT 06612 Office: 304 Seaview Ave Bridgeport CT 06607

NOWELL, LUCILLE (LUCY) TERRY, costume designer, educator; b. Leeds, Ala., Sept. 24, 1951; d. Thomas Daniel and Martha Dowdy (Thomason) Terry; B.A., U. Ala., 1972, M.A. (Grad. Council fellow), 1974; postgrad., U. New Orleans, 1982—; m. Thomas Ruffin Nowell, May 4, 1974; 1 dau., Jessica Marian. Guest artist U. Montevallo (Ala.), 1974-76; asst. prof. dramatic arts Lynchburg (Va.) Coll., 1976—. Sec. women's rights com. LWV, Lynchburg, 1981. Mem. Southeastern Theatre Conf. (adv. bd. dirs. 1981—), U.S. Inst. for Theatre Tech. (dir. 1982—). Mem. Disciples of Christ Ch. Costumer designer for 23 plays and mus. in ednl. theatre, 1974—. Home: 7108 Richland Dr Lynchburg VA 24502 Office: Dramatic Arts Lynchburg Coll Lynchburg VA 24501

NOWICKI, MARILYN FRANCES, veterinarian; b. Stambaugh, Mich., Oct. 4, 1953; d. Frank Anthony and Leona Ann (Dedo) Nowicki; B.S., Mich. State U., 1974, D.V.M., 1976. Asso. veterinarian Curley Animal Clinic, Lapeer, Mich., 1976-77; mgr., asso. veterinarian Zeeb Animal Hosp., Lansing, Mich., 1977-79, Haslett Animal Hosps., Lansing, 1977-79; veterinarian Biscayne Animal Hosp., Miami, Fla., 1979-80; owner veterinarian Animal Care Animal Hosp., North Dade and Davie, Fla., 1980—, also Animal Care Mobile Veterinary Clinic of Broward and Dade, Miami, Animal Care Animal Hosp. Mem. AVMA, South Fla. Vet. Med. Assn., North Dade C. of C. Office: 7395 Davie Rd Extension Hollywood FL 33024

NOWICKI, SUSAN ANN, profl. assn. exec.; b. Detroit, Sept. 30, 1945; d. Carl Louis and Mary Louise (Waitz) N.; A.A., Highland Park Coll., 1967; B.S., Mich. State U., 1974. Writer communications div. United Dairy Industry Assn., Rosemont, Ill., 1975-78; asst. dir. dept. communications Am. Acad. Orthopaedic Surgeons, Chgo., 1978—, editor bull., 1978—. Mem. Public Relations Soc. Am., Women in Communications (dir. Chgo. chpt. 1981-82, treas. 1981-82, co-chmn. Coll. Career Conf. 1981, fund raising v.p. 1982-83), Internat. Assn. Bus. Communicators. Democrat. Presbyterian. Home: 720 Gordon Terr Apt 18-J Chicago IL 60613 Office: Am Acad Orthopaedic Surgeons Suite 1500 444 N Michigan Ave Chicago IL 60611

NOXON, MARGARET WALTERS (MRS. HERBERT RICHARDS NOXON), community vol.; b. Detroit, Dec. 16, 1903; d. George Alexander and Ethelwyn (Taylor) Walters; grad., Liggett Sch. for Girls, Det., 1922; life teaching certificate Wayne State U., 1925; student Columbia Tchrs. Coll., 1939-40; m. Herbert Richards Noxon, July 15, 1926 (dec. Aug. 4, 1971). Bd. dirs. Coll. Club, Detroit, 1925-30; mem. Salvation Army Aux., Detroit, 1926—; mem. Coll. Club, Summit N.J., 1941—; historian D.A.R., N.Y.C., 1943-46, vice regent, 1946-49; dir. New Eng., Women, 1961-64; dir. Woodycrest-Five Points Child Care, 1961-77; bd. dirs. ARC, Summit, N.J., service com. chmn. uniforms and insignias, 1943-45; v.p. N.Y. Infirmary Aux., N.Y.C., 1948-58, bd. dirs., 1959-80. Recipient award for meritorious personal service ARC, 1945. Mem. Nat. Inst. Social Scis., Grand Jury Assn. N.Y. County, D.A.R. (dir. 1950-70), St. David's Soc. State N.Y., English-Speaking Union, Daus. Am. Colonists, AAUW, Southampton Colonial Soc., Nat. Woman's Farm and Garden Assn. (dir. met. br. 1975—, dir. N.Y. State div. 1978-80, mem. nat. council 1978-80), Alpha Sigma Tau. Republican. Presbyterian. Clubs: Southampton (N.Y.) Bath and Tennis, City Gardens (dir. 1963-68, mem. adv. com. 1968-74, dir. 1974-80, adv. bd. 1980—), York (bd. govs. 1965-66, 73-77), Barnard (trustee 1979-81), Sorosis (v.p. 1979-81), Regency Whist (N.Y.C.). Home: 1100 Madison Ave New York NY 10028

NUDELMAN, JUDI LOIS, mfg. co. exec.; b. Chgo., Feb. 6, 1940; d. Hyman and Sally (Saltzberg) Weiss; B.S., Northwestern U., 1960; m. Harvey Banet Nudelman, June 23, 1968; children—Scott Perry, Lee Drew. Speech therapist, Highland Park, Ill., 1960; systems engr. IBM Corp., Chgo. and Houston, 1961-77, adv. mktg. rep., Houston, 1978—; data processing coordinator Frost Nat. Bank, San Antonio, 1977-78. Recipient Mktg. award IBM Corp., 1979. Mem. Nat. Assn. Female Execs., Assn. Women in Sci. (treas. 1977). Home: 4062 Leeshire St Houston TX 77025 Office: IBM Corp 1 Riverway Houston TX 77056

NUDGE, MARJORIE SNYDER, editor, photojournalist; b. Reading, Pa., July 19, 1938; d. Robert Richardson and Mary Josephine (Lessig) Snyder; student Penn State U., 1956-57, Indiana U. Pa., 1958; B.A. in Liberal Studies, U. Del., 1976; m. Joseph Allen Nudge, June 8, 1958; children—Laurilei Renee Paoli, Kimberly Jo, Joseph Robert, Joshua Daniel. Editor Tri-State Trade Exchange, Del., Md. and Pa., 1978-79, Del. Humanities Forum, Wilmington, 1979-80; freelance photojournalist, 1970—; feature editor Newark (Del.) Post, 1980—; freelance pub. relations and journalistic communications cons., 1970—; publicity dir., communications specialist Compleat Communications, 1980; tchr. Del. schs., 1976-80. Coordinator Public TV Ann. Auction, 1976; v.p. Kimberly Internat., 1980. Recipient Literary Grant U. Del., 1975. Mem. Del. Press Women, Nat. Fedn. Press Women, Kappa Delta (alumni assn. Beta Theta chpt.). Republican. Clubs: Newark Republican Women's, Christian Women's (exec. bd. 1970-74) (Newark). Home and Office: 238 Penn Wood Dr Newark DE 19713

NUGARIS, JUDITH LEE JONES, psychotherapist; b. Terre Haute, Ind., Sept. 2, 1937; d. Stanley Calvert and Naomi Mae (Simpson) Jones; B.A., No. Ill. U., 1960; M.S.W., U. Denver, 1964; m. Charles Joseph Nugaris, June 1964 (div. 1967). Social worker U. Colo. Med. Center, Denver, 1966-73, Arapahoe Mental Health Center, Englewood, Colo., 1973-75; asso. Denver Psychotherapy Assos., 1972—; a founder, dir. Reality Therapy Assos. Colo., Inc., Colorado Springs, 1978—; social worker Luth. Service Soc., Denver, 1960-62; pvt. practice psychotherapy, Denver, 1972—. Bd. dirs. Big Sisters Colo., 1976-81, v.p., 1979-80; Mem. NOW (v.p. S. Met. Denver 1979-80), Nat. Assn. Social Workers (dir.). Democrat. Episcopalian. Contbr. chpt.: What Are You Doing? How People Are Helped through Reality Therapy, 1980. Office: 5590 E Yale Ave Denver CO 80222

NUGENT, CHRISTINE MURPHY, food co. sales analyst; b. Suffern, N.Y., Nov. 30, 1951; d. Thomas William and Kathleen Christina (Connors) Murphy; A.A., Edward Williams Coll., 1975; B.S., Fairleigh Dickinson U., 1978, M.B.A., 1982; m. William R. Nugent, Jan. 30, 1971. Adminstrv. asst. to dir. product mgmt. Thomas J. Lipton, Inc., Englewood Cliffs, N.J., 1972-75, adminstrv. asst. to exec. v.p. mktg., 1975-79, consumer promotions adminstr., 1979, sales promotion analyst, 1979—. Republican. Roman Catholic. Office: Thomas J Lipton Inc 800 Sylvan Ave Englewood Cliffs NJ 07632

NUGENT, JANE ELLEN, health care exec.; b. Boston, Nov. 26, 1945; d. Charles Edward and Marjorie Elizabeth (Sloane) N.; B.A. in History, U. N.H., 1967; M.Ed. in Ednl. Research (NEASA Title IV fellow 1969-71), Northeastern U., 1971; M.B.A. (TRW Found. fellow 1975), Stanford U., 1977. Adminstrv. asst. to dir. office of planning and program coordination Commonwealth of Mass., Boston, 1968-69; research asst. Bd. Higher Edn., City U. N.Y., N.Y.C., 1971-72; fin. analyst and researcher McKinsey and Co., N.Y.C., 1973-75; sr. fin. analyst internat. fin. planning Baxter Travenol Labs., Deerfield, Ill., 1977—, market devel. mgr., 1978-79, dir. mktg. Cardiopulmonary Products div., 1979-81, dir. corp. devel., 1982—; cons. to small bus. Mem. Am. Mgmt. Assn., Assn. M.B.A. Execs., Stanford Alumni Assn. (dir. Chgo. chpt.), Assn. Corp. Growth, Chgo. Council Fgn. Relations, Women in Health Care. Home: One E Schiller St Chicago IL 60610 Office: One Baxter Pkwy Deerfield IL 60015 also Hayes Gate House Uxbridge Rd Hayes Middlesex UB4 0JN England

NUGENT, NELLE, theatrical producer; b. Jersey City, May 24, 1939; d. John Patrick and Evelyn Adelaide (Stern) N.; B.S., Skidmore Coll., 1960, H.H.D. (hon.), 1981; m. Jolyon Fox Stern, Apr. 7, 1982. Stage mgr. off-Broadway, N.Y.C., 1960-63, Broadway, 1964-69; v.p. prodn. services Theatre Now, Inc., N.Y.C., 1968-70; asso. mng. dir. Nederlander Orgn., N.Y.C., 1970-76; chmn. McCann and Nugent Prodns., Inc., N.Y.C., 1976—, producers of Dracula, The Elephant Man, Mornings at Seven, Home, Amadeus, Piaf, Rose, Nicholas Nickleby, The Dresser, Mass Appeal, Pilobolos. Voting mem. Blue Cross-Blue Shield; mem. bd. visitors Syracuse U.; bd. dirs. League N.Y. Theatres. Recipient Tony awards for Dracula, the Elephant Man, Mornings at Seven, Amadeus, Nicholas Nickleby; N.Y. Drama Critics award for The Elephant Man, Nicholas Nickleby; Drama Desk awards for Amadeus, The Elephant Man, Nicholas Nickleby; Los Angeles Critics awards; Entrepreneurial Woman of Yr. award, 1981. Office: 1501 Broadway New York NY 10036

NUMEROF, RITA ELLEN, psychotherapist, educator; b. Phila., Dec. 24, 1947; d. Paul and Claire Selma (Slachowitz) N.; B.A. magna cum laude, Syracuse U., 1969; M.S.S., Bryn Mawr Coll., 1971; Ph.D., 1979; m. Michael Norman Abrams, July 20, 1980. Psychol. cons., Pa. Dept. Health, 1972; acting dir. adolescent services, clin. supr. Harrisburg (Pa.) Hosp. Community Mental Health Center, 1972-75, dir. adolescent and children's services, 1975-76; pvt. psychotherapy practice, 1975—; asst. prof. orgn. behavior and mgmt., coordinator health care adminstrn. program LaSalle Coll., Phila., 1978-79; asst. prof. psychodynamic methods and group process Washington U., St. Louis, 1979—; adj. prof. Estes Park Inst., Englewood, Colo., 1980—; pres. Numerof & Assos., Inc., mgmt. cons., St. Louis, 1981—. NIMH grantee, 1969-71, 76; Joan Sall Rivitz fellow, 1977-79. Fellow Soc. Clin. Social Work; mem. Am. Orthopsychiat. Assn., Acad. Mgmt., Am. Hosp. Assn., Nat. Assn. Social Workers, Am. Psychol. Assn., Phi Beta Kappa, Psi Chi, Phi Kappa Phi. Jewish. Author: Accent on People, 1980; The Practice of Management for Health Care Professionals, 1982; contbr. articles to profl. jours. Home: 7031 Stanford Ave University City MO 63130 Office: Box 1196 Washington U St Louis MO 63130

NUMRICH, CAROL JEAN, univ. adminstr.; b. Aurora, Ill., July 29, 1934; d. Frederick and Jessie Belle (Knickerbocker) N.; B.A. in English, Calif. State U., Los Angeles, 1968, M.A. in Ednl. Psychology, 1982. Mem. adminstrv. staff Calif. State U., Los Angeles, 1961-66, 68—, dir. alumni, 1968-73, dir. univ. devel. and alumni, 1973—, mem. archival com., 1980—; pres. statewide alumni council Calif. State U. and Colls., 1977; bd. dirs. region VII, Council Advancement and Support Edn., 1979—. Bd. dirs., mem. exec. com. Solheim Home, Los Angeles, 1982—. Recipient alumni award merit Calif. State U., Los Angeles, 1981. Mem. Nat. Soc. Fund Raising Execs., Delta Theta Chi. Republican. Lutheran. Club: University (pres. 1979). Office: 5151 State University Dr Los Angeles CA 90032

NUNEZ, JOSEPHINE OROZCO, coll. ofcl.; b. San Antonio, Oct. 29, 1932; d. Joe M. and Juanita (Linares) Orozco; student St. Mary's U., 1969, Dyer Sch. Real Estate, 1969, Our Lady of the Lake U., 1976; m. Ruben R. Nunez, May 13, 1978; children—Pete, Michael Anthony, Mary Elizabeth Mazuca. With A.B. Frank Wholesale, San Antonio, 1951-55; sec. Fireman & Policeman Assn., San Antonio, 1961-62, Teamsters Local 657, San Antonio, 1962-65, Cath. Chancery Office, San Antonio, 1965-68; with St. Mary's U., San Antonio, 1968-71, exec. sec. Office Mex.-Am. Studies, also asst. coordinator new careers program, 1969-70; with Our Lady of the Lake U., San Antonio, 1971—, adminstrv. asst., 1978—; bookkeeper Title XX, Tex. Dept. Human Resources Project, 1978-81, adminstrv. asst., 1982—. Active Democratic Women of Bexar County, 1962-68, Our Lady of Pillar Christian Renewal Center, 1966-70; exec. dir. Addiction Research Commn., Our Lady of Mt. Carmel Hosp., Austin, 1972-73; treas. Archdiocesan Credit Union, 1975-76; bd. dirs. King William Assn., San Antonio, 1978—, treas., 1981—; mem. Our Lady of the Lake U. Non-Acad. Personnel Council, 1977-78, staff orgn., 1971—; active United Way. NIH grantee, 1971. Roman Catholic. Home: 325 Madison San Antonio TX 78204 Office: Worden Sch Social Service 411 SW 24th St Worden Sch San Antonio TX 78285

NUNEZ, LORENA KAY PRATT, savs. and loan exec.; b. Valparaiso, Ind., Mar. 7, 1941; d. Edward Carter and Marguerite (Krudup) Pratt; student Burroughs Systemic Banking Sch., Chgo., 1960, Savs. and Loan Inst., Cupertino, Calif., 1970-71; m. Moses Nunez, Dec. 1, 1961 (div. 1969); 1 dau., Deserie Alexandria. Note teller Wells Fargo Bank, Gilroy, Calif., 1961-62; supr. Salinas Valley Savs., Gilroy, 1962-66; with No. Calif. Savs., Palo Alto, Calif., 1969—, ops. officer, 1971-73, v.p., mgr., 1974—. Exec. dir. YMCA of Monterey, 1975-78. Recipient Service award Pacific Grove Unified Sch. Dist., 1976; Investment and Security award Loma Prieta Dist. 9, 1977; Service award YMCA, 1978; Top Hat award Monterey Peninsula, Calif. Bus. and Profl. Womens Club, 1981. Mem. Gen. Fedn. Women's Clubs, Pacific Grove C. of C. (exec. dir. 1974-78, service award 1977). Republican. Episcopalian. Office: No Calif Savs 170 Country Club Gate Pacific Grove CA 93950

NUNLEY, JOYCE ELAINE NEAL, fin. exec.; b. Dayton, Tenn., Mar. 17, 1947; d. John Thomas and Cora Geneva (Collins) Neal; student Career Tng. Inst., 1969-71, Chattanooga State Tech. Inst., 1973-75; m. Sherman Allen Nunley, Nov. 15, 1975. Sec. to plant engr. Oster Mfg. Co., Dayton, Tenn., 1966-68; adminstrv. sec. Tenn. Food Products, Dayton, 1968-70; bookkeeper Sequatchie Valley Equipment Co., Dunlap, Tenn., 1970-72; exec. sec. Allied Paper Co., Chattanooga, 1972-74; fin. adminstr., sec. Progress for People, human resource agy., Dunlap, Tenn., 1974—; exec. sec. Fletcher Trucking Co., Dunlap; dir. Energy Crisis Assistance Program. Mem. Tenn. Assn. Community Action. Republican. Clubs: Order Rainbow Girls. Office: PO Box 62 Dunlap TN 37327

NUNLEY, LORENE WEDDINGTON, mental retardation habilitation specialist; b. Sayersville, Ky.; d. Crit and Ella (Stanley) Weddington; B.S. in Vocat. Home Econs., Tex. Woman's U., 1970; postgrad. U. Cin., 1977—; children—Stephen Leonard, Angela Kaye. High Sch. tchr., Aubrey (Tex.) Ind. Sch. Dist., 1974-75; tchr. Clermont County (Ohio) High Schs., 1975, 76; mental retardation habilitation specialist Clerco Inc., Owensville, Ohio, 1977—. Mem. Profl. Assn. Retardation. Mem. Unity Ch. Office: Clerco Inc PO Box 331 Owensville OH 45160

NUOVO, BETTY ANNE, lawyer; b. Englewood, N.J., Dec. 10, 1931; d. Charles H. and Edna Z. (Ruch) Stagg; student East Stroudsburg (Pa.) State Tchrs. Coll., 1949-50; B.S.Ed., Bucknell U., 1953; m. Victor L. Nuovo, June 7, 1953; children—Victor, Thomas. Tchr., Mich., 1953-54, N.Y., 1954-57; law clk. firm Langrock Sperry Parker & Stahl, Middlebury, Vt., 1968-73, William K. Sessions, Middlebury, 1974; admitted to Vt. bar, 1974; individual practice law, Middlebury, 1974—. Mem. Vt. Ho. of Reps., 1981-82; chmn. Middlebury Planning Commn., 1978-80; mem. Addison County Regional Planning Commn., 1975-78, exec. bd., 1976-78; bd. dirs. Addison County Econ. Devel. Corp., 1976-79; mem. state bd. Vt. Democratic Com., 1977—; mem. Addison County Dem. Com., 1971—, chmn., 1977-81; bd. dirs. Addison County Community Action Group. Mem. Vt. Bar Assn., Addison County Bar Assn., Addison County C. of C. (dir. 1977-80, treas. 1979-80), LWV (chpt. pres. 1968, state bd.), Bus. and Profl. Women. Congregationalist. Home: RD 1 Middlebury VT 05753 Office: PO Box 347 Middlebury VT 05753

NURSE, CROSBY LLEWELLE GRANT (MRS. WILLIAM NURSE), nurse; b. Glace Bay, N.S., Can., Apr. 23, 1928; d. Walter Cyril and Llewelle Isette (Estwick) Grant; R.N., New Waterford (N.S.) Gen. Hosp., 1949; B.A., St. Francis Xavier U., Sydney, N.S., 1976; B.Adminstrn. in Health Services, Can. Sch. Mgmt. and Northland Open U., Toronto; m. William Nurse, Nov. 27, 1952; children—Charlotte (Mrs. George Brown), David. Staff nurse, relief supr. New Waterford Gen. Hosp., 1949-50, staff nurse, 1951-53; staff nurse, charge nurse Univ. Heights Hosp., Bronx, N.Y., 1950-51; mem. staff St. Rita Hosp., Sydney, 1953—, dir. nursing service, 1967-78, supr. nursing service and staff devel., 1978—. Mem. Am. Soc. Hosp. Nursing Service Adminstrs., Registered Nurses Assn. N.S. Home: Grand Lake Rd Rural Route 4 Site 8 Box 2 Sydney NS B1P 6G6 Canada Office: 409 King's Rd Sydney NS B1S 1B4 Canada

NURSS, JOANNE RUTH, educator; b. Peoria, Ill., Sept. 13, 1937; d. Edwin Dean and Grace Agnes (Thompson) N.; B.A., Beloit (Wis.) Coll., 1958; M.A., Columbia U. Tchrs. Coll., 1962; Ph.D., Columbia U., 1966. Tchr., Denver pub. schs., 1958-63; asst. prof. edn. and psychology Emory U., 1967-69; mem. faculty Ga. State U., Atlanta, 1969—, prof. early childhood edn., 1977—, chmn. dept., 1969-74, asso. dean acad. programs Coll. Edn., 1974-77. Author: Metropolitan Readiness Tests, 1976; Handbook of Skill Development Activities, 1977. Address: Dept of Childhood Edn Ga State Univ University Plaza Atlanta GA 30303 *

NURU, NJERI, univ. dean; b. Richmond, Va., May 16, 1947; d. Ira A. and Marinda (Morgan) Kyles; B.A., Howard U., 1969, M.A., 1971; Ph.D., U. Md., 1975; children—Amani, Aja. Clin. audiologist, coordinator audiology clinic St. Elizabeth's Hosp., Washington, 1971-76; cons. to med. dir. U.S. Consumer Product Safety Commn., Washington, 1976;

asst. prof., clin. supr. dept. communication arts and scis. Howard U., Washington, 1977-78, asso. prof. dept. communication arts and scis., asso. dean Sch. Communications, 1979—; asso. prof. dept. communication scis. U. D.C., Washington, 1977-78; cons. Contract Research Corp., Boston, 1976-78, Sensory Disorders Unit, Indian Health Service, HEW, Albuquerque, 1976-78, NIH, Nat. Inst. Neurol. and Communicative Disorders and Stroke, Bethesda, Md., 1979; project dir. Career Info. for Students of Ethnic Minority Groups, HEW, 1977-78, Noise Outreach Info. System and Evaluation, EPA, 1977-78, others; dir. urban and ethnic program Am. Speech and Hearing Assn.; dir. spl. edn. project Council of Chief State Sch. Officers, Washington, 1978-79; guest lectr. dept. hearing and speech sci. U. Md., College Park, 1974-76; clin. research asst., instr. Howard U., Washington, 1970-71; clin. trainee Easter Seal Treatment Center for Crippled Children and Adults, Rockville, Md., 1971; adv. council Howard U. Sch. Communications, 1975-79; nat. adv. bd. Contract Research Corp., 1976-77; communications coordinator Nationhouse Positive Action Center, 1978-81, editor Nation Times, 1979-81. Outstanding Woman Doctoral Grad., U. Md., 1976; John Hay Whitney fellow, 1969-71. Fellow Am. Speech-Lang.-Hearing Assn. (mem. clin. certification bd. 1973-76), Acoustical Soc. Am., Amnesty Internat., D.C. Speech and Hearing Assn., Md. Speech and Hearing Assn., Am. Inst. Physics, Nat. Black Assn. for Speech Lang. and Hearing (bd. dirs. 1978-80, exec. dir. 1980-82), Nat. Assn. Personnel Workers, Transafrica. Contbr. articles to profl. jours.; poet. Home: 1330 Geranium St NW Washington DC 20012 Office: Howard Univ Sch Communications Washington DC 20059

NUSBAUM, ADELE HELEN, govt. ofcl.; b. Toronto, Ont., Can., Apr. 26, 1918; d. Louis J. and Edith Nusbaum; B.A. magna cum laude, U. Rochester (N.Y.), 1940; M.A., Columbia U., 1942; postgrad. Am. U., 1971. Info. specialist War Food Adminstn., 1942-45; successively staff asso. C.M. Bayer Public Relations, Sally Dickson Assos., United Jewish Appeal, N.Y.C., 1945-55; dir. public relations United Jewish Fedn., Pitts., 1955-64, B'nai B'rith Women, Washington, 1964-68; communications cons. urban affairs, 1968-69; sr. writer div. physician manpower NIH, Washington, 1969-71, dir. fed. women's program, 1971-74; program dir. communications devel. Nat. Cancer Inst., 1974—. Mem. Public Relations Soc. Am., Nat. Assn. Govt. Communicators (sec.), Am. Soc. Public Adminstrn., Am. Newspaper Women's Club, Phi Beta Kappa. Home: 2829 Connecticut Ave NW Washington DC 20008 Office: 8300 Colesville Rd Silver Spring MD 20910

NUSS, CAROL ANN, real estate exec.; b. Cleve., May 7, 1951; d. Walter and Mary (Martinko) N.; A.A. in English, Santa Ana Coll., 1975; grad. Realtors Inst. Calif., 1981. Exec. sec., mgr. Cal-West Engring. and Constrn., Santa Ana, Calif., 1972-75; mgr. Tarbell Realtors, Tustin, Calif., 1975-80; owner, mgr. Redhill Realty, Tustin, 1980—; mktg. cons. small bus.; cons. Garden Habitats, Costa Mesa, Calif.; lectr. on sales motivation; free lance writer. Mem. East Orange County Investments, Irvine Bd. Realtors (building com.), Nat. Assn. Female Execs. Democrat. Roman Catholic. Home: 690 Ranchroad Dr Orange CA 92669 Office: 18002 Irvine St Tustin CA 92680

NUSSBAUM, DIANE RESNICK, clin. psychologist; b. Phila., July 22, 1931; d. Michael Edward and Celia (Richter) Resnick; student Hebrew edn. Gratz Coll., 1948; student Temple U., 1963-65, Beaver Coll., 1970; B. Edn., Antioch Coll., 1971, M.Ed., 1974; m. Milton Nussbaum, Oct. 15, 1950; children—Merle, Freddie, Nina. Instr., mem. credential com. Phila. Center of Antioch Coll., Yellow Springs, Ohio, 1969-71; tchr. Phila. Sch. Dist., 1967-71, guidance counselor, 1976—; founder, coordinator, counselor Continuing Edn. for Women Program, Montgomery County Community Coll., 1974-77; clin. psychologist Center for Creative Devel., Phila., 1979-81; clin. psychologist, dir. Center for Personal Potential, Phila., 1981—; adj. instr. Marywood Coll. Women Reentering Coll. and Work Force grantee; lic. psychologist, Pa. Mem. Am. Psychol. Assn., Am. Counselors Assn., Pa. Personnel and Guidance Assn., Personnel and Guidance Assn. Greater Phila. Republican. Jewish. Home: 7809 Louise Ln Philadelphia PA 19118 Office: 4125 Daisy Ln Plymouth Meeting PA 19462

NUSSDORF, GERRIE E., psychologist; b. Bklyn., Feb. 2, 1944; d. Oscar and Edith (Posner) N.; Ph.D. in Psychology, Fordham U., 1975; cert. psychoanalysis and psychotherapy Postgrad. Center for Mental Health, 1981. Computer programmer, 1966-69; psychology intern Fairfield Hills Hosp., Newtown, Conn., 1972-73; staff psychologist Nyack (N.Y.) Cons. Center, 1975-78; asso. psychologist Rockland Psychiat. Center, Orangeburg, N.Y., 1978-80; therapist, tng. candidate adult program Postgrad. Center Mental Health, N.Y.C., 1977-81; prin. psychologist Manhattan Psychiat. Center, N.Y.C., 1980—; pvt. practice, N.Y.C., 1981—; adj. instr. psychology Marymount Manhattan Coll., 1974; tri-state coordinator Assn. Women in Psychology, 1975, 76. NDEA Title IV teaching fellow, 1969-72; Regents scholar, 1961-65. Mem. Am. Psychol. Assn., Assn. Women in Psychology, Eastern Psychol. Assn., Postgrad. Center Mental Health Psychoanalytic Soc., Austin Healey Club Am., Sports Car Club Am. Home: 305 W 13th St New York NY 10014 Office: Dept Psychology Manhattan Psychiatric Center Wards Island New York NY 10035

NUTLEY, GRACE STUART (MRS. CYRIL ARTHUR NUTLEY), educator; b. Alameda, Calif.; d. Samuel Vernon and Marie Belle (Eubank) Stuart; B.E., U. Wash. 1922; M.A., N.Y. U., 1938, Ph.D., 1945; m. Cyril Arthur Nutley, Aug. 22, 1925; 1 dau., Jean Margaretta (Mrs. Dudley Ives Ferris). Asso. prof. English, Pratt Inst., 1936-46, U. State N.Y., 1938-46; instr. English, N.Y. U., 1944-46; asso. prof. English, Bklyn. Coll., 1946—; lectr. adult edn. YWCA, Bklyn., 1935-50, Federated Women's Clubs, 1952—, N.Y. Times & Herald Tribune Lecture Bur., 1952-58, Friends of UN, 1957—; Smith-Mundt prof. English, State Dept., Philippines, 1950-52; Fulbright lectr. Annamalai U., India, 1959-61; tchr. English, Japan, Taiwan, Manila, 1967. Fulbright lecture grantee 1959-61, 67-68, Am. Specialist grantee, 1964, 67, 68. Fellow Am. Studies Assn.; mem. Mem. Friendly Vistors (pres. 1956-59), AAUW (chmn. art com. 1953-55, dir. 1954-57). N.Y. Coll. English Assn. (pres. 1954-55, dir. 1955-59), Pan Pacific S.E. Asia Women's Assn. (nat. pres. 1963-67, internat. v.p. 1968-75, pres. 1975-78), Asia Soc. (mem. Burma council 1962-72). AAUP, Modern Lang. Assn., Coll. English Assn. (nat. chmn. com. on acad. status of women 1968-72), Nat. Council Tchrs. English, Coll. Conf. Composition and Communication, Nat. Council Women, Assn. Higher Edn., Adult Edn. Assn. U.S.A., Am. Acad. Polit. and Social Sci., UN Assn. U.S.A. (pres. N.W. Maricopa County chpt. 1970—, pres. Ariz. div. 1972—), Internat. Platform Assn., Kappa Delta, Mortar Bd., Pi Lambda Theta (pres. N.Y. chpt. 1955-57, dir. 1957-59). Clubs: Foreign Service; Pilot (pres. N.Y. 1955-56, dist. gov. 1958-59). Contbr. articles to profl. jours. Home: 9407 109th Dr Sun City AZ 85351

NUTT, BETTY JAMES VAN METER, crime prevention cons.; b. Hodgenville, Ky., Nov. 22, 1930; d. John James Van Meter and Mary James (McConnell) Van Meter Harper; student Transylvania U., 1948-51, U. Ky., 1951-52; now student Iowa Central Community Coll.; Tex. Crime Prevention Inst., S.W. Tex. U., 1980; m. Van Winston Nutt, Oct. 1, 1955 (dec. Jan. 1981); children—Kathleen Louise, Van Winston, Rose Marie and Robert Lee (twins). Civilian employee Dept. Army, Ft. Knox, Ky., 1951-56; public relations sec. Morningside Coll., Sioux City, Iowa, 1967-68; Area 4 staff cons. Iowa Crime Prevention Coalition, Dept Public Safety, Des Moines, 1980-81. Chmn. public relations com. Sioux Trails council Girl Scouts U.S.A.; publicity chmn. YWCA; pres./coordinator Siouxland Crime Prevention Coalition, 1978-80; sec. Gateway Coalition, 1977-80; committeewoman Precinct 33, Woodbury County Democratic Com., 1976-79; mem. CWF Commn., Christian Ch. in the Upper Midwest. Mem. Internat. Soc. Crime Prevention Practitioners, Tex. Crime Prevention Assn., Iowa Fedn. Womens Clubs (chmn. community concerns div.), Woodbury County Geneal. Soc., Christian Women's Fellowship (pres.). Mem. Christian Ch. (Disciples of Christ). Clubs: Sioux City Woman's (pres. 1976-78), Lit. Outlook (pres.), Order of Eastern Star (past matron). Office: 1414 N 10th St Fort Dodge IA 50501

NUTTELMAN, DORIS LOUISE, nursing educator, cons.; b. Williamsburg, Mass., Apr. 20, 1930; d. Ernest Henry and Ruth Katherine (Tetro) Graves; R.N., Lynn Hosp. Sch. Nursing, 1968; B.S., Springfield Coll., 1971; M.A.T., U. Mass., 1973, M.S., 1975; postgrad. Case Western Res. U., 1977; m. David A. Nuttelman, May 5, 1951; children—Melissa Ann, Seth David. Staff, Smith Coll. Health Service, Northampton, 1951-52, 66-68; pvt. nursing service, Northampton, 1968-70; instr., Holyoke Community Coll., 1971-74; dir. div. nursing Am. Internat. Coll., 1969-77; research asst. Univ. Hosps., Cleve., 1978; chmn. dept. nursing Colby Sawyer Coll., New London, N.H., 1980—. Bd. dirs. Hampshire Regional YMCA, 1971-77. Mem. Am. Nurses Assn., Mass. Nurses Assn., N.H. Nurses Assn., Am. Assn. Nurse Anesthetists, Am. Public Health Assn., Nurses Coalition for Action in Politics, Sigma Theta Tau, Beta Zeta. Contbr. articles to profl. jours. Home: 331 Burts Pit Rd Northampton MA 01060

NYCHIS, AMELIA J. BOTSARIS, coll. adminstr.; b. Sharon, Pa., Feb. 9, 1931 d. John M. and Smaragda G. (Moscovitis) Botsaris; B.A., Chatham Coll., 1953; M.A., Cornell U., 1957; m. Peter V. Nychis, Aug. 16, 1969; children—Panetha, Caylee. Asst., Cornell U. 1953-55, head resident 1956-57; asst. dean, registrar, dir. fin. aid Chatham Coll., 1957-69; fin. aid cons. Wheelock Coll. 1970; dir. fin. aid and student employment Wellesley Coll. 1970—; cons. HEW; mem. various coms. Coll. Scholarship Service. Formerly active Women's Community League, Weston, Mass., Weston PTO; trustee Chatham Coll., Mt. Ida Coll. Mem. Mass. Assn. Student Fin. Aid Adminstrs. (pres. 1976-78), Nat. Assn. Student Fin. Aid Adminstrs., U.S. Nat. Student Assn. (v.p. 1953-54), Western Pa. Scholarship Assn. Allegheny County Scholarship Assn., Fin. Aid Assn. Ind. Womens Colls., Pitts. Area Fin. Aid Officers Assn., Eastern Assn. Fin. Aid Adminstrs. Home: 17 Apple Crest Rd Weston MA 02193

NYCUM, SUSAN HUBBELL, lawyer; B.A., Ohio Wesleyan U., 1956; J.D., Duquesne U., 1960. Admitted to Pa. bar, 1962, Calif. bar, 1974, U.S. Supreme Ct. bar, 1967; individual practice law, Pitts., 1962-65; dir. computerized research systems for lawyers U. Pitts./Aspen Systems Corp., Pitts., 1965-68; mgr. ops. and user services Carnegie Mellon U. Computer Center, 1968-69; dir. Stanford U. Computer Center, 1969-72; law and computer fellow Stanford U. Law Sch., 1972-73; cons. computers and law, San Francisco, 1973-74; asso. firm MacLeod Fuller Muir & Godwin, Los Altos, Calif., 1974-75; partner firm Chickering & Gregory, practicing gen. bus. law with emphasis on computers, San Francisco, 1975-80; partner firm Gaston Snow & Ely Bartlett, Boston, Palo Alto, Miami, N.Y.C. and Washington, 1980—; co-prin. investigator study on computer abuse NSF, 1972—; mem. adv. bd. for math. and computer sci. NSF; area dir. all law related session Nat. Computer Confs., 1975, 78, 80, 81; lectr. Practising Law Inst., 1975—; mem. panel on transborder data flow Am. Fedn. Info. Processing Socs., 1979-80; chmn. Office Tech. Assessment Task Force on Nat. Info. Systems, 1979-80. Chmn. evening div. Jr. League Palo Alto (Calif.), 1975-76; mem. Town of Portola Valley (Calif.) Open Space Acquisition Com., 1977. Mem. Am. Bar Assn. (chmn. sect. sci. and tech. 1979-80), Internat. Bar Assn., Assn. Computing Machinery (chmn. standing com. legal issues 1975—, mem.-at-large council 1976—, nat. lectr. 1977—), Computer law Assn. (dir. 1975—), Calif. State Bar Assn. (chmn. com. law and computers 1977-78, founder and 1st chmn. sect. econs. of law 1978-79), EDUCOM (trustee 1978—), Nat. Conf. Lawyers and Scientists, Peninsula Profl. Women's Network, DAR, Mortar Bd., Phi Beta Kappa, Delta Sigma Rho, Pi Sigma Alpha, Pi Delta Epsilon. Author: Your Computer and the Law, 1975; Forms for Data Processing Contracts, 1981; Protection of Proprietary Interests in Computer Software, 1981; contbr. articles to profl. jours. Office: 2 Palo Alto Sq Palo Alto CA 94304

NYE, MIRIAM MAURINE BAKER, writer; b. Castana, Iowa, June 14, 1918; d. Horace Boies and Hazel Dean (Waples) Hawthorn; B.A., Morningside Coll., 1939, postgrad., 1957-58; postgrad. U. Ariz., 1973, U. S.D., 1975-77, New Coll., U. Edinburgh (Scotland), 1974; m. Carl E. Baker, June 21, 1941 (dec. 1970); children—Kent Alfred, Dale Hawthorn; m. 2d, John Arthur Nye, Dec. 25, 1973. Tchr. jr. high sch., Rock Falls, Ill., 1939-41, Moville (Iowa) Community Sch., 1957-62, Woodbury Central Community Sch., Climbing Hill, Iowa, 1962-64; homemaking columnist Sioux City (Iowa) Jour.'s Farm Weekly, 1953-81; author: Recipes and Ideas From the Kitchen Window, 1973; But I Never Thought He'd Die: Practical Help for Widows, 1978; speaker, Iowa, Nebr., Minn., S.D. Counselor, Iowa State U., 1972—; county adv. Iowa Children's and Family Services, 1980—; mem. public relations com. Farm Bur., Woodbury County, 1980—; lay del. Iowa United Meth. Conf., 1981—. Recipient Alumni award Morningside Coll., 1969, Service award Woodbury County Fair, 1969, Friend of Extension award Iowa State U., 1981. Mem. AAUW, Iowa Fedn. Women's Clubs (dist. creative writing chmn. 1978-80), Common Cause, Alpha Kappa Delta, Sigma Tau Delta. Methodist. Home and Office: Box 193 Route 2 Moville IA 51039

NYSTROM, IRENE ALSCHULER, psychologist; b. Sandy, Utah, Mar. 30, 1939; s. August and Irene N.; B.S., U. Utah, 1961; M.A., Stanford U., 1963; M.A., San Francisco State Coll., 1965; Ed.D., SUNY, Albany, 1973; postgrad. Harvard U., 1974; cert. psychology U. Oreg., 1979; m. Alfred Alschuler, June 19, 1964; children—Lisa Carol, Brigette Ann, Alfred August. Tchr., Redwood City (Calif.) Sch. Dist., 1862-63; tchr. spl. edn. Children's Health Council, Palo Alto, Calif., 1963-65; instr. in spl. edn. Boston U., 1965-66; tchr. campus sch. Brandeis U., 1967-69; asst. adminstr. Smith Coll Campus Sch., 1973-74; asst. prof. early childhood edn., dir. lab. sch. Coll. Edn., U. Mass., Amherst, 1974-79; psychologist, dir. spl. edn. Palmer (Mass.) Public Schs., 1979-81; psychologist Jordan Sch. Dist., Sandy, Utah, 1981-82; asst. prof. ednl. studies U. Utah, 1981-82; ednl. coordinator Northampton (Mass.) Center for Children and Families, 1982—; pvt. practice family and child therapy; cons. presch. edn. Vol. polit. fundraising activities Democratic Party. Recipient Coop. Edn. Hon. award State Mass., 1979; NIMH research grantee, 1962-64; NIMH tng. grantee, 1965-66; cert. elem., secondary and spl. edn. tchr., psychology, public sch. adminstr., Mass. Mem. Nat. Assn. Edn. Young Children, Am. Ednl. Research Assn., Jean Piagetian Soc., Nat. Assn. Sch. Psychologists. Research, publs. in field. Home: 57 Harkness Rd Pelham MA 01002

OAKAR, MARY ROSE, congresswoman; b. Cleve., Mar. 5, 1940; d. Joseph and Margaret Oakar; B.A. in English, Speech and Drama, Ursuline Coll., Cleve., 1962; M.A. in English, John Carroll U., Cleve., 1966; postgrad. Royal Acad. Dramatic Arts, London, Eng., Westham Adult Coll., Warwickshire, Eng., Columbia U. Instr. English and drama Lourdes Acad., Cleve., 1963-70; asst. prof. English, speech and drama Cuyahoga Community Coll., Cleve., 1968-75; mem. 95th Congress from 20th Ohio Dist., mem. Banking, Fin. and Urban Affairs Com., chmn. Select Com. on Aging, Post Office and Civil Service Com.; mem. Nat. Commn. on Unemployment Compensation. City councilwoman, Cleve., 1973-76; Democratic state central committeewoman 20th Dist., 1974-76; trustee Fedn. for Community Planning, Health and Planning Commn., Community Info. Service, Soc. for Crippled Children, Nationalities Services Center, YWCA. Recipient Outstanding Service award OEO, 1973-75, Community Service awards Am. Indian Center, 1973, Nationalities Services Center, 1974, Club San Lorenza, 1976; named Ursuline Coll. Alumni of Yr., 1977, Cuyahoga County Dem. Woman of Yr., 1977, knight Order St. Ladislaus, 1980. Home: 1892 W 30th St Cleveland OH 44113 Office: 107 Cannon House Office Bldg Washington DC 20515

OAKEN, MARY RAY, utility assn. ofcl.; b. Madisonville, Ky., Feb. 23, 1936; d. Clarence Arnett and Gaynelle (Teague) Stum; B.S., Western Ky. U., 1960, M.A., 1962; postgrad. Murray State U., 1964-66; m. Arnold S. Oaken, June 4, 1955; 1 son, Dean Arnold. Tchr. in public schs. of Ky., 1957-75; mem. Ky. Personnel Bd., 1976; commr. Ky. Public Service Commn., 1977-79; commr. Ky. Utility Regulatory Commn., Frankfort, 1979—; 1st v.p. Southeastern Regulatory Commrs., 1979-80. Bd. dirs. Ky. Rural Med. Scholarship Fund, 1974-77, Ky. Arthritis Found., 1975-76, Ky. Heart Assn., 1977—, mem. exec. com., 1979—. Named Outstanding Citizen, Trigg County, Ky., 1974, named Bus. Woman of Year, Trigg County, Ky., 1972; recipient numerous outstanding achievement awards from various clubs, Ky. Heart Assn. and Trigg County C. of C. Mem. Nat. Assn. of Regulatory Commrs., Southeastern Assn. Regulatory Commrs., Nat. Fedn. of Bus. and Profl. Women's Clubs, Ky. Fedn. of Bus. and Profl. Women's Clubs (pres. 1974-75, award 1977), Ky. C. of C. Democrat. Methodist. Home: PO Box 327 Woodlawn Estates Cadiz KY 42211 Office: 730 Schenkel Ln Frankfort KY 40602

OAKES BUTLER, SHIRLEY LEWIS, lawyer; b. Toronto, Ont., Can., Apr. 10, 1929; d. Harry and Eunice (McIntyre) O.; A.B. with honors, Vassar Coll., 1951; postgrad. Institut d'Etudes Politique, U. Paris, 1949-50; LL.B., Yale, 1954, J.D., 1971; LL.M., Columbia U., 1976. Law clk. Davidson, Dawson & Clark, N.Y.C., 1954-56; asst. sec. fgn. dept. Empire Trust Co., N.Y.C., 1957-59; v.p., dir. Brit. Colonial Hotel Co., Ltd., Nassau, Bahamas, 1956—; co-founder, dir. Butlers Bank Ltd. and asso. cos., Nassau, 1962-72; pres., dir. Golf Course, Ltd., Nassau, 1963-68; registered rep. Bache & Co., Inc., 1967-69; pres., dir. Bache & Co. (Nassau) Ltd., 1967-69; chmn. bd., pres. Gen. Bahamian Cos. Ltd., 1980—; pres. Westminster Mgmt. Co. Ltd.; dir. Carib Ins. Ltd., others. Pres. Asso. Alumnae Vassar Coll., 1963-66; mem. extra-mural adv. com. for Bahamas, U. West Indies, 1967; chmn. crippled children's com. Council for Handicapped, Nassau; mem. Bahamas nat. com. Internat. Women's Year; bd. dirs. Yale Law Sch. Fund; trustee Vassar Coll., Poughkeepsie, N.Y., 1970-78. Mem. Grays Inn (London), Yale Law Sch. Assn. (v.p. 1975-77), Phi Beta Kappa. Clubs: River, Cosmopolitan, Vassar (N.Y.C.); Lyford Cay, Gym Tennis (Nassau). Home: Jacaranda House PO Box N 4865 Nassau Bahamas Office: Westminster Mgmt Co Ltd PO Box N 4865 Nassau Bahamas

OAKLEY, DEBORAH JANE, researcher, educator; b. Detroit, Jan. 31, 1937; d. George F. and Kathryn (Willson) Hacker; B.A., Swarthmore Coll., 1958; M.A., Brown U., 1960; M.P.H., U. Mich., 1969, Ph.D., 1977; m. Bruce Oakley, June 16, 1958; children—Ingrid Andrea, Brian Benjamin. Dir. teenage and adult programs YWCA, Providence, 1959-63; editorial asst. Stockholm U., 1963-64; research investigator, lectr. dept. population planning U. Mich., 1971-77; asst. prof. community health programs U. Mich., Ann Arbor, 1977-79, asst. prof. nursing research, 1979-81, asso. prof., 1981—. Trustee, Womens Health Research Inst., 1981—. Recipient Margaret Sanger award Washtenaw County Planned Parenthood, 1975; Outstanding Young Woman of Ann Arbor award Jaycees, 1970. Mem. Am. Public Health Assn. (chmn. population sect. council), Internat. Union Sci. Study Population, Midwest Nursing Research Soc., Population Assn. Am., Delta Omega. Democrat. Author: (with Leslie Corsa) Population Planning, 1979; contbr. articles to profl. jours. Home: 1709 Pontiac Trail Ann Arbor MI 48105 Office: Sch Nursing U Mich Ann Arbor MI 48109

OANA, KATHERINE DEME, counselor, author, educator; b. Akron, Ohio, Aug. 29, 1929; d. William and Florence Deme; B.S., U. Akron, 1951, M.S., 1956, postgrad., 1956—; m. Larry Oana, July 22, 1954; 1 dau., Patty. Tchr. bus., guidance counselor Akron Public Schs., 1960—; spl. instr. U. Akron Community and Tech. Coll., 1960—; author numerous children's books, including: Bobby Bear and the Blizzard, Timmy Tiger and the Masked Bandit; author: Opportunities in Guidance and Counselling, 1979; Women In Their Own Business, 1982; assoc. editor Oddo Pub. Co.; cons. to editors. Mem. Am. Personnel and Guidance Assn., Author's Guild, Soc. Children's Book Writers, NEA, Ohio Edn. Assn., Akron Edn. Assn., Akron Area Bus. Tchrs. Assn., Delta Kappa Gamma. Episcopalian. Clubs: Jr. Women's Civic, Rotary Anns, Portage Country.

OATES, JOYCE CAROL, author; b. Lockport, N.Y., June 16, 1938; d. Frederic James and Caroline (Bush) Oates; B.A., Syracuse U., 1960, M.A., U. Wis., 1961; m. Raymond Joseph Smith, Jan. 23, 1961. Prof. English, U. Detroit, 1961-67, U. Windsor, Ont., Can., 1967—; vis. prof. English, Princeton U., 1978—. Mem. Am. Acad. and Inst. Arts and Letters. Recipient O. Henry Prize Story award, 1967-68. Guggenheim fellow, 1967-68. Author: (stories) By The North Gate, 1963; (play) The Sweet Enemy, 1965; (novel) With Shuddering Fall, 1965; (stories) Upon the Sweeping Flood, 1966; (novel) A Garden of Earthly Delights, 1967; (poems) Women in Love, 1968; Expensive People, 1968; Them, 1969; (poems) Anonymous Sins, 1969; (stories) The Wheel of Love, 1970; (poems) Love and its Derangements, 1970; (novel) Wonderland, 1971; (essays) The Edge of Impossibility, 1971; (stories) Marriages and Infidelities, 1972; (poems) Angel Fire, 1973; (novel) Do With Me What You Will, 1973; (play) Sunday Dinner, produced at Am. Place Theatre, 1970; (essays) The Hostile Sun; The Poetry of D.H. Lawrence, 1973; (poems) Dreaming America, 1973; (stories) The Hungry Ghosts, 1974; (stories) The Goddess and other Women, 1974; (essays) New Heaven, New Earth, 1974; (play) Miracle Play, 1974; (stories) Where Are You Going, Where Have You Been, 1974; (stories) The Poisoned Kiss and Other Portuguese Stories, 1975; (stories) The Seduction and Other Stories, 1975; (novel) The Assassins, 1975; (stories) Crossing the Border, 1976; (novels) Childwold, 1976, The Triumph of the Spider Monkey, 1977; (stories) Night-Side, 1977; (novel) Son of the Morning, 1978; Unholy Loves, 1979; Bellefleur, 1980; (play) Daisy (prod. Cubioulo Theatre N.Y.C.) 1980; A Sentimental Education, 1981; Contraries: Essays, 1981; (novel) Angel of Light, 1981; editor: Scenes from American Life, 1973, Ont. Rev.; The Best American Short Stories, 1979; also fiction in nat. mags. Office: Princeton U Creative Writing Program 185 Nassau St Princeton NJ 08540 *

OATEY, JENNIFER SUE, recreational sports adminstr.; b. Rochester, Minn., Aug. 30, 1949; d. Elwyn Brown and Phyllis Eileen (Quammen) Larson; B.A., N. Mex. State U., 1973, M.A., 1973; Ph.D. in Edn., U. Minn., 1981; m. William Baier Oatey, Aug. 19, 1978. Asst. dir. recreational sports U. Mich., Ann Arbor, 1976-77; intramural supr. Stephen Austin State U., Nacogdoches, Tex., 1975-76; campus center coordinator Brainerd (Minn.) Community Coll., 1974-75; phys. edn. instr., asst. intramural dir. N. Mex. State U., Las Cruces, 1973-74; assoc. dir. recreational sports U. Minn., Mpls., 1977—; exec. v.p. Consultants ET CETERA. Bd. dirs. Univ. YWCA, 1981-83. Mem. Nat. Intramural-Recreational Sports Assn. (dir. Minn. 1977-81, mem. editorial bd. Jour., 1981—), Can. Intramural Recreation Assn., Sons of Norway, U. Minn. Alumni Assn., Phi Theta Kappa. Lutheran. Home: 333 Oak Grove Apt

308 Minneapolis MN 55403 Office: 108 Cooke Hall U Minn Minneapolis MN 55455

OATMAN, ELINOR SAVAGE, banker; b. San Diego, Aug. 21, 1916; d. Basil Henderson and Dorothy Anne (Knox) Savage; student UCLA, 1932-33; m. Jack L. Oatman, Nov. 2, 1938; children—Jack L., Christine, Homer. Editor women's page San Diego Evening Tribune, 1937-43; dir. San Diego Trust & Savs. Bank, 1973—. Bd. dirs. Children's Hosp., San Diego, 1960-76, Rest Haven Preventorium, San Diego, 1971—; mem. bd. overseers U. Calif., San Diego, 1975—; bd. govs. San Diego Community Found. Mem. San Diego Mus. Art (pres. 1974-77, trustee), Jr. League San Diego (pres. 1948-49). Republican. Episcopalian. Home: 3170 Curlew St San Diego CA 92103 Office: San Diego Trust & Savings Bank 540 Broadway St San Diego CA 92101

O'BANNION, MINDY MARTHA MARTIN, nurse; b. Cushing, Okla., Aug. 19, 1953; d. John William and Martha Florence (Vineyard) Martin; student Okla. State U., 1971-73, Oscar Rose Jr. Coll., 1973; grad. St. Anthony Sch. Nursing, 1975; m. William Neal O'Bannion, Oct. 9, 1976; 1 dau., Mindi Martha Mae. Nursing asst. Cushing Mcpl. Hosp., 1973-75, head nurse surg. floor, 1975-76, charge nurse med. unit, 1978-79. Mem. social com. Royal Haven Bapt. Ch. Women's Missionary Union, Cushing, 1977-78; mem. extension dept. nursery First Bapt. Ch., Cushing, 1979-82, extension dept. presch., 1982—. Mem. Am., Tex., Okla. State nurses assns., St. Anthony Hosp. Sch. Nursing Alumnae, Alpha Xi Delta (corr. sec. 1973), Tau Beta Sigma. Baptist. Club: Studebaker Drivers. Home: 850 E Moses St Cushing OK 74023

O'BANNON, DONA CAROLE, cons. firm exec.; b. Washington, Apr. 13, 1943; d. H.A. and E. Kay (Kessel) O.; B.S. in Fgn. Service cum laude, Georgetown U., 1965. Spl. asst. to Congressman Sam Gibbons from Fla., 1963-74; partner Alcalde, Henderson & O'Bannon, govt. and public affairs cons. firm, Rosslyn, Va., 1974—. Mem. adv. council Cornell U. Grad. Sch. Bus. and Public Adminstrn. Mem. Nat. Assn. Women Bus. Owners (named Entrepreneur of Year 1977, pres., 1977-78), AAUW, Phi Beta Kappa. Club: Nat. Press. Contbr. articles to profl. mags. Home: 3409 Prospect St NW Washington DC 20007 Office: 1901 N Fort Myer Dr Suite 1204 Rosslyn VA 22209

O'BANNON, HELEN BOHEN, state ofcl.; b. Ridgewood, N.J., Aug. 15, 1939; d. Arthur C. and Lillian (McNamara) Bohen; B.A., Wellesley Coll., 1961; M.A., Stanford U., 1962; m. George W. O'Bannon, Sept. 15, 1962; children—Patrick, Colin, Sean, Casey. Research economist U.S. Treasury, Washington, 1963, 64-65; instr. econs. Robert Morris Coll., Pitts., 1970-72; lectr. Chatham Coll., Pitts., 1975; lectr. program execs. Bryn Mawr (Pa.) Coll., 1980, lectr., 1981; asst. and assoc. dean Carnegie-Mellon U., Pitts., 1973-76, lectr. program execs., 1978-82; mem. Pa. Pub. Utility Commn., Harrisburg, 1975-79; sec. pub. welfare Commonwealth of Pa., Harrisburg, 1979—. Bd. dirs. Job. Adv. Service, Pitts., 1977—, Women in Govt., Carlow Coll., Pitts., 1980—; mem. adv. council Women's Polit. Caucus Allegheny County, 1980—; trustee Wellesley Coll., 1982-85. Named Disting. Dau. Pa. by Gov. of Pa., 1977; recipient Woman in Govt. award AAUW, 1979, Alumnae Achievement award Wellesley Coll., 1980. Mem. Nat. Assn. Regulatory Commrs. (exec. bd. 1977-79). Contbr. articles to profl. jours. Home: 3501 N 2d St Harrisburg PA 17110 Office: 333 Health and Welfare Bldg Harrisburg PA 17120

OBERLANDER, SUZANNE MORRIS, staff asst. sci. orgn.; b. Salisbury, Md., Aug. 22, 1945; d. Henry Sanford and Martha (Adams) Morris; student Am. Inst. Banking, 1963-68, American U., 1977, Montgomery Coll., 1979; m. George Hans Felix, Oct. 14, 1978; stepchildren—Michael B., Sylvia R. Sec. trust dept. First and Mchts. Nat. Bank, Newport News, Va., 1963-68, Dow Badische Co., Williamsburg, Va., 1968-71, Newport News (Va.) Shipbldg. and Dry Dock Co., 1971-72; sr. sec. Sperry Univac, Washington, 1972-74; mortgage analyst Walker and Dunlop, Inc., Washington, 1974-79; adminstrv. asst. Nat. Acad. Scis., Washington, 1980-81, staff asst. elections, 1982—. Bd. dirs. Push Literacy Action Now, 1978—. Mem. Sisterhood Temple Beth Ami. Clubs: Altrusa Internat. (editor dist. service bull. 1980-82, chmn. astra com. Dist. Two 1982-84, pres. Washington chpt. 1982-83). Office: 2101 Constitution Ave NW Washington DC 20418

OBLINGER, JOSEPHINE KNEIDL HARRINGTON (MRS. WALTER L. OBLINGER), state legislator; b. Chgo., Feb. 14, 1913; d. Thomas William and Margaret (Kneidl) Harrington; B.S., U. Ill., 1933; LL.B., U. Detroit, 1943, J.D., 1977; L.H.D., Sioux Empire Coll., 1966; m. Walter L. Oblinger, Apr. 27, 1940; 1 son, Carl D. Tchr. Lanphier High Sch., Springfield, Ill., 1951-62; clk. Sangamon County, assessor Capital Twp., Springfield, 1962-69; asst. dir. Ill. Dept. Registration and Edn., Springfield, 1970—; mem. Ill. Ho. of Reps., 1978—; exec. dir. Gov.'s adj. Prof. gerontology Sangamon State U.; on Voluntary Action, 1970-73; asst. to 97 pres. Lincoln Land Community Coll., 1973-77; dir. Ill. Dept. on Aging, 1977-78; adj. prof. gerontology Sangamon State U.; mem. Ill. Council on Aging; rep. nat. bd. Nat. Assn. State Units on Aging, HEW. Sec. Springfield and Sangamon County Community Action, 1965-70, pres., 1970-75, treas., 1975—; mem. fin. com. Child and Family Service, Springfield, 1965-71; mem. Sangamon County planning com. United Community Services, 1971—; mem. Urban League, 1955—, Nat. Com. for Day Care of Children, 1960—; bd. dirs. Nat. Center for Voluntary Action, 1971-77, RSVP (Ret. Sr. Vol. Program), Sangamon County Salvation Army, Ill. Council Continuing Higher Edn.; officer, Republican Women's Luncheon Club, 1959—, pres., 1963—; chmn. Sangamon County Rep. com., 1965—; 1st v.p. Ill. Fedn. Rep. Women, 1972, pres., 1974-76; del. Rep. Nat. Conv., 1972; del., chmn. older women's concerns com. White House Conf. on Aging, 1981; mem. Fed. Council on Aging, 1981; bd. dirs., pres. Sangamon County Council on Alcoholism and Drugs, 1973-74; pres. Planning Consortium for Services to Children in Ill. Continuing Higher Edn., 1978; mem. Ill. Nutrition Adv. Council, Sangamon County Mental Health Bd; chmn. Sangamon County March of Dimes; mem. Ill. interagy. coordinating com. Ill. Employment and Tng. Council; mem. Springfield Women's Polit. Caucus, Sangamon County Mental Health Bd.; hon. mem. bd. Sojourn House. Mem. Ill. Assn. County Clks. and Recorders (pres.), Am. Bus. Women's Assn., Ill., Sangamon County bar assns., NAACP (exec. bd.), U. Ill. Alumni Assn., Nat. Assn. Counties, Nat. Assn. Recorders and Clks., Ill. Fedn. Tchrs. (pres. 1959-63, parliamentarian, 1963—), Conf. Women Legislators, Sangamon County Hist. Soc., P.E.O., Am. Assn. Vol. Services Coordinators (chmn. public policy com., 1st v.p. 1975), Ill. Assn. Sr. Centers, Bus. and Profl. Women's Club, Kappa Delta Pi, Sigma Delta Pi, Delta Delta Delta. Clubs: Riverton (Ill.) Women's; Altrusa (pres. 1967-68, legal advisor, dir.) (Springfield). Office: 117 W State St Nokomis IL also Stratton Bldg Springfield IL

OBLINGER, NANCY LEE, communications exec.; b. Fort Sill, Okla., May 18, 1945; d. Richard Lee and Jane Catherine (Fleig) O.; student U. Calif., Santa Barbara, 1963-64, Kent State U., 1964-65. Adminstrv. asst. VanBarneveld & Ellis Public Relations, Los Angeles, 1965-67, Md. Casualty Co., Los Angeles, 1968-72; asst. v.p. Foremark Corp., Swett & Crawford Group, Los Angeles, 1972—, asst. v.p., mgr. corp. communications, 1976—. Recipient awards Am. Inst. Graphic Arts Show, 1978, Communication Arts Soc. Show, 1979. Mem. Internat. Assn. Bus. Communicators, Ins. Advt. Conf. (award of excellence 1980), Insurers Public Relations Council, So. Calif. Bus. Communicators (award of excellence 1978). Republican. Episcopalian. Club: Toastmasters. Home: 3302 Griffith Park Blvd Los Angeles CA 90027 Office: 4201 Wilshire Blvd Los Angeles CA 90010

OBOLENSKY, MARILYN WALL (MRS. SERGE OBOLENSKY), metals co. exec.; b. Detroit, Aug. 13, 1929; d. Albert Fraser and Christine (Frischkorn) Wall; student Duschesne Jr. Coll., 1947; children—Albert F. Wall and Carl Breer II (twins); m. Serge Obolensky, June 3, 1971. Chmn. bd. Wall-Colmonoy Corp., Detroit, 1959-61, dir., 1961-65, sec., 1961—; pres. Serge Obolensky Assos., 1979—. Bd. dirs. Heart and Lung Found., N.Y.C. Republican. Roman Catholic. Club: Bathing Corporation (Southampton, N.Y.). Home: 465 Park Ave New York NY 10022 also 45 Preston Pl Grosse Pointe Farms MI 48236

O'BRIAN, THERESE DE STE. MARTHE MCGINNIS, translator, interpreter; b. Phila., Dec. 30, 1942; d. Maurice G. and Marie Antoinette (de Ste. Marthe) McGinnis; A.B. summa cum laude, Cath. U. Am., 1960; M.A., Columbia U. Tchrs. Coll., Ed.D. summa cum laude, 1962; M.S. in Journalism, Columbia U., 1963; Ph.D. summa cum laude in Psychology, Harvard U., 1964; Ph.D. summa cum laude in Langs., Sorbonne, Paris, 1965; student (Rhodes scholar) Oxford U.; m. Brian K. O'Brian, Jr., June 18, 1964 (dec. 1969); children—Brian K., III (dec.), Maureen Karen (dec.). Tchr. English, langs. and journalism; editor for mags. and pub. houses; tchr. Spanish and journalism Columbia U. Coll. Physicians and Surgeons, translator, interpreter for UN, 1972—; tchr. Berlitz Sch. Langs., 1960-64; cons. N.Y. State Dept. Edn. Mem. Am. Soc. Profl. and Exec. Women, AAUW, NOW, NEA, Am. Assn. Artists and Writers, Exec. Female, N.Y. State Tchrs. Union, United Fedn. Tchrs., Mensa, Internat. Platform Assn., Smithsonian Assos., Phi Beta Kappa, Kappa Tau Alpha, Delta Kappa Gamma. Democrat. Roman Catholic. Clubs: Aspen, Lake Tahoe, Elmridge Bath and Tennis, Lake Placid. Author articles for mags., newspapers. Home: Box 894 Tannersville NY 12486 also Riverdale NY 10471

O'BRIEN, ANNA MAE, home economist; b. Chgo., Mar. 25, 1930; d. Frank Joseph and Ella Mary (McNicholas) O'B.; B.A. in Home Econs. and Human Devel., Mundelein Coll., Chgo., 1971; postgrad. U. Wis., Madison, No. Ill. U. Sec., office mgr. housewares div. Gen. Electric Co., Chgo., 1951-60, region home economist, 1960—, retail sales specialist housewares and audio bus. div., 1980—. Mem. Am. Home Econs. Assn., Home Economists in Bus., Electric Women's Round Table, Am. Women in Radio and TV. Roman Catholic. Home: 1415 Carol St Park Ridge IL 60068 Office: 2300 E Devon St Suite 171 Des Plaines IL 60018

O'BRIEN, CAROL MARIA, psychiat. nurse, army officer; b. Mobile, Ala., Aug. 19, 1948; d. George I. and Leona J. (Balasa) Moleski; B.S., Walter Reed Army Inst. Nursing, U. Md., 1970; M.S., Ariz. State U., 1975; m. Robert Michael O'Brien, Jan. 30, 1982. Commd. 1st lt. U.S. Army, 1970, advanced through grades to maj., 1979; psychiat. head nurse, Ft. Gordon, Ga., 1971-72; psychiat. nurse clinician Brooke Army Med. Center, San Antonio, 1972-73; instr. Walter Reed Army Inst. Nursing, Washington, 1976; dir. psychiat. day hosp. Beaumont Army Med. Center, El Paso, 1977-79; psychiat. nurse clinician 121st Evacuation Hosp., Seoul, Korea, 1979-80; cons. in drug and alcohol rehab. Office of Army Surgeon Gen., Pentagon, 1980—. Decorated Army Commendation medal, Meritorious Service medal. Mem. Assn. Mil. Surgeons, Am. Nurses Assn., Nat. League for Nursing, Council Advanced Practitioners in Psychiat.-Mental Health Nursing, Sigma Theta Tau. Mem. Disciples of Christ Ch. Contbg. author: Risk Taking in Groups, 1980. Home: 3012 Whisper Fern Dr San Antonio TX 78230 Office: Room 2 D 520 Pentagon Washington DC 20310

O'BRIEN, (DOROTHY) MERRIE, public relations and advt. exec.; b. Stanchfield, Minn., Apr. 5, 1936; d. Theodore Eric and Gladys Ione (Mongsene) Peterson; ed. public schs., community coll.; m. Dean Owen O'Brien, Nov. 20, 1954; children—Patrick, Peggy O'Brien Zamora, Kelly, Kerry, Kevin. Columnist, writer, community editor Green Sheets and The World, 1970-82; Community Quips columnist Sacramento Bee, 1978; owner, operator Aries Agy., Public Relations and Advt., North Highlands, Calif., 1975—. Mem. Calif. State Democratic Central Com., 1979-82; founder North Highlands Moonwalk Parade and Festival; bd. dirs. North Highlands Recreation and Park Dist., 1978; trustee Grant Joint Union High Sch. Dist., 1981. Nominee for Outstanding Businesswoman award Sacramento Met. C. of C., 1980. Mem. Calif. Elected Women's Assn. Edn. and Research, North Highlands C. of C. (Outstanding Citizens award). Lutheran. Home: 6713 Stoneman Dr North Highlands CA 95660

O'BRIEN, GRACE WILHELMINA EHLIG, psychologist, ednl. adminstr., co-owner travel bur.; b. Los Angeles, Aug. 27, 1922; d. Max Carl and Janette (Rentchler) Ehlig; A.A., Pasadena City Coll., 1942; A.B., UCLA, 1944, postgrad., 1944-46; postgrad. Riverside City Coll., 1946; postgrad. Calif. State Coll. at Los Angeles, 1954-66, 68-78, M.A. in Guidance, 1964; m. Louis J. O'Brien, Nov. 8, 1947; children—Carol Jean, Lawrence John, Perry Lewis. Tchr., Perris (Calif.) Union High Sch., 1945-46; tchr., counselor, psychometrist Los Angeles City Schs., 1946-66, cons. counselor, sch. psychologist Elem. Secondary Edn. Act, Edn. and Guidance program, 1966-68; head counselor, asst. prin. Garden Gate Opportunity Sch., 1968-73; vice prin. Markham Jr. High Sch., 1973, Belvedere Jr. High Sch., 1974; asst. prin. Garfield High Sch., 1974-75, Mt. Vernon Jr. High Sch., Los Angeles, 1975-76; prin. Garden Gate High Sch., 1977-80, Johnson High Sch., 1980—. Den mother chmn. Cub Scouts, 1964-66. Recipient spl. service award Boy Scouts, 1964. Mem. UCLA Alumni Assn., Sr. High Prins. Assn., Los Angeles Assn. Sch. Adminstrs., Calif. Assn. Sch. Adminstrs., Phi Delta Kappa Pi Lambda Theta, Chi Delta Phi. Presbyterian (supt. Sunday sch. 1953-54). Home: 3880 Shadow Grove Rd Pasadena CA 91107 Office: 900 E 42d St Los Angeles CA 90011

O'BRIEN, JEAN CHARLOTTE, mktg. cons.; b. N.Y.C., Apr. 7, 1922; d. John E. and Georgiana H. O'B.; B.S., Coll. of St. Elizabeth, 1943. Dir. nutrition service Beech-Nut Packing Co., N.Y.C., 1944-57; product rep. asst. mgr. new products mktg., 1957-62; mktg. mgr. new products Nabisco, Inc., N.Y.C., 1962-65; exec. v.p. Dunham & Luttman, Inc., Chappaqua, N.Y., 1965—. Mem. Am. Home Econs. Assn., Home Economists in Bus., Inst. Food Technologists. Republican. Roman Catholic. Home: Nosband Ave White Plains NY 10605 Office: 24 N Greeley Ave Chappaqua NY 10514

O'BRIEN, LIBBY ATKINS, public relations exec.; b. N.Y.C., Mar. 17, 1913; d. Richard Travis and Alice Gordon (Quigley) Atkins; grad. Kendall Hall, 1931; m. Richard Thomas O'Brien, June 25, 1935 (dec.); children—Francis DeSales, Sarah Jane O'Brien Prezalor. Car rep. Brady Stannard Motors, Brewster, N.Y., Blanchard Motors, Greenwich, Conn., and Tolm Motors, Darren, Conn., 1940-46; producer TV show Libby O'Brien's Table Toppers, 1946-48; commentator, dir. women's programs WLAD, Danbury, Conn., 1948-51, WSTC, Stamford, Conn., 1951-53; asst. dir. public relations Save the Children Fedn., 1954-55; advt. mgr. Roux Distbg. Corp., 1956-57; public relations mgr. Lily Tulip Cup Corp., 1957-64; owner, mgr. Libby O'Brien Enterprises, Inc., 1964-69; owner, breeder, exporter O'Brien Donkey Farm, promoter of tourism in Kenmare, Ireland, 1969-76; book collaborator; active Utilizing Sr. Energy, Know Your Body-Am. Health Orgn.; publicity chmn. Greenwich Meals on Wheels. Collector, seller old N.Y.C. st. signs. Mem. Am. Women in Radio and TV, Public Relations Assn., Public Relations Inst. U.K. Republican. Home: 44 Arcadia Rd Old Greenwich CT 06870

O'BRIEN, MARY THERESA, social worker; b. Pottsville, Pa., May 9, 1953; d. Vincent J. and Mary (Dudick) O'B.; B.A. cum laude, Bloomsburg State Coll., 1975; M.S.W., St. Louis U., 1977. Dir. social services Good Samaritan Hosp., Pottsville, Pa., 1977—. Mem. Schuylkill County Hospice Steering Com. NIMH grantee, 1975-76. Mem. Acad. Cert. Social Workers, Nat. Assn. Social Workers, Soc. for Hosp. Social Work Dirs., Central Pa. Health and Hosp. Social Workers, Social Work Oncology Group. Home: 48 S Nichols St Saint Clair PA 17970 Office: Good Samaritan Hosp E Norwegian and Tremont Sts Pottsville PA 17901

O'BRIEN, MAUREEN, investment banker; b. Waterbury, Conn., Mar. 9, 1952; d. Donald and Lorraine O'B.; B.A., Rutgers U. Br. mgr. First Jersey Nat. Bank, Jersey City, 1974-77; dir. loans and grants Jersey City Redevel. Agy., 1977-79; 2d v.p. Matthews & Wright, Inc., N.Y.C., 1979—; cons. HUD, Nat. Assn. Housing and redevel. Ofcls. Vice-pres., Van Vorst Park Assn., 1978. Mem. N.J. Assn. Elected Women Ofcls., Council Urban and Econ. Devel., Nat. Assn. Housing and Redevel. Ofcls. Office: 14 Wall St New York NY 10005

O'BRIEN, MILDRED MAE, mfg. co. exec.; b. Birmingham, Ala., Sept. 28, 1923; d. James Garshore and Elizabeth (Hitchfield) Foster; student Birmingham So. Coll., 1940-41; m. William Donald O'Brien, May 5, 1942 (div. 1956); 1 son, William Foster. Sec., acct. The Re-Print Co., Birmingham, 1941-46; exec. sec. Firestone Tire and Rubber Co., Birmingham, 1947; sec.-treas., office mgr. Fly Ash Arrestor Corp., Birmingham, 1947-67, asst. sec., personnel mgr., mgr. adminstrv. services Air Systems div. Zurn Industries, Inc., 1967—. Mem. Birmingham Personnel Assn., Bus. and Profl. Women's Club (editor monthly bull. 1957-61, corr. sec. 1961-63, sec. 1963-64, treas. 1964-65, auditor 1965-66). Mem. Ch. of the Nazarene. Home: 1500 Steven Dr Birmingham AL 35226 Office: 245 N Center St Birmingham AL 35204

O'BRIEN, PATRICIA, social worker; b. Balt., July 5, 1929; d. Francis P. and Ellen A. (Bohn) O'B.; B.A., Marywood Coll., Pa., 1954, M.S. in Counseling, 1966; M.S.W., U. Md., 1973. Joined Sisters of I.H.M., Scranton, Pa., Roman Catholic Ch., 1947; tchr. St. Paul High Sch., Scranton, 1959-60, Marywood Sem., Scranton, 1960-62, Cathedral High Sch., Scranton, 1962-67, Archbishop Neale High Sch., La Plata, Md., 1967-70; guidance counselor, 1966-70; tchr. St. Agnes Elem. Sch., Balt., 1970-71; group therapist Essex Mental Health Clinic, Balt., 1973-75; clin. social worker, group therapist, supr. Spring Grove Hosp. Center, Catonsville, Md., 1973-75, 76—; prin. Archbishop Neale Grade and High Sch., La Plata, 1975-76; evaluator St. Mark's Guidance of Cath. Charities, La Plata, 1975-76. Lic. and cert. social worker, Md.; cert. tchr., N.Y., Pa.; cert. therapist. Mem. Nat. Assn. Social Workers, Profl. Social Workers Assn., U. Md. Sch. Social Work Alumni Assn. Author poetry. Home: 1201 Caton Ave Baltimore MD 21227 Office: Spring Grove Hosp Center Wade Ave Catonsville MD 21228

O'BRIEN, PATRICIA FLORENCE, real estate and appraisal co. exec., educator; b. Truro, N.S., Can., Sept. 15, 1914; d. Clarence Osborne and Florence Isabel (Ripley) Davidson; B.S., Marquette U., Milw., 1958, M.A. in Spanish, 1961; M.A. in English Lit., U. Alta., 1966; m. Cyril Cornelius O'Brien, July 27, 1957; stepchildren—Maureen Louise, Terry Michael, Christopher Joseph. Social worker, Halifax, N.S., 1933-42; public sch. tchr., 1942-52; chmn. dept. English English Cath. Coll., La Paz, Bolivia, 1952-56; instr. Spanish Carroll Coll., Waukesha, Wis., 1959-60, Mt. Mary Coll., Milw., 1960-62; tchr. math. and Spanish Solomon Juneau High Sch., Milw., 1962-63; instr. English U. Alta., Edmonton, 1965-70; sec.-treas. Adan Research Co. Ltd., Edmonton, 1969—; pres. Patra Real Estate and Appraisal Co. Ltd., 1975—; instr. art Lakeland Coll., Vermilion, Alta.; sec. Prince of Peace Research Inst., Mundare, Alta., 1980—. Decorated Lady Equestrian Order Holy Sepulchre Jerusalem, 1979, Lady Magistral Grace Mil. Order Most Holy Savior and St. Bridget of Sweden, 1982. Mem. Assn. Pontifical Knights, Royal Soc. Arts, Marquette U. Faculty Wives Assn. (past dir.), Phi Delta Gamma (pres. 1960-62), Sigma Delta Pi (sec. 1960-61), Pi Mu Epsulon, Phi Delta Phi, Alpha Mu Gamma. Club: Laura Reid Art (pres. 1976-78) (Vegreville, Alta.). Author papers in field, also poetry. Address: PO Box 503 Clandonald County of Vermilion River AB ROB OXO Canada

O'BRIEN, ZINA KRAKOWSKY, restaurant/gift shop owner; b. San Pedro, Calif., July 7, 1944; d. Henry Hyman and Frances (Kurtzman) Krakowsky; A.A., Vallejo Jr. Coll., 1964; student U. Mo., Columbia, 1963, (scholar) San Francisco Acad. Art, 1964, Calif. Coll. Arts and Crafts, 1966. Grocery checker Safeway and Lucky Stores, Vallejo, Concord, Calif., 1964-66; owner feather flower bus., Tahoe, 1966-70; cashier, waitress, cook, cocktail waitress, mgr. various restaurants, Tahoe-Squaw Valley area, 1966-70; developer, owner, operator O'B's Board Restaurant, Truckee, Calif., 1970-80, C. B. White's Restaurant, Catering, Antiques & Gifts, Truckee, 1979—. Mem. Truckee Downtown Mchts. Assn., Truckee Hist. Soc. Democrat. Jewish. Home: 13059 Donner Pass Rd Donner Lake CA 95734 Office: PO Box 396 10292 Donner Pass Rd Truckee CA 95734

OBST, MARLENE KRUSE, extension agt.; b. Ft. Wayne, Ind., Mar. 20, 1937; d. Gustav H. and Velma M. (Bultemeier) Kruse; B.S., Grand Canyon Coll., Phoenix, 1972; m. Richard C. Obst, Dec. 27, 1958; children—Richard C., Jonathan, Timothy, Christopher. Elem. sch. tchr., Toledo, 1956-60; dir. Am. Pre-sch. and Day Care Center, Phoenix, 1972-73; 4-H extension agt. Maricopa County, Coop. Extension Service, Phoenix, 1977—. Mem. Nat. Assn. Extension 4-H Agts. Home: 5928 S JenTilly St Tempe AZ 85283 Office: 4341 E Broadway Phoenix AZ 85040

O'BYRNE, NATALIE KWASNESKI, psychiatrist; b. Bklyn., Nov. 29, 1933; d. Julian Leon and Jeannette Pauline (Kowalski) Kwasneski; B.S. in Chemistry cum laude, St. John's U., 1955; M.D., State U. N.Y., Bklyn., 1959; m. William O'Byrne, June 13, 1959; children—Cecily, Matthew, Stephanie, Gabrielle, Luke. Intern, Kings County Hosp., N.Y.C., 1960-61; resident in pediatrics Children's Hosp., San Francisco, 1962-63, adolescent medicine fellow, 1963-64; resident in adult psychiatry St. Mary's Hosp., San Francisco, 1964-66, in child psychiatry, 1966-68; practice medicine specializing in adult, child and adolescent psychiatry, San Anselmo, Calif., 1968—; asst. clin. prof. U. Calif. (San Francisco); sr. supervising psychiatrist Langley-Porter Children's Service; cons. Hanna Boys Center, Sonoma, Calif., San Francisco Theol. Sem.; lectr. to parent groups, high sch. and univ. students. Diplomate Am. Bd. Psychiatry and Neurology. Fellow Am. Psychiat. Assn., Am. Acad. Child Psychiatry; mem. AMA, Calif. Med. Assn., Marin, San Francisco med. socs., No. Calif. Psychiat. Assn., Regional Orgn. Child-Adolescent Psychiatry, Nat. Guild Cath. Psychiatrists (dir.). Roman Catholic. Home: 715 Butterfield Rd San Anselmo CA 94960 Office: Box 457 San Anselmo CA 94960

O'CALLAGHAN, AILEEN, mgmt. cons.; b. N.Y.C., Mar. 2, 1947; d. Patrick Francis and Catherine Mary (Gallagher) O'C.; B.A., SUNY, New Paltz, 1968. With Citibank, N.Y.C., 1968-75, sr. job analyst, 1972-74, personnel specialist, 1974-75; with Hay Assos., Phila., 1975—, sr. asso., 1976-77, prin., 1977—. Office: 229 S 18th St Philadelphia PA 19103

OCASIO, JOSEFA, nurse; b. Mayaguez, P.R., Nov. 4, 1940; came to U.S., 1949; d. José Ocasio and Josefina (Jorge) O.; L.P.N., Bellavista Hosp., 1964; R.N., Manhattan Community Coll., City U. N.Y., 1978; B.A. in Hosp. Adminstrn., CCNY, 1981; cert. in childbirth Council Childbirth Educators, 1978; divorced; children—Brenda, Joey. Office nurse, 1964-66; mem. nursing staff Columbia-Presbyn. Med. Center, N.Y.C., 1966—; parent educator Lamaze Inst., Lenox Hill Hosp.,

1980-81; Lamaze instr., 1978—; public health nurse N.Y.C. Bur. Child Welfare, 1980-81; founder, 1976, since dir., tchr. pregnancy prevention Washington Heights Youth Outreach Program; bd. dirs. East Harlem Health Council, 1980—; sec. gen. Hispanic Health Congress No. Manhattan, 1980—; mem. program planning and facilities com. Presbyn. Hosp. Community Health Council, 1979—. Mem. Am. Nurses Assn., Nat. Assn. Female Execs., Women's Health Network, Internat. Childbirth Assn., N.Y. State Nurses Assn., Met. Childbirth Assn. N.Y.C., Nat. Astrological Soc., Internat. Coll. Astrology. Address: 600 W 178th St New York NY 10033

OCHAL, BETHANY JACQUITA, library dir.; b. Flint, Mich., Dec. 2, 1917; d. Llewellyn Lane and Idah B. (Stewart) Ziegler; A.B., Wayne State U., 1944, J.D., 1945; m. Edward Louis Ochal, July 1, 1944; children—Myrna Irene, Edward Llewellyn. Admitted to Mich. bar, 1945; practiced in Detroit, 1945-52; reference librarian Detroit Bar Assn. Library, 1952-60, librarian, 1960-61; law librarian Wayne State U. Law Sch. Library, Detroit, 1961-72; dir. Orange County (Calif.) Law Library, Santa Ana, 1972—; mem. faculty rotating insts. Am. Assn. Law Libraries, 1972, 73, 75, 79. Mem. State Bar Mich. (chmn. legal publs. com. 1968-70), Women Lawyers Assn. Mich. (pres. 1966-67), Am. Assn. Law Libraries (chmn. membership com. 1965-67, chmn. chpts. com. 1968-70, chmn. audiovisual com. 1970-71, 81-82), Ohio Regional Assn. Law Libraries (pres. 1969-70), Internat. Assn. Law Libraries, Nat. Micrographics Assn. Republican. Club: Soroptimist. Contbr. to Law Library Jour. Home: 2541 N Alona Santa Ana CA 92706 Office: 515 N Flower Santa Ana CA 92703

OCHOA, SALLYANN, state ofcl.; b. Dodge City, Kans., Feb. 10, 1947; d. Norman Elmo and Rosa Laura (Scheib) Nimmo; student Wichita State U., 1965-69, Northwestern State U., Alva, Okla., 1969-70, Garden City (Kans.) Jr. Coll., 1978—; m. Joe Ochoa, Dec. 25, 1979; 1 dau. by previous marriage—Skye LeAnn McCue. Music tchr., Wilmore, Kans., 1969-70; sec. Lakin Feeders (Kans.), 1970-71; dental asst. Dennis Parsons, D.D.S., Garden City, 1971-73; dep. treas. Kearny County, Lakin, 1973-76; ct. services officer Finney County, 1976-79, State of Kans., Topeka, 1979—. Mem. Lakin City Council, 1971-79; vice mayor City of Lakin, 1976-79; Republican chmn. Kearny County, 1976; mem. S.W. Regional Planning Commn., 1971-79, sec., vice chmn., 1975, 79, recipient service awards. Mem. Kans. Probation Officers Assn. Presbyterian. Home: Box 721 Lakin KS 67860 Office: 504 Saint John Garden City KS 67846

OCHSNER, PEGGY, designer; b. N.Y.C., June 27, 1940; d. Edward and Margaret Hessberg; A.A., Boston U., 1960; postgrad. Boston U., 1961-62, Long Beach State U., 1962-63, N.Y. Sch. Interior Design, 1967-68; m. Robert Carr Ochsner, May 4, 1971; children—Edward Kenneth and Thomas Michael Covell. Fabric and design sales rep., 1965-67; freelance designer, Charleston, S.C., 1967-71, N.Y.C., 1971-72; pres., dir. Peg'O, Inc., Atlanta, 1972—; dir. Ray Sorrell Travel Co., Edmarg, Inc. Mem. Republican Nat. Com. Mem. Nat. Assn. Female Execs., Soc. Profl. Women, Fashion League, LWV, Women's Commerce Club Atlanta, Buckhead Bus. Assn. Photoessayist, works featured in mags. Home: 1665 W Wesley Rd NW Atlanta GA 30327 Office: 2985 Grandview Ave NE Atlanta GA 30305

OCKENDEN, KATHRINE MARGARET, fund raising exec.; b. Northampton, Mass., May 13, 1932; d. Albion Charles and Kathrine Mathilde (Abkarian) O.; B.A., Smith Coll., 1953. Sec. to adminstr. Sloan Scholarship Program, Alfred P. Sloan Found., Inc., 1954-58; exec. sec. to personnel mgr. Arthur D. Little, Inc., 1958-62; asst. to dir. Center for Internat. Studies, M.I.T., 1962-68; researcher fin. com. Rockefeller for Pres. Hdqrs., 1968; coordinator Internat. Univ. Choral Festival, Lincoln Center Performing Arts, Inc., 1968; asst. to chmn. bd. Marine Midland Bank, N.Y.C., 1969-73; dir. endowment campaign WNET/Channel 13, N.Y.C., 1973-77; dir. devel. N.Y. Philharm. Symphony Soc., Inc., N.Y.C., 1977—. Mem. com. Harlem Sch. Arts. Mem. Accion Internat. (dir.), English Speaking Union, Fin. Women's Assn. N.Y., LWV, Fgn. Policy Assn., Lower Manhattan Cultural Council. Democrat. Episcopalian. Clubs: Smith Coll., Cosmopolitan. Home: 157 E 72d St New York NY 10021 Office: 65th and Broadway New York NY 10023

OCKER, DELLA MAE, newspaper exec.; b. Ottumwa, Iowa, July 25, 1936; d. Charles Leo and Alla Maude (Denny) Brumbaugh; student pub. schs.; m. Samuel Eugene Ocker, Mar. 28, 1954; children—Charles Eugene, Enid Roxiann, Della Irene, M. GeoAlla. Keypunch operator State of Iowa, Des Moines, 1966-71, Bankers Life Ins. Co., Des Moines, 1973-75; typesetter Prairie City (Iowa) News, 1975-78, pub., 1978—. Vol. ambulance attendant and driver, 1978—. Mem. Nat. Fedn. Ind. Bus., Iowa Press Assn. Home: 501 E 5th St Prairie City IA 50228 Office: Prairie City News 106 N Main St Prairie City IA 50228

O'CONNELL, ANNA PORRECA, biologist; b. Phila., Apr. 26, 1937; d. Francis Paul and Anna Agnes (Donatucci) Porreca; A.B., Temple U., 1959. Mem. staff Inst. Cancer Research, Phila., 1959—, research asso., 1972-81, sr. research asso., 1981—. Mem. Am. Soc. Microbiology, Pa. Soc. Microbiology. Author papers in field. Office: 7701 Burholme Ave Philadelphia PA 19111

O'CONNELL, KATHLEEN ROSEMARY, psychologist; b. Boston, Jan. 23, 1950; d. William Edward and Anne Veronica (Beinert) O'C.; A.A. in Nursing, Cabrillo Coll., 1973; B.A. in Psychology, Am. U., Washington, 1975; M.P.H., Tulane U., 1977; Ph.D., Paideia U., 1981; m. Don James Mohle, Aug. 16, 1976; 1 dau., Joel Christine. With Community Action Bd., Santa Cruz, Calif., 1973-74; psychotherapist Kaiser Permanente Health System, George Washington Med. Center, Washington Hosp. Center, 1973-75; clin. mgr. Rock Creek Found. for Mental Health, Bethesda, Md., 1975-76; cons. to psychiat. hosps. and fed. govt., Santa Cruz, Calif., 1976—. Mem. Am. Public Health Assn., Mental Health Adminstrs. Assn., Nat. Assn. Female Execs., Nat. Women's Polit. Caucus. Club: Washington Women's Network. Home and Office: 1803 Mission St Santa Cruz CA 95060

O'CONNELL, SHEILA J., banker; b. Washington, Dec. 22, 1942; d. Joseph James and Hazel (Ashmore) O'C.; B.A., Newton Coll. Sacred Heart, 1964. With N.Y. Life Ins. Co., N.Y.C., 1964-66, Burr, Lucey & Co., N.Y.C., 1966-69; with Morgan Guaranty Trust Co., N.Y.C., 1969—, now v.p. Home: 80 East End Ave New York NY 10028

O'CONNOR, CONSTANCE, publisher; b. N.Y.C., Sept. 24, 1927; d. Thomas J. and Constance D. (Egan) Reilly; B.S., Fordham U., 1948; m. James T. Sutter, 1944 (div. 1963); children—Valerie Sutter-Remy, Meredith McGraw, John W. Sutter, Russell J. Sutter; m. 2d, John J. O'Connor, 1968. Editor Spectator, house organ Standard & Poor's, N.Y.C., 1948; owner Sutter Agy., public relations, Mt. Vernon, N.Y., 1963-66; dir. publicity N.Y. State Pavilion, Worlds Fair, N.Y.C., 1964-66; founder, editor Yankee Trader, Port Jefferson, N.Y., 1966—; pres. Osprey Publs. Inc., 1966—, Yankee Ad-Pak Corp., 1981—; pub. Harbor Chronicle Weekly News, 1980—; mem. Brookhaven Small Bus. Adv. Council. bd. dirs. Postal Customers Club L.I. Served with WAC. Mem. N.Y. State Advt. Pubs. Assn., L.I. Pubs. Assn., L.I. Advt. Club, Ameral de Grasse Soc., Decisions, Women in Commerce, Am. Legion. Republican. Roman Catholic. Clubs: Overseas Press (N.Y.C.); L.I. Press, Old Field. Home: 153 Quaker Path Setauket NY 11733 Office: 1110 Route 25A Port Jefferson Station NY 11776

O'CONNOR, EILEEN CECELIA, lawyer; b. Edina, Mo., Sept. 16, 1917; d. William Francis and Mary Ellen (Maloney) O'C.; A.B., Coll. St. Elizabeth, 1938; J.D., George Washington U., 1941. Admitted to D.C. bar, 1941, U.S. Supreme Ct. bar, 1948; atty. Office of Gen. Counsel, Dept. Treasury, Washington, 1942-74; individual practice law, Washington, 1975—; pres., dir. Treasury Dept. Fed. Credit Union, 1954-63. Mem. adv. bd. legal asst. program continuing edn. for women center George Washington U., 1978—; mem. D.C. Internat. Women's Year Com., 1977; pres. St. Matthew's Cathedral Parish Council, 1978. Mem. Fed. Bar Assn. (pres. D.C. chpt. 1977-78, v.p. D.C. circuit 1979-80), Inter Am. Bar Assn. (asst. sec. 1975-79, mem. council 1979—), D.C. Bar Assn. Democrat. Roman Catholic. Clubs: Zonta (pres. Washington 1979-81), Nat. Lawyers. Editor: Fed. Bar News, 1978-80. Address: 1 Scott Circle NW Washington DC 20036

O'CONNOR, HELEN SULLIVAN (MRS. LAWRENCE CHARLES O'CONNOR), educator; b. Boston, Jan. 28, 1931; d. Timothy and Ellen (Ahern) Sullivan; B.S. in Edn., Framingham (Mass.) Coll., 1952; M.Ed., Boston U., 1960; m. Lawrence Charles O'Connor, July 9, 1955. Tchr., Quincy (Mass.) Public Schs., 1952-57, Scituate (Mass.) Public Schs., 1957-61, Santa Clara Sch. Dist., Sunnyvale, Calif., 1961-62; dir. USAF Inst., Camp Roberts, Calif., 1962-63; supr. secondary edn., Brindisi, Italy, 1963-64; tchr. USAF Inst., Misawa, Japan, 1964-65; chairperson reading and lang. dept. Scituate Public Schs., 1965-73; asso. prof. humanities, dir. devel. studies Cape Cod Community Coll., West Barnstable, Mass., 1973—; cons. Holt, Rinehart, Winston Pub. Co., 1973-75. Cert. reading specialist, sch. psychologist, Mass. Mem. NEA, Mass. Tchrs. Assn., Internat. Reading Assn. Office: Cape Cod Community College West Barnstable MA 02668

O'CONNOR, JEAN SMITH, poet, author; b. nr. Hamlin, W.Va.; d. Oscar French and Florence (Adkins) Smith; grad. W.Va. Bus. Coll.; m. Gerald Francis O'Connor, Aug. 3, 1929; children—Joan Florence (Mrs. Alfred James Dickerson, Jr.), Peggy Frances (Mrs. Lanny J. Pixley), Geraldine Phyllis (Mrs. Philip James Barrons). Mem. editorial staff Echoes of W.Va., Charleston, 1952-56; v.p., sec.-treas. Line Creek Coal Corp., Charleston, 1962-66. Mem. W.Va. Poetry Soc. (organizer Charleston chpt. 1968, state pres. 1968-69), Acad. Am. Poets (affiliate), Nat. League Am. Pen Women (state pres. 1964-66, organizer Huntington br. 1966, nat. poetry chmn. 1970-72, W.Va. letters chmn. 1980-82), Cath. Daus. Am., Huntington Poetry Guild. Democrat. Roman Catholic. Club: St. Agnes Garden. Author: The Quiet Hills, 1963. Editor: Poets' Crossroads, 1953-76. Home: Apt 4K Plaza East 4300 N Ocean Blvd Fort Lauderdale FL 33308

O'CONNOR, JOYCE MARIE, artist, educator; b. Oklahoma City, Apr. 1, 1934; d. Neal William and Oleighla Julia (Osborne) Taylor; B.S. in Bus. Adminstrn., Calif. State U., Sacramento, 1982; m. Kelly J. O'Connor, Aug. 29, 1953; children—Dana Price, Mary Kellyeen O'Connor Davis. Bookkeeper First Nat. Bank, Burns, Oreg., 1956-57; with Peoples Nat. Bank of Moses Lake (Wash.), 1958-59; legal stenographer to judge, Stigler, Okla., 1960-62; loan counselor United Credit Union, Misawa, Japan, 1967-68; cashier McClellan Non-Commd. Officers Club, McClellan AFB, Sacramento, 1969-70; fine and applied arts tchr. adult edn. Grant Sch. Dist., Sacramento, 1977—; tchr. N. Highlands Dist., various orgns. Mem. Soc. Western Artists, Calif. Arts League, Highlands Artists Guild. Democrat. Methodist. Clubs: Non-Commd. Officers Wives (past officer AFB bases). Home and Office: 5636 Sapunor Way Carmichael CA 95608

O'CONNOR, JUDITH G., state legislator; b. St. Louis, Dec. 1, 1936; student U. Mo., St. Louis; m. Patrick J. O'Connor, 1959 (dec.); 4 children. Mem. Mo. Ho. of Reps., 1971—. Past mem. Gov.'s Adv. Council on Higher Edn. Recipient meritorious award Globe Democrat., 1979. Democrat. Office: Mo State Ho of Reps Jefferson City MO 65101 *

O'CONNOR, KATHLEEN MARY, collection firm exec.; b. Orange, N.J., Dec. 30, 1939; d. James J. and Ann E. (Kievning) O'C.; grad. public schs., Maplewood, N.J. Sec., Prudential Ins. Co., Newark, 1958-65; fgn. service sec. Dept. State, Washington, 1965-69; v.p. CTC Collections, West Orange, N.J., 1972-77; pres. O'Connor-Ravell Assos., East Orange, N.J., 1977—. Mem. Comml. Law League Am., N.J. Assn. Credit Execs., N.J. Creditwomen's Group, N.J. Bus. and Industry Assn., N.J. Assn. Women Bus. Owners Office: 715 Park Ave East Orange NJ 07017

O'CONNOR, LAURA JEAN, railroad ofcl.; b. Greeley, Nebr., Dec. 14, 1932; d. Everett George and Hazel Irene (Nelson) Caudill; A.B.A. in Arts and Scis., Laramie County Community Coll., Cheyenne, Wyo., 1976; divorced; children—LaShara Marie, LaRayne Larie, Timothy Richard, Mark Thomas, Deanna Lynn, Rose Ann. Elementary sch. tchr., Greeley County, Nebr., 190-52, Merrick County, Nebr., 1957-59; receptionist, secretarial positions, 1952-57, 62-65; with communications dept. Union Pacific R.R., 1964—, program devel. specialist tech. tng., personnel dept., Omaha, 1978—. Mem. planning commn., Papillion, Nebr., 1975-78, chmn., 1978-79, mem. city council, 1979—. Mem. Union Pacific Jr. Old Timers (chpt. aux. pres. 1969-70), Beta Sigma Phi (past chpt. pres.). Roman Catholic. Home: PO Box 34 924 S Madison St Papillion NE 68046 Office: 1416 Dodge St Room 111 Omaha NE 68179

O'CONNOR, SISTER, MARY CONSOLATA, coll. pres.; b. Waterbury, Conn.; d. John Joseph and Nora (Perkinson) O'Connor; B.A., St. Joseph Coll., 1939; M.A., Cath. U. Am., 1951, Ph.D., 1955. Tchr. St. Peter's Sch., Hartford, Conn., 1942-46, Cathedral High Sch., Hartford, 1946-50; prof. history St. Joseph Coll., West Hartford, Conn., 1954-67, dean of students, 1954-58, acad. dean, 1958-69, pres., 1969—; mem. exec. com. Conn. Council Higher Edn., 1971—, v.p., 1973-74, pres., 1974-75; sec.-treas. Conn. Conf. Ind. Colls., 1975-76, exec. com., 1979—; sec. Greater Hartford Consortium for Higher Edn., 1972-76, v.p., 1976—; mem. Edn. Commn. of the States, 1980—; trustee Soc. for Savs. Mem. Am., New Eng. hist. assns. Home and office: St Joseph College 1678 Asylum Ave West Hartford CT 06117

O'CONNOR, MARY SCRANTON, public relations and advt. agy. exec.; b. New Haven, May 9, 1942; d. James T., Jr. and Mary Elizabeth (Scranton) O'C.; B.A., Manhattanville Coll., Purchase, N.Y., 1964; postgrad. neuropsychology, U. Hartford (Conn.). Reporter, Hartford Times, 1964-65, women's editor, 1965-68; from public relations account exec. to v.p., dir. public relations Wilson, Haight & Welch, Inc., Hartford, 1968-75; ind. public relations cons., 1975-76; v.p. public relations Lowengard & Brotherhood, Hartford, 1976-78, pres., 1978—; instr. Manchester (Conn.) Community Coll., 1975. Bd. dirs. Child and Family Services Hartford, 1980—, Hartford Better Bus. Bur., 1980—, Intensive Edn. Center, Hartford, 1981—, Criminal Justice Edn. Center, Hartford, 1980-81, Family Service Soc. Hartford, 1978-80. Recipient Women in Leadership award Hartford YWCA, 1981. Mem. Public Relations Soc. Am., Internat. Assn. Bus. Communicators. Office: 12 Charter Oak Pl Hartford CT 06106

O'CONNOR, MICHOL, lawyer; b. Houston, Nov. 30, 1942; d. Charles Cary and Ida Mae (Mueller) Baird; B.A., U. Tex., Austin, 1966; J.D., U. Houston, 1973; 1 son, Baird James Craft. Admitted to Tex. bar, 1973; law clk. 1st Ct. Civil Appeals, Houston, 1974-75; asst. dist. atty. Harris County Dist. Attys. Office, Houston, 1975-76; asso. firm Kronzer, Abraham & Watkins, Houston, 1976-78; asst. U.S. atty. U.S. Atty.'s Office, So. Dist. Tex., Houston, 1978-81; corp. counsel Century Devel. Corp., 1981—. Recipient award for jour. article, Tex. Bar Found., 1978. Mem. Am. Bar Assn., Tex. Bar Assn. (chmn. adminstrn. justice com.), Houston Bar Assn. (dir. 1977-79), Houston Young Lawyers (dir. 1975-76, Outstanding Contbn. award 1975), Order of Barons. Democrat. Contbr. articles to profl. and polit. jours. Office: 5 Greenway Plaza Suite 1700 Houston TX 77046

O'CONNOR, NINA LOUISE, nurse; b. Long Beach, Calif., Mar. 10, 1934; d. Quincy Arthur and Evie Lorraine (Boykin) Roberts; A.A., R.N., Pasadena City Coll., 1976; children—Dennis E., Michael H., Patricia S. Nurse surg. service Meth. Hosp. of So. Calif., Arcadia, 1976, staff nurse surg. ICU, 1977-79, head nurse surg. ICU, 1979—; rev. mgr. PSRO, 1980-81, dir. profl. services, 1981-82. Youth coordinator Pasadena (Calif.) council Girl Scouts U.S.A., 1964-74; mem. Pasadena Election Bd., 1964-82. youth leader Congl. Ch., 1964-74. Cert. advanced life support in CPR, critical care R.N. Mem. Assn. Critical Care Nurses, Nat. Critical Care Inst., Alpha Gamma Sigma, Delta Gamma Omega, Sigma Phi Nu. Congregationalist. Home: 3870 Mayfair Dr Pasadena CA 91107

O'CONNOR, PATRICIA WALKER, educator; b. Memphis, Apr. 26, 1931; d. Shade Wilson and Lillie (Mullins) Walker; student Fla. State U., 1949-51, U. Havana, 1949; B.A. in Edn., U. Fla., 1953, M.A., 1954, Ph.D., 1962; m. Anthony M. Pasquariello; children—Michael P., Erin A. Instr. dept. Romance langs. and lit. U. Cin., 1961-62, asst. prof., 1962-66, asso. prof., 1966-72, prof., 1972—. Am. Philos. Soc. grantee; Taft research grantee. Mem. MLA, Midwest MLA, Am. Assn. Tchrs. of Spanish and Portuguese, AAUP, Phi Beta Kappa. Author: Women in the Theater of Gregorio Martínez Sierra, 1966; Gregorio and María Martínez Sierra, 1977; Contemporary Spanish Theater, 1980; Plays of Protest from the Franco Era, 1981. Office: Dept Romance Langs and Lit U Cin Cincinnati OH 45221

O'CONNOR, SALLY ANNE, bank exec.; b. Newton, Mass., Mar. 12, 1942; d. Frank Martin and Mary O'Connor; student Newton Coll., 1960-62; A.S. with honors, Garland Coll., 1964. Vice pres., gen. mgr. Hampshire House, Boston, 1971-79; dir. mktg. Coopers of Boston, 1980-81; mgr., spl. events mgr. 1st Nat. Bank of Boston, 1981—. Bd. dirs. Public Action for Arts; trustee Boston Ballet. Mem. Jr. League Boston. Republican. Club: Woman's City. Home: 1284 Beacon St Brookline MA 02146 Office: 100 Federal St HO-17 Boston MA 02110

O'CONNOR, SANDRA DAY, supreme ct. justice; b. El Paso, Tex., Mar. 26, 1930; d. Harry A. and Ada Mae (Wiley) Day; B.A., Stanford U., 1950, LL.B. (bd. editors Law Rev.), 1952; m. John Jay O'Connor, III, Dec. 1952; children—Scott, Brian, Jay. Admitted to Calif. bar, 1952, Ariz. bar, 1957; dep. county atty., San Mateo, Calif., 1952-53; civil atty. Q.M. Market Center, Frankfurt/Main, W.Ger., 1954-57; pvt. practice law, Phoenix, 1959-65; individual practice, Maryvale, Ariz., 1959-60; asst. atty. gen., Ariz., 1965-69; mem. Ariz. Senate, 1969-74; judge Superior Ct., Maricopa County, Ariz., 1974-79, Ariz. Ct. Appeals, Phoenix, 1979-81; asso. justice supreme ct. U.S., 1981—; juvenile ct. referee, 1962-64; chmn. vis. bd. Maricopa County Juvenile Detention Home, 1963-64; chmn. com. to reorganize lower cts. Ariz. Supreme Ct., 1974-75; mem. Anglo-Am. Legal Exchange, 1980 Maricopa County Supreme Ct. Judges Tng. and Edn. com.; faculty Robert A. Taft Inst. Govt.; vice chmn. Select Law Enforcement Rev. Commn., 1979-80. Mem. Ariz. Senate, 1969-75, chmn. state, county and mcpl. affairs com., 1972-73, majority leader, 1973-74; past Rep. dist. chmn.; mem. Maricopa County Bd. Adjustments and Appeals, 1963-64, Ariz. Personnel Commn., 1968-69. Nat. Def. Adv. Com. Women in Services, 1974-76; dir. Lazy B Cattle Co. Mem. nat. bd. Smithsonian Assos., 1981—; Ariz. State Personnel Commn., 1967-69; trustee Stanford U., 1976-80; bd. dirs. Ariz. Acad.; pres. Heard Mus., 1980-81; bd. dirs. Phoenix Hist. Soc., 1974-77; adv. bd. Salvation Army, 1975-19; Mem. State Bar Ariz., Am. Bar Assn. Named Phoenix Woman of Year, Advt. Club, 1972; recipient award, NCCJ, 1975, Disting. Achievement Award Ariz. State U., 1980. Office: Supreme Ct of US 1 1st St NW Washington DC 20543 *

O'CONNOR, SARA ANDREWS, repertory theater co. exec.; b. Syracuse, N.Y., Apr. 5, 1932; d. Harlan Francis and Ethel (Hoyt) Andrews; B.A. with high honors in Fine Arts, Swarthmore Coll., 1954, M.A. in Drama, Tufts U., 1955; m. Boardman O'Connor, Aug. 26, 1955 (div. 1969); children—Ian, Douglas. Assoc. producer Co. of the Four, Chgo. 1959-64; assoc. producer Theatre Co. Boston 1965-68, producer, 1969-71; pub. relations dir. Repertory Theatre, New Orleans 1968-69; mng. dir. Cin. Playhouse in the Park 1971-74; mng. dir. Milw. Repertory Theater 1974—; cons. in field. Recipient Rotary Club Milw. citation for service 1980. Mem. Dramatists Guild, Am. Arts Alliance (dir. 1982—), League Resident Theatres (v.p. 1971-78), Theatre Communications Group (pres. 1980-82), Internat. Theatre Inst. (dir. 1980), Milw. Artists Found. (dir. 1981—), Amnesty Internat., Performing Artists for Nuclear Disarmament, ACLU. Translator: The Workroom 1980; At Fifty, She Discovered the Sea 1982. Office: 929 N Water St Milwaukee WI 53202

O'DANIEL, ROSEMARY, nurse; b. Quincy, Ill., May 19, 1950; d. James Andrew and Stella Mae (Cain) Statler; L.P.N., Carl Sandburg Coll., 1977, A.A., 1981; m. William Edward O'Daniel, July 3, 1970; children—Tracy Lynn, John Thomas. Nurse, Community Meml. Hosp., Monmouth, Ill., 1977-82; nurse Warren County Project Help/Western Ill. Home Health Care, 1982—. Mem. Internat. Bus. and Profl. Women. Baptist. Club: Altrusa (grantee 1981). Home: 620 S 9th St Monmouth IL 61462 Office: 304 S Main St Monmouth IL 61462

O'DAY, REY, choreographer, artistic services co. exec., entertainment co. exec.; b. Honolulu, June 23, 1947. Singer-dancer throughout U.S., to 1970; mem. dance faculty Citrus Coll., Los Angeles, 1975—; founder Diamond Bar Children's Theatre, 1971-74; dir., choreographer Golden California Singers, 1975-80; writer, dir. stage shows; exec. dir. Mickey Rooney's Talent Town, U.S.A., 1982—; dir., co-owner Wings of Fame Prodns., Los Angeles, 1975—; entertainment mgr. Busch Gardens, Los Angeles, 1974-77. Author: Theatre of the Spirit, 1980; also articles. Address: 215 E 24th St Apt 712 New York NY 10010 also PO Box GC Azusa CA 91702

ODDE, MARY ELLES MCBEATH, edn. assn. exec., state legislator; b. Rochester, Tex., Feb. 18, 1918; d. Charles Cleveland and Mary Rebecca Ann (Crawford) McBeath; B.A., U. Wyo., 1961; postgrad. DePauw U., 1966; M.A., Idaho State U., 1971; m. Harold S. Odde, Oct. 17, 1941; 1 dau., Ruth Joyce Odde Hartman. Sch. tchr. rural schs., Wyo., 1941-43; sec. to supt. schs., Thermopolis, Wyo., 1944-45; sec. Registrar, N.W. Community Coll., Powell, Wyo., 1947-55; sec. U.S. Bur. Reclamation, Boysen, Wyo., 1956-57; tchr., Shoshoni, Wyo., 1958-78; field dir. UniServ, Wyo. Edn. Assn., Shoshoni, 1978—; instr. field adult edn. U. Wyo., 1971—; mem. Edn. Commn. States, 1981—, Wyo. Travel Commn., 1978-80; mem. Wyo. Dept. Edn. Profl. Standards Bd., 1977-81; mem. Wyo. Ho. of Reps., 1980—. Mem. NEA, PTA (life), Future Farmers Am. (life, hon.), Wyo. Edn. Assn. (pres., bd. dirs.), Delta Kappa Gamma. Republican. Presbyterian. Home: 621 California St Shoshoni WY 82649

O'DEA, CONSTANCE LOUISE, state agy. exec., educator; b. N.Y.C., June 27, 1946; d. John W. J. and Valerie C. O'Dea; B.A. (Durant scholar), Wellesley Coll., 1968; M.A., Harvard U., 1973. Asst. coordinator systems analysis group Inst. Space Research, Nat. Research Council of Brazil, Sao Paulo, 1973-74; vis. prof. Tech. Inst. Aeros., Sao Paulo, 1974; instr. Am. Sch., Rio de Janeiro, Brazil, 1975-77, coordinator research and devel. planning N.J. Dept. Edn., Trenton, 1978—; cons. in field. Rep. for Rio de Janeiro-Belo Horizonte to Wellesley (Mass.) Coll., 1976-77. Ford Found. fellow Harvard U., 1969-73; Fanny Bullock Workman fellow Wellesley Coll., 1969-70. Mem. Phi Beta Kappa. Clubs: N.Y. Wellesley, St. Bartholomew Community. Editor, collaborator: The Social Economy of the Future, 1979. Home: 141 Red Hill Rd Princeton NJ 08540 Office: 225 W State St Trenton NJ 08625

O'DELL, LYNN MARIE LUEGGE, librarian; b. Berwyn, Ill. Feb. 24, 1938; d. George Emil and Helen Marie (Pesek) Luegge; student Lyons Twp. Jr. Coll., La Grange, Ill., 1957; student N. Ill. U., Elgin Community Coll., U. Ill.; m. Norman D. O'Dell, Dec. 14, 1957; children—Jeffrey, Jerry. Sec. Martin Co., Chgo., 1957-59; librarian, Carol Stream (Ill.) Public Library, 1964—; exec. com. Du Page County Library System, 1967, 68, 71—, v.p. automation governing com. Active Carol Stream unit Central DuPage Hosp. Aux.; sec. Carol Stream Bicentennial Commn. Named Woman of Year, Wheaton Bus. and Profl. Woman's Club, 1968. Mem. ALA, Ill. Library Assn., Library Adminstrs. Conf. No. Ill., Carol Stream Hist. Soc. (1st v.p.). Club: Carol Stream Woman's (sec. 1968, 1st v.p. 1969). Lutheran (organist). Home: 182 Yuma Ln Carol Stream IL 60187 Office: 616 Hiawatha Dr Carol Stream IL 60187

O'DELL, MARGOT NUMAN, life ins. co. exec.; b. Green Bay, Wis., Feb. 26, 1942; d. Garno Orange and Geraldine Mae (Farrell) Numan; B.S. in Bus. Adminstrn., Franklin U., Columbus, Ohio, 1974; m. Willard Gerald Hill, II, Aug. 25, 1979; 1 dau., Kathleen. Dept. mgr. Donaldson's Dept. Store, Mpls. and Rapid City, S.D., 1962-67, Lerner Shop, N.Y.C., 1967-68; buyer Hislop's Dept. Store, Auburn, N.Y., 1969-71; asst. mgr. Gentlemen's Clothing, Columbus, Ohio, 1972-74; agt. Aetna Life Ins. Co., Columbus, 1974-78, brokerage supr., 1978-80; pres. O'Dell Ins. Agy., Inc., Gahanna, Ohio, 1980—. Named Bus. Woman of Year, Columbus Profl. and Bus. Women, 1979; mem. Women's Leaders Round Table, 1976-78, Leading Producers Round Table, 1974-80; C.L.U., 1979. Mem. Nat. Assn. Health Underwriters (nat. pres. trustees Leading Producers Round Table 1980), Nat. Assn. Life Underwriters, Am. Soc. C.L.U.s, Ohio Assn. Health Underwriters (pres. 1980). Republican. Episcopalian. Home: 129 N Stygler Rd Gahanna OH 43230 Office: 129 N Stigler Rd Gahanna OH 43230

O'DELL, MARY B., assn. exec., polit. cons.; b. Columbus, Nebr., Aug. 28, 1930; d. Harry C. and Helen (Cherny) Brown; B.A. in Elem. Edn., U. Colo., 1952; m. R.A. O'Dell (div.); children—Christopher Craig, Mark Kendall, Paul John. Kindergarten tchr., Kirkwood, Mo., 1952-55; news editor, city reporter, acting bus. mgr. Aurora (Colo.) Sun, 1972-76; free lance polit. cons. and public relations work, 1972—; exec. dir. Colo. Assn. Tobacco and Candy Distbrs., Aurora, 1977—; exec. dir. Colo. Assn. Temporary Services, 1981—; campaign office mgr. U.S. Rep. William L. Armstrong, 1976, asst. to fin. dir. Armstrong Com., 1978; dep. campaign mgr. Eckelberry for Congress Com., 1978; scheduling dir. Cogswell for Senate Com., 1980; advisor to Denver Research Inst., 1975. Apptd. to Colo. Commn. on Status of Women, 1974; chmn. bd. dirs. Met. Denver Sewage Disposal Dist. 1, 1974-76; chmn. Mothers' March of Dimes, 1961; mem. citizens adv. budget com. to Aurora City Council, 1980—; mem. Arapahoe County Republican exec. com., 1974-81; pres. Aurora Rep. Women's Club, 1974-76. Recipient Key to City of Aurora, 1976; Ernest J. O'Brien award Nat. Assn. Tobacco Distbrs., 1981. Mem. Am. Soc. Assn. Execs., Colo. Soc. Assn. Execs., Pi Lambda Theta, Tau Beta Sigma. Presbyterian. Clubs: PEO, Aurora JayCee-ettes (pres. 1960-61). Subject of feature story Denver Post, 1976. Office: PO Box 31308 Aurora CO 80041

ODEN, LAURA JUANITA BURTON, personnel exec.; b. Newark, Jan. 21, 1947; d. Herman L. and Iola (Brnatley) Burton; B.A., Seplman Coll., 1968; postgrad. Control Data Inst., 1970; m. Jerry Oden, Sept. 4, 1970. Social worker Los Angeles County Public Social Services, 1968-70; chief personnel tng., 1970-72, personnel analyst with personnel dept., 1972-74, team leader, 1974-77, community devel. analyst, 1974-77, now personnel analyst III. Pres., Black Women's Network; mem. Inter-Alumni Council United Negro Coll. Fund. Mem. Calif. Personnel Mgmt. Assn., Am. Soc. Personnel Mgmt., Am. Soc. Public Adminstrn. Presbyterian. Home: 1222 S Alvira St Los Angeles CA 90035 Office: 222 N Grand Ave Los Angeles CA 90012

ODENDAHL, ANNE LOUISE HITCH, writer, editor, pub. relations cons.; b. Dayton, Ohio, June 7, 1939; d. James Leonard and Frieda Engelke Hitch; B.A., Ohio State U., 1961; m. Alan Odendahl, July 21, 1968; children—Laura Jean, Cynthia Leonard. Reporter, Dayton Jour. Herald, 1961-63, Balt. Sunpapers, 1964-66; pub. relations dir. Md. Inst. Coll. Art, 1966, Balt. Mental Health Assn., 1967-68; account exec. Compton Jones Advt., Washington, 1969-71; free lance writer, pub. relations cons., Washington, 1971—; dir. news bur. Cath. U. Am., Washington, 1976-78. Mem. D.C. City Panhellenic Assn. (v.p. 1976-77), Zeta Tau Alpha. Democrat. Unitarian. Club: Woman's Nat. Democratic. Home: 14828 Fireside Dr Silver Spring MD 20904 Office: PO Box 177 Burtonsville MD 20866

ODIORNE, ALICE SOULEK, lawyer; b. Newport News, Va., Apr. 27, 1953; d. Dale Sinclair and Lucy (Bishop) Soulek; B.A. with honors, Baylor U., 1975, J.D., 1978; m. James T. Odiorne, Apr. 26, 1980; 1 son, James Michael; 1 son by previous marriage, Toby Aaron Quinn. Admitted to Tex. bar, 1979; ptnr. firm James T. Odiorne, Bastrop, Tex., 1978—. Bd. dirs. Bastrop Opera House, 1979-80. Mem. Bastrop County Bar Assn. (pres. 1980-81), Tex. State Bar (criminal law sect.), Am. Bar Assn., Tex. Young Lawyers Assn., Nat. Assn. Female Execs. Democrat. Methodist. Office: 710 Chestnut St Bastrop TX 78602

ODOM, MARJORIE MILDRED MORGAN, librarian; b. Lavernia, Tex., July 22, 1924; d. Andrew Jackson and Estella Fledia (Phillips) Morgan; cert. in cosmetology C.J. Walker Beauty Coll., 1943; B.A. in Library Sci., Our Lady of Lake Coll., San Antonio, 1964, M.A. in Edn., 1979; m. Steven Odom, Jr., June 25, 1944 (dec.). Mgr., Mme. C.J. Walker Beauty Salon, San Antonio, 1944-52; propr. Ross Hotel Beauty Salon, San Antonio, 1952-63; asst. supr. children's dept. San Antonio Main Public Library, 1964-65; secondary sch. librarian San Antonio Ind. Sch. Dist., 1965—; sponsor Library Reading Club. First asso. supt. ch. sch. New Mt. Pleasant Baptist Ch., San Antonio, 1974—, tchr. jr. boys class 1967—, dir. Christian edn., 1978—, chmn. library com., 1978—; mem. Tex. Senator's adv. council on legis. affairs. Recipient outstanding award analysis and design Kappa Pi Sigma, 1978. Mem. NEA (life), Tex. Tchrs. Assn., Tex. Classroom Tchrs. Assn., San Antonio Ind. Sch. Dist. Librarians Assn., Bexar Library Assn., PTA, San Antonio Tchrs. Council. Democrat. Home: PO Box 8374 San Antonio TX 78208

O'DONNELL, ALICE LOUISE, govt. ofcl.; b. Stanwood, Wash.; d. John James and Jeannette May (Anderson) O'Donnell; student U. Wash., 1932, U. So. Calif., 1943-44; student George Washington U, 1940-42, J.D., 1954. Admitted to U.S. Dist. Ct. bar for D.C., U.S. Supreme Ct. bar, U.S. Ct. of Appeals bar for D.C. Circuit; with staff Atty. Gen. U.S., 1945-49; mem. staff Justice Clark, Supreme Ct. of U.S., Washington, 1949-67; lawyer Fed. Jud. Center, Washington, 1968—, dir. div. inter-jud. affairs and info. services, 1971—; sec.-treas. Nat. Center for State Cts., 1971-81. Vice-chmn. bd. dirs. Potomac Law Sch., Washington, 1975-79. Fellow Inst. Jud. Adminstrn.; mem. Am. (mem. div. jud. adminstrn., chmn. 1973-74), Fed. (mem. nat. council) bar assns., Nat. Assn. Women Lawyers, Am. Judicature Soc., Nat. Lawyers Club Washington (bd. govs.), Supreme Ct. Hist. Soc. (1st v.p.), Phi Alpha Delta. Roman Catholic. Home: The Towers 4201 Cathedral Ave NW Washington DC 20016 Office: Dolley Madison House 1520 H St NW Washington DC 20005

O'DONNELL, MARY ANNE, coll. adminstr.; b. Bryn Mawr, Pa., Mar. 15, 1954; d. Charles S. and Anne Catherine O'D.; B.S., Bloomsburg State Coll., 1976; M.S., Shippensburg State Coll., 1979. Grad. asst. Bloomsburg (Pa.) State Coll., 1976-77; grad., counselor Shippensburg (Pa.) State Coll., 1977-79; residence dir. St. Mary's Coll., Notre Dame, Ind., 1979-80, dir. student activities, 1980—. Mem. Nat. Assn. Student Personnel Adminstrs., Nat. Entertainment and Coll. Activities Assn., Nat. Assn. Orientation Dirs., Am. Coll. Unions Internat. Home: 439 LaMonte Terr South Bend IN 46616 Office: Saint Mary's College 166 LeMans Hall Notre Dame IN 46556

O'DONOGHUE, MARY ANN MCDEVITT, psychologist; b. Drexel Hill, Pa., Apr. 24, 1929; d. Thomas F. and Anna (McHugh) McDevitt; B.A., Trinity Coll., Washington, 1959; M.A., Cath. U., 1966, Montclair State Coll., 1974; Ph.D., Hofstra U., Hempstead, N.Y., 1979; m. Joseph O'Donoghue, Jan. 10, 1975. Tchr., Sisters of Notre Dame, 1951-69; mem. faculty Kenyatta Coll., Nairobi, Kenya, 1969-71, Westchester (Pa.) State Coll., 1971-73; dir. Marjoe Research Cons., Inc., N.Y.C., 1973-79; mem. faculty Molloy Coll., Rockville Center, N.Y., 1979-82; project dir. Marjoe Cons., Lido Beach, N.Y., 1982—; cons. female promotional patterns to Japanese and Am. firms; psychologist internat. Japanese and Am. exchange program; dir. summer seminars for orientation of Japanese students in U.S. Recipient Spl. Service award Japan Engr. Devel. Co., 1981; Irish-Am. Research fellow, 1982. Mem. Am. Psychol. Assn., Japan Engr. Devel. Assos. Democrat. Roman Catholic. Club: Faculty Women of U.S. and Japan. Author: Love as Concern, 1974. Home and office: 66 Leamington St Lido Beach NY 11561

O'DWYER, JOANNE INEZ, data processing exec.; b. Chgo., Oct. 13, 1936; d. John A. and Emmy (Schneckenberger) Bruland; B.A., U. Colo., 1954-58. Acct. rep. Royal Globe Ins. Cos., Chgo., 1961-64; various office positions Milw. Gear Co., 1965-70, data processing mgr., 1970-72; partner AIS Computer Services, Milw., 1972-73, Ozauk Computer Services, Grafton, Wis., 1973-75; pres. Moraine Data Services, Inc., Hartford, Wis., 1975—. Mem. adv. council Trees For Tomorrow Environ. Center, 1975—; treas. Friends For Battered Women of Washington County, 1979-81; mem. crime prevention com. Richfield Twp., 1975-77; pres. Niles Twp. (Ill.) Young Republican Orgn., 1960-62, co-chmn. Cook County 1961-62; mem. Washington County (Wis.) Rep. Orgn., 1976—. Mem. Data Processing Mgmt. Assn. (dir. Milw. chpt. 1977—, sec. 1977-79), Wis. Fedn. Women's Clubs (charter pres. Richfield-Hubertus 1970-71, pollution chmn. 1971-72, conservation chmn. 1972-74, 79-80, public affairs chmn. 1974-76, internat. affairs chmn. 1976-77, home life chmn. 1977-78, pres. 1978-79, del. gen. conv. 1973-74, 76—, dist. conservation chmn. 1976-82, state jr. conservation chmn. 1972-74, state gen. conservation chmn. 1974-76, corr. sec., state project selection chmn. 1976-78, state 2d v.p. 1978-80, 1st v.p. 1980-82, pres. 1982—), Nat. Assn. Women Bus. Owners, Alpha Omicron Pi (dist. dir. Ill. 1960-62, chpt. adv. 1962-67). Lutheran. Home: 3428 Lovers Ln Slinger WI 53086 Office: 51 E Sumner Hartford WI 53027

OEHLERT, ALICE GREENE, civic worker; b. Munson, Pa., May 17, 1912; d. Hugh R. and Elva (Howe) Greene; grad. Thomas W. Evans Dental Inst., U. Pa., 1931; m. Benjamin H. Oehlert, Mar. 27, 1937; children—Benjamin H. III, Wendy Howe. Bd. dirs. Henry St. Settlement, N.Y.C., 1956-68, Browse Gallery of Atlanta Art Assn., 1959-61, Palm Beach (Fla.) Community Chest, 1971-73; sec. Bargain Box, Inc., N.Y.C., 1956-69; trustee Atlanta Art Assn., 1966-67; mem. adv. council Young Women's Community Club, Orlando, Fla., 1963-64; bd. dirs. Orange County chpt. Nat. Found., 1962-64; mem. women's aux. Piedmont Hosp., Atlanta, 1965-67; mem. adv. bd. jr. adv. com. High Mus. Art, Atlanta, 1965-67; v.p. Loch Haven Art Center of Orlando Art Assn., 1963-64, trustee, 1964-65; chmn. cultural affairs Greater Orlando C. of C., 1964-65; hon. pres. Am. Women's Club, Islamabad, Pakistan, 1967-69; chmn. 1st Designer Showcase, Islamabad, 1967-69; Am. dir. to all Pakistan Women's Club, Islamabad, 1967-69; bd. dirs. picture program Good Samaritan Hosp., West Palm Beach, Fla., 1969-70, mem. adv. bd. fund raising com. for women's aux., 1970-73, chmn. Ball Jour., 1978-82; chmn. Palm Beach ARC Designers Showcase, 1976. Recipient commendation ARC, 1976, Palm Beach Garden Club Showcase, 1973. Mem. DAR. Republican. Presbyterian.

OFARIM, DIANE, psychotherapist; b. Chgo., Feb. 25, 1944; d. Gustave and Freidella (Reiff) Platt; M.A. in Clin. Psychology, Pepperdine Coll., 1966; postgrad. U. So. Calif., 1966-71; 1 dau., Monica. With various social service agys. including juvenile probation, family and group therapy Los Angeles Dept. Public Aid, 1962-70, Cook County Juvenile Ct., Chgo., 1970-75, pvt. practice psychotherapy, specializing in psychoanalytically oriented, interpersonal relationships, individuals, couples and group therapy, Evanston, Ill., 1975—; Mem. Assn. for Humanistic Psychology, Am. Psychol. Assn., Am. Personnel and Guidance Assn., Psi Chi. Office: 1603 Orrington Suite 1044 Evanston IL 60201

O'FARRELL, LUCY SHELTON, real estate co. exec.; b. Warrenton, Ga., Dec. 25, 1918; d. Bennett Gordon and Mary VanDella (Dye) Shelton; student Ga. State Women's Coll., 1936-37, Hurst Bus. Coll., 1937-38; m. Oscar Cameron O'Farrell, July 21, 1941; 1 dau., Carol Lynn. Sec., Lockhart Ins. & Realty Co., Atlanta, 1939-41; sec., rater, office mgr., agent Gen. Ins. Merritt & McKenzie, Atlanta, 1941-71; sales asso. Clover Realty Co., Atlanta, 1971-75, br. mgr., v.p., 1975—. Cert. real estate broker. Mem. Nat. Assn. Realtors, Ga. Assn. Realtors, Atlanta Bd. Realtors, Womens Council Realtors, Sales Mgrs. Club, Ga. Assn. Parliamentarians, Nat. Assn. Parliamentarians, Atlanta Ins. Women. Democrat. Baptist. Club: Toastmasters. Home: 7264 Selkirk Dr NE Atlanta GA 30328 Office: Clover Realty Co 3456 Piedmont Rd NE Atlanta GA 30328

OFFERMAN, MURIEL KRAMER, merchant; b. Wilmington, N.C., July 22, 1935; d. Harry Edward and Vivian Freda (Katzoff) Kramer; student Smith Coll., 1953-56; B.A., U. Chgo., 1957; m. Max Offerman, July 29, 1956; children—Mark Allen, Sheri Cay, Lori Lynn. Tchr., Chestnut St. Jr. High Sch., Wilmington, 1957-58; with Kramer's Dept. Store, Wallace, N.C., 1966—, pres., 1976—; dir. Bank of N.C. Pres., treas. Crossroads Playhouse, 1961-69; pres. Elem. Sch. PTA, Wallace, 1967, Charity PTA, 1977; mem. Duplin County Sch. Adv. Com., 1967—; adv. com. health careers James Sprunt Tech. Coll., 1979—; vice-chmn. Rockfish Democratic Precinct. Mem. N.C. Assn. Jewish Women, Am. Bus. Women's Assn., Wallace C. of C. (2d v.p.), Smith Coll. Alumni Assn., Tar Heel Fine Arts Soc. (v.p. 1973-75). Jewish. Clubs: Hadassah (pres. 1960-62), Wallace Jr. Women's (pres. 1960-61), Evergreen Garden (pres. 1965). Home: 500 N Harrell St Wallace NC 28466 Office: Rockfish Plaza Wallace NC 28466

OFFIR, CAROLE WADE, psychologist, educator; b. Mpls., Mar. 7, 1941; d. Robert and Rose Wade; B.A., UCLA, 1963; Ph.D., Stanford U., 1973; children—Jessica, Jason. Asst. prof. psychology U. N.Mex., Albuquerque, 1972-73; asso. editor Psychology Today Mag., Del Mar, Calif., 1973-75; prof. psychology San Diego Mesa Coll., 1975—; social sci. writer. Mem. Am. Psychol. Assn., NOW. Author: (with Carol Tavris) The Longest War: Sex Differences in Perspective, 1975; Human Sexuality, 1982. Office: Behavioral Scis Dept San Diego Mesa Coll San Diego CA 92111

OFFNER, MARY ELLEN, budget analyst; b. St. Louis, Aug. 10, 1954; d. Lawrence Joseph and Audre June (Cooper) O.; B.S. in Biology, Maryville Coll., 1976. Research asst. Washington U. Sch. Medicine, St. Louis, 1976-77; salesperson Creativity Unltd., St. Louis, 1977-78; budget analyst McDonnell Douglas, St. Louis, 1978—. Fin. adviser Jr. Achievement, 1980—. Mem. Toastmasters Internat., Women's Polit. Caucus of St. Louis, Women's Commerce Assn. St. Louis, Delta Epsilon Sigma. Roman Catholic. Club: Blue Army. Office: McDonnell Douglas PO Box 516 Saint Louis MO 63166

OGDEN, ELIZABETH KOHNSTAMM, social worker; b. N.Y.C., Dec. 13, 1920; d. Lothair S. and Madeline (Peck) Kohnstamm; B.A., Russell Sage Coll., 1942; M.S.W., N.Y. U., 1968; m. Leslie Pantin Ogden, June 24, 1941; children—Thomas H., Richard L. Sec., Vocat. Adv. Service, N.Y.C., 1944; social worker Home Service div. ARC, Bklyn., 1945; clin. social worker Scarsdale (N.Y.) Family Counseling Service, 1968-77; pvt. practice psychotherapy, Harrison, N.Y., 1977—; dir. H. Kohnstamm Inc., mfg. chemists, 1979-81. Bd. dirs. Harrison Ave. PTA, 1953-57; bd. dirs. LWV, Harrison, 1955-59, 1st v.p., 1959-61, pres., 1961-63; alumnae leadership chmn. Russell Sage Coll. capital fund, 1982. Fellow N.Y. State Soc. Clin. Social Work Psychotherapists; mem. Nat. Assn. Social Workers, Am. Orthopsychiat. Assn. Home and office: Winfield Ave Harrison NY 10528

OGDEN, VALERIA JUAN, mgmt. cons.; b. Okanogan, Wash., Feb. 11, 1924; d. Ivan Bodwell and Pearle (Wilson) Munson; B.A. magna cum laude, Wash. State U., 1946; m. Daniel M. Ogden, Jr., Dec. 28, 1946; children—Janeth Lee Ogden Martin, Patricia Jo Ogden Hunter, Daniel Munson. Exec. dir. Potomac Camp Fire Girls, Washington, 1964-68, Ft. Collins (Colo.) United Way, 1969-73, Designing Tomorrow Today, Ft. Collins, 1973-74, Poudre Valley Assn. Community Edn., Ft. Collins, 1975-77; acting exec. dir. Golden Gate Council Camp Fire Girls, San Francisco, 1978, Camp Fire Council Chesapeake, Balt., 1978-79, St. Paul Council Camp Fire Girls, 1979; pres. Valeria M. Ogden, Inc., mgmt. cons. and trainer not-for-profit orgns., Kensington, Md., 1979—; exec. dir. YWCA, Nat. Capital Area, 1981—; mem. nat. vol. staff Camp Fire, Inc., 1976-81; lectr. Lewis and Clark Coll., Portland, Oreg., 1978—; mem. Colo. Social Work Lic. Bd., 1974-77. Chmn., Larimer County (Colo.) Democratic Com., 1974-76; pres. Ft. Collins Council Arts and Humanities, 1974-76; mem. nat. coll. and univ. bd. YWCA, 1960-66. Named Citizen of Yr., Ft. Collins Realtor's Assn., 1973; recipient Gulick award Camp Fire Girls, Lewiston, Idaho, 1956. Mem. PEO, Mortar Board (nat. sec. 1973-76, v.p. 1976-79), Phi Beta Kappa. Democrat. Unitarian. Address: 3333 University Blvd Kensington MD 20895

O'GORMAN, PATRICIA ALICE, psychologist; b. N.Y.C., May 27, 1946; d. Patrick M. and Mary L. (Kohut) O'G.; B.A., CCNY, 1968, M.S., 1970; Ph.D., Fordham U., 1975; m. Robert Allen Ross, Aug. 12, 1979. Clin. Asst. dept. sch. psychology Bklyn. Coll., 1973-74, adj. lectr., 1974; dir. dept. prevention and edn. Nat. Council on Alcoholism, N.Y.C., 1974-79; clin. instr. dept. psychiatry N.Y.U., N.Y.C., 1976-79; dir. div. prevention Nat. Inst. Alcohol Abuse, Rockville, Md., 1979-81; chief psychologist Berkshire Farm Ctr. and Services for Youth, Canaan, N.Y., 1981—; pvt. practice psychology East Greenbush, N.Y., 1981—; nat. and internat. lectr. on alcoholism prevention; also spokesperson on radio, TV and press; cons. VA Hosp., Albany, N.Y., 1978-79, SUNY, Albany, 1979, 81, N.Y. Council on Children and Families, Albany, 1979, Ministry Labour and Social Affairs, Israel, 1981; mem. grad. edn. nat. adv. com. project Physician Requirements for 1990's, 1982. Mem. Pres. Carter's Transition Task Force on Health, 1976; mem. N.Y. Gov.'s Transition Task Force on Alcohol and Substance Abuse, also chmn. com. on prevention, 1976; mem. adv. subcom. on alcoholism N.Y. State Senate, 1977-79; mem. alcohol and drug work group for promoting health and preventing disease Objectives for Nation, 1979; nat. adv. bd. Women in Crisis Conf., 1981-82. Mem. Am. Psychol. Assn., Am. Pub. Health Assn., Research Soc. on Alcoholism. Democrat. Author: (with P. Finn) Teaching About Alcohol, 1981; also articles. Editorial bd. Focus on Women: Jour. of Addiction and Health, 1981-82. Home: Rural Delivery Box 300 East Chatham NY 12060 Office: Berkshire Farm Ctr Canaan NY 12029 also 568 Columbia Turnpike East Greenbush NY

O'HAGAN, MIMI (EUGENIE J.), hosp. exec.; b. Bklyn., Mar. 19, 1930; d. John F. and Chrystal (Byrne) O'Hagan; B.A., Newton Coll. of the Sacred Heart, 1951. Asst. Campaign dir. advance man Citizens for Eisenhower, 1956; advt. and pub. relations dir. Schweppes Ltd., N.Y.C., 1957-63; nat. publicity dir. Project HOPE, N.Y.C., 1963-65; partner Murphy O'Hagen Coordinated Communications, N.Y.C., 1965-79; public affairs dir. Kero-Sun, Inc., Kent, Conn., 1979-80; partner Murphy O'Hagan, N.Y.C., 1981-82; dir. public and community relations Danbury (Conn.) Hosp., 1982—; founder and co-adminstr. Entente Sacre Coeur, 1966. Mem. adv. bd. Alumnae Assn. of the Sacred Heart, N.Y.; v.p. bd. trustees Acad. of Sacred Heart. Mem. Council of Independent Secondary Schs., Kappa Gamma Pi. Republican. Roman Catholic. Author series of study skill booklets, 1973-79. Home: Box 374 RR 1 Kent CT 06757

O'HAIR, MADALYN, author, orgn. exec.; b. Pitts., Apr. 13, 1919; d. John I. and Lena C. (Scholle) Mays; B.A., Ashland Coll.; LL.B., J.D., S. Tex. Coll. Law; Ph.D., Minn. Inst. Philosophy; m. Richard F. O'Hair; children—William J., Jon Garth Murray, Robin Murray-O'Hair. Founder Soc. Separationists; founder Am. Atheist Library and Archives, Austin, Tex.; founder Am. Atheist Radio Series, Am. Atheist Center, Am. Atheist TV Series, United World Atheists, Am. Atheist Women; founder, editor Am. Atheist Mag. Bd. dirs. Am. Humanist Assn. Author: Freedom Under Siege; What on Earth is An Atheist?; The Atheist World; Atheists Speak; Atheists Believe; Why I Am An Atheist; An Atheist Epic; All About Atheists; Atheism, Its Viewpoint; Jesus Christ, Super Fraud; An Original Theory in Respect to the Origin of Religion; Religious Games People Play; An Atheist Primer; All the Questions You Ever Wanted to Ask American Atheists; War in Vietnam: The Religious Connection. Adv. editor to N.Y. Times. Litigant in Murray vs. Curlett case U.S. Supreme Ct. to remove prayer from pub. schs., 1963. Office: 2210 Hancock Dr Austin TX 78756

O'HALLAREN, MAUREEN THERESE (MRS. ANDREW COUBROUGH, JR.), marriage and family therapist; b. Chgo., Oct. 3, 1940; d. Bernard James and Josephine Frances (White) O'H.; B.A., Siena Heights Coll., 1963; M.A., U. Detroit, 1970; cert. Inst. Religion and Human Devel., Houston, 1973; m. Andrew Coubrough, Jr., Oct. 15, 1977; children—Andrew Coubrough III, Heather Arlene. Tchr. English, Sts. Peter and Paul High Sch., Ruth, Mich., Dominican High Sch., Detroit, 1965-71; chaplain Hermann Hosp. Tex. Med. Center, Houston, 1971-72; dir. Ecumenical Counseling Center, Webster, Tex., 1972-73; pvt. practice psychol. counseling, Houston, 1973-75; alcoholism therapist Henry Ford Hosp., Detroit, 1975-76, dir. outpatient alcoholism treatment program, Troy, Mich., 1975-76; health counselor Ford Motor Co., Detroit, 1976—; pvt. practice psychol. counseling, Birmingham, Mich., 1976—. Mem. Mich. Interprofl. Assn., Nat. Inst. Alcohol Abuse and Alcoholism, Assn. Labor-Mgmt. Adminstrs. and Cons. on Alcoholism, Am. Assn. Marriage and Family Therapists. Roman Catholic. Office: 111 S Woodward Suite 250 Birmingham MI 48011

O'HALLORAN, (LAVERNE M.) KATHLEEN (MRS. JOHN R. O'HALLORAN, JR.), realtor; b. Laurium, Mich., Nov. 15, 1921; d.

Joseph Wilfred and Della K. (Gervais) Shaffer; student Fond Du Lac Comml. Coll., 1938-40, Fresno City Coll., 1965-66; m. John Richard O'Halloran, Jr., July 15, 1942; children—Sheila Ann O'Halloran Stoll, Gregory, Michael, Maureen O'Halloran Benelli, Sean, Margaret O'Halloran Johnson. Co-owner Hamlin Hotel, San Francisco, 1946-48, Lazy F Guest Ranch, Ellensburg, Wash., 1948-50; real estate broker, Fresno, 1965—. Charter mem. Infant of Prague Adoption Agy. Aux., 1954—, sec., 1955; mem. Mayor's Com. Community Devel., 1963-64; pres. Sacred Heart Mothers Club, 1959; pres. Calif. Citizens for Decent Lit., 1961-63, Central Calif. Citizens for Decent Lit., 1959-64; sec. Sacred Heart Altar Soc., 1976-78; precinct chmn. Goldwater campaign, 1964; chmn. Fresno County United Republicans Calif., 1962; area coordinator Clean Campaign Ballot Initiative, 1966; candidate Fresno City Council, 1961. Mem. Fresno Bd. Realtors, Nat. Assn. Real Estate Bds. Roman Catholic. Home: 3503 N Bond St Fresno CA 93726

OHANESIAN, JOANNE MARIAM, career placement agy. exec.; b. Selma, Calif., July 21, 1943; d. John Malcolm and Satrig Hazel (Shabasian) O.; grad. parochial schs. Real estate, property mgmt. exec., Fresno, Calif., 1961-67; vice-pres. Lynn Carol, Inc., Los Angeles, 1967-79; pres. Ohanesian and Assos., Inc., Beverly Hills, Calif., 1979—. Mem. Western Regional C. of C., Beverly Hills C. of C., Los Angeles C. of C., Women In Bus., Nat. Assn. Women Bus. Owners. Contbr. articles to Los Angeles Times, Santa Monica Evening Outlook, Executive Mag., others. Office: 9107 Wilshire Blvd Beverly Hills CA 90213

OHANJANIAN, SANDRA CAROL (SANDRA OHAN), welding co. exec.; b. Chgo., Oct. 22, 1955; d. Nick Haig and Josephine (Alexanoff) O.; B.A. in Philosophy, Roosevelt U., 1978. Dir. bus. ops. Diamond Toymakers, Skokie, Ill., 1976-79; pres. Ohan Enterprises, Inc., Chgo., 1979-81; v.p. Precision Welding, Inc., Chgo., 1981—. Mem. Nat. Assn. Female Execs., Internat. Trade Club Chgo. Club: Order Eastern Star. Office: 3054 W Belmont Ave Chicago IL 60618

O'HARA, KATHY MARLEEN, physician; b. Bridgeport, Conn., Feb. 22, 1951; d. Walter Edgar and Grace Dorothy (Potter) Magill; B.S. cum laude in Biology, Oral Roberts U., Tulsa, 1973; D.O., Coll. Osteo. Medicine and Surgery, Des Moines, 1977. Intern, Des Moines Gen. Hosp., 1977-78; emergency room physician Salem County Meml. Hosp., Salem, N.J., 1981—; guest speaker. Served with USN, 1978-80. Mem. Am. Osteo. Assn., Am. Med. Women's Assn., Christian Med. Soc., Assn. Mil. Osteo. Physicians and Surgeons, AAUW, Sigma Sigma Phi. Republican. Mem. Assembly of God. Home: Laura's Glen Apt F-8 Pennsville NJ 08070 Office: Salem County Memorial Hospital Salem NJ 08079

O'HEARN, MARYALICE, reading resource specialist; A.B. cum laude, Emmanuel Coll., Boston, 1965; M.Ed. with distinction, Boston Coll., 1975. Dir., Project Head Start Spanish Speaking Center, Boston, summers 1965, 66; tchr. Dept. Def. Overseas Tng. Program, Philippines, 1967-68, Yokota, Japan, 1968-69, Yokosuka, Japan, 1969-70; tchr., Vietnam, 1967-69; instr. Sony Industries, Tokyo, part time 1968-70; transition tchr. Title I Program, Brockton (Mass.) Sch. System, 1970-72; reading resource specialist, 1972—; cons. Stonehill Coll., North Easton, Mass., part time 1977—; sr. cons. Holt, Rinehart and Winson, N.Y.C., 1977—. Mem. World Forum Com., World Affairs Council; mem. policy com. Center for Internat. Visitors; ambassador, host Friendship Force. Mem. AAUW, NEA, Mass. Tchrs. Assn., Internat. Reading Assn., Japan Soc., Emmanuel Coll. Alumnae Assn., Boston Coll. Alumnae Assn. Address: 105 Sea Ave Quincy MA 02169

O'HERN, ELIZABETH MOOT, microbiologist, health adminstr.; b. Richmondville, N.Y., Sept. 1, 1913; d. Carl Melvin and Margaret Esther (Dibble) Moot; B.A., U. Calif., Berkeley, 1945, M.A., 1947; Ph.D., U. Wash., Seattle, 1956; m. William J. O'Hern, Jan. 4, 1952. Fellow, U. Wash., 1951-56; instr. State U. N.Y. Med. Center, Bklyn., 1957-62; asst. prof. George Washington U., 1962-65; research adminstr. Bionetics Inc., 1965-68; health sci. adminstr. NIH, 1968—. spl. asst. to dir. 1975-78; mem. bd. examiners in basic scis. Commn. Licensure to Practice Healing Art D.C., 1974. Established Mary Church Terrel scholarship for D.C. women, 1969. Mem. Am. Soc. Microbiology (chmn. com. status of women 1975-78, bd. dirs. Found. for Microbiology 1975-77), Am. Acad. Microbiology, AAAS, Am. Inst. Biol. Scis., AAUW (pres. Washington br. 1967-69, trustee Ednl. Found. 1977-81), Am. Soc. Cell Biology, Am. Soc. Microbiology, Med. Mycology Ams., N.Y. Acad. Sci., Washington Acad. Sci., Grad. Women in Sci. (nat. sec. 1974-77). Contbr. numerous articles to profl. jours. Home: 633 G St SW Washington DC 20024 Office: NIH Westwood Room 952 Bethesda MD 20205

O'HERN, LINDA KAREN, marriage and family therapist; b. Denver, Oct. 2, 1946; d. Forbes W. and Bertha (Hylen) Van Scoyk; B.A. in Elem. Edn., U. Ariz., 1968; M.Ed. in Counseling, 1977, postgrad., 1977—; m. Frank R. Williams, Jan. 27, 1979; children by previous marriage—Christopher M., Jeffrey P. Campus ministry coordinator Am. Baptist Chs. Ariz., 1975-77; program asst. continuing edn. U. Ariz., 1977-78, dir. PHASE, 1978-80, grad. asst. counseling dept., 1980-82, instr. women's studies, 1979-81; ind. practice marriage and family therapy, Tucson, 1980—; organizer, trainer Divorce Recovery Project, 1978-82; county chmn. White House Conf. Families, 1980; organizer Ariz. Stepfamily Assn., 1981-82. Bd. dirs. Tucson YWCA, 1978—, pres., 1982-83; organizer, mem. steering com. Exec. Women's Council Tucson, 1979-81. Recipient Creative Programming award Nat. U. Extension Assn., 1978; Middle Yrs. Humanities grantee, 1977; Vocat. Edn. Adminstrn. grantee, 1978-80. Mem. Alderian Soc. Ariz., N. Am. Soc. Adlerian Psychology, Am. Assn. Marriage and Family Therapy (asso.), Nat. Council Family Relations, Am. Personnel and Guidance Assn., Ariz. Personnel and Guidance Assn., Family Mediation Assn. Democrat. Baptist. Author articles in field. Home: 4757 E 2d St Tucson AZ 85711 Office: 1160 N Craycroft St Tucson AZ 85712

OHM, JEAN, collection agy. exec.; b. Marietta, Minn., July 4, 1928; d. J. Earl and Myrtle (Stone) Ruby; student U. Minn., 1946; m. Albert Ohm, Oct. 30, 1947 (dec.); children—Albert Randall, Kevin Jay. Telephone operator Northwestern Bell Telephone Co., Marietta, 1940's; mgr. Huron Collection Agy. (S.D.), 1965—; tchr. classes on money mgmt. N.W. Coll. Commerce. Mem. Parish Edn. Bd., Lutheran Ch., 1964-68; mem. S.D. State Fair Bd., 1970—, pres., 1974-75; pres. Nat. Fedn. Democratic Women, 1977-80. Named Dem. Woman of Year in S.D., 1973. Mem. Bus. and Profl. Women, Am. Legion Aux. Club: Altrusa Internat. Contbr. articles to Lutheran Standard, 1958-63. Home: 345 6th St SW Huron SD 57350 Office: 337 Dakota St Huron SD 57350

OJANLATVA, ANSA TERTTU TELLERVO, lecturer; b. Piippola, Finland, Mar. 19, 1948; came to US., 1973; s. Leevi Johannes and Kerttu (Helmi) O.; M.S., U. Ill., 1975; Ph.D. (teaching asst.), So. Ill. U., 1977; grad. U. Jyvaskyla (Finland), 1971. Asst. prof. U. Houston, 1978-81; lectr. Calif. State Coll., San Bernardino, 1981—; cons. family life edn. San Diego State U., 1981; chmn. health edn. profl. edn. sect. Tex. Assn. Health, Phys. Edn. and Recreation, 1981; mem. Houston steering com. Internat. Yr. of Disabled Persons, 1981. Am.-Scandinavian Soc. grantee, 1976-77; cert. sex educator. Mem. Am. Assn. Sex Educators, Counselors and Therapists (continuing edn. com. 1982—), Nat. Rehab. Counseling Assn. (task force sexuality and disability 1982—), Internat. Union Health Edn., Nat. Assn. Female Execs., Eta Sigma Gamma, Phi Delta Kappa. Contbr. articles to profl. jours. Office: Calif State Coll San Bernardino CA 92407

O'KANE, COLLEEN RILEY, advt. agy. exec.; b. Whidby Island, Wash., Oct. 12, 1948; d. Jack and Marjorie (Webel) Riley; B.A., Queen's U., Belfast, No. Ireland, 1969. Media planner, buyer Leo Burnett, Chgo., 1970-76; media planning dir., partner Tatham-Laird & Kudner, Chgo., 1976—. Mem. Chgo. Advt. Club, Broadcast Advt. Club Chgo., NOW, Nat. Assn. Female Execs. Office: Tatham-Laird & Kudner 625 N Michigan Ave Chicago IL 60611

O'KEEFE, BETH EGAN, psychologist; b. Springfield, Ill., Aug. 27; d. James Michael and Margaret M.L. (Kuhn) Egan; A.A., Sacred Heart Coll., Ala., 1965; A.B. cum laude, Mt. St. Scholastica Coll., Kans., 1967; M.S., St. Louis U., 1970, Ph.D., 1971; m. Rip L. O'Keefe, June 27, 1969; children—Kelly Egan, Casey Egan, Quinn Egan. Trainee, Jefferson Barracks (Mo.) VA Hosp., 1968-70; John Cochran VA Hosp., St. Louis, 1970-71; staff psychologist Comprehensive Community Mental Health Center Rock Island and Mercer Counties, Rock Island, Ill., 1971-72; coordinator psychology services, 1972-82; pvt. practice, 1973—. Mem. Am. Psychol. Assn., Ind. Psychologists Assn. of Quad Cities (v.p. 1980-82), Assn. Advancement Psychology, Ill. Psychol. Assn., Rock Island County Psychol. Assn. (v.p. 1978—). Office: Southpark Psychology Center 1601 52d Ave Suite 3 Moline IL 61265

O'KEEFE, WANDA LYDIA, retail food co. exec.; b. North Bergen, N.J., Aug. 8, 1926; d. David Charles and Ida Josephine (Del Nero) Viola; grad. public schs., Englewood, N.J.; m. Arthur R. O'Keefe, Nov. 6, 1948; children—Arthur R., Barbara Ann, Charles James. Asst. to frozen food buyer N.Y. region Grand Union Co., Elmwood Park, N.J., 1964-68, sec. to mdse. mgr., N.Y. region, 1968-71, mgr. customer relations, 1971-75, mgr. customer communications, 1975—. Mem. Soc. Consumer Affairs Profls., Nat. Assn. Food Chains (mem. steering com. consumer affairs), N.J. Food Council (mem. consumer affairs com.), N.Y. State Food Mchts. Assn. (mem. consumer affairs com.). Home: 209 Wilson St Saddle Brook NJ 07662 Office: 100 Broadway Elmwood Park NJ 07407

O'KEEFFE, GEORGIA, artist; b. Sun Prairie, Wis., Nov. 15, 1887; d. Francis and Ida (Totto) O'Keeffe; student Art Inst. Chgo., 1904-05, Art Students' League, N.Y.C., 1907-08, U. Va., summer 1912, Columbia U., 1914-1916; D.F.A. (hon.), Coll. William and Mary, 1938, U. N.Mex., 1964, Brown U., 1971, Minn. Coll. Art and Design, 1972; Litt.D., U. Wis., 1942, Mills Coll., 1951, Mt. Holyoke Coll., 1971; D.H.L., Columbia, 1971; D.Arts, Harvard U., 1973; m. Alfred Stieglitz, Dec. 11, 1924. Began as illustrator for advt. cos., 1929; supr. art pub. schs., Amarillo, Tex., 1912-14; instr. art U. Va., summers, 1913-16; head art dept. West Tex. State Normal Coll., Canyon, 1916-18; became one of group sponsored by Alfred Stieglitz; paintings first exhibited by him at 291, N.Y.C., 1916-17, Anderson Galleries, 1923, 24, 25; ann. one-man shows at Intimate Gallery, An American Place till 1946, N.Y.C.; retrospective exhbn. Art Inst. Chgo., 1943, Mus. Modern Art, N.Y.C., 1946, Worcester (Mass.) Art Mus., 1960, Amon Carter Mus., Ft. Worth, 1966, Mus. Fine Arts, Houston, 1966, U. N.Mex., 1966, Whitney Mus. Am. Art, 1970, Art Inst. Chgo., 1971, San Francisco Mus. Art, 1971; represented in major museums throughout U.S. Recipient Creative Arts award Brandeis U., 1963, Gold Medal for painting Nat. Inst. Arts and Letters, 1970, M. Carey Thomas award Bryn Mawr Coll., 1971, Edward MacDowell medal MacDowell Colony, 1973, award Skowhegan Sch. Painting and Sculpture, 1973; Presdl. Medal of Honor, 1977. Mem. Nat. Inst. Arts and Letters, Am. Acad. Arts and Letters, Am. Acad. Arts and Scis. Author: Georgia O'Keeffe Drawings, 1968; Georgia O'Keeffe, 1976. Home: Abiquiu NM 87510

O'KELLEY, PATRICIA FERRANTE, assn. exec.; b. Lawrence, Mass., July 22, 1937; d. Leo Peter and Josephine Rita (Pulverenti) Ferrante; B.A., DePaul U., 1980; diploma Carol Nashe Sch., Boston, 1965, Pierce Bus. Sch., 1956, Tng. Course Montessori Tchrs., Clarendon Hills, Ill., 1974; m. James W. O'Kelley, Jr., Dec. 4, 1961; children—Meg, Jimmie, Patricia. Exec. sec. Avco Corp., Wilmington, Mass., 1956-65; mgr. Fashion Two Twenty Cosmetics, Haverhill, Mass., 1964-72; instr. personal devel. Malden Bus. Sch. (Mass.), 1969-72; employee activities coordinator, exec. sec. to pres. IUDS Midwest, Inc., Hillside, Ill., 1975-77; office mgr. Beatrice Foods Co., Oak Brook, Ill., 1977-79; mgr. Lioness Clubs dept. Internat. Assn. Lions Clubs, Oak Brook, 1979—. Mem. Bd. Edn. Dist. 106 LaGrange, Ill., 1978, bd. sec., chmn. edn. com.; chmn. personnel com.; program chmn. Camp Fire Girls, Melrose, 1970-71, town chmn., 1971-72. Recipient Ann Curley Service award Pilot Club, 1971. Mem. Women in Mgmt. (membership chmn. Oak Brook chpt.), Highlands Sch. Parent Tchr. Council, Lyons Twp. Home Sch. Council, Nat. Assn. Female Execs. Republican. Roman Catholic. Club: Villa Park Lioness. Home: 13 Sweetwood Ct Indian Head Park IL 60525 Office: 300 22d St Oak Brook IL 60570

O'KELLY, PATRICIA JANE, orch. adminstr.; b. Memphis, Apr. 15, 1953; d. William Benjamin and Dorothy (Muckleroy) O'K.; B.M.E., Miss. State U., 1975; postgrad. U. Md., 1975—. Mgr., U. Md. Chorus, 1975-76; program asst. Nat. Symphony Orch., Washington, 1976-78, programs, publicity asst., 1979-81, assoc. dir. public relations, 1981—, programming coordinator, 1981—; freelance writer, 1977—. Methodist. Office: John F Kennedy Center Washington DC 20566

OKEN, JEANNE MAKOVER, social worker; b. Balt., Oct. 6, 1919; d. Abraham Bernard and Celeste (Greenberg) Makover; B.A., U. Md., 1941, M.S.W., 1967; m. Jack Oken, Dec. 23, 1945; children—Robert M., Harry Andrew, Celeste Katie. Caseworker, Balt. Dept. Social Services, 1941-42; editorial asst. U.S. Army Ordnance Corps, Camp Holabird, Md., 1942-43; employment interviewer U.S. Employment Service, Balt., 1943-46; social worker Sinai Hosp., Balt., 1967—, chief med. social worker, 1973—, coordinating supr. dept. social work, 1967—. Mem. Nat. Assn. Social Workers, Acad. Cert. Social Workers. Democrat. Jewish. Home: 3216 Timberfield Ln Baltimore MD 21208 Office: Sinai Hosp Greenspring and Belvedere Ave Baltimore MD 21215

OKEREKE-ONYIUKE, NDI, stock exchange exec.; b. Port-Harcourt, Nigeria, Nov. 2, 1950; came to U.S., 1971, naturalized, 1979; d. Daniel Ernest and Kalaya Augusta (Long-John) Okereke; B.B.A., Bernard M. Baruch Coll., City U. N.Y., 1974, M.B.A., 1977; post-M.B.A. profl. cert. Columbia U., 1978; Ph.D., City U. N.Y., 1980; m. Okey Charles Onyiuke, Aug. 30, 1976. Export mgr. Fortuna Fisheries, Inc., N.Y.C., 1973-75; chancery officer Mission of Nigeria to UN, 1975-76; systems mgr. The N.Y. Stock Exchange, N.Y.C., 1977—; adj. prof. Bernard Baruch Coll. of City U. N.Y., 1977-79; mktg. cons. Chieke Internat. Corp., N.Y.C., 1979—; asst. lectr. Manhattan Community Coll., 1976-77. Mem. Mayor's Exec. Vols., N.Y.C., 1979-80; UN hospitality com. mem., 1975-76; evening dir. coll. aide activities Model Cities Tutorial Program of N.Y., 1975-76; mem. Pres.'s Commn. on Exec. Exchange, 1980. City U. Grad. Research award/teaching fellow, 1978-79; Research award U. Paris-IX, Dauphine, summer 1975; Goldman Research award Cambridge (Eng.) U., 1977; Chase Manhattan Bank M.B.A. fellow, 1979. Mem. Nat. Assn. Female Execs., Assn. M.B.A. Execs., Am. Mgmt. Assn., Am. Mktg. Assn., Educators to Africa Assn., Fraternal Order Police (com.), Beta Gamma Sigma. Club: Sales Execs. Editor: (with others) Nigeria at the United Nations, 1976; author article. Home: 40 Harrison St New York NY 10013

OKERLUND, ARLENE NAYLOR, univ. dean; b. Emmitsburg, Md., Oct. 13, 1938; d. George Wilbur and Ruth Opal (Sensenbaugh) Naylor; B.A., U. Md., 1960; Ph.D., U. Calif., San Diego, 1969; 1 dau., Linda Susan. Instr. sci. Mercy Hosp. Sch. Nursing, Balt., 1959-63; prof. English, San Jose (Calif.) State U., 1969-80, dean Sch. Humanities and Arts, 1980—. Mem. MLA, Philol. Assn. Pacific Coast (sec.-treas. 1975-78), Calif. Women Higher Edn. Author articles in field. Address: Sch Humanities and Arts San Jose State U San Jose CA 95192

OKOSHI, EUGENIA SUMIYE, artist; b. Seattle; d. Masanari and Riyoko (Fukoda) Ushiyama; student Seattle U., 1954-57, Henry Fry Mus. Modern Art, Seattle, 1957-59; m. George Mukai, Mar. 21, 1976. One-woman shows: Gallery Internat., N.Y.C., 1970, Miami Mus. Modern Art, 1970, Westbeth Courtyard Gallery, N.Y.C., 1972, Galerie Salson, Tokyo, 1982; exhibited in group shows: Met. Mus. Art, N.Y.C., 1977, World Trade Center, N.Y.C., 1979, Tokyo Nat. Mus., 1979, Pace U. Gallery, Briarcliff, N.Y., 1981, Joslyn Center Arts, Torrance, Calif.; represented in permanent collectiosn at Miami Mus. Modern Art, Low Gallery, U. Maimi, Nat. Women's Edn. Center, Japan. Mem. Burr Artists, Hudson River Artists Assn., Japanese Artists Assn. N.Y. Episcopalian. Address: 155 Bank St New York NY 10014

OKUM, MARJORIE ELLEN, child psychologist; b. Balt., Oct. 8, 1948; d. Alfred Joseph and Fanny Mae (Neuburger) Okum; B.S., U. Md., 1970; Ph.D. in Clin. Psychology (VA fellow), Cath. U. Am., 1975. Psychology intern Springfield Hosp. Center, Sykesville, Md., 1973-74, Perry Point (Md.) VA Hosp., 1973-74; chief psychologist Walter P. Carter Community Mental Health Center, Balt., 1980—, coordinator children's and adolescents' services, 1978—; clin. instr. psychiatry U. Md. Sch. Medicine, Balt., 1978—; pvt. practice clin. psychology, Balt. Mem. Am. Psychol. Assn., Md. Psychol. Assn. (sec.-treas. div. II psychologists in public service), Am. Orthopsychiat. Assn., Balt. Assn. Cons. Psychologists, Phi Beta Kappa, Psi Chi, Phi Kappa Phi. Democrat. Jewish. Home: 111 Hamlet Hill Rd Baltimore MD 21210 Office: 630 W Fayette St Baltimore MD 20201

OLAETA, JULIA O'KEEFFE MCCURRY, ednl. adminstr.; b. Silver Lake, Oreg., Jan. 26, 1923; d. Cornelious M. and Myrtle Alice (McKune) O'Keeffe; B.A., Oreg. State Coll., 1944; M.A., Fresno State Coll., 1961; m. Franklin P. McCurry, Dec. 30, 1944 (dec.); children—Mary Alice McCurry Barber, Ann McCurry Lang, Paul McCurry, Patricia McCurry Williams; m. 2d, Thomas Olaeta, June 24, 1978. Tchr. public schs., Portland, 1944-45; tchr. demonstration nursery sch. Oreg. State U., Corvallis, 1945-46; tchr. public schs., Atwater, Calif., 1956-66, prin. elementary sch., 1966—. Active Am. Cancer Soc., 1974—. Mem. Am., Calif. assns. sch. adminstrs., Nat. Assn. Elem. Schs., AAUW, Kappa Delta Pi, Delta Kappa Gamma, Beta Sigma Phi, Mu Beta Beta. Republican. Roman Catholic. Home: 2115 3d St Atwater CA 95301 Office: PO Box 775 Atwater CA 95301

OLAFSON, FREYA, public health educator, found. exec.; b. Ithaca, N.Y., Apr. 3, 1940; d. Peter and Harriette Elizabeth (Smith) Olafson; B.A., U. Calif., Berkeley, 1964, M.P.H., (USPHS fellow), 1968; m. William J. Bicknell, Nov. 10, 1971 (dir. 1981). Vol., Peace Corps, Paraiba, Brazil, 1964-66, mem. Peace Corps tng. staff, 1966-67; biomed. project adminstr. Sch. Public Health, U. Calif., Berkeley, 1969, coordinator health center seminar program, 1969-73; program dir. info. and referral services Mass. Planned Parenthood League, Newton, 1973; community health asso. The Med. Found. Inc., 1974; dir. info. edn. and communications The Pathfinder Fund, Boston, 1974-77, chief Women's Programs div., 1977—; vis. lectr. U. Calif., Berkeley, Boston U.; cons. in field. Bd. dirs. Greater Boston YWCA, 1973-75; mem. edn. com. Boston Sickle Cell Center, 1973-75; mem. social services task force Boston Women's Collective, 1974. Mem. Am. Public Health Assn., Soc. Public Health Educators, Women's Network for Population and Devel. (exec. com., adv. bd.), Delta Omega. Author: Confidentiality: A Guide for Neighborhood Health Centers; editor: Sickle Cell Anemia—the Neglected Disease, 1973; author papers on family planning. Home: 62 Pinckney St Apt 2 Boston MA 02114 Office: The Pathfinder Fund 1330 Boylston St Chestnut Hill Boston MA 02167

OLAH, JUDITH AGNES, chemist; b. Budapest, Jan. 21, 1929; came to U.S., 1964, naturalized, 1969; d. Janos and Magaret (Kraus) Lengyel; M.S. in Chemistry, Tech. U. Budapest, 1955; m. George A. Olah, July 9, 1949; children—George John, Ronald Peter. Research chemist Central Research Inst., Hungarian Acad. Scis., 1955-56; research asso. Case Western Res. U., Cleve., 1966-77; adj. asst. prof. chemistry U. So. Calif., 1977-79, adj. asso. prof., 1979—. Mem. Iota Sigma Pi. Contbr. articles on organic chemistry to profl. jours., chpts. in books. Home: 2252 Gloaming Way Beverly Hills CA 90210 Office: Dept of Chemistry University of Southern California University Park Los Angeles CA 90007

OLAH, SUSAN ROSE, artist; b. Budapest, Hungary, June 14, 1947; d. Joseph and Emma (Hupcsak) Olah; came to Can., 1957, naturalized, 1962; student Art Instrn. Sch., Mpls., 1966-69. Tchr. art Wascana Hosp., Regina, Sask., Can., 1969-72, art cons., talent evaluator, 1970-72; exhibited in one woman shows at Gallery of Roof, Regina, 1973, Galerie Mouffe, Paris, 1977, Galerie Vallombreuse, Biarritz, France, 1977. Recipient awards Regina Exhbn., 1960, Mpls. award for painting, 1967, cert. of attainment Art Instrn., Sch., Mpls., 1969, gold medal in art Accademia Italia Belle Arti e del Lavoro, 1979; diploma of merit Universita delle Arti, Parma, Italy, 1982; Golden Centaur, Accademia Italia, 1982. Mem. Internat. Order Vols. for Peace (Italy). Home: 37 Haultain Crescent Regina SK S4S 4B4 Canada

OLANDER, HELEN LINNEA, educator; b. Singapore, Sept. 1, 1923 (parents Am. citizens); d. Carl Harold Gideon and Lydia Elizabeth Olander; A.B., Alma (Mich.) Coll., 1944; M.S.W., U. Mich., 1948; D.S.W., U. So. Calif., 1964; m. Jacob Jupiter, Sept. 3, 1953 (div.). Social worker in Detroit and Los Angeles, 1947-51; chief welfare specialist, then asst. area dep. Calif. Dept. Social Welfare, Los Angeles, 1951-59; asst. prof. U. So. Calif. Sch. Social Work, 1961-64, UCLA Sch. Social Welfare, 1964-69; asso. dir. Health Tng. Center, Calif. Dept. Mental Health, 1969-79; ednl. cons. in mental health, 1980—; mem. San Bernardino County Mental Health Adv. Bd., 1980—, chmn., 1981-83; chmn. personnel com. Internat. Inst. Los Angeles, 1977-81; mem. continuing edn. rev. com. NIMH, 1975-79. Named Outstanding Alumna, U. So. Calif., 1975. Mem. Nat. Assn. Social Workers (named Social Work Educator of Yr., Calif. chpt. 1979), Acad. Cert. Social Workers, Council Social Work Edn. Address: 62395 Holiday Way Joshua Tree CA 92252

OLDEN, ANNA BEATRICE, educator; b. Pinehurst, N.C., Mar. 15, 1931; d. Allen and Anna (Wallace) Bethea; B.A., Bennett Coll., 1952; postgrad. Bank Street Coll., N.Y.C., Am. U., Mary Wood Coll.; m. Simon J. Olden, June 12, 1953 (div.); children—Darryl Craig, Pamela Lynette, Brian Kevin. Tchr. Kannapolis (N.C.) Public Schs., 1952-53, Carousel Sch., Jamaica Estates, N.Y. and Headstart tchr., curriculum coordinator, supr., St. Albans, N.Y., 1955-69; tchr. Cecil County (Md.) Public Schs., 1969—. Mem. NEA, Md. Tchrs. Assn., Cecil County Tchrs. Assn., Internat. Reading Assn. Methodist. Home: 1 Bristal Way New Castle DE 19720

OLDENBURG, DEBORAH LYNN, nurse, educator; b. Benton Harbor, Mich., Dec. 2, 1954; d. Howard Elton and Joan Kay (Ackerman) O.; B.S. in Nursing, U. Mich., 1977; M.S. in Nursing, Vanderbilt U., 1980. Staff and charge nurse Meml. Hosp., St. Joseph, Mich., 1977-78; traveling collegiate sec. Alpha Delta Pi Sorority, Atlanta, 1978-79; part-time staff nurse Vanderbilt U. Hosp., Nashville, 1980, Greenview Hosp., Bowling Green, Ky., 1982—; asst. prof. nursing Western Ky. U., Bowling Green, 1980—, mem. faculty senate, 1982—. Mem. steering com. Coronary Club affiliate Am. Heart Assn., 1982. Recipient Dorothy

Shaw Leadership award Alpha Delta Pi, 1977; U. Mich. Regents Alumni scholar, 1973; Sawyer Community Assn. scholar, 1974, 75, 76; Panhellenic Achievement Award scholar, 1976; Alpha Delta Pi 125th Anniversary scholar, 1979; Vanderbilt U. Sch. Nursing trainee, 1979-80. Mem. Am. Nurses Assn., Ky. Nurses Assn., Nat. League for Nursing, Sigma Theta Tau, Alpha Delta Pi (pres. U. Mich. chpt. 1975-76). Home: 1040 Shive Ln Apt C-16 Bowling Green KY 42101 Office: Dept Nursing Western Ky U Bowling Green KY 42101

OLDFATHER, PAULA MARIE, computer co. exec.; b. Rosenberg, Tex., Aug. 3, 1940; d. Theron Andrew and Pansy Blossom (Carpenter) O.; B.S. with honors in Math., UCLA, 1966. Mem. tech. staff RAND Corp., Santa Monica, Calif., 1964-67; analyst, programmer Auerbach Assos., Phila., 1967-69; mgr. systems and programming CARA Corp., Phila., 1969-71, v.p., 1975-82; pres. Belmont & Oldfather, Inc., Glen Mills, Pa., 1982—; tchr. SIMSCRIPT programming USAF, 1965-67. Mem. Assn. Computing Machinery, Data Entry Mgmt. Assn., Soc. Ambulatory Med. Systems, Nat. Assn. Female Execs. Author computer materials. Home: 21 Winding Way RD 5 Glen Mills PA 19342 Office: Baltimore Pike and Cheyned Rd Concord Village Shops Glen Mills PA 19342

OLDHAM, VIRGINIA ALDRIDGE, economist, govt. ofcl.; b. Adsit, Va.; d. Zebedee and Jennie (Ridley) Aldridge; B.A., Howard U., 1959; m. Archie W. Johnson, Sept. 4, 1937 (dec. Sept. 1939); m. 2d, M. Brent Oldham, Aug. 27, 1949; 1 son, Brent Aldridge. Clk., War Dept., 1942-43, War Manpower Commn., 1943; acctg. clk. OPA, 1943-46, fin. analyst, 1946-47; payroll clk. Dept. Labor, 1947-51, 1953-55; statis. clk. NPA, 1951-52, clk., 1953-54; statis. clk. Bur. Comml. Fisheries, Dept. Interior, 1956-58, industry economist, 1958-64, economist Bur. Indian Affairs, 1964-66, staff asst. personnel (all Washington); staff asst., recruit specialist, employee counselor, part-time human relations instr. mgmt. and systems service VA, Washington, 1966-72, fed. women's program coordinator, 1970—, personnel mgmt. specialist, 1972-73; equal opportunity specialist, 1973—, spl. asst. to asst. adminstr. for personnel, 1975-77, fed. women's program mgr. and spl. asst. to asst. adminstr. Office Human Goals, 1978—. Coordinator Fed. Savs. Bonds Program, 1969-73. Mem. invitations and tickets com. Presdl. Inaugural, 1965, 69, 73, 77, 81; mem. Hospitality and Info. Service, Washington, 1964—; rep. Parents Council Washington, 1964-65. Mem. LWV, Ams. for Democratic Action (v.p. Washington chpt. 1962, mem. exec. bd. 1959), Nat. Council Negro Women, Am. Econ. Assn., Assn. Fed. Woman's Award Recipients (rec. sec. 1976—), Internat. Personnel Mgmt. Assn., Delta Sigma Theta. Clubs: Howard U. Faculty Wives, Howard U. Women's, Capital City Links (chpt. chmn. nat. trends and services com. 1979—). Author: (with others) New England Groundfish Situation Reports, 1962, 63. Research on relative position fishing industry in domestic economy, 1961; on early rehab. housing program Am. Indians in 1930s, 1964. Home: 4325 20th St NE Washington DC 20018 Office: VA 810 Vermont Ave NW 09B Washington DC 20420

OLDING, DOROTHY (MCKEOWN), lit. agt.; b. N.Y.C., Apr. 12, 1910; d. Addington Eric and Seraphine (Theodor) O.; student Columbia U., 1927-29; m. Edward V. McKeown, Aug. 14, 1946 (dec. 1951). Asst. fiction editor Am. mag., N.Y.C., 1929-38; with Harold Ober Assocs. Inc., lit. agy., N.Y.C., 1938—, partner, then exec. v.p., 1949-72, pres., 1972—. Home: 447 E 57th St New York NY 10022 Office: 40 E 49th St New York NY 10017

OLDOW, PAMELA FLORENCE, charter boat capt.; b. Victoria, B.C., Can., July 6, 1932; came to U.S., 1967, naturalized, 1972; d. William Hall and Pamela Ida (Knowles) Paine; student Royal Bus. Coll., Victoria, 1949-50, Victoria Community Coll., 1965-66; m. Donald J. Oldow, July 8, 1967; children—Bruce William, Bryan Charles, Linda-Rae, Richard Owen. Sect. mgr. Can. Govt. Dept. Hospitalization, Victoria, 1950-52; house bldg. contractor Clarke's Constrn., 1956-62; auditor Can. Stock Audit, Vancouver, B.C., 1964-65; sec. public schs., Victoria, 1965-67; legal sec. firm Reasor, Tunley & Ross, Seward, Alaska, 1970-74; deckhand charter boat Shaman, Seward, 1974-77, capt., owner Shaman, Seward, 1982—. Treas. bd. dirs. Seward Gen. Hosp., 1971-72; mem. Seward Planning and Zoning Commn., 1973-74; mem. Seward City Council, 1974-77; assemblyman Kenai Borough (Alaska) Assembly, 1975-77; treas. Seward C. of C., 1978-81. Home: 315 2d Ave PO Box 881 Seward AK 99664

OLDS, VICTORIA, social worker, emeritus educator; B.A., U. Pitts., 19 ; M.S. in Social Work, Case Western Res. U., 1935; D.S.W., Columbia U., 1966; m. Edward Olds (dec.). Prof. social work, dir. field work, Sch. Social Work, Howard U., Washington, 1955-67; cons. on faculty recruitment and devel. of new faculty Council on Social Work Edn., 1967-68; prof. social work, Grad. Sch. Social Work, Fordham U., N.Y.C., 1969-81, prof. emeritus, 1981—, coordinator Brookdale Scholarship Com., Fordham U., 1976, asso. dir. Center on Gerontology, 1977-78, project dir. Adminstrn. on Aging tng. grant, 1978-79, project dir. planning grant, 1977-78, coordinator field work placements; designer, participant seminars, insts., programs in field; presented testimony Select Com. on Aging, U.S. Ho. of Reps., 1978. Adv. com. and advocacy for minority elderly project Nat. Urban League. Mem. Nat. Assn. Social Workers (charter, v.p. N.Y.C. chpt. 1975-76, del. nat. assembly 1975, 77), Acad. Cert. Social Workers, Council of Social Work Edn., Am. Public Welfare Assn. (mem. com. on revisions of social security provisions), Internat. Congress of Schs. of Social Work, Internat. Conf. Social Welfare, Am. Pub. Health Assn., AAUP, N.Y. State Assn. Gerontol. Educators (pres. 1981-82, exec. com. 1973-81, charter mem., com. chmn.), Gerontol. Soc., Nat. Council Sr. Citizens, Nat. Council on the Aging, Assn. for Gerontology in Higher Edn. Panelist, contbr. papers to profl. confs. in field; contbr. articles, book rev. to publs.; editor proceedings profl. confs. Home: 444 E 82d St New York NY 10028 Office: Lincoln Center Campus Fordham Univ 113 W 60th St New York NY 10023

OLEKSIUK-VELEZ, ADRIANA BERNADETTE, speech and lang. pathologist; b. Bklyn., Apr. 14, 1950; d. Roman and Luba Maria (Krystyniak) Oleksiuk; B.A., Hofstra U., 1971; M.A. (fellow), Queens Coll., CUNY, 1973, postgrad. (fellow) Grad. Sch. and Univ. Center, 1974—; m. Andrew P. Velez, Aug. 24, 1974. Lang. and speech clinician Stamford (Conn.) Public Schs., 1972-74; lang and speech pathologist St. Joseph's Sch. for the Blind, Jersey City, N.J., 1974-75; adj. lectr. Bklyn. Coll., 1975-76; research asst. communication skills of deaf children St. Francis de Sales Sch. for Deaf, Bklyn., 1975-76; cons. Nat. Tech. Inst. for Deaf, 1978-80; adj. lectr. Hunter Coll., 1981, Queens Coll., 1981-83. Cert. speech pathologist, N.Y. Mem. Am. Speech, Lang., and Hearing Assn., N.Y. State Speech, Lang., and Hearing Assn., N.Y.C. Speech, Hearing, and Lang. Assn., Internat. Assn. for Study Child Lang., N.Y. State Outdoor Edn. Assn., N.Y. Acad. Scis. Roman Catholic. Office: 33 W 42d St New York NY 10036

OLENDER, TERRYS T. (MRS. EDWARD GLICK), lawyer, author; b. San Francisco; d. Julius and Mollie Olender; B.A., U. Calif. at Berkeley; postgrad. U. So. Calif. Law Sch.; m. Edward Glick, May 26, 1952. Admitted to Calif. bar, 1932, Fed. bar, 1932; practiced law in Los Angeles, 1933-41, 50—, San Francisco, 1942-49; dep. dist. atty. Los Angeles County, 1933-38; fgn. corr. Overseas News Agy., Mediterranean area, 1949-50; land subdivider, developer, 1955—; program coordinator radio and TV, producer, 1959—; feature columnist, editorial writer Citizen News, 1971—, also Athens (Greece) Daily Post; guest numerous interview and panel shows. Del. of Internat. Fedn. Women Lawyers to ECOSOC, Geneva, 1962; del. to UN Meeting on criminal law, Tokyo, 1960; public service legal Coordinator Hollywood Mus. Mem. mayor's adv. com. Juvenile Delinquency and Narcotic Committees; pres.'s com. to Maintain Hotel Rent Control, San Francisco, 1948; an organizer, liaison officer No. Calif. br. Am. Christian Palestine Com., 1947-49, liaison officer, Los Angeles, 1950-59. Founder, pres. Olender Found.; trustee Inst. Cancer and Blood Research. Recipient joint awards Los Angeles Bd. Suprs. and Los Angeles City Council, 1961; Western mem. adv. bd. U.S. Wheelchair Sports Fund; sponsor Cal. Wheelchair Athletic Club. Named Women of Year, Zionist Orgn. Am., 1964; recipient award Israel Found. for Handicapped Children, 1968; named Woman of Achievement, Calif. Press Women, 1968. Mem. Am. Bar Assn., Hollywood Bar Assn., Los Angeles County Bar Assn., Los Angeles Bar Assn., So. Calif. Women Lawyers, Internat. Fedn. Women Lawyers, Acad. Television Arts and Scis. (judge Emmy awards Los Angeles area 1964), Radio and TV Women So. Calif., Nat. Fedn. Press Women, Calif. Fedn., Press Women, Profl. Writers League, World Affairs Council, Calif. State Bar, Brit. Anti-Slavery Soc., Nat. Assn. Women Lawyers, Am. Women Radio and Television, UN Assn. U.S.A. (dir. Los Angeles). Democrat. Clubs: Greater Los Angeles Press, Hollywood (Calif.) Foreign Press. Author: For The Prosecution: Miss Deputy D.A.; Delitto Prequidizio; My Life in Crime (autobiography, 1st prize Calif. Press Women Writing contest 1967), 1966. Legal tech. adviser motion picture The Long Rope, 1961. Contbr. articles newspapers, mags.; feature columnist Los Angeles Daily Jour.; syndicated column, Hollywood Oddities, World Union Press. Address: 450 N Rossmore Ave Los Angeles CA 90004

OLIN, VIOLET STRAHAN, acct.; b. Natchez, Miss., Mar. 21, 1932; d. Lonzo Lawrence and Maudie Lee (Sanders) Strahan; student Hinds Jr. Coll., 1973-76; m. B.J. Bliss, Nov. 12, 1947 (dec.); children—Beverly Diane Bliss Kavanaugh, Valerie R. Bliss Hiddle; m. 2d, Gary S. Olin, Mar. 8, 1971 (div.). Acct., Gold & Levi Accts., 1955-60, Vicksburg Frozen Food Center, Inc. (Miss.), 1962—; auditor, staff acct., mgmt. analyst Lower Miss. Valley div. C.E., U.S. Army, Vicksburg, 1964—; pvt. practice acctg., 1960—. Mem. Nat. Assn. Accts., Federally Employed Women (past chpt. pres.), Bus. and Profl. Women (chmn. fin. com.). Presbyterian. Office: PO Box 80 Vicksburg MS 39180

OLINCY, MARGARET MARY, trade pub. co. exec.; b. Chgo., July 19, 1947; d. Walter Haworth, Jr. and Mary Louise (Richards) Faget; B.A., Mich. State U., 1969; M.A., 1970, M.B.A., 1974; m. Stephen Robert Olincy, Nov. 26, 1977; 1 dau., Mary Elizabeth. Sales rep. Scott Periodicals, Elmhurst, Ill., 1975—, sec., dir., 1976—; sec. Constrn. Industry Press, 1976—. Mem. Nat. Assn. Female Execs. Home: 752 Beverly Pl Lake Forest IL 60045 Office: 135 Addison St Elmhurst IL 60126

OLIVER, HARRIET BOUGEN, lawyer; b. N.Y.C., Oct. 12, 1939; d. Max David and Pauline (Steinman) Bougen; B.A., Bennington Coll., 1960; M.A. in Physics, Columbia U., 1963; M.S.W. (N.Y. State Mental Hygiene fellow 1965-66), Adelphi U., 1966; J.D. cum laude, Albany Law Sch., 1981; m. Lewis B. Oliver, Jr., May 18, 1973; children—Gideon Orion, Naomi Grace. Clin. social worker Manhattan VA Hosp., N.Y.C., 1966-69; supervising social worker Spence-Chapin Services to Families and Children, N.Y.C., 1969-76, Albany (N.Y.) Jewish Family Services, 1977-78; admitted to N.Y. bar, 1982; pvt. practice law, 1982—. Cert. social worker, N.Y. Mem. Nat. Assn. Social Workers, Acad. Cert. Social Workers, Justinian Soc. Home: 31 Barclay St Albany NY 12209

OLIVER, JEAN WEST (MRS. BENSON G. OLIVER), assn. exec.; b. Jasper, Ala., Dec. 8, 1920; d. John Mason and Lillie Lorene (O'Rear) West; student Del Mar. Coll., 1962; m. Benson Gordon Oliver, Mar. 6, 1937; children—Gloria Diane (Mrs. George Meerdink), John Gordon, James Moreland. Exec. sec. Nueces County Med. Soc., Corpus Christi, Tex., 1960—; cons. to membership com. Tex. Med. Assn.; med. librarian Meml. Med. Center, 1960-71, art coordinator, 1964-70. Active PTA, 1945-68, Boy Scouts Am., 1957-60; vol. Am. Cancer Soc., 1971—. Mem. Am. Assn. Med. Execs., Women in Communications. Clubs: Aurora Study (San Benito, Tex.); Corpus Christi Press, Junior Woman's, Woman's, Knife and Fork. Mem. editorial bd., editorial sec. Coastal Bend Medicine. Home: 430 Peerman Pl Corpus Christi TX 78411 Office: 2606 Hospital Blvd Corpus Christi TX 78405

OLIVER, JULIA JERVEY (MRS. JOHN P. OLIVER), social services agy. adminstr.; b. Albany, Ga.; d. Francis Weston and Irene Mercer (Tift) Smith; A.B., U. Ala., 1947; M.S.W., Fla. State U., 1969; m. John Percival Oliver, Sept. 4, 1946; children—John P., (dec.), Frances Weston (dec.), Edward Banks, William Houston. Tchr., Dadeville (Ala.) Public Schs., 1950; with Tallapoosa County Dept. Pensions and Security, 1954-71, dir., 1971; asst. dir. Bur. Info. Service, Govt. of Ala., 1971, dir., 1971-72, external adminstr. Dept. Pensions and Security, 1972-74, commr., 1974-76, spl. asst. to commr., 1976-81, state social services adminstr., 1981—. Mem. Am. Public Welfare Assn. (past nat. v.p.), Ala. Conf. Social Work (past pres.), Nat. Mental Health Assn. (v.p.), Ala. Mental Health Assn. (pres.), Acad. Cert. Social Workers, Nat. Assn. Social Workers, Ala. Assn. County Dirs. Pensions and Security (past pres.). Episcopalian. Home: PO Box 277 112 Oliver Grove Dadeville AL 36853 Office: 64 N Union St Montgomery AL 36130

OLIVER, MARY, poet; b. Cleve., Sept. 10, 1935; d. Edward William and Helen Mary (Vlasak) O.; student Ohio State U., 1955-56, Vassar Coll., 1956-57. Mather vis. prof. Case Western Res. U., 1980, 82; author: No Voyage and Other Poems, 1965; The River Styx, Ohio, 1972; The Night Traveler, 1978; Twelve Moons, 1979; American Primative, 1983; also poems in various mags. Recipient Shelley Meml. award, 1972, Castagnola award, 1973; fellow Nat. Endowment Arts, 1972-73, Guggenheim Found., 1980-81. Mem. Poetry Soc. Am., PEN. Address: Box 338 Provincetown MA 02657

OLIVER, MARY ANN URSO, lawyer; b. Tampa, Fla., Aug. 25, 1948; d. Philip and Mary (Frisco) Urso; B.A. magna cum laude, U. Mass., 1970; J.D., Boston Coll., 1973; m. Richard Allen Oliver, May 23, 1972; children—Edward Raymond, Robert Philip. Admitted to D.C. bar, 1973, Va. bar, 1975, U.S. Supreme Ct. bar, 1980; atty. electric and telephone div. U.S. Dept. Agr., Washington, 1973-77; atty. SEC, Washington, 1977-80, dep. asst. dir. div. corp. regulation, 1980—. Mem. Am. Bar Assn., D.C. Bar Assn., Boston Coll. Alumni Assn., Phi Beta Kappa, Phi Kappa Phi. Office: SEC 500 N Capitol St NW Washington DC 20549

OLIVER, MARY WILHELMINA, law librarian, educator; b. Cumberland, Md., May 4, 1919; d. John Arlington and Sophia (Lear) Oliver; A.B., Western Md. Coll., 1940; B.S. L.S., Drexel Inst. Tech., 1943; J.D., U. N.C., 1951. Asst. circulation librarian N.J. Coll. Women, 1943-45; asst. in law library U. Va., 1945-47; asst. reference, social sci. librarian Drake U., 1947-49; research asst. Inst. Govt., U. N.C., 1951-52, asst. law librarian, 1952-55, asst. prof. law, law librarian, 1955-59, asso. prof. law, law librarian, 1959-69, prof. law, law librarian, 1969—; admitted to N.C. bar, 1951. Mem. Internat. Assn Law Libraries, Am. Assn. Law Libraries (pres.) Spl. Libraries Assn., Am., Bar Assn., N.C. Bar Assn., Assn. Am. Law Schs. (exec. com. 1979-81), Am. Soc. Legal History, Law Alumni Assn. U. N.C., Seldon Soc., Order of Coif. Home: Box 733 Chapel Hill NC 27514 Office: U NC Law Library Chapel Hill NC 27514

OLIVER, PAMELA MASON, audiologist; b. Washington, July 15, 1952; d. Jeremy Eldridge and Margaret (Walton) Mason; B.A., Mary Washington Coll., 1974; M.Ed., U. Va., 1975; m. Craig John Oliver, Sept. 22, 1979. Mgr. career info. Am. Speech and Hearing Assn., Washington, 1975-76; clin. audiologist NIH, Bethesda, Md., 1976-79; clin. audiologist Catholic U. Am. Speech and Hearing Center, 1979—; cons. NIH; mem. Met. Council of Govts. Noise Tech. Com., 1976—; mem. Montgomery County (Md.) Noise Control Adv. Bd., 1976-77. Mem. Am. Speech and Hearing Assn. (cert. clin. competence). Research in ototoxic drugs; also articles. Home: 2328 Ashmead Pl Apt 1 Washington DC 20009 Office: Catholic U Speech and Hearing Center 4001 Harewood Rd NE Washington DC 20064

OLIVER, PHYLLIS RYBINSKI, contract specialist; b. Lakeland, Fla., Sept. 3, 1953; d. Marion Michael and Estelle Barbara (Ogorzelec) Rybinski; B.A. in Internat. Affairs, Fla. State U., 1975. Mem. adminstrv. staff Ga. Inst. Tech., Atlanta, 1975—, contracting officer, 1979-81, asst. to dir. Sch. Chemistry, 1981-82; sr. contract adminstr. Metric Systems Corp., Fort Walton Beach, Fla., 1982—. Counselor, Cobb County Rape Crisis Center; mem. Cobb County Coalition ERA. Mem. AAUW, Nat. Council U. Research Adminstrs., Ga. Women's Polit. Caucus, Atlanta Friendship Force Club, Bus. and Profl. Women's Club, Nat. Contract Mgmt. Assn. Republican. Roman Catholic. Home: 3458 Sabrina Ct Marietta GA 30066 also 129 Newcastle Circle Fort Walton Beach FL 32548 Office: 736 N Beal St Fort Walton Beach FL 32548

OLIVER, SANDRA JO HURST MILLHOUSE, ednl. adminstr.; b. Niles, Mich., Aug. 25, 1934; d. Kenneth Dean Hurst and Helen Mae (Holm) Hurst Morris; B.A., Western Mich. U., 1956; M.A., Andrews U., Berrien Springs, Mich., 1964; adminstrn. cert. Nat. Coll. Edn., Evanston, Ill., 1980; children—Douglas Kirk Millhouse Oliver, Scott Tracy Millhouse Oliver, Kirsten Anne Oliver. Elem. sch. tchr., Ill. and Mich., 1957-59, 63-65; jr. high sch. guidance counselor Fair Plain Public Schs., Benton Harbor, Mich., 1965-67; reading specialist/home-hosp. tutor Oak Park (Ill.) Elem. Schs., 1967-69, learning disabilities tchr., 1971-75, coordinator spl. edn., 1974-78, dir. spl. edn., 1978—; jr. high sch. guidance counselor/home-hosp. tutor Wheeling and Arlington Heights, Ill., 1969-71; lectr. in field. Mem. Council Exceptional Children, Ill. Council Adminstrs. Spl. Edn., Ill. Women Adminstrs., Ill. Council Pupil Personnel Adminstrs., Ill. Adminstrs. Spl. Edn., West Suburban Learning Disabilities Assn.

OLIVER-FELCHLIN, DIANE GORDON, pathologist; b. Long Beach, Calif., July 21, 1937; d. William C. and Mary Valerie (Voros) Gordon; A.B., U. Calif., Berkeley, 1959; M.D., U. Calif., San Francisco, 1963; m. James A. Felchlin, Oct. 3, 1975; children—Lauren Michelle, Giffin Marie, Anita Louise, Dare Valerie. Intern, San Francisco Gen. Hosp., 1963-64, resident, 1964-66; resident U. Calif., San Francisco, 1966-68; NIH fellow, 1968-69; pres., med. dir. Comprehensive Health, Inc., San Francisco, 1969-77; med. dir. research Flow General Inc., San Bruno, Calif., 1977—, dir., 19—. Mem. Am. Soc. Clin. Pathologists, Coll. Am. Pathologists. Office: Flow General Inc 1057 Sneath Ln San Bruno CA 94066

OLIVEROS, PAULINE, composer; b. Houston, 1932; studied composition with Erickson and Nee. Mem. San Francisco Tape Music, Center, Mills Coll., 1961-67; dir. Tape Music Center, Mills Coll., 1966; prof. music. U. Calif., San Diego; dir. Center for Music Experiment, U. San Diego. Recipient Beethoven prize City of Bonn, 1977; Guggenheim fellow, 1972-73. Composer: I of IV, 1966; Sonic Meditations; El Relicario de los Animales; Tashi Gomang for orch. (premier Cabrillo Music Festival, 1981); The Well, 1982; recs. Horse Sings from Cloud, Rattlesnake Mountain, 1982. Address: PO Box 164 Mount Tremper NY 12457

OLIVETI, SUSAN GAIL, communications co. mgr.; b. Bklyn., Nov. 1, 1938; d. Peter and Nancy (Wolk) Randolph; student CCNY, Bklyn. Jewish Hosp. Sch. Nursing, 1956-58, 1958-60, N.Y. U., 1967-68; m. Fosco Oliveti, Sept. 18, 1970; children—Lois, Peter, Elizabeth. Estimator, Ogilvy & Mather, N.Y.C., 1966-68; adminstrv. asst. Adam Young, N.Y.C., 1968-69, Paramount Pictures, N.Y.C., 1969-80; mgr. conv. and media events Warner Amex Satellite Entertainment Co., N.Y.C., 1980—. Recipient award United Airlines, 1978. Mem. Cable TV Assn., Nat. Cable TV Assn., Women in Cable, Meeting Planners Internat. Office: 1211 Ave of Americas New York NY 10036

OLIVIERI, LINDA R., banker; b. Chgo., Feb. 25, 1953; d. Joseph John and Adelaide Teresa (Leonard) O.; B.A., Elmhurst Coll., 1976. Personnel, mktg. dir. East Side Bank & Trust Co., Chgo., 1977—. Mem. Nat. Assn. Female Execs., Nat. Assn. Bank Women, Am. Inst. Banking. Club: Southwest Archdiocese Singles. Office: 10635 Ewing St Chicago IL 60617

OLLIS, HESTER GREY, ins. agency exec.; b. Eldorado, Okla., Mar. 19, 1914; d. Embry G. and Gladys Gertrude (Wood) West; m. Lawrence Woodbridge Ollis, Oct. 21, 1934; children—Ronald Arkwright, Hester Elizabeth Ollis Massey. Partner, sec. Ollis and Co., Springfield, Mo., 1955-60, v.p., 1960-70, pres., 1970-72, v.p., dir., 1972—, semi-ret. Treas. steering com. Goals for Springfield, 1972-73; membership chmn. Community Concert Assn., 1970-71; pres. St. Anne's Guild, St. John's Episcopal Ch. Mem. Springfield Assn. Ind. Ins. Agts (sec. treas.), P.E.O. (treas. chpt. FU). Republican. Club: Soroptimists Internat. Home: 3745 E Monroe St Springfield MO 65804 Office: 2274 E Sunshine St Springfield MO 65804

OLLIVIERRE, MURIEL MARY, ednl. adminstr.; b. N.Y.C., Mar. 15, 1940; d. Vincent Leslie and Muriel Ann (DuJon) O.; B.S., Fordham U., 1962; M.A., U. Utah, 1976. Br. mgr. Opportunities Industrialization Center N.Y., N.Y.C., 1968-70; dir. program ops. and mgmt., public service employment programs N.Y.C. Human Resources Adminstrn., 1972-78; asst. to chancellor N.Y.C. Bd. Edn., 1979-80, adminstrv. mgr. industry-sch. programs, 1981—; cons. in field. Grantee NSF, 1964. Mem. Nat. Assn. Female Execs., NOW, NAACP. Democrat. Roman Catholic. Office: 110 Livingston St Brooklyn NY 11201

OLM, JANE GRAY, librarian; b. Van Horn, Tex., Nov. 5, 1925; d. Robert Lee and Mary Louise (Lightfoot) Gray; B.B.A., U. N.Mex., 1948; M.L.S., U. Tex., Austin, 1966. High sch. librarian, Austin, Tex., 1963-66; reference librarian U. N.Mex. Zimmerman Library, 1966-67; asst. law librarian U. Tex. Law Library, Austin, 1967-71; assoc. librarian Tex. State Law Library, Austin, 1971-75; asst. law librarian Tex. Tech U. Sch. Law, Lubbock, 1975-78, head law librarian, 1978—; cons. county law libraries, law firms, Tex. Mem. Am. Assn. Law Libraries, Southwestern Assn. Law Libraries (pres. 1979-80), Tex. Council State Univ. Libraries (chmn. 1982-84). Editor: Directory of Law Libraries, 1982. Home: 4917 59th St Lubbock TX 79414 Office: Sch Law Library Tex Tech U Lubbock TX 79409

OLMSTED, PATRICIA PALMER, ednl. researcher; b. Chgo., Sept. 19, 1940; d. Richard O. and Marion E. (Huffman) Palmer; B.A. in Psychology, Mich. State U., 1962; postgrad. Stanford U., 1962-63; M.A., Columbia U., 1965; Ph.D., U. Fla., 1977. Grad. research asst. Columbia U., N.Y.C., 1964, public health trainee in psychopathology, 1964-65; asso. research scientist dept. med. genetics Psychiatric Inst., N.Y.C., 1965-66; asst. research coordinator Merrill-Palmer Inst., Detroit, 1966-68, instr., 1966-69, research coordinator, 1966-69; instr. Coll. Edn., U. Fla., Gainesville, 1969-71, asst. in edn., 1971-73, asso. in edn., 1973-77; clin. asst. prof. Sch. Edn., U. N.C., Chapel Hill, 1977—, dir. parent edn. follow through program, 1977—; cons. various public schs., 1969—.

Office of Edn. grantee, 1977-82. Mem. Soc. for Research in Child Devel., Am. Ednl. Research Assn., Nat. Assn. for Edn. of Young Children, Phi Delta Kappa. Contbr. articles on research in edn. to profl. publs.; contbr. chpts. to books on edn. Home: 49 Cedar Terrace Rd Chapel Hill NC 27514 Office: School Education Univ North Carolina Chapel Hill NC 27514

OLNEY, DONNA MAE, civic worker, former educator; b. Three Oaks, Mich., Mar. 29, 1914; d. Jesse J. and Mae Frances (Myers) Richardson; B.A., Eastern Mich. U., 1945; M.A., Western Mich. U., 1957; student U. Colo., 1934, No. Ariz. U., 1966, Andrews U., 1972, U. Ariz., 1973, Ariz. State U., 1957; m. Nov. 21, 1936. Tchr. rural schs., Berrien County, Mich., 1934-36, 43-44; tchr. music and art, schs., Berrien Springs, Mich., 1944-51; elementary tchr. including music, Morenci, Ariz., 1951-79, ret., 1979; mem. Ariz. State Music Com., 1973. Choir dir. Shepherd of the Hills Ch., Morenci, 1953-72, 74-76. Mem. NEA, Ariz. Edn. Assn. (exec. bd. 1956-57, state mental health chmn. 1958-59), United Meth. Women, Delta Kappa Gamma (state parliamentarian 1957-58, 2d v.p. 1959-61). Republican. Clubs: Bus. and Profl. Women (Woman of Year 1978-79) (Clifton, Ariz.), Safford Hosp. Aux., Berrien Gen. Hosp. Aux., Republican Women of Graham County (corr. sec. 1980-81), Morenci Women's. Composer prize winning song Delta Kappa Gamma, 1974, bicentennial song: America Calling, featured state and SW regional convs., 1976. Contbr. articles to profl. jours. Home: 2872 Hoopes Ave Thatcher AZ 85552

OLSCHEFSKY, CECILIA FRANCES, med. technologist; b. Detroit, Nov. 4, 1919; d. Joseph and Cecilia (Wolschon) O.; B.S. in Chemistry, U. Detroit, 1945. Med. technologist Grace Hosp., Detroit, 1942-43; exec. dept. head med. lab. Saratoga Gen. Hosp., Detroit, 1943-51, North Detroit Gen. Hosp., 1951-58; exec. head med. lab. dept. Dearborn (Mich.) Med. Centre Hosp., 1959—; bd. dirs., v.p., treas. Detroit Blood Bank, 1954-72. Com. mem. Grosse Pointe Symphony Women's Assn., Women's Assn. for Detroit Symphony Orch., 1959—. Mem. Am. Soc. Med. Technologists, Am. Soc. Clin. Pathologists, Mich. Soc. Med. Technologists, AAUW, Alumni Assn. U. Detroit (life), League Cath. Women. Clubs: Detroit Boat, Detroit Women's City, Terrapin Swim (corr. sec., pres. 1969-72), Dolphin Swim (dir., treas. 1977-79). Address: 359 Washington Rd Grosse Pointe MI 48230

OLSEN, CHERYL OLIVAR, human resources specialist; b. Manila, Philippines, Sept. 22, 1945; d. George Ramesola and Celia Castro (Bocobo) Olivar; B.A. cum laude, U. Philippines, 1966; M.P.A., U. Mich., 1971; m. Edward Tait Olsen, Aug. 12, 1969. Instr., U. Philippines, 1966-68; account exec. Philippine Advt. Counselors, Manila, 1967-68; researcher Inst. Social Research, Ann Arbor, Mich., 1969-71; media buyer Russ Reid Co., Pasadena, Calif., 1973-75; program coordinator Women's Career Devel. Program, YWCA, Van Nuys, Calif., 1977; equal opportunity programs adminstr. Bunker Ramo Electronic Systems, Westlake Village, Calif., 1977-79, equal opportunity programs mgr., 1979-80; equal opportunity programs mgr. Electronics div. Xerox Corp., El Segundo, Calif., 1980-81, mgr. equal employment opportunity programs and personnel info. systems, 1981—. Mem. adv. bd. Los Angeles Human Relations Commn., Los Angeles Mayors Com. on Handicapped; mem. industry adv. bd. Center for Employment Tng. (Ventura County); co. coordinator Youth Motivation Task Force. Mem. Greater Los Angeles Urban League, Internat. Assn. Personnel Women, Asian-Pacific Women's Network, Asian-Pacific Personnel Assn., Los Angeles Basin Equal Opportunity League (v.p.), Aerospace Industry Equal Opportunity Com., Am. Electronics Assn. (equal employment opportunity task force), AAUW, NOW, YWCA, Nat. Assn. Female Execs., Calif. Karate Assn., Northridge Bus. and Profl. Women's Club (corr. sec.), Pacificulture Found. Office: 701 S Aviation El Segundo CA 90245

OLSEN, INGER ANNA, psychologist; b. Copper Mountain, B.C, Can., Dec. 25, 1926; d. Arthur I.J. and Dagmar O.; B.S., Wash. State U., 1954, M.S., 1956, Ph.D., 1962. Psychiat. nurse Provincial Mental Health Services B.C., 1947-51, psychologist, 1956-58; psychologist Vancouver (B.C.) City Met. Health Services, 1958-60, Wash. State U. Student Counseling Center, Pullman, 1960-62; sr. psychologist Met. Health Services, Vancouver, 1962-66; instr. psychology Vancouver Community Coll., 1966—; docent Vancouver Aquarium Assn. Bd. dirs. Second Mile Soc., 1975—. Mem. Assn. Childhood Edn. Internat., Am. Psychol. Assn., B.C. Psychol. Assn., Gerontol. Soc., Can. Assn. Gerontology, B.C. Assn. Gerontology, Phi Beta Kappa, Sigma Xi, Alpha Kappa Delta. Contbr. articles to profl. jours. Home: 1255 Bidwell St Apt 1910 Vancouver BC V6G 2K8 Canada Office: 100 W 49th Ave Vancouver BC V5Y 2Z6 Canada

OLSEN, KIRSTEN, broker; b. Copenhagen, Nov. 5, 1942; came to U.S., 1948, naturalized, 1956; d. Jens Peder and Else Emilie (Jorgensen) Jensen; student Coll. San Mateo, 1964; grad. Stanford U. Exec. Inst., 1976; m. Thomas Allen Skornia, May 22, 1976; 1 dau., Erika Skornia-Olsen. Asst. to pres. Drexler Tech., Palo Alto, Calif., from 1968, mgr. public relations, to 1973; investment broker Merrill Lynch, San Jose, Calif., 1973, Palo Alto, to 1977, Paine Webber Jackson & Curtis, Palo Alto, 1977-80, Smith Barney Harris Upham, Menlo Park, Calif., 1980—. Mem. San Francisco Bay Conservation and Devel. Commn.; bd. dirs. Miramonte Health Center, Palo Alto. Mem. Peninsula Profl. Women's Network, Calif. Elected Women. Democrat. Lutheran. Club: Peninsula Stock and Bond (pres.) (Palo Alto). Home: 1601 Stone Pine Ln Atherton CA 94025 Office: 3000 Sand Hill Rd Bldg 3 Menlo Park CA 94025

OLSEN, LINDA ELAINE, clin. psychologist; b. Oregon City, Oreg., Jan. 16, 1947; d. Clarence A. and Marilyn M. (Roppell) O.; B.A., Vassar Coll., 1968; Ph.D. (Margaret Floy Washburn fellow 1968), U. Chgo., 1975. Psychologist, Chgo. Counseling and Psychotherapy Center, 1968-73, Calif. Sch. Profl. Psychology, Los Angeles, 1973-76; clin. psychologist Los Angeles Family Inst., 1975—; asst. clin. prof. psychiatry UCLA, 1981—. USPHS trainee, 1970-71. Mem. Am. Psychol. Assn. (editorial bd. Jour. Psychotherapy 1973-76), Calif. State Psychol. Assn., Am. Family Therapy Assn. (charter). Author workbook and cassette tapes: Experiential Focusing Training Program, 1975. Office: 1315 Westwood Los Angeles CA 90024

OLSEN, MARGARET ANN, numismatist, retail exec.; b. Chgo., July 22, 1944; d. Carl Johan and Ruth Vera Olsen; R.N., Swedish Covenant Hosp., Chgo., 1965; B.S., No. Ill. U., 1968. Mem. nursing staff hosps. in Ill. and Colo., 1962-74; cons. Adams County Mental Health Center, Commerce City, Colo., 1973-74; fin. dir., instr. Rocky Mountain Transactional Analysis Inst., Littleton, Colo., 1974-76; cons. Rimel Assos. in Psychiatry, P.C., Denver, 1974-75; therapist Profl. Counseling Assos., Littleton, Colo., 1974-77; instr. Profl. Tng. Center, Littleton, 1975-77; therapist Denver Mental Health Group, 1977-80; pres. Westminster Coin & Jewelry, Ltd., also mgr., v.p., pres. Westminster Coin Co. (Colo.), 1974—. Bd. govs. Adelphi U., Garden City, N.J., 1982—. Mem. Inst. Numismatic and Philatelic Studies, Internat. Trasactional Analysis Assn. (dir. Rocky Mountain chpt.), Am. Nurses Assn., Am. Numismatic Assn., Nat. Assn. Coin and Precious Metals Dealers, Nat. Assn. Female Execs., Fla. United Numismatists Inc., Internat. Soc. Appraisers, Token and Medal Soc., Soc. Paper Money Collectors, Facts Trading Info. System, Colo. Wyo. Numismatic Assn., Colo. Ednl. Numismatic Assn. Office: 3489 W 72d Ave Suite 100 Westminster CO 80030

OLSEN, MARTHA BROWN, state ofcl.; b. Cookeville, Tenn., June 6, 1948; d. Raymond and Mary Elizabeth Brown; B.S., Tenn. Technol. U., 1970; postgrad. U. Western Australia, 1970-71, Tenn. State U., 1977-78, Harvard U., 1979; m. Robert J. Olsen, Sept. 15, 1972. Asst. commr. revenue Tenn. Dept. Revenue, Nashville, 1979-80, commr., 1980—; exec. asst. to chancellor U. Tenn., Nashville, 1975-79, dir. devel. and alumni relations, 1974-75. Republican. Mem. Christian Ch. Office: Dept Revenue Room 927 Andrew Jackson Bldg Nashville TN 37242

OLSEN, NEVA FOSTER, educator; b. Natchitoches, La., Nov. 12, 1927; d. George W. and Pearl (Carver) Foster; B.S., La. Tech. U., 1947; M.S., La. State U., 1961; Ph.D., Tex. Woman's U., 1976; m. Leonard J. Olsen, June 1, 1948 (dec.); children—Catherine Dianne, Brenda Susan. Tchr. home econs. and chemistry secondary schs., Arcadia, La., 1947-49, Haynesville, La., 1949-51, Lake Charles, La., 1955-58, Lafayette, La., 1958-60; prof. textile sci., dir. Sch. Home Econs., La. State U., Baton Rouge, 1961—; textile cons. ednl. orgns., state and consumer agys.; leader textile research projects La. Agrl. Expt. Station, U.S. Dept. Agr. Mem. Am. Home Econs. Assn., Am. Assn. Textile Chemists and Colorists, ASTM, Assn. Coll. Profs. Textiles and Clothing, Gamma Sigma Delta, Phi Lambda Pi. Methodist. Club: Camelot. Contbr. articles on textile research to profl. jours. Home: 6969 Highland Rd Baton Rouge LA 70808 Office: Louisiana State Univ Baton Rouge LA 70803

OLSEN, SALLIE MULLIKEN, psychologist, nurse, educator; b. Urbana, Ill., July 16, 1942; d. Wallace Mulberry and Jean (Forrest) Mulliken; B.S., U. Wis., 1965; M.S., U. Ill., Chgo., 1968; Ph.D., Saybrook Inst., San Francisco, 1980; m. Richard L. Olsen, June 11, 1966; children—Erik Wallace, Kristin Mahloch. Clin. specialist nurse City and County of San Francisco, 1968-70; pvt. practice psychotherapy, San Francisco, 1972—; asst. prof. U. Calif., San Francisco, 1975-80; lectr. Calif. State U., Hayward, 1981; dir. community and nursing edn. Mt. Diablo Hosp., Concord, Calif., 1981-82; tchr. U. Calif., San Francisco, Santa Cruz, Fresno and Davis extensions; cons. Mt. Diablo Hosp. Med. Center, Children's Hosp., San Francisco, Mt. Zion Hosp., San Francisco. Pres., treas. Miraloma Coop. Nursery, 1973-75. Mem. Am. Nurses Assn., Am. Psychol. Assn., Am. Soc. Tng. and Devel. Home: 350 Urbano Dr San Francisco CA 94127 Office: 203 Clement St San Francisco CA 94118

OLSEN, SALLY, state legislator; B.A., Met. State U.; postgrad. Hamline U. Law Sch.; m. Vernon Olsen; children—Richard, Roxanne, Susan. Mem. Minn. Ho. of Reps., St. Paul, 1978—, mem. edn., gen. legis. and vets. affairs, taxes coms. Chairperson bd. govs. Golden Valley (Minn.) Health Center; gov. Health Central, Inc.; mem. Council on Econ. Status of Women; mem. Minn. Gov.'s Statewide Adv. Council on Community Edn.; mem. Minn. Edn. Council; mem. St. Louis Park (Minn.) Sch. Bd.; bd. dirs. Minn. Sch. Bds. Assn., Minn. State High Sch. League; pres. St. Louis Park LWV; sec. Minn. LWV; bd. dirs. Suburban Hennepin County (Minn.) Vocat. Tech. Schs. Office: 329 State Office Bldg Saint Paul MN 55155 *

OLSEN, SHIRLEY ANNE, educator; b. Springfield, Ohio, Mar. 21, 1939; d. Ernest and Shirley Isabel (Daniels) O.; B.F.A., Ohio State U., 1961; M.A., 1964; children by previous marriage—Margaret Alyssa Jones, Murray Christopher Jones. Graphic designer Westinghouse Electric Corp., Pitts., 1967-69; graphic design cons. Paul Arthur & Assos., Toronto, 1969; lectr. York U., 1970; asst. prof. indsl. design Ohio State U., Columbus, 1970-75, asso. prof., 1975—; design cons. Mgmt. Graphics Inc., Worthington, Ohio, 1981-82. Recipient grants Ohio State U., 1975, 78. Editor: Group Planning and Problem Solving Methods in Engineering Management, 1982. Home: 221 E Schreyer Pl Columbus OH 43214 Office: Dept Indsl Design Ohio State U Columbus OH 43210

OLSEN, THEODORA EGBERT PECK (MRS. SEVERT ANDREW OLSEN), artist; b. Union, N.J., Sept. 6, 1909; d. Edward Egbert and Theodorea G. (Tucker) Peck; student N.Y. Sch. Design, 1928-29, Pratt-Phoenix Sch. Design, N.Y.C., 1929-32, Coll. City N.Y., 1955, Wagner Coll., summer 1965; m. Ray Sheldon Wilbur, Sept. 8, 1933 (dec. 1966); 1 dau., Margaret Anne (Mrs. Prudhomme); m. 2d, Severt Andrew Olsen, July 17, 1967 (dec. Feb. 1975); stepchildren Arlene Christine, Severt Eugene (dec.). Exhibited at Contemporary Gallery, Newark, 1932, S.I. Mus., 1947-65, N.Y.C. Fedn. Women's Clubs exhibit, 1961, Island Art Center Gallery, New Dorp, S.I., 1961, 33d N.J. Exhbn., Montclair Art Mus., 1964, Summit (N.J.) Art Center, 1965; outdoor shows at Sailors Snug Harbour, S.I., 1956-63, Greenwich Village, N.Y.C., 1961-64, Southhampton and Westhampton (L.I.) Beach, 1964, Summit Art Center, N.J., 1967, Spring Festival Arts, Staten Island, 1968; represented in permanent collection at Wagner Coll., S.I.; prin. works include View From Guild Hall, Show Case, Variation on Theme VIII, Long Island Expressway, Seed Pods, Emergence from Chrysalis. Cons., lectr., pvt. tchr., 1934—; tchr. painting YWCA, S.I., 1968-72. Active fund-raising Richmond Mem. Hosp., 1946-54, com. to beautify halls Tottenville (S.I.) High Sch., 1958-60. Recipient S.I. Mus.-Wagner Coll. Purchase award, 1958—; Julius Weisglass award S.I. Mus., 1960, 65; 1st prize and Honorable mention N.Y.C. Fedn. Women's Clubs competition, 1961. Founder, hon. life mem. South Shore Artists Group (pres. 1946-47, 49-61, 2d v.p. 1965-66); mem. S.I. Inst. Arts and Scis., S.I. Hist. Soc. Women's Aux., S.I. Hist. Soc., Nat. Assn. Mil. Widows, Pratt-Phoenix Sch. Design Alumni (jury awards 1949), Epsilon Nu Sigma. Clubs: Prince Bay Women's (pres. 1969-71); Coast Guard Officer's Wives. Home: 72 Bayview Ave Prince Bay Staten Island NY 10309

OLSEN, TILLIE, author; b. Nebr., Jan. 14, 1912; d. Samuel and Ida (Beber) Lerner; grad. high sch.; D.Arts and Letters (hon.), U. Nebr., 1979; Litt.D. (hon.) Knox Coll., 1982; m. Jack Olsen; children—Karla, Julie, Kathie, Laurie. Author: Tell Me A Riddle (title story received O'Henry 1st Prize award, 1961 (film version 1980), 1962; Yonnondio: From the Thirties, 1974; Rebecca Harding Davis: Life in the Iron Mills, 1973; Silences, 1978; film made of I Stand Here Ironing, 1980, 81, also other dramatizations of work, 1975-81; short fiction pub. in 61 anthologies. Writer-in-residence or vis. faculty English, Amherst Coll., 1969-70, Stanford U., 1972, M.I.T., 1973-74, U. Mass., Boston, 1974; internat. vis. scholar, Norway, 1980; cons. on lit.; reader and lectr. Recipient Nat. Endowment for Arts award, 1967; Am. Acad. Nat. Inst. award for disting. contbn. to Am. letters, 1975; Ministry to Women award Unitarian Universalist Fedn., 1980; Brit. Post Office and B.P.W. award, 1980; Tillie Olsen Day proclaimed May 18, 1981 by mayor of San Francisco; Ford Found. grantee, 1959, Stanford writing fellow, 1956, Radcliffe Inst. fellow, 1962-64, Guggenheim fellow, 1975-76; Copeland fellow Amherst Coll., 1977; Regents lectr. U. Calif. at San Diego, 1977. Mem. Authors Guild, PEN. Home: 1435 Laguna St San Francisco CA 94115

OLSHANSKY, PHYLLIS MACKLIN, clin. psychologist; b. N.Y.C., July 19, 1929; d. Joseph and Dorothy (Chasnoff) Macklin; B.A., N.Y. U., 1950, M.A., 1961, postgrad., 1977; M.A., Yeshiva U., 1963, Ph.D., 1971; m. Murray Olshansky, Mar. 26, 1950; children—Brian, Emily, Nicolas. Therapist, Jewish Family Service Center, Bronx, N.Y., 1966-67; lectr. Iona Coll., New Rochelle, N.Y., 1967-68; psychologist Westchester County Community Mental Health Bd., Mt. Vernon, N.Y., 1967-70; Guidance Center of New Rochelle, N.Y., 1969—, dir. day hosp., 1975—. NIMH fellow, 1964-65. Diplomate in clin. psychology Am. Bd. Profl. Psychology. Mem. Am. Psychol. Assn., N.Y. Psychol. Assn., Westchester County Psychol. Assn., Assn. Day Hosps. of N.Y., Phi Beta Kappa. Democrat. Home: 60 Lakeview Rd New Rochelle NY 10804 Office: Guidance Center 70 Grand St New Rochelle NY 10801

OLSON, BETTY LEE, controller; b. Anadarko, Okla., Feb. 4, 1932; d. Joseph Oscar and Lillie Belle (Brush) McClure; student U.S. Dept. Agr. Grad. Sch., 1977-78, 81-82; m. Harold L. Olson, May 14, 1949. Bookkeeper-cashier Southwestern Pub. Service Co., Clovis, N.Mex., 1953-59; bookkeeper-partner C & S Oil Co., Portales, N.Mex., 1960-61; sec. Erath County Electric Coop. Assn., Stephenville, Tex., 1962, data processing supr., 1969, office mgr., 1974, controller, 1977—. Chmn., Woman of Yr. Com., Stephenville 1979—. Mem. Stephenville C. of C., Tex. Electric Coop. Acctg. Assn. (chmn. Group IV 1979-80, sec. state assn. 1981-83). Club: Cross Timbers Bus. and Profl. Women's (pres. 1977-78). Home: Route 3 Box 95 Stephenville TX 76401 Office: PO Box 290 Stephenville TX 76401

OLSON, BEVERLY JO ELICERIO, chemist; b. St. Paul, Nov. 13, 1952; d. Felix Istores and Virginia Mae (Jurecki) Elicerio; student Iowa State U., 1970-72; student U. Minn., Duluth, 1972-74, U. Minn., Mpls., 1975-77; m. George T. Olson, Sept. 6, 1975. Sr. lab technician H. B. Fuller Co., St. Paul, 1974-78, lab. specialist, 1978-80, chemist, 1980—. Congregationalist. Patentee in field. Office: 2267 Como Ave Saint Paul MN 55108

OLSON, BONNIE WAGGONER BRETERNITZ, civic worker; b. North Platte, Nebr., May 30, 1916; d. Floyd Emil and Edith (Waggoner) Breternitz; A.B., U. Chgo., 1947; m. O. Donald Olson, May 17, 1944; children—Pamela Lynne, Douglas Donald. Dep. clk. Dist. Ct., Lincoln County, Nebr., 1940-42; advt. researcher Burke & Assos., Chgo., 1942; contbg. newspaper columnist Chgo. Herald-Am., 1943; social worker ARC, Chgo., 1942-44; exec. sec. Econometrica, Cowles Commn. for Research in Econs., Chgo., 1945-47. Active Chgo. Maternity Center Fund Drive, 1953; mem. Colo. Springs Community Council, 1956-58, chmn. children's div., 1956-58, mem. exec. bd., 1956-58, mem. budget com., 1957-58; mem. Colorado Springs Charter Assn., 1956-60, mem. exec. bd., 1957-59, sec., 1958; chmn. El Paso County PTA, Protective Services for Children, 1959-61; chmn. women's div. fund drive ARC, 1961; mem. LWV, 1957—, mem. state children's law com., 1961-63; chmn. ad hoc com. El Paso County Citizens Com. for Nat. Probation and Parole Survey, Juvenile Ct. Procedures and Detention, 1957-61; mem. children's adv. com. Colo. Child Welfare Dept., 1959-63, chmn., 1961; del. White House Conf. on Children and Youth, 1960, 70; sec. Citizens Ad Hoc Com. for Comprehensive Mental Health Clinic for Pikes Peak Region, 1966—; mem. Colorado Springs Human Relations Commn., 1968-71; sustaining mem. Symphony Guild, 1970-72, Fine Arts Center, 1957—; bd. dirs. Pikes Peak Mental Health Center, 1964-67; del. Colo. Gov.'s Conf. on Aging, 1980; observer White House Conf. on Aging, 1981. Recipient Lane Bryant Ann. Nat. Awards citation, 1961; alumni citation for public service U. Chgo., 1961. Mem. Am. Acad. Polit. and Social Sci., Council on Religion and Internat. Affairs. Episcopalian. Clubs: Quadrangle, University (Chgo.); Broadmoor Golf, Garden of the Gods, ENT Officers Wives (hon.) (Colorado Springs). Home: 2110 Hercules Dr Colorado Springs CO 80906

OLSON, CAROL ANNE BATES, exec. suite complex exec.; b. Bournemouth, Eng., Dec. 24, 1935; came to U.S., 1959; d. William Henry and Margaret (Johnson) Bates; student Brit. schs.; m. Robert Carroll Olson, Nov. 14, 1959 (dec. Dec. 1975); children—David William Michael, Rand Patrick Carroll. Pres.; Exec. Row, Inc., Newport Beach, Calif., 1977—, also Exec. Row (Internat.), Inc.; v.p. BASIC (Commodities), Ltd.; dir. Evans & Assos., Underwater Ways. Named Entrepreneural Woman of Year in Orange County, Careers for Women, 1979. Mem. Am. Soc. Profl. and Exec. Women, Am. Entrepreneurs Soc., Am. Mgmt. Assn., Black Africa Soc. Internat. Cooperation (v.p.), Newport Harbor C. of C. Clubs: Newport Harbor Bayview Yacht, Sporting House. Home: 6291 Sierra Bravo Irvine CA 92715 Office: 3901 MacArthur Blvd Suite 211 Newport Beach CA 92660

OLSON, CHARLOTTE GRETHEL ELKINS, med. records adminstr.; b. Gilbert, W.Va., Sept. 14, 1922; d. Rush and Mary Ellen (White) Elkins; B.A., Goddard Coll., 1968; grad. Sch. for Med. Record Adminstrs., USPHS Hosp., 1969. Chief med. info. sect. VA Hosps. at Martinsburg, W.Va., 1970-71, West Side Chgo., 1971-72, Durham, N.C., 1972-74, Bay Pines, Fla., 1975-76, Martinsburg, W.Va., 1976-80, Mountain Home, Tenn., 1981—; with Project Hope Agencia, Brazil, S.Am., 1974; vol. Sage Meml. Hosp., Ganado, Ariz., 1971. Recipient Cert. of Appreciation, Project Hope. Mem. Am. Med. Record Assn., Tenn. Med. Record Assn. (pres.-elect 1980-81), AAUW (treas. Chgo. br. 1972). Republican. Presbyterian. Club: Order Eastern Star. Home: Route 5 PO Box 606 Elizabethtown TN 37643

OLSON, DANA LEHMAN, clin. psychologist; b. N.Y.C., Jan. 31, 1942; d. Lloyd George and Pearl Lorean (Ellis) Dence; A.B., Bethany (Okla.) Coll., 1965; M.A., Oklahoma City U., 1966; Ph.D. (Inst. Advanced Study Rational Psychotherapy fellow), Okla. State U., 1974; m. Phillip Coy, Feb. 14, 1980. Psychologist, Family Cons. Center, Burnsville, Minn., 1974-78, St. Louis Park (Minn.) Med. Center, 1978-79; pvt. practice psychology, Edina, Minn., 1979—; mem. Bloomington (Minn.) Adv. Bd. Health, 1982; mem. profl. adv. bd. Women's Resource Center, Bloomington, 1982; cons. in field. Mem. Am. Psychol. Assn., Minn. Psychol. Assn., Minn. Psychologists in Pvt. Practice. Author chpts. in books. Home: 9550 Collegeview Rd Bloomington MN 55437 Office: 6950 France St Room 204 Edina MN 55437

OLSON, DONNA RAE, med. technologist; b. St. Louis, Oct. 20, 1946; d. Roy William and Ann Elizabeth (O'Donnell) O.; B.A. in Biology, Cath. U. Am., 1964, B.S. in Med. Tech., 1966, M.A. in Ednl. Tech., 1973; M.A. in Health Care Mgmt. and Supervision, Central Mich. U., 1981. Clin. chemistry supr. Washington Hosp. Center, 1965-69, teaching coordinator Sch. Med. Tech., 1969-72; clin. chemistry technologist NIH, Bethesda, Md., 1972—. Recipient various govt. awards. Mem. Am. Soc. Clin. Pathologists (affiliate), Am. Soc. Med. Technologists, Am. Mgmt. Assn., Clin. Lab. Mgmt. Assn., D.C. Soc. Med. Tech. (ednl. coordinator 1979-81). Home: 6001 Landon Ln Bethesda MD 20817 Office: Clin Chem Service NIH Bethesda MD 20814

OLSON, DORISE EVELYN (MRS. RAUL J. MINA-MORA), artist; b. N.Y.C., June 8, 1932; d. Athur C. and Anna (Carlson) Olson; student Art Student's League, L.I. Art League, Woodstock, N.Y., Traphagen Sch. Design, N.Y.; m. Raul J. Mina-Mora, Oct. 27, 1967. One-man shows at Caravan House Galleries, Lord & Taylor's Galleries, Different Drummer Gallery, 1976, Nat. Art League, Wickford Art Gallery; exhibited in group shows at Bklyn. Mus., Nat. Arts Club, Nat. Acad., Nat. Acad. Fine Arts, Met. Mus. Arts, Community Gallery with Burr Artists, 1977, Goldsboro (N.C.) Art Mus., 1977, Parrish Art Mus., 1970, 72, Springfield (Mass.) Art Mus., Stony Brook U., Cork Gallery, Avery Fisher Hall, Lincoln Center, 1980; represented in pvt. collections; tchr. painting Islip Art Mus. Demonstrator watercolor for various schs. and pvt. clubs. Recipient award Bus. and Profl. Women's Club, N.Y.C., 1967; gold medal Knickerbocker Artists, 1968; Hydenryk award Catherine Lorillard Wolfe Art Club, 1969; 1st place award in watercolor Bklyn. Mus. competition, 1966, 67, 69, Windsor and Newton award, Nat. Arts League Gold medal, 70, Grumbacher award 1971, 1st prize for watercolor Malverne Artists, 1973, best watercolor award Burr Artists, 1974, Forbes award, 1981, Newman award Nat. Soc. Painters in Casein and Acrylic, 1981, others. Mem. Am. Artists Profl. League (award 1979), Allied Artists Am., Catherine Lorillard Wolfe Art Club,

Nat. Soc. Painters in Casein and Acrylic, Knickerbocker Artists (award 1979), Nat. Arts Club, Audubon Artists. Address: 87 Central Blvd Oakdale NY 11769

OLSON, GLORIA ANNE SONDRA, army officer; b. Rome, N.Y., May 7, 1928; d. John S. and Mary (Pardi) O.; B.S., SUNY, Oswego, 1951; M.S., Syracuse U., 1953. Enlisted in U.S. Army, 1953, advanced through grades to col., 1979; chief radio-TV br. Def. Info. Sch., Fort Benjamin Harrison, Ind., 1964-67; chief TV br. Office Public Affairs, Pentagon, Washington, 1967-68; photojournalist, command info. officer personal staff Gen. Creighton W. Abrams, Vietnam, 1968-69; chief recruiting 12-state area, New Eng., Va., 1970-72; action officer Policy and Planning Div. Public Info., Pentagon, 1972-74; public relations dir. U.S. Army Hosps., Fort Sam Houston, Tex., 1981—. Decorated Air medal, Bronze Star, 15 meritorious medals. Office: Hdqrs HSC Fort Sam Houston TX 78234

OLSON, ILYNE MCJIMSEY (MRS. KENNETH VERDERE OLSON), educator; b. Kerrville, Tex., Apr. 16, 1919; d. Albertus and Laura (Wilson) McJimsey; B.J., U. Tex., 1941, postgrad., 1953; postgrad. U. Tenn., 1963, Incarnate Word Coll., 1967; m. Kenneth Verdere Olson, June 21, 1942; children—Daniel Verdere, Sharon Kathlyne (Mrs. Wilson James Ramsey, Jr.), John Laurence. Advt. copywriter Sears Roebuck & Co., 1941-42; advt. mgr. Stowers Furniture, San Antonio, 1942-43; tchr., St. Michael Episcopal Sch., Dallas, 1965-66; tchr. Alamo Heights Sch. Dist., San Antonio, 1966-68, N.E. Ind. Sch. Dist., San Antonio, 1968-69; tchr. history W.T. White High Sch., Dallas Ind. Sch. Dist., 1970-72; tchr. journalism Alief Ind. Sch. Dist., Houston, 1972-74. Creator ednl. games Internat. Travel Mate, Addison, Tex., 1971, Kenworthy Ednl. Service, Buffalo, 1974, T.S. Denison & Co., Inc., Mpls., 1977. Mem. Women in Communications, Sigma Delta Chi. Home: 6407 Redding Rd Houston TX 77036

OLSON, JOSEPHINE EVA, economist, educator; b. Bronxville, N.Y., Aug. 25, 1942; d. Reinhold S. and Elizabeth S. (Deacon) O.; A.B., Wellesley Coll., 1964; Ph.D. in Econs. (Ford Found. fellow, NSF fellow), Brown U., 1970; m. Jerome A. Spieckerman, May 24, 1980; 1 stepdau., Julia L. Asst. prof. econs. and fin. Bernard M. Baruch Coll., CUNY, 1969-71; asst. prof. bus. adminstrn. U. Pitts., 1971-75, asso. prof., 1975—; trustee Tchrs. Ins. and Annuity Assn., N.Y.C., 1974—. Bd. dirs. Penn Group Health Plan, Pitts., 1977—. Mem. Am. Econ. Assn., Transp. Research Forum. Democrat. Office: Graduate School of Business University of Pittsburgh Pittsburgh PA 15260

OLSON, KAREN MARIE, acct.; b. Elmhurst, Ill., July 25, 1950; d. Richard Steven and LaVerne Marie (Voss) O.; B.S. in Accountancy, U. Ill., Urbana, 1972. Jr. acct. Easterling-Cordcraft, Wheaton, Ill., 1972; acctg. asst. First Fed. Savs. & Loan of Aurora (Ill.), 1972-73; audit mgr. Glenn Ingram & Co., Chgo., 1973—. Mem. Am. Inst. C.P.A.s, Ill. C.P.A. Soc., Am. Women's Soc. C.P.A.s, Chgo. Soc. Women C.P.A.s. Home: 375 Windsor Ave Glen Ellyn IL 60137 Office: Glenn Ingram & Co 150 N Wacker Dr Chicago IL 60606

OLSON, MARGARETTE ADELINE, clin. psychologist; b. Minn.; B.S., U. N.D., 1944, M.S., 1948, Ph.D., 1951; postgrad. Columbia U., 1956, Okla. State U., 1965-66, U. S.D., 1974-75, U. Minn., 1976-77; m. Alfred O. Olson, Jan. 1, 1942; 1 son, Mark David. Prin., field supt. Gulf Coast Bus. Schs., Bay City, Tex., 1945-47; chmn. dept. bus. edn. U. N.D., 1947-56; prof., chmn. dept. bus. edn. State Coll., Mayville, N.D., 1956-62; dean of women, asso. dean of students Nebr. State Coll., Chadron, 1962-65; resident in clin. psychology State Hosp., Hastings, Nebr., 1965-66; prof. psychology SW State Coll., Weatherford, Okla., 1966-71; clin. psychologist S.D. Human Services Center, Yankton, 1971—; psychol. cons. Okla. Gen. Hosp., Concho Indian Sch., Clinton Indian Hosp.; tchr. continuing and adult edn. Mount Marty Coll., Yankton Public Schs. Mem. Gov.'s Com. on Children and Youth, 1958-61, Gov.'s Com. on Aging, 1960-61, Gov.'s Com. on Edn. and Research in Aging, 1961-62; del. White House Conf. on Children and Youth, 1960, White House Conf. on Aging, 1961; mem. Com. of Concern for Alcoholism, 1967-71, vice-chmn., 1968-70. Mem. Am. Psychol. Assn., So. Psychol. Assn., Midwestern Psychol. Assn., S.D. Psychol. Assn. (sec.-treas. 1978-80), Bd. Examiners for Psychologists (sec.-treas. 1979-81, pres. 1981—), Nebr. Council Adminstrv. Women, N.D. Federated Women's Clubs (state chmn. statue of women 1962-63), AAUW (pres. state div. 1958-60), Bus. and Profl. Women's Club (pres. 1980-81). Republican. Methodist. Clubs: Zonta, Soroptimist, Woman's, Extension, VFW Aux. Home: 2307 Mulberry St Box 76 Yankton SD 57078 Office: Box 76 Yankton SD 57078

OLSON, MARIAN KATHERINE, govt. ofcl.; b. Tulsa, Oct. 15, 1933; d. Sherwood Joseph and Katherine M. (Miller) Lahman; B.A. in Polit. Sci., U. Colo., 1954, M.A. in Elem. Edn., 1962; Ed.D. in Ednl. Adminstrsn., U. Tulsa, 1969; m. Ronald Keith Olson, Oct. 27, 1956. Tchr. public schs., Wyo., Colo., Mont., 1958-67; teaching fellow, adj. instr. edn. U. Tulsa, 1968-69; asst. prof. edn. Eastern Mont. State Coll., 1970; program asso. research adminstrn. Mont. State U., 1970-75; on leave with Energy Policy Office of White House, then with Fed. Energy Adminstrn., 1973-74; with Dept. Energy, and predecessor, 1975—, program analyst, 1975-79, chief planning and environ. compliance br., Bartlesville, Okla., 1979—; pres. LNG Resources, Inc. Grantee Okla. Consortium Higher Edn., 1969, NIMH, 1974. Mem. Am. Assn. Budget and Program Analysis, Women in Energy, Oklahomans for Energy and Jobs, Kappa Delta Pi, Phi Alpha Theta, Kappa Alpha Theta. Republican. Author articles in field. Home: Route 2 Box 142KK Bartlesville OK 74003 Office: PO Box 1398 Bartlesville OK 74003

OLSON, MARY LEVIA, art gallery exec.; b. Sterling, Ill., Mar. 4, 1941; d. Harold E. and Virginia E. (Brittenham) Olson; student Iowa Wesleyan Coll., 1959-61, pvt. student Art, 1975-79. With fleet dept. Pyrofax Corp., Houston, 1964-69; asst. dir., corp. sec. R.H. Love Galleries, Chgo., 1969-79, dir. mktg./sales, corp. sec., 1981—; mgr. portrait photography studio PCA Internat., Chgo., 1979; export mgr., agt. Air-Line Air Freight, Ltd., Bensenville, Ill., 1980-81. Mem. Nat. Assn. Female Execs. Designer, preparer art catalogs: American Paintings, 1977, Harriet Randall Lumas, 1870-1953, 1977, William Chadwick, An American Impressionist, 1879-1962, 1978; project coordinator John Barber: The Artist, the Man; researcher Cyclopedia of Am. Impressionism. Office: 100 E Ohio St Chicago IL 60611

OLSON, NANCY SUZANNE, fashion co. exec.; b. Crookston, Minn., Feb. 22, 1938; d. Solon Hubert and Orpha Florence (Love) Gullickson; B.A., Concordia Coll., Moorhead, Minn., 1960; M.S., U. Minn., 1968; m. Arvid L. Olson, Nov. 26, 1960; children—Daniel, David. Tchr. home econs. dept. Circle Pines Jr. High Sch., 1960-61; home econs. tchr. Minnetonka East Jr. High Sch., 1966-68; chmn./coordinator apparel specialist program Anoka (Minn.) Vocat. Tech. Inst., 1968-72; pres. Fashion Services, Inc., Mpls., 1972—; cons. sewing notions div. 3M Co., 1972-73; instr. creative learning center Control Data Corp., 1972-73. Bd. dirs., officer Minn. Montessori Found., 1968-74. Mem. Am. Home Sewing Assn., Am. Home Econs. Assn., The Fashion Group, Am. Fedn. Radio and TV Artists. Lutheran. Author: Patterngrams, 2d edit., 1980; patentee in field. Home: 412 Arthur St Edina MN 55343 Office: 600 1st Ave N Minneapolis MN 55403

OLSON, SANDRA FORBES, physician, educator; b. East Chicago, Ind., Jan. 8, 1938; d. James Cornelius and Mabel Elizabeth (Newman) Forbes; student St. Mary's of Notre Dame, 1955-56; B.S., Purdue U., 1959; M.D., Northwestern U., 1963; m. Ronald W. Olson, Sept. 2, 1967; children—Ronald W., Kirsten Ann. Chief of staff Northwestern Meml. Hosp., Chgo.; assoc. prof. dept. neurology Northwestern U. Med. Sch. Mem. Am. EEG Soc., Chgo. Neurol. Soc., AMA, Am. Epilepsy Soc., Am. Acad. Neurology, Sigma Xi, Psi Iota Xi, Phi Beta Phi. Roman Catholic. Club: Women's Athletic. Office: 251 E Chicago Ave Chicago IL 60611

OLSON, SUE, banker; b. Cheyenne, Okla., July 16, 1940; d. Albert Franklin and Stella Lee (Bradford) Davis; student Okla. Intermediate Sch. Banking; m. Benjamin Carl Olson, Dec. 22, 1956; children—Albert Leon, Lonnie Dean. Bookkeeper, City Nat. Bank of Sayre (Okla.), 1967-70, teller, 1970-76, asst. cashier, 1976-79, cashier, 1979—. Mem. Nat. Assn. Bank Women (publicity chmn. Western Plains Group 1980, sec. 1981). Home: Route 1 PO Box 96 Cheyenne OK 73628 Office: PO Box 310 128 E Main St Sayre OK 73662

OLSTEIN, NAOMI (AMI), editor; b. San Martin, Argentina, Dec. 29, 1944; came to U.S., 1945, naturalized, 1951; d. Leon and Dvora (Silverstein) Olstein Mintz; B.A., Glassboro State Coll., 1966; M.A., N.Y. U., 1970. Vocat. counselor, manpower devel. tng. program N.Y. State Dept. Labor, N.Y.C., 1970-73; vocat. counselor CETA, N.Y.C., 1973-74; dir. counseling, fin. aid counselor Apex Tech. Sch., N.Y.C., 1976-77, Monroe Bus. Inst., 1977-78, Pvt. Vocat. Schs. Assn. Manpower Tng. Program, 1975-76; exec. dir. The Writing Workshop, N.Y.C., 1978-81; freelance writer, editor, film editor, 1981—. Mem. Am. Personnel and Guidance Assn., Am. Soc. Tng. and Devel., Nat. Assn. Female Execs., Am. Film Inst.

OLSTON, MARY KAY, psychologist; b. Milw.; d. Gordon Rhodes and Mary Anne (Popp) O.; B.A., Carroll Coll., 1970; M.S., U. Wis., Milw., 1971. Asso. sch. psychologist Milw. Public Schs., 1971-74, sch. psychologist, 1974—; research asst. U. Wis., Madison, 1973-76. Lic. sch. psychologist, Wis. Mem. Am. Psychol. Assn., Wis. Sch. Psychologist Assn., Nat. Assn. Sch. Psychologists, Milwaukee County Psychol. Assn. (treas. 1982—), Milw. Area Assn. Psychologists in Schs., Alliance Française (librarian 1980-82). Home: 10541 W Woodward Ave Wauwatosa WI 53222 Office: 5225 W Vliet St Milwaukee WI 53201

OLUFSON, EDNA MAE KATHLEEN, nurse; b. Dunseith, N.D., July 30, 1940; d. Abraham C. and Mary (Evanstad) Nelson; R.N., Lutheran Deaconess Hosp., Mpls., 1961; B.S., City Coll., Seattle, 1979; m. David Olufson, July 17, 1965; children—Philip David, Julie Christine. Operating room nurse Luth. Deaconess Hosp., 1961-65; supr. operating room Dakota Hosp., Fargo, N.D., 1965-68; nursing supr., asst. adminstr. Good Samaritan Nursing Center, East Grand Forks, Minn., 1968-75; part-time nurse instr. Good Samaritan Nursing Center, Green Acres, Wash., 1975-76; asst. staff devel. coordinator Foss Home, Seattle, 1976—; health programs coordinator City Coll., 1979—; workshop instr. nursing asst. cert. Organist, Trinity Luth. Ch., Lynnwood, Wash., 1977—. Mem. Am. Coll. Nursing Home Adminstrs., Am. Nurses Assn., King County Nurses Assn. (chmn. gerontology group), Council Nursing Home Nurses, Am. Guild Organists, Am. Coll. Musicians. Republican. Author manual, workbook. Home: 710 10th Pl S Edmonds WA 98020 Office: 13023 Greenwood Ave N Seattle WA 98133

OLYMPIA, JOSIE LIM, psychiatrist; b. Or. Mindoro, Philippines, Feb. 9, 1944; came to U.S., 1968; B.S., U. Philippines, 1962, M.D., 1967. Rotating intern Mt. Sinai Hosp., Milw., 1968; resident in psychiatry Buffalo Psychiat. Center, 1968-71, psychiatrist I, II, III, 1971-77, dir. med. edn., 1977—; asst. chief psychiatry service Buffalo VA Med. Center, 1981—; assoc. clin. prof. psychiatry SUNY, Buffalo; cons. Mental Health Corp. II, Erie County, N.Y., Niagara Falls Meml. Med. Center, N.Y. Bur. of Disability. Served to maj. USAR. NEH grantee, 1979. Mem. Am. Psychiat. Assn., Am. Orthopsychiat. Assn. Roman Catholic. Office: VA Med Center 2495 Bailey Ave Buffalo NY 14215

OLZENDAM, HARRIETT STEELE, ret. lawyer; b. Dover, N.H., Aug. 5, 1914; d. Enoch Ned and Lena Marion (Steele) Olzendam; B.A., Wellesley Coll., 1936; M.A., Trinity Coll., 1942; J.D. with distinction, U. Conn., 1946. Admitted to Conn. bar, 1946, Fed. Dist. bar, 1948; with The Travelers Ins. Co., Hartford, Conn., 1937-79, chief contract underwriter, 1951-61, asst. sec., 1961-69, sec., 1969-79. Mem. residence com. YWCA, Hartford, Conn., 1964-79, dir., 1971-77, sec., 1972-74, v.p., 1974-75, pres., 1975-77, mem. fin. com., 1975-79, personnel com., 1979—. Mem. Am., Hartford County bar assns., Am. Judicature Soc., Mental Health Assn. Conn. (nominating com. 1976-78, trustee 1979—), Conn. Ins. Assn. (group com.), Conn. Health Reins. Assn. (chmn. forms com.), Soc. Group Contract Analysts, Wellesley Coll. Alumnae Assn., U. Conn. Sch. Law, Trinity Coll. alumni assns., Mark Twain Meml., Wadsworth Atheneum, Antiquarian and Landmarks Soc. Conn., Nat. Audubon Soc., Nat. Wildlife Fedn., Smithsonian Assos., Hartford Easter Seal Rehab. Center. Republican. Conglist. Clubs: Wellesley (fin. chmn. 1975-77, 1st v.p. 1977-79), Quota (corr. sec. Hartford 1970-78, 1st v.p. 1978—), Town and County (gov. 1978-82, rec. sec. 1979-80, personnel com. 1978-82, exec. com. 1979-82, chmn. exec. com. 1979—). Address: 2012 Blvd West Hartford CT 06107

OMAGGIO, ALICE CATHERINE, educator; b. Phila., Nov. 24, 1947; d. William Edward and Alice Marie (Able) Burns; B.S., Pa. State U., 1969; M.A., Ohio State U., 1973, Ph.D., 1977. Asso. dir. ERIC Clearinghouse on langs. and linguistics Center for Applied Linguistics, Washington, 1977-79; asst. prof. French, U. N.Mex., Albuquerque, 1979-80, U. Ill., Urbana, 1980—. Mem. Am. Council Teaching Fgn. Langs., Am. Assn. Tchrs. French, Am. Assn. Univ. Supervisors and Coordinators Fgn. Lang. Programs, Ill. Fgn. Lang. Tchrs. Assn. Home: 2510 Sheridan Dr Champaign IL 61820 Office: French Dept 707 S Mathews University of Illinois Urbana IL 61801

O'MALLEY, HONOR, audiologist, educator; b. N.Y.C., Oct. 11, 1949; d. Thomas and Josephine (Navoni) O'M.; B.A. magna cum laude, Marymount Manhattan Coll., 1971; M.S., Purdue U., 1973, Ph.D., 1977; m. Roger N. Anderson, Oct. 2, 1982. NSF, Nat. Needs postdoctoral research fellow Auditory Research Labs., Northwestern U., Evanston, Ill., 1978; asst. prof. audiology Columbia U., N.Y.C., 1978—. Mem. Am. Speech, Lang. and Hearing Assn., AAAS, Acoustical Soc. Am. Home: 106 Morningside Dr New York NY 10027 Office: Columbia U Teachers College Box 145 525 W 120th St New York NY 10027

O'MALLEY, KAREN FORDINA LAY (MRS. JOSEPH PATRICK O'MALLEY), data processing exec.; b. Bell, Calif., Mar. 2, 1940; d. Thomas Riley and Verena Fordina (Cokely) Lay; B.S., Calif. State U., Long Beach, 1962; m. Joseph Patrick O'Malley, Dec. 22, 1962; children—Thomas Owen, Patrick Sean. Programmer, Project Apollo, N. Am. Aviation, Downey, Calif., 1959-63; programmer analyst Control Data Corp., Los Angeles, 1963-65; analyst, mgr. Meml. Med. Center of Long Beach, 1969-74; mgr. Calif. State U. and Colls., 1975-77; dir. data processing Hoag Meml. Hosp., Newport Beach, Calif., 1977-78; sr. edn. specialist Sperry Univac, Los Angeles, 1978—. Mem. Am. Mgmt. Assn., Nat. Assn. Female Execs., Calif. Ednl. Computer Consortium, Women U.S.A., Nat. Audubon Soc., Data Processing Mgmt. Assn., Affiliated Network of Exec. Women. Democrat. Congregationalist. Home: 17523 Roslin Ave Torrance CA 90504 Office: 10920 Wilshire Blvd Suite 210 Los Angeles CA 90024

O'MALLEY, MARJORIE GLAUBACH, financial co. exec.; b. N.J., Apr. 28, 1950; d. Robert M. and Joanne M. (Weil) Glaubach; B.A. in Econs., U. Pa., 1969; m. Charles A. O'Malley, III, Dec. 27, 1969; 1 son, Gregory Robert. With Old Stone Bank, Providence, 1970-80, sr. v.p., treas., 1977-80; with Old Stone Corp., Providence, 1970-80, v.p., 1977-80, treas., 1978-80; dir. corp. fin. Conn. Gen. Life Ins. Co., Bloomfield, 1980-81, dir. mktg. and strategic planning, group pensions, 1981—. Mem. R.I. Statewide Planning Council, 1978-80; bd. dirs., v.p. Health Planning Council of R.I., 1977-80; bd. dirs., treas. New Eng. Econ. Project, 1974-76; mem. planning com. Health Systems Agy. N. Central Conn., 1981—. Mem. Fin. Execs. Inst. Home: 47 Old Wood Rd Avon CT 06001 Office: 900 Cottage Grove Rd Bloomfield CT

O'MEARA, SARA BUCKNER, children's care centers exec.; b. Knoxville, Tenn., Sept. 9, 1934; d. Claude and Lily Buckner; student Briarcliff (N.Y.) Jr. Coll., 1954; B.A. in Theatre Arts, Sorbonne, Paris, 1956; student Pasadena (Calif.) Playhouse; children—John Leland Hopkins, Charles Stanford Hopkins. Co-founder Internat. Orphans, Inc., 1960, nat. bd. chmn., 1960's; co-founder Children's Village, Beaumont, Calif., 1978, later Children's Village, U.S.A., Woodland Hills, Calif.; bd. Nat. Alliance for Prevention and Treatment of Child Abuse and Maltreatment, Inc.; lectr. Drug Abuse Centers, Calif. Pres. Spastic Children's League; rec. sec. Assistance League So. Calif.; mem. Mayor's Adv. Bd.; mem. adv. bd. Ednl. Film Co. Recipient Sertoma Humanitarian award, 1966, Victor M. Carter Diamond award, Japan-Am. Soc., 1970, Cross of Merit, Knightly Order of St. Brigitte, 1967, Dame Cross of Merit, Order of St. John of Denmark, 1980, Halo award, So. Calif. Motion Picture Council, 1981, Woman of Achievement award Career Guild, 1982, citations include Japanese Consul Gen., 1965, USMCR, 1966, III Marine Amphibious Force, 1966, Los Angeles County Bd. Suprs., 1970, Gov. of Calif., 1979, Mayor and City Council of Los Angeles, 1980. Mem. Internat. Platform Assn., World Affairs Council. Address: 6463-65 Independence Ave Woodland Hills CA 91367

OMOHUNDRO, DELIGHT DIXON, pub. co. exec., writer; b. Fairfield, Conn.; d. DeLoss F. and Virginia L. Dixon; B.A. (nat. scholar), Cornell U., 1954; M.S., U. Bridgeport, 1979; m. William A. Omohundro, July 27, 1957; children—William, Jeffrey, Robert. Dir. advt. Warnaco, Bridgeport, Conn., 1960-68; pres. Delight Dixon Assos., Westport, Conn., 1968-78; syndicated columnist Chgo. Tribune, 1974; v.p. Carthage Community Press, Inc. (N.Y.), 1982—; mktg. cons. U.S. and Can. cos. Recipient Andy award N.Y. Advt. Club, 1967, 69. Mem. Fashion Group, Am. Mktg. Assn., Am. Women in Radio and TV. Author: Hbw to Win the Grocery Game, 1973; Cost of Living Cookbook, 1974.

O'MORE, ELOISE PITTS, designer; b. Fayetteville, Tenn., June 7, 1911; d. William Woodruff and Josephine Martin (Diemer) Pitts; student Ward-Conley Art Sch., 1928-30, Ward-Belmont Coll., 1930-32; Baccalaureat d'Art Decoratif, Le College Feminin, Paris, 1937; m. James Robert Muratta, Oct. 4, 1929; 1 dau., Donna Maria; m. 2d, Rory O'More, IV, Dec. 26, 1940; 1 son, Rory V. Self-employed designer and muralist, 1938-60; dir. of design Stoddards Office Designs, Nashville, 1960-66; partner Mitchell & O'More, designers, Nashville, 1966-69; founder, dir. O'More Sch. of Design, Franklin, Tenn., 1970—; executed historic murals 3d Nat. Bank, Nashville, 1963, First Franklin Fed., 1964, First Nat. Bank, Centerville, 1972, United Am. Bank, Nashville, 1972, Harpeth Nat. Bank, Franklin; lectr. design and decoration for various schs., clubs and bus. orgns. Bd. dirs. Heritage Found. Franklin; mem. Cheekwood Fine Arts Center, Nashville; mem. Nashville Hist. Commn. Mem. Am. Soc. Interior Designers, Nat. Trust for Historic Preservation, Williamson County Hist. Soc., Societe des Arts, Alliance Francaise. Roman Catholic. Office: 423 S Margin St Franklin TN 37064

ONASSIS, JACQUELINE BOUVIER KENNEDY, former wife of 35th Pres. of U.S., b. Southhampton, L.I. N.Y., July 28, 1929; d. John Vernou III and Janet (Lee) Bouvier; grad. Miss Porter's Sch., Farmington, Conn., 1947; student Vassar Coll., 1947-48; The Sorbonne, Paris, France, 1949; B.A., George Washington U., 1951; m. John Fitzgerald Kennedy, Sept. 12, 1953 (35th Pres. U.S.A.) (dec. Nov. 22, 1963); children—Caroline Bouvier, John Fitzgerald, Patrick Bouvier (dec.); m. 2d, Aristotle Onassis, Oct. 20, 1968 (dec. Mar. 1975). Inquiring photographer Washington Times-Herald (now Washington Post and Times Herald). 1952; cons. editor Viking Press, 1975-77; asso. editor Doubleday & Co., 1978—. Planned and conducted restoration decor of White House, 1961-63. Trustee Whitney Mus. Am. Art. Recipient Prix de Paris, Vogue mag., 1951; TV Emmy award for pub. service 1962. Office: 1040 Fifth Ave at 85th St New York NY 10028 *

ONDUE, AMY NAGAYAMA, sales exec.; b. Lanai City, Lanai, Hawaii, June 2, 1937; d. William Tokuichi and Setsuyo (Imamura) Nagayama; grad. Hilo Comml. Coll., 1957; m. George Toshimi Ondue, June 1, 1957; children—Steven, Lynn, Mavis, Glenn, Gail. Sec. to mgr. Von Hamm Young Drug Wholesale, 1957; Golden Galaxy mgr. Tupperware Home Parties, 1961-75; exec. sr. state area mgr. Jewels by Parklane, 1975-76; area mgr. Hawaii, Celebrity Jewels, 1976-77; corp. pres. Toriam, Inc., Honolulu, 1977-82; regional mgr. Cher Beli Creations, 1982—. Bd. dirs., sec. Family Community Leadership Project; cultural arts chmn., Univ. Extension, pres. Univ. Extension West Council, 1979-80, state historian, 1981-83, chmn. public realtions-community outreach, 1981-83, Outstanding Woman of Yr., 1979. Mem. Hawaii Extension Homemakers Council. Home: 1836 Ala Noe Pl Honolulu HI 96819 Office: 2046 N King St Honolulu HI 96819

O'NEAL, BARBARA LYNNE, educator; b. Washington, May 4, 1939; d. Orton Thomas and Edna Earle (Ryals) Campbell; B.A., Baylor U., 1973; children—Kai Lynne, Carlton Clay, John F. Legal sec. Carlton Smith, Waco, Tex., 1960-62, John F. O'Neal, Hamilton, Tex., 1962-66; tchr. Waco Ind. Sch. Dist., 1973—. Sec. McLennan County Dem. Conv., 1978; del. Dem. Nat. Conv., 1980. Named outstanding tchr. of Tex., 1975. Mem. NEA, Tex. Tchrs. Assn. (pres., 1982—), Waco Classroom Tchrs. Assn. (pres., 1977-78), Alpha Delta Kappa. Baptist. Home: 7333 Brentwood Circle Waco TX 76710

O'NEAL, JERRY AVALENE, nutritionist, cosmetic co. exec.; b. Fulton County, Ill., July 26, 1921; d. Benjamin Harrison and Maye Mary (Smith) Powell; B.S., Warner Coll., 1943; Ph.D., U. Mex., 1979; m. Phillip Harold Churpek, Nov. 8, 1968. Founder, pres. Jeneal Internat. Inc., Houston, 1949—, chmn. bd., pres. Treasure of Jeneal Studios, Inc. Active Houston Women's Fund. Mem. Holistic Health Soc., Nat. Fedn. Ind. Businessmen. Methodist. Club: Order of Eastern Star. Home: 1 Tree Frog Ln Houston TX 77074 Office: 2721 Hillcroft St Houston TX 77057

O'NEIL, EMILY JEAN, bank exec.; b. Jamaica, N.Y., Jan. 8, 1948; d. James Coyle and Emily (Olff) O'N.; A.A., Suffolk County Community Coll., 1968; B.S., SUNY, Stony Brook, 1970; M.A., Adelphi U., 1975, cert. mgmt., 1977, M.B.A., 1980. Sales-person/cashier Rainbow Shops, Port Jefferson Station, N.Y., 1966-70; tchr. Sachem Sch. Dist., Holbrook, N.Y., 1970-72; tax examiner IRS, Holtsville, N.Y., 1973-77; adminstrv. systems analyst Nat. Bank N.Am., N.Y.C., 1977-80, mgr. adminstrv. services, planning officer, 1980—. Committee person Suffolk County Democratic Party, 1972-73; treas. Com. of People for Lutz, Brookhaven Twp., N.Y., 1978—; mem. com. Citizens Adv. Com., Brookhaven Twp., 1975-76; mem. Brookhaven Town Adv. Com. on Youth, 1976-77; mem. Brookhaven Town Youth Bur. Bd., 1977—. Mem. Nat. Assn. Bank Women, Nat. Assn. Female Execs. Roman Catholic. Club: Nassau Hiking and Outdoor. Home: 17 MaryAnne Ave Port Jefferson Station NY 11776 Office: 3 Huntington Quadrangle Melville NY 11743

O'NEIL, KATHERINE BRENNAN, educator; b. Phila.; d. Robert and Katherine (McGuigan) Brennan; A.B. summa cum laude, Mundelein Coll., 1934; A.M., Loyola U., Chgo., 1936; postgrad. U. N.C., 1968, Villanova U., 1963; m. Charles Joseph O'Neil, Dec. 28, 1935; children—Rickard, Stephen, Mary O'Neil Gericke (dec.), Maureen. Tchr. pvt. schs., Ill., Wis., 1947-61; adminstrv. asst. Loyola U., Chgo., 1944-46; exec. sec. Nat. Home and Sch. Service, Washington, 1961-64; prof. behavioral scis. Harcum Jr. Coll., Bryn Mawr, Pa., 1964—. chmn. dept., 1967—; Wis. del. White House Conf. on Children and Youth, 1960; mem. task force on health and welfare Pres.'s Commn. on Status of Women, 1966-67. Mem. round table Nat. Orgns. for Better Schs., 1960-68; mem. Shorewood Civic Study Group and Neighborhood Council, 1956-60; internat. expert Internat. Lay Congress, Rome, 1967; cons. home and sch. Nat. Council Cath. Women, 1964-66. Mem. Common Cause, AAUP, Am., Am. Cath. hist. assns., Nat. Council Family Relations, Am. Sociol. Assn., Assn. Women in Community and Jr. Colls., Easter Community Coll. Social Sci. Assn., Mundelein Coll. Alumnae (past pres.). Democrat. Roman Catholic. Home: 17 S Roberts St Bryn Mawr PA 19010 Office: Harcum Jr Coll Bryn Mawr PA 19010

O'NEILL, BARBARA MAXWELL, co. mgr.; b. St. Louis, Mar. 6, 1936; d. Robert Joseph and Audrey Leona (Knueppe) Maxwell; B.J., U. Mo., 1958; m. Kelly O'Neill, Nov. 21, 1964. Asst. promotion dir. KMOX, St. Louis, 1958-60; jr. account exec. Merchandising Group, N.Y.C., 1960-61; asst. to Congressman Melvin Price, Washington, 1961; advt. copywriter Gold Agy., St. Louis, 1962-63, 66; promotion prodn. asst. Am. Heritage Pub. Co., N.Y.C., 1963, book prodn. mgr., 1964-65; tchr. Head Start, Vista Programs, St. Louis, 1967-72, also publicity, promotion writer Human Devel. Corp.; chmn. Nat. Conf. Endangered Species, Wild Canid Survival and Research Center, St. Louis, 1973; adminstr. Am. Soc. Mag. Photographers, N.Y.C., 1974-79; incentive and group mgr. Gulliver's Inc., Los Angeles, 1980—. Mem. Expt. in Internat. Living, Women in Communications, Outward Bound Survival Sch., Delta Gamma, Kappa Tau Alpha. Office: 6916 Hollywood Blvd Los Angeles CA 90028

O'NEILL, CHRISTINA MARIE, lawyer, state legislator; b. Pitts., May 15, 1953; d. James Daniel and Stella Anne (Glowacz) O'N.; A.B., Dartmouth Coll., 1976; J.D., U. Miami, 1979. Admitted to N.H. bar, 1979; individual practice law, Laconia, N.H., 1979—; mem. N.H. Ho. of Reps., 1980—, mem. judiciary com., clk. Belknap County del. Mem. Belknap County Bar Assn., Am. Bar Assn., N.H. Humane Soc. Republican. Roman Catholic. Club: Altrusa. Home and Office: 35 Academy St Laconia NH 03246

O'NEILL, CLAIRE BERNADETTE, security services corp. ofcl.; b. Chgo., Sept. 29, 1943; d. Harold William and Clara Jeannette (Pape) Glavin; student Immaculata Sch., Chgo.; m. Patrick F. O'Neill, Sept. 30, 1961; children—Kathleen Claire, Patrick Sean. Asst. service mgr. Jewel Food Stores, Chgo., 1961-65; civil service examiner Chgo. Park Dist., 1969-79; dist. mgr. Burns Internat. Security Services, Inc., Hinsdale, Ill., 1979-80, asst. mgr. nuclear unit, Bensenville, Ill., 1980-81, nuclear personnel specialist, 1981—. Active Chgo. Park Dist. Air and Water Show, 1971—, awards, 1977, 78; active 47th Ward Regular Dem. Orgn.; mem. Ravenswood Conservation Com., 1975-78. Mem. Am. Soc. Indsl. Security, Chgo. Park Dist. Employees Assn. (dir., chmn. publicity com. 1976-79), Nat. Assn. Female Execs., Am. Soc. Profl. and Exec. Women, Chgo. Police Wives Assn. (sec. 1969-70). Roman Catholic. Creator, writer column Park Pal, Parkways, 1977-79. Office: 252 James St Bensenville IL 60106

O'NEILL, MARY JANE, health agy. exec.; b. Detroit, Feb. 24, 1923; d. Frank Roger and Kathryn (Rice) Kilcoyne; Ph.B. summa cum laude, U. Detroit, 1944; postgrad. U. Wis., 1949-50; m. Michael James O'Neill, May 31, 1948; children—Michael, Maureen, Kevin, John, Kathryn. Editor, East Side Shopper, Detroit, 1939-45; club editor Detroit Free Press, 1946-48; reporter UP, Milw. and Madison, Wis., 1949; dir. public relations Fairfax-Falls Church (Va.) Community Chest, 1955-60; copy editor Falls Ch. Sun-Echo, 1958-60; free-lance writer, Washington, 1960-63; asso. editor Med. World News, Washington, 1963-66; dir. public relations Westchester Lighthouse, N.Y. Assn. for Blind, 1967-71; dir. public edn. The Lighthouse, N.Y.C., 1971-73, dir. public relations, 1973-80; exec. dir. Eye-Bank for Sight Restoration, Inc., 1980—. Mem. Women in Communications (pres. N.Y. chpt. 1980-81), Eye-Bank Assn. Am. (lay adv. bd. 1981—), Public relations Soc. Am., Publicity Club. Club: Cosmopolitan. Office: 210 E 64 St New York NY 10021

O'NEILL, PATRICIA, med. social worker; b. Bklyn., Apr. 6, 1934; d. Charles Gerard and Virginia Dolores (Fortier) O'N.; B.A. in History, St. Francis Coll., Bklyn., 1964; M.S.W., Fordham U., 1976. Joined Sisters of Mercy, Roman Catholic Ch., 1953; elem. sch. tchr., Bklyn., 1956-72; caseworker Catholic Charities, Bklyn., 1972-75, med. social worker, 1976—; community organizer Sr. Citizens Md., summer 1974; bd. dirs., treas. Crown Heights Community Corp., Bklyn., 1970-77; mem. Crown Heights Clergy Council, 1968-76; exec. bd., pres. Sisters Senate, Bklyn., 1970—. Mem. Nat. Assn. Social Workers, Network, NOW, Nat. Assembly Women Religous. Democrat. Home: 462A 17th St Brooklyn NY 11215 Office: 310 Prospect Park W Brooklyn NY 11215

O'NEILL, SALLIE BOYD, educator; b. Ft. Lauderdale, Fla., Feb. 17, 1926; d. Howard Prindle and Sarah Frances (Clark) Boyd; A.A., Stephens Coll., 1945; m. Roger H. Noden, July 8, 1945; children—Stephanie Ann Ballard, Ross Hopkins Noden; m. 2d, Russell R. O'Neill, June 30, 1967. With UCLA Extension, 1960-66, program rep., 1966-72, specialist continuing edn. dept. human devel., 1972—; edn. cons. to bus.; v.p., dir. Women in Bus., Inc. HEW Women's Edn. Equity grantee, 1976-77. Mem. Nat. Univ. Extension Assn. (Outstanding Program award div. women's edn. 1980), UCLA Assn. Acad. Women, NOW. Home: 15430 Longbow Dr Sherman Oaks CA 91403 Office: 10995 Le Conte Los Angeles CA 90024

O'NEILL BARBER, KATHLEEN MARIE, educator; b. Flushing, N.Y., Oct. 5, 1954; d. John Francis and Anne (McMahon) O'Neill; A.A., Suffolk Community Coll., 1974; B.A., SUNY-Stony Brook, 1975; M.S., C.W. Post U., 1977; postgrad. Boston U.; m. James J. Barber, Sept. 18, 1982. Spl. educator Centereach (N.Y.) Middle Country Sch. Dist., 1977-79; research asst. Boston U., 1979; adminstrv. intern Arlington (Mass.) Spl. Edn. Dept., 1980; clin. counselor, Stoneham, Mass., 1980—; spl. educator, Chelsea, Mass., 1981-82; active Spl. Olympics program. United Travelers Am. scholar, 1977; Lambda Theta scholar, 1980-81. Address: 16 Walnut St Montvale NJ 07645

ONESTO, SERENE PANAMA, educator; b. Chgo., Aug. 28; d. Harold and Bess Blanche (Lorber) Panama; B.A., DePauw U., 1948; M.S. in Edn., Ill. Tchrs. Coll., 1966; Ed.D., No. Ill. U., 1975; m. Joseph E. Onesto, Aug. 28, 1961. Tchr., librarian Chgo. Bd. Edn., 1960-67; head Instructional Materials Center, Chgo. State U., 1967-73, head Div. Learning Resources, 1973—, prof., 1980—. Judge, Am. Film Festival, 1979-82. Recipient Service award Chgo. State U., 1979. Mem. Assn. Ednl. Communication and Tech., Ill. Assn. Ednl. Communication and Tech., No. Ill. Media Assn. (pres. 1977-78), Nat. Council Adminstrv. Women in Edn., Nat. Assn. Am. Pen Women, Phi Delta Kappa, Delta Kappa Gamma, Pi Lambda Theta. Contbr. in field. Home: 1055 D Peterson St Park Ridge IL 60068 Office: 95th St at King Dr Chicago IL 60628

ONGKEKO-DOYLE, GILDA, psychiat. social worker; b. Quezon City, Philippines, Apr. 3, 1954; came to U.S., 1965, naturalized, 1973; d. Hermenegildo T. and Lourdes (Astraquillo) Ongkeko; B.S.W., U. So. Calif., 1976, M.S.W., 1977; m. J. Michael Doyle, Aug. 7, 1976. Adminstrv. asst. U. So. Calif. Safety Center, 1973-75; project dir. Optimist Boys Home and Ranch, Los Angeles, 1977-78; psychiat. social worker Central City Community Mental Health Center, Los Angeles, 1978; clin. social worker UCLA Med. Center, Los Angeles, 1978-81; psychiat. social worker Neuropsychiat. Inst., UCLA, 1981—; mem. Calif. Clin. Social Worker Exam. Bd., 1979—. Mem. adv. bd. Asian Am. Community Mental Health Tng. Center. Child Welfare scholar Child Welfare Assn., 1976; NIMH scholar, 1977. Mem. Nat. Assn. Social Workers, Nat. Bus. and Profl. Women's Clubs, Asian Am. Social Workers. Home: 2225 Ocean Park Blvd Apt 6 Santa Monica CA 90405 Office: Neuropsychiat Inst UCLA Los Angeles CA 90024

ONLEY, NONA SUE, chem. co. exec.; b. Rockford, Ill., June 20, 1949; d. Kenneth John and Elaine Marie (Poliska) Peters; student public schs., Ill. With Filter Dynamics, Inc., Santa Ana, Calif., 1974-76; Western regional sales mgr. Armor All Products, Irvine, Calif., 1977-80; v.p. Espree Products, Salt Lake City, 1980—. Mem. Nat. Assn. Female Execs. (network dir.), Auto Parts and Accessories Assn., Splty. Equipment Mfrs. Assn. Home: 28129 Peacock Ridge Dr Rancho Palos Verdes CA 90274 Office: PO Box 27157 Salt Lake City UT 84127

ONYEALI, BARBARA ANN, educator; b. Chgo., Mar. 8, 1935; d. Elmer and Maude Mary (Elder) Page; B.Ed., Chgo. Tchrs. Coll., 1963; M.E., Erikson Inst. for Early Childhood Edn., Loyola U., Chgo., 1973; children—Amaechi Samuel, Elkanah Okwudili. Dictaphone operator, mental health centers, Chgo., 1953-60; tchr. kindergarten Medill Primary Sch., Chgo., 1963-69, Head Start tchr., 1972-75; parent resource tchr. Cockrell Child Parent Center, Chgo., 1975—; also tchr. dance, dir. day camp, workshop leader, instr. jr. coll., supr. Sunday sch. Sec., Tchrs. div. Operation P.U.S.H., Chgo., 1970-72; leader Cub Scout program, Chgo., 1977-80, com. chmn., 1981-82. HEW Head Start Leadership Tng. grantee, 1971-73. Mem. Am. Fedn. Tchrs., Nat. Assn. Edn. Young Children, Field Museum Natural History. Club: Chgo. Health and Racquetball. Office: 30 E 61st St Chicago IL 60637

ONYSHKEVYCH, LARISSA MARIA LUBOV ZALESKA, researcher, editor, educator; b. Ukraine; came to U.S., 1961, naturalized, 1966; d. Thaddeus and Maria W. (Shankovska) Zalesky; diploma Ryerson Poly. Inst., Toronto, Ont., Can., 1954; B.A., U. Toronto, 1963; M.A., U. Pa., 1969, Ph.D. (fellow 1972-73), 1973; m. Lubomyr Onyshkevych, June 3, 1961; children—Vsevolod, Boyan, Lada. Chem. technologist Connaught Med. Research Labs., U. Toronto, 1956-61; free lance tech. translator, 1961-65; dir. Sch. for Ukrainian Studies, 1972-81; vis. lectr. Slavic dept. Rutgers U., New Brunswick, N.J., 1974-76, adj. asst. prof., 1976-78; free lance editor, researcher George W. Ball Inst., Princeton, N.J., 1979-81; acad. researcher Inst. for Advanced Study, Princeton, 1981—; guest lectr. various univs. in U.S., 1972—; cons. Slavic and East European langs. to various publs., 1973-76 mem. adv. bd. gifted and talented programs Lawrence Twp. (N.J.) Schs., 1977-80. NDEA fellow, 1971-72. Mem. MLA, Am. Assn. for Advancement Slavic Studies, Am. Assn. Tchrs. Slavic and East European Langs., AAUP, Ukrainian Acad. Scis. in U.S., Schevchenko Sci. Soc. (dir. 1980—), Rutgers Inst. For Women's Studies, Plast Internat. (dir. 1977—, editor quar. for teenage councillors 1973—). Eastern Catholic. Co-author: Ethnic Theater in America, 1982; editor: Yunak monthly mag., 1963-69; Kontrasty (anthology of poetry), and prose by teenagers 1970; Lambda Letter, U. Pa., 1971-73; editor, contbr. intro. to abridged edit. of Tyhrolovy (Ivan Bahryanyi), 1969; editorial bd. Plastovyi Shlyakh, 1967-72, 79-80; contbr. intros. to A Dictionary of Ukrainian Family Names in Canada, 1974; Vohon Kupala (Ihor Kalynets), 1975. Home: 9 Dogwood Dr Lawrenceville NJ 08648

OOSTING, MARY, artist; b. Chattanooga, Sept. 6, 1910; d. James Bright and Gertrude (Weber) Robinson; diploma Sarah Lawrence Coll., 1932, B.A., 1963; student U. Chattanooga, 1928-29, U. N.Mex., 1930, L'École de Chaumière, Paris, 1929-30; m. Gerard Barber, 1937; children—Ann, Helen, Gerard, Bruce; m. 2d, Henry Oosting, 1970 (dec. 1979). Designer and mural painter, N.Y.C., 1937-53; one-woman shows of tapestries which combine techniques of painting and sewing, collage and crewel: Garden Cafe Gallery, Burlingame, Calif., 1975, Honolulu Hale, 1975, Arden Wood Gallery, San Francisco, 1976, Renaissance Gallery, Ukiah, Calif., 1978; 2-person shows include: Octagon Gallery, Daly City, Calif., 1976, Corridor Gallery, Redwood City, Calif., 1976, Twin Pines Gallery, Belmont, Calif., 1977, Sundance Gallery, San Mateo, Calif., 1977; represented in permanent collections: Art Gallery of City and County of Honolulu, San Mateo County Art Council at Twin Pines Gallery, Shelby Cullum Davis Collection, N.Y.C., Gilberto Mungua Collection, San Francisco, Mildred Kimball Collection, Sedalia, Colo., also numerous pvt. collections. Mem. San Francisco Women Artists, Assn. Honolulu Artists, Nat. League Am. Pen Women. Home: 857 S Oak St Ukiah CA 95482 also 2999 Kalakaua Ave Apt 402 Honolulu HI 96815

OPALKA, JOYCE ANNE, retail exec.; b. Phila., June 9, 1947; d. John Joseph and Josephine (Wielehowski) Tomczyszyn; cert. bus. mgmt. Am. Mgmt. Assn., 1978; corr. student Pa. State U., 1974-77; m. John Opalka, Sept. 14, 1968. Sec., U.S. Food Equipment Co., Phila., 1965-66; sec. Acme Markets, Inc., Phila., 1966-73, adminstrv. asst. data processing, 1973-79, supr. data processing adminstrv. services, 1979-81, M.I.S. adminstr., 1981—. Mem. Nat. Assn. Female Execs., Am. Mgmt. Assn., Am. Soc. Profl. and Exec. Women, Am. Soc. for Tng. and Devel., Am. Assn. Individual Investors, Am. Biog. Inst. Home 542 7th Ave Warminster PA 18974 Office: 124 N 15th St Philadelphia PA 19101

OPENSHAW, LINDA LEEK, social worker; b. Provo, Utah, Oct. 30, 1948; d. Kenneth Frank and Della Mae (Williams) Leek; B.A. in English, U. Utah, 1971, M.S.W., 1974, D.S.W., 1981; m. David Byron Openshaw, July 10, 1975; children—Amy Elizabeth, Alison Rebecca. Tchr. English, Strategakis Sch., Athens, Greece, 1972; psychiat. social worker Stanislaus Mental Health, Brief Treatment Program, Modesto, Calif., 1974-76; instr. Chapman Coll., Merced, Calif., 1975; psychiat. social worker Weber Mental Health, Intake Team, Ogden, Utah, 1976-77; women's group coordinator YWCA, Ogden, 1976-77; juvenile ct. alcohol sch. instr., Salt Lake City, 1978-80; sch. social worker East High Sch., Salt Lake Sch. Dist., Salt Lake City, 1977-80; trainer for tchrs. Salt Lake Sch. Dist., 1979-80, for Utah Div. Alcohol and Drugs, 1982—. Del., Utah Democratic Conv., 1974. Recipient spl. recognition Utah Sch. Social Workers, 1979.; lic. clin. and cert. social worker, Utah. Mem. Utah Council of Sch. Social Workers (pres. 1979-80), Nat. Assn. Social Workers, Acad. Cert. Social Workers. Democrat. Mem. Ch. of Jesus Christ of Latter-day Saints. Home: 3184 South 2000 East Salt Lake City UT 84109

OPOKU, LOUISE MIDECHA, educator; b. Kaimosi, Kenya, Oct. 4, 1956; came to U.S., 1975; d. David and Salome Nolega (David) Mbarani; B.A. in French (Layman Meml. scholar), Berea Coll., 1978; M.A. in French, Tex. Tech U., 1982; m. Jacob Opoku, Dec. 30, 1978; 1 dau., Melissa. Guide, interperter, Kenya, 1973; tchr. Kibabi High Sch., Bugoma, Kenya, 1974; tchr. French, Ohio U., 1978-79; tchr. asst. Tex. Tech U., Lubbock, 1980—; tutor in French. Recipient Dubois-Nyerere award Black Students Assn.; named Outstanding Woman in French, Alpha Sigma Chi chpt. Mortar Bd., 1978. Mem. Fleur De Lys, Pi Delta Phi. Presbyterian. Home: 5501 48th St Apt 127 Lubbock TX 79414

OPOTOWSKY, BARBARA BERGER, lawyer, non-profit corp. exec.; b. N.Y.C., Aug. 31, 1945; d. Alexandre and Adele (Brooks) Berger; B.A., U. Pa., 1967; J.D., Fordham U., 1971; m. Stuart Berger Opotowsky, Aug. 3, 1972; children—Sasha. Admitted to N.Y. bar, 1972; assoc. firm Stroock & Stroock & Lavan, 1971-74; asst. commr. N.Y.C. Dept. Consumer Affairs, 1974-78; pres. Better Bus. Bur. Met. N.Y., 1978—. Mem. Bar Assn. City N.Y., N.Y. State Bar Assn. (chmn. regulatory reform project). Home: 115 Central Park W New York NY 10023 Office: 257 Park Ave S New York NY 10010

OPPENHEIMER, SELMA LEVY (MRS. REUBEN OPPENHEIMER), artist; b. Balt.; d. William and Beatrice (Stern) Levy; A.B., Goucher Coll., 1919; student Md. Inst., 1920-22; m. Reuben Oppenheimer, June 26, 1922; children—Martin J., Joan (Mrs. Stanley Weiss). One-man show Har Sinai Synagogue, 1977, McDonough Sch., Balt., 1978; exhibited in group shows at Balt. Mus. Art, 1935-61, also invitational exhbn., 1968, Peale Mus., 1938-66, Phila. Art Alliance, 1940, So. State, 1947, Hagerstown Mus. Fine Arts, Pa. Acad., 1938, Chgo. Art Inst., 1952, Phillips Meml. Gallery, 1938, Corcoran Gallery, 1941-47, 51, 56, 57, 60, Va. Mus. Fine Arts, 1938, Ringling Mus. Art, 1960, Calif. Palace Legion Honor, San Francisco, 1938, Mus. Modern Art, N.Y.C., 1933, Smithsonian Instn., 1956, N.A.D., N.Y.C., 1938-66, Royal Acad. Galleries, Edinburgh, Scotland, 1963, Royal Birmingham (Eng.) Soc. Artists Galleries, 1963, Johns Hopkins Med. Residence Hall, 1961, Goucher Coll., 1965, 76, Jewish Community Center Retrospective Exhibit, 1967; with traveling exhbn. U.S., 1963-65, Scotland (Edinburg), 1964, France, 1965; represented in permanent collection Balt. Pub. Schs., U. Md., Loyola Coll. Chmn. art com. Jewish Community Center, Balt., 1958-65, bd. dirs., 1958-64; corr. sec. Balt. br. Council Jewish Women; publicity chmn. Md. Fedn. Women's Clubs; sec.-treas. Balt. Art Festival; vice chmn. artists com. Balt. Mus. Art, 1950, artists com., trustee, 1961-72, chmn. classical arts accessions com., 1969—. Recipient medal Md. Inst., 1933, Balt. Mus. Art, 1935, 38, Balt. Water Color Club, 1959, award oil painting Nat. Assn. Women Artists, 1952, 60, 65, purchase award Loyola Coll., 1967. Mem. Nat. Assn. Women Artists, Artists Equity Assn. (past pres. Md. chpt.), Am. Fedn. Arts, Balt. Watercolor Club. Clubs: Hamilton Street (Balt.); Suburban (Pikesville, Md.). Address: 7121 Park Heights Ave Baltimore MD 21215

ORDIN, ANDREA SHERIDAN, U.S. atty.; A.B., UCLA, 1962, LL.B., 1965; m. Robert L. Ordin; 1 dau., Maria; stepchildren—Allison, Richard. Admitted to Calif. bar; dep. atty. gen. Calif., 1965-72; So. Calif. legal counsel Fair Employment Practices Commn., 1972-73; asst. dist. atty. Los Angeles County, 1975-77; U.S. atty. for Central Dist. Calif., Los Angeles, 1977—. Mem. Los Angeles County Bar Assn. (past dir.). Address: US Attys Office 312 N Spring St Los Angeles CA 90012 *

ORDONEZ, CECILIA BEATRIZ, dentist; b. Cuenca, Ecuador, May 15, 1949; came to U.S., 1952, naturalized, 1967; d. Generno and Estela Laura (Aguilar) O.; A.A., U. Fla., 1970, B.S. in Biology, 1971; D.D.S., UCLA, 1977; m. Robert Lietzow, Feb. 23, 1980; 1 son, Nicholaus Victor. Dentist in group practice, Rosemead, Calif., 1977-78; prof. community dental health U. Santa Barbara (Calif.), 1978-79; gen. practice dentistry, Isla Vista, Calif., 1978—; dental cons. Santa Barbara County, 1979-80; mem. dental health subcom. State of Calif., 1979—. Project dir. for Senate Bill 111, Santa Barbara County, 1979-80. Mem. ADA, Calif. Dental Soc., Ventura-Santa Barbara Dental Assn., Johanson Dental Study Group. Home: 35 Romaine Dr Santa Barbara CA 93105 Office: 970 Embarcadero del Mar Isla Vista CA 93017

O'REILLY, EUGENIA NICKS, educator; b. Dallas, May 11, 1910; d. B.A. and Sarah Elisabeth (Harrison) Nicks; A.S., U. Tex., Arlington, 1929; student So. Meth. U., 1937-48, Southwestern Conservatory, 1940-41, Ind. U., summer 1969; studied under Paul Van Katwijk, Fritz Fall, Isabelle Hutcheson, Alfred Mirovitch, Gyorgy Sandor; m. Oren Patrick O'Reilly, May 5, 1930 (dec.); 1 dau., Sally. Pvt. tchr. piano, Dallas; lectr. Brook Haven Coll., 1981, East Tex. State U., 1981, Tex. Christian U., 1981; condr. workshop Music Tchrs. Nat. Conv., New Orleans, Richardson, Garland and Irving (Tex.) music tchrs. assns. Mem. Music Tchrs. Nat. Assn., Tex. (past dir.), Dallas (past pres.) music tchrs. assns., Dallas Piano Forum (exec. dir.), Nat. Guild Piano Tchrs. (Hall of Fame), Nat. Fedn. Music Clubs, Van Katwijk Club, Sigma Alpha Iota, Phi Kappa Theta. Home: 2232 Elder Oaks Ln Dallas TX 75232

O'REILLY, JANE, writer; b. St. Louis, Apr. 5, 1936; d. Archer and Mary Margaret (Conway) O'R.; B.A., Radcliffe Coll., 1958; 1 son, Jan Fischer. Free-lance writer, 1960—; contbg. editor N.Y. mag., 1968-75; syndicated columnist Newspaper Enterprise Assn., 1976-78; contbr. Time mag., 1978—; The Girl I Left Behind, 1980. Recipient Penny-Mo. mag. awards, 1971; award Women's Equity Action League, 1978. Mem. Nat. Book Critics Circle, Washington Ind. Writers, Soc. Am. Travel Writers, Writers Guild Am. Home: New York NY

O'REILLY, MARYLEA, pub. co. exec.; b. N.Y.C., Aug. 23, 1947; d. John Russell and Margaret (Cronin) O'Reilly; B.A., Marymount Coll., 1969; postgrad. Seton Hall U., 1969-70; m. William M. Schmidt, Sept. 20, 1980. Supr. prodn. Viking Press, N.Y.C., 1970-74; mgr. prodn., spl. projects Alfred A. Knopf, N.Y.C., 1974-79; mgr. prodn. dept. adult trade div. Random House, Inc., N.Y.C., 1979—; faculty N.Y. U., 1974. Asst. prodn. mgr. Sr. Summary mag., 1981, The Jr. League of N.Y., 1978—; properties mgr. The Blue Hill Troupe, Ltd., 1980, program mgr., 1981. Seton Hall U. grad. fellow in history, 1969-70. Mem. Bookbinders of N.Y., Am. Assn. Pubs., Women in Prodn., Am. Soc. Profl. and Exec. Women, Nat. Assn. Female Execs. Roman Catholic. Clubs: St. Bartholomew Community, New Neighbors of Westport. Home: 89 Partrick Rd Westport CT 06880 Office: 201 E 50th St New York NY 10022

O'REILLY, SALLY, violinist, pianist; b. Dallas, Oct. 23, 1940; d. Oren Patrick and Eugenia (Nicks) O'Reilly; B.S., Tex. Women's U., 1963; M.Mus. with performer's certificate, Ind. U., 1965; postgrad. Royal Conservatory Music, Brussels, N. Tex. State U., Curtis Inst. Music, Phila.; pupil of Marjorie F. Harrell, Jack Roberts, Ivan Galamian, Josef Gingold, Carlo Von Neste. Solo debut with Dallas Symphony, 1957; concertmaster, soloist Internat. String Congress, P.R., 1960; orchtl. soloist, recitalist in U.S., Europe and Can., 1962—; mem. faculty Manhattan Sch. Music, N.Y.C., 1972-81; asso. prof. La. State U., Baton Rouge, 1981—; sr. Fulbright lectr. Nat. Conservatory, Montevideo, Uruguay, 1982; founding mem. Caecilian Trio, 1976. Home: 827 N Allyson Dr Baton Rouge LA 70815

ORIN, DENISE CAROL, occupational therapist; b. Flint, Mich., Oct. 14, 1953; d. John and Dorothy Agnes (Hritz) M.; B.S. in Occupational Therapy, Eastern Mich. U., 1975; m. Donald Roe Orin, Jr., Feb. 21, 1981. Staff occupational therapist Physician's Phys. Therapy Service, Gary, Ind., 1976-77, dir. occupational therapy, 1977-78; occupational therapist Oakdale Regional Center, Mich. Dept. Mental Health, Lapeer, 1978—; cons. Physician's Phys. Therapy Service in contract negotiations with health care agys. Mem. St. Michael's Ladies Altar Guild, Flint. Recipient Prin.'s Leadership award Flint Community Schs., 1951; Nat. Merit scholar, 1971; Bd. Regents award Eastern Mich. U., 1971. Mem. Am. Occupational Therapy Assn., Ind. Occupational Therapy Assn., Mich. Occupational Therapy Assn., Sigma Sigma Sigma. Home: 5142 Jennings Rd Flint MI 48507 Office: 2995 N Genesee St Lapeer MI 48446

ORION, GERTRUDE FELDSHER, educator; b. Bklyn.; d. Hyman and Dora Feldsher; B.A., Bklyn. Coll., 1961; M.A., Queens Coll., 1967;

Ed. D., Nova U., 1976; m. Henry Orion, Aug. 19, 1952; 1 dau., Doreen. Tchr. speech improvement N.Y.C. Bd. Edn., 1965-67; asso. prof. speech communications and theatre arts Queensborough Community Coll. CUNY, 1967—. Lic. speech-lang. pathologist, N.Y. Mem. Am. Speech, Lang. and Hearing Assn. (cert. clin. competence), N.Y. State Speech Hearing and Lang. Assn., N.Y.C. Speech, Hearing and Lang. Assn. Home: 1 Fifth Ave New York NY 10003 Office: Bayside NY 11364

ORITO, MARY ALICE, fashion designer; b. Kansas City, Kans., July 10, 1941; d. John and Alice McNamara; student Emporia State Tchrs. Coll., Sch. Visual Arts, Parsons Sch. Design, New Sch. Social Research; m. Hiroshi Orito, Aug. 1963 (div. 1972). Designer, Aileen Girl, 1964, Petite League, 1965-67, Jack Winter, 1968-71, Hang Ups Sportswear, 1971-74; exec. design dir. Clyde Sportswear, 1975-78; designer/cons. Bagatelle Internat. Ltd., N.Y.C., 1978-81; costume designer Search for Tomorrow, CBS-TV, N.Y.C., 1981—; costume designer for off-off Broadway plays, summer stock. Merit scholar, 1961-64. Mem. United Scenic Artists, Nat. Acad. TV Arts and Scis., Am. Theatre Assn. Democrat. Mem. Unity Ch.

ORJIAS, BETTY KYZAR, banker; b. Tallulah, La., Aug. 27, 1935; d. Autie James and Annie Marjorie (Mills) Kyzar; student pub. schs., Tallulah; m. Theodor Orjias, Jan. 15, 1956; children—Autie Theodor, Arthur Christian, Susan Stephanie. Operator South Central Bell Tel. Co., Tallulah, 1955, New Orleans, 1956, service asst., directory clerk, operator-supr. tng., 1959; teller So. Nat. Bank, Tallulah, 1970-75, head teller, 1975-76, asst. cashier, 1976—. Den mother Cub Scouts; adviser 4-H Club, tchr.; treas. Tallulah High Sch. Band Boosters, 1969—; active Tallulah Acad. Parents Club, 1970-81; treas. March of Dimes, 1977-80; scorekeeper Little League Baseball, 1965-68. Republican. Baptist. Club: Madison Parish Home Demonstration. Home: 910 Madison St Tallulah LA 71282 Office: 500 Askew St Tallulah LA 71282

ORKOW, BONNIE MARIE, state social services adminstr.; b. Natrona Heights, Pa., June 11, 1945; d. Ralph William and Helen Frances (Rakowski) Bole; B.A., Coll. Wooster, 1967; M.S.W. (scholar), Washington U., St. Louis, 1970; m. Alex Frank Orkow, Jan. 24, 1970. Med. social worker City Hosp. #1, St. Louis, 1970-71; office social worker Tri-County Dist. Health Dept., Englewood, Colo., 1971-77, dir. dept. social work, 1977-81; chief Office of Evaluation, Colo. State Dept. Social Services, Denver, 1981—; lectr. med. schs., nursing schs., community colls; field instr. Denver U. Sch. Social Work, 1975-80; cons. on Block Grant in primary health care, 1981; chmn. commn. on Youth & Culture for forum F.D.R. U.S.-Soviet Dialogue, Tallinn, Estonia (USSR), 1981 and others. Mem. Arapahoe County Child Protection Council, 1975-80, v.p., 1976, pres., 1977; mem. adv. council Human Services Inc., 1976-77, chmn., 1977. Mem. Acad. Cert. Social Workers, Nat. Assn. Social Workers, Orgn. Program Evaluators in Colo. Contb. of publs. Home: 1450 S Filbert Way Denver CO 80222 Office: State Dept Social Services 1575 Sherman St Room 709 Denver CO 80203

ORLICH, MARGARET ROBERTA CARLSON, educator; b. Duluth, Minn., Feb. 27, 1917; d. Henry J. L. and Anna E. (Westerman) Carlson; student Duluth Jr. Coll., 1935-37; B.S., U. Minn., 1939, M.A., 1954, postgrad. 1979; m. Eli Orlich, Apr. 5, 1941. Asst. librarian Duluth Public Library, 1939-41; high sch. prin. and supt. schs. Wrenshall, Minn., 1941-44; prin. Hermantown High Sch., Duluth, Minn., 1945-51; instr. Central High Sch., Duluth, 1955-77; supervising tchr. edn. dept. U. Minn., 1978-80; instr. U. Wis., Superior, 1977-80; instr. comparative govt. and econs. Coll. of St. Scholastica, Duluth, 1978—; faculty safety edn. dept. indsl. and tech. studies U. Minn., Duluth, 1979—; organizer Model UN in schs. and univs., 1975-80; founder Head of the Lakes UN Assn., 1962; founder Head of the Lakes World Affairs Council, 1970, pres., 1973-75. Mem. Internat. Com. YMCA, 1977—. Recipient Disting. Service award Mayor of Duluth, 1965, 67, 70, 73, 75; UN Fellowship award, 1970, UN Peace award, 1975. Mem. NEA, Am. Fedn. Tchrs., Nat. Council of Social Studies, Am. Acad. Social and Polit. Scis., AAUW, League of Women Voters, AAUW, Gen. Fedn. Women's Clubs (local pres. 1980-82, dist. v.p.), Nat. Council Women (nat. pres. 1978-80), Minn. Assn. Women Hwy. Safety Leaders (v.p. 1978—), Nat. Assn. of Women Hwy. Safety Leaders (dir. 1970-80), Nat. Fedn. of Bus. and Profl. Women's Clubs, Nat. Council of Women, St. Louis Hist. Soc., Alpha Delta Kappa (nat. pres. 1971-73, internat. pres. 1971-73, internat. field dir. 1977—). Clubs: Order Eastern Star, Daus. of the Nile, Duluth Women's, Anderson Road Garden. Author: (with R. Golden) History of Alpha Delta Kappa, 1974; contbr. articles to ednl. and bus. jours.; editor (film) Glimpses of the Orient, 1970. Home and Office: 421 Anderson Rd Duluth MN 55811

ORLING, ANNE, art cons. and appraiser; b. N.Y.C.; d. Joseph and Bertha (Elsner) Acks; B.S., in Art Adminstrn., SUNY, Old Westbury, 1977; art student Art Students League, also studied art with pvt. tchrs.; m. Michael Orling; children—Merry, Jeffrey, Alan. One-woman shows include: Silvermine Guild, Lafayette (Ind.) Art Center, U. Ariz., Tucson, Pa. State U., Hazleton, Baldwin Wallace Coll., Berea, Ohio, U. Idaho, Moscow, U. Fla., Gainesville; group shows include: Hofstra U., Hempstead, N.Y., L.I.U., Bklyn., N.Y. World's Fair Fine Arts Pavilion, Silvermine Guild, New Canaan, Conn., N.Y.C. Center, Provincetown Art Assn., NAD, Hofstra U., Heckscher Mus., Adelphi U., Fordham U., Bklyn. Coll., UN Plaza, Royal Acad., Stockholm; represented in permanent collections UN, C.W. Post Coll., many pvt. collections; former mem. staff North Shore Community Arts Center. Recipient 1st prize Hofstra U., 1960, Heckscher Mus., 1960; award Silvermine Guild, 1960, East Hampton Guild, 1960, Winners Show at Hofstra U., 1964, 65; 2d prize Lincoln House, 1965. Mem. Appraisers Assn. Am., Profl. Artists Guild (pres.). Home: 69 Shelter Ln Roslyn Heights NY 11577

ORLOFF, LYNDA KESTENBAUM, mfg. co. exec.; b. Pitts., Sept. 22, 1951; d. Louis and Gertrude (Kallus) Kestenbaum; student Tel-Aviv U., 1969-70, Calif. State U., Northridge, 1970-73. With Elkay Plastics Co., Inc., Los Angeles, 1965—, exec. v.p., 1978—. Mem. Calif. Film Extruders and Converters Assn., Shelters for Israel, Women's Am. ORT. Office: 2320 E 49th St Los Angeles CA 90058

ORLOFF, SUSAN NESSA-SCHRIBER, occupational therapist; b. Washington, Aug. 25, 1946; d. Max and Lillian (Levinson) Schriber; student Am. U., 1964-65; B.S. in Edn., U. Md., 1969; grad. cert. in occupational therapy U. Pa., 1971; m. David Orloff, June 18, 1972; children—Jenny Rebecca, Rachel May. Tchr. spl. edn. Meeting Individual Needs Daily program Washington Public Schs., 1969; staff therapist Friends Hosp., Phila., 1971; staff therapist Norristown (Pa.) State Hosp., 1971-72, supr. occupational therapy, admissions bldg., 1972-73; supr. adult services Lafayette Clinic, Detroit, 1973-74; occupational therapist, 1974—; chief occupational therapy services Crafts-Farrow State Hosp., Columbia, S.C., 1981—; cons. Capital Convalescent Center, 1975-76, Midlands Center for Retarded Children, Columbia, 1975, J.F. Hawkins Nursing Home, Newberry, S.C., 1975-76, Barnwell County Hosp., Barnwell, S.C., 1975-76, Rikard Nursing Homes, Lexington, S.C., 1975-77, Hopewell Intermediate Nursing Home, Sumter, S.C., 1976-79, Williamsburg Skilled Nursing Facility, Sumter, S.C., 1975-79, Lowman Home, White Rock, S.C., 1975—, Babcock Center for Retarded Children, Columbia, 1975-79, S.C. Public Schs., 1979—, Wm. S. Hall Psychiat. Inst., Columbia, 1980-81; Mem. Jewish Welfare Bd., 1975—; vol. Jewish Community Center, 1975; mem. adult edn. com. Tree of Life Congregation, 1976; mem. Columbia Women's Symphony Assn., 1977. Danforth asso., 1977; recipient Outstanding Educator award S.C. Occupational Therapy Assn., 1981. Mem. Am., S.C. (dist. chmn. 1976, licensure chmn. 1977—, v.p. 1978-79) occupational therapy assns., Hadassah. Jewish. Contbr. articles to profl. jours. Office: Wm S Hall Inst Occupational Therapy Dept Columbia SC 29002

ORMAN, BETTY, social worker, adminstr.; b. Detroit, Nov. 24, 1928; d. Robert Israel and Lillian (Aberson) Fleiss; B.A., Wayne State U., 1950; M.S.W. Ariz. State U., 1973; m. Bernie Orman, Oct. 22, 1950; children—Rodger, Marc. With State of Mich., 1952-56; caseworker Jewish Family Service, Tucson, 1961-71, social worker, 1973-79, asst. exec. dir., 1979—; asso. prof. Pima Community Coll., 1979—; mem. field faculty Ariz. State U., 1977-79. Mem. Family and Social Service Task Force, City of Tucson, 1975-77. Mem. Nat. Assn. Social Workers (nominating com. 1979—), Acad. Cert. Social Workers, Nat. Registry Clin. Social Workers. Jewish. Home: 7358 E Kenyon Dr Tucson AZ 85710 Office: 102 N Plumer St Tucson AZ 85719

ORME, JEAN MARIE, elec. contractor; b. Webb City, Mo., Oct. 8, 1935; d. James Thomas and Muriel Cecelia (Loesche) Hardy; student public schs., Webb City, Mo. and Miami, Fla.; m. Harold D. Orme, Jr., Apr. 23, 1960; children—Linda Marie, Kenneth Michael. With First Nat. Bank Miami, 1953-60, head teller installment loan dept., 1957-60, asst. supr. of tellers, installment loan dept., 1960; vol. asst. librarian St. Rose of Lima Sch., Miami Shores, Fla., 1973-79; pres., sec., bookkeeper Orme Electric, Inc., Miami, 1978—. Active North Miami Community Concert Band. Roman Catholic. Home and Office: 284 NE 118th Terr Miami FL 33161

O'ROAKE, DEBBY LOUISE, public relations rep.; b. Merced, Calif., Sept. 24, 1953; d. Patrick T. and Louise Mary (Baptista) O'Roake; student Cerritos Jr. Coll., 1972-76; B.A. in Journalism and Public Relations, Calif. State Univ., Lynwood, 1980. Sec., Bur. Social Services, Foster Care Unit, Los Angeles County, Calif., 1973-77; coordinator vol. services dept. St. Francis Med. Center, Lynwood, Calif., 1977-81, community affairs coordinator, public relations rep., 1981—; sales rep. Jafra Skin Care Co., 1971-78. Named Employee of Month, St. Francis Med. Center, 1980. Mem. Women in Communications (mem. bd.) Soc. Hosp. Public Relations. Office: 3630 E Imperial Hwy Lynwood CA 90262

OROPILLA, TERESITA BACANI, psychiatrist; b. Naga City, Philippines, Mar. 17, 1929; came to U.S., 1973, naturalized, 1979; d. Gerardo Ramos and Policarpia (Ruivivar) Bacani; A.A., U. Santo Tomas, Manila, 1950, M.D. cum laude, 1956; m. Ricardo Oropilla, Oct. 29, 1960; children—Joseph Marius, Teresa Ann. Intern, U. Santo Tomas, 1955-56; rotating intern U. Louisville, 1956-57, resident in pediatrics, 1957-58, resident in psychiatry, 1976-79, asst. prof., 1980—; practice medicine specializing in pediatrics, Philippines, 1959-73; staff physician Children's Treatment Service, Louisville, 1973-78; mem. psychiat. staff, charge mental hygiene clinic VA Med. Center, 1980—; vol. med. missions, Guatemala, 1976. Diplomate Am. Bd. Psychiatry and Neurology. Mem. Jefferson County Med. Soc., Ky. Med. Assn., Filipino-Am. Soc., Philippine Med. Assn. Ky. Roman Catholic. Home: 2517 Stonehurst Dr Louisville KY 40222 Office: 800 Zorn Ave Louisville KY 40202

OROSZ, JUDY INEZ, pediatrician; b. Woodbury, Ga., July 16, 1945; d. Joseph Michael and Ruby Inez (Brown) Orosz; student U. Ga., 1963-64; B.S. in Biology, Ga. State U., 1967; M.D., Med. Coll. Ga., 1971. Intern, Baroness Erlanger Hosp., Chattanooga, Tenn., 1971-72; resident T.C. Thompson Children's Hosp., Chattanooga, 1972-74, chief resident, 1973-74; pvt. practice medicine specializing in pediatrics, Cartersville, Ga., 1974-79; mem. staff Gracewood (Ga.) State Sch. and Hosp., 1979-81; asst. prof. pediatrics Med. Coll. Ga., Augusta, 1980—, dir. ambulatory pediatrics, 1980—; pres. med. staff Sam Howell Meml. Hosp., 1977,78. Mem. adv. bd. Bartow County Tng. Center, 1974-76; active Nat. Found. March of Dimes, 1976-77. Named Dept. Pediatrics Tchr. of Yr., Med. Coll. Ga., 1981. Mem. Richmond County Med. Soc., Med. Assn. Ga., AMA, Am. Acad. Pediatrics, Bapt. Med.-Dental Fellowship, Nat. Perinatal Assn. Baptist. Contbr. articles to profl. jours. Home: 4451 Forrest Dr Martinez GA 30907 Office: 1350 Walton Way Augusta GA 30910

O'ROURKE, ALICE ANNA, coll. pres.; b. Downs, Ill., Aug. 23, 1923; d. Martin and Mary (Hickey) O'R.; B.A., Rosary Coll., 1949; M.A., U. Notre Dame, 1958; Ph.D., U. Calif., Berkeley, 1963. Joined Sinsinawa Dominican Religious Congregation, Roman Catholic Ch.; tchr., high schs., 1951-57; instr. history Rosary Coll., 1957-60, asst. prof., assoc. prof., 1963-67, prof., 1973-77; assoc. prof. Saginaw Valley Coll., 1969-73; pres. Edgewood Coll. Madison, Wis., 1977—. Mem. Orgn. Am. Historians, Ill. Hist. Soc., Wis. Hist. Soc., Assn. Cath. Colls. and Univs. Author: Good Work Begun: Centennial History of Peoria Diocese, 1977. Office: 855 Woodrow St Madison WI 53711

O'ROURKE, MARGARET MARY, govt. ofcl.; b. East Chicago, Ind., Nov. 2, 1945; d. Edward J. and Helen M. (Saprony) Savage; B.A., Marygrove Coll., Detroit, 1967; M.P.A., George Washington U., Washington, 1980; m. John E. O'Rourke, May 16, 1969. Import specialist U.S. Customs Service, Detroit, 1967-71, systems analyst, Washington, 1971-76, chief mgmt. info. br., 1976-77, spl. asst. to commr. data processing, 1977-79, dir. office mgmt. insp., 1979-82, dir. office trade ops., 1982—. Recipient Outstanding Performance award U.S. Customs Service, 1977. Mem. Am. Soc. Public Adminstrn. Roman Catholic. Home: 1211 Tulane Dr Alexandria VA 22307 Office: 1301 Constitution Ave NW Washington DC 20229

O'ROURKE, MARGUERITE PATRICIA, comml. property mgmt. exec.; b. N.Y.C., May 10, 1950; d. William Lawrence and Olive Rose (Ponte) O'R.; B.A. in Polit. Sci. (Ednl. Opportunity grantee, N.J. State scholar), Am. U., 1972. Adminstrn. asst. Asso. Merchandising Corp., Washington, 1972-73; various positions Savage/Fogarty Co., Inc., Alexandria, Va., 1973-79; property mgr. Community Mgmt. Corp., Reston, Va., 1979-80; property mgr. Braedon Cos., Washington, 1980-81, dir. property mgmt., 1981-82; v.p. bldgs. adminstrn. Smithy Braedon Property Co., Washington, 1982—; corp. sec. Savage/Fogarty Co., Inc., 1978-79. Intern Senator Claiborne Pell, R.I., 1971. Mem. Inst. Real Estate Mgrs., Building Owners and Mgrs. Assn., Property Mgrs. Assn., Washington Bd. Realtors, Nat. Assn. Female Execs., NOW, Audubon Soc., Environ. Def. Fund, Union Concerned Scientists, Cousteau Soc., Nat. Trust for Historic Preservation, Smithsonian Instn., Am. Film Inst. Office: 1110 Vermont Ave Suite 200 Washington DC 20005

OROVITZ, MARCIA CAROL, newspaper pub.; b. Miami Beach, Fla., June 28, 1947; d. Maurice and Adele (Rabinowitz) O.; B.S. in Journalism, Northwestern U., 1969. Copywriter, Jordan Marsh Co., Boston, 1969-71; sales coordinator, asst. to pub., supplements editor, mng. editor Boston Phoenix, 1971-74, asst. pub., 1976—; editor, pub. Miami (Fla.) Phoenix, 1974-76; v.p. Boston Phoenix Inc., 1981—; bd. trustees Articulture, 1978-81. Mem. Advt. Club Boston. Home: 118 Saint Paul St Apt 6 Brookline MA 02146 Office: 100 Massachusetts Ave Boston MA 02115

ORPHAN, BECKY STAIKOS, ednl. adminstr.; b. Chgo., Feb. 23, 1931; d. Demetrios N. and Pelagia N. (Savopoulos) Staikos; B.S., Chgo. Tchrs. Coll., 1957, M.Ed., 1963; Specialist in Edn., Fla. State U., 1979. Tchr. public schs., Chgo., 1957-69, prin. Mason Primary Sch., 1969-71, prin. Budlong Sch., 1971—; instr. bilingual edn. Chgo. State U., 1974-76; mem. Ill. Bilingual Adv. Council, 1978—, chmn., 1982—; cons. desegregation seminar Northeastern U., 1982—. Mem. Chgo. Prins. Assn. (pres. AUX I, 1972-81), Hellenic Council on Edn. (past v.p.), Am. Hellenic Progressive Assn., Daus. of Penelope. Greek Orthodox. Author Greek bilingual govt. proposal, 1972; designer curriculum. Office: 2701 W Foster Chicago IL 60625

ORR, COLLENE JOYCE, investment and research cons. co. exec., gem co. exec., fund-raising co. exec.; b. Torrance, Calif., Nov. 26, 1951; d. Sheldon William and Arlene M. (Russell) Branagan; student Mt. San Antonio Coll., 1975-76; m. Luther Allen Orr, Dec. 3; children—Craig Allen, Keith Michael. Fin. controller West End Council Human Services, Ontario, Calif., 1976-77; ind. agt. Cal-So, Ins., Pasadena, Calif., 1977-78; owner, mgr. Orr & Assos., Los Angeles, 1978—; pres. bd. and corp. Investment Ltd., Grand Caymen, Caymen Islands, and Switzerland, 1979—; regional dir. GC Investments, Century City, Calif., 1982—. Adv., Am. Cancer Soc.; v.p. Stork Sch. Bd., Alta Loma, Calif., 1981-82; v.p. bd. dirs. House of Ruth, shelter for abused women and children, Pomona, Calif., 1981-82. Recipient Leader award Girl Scouts U.S.A., 1979, Parents Coalition award, 1981. Mem. Women's Network (Top Achiever plaque 1981), Women Achievers, Nat. Assn. Female Execs., Orange County Profl. Women's Network, Parents Coalition (founder, pres. 1981), Nat. Film Inst. Republican. Mem. Chs. of Christ. Clubs: Four Winds Yacht, Islanders (owner, pres. 1979), Beverly Hills Gun, Playboy, Tennis, Holiday Spa Health, Beverly Hills Unlisted (founder, pres.). Research on internat. armament, women through history. Office: 446 N Palm Canyon Dr Palm Springs CA 92262 also 2049 Century Park E Century City CA

ORR, LYNNE JOY, ins. broker; b. Corning, N.Y., Sept. 25, 1948; d. William Henry and Cleo Ann (Williams) Prentice; A.A., Foothill Coll., 1969; ins. studies IIAAC, IEA, WAIB; m. George W. Orr, Nov. 1, 1975; children—Lisa, Sharon. Account exec. Sardine Ins. Brokers, Inc., San Francisco, 1979-83; tchr. ins. seminars. C.P.C.U. Mem. Western Ins. Brokers, Underwriters Forum, Ins. Forum. Methodist. Democrat. Office: 50 Francisco St San Francisco CA 94133

ORR, PRUDIE LUTHER, psychologist; b. Dallas, Nov. 7, 1937; d. Joseph Bailey and Christeen (Chitwood) Luther; A.S.N., E. Tex. State U., 1964, B.S., 1971; M.A. (Kappa Alpha Theta fellow), U. Ark., 1974, Ph.D., 1977. Chief psychiat. nurse Ozark Guidance Center, Fayetteville-Springdale, Ark., 1973-74; nursing cons. VA Hosp., Fayetteville, Ark., 1974-75; intern in clin. psychology U. Tenn. Med. Sch., Memphis 1975-76; clin. dir. Frayser Mental Health Center, Memphis, 1976-79; pvt. practice psychology, Memphis, 1977—; dir. Area Clin. Assos., Memphis and Millington, Tenn., 1981—; clin. faculty dept. psychiatry U. Tenn.; adj. asso. prof. nursing, Memphis State U. Mem. Am. Psychol. Assn., Am. Nurses Assn., Tenn. Psychol. Assn., Tenn. Nurses Assn., Southeastern Psychol. Assn. Home: 3590 Joslyn St Memphis TN 38128

ORRALL, CHARLOTTE CROSIER, mental health worker, home economist, educator; b. Holyoke, Mass., July 24, 1927; d. Walter Earl and Bessie E. (Robinson) Crosier; B.S. in Edn., Framingham State Coll., 1949; m. John H. Orrall, July 9, 1949; children—John Peter, Nancy Crosier, Judith Anne. Substitute tchr. Winthrop (Mass.) Public Schs., 1949-50; paraprofl. vol. Greater Lynn (Mass.) Mental Health, 1974-81, staff, 1981—. Leader Bay Shore council Boy Scouts Am., 1958-59, Hawthorne council Girl Scouts U.S.A., 1960-62. Recipient Vol. of Yr. award Greater Lynn Mental Health Assn., 1980. Mem. Am., Mass. (dir.) home econs. assns. Republican. Home: 7 Norris Rd Lynnfield MA 01940 Office: Greater Lynn Mental Health Community Day Treatment Union Hosp 500 Lynnfield St Lynn MA 01904

ORRICK, SUE STEINBERG, speech therapist; b. Albany, N.Y., June 2, 1946; d. David Jacob and Florence Swire Steinberg; B.S. in speech Pathology, Emerson Coll., 1968; M.S. in Speech Pathology and Audiology, SUNY, Albany, 1970; m. David W. Orrick, Sept. 15, 1973; children—Michael Benjamin, Sarah Rachel. Speech therapist Fairfax County Sch. System, Alexandria, Va., 1968-69; speech therapist dept. otolaryngology Albany (N.Y.) Med. Center, 1970-71; chief speech therapist Royal Victoria Hosp., Montreal, Que., Can., 1971-74; speech and lang. pathologist Barre (Vt.) City Schs. System, 1974-78; pvt. practice speech therapy, Montpelier, Vt., 1979—. Named Outstanding Young Educator in Greater Barre, Jaycees, 1977. Mem. AAUW (1st v.p. Montpelier br. 1977-79, dir. 1975—), Am. Speech-Lang. and Hearing Assn. (cert. of clin. competence), Vt. Speech and Hearing Assn. Jewish. Founder: Beth Jacob Bull., 1975. Home and Office: 9 Bailey Ave Montpelier VT 05602

ORSBY, LULA JEAN, educator; b. Jonestown, Miss., Mar. 10, 1950; d. Oscar Samuel and Rosie Lee (Greer) Orsby; B.A., Delta State U., 1971, M.Ed., 1977. English, social studies and speech tchr. Lake Wales (Fla.) Schs., 1972-73; English tchr. Liberty (Miss.) Attendance Center, 1973-74; English, social studies and reading tchr. Elaine (Ark.) Elem. Sch., 1974-78; English and reading tchr. Marvell (Ark.) Middle Sch., 1978—. Leader, Troop 45, Girl Scouts Am., Marvell, 1981-82; judge Phillips County Spelling Bee, 1979. Mem. Ark. Edn. Assn. (mem. credentials com.), Elaine Edn. Assn., (pres.), Tri-County Ark. Reading Council (pres. 1981-82), Marvell Edn. Assn. (editor newsletter), Ark. Black Social Workers (chpt. sec. Phillips County), Internat. Reading Assn., Nat. Council Tchrs. English, Assn. Supervision and Curriculum Devel., NEA, Ark. Athletic Assn. Roman Catholic. Home: 509 W Russell St West Helena AR 72390 Office: Marvell Middle Sch Willis Dr Marvell AR 72366

ORT, VIRGINIA LEE, metal stamping co. exec.; b. Little Rock, June 1, 1939; d. Delmo Lee and Evelyn Louise (Owens) Page; student Defiance Coll., U. Toledo; m. Wayne Richard Ort, June 11, 1961; 1 dau., Page Elizabeth. Exec. sec. Defiance Pub. Co. (Ohio), 1957-77; office mgr. Safe-Way Plating Div., Defiance, 1977-78; co-ordinator Crow, Inc., Toledo Express Airport (Ohio), 1978; exec. sec. Winzeler Stamping Co., Montpelier, Ohio, 1978—. Program dir. Jr. Achievement Northwestern Ohio, Inc., 1979—. Sec. public relations Defiance County March of Dimes, 1962-63; sec. Defiance Youth Center, Inc., 1977-80. Mem. Bus. and Profl. Women, Defiance Hosp. Aux. Republican. Presbyterian. Home: Oakwood St Bryan OH 43506 Office: 129 Wabash Ave Montpelier OH 43543

ORTEGA, CLAUDIA, Hispanic center adminstr.; b. N.Y.C., Nov. 19, 1952; d. Louis Garcia and Antoinette (Bascelli) Ortega; student Ditzer Coll., 1970-71, 74-75, U. Hartford, 1972-74; Model, N.Y.C., Calif., 1971-75; personnel counselor Staff Builders, N.Y.C., 1976, Career Employment, Inc., Hartford, Conn., 1976, Gilbert Lane, Hartford, 1977-78; job search counselor C.A.G.M., Middletown, Conn., 1978-79, program supr. Hispanic program, 1979; dir. devel. San Juan Center, Hartford, 1979—; acting dir. Yukiyu Arts Center, 1980—; cons. in field; mem. Capitol Region Council Govts., Hartford, 1981—; co-host, co-producer, bd. dirs. Adelante TV program; feature writer Canales mag., Que Pasa mag.; instr. Karate class. Recipient Outstanding Community Service award, Que Pasa mag., 1981; Sangamon State U. scholar, 1980. Mem. Nat. Assn. Hispanic Arts Advocates (co-founder, chmn. 1981—), Asociacion de Cronistas de Espectaculas, Bus. and Profl. Women. Democrat. Jewish. Contbr. articles to profl. jours. Home: 60-62 Niles St Hartford CT 06105 Office: 1293 Main St Hartford CT 06103

ORTEN, BETTY, state legislator; b. Washington, Feb. 3, 1927; B.A., U. Colo., 1949; postgrad. Denver U.; m. Russell Orten; children—Rusty,

Jerry, Frank, Bruce. Mem. Colo. Ho. of Reps., mem. fin., health, environ., welfare and instns., rules coms., chmn. Democratic house caucus. County vice chmn., state vice chmn. Democratic Party. Presbyterian. Office: Colo Ho of Reps State Capitol Denver CO 80203 *

ORTH, ARDEAN SYLVIA, nurse; b. Racine, Wis., Oct. 5, 1947; d. Alfons and Evelyn Florence (Hahnefeld) O.; R.N., Deaconess Hosp., Milw., 1968; B.S., Evangel Coll., Springfield, Mo., 1973; M.S., U. Wis., Milw., 1980. Staff nurse, then head nurse Milw. County Mental Health Center, 1968-72, 76-77; head nurse Lutheran Hosp., Milw., 1973-75; dir. Community Mental Health Nursing, Waukesha, Wis., 1977—; workshop leader, 1979—; adv. com. Mental Health Assn. Waukesha County, 1979—. Mem. Nat. League Nursing, Evangel Coll. Alumni Assn. Republican. Baptist. Home: 8510-8 W Waterford Ave Greenfield WI 53228 Office: 25042 W Northview Rd Waukesha WI 53186

ORTIZ, DOLORES MILDRED, newspaper editor; b. Montclair, N.J., Nov. 7, 1932; d. Rocco Lawrence and Lena Alta (Christian) Cardell; R.N., Englewood Hosp. Sch. Nursing, 1953; student Montclair State Coll., 1953-54; m. Milton Anthony Ortiz, Aug. 21, 1955; children—Richard Michael, Kimberly Ann Ortiz Hynson, Tracey Lee, Robert Milton. Staff nurse Montclair (N.J.) State Coll., 1953-54, Mountainside Hosp., Montclair, 1954-55; nurse Vis. Nurses Assn., Bloomfield, Glen Ridge, N.J., 1955-56; pvt. duty nurse, Lawton, Okla., 1957-58; staff nurse Mountainside Hosp., Montclair, 1959; tchr. pre-natal classes Baby Service, Inc., Irvington, N.J., 1960-62; nurse Welkind Neurol. Hosp., Chester, N.J., 1969-71; writer West Morris Star Jour., Ledgewood, N.J., 1963—, asst. editor, 1977-78, mng. editor, 1978—; editor News Leader, Netcong, N.J., 1980—. Vice-pres., pres. Roxbury Elem. PTA, Roxbury Twp., N.J., 1966-68; chmn. PTA Pres. Council, Roxbury Pre-Sch., 1970-71; dir. public relations Girl Scouts U.S.A. 1964-71, PTA, 1963-64, Morris County Council PTAs, 1964-68; regional dir. County PTA, 1968-72, v.p., 1972-76; trustee Welkind Neurol. Hosp., Chester, 1973, 74, 75, pres., 1975; trustee Sprow Meml. Found., 1980—; mem. lay adv. com. sex, edn. com. Roxbury High Sch. Expansion, 1970; mem. Morris County Prosecutor's Task Force on Sch. Crime, 1979—, Morris County Vo-Tech Adult Edn. Adv. Council, 1982—. Mem. N.J. Presswomen's Assn., Mt. Olive C. of C. (trustee), Roxbury Area C. of C., N.W. Morris Bus. and Profl. Women's Club. Roxbury Twp. Hist. Soc. Republican. Roman Catholic. Club: Uncontrollable Women. Home: 164 Route 10 Succasunna NJ 07876 Office: Ledgewood Mall Rt 10 Ledgewood NJ 07852 also Main St Netcong NJ 07857

ORTIZ, MARIA ELENA, educator; b. Cuidad Acuna, Coahuila, Mex. (parents Am. citizens); d. Isaias and Margaret (Muro) Ortiz; A.S., San Antonio Coll., 1966; B.S., S.W. Tex. State U., 1968, M.A., 1970; Ph.D., Tex. Woman's U., 1973; m. George N. Knecht, Dec. 22, 1976. Lab. instr. S.W. Tex. State U., San Marcos, 1966-70, Tex. Woman's U., Denton, 1970-72; asso. prof. biology Calif. Poly. State U., San Luis Obispo, 1972—; research participant Argonne Nat. Lab., summer 1975, Oak Ridge Nat. Lab., summer 1976, Battelle N.W. Lab., 1977 Lab. Biomed. and Environ. Scis., UCLA, summer 1981. NSF summer research trainee, 1971. Mem. AAAS, Am. Soc. Zoologists, Nat. Geog. Soc., Sigma Tau Sigma, Kappa Delta Pi, Beta Beta Beta. Home: 7755 Del Rio Rd Atascadero CA 93422 Office: Biol Scis Calif Poly State U San Luis Obispo CA 93407

ORTMAN, MARY MARGARET, nurse; b. New Lebanon, Ohio, June 29, 1927; d. William and Alma Norris; R.N., Middletown (Ohio) Hosp. Sch. Nursing, 1948; m. Charles L. Ortman, Sept. 4, 1948; children—Lee, Mike, Cindy, Judy. Staff nurse Middletown Hosp., 1968-73; nurse Lebanon (Ohio) Correctional Instn., 1973-75; asst. dir. nursing Barbara Park Convalescent Center, Middletown, 1975-81; staff nurse St. Elizabeth Med. Center, Dayton, Ohio, 1981—. Mem. Am. Nurses Assn. Methodist. Home: 2840 Burbank St Middletown OH 45042

ORULLIAN, B. LARAE, bank exec.; b. Salt Lake City, May 15, 1933; d. Alma and Bessie (Bacon) O.; cert. Am. Inst. Banking, 1961, 63, 67; grad. Nat. Real Estate Banking Sch., Ohio State U., 1969-71. With Tracy Collins Trust Co., Salt Lake City, 1951-54; sec. to exec. sec. Union Nat. Bank, Denver, 1954-57; exec. sec. Guaranty Bank, Denver, 1957-64, asst. cashier, 1964-67, asst. v.p., 1967-70, v.p., 1970-75, exec. v.p., 1975-77, also dir.; pres., chief exec. officer, dir. The Women's Bank N.A., Denver, 1977—, Equitable Bankshares of Colo., 1980—; instr. Am. Inst. Banking; lectr. Nat. treas. Girl Scouts U.S.A., 1981. Mem. Bus. and Profl. Women Colo. (3d Century award 1977), Denver C. of C. (energy task bd.), Am. Inst. Banking, Nat. Assn. Bank Women, Colo. Bankers Assn., Women in Bus. Assn. Republican. Mormon. Clubs: Zonta, Soroptimist, Denver. Office: PO Box 8770 Denver CO 80201

ORZACK, MARESSA HECHT, psychologist; b. Boston; d. Selig and Cecilia (Heubschman) Hecht; B.A., U. Rochester (N.Y.), 1945; M.A., Columbia U., 1947, Ph.D., 1951; m. Louis H. Orzack, Sept. 4, 1947; children—Deborah, Steven, Elizabeth. Instr., U. Wis., 1956-58; research psychologist Central Wis. Colony and Tng. Sch., 1959-61; research asso. Boston U. Med. Sch., 1959-61, asst. prof. to asso. prof. psychology, 1967-79, dep. to prin. investigator Psychosurgery Evaluation Research Project, 1975-79; dir. drug abuse liability project, asso. psychologist McLean Hosp.-Harvard U. Med. Sch., Boston, 1979—; trustee Boston Mental Health Found., 1970—; mem. exec. bd., clk., bd. dirs. Public Responsibility in Medicine and Research, 1977—; mem. instl. rev. bd. Boston U. Med. Sch., 1977-80; workshop leader in field. Mem. Am. Psychol. Assn., Am. Coll. Neuropsychopharmacology, Assn. for Advancement of Behavior Therapy, Eastern Psychol. Assn., Internat. Congress Psychologists, Mass. Psychol. Assn. Author articles in field. Home: 7 Bunny Circle Newton MA 02158 Office: McLean Hosp 115 Mill St Boston MA 02178

OSBORN, MARY JANE MERTEN, biochemist; b. Colorado Springs, Colo., Sept. 24, 1927; d. Arthur John and Vivien Naomi (Morgan) Merten; B.A., U. Calif., Berkeley, 1948; Ph.D., U. Wash., 1958; m. Ralph Kenneth Osborn, Oct. 26, 1950. Postdoctoral fellow N.Y.U. Med. Sch., 1959-61, instr., then asst. prof., 1961-63; asst. prof., then asso. prof. Albert Einstein Coll. Medicine, Bronx, N.Y., 1963-68; prof. microbiology U. Conn. Health Center, Farmington, 1968—, chairperson, 1980—; mem. bd. sci. counselors Nat. Heart, Lung and Blood Inst., 1975-79; mem. Nat. Sci. Bd., 1980—. NIH fellow, 1959-61, grantee, 1962—; grantee NSF, 1965-68, Am. Heart Assn., 1968-71. Fellow Am. Acad. Arts and Scis., Nat. Acad. Scis.; mem. Am. Chem. Soc. (chmn. div. biol. chemistry 1975-76), Am. Soc. Biol. Chemists (pres. 1981-82), Am. Soc. Microbiologists. Democrat. Asso. editor Jour. Biol. Chemistry, 1978-80; contbr. articles profl. jours. Office: Dept Microbiology Univ Conn Health Center Farmington CT 06032

OSBORN, RUTH HELM, psychologist, former coll. dean; b. Great Falls, Mont., Feb. 17, 1919; d. Clarence A. and Alma M. (Hawkinson) Helm; B.S., U. Minn., 1940; M.A., George Washington U., 1946, Ed.D., 1963; m. James M. Osborn, Oct. 12, 1946. Secondary sch. tchr., Carleton County, Minn., 1940-41; asst. to dir. personnel Capital Transit Co., Washington, 1941-46; asst. to dir. Inst. Correctional Adminstrn., George Washington U., 1952-55, instr., 1960-63; research asso. Am. Personnel and Guidance Assn., Washington, 1963-65, Nat. Acad. Sci., Washington, 1963-65; dir. continuing edn. for women George Washington U., Washington, 1965-73, asst. dean Coll. Gen. Studies for Continuing Edn. for Women, 1973-79, coordinator women's studies Grad. Sch. Arts and Scis., 1973-75; guest speaker at various colls. and univs. Recipient Contbns. to Continuing Edn. citation Alverno Coll., 1968, Outstanding Va. Woman award Madison Coll., 1975; Contbn. to Advancement of Human Rights citation UN Assn. U.S., 1972; Phi Delta Kappa Disting. Service award, 1975; Alumni Achievement award George Washington U. Sch. Edn., 1979. Mem. Am. Psychol. Assn., Nat. Vocat. Guidance Assn., Am. Personnel and Guidance Assn., Assn. Measurement and Evaluation in Guidance Counseling, Assn. Counselor Educators and Suprs., Phi Delta Gamma (nat. achievement award 1980), Pi Lambda Theta. Clubs: Zonta of Washington (pres. 1976-77); Columbian Women (pres. 1979-81); Woodstown (N.J.) Women's (pres. 1948-50), Washington Forum (pres. 1980-81). Author: Developing New Horizons for Women, 1970. Contbr. numerous articles on continuing edn. to profl. jours. Home: 908 Crescent Dr Alexandria VA 22302

OSBORN, (VELVA) JEANNE, librarian, educator; b. Revere, Mo., Apr. 25, 1918; d. Earl Orlando and Zola Esther (Christy) O.; B.S. in Edn., Kans. State Tchrs. Coll., Emporia, 1939; M.A., U. Chgo., 1944; M.A., U. Ill., Urbana, 1962, Ph.D., 1965. Asst. librarian Kansas City (Kans.) Public Library, 1939-42; cataloger Chgo. Tchrs. Coll., 1942-45; cataloger, reference librarian Columbia U., N.Y.C., 1945-52, Midwest Inter-Library Center, Chgo., 1952-54; head catalog dept. Western Ill. U., 1954-67; assoc. prof. library sci. No. Ill. U., 1967-71; prof. library sci. U. Iowa, Iowa City, 1971—. Research fellow Lyndon B. Johnson Presdl. Library, Austin, 1974. Mem. ALA, Spl. Libraries Assn., NEA, Am. Soc. Info. Sci. Democrat. Presbyterian. Author: Dewey Decimal Classification: A Study Manual, 19th edit., 1982. Home: 1434 Franklin St Iowa City IA 52240 Office: Main Library 3076 U Iowa Iowa City IA 52242

OSBORNE, CAROL ANN, lawyer; b. Erie, Pa., Aug. 26, 1938; d. Clarence Henry and Grace Louise Bronson; LL.B., Western State U., 1977, J.D., 1978; m. Dwight E. Osborne, Jr., Jan. 1, 1965; children—Dwight E., Joy Louise. Legal sec., Orange County, Calif., 1967-78; admitted to Calif. bar, 1978; individual practice law, Orange, Calif., 1978—. Active PTA Kraemer Jr. High Sch. and Van Buren Elem. Sch.; treas. Kraemer Parent Booster Club, 1979-80. Mem. Am. Bar Assn., Calif. Bar Assn., Orange County Bar Assn., Calif. Trial Lawyers Assn., Orange County Trial Lawyers Assn., Am. Bus. Women's Assn. (chpt. officer), Western State U. Alumni Assn., Nu Beta Epsilon. Republican. Office: PO Box 702 Yorba Linda CA 92686

OSBORNE, CHRISTINE, artist; b. Bklyn.; B.A. in Fine Arts cum laude, Adelphi U., Garden City, N.Y., 1973; pupil of Frances Avery, Rudolf Schaefer, Richard Vaux, Leo Manso, Paul Wood. One-woman exhbns. include N. Bellmore (N.Y.) Art Council, 1975, East River Bank, Massapegua, N.Y., 1976, Equitable Bank, E. Northport, N.Y., 1976, Huntington (N.Y.) C. of C., 1976, Mallette Gallery, Garden City, 1977; group exhbns. include Ruth S. Harley Univ. Center, Garden City, 1971, 72, Nat. League Am. Pen Women, 1975, Syosett (N.Y.) Pub. Library, 1975, N. Bellmore Arts Council, 1975, Captri Gallery, Long Beach, N.Y., 1975; juried shows include C.P. Art Show, Garden City, 1974, 75; S.A.L. Cultural Arts Div., Oyster Bay, N.Y., 1974, Community Arts Council S. Shore, Hewlett, N.Y., 1974, Island Guild, Hempstead, N.Y., 1975, S. Shore Art League Open, Merrick, N.Y., 1975, Black Artists Assn. Open, Hempstead, 1975, Smithtown Twp. Arts Council Open, Hauppauge, N.Y., 1975, Long Beach Art Assn. Open, 1975, Nat. Art League Open, Douglaston, N.Y., 1975, 17th Ann. Open Suburban Art League, Syosset, 1975. Recipient award excellence Town of Hempstead, 1974; 1st pl Village Art Club, N.Y.C., 1975, 2d pl., 1975; 3d pl. Town of Islip Art and Cultural Festival, 1975. Mem. Nat. League Am. Pen Women, Village Art Club, Ind. Art Soc., S. Shore Art League, Long Beach Art Assn., Kappa Pi Address: 2740 Sunset Dr Largo FL 33540

OSBORNE, MARGARET MARY, elec. engr.; b. Detroit, Dec. 30, 1955; d. James Martin and Helen Mary (Brabson) O.; B.S. in Elec. Engring., Marquette U., Milw., 1979. With AC Spark Plug div. of Gen. Motors, 1976-79, field service engr. Delco Electronics div., Saddle Brook, N.J., 1979-82, reliability engr. Pontiac Motor div. (Mich.), 1982—. Mem. IEEE, Nat. Assn. Female Execs., Vocat./Indsl. Club, Am., Soc. Automotive Engr., Marquette U. Alumni Assn. Republican. Roman Catholic. Home: 60 Island Dr Merrimack NH 03054 Office: 1 Pontiac Plaza Pontiac MI 48053

OSBORNE, PATRICIA HANNERS, banker; b. Guntersville, Ala., Dec. 23, 1945; d. Bill and Madeliene Jane (Conway) Hanners: A.S., Gadsden State Coll., 1967; I.E., U. Ala.; m. Bill G. Osborne, Aug. 21, 1965; children—Wessley Hanners, Calvin Paxton. Adminstrv. dir. computer sci. dept. Gadsden (Ala.) Coll., 1967-72; v.p., lending officer Ala. City Bank, Gadsden, 1972—; mem. tech. adv. bd. Gadsden State Coll., 1976-78. Mem. Nat. Assn. Bank Women, EDP Auditors Found. Methodist. Home: PO Box 4283 Gadsden AL 35904 Office: 201 Wall St Gadsden AL 35904

OSBORNE, SALLY RUTH, psychologist; b. St. Anthony, Nfld., Can., Nov. 2, 1932; came to U.S., 1950, naturalized, 1955; d. Frederick Gilbert and Margaret Ruth (Heidger) O.; B.S. with distinction and honors in Psychology, U. Iowa, 1966; Ph.D. in Clin. Psychology SUNY, Stony Brook, 1971. Psychology intern VA Hosp., Northport, N.Y., 1969-71, staff clin. psychologist, 1971-74, alcohol and drug Clinic, Manchester, N.H., 1974-77, Mental Health Outpatient Clinic, 1977—. Served with WAC, 1954-63. Mem. Am. Psychol. Assn., Canadian Psychol. Assn., N.H. Soc. Psychologists, ASPCA, Internat. Platform Assn., ACLU, Nat. Wildlife Assn., Fortune Soc. Club: Mensa. Home: 11 Ray Dr Hooksett NH 03106 Office: VA Medical Center Smyth Ave Manchester NH 03104

OSBORNE, SHEILA AMELIA, educator; b. Panama, Republic of Panama, May 10, 1946; came to U.S. 1966; d. Alfred E. and Ditta S. Osborne; A.A., Canal Zone Coll., 1966, B.A. in Biology, Mills Coll., 1968; M.A. magna cum laude, Pa. State U., 1975. Tchr., Instituto Alberto Einstein, Panama 1969; prof. lang. Centro Cultural Panameno Norteamericano, Panama 1969-75; lang. specialist Orange (Calif.) Unified Sch. Dist. 1975-79, Title I coordinator Prospect Elem. Sch. 1979—. Sec. Local Spiritual Assembly of Bahais of Panama 1973-75, editor Bahai Happenings/Acontecimientos Bahai 1973-75, sec. Fullerton, Calif. 1976-78, treas. Seal Beach, Calif. 1979-81, sec. 1981—. Mem. Calif. Tchrs. Assn., NEA, Orange Unified Educators Assn., Internat. Reading Assn., Calif. Reading Assn., Orange County Reading Assn., Orange County Assn. English as a Second Lang./Bilingual Edn., Calif. Assn. Tchrs. English to Speakers of Other Langs., Nat. Assn. Female Execs. Inc. Club: Anaheim Hills Lioness (3d v.p. 1981-82, 1st v.p. 1982—, chmn. pub. relations 1982—). Office: 370 N Prospect St Orange CA 92669

OSERO, GLORIA JEAN, ednl. program adminstr.; b. Red Wing, Minn., Feb. 27, 1950; d. Bernard Walwin and Alice Mathilda (Peterson) Freier; B.S. in Elem. Edn., U. Wis., River Falls, 1972, B.S. in Speech, 1972; m. Kenneth L. Osero, Apr. 7, 1979; 1 son, Ryan Blake. Tchr., Reedsburg (Wis.) Dist. Schs., 1972-73; tchr. Archdiocese of St. Paul and Mpls., St. Paul, 1973-78, lang. arts curriculum dir., 1975-76, lang. arts chmn., 1976-77; tchr. West St. Paul Dist. Schs., 1978-79; case mgr. spl. edn. program Roseville (Minn.) Dist. Schs., 1979—. Speech scholar, 1969, Gamma Phi Beta scholar, 1971-73, Pi Kappa Delta scholar, 1969-72. Mem. NEA, Minn. Edn. Assn., Minn. Educators of Emotionally Disturbed, Roseville Edn. Assn. Mgmt. Asst. Assn. (mem. exec. bd. and treas. 1979-80). Lutheran. Contbr. articles to profl. publs. Home: 2855 Rice St 1214 Roseville MN 55113 Office: Little Canada Sch 400 Eli Rd Little Canada MN 55117

OSHINS, GLADYS BERNSTEIN, advt. agy. exec.; b. Bronx, N.Y., Sept. 10, 1935; d. Louis and Dorothy (Greenberg) Bernstein; B.A., Bklyn. Coll., 1956; m. Elliot Oshins, Apr. 4, 1965. Media planner Zlowe Co. Inc., N.Y.C., 1959-69; v.p., asso. media dir. Marsteller, Inc., N.Y.C., 1969-80; v.p., media dir. Intermarco Advt. Inc., N.Y.C., 1980—. Home: 660 Willow Rd Franklin Square NY 10010 Office: 4 W 58th St New York NY 10019

OSINSKI, (BONNIE) ELIZABETH, grants mgmt. cons.; b. Buffalo, Apr. 19, 1941; d. Henry J. and Antoinette R. (Lopian) O.; B.A., Mercyhurst Coll., 1962; M.P.A., N.Y. U., 1981. Social worker Cath. Charities of Buffalo, 1962-64; media analyst A.C. Nielsen Co., N.Y.C., 1964-66, WNEW-TV, N.Y.C., 1966-68, WOR-TV, N.Y.C., 1968-70, The Marschalk Co., N.Y.C., 1970-73, Ted Bates Advt., N.Y.C., 1973-75; program officer, cons. N.Y. region ACTION, 1975-77; owner, pres. Project Planning Perspectives, N.Y.C., 1979—; grantsmanship and project devel. cons. Legal Services Corp., Washington, 1977—J.O.B. Inc., N.Y.C., 1979—, Nat. Consumer Law Center, Boston, 1981—, Am. Mgmt. Assn., N.Y.C., 1981—, Hebrew Union Coll., N.Y., 1981—, Nat. Econ. Devel. and Law Center, 1979—, City of N.Y., 1981—; lectr. Grad. Sch. Public Adminstrn., N.Y. U., 1979—; trainer Center Mgmt. Devel. and Orgn. Research, Baruch Coll., 1980—; dir. grant resources Am. Lung Assn., N.Y.C., 1982—. Mem. Grad. Sch. Public Adminstrn. Alumni Assn. (dir. 1981—), Am. Soc. Public Adminstrn., Nat. Assistance Mgmt. Assn., Women Bus. Owners N.Y.

OSKEY, D. BETH, banker; b. Red Wing, Minn., Dec. 23, 1921; d. Alvin E. and Effie O. (Thompson) Feldman; student U. Wis., River Falls, 1939-41; B.A., Met. State U., Minn., 1975; grad. degree in banking, U. Wis., 1973, postgrad. in banking, 1977; student in interior decorating LaSalle Extension U., Chgo., 1970; m. Warren B. Oskey, Sept. 27, 1941; children—Jo Cheryl, Warren A., Peter (dec.), Jeffrey L. Officer, Hiawatha Nat. Bank, Hager City, Wis., 1959—, cashier, 1978-79, pres., 1979, exec. v.p., dir., sec. bd. dirs., 1959—, sec., mem. discount com.; with First Nat. Bank of Glenwood, Glenwood City, Wis., 1965— pres., exec. v.p. 1979—, dir., sec. bd., 1965—, sec., mem. discount com.; speaker on women in banking. Banking com. Vo-Tech Sch., Red Wing, Minn.; former officer civic orgns. Mem. Ind. Bankers Am., Wis. Bankers Assn., Am. Bankers Assn. Republican. Lutheran. Club: Minn. Fedn. Women's Clubs (treas., pres. dist. III, 1978—). Home: 1022 Hallstrom Dr Red Wing MN 55066 Office: Hiawatha National Bank Hager City WI 54014

OSLER, DOROTHY K., state legislator; b. Dayton, Ohio, Aug. 19, 1923; d. Carl M. and Pearl A. (Tobias) Karstaedt; B.S. cum laude in Bus. Adminstrn., Miami U., Oxford, Ohio, 1945; m. David K. Osler, Oct. 26, 1946; children—Scott C., David D. Mem. Conn. Ho. of Reps., 1973—. Mem. Greenwich (Conn.) Rep. Town Meeting, 1968—, Eastern Greenwich Women's Rep. Club, 1970—; sec. Conn. Student Loan Found., 1973—; mem. Spl. Edn. Cost Commn., 1976-77, Sch. Fin. Adv. Panel, 1977-78, Edn. Equity Study Com., 1980-81, Commn. on Goals for U. Conn. Health Center, 1975-76; bd. dirs. ARC, 1975. Mem. LWV (pres. Greenwich chpt. 1965-67, sec. Conn. chpt. 1967-72), AAUW (dir. 1971-73), Mortar Board, Phi Beta Kappa, Alpha Omicron Pi. Republican. Christian Scientist. Bi-weekly columnist local newspaper, 1973—.

OSMENA, LETICIA LLACUNA, med. technologist; b. Santo Domingo I. Sur, Philippines, Jan. 26, 1941; came to U.S., 1963; d. Juan Tomas and Estefania Tenoso (Tremor) Llacuna; B.S. in Pharmacy, B.S. in Med. Tech., Manila Central U., 1961; B.S. in Med. Tech., Durfee Coll.-Truesdale Hosp., Fall River, Mass., 1964; m. Divino Osmena, Jan. 6, 1965; children—Mary Jane, Divina. Pharmacist, Mercury Pharm. Co., Manila, 1961-63; med. technologist intern Truesdale Hosp., 1963-64; sr. research technologist Columbia U. Coll. Physicians and Surgeons, 1964-67; med. technologist St. Therese Hosp., Waukegan, Ill., 1967-69; hematologist Newport (R.I.) Hosp., 1969—; instr. coagulation. Mem. Am. Soc. Clin. Pathologists, Philippine Pharm. Assn., Philippine Am. Assn. (sec. 1979-80 v.p. 1981-82). Roman Catholic. Office: Newport Hosp Lab Friendship St Newport RI 02840

OSOFSKY, JOY DONIGER, psychologist; b. N.Y.C., Sept. 9, 1944; d. Harry Eliot and Marion (Sterngold) Doniger; B.A., Syracuse U., 1966, M.A., 1967, Ph.D., 1969; m. Howard Osofsky, Sept. 1, 1963; children—Hari, Justin, Michael. Asst. prof. human devel. Cornell U., Ithaca, N.Y., 1969-71; asst. prof. psychology Temple U., Phila., 1971-72, asso. prof., 1972-75; postdoctoral fellow Judge Baker Guidance Center and Children's Hosp., Boston, 1975-76; postdoctoral fellow Menninger Found., Topeka, 1976-78, research and staff psychologist, 1978—; adj. asso. prof. human devel. U. Kans., 1978—; NIMH grantee, 1982-87. Fellow Am. Psychol. Assn., Am. Orthopsychiat. Assn.; mem. Soc. for Research in Child Devel., AAAS. Jewish. Editor, Newsletter of Soc. for Research in Child Devel.; cons. editor Child Devel., 1974—; editor: Handbook of Infant Devel., 1979; editor: (with H. Osofsky) The Abortion Experience, 1973; author (with H. Osofsky) Answers for New Parents: Adjusting to Your New Role, 1980. Home: 521 Danbury Ln Topeka KS 66606 Office: Menninger Found PO Box 829 Topeka KS 66601

OSSEN, CAROL MAE GOLDSTEIN ADELMAN, sch. counselor; b. N.Y.C., Mar. 2, 1925; d. Henry and Rose (Steierman) Goldstein; B.A., Hunter Coll., 1946, M.A., Bklyn. Coll., 1969; M.S., L.I. U., 1972; m. Pincus Adelman, June 18, 1946 (dec. 1973); children—Anne Adelman Stein, Nancy Adelman Covucci, Joan P. Adelman Kleiner; m. 2d, Morris Ossen, Aug. 5, 1973. Tchr. English, J.J. Reynolds Jr. High Sch., Bklyn., 1965-70, grade advisor, 1971-75; summer youth counselor N.Y. State Employment Service, 1972; adj. counselor Spl. Baccalaureate Degree Program for Adults, Bklyn. Coll., 1973-75; vocat. counselor N.Y.C. Adult Tng. Program, 1975-77; guidance counselor George Westinghouse Vocat., Tech. High Sch., Bklyn., 1977—. Vice pres., PTA, Bklyn., 1960-65, mem. liaison com., 1969-73. Mem. Am. Personel and Guidance Assn., N.Y. State Personnel and Guidance Assn., N.Y.C. Personnel and Guidance Assn. Jewish. Office: 105 Johnson St Brooklyn NY 11201

OSSENBERG, HELLA SVETLANA, psychoanalyst; b. Kiev, Russia, June 10, 1930; came to U.S., 1957, naturalized, 1964; d. Anatole E. and Tatiana N. (Dombrovski) Donath; diploma langs. and psychology, U. Heidelberg (W. Ger.), 1953; M.S., Columbia U., 1968; cert. Nat. Psychol. Assn. Psychoanalysis, 1977; m. Carl H. Ossenberg, June 7, 1958. Sr. psychiat. social worker VA Mental Hygiene Clinic, N.Y.C., 1968-80, pvt. practice psychoanalysis, N.Y.C., 1975—; mem. Theodor Reik Cons. Center, 1978—; field instr. Columbia U., Fordham U. schs. social work. Mem. Nat. Assn. Social Workers, Acad. Cert. Social Workers, Nat. Psychol. Assn. Psychoanalysis, Nat. Assn. Advancement Phychoanalysis (Am. Bds. Accreditation and Certification), Council Psychoanalytic Psychotherapists. Home: 820 West End Ave New York NY 10025 Office: 345 W 58th St New York NY 10019

OSSOFSKY, HELEN JOHNS (MRS. ELI OSSOFSKY), physician; b. Phila., Dec. 7, 1921; d. William Calloway and Gertrude (Schindele) Johns; A.B., Mt. Holyoke Coll., 1943; student Women's Med. Coll. Pa., 1950-52; M.D., Johns Hopkins U., 1954; m. Eli Ossofsky, Aug. 8, 1950, (dec. Oct. 1950). Research asso. Johns Hopkins Sch. Hygiene and Pub. Health, 1957-59; asst. prof. Georgetown U. Sch. Medicine, 1959-66, asso. prof. pediatrics, 1966-79; supervisory med. officer D.C. Dept. Pub. Health, 1959-62, med. cons. div. mental retardation, 1967-69; child psychiatry consultation practice, McLean, Va., 1966—. Cons., Inst. Child Health and Human Devel., NIH, Bethesda, Md., 1962-63; cons. in med. tng. div. chronic diseases USPHS, 1964-65; cons. Va. Assn.

Children with Learning Disabilities, Psychiatric Inst. Washington, 1972—; lectr. Cath. U. Sch. Cardiovascular Nursing, 1959—; mem. advisory council Cybernetic Research Inst. Mem. Fairfax County Med. Soc., AMA, Washington Psychiat. Soc., Am. Psychiat. Assn., Johns Hopkins Med. and Surg. Assn., Phi Beta Kappa. Author: Tumors of the Eye and Adnexa in Infancy and Childhood, 1962; also articles in profl. jours. Address: 1333 Merrie Ridge Rd McLean VA 22101

OSTAP, MARTINE ELIZABETH, educator; b. New Brunswick, N.J., Mar. 31, 1959; d. Helen M. O.; B.A. with honors, U. Wyo., 1981; postgrad. U. Tex., El Paso, 1981—. Instr. English U. Tex., El Paso 1981—, research asst. English composition, 1982. Mem. Omicron Delta Kappa. Home: 1271 N 17th St Laramie WY 82070 Office: University of Texas El Paso 318 Hudspeth Hall El Paso TX 79968

OSTBY, ROSE MARY, personnel/adminstrv. bus. cons.; b. N.Y.C., Jan. 26, 1932; B.A., 1957; student Juilliard Sch. Music, 1950-51, Hunter Coll., 1951-52; m. Kenneth A. Ostby, Sept. 3, 1971; children—Kevin, Kyle, Jeffrey (by previous marriage). With Rich's, N.Y.C., 1945-50; asst. bookkeeper Norman D. Waters Advt. Co., N.Y.C., 1952-53; with Hemline Suite & Coat Co., Bklyn., 1950-52; with William Ewart & Sons, N.Y.C., 1953-66, office mgr./personnel, 1962-66; office mgr./personnel Carewell Convalescent Hosp., Van Nuys, Calif., 1966-67; asst. adminstr., 1967-69; employment counselor Snelling & Snelling Employment Agy., Salem, Oreg., 1970-71, Action Personnel Agy., Albany, Oreg., 1971-72; owner Wise Personnel Agy., Corvallis, Oreg., 1973-79, Rose M. Ostby Bookkeeping Service, 1973-75, Temporaries Unltd., 1974-78, Rose M. Ostby Secretarial Typing Service, Corvallis, 1974-79, Rose M. Ostby Personnel & Adminstrv. Bus. Cons., Corvallis, 1973—; singer St. Andrews & St. Paul Ch., N.Y.C., 1947-50; singer, actor Davenport Theater, N.Y.C., 1948-49; leading roles in operettas: Naughty Marietta, The Student Prince, Show Boat, Kismet, Oklahoma, Carousel, Kiss Me Kate, My Fair Lady, The Desert Song; mem. employment agy. adv. bd. Oreg. Bur. Labor, Portland, 1976-80, implementation of counselor validation testing program, 1978. Bd. dirs. Jr. Achievement, Corvallis, 1977-81, spl. activities v.p., 1979-81; adv. com. Dist. 4 Manpower Planning Bd., Corvallis, 1977, chmn. goals com., 1978, exec. bd. dirs., 1978-80; mem. Benton County Greivance Bd., 1974-75; adv. com. Linn-Benton Community Coll., 1974-75; mem. Tax Base Election Bd., 1979-80, Corvallis Planning Commn., 1981—; candidate Corvallis City Council, 1982. Recipient George award C. of C., 1976, Pres.'s award, 1978; Progress and Prosperity award, 1978. Mem. Albany C. of C., Am Bus. Women's Assn. Credit Women Internat. (pres. 1973-74), Nat. Fedn. Bus. and Profl. Women's Clubs, (pres. 1973-74), Pacific N.W. Personnel Mgmt. Assn. Clubs: Lady Elks, Lady Moose. Contbr. articles to profl. jours. Home: 1832 NW Douglas Pl Corvallis OR 97330 Office: 621 SW 11th St Corvallis OR 97333

OSTER, ROSE MARIE GUNHILD, univ. adminstr.; b. Stockholm, Feb. 26, 1934; d. Herbert Jonas and Emma Wilhelmina (Johnson) Hagetorn; came to U.S., 1958; Fil. mag., U. Stockholm, 1956; D. Phil., Kiel (Germany) U., 1958; m. Ludwig F. Oster, May 17, 1956; children—Ulrika, Mattias. Postdoctoral research fellow linguistics Yale U., 1958-60, research fellow Germanic langs., 1960-64, lectr. Swedish, 1964-66; mem. faculty U. Colo., Boulder, 1966-80, asso. prof. Germanic langs. and lits., 1970-77, prof., 1977-80, chmn. dept., 1972-75, asso. dean Grad. Sch., 1975-79, asso. vice chancellor for grad. affairs, 1979-80; dean for grad. studies and research U. Md., College Park, 1980—, prof. Germanic langs. and lits., 1980—. Mem. Fulbright Nat. Screening Com. Scandinavia, 1973; cons. panelist Nat. Endowment for Humanities, 1975—, mem. bd. cons., 1980—; state coordinator Am. Council on Edn., Colo., 1978-80, Md., 1981—; mem. exec. com. Assn. Grad. Schs., 1980—; cons. in field. Carnegie fellow, 1974; grantee Swedish Govt., Am. Scandinavian Found. Mem. Soc. Advancement Scandinavian Studies (pres. 1979-80), Rocky Mountain Modern Lang. Assn., Am. Scandinavian Found., Am. Assn. Higher Edn., AAUP, NOW. Contbr. articles and revs. to profl. publs. Home: 7511 Vale St Chevy Chase MD 20015 Office: South Adminstrn Bldg U Md College Park MD 20742

OSTERBERG, SUSAN SNIDER, dramatist; b. Balt.; d. Ray S. and Helen T. Snider; B.S., Northwestern U.; M.S., So. Ill. U.; Ed.D., U. Houston, 1980; m. Edward C. Osterberg, Jr., Aug. 26, 1967. Dir.'s asst., editor Opera Houston Grand Opera Assn., 1971-74; lectr. U. Houston, 1967-73; drama dir. Contemporary Arts Mus., Houston, 1975-76; dir. drama Elem. Sch. for Creative and Performing Arts, Houston, 1976-78; dir., writer, instr. Alley Theatre, Children's Theatre, Houston, 1970-82; dist. talent show cons. Houston Ind. Sch. Dist., 1975-77. Bd. dirs. Community Children's Theatre, 1973-74; bd. dirs. Houston Area Feminist Credit Union, 1977-78; communications com. Women's Polit. Caucus, 1975-76. Mem. Am. Theatre Assn. (chmn. theatre mgmt./arts adminstrn. program), Assn. Supervision and Curriculum Devel., Children's Theatre Assn. Am., Internat. Reading Assn., Internat. Assn. Theatre for Children and Youth, Tex. Assn. Improvement of Reading, AAUW (dir. 1976-78, 82-83), Chi Omega Alumnae (pres. 1972-73). Clubs: Northwestern U. Alumni (pres. 1979—), Ramada, Metropolitan Racquet, Houston Center (Houston). Author 4 plays. Home: 11222 Wilding Ln Houston TX 77024

OSTMANN, BARBARA GIBBS, journalist; b. Berryville, Ark., Dec. 25, 1948; d. Rex and Virginia Dell (Oliver) Gibbs; A.A. with honors, Christian Coll., 1969; B.J., U. Mo., Columbia, 1971, M.A., 1974; French cert. U. Neuchatel (Switzerland), 1973; m. Wilfred C. Ostmann, Apr. 3, 1976. Bilingual sec. Internat. Union for Conservation of Nature, Morges, Switzerland, 1973; journalism and English, Coll. of Chinese Culture, Taipei, Taiwan, 1974; asst. women's editor, grad. teaching asst., Columbia Missourian, 1970-71, 73-74; food editor St. Louis Post-Dispatch, 1975—; judge various cooking contests; lectr. Swimming instr. ARC; mem. scholarship selection com. Union High Sch., 1979. Recipient Vesta award Am. Meat Inst., 1978, 79, cert. of merit, 1980, 81; Rotary Internat. fellow, 1971-72; 1st place Golden Carnation award for nutrition writing Carnation Co., 1981; Mott fellow, 1973-74. Mem. Women in Communications (hon. mention Ruth Philpott Collias award St. Louis chpt. 1981), Nat. Food Editors and Writers Assn. (regional dir. 1981-82, cookbook chmn., co-chmn. 1981 ann. meeting St. Louis), Alumni Assn. U. Mo.-Columbia, Smithsonian Instn. Methodist. Office: St Louis Post-Dispatch 900 N Tucker Blvd Saint Louis MO 63101

OSTRANDER, DORIS BRANSON, machine mfg. co. exec.; b. Glen Cove, N.Y., Feb. 17, 1929; d. Victor Edward and Isabelle Ida (Sommer) Branson; cert. in personnel adminstrn./labor relations Internat. Corr. Schs., 1972, cert. in indsl. psychology, 1975; m. Sherman H. Ostrander, Aug. 18, 1972; children by previous marriage—Kenneth W. Worden, Charles E. Worden, Steven C. Worden, Linda W. Hersey. Exec. sec. to gen. mgr. Sta. WNBF, Triangle Publ., Binghamton, N.Y., 1965-69; office mgr. Steuben Broadcasting, Inc., Hornell, N.Y., 1969-70; personnel coordinator F.L. Smithe Machine, Inc., Duncansville, Pa., 1970—. Mem. gen. adv. council Altoona Area Vocat. Tech. Sch. Mem. Indsl. Relations Assn. Blair County (past pres.). Home: Rural Delivery 3 Box 464 Duncansville PA 16635 Office: F L Smithe Machine Co PO Box 36 Duncansville PA 16635

OSTRANDER, NANCY, ambassador; b. Indpls., Oct. 25, 1925; d. Joseph and Guinevere (Ham) O.; A.B., Butler U., Indpls., 1947; postgrad. Nat. War Coll., 1974. Commd. fgn. service officer Dept. State, 1947; adminstrv./consular officer, Antwerp, Belgium, 1957-61; personnel placement officer Washington, 1961-64; asst. chief VISA sect., Mexico City, 1964-67; chief consular officer, Kingston, Jamaica, 1967-70; chief fgn. ops. div. VISA Office, Washington, 1970-73; examiner Fgn. Service Bd. Examiners, 1974-75; career devel. counselor, chief Consular Officer Program, 1975-76; personnel/placement officer Sr. Officer Div., 1976-78; ambassador to Suriname, 1978-80; mem. Dept. of State Exec. Seminar in Fgn. Policy, 1980—. Decorated Order of Palm (Suriname); recipient Superior Honor award Dept. State, 1970. Mem. Am. Fgn. Service Assn., Soc. Ind. Pioneers, Irvington Hist. Soc. (Indpls.), Kappa Kappa Gamma Outstanding Woman 1980. Episcopalian. Office: care Fgn Service Inst Dept State Washington DC 20520

OSTROFF, JUDITH RUBINOW, speech pathologist; b. Scranton, Pa., Aug. 31, 1948; d. Harold and Ruth Barbara (Levy) Rubinow; Rotary Internat. exchange student, Japan, 1965-66; B.S., Pa. State U., 1971; M.Ed. (grantee), Northeastern U., 1973; m. Nathan Litman Ostroff, Aug. 7, 1977; children—Carli Sara, Loren Garrett. Speech clinican Capitol Area, Harrisburg (Pa.) Schs., 1971-72, Lancaster (Pa.) Sch. Dist., 1973-74, 74-75, Sch. Dist. Phila., 1975—. Mem. Pa. Speech and Hearing Assn., Am. Speech and Hearing Assn. (cert. in clin. competence). Jewish. Clubs: Women's Am. ORT, Hadassah. Office: 104 Stevens Adminstrn Bldg Speech and Hearing Office 13 and Spring Garden Sts Philadelphia PA 19123

OSTROM, JACQUELYN RENEE, public relations exec.; b. Lockport, N.Y., Dec. 14, 1950; d. Elmer Van and Helen Louise (Cain) Ostrom; B.A., Ohio State U., 1973; postgrad. U. Fla., 1978; m. Theodore P. Remley, Jr., Dec. 30, 1977 (div. Apr. 1982). Congressional intern Rep. Henry P. Smith, III, Washington, 1970; floor dir. Sta. WLWC-TV, Columbus, Ohio, 1973; reporter/producer Sta. WSVA-TV-AM, Harrisonburg, Va., 1973-75; reporter/anchor Sta. WDBJ-TV, Roanoke, Va., 1975-76; public relations adminstr. and tng. asst. Dominion Bankshares Corp., Roanoke, 1976-77; writer/producer Health Ctr. Communications Office, U. Fla., Gainesville, 1978; asso. dir. media edn. and producer U.S. C. of C., Washington, 1978-79; dir. public relations Nat. Health Agys. for Combined Fed. Campaign, Alexandria, Va., 1979—; cons., lectr. Pres. bd. dirs. Arlington Homeowners Assn., 1981—; chmn. Arlington Archtl. Control Com., 1980-81; sec. bd. dirs. First United Meth. Ch., Salem, Va., 1976-77; mem. Annandale United Meth. Ch., 1981—. Mem. Women in Communications, Public Relations Soc. Am., Ohio State U. Alumni Assn., Sigma Delta Chi. Club: Washington Ski. Contbr. articles to profl. jours. Home: 2737-D S Walter Reed Dr Arlington VA 22206 Office: 4900 Leesburg Pike Suite 203 Alexandria VA 22302

O'SULLIVAN, ELLEN PATRICIA, educator; b. Cork City, Ireland, Mar. 8, 1922; came to U.S., 1947, naturalized, 1954; d. Daniel and Margaret (O'Mahony) O'Sullivan; B.Sc., Marywood Coll., 1960; M.A., Ball State U., 1971, Ed.D. (fellow), 1973. Tchr. parochial schs., N.C. Wilmington, Del., L.I., N.Y., 1950-71; coordinator elem. edn. Curry Coll., Milton, Mass., 1973-77; prin. St. Lawrence Sch., Muncie, Ind., 1977-80; ednl. dir. Delaware Juvenile Detention Center, Muncie, 1977—; prof. Ball State U., Muncie, 1981—. Recipient award for services in promotion of literacy Internat. Reading Assn., 1982. Mem. Nat. Math. Tchrs. Assn., Phi Lambda Theta, Phi Delta Kappa. Clubs: Soroptimists, Daus. of Isabella. Office: 101 W Gibert St Muncie IN 47303

OTA, MARLENE MAE, cytotechnologist; b. Ephrata, Wash., Nov. 4, 1948; d. Chisato and Aiko (Osumi) Omori; cert. in cytology U. Wash., 1971; B.S. in Bus. Adminstrn., U. Redlands (Calif.), 1981; m. Koichi R. Ota, Nov. 13, 1971. Cytotechnologist, Western Clin. Lab., Roseville, Calif., 1972-74, North Area Cytology Lab. Sacramento, part-time 1972-74, St. Bernardino Hosp., San Bernardino, Calif., part-time 1974-76, Parkview Hosp., Riverside, Calif., 1980—; program dir. Sch. Cytotech., supt. cytotech. dept. Loma Linda (Calif.) U. Med. Center, 1975—, instr. Sch. Cytology, 1975—. Mem. Am. Soc. Clin. Pathologists (assoc.), Am. Soc. Cytology, Am. Soc. Cytotech., Calif. Assn. Cytology. Office: Loma Linda U Anderson/Barton Rd Loma Linda CA 92354

OTEY, RHEBA LOUISE, librarian; b. Xenia, Ohio, Sept. 26, 1920; d. E. Byron and Lottie (Myers-Jenkins) Washington; A.B. cum laude, Wilberforce U., 1942; cert. in library Ohio Dominican Coll., Columbus, 1964; M.A. in English, Ohio State U., 1969, Ph.D. 1971; m. Robert C. Otey, Sept. 12, 1947; 1 son, James Edward. Lectr., coordinator job devel. Bur. of Employment State of Ohio, 1956-62; with Columbus Public Schs., 1964—, now head librarian; columnist Ohio Sentinel, 1960-64, Columbus Call and Post, 1970—; partner Assos. Resource Inst. Inc., Columbus, 1970-73; delegate Ohio White House Conf. on Library and Info. Services, 1979; mem. middle sch. curriculum com. Library Academics, 1980-81; speaker in field. Recipient State of Ohio Gov.'s Proclamation award for Outstanding Community Service, 1971. Mem. Ohio Edn. Library Media Assn., Nat. Council Tchrs. English, MLA, NEA, Ohio Edn. Assn., Columbus Edn. Assn., Women in Communications, Phi Delta Kappa. Roman Catholic. Club: Continental Socs., Inc. (nat. public relations dir. 1976—). Author: Progress and Providence; The Myth of Time in Emerson and Hawthorne, 1969; Mercury Identified: A Study of the Nature of Man, 1970; Toward a Definition of Nature in Pope's Essay on Criticism, 1970; The Eye of Grace in Flannery O'Connor's Fiction, 1977; The Theme of Isolation in Literature About Black Youth: A Comparative Study, 1978. Home: 2142 Oriole Pl Columbus OH 43219

OTIS, ELAINE ELESE PITT, educator; b. Glendale, Calif., Sept. 16, 1942; d. William Granger and Marian Elese (Calhoun) Pitt; B.A. in Psychology, Lake Forest Coll., 1964; m. James Richard Otis, June 18, 1966; children—Christine, Rebecca. Tchr., Hawthorn Sch., Mundelein, Ill., 1964-70, Sch. Dist. 47, Crystal Lake, Ill., 1978—. Vice-chmn. Citizen's Adv. Council Dist. 47, 1979-80, chmn., 1980-81, mem. career edn. com., 1978—; mem. West Elem. Citizen's Adv. Network, 1975—; election judge, 1980—; v.p. West Parents Orgn., 1980-81; organizer Girl Scouts U.S.A., 1979—. Mem. AAUW (pres. Crystal Lake br. 1977-79). Methodist.

OTIS, GERTRUDE ANNE, educator; b. Wesley, Iowa, July 10, 1922; d. James Henry and Mary Martha (Schwiderski) O.; B.A., St. Mary's Coll., Notre Dame, Ind., 1952, M.A., 1955, Ph.D., 1960. Joined Congregation of Sisters of Holy Cross, 1946; adminstr. St. Mary's Coll., 1950-63; tchr. Cardinal Cushing Coll., Boston, 1967-72; asst. dean Sch. Religious Studies, Cath. U., 1974-76; dir. pastoral care dept. St. Joseph Hosp., South Bend, Ind., 1976-78; prof. religious studies Barry U., Miami Shores, Fla., 1978—, chmn. dept. philosophy and religious studies, 1980—. Mem. Coll. Theology Soc., Cath. Bibl. Assn., Nat. Assn. Cath. Chaplains, Nat. Assembly Women Religious. Office: 11300 NE 2d Ave Miami Shores FL 33161

OTIS, JEANNE ALICE, ceramic artist, educator; b. Hackensack, N.J., Jan. 13, 1940; d. James Arthur and Carrie May (Dilkes) Edmonds; B.A., DePauw U., 1961; B.F.A., Denison U., 1973; M.F.A., Ohio State U., 1974; m. Robert D Fronske, Feb. 26, 1976; children—Kimberly Anna, Lisa Marie. One-woman shows: Gallery 200, Columbus, Ohio, 1974, Triad Gallery, San Diego, 1976; group shows include: Huntington Gallery, Columbus, 1974, Elaine Horwitch Gallery, Scottsdale, Ariz., 1975, Plymouth State Coll. Gallery, 1976, Krannert Gallery, U. Evansville, Ind., 1977, Tweed Mus. Art, Duluth, Minn., 1977, Pratt Inst. Gallery, Bklyn., 1979, Renwick Gallery, Smithsonian Instn., 1980-81, Grossmont Gallery, Grossmont Coll., 1981; Represented in permanent collections: Valley Nat. Bank, Payson, Ariz., Ohio State U., Columbus; instr. art San Diego State U., 1975; asst. prof. art ceramics Ariz. State U., Tempe, 1975—. Office: Sch Art Ariz State U Tempe AZ 85287

OTT, BELVA JOLEEN, state legislator; b. Wichita, Kans., June 5, 1940; d. Kenneth Theodore and Vera Esther (Harvey) Massey; student Wesley Med. Center Sch. Nursing, 1958-59, Wichita State U. Precinct committeewoman Sedgwick County Republican Party, 1972—, ward chmn., 1973—, del. 4th Dist. Republican Party Conv., 1976, alt. del. Kans. State Rep. Conv., 1976; mem. Kans. Ho. of Reps. from 92d Dist., 1977—, chmn. ho. election com., 1979—. Mem. Mid-Am. Heart Assn., LWV, Kans. Fedn. Republican Women, Sedgwick County Republican Women's Club, Women's Polit. Caucus (sec.), Am. Council Young Polit. Leaders. Methodist. Office: Kans Ho of Reps State Ho Topeka KS 66612 *

OTT, ELIZABETH KARG, psychologist b. Akron, Ohio, Aug. 11, 1929; d. Bert George and Mary Magdelen (Sadler) Karg; B.A., Western State Coll. Colo., 1969; M.A., U. Akron, 1971, Ph.D., 1974. children—Christine, Mary Catherine. Tchr. elem. schs., Akron, 1958-65; coordinator tng. profl. staff State of Ohio, Columbus, 1974; asst. prof. psychology Marywood Coll., Scranton, Pa., 1974-77; clin. dir. psychology internship tng. program N.E. Ohio U. Coll. Medicine, Cuyahoga Falls, 1977—, asso. prof., 1981—; pvt. practice, Cuyahoga Falls, 1974—; dir. psychology Fallsview Psychiat. Hosp. Bd. dirs. Big Bros. and Big Sisters. Mem. Am. Psychol. Assn., Ohio Psychol. Assn., Cleve. Psychol. Assn., State Assn. Psychologists and Psychol. Assts., Soc. Clin. and Exptl. Hypnosis. Roman Catholic. Home: 1856 11th St Cuyahoga Falls OH 44221 Office: 2125 Front St Cuyahoga Falls OH 44221

OTT, IRENE MAE, home economist; b. Albert Lea, Minn., May 26, 1931; d. J. Cyrus and Gladys Marie (Horning) O.; B.S. in Home Econs., U. Minn., 1958, M.S. in Home Econs. and Family Social Sci., 1968. County extension home economist U. Minn., Martin and McLeod Counties, 1954-67; instr. home mgmt. U. Minn., Duluth, 1967-68; county extension home economist Mich. State U., Genesee County, 1968-72; program leader in family living edn., regional supr. coop. extension service, Mich. State U., East Lansing, 1972-80; state program leader in home econs./family living, agrl. extension service, U. Minn., St. Paul, 1980—. Mem. archtl. control com. Arden Hills North Homes Assn., St. Paul; mem. intergenerational com. Centennial United Methodist Ch., St. Paul. Cert. profl. mgr.; Farm Found. grantee, 1978. Mem. Am. Home Econs. Assn., Minn. Home Econs. Assn., U. Minn. Home Econs. Alumni Soc. (dir.), Alumnae Assn. Beta of Clovia (dir.), Phi Upsilon Omicron, Epsilon Sigma Phi. Home: 1394 Arden View Dr Saint Paul MN 55112 Office: 48D McNeal Hall U Minn Saint Paul MN 55108

OTT, KATHLEEN GALIHER, info. services exec.; b. Washington, Oct. 21, 1949; d. Richard Wilkinson and Phyllis Adeline (Sullivan) Galiher; B.A., Regis Coll., Weston, Mass., 1971; French cert. U. Fribourg (Switzerland), 1970; M.S., Georgetown U., 1973; M.P.A., George Washington U., 1979; m. Charles Michael Ott, Dec. 27, 1980. Tchr., Am. Lang. Inst./Cath. U., Washington, 1973-74; personnel asst. Pan Am/WHO, Washington, 1974-76; staff asst. fed. relations TRW Inc., Washington, 1976-78, mgr. info. services, 1978—. Bd. dirs. Women's Equity Action League, 1981—; chmn. community research com. Jr. League Washington, 1981-82; mem. Rally Program, Regis Coll. Mem. Women in Govt. Relations, Inc., Spl. Libraries Assn., Am. Soc. Public Adminstrn., Info. Industry Assn., Pi Alpha Alpha. Club: Regis Coll. (Washington). Office: TRW Inc Suite 2700 1000 Wilson Blvd Arlington VA 22209

OTT, MARGARET EDNA HAGENAH, nurse, nutrologist, cosmetologist, educator; b. Ada, Minn., Apr. 11, 1916; d. Harry Christian and Ruby Luella (Bailey) Hagenah; grad. Mont. Deaconess Sch. Nursing, 1932; B.Ed., Colo. State U., 1964, M.Ed., 1968; grad. Volkman Acad. Beauty Culture; le. Ott, June 28, 1947; 1 adopted dau., Sandra Dewing Ott Bright; foster children—Norma Pospisil Weingart, Evelyn Pospisil Vogl. Supr. of 1st. aid, Columbus Hosp., Great Falls, Mont., 1933-35, 39-41; emergency nurse St. Peter's Hosp., Helena, Mont., 1935-36; pub. health nurse U. Minn., 1936, Mont., 1937; civilian head nurse Bomber Command, Ferry Command, Hdqrs. Unit, Great Falls, 1943; propr., cosmetologist Pondera Salon, Conrad, Mont., 1945-47; state insp. beauty salons Mont. Bd. Cosmetology, Helena, 1953-56; instr. dept. cosmetology No. Mont. Coll., Havre, 1956-61, asst. prof., 1961-64, asso. prof., 1965-76, asso. prof. emeritus, 1977—. Mem. Fergus County (Mont.) Sch. Bd., 1952-53; choir dir. Denton (Mont. Methodist Ch., 1949-54. Mem. NEA, Mont. State Cosmetologists Assn. (exec. sec. 1975-76), Educators Fed. Credit Union (dir. 1972-76), Nat. Hairdresser's and Cosmetologist's Assn., Mont. Deaconess Sch. of Nursing Alumni Assn., Tchrs. Edn. Council, Colo. State U. Alumni Assn., Assiniboine Geneal. Soc. (charter). Clubs: Internat. Toastmistress (regional supr. 1956, internat. dir. 1957-58), Order Eastern Star, Daus. of Nile, Internat. Toastmasters. Author poetry. Home: PO Box 522 Havre MT 59501 Office: Vo-Tech Office ETIA Bldg Northern Montana College Havre MT 59501

OTTE, DORIS MINNIE, graphic arts co. rep.; b. Iowa, May 22, 1928; d. LeRoy and Minnie Elizabeth (Swanson) Johnson; student public schs.; m. Darrel Paul Otte, Sept. 7, 1947; children—Curtis Darrel, Marianne Doris. With Cramer's Jewelry, Clarinda, Iowa, 1940-56; dir. vols. Iowa Mental Health, 1956-61; with Black Dot, graphic arts, Crystal Lake, Ill., 1967—, customer service rep., 1971—; editorial cons. tchr. typesetting markup. Past mem. and leader 4-H Club. Mem. Bus. and Profl. Women (chpt. pres. 1960), Am. Bus. Women's Assn. (organizer chpt. 1978, pres. 1978-79; Woman of Yr. award 1979). Lutheran. Club: China Painters. Editor: Coal Mining and Yesterday, 1979. Home: 431 Linn St Crystal Lake IL 60014 Office: Crystal Lake IL 60014

OTTENHEIMER, HARRIET JOSEPH, anthropologist, educator; b. Bklyn., June 11, 1941; d. William and Belle (Gartner) Joseph; B.A., Bennington Coll., 1962; Ph.D. (NIMH fellow), Tulane U., 1973; m. Martin Ottenheimer, June 15, 1962; children—Afan Joseph, Davi Ben. Spl. lectr. anthropology La. State U., New Orleans, 1966; asst. prof. anthropology Kans. State U., Manhattan, 1969-80, asso. prof., 1980—. Grantee, Kans. State U. 1978—. Fellow Am. Anthrop. Assn.; mem. Soc. Ethnomusicology, Current Anthropology, So. Anthrop. Soc., Kans. Anthropologists, La. Folklore Soc., African Music Soc. Club: Blue Valley Yacht (sec. newsletter 1978-79). Office: Dept Sociology Anthropology and Social Work Kans State U Manhattan KS 66506

OTTO, EVA POLLARD, ednl. media specialist; b. Polo. Mo., Feb. 17, 1917; d. John Stephen and Clara Belle (Yoho) Pollard; B.A. in Elem. Edn., U. No. Colo., 1955; M.A. in History, Western State Coll., 1967; postgrad. in media Adams State Coll., 1971-74, U. Colo. 1970-71; m. Gerald Milburn Otto, Aug. 17, 1958; 1 dau., Judy Patricia Otto Osipovs. Tchr., Washington County (Colo.) Schs., 1937-46; ednl. sec. Denver Public Schs., 1946-50; tchr., librarian, media specialist Pueblo (Colo.) Public Schs. Dist. 60, 1950-78, ret., 1978; condr. media workshops, 1978—; off-campus instr. in media Adams State Coll., 1975—; chmn. media com. North Central Assn. Evaluation of Trinidad (Colo.) High Sch., 1974; chmn. steering com. North Central Assn. Evaluation of Central High Sch., Pueblo, 1975. Election campaign asst. Democratic Hdqrs., Pueblo. Recipient Sunshine award Pueblo Civic Assn., 1977, commendation for career edn. U.S. Army Recruiting Program, 1977, cert. merit Silver State Lodge Masons, 1978. Mem. NEA (life), AAUW, Nat. Ret. Tchrs. Assn., Colo. Ret. Tchrs. Assn., Phi Alpha Theta. Methodist. Club: Heather Ridge Country. Home: 2397 S Xanadu Way Aurora CO 80014

OTTO, SISTER, MARY VINCENT, counselor, nun; b. Scotland, Tex., Aug. 5, 1932; d. Edward H. and Margaret M. (Meurer) O.; B.A., Our Lady of the Lake U., San Antonio, 1965, M.S. in Clin. Counseling, 1979. Joined Sisters of St. Mary of Namur, Roman Cath. Ch., 1949; Sisters for Christian Community, 1981; various teaching and adminstrv. positions in parochial elem. and jr. high schs. Sisters of St. Mary, Tex. and Calif., 1949-75; asst. prin. Resurrection Sch., Houston, 1954-58, prin., 1969-73; field dir. Office of Camp Fire Girls, Wichita Falls, Tex., 1968-69; dir. family life services St. Martin's Ch., La Mesa, Calif., 1981—; guest lectr. on mental health to civic and ch. groups, participant in media presentations, 1976—; pvt. practice family and rehab. counseling, Houston, 1979-81. Vol. SW unit, bd. dirs. Bexar County (Tex.) Mental Health Assn., 1977-79; bd. dirs Vol. Services Council, San Antonio State Hosp., 1978-79, bd. sponsors Houston Holistic Health Assn., 1979-81; bd. dirs. Mental Health Assn. San Diego County, 1982—. Mem. Assn. Religious and Value Issues in Counseling, Am. Mental Health Counselors Assn., Mental Health Assn. San Diego County, Am. Personnel and Guidance Assn., Calif. Personnel and Guidance Assn., Am. Orthopsychiat. Assn., Nat. Assembly Women Religious, Nat. Rehab. Counseling Assn. Address: 8633 La Mesa Blvd Apt 80 La Mesa CA 92041

OTTO, SARA VIRGINIA, molluscan histopathologist; b. Pitts., Sept. 2, 1942; d. Oscar Francis and Helen Virginia (Shook) O.; A.B., MacMurray Coll., 1964. Histotechnician, chemistry lab. technician Biol. Lab., Dept. of Interior, Oxford, Md., 1964-65; charge project lab. dept. pathobiology, tissue culture technician Johns Hopkins U., 1965-66; leader marine animal disease investigations Tidewater Adminstrn. Lab. Unit. Md. Dept. Natural Resources, Annapolis, 1967—; cons.; guest lectr. zoology U. Md. Former pres. Talbot Little Theatre. Mem. AAAS, Crustacean Soc., N.Y. Acad. Scis., Alliance Francaise, Sigma Xi. Club: Eastern Star (past matron). Editor Jour. Nat. Shellfisheries Assn., 1973-74; contbr. articles to profl. jours. Office: Maryland Dept Natural Resources Tawes State Office Bldg C 2 Annapolis MD 21401

OTZMAN, ROSEMARY KATHERINE, editor; b. Detroit, Feb. 15, 1937; d. Stephen John and Marian Ann (Silvenis) Kuchta; B.A., Albion Coll., 1958; postgrad. Mich. State U., U. Mich., Wayne State U., U. No. Colo.; m. Gerald Otzman, June 9, 1958 (div.); children—Gerald (dec.), William Robert, James Harold; m. 2d, Joseph Zurakowski, Jan. 19, 1975. Free-lance writer, 1965-74; spl. writer Detroit News, 1971-74; editor The Review, Richmond, Mich., 1974—; newscaster WSMA Radio, Marine City, Mich., 1971—; mng. editor Sommerville Communications, Inc., Richmond, 1976—. Mem. exec. bd. Otsikita council Girl Scouts Am., 1971, Humanity House Alcoholic Treatment Center, 1972-73; mem. North Macomb Crime Prevention Exec. Bd., 1977-78. Recipient Communicators award 4-H Clubs, 1977; Communicator of Yr. award Farm Bur. Macomb County, 1978. Home: 11974 Sharon Lee St Romeo MI 48065 Office: 68830 Main St Richmond MI 48062

OUSTECKY, MARIANNE J., public relations exec.; b. Greenville, Miss., Jan. 1, 1943; d. Nathaniel J. and Amelia (Silverman) Stewart; B.S., U. Md., 1965; postgrad. Syracuse U. 1978. Editorial asst. Sci. Am., N.Y.C., 1965-68; editor Gregg div. mags. McGraw Hill, N.Y.C., 1968-72; editor-in-chief Investors Forum, N.Y.C., 1972-73; asst. v.p., public relations Alexander & Alexander, N.Y.C., 1973-79; account exec. Hill and Knowlton, N.Y.C., 1980-82; account supr. Makovsky & Co., N.Y.C., 1982—. Active United Way, March of Dimes. Office: 370 Lexington Ave New York NY 10017

OVERDEER, PATRICIA MILLER, mathematician, educator; b. San Mateo County, Calif., Nov. 30, 1922; d. Herman Potts, Jr. and Nancy (Lewis) Miller; B.A. in Edn., Montclair (N.J.) State Coll., 1943; M.S. in Math., U. Del., 1949; postgrad. Bryn Mawr Coll., Villanova (Pa.) U.; children—Lynn Randall, Nancy O. Daly, Louise O. Hettema. Tchr., New Providence (N.J.) Public Schs., 1943-44; grad. asst., then part-time instr. U. Del., 1946-50; mem. faculty Pa. State U., Ogontz campus, Abington, 1956—, prof. math., 1976—. Mem. Jenkintown Borough Sch. Bd., 1960-72. Named Outstanding Tchr., Ogontz campus, 1973. Mem. Math. Assn. Am., Nat. Council Tchrs. Math., Pi Mu Epsilon. Home: 2031 Harmony Ln Glenside PA 19038 Office: Pa State U Ogontz Campus Abington PA 19001

OVERLAND, SHIRLEY MAE HUEBNER, multipurpose sr. center adminstr.; b. Postville, Iowa, Jan. 8, 1920; d. Rudolph Carl and Estelle Louise (Zieman) Huebner; student U. No. Iowa, 1937-39, Upper Iowa U., 1939, U. Mich., 1976; m. Ernest Olaf Overland, Sept. 19, 1942; children—Dianne Elizabeth (dec.), Mary Lee, Deborah Jo. Tchr. public schs., Sheffield, Iowa, 1940-43, Postville, Iowa, 1943-44; evangelism dir. Am. Luth. Ch., Huron, S.D., 1956-62; dir. parish edn. Luth. Ch. of the Master, Omaha, 1964-70; exec. dir. Huron Area Sr. Center, Inc., 1972—; adj. prof. gerontology Huron Coll., 1979, 80; mem. U.S. commr.'s task force on sr. center devel. Adminstrn. on Aging, 1978; regional del., mem. del. council Nat. Inst. Sr. Centers; founder Area Coalition on Aging, 1981, Adult Day Care program, Huron, 1982. Recipient merit award Gerontology Assn. for Tng. and Edn., 1977; Farmers' Home Adminstrn. grantee; HUD grantee. Mem. Nat. Council on Aging, Nat. Inst. Sr. Housing (founding), Western Gerontol. Soc., S.D. Assn. Sr. Citizens (Outstanding Service award 1979), C. of C., Bus. and Profl. Women's Club (Woman of Yr. 1975), Beadle Sr. Citizens Assn. (founder), 100,000 Club. Republican. Lutheran. Home: 616 Dakota St S Huron SD 57350 Office: Huron Area Sr Center Inc 7th and Ohio St SW Huron SD 57350

OVERLAND, WANDA IDELLE, YMCA ofcl.; b. Harvey, N.D., Sept. 15, 1953; d. Ingwald T. and Edna M. Overland; B.S., N.D. State U., 1975, M.S., 1982. Tchr. home econs. N.H. high schs., 1975-78; head resident residential life/housing N.D. State U., 1978-81, adminstrv. asst. Coll. Home Econs., 1978-81; dir. YMCA at N.D. State U., 1981—, tchr. adult edn. courses; speaker, cons., workshop leader in field. Chmn. N.D. State U. Campus Equity, 1982. Christine Finlayson scholar, 1978-80; Elsie Stark Martin scholar, 1974; named Hillsboro Outstanding Young Educator, 1978. Mem. Am. Personnel and Guidance Assn., Am. Home Econs. Assn., Kappa Delta Pi, Phi Upsilon Omicron. Republican. Lutheran. Club: N.D. State U. Women's. Home: 1221 10th Ave N Fargo ND 58102 Office: Box 5512 Univ Sta Fargo ND 58105

OVERMAN, FRANCES ELIZABETH HENSON, writer, civic worker; b. Eddyville, Ky.; d. John Napoleon and Ida Belle (Koon) Henson; student Union U., 1930-32; A.B., Murray State U., 1937; postgrad. Northwestern U., 1940, U. Wis., 1941, 44; m. Ralph Theodore Overman, June 30, 1945 (div. Jan. 1968); children—Ralph Theodore, Ann Frances. Tchr. elem. schs., Ballard County, Ky., secondary schs., LaCenter, Cadiz, Maysville, and Benton, Ky., 1937-44; tchr. Oak Ridge Schs., 1944-45, 57-59; freelance writer. Active, Cub Scouts, Brownies; adviser Y-Teens; active Oak Ridge Civic Music Assn., Oak Ridge Community Playhouse, Oak Ridge Community Art Center. Recipient Community Service award, 1972. Fellow Intercontinental Biog. Assn.; mem. Internat. Platform Assn., League Women Voters, Centro Studi E Scombi Internazionali (internat. com. fine arts 1970-71), Internat. Acad. Leonardo Da Vinci, Tau Kappa Alpha. Contbr. articles to profl. jours. Address: 107 E Vanderbilt Dr Oak Ridge TN 37830

OVERS, BARBARA QUANE, mfg. co. exec.; b. Batavia, N.Y., Apr. 14, 1933; d. Albert and Winifred Quane; m. Ronald R. Overs, Dec. 5, 1969; children—April Anne, Randall Mark. Vice pres. Overs Assos., Williamsville, N.Y., 1970-72; pres. Overs Ltd., Toronto, Ont., Can., 1974—; v.p. EMSCO Electronics Co., Buffalo, 1974-76, sec.-treas., 1976—; sec.-treas. Electro Marine Systems Inc., East Amherst, N.Y., 1970—, Electro Marine Systems Internat. Inc., 1973—; dir. RB II, 1976—; asst. treas., dir. Coterie Inc., 1980—. Mem. Boating Industry Assn., Nat. Fedn. Bus. and Profl. Women, Nat. Assn. Female Execs., Cessna Skylane Owners Assn., Aircraft Owners and Pilots Assn., 99's Internat. Women's Pilots Assn., Exptl. Aircraft Assn., Smithsonian Instn., Albright Knox Art Gallery. Clubs: Buffalo Yacht, Buffalo Canoe, Amherst Dance. Address: 96 Fox Hunt Ln East Amherst NY 14051

OVERSTREET, BONARO WILKINSON, author, lectr.; b. Geyserville, Calif., Oct. 30, 1902; d. Edward and Margaret Elizabeth (Bonar) Wilkinson; A.B., U. Calif., 1925, tchr.'s cert., 1926; m. Harry Allen Overstreet, Aug. 23, 1932. Research asso. Am. Assn. Adult Edn., 1939-40; instr. adult edn. Claremont County. Calif., summer, 1940, Mills Coll., Calif., summer, 1941, U. Mich. Extension Service, 1945-46, 49, U. Calif. extension div., 1948; instr. U. Va. Continuation Center. Mem. Am. Assn. for Adult Edn., Sigma Delta Pi, Phi Beta Kappa, Theta Sigma Phi. Clubs: Nat. Press, International (Washington). Author: Poetic Way to Release, 1931; Footsteps on the Earth, 1934; Search for a Self, 1938; Brave Enough for Life, 1941; (with H.A. Overstreet) Town Meeting Comes to Town, 1938; Leaders for Adult Education (Am. Assn. Adult Edn.), 1940; American Reasons, 1943; Courage for Crisis, 1943; Freedom's People, 1945; How to Think About Ourselves, 1948; Understanding Fear: in Ourselves and Others, 1951; The Mind Alive (with H.A. Overstreet), 1954; Hands Laid Upon the Wind, 1956; The Mind Goes Forth 1956, What We Must Know About Communism, 1958 (with H.A. Overstreet); The War Called Peace; (with H.A. Overstreet) Krushchev's Communism 1961, The Iron Curtain, 1963; The Strange Tactics of Extremism, 1964; The FBI in Our Open Society, 1969; Signature, 1978; contbr. to jours. Home: 3409 Fiddler's Green Falls Church VA 22044

OVERSTREET, DEBORAH PATRICIA ELLA, social worker; b. Detroit, May 10, 1951; d. Murrel Edward and Dorothy Inez (Hayes) O.; B.A., Wayne State U., Detroit, 1974, M.S.W., 1978. Social worker Lula Belle Syewart Center, Detroit, 1974-76; asst. to dir. minority recruitment Wayne State U., 1976-78; social worker Harper Grace Hosp., Detroit, summer 1977; social worker teenage parent program Children's Center Wayne County, Detroit, 1978-79, dir. program, 1978-82, dir. adolescent program, 1982—; crisis intervention worker. Pepsi Cola scholar, 1973; Social Services Edn. Grantee, 1976-78. Mem. Nat. Assn. Social Workers, Nat. Assn. Black Social Workers, NAACP, Nat. Assn. Female Execs., Nat. Black Child Devel. Assn., Mich. Assn. Social Workers, Detroit Assn. Black Social Workers. Democrat. Club: Zonta. Office: 101 E Alexandrine St Detroit MI 48201

OVERSTREET, KATHLEEN, journalist; b. Savannah, Ga., July 19, 1951; d. Edward Kinchley and Evelyn (Griner) O.; student Wesleyan Coll., 1969-71; B.A. in Speech/Journalism, Ga. Southern Coll., 1973. Library asst. San Antonio Light, 1973-74, staff writer, 1974-81, asst. editor —Slot—, 1981-82, TV editor, 1982—. Founder Bexar County Women's Center, 1977, sec. bd. dirs., 1977-78, 82—, chmn. bd. dirs., 1978-80. Recipient Feature Writing award UPI, 1980, 1978. Mem. Women in Communications (dir.), San Antonio Press Club (dir.), Tex. Press Women, Local 25 Newspaper Guild, Sigma Delta Chi. Democrat. Home: 218 Adams St San Antonio TX 78210 Office: PO Box 161 San Antonio TX 78291

OVERTON, ANITA FAYE, mortgage banking exec.; b. Enid, Okla., Oct. 30, 1943; d. Carl J. and Audine G. (Leser) Eisele; student Enid Bus. Coll., 1961-62, Los Angeles Valley Jr. Coll., 1963-64, Lumbleau Real Estate Sch., 1978, Lane Community Coll., 1981-83; 1 dau. by previous marriage, Elena Suzanne Overton. Loan processor Investor's Mortgage Service Co. Los Angeles, 1964-66, Colonial Assos., Inc., Sherman Oaks, Calif., 1967-68; office mgr. Century Mortgage Co., Los Angeles, 1968-69; office mgr. The Colwell Co., Inglewood, Calif., 1969-71, asst. sec. of corp., 1969-71; adminstrv. asst. Kassler & Co., Encino, Calif., 1971-72; supr. Crenshaw Mortgage Co., Inglewood, 1972-74; loan rep. Imperial Bank Mortgage, Inglewood, 1974; office mgr. Cal Fed Mortgage Co., Northridge, Calif., 1974-75; v.p. and corp. sec. Funders Mortgage Co., Inc., Northridge, 1975-78; v.p. and corp. sec. Funders Mortgage Co., Inc., Reseda, Calif., 1978—, also dir.; corp. sec. Funders Home Loan Co., Inc., 1978—; dir. Funders Ins. Agy., Inc.; corp. sec. Funders Ins. Co., 1978-80. Lic. income tax preparer. Mem. Nat. Assn. Female Execs., Assn. Profl. Mortgage Women, Calif. Escrow Assn., Phi Theta Kappa.

OVERTON, DEBRA YVONNE, auditor; b. Phila., Sept. 7, 1954; d. Willie and Bessie (Edgerton) O.; B.A. in Bus. Adminstrn., Lincoln U., 1976; postgrad. Temple U., 1979. Corporate staff auditor RCA, Cherry Hills, N.J., 1977—. Mem. Assn. M.B.A. Execs., Nat. Assn. Female Execs. Democrat. Baptist. Home: 4425 N 18th St Philadelphia PA 19140 Office: RCA Cherry Hill NJ 08358

OVERTON, ELLEN STERN, govt. agy. adminstr.; b. Hamburg, Ger., Jan. 10, 1925; came to U.S., 1940, naturalized, 1946; B.A. magna cum laude, Mt. Holyoke Coll., 1946; M.A., Yale U., 1949; m. June 4, 1955; children—Roger W., Michael P. Polit. analyst U.S. Govt., Washington, 1949-57; info. center adminstr. and trainer Washington Opportunities for Women, 1966-73, also dir.; pvt. practice career counseling, Washington, 1973-77; dir. Vol. and Intern program Women's Equity Action League, Washington, 1973-74, pres. nat. capital chpt., 1975-76, study dir. Ednl. and Legal Def. Fund, 1975-76, corr. sec., 1976-77; Washington, fed. women's program mgr. Nat. Oceanic and Atmospheric Adminstrn. Dept. Commerce, Washington, 1977—. Mem. Clearinghouse on Women's Issue (v.p.), Am. Soc. Public Adminstrn., Federally Employed Women, Inc., Fedn. Orgns. Profl. Women, Nat. Women's Polit. Caucus, Nat. Council Career Women, Washington Women's Network, Nat. Assn. Women Bus. Owners, Nat. Council on Alternative Work Patterns (v.p., conf. coordinator 1976-77, dir.), Phi Beta Kappa. Clubs: Women's Nat. Democratic, Yale of Washington, Mt. Holyoke of Washington, Edgemoor. Home: 4820 W St Washington DC 20007 Office: Rockwall Bldg 11400 Rockville Pike Rockville MD 20852

OVERTON, HELEN PARKER (MRS. SAMUEL WATKINS OVERTON), Realtor; b. Memphis, Dec. 30, 1920; d. William and Pearl (Pinkston) Parker; m. Samuel Watkins Overton, Sept. 3, 1952; children—Helen Parker (Mrs. William Barron Brown), Napoleon Hill. Exec. sec. Memphis State U., 1941-43, Chgo. and So. Air Lines, 1943-46, Memphis Bd. Edn., 1948-50; dir. women's programs Sta. WHBQ-TV, Memphis, 1950-52. Pres., Beethoven Club, 1960-66, 72-78, Mid-South Opera Guild, 1967—; dir. auditions Mid-South region Met. Opera, 1960-71, mem. nat. council, 1960-71; chmn. Tenn. Arts Commn., 1968-70; bd. dirs. Opera Memphis, Arts Appreciation, Tenn. Arts Commn., 1967-74. Mem. Sigma Alpha Iota, Alpha Gamma Delta. Clubs: Memphis Country (Memphis). Home: 5476 Collingwood Cove Memphis TN 38117

OVERTON, MEREDITH ANN, educator; b. Kansas City, Mo., Jan. 4, 1947; d. James Howard and Viola May (Moats) Holloway; B.S. in Home Econs., Kans. State U., 1969; M.S., U. Kans., 1973; postgrad. U. Mo., 1974-75; m. Richard Orion Overton, May 19, 1975. Dietetic intern Houston VA Hosp., 1969-70; admistrv./clin. dietitian Mpls. VA Hosp., 1970-71; dietitian coordinator for nutrition edn. med. students U. Kans. Med. Center, 1972-74, clin. dietitian, instr., 1973-74; clin. dietitian/trainee counselor Good Samaritan Hosp. and Med. Center, Portland, Oreg., 1975-76; sales rep. nutritional div. Mead Johnson, Portland, 1976-78; asst. prof., dir. dietetic internship Oreg. Health Scis. U., Portland, 1978—; faculty Clackamas Community Coll., 1976-78, Portland State U., 1978-81. Active March of Dimes, Hawaii Dietetic Assn., Multiple Sclerosis. AAUW scholar, 1966-67; Midwest Fish & Frozen Seafood scholar, 1967-68; Martha S. Pittman scholar, 1968-69; Bessie Brooks West scholar, 1968-69. Mem. Am. Dietetic Assn., Am. Soc. Profl. and Exec. Women, Oreg. Dietetic Assn., Portland Dietetic Assn., Am. Council Sci. and Health, Western Region Coll. and Univ. Tchrs. of Foods and Nutrition, Soc. Nutrition Edn., Oreg. Nutrition Council, Am. Soc. Parenteral and Enteral Nutrition, Am. Home Econ. Assn., Phi Kappa Phi, Omicron Nu, Phi Upsilon Omicron, Alpha Lambda Delta. Methodist. Author: (with B. P. Lukert) Clinical Nutrition-A Physiologic Approach, 1977. Home: 10565 S Bremer Rd Canby OR 97013 Office: UHN 3116 3181 SW Sam Jackson Park Rd Portland OR 97201

OVERTON, ROSILYN GAY HOFFMAN, stockbroker, economist; b. Corsicana, Tex., July 10, 1942; d. Billy Clarence and Ima Elise (Gay) Hoffman; B.S. in Math., Wright State U., Dayton, Ohio, 1972, M.S. in Applied Econs. (fellow), 1973; postgrad. N.Y. U. Grad. Sch. Bus., 1974—; m. Aaron Lewis Overton, Jr., July 2, 1960 (div. Mar. 1975); children—Aaron Lewis III, Adam Jerome. Research analyst Nat. Security Agy., Dept. Def., 1962-67; bus. reporter Dayton Jour.-Herald, 1973-74; economist First Nat. City Bank, N.Y.C., 1974, AT&T, 1974-75; broker Merrill Lynch, N.Y.C., 1975-80; asst. v.p. E.F. Hutton & Co., Inc., N.Y.C., 1980—; adj. faculty Marymount Manhattan Coll., 1977—. Active spl. gifts com. Channel 13 (WNET). Named Businesswoman of Yr., N.Y.C., 1976. Mem. Met. Econ. Assn., Nat., N.Y. assns. bus. economists, Nat. Fedn. Bus. and Profl. Women, Nat. Economists Club, Bus. and Profl. Women's Clubs N.Y. State (asst. dir. dist. I, state dir., chmn. Status of Women), Wright State U. Alumni Assn. (dir.), Mensa. Methodist. Clubs: Zonta, Women's Nat. Republican. Author: (with John Treacy) Measuring Externalities of Strip Coal Mining via Property Tax Assessment, 1973; editor: Monthly Economic Letter, First Nat. City Bank, 1974; contbr. articles to profl. jours. Home: 115 E 9 St New York NY 10003 Office: 345 Park Ave New York NY 10154

OVERTURF, JOAN DEWITT, social worker; b. Oklahoma City, June 20, 1932; d. Willard Minton and Louise (De Witt) Lay; B.A., Pomona Coll., 1955; M.S.W., U. So. Calif., 1958, D.S.W., 1978; m. Jack Carson Overturf, June 20, 1952; children—Kristen Leigh, Heidi Louise. Family counselor Family Service Assn., Pomona Valley, Calif., 1967-72; psychiat. social worker Calif. State Dept. Health, Pomona, 1970-74; instr. Chaffey Coll., Alta Loma, Calif., 1973, U. Calif. at Riverside, 1974; clin. prof. U. So. Calif., Los Angeles, 1970-74, lectr., 1976-78; pvt. practice social work, Claremont, Calif., 1972—. Mem. Nat. Assn. Social Workers, Am. Assn. Marriage and Family Therapists, Acad. Cert. Social Workers, So. Calif. Soc. Clin. Hypnosis, Alpha Kappa Delta. Office: 219 N Indian Hill Blvd Claremont CA 91711

OVSAK, SHELLEY JEAN, flight attendant; b. N.Y.C., Apr. 14, 1951; d. Jan and Elinor (Katrak) Ovsak; diplomas Grace Downs Model and Air Career Coll., 1970; A.A., Pensacola (Fla.) Jr. Coll., 1974; B.S., U. West Fla., 1976, M.S., 1977; M.A., Central Mich. U., 1981; postgrad. in health care mgmt. Calif. Western U., 1981—. Served with WAVES, U.S. Navy, 1970-73, U.S. Air Force, 1979—; spl. air missions flight attendant, Andrews AFB, Camp Springs, Md., 1981—. Vol. ARC, Malcolm Grow Med. Center, Andrews AFB, 1981—. Mem. AAPHER, Assn. Advancement Health Edn., Nat. Assn. Sport and Phys. Edn., AAUW, Nat. Recreation and Parks Assn., Am. Home Econs. Assn., Delta Chi Omega, Alpha Delta Pi, Chi Gamma Iota, Sigma Iota Epsilon, Phi Epsilon Kappa. Republican. Roman Catholic. Home: 219 E 89th St New York NY 10028 Office: PSC 1 Box 786 Andrews AFB Camp Springs MD 20331

OWEN, ALYCE CHASSE, computer cons.; b. Mass., Sept. 26, 1946; d. Gerard Henry and Rose Virginia (Monaco) Chasse; B.A. in Math., Trinity Coll., Washington, 1968. Computer programmer H.P. Hood & Son, Boston, 1968-71, Transam. Corp., San Francisco, 1972-74; tng. and recruiting coordinator Pacific Gas & Electric Co., San Francisco, 1974-79; computer cons., seminar leader on computer literacy; instr. data processing jr. coll. Mem. Data Processing Mgmt. Assn., Am. Soc. for Tng. and Devel., AAUW. Home: 3271 Hidden Valley Dr Santa Rosa CA 95404

OWEN, BLYTHE, composer; b. Bruce, Minn., Dec. 26, 1898; d. Herbert Lee and Minnie Belle (Perkins) O.; B.M., Chgo. Musical Coll., 1941; M.M., Northwestern U., 1942; Ph.D. in Composition, Eastman Sch. Music, Rochester, N.Y., 1953; D.M. (hon.), Andrews U., 1980; pvt. studies in piano and composition. Mem. faculty Hull House Music Sch., Chgo., 1926-29, Walla Walla Coll., 1919-22, 61-65, Northwestern U., 1942-50, Cosmopolitan Sch. Music, Chgo., 1943-61, Roosevelt U., 1950-61; prof. music, chmn. composition Andrews U., from 1965, now emeritus; adjudicator Nat. Guild Piano Tchrs.; performer St. Joseph (Mich.) Symphony Orch., 1967-78; composer for orch., chamber groups, chorus, piano, organ and band; works include: State St. Suite (2d place Henry P. Lytton award), 1946, Concerto for Piano and Orch. (Mu Phi Epsilon Biennial award), 1955, Concerto Grosso for Strings, Oboes, Horns and Bassoons (Mu Phi Epsilon Biennial award), 1961, Sonata Fantaisie for Cello and Piano (Mu Phi Epsilon Biennial award), 1940, Quintet for Piano and String Quartet (Delta Omicron award), 1944, Sonata for Violin and Piano (Mu Phi Epsilon Biennial award), 1946, Trio for Oboe, Clarinet and Bassoon (Mu Phi Epsilon Biennial award, hon. mention Gedok Competition, Germany), 1950, Quartet for String No. 2 (Mu Phi Epsilon Biennial award), 1951, Trio for Flute, Clarinet and Piano (1st prize Musicians Club of Women), 1959, Trio for Violin, Cello and Piano (spl. merit citation Mu Phi Epsilon), 1962, Two Inventions for Woodwinds (spl. merit citation Mu Phi Epsilon), 1964, Awake O Zion (1st prize Am. Pen Women Chgo.), 1952, Blessed Be The God and Father (1st hon. mention Friends of Harvey Gaul Contest), 1950, Sonatina in A (2d prize Mu Phi Epsilon Biennial Contest), 1939, Sonata No. 1 (1st prize Lakeview Musical Soc.), 1948, Toccata (Mu Phi Epsilon Biennial award) 1950. Named Mich. Composer of Yr., 1980-81. Mem. Am. Soc. Univ. Composers, Mich. Music Tchrs. Assn., Musicians Nat. Tchrs. Assn., Nat. Guild Piano Tchrs., Am. Women Composers, Mu Phi Epsilon, Pi Kappa Lambda. Democrat. Seventh-day Adventist. Club: Monday Musical (St. Joseph). Office: Andrews University Berrien Springs MI

OWEN, CAROL THOMPSON (MRS. JAMES E. OWEN), artist, educator; b. Pasadena, Calif., May 10, 1944; d. Sumner Comer and Cordelia (Whittemore) T.; student Pasadena City Coll., summer 1963; B.A. with distinction, U. Redlands, 1966; postgrad. Stanford U., summer 1966; M.A., Calif. State U. at Los Angeles, 1967; M.F.A., Claremont Grad. Sch. and Univ. Center, 1969; m. James Eugene Owen, July 19, 1975; children—Kevin Christopher, Christine Celese. Student asst. Calif. State U., 1966-67; head resident Pitzer Coll., Claremont, Calif., 1967-70; instr. art Mt. San Antonio Coll., Walnut, Calif., 1968—, dir. coll. art gallery, 1972-73; exhibited one-person show M.F.A. Exhbn., Scripps Coll., Claremont, 1969, Covina Pub. Library, 1971; exhibited in shows: U. Redlands, 1964, 65, 70, 78, Sr. Thesis Exhibit, U. Redlands, 1966, Calif. State Coll., 1967, Rio Hondo Coll. Design div. Am. Ceramic Soc., 1968, faculty exhibits Mt. San Antonio Coll., 1968, 70, 72, 74, Am. Ceramic Soc. Design Div. Mem. Show, 1969, Calif. State Poly. Coll., Pomona, 1972; reader Henry E. Huntington Library and Art Gallery, 1967-68. Recipient Curved Bar award Girl Scouts U.S.A., 1958, Forensic award Lions Club, Region finalist, 1962; Woman's Aux. Am. Legion scholar Alhambra Post, 1962, Calif. State Grad. fellow, 1968. Mem. Calif. Scholarship Fedn. (life), Faculty Assn. Mt. San Antonio Coll.,

Am. Ceramic Soc., Coll. Art Assn. Am., Calif. Tchrs. Assn., Friends Huntington Library, Los Angeles County Mus. Art, Heard Mus. Assn., Internat. Platform Assn., Sigma Tau Delta. Republican. Presbyterian. Home: 534 S Hepner St Covina CA 91723 Office: Mt San Antonio Coll Grand Ave Walnut CA 91789

OWEN, FREYA WEAVER, educator; b. Palo Alto, Calif., May 27, 1921; d. Clarence Eugene and Monica Ting Weaver; B.A., Santa Barbara Coll., 1944; M.A., Stanford U., 1954, Ph.D., 1961; postgrad. Maudsley Hosp., London, 1962; m. Cramer Hill Owen, Mar. 23, 1941 (div. 1969); children—Cramer Hill II, Indira Rimkiet, Ellen Mohn. Tchr. pub. schs., Santa Barbara, Calif., 1946-51; tchr. Children's Hosp., Stanford U., 1953, psychologist, 1954-61; coordinator educationally and mentally handicapped Palo Alto Unified Sch. Dist., 1965-76, coordinator spl. edn., 1976—; lectr. dept. psychiatry and behavioral scis. Stanford U. Med. Sch., 1976—; mem. profl. adv. com. Peninsula Children's Center, Children's Health Council; chmn. North Santa Clara County Comprehensive Plan for Spl. Edn., 1975-77. Lic. psychologist, Calif. Mem. Am. Psychol. Assn., Soc. for Research in Child Devel. Office: Palo Alto Unified Sch Dist 25 Churchill Ave Palo Alto CA 94306

OWEN, PATRICIA ANN, telephone co. exec.; b. Madison, Wis., Apr. 4, 1941; d. Donald Vincent and Evelyn Mary (Bauer) Doyle; B.S., Platteville State U., 1963; m. Arthur Owen, Aug. 26, 1967; 1 dau., Anne Margaret. Tchr. math. public schs., West Bend, Wis., 1963-64, Watertown, Wis., 1964-65, Wautoma, Wis., 1965-66; asst. engr. Northwestern Bell Telephone Co., St. Paul, 1966-72, engr., 1972-74, mgr., 1974-75, tng. supr. engring., 1975-77, personnel supr., 1978, mgr. distbn. engring., Brooklyn Center, Minn., 1978-81, mgr. distbn., St. Paul, 1981, mgr. assignments, 1981—. Parent del. Child Care Council of Ramsey County, Minn., 1979-81; St. Rose del. Twin City Orgn., 1977-78. Mem. Minn. Mgmt. Women, LWV. Home: 1506 18th St NW New Brighton MN 55112 Office: 6540 Shingle Creek Brooklyn Center MN 55430

OWEN, SUZANNE, savs. and loan exec.; b. Lincoln, Nebr., Oct. 6, 1926; d. Arthur C. and Hazel E. (Edwards) O.; B.S. in Bus. Adminstrn., U. Nebr., Lincoln, 1948. With G.F. Lessenhop & Sons, Inc., Lincoln, 1948-57; with First Fed. Lincoln, 1963—, v.p., dir. personnel, 1975-81, 1st v.p., 1981—. Mem. Adminstrv. Mgmt. Soc. (dir. local chpt.), Lincoln Personnel Mgmt. Assn., Phi Chi Theta. Republican. Christian Scientist. Clubs: Altrusa, Wooden Spoon, Twig Daniels Network, Exec. Women's Breakfast Group, Pi Beta Phi Alumnae, Order of Eastern Star (Lincoln). Office: First Fed Lincoln 13th and N Sts Lincoln NE 68508

OWENS, A. ANNE, lawyer; b. Santa Maria, Calif., Nov. 26, 1943; d. Luther Edward and Alice Iola (Wentworth) O.; student Hanover Coll., 1962-64; B.A., Ohio State U., 1966; M.A., U. South Fla., 1974; J.D. with honors, U. Fla., 1979. Social worker Franklin County Welfare Dept., Columbus, Ohio, 1966-68; social worker Dept. Social and Econ. Services, St. Petersburg, Fla., 1968-73; social worker Cath. Social Services, St. Petersburg, 1974-77; admitted to Fla. bar, 1979; asso. atty. Holland & Knight, Lakeland, Fla., 1979-81; asso. firm Canan & Murphy, P.A., Lakeland, 1981—. Mem. Big Sisters of Pinellas County, 1971-78; Vietnamese resettlement coordinator U.S. Cath. Conf., St. Petersburg Diocese, 1975-76. Mem. Am. Bar Assn., Fla. Bar Assn., Lakeland Bar Assn., Phi Delta Phi, Phi Kappa Phi. Republican. Presbyterian. Exec. editor: U. Fla. Law Rev., 1979. Contbr. articles to profl. jours. Home: 3555 Raintree Way Lakeland FL 33803 Office: PO Box 6558 5001 S Florida Ave Lakeland FL 33803

OWENS, DEBRA ANN, assn. exec.; b. Oak Park, Ill., Oct. 15, 1951; d. Raymond L. and Elaine G. (Nowotarski) Zeason; B.S. in Biology, Millikin U., 1975; Med. Technologist, St. Therese Hosp., 1975; m. Stephen K. Owens, Jan. 6, 1978; 1 son, Stephen. Med. technologist, clin. supr. Victory Meml. Hosp., Waukegan, Ill., 1975-77; quality control supr. Travenol Labs., Mundelein, Ill., 1977-79; asst. tech. dir. Am. Soc. Quality Control, Milw., 1979-81, tech. dir., 1981—. Mem. Am. Soc. Quality Control. Roman Catholic. Author column Quality Progress Mag. Home: 803 Flossmoor St Waukegan IL 60085 Office: 230 W Wells St Milwaukee WI 53203

OWENS, ERMA JEAN, educator; b. Ft. Worth, July 27, 1939; d. James Ellis and Jetrenee (Parks) Jones; B.S., Calif. State U., Hayward, 1971, M.S., 1975, Ph.D., 1977; m. Theopris Owens, Dec. 12, 1960; children—William Curtis Venters, Cathy Venters, Jetrenee Owens, Cheryl Owens. Tchr. elem. schs. Roman Cath. Diocese schs., Oakland, Calif., 1968-72, Oakland Unified Sch. Dist., 1972—; kindergarten tchr., choir dir. Garfield Elem. Sch., 1976—; founder, dir. Youth on Move, Oakland, 1966; exec. dir. Uncle K's Kiddie Kollege; gen. mgr. Connections Unltd. Travel Agy. Mem. Assn. Supervision and Curriculum Devel., Exec. Women, Beta Pi Sigma, Delta Sigma Theta. Democrat. Baptist. Clubs: Crescent Ettes Social, Order Eastern Star. Home: 526 Berry St Hayward CA 94544 Office: 10823 MacArthur Blvd Oakland CA 94605

OWENS, EVALYN BERGSTRAND, former educator; b. Danville, Ill., Sept. 9, 1907; d. John Ivard and Esther (Jernberg) Bergstrand; B.S., U. Minn., 1928, postgrad., 1939-41; M.S., Iowa State Coll., 1936; m. Emery E. Owens, Dec. 1948 (dec. 1978). Nutritionist, Nassau County (L.I.) Com. Tb and Public Health, 1928-29, Freeport (L.I.) public schs., 1929-30; tchr. home econs., Frederic, Wis. 1930-32, Waupaca (Wis.) High Sch., 1932-35; teaching grad. asst. home econs. Iowa State Coll., 1935-36; instr. home mgmt., child devel. Mich. State Coll., 1936-39, asst. prof., 1941-42; instr. home econs. U. Minn., 1939-40; dean home econs. U. Conn., 1942-49; instr. home mgmt., child devel. Iowa State Coll. summer 1937, acting head home mgmt. dept., summer 1938, 39. Exec. com. Family Service Agy. Waukesha County; mem. Waukesha County Council Child Welfare, Social Agys. Council; mem. bd. vistors U. Wis., 1950-60; mem. research adv. com. U.S. Dept. Agr., 1954-60. Recipient outstanding achievement award, U. Minn., 1956. Mem. Am. (treas. 1952-54), Tex. home econs. assns., Omicron Nu, Phi Upsilon Omicron, Pi Lambda Theta, Iota Sigma Pi, Kappa Alpha Theta. Republican. Lutheran. Address: 212 N 40th St McAllen TX 78501 also 5300 Vernon Ave Apt 313 Mineapolis MN 55436

OWENS, JOAN D., writer, producer; b. Los Angeles, June 2, 1942; d. Albert Lazar and Esther (Lipson) Kaplan; B.A. in History, U. Calif., Berkeley, 1964, postgrad., 1965; postgrad. Sorbonne, Cours de Civilisation Français, 1964. Assoc. producer public affairs KHJ-TV, Los Angeles, 1965-66; assoc. producer David L. Wolper Prodns., 1967-68, producer, writer, 1970-73; assoc. producer, writer Metromedia Producers Corp., 1969; producer Alan Landsburg Prodns., 1972; producer, writer, dir. CRM Prodns., 1974; writer Alan Sloan Prodns., Los Angeles, 1975; writer CBS and ABC network children's programming, Hollywood, Calif., 1976-82; exec. producer KOCE-TV, 1982—. Recipient Gold medal Internat. Film and TV Festival N.Y., 1975; Chris Bronze plaque Columbus Film Festival, 1975; Bronze medal V.I. Internat. Film Festival, 1975; award for creative excellence U.S. Internat. Film Festival, 1975. Mem. Women in Film (dir. 1976-78), Writers Guild Am.-West. Writer, producer numerous television documentaries and ednl. films including Say Goodbye (asso. producer), 1971; It Takes a Lot of Love, 1972; The Explorers, 1973; CBS pilots The Magic Land of Zo, 1977, Bill Cosby and the Clubhouse Kids, 1977; exec. producer U.S., French nat. TV spls.; writer McGraw Hill Co., 1979, Disney Telecommunications, 1981.

OWENS, LORRAINE LUCILLE, handwriting analyst, cons.; b. Pettus, Tex., Sept. 19, 1927; d. Bernard Phillip and Lucille Lillian (Newman) Hopkins; B.A. in Psychology, Ottawa (Kans.) U., 1977; m. George Erwin Owens, Feb. 5, 1947; children—Janet Lucille, George Erwin, David M., Lynn L. Partner, Allen and Owens, Kansas City, Mo., 1970-80; pres. Kaleidoscope Corp., Kansas City, Mo., 1980—; psychology instr. Graphoanalysis Congress, Chgo., 1978-81; cons. with psychologist Lansing State Prison, Marillac Sch. Bd. dirs. Marillac Sch., Kansas City, Mo., 1977-82; troop, troop organizer Mid Continent council Girl Scouts U.S.A., 1962-72. Mem. Internat. Graphoanalysis Soc. (certificate of merit, 1979). Republican. Unity Ch. Author: Different Ways to Describe Traits, 1976; Handwriting Analysis Dictionary, 1981. Home: 6300 Verona Shawnee Mission KS 66208 Office: 1524 Crystal Kansas City MO 64126

OWENS, MARY LOUISE, artist; b. Des Moines; d. John David and Ruth Kathryn (Colvin) O.; student Albright-Knox Art Sch., 1953-54; B.S., SUNY, 1957; m. John Robert Schnore, July 4, 1971. Dealer, Janus Gallery, Los Angeles; one-woman show Janus Gallery, Los Angeles, 1976; group shows include: Nat. Watercolor Soc., Laguna Beach (Calif.) Mus. Art, 1976, Springville (Utah) Mus. Art, 1977, Springfield (Mo.) Art Mus., 1977, Rocky Mountain Nat. Watermedia Exhibition, Golden, Colo., 1977, Calif. State U., Northridge, 1977, Foyer Gallery, Brand Art Galleries, Glendale, Calif., 1977, Springville Mus., 1978, Bard Hall Gallery, San Diego, 1979, NAD Galleries, N.Y.C., 1979; represented in permanent collections: Fluor Corp., Irvine, Calif., City Bank Internat., San Francisco, SUNY, Buffalo, Los Angeles Dept. Water and Power Credit Union Corp. Hdqrs. Recipient Golden C. of C. cash award, 1977. Mem. Nat. Watercolor Soc. Address: 2443 Yosemite Dr Los Angeles CA 90041

OWENS, ROCHELLE, playwright, poet; b. Bklyn., Apr. 2, 1936; d. Maxwell and Molly (Adler) Bass; student N.Y.C. public schs.; m. George D. Economou, June 17, 1962. Author 11 books of plays and poetry, 1961—, latest collections being The Joe 82 Creation Poems, 1974; The Joe Chronicles Part 2, 1979; Shemuel Poetry, 1979; The Karl Marx Play and Others, 1974; Emma Instigated Me, 1978; Chucky's Hunch, 1982. Recipient Obie Best Play award, 1967; fellow Ford Found., 1965, Guggenheim Found., 1972, Creative Artists Public Service, 1974, Rockefeller Found., 1976, Nat. Endowment for Arts, 1978. Mem. Dramatists Guild, Authors Guild, ASCAP, PEN. Address: 606 W 116th St New York NY 10027

OWENS-POTE, KAREN ASKEY, nutrition cons.; b. Indiana, Pa., Dec. 3, 1945; d. William Anthony and Cleo Margaret (Lyons) Askey; B.S. in Home Econs., Indiana U. of Pa., 1967; M.S. in Food and Nutrition, Va. Poly. Inst. and State U., 1970; postgrad. in bus. mgmt. Pepperdine U., 1979-80; m. Wilfred D. Pote, Feb. 14, 1981. Dir. dietetics and food service Somerset (Pa.) Community Hosp., 1970; food mgr. supr. Restaurant-Hotel div. Stouffer Food Corp., Cleve., 1967-68; allied health nutritionist, sr. dietitian City of Hope Nat. Med. Center, Duarte, Calif., 1970-71; chief nutritionist U. Calif. Med. Center-Irvine, Orange, Calif., 1971-74; prin. K.A. Owens Assos., Sierra Madre, Calif., 1972-80; pres. K.A. Owens & Assos., Inc., St. Paul, 1981—; mgr. nutritional affairs Gen. Foods Corp., White Plains, N.Y., 1980-81; instr. public health nutrition U. Minn., Mpls., 1981—; chmn., asst. prof. home econs. and dietetics Pepperdine U., Malibu, Calif., 1974-80; adj. prof. social ecology U. Calif., Irvine, 1972-74; lectr., researcher in human nutrition Va. Poly. Inst. and State U., Blacksburg, 1968-70; condr. ednl. seminars in field, Calif., Idaho, Minn.; cons. Northwoods Exec. Fitness Program, Kane-Miller Corp., Anderson-Hendrickson & Co., Van de Kamp Frozen Foods, Pillsbury Co., Robert Marston and Assos., Inc., Hunt-Wesson Foods, Inc., Dinah's Place, NBC-TV, Longevity Centers, Inc., Glass Packaging Inst., Home Savs. and Loan Assn., various public relations and advt. agencies, profl. assns. and firms, utilities, hosps., govt. and civic groups. Vol. public radio and TV, Los Angeles, Mpls., St. Paul; chmn. fundraising for program in nutrition adminstrn. U. Minn.; chmn. neighborhood protection Summit Hill Assn.; active fundraising for symphony orch. Registered dietitian. Mem. Am. Dietetic Assn., Home Economists in Bus., Soc. Nutrition Edn., Inst. Food Tenhnologists, Am. Home Econs. Assn., Am. Soc. Tng. and Devel., Am. Fedn. TV and Radio Artists, Phi Tau Sigma, Kappa Omicron Phi. Republican. Methodist. Clubs: St. Paul Athletic, Sigma Sigma Sigma. Office: 728 Goodrich St Suite A Saint Paul MN 55105

OWNBEY, VIRGINIA KAY, architect; b. Miami, June 2, 1946; d. Hal Norwood and Mary Virginia (Williams) Buchanan; B.Arch., Okla. State U., 1970; m. Charles Lewis Ownbey, Aug. 11, 1974; children—Christine Vanessa, Wade Preston. Archtl. draftsperson Frank L. Hope & Assos., Santa Ana, Calif., 1970-73, Am. Devel., Torrance, Calif., 1973-74, J. Ward Dawson, Architect, Tustin, Calif., 1975-76; architect Archi & Tekton, Newport Beach, Calif., 1977-79; individual practice, Tustin, 1979—. Nat. Endowment Arts grantee, 1969. Mem. Womens Archtl. League, Methodist. Address: 1522 Garland St Tustin CA 92680

OXLEY, ANN, TV exec.; b. Canton, Ohio, Aug. 3, 1924; d. Edward and Dorothy (Duffy) Adang; B.A. with distinction, Ind. U., 1974, M.P.A., 1982; m. Jack Raymond Oxley, Aug. 10, 1946; children—Kathleen Oxley Wiggins, Maureen Oxley Gaff, Joseph, Jeffrey, Christeen Oxley Rhodes, Daniel, Julianne, Jamie, Kevin, Valerie, Amy. Advt. account salesperson Ft. Wayne (Ind.) Jour. Gazette, 1945-47; office mgr. Ind. Equestrian Assn., Ft. Wayne, 1971-73; research dir. Taxpayers Research Assn., Ft. Wayne, 1974-76; exec. dir. Ft. Wayne Pub. TV Inc., 1976—. Active Bicentennial Com., 1976; adviser Media Arts Panel Ind. Arts Commn. Mem. AAUW, Internat. Assn. Bus. Communicators, Women in Communications, Ind. Pub. Broadcasters Soc. (dir.), Mensa Internat., C. of C. (cultural com.), Phi Alpha Alpha. Roman Catholic. Home: 4035 Arlington St Fort Wayne IN 46807 Office: 227 E Washington Blvd Fort Wayne IN 46802

OXLEY, GERALDINE MOTTA, life ins. co. exec.; b. Hoboken, N.J., June 25, 1930; d. Edward Joseph and Mary Ellen (Green) Motta; B.S. in Math., Coll. Mt. St. Vincent, 1951; postgrad. N.Y. U., 1955-59; m. John Edward Oxley, Sept. 19, 1953. Mem. coll. trainee program N.Y. Life Ins. Co., N.Y.C., 1951-54, data processing programmer, 1954-59, mgr. systems programming, 1959-68, dir. electronics research, 1968-73, asst. v.p., 1973-75, 2d v.p., 1975-78, v.p., 1978—. Mem. Assn. Computer Machinery, Coll. Mt. St. Vincent Alumnae Assn. (pres. 1969-71, fund dir. 1975-76). Office: NY Life Ins Co 51 Madison Ave New York NY 10010

OXTOBY, LILLIAN ROSEN, educator; b. Portland, Maine, Feb. 12, 1926; d. Benjamin and Bella (Kaufman) R.; B.S., Coll. City N.Y., 1949; M.A., Columbia U., 1952, M.Ed., 1972; m. Toby Ewing Oxtoby, Aug. 3, 1952; 1 step-son, John, 1 son, Kenneth. Child welfare program specialist Calif. State Dept. Social Welfare, Los Angeles, 1953-56; dir. East Tremont Child Care Center, N.Y.C., 1961-70; guest lectr. Lehman Coll., 1968-73; asst. prof. edn. N.Y.C. Community Coll., 1970-71, chmn. child care-early childhood edn. program., 1971—; vis. prof. Fordham U., 1973—. Bd. dirs. East Tremont Child Care Center, Urban Child Devel. Center, Clinton Pre-Sch. Mem. Profl. Day Care Dirs. Assn. (pres. 1967-69), Nat. Assn. Social Workers, Assn. Childhood Edn. Internat., Nat. Assn. Edn. Young Children, Nat. Froebel Found., Organisation Mondiale pour L'education préscolaire, East Tremont Neighborhood Assn. Author: (with others) Early Childhood Education; Day Care It's Implication on Divorce and Separation. Producer, dir. film East Tremont Welcomes You, also slide and sound presentation on day care. Home: 170 West End Ave New York City NY 10023 Office: Borough of Manhattan Community College CUNY 199 Chambers St New York City NY 10007

OYLER, SUSAN DEBORAH, microbiologist; b. Roanoke, Va., Apr. 21, 1950; d. Dalton Oliver and Margaret Clay (Waldron) O.; B.A. in Biology, U. Va., 1972; Med. Technologist, Duke U., 1973; M.S. in Microbiology (A.D. Williams fellow 1973-74, NIH grantee 1974-76), Med. Coll. Va., 1976. Mgr. lab. Family Med. Center, Richmond, Va., 1975-76; gen. lab. supr. Physicians Clin. Labs., Richmond, 1976-78; supr. biol. formulation Technicon Corp., Middletown, Va., 1978-80; specialist fermentation tech. support Abbott Labs., N. Chicago, Ill., 1980—; mem. faculty J. Sargeant Reynolds Community Coll., Richmond, 1976-77. Regional rep. Va. Democratic Conv., 1976. Mem. Am. Soc. Clin. Pathologists, Am. Mgmt. Assn., Nat. Assn. Female Execs. Home: 1293 Bristol Ln Buffalo Grove IL 60090

OZICK, CYNTHIA, author; b. N.Y.C., Apr. 17, 1928; d. William and Celia (Regelson) Ozick; B.A. cum laude with honors in English, N.Y. U., 1949; M.A., Ohio State U., 1950; m. Bernard Hallote, Sept. 7, 1952; 1 dau., Rachel Sarah. Author: Trust, 1966; The Pagan Rabbi and Other Stories, 1971; Bloodshed and Three Novellas, 1976; Levitation: Five Fictions, 1982; Art and Ardor: Essays, 1983; fiction, poetry, criticism, revs., translations, 100 essays in numerous periodicals and anthologies. Mem. Phi Beta Kappa. Office: care Alfred A Knopf Co 201 E 50th St New York NY 10022

OZOLS, LIA, med. technologist; b. Riga, Latvia, Jan. 4, 1929; came to U.S., 1950, naturalized, 1959; d. Karlis and Olga Rozenfelds; B.S., U. Minn., 1957; postgrad. Metro State U., Minn., 1980; m. Laimons Ozols, Mar. 19, 1956; children—Ingemars, Arnis. Med. technologist U. Minn. Hosps., 1957-61; chief adminstrv. technologist Abbott Hosp., Mpls., 1957-77; administrv. lab. dir. Abbott-Northwestern Hosp., 1977-79; dir. Les Soeurs Orgn., Mpls., 1979—. Vice chair adv. bd. City of Richfield (Minn.) Dept. Health. Mem. Am. Soc. Clin. Pathologists, Am. Soc. Med. Technology, Minn. Microbiologists, Minn. Soc. Med. Technology, Minn. LWV, Women's Equity Action League (v.p. 1981-82), Women's Consortium, Good Old Girls, Exec. Females. Club: Selga (pres. 1981-82). Home: 2012 W 68th St Minneapolis MN 55423

PAASO, GRACE SPILLER, assn. exec.; b. St. Augustine, Fla., Sept. 3, 1946; d. Albert William and Gina (Versaggi) Spiller; B.S. in Journalism, U. Fla., 1968. Mgr. D. Marino, Inc., Boston, 1973-77; area dir. Am. Cancer Soc., Boston, 1978-81; nat. adminstr. Nat. Assn. Emergency Med. Technicians, Newton Highlands, Mass., 1981—; exec. sec. Joint Rev. Com. on EMT-Paramedic Program Accreditation, Newton Highlands, 1981—. Trustee, Leukemia Soc. Am., 1973-80. Mem. Women in Communications, Am. Soc. Assn. Execs., Internat. Chili Soc. Am. Democrat. Roman Catholic. Home: 359 Tappan St Brookline MA 02146 Office: PO Box 334 Newton Highlands MA 02161

PACCIONE, CATHERINE, artist; b. Bklyn., Feb. 12, 1955; d. John and Josephine (Corella) Paccione; m. Steven Thiem, May 22, 1983. Free-lance artist. Mem. Boston Mus. Fine Arts, Met. Mus.

PACE, DENISE KATHLEEN GOODWIN, editor; b. Wilkes-Barre, Pa., Jan. 17, 1954; d. John Arthur and Joan Patricia (McGeehan) G.; B.A. in English, King's Coll., Wilkes-Barre, Pa., 1975. Reporter, Wyoming Valley Observer, Wilkes-Barre, 1975; asso. editor Mount Washington Press, Cin., 1976; mng. editor Appleton-Century-Crofts, N.Y.C., 1977-81, Visual Info. Systems, N.Y.C., 1981-82; pres. Goldenwords, Northport, N.Y., 1982—. Democrat. Roman Catholic. Mng. editor Jour. Nat. Med. Assn., 1979-81. Home and Office: 22 Bayview Ave Northport NY 11768

PACE, DORIS HESTER, town justice; Seneca Falls, N.Y., Mar. 9, 1912; d. Pierson and Jessie (Keane) Bell; B.S., Keuka Coll., 1932; m. Clifford E. Pace, Aug. 17, 1964; children from previous marriage—Mary Rosalind, Samuel Kepner, Cecilia Jane Nester. Owner, operator Nester Petroleum Co.; town justice, Torrey, N.Y. Republican. Episcopalian. Home: 1240 Rockhaven Beach Rd Dresden NY 14441

PACE, NORMA, assn. exec., economist; grad. Hunter Coll., 1941; grad. study Columbia U.; Ph.D. (hon.), Mich. Technol. U., Poly. Inst. N.Y., Cedar Crest Coll., Grove City Coll., CCNY. Staff, Econometric Inst.; with U.S. Economics Corp., bus. adv. cons. service, 1944-71, pres., dir., dir. research, 1969-71; v.p., dir. indsl. econs. Lionel D. Edie & Co., N.Y.C., 1971-73; sr. v.p. Am. Paper Inst.; asst. devel. visual aids for teaching econs. Columbia Visual Lab.; dir. Sears, Roebuck & Co., Sperry Corp., Minn. Mining and Mfg. Co., Milton Bradley Co., Vulcan Materials Co., ABC. Mem. adv. council Stanford U.; mem. Econ. Forum, Conf. Bd.; mem. econs. adv. bd. Columbia U. Grad. Sch. Bus.; trustee Com. for Econ. Devel.; mem. Pres.s Commn. on Employment Policy. Named to Hunter Coll. Hall of Fame, 1973. Address: Am Paper Inst 260 Madison Ave New York NY 10016

PACE, SHELIA DIANE, acctg. co. exec.; b. Marion, S.C., Aug. 15, 1955; d. Woodrow Edward and Bobbie Jean (Byrd) P.; B.S. in Bus. Adminstrn. summa cum laude, Coll. Charleston, 1977. Mgr., McKnight, Frampton, Buskirk and Co., C.P.A.s, Charleston, S.C., 1977—. Mem. Trident C. of C. Small Bus. Council, Charleston; team capt. United Way, Charleston. C.P.A., S.C. Mem. Am. Inst. C.P.A.s, S.C. Assn. C.P.A.s, Nat. Assn. Accts. Baptist. Office: 155 King St Charleston SC 29401

PACE, SHIRLEY LOVON, pvt. edn. adminstr.; b. Madison County, Tex., Oct. 7, 1950; d. Henry and Lillie Mae (Brown) Nealey; M.A., Southwestern U., 1974; m. Roy Pace, May 2, 1970; children—Julia, Sheretta. Pres., La Rochelle Acads., Houston, 1971—; exec. dir. Larochelle Community Devel. Inc., Houston, 1973—, La Rochelle Community Devel. Inc., Houston, 1980—; cons. bus. Mem. Civic Com., Houston, 19 —, pres., 1979-80. Named Outstanding Employer, 1980, 81. Mem. Nat. Assn. Female Execs., Tex. Lic. Child Care. Mem. Ch. of Christ. Club: Meadows Garden. Office: 2600 S Loop W Suite 250 Houston TX 77054

PACK, PHOEBE KATHERINE FINLEY, civic worker; b. Portland, Oreg., Feb. 2, 1907; d. William Lovell and Irene (Barnhart) Finley; student U. Calif., Berkeley, 1926-27; B.A., U. Oreg., 1930; m. Arthur Newton Pack, June 11, 1936; children—Charles Lathrop, Phoebe Irene. Layman referee Pima County Juvenile Ct., Tucson, 1958-71; patron Menninger Found., Topeka; mem. Alcoholism Council So. Ariz., 1960—; bd. dirs. Kress Nursing Sch., Tucson, 1957-67, Pima County Assn. for Mental Health, 1958—, Ariz. Assn. for Mental Health, Phoenix, 1963—, U. Ariz. Found., Casa de los Niños Crisis Nursery; co-founder Ariz.-Sonora Desert Mus., Tucson, 1975—, Ghost Ranch Found., N.Mex. bd. dirs. St. Mary's Hosp., Tucson, Tucson Urban League, Tucson YMCA Youth Found. Mem. Mt. Vernon Ladies Assn. Union (state vice regent, 1962—), Alpha Phi. Home: 8579 N Calle Tioga Tucson AZ 85704

PACKARD, BETTY JANE, mgmt. cons.; b. Indpls., Oct. 1, 1937; d. Raymond Roy and Juanita Doris (Copeland) Reed; B.A., Franklin (Ind.) Coll., 1967; m. Stephen M. Voris, Sept. 26, 1975; children by previous marriage—Lisa Lynn Packard Beaudry, James Russell Packard III. Reporter, Indpls. Star, 1955, Franklin Evening Star, 1955-57; dir. journalism Ben Davis High Sch., Indpls., 1967-69; editor nat. ins. trade mags. Research & Rev. Service Am., Inc., Indpls., 1969-75; pres. Packard Consulting, Speedway, Ind., 1975—; cons. life ins. tng. courses;

del. World Conf. Women Journalists, Seoul, Korea, 1978. Active numerous polit. and civic orgns., including Cystic Fibrosis Found., Heart Assn., Women's Polit. Caucus, Ind. Addiction Services Commn., Ind. Bus./Industry Project Bd., Dept. Mental Health; mem. vol. council Ft. Ord chpt. ARC and Dist. XII, ARC; lobbyist for women's rights; mem. Nat. Security Forum, 1975; bd. journalism trustees Franklin Coll. Recipient numerous awards including 63 Ind. Women's Press Club writing awards, 10 Nat. Fedn. Press Clubs writing awards, Adela Rogers St. John Honeycomb award as outstanding Ind. Woman in Journalism, 1975. Mem. Nat. Assn. Life Underwriters, Nat. Fedn. Press Women, World Assn. Women Writers, Nat. Women's Polit Caucus, Women in Communications, Nat. Press Club, Indpls. Press Club, AAUW. Republican. Mem. Christian Ch. (Disciples of Christ). Clubs: Order Eastern Star: Officers Wives (Ft. Ord, Calif.). Author: I Love You, 1975; When Someone Is Crying, 1976. Home: 252 Ardennes Circle Fort Ord CA 93941 Office: 4918 W 15th St Speedway IN 46224

PACKARD, RUTH MCCREA, social worker; b. Cashmere, Wash., May 3, 1920; d. Donald Preston and Maude Maggie Adelaide (Richardson) McCrea; B.A. magna cum laude, U. Puget Sound, 1942; M.S.W., U. Wash., 1964; m. Gail Vernard Packard, Aug. 8, 1944; children—Margaret, Mary, Martha, Melinda. Sr. social worker Long Beach (Calif.) Gen. Hosp., 1964-68, supr. M.S.W., 1970-81; supervising med. social worker Ranchos Los Amigos Hosp., Downey, Calif., 1968-69; supr. M.S.W. program, U. Oreg. Med. Sch., Portland, 1969-70; dir. Social Work div. Los Angeles County, Calif. Children's Services, 1981—; field instr. social work UCLA, 1972-73, U. So. Calif., 1973-74, Calif. State U., Long Beach, 1971-81. Lic. clin. social worker, Calif. Mem. Nat. Assn. Social Workers, Acad. Cert. Social Workers. Mem. Ch. of Religious Sci.

PACKER, MARQUERITE JUNE, assn. exec.; b. Seattle, Mar. 30, 1929; d. Frank Elizah and Susan Veronica (Grue) Thomas; student public schs., Seattle; m. George Albany Packer, Feb. 15, 1969; children—Edward Thomas Jones, Blake Reid Jones. Clk., Columbia br. Seattle Public Library, 1943-45, main br., 1946-54, in charge delinquent dept., 1950-54; clk., asst. librarian Puyallup (Wash.) Public Library, 1962-67; photo librarian Am. Plywood Assn., Tacoma, 1967-68, supr. central files, 1968-69, co-mgr. Records Center, 1969-74, records mgr., 1974—. Mem. edn. com., bd. dirs. Westop Credit Union, Tacoma, 1975—; active edn. groups United Meth. Ch., Puyallup, 1974—. Recipient Golden Acorn award PTA, 1969. Democrat. Club: Elks. Home: 15409 100th Ave E Puyallup WA 98373 Office: 7011 S 19th PO Box 11700 Tacoma WA 98411

PACKETT, JESSIE HILLYARD, assn. exec.; b. Balt., Jan. 15, 1918; d. Gardner Bennett and Mollie Harmon (Haines) Hillyard; student George Washington U., 1952-54, San Antonio Coll., 1978, Ball State U., 1979, Drake U., 1980. Sec., office mgr. Comml. Loan Co., Winchester, Va., 1936-44; sec. office mgr. Chain Belt Co., Washington and Phila., 1944-48; sec. to treas. George Washington U., Washington, 1948-53, asst. to treas., 1953-63, asst. dir. Office Fin. Aid, 1963-72; sec. Dairy Council Upper Chesapeake Bay, Towson, Md., 1972-73, communications coordinator, 1973—, sec. bd. dirs., 1973—. Mem. Nat. Fedn. Press Women (credentials dir. 1979-83), Md. Press Women (founder, 1st pres.), Md. Del. D.C. Press Assn., Nat. League Am. Pen Women (pres. Balt. chpt. 1981-83), Nat. Hist. Soc., Nat. Trust for Historic Preservation, Nat. Wildlife Fedn., Smithsonian Instn., Md. Center for Broadcasting, U.S. Olympic Soc., DAR, United Daus. of Confederacy, Beta Sigma Phi. Club: Towson. Home: 8 Club Rd Baltimore MD 21210 Office: 202 Carroll Bldg 8600 LaSalle Rd Towson MD 21204

PADBERG, HELEN SWAN, violinist; b. Shawnee, Okla., May 3, 1919; d. Frank Pusey and Birdie B. (Rudell) Swan; A.A., Stephens Coll., 1938; Mus.B., U. Okla., 1940; Mus.M., Northwestern U., 1941; student Jacques Gordon; m. Frank Padberg, Feb. 6, 1943; children—Frank, Kristen. Solo performances and concerts, 1932—; mem. faculty string quartet and symphony soloist Stephens Coll., 1937-38; violinist Oklahoma City Symphony Summer Concerts, 1940; soloist Northwestern U. Symphony, 1941; mem. and soloist USO Orch., 1941-44; violinist Nat. Orchestral Assn. and Am. Youth Orch., N.Y.C., 1944-46; tchr. strings Public Schs. Maywood (Ill.), 1946-47; asst. concertmaster West Suburban Symphony, Chgo., 1947-48; mem. Chgo. Women's Symphony, Chgo. Civic Orch. and chamber music groups, 1947-51; violinist Ark. String Trio, 1952-58; concertmaster Ark. Symphony and Little Rock Philharmonic, 1953-57, Marjorie Lawrence TV Series, Ark., 1953-54; pvt. tchr. violin, Little Rock, 1953-66; accompanist and performer on piano, harp. Pres., Ark. Med. Soc. Aux., 1962-63, historian, 1963—. Mem. Am. Harp Soc., Chgo. Harp Soc. (sec. 1979—), Am. Fedn. Musicians, Am. Opera Soc. (v.p. and program chmn. Chgo. chpt. 1981-82), Pi Kappa Lambda, Mu Phi Epsilon, Pi Beta Phi (pres. Little Rock Alumnae Club). Presbyterian. Clubs: Aesthetic (pres. Little Rock); Woman's Athletic of Chgo. Home: 175 E Delaware Pl Chicago IL 60611

PADDOCK, SUSAN C., coll. adminstr.; b. Madison, Wis., Sept. 23, 1947; d. Robert H. and Elizabeth Isabelle (Church) P.; B.A., U. Wis., Madison, 1969; M.A.T., U. Mass., Amherst, 1971; Ph.D., (Mott Found. fellow), U. Oreg., 1977. Info. specialist U. Mass., Amherst, 1970-71; tchr. secondary schs. Atlantic City, 1971-74, Eugene, Oreg., 1974-76; research asso. U. Oreg., Eugene, 1976-77; research asso. Southwest Community Edn. Center, Ariz. State U., Tempe, 1977-81, dir. advanced govt. tng., 1981—, acting dir. staff devel. and tng. State of Ariz., 1982—. Mem. Neighborhood Exec. Com. Eugene, 1976, Rio Salado Commn., Tempe, 1981. U. Denver fellow, 1969-70; HEW grantee, 1980, 81. Mem. Nat. Community Edn. Assn. (chmn. com.), Ariz. Community Edn. Assn. (treas. 1978-80), Am. Ednl. Research Assn., Am. Assn. Sch. Adminstrs., Am. Soc. Tng. and Devel., Am. Soc. Public Adminstrn. Democrat. Presbyterian. Author: Management Implications of Team Teaching, 1977; Planning Handbook, 1980; Process Evaluation, 1980; editor JEEL, 1980-83; research editor CE Jour., 1980—. Office: Wilson Hall Ariz State U Tempe AZ 85287

PADFIELD, MARIANNE NINA, psychologist; b. New Haven, Nov. 14, 1930; d. Arthur B. and Evelyn L. (Mettel) Carter; student San Diego State U., 1948-50; B.A. with distinction, Ariz. State U., 1952; M.Ed., U. Ariz., 1970, Ph.D., 1975; children—Charisse, Ravena, Jesse. Tchr., Nat. City (Calif.) Jr. High Sch., 1952-54; co-dir. St. Francis Boys' Home, Salina, Kans., 1954-55; program dir. Pima and Pinal counties Ariz. Migrant Ministry, 1956-62; tchr. Laguna (Ariz.) Elem. Sch., 1962-64, Spring Jt. High Sch., Tucson, 1964-69; recreation therapist Mathari Valley Mental Hosp., Kenya, Africa, 1970-71; tchr. Western Ch. Leadership Sch., Oreg. State U., 1974-76; pvt. practice clin. psychology, Corvallis, Oreg., 1975—; mem. faculty div. humanities and social services Linn-Benton Community Coll., 1976—; affiliate mem. med. staff Good Samaritan Hosp., Corvallis, Albany (Oreg.) Gen. Hosp.; chmn. Linn-Benton Treatment Com. on Sexual Abuse in Family Environment; mem. ad hoc com. oral exams. Bd. Psychol. Examiners, State of Oreg. Recipient Social Sci. award Chi Omega, 1952; lic. psychologist, Oreg. Mem. Am. Personnel and Guidance Assn., Am. Psychol. Assn., Oreg. Psychol. Assn., Benton County Med. Assn., Am. Assn. Sex Educators, Counselors and Therapists, Benton County Mental Health Assn., Assn. Advancement Psychology, Oreg. Acad. Profl. Psychologists, Pi Lambda Theta, Kappa Delta Pi. Democrat. Episcopalian. Clubs: Altrusa, Corvallis, Women of Moose. Office: 548 SW 3d St Corvallis OR 97330

PADGETT, RUTH ELIZABETH MONTEITH, nurse; b. Hartford, May 13, 1946; d. Robert Birdsall and Ruth Mavis (Gosselin) Monteith; B.S. in Nursing, U. Vt., 1968; M.S. candidate Troy State U.; m. Thomas Goodwin Brown, Dec. 31, 1968 (div.); children—Catherine Elizabeth, Matthew Thomas; m. 2d, Garland Padgett, Jr., Mar. 1978; children—Eric Christopher, Michael West. Pediatric staff nurse Meml. Hosp., Colorado Springs, 1968; instr. practical nursing Robeson Tech. Inst., N.C., 1969-70; staff nurse Providence Hosp., Anchorage, 1970-72; staff and charge nurse spl. care unit Tacoma (Wash.) Gen. Hosp., 1973; patient care coordinator rehab. Good Samaritan Hosp., Puyallup, Wash., 1973-75; clin. project coordinator research U. Ark., Little Rock, 1976-78; instr. practical nursing, Tucson, 1978-79; coordinator nursing home, Las Vegas, 1980; supr. St. Rose de Lima Hosp., Henderson, Nev., 1981; vis. nurse Mid South Home Health Agy., Montgomery, Ala. Mem. Kappa Delta Pi, Gamma Beta Phi. Lutheran.

PADNOS, DONNA MOTEL, hosp. adminstr.; b. Chgo., Oct. 12, 1941; d. Sidney Benjamin and Beatrice (Sachs) Motel; B.S., U. Ill., 1962, M.S., 1978; M.B.A., U. Chgo., 1982; m. Richard D. Padnos, Aug. 27, 1961; children—Stephen, Beth, Gerald. Teaching asst., research asst. U. Ill., Chgo., 1973-77; pediatric research technician Michael Reese Med. Center, Chgo., 1977-80, adminstrv. asst., 1980—. Membership chmn. LWV, Chgo., 1969-70, land use chmn., 1971-73, health care com. mem., 1978—. Mem. Chgo. Health Execs. Forum, Ill. Soc. Anesthesiologists (exec. sec. 1981—), Women's Health Exec. Network. Contbr. articles to profl. jours. Home: 4741 S Kimbark Ave Chicago IL 60615 Office: 29th St and Ellis Ave Chicago IL 60616

PAFFENROTH, SANDRA LEA, oil co. public affairs writer; b. Cleve., June 14, 1947; d. Herman E. and Janet M. (Friedrich) P.; A.A.S., City U. N.Y., 1968; student U. Wis., Oshkosh, 1965-67; B.S., Northwestern U., 1975. Polit. research analyst Bus. Econs., Chgo., 1969-70; editor spl. publs., speech writer Standard Oil Co. (Ind.), Chgo., 1970—; lectr. speechwriting skills and careers in corp. communications. Recipient Leadership award Met. Chgo. YWCA, 1976. Home: 247 E Chestnut St Chicago IL 60611 Office: 200 E Randolph Dr Chicago IL 60601

PAGE, ABBIE COLLINGWOOD, energy cons.; b. N.Y.C., Oct. 10, 1942; d. Albert Edward and Beatrice Cuthbert (Collingwood) Miller; B.S. in Chemistry, Brown U., 1964; M.S. in Biology, Purdue U., 1969; m. David S. Page, Sept. 30, 1964; children—David C., Vivian W.; m. 2d, Michael A. McMillen, Feb. 14, 1980. Environ. cons. and farmer, 1971-73; resource planner, Maine Planning Office, 1973-75; dir. Maine Energy Office, 1975-77; mem. tech. staff MITRE Corp., Bedford, Mass., 1977-78, group leader regional energy systems, 1978-81; project mgr. Weston Designers/Cons., 1981—; Mem. New Eng. Energy Facility Siting Task Force; corp. asso. Resource Policy Center, Dartmouth Coll. Founder, Lafayette (Ind.) Environ. Action Fedn., 1969; founder, sec., v.p. farming Maine Organic Farmers and Gardeners Assn., 1971-72; mem. Androscoggin Valley (Maine) Regional Planning Commn., 1972-74; chmn. Poland (Maine) Planning Bd., 1973-74. David Ross grad. research fellow, 1966. Mem. AAAS, Nat. Assn. Female. Execs., New Eng. Energy Congress. Contbr. articles to profl. publs. Office: Weston Inc 111 S Bedford St Suite 206 Burlington MA 01803

PAGE, HELEN MAE HAMMER (MRS. MARIUS CURT PAGE, JR.), sales person; b. Scales Mound., Ill., Nov. 20, 1941; d. Elmer George and Margaret (Kendall) Hammer; grad. St. Mary's Sch. Radiologic Tech., 1961; student music U. Wis. at Sauk County campus; m. Marius Curt Page, Jr., Sept. 22, 1962; children—Michael Charles, Robin Joan. Asst. to chief technologist St. Mary's Ringling Hosp., Baraboo, Wis., 1961-62, chief technologist, 1962, asst. to chief technologist St. Clare's Hosp., Baraboo, Wis., 1963-65; radiologist Med. Assos. Baraboo, 1968—; advt. rep. Baraboo News Pub. Co., Lavine Media, Inc., 1972—; salesperson Glacier Valley Ford-Mercury-Subaru, Inc., Baraboo. Observer Ontario Cancer Found., Ottawa, Ont., Can., 1961. Ward co-chmn. St. Mary's Ringling Manor Bldg. Fund, 1967; dir. St. Joseph's Guitar Choir; asst. treas. Sauk County Assn. for Mental Health, 1966—; mem. St. Joseph's Parish Council, 1976-79, chmn. ecumenical commn., 1977-79. Mem. Am. Registry of Radiologic Technologists, Am., Wis. socs. radiologic technologists. Roman Catholic (v.p., program chmn. Our Lady of Grace Sodality, pres. 1969). Club: Baraboo Country (asst. handicap chmn. 1968—). Contbr. articles to profl. jours. Home: 1009 3d St Baraboo WI 53913 Office: 615 South Blvd Baraboo WI 53913

PAGE, JANE BICKERTON, audiologist; b. Bklyn., Mar. 9, 1941; d. Cornelius Edward and Jean Ann (Meehan) Bickerton; A.B., Hunter Coll., 1962; M.S., U. Mich., 1964; m. John McCue Page, Sept. 3, 1966; children—Ann Jennifer, Matthew John. Audiologist, A.J. Woodring, M.D., Bryn Mawr, Pa., 1974-75; audiologist ENT Assos. Lehigh Valley, Allentown, Pa., 1975-76; audiologist, speech pathologist Lehigh Valley Soc. Crippled Children and Adults, Bethlehem, Pa., 1976—. Bd. dirs. Whitehall Twp. Public Library, 1977—, treas., 1977-78, v.p., 1978-80, pres., 1980-82. Mem. Am. Speech, Lang., and Hearing Assn. (cert. in clin. competence in speech/audiology). Roman Catholic. Home: 325 7th St Whitehall PA 18052 Office: 2200 Industrial Dr Bethlehem PA 18017

PAGE, JANET LOUISE, accountant; b. Monterey Park, Calif., Feb. 4, 1944; d. John Lester and Maxine (Clift) P.; B.S., Brigham Young U., 1966. Auditor, Peat, Marwick, Mitchell & Co., Los Angeles, 1966-71; controller H.F. Ahmanson & Co., Los Angeles, 1971-74, dir. internal audit, 1974-81, v.p., controller, 1981—. C.P.A., Calif. Mem. Am. Inst. C.P.A.s, Am. Mgmt. Assn., Calif. Soc. C.P.A.s. Republican. Mormon. Office: 3731 Wilshire Blvd Suite 640 Los Angeles CA 90010

PAGE, MARTHA POITEVIN, editor, publisher; b. Idaho Falls, Idaho, May 24, 1948; d. John Joseph and Doris Clare (Gregory) P.; student U. Idaho, 1965-66, Coll. San Mateo, 1967-68; B.A., U. Calif., Berkeley, 1970; m. Curtis Matthewson Page, Feb. 12, 1977; 1 dau., Allison Rose. News dir. Sta.-KSKI-AM, Hailey, Idaho, 1973-74; advt. sales mgr. Ketchum (Idaho) Tomorrow, 1974; founder, advt. sales Idaho Mountain Express weekly, Ketchum, 1974—, editor, 1977-80; pres. Express Publ. Inc., Ketchum, 1979—; editor, pub. L.A. Kid newspaper, 1981—. Mem. Ketchum City Council, 1974-77, pres., 1976-77; mem. Blaine County Planning and Zoning Commn., 1974-75. Democrat. Presbyterian. Home: 19955 Lanark St Canoga Park CA 91306 Office: PO Box 1013 Ketchum ID 83340

PAGE, RUTH, dancer; b. Indpls.; d. Lafayette and Marian (Heinly) Page; student Tudor Hall, Indpls., N.Y.C. L.H.D., DePaul U., 1980, Ind. U., 1981; m. Thomas Hart Fisher, Feb. 8, 1925 (dec.). Dancer with Pavlowa at age of 15; performed in leading role of J. Alden Carpenter's The Birthday of the Infanta, produced by Chgo. Opera Co., 1919, later in N.Y.C.; toured U.S. as prin. dancer with Adolph Bolm's Ballet, later appeared in London with Mr. Bolm; premiere danseuse 2d Music Box Revue, N.Y.C., 1921-23, Chgo. Allied Arts performances, 1924, 25, 26; studied under Enrico Cecchetti at Monte Carlo, 1925; premiere danseuse Mcpl. Opera Co., Buenos Aires, Ravinia Opera Co., 1926-31; guest soloist with Met. Opera Co., 1926-28; guest artist at enthronement ceremonies for Emperor Hirohito, Japan, 1928; performed series of Am. dances before Sophil Soc., Moscow, 1930; ballet dir. Chgo. Opera 1934-37, 42-43, 45; dir. Fed. Theatre Dance Project, Chgo., 1938-39; S. Am. tour with first dance group as co-dir. Page-Stone Ballet, 1940; guest choreographer with Bentley Stone, dancer Frankie and Johnny for Ballet Russe de Monte Carlo, 1945; guest choreographer, dancer The Bells for Ballet Russe de Monte Carlo, 1946, Billy Sunday, 1948; Impromptu au Bois, and Revanche, Les Ballets des Champs-Elysees, 1951, Royal Festival Ballet, Vilia, 1953; co-dir. Les Ballets Americains, Theatre des Champs Elysees, Paris, 1950; ballet mistress Chgo. Lyric Opera, 1954-69; choreographer, dir. Ruth Page's Chgo. Opera Ballet, 1956-66, Ruth Page's Internat. Ballet, 1966-70; choreographer Merry Widow Ballet, 1956, Susanna and the Barber, 1957, Salome, 1957, Triumph of Chastity, 1958, El Amor Brujo, 1958, Camille, 1958, Carmen, 1959, Fledermaus, 1960, Concertino, 1961, Mefistofela, 1962, Bullets or Bon-Bons, 1965, Nutcracker, 1965-81, Carmina Burana, 1966, Bolero, 1967, Dancer's Ritual, 1968, Alice in the Garden, 1970, also Alice in Wonderland and Alice Through the Looking Glass at Pitts. Ballet Theatre, 1971, Catulli Carmina, 1973, Chain of Fools, 1973, Alice in Wonderland, 1978, Frankie and Johnny (produced by Dance Theater of Harlem), Covent Garden, 1981, New York, 1982; lectr. tour Ruth Page's Invitation to the Dance, 1971-72. Recipient award Adult Council Greater Chgo., 1963; citation outstanding service Ballet Guild Chgo. Mem. Chgo. Nat. Assn. Dance Masters (hon.). Clubs: Arts, Friday, Racquet (Chgo.). Contbr. to mags. Address: Ruth Page Found Sch Dance 1016 N Dearborn St Chicago IL 60610

PAGE, SALLY JACQUELYN, univ. adminstr.; b. Saginaw, Mich., July 8, 1943; d. William Henry and Doris Effie (Knippel) P.; B.A., U. Iowa, 1965; M.B.A., So. Ill. U., 1973. Copy editor, C.V. Mosby Co., St. Louis, 1965-69; editorial cons. Editorial Assos., Edwardsville, Ill., 1969-70; research adminstr. So. Ill. U., 1970-74, asst. to pres., affirmative action officer, 1974-77; civil rights officer U. N.D., Grand Forks, 1977—, lectr. mgmt., 1978—, mem. women's equity com., 1980—, handicapped facilities com., 1981—. Pres., Pine to Prairie council Girl Scouts U.S.A., 1980—; mem. Grand Forks Civil Service Task Force; mem. employment com. Ill. Commn. on Status of Women, 1976-77; mem. Bicentennial Com. Edwardsville, 1976, Bikeway Task Force Edwardsville, 1975-77. Mem. AAUW (dir. Ill. 1975-77), Am. Assn. Affirmative Action, Soc. Research Adminstrs., M.B.A. Assn. Republican. Presbyterian. Home: 3121 Cherry St Grand Forks ND 58201 Office: Univ ND Grand Forks ND 58202

PAGE, SARA MARIE, social worker; b. Wheeling, W.Va., Oct. 25, 1940; d. Dominic R. and Josephine L. (Giardino) Page; B.A. cum laude, Muskingum Coll., 1963; M.S.W., Case Western Res. U., 1965; 1 dau., Eve Marie. Sr. psychiat. social worker Akron (Ohio) Child Guidance Center, 1965-71; chief social worker, children's unit Ga. Mental Health Inst., Atlanta, 1972-75, program dir., children's unit, 1975-77; pvt. practice psychiat. social work, Atlanta; field instr. grad. social work Western Res. U., U. Ga. Mem. Nat. Assn. Social Workers, Acad. Cert. Social Workers, Atlanta Mental Health Assn. Home: 5465 Mt Vernon Pkwy NW Atlanta GA 30327 Office: 6627 Vernon Woods Dr Atlanta GA 30327

PAGE-JONES, SUZANNE BERGER, fin./mgmt. cons.; b. Bklyn., Jan. 12, 1955; d. Robert Lee and Helene (Tice) Berger; B.S., U. Pa., 1976; postgrad. City U. N.Y., 1977-81. Fin. analyst Securities Industry Automation Corp., N.Y.C., 1977-79; EDP auditor Chem. Bank, N.Y.C., 1979-80; sr. staff analyst Ins. Services Office, N.Y.C., 1980-81; proprietor Witan Cons., Federal Way, Wash., 1981—. Mem. Nat. Assn. Female Execs., Assn. Women in Computing, AAUW, South Seattle Women's Bus. League. Office: Witan Cons PO Box 4804 Federal Way WA 98003

PAGELS, ELAINE HIESEY, historian of religion, educator; b. Palo Alto, Calif., Feb. 13, 1943; d. William McKinley and Louise Sophia (Boogaert) Hiesey; B.A., Stanford, 1954, M.A., 1965; Ph.D., Harvard, 1970; m. Heinz R. Pagels, June 7, 1969. Asst. prof. history of religion Barnard Coll., Columbia, 1970-74, from asso. prof. to prof., chairperson dept. religion, 1974-82; Harrison Spear Paine prof. religion Princeton U., 1982—. Nat. Endowment Humanities grantee, 1973; Mellon fellow Aspen Inst. Humanistic Studies, 1974, Hazen fellow, 1975; Rockefeller fellow, 1978-79; Guggenheim fellow, 1979—; MacArthur prize fellow, 1981—. Mem. Soc. Bibl. Lit., Am. Acad. Religion. Episcopalian. Club: Bibl. Theologians. Author: The Johannine Gospel in Gnostic Exegesis, 1973; The Gnostic Paul, 1975; The Gnostic Gospels, 1979.

PAGONES, MIA PAULA, educator; b. Poughkeepsie, N.Y., July 2, 1954; d. George L. and Stemi Pagones; B.A., Hartwick Coll., 1976; M.A., SUNY, New Paltz, 1980. Process operator IBM, East Fishkill, Hopewell Junction, N.Y., 1976-77; French/Spanish tchr. Arlington Central Sch. Dist., Poughkepsie, N.Y., 1977—. Mem. N.Y. State United Tchrs., N.Y. State Fgn. Lang. Tchrs. Greek Orthodox. Home: 146B Rhobella Dr Poughkeepsie NY 12603 Office: Arlington Middle Sch 5 Dutchess Turnpike Poughkeepsie NY 12603

PAGTAKHAN-SO, LEONOR, pediatrician, allergist; b. Philippines, June 28, 1941; d. Bartolome Reyes Pagtakhan and Rosario Salamanca; M.D., Manila Central U., 1965; m. Ojien Hwat So; children—Rosalinda Ann, Robert Emerson. Intern, Springfield (Mass.) Hosp., 1971, resident, 1972-73; house physician Northampton (Mass.) State Hosp., 1968-70; fellow in pediatrics St. Clare's Hosp., Schenectady, 1974-75; practice medicine specializing in pediatrics and allergy, Pikeville, Ky., 1975—. Diplomate Am. Bd. Pediatrics. Mem. AMA, Pike County Med. Soc., Ky. Med. Assn. Democrat. Roman Catholic. Address: Island Creek Med Bldg Box 2229 Pikeville KY 41501

PAIGE, RUTH ULLMANN, psychologist; b. Germany, May 4; came to U.S., 1938, naturalized, 1946; d. Adolf and Else (Heumann-Abraham) Ullmann; B.A., Bklyn. Coll., 1956; M.S. (scholar), CUNY, 1957; postgrad. U. Kans., Lawrence, 1957-60; Ph.D., U. Oreg., Eugene, 1978; m. Albert B. Paige, Mar. 20, 1954; children—David, Elizabeth, Rebecca. Teaching and research asst. counseling psychology U. Kans., 1957-58; sch. psychologist, Shawnee, Kans., 1958-59; remedial reading instr., also pvt. practice, Lawrence, 1957-63; psychologist Lawrence-Douglas County Mental Health Clinic, 1959-63; psychology research asst. Menninger Clinic, Topeka, 1963; psychology research asst. VA Hosp., Leavenworth, Kans., 1964-65; counselor Group Processes, Inc., Seattle, 1969-72; psychologist intern Snohomish County Mental Health Clinic, Everett, Wash., 1973-74, Highline-West Seattle Mental Health Center, 1974-75; dir. Counseling Center programs North Seattle Community Coll., 1979—; cons. family mediation King County Family Ct., 1978—; instr. Lane Community coll., 1972-73; vol. instr. U. Oreg., 1972-73; mem. affirmative action com. Bellevue Sch. Dist. Mem. Am. Psychol. Assn., Western Psychol. Assn., Wash. State Psychol. Assn. (pres. div. personal and human rights 1979), Assn. Women in Psychology, Counseling and Guidance Dirs. Assn. Wash. Community Colls. (pres. 1981-82), N.W. Family Therapy Inst. Contbr. articles to profl. jours. Home: 13436 NE 47th St Bellevue WA 98005 Office: 9600 College Way N Seattle WA 98103

PAINTER, CHARLOTTE LOUISE PORTER, glass products mfg. co. exec.; b. N.Y.C., Dec. 16, 1949; d. Ralph L. and Janet L. (Weaver) Porter; B.S., N.C. State U., 1971; M.S. in Indsl. Mgmt., Frostburg State Coll., 1975; m. Mar. 21, 1981. Student records coordinator Guilford Tech. Inst., Jamestown, N.C., 1971-73; shift supr. Corning Glass Works, Martinsburg, W.Va., 1973-77, buyer and purchasing agt., 1977—. Mem. Am. Prodn. and Inventory Control Soc., AAUW. Republican. Mem. Christian Ch. Home: Rt 7 904 Penn St Martinsburg WV 25401 Office: Corning Glass Works Route 11 South Martinsburg WV 25401

PAINTER, GENEVIEVE, clin. psychologist; b. Chgo., Sept. 5, 1919; d. Max and Amelia (Swartz) Berkowitz; B.S., U. Ill., 1963, M.S., 1964, Ed.D. (U.S. Office Edn. fellow), 1967; cert. in psychotherapy Alfred Adler Inst., Chgo., 1969; m. John Paul Painter, July 20, 1960 (dec.); children—Bruce Schneidman, Terry. Music tchr., Chgo., 1950-64; asst. prof. psychology U. Ill., Champaign, 1967-68; pvt. practice clin. psychology, Champaign, 1968-73, Honolulu, 1973—; founder, dir.

Family Edn. Assn., Champaign, 1967-73; instr. family counseling U. Hawaii, Honolulu, 1973-76; instr. on radio Hawaii Pacific Coll., 1975—; dir. Assos. for Human Devel., Honolulu, 1975—; cons. to schs. systems, Hawaii, 1974—; tchr. infant edn. dept. social medicine Hebrew U., Jerusalem, 1977; instr. U. Vt. Summer Sch., 1980. Chmn. profl. standards com. Family Edn. Centers Hawaii, 1974—. Mem. Am. Psychol. Assn., Hawaii Psychol. Assn., N. Am. Soc. Adlerian Psychology, Assn. for Humanistic Psychology, Nat. Registry for Health Providers in Psychology. Author: Infant Education, 1968; Teach Your Baby, 1971, 2d edit., 1982; ABC's for Baby, 1977; co-author: The Practical Parent, 1975; co-editor: Alfred Adler As We Remember Him, 1977. Home: 2333 Kapiolani Blvd Apt 3214 Honolulu HI 96826 Office: 750 Amana St Suite 205 Honolulu HI 96814

PAINTER, JANET MARIE (CARTE), banker; b. Carleston, W.Va., June 29, 1938; d. James Monroe and Breman Erlene (Means) Carte; student Marshall U., 1968; grad. Charleston Sch. Commerce, 1957, W.Va. Sch. Banking, 1979; m. Doyle Eugene Painter, Nov. 21, 1958; children—Leigh Ann, Lane Ashley, Leslie Amber. Title service rep. public relations Chesapeake and Potomac Tel. Co., Charleston, 1957-72; ops. officer, asst. cashier Citizens Nat. Bank, St. Albans, W.Va., 1975—. Past pres. St. Albans Jr. Women's Club; leader Girl Scouts U.S.; active Band Booster Club, Hayes Jr. High Sch., Athletic Boosters Hayes Jr. High Sch., PTO, Lakewood Elem. Sch. Home: 114 Heritage Dr St Albans WV 25177 Office: 603-613 MacCorkle Ave St Albans WV 25177

PAINTER, MARY ELLA, editor; b. Tulsa, July 15, 1920; d. Ernest Balf Parker and Maggie Mae (Renaud) P.; B.A., Oklahoma City U., 1943; postgrad. Columbia U., 1944; m. Charles J. Yarbrough, Apr. 7, 1946; children—Kirby John, Kevin Lee. Editorial asst., feature writer Office War Info., 1943-46; feature writer, news editor U.S. Dept. State, 1946-53; with USIA, Washington, 1953-78, editor of USIA World, 1967-78; with U.S. Internat. Communications Agy., Washington, 1978-80, editor USICA World, 1979-80; with Food Policy Center, Washington, 1981—; with World Hunger Yr., N.Y.C. and contbg. editor Food Monitor, 1981—. Recipient award for meritorious service USIA, 1964, spl. commendation, 1974, Dir.'s award for outstanding creativity Internat. Communications Agy., 1980. Mem. Women's Action Orgn., Am. Fgn. Service Assn., Assn. Am. Fgn. Service Women. Democrat. Baptist. Home: 12232 Quorn Ln Reston VA 22091 Office: 438 7th St SE Washington DC 20003 also 350 Broadway Suite 209 New York NY 10013

PAIR, JOYCE MORROW, educator; b. Newnan, Ga., July 1, 1931; d. Glenn Moore and Catherine McGee (Buchanan) Morrow; B.A., Ga. State U., 1973, M.A., 1975, Ph.D.; 1 dau., Vicki Lyn. With Chrysler Motors Corp., Atlanta, 1957-68; with Aetna Life Ins. Co., Atlanta, 1968-69; instr. English, DeKalb Community Coll., 1978—. Mem., Atlanta High Mus. Art. Recipient George M. Sparks Fellowship award, 1974. Mem. DeKalb Coll. Women's Profl. Assn., South Atlantic Modern Lang. Assn., Coll. English Assn. Democrat. Home: 464 Princeton Way NE Atlanta GA 30307 Office: 3251 Panthersville Rd Decatur GA 30034

PAIS, CLAUDETTE RACHEL, horse-racing cons.; b. Timmins, Ont., Can., Aug. 11, 1941; came to U.S., 1962, naturalized, 1975; d. Patrick Xavier and Jeannette Marie (Labelle) Bigras; student U. Toronto, 1959-61, extension courses UCLA, 1981; m. Alfred Frank Pais, May 5, 1965; children—Louise, Frank. Co-owner Pais Properties, Santa Monica, Calif., 1965—; founding pres. Golden Bear Raceway, Sacramento, 1975-76, Standardbred Owners Calif., Santa Monica, 1977-78; organizer stockholder relations Hollywood Park, Inc., Inglewood, Calif., 1978-82; mem. Calif. Horse Racing Bd. Com. and Subcom. Off-Track Wagering Calif., 1975—. Mem. citizens adv. com. City Santa Monica, 1976; commr. Parks and Recreation, City Santa Monica, 1977-79; dir., sec. Girls Club Santa Monica Bay Area, Inc., 1978-80; asso. Pepperdine U., 1980—; bd. dirs. Santa Monica Coll. Assos., 1982—; vol., cons. polit. campaigns. Recipient award City of Santa Monica, 1977, 79; named Ky. Col. Mem. Nat. Cowboy Hall Fame. Clubs: Santa Monica Republican (life). Home: 1115 14th St Suite 306 Santa Monica CA 90403 Office: 1400 California Ave Santa Monica CA 90403

PALACIOS, VICTORIA JEAN, educator; b. Standardville, Utah, Sept. 5, 1947; d. Joseph and Mary Isaura (Martinez) P.; student Weber State Coll., 1970-72; student U. Utah, 1972-74; J.D., U. Nebr., 1975; m. Robert LeRoy Johnson, July 30, 1966 (dec.); children—Trisha, Jessica. Teaching asst. Council Legal Edn. Opportunity, U.N. Mex., 1974; tutor Law Sch., U. Utah, Salt Lake City, 1972-73, lectr., dir. spl. programs, 1977-79, asso. prof. law, 1979—; Hastie fellow U. Wis., Madison, 1975-77; temporary hearing examiner EEO, Washington, 1977-79, Utah State Personnel Review Bd., 1979-81. Mem. Utah State Bd. Pardons, 1980—. Mem. Am. Correctional Assn., Utah Prison Assn. Democrat. Roman Catholic. Home: 1140 Laird Ave Salt Lake City UT 84105 Office: University of Utah College of Law Salt Lake City UT 84112

PALADINO, JEANNETTE E., advt./pub. relations exec.; b. Bklyn.; d. Albert E. and Jennie Paladino; B.A., Hofstra U., 1962; m. Charles Antin, June 5, 1976. Reporter, L.I. Comml. Rev., 1961-63; pub. relations account supr. Batten, Barton, Durstine & Osborn, Inc., 1963-68; pub. relations dir./advt. account exec. Warwick, Welsh & Miller, Inc., 1968-72; pub. relations officer Econ. Devel. Adminstrn. Commonwealth P.R., N.Y.C., 1972-76; pub. relations mgr. Anaconda Co., N.Y.C., 1976-78; sr. v.p. corp. communications Marsh & McLennan, Inc., N.Y.C., 1978—. Recipient Matrix award N.Y. Women in Communications, 1982. Mem. Internat. Radio and TV Soc., N.Y. Women in Communications, Pub. Relations Soc. Am. Office: 1221 Ave of the Americas New York NY 10020

PALAPIS, MARTHA MARCELLA, mfg. co. exec.; b. Waterbury, Conn., Aug. 30, 1924; d. Peter Phillip and Magdalene (Tamosaitis) P.; student Coll. Advanced Traffic of Chgo., 1975-76. Owner, operator Palapis Smoke Shop, Waterbury, Conn., 1956-62; with Timex Corp., Waterbury, 1966—, supr. freight rates, 1978—. Mem. Am. Soc. Notaries, Postal Commemorative Soc., Internat. Platform Assn., Am. Collectors Club, Nat. Audubon Soc. Clubs: Rosicrucian Order. Home: 99 Cherry Ave Watertown CT 06795 Office: PO Box 2126 Waterbury CT 06720

PALASZEWSKI, RUTH, computer scientist, educator; b. Clifton, N.J., Feb. 8, 1952; d. Joseph Stanley and Emma (Kratochvil) P.; B.A. in Humanities and Langs., Hofstra U., 1973, M.A. in Linguistics, N.Y. U., 1977, Ph.D., 1983. Systems mgr. Predex Corp. N.Y.C. 1977—; adj. asst. prof. data processing City U. N.Y. 1977-79, asst. prof. 1978-79, research assoc. Research Found. 1977-78; instr. computer sci. Boston Coll. 1979—; v.p. Green Turtle Corp. N.Y.C. 1981-82; cons. C.S.P. Electronics N.Y.C.; dir. Internat. Computer Systems and Services Boston. Mem. Assn. Computing Machinery, IEEE, Linguistic Soc. Am., North-East Linguistics Soc., N.Y. Acad. Sci., Assn. Computational Linguistics, Acoustics Speech and Signal Processing Soc., Info. Theory Soc. Club: Cornell. Home: 334 Beacon St Boston MA 02116 Office: 1345 Ave of the Americas New York NY 10019

PALEY, GRACE, author; b. N.Y.C., Dec. 11, 1922; d. Isaac and Mary (Ridnyik) Goodside; ed. Hunder Coll., N.Y. U.; m. Jess Paley, June 20, 1942; children—Nora, Dan; m. 2d, Robert Nichols. Formerly tchr. Columbia Syracuse U.; now mem. lit. faculty Sarah Lawrence Coll. Sec., N.Y. Greenwich Village Peace Center. Recipient Lit. award for short story writing Nat. Inst. Arts and Letters, 1970; Guggenheim fellow. Mem. Acad. Am. Letters. Author short stories: The Little Disturbances of Man, 1959; Enormous Changes at the Last Minute, 1975; stories pub. in Atlantic, Esquire, Ikon, Genesis West, Accent, New Yorker, others. Home: 126 W 11th St New York NY 10011 Office: Sarah Lawrence Coll Bronxville NY 10708

PALLADINO, LUCY JO, psychologist; b. N.Y.C., Oct. 13, 1950; d. John Michael and Lucy Nancy (Caravella) P.; B.S., Fordham U., 1972; M.A., Ariz. State U., 1975, Ph.D., 1978; m. Arthur Achilles Cormano, July 1, 1979. Tchr. math. public schs., N.Y.C., 1971-73; research asst. Ariz. State U., 1973-74; research asso. Ariz. State Hosp., Phoenix, 1974; clin. psychology intern Good Samaritan Hosp., Phoenix, 1974-76, 77-78; clin. psychology fellow Southwestern Med. Sch., 1976-77; pvt. practice clin. psychology, Tucson, 1978—; lectr. U. Ariz. Med. Sch., 1979—. Mem. Am. Psychol. Assn., Am. Congress Rehab. Medicine, Biofeedback Soc. Am., Soc. Psychol. Study Social Issues, Ariz. State Psychol. Assn., So. Ariz. Psychol. Assn., Phi Beta Kappa. Editorial asst. Rehab. Psychology, 1975-78. Home: 6502 East Calle Altair Tucson AZ 85710 Office: 2221 E Broadway Suite 200 Tucson AZ 85719

PALLASCH, MAGDALENA HELENA (MRS. BERNHARD MICHAEL PALLASCH), artist; b. Chgo., Sept. 6; d. Frank and Anna (Meier) Fixari; student Chgo. Acad. Fine Arts, 1922-26, Am. Acad. Fine Arts, 1926-30, U. Chgo., 1960, Art Inst. Chgo.; pvt. study with Joseph Allworthy, 1935-38; m. Bernhard Pallasch, Nov. 26, 1931; children—Bernhard Michael, Diana Pallasch Miller. Contbr. two murals and ten life size figures for Century of Progress Exhbn., Chgo., 1933-34; free-lance portrait artist, Chgo., 1958—; represented in permanent collections Loyola U., Chgo., Barat Coll., Lake Forest, Ill., Internat. Coll. Surgeons, Chgo., Columbus Hosp. Med. Library, Chgo. Roman Cath. Archdiocese Office, Cardinal Newman Coll., St. Louis. Mem. Presentation Ball Aux.; mem. President's Club, Loyola U., also mem. women's bd., permanent mem. bd. dirs. Parents Assn. Recipient first award for still life, Arts Club, N.Y.C., 1960; First award, Washington, D.C. Nat. League of Am. Pen Women, 1972; 1st place and best of show State Exhibit, Springfield, Ill., 1973; 1st award Chgo. Womans Club, 1978. Mem. Nat. League of Am. Pen Women (v.p. Chgo. branch 1966-68, art chmn. 1978-80, Margaret Dingle Meml. award 1979), Friends of Austria, Friends of D'Arcy Gallery of Medieval and Renaissance Art, Am. Soc. Arts and Letters, Cenacle. Clubs: Illinois Club for Cath. Women (gov. 1979—), Cuneo Meml. Hosp. Aux. (bd. mem.), Fidelitas (bd. mem.). Home and studio: 723 Junior Terr Chicago IL 60613

PALMATIER, MARION BABILLA, dispatcher; b. Gary, Ind., Nov. 18, 1925; d. Sam L. and Theresa Marie Babilla; student Ind. U., 1944-46, Western Ky. State Tchrs. Coll., 1946, Western Mich. Coll., 1946-47; m. Robert A. Palmatier, Dec. 21, 1946; children—David Eugene, Denise Marie. Receptionist, switchboard operator Progressive Welder, Vicksburg, Mich., 1950-53; transp. clk. Western Mich. Univ., Kalamazoo, 1961-68, work order clk., radio dispatcher, 1968-73, cost and billing clk. phys. plant, 1973-75, sec., billing clk. communication and transp., 1975-77, dispatcher, 1977—. Mem. Adminstrv. Profl. Assn., Woman's Commn. Western Mich. U. Presbyterian. Home: 1326 Hardwick Kalamazoo MI 49002 Office: Physical Plant Oakland Dr Kalamazoo MI 49008

PALMER, ADA MARGARET, computer exec.; b. Arkansas City, Kans., Feb. 8, 1940; d. Mark Lloyd Palmer and Eunice Elizabeth (Thompson) Palmer Schnitzer; A.A., Colo. Woman's Coll., 1960; B.A., George Washington, U., 1962. Adv. sr. programmer Merrill Lynch, N.Y.C., 1969-72; systems analyst Tchrs. Ins. & Annuity, N.Y.C., 1972-77; systems specialist N.Y. Times, N.Y.C., 1977-81; mktg. dir. Applied Systems Resources, Inc., N.Y.C., 1981—. Vol. info. center, guide Met. Opera House, N.Y.C., 1975-79. Republican. Methodist. Home: 201 W 85th St Apt 11 A New York NY 10024 Office: 1133 Broadway St Suite 532 New York NY 10010

PALMER, BEVERLY BLAZEY, psychologist, educator; b. Cleve., Nov. 22, 1945; d. Lawrence Edwin and Mildred Marie Blazey; B.A. in Psychology, U. Mich., 1966; M.A. in Counseling Psychology, Ohio State U., 1969, Ph.D., 1972; m. Richard Cletus Palmer, June 24, 1967; 1 son, Ryan Richard. Research psychologist Health Services Research Center, UCLA, 1971-77; prof. dept. psychology Calif. State U., Dominguez Hills, Carson, 1973—; reviewer manuscripts coll. textbook pubs. Public health commr., Los Angeles, 1978-81. Mem. Am. Psychol. Assn., Am. Personnel and Guidance Assn., Assn. Humanistic Psychology. Contbr. articles in field to profl. jours. Office: Dept Psychology Calif State U Dominguez Hills Carson CA 90747

PALMER, KATHLEEN LEE, speech and lang. pathologist; b. Munich, W.Ger., June 18, 1951; d. Leland Harvard and Gertrude (Woelfel) P.; B.S. in Speech Pathology and Audiology, U. Tex., 1972; M.A., La. State U., 1974. Speech pathologist Speech Pathology Center, Baton Rouge, 1974-76; speech/lang. pathologist Speech, Hearing and Lang. Center, Tufts-New Eng. Med. Center Hosp., Boston, 1976-81, master speech/lang. pathologists, 1981—. coordinator communication disorders seminar series, 1978—. Mem. Am. Speech/Lang. and Hearing Assn. (cert. of clin. competence), Mass. Speech/Lang. and Hearing Assn., Boston Area Clin. Aphasiology Group. Asso. editor: News of Assn. Service Programs in Communicative Disorders, 1978—; mem. editorial staff Mass. Speech and Hearing Assn. Newsletter, 1977-79. Home: 86 Marlbourgh St Boston MA 02116 Office: 185 Harrison Ave Boston MA 02111

PALMER, LILLI, actress; b. Posen, Germany, May 24, 1914; came U.S., 1945; d. Alfred Peiser and Rose Lismann Palmer; student Hohenrollern Gymnasium, Berlin, 1932; m. Rex. Harrison, Jan. 25, 1943 (div. Feb. 6, 1957); 1 son, Carey; m. 2d, Carlos Thompson, 1957. Plays include: Little Ladyship, 1939; No Time for Comedy, 1940 (both Eng.), My Name is Aguilon, 1949; Cesar and Cleopatra, 1950; Bell, Book and Candle, 1951 (all N.Y.C.); motion pictures include: Great Barrier, 1937, Thunderrock, 1942, Notorious Gentleman, 1944 (all Eng.), Cloak and Dagger, 1946; Body and Soul, 1947, The Four Poster, 1951; Main Street to Broadway: Is Anna Anderson Anastasia?, 1956, But Not For Me, 1959, Conspiracy of Hearts, 1960, Counterfeit Traitor, 1962, The Pleasure of His Company, 1961, Adorable Julia, 1964, The Flight of the White Stallions, 1964, The Great Spy Mission, Murders in the Rue Morgue, 1971, The House That Screamed, 1971, Lotte in Weimar, 1977, The Boys from Brazil, 1978; appeared in TV series Zoo Gang, 1975. Author: The Autobiography of Lilli Palmer, 1975; The Red Raven, 1978; A Time to Embrace, 1980. Office: care Macmillan Inc 866 3d Ave New York NY 10022 *

PALMER, (LLOYD) FERN, author, musician; b. Snyder, Okla., May 25, 1913; (d. George Monroe and Mabel Claire (Sammons) Martin; student Rio Hondo Coll., 1974-79; m. Eugene Earl Palmer, Jan. 18, 1936; children—Jean Joan, Gene Paul, Kim. Freelance writer of poetry, articles, and radio scripts, 1948—; books include: On This Rock: An Unconventional Interpretation of Jesus' Teachings Based on the Greek Language Rather Than the Aramaic Language, 1966; tchr. piano, Denver, 1934-39; pianist, composer, arranger, singer, Los Angeles, 1939—; public appearances include: Replier Bowl, Banning, 1973, women's clubs and lodges, Sacramento, 1975, 76, Eureka Springs, Ark., 1977, 78, Hartford, Conn., 1977, Chgo., 1979; pianist, singer Chico's, Lynwood, Calif., 1969—; composer 14 musical compositions, pop songs and westerns; lectr. writing, religion and human rights for TV, radio, clubs and schs., 1965—. Co-founder SE Los Angeles/Whittier chpt. NOW, pres., 1972-74, 76-78; bd. dirs. Women's and Children's Crisis Shelter, Inc., Whittier, 1977-78. Mem. Humanist Assn. Los Angeles. Club: Writers of Whittier (pres. 1976-78).

PALMER, MARILYN JOAN, educator; b. Mahoning County, Ohio, Mar. 3, 1933; d. Rudolph George and Marian Eleanor Wynn; phys. therapy cert. UCLA, 1954, B.S., 1955; M.A. in Philosophy, Ohio State U., 1969; postgrad. U. Okla., 1981—; m. Richard Palmer, Nov. 10, 1956 (div. 1972); children—Ricky, Larry, Kevin. Phys. therapist Neil Ave. Sch. for Handicapped, Columbus, Ohio, 1968-69; instr. philosophy Ohio State U., Columbus, 1969; instr. English, Youngstown (Ohio) State U., 1970-71; writer, editor The Economy Co., ednl. publs., Oklahoma City, 1977-81; grad. asst. in English, U. Okla., Norman, 1981—; free-lance editing and cons. Fund-raiser Easter Seal Soc., 1965-68; den mother coordinator Boy Scouts Am., 1966, 67. Dept. Energy grantee, 1976. Mem. AAUP, Am. Phys. Therapy Assn., Soc. for Women in Philosophy, Alpha Xi Delta. Editor: Kindergarten Keys Teacher's Guidebook, 1982, author parochial supplement, 1982. Office: 760 Van Fleet Oval Norman OK 73069

PALMER, PATRICIA TEXTER, educator; b. Detroit, June 10, 1932; d. Elmer Clinton and Helen (Rotchford) Texter; B.A., U. Mich., 1953; M.Ed., Nat. Coll. Edn., 1958; M.A., San Francisco State U., 1966; postgrad. Stanford U., 1968, Hayward State U., 1968-69; m. David Jean Palmer, June 4, 1955. Chmn. speech dept. Grosse Pointe (Mich.) Univ. Sch., 1953-55; tchr. South Margarita Sch., Panama, C.Z., 1955-56, Kipling Sch., Deerfield, Ill., 1956-57; chmn. Rio San Gabriel Sch., Downey, Calif., 1957-59; tchr. devel. reading, journalism advisor Roosevelt High Sch., Honolulu, 1959-62; tchr. English, speech, journalism advisor El Camino High Sch., South San Francisco, Calif., 1962-68; tchr., dept. chmn. English as a 2d lang. South San Francisco Unified Sch. Dist., 1968-81; dir. English as a 2d lang. Inst., Millbrae, Calif., 1978—; master tchr. for Calif. in English as 2d lang. Calif. Council Adult Edn., 1979-81. Precinct chmn. North San Mateo (Calif.) Republican Com., 1963-64, asst. div. chmn., 1963-64; mem. San Mateo County Aviation Com. Recipient Concours de Francais prix, 1947; Jeannette M. Liggett Meml. award for excellence in history, 1949; commendation for journalism Hawaii State Legislature, 1962. Mem. TESOL, Calif. Council Adult Edn., Calif. Tchrs. Assn., NEA, Internat. Platform Assn., U. Mich. Alumnae Assn., Nat. Coll. Edn. Alumnae Assn., Chi Omega. Republican. Roman Catholic. Home: 2917 Franciscan Ct San Carlos CA 94070 Office: 450 Chadbourne Ave Millbrae CA 94030

PALMER, RUTH A(LICE), govt. purchasing exec.; b. Houlton, Maine, Nov. 21, 1924; d. Orrin C. and Beatrice W. P.; student public schs., Houlton. With Vets. Canteen Service, VA, 1947—, chief, Northport, N.Y., 1971-75, buyer, Washington, 1975-80, asst. chief procurement, 1980—. Vol., Opportunity Shop, St. John's Ch., Bethesda, Md. Episcopalian. Home: 5480 Wisconsin Ave Chevy Chase MD 20815

PALMER, WINTHROP BUSHNELL, writer; b. N.Y.C., Sept. 14, 1899; d. Ericsson Foote and Bertha Tudor (Thompson) Bushnell; student Barnard Coll., Columbia U., N.Y. U.; Litt.D. (hon.), L.I. U., 1956; m. Carleton H. Palmer, Oct. 2, 1919; children—Carleton H., Lowell M. II (dec.), Winthrop (Mrs. James Boswell), Rosalind (Mrs. Henry G. Walter Jr.). Pres. Nat. Assn. Jr. Leagues Am., 1926-28; rep. New Eng. states Eleanor Roosevelt's Reporter Plan Com., 1932; asso. editor Dance News, N.Y.C., 1940; faculty English, C.W. Post Center, L.I.U., Brookville, N.Y., 1956-74; trustee L.I. U., 1969-74, chmn. bd. trustees, 1974-75, chmn. emerita, 1975—; lectr. in field. Mem. PEN, Poets and Writers, Poetry Soc. Am., Acad. Am. Poets, Joyce Soc., Alliance Française. Clubs: Piping Rock, Seawanhaka, Met. Author: Theatrical Dancing in America, 1945, rev. edit., 1978; The New Barbarian, 1951; Beat the Wind, 1960. Asso. editor Confrontation, 1973—. Home: 502 Centre Island Rd Oyster Bay NY 11771

PALMERI, LUCILLE, retail exec.; b. Bklyn., July 25, 1941; d. James I. and Laura (Miserandino) P.; B.F.A., Hunter Coll., N.Y.C., 1970. Personnel asst. Goldsmith Bros., N.Y.C., 1967-69; personnel mgr. Barney's, N.Y.C., 1969-70; personnel mgr. King's Plaza store Alexanders Dept. Stores, Bklyn., 1971-76; Washington metro personnel mgr. Zayre Corp., 1976—; instr. Kingsborough Community Coll., Bklyn., eves. 1974-75. Mem. Nat. Assn. Female Execs., Greater Washington Bd. Trade. Office: 7690 Richmond Hwy Alexandria VA 22306

PALMER-LITCHFIELD, BARBARA, counseling services adminstr.; b. Bklyn., Aug. 31, 1938; s. Harold Palmer and Elsie E. (De Peyster) Palmer Hatton; B.A., Bklyn. Coll., 1962; postgrad. Rutgers U., 1975; M.A., Goddard-Cambridge Inst., 1980; m. Joseph L. Litchfield, Apr. 18, 1975. Dir., Family Life Service Center, Bklyn., 1965-70; coordinator staff inservice Bklyn. Devel. Services, 1970-71, community services specialist, 1971-73; cons. John C. Corrigan Mental Health Center, Fall River, Mass., 1973-74; dir. Driving While Intoxicated Program, Cape Cod, Mass. and Islands, 1974-75; pvt. practice counseling, 1974-75; founder, pres. The Cape Shelter, Hyannis, Mass., 1976-79, Network of Women of Color in Therapeutic Community, 1981—; clin. dir. I Can Network, Somerville, Mass., 1980—; cons. to govt. agys., various bus. firms, 1976—. Bd. dirs. Third World Coalition, 1975—. Cert. Alcohol counselor, Mass.; lic. pvt. tchr., N.Y. Mem. Am. Personnel and Guidance Assn., Assn. Women in Psychology, Am. Black Psychologists Assn., Nat. Assn. Female Execs., Nat. Coalition Battered Women's Service Providers, AAU. Buddhist. Club: Hyannis Community. Home: 2 Adams Rd West Yarmouth MA 02673 Office: 32 Cogswell Ave Suite 2 Cambridge MA

PALMORE, MARY KATE, obstetrician and gynecologist; b. Chgo., July 24, 1952; d. Richard Eugene and Mary Kate (Mann) P.; B.A. in Biology, Hampton Inst., 1974; M.D., Rush Med. Coll., 1978. Community rep. Chgo. Dept. Human Resources, summers 1976, 76; resident in ob-gyn Presbyn.-St. Luke's Med. Center, Chgo., 1978-82, also adj. attending staff, instr. Rush Med. Coll., 1981-82; obstetrician and gynecologist Kaiser Permanente of Tex., Dallas, 1982—. Mem. Am. Med. Women's Assn., AMA, Nat. Med. Assn. Democrat. Mem. United Ch. of Christ. Office: 7777 Forest Ln Suite 2-333 Dallas TX 75230

PALUCKI, LOIS EILEEN, data processor; b. Los Angeles, Mar. 2, 1944; d. Robert Erest and Evelyn Nora (Frase) Hoyer; B.S., U. Wis., Madison, 1966; m. Drew Michael Palucki, June 12, 1976. Program analyst Allegheny Airlines, Washington, 1967-69; systems programer Kemper Ins. Co., Long Grove, Ill., 1969-72; tech. specialist A.G. Becker Co., Chgo., 1972-73; div. mgr., systems officer No. Trust Co., Chgo., requirements chmn. CME Project, SHARE, Inc. Mem. Computer Measurement Group, Surburban Aquarist Soc. (treas. 1980-81). Club: Order Eastern Star. Home: 1364 Court Tiburon Hanover Park IL 60103 Office: 125 S Wacker Dr Chicago IL 60675

PALUTIS, ANNETTE HELEN, educator; b. Scranton, Pa., Mar. 31, 1937; d. Alexander and Helen Talkevich; B.M., Marywood Coll., 1959; student U. Scranton, 1963-64, Pa. State U., 1970-71, Am. Acad. Dramatic Arts, 1974-75; m. Bernard Palutis, Jr., Nov. 26, 1960; 1 son, Alexander Joseph. Tchr. speech and drama and English, Scranton Sch. Dist., 1959—, dir. plays including Bye Bye Birdie, Oliver, Li'l Abner, Annie Get Your Gun, Gypsy, The Music Man, Wizard of Oz. Chmn., Lackawanna County Cancer Crusade, 1977-78; bd. dirs. Lackawanna County unit Am. Cancer Soc. Mem. Scranton Edn. Assn. (pres.), Pa. Edn. Assn. (dir.), NEA (legis. com.), Pa. Reading Assn., Scranton

Philharm. Soc., Friends of Scranton Public Library. Roman Catholic. Club: Scranton Women Tchrs. Home: 703 N Rebecca Ave Scranton PA 18504 Office: 1539 N Main Ave Scranton PA 18508

PALUZZI, JEANNE GERRITSEN, public relations counselor; b. Zeeland, Mich., Sept. 18, 1934; d. Gerrit John and Mary (Staal) Gerritsen; student Calvin Coll., Grand Rapids, Mich., 1952-53, Wayne State U., 1970-76; m. Rocco Paluzzi, Apr. 7, 1956 (div. Apr. 8, 1971); children—Jeanna Marie, Nicholas, Paul, Karen Adele. Asst. to dir. public affairs Smith Hinchman & Grylls, Inc., Detroit, 1972-73; co-mgr. public relations Albert Kahn Asso., Detroit, 1973-74; owner Jeanne Paluzzi & Co., Detroit, 1974-76; public relations exec. Young & Rubicam, Inc., Detroit, 1976-79; pres. JGP Public Relations, Inc., Detroit, 1979—; mem. Livonia Indsl. Devel. Commns. Bd. dirs. Met. Detroit YWCA; mem. Wayne 2d Dist. Republican Exec. Com., 1981-83; bd. dirs. Mich. Rep. Women's Task Force, 1982-84; mem. nat. adv. council SBA. Recipient Demmy award, 1976; United Found. award, 1977; SBA Women in Bus. Adv. of Yr., Mich. award, 1981. Mem. Public Relations Soc. Am. (accredited), Women In Communications (program chmn. nat. conv. 1978, chmn. fin. com. 1977-78, 1st v.p. Detroit chpt. 1978-79, v.p. chpt. public relations 1980-82), Nat. Assn. Women Bus. Owners (v.p. public relations Mich. chpt. 1980-82, pres. elect 1981, pres. 1982), Bus./Profl. Advt. Assn., Livonia C. of C. (dir. 1980-83, bus. and econ. devel. council). Clubs: Renaissance, Detroit Press, Women's Econ. of Detroit. Home and Office: 17315 Rougeway St Livonia MI 48152

PALZER, DORIS MAWHINNEY, home economist; b. Phila., May 17, 1925; d. John A. and Anne Evelyn (Gledhill) Mawhinney; B.S., Pa. State U., 1947; M.S., Cornell U., 1955; Ed.D., Temple U., 1978; m. E. Watson, Palzer, Apr. 27, 1957; children—Ellen Ann, Jeffrey Eric. Tchr. home econs. public schs., Phila., 1947-50, Neshaminy Sch. Dist., 1952-54, Pennsbury Sch. Dist., 1966-70, 73-74, Hopewell Valley Sch. Dist., Pennington, N.J., 1975-76; mem. faculty Glassboro (N.J.) State Coll., 1976—, chmn. dept. home econs., 1977—; chemist Kessler Chem. Co., Phila., 1950-51. Zeta Tau Alpha grantee, 1974-75; Glassboro State Coll. grantee. Mem. AAUW (rep., state parliamentarian Pa., pres. br., scholarship grant named in her honor), Am. Home Econs. Assn., N.J. Home Econs. Assn., Am. Vocat. Assn., N.J. Vocat. Edn. Assn., Nat. Council Adminstrs. Home Econs., Nat Assn. Parliamentarians, Pa. State U. Alumni Assn., Cornell U. Alumni Assn., Phi Delta Kappa, Kappa Omicron Phi, Zeta Tau Alpha. Home: 909 Fernwood Rd Moorestown NJ 08057 Office: Dept Home Econs Glassboro State Coll Glassboro NJ 08028

PANEHAL, FRANCINE MARY, state legislator; b. Cleve., Oct. 10, 1925; d. James Francis and Georgia Mary (Beyer) McAllister; B.A., Ursuline Coll., H.H.D. (hon.), 1979; m. Robert Panehal, 1948; children—Kathleen, Elise, Alexandria, Robert, Georgiana. Mem. Ohio Ho. of Reps., Dist. 5, 1975—, majority whip. Mem. Cleve. City Planning Commn., 1966-71; councilman Ward 1, Cleve., 1972; exec. com., cabinet Cuyahoga County Dem. Party; pres. Ward 1 Dem. Club; 1st v.p. Cleve. LWV; active Cuyahoga County Women's Polit. Caucus, Women Space. Named Outstanding Legislator, Ohio Nurses Assn., Ohio Regional Council on Alcoholism, Ohio Peri-Natal Assn., Ohio Women's Polit. Caucus, 1979, 80, Ohio Regional Tourist Authority. Roman Catholic. Clubs: W. Side Irish Am., Slovak Radio. Office: State House Columbus OH 42315

PANEK, JERI HERNDON, computer/public relations exec.; b. Salt Lake City, June 15, 1939; d. Norman C. and Geraldine E. (Griffin) Herndon; ed. U. Utah; m. Larry H. Panek, Sept. 20, 1958 (div.); 1 son, Brad. Public relations asst. Univac, Salt Lake City, 1961-69; dir. communications U. Utah, Salt Lake City, 1969-73; coordinator communications Sperry-Univac, Salt Lake City, 1973-74; electronic data processing communications coordinator Singer Bus. Machines Internat. Div., Brussels, Belgium, 1974-76; public relations and corp. planning mgr. Beehive Internat., Salt Lake City, 1977-80; program mgr., sales rep. Digistar computer graphics Evans & Sutherland Computer Corp., Salt Lake City, 1980—. Mem. Public Relations Soc. Am. (chmn. membership com., editor newsletter, chpt. treas. 1968—, v.p., immediate pas pres.), Assn. Computing Machinery (mem. conf. and symposia com. 1972-74), Internat. Planetarium Soc., Planetarium Assn. Can., C. of C. (aviation com.). Home: 471 Harrison St Midvale UT 84047 Office: 580 Arapeen Dr Salt Lake City UT 84108

PANEK, MARGARET MILDRED MARY, collection agy. exec.; b. Elizabeth, N.J., Feb. 20, 1944; d. Roy R. and Margaret Concetta (Clemintone) Lenois; student Middlesex County Coll., Edison, N.J., 1973—; m. Richard William Panek, Nov. 18, 1961; children—Richard John, Gary William, Robert Roy, William Dominic. Asst., Dr. Fermin Ano, Daytona Beach, Fla., 1974-75; asst. Dr. Jon Mandell, Edison, N.J., 1976-78; exec. sec. N.J. Movers Tariff Bur., Highland Park, 1976-77; sec. Nissan Motor Corp., Piscataway, N.J., 1978; support sec. AT & T Long Lines, Bedminster, N.J., 1978-79; fin. sec. Drs. Portnoff and Sklar, Edison, N.J., 1979; owner mgr. East Coast Collection Service, Edison, 1979-80; owner, mgr. East Coast Counseling Service, Edison, 1979-80; pres. Lenois Enterprises, Edison, 1980—; lectr. in field. Mem. Internat. Toastmasters Assn. Republican. Roman Catholic. Contbr. articles in field. Home: 71 Union Ave Edison NJ 08817

PANKEY, VIVIAN WHITESIDE, nurse; b. Cameron, Tex.; d. Albert and Paraline (Woodward) Whiteside; B.S. in Nursing, Incarnate Word Coll., 1968; Family Nurse Practitioner, U. Tex., 1975; m. Cecil Yancey, Aug. 9, 1950 (div. 1971); children—Cecil, Clark; m. 2d, Franzell Pankey, Sept. 1, 1979. Dir. nurses Iglehart Nursing Home, San Antonio, 1968-75; family nurse practitioner Audie Murphy VA Hosp., San Antonio, 1975—; Black program mgr., 1980-81. Mem. San Antonio Citizens for Justice. Mem. Blacks in Govt., Black Council Fed. Employees of San Antonio, Am. Heart Assn., Am. Nurses Assn., Family Nurse Practitioner Assn. Club: Lackland Air Force Base Officers. Home: 6136 Stirrup Ln San Antonio TX 78240 Office: 7400 Merton Minter Suite 118 San Antonio TX 78284

PANKIW, HALYNA (HANNA CHERIN), librarian, writer; b. Ukraine, Apr. 29, 1924; d. Ivan and Iuliia (Levycka) Hrybinsky; came to U.S., 1949, naturalized, 1959; M.A. in Linguistics, U. Chgo., 1953, M.A. in L.S., 1966; m. Stephan Pankiw, July 21, 1957; 1 dau., Inna. Asst. Slavic librarian U. Chgo. Library, 1967—; editor children's dept. Our Life, 1963-66, Ind. Ukraine, 1974—. Recipient Mary V. Beck Lit. Competition, 1962, 65, 68, 71, 73, 81, 1st prize Internat. Competition for Children's Story, 1979. Mem. Ukrainian Writers Assn., Slovo, Assn. Ukrainian Librarians, Ukrainian Gold Cross. Ukrainian Orthodox Ch. Author 19 books including: Chornozem (poems), 1962; Id'mo zi mnoiu (travelog), 1965; Nebesni virshi (poems), 1970; Khytra Makitra (stories), 1974; Slova (novel in verse), 1980. Contbr. numerous articles to various publs. Office: Library U Chgo 1100 E 57th St Chicago IL 60637

PANOZZO, DIANE JEAN, bus. exec.; b. Chgo., Dec. 16, 1937; d. Anthony Muffy and Genevieve Phyllis (Coffero) P.; B.A., Coll. St. Francis, Joliet, Ill., 1959. Mgr., Variety Personnel Service, Chgo., 1959-71; adminstrv. asst. Finn. Industries div. Potlatch Forests, Inc., Chgo., 1971-72; exec. asst. to chmn., pres. Chemetron Corp., Chgo., 1972-79; adminstrv. asst. Price Waterhouse & Co., Chgo., 1979-80; adminstrv. sec. Chgo. Sch. Fin. Authority, 1980-81; exec. asst. to chmn. Telemedia, Inc., Chgo., 1981—; v.p. fin. Jonpir, Inc., Hinsdale, Ill., 1981—. Mem. Nat. Assn. Female Execs. Club: Executives (Chgo.). Home: 1455 Sandburg Terr #1602 Chicago IL 60610 Office: 310 S Michigan Ave Chicago Il 60604

PANTANO, LYNN THERESA, clin. psychologist; b. Detroit, Sept. 1, 1949; d. Guy Dewey and Lois Ulin (Buchanan) Pantano; B.A. in Psychology with honors, Wayne State U., 1971, M.A. (grad. scholar), 1975, Ph.D. in Clin. Psychology, 1979; m. Kenneth Andrew Skuzenski, July 20, 1979. Neuropsychology clin. asst. Harper Hosp., Detroit, 1971-72, neuropsychology intern, 1975-76; psychology clin. asst. Lafayette Clinic, Detroit, 1972-74, psychology intern, 1974-75; psychologist, unit coordinator Northeast and Northwest Centers, Detroit Psychiat. Inst., 1976-79, Northwest Center, Northville Regional Psychiat. Hosp., Detroit, 1979-81; psychologist Alt. Living Service, Southgate (Mich.) Regional Center, 1981-82; chief psychologist Kingswood Hosp., Ferndale, Mich., 1982—; clin. psychologist E. Pointe Mental Health Assn., Harper Woods, Mich., 1981—; clin. instr. Sch. of Osteopathy, Mich. State U., Lansing., 1982—. NSF grantee, 1970, USPHS grantee, 1971-72. Mem. Am. Psychol. Assn., Midwestern Psychol. Assn., Mich. Psychol. Assn., Mich. Soc. Lic. Psychologists, Internat. Neuropsychology Soc., Phi Beta Kappa, Psi Chi. Roman Catholic. Contbr. articles in field to profl. publs. Home: 19228 Linville Ave Grosse Pointe Woods MI 48236 Office: 10300 W Eight Mile St Ferndale MI 48220

PANTELEAKOS, EILEEN ANN, nursing home adminstr.; b. Bklyn., Conn., Jan. 9, 1937; d. Thomas Frank and Helen Josephine (Gorman) Harrington; student Windham Regional Tech. Sch. of Practical Nursing, 1969, U. Conn., 1972-73, Quinebaug Valley Community Coll., 1976—; m. Arthur Panteleakos, Apr. 8, 1954; children—Timothy, Pamela, Cynthia, David, Stephen. Asst. adminstr. Colchester Convalescent Home, Colchester, Conn., 1970-73; adminstr. Valley View Convalescent Center, Willimantic, Conn., 1973-74; cons. adminstr. for Joseph Strauss, 1974-75; adminstr. Westview Convalescent Center, Dayville, Conn., 1975—. Adv. bd. Windham Regional Tech. Sch. Practical Nursing, 1978—, Conn. Dept. Social Services "Project Find", 1976-79; mem. Killingly Water Pollution Control com., 1974-75; mem. Killingly Town Council, 1975—. Named Woman of the Yr., Northeastern Conn. Bus. and Profl. Woman and Conn. Fedn. Bus. and Profl. Women, 1978. Mem. Assn. of Health Care Facilities of Conn., Northeastern Conn. Bus. and Profl. Women (charter pres. 1974-75), Conn. Fedn. Bus. and Profl. Women (treas. 1976-77), Am. Coll. Nursing Home Adminstrs., Am. Health Care Assn., Conn. Assn. Health Care Facilities. Democrat. Greek Orthodox. Address: Westview Convalescent Center Inc RFD 1 Dayville CT 06241

PANTLE, WANDA TINDALL, psychiat. social worker; b. Kansas City, Mo., Oct. 3, 1942; d. Guy Russell and Irma Mae (Transue) Tindall; B.S., U. Oreg., 1966; M.S.W., U. Kans., 1969; m. James Ernest Pantle, June 16, 1963. Psychiat. social worker Brook Ln. Psychiat. Center, Hagerstown, Md., 1969-78; pvt. practice social work Antietam Psychiat. Assos., Hagerstown, Md., 1978—; lectr. and cons. in field. Mem. guild Millbrook Found. for Performing Arts. Mem. Nat. Assn. Social Workers, Acad. Cert. Social Workers, Smithsonian Assos. Democrat. Home: 305 W German St Shepherdstown WV 25443 Office: 138 E Antietam St Hagerstown MD 21740

PANZER, MARY E., state legislator; b. Waupun, Wis., Sept. 19, 1951; B.A., U. Wis., Madison. Legis. analyst Wis. State Senate; mem. Wis. Ho. of Reps., 1980—. Mem. Wis. Farm Bur., New Republican Conf. (past legis. chmn.), Order Women Legislators. Office: Wis Ho of Reps Room 335-C N State Capitol Madison WI 53702

PAO, MIRANDA HAU-YUNG LEE, educator; b. Shanghai, China, Feb. 14, 1936; d. Wai-sin and Yuk (Lau) Lee; came to U.S., 1956, naturalized, 1967; B.S., Julliard Sch. Music, 1960, M.S., 1961; M.S. in L.S., Case-Western Res. U., 1970, Ph.D., 1972; m. Richard H.F. Pao, June 10, 1961. Tchr. piano pvt. lessons, Terre Haute, Ind., 1961-67; piano recitalist, Terre Haute, 1963, 64, 66, Hong Kong, 1964; instr. piano Cleve. Inst. Music, 1967-76; lectr. library sci. Case-Western Res. U., Cleve., 1972-73, asst. prof., 1973-79, asso. prof., 1979—; mem. adv. com. biomed. library rev. com. Nat. Library of Medicine. Mem. Music Library Assn., Assn. Am. Library Schs., Am. Soc. Info. Sci. (ednl. com.), Sigma Alpha Iota, Beta Phi Mu. Contbr. articles to profl. jours. Office: Sch Library Sci Case Western Res U Cleveland OH 44106

PAOLI, GLORIA, pediatric ophthalmologist; b. Dominican Rep., Oct. 13, 1946; d. Rafael T. and Milagros (Fernandez) P.; B.S., Columbia U., 1974, M.D., 1978; children—Ryan, Damaris. Intern, Roosevelt Hosp., N.Y.C.; resident in ophthalmology Harlen Hosp., Columbia U.; fellow in pediatrics and strabismus, Columbia U., 1982—. Trustee, Broadway Methodist Ch. Mem. AMA, Acad. Ophthalmology, Dominican Med. Orgn., N.Y. Med. Soc.

PAOLINI, SHIRLEY JOAN, univ. dean; b. Cleve.; d. James and Anne D. (Jurist) Burke; B.A., Mount St. Mary's Coll., Los Angeles; postgrad. (Swiss Govt. fellow), U. Lausanne; M.A., Calif. State U., Fullerton, 1966; Ph.D., U. Calif., Irvine, 1973; m. Maurizio Paolini; children—Kenneth, Marco, Angela, Laura. Tchr., Whittier (Calif.) High Sch., 1966-67; asst. dir. edn. Nat. Systems Corp., Newport Beach, Calif., 1971-73; asst. prof. English, asst. specialist U. Hawaii, Honolulu, 1973-75; dir. planning Chaminade U., Honolulu, 1975-78; art-reach dir. Anchorage Arts Council, 1978-79; asso. prof. humanities, dean univ. affairs Alaska Pacific U., Anchorage, 1979—; ednl. cons., Hawaii, Alaska, 1973—. Project dir. Nat. Endowment for Humanities Grants, 1977-82, Strengthening Developing Instns. grant coordinator, 1975-81. Recipient Los Angeles Consulate award French Govt. Mem. MLA, Am. Comparative Lit. Assn., Pacific Philol. Assn., Council for Advancement Exptl. Learning (asso.), World Affairs Council (Anchorage). Democrat. Roman Catholic. Author: Confessions of Sin and Love in the Middle Ages - Dante's Commedia and St. Augustine's Confessions, 1982. Editor: Hawaii Open Program Courses, 1974-75. Home: 1242 St Gotthard Ave Anchorage AK 99504 Office: Dean Univ Affairs Alaska Pacific U Anchorage AK 99504

PAOLUCCI, ANNE ATTURA, educator, author; b. Rome; d. Joseph and Lucy (Guidoni) Attura; B.A., Barnard Coll.; M.A., Columbia U.; Ph.D.; Fulbright scholar U. Rome; m. Henry Paolucci. Mem. faculty Brearley Sch., N.Y.C. 1957-59, CCNY, 1959-69; univ. research prof. St. John's U., Jamaica, N.Y., 1969-77, prof. English, 1977—, acting head dept. English lit., 1974, chmn. dept. English, 1982—; Fulbright lectr. Am. drama U. Naples, 1965-67; spl. lectr. Renaissance Inst., Ashland, Oreg., 1973, 74; founder, editor Rev. Nat. Lits., 1970—; founder, exec. dir. Council Nat. Lits., 1974—; writer in residence Yaddo, 1965; vis. fellow Humanities Research Center, Australian Nat. U., Canberra, 1979; U.S. rep. Internat. Poetry Festival, Struga, Yugoslavia, 1981; dir. Shakespeare and The World series of bilingual dramatic readings, summer 1981; author: Pirandello's Theater: The Recovery of the Modern Stage for Dramatic Art, 1974; From Tension to Tonie: The Plays of Edward Albee, 1972; Hegel on Tragedy, 1962; Machiavelli's Mandragola, 1962; Poems Written for Sbek's Mummies, Marie Menken and Other Important People, Places and Things, 1977; Eight Short Stories 1977; (one-act play) Minions of the Race, 1978; (poems) Riding the Mast Where It Swings, 1980. Garibaldi scholar 1948-50; grantee Columbia U. 1963, 64, 65; Woodbridge fellow 1961-62; recipient Drama award Medieval and Renaissance Inst. 1972; named Disting. Alumna in News Barnard Coll. mag. 1973; Woman of Yr., Dr. Herman Henry Scholarship Found., 1973; Women of Yr., AMITA, 1970; Elena Cornaro award N.Y. State OSIA, 1980; Educator's award Bklyn. Coll., 1982, City-Wide Italian Heritage Week award, 1982, other citations and awards. Mem. Dante Soc. Am., Pirandello Soc. Am. (pres. 1979—), World Centre Shakespeare Studies, Conf. Editors Learned Jours., Nat. Soc. Lit. and Arts, Internat. Shakespeare Assn., Shakespeare Assn. Am., Renaissance Soc. Am., Renaissance Inst. Japan, Internat. Comparative Lit. Assn., Am. Comparative lit. Assn., Am. Byron Soc., Internat. Byron Soc., PEN. Office: St John's University Jamaica NY 11439

PAOLUCCI, BARBARA ANN, consumer products co. mgr.; b. Bklyn., Oct. 8, 1945; d. Theodore John and Madeline Louise (Lobasso) P.; student public schs.; divorced; 1 dau., Janine. Adminstr., L.A. Rader and Assos., Inc., Shareholders Mgmt. Corp., Kohlmeyer & Co., also T.P.O., Inc., N.Y.C., 1966-74; office mgr. Linden Trimmings, Inc., N.Y.C., 1974-78; office mgr. acctg. and adminstrn. Met. Calculator Systems, Inc., N.Y.C., 1978-80; controller Holiday Temp. Services, N.Y.C., 1980-81; mgr. personnel systems, records and relocation United Brands Co., N.Y.C., 1981—. Mem. Republican Presdl. Task Force. Mem. Employee Relocation Council, Northeast Users Payroll and Personnel Systems, Nationwide Users Payroll and Personnel Systems, Assn. Computer Users, Nat. Assn. Female Execs., Am. Mgmt. Assn. Roman Catholic. Office: 1271 Ave Americas New York NY 10020

PAONESSA, ROSE ELIZABETH, educator; b. Gimigliano, Italy, Nov. 19, 1939; brought to U.S., 1940, naturalized, 1963; d. Salvatore and Assunta Mary (Curcio) Paonessa; B.S. in Elem. Edn., Western Conn. State Coll., 1961; M.A. in Classroom Teaching, Fairfield U., 1965; M.A. in Student Personnel Adminstrn. in Higher Edn., Columbia U., 1972. Tchr. elem. schs. Bethel (Conn.) Bd. Edn., 1961-63; tchr. elem. and secondary sch. Danbury (Conn.) Bd. Edn., 1963-66, 68-71, 72—; tchr. English, Dependents Schs., Heilbronn, W.Ger. and Iraklion, Crete, 1966-68; cooperating tchr. student tchrs. Western Conn. State Coll., 1963-64, 72-75, 78-79, 81; intern U. Bridgeport, 1971-72. Vol. Danbury Hosp., 1969-71, Community Caregivers, 1973-75. Mem. Nat., Conn., Danbury (mem. rep. council 1977-79) edn. assns., Western Conn. State Coll. Alumni Assn. (editor Newsletter 1962-65, v.p. 1963-64), Phi Delta Kappa (v.p. chpt. 1982-83). Home: 47 Olcott Way Ridgefield CT 06877 Office: Broadview Jr High Sch Hospital Ave Danbury CT 06810

PAPA, GRACE JOYCE, assn. exec.; b. Bronx, N.Y., Sept. 12, 1952; d. Salvatore Joseph and Stella (Colucci) P.; student N.Am. Sch. Animal Scis., 1971-73. Staff, Paradise Kennels, Bronx, N.Y., 1973-74, Yonkers (N.Y.) Humane Soc., 1973-74; receptionist Swiss Ct. Motel, Upper Saddle River, N.J., 1974-76; gen. mgr. Nat. Cat Protection Soc., Spring Valley, Calif., 1976-82; founder, pres. The Cat Factory, 1982—. Mem. Humane Soc. U.S., Voice of Voiceless (Humane award, 1978), Feline Defenders (Humane award 1977). Office: 9031 Birch St Spring Valley CA 92077

PAPA, PHYLLIS MARYANN, ballet dancer, adminstr., choreographer, educator; b. Trenton, N.J., Jan. 30, 1950; d. Armando Carmen and Mary (Grace) P.; student ballet Royal Ballet Centre, 1955-62, Am. Ballet Center, N.Y.C., 1962-65, Harkness House for Ballet Arts, N.Y.C., 1965-68; m. Thomas E. de Ment, Jr., Sept. 2, 1979. Dancer, Princeton (N.J.) Ballet Co., 1963-68, Harkness Youth Co., N.Y.C., 1965-68, Am. Ballet Theatre, N.Y.C., 1968-70, Royal Danish Ballet, Copenhagen, 1970-72; founder Mercer Ballet (formerly W. Jersey Ballet Co.), Mooretown, N.J., 1972—, artistic dir., 1972—; founder, artistic dir., Ballet Concertante, chamber ballet, Mooretown, 1975—; artistic dir., ballet mistress, prin. dancer Stars of Am. Ballet, N.Y.C.; prin. dancer Atlanta Ballet Co., 1978—; tchr. Royal Dance Centre, Royal Ballet Centre, Mercer County Community Coll.; founder Am. Internat. Ballet, Inc., N.Y.C., 1979—, choreographer, prin. dancer S.E. Asia tour, 1980; prin. dancer, ballet mistress Ballets Elan, 1980; artistic dir. Atlantic City Ballet, 1981—; cons. in field; choreographer over 20 ballets for regional and profl. cos. Grantee N.J. State Council of Arts and Nat. Endowment on Arts, 1975-76, 82.

PAPALIA-FINLAY, DIANE ELLEN, educator; b. Englewood, N.J., Apr. 26, 1947; d. Edward Peter and Madeline (Borrin) Papalia; A.B., Vassar Coll., 1968; M.S., W.Va. U., 1970, Ph.D. (NSF fellow), 1971; m. Jonathan Finlay, June 19, 1976. Asst. prof. child and family studies U. Wis., Madison, 1971-75, assoc. prof., 1975-78, prof., 1978—, assoc. dean grad. studies and research Sch. Family Resources and Consumer Scis., 1982—. Am. Council Edn. fellow, 1979-80; U. Wis. grantee. Fellow Gerontol. Soc.; mem. Am. Psychol. Assn., Soc. Research in Child Devel., Nat. Council Family Relations, Psi Chi. Author: (with Sally W. Olds) A Child's World: Infancy through Adolescence, 1975, 79, 82; Human Development, 1978, 81; contbr. articles to profl. jours. Home: 606 Blue Ridge Pkwy Madison WI 53705 Office: 1430 Linden Dr Madison WI 53706

PAPARELLI, JUDITH MARIE, broadcaster; b. Yonkers, N.Y., Jan. 8, 1954; d. Joseph Anthony and Immaculate (Cimino) P.; student Tufts U., 1971-76. With public relations dept. 1st Nat. Bank Boston, 1975; host daily talk show, continuity dir. public relations Sta. WLNH-AM-FM, Sconnix Group Broadcasting Corp., Laconia, N.H., 1977-79, public relations dir., on-air feature editor Sta. WTMA-WPXI, Charleston, S.C., 1979-81; freelance radio and TV interviewer, Charleston, 1980-81; talk show host Sta. WRNG, Atlanta, 1982—; pianist. Bd. dirs., publicity dir. Lakes Region United Way, N.H., 1979; adv. Youth Service Bur., Juvenile Justice Bd., Laconia, 1979. Named Young Career Woman, Charleston, 1981. Mem. N.H. Bus. and Profl. Women's Assn., Atlanta Press Club, Tennis League. Democrat. Roman Catholic. Home: 8111C Colquitt Rd Atlanta GA 30338

PAPAVERO, ANNA LOUISE MARIE, funeral dir.; b. New Brunswick, N.J., June 30, 1943; d. Anthony C. and Frances (Pellicane) Bongiovi; diploma mortuary sci., Am. Acad. McAllister Inst., N.Y.C., 1962; m. Anthony J. Papavero, Oct. 20, 1963; children—Anthony J., Jason C. Mgr., operator Bongiovi Funeral Home, Raitan, N.J., 1962—, co-owner, 1980—; counselor, instr., lectr. death edn. Past pres. St. Ann's Altar-Rosary Soc.; past v.p. St. Ann's PTA. Mem. Nat. Funeral Dirs. Assn., N.J. State Funeral Dirs. Assn. (pres.-elect 1980-81, pres. 1981—, originator ann. Talisman Conf., program exclusively for women funeral dirs.), Middlesex-Somerset County Funeral Dirs. Assn. (pres. 1977-78), Order Golden Rule. Roman Catholic. Clubs: Raitan Lions Aux. (pres. 1968, 78), Zonta. Home: 820 Rhine Blvd Raritan NJ 08869 Office: Bongiovi Funeral Home Bell Ave and Anderson St Raritan NJ 08869

PAPICH, ANITA CAMILLE, sch. adminstr.; b. Blue Island, Ill., Feb. 28, 1941; d. Joseph John and Josephine Cecilia (Groszek) Kracik; B.S. in Edn., No. Ill. U., 1962; M.A.T., Rockford Coll., 1970; children—Jeffrey, Jennifer. Tchr. Guilford High Sch., Rockford, 1963-64; tchr. math. Keith Country Day Sch., Rockford, Ill., 1965—, head dept. math., 1967—, dir. devel. and alumni affairs, 1981—. Pres., Divorced Cath. Group, Rockford, 1977-79, bd. dirs., 1981—. Mem. Nat. Council Tchrs. Math., Archeol. Inst. Am., Council Advancement of Secondary Edn., Alpha Xi Delta, Sigma Zeta. Roman Catholic. Home: 3323 Landstrom Rd Rockford IL 61107 Office: 1 Jacoby Pl Rockford IL 61107

PAPO, JEAN KAY, retail stores exec.; b. Spencer, Iowa, Sept. 14, 1946; d. George Henry and Mary Elsie (Stuart) Williams; student Rollins Coll., 1964-65, U. Iowa, 1965-67, Sorbonne, U. Paris, 1967-68, U. San Francisco, 1970-71; bus. mgmt. diploma Minn. Sch. Bus., Mpls., 1969; B.A. in French with honors, U. Calif., Berkeley, 1972; postgrad. Hastings Law Sch., 1972-73; m. Claudius L. Papo, June 15, 1968 (dec.).

Street artist, San Francisco, 1975-77; partner, pres. The Leather Box, San Francisco, 1978—, Buckle Up, San Francisco, 1976—. Mem. Mechanics Inst., Women Entrepreneurs, Am. Entrepreneurs Assn., Nat. Fedn. Ind. Bus., Assn. Women Architects, Menswear Retailers Am., Am. Contract Bridge League (life master). Home: 1605 Manzanita Ave Belmont CA 94002 Office: 1125 Grandview Dr S San Francisco CA 94080

PAPON, NADINE MARSHA DAILY, architect; b. Akron, Ohio, Sept. 17, 1940; d. Robert Marsh and Ellen J. (Susko) Daily; B.A., U. Akron, 1962; B.Arch., M.Arch., Columbia U., 1967; m. Robert Donald Papon, Oct. 3, 1975; 1 dau., Lucienne Claire. Designer, Warner Burns Toan & Lunde, N.Y.C., 1967-69, asst. job capt., 1969-70; designer Robert McMillan Assos., N.Y.C., 1971, Wong & Tung, Atlanta, 1972-73; staff architect Hilton Internat., N.Y.C., 1974-79; asso., project architect David Jacobson Assos., Atlantic City, 1979-80; hotel architect Holiday Inns Inc., Memphis, 1980—. William Kinne Fellows travelling fellow, 1966; registered architect, N.Y. State, N.J. Mem. AIA, Assn. Women in Architecture, Nat. Assn. Female Execs. Republican. Episcopalian. Club: Illuminati (council). Designer Goat Island Sheraton Inn, Newport, R.I., 1968; project architect Claridge Hotel/Casino Atlantic City, 1979; hotel architect New Orleans Poydras Holiday Inn, 1981. Office: 3645 Lamar Ave Memphis TN 38195

PAPPAS, EVA, psychologist/psychoanalyst; b. N.Y.C.; B.A. (scholar 1958-62), Pace U., 1962; M.A., N.Y.U., 1965, Ph.D., 1973. Tchr. pub. schs., N.Y.C., 1963-65; counselor P.A.L. Project, 1965-66; instr. psychology dept. edn. Adelphi U., 1966-69; sr. staff psychologist Goldwater Meml. Hosp., N.Y.C., 1973-76; fellow Postgrad. Center for Mental Health, N.Y.C., 1976-78, asso. staff, 1976-80, staff, 1980—, co-teaching staff, 1982—; psychologist/psychoanalyst in pvt. practice, N.Y.C., 1976—. Lic. psychologist, N.Y. State. Mem. Am. Psychol. Assn., Nat. Registry Health Service Providers in Psychology, N.Y. Soc. Clin. Psychologists. Office: 82 W 12 St New York NY 10011

PAPPAS, VIRGINIA MARIE, assn. exec.; b. Bklyn., June 8, 1953; d. Vincent and Rose Margaret Janucci; B.A., Baruch Coll., 1976; m. William Pappas, Oct. 20, 1971; 1 son, Anthony. Mgr., Cabrini Health Care Center, N.Y.C., 1975-78; admintr. technologist sect. Soc. Nuclear Medicine, N.Y.C., 1978—. Mem. Am. Soc. Assn. Execs., Am. Soc. Allied Health Professions, N.Y. Soc. Assn. Execs., Nat. Assn. Female Execs. Home: 144 Bay 8 St Brooklyn NY 11228 Office: 475 Park Ave S New York NY 10016

PAPPENHEIM, HARRIET JOYCE, social worker, psychotherapist; b. N.Y.C., Oct. 4, 1934; d. Max and Bertha (Katz) Wilner; B.A., Barnard Coll., 1956; M.S.W. (NIMH grantee 1963-64), Yeshiva U., 1964; cert. psychoanalysis (NIMH grantee 1968), Postgrad. Center Mental Health, N.Y.C., 1973; m. Wolf Pappenheim, 1969; 1 dau., Meghan. Staff therapist Jewish Bd. Guardians, N.Y.C., 1965-68; pvt. practice therapy and marriage counseling, 1970—; staff therapist, supr. Postgrad. Center Mental Health, 1978-79; mem. faculty Adelphi U. Sch. Social Work, Garden City, N.Y., 1973-76; founder, co-dir. Parents Center Inc., N.Y.C., 1978—. Diplomate N.Y. Soc. Clin. Social Work Psychotherapists. Mem. Nat. Assn. Social Workers, Am. Assn. Marriage and Family Counselors, Am. Orthopsychiat. Assn., N.Y. Soc. Clin. Psychologists. Jewish. Club: Barnard Coll. Profl. Women's. Home: 330 E 79th St New York NY 10021 Office: 250 E 87th St New York NY 10028

PAQUETTE, JACQUELINE PETERS, molded and styrene products co. fin. exec.; b. Waterville, Maine, Dec. 26, 1939; d. Peter J. and Jessie M. Peters; student Thomas Coll., 1975-77; m. Robert Paquette, July 4, 1958 (dec. June 1975); children—Kelly, Randall Scott. With Keyes Fibre div. Van Leer Packaging Co., Waterville, 1963—, sec., asst. to asst. v.p. fin., 1974-76, mgr. gen. acctg., 1976-79, plant comptroller, 1979—. Home: RFD #2 Clinton ME 04927 Office: Keyes Fibre College Ave Waterville ME 04901

PARBERRY, ELIZABETH CIESLIK, strategic planner; b. Phila., Aug. 11, 1939; d. Charles Joseph and Elizabeth Marguerite (Anderson) Cieslik; B.S. in Psychology summa cum laude, St. Joseph's U., 1979, M.B.A., 1982; m. Donald Edward Parberry, Sept. 28, 1963; 1 son, Stephen. Asst. to v.p. bus. planning and devel. Sperry Univac, Blue Bell, Pa., 1973-79, bus. analyst, 1979—. Recipient psychology award, St. Joseph's U., 1979. Mem. N.Am. Soc. Corp. Planning (pres. Phila. chpt., 1982-83, mem. nat. bd. dirs., 1982-83), Psi Chi, Alpha Sigma Lambda. Home: 3568 Indian Queen Ln Philadelphia PA 19129 Office: PO Box 500 Blue Bell PA 19424

PARDEE, MARGARET ROSS, violinist, violist, educator; b. Valdosta, Ga., May 10, 1920; d. William Augustus and Frances Ross (Burton) P.; diploma Inst. Mus. Art, Juilliard Sch. Music, 1940, grad. diploma, 1942, diploma Juilliard Grad. Sch., 1945; m. Daniel Rogers Butterly, July 5, 1944. Instr. violin and viola Manhattanville Coll. Sacred Heart, N.Y.C., 1942-54, Juilliard Sch., N.Y.C., 1942—, Meadowmount Sch. Music, Westport, N.Y., 1956—; concert master Great Neck (L.I.) Symphony, 1954—; adj. asso. prof. music Queens Coll., Flushing, N.Y., 1978—; adj. asso. prof. Adelphi U., Garden City, N.Y., 1979—; adj. prof. SUNY, Purchase, 1980— debut N.Y. Town Hall, 1952; toured U.S. as soloist and in chamber music groups; soloed with symphony orchs. in Miss., N.J., D.C. and N.Y.; mem. jury for internat. competitions. Bd. dirs. Meadowmount Sch. Music. Mem. Soc. for Strings (dir. 1965—), Associated Music Tchrs. League N.Y. (cert.), N.Y. State Music Tchrs. Assn. (cert.), Music Tchrs. Nat. Assn., Am. Fedn. Musicians, Viola Research Soc. Office: care Juilliard Sch Lincoln Center Plaza New York NY 10023

PARDO, MARIAN URSULA, trust co. exec.; b. Rockville Centre, N.Y., Sept. 23, 1946; d. Francis V. and Dorothy E. (Bellidora) P.; B.A., Barnard Coll., 1968; m. Michael S. Toonkel. With Morgan Guaranty Trust Co. N.Y., N.Y.C., 1968—, v.p. investment div., 1978—. Bd. dirs., pres. Opportunity Resources for Arts. Past mem. Robert Morris Assos. (gov. N.Y. chpt. 1977-79). Office: Morgan Guaranty Trust Co NY 9 W 57th St New York NY 10019

PARDUE, AYTEN SUREREKER, hematologist-oncologist; b. Istanbul, Turkey, Aug. 28, 1932; d. Kemalettin and Ruhiye Surereker; M.D., Ankara (Turkey) U., 1955; m. Frank S. Pardue, May 8, 1976; children—Suzan, Donald, Gregory, Semra MacLellan. Instr. physiology Ankara U. Faculty Medicine, 1955-56; intern Albany (N.Y.) Meml. Hosp., 1956-57; resident in pediatrics Columbia (S.C.) Gen. Hosp., 1957-58; resident in pediatrics Tex. Children's Hosp., Houston, 1958-60, fellow in pediatric hematology, 1960-61; fellow in clin. hematology J.K. and Susie L. Wadley Research Inst. and Blood Bank, Dallas, 1961-64; practice medicine specializing in pediatrics, Garland, Tex., 1964-65; hematologist-oncologist Wadley Insts. Molecular Medicine, Granville C. Morton Cancer and Research Hosp., Dallas, 1965—, assoc. to dir. pediatrics, 1965—, chief pediatrics, 1969—; asst. attending staff Children's Med. Center, Dallas, 1969—; assoc. attending physician dept. pediatrics Baylor U. Med. Center, Dallas; clin. instr. pediatrics U. Tex. Southwestern Med. Sch., Dallas, 1969—; mem. med. adv. bd. Dallas chpt. Nat. Hemophilia Found., 1970—. Mem. AMA, Tex. Med. Assn., Dallas County Med. Soc., Am. Soc. Clin. Oncology, Am. Soc. Hematology, Internat. Soc. Hematology, Internat. Soc. Exptl. Hematology, So. Clin. Soc., Dallas So. Clin. Soc., Dallas Internist Club, Islamic Assn. North Tex. Club: Ridglea Country. Contbr. numerous articles to med. jours.

PARENT, GAIL, writer; b. N.Y.C., Aug. 12, 1941; d. Theodore and Ruth Kostner; B.S., N.Y.U. m. Peter Wylan, Feb. 28, 1981; children—Kevin, Gregory. Writer, The Carol Burnett Show; author: (novels) Sheila Levine is Dead and Living in New York: David Meyer is a Mother, the Best Laid Plains; co-creator Mary Hartman, Mary Hartman; (with Andrew Smith) (film) The Main Event. Recipient Emmy for Carol Burnett Show. Mem. Writers Guild Am., Lit. Guild, AFTRA, Screen Artists Guild, Am. Soc. Composers, Authors and Pubs.

PARENT, LILLIAN M., state legislator, banker; b. Fountain County, Ind., Oct. 21, 1922; d. Eston B. and Mabel Jane (Marks) Cox; student in banking Ind. U., 1950; m. William D. Parent, Aug. 11, 1941; 1 son, David Lee. With Danville (Ind.) State Bank, 1950—, cashier, 1978—; county treas. Hendricks County (Ind.), 1969-77; mem. Ind. Ho. of Reps., 1978-79, Ind. Senate, 1979—. Committeeman, Republican Precint; del. Rep. State and Nat. Conv. Recipient Golden Rule award. Methodist. Mem. Ind. County Treas.'s Assn. (pres.), Assn. Ind. Counties (sec.-treas.), Bus. and Profl. Women's Club (pres.). Clubs: Rep. Women's, Order Eastern Star. Office: Indiana Senate State Capitol Indianapolis IN 46204 *

PARENT, MYRTLE MABLE, accountant; b. Salt Lake City, Oct. 4, 1929; d. Richard Earl and Mabel (Mills) Clayton; acctg. degree LaSalle Extension U., 1960; m. Herbert Parent, Dec. 20, 1979; children—Gary Lee Smith, Teresa Vee Dutcher, Marvin Dee Smith; stepchildren—Claudia Wells, Karen Boatwright, Steve Parent. Acct., White Bros., 1950-60; head acct. Cobain Bros., 1952-54; from clk. to acting office mgr. Walla Walla County (Wash.) Agr. and Stblzn. Office, 1954-59; acct. W.R. Williams C.P.A., 1960-62, Walla Walla Grain Growers, 1962-64; mgr., owner Myrtle Parent, C.P.A., Walla Walla, 1961—. C.P.A., Wash. Mem. Am. Women's Soc. C.P.A.s, Am. Inst. C.P.A.s, Am. Bus. Women's Assn., Wash. Soc. C.P.A.s. Mormon. Address: 1475 S 2d St Walla Walla WA 99362

PARENTEAU, IRENE FORCIER, controller; b. Coventry, R.I., Dec. 23, 1933; d. Regis and Evelyn (Levesque) P.; A.S., Leiscester Jr. Coll., 1953; student U. R.I., 1978-80, Bryant Coll., 1981-82; 1 dau., Renee Edith. Acct., Carley & Nardella, West Warwick, R.I., 1962-65, Golden Lantern, Warwick, R.I., 1966-67; controller Coventry Narrow Fabrics, Inc., Coventry, 1967—. Mem. Am. Inst. Corp. Controllers. Roman Catholic. Office: Coventry Narrow Fabrics Inc 624 Washington St Coventry RI 02816

PARHAM, GERALDINE T., ednl. cons.; b. Pilot Mountain, N.C., May 11, 1936; d. Oscar M. and Essie (Smith) Taylor; B.S., Philander Smith Coll., 1957; M.S.W., U. Pa. Sch. Social Work, 1963; m. Wallace L. Parham; children—Ilene (Mrs. Stephen Pritchett), Wallace T., Keith L. Caseworker, intake worker Phila. County Bd. Assistance, 1958-64; caseworker/supr. Camden (N.J.) Home for Children, 1964-66; sch. social worker Camden City Public Schs., 1966-68; counselor parents of handicapped children Assn. Children with Learning Disabilities, Cherry Hill, N.J., 1968-70; cons. Br. Spl. Edn., N.J. State Dept. Edn., Trenton, N.J., 1968—; adj. instr. Camden County Coll., 1981—. Mem. Camden County Ethic Com., 1979-82; organizer, pres. New Mickle Bapt. Ch. Scholarship Club. Mem. Nat. Assn. Social Workers, Acad. Cert. Social Workers, Mem. Nat. Com. for Prevention of Child Abuse (mem. advisory council), N.J. Assn. Sch. Social Workers, Delta Sigma Theta. Baptist. Clubs: Links, Inc., Jack and Jill of Am. Inc. Co-author IEP Parent Involvement Tng. Guide; also articles. Home: 1746 Country Club Dr Cherry Hill NJ 08003 Office: 225 W State St Trenton NJ 08625

PARHAM, RUBY INEZ MYERS, civic worker, former educator; b. Tamaha, Okla., Nov. 4, 1914; d. Ola T. and Bursha Bell (Culver) Myers; B.S. in Edn., Northeastern State Coll., 1940, M.Teaching, 1955; m. Rufus K. McCollum, Dec. 31, 1937 (dec. Oct. 1966); m. 2d, Jewell A. Parham, June 10, 1973; stepchildren—Bill, Donal E., Ann (Mrs. Everett George), Garry. Tchr. rural schs., Haskell County, Stigler, Okla., 1934-38, Adair County, Stilwell, Okla., 1946-50, Cherokee County, Tahlequah, Okla., 1939-46, 50-66; tchr. Westville (Okla.) Jr. High Sch., 1966-77, ret., 1977. Vol., Tahlequah City Hosp. Aux., now pres.; vice chmn. Ester Circle, Bapt. Women's Missionary Union. Recipient Oklahoma Bankers award, 1965. Mem. Nat., Okla. edn. assns., Sr. Citizens, Nat. Ret. Tchrs. Assn., Okla. Ret. Tchrs. Assn., Am. Legion Aux., Northeastern State U. Alumni Assn. (life), Nat. Wildlife Assn., Kappa Kappa Iota (royal high lady Tahlequah, Okla., 1953-55), Delta Kappa Gamma. Republican. Clubs: Rebekah (noble grand 1959-60, jr. noble grand 1960-61, lodge dep. 1961-63, musician), Order Eastern Star (organist, conductress, worthy matron 1979, chmn. Estarol com. Dist. 18). Home: 215 S College St Tahlequah OK 74464

PARIS, DORIS FORT, chemist; b. Roanoke, Va., July 3, 1924; d. Richard Hubert and Mary Louise (Hardy) Lowe; student Longwood Coll., 1940-42; B.S. Chemistry, U. Va., 1946; M.S., U. Ga., 1966; m. Marion Kirkland Fort, Apr. 7, 1945 (dec. 1964); children—Mary Susan Fort Donnelly, John Kirkland; m. 2d Frederic David Paris, Nov. 25, 1967. Med. technologist U. Va. Hosp., 1943-45; research chemist Environ. Research Lab., EPA, Athens, Ga., 1966—. Sec. Otaki council Girl Scouts U.S.A., 1958-61; pres. Women of Central Presbyterian Ch., Athens, 1960-62; chmn. heart clinic Athens Jr. Assembly, 1962-63; bd. dirs. Univ. Community Concert Assn., Athens, 1962-65, 73-75, Athens Mental Health Assn., 1965-66. Recipient Outstanding Performance rating and award Civil Service Commn., 1967. Mem. Am. Soc. Microbiology, Am. Chem. Soc. (N.E. Ga. council 1977—), Lychnos Hon. Soc., Sigma Xi. Clubs: Athens Country, U. Ga. Women's (pres. 1962-63). Research, publs. in biochemistry of microorganisms and pollutant degradation. Home: 145 Meadowview Rd Athens GA 30606 Office: ERL EPA College Station Rd Athens GA 30605

PARISEAU, JUDY L., state legislator; b. Manchester, N.H., Jan. 12, 1941; d. John J. and Marie Anne (Duplessis) Vercauteren; m. Robert J. Pariseau, Aug. 22, 1964; children—John, Gregory, Gary, Lynn. Mem. N.H. Ho. of Reps., 1981—. Republican. Roman Catholic. Home: 93 Rosedale Ave Manchester NH 03103

PARK, ALICE MARY, genealogist; b. Loda, Ill., Oct. 4, 1901; d. Frederick Adam and Sarah Elizabeth (Clemens) Crandall; B.S., U. Chgo., 1924; m. Lee I. Park, Aug. 29, 1925; children—Lee C., Nancy (Mrs. John W. Kern, III). Geneal. researcher, 1965-74; tchr. U. Chgo. Lab. Sch., 1924-25. Pres. Falls Church (Va.) PTA, 1941-42. Mem. League Women Voters (pres. Fairfax County 1947-48). Author: (hist. genealogy) Park/e/s and Bunch on the Trail West, 1974, rev. edit., 1982. Home: 4200 Cathedral Ave NW Washington DC 20016

PARK, CAROLE ROPER, state legislator; b. Kansas City, Sept. 18, 1939; student U. Miami (Fla.), U.Kans.; B.A., U. Mo.-Kansas City, also postgrad.; 1 dau. Former tchr. pub. schs.; mem. Mo. Ho. of Reps., 1976—. Bd. dirs. United Eastern Democrats. Mem. Sugar Creek Bus. and Civic Club, U. Mo.-Kansas City Alumni Assn., Sugar Creek Hist. Soc., Jackson County C. of C., Independence C. of C., Kappa Kappa Gamma Alumni Assn. Roman Catholic. Office: Mo State Ho of Reps Jefferson City MO 65101 *

PARK, DOROTHY GOODWIN DENT (MRS. ROY HAMPTON PARK), broadcasting, newspaper exec.; b. Raleigh, N.C.; d. Walter Reed and Mildred (Goodwin) Dent; student Peace Jr. Coll., 1925-33; A.B., Meredith Coll., 1936; m. Roy Hampton Park, Oct. 3, 1936; children—Roy Hampton, Adelaide Park Gomer. Sec., dir. RHP, Inc., Ithaca, N.Y., 1945—, Roy H. Park Broadcasting of Va., Inc., Sta. WTVR-TV-AM-FM, Richmond, 1965—, Roy H. Park Broadcasting of Tri-Cities, Inc., Sta. WJHL-TV, Johnson City, Tenn., 1964—, Roy H. Park Broadcasting of Tenn., Inc., Sta. WDEF-TV-AM-FM, Chattanooga, 1963—, Park Broadcasting, Inc., Ithaca, 1942—, Roy H. Park Broadcasting, Inc., Sta. WNCT-TV-FM, Greenville, N.C., 1962—, Roy H. Park Radio, Inc., Sta. WNCT-AM, Greenville, 1963—, Park Found., Inc., Greenville, 1966—, Cobb House of Rock Hill, S.C. Inc., 1967—, Roy H. Park Broadcasting of Midwest, Inc., Sta. WNAX-AM, Yankton, S.D., 1968—, Roy H. Park Broadcasting of Roanoke, Inc., Sta. WSLS-TV, 1969—, Roy H. Park Broadcasting of Utica-Rome, N.Y., Inc., Sta. WUTR-TV, 1969—, Park Newspapers, Inc., Ithaca, 1972—, Park Outdoor Advt. of Scranton-Wilkes-Barre, Inc., Park Newspapers of Ga., Inc., 1972—, KWJJ-AM, Portland, Ore., 1973—, RHP Newspapers, Inc., Ithaca, 1973—, Roy H. Park Broadcasting of Birmingham (Ala.), Inc., 1973—, Park Newspapers Va., Inc., 1973—, Birmingham TV Corp., Sta. WBMG-TV, 1973—, Lockport Publs., Inc., Ithaca, 1973—, Lockport (N.Y.) Union Sun & Jour. Inc., 1973—, Prince William Pub. Co., Inc., Manassas, Va., 1973—, Roy H. Park Broadcasting of Lake County, Inc., Sta. KJJO, St. Louis Park, Minn., 1974—, Roy H. Park Broadcasting of Minn., Inc., Sta. KRSI-AM, St. Louis Park, 1974—, Contemporary FM, Inc., Sta. KJIB-FM, Portland, 1974—, Roy H. Park Broadcasting of Syracuse, Inc., 1976—, Roy H. Park Broadcasting of Wash., Inc., Sta. KEZX-FM, Portland, 1975—, Park Newspapers of Neb., Inc., Ithaca, 1975—, Press Printing Co., Nebraska City, Neb., 1975—, Park Newspapers of Fla., Inc., Brooksville, 1975—Roy H. Park Broadcasting of Syracuse, Inc., WHEN-AM, 1976—; Roy H. Park Broadcasting of Finger Lakes, Inc., WRRB-FM, 1977—, Park Newspapers of St. Lawrence, Inc., Ithaca, 1975—, Northern. N.Y. Pub. Co., Odensburg, 1975—, Courier-Freman, Inc., Potsdam, N.Y., 1975—, Massena (N.Y.) Observer Pub. Co., 1975—, St. Lawrence Plaindealer, Inc., Canton, N.Y., 1975—, Park Newspapers of Ill., Inc., 1979—, State & Aurora, Inc., Broken Arrow, Okla., 1979—, Southside Publs., Inc., 1979—, WND, Inc., Sapulpa, Okla., 1979—, Park Newspapers of Newton, Inc., 1979—, Park Newspapers of Morganton, Inc., 1979—, Park Newspapers of Statesville, Inc., 1979—, Park Newspapers of Concord, Inc., 1980—, Park Newspapers of Perry, Ga., Inc., 1980—, Park Newspapers of Michigan, Inc., 1980, Park Newspapers of Ark., Inc., 1981, Park Newspapers of Lumberton, N.C., 1982, Park Newspapers of Moore County, N.C., Inc., 1982, Park Newspapers of Devils Lake, N.D., Inc., 1982. Bd. visitors Peace Coll., Raleigh, 1968—. Mem. DAR (1st vice regent 1955-57), Daus. Am. Colonists, Nat. Soc. Magna Charta Dames, Sovereign Colonial Soc. Ams. Royal Descent, Descs. Knights of Garter, Colonial Order of Crown, Service League Ithaca, LWV. Presbyterian. Clubs: Garden (Ithaca), Ithaca Woman's. Home: 205 Devon Rd Ithaca NY 14850 Office: Terrace Hill Ithaca NY 14850

PARK, MARILYN EARLEY, interior design co. exec.; b. San Francisco, Jan. 29, 1937; d. James Lynn and Rita Elva (Valento) Earley; B.A. cum laude, U. Pacific, 1958; m. Dean Howard Park, Feb. 12, 1961; children—Catherine, Margaret, Suzanne, James. Personnel mgr. Hale's Dept. Stores, Sacramento, 1958-62; credit mgr. Wilsons Contemporary Furniture, Sacramento, 1975-77; mng. partner Design Showroom, Sacramento, 1977—; mem. adv. bd. Meridian Bank. Del., Capitol to Capitol Trip to Washington, 1981; Named Vol. of Year United Cerebral Palsy of Sacramento, 1980; bd. dirs. Sacramento Opera Assn., Cerebral Palsy Guild, Encore of Sacramento Symphony. Mem. Soc. for Mktg. Profl. Services, Sacramento Met. C. of C. (dir., pres. Women's Council; named Businesswoman of Yr. 1981), Delta Gamma Alumni. Democrat. Roman Catholic. Home: 1081 38th St Sacramento CA 95816 Office: 2560 Marconi Ave Sacramento CA 95821

PARKAS, IVA RICHEY, educator, historian, curator, paralegal; b. Comanche County, Tex., June 28, 1907; d. Andrew Jackson and Pearl Lucretia (Kennedy) Richey; grad. Wayland Coll., 1927; B.A., Tex. Tech. U., 1935; M.Litt., U. Pitts., 1950; postgrad. UCLA, 1960, Pa. State U., 1961, U. Calif., Berkeley, 1962, Duquesne U., 1963, Carnegie-Mellon U., 1968; m. George Eduardo Parkas, May 5, 1945. Curator, historian Fort Pitt Blockhouse, Pitts., 1946-52, now asst. curator, historian; tchr. U.S. history Pitts. public schs., 1953-72; with Allegheny County (Pa.) Law Dept., 1977—. Del., White House Conf. on Children and Youth, Washington, 1960, 70, World Food Conf., Rome, 1974. Named Disting. Alumnae, U. Pitts., 1978—; recipient Valley Forge Classroom Tchr.'s medal, 1960. Henry Clay Frick Ednl. fellow; NDEA grantee; Greater Pitts. Air Force Squadron scholar. Mem. NEA (life), AAUW (pres. Pitts. br. 1974-76), Hist. Soc. Western Pa., Western Pa. Council for Social Studies (pres. 1969-71), U. Pitts. Alumnae Assn. (dir., sec. 1978—), Pa. Ret. Public Sch. Employees Assn. (life, bicentennial chmn. 1974-76), DAR, Delta Kappa Gamma, Phi Alpha Theta. Editor: So Your Children Can Tell Their Children, 1976. Contbr. articles on hist. subjects to newspapers, mags. Home: 5520 Fifth Ave Pittsburgh PA 15232

PARKE, PRISCILLA ANN, clothing mfg. co. exec.; b. Uniontown, Pa., Sept. 25, 1950; d. Allen Jones and Auberta Ann (Crawford) P.; B.F.A., Pratt Inst., 1972. Asst. buyer Abraham & Straus, Bklyn., 1972-73, dept. mgr., Huntington, N.Y., 1973-75; salesperson Burlington Industries, N.Y.C., 1975-77, sales mgr., 1977-81; merchandising mgr. Espresso div. Chestnut Ridge Industries, N.Y.C., 1981—. bus. cons. clothing mfrs. Mem. Nat. Assn. Female Execs. Research on finishes for rainwear. Home: 184 73d St Brooklyn NY 11209 Office: 1411 Broadway New York NY 10018

PARKER, ADAJUNE, consumer specialist; b. Oak Hill, Ill., Mar. 15, 1938; d. Delbert Vernon and Nellie Adelaide (Hayes) Helle; B.S. in Home Econs., Bradley U., 1961; postgrad. No. Ill. U., 1973, 74; m. William Robert Parker, June 18, 1961; children—Rebecca June, Phyllis Ann. Asst. dept. mgr. Marshall Field and Co., Oak Park, Ill., 1961; home econs. tchr. Forest Park (Ill.) Jr. High Sch., 1962-64, Glenbard East High Sch., Lombard, Ill., 1964-65; vocat. foodservice and home econs. tchr. Lisle (Ill.) Community High Sch., 1969-74; extension advisor Licking County Coop. Extension Service, Newark, Ohio, 1975-76; consumer specialist, dir. home environ. lab. program Underwriters Labs., Inc., Northbrook, Ill., 1976-80, sec. consumer adv. council, sponsor rep. to Chgo. Area consumer sounding-board; lectr., speaker consumer product safety and foodservice sanitation; instr. Chgo. City-Coll., 1976-79; ind. consumer specialist and cons., Newark, Ohio, 1980-81; interior designer Price Enterprises, Granville, Ohio, 1981-82; foodservice cons. Dupage Area Vocat. Edn. Authority, 1974. Mem. Licking County Health Dept. steering com. Orchard-brook Homeowners Assn., 1976; Bicentennial Commn. Licking County, 1975-76; 4-H Program Rev. Com., 1975-76, county fair advisor/judge, 1975; active Walkathon Communications, March of Dimes, 1973, 74; reporter foodservice div. adv. council Dupage Area Vocat. Edn. Authority, 1969-74; vol. hot lunch coordinator Bethany Luth. Sch., Naperville, Ill., 1966-68; Brownie leader, Woodridge, Ill., 1969-71. Recipient disting. service award Nat. Inst. for Foodservice Industry, 1977. Mem. Elec. Womens Roundtable (sec. Chgo. chpt., 1978-79, treas., 1979-80, nat. conf. program co-chmn., 1979), Am. Home Econs. Assn., Home Economists in Bus., Internat. Microwave Power Inst.-Cooking Appliance Sect., Ill. Home Econs. Assn., Soc. Consumer Affairs Profls., Kappa Omicron Phi. Methodist. Clubs: Newcomers Bridge, Orchard-brook Assn. Editor consumer adv. council bull., 1977-80; contbr. consumer articles, Newark Advocate, 1974-76; editor monthly newsletter for coop. extension service, 1975-76; editor UL Trends, 1980; participant in Homemakers Cues and Clues program, sta. WCLT, Newark, 1974-76; contbr. research papers, news releases, articles to publs. in field. Home: 52 Victoria Dr Newark OH 43065 Office: PO Box 2173 Newark OH 43055

PARKER, BOOTS FARTHING, mgmt. cons., public relations exec.; b. Boone, N.C., Dec. 25, 1929; d. Joseph Edward and Polly Ida (Harmon) Farthing; student Ohio State U., 1948; m. Paul Hixson, Dec. 31, 1949 (dec. 1968); m. 2d, W. Dale Parker, Sept. 13, 1968; 1 adopted dau., Jacquelyn Susan. With Greenpark Hotel, Blowing Rock, N.C., and Sea Ranch Hotel, Ft. Lauderdale, Fla., 1947-48, O'Neil Co., Akron, Ohio, 1948-67; chief Firestone's United Trading Co., also ofcl. hostess, chief of protocol Firestone Internat., Monrovia, Liberia, 1958-61; with Holiday Inns. Am., F.W. Woolworth, Fla., 1967-72; pres. Multiple Services, Titusville, Fla., 1972—; art collector. Former mem. Democratic Exec. Com. Recipient Internat. Humanitarian award, London, 1972, Disting. Service award Fla. Sheriff's Assn., 1976; hon. col. Ala. State Militia; named hon. navy recruiter U.S. Navy Dept., 1977. Mem. N.Y. Vets. Police Assn., Va. Sheriffs Assn. Clubs: Royal Oak Golf and Country, Hound Ears Golf and Country, Order of Does, Fla. Fraternal Order Police. Home: PO Box 246 Deck Hill Boone NC 28607 Office: PO Box 144 Titusville FL 32780

PARKER, CAROLE JUNE (MRS. MARTIN M. PARKER), psychotherapist; b. Oak Park, Ill.; d. Paul Larsen and June Lillian (Timmer) Fager; B.A., Roosevelt U., 1970, M.A. (grad. scholar), 1974; postgrad. Ill. Inst. Tech., Chgo. Inst. Psychoanalysis; m. Martin Michael Parker, June 16, 1974; children—Marty, Heather. Child guidance counselor Pritzler Psychiat. Hosp., Chgo., 1969-70, spl. edn. dept. Chgo. Bd. Edn., 1970-77; therapist Berwyn Family Service, 1974-76; pvt. practice psychotherapy, Northbrook, Ill., 1976—; head dept. psychol. diagnostic testing Ravinia Circle, Ltd., 1976—; instr. Triton Jr. Coll.; instr., cons. dept. mgmt. devel. Arthur Andersen & Co. Cert. alcohol counselor. Mem. Am. Psychol. Assn., (asso.), Ill. Psychol. Assn., Midwestern Psychol. Assn. Home: 542 Pinewood Dr Glencoe IL 60022 Office: 500 Skokie Blvd Northbrook IL

PARKER, CATHERINE MARILYN, state legislator; b. Bridgeport, Conn., July 27, 1921; d. Peter F. and Beatrice E. (Cassidy) Moore; m. J. Kenneth Parker, June 5, 1943; children—Phyllis K. Miller, Diane P. Cavallo, Lawrence D. Alderwoman, City of Bridgeport, 1971-76; pres. Common Council Bridgeport, 1976; mem. Conn. Ho. of Reps., 1977—; corp. sec. Met. Life Ins. Co., Bridgeport. Democrat. Roman Catholic.

PARKER, DOROTHY, author; b. Reading, Mass., Dec. 8, 1922; d. Robert Emerson and Edith Lynwood (Ives) P.; B.A., U. N.H., 1944; m. Alvin J. Slep, 1946 (div. 1954); 1 son, Peter A.; m. 2d, Saul Maloff. Editor, McGraw-Hill Book Co., N.Y.C., 1944-52, Popular Library, N.Y.C., 1952-57; mem. faculty Columbia U., N.Y. U., New Sch. Social Research, Pratt Inst., 1957-62; sr. editor Atheneum Pubs., N.Y.C., 1959-76; tchr. workshops, writers' confs., 1944-78; freelance cons. editor, writer, reviewer, 1976—; author: The Wonderful World of Yogurt, 1972, Feeling Fine, Looking Great, 1974, Home Preserving Made Easy, 1975, Ms. Pinchpenny's Book of Kitchen Magamement, 1977, Ms. Pinchpenny's Book of Interior Design, 1979. Mem. Women's Nat. Book Assn., Young People in Book Pub. Clubs: Editors Lunch, Appalachian Mountain. Address: Second Hill Rd Bridgewater CT 06752

PARKER, ELINOR MILNOR, editor; b. Jersey City, Mar. 20, 1906; d. Charles Wolcott and Emily (Fuller) P.; A.B., Bryn Mawr Coll., 1927. Gen. asst. The Bookshop, Morristown, N.J., 1928-38; head children's books, then asst. mgr. Scribner Book Store, N.Y.C., 1938-53; editor trade books Charles Scribner's Sons, 1953-79, dir., 1966-79, asst. sec., 1970-79, v.p., 1973-79, editorial cons., 1979—. Mem. Nat. Soc. Colonial Dames. Episcopalian. Club: Cosmopolitan (N.Y.C.). Author: Cooking for One, 1949; Some Dogs, 1950; Entertaining Singlehanded, 1952; Most Gracious Majesty, 1953. Compiler: A Birthday Garland, 1949; 100 Story Poems, 1951; 100 Poems About People, 1955; I Was Just Thinking, 1959; 100 More Story Poems, 1960; The Singing and the Gold, 1962; Poems of William Wordsworth, 1964; Here and There, 1967; Four Seasons Five Senses, 1974; Poets and the English Scene, 1975; Echoes of the Sea, 1977; Letters and Numbers for Needlepoint, 1978. Home: 30 E 72d St New York NY 10021

PARKER, ELLEN, arts cons.; b. Columbus, Ohio, Feb. 18, 1949; d. Milton Marvin and Harriet Sylvia (Hyman) Parker; student N.C. Sch. Arts, 1967-68, U. Pa., 1970; cert. Inst. Arts Adminstrn., Harvard U., 1976; B.A. (Univ. Honors scholar), N.Y. U., 1978, M.P.A. (Lesley Jane Rosen scholar), 1981; Ph.D. Candidate N.Y.U., 1982; m. Zev W. Chayes, Aug. 29, 1981. Dancer, Pa. Ballet, 1968-72; adminstr. Manhattan Sch. Music Summer Chamber Music Center, 1972, 73; 1st intern dance program Nat. Endowment Arts, Washington, summer 1974; asst. to dir. for performance Manhattan Sch. Music, 1973-76; dir. continuing edn. and community services Minskoff Cultural Center, N.Y.C., 1976-77; performing arts cons. N.Y. State Council Arts, 1975—; cons. project for profl. tng. in performing arts Nat. Endowment for Arts, 1979; bd. dirs., sec. Performing Arts Dance Fund, N.Y.C., 1977—; sec., bd. dirs. Pauling Koner Dance Consort, N.Y.C., 1976—. Mem. Nat. Assn. Regional Ballet, Am. Dance Guild, Am. Council for Arts, Dance History Scholars. Author articles in field. Address: 175 W 79th St New York NY 10024

PARKER, ETHEL MAX, assn. exec.; b. Sheboygan, Wis.; d. Mayer and Jennie (Zion) Max; B.A., U. Wis., 1928, M.A., 1951; m. Cedric M. Parker, Aug. 19, 1951. Tchr. elementary sch., Cudahy, Wis., Sheboygan, 1921-25; columnist, feature writer Capital Times, Madison, Wis., 1926-33; tchr. secondary schs. and adult edn. Public Schs. Sheboygan, 1934-49; dir. public info. ARC, Madison, 1952-66; vol. public info. cons. Wis. Capital div. ARC, Madison, 1966—, sec., 1972—, chmn., 1976—. Chmn. public policy com. for establishment of child treatment center Wis. Mental Health Assn., 1958-59. Recipient Writers Cup Theta Sigma Phi, 1961. Mem. Women in Communications, Wis. Acad. Scis., Arts, and Letters (life), Wis. Alumni Assn., AAUW, Pi Lambda Theta. Club: Madison Press (v.p. with husband 1976). Home: 2810 Waubesa Ave Madison WI 53711 Office: 1202 Ann St Box 603 Madison WI 53711

PARKER, EVELYN CAMILLE HILL KILLIAN, physician, surgeon; b. Columbus, Ohio, June 28, 1918; d. John Vincent and Myrtle (Kagy) Hill; student U. Chgo., 1942-43; B.S., U. Ill., 1945, M.D., 1946; postgrad. in ophthalmology Northwestern U., 1947-48; m. E.W. Killian, Apr. 25, 1943 (dec.); children—Paul Wesley, Clyde Bernard; m. 2d, Francis W. Parker, Dec. 7, 1958. Intern, Wesley Meml. Hosp., Chgo., 1946-47; resident in ophthalmology Ill. Eye and Ear Infirmary, Chgo., 1949-51; practice medicine specializing in med. and surg. ophthalmology, Logansport, Ind., 1951—; sec. staff Meml. Hosp., Logansport, 1959; pres. med. staff St. Joseph Hosp., Logansport, 1965. Pres. Logansport Council for Public Schs., 1961-62; chmn. social concern Methodist Ch., 1963-65, ofcl. bd., 1961-65. Recipient Service award Culver Mil. Acad., 1969. Diplomate Am. Bd. Ophthalmology. Fellow Am. Acad. Ophthalmology and Otolaryngology; mem. Soc. Eye Surgeons (charter), AMA (physicians recognition award 1971, 75, 79, 82), Logansport C. of C., Cass County Med. Soc. (pres. 1971), Ind. State Med. Assn., Ind. Acad. Ophthalmology and Otolaryngology (pres. 1979-80). Republican. Clubs: Altrusa (v.p. 1967-69), Culver Mothers (pres. 1968-69). Home and Office: 2500 E Broadway Logansport IN 46947

PARKER, HAPPY NORMA, psychologist; b. Bakersfield, Calif., Sept. 23, 1929; d. Charles Edward and Ruth (Swindell) Radebaugh; A.A., Mesa Coll., 1965-67; B.A., San Diego State U., 1970, M.S., 1972; Ph.D., U.S. Internat. U., 1974; postgrad. U. Calif., San Diego, 1972-76, U. Wash., summer 1975; m. Lee E. Parker, Jan. 17, 1960; 1 son, Charles Edward. Asst. to dir. clin. studies Clin. Tng. Center, San Diego State U., 1970-76, dir. 1975; adj. prof. San Diego State U., 1973-76; pvt. practice marriage, family and child counseling, San Diego, 1974-78; instr. psychology Mesa Coll., San Diego, 1974-75, Pepperdine U., Los Angeles, 1976-77, Chapman Coll., San Diego, 1977, La Verne U., N. Island, Calif., 1976-77; psychologist Mental Health Services, Lake County, Lakeport, Calif., 1978, chief psychologist, 1978—, now dir. mental health; mediator Superior Ct., Lake County; vis. guest lectr. Grossmont Coll., 1975; faculty Yuba Coll., 1979—. Lic. marriage, family and child counselor, Calif. Mem. Am. Psychol. Assn., Psychology-Law Assn. San Diego, Western Psychol. Assn., Psi Chi. Club: Order Eastern Star.

PARKER, HARRIET MASHBURN, univ. adminstr.; b. Jackson County, N.C., June 26, 1935; d. Avery Richard and Lydia (Higdon) Mashburn; B.S.Ed., Western Carolina U., 1957; m. Grady C. Parker, Sept. 3, 1955; children—Greg, Doug, Tony. Asst. registrar Western Carolina U., 1957-69, registrar, 1970—. Named Boss of Yr., Western Carolina chpt. N.C. Assn. Ednl. Office Personnel, 1979, Dist. Boss of Yr., 1980; cert. tchr. bus., health and phys.edn., N.C. Mem. Am. Assn. Collegiate Registrars and Admissions Officers, So. Assn. Collegiate Registrars and Admissions Officers, Carolinas Assn. Collegiate Registrars and Admissions Officer, N.C. State Employees Assn., AAUW (pres. 1982-83), Jackson County C. of C., Jackson County Bus. and Profl. Women (pres. 1982-83), Camp Lab Parent-Tchr. Orgn. Baptist. Club: Order Eastern Star (past matron, dist. dep.). Home: Route 66 Box 40 Cullowhee NC 28723 Office: Room 206 UA/MHC Western Carolina U Cullowhee NC 28723

PARKER, ILA DARLENE FOLTZ, home economist; b. Winston-Salem, N.C., Mar. 21, 1944; d. Howard Gilbert and Alta Bertha (Mendenhall) Foltz; B.S. in Home Econs., Campbell U., 1966; m. Burke Henry Parker, Dec. 23, 1969. Asst. home econs. extension agt. N.C. Agrl. Extension Service (Martin County), Williamston, N.C., 1966-69, asso. home econs. extension agt., 1969-73, home econs. extension agt., 1973—. Mem. N.C. Assn. Extension Home Economists (outstanding young agt. award 1975), Nat. Assn. Extension Home Economists (disting. service award 1979), Am. Home Econs. Assn., N.C. Home Econs. Assn., N.C. Assn. Coop. Extension Assns., Epsilon Sigma Phi. Methodist. Club: Williamston Jr. Woman's (rec. sec. 1977, com. chmn. 1979). Home: 203 E Main St Williamston NC 27892

PARKER, JANE, social worker; b. Laurel, Miss., Dec. 20, 1951; d. Thomas Watson and Sarah Kathryn (Murphy) Parker; A.A., Jones County Jr. Coll., 1971; B.A., Miss. State U., 1973; M.S.W., U. So. Miss., 1979. Dir. youth ministry Parkway Heights United Meth. Ch., Hattiesburg, Miss., 1974-77; resdl. social worker Ellisville (Miss.) State Sch., 1977-79; clin. social worker, therapist Pine Belt Mental Health Center, Laurel, Miss., 1979—; cons. agys., civic groups. Mem. Miss. Conf. Bd. Ch. and Society, United Meth. Ch. Mem. Nat. Assn. Social Workers, Miss. Conf. Social Welfare, Am. Humane Soc., NOW, Bus. and Profl. Women's Club, Acad. Cert. Social Workers, Phi Alpha, Phi Theta Kappa, Phi Kappa Phi. Office: PO Box 113 Laurel MS 39440

PARKER, JEANETTE PLAUCHE, educator; b. Lake Charles, La., Oct. 14, 1934; d. Stephen Eugene and Jeanette M. (Vitello) Plauche; student Nat. U. Mexico, 1952; B.A., La. State U., 1955; M.A., U. Southwestern La. 1971; Ednl. Specialist, U. South Fla., 1977; Ed.D., U. Ga., 1979; m. Luther George Parker, Aug. 14, 1954; children—James Stephen, Robert William, George Thomas. Founder, adminstr., headmistress of Ascension Episcopal Day Sch., Lafayette, La., 1959-68; tchr. Edgar Martin Elem. Sch., 1969-75, gifted program tchr., 1975-78; asst. prof. edn., coordinator gifted programs U. Southwestern La., Lafayette, 1979—. Trustee, Episcopal Sch. of Acadiana, 1982—. Mem. Nat. Assn. for Gifted Children, Assn. for Gifted and Talented Students, World Future Soc., Creative Edn. Found., Phi Delta Kappa, Phi Kappa Phi, Alpha Delta Pi. Contbr. articles to profl. jours. Office: Univ of Southwestern Louisiana PO Box 43251 Lafayette LA 70504

PARKER, JERI, educator, writer; b. Rexburg, Idaho, Oct. 28, 1939; d. Elbert and Shirley (Stoddard) P.; B.A., Brigham Young U., 1957; M.A., U. Utah, 1970, Ph.D. (Pres. Research fellow), 1973; postgrad., Am. U., Beirut, summer 1962, U. Grenoble, summer 1963. Dir. Women's Center, Westminster Coll., Salt Lake City, 1975-79; dir. Summer Writing Workshop, U. Utah, Salt Lake City, 1980-81, instr. English, 1979—; tech. writing cons. Utah Power and Light Co., grant writing cons. Mt. Fuel Programs; bd. advs. Network Publs., Odyssey House, 1979. Mem. Delta Kappa Gamma. Republican. Mormon. Club: Literary. Author: Uneasy Survivors: Five Women Writers, 1975, also tech. writing manuals for engrs.; contbr. theatre revs., poems, short stories to various publs. Home: 956 Browning Ave Salt Lake City UT 84105

PARKER, JUDITH KOEHLER, educator; b. Dalhart, Tex., May 12, 1940; d. James Albert and Mildred Zimlich K.; B.S., St. Louis U., 1962; M.A., Washington U., 1979; m. Gerald E. Parker, Dec. 30, 1964; children—James E., G. Michael. Head bacteriologist St. Louis U. Hosp., 1962-63; bacteriologist N.Mex. Pub. Health Dept., 1963-64; instr., head bacteriologist St. Louis U. Hosp., 1964-66; med. technologist S.W. Med. Center, St. Louis County, Mo., 1966-72; adj. instr. Maryville Coll., Sunset Hills, Mo., 1981—; propr. Splty. Retail Shop, 1981—. Dir. bd. edn. St. Louis County Spl. Sch. Dist., 1982; Bonhomme Democratic committeewoman, 1979—; mem. Mo. State Dem. Com., 1980—; del. Nat. Dem. Conv., 1980, Mo. State Conv., 1980. Mem. Am. Soc. Clin. Pathologists (affiliate), Mo. Assn. Children with Learning Disabilities, Gamma Pi Epsilon, Pi Lambda Theta. Roman Catholic. Home: 53 Forest Knoll Fenton MO 63026

PARKER, KATHLYN A., chemist, educator; b. Chgo., Jan. 28, 1945; d. Harry and Pearl Kathlyn (Clark) P.; student Columbia U., 1971-73; B.A., Northwestern U., 1966; Ph.D., Stanford U., 1971. Asst. prof. chemistry Brown U., Providence, 1973-79, assoc. prof., 1979-82, prof., 1982—; mem. study sect. medicinal chemistry NIH. Sloan fellow; Camille and Henry Dreyfus tchr. scholar. Mem. Am. Chem. Soc. Office: Box H Brown U Providence RI 02912

PARKER, LESLIE WILEY, personnel cons.; b. Guam, July 31, 1950; d. Alfred E. and Gloria C. (Harris) Wiley; student pub. schs., Altus, Okla.; m. William S. Parker, May 30, 1981; children—Mandi Jo, Pauline Elizabeth, Jennifer Lynn. Property mgr. Wallace/Bell & L.M. & M. Mgmt., Baton Rouge, 1973-76; mgr. Spencer Gifts, Baton Rouge, 1976-78; employment counselor Snelling & Snelling, Baton Rouge, 1978-81; owner, operator Parker Personnel Services, Baton Rouge, 1981—. Cert. personnel cons., La. Mem. La. Assn. Bus. and Industry, Am. Bus. Women's Assn., Baton Rouge C. of C., Baton Rouge Better Bus. Bur. Office: 930 Shadowbrook Ave Denham Springs CA 70726

PARKER, LOIS PROCTOR, educator; b. Takoma Park, Md., Dec. 31, 1927; d. Frank Baker and Margaret Elizabeth (Faulconer) Proctor; A.B., Washington Coll., 1949; M.A., George Washington U., 1956; m. James W. Parker, Dec. 28, 1948 (div.); 1 dau., Robin E. Parker. Tchr. jr. high sch., Takoma Park, 1949-53, tchr.-coordinator coop. work programs, 1953-57; vocat. counselor Montgomery Blair High Sch., Silver Spring, Md., 1960-61; spl. dept. research Montgomery County (Md.) Public Schs., 1961-67, specialist in work experience programs, 1967-69, supr. curriculum and instrn., 1969-75, coordinator career edn., ednl. cons., 1975—. Mem. TV curriculum council Sta. WETA, Washington, 1969-73; mem. TV com. Md. Dept. Edn., 1975—; mem. Citizens' Adv. Com. Career and Vocat. Edn., 1974—; chmn., bd. dirs. Montgomery County Jr. Achievement, 1980-81; coordinator C. of C. Adopt-A-Sch. Program, 1977—. Recipient award Women's Am. ORT, 1980-81. Mem. Nat. Tchrs. Assn., Md. State Tchrs. Assn., Montgomery County Tchrs. Assn., Am. Vocat. Assn., Montgomery County Assn. Adminstrv. and Supervisory Personnel, Alpha Chi Omega. Democrat. Episcopalian. Contbr. articles to profl. jours., also author TV scripts and curriculum guides. Home: 3612 Patrick Henry Dr Olney MD 20832 Office: 850 Hungerford Dr Rockville MD 20850

PARKER, LUCY ULMAN, psychologist; b. Vienna, Austria, Jan. 21, 1933; came to U.S., 1939, naturalized, 1945; d. Joseph and Maria (Tauber) Thimann; B.S., Boston U., 1958, M.Ed., 1965, Ed.D., 1974; Ph.D., Heed U., 1973; m. Robert Alan Parker, Feb. 1, 1980; children by previous marriage—Karen Sue, Janet Lee, Geoffrey Samuel, Linda Ann. Elem. tchr. Bellingham (Mass.) Public Schs., 1958-59; tchr. jr. high sch. Temple Shalom, Newton, Mass., 1962-64; sch. adjustment counselor Needham (Mass.) Public Schs., 1964-67; pvt. practice psychotherapy, crisis intervention, Waban, Mass., 1965-72; counseling psychologist Leslie B. Cutler Child Guidance Clinic, Norwood, Mass., 1967-70, Walker Home for Children, Needham, 1968-72; clin. dir. Chestnut Hill (Mass.) Psychotherapy Assos., 1971—; lectr. in psychology Northeastern U. Grad. Sch. Edn., 1966-67; asst. prof. edn. Lesley Coll., 1967-72; asso. prof. psychology and edn., New Eng. coordinator, Heed U., 1972-74, prof., 1974-78; asso. prof. edn. Newton Coll., 1972-75; guest lectr. colls., univs., 1966-78; research asso. in behavioral scis. Mass. Coll. Optometry, 1973-75; sensitivity group trainer, cons. human relations Nat. Tng. Labs., 1968-79; cons., condr. seminars and workshops in field. Bd. dirs. Washingtonian Hosp., Jamaica Plain, Mass., 1967-77. Lic. psychologist, cert. elem. tchr., guidance counselor, dir. guidance, sch. adjustment counselor, Mass.; diplomate Am. Acad. Behavioral Medicine. Fellow Am. Acad. Optometry, Am. Acad. Scis., Internat. Council Sex Edn. and Parenthood; mem. Am. Psychol. Assn., AAUP, Am. Soc. Clin. Hypnosis, Am. Assn. Sex Educators and Counselors, Am. Assn. Marriage and Family Counselors, Am. Personnel and Guidance Assn., Mass. Psychol. Assn. Research, publs. in field. Office: 25 Boylston St Chestnut Hill MA 02167

PARKER, LYNDA MICHELE, psychiatrist; b. Phila., Sept. 28, 1947; d. Albert Francis and Dorothy Thomasinia (Herriott) P.; B.A., C. W. Post Coll., 1968; M.A. (Martin Luther King Jr. scholar 1968-70), N.Y.U., 1970; M.D., Cornell U., 1974; postgrad. N.Y. Psychoanalytic Inst., 1977-82. Intern, N.Y. Hosp., N.Y.C., 1975; resident in psychiatry Payne Whitney Clinic, N.Y.C., 1975-78; psychiatrist in charge day program Cabrini Med. Center, N.Y.C., 1978-79, attending psychiatrist, 1978—; admitting psychiatrist inpatient psychiat. treatment Payne Whitney Clinic, N.Y.C., 1978—, supr. psychiatry residents, 1978—, supr. long-term psychotherapy, 1980-82; attending psychiatrist N.Y. Hosp., Cornell Med. Center, 1979—; practice medicine specializing in psychiatry, N.Y.C., 1979—; instr. psychiatry Cornell U. Med. Coll., 1977—, N.Y. Med. Coll., 1978—. Recipient Ethel B. Cohen award in biology C.W. Post Coll., 1968; Charles E. Horn prize Cornell U. Med. Coll., 1970. Mem. Am. Psychiat. Assn. Episcopalian.

PARKER, MARGERY ELEANOR, sales rep.; b. Scranton, Pa., Sept. 24, 1946; d. Roswell James and Margery Elizabeth (Thomas) Parker; B.S. in Med. Tech., Temple U., 1968. Research technologist Temple U. Sch. Medicine, Phila., 1968-76; instr. Coulter Electronics, Islamorada, Fla., 1976-77; sales rep. Curtin Matheson Sci., Easter, Pa., 1977-80, Calbiochem-Behring Corp., Allentown, Pa. 1980—. Mem. Am. Soc. Clin. Pathologists. Republican. Presbyterian. Address: 108 E Village Round Allentown PA 18106

PARKER, MARILYN MORRIS, corp. exec.; b. St. Louis, Jan. 2, 1935; d. Walter Louis and R. Viola (Morris) Priebe; B.B.A., Washington U., 1954, M.B.A., 1955; m. H. Virgil Parker, Mar. 11, 1971. With IBM Corp., various locations, 1957—, mgr. IBM Aids, Los Angeles, 1971-75, mgr. performance evaluation, San Jose, Calif., 1976-79, tech. asst. to mgr. performance and tech., 1979-80, mgr. IBM Los Angeles Sci. Center, 1981—; v.p. Cherokee Creek Enterprises, Los Angeles and San Jose, 1973—. Co-founder, pres. Am. Indian Scholarship Fund, 1971-76, No. Calif. regional dir., 1977-80, exec. dir., 1981—; mem. Santa Clara County Alcoholism Adv. Bd., 1977; bd. dirs. Try Found., 1977-78. Named KNX Newsradio Citizen of the Week, Feb. 1974; recipient City of Los Angeles Cert. of Merit, 1976, others. Mem. Cherokee Confederacy, Am. Indian Edn. Assn., Washington U. Alumni Council, Am. Harp Soc. Lutheran. Office: 9045 Lincoln Blvd Los Angeles CA 90045

PARKER, MARION DEAN HUGHES, home care service exec.; b. Greenwich, Conn., July 21, 1911; d. Walter A. and Marion K. (Dean) Hughes; B.A., UCLA, 1932; m. Conkey P. Whitehead, Nov. 14, 1929 (div. Aug. 1933); m. 2d, Andrew Granville Pierce III, Oct. 21, 1933; m. 3d, Willard Parker, Oct. 5, 1939 (div. 1951); 1 son, Walter van Eps. Actress appearing in Broadway prodns. New Faces, Three Waltzes, I Must Love Someone, on tour in The Women, The Man Who Came to Dinner, Lady in the Dark; various night club engagements; appeared in motion picture All About Eve; TV appearances; owner, mgr. Marion Parker's Guys & Dolls, Scottsdale, Ariz., 1951-59; mng. dir., purchasing agt. shipboard gift and accessory shops Am. Export Lines, 1960-64; dir. spl. events ITT, N.Y.C., 1965-66; exec. dir. Assn. Operating Room Nurses, N.Y.C., 1966-68; pres. Home Care-Ring Service, N.Y.C., 1968—; staff Park East Real Estate; asst. to v.p. in charge devel. Bennett Coll., Millbrook, N.Y., 1970; public relations cons., 1970—. Mem. Women's Nat. Republican Club, N.Y.C., Manhattan East Rep. Club, N.Y.C. Mem. Screen Actors Guild. Address: 301 E 78th St New York City NY 10021

PARKER, MARY EVELYN DICKERSON (MRS. W. BRYANT PARKER), state ofcl.; b. Fullerton, La., Nov. 8, 1920; d. Racia E. and Addie (Graham) Dickerson; B.A., Northwestern State Coll., 1941; diploma of social welfare, La. State U., 1943; m. W. Bryant Parker, Oct. 31, 1954 (dec. May 1965); children—Mary Bryant, Ann Graham. Social worker, Allen Parish, La., 1941-42; personnel adminstr. War Dept., Camp Claiborne, La., 1943-47; editor Oakdale (La.) Jour., 1947-48; exec. dir. La. Dept. of Commerce and Industry, Baton Rouge, 1948-52; with Mut. of N.Y., Baton Rouge, 1952-56; chmn. State Bd. of Pub. Welfare, Baton Rouge, 1950-51; commr. La. Dept. of Pub. Welfare, Baton Rouge, 1956-63; commr. Div. of Adminstrn., State of La., Baton Rouge, 1964-67; treas. State of La., Baton Rouge, 1968—. Chmn. White House Conf. on Children and Youth, 1960; pres. La. Conf. of Social Welfare, 1959-61; nat. Democratic Committeewoman, 1948-52; bd. dirs. Womans Hosp., Baton Rouge; trustee Episcopal High Sch., Baton Rouge, Baton Rouge Gen. Hosp. Found.; mem. adv. council Coll. Bus., Tulane U., New Orleans. Named Baton Rouge Woman of Yr., 1976. Baptist. Home: 9309 Hill Trace Ave Baton Rouge LA 70809 Office: PO Box 44154 Capitol Sta Baton Rouge LA 70804

PARKER, MARYLAND (MIKE), radio announcer; b. Oklahoma City, Feb. 5, 1926; d. Clarence N. and Minzola (Perkins) Davis; student U. Ark., Pine Bluff, 1970-71; student Marymount Coll., 1974-77; m. John Harrison Parker, Nov. 25, 1944 (dec.); children—Norma Jean Parker Brown, Janice Kay Parker Shelby, Joyce Lynn, John H., Cherie D. Parker Hite, Patrick Scott, Charles Roger. Beautician, Maryland's Ho. of Beauty, Salina, Kans., 1964-69; youth advisor NAACP, Salina, 1970-72; newspaper reporter B.A.C.O.S. Newsletter, Salina, 1971-77;

radio announcer Kina's B.A.C.O.S. Report, Salina, 1973—. Mem. Saline County Democratic Women, 1960—; part-time vol. Salvation Army, Salina, 1979—; bd. dirs. Salina Child Care Assn. Mem. Internat. Platform Assn., NAACP (life), Nat. Fedn. Press Women, Kans. Press Women, VFW Aux., Am. Legion Aux., YWCA. Mormon. Home: 920 Birch Dr PO Box 705 Salina KS 67401 Office: PO Box 778 Salina KS 67401

PARKER, NANCY SNOWDEN DEUPREE, artist; b. Memphis, Jan. 15, 1934; d. William Williams and Mary Evelyn (Cavett) Deupree; student Southwestern at Memphis, 1952-55, Boston Museum Sch., 1965, Furman U., 1960, Memphis Acad. Art, 1963, Harvard Adult Sch., 1964, Houston Mus. Sch. Art, 1978; divorced; children—Michael Lloyd-Cavett Crisamore, Madeline Penn Crisamore. Portrait artist, 1968—; one-women exhbns. include: Front St. Gallery, Lahaina, Maui, Hawaii, Menemsha Gallery, Martha's Vineyard, Mass., Sycamore Gallery, Memphis, Carlen's Gallery, Atlanta, Lantern Lane Gallery, Houston, High Mus. Art, Atlanta, Columbus (Ga.) Mus. Art; owner Nancy D. Parker Art Collection, 1980—; art show judge, 1975—. Chmn. Atlanta chpt. LWV, 1969. Recipient 1st prize for slum ghetto project Atlanta Women's C. of C., 1968. Mem. Artists Equity. Republican. Episcopalian. Club: Houstonian. Address: 170 Haversham Dr Houston TX 77024

PARKER, NANCY WINSLOW, writer, illustrator; b. Maplewood, N.J., Oct. 18, 1930; d. Winslow Aurelius and Beatrice McCelland (Gaunt) P.; B.A., Mills Coll., Calif., 1952; postgrad. Art Students League, N.Y.C., Sch. Visual Art, N.Y.C. Sec., Nat. Broadcasting Co., N.Y.C., 1956-60; TV-radio promoter N.Y. Soccer Club, 1961-63; syndicated sales clk. RCA Victor Record div. Radio Corp. Am., 1964-67; art dir. Appleton, Century, Crofts div. Meredith Corp., N.Y.C., 1968-70; staff designer Holt, Rinehart and Winston, Inc., N.Y.C., 1970-73; author and illustrator: The Man with The Take-Apart Head, 1974, The Party At The Old Farm, 1975, Mrs. Wilson Wanders Off, 1976, Love From Uncle Clyde, 1977, The Crocodile Under Louis Finneberg's Bed, 1978, The President's Cabinet, 1978; The Ordeal of Byron B. Blackbear, 1979, Puddums, the Cathcarts' Orange Cat, 1980, Poofy Loves Company, 1980, The Spotted Dog, 1980, The President's Car (hon. mention N.Y. Acad. Sci. 1981), 1981, Cooper, The McNallys' Big Black Dog, 1981; illustrator books: Oh, A Hunting We Will Go!, 1974, Warm as Wool, Cool as Cotton, The Story of Natural Fibers, 1975, The Goat in the Rug, 1976, Willy Bear (Christopher award), 1976, Sweetly Sings the Donkey, 1976; The Substitute, 1977, Hot Cross Buns and Other Old Street Cries, 1978, No Bath Tonight, 1978, My Mom Travels a Lot (Christopher award AIGA), 1981. Sec.-treas. E. 74th St Block Assn. Jane Tinkham Broughton fellow, 1975. Mem Graphic Artists Guild, Soc. Illustrators, Author's Guild. Club: Mantoloking Yacht. Home: 51 E 74th St New York NY 10021

PARKER, PATRICIA EVANS, bus. machines co. exec.; b. Nashville, June 25, 1954; d. Robert Carlton and Martha Elizabeth (Leyhew) Evans; student Vol. State Community Coll., Belmont Coll., 1972-74; m. James F. Parker, Jr., Sept. 5, 1975; 1 dau., Angela Beth. Acctg. clk. Jenkins & Tallent, Nashville; now exec. v.p., sec.-treas. Bus. Machines, Inc., Nashville; also notary public, Tenn. Mem. Exec. Women Internat., Beta Sigma Phi. Democrat. Baptist. Home: 112 Overbrook Point Ct Brentwood TN 37027 Office: PO Box 110376 304 Space Park S Nashville TN 37211

PARKER, PEGGY BONNER, graphic designer; b. Princton, W.Va., May 23, 1937; d. Claude Marion and Mabel Ann (Bragg) Bonner; B.S. in Art Edn., Concord Coll., Athens, W.Va., 1958; postgrad. Cath. U. Am., Parsons Sch. Design; m. Thomas Curtis Parker, Feb. 21, 1968. Secondary art tchr., Fairfax, Va., 1958-61; art edn. cons., N.Y.C., 1964-66; art dir. Opera News mag., N.Y.C., 1966-69; art dir., designer Sch. Times, 1970-71; freelance graphic designer cosmetic related industries, 1971—. Recipient design awards for packaging perfumes and cosmetics Art Dir.'s Show. Mem. Soc. Illustrators, N.Y. Art Dir.'s Club.

PARKER, ROSEMARY KRIEGUER, educator; b. Serena, Ill., Aug. 5, 1922; d. Fred G. and Rose M. Krieguer; B.S., U. Ill., 1944; M.S., Iowa State U., 1953; cert. advanced study No. Ill. U., 1975; m. Robert E. Parker, Dec. 23, 1954; children—Anne, Elizabeth, Jane Susan. High sch. tchr. in Ill., 1944-59; tchr. home econs. Ill. Valley Community Coll., Oglesby, part-time 1967—; instr. home econs. part-time No. Ill. U., 1981; extension vol. instr. Tailoring cons. LaSalle County 4-H Clubs; judge 4-H Fairs, Grange contests; mem. Sandwich (Ill.) Hosp. Aux. Mem. Craft Guild, Joliet Weavers Guild, Pi Lambda Theta. Clubs: Serena Improvement, Midwest Weavers. Home: Rural Route 1 Box 2 Serena IL 60549 Office: Ill Valley Community Coll Oglesby IL 61348

PARKER, TERRY MARIE, lawyer, city ofcl.; b. Higginsville, Mo., Apr. 16, 1948; d. Elvis Wyatt and Lola Mae (Jennings) P.; B.A., U. Mo., Kansas City, 1970; J.D., U. Kans., 1973; postgrad. in public adminstrn. Ariz. State U.; m. Robert David Sparks, Jan. 3, 1980. Admitted to Kans. bar, 1973; staff atty. Ariz. Legis. Council, Phoenix, 1973-78; mgmt. asst., mgmt. and budget dept. City of Phoenix, 1978-80, cable communications officer Office Cable Communications, 1980—. Mem. Am. Bar Assn., Kans. Bar Assn., Internat. City Mgmt. Assn., Ariz. Mcpl. Mgmt. Assts. Assn., Am. Soc. Public Adminstrn., Nat. Assn. Telecommunications Officers and Advisors (exec. com.), Women in Cable (dir. Ariz. chpt.). Office: 251 W Washington 9th Floor Phoenix AZ 85003

PARKER, VIRGINIA ANNE, ranch adminstr.; b. Brockton, Mass., Apr. 24, 1918; d. John and Jennie (Krusas) Salus; student Bryant Stratton Coll., Boston, 1938, Columbia U., 1941; m. John Glendon Parker, Feb. 1942 (div. 1952); one dau., Deborah Anne. Sales supr. Reuben H. Donnelley Corp., N.Y.C., 1944-46; traveling sales rep. Elizabeth Arden Inc., N.Y.C., 1946-47; advt. salesperson Park East Pub. Co., N.Y.C., 1947-48; point of sale display work Parker Kleinhans Assos. and V.A. Parker Co., N.Y.C., 1950-55; merchandising coordinator WGBS Radio Sta., Miami, 1957-59; lighting cons. Verd-A-Ray Corp., Miami, 1960-63; string writer, advt. salesperson Palm Beach (Fla.) Post Times, 1963-65; advt; advt. salesperson Avon Park (Fla.) Sun and Sebring (Fla.) News, 1965-67; sales mgr. radio sta. WJCM, Sebring, and advt. salesperson radio sta. WIPC, Lake Wales, Fla., 1967-69; office mgr., trustee asst., exec. sec. Griffith Ranch Inc., Okeechobee, Fla., 1969-80, semi-ret., 1980. Mem. Bus. and Profl. Women Miami (2d v.p., rec. sec. 1958-60, state award for nat. security 1960), Parents Without Partners Fla. (news editor 1962-63). Club: Advt. Miami. Address: 415 Mat-Lo Ave PO Box 1112 Sebring FL 33870

PARKER, YETTA BRANDWINE, ret. assn. ofcl.; b. Bklyn., Oct. 25, 1918; d. Max and Frieda (Orling) Brandwine; B.S. in Bus., C.W. Post Coll., 1968; M.L.S., SUNY, Stony Brook, 1974; children—Robert Alan, Steven Paul. Adminstrv. asst. to chief scientist Cutler-Hammer Inc., Melville, N.Y., 1957-71, asst. to chmn. dept. music, 1973-76, asst. to chmn. elec. engring., 1971-73; adminstrv. asst. to mng. editor Phys. Rev., Am. Phys. Soc., Ridge, N.Y., 1976-81. Club: Hadassah (v.p. 1974). Home: 7005 Toledo Rd Spring Hill FL 33526

PARKER-KLEIN, KAREN CROMWELL, psychologist; b. Stamford, Conn., Aug. 26, 1946; d. Blakeslee Barnes and Doris Grace (Knutson) Parker; B.A., Lake Erie Coll., 1968; B.A., U. Md., 1973; M.A., Western Res. U., 1977, Ph.D., 1978; m. Ronald Marvin Klein, July 12, 1980; 1 dau., Halle Elizabeth. Psychol. fellow Cleve. Clin., 1975-76; psychol. intern VA Hosp., Cleve., 1976-78, Loma Linda, Calif., 1976-78, pain unit, 1979—; instr. Fuller Theol. Sem., 1979—; lectr. Loma Linda U. Recipient Alumni award Case Western Res. U., 1977; superior performance award VA, 1980, 82; Hadassah award, 1982. Mem. Am. Psychol. Assn. Democrat. Episcopalian. Office: VA Hosp 11201 Benton St Loma Linda CA 92367

PARKER-MADISON, ISABEL WALSH, gerontologist; b. Pittsfield, Mass., Sept. 22, 1929; d. Joseph F. and Ada Francis (Bauer) Walsh; B.S., Hobart Coll., Geneva, N.Y., 1949; M.S., North Adams (Mass.) Coll., 1966; gerontology cert. U. R.I., 1973; m. Earl Madison, Aug. 22, 1975; children—David, Faith, Stephen Parker. Dir., Hobart News Bur., 1946; editorial writer Brit. Info. and Press Service, N.Y.C., 1945-46; editor Gen. Electric News, Pittsfield, 1947; script writer, program coordinator, announcer Sta. WBRK-TV, Pittsfield, 1948-54, 1960-78; dir. aging program, Pitts., 1957-80; tchr. English, Berkshire Community Coll., Pittsfield, 1966-81; assoc. editor ABC, N.Y.C., 1978—; dir. Council on Aging, Mass. Evaluation Com. Aging; mem. bd. Vis. Nurses Assn., 1975-80; initiator program on aging, Mass., del. White House Conf. on Aging. Mem. Pittsfield Bicentennial Commn., 1975-76; pres. Berkshire Social Services Commn., 1972-73; active United Community Services; mem. Town Players. Recipient Bradford Arms award Berkshire Housing Corp., 1973, Community Coordinator award Mass. Dept. Elder Affairs, 1973; award Rotary Club, Kiwanis Club; Mass. Library dept. grantee, 1979; NEA grantee, 1976-80. Mem. Western Mass. Assn. Councils Aging (pres. 1971-79), Mass. Center Dirs. Assn. (pres. 1975-78), Mass. Assn. Older Ams., Nat. Recreation and Parks Soc., Nat. Council on Aging (charter), Gerontol. Soc., Bus. and Profl. Women's Club. Clubs: Quota, Women's, Pittsfield Coll. Author column Berkshire Eagle, 1960—; contbr. articles on gerontology to profl. jours.

PARKEY, EDITH MAGILL LAMPKIN, clergywoman, guidance counselor; b. Cin., Jan. 14, 1921; d. Roland and Edith (Mehan) Magill; B.A., U. Cin., 1937; postgrad. Temple U., 1965; Ph.D., Coll. Divine Metaphysics, Indpls., 1969; postgrad. TEC, Antioch/West, Seattle, 1980; m. Eugene E. Lampkin, Feb. 2, 1936 (div. 1952); children—Curtis, James, Sharon Louise; m. 2d, Otis Parkey, Oct. 20, 1959 (dec. 1963). Archtl. designer Arnold Voss, N.Y.C., 1959-64, U.S. Post Office, Phila., Cin., 1964-71; ordained to ministry Ch. of Divine Metaphysics, 1969; pastor 1st Ch. Divine Metaphysics (now New Thought Seminar Arts and Scis. of Living), Cin., 1969-73; columnist Cin. Post, 1970; dir. Human Potential Specialists-Consultants and Trainers, Seattle, 1978. Asso. founder, pres. Cin. Council on Status of Women, 1970-76. Mem. Federally Employed Women (founder chpt. 1, 1969), Huxley Inst. BioSocial Studies, Internat. Hypnosis Assn., Nat. Geocosmic Research Assn., Am. Fedn. Astrologers (life), Bus. and Profl. Women, Women in Communication, Internat. Platform Assn., Nat. Astrological Research and Delineation Assn. (past pres.), many others. Author: Sages Secrets - Ten Lessons in Meditation Techniques, 1973; Ye Pray Amiss: Prayer Is a Science, 1975; Modern Professional Astrology, Vol. 1, 1976.

PARKHURST, ELEANOR, editor, historian; b. Chelmsford, Mass.; d. George Thomas and Ednah Florence (Byam) P.; B.A., Wellesley Coll., 1931, M.A., 1933; postgrad. U. Chgo. Asst. to dean grad. studies, asst. to head dept. English lit. Wellesley Coll., 1931-34; asst. in home econs. Iowa State Coll., 1934-35; adminstrv. asst. Sch. Social Service Adminstrn., U. Chgo., 1935-39; psychiat. case worker, home finding supr. R.I. Children's Friend Soc., Providence, 1939-42; psychiat. social worker Family Welfare Soc., Providence, 1942-44; editor Chelmsford-Westford-Tyngsboro Newsweekly, Inc., 1960—; cons. in public relations. Trustee, Old Chelmsford Garrison House Assn., 1953—; curator Chelmsford Hist. Soc., 1956-58; asso. Chelmsford Republican Town Com., 1980. Recipient cert. of appreciation Am. Legion, 1962. Mem. Nat. Acad. Cert. Social Workers, AAUW, NOW, Inst. Gen. Semantics, Internat. Soc. Gen. Semantics, Chelmsford Art Soc., Sigma Delta Chi. Episcopalian, Club: Chelmsford Garden (hon.). Home: 51 Acton Rd Chelmsford MA 01824 Office: 5 North Rd Chelmsford MA 01824

PARKHURST, VIOLET KINNEY, artist; b. Derby Line, Vt., Apr. 26, 1926; d. Edson Frank and Rosa (Beauchene) Kinney; student Mus. Fine Arts, Boston, 1941-42, Baylor Coll., 1942-43, Calif. State U., Los Angeles, 1955-56; m. Donald W. Parkhurst, Apr. 10, 1948. Fgn. corr. Brazilian mags., 1944-51; tech. illustrator Douglas Aircraft, 1952-53; one-woman shows include: Biltmore Galleries, Los Angeles, 1975-76, Saddleback Gallery, Santa Ana, Calif., 1977; group shows include: Cultural Exchange Tour of European Museums, 1962-67, Laguna Art Festival, 1964, Catalina Invitational, 1975-77; owner galleries Ports of Call, Los Angeles, Laguna Beach, Calif., Seaport, Long Beach, Calif., Queen Mary, Long Beach. Fellow Am. Inst. Fine Arts. Author: Parkhurst on Seascapes, 1973; Parkhurst Painting at the Seashore; Parkhurst on Sunsets. Home: 2300 Daladier Dr Rancho Palos Verdes CA 90274

PARKO-KOZUCH, DONNA, psychologist; b. Conemaugh, Pa., July 12, 1937; d. Frank J. and Catherine (Podgorney) Parko; B.S., Indiana U. of Pa., 1959; M.Ed., Pa. State U., 1961; Ph.D., Am. U., 1977; m. James R. Kozuch, Jan. 25, 1964; children—James R., Benjamin P. Dir. guidance Johnstown (Pa.) Public Schs., 1961-64; sch. psychologist Moutgomery County (Md.) Schs., 1977-78; staff psychologist D.C. Inst. Mental Hygiene, 1977-81; psychologist disability determination div. State of Md., Balt., 1981-82; pvt. practice psychology, Bethesda and Chevy Chase, Md., 1981—; cons. in field. Lic. psychologist, Md., D.C. Mem. Am. Psychol. Assn., Md. Psychol. Assn., D.C. Psychol. Assn., Assn. Practicing Psychologists of Montgomery and Prince Georges County. Club: Carderock Springs Swim and Tennis. Home: 8025 Thornley Ct Bethesda MD 20817 Office: 35 Wisconson Circle Suite 515 Chevy Chase MD 20814

PARKS, ARLENE GARVERICH, ceramist, educator; b. Harrisburg, Pa., May 18, 1930; d. Charles and Thelma (Stambaugh) Garverich; student Wilson Coll., 1948-50; B.S., Johns Hopkins U., 1952; B.F.A, Md. Inst. Art, 1952; postgrad. Towson State U., 1974-75, Johns Hopkins U., 1952; B.F.A., Antioch Coll., Columbia, Md., 1982; m. H. Emslie Parks, June 14, 1952; children—Douglas Wayne, Cinda Lee, Donna Lynn. Tchr. art, Catonsville (Md.) High Sch., 1952-53; elementary art adviser Md., 1953-54; adviser to occupational therapist Summitt Nursing Home, Bd. Edn. Baltimore County, 1969-70; tchr. ceramics, adult edn., Baltimore County, 1959-64, 68-82; tchr. pottery Coll. Bahamas, Abaco Island, 1981—. Adviser, Girl Scouts, 4H; edn. chmn. Baltimore County Hosp. Aux., 1970-72. Recipient grand award Middle Atlantic Ceramics Assn., 1973, 1st prize Md. Biennial of Crafts. Nat. League Am. Pen Women, 1973. Mem. Alumnae Assn. Johns Hopkins U., Alumnae Assn. Md. Inst., Nat. League Am. Pen Women (2d v.p. Carroll br. 1978, pres. 1982—), Md. Art League, Rehobeth Art League, Chesapeake Potters Assn. Episcopalian. Home: Granite Rd Woodstock MD 21163 also Marsh Harbor Abaco Bahamas

PARKS, BETTY JEAN, retail exec.; b. Oklahoma City, July 2, 1926; d. Claude LeRoy and Minnie Pauline (Samara) Rash; student N.Mex. State U., 1963-65, Sierra Coll., 1977-80; m. William VanZant Parks, June 3, 1946 (dec. 1982); 1 dau., Claudia Juliet. Asst. mgr. post exchange, 1944; civil service employee, 1945-46; owner, operator bookkeeping service, 1947-49; mem. personnel and payroll staff Officers Club, Ft. Sill, Okla., 1952-53; owner, mgr. Wilbets Maternity Shop, Ozak, Ala., 1954-59; mgr. Vanity Fair Jr. Dept. Store, Sierra Vista, Ariz., 1962; rental-leasing agt. Paul Leggi Realty Co., El Paso, Tex., 1967-69; mgr. Beno's Family Apparel, Auburn, Calif., 1974-82; dist. mgr. The Gamekeepers, Goleta, Calif., 1982—. Bd. dirs. Regional Occupational Program; mem. Community Council, White Sands Missile Range, N.Mex., 1963-64; past leader, trainer Rio Grande council Gril Scouts U.S.A.; mem. ad hoc com. Sierra Coll., Pocklin, Calif. Named Mgr. of Yr., Beno's Family Apparel, 1978. Mem. Nat. Assn. Female Execs., Auburn C. of C. (dir.), Auburn Ravine Mchts. Assn. (v.p.). Clubs: Order Eastern Star, White Shrine of Jerusalem. Office: 35 S Patera Ln Goleta CA 93117

PARKS, JULIA ETTA, educator; b. Kansas City, Kans., Apr. 5, 1923; d. Hays and Idella Long; B.Ed., Washburn U., 1959, M.Ed., 1965; Ed.D., U. Kans., 1980; m. James A. Parks, Aug. 10, 1941; 1 son, James Hays. Tchr., Lawman Hill Elem. Sch., 1959-64; faculty Washburn U., Topeka, Kans., 1964—, asso. prof. edn. 1981—, mem. pres.'s adv. council, 1981—; mem. vis. teams Nat. Council for Accreditation of Tchr. Edn., 1974—. Bd. dirs. Children's Hour, 1981—, Mulvane Art Center, 1974-78. Mem. Internat. Reading Assn., Kans. Reading Assn., Kans. Reading Profls. Higher Edn., Delta Kappa Gamma, Phi Delta Kappa. Methodist. Office: Washburn University Dept Education 1700 College Ave Topeka KS 66621

PARKS, SALLIE ANN RENNIE, community relations specialist; b. Mich., Sept. 5, 1936; d. Bertram Alexander and Edna Vera (Lampman) Rennie; B.S., Central Mich. U., 1959; children—Sheri Lynn, Steven Rennie. Tchr. public schs. in Mich. and Fla., 1959-75; editor newsletter Pinellas Classroom Tchrs. Assn., 1967-73; exec. dir. Pinellas County Arts Council, Clearwater, Fla., 1976-81; dir. community relations Mease Hosp. and Clinic, Dunedin, Fla., 1981—; bd. dirs. Performing Arts Center and Theatre, Clearwater, 1978-81; cons. in field. Mem. Clearwater Community Devel. Adv. Bd.; chmn. Clearwater Planning and Zoning Bd., 1980, 81; bd. dirs. Mental Health Assn. Pinellas County; active Leadership Pinellas. Mem. Nat. Soc. Arts and Letters, Am. Council Arts, Women in Communications, Inc., Am. Soc. Hosp. Pub. Relations, Fla. Pub. Relations Assn., Pub. Relations Council, Fla. Hosp. Assn., PEO, LWV (pres. Clearwater area 1971-72), Alpha Chi Omega, Pi Kappa Delta. Republican. Presbyterian. Office: Mease Hosp and Clinic 833 Milwaukee Ave Dunedin FL 33528

PARKS, SUZANNE LOWRY, psychiat. nurse, educator; b. Columbus, Ohio, Feb. 29, 1936; d. Frank Carson and Mabel (Brown) Lowry Morris; B.S., Emory U., 1958; M.S., U. Md., 1959; children—Jennifer, Kristin, Greg. Asst. prof. psychiat. nursing U. Va., 1959-61, U. N.C., Chapel Hill, 1961-63, grad. faculty, 1975-81; asst. prof., dir. div. psychiat. nursing Duke U., 1964-67; clin. instr. psychiatry Sch. Medicine, Emory U., Atlanta, 1968-71; asst. prof., nursing coordinator Appalachian Area Nursing Inservice project Clemson (S.C.) U., 1973-75; clin. staff Northside Mental Health Center, 1975-81; dir. staff devel. Hawaii State Hosp., Kaneoke, 1981—. Mem. Am., N.C. nurses assns., Am. Guild of Hypnotherapists, Parents Without Partners, Triangle (dir. chpt. 1977-78), Mental Health Assn., PTA. Home: 45-535 Luluku Rd Apt K5 Kaneoke HI 96744

PARLATO, LINDA GAE, painter; b. Aurora, Ill., Dec. 20, 1939; d. Gaylord Major and Sophie Lucille (Baskovich) Renz; B.A., Milw. Downer Coll., 1960; postgrad. Drury Coll., 1972, SUNY, Buffalo, 1979; m. George S. Parlato, June 25, 1960; children—Marcella, Salvatore, Gae Lynn, Gina Lee. One-woman show; Gallery Upstairs, Orchard Park, N.Y., 1976; group shows include: Mid-South Exhibit, Memphis, 1971, 72, Watercolor U.S.A., Springfield, Mo., 1973, St. Louis Art Mus., 1974, Mid-Am. V Nelson Gallery Kansas City, 1974, Am. Watercolor Soc., 1976, NAD, 1977, AAO Gallery, Buffalo, 1980, 81; represented in permanent collections: Lawrence U., Spiva Art Center of So. Mo. Coll., Sch. of Ozarks; co-owner Park Central Art Gallery, Springfield, Mo., 1972-75, instr., 1974-82. Mem. Am. Watercolor Soc. (asso.), East Aurora Art Soc., Women's Caucus for Art. Republican. Roman Catholic. Home and Studio: 3 Red Brick Rd Orchard Park NY 14127

PARLETTE, CAROL HOLLAND, assn. exec.; b. Springfield, Mo., Feb. 21, 1944; d. Marvin Benjamin and Georgia Genevieve (Hagar) Holland; B.S. in Edn., SW Mo. State U., 1966; M.P.H., U. Calif., Berkeley, 1974; m. George Nicholas Parlette, May 23, 1975. Tchr. English and speech Lockwood (Mo.) High Sch., 1967-68; program asst. continuing edn. in public health Am. Public Health Assn., San Francisco, 1968-71; exec. dir. Calif. Soc. Internal Medicine, San Francisco, 1972—. Bd. dirs. Redwood Hills Assn. Regents scholar, 1962. Mem. Profl. Conv. Mgmt. Assn., Am. Assn. Med. Soc. Execs., Am. Soc. Assn. Execs., No. Calif. Soc. Assn. Execs. (dir.) Bay Area Exec. Women's Forum (dir.). Club: Commonwealth (San Francisco). Office: 703 Market St Suite 1412 San Francisco CA 94103

PARMAN, MICKEY (MARJORY JEAN), journalist, news editor; b. Harrisonville, Mo., Sept. 13; d. Albert Denton and Eva Buriella (Kerrens) Matteson; grad. public schs.; m. Keith Charles Parman, Oct. 12, 1947; children—Bruce Matteson, Anthony Ray, Wendy Lee, Trudy Jane. Cub reporter St. Joseph (Mo.) News Press, 1945-46, feature writer, 1946-52, downtown, conv. reporter, 1946-48, state editor, 1948-50, asst. city desk, 1950-52; exec. sec. NW Mo. Heart Assn., St. Joseph, 1955-57; editor plant organ, The Headlight, Locomotive Finished Materials, Atchison, Kans., 1953-57; freelance writer Kansas City Star, 1957-66; sports editor Atchison Daily Globe, and columnist The Sports Roamer, 1966-81, news editor, columnist It's My World, Too, 1981—. Recipient numerous awards including 1st pl. awards in news, features, poetry, publicity, editorials and columns Mo. Women's Press Assn., 1946-52; feature award Nat. Amateur Softball Assn., 1977. Mem. Nat. Affiliation Press Women (1st pl. awards in news and sports 1972), Kans. Press Assn., NW Mo. Press Assn., Kans. Women's Press Assn. (1st pl. awards in sports, features, columns, news 1967-76). Presbyterian. Editor: Globe Football, 1979-81, Globe Cookbook, 1979—. Home: 1146 Kearney St Atchison KS 66002 Office: 1015 Main St Atchison KS 66002

PAROWSKI, SANDRA FRANCES, public relations exec.; b. Norwalk, Conn., Nov. 20, 1939; d. Peter John and Mary Elizabeth (Sudell) Ventrella; student Berkeley Bus. Sch., 1960, Fairfield U., 1978, Sacred Heart U., 1978—; m. Albert Parowski, Oct. 15, 1960; children—Karen, Alan. Adminstrv. asst. Info. Dept., IBM, White Plains, N.Y., 1959-61; editorial asst. Westport (Conn.) News, 1964; platform tennis editor Serve and Volley Mag., Trumbull, Conn., 1976; mgr. public relations, public relations rep. T-Bar, Inc., Wilton, Conn., 1970—. Mem. Public Relations Soc. Am., Conn. Press Women (pres.), Nat. Investor Relations Inst., Alpha Sigma Lambda. Club: Norwalk Jr. Women's (1st v.p. 1972-73).

PARRIS, ETHEL STEINBERG, probation officer; b. Bklyn., Dec. 31, 1923; s. Charles and Rose (Segherman) Steinberg; B.A., Bklyn. Coll., 1945; M.S.W., U. Pitts., 1947; m. Chester Parris, June 4, 1950; children—Roger, Donna, Carolyn, Elizabeth. Supr. jr. program Brownsville YM-YWHA, Bklyn., 1947-50; day camp dir. Morris County Guidance Center, Morristown, N.J., 1969-77; staff social worker Morristown Meml. Hosp., 1974-79, Morris County Probation Dept., Morristown, 1978—, probation officer 1978—. Irene Kaufmann Settlement fellow, 1945. Mem. Acad. Cert. Social Workers, Nat. Assn. Social Workers. Jewish. Club: Hadassah Women's Am. Orgn. Office: Morris County Probation Dept Hall of Records Morristown NJ 07960

PARRISH, CONSTANCE DIANE, conservationist; b. Chgo., Apr. 28, 1938; d. William Phillip and Dorothy Virginia (Gulbrandsen) Brand; B.S. with honors, U. Ill., 1961; m. Earl Harrison Parrish, Jan. 25, 1959 (div. 1967); children—Lisa Ann, Julia Katherine. Reporter, Rochester (N.Y.) Democrat and Chronicle, 1966-67; alumni sec. Telluride Assn., Ithaca, N.Y., 1967-68; public info. officer Save-the-Redwoods League,

San Francisco, 1969; conservation staff Friends of the Earth, San Francisco, 1969—, Calif. rep., 1973—. No. Calif. campaign coordinator Conservationists for Carter, 1976, 80. Mem. Alpha Omicron Pi, Theta Sigma Phi. Democrat. Lutheran. Home: 90 Mountain Ln Mill Valley CA 94941 Office: 1045 Sansome St San Francisco CA 94111

PARRISH, NANCY ELAINE, Kans. state senator; b. Cedar Vale, Kans., Nov. 9, 1948; d. Julian Milton and Vergie (Bryant) Buchele; B.S., Kans. State U., 1970; M.S., U. Kans., 1974; m. Jim Parrish, 1970; 1 dau., Leslie Elgin. Mem. Kans. State Senate, 19th Dist., 1980—; mem. Ednl. Task Force, Midwestern Conf. Council State Govts., 1981—. Pres., Council for Exceptional Children, Topeka, 1978-79; bd. dirs. Boys Club of Topeka; bd. dirs. Mental Health Assn.; bd. advs. Sch. Future. Mem. LWV, Topeka Foster Parent Assn. Office: Kans State Senate State Capitol Topeka KS 66612 *

PARRISH, PATRICIA ANN, housing authority cons.; b. Rush City, Minn., July 9, 1948; d. Chester Bryce and Dorothy Mae P.; student St. Cloud State U., 1966-68; B.S.B.A., U. Minn., 1982. Sec., Mpls. Housing Authority, 1969-72; adminstrv. asst. South St. Paul Housing Authority, 1972-74, asst. exec. dir., 1974-79, exec. dir., 1979-81, cons., 1981—. Mem. Nat. Assn. Housing and Redevel. Ofcls. (Minn. exec. bd., v.p. community revitalization/devel., regional exec. bd., nat. energy sub-com.), Minn. Women in Housing, Nat. Assn. Female Execs., C. of C. (bus. devel. council). Panelist profl. conf., 1977. Home: 1811 Upton Ave N Minneapolis MN 55411

PARRISH-HARRA, CAROL WILLIAMS, clergywoman, author, lectr.; b. Nettleton, Ark., Jan. 21, 1935; d. Claremce Elmer and Corinne (Parrott) Williams; student public schs.; m. Charles Clayton Harra, Dec. 2, 1975. Accounts control mgr. Caledesi Nat. Bank, Dunedin, Fla., 1963-66; analysis coordinator Capital Formation Counselor Co., Clearwater, Fla., 1966-71; ordained Spiritual Center St. Petersburg (Fla.), 1971; asso. minister Temple of Living God, St. Petersburg, 1971-75; pres. Fla. Humanistic Inst., St. Petersburg, 1974-75; dir. Villa Serena Spirtual Community, Sarasota, 1976-81; pres. Light of Christ Community Ch., Tahlequah, Okla., 1981—; mem. faculty Internat. Coll. Nat. Health Scis., 1977—; moderator, speaker Sarasota chpt., NCCJ; workshop leader, lectr. retreats Spiritual Frontiers Fellowship; trustee Nat. Council Community Chs. Mem. Am. Bus. Women's Assn., NOW. Democrat. Author: New Age Handbook on Death and Dying, 1982. Address: PO Box 1274 Tahlequah OK 74464

PARRIS-MILLER, JUNE HAZEL FRANCES, counselor; b. Golden Groves, Guyana, June 12, 1954; came to U.S., 1973; d. Carmel St. John and Leila Winifred (Parris) Miller; A.A., Finch Coll., 1975; B.A., Marymount Manhattan Coll., 1977; M.A., Columbia U. Tchrs. Coll., 1978, Ed.M., 1979; postgrad. Inst. for Moral Edn., Harvard U., summer 1980. Dir. guidance St. Mark's Day Sch., sch. for immigrant students, Bklyn., 1979-81; counselor higher edn. opportunity program Le Moyne Coll., 1981—. Recipient cert. appreciation Project Double Discovery, Columbia U., 1979, Across Culture Caribbean Am., 1978. Lic. guidance counselor, N.Y. State. Mem. World Council for Curriculum and Instrn., AAUW, Am. Personnel and Guidance Assn., Nat. Assn. Women Deans, Adminstrs. and Counselors. Mem. Moravian Ch. Office: Le Moyne Coll Le Moyne Heights Syracuse NY 13214

PARRO, NOEL LOUISE, educator; b. Kansas City, Mo., Dec. 15, 1944; d. Louis Eugene and Ruth (McGannon) Robichaux; B.S., Lamar State U., 1968; m. James Parro, Dec. 18, 1972; children—Louise Adele, Jean-Francois. Tchr., Lafourche Parish Schs., Lockport, La., 1970—. Pres., Thibodaux Playhouse, 1979—, bd. dirs., 1974—; pres. Lafourche Assumption Terrebonne Ballet Allegro, 1975—. Home: 1328 Louisiana 1 S Raceland LA 70394 Office: 1421 Crescent Ave Lockport LA 70374

PARRY, CAROL JACQUELINE, banker; b. Chgo., Apr. 12, 1941; d. Ralph Geoffrey and Estelle (Hoffman) Newman; student UCLA, 1959-61; B.A., Tufts U., 1964; M.S.W. (NSF fellow), U. Conn., 1969. Dir. program planning N.Y.C. Agy. Child Devel., 1971-72; assoc. McKinsey & Co., N.Y.C., 1972-74; asst. commr. City N.Y. Dept. Social Services, 1974-77; sr. v.p. in charge middle market in Manhattan, Chem. Bank, N.Y.C., 1978—. Mem. bd. advs. Sta. WNET, N.Y.C., 1979—; bd. dirs. N.Y. Urban Coalition, N.Y.C.; treas. Nat. Child Labor Com. Office: 11 W 51st St New York NY 10019

PARRY, JEANNE HOBGOOD, public relations exec.; b. Basin, Wyo., June 18, 1920; d. Guy and Irene Antoinette (Haines) Hobgood; B.A., Wasatch Acad., 1941; postgrad. UCLA, 1950-52; m. C. J. Robert Coulter McReynolds, 1941; 1 son, Robert C. McReynolds; m. 2d, David Fisher Parry, Dec. 23, 1969. Sch. tchr. Jicarilla Apache Reservation, Dulce, N.Mex., 1949; fashion coordinator May Co., Los Angeles, 1953-54; freelance public relations, 1954-55; asso. editor Fortnight Mag., Los Angeles, 1955-57; account exec. Barton Stebbins Advt. Agy., Los Angeles, 1958; dir. women's div. mktg. Western Airlines, Los Angeles, 1959-63; Western area mgr. public relations Scandinavian Airlines, Los Angeles, 1963-74, public relations counsel, 1974—; v.p. David Parry & Assos., Los Angeles, 1974—. Recipient Los Angeles Advt. Women's Achievement award, 1966. Mem. Soc. Am. Travel Writers, Women in Communication. Home: 5903 W Colgate St Los Angeles CA 90036 Office: 5900 Wilshire Blvd Los Angeles CA 90036

PARRY, NANCY, physician, surgeon; b. Salt Lake City, Dec. 20, 1940; d. Nathaniel Edmunds and Dortha Nell (Harris) P.; B.S., U. Utah, 1963; M.D., U. Calif., Irvine, 1967. Intern, Latter-Day Saints Hosp., Salt Lake City, 1967-68; gen. practice medicine and surgery, Anaheim, Calif., 1969—; mem. staff Martin Luther Hosp., Anaheim, Anaheim Meml. Hosp., West Anaheim Community Hosp.; originator, developer, pres. Parry Devel. Co., Sun Valley, Idaho, Maui, Hawaii, Anaheim and Carlsbad, Calif., 1973—; developer, mng. gen. partner Med. Arts East, Anaheim, 1974—; developer Parry Profl. Bldg.; pres. Breast Inst.; pres. Profl. Edn. Services, Anaheim, 1975—; mem. gen. practice com. Martin Luther Hosp. Bd. dirs. Martin Luther Hosp. Found., 1982—. Orange County Med. Assn. Found. Diplomate Am. Bd. Family Practice. Fellow Acad. Family Physicians; mem. Am. Coll. Emergency Physicians, AMA, Am. Women Med. Assn., Orange County Women in Bus. (dir.), Calif. Med. Assn., Orange County Med. Assn. Address: 1801 W Romneya Dr #601 Anaheim CA 92801

PARRY, RANDINE ELIZABETH, psychologist; b. Hartford, Conn., Sept. 6, 1947; d. William Brown and Mary Elizabeth (Caton) P.; A.B., Mt. Holyoke Coll., 1968; Ph.D. (USPHS fellow, 1968-72), U. Chgo., 1977; m. Stanley A. Cruwys; children—Robert W. Parry-Cruwys, Brendon C. Parry-Cruwys. Staff psychologist behavior analysis research lab., dept. psychiatry, U. Chgo., 1971-74, dir. fluency clinic, 1974-77; dir. psychology Walter Fernald State Sch., Waltham, Mass., 1977-80, chief psychologist, 1980—; lic. psychologist SE Counseling Assos., Norwood, Mass., 1980—; vis. asst. prof. Northeastern U., Boston, 1977-80; cons. Human Resource Inst. of Franklin, Mass., 1979-81. Active NOW, 1974—, chmn. ERA com., Chgo. chpt., 1974-77; mem. Women's Polit. Caucus, 1977—, ACLU, 1978—, Nat. Abortion Rights Action League, 1977—, Friends of Family Planning, 1981—, Friends of Sturbridge Village, 1981—, N.E. Aquarium, Mus. Fine Arts, Mus. Sci., Boston, 1979—. Mem. Am. Psychol. Assn., Eastern Psychol. Assn., New Eng. Psychol. Assn., Mass. Psychol. Assn., Assn. for Applied Behavior Analysis, Assn. for Advancement of Behavior Therapy, Assn. for Advancement of Psychology, Assn. for Women in Psychology, Boston Behavior Therapy Interest Group. Club: Corinthian Yacht (Marblehead, Mass.). Contbr. papers to profl. confs. Home: 15 Cherry Oca Ln Framingham MA 01701 Office: Dept Psychology Walter Fernald State Sch 200 Trapelo Rd Waltham MA 02154

PARSON, PATRICIA (TRISHA) JEAN, mktg. exec.; b. San Angelo, Tex., Nov. 4, 1939; d. Hugh L. and WyNama (Wilemon) Mason; B.A. in Mgmt., DePaul U., Chgo., 1977; 2 children. Personnel asst. Sears, Roebuck & Co., San Angelo, 1958-60; asst. to pres. McAx Corp., Waco, Tex., 1962-64; adminstrv. asst. Ethicon, Inc., San Angelo, 1964-69; personnel adminstr. Maremont Corp., Chgo., 1970-71; pres. Parson Assos., Inc., 1971-77; sr. asso. Sales and Mgmt. Search, Inc., 1974-77; gen. mgr. Metro Bus. Assos., Inc., Washington, 1977-78; v.p. MBA Exec. Group, 1978-80; v.p. mktg. MBA Mgmt., Inc., 1980—; lectr. in field; adj. prof. George Washington U.; vis. lectr. Am. U. Mem. Internat. Orgn. Women Execs. (chairperson 1980-81), Washington Indsl. Round Table, Nat. Council Career Women (dir. 1980—), Greater Washington Bd. Trade, Nat. Assn. Personnel Cons. Home: 12126 Quorn Ln Reston VA 22091

PARSON, SUE CAROLYN, asst. controller; b. Indpls., Aug. 1, 1940; d. Henry Howard and Nettie Rebecca (Webster) Walton; student Indpls. Bus. Coll., 1978, Ind. U.-Purdue U., 1977, Clark Coll., 1980—; m. Leon Parson, Sept. 20, 1958 (div.); children—Leon, Timothy, Justina Marie. With RCA, Indpls., 1966-77, key operator, Legal Services Orgn. Ind., Inc., 1977, receptionist, 1977-78, acctg. clk., 1978-79, asst. to bus. mgr., 1979-81, asst. controller, 1981—. Treas. Concerned Citizens for Legal Services, 1980-81; pres. N.E. Mothers Club, 1967-72; den mother Cub Scouts Am., 1965-68; counselor Camp Fire Girls, 1968-72. Mem. Nat. Legal Aid Defenders Am., Alpha Pi Chi. Democrat. Baptist. Home: 6133 Beech St Indianapolis IN 46224 Office: 107 N Penna St Suite 300 Indianapolis IN 46204

PARSON, TERESIA ANN, banker; b. Roswell, N.Mex., Apr. 19, 1947; d. Sidney Allen and Syble Nell (Painter) Emerson; student public schs., also various banking schs.; m. Gary L. Parson, Feb. 19, 1966; children—Kimberly Dawn, Stephen Garrett. Sec., Valley Nat. Bank, Phoenix, 1967-68; collection and exchange teller First Nat. Bank, Alamogordo, N.Mex., 1968-69; br. teller First Nat. Bank of Clovis, 1969-70; sec., then loan operation officer Roswell (N.Mex.) State Bank, 1970-79, loan rev. officer, 1979-81; asst. v.p. First Interstate Bank of Roswell, 1981—. Residential chmn. Roswell chpt. Am. Cancer Soc. drive, 1980. Mem. Am. Inst. Banking (dir., pres. Tres Rios chpt. 1980—). Mem. Am. Inst. Banking, Am. Bus. Women's Assn. Democrat. Baptist. Home: 1618 S Kansas St Roswell NM 88201 Office: PO Box 2057 Roswell NM 88201

PARSONS, ESTELLE, actress; b. Lynn, Mass., Nov. 20, 1927; d. Eben and Elinor (Mattson) Parsons; B.A. in Polit. Sci., Conn. Coll. Women, 1949; student Boston U. Law Sch., 1949-50; m. Richard Gehman, Dec. 19, 1953 (div. Aug. 1958); children—Martha and Abbie (twins). Stage appearances include Happy Hunting, 1957; Whoop Up, 1958; Beg, Borrow and Steal, 1960; Threepenny Opera, 1960; Mrs. Dally Has a Lover, 1962; Ready When You Are C.B., 1964; Malcolm, 1965; Seven Descents of Myrtle, 1968; And Miss Reardon Drinks a Little, 1971; Mert and Phil, 1974; The Norman Conquests, 1975-76; Ladies of the Alamo, 1977; Miss Margarida's Way, 1977-78; Pirates of Penzance, 1980-81; film appearances include Bonnie and Clyde, 1966; Rachel, Rachel, 1967; I Never Sang for My Father, 1969. Recipient Theatre World award, 1962-63, Obie award, 1964, Motion Picture Acad. Arts and Scis. award, 1967, Conn. Coll. medal of honor, 1969. Home: 505 West End Ave New York NY 10024

PARSONS, JOYCE COLLEEN, mgmt. cons., educator; b. Grand Rapids, Mich., Jan. 25, 1946; d. Robert Lewis and Mary Jane (Manning) Stephens; B.S., SUNY, 1979; M.B.A. (Comerco scholar), U. Puget Sound, 1980; m. Robert G. Parsons, II, Aug. 26, 1973; children—Julia C., Jeffery T., Colleen M. Mktg. research asst. MNO, Inc., Ann Arbor, Mich., 1971-75; personnel specialist Dept. Navy, San Francisco, 1975-77; regional adminstr. U. No. Colo., Greeley, 1977-78; acad. advisor, asst. adminstr. U. Puget Sound, Tacoma, Wash., 1978-79, prof. bus., 1981—; mktg. specialist Econ. Devel. Bd., Tacoma, 1980-81; cons. Puget Sound Learning Inst., Tacoma, 1980—; pvt. practice mgmt. cons., Tacoma, 1980—. Speech coach for profl. women MS Downtown Tacoma, 1981. Mem. M.B.A. Execs. Assn., Nat. Assn. Female Execs., Sales and Mktg. Execs., Am. Mgmt. Assn., South Sound Women's Network (co-founder, dir.), University Pl. C. of C. (chmn. govt. affairs task force, edn. task force). Unitarian. Club: Toastmasters. Home: 5202 96th Ave Ct W Tacoma WA 98467

PARSONS, LEONA MAE, hosp. adminstr.; b. Newark, Ohio, Sept. 13, 1932; d. Enos Andrew and Emma Mae (Simmers) Chew; R.N., Andrews U., 1960; B.S. in Nursing, So. Missionary Coll., 1980; m. David J. Parsons, June 14, 1953; children—Davona Joy, Cynthia Carol, David J. Operating room supr. Bongo Hosp., Angola, Africa, 1961-68; dir. nurses Bongo Mission Hosp., Angola, 1968-75; nurse in charge refugee camps S. African Govt., Windhoek, S.W. Africa, 1975-76; matron, dir. nurses Windhoek (S.W. Africa) State Hosp., 1976-79; asst. v.p. Fla. Hosp., Orlando, 1980—. Mem. Assn. Seventh-day Adventist Nurses, Am. Soc. Psychoprophylaxis in Obstetrics, Assn. Operating Room Nurses, Fla. Soc. Hosp. Nursing Service Adminstrs., Nat. Assn. Female Execs., S. African Nurses Assn., Orange County Med. Soc. Aux., Am. Med. Assn. Aux.

PARSONS, LUCY LYNN, town ofcl.; b. W. Bloomfield, N.Y., Apr. 23, 1925; d. Hugh and Mary (Rowlinson) Lynn; student Rochester Bus. Inst., 1941-42; m. May 21, 1949; children—William, Lynn, Stephen. Sec., U.S. Ordnance Dept., Rochester, N.Y., 1942-45; sec. Eastman Kodak Co., Rochester, 1945-50; councilman Town of Rush (N.Y.), 1974-77, supr., 1978—. Trustee Rush Pub. Library, 1960-73. Mem. Suprs. Assn. Monroe County, PTA. Republican. Baptist. Home: 2782 Pinnacle Rd Rush NY 14543 Office: 5977 E Henrietta Rd Rush NY 14543

PARSONS, PATRICIA ANN, educator; b. Byron, Mich., Jan. 17, 1952; d. Donald Robert and K. Lucille (Wakeman) Hudson; B.A., Spring Arbor Coll., 1973; M.A., Central Mich. U., 1982; m. J. Mark Parsons, Oct. 14, 1972; 1 child, Caleb Joseph. Tchr., Evart (Mich.) High Sch., 1974-75; media specialist Evart Public Schs., 1975-81, elem. sch. tchr., 1981—. Mem. Evart Edn. Assn., Mich. Edn. Assn., NEA, Mich. Assn. Media In Edn., Mich. Cheerleading Coaches Assn. (dir. 1978-80, v.p. 1980-81, 82-83, state championship com. mem. 1979-83), Evart Prof. and Bus. Women. Methodist. Contbr. articles in field to profl. publs. Home: 624 N Main St Evart MI 49631 Office: Evart Public Sch 515 N Cedar St Evart MI 49631

PARSONS, PURNA LYNN, acct.; b. Sandusky, Ohio, June 15, 1954; d. Carl Ray and Elise Purna (Snowden) P.; B.S.B.A., Ohio State U., 1976. Jr. acct. Gen. Motors Corp., Detroit, 1976-77; acct. Okla. Steel Castings, Tulsa, 1977-78; controller Broadcasting Assos., Inc., Tulsa, 1979; internal auditor Mapco Inc., Tulsa, 1979-81; revenue acct. Cotton Petroleum Co., Tulsa, 1981—. Mem., vol. Theatre Tulsa. Mem. Nat. Fedn. Bus. and Profl. Women (fin. com. co-chmn.), Ohio State U. Alumni Assn. (meetings and program chmn.), Beta Gamma Sigma. Home: PO Box 4551 Tulsa OK 74104 Office: One Williams Center Suite 4200 Tulsa OK 74119

PARTEE, BARBARA HALL, linguist, educator; b. Englewood, N.J., June 23, 1940; d. David Brewer and Helen Mar Hall; B.A. with high honors in Math., Swarthmore Coll., 1961; Ph.D. in Linguistics, M.I.T., 1965; m. Morriss Henry Partee, 1966 (div. 1971); children—Morriss Mark, David Matthew, Joel Timothy; m. 2d, Emmon Bach, Nov. 2, 1973. Asst. prof. UCLA, 1965-69, asso. prof., 1969-73; asso. prof. linguistics and philosophy U. Mass., Amherst, 1972-73, prof., 1973—; mem. Linguistic Inst., UCLA, 1966, Calif. Linguistics Inst., Santa Cruz, 1973, Linguistic Inst., U. Mass., 1974. NSF grantee, 1973-75, 1979-81; Sloan found. grantee, 1978-83; fellow Center for Advanced Study in the Behavioral Scis., 1976-77; U. Mass. faculty fellow, 1981-82; Nat. Endowment for Humanities fellow, 1982-83. Mem. Linguistic Soc. Am. (chmn. nominating com. 1979-80), Am. Philos. Assn., Assn. for Computational Linguistics, Sigma Xi (asso.). Author: (with R. P. Stockwell and P. Schachter) The Major Syntactic Structures of English, 1972; Fundamentals of Mathematics for Linguistics, 1979; editor: Montague Grammar, 1976; mem. editorial bd. Lang., 1967-73, Linguistic Inquiry, 1972-79, Theoretical Linguistics, 1974—, Linguistics and Philosophy, 1977—. Home: 50 Hobart Ln Amherst MA 01002 Office: Linguistics Dept South Coll U Mass Amherst MA 01003

PARTON, DOLLY, singer, composer; b. nr. Sevierville, Tenn., Jan. 19, 1946; d. Robert Lee and Avie Lee (Owens) Parton; grad. high sch.; m. Carl Dean, May 30, 1966. Country music singer, composer, radio and TV personality; radio appearances include Grand Ole Opry, WSM Radio, Nashville, Cass Walker program, Knoxville; TV appearance include Porter Wagoner Show, from 1967, Cass Walker program, Bill Anderson Show, Wilburn Bros. Show; Tonight Show, Merv Griffin Show, Mike Douglas show, Acad. Awards Telecast; film actress Nine to Five, Best Little Whorehouse in Texas rec. artist Mercury, Monument, RCA record cos. Recipient (with Porter Wagoner) Vocal Group of Year award 1968, Vocal Duo of Year award, all Country Music Assn., 1970, 71; Dolly Parton Day, Sevier County, Tenn., designated Oct. 7, 1967; Nashville Metronome award, 1979; Grammy award, 1979, 81; named Female Vocalist of Yr., Country Mus. Assn., 1976, 77; Country and Western Star of Yr., 1977; Entertainer of Yr., Acad. Country Mus., 1978. Recordings include Dumb Blonde, Something Fishy, I Couldn't Wait Forever, Daddy Was an Old Time Preacher Man, Joshua, Jolene, Here You Come Again, New Harvest, First Gathering (Am. Music award 1977), It's All Wrong, But It's Alright, Best of Dolly Parton, Heartbreaker, Dolly, Dolly, Dolly. Composer: Dumb Blonde, Something Fishy; (with others) I'm in No Condition, Ol' Handy Man, Friends Tell Me, Put It Off Until Tomorrow, The Company You Keep, You Know How to Hurt A Guy, Two Doors Down, 9 to 5, Heartbreak Express, Do I Ever Cross Your Mind?, Hollywood Potters, Act Like a Fool, My Blue Ridge Mountain Boy, As Much as Ever, Prime of Our Love, Barbara on Your Mind, numerous others. Address: care Katz-Gallin-Morey 9255 Sunset Blvd Los Angeles CA 90069

PARTYKA, DIANE LOUISE, diversified co. exec.; b. Mineola, N.Y., June 5, 1951; d. Robert James and Irene (Malinowski) P.; A.A. in Liberal Arts, Union Coll., Cranford, N.J., 1971; cert. advt. Spectrum Inst. Advt. Arts, 1974; B.S. in Mktg., Rutgers U., 1980. Asst. store mgr. The Stitchery Ltd., Somerville, N.J., 1971-72, advt. mgr., Menlo Park, N.J., 1972-74; art dir. Rahn Studio, Bernardsville, N.J., 1974-75; media buyer Black-Russell-Morris, Union, N.J., 1975; self-employed, 1975-76; mgr. mktg. communications Stork Bowen Enging. Inc., Somerville, N.J., 1976-80; advt. mgr. Pennwalt Corp., Phila., 1980—; dir. Coll. Ave. Tavern Assos., 1976-78. Mem. Phi Chi Theta (chpt. pres. 1978-80, nat. councillor 1978), Alpha Sigma Lambda. Club: Middlesex County Trotting (hon.). Home: 28E Village of Pine Run Blackwood NJ 08012 Office: Three Pkwy Philadelphia PA 19102

PASCHAL, ANNE BALES, educator; b. Runnels County, Tex., Oct. 10, 1929; d. Wirt Samuel and Lora Louise (Corum) Bales; B.S. Angelo State U., 1970, M. Sch. Adminstrn., 1983; m. Bill Paschal, Dec. 16, 1946; children—William Douglas, Susan Louise Paschal Spates, Paul Neal. Tchr. math. Central High Sch., San Angelo, Tex., 1970—; workshop presenter; dir. Concho Educators Fed. Credit Union, 1975-80, pres. bd., 1979-80. Recipient Leadership and Scholarship award Angelo State U., 1970. Acad. Excellence awards, 1968, 69, Leadership and Achievement award Angelo U., 1969, 70; named Outstanding Tchr., Central High Sch., 1977, Tchr. of Yr., 1978. Mem. Nat. Council Tchrs. of Math., San Angelo Council Tchrs. of Math (v.p. 1975), NEA, Tex. Tchrs. Assn., (local treas. 1978-79), Tex. State Classroom Tchrs. Assn. (treas. 1978-79), Kappa Delta Pi, Delta Kappa Gamma, Pi Mu Epsilon, Sigma Tau Delta, Alpha Chi. Republican. Home: 801 W Ave D San Angelo TX 76901 Office: 100 Cottonwood St San Angelo TX 76901

PASCHAL, L. TERESA, univ. dean; b. Langdale, Ala., Aug. 30, 1952; d. Thomas W. and Sara (Crutchfield) P.; B.S., Auburn U., 1974; M.Ed. in Student Personnel in Higher Edn., U. Ga., 1979. Tchr. vocat. home econs., LaGrange, Ga., 1974-75, Hamilton, Ga., 1976-77; edn. coordinator Up With People, Tucson, 1975-76; grad. supr. U. Ga., 1977-79; program adviser Ill. State U., Normal, 1979-80; asst. dean student life Clemson (S.C.) U., 1980—. Mem. Oconee Community Theatre, Anderson Community Theatre Episcopal Ch. choir. Mem. Nat. Panhellenic Council, Nat. Assn. Women Deans, Adminstrs. and Counselors, So. Assn. Coll. Personnel Adminstrs., U. Ga. Alumnae Assn., Auburn Alumnae Assn., Alpha Lambda Delta, Kappa Delta Pi, Phi Delta Kappa, Delta Gamma.

PASCHALL, AMY KING, editor; b. Atlanta, Feb. 9, 1951; d. Walter Goode and Eliza (King) P.; B.A. in Communications, Grinnell Coll., 1973. With Ga. Dept. Labor, Atlanta, 1973—, public relations and info. specialist, 1974—; mem. Gov.'s Council on Deaf, 1978—; cons.; freelance writer, photographer, 1975—. Co-chmn. publicity com. Metro Atlanta Task Com. on Handicapped, 1981, chmn., 1982. Named Handicapped Profl. Woman of Yr., Decatur (Ga.) Pilot Club, 1981. Mem. Internat. Assn. Personnel Employment Security (recipient writing awards, com. chmn. 1973—), Women in Communications, Inc. Office: Room 658 State Labor Bldg Atlanta GA 30334

PASCHALL, PAMELA GENELLE, public accountant; b. Pasadena, Calif., June 18, 1949; d. James Edward and Mary Anita (Butler) P.; B.S., U. So. Calif., 1976. Asst. dir. fiscal services Pasadena (Calif.) Unified Sch. Dist., 1972-78; staff acct. George C. Troutman, C.P.A., Louisville, 1978-80; sr. staff acct. Celanese Corp., Louisville, 1980—. Mem. Ky. Soc. C.P.A.s, Nat. Acctg. Assn., Am. Inst. C.P.A.s, River City Bus. and Profl. Women's Club. Home: 3603 Stanton Blvd Louisville KY 40220 Office: 1 Riverfront Plaza Louisville KY 40202

PASCHKES, ANDREA, psychologist; b. Bklyn.; d. Harry and Helen (Podolnick) Harstein; B.A., Lehman Coll., City U. N.Y., 1970; M.A., Fordham U., 1972, Ph.D. (fellow), 1979; m. B. Michael Paschkes, Aug. 28, 1954; children—Jacqueline Sue, Benjamin Neil. With Kirby Block Distbg. Corp., 1953-59; export mktg. cons., N.Y.C.; 1963-65; amanuensis to Bel Kaufman, 1966-67; research asst. to neurosurgeon, Bronx, N.Y., 1970-72; pvt. practice psychotherapy, hypnotherapy, N.Y.C., 1976—; cons. Center for Emotional Re-Edn., N.Y.C., 1974—. Mem. Am. Psychol. Assn., Alumni Assn. Fordham U. Jewish. Office: 110 E 87th St New York NY 10028 also 5900 Arlington Ave Bronx NY 10471

PASCUAL, MARGARITA FRANCISCA CANDIDO, physician, internist, cardiologist; b. Manila, Sept. 17, 1938; came to U.S., 1964, naturalized, 1977; d. Manuel and Carmen (Galvez) Candido; A.A., U. San Tomas, 1956, M.D., 1961; m. Dominador Pascual, June 21, 1964;

children—Christine, Susan, David, Catherine, Daniel, Darren, Dominador III. Rotating intern U. Santo Tomas Affiliated Hosps., 1960-61; resident in ob-gyn, internal medicine, surgery and pediatrics St. Anne's Hosp., Manila, 1961-64; rotating intern N.Y. Polyclinic Hosp., N.Y.C., 1964-65; resident in internal medicine Bklyn. Jewish Hosp., 1965-66, Lincoln-Albert Einstein Coll. Medicine, N.Y.C., 1966-68; fellow in cardiology Bklyn. Jewish Hosp., 1968-69; fellow in cardiology Beth Israel Med. Center, Manhattan, 1969-70, cardiopulmonary fellow, 1970-71; cardiopulmonary fellow Kings County (N.Y.) Downstate Med. Center, 1971-72; practice medicine specializing in internal medicine and cardiology, N.Y.C., 1972-73, Brentwood, N.Y., 1973—; mem. staffs Southside, Good Samaritan, Smithtown Gen. hosps., St. James Plaza, St. James Nursing Home, Sunrise Manor Nursing Home, Berkshire Nursing Center; sch. physician Half Hollow Hills Sch. Dist. Mem. Suffolk, N.Y. State med. socs., Am. Soc. Internal Medicine, Suffolk, N.Y. heart assns. Office: 16 Washington Ave Brentwood NY 11717 also 210 Ronkonkoma Ave Lake Ronkonkoma NY 11779

PASICATAN, SUSANA TAYAN-BATCAGAN, psychiatrist; b. Philippines, Dec. 14, 1941; d. Lino M. and Avelina (Tayan) Batcagan; grad. U. East, Philippines, 1962; M.D., U. East, Ramon Magsaysay Meml. Med. Center, 1968; m. Alfonso A. Pasicatan, June 29, 1974; children—Michelle, Marco, Marcel (dec.), Marvel. Intern, U. East Ramon Magsaysay Meml. Med. Center, 1967-68; resident in psychiatry St. Luke's Hosp., Quezon City, Philippines, 1968-71, Rollman Psychiat. Inst., U. Cin., 1974-77; adminstr. psychiatry dept. ABM Sison Hosp., Philippines, 1972-73; staff psychiatrist Longview State Hosp., Cin., 1977-79, S.C. State Hosp., Columbia, 1979—. Diplomate Am. Bd. Psychiatry and Neurology. Mem. Am. Psychiat. Assn. Office: 2100 Bull St Columbia SC 29202

PASS, CAROLYN JOAN, dermatologist; b. Balt., May 14, 1941; d. Isidore Earl and Rhea (Koplowitz) P.; B.S., U. Md., 1962, M.D., 1966; m. Richard Malcolm Susel, June 23, 1963; children—Steven, Gary. Rotating intern USPHS Hosp., Balt., 1966-67; med. resident St. Agnes Hosp., Balt., 1967-71; dermatology resident and fellow U. Md. Sch. Medicine Hosps., 1971—; pvt. practice specializing in dermatology, Balt. and Ellicott City, Md., 1971—; mem. staff James Lawrence Kernan, St. Agnes, South Balt. Gen. and Bon Secours hosps.; vol. dermatology clinics U. Md., St. Agnes hosps.; asst. prof. medicine U. Md. Sch. Medicine, 1971—; mem. exec. com. adv. bd. Nat. Program in Dermatology, 1975. Diplomate Am. Bd. Dermatology. Mem. AMA, Med. and Chirurg. Faculty Md., Balt. City Med. Soc. (del. 1974), Am. Women's Med. Assn., Am. Acad. Dermatology (award exhibit 1970), Soc. Investigative Dermatology, Md. Dermatology Soc. (sec.-treas. 1974-76, pres. 1976-77), Dermatology Found., Soc. Contemporary Medicine and Surgery, Cowpet Bay Gourmet Soc. Jewish. Clubs: Suburban Country (Balt.); Country Garden, Gourmet-SSS. Contbr. articles to profl. jours. Home: Timberlane 8410 Park Heights Ave Pikesville MD 21208 Office: Suite 301 Pine Heights Med Center 1001 Pine Heights Ave Baltimore MD 21229 also Howard County Med Center Chevrolet Dr and Saint John's Ln Ellicott City MD 21043

PASSAMANECK, RANDI LEA, health service exec.; b. Richmond, Va., May 18, 1942; d. Yale and Ann (Berman) Passamaneck; B.S. in Med. Tech., U. N.C., 1964; postgrad. Johns Hopkins Hosp., 1972-73; Research technologist USPHS Hosp., Balt., 1964-65; lab. scientist U. Md. Hosp., Balt., 1965-72, tech. and adminstrv. specialist, 1973-74; lab. assoc. Johns Hopkins Hosp., Balt., 1972-73; dir. tech. services ARC Blood Services, Cheapeake region, Balt., 1974—. Mem. bd. Mid-Atlantic Assn. Blood Banks, 1976-81, pres., 1979-80; mem. tech. workshop com. Am. Assn. Blood Banks, 1976-78; v.p. Washington-Balt. Blood Study Group, 1975-76; guest speaker South African Congress Blood Transfusion, East London, 1981. Mem. Am. Soc. Clin. Pathologists, Am. Soc. Med. Tech., Internat. Soc. Blood Transfusion, Md. Soc. Med. Tech., Pa. Assn. Blood Banks. Democrat. Jewish. Office: American Red Cross Blood Services 2701 N Charles St Baltimore MD 21218

PASSARELLE, L(IDIA) MARISA, sales exec.; b. New Rochelle, N.Y., May 19, 1953; d. Joseph Peter and Olivia C. (Sacco) P.; B.A., Vassar Coll., 1975; postgrad. N.Y.U., 1977-79. Research biochemist Sloan-Kettering Inst. Cancer Research, N.Y.C., 1975-76, Albert Einstein Coll. Medicine, N.Y.C., 1976-79; brokerage cons. AT&T Long Lines, N.Y.C., 1979-81; sales exec. fin. and legal printing sales R. R. Donnelley & Sons, Co., Inc., N.Y.C., 1981—. Mem. Network Assn. Women in Bus., Nat. Orgn. Italian-Am. Women, Vassar Alumnae Assn. Author articles, tng. manuals. Home: 250 Garth Rd Scarsdale NY 10583 Office: 80 Pine St New York NY 10005

PASSARO, JOAN BERNADETTE, personnel exec.; b. Paterson, N.J., Apr. 15, 1939; d. John and Anna (Druther) Osekowski; A.A. in Bus., Wheeler Sch., 1978; student Robert Morris Coll.; m. Robert J. Passaro, June 17, 1961. Sec. to security officer Bunker-Ramo Corp., Silver Spring, Md., 1964-66; asst. to pres. Treasure House, Pitts., 1966-68; sec. inside sales George P. Dempler Co., Bridgeville, Pa., 1968-79; sec. Miller Printing Equipment Corp., Pitts., 1979-80, personnel supr. indsl. relations dept., 1980—. Campaign chmn. United Fund. Mem. Nat. Assn. Female Execs., Am. Soc. Personnel Adminstrn., Pitts. Personnel Assn. Home: 251 Twin Hills Dr Pittsburgh PA 15216

PASSELA, ELIZABETH MCCASLIN, banker; b. Chattanooga, Nov. 24, 1945; d. John J. and Elizabeth D. (Johnson) McCaslin; B.A. in Econs., Conn. Coll., 1967; M.B.A., U. Pa., 1974; m. George W. Passela, 1978; children—Christopher A. Battles, Hadley Passela. Stockbroker, Goodbody & Co., Phila., 1967-70, DeHaven & Townsend, Crouter & Bodine, Phila., 1970; trust investment officer S.E. Banks Trust Co., Miami, Fla., 1974-76; div. v.p. Royal Trust Bank of Miami, 1976-77; v.p. Biscayne Bank, Miami, 1977—. Treas., Phila. Mus. of Art Vol. Guides, 1972; bd. dirs. Dade Heritage Trust, Inc., 1978, treas., 1978. Mem. Econ. Soc. South Fla., Miami Bond Club. Congregationalist. Club: Miami Forum. Office: Biscayne Bank 350 Biscayne Blvd Miami FL 33132

PASSONNEAU, JANET VIVIAN, biochemist; b. Crosby, Minn., June 22, 1924; d. Stansmore Neal and Lillian Ingeborg (Tingstad) Vivian; B.A., U. Minn., 1945; M.A., Radcliffe Coll.-Harvard U., 1946, Ph.D., 1949; m. Joseph Russell Passonneau, Apr. 21, 1948; children—Christopher, Rebecca, Polly, Sarah. Biochemist, Argonne (Ill.) Nat. Lab., 1949-52, Oak Ridge Nat. Lab., 1952-55, VA Hosp., St. Louis, 1955-56; mem. faculty Washington U., St. Louis, 1956-58, Washington U. Sch. Medicine, 1968-68; vis. asso. prof. Northwestern U., 1968-69; chief lab. neurochemistry Nat. Inst. Neurol. and Communicable Disorders and Stroke, NIH, Bethesda MD, 1968—; mem. study sect. VA. Recipient Borden award, 1966. mem. Am. Soc. Neurochemistry, Am. Soc. Biol. Chemists, Am. Soc. Pharmacology and Exptl. Therapeutics, Internat. Soc. Neurochemistry, Phi Beta Kappa. Democrat. Office: NINCDS NIH Bldg 36 Room 4D-20 Bethesda MD 20205

PASTEN, LAURA JEAN, veterinarian; b. Tacoma, May 25, 1949; d. Frank Larry and Jean Mary (Slavich) Brajkovich; student Stanford U., 1970; B.A. in Physiology, U. Calif., Davis, 1970, D.V.M. (regents scholar), 1974; postgrad. Cornell U., 1975. Veterinarian, Nevada County Vet. Hosp., Grass Valley Calif., 1975-80; pvt. practice vet. medicine; owner Mother Lode Vet. Hosp., Grass Valley, 1980—; lectr. in field. Recipient Internat. award Vet. Econs., 1982. Mem. AVMA, Calif. Vet. Med. Assn., Mother Lode Vet. Assn., Am. Animal Hosp. Assn. (Mother Lode Vet. Hosp. cited for excellence), Nat. Ophthal. Soc., Nat. Pygmy Goat Assn., Nat. Appaloosa Soc., Nat. Assn. Underwater Instrs., Sacramento Valley Vet. Assn., Denver Area Med. Soc., Internat. Vet. Assn. Am., Endurance Riding Soc. Republican. Lutheran. Club: Grass Valley Bus. Women. Author: (with Dr. Muller) Canine Dermatology, 1970; contbr. articles to profl. jours. Home: 15978 Shebley Rd Grass Valley CA 95945 Office: 11509 La Barr Meadows Rd Grass Valley CA 95945

PASTERNAK, EUGENIA, instn. adminstr.; b. Ukraine, Jan. 8, 1919; d. Mychail and Maria (Okonska) Nowakiwsky; student philosophy Goethe U., Germany, 1945-47; cert. Shaw Bus. Coll., Toronto, Ont., Can., 1956; diploma McMaster U., 1971; m. Eugene Pasternak, July 19, 1944. Came to Can., 1948, naturalized, 1955. Tchr., prin. jr. coll., Galitzia, Ukraina, 1939-42; exec. relief coms., also ARC during and after World War II; exec. Multiblitz Photog., Toronto, 1955-57; acct. Legal Humeniuk and Romanko, Toronto, 1958-63; pres. Ukrainian Home for Aged, Toronto, 1961-73; dir., adminstr. Ivan Frankso Home, Toronto, 1964—. Mem. Ont. Internal Group Com.; commr. for taking affidavits Province Ont. Recipient medal and scroll Ukrainian Can. Com., 1962, Free Cossacs of Ukraine, 1978; citation and medal Union for Freedom of Ukraine in Australia, 1977. Mem. Internat. Platform Assn., Gerontol. Soc., Can. Assn. Gerontology. Clubs: Ukrainian Pensioners (pres.), Ukrainian Arts, Crafts and Hobbies. Address: 767 Royal York Rd Toronto ON M8Y 2T3 Canada

PASTERNAK, JAN, packaging co. exec.; b. Houston, Apr. 27, 1953; d. Aaron and Helen (Shoob) Pasternak; B.S. in Recreation, Ariz. State U., 1975-76. Profl. racquetball player Jewish Community Center, St. Louis, 1975-76; head profl., mgr. Westside Racquetball Center, Houston, 1978-80; owner, operator Pack N'Ship, Houston, 1981—. Singles and Doubles Women's Nat. Racquetball Champion, 1971. Home: 2612 Arbuckle St Houston TX 77005 Office: 6305 Skyline Dr Suite D Houston TX 77057

PASTOR, JOAN FAYE, psychotherapist, trainer; b. Detroit, Aug. 9, 1954; d. Manuel and Esther C. (Razzman) P.; B.A. in Social Scis. and Religious Studies, U. Mich., 1975; M.A. in Religious Studies, Temple U., 1979, M.A. in Community Psychology, 1979. Instr., Washtenaw Community Coll., 1976; research scholar Temple U., 1976-77, teaching scholar, 1977-79; facilitator/trainer Women's Sch., Phila. 1977—; therapist/trainer Eagleville Hosp. and Rehab. Center, Norristown, Pa., 1979-80; therapist/coordinator Community Coll. Phila., 1980-81; pvt. practice psychotherapy with Bucks County Inst., Mt. Airy, Pa., Phila., 1980-81, asso. Options, 1981—; co-dir. Bootstraps Seminars, tng. and public speaking, N.Y.C. and Phila., 1981—; seminar leader Inst. Awareness, Phila., 1980-82; instr. Temple U., Center City, 1981, Cheltenham (Pa.) Adult Sch., 1981-82; appearances on radio, TV talk shows; commentator on affairs of psychol. interest Sta. WXPN-FM, Phila., 1980—. Vol. tchr. nutrition and public health Coop. Extension Services Washtenaw County (Mich.), 1973-75; asst. co-coordinator Program for Festival of Life, Office Ethics and Religion, U. Mich., 1973-75; researcher Women Organized Against Rape, Phila., 1979-80. Recipient Hon. citation Mich. Competitive Scholarship Exams, 1972. Mem. Am. Psychol. Assn., Assn. Humanistic Psychology (chairwoman com. publicity Eastern Regional Network Br. 1977—), Internat. Imagery Assn., Nat. Speaker's Assn., Women in Psychology, Interlochen Nat. Music Camp Alumni, Women's Referral Service, Inc., Phi Beta Kappa. Home: 332 W Hortter St Philadelphia PA 19119 Office: 1900 Spruce St Philadelphia PA 19103

PASTOR, MILLIE A., interior designer; b. Wayne County, Mich.; d. Martin Joseph and Bessie B. Kloka; student U. Detroit, 1947-48; B.S.N.E., R.N., Mercy Coll., 1951; m. Robert Henry Pastor, Sept. 29, 1951; children—Robert Henry, George H., Patricia C., Karen M. R.N., Mercy Hosp., Detroit, 1953-58; founder, pres. Pastor Interiors, Inc., Bloomfield Hills, Mich., 1965—; cons. URI, Nashville; cons., speaker, mem. nat. women's bd. Northwood Inst. Pres., Project Hope, 1973-75; commr. Mich. Am. Revolution Bicentennial, 1972-78; mem. exec. bd. March of Dimes; bd. dirs. Christ Child Soc., 1960-68, Mich. Artrain; pres. Am. Lung Assn. Southeastern Mich., March of Dimes Action Group, 1980-82. Recipient Outstanding Contbn. award March of Dimes, 1977-79; Outstanding Fund Raising Vol. award Nat. Soc. Fund Raising Execs., 1982; named Women of Yr., Boys Town of Italy, 1980. Mem. Nat. Home Fashions League (Image Maker award, Mich. chpt. 1979, v.p.) Am. Soc. Interior Designers, Design Lighting Inst., Detroit Zool. Soc. Republican. Club: Women's Econ.

PATAKY, MARIE ANN, acct.; b. Wilkensburg, Pa.; d. John Andrew and Elizabeh Ann (Koaka) P.; B.S. in B.A., Robert Morris Coll., 1974; A.S. in Data Processing, Community Coll. Allegheny County, Pitts., 1970. Auditor, Peat, Marwick, Mitchell & Co., Pitts., 1974-76; tax acct. G.L. Roteman & Assos., Pitts., 1976-77; acctg. cons. Career & Life Planning Inst., Pitts., 1977-78; tax acct. Westinghouse Electric, Pitts., 1978-80; internal auditor Johnson & Johnson, New Brunswick, N.J., 1980-81; tax supr. Interpublic Group of Cos., Inc., N.Y.C., 1981—; fin. cons., dir. Contrarian Investment Inst., Princeton, N.J., 1981—. Treas.' Children's Hosp. Fund., 1979-80. C.P.A., Pa.; Robert Morris scholar, 1972-74. Mem. Am. Inst. C.P.A.s, Pa. Inst. C.P.A.s, Nat. Assn. Accts., Assn. M.B.A. Execs., Am. Women's Soc. C.P.A.s, Inst. Cert. Fin. Planners, Internat. Inst. Fin. Planning. Club: Toastmistress (treas. 1979-80). Address: Box 1442 Palmer Sq Princeton NJ 08540

PATASINI, LOUISE LAVERNE, banker; b. San Antonio, June 11, 1931; d. Albert J. and Ethel Reinsch; A.A. in Banking, LaSalle Extension U., 1979; m. Lester Patasini, Mar. 15, 1956; children—Russell, Kenneth, Gloria, Donna, Leslie. With Bell Telephone Co., 1950-55, Atlas Tack Corp., 1955-65; with Fairhaven Savs. Bank (Mass.), 1965—, head teller, 1966-75, asst. treas., 1975—. Mem. Savs. Bank Women Mass. (past sec.). Home: 202 Farmfield Ct Fairhaven MA 02719 Office: Fairhaven Savs Bank Box 87 Fairhaven MA 02719

PATCH, LORRAINE MARIE, investment systems consultant; b. Revere, Mass., Feb. 21, 1947; d. William Albert and Mary Rita (Gelardi) P.; B.A. magna cum laude in Mgmt. (Coll. Profl. Studies prize 1978), U. Mass., Boston, 1978; M.B.A., Suffolk U., 1981; 1 son, Derek Scott Burke. Benefits coordinator, money market bookkeeper State St. Bank and Trust Co., Boston, 1968-76; freshmen adv. U. Mass., Boston, 1976-77; customer service rep. First Nat. Bank Boston, 1977-78; analyst investment systems group TMI Systems Corp., Lexington, Mass., 1980-81, staff cons., sect. mgr., 1981—. Mem. search com. for chancellor U. Mass., 1979. Mem. Female Execs. Assn., M.B.A. Assn., Assn. Women in Computing, Women in Mgmt. Network Assn. (co-founder 1981, treas. 1981—), U. Mass. Alumni Assn. Suffolk U. Alumni Assn., Mass. Fair Share. Home: 30 Bradford Rd Natick MA 01760 Office: 83 Hartwell Ave Lexington MA 02173

PATCH, OLIVIA ESTHER, physician; b. Chgo., June 6, 1954; d. Manuel and Annie Patch; B.S., U. Ill., 1975, M.D., 1979. Resident in internal medicine Cook County Hosp., Chgo., 1979-82, chief resident, 1982-83, v.p. staff assn., 1980-82. Recipient Bruno J. Epstein intern of year award, 1980. Mem. A.C.P. (asso.), Sigma Gamma Rho. Home: 746 E 79th St 217 Chicago IL 60619 Office: Cook County Hosp 1825 W Harrison Chicago IL 60612

PATE, JACQUELINE HAIL, facilities adminstr.; b. Amarillo, Tex., Apr. 7, 1930; d. Ewen and Virginia Smith (Crosland) Hail; student Southwestern U., Georgetown, Tex., 1947-48; children—Charles (dec.), John Durst, Virginia Pate Edgecomb, Christopher. Exec. sec. Western Gear Corp., Houston, 1974-76; adminstr., treas., dir. Aberrant Behavior Center, also dir. Personality Profiles, Inc., Corp. Procedures, Inc., Dallas, 1976-79; br. facilities mgr. Digital Equipment Corp., Dallas, 1979—. Active PTA, Dallas, 1958-73. Mem. Farmers Branch Bus. C. of C. (dir.). Methodist. Club: Soroptimist (treas. Carrollton-Farmers Branch). Home: 3519 Casa Verde Apt 268 Dallas TX 75234 Office: 12100 Ford Rd Suite 200 Dallas TX 75234

PATE, LUCILLE IVA, real estate broker; b. Tuckerman, Ark., Dec. 22, 1920; d. Elmer L. and Josie W. (Spence) SHownes; grad. Chillocothe Bus. Coll., 1939; grad. Realtor Inst., 1980; m. Virgil C. Pate, Aug. 18, 1940; 1 dau., Cynthia L. Comml. tchr. Leachville (Ark.) High Sch., 1941-45; owner, mgr. Pate's, Leachville, Ark., 1946-55; acct., office mgr. Secretarial and Office Services, Inc., West Memphis, Ark., 1963—, owner Pate Real Estate, Inc., West Memphis. Leader, Girl Scouts U.S.A., 1946-50; pres. Crittenden County unit Am. Cancer Soc., 1981-82. Mem. West Memphis Bd. Realtors (sec. 1977-78, pres. 1980), Ark. Assn. Realtors, Nat. Assn. Realtors, West Memphis C. of C. Methodist. Club: Bus. and Profl. Women's. Home: 501 S Roselawn St West Memphis AR 72301 Office: 110 E Thompson St Suite 204 West Memphis AR 72301

PATE, MARTHA B. LUCAS, educator; b. Louisville, Nov. 27, 1912; d. Robert H. and Gertrude W. (Lasch) Lucas; student Vassar Coll., 1931-32; A.B., Goucher Coll., Balt., 1933, LL.D., 1946; A.M., George Washington U., 1935; Ph.D., U. London, 1940; LL.D., Ala. Coll., 1946, Atlanta U., 1972; L.H.D., U. Louisville, 1950, Smith Coll., 1971; m. Maurice Pate, Oct. 1961 (dec. 1965). Asso. prof. philosophy and religion, dean of students U. Richmond (Va.), 1941-44; asso. dean Radcliffe Coll., 1944-46; pres., prof. philosophy of religion Sweet Briar Coll. (Va.), 1946-50; exec. dir. office of univ. and coll. relations Inst. Internat. Edn., 1961-62; chmn. coll. and sch. div. United Negro Coll. Fund, 1962—, bd. dirs., 1967—, chmn. Dana Fellowship com., 1971—, chmn. Annenberg Fund selection com. for scholarships; bd. dirs. Fgn. Policy Assn., 1963—, mem. gen. ops. com., 1973—, also exec. com., nominations com.; bd. dirs. Rec. for the Blind, 1962-76, chmn. planning and devel. com., 1963—, v.p., 1967—, chmn. nat. scholastic awards, 1968—; mem. nat. selections com. for Fulbright Scholarships, 1948-50, U.S. del. UNESCO Prep. Conf. of Univ. Reps., Utrecht, Netherlands, 1948, 4th Gen. Conf. UNESCO, Paris, 1949; mem. Adv. Council for Jr. Year in France, 1947-50; mem. bd. dirs. Assn. Am. Colls., 1949-50, v.p. So. U. Conf. and chmn. com. on improvement of coll. teaching, 1949-50; 2d vice chmn. Am. Council Edn., 1949-50; mem. adv. council on health careers United Hosp. Fund; adv. council Columbia U. Sch. Social Work, 1967-80, chmn. nominations com., 1970—; mem. U.S. Nat. Adv. Commn. Internat. Edn. and Cultural Affairs, 1970-73; mem. Nat. Com. U.S.-China Relations, 1971—; public mem., selection panel fgn. service officers USIA, 1973; mem. commn. accrediting Assn. Theol. Schs. U.S. and Can., 1978-81. Trustee N.Y. Med. Coll. 1967—, Fund for Peace, 1967—, N.Y. Sch. Psychiatry, 1971—, Fund Theol. Edn., Inc., 1969—; bd. dirs. Westchester Med. Center Found., 1969-75, dir., chmn. ednl. planning com., 1975—; bd. dirs. N.Y. met. com. UNICEF, 1972—, incorporator nat. com., 1975—; trustee L.I. U., 1969—, chmn. acad. policies com. 1970—, mem. nominations com., 1976—; trustee Pierce Coll., Athens, Greece, 1962-69, chmn. acad. affairs com., 1962-69, hon. trustee, 1969—; alumnae trustee Goucher Coll., 1968-71; bd. regents Georgetown U., 1974-75, bd. dirs., 1975—, mem. Med. Coll. com., 1976—, exec. com., 1978—; bd. dirs., chmn. univs. and colls. com. Ralph Bunch Meml. Project, 1976—; trustee St. Stephen's Sch. in Rome, 1977-81, mem. nominations com., 1978—, mem. future planning and devel. com.; bd. advs. Inst. for Study World Politics, 1977—, Center for Def. Info., 1979—, Global Perspectives in Edn., 1979—, New Dramatists, Inc., Inst. for Bio-Ethical studies of Georgetown U.; bd. dirs., chmn. Univs. Commn., also Fgn. Planning Commn., 1975—; bd. dirs. Am. Council for Internat. Women's Affairs, 1982—Decorated chevalier French Legion of Honor, 1948; recipient George Washington U. Alumni Citation, 1947; citation Internat. Women's Yr., State of Conn., 1975; Disting. Service award in internat. edn. Sweet Briar Coll., 1975; Patrick Healy award Georgetown U. Alumni, 1981. Fellow Soc. Religion in Higher Edn. (dir. 1976—); mem. Am. Philos. Assn., Nat. Inst. Social Scis., Council Religion and Internat. Affairs (trustee 1968—, chmn. 60th anniversary com. 1970-74), Acad. Religion and Mental Health, Am. Acad. Polit. Sci., Phi Beta Kappa (Bicentennial fellow 1976). Clubs: Faculty (New Haven); Vassar, Cosmopolitan (N.Y.C.). Episcopalian. Author: (with others) Religious Faith and World Culture, 1951. Lectr. on internat. edn., philosophy and pub. affairs. Home: Godstow RFD 1 West Redding CT 06896 Office: 330 E 49th St New York NY 10017

PATE, NANCY BLUM, veterinarian; b. Coffee County, Tenn., Dec. 2, 1943; d. Preston Henry and Cecile Mae (Eggleston) Blum; B.S., N.C. State U., Raleigh, 1967; D.V.M., Okla. State U., 1969; M.P.H., U. Okla., 1976; m. Don Saine Pate, Apr. 12, 1968 (dec.); 1 son, John Preston. Small animal vet. practice, Fayetteville, N.C., 1969-70, 72-74, Whidbey Island, Wash., 1971-72, Atlanta, 1974-75; drug reviewer Bur. Vet. Medicine, FDA, Washington, 1976-78; commd. health officer USPHS, 1977—; environ. health specialist Office Air Quality Planning and Standards, EPA, Research Triangle Park, N.C., 1978—. Sec. com. Cub Scouts, 1978-82; sec.-treas. com. Boy Scouts Am., 1982—. Mem. N.C. Bicycle Tng. Soc., Am. Assn. Zoo Veterinarians, AVMA, Am. Public Health Assn., N.C. Vet. Med. Assn., Nat. Assn. Exec. Females, Womens Vet. Med. Assn., Wash. Vet. Med. Assn., Commd. Officers Assn., Nat. Rifle Assn., League Am. Wheelmen, Am. Youth Hostles, N.C. Bicycle Club, Bikecentennial.

PATON, MARY MARGARET, corp. exec.; b. St. Louis, Feb. 18, 1918; d. William L. and Margaret (Brown) Paton; student pub. schs. Clk. typist Dun & Bradstreet, St. Louis, 1935-36; clk. typist, sec. Wm. A. Streub, Inc., Clayton, Mo., 1936-44, sec. to pres., 1947-53, corp. sec., 1950—, buyer, 1963—, supr. restaurant ops., 1953-72; with U.S. Civil Service, Army Air Base, Tonopah, Nev., 1944-46; sec. Parkside Realty Co., Clayton, 1950—; pres. Pro-Mir Garments, Ltd., St. Louis, 1971—. Presbyterian. Home: 8845 Burton Ave Saint Louis MO 63114 Office: 8282 Forsyth Blvd Clayton MO 63105

PATRICK, BETTY RUTH, ins. agt.; b. Vanceburg, Ky., May 28, 1934; d. William E. and Opal (McGlosson) Lewis; student public schs., Portsmouth, Ohio; m. May 14, 1954; children—Kimberly, Lisa. Sec., Powell Ins. Agy., New Boston, Ohio, 1965-67, officer mgr., 1967-72, owner, agt., 1972—. Mem. Nat. Fedn. Ind. Bus., Ind. Mut. Ins. Agts. Democrat. Baptist. Club: Order Eastern Star. Office: 4057 Rhodes Ave New Boston OH 45662

PATRICK, ELIZABETH LEAHY, personnel search co. exec.; b. Kingston, N.Y., Dec. 22, 1952; d. Thomas F. and Lucy G. (Dunn) Leahy; B.A. in Psychology cum laude, Marist Coll., 1974. Prin. dancer, instr. Deborah Vinton Sch. Ballet, New Paltz, N.Y., 1974-78; tech. placement cons. Perry-White Assos., San Francisco, 1978-79; pres. cert. employment specialist, software engring. placement Patrick and Co. Personnel Service, Sunnyvale, Calif., 1980—. Mem. Nat. Assn. Female Execs., Nat. Assn. Personnel Cons., Calif. Assn. Personnel Cons. (dir.), Women in Electronics, Am. Sales Assn., Women in Info. Processing, Am. Assn. Individual Investors. Republican. Home: 324 Innisfree Dr Daly City CA 94015 Office: 333 Cobalt Way Suite 106 Sunnyvale CA 94086

PATRICK, GEORGIA O'BRIEN LAKAYTIS, communications exec.; b. Dallas, July 2, 1945; d. Jack Dallas and Jane (Childs) O'Brien; B.J.,

U. Mo., 1967; m. Thomas Donald Patrick, Oct. 23, 1981. Tech. writer Mo. Regional Med. Programs, Columbia and Kansas City, 1967-69; public relations dir. Center for Student Life, U. Mo., Columbia, 1969-76; communications dir. Am. Home Econs. Assn., Washington, 1976-81; exec. v.p. The Communicators, Inc., Washington, 1981—. Mem. Am. Soc. Assn. Execs., Internat. Assn. Bus. Communicators, Pub. Relations Soc. Am., Washington Bus. Communicators (v.p. 1981—). Contbr. articles to profl. jours. Home: Blue Ridge Acres Box 11 Harpers Ferry WV 25425 Office: 966 Hungerford Dr Suite 14 Rockville MD 20850

PATRICK, GRACIE MAE, nurse; b. Jones County, Miss., Sept. 15, 1933; d. Richard Franklin and Margaret Corinne (Upchurch) Bonner; diploma South Miss. Charity Hosp., 1956; B.S.N., William Cary Coll., 1982; m. Joe Neil Patrick, Dec. 27, 1952; children—Joe Neil, Debra Elaine. Nurse, various hosps., U.S., 1956-65; nurse VA Hosp., Biloxi, Miss., 1965—, head nurse, 1970—. Mem. Am., Miss. nurses assns., Internat. Urol. Scis. Inc. Home: 224 Holly Hills Dr Biloxi MS 39532 Office: VA Hosp Biloxi MS

PATRICK, RUTH (MRS. CHARLES HODGE), limnologist, diatom taxonomist; b. Topeka, Kans.; d. Frank and Myrtie (Jetmore) Patrick; B.S., Coker Coll., 1929; M.S., U. Va., 1931, Ph.D., 1934; D.Sc., Beaver Coll., 1970, PMC Colls., 1971, Phila. Coll. Pharmacy and Sci., 1973, Cedar Crest Coll., 1974, Wilkes Coll., 1974, Hood Coll., 1975, Med. Coll. Pa., 1975, Drexel U., 1975, Swarthmore Coll., 1975, U. New Haven, 1975, Bucknell U., 1976, Rensselaer Poly. Inst., 1976, St. Lawrence U., 1978; LL.D., Coker Coll., 1971; L.H.D., Chestnut Hill Coll., 1974; m. Charles Hodge IV, July 10, 1931; 1 son, Charles V. Asso. curator microscopy Acad. Natural Scis., Phila., 1939-48, curator Leidy Micros. Soc., 1937-48, curator limnology, 1948—, chmn. dept limnology, 1948-73, holder Francis Boyer Research Chair, 1973—, chmn. bd. trustees, 1973-76, hon. chmn., 1976—; prof. biology dept. U. Pa., 1970—; guest fellow Saybrook, Yale U., 1975; leader Catherwood Amazon Expdn. to headwaters of Amazon River, 1955; U.S. del. to Internat. Limnological Congress, 1953; mem. Internat. Com. on Nomenclature of Algae, 1949-59. Mem. subpanel on water blooms Pres.' Sci. Advisory Com., 1966; mem. panel on water resources and water pollution Gov.'s Sci. Advisory Com., 1965, mem. panel on pollution, 1967-68; mem. nat. tech. advisory com. on water quality requirements for fish, and other aquatic life and wildlife Dept. Interior, 1967-68; mem. citizen's advisory council Pa. Dept. Environ. Resources, 1971-73; mem. hazardous materials adv. com. EPA, 1971-74, mem. exec. adv. com., 1974-79, chmn. panel on ecology, 1974-76; mem. Pa. Gov.'s Sci. Advisory Com., 1972-78; mem. adv. council Electric Power Research Inst., 1973—, NSF, 1973-74; mem. com. human resources NRC, 1975-76; mem. adv. council dept. biology Princeton U., 1975—; mem. gen. adv. com. ERDA, 1975-77; mem. univ. council com. Yale Sch. Forestry and Environ. Studies, 1978—; mem. U.S. sci. adv. council World Wildlife Fund, 1978—; vis. com. dept. energy and environ. Brookhaven Nat. Lab. of Asso. Univs., 1979—; mem. air and water tech. adv. com. Pa. Dept. Environ. Resources, 1979—. Trustee Aquarium Soc. Phila., 1951-58, Lacawac Sanctuary Found. Recipient Distinguished Dau. of Pa. award, 1952; Richard Hopper Day meml. medal Acad. Natural Scis., 1969; Gimbel Phila. award, 1969; Gold medal YWCA, 1970; Lewis L. Dollinger Pure Environment award Franklin Inst., 1970; Pa. award for excellence in sci. and tech., 1970; Eminent Ecologist award Ecol. Soc. Am., 1972; Phila. award, 1973; Gold medal Pa. State Fish and Game Protective Assn., 1974; 2d ann. Internat. John & Alice Tyler Ecology award, 1975; Gold medal Phila. Soc. for Promoting Agr., 1975; Gold Plate award Am. Acad. Achievement, 1975; Pub. Service award Dept. Interior, 1975; Iben award Am. Water Resources Assn., 1976; Outstanding Alumni award Coker Coll., 1977; Frances K. Hutchinson medal Garden Club Am., 1977; Golden medal Royal Zool. Soc., Belgium, 1978; Green World award N.Y. Bot. Garden, 1979; Hugo Black award U. Ala., 1979. Fellow AAAS; mem. Nat. Acad. Scis. (nominating com. 1973-76, chmn. sect. on population biology, evolution and ecology 1980—), Water Pollution Control Fedn. (hon.), Bot. Soc. Am. (mem. Darbarker prize com. 1956, merit award 1971), Phycological Soc. Am. (pres. 1954), Internat. Limnological Soc., Internat. Soc. Plant Taxonomists, Am. Soc. Plant Taxonomy, Am. Soc. Limnology and Oceanography, Pa. Zool. Soc., Colonial Dames Am., Soc. Study Evolution, Water Resources Assn. Del. River Basin, Am. Soc. Naturalists (pres. 1975), Ecol. Soc. Am., Franklin Inst. (com. on sci. and arts 1978—), Smithsonian Instn. (advisory council), Am. Inst. Biol. Scis., Internat. Phycol. Soc., Am. Philos. Soc., S.C. Acad. Scis. (hon.), Am. Acad. Arts and Scis., Sigma Xi. Presbyterian. Author: (with Dr. C.W. Reimer) Diatoms of the United States, Vol. I, 1966, Vol. II, Part I, 1975. Contbr. articles to profl. jours. Office: Acad Natural Scis 19 & Benjamin Franklin Pkwy Philadelphia PA 19103 *

PATRICOF, PAT ESTHER, writer, public relations exec.; b. Middletown, Ohio, July 13, 1910; d. Leon and Dora (Rosenfeld) Patricof; B.S., Ohio State U., 1932; postgrad. N.Y. Inst. Fin., 1958. Writer publicity, spot commls. Benton & Bowles Advt. Agency, N.Y.C., 1933-36; account exec. Radio Features, N.Y.C., 1936-40; publicity dir. WGN Concert Bur., N.Y.C., 1940-42; editor WGN Concert News mag.; account exec. Steve Hannagan Assos., N.Y.C., 1942-54, Jules Berens Orgn., N.Y.C., 1955-57, M. Silver Assos., N.Y.C., 1957-75; dir. public relations, publicity writer Finland Nat. Tourist Office N.Am., N.Y.C., 1975—; free lance mag. and radio script writer. Decorated knight Order of White Rose (Finland); recipient Excellence in Press Relations award N.Am. Precis Syndicate, 1975. Mem. Publicity Club N.Y. (charter), Women in Communications, Ohio State U. Alumni of N.Y. (bd. govs.). Home: 319 E 50th St New York NY 10022

PATRON, JUNE EILEEN, govt. ofcl.; b. N.Y.C., May 15; d. Irving B. and Mollie Patron; A.B. in Govt. with honors, Clark U., Worcester, Mass., 1965; M.A., Am. U., 1967. With U.S. Dept. of Labor, 1966—, head Black Lung benefits program, 1976-79, asst. adminstr. pension and welfare benefit programs, 1979—; mem. Sr. Exec. Service. Recipient various awards Dept. Labor. Office: 200 Constitution Ave NW Washington DC 20210

PATTEN, BEBE HARRISON, clergyman, coll. pres.; b. Waverly, Tenn., Sept. 3, 1913; d. Newton Felix and Mattie Priscilla (Whitson) Harrison; D.D., McKinley-Roosevelt Coll., 1941; D.Litt. (hon.), Temple Hall Coll. and Sem., 1943; m. Carl Thomas Patten, Oct. 23, 1935 (dec. 1958); children—Bebe Rebecca and Priscilla Carla (twins), Carl Thomas. Ordained to ministry Ministerial Assn. of Evangelism, 1935; evangelist in nationwide campaigns, 1933-50; founder, pres. Christian Evang. Chs. of Am., Oakland, Calif., 1944—; founder, pres. Patten Bible Coll., Oakland, 1945—; founder program daily nation-wide radio ministry The Shepherd Hour, 1934—, daily TV telecast, 1976—, nat telecast, 1979—; founder, pres. Acad. Christian Edn., 1944—; pastor Christian Cathedral, Oakland, 1950—. Recipient numerous awards including medallion for religious affairs Israeli Fgn. Ministry, 1969, medal Govt. Press Office, Jerusalem, 1971, Gentile honoree Jewish Nat. Fund, 1975, Hidden Heroine award San Francisco Bay council Girl Scouts U.S.A., 1976, medallion Ben Gurion Research Inst., 1977; resolution of commendation Calif. Senate Rules Com., 1978; hon. fellow Bar-Ilan U., Israel. Mem. Am. Assn. Pres. Ind. Colls. and Univs., Zionist Orgn. Am., Am. Jewish Hist. Soc., Am. Acad. Religion, Soc. Bibl. Lit., Am. Assn. Higher Edn., Religious Edn. Assn., Bar-Ilan U. Assn. (exec. bd.). Author: Give Me Back My Soul (in English, Japanese, Spanish and Chinese), 1973; editor-in-chief The Trumpet Call, 1953—; composer 20 Gospel Songs, 1945; chair in social action established in her name at Bar-Ilan U., 1981. Address: 2433 Coolidge Ave Oakland CA 94601

PATTEN, ELLEVA JOSLYN, psychologist; b. Lynn, Mass., Dec. 15, 1916; d. Arthur Everett and Clare Jean (Allen) Joslyn; student Lewis Inst., 1933-34, Internat. People's Coll., Elsinore, Denmark, 1934-35; S.B., U. Chgo., 1938; M.A., Columbia U., 1939; B.S., U. Ill., 1947; m. Sheldon Leroy Patten, June 13, 1948; children—Arthur, Joslyn, David Allen, Jonathan Neil. Psychologist, Inst. for Juvenile Research, Chgo., 1940-42, Cook County Juvenile Ct., 1942-45, Ill. Neuropsychiat. Inst., 1945-47, Mental Health Clinic, Women's and Children's Hosp., 1947-56, U. Chgo. Clinics, 1948-49, Chgo. Community Clinic, 1949-51, Michael Reese Hosp., 1957, Villa Park (Ill.) Sch. Dist., 1959-66, Elmhurst (Ill.) Sch. Dist., 1966—; pvt. practice, 1949—. Vice pres. York Center Community Coop., 1961, 78—. Mem. Am. Psychol. Assn., Ill. Psychol. Assn., Nat. Assn. Sch. Psychologists, Internat. Transactional Analysis Assn., West Suburban Psychologists. Home: 519 E 14th St Lombard IL 60148 Office: 145 Arthur St Elmhurst IL 60126

PATTEN, FLORENCE WOODWORTH, cytotechnologist; b. Albany, Oreg., Jan. 27, 1935; d. Marshall Melvin and Grace Janet (Chalmers) Woodworth; B.S., U. Oreg., 1957, postgrad., 1958, 59; m. Stanley Fletcher Patten, Jr., Oct. 20, 1979. Chief cytotechnologist U. Wash., Seattle, 1959-65; cytology supr. U. Oreg. Med. Sch., Portland, 1966-70; chief cytotechnologist and ednl. coordinator U. Rochester (N.Y.) Med. Center, 1970-80, asst. prof. pathology, 1977-80, clin. asst. prof. pathology and sr. tech. assoc. obstetrics/gynecology, 1980—; mem. faculty-tutorials in clin. cytology Internat. Acad. Cytology and U. Chgo., 1971—. Recipient Internat. Acad. Cytology Cytotechnologist award, 1977; Am. Soc. Cytology Cytotechnologist of the Yr. award 1979, Cert. of Merit, 1980. Mem. Am. Soc. Cytology, Am. Soc. Clin. Pathologists, Internat. Acad. Cytology, Am. Soc. Cytotechnology, Phi Beta Kappa, Alpha Chi Omega. Club: P.E.O. Editor, The Cytotechnologist Bull., 1973-80; asst. editor Acta Cytologica, 1982—. Office: PO Box 668 601 Elmwood Ave Rochester NY 14642

PATTEN, LINDA FRANK, banker; b. Chgo., Sept. 5, 1949; d. Eugene T. and Annette (Fell) Frank; B.A., St. Olaf Coll., 1971; M.B.A., So. Meth. U., 1977; m. Clark W. Patten, May 17, 1975. Successively computer programmer, mgr. adminstrn., personnel cons., mgr. staffing Res. Life Ins. Co., Dallas, 1975-77; compensation analyst-internat., Bank of Am., San Francisco, 1977-78, tng. officer South, Los Angeles, 1979-80; head mgmt. tng., 1980-81, asst. v.p., head tng. dept., 1981-82, v.p. human resource planning and adminstrn., San Francisco, 1982—. Served with U.S. Army, 1970-74. Decorated Army Commendation medal with oak leaf cluster. Mem. Am. Soc. for Tng. and Devel., Internat. Assn. Personnel Women, Nat. Assn. Female Execs., Am. Soc. Personnel Adminstrs. Republican. Lutheran. Home: 3545 Perada Dr Walnut Creek CA 94598 Office: 555 California St San Francisco CA 94104

PATTERSON, CAROL HELEN, accountant; b. Portland, Oreg., Nov. 11, 1943; d. Dean Lamont Pugh and June Elizabeth Patterson; B.A. in Microbiology, San Jose State U., 1966; M.B.A., U. Calif., Berkeley, 1975; postgrad. Golden Gate U., 1982—. Sr. med. technologist Kaiser Hosp., San Francisco, 1971-79; health plan controller French Hosp., San Francisco, 1976; sr. acct. Sallmann & Jones, Oakland, Calif., 1977-79; internal audit mgr. Bendix Forest Products Corp., San Francisco, 1979-81; sr. ops. analyst Crown Zellerbach, San Francisco, 1981—. Mem. Am. Inst. CPAs, Calif. Soc. CPAs, Am. Soc. Women Accts., Calif. Assn. Clin. Lab. Tech., Am. Soc. Clin. Pathologists. Presbyterian. Clubs: Dolphin S. End Runners (San Francisco); U.S. Ski Assn. Home: 497 Crestmont Dr San Francisco CA 94131 Office: One Bush St San Francisco CA 94104

PATTERSON, ELIZABETH JOHNSTON, state senator; b. Columbia, S.C., Nov. 18, 1939; d. Olin DeWitt and Gladys (Atkinson) Johnston; B.A., Columbia Coll., 1961; postgrad. in polit. sci. U. S.C., 1961, 62, 64; m. Dwight Fleming Patterson, Jr., Apr. 15, 1967; children—Dwight Fleming, Olin DeWitt, Catherine Leigh. Pub. affairs officer Peace Corps, Washington, 1962-64; recruiter VISTA, OEO, Washington, 1965-66; state coordinator Head Start and VISTA, OEO, Columbia, 1966-67; tri-county dir. Head Start, Piedmont Community Actions, Spartanburg, S.C., 1967-68; adminstrv. asst. Congressman James R. Mann, Spartanburg, 1969-70; mem. Spartanburg County Council, 1975-76; mem. S.C. State Senate, 1979—. Trustee, Wofford Coll.; bd. dirs. Charles Lea Center, Spartanburg Council on Aging; pres. Spartanburg Democratic Women, 1968; v.p. Spartanburg County Dem. party, 1968-70, sec., 1970-75. Mem. Bus. and Profl. Women's Club, Alpha Kappa Gamma. Methodist. Home: 1275 Partridge Rd Spartanburg SC 29302 Office: 508 Gressette Bldg Columbia SC 29202

PATTERSON, JANET DOERR, bank exec.; b. Rochester, Minn., Oct. 7, 1941; d. Rudy Ernest and Mary Leone (Wilkes) Doerr; student U. Iowa, 1959-61; m. Walter Patterson, Apr. 22, 1978. Dir. mktg. The Drovers Nat. Bank of Chgo., 1976-78; dir. mktg. Lawndale Trust and Savs. Bank, Chgo., 1978, v.p. comml. banking group, 1978-79, pres., chief exec. officer, 1979—. Episcopalian. Clubs: Econ. of Chgo., PEO. Office: 3333 W 26th St Chicago IL 60623

PATTERSON, JUDITH ELAINE BONDS, mfg. co. personnel exec.; b. Columbia, S.C., Oct. 17, 1952; d. Edgar and Mary Evelyn (Heath) Bonds; grad. Aiken County Sch. Nursing, 1972; student Aiken Tech. Coll., 1976-78, U. S.C., Aiken, 1981—; m. William Kim Patterson, Sept. 21, 1975; children—William Richard Holley II, Amber Elizabeth Leigh. Operating room nurse Aiken County Hosp., Aiken, S.C., 1972-74; indsl. nurse Harvey Hubbell, Inc., Aiken, 1974-78; personnel adminstr. Beecham Products, Aiken, 1978—. Mem. budget and evaluation com. United Way Aiken County, 1981-82, in-plant chmn., 1976, 77, 79, 80, 81; chmn. public edn. Aiken County chpt. Am. Cancer Soc., 1975. Aiken Bus. and Profl. Women's Club ednl. grantee, 1971. Mem. Am. Soc. Personnel Adminstrs., Nat. Assn. Female Execs., Beta Sigma Phi (Girl of Yr. 1979). Baptist. Home: 12 Lander Ln Aiken SC 29801 Office: 65 Windham Blvd Aiken SC 29801

PATTERSON, KAREN ANN, educator; b. Los Angeles, Oct. 29, 1947; d. Dow and Miriam Elizabeth (Brown) Patterson; student Pasadena City Coll., 1965-68; B.S., Tex. Christian U., 1970; M.S., North Tex. State U., 1973; postgrad. Memphis State U., 1978—. Speech, lang. and hearing therapist Ft. Worth Ind. Sch. Dist., 1970-77; cons. speech pathologist Otolaryngology Assocs., Arlington, Tex., 1975-76; staff audiologist U. Tenn. Coll. Health Sci., Memphis, 1978-80; audiology supr. Memphis State U., 1980; instr. speech pathology/audiology Ark. State U., Jonesboro, 1981—; cons. Mississippi County Head Start, Blytheville, Ark., 1982. Mem. Am. Speech and Hearing Assn., Tenn. Speech and Hearing Assn. Home: 1705 Brookhaven Jonesboro AR 72401 Office: PO Box 2773 State University AR 72467

PATTERSON, LUCY PHELPS, educator; b. Dallas, Tex., June 21, 1931; d. John C. and Florence L. (Harllee) Phelps; A.B., Howard U., 1950; M.S.W., U. Denver, 1963; m. Albert S. Patterson, Nov. 25, 1950; 1 son, Albert Harllee. Tabulating machine operator supr. Dept. Commerce, Bur. Census, Washington, 1950-52, Dept. Navy, Bur. of Ships, Washington, 1952-54; caseworker dept. public welfare Dallas, 1954-61, casework supr., 1963-68; dir. Interagy. Project, Dallas, 1968-71; exec. dir. Dallas County Child Care Council, 1971-73; planning dir. Community Council of Greater Dallas, 1973-74; asst. prof. and field work coordinator N. Tex. State U., 1974-78; Ethel Carter Branham prof. Bishop Coll., Dallas, 1978—, dir. social work, 1978—; cons. to Creative Learning Center, Rhodes Terrace Pre-sch., Head Start Consultation Register, Inst. Urban Studies, So. Meth. U. Councilwoman, City of Dallas, 1973-80. Recipient Outstanding Woman award Women's Center of Dallas, 1978, Public Service award Elite Newspaper, 1978; named Mother of Yr., 1979. Mem. Nat. Assn. Social Workers, Acad. Cert. Social Workers, Council on Social Work Edn., Tex. Assn. Coll. Tchrs., Nat. Assn. Black Social Workers, Dallas County Mental Health Assn., NOW, Tex. Black Polit. Caucus, Tex. Assn. of Women Elected Ofcls., Women's Council of Dallas County, LWV, Nat. Council of Negro Women, Council on Consumer Edn., Alpha Kappa Alpha. Republican. Methodist. Club: Altrusa. Weekly columnist Post Tribune, 1973-80, The Dallas Weekly, 1973-80. Home: 2779 Almeda Dr Dallas TX 75216 Office: 3837 Simpson Stuart Rd Dallas TX 75241

PATTERSON, MARIA JEVITZ, microbiologist; b. Berwyn, Ill., Oct. 23, 1944; d. Frank Jacob and Edna Frances (Costabile) Jevitz; B.S., M.T., Coll. St. Francis, Joliet, Ill., 1966; Ph.D. in Microbiology, Northwestern U., Chgo., 1970; postdoctoral fellow in clin. microbiology, U. Wash., Seattle, 1970-72; m. Ronald James Patterson, Aug. 22, 1970; children—Kristin Lara, Kier Nicole. Asst. prof. microbiology and public health Mich. State U., East Lansing, 1972-77, asso. prof. microbiology, public health and pathology, 1977—, staff microbiologist, clin. labs., 1978—; staff microbiologist Lansing Gen. Hosp., 1972-75. Recipient award for teaching excellence Coll. Osteo. Medicine, Mich. State U., 1977, 79; Disting. Faculty award Mich. State U., 1980; Cert. of Recognition YWCA, 1980; grantee Mich. Dept. Public Health, Renal Disease div., 1976—. Mem. Am. Soc. Microbiology, Am. Soc. Clin. Pathologists, S. Central Assn. Clin. Microbiology. Roman Catholic. Contbr. articles to profl. jours., chpt. to book. Office: Dept Microbiology and Public Health Mich State U East Lansing MI 48824

PATTERSON, MARY ELIZABETH, banker; b. Balt., Nov. 7, 1946; d. Howard W. and Mary Elizabeth (Schaefer) Patterson; B.S., Old Dominion U., 1968; diploma Va. Sch. Bank Mgmt., 1978. With Va. Nat. Bank, Norfolk, 1968—, public relations officer mktg., 1974-79, v.p. public relations/mktg., 1979—. Bd. dirs. Canterbury House, Old Dominion U., 1978-81, Vol. Action Center, Norfolk, 1979—; mem. Norfolk Clean Community Com., 1979, Norfolk Rev. Com., 1979; mem. edn. bd. Old Dominion U., 1979—. Mem. Va. Bankers Assn. (chmn. public info. and mktg. com. 1978-79), Va. Press Women, Norfolk C. of C. (chmn. free enterprise com. 1979—). Episcopalian. Office: 1 Commercial Pl Norfolk VA 23510

PATTERSON, PAMELA DOROTHY MESSMORE, mfg. co. exec.; b. N.Y.C., Dec. 24, 1946; d. Francis B. and Dorothy H. Weeks (Heckle) Messmore; B.A. in Econs. summa cum laude, Fordham U., 1976, M.B.A. in Mgmt. Acctg., 1978; separated. Fin. analyst Eastern Air Lines, Inc., Miami, Fla., 1979-81; asst. mgr. pension fund trusts and investments ITT Corp., N.Y.C., 1977-79; v.p. Messmore & Damon, Inc., N.Y.C., 1981—. Mem. Fordham U. Alumni Assn., DAR, Japan Soc. Republican. Office: 530 W 28th St New York NY 10001

PATTERSON, PAMELA JANE, audiologist; b. Passaic, N.J., Feb. 26, 1951; d. Robert and Marian M. Patterson; B.S., Ohio State U., 1973, postgrad., 1973-74; M.A., Kent State U., 1976. Audiologist, E.N.T. Head and Neck Surgeons, Columbus, Ohio, 1975-76; audiologist Arnold D. Rubenfield M.D. & Assos., New Kensington, Pa., 1976-80, bus. mgr., 1978-80; dir. audiological services Hearing Cons. for Industry, New Kensington, 1977-80; audiologist Central Ohio Hearing Aid Center, Reynoldsburg, 1980—. Mem. Am. Speech and Hearing Assn. Republican. Presbyterian. Home: 1000 W Main St West Jefferson OH 43162 Office: 1607 Brice Rd Reynoldsburg OH 43068

PATTERSON, PATRICIA BERNADETTE, bank data processing ofcl.; b. Phila., May 14, 1955; d. Daniel David and Mary Theresa (Kearney) Kenney; student in Bus. Mgmt., St. Joseph's U., Phila.; m. Thomas J. Patterson, Jr., Mar. 11, 1978. Clk. programming and systems dept. Continental Bank, Fort Washington, Pa., 1974-75, programmer trainee, 1975-76, programmer, 1976-78, programmer analyst, 1978-79, lead programmer, 1979-80, project leader, programming dept., 1980—. Mem. Am. Soc. Profl. and Exec. Women, Nat. Assn. Female Execs., Data Processing Mgmt. Assn. (dir. membership directory Montgomery County chpt. 1981, 82). Roman Catholic. Home: 151 E Phoenix Dr Phoenixville PA 19460 Office: 515 Pennsylvania Ave Fort Washington PA 19034

PATTERSON, PEGGY JEAN, real estate broker; b. Macon County, N.C., Nov. 10, 1940; d. Jay B. and Agnes Aletha (Saunders) Moore; student Southwestern Tech. Coll., 1974; m. Morris Patterson, Aug. 23, 1970; children—Kenneth Douglas, Aletha Darlene. Sec., John Phelan Real Estate, Highlands, N.C., 1973-74; broker Jones Real Estate, Franklin, N.C., 1974-75; owner, pres., sec. Patterson Realty, Inc., Franklin, 1977—. Recipient Membership award Franklin Area C. of C., 1980; Beautification award Franklin Garden Club, 1980. Mem. C. of C. (dir. 1980), Better Bus. Bur., N.C. Assn. Realtors (dir. 1981—), Franklin Bd. Realtors (sec. 1979, pres. 1981), Nat. Assn. Female Execs., Nat. Assn. Realtors. Republican. Baptist. Clubs: Merchants Assn., Bus. and Profl. Women's. Home: Route 1 PO Box 76 Otto NC 28763 Office: 146 Palmer St Franklin NC 28734

PATTERSON, PEGGY LOU, army officer; b. Weleetka, Okla., June 21, 1944; d. Walter and Cinderella (Johnson) P.; B.A., Golden Gate U., 1979; 1 dau., Kiila Michelle. Englisted U.S. Army, 1965, commd. 2d lt. 1971; served in Vietnam; comdr. 9th Inf. Div. Mil. Police Co., 1976-77; asst. prof. mil. sci. La. State U. Decorated Bronze Star, Army Commendation medal. Mem. Assn. U.S. Army. Baptist. Home: PO Box 572 Weleetka OK 74880 Office: USMCA Zweibrucken West Germany APO NY 09052

PATTERSON, POLLY REILLY, ret. communications co. exec., civic worker; b. Wilkinsburg, Pa.; d. Thomas L. and Margaret (Coughey) Reilly; student U. Pitts.; m. W. Ray Patterson, Sept. 2, 1943. With Bell Telephone Co. of Pa., Pitts., 1925-71, beginning as clk., successively various mgmt. positions, 1935-64, staff asso. pub. relations staff, 1965-71; dir. Chatham Village Homes, Inc., 1973-76. Asst. treas. Allegheny County Soc. for Crippled Children, 1962-66, v.p., 1966-70; bd. dirs. Jr. Achievement, Inc. of S.W. Pa., 1950-71, Pitts. YWCA, 1964-72, Pa. Soc. Crippled Children and Adults, 1960-68; mem. nat. ho. of dels. Nat. Soc. for Crippled Children and Adults, 1965-67. Named One of Pitts.'s Ten Outstanding Women, Pitts. Sun Telegraph, 1959, Pitts. Advt. Woman of Yr., 1958; recipient Crystal Prism award Am. Advt. Fedn., 1972, 75. Mem. Assn. Pitts. Clubs (dir. 1946-81, pres. 1953), Altrusa Internat. (pres. Pitts. club 1950-51), Pitts. Advt. Club (v.p., sec. 1929-69), Bus. and Profl. Women's Club Pitts., Telephone Pioneers. Home: 402 Olympia Rd Pittsburgh PA 15211

PATTERSON, ROSALYN VICTORIA MITCHELL, biologist; b. Madison, Ga., Mar. 25, 1939; d. Walter Melvin and Hazeltine Virginia (Jones) Mitchell; B.A., Spelman Coll., 1958; M.S., Atlanta U., 1960; Ph.D. Univ. fellow, Emory U., 1967; m. Joseph William Patterson, June 1, 1961; children—Hazelyn Mamette, Joseph William II, Rosman Victor Melvin. Instr. to prof. biology Spelman Coll., 1960-70; So. Fellowship Funds postdoctoral fellow Ga. Inst. Tech., 1969-70; staff specialist to commr., cons. Bur. Reclamation, Dept. of Interior, Washington, 1970-71; coordinator nat. environ. edn. devel. program Nat. Park Service, Dept. of Interior, 1971-72; NIH postdoctoral fellow exptl. cytology br. NIH and Bur. Biologics, FDA, Bethesda, Md., 1972-73; asso. prof. biology Ga. State U., 1974-76; prof., chmn. dept. biology

Atlanta U., 1977—; cons. Dept. Interior, 1970-71. Mem. AAAS, Am. Soc. Cell Biology, Soc. Devel. Biology, Sigma Xi, Phi Sigma. Baptist. Research on mammalian chromosomes in cell culture. Home: 109 Burre Ln SW Atlanta GA 30331 Office: 223 Chestnut St SW Atlanta GA 30314

PATTERSON, VIRGINIA GOODWIN, social worker; b. Nashville, Feb. 21, 1917; d. Marsh and Lena Grace (Givens) Goodwin; B.S., Peabody Coll., 1968; M.S.W., U. Tenn., 1970; m. Fletcher Woodall Patterson, June 17, 1940; 1 dau., Judith Ellen Patterson Murphy. Various secretarial positions, 1934-43; dir. day camp Cumberland Valley Girl Scout council, Nashville, summers 1953-62; sec. Centenary Methodist Community Center, Nashville, 1961-64; dir. resident camp Sycamore Hills, Ashland City, Tenn., summers 1963-65; case worker United Methodist Community Center, 1970-71; social case worker, dir. day care for elderly Sr. Citizens, Inc., Nashville, 1971—; v.p. Cumberland Valley Girl Scout council, 1963-64; youth tchr., counselor Dalewood Meth. Ch., 1950—, pres. Women's Soc. Christian Service. Pres. Isaac Litton High Sch. PTA, Nashville, 1959-61. Recipient Thanks badge Girl Scouts, 1961. Mem. Nat. Assn. Social Workers (past chpt. registrar, corr. sec.), Am. Camping Assn., Nat. Gerontol. Assn., Tenn. Fedn. Aging (pres. 1982—), Nat. Council Aging, Pi Gamma Mu (past chpt. sec.). Republican. Contbr. articles to profl. jours. Home: 1709 Sherwood Ln Nashville TN 37216 Office: 1801 Broadway Nashville TN 37203

PATTERSON, VIVIAN ROGERS, banker; b. Wake County, N.C., June 2, 1924; d. Lattie Raymond and Dala Earnal (Prince) Rogers; B.S.C., N.C. Coll., 1951, M.S.C., 1961; postgrad. Stonier Grad. Sch. Banking, Rutgers U., 1978, Cannon's Trust Sch., U. N.C., 1981; m. Cecil L. Patterson, Apr. 1, 1956. With Mechanics and Farmers Bank, Durham, N.C., 1944—, asst. v.p., 1967-68, v.p., 1968—, corp. sec., 1979—, trust officer, 1980—; mem. adv. council Sch. Bus., N.C. Central U., Durham; dir. REMCA, Inc. Past mem. fin. com. Harriet Tubman br. YWCA, Durham; past sec., 1st v.p. Durham chpt. Am. Cancer Soc.; past unit leader Durham United Fund; mem. vestry St. Titus Episcopal Ch., Durham; active Durham chpt. ARC; Ch. Women del. Gen. Conv., Episcopal Ch., 1973, lay del., 1982. Mem. Am Inst. Banking, Nat. Assn. Bank Women, Durham Council Estate Planning, Durham Bus. and Profl. Women's Club, NAACP, N.C. Central U. Alumni Assn., Delta Sigma Theta. Clubs: Lawson St. Community, Downtown. Home: 409 Lawson St Durham NC 27707 Office: PO Box 1932 Durham NC 27702

PATTERSON, ZELLA JUSTINA BLACK, home economist, historian; b. Coyle, Okla., May 20, 1909; d. Thomas and Mary Elizabeth (Horst) Black; B.S. in Home Econs. Edn., Langston (Okla.) U., 1937; M.S., Colo. State U., Ft. Collins, 1941; postgrad. U. Calif., Berkeley, Okla. State U.; m. George W. Patterson, Dec. 24, 1946 (dec.). Elem. sch. tchr., 1931-34; extension worker, 1934-36; vocat. home econs. tchr., supervising tchr., 1937-60; mem. faculty Langston U., 1937-46, 60-72, prof. home econs. and home econs. edn., 1965-72, chmn. dept., 1965-72; family living specialist coop. extension Okla. State U.-U.S. Dept. Agr., 1972-74; mem. Langston Community Edn. Adv. Com.; bd. dirs. Logan County Hist. Soc.; mem. Diamond Jubilee Commn. Okla.; mem. Okla. Hist. Soc. Black Heritage adv. com. to exec. com.; author: Langston University: A History, 1979, A Garden of Poems, 1978; also family histories. Recipient Honor Alumna award Colo. State U., 1976, Outstanding Woman award Langston U., 1979; named ambassador of Good Will. Mem. Okla. Edn. Assn. (Outstanding Educator Recognition award 1973), Am. Home Econs. Assn., Okla. Home Econs. Assn., Okla. Ret. Soc., Nat. Ret. Tchrs. Assn., Alpha Kappa Alpha. Republican. Baptist. Clubs: Langston Beautiful, Order Eastern Star, Langston-Coyle Bus. and Profl. Women's. Author: Churches of Langston. Contbr. poem to anthology. Address: PO Box 96 Langston OK 73050

PATTISON, POLLY CLAIRE, publ. designer; b. Mpls., Aug. 4, 1932; d. Ralph Bigelow and Theone (Bonney) Beal; B.A. in Internat. Relations, Stanford U., 1954; postgrad. Sch. Visual Arts, N.Y.C., Art Center Coll., Pasadena, Calif.; m. Robert A. Pattison, June 13, 1970. Design and public relations work with MRA Prodns., 1960-64; designer, prodn. mgr., personnel mgr. PACE Publns., Los Angeles, 1964-70; freelance publ. designer, Westminster, Calif., 1970—; condr. seminars in field. Recipient various design awards Internat. Assn. Bus. Communicators, Soc. Publ. Designers, Calif. Press Women, Orange County Advt. Assn. Mem. Internat. Assn. Bus. Communicators, Women in Communication, Orange County Press Women, Soc. Calligraphy, Soc. Publ. Designers, Nat. Speakers Assn. Address: 5092 Kingscross Rd Westminster CA 92683

PATTON, CELESTEL HIGHTOWER, educator; b. Nacogdoches, Tex., July 14, 1912; d. Felix and Martha Jane (Turner) Hightower; grad. in Dental Tech., Meharry Med. Coll., 1947; B.S. in Health Edn., Tenn. State U., 1952; M.A., Columbia U. Tchrs. Coll., 1958; M.A. in Spanish, Universidad Interamericana, Saltillo, Coah, Mex., 1964; certificate in Spanish, U. Madrid, 1965; m. Ural Leonard Patton, Jan. 31, 1930. Dental hygientist Tex. Pub. Sch. System, 1947-52; dean women, instr. health and phys. edn. Bishop Coll., Marshall, and Dallas Tex., 1954-60; dir. phys. edn. for women Wilberforce U., 1960-62; asso. prof. health edn. So. U., Baton Rouge, 1962—. Recipient Pres. award Meharry Med. Coll., 1972; Alumns award, 1972. Mem. Am., Tex. pub. health assns., Southwestern Sociol. Assn., Am. Tex. dental hygienist assns., AAH PER, AAUP, AAUW, Dallas Dental Hygienist Group, S. Dallas Bus. Women's Club, Zeta Phi Beta. Democrat. Mem. Christian Ch. Home: 4934 Echo Ave Dallas TX 87215 Office: PO Box 9922 Southern U Baton Rouge LA 70813

PATTON, CONNIE GARCIA, educator; b. Luarca, Spain, Nov. 7, 1941; d. Antonio Garcia and Palmira Garcia (Lavin) Mendez; B.A., U. N.Mex., 1964, M.A., 1966; m. Michael G. Patton, July 5, 1970; children—Michael Anthony, Ryan Blake. Instr., Peace Corps, 1964-66; asso. prof. fgn. lang. Emporia (Kans.) State U., 1966—; court translator Lyon County Courthouse, 1974—. Bd. dirs. Sexual Offense Services, 1974-78; v.p. Big Bro.-Big Sister, 1977-79. Ford Found. grad. fellow, 1963-66; Nat. Endowment for Humanities grantee, 1976, 78; named Outstanding Young Kansan, Jaycees, 1977. Mem. Am. Assn. Tchrs. Spanish and Portuguese, MLA, AAUP, Sigma Delta Pi. Author: Spanish Vocabulary Units, 1975. Home: 2323 DeLane St Emporia KS 66801 Office: 1200 Commercial St Emporia KS 66801

PATTON, DIANA LEE WILKOC, artist; b. New Rochelle, N.Y., June 28, 1940; d. August E. and Meta Diane (Neuburg) Wilkoc; A.B. cum laude (Elisha Benjamin Andrews scholar 1960), Brown U., 1962; postgrad. Pan-Am. Art Inst., 1962-63; m. Gardner C. Patton, Aug. 10, 1963; children—Michael, Talryn, Shawn. Service mgr. Lord and Taylor, N.Y.C., 1962-63; tchr. adult edn., Mountain Lakes, N.J., 1972-74; tchr. Somerville Adult Sch., 1978-81, Bridge-water-Raritan (N.J.) Adult Sch., 1982—; artist in watercolors, pen and ink; exhibitor one-woman and group shows NE and SW U.S., Perth, Australia, 1977, spl. bicentennial exhibit, Trenton, N.J., 1976; work represented pvt. and public collections U.S., Australia, N.Z., Europe, Japan; instr. in field; developer art appreciation courses for children and adults; toymaker, 1973-76. Active PTA, PTO, Welcome Wagon. Winner bronze medal in watercolor Nat. Mystic (Conn.) Outdoor Art Festival, 1977; Mayor's Purchase prize Franklin Twp., 1976; watercolor award Somerset County Coll. Tri-State Show, 1978; winner awards, ribbons. Mem. Garden State Watercolor Soc. (Princeton Bank award 1979) N.J. Miniature Art Soc., AAUW (life, various offices 1963-73), art assns. Raritan Valley (best in show award 1978, pres. 1980-82), Somerset, Princeton, Summit, Mystic, North Haven. Presbyterian. Clubs: Hanover Squares (co-pres., 1972-73), Morris County Folk Dancers (co-pres. 1963). Home and studio: 497 Stony Brook Rd Bridgewater NJ 08807

PATTON, JESSICA, designer; b. N.Y.C., July 13, 1920; d. Frederick Henry and Jessie Davis (Woolley) P.; A.B., Stephens Coll., 1939; B.A., Mich. State U., 1941; postgrad. Am. Acad. Dramatic Art, 1941-42; m. George Barkentin, Apr. 21, 1942; children—Perii Alexandra, Pamela Meredith. Fashion model, 1942-47; fashion cons. for films Stage Door Canteen, 1943, Cover Girl, 1944; fashion editor Jr. Bazaar, 1947-48, Good Housekeeping, 1949-51; fashion cons. Mademoiselle mag., 1947-53; prodn. designer for advt. and indsl. films, 1951-61; partner Van Glintenkamp Enterprises, prods. docu-dramas and indsl. films, N.Y.C., 1961—; v.p. White O'Morn Film Corp., 1977—. Recipient Silver Phoenix for film Zebra, Atlanta Film Festival, 1975, Gold medal for Nanette: An Aside, V.I. Internat. Film Festival, 1978. Mem. Am. Soc. Mag. Photographers, Salmagundi Club, Nat. Arts Club. Office: 5 E 16th St New York NY 10003

PATTON, JOANNA, advt. agy. exec.; b. Quincy, Ill., Dec. 20, 1946; d. John H. and Jane Vandike P.; student Stetson U., 1964-66, Fla. State U., 1966-67. Para legal, Miami, Fla., 1968-74; exec. sec. Louis Nizer, Atty., N.Y.C., 1974-77; adminstrv. asst. to pres. Cosmair, N.Y.C., 1977-78, mgr. public relations, 1978, dir. public relations, 1978-79, mktg. dir., 1980-81; owner Joanna Patton Advt., N.Y.C., 1982—. Mem. Fashion Group, Advt. Women N.Y. Office: 320 E 46th St New York NY 10017

PATTON, MARY FRANCES, state probation adminstr.; b. Ralph, Ala., June 22, 1951; d. Tyson Wendell and Lee Dell (McKinney) P.; B.S., U. Wis., 1973, M.S. (Univ. grantee and scholar 1969-73, Grad. Sch. Advanced Opportunity fellow 1974-75), 1975. Teaching asst. U. Wis., Madison, 1973-74, project asst., 1974; substitute houseparent Orchard Hill, home for mentally retarded, Madison, 1974-75; youth devel. worker I Oak Hill Homes, Fulton County (Ga.) Dept. Family and Child Services, Atlanta, 1976; probation supr. II. Ga. Dept. Offender Rehab., Jonesboro, 1977—. Mem. Ga. Probation and Parole Assn. Home: 4122 Herschel Park Dr Apt A-8 College Park GA 30337 Office: Room 301 Courthouse Jonesboro GA 30236

PATUSKY, KATHLEEN LAURA, nurse; b. Bridgeport, Conn., Aug. 29, 1949; d. Peter Paul and Laura Kathleen (Cwikla) P.; B.S.N. with honors and distinction, U. Conn., 1971; M.A. in Counseling, Nat. U., 1981; postgrad. U.S. Internat. U., 1982—. Commd. ensign, Nurse Corps, U.S. Navy, 1970, advanced through grades to lt. comdr., 1979; staff nurse, charge nurse dept. psychiatry U.S. Naval Regional Med. Center, Oakland, Calif., 1971-74, charge nurse dept. obstetrics, Guam, 1974-76; charge nurse dept. psychiatry, Long Beach, Calif., 1976-79; charge nurse dept. obstetrics Naval Regional Med. Center, Camp Pendleton, Calif., 1979-82. Mem. Am. Nurses Assn., Calif. Nurses, Am. Holistic Nurses Assn., Sigma Theta Tau. Home: 160 Madison St Oceanside CA 92056 Office: 2885 Hope Ave Carlsbad CA 92008

PAUL, BETTY BYFIELD, social worker; b. N.Y.C., Nov. 23, 1925; d. Robert Sigmund and Janice (Weil) Byfield; B.A., Bryn Mawr Coll., 1947; M.S.W., Simmons Sch. Social Work, 1966; m. Norman Leo Paul, June 8, 1951; children—Marilyn, David. Asst. to dir. N. Y. Times Youth Forums, 1950-51; family systems specialist Arlington (Mass.) Pub. Schs., 1967-81; pvt. practice social work, Lexington, 1972—; mem. faculty, Center for Parenting Studies, Wheelock Coll., 1979-82, New Eng. Center for Study of Family, 1980-82; numerous TV appearances on marriage and divorce. Reporter, White House Conf. on Children, 1970; bd. dirs. Friends of Mass. Mental Health Center, Boston, 1954-60, pres., 1960-62. Mem. Nat. Assn. Social Workers, Register Clin. Social Workers, NEA, Acad. Cert. Social Workers, Am. Family Therapy Assn. (charter). Jewish. Club: Bryn Mawr of Boston (v.p. 1977-79, pres. 1979-80). Author: (with Norman L. Paul) A Marital Puzzle, 1975, also German edit., 1977. Home: 26 Barberry Rd Lexington MA 02173 Office: 442 Marrett Rd Lexington MA 02173

PAUL, ELLEN LOUISE, USO ofcl.; b. Seoul, Korea, Feb. 18, 1948; d. Albert Ernest and Louise (Wilson) Croft; B.A., U. Md., 1969, M.A., 1974; m. Stephen A. Pettit, Sept. 25, 1975. Advt. asst. Dart Drug Corp., Washington, 1969-70, Grand Union Co., Landover, Md., 1970-73; dir. communications Salvation Army, Nat. Capital and Virginias div., 1973-77; nat. dir. communications Am. Assn. Blood Banks, Washington, 1977-78; asst. world dir. public info. USO World Hdqrs., Washington, 1978-81, dir. direct mail mktg., 1981—; v.p. Image Makers, Inc., Upper Marlboro, Md., 1977—. Recipient Freedom Found. award, 1980. Mem. Religious Public Relations Council (Paul M. Hinkouse award 1973, Hinkhouse-DeRose award 1975; pres. Washington chpt. 1977), Internat. Assn. Bus. Communicators (v.p. D.C. chpt. 1978-79; award for writing and prodn. multi-media presentations 1976, awards for visual communications, photography, print communications 1980), Public Relations Soc. Am. (Toth award for spl. events 1979, Silver Anvil award for spl. events 1979). Democrat. Methodist. Co-author 2 books on folklore of Md., 1973-75; contbr. articles various mags., revs.; producer weekly program Armed Forces Radio Network. Home: 2 Blaketon Ct Upper Marlboro MD 20772 Office: 1146 19th St NW Washington DC 20036

PAUL, EVE W., lawyer, assn. exec.; b. N.Y.C., June 16, 1930; d. Leo and Tamara (Sogolow) Weinschenker; A.B., Cornell U., 1950; J.D., Columbia U., 1952; m. Robert D. Paul, Apr. 9, 1952; children—Jeremy Ralph, Sarah Elizabeth. Admitted to N.Y. bar, 1952, Conn. bar, 1960; asso. Botein, Hays, Sklar & Herzberg, N.Y.C., 1952-54, Bernard D. Cahn, N.Y.C., 1954-56; pvt. practice law, Stamford, Conn., 1960-70; staff atty. Legal Aid Soc., N.Y.C., 1970-71; asso. Greenbaum, Wolff & Ernst, N.Y.C., 1972-78; gen. counsel Conn. Women's Bank, Greenwich, 1974-77; v.p. legal affairs Planned Parenthood Fedn. of Am., N.Y.C., 1979—; lectr. in field. Trustee, Cornell U., 1979—; mem. Stamford Planning Bd., 1967-70. Mem. N.Y.C. Bar Assn., Am. Bar Assn., Conn. Bar Assn., Stamford Bar Assn., N.Y. County Lawyers Assn., Nat. Assn. Women Lawyers. Democrat. Jewish. Contbr. articles to profl. jours. Home: 500 E 77 St New York NY 10021 Office: 810 7th Ave New York NY 10019

PAUL, GRACE, ret. med. technologist, author; b. Liberal, Kans., Mar. 12, 1908; d. David and Myrtle Helen (Brewer) P.; student Tulsa U., 1930-36, Auburn U., 1948, Columbia U., 1949-51. Med. technologist St. Johns Hosp., Tulsa, 1930-36, VA Hosp., Wadsworth, Kans., 1947-48; plant quarantine insp. U.S. Dept. Agr., N.Y.C., 1948-51; claims examiner Social Security Adminstrn., Balt., 1956-71; market research interviewer Response Analysis, Princeton, N.J., 1973-76. Vol. worker United Way of Temple (Tex.), 1974—, Cultural Activities Center, Youth Services Bur., Ret. Sr. Vol. Program; active CAC Humanities Council of Temple, 1972-76. Served with WAC, 1944-46. Mem. Am. Soc. Med. Technologists, Entomol. Soc. Am., Internat. Platform Assn. Presbyn. Club: Business and Professional Women's. Author: Your Future in Medical Technology, 1962; A Short Course in Skilled Supervision, 1965; contbr. to Environ. Engr.'s Handbook, vol. III, 1975. Address: 705 N Main St Temple TX 76501

PAUL, JOYCE WERTHMAN, mgmt. cons.; b. Detroit, Oct. 31, 1941; d. Alfred J. and Mary L. (Janssen) Werthman; student public schs., Warren, Mich.; m. Robert A. Paul, Sept. 23, 1961; children—Kathleen, Carol, Brian. Sales mgr. Tupperware Home Parties, Detroit, 1964-71; distbr. Act II Jewelry Co., Orlando, Fla., 1974-76; sales mgr. Deco Plants Co., Detroit, 1976-79, nat. sales counselor, St. Louis, 1979-81; mgmt. cons. The Joyce Paul Co., Rochester, Mich., 1981—; motivational speaking specialist. Vol., Mich. Spl. Olympics, 1978-82. Mem. The Direct Selling Assn. Author: The Unit Leaders Growing Guide, 1980, others. Address: 53655 Pappy Ln Rochester MI 48063

PAUL, VIRGINIA OTTO, former orgn. exec.; b. Easton, Wash., Mar. 18, 1917; d. Clarence and Anne Marie Otto; diploma in bus. adminstrn., communications Peterson's Tech. Sch., 1938; m. Philip Henry Paul, May 19, 1940; children—Philip O., J. Stephen, Joseph H., Jeananne. State sec. Wash. Farm Bur. Fedn., 1957-62, Wash. Cattlemen's Assn., 1962-65; sec.-treas., dir. communications program Wash. State Beef Council, 1962-69; exec. sec. Wash. State Beef Commn., 1969-80; exec. dir. United Good Neighbors, Kittitas County, Wash., 1968-69; speaker in field, 1950—, promotion chmn. Wash. Cowbelle Orgn., 1955, publicity chmn., 1956-74. Recipient Outstanding Service award Home and Family Life Tchrs. of Wash., 1980. Mem. Am. Women in Radio and TV (pres. Wash. chpt. 1977), Nat. Fedn. Press Women (1st pl. award non-fiction book 1974), Wash. Press Assn. (1st pl. award publicity and promotion 1970-73, Outstanding Achievement award 1970, Woman of Achievement award 1979), Author: (pictorial histories) This Was Cattle Ranching, 1973, This Was Sheep Ranching, 1976; The Homestead Cookbook, 1976. Home: 109 N Anderson St Ellensburg WA 98926

PAULEY, JANE, TV journalist; b. Indpls., Oct. 31, 1950; B.A. in Polit. Sci., Ind. U., 1971. Reporter, WISH-TV, Indpls., co-anchor mid-day news reports and anchor weekend news reports; co-anchor nightly news WMAQ-TV, Chgo., 1975-76; on-air staff The Today Show, 1976—; a prin. newscaster NBC News Update, 1977—; co-anchor Early Today (NBC News); prepares and delivers Money Matters (NBC); Monday-Friday anchor NYT News, NBC Radio Network. Office: care NBC News Today 30 Rockefeller Plaza New York NY 10020 *

PAULI, LYDIA LYGIA BOKS (MRS. BENNO PAULI), physician; b. Vladivostok, Russia; d. Alois and Tatiana (Sapilov) Boks; B.S., Gymnasium, Czechoslovakia; M.D., U. Graz, Austria, 1950; m. Benno Pauli, Oct. 11, 1952. Rotating intern St. Johns Episcopal Hosp., N.Y.C., 1950-51; pediatric intern Johns Hopkins Hosp., Balt., 1951-53, asst. resident, 1953-54, fellow in pediatrics, 1954-57, asso. Epilepsy Clinic, 1955-57, asso. dir., 1957-73, cons. convulsive disorders for comprehensive health care, 1967-70; instr. pediatrics Johns Hopkins Sch. Medicine, Balt., 1957-63, asst. prof., 1963—, asso. dir. Samuel Livingston Epilepsy Diagnostic and Treatment Center, 1973—. Cons. on convulsive disorders Md. Dept. Health, 1957—; cons. Md. Dept. Vocat. Rehab., 1957-77. Bd. dirs. Chesapeake Assn. for Epilepsy. Recipient 1st prize of exhibit Am. Acad. Neurology, 1962, Gold award Am. Psychiat. Assn., 1967 Citation for outstanding service Gov. Md., 1981. Mem. AMA, N.Y. Acad. Scis., Am. Epilepsy Soc., Md. Soc for Research, Balt. Med. and Chirurg. Soc.; asso. Am. Acad. Neurology, Am. Acad. Pediatrics, Balt. Neurol. Soc. Research and publs. on exptl. anti-convulsive drugs, heredity in epilepsy, socio-econ. aspects and employment in epilepsy. Contbg. author: Comprehensive Textbook of Psychiatry, 1967, 3d rev. edit., 1980. Home: 6651 Loch Hill Rd Baltimore MD 21239 Office: 1039 St Paul St Baltimore MD 21202 also CMSC-POPS Johns Hopkins Hosp Baltimore MD 21205

PAULINE, TERRI JO, mfg. co. exec.; b. Atlanta, July 13, 1954; d. Henry Michael and Jacquelyn (Cleveland) P.; B.S. in Engring., Princeton U., 1976; m. William LaRon Slocum, June 16, 1979; 1 dau., Christina Marie Pauline. Field sales engr. semicondr. div. Tex. Instruments Co., Sunnyvale, Calif., 1976-77; sales engr. test and measurement group Tektronix Co., Santa Clara, Calif., 1977-81; co-owner T.R. Graphics & Printing Co., San Jose, Calif., 1979—. Mem. Peninsula Profl. Women's Network. Home: 685 Dotey Ct San Jose CA 95111

PAULSEN-ASKINS, NANCY ELLEN, fin. co. exec.; b. St. Paul, Nov. 2, 1948; d. Charles A. and Stasia (Sawicki) Paulsen; B.S.H.Ec., U. Cin., 1970. B.S.Ed., 1971, M.Ed., 1972; postgrad. SUNY, Buffalo, 1974-76; student C.L.U. program 1979-81, Inst. Fin. Edn., 1982—, mgmt. program. Am. Mgmt. Assn./Monmouth Coll., 1982—; m. Arthur J. Askins, Apr. 28, 1979. Camp counselor, Girls Scouts U.S.A., summers 1966, 67; asst. aquatic supr. Cin. Recreation Commn., 1969-72; student affairs adminstr., mem. faculty U. Cin., 1970-72, Tex. Luth. Coll., 1972-73, SUNY, Geneseo, 1974-76, Temple U., 1976-78; tchr., drug awareness coordinator Harlandale Schs., San Antonio, 1973-74; career life ins. agt., fin. planning cons. Phoenix Mut. Life Ins. Co., Phila., 1978-81; registered rep., securities agt. Phoenix Equity Planning Corp., Phila., 1980-81; owner Paulsen-Askins Fin. Services, Somers Point, N.J., 1980-81; mem. women's task force Phoenix Cos., 1980-81; tng. services coordinator Collective Fed. Savs. & Loan Assn., Egg Harbor City, N.J., 1981—, asst. v.p., 1982—; facilitator Assertiveness Tng. Group, Interpersonal Communications Group; sales adv. Jr. Achievement; instr. Inst. Fin. Edn., 1982—; Agy. chmn. United Way Campaign, Phila., 1979, 80; active ann. Muscular Dystrophy Telethon, Phila.; active Girl Scouts U.S.A., 1956-74; mem. parish council, choir St. Joseph Roman Cath. Ch., Somers Point, N.J., 1979—. Recipient Blue Vase sales achievement award Phoenix Mut. Life Ins. Co., 1978, named Asso. of Month, 1979. Mem. Greater Camden Assn. Life Underwriters (chmn. Life Ins. Week for South Jersey 1978-79, dir. 1979-81, public relations chmn. 1979-81, chmn. state edn. 1981), Greater Mainland C. of C. (v.p. treas., membership coordinator 1980—), U. Cin. Alumni of Greater Phila. Area. (pres. 1980—), Alliance, The Women's Network. Democrat. Club: Soroptomist Internat. Home: PO Box 800 Somers Point NJ 08244 Office: 200 Philadelphia Ave Egg Harbor City NJ 08215

PAULSON, LYNDA ROSE, tng. specialist; b. Indpls., Oct. 18, 1939; d. Alfred E. and Mary Louis (Gladden) Fitch; B.A., Ind. U., 1961; m. Bernard N. Mariano, Dec. 10, 1975; children by previous marriage—Phillip Todd, Paige Anne Paulson. Mgr., Margie's Bridal Salon, Melrose Park, Ill., 1967-68; account exec. Sheraton Hotel, Oak Brook, Ill., 1968-70; regional sales mgr. Dale Carnegie Inst., Westchester, Ill., 1970-79; pres., founder Success Strategies, Inc., Clarendon Hills, Ill., 1979—; developer retail sales and people mgmt. seminars; designer Exec. Speaking Seminars; speech coach; instr. Am. Mgmt. Assn., Dale Carnegie courses. Recipient awards for prodn. Dale Carnegie Inst., 1976-79, awards for profl. instrn., 1977-79; named Entrepreneur of Yr., Women in Mgmt., 1981, Who to Look for in '81, Entree mag., 1981. Mem. Nat. Assn. Women Bus. Owners, Women in Mgmt., Am. Mgmt. Assn., Young Pres. Orgn. Republican. Clubs: Executives, Chgo. Health (Chgo); Willowbrook Racquet, Oak Brook Racquet, Sports Fitness Inst. Home and office: 23 Kane Ct Clarendon Hills IL 60514

PAULSTON, CHRISTINA BRATT, educator; b. Stockholm, Dec. 30, 1932; came to U.S., 1951, naturalized, 1960; d. Lennart and Elsa (Facht) B.; B.A., Carleton Coll., 1953; M.A., U. Minn., 1955; Ed.D., Columbia U., 1966; m. Rolland Paulston, July 26, 1963; children—Christopher, Ian. Tchr. Clara City and Pine Island (Minn.) High Schs., 1955-60, Am. Sch. Tangier (Morocco), 1960-62, Katrineholm Allmanna Laroverk, Katrineholm, Sweden, 1962-63; circulation librarian East Asian Library, Columbia U., 1963-64, asst. instr. Tchrs. Coll., 1964-66; prof. Pontificia Universidad Catolica del Peru, Lima, 1966-67; cons. Instituto Linguistico de Verano, Lima, 1967-68; asst. dir. English Lang. Inst., U. Pitts., 1969-70, dir., 1970—, prof. linguistics, 1969—, acting chmn. dept. gen. linguistics, 1974-75, chmn., 1975—. Recipient Research award Am. Ednl. Research Assn., 1980. Democrat. Episcopalian. Contbr. articles to profl. jours. and books. Office: Linguistics CL 2801 U Pitts Pittsburgh PA 15260

PAULU, FRANCES BROWN, orgn. exec.; b. Hastings, Minn., June 22, 1920; d. Thomas Andrew and Florence Ida (Tuttle) Brown; B.A. magna cum laude, U. Minn., 1940, postgrad. Sch. Social Work, 1942-44; m. Burton Paulu, June 29, 1942; children—Sarah Leith Paulu-Boittin, Nancy Jean, Thomas Scott. Case worker Family Welfare Assn. Mpls., 1943-45; interviewer Community Health and Welfare Council, Mpls., 1963; sch. social worker Project Head Start, Mpls., 1966; program dir. Minn. Internat. Center, Mpls., 1970-72, exec. dir., 1972—. Pres. UN Rally, 1970-72; chmn. Mpls. Charter Commn., 1972-74; bd. dirs. Urban Coalition of Mpls., 1967-70, Minn. World Affairs Center, 1972—; mem. tourism adv. com. City of Mpls., 1976—; dir. Minn. World Trade Week, 1977-81; mem. mgmt. team Minn. Awareness Project, 1982—. DeWitt Jennings Payne scholar, 1939-40. Mem. Nat. Council for Internat. Visitors (officer and/or exec. com. mem. 1975-81), Nat. Assn. for Fgn. Student Affairs, LWV (pres. Mpls. 1967-69), UN Assn. Minn. (adv. council 1979—), Mpls.-St. Paul Com. on Fgn. Relations, Phi Beta Kappa, Alpha Omicron Pi, Lambda Alpha Psi. Home: 5005 Wentworth Ave Minneapolis MN 55419 Office: Minn Internat Center 711 East River Rd Minneapolis MN 55455

PAULUS, NORMA JEAN PETERSEN (MRS. WILLIAM G. PAULUS), sec. state Oreg.; b. Belgrade, Nebr., Mar. 13, 1933; d. Paul Emil and Ella Marie (Hellbusch) Petersen; LL.B., Willamette Law Sch., 1962; m. William G. Paulus, Aug. 16, 1958; children—Elizabeth, William Frederick. Sec. to Harney County Dist. Atty., 1950-53; legal sec., Salem, Oreg., 1953-55; sec. to chief justice Oreg. Supreme Ct., 1955-61; admitted to Oreg. bar, 1962; of counsel Paulus and Callaghan, Salem, mem. Oreg. Ho. of Reps., 1971-77, former mem. judiciary com., environ. and land use com., profl. responsibility com., criminal law revision com., Rep. floor leader, mem., vice chmn. elections com., mem. revenue com., chmn. Oreg. Solid Waste Mgmt. Citizen's Adv. Com.; sec. state State of Oreg., Salem, 1976—. Fellow Eagleton Inst. Politics, 1971; trustee Willamette U., 1978—; bd. dirs. Benedictine Found. of Oreg., 1980—. Mem. Salem Human Relations Commn., 1967-70, Marion-Polk Boundary Commn., 1970-71. Recipient Golden Torch award Bus. and Profl. Women Oreg., 1971; Distinguished Service award City of Salem, 1971; named One of 10 Women of Future, Ladies Home Jour., 1979. Mem. Nat. Order Women Legislators, Nat. Soc. State Legislators (dir. 1971-72), Oreg. State Bar, Bus. and Profl. Women's Club, Zonta Internat., Delta Kappa Gamma. Office: Office Sec State 136 State Capitol Salem OR 97310 *

PAUTH, PATRICIA RUTH, librarian; b. Rochester, N.Y., Feb. 14, 1936; d. Frank Alvin and Ruth Rose (Vose) P.; student Wittenberg U., Springfield, Ohio, 1953-56. Library asst. periodicals dept. Rush Rhees Library, U. Rochester (N.Y.), 1956-59; with Price Waterhouse & Co., N.Y.C., 1959—, purchasing asst., 1959-63, reference librarian, 1963-72, asst. librarian, 1972-74, head librarian, 1974—. Mem. Spl. Libraries Assn., Am. Soc. for Info. Sci., DAR, Union Street Gardens Assn. (past treas., pres.). Home: 376 Union St Brooklyn NY 11231 Office: 153 E 53d St New York NY 10022

PAUTSCH, DELORES ALMA, distbg. co. exec.; b. Fond du Lac, Wis., Oct. 30, 1928; d. William Frederick and Alma Pauline (Schmidt) Mielke; student Fond du Lac Bus. Coll., 1945-46; m. Milton Gustave Pautsch, Nov. 5, 1949; children—Floyd A., Joy Faye, Bonnie Mae and Betsy Mae (dec.)(twins). With Nat. Rivet Co., 1946-47, Johnson Truck Service, 1947-49, Milt's Service Sta., 1949-52, Nash Waupun, 1952-57, Peters Oil Co., 1957-62; self-employed floral designer, 1963-75; owner, pres. Pautsch Distbg. Co., Waupun, Wis., 1975—. Home: 734 S Madison St Waupun WI 53963 Office: Pautsch Distbg Co 735 S Madison St Waupun WI 53963

PAUWELS, COLLEEN KRISTL, library adminstr.; b. Chgo., Jan. 25, 1946; d. Frank Robert and Alyce Louise (Wear) Kristl; B.A., Barat Coll., 1968; M.L.S., Ind. U., 1975; m. Gerard W. Pauwels, Aug. 21, 1971; 1 dau., Erin Kristl. Public services librarian Ind. U.-Bloomington Law Library, 1975-78, acting dir., 1978-81, dir., 1981—, instr. legal bibliography, law library adminstrn. Sch. Library and Info. Sci., 1977—. Mem. Am. Assn. Law Libraries. Roman Catholic. Home: 3442 Longview Dr Bloomington IN 47401 Office: Ind U Sch Law Library Law Bldg Bloomington IN 47405

PAVELKA, ELAINE BLANCHE, mathematician, educator; b. Chgo.; d. Frank Joseph and Mildred Bohumila (Seidl) P.; B.A., M.S., Northwestern U.; Ph.D., U. Ill. With Northwestern U. Aerial Measurements Lab., Evanston, Ill.; tchr. Leyden Community High Sch., Franklin Park, Ill.; prof. math. Morton Coll., Cicero, Ill.; speaker 3d Internat. Congress Math. Edn., Karlsruhe, Germany, 1976. Recipient sci. talent award Westinghouse Elec. Co. Mem. Am. Edn. Research Assn., Am. Math. Assn. 2-Year Colls., Am. Math. Soc., Assn. Women in Math., Can. Soc. History and Philosophy of Math., Ill. Council Tchr. of Math., Ill. Math. Assn. Community Colls., Math. Assn. Am., Math. Action Group, Ga. Center Study and Teaching and Learning Math., Nat. Council Tchrs. of Math., Sch. Sci. and Math. Assn., Soc. Indsl. and Applied Math., Northwestern U. Alumni Assn., U. Ill. Alumni Assn., Am. Mensa Ltd., Intertel, Am. Youth Hostel, Sigma Delta Epsilon, Pi Mu Epsilon. Home: 1900 Euclid Ave Berwyn IL 60402 Office: 3801 S Central Ave Cicero IL 60650

PAVIL, MARY CAROLYN, health corp. exec.; b. Bethel, Alaska, May 22, 1943; d. Max E. and Sophie P. (Anaruk) Lieb; ed. Knapp Bus. Coll., Kuskokwim Community Coll.; m. Howard Pavil, Apr. 26, 1963; children—Kelly, Eric, Jeffrey, Howard. Nors monitor 21st Supply Sq., Elmendorf AFB, 1967-68, 70-71; sec. Yukon Kuskokwim Health Corp., Bethel, 1972-73, supply clk., 1973-74, health aide, 1974-76, services coordinator, 1976-77, adminstrv. asst., 1977-78, exec. dir., 1979—. Mem. Bethel City Council, 1981—. Recipient Outstanding Performance award USAF, 1969. Mem. Am. Soc. Circumpolar Health, Am. Health Planning Assn., Assn. Regional Health Dirs. Moravian. Home: 8023 Mallard Ln Bethel AK 99559 Office: PO Box 528 Bethel AK 99559

PAVONE, SHARON LYNN, mfg. co. exec.; b. Chgo., June 30, 1950; d. Erwin John and Frances Louise (Mieszcak) Beilke; student So. Ill. U., Carbondale, 1968-70; m. J.T. Pavone, Aug. 24, 1975 (dec.); 1 dau., Candy Lynn. V.p. Exec. Accounts Mgmt., Los Angeles, 1980-81; credit mgr. Victrex Sales, Culver City, Calif., 1978, Cal Custom Hawk, Carson, Calif., 1978-80, Albrass Enterprises, Los Angeles, 1981—. Mem. Credit Mgrs. Assn. (chmn. 1979-80), Export Mgrs. Assn., Calif. Check Investigators Assn., Nat. Assn. Female Execs., Calif. Furniture Mfrs. Assn. Office: 2801 E 11th St Los Angeles CA 90023

PAWLAK, ANN LOUISE, exec. recruiter; b. St. Paul, May 17, 1947; d. John Thomas and Faith Joy-Grace (Heidinger) P.; B.A., Macalester Coll., 1969; M.A., Syracuse U., 1971. Lectr. dept. English, Otterbein Coll., Columbus, Ohio, 1972-74; fiscal analyst appropriations com. Minn. Ho. of Reps., St. Paul, 1974-76; program mgr. personnel, budget, planning Minn. Energy Agy., St. Paul, 1976-77; market research coordinator Jefferson Lines, Mpls., 1977-78; owner Ann Pawlak & Assos., Inc., St. Paul, 1978-82; corp. recruiter (EDP), Mgmt. Search, Mpls., 1982—. Mem. Nat. Assn. Female Execs., Nat. Assn. Women Bus. Owners, Women's Network, Phi Beta Kappa. Democrat. Home: 2417 Como Ave SE Minneapolis MN 55414 Office: Suite 366 400 Shelard Plaza S Minneapolis MN 55426

PAXSON-STEINFALS, GEORGIA KAY, employment services co. exec.; b. Floresville, Tex., Sept. 8, 1944; d. George Frederick and Mary Catherine Berger; student public schs., Linwood, N.J.; m. Chris Steinfals, Aug. 11, 1982; children—Robert S., Alyssa N. Legal adminstrv. asst. McGahn & Friss, Atlantic City, 1966-76; pres., owner Paxson Ford Assos., Inc., Atlantic City, 1977—; cons. Resorts Internat. Hotel/Casino. Coordinator campaigns McGahn for Senate, 1971, 73, 77, campaign dir., 1981; coordinator Miss Atlantic City Pageant, 1980. Mem. Atlantic City Womens C. of C. (1st v.p. 1981), Atlantic City Hotel/Motel Assn., Nat. Assn. Female Execs. Democrat. Lutheran. Office: 1421 Atlantic Ave Atlantic City NJ 08401

PAXTON, ALICE ADAMS, artist, designer; b. Hagerstown, Md., May 19, 1914; d. William Albert and Josephine (Adams) Rosenberger; student Peabody Inst. Music, Balt., 1937-38; grad. Parson's Sch. Design, N.Y., 1940; studied portrait painting with J. Laurie Wallace, 1944-46; studied with Augustus Dunbier, 1947-48, Sylvia Curtis, 1949, Milton Wolsky, 1950, Frank Sapousek, 1951; m. James Love Paxton, Jr., June 26, 1942 (div.); 1 son, William Allen III. Free-lance work archtl. renderings and interior design for various N.Y. interior decorators, 1937-40; interior designer, spl. furnishings designer and muralist Orchard and Wilhelm, furniture store, Omaha, 1940-42; designer interior Chapel Boys' Town, Nebr., 1942; tchr. art classes Alice Paxton Studio, Omaha, 1957-64; dir. Paxton-Mitchell Co., Omaha; tchr. mech. drawing, archtl. rendering, mech. perspective Parson's Sch. Design, N.Y., 1937-40; one-man show of archtl. renderings, Washington County Mus. Fine Arts, Hagerstown, 1944; exhibited group shows at Joslyn Mus., Omaha, 1943, 44, Ann. Exhbn. Cumberland Valley Artists, Hagerstown, Md., 1945; represented permanent collections at No. Natural Gas Co. Bldg., Omaha, Swanson Found., Omaha, also pvt. collections. Vol. designer, decorator recreation room Omaha Blood Bank, A.R.C., 1943, recreation room Creighton U., 1943, lounge psychiat. ward Lincoln (Nebr.) Army Hosp., 1944; planner color coordinator Children's Hosp., Omaha, 1947, painted murals, 1948, decorated dental room, 1950; also numerous other vol. profl. activities for civic orgns., hosps., clubs, chs., also community playhouse. Co-chmn. camp and hosp. coms. A.R.C., 1943-45, county com. select and send gifts servicemen, 1943-46; mem. Ak-Sar-Ben Ball com., Omaha, 1946-48; judge select Easter Seal design, Joslyn Mus., 1946; mem. council Girl Scouts U.S.A., Omaha, 1943-47; spl. drs. chmn. Jr. League, Omaha, 1947-48, chmn. Jr. League Red Cross, fund dr., 1947-48; bd. dirs., vol. worker Creche, Omaha, 1954-56; chmn. Jr. League Community Chest Fund Dr., 1948-50; co-chmn. Infantile Paralysis Appeal, 1944. Recipient three teaching scholarships Parson's Sch. Design, 1937-40; presdl. citation A.R.C. activities, 1946; 1st prize Ann. Midwest Show Joslyn Mus., 1943; painted and decorated straw elephant bag which was presented to Mrs. Richard Nixon, 1960. Contbr. articles and photographs Popular Home mag., 1958. Mem. Asso. Artists Omaha (charter), Jr. League Omaha, Am. Security Council (nat. adv. bd.), Internat. Platform Assn., U.S. Hist. Soc. Republican. Episcopalian. Club: Fountain Head Country. Home: 2001 Greenfield Rd Hagerstown MD 21740

PAXTON, CAROL JEANNE, environ. engr.; b. Richmond, Ind., May 5, 1928; d. Elbert Raymond and Lenora Ione (Watkins) Belcher; B.S. in Mech. Engring., Trinity U., San Antonio, 1948; M.B.A., Iowa State U., 1975; student environ. mgmt. and engring. U. Va., 1975; m. William Clark Paxton, Sept. 1, 1946; children—James, Joan, Sandra, Patricia, Dale, Mark, Dana. Mgr. fin. planning and contracts Aerojet-Gen. Corp., 1949-63; owner Carol's Engring. Cons., Huntington Beach, Calif., 1965-68; lab. supr. Mason & Hangar-Silas Mason Co., Inc., Burlington, Iowa, 1968-77; engring. scientist, OSHA compliance officer State of N.Mex., 1977; environ. engring. supr. Zia Co., Los Alamos, 1977—; cons., lectr. in field. Pres., Mediapolis (Iowa) United Way, 1970-72; chmn. Mediapolis Mothers March of Dimes, 1972-73; v.p. Mediapolis Mchts. Assn., 1973-74; pres. bd. dirs., treas., project coordinator N.Mex. State Employees Commuters Assn., Inc., 1977—; nat. membership chmn. Am. Rideshaing Profls., 1981. Recipient Sec. Def. award, 1976. Mem. Soc. Women Engrs., N.Mex. Network Women in Sci. and Engring., LWV, Women's Polit. Caucus. Democrat. Methodist. Office: Zia Co PO Box 1539 Los Alamos NM 87544

PAXTON, JUANITA WILLENE, univ. ofcl.; b. Birmingham, Ala., Oct. 30, 1930; d. Will and Elizabeth P.; A.B. (Jr. League scholar), Birmingham So. Coll., 1950; M.A., Mich. State U., 1951; Ed.D., Ind. U., 1971. Dormitory dir. Tex. Tech U., Lubbock, 1951-53; asst. dean students State U. Tchrs. Coll., Fredonia, N.Y., 1953-56, assoc. dean students, 1956-57; asst. dean women U. N.Mex., Albuquerque, 1957-63; dean women East Tenn. State U., Johnson City, 1963-68, 70-78, dir. Counseling Ctr., 1978—. Sec. adminstrv. bd. Munsey Meml. Methodist Ch., Johnson City, 1977-81; v.p. bd. dirs., chmn. tng. com. Washington, Carter and Greene Counties, Contact Teleministries. NDEA grantee, 1965; Ednl. Profl. Devel. Act grantee, 1968-69. Mem. Tenn. Assn. Women Deans and Counselors (v.p. 1964-66, pres. 1966-68, chmn. conv. program 1972-77), East Tenn. Edn. Assn. (chmn. guidance div. 1967), Watauga Personnel and Guidance Assn. (sec. 1966-67, pres.-elect 1967-68, program chmn. 1973), Am. Coll. Personnel Assn. (media bd. 1978-80), Tenn. Personnel and Guidance Assn., Nat. Assn. Women Deans, Adminstrs. and Counselors, Assn. Counselor Educators and Suprs., Am. Assn. Higher Edn., So. Assn. Counseling Center Personnel, So. Coll. Personnel Assn., Delta Kappa Gamma (chpt. pres. 1975-76, state sec. 1977-78, state 1st v.p. 1979-81). Clubs: Monday Club Aux. (pres. 1980-81, 2d v.p. 1982-83). Contbr. articles to profl. publs. Office: East Tenn State Univ Counseling Center PO Box 24-220A Johnson City TN 37614-0002

PAYMAR, PATRICIA ANN, cosmetic sales co. exec.; b. Battle Creek, Mich., Sept. 19, 1936; d. Norman Elmer and Alice Margaret (Buettner) Douthwaite; student public schs., Jackson and Battle Creek, Mich.; m. Darrell Myron Paymar, Dec. 23, 1963; children—Willard, Susan, Sandra, Kathleen. Head cashier Assos. Loan Co., Jackson, 1958-64; bookkeeper, office mgr. Kitchen Shoppe, Jackson, 1966-69; owner, mgr. Mary Kay Cosmetics, Niles, Mich., 1976—; condr. sales seminars. Chmn. TV com. Pawating Hosp. Aux. Assn., Niles, 1977-78. Mem. Nat. Assn. Female Execs. Club: Star, White Shrine of Jerusalem. Home and Office: 4054 Blossom Ct Brunswick OH 44212

PAYNE, BETTIE SELDEN WATFORD, health assn. exec.; b. Texas City, Tex., June 20, 1948; d. Wilbur Horsley and Bettie Selden (Friedell) Watford; B.J., U. Tex., Austin, 1970; m. John Howard Payne, III, Jan. 24, 1970 (div. July 1981). Public relations dir. Lyndon B. Johnson Sch. Public Affairs, U. Tex., Austin, 1971-72; public info. officer Area II Regional Med. Program, U. Calif. Med. Sch., Davis, 1972-73, asst., then acting info. officer med. sch., 1973-74; congressional staff asst., Washington, 1975-76; dir. public relations Nat. Soc. Med. Research, 1976-79; dir. Office Communications and Public Affairs, Group Health Assn., Inc., 1979—. Mem. public affairs adv. com. Washington chpt. ARC. Recipient Achievement awards for brochures and newsletters Soc. Tech. Communication, 1977. Mem. Nat. Fedn. Press Women (nat. bd. 1977—), Am. Med. Writers Assn., Hosp. Council Nat. Capital Area, Alpha Omicron Pi. Democrat. Episcopalian. Home: 2420 N Florida St Arlington VA 22207 Office: 2121 Pennsylvania Ave NW Washington DC 20037

PAYNE, ELAINE WORLEY, blanket mfg. co. ofcl.; b. Asheville, N.C., June 10, 1941; d. McKinley Clenon and Katherine (Plemmons) Worley; student Asheville-Buncombe Tech. Coll., 1968, 80, U. N.C., Asheville, 1978; m. Leonard E. Payne, Sept. 28, 1957; children—Clint, Michael, Phyllis. Sewing machine operator Beacon Mfg. Co., Swannanoa, N.C., 1959-74, large blanket sewing dept. supr., 1977-79, mgr. large blanket sewing and baby blanket depts., 1979—. Adviser Jr. Achievement 1980-81; treas. Black Mountain Com. Better Sports, 1973-74. Democrat. Baptist. Club: Big O. Home: PO Box 172 Rainbow Terr Black Mountain NC 28711 Office: 202 Whitson Ave Swannanoa NC 28778

PAYNE, GAIL ANN CURTIS, radio sta. exec.; b. Stonewall, Okla., July 3, 1940; d. William Raymond and Thelma May (Schwandt) Curtis; B.A. in English Edn., Central State U., Edmond, Okla., 1963; m. William Haydon Payne, July 3, 1960; children—Anne M., Kelly Gail, Haydon Michelle, William Haydon II. With Sta. KWHP, Edmond, 1962-79, news reporter, 1962-72, pub. relations dir., corp. sec., 1972-79; v.p. Central Broadcast Co., Inc., Tulsa, 1977—; real estate sales asso. Bob Turner and Assos., Edmond, 1977-81; part-time sec. Louis Holshouser Advt., Edmond, 1979-81. Chmn. Cerebral Palsey, Edmond. Mem. Nat. Assn. Broadcasters, Greater Oklahoma City FM Broadcasters, Edmond Bd. Realtors, Okla. Bd. Realtors, Edmond C. of C., Town and Country Homemakers Extension Group (past pres.). Democrat. Club: Merry Modern Mother's (sec.). Office: Central Broadcast Co Inc 5840 S Memorial St Suite 103 Tulsa OK 74145

PAYNE, KERRY HANCOCK, civic worker, calligrapher; b. Jackson, Miss., Aug. 12, 1944; d. Herman Huffman and Katie Maxine (Moore) Hancock; A.B., Ala. Coll., 1966; m. Gillis Lavelle Payne, Jr., July 3, 1966 (div. Sept. 1981); 1 son, Andrew Christian. Dental asst. Dr. Richard Perryman, Bessemer, Ala., 1960-65; tchr. Elyton Elem. Sch., Birmingham (Ala.) Public Schs., 1966-68, Lakeview Elementary Sch., Nashville Public Schs., 1968-69. Tour guide Landmarks Found., Montgomery, Ala., 1975-78; pres. Montgomery-Autauga Med. Aux., 1978-79; active Jr. League Montgomery, Montgomery Guild Performing Arts. Mem. DAR. Methodist. Home: 501 Martha St Montgomery AL 36104

PAYNE, MARGARET ANNE, parks and recreation adminstr.; b. Ithaca, N.Y., May 25, 1942; d. Douglass M. and Jean L. (Linklater) P.; B.S., SUNY, Cortland, 1964; M.A., N.Y. U., 1970; m. John P. Clements, May 19, 1979. Recreation supr. Oceanside (N.Y.) Sch. Dist., 1964-66; with Nassau County (N.Y.) Dept. Recreation and Parks, 1966-75, regional park supr., 1970-75; commr. parks, recreation and youth services Town of Greenburgh, N.Y., 1975-76; asst. commr. for recreation N.Y. State Office of Parks and Recreation, Albany, 1976—. Mem. N.Y. State Recreation and Park Soc., Nat. Recreation and Park Assn., World Leisure and Recreation Assn., Am. Dance Guild, Nat. Assn. Female Execs., Nat. Parks and Conservation Assn., N.Y. State Outdoor Edn. Assn. Democrat. Home: 2 Chaucer St Hartsdale NY 10530 Office: NY State Office of Parks and Recreation Empire State Plaza Albany NY 12238

PAYNE, MARGARET RALSTON, coll. dean; b. Louisville, Jan. 31, 1946; d. Henry Morris and Rena Belle (Owens) Ralston; B.A., Kalamazoo Coll., 1968; M.A., Kent State U., 1971, postgrad., 1972—; student U. Sierre Leone, 1966-67; m. James Edward Payne, Dec. 11, 1976. Asst. prof. psychology Kent (Ohio) State U., 1972-78, adj. asst. prof., 1978—, asst. dean devel. services, 1974—; cons. Portage County Headstart, 1974-79. Bd. dirs. Portage County Community Action Council, 1979—. Ohio Rehab. Services Commn. grantee, 1974, 75; HEW grant, 1974, 78, 79, 80, 81. Mem. Am. Psychol. Assn., Midwestern Psychol. Assn., Nat. Assn. Black Psychologists, Am. Assn. Higher Edn., Nat. Assn. Women Deans, Adminstrs. and Counselors, Midwestern Assn. Equal Opportunity Program Personnel, Ohio Assn. Equal Opportunity Program Personnel, Ohio Assn. Women Deans, Adminstrs. and Counselors. Home: 237 Rellim Dr Kent OH 44240 Office: Dept Devel Services Kent State U Kent OH 44242

PAYNE, MARTHA LEE HARVEY, interior designer; b. Oakland, Calif., Sept. 29, 1944; d. Ira Omar and Dorothy (Page) Harvey; B.A., So. Meth. U., 1966; postgrad. UCLA, 1975; children—Gregory Thomas, Alysha Carol, David Lee Harvey. Retail trainee Neiman-Marcus, Dallas, 1964-65; interior designer Jan Grierson, Austin, Tex., 1970; owner, operator Inside-Out Interior Design, Pacific Palisades, Calif., 1974—; fabric buyer, furniture designer Elite Upholstery Co., City of Industry, Calif., 1975; West coast area mgr. decorative fabrics Milliken & Co., Los Angeles, 1976-78; Calif. ter. mgr. Design Resources, Los Angeles, 1978-80; account exec. Pindler & Pindler, Los Angeles, 1980-81; nat. account mgr. Coral of Chgo., 1981-82. Chmn. fund-raising com. YMCA, 1975-76, football coach YMCA, 1975-79. Mem. Am. Soc. Interior Designers (West Coast nat. v.p. 1976), S.W. Furniture Mfrs. Assn., So. Meth. U. Alumni Assn. Republican. Office: Dallas TX

PAYNE, MARY ELIZABETH, accountant; b. Chgo., Dec. St Rd 1942; d. Harry Stone and Virginia (Frazer) Walsh; student So. Ill. U., 1961-63; B.S., U. Ill., 1966; m. Frank Edward Payne, Sept. 9, 1972. Audit asst. Arthur Andersen & Co., Chgo., 1966-69, audit sr., 1969-72, audit mgr., 1972-75; corporate controller I.D.C. Services, Chgo., 1975-77; practice public acctg., Hinsdale, Ill., 1977—. C.P.A., Ill. Mem. Am. Inst. C.P.A.s, Ill. Soc. C.P.A.s, Hinsdale Bus. and Profl. Women's Club. Office: 907 N Elm St Rd Hinsdale IL 60521

PAYNE, MARY LIBBY BICKERSTAFF, lawyer; b. Gulport, Miss., Mar. 27, 1932; d. Reece Orville and Emily (Cook) Bickerstaff; B.A., U. Miss., 1954, J.D., 1955; m. Bobby Ray Payne, Dec. 20, 1955; children—Reece Allen, Glenn Russell. Admitted to Miss. bar, 1955; pvt. practice, Gulfport, Jackson and Brandon, Miss., 1955-68; draftsman Miss. Ho. of Reps., part-time 1964-68, full-time 1970-72; exec. dir. Miss. Judiciary Commn., 1969-70; asst. atty. gen., 1972-75; mem. faculty Miss. Coll. Sch. Law, 1975—, dean assoc. prof., until 1978, prof. law, 1978—; mem. Miss. Jud. Selection Commn., 1981; v.p. 1st Fin. Corp., 1963-68; pres. Rankin County Bar Assn., 1968-69. Mem. Pearl (Miss.) Planning Commn., 1974; bd. govs. Jackson Youth for Christ, 1977-80. Fellow Am. Bar Found.; mem. ABA, Am. Judicature Soc., Miss. State Bar, Hinds County Bar Assn., Scribes. Home: 3617 Wilcox Dr Pearl MS 39208 Office: 151 E Griffith St Jackson MS 39201

PAYNE, PAULA DAVIS, utility exec.; b. Madison County, Tenn., Nov. 4, 1943; d. John Herbert and Leilah (Moore) Davis; B.A., U. Miss., 1965, postgrad., 1968; postgrad. Memphis State U., Memphis Acad. Arts; m. Joel L. Payne, Dec. 18, 1971. Tchr., Memphis schs., 1965-68; med. illustrator St. Jude Children's Research Hosp., Memphis, 1968-69; with Memphis Light, Gas and Water Co., 1970—, supr. communication services, 1975-77, mgr. communication services, 1977—. Adv. com. Skills Center Vocat. Sch., Memphis, 1979—; bd. dirs. Greater Memphis State U., 1981—, Memphis Travelers Aid, 1980—, Memphis United Way, 1980-81; v.p. Episcopal Churchwomen, Christ Episcopal Ch., Memphis, 1981. Mem. Internat. Assn. Bus. Communicators, Public Relations Soc. Am. (officer Memphis chpt.; Silver Quill award Memphis chpt. 1981), Memphis Area C. of C. (communications com.). Republican. Home: 2086 Florette St Memphis TN 38116 Office: 220 N Main St Memphis TN 38101

PAYNE, SUSAN F., assn. exec.; b. N.Y.C., Feb. 17, 1941; d. Frederick and Caroline (Campbell) Frantz; student SUNY, Oswego, 1960; B.S., Simmons Coll., 1963; postgrad. U. Hartford, 1978, Smithsonian Inst. Mus./Sch. Relations Workshop, 1979; also craft workshops; m. John H. Payne III, Aug. 24, 1963; children—John IV, Sarah. Trainee, Design Research Inc., Cambridge, Mass., 1962; service rep. Va. Tel & Tel., 1963; sec. McGuffey Reading Clinic, U. Va., 1963-64; office mgr. admissions U. Hartford (Conn.), 1964-66; with Am. Indian Archaeol. Inst., Washington, Conn., 1976—, dir. edn., 1977, chmn. collection com., 1978—, dir. devel., 1981—, editor instn. publs., exec. v.p., 1982—. Bd.

dirs. Washington Montessori Sch., 1970-71; chmn. film benefits Washington Art Assn., 1970, 73; chmn. uniforms com. Washington-Gunnery Hockey and Skating Assn., 1976; treas. Nettleton Hollow Assn., 1972-78; gov. Washington Club, 1976-78; chmn. for arts Bicentennial Com. Town of Washington, 1974-76; bd. dirs. Montessori Sch. Northwestern Conn., 1974-76; chmn. Historic Dist. Commn., Washington, 1976-81. Mem. Am. Assn. Mus., Am. Indian Archaeol. Inst., Gunn Meml. Hist. Mus., New Eng. Mus. Assn., Smithsonian Instn., Washington Art Assn. Address: Nettleton Hollow Rd Washington CT 06793

PAYNICH, MARY LOUISE, nurse-sociologist; b. Copper City, Mich.; d. George Acacie and Justine (Chopp) Paynich; R.N., U. Mich. Sch. Nursing, 1934, B.S., Sch. Pub. Health, 1944; M.S., Cath. U. Am., 1953, Ph.D., 1961. Staff nurse U. Mich. Hosp. and Health Service, Ann Arbor, 1934-39; health counselor Longfellow Camp for Boys, Annapolis, Md. summer 1939; pub. health staff nurse Md. Health Dept., Balt., 1940-42; pub. health nurse and field tchr. Kellogg Found., Battle Creek, Mich., 1944-47; nursing cons. Am. Nat. Red Cross, 1947-51; asst. prof. Cath. U. Am., Washington, 1952-56; research asso., supr. N.Mex. Health Dept., Santa Fe, 1961-63; research cons., asst. prof. Mercy Coll. of Detroit, 1963-64; asso. prof., U. S.C. Sch. Nursing, Columbia, 1964-67; prof., chmn. pub. health nursing dept. sch. nursing, Med. Coll. Va., Richmond, 1967-70; now prof. emeritus Nazareth Coll., Kalamazoo; engaged in writing, Paw Paw, Mich. Lt. comdr. USPHS, Res. Fellow USPHS; mem. Am. Sociol. Assn., Am. Nurses Assn., Am. Assn. U. Profs., Am. Assn. U. Women, Am. Acad. Polit. and Social Sci., Nat. League for Nursing, Am. Acad. Scis., Sigma Theta Tau, Pi Gamma Mu. Contbr. articles to profl. jours. Home: 28980 42d Ave Paw Paw MI 49079

PAYSON, MARY REEF, nurse; b. Mt. Carmel, Ill., Nov. 1, 1920; d. Evert Reef and Fern (Hawkins) Snyder; R.N., Welborn Walker Sch. Nursing, 1942; B.S. cum laude, Boston Coll., 1961; M.Ed., Mass. State Coll. at Framingham, 1965, postgrad., 1980—. With Medfield (Mass.) State Hosp., 1956—, dir. nurses, 1978—; spl. cons. Tech. Program Assistance Br., NIMH, 1968; nurse cons. in group work Brockton VA, 1977; hosp. coordinator Medfield-Norfolk Prison Project, 1970. Served with U.S. Navy, 1943-46. Mem. Am. Nurses Assn. (cert. nursing adminstr.), Am. Legion, Mass. Mental Health Nurses Assn. (pres. 1975-78), Sigma Theta Tau. Contbr. articles to profl. jours. Office: 45 Hospital Rd Medfield MA 02052

PAZANT, ROSALIE FRAZIER, educator; b. Beaufort, S.C., Nov. 19, 1918; d. William Bradford and Lauretta Lurene (Grayson) Frazier; B.A., Savannah State Coll., 1937; student Temple U., 1964, N.C. A&T U., 1969, Rutgers U., 1967; M.S., S.C. State U., 1957; m. Edward Theodore Pazant, Dec. 25, 1936; children—Lauretta, Edward Theodore, Alvin, DaRenne, Lolita, Charlotte, Reba. Chmn. English dept. Robert Smalls High Sch., Beaufort, 1950-70; chmn. English dept. Beaufort High Sch., 1970-73; chmn. English dept. Battery Creek High Sch., Beaufort, 1973-77; English coordinator div. developmental studies Savannah State Coll., 1977—, asst. prof., 1977-82, asso. prof., 1982—. Mem. S.C. State Textbook Adoption Com., 1975. Mem. Internat. Reading Assn., Exec. Woman, Nat. Edn. Assn., Nat. Council Tchrs. English, Ga. Assn. Educators, Council Coll. Composition and Communications, S.C. Council Tchrs. of English, Delta Sigma Theta, Iota Phi Lambda. Democrat. Baptist (organist, sec., chmn. women's day). Club: Order Eastern Star. Home: 803 Green St Beaufort SC 29902 Office: Savannah State Coll Savannah GA 31404

PEACE, BARBARA ELLEN, banker; b. Santa Rita, N.Mex., Feb. 17, 1942; d. Roland Daniel and Ellen Ellenore (Dickinson) Beach; student Nat. Assn. Bank Women, Am. Inst. Banking; m. Roy E. Peace, June 14, 1960; children—Robin Marie, Kristi Anne. IBM proof operator, stenographer, sec. First Nat. Bank Ariz., Phoenix, 1960-61; clk. credit checking and ratings Valley Nat. Bank Ariz., 1962-64, ins. clk., loan disbursement, sec., 1966-67; new accounts sec., br. sec. United Bank Ariz., Phoenix, 1969-72, br. ops. asst., 1972-73, asst. mgr., ops. officer Camelback office, 1973-75, ops. officer II downtown office, 1975-77, asst. v.p., adminstrv. ops. officer, 1977-78, v.p. adminstrv. ops. officer, 1978—; tchr. Am. Inst. Banking, Rio Salado Community Coll., 1979-80. Mem. Glendale Elem. Sch. Bd. Trustees, 1975-77, clk., pres., 1975-77. Mem. Nat. Assn. Bank Women, Bank Adminstrn. Inst. Republican. Methodist. Office: 100 W Van Buren St Phoenix AZ 85003

PEACE, CORINNE, tourism commn. adminstr., journalist; b. St. Augustine, Fla.; d. George Joseph and Lila Marie Peace; student McNeese State U., Lake Charles, La., L'Institut Catholique, Paris, summer, 1972. Soc. editor Morgan City (La.) Rev., 1945-62; feature writer and food editor Lake Charles Am. Press, 1962—; exec. dir. Atchafalaya Delta Tourist Commn., Morgan City, 1982—. Mem. Salvation Army adv. bd.; mem. Lake Charles Bicentennial Commn.; adv. Council for Devel. of French in La.; mem. La. Trails Adv. Council, 1975; pres. S.W. La. Hist. Assn., 1975-76, founder, organizer Gingham Ladies, aux. unit. 1976; mem. Lake Charles Little Theatre, Vis. Artists Group and France-Amerique de Lake Charles. Named Press Woman of Yr., La., 1976. Mem. La. Press Women (pres. 1968-69, bicentennial chmn. 1976), Nat. Fedn. of Press Women (nat. conv. chmn. New Orleans 1970), Calcasieu Hist. Preservation Soc., S.W. La. Geneal. Soc. (charter mem.), La. Preservation Alliance (charter mem., dir.), Art Assos. of Lake Charles, Greater Lake Charles C. of C. (communications com.). Contbr. articles in field to profl. jours. Office: PO Box 2332 Morgan City LA 70381

PEACE, MIRIAM SISKIN, cytotechnologist, lawyer; b. Winnipeg, Man., Can., Feb. 13, 1931; d. David L. and Rissa (Ghitter) Siskin; cert. Sch. of Cytology, Med. Coll. of Ga., 1951; L.L.B., John Marshall Sch. Law, 1972; children—Brian Smiley, Carl Smiley, Janice Smiley Hazelhurst, Vickie Smiley, Rissa Peace. Cytologist Med. Coll. of Ga., Augusta, 1951-52, Grady Hosp., Atlanta, 1956-57; supr. St. Joseph's Infirmary, Atlanta, 1957-62, Peace Labs., Atlanta, 1962-69; cytotechnologist Peachtree Lab., Atlanta, 1969—; supr. Piedmont Hosp., Atlanta, 1979—; admitted to Ga. bar, 1973; individual practice law, Atlanta, 1974-75. Precinct co-chmn. Andrew Young campaign for Congress, 1970, 72. Mem. Am. Soc. Clin. Pathologists (registered cytotechnologist, charter mem.), Am. Soc. for Cytotechnology, State Bar of Ga. Democrat. Jewish. Home: 6951 F Roswell Rd Atlanta GA 30328 Office: 1968 Peachtree Rd NW Atlanta GA 30309

PEACOCK, LARITA WILLIAMS, corp. mgr.; b. Madisonville, Ky., Mar. 24, 1954; d. Charles Eugene and Clara Bell (Smith) Williams; B.A. in Math., Princeton U., 1973; M.B.A., Stanford U., 1975; m. Hubert Leonard Peacock, Jr., Aug. 30, 1980. Systems analyst Exxon Corp., Florham Park, N.J., 1976-77, Exxon Chem. Co. U.S.A., Houston, 1977-79; project mgr. info. systems dept. Marriott Corp., Bethesda, Md., 1980—. Mem. Nat. Assn. Female Execs. Club: Miladi's Social (treas. 1981—). Address: 899 Clopper Rd Apt T2 Gaithersburg MD 20878

PEARCE, BARBARA FLETCHER (BURTON), personnel ofcl.; b. Carroll County, Ga., Dec. 26, 1932; d. Grady Franklin and Grace Irene (Camp) Fletcher; student Ga. State U., 1947-48; m. William Burton Jr., Sept. 13, 1950 (div. 1970); Pearce, Nov. 28, 1974; children—Barbara Burton Punkey, Betina Burton Partain; m. 2d, David Lee Pearce, Nov. 28, 1974. Office supr. J. C. Penney Co., Atlanta, 1961-66, personnel asst., 1966-73, mgr. personnel services regional area, 1973-79, personnel mgr., Morrow, Ga., 1982—; cons. in field. Vice pres. Glenwood Jaycettes, 1968; pres. Miss DeKalb County Scholarship Pageant, 1974-82; pres. Toney Valley Civic Club, 1968-71. Mem. Am. Soc. Personnel Adminstrn. (dist. dir., v.p., pres. Atlanta chpt., recipient superior merit award), Ga. C. of C. (mem. employer-employee council). Republican. Baptist. Home: 144 Rue Fontaine Decatur GA 30038 Office: 6840 Barton Rd Morrow GA 30260

PEARCE, DORIS PARSONS, educator; b. Jonesboro, Tenn., Aug. 30, 1929; d. William Vines and Annie Margaret (Cooper) Parsons; B.A. in Psychology, Berea Coll., 1950; M.S. in Home Econs., Okla. State U., 1952; Ph.D., Fla. State U., 1963; m. Ralph James Pearce, June 15, 1950 (dec. June 1958); children—William Fred, Virginia Dale. Instr., Okla. State U., 1952-53; asst. prof. Carson Newman Coll., Jefferson City, Tenn., 1955-61, Ohio U., 1963-65; asso. prof. home econs. U. Ky., 1965-66; asso. prof. Ga. So. Coll., Statesboro, 1966—, dir. home econ. nursery sch., 1972—; vis. prof. U. Tenn., summer 1964; Head Start tng. dir. Ohio U., summer 1965; cons. public and pvt. day care; instr. specialist ARC, 1976—. Mem. Soc. Research Child Devel., Nat. Council Family Relations, AAUP, Nat., Ga. assns. young children. Home: 207 Donaldson St Statesboro GA 30458 Office: Landrum Box 8021 Ga So Coll Statesboro GA 30460

PEARCE, ELIZABETH ANN (BETSY), social worker; b. Royal Oak, Mich., May 15, 1949; d. Gordon James and Elizabeth Ann (McRae) McMullen; A.A., Monticello Coll., 1969; B.A., Washington U., St. Louis, 1971; M.S.W., U. Mich., 1974; m. Roger Norman Pearce, Mar. 2, 1973; children—Katy Elizabeth and Emily Jean (twins). Clin. social worker Livingston County Community Mental Health Center, Howell, Mich., 1974-79; pvt. practice clin. social work, East Lansing, Mich., 1976—. Mem. com. Council of Child Abuse and Neglect, 1978-79. Mem. Nat. Assn. Social Workers, Acad. Cert. Social Workers. Home: 4750 N Zimmer Rd Williamston MI 48895 Office: Suite 210 5000 Northwind Rd East Lansing MI 48823

PEARCE, JANE, psychiatrist; b. Austin, Tex., Jan. 13, 1914; d. James Edward and Belinda (Doppelmayer) P.; student Radcliffe Coll., 1931-32; B.A. cum laude, U. Tex., Austin, 1934; M.D., U. Chgo., 1941, Ph.D., 1941; student Washington Sch. Psychiatry, 1947-48; grad. William A. White Inst., N.Y.C., 1944-49; student Inst. Individual Psychology, Chgo., 1936-41; children from previous marriage—Sarah, Robert, Paul, Christopher. Intern, Harriet Lane Hosp., Balt., 1942, Albany (N.Y.) Hosp., 1942-43, resident in psychiatry, 1943; resident N.Y. State Psychiat. Inst., N.Y.C., 1943-44, 48-49; pvt. practice psychoanalysis, N.Y.C., 1944—; tng. analyst William Alanson White Inst., 1946-57, faculty, 1950-57; co-founder, asst. dir., research dir., supr. Sullivan Inst. Research in Psychoanalysis, N.Y.C., 1957-77; mem. faculty N.Y. U., 1951-53; co-founder, clin. dir. North Side Center, N.Y.C., 1945-46. Diplomate Am. Bd. Psychiatry and Neurology. Fellow Am. Assn. Social Psychiatry; mem. AMA, Am. Psychiat. Assn., Physicians for Social Responsibility, Phi Beta Kappa, Sigma Xi, Kappa Kappa Gamma. Democrat. Author: (with Saul Newton) The Conditions of Human Growth, 1963; contbr. articles to profl. jours. Home: 332 W 77th St New York NY 10024 Office: 332 W 77th St New York NY 10024

PEARCE, JANICE, educator; b. Salt Lake City, Aug. 8, 1931; d. Kelley Bradford and Thyra (Morgan) Pearce; B.S., U. Utah, 1952; M.S., Wash. State U., 1959; postgrad. Stanford U., 1966-67; Ph.D., U. Utah, 1974. Tchr., Arrowview Jr. High Sch., San Bernardino, Calif., 1952-53, Olympus High Sch., Salt Lake City, 1953-56; teaching asst. Wash. State U., Pullman, 1956-57; mem. faculty Utah State U., Logan, 1957—, prof., chmn. health edn. program, 1980—; lectr. in field. Trustee, Cache Valley Health Care Found., 1977-82; mem. Bear River Assn. of Govt.'s Human Services Bd., 1978-82; mem. Bear River Adv. Council on Alcoholism and Other Drug Dependencies, 1973-80, council chmn., 1974-75; mem. steering com. Ind. and Republicans—Matheson for Gov., 1976; mem. adv. bd. Planned Parenthood of Logan, 1978; pub. edn. chmn. Cache County chpt. Utah Cancer Soc., 1977-79; bd. dirs. Hospice of Cache Valley, 1979-81; chmn. Utah Gov.'s Bd. on Alcoholism and Drugs, 1982-83, others. Recipient Disting. Service award, Am. Sch. Health Assn., 1980; honor award S.W. dist. AAHPER, 1979; Woman of Yr. award Logan Bus. and Profl. Women's Club, 1976. Fellow Am. Sch. Health Assn. (pres. 1982-83); mem. Nat. Assn. for Girls and Women in Sport, AAHPER, Assn. for Advancement of Health (editorial bd. 1979-81), Utah Assn. Health, Phys. Edn. and Recreation (v.p. health 1970-71, editor, bus. mgr.), Western Soc. for Phys. Edn. of Coll. Women (chmn. legis. com. 1958-61), Consortium of Utah Women in Higher Edn., Utah Fedn. Bus. and Profl. Women (pres. 1981-82), Nat. Assn. Parliamentarians, Mortar Bd., Alpha Lambda Delta. Mormon. Author: Tennis, 1971; mem. editorial bd. Jour. Early Adolescence, 1981—; contbr. articles to profl. jours. Home: 282 N 4 E Hyde Park UT 84316 Office: Dept Health Phys Edn and Recreation UMC 70 Utah State Univ Logan UT 84322

PEARCE, MARIA DEL CONSUELO QILANTAN, lang. devel. program supr.; b. Monterrey, N.L., Mexico, Aug. 14, 1944; d. Antonio and Ascension (Garcia) Quilantan; B.A. in Edn., Idaho State U., 1970; M. in Elem. Edn. Reading, Boise State Univ., 1980; m. Francis L. Pearce, Sept. 11, 1965; children—Krystal Ana, Jwon Antonio, Kalynda Jaynina. Migrant labor worker, 1952-64; tutor Idaho State Univ., 1964-69; psychiat. aide Eastern Oreg. Hosp., Pendleton, 1972; tchr. Pendleton High Sch., 1972-73; English as a second lang. tchr. Blue Mountain Community Coll., Pendleton, 1973; ednl. cons. migrant edn. Sch. Dist. 131, Nampa, Idaho, 1973-75, bilingual edn. curriculum supr., 1977-80, supr. lang. devel. program, 1980—; spl. lectr. tchr. edn. Boise State U., 1975-76, spl. lectr., 1975-80; edn. cons., 1976-78; supr. tchr. bilingual edn. Northwest Nazarene Coll., Nampa, 1980-81. Commr., Idaho Human Rights Commn., 1976—, pres., 1980—. Mem. Idaho Assn. Bilingual Edn. (mem. exec. bd. 1978-81; pres. 1981), Valley Reading Assn., Idaho Reading Assn., Internat. Reading Assn., Nat. Assn. Bilingual Edn. (del.), Idaho Assn. Bilingual Edn., Delta Kappa Gamma, Phi Delta Kappa. Democrat. Roman Catholic. Home: 847 W Iowa St Nampa ID 83651 Office: 619 S Canyon St Nampa ID 83651

PEARCE, MARTHA VIRGINIA, educator; b. Wilmington, Del., Sept. 26, 1929; d. Alva Elmer and Mary Rickards (Clark) P.; B.S., Columbia U., 1958; M.S., Boston U., 1965; Ed.D., Ariz. State U., 1980. Faculty asso. Ariz. State U., Tempe, 1977-81, asst. prof. aero. tech., 1981—. Served with Nurses Corps, USN, 1954-75. Mem. Nat. Assn. Flight Instrs., Soaring Soc. Am., Ninety-Nines, Inc., Ariz. Adult Edn. Assn., Pi Lambda Theta, Alpha Eta Rho. Home: 2331 E Aspen Dr Tempe AZ 85282 Office: Ariz State U Tempe AZ 85281

PEARCE, MARY SHARROCK, educator; b. Palava, Tex., Aug. 8, 1937; d. Oran Lee and Eavvie Hector Sharrock; B.A., Ariz. State U., 1968, M.A., 1970; m. Philip Edward Pearce, July 26, 1957; children—Phyllis, Laurie, Philip. Tchr., Tempe (Ariz.) Elem. Schs., 1968; tchr., reading specialist, chmn. reading dept. Carson Jr. High Sch., Mesa, Ariz., 1968-74; faculty assoc. Ariz State U., 1977-81; tchr., reading specialist, reading coordinator Tempe (Ariz.) Union High Sch., 1974—; reading cons. Mem. Internat. Reading Assn., Ariz. Reading Council Nat. Reading Conf., Am. Edn. Research Assn., NEA, Ariz. Edn. Assn., Tempe Secondary Edn. Assn., Delta Kappa Gamma (rec. sec.). Democrat. Home: 111 E Geneva Dr Tempe AZ 85282 Office: 1730 S Mill Ave Tempe AZ 85281

PEARCE, PHYLLIS LOIS YOCUM, archtl. firm exec.; b. East Chicago, Ind., June 18, 1938; d. Elmer A. and Ledora (McSwain) Yocum; grad. cum laude Hammond (Ind.) Bus. Coll., 1957; student spl. courses Ind. U., U. Wis.; m. Alton Pearce, Jr., Aug. 4, 1957; children—Dawn Alane, Alton III. Adminstrv. asst. to exec. dir. Purdue-Calumet Devel. Found., East Chicago, 1957-66; office mgr. Wendell Campbell Assos., Inc., Chgo., 1966-71, Campbell & Macsai Architects, Inc., Chgo., 1971-75; asst. to pres., chief profl. mgr. Wendell Campbell Assos., Inc., 1975—; mktg. and sales cons.; public relations cons. Life mem. NAACP, sec. Gary br., 1977-78, 81-82. sec. Ind. Conf. Branches labor and industry com., 1977-78, mem. Conf. Black Politics, 1978, recipient Meritorious Service citation and plaque NAACP, 1977. Progressive Literary and Art Club scholar. Mem. Am. Mgmt. Assn., Profl. Service Mgmt. Assn., Coalition of Black Feminists, Am. Soc. Profl. and Exec. Women. Baptist. Clubs: Ida M. Walker Household of Ruth, Odd Fellows. Organist, pianist. Home: 688 Cass Ct Gary IN 46403 Office: 1321 S Michigan Ave Chicago IL 60601

PEARCY, CYNTHIA ANN, nurse; b. Providence, May 31, 1946; d. William Frances and Marcella Rose Ferris; R.N., Grace Hosp., Detroit, 1967; divorced; children—Shawn Michael, Ryan Robert. Staff nurse Grace Hosp., 1967-68; head nurse ICU, Martin Place Hosp., Warren, Mich., 1968-69; charge nurse intensive cardiac care S. Macomb Hosp., Warren, 1971-73; head nurse intensive care stepdown St. Joseph Hosp., Mt. Clemens, Mich., 1975-80, edn. coordinator critical care services, 1980—, also instr. coronary care. Mem. Nat. Assn. Female Execs., Am. Assn. Critical Care Nurses. Roman Catholic. Home: 37342 Glenbrook Mount Clemens MI 48043 Office: 215 North Ave Mount Clemens MI 48043

PEARLMAN, FLORENCE SADOFF, social worker; b. N.Y.C., Dec. 26, 1928; d. Sam and Eva (Brunstein) Sadoff; B.A., Barnard Coll., 1950; M.S.W., Wurzweiler Sch. Social Work, 1971; m. Donald Pearlman, June 22, 1947 (div. Feb. 1971); children—David J., Erica Lee (dec.). Editorial staff profl. jours., 1951-54; alumnae sec. Briarcliff Coll., Briarcliff Manor, N.Y., 1966-67; psychiat. social worker Yonkers (N.Y.) Mental Health Clinic, 1971; supr. Alcoholism Clinic, Yonkers, 1974-75. Mem. coms. Planned Parenthood-World Population, 1965-75, bd. dirs., 1966-72; active Planned Parenthood Westchester, 1962-80; bd. dirs. Assoc. Alumnae of Barnard Coll., 1975-78. Mem. Acad. Cert. Social Workers, Nat. Assn. Social Workers, Assn. Amateur Chamber Music Soc., Am. Orthopsychiat. Assn. Democrat. Jewish. Home: 17 Cedar Road S Katonah NY 10536

PEARSALL, PATRICIA MOODY, edn. program specialist; b. Detroit, Dec. 10, 1934; d. Rayford Moody and Lily Moody Walden; B.A., Spelman Coll., 1956; M.A., U. Mich., 1957; m. Gurney Pearsall, June 21, 1958; children—Lisa Renee, Gurney Fields, Stacy Louise, Joel Patrick. Counselor-psychometrist Fisk U., Nashville, 1957-58; asst. prof. Detroit Inst. Commerce, 1961-64; edn. program specialist Met. Transit Authority, Houston, 1979—; bd. dirs. Harris County Child Welfare, 1976—; dir., exec. com. Houston Festival; mem. St. James Sch. Bd. Mem. Am. Mktg. Assn., Am. Personnel and Guidance Assn., Adult Edn. Assn., NEA, Tex. State Tchrs. Assn., Nat. Alumnae Assn. of Spelman Coll. (pres. 1978-82), Nat. Coalition of 100 Black Women (v.p.), Delta Sigma Theta. Episcopalian. Home: 10822 Riverview St Houston TX 77042 Office: PO Box 61429 Houston TX 77208

PEARSALL, PENNY LEA, cosmetic co. exec.; b. Fayetteville, N.C., Jan. 14, 1942; d. Arthur H. and Ruby Mae P.; A.A., Lees-McRae Coll., 1962; student med. record library sci. N.C. Baptist Hosp., Winston-Salem, N.C., 1963. Med. record adminstr. Med. Coll. Va. Hosp., 1963-65; dir. med. records Westbrook Psychiat. Hosp., Richmond, Va., 1965-70; dir. med. record consulting Am. Health Services, Richmond, 1970-72; dir. med. records Henrico Doctor's Hosp., Richmond, 1976-81; ind. sales dir. Mary Kay Cosmetics, Glen Allen, Va., 1975—; cons. to nursing home facilities. Recipient Cadillac, Mary Kay Cosmetics, 1980, 82, named to 250,000 Club, 1981, 350,000 Club, 1982, 500,000 Club, 1982, Sammy award, Richmond, 1982. Mem. Am., Va. med. record assns., Sales and Mktg. Execs. Richmond. Home and Office: 10512 Glencoe Rd Glen Allen VA 23060

PEARSON, DOROTHY MARIE, social worker, educator; b. Darbun, Miss., June 22, 1937; d. Wallace and Annie Bell (Stovall) P.; B.A. magna cum laude (La. Legis. scholar), So. U., 1958; M.S., U. Wis., 1960, Ph.D., 1973; cert. grad. program in mgmt. Simmons Coll., 1979. Psychiat. social worker Milw. County (Wis.) Mental Health Center, 1960-64; asst. prof. Sch. Social Welfare, U. Wis., Milw., 1964-70; pres. Urban Resources, Inc., Milw., 1970-73; asst. prof. Sch. Medicine, U. Miami (Fla.), 1973-75; adj. prof. Sch. Social Work, Barry Coll., Miami, 1973-75; asso. dean, prof. Sch. Social Work, Howard U., Washington, 1975—, founding dir. doctoral program, 1976, chmn. Conf. on Women, 1979; co-founder Bogalusa (La.) Tng. Center, 1954, Wis. Assn. Black Social Workers, 1972; charter mem. Wis. Assn. Social Workers for the Retarded, 1966; treas. Wis. Rehab. Assn., 1971-72; cons. Jewish Vocat. Service, Milw., 1966-73, Opportunities Industrialization Center, Milw., 1968-70; advisor Nat. Study of Black Americans, Mich., 1978, Women in Crisis Conf., N.Y., 1980; evaluator Middle States Assn. Secondary Schs. and Colls., 1981. Recipient service awards Bogalusa Tng. Center, 1955, Barry Coll. Assn. Black Student Social Workers, 1973; NIMH trainee, 1970-73, tng. grantee, 1976-80. Mem. Council on Social Work Edn. (chmn. Black Caucus, commr. on ednl. planning), Nat. Assn. Social Workers (v.p. Met. D.C. chpt., chmn. labor task force), Am. Orthopsychiat. Assn., Acad. Certified Social Workers, Alpha Kappa Mu. Club: Black Women's Agenda. Contbr. sect. to publ. in field. Office: School Social Work Howard Univ Washington DC 20059

PEARSON, LESLEY AGNES JOAN (MRS. ERNST ALFRED SIEMSSEN), advt. exec.; b. Aberdeen, Scotland, May 27, 1918; d. Gerald Hamilton Jeffery and Mary Agnes (Mackenzie) P.; came to U.S., 1924; student Drexel Inst., 1936-37; m. Louis Joseph Fridenberg, July 3, 1945 (dec. Jan. 1970); m. 2d Ernst Alfred Siemssen July 11, 1980. Free-lance advt. cons., Phila., 1941-49; sales promotion dir. Dewees Splty. Store, Phila., 1949-64; chief all fashion advt. Gimbels Stores, Phila., 1964-76; cons., 1976—; instr. fashion merchandising Temple U., 1961, 63. Chmn. splty. stores div. United Fund, 1960. Mem. Phila. Club Advt. Women, Fashion Group. Club: Cosmopolitan. Home and Office: West Lamplighter Ln Gwynedd PA 19436

PEARSON, LOUISE MARY, mfg. co. exec.; b. Inverness, Scotland, Dec. 14, 1919 (parents Am. citizens); d. Louis Houston and Jessie M. (McKenzie) Lenox; grad. high sch.; m. Nels Kenneth Pearson, June 28, 1941; children—Lorine Pearson Walters, Karla. Dir. Wauconda Tool & Engring. Co., Inc., Algonquin, Ill., 1950—; reporter Oak Leaflet, Crystal Lake, Ill., 1944-47, Sidelights, Wilmette, Ill., 1969-72, 79-82. Active Girl Scouts U.S.A., 1955-65. Recipient award for appreciation work with Girl Scouts, 1965. Clubs: Antique Automobile of Am. (Hershey, Pa.); Veteran Motor Car (Boston); Classic Car of Am. (Madison, N.J.). Home: 125 Dole Ave Crystal Lake IL 60014

PEARSON, MARY LYNN, med. technologist; b. Milw., Dec. 13, 1944; d. Arvid Robert and Mary (Haven) Pearson; B.S., U. Wis., Madison, 1967. Med. technologist St. Michael Hosp., Milw., 1970-73, 74, Comprehensive Drug Program of Dade County, Miami, Fla., 1973; supr. clin. toxicology, dept. pathology Milw. County Med. Complex, 1974—. Mem. Am. Soc. Clin. Pathologists, Am. Soc. Med. Technologists, Madison-Chgo.-Milw. Mass Spectrometry Discussion Group. Lutheran. Contbr. articles to profl. jours. Office: 8700 W Wisconsin Ave Milwaukee WI 53226

PEARSON, PHYLLIS MAE MANNEL, social worker; b. Denver, Feb. 28, 1943; d. Sydney Byron and Molly Mannel; B.S., U. Ill., 1967; M.S., L.I. U., 1974; M.S.W., Calif. State U., Fresno, 1977; m. Phillip Roger Pearson, June 9, 1968. Editorial asst. Prairie Farmer Pub. Co., Chgo., 1967; copywriter Goldblatt's Dept. Stores, Chgo., 1967-68, Sta. WRIT, Milw., 1968-69; substitute tchr. Brevard County Sch. Bd., Titusville, Fla., 1970-71; coordinator vols. Involvement Corps, Los Angeles, 1974-75, asst. to pres., 1977; psychiat. social worker Hathaway Home for Children, Lake View Terrace, Calif., 1977-80; pvt. practice clin. social work, 1980—; counselor Suicide Prevention Center, Los Angeles, 1973-75; counselor Narcotics and Drug Abuse Rehab. Program, Los Angeles, 1973-74. Lic. clin. social worker. Mem. Nat. Assn. Social Workers, Soc. Clin. Social Work, Acad. Cert. Social Workers, AAUW. Office: 18075 Ventura Blvd Suite 221 Encino CA 91316

PEARSON, SUSAN WINIFRED, guidance counselor; b. Wasco, Calif., Oct. 8, 1941; d. Gerald Thomas and Maxine (Jensen) P.; B.S., Tex. Christian U., 1963, M.Ed., 1971; postgrad. U. Houston, 1982. Tchr. history, chmn. dept. Spring Branch Ind. Sch. Dist., Houston, 1963-68; personnel asst. Tenneco Inc., Houston, 1969-70; grad. asst. Tex. Christian U., 1970-71; dir. student activities Navarro Jr. Coll., Corsicana, Tex., 1972-73; dir. counseling services North Harris County Coll., Houston, 1973—. Mem. Am. Personnel and Guidance Assn., Am. Coll. Personnel Assn., Nat. Assn. Women Deans, Adminstrs. and Counselors, So. Coll. Personnel Assn., Tex. Assn. Women Deans, Adminstrs. and Counselors, Tex. Assn. Coll. and Univ. Student Personnel Adminstrs., Phi Kappa Phi, Delta Gamma. Presbyterian. Author articles in field. Office: 2300 W Thorne Dr Houston TX 77073

PEASE, BARBARA BUCKLEY, social worker; b. Memphis, Oct. 23, 1926; d. John Blair and Bonnie S. (Hart) Buckley; B.J., U. Mo., 1947, B.A., 1949; M.S.W. (Scholastic award 1967, Outstanding Sr. award 1967, Alumni Cert. of Merit 1967), La. State U., 1967; postgrad. Tulane U., 1976; m. Bryden Pease, Jr., Sept. 2, 1947; children—Barbara Hart Pease Hammer, Mary Bryden Pease Teekell. Social worker Miss. Dept. Public Welfare, 1954-71, dist. supr., Gulfport, 1967-71; social worker VA Med. Center, Biloxi, Miss., 1971-73, supervisory social worker, 1973—; faculty adv. Sch. Social Work, U. So. Miss., Gulf Park br., 1979—, field instr., 1975—; spl. lectr. La. State U. Sch. Social Work, 1973-75. Dir. vocat. guidance Westminster United Presbyn. Ch., Gulfport, 1969-74; bd. dirs. Goodwill Industries So. Miss., Miss. Gulf Coast Help Line Assn. Mem. Acad. Cert. Social Workers, Nat. Assn. Social Workers (Social Worker of Yr., Miss. Gulf Coast chpt. 1975, pres. Miss. chpt. 1981—), Miss. Conf. Social Welfare (pres. 1978-79), Child Welfare League Am., Am. Public Welfare Assn., Council Social Work Edn., Mental Health Profls. S. Miss., Miss. Assn. Women in Higher Edn., Ala./Miss. Social Work Educators Assn., Mental Health Assn. Harrison County, Family Planning Assn. Harrison County (charter bd. dirs. 1967-75), Phi Kappa Phi, Delta Delta Delta. Home: 3903 Washington Ave Gulfport MS 39501 Office: VA Hosp Gulfport MS 39501

PEASLEE, CHARLOTTE HOFFMAN, editorial service co. exec., b. N.Y.C. July 13, 1931; d. Edmund Witherbee and Emily (Delafield) P.; student Radcliffe Coll., 1949-52; B.J., U. Mo., 1958. Reporter, Paterson (N.J.) Morning Call, 1958; editorial asst. Electronic and Appliance Specialist, N.Y.C., 1958-60, Palmerton Pub. Co., N.Y.C., 1960-61; asst. editor in charge prodn. Sci. Digest, Hearst Mag. div., N.Y.C., 1961-64; writer Consol. Edison Co., N.Y.C., 1964-69; tech. editor Nat. Elec. Mfrs. Assn., N.Y.C., 1969-70; free-lance writer, copy editor, 1970-71; mng. editor Lady's Circle mag. Lopez Publs., N.Y.C., 1971-75; cons., owner editorial service Special Projects by Charlotte Peaslee, N.Y.C., 1976—. Mem. Women in Communications, NOW (N.Y. exec. v.p. 1972, dir. 1973), N.Y. Assn. Women Bus. Owners, Women's Econ. Round Table, Publicity Club N.Y., Kappa Tau Alpha, Kappa Alpha Mu, Overseas Press Club. Home: 165 E 72d St New York NY 10021

PEAY, JULIA ANNE, employment agy. exec.; b. Chgo., July 24, 1952; d. Oliver Wendell and Betty Jane (Nichols) Armstrong; B.S. in Bus. Adminstrn., William Woods Coll., 1973; m. Gregory V. Peay, June 18, 1977; children—Juddson, Sarah. With Careers, Ltd., Denver, 1974—, v.p., 1978—. Mem. consumer complaint arbitration com. Better Bus. Bur. Denver. Mem. Denver C. of C., Alpha Phi. Republican. Presbyterian. Home: 62 Paradise Rd Golden CO 80401 Office: 1390 Logan St Suite Denver CO 80203

PECARICH, PAMELA JAE, mem. congressional staff; b. Grand Island, Nebr., Nov. 11, 1943; d. A.J. and Lorraine Hanway; student U. Calif., Berkeley, 1961-62; B.S. with honors, Calif. State U., 1969; postgrad. in acctg. U. Wash., 1971-72; m. Frank J. Pecarich, Apr. 13, 1965; 1 son, Jason Dean. Sr. cons. revenue and taxation com. Calif. State Assembly, 1969-74; cons. U.S. Adminstrv. Conf., Washington, 1974-75; dir. Office Policy and Planning, Commodity Futures Trading Commn., 1975-77; staff dir. subcom. on oversight U.S. Ho. of Reps. Ways and Means Com., 1977-81, chief tax policy analyst, 1981—. Mem. Am. Soc. Public Adminstrn., Beta Alpha Psi, Beta Gamma Sigma, Phi Kappa Phi. Office: Room 1136 Longworth House Office Bldg Washington DC 20515

PECK, ANNE ELLIOTT ROBERTS, estate planner, trust banker; b. N.Y.C., Dec. 17, 1935; d. James Ragan and Jane Ziegler (Elliott) Roberts; B.A. with honors in English, Wellesley Coll., 1957; M.A. with honors in Comparative Lit., Columbia U., 1966; postgrad. Villanova U., 1979, 80; m. George Linn Davis, May 29, 1955 (div. Aug. 1967); children—James Roberts, Elliott Britton, George Linn, William Vaughn; m. 2d, Robert Gray Peck 3d, Oct. 24, 1969; children—Andrew Adams, Matthew Canfield Roberts. Contbg. editor Newsfront mag., 1960-63; English tchr. The Masters Sch., Dobbs Ferry, N.Y., 1963-65; sports feature writer Westchester-Rockland newspapers, Gannett chain, White Plains, N.Y., 1969—; corr., weekly column Knickerbocker News-Union Star, Capital Newspapers, Hearst chain, Albany, N.Y., 1971-73; public tax preparer H & R Block, Inc., Wayne, Pa., 1976-79; bookkeeper Shop of John Simmons, Bryn Mawr, Pa., 1979; estate planning officer trust div. Provident Nat. Bank, Phila., 1981—. Mem. art com., bd. Schenectady Mus. Art and Sci.; bd. dirs. Scarsdale (N.Y.) Jr. League, 1960-61; asst. producer Poetry, Channel 25-TV, N.Y.C.; bd. dirs., legis. chmn. Greenacres Sch. PTA, 1968-69; public relations chmn. Planned Parenthood League, Schenectady; sec., parliamentarian N.Y. State Legis. Forum, 1971-73; editor directory St. David's Ch., 1976, mem. exec. com. every-member canvass, 1977; fair gates-keeper Episcopal Ch., 1974-80; on-screen TV panel moderator Access, public Channel 17, Albany-Troy-Schenectady area; maj. gift solicitor Planned Parenthood Southeastern Pa., 1975-76; mem. plant sale exec. com. Haverford Sch., 1976, 77; Republican pollchecker Tredyffrin Twp., 1978, 79 majority insp. of elections, 1981—; bd. dirs. Del. Learning Center, Wilmington, 1981—; bd. dirs., past treas. Paoli Parties Inc.; rep. Merion Deanery, Protestant Episcopal Ch., 1981—; bd. dirs. Willpower fund raising com. Summer Shakespeare Theatre, Villanova U., 1981—; alumna rep. to council Wellesley Coll. Recipient prize Coll. Bd. Contest Mademoiselle mag., 1954; Prix de Paris, Vogue mag., 1957. Mem. DAR (bd. mgrs.-public relations Phila. chpt.), AAUW (dir. Schenectady 1971-76, legis. chmn.), N.Y. State Women's Press Club (Capital dist. br.), Art Alliance Phila., Phila. Estate Planning Council, Jr. League Phila. (edn. com., child abuse center com., bicentennial cookbook com.), Bucks County Estate Planning Council. Republican. Clubs: Schenectady Curling, Mohawk Golf (Schenectady); Shenorock Shore (Rye, N.Y.); Merion Cricket (Haverford, Pa.); Wellesley Alumnae (Phila.). Address: 100 Steeplechase Rd PO Box 356 Devon PA 19333

PECK, DIANNE KAWECKI, architect; b. Jersey City, June 13, 1945; d. Thaddeus Walter and Harriet Ann (Zlotkowski) Kawecki; B.A. in Arch., Carnegie Mellon U., 1968; m. Gerald Paul Peck, Sept. 1, 1968; children—Samantha Gillian, Alexis Hilary. Architect, P.O.D. Research & Devel., 1968, Kohler-Daniels & Assos., Vienna, Va., 1969-71, Beery-Rio & Assos., Annandale, Va., 1971-73; partner Peck & Peck Architects, Occoquan, Va., 1973-74, Peck, Peck & Williams, Occoquan, 1974-81; corp. officer Peck Peck & Assos., Inc., Woodbridge, Va., 1981—. Vice pres. Vocat. Edn. Found., 1976; chairwoman architects and engrs. United Way; mem. Health Systems Agy. of No. Va., commendations, 1977; mem. Washington Profl. Women's Coop.; chairwoman Indsl. Devel. Authority of Prince William, 1976, vice chair, 1977, mem., 1975-79. Recipient commendation Prince William Bd. Suprs., 1976. Mem. Prince William C. of C. (dir.). Republican. Roman Catholic. Club: Soroptimist. Research on inner-city rehab. Office: 1924 Opitz Blvd Woodbridge VA 22191

PECK, ELLEN, author, editor; b. Fairbury, Ill., Aug. 24, 1942; d. Carlton and Genevieve (Doran) Remsburg; student Northwestern U., 1960-61, Loyola U., Chgo., 1963-64; B.S. in Edn., Ill. State U., 1965; m. William Allen Peck, June 12, 1965. Tchr. pub. schs., Balt., 1966-69; columnist Chgo. Tribune/N.Y. News Syndicate, 1969-74; founder Nat. Orgn. for Non-Parents, Balt., 1972, officer, 1972—; founder Consortium on Parental Aptitude, 1976, officer, 1976—; contbg. editor Pageant, 1972-74; editor Jour. Sex Edn. and Therapy, from 1975; cons. continuing edn. div. Am. Coll. Obstetricians and Gynecologists, from 1974, Negative Population Growth, 1976. Bd. dirs. Zero Population Growth. Mem. Planned Parenthood/World Population, Environ. Action, Cleveland Amory Fund for Animals, Population Inst., NOW (adv. com. task force on media). Democrat. Author: The Baby Trap, 1971; Sex and Birth Control: A Guide for the Young, 1973; Pronatalism: The Myth of Mom and Apple Pie, 1974; A Funny Thing Happened on the Way to Equality, 1975; The Joy of the Only Child, 1977; The Parent Test: How to Measure and Develop Your Aptitude for Parenthood, 1978. Address: 177 E 77th St New York NY 10021 *

PECK, ELLIE ENRIQUEZ, state consumer affairs cons.; b. Sacramento, Oct. 21, 1934; d. Rafael Enriquez and Eloisa Garcia Rivera; student polit. sci. Sacramento State U., 1974; m. Raymond Charles Peck, Sept. 5, 1957; children—Reginaldo, Enrico, Francisca Guerrero, Teresa, Linda, Margaret, Raymond Charles, Christina. Tng. services coordinator Calif. Div. Hwys., Sacramento, 1963-67; tech. and mgmt. cons., Sacramento, 1968-78; expert examiner Calif. Personnel Bd., 1976-78; tng. cons. Calif. Personnel Devel. Center, Sacramento, 1978; spl. cons. Calif. Commn. on Fair Employment and Housing, 1978; community services rep. U.S. Bur. of Census, No. Calif. counties, 1978-80; spl. cons. Calif. Dept. Consumer Affairs, Sacramento, 1980—, project dir. Golden State Sr. Discount Program, 1980—; chairperson Calif. Suprs.' Forum, 1966. Trustee, Stanford Settlement, Inc., Sacramento, 1975-79, hon. life trustee, 1979—; bd. dirs. Sacramento Emergency Housing Center, 1974-77; del. Democratic Nat. Conv., 1976; co-chairperson rules com., mem. exec. bd. Calif. Dem. Central Com. Recipient numerous awards, including Outstanding Community Service award Comuicaciones Unidos de Norte Atzlan, 1975, 77, Outstanding Service award, Chicano/Hispanic Dem. Caucus, 1979, Vol. Service award Calif. Human Devel. Corp., 1981. Mem. NAACP, Nat. Coalition Hispanic Orgns., Nat. Women's Polit. Caucus, Comision Femenil Mexicana Nacional de Sacramento Inc. (nat. exec. bd. 1979-81, chpt. pres. 1981-83). Club: Hispanic Dem. Sacramento County (v.p. 1982-83). Author U.S. Office Consumer Edn. publ., 1982, Calif. Dept. Consumer Affairs publ., 1981. Home: 2667 Coleman Way Sacramento CA 95818

PECK, GAYLE LOUISE, med. technologist; b. Yonkers, N.Y., Mar. 14, 1948; d. Joseph John and Jean Elizabeth Canepi; B.S., Quinnipiac Coll., Hamden, Conn., 1970; diploma in med. tech. Hosp. of St. Raphael, New Haven, 1970; m. Laurance Edward Peck, Oct. 13, 1973. Supr. chemistry Mt. Sinai Hosp., Hartford, Conn., 1971-72; mem. lab. staff VA Med. Center, Palo Alto, Calif., 1972—, asst. supr. blood bank, 1976—; instr. Sch. Med. Tech., San Francisco State U., 1979—. Mem. Am. Soc. Clin. Pathologists (asso.), South Bay Immunology Club (pres. 1979). Office: VA Med Center 3801 Miranda Ave Palo Alto CA 94304

PECK, JOSEPHINE GRACE, nurse; b. Lawrence, Mass., May 24, 1918; d. Carmello and Mary (Zangri) Sciuto; R.N., Boston City Hosp. Sch. Nursing, 1940; B.S., Boston U., 1948; postgrad. Tufts U., 1967; m. Joseph N. Peck, Aug. 22, 1948; children—Robert C., James J. Head nurse Boston City Hosp., 1940-41; supr. Boston State Hosp., 1941-42; dir. nursing Medfield (Mass.) State Hosp., 1948-50; owner, operator Hillcrest Retreat, Haverhill, Mass., 1954-67; dir. staff devel. Danvers (Mass.) State Hosp., 1967-69; asst. dir. nursing Hogan Rehab. Center, Danvers, 1969-70; clin. instr. psychiatric nursing No. Essex Community Coll., 1973; dir. nursing H.C. Solomon Mental Health Center, Lowell, Mass., 1970-76; supr. nursing Country Manor Nursing Home, Newburyport, Mass., 1977-78; dir. nursing Greenleaf Nursing Home, Salisbury, Mass., 1979—. Served with Nurse Corps, U.S. Army, 1942-46; PTO. Mem. Am. Nurses Assn. Republican. Roman Catholic. Clubs: Soroptimist, Civic Women's. Home: 60 Main St Atkinson NH 03811 Office: 335 Elm St Salisbury MA 01950

PECK, MARIAN JOSEPHINE, educator, fin. mgmt. co. exec.; b. Mpls., June 24, 1930; d. Carl Millard and Josephine Christine (Knuteson) Knudson; B.S., U. Minn., 1952, M.A., 1964; m. William Ross Peck, Nov. 25, 1956; children—Richard Ross, Robert William. Tchr., Isaac Public Schs., Phoenix, 1953-56; instr. U. Minn., 1956-61; team leader/dept. head Chaska (Minn.) Public Schs., 1975-81, tchr., 1962—; exec. dir., owner Wise Money Mgmt., Excelsior, Minn., 1980—. Bassoonist, Tucson Symphony Orchestra, 1952-53. Mem. Chaska Edn. Assn., Minn. Edn. Assn., NEA, Minn. Music Edn. Assn., Nat. Assn. Female Execs., Delta Kappa Gamma. Congregationalist. (organist, choir dir. 1957-60). Club: Minnetonka Country. Home: 2763 Pine Circle Excelsior MN 55331 Office: Chanhassen Elem Sch 7600 Laredo Dr Chanhassen MN 55317

PECK, MARY CATHERINE, interior designer; b. Pitts., May 24, 1916; d. Howard Elon and Mary Sabra (Haldeman) Way; student U. Calif., San Francisco, 1936-37; m. Jerome N. Peck, Aug. 31, 1941 (div.); children—Joanne, John, Jerry, Jim, Mary. With Edmund Lowey, San Francisco, 1938; asst. Carolyn Kelsey Splty. Shop, 1939-40; asst. bridal cons. The Emporium, San Francisco, 1941-42; interior designer, owner Mary C. Peck Interiors, Menlo Park, Calif., 1942—; affiliate Coyote Point Mus., San Mateo, Calif. Mem. Beautification Com. Menlo Park, 1978-79. Mem. Am. Soc. Interior Designers, Menlo Park C. of C. Episcopalian. Club: Palo Alto Golf and Country. Home: 62 Lupin Ln Atherton CA 94025 Office: 1340 El Camino Real Menlo Park CA 94025

PECK, MARYLY VANLEER, univ. dean; b. Washington, June 29, 1930; d. Blake Ragsdale and Ella Lillian (Wall) VanLeer; B.Chem.Engring. magna cum laude, Vanderbilt U., 1951; M.S. in Engring., U. Fla., 1955, Ph.D. (NSF fellow), 1963; m. Jordan B. Peck, Jr., June 15, 1951; children—Jordan B., III, Blake VanLeer, James Tarleton VanLeer, Virginia Ellaine. Chem. engr. Naval Research Lab., Washington, 1951-52; chem. engr. Med. Field Research Lab., Camp LeJeune, N.C., 1952; assoc. in research and instrn. U. Fla., Gainesville, 1954-55; chem. engring. research assoc. Ga. Inst. Tech. Expt. Sta., Atlanta, 1956-58; lectr. Ga. State Coll., Atlanta, 1957-58; lectr. math. East Carolina U. Extension, Camp LeJeuone, 1959; sr. research engr. Rocketdyne div. N.Am. Aviation Co., 1961-63; ind. lectr., U.S., 1963; assoc. prof. Campbell Coll., Buie's Creek, N.C., 1963-66; acad. dir. St. John's Episcopal Sch., Upper Tumon, Guam, 1966-68; prof. phys. scis., chmn dept. U. Guam, Agana, 1968-73, dean Coll. Bus. and Applied Tech., 1973-74, dean Community Career Coll., 1974-77; pres. Cochise Coll., Douglas, Ariz., 1977-78; systems planning analyst Urban Pathfinders, Inc., Balt., 1978-79; dean undergrad. studies Univ. Coll., U. Md., College Park, 1979—. Recipient Golden Plate of Achievement, Dell Webb Found., 1962. Mem. Am. Inst. Chem. Engrs., Am. Chem. Soc., Soc. Women Engrs. (v.p. 1962-63), Nat. Soc. Profl. Engrs., Am. Assn. for Higher Edn., Am. Assn. Community and Jr. Colls., Am. Assn. Univ. Adminstrs., Md. Assn. Higher Edn., Am. Women in Sci., AAUW, Sigma Xi, Tau Beta Pi (Women's badge 1950), Chi Omicron Gamma, Phi Kappa Phi. Episcopalian. Club: U. Md. (pres. 1982). Home: 1971 13th St NW Winter Haven FL 33880 Office: Polk Community Coll Winter Haven FL 33880

PECK, PAULINE CLAIRE, editor; b. Boston, Sept. 30, 1927; d. Elmer Vernald and Eileen Marie (Fay) Brooks; B.S., Boston State Coll., 1947; postgrad. Northeastern U., Boston, 1959-60; m. David Tebbutt Peck, Mar. 17, 1962; children—Kathleen R. Ross, William L. Ross, Sharon M. Ross. Elem. sch. tchr., Boston, 1947-49; social worker, Boston, 1949; elem. sch. tchr., Mass., Maine, 1953-55; mgr., bookkeeper Armour & Co., Searsport, Maine, 1955-58; elem. sch. tchr., Lynnfield and Gloucester, Mass., 1958-61; editor Xerox Edn. Publs., Middletown, Conn., 1961-72, sr. editor, 1972—; career adv. Wesleyan U., Conn., 1976-82. Recipient Ed Press award Ednl. Press Assn. Am., 1968, 69, 77, 82; named Alumnus of Yr., Boston State Coll., 1970. Mem. Internat. Reading Assn., Women in Communications, Inc., Nat. Soc. Poets. Author: Liberty B. Mouse Goes to a Party, 1978; The Ghastly Green Ghost, 1979; Buddy Bear and the Big Scare, 1980; Buddy's No-Cook Cookbook, 1980; Buddy's ABC Coloring Book, 1980; The Day Buddy Bear Ran Away, 1981; Liberty B. Mouse Comes to America, 1977; Performable Poems, 1981. Home: 825 Randolph Rd Middletown CT 06457 Office: 245 Long Hill Rd Middletown CT 06457

PECK, RENEE BRANDT, journalist; b. Houston, Dec. 22, 1953; d. Edward Dupree and June (West) Brandt; B.A. in English Lit., Kenyon Coll., 1975; m. Stewart Foster Peck, Aug. 23, 1975. Asst. archivist, curatorial asst. Hist. New Orleans Collection, 1975-77; food editor The Times Picayune-The States-Item, New Orleans, 1977—. Bd. dirs. Pan Am. Culinary Olympics. Recipient Vesta Award for food reporting Am. Meat Inst., 1981. Mem. Newspaper Food Editors and Writers Assn. Democrat. Editor: Degrees of Discovery-From New World to New Orleans, 1977. Office: 3800 Howard Ave New Orleans LA 70140

PECK, SHEILA, securities analyst; b. Grosse Pointe, Mich., Oct. 9, 1957; d. Rankin Philip and Elaine (Zimmerman) P.; B.A. in Bus. Adminstrn., Rollins Coll., 1979. Securities analyst, office equipment industry Standard & Poor's Corp., N.Y.C., 1979—. Mem. N.Y. Soc. Security Analysts, Sigma Gamma Assn., Kappa Kappa Gamma. Republican. Roman Catholic. Club: Apple Platform Tennis. Home: 329 E 63d St New York NY 10021 Office: 25 Broadway New York NY 10004

PECKHAM, ANETTA DE VRIENDT, drug prevention adminstr.; b. Maracaibo, Venezuela, Aug. 27, 1932; came to U.S., 1952, naturalized, 1964; d. Everhart F. Hendrick and Lucie (Kraaijenhagen) de Vriendt; B.A., Swarthmore Coll., 1955; postgrad. Georgetown U., 1956, LaVerne U., 1966; M.S. in rehab. Calif. State U., Los Angeles, 1969; M.P.A., Calif. State U., Long Beach, 1977; m. Ronald W. Peckham, Dec. 19, 1959. Adult activities dir. Internat. Center, Balt., 1959-60; exec. dir. YWCA's, Fontana, Glendora and greater Bonita, Calif., 1963-67; community services coordinator Los Angeles County Mental Health Dept., Norwalk, Calif., 1969-74; regional planner Los Angeles County Dept. Health Services, Long Beach, 1974-75; head prevention, edn., tng. and tech. assistance Los Angeles County Drug Program, Los Angeles, 1976—. Mem. AAUP, Phi Kappa Phi. Republican. Mem. Dutch Reform Ch. Office: 840 S Broadway 11th Floor Los Angeles CA 90014

PECKMAN, AUDREY KERN, cons., counselor, educator; b. Bklyn., Jan. 14, 1936; d. Max Irwin and Matilda (Patrick) Kern; student Skidmore Coll., 1953-54; B.A., Columbia U., 1957; m. Paul Peckman, June 10, 1956 (div. 1975); children—Glenn, Jodi. Rep., Nightingale-Conant Corp., Chgo., 1975—; columnist personal devel. Womensweek newspaper, N.Y.C., 1976-78; self-employed cons., program dir. human resources devel., N.Y.C., 1977—; mem. faculty Parsons div. New Sch., Manhattan, N.Y., 1979—; instr. workshops personal growth YWCA, N.Y.C., 1980—. Pres. women's div. Lawrence Village Park Recreational Facility, 1971-73. Mem. Women Bus. Owners N.Y. (dir.), Women in Communications. Contbr. column Downtown Manhattan, 1978—. Home and Office: 30 E 70th St New York NY 10021

PECSOK, MARILYN WIEGAND, civic worker; b. Indpls., Nov. 19, 1929; d. Homer Louis and Florence (Randel) Wiegand; A.B. in Romance Langs., De Pauw U., 1951; M.S. in Edn., Butler U., 1955; m. John Gilbert Pecsok, July 14, 1962. Tchr. elem. grades, supr. student tchrs. Indpls. Pub. Schs., 1951-62. Advt. coordinator 500 Festival Program, 1978; vice precinct committeewoman Noblesville Republican Com., 1963-66; chmn. adv. council Vol. Bur., 1969-72; v.p. Hoosier Capital council Girl Scouts U.S.A., 1969-72; v.p. community projects Jr. League, Indpls., 1968-69; sch. vol. council Indpls. Public Schs., 1972-74; sec., v.p. Ind. chpt. Cystic Fibrosis Research Found., 1972-75; pres. United Way League, 1978-79; chmn. residential div. United Way, 1979, mem. admissions com., 1978-81: chmn. local arrangements Ind. Gov.'s Conf. on Libraries and Info. Services, 1979; bd. dirs. Indpls. chpt. ARC, Community Service Council; treas. Children's Bur. Aux., 1979-81, v.p., 1981-82, pres., 1982-83; mem. Indpls. Day Nursery Aux. Bd., 1975-81, pres.-elect, 1981-82; pres. Breath of Life Guild, 1973-74, 81-82; alumni bd. Butler U., 1979-83, sec., 1981-82; bd. dirs. North Group, Ind. State Symphony Soc., 1981-83. Recipient hon. award Gov. of Ind., 1976, Those Spl. People award Women in Communications, 1969. Mem. AAUW (pres. Indpls. br. 1962-64, state bd., library chmn. 1964-68), DAR (regent Jonathon Jennings chpt. 1968-70), Women's Archtl. League (pres. 1965-66), Classic Car Club (sec.-treas. Ind. region 1976-78), Milestone Car Soc. (exec. sec. 1977-79), Mortar Bd. (pres. alumnae 1965), Phi Beta Kappa (pres. Ind. Alpha chpt. 1970-72), Theta Sigma Phi, Delta Kappa Gamma (pres. Beta Gamma chpt. 1966-68, pres. Indpls. council), Kappa Kappa Kappa (chpt. pres. 1971-72, state chmn. 1973-83), Pi Beta Phi (pres. house corp. 1955-62, pres. Indpls. alumnae 1966-68, chmn. alumnae adv. council 1978-79). Presbyterian. Home: 4716 E 75th St Indianapolis IN 46250

PEDDICORD, MARY EVELYN HILL, ednl. adminstr.; b. Laurens, S.C., Oct. 21, 1932; d. Robert Lee and Eunice Lenora (Culbertson) Hill; A.A. summa cum laude, Anderson Coll., 1969; A.B. with honors, Clemson U., 1971; M.S., U. So. Miss., 1972, Ph.D. (Grad. fellow 1976-77), 1980; m. Herschel Q. Peddicord, Jr., June 1, 1949; children—Herschel Q., Wallace D. Tchr., Laurel (Miss.) City Schs., 1972-74, Hattiesburg (Miss.) City Schs., 1974-75; instr. U. So. Miss., Hattiesburg, 1976-77; instr., chmn. humanities dept. Pearl River Jr. Coll., Poplarville, Miss., 1977—. Mem. Nat. Council Tchrs. English, SE Conf. on English in Two Year Coll., South Central Modern Lang. Assn., English Commn. for Miss., Kappa Delta Pi. Baptist. Club: Kappa Kappa Iota. Home: 109

Tanglewood Dr Hattiesburg MS 39401 Office: Academic Bldg Office 133 Pearl River Junior College Poplarville MS 39470

PEDDIE, ELIZABETH BELL, pub. co. exec.; b. Washington, Feb. 4, 1923; d. Ulric Joseph and Helen Corinne (Kennedy) Bell; A.B., Wellesley Coll., 1943; m. David Donald Peddie, Mar. 4, 1944; children—Donna Elizabeth, Sandra Joan, Monica Jean. Reporter, Raleigh (N.C.) News & Observer and Columbus (Ohio) Dispatch, 1943-48; editor Minn. Pharmacist, St. Paul, 1948; reporter Suburban Sun, Hopkins, Minn., 1953; writer, editor Finney Pub. Co., Mpls., 1960—; publs. editor Bush Leadership Fellows Program, Bush Found., St. Paul, 1971—. Mem. Minn. Press Club. Republican. Home: 4612 Lakeview Dr Edina MN 55424 Office: Finney Co 3350 Gorham Ave Minneapolis MN 55426 Bush Found E900 First Nat Bank Bldg St Paul MN 55101

PEDEN, LOIS GRACE, univ. ofcl., acct.; b. Fountain Inn, S.C., Oct. 21, 1928; d. John Otis and Mae Bell (Leopard) P.; B.A. in Journalism, Winthrop Coll., 1948, postgrad., 1961-62. Reporter, Greer (S.C.) Citizen, 1948; sec. Rock Hill (S.C.) Evening Herald, 1949-50; with Winthrop Coll., Rock Hill, 1950—; tchr. York (S.C.) Elem. Sch., 1962-63. Pres. women's div. St. John's United Methodist Ch., Rock Hill, 1979-80. Mem. Rock Hill Bus. and Profl. Women's Club (pres. 1976-77, 78-79), S.C. Employees Assn. (dir. 1966-69, 79—). Democrat. Home: 2185 India Hook Rd Rock Hill SC 29730 Office: Winthrop College Oakland Ave Rock Hill SC 29730

PEDERSEN, ANN MARIE, social worker; b. Framingham, Mass., Nov. 29, 1933; d. Charles F. and Mary A. (Smith) Ahern; grad. Newton-Wellesley Hosp. Sch. Nursing, 1951-53; student Union Coll., 1974-75; B.A. magna cum laude, Kean Coll., 1977; M.S.W., Rutgers U., 1979; m. Carl R. Pedersen; children—Nancy, Robert, Kevin, Thomas, Melissa. Physician's asst. Marvin Winell, Plainfield, N.J., 1972; counselor Union County Probation Dept., Elizabeth, N.J., 1973-75; social worker Mountainside Hosp., Montclair, N.J., 1976-77; adolescent social work specialist Muhlenberg Hosp., Plainfield, N.J., 1978-81; pvt. cons., Hagerstown, Md., 1981—. Mem. Soc. Adolescent Medicine, Nat. Assn. Social Workers, Alpha Delta Mu, Psi Chi. Roman Catholic. Home: 100 Overhill Dr Hagerstown MD 21740

PEDIGO, SKIP MARCHEL, public relations exec.; b. Sharon, Tenn., May 30, 1933; d. Ocie D. and Nellie Lee (Garrett) Cooley; B.A., Calif. State U., 1970; m. Jerry L. Pedigo, Dec. 10, 1977; 1 dau., Alison. Copywriter/account supr. Chris Art Studio, Costa Mesa, Calif., 1971-73; mktg. dir. Pacific City Bank, Huntington Beach, Calif., 1973; promotion/mktg. dir. for Westminster (Calif.) Mall, Homart Devel. Co., 1974-76; editor Orange Coast mag., Newport Beach, 1976-78, Sr. Life mag., Newport Beach, 1978, HomeBuyer's Guide, Newport Beach, 1979; pres. Pedigo Public Relations, Newport Beach, 1979-80; owner/partner Coombe & Pedigo Public Relations, Newport Beach, 1980—; lectr. in field. Bd. dirs. The Rap Center, Tustin, Calif., 1973-74; mem. spl. events bd. City of Huntington Beach, 1979. Mem. C. of C., Nat. Council Shopping Centers, Women Can Win, Nat. Assn. Female Execs., Orange County Coast Assn., Am. Soc. Profl. and Exec. Women. Contbr. articles to profl. jours. Home: 6652 Luciento Dr Huntington Beach CA 92647 Office: 359 San Miguel Dr Suite 305 Newport Beach CA 92660

PEDTKE, MARY MARJORIE, educator; b. DuBois, Ill., Oct. 7, 1929; d. Oscar Diedrich and Katherine I. (Schwind) Peeck; B.S. in Edn., So. Ill. U., 1957; m. Anthony Pedtke, June 27, 1959; 1 dau., Tina Katherine. Tchr. rural schs. Perry County Ill., 1948-51, Tamaroa (Ill.) Grade Sch., 1951—, supt., 1964-69. Treas. DuBois Methodist Ch., 1954-75; supt. United Meth. Sunday Sch., Ashley, Ill., 1978-82. Mem. Perry County Tchrs. Assn. (v.p. 1958-59), Nat., Ill., Tamaroa edn. assns. Home: Route 1 Box 163A DuBois IL 62831

PEEBLES, ALLENE KAY, manufactured home mktg. co. exec.; b. Waukegan, Ill., Feb. 9, 1938; d. Allan Laverne and Kathryn Bernice (McGill) Sedlmayr; B.S. with high honors, U. Wis., 1960, M.S., 1967, postgrad. 1968; m. William Ross Peebles, July 9, 1960; children—Ross William, Robb Allen, Raymond John, Renda Kay. Tchr. public schs., Horicon, Wis., 1960-61, Oconomowoc High Sch., 1961-67; freelance writer newspapers, nat. mags., 1967-70; v.p. Luxury Homes, Inc., Watertown, Wis., 1970—, Plus Devel. Inc., Watertown, 1977—; partner Hidden Meadows Community, Watertown, 1976—; lectr. in field; chmn., moderator public seminars on manufactured housing. Active various charitable orgns.; lay preacher, chmn. adminstrv. bd. United Meth. Ch., 1974-77, co-chmn. ministries for families, 1976-79; active Boy Scouts Am., 1974—, merit badge counselor, 1974—, cubmaster, 1976-79, dist commr., 1980—; chmn. local campaign area Congressman Kasten for Gov., 1978; mem. Gov.'s Conf. on Children and Families, 1980, Gov.'s Milw. Regional Council on Children and Families, 1980—. Mem. Wis. Home Econs. Assn., Am. Home Econs. Assn., Nat. Home Economists in Bus., Wis. Home Economists in Bus. (public relations chmn. 1978-79, sec. 1980—), AAUW (pres. 1980—), Wis. Manufactured Housing Assn. (state bd. dirs. 1979—), Waukesha County Bd. Realtors, Wis. Assn. Realtors, Nat. Assn. Realtors, Phi Kappa Phi. Methodist. Home: 37788 Mapleton Rd Oconomowoc WI 53066 Office: Hidden Meadows Pkwy Watertown WI 53094

PEENEY, GEORGIANA HARRIET, engr.; b. Evanston, Ill., Oct. 9, 1906; d. Edward Anderson and Clara Matilda (Schnell) P.; B.S. in Civil Engring., M. Indsl. Engring., Northwestern U., 1929. Engr., Curtis Lighting, Inc., Chgo., 1929-32, Victor Pearlman Co., Chgo., 1932-33; free lance drafting and engring., 1933-36; engr. Dept. Pub. Works, Evanston, Ill., 1936-42, 46-47, Office Chief Ordnance, U.S. Army, 1942-46, Lansing B. Warner, Inc., Chgo., 1947-74; pvt. practice, 1974—; mem. Ill. Profl. Engring. Exam. Com., 1976-77. Recipient silver medal, award of merit Soc. Am. Mil. Engrs., 1945; Alumni Merit award Northwestern U., 1949. Registered profl. engr., Ill. Mem. Ill. Soc. Profl. Engrs., Nat. Soc. Profl. Engrs., Western Soc. Engrs. (life mem.; chmn. profl. women's div., vice chmn. publs. com.), Soc. Am. Mil. Engrs., Am. Ordnance Assn., Soc. Women Engrs. (nat. public relations chmn.), AAUW, Bus. and Profl. Women's Club of Evanston (chmn. radio and TV com., news service com.), Northwestern U. Alumni Assn. (dir. 1959-62), Evanston Hist. Soc., Sigma Sigma Delta. Republican. Presbyterian. Home: 2226 Colfax St Evanston IL 60201

PEEVERS, BARBARA HOLLANDS, sociologist, social psychologist, educator; b. Mpls., Sept. 30, 1930; d. Harold Fuller and Rachel Josephine (Steiber) Hollands; student U. Oreg., 1948-49, Sorbonne, 1949-50; B.A. with distinction, Stanfurd U., 1953; Ph.D. in Social Psychology, U. Nev., 1970; children—Richard Hollands, Michael James. NIH grad. trainee, 1966-69; research asso., lectr. dept. psychology U. Nev., Reno, 1970-73; lectr. dept. sociology Calif. State U., Chico, 1973-75, asst. prof., 1975-77, asso. prof., 1977—. Mem. Am. Psychol. Assn., Am. Sociol. Assn., Western Psychol. Assn., Pacific Sociol. Assn., Soc. for Research in Child Devel., AAUW (pres. Reno br. 1963-64), Sigma Xi, Phi Kappa Phi. Contbr. articles to profl. jours. Home: 456 Madrone Ave Chico CA 95926 Office: Dept Sociology Calif State U Chico CA 95929

PEGG, MARY NORWOOD, state legislator; b. Richmond County, N.C., June 24, 1938; d. Stephen Garland and Katherine Louise (Patrick) Norwood; student U. N.C., Greensboro, 1956-77, Wingate Coll., 1957-58; degree LaSalle Interior Design, 1973; m. Jabez Gilbert Pegg, June 28, 1958; children—Elizabeth, Stephen, Jennifer. Tchr. public schs., Bordentown, N.J., 1958-59; faculty Alamance Tech. Inst., Burlington, N.C., 1972-73; mem. N.C. Ho. of Reps., 1979—. Bd. dirs. Council on Drug Control, Alamance County Mental Health Dept., 1970-71; chmn. N.C. Internat. Women's Yr. Citizens' Rev. Com., 1977-78; active Extension Homemakers Club, Winston-Salem Symphony Guild, Little Theatre Guild, Reynolda House Docents, Forsyth County Rep. Women's Club, Southeastern Center of Contemporary Art, church orgns. Recipient Eagle award, 1979, legis. award N.C. Conservative Union, 1979; named Young Woman of Yr. for Alamance County, 1971. Methodist. Club: Jr. Woman's. Testified before ad hoc congressional hearings.

PEIRCE, CAROL MARSHALL, educator; b. Columbia, Mo., Feb. 1, 1922; d. Charles Hamilton and Helen Emily (Davault) Williams; A.B., Fla. State U., 1942; M.A. (McGregor fellow, DuPont fellow), U. Va., 1943; Ph.D. (Harvard tutor, Anne Radcliffe traveling fellow), Radcliffe Coll./Harvard U., 1951; m. Brooke Peirce, July 12, 1952. Head English dept. Fairfax Hall, Waynesboro, Va., 1943-44; instr. English Cedar Crest Coll., Allentown, Pa., 1944-46; instr. English, Harvard U., 1952-53; asst. dean instrn. Radcliffe Coll., Cambridge, 1950-53; head English extension homestudy U. Va., Charlottesville, 1953-54; asst. dir. admissions Goucher Coll., Towson, Md., 1956-62; prof. and chmn. English, U. Balt., 1968—, holder Disting. Teaching chair Coll. Liberal Arts, 1981-82, chmn. humanities div., 1972-80; chmn. bd. New Poets Series, 1975—; vis. scholar Lucy Cavendish Coll., U. Cambridge (Eng.), 1977-78. Mem. Edgar Allen Poe Soc. (dir. 1973-77), Lawrence Durrell Soc. (nat. pres. 1980-82), MLA, Md. Assn. English Depts., Chi Delta Phi, Phi Alpha Theta, Phi Kappa Phi, Phi Beta Kappa. Author: (with Brooke Peirce) A Study of Literary Types and An Introduction to English Literature from Chaucer to the Eighteenth Century, 1954, A Study of Literary Types and An Introduction to English Literature from the Eighteenth Century to the Present, 1954. Office: Dept English U Balt Baltimore MD 21201

PEKAR, CATHERINE DUSEK, nurse; b. Chgo., Aug. 4, 1951; d. Anton J. and Rose Mary (Zielonka) Dusek; B.S. in Nursing, St. Xavier Coll., Chgo., 1973; M.S.N., Loyola U., Chgo., 1978; m. Dennis J. Pekar, May 28, 1978. Staff nurse birth unit and women's ambulatory care clinic Rush-Presbyn.-St. Luke's Med. Center, Chgo., 1973-75; maternal/child health instr. Meml. Hosp. DuPage County, Elmhurst, Ill., 1975-77; head nurse, clin. nursing instr. U. Chgo. Med. Center, 1977-80; dir. maternal/child nursing St. Joseph Hosp., Chgo., 1980—; instr. LaMaze childbirth edn., 1980—; CPR instr. Am. Heart Assn., 1980—. Mem. Internat. Childbirth Edn. Assn., Am. Nurses Assn., Nurses Assn. of Am. Coll. Ob-Gyn, Parent and Child Edn. Soc., Midwest Parentcraft Center, Ill. Soc. Nurse Adminstrs., Ill. Nurses Assn. (dist. program chmn. 1976-77), Sigma Theta Tau. Republican. Roman Catholic. Office: 2900 N Lake Shore Dr Chicago IL 60657

PELÁEZ, ARMANTINA R., religious educator; b. Havana, Cuba, Apr. 21, 1948; came to U.S., 1962, naturalized, 1968; d. Armando and Argentina (Pérez) P.; B.A., Ladycliff Coll., Highland Falls, N.Y., 1973; M.A. in Religious Edn., Fordham U., 1977. Asst. child care worker St. Joseph's Home of Peekskill (N.Y.), 1968-70; asso. dir. religious edn. St. Joseph's of Palisades Parish, West New York, N.J., 1973-75; sec. of evangelization Diocese of Paterson (N.J.), Roman Catholic Ch., 1975-80, Hispanic Apostolate coordinator, asst. adminstr. to vicar of Hispanic Ministries, 1980—. vol. team mem. pastoral Hispanic youth ministry St. Augustine's Parish, Union City, N.J., 1979—; cons. Latin Am. program Wilson Center, Washington, 1982, CARA/Center for Applied in Apostolate, 1981; authorized instr. parent and tchr. effectiveness tng. N.J. chm. Cuban Nat. Planning Council, 1974-75, nat. bd. dirs., 1974-75. Mem. Nat. Assn. for Women Religious, Found. of Thanatology (assoc.), Am. Soc. Psychical Research, Las Hermanas Nat. Orgn. (N.Y. coordinator 1970-72, N.Y. Upstate coordinator 1972-73, N.J. coordinator 1978-79). Clubs: N.Y. Road Runners, N.Y. Race Walking, N.J. Shore Athletic, N.J. Athletics Congress. Contbr. articles to Spanish lang. newspapers, jours. Home: 4009 Palisade Ave Union City NJ 07087 Office: 777 Valley Rd Clifton NJ 07013

PELLEGRINI, ANNA MARIA, soprano; b. Pretoro, Chieti, Italy; d. Vincenzo and Giuseppina (Pietrantonio) P.; student U. Toronto Opera Sch., 1964-67; m. Steven Thomas, Aug. 13, 1973; 1 son, Vincent Thomas. Can. debut as Gilda in Rigoletto, 1965; appearances with Sadlers' Wells, Royal Opera House, Covent Garden, also in Parma, Bologna and Palermo, Italy, Pitts., Can., N.J., Toronto, Vancouver and Winnipeg; roles include: Mimi in La Bohème, Liu in Turandot, Nedda in I Pagliacci, Chrysothemis in Elektra, title roles of Manon Lescaut and Madama Butterfly; star CBC prodn. of Madama Butterfly. Recipient Caravello d'Oro (Italy); winner Met. Opera Nat. Auditions. Mem. Can. Actors Equity, Brit. Equity, Am. Guild Mus. Artists, Assn. Can. TV and Radio Actors. Office: Robert Lombardo Assos 61 W 62d St New York NY 10023

PELLERIN, MARY ANN, educator; b. Rochester, N.H., Nov. 23, 1934; d. Jesse Lee and Cora Eugenia (Stacy) P.; B.Ed., Keene (N.H.) State Tchrs. Coll., 1956; M.S., Central Conn. State Coll., 1963, cert., 1970; D.Min., Christian Internat. U., 1976; diploma U. Conn., 1979, then. postgrad. Elem. tchr. Richards Sch., Newport, N.H., 1956-60, Barkhamsted Sch., Pleasant Valley, Conn., 1960-64; instr., supervising tchr. Locust Ave Sch. and Western Conn. State Coll., 1964-67; substitute tchr. Lebanon (N.H.) Sch. Dist., 1967-68; instr. to asst. prof. Stanley Sch., Central Conn. State Coll., New Britain, 1968-77, asst. prof., media specialist, 1977—; cert. lay minister Am. Baptist Chs. of Conn. Pres. Greater Bristol Conf. Congregations, 1977-79. Mem. NEA, Conn. Edn. Assn., Assn. Supervision and Curriculum Devel., Conn. Ednl. Media Assn., Assn. Ednl. Communications and Tech. (1982 Meml. Scholar award), ALA, Am. Sch. Library Assn., Assn. Multi-Image, New Eng. Media Assn., Phi Delta Kappa, Pi Lambda Theta. Author: Hexagames for Language Arts, 1972; contbr. article to profl. jour. Home: 228 Morningside Dr E Bristol CT 06010 Office: CIM Willard Hall 1615 Stanley St New Britain CT 06050

PELLETIER, EDITH J. TERCASIO (MRS. GEORGE PELLETIER), business exec.; b. N.Y.C.; d. John and Rose (Graziosa) Tercasio; grad. high sch.; Ph.D. (hon.), Colo. Christian Coll., 1973; m. George Pelletier, Apr. 27, 1927; 1 dau., Anne Pelletier De Cristofaro. Rep., Elizabeth Arden, 1930-32; sales rep. Reefer & Galler, 1932-45; established (with husband) Columbia Loose Leaf Corp., N.Y.C., 1945, exec. sec., treas., 1945—, now pres. Mem. Arcana, St. Johns U. Ladies Aux. Home: 26 Rampasture Rd Hampton Bays NY 11946 Office: 32 Fairway Dr Manhasset Long Island NY 11030

PELOWSKI, BARBARA GOULD, educator; b. Seneca Falls, N.Y., Apr., 23, 1942; d. Seabury Smith and Elizabeth (Loomis) Gould; B.A., Lake Erie Coll., 1964; M.A. (grad. asst.), Syracuse U., 1966; Ph.D. (grad. asst.), Mich. State U., 1981; m. James Forney Pelowski, Jan. 29, 1966; 1 dau., Elizabeth Clarke. Head resident Syracuse (N.Y.) U., 1964-66; head resident counselor U. Cin., 1966-69; dean students Lake Erie Coll., 1971-78; adj. faculty Findlay (Ohio) Coll., 1981—; cons. to ednl./religious orgns.; lectr. in field. Mem. Diocesan Bd. Rev. in Higher Edn. Episcopal Ch., 1966-69, mem. parish vestry, 1978, mem. edn. div., 1981—; mem. lifelong learning adv. council Findlay Coll., 1981—, chmn., 1982; fundraiser Cleve. Symphony Orch., 1977-79. Mem. Ohio Assn. Women Deans, Adminstrs. and Counselors (exec. bd. 1981-82), Nat. Assn. Women Deans, Adminstrs. and Counselors, Findlay Area Personnel Assn., Am. Soc. Tng. and Devel., Delta Kappa Gamma. Clubs: William Shakespeare Soc., Women's of Findlay College, Findlay Country, Mentor Harbor Yacht. Home: 1304 S Main St Findlay OH 45840 Office: 2703 N Main St Findlay OH 45840

PELUSO, CAROL ANN, broadcasting exec.; b. Auburn, N.Y., Feb. 28, 1941; d. Joseph N., Sr., and Georgianna (Wood) Peluso; student Auburn public schs. Clk.-typist, receptionist McCulley Adjustment Co., Shreveport, La., 1962-65; office mgr. KJOE Radio, Shreveport, 1965-70; adminstrv. asst. Dynamic Broadcasting, Austin, Tex., 1970-72; ops. mgr. KTRM AM-FM, Beaumont, Tex., 1972-74; gen. mgr. KJOE Radio, Shreveport, 1974-75; v.p., ops. mgr. KRBE Radio, Houston, 1975—. Served with USAF, 1959-62. Mem. Nat. Assn. Female Execs., Houston Assn. Credit Mgrs. Roman Catholic. Home: 12058 Spring Grove Dr Houston TX 77099 Office: 9801 Westheimer Rd Houston TX 77042

PELUSO, SUSAN LINDA, research chemist; b. N.Y.C., Jan. 15, 1952; d. Patrick James and Ida Angela (Vitarelli) P.; B.A. in Chemistry and Biology, Hofstra U., Hempstead, N.Y., 1975; Ph.D. in Chemistry (teaching asst. 1975, fellow 1976-79), Brown U., 1980. Research chemist E.I. du Pont de Nemours & Co., Inc., Wilmington, Del., 1979—. Tchr. Christian doctrine Immaculate Heart of Mary Roman Cath. Ch., Wilmington, 1981—. Mem. New Eng. Catalysis Soc., Northeastern Electron Spectroscopy for Chem. Analysis Users Group, Am. Chem. Soc. Club: Toastmasters. Contbr. articles to profl. jours. Home: 814 Bezel Rd Wilmington DE 19803 Office: Polymer Products Dept Exptl Sta du Pont Co Wilmington DE 19898

PELZ, CAROLINE DUNCOMBE, ednl. adminstr.; b. White Plains, N.Y.; d. David Sanford and Helena (Ebert) Duncombe; A.B., Barnard Coll., 1940; m. Edward Joseph Pelz, July 11, 1942; children—Caroline Pelz Elbow, Margaret L. (dec.), Patricia Pelz Hart, Sanford M. Adjustments supr. R.H. Macy & Co., N.Y.C., 1940-42; admissions interviewer Barnard Coll., 1960-63; alumni sec. Allen-Stevenson Sch., N.Y.C., 1967-70, admissions asst., 1969-70; adminstrv. asst. Ednl. Records Bur., N.Y.C., 1970-72; dir. admissions Grace Church Sch., N.Y.C., 1972—. Trustee Barnard Coll., 1963-67. Mem. Barnard Coll. Alumnae Assn. (pres. 1963-66), English-Speaking Union. Republican. Episcopalian. Home: West St Stephentown NY 12168 also 55 E 87th St New York City NY 10028 Office: 86 4th Ave New York City NY 10003

PEMBERTON, ACQUILINA DOREATHA, govt. ofcl.; b. Tallahassee, Fla., Dec. 30, 1938; d. Moses and Mary (Porter) P.; B.S., Fla. Agrl. and Mech. U., 1960. Librarian, Middleton Sch., Crescent City, Fla., 1960-63, Morgan County Schs., Madison, Ga., 1964-75; sec. Fla. Dept. Revenue, Tallahassee, 1980—. Mem. AAUW, Fla. A. and M. U. Alumni Assn., NAACP, Sigma Gamma Rho, Beta Delta Sigma. Baptist. Editor: Insight Newsletter, 1979-80. Home: 1015 Volusia St Tallahassee FL 32304 Office: State of Florida Dept Revenue Fletcher Blvd Tallahassee FL 32304

PEÑA, MICHI E., systems engr.; b. Chgo., July 16, 1955; d. Severo George and Mildred M. (Salmeron) P.; B.A., North Park Coll., 1975; M.B.A., Roosevelt U., 1978; postgrad. Northwestern U., 1981—. Office mgr., bookkeeper Airways Broadcasting Sales, Niles, Ill., 1974-76; systems engr. IBM, Chgo., 1977-82; systems engr. Paradyne Corp., Rosemont, Ill., 1982—. Mem. Nat. Assn. Female Execs., NOW, ACLU. Home: 1106 S Elmwood St Oak Park IL 60304 Office: 9801 Higgins Rd Rosemont IL 60018

PENACHIO, MADELINE MARY, social worker; b. N.Y.C., Mar. 10, 1944; d. Thomas A. and Lillian Penachio; B.A., Ursiline Coll., 1966; M.S.W., Fordham U., 1971; m. Alan J. Konigsberg, May 19, 1973. Social worker Cath. Charities, N.Y.C., 1971-72; social work cons. N.Y. State Dept. Health, 1972-75, patient adv. N.Y.C. region, 1976—; dir. social services Kings Harbor Health Care Center, Bronx, N.Y., 1975-76; psychotherapist Social Psychiatry Inc., N.Y.C., 1975—. Cert. social worker, N.Y. State. Mem. Nat. Assn. Social Workers, Acad. Cert. Social Workers, Women in Govt., Nat. Assn. Patient Representatives. Home: 340 E 64th St New York NY 10021 Office: NY State Dept Health 1 Penn Plaza 2d Floor New York NY 10001

PENALUNA, JUDITH KAYE, truck line exec.; b. Hampton, Iowa, Aug. 5, 1949; d. LaVerne Grover and Mildred Emma (Olk) Harris; student Ellsworth Jr. Coll., Iowa Falls, Iowa, 1967-68; m. Joel Patrick Penaluna, May 4, 1968; children—Darci Diann, Michael Patrick. Sec.-bookkeeper Penaluna Transfer Co., Iowa Falls, Iowa, 1968—, Pen-Bros., Iowa Falls, 1979—. Co-founder crisis line Hardin County (Iowa) Alcohol and Drug Abuse Center; 2d v.p. Ellsworth Hosp. Aux., Iowa Falls, 1981-83. Recipient 2d place award Today's Woman essay contest. Mem. Iowa Falls Jaycee-Ettes (charter pres. 1978-79, pres. 1979-80, chmn. bd. 1980-81, sec. 1981-82, state dir. 1982-83, regional dir., mem. Iowa exec. council 1980-81; Rookie Region G Pres. award 1979, Keywoman award 1979-80). Lutheran. Home: Rural Route 4 Twin Hills Iowa Falls IA 50126 Office: Box 354 Rural Route 3 Iowa Falls IA 50126

PENCE, JUDITH ANN, oboist; b. Springfield, Ohio, Apr. 1, 1933; d. Lowell David and Thelma Marcellite (Kelsey) Isenbarger; B.M., Butler U., 1955; M.A., Ball State U., 1966; m. Homer Charles Pence, July 16, 1955; children—Terry Alan, Kristin Ilona. Oboist, Indpls. Symphony Orch., 1955-56, 71—, soloist, 1972; instr. music Ball State U., 1958-70, Butler U., 1972-78; oboist Musical Arts Quintet, 1960-70, Sebago Long Lake Region Chamber Music, summers 1972—; recitalist Carnegie Hall, 1963, 66; rec. artist Musical Arts Quintet, Indpls. Symphony Orch. Mem. Internat. Conf. Symphony and Opera Musicians.

PENCHANSKY, MIMI BLACK, librarian; b. N.Y.C., Oct. 17, 1925; d. Isidor and Lillian (Schwartz) Black: B.A., Queens Coll., 1962; M.S. in Library Sci., Columbia U., 1964; M.A. in Media Ecology, N.Y.U., 1975; m. Charles Penchansky, Feb. 27, 1949; 1 son, David. Instr. English, Joseph Pulitzer Jr. High Sch., Jackson Heights, N.Y., 1962-64; interlibrary loan librarian Queens Coll. Library, City U. N.Y., Flushing, 1962—, asso. prof., head gen. reference dept. Paul Klapper Library, 1976—; mem. SUNY OCLC Interlibrary Loan Adv. Group, Met. Com. to Study NYSILL. Mem. ALA (coordinator social responsibilities roundtable task force on alternatives in print, feminist task force mem. MARS bibliog. databases and datafiles com.), Assn. Coll. and Research Libraries, Library Assn. CUNY, Profl. Staff Congress, Women Library Workers, N.Y. Met. Reference and Research Library Agy. Reference Librarians Discussion Group, Internat. Soc. for Gen. Semantics, Internat. Communication Assn., Phi Beta Kappa. Club: B'nai B'rith Women. Editor, compiler: Management, Instruction and Technology in the Academic Library, 1972, Publishing: Alternatives and Economics, 1974, The Library as Consumer: Problems and Prospects of Libraries as Consumers, 1975, New Realities in Librarianship-Making the Most of Human Resources, 1976; compiler Media Integration in Academic Libraries, 1973, Libraries and Librarians: the Next Generation, 1977, Libraries On-Line, 1978. Coordinator, Alternatives in Print, 2d edit., 1972, 5th edit., 1977, sr. editor 6th edit., 1980. Mem. editorial bd. Serials for Libraries: an annotated guide to annuals, directories, yearbooks and other non-periodical serials, 1978. Home: 172-90 Highland Ave Jamaica NY 11432 Office: Queens Coll City U NY Paul Klapper Library Flushing NY 11367

PENDERY, JOANN, newspaper editor; b. Brunswick, Ga., May 17, 1935; d. Robert James and Maude Lorraine (Strickland) Gilks; grad. Glynn Acad., 1953; student photojournalism workshops in Fla., U. Okla.; m. William Paul Pendery, July 23, 1966. Glynn County area photojournalist Sta. WJXT-TV, Jacksonville, Fla., 1961-75; freelance journalist area TV stas. including WSB-TV, Atlanta, 1961-75; women's editor Brunswick (Ga.) News, 1975—. Charter mem. Friends of Brunswick Regional Library. Recipient public service cert. Ga. Forestry Assn., 1968, Northside Kiwanis Club, 1973, Am. Cancer Soc., 1969. Mem. Ga. Press Assn., Golden Isles C. of C. Democrat. Baptist. Clubs: Brunswick Jr. Woman's (past v.p., public service cert. 1979, 81), Sea Oats Garden. Home: 136 Belle Point Pkwy Brunswick GA 31520 Office: PO Box 1557 Brunswick GA 31521

PENDLETON, IRENE PATRICIA, govt. ofcl.; b. Merriam, Kans., Oct. 26, 1940; d. Wayne S. and Fern Geneva (Gilmore) Provence; B.A., West Oahu Coll., U. Hawaii, 1979; postgrad. Pepperdine U., 1980, U. So. Calif., 1980—; m. John D. Pendleton, Feb. 28, 1959; children—Tamara Marlane, David Andrew, Kowena Lorraine. Office draftsman, public works engring. NAS Memphis, Millington, Tenn., 1966-69; adminstrv. asst. COMTHIRDFLT, Pearl Harbor, Hawaii, 1969-71; adminstrv. officer, Fleet Tng. Group, Command Support Dept., Pearl Harbor, 1976-79, tng. resources mgmt. officer, 1979-81, staff edn. specialist COMOCEANSYSPAC, 1981—. Mem. Nat. Assn. Female Execs. Republican. Lutheran. Clubs: Beta Sigma Phi, Sertoma (gov. Los Angeles-Hawaii Dist., 1977-78, regional dir. Pacific Southwest 1978-80, internat. rec. sec. 1980-81, internat. treas. 1981-82), Order Eastern Star, Zonta. Home: 98-1369 Akaaka St Aiea HI 96701 Office: COMOCEANSYSPAC Code NZA Pearl Harbor HI 96860

PENDLETON, JANET HUNTER, oil co. exec.; b. Westerly, R.I., Dec. 25, 1945; d. Stuart Nicol and Emilie Gruzdis Pendleton; B.A. in Math., Hood Coll., 1967. Planning and engring. analyst New Eng. Telephone, Boston, 1973-74; plant supr. AT&T Long Lines, White Plains, N.Y., 1975-76, sr. internal auditor, 1974-75; with Mobil Oil, Scarsdale, N.Y., 1976—, ops. exec. NE region, 1977-79, credit control mgr. NE region, 1981-82, asst. pricing mgr. New Eastern region, 1982—. Mem. Bus. and Profl. Women, Nat. Assn. Female Execs. Office: PO Box 839 Valley Forge PA 19482

PENDLETON, THELMA BROWN, phys. therapist, health service adminstr.; b. Rome, Ga., Jan. 30, 1911; d. John O. and Alma (Ingram) Brown; diploma Provident Hosp. Sch. Nursing, 1931; cert. Loyola U., 1942, Northwestern U., 1946; m. George W. Pendleton, Mar. 2, 1946; 1 son, George William. Pediatric nurse Rosenwald Found., Chgo., 1931-32; staff nurse Vis. Nurse Assn., Chgo., 1932-45; chief phys. therapy Provident Hosp., Chgo., 1946-55; phys. therapy cons. Parents Assn., Inc., Chgo., 1956-60; cons. United Cerebral Palsy of Greater Chgo.'s Pipers Portal Schs., 1961-63, dir., 1963-64; dir. phys. therapy services LaRabida Children's Hosp. and Research Center, Chgo., 1964-75; mem. nat. com. Joint Orthopedic Nursing Adv. Services, 1947-55; clin. supr., instr. programs in phys. therapy Northwestern U. Med. Sch., Chgo., 1947-55, 64-75; cons. United Cerebral Palsy, 1970-75; lectr. Japanese service com. on Cerebral Palsy, 1970; mem. Ill. Phys. Therapy Exam. Com., 1952-62. Recipient cert. of commendation CSC Cook County (Ill.), 1961, Citation of Merit, Wands Cerebral Palsy Unit, 1961. Mem. Am., Ill. phys. therapy assns., Ill. League Nursing, Provident Hosp. Nurses Alumni Assn. Democrat. Clubs: Washington Park Swimming, Tu-Fours Bolivia. Author: Low Budget Gourmet, 1977; (booklet) Patient Positioning, 1981; contbr. articles on phys. therapy to profl. jours. Address: 2631 S Indiana Ave Chicago IL 60616

PENDLEY, EVELYN HOGE (MRS. WALTER O. PENDLEY), author; b. Rome, Ga., June 24, 1918; d. Edward Herman and Caroline (Bostick) Hoge; A.B., Berry Coll., 1938; M.A., Emory U., 1941; spl. study Shorter Coll., Converse Coll., Winthrop Coll.; m. Walter O. Pendley, Nov. 14, 1943; children—Joyce Bernadette, Lee Hoge. Tchr. pub. high sch., Ga., 1939-41, 45; sec. to treas. Emory U., 1942-43; instr. English, Memphis State Coll., 1949-50; instr. Berry Coll., Mt. Berry, Ga., 1959-62, asst. prof. English, asst. coll. supr. student tchrs., 1962-76, asso. prof., 1976—; med. sec. to Dr. Pendley, 1954-75. Pres. Open Door Home Bd., Rome, Ga., 1953-55. Mem. Ga. Poetry Soc., Berry Alumni Assn., AAUW, Women's Auxiliary to Med. Assn. Ga., South Atlantic MLA, Mental Health Assn. of Floyd County, Salvation Army Aux., Martha Berry Soc., Rome Heritage Found., Nat. Council Tchrs. English, Ga. Assn. Tchr. Educators, Soc. Study So. Lit. Presbyn. Club: Three Rivers Garden. Author: Sketches of the Life of Martha Berry, 1945; Mountain Top Moments, 1953; Growing Pleasures, 1956; Angel Wings, 1957; A Golden Chain (poems), 1962; Sixty Years of Education for Service, 1964; A Lady I Loved, 1966; (poetry) Open Before Christmas, 1967; As One, 1972; The Lesson Lingers On, 1974; More Years of Education for Service, 1977; (poetry) Doctor on Call, 1976, A Diamond Jubilee Review, 1977, For the Dozen Days of Christmas, 1977; A Berry Cavalcade, 1981. Home: Sequoia Acres Rome GA 30161 Office: Berry Coll Mount Berry GA 30149

PENFOUND, MARY ELEANOR SHARON, nurse; b. Chatham, Ont., Can., Jan. 28, 1942; d. John Henry and Bernice Eileen (Deighton) P.; came to U.S., 1965, naturalized, 1971; R.N., Providence Hosp., Detroit, 1973; student U. Detroit, 1975—. Head nurse Henry Ford Hosp., Detroit, 1975-77, project nurse, 1977, supr. dept. emergency medicine, 1978-79; asst. adminstr. nursing Bapt. Med. Center, DeKalb, Ala., 1979—. Mem. Emergency Dept. Nurses Assn., Am. Nurses Assn., Am. Hosp. Assn. Nurse Adminstrs. Baptist. Designer peritoneal dialysis delivery system utilizing Gorman-Rupp blood warmer. Home: 2905 Forrest N Fort Payne AL 35967

PENICK, ELIZABETH CARNEL, psychologist, educator; b. New Orleans, July 17, 1934; d. Rawley Martin and Marie (Sells) P.; B.A., Sophie Newcomb Coll., 1957; postgrad. U. London, 1958; M.Sc., Tulane U., 1960; Ph.D., Washington U., 1975. Intern in clin. psychology Washington U., St. Louis, 1962-63, research asst., 1960-62, instr., 1966-74; dir. psychology lab. St. Louis Children's Hosp., 1964-68; pvt. practice, cons. to local schs., St. Louis, 1968-69; clin. psychologist III, coordinator Community Psychol. Services, Malcom Bliss Mental Health Center, St. Louis, 1969-74; research project dir. dept. psychiatry U. Ky., Lexington, 1974-77, Research Service, VA Hosp., Kansas City, Mo., 1977-78, coordinator Alcohol Dependency Treatment Unit, 1978-80; dir. div. psychology, dept. psychiatry Kans. U. Med. Center, Kansas City, 1980—; asst. prof. dept. psychiatry U. Ky. Med. Center, Lexington, 1976-77; asso. prof. dept. psychiatry Kans. U. Med. Center, Kansas City, 1977—. Mem. profl. adv. bd. Judevine Found. for Autistic Children, St. Louis, 1970-74; adv. bd. Head Start, Health Services, Human Devel. Corp., St. Louis, 1972-74; adv. bd. Home Study Project, Central Inst. for Deaf, St. Louis, 1969-74; invited mem. Lt. Gov.'s Task Force on Mental Health Problems in Times of Disaster, 1973-74; mem. Kansas City Nat. Council on Alcoholism, 1978—. Recipient Chi Omega prize in psychology, 1957; Spl. Office Drug and Alcohol Programs grantee, 1974-77; Nat. Inst. Drug Abuse grantee, 1978—; NIMH research fellow and research trainee Washington U. Sch. Medicine, 1963-64. Mem. Am. Psychol. Assn., Evaluation Research Soc. Episcopalian. Contbr. articles to profl. jours. Home: 4725 Black Swan Dr Shawnee KS 66216 Office: Dept Psychiatry Kansas U Med Center 39th and Rainbow Blvd Kansas City KS 66103

PENN, FLOY LIVINGSTON (MRS. C.J. PENN), educator, cons.; b. nr. Six Mile Run, Pa.; d. Charles A. and Sarah (Whited) Livingston; B.S., Calif. State Coll., 1933; M.Ed., U. Pitts., 1938, Ph.D., 1953; m. Calvin J. Penn, Mar. 14, 1942 (dec. 1968). Tchr. pub. sch., Allegheny County, Pa., 1922-29; classroom tchr. Mt. Lebanon, Pa., 1929-38, remedial tchr., 1938-48, public sch. psychologist, 1948-54, dir. instrn., 1954-70; ednl. cons. Nat. Drug Abuse TV Project, 1970-71; dir. spl. services Washington County Bd. Edn., 1971-72, coordinator spl. services, Intermediate Unit I, 1972; exec. dir. Wesley Inst., 1972-76. Curriculum com. Ednl. TV Sta. WQED, Pitts.; 1957-70, chmn., 1968-70; lectr. U. Pitts., summer 1963. Pres. Western Pa. chpt. Council Exceptional Children, 1949, 57; scholarship com. United Mental Health Services, Pitts., 1960-68; edn. com. Sch. of Nursing, South Side Hosp., Pitts., 1957-70. Trustee South Hills Child Guidance Center, 1957-68; bd. dirs. Wesley Inst., 1965-76, pres., 1972-76; bd. dirs. Meth. Home, Mt. Lebanon, 1974—, sec., 1980-82; mem. Pacesetter Energy Project, 1977-79. Named Illustrious Californian, 1975; recipient Meritorious Profl. Achievement award U. Pitts., 1978; bldg. named in her honor Wesley Inst., 1982. Mem. AAUW, Assn. for Supervision and Curriculum Devel., Nat. Soc. for Study Edn., NEA, Pa. State Ednl. Assn., Am., Pa., Pitts. psychol. assns., Adminstrv. Women in Edn. (pres. Pitts. 1959-61), Pitts. Doctoral Assn. of Educators (treas. 1966-78; Meritorious Service award 1981), Cum Laude Soc., Pa. PTA, Delta Kappa Gamma (sec. 1956-58), Pi Lambda Theta (pres. Western Pa. alumnae chpt. 1974-78). Methodist (adminstrv. council). Clubs: South Hills Coll., Pitt. Coll. Editor Scribe, 1964-66. Home: 7 Dorchester Dr Apt 410 Pittsburgh PA 15241

PENN, JANICE, nurse, educator; b. Bronx, N.Y., May 2, 1941; d. Leonard and Eva Willis (Chandler) Penn; B.S., State U. N.Y. Downstate Med. Center, 1973; M.A., N.Y. U., 1975; Ph.D., Tex. Women's U., Denton, 1982; 1 son, Jose Gonzalez. Nurse, Albert Einstein Coll. Hosp., Bronx, 1973, Bronx Montefiore Morrisania Hosp., 1973-74, Bronx VA Hosp., 1974; mem. faculty U. Albuquerque, 1975-76; supr. Bernalillo County Med. Center, Albuquerque, 1975-76; mem. faculty, mem. advanced psychiat. council faculty U. N.Mex., Albuquerque, 1976-78; faculty U. Tex., Arlington, 1980—. Mem. Am., N.Mex. nurses Assns., Alaska Native Nurses Assn., Sigma Theta Tau. Democrat. Home: Twin Lakes Route 5 Stuart Rd Box 268 Denton TX 76201

PENNA, CAROLINE E., cosmetic co. exec.; b. Springfield, Mass., Feb. 15, 1953; d. George Joseph and Esther Ann (Colapietro) P.; student Royal Acad. Dramatic Art, U. London, 1973; B.A., Marymouth Coll., 1974; m. Kevin Kean Murphy, Dec. 26, 1981. Actress, 1974-75; coordinator Beauty Advisor Center, Estee Lauder, N.Y.C., 1975-76; product mgr. Revlon, asst. mktg. mgr., N.Y.C., 1977-80; mktg. mgr. Andrea Raab Corp., Bklyn., 1980—; cons. to children's cosmetic line Fresh n' Fancy, Hasbro Toys. Mem. Fashion Group. Clubs: St. Bartholomew Community (N.Y.C.), Airline Theatre Wing, Playwright's Collective Theatre. Contbr. to: Look Super for Less, 1981. Home: 215 E 80th St New York NY 10021 Office: 4702 Glenwood Rd Brooklyn NY 11234

PENNE, CAROL BLAKE, librarian, econ. analyst; b. Marietta, Ohio, Dec. 5, 1949; d. Charles Ledger and Garnett Fern (Pryor) Blake; B.A., Earlham Coll., 1971; M.L.S., U. Md., 1974. Asst. buyer, Bloomingdales Dept. Store, N.Y.C., 1971-73; librarian, econ. analyst Nat. Econ. Research Assos., Washington, 1974-78; asst. dir. library Am. Bankers Assn., Washington, 1978—; del. D.C. Pre-White House Conf. on Libraries and Info. Sci. Mem. Spl. Libraries Assn., Law Librarians Soc., Beta Phi Mu. Home: 1913 Yorktown Rd NW Washington DC 20012 Office: 1120 Connecticut Ave NW Washington DC 20036

PENNELL, FRANCES, mgmt. cons.; b. Boston, Aug. 6, 1951; d. Walter Francis and Helen (Redmond) P.; B.S., Simmons Coll., 1973; M.P.H. in Health Adminstrn., Columbia U., 1978; postgrad. N.Y.U. Grad. Sch. Bus., 1982—. Emergency room med. technologist Martha's Vineyard Hosp., Mass., 1973; med. technologist, ednl. in-service coordinator Park Med. Lab., Brookline, Mass., 1974-76; mgmt. cons. Macro Systems, Inc., Silver Spring, Md., 1977; program and fin. analyst N.Y.C., Health and Hosp.'s Corp., Office Med. and Profl. Affairs, 1978-80; supervising mgmt. cons. Coopers & Lybrand, N.Y.C., 1980—. Mem. Hosp. Fin. Mgmt. Assn., Am. Soc. Clin. Pathologists (registered med. technologist). Contbr. articles on health care industry to profl. jours. Home: 105 W 70th St Apt 5R New York NY 10023 Office: 1251 Ave of the Americas New York NY 10020

PENNEY, SHERI LAYNE, diversified corp. exec.; b. Logan, Utah, July 24, 1943; d. Darwin Reuben and Billie Bryan (Perry) Penney; B.A., U. Utah, 1966. Tech. writer Computer Sci. Corp., El Segundo, Calif., 1969-70, customer systems rep., 1970-71; programmer/analyst Wm. O'Neil & Co., Westwood, Calif., 1971-73; tech. rep. Nat. CSS, Los Angeles, 1976-79, sales rep., 1979; users' group analyst Xerox Corp., El Segundo, 1973-75, sales promotions mgr., 1979—. Mem. Nat. Assn. Female Execs. Democrat. Club: Beach Cities Ski. Editor: Exchange User's News, 1973-75, Weekly Briefing, 1974-75, Output, 1979-80, Insider, 1982, Xerox newsletters, brochures and films. Office: 880 Apollo St P1-62 El Segundo CA 90245

PENNICK, AURIE ALMA, orgn. exec.; b. Chgo., Dec. 22, 1947; d. Aurie Alma Watts Pennick; B.A., U. Ill., M.A. in Adminstrn. of Justice, 1981; divorced; children—Faith, Keidra. Exec. dir. Coalition Concerned Women in War on Crime, 1976-78; founding exec. dir. Chgo. Abused Women, 1978-81; exec. dir. Citizens Alert, police and law enforcement watchdog, Chgo., 1981-82; bd. dirs. Planned Parenthood Chgo.; mem. regional minority women's conf. com. Women's Bur., Dept. Labor. Pres. Lutheran Career Devel. Corp., 1976, Englewood Health Services, 1975. Recipient Community Service award United Block Clubs Englewood, 1979; cert. recognition Women's Bur., Dept. Labor, 1981; Chgo. Community Trust fellow, 1982-83. Mem. Nat. Hook-up Black Women, Nat. Assn. Female Execs., Internat. Women's Econ. Devel. Corp., Inst. Criminal Justice Ethics. Lutheran. Office: 208 S La Salle St Suite 850 Chicago IL 60605

PENNINGER, FRIEDA ELAINE, educator; b. Marion, N.C., Apr. 11, 1927; d. Fred Hoyle and Lena Frances (Young) Penninger; A.B., Woman's Coll. of U. N.C., 1948; M.A., Duke U., 1950, Ph.D., 1961. Copywriter, Sta. WSJS, Winston-Salem, N.C., 1948-49; asst. prof. English, Flora Macdonald Coll., Red Springs, N.C., 1950-51; tchr. English, Barnwell, S.C., 1951-52, Brunswick, Ga., 1952-53; instr., U. Tenn., Knoxville, 1953-56; instr., asst. prof. Woman's Coll. of U.N.C., Greensboro, 1956-58, 60-63; asst. prof., assoc. prof. U. Richmond (Va.), 1963-71, chmn. English dept. Westhampton Coll., 1970-77, prof., 1971—. Fellow Southeastern Inst. Medieval and Renaissance Studies; mem. Mediaeval Acad. Am., New Chaucer Soc., South Atlantic Modern Lang. Assn., AAUP. Democrat. Presbyterian. Author: English Drama to 1660, 1976; William Caxton, 1979; editor: A Festschrift for Prof. Marguerite Roberts, 1976. Home: 4312 Kensington Ave Richmond VA 23221 Office: English Dept U Richmond Richmond VA 23173

PENNINGTON, DORIS ETHEL, assn. adminstr.; b. Gibson County, Tenn., Aug. 15, 1933; d. Jesse Curn and Wreatha Sedoris (Malugen) Buckingham; student Wesley Theol. Sem., 1969-71, George Washington U., 1981—; m. Philip Wayne Pennington, Nov. 29, 1951; children—Philip Michael, Richard Wayne. Clk., FBI, Washington, St. Louis, 1951-52, 53-55; adminstrv. asst. Foundry United Meth. Ch., 1965-70; sec./office mgr. Hughes and McCloskey Law Offices, Washington, 1971-75; sales asso. Routh Robbins Realtors, Alexandria, Va., 1975-78; adminstrv. asst. to pres. Computer and Bus. Equipment Mfrs. Assn., Washington, 1977, Electronic Industries Assn., Washington, 1977—; realtor asso. Laughlin Realtors, McLean, Va., 1979—. Mem. Am. Soc. Assn. Execs., Exec. Female, Nat. Assn. Realtors, No. Va. Bd. Realtors. Democrat. Club: Order Eastern Star. Home: 6656 Madison of McLean McLean VA 22101 Office: 2001 Eye St NW Washington DC 20006

PENNY, JOSPHINE B., banker; b. N.Y.C., July 7, 1925; d. Charles and Delia (Fahey) Booy; student Columbia U., Am. Inst. Banking; grad. Sch. Bank Adminstrn. U. Wis., 1975; m. John T. Penny, July 15, 1950 (div.); children—John T., Charleen Penny DeMauro, Patricia Penny Paras. With Prentice-Hall, N.Y.C., 1942-43; with Trade Bank & Trust Co., 1943-52, 61-70; with Nat. Bank N.Am., 1970—, dep. auditor, 1978—. Mem. Bank Adminstrn. Inst. (dir.), Nat. Assn. Bank Women. Home: 29 Crescent Ave Staten Island NY 10304 Office: 44 Wall St New York NY 10005

PENNYWITT, ANN HOLMES, investment broker, fin. planner; b. Charlotte, N.C., June 20, 1955; d. Cameron Parker and Katy Wells (Spruill) Holmes; A.A., Wingate Coll., 1975; B.A., U. N.C., Chapel Hill, 1977; m. Neil Charles Pennywitt, July 8, 1978. Program analyst N.C. Dept. Human Resources, Raleigh, 1975-77; media coordinator Forsyth County Retarded Citizens Workshop, 1976-77, media coordinator Runaway Hotline Program N.C., 1975-76; account exec. Village Advocate, Chapel Hill, N.C., 1977-80; investment broker, fin. planner Bache Halsey Stuart & Shields, Durham, N.C., 1980—. Mem. media staff Ford Com. 1976 Republican Nat. Conv.; mem. publicity staff Chapel Hill United Fund, 1979; media advisor Assn. for Retarded Citizens, 1979-80. Mem. Assn. Women Students, Women in Communications. Home: 1000 Lamond Durham NC 27701 Office: First Federal Bldg 400 E Main St Durham NC 27702

PENROD, ALYCE JEAN, nurse; b. South Whitley, Ind., Feb. 10, 1933; d. Dale and Mary Helen (Sherer) Parker; diploma Meth. Hosp. Indpls., 1955; grad. Famous Artist Sch., 1970; m. John L. Penrod, Feb. 26, 1955; children—J. Mark, Ruth, Roberta, David, Violet, Tom, Jean. Staff nurse Wabash (Ind.) County Hosp., 1960, asst. supr., 1960-74, supr., 1974-77, asst. dir. nursing, 1977—. Pres., Wabash Art Guild, 1976-79. Democrat. Mem. Ind. Fedn. Art Clubs (dir. 1980, 2d v.p. 1981, 1st v.p. 1982-83). Mem. Brethren Ch. Clubs: Country Women's (asst. treas. 1980), Wabash County Choral. Home: Route 1 North Manchester IN 46962 Office: 670 N East St Wabash IN 46992

PENTA, IRENE PLATT, nurse, club woman; b. Concord, N.H., Jan. 2, 1920; d. Frank Bishop and Ida Louisa (Cable) Platt; student Portland Jr. Coll., 1939; R.N., Dr. Drummond's Hosp. Nursing Sch., Portland, Maine, 1942; m. Walter E. Penta, Sept. 25, 1943; 1 son, Donald Platt. Nurse, Maine Med. Center, Portland, 1942-43, Mercy Hosp., Portland, 1943, Boston City Hosp., 1943-44, Beth Israel Hosp., Boston, 1944, Mass. Gen. Hosp., Boston, 1944, Deaconess Hosp., Boston, 1943, Meth. Hosp., Dallas, 1944-45, Med. Arts, Dallas, 1944-45, So. Bapt. Hosp., Dallas, 1944-45. Sec., Woman's Aux. Maine Med. Assn., Portland, 1955-56, v.p., 1956-57, pres.-elect, 1957-58, pres., 1958-59, bd. dirs., 1955—, chmn. internat. health-womans aux. 1967—; v.p. Ladies of Kiwanis, Portland, 1958, pres., 1959, bd. dirs., 1957—; active aux. Maine Med. Center; mem. organizational com. Tri-State Health Careers Research Group, Portland, 1960-61; rural health chmn. region one, Woman's Aux. to AMA, 1960-65, Maine internat. health chmn. Mem. Maine Nurses Assn., Dr. Drummonds Hosp. Alumni Assn. (pres. 1964-66, 82—), Maine Hist. Soc., Internat. Platform Assn., Wives Wing of Aerospace Med. Assn., Nat. Soc. Daus. of Founders and Patriots Am., Nat. Soc. Women Descs. Ancient and Honorable Arty. Co. (v.p. Maine chpt. assts. 1972—). Congregationalist (pres. Jr. Guild 1956). Club: Woodfords (Portland). Home: 316 Woodford St Portland ME 04103

PENT LAND, SUE-BYRD, ballerina; b. Sioux City, Iowa, Mar. 25, 1928; d. Edgar O. and Mabel (French) Hill; student Ark. U., 1943; m. Ernest Edward Roberts, June 10, 1944 (dec. Sept. 1960); 1 son, William-Hill; m. 2d, Robert Pentland, Jr., Jan. 25, 1963 (dec. July 1979). Formerly prima ballerina Miami Ballet; tchr. acad. classical ballet technique St. Stephen's Episcopal Day Sch., Coconut Grove, Fla., 1959-62. Active USO; prin. dancer, soloist The Iham Follies for crippled children, 1953-61; mem. Debutante Com., Opera Guild Greater Miami. Recipient gold medal U.S.O.; Queen of Hearts award Variety Internat. Club, 1971, Great Gal award, 1972. Mem. U.D.C., Dance Masters Am., Internat. Platform Assn., Soc. Univ. Founders. So. Democrat. Episcopalian. Clubs: Miami Woman's (perpetual mem., chmn. ballet, drama and music div. fine arts dept., 1958-60, 61-62), Hibiscus Garden; U. Miami Woman's; Indian Creek Country, Surf; Golden Hills Turf and Golf Country (Ocala, Fla.); Brookfield West, Country (Roswell, Ga.). Home: Quarter Mile Farms S Ocala FL 32670 also 12173 Mountain Laurel Dr Brookfield West Roswell GA 30075

PEPITONE-ARREOLA-ROCKWELL, FRANCES MARIE, clin. psychologist; b. San Mateo, Calif., June 3, 1941; d. Joseph and Hope Norma (Arreola) Pepitone; R.N., Highland Sch. Nursing, 1961; B.A., Calif. State U., 1966, M.A., 1971; Ph.D., Calif. Sch. Profl. Psychology, 1974; m. Don A. Rockwell, Dec. 23, 1965; children—Grant Arthur, Chad Arthur. Psychiat. nurse VA Hosp., Palo Alto, Calif., 1961-62; Glenside Hosp., Jamaica Plain, Mass., 1962-63; Langley Porter Neuropsychiat. Inst., U. Calif., San Francisco, 1964-66; Center for Spl. Problems, San Francisco, 1966-67; problem pregnancy counselor Planned Parenthood Assn., Sacramento, Calif., 1970-71; asst. prof. dept. psychiatry Sch. Medicine, U. Calif., Davis, 1974—, acting acad. dir., 1977-78, dir. Women's Resources and Research Center, 1978—. Bd. dirs. Yolo County Sexual Assault Center, 1976-78; rape adv. panel Office of Criminal Justice, 1977. Mem. Am. Psychol. Assn., Calif. State Psychol. Assn., Sacramento Soc. Clin. Psychologists, Sacramento Valley Psychol. Assn. (dir. 1975-76), Nat. Assn. for Women Deans, Adminstrs. and Counselors, Council for Nat. Register of Health Service Providers in Psychology. Club: The Tennis (Davis, Calif.). Contbr. articles to profl. jours. Office: Women's Resources and Research Center U Calif TB 124 Davis CA 95616

PEPPER, ADELINE ELIZABETH, advt. service exec., writer, photographer; b. Madison, Wis.; d. John and Emmeline (Able) Pepper; B.A., U. Wis. Med. writer AMA, ACS; asst. advt. mgr. Mead Johnson & Co., Evansville, Ind., publicity dir. Com. on Care of Children in Wartime, Evansville, 1945; radio advt. writer Knox Reeves, Inc., Mpls.; pub. relations Pa. R.R. Centennial, 1946; advt. writer L. W. Frohlich Agy., N.Y.; med. advt. writer and designer E. R. Squibb & Sons, Ciba Pharm.; owner Pep, Inc., advt. service, 1956—. Judge for N.J. Community Improvement Program, 1976. Mem. Authors League Am., Am. Med. Writers Assn., Phi Kappa Phi. Author: Tours of Historic New Jersey (N.J. Tercentary medal 1964), 1965, rev. edit., 1973; N.J. vol. Fodor's Guide to the U.S.A., 1966; The Glass Gaffers of New Jersey (Art History award N.J. Assn. Tchrs. English 1972, award of Merit Am. Assn. State and Local History 1972). Contbr. articles on travel, history, and decorative arts to mags. and maj. met. newspapers. Address: Roselle Park NJ 07204

PEPPERELL, ELISABETH MARY, banker; b. Eng., Jan. 26, 1949, came to U.S., 1953, naturalized, 1970; d. Gerald V.S. and Margaret (Thomas) P.; B.A., Wheaton Coll., Norton, Mass., 1970. Internat. corp. banker Mfrs. Hanover Trust Co., N.Y.C., 1970-76, v.p., 1976—, dist. head charge maj. oil cos. in Energy Group, 1982—. Republican. Episcopalian. Home: 333 E 56th St New York NY 10022 Office: 270 Park Ave New York NY 10022

PEPPLE, RUTH ANN, housing referral service exec.; b. Keokuk, Iowa, Apr. 27, 1943; d. John W. and Doris E. Pepple; B.A., U. Iowa, 1965; broker's lic., Mo. Real Estate Sch., 1971. Spl. activities coordinator Hallmark Cards, Kansas City, Mo., 1965-70; personnel asst. Kansas

City Power & Light Co. (Mo.), 1970-71; v.p. ops. Inter-community Relocation, Inc., Kansas City, Mo., 1971—; mem. editorial liason group Employee Relocation Council, 1980. Mem. Nat. Assn. Realtors, Am. Soc. Assn. Execs., Mo. Assn. Realtors, Kansas City Bd. Realtors, Mensa. Club: Kansas City Ski. Home: 5015 Walnut St Kansas City MO 64112 Office: 8301 State Line St Kansas City MO 64114

PEPPLER, ALICE STOLPER, publishing co. ofcl.; b. Saginaw, Mich., Mar. 14, 1934; d. Lothar E. and Hulda M. (Koenig) Stolper; B.S., Concordia Tchrs. Coll., River Forest, Ill., 1956; postgrad. U. Ill., 1966-67; children—Jeanne, Jon, Jan. Elem. sch. tchr., librarian, music dir. Bethany Luth. Sch., Chgo., 1956-63; editor lang. arts materials Scott, Foresman & Co., Chgo., 1963-71; sr. editor lang. arts materials Lyons & Carnahan, Chgo., 1972-74; mktg. dir. lang. arts, fgn. langs. and social studies Rand McNally & Co., Chgo., 1974-77; mktg. dir. lang. arts Scott, Foresman & Co., Chgo., 1977—; piano tchr., 1956-63. Organist, music dir. First Luth. Ch. of Trinity, 1967-76; organist, choir dir. Mt. Olive Luth. Ch., Chgo., 1976—; leader singles seminars and workshops, 1975—. Mem. Internat. Reading Assn., Nat. Council Tchrs. English, Nat., Luth. edn. assns., Evang. Luths. in Mission. Author: Bible Children I Know, 1971; God's Love for Everyone, 1971; Why Jesus Came, 1972; Divorced and Christian, 1974; Who Put the Finger on God?, 1975; Single Again—This Time with Children, 1982; also articles, poems, monograph; editor Luth. Edn. Assn. Yearbook, 1972-74. Home: 5851 W Henderson St Chicago IL 60634 Office: 1900 E Lake Ave Glenview IL 60025

PERA, ISABELLA, sculptor; b. Trivero, Italy, Sept. 24, 1945; d. Gino and Lucia (Barberis) P.; came to U.S., 1967, naturalized, 1974; B.A., SUNY, Cortland, 1973; M.F.A., U. Ill., Champaign-Urbana, 1977; m. Chris Cusano, Aug. 7, 1974. One man shows include: Gilman Galleries, Chgo., 1977, Freeport (Ill.) Art Mus., 1979, Sheldon Swope Art Mus., Terre Haute, Ind., 1980, Italian Cultural Center, Chgo., 1980, Burpee Art Mus., Rockford, Ill., 1981, Western Ill. U. Art Gallery, Macomb, 1982; group shows include: Evansville (Ind.) Mus. Art and Sci., 1978, Laguna Gloria Art Mus., Austin, Tex., 1979, Foothills Art Center, Golden, Colo., 1979, Butler Inst. Am. Art, Youngstown, Ohio, 1980, Coos Art Mus., Coos Bay, Oreg., 1981, New Artists at Madison Square Garden, N.Y.C., 1981, Gallery New World, Washington, 1982; represented in permanent collections including Sheldon Swope Art Mus., Del Mar Coll. Gallery, Corpus Christi, Tex., Millikin U., Decatur, Ill., Almidones Mejicanos Bldg., Guadalajara, Mex., Santuario di Oropa (Italy), Italian Cultural Center. Leader, Girl Scouts U.S.A., 1967-69. Recipient nat. sculpture awards; Ill. Art Council grantee, 1980. Roman Catholic. Home: 1303 Belmeade Dr Champaign IL 61820

PERCIA, VALERIE CHASE, speech, hearing and lang. specialist; b. Bklyn., Nov. 17, 1950; d. Benjamin Joseph and Rosemary Jacqueline (Sullivan) Chase; B.A. summa cum laude, St. John's U., 1972; M.Ed. magna cum laude, Bridgewater State Coll., 1975; m. Salvatore Charles Percia, June 10, 1972; children— Elizabeth Diane, Benjamin John. Research asst. Queens Children's Hosp., St. John's U., N.Y.C., 1971-72; tchr. deaf and aphasic children Little People's Sch., West Newton, Mass., 1972-75; speech and lang. specialist Leominster (Mass.) Public Schs., 1975-80, designer pre-sch. lang. devel. program; cons. devel. service unit Fitchburg (Mass.) Mental Health Dept., 1980—. Cert. tchr. speech and hearing handicapped, Mass.; cert. tchr. learning disabled, Mass. Mem. Am. Speech, Hearing and Lang. Assn. (cert. clin. competence), Sigma Alpha Eta. Home: 46 Kendall Hill Rd Sterling Junction MA 01565 Office: 16 Cross St Leominster MA 01453

PERDUE, JEANETTE DEEVERS, social worker/adminstr.; b. Clarksville, Ark., Aug. 30, 1948; d. Leon Joe and Lou Verdell Deevers; student U. Ark., Fayetteville, 1966-67, Ark. Tech. U., 1967-69; B.A., U. Ark., Little Rock, 1970, M.S.W., 1972; m. Gary Wayne Perdue, June 29, 1969; 1 dau., Allison Suzanne. Psychiat. social worker Ark. State Hosp., Little Rock, 1972-73, psychiat. social work supr., 1973-79; dir. health implementation program Dept. Health State of Ark., Little Rock, 1979; dir. social work Ark. Children's Hosp., Little Rock, 1979—; cons. and lectr. in field. Registered social worker, Ark.; lic. social worker, Ark. Mem. Nat. Assn. Social Workers, Acad. Cert. Social Workers, Ark. Council on Child Protection, Ark. Advs. for Families and Children, Soc. for Hosp. Social Work Dirs., Assn. for Care Children's Health. Methodist. Home: 10815 San Joaquin Valley Ln Little Rock AR 72212 Office: 804 Wolfe St Little Rock AR 72201

PEREIRA, JORGINA ANTUNES, systems analyst; b. Rio De Janeiro, Brazil, Aug. 12, 1944; came to U.S., 1974; d. Rafael and Maria Dolores Antunes Pereira; B.A., Social Service Sch. Rio De Janeiro, 1970; B.G.S. with emphasis in Computer Sci., Roosevelt U., 1978; m. Mark Louis Branham, Dec. 31, 1980. Head social work programs Paroquia Santa Cruz De Copacabana, Rio De Janeiro, 1971-73; mem. council of internat. program Jane Addams Grad. Sch. Social Work, U. Ill., Chgo., 1974-75; trainee No. Trust Bank, Chgo., 1977-78, programmer, 1978-79, sr. programmer, 1979-80, tech. analyst, 1980-82, systems analyst, 1982—. Bd. dirs. Council of Internat. Program for Social Workers, Chgo., 1979-81. Mem. Library Computer and Info. Scis., Franklin Honor Soc. Home: 643 W Roscoe Chicago IL 60657 Office: 125 S Wacker Chicago IL 60606

PEREIRA, TERESINKA ALVES, educator; b. Belo Horizonte, Brazil, Nov. 1, 1934; came to U.S., 1960, naturalized, 1978; d. Pindaro de Paula and Maria-Albertina (Alves) P.; Ph.D. in Spanish, U. N.Mex., 1972; m. Pedro Melendez, Mar. 2, 1978; 1 son, Pedro-Alberto; children by previous marriage—Luzia Martins, Emilia Martins. Instr. Portuguese, Tulane U., 1962-68, Stanford U., 1968; assoc. prof. Spanish and Portuguese, U. Colo., Boulder, 1975—; vis. prof. Georgetown U., 1974-75; dir. lit. mag. Internat. Poetry, 1976—. Mem. Asociacion de Escritores de Mex., World Poetry Soc., Can. Soc. Poets (Poet of Yr. award 1977), Sociedad Argentina de Letras, Artes y Ciencias, Uniao Brasileira de Trovadores, Academia Literaria de Felgueiras, Accademia Universale G. Marcone, Club Internat. de Vol Libre. Author: Tienda de Rondas, 1971; Torre de Mitos, 1973; El amor de los narcisos, 1974; A Rosa no Tempo das Cerejeiras em Flor, 1974; Pa Mina Landflyktiga, 1976; La alegria esta en huelga, 1978. Office: Department of Spanish and Portuguese University of Colorado Boulder CO 80309

PERET, KAREN KRZYMINSKI, nursing adminstr.; b. Springfield, Mass., Mar. 8, 1950; d. Edward Stanley and Doris Lena (Beaudry) Krzyminski; B.S. in Nursing, St. Anselm's Coll., 1972; M.S. in Nursing Adminstrn., Boston U., 1980; m. Robert J. Peret, June 19, 1971; children—Heather Lee, James Edward, Kaitlin Elizabeth. Staff nurse Boston VA Hosp., 1972-73; staff nurse Harrington Meml. Hosp., Southbridge, Mass., 1973-74, instr., 1974-75; continuing edn. dir. Central Maine Med. Center, Lewiston, 1975-76; asst. dir. nursing Monson Devel. Center, Palmer, Mass., 1977—. Mem. sch. com. Town of Holland, Mass., 1981, ambulance com., 1981; mem. Emergency Med. Services Adv. Bd. Mass., 1980—. Mem. Am. Nurses Assn., Council Nurse Adminstrs. of Mass., Nurses Assn., Mass. Soc. Nursing Service Adminstrs., Nat. Assn. Female Execs., Sigma Theta Tau. Home: Sturbridge Road Holland MA 01550 Office: State Ave Palmer MA 01069

PERETTI, ELSA, jewelry designer; b. Florence, Italy, May 1, 1940. Tchr. French, Italian pvt. schs.; mem. staff Dado Torrigiani, Architect, Milan, Italy; fashion model, Spain, France, Gt. Britain, U.S.; jewelry designer. Recipient Coty award, 1971. Office: care Tiffany & Co 727 Fifth Ave New York NY 10022 *

PEREZ, BETTY JONES-LENZ, speech pathologist; b. Ogdensburg, N.Y., May 24, 1931; d. Bruce Clark and Laura K. (Schermerhorn) Bellinger; B.S., Ithaca (N.Y.) Coll., 1952; M.S., State Univ. Coll., Buffalo, 1964; postgrad. SUNY, Buffalo; m. Joseph A. Perez, Oct. 25, 1975; 1 dau., Susan M. Jones MacVittie. Speech-lang. pathologist Bd. Coop. Ednl. Services, Erie County (N.Y.) Sch. Dist. 1, 1956-61, Clarence (N.Y.) Central Sch., 1961—; supr. student tchrs., condr. workshops in field. Mem. Am. Speech and Hearing Assn., N.Y. State Speech and Hearing Assn., Speech and Hearing Assn. Western N.Y., N.Y. State United Tchrs. Union, Erie County Tchrs. Assn., Clarence Tchrs. Assn., Ithaca Coll. Alumni Assn., Buffalo State Coll. Alumni Assn., DAR. Presbyterian. Office: Clarence Central Schs Box T Clarence NY 14031

PEREZ, EDITH ADALJISA, physician; b. Humacao, P.R., Apr. 30, 1956; d. Ruben and Edith (Maldonado) Perez; B.A., U. P.R., 1975, M.D., 1979. Resident in internal medicine Loma Linda U., 1979-82; physician Nat. Health Service Corps, 1982—. Mosby scholar, 1975. Mem. AMA, ACP. Office: 245 S Fetterly Ave Los Angeles CA 90022 *

PERINE, MAXINE HARRIET, educator; b. Worth County, Mo., May 11, 1918; d. Robert Rozwell and Della Dale (Martin) P.; B.S. in Edn., Central Mo. State U., 1944; M.A., Columbia U., 1954, profl. diploma, 1960, Ed.D., 1977. Tchr., Worth County schs., 1935-44, Kansas City (Mo.) public schs., 1944-59; reading cons. Kansas City (Mo.) public schs., 1959-64; editor Holt, Rinehart, Winston, N.Y.C., 1964; mem. faculty U. Mich., Flint, 1964—, prof. specializing in reading, dept. edn., 1972—; vis. scholar Columbia U., 1978. Mem. Internat. Reading Assn., AAUP, Kappa Delta Pi (chpt. founding counselor 1980—), Delta Kappa Gamma (named Woman of Distinction 1972). Presbyterian. Author, editor in field. Office: 1321 E Court St Flint MI 48503

PERKIN, ETHEL MURPHY (MRS. FRANK SCOTT PERKIN), clubworker; b. Chgo., July 21, 1916; d. John F. and Ethel (Howden) Murphy; student Highland Park Jr. Coll., 1935-37; A.B. in English Edn., Wayne U., 1939; m. Frank Scott Perkin, Feb. 27, 1942 (dec. Nov. 1973); children—Linda Josephine, John Francis, Sandra Ethel. Tchr. elem. English, lit., gen. lang., Detroit, 1941-45; personnel counselor women Plymouth plant Chrysler Corp., Detroit, 1943; asst. sec., dir. Murphy Ventures Corp., Grosse Pointe, Mich., 1956—. Chmn. membership Harper Hosp. Aux., Detroit, 1951, chmn. publicity, 1961; treas. Maire Sch. PTA, Grosse Pointe, 1960-62, mem. PTA Council, 1960-62; mem. bd. Mich. Humane Soc.; 2d v.p. Women's City Club of Detroit, 1969-71, bd. dirs., 1964-67, 74-77, nominating com., 1972-73; mem. women's aux. Wayne County Med. Soc., 1942—; mem. women's com. Grosse Pointe Symphony Orch.; life mem. Women's Assn. Detroit Symphony Orch.; life mem. women's div. Project Hope. Mem. Detroit Hist. Soc. (life), Internat. Platform Assn., Art Founders' Soc., Archives Am. Art, Detroit, AAUW, Detroit Rev. Club (pres. 1974-75), Liggett Sch. Parents Assn. (bd. 1965-66), Woman's Nat. Farm and Garden Assn. (Grand Marais br.), Alpha Gamma Delta. Club: Colony Town (dir. 1975—). Address: 1709 Shore Club Dr Saint Clair Shores MI 48080 also Yacht Club Terr 44-121-4 Laha St Kaneche HI 96744

PERKINS, ANNE SCARLETT, state legislator; b. Balt., Sept. 29, 1937; student Bryn Mawr Sch., 1949-55; B.A., Boston U.; 1949, J.D., U. Balt., 1978. Admitted to Md. bar, 1978; atty. Md. Advocacy Unit for Developmentally Disabled, Balt., 1979-81; mem. Md. Ho. of Dels., 1979—; mem. Gov.'s Commn. to Study Adoption Laws, State Adv. Council for Coordination of Services to Handicapped; alt del. Democratic Nat. Conv., mem. nat. rules com., 1972; mem. Dem. State Central Com., 1973-74; mem. citizens adv. bd. Mayor's Coordinating Council on Criminal Justice, 1974-75; pres. Md. Conf. Social Concern, 1973-75, New Dem. Club 2d Dist., 1976-77; bd. dirs. Md. Inst., Coll. Art, Citizens Planning and Housing Assn., Balt. City Fair, Balt. Center for Victims of Sexual Assault, Met. Sr. Citizens Center, Family and Children's Soc., Greater Hampden Task Force on Youth. Mem. Am. Bar Assn., Md. State Bar Assn., Balt. City Bar Assn. Office: 316 Lowe Bldg Annapolis MD 21401

PERKINS, CATHY ASHLEY, fashion advisor, public relations specialist; b. Ogden, Utah, Aug. 18; d. Darrell Joseph and Delores Irene (Coates) Perkins; A.S., Weber State Coll., 1978; student U. Utah, 1979, U. Calif., San Diego, 1980, Am. Inst. Fgn. Study, 1976; 1 dau., Marlee. Radio-TV and newspaper copywriter The Bon Dept. Stores, Allied Mktg. Corp., 1974-75, asst. buyer, 1975-76, fashion coordinator, 1977-78; presdl. asst. public relations Intermountain Fin. Cons., Reno, 1978-79; European adv. Fgn. Study League, Greenwich, Conn., 1976; program coordinator Weber County (Utah) Schs., Ogden, 1975-77; profl. model and actress; corp. pres., founder, dir. The Stepping Stone, Modeling and Finishing Studios, Inc., 1977—; lectr., cons. in field. Mem. adv. bd. Weber State Coll.; Recipient Dean's Spl. Services award Weber State Coll., 1977; Spl. Contbn. award Distributive Edn. Clubs Am., 1978. Mem. Nat. Retail Mchts Assn., C. of C., Nat. Assn. Female Execs., SAG, Internat. Fashion Models Assn., Women's Network, World Models Assn., AFTRA, Utah Assn. Motion Picture and TV Artists. Contbr. articles to profl. jours. Office: PO Box 2762 Van Nuys CA 91404

PERKINS, CHARLOTTE MARIE, social worker; b. Magnolia, Ark., Oct. 7, 1943; d. Paul Jack and Cora Faye (Pearce) Jones; B.A. in Sociology, So. Ark. U., 1965; M.S.W., U. Denver, 1967; m. William E. Perkins, Sept. 4, 1966; children—Paul Ivan, Jonathan William. Social worker child welfare Boulder County Dept. Public Welfare, Boulder, Colo., 1967-72, social service dept. Beth Israel Hosp., Boston, 1972-74; psychotherapist Psychiat. Clinics of Ind., Anderson, 1977—; nursing home cons. Pres., E. Central Ind. chpt. Sudden Infant Death Syndrome. Mem. Nat. Assn. Social Workers, Acad. Cert. Social Workers. Baptist. Office: 619 Citizens Bank Bldg Box 724 Anderson IN 46016

PERKINS, DEBORAH ELAINE, banker; b. Memphis, Dec. 23, 1951; d. Fred L. and Florine (Franklin) P.; A.B. in Math. Econs., Brown U., 1973. Asst. treas. Chase Manhattan Bank, N.Y.C., 1973-76; sr. credit analyst Fed. Res. Bank N.Y., 1976-77; asst. v.p. Bank of N.Y., 1977—; cons. in field. Mem. Nat. Assn. Female Execs. Assoc. Black Alumni Brown U. (sec.-treas., dir. N.Y. chpt. 1976-78). Home: 264 Clermont Ave Brooklyn NY 11205 Office: Bank of NY 48 Wall St New York NY 10015

PERKINS, ESTHER ROBERTA, literary agt.; b. Elkton, Md., May 10, 1927; d. Clarence Roberts and Esther Crouch (Terrell) P.; student West Chester State Tchrs. Coll., 1945-47, U. Del. Acct., E. I. duPont de Nemours & Co., Inc., Wilmington, Del., 1947-65; records specialist U. Del., 1966-78; partner Holly Press, Hockessin, Del., 1977—; owner Esther R. Perkins Lit. Agy., Childs, Md., 1979—; author's agt. Mem. Authors Guild, Nat. Assn. Female Execs., Nat. Writer's Club, DAR. Republican. Methodist. Author: Backroading Through Cecil County Maryland, 1978; Things I Wish I'd Said, 1979. Home and Office: PO Box 48 Childs MD 21916

PERKINS, HELEN IRENE, home economist; b. Swanville, Minn., May 6, 1923; d. Nicholas William and Verbena Sophia (Hildebrandt) Truog; B.S. in Home Econs. Edn., U. Minn., 1944; m. Donald Harrison Perkins, June 18, 1944; children—Robert Jay, Ann Marie, Carin Irene, Donald Richard, Edward Nicholas, Faye Jean, Gretchen Lu. Home econs. tchr., Anoka, Minn., 1944-45; Luth. student exec. sec. Iowa State U., Ames, 1946-47; extension home economist, Howard and Winneshiek Counties, Iowa, 1969—. Leader 4-H, 1963-69. Mem. Nat. Home Econs. Assn., Extension Home Economists (Disting. Service award 1980), Phi Upsilon, Omicron Nu. Republican. Lutheran. Clubs: Federated, Legion Aux. Home: Route 1 Cresco IA 52136 Office: 218 N Elm St Cresco IA 52136

PERKINS, JILL ANN HIGBEE, postal service worker, home econs. cons.; b. Omaha, Apr. 11, 1954; d. Byron Ellsworth and Dorothy Maude (Kidder) Higbee; B.S. in Home Econs. and Bus., N.Mex. State U., 1976; m. James Michael Perkins, July 9, 1979. Extension home agt. S.D. Extension Service, Cheyenne River Reservation, Eagle Butte, 1977-79; asst. mgr. McDonalds Restaurant, Craig, Colo., 1979; free-lance home economist, Rock Springs, Wyo., 1979—; tchr., cons. Cheyenne River Community Coll., Eagle Butte, 1978-79; asst. mgr. Thrifty Drugstores Inc., Rock Springs, 1980-81; letter carrier U.S. Postal Service 1981—. Named outstanding 4-H agt. Yankton (S.D.) Daily Press, 1979. Mem. Nat. Assn. 4-H Agts., Am. Home Econs. Assn., Nat. Assn. Extension Home Economists, Minne Coujou Sioux Cultural Soc., Jaycees. Democrat. Baptist. Club: Order of Eastern Star. Home and Office: 724 N St Rock Springs WY 82901

PERKINS, MARTHA LOUISE, banker; b. Elkton, Ky., Aug. 24, 1915; d. Sterling and Sallie (Chesnut) P.; student public schs., Elkton. With Elkton Bank & Trust Co., 1937—, past pres., now chmn. bd., dir. Trustee, Petrie Meml. Methodist Episcopal Ch.; treas. City of Elkton, 17 yrs.; treas. Todd County Bd. Edn., 25 yrs. Address: Elkton Bank Trust Co Public Sq Elkton KY 42220

PERKINS, NANCY JANE, indsl. designer; b. Phila., Nov. 5, 1949; d. Gordon Osborne and Martha Elizabeth (Keichline) P.; student Ohio U., 1967-68; B.F.A. in Indsl. Design, U. Ill., Champaign, 1972. Indsl. designer Peterson Bednar Assos., Evanston, Ill., 1972-74, Deschamps Mills Assos., Bartlett, Ill., 1974-75; dir. graphic design Cameo Container Corp., Chgo., 1975-76; indsl. designer Sears Roebuck & Co., Chgo., 1977—; planning, devel. and design cons. for products, graphics and packaging programs, 1972—; instr. grad. design Seminar U. Ill. at Chgo. Circle, 1982; Keynote Speaker Soc. Automotive Engrs., 1980, Women in Design, 1982. Co-leader Cadette troop DuPage County council Girl Scouts U.S.A., 1978-79. Recipient Outstanding Alumni award U. Ill. Alumni Jour., 1981. Mem. Indsl. Designers Soc. Am. (treas. Chgo. chpt. 1977-79, vice chairperson chpt. 1979-80, chmn. 1981, dist. membership 1982, ann. conf. com. 1983; Kudos award 1978). Presbyterian. Patentee marine galley, 1974, auto battery, 1982. Home: 1926 Prairie Square 227 Schaumburg IL 60195 Office: BSC 23-23 D/817 Sears Tower Chicago IL 60684

PERKS, BARBARA ANN MARCUS, psychologist; b. Wilson, Pa., July 1, 1937; d. Alfred M. and Lillian (Reibman) Marcus; B.S., Pa. State U., 1959; M.A., Columbia U., 1963; cert. in ednl. psychology Oxford (Eng.) U., 1965; postgrad. (Univ. fellow, Dr. MacKenzie Am. Alumni scholar), U. B.C., 1976—; m. Anthony Manning Perks, Sept. 9, 1963. Tchr. gifted Hamden (Conn.) Sch. Dist., 1959-62; reading cons. Oxfordshire County, Littlemore, Eng., 1964-65; sch. psychologist Vancouver (B.C., Can.) Sch. Bd., 1972-76; supr. student tchrs. U. B.C., Vancouver, 1977-78, cons. Research Center, 1978-79, ednl. psychologist, child and family unit child psychiatry Health Scis. Centre Hosp., 1979—, lectr., 1977—. Recipient Can. Daus. League award; Provincial Council of B.C. award, 1981, U. B.C. award, 1980; U. B.C. summer scholar, 1982; cert. psychologist, B.C. Mem. Am. Psychol. Assn., B.C. Psychol. Assn., Assn. Humanistic Psychology, Nat. Assn. Sch. Psychology, Am. Ednl. Research, N.Am. Soc. Adlerian Psychology, Am. Orthopsychiat. Assn., Mortar Bd., Pi Sigma Alpha, Pi Lambda Theta, Kappa Delta Pi. Clubs: Figure Skating (Vancouver, B.C., New Haven, Conn., Allentown, Pa.). Author research papers. Home: 4570 Glenwood Ave North Vancouver BC V7R 4G5 Canada Office: U BC Dept Ednl Psychology Faculty of Edn 2125 Main Mall U BC Vancouver BC V6T 1Z5 Canada

PERLMAN, EILEEN ELEANOR, civic worker, former restaurant chain exec.; b. Chgo., Oct. 31, 1935; d. Bennett Viggo and Eleanor Lucille Christensen; student Northwestern U., nights 1954, Patricia Stevens Modeling Sch., 1955, Liberty Baptist Coll., 1977-79; m. Clifford Seely Perlman, July 30, 1959 (div. 1969); children—Jason, Clayton, Ivy. Co-founder, Lum's, Inc., Miami Beach, Fla., 1958; fin. sec., treas. Christian Womens Club, South Fla., 1973-75; visitation chmn. Granada Presbyn. Ch., 1973-75, circle chmn., 1978; active Protect Our Children, Anti-ERA campaign, ARC, Women for Responsible Legis. and Polit. Action (dir., corr. sec. 1979-80), Floridians Against Casino Takeover, Christian Broadcasting Network, Inc., 700 Club, Old Time Gospel Hour, Faith Partners, Moral Majority; mem. transp. com., scholarship fund com. Westminster Christian Sch.; com. mem. Jews for Jesus; nat. adv. com. Am. Security Council; program chmn. Fla. So. dist. Concerned Women for Am., 1980—; sustaining mem. Republican Party; sponsor Rep. Victory Fund, 1980. Mem. U.S. Lawn Tennis Assn., U.S. Figure Skating Assn. (dir. Miami chpt.), Interfaith Comm. Against Blasphemy, Am. Bridge Club, Internat. Platform Assn., Nat. Fedn. Rep. Women. Republican. Presbyterian. Clubs: Century (Miami Christian U.); California (N. Miami). Home: 6401 Cellini St Coral Gables FL 33146

PERLMAN, MARILYN COHEN, artist; b. Lynn, Mass., Oct. 1, 1925; d. Eli A. and Bessie (Beevman) Cohen; B.A., Smith Coll., 1945; M.S., Simmons Sch. Social Work, Boston, 1947; m. Jack Perlman, June 20, 1948 (dec. 1969); children—Meg, Adam, Noah, Beth, Adam (dec.). One women shows: Spectrum Gallery, N.Y.C., 1969, Fourteen Sculptors Gallery, 1973, Bodley Gallery, 1980; group shows include: Jersey City Mus., 1971, Fourteen Sculptors Gallery, 1972-76, Mus. Modern Art, 1973-75, Bklyn. Mus., 1975, Women's Inter Art Center, 1976; represented in permanent collections: Harvard Smithsonian Obs., Rose Art Mus., Brandeis U., Fogg Art Mus., Harvard U. Recipient Goldie Paley award, 1978. Mem. Artists Equity Assn. N.Y., Art Students League N.Y.C. Democrat. Jewish. Home: 20 W 64th St New York NY 10023 Office: 106 E 19th St New York NY 10003

PERLMAN, SUSAN GAIL, orgn. exec.; b. N.Y.C., Dec. 29, 1950; d. Philip and Pearl Perlman; ed. Hunter Coll., N.Y.C., 1967-71. Copywriter, Blaine Thompson Advt., N.Y.C., 1968-71; copywriter J.C. Penney Co., N.Y.C., 1971-72; exec. info. officer Jews for Jesus, San Francisco, Co., 1972—, also editor Issues mag.; speaker, cons. in field; asst. coordinator Lausanne Com. Task Force Jewish Evangelism; mem. Internat. Council Bibl. Inerrancy, Congress on Bible Com.; del. Conservative Baptist Assn. Am. Democrat. Baptist. Author articles in field. Office: 60 Haight St San Francisco CA 94102

PERLOFF, MARJORIE GABRIELLE, educator; b. Vienna, Austria, Sept. 28, 1931; d. Maximilian and Ilse (Schueller) Mintz; B.A., Oberlin Coll., 1953; M.A., Cath. U., 1956, Ph.D., 1965; m. Joseph K. Perloff, July 31, 1953; children—Nancy, Carey. Asst. prof. English, Cath. U., Washington, 1965-68; asso. prof. U. Md., College Park, 1968-71, asso. prof., 1971-73, prof., 1973-77; Florence Scott prof. English and comparative lit. U. So. Calif., Los Angeles, 1977—; cons. Nat. Endowment for Humanities, 1978. John Simon Guggenhein fellow, 1981-82. Mem. MLA (mem. exec. council), AAUP, Am. Comparative Lit. Assn., Phi Beta Kappa. Author: Rhyme and Meaning in the Poetry of Yeats, 1970; The Poetic Art of Robert Lowell, 1973; Frank O'Hara Poet Among Painters,

1977; The Poetics of Indeterminacy: Rimbaud to Cage, 1981. Home: 1467 Amalfi Dr Pacific Palisades CA 90272 Office: Taper Hall of the Humanities Dept of English Univ of So Calif Los Angeles CA 90089-0345

PERLOV, DADIE, orgn. exec.; b. N.Y.C., June 8, 1929; d. Aaron and Anna Heitman; B.A., N.Y.U., 1950; postgrad., Vanderbilt U., 1973; m. Norman Perlov, May 29, 1950; children—Nancy, Jane, Amy. Exec. dir. Operation Open City, N.Y.C., 1962-64; dir. field services Nat. Council Jewish Women, Inc., N.Y.C., 1968-74, exec. dir., 1981—; exec. dir. N.Y. Library Assn., 1974-81. Mem. panel Sch. Bd. Dist. 26, 1967. Cert. assn. exec., 1978. Mem. N.Y. Soc. Assn. Execs. (dir. 1980-82, Exec. of Yr. 1980), Internat. Platform Assn., Am. Soc. Assn. Execs., Nat. Assembly Voluntary Health and Social Welfare Orgns. (dir. 1981-82), Internat. Council Library Assn. Execs. (v.p. 1979-81), Nat. Jewish Community Relations Council and Conf. of Pres., LWV (chpt. pres. 1960-62). Home: 262 Central Park W New York NY 10024 Office: Nat Council Jewish Women 15 E 26th St New York NY 10010

PERNALETE, PATRICIA BERRY, educator; b. Norman, Okla., Sept. 5, 1923; d. Fred Andrew and Margaret (Cochran) Berry; B.A., Oklahoma City U., 1962; M.A., U. Okla., 1967; m. Gaston Pernalete, Nov. 5, 1943; children—Franz F., Margaret Pernalete Youngblood. Tchr. English as a second lang. Creole Oil Co., Venezuela, S.Am., 1950-52; tchr. John Marshall High Sch., 1962-65; asst. prof. Spanish Okla. Bapt. U., Shawnee, 1965—; cons. Behavioral Objectives Seminar, U. Okla., 1968; cons. curriculum re-evaluation com. for fgn. langs. Okla. State Dept. Edn., 1967-68. Recipient research devel. award Okla. Consortium, 1968. Mem. Am. Assn. Tchrs. Spanish and Portguese (chpt. pres.), Okla. Fgn. Lang. Assn. (dir.), Am. Council Fgn. Lang. Tchrs. (dir.), AAUP, Baptist. Club: Altrusa (Pres. 1977) (Shawnee, Okla.). Author: The Latin American Hero of Rómulo Gallegos, 1968; translator short stories by Uslar Pietri, biography of Gumersindo Torres by Aníbal Martínez.

PERNELL, BETSY LEONARD, educator; b. Franklin County, N.C., June 26, 1931; d. Quinton Samuel and Sallie Louise (Wood) Leonard; A.A., Louisburg Coll., 1956; A.B., Atlantic Christian Coll., 1957; postgrad. East Carolina U., 1961; m. John Cleveland Pernell, Sept. 3, 1950; children—John Cleveland, Rebecca Ellen. Formerly tchr. Bunn (N.C.) High Sch.; now prof. bus. Louisburg (N.C.) Coll. Mem. Franklin County Commn., 1970-78; active Louisburg LWV. Mem. Nat. Bus. Tchrs. Assn., N.C. Bus. Tchrs. Assn., Delta Kappa Gamma. Democrat. Baptist. Home: Rt 5 Box 100 Louisburg NC 27549 Office: Box 796 Louisburg College Louisburg NC 27549

PERNICE, SUSANNE, educator; b. Warren, Ohio, Apr. 16, 1930; d. Chester Anthony and Mary (Lazor) P.; B.S., Kent State U., 1955; M.A., U. Minn., 1959; Ph.D., U. Iowa, 1972. Tchr. pub. schs., Youngstown, Ohio, 1955-58; instr. Pa. State U., 1959-65; asst. prof. phys. edn. Ind. State U., Terre Haute, 1965-71, assoc. prof., 1972-77, prof., 1977—, coach field hockey, 1968—. Mem. Coll. Frat. Editors Assn., U.S. Field Hockey Assn., AAHPER and Dance, Ind. Assn. Health, Phys. Edn., Recreation and Dance, Assn. Intercollegiate Athletics for Women (Midwest regional rep.), Delta Psi Kappa (nat. pres. 1980-82). Office: Dept Phys Edn Ind State U Terre Haute IN 47809

PERNICK, SANDRA ROSE, educator; b. Chgo., Oct. 7, 1942; d. Karl and Diana (Matlin) Witt; B.A., Roosevelt U., Chgo., 1964; m. Steven L. Pernick, Oct. 11, 1964; children—Kevin Michael, Kelly Andrew. Corr., Time, Inc., 1964-66; tchr. emotionally handicapped children Chgo. pub. schs., 1966-68; pres. bd. dirs. Orchard Village Skokie, Ill., 1976—. Adviser Assn. Spl. Edn., Skokie; mem. mental health com. Nat. Council Jewish Women. Mem. Nat., Ill. assns. retarded citizens. Home and Office: 433 Sunset Dr Wilmette IL 60091

PERNICONE, MARGARET MARY, advt. agy. exec.; b. Omaha, Jan. 10, 1951; d. I.J. and Marian (Bergman) P.; student Ariz. State U., 1969-71. Copywriter/producer Bozell & Jacobs, Inc., Omaha, 1972-76; freelance copywriter/producer, Omaha, 1976-77; sr. copywriter/producer Bernstein/Rein, Kansas City, Mo., 1977-78; sr. copywriter/broadcaster prodn. mgr. Barrett-Yehle, Kansas City, 1978-81; v.p., creative dir. Smith & Yehle, Inc., Kansas City, 1981—; tchr. advt. Nettleton Bus. Coll., Omaha, 1975-76. Recipient numerous advt. awards. Mem. Nat. Assn. Female Execs. Office: 3217 Broadway Kansas City MO 64111

PERRAULT, ANNA HEMER, librarian; b. Biloxi, Miss., Sept. 28, 1944; d. Harold Henry and Margie (Williams) Hemer; B.A., U. Miss., 1965; M.A. in English Lit., La. State U., 1967, M.S. in Library Sci., 1969; m. Joseph A. Perrault, Jr., Dec. 31, 1966; children—Jean-Paul, André. Mem. staff La. State U. Library, Baton Rouge, 1969—, humanities bibliographer, 1976—; mem. Arts and Humanities Council Baton Rouge; sec. Friends La. State U. Library, 1980—. Grantee, La. Com. Humanities. Mem. ALA, Assn. Coll. and Research Libraries, La. Library Assn., MLA, Phi Kappa Phi, Beta Phi Mu. Roman Catholic. Clubs: La. State U. Faculty, La. State U. Women's Faculty. Author papers in field. Home: 5609 Valley Forge St Baton Rouge LA 70808 Office: La State U Library Baton Rouge LA 70803

PERRET, NELL FOSTER, artist; b. Bklyn., Dec. 22, 1916; d. Charles Andrew and Ethel (Churchwell) Foster; student Pratt Inst., 1934-36, Art Students League, 1936-38; m. George Albert Perret, June, 1947; children—Gabriel Aime, Nellie Maude Perret-Pomerance. Exhibited in group shows Riverside Mus., N.Y.C., also major mus.; adj. prof. Southampton Coll., 1968-70. Mem. N.Y. Artists Equity, Audubon Artists (treas. 1977-81), Guild Hall, N.J. Soc. Artists and Sculptors, Westbeth Graphics Workshop. Author, illustrator: Little Seal, 1943; illustrator: Tales of Mohawk, 2 vols., 1968. Address: 463 West St Apt 628A Westbeth New York NY 10014

PERRETTI, SERENA, fed. magistrate; b. Passaic, N.J., Oct. 3, 1928; d. Peter N. and Jessie (Ingram) P.; A.B., Vassar Coll., 1948; J.D. with honors, Rutgers U., 1954; postgrad. dept. religious studies Seton Hall U., 1982; m. Richard S. Benson, Mar. 27, 1962; children—Thane, Serena, Peter. Admitted to N.J. bar, 1955; individual practice law, Passaic, 1955-76; U.S. magistrate, Newark, 1976—; panelist, participant seminars. Sec., Passaic County Ethics Com., 1969, mem., 1969-71, 75-76; mem. Passaic Bd. Edn., 1956-59. Mem. Passaic County Bar Assn. (sec. 1976, trustee 1973-76), Assn. Fed. Bar N.J., Nat. Assn. Women Judges. Republican. Mem. United Ch. of Christ. Mng. editor Rutgers Law Rev., 1953, editor-in-chief, 1954; contbr. articles to profl. publs. Office: US Court House and Post Office Newark NJ 07101

PERRIN, ELIZABETH ANN, glass co. ofcl.; b. Cleve., Apr. 16, 1951; d. Alfred Emerson and Monzell (Moore) Jackson; grad. cum laude Point Park Coll., Pitts., 1975; m. David T. P. Perrin, Aug. 25, 1973; children—Caleb, Quianee. Account rep. Gen. Electric Co., Boston, 1975-77; career counselor/coordinator programs Tom Skinner Assos., Howard U., Washington, 1978-80; dir. career counseling and placement Engine Co. No. 2, an ednl. orgn., Washington, 1980-81; minority and women program specialist Corning Glass Works (N.Y.), 1981—. Adv., NAACP Youth Group, Elmira, N.Y.; chairperson com. for social justice Friendship Baptist Ch., Corning. Recipient Cleve. Scholarship award, 1969. Mem. Soc. Black Profls. (mem. com. profl. image), Black Career Women, Soc. Women Engrs. (asso.), Am. Personnel and Guidance Assn., Am. Soc. Personnel Adminstrn., Am. Soc. Tng. and Devel., Nat. Assn. Female Execs. Office: HP-CB-1 Corning NY 14831

PERRIN, ELLEN HAYS, coll. dean; b. Buckhannon, W.Va.; d. Charles Gilbert and Geraldine Sexton (Hays) P.; B.S. in Music Edn., Duquesne U., 1946; M.Edn., U. Pitts., 1952, Ph.D., 1974. Tchr. music West Mifflin (Pa.) Dist. Schs., 1947-61, counselor, 1961-64; dean women Slippery Rock (Pa.) State Coll., 1965-70, asst. to v.p. for student affairs, 1970-72, dir. counseling and career services, 1972-74, dean students, 1974—; mem. supts. adv. com. West Mifflin Dist. Schs., 1955-60. Mem. steering com. Pitts. Fgn. Affairs Forum, 1959-60; mem. com. on edn. Pa. Gov.'s Commn. on Status of Women, 1965-66; mem. Pitts. Bicentennial Assembly, 1958-59. Mem. NEA, Pa. Edn. Assn. (pres. West Mifflin br. 1962-64, exec. com. west region 1963-64, v.p. assn. ind. sch. dists. Allegheny County 1963-64), AAUW (pres. Pitts. br. 1958-62, Pa. div. chmn. status of women 1962-63, chmn. cultural interests 1963-64, area rep. for edn. 1964-66, chmn. edn. projects for state div., chmn. topic of study 1967-69, fellowship award named in her honor 1970), Nat. (parliamentarian 1975-76, 77-78, nat. treas. 1981—), Pa. (parliamentarian 1969-72, 2d v.p. 1972-74, legis. chmn. 1976-78, pres. 1979-81), Western Pa. (sec. 1970-71) assns. women deans, adminstrs. and counselors, DAR (conservation chmn. local chpt. 1959-62, chpt. chaplain 1963-65), Nat. Soc. U.S. Daus. of 1812, Nat. Soc. Daus. Colonial Wars, Daus. Am. Colonists, Nat. Soc. Women Descs. of Ancient and Hon. Arty. Co., Colonial Dames XVII Century (bylaws chmn. local chpt. 1978-80, state corr. sec. 1981—, 2d v.p. local chpt. 1981-83) Nat., Pa. (membership chmn. 1972) assns. student personnel adminstrs., Doctoral Assn. U. Pitts., Phi Delta Kappa. Presbyterian. Clubs: South Hills Coll. (Pitts.); Women's (chmn. edn. com. 1970-72) (Slippery Rock); Zonta Internat. (organizing pres. Slippery Rock-New Wilmington-Grove City area 1980-81, parliamentarian dist. IV 1974-76); Order Eastern Star (Grove City, Pa.). Home: 140 Longue Vue Dr Mt Lebanon Pittsburgh PA 15228 Office: Slippery Rock State Coll Slippery Rock PA 16057

PERRIN, SARAH ANN, lawyer; b. Neoga, Ill., Dec. 13, 1904; d. James Lee and Bertha Frances (Baker) Figenbaum; LL.B., George Washington U., 1941, J.D., 1964; m. James Frank Perrin, Dec. 24, 1926. Admitted to D.C. bar, 1942; asso. atty. Mabel Walker Willebrandt, law office, Washington, 1941-42; atty. various fed. housing agys., 1942-69, asst. gen. counsel FHA, Washington, 1959-60, asst. gen. counsel HUD, Washington, 1960-69; sec. Nat. Housing Conf., Washington, 1970-79; research cons. housing and urban devel., Palmyra, Va., 1970—; acting sec. Nat. Housing Research Council, Washington, 1973—; bd. dirs. Nat. Housing Conf., 1972—. Trustee Found. for Coop. Housing, 1975-82. Mem. ABA, Fed. Bar Assn., Women's Bar Assn. D.C. (pres. 1959-60), Nat. Assn. Women Lawyers, Fluvanna County Hist. Soc. (pres. 1973-75), Phi Delta Delta (internat. pres. 1955-57) Presbyterian (div. Presbytery Mission, Blue Ridge Presbytery 1978-79). Club: Order Eastern Star. Home: Solitude Plantation Palmyra VA 22963

PERRINE, REBECCA ANN, retail exec.; b. Lyons, Ga., Dec. 14, 1934; d. Julius Russell and Martha Inez (Horton) Clark; student Accounting Manatee Jr. Coll., 1960-62; m. Gary Raymond Perrine, June 12, 1962; 1 son, Raymond Clark. Acct., Electro Mech. Systems, Titusville, Fla., 1963-66; head internal acctg. dept., Kelley, Drye, Newhall, McGuiness & Warren, 1967-70; co-owner, mgr. Perrine Mobile Homes Sales, Naples, Fla., 1972—, Palm River Mobile Home Park, Naples, 1971—, Chokoloskee Island Park (Fla.), 1972—, Shady Acres Travel Park, Estero, Fla., 1977—, Harmony Shores Mobile Home Port, also Bullfrog Creek Mobile Home Park, Gibsonton, Fla., 1981—. Republican. Home: 2470 Tarpon Rd Naples FL 33942 Office: 3078 Tamiami Trail S Naples FL 33942

PERRUZZI, GLORIA ANN, food cons.; b. Washington, Feb. 9, 1946; d. Paul Raymond and Catherine Loretta (Sweeney) Perruzzi; student Hunter Coll., 1971-73, Queensboro Community Coll., 1973-75. Passenger service agt. United Airlines, N.Y.C., Newark, and San Francisco, 1966—, friendship service dir. LaGuardia Airport, N.Y.C., 1974-76; pres., owner, founder Cuisine Elegante, Foster City, Calif., 1980—. Mem. Nat. Assn. Female Exec., Am. Bus. Women's Assn. Republican. Roman Catholic. Home and office: 865 Cabot Ln Foster City CA 94404

PERRY, ANNE MARIE LITCHFIELD, educator; b. LaJunta, Colo., May 20, 1943; d. Robert Silas and Anne (Kennedy) Hovey; B.S. in Edn., Drake U., 1966; M.A., U. Tex., Austin, 1969; Ph.D., Tex. A&M U., 1977; m. Franklin Haile Perry, Dec. 21, 1968; children—Kristina Marie, Tad Kennedy. Grade sch. tchr., San Antonio, 1966-67, Austin, 1967-68; research asso. Research and Devel. Center, U. Tex., Austin, 1968; grad. asst., instr. Tex. A&M U., 1969-70; kindergarten tchr., 1970-72; instr. U. St. Thomas, 1973-74; spl. edn. tchr., supr. Cypress-Fairbanks Ind. Sch. Dist., Houston, 1974-77, supr. gifted/talented, bilingual, English lang. devel. programs, 1977-80; mem. adj. grad. faculty U. Houston, 1979—; lower sch. dir. curriculum and ednl. resources Kinkaid Sch., Houston, 1980—; cons. gifted/talented edn., 1978—. Named Tchr. of Yr., Hancock Elem. Sch., 1975. Mem. Nat. Assn. Gifted Children, Tex. Assn. for Gifted and Talented, Houston Area Assn. Gifted and Talented, Assn. Supervision and Curriculum Devel., Tex. Assn. Planning, Evaluation and Research, Puppeteers of Am., Greater Houston Puppetry Guild. Presbyterian.

PERRY, BLANCHE BELLE, phys. therapist; b. New Bedford, Mass., Sept. 2, 1929; d. Joseph Rudolph and Beatrice Andrews; B.S., Ithaca (N.Y.) Coll., 1951; M.A., Assumption Coll., Worcester, Mass., 1977; m. Louis Perry, Nov. 26, 1953; (dec. 1980); children—Marcia, Susan, Tracey, Evelyn. Office and hosp. phys. therapist, Mass. and N.Y., 1961-65; dir. rehab. services St. Luke's Hosp., New Bedford, 1967—; chmn. public edn. Greater New Bedford area chpt. Am. Cancer Soc., 1980; profl. adv. com. Vis. Nurse Assn. Wareham, 1980; corporator New Bedford Five Cents Savs. Bank./Chmn. Mattapoisett Sch. Com., 1970; vice chmn. Mass. Sch. Commn. Area IV, 1972-75; sec. Old Colony Regional Vocat. Sch. Com., 1973—; trustee Abner Pease Scholarship Found.; bd. dirs. New Bedford YWCA. Grantee Elks Nat. Found., 1965. Mem. Am. Phys. Therapy Assn., Nat. Rehab. Adminstrs. Assn., Wareham Bus. and Profl. Women's Club, Delta Kappa Gamma. Republican. Club: Mattapoisett Women's. Home: 41 Aucoot Rd Mattapoisett MA 02739 Office: 101 Page St New Bedford MA 02740

PERRY, CAROLE JOAN, mfg. co. exec.; b. Bklyn., Aug. 12, 1942; d. Allen and Ruth (Dworkin) Marcus; B.A., Bklyn. Coll., 1964; M.S., Richmond Coll., 1974; m. Lawrence Perry, Aug. 29, 1966; children—Jeffrey, Lori. Tchr., Public Sch. 244, Bklyn., 1954, Gladstone St. Sch., Azusa, Calif., 1966-68, sci. enrichment tchr., 1967-68; tchr. Public Sch. 22, S.I., N.Y., 1972; v.p. Avant-Guard Devices, Bklyn., 1972—, Rapidcircuit, Inc., 1972—, also dir. product mktg.; v.p., sec. Designalarm, Inc., 1982—; sec. Microtech Industries, Bklyn., 1982—. electronics tchr. S.I. Public Schs., 1982—. Leader, Brownies, S.I., 1976-77. Mem. Am. Radio Relay League. Club: S.I. Tennis. Author tech. articles on energy saving devices. Home: 10 Berglund Ave Staten Island NY 10314 Office: 5721 18th Ave Brooklyn NY 11204

PERRY, CARRIE SAXON, state legislator; b. Hartford, Conn.; d. Mabel Saxon; student Howard U. Exec. dir. Amistad House, Inc., Hartford, 1971—; mem. Conn. Ho. of Reps., asst. minority leader, 1980—. Mem. Legis. Black Caucus, Conn. Caucus Black Women for Polit. Action. Club: Greater Hartford Black Democratic. Office: 5 Clark St Hartford CT 06120

PERRY, C(ONSTANCE) ELEANOR, market research exec.; b. Boston, Sept. 18, 1947; d. Dolan Ray and Constance Eleanor (Krancer) P.; B.A., Mary Washington Coll., 1969; M.B.A., Pepperdine U., 1980. Sr. research asso. Behavior Sci. Corp., Los Angeles, 1971-73; project dir. Ogilvy & Mather Advt., Los Angeles, 1973-74; research analyst Max Factor, Hollywood, Calif., 1974-76; market research project mgr. Nissan Motor Corp., Carson, Calif., 1976-82; consumer research mgr. Mattel Toys, Hawthorne, Calif., 1982—. Vol. coordinator Los Angeles White House Advance Office, 1976. Mem. Am. Mktg. Assn. (dir. So. Calif. chpt. 1978-82, seminar chmn. 1982, program chmn. 1978-80, chmn. membership analysis com. 1976-77, chmn. membership survey 1976-77), Women in Bus. of Los Angeles. Club: Mensa. Office: Mattel Toys 5150 Rosecrans Ave Hawthorne CA 90250

PERRY, CYNTHIA LEE, nurse; b. Madison, Wis., Mar. 13, 1953; d. Dan Ervin Oliver and Marcia Mae (Songer) Moore; A.S., Ind. Central U., 1974; student Ball State U., 1981—; m. John Junior Perry, June 24, 1973; 1 dau., Melissa Ann. Staff nurse pediatrics Community Hosp., Anderson, Ind., 1974-75, intensive and coronary care unit, 1975-77; in-service dir. New Castle (Ind.) Healthcare Ctr., 1977-78, dir. nursing 1978-79; staff nurse St. John's Med. Center, Anderson, Ind., 1979-81, asst. dir. nursing service, 1981—. Mem. Golden Key Nat. Honor Soc. Office: 2015 Jackson St Anderson IN 46014

PERRY, ELYCE DORATHY, med. technologist; b. Chgo., Oct. 18, 1945; d. Roy Earl and Dorathy Mary (Ziegler) Hall; B.S., Coll. St. Francis, Joliet, Ill., 1967; m. Allan E. Perry, Nov. 21, 1970; children—Mara Élan, Max Joshua. Bench technologist St. James Hosp., Chicago Heights, Ill., 1967-69; mem. staff St. Francis Hosp., Blue Island, Ill., 1968—, chem. supr., 1972-73, tech. supr., 1973—; saleswoman McNulty Real Estate, 1979—. tchr. immunology, 1971-72, 73-77. Active local Girl Scouts U.S.A. Mem. Am. Soc. Clin. Pathologists. Roman Catholic. Home: 2505 Burr Oak St Blue Island IL 60406 Office: 12935 Gregory St Blue Island IL 60406

PERRY, EMMA BRADFORD, educator; b. Hodge, La., Dec. 25, 1942; d. Ibe and Mattie Bradford; B.S., Grambling State U., 1965; M.S. in L.S., Atlanta U., 1967; Ed.S., Western Mich. U., 1974; m. Huey L. Perry, Aug. 26, 1972; children—David, Jeff. Head librarian Sevier Elem. Sch., Ferriday, La., 1965-66; instr., coordinator library edn. program Grambling State U., 1967-70; head br. library Evanston (Ill.) Pub. Library, 1972-76; asst. prof., head circulation div. Tex. A&M U. Library, College Station, 1977—. Bd. dirs. Brazos Girls Club, 1980-82, v.p., 1978-80. Martin Luther King grantee, 1970-71. Mem. ALA, Tex. Library Assn., Tex. Assn. Coll. Tchrs., So. Conf. Afro-Am. Studies, Beta Phi Mu, Alpha Kappa Alpha. Baptist. Office: Head Circulation Division Texas A&M University Library College Station TX 77843

PERRY, EMMA NANCY, postal service ofcl.; b. Little Rock, Dec. 15, 1937; d. Levi Steven and Mildred (Smith) Overall; student Lincoln U., Jefferson City, Mo., 1956-57, U. Ark., Little Rock, 1972-73; B.A., Philander Smith Coll., Little Rock, 1975; postgrad. U. Ark., 1980-81; children—Michael Andre, Reginald Louis. Accounting clk. gen. office, acting housing mgr. Little Rock Housing Authority, 1962-65; distbn. clk.-career, job instr. mail processing unit Little Rock Postal Service, 1966-69, distbn. clk.-machine operator, acting operator trainer-mail processing unit, 1969-73, Postal Employment Devel. Center tng. technician employee and labor relations unit, 1973—, 204B detailed acting supr. customer services and collections and delivery units, 1980, publicity mgr., resource person EEO adv. council, 1981—, chmn. adv. com. Adv. bd. Urban League Guild Greater Little Rock, 1982-84; supporting mem. Arkansans for the Arts, 1981—. Recipient Quality Step Increase award Little Rock Postal Service, 1974. Mem. Nat. Assn. Female Execs., Nat. Tchrs. Assn., Ark. Tchrs. Assn., Philander Smith Coll. Alumni Assn., Delta Sigma Theta. Mem. A.M.E. Ch. Home: 1123 Appianway Little Rock AR 72204 Office: US Postal Service Postal Employment Devel Tng Room 201 Gen Mail Facility North Little Rock AR 72231

PERRY, GERI, hosp. adminstr.; b. Vancouver, Wash., June 18, 1945; d. Hazel G. Maloney; B.S., San Francisco State U., 1966; B.A., St. Mary's Coll., 1981; m. Michael W. Perry, July 2, 1975; 1 son, Sebastian. Ward clk. St. Luke's Hosp., San Francisco, 1970-74; admissions rep. Community Hosp., Santa Cruz, Calif., 1974-76, supr. admissions, 1976, now dir. admissions; cons. in field. Mem. Nat., Calif. assns. hosp. admitting mgrs. Orthodox Christian. Club: Valley Gardens Golf. Home: PO Box 938 Ben Lomond CA 95005 Office: 610 Frederick St Santa Cruz CA 95062

PERRY, GWENDOLYN JUSTICE, govt. agy. adminstr.; b. Durham, N.C.; d. Mack B. and Lola M. Justice; B.S., N.C. Agrl. and Tech. Coll.; M.A., U. Bridgeport (Conn.). Tchr., Stamford (Conn.) Pub. Schs., 1967-71; contract officer N.Y. State Div. Substance Abuse Services, N.Y.C., 1977—. Vice chmn. bd. trustees Antioch Bapt. Ch., Corona, N.Y. Mem. NAACP, Women's Athletic Assn. Baptist.

PERRY, JACQUELINE CHERYL, govt. ofcl.; b. Bronx, N.Y., Aug. 29, 1947; d. James Edward and Jessie Mae (Footmon) P.; B.A., CUNY, 1970; M.S., U. Utah, 1976. Mgmt. trainee Gen. Services Adminstrn., N.Y.C., 1970-71, inventory mgmt. specialist, 1971-72, equal opportunity specialist, 1972-78, supervisory equal opportunity specialist, 1978-79, regional EEO officer, 1979, equal opportunity specialist central office, Washington, 1979—, acting dir. complaints, compliance and investigation div. Office of Civil Rights, 1980—; supervisory equal opportunity specialist Dept. Labor, Office of Fed. Contract Compliance Programs, N.Y.C., 1978-79; equal opportunity staff officer U.S. Army Res., 1977—. NSF grantee, 1969. Mem. Am. Soc. Public Adminstrn., Conf. Minority Public Adminstrs., Am. Personnel and Guidance Assn., Assn. Non-White Concerns in Personnel and Guidance, Res. Officers Assn. (life), Federally Employed Women, Inc. (regional coordinator 1975), WAC Mus. Soc. (life), Nat. Council Negro Women, Inc., Fed. Mgrs. Assn., Nat. Council Career Women. Office: Gen Services Adminstrn Bldg 18 and F Sts Washington DC 20405

PERRY, JEAN LOUISE, educator; b. Richland, Wash., May 13, 1950; d. Russell S. and Sue W. Perry; B.S., Miami U., Oxford, Ohio, 1972; M.S., U. Ill., Urbana, 1973, Ph.D., 1976. Cons. ednl. placement office U. Ill., 1973-75, adminstrv. intern Coll. Applied Life Studies, 1975-76, asst. dean, 1976-77, asso. dean, 1978-81; asst. prof. dept. phys. edn., 1976-81; asso. prof. phys. edn. San Francisco State U., 1981—, chmn. dept., 1981—. Named to excellent tchr. list, U. Ill., 1973-79. Mem. AAHPER and Dance (fellow research consortium), Am. Assn. Higher Edn., Am. Ednl. Research Assn., Nat. Assn. Phys. Edn. in Higher Edn., Nat. Assn. Women Deans, Adminstrs. and Counselors, Nat. Assn. for Girls and Women in Sports (guide coordinator), Delta Psi Kappa, Phi Delta Kappa. Home: 370 Park St San Francisco CA 94110 Office: San Francisco State U 1600 Holloway Ave San Francisco CA 94132

PERRY, KATHARINE BROWNE, agrl. meteorologist; b. Washington, Mar. 19, 1952; d. Arthur Vincent and Mary Elizabeth (King) Browne; B.S., Pa. State U., 1974, M.S., 1976, Ph.D., 1979; m. Steven Gerard Perry, Oct. 2, 1976; children—Matthew Thomas, James Arthur. Research asst. Pa. State U., State College, 1979-80; extension specialist N.C. State U., Raleigh, 1980-81, asst. prof., 1982—. Mem. Am. Meteorol. Soc., Am. Soc. for Hort. Sci., Nat. Weather Assn., Sigma Xi, Alpha Zeta, Gamma Sigma Delta. Home: 1226 Kilmory Dr Cary NC 27511 Office: 123 Kilgore Raleigh NC 27607

PERRY, KATHRYN MARGARET, security exec.; b. Milw., Aug. 15, 1950; d. Lewis Gordon and Margaret Joyce (Bryner) P.; B.A., U. Wis., Green Bay, 1976; M.A., Pepperdine U., 1979. Commd. 2d lt. U.S. Army, 1968, advanced through grades to 1st lt., 1980; platoon leader 511th Mil. Police Corps, Ft. Dix, N.J., 1976-77; exec. comdr. 532d Mil. Police Corps, Ft. Dix, 1977-78; detachment comdr. 759th Mil. Police Corps, Ft. Dix, 1978-79; 1st lt. USAR; supr. security Kodak Co., Rochester, N.Y., 1979—. Religious edn. tchr. St. Joseph's Parish, Penfield, N.Y.; recorder Northeast Region Exec. Com., Diocese of Rochester. Decorated Army Commendation medal with 2 oak leaf clusters, Cert. protection profl. Am. Soc. Indsl. Security. Mem. Nat. Inst. Law Enforcement and Criminal Justice, Nat. Assn. Female Execs. Democrat. Home: 718 Shanlee Dr Webster NY 14580 Office: 901 Elm Grove Rd Rochester NY 14650

PERRY, LINDA MAE, acct.; b. Yakima, Wash., Nov. 21, 1943; d. William P. and Bonnie J. (McCord) Broom; B.A. in Sociology, Wash. State U., 1965; postgrad. U. Calif., Berkeley, 1964-65, De Paul U., Chgo., 1967-69; M.Bus. Taxation, U. So. Calif., 1978. Tax technician IRS, San Francisco, 1967, Chgo., 1967-69, appellate auditor, 1969, tax technician, Seattle, 1969-71, appellate auditor, Seattle, 1971-74, chief appellate audit sect., Los Angeles, 1974-77, appeals officer, 1977-78; owner L.M. Perry, P.S., C.P.A., Seattle; guest lectr. various civic groups, TV, Chgo., 1967-69, Seattle, 1980, 82; instr. tax courses Edmonds Community Coll., Lynnwood, Wash., 1973, 79, Los Angeles, 1974-78, Pasadena, 1977, UCLA, 1976, U. Wash., 1980, Edmonds Community Coll., 1978-82. C.P.A., Wash. Mem. Am. Inst. C.P.A.s, Wash. Soc. C.P.A.s, Assn. Women C.P.A.s, IRS C.P.A.s (treas. 1976, v.p. 1977). Contbr. book chpts. on acctg. Office: 2150 N 107th St Seattle WA 98133

PERRY, MARGARET, librarian, writer; b. Cin., Nov. 15, 1933; d. Rufus Patterson and Elizabeth Munford (Anthony) P.; A.B., Western Mich. U., 1954; M.S.L.S., Cath. U. Am., 1959. Asst. dir. libraries for reader services U. Rochester (N.Y.), 1975-82, edn. librarian, 1970-75, asst. prof. English, 1972-75, asso. prof., 1975-82; dir. libraries Valparaiso U. (Ind.), 1982—; speaker profl. meetings; books include: A Bio-Bibliography of Countee P. Cullen 1903-1946, 1971; Silence to the Drums: A Survey of the Literature of the Harlem Renaissance, 1976; The Harlem Renaissance, an Annotated Bibliography and Commentary, 1982; asso. editor U. Rochester Library Bull., 1970-73; contbg. editor: Afro-Americans in New York Life and History, 1978; contbr. to What Black Librarians Are Saying, 1973; contbr. articles, stories and revs. to history and library jours., lit. jours. Former bd. dirs. Urban League Rochester. Recipient 1st prize Armed Forces Writers League Short Story Contest, 1965; 2d prize Frances Steloff Fiction Prize, 1968. Mem. ALA, Modern Lang. Assn. Democrat. Roman Catholic. Home: 1200 Wood St Valparaiso IN 46383 Office: 219 Moellering Library Valparaiso University Valparaiso IN 46383

PERRY, MARY JANE, oceanographer; b. N.Y.C., Mar. 30, 1948; d. William Joseph and Alice Margaret (Tierney) P.; B.A., Coll. New Rochelle (N.Y.), 1969; Ph.D., U. Calif., San Diego, 1974; m. Peter Jumars, 1976. Mem. faculty Washington U. Med. Sch., St. Louis, 1974-76, U. Wash., Seattle, 1976-80; oceanographer, program dir. astron., astomospheric, earth and ocean scis. NSF, 1980—. Mem. Am. Geophys. Union, Am. Soc. Limnology and Oceanography, AAAS, Am. Inst. Biol. Scis., Ecol. Soc. Am., Assn. Women in Sci. Editorial bd. Jour. Marine Research. Home: 13730 39th Ave NE Seattle WA 98125 Office: Ocean Scis Div NSF Washington DC 20550

PERRY, NANCY AMES NICHOLS, social services supr.; b. Salem, Mass., June 20, 1942; d. Richard Lesquereux and Mary (Wakefield) Nichols; B.S. in Phys. Edn. cum laude, U. Mass., 1964; M.Ed. in Counseling, Antioch U., 1980; m. Allan Robertson Perry, Aug. 7, 1969. Tchr. phys. edn. schs. in Mass. and Eng., 1964-68; social worker Mass. Dept. Public Welfare, Lawrence, 1969-73, homefinder, 1973-77, supr. social service, Beverly and Haverhill, 1977-80; family resource supr. Mass. Dept. Social Services, 1980—; mem. Gov. Mass. Task Force on Adoption; bd. dirs. Children's Aid and Family Soc., Haverhill, 1973-81, pres., 1978-80; tech. adv. bd. Mass. Adoption Resource Exchange, 1972. Mem. AAHPER, Nat. Assn. Social Workers, Mass. Social Workers Guild, New Eng. Homefinders Assn., Women's Sports Found., Mingra Softball League (pres. 1972-74), Georgetown Women's Bowling League (treas. 1969-79). Home: 809 Salem St Groveland MA 01834 Office: 200 Main St Haverhill MA 01830

PERRY, NANCY ESTELLE, psychologist; b. Pitts., Oct. 30, 1934; d. Simon Warren and Estelle Cecelia (Zaluski) Reichard; B.S., Ohio State U., 1956, M.A. in Psychology, 1969, Ph.D. edn. in Psychology (EPDA fellow), 1973; m. John Cleveland; children—Scott, Karen, Elaine. Nurse, various locations, 1956-63; sch. psychologist Public Schs. Columbus (Ohio), 1970-72; human devel. specialist Madison County (Ohio) Schs., 1972-75; pvt. practice clin. psychology, cons. psychology, Worthington, Ohio, 1975-80; tchr. U. Wis. Sch. Nursing, Milw., 1980—; pvt. practice with Milw. Devel. Center, 1980—. Ohio Dept. Edn. grantee, 1973-76. Mem. Am. Nurses Assn., Wis. Nurses Assn., Am. Psychol. Assn., Ohio Psychol. Assn., Orgnl. Devel. Network, Internat. Assn. Applied Social Scientists, Am. Assn. Marriage and Family Counselors. Home: 2210 Charter Mall Mequon WI 53092 Office: 1500 E Capital Dr Milwaukee WI 53211

PERRY, NANCY JO, investment co. exec.; b. Olean, N.Y., Dec. 12, 1931; d. Thomas Bronson and Doris Marjory (Bacon) White; student Gustavus Adolphus Coll.; grad. Bethesda Hosp. Sch. Nursing, St. Paul, 1952; m. Charles Robert Perry, Apr. 9, 1955; children—Elizabeth Perry Sewell, Charles Thomas, Nancy Marie. Asst. head nurse U. Colo. Gen. Hosp., 1953-55; co-owner, dir. Perry Gas Co., Perry Energy Co., Odessa, Tex., 1967-82; v.p. Perry Investments, Perry Found., 1982—; past sec.-treas. Perry Energy Co., Perry Gas Processors, Perry Gas Transmissions, Inc., PGP Gas Products, Inc., Rockies Oil and Gas Corp. Bd. dirs. Odessa Council on Alcoholism, Task Force on Women; pres. bd. dirs. West Tex. Pastoral Counseling Center. Presbyterian (elder). Home: 9 San Miguel Sq Odessa TX 79762 Office: 621 State National Plaza Odessa TX 79762

PERRY, SHIRLEY BIRD, univ. adminstr.; b. Stockdale, Tex., Aug. 18, 1936; d. Homer S. and Laura B. (Stevenson) Bird; B.S., U. Tex., 1958, M.A., 1967; m. Sam R. Perry, July 13, 1963. Program dir. Tex. Union, U. Tex., Austin, 1958-59, 60-73, dir. Tex. Union, 1973-76, asst. to pres., coordinator centennial program activities, 1979-81, v.p., coordinator centennial programs, 1981—; coordinator ednl. programs and services Assn. Coll. Unions Internat., 1976-79; tchr. Cajon Valley Ind. Sch. Dist., El Cajon, Calif., 1959-60; cons., lectr. in field. Mem. U. Tex. Pres.'s Assos. Mem. Assn. Coll. Unions Internat. (v.p. 1969-70, pres. 1972-73, chmn. ednl. program com. 1975-76, Butts-Whiting award 1976), Council Student Personnel Assns. in Higher Edn. (exec. com. 1971-75), Am. Coll. Personnel Assn., Am. Personnel and Guidance Assn., U. Tex. Ex-Students Assn. (council 1977—), U. Tex. Chancellor's Council, English Speaking Union. Democrat. Methodist. Contbr. articles to profl. publs. Home: 1906 Matthews Dr Austin TX 78703 Office: care Office of Pres U Tex at Austin Austin TX 78712

PERRY, SHIRLEY MAE, personnel service exec.; b. Houston, May 25, 1932; d. Raymond E. and Etta Mae (Davidson) Henry; student Brazosport Coll., 1970-77; m. Bryan L. Perry, June 28, 1952 (div.); children—Mary Lynn, Bryan Lamar III. Ins. clk. Adams & Porter Ins. Co., 1951-53; office mgr. Freeport Party Boats (Tex.), 1973-74; founder, owner, mgr., pres. Gulf Coast Employment Service, Freeport, 1974—; speaker in field sch. and civic groups. Active Domestic Violence Task Force; vol. Crisis Hotline, 1978; sec. Brazosport Youth Employment, 1981; v.p., mem. exec. com. Brazosport Fine Arts Council, 1982; v.p. Brazosport Music Theater, 1982; chmn. Drill Team Com., 1970; ch. choir dir., soloist, 1970, Sunday sch. tchr., dir. Bible Sch., 1959-67; sec. PTA, 1962; troop leader, cons., organizer South Tex. council Girl Scouts U.S.A., 1963-66; mem. Pres. Club, 1980-81. Mem. Tex. Assn. Personnel Cons., Houston Area Assn. Personnel Cons., Brazosport C. of C., Asso. Builders and Contractors, Freeport League. Presbyterian. Clubs: Bus. and Profl. Women's (pres. 1981, Woman of Yr. Dist. 3, Tex. Fedn. 1980), Soroptimist Internat. (corr. sec., 1982). Home: 19 Hickory Ct Richwood TX 77531 Office: 26A Brazosport Savings Center Freeport TX 77541

PERSIANO, PATRICIA ANN, real estate co. exec., broker; b. Niles, Ohio, Mar. 5, 1933; d. Jerome P. and Beatrice A. (Wingrove) Kramer; B.S., Fenn Coll., 1954; grad. Realtors Inst., 1972; m. George P. Persiano, Apr. 24, 1953; children—Geraldine A., George P., Kathleen A. Real estate sales asso. Hilltop Realty Inc., Cleve., 1967, mgr., asst. v.p., 1972-75, mgr., v.p., 1975—. Bd. dirs. S. Euclid-Lyndhurst LWV, 1959-66; sec. Cuyahoga County LWV, 1966-68, pres., 1968-70. Million dollar sales club award, 1970-79. Mem. Nat. Assn. Realtors, Ohio Assn. Realtors (trustee), Cleve. Area Bd. Realtors (chmn. grievance com.), Realtors Nat. Mktg. Inst. (instr.), Internat. Real Estate Fedn. Roman Catholic. Home: 6442 Foxboro Dr Mayfield Village OH 44143 Office: 5035 Mayfield Rd Cleveland OH 44124

PERSON, JOYCE HUMPHREYS, civic worker; b. Cleve., Apr. 18, 1936; d. Frederick Warwick and Dorothy Waid (Wray) Humphreys; student Monmouth Coll., 1954-55; m. Leland E. Person, June 24, 1969. Former chpt. officer PEO Sisterhood, Hinsdale, Ill; pres. Western Springs (Ill.) Garden Club; life mem. Women's Aux., Community Meml. Gen. Hosp., LaGrange, Ill.; mem. Naval Air. Sta. of Glenview Officers' Wives Clubs, Jr. Woman's Club Western Springs; dist. officer, dir. Garden Clubs of Ill., legis. officer, 1981-82, 3d v.p., 1982-84, also life mem.; chmn. Altar Guild, Union Ch. of Hinsdale, mem. bd. edn., 1959. Runner-up design competition for flag for Village of Western Springs, 1976. Republican. Home: 5028 Lawn Ave Western Springs IL 60558

PERSONETT, ANDREA GARNER, mktg. exec.; b. Atlanta, Feb. 4, 1949; d. Andrew Coatsworth and Betty Jean (Deckner) Garner; B.A., Fla. State U., 1970; 1 son, Erin Louis. Promotions dir. sta. WFSU TV, Tallahassee, 1968-69; writer, film editor Peter Barton Prodns., Tallahassee, 1968-71; producer, writer, promotions dir. KKTV, Colorado Springs, 1971-73; producer, writer Kohen & Williams Advt. Co., Colorado Springs, 1973-74; account exec., producer, writer Shockey-Hester Advt. Inc., Colorado Springs, 1974-77; dir. advt. Ridgewood Realty, Denver, 1977—; v.p. mktg. Mid-States Bank, Fidelity Bank & Trust, 1st Nat. Bank of Lakewood, Denver, 1979—. Recipient award Southeastern Art Dirs., 1970, Colo. Broadcasters, 1972, Pikes Peak Ad Fedn., 1973, 76, 77. mem. Nat. Bank Mktg. Assn., Denver Advt. Fedn. Contbr. articles to various publs. Home: 5841 Lowell Blvd Littleton CO 80123 Office: 6350 Coal Mine Rd Littleton CO 80123

PERSONS, PATRICIA NIVER, clothing mfg. co. exec.; b. Bennington, Vt., Oct. 4, 1927; d. Bertram John and Phyllis Woolsey (Shattuck) N.; B.A. in Sociology magna cum laude, Tex. Woman's U., Denton, 1949; M.A., 1951; m. Robert H. Persons, Sept. 8, 1951; children—David Eric, Amy Sarah. Instr. sociology Tex. Woman's U., 1949-51; personnel asst. Container Corp. Am., Ft. Worth, 1949-50, 51-53; acting exec. dir. YWCA, Ft. Worth, 1977-78; v.p. personnel Niver Western Wear, Inc., Ft. Worth, 1979—. Bd. dirs. Tex. United Community Services, 1976—; chmn. for Tarrant County, First Lady's Vol. Program, 1977-79, Tarrant County com. UNICEF, 1970-78, Vol. Center com. United Way Tarrant County, 1976-77; mem. Mayor Ft. Worth Com. Status Women, 1976-77; pres. Ft. Worth YWCA, 1973-75; editor Tex. Ch. Woman, 1967-70. Recipient Nat. Vol. award, 1974, Inst. of Women Today award, 1978. Mem. Am. Soc. Personnel Adminstrs. Presbyterian. Home: 4712 Westlake Dr Fort Worth TX 76132 Office: 1221 Hemphill St Fort Worth TX 76104

PERUNKO, MARCELLA ANN, nursing mgmt. cons. exec.; b. Warren, Ohio, Aug. 3, 1937; d. Cyril Matthew and Stephania (Wenckowski) P.; B.S. in Nursing, U. Cin., 1959; cert. in Hemodialysis Nursing, U. Wash., Seattle, 1964; cert. in home nursing instrn. ARC, Warren, Ohio, 1965; M. Health Sci., Governors State U., Park Forest South, Ill., 1979. Staff nurse, team leader, charge nurse, head nurse VA Hosps., Cin., San Francisco, and Cleve., 1959-65; supr. Albert Einstein Med. Coll. Hosp., Bronx, N.Y., 1966; staff nurse, charge nurse, team leader, asst. head nurse, head nurse, instr. Trumbull Meml. Hosp., Warren, Ohio, 1965-66, 67-73; asst. dir. nursing Hillside Hosp., Warren, 1973-74; asso. dir. nursing Akron (Ohio) Gen. Med. Center, 1974-76; dir. nursing South Suburban Hosp., Hazel Crest, Ill., 1976-77; dir. nursing St. Mary Med. Center, Gary, Ind., 1977-78; owner, dir. Nursing Mgmt. Seminars and Workshops, Park Forest, Ill., 1979—; owner, dir. Nursing Mgmt. Consultation Services, Park Forest, 1979—; mgr. edn., eval. and research dept. nursing Louis A. Weiss Meml. Hosp., Chgo., 1981—. community prof. Governors State U., 1980, mem. steering com. health services adminstrn. program, Sch. Health Professions, 1981-82; instr. Inst. Continuing Edn. Purdue U., Hammond, 1980; guest lectr. numerous univs. instr., cons. div. nursing Am. Hosp. Assn., 1980—. Bd. dirs. Found. I Center for Human Devel., Harvey, Ill., 1980-81. Mem. Nat. League for Nursing, Ill. League for Nursing, Am. Nurses Assn., Ill. Nurses Assn. (reviewer continuing edn. approval and recognition program 1979-81, com. on nominations 1981—, mem. dist. commn. on adminstrn. 1979—), Governors State U. Sch Health Professions Alumni Assn. (dir. 1980-82), Mensa. Author manual: Controlling Absenteeism in a Nursing Dept.; media cons. Jour. Nursing Adminstrn., 1980-81; book reviewer Nursing Outlook, 1980—. Office: 111 Forest Blvd Park Forest IL 60466

PERVI, SUSAN DENISE, coll. dean; b. Roslyn, N.Y., Feb. 13, 1952; d. Frederick A. and Amelia (Forino) Goldsmith; B.A., SUNY, Geneseo, 1974; M.A., Bowling Green (Ohio) State U., 1975; m. Peter A. Pevi; 1 dau., Kristina D. Resident dir. Bowling Green State U., 1974-75; resident dir., asst. dir. summer housing Georgetown U., Washington, 1975-76, asst. dean residence life, dir. summer and spl. programs, 1976-78, asso. dean residence life, 1978-82; dir. resident life and food services Cath. U. Am., Washington, 1982—; cons. in field. Mem. Am. Coll. Personnel Assn., Am. Personnel and Guidance Assn., Nat. Assn. Women Deans, Adminstrs. and Couselors, Am. Assn. Higher Edn., Nat. Assn. Student Personnel Adminstrs., Assn. Coll. and Univ. Housing Officers. Home: 951 Deer Creek Run Arnold MD 21012 Office: Monroe Hall Cath U Am Washington DC 20064

PESCOW, DONNA GAIL, actress, singer; b. Bklyn., Mar. 24, 1954; d. Irving Martin (stepfather) and Rhoda Sydelle (Goldress) Epstein; grad. Am. Acad. Dramatic Arts, 1975, Lee Strassberg Theatre Inst., 1976, Appeared in play Ah Wilderness, 1975, Body-Bags, 1981; TV appearances include: One Life To Live; star of ABC-TV's Angie; TV films include Human Feelings, Rainbow, Advice to the Love Lorn, The Day the Bubble Burst appeared in films Saturday Night Fever, Rainbow, Human Feelings.; also night-club acts. Office: care Creative Artists Agy Inc 1888 Century Park E Los Angeles CA 90067 *

PESIN, BARBARA M., cosmetic co. exec.; grad. Principia Coll., Ill. Copywriter J. Walter Thompson, 1961-62, Foote, Cone & Belding, 1962-65, Leo Burnett, 1965-66; copy supr. Ogilvy & Mather, 1969; group creative dir. Dreher Advt., 1969-72; assoc. creative dir. Needham, Harper & Steers, 1973; v.p. Grey Advt., 1967-69, 73-75; dir. advt. Avon Products, Inc., N.Y.C., 1975—, v.p. advt., 1977—. Office: Avon Products Inc 9 W 57th St New York NY 10019 *

PETER, LILY, plantation operator, writer; b. Marvell, Ark.; d. William Oliver and Florence (Mobrey) Peter; B.S., Memphis State U., 1927; M.A., Vanderbilt U., 1938; postgrad. U. Chgo., 1930, Columbia U., 1935-36; L.H.D. (hon.), Moravian Coll., Bethlehem, Pa., 1965; LL.D. (hon.), U. Ark., 1975. Owner, operator plantations, Marvell and Ratio, Ark.; writer poetry, feature articles pub. in SW Quar., Am. poetry Mag., Etude, Silhouettes, Am. Weave, others; mem. staff S.W. Writers Conf., Corpus Christi, Tex., 1954—, sponsor Ark. Writers' Conf. Chmn. Poetry Day in Ark., 1953—; state coordinator Ark. Bicentennial Music, 1975-76. Hon. trustee Moravian Music Found.; mem. nat. council Met. Opera Assn., N.Y.C.; bd. dirs. So. Ginners Assn., Nat. River Acad., Helena, Ark., Ark. State Festival Arts, Ark. Symphony Orch., Ark. Opera Theatre; mem. Circle of 15, 1974. Recipient Moramus award, Friends of Moravian Music, 1964; Distinguished Alumni award Vanderbilt U., 1964; named Ark. Democrat Woman of Year, 1971; Liberty Bell award Phillips County Bar Assn., 1971; Kenneth Beaudoin Gemstone award, 1967; named poet laureate of Ark., 1971, Ark. Conservationist of Year, 1975; highest honor in conservation Nat. Wildlife Fedn., 1976. Mem D.A.R. (hon. state regent), Nat. League Am. Pen Women, Ark. Authors and Composers Soc. (Gold Cup of Achievement 1965), Poets' Roundtable Ark. (C.C. Allard award 1962), Nat. Fedn. Music Clubs (Ark. state chmn. bicentennial 1973-75), Poetry socs. of Tenn., Tex., Ga., Okla. (Gold Cup 1967), Big Creek Protective Assn. (chmn. 1974—), Sigma Alpha Iota. Democrat. Methodist. Clubs: Pacaha (Helena, Ark.); Woman's City (Little Rock, Ark.). Author: The Green Linen of Summer, 1964; The Great Riding, 1966; The Sea Dream of the Mississippi, 1973. Home: Route 2 Box 69 Marvell AR 72366

PETERKIN, BETTY B., govt. ofcl.; b. Gosport, Ind., Oct. 28, 1921; d. Ernest F. and May C. (Cherry) Brown; B.S., Purdue U., 1942; m. Ernest W. Peterkin, July 18, 1948; children—Janet L. Peterkin Brock, Nancy J. Peterkin Standish, Lucy A. Food economist U.S. Dept. Agr., Washington, 1943-50, research leader, Washington and Hyattsville, Md., 1961-80, dep. dir. Consumer Nutrition Center, Hyattsville, 1981—. Mem. Am. Inst. Nutrition, Am. Public Health Assn., Am. Home Econs. Assn., Soc. Nutrition Edn. Contbr. articles in field to profl. jours. Home: 7118 Westhaven Dr Camp Springs MD 20748 Office: US Dept Agriculture Federal Bldg Hyattsville MD 20782

PETERMAN, DONNA COLE, retail co. exec.; b. St. Louis, Nov. 9, 1947; d. William H. and Helen Cole; B.J., U. Mo., 1969; m. John Andre Peterman, Feb. 7, 1970. Editor, employee publs. Edison Bros. Stores, Inc., St. Louis, 1969-72; dir. public relations Ron Katz & Assos., St. Louis 1972-73; editor St. Louis Realty & Investment, 1973-74; chmn. statewide polit. campaign Citizens for Ashcroft, Mo., 1974; asst. media dir. DeKalb County, Ga., 1975; writer Atlanta Mag., 1975; dir. internal communications, exec. speechwriter Sears Roebuck and Co., Atlanta, 1976-80; dir. public affairs Seraco Group-Homart Devel. Co., Chgo., 1980-82; dir. corp. editorial services Sears Roebuck and Co., Chgo., 1982—. Mem. Internat. Assn. Bus. Communicators, Public Relations Soc. Am., Nat. Assn. Corp. Real Estate Execs., Internat. Council Shopping Centers, Kappa Tau Alpha, Alpha Chi Omega. Republican. Roman Catholic. Club: Columbia Yacht. Office: Sears Roebuck and Co Dept 903 BSC 51-20 Sears Tower 33d Floor Chicago IL 60684

PETERS, B. JEANNE, personnel exec.; b. Chgo., May 26, 1940; d. James William and Evelyn (Short) Hill; B.A., No. Ill. U., 1962; postgrad. U. Ill., Northwestern U.; children—Lisa L., Krylyn G. Tchr., ednl. writer suburban sch. dists., Ill., 1962-74; pres. Affirmative Action Cons., Wheeling, Ill., 1974-77; employee relations adminstr. Motorola, Inc., 1978-79, corporate dir. affirmative action and compliance, 1979—; tech. adv. mem. U.S. Employer Del. ILO, 1981, 82. Bd. dirs. Minority Econ. Resources Corp., Des Plaines, Ill., Operation Uplift, Maywood, Ill.; mem. council Northwest Cook County Girl Scouts U.S.A. Recipient award YWCA, 1978. Mem. Am. Soc. Personnel Adminstrs. Unitarian. Home: 711 Greenwood Ct Palatine IL 60067 Office: 1303 E Algonquin Rd Schaumburg IL 60196

PETERS, BERNADETTE (BERNADETTE LAZZARA), actress; b. Queens, N.Y., Feb. 28, 1948; d. Peter and Marguerite (Maltese) Lazzara; student Quintano Sch. Young Profls., N.Y.C. Regular on TV series All's Fair, 1976-77; frequent guest appearances on TV; films include: The Longest Yard, 1974, Silent Movie, 1976, Vigilante Force, 1976, W.C. Fields and Me, 1976, The Jerk, 1979, Pennies From Heaven, 1981, Heart Weeps, 1981, Tulips, 1981; stage appearances include: The Most Happy Fella, 1959, Gypsy, 1961, This is Google, 1962, Riverwind, 1966, The Penny Friend, 1966, Curly McDimple, 1966, Johnny No-Trump, 1967, George M!, 1968, Dames at Sea, 1968, La Strada, 1969, W.C., 1971, On the Town, 1971, Tartuffe, 1972, Mack and Mabel, 1974; nightclub singer, rec. artist MCA Records. Recipient Drama Desk award for Dames at Sea, 1968. Office: care Agy for the Performing Arts Inc 9000 Sunset Blvd Suite 315 Los Angeles CA 90069 *

PETERS, CAROL BEATTIE TAYLOR, mathematician; b. Washington, May 10, 1932; d. Edwin Lucius and Lois (Beattie) Taylor; B.S., U. Md., 1954, M.A., 1958; m. Frank Albert Peters, Feb. 26, 1955; children—Thomas, June, Erick, Victor. Group mgr. Tech. Operations, Inc., Arlington, Va., 1957-62, sr. staff scientist, 1964-66; supervisory analyst Datatrol Corp., Silver Spring, Md., 1962; project dir. Computer Concepts, Inc., Silver Spring, 1963-64; mem. tech. staff Informatics Inc., Bethesda, Md., 1966-67, tech. dir. advanced tech., 1967-76; sr. tech. dir. Ocean Data Systems, Rockville, Md., 1976—. Mem. Assn. Computing Machinery, IEEE Computer Group. Home: 12321 Glen Mill Rd Potomac MD 20854 Office: 6000 Executive Blvd Rockville MD 20852

PETERS, CASSANDRA ALETHA, speech pathologist; b. Atlanta, Sept. 1, 1948; d. William McKinley and Jocelyn (Carter) P.; B.A., Mt. St. Agnes Coll., 1970; M.Ed., Northeastern U., 1971; postgrad. Howard U., 1976—. Speech pathologist The Davison Sch., Atlanta, 1971-74; pvt. practice speech therapy, 1973-76; instr., coordinator speech program Morehouse Coll., Atlanta, 1974-76; clin. supr., grad. teaching and research asst. Howard U., Washington, 1976-79, NSF fellow, 1979-82; speech pathologist Montgomery County Public Schs., 1981-82. Mem. Am. Speech, Lang. and Hearing Assn., Speech Communication Assn., D.C. Speech and Hearing Assn., D.C. Assn. Retarded Citizens. Methodist. Home: 1912 Beecher Rd SW Atlanta GA 30310 Office: 6024 8th St NW Suite C-5 Washington DC 20011

PETERS, DIANE PECK, painter; b. Corpus Christi, Tex., May 14, 1940; d. Wilfred John and Mayme Alice (Mitchell) Peck; student U. Okla., La. Tech. U., Del Mar Coll.; m. George Peters, Dec. 20, 1958; children—George, Louise Irene, Marie Diane, Wilfred John. Designer in stained glass Olszewski Stained Glass Studio, Corpus Christi, 1969-73; operator art studio, Corpus Christi, 1973—; one-woman exhbns. include: Corpus Christi Mus., Bayfront Plaza Auditorium, Corpus Christi, Kottler Galleries, N.Y.C.; group exhbns. include McNay Art Inst., San Antonio, 1979, Birmingham (Ala.) Mus. Art, 1979, Owensboro (Ky.) Mus. Fine Arts, 1979, Nat. Acad. Galleries, N.Y.C., 1979, Raymond Duncan Galleries, Paris, 1980; represented in permanent collection Corpus Christi Mus.; mural Tex. Wildflower commd. by Olszewski Stained Glass Studio 1973, Stations of Cross, 1971. Recipient Merchants watercolor award Okla. 3d ann. Nat. Open Exhbn., 1977. Mem. Tex. Watercolor Soc. (John Herweck award 1977), So. Watercolor Soc., Southwestern Watercolor Soc., Western Fedn. Watercolor Socs., Ky. Watercolor Soc., La. Watercolor Soc., Ala. Watercolor Soc., Watercolor Soc. S. Tex.; asso. mem. Allied Artists Am., Am. Watercolor Soc., Audubon Artists.

PETERS, DOROTHY MARIE, educator; b. Sutton, Nebr., Oct. 23, 1913; d. Sylvester and Anna (Olander) Peters; A.B. with high distinction, Nebr. Wesleyan U., 1941; M.A., Northwestern U., 1957; Ed.D., Ind. U., 1968. Tchr. Nebr. pub. schs., 1931-38; caseworker Douglas County Assistance Bur., Omaha, 1941; hosp. field dir., gen. field rep. ARC, 1941-50; social worker Urban League, Meth. Ch., Washington, 1951-53; asst. prin., dir. guidance, Manlius (Ill.) Community High Sch., 1953-58; dean of girls, guidance dir. Woodruff High Sch., Peoria, Ill., 1958-66; vis. prof. edn. Bradley U., Peoria, 1959-77; coordinator, dir. Title I programs Peoria Public Sch. System, 1966-68, dir. pupil services, 1968-72; dir. counseling and evaluation Title I Programs, 1972-73; vol. dir. youth service programs, vol. program cons. Central Ill. chpt. and Heart of Ill. div. ARC, Peoria, 1973-77; owner, operator Ability-Achievement Unlimited Cons. Services, Saratoga Springs, N.Y., 1978-81; spl. cons. Courage Center, Golden Valley, Minn., 1981—; mem. sr. adv. bd. F&M Marquette Nat. Bank, 1981—. Bd. dirs, home service com. disaster com. Peoria chpt. ARC, 1958-73; pres., bd. dirs. Ct. Counselor Program; mem. Mayor's Human Resources Council, City of Peoria; chmn. met. adv. com. transp. for handicapped; ednl. dir., prin., bd. dirs. Catalyst High Sch., 1975-77; hon. life bd. mem. Am. Nat. Red Cross; mem. Saratoga Springs Hosp. Bldg. Rehab. Com.; founder, steering com. Open Sesame, Saratoga Springs, 1978-81; appointee N.Y. State Employment and Tng. Council, 1979-81, Saratoga County Employment and Tng. Com., 1979-81; bd. dirs. Unlimited Potential, 1979-81; mem. Metro Mobility Adv. Task Force, Mpls., 1981—. Mem. Peoria Edn. Assn. (v.p. 1962-64), Ill. Guidance and Personnel Assn. (v.p. Area 8, 1963-64), NEA, Ill. Edn. Assn. (del. 1962-64), Am. Personnel and Guidance Assn., Am. Sch. Counselors Assn., Nat. Assn. Women Deans and Counselors (K-12 task force chmn. 1974—, editorial bd. Jour.), Ill. Vocat. Guidance Assn. (dir.), Ill. Assn. Women Deans and Counselors, Phi Kappa Phi, Psi Chi, Pi Gamma Mu, Pi Lambda Theta, Delta Kappa Gamma, Alpha Gamma Delta. Address: 7201 York Ave So Apt 703 Edina MN 55435

PETERS, EDNA LUCILLE, nurse; b. Sand Lake, Minn., Dec. 1, 1933; d. Cleo Bailey and Mae Evelyn (Johnson) P.; R.N., Children's Hosp., San Francisco, 1956; B.S., U. Oreg., Portland, 1965; M.S., U. Md., 1973. Sec., Aetna Inst. Co., San Francisco, 1951-53; charge nurse Sacred Heart Hosp., Medford, Oreg., 1956-58; commd. ensign Nurse Corps, USN, 1959, advanced through grades to capt., 1980; staff nurse Naval Hosp., Great Lakes, Ill., 1959; charge nurse EENT clinic and operating room, 1959-62, clinic nurse Boot Camp, 1962-63; charge nurse mil. ward, supr. med. ward Naval Hosp., Guam, 1965-66; instr. Hosp. Corps Sch., San Deigo, 1966-69; charge nurse gyn ward Naval Hosp., Portsmouth, Va., 1969-70, instr. B. Sch., 1970-71; med. area coordinator, Phila., 1973-76; nursing service adminstr. patient care coordinator, asst. officer-in-charge Naval Regional Med. Clinic, Iwakuni, Japan, 1976-79, officer in charge, 1977-78; chief nursing service Naval Regional Med. Clinic, Port Hueneme, Calif., 1979-82; ret., 1982; instr. nursing dept. Ventura (Calif.) Coll., 1981—. Local rep. Officer's Christian Fellowship. Recipient Outstanding Woman of Year award Navy League, Port Hueneme, Calif., 1980. Mem. Am. Soc. Nursing Service Adminstrs., NOW, Nat. League Nursing, Am. Nurses Assn., Nat. Assn. Female Exec., Ventura County Dirs. Nurses. Nazarene. Home: 1426 Gina Dr Oxnard CA 93030

PETERS, ELIZABETH ANNE, educator; b. Hebron, Ill., June 9, 1940; d. Tibbets E. and Ruby Marie (Giddens) Rolls; B.S., U. Ill., 1962, M.S., 1967; postgrad. U. Ill., 1970-74, Iowa State U., 1974, Northwestern U., 1980; div. Tchr., Bremen High Sch., Midlothian, Ill., 1962-65, Waller High Sch., Chgo., 1965-67, Evanston (Ill.) High Sch., 1967-70; instr., coordinator food service adminstrn. and hotel mgmt. Coll. DuPage, Glen Ellyn, Ill., 1970-75; clin. dietitian U. Chgo. Hosps. and Clinics, 1975; asst. restaurant mgr. Hyatt Regency, Chgo., summer 1980; prof., coordinator hospitality mgmt. program Chicago City-Wide Coll., 1976—; cons. bds. health, colls. Mem. adv. com. No. Ill. U.; judge various food contests; mem. Chgo. Council on Fgn. Relations; mem. Chgo. Lyric Opera Guild, Alliance of Art Inst.; trustee Three Arts Club Chgo. Recipient Nat. Restaurant Assn. Fellowship award, 1980; Master Tchrs. Seminar Fellowship award, 1974; Nat. Leadership Devel. Fellowship award, 1975. Registered Dietitan. Mem. Nat. Restaurant Assn., Ill. Restaurant Assn., Chgo. Restaurant Assn., Am. Dietetic Assn., Ill. Dietetic Assn., Chgo. Nutrition Assn., Ill Nutrition Com., Chgo. Dietetic Assn. (dir.), Soc. Nutrition Edn., Inst. Food Technologists, Restaurant Women's Club Chgo. (dir.), Council on Hotel-Restaurant Edn. Clubs: Flossmoor Country, Lake Geneva Yacht, Canyon. Home: 215 E Chestnut St Chicago IL 60611 Office: 185 N Wabash Ave Chicago IL 60601

PETERS, ELLEN ASH, justice Supreme Ct. Conn.; b. Berlin, Mar. 21, 1930; naturalized citizen U.S.; B.A. cum laude, Swarthmore Coll., 1951; LL.B. cum laude, Yale U., 1954, M.A. (hon.), 1964. Law clk. to U.S. Circuit Ct. Judge Charles E. Clark, 1954-55; asso. in law U. Calif., Berkeley, 1955-56; faculty Yale U. Sch. Law, New Haven, 1956—, now adj. prof.; currently justice Supreme Ct. Conn.; mem. Conn. Law Revision Commn., Conn. Commn. Public Legis. Trustee, Yale New Haven Hosp. Author: Commercial Transaction, Cases, Text and Problems, 1971; A Negotiable Instruments Primer, 1974; contbr. numerous articles to legal jours. Office: Supreme Court Bldg 231 Capitol Ave Hartford CT 06106

PETERS, EUNICE SARAH BATES LOWERY, artist; b. Chelsea, Mass., Oct. 18, 1906; d. William Edgar and Eunice Hall (Fergusson) Lowery; grad. Famous Artists Sch., Mind Psi-Genics; M. Psycho-Cybernetics, Am. Inst. Motivational Sci.; m. William J. Peters, June 3, 1927 (dec. June 1967); children—Eunice L. Peters Harrington, William J. Exhibited in one-woman shows at Alhambra (Calif.) Library, 1976; group shows: Pasadena Soc. Artists, San Gabriel Soc. Arts; sec., dir. Trail Chem. Corp., El Monte, Calif., 1947. Mem. Pasadena Arts Council, Pasadena Artists Assn., San Gabriel Fine Arts and Culture Assn., Pasadena Artists, Nat. League Am. Pen Women (pres. Pasadena br. 1972-74), Composers and Artists (Pasadena br.). Home: 1315 Monterey Pl San Marino CA 91108 Office: 9904 Gidley St El Monte CA 91731

PETERS, GLORIA CACHE POINDEXTER, civic worker; b. Walters, Okla., Apr. 5, 1907; d. Samuel Clifford and Maude Lucinda (York) Poindexter; B.S. in Psychology, U. Miami, Coral Gables, 1950, postgrad., 1952; m. Wirt L. Peters, Sept. 6, 1925. Asst. to dean Coll. Fine Arts, U. Okla., Norman, 1932-42; employee relations officer Gt. Lakes Div., C.E., Chgo., 1944-45. Mem. adv. council Fla. Internat. U., 1969-78, Gov's. Com. for Rehab. of Handicapped. Mem. AAUW (nat. bd. 1965-71; pres. State of Fla., 1974-76, established Gloria Peters endowment 1967, editor Miami Br. Bull. INFORMat, 1957-60), Fla. Psychol. Assn. (charter, bull. editor 1950), DAR, Magna Charta Dames, Psi Chi. Democrat. Methodist. Clubs: Women's Com. of 100, Miami. Editor Faculty Wives Bull. DISTAFF, 1954-55; regular contbr. nat. mag., Boston, 1962-68. Home: 3305 Alhambra Circle Coral Gables FL 33134

PETERS, GRETA BARKSDALE, computer systems engr.; b. Indpls., Jan. 27, 1945; d. Bruce Ford and Sarah Catherine (Cunningham) Brown; student Sweet Briar Coll., 1962-65; B.S. in Theoretical Physics, Butler U., 1967; m. Charles T. Peters, Feb. 3, 1968; 1 son, Charles Taft, III. Physicist, Bur. of Weapons, Dept of Navy, 1967-68; dept. pathology Med. Coll. Va., 1968-69; computer systems programmer Va. Employment Commn., Richmond, 1969-72; systems software engr. Computer Software Co., Richmond, 1972-77; tech. cons. Reynolds Metals Co., Richmond, 1977—; cons. on computerization to pvt. cos. Chairperson various coms. Fan Dist. Civic Assn., Richmond, 1968-78; chmn. profls. bd. mgrs. Jr. League of Richmond, 1976-77, treas., 1978-80; mem. budget and allocations com. United Way of Greater Richmond, 1980-83. Mem. Data Processing Mgmt. Assn., MENSA, Va. Fan Dist. Assn., Common Cause. Republican. Presbyterian. Home: 2103 Park Ave Richmond VA 23220 Office: MIS 6605 W Broad St Richmond VA 23261

PETERS, HELEN FRAME, fin. exec.; b. Richmond, Eng., Mar. 22, 1948; d. Harold Mayne and Helen (Frame) Peters; B.A., U. Pa., 1970, M.A., 1974; Ph.D., Wharton Sch., U. Pa., 1979; m. Judson Parker, Jan. 8, 1972; 1 son, Coleman Parker. Mgr. dept. research, economist Fed. Res. Bank of Phila., 1976-79; asst. v.p. Phila. Saving Fund Soc., 1979-80; mgr. Merrill Lynch, Phila., 1980-81, v.p. mortgage backed securities, 1981-82, mng. dir. debt strategy group, N.Y.C., 1982—; adj. prof. fin. U. Pa., Phila., 1980—; mem. Fed. Savs. and Loan Adv. Council, 1982—. Mem. Mayor's task force on appointing women to cabinet positions, 1979; bd. dirs., exec. com. Pa. Economy League, 1980—; active Community Leadership program, 1979—. Rodney L. White Research fellow, 1971-72. Mem. Am., Phila. (pres. 1980-81, dir. 1980-81) fin. assns., Nat. Assn. Bus. Economists, Kappa Alpha Theta. Office: 165 Broadway New York NY

PETERS, JUDITH ROCHELLE, pharmacy exec.; b. Phila., July 16, 1951; d. John Bernard and Priscilla Jo (Johnson) P.; B.S. (Senatorial scholar), Pa. State U., 1973; postgrad. Temple U. Sch. Pharmacy, 1975-77; M.B.A., H.H.S.A., Cornell U., 1977. Supr., lifeguard Phila. Dept. Recreation, 1971-74; pharmacy intern Needle & Boonin, Zachian Bros. and Bell Family Pharmacies, Phila., 1976-79; mgr., partner Adero Pharmacy, Phila., 1980—; sci. specialist Phila. Bd. Edn., 1978—. Vol., Big Sisters Am., ARC, Phila.; deacon Lombard Central United Presbyterian Ch., Phila. Mem. Nat. Assn. Health Services Execs., Am. Public Health Assn., Internat. City Mgmt. Assn., United Presbyn. Women. Club: United Soul Ensemble. Office: 2267 N 19th St Philadelphia PA 19132

PETERS, MARJORIE YOUNG, state legislator; b. Bklyn., Dec. 6, 1928; d. Willard Voornees and Matilda (Miller) Young; m. C. Oswald Peters, Sept. 20, 1952; children—Clark Voorhees, Charles Young, Matilda Peters Norton. Mem. N.H. Ho. of Reps. from Hillsborough Dist. 9, 1975—, vice chmn. ways and means com., 1980. Mem. Bedford (N.H.) Bicentennial Com., 1976; bd. dirs. Bedford Friends of Library, 1982. Mem. Nat. Order Women Legislators, N.H. Fedn. Republican Women, Bedford Hist. Soc. Presbyterian. Office: State House Concord NH 03301

PETERS, MARSHA, social worker; b. Brigham City, Utah, Oct. 9, 1949; d. Paul Madsen and Enid (Fishburn) P.; B.S., U. Utah, 1973, M.S.W., 1975. Social worker Utah State Div. Services for the Visually Handicapped, Salt Lake City, 1975—; clin. asst. prof. Grad. Sch. Social Work, U. Utah. Bd. dirs. Women's State Legis. Council of Utah, 1979—. Mem. Nat. Assn. Social Workers (dir. Utah chpt. 1976—, Social Worker of Yr., Utah chpt. 1979), Am. Soc. Public Adminstrn., Utah Public Employees Assn., Am. Assn. Workers for the Blind, Beta Sigma Phi. Home: 826 16th Ave Salt Lake City UT 84103 Office: 309 E 1 S Salt Lake City UT 84111

PETERS, MERCEDES, psychoanalyst; b. N.Y.C.; B.S., L.I. U., 1945; postgrad. Columbia U., 1944-45; M.S., U Conn., 1953; tng. in psychotherapy Am. Inst. Psychotherapy and Psychoanalysis, 1960-70; grad. Postgrad. Center Mental Health. Social worker various agys., pub. instns., 1945-63; staff affiliate, sr. psychotherapist Community Guidance Service, 1960-75; affiliate Postgrad. Center for Mental Health, 1974-76; pvt. practice psychotherapy, Bklyn., 1961—. Certified psychoanalyst Am. Examining Bd. Psychoanalysis; certified mental health cons. Fellow Am. Orthopsychiat. Assn.; mem. Nat. Assn. Social Workers, LWV, NAACP, Brooklyn Heights Mus. Soc. (v.p.). Office: 142 Joralemon Brooklyn NY 11201

PETERS, PATRICIA ELAINE, bank mgr.; b. Chgo., Oct. 14, 1941; d. Lawrence and Kathlee R. (Lyons) P.; B.A., Marycrest Coll., Davenport, Iowa, 1963; m. James Stanley Carter, Jan. 1, 1982. With Morgan Guaranty Trust Co., N.Y.C., 1969—, mgr. N.Am. research unit, 1978-81, instl. portfolio mgr., 1981—. Mem. Fin. Women's Assn., N.Y. Soc. Security Analysts. Office: 9 W 57th St New York NY 10019

PETERS, ROBERTA, soprano; b. N.Y.C., May 4, 1930; d. Sol and Ruth (Hirsch) Peters; ed. privately; Litt.D. Elmira Coll., 1967; Mus. D., Ithaca Coll., 1968, Colby Coll., 1980; L.H.D., Westminster Coll., 1974, Lehigh U., 1977; m. Bertram Fields, Apr. 10, 1955; children—Paul, Bruce. Met. Opera debut as Zerlina in Don Giovanni, 1950, also appeared in Rigoletto, The Magic Flute, The Barber of Seville, The Marriage of Dallas. Lucia di Lammermoor, Die Fledermaus, Don Pasquale, L'Elisir d'Amore Lakme, Cosi ops., Tutte, La Sonnambula, Martha, Richard Strauss' Ariadne auf Naxos; recorded numerous operas; appeared motion pictures Tonight We Sing, Barber of Seville; frequent appearances radio and TV; sang at Royal Opera House, Covent Garden, London, Eng., summers 1951-60, Cin. Opera, summers 1952-53, 58, Vienna State Opera, 1963, Salzburg Festival, 1963, 64; debuts at festival in Vienna and Munich, 1963, 64; concert tours in U.S., Soviet Union, Scandinavian countries, Isreal; debut Kirov Opera, Leningrad, USSR, 1972, Bolshoi Opera, Moscow, 1972. Named Women of Yr., Fedn. Women's Clubs, 1964; 1st Am. to receive Bolshoi medal. Author: Debut at the Met. Home: Scarsdale NY 10583 Office: ICM Artists Ltd 40 W 57th St New York NY 10019

PETERS, ROSALIE DAVIS, needlework designer; b. Gainesville, Tex., Feb. 22, 1939; d. Marvin Oliver Frank and Agnes (Whaley) Davis; student Tex. Wesleyan U., 1956-57, North Tex. U., 1957-58; m. May 28, 1958; children—Diane Louise, Sharon Ann. Sec., Tex. Instruments, Dallas, 1959-62; pres. Shariane Designs, Tucker, Ga., 1971—, Masterpiece Publs., Ltd., Tucker, 1979—; tchr., lectr. in field. Recipient cert. of appreciation Distributive Edn., 1979. Mem. Nat. Council Am. Embroiderers, Am. Needlepoint Guild, Embroiderers Guild Am., Nat. Assn. Female Execs., Women Bus. Owners, Nat. Needlework Assn., Callanwolde Guild, DAR. Methodist. Author, co-author various booklets on needlepoint and cross stitch. Home: 994 Willow Run Stone Mountain GA 30088 Office: 4764C Hammermill Rd Tucker GA 30083

PETERS, SUSAN TAYLOR, univ. adminstr.; b. Harrodsburg, Ky., Apr. 15, 1953; d. Charles Clyde and Leah Wood (Taylor) P.; B.Ed. in Phys. Edn., U. Miami (Fla.), 1975, M.Ed., 1977. Grad. asst. campus sports and recreation, acting dir. women's intramurals U. Miami, 1975-77, asso. dean personnel, 1977—, Panhellenic adv., 1981—. Recipient Pres.' Phys. Fitness award, 1982. Mem. Am. Coll. Personnel Assn., So. Coll. Personnel Assn., Southeastern Panhellenic Conf., Fla. Assn. Women Deans, Adminstrs. and Counselors, Assn. Frat. Advisers, Kappa Kappa Gamma (Alumni pres. 1981), Omicron Delta Kappa. Phi Kappa Phi. Republican. Presbyterian. Home: 6514 SW 114th Pl Unit D Miami FL 33173 Office: PO Box 248106 Coral Gables FL 33124

PETERS, VERA CONSTANCE ASTER HESS, real estate exec.; b. Bklyn., Apr. 3, 1945; d. Charles H. and Erna Anna (Schoen) Aster; student Latter-day Saints Bus. Coll., 1958, U. Utah, 1961; m. Ted Peters, Nov. 23, 1980; children by previous marriage—Troy Dee, Tyrone Chad. Legal sec., office mgr. Gordon I. Hyde, Salt Lake City, 1969-71; adminstrv. asst. Flying Diamond Oil Corp., Salt Lake City, 1971-74, also exec. sec. to chmn. bd.; sec. treas. Shuhart Industries, Inc., Salt Lake City, 1974-77; Realtor, 1977-80; broker, 1980—; owner, pres. Market Realty, Inc., 1980—. Mem. Nat. Assn. Realtors, Salt Lake Bd. Realtors, Women's Council Realtors, LWV. Lutheran. Home: 1865 Wasatch Dr Salt Lake City UT 84108

PETERS, VIRGINIA LEE, educator; b. Drumright, Okla., June 15, 1934; d. Carl William and Virginia Alice (Gorman) P.; B.S. in Health and Phys. Edn., Central State Coll., Edmond, Okla., 1957; M.S., U. Colo., 1962; Ph.D. (NDEA fellow), Fla. State U., 1968. Tchr., John Marshall Jr.-Sr. High Sch., Oklahoma City, 1957-58; prof. health, phys. edn. and recreation Central State U., Edmond, 1958—, chmn. dept., 1973—, dir. women's athletics, 1970—, also coach women's field hockey, basketball and fencing; tchr. inservice courses' speaker in field; dir. Okla. Spl. Olympic. Chmn. parish council St. John's Roman Cath. Ch., Edmond, 1981-82. Recipient Disting. Former Student award Central State U., 1980, named Outstanding Woman Faculty Mem., 1971; named to Jim Thorp Okla. Athletic Hall of Fame, 1975. Mem. AAHPER (v.p. So. dist. 1976), AAUP, Okla. Assn. Health, Phys. Edn. and Recreation (Honor award 1977), Okla. Assn. Phys. Edn. Women, Phi Delta Kappa, Delta Kappa Gamma, Delta Psi Kappa, Phi Kappa Phi. Democrat. Author papers in field. Home: 2012 Rolling Creek St Edmond OK 73034 Office: 100 N University St Edmond OK 73034

PETERSEN, BARBARA KATHRYN, utility co. exec.; b. Mason City, Iowa, Aug. 12, 1947; d. Charles Michael and Elizabeth Mary (Brandeker) Foldesi; A.A., N. Iowa Area Community Coll., 1967; B.A., U. Iowa, 1969; m. O. Keith Petersen, Jan. 3, 1981; 1 dau., Heather Kristine Graham. Broadcast journalist Sta. WSUI, Iowa City, Iowa, 1968-69, Sta. KGLO TV-Radio, Mason City, Iowa, 1969, Sta. KCRG TV-Radio, Cedar Rapids, Iowa, 1970; tchr. Austin-Del Valle (Tex.) Public Schs., 1972; reference librarian, writer, Austin, Tex., 1973-74; editor Office of Research Mgmt., U. Tex. System, Austin, 1974-75, coordinator public info. Center for Energy Studies, 1975-77; supr. Public Affairs Research Center, Consumers Power Co., Jackson, Mich., 1977—. Mem. Nat. Assn. Female Execs., Women in Communications Inc. (dir. Lansing chpt. 1979—). Home: 1744 Sevenoaks Rd Jackson MI 49203 Office: 212 W Michigan Ave Jackson MI 49201

PETERSEN, EDIE, mktg. exec.; b. N.Y.C., Feb. 21, 1943; d. John and Herta Marie (Link) Petersen; B.A. magna cum laude in Speech, Hofstra U., 1972; children—John, Richard Paul, James Thomas. Mktg. rep. Xerox Corp., N.Y.C., 1973-74, mktg. exec., Pensacola, Fla., 1974-76, med. market exec., 1977-78, sales tng. mgr., 1978-79, mktg. mgr., Jackson, Miss., 1979-82; computer software mktg. exec. Cutler-Williams, Dallas, 1982—. Mem. Nat. Assn. Female Execs., Smithsonian Assocs. Lutheran. Club: Pres.'s (Xerox). Home: 3917 Harvest Hill Rd Dallas TX 75234 Office: 2655 Villa Creek Dr Dallas TX 75234

PETERSEN, MAUREEN ANNE, instrument co. fin. exec.; b. Bklyn., June 26, 1953; d. Peter Thomas and Rosemary Anne (Manning) P.; student Nassau Community Coll., Uniondale, N.Y., 1972, 78. Buyer, asst. mgr. Womrath Bookstore, Hempstead, N.Y., 1972-74; with A & M Instrument, Inc., Rockville Centre, N.Y., 1974—, asst. controller, 1977, controller, 1977—. Mem. Am. Prodn. and Inventory Control Soc., Inst. Mgmt. Edn. Roman Catholic. Home: 2930-10 Rockaway Ave Apt 82 Oceanside NY 11572 Office: 5 Nassau St Rockville Centre NY 11570

PETERSEN, MRS., WILLIAM J. (BESSIE RASMUS PETERSEN), orgn. exec., club woman; b. Cherokee, Iowa, June 30, 1902; d. Andrew John and Singni (Nystedt) Rasmus; B.A., State U. Iowa, 1926, M.A., 1930; m. William John Petersen, Sept. 25, 1937. Speech pathologist Rockefeller Found. Mental Hygiene Clinic for Iowa, Iowa City, 1926-28; instr. speech, phonetics U. Iowa, 1928-37; organizer, dir. U. Iowa, Articulatory Speech Clinic, 1928-37; lectr., speech pathology U. Nebr., summers 1931, 37, 38, 39, 40, 41; lectr. Butler U., summer 1937; cons. spl. edn. Iowa Dept. Pub. Edn., 1948-50; asst. dir. Iowa State Hist. Soc. Tours, 1948—. Mem. com. White House Conf. on Spl. Edn., 1929. Mem. Girl Scout Council, 1938-41. Mem. Needlework Guild of Am. (pres. 1939), AAUW (pres. 1940), Iowa Speech and Hearing Assn., Iowa Bus. and Profl. Women's Club, Iowa State Hist. Soc., League Women Voters Iowa Fedn. Women's Clubs, Sigma Xi, Chi Omega. Mem. Order Eastern Star. Club: University. Home: 329 Ellis Ave Iowa City IA 52240

PETERSON, ANN SULLIVAN, physician, univ. adminstr.; b. Rhinebeck, N.Y., Oct. 11, 1928; B.A., Cornell U., 1950, M.D., 1954, M.S. (Alfred P. Sloan fellow), M.I.T., 1980. Intern, resident in medicine Cornell U. Div. Bellevue Hosp., N.Y.C., 1954-57; fellow in medicine and physiology Meml.-Sloan Kettering, Cornell U. Med. Coll., 1957-60; instr. to asst. prof. medicine, asst. dir. clin. research unit Georgetown U., 1962-69; asso. prof. medicine, asso. dean U. Ill., 1969-72; asso. prof. medicine Coll. Physicians and Surgeons, Columbia U., 1972-80, asso. dean, 1972-79; asso. prof. medicine, asso. dean Cornell U. Med. Coll., 1980—. John and Mary R. Markle scholar in acad. medicine. Diplomate Am. Bd. Internal Medicine. Fellow ACP; mem. Am. Fedn. Clin. Research, Assn. Am. Med. Colls., AMA (asst. sec. liaison com. on med. edn.), Alpha Omega Alpha. Contbr. articles to sci. jours. Office: 1300 York Ave New York NY 10021

PETERSON, ARLENE JULIETTE, constrn. co. exec.; b. Winner, S.D., Apr. 27, 1936; d. Elwood Lloyd and Geneva Carolyn (Mayes) Miller; B.S., Black Hills State Coll., 1968; children—Richard Allen, Dean Allen. Tchr. pub. schs., Meade County, S.D., 1959-60; spl. edn. tchr. Title I Program, New Underwood, S.D., 1960-72; office mgr. Overhead Dr. Co., Rapid City, S.D., 1972-75; office mgr. Dean Kurtz Constrn. Co., Rapid City, 1975—, sec.-treas., 1976—, dir., 1979—. Mem. Asso. Gen. Contractors Am., Women in Constrn. Republican. Lutheran. Home: 2110 6th Ave Rapid City SD 57701 Office: PO Box 1917 Rand Rd Rapid City SD 57709

PETERSON, CYNTHIA NANCE, architect; b. New Rochelle, N.Y., Mar. 6, 1937; d. Alfred George and Brenda (Wild) Peterson; B.A., Brown U., 1958; B. Arch., Yale U., 1965, M. Arch., 1965. With Douglas Orr, Architect, New Haven, 1958-60; with Canbilis Joseit Woods, Paris, 1962-63, Ludquist & Stonehill, N.Y.C., 1966-67, Davis, Broady & Assocs., 1968-75; self employed architect, 1975-82; archtl. engr., project architect Robert Lamb, Architects and Planners, 1982—; adj. prof. CUNY, 1973—; vis. critic Cooper Union. Registered architect, N.Y. Mem. Archtl. League N.Y., Alliance of Women in Architecture. Democrat. Episcopalian. Home: 333 E 30th St New York NY 10016

PETERSON, DEBORAH LYNN, comml. investment realtor; b. Chgo., Dec. 30, 1950; d. Robert Alexander and Betty Jean Easton; student U. Nev., 1968-69, Ill. Realtors Inst., 1975-77, Realtors Nat. Mktg. Inst., 1976-81, Coll. Fin. Planning, 1982; m. William H. Fitzsimmons, Feb. 14, 1981. Real estate broker Mel Foster Co., Moline, Ill., 1974-77; realtor Comml.-Investment div. Weiner & Assos., Inc., Moline, 1977-79; project mgr. Comml.-Investment div. Boeye Realtors, Inc., Rock Island, Ill., 1979—. Pres., club adv., treas. Jr. Women's Club East Moline, 1974-79; chmn. Realtors' Polit. Action Com., 1976-78; adv. com. Black Hawk Coll., 1979—. Cert. comml. investment mem.; grad. Realtors Inst.;

recipient Arthur Bud Hill award, 1978. Mem. Cert. Comml. Investment Mems., Nat. Assn. Female Execs., Rock Island County Bd. Realtors (dir., past treas.), Nat. Assn. Realtors, Ill. Assn. Realtors, Realtors Nat. Mktg. Inst., Inst. Cert. Fin. Planners, Gamma Phi Beta. Republican. Presbyterian. Home: 2101 31st St Rock Island IL 61201 Office: 3900 18th Ave Rock Island IL 61201

PETERSON, DONNA, state legislator; B.A. in Anthropology, U. Minn. Mem. Minn. Ho. of Reps., 1980—, vice chmn. gen. legis. and vets. affairs coms., mem. commerce and econ. devel., reapportionment and elections, taxes coms. Office: 254 State Office Bldg Saint Paul MN 55155 *

PETERSON, DORA ELVIRA, soft drink co. exec.; b. Ravenna, Mich.; d. Clarence and Bertha Patterson; diploma Muskegon (Mich.) Bus. Coll.; m. Paul Miller; children—Lois Miller Frausto, Donald; m. 2d, Gerald Peterson, Mar. 20, 1954. Asst. to service mgr. Sealed Power Corp., Muskegon, 1921-27; with Coca Cola Bottling Co. Muskegon, 1943—, pres., 1945—; dir. Muskegon Bank & Trust Co., 1975-80. Named Bus. Woman of Year, 1972. Mem. Mich. Soft Drink Assn. (dir. 1975—, pres. 1980-81), Nat. Soft Drink Assn., Muskegon C. of C., Nat. C. of C., Mich. C. of C. Episcopalian. Club: Muskegon Zonta. Address: Coca Cola Bottling Co 1770 E Keating St Muskegon MI 49442

PETERSON, DORIS LORRAINE COX, counselor; b. Newark, Apr. 30, 1924; d. Henry Alfred and Flora Belle (Smith) Cox; B.S. magna cum laude, Syracuse U., 1946; M.S., Cornell U., 1949; postgrad. Purdue U., 1979—; children—Ross Erik, Kendall Cox, Gunnar Bradford. Sr. lectr. Bklyn. Union Gas Co., 1946-48; asst. prof. Pratt Inst., Bklyn. and Montclair (N.J.) State Coll., 1953-54, 1962-65; direct sales rep. Sanna Dairies, Madison, Wis., 1949-52; con. market research, N.Y.C., Syracuse and Gloversville, N.Y., Allentown, Pa., 1952-53; tchr. chemistry Wequahic High Sch., Newark, 1970-72; extension home economist Rutgers State U., New Brunswick, N.J., 1972-74; consumer edn. workshop dir. Marywood Coll., Scranton, Pa., 1964; sr. adv. Culver Mil. Acad., Ind., 1974-76; curriculum project coordinator for State of Mich., seminar prof. Eastern Mich. U., Ypsilanti, 1976-78; geosci. counselor Purdue U., West Lafayette, Ind., 1978-80, counselor dept. bldg. constrn. and contracting, 1980—, Ind. State rep. Region V Adv. Council of Displaced Homemaker's Nat. Network, Inc., 1980—. Mem. Maplewood Symphony, 1939-42, Syracuse Symphony, 1942-46; chmn. Friends of the Maplewood Library, 1960-62; chmn. mothers' com. jr. cavalvry unit Jr. Essex Troop, N.J. 1968-69. Mem. AAUW, Nat. Assn. Women Deans, Adminstrs. and Counselors, N.J. Home Econs. Extension Assn., N.J. Home Econs. Assn. (acting coordinator), Eastern Regional Conf. of Coll. Nutrition Tchrs. (sec.), Home Econs. Women in Bus., No. N.J. Home Economists in Homemaking (past pres.), Nat. Home Econs. Assn. (N.J. del. and curriculum showcase presenter convs.), No. N.J. Chi Omega Alumni, Phi Delta Kappa, Kappa Delta Pi, Eta Pi Upsilon, Omicron Nu, Kappa Kappa Kappa, Chi Omega (officer). Republican. Methodist. Club: Lafayette Tennis. Contbr. articles in field to profl. jours.; textbook reviewer MacMillan Pub. Co., 1977-79. Home: 122 1/2 Marstellar St West Lafayette IN 47906 Office: SCC-A Dept Bldg Constrn Sch Tech Purdue U West Lafayette IN 47907 also Woodland Shores Bridgman MI 49106

PETERSON, HAZEL AGNES, cons. petroleum geologist; b. Houston; d. Howard Lynn, Sr., and Carrie Rice (Brown) P.; B.A. in Geology, N.Y. U., 1939; M.A. in Geology, U. Tex., 1942; postgrad. various univs. Jr. subsurface geologist Shell Oil Co., Houston, 1942; subsurface geologist Texaco, Houston and Tulsa, 1942-44, Sun Oil Co., Dallas and Corpus Christi, Tex., 1944-52; supervising geologist Seaboard Oil Co. of Del., Dallas, 1952-54; pvt. practice cons. petroleum geologist, Dallas, Commerce and Denton, Tex., 1952—; asst. prof. E.Tex. State U., Commerce, 1958-78; former water resources adv. City of Commerce. Mem. City of Commerce Planning and Zoning Commn., 1977-82. Research grantee, U.S. Nat. Park Service, 1959-61; faculty research grantee E.Tex. State U., 1960s. Mem. Am. Assn. Petroleum Geologists (cert. petroleum geologist), Dallas Geol. Soc., Sigma Xi (hon.). Methodist. Clubs: DAR (vice regent Benjamin Lyon chpt., 1955-57, acting regent 1956-57), Soc. New Eng. Women (corr. sec. Tex. Colony), Huguenot Soc. of Founders of Manakin (Tex. Br.), Delta Zeta. Condr. research profl. fields and local history; contbr. articles to various publs. Home and Office: 820 Hillcrest Denton TX 76201

PETERSON, JIMMIE RUTH, savs. and loan exec.; b. Tenaha, Tex., Jan. 7, 1922; d. Fred Sue and Jimmie Jewell (Currie) Stillwell; student Garner Bus. Sch. and Inst. Fin. Edn., New Orleans, 1974-75; m. Oscar Isidore Peterson, Dec. 15, 1941; 1 son, Fred Stillwell. With Central Savs. and Loan Assn., New Orleans, 1950—, loan clk., cashier, 1950-66, asst. v.p., 1966-71, v.p., 1971-73, exec. v.p., 1973-74, pres., 1974-78, dir., 1971—, chmn. bd. dirs., 1978-81, cons., 1981—. Tchr., St. Bernard United Meth. Ch., 1955-75; cubs den mother Pack 277 New Orleans Area council Boy Scouts Am., Chalmette, La., 1960-69; mem. Urban League Task Force, New Orleans. Mem. Home Builders Assn. Greater New Orleans (dir., 1978-81; dir. Ladies Aux. 1979; recipient Spike award 1979, 80, Spikette award 1979), New Orleans Realtors (dir. Women's Council 1979), Internat. House (World Trade Center, New Orleans), U.S. League of Savs. and Loan Assns., La. State League Savs. Assns., League of Savs. and Loan-Homestead Assn. Met. New Orleans, Greater New Orleans Exec. Assn., Inst. Fin. Edn. Democrat. Clubs: Carolyn Park Garden (Chalmette), Pandora Carnival (New Orleans), Order Eastern Star, Daus. of Desert, Daus. of Nile, Jerusalem Temple Clownettes. First woman to serve on bd. dirs. Central Savs. and Loan Assn. and on bd. of Home Builders Assn. Greater New Orleans; winner nat. and local flower shows. Office: 710 Canal St New Orleans LA 70130

PETERSON, JO, drafting service co. exec.; b. Palo Alto, Calif., Dec. 9, 1951; d. Ellsworth Woodrow and Henrietta Marcella (Erasmy) Peterson; student De Anza Coll., 1970-71, West Valley Coll., 1972-75. Civil engring. draftsperson Charles S. McCandless & Co., Palo Alto, 1969-74, archtl. design cons., owner Lines Unltd., Palo Alto, Calif., 1974—. Recipient Bank of Am. Achievement award in Trades and Indsl. Arts., 1970. Mem. Am. Inst. Bldg. Design, Inst. for Cert. of Engring. Technicians, Constrn. Specifications Inst., Nat. Assn. Female Execs., Nat. Fedn. Ind. Bus. Democrat. Home and office: 695 Arastradero Rd Palo Alto CA 94306

PETERSON, JUDITH ELIZABETH, educator, mgmt. cons.; b. White Plains, N.Y., Mar. 25, 1946; d. Leroy and Etta (Tate) Peterson; B.A., Utica Coll., Syracuse U., 1968; M.Ed., U. Mass., 1972, postgrad., 1972-76. Tchr. French, Whitesboro Jr. High Sch., Whitesboro, N.Y., 1968-71; exec. sec. Five Coll. Black Studies Exec. Com., Amherst, Mass., 1974-76; cons. Aetna Life and Casualty, Hartford, Conn., 1977-78, sr. cons., 1978-80, adminstr., 1980; 2d v.p. Chase Manhattan Bank, N.Y.C., 1980—; youth motivation task force cons. Nat. Alliance Bus., 1980—. First v.p. NAACP, Amherst, 1976. W. K. Kellogg Found. fellow, 1973-74; Ford Exec. Leadership Program, fellow, 1972-73; Nat. Fellowships Fund fellow, 1973-74. Mem. AAUW, Am. Soc. Tng. and Devel., Human Resources Planning Soc., Nat. Assn. Female Execs. (network dir.), Urban League. Home: 143 Hoyt St Stamford CT 06905 Office: 80 Pine St 20th Floor New York NY 10081

PETERSON, MARCIA WRAITH, nursing adminstr.; b. Robinson, Ill., Aug. 5, 1953; d. George Bernard and Helen (Wheeler) Wraith; R.N., Harris Coll. Nursing, 1977; B.S.N., Tex. Chrisitan U., 1977; m. Timothy Alan Peterson, July 6, 1975; 1 dau., Mindy Anne. Staff nurse labor and delivery Harris Hosp. Meth., Fort Worth, 1977-78; dir. med. services Lena Pope Home, Fort Worth, 1978; coordinator maternity edn. Harris Hosp. Meth., Fort Worth, 1978-80; nurse adminstr. Edna Gladney Home, Fort Worth, 1980—. CPR instr. trainer Am. Heart Assn.; first aid instr. ARC. Mem. Nurses Assn. of Am. Coll. Ob-Gyn., Tex. Hosp. Assn., Tex. Soc. Hosp. Nursing Service Adminstrs., Tex. Soaring Assn., Soaring Soc. Am. Home: 3620 Willowbrook St Fort Worth TX 76133 Office: 2308 Hemphill St Fort Worth TX 76110

PETERSON, MARGARET MARY, radiation therapist, cons.; b. Newark, July 25, 1948; d. Andrew Joseph and Margaret Mary P.; student in X-ray tech. USPHS Hosp., S.I., N.Y., 1966-68; student in radiation tech. Los Angeles County/U.So. Calif. Med. Center, 1969-70; A.A. in Bus. Adminstrn., San Mateo City Coll., 1978, U. Phoenix, 1982. Staff technician, dosimetrist Los Angeles County/U. So. Calif. Med. Center, 1969-71; dosimetrist City of Hope Nat. Med. Center, Duarte, Calif., 1971-74; radiation therapy technologist So. Bay Hosp., Redondo Beach, Calif., 1974-76; dept. mgr., dosimetrist Peninsula Hosp. and Med. Center, Burlingame, Calif., 1976-81; clin. cons. ATC Med. Technology, Sunnyvale, Calif., 1981-82; cons. in field. Supervisory com. Peninsula Hosp. Credit Union, 1979-83, mgmt. steering com., 1980-81, vice chmn., 1981. Grantee, State of Calif., 1980-83; lic., cert. radiology and radiation therapy. Mem. Am. Assn. Med. Dosimetrists (pres., 1979-81), Assn. Univ. Radiol. Technologists, Am, Soc. Radiol. Technologists, Calif. Soc. Radiol. Technologists (joint rev. com. therapeutic radiologists com. on tech. and edn. com. Am. Assn. Med. Dosimetrists), No. Calif. Soc. Radiation Therapy Technologists (pres.). Home: 645 Topaz St Redwood City CA 94061

PETERSON, MARTHA, coll. pres.; b. Jamestown, Kans., June 22, 1916; d. Anton R. and Gail (French) Peterson; A.B., U. Kans., 1937, M.A., 1943, Ph.D., 1959; postgrad. Northwestern U., Columbia U.; L.H.D., Chatham Coll., 1968, Med. Coll. Pa., 1970, Molloy Coll., 1971, Mundelein Coll., 1972, Pace Coll., 1974, U. Wis., 1975, Temple U., 1975, W.Va. Wesleyan Coll., 1976; D.Pedagogy (hon.), R.I. Coll., 1975; LL.D., Columbia, 1968, Douglass Coll., 1968, Hofstra U., 1969, Austin Coll., 1972, Hamilton Coll., 1974, Drury Coll., 1975, Beaver Coll., 1977. Instr. U. Kans., 1942-46, asst. dean women, 1946-52, dean women, 1952-56; dean women U. Wis., 1956-63, asst. to pres., 1963, univ. dean for student affairs, 1963-67; pres. Barnard Coll., N.Y.C., 1967-75, Beloit (Wis.) Coll., 1975—; dir. Exxon, Met. Life Ins. Co., United Banks Ill., R.H. Macy & Co., 1st Wis. Corp. Mem. adv. council presidents Assn. Governing Bds. Univs. and Colls.; mem. Pres.'s Commn. on White House Fellowships; vice chmn. Wis. Gov.'s Adv. Commn. Tax Reform, 1978-79; trustee Chatham Coll., Pitts., 1965-79, U. Notre Dame, 1976—, Coll. Entrance Exam. Bd. Recipient Disting. Alumni award, U. Kans., 1968; medalist award N.Y. Acad. Public Edn., 1974; Charles Evans Hughes award, 1975; Spirit of Achievement award Albert Einstein Coll. Medicine, 1975. Mem. Am. Council Edn. (student personnel commn. 1956-59, exec. com. 1971-72), Nat. Assn. Women Deans and Counselors (exec. bd. 1959-61, pres. 1965-67), Intercollegiate Assn. Women Students (nat. adviser 1953-55, 59-61, Am. Personnel and Guidance Assn., Am. Arbitration Assn. (dir.), Mortar Bd., Phi Beta Kappa, Sigma Xi, Pi Lambda Theta, Phi Kappa Phi. Office: Beloit College Beloit WI 53511 *

PETERSON, MARTHA E., coll. pres., corp. dir.; b. Jamestown, Kans., 1916; B.A., M.A., Ph.D., U. Kans. Pres. Beloit (Wis.) Coll.; dir. Met. Life Ins. Co., Exxon Corp. Office: Office of the Pres Beloit Coll Beloit WI 53511 *

PETERSON, MARY LOUISE, trucking co. exec.; b. New Orleans, Dec. 20, 1940; d. Edmond Adam's and Dorethea (Fletcher) Peterson; children—DeVon Daniel, Danita Daniel, Michelle Johnson, Mitchel Johnson. Owner, mgr. Agee's 24 Hour Moving & Storage Co., Los Angeles, 1970—. Home: 1837 S Bronson St Los Angeles CA 90019 Office: Agee's 24 Hour Moving & Storage Co 3556 S Western Ave Los Angeles CA 90018

PETERSON, MAUREEN ANNE, psychologist; b. Jersey City, N.J., May 18, 1942; d. George James and Winifred Theresa (Burns) P.; M.S., Villanova U., 1966; Ph.D., N.Y. U., 1981. Research analyst Grey Advt., N.Y.C., 1966; asst. prof. psychology Fairleigh Dickinson U., Teaneck, N.J., 1966-76, asso. prof., 1976—; psychologist S. Bergen Mental Health Center, Lyndhurst, N.J., 1972—. Bd. trustees, Urban Crisis Council, Passaic, N.J., 1968-71; mem. S. Bergen Human Rights com., 1970-73. Mem. Am. Psychol. Assn., N.J. Psychol. Assn., Psi Chi. Home: 702 Bloomfield St Hoboken NJ 07030 Office: Edward Williams Coll Fairleigh Dickinson Univ 150 Kotte Pl Hackensack NJ 07601

PETERSON, MILDRED OTHMER, lectr., photographer, writer, librarian, civic leader, world traveller; b. Omaha, Oct. 19, 1902; d. Frederick George and Freda Darling (Snyder) Othmer; student U. Nebr., U. Iowa, U. Chgo., Northwestern U.; m. Howard R. Peterson, Aug. 25, 1923 (dec. Feb. 1970). Asst., Central High Sch. Library, Omaha, 1915-19, Tech. High Sch. Library, 1919-20, U. Nebr. Library, 1921-23; dir. public relations and gen. asst. Des Moines Public Library, 1928-35; broadcaster weekly book programs WHO and other Iowa radio stas.; columnist, writer Mid-West News Syndicate, Des Moines Register and Tribune, editor Book Marks, 1929-35; editor Adelphean of Alpha Delta Pi, 1938-39; writer and spl. asst. ALA, 1935—, Chgo. Tribune, 1941—; lectr. on travel, fgn. jewelry and internat. relations, 1940—; lectr. S.S. Rotterdam of Holland Am. Line, 1971, Illini Girls State, 1975; del. 1st Assembly Librarians of Americas, Washington, 1947. Chgo. chmn. India Famine Relief, 1943; a founder, pres. Pan. Am. Bd. Edn., 1955-58, Internat. Visitors Center, 1954-58; Chgo. rep. State Dept. Founding Conf. on Community Services to Fgn. Visitors, Washington, 1957; mem. Mayor's Com. on Chgo. Beautiful, cited by Chgo. Sun and Ill. Adult Edn. Council; bd. dirs. YWCA; mem. 75th and 100th anniversary coms. Hyde Park Union Ch., also mem. mission bd., council; bd. dirs. Friends of Channel 11, PBS, 1982—. Recipient world understanding merit award Chgo. Council Fgn. Relations, 1955; named Woman of Yr. for U.S. and Can., Alpha Delta Pi, 1955; Disting. Service award Pan-Am Bd. Edn., 1966, also founders award, 1968; Uruguayan medal, 1952; Internat. Eloy Alfaro medal, 1952, medal Order of Carlos Manuel de Cespedes, 1956 (Cuba); medal Order of Vasco Nunez de Balboa (Panama), 1956; Internat. Friendship award Girl Scouts of Philippines, 1971; Simon Bolivar trophy Fedn. Latin Am. Orgns., 1976; Outstanding Service award Nat. Council for Community Service to Internat. Visitors, 1977; named Woman of Yr., Friends Chgo. Sch. and Workshop for the Retarded, 1975; Disting. Service award U. Nebr., 1955. Fellow Am. Internat. Acad. (life); mem. Nat. Council Women U.S., Pan-Am Bd. Edn., U.S. Capitol, Ill., Nebr., Chgo. hist. socs., Chgo. Natural History Mus., Citizenship Council Met. Chgo., Oriental Inst., Chgo. Mus. Sci. and Industry, Am. Heritage Council, ALA, Ill. Library Assn., Friends Chgo. Public Library, Chgo. Opera Guild, Chgo. Hort. Soc., Am. Security Council, Lincoln Park Zool. Soc., Mus. Contemporary Art, Crossroads Student Center, Hyde Park-Kenwood Community Conf., Internat. House Assn. (dir., v.p.), Japan-Am. Soc., Soc. Woman Geographers (chpt. pres.; nat. v.p.), Ill. Partners of Ams. (gov.'s com. Sao Paulo, Brazil), Council Fgn. Relations (speakers bur.), Pan Am. Council (a founder, disting. service award 1966), Library Internat. Relations (consular ball com. 18 yrs.), U. Nebr. Alumni Assn. (past pres. local chpts., Disting. Achievement award), U. Nebr. Found., Chgo. Symphony Orch. Soc., Chgo. Art Inst. (Disting. Service award 1979), U. Chgo. Service League (dir.), Am. Legion Aux. (state bds. Iowa and Ill.), AAUW, LWV, Children's Benefit League, United Negro Coll. Fund Bd., Renaissance Soc., Peruvian Arts Soc., U.S.-China People's Friendship Assn., Hispanic Soc. Chgo., Chgo. Acad. Scis. (woman's bd.) Chgo. Chamber Orch. Assn., John G. Shedd Soc., Internat. Platform Assn., Friends of Parks, Internat. Platform Assn., Cook County Hosp. Aux., Grant Park Concert Soc., English Speaking Union, Alpha Delta Pi (past pres. local alumnae chpts.), Xi Delta. Clubs: Order Eastern Star, College, Quadrangle, Ill. Athletic, U. Chgo. Dames, Iowa Authors, Lakeside Lawn Bowling, Hyde Park Neighborhood, Travelers' Century. Contbr. articles to newspapers, periodicals, encys. and yearbooks. Visited and photographed over 230 fng. countries; travels and lectures on fgn. countries; unofcl. attendant numerous internat. confs. Address: 5834 Stony Island Ave Chicago IL 60637

PETERSON, PATRICIA ELIZABETH, govt. ofcl.; b. Washington, Mar. 2, 1941; d. John David and Elsie May (Dickerson) Aldridge; student public schs.; m. Robert Vincent Peterson, May 22, 1976; children—Mark Lee, David Talmadge, Tina Lynn, Tuesday Louise, Sheila Anne, Victoria Elizabeth. Sec., United Security Ins., Washington, 1962-65; sec./receptionist Vlastimil Koubek, AIA, Washington, 1965-72; sec. Met. Washington Area Transit Authority, 1972, exec. sec., 1972—. Mem. Nat. Assn. Female Execs., Nat. Secs. Assn. Club: Met. Toastmistress (past pres.). Home: 212 Aragona Dr Oxon Hill MD 20022 Office: 600 5th St NW Washington DC 20001

PETERSON, SANDRA LEE, pilot; b. St. Paul, June 17, 1947; d. Ralph Edward and Emily Emma Peterson; student U. Minn., Metro State U., St. Paul; grad. various flight schs.; divorced; children—Todd Eric Sirbasku, Mark Allen Sirbasku. Securities agt. Inland Realty Investments, Edina, 1971-73; broker S.L. Peterson Real Estate, St. Paul, 1971—; flight instr., asst. chief pilot Thunderbird Aviation, Eden Prairie, Minn., 1975—, now charter pilot; corp. pilot, asst. chief pilot Proform Inc., Bloomington, Minn., 1976-80; asst. air traffic controller Mpls. Ctr., Farmington, Minn., 1981—; pres. Profl. Pilots, Inc., St. Paul, 1980—; cons., tchr. in field. Lic. airline transport pilot. Grantee Career Guidance and Tng. Center, St. Paul, 1976. Mem. Nat. Assn. Women Bus. Owners, Nat. Assn. Female Execs., Minn. Women's Network. Address: 43 Battle Creek Pl St Paul MN 55119

PETERSON, SARAH JEAN, mfg. co. employee benefits mgr.; b. Lamberton, Pa., Nov. 21, 1926; d. Harry Franklin and Ethel (Hails) Momeyer; student Drake Bus. Sch., 1944-46; m. Richard J. Peterson, Dec. 7, 1979; children by previous marriage—Andrew John, Francis John, Mary John. Sec., John & John, Uniontown, Pa., 1944-49, Mut. of N.Y., Plainfield, N.J., 1957-59; sec. Mack Trucks, Inc., Plainfield and Bridgewater, N.J., 1960-73, supr. personnel services, Bridgewater, 1973-77, mgr. personnel, Allentown, 1977-79, corp. mgr. employee benefits, 1979—. Industry rep. Somerset County (N.J.) Adv. Council, 1966-67; mem. Employer's Adv. Council, Allentown, Pa., 1977-79; mem. Lehigh Valley (Pa.) Manpower Assn., 1977-79; mem. Mayor's Council for Employment of Youth, Allentown, 1977-79; bd. dirs. Women's Correctional Inst., Clinton, N.J., 1974-77; loaned exec. United Way of Somerset Valley, 1975; bd. dirs. Sheltered Workshops, 1975-79, Valley Youth House, Bethlehem, Pa., 1979—. Mem. Community Indsl. Relations Orgn., Allentown C. of C. Personnel Forum. Clubs: Suburban Women's, Beaver Brook Country, Arrowhead Lake Country. Home: 2 Gerrish House The Wawbeek Melvin Village NH 03850 Office: 2100 Mack Blvd Allentown PA 18105

PETERSON, SHIRLEY MARACE, journalist; b. Eugene, Oreg., Sept. 13, 1936; d. William Horace Donald and Catherine Harriet (Gribble) Neely; B.A., Lewis and Clark Coll., 1958; M.S., U. Cin., 1968; m. Jerry R. Peterson, Sept. 5, 1959; children—Kerstin Day, Jon Jeffrey. Tchr., Coll. Prep. Sch., Cin., 1970-71; lectr. biology No. Ky. State Coll., 1971-72, West Valley Coll., Saratoga, Calif., 1973-74; owner, operator Burnt Hills Books (N.Y.), 1977-82; book rev. columnist Schenectady Gazette, 1978—, Suburban Publs., Wayne, Pa., 1982—. Bd. dirs. Homeowner and Taxpayer Assn. Pride's Crossing, Saratoga, 1973-75; pres. Charlton (N.Y.) Hist. Soc., 1978-79. NSF grantee, 1958. Office: Schenectady Gazette 332 State St Schenectady NY 12301 also 134 N Wayne Ave Wayne PA 19087

PETERSON, SUSAN JANE, educator; b. Crookston, Minn., June 29, 1950; d. Bruce Higinbotham and Lois Margaret (Fellman) Higinbotham; A.A., N.D. State Sch. Sci., 1970; B.S., No. Ariz. U., 1976, M.A., 1979, postgrad, 1980—; m. Larry John Peterson, Aug. 5, 1972. Dental hygienist Dr. Roger Zehren, Winona, Minn., 1970-74, Dr. A. Dalpiaz and Dr. Terry Morris, Flagstaff, Ariz., 1974-76; asst. prof. dental hygiene No. Ariz. U., Flagstaff, 1974—, clin. dir., 1979-82, now dept. chmn. Mem. Am. Dental Hygienist Assn., Am. Assn. Dental Schs., Am. Acad. Periodontology, No. Ariz. Dental Hygiene Assn., Phi Kappa Phi. Presbyterian. Club: Expanded Functions Study, Elks. Office: No Ariz U Box 15065 Flagstaff AZ 86011

PETERSON, VIVIAN ALICE, librarian; b. Blooming Prairie, Minn., Oct. 15, 1919; d. Hans and Alice Marie (Hansen) P.; B.A., Augsburg Coll., Minn., 1941; M.A., U. Denver, 1949; cert. advanced study, Columbia U., 1971. Tchr., Minn., 1941-48; asst. librarian U. Colo. Med. Sch., 1948; catalog librarian Iowa State Coll., 1949-52, Luther Coll., Iowa, 1952-60; library dir. Midland Luth. Coll., Nebr., 1960-74; dir. library services Concordia (Nebr.) Tchrs. Coll., 1974—. Luth. Edn. Fund grantee, 1966; Comparative Internat. Edn. Soc. and Phi Delta Kappa field study seminar grantee, 1972. Mem. ALA (council 1975-79), Mountain Plains Library Assn., Nebr. Library Assn. (pres. 1972-73, pres. coll. and univ. sect. 1982-83), AAUW, Gen. Fedn. Women's Club, Common Cause, Seward Arts Council. Lutheran. Club: Seward Women's. Author articles in field. Home: 1103 Kolterman St Seward NE 68434 Office: Link Library Concordia Tchrs Coll 800 N Columbia St Seward NE 68434

PETERSON-FALZONE, SALLY JEAN, speech pathologist; b. Paxton, Ill., Feb. 22, 1942; d. Clarence Eugene and Dorothy Lucille (Stine) Peterson; B.S., U. Ill., 1964, M.A., 1965; Ph.D., U. Iowa, 1971; m. Nicholas R. Falzone, May 17, 1975. Research asso. Audiology Cleft Palate Clinic and dept. otolaryngology U. Ill. Coll. Medicine, Chgo., 1965-67, asso. prof. otolaryngology, project dir. speech and hearing Center Craniofacial Anomalies, 1971—; sr. speech pathologist Inst. Phys. Medicine and Rehab., Peoria, Ill., 1970-71; adj. asso. prof. Purdue U., 1977. Mem. Am. Speech, Lang. and Hearing Assn., Am. Cleft Palate Assn., Am. Cleft Palate Ednl. Found., Internat. Assn. Logopedics and Phoniatrics, AAAS, Soc. Ear-Nose-Throat Advancements in Children, Phi Beta Kappa, Sigma Xi, Phi Kappa Phi, Zeta Phi Eta. Author articles in field. Editorial ... profl. jours. Office: 808 S Wood St Chicago IL 60612

PETERY, MARY ANN, mfg. co. exec.; b. Portland, Oreg., June 1, 1936; d. Walter H. and Ida May (Hartzell) Bauer; grad. Smaller Co. Mgmt. Program, Harvard U., 1977; m. Yuergen E. Schuessler, 1980; children—Melinda, Lorri. With Selma Pressure Treating Co., Inc. (Calif.), 1961-81, chief exec. officer, 1977-81; chief exec. officer Sierra Constrn. Supply, Inc., 1981—; corp. officer Selma Leasing Co., Inc., 1971-76. Bd. dirs. Better Bus. Bur., Pvt. Industry Council; del. White House Conf. on Small Bus.; bus. adv. council Calif. State U., Fresno; adv. council forest products dept. U. Calif.; fund agt. Harvard U. Sch. Bus., 1979-80, 81, 82; Fresno adv. council Region IX, SBA. Mem. Am. Wood Preservers Assn. (gov.), DAR, Colonial Dames XVII Century. Clubs: Harvard Bus. Sch., Harvard. Home: 4355 N Palm Ave Fresno CA 93704 Office: PO Box 13219 Fresno CA 93795

PETHTEL, LILLIAN GISH, journalist; b. Stettler, Alta., Can., Mar. 24, 1912; d. Carl Albert and Alice Myrtle (McMullen) Gish; student Links Sch. Bus., 1930; m. Tom M. Pethtel, Feb. 24, 1931; children—Thomas LeRoy, Reta Joan. Head credit dept. C.C. Anderson Co., Boise, Idaho, 1930-31; sec. firm W.B. Davidson, 1931-33; journalist Lewiston (Idaho) Morning Tribune, 1947-72, Spokane (Wash.) Chronicle, 1965-75; garden editor Idaho County Free Press, Grangeville, 1977—; sec.-treas., acct., dir. Charles E. Burkhart Homes, Inc., 1978-81; master flower show judge, horticulture instr.; pres. Arboretum Assos., U. Idaho, 1978-80, sec., 1980—. Recipient Environ. award U.S. Forest Service, 1973. Mem. Nat. Council State Garden Clubs (nat. affiliates chmn. 1977-81, improved cultivar chmn. 1981—, dir. 1971-79), Idaho Fedn. Garden Clubs (past pres. 1971-73), Idaho Press Women, Nat. Fedn. Press Women, Flower Show Judges Council (pres. 1978-80), Garden Writers Am., Lewis County Hist. Soc. (sec. 1977-79, chmn. archives com. 1980—), Kamiah C. of C., Kamiah Grange. Roman Catholic. Home: Route 2 Box 10 Kamiah ID 83536

PETITE, JEANNETTE ALESSIO, civic worker; b. Akron, Ohio, July 15, 1940; d. Ernest David and Teresa (Petrini) Alessio; B.S., Ohio State U., 1962; m. Michael James Petite, Apr. 27, 1963; children—Christopher, Jennifer. Staff occupational therapist, tchr. Ohio State U. Hosp., Columbus, 1962-63; staff occupational therapist Glendale (Md.) Hosp., 1963-64; art tchr. Florence Crittenton Home, Washington, 1969-74; art cons., Washington, 1974—. Bd. dirs. Montgomery County Sch. PTA, Bethesda, Md., 1972-73; bd. dirs. Lung Assn. Mid-Md., 1973-81, program chmn. Women's Guild, 1972-73, v.p., 1973, pres., 1974; docent Corcoran Gallery Art, 1971-81, asst. chmn., 1973-75, chmn., 1976, women's com., 1979—. Recipient Service award Women's Guild, 1975. Mem. Med. Wives-Georgetown U. Hosp. (pres. 1967), Am. Occupational Therapy Assn., Nat. Soc. Arts and Letters (program chmn. Washington chpt.), Art Barn Assn. (benefit chmn. 1982), Alpha Delta Pi. Home: 5508 Pembroke Terr Bethesda MD 20034

PETKOFF, RUTH LINKSMAN, educator; b. Bklyn., Nov. 27, 1924; d. Morris and Miriam (Schiff) Linksman; B.A., L.I.U., 1946; M.A. in Ednl. Adminstrn., Fed. City Coll., Washington, 1975; m. Leonard Petkoff, Apr. 20, 1969; children—Marcy, Carrie. Contract adminstr. Linochine Products Co., N.Y.C., 1949-59; v.p. Boraca Corp., P.R., 1959-69; instr. lang. and culture, Seoul, Korea, 1969-71; cons. continuing edn. women Fed. City Coll., also U. Va., Falls Church, 1973-74; career counselor Washington Opportunities Women, 1973-75; career devel. coordinator Arlington (Va.) Career Center, 1974-76; supr. CETA Tng. Center, Arlington, 1975—; co-dir. Career Edn. Project Handicapped, 1975-76; lectr. vocat. rehab. Trinity Coll., Washington, 1978—; mem. Arlington Coalition Career Edn., 1979—; also Title IX Coordinating Com.; mem. vocat. com. Va. Mental Health and Mental Retardation Services Bd.; cons. in field Mem. Am. Vocat. Assn., Nat. Skill Center Adminstrs. Assn., Adult Edn. Assn., Nat. Assn. Female Execs., Nat. Employment and Tng. Assn., Va. Employment and Tng. Assn. (pres. 1981), Va. Vocat. Assn. (v.p. 1981), Arlington Bus. and Profl. Women, Women's Am. ORT. Author curriculum materials, papers in field. 22101 Office: 818 S Walter Reed Dr Arlington VA 22204

PETRAITIS, KAREL COLETTE, lawyer; b. Chgo., Apr. 4, 1945; d. Ferdinand John and Dolores (Karroll) P.; B.A., U. Md., 1967, postgrad., 1967-68; J.D., George Washington U., 1971. Admitted to Md. bar, 1972, U.S. Supreme Ct., 1977; law clk. Prince George's County Office of Law (Md.), 1971-72, atty., 1972-80; real estate agt. Harloff & Perkins, Riverdale, Md., 1978—; individual practice law, College Park, Md., 1980—. Bd. dirs. College Park Bd. of Trade, 1981—; youth coordinator Agnew for Gov., 1966, Mathias for Senate, 1968, Beall for Senate, 1970; nat. committeewoman Md. Young Republicans, 1971-79, dir., 1979-81, legal counsel, 1972-79. Recipient cert. appreciation Prince George County Circuit Ct., 1979; cert. public service Prince George County, 1980. Mem. Am. Bar Assn., Md. Bar Assn., Prince George County Bar Assn., AAUW, College Park Bus. and Profl. Women, Prince George's County Bd. Realtors, Elizabeth Seton Alumni Assn., George Washington Law Alumni Assn. (dir. 1979-81, sec. 1982—), U. Md. Alumni Assn. (pres. young alums 1978-80). Roman Catholic. Home: 7307 Radcliffe Dr College Park MD 20740 Office: 4321 Hartwick Rd L201 College Park MD 20740

PETRAKIS, LORRAINE MARDELL TECKLENBURG, univ. adminstr.; b. Armour, S.D., Jan. 16, 1933; d. Alvin Fred and Bertha Kathryn (Boettcher) Tecklenburg; state tchrs. cert. U. S.D., 1952; student Calif. State U., San Francisco, 1973-74, 76; children—Tina Diane, Sonya Lee. Tchr. pub. schs., Canton, S.D., 1952-53; office mgr. Blue Cross, Champaign, Ill., 1953-54; acct. U. Ill., Urbana, 1954-57, Hunzicker Bros., Oklahoma City, 1957-58; office mgr., hosp. adminstrn. U. Calif.-San Francisco Med. Center, 1959, acct., AID overseas contract, 1960-61, adminstrv. asst. contracts and grants adminstrn., 1961-67, contracts and grants officer, contracts and grants adminstrn., 1967-78, asso. dir., contracts and grants adminstrn. and gifts and endowments, 1978—. Mem. Soc. Research Adminstrs., Western Assn. Coll. and Univ. Bus. Officers, Assn. Am. Med. Colls. Democrat. Unitarian. Home: 126 E Vista Ave Daly City CA 94014 Office: U Calif-San Francisco Med Center 1483 4th Ave San Francisco CA 94143

PETRINI, MARCIA AGNES, nurse, educator; b. Sharon, Pa., Oct. 21, 1941; d. Victor Leo and Patricia Agnes (Biggins) P.; B.S. in Nursing, Cath. U. Am., 1963; M.S. (USPHS Title II grantee, 1964-65), U. Calif., San Francisco, 1965; Ph.D., SUNY, Buffalo, 1977; children—Colleen, Theresa, Moira. Faculty St. Joseph's Coll., Emmittsburg, Md., 1963-64, SUNY, Buffalo, 1965-77, Cath. U. Am., Washington, 1977-79; grad. faculty, chmn. dept. parent child nursing, U. Cin., 1979—; prof., dir. nursing program Thiel Coll., Greenville, Pa., 1981—. Allocation Bd., United Way, 1975-77; mem. Chgo. Mus. Health and Human Services grantee, 1980-82, Area Health Edn. Council grantee, 1979-80, 81-83. Mem. Am. Nursing Assn., Nat. League for Nursing (grantee, 1974), Assn. for Supervision and Curriculum Devel., Hastings Center, Smithsonian Instn., Alumnae Assn., Assn. for the Care of Children's Health, Nat. Assn. for the Edn. of Young Children, Day Care Council of Am., Nat. Assoc. of Pediatric Nurse Associates/Practitioners. Clubs: Suburban Study (pres., 1973-74), Garden. Contbg. author article to profl. publ. Office: Thiel College Greenville PA 16125

PETRO, FRANCES CHRISTINE SIMONAITIS, indsl. cabinet mfg. co. exec.; b. Kingston, Pa., Sept. 6, 1939; d. Frank and Helen Christine (Grazaitis) Simonaitis; student Coll. Misericordia, 1957-59, Wilkes Barre Bus. Coll., 1959-60, Cedar Crest Coll.; m. Robert Bernard Petro, Sept. 5, 1964; 1 son, Justin Boyd. Lab. technician Duplan Silk Mills, 1959-60; cost estimator, asst. to plant mgr. Linear Inc., Dallas, Pa., 1960-64; buyer Hess's Dept. Store, 1964-65; with Stanley-Vidmar Inc., 1965—, mgr. purchasing. Chmn. Bicentennial Com. Upper Saucon Twp.; chmn. adv. com. at local community colls., 1979—. Cert. purchasing mgr. Nat. Assn. Purchasing Mgmt. Mem. Am. Prodn. and Inventory Control Soc., Purchasing Mgmt. Assn. Lehigh Valley (officer), Lehigh Valley Purchasing Assn. (pres.). Roman Catholic. Home: Wethersfield RD #1 Center Valley PA 18034 Office: Stanley-Vidmar Inc 11 Grammes Rd Allentown PA 18103

PETRO, VIVIAN HAZEL, wallcovering sales co. exec.; b. Plainfield, N.J., Nov. 13, 1921; d. Victor and Hazel (Vaughn) Petersen; student Pasadena Bus. Coll., 1943-44, Middlesex County Coll., 1972-73; m. Albert R. Petro, Aug. 3, 1947; children—Robert, Edward, Donna. Office mgr. Central Cutter Corp., Somerset, N.J., 1965-73; head dept. teller tng. Franklin State Bank, 1973-78; pres. Wallpaper Factory, Point Pleasant, N.J., 1978—; instr. in banking to Spanish-speaking class Union County Coll., 1977. State Commr. N.J. Bd. Pharmacy, 1973-78; pres. scholarship com. Assn. PTAs of Edison, 1965-68; pres. Edison (N.J.) Republican Club, 1967-68; pres. PTA, Stelton Sch., Thomas Jefferson Jr. High Sch., Edison; pres. Edison Council PTA, 1968-69. Club: Midstreams Women's (sec.). Office: 2807 Bridge Ave Point Pleasant NJ 08742

PETROS, SOPHIE KARIPIDES (MRS. THOMAS S. PETROS), home economist, dir. pub. relations; b. Canton, Ohio, Nov. 4, 1932; d. Constantine N. and Martha (Sideropoulos) Karipides; student Ohio State U., 1950-52; B.S. in Journalism, Northwestern U., 1954; m. Thomas S. Petros, Jan. 10, 1960; 1 son, Dean. Tchr. home econs. St. Charles Borromeo Environ. House, Chgo., 1958; publicity-promotion asst. Toni Co., Chgo., 1954-55; TV account exec. Yardis Advt. Co., Phila., 1955-56; TV writer, demonstrator Crestline Co., Chgo., 1957; home service rep. Peoples Gas Light & Coke Co., Chgo., 1957-62; dir. pub. relations and advt., sec. Dial On Corp., Milw., 1962—; condr. gourmet cooking show Sta. WISN-TV, Milw., 1971—; owner-mgr. Sophie Kay's Restaurant, 1980, Sophie Kay's Fine Dining, Hales Corners, Wis., 1980—; free-lance food demonstrator; free-lance TV commls., 1956—. Chmn., Hope for Hope Fund, Canton, 1954. Recipient debate award Nat. Forensic League, 1950. Mem. AFTRA, Am. Home Econs. Assn., Home Econs. in Bus., Northwestern U. Alumni Assn., Theta Sigma Phi, Alpha Xi Delta. Greek Orthodox. Club: Annunciation Women's. Author: Sophie Kay's Step-by-Step Cook Book, 1972; Sophie Kay's Family Cookbook, 1975; Jr. Chef Cookbook, 1977; Sophie Kay's Yogurt Cookery, 1978; Sophie Kay's Pasta Cookery, 1979; The Chicken Cookbook, 1981. Home: 15325 Westover Rd Elm Grove WI 53108

PETROVSKA, MARIJA, French scholar, educator; b. Zagreb, Yugoslavia; d. Frantisek and Marija P.; B.A. in Drama, Conservatory Dramatic Arts, Prague, Czechoslovakia; diploma Institut Hautes Etudes d'Interpretariat, Milan, Italy, 1954; M.A. in French, U. Tenn., 1965; Ph.D. in French, U. Ky., 1972. Profl. actress, Czechoslovakia, 1946-50; free-lance translator, interpreter, journalist, Italy, 1950-63; instr. French and Italian, U. Tenn., Knoxville, 1963-72, asst. prof. French and Czech, 1972-76, asso. prof. French and comparative lit., 1976-81, prof., 1981—. Fellow, Seminar in American Studies, Salzburg, Austria, 1960; Haggin grad. fellow, U. Ky., 1969-70. Mem. MLA, So. Assn. MLA, Czechoslovak Soc. Arts and Scis. in Am. Author: Victor Hugo, l'écrivain engagé en Bohême, 1977; Prague Diptych, a Novel, 1980; contbr. articles to scholarly jours. France and U.S. Home: 3617 Southwood Dr Knoxville TN 37920 Office: Univ Tennessee Knoxville TN 37916

PETTERSON, SYLVIA ROYSENE, radiologist; b. Worcester, Mass., Aug. 21, 1944; d. Roy Gustav Adolphus and Miriam Sylvia (Anderson) Petterson; B.S. with honors, Fla. So. Coll., 1966; M.D., U. Miami (Fla.), 1970. Intern in surgery St. Vincent Hosp., Worcester, Mass., 1970-71, resident in pathology, 1971-72, radiology, 1972-75, chief resident, 1974-75; staff. radiologist Indian River Meml. Hosp., Vero Beach, Fla., 1976-79, Sebastian River Med. Center, Sebastian, Fla., 1976-79, Fla. Med. Center, Ft. Lauderdale, Fla., 1979-80, St. Francis Hosp., Miami Beach, Fla., 1979-80, Broward Med. Center, Ft. Lauderdale, 1980—, Imperial Point Hosp., Ft. Lauderdale, 1980—, North Broward Hosp., Ft. Lauderdale, 1980—; partner W.W. McCorkle M.D. and W. B. Whittiker, M.D., Vero Beach, 1976-79, Cunningham and Rasken, M.D., P.A., Tamarac, Fla., 1979-80; asso. North Broward Radiologists, Ft. Lauderdale, 1981—; advisor Radiol. Technologist tng. program Indian River Community Coll., Ft. Pierce, 1976—, Broward Community Coll., Fort Lauderdale, 1980—. Named Young Alumnus of the Year, Fla. So. Coll., 1973. Mem. AMA (Physician Recognition award, 1973, 76, 79), Fla. Med. Assn., Broward County Med. Assn., New Eng. Roentgen Ray Soc., Am. Med. Women's Assn., Radiology Soc. N. Am., Am. Assn. Women Radiologists. Republican. Methodist. Contbr. articles in field to med. jours. Home: 2430 Deer Creek Country Club Blvd Deerfield Beach FL 33441 Office: Broward Gen Med Center 1600 S Andrews Ave Fort Lauderdale FL 33316

PETTETT, BARBARA VIRGINIA, computer specialist; b. Cin., Sept. 18, 1938; d. Philip Wayne and Virginia Bird (Handley) P.; student Sinclair Coll., Tulane U.; 1 son, Daniel Frederick Reasor, Jr. Owner, mgr. Honeysuckle Pet Shop, Tipp City, Ohio, 1970-76; office mgr. Doody & Doody, C.P.A.s, New Orleans, 1976-77, computer ops. mgr., 1979—; office mgr. San Diego Yacht Club, 1977-79. Mem. DECUSERS Assn. Republican. Lutheran. Home: 320 W Wm David Metairie LA 70005 Office: 1160 Commerce Bldg New Orleans LA 70112

PETTIJOHN, JOYCE LORRAINE, pharmacist; b. Portland, Oreg., Jan. 7, 1955; d. Elzo Irving and Verona Muriel (McKittrick) Pettijohn; B.S. in Pharmacy, Oreg. State U., 1978. Staff pharmacist Evergreen Pharm. Services, Kirkland, Wash., 1979-80, sr. staff pharmacist, 1981—; dir. Health Products, Inc., Kirkland. Lic. pharmacist, Wash., Calif., Oreg. Mem. Am., Wash. State pharm. assns. Office: 200 Kirkwood Mall Kirkland WA 98033

PETTIROSS, VIRGINIA ELISE, educator; b. Ludlow, Mass., Oct. 7, 1940; d. William Rettew and Lea Roseanne (LaFave) Albanese; B.S., Central Conn. State Coll., 1960, M.S., 1965; C.A.G.S., U. Conn., 1976. Tchr. social sci. dept. Valley Regional High Sch., Deep River, Conn., 1960-66; tchr. Durham (Conn.) High Sch., 1966-68; faculty social sci. dept. Project DISCUSS, Durham, 1968-69; mem. adminstrv. staff Middlesex Community Coll., Middletown, Conn., 1969-74, coordinator cable telecommunications, 1974—. Chairperson Middletown Cable TV Advisory Bd., 1973-78, 5-Town Regional Cable Advisory Council, 1977—; mem. State Commn. on Ednl. and Informational Uses of Cable Telecommunications, 1974-75. Mem. Nat. Cable TV Assn., Assn. Ednl. Communications and Tech., Conn. Higher Edn. TV Assn., Cable TV Higher Edn. Telecommunications Assn. Democrat. Home: 124 Crystal Lake Rd Middletown CT 06457

PETTIT, MARGARET ESTA, broadcasting exec.; b. Provo, Utah, July 22, 1926; d. Howard Hammil and Edith Susan (Cummins) Cain; student public schs.; m. Claud Martin Pettit, July 30, 1948; children—Ruth Elaine, Paul Martin. Co-owner, office supr. Sta. KEOS, Flagstaff, Ariz., 1960-61; co-owner, bookkeeper Sta. KWIV, Douglas, Wyo., 1965-74; co-owner, bookkeeper, program dir., office supr. Sta. KCMP, Brush Colo., 1976-82; dir. Custom Broadcasting Co., Denver; sec.-treas., dir. Ranchland Broadcasting Co. Bd. dirs. Jefferson Park Community Activity Assn., Denver, 1981—. Mem. Model T Ford Club. Baptist. Home: 2761 E 93d Pl Thornton CO 80229 Office: 2761 E 93d Pl Thornton CO 80229

PETTY, MARILYN, banker; b. N.Y.C., Sept. 3, 1932; d. Henry and Rosemarie (Fahner) Wahl; B.A., Queens Coll., 1959, M.B.A., 1981. With Mfrs. Hanover Trust Co., N.Y.C., 1950-72, asst. mgr., 1964-72; investment asst. Bank of Bermuda, Ltd., Hamilton, 1963-64; ops. officer Beverly Hills Nat. Bank (Calif.), 1972-74; trust ops. officer Palmer 1st Nat. Bank, Sarasota, Fla., 1976; investment officer Savs. Bank Trust Co., N.Y.C., 1976—; tchr. Am. Inst. Banking. Children's com. L.I. Jewish Med. Center. Mem. Savs. Banks Assn. for Women, Investment Officers Assn. Savs. Banks. Office: 200 Park Ave New York NY 10166

PETTY, RUTH ROBERTS, ins. co. exec.; b. Greensboro, N.C., Aug. 12, 1947; d. David Herbert and Virginia (Ketner) P.; B.A., Wheaton Coll., 1969; M.A., Calif. State U., Sacramento, 1977; 1 son, David Petty. Instr., Calif. Community Colls., 1976-81; real estate exec. Jones, Brand & Hullin-Coldwell Banker, Sacramento, 1977-82; rep. Equitable Life Assurance Soc., Richmond, Va., 1981—; cons. fins., mgmt. Pres., Crosswoods Homeowners Assn., Citrus Heights, Calif., 1976-77, v.p., 1977. Mem. Am. Bar Assn., Am. Sociol. Assn., Pacific Sociol. Assn., Am. Mgmt. Assn., Nat. Assn. Life Underwriters. Author: (with others) Sociology With a Human Face, 1977. Office: PO Box 8703 1801 Libbie Ave Richmond VA 23226

PETTYJOHN, SHIRLEY ELLIS, lawyer, real estate exec.; b. Liberty, Ky., Aug. 16, 1935; d. Wesley Barker and Ada Lou (Bryant) Ellis; B.S. in Commerce, U. Louisville, 1974, J.D., 1977. m. Flem D. Pettyjohn, Sept. 24, 1955; children—Deena Reneé, Ellisa Denise. Pres., Pettyjohn, Inc., real estate brokering service operating in Ky. and Ind.; admitted to Ky. bar, 1978; individual practice law, Louisville, 1978—. Commr., vice chmn. Louisville and Jefferson County Planning Commn., 1971-75; participant Gov.'s Conf. on Edn., 1977. Mem. Am. Bar Assn., Ky. Bar Assn., Louisville Bar Assn., Am. Judicature Soc., Am. Inst. Planners, Council Women Pres. (Woman of Achievement award 1974), Women's C. of C. of Ky., Sigma Delta Kappa. Recipient Mayor's Cert. of Recognition for community service, 1974; Mayor's Fleur de Lis award for outstanding service to City of Louisville, 1969-73; jud. nominee, 1981. Clubs: Am. Legion Aux., Fraternal Order Police Assos. Home: 6924 Norlynn Dr Louisville KY 40228 Office: 606 S 3d St Louisville KY 40202

PETZEL, FLORENCE ELOISE, educator; b. Crosbyton, Tex., Apr. 1, 1911; d. William D. and A. Eloise (Punchard) P.; Ph.B., U. Chgo., 1931, A.M., 1934; Ph.D., U. Minn., 1954. Instr., Judson Coll., 1936-38; vis. instr. Tex. State Coll. for Women, 1937; asst. prof. textiles Ohio State U., 1938-48; asso. prof. U. Ala., 1950-54; prof. Oreg. State U., 1954-61, 67-75, 77; prof. emeritus, 1975—, dept. head, 1954-61, 67-75; prof., div. head U. Tex., 1961-63; prof. Tex. Tech. U., 1963-67; vis. prof. Wash. State U., 1967. Effie I. Raitt fellow, 1949-50. Mem. Sigma Xi, Phi Kappa Phi, Omicron Nu, Iota Sigma Pi, Sigma Delta Epsilon, Am. Assn. Ret. Persons. Author articles in field. Home: 730 NW 35th St Corvallis OR 97330

PEUGH, SARAH LOUISE PEARSON (MRS. WALTER STEPHEN PEUGH, SR.), freelance writer; b. Houston, Miss., Oct. 4, 1924; d. Edd Monroe (dec.) and Mattie (Shivers) (dec.) Pearson; student Trevecca Coll., 1941-43, Miss. state Extension, 1964, Auburn U., 1970, student Itawamba Jr. Coll., 1970; m. Walter Stephen Peugh, Sr., Dec. 20, 1947; children—Sarah Peugh Franks, Mary Jo Peugh Ayres, Steve, Bob. Clk., teller First Nat. Bank, Phila. and San Diego, 1944; owner Town House Restaurant, Aberdeen, Miss., 1952-62; owner, grad., bridal cons. Wedding Services, Aberdeen, 1969-76; columnist Aberdeen Examiner, 1970-74, 77; Aberdeen News Herald, 1974-75. Exec. sec. ARC, Aberdeen, 1972-73, bd. dirs. 1973-77; bd. dirs. Miss. YMCA, 1974-78, Miss. for Ednl. TV, 1978-80; chmn. Council Clubs and City Beautiful Commn., 1974-76; area rep. Keep Miss. Beautiful, 1974-76; initiator Butterfly scholarship Miss. Fedn. Women's Clubs, 1978, Amblin scholarship, 1976, organizer 1st Juniorette Club, 1974. Miss. YMCA, Youth Gov. scholarship, 1977. Named Most Outstanding Woman, Jr. Aux. Charity Ball, Aberdeen, 1972. Mem. Aberdeen C. of C., Miss. Press Women, Miss. Fedn. Women's Clubs (Outstanding Woman of Yr. 1981), Nat. Fedn. Press Women, Miss. Poetry Soc. (organizer North Branch, Miss. chpt. 1979), Public Relations Assn. of Miss., N.E. Miss. Tourism Council, Am. Legion Aux. Clubs: Woman's (pres. 1973-74), Home and Garden, Gourmet (founder), Miss. Fashion Women (founder, exec. dir.). Editor: The Glencoe Story, 1967; contbr. poetry to various publs. Address: 205 Hillcrest St Aberdeen MS 39730

PEVEAR, ROBERTA CHARLOTTE, state legislator; b. Bethel, Maine, July 4, 1930; d. Frank Albert and Thirza Estelle (Hickford) Gibson; student pvt. schs., Bethel Maine; m. Edward Gordon Pevear, Aug. 21, 1971. Legal and exec. sec. Johnson & Johnson, New Brunswick, N.J., 1959-66; exec. sec., adminstrv. asst. Sears, Roebuck & Co., 1967-77; sec. Southeastern N.H. Regional Planning Commn., 1978-79; mem. N.H. Ho. of Reps., 1979—, com. on agr. and environ., also various subcoms.; exec. bd. Rockingham County. Dir. CD, Hampton Falls, N.H. Mem. N.H. Order Women Legislators, Nat. Order Women Legislators, Gen. Fedn. Women's Clubs, Hampton Falls Fire Dept. Aux., VFW Aux., Am. Legion Aux., DAR (vice regent Ranger chpt.). Republican. Club: Hampton Monday.

PEVELER, SARAH KATHRYN FESSLER, personnel ofcl.; b. Mt. Vernon, Ill., Feb. 21, 1947; d. Floyd Roscoe and Mildred Faye (Carson) Fessler; B.A., Emory U., 1969; postgrad. U. South Sch. Theology, 1980—; m. R. David Peveler, June 14, 1969 (div. Aug. 1981). Tng. dir. Ill. Shore council Girl Scout U.S.A., Wilmette, Ill., 1970-73, Abnaki council, Brewer, Maine, 1973-75, tng. dir., dir. field services Shawnee council, Martinsburg, W.Va., 1976-77; personnel dir. Seamen's Ch. Inst. N.Y. and N.J., N.Y.C., 1978-80; personnel dir. Trinity Ch., N.Y.C., 1980—; owner, propr. The Uncommon Resume, cons. firm. Personnel com. Greater N.Y. council Girl Scouts U.S.A.; sec. Lower Manhattan Interparish Council, 1979—; adminstrv. com. Irish Arts Center. Mem. Am. Soc. Personnel Adminstrn., N.Y. Personnel Mgmt. Assn., Phi Mu. Club: St. Bartholomew's City. Office: 74 Trinity Pl New York NY 10006

PEVEN, DOROTHY ESTELLE SPINKA, psychiat. social worker; b. Chgo.; M.S.W. (NIMH grantee), Jane Addams Sch. Social Work, U. Ill., Chgo., 1969; cert. in psychotherapy Alfred Adler Inst., Chgo., 1972. Psychotherapist in group pvt. practice, Chgo., 1969—; mem. faculty, tng. therapist Alfred Adler Inst., Chgo.; allied health profl. St. Joseph Hosp., Chgo., also cons. In-Patient Service Community Mental Health, 1972—; cons., lectr. Alfred Adler Insts., St. Louis, Vancouver, B.C., Cleve., Toronto; lectr. N. Am. Soc. Adlerian Psychology, N.Y.C., Congress of Internat. Assn. Individual Psychology, Zurich, Switzerland, Vienna Austria, Amsterdam, Netherlands. Mem. Acad. Cert. Social Workers, Nat. Assn. Social Workers, N.Am. Soc. Adlerian Psychology (officer), Am. Assn. Marriage and Family Therapy, Internat. Assn. Individual Psychology (council). Contbr. articles to profl. jours. Office: 2913 N Commonwealth Ave Suite 617 Chicago IL 60657

PEYTON, LORETTA ANNE, educator; b. Richmond, Va., May 31, 1949; d. Welford Michael and Mary Alice (Burt) Childress; student Longwood Coll., 1967-69; B.A., Westhampton Coll. of U. Richmond, 1971; postgrad. Va. Commonwealth U., 1977; m. Peter Mark Peyton, Mar. 24, 1978; 1 dau., Mary Lauren. Ednl./vocat. counselor Army Edn. Center, Herzo Base, W. Ger., 1971-72; social worker Palo Alto Mental Health Center, Mineral Wells, Tex., 1973; PREP coordinator Monterey (Calif.) Peninsula Unitied Sch. Dist., 1974-76; adult basic edn. tchr. Henrico County Schs., Richmond, Va., 1976-81; dir. edn./dean students Smithdeal-Massey Bus. Coll., Richmond, 1981—; cons. Va. State Dept. Edn., 1981—; adult edn. tchr. Mem. Forest Hill Civic Assn., 1982—; vol. worker Am. Heart Assn., 1982—. Recipient Cert. of Achievement, Army Edn. Center, W. Ger., 1972. Mem. Adult Edn. Assn. Va. (legis. com. 1981-82), Westhampton Alumnae Assn., Psi Chi, Kappa Delta Alumnae. Republican. Baptist. Home: 1204 W 45th St Richmond VA 23225 Office: 300 W Grace St Richmond VA 23220

PEZZULLO, MARY ANN, mktg. research cons.; b. Boston, Dec. 15, 1937; d. George William and Angela Rita (Crescio) O'Donnell; B.S. in Bus. Adminstrn., Emmanuel Coll., 1958; M.A. in Econs., Boston Coll., 1967; m. Joseph Pezzullo, Dec. 14, 1969. Instr. in econs., fin. aid officer Emmanuel Coll., 1965-68; research asso. Inst. Human Scis., Boston

Coll., 1968-69, research asso. United Jersey Banks, Princeton, N.J., 1972-74, mgr. mktg. research, 1974-78, v.p., dir. mktg., 1978-81; asso. RL Assos., Princeton, 1981—. Mem. Bank Mktg. Assn. (pres. Pa./N.J./Del. chpt., speaker conv. 1979), Am. Mktg. Assn. Roman Catholic. Author: Marketing for Bankers, 1982 Office: 15 Chambers St Princeton NJ 08540

PFAELZER, MARIANA R., fed. judge; b. 1926; A.B., U. Calif.; LL.B., UCLA Sch. Law. Admitted to bar, 1958; judge U.S. Dist. Ct. for Dist. Central Calif. Mem. Am. Bar Assn. Office: US Dist Ct 312 N Spring St Los Angeles CA 90012 *

PFAFF, SANDRA JEAN, health consortium ofcl.; b. Somerville, N.J., May 24, 1946; d. Ernest Kenneth and Hester Elizabeth (Tichenor) P.; B.S. in Nursing, DePauw U., 1968. Med.-surg. charge nurse Newton (N.J.) Meml. Hosp., 1972-73, infection control nurse, central supply supr., 1973-74; infection control practitioner St. Joseph's Hosp., Milw., 1974-79; nursing cons. South Fla. Hosp. Consortium for Infection Control, 1979-81, asso. dir., 1981—; cons. Center for Disease Control, 1981—; cons., writer, lectr. in field. Served with Nurse Corps. U.S. Army, 1968-72. Mem. Assn. Practitioners Infection Control (pres. Greater Milw. chpt. 1977, dir. chpt. 1978, chmn. nat. edn. com. 1978-80, nat. dir. 1979-80). Office: S Fla Hosp Consortium for Infection Control 1295 NW 14th St Suite M Miami FL 33125

PFAFFENROTH, SARA BEEKEY, educator; b. Reading, Pa., Dec. 2, 1941; d. Cyrus Ezra and Viola Bessie (Sweigart) Beekey; A.B., Bryn Mawr Coll., 1963; M.A., Ind. U., 1964; m. Peter Albert Pfaffenroth, June 26, 1966; children—Elizabeth Kilmer, Peter Cyrus, Catherine Genevieve. Instr. English, Northwestern Mich. Coll., Traverse City, 1964-66, Middlesex County Coll., Edison, N.J., 1966-68; prof. English, County Coll. of Morris, Randolph, N.J., 1968—; grants cons., 1979-82. Recipient poetry award Bryn Mawr Arts Council, 1963, Gertrude Saucier Hist. Poetry award, 1970. Mem. N.J. Poetry Soc. (trustee), MLA, Coll. English Assn., Jane Austen Soc. N.Am. Lutheran. Editor anthologies: Beyond Tether, 1975; A Palette of Poets, 1976; Endless Waters Welling Up, 1977; From Rim to Rim, 1978; Crystal Cadences, 1980. Home: Box 429 Chester NJ 07930 Office: County College of Morris Randolph NJ 07801

PFEFFER, JANICE MARIE, physiologist; b. Rockford, Ill., Oct. 31, 1943; d. William and Mary Frances (Olszewski) Sikorski; B.A. Rockford Coll., 1969; Ph.D., U. Okla., 1977; m. Marc Alan Pfeffer, Aug. 22, 1970. NIH post-doctoral fellow Harvard Med. Sch., Boston, 1977-80, instr. medicine, 1980-81, asst. prof. medicine, 1981—. Recipient Young Investigators Research award NIH, 1980-83, Mem. Am. Heart Assn., Am. Physiol. Soc., Internat. Soc. Hypertension, Internat. Soc. Heart Research, Am. Fedn. Clin. Research. Contbr. articles to various publs. Home: 30 Broadlawn Dr Chestnut Hill MA 02167 Office: Dept of Medicine Brigham and Women's Hosp 75 Francis St Boston MA 02115

PFEIFER, ELLEN CLAIRE, journalist; b. St. Louis, June 23, 1947; d. George Edwin and Audrey Louise Pfeifer; student U. Colo., 1964-65; B.S. in Journalism, Northwestern U., 1968; postgrad. U. So. Calif., 1968-70; m. Daniel M. Polvere, Apr. 8, 1973. Asst. music critic Boston Globe, 1970-72; music critic Boston Herald Am., 1972—. Sec., Charlestown (Mass.) Preservation Soc., 1976-78. Rockefeller Found. Project for Tng. Music Critics fellow, 1969-71. Mem. Music Critics Assn. Contbr. articles to music mags. Office: 300 Harrison Ave Boston MA 02106

PFEIFFER, JANE CAHILL, former broadcasting co. exec., cons.; b. Washington, Sept. 29, 1932; d. John Joseph and Helen (Reilly) Cahill; B.A., U. Md., 1954; m. Ralph A. Pfeiffer, Jr., June 3, 1975. With IBM Corp., Armonk, N.Y., 1955-76, sec. mgmt. rev. com., 1970, dir. communications, 1971, v.p. communications and govt. relations, 1972-76, bus. cons., 1976-78; chmn. NBC, Inc., N.Y.C., 1978-81; bus. cons., 1981—; dir. Chesebrough-Ponds, Inc., Internat. Paper Co., J.C. Penney Co. Participant, White House Fellows program, 1966; mem. Council on Fgn. Relations, Overseas Devel. Council, Pres.'s Commn. Mil. Compensation, 1978-79, Pres.'s Commn. White House Fellows, 1976-81. Trustee, Rockefeller Found., U. Notre Dame. Office: Field Point Circle Greenwich CT 06830 *

PFEIFFER, PHYLLIS KRAMER, pub.; b. N.Y.C., Feb. 11, 1949; d. Jacob N. and Estelle G. Rosenbaum-Pfeiffer; student Harvard U., 1967, N.Y.U., 1968, 72, Ithaca Coll., 1969; B.S., Cornell U., 1970; postgrad. U. San Diego, 1976-78; m. Stephen M. Pfeiffer, Dec. 21, 1969. Instr., Miss Porter's Sch., Farmington, Conn., 1970; tchr. N.Y.C. Bd. Edn., Dewey Jr. High Sch., 1970-73; research Hunter Coll., N.Y., 1971-72; account exec. La Jolla (Calif.) Light, 1973-75, advt. dir., 1975-77, gen. mgr., 1977-78, pub., 1978—; dir. communications center San Diego State U., 1980—. Bd. dirs. La Jolla Cancer Research Found., 1979—, Alvarado Hosp., 1981—; co-chmn. Operation USS La Jolla, U.S. Navy, 1980—; mem. mktg. com. United Way, 1979-81; bd. dirs. YMCA, San Diego Ballet, 1980; trustee La Jollan's Inc., 1975-78. N.Y. Bd. Edn. grantee, 1971-72. Mem. Am., Calif. newspaper pubs. assns., Women in Communications, Chancellor's Assn. U. Calif. San Diego, Calif. Newspaper Advt. Execs. Assn. Club: Tennis of La Jolla. Home: 6024 Avenida Cresta La Jolla CA 92037 Office: PO Box 1927 450 Pearl St La Jolla CA 92038

PFINGSTAG, NANCY LEE, educator; b. Chgo., Apr. 2, 1946; d. George and Celeste Mary (Maher) Sammet; B.A., SUNY, Binghamton, 1976; M.A., U. N.C., Charlotte, 1979; m. Benjamin Nelson Pfingstag, Jan. 9, 1970; children—Thomas Dylan, Constance Shannon. Lectr., Central Peidmont Community Coll., Charlotte, N.C., 1976-77, Queens Coll., Charlotte, 1978-79; instr. English lang. tng. inst. U. N.C., Charlotte, 1979—; English as a second lang. cons. Charlotte-Mecklenburg Public Sch. System, Charlotte. Mem. Assn. Tchrs. of Advanced Composition, Nat. Council Tchrs. of English, Tchrs. of English to Speakers of Other Langs., Mecklenburg Literacy Council, AAUW, Phi Beta Kappa. Democrat. Roman Catholic. Contbr. articles on English edn. to profl. jours. Home: 2400 Kimway Dr Matthews NC 28105 Office: Center for Internat Studies U NC Charlotte NC 28223

PFLAGER, RUTH WOOD, communications coordinator; b. Springfield Mass., Mar. 3, 1917; d. Walter Guy and Mabel (Munson) Wood; B.S., U. Mass., 1938; postgrad. Northwestern U., 1939-40; m. Miller S. Pflager, Aug. 31, 1940; children—Sandra P. Wischmeyer, Charlene P. Balistrere, William Wood, Jessie Ruth. Program chmn., v.p. Radio and TV Council Greater Cleve., Inc., 1973-75, pres., 1975-77, exec. dir., 1977-79. Mem. Communications Commn., Greater Cleve. Interchurch Council, 1972—, vice chmn. 1981—; chmn. Community Mental Health Inst., 1981-82; communications coordinator Ch. Women United in Cleve., 1974—, bull. editor, 1974-78, honor award, 1980; chmn. media concerns Ch. Women United in Ohio, 1979—. Recipient Outstanding Service award Radio-TV Council, 1977. Mem. AAUW (br. pres. 1977-79, com. on women Ohio div. 1979-81, chmn. media concerns task force), Am. Council Better Broadcasts (life mem., sec. 1979-80 v.p. 1980—), Nat. Assn. Better Broadcasting, Nat. Citizens Com. for Broadcasting, Orange Hist. Soc. Methodist. Club: Women's City (mem. mental health com. 1974—) (Cleve.). Home: 4349 S Hilltop Dr Chagrin Falls OH 44022 Office: Room 1219 University Tower Cleveland OH 44115 also 2230 Euclid Ave Cleveland OH 44115

PHAGAN, PATRICIA ANN, educator; b. St. Louis, July 9, 1946; d. Charles Patrick and Veronica Rose (Callahan) Coyne; B.S., Loyola U., Chgo., M.Ed. (HEW scholar 1974), Ed.D. in Adminstrn. and Supervision; married Oct. 15, 1977; 1 son, Peter. Part-time dental hygienist, Deerfield, Ill., 1970-75; office asst. Loyola U. Dental Sch., 1975-77; mem. faculty Northwestern U. Dental Sch., 1974—, prof. dental hygiene and adminstrn., 1980—, div. chmn. dental hygiene and aux. programs, 1979—. Mem. Am. Dental Hygienists Assn. (scholarship 1969-70), N. Suburban Dental Hygienists Soc. (pres. 1972-73), Ill. Dental Hygienists Assn. (dir. 1972-79, chmn. com. dental health edn. and public info. 1973-78), Chgo. Dental Soc., Orgn. Tchrs. Dental Practice Adminstrn. (exec. council 1977—), Ill. Dirs. Dental Hygiene Assn. (chmn. 1977-79), Nat. Dirs. Dental Hygiene Assn., Ill. Dental Soc., Am. Assn. Dental Schs., ADA, Nat. Soc. Prevention Oral Disease (dir. 1981-82), Sigma Phi Sigma (chpt. pres. 1973-77), Phi Delta Kappa, Alpha Sigma Nu. Democrat. Roman Catholic. Author articles in field. Office: 240 E Huron St Chicago IL 60611

PHARIS, MARY MARGARET EVANS, psychologist, psychiat. social worker; b. Milw., July 3, 1938; d. Silas McAfee and Lorraine (McManamy) Evans; student Stanford U., 1956-58; B.S. with sr. honors, U. Wis., 1960; M.A. (Univ. fellow 1961-62), U. Chgo., 1962; Ph.D., U. Tex.-Austin, 1978; m. David Bunsen Pharis, Aug. 6, 1966; children—Christopher Eugene, Michael Jonathon. Caseworker Scholarship and Guidance Assn., Chgo., 1962-66; social work supr., psychiat. services Michael Reese Hosp., Chgo., 1966-68, coordinator student program, psychiat. social work dept., 1967-68; spl. services social worker Lab. Sch., Evanston, Ill., 1968-69; instr. MacMurray Coll., 1972-74, Ill. Coll., 1972-74; psychology intern U. Tex. Counseling-Psychol. Services Center, 1978-79; Congl. Sci. fellow U.S. Congress, 1979-80; spl. asst. to chief Mental Health Study Center, NIMH, 1980-81; pvt. practice, 1982—; adj. asst. prof. dept. psychology, also asst. prof. Sch. Social Work, U. Tex. at Austin, 1982—; cons. Settlement Club Home, 1982—; therapist dept. clin. services Family Ct. of Cook County, 1964-66; field work instr. U. Chgo. Sch. Social Service Adminstrn., 1966-68, Smith Coll. Sch. Social Work, Northampton, Mass., 1967-68; research asso. U. Tex., Austin, 1975; cons. Loretto Hosp., Chgo., 1969, Ill. Law Enforcement Commn., 1970. Bd. dirs. Jacksonville Area Council on Alcoholism, Morgan County Big Bro.-Big Sister Assn. Recipient Lindsey Barbee fellowship AAUW, 1960-61; NIMH trainee, 1974-75, research fellow, 1976-78. Mem. Am. Psychol. Assn., Nat. Assn. Social Workers, Acad. Certified Social Workers, Soc. Research in Child Devel., Am. Orthopsychiat. Assn., Phi Kappa Phi. Co-author: Profiles in Social Work, 1976. Club: Service of Milw. Contbg. editor: Clin. Social Work Jour., 1972—. Contbr. to profl. jours. Address: 13412 Lois Ln Austin TX 78750

PHARIS, RUTH MCCALISTER, banker; b. San Diego, Feb. 13, 1934; d. William L. and Mary E. (Beuk) McC.; student Del Mar Coll., Corpus Christi, Tex.; m. E. Edwin Pharis, Mar. 14, 1953; children—Beth, Tracey, Todd. Asst. cashier Parkdale State Bank, Corpus Christi, 1970-72, asst. v.p., 1972-76, v.p., 1976-79: v.p. Cullen Center Bank & Trust, Houston, 1979-81, sr. v.p., 1982—; instr. Am. Inst. Banking, 1977-79. Mem. Am. Soc. Personnel Adminstrs., Bank Adminstrn. Inst. (v.p. Coastal Bend chpt.), Nat. Assn. Bank Women (ednl. chmn. Coastal Bend group), Am. Inst. Banking (rep.), Coastal Bend Personnel Soc. (v.p.), Houston Personnel Assn., Corpus Christi C. of C. (mem. women's com. 1976-79). Republican. Baptist. Club: Order Eastern Star. Home: 5102 Wightman Ct Houston TX 77069 Office: 600 Jefferson St Houston TX 77001

PHELAN, CAROL HADLEY, nurse; b. Mikado, Mich., Dec. 20, 1936; d. Daniel Everett and Fern Olive (Door) Hadley; R.N., Henry Ford Hosp., Detroit, 1958; B.S. summa cum laude, Central Mich. U., 1977; M.A. summa cum laude Mich. State U., 1980; m. Richard Paul Phelan, July 10, 1960; children—Patricia Lee, Richard Eric, Alina Mari. Staff nurse hosps. in Mich. and Calif., 1958-64; indsl. nurse Oldsmobile div. Gen. Motors Corp., Lansing, Mich., 1964-67; clinic nurse No. Ill. U. Med. Center, DeKalb, 1967-69; dir. edn. Ingham Med. Center, Lansing, 1970-74, cardiac rehab. supr., 1974-77; clin. nursing instr., adminstrv. asst. Lansing Community Coll., 1974-77, dir. continuing health edn. and community services program, 1977—; mem. coms. Mich. div. Am. Cancer Soc.; speaker, mem. edn. com. Mich. Hospice Orgn.; bd. dirs. Tri County unit Mich. Heart Assn. Mem. Am. Soc. Health Manpower Edn. and Tng. (charter), Mich. Soc. Health Manpower Edn. and Tng. (charter, past pres.), Mich. Community Coll. Service Assn. Congregationalist. Club: Charlotte Country. Home: 1400 Battle Creek Rd Charlotte MI 48813 Office: 419 N Capitol St Box 40010 Lansing MI 48901

PHELAN, F. ADELE, coll. pres.; b. Denver, Nov. 15, 1935; d. Frank Adam and Della Catherine (Pigotti) Muto; B.A. in English, Webster Coll., 1959; M.A. in English (Woodrow Wilson fellow), St. Louis U., 1962; M.A. in Ednl. Psychology (NDEA Inst. fellow), U. Minn., 1974; m. Gerry Phelan, Oct. 9, 1971. Chmn. English dept. Machebeuf High Sch., Denver, 1961-67; mem. faculty English dept. Loretto Heights Coll., Denver, 1967-68, dir. counseling, 1968-70, dean of students, 1970-74, pres., 1975—; asst. to dean of students U. Denver, 1974-75; dir. 1st Nat. Bank of Denver; evaluator North Central Assn. Colls. and Secondary Schs. Vice pres. bd. dirs. ELDERHOSTEL, 1981; Sec. bd. trustees Swedish Med. Center; mem. council Public TV-Channel 6; bd. dirs. Tech. Assistance Center, Women's Forum Colo., 1980, Inst. Health. Recipient Ann. Salute to Women award, 1982. Mem. Am. Council Edn., Assn. Am. Colls., Nat. Assn. Ind. Colls. and Univs. Office: 3001 S Federal Blvd Denver CO 80236

PHELAN, MARY BENEDICT, educator; b. Galesburg, Ill., Mar. 4, 1902; d. John Francis and Ellen Victorine (Malone) P.; B.A., Clarke Coll., 1924, Ll.D. (hon.), 1974; M.A., U. So. Calif., 1928; Ph.D., Catholic U. Am., 1940; Litt.D. (hon.), Looras Coll., 1967; Ll.D. (hon.), U. Dubuque, 1969. Joined Sisters of Charity, 1931; adminstr., tchr. Burbank (Calif.) Pub. Schs., 1925-31; prof., chairperson dept. psychology and edn. Mundelein Coll., Chgo., 1940-57; pres. Clarke Coll., 1957-69; corp. rep. Sisters Charity, 1970-80; mem. Govs. Commn. Status of Women, 1964-68. Recipient George Washington Honor Medal award Freedoms Found., 1965; spl. merit award Am. Alumni Council, 1969; Disting. Civic Service award Debuque Area C. of C., 1967. Mem. Am. Psychol. Assn., AAUW, Pi Lambda Theta. Roman Catholic. Contbr. in field. Home and office: 6364 N Sheridan Rd Chicago IL 60660

PHELPS, BETTY JEANE POTTENGER, civic worker, farmer; b. Warsaw, Ind., Oct. 20, 1921; d. Royal and Erba Ermal (Hinkson) Pottenger; A.B., Manchester Coll., 1943; registered Occupational Therapist, Washington U., St. Louis, 1952; m. Charles Puterbaugh Phelps, June 5, 1955 (dec. 1969); children—Carl James, Rebecca Susan. Tchr., Richland Center Sch., Rochester, Ind., 1943-44, Lakeview Sch., Tulia, Tex., 1944-45; staff therapist, student supr. Indpls. Gen. Hosp., 1953; dir. occupational therapy James O. Parramore Hosp., Crown Point, Ind., 1954-55; cons. occupational therapy Miller's Merry Manor, Peru, Ind. Vol. worker Meals-on-Wheels, 1972-80; bd. dirs. Campaign for UN Reform; local adv. Hunger Task Force, Presbyn. Ch.; local contact person Hoosiers for Equal Rights Amendment; active Cancer Soc., March of Dimes. Mem. Universal Esperanto Assn. (del.), Common Cause, World Federalists (v.p. Ind.), UN Assn., Internat. Platform Assn., Wilderness Soc., SANE, Internat. Order Vols. for Peace, Internat. Soc. Friendship and Good Will (hon.). Democrat. Presbyterian. Home: 18 E 2d St Peru IN 46970

PHELPS, DIANA JAYNE, nurse; b. Louisville, Sept. 25, 1941; d. James Windsor and Victoria Burt (Sappio) Deeble; R.N., St. Mary's Sch. Nursing, 1962; m. Marshall Lyons Phelps, Jan. 25, 1963; children—Peter Marshall, Deborah Lynn, Sarah Victoria, Rebecca Lynn. Charge nurse pediatrics Meml. Hosp., Worcester, Mass., 1964-66; nursery and pediatric nurse Grossmont Hosp., La Mesa, Calif., 1968-72; water safety instr. San Diego and Tustin, Calif., 1974-77; exec. dir. Orange County Apple Sch., Costa Mesa, Calif., 1977-80; child birth educator Shaw Health Center, Los Angeles, 1980—; lectr. in field. Chmn. bd. dirs. Orange County Apple Sch., 1977-80; adv. Com. on Pub. Health and Safety, 1981; vol. aide program Elem. Sch. Reading, La Mesa, 1972-73; pres. San Diego chpt. Children's Asthma Research Inst. & Hosp., 1970-72; ordained minister Ch. of Scientology. Recipient Pub. Service award Am. Acad. Husband-Coached Childbirth, 1976. Mem. Am. Cultural Assn. (v.p. 1980-81), Internat. Profl. Assn. (pres. 1979), La Leche League Internat., Internat. Childbirth Educators Assn., Soc. for Protection of Unborn Through Nutrition, Nat. Assn. Parents and Profls. for Safe Alternative in Childbirth. Author: How Natural Childbirth Can Protect You and Your Baby, 1979; producer: Welcome to Our World, movie, 1976. Address: 1401 Bryan Ave Tustin CA 92680

PHELPS, EDITH BLAKESLEE, orgn. exec.; b. Worcester, Mass., June 23, 1917; d. George Hubbard and Edna (Day) Blakeslee; grad. Smith Coll., 1938; Litt.D. (hon.), Emerson Coll., 1973; m. William Griswold Phelps, Sept. 5, 1941 (dec.); children—Judith Phelps Felton, Lisa, Catherine. Head history dept. Riverdale Country Sch. Girls, 1939-43; instr. history, cadet tng. detachment USAAF, Coll. Idaho, 1943-44; lectr. Council Fgn. Affairs, Boston, 1946-51; head history dept. Concord Acad., 1958-59, asst. headmistress, 1959-63; prin. Dana Hall Sch., Wellesley, Mass., 1963-73; edn. cons. Nat. Assn. Ind. Schs., 1973-74; nat. exec. dir. Girls Clubs Am., Inc., 1974—; mem. nat. adv. bd. Center for Early Adolescence, 1977—. Mem. vis. com. student affairs M.I.T. Corp., 1965-68; chmn. Nat. Collaboration for Youth, 1976-78; trustee Brimmer-May Sch., 1960-63, Smith Coll., 1974-80, Middlesex Sch., 1973-76. Aspen Inst. fellow, 1979. Recipient Smith medal, 1971. Mem. Nat. Assn. Ind. Schs. (dir. 1965-68;), Nat. Assn. Prins. Schs. for Girls, New Eng. Assn. Coll. and Secondary Schs. (dir. 1965-74, pres. 1969-71), Nat. Assembly Nat. Health and Social Welfare Agys. (dir.). Contbr. articles to profl. jours. Home: 200 E 66th St New York NY 10021 Office: 205 Lexington Ave New York NY 10016

PHELPS, FLORA L(OUISE) LEWIS, editor, anthropologist, photographer; b. San Francisco, July 28, 1917; d. George Chase and Louise (Manning) Lewis; student U. Mich. A.B. cum laude, Byrn Mawr Coll., 1938; A.M., Columbia U., 1954; m. C(lement) Russell Phelps, Jan. 15, 1944; children—Andrew Russell, Carol Lewis, Gail Bransford. Acting dean Cape Cod Inst. Music, East Brewster, Mass., summer 1940; asso. social sci. analyst, U.S. Govt., 1942-44; co-adj. staff instr. anthropology Univ. Coll., Rutgers U., 1954-55; mem. editorial bd. Americas, Pan Am. Union, Washington, 1960—, sr. editor, 1963-71, editor English edition, 1971—, mng. editor, 1974—. N.J. vice chmn. Ams. Democratic Action, 1950; mem. Dem. County Com. N.J., 1948-49. Mem. Am. Anthrop. Assn., Anthrop. Soc. Washington, Soc. for Am. Archaeology, AAAS, Soc. Woman Geographers. Club: Woman's Nat. Democratic. Author articles in field of anthropology, art, architecture, edn., travel. Office: Gen Secretariat OAS Washington DC 20006

PHELPS, NELL JOHNNIE, lithographer, civic worker; b. Raleigh, N.C., Apr. 4, 1922; student Calif. Poly. State U., 1974-76, UCLA, 1975-76; m. Dillard Jasper Phelps, June 1, 1938. Graphic designer, 1951-70; alcoholism counselor Public Inebriate Program, Alcoholism Center for Women, 1970-76; owner, operator Graphic Expression, Inc., Valinda, Calif., 1976—. Bd. dirs. Calif. NOW; chmn. Lesbian Rights Task Force; feminist, activist; mem. Status of Women Commn., Criminal Justice Com. Served with WAC, U.S. Army, 1942-48. Mem. Nat. Women's Polit. Caucus, Calif. Human Rights Advs., DAV (life), NOW, Nat. Gay Task Force, Nat. Lesbian Rights Com. Home and Office: 16047 Maplegrove St Valinda CA 91744

PHIBBS, SUSAN BERNICE, ednl. adminstr.; b. Lombard, Ill., Sept. 19, 1943; d. Vincent D. and Bernice E. (Hammerschmidt) Condella; B.S., U. Wis., 1965; Ed.M., Ga. State U., 1969; Ph.D. in Ednl. Adminstrn., Ga. State U. 1979; m. Ernest E. Phibbs, Sept. 3, 1966. Tchr. public schs., Flint, Mich., 1965-66, Atlanta, 1966-72; dir. Grady Hosp. Child Care Center, Atlanta, 1972-76; research asst. Ga. State U., 1976-79; edn. coordinator Ga. Dept. Edn., Atlanta, 1979—; partner Orgnl. Enrichment Assos., Atlanta, 1979—. Mem. Am. Assn. Sch. Adminstrs., Am. Ednl. Research Assn., Assn. for Supervision and Curriculum Devel., Nat. Assn. for Women Deans, Counselors and Adminstrs., Phi Delta Kappa. Contbr. articles on edn. to profl. publs. Home: 1383 Northview Ave NE Atlanta GA 30306 Office: Suite 2054 Twin Towers East Atlanta GA 30334

PHILLIP, JANE JONES, health technologist; b. N.C., Nov. 24, 1935; d. William and Margie (Copes) Jones; student Duke U., 1970; cert. EEG tech. Northwestern Sch. Sci., 1979, B.S., 1979; m. Leon Phillip, Dec. 2, 1974; children from previous marriage—Kenneth, Kimberly. Bookkeeper, Acme Service Co., Newark, 1958-60; clk. N.J. Mediation Bd., 1961-62; sec. D.J. Flicker, M.D., Newark, 1962-65; sec., EEG technician St. Michael's Med. Center, Newark, 1965-71; health technologist N.J. Coll. Medicine and Dentistry, Newark, 1971-81, neurophysiologist technologist, 1980-81; paramed. examiner various ins. cos., 1982—; instr. First Sch. Secretarial Sci., 1979-80; ordained to ministry Baptist Ch., 1970. Mem. Am. Soc. EEG Technologists, Nat. Assn. Female Execs. Club: Mayan Soc.

PHILLIPS, ANNE MARIE, clin. psychologist; b. Staten I., N.Y., Aug. 7, 1949; d. Michael Joseph and Mary Agnes (Conneely) Boyle; B.S., Fordham U., 1971; M.S., U. S.D., 1973, Ph.D., 1976; m. Walter M. Phillips, July 3, 1971. Psychologist Lewis and Clark Mental Health Center, Yankton, S.D., 1974-76; clin. psychologist Inst. of Living, Hartford, Conn., 1976-79, sr. clin. psychologist, 1979—. Mem. Am. Psychol. Assn., Conn. Psychol. Assn., Assn. for Advancement of Psychology, Phi Beta Kappa. Democrat. Home: 82 Cider Brook Rd Avon CT 06001 Office: 400 Washington St Hartford CT 06106

PHILLIPS, BETTY JANE TOMANEK, credit union exec.; b. Akron, Ohio, Mar. 31, 1931; d. Michael and Mary Cecilia (Kucera) Tomanek; student Akron U., 1951; m. Harvey G. Phillips, June 19, 1965; 1 dau., Ann Marie. Title and mortgage clk. Folk Chevrolet, Inc., Akron, 1949-54; teller BFG Employees Fed. Credit Union, Akron, 1958-60, asst. mgr., 1961-67, mgr., 1968-78, gen. mgr., 1979—; cons. B.F. Goodrich Credit Union Computer System, various credit unions. Mem. Credit Union Exec. Soc., Nat. Credit Union Mgmt. Assn., Am. Bus. Women's Assn., Summit County Credit Union Mgrs. Assn. Office: 500 S Main St Akron OH 44318

PHILLIPS, CAROLYN LYNN, personnel exec.; b. Anniston, Ala., Sept. 13, 1939; d. James Franklin and Dorothy Mae (Dill) Campbell; student Ind. U., Gary, 1965; m. Standley Lee Phillips, Nov. 27, 1958; children—Cole Gray, Stacey Lee, Blake Lee. Mgr. savs. dept. Comml. Bank, Crown Point, Ind., 1969-72; dir. personnel and tng. First Nat. Bank, Dothan, Ala., 1972-77; EEO and tng. mgr. Akwell Industries, Inc., Dothan, 1977-80, dir. personnel, 1980—; tchr. EEO, George C. Wallace Jr. Coll. Bd. dirs. United Fund Dothan, 1979; mem. adv. com. State Employment Job Assistance Program, 1980; mem. State Adv. Bd. Gov's. Employment and Tng. Initiative for Women, 1980; North area chmn. United Fund Dothan, 1981; mem. Advs. Network for Mgmt. Devel. Programs, Div. Continuing Edn., U. Ala., 1981; mem. Personnel

Bd., City of Dothan, 1981—. Mem. Am. Soc. Personnel Adminstrs., Wiregrass Personnel Assn. Democrat. Baptist. Home: 635 Wimbledon Dr Dothan AL 36301 Office: Industrial Rd Dothan AL 36303

PHILLIPS, DEBORAH LEE, nurse; b. East Liverpool, Ohio, June 10, 1950; d. Thomas Eugene and Phyllis (Bair) P.; R.N., Presbyterian. U. Hosp. Sch. Nursing, Pitts., 1971; cardiovascular nurse specialist cert. Tex. Heart Inst., 1976. Public health nurse trainee Allegheny County (Pa.) Health Dept., 1972; staff nurse coronary care unit U. Calif. at San Diego Hosp., 1972-73; staff nurse intensive care unit Stanford U. Hosp., Palo Alto, Calif., 1973-76; clin. supr. critical care St. Luke's Hosp., San Francisco, 1976-79; cardiovascular nurse cons., specialist in cardiac rehab., 1979—; instr. continuing edn. in nursing, 1976—. Mem. Nat. Critical Care Inst., Am. Heart Assn., Calif. Soc. Cardiac Rehab., Am. Assn. Critical Care Nurses, Am. Soc. Profl. and Exec. Women. Democrat. Club: Job's Daus. Home: 576 Martin St Oakland CA 94609 Office: Valley Meml Hosp 1111 E Stanley Blvd Livermore CA 94550

PHILLIPS, ELEANOR LILLIAN, travel agt.; b. Marlborough, Mass., Apr. 17, 1923; d. Loni Peter and Anna Marie (Mueller) Peristere; diploma Worcester (Mass.) Sch. Bus., 1942; cert. travel counselor, Inst. Cert. Travel Agts., 1981; m. Oscar V. Phillips, Sept. 10, 1950; children—Glenn L., Pamela R. Mgr. payroll Reed Small Tool Co., Worcester, 1944; officer mgr. London Display Co., Worcester, 1947-49; bookkeeper Sessions Casket Mfg. Co., Worcester, 1949-50; owner Dotel Ceramics Inc., Trumbull, Conn., 1970; pres., mgr. Phillips Internat., Trumbull, 1976—; pres. E.L.P. Corp., Southbury, Conn., 1975; adv. bd. Pan Am. Air Lines. Mem. Assn. Travel Agts., Inst. Cert. Travel Agts. Mem. Albanian Orthodox Ch. Clubs: Bridgeport (Conn.) Quota (asst. treas. 1980), Order Eastern Star. Home: 192 Edison Rd Trumbull CT 06611 Office: 34 Quality St Trumbull CT 06611

PHILLIPS, ELIZABETH REED, psychologist, educator; b. N.Y.C., June 2, 1947; d. Glenn and Aida (Palermo) Reed; B.A., U. Fla., 1969; M.S., Fla. State U., 1974, Ph.D., 1977; postgrad. (scholar) Rudolf Dreikurs Summer Inst., Zurich, Switzerland, 1979. Human resource cons., U.S. and Europe, 1976-79; prof. counseling Fla. State U., Tallahassee, 1977-78; prof. psychology overseas program Boston U., Munich, W. Ger., 1978-79; asst. to vice-chancellor acad. programs State Univ. System, Tallahassee, 1979—. Del., Democratic Nat. Conv., 1972; mem. Jacksonville Community Relations Commn., 1973, Fla. Commn. on Human Relations, 1974; founding mem., bd. dirs. Jacksonville Rape Crisis Center, since 1972—. Mem. Am. Soc. Clin. Hypnosis, Am. Psychol. Assn., Am. Personnel and Guidance Assn. Home: 3253 Majestic Prince Trail Tallahassee FL 32308 Office: 107 W Gaines St Tallahassee FL 32301

PHILLIPS, HELEN WHITELY, optician; b. Whitesville, Ky., Nov. 25, 1922; d. Wilbur Hayward and Amby Rea (Haynes) P.; R.N., Sch. Nursing, 1944. Office nurse Dr. N.H. Burkhead, Owensboro Ky., 1944; nurse Oak Ridge (Tenn.) Hosp., 1945-47; ophthalmic asst., office mgr. Raymond A. Johnson, M.D., Oak Ridge, 1947-81; optician, mgr. Optical Center, Jack C. Eckerd Corp., Chattanooga, 1981—. Mem. Tenn. Dispensing Opticians Assn. Republican. Presbyterian. Home: 3917 Quail Ln N Chattanooga TN 37415 Office: Northgate Mall Chattanooga TN 37415

PHILLIPS, INEZ EVALYN, commodity broker; b. Lakin, Kans., Oct. 9, 1919; d. Charles Winfield and Hannah Alida (Johnson) Rosebrook; student Salt City Bus. Coll., 1936-38; m. Frank Phillips, 1936 (dec. 1966); children—Kelley, Terry, Kerry, Vicki, Kirby. Exec. dir. Western Kans. counties Nat. Multiple Sclerosis Assn., Garden City, 1967-69; commodity broker, stock broker Goffe-Carkener Blackford, Garden City, 1969-72; account exec., br. mgr. Heinold Commodities and Heinold Securities, Garden City, 1972—; dir. Western State Bank, Garden City; tchr. Garden City Community Coll. County chmn., vice chmn., precinct committeewoman Democratic Party; dir. Garden City Logopedics Bd., 1982—, Beef Empire Bd., 1982—. Mem. Nat. Bus. Women, Garden City C. of C. (dir.), Am. Legion Aux. Presbyterian. Home: 1602 Belmont Pl Garden City KS 67846 Office: 403 Campus Dr Garden City KS 67846

PHILLIPS, JEAN BROWN (MRS. JOHN T. PHILLIPS), bus. exec.; b. Phila.; d. Harold T. and Elizabeth (Ulrich) Brown; B.S. in Home Econs. and Journalism, Drexel U.; postgrad. U. Pa.; m. John T. Phillips; 1 dau., Barbara Jean. Former producer, broadcaster WTVT-TV, Tampa, Fla.; mgr. pub. relations Frank G. Shattuck Co., N.Y.C.; account supr. Dickson-Basford, Inc., N.Y.C.; editor Good Food mag.; now pres. Phillips Communications, Inc. Mem. Am. Home Econs. Assn., Am. Women in Radio and TV, Am. Acad. TV Arts, Pub. Relations Soc. Am., Advt. Women N.Y., Soc. Consumer Affairs Profls. in Bus., N.Y. Assn. Women Bus. Owners (founder), Overseas Press Club. Address: 250 W 57th St New York NY 10019

PHILLIPS, JOAN KARIN, hosp. adminstr., humanist counselor; b. Chgo., May 27, 1932; d. Ben and Vivien Dorothy (Federman) Rosenfield; B.A. in Communication Arts, Columbia Coll., 1970; M.A. in Cultural Studies, Governors State U., 1973, M.A. in Human Learning and Devel., 1974; Ph.D. in Psychology, Northwestern U., 1978. Tchr., performing artist, piano, voice, folk guitar, Chgo., 1962—; exec. mgr. Chgo. offices Boys Town of the Desert, 1966-69; asst. registrar Columbia Coll., Chgo., 1969-70, dir. admissions, fgn. student adviser, records evaluator, 1970-76; coordinator Learning Exchange, Evanston, 1973; founder, dir. Humanist Center, New Directions, Chgo., 1973-79; human relations cons. Communications Labs., Tinley Park, Ill., 1974—; edn. and pub. relations coordinator, instr. Samuel and Melvin A. Kopp Center for Continuing Edn., Honey Creek, Wis., and Evanston, Ill., 1975-79; Tai Chi instr., Chgo., 1975-79; convenor, activities coordinator TORI Assos., Midwest, Chgo., 1975-79; freelance tech. and public relations writer, Chgo., 1975—; adminstr. Rush-Presbyn.-St. Luke's Med. Center, 1976—; cons., writer Kornhaber, Manka & Assos., Community Therapists, Crestwood, Ill., 1979—. Performer, dir. publicity Hemenway Players Theater Co., Evanston, 1982—; sign lang. interpreter Chgo. Soc. for Deaf, 1981—. Mem. Nat. Assn. Women Deans, Adminstrs. and Counselors, Ill. Assn. Coll. Admissions Counselors, Assn. for Humanistic Psychology, Am. Humanist Assn., Ethical Humanist Soc., Nat. Assn. Fgn. Student Affairs, Am., Ill. assns. collegiate registrars and admissions officers, Oasis, Midwest Center for Human Potential, NOW, Profl. Women's Network (chief coordinator), Chgo. Mus. Contemporary Art, Field Mus. Natural History, Lincoln Park Zool. Soc., Costeau Soc., S.W. Suburban Women's Coalition, TORI Assos. Internat., Chgo. Chamber Choir, Grant Park Symphony Chorus, Rush-Presbyn.-St. Luke's Med. Center Choir. Episcopalian. Contbg. editor News Rounds, publ. Rush-Presbyn.-St. Luke's Med. Center, Chgo., 1977—.

PHILLIPS, JUDITH PARKER, interior designer; b. Guantanamo Bay, Cuba, Sept. 16, 1954; d. John Adams and Frances Adeline (Zaino) Parker; B.S., U. Conn., 1976; m. Nicholas William Phillips, III, Apr. 14, 1978. Designer, Clark Contract Interiors, Hartford, Conn., 1976-78; project designer Contract Interiors, Detroit, 1978-79, Silvers, Inc., Detroit, 1980; sr. project designer Interiors Internat., Inc., Grand Rapids, Mich., 1980-81, design mgr., 1982—; works include: sports complexes, schs. and housing in Saudi Arabia; freelance designer pvt. residences. Worthy advisor Rainbow Girls, Order Eastern Star, 1976—, recipient Grand Cross of Color; organizer glass recycling center, 1972. Recipient 1st prize student competition Inst. Bus. Designers, 1976. Mem. Inst. Bus. Designers (affiliate), Profl. Women's Network, Mgrs. and Suprs. Am. Seating Club, Blodgett Area Neighborhood Assn. Republican. Congregatinalist. Office: 678 Front St NW Grand Rapids MI 49504

PHILLIPS, LINDA JANE, software engr.; b. Pitts., Mar. 12, 1948; d. Henery Albert and Frances Helen (Moore) P.; B.S. in Math, U. Mass., Amherst, 1971; now postgrad. Rensselaer Poly. Inst. Tchr. Stoneleigh-Burnham Sch., Greenfield, Mass., 1971-73, Assabet Valley Regional Vocat. High Sch., Marlborough, Mass., 1973; supr. software devel. Gerber Sci. Instruments, South Windsor, Conn., 1974-78; mgr. design software Gerber Systems Tech., Inc., South Windsor, 1979-80; mgr. software engring. Nova Robotics, East Hartford, Conn., 1981—. Gerber rep. to working com. Initial Graphics Exchange Specification, Nat. Bur. Standards, Gaithersburg, Md., 1980. NSF grantee, 1979. Mem. Nat. Assn. Female Execs., Computer and Automated Systems Assn. (Sr.), Alpha Gamma Delta. Office: 262 Prestige Park Rd East Hartford CT 06108

PHILLIPS, LOIS GAIL, exotic bird breeder; b. Detroit, June 21, 1939; d. John Patrick and Leona Victoria (Wagner) P.; B.S. in Chemistry, Fresno (Calif.) State Coll., 1962. Radiol. chemist Nat. Canners Assn., Berkeley, Calif., 1963-64; tchr. Progress Sch., Long Beach, Calif., 1966-67; vol. Peace Corps tchr., Nepal, 1967-69; univ. extension tchr. Nepal tng. programs, Davis, Calif., 1969-71; nursery employee Valley Gardens, Woodland, Calif., 1971-74, Farrell's Garden Center, Sonoma, Calif., 1974-75; mgr. 7-Eleven Store, Petaluma, Calif., 1977—; owner Bodega Birds. Bd. dirs. Sonoma County People Econ. Opportunity, 1978—, sec. to bd., 1978-79. Mem. ACLU, Am. Fedn. Aviculture, Nat. Audubon Soc., Sierra Club. Home: 1821 Lakeville St Apt 2 Petaluma CA 94952 Office: 860 Perry Ln Petaluma CA 94952

PHILLIPS, MARGARET JEAN, psychologist, educator; b. Denver, July 17, 1926; d. Robert Barton and Mildred Dorothy (Rogers) Kelso; B.S. cum laude, U. Wyo., 1954, M.A. (NDEA fellow), 1960, Ph.D., 1962; m. Arlin Dee Phillips, Oct. 4, 1946; children—Margaret Dee, Robert Arlin. Tchr. home econs. Sheridan (Wyo.) High Sch., 1954-59; mem. faculty U. Ill., Champaign-Urbana, 1962—, assoc. prof. ednl. psychology, 1972—, assoc. chmn. dept., 1975-80, dir. research univ. honors programs, 1971-74; exec. sec.-treas. Nat. Collegiate Honors Council, 1971-74. Mem. Am. Psychol. Assn., Am. Personnel and Guidance Assn., Am. Research in Edn. Assn. Author numerous articles in field. Home: 2001 Cypress St Champaign IL 61820 Office: 226 Education Bldg U Ill Champaign IL 61820

PHILLIPS, MARGARET JOSEPHINE, educator, calligrapher; b. Sandusky, Ohio, Mar. 19, 1943; d. Armenio and Lidia (Arduini) Phillips; B.S., Bowling Green State U., 1965; M.A., George Washington U., 1969; postgrad. Firelands Coll., part-time. Tchr. 6th grade Randolph Village Elem. Sch., Landover, Md., 1965-68, tchr. learning disabilities, 1968-69; tchr. 6th grade Bataan Elem. Sch., Port Clinton, Ohio, 1969-70; tchr. learning disabilities Portage Elem. Sch., Gypsum, Ohio, 1970-77; English tchr. Port Clinton High Sch., 1977—. Trustee, Ottawa County Vol. Juvenile Probation Officers, Inc.; mem. Immaculate Conception Sch. Bd. Edn., 1978-80. Mem. Port Clinton (exec. bd. 1970-74), N.W. Ohio, Ohio edn. assns., Am. Fedn. Tchrs., Nat. Hist. Soc., Nat. Council Tchrs. of English, Ohio Council Tchrs. of English and Lang. Arts, George Washington U. Gen. Alumni Assn., Bowling Green State U. Found., AAUW (2d v.p. 1976-78), Port Clinton Area C. of C., Delta Kappa Gamma. Democrat. Roman Catholic. Home: 311 11th St Port Clinton OH 43452 Office: Port Clinton High Sch 821 Jefferson St Port Clinton OH 43452

PHILLIPS, MARGARITA GÓMEZ, microbiologist; b. Jerez, Zacatecas, Mex., July 20, 1942; came to U.S., 1964, naturalized, 1972; d. José Gómez and Guadalupe Lamas (de la Torre) Lozano; diploma Adult Tech. Sch., 1967; B.A. in Microbiology, U. S. Fla., 1972; m. Perry Lineal Phillips, Jan. 13, 1962; 1 son, José. Med. lab. technician Manatee Meml. Hosp., Bradenton, Fla., 1967-68; med. technologist Community Hosp., New Port Richey, Fla., 1973-74, head microbiology, 1974-75, asst. to mgr., 1975-80; microbiologist Smith Kline Clin. Labs., Tampa, Fla., 1980-82; chief technologist, mgr. Internat. Clin. Labs., Inc., New Port Richey, 1982—. Mem. Am. Soc. Clin. Pathologists, Am. Soc. Microbiology, Am. Soc. Med. Technology, Soc. Applied Anthropology, Nat. Cert. Agy. Lab. Personnel, Fla. Assn. Blood Banks, U. South Fla. Alumni Assn. Democrat. Roman Catholic. Home: 912 Linwood Terr Lutz FL 33549 Office: Colonial Med Center 151 Sunset Blvd Suite 6 New Port Richey FL 33552

PHILLIPS, MARILYN MILLER, ch. adminstr.; b. N.Y.C., Feb. 28, 1933; d. Wilbert John and Edith (Hisnay) Miller; B.S., Columbia U., 1958; m. George W. Phillips, Sept. 6, 1958; children—Elizabeth M., John W. Various secretarial and bookkeeping positions, 1953-76; adminstr. Round Hill Community Ch., Greenwich, Conn., 1976—. Mem. Jr. League Greenwich. Clubs: Garden of Old Greenwich (treas. 1972-74). Home: 94 Deer Hill Dr Ridgefield CT 06877

PHILLIPS, MARION GRUMMAN, author, civic worker; b. N.Y.C., Feb. 11, 1922; d. Leroy Randle and Rose Marion (Werther) Grumman; student Mt. Holyoke Coll., 1940-42; B.A., Adelphi U., 1981; m. Ellis Laurimore Phillips, Jr., June 13, 1942; children—Valerie Rose (Mrs. Adrian Parsegian), Elise Marion (Mrs. Edward E. Watts III), Ellis Laurimore III, Kathryn Noel (Mrs. Philip Zimmermann), Cynthia Louise. Civic vol. Mary C. Wheeler Sch., 1964-68, Historic Ithaca, Inc., 1972-76; vol. Ellis L. Phillips Found., 1960—, now v.p.; bd. dirs. North Shore Jr. League, 1960-61, 64-65, 68-69, Family Service Assn. Nassau County, 1963-69, Homemaker Service Assn. Nassau County, 1959-61; writer; books include: (light verse) A Foot in the Door, 1965; The Whale-Going, Going, Gone, 1977; Doctors Make Me Sick (So I Cured Myself of Arthritis); Richard and Rhoda, Letters from the Civil War, 1982; editor Jr. League Shore Lines, 1960-61; contbr. articles on fund raising to mags. Episcopalian. Clubs: Creek, Mt. Holyoke of N.Y., PEO Sisterhood, Matinocock Garden. Home: Point of View Sharon VT 05065

PHILLIPS, MARY LOUETTA, comml. real estate firm exec.; b. Hoxie, Ark., Aug. 18, 1933; d. Sidney William and Christina Mardel (Golden) Steele; student pub. schs.; children—Jeanne, Susan, Sidney, David. Mail clk. Bemis Brothers Bag Co., St. Louis, 1951-52; accounts payable clk. Prince Gardner, St. Louis, 1952-55; mktg. acctg. clk. Exxon Corp., Houston, 1962-69; leasing agt. Shindler/Cummins, Houston, 1972-77; owner, pres. Phillips Internat. Co., Houston, 1978—; mem. Spl. Task Force for Women, Washington, 1980. Pres., Women's Missionary Council, 1969; bd. dirs. SALT. Mem. Nat. Assn. Women in Comml. Real Estate (founder), League Women Voters, Houston Bd. Realtors, Tex. Assn. Realtors, Realtors Nat. Marketing, Tex. Real Estate Action Com., Am. Bus. Women's Assn., Nat. Assn. Women Bus. Owners, C. of C., Houston Entrepreneurship Council (dir.). Office: 1700 W Loop Pl #370 Houston TX 77027

PHILLIPS, NANCY, guidance counselor; b. Camden, N.J., Oct. 17, 1946; d. Albert Raymond and Henrietta (Reichenbach) Miller; B.A., teaching cert., Montclair (N.J.) State Coll., 1970; M.A., pupil personnel credential, Calif. State U., San Bernardino, 1979; adminstrv. credential Calif. State U., Fullerton, 1982; divorced; 1 dau., Jennifer. Head home econs. dept. Kamuli Coll., Uganda, 1970-73; supr. food service Canyon Gen. Hosp., Anaheim, Calif., 1974; supr. food service, tchr. Riverside (Calif.) Unified Sch. Dist., 1977-79; instr. San Bernardino Valley Coll., summers 1977-79; counselor Palo Verde High Sch., also Palo Verde Coll., Blythe, Calif., 1979—; mem. Palo Verde High Sch. Site Council, 1979-80. NSF grantee, summer 1981. Mem. Am. Personnel and Guidance Assn., Assn. Calif. Sch. Adminstrs., Calif. Sch. Counseling Assn., Palo Verde Schs. Mgmt. Assn. (v.p. 1980-81). Office: 689 N Lovelein Blvd Blythe CA 92225

PHILLIPS, NANCY CHAMBERS, social worker; b. Danville, Ky., Oct. 11, 1941; d. Alvia Jackson and Virginia Oradell Chambers; B.A., Georgetown Coll., 1962; M.S.W., U. Denver, 1968; postgrad. Tulane U., 1981—; m. Eldon Franklin Phillips, Nov. 27, 1968. Tchr., Hazard (Ky.) High Sch., 1962; social worker Ky. Dept. Econ. Security, 1964-71; rehab. counselor Ky. Bur. Vocat. Rehab., 1971-72; team leader Cath. Social Services, Bureau, Ky., 1972-74; instr. U. Cin., 1972-77; vis. asst. prof. Fla. Internat. U., 1977-79; asst. prof. social work Idaho State U., Pocatello, 1979-81; research asst. Child Welfare Tng. Center Region VI, Tulane U., New Orleans, 1981—; former mem. profl. adv. bd. Fla. Soc. Autistic Children, South Fla. Soc. Autistic Children, Ohio State U. Community Edn. Unit Adv. Council. Formerly active children's subcom. Dade and Monroe Counties Mental Health Bd., United Family and Children's Services, Family and Child Advocacy in Action Group. Recipient ednl. stipend Ky. Dept. Econ. Security, 1966-68; named Ky. col. Mem. Nat. Assn. Social Workers, Council Social Work Edn., South Fla. Soc. Autistic Children (hon., nat. cert. of recognition 1979, Disting. Service award 1979). Home: 2233 St Charles Ave Apt 101 New Orleans LA 70130 Office: Sch Social Work Tulane U New Orleans LA 70118

PHILLIPS, PRISCILLA MOULTON (MRS. WARREN DAVIS PHILLIPS), educator; b. Lewiston, Maine, Nov. 6, 1918; d. Clement Richmond and Myrtle (Marston) Moulton; student Auburn (Maine) Sch. Commerce, 1939-42; B.S., Boston U., 1947, M.S., 1948, certificate Advanced Grad. Study, 1962, Ed.D., 1965; m. Warren Davis Phillips, June 20, 1964. Tchr. bus. dept. Edward Little High Sch., Auburn, 1942-47; summer demonstration tchr. Sch. Edn. Boston U., 1948, Tchrs. Coll., Columbia, 1949; supr. secretarial studies Bryant Coll., Smithfield, R.I., 1948-65, asst. dean secretarial sci. dept., bus. tchr. edn. dept., 1965-68, chmn. edn. dept., 1968—; mem. tchr. cert. com. R.I. State Dept. Edn.; corporator Citizens Bank R.I. Bd. dirs. St. Mary's Home for Children, North Providence, R.I., St. Elizabeth Home, Providence; mem. vestry St. Stephen's Episcopal Ch. Mem. Eastern Bus. Edn. Assn., New Eng. Bus. Educators Assn. (past pres.), Eastern States Assn. Tchr. Edn. (past pres.), Pottery and Porcelain (past pres.), Travelers Aid Soc. R.I. (past pres.), Pi Lambda Theta, Delta Pi Epsilon. Clubs: Agawam Hunt; Colonial Dames R.I., Providence Art (dir.), Providence County Garden. Contbg. editor: The Shorthand Corner in Business Education World, 1962-64, co-author column The Chalkboard, 1969-77. Contbr. articles to profl. mags. Home: 72 Prospect St Providence RI 02906 Office: Bryant Coll Smithfield RI 02917

PHILLIPS, ROBERTA ANNE, nurse, nursing home adminstr.; b. Savannah, Ga., Aug. 11, 1943; d. Robert Nelson and Bertis Dorothy (Phillips) P.; R.N. diploma, Crawford W. Long Sch. Nursing, Emory U., 1965; B.A. in Psychology, Ga. State Coll., Atlanta, 1965; student rehab. nursing Chgo. Rehab. Inst., Northwestern U. Med. Center, 1979. Charge nurse ICU, Crawford Long Hosp., Atlanta, 1965-66; asst. head nurse ICU, Bapt. Meml. Hosp., Jacksonville, Fla., 1966-67; charge nurse cardiac ICU, Riverside Hosp., Jacksonville, 1967-69, evening supr., 1969-71; staff nurse surg. ICU Meml. Hosp., Jacksonville, 1971-72; supr. phlebotomy unit Ocean Plasma Corp., Jacksonville, 1972-75; staff nurse ICU, intravenous therapy Meth. Hosp., Jacksonville, Fla. 1976-77; dir. nursing Wincrest Nursing Home, Chgo., 1979—; instr. CPR, Am. Heart Assn. Recipient Outstanding Service award Ocean Plasma Corp., 1974. Mem. Am. Nurses Assn. Home: 5600 N Sheridan Rd Apt 6B Chicago IL 60660 Office: 6326 N Winthrop Chicago IL 60660

PHILLIPS, SUSAN MEREDITH, govt. economist; b. Richmond, Va., Dec. 23, 1944; G.A., Agnes Scott Coll., 1967; M.S., La. State U., 1971, Ph.D., 1973. Asst. prof. La. State U., 1973-74; asst. prof. fin. U. Iowa, 1974-78, assoc. prof., 1978-82, interim asst. v.p. fin. and univ. services, 1979-80, assoc. v.p. fin. and univ. services, 1980-82; fellow in econ. policy Brookings Inst., 1976-77; econ. fellow SEC, 1977-78, dir. econ. and policy research; commr. Commodity Futures Trading Commn., Washington, 1982—. Office: 2033 K St NW Washington DC 20036 *

PHILLIPS, VIRGINIA GAIL, oil co. exec.; b. Phillipsburg, Kans., Feb. 1, 1952; d. Boyd D. and JoAnn (Larimore) Phillips; B.A. in Polit. Sci., Okla. State U., 1974; M.B.A., Phillips U., 1978. Social worker HEW, Enid (Okla.) State Sch., 1975-76, coordinator vol. services, 1976; office mgr. Phillips Oil Operating Co., Enid, 1976—; pres. Ra-Gale Ltd. Petroleum Investment Co., Enid, 1976—; asst. to pres. and v.p. Eagle Petroleum Corp., Oklahoma City, 1978; title analyst Grace Petroleum Corp., Oklahoma City, 1979; co-owner Ra-Gale Trucking, 1981—. Contact worker Christian Telephone Ministry, Enid, 1975; worker United Fund Dr., Enid, 1975; mem. aquatics com. YMCA, Enid, 1976; bd. dirs. YWCA, 1981—. Selected as overseas student in Sweden, Phillips U., 1974, 1st female grad. of M.B.A. program, 1978; Mem. Nat. Polit. Sci. Orgn., Desk and Derrick Nat. Women's Petroleum Industry Assn. (Enid chpt. membership chmn. 1978), Phillips U. Geol. Soc., Phillips U. Masters of Bus. Assn., Alpha Phi (v.p. 1972). Club: Altrusa (Mem. of Year 1982). Author: Requirements for Small Business Policy manual, 1978. Office: PO Box 1728 Enid OK 73701

PHILPOTT, BETTE WALKER, real estate investment co. exec.; b. Loma Linda, Calif., Mar. 6, 1941; d. Reed Clemens and Dortha (Pace) Walker; B.A. in Psychology, UCLA, 1964; children—Jane, Anne, James, Daniel. Personnel testing specialist N.Am. Aviation, El Segundo, Calif., 1964; kindergarten tchr. Am.-Nicaraguan Sch., Managua, Nicaragua, 1975-76; real estate salesperson Ackerman Real Estate Services, Washington, 1976-78; v.p. Internat. Investment Counsel, Los Angeles, 1978—. Mem. AAUW, Assn. Am. Fgn. Service Women. Home: 105 Via Ravenna Newport Beach CA 92663 Office: 3 Brookhollow Dr Santa Ana CA 92705

PHILPOTT, EMALEE ISOLA EWING, librarian; b. Charlotte, N.C., Dec. 19, 1921; d. David Weldon and Ada (Gilliam) Ewing; A.B., Coll. William and Mary, 1942; postgrad. George Washington U., 1945-47; M.Ed., U. Ariz., 1955; postgrad. U. N.C., 1968; m. Earl Russell Philpott, Apr. 8, 1950. Profl. asst. to librarian Hollins (Va.) Coll., 1942-43; librarian Corey Meml. Library, Oceana (Va.) Pub. Schs., 1943-44; post librarian Army Library Service, Camp Pendleton, Va., 1944; hosp. librarian Ft. Story (Va.) Canvalescent Hosp., 1944-45; post librarian Camp Pickett, Va., 1945; profl. reference librarian Gen. Reference and Bibliography div. Library of Congress, Washington, 1945-47; cataloger Indsl. Coll. Armed Forces, Nat. War Coll., Ft. Leslie J. McNair, Washington, 1947-48; chief of libraries Engr. Research and Devel. Labs., Ft. Belvoir, Va., 1948-50; sec., tchr. Spanish, history, social studies Duncan (Ariz.) Union High Sch., 1950-52; librarian, English tchr. Pima (Ariz.) pub. schs., 1952-55; librarian Thatcher (Ariz.) High Sch., 1955—; jr. partner Philpott & Son, wholesale distbrs., Duncan, 1950—; asso. in edn. dept. Library sci. Ariz. State U., Tempe, summer 1961, 66, 67; librarian, dir. Instrnl. Materials Center; attended NDEA Inst. U. N.C., summer 1968; mem. Ariz. Adv. Council on Libraries, 1971-76, chmn., 1975-76; mem. Cons. Cadre, Ariz. Dept. Edn. Merit badge counselor Graham County council Boy Scouts Am., 1952—. Named Master Tchr., Ariz. Dept. Edn. Mem. AAUW (br. arts chmn. 1959-64), ALA (life), NEA, Ariz. Edn. Assn., Ariz. Library Assn. (chmn. state recruitment com. 1958-60, editor Ariz. Librarian 1960-62, pres. 1963-64, state policy chmn., 1964-65; state policy chmn. sch. libraries div.

1965-66; chmn. SLAA adv. com.; chairperson intellectual freedom com. 1976-78) Student Library Assn. Ariz. (founder; state sponsor 1969-70, 71-73, 74-76), Dept. Audio Visual Instruction, Assn. Ednl. Communications and Tech. (nat. legis. com. 1970-74), Internat. Platform Assn., Ariz. Assn. Audio Visual Edn. (state legis. com.), Am. Assn. Sch. Librarians (intellectual freedom com. 1977-79), Ariz. Coalition for Intellectual Freedom, Beta Sigma Phi. Methodist. Mem. Order Eastern Star (worthy matron 1969). Contbr. articles to profl. jours. Home: PO Box 233 Duncan AZ 85534 Office: Thatcher High Sch Thatcher AZ 85552

PHITAKSPHRAIWAN, PHUANGNOI, child neurologist; b. Trang, Thailand, Sept. 19, 1927; d. Phra and Amphorn P.; came to U.S., 1962; M.D., Siriraj Med. Sch., Bangkok, Thailand, 1951; m. Wisutr Yontwises, Dec. 27, 1966. Intern, Siriraj Hosp., Bangkok, 1951-52; resident in pediatrics St. Louis Children's Hosp., 1955-56, Driscoll Found. Children's Hosp., Corpus Christi, Tex., 1962-63; mem. pediatric staff Children's Hosp., Bangkok, Thailand, 1956-62; fellow in neonatology Baylor U. Med. Coll., Houston, 1963-64, in pediatric neurology U. Okla. Med. Center, Oklahoma City, 1964-65; resident in neurology U. Miss. Med. Center, Jackson, 1967-68; staff physician, cons. neurologist Denton (Tex.) State Sch., 1969-74; instr. pediatrics U. Tex. Health Scis. Center, Dallas, 1975-76, asst. prof., 1976-80 pediatric dir. univ. affiliated facility, 1976-80; staff Lanterman State Hosp., Pomona, Calif., 1980—; cons. pediatric neurologist Ft. Worth State Sch., 1978-79. Fulbright scholar, 1954-55. Mem. Am. Acad. Neurology (asso.), Am. Assn. Mental Deficiency, AMA, Tex., Dallas County med. assns. Home: 23819 Country View Dr Diamond Bar CA 91765 Office: 3530 W Pomona Blvd Pomona CA 91786

PIACENTINI, PATRICIA RUTH YOUNG, sch. psychologist; b. Glen Ridge, N.J., Oct. 25, 1950; d. William Vernon and Elaine (Engelbrecht) Young; B.A., U. Va., 1972; M.A., Seton Hall U., 1975; m. Michael J. Piacentini, Nov. 27, 1976; children—Michael, Timothy, Matthew. Sch. psychologist Point Pleasant Beach (N.J.) Public Schs., 1976-78; dir.-psychologist Stafford Twp. Project, 1975-79; sch. psychologist Manchester Twp., N.J., 1977—, also Ridgeway Sch., Lakehurst, N.J.: cons. psychologist Project Gain, Tuckerton Pre-Sch. for Handicapped, 1979-80. Mem. exec. bd. Ocean County Unit for Retarded Citizens, 1975-77. Mem. N.J. Psychol. Assn., Ocean County Coalition for Pre-Sch. Edn., Nat. Assn. Sch. Psychologists, Am. Psychol. Assn., Monmouth County Med. Aux., Ocean County Med. Aux., N.J. Assn. Sch. Psychologists, Freehold Area Drs. Wives Assn. Presbyterian. Club: Manasquan River Yacht. Home: 810 Schoolhouse Rd Brielle NJ 08730 Office: Ridgeway Sch Route 571 Lakehurst NJ 08759

PIANETTI, CATHERINE NATALIE, occupational therapist; b. Rock Spring, Wyo., June 4, 1909; d. Anthony and Anna Mary (Picco) P.; diploma Seattle Pacific Coll., 1932; B.A. in Edn., Central Wash. U., 1938; postgrad. U. Wash., 1940; cert. of proficiency in occupational therapy Mills Coll., 1945. Tchr., Wash. Public Schs., 1936-45; chief occupational therapist Marion (Ind.) VA Hosp., 1948-50, 54-69; head occupational therapist NP sect. Walter Reed Army Hosp., 1950, Valley Forge Army Hsop., 1952-53; chief occupational therapist Downey (Ill.) VA Hosp., 1953-54; ret., 1969; lectr. Ball State U., Purdue U., Marion and Anderson colls. Bd. dirs., sec., v.p. Family Service Orgn.; bd. dirs., treas., v.p. Grant County Mental Health Assn.; bd. dirs. Blind Assn., Retarded Children Assn. Served from 1st lt. to capt., Womens Med. Specialists Corps., U.S. Army, 1950-53. Recipient Excellence in Communications with Pub. award, 1969, Mgrs. commendation on retirement, 1969. Mem. Am., Ind. occupational therapy assns., Am. Legion Aux. (1st and 2d vice comdr. Rainier Valley Post 139, 1971-72, comdr. 1976, and comdr. Service Girls Post 1977, comdr. 1st Seattle Dist. 1978-79), 20 and 4, 8 and 40 (pres. 1976, chmn. 1979—), Pioneers of Columbia, Nat. Assn. Fed. Employees. Roman Catholic. Clubs: Seattle Womens Century (publicity chmn. rec. sec. Past Pres.'s Assembly 1974-75, treas. 1975-77, v.p. 1976-78, pres. 1979-81), DAV, Gen. Fedn. Womens' Clubs. Contbr. articles to profl. jours. Home: 4221 47th Ave S Seattle WA 98118

PIANTADOSI, JEANETTE KEMCHICK, ednl. cons.; b. Point Pleasant, N.J., Sept. 2, 1954; d. Patrick John and Gloria Edith (Stensland) Kmiechick; B.A. magna cum laude in Sociology, Am. U., 1977, M.Ed. in Student Devel., 1979; postgrad. (Charles Revson fellow) George Washington U., 1981; m. William Jay Collard, Mar. 12, 1982. Dir., Office of Fin. Aid Am. U., Washington, 1977-81; legis. aide (as Charles Revson fellow) Rep. Patricia Schroeder, Washington, 1981-82; dir. fed. and state relations Systems Research Inc., Washington, 1981-82; v.p. mktg. Sigma Systems Inc., 1982—; lectr., cons. Asst. cheerleading coach Spring Lake Elem. Sch., 1971-72; cheerleading coach St. Dominic's Elem. Sch., 1972-75, Catholic Youth Orgn., 1972-75; Mem. Del. Assn. Student Fin. Aid Adminstrs., D.C. Assn. Student Fin. Aid Adminstrs., Md. Assn. Student Fin. Adminstrs., NE Assn. Student Employment Adminstrs. (sec. 1981-82), Eastern Assn. Student Fin. Aid Adminstrs. (exec. council, ex-officio mem. 1980-81) rep. to exec. bd. Washington 1978-81, pres. Washington 1980-81), Nat. Assn. Student Fin. Aid Adminstrs., Nat. Assn. Women Deans, Adminstrs. and Counselors, Fedn. Orgns. Profl. Women (liaison 1981-82), NOW, AAUW, Nat. Assn. Coll. Admissions Counselors, Phi Theta Kappa, Phi Kappa Phi. Democrat. Roman Catholic. Home: 12115 San Vicente Blvd #311 Los Angeles CA 90049 Office: 1650 Westwood Blvd Suite 202 Los Angeles CA 90024

PIATNEK-LEUNISSEN, DOROTHY ANN, physician; b. Lawrence, Pa., Feb. 8, 1928; d. Andrew Paul and Mary Theresa (Batrla) Piatnek; B.A., Seton Hill Coll., 1949; M.A. (grad. asst.), Mt. Holyoke Coll., 1951; Ph.D., U. Pitts., 1956; M.D., Med. Coll. Pa., 1974; m. Reinhard L. A. Leunissen, May 12, 1962. Research asst. Jefferson Med. Coll., Phila., 1951-53; research assoc. U. Pitts., 1956-62, USPHS fellow, 1956-57; research asst. prof. medicine, asst. prof. physiology, NIH grantee Hahnemann Med. Coll., Phila., 1962-69; intern in medicine Bryn Mawr (Pa.) Hosp., 1974-75, resident in medicine, 1975-76; practice medicine specializing in internal medicine, Media, Pa., 1976—; mem. staff Riddle Meml. Hosp., Media. Fellow Am. Inst. Chemists; mem. Am. Assn. Physiology, N.Y. Acad. Scis., AAAS, AMA, Pa. Med. Soc., Del. County Med. Soc., Brandywine Conservancy, Sigma Xi. Democrat. Roman Catholic. Author articles in field. Office: Suite 209 Riddle Health Care Center 1048 Baltimore Pike Media PA 19063

PIAZZA, DEBRA JEAN, banker; b. Mineola, N.Y., Apr. 14, 1955; d. Frank V. Tobia and Euphemia A. Stepelton; A.S. in Bus. Adminstrn., SUNY, 1980; postgrad. Adelphi U., 1980; m. John Piazza, Aug. 31, 1974. Sec., Franklin Nat. and European Am. Bank, Westbury, N.Y., 1973-79; asst. sec. European Am. Bank, Westbury, 1979-80; asst. v.p. Marine Midland Bank, N.Y.C., 1980—; speaker various cash mgmt. related confs., 1981—. Bd. dirs. N.Y. Diabetes Assn., 1977—, sec. bd., 1977-78, chmn. membership, 1981. Mem. Nat. Assn. Female Execs., Nat. Corporate Cash Mgmt. Assn., Cash Mgmt. Inst. Office: 140 Broadway New York NY 10015

PIAZZA, MARGUERITE, opera singer, actress, supper club entertainer; b. New Orleans, May 6, 1926; d. Albert William and Michaela (Piazza) Luft; Mus.B., Loyola U. of South; Mus.M., La. State U.; D.Mus. (hon.), Christian Bros. Coll., Memphis, 1973; L.H.D. honoris causa, Loyola U. at Chgo., 1975; m. William J. Condon, July 15, 1953 (dec. Mar. 1968); children—Gregory, James (dec. Oct. 1975), Shirley, William J., Marguerite P., Anna Becky; m. 2d, Francis Harrison Bergtholdt, Nov. 8, 1970. Soprano, N.Y.C. Center Opera, 1948, Met. Opera Co., 1950; TV artist Show of Shows, NBC, 1950-54; founder Marguerite Piazza Thanksgiving Gala for the benefit of St. Jude's Hosp., 1976. Dir. Cemrel, Inc. Bd. dirs. St. Jude Found., Found. World Literacy, NCCJ, Memphis Symphony Orch. Nat. chmn. Soc. for Cure Epilepsy; nat. crusade chmn. Am. Cancer Soc., 1971. Recipient Sesquicentennial medal for Carnegie Hall Concert, 1952; service award Chgo. Heart Assn., 1956, Fedn. Jewish Philanthropies of N.Y., 1956; named Queen of Memphi, Memphis Cotton Carnival, 1973, Person of the Year Louisianna Council for Performing Arts, 1975. Mem. Woman's Exchange, Beta Sigma Omicron, Phi Beta. Roman Catholic. Clubs: Memphis Country, Memphis Hunt and Polo, New Orleans Country. Home: 1720 Central Ave Memphis TN 38104

PICARDI, SHIRLEY MAE, univ. adminstr.; b. Margaretville, N.Y., Feb. 20, 1948; d. Clifford Daniel and Edna Rose (Moore) Ives; A.B. summa cum laude in chemistry, Radcliffe Coll., 1970; M.S., M.I.T., 1972, Ph.D. in Food Sci., 1976, M.S. in Mgmt., 1981; m. Anthony Charles Picardi, Sept. 4, 1970. Indsl. liaison officer M.I.T., Cambridge, 1976-79, asst. dir. Indsl. Liaison Program, 1979-80, spl. asst. to v.p. for resource devel., 1981, sec. Alumni Assn. 1981—; lectr. in field. NSF grad. fellow, 1970-73; Nestle Co. fellow, 1973-74; Nutrition Found. fellow, 1974-75; Alfred P. Sloan fellow, 1980-81. Mem. Inst. Food Technologists, Soc. for Nutrition Edn., Phi Beta Kappa, Sigma Xi. Contbr. articles to profl. jours. Office: Alumni Assn MIT Room 10-110 Cambridge MA 02139

PICCARD, ELIZABETH JANE, social worker, educator; b. St. Paul, Jan. 10, 1925; d. James John and Mary Hilarian (Brennan) Koalska; B.A. cum laude, U. Minn., 1945, M.A., 1948; m. Paul J. Piccard, Aug. 1, 1947; children—Robert, Jane, John, Mary, Ann. Caseworker, Mpls. Travelers Aid Soc., summers 1953, 55, 56; exec. Leon County Mental Health Assn., Tallahassee, 1963-69; mem. faculty Fla. State U., Tallahassee, 1969—, assoc. prof. social work, 1976—, dir. undergrad. program social work, 1975-82. Served with WAVES, 1945-46. Mem. Nat. Assn. Social Workers (chpt. pres. 1972), Council Social Work Edn., Assn. Baccalaureate Program Dirs., LWV. Roman Catholic. Author: Introduction to Social Work: A Primer, 3d rev. edit., 1982. Home: 404 Terrace St Tallahassee FL 32308 Office: Sch Social Work Fla State U Tallahassee FL 32306

PICHETTO, CHRISTA BARBARA, educator, nurse; b. New Haven, June 26, 1949; d. Elmer E. and Hannelore (Bareis) Hallinger; B.S. in Nursing, U. Calif., San Francisco, 1972, M.S., 1973; counseling credential Calif. State U., 1975. Nursing supr., inservice edn. coordinator dept. psychiatry Highland Hosp., Oakland, Calif., 1973-75; health educator, sch. nurse Miramonte High Sch., Orinda, Calif., 1975-78; mental health cons. Center for Human Devel., Lafayette, Calif., 1978-79; instr. psychiatric nursing Coll. Nursing, Merritt Hosp., Oakland, 1979-81, coordinator acad. advisement, community relations, 1981—. NIMH grantee, 1972-73. Mem. Nat. League Nursing, Psychiat.-Mental Health Nursing Interest Group, Sigma Theta Tau. Contbr. author: Tribes 1979. Office: Merritt Hosp Coll of Nursing Hawthorne and Webster Sts Oakland CA 94609

PICHT, KATHRYN ANNETTE, cellist; b. Ft. Dodge, Iowa, May 31, 1953; d. Melvin Ross and Norma Jean (Nicoll) P.; student U. Wis., 1971-73; B.M., U. Ill., 1975, M.M., Boston U. 1977; student of George Neikrug. Cellist summer festivals Congress of Strings, 1971, Colby Coll. Summer Sch. Music, 1972, Banff Sch. for Arts, 1973, Claremont Music Festival, 1974; mem. string quartet in residence, Battle Creek, Mich. 1977-78; prin. cellist Des Moines Metro Summer Festival of Opera, 1979; cellist Phila. Orch., 1979—; tchr. New Sch. Music, 1981. Mem. Phila. Mus. Soc., Am. Fedn. Musicians, Sigma Alpha Iota. Methodist. Office: 1420 Locust St Philadelphia PA 19102

PICKARD, BARBARA GILLESPIE, biologist, educator; b. Charleston, W.Va., Feb. 24, 1936; d. Rollin Wilson and Helen Claire (Schregardus) Gillespie; B.A., Stanford U., 1958, M.A., 1959; Ph.D., Harvard U., 1963, postdoctoral 1963-64; postdoctoral student 1964-66; m. William F. Pickard, Apr. 1963; children—K. Koré, William F. Mem. faculty Washington U., St. Louis, 1966—, assoc. prof. plant biology, 1973—. Guggenheim fellow, 1974-75. Mem. Am. Soc. Plant Physiologists, Am. Inst. Biol. Scis., Am. Chem. Soc., Soc. Gen. Physiology, Am. Women in Sci. Contbr. articles to profl. jours. Home: 6925 Princeton Ave University City MO 63130 Office: Dept Biology Washington U Saint Louis MO 63130

PICKERING, ANN MARIE, ins. co. rep.; b. Mpls., June 10, 1947; d. Harold Christian and Mary Genevieve (Schallau) Heisler; R.N., Mercy Hosp. Sch. Nursing, Cedar Rapids, Iowa, 1968; m. Robert Allen Pickering, Aug. 17, 1968; children—Amy Marie, Paul Robert. Office nurse D.A. Dutton, M.D., Van Horne, Iowa, 1968-79; staff nurse Virginia Gay Hosp., Vinton, Iowa, 1968-77, asst. dir. nursing service, 1978-79; state hosp. risk mgmt. rep. St. Paul Fire and Marine Ins. Co., 1979-80, Cedar Rapids, 1979—. Mem. Benton County Mental Health Bd., 1977-79. Mem. Am. Operating Room Nurse Assn., Am. Nurses Assn., Nat. League Nursing. Democrat. Roman Catholic. Home: Rural Route 1 Keystone IA 52249 Office: St Paul Ins Cos Cedar Rapids IA

PICKERING, KATHLEEN CUMINGS, assn. exec.; b. Neenah, Wis., Mar. 3, 1943; d. John Billings and Grace Ruth (Wenban) Cumings; B.A., U. Wis., Eau Claire, 1965; postgrad. U. Minn., 1968-69, St. Thomas U., 1979, Harvard U., 1979; m. William A. Pickering, Aug. 18, 1978. Mgmt. trainee Sears-Reobuck Co., Denver, 1965-66; field dir. St. Croix Valley council Girl Scouts U.S.A., St. Paul, 1966-72, dir. fin., 1972-74, exec. dir. Lac Baie council, Green Bay, Wis., 1974-77, exec. dir. Miss. Valley council, 1977-78, exec. dir. Greater Mpls. council, 1979—. Bd. dirs. United Way Council, Green Bay, Wis., 1976-77; vice-chmn. council agy. execs. United Way Mpls., 1982—; mem. employment review bd., State of Minn., 1967-73. Mem. Am. Mgmt. Assn., Assn. Girl Scouts Execs., AAUW, Mpls. C. of C. Republican. Lutheran. Clubs: Women's of Mpls., Zonta.

PICKETT, BETTY RUTH HORENSTEIN, psychologist; b. Providence, Feb. 15, 1926; d. Isadore S. and Etta (Morrison) Horenstein; A.B., Pembroke Coll., Brown U., 1945; M.S., Brown U., 1947, Ph.D., 1949; m. James McPherson Pickett, Mar. 10, 1952. Asst. prof. psychology U. Minn., Duluth Br., 1949-51, U. Nebr., 1951; lectr. psychology U. Conn., 1952; profl. asso. Bio-Scis. Info. Exchange, Smithsonian Instn., Washington, 1953-57; exec. sec. behavioral scis. study sect., div. research grants NIH, Bethesda, 1957-59, exec. sec. expt. psychology study sect., 1959-62; cons. NIMH Research Grants, HEW, region 1, Boston, 1962-63; exec. sec. research career program NIMH, Bethesda, 1963-66, chief cognition and learning sect., behavioral scis. research br., 1966-68, dep. dir. div. extramural research programs, 1968-74, dir. div. spl. mental health programs, 1974-75, acting dir. div. extramural research program, 1975-77; asso. dir. extra mural and collaborative research program Nat. Inst. Aging, 1977-79; dep. dir. Nat. Inst. Child Health and Human Devel., Rockville, 1979-81, acting dir., 1981-82, dir. div. research resources, 1982—. Mem. Am., Eastern psychol. assns., Psychonomic Soc., Assn. Women in Sci., Phi Beta Kappa, Sigma Xi. Contbr. articles to profl. jours. Home: 2561 Waterside Dr NW Washington DC 20008 Office: Div Research Resources Bldg 31 Rm 5B-03 Bethesda MD 20205

PICKETT, JOCELYN KAY, educator; b. Chgo., Dec. 8, 1955; d. Jeremiah and Earlene (Oliphant) P.; B.A. in Edn., Roosevelt U., 1977, postgrad., 1977-78; student Chgo. Conservatory of Music, 1978-79, Chgo. Musical Coll., Roosevelt U., 1981—. Tchr., St. Peter Luth. Sch., Chgo., 1977-79, Emmanuel Christian Sch., Chgo., 1979—. Active, St. Luke Ch. of God in Christ. Composer mus. compositions: Come Unto Me (I Will Give You Rest), 1978; To The Glory of God, 1979. Office: 8301 S Damen Ave Chicago IL 60620

PICKETT, JOYCE BETH, home economist; b. Tioga, La., Dec. 12, 1937; d. Thomas Allen and Louise (Gorham) Maxwell; B.S., Northwestern State U., 1959; M.S., La. State U., 1968; m. John Roderick Pickett, June 3, 1960; children—Nina Monique, JoLisa Beth. Tchr. home econs. public schs. Rapides Parish, Plainview, La., 1959-60; 4-H agt. La. State U. Coop. Extension Service, Sabine, 1961-62; Terrebonne, 1963-73, Sabine, 1973—. Mem. Am. Home Econs. Assn., La. Home Econs. Assn., Nat. Assn. Extension Home Economists, La. Assn. Extension Home Economists, La. Bus. and Profl. Womens Club (Woman of Yr., Many 1980). Baptist. Home: PO Box 1157 130 Lawrence St Many LA 71449 Office: PO Box 347 300 Main St Many LA 71449

PICKETT, MARGARET ANN, banker; b. Newton, Kans., Aug. 28, 1936; d. Theodore Edward and Cleta Edna (Worline) Frerking; student El Dorado Jr. Coll., 1954-56; student Kans. State U., 1956-58; m. Dirk A. Pickett, Dec. 22, 1959; 1 son, Kirk Dean. Bookkeeper, First Nat. Bank, Manhattan, Kans., 1964-66, teller, 1966-72, discount teller, 1972-78, comml. loan officer, 1978-80, asst. v.p. real estate lending, 1980—. Treas., Troop 76, Coronado Area Council Boy Scouts Am., 1972—; mem. City of Manhattan Zoning Appeals Bd., 1980-82; treas. Riley County Cancer Soc. Mem. Manhattan Homebuilders Assn. (dir.), Manhattan Bd. Realtors, Nat. Assn. Bank Women (chmn. Blue Valley chpt.), Bank Adminstrn. Inst. (past pres. chpt.), Am. Bus. Womens Assn. (past treas. chpt.). Christian. Mem. Order Eastern Star (past worthy matron), Eagles Aux. (past pres.). Home: 2109 Lawarence Rd Manhattan KS 66502 Office: 701 Poyntz St Manhattan KS 66502

PICK-JACOBS, ELLEN MARIE (ELLY), public relations exec.; b. Rochester, Minn., May 22, 1949; d. James William and Elizabeth (Peters) Pick; B.A. in Journalism, U. Wis., 1972; m. Charles Henry Jacobs, Sept. 15, 1979. Reporter, West Bend (Wis.) Daily News, 1972; asst. editor Lady Com. mag., Chgo., 1972-74; mgr. public relations and advt. Tiger Leasing Group, Chgo., 1974-78; account exec. New Dimensions Mktg. Inc., Chgo., 1978-79, Hill & Knowlton, Inc., Chgo., 1979-80; dir. public relations Manpower, Inc., Milw., 1980—. Bd. dirs. Penfield Children's Center; adv. Mt. Mary Coll., Wauwautosa, Wis.; chmn. spl. events Lakefront Festival of Arts, 1981, chmn. silent auction, 1982. Mem. Women in Communications (treas. 1971), Wis. Sr. Public Relations Forum, Public Relations Soc. Am. Chgo. Women's Network (founder, dir.), TEMPO (dir.), Chgo. Headline Club. Republican. Roman Catholic. Clubs: Women's Athletic of Chgo.; Jr. League (Milw.); Freeport Resort & Tennis (Bahamas), Contbr. articles in field to profl. jours. Home: 4611 N Wildwood Ave Whitefish Bay WI 53211 Office: Manpower Inc 5301 N Ironwood Rd Milwaukee WI 53217

PICKLER, MARILYNN ROBINSON, real estate co. exec.; b. Jonesboro, Ark. Dec. 24, 1937; d. Henry Lucius and Virginia Arabella (Barton) Robinson; B.M.E., Ark. State U., 1961; m. Roger Pickler, Sept. 1, 1957; children—David Anthony, Anita Carol, Jennifer Ann. Tchr. elementary schs., Walnut Ridge and Hoxie, Ark., 1958-63; pvt. practice real estate sales, Jonesboro, 1974-76; pres. Viking Realty & Devel., 1975—; soloist N.E. Ark. Community Chorus, 1976-82, also Lindsay Meml. Presbyn. Ch., mem. Richardson (Tex.) Women's Chorus, Dallas Civic Opera Chorus; appeared in summer musicals Jonesboro Fine Arts Council, 1971-81. Co-chmn. Miss Jonesboro Pageant, 1981-82. Mem. Nat. Assn. Builders, Jonesboro Bd. Realtors; Nat. Bd. Realtors, Ark. Bd. Realtors, Altrusa Internat., NEA, Ark. Edn. Assn., Alpha Gamma Delta. Democrat. Presbyterian. Clubs: DAR, Regent, Cynthia Crowley, Treble Clef Music Club, Noctourne Music, Ark. State U. Indian, Etude, Chorale; Beethoven (Memphis). Home and Office: 902 Valhalla Sr Jonesboro AR 72401

PICOW, LINDA HELMAN, respiratory therapist; b. Spring Valley, N.Y., May 5, 1942; d. Joseph George and Jean (Foxman) Helman; B.A. with high honors in Edn., U. S.C., 1970; A.S. with high honors in Respiratory Therapy, Midlands Tech. Coll., Columbia, S.C., 1974; divorced; children—Rene Cheryl, Natalie Beth. Bookkeeper, accountant Allan's Dept. Store, Columbia, S.C., 1961-67; sportswear designer Swansea Mfg. Co. (S.C.), 1967-74; tchr. Richland County Dist. 1, Columbia, 1970-72; instr., coordinator Midlands Tech. Coll., 1974-78, head dept. respiratory therapy, 1978—; cons. in field. Cert. respiratory therapy technician; registered respiratory therapist. Mem. Am. Assn. Respiratory Therapy (del. 1978-82), S.C. Soc. Respiratory Therapy (del. 1978-80), Am. Heart Assn., Am. Lung Assn., S.C. Lung Assn. (dir.). Democrat. Jewish. Office: PO Box 2408 Midlands Tech Coll Columbia SC 29202

PIEL, ELEANOR JACKSON, lawyer; b. Santa Monica, Calif., Sept. 22, 1920; d. Louis Harris and Blanche Melicent (Virden) Jackson; student U. Calif. at Los Angeles, 1936-39; B.A., U. Calif. at Berkeley, 1940, LL.B., 1943; postgrad. U. So. Calif., 1940-41; m. Gerard Piel, June 24, 1955; 1 dau., Eleanor Jackson. Admitted to Calif. bar, 1943; N.Y. bar, 1957; law clk. U.S. Dist. Ct., San Francisco, 1939, 44; dep. atty. gen. State of Cal., 1944; clk. U.S. Senate Civil Service Com., 1945; legal adviser Supreme Command Allied Powers, Japan, 1945-48; practice law in Los Angeles, 1948-55 atty. Legal Aid. Soc., N.Y.C., 1957-58; practice in N.Y.C., 1957—. Trustee, N.Y. U. Med. Center, 1967—. Fellow Am. Bar Assn., Com. for Public Justice; mem. Assn. Bar City N.Y. (mem. spl. com. to revise criminal code 1970—, com. on penology 1971—, grievance com. 1973—, vice chmn.). Clubs: Cosmopolitan, Women's City (counsel). Home: 320 Central Park West New York NY 10025 Office: 36 W 44th St New York NY 10036

PIEPENBRINK, NANCY LEA, nurse; b. Morrison, Ill., Nov. 4, 1948; d. Albert L. and Arlene E. (Montgomery) Benedict; B.S. Nursing, Ill. Wesleyan U., 1970; m. Harold C. Piepenbrink, Aug. 4, 1972; 1 dau., Alison Lea. Nurse, Ill. Dept. Med. Health, Chgo., 1970-73; head nurse VA Research Hosp., Chgo., 1973-75, VA Hosp., Bklyn., 1975-76, Ohio State Univ. Hosp., Columbus, 1976-77; nurse cons. on accrediation Ohio Dept. Mental Health, Columbus, 1977-78; dir. nursing Longview State Hosp., Cin., 1978—. Mem. Am. Nurses Assn., Ohio Nurses Assn., Dirs. of Nursing of Ohio Mental Health and Retardation Hosps. (v.p.), Dirs. of Nursing of Greater Cin. Area, Assn. Mental Health Adminstrs. Home: 9499 Mapleknoll Cincinnati OH 45239

PIEPER, SISTER, BERNADINE ELIZABETH, assn. exec.; b. Lee County, Iowa, Feb. 21, 1918; d. Frank William and Mary Adelaide (Nichting) P.; B.S., Marycrest Coll., 1942; M.S., St. Louis U., 1944; Ph.D., U. Iowa, 1952. Joined Congregation of Humility of Mary, Roman Catholic Ch., 1938; instr. to prof. Marycrest Coll., Davenport, Iowa, 1944-66; pres. Congregation of Humility of Mary, Ottumwa, Iowa, 1966-76, Ottumwa Heights Coll., Ottumwa, 1976-80; exec. sec. Am. Friends Service Com., North Central Region, Des Moines, 1980—; mem. Des Moines Cath. Diocese Bd. Edn. Active, Iowa Civil Liberties Union; mem. Network; chmn. bd. dirs. New Horizons, 1977—. Danforth scholar, 1953; NSF grantee, 1962. Mem. Des Moines Ministerial Assn., Nat. Assn. Women Religious, Sigma Xi, Phi Theta Kappa. Author: Footprints, 1978; contbr. articles to sci. and cath. jours.

PIEPER, HELEN FISHER, social worker; b. St. Louis, Jan. 7, 1932; d. Gordon and Helen (Diehm) Fisher; student Duke U., 1950-51; A.B.,

U. Ariz., 1954; M.S.W., Washington U., St. Louis, 1968; m. Karl Bailey Pieper, Dec. 15, 1956 (dec. Feb. 1965); children—Karl Gordon, Kenneth Robert, Kathryn Bernays. Dir. publicity Chase Park Plaza Hotels, St. Louis, 1954-56; social worker St. Louis County Spl. Sch. Dist., 1968—, supr. social work, 1978—. Mem. Nat. Assn. Social Workers, Acad. Certified Social Workers, Registry Clin. Social Workers, Mo. Assn. Children with Learning Disabilities, Mo. State Tchrs. Assn., Council Exceptional Children, Alpha Chi Omega. Episcopalian. Home: 1024 Dutch Mill Dr Saint Louis MO 63011 Office: 12110 Clayton Rd Town and Country MO 63131

PIEPER, JANET LEAH, state ofcl.; b. Norfolk, Nebr., Feb. 12, 1932; d. Walter Arthur Arnold and Alma Eulalia (Heintzelman) Steffen; B.Sc., U. Nebr., 1954; postgrad. Omaha U., 1957-58, Butler U., 1965-66; M.A., U. Nebr., 1969, Ph.D., 1976; m. Donald R. Pieper, June 20, 1954; children—David Richard, James Steffen, Steven Donald. Math., English and journalism tchr. Stanton (Nebr.) High Sch., 1954-56; instr. English, Omaha U., 1956-58; asst. dir., editor Study Commn. Undergrad. Edn., U. Nebr., Lincoln, 1972-75, adminstrv. asst. to dean, 1976-78; dir. dept. personnel State Nebr., Lincoln, 1978—. Chmn., Savs. Bond Dr. State Employees, 1978-81. AAUW Ednl. Found. Project grantee, 1979-80, AAUW individual project grantee, 1973-74, Johnson fellow, 1971-72. Mem. AAUW (edn. chmn. state div. 1968-79), Nat. Assn. State Personnel Execs., Internat. Personnel Mgmt. Assn., Lincoln Personnel Mgmt. Assn., Mortar Bd. Alumni Assn. (pres. 1978-79), Phi Beta Kappa, Pi Lambda Theta, Pi Mu Epsilon, Delta Phi Alpha, Gamma Phi Beta, PEO. Club: Sweet Adelines. Home: 2955 Park Pl Dr Lincoln NE 68506 Office: PO Box 94905 Lincoln NE 68509

PIEPER, PATRICIA R., artist, photographer; b. Paterson, N.J., Jan. 28, 1923; d. Francis William and Barbara Margareth (Ludwig) Farabaugh; student Baron von Palm, 1937-39, Deal (N.J.) Conservatory, summers 1939, 40, Utah State U., 1950-52; m. George F. Pieper, July 1, 1941 (dec. May 3, 1981); 1 dau., Patricia Lynn. One-woman shows: Charles Russell Mus., Great Falls, Mont., 1955, Fisher Gallery, Washington, 1966, Tampa City Library, 1977, 78, 79, 80, 81; exhibited in group shows: Davidson Art Gallery, Middletown, Conn., 1968, Helena (Mont.) Hist. Mus., 1955, Dept. Commerce Alaska Statehood Show, 1959, Joslyn Mus., Omaha, 1961, Denver Mus. Natural History, 1955, St. Joseph's Hosp. Gallery, 1980; represented in pvt. collections. Pres., Bell Lake Assn., 1976-78, 79. Winner photog. competition Gen. Telephone Co. of Fla., 1979. Mem. Pasco County (Fla.) Water Adv. Council, 1978—, chmn. 1979-82; gov.'s appointee to SW Fla. Water Mgmt. Dist., Hillsboro River Basin Bd., 1981-82; active Save Our Rivers program, 1981-82; adv. bd. Tampa YMCA, 1979-80. Mem. Nat. League Am. Pen Women (v.p. Tampa 1976-78, Woman of Yr. award 1977-78), Tampa Art Mus., Land O' Lakes C. of C. (dir. 1981-82, outstanding service award 1980), Fla. Geneal. Soc. Clubs: Lutz, Land O' Lakes Women's. Home and Studio: PO Box 15 Land O' Lakes FL 33539

PIEPHO, SUSAN BRAND, chemist; b. Pound Ridge, N.Y., Apr. 28, 1942; d. Byron Alexander and Katherine F. (Brammer) Brand; B.A. summa cum laude with honors in Chemistry, Smith Coll., 1964; M.A. in Sci. Edn., Columbia U., 1965; Ph.D. in Phys. Chemistry (NDEA fellow 1968-70, A.T. Gwathmey Meml. award 1970), U.Va., 1970; m. Edward Lee Piepho, June 13, 1964. Secondary sch. tchr., N.Y.C. and Charlottesville, Va.,1965-67; asst. prof. chemistry Sweet Briar (Va.) Coll., 1971-73; postdoctoral research asso. U. Va., 1973-75; NATO postdoctoral fellow Oxford (Eng.) U., 1975-76; postdoctoral fellow U.So. Calif., 1976; asst. prof., then asso. prof. chemistry Randolph-Macon Woman's Coll., Lynchburg, Va., 1977-81; asso. prof. chemistry Sweet Briar Coll., 1981—. NSF grantee, 1979, 82. Mem. Am. Chem. Soc., Am. Phys. Soc., AAAS, AAUP, ACLU (chmn. Lynchburg chpt. 1977-81), Common Cause (coordinator Amherst County, Va. 1979-82), Phi Beta Kappa, Sigma Xi. Democrat. Episcopalian. Club: Village Garden (treas. 1980-82). Author papers in field. Home: Box AM Briarhurst Dr Sweet Briar VA 24595 Office: Dept Chemistry Sweet Briar Coll Sweet Briar VA 24595

PIERCE, CAROL ANN SMITH, psychologist; b. New Braunfels, Tex., Oct. 5, 1945; d. Charlie Robert and Pearly Joyce (Koch) Smith; B.S. in Edn., S.W. Tex. State U., 1969; M.A. in Psychology and Counseling, East Tex. State U., 1975, Ph.D. in Psychology, 1979; m. Max Pierce, June 20, 1979; children—Scott Orin, Zachary Ivan. Middle sch. tchr. Springfield Ind. Sch. Dist., 1969-73; mem. faculty East Tex. State U., 1975-79; staff psychologist East Tex. Mental Health/Mental Retardation Center, 1979-80; dir. Grayson County Guidance Clinic, Denison, Tex., 1980-82; pvt. practice psychology Sherman Psychol. Services (Tex.), 1982—; cons., clin. supr. Grayson County Guidance Clinic; instr. continuing edn. Sherman Ind. Sch. Dist. Adv. bds. spl. edn. Sherman and Denison Ind. Sch. Dists. Mem. Am. Psychol. Assn., Southwestern Psychol. Assn., Tex. Psychol. Assn., Texoma Psychol. Assn., Grayson County Social Services Assn. Episcopalian. Office: 2511 N Travis St Sherman TX 75090

PIERCE, DIANE, artist, sculptor; b. Lakewood, Ohio; d. William Henry and Ramona (Phipps) P.; diploma Cleve. Inst. Art, 1957-61; B.A., Western Res. U., 1962. Freelance wildbird artist, 1965—; wildlife prints pub. in limited edition; lectr. in field, 1973—; illustrator numerous books in field to ornithology, also jours. and mags.; paintings represented in Ind. State Mus., Ind. Ward Found. Art Mus., pvt. collections, U.S., Can., Europe; exhibited Internat. Exhibit Wildbird Artists, Woodson Art Mus., 1976-82; judge World Championship Wildfowl Carving Competition, 1979. Winner Ind. Waterfowl Stamp Contest, 1979, L.I. Waterfowl Stamp Contest, 1980. Mem. Soc. Animal Artists, Nat. Audubon Soc., World Wildlife Fund, Nature Conservancy, Outdoor Writers Assn. Am. Club: Salmagundi (N.Y.C.). Home and Studio: Edge of the Wild Spring Creek Rd Bonita Springs FL 33923

PIERCE, ELIZABETH GAY, club woman; b. N.Y.C., Mar. 26, 1907; d. Martin and Julia DeWitt (Stone) Gay; B.A., Barnard Coll., 1929; m. William Curtis Pierce, June 19, 1929; children—Martin Gay, William Curtis (dec.), Elizabeth Gay, Josiah. Vol. worker Boston City Hosp., 1929-30, Community Service Soc., 1931-32; mem. dependent children's sect. Welfare Council, N.Y.C., 1939-40; bd. dirs. Half Orphan Home (now Windham House), 1939-40; chmn. house com. North Shore Holiday House, Huntington, N.Y., 1944, pres., 1945; co-chmn. thrift shop com. Knickerbocker Hosp., N.Y.C., 1957-64; mem. exec. com. of women's com. Legal Aid Soc., N.Y.C., 1958; mem. exec. com. Women's Aux. Knickerbocker Hosp., 1960-64; bd. mgrs. Nat. Soc. Colonial Dames in State N.Y., 1962-67, corr. sec., 1965-67, pres., 1967-70; nat. pres. Nat. Soc. Colonial Dames Am., 1972-76, hon. pres., 1976—. Mem. Soc. Mayflower Descs. in State N.Y. (bd. assts., chmn. house com.), Nat. Soc. Daus. Founders and Patriots, Soc. Preservation New Eng. Antiquities (Maine council 1976-82, mem., past chmn. Marrett House com.), Grange. Episcopalian. Club: Colony. Home: Box 352 Route 1 West Baldwin ME 04091

PIERCE, GRACE WAGNER, environmentalist; b. Coatesville, Pa., May 9, 1926; d. Jacob and Grace Anne (Wallace) Wagner; student Goldey Coll., 1944, Wesley Jr. Coll., 1970, 73; pupil art Howard Schroder, Loren Kohut, Lon Fluman; m. W. Lemar Pierce, Dec. 15, 1945 (dec.); children—Linda Pierce Dolan, Barry Wallace Clark Pierce, Susan Pierce Gottfried. Owner, Pierce's Pharmacy, Inc., Dover, Del., 1962—; issues specialist Wilderness Soc., Washington, 1975-78; chmn. Watch Our Waterways, 1978-80; nat. environ. dir. Nat. Unity Campaign for John Anderson, 1980. Republican committeewoman 29th dist. Kent County, Del., 1966-69; chmn. vols. Kent County Rep. campaign, 1968; del. Rep. Nat. Conv., 1968; program chmn. Del. Fedn. Rep. Women, 1968-69; vice chmn. Kent County Rep. Com., 1969-72, vice chmn. edn. com., 1973—; pres. Fedn. Rep. Women Del., 1970-72; Rep. committeewoman 31st dist. Kent County, 1973—; chmn. Kent County campaign Gov. R.W. Peterson, 1972; candidate Del. Ho. of Reps., 1974. Pres. jr. bd. Kent Gen. Hosp., 1960-62; work with presch. children Capitol Green Community Center, 1970-71; chmn. East Coast Environ. Leadership Conf., 1974; mem. women's study com. Del. Tech. and Community Coll. Bd. dirs. Kent Gen. Hosp., 1971-76, Delawareans for Orderly Devel.; mem. Del. Water Quality Awareness Com., 1975-80; bd. dirs. Del. Audubon Soc., 1981—; treas. City Council of Slaughter Beach, 1981—. Mem. Rehoboth Art League. Home: 535 American Ave Dover DE 19901 Office: 3255 K St NW Washington DC 20007

PIERCE, JANIS VAUGHN, ins. exec., cons.; b. Memphis, Dec. 23, 1934; d. Jesse Wynne and Dorothy Arnette (Lloyd) Vaughn; B.A., U. Miss., 1956, M.A. (univ. scholar), 1964; m. Gerald Swetnam Pierce, May 27, 1956; children—Ann Elizabeth Swetnam, John Willard. High sch. tchr., 1957-58; mem. faculty Memphis Univ. Sch., 1964-66, Memphis State U., 1968-75; agt. Aetna Life Ins. Co., Memphis, 1977-80, career supr., 1980—, chmn. Aetna Women's Task Force, 1980—; v.p., dir. Consultants System, Inc., bus. cons., 1975—. Pres., Women's Resources Center, Memphis, 1974-77; sec. Tenn. chpt. Women's Polit. Caucus, 1975-76; bd. dirs., treas., mem. exec. com. Memphis YWCA, 1979—; mem. Memphis Area Transit Authority; mem. Tenn. adv. com. U.S. Civil Rights Commn., 1980—. Named Aetna Regionnaire, 1977-82, First Year Top Achiever, 1977; mem. Leadership Memphis C.L.U. Mem. Million Dollar Roundtable, 1978, 79, Women Leaders Roundtable, 1978—. CLU. Mem. Nat. Assn. Life Underwriters, Tenn. Life Underwriters Assn., Memphis Life Underwriters Assn., Memphis PTA (council 1971-72), Memphis Soc. CLUs, LWV, AAUW, Mortar Bd. (regional coordinator 1972-78), Memphis C.L.U. Assn., Alpha Lambda Delta, Sigma Delta Pi. Republican. Episcopalian. Club: Le Bonheur (dir.). Home: 4743 Park Ave Memphis TN 38117 Office: 1355B Lynnfield Rd Suite 109 Memphis TN 38138

PIERCE, MARAH GAYLE, computer co. exec.; b. Franklinton, La., Apr. 1, 1938; d. Woodrow and Melba (Jenkins) Pierce; student Houston Conservatory Music, 1957-59, U. Houston, 1960-62, Thomas A. Edison Coll., 1977-78. Exec. sec. Gt. So. Life Ins. Co., Houston, 1958-62, computer programmer, 1962-64; programmer/analyst United Services Automobile Assn., San Antonio, 1964-69; research analyst computer div. RCA, Houston, 1969-70, project mgr., 1970, edn. mgr., 1970-71; systems mgr. Sperry Univac, Bellaire, Tex., 1972, So. ops. edn. mgr., 1972-75, sr. sales rep., 1975-77, account exec., 1977—. Recipient Superior Systems Performance award RCA, 1969, Mktg. Achievement Club award, 1970, 71, Tiger Club award Univac SW region, 1972, Mktg. Quota Achievement Club awards, 1976-83; mem. Univac Million Dollar Club, 1976-83. Mem. Data Processing Mgmt. Assn., Life Office Mgmt. Assn., NOW, Tex. Women's Polit. Caucus. Home: 10622 Braewick St Houston TX 77096 Office: 6700 W Loop S Suite 200 Bellaire TX 77401

PIERCE, MARCELLA BULLARD, accountant; b. Little Rock, Sept. 4, 1950; d. William Richard and Vera Darlene (Stipp) Bullard; B.S., Ark. State U., 1972; m. Michael E. Pierce, Nov. 28, 1969; 1 dau., Candace Lea. Mem. acctg. staff Enterprise Products Co., Inc., Stuttgart, Ark., 1972-73; sec.-treas., acct., computer programmer Gravis Concrete Co., Inc., Stuttgart, 1973—, MIP Trucking Inc., 1975—; acct., computer programer, Irven Pierce Constrn. Co., Inc., 1977—. Mem. Beta Sigma Phi. Episcopalian. Club: Stuttgart Jr. Woman's (treas. 1982-83). Home: 304 Roosevelt Pl Stuttgart AR 72160 Office: 209 N Buerkle St Stuttgart AR 72160

PIERCE, MILDRED D., tourist agy. ofcl.; b. N.Y.C., Aug. 23, 1923; d. Albert and Betty (Kadish) Dreyer; B.A., N.Y.U., 1944; children—Elizabeth F., Jeanne S., John G. Pres., University Study Tours, Inc. (Adler, Duncan & Pierce), San Francisco, 1967-71; dist. sales mgr. Gogo Tours, Inc., San Francisco, 1972-76; regional sales mgr. Haley Corp./Caribbean Holidays Inc., San Francisco, 1976-81; dist. sales mgr. Bahamas Tourist Office, San Francisco, 1981—; bd. advisors Gt. World Travel Coll. Cert. travel counselor Inst. Cert. Travel Assos. Mem. Am. Soc. Travel Agts., Travellarians of Calif. (San Francisco pres., 1974-75, 76-77), Internat. Fedn. Womens Travel Orgns. (program chmn., 1979-80), Nat. Assn. Female Execs., Sacramento Soc. Assn. Execs., Pacific Area Travel Assn. Office: 209 Post St Suite 715 San Francisco CA 94108

PIERCE, PATRICIA JADINE, med. librarian; b. Syracuse, N.Y., Apr. 15, 1950; d. Jack Edward and Nadine Lucille (Sparks) Pierce; B.A. with honors, U. Calif., San Diego, 1972; M.L.S., UCLA, 1974. Librarian, Naval Undersea Center, San Diego, 1973; library intern edn./psychology library UCLA, 1973-74; asst. librarian Kelco, div. Merck & Co., Inc., San Diego, 1975-76; med. library and continuing med. edn. coordinator Scripps Meml. Hosp., San Diego, 1976—. Pub. relations rep. com. orgn. Olympic Games, Munich, W. Ger., 1972. Mem. Med. Library Assn. (cert. health scis. librarianship 1974, 83), Ariz., Nev., So. Calif., med. library groups, U. Calif. Library Schs. Alumni Assn. Club: Mission Bay Yacht. Contbg. editor SMH Physician, 1976-78. Home: 2335 Cowley Way San Diego CA 92110 Office: Scripps Meml Hosp 9888 Genessee Ave La Jolla CA 92037

PIERCE, PATRICIA JOBE, art dealer, historian, lit. agt., appraiser; b. Seattle, May 18, 1943; d. Leonard Carl and Ruth Hazeltine (Baten) Jobe; student U. Conn., summers 1963, 64; B.F.A., Boston U., 1965; m. Norman Brayton Pierce, June 26, 1965; children—Christine Ruth, Matthew Jobe. Actress, Southbury (Conn.) Playhouse, Conn. Playmakers, Greenwich, Glendale (Calif.) Centre Theatre, Shubert Theater, Boston, Boston U. Playhouse, 1957-65; mktg. dir. Kelly Services, Boston, 1965-66; tchr. English-drama high sch., Wareham, Mass., 1967-68; pres. Pierce Galleries, Inc., Hingham, Mass., 1968—; lit. agt. Kahlil Gibran properties, 1979—; agt. for Samuel Rose, Roy Thompsen, A.C. Savrann, Lawrence Kupferman; owner, v.p. Pierce Galleries Pub. Co., 1980—; lectr. colls., mus.; mem. New Eng. adv. com. Archives on Am. Art. Fund raising chmn. Elma Lewis Afro-Am. Center, Roxbury, Mass., 1973-74; chmn. stewardship Meth. Ch., East Bridgewater, Mass., 1974. Boston U. acting scholar, 1961-65, 67. Mem. Appraisers Assn. Am., Internat. Acad. Poets, Boston Athenaeum, Boston Mus. Fine Arts, Brockton Art Center, Frick Art Reference Library, Smithsonian Instn. Author: John Joseph Enneking, American Impressionist Painter, 1972; Living Painters Trained in Boston, 1975; The Ten (American Painters), 1976; I Am Who I Am; They Who Touch the Earth, 1977; The King Who Lost His Pride, 1977; My Name's Imagination, 1977; Edmund C. Tarbell and the Boston School, 1981; The Watercolored World of J.W.S. Cox, 1981; Richard Earl Thompson, American Impressionist, 1982; Introduction to Jane Peterson, American Patriot; contbr. articles to profl. jours.; profl. Karate coach. Home and Office: 721 Main St Route 228 Hingham MA 02043 also Plymouth MA

PIERCE, PHYLLIS HARWARD, clin. psychologist; b. Chgo., July 10, 1947; d. Albert and Naomi Josephine (Markee) Harward; B.A., Ariz. State U., 1969; M.S., Fla. State U., 1972, Ph.D. in Clin. Psychology, 1976; m. Roger Clarke Pierce, Nov. 27, 1972. Clin. intern St. Elizabeths Hosp., Washington, 1972-73, research intern, 1973-74; outpatient clin. psychologist Rutland (Vt.) Mental Health Services, 1975—, chmn. inservice tng. com., 1976-78, chmn. quality assurance com., 1979—; adj. prof. Coll. St. Joseph The Provider, Rutland, 1978—. Chmn. Rutland County Task Force on Women and Alcoholism, 1978-80. Mem. Am. Psychol. Assn., Vt. Psychol. Assn. Home: Box 191 East Wallingford VT 05742 Office: 78 S Main St Rutland VT 05701

PIERCE, SYLVIA YELLIN, social work adminstr.; b. Bklyn., May 31, 1926; d. Nathan and Tillie Spector; B.S.W., Adelphi U., 1974, M.S.W., 1975; children—Marion Yellin Bilich, Ronnie Yellin Charme. Staff social worker Glen Cove (N.Y.) Hosp., 1976-78; dir. social work dept. Community Hosp. Glen Cove, 1978—; pvt. practice marital and bereavement counseling Floral Park, N.Y., 1978—. Recipient Public Service award Anti-Defamation League, 1964. Mem. Glen Cove Inter-Agy. Council, Nat. Assn. Social Workers, Hosp. Dirs. Social Work, Soc. Clin. Social Work Psychotherapists, Acad. Cert. Social Workers, Nassau County Dirs. Hosp. Social Work, Nat. Assn. Social Workers. Home: 270-29E Grand Central Pkwy Floral Park NY 11005 Office: Community Hosp at Glen Cove Saint Andrews Ln Glen Cove NY 11542

PIERCY, MARGE, poet, novelist; b. Detroit, Mar. 31, 1936; d. Robert and Bert P.; A.B., U. Mich., 1957; M.A., Northwestern U., 1958. Author novels: Small Changes, 1973; Woman on the Edge of Time, 1976; The High Cost of Living, 1978; Vida, 1980; Braided Lines, 1982; author books of poetry: Living In The Open, 1973; To Be of Use, 1976; Twelve-Spoked Wheel, 1978; The Moon Is Always Female, 1980; Circles on the Water, 1982; contbr. essays, revs. to various publs.; mem. vis. faculty Women's Writers Conf., Cazenova Coll., 1978-80; mem. staff Writer's Conv., Ind. U., Bloomington, 1977, 80; fiction writer-in-residence Holy Cross U., 1976; mem. staff Fine Arts Work Center, Provincetown, Mass., 1976-77; speaker in field. Winner, Avery Hopwood Contest, 1957; recipient Orion Scott award in humanities; Lit. award Mass. Gov.'s Com. on Status of Women, 1974; James B. Angell scholar; Nat. Endowment for Arts grantee, 1978. Mem. Authors Guild, Authors League, PEN, Poetry Soc. Am., Women's Inst. for Freedom of Press. Office: PO Box 943 Wellfleet MA 02667

PIERCY, SANDRA SUE, pub. co. exec.; b. Iaeger, W.Va., Jan. 3, 1944; d. Andrew Larkin and Lois Catherine (Harman) Christian; student public schs., Iaeger; children—Regennol Edward Piercy, Cynthia Allison Piercy. Controller, clothing designer Amerex Corp., Los Angeles, 1971-74; asst. controller, office mgr. K-B Mgmt., Co., Los Angeles, 1974-75, Tristar Western Co., Los Angeles, 1975-76; tax acct. Deloitte Haskins & Sells, C.P.A.'s, Los Angeles, 1976-78; co-pub., gen. mgr., fin. officer Claude Hall's Internat. Radio Report Co., Los Angeles, 1978—. Mem. Nat. Assn. Female Execs. Methodist. Clubs: Los Angeles Athletic, Calif. Yacht, Order Eastern Star. Home: 203 S Lucia St Redondo Beach CA 90277 Office: 1 Wilshire Blvd Suite 1900 Los Angeles CA 90017

PIERORAZIO, HELENA MARIA, automotive co. exec.; b. Yonkers, N.Y., June 26, 1952; d. Nicholas Paul and Mary (Malotz) P.; student Westchester Community Coll., 1970; B.A., Queens Coll., 1981. Controller, Queensboro Porsche Audi, L.I., N.Y., 1971-75, Porsche Audi of Queens Inc., Jamaica, N.Y., 1975-80; controller Walters-Donaldson Volkswagen, Inc., Walters-Donaldson Porsche Audi Inc., Wal-Don Enterprises, Inc. and wholly-owned subsidiaries, Hicksville, N.Y., 1980—. Mem. Nat. Assn. Female Execs. Democrat. Roman Catholic. Home: 21 Pantzer St Smithtown NY 11757

PIERPONT, GLENNA GAIL, energy/gas pipe line co. exec.; b. Bellville, Tex., Mar. 21, 1950; d. Steve A and Eunice S. Gindorf; B.S., Stephen F. Austin State U., 1972; m. William G. Pierpont, June 25, 1972. With, Transco Cos., Inc., 1973—, staffing supr. personnel dept., Houston, Tex., 1981—. Mem. Am. Soc. Personnel Adminstrs., Houston Personnel Assn., Sigma Kappa. Republican. Presbyterian. Club: Knife and Fork. Home: 4206 Southwestern St Houston TX 77005 Office: Transco Cos Inc PO Box 1396 Houston TX 77251

PIERSON, ANNA META, ret. food supplements and cosmetic distbr.; b. Ft. Smith, Ark., Dec. 22, 1919; d. Charles Henry and Meta Henrietta (Kahrs) Weller; student Citrus Coll., Azusa, Calif., 1963-65, U. Okla., 1937-38; m. John Howard Pierson, June 5, 1938; children—John Howard, James Henry, Nancy Ann Pierson Scoble, William Jay; m. 2d, Hugh R. Green, Jr., Oct., 1980. Asst. bookkeeper W.E. Logan, Muskogee, Okla., 1950-52; ins. underwriter AAA Motor Club, Oklahoma City, 1953-55; nat. underwriter Abstainers Nat. Ins. Co., Oklahoma City, 1956-58; fin. sec. John Marshall High Sch., Oklahoma City, 1959-60; underwriter, mgr. Paul Kautz Ins. Agy., Arlington, Tex., 1960-63; partner The Pierson Co., 1967-70; pres., owner, fin. dir. The J. Pierson Co., Orange, Calif., 1970-76, v.p., fin. dir., sec.-treas., fin. dir., part-owner, 1976—, dir., 1970-81; distbr. Anna M's Cosmetics, until 1981. Pres. Women's Aux. VFW, 1946-48. Mem. Nat. Nutritional Foods Assn., Golden West Nutritional Foods Assn. Republican. Methodist. Clubs: Soroptimist Internat. (pres. San Clemente, Calif. 1980-81), Order Eastern Star. Oil painter, works exhibited juried art shows; organist. Home: 27703 Ortega Hwy Apt 138 San Juan Capistrano CA 92675 Office: 995 Enterprise Way Orange CA 92667

PIERSON, EILENE CRAWLEY, educator; b. Kane, Pa., Oct. 28, 1927; d. Norbert Michael and Lucille Lillian (Warner) Crawley; B.A., Villa Maria Coll., 1949; postgrad. Yale, 1947-48, U. Md., 1955-56, Bethany Coll., 1958-59, U. Hawaii, 1967-68, Fla. Atlantic U., 1969-70, East Carolina U., 1974—; M.A., U. N.C., 1975; children—Robert Blaise, Maureen Louise, Sharon Gay, Deirdre Kathleen. Fashion model dept. stores and specialty shops, 1949—, Ft. Lauderdale, Fla., 1975—; comml. artist Halle Bros. Dept. Store, Erie, Pa., 1950-52; dancer Arthur Murray Studio, Washington, 1954-55; commentator Sta. WTRF-TV, Wheeling, W.Va., 1956-57; comml. artist, fashion coordinator Horne's Dept. Store, 1956-57; instr. drama Bethany (W.Va.) Coll., 1957-61; instr. speech Broward Jr. Coll., Ft. Lauderdale, 1968-69, 75—; asst. prof. speech and English, coordinator theater program Coll. Boca Raton (Fla.); model, fashion coordinator Edna Oliver Shops, Honolulu, 1965-67; dean Smith Coll. for Women, Ft. Lauderdale, 1969-70; instr. humanities Coastal Carolina Community Coll., Jacksonville, N.C., 1970-75; drama cons. pub. schs. Vol. tchr. Bethesda (Md.) Naval Hosp., 1954-55; dir. Quantico (Va.) Community Theatre, 1963-65; actress Honolulu Community Theatre, 1965-67; bd. dirs. Jacksonville (N.C.) Community Concert Series, 1973-75. Mem. N.C. Fine Arts Assn. (steering com. 1972-75), Yale Alumnae Assn., Smithsonian Nat. Assn., Internat. Wives Club. Club: Coastal Carolina Community Coll. Women's (pres. 1972-73). Republican. Home: 1413 NE 57th Ct Fort Lauderdale FL 33334

PIERSON, JUANITA THOMAS, educator; b. Shreveport, La., Oct. 28, 1921, d. Henry and Rodessa (Scott) Thomas; B.A., Wiley Coll., 1956; M.S., La. Tech., 1975; postgrad. Northwestern U., 1972-74, So. U., 1968-69, Prairie View A&M U., 1969-70, U. Md., 1965-66, Centenary Coll., 1967-68, Santa Clara U., 1974; m. Floyd Allen Pierson, Sept. 18, 1938; children—Annette Marilyn Pierson Poulard, Frederick Allen. Sec., Mooretown Sch., Shreveport, 1957-67; elem. music specialist Caddo Parish Schs., La., 1967-70, secondary tchr., 1970—; partner Pierson's Allendale Plaza, Shreveport, 1979—; instr. Christian Edn., Shreveport, 1970—; organist Shiloh Bapt. Ch., Shreveport, 1975-78; bookkeeper F & F Food Store, Shreveport, 1978—. Mem. ways and means com. Greenwood Acres Civic Club, 1975-81; mem. Greenwood Acres Econ. Devel. and Planning com., 1980-81. Names Educator of Yr., Caddo Parish Sch. Bd., 1978; hon. state senator, La., 1980-81. Mem. Shreveport C. of C., Leadership Shreveport Council, NEA, Nat. Council Tchrs. English, Shreveport Symphony Soc., Shreveport Regional Arts

Council, La. Council Tchrs. English, Phi Delta Kappa, Sigma Gamma. Rho. Baptist. Address: Route 6 Box 262 Shreveport LA 71119

PIERSON, LOWANDA, nurse; b. Berkeley, Calif., Dec. 8, 1952; d. Frank Paul and Lela (Huggins) Smith; B.S. in Nursing, San Jose State U., 1975; m. Willie C. Pierson, June 22, 1974; children—Rukiya J., Anesah Naemah. Profl. interviewer Field Research, San Francisco, 1973; staff nurse Choppe Hosp., San Mateo, Calif., 1975-76; staff nurse, asst. head nurse Children's Hosp. Med. Center, Oakland, Calif., 1976-78; head nurse O'Connor Hosp., San Jose; Calif., 1980; staff nurse med. ICU, Valley Med. Center, San Jose, 1981—. Mem. Calif. Nurses Assn., Critical Care Nurses Assn., Registered Nurses Profl. Assn. Democrat. Home: 1880 MacDuee Way San Jose CA 95121

PIESTRAK, LORRAINE HELEN, chemist; b. Wilkes Barre, Pa., Nov. 8, 1953; d. Henry J. and Helen A. (Mikala) P.; B.S. in Criminalistics, Mich. State U., 1975. With E.I. duPont de Nemours & Co., Inc., 1976—, quality control chemist, Wilmington, Del., 1979—. Adv., Jr. Achievement, 1980. Mem. Nat. Orgn. Female Execs., NOW.

PIETREWICZ, ALEXANDRA THERESA, psychologist, educator; b. Worcester, Mass., Aug. 13, 1949; d. Edward Stanley and Alexandra Elizabeth (Rydzewski) P.; B.S. with honors, U. Mass., 1972, M.S., 1975, Ph.D., 1977; m. Johnson Eugene Mauldin, July 11, 1981. NIH exptl. trainee, U. Mass., Amherst, 1973-75, vis. lectr. in psychology, 1976-77; asst. prof. psychology Emory U., Atlanta, 1977—. Co-prin. investigator NSF research grant, 1977-79; research grantee Emory U., 1977-78, 1979-80. Mem. Am. Psychol. Assn. (div. comparative and physiol. psychology), Animal Behavior Soc., N.Y. Acad. Scis., Southeastern Psychol. Assn. Researcher predator-prey relationships, foraging strategies; contbr. sect. to book in field; also articles. Address: 116 Psychology Bldg Emory University Atlanta GA 30322

PIETRO, DEBORAH LOIS, data processing co. exec. b. Worcester, Mass., Nov. 9, 1950; d. Lawrence Foss and Ellen (Syrene) Seal; B.A. in Edn., Worcester State Coll., 1972; M.Natural Sci., Worcester Poly. Inst., 1978. Tchr. biology Kennedy Jr. High Sch., Natick, Mass., 1972-78; coordinator info. support services Mid-Coast Tchr. Center, Rockport, Maine, 1979-80; mgr. edn. services group, dir. sch. practices info. network Bibliog. Retrieval Services, div. Indian Head Co., Latham, N.Y., 1980—; cons. in field. Recipient various certs. appreciation. Democrat. Designer computer programs. Office: BRS 1200 Route 7 Latham NY 12110

PIETTE, MICHELLE ELLEN, educator; b. Appleton, Wis., July 10, 1952; d. Norbert L. and Rosemarie P.; B.S., U. Wis., LaCrosse, 1975, M.S., 1980. Phys. edn. instr., Dodgeville, Wis., 1976-79; grad. asst. U. Wis., LaCrosse, 1979-80; asst. prof., athletic tng. program dir. Ariz. State U., Tempe, 1980—. Mem. Nat. Athletic Trainers Assn., Ariz. Athletic Trainers Assn. (chmn. profl. edn. com.), Ariz. Assn. Health, Phys. Edn., Recreation and Dance. Office: PEBE 146 Ariz State U Tempe AZ 85287

PIGG, CLAIRE CHARLENE, chamber of commerce exec.; b. Duncan, Okla., June 17, 1927; d. Odus Arthur and Ruby Julia (Cannon) Russell; student public schs.; children—Lisa, Marc, Scott, Eric, Steve. Various secretarial and office positions, 1945-70; asst. sec. Litchfield (Ill.) C. of C., 1971-73, exec. sec., 1973—; sec. bd. dirs. Litchfield C. of C. Civic Pride Assn., Litchfield Community Devel. Assn. Sec., Litchfield 4th of July Assn., 1970-79, Litchfield Bicentennial Commn., 1974-77. Recipient service awards Litchfield 4th of July Assn. Mem. Ill. Assn. C. of C. Execs., Am. Legion Aux., Beta Sigma Phi. Club: Women of Moose. Home: 1410 N Jefferson Litchfield IL 62056 Office: 115 E Ryder St Litchfield IL 62056

PIGGOTT, EILEEN MARIE, mfg. co. exec.; b. Chgo., Jan. 9, 1949; d. Thomas William and Mary Margaret (Stocker) Pender; B.A. in Sociology, Loyola U., Chgo., 1971; 1 dau., Katherine Nora. With Bell & Howell Co., Chgo., 1973—, mem. corp. staff manpower planning, 1979-80, mgr. employment and orgn. planning, 1980—. Mem. Human Resource Planning Soc., No. Ill. Indsl. Assn., Employee Relocation Council. Office: 7100 McCormick Rd Chicago IL 60645

PIKE, NANCY BROOKS, med. technologist; b. McComb, Miss., Oct. 22, 1952; d. James Hilton and Maxine (Arnold) Brooks; B.S., La. State U., 1975; m. Michael Alan Pike, Apr. 6, 1974; 1 son, Nathan Alan. Staff technologist Our Lady of the Lake Med. Center, Baton Rouge, La., 1975-76, Texoma Med. Center, Denison, Tex., 1976-80, asso. dir. labs., 1980—; med. lab. technician clin. coordinator Grayson County Coll. and various hosp. coms.; lectr. in field. Vol. worker Cystic Fibrosis, Multiple Sclerosis, March of Dimes; Acteen leader First Baptist Ch. Mem. Am. Soc. Clin. Pathologists (cert. med. technologist, specialist in hematology), Phi Mu, Beta Sigma Phi, Lambda Tau. Democrat. Club: Denison Rod & Gun. Home: 3009 Francis St Denison TX 75020 Office: 1000 Memorial St Denison TX 75020

PIKE, PRISCILLA RAE, ct. reporter, bus. propr.; b. Los Angeles, Dec. 7, 1930; d. Raymond Bruce and Amy Elizabeth (Dunaway) Linganfield; student schs. Glendale, Calif.; m. William F. Pike, Aug. 7, 1949; children—Pamela R. Pike Plowman, Lauri E. Pike Miller, Gary W., Thomas C. Various positions Ventura County (Calif.) dist. atty's office, superior ct.; county clk. Ventura County Bd. Suprs., 1970-75; hearing reporter Calif. Coastal Commn., Ventura, 1977—; founder Priscilla Pike Hearing Reporter Services, Ventura, 1978—, conf. planner, author, participant confs. U.S., Can. Republican. Mem. Nat. Ct. Reporters Assn., Calif. Ct. Reporters Assn., Nat. Assn. Female Execs. Christrian Scientist. Home and Office: 6367 Swallow St Ventura CA 93003

PILAO, LEONORA CARRIAGA, nurse; b. Lucena City, Philippines, Feb. 20, 1951; came to U.S., 1973, naturalized, 1981; d. Norberto Pamposa and Natalia Laloon (Carriaga) P.; B.S. in Nursing, U. of the Philippines, 1972; postgrad. in gerontology Rutgers U., 1976, U. Pa., 1980. Head nurse Senator Convalescent Center, Atlantic City, 1973-74; nursing supr. Senator Manor Nursing Home, Atlantic City, 1974-75; dir. in-service edn. Shore Manor Nursing Home, Atlantic City, 1975-76, asst. dir. nursing, 1976-77; dir. nursing services SCA Intermediate Care Facility, Atlantic City, 1977—; mgmt. cons. Golden Crest Convalescent Center, Atlantic City, 1978-80; chmn. com. investigating impact of casino industry to health care delivery Atlantic County, 1980; participant Kellogg Found. nursing adminstrn. tng. program U. Pa., 1982, Soviet-Am. Gerontol. Nursing Study Tour, 1982; guest speaker civic orgn. Mem. Am. Nurses Assn., N.J. Assn. In-Service Edn. and Tng., N.J. League of Nursing, Nat. Assn. Female Execs. Condr. research on efficacy of influenza vaccine among elderly, 1980. Home: Somers Point NJ 08244 Office: 166 S South Carolina Ave Atlantic City NJ 08401

PILIAVIN, JANE ALLYN, social psychologist, educator; b. Montclair, N.J., Feb. 21, 1937; d. Horace Warren and Mary Elizabeth (Young) Allyn; B.A. in Psychology with high honors, U. Rochester, 1958; Ph.D. in Social Psychology, Stanford U., 1962; m. Irving M. Piliavin, Dec. 27, 1968; 1 dau., Elizabeth Elaine; 1 son by previous marriage, Allyn Henry Hardyck. Research psychologist, lectr. U. Calif., Berkeley, 1962-66; vis. asst. prof. psychology Mills Coll., Oakland, Calif., 1966-67; asst. prof. psychology U. Pa., Phila., 1967-70; assoc. prof. Sch. Family Resources and Consumer Scis., U. Wis.-Madison, 1970-73, prof., 1973-77, prof. sociology, 1977—, assoc. chmn. dept. sociology, 1979-82; mem. NSF review panel on social and devel. psychology, 1981—. NSF grantee, 1967-72; NIH grantee, 1979—. Mem. Am. Psychol. Assn., Am. Sociol. Assn., AAAS, Soc. Exptl. Social Psychology, NOW, Nat. Women's Polit. Caucus. Author: (with Charles Y. Glock, Robert Wuthnow and Metta Spencer) Adolescent Prejudice, 1975, (with John Dovidio, Samuel Gaertner and Russell D. Clark III) Emergency Intervention, 1981. Home: 2703 Mason St Madison WI 53705 Office: Dept Sociology Univ Wis Madison WI 53706

PILIKOWSKI, ANNE CECILE, librarian, nurse; b. Prince Albert, Sask., Can., Feb. 3, 1924; d. William and Josephine (Klamantoski) P.; R.N., Holy Family Hosp., Prince Albert, 1947, R.R.L., 1960. Asst. dir. med. records Holy Family Hosp., Prince Albert, 1960-71; chief record librarian Norfolk Gen. Hosp., Simcoe, Ont., Can., 1971-73; record librarian Victoria Hosp., London, Ont., 1973—. Cert. health record adminstr. Mem. Ont. Health Record Assn., Can. Assn. Med. Records Librarians. Address: 500 Gordon Ave Apt 902 London ON N6J 2V8 Canada

PILL, CYNTHIA JOAN, social worker; b. N.Y.C., Mar. 30, 1939; d. Alfred and Edna (Strauss) Fruchtman; B.S. cum laude, Jackson Coll., Tufts U., 1961; M.S., Sch. Social Work, Simmons Coll. 1963; m. Robert Pill, July 29, 1961; children—Laura, Daniel, Karen. Clin. social worker Concord (Mass.) Family Service, 1965-78; coordinator family life edn. Family Counseling Service, Newton, Mass., 1979—; pvt. practice clin. social work, Newton, Mass., 1979—; co-founder, clin. social worker Remarriage Counseling Collaborative, Newton, Mass., 1981—; cons. Hospice of the Good Shepherd Inc. Lic. ind. clin. social worker. Mem. Mass. Acad. Psychiat. Social Work, Nat. Assn. Social Workers, Soc. Family Therapy and Research, Nat. Assn. Social Workers, Register Clin. Social Workers. Contbr. to profl. publs. Address: 14 Mason Rd Newton Center MA 02159

PILLAI-MASSEY, SARALA DEVI, psychiatrist; b. Kuala Kangsar, Malaysia, Jan. 11, 1944; came to U.S., 1975; d. K. V. Balakrishna and Kamalakshi B. Pillai; pre-univ. degree Stella Maris Coll., Madras, India, 1962; M.B., B.S., Kasturba Med. Coll., Mysore, India, 1970; m. Johnson Pervez Massey, Oct. 10, 1978; children—Kala, Alka; 1 stepdau., Ann. Intern in medicine Govt. Gen. Hosp., Madras and Govt. Gen. Hosp., Ipoh, Malaysia, 1971-72; med. officer Govt. Gen. Hosp., Ministry Health Malaysia, 1972-74; clin. physician Napanoch and Fishkoll (N.Y.) correctional facilites, 1977-78; resident in psychiatry Hudson River Psychiat. Center, Poughkeepsie, N.Y., 1978-79, N.Y. Med. Coll., 1979-82; attending psychiatrist, Bronx, N.Y., 1982—; cons. psychiatry; leader multidisciplinary team in patient care. Mem. AMA, Am. Women's Med. Assn., Psychiat. Soc. Westchester, World Med. Assn.

PILLON, SHARON THERESA, nurse, hosp. adminstr.; b. Ont., Can., Mar. 8, 1949; came to U.S., 1973; d. Joseph Adolph and Marion Elizabeth (Bondy) Pillon; R.N. diploma, Hotel Dieu Hosp. Sch. Nursing, Windsor, Ont., 1970; B.S. in Mgmt., Pacific Christian Coll., 1980. Pres., Calif. Med. Careers, Inc., Redondo Beach, 1978-79; dir. edn. La Mirada (Calif.) Community Hosp., 1978-80, Westside Hosp.-Am. Med. Internat., Inc., Los Angeles, 1980—; dir. nursing Meml. Hosp., Hawthorne, Calif., 1981—; instr. basic cardiac life support Am. Heart Assn.; Harbor Area dir. Nursing Council; active Health Fair Expo. Mem. Nat. Assn. Female Execs. Roman Catholic. Office: 13300 S Hawthorne Blvd Hawthorne CA 90250

PINCKNEY, CATHERINE LARKUM, author, consumer reporter; b. N.Y.C.; d. Edward S. and Isolde (Illian) Larkum; student N.Y. U., 1942-44, 48, Syracuse U., 1946-48, New Sch. Social Research, 1949, U. Calif.-Berkeley, 1969-70; m. Edward R. Pinckney, Sept. 18, 1944; 1 dau., Cathey Lee. Writer various stories Ben Casey, TV series; co-writer daily and Sunday column Mirror of Your Mind pub. in U.S., fgn. newspapers, 1967—; book reviewer Parade of Books, 1965—; contbg. editor Consumer Newsletter; spl. editorial cons. The Pocket Book Family Med. Ency., 1976; health, food and restaurant editor Consumer News for Cable TV, 1980—. Mem. Writers Guild Am., Authors League. Author: The Fallacy of Freud and Psychoanalysis, 1964; Medical Encyclopedia of Common Illnesses, 1962; Granny's Hillbilly Cookbook, 1966; The Cholesterol Controversy, 1973; A Consumer's Guide to Common Medical Dilemmas, 1975; The Restaurant Book, 1977; Ency. of Medical Tests, 1978, 2d revised edit., 1982; A Patient's Guide to Medical Tests, 1983; contbg. editor Media & Consumer; contbr. articles to publs. Office: PO Box P Beverly Hills CA 90213

PINCUS-STROM, DIANE GAIL, psychiat. social worker; b. N.Y.C., Feb. 23, 1949; d. Morris and Emma Blanche (Mencher) Pincus; B.A., CCNY, 1970; M.S.W., N.Y. U., 1976; postgrad. N.Y. Center Psychoanalytic Tng., 1976-79. Pediatric group worker Bronx-Lebanon Hosp., Bronx, N.Y., 1970-74, hemodialysis social worker, 1976—; pvt. practice psychotherapy, N.Y.C., 1978—; group worker, cons. CCNY, 1976—; clin. asso. Lehman Coll., Bronx, N.Y., 1980—. Mem. Acad. Cert. Social Workers, Nat. Assn. Social Workers, Council Nephrology Social Workers, Nat. Assn. Patients on Hemodialysis and Transplantation, Nat. Kidney Found., CCNY Alumni House Plan Assn. Jewish. Home: 5650 Netherland Ave Bronx NY 10471 Office: Dept Social Work Bronx Lebanon Hosp 1276 Fulton Ave Bronx NY 10456 also 1651 3d Ave Suite 201 New York NY 10028

PINE, ANN SALLET, costume designer; b. Malden, Mass., Sept. 23, 1946; d. George John and Jeanette Evelyn (Murphy) Sallet; cert. Mass. Mus. Sch. Art, 1964, M.I.T., 1967; m. Roger William Pine, III, July 25, 1969. Draftsman, Sylvania Elec. Co., 1965; sr. tech. artist Lincoln Lab., M.I.T., 1966-67; sr. artist illustrator Honeywell Corp., San Diego, 1968-74; display mgr. Walker Scott Co., Calif., 1978; children's clothing designer Dorsey Co., 1979; costume designer San Diego Costume Co., 1979, TV pilots for Fractured Funnies, 1982, Jack Diamond Pvt. Eye, 1982, Lord Geoferys Manor, 1982; self-employed costume designer, Poway, Calif., 1979—; co-owner antastic Fantastic Fantasy Factory (costume shop), Weddings-R-Us; wardrobe designer Ace Diamond, Pvt. Eye, TV pilot, 1980, On the Line, TV pilot, 1981, Father Forgive Me, motion picture, 1981; pres. Art and Adult Sch. Theatre, 1980-81; art dir. Firemen's Follies, San Diego, 1979; artistic cons. Mt. Carmel High Sch. Pop Ensemble, 1980-81; costume designer San Diego Head Dress Ball, 1978. Recipient 1st place award Nat. Fair Housing Assn., 1964; Cleo award, 1979. Mem. Nat. Thespian Soc., Poway Firemen's Bldg. Orgn., San Diego C. of C. Office: 13380 Poway Rd Poway CA 92064 also PO Box 332 Poway CA 92064

PINEAU, SISTER, NICOLE MARIE, social worker; b. Paris, Dec. 4, 1924; came to U.S., 1964, naturalized, 1976; d. Henri Raymond Pierre and Caroline Marie Rose (Morel D'Arleux) P.; student Ecole de la Croix Rouge, 1945; B.A., U. Southwestern La., 1967; M.S.W., Tulane U., 1967. Joined Dominican Rural Missionaries, Roman Cath. Ch., 1951; missionary in rural France, 1951-64; vol. Head Start, Abbeville, La., 1967-68; social worker Vermilion Parish Community Action, Kaplan, La., 1968-69; social worker, health coordinator Jeff Davis Community Action Head Start, Jennings, La., 1969—; social worker S.W. La. State Sch. for Mentally Retarded, 1982—. Active Alcoholics Anonymous, Al-Anon. Recipient cert. So. U. Alcoholism Counselor Tng. Program, 1969, Crowley Mental Health Center, 1972. Mem. Nat. Assn. Social Workers, Nat. Assn. Women Religious, NAACP, Bread for the World. Democrat. Home: 1321 S Lake Arthur Ave Jennings LA 70546 Office: PO Box 1106 Jennings LA 70546

PINES, AYALA MALACH, psychologist; b. Russia, July 19, 1945; d. Zeev and Judith Malach; B.A., Hebrew U. Jerusalem, 1967; M.A., Boston U., 1971, Ph.D., 1973; m. Alexander Pines, Aug. 31, 1967; children—Itai, Shani. Researcher, Research Inst. Ednl. Problems, Harvard U. Med. Sch., 1968-69; lectr. dept. psychology Center Applied Behavioral Scis., Boston U., 1969-72; lectr., research asso. U. Calif., Berkeley, 1973-80, research asso., 1980—; cons. on coping with burnout. Served with Israeli Army, 1967-68. Mem. Am. Psychol. Assn., Soc. Psychol. Assn., Soc. Psychol. Study Social Issues, AAUP, Assn. Women in Psychology. Democrat. Jewish. Author: (with C. Maslach) Experiencing Social Psychology, 1979; (with E. Aronson) Burnout: From Tedium to Personal Growth, 1981; contbr. articles to profl. jours. Home: 136 Purdue Ave Kensington CA 94708 Office: Dept Psychology U Calif Berkeley CA 94720

PINGREE, DIANNE HAYS, publisher; b. Dallas, B.F.A. magna cum laude, So. Meth. U., 1976; A.A. summa cum laude, Richland Coll., 1974; m. Harlan Pingree. Freelance journalist, 1974-76; editor, pub. Tex. Woman Mag., Dallas, 1977-80; pres. Tex. Woman, Inc., Dallas, Dianne Pingree Enterprises, Dallas, 1980—. Recipient Women Helping Women award Women's Center Dallas, 1980. Mem. Women in Communications (Matrix award 1979), Exec. Women Dallas (sec., bd. mem. 1981, v.p. 1982), Dallas Communications Council, Dallas Press Club (Gridiron Show award 1982), Sigma Delta Chi. Office: 5551 Yale Blvd Dallas TX 75206

PINKERTON, ANN BARHAM, accountant; b. Abilene, Tex., May 2, 1945; d. Harold Nathan and Georgia Fay (Griffin) Barham; B.S. in Acctg., Tex. Technol. U., 1978; m. William Edmond Pinkerton, Dec. 27, 1964; children—Deborah Page, William Edmond, James Douglass, John Mark. Bookkeeper, Pinkerton Farms, Edmonson, Tex., 1970-78, Tex. Tech. U. Theater, Lubbock, 1978; acct. Armstrong & Armstrong, C.P.A.s, Lubbock, 1979—; asst. dir. acctg. W. Tex. State U., Canyon, 1980—; cons. in field. 4-H project leader Edmonson, Tex., 1979-80; leader Girl Scouts U.S.A., Edmonson, 1971-73; Republican precinct chmn., fund raiser, 1959-63; choir leader, Sun. Sch. tchr. Halfway Meth. Ch., 1971-75; water safety instr. ARC. Nat. Aquatic Sch. scholar, 1963; C.P.A., Tex. Mem. Tex. Technol. U. Acctg. Soc. (sec. 1975-78, Appreciation award 1978), Randall County Profl. Republican Women, Amarillo Women's Network (audit chmn. 1982), Beta Alpha Psi. Republican. Methodist. Home: 1201 Brookhaven Canyon TX 79015 Office: Box 999 Canyon TX 79015

PINKERTON, PATRICIA ELLEN, boatbldg. co. exec.; b. Lamar, Colo., Aug. 23, 1951; d. William Thomas and Billie Joy (Shepard) P.; B.A., San Diego State U., 1976. Repair clk. customer services Pacific Telephone, San Francisco, 1971-78; mgr., tech. advisor Composite Engrng., Inc., Winchester, Mass., 1978—; sportscaster Sta. WQTV, Boston, 1979-80. Mem. Nat. Assn. for Female Execs., U.S. Rowing Assn., Nat. Women's Rowing Assn. (pres. 1982—), New Eng. Bicycle Club, Cambridge Sports Union. Clubs: Cambridge Boat, Riverside Boat, Eastern Devel. Camp (pres. 1979-81.). Nat. medalist Women's Nat. Rowing Championships, 1975-82; contbg. author The Oarsman, 1976—. Office: 742 Main St Winchester MA 01890

PINKERTON, VIRGINIA BROWN, editor, publisher, writer; b. St. Louis, Apr. 10, 1926; d. Grover Cleveland and Beulah Anise (Gibson) Brown; student U. Va., No. Va. Community Coll.; m. Forest Pinkerton, Aug. 17, 1970; children—Marion Nuckols, Bonnie Brady, Mark Dooley, John Dooley, Carolyn Dooley. Editor, Auto-Call Mag., Alexandria, Va., 1975—; public relations asst. Am. Radio Relay League, Newington, Conn., 1975—; contbr. articles to amateur radio mags.; author: How To Be Pain-Free Without Drugs, 1979. Mem. Assn. to Advance Ethical Hypnosis, Internat. Platform Assn., Found. Amateur Radio, Nat. Writers Club, Washington Area Young Ladies Amateur Radio Club, Hypoglycemia Soc. Address: 7223 Wickford Dr Alexandria VA 22310

PINKHAM, ELEANOR HUMPHREY, univ. librarian; b. Chgo., May 7, 1926; d. Edward Lemuel and Grace Eleanor (Cushing) Humphrey; A.B., Kalamazoo Coll., 1948; M.S. in Library Sci. (Alice Louise LeFevre scholar), Western Mich. U., 1967; m. James Hansen Pinkham, July 10, 1948; children—Laurie Sue, Carol Lynn. Public services librarian Kalamazoo Coll., 1967-68, asst. librarian, 1960-70, library dir., 1971—; vis. lectr. Western Mich. U. Sch. Librarianship, 1970—, mem. adv. bd., 1977-81, also adv. bd. Inst. Cistercian Studies library, 1975-80. Mem. ALA, Mich. Library Assn. (chmn. acad. div. 1977-78), Mich. Library Consortium (exec. council 1974-82, chmn. 1977-78), AAUP, Beta Phi Mu. Presbyterian (elder 1969—). Home: 2519 Glenwood Dr Kalamazoo MI 49008 Office: 1200 Academy St Kalamazoo MI 49007

PINKHAM, ROBIN REMICK, steel co. exec.; b. Bridgeport, Conn., May 5, 1944; d. Irving Grant and Theresa Helena (Busci) Pinkham; A.B. in English, Conn. Coll. Women, 1965; postgrad. N.Y. Inst. Fin., 1965-66. Sales asst. Paine, Webber, N.Y.C., 1965-68; Dean, Witter, N.Y.C., 1969; adminstr. Scudder, Stevens & Clark, N.Y.C., 1969-72; asst. to dir. fin. planning Wood Walker, N.Y.C., 1972-73; pension fund investment mgr. Nat. Forge Co., N.Y.C., 1973—. Vol., Lighthouse for the Blind, 1966-68. Registered investment counsellor. Mem. N.Y. Soc. Security Analysts, Fin. Analysts Fedn. Republican. Home: 245 E 63d St Apt 1127 New York NY 10021 Office: 110 W 51st St Suite 3700 New York NY 10020

PINKNEY, HELEN LOUISE, librarian, curator; b. Decatur, Ill., May 4, 1911; d. Charles DeWitt and Anna (Fisk) P.; 4 yr. diploma Dayton (Ohio) Art Inst., 1940. Librarian, registrar of collections, then gen. curator, librarian Dayton Art Inst., 1936-59, librarian, curator textiles, 1959—, tchr. textile design and printing, 1945-46. Mem. Spl. Libraries Assn., Art Libraries Soc. N.Am., Am. Assn. Mus., Ohio Mus. Assn., DAR. Author collection catalogues. Home: 37 Stoddard Ave Dayton OH 45405 Office: Dayton Art Inst PO Box 941 Dayton OH 45401

PINKSTAFF, MARLENE ARTHUR, tng. and devel. cons.; b. Alma, Ark., Sept. 21, 1936; d. James Alexander and Ruby Jo (Fitzgerald) Arthur; A.A., Claremore Coll., Okla., 1976; B.S., U. Tulsa, 1979; m. Richard E. Pinstaff, Sept. 2, 1955; children—Mark Richard, Jay Ralph. Records analyst A.S. Aloe Co., St. Louis, 1955-57; office mgr. McKendree Coll., Lebanon, Ill., 1957-58; exec. sec. Tri-State Ins. Co., Tulsa, Okla., 1958-59; exec. sec. A.E. Staley Mfg. Co., Decatur, Ill., 1959-62; sr. cons. Dick Pinkstaff Associates, Tulsa, 1970-79; prin. Pinkstaff, Pinkstaff, Wilkinson & Koepernik, Tulsa, 1980, pres. PPW Cons. Group, Inc., 1981—; cons., dir. Aldersgate Pre-Sch., 1973-77. Mem. Am. Soc. Profl. Cons., Am. Soc. Tng. and Devel., Adminstrv. Mgmt. Soc., Phi Theta Kappa. Methodist. Author: Women at Work, 1979; Personal Skill Building for the Emerging Manager, 1979. Home: 4230 E 78th St Tulsa OK 74136 Office: 7030 S Yale Tulsa OK 74177

PINNEY, ANN WEBSTER, productivity improvement co. exec.; b. Manchester, Conn., Sept. 25, 1952; d. Charles Arthur and Ann Miriam P.; B.A., N.Mex. State U., 1974, M.A., 1975; postgrad. U. Denver, 1977—; m. Gerald T. McPhee, Mar. 1, 1980. Psychologist, Pikes Peak Mental Health Center, Colorado Springs, Colo., 1975-77; research analyst Colorado Springs C. of C., 1977-78; program dir. Performance Systems Improvement, Tustin, Calif., 1978-81; pres. AWP. Performance Improvement, Denver, 1981—; cons. in field. Recipient Honorary Datum Employee award Datum, Inc., 1979. Mem. Am. Psychol. Assn., Colo. Mining Assn., Rocky Mountain Coal Mining Inst., Women in Mining, Am. Personnel and Guidance Assn., Denver Center for Performing Arts Assn., AAUW. Republican. Clubs: Denver Coal,

Parker Book Review. Author: Training Manual for Improving Performance, 1981. Office: 8911 Thunderbird Rd Parker CO 80134

PINSKER, ESTHER JILL, social worker; b. N.Y.C., Oct. 29, 1940; d. David Aaron and Claire (Sohn) Silver; B.S. (Coll. scholar), Emerson Coll., 1961; M.A., N.Y. U., 1966; M.S.W., U. Houston, 1978; m. Harold M. Pinsker, July 2, 1967; 1 dau., Annie Love. Speech correctionist Elmont (N.Y.) Meml. High Sch., 1962-66; TV tchr., performer and script writer New Hyde Park (N.Y.) Schs., 1964; speech pathologist Rusk Inst. Rehab. Medicine, N.Y. U., 1966-68, dir. children's speech service, 1968-72; jail motivation program co-founder and coordinator for Galveston County, Gulf Coast Mental Health-Mental Retardation, Galveston, Tex., 1977—; pvt. practice psychotherapy; dir., founder Jail Theatrical Group. Convenor, pres. Galveston County NOW, 1974-75; performer in community and profl. theater, Galveston, 1979. Recipient Best Actress award Galveston Coll. Upper Deck Theater, 1980; Vocat. Rehab. fellow, 1961; Kappa Kappa Gamma fellow, 1966. Mem. Assn. Cert. Social Workers, Am. Assn. Marriage and Family Therapists (clin.), Internat. Assn. Transactional Analysis, NOW, Nat. Assn. Social Workers, Internat. Soc. Profl. Hypnosis. Democrat. Jewish. Home: 2118 1/2 Strand #A Galveston TX 77550 Office: 2306 Ave P Galveston TX 77550

PINSON, MARGUERITE LORETTA, ednl. cons.; b. Willard, N.Mex., May 25, 1912; d. Ephriam Eastlan and Lucy Ethlyn (Angle) Berry; B.S. in Edn., Ark. State Coll., Conway, 1948; M.S., U. Ark., Fayetteville, 1951; children—Ralph Young, Sue Young Wilson. Tchr., Little Rock Schs., 1943-53; tchr. Anaheim (Calif.) Elem. Sch., 1953-57; dir. elem. edn. Chapman Coll., Orange, Calif., 1957-59; cons. Orange County (Calif.) Dept. Edn., Santa Ana, 1959-77; program rev. cons. Calif. State Dept. Edn., 1977-82; mem. adv. panel Nat. Affiliation for Literacy Advance, 1980—. Mem. NEA, Calif. Tchrs. Assn., Fgn. Lang. Assn., Phi Theta Kappa, Alpha Chi, Kappa Delta Pi, Delta Kappa Gamma. Democrat. Methodist. Home: 2744 Lorenzo Ave Costa Mesa CA 92626

PINTA, WANDA BOHAN (MRS. R. JACK PINTA), home economist; b. Greenfield, Iowa, Sept. 11, 1918; d. Edward Philip and Stella (Plymesser) Bohan; B.S., Iowa State U., 1943; postgrad. Calif. State U., Los Angeles, 1956-59; m. R. Jack Pinta, Apr. 17, 1948. Tech. writer, editor Gen. Motors Corp., Milford, Mich., 1943-45; sr. home economist Los Angeles Dept. Water and Power, 1956-61, dir. consumer services, 1961—, supr. ednl. services, 1981—. Pub. relations dir. LWV, Des Moines, 1953-55; sec. Assn. for UN, Des Moines, 1953-55. Recipient Laura McCall Home Service Achievement award, 1960, Alma award Assn. Home Appliance Mfrs., 1971, 73. Mem. Am. (mem. consumer interests com.), Calif. (pres. Los Angeles 1966-67) home econs. assns., Los Angeles Home Economist in Bus., Elec. Women's Round Table (nat. dir., nat. pres. 1978-80), Soc. Consumer Affairs Profls. (sec. So. Calif. chpt. 1978-79), Los Angeles City/County Energy Edn. Council (newsletter editor 1981—), Los Angeles World Affairs Council, Town Hall. Episcopalian. Mem. Order Eastern Star. Club: Pilot (pres. Van Nuys 1962-63). Home: 5744 Vantage Ave North Hollywood CA 91607 Office: 111 N Hope St Los Angeles CA 90012

PINTO, GINA SIDDI, educator; b. Elbert, W.Va., Jan. 14, 1930; d. Severino F. and Teresa M. (Flavia) Siddi; B.S. in Bus. Edn., W.Va. U., 1951, M.A. in Econ. Edn., 1954; postgrad. Eastern Ill. U., Sagamon State U.; m. Frank James Pinto, Jr., Aug. 25, 1956; 1 dau., Mary Kathryn Pinto Thompson. Tchr. high schs., W.Va., 1951-52, 53-56; instr. W.Va. U., 1952-53; asst. prof. Fairmont (W.Va.) State Coll., 1956-67; tchr. West Hills Secondary Sch., Owen Sound, Ont., Can., 1967-69; asso. prof. bus. Richland Community Coll., Decatur, Ill., 1972-79, prof., 1979—. Active in working for restoration hist. sites; active United Way, Decatur Arts Council, YWCA, Mental Health Assn. Mem. Am. Bus. Woman's Assn. (pres., 1977-78, named Bus. Woman of Yr., Monarch chpt. 1977-78), AAUW (sec., 1970-71), Civic Exchange C. of C., Nat. Bus. Edn. Assn., Ill. Bus. Edn. Assn., Am. Vocat. Assn., Ill. Vocat. Assn., W.Va. Bus. Edn. Assn. (past pres.), NEA (life), Internat. Bus. Edn. Assn., Delta Zeta. Roman Catholic. Club: Zonta (pres. Decatur chpt. 1979-81). Home: 325 S Westlawn Ave Decatur IL 62522 Office: Richland Community Coll 2425 Federal Dr Decatur IL 62526

PIOMELLI, MARIA-ROSARIA, architect; b. Naples, Italy, Oct. 24, 1937; d. Alberto and Giuseppina (Trapanese) Angrisano; came to U.S., 1957; B.Arch., M.I.T., 1960; M.Art Accademia d'Arte, Naples, 1955; m. Sergio Piomelli, M.D., Apr. 25, 1956; children—Ascanio Alberto, Fosca Francesca. Designer, Warner Burns Toan & Lunde, Architects, N.Y.C., 1963-69; asso. architect E.H. Grosmann Architect, Rotterdam, Netherlands, 1969-70; project architect I.M. Pei & Partners, N.Y.C., 1971-74; prin. Rosaria Piomelli, Architect, N.Y.C., 1971—; tchr. design and bldg. systems tech. Pratt Inst., CCNY, 1971-76, chmn. faculty Pratt Inst. Sch. Architecture, Bklyn., 1975-79; dean Sch. Architecture, CCNY, 1980—; organizer exhibit Women in Architecture, 1974. Chmn., N.Y.C./AIA Equal Opportunity Com., 1973-75. Recipient HEW design award for Brown U. Sci. Library, 1966; Mudd Found. design award for Oberlin Coll. Learning Center, 1973. Mem. AIA (dir. exec. com. N.Y. chpt. 1977-79). Home: 390 W Broadway New York NY 10012

PIPER, ROBERTA BICKNELL, psychologist; b. Chelsea, Vt., Aug. 3, 1928; d. Maurice Slack and Neva (Bohanon) Bicknell; B.A., U. Vt., 1950; M.A., Columbia U., 1952; M.S., So. Ill. U., 1975, Ph.D., 1978; m. Henry Dan Piper, July 2, 1953; children—Andrew Dan, Jonathan Bicknell. Instr., So. Ill. U., Carbondale, 1965-66, intern Counseling Center, 1976-78; pvt. practice clin. psychology, Carbondale, 1978—. Bd. dirs., v.p. Women's Center, Carbondale, 1977-80, initiator counselor program, 1972-75. So. Ill. U. fellow, 1975-76. Mem. Am. Psychol. Assn., Am. Personnel and Guidance Assn. Author: Little Red, 1964; contbr. articles to profl. jours. Home and Office: Route 1 Box 160 Murphysboro IL 62966

PIPITONE, PHYLLIS LUIS, psychologist; b. Chgo.; d. Max and Antoinette Walkey; student Chgo. Conservatory Music, 1941-44, Peabody Conservatory Music, 1945, Chgo. Tchrs. Coll., 1946-47, So. Meth. U., 1951-52; M.A., U. Akron, 1967; Ph.D. (NIMH grantee, HEW Child Devel. fellow), Kent State U., 1974; m. S. Joseph Pipitone, Aug. 28, 1948 (dec.); children—Guy, Daniel, Paul; m. 2d, Thomas A. Cox, Jan. 3, 1980. With B.S. & H. Advt. Agy., Chgo., 1941-43; instr. piano and theory Music Acad. Chgo.; psychologist, instr. U. Akron and Kent State U., 1970-79; pvt. practice psychology, Akron, Ohio, 1967—; lectr. Served with WAC, AUS, 1944-46. Mem. Am. Psychol. Assn., Nat. Assn. Sch. Psychologists, Mensa, Council Exceptional Children, Am. Hypnosis Soc., Psi Research Group. Clubs: Tuesday Musical, Weathervane Theatre, Akron Women's City, Wadsworth Women's. Home: 224 Pheasant Run Wadsworth OH 44281

PIRATZKY, JOANNE HAZEL, cytotechnologist; b. Hackensack, N.J., May 23, 1951; d. Albert Richard and Johanna Josephine (Gaccione) P.; B.A., Duke U., 1973; M.S., Fairleigh-Dickinson U., 1978; C.T., Duke U., 1974; postgrad. N.Y. U., 1981—. Cytotechnologist, Duke U. Med. Center, Durham, N.C., 1973-75; cytotechnologist GYN Cytology & Pathology Assoc., Englewood, N.J., 1975-76; sect. head cytology lab. Hackensack (N.J.) Med. Center, 1976—; asst. prof. Sch. Cytotechnology, Coll. of Medicine & Dentistry of N.J., 1981—. Bd. dirs. Planned Parenthood of Bergen County, 1980—. Mem. Internat. Acad. Cytology, Am. Soc. Cytology, Am. Soc. Clin. Pathologists, Greater N.Y. Assn. Cytotechnology, Am. Soc. Cytotechnologists. Roman Catholic. Home: 145 Clinton Pl Apt 9A Hackensack NJ 07601 Office: Dept Labs Hackensack Med Center Hackensack NJ 07601

PIRSCH, CAROL MCBRIDE, telephone co. community relations supr., state senator; b. Omaha, Dec. 27, 1936; d. Lyle Erwin and Hilfrie Louise (Lebeck) McBride; student U. Miami, Oxford, Ohio, U. Nebr., Omaha; m. Allen I. Pirsch, Mar. 28, 1954; children—Pennie Elizabeth, Pamela Elaine, Patrice Eileen, Phyllis Erika, Peter Allen, Perry Andrew. Former mem. data processing staff Omaha Public Schs.; wage practices Western Electric Co., Omaha; legal sec., Omaha; office mgr. Pirsch Food Brokerage Co., Inc., Omaha; employment supr. Northwestern Bell Telephone Co., Omaha, now supr. community relations; mem. Nebr. Senate. Former bd. dirs. Adams Sch. PTA; bd. dirs. U. Nebr. at Omaha Parents Assn., Nebr. chpt. Cystic Fibrosis Found., Developmental Disabilities Council; Brownie leader Girl Scouts U.S.A.; mem. Mayor's Commn. on Status of Women; del. White House Conf. on Families; mem. Republican County Central Com.; del. state and county Rep. convs.; justice of the peace; deacon Benson Presbyn. Ch. Recipient Golden Elephant award; Outstanding Legis. Leadership award Nat. Orgn. Victim Assistance. Mem. Orgn. Women Legislators, Tangier Women's Aux. Clubs: Pilot, Omaha Women's, N.W. Civic, Benso Republican Women's. Office: Dist 10 Room 1126 State Capitol Bldg Lincoln NE 68509

PIRTLE, MAXINE KAY, Boy Scout exec.; b. Wichita, Kans., Oct. 19, 1945; d. Thomas Arthur and Geraldine Fern (Miller) P.; B.A. in Journalism, Tex. Christian U., 1977. Public relations asst. Tex. Refinery Corp., 1966-69; staff writer Quarter Racing Record mag., 1977; dir. public relations Longhorn council Boy Scouts Am., 1977-79, nat. communications editor, Irving, Tex., 1979—, asst. adv. Journalism Explorer Post, 1981. Mem. Internat. Assn. Bus. Communicators, Women in Communications (sec. 1975-77), Sigma Delta Chi. Club: Ft. Worth Press. Address: 1325 Walnut Hill Ln Irving TX 75062

PISCOPO, MARIAN LOUISE, health care exec.; b. Chgo., Nov. 14, 1950; d. John Michael and Marjorie Maxine (Sadler) P.; student U. Ill., St. Xavier Coll.; m. Robert J. O'Brien, Jan. 8, 1982. Various secretarial positions, 1968-79; mgr. Women's Health Cons., S.C., Chgo., 1979—; system mgr. Health Computer Assos., Chgo., 1979—; guest lectr. Triton Coll., River Grove, Ill., 1981—. Mem. Nat. Assn. Female Execs., Group Practice Mgmt. Assn., MUMPS Users Group, COSTAR Users Group, Am. Horse Show Assn., U.S. Dressage Assn., U.S. Combined Tng. Assn., Ill. Dressage Assn. Republican. Roman Catholic. Author articles on dressage. Home: 6 Cinnamon Creek Dr Palos Hills IL 60465 Office: 1725 W Harrison St Suite 450 Chicago IL 60612

PITCHER, BARBARA, psychometrician; b. Poughkeepsie, N.Y., May 22, 1929; d. Hubbard McKenzie and Ruth (McCulloch) P.; A.B., Vassar Coll., 1951; M.A., Syracuse U., 1952; postgrad. U. Mich., 1952-53. Stat. asst. Ednl. Testing Service, Princeton, N.J., 1953-58, head computing unit, stats. analysis, 1958-65, head stats. service sect., test programs research and stats., 1965-71, sr. stat. asso., 1971-79, sr. measurement statistician, higher edn. and career programs, 1979—. Margaret Floy Washburn fellow, 1951-53. Mem. AAAS, AAUW, Am. Ednl. Research Assn., Am. Psychol. Assn., Nat. Council Measurement in Edn., Psychometric Soc. Unitarian. Office: Ednl Testing Service Rosedale Rd Princeton NJ 08541

PITCHER, GLADYS, music editor, composer, arranger; b. Belfast, Maine, Dec. 11, 1890; d. Elbridge S. and Emma B. (Pitcher) P.; grad. with honors New Eng. Conservatory Music, 1911, postgrad., 1911-12; spl. work in orchestration and composition Frederick S. Converse, 1922. Tchr. theory and harmony high sch., Chelsea, Mass., 1912-13; mem. music dept. and acting dean of women Beloit (Wis.) Coll., 1917-19; harmony dept. Am. Inst. Normal Methods, Auburndale, Mass., summers 1922-25; tchr. pub. sch. music, Passaic, N.J., 1920-21, Bennington, Vt., 1922-24, Manchester, N.H., 1924-25; editorial staff C.C. Birchard and Co., Boston, 1925-46, editor-in-chief, 1946-57; free-lance composer, arranger and editor, 1957—. Chmn. Boston Bookbuilders, 1941-42, Bookbuilders Workshop, 1950-52; mem. bd. mgrs. Boston Port and Seamen's Aid Soc., 1958-63. Mem. Am. Musicol. Soc., Nat. Music Educators Assn., Mass., Maine music educator's confs., Plimoth Plantation, Victoria Soc. of Maine Woman, Belfast Hist. Soc., Organ Hist. Soc. Pi Kappa Lambda, Alpha Chi Omega. Republican. Conglist. Clubs: Belfast Business Women's, Travellers' of Belfast (Me.) (pres. 1966-68). Author: A Singing School, series music books for children. Composer, arranger many works for chorus. Cons. This Is Music series, music textbooks. Address: 1 Northport Ave Belfast ME 04915

PITCHER, VIRGINIA LEA, assn. exec.; b. Marshalltown, Iowa, July 16, 1947; d. Milo Shields and Elsie Fredricka (Zelle) P.; B.S. in Edn., Drake U., Des Moines, 1969; M.A. in Guidance and Counseling, U. Iowa, 1972. Secondary sch. math. tchr. Midland Community Schs., Wyoming, Iowa, 1969-72; social security disability examiner State of Tenn., 1973-74; legis. asst. Health Ins. Assn. Am., Washington, 1974-76; staff asst. Met. Life Ins. Co., Washington, 1976-79; Washington asst. ACS, 1979—. Mem. Women in Govt. Relations, Am. Soc. Assn. Execs., Health on Wednesday, Founders Park Community Assn., Alpha Lambda Delta, Pi Omega Pi. Republican. Methodist. Club: Capitol Hill. Home: 111 Quay St Alexandria VA 22314 Office: 1919 Pennsylvania Ave NW Suite 300 Washington DC 20006

PITKIN, JOAN B., state legislator; b. N.Y.C.; ed. U. Vt., Columbia U.; married; 4 children. Mem. Md. Ho. of Dels., 1979—, mem. Joint Com. on Investigations, Joint Com. of Hospice Reimbursement, Ho. Environ. Matters Com. Past dir. Bowie Health Center, Bowie Cultural Arts Commn.; co-founder Belair Cooperative Nursery Sch.; mem. Gov.'s Adv. Com. for Office of Children and Youth; past chairperson Prince George's County Office of Children and Youth; mem. Council on Toxic Substances, State Dept. Edn. Energy Task Force. Mem. Bowie State Coll. Fine Arts Soc. (past dir.). Club: Bowie Woman's. Office: 208 Lowe Bldg 21401 Annapolis MD 21401 *

PITMAN, JUDITH LYNNE, ednl. mktg. exec.; b. Pueblo, Colo., Jan. 30. 1945; d. Leonard Lynn and Maxine Ruth Pitman; B.S., U. Ariz., 1967; M.B.A., Pepperdine U., San Diego, 1977. Med. technologist supr. Mills Hosp., San Mateo, Calif., 1966-69; mgr. San Diego Analytical Labs., 1969-74; mgr. Immunodiagostics, San Diego, 1974-76; mktg. planning mgr. Beckman Instruments, Inc., 1976-78; mktg. dir. Central Fed. Savs. & Loan Assn., 1978-81; pres., co-owner Bank-Ed, Inc., San Diego, 1981—. Mem. Savs. Instns. Mktg. Soc., Bank Mktg. Assn., Am. Mgmt. Assn. Republican. Club: City. Office: 1133 G St San Diego CA 92101

PITRONE, JEAN MADDERN, author; b. Ishpeming, Mich., Dec. 20, 1920; d. William Courtney and Gladys May (Beer) Maddern; student Detroit Inst. Musical Art, 1955-56; m. Anthony Pitrone, Oct. 26, 1940; children—Joseph, Jill, Anthony, Joyce, John, Janet, Julie, Jane, Cheryl. Columnist, Detroit Purchasor, 1958-65; editorial assoc., instr. short story writing Writer's Digest, Cin., 1969-82, editorial assoc., 1969—; tchr. writing classes Wayne County Community Coll., Detroit, others; author: (biographies) Trailblazer, Negro Nurse in the American Red Cross (1st pl. award Friends Am. Writers 1970), 1969; The Touch of His Hand, 1970; Chavez: Man of the Migrants, 1971; Myra: Life and Times of Myra Wolfgang, Trade Union Leader, 1980; The Dodges: The Auto Family Fortune and Misfortune, 1981. Mem. Trenton (Mich.) Cultural Commn., 1980-81, Trenton Cable TV Commn., 1982—; organist St. Anselm Roman Cath. Ch., Dearborn Heights, Mich., also Our Lady of Grace Roman Cath. Ch., Dearborn Heights, 1955-74; music dir. St. Alfred Roman Cath. Ch., Taylor, Mich., 1974-81. Mem. Detroit Women Writers (past pres.). Address: 3878 Pare Ln Trenton MI 48183

PITTARI, LINDA, brokerage firm exec.; b. Bklyn., Nov. 22, 1944; d. Edward and Grace Pittari; B. Profl. Studies with distinction, Pace U., 1978; M.S. in Human Resource Mgmt., New Sch. Social Research, 1982. Sec., Merrill Lynch, N.Y.C., 1962-72, exec. sec., 1972-76, tng. adminstr., 1976-78, adminstrv. mgr., 1978-80, asst. v.p., mgr. resources, 1980-82, v.p., mgr. Manpower resources, 1982—. Cert. profile assessment center adminstr. Devel. Dimension Internat. Mem. Career Planning and Adult Devel. Network, Am. Soc. Tng. and Devel. Office: 1 Liberty Plaza 165 Broadway New York NY 10080

PITTMAN, ELIZABETH DAVIS, judge; b. Council Bluffs, Iowa, June 3, 1921; d. Charles F. and Mabel (Adams) Davis; student U. Nebr., 1938-40; B.S., Creighton U., 1944, LL.B., 1947; LL.D. (hon.), Creighton U., 1973; m. Arthur Basil Pittman, Dec. 25, 1942 (div. 1957); 1 dau., Antoinette Marguerite. Admitted to Nebr. bar, 1948; mem. firm Davis & Pittman, Omaha, 1948—; now judge. Aux. faculty John F. Kennedy Coll. Mem. Omaha Bd. Edn., 1951; mem. Soc. Liberal Arts Joslyn Mus., Omaha; mem. Iowa-Nebr. Fedn. Settlement; formerly pres. Nat. Fedn. Settlements; mem. Omaha Urban League Guild, Omaha YWCA, Woodson Center Settlement House, Omaha; mem. pres.'s council of women Creighton U.; mem. adv. bd. Salvation Army; mem. chancellor's adv. bd. U. Nebr., Omaha. bd. dirs. Nat. Assembly on Social Policy and Devel., Nat. Conf. Social Work; nat. bd. dirs. City of Hope, area bd. dirs. City of Hope Hosp. Recipient award of merit Omaha Urban League, 1948; United Community Services Career award, 1963; citizenship award B'nai B'rith, 1965; award of merit Women Lawyers of Nebr., 1971; Myrtle Wreath award Omaha chpt. Hadassah; named Woman of Yr, Omaha Bus. and Profl. Women, 1971. Mem. N.Am. Trial Judges Assn., Am. Judicature Soc., ABA, Nebr., Omaha bar assns., NAACP (dir. Omaha), Omaha Urban League (dir.), Omaha Women Lawyers Guild (pres. 1953), Links, Inc. (chpt. pres.), Gamma Pi Epsilon, Alpha Kappa Alpha (basilous Omaha 1949), Phi Delta Gamma (hon.), Omicron Delta Kappa, Alpha Sigma Nu. Democrat. Episcopalian (del. gen. conv. 1949). Club: Elks. Home: 3000 Farnam St Omaha NE 68131 Office: Hall of Justice Omaha-Douglas Civic Center Omaha NE 68102

PITTMAN, JOYCE JANITA, real estate devel. co. exec.; b. Dallas, Aug. 31, 1940; d. O. B. and Thelma Louise Howard; student So. Methodist U., 1961-64, Dallas Baptist U., 1977-78; M.A. in Civic Affairs, U. Dallas, 1980; m. Clyde H. Pittman, Nov. 7, 1958; children—Craig Howard, Clarissa Dawn. Exec. sec., 1960-67; owner, operator Curiosity Corner, Irving, 1969-71; v.p., co-owner Epic Cos., Dallas, 1975—; cons. North Tex. Commn.; adv. dir. Am. Bank & Trust. Mem. Irving City Council, 1974-77; pres. Irving chpt. Am. Heart Assn., 1978; dist. dir. Tex. Republican Women's Orgn., 1974-77. Named Outstanding Council Woman, Irving, 1976, Outstanding Republican Woman Tex., 1977. Mem. Irving C. of C. Methodist. Club: Irving Rep. Women's (sec.-treas. 1968-70, pres. 1971-72). Home: 1401 Colony Irving TX 75061 Office: 8585 N Stemmons Freeway Dallas TX 75247

PITTMAN, MARIE ESTELLA MCGHEE (MRS. LOUIE CLARK PITTMAN), univ. librarian; b. Mt. Olive, Miss., Apr. 17, 1923; d. Neal and Maggie (Minor) McGhee; B.S., N.C. Central U., 1952; M.S. in L.S. (univ. scholar), Atlanta U., 1959; postgrad. N.C. Agrl. and Tech. U., 1967—; m. Louie Clark Pittman, Mar. 10, 1940 (dec. May 1963); children—Louie Clark, Joyce Lavonne. Library asst. N.C. Central U., Durham, 1952-57, asst. catalog librarian, 1958-59, music librarian, 1959-64; asst. prof., head catalog librarian, N.C. Agrl. and Tech. State U., Greensboro, 1964-69, asst. prof. library edn., 1969-72, head circulation librarian, 1972-75, research asso.-bibliographer, from 1975, now asst. prof., reference librarian. Chmn., Guilford County (N.C.) Com. Black and African Arts and Culture, 1972—. Mem. ALA, N.C. Library Assn., Guilford Library Club, Nat. Council Negro Women, Nat. Assn. Negro Bus. and Profl. Women's Clubs (pres. Reidsville 1978—, treas. S.E. dist. 1980—), Nat. Epicureans, Delta Sigma Theta (May Week 1972, rec. sec. 1959-64, 70-72). Democrat. Methodist. Home: 415-B Lindsay St Greensboro NC 27401 Office: F D Bluford Library NC A&T State U Greensboro NC 27411

PITTMAN, MARY ANN, interior designer, restaurateur, cattle breeder; b. Commerce, Tex., May 21, 1922; d. Clyde B. and Lillian (Craig) Ketron; student East Tex. State U., Commerce, 1940-42; m. James Porter Pittman, June 3, 1961; children—DeAnn, Mary Robin. Owner, broker Suburban Realty, Richardson, Tex., 1955-62; owner, interior designer Mary Pittman's Decorator & Gift Nook, Richardson, 1962-78, Dallas, 1968-78; owner, mgr. Mary Pittman's Tea House, Van Alstyne, Tex., 1978—; co-owner, Greenbriar Charolais Cattle Farms, Van Alstyne, 1964—. Mem. Richardson Service League (1st pres. 1966, 2d pres. 1967, name changed to Richardson Jr. League 1980), Methodist. Club: Richardson Woman's (founding mem. 1955). Author: Collectibles Cookbook, 1980, 2d and 3d edit., 1981. Home: Route 2 Greenbriar Farms Van Alstyne TX 75095 Office: 216 W Jefferson St PO Box 1008 Van Alstyne TX 75095

PITTMAN, VERONICA KING, educator; b. Talbot County, Ga., Nov. 26, 1947; d. Freddie and Wessie B. King; B.S., Ft. Valley (Ga.) State Coll., 1969; M.S. (Early Childhood Edn. fellow 1969-72), Ala. A. and M. U., 1973; m. Milton C. Pittman, Aug. 16, 1977. Kindergarten tchr., then 3d grade tchr. Wesley Heights Elementary Sch., Columbus, Ga., 1974-80; instr. child devel., nursery sch. dir. Ft. Valley State Coll., 1974-80; child devel. specialist Albany (Ga.) Area Vocat. Tech. Sch., 1980—. Mem. Peach County Hosp. Aux., Ft. Valley; bd. dirs. Mission Bible Camp. Mem. Nat. Home Econs. Assn., Nat. Assn. Edn. Young Children, Assn. Childhood Edn. Internat., So. Assn. Children Under Six. Home: 109 Mathews St Fort Valley GA 31030 Office: 1021 Lowe Rd Albany Area Tech Albany GA 31708

PITTS, ELAINE RUTH HALLEAD (MRS. PAUL ELBERT PITTS), co. exec.; b. Chgo., June 20, 1917; d. Harry Albert and Ethel Mae (Waring) Hallead; student Ill. Inst. Tech., 1948-49, Art Inst. Chgo., 1947-48, N.Y.U., 1976-78; m. Paul Elbert Pitts., Aug. 25, 1945. Packaging engr. Aldens, Inc., Chgo., 1943-46; sr. packaging engr. Spiegel, Inc., Chgo., 1946-52; mgr. package engring. Sperry & Hutchinson Co., Chgo., 1953-59, mgr. consumer relations, N.Y.C., 1959-70, dir. consumer affairs, N.Y.C., 1970, v.p. corp. relations, 1970-79; partner Dalton/Pitts Assos., San Mateo, Calif., 1979—; lectr. M.I.T., U. Wis., Purdue U., UCLA, Ill. Inst. Tech., U. Ill. Nat. adv. bd. Distributive Edn. Clubs Am., 1962—, vice chmn., 1964, chmn., 1965; bd. dirs. S and H Found., 1974-79; mem. Ariz. State U. packaging adv. bd. Mem. Secs. Guild Chgo. Boys' Clubs (pres. 1963), Bus. and Profl. Women's Club, Soc. Packaging and Handling Engrs. (chpt. pres. 1957, nat. chmn. bd. 1966-67), Office Edn. Assn. (dir.), Soc. Women Engrs. (exec. com. 1968-69, 77-80), Am. Women Radio and TV (v.p. 1969-70, pres. 1973-74), Public Relations Soc. Am., U.S. C. of C. (consumer affairs com.). Home: 1081 Beach Park Blvd Apt. 214 Foster City CA 94404 Office: 307 S B St San Mateo CA 94401

PITTS, JEANETTE JOHNSON, telephone co. staff; b. Opelousas, La., Oct. 4, 1943; d. Johnny and Audria Marie (Fontenot) Johnson; student Miami-Dade Jr. Coll., 1970-73; 1 dau., Nichol. Dietary aide Opelousas Gen. Hosp., 1961-62, food service supr., 1962-66; long distance operator So. Bell Telephone Co., Miami, Fla., 1967-68, recruiting supr., 1969-69, group chief operator, 1969-75, assessor, 1975, service adv., 1975, separations studies supr., 1975-78, asso. staff mgr., 1978—. Sun Sch. tchr. Bapt. Ch., Miami, 1980-81. Mem. Nat. Assn. Female Execs., NAACP, Democrat. Baptist. Office: 666 Northwest 79 Ave Miami FL 33126

PITTS, MARGARET JANE, chemist; b. Spokane, Wash., Aug. 10, 1923; d. Herbert Ryder and Gladys (Burchett) P. B.S. in Chemistry, Wash. State U., 1946. Chemist, Electrometall. Co., Spokane, 1943-44, div. indsl. research Wash. State U., Pullman, 1945-46, Hayne Stellite Co., Kokomo, Ind., 1946-51, Pacific NW Alloys, Spokane, 1951-53, Pitts. Testing Labs., Portland, 1954-56, Boeing Co., Seattle, 1956-60, U. Wash., Seattle, 1960-63, Comml. Chems., Inc., Seattle, 1964-66, Puget Sound Naval Shipyard, Bremerton, Wash., 1966-77, Naval Undersea Warfare Engring. Station, Keyport, Wash., 1977—. Mem. Am. Chem. Soc., AAAS, ASTM, Soc. for Applied Spectroscopy, AAUW, Federally Employed Women. Republican. Club: Bus. and Profl. Women. Home: 1717 E 16th St Apt 105 Bremerton WA 98310 Office: Code 312 Naval Undersea Warfare Engring Station Keyport WA 98345

PIZZOLATO, MARY ANN ROSE, chem. engr.; b. Newark, Apr. 23, 1953; d. Benjamin and Jennie (Lombardino) P.; B.S.Ch.E., Rutgers U., 1976. Process engr. FMC Corp., Carteret, N.J., 1976, asst. area supr., 1977-78; chem. engr. Gulf Oil Co.-U.S.A., Phila., 1978-80, sr. refining analyst, Houston, 1980—. George Auchter scholar, 1974-76; Ross scholar, 1974-76. Mem. Am. Inst. Chem. Engrs., Rutgers Alumni Assn., Rutgers Engring. Soc., Nat. Assn. Female Execs., Soc. Women Engrs. Roman Catholic. Home: 7503 Live Oak Dr Humble TX 77338 Office: PO Box 3915 Houston TX 77253

PLANCK-KUPFERER, LYNNETTE, cons.; b. Dallas, Feb. 29, 1948; d. Paul Grayson and Marilyn Lois (Schmidt) Planck; student Colo. State U., 1965-66, Colo. U., Denver, 1968—; m. Marvin Theodore Kupferer, Jr., Oct. 4, 1980; 1 dau., Chantel Planck. Profl. model, Denver, 1966-75; store model, fashion coordinator Neusteters Dept. Store, Denver, 1969-72; office mgr. George Epcar Co., Denver, 1972-75; adminstrv. asst. Cryovac div. W.R. Grace & Co., Lakewood, Colo., 1975-79; office cons., 1980—; spl. events mgr. Denver Dept. Store, 1979-80; modeling tchr., asst. to dir. J. F. Images, Inc., Englewood, Colo., 1970. Mem. Nat. Assn. Female Execs. Episcopalian. Club: Secretary (Denver).

PLANTHOLD, MILDRED ANN, assn. exec., mayor; b. St. Louis, Mar. 3, 1913; d. Frederick F. and Amanda-Marie Ann (Rook) P.; student N.Y. U., 1935-36, Washington U., St. Louis, 1936-37; m. Louis Cardinal Michie, Apr. 23, 1955 (dec.). Instr. speech Chautauqua (N.Y.) Summer Schs., 1937-38; speech instr. Notre Dame Acad., Quincy, Ill. and Belleville, Ill., also women's editor St. Louis Register, 1940-41; ch. editor St. Louis Globe-Democrat, 1941-43, women's editor, fashion and food editor, 1941-56; exec. sec. Allied Florists of Greater St. Louis, 1956-78; exec. sec. Profl. Florists of Mississippi Valley, St. Clair, Mo., 1978—. Mem. adv. com. hort. div. East Central Coll., Union, Mo., 1976—; mayor Town of Piney Park (Mo.), 1954-58, 79—; bd. trustees Scenic Regional Library System, 1971-73. Named St. Louis Woman of Achievement, 1948; recipient award Am. Meat Inst., 1950; Sterling trophy Netherlands Flower-Bulb Inst., 1965; John Walker award Soc. Am. Florists, 1982. Mem. Nat. Fedn. Press Women (life, pres. 1969-71), Mo. Press Women (life, pres. 1975-77), Women in Communications (30 yr. commendation 1980), Soc. Am. Florists Assn. Execs. Div. (chmn. 1966-70). Author, dir. documentary film on convent life, 1953. Home: Rural Route 1 Saint Clair MO 63077

PLATO, CANDACE ELLEN HUNTER, research chemist, computer systems analyst, real estate investor; b. Tampa, Fla., Feb. 9, 1936; d. Melville Gunby and Grace Florence (Robinson) Hunter; B.S. in Chemistry, Stetson U., DeLand, Fla., 1957; M.S. in Organic Chemistry, George Washington U., 1968; m. Robert Gene Plato, Dec. 17, 1955 (div. 1965). Public sch. tchr., Tampa, 1957-58; supr. chemistry labs. Stetson U., 1958-59; biochemist Nat. Inst. Arthritis and Metabolic Diseases, NIH, Bethesda, Md., 1960-66; analytical chemist pesticides standards FDA, Washington, 1966-74, computer systems analyst Bur. Foods, FDA, Washington, 1974—; partner Wiencke & Plato, Chevy Chase, Md., 1972—; tchr. seminars on differential scannings calorimetry U. Md. and George Washington U.; tchr. computer programming. Mem. Am. Chem. Soc., Psi Chi, Gamma Sigma Epsilon. Republican. Home: 6807 Brennon Ln Chevy Chase MD 20815 Office: Computer Systems Group HFF 33 Bureau of Foods FDA 200 C St SW Washington DC 20204

PLATT, ELLEN VALBORG, personnel cons.; b. Rockford, Ill., May 24, 1934; d. Sven August and Sigrid Potentia (Kristianson) Lundh; A.A., Emmetsburg Jr. Coll., 1955; B.S., Drake U., 1964; M.A., No. Ill. U., 1974; m. George Warren Platt, June 9, 1957; 1 dau., Susan Ellen. Elem. tchr. Britt Elem. Sch., Britt, Iowa, 1959-62, Williamsburg (Iowa) Elem. Sch., 1962-64, Des Moines, 1965-66, Momence (Ill.) Elem. Sch., 1970-71; sr. v.p. Met. Personnel, Wayne, Pa., 1974-81, corp. dir., 1978-81; personnel cons. Vanguard Group, Inc., Wayne, Pa., 1982—; cons. in field. HEA fellow, 1968-69; cert. personnel cons. Mem. Nat. Assn. Personnel Cons. Republican. Lutheran. Home: 121 Shaffer Rd King of Prussia PA 19406 Office: Suite 340 8 Valley Forge Exec Mall Wayne PA 19087

PLATT, JANICE KAMINIS, county ofcl.; b. St. Petersburg, Fla., Sept. 27, 1936; d. Peter Clifton and Adele (Diamond) Kaminis; B.S., Fla. State U., 1958; postgrad. U. Fla. Law Sch., 1958-59, U. Va., 1962, Vanderbilt U., 1964; m. William R. Platt, Feb. 8, 1963; 1 son, Kevin Peter. Tchr. public schs., 1959-60; field dir. Girl Scouts U.S.A., Tampa, Fla., 1960-62; mem. Tampa City Council, 1974-78; chmn. Hillsborough County (Fla.) Commn., 1979—; chmn. Hillsborough County Environ. Protection Commn., Council of Govts.; chmn. Tampa Bay Regional Planning Council; mem. Fla. Constitution Revision Commn., Tampa Area Com. on Fgn. Affairs. Pres., Suncoast council Girl Scouts U.S.A., Citizens Alert, Tampa; v.p. Hillsborough County Bar Aux.; bd. dirs. Fla. Gulf Coast Symphony, New Place, Tampa. Recipient Athena award Women in Communications, 1976; Spessard Holland meml. award in county govt. Tampa Bay Com. for Good Govt., 1979-80; Humanitarian award Nat. Orgn. for Prevention of Animal Suffering; named 1st Lady of Yr., Beta Sigma Phi. Mem. Fla. Council on Aging, Am. Public Works Assn., Fla. State Assn. County Planning and Zoning Dirs., LWV, AAUW, Phi Beta Kappa, Pi Sigma Alpha, Phi Kappa Phi, Alpha Lambda Delta. Democrat. Episcopalian. Office: PO Box 1110 Tampa FL 33601

PLATUS, LIBBY, artist, sculptor; b. Los Angeles, Aug. 18, 1939; d. Benjamin Lyon and Gertrude Goldman; B.A., UCLA, 1961; children—Julie Linda, Diana Lisa. Group shows: Richmond (Calif.) Designer Craftsmen, 1971, E. B. Crocker Gallery, Sacramento, 1973, Comsky Gallery, Beverly Hills, Calif., 1973, Galeria del Sol, Santa Barbara, Calif., 1973, Laguna Beach (Calif.) Mus. Art, 1973, Riverside (Calif.) Art Center, 1974, Calif. State U. Northridge, Los Angeles, 1974, Calif. State U., Fullerton, 1974, Calif. Design '76, Los Angeles, 1976, Cleve. Mus. Art, 1977; represented in collections: Tex. Christian U., Faberge Hdqrs., N.Y.C., numerous other public and pvt. collections; commd. works: Big Canyon Country Club, Newport Beach, Calif., Carolando Hyatt Hotel, Orlando, Fla., Mc Culloch's Silver Lakes Resort Hotel, Victorville, Calif., Blue Cross So. Calif., Los Angeles; lectr., condr. workshops numerous internat., nat., regional and state meetings, including World Craft Conf., Kyoto, Japan, 1978, Vienna, Austria, 1980, Glasgow (Scotland) Sch. Art, 1980, Loughborough (Eng.) Coll. Art, 1980; mem. Los Angeles Olympics 1984 Cultural and Fine Arts Commn., 1980-84, Los Angeles Olympics 1984 Citizens Adv. Commn. 1980-84; mem. Los Angeles County Museum Art Costume Council; mem. Craft and Folk Art Mus. Contemporary Craft Council. Recipient Graphic Achievement award Fox River Paper Corp., 1974; winner Tex. Christian U. Nat. Invitational Fiberwork Competition, 1977. Mem. Artists Equity (adv. bd. Los Angeles chpt.), Women In Bus., Am. Crafts Council, Calif. Design, Handweavers Guild Am., Women's Caucus for Art. Home and Office: 1359 Holmby Ave Los Angeles CA 90024

PLAXE, RENA KESSEL, city ofcl.; b. Newark, Sept. 10, 1942; d. Louis and Beatrice (Drosness) Kessel; m. Jerome Plaxe, Oct. 8, 1962; children—Laurence Scott, Daniel Marc. Research asst. Gartenoff & Ellenberg Esqs., N.Y.C., 1965-66; tchr. liberal arts Parsippany (N.J.) Troy Hill Bd. Edn., 1972-74; dir. consumer affairs Parsippany Troy Hills Office Consumer Affairs, 1974—; teaching cons. Morris County Community Coll. Mem. Lake Hiawatha Civic Assn., 1970-72, Garden State Arts Council, 1972-73, Consumer Product Safety Commn., 1975-78, Washington Product Safety Adv. Council, 1975-78, Parsippany Bd. Edn. Adv. Councils, 1965-70, Lake Hiawatha Civic Assn., 1975-77. Adv. com. Underwriters Lab., N.J. Bell Telephone, Public Service Electric & Gas; advt. and mktg. adv. council Dept. Energy. Mem. Am. Arbitration Assn., County and Municipal Consumer Affairs Agys. N.J. (v.p.), North Jersey Profl. Woman's Orgn., AAUW, Orgn. Women for Legal Awareness, Consumer Fedn. Am., Bus. and Consumer Coalition. Club: Deborah. Producer, editor consumer protection books and pamphlets. Contbr. articles to mag. Caveat Emptor. Home: 14 Ashwood Pl Parsippany NJ 07054 Office: 120 Cherry Hill Rd Parsippany NJ 07054

PLAYER, THELMA B., librarian; b. Owosso, Mich.; d. Walter B. and Grace (Willoughby) Player; B.A., Western Mich. U., 1954. Reference asst. USAF Aero. Chart & Info. Center, Washington, 1954-57; reference librarian U.S. Navy Hydrographic Office, Suitland, Md., 1957-58; asst. librarian, 1958-59; tech. library br. head U.S. Navy Spl. Project Office, Washington, 1959-68, Strategic Systems Project Office, 1969-76. Mem. Spl. Libraries Assn., D.C. Library Assn., AAUW, English-Speaking Union, Nat. Geneal. Soc., Internat. Soc. Brit. Genealogy and Family History, Smithsonian Assos., Royal Oak Found., Friends Folger Library. Episcopalian. Home: 2021 Brooks Dr Apt 406 Forestville MD 20747

PLEASANT, DONNA MARIA, nurse, health care service exec.; b. Temple, Tex., May 11, 1950; d. John Herbert and Zetha (Poss) Mattes; A. Nursing, McLennon Commmunity Coll., 1972; B.S. with honors, S.W. Tex. State U., 1982; postgrad. in gerontology Baylor U.; m. Mark Edward Pleasant, July 14, 1978; 1 son, William Eric. Charge nurse, Providence Hosp., Waco, Tex., 1972-74, instr. edn. and outpatient/staff tchr., 1975-81, dir. edn., 1979-81; mng. service dir. Upjohn Health Care Services, Waco, 1981-82; instr. coordinator McLennan Community Coll., Waco, 1982—; staff nurse Harris Hosp., Ft. Worth, 1974. Bd. dirs. am. Heart Assn., Waco; mem., chmn. Task Force for Mass CPR training Project, Waco, 1980—; CPR affiliate faculty Am. Heart Assn., Mem. Waco Heart Assn., Tex. Heart Assn., Am. Heart Assn., Am. Bus. Women's Assn. Democrat. Roman Catholic. Club: Altrusa. Home: 2301 Parrott Ave Waco TX 76707 Office: 1400 College Dr Waco TX 76708

PLECK, ELIZABETH, historian; b. N.Y.C., Sept. 20, 1945; d. Fred and Leah Hafkin; B.A., Brandeis U., 1967, M.A., 1969, Ph.D., 1973; Asst. prof. history U. Mich., 1973-78; research assoc. Center for Research on Women, Wellesley, Mass., 1978—; vis. assoc. prof. M.I.T., 1982, Wellesley Coll., 1982. Ford Found. fellow, 1975-76. Mem. Am. Hist. Assn. (nominating com. 1982—), Social Sci. History Assn. (exec. bd. 1979-82), Am. Hist. Assn., Orgn. Am. Historians. Editor: Black Migration and Poverty: 1865-1900, 1979; (with Nancy F. Cott) A Heritage of Her Own: Towards New Social History of American Women, 1979; (with Joseph Pleck) The American Man, 1980; Series in American Social History, 1980—. Home: 25 Trowbridge St Newton Center MA 02159

PLEMING, LAURA CHALKER, educator; b. Sheridan, Wyo., May 25, 1913; d. Sidney Thomas and Florence Theresa (Woodbury) Chalker; B.A., Long Beach State Coll. (now Calif. State U., Long Beach), 1953, M.A. in Speech and Drama, 1954; postgrad. U. So. Calif., 1960-63; Rel.D., Sch. Theology, Claremont, Calif., 1968; m. Edward Kibbler Pleming, Aug. 25, 1938; children—Edward Kibbler, Rowena Pleming Chamberlin, Sidney Thomas. Profl. Bible tchr., 1953—; lectr. Calif. State U., Long Beach, 1960-66, U. So. Calif., 1963-65; Bible scholar for teaching Scriptures Program, First Ch. of Christ Scientist, Boston, 1970-75; freelance Bible lectr., tchr., resource person for adult seminars, 1954—; active in summer teaching for young people, 1963-68; tchr. adult edn. Principia Coll., summers 1969-71; tour lectr. to Middle East, yearly, 1974—; mem. archaeol. team, Negev, Israel. Mem. Am. Acad. Religion, AAUP, Soc. Bibl. Lit. and Exegesis, Am. Schs. Oriental Research, Inst. Mediterranean Studies, Religious Edn. Assn., Internat. Congress Septuagint and Cognate Studies, Gamma Theta Upsilon, Zeta Tau Alpha, Phi Beta. Republican. Christian Scientist. Author: Triumph of Job, 1979; editor Bibleletter, 1968, 76, 82—. Home: 2999 E Ocean Blvd Apt 2020 Long Beach CA 90803

PLENK, AGNES MERO, psychologist; b. Budapest, Hungary, Jan. 28, 1916; came to U.S., 1938, naturalized, 1944; d. Julian and Rose (Szesci) Mero; B.A., Northwestern U., 1945, M.A., 1947; Ph.D., U. Utah, 1967; m. Henry P. Plenk, June 17, 1938; children—Bruce, Penny Plenk Dalrymple, Timothy. Ind. practice psychology, 1950-62; founder, dir. Holladay Community Nursery Sch., Salt Lake City, 1953-62; founder, 1962, since exec. dir. Children's Center, Salt Lake City; tchr. grad. classes psychology U. Utah, 1972—. Recipient Jane Addams award, 1968. Mem. Am. Orthopsychiat. Assn., Am. Assn. Psychiat. Services Children, Am. Psychol. Assn., Utah Psychol. Assn. (pres. 1976), Utah Assn. Mental Health (dir.). Congregationalist. Clubs: Cottonwood, Salt Lake City Tennis, Bonneville Knife and Fork (dir.). Author articles in field. Home: 2169 Pheasant Way Salt Lake City UT 84121 Office: 1855 Medical Circle Salt Lake City UT 84112

PLESHETTE, SUZANNE, actress; b. N.Y.C., Jan 31; d. Eugene Pleshette and Geraldine Pleshette (Rivers); student Syracuse (N.Y.) U., Finch Coll., N.Y.C.; m. Thomas Joseph Gallagher, III, Mar. 16, 1968. Star in Broadway prodns. Compulsion, Cold Wind and The Warm, The Golden Fleecing, Two for the Sea-Saw, The Miracle Worker, Special Occasions, star numerous TV prodns. latest being Rob Newhart Show, 1972-78; star 30 feature films; including The Power, 1968, If It's Tuesday This Must Be Belgium, 1969, Suppose They Gave a War and Nobody Came, 1969, Support Your Local Gunfighter, 1971, The Shaggy D.A., 1976, Hot Stuff, 1979, Oh God! Book II, 1980; TV movie Flesh and Blood, 1979, If Things Were Different, 1979, various others. Office: PO Box 1492 Beverly Hills CA 90213 *

PLETCHER, VERA EDITH CROSBY, educator; b. Plainview, Nebr., Nov. 6, 1916; d. William Edward and Lula (Partridge) Crosby; student U. Kans., 1947-51; B.S. cum laude, Kans. State U., 1956, M.A. (Mueller scholar 1958-59), 1960; postgrad. Pa. State U., 1967; m. Blaine F. Pletcher, Sept. 9, 1936; children—Patricia Louise (Mrs. James E. Carlson), Janet Sue (Mrs. Jack Carlson), Sharon Lee (Mrs. James Hurt). Tchr. elementary schs., Kans., 1935-37, 44-54, secondary schs., Kans., 1956-57; mem. faculty Kans. State U., Manhattan, 1959-67, instr. history and social scis., 1962-67; instr. Manhattan Sr. High Sch., 1966-69, head social sci. dept., 1969-76, dir. advanced placement and ind. study, 1974—. Counselor, Wamego Rural High Sch., 1959-62; instr. U. Kans. Ind. Study Center, 1965-70; Mem. Riley County Bicentennial Com.; planner, adminstr. state advanced placement program; Kans. NDEA grantee, 1960, 67; Nat. Edn. grantee, 1969; Grad. Coe fellow Inst. Internat. Studies SUNY, Stonybrook, 1975. Named Woman of Year, Rho chpt. Phi Delta Gamma, 1967; recipient Meritorious Teaching award Nat. Council Geog. Edn., 1971. Mem. NEA, Kans. State Tchrs. Assn., Kans. Assn. Women Deans and Counselors (sec.-treas. 1962-64), Am. Personnel and Guidance Assn., Kans. State Alumni Assn., Kans. State Hist. Soc. (bd. dirs. 1972—), Am. Hist. Assn., Bus. and Profl. Women, Nat. Hist. Soc. (charter), Kans. State U. Hist. Soc. (charter), Phi Kappa Phi, Phi Alpha Mu, Phi Alpha Theta, Delta Kappa Gamma, Phi Delta Gamma (chpt. pres. 1966, 72, nat. treas. 1966-68, nat. council rep. 1966-70, nat. conv. chmn. 1972-74, nat. v.p. 1976-78, nat. pres. 1978-80, Bicentennial Jour. award 1976). Mem. Christian Ch. Mem. Order Eastern Star, Jobs Daus. (guardian 1971-74). Contbr. articles to profl. jours. Home: Route 5 Box 129 Manhattan KS 66502

PLEWINSKI, TERESA MARIA SAUER, physician; b. Poland; d. Gustav and Jadwiga (Bedynski) Sauer; naturalized, 1974; M.D., Wroclaw and Warsaw Med. Sch., 1951, Ph.D., 1966; m. Gustav L. Plewinski, Apr. 5, 1949; children—Magdalena, Michael. Intern, resident in internal medicine Columbus Hosp., N.Y.C., 1969-73; dep. surgeon-in-chief Children's Hosp., Warsaw, Poland, 1958-67; pediatric surgeon-in-chief Regional Hosp., Ho, Ghana, 1968; attending physician Cabrini Med. Center, N.Y.C., 1973—. Recipient Physician's Recognition award AMA, 1972, 75, 78. Fellow A.C.P., Am. Acad. Family Practice; mem. N.Y. Acad. Scis., Polish Inst. Arts and Scis. in Am. Research and publs. in med. field. Home: 10 Waterside Plaza New York NY 10010 Office: 242 E 19th St New York NY 10003

PLIMPTON, PAULINE AMES, civic worker; b. N. Easton, Mass., Oct. 22, 1901; d. Oakes and Blanche Ames; B.A., Smith Coll., 1922; m. Francis T.P. Plimpton, June 4, 1926; children—George Ames, Francis T.P., Oakes Ames, Sarah Gay. Pres., House of Industry, 1940-48; bd. dirs. Inst. World Affairs, 1940-74, Pub. Edn. Assn., 1933-44; chmn. United Campaign Fund for Planned Parenthood of Manhattan and Bronx, 1946-49; chmn. Planned Parenthood Fedn. Am. campaign, 1959-60, bd. dirs. 1959-67, 70-73; chmn. United Campaign, 1964; bd. dirs. Planned Parenthood of N.Y.C., 1965-74; rep. Western Hemisphere region Internat. Planned Parenthood Fedn., 1970-73; fund raiser Ladies' Aux. Philharmonic Symphony Soc. N.Y., N.Y. Legal Aid Soc., ARC. Recipient Planned Parenthood award for devoted service, 1969. Republican. Unitarian. Clubs: Cosmopolitan, River (N.Y.C.); Ausable (Adirondacks). Contbr. author, editor, compiler Orchids at Christmas, 1975; The Ancestry of Blanche Butler Ames and Adelbert Ames, 1977; Oakes Ames—Jottings of a Harvard Botanist, 1979. Home: 131 E 66th St New York NY 10021 also 168 Chichester Rd West Hills Huntington NY 11743

PLITT, JEANNE GIVEN, librarian; b. Whitehall, N.Y., Aug. 27, 1927; s. Charles Russell and Anna Marie (Noyes) Given; student St. Lawrence U., 1945-47; A.B., U. Md., 1940; postgrad. Am. U., 1960-61; M.L.S., Cath. U. Am., 1968; m. Ferdinand Charles Plitt, Jr., Jan. 19, 1952; children—Christine, Marie, Charles Randolph. Library asst. Spl. Services div. U.S. Army, 1949-51; tchr. secondary schs., Md. and Va.; reference librarian Alexandria (Va.) Library, 1967-68, asst. dir., 1968-70, dir., 1970—; chmn. librarians' tech. com. Council Govts., Washington, 1971-72, 80-81; chmn. No. Va. Library Networking Com. Active Little Theatre Group, Alexandria. Recipient Alexandria Pub. Service award, 1964, 74. Mem. ALA, Va. Library Assn., Manuscript Soc., PTA, U. Md., Cath. U. alumni assns., Alexandria Assn., Urban League, Alexandria Hist. Soc. (dir. 1974—). Roman Catholic. Club: Zonta (sec. chpt. 1972-73, dir. 1973-74). Office: Alexandria Library 717 Queen St Alexandria VA 22314

PLONA, SISTER, MARY LAETITIA, nurse administr., educator; b. Gardner, Mass., Dec. 31, 1906; d. Alexander and Alexandra (Wiski) Plona; B.S. in Nursing Edn., Catholic U. Am., 1946; M.S., Boston Coll., 1963. Dir. nursing service St. Joseph Hosp., Bangor, Me., 1947-54; dir. sch. practical nursing Okla.-Blackwell Gen. Hosp., 1954-55; infirmarian Our Lady of Angels Infirmary, Enfield, Conn., 1955-57; dir. nursing service St. Joseph Hosp., Bangor, 1957-66, adminstr., 1958-60, 62-64, dir. Sch. Practical Nursing, 1963-72, dir. program in diploma nursing, 1973-82, now dir. emeritus Sch. Nursing; appointee Maine State Bd. Nursing, 1977-82. Mem. Am. Nurses Assn., Maine Nurses Assn. (dir.), Sigma Theta Tau. Contbr. articles to profl. jours. Address: 297 Center St Bangor ME 04401

PLOTNER, TERRY LEE, retail store mgr; b. Youngstown, Ohio, Jan. 26, 1948; d. Glenn Stephen and Gladys (Stevenson) Shingledecker; student Youngstown State U., 1966-70; m. Robert R. Plotner, June 1, 1968; children—Christy Lee, Shawn Thomas Alan. With Spencer Gifts, Inc., So. Park Mall, Youngstown, Ohio, 1971-73, store mgr. Eastwood Mall, Niles, Ohio, 1974-75, Beaver Valley Mall, Monaca, Pa., 1975-78; with F.W. Woolworth Co., Eastwood Mall, Niles, 1973-74; mgr. Altmeyer Home Stores, No. Lights Shopping Center, Baden, Pa., 1980—. Mem. Nat. Assn. Female Execs. Democrat. Presbyterian. Home: 135 Knollwood Dr Industry PA 15052 Office: 1642 State St W Baden PA 15005

PLOUS, LOIS MICHEL, state legislator; b. Milw., Aug. 14, 1938; d. LeRoy Michel and Ruth Plotkin; B.S., U. Wis., Milw., 1966, M.S. (fellow), 1973; children—Wendy, Scott. Learning disabilities tchr. Shorewood Pub. Sch., 1973-75; learning disabilities diagnostic tchr. Milw. pub. schs., 1975-76, supr. exceptional edn., 1976-80; mem. Wis. Ho. of Reps., 1980—, vice chmn. justice and pub. safety com., mem. edn. com., children and human devel. com., joint legis. council. Mem. Jr. Acad. Medicine (dir.), Nat. Order Women Legislators, Wis. Women's Network, LWV, Delta Kappa Gamma, Delta Tau Kappa. Club: Sierra. Office: State Capitol Madison WI 53702 *

PLOWMAN, LOIS REBECCA, educator; b. Aztalan, Wis., Apr. 2, 1920; d. John Waterbury and Joy Lucretia (Hall) Mansfield; B.Ed., U. Wis., 1941; M.S., U. So. Calif., 1960; m. Earl Robert Plowman, June 30, 1945; children—Earl Robert, Rebecca, John, Barbara, James, Darryl. Tchr., Muscoda (Wis.) High Sch., 1941-42; adjudicator War Dept., Newark, 1942-45; crew leader U.S. Census, Wis., 1950; tchr. Hustisford (Wis.) High Sch., 1954-56, Leuzinger (Calif.) High Sch., 1957-59, Compton (Calif.) High Sch., 1959-65, bus. edn. dist. chmn., 1959-65; prof. Cerritos (Calif.) Coll., 1965—, chmn. office occupations, 1978-79. Mem. Calif. Bus. Edn. Assn., Soc. Tech. Writers, Nat. Assn. Legal Assts., LWV, Nat. Certifing Bd. Legal Assts., Mayflower Soc., Colonial Dames XVII Century, Magna Charta Dames, Daus. of Am. Colonists, New Eng. Women, DAR, Daus. of 1812, Daus. of Colonial Wars, Dames of Ct. of Honor, Women Descs. of Ancient and Honorable Arty., Delta Pi Epsilon. Democrat. Presbyterian. Contbr. articles to profl. jours. Office: 11110 Alondra Blvd Norwalk CA 90650

PLUCHINSKY, NADINE, educator; b. Johnstown, Pa., Oct. 10, 1948; d. Thomas Francis and Diana (Moncilovich) P.; B.S. in Edn., Indiana U. of Pa., 1970; M.S. in Edn., Simmons Coll., 1974; m. Marcial Cruz-Galvez, June 6, 1980; 1 son, Thomas Andrés. Dietary supr. Children's Hosp. Med. Center, Boston, 1970; tchr. home econs. Boston Public Schs., 1970—, founder, developer, tchr. women's studies course, 1975, cons. and workshop leader for labor and feminist issues, 1977—. Mem. ednl. task force Gov.'s Commn. on Status of Women, 1976; public speaker on labor and feminist issues in Boston Met. Area, 1977—. Mem. Am. Fedn. Tchrs., Home Econs. Assn., Coalition of Labor Union Women (conf. dir.).

PLUMB, PAMELA PELTON, mayor; b. St. Louis, Oct. 26, 1943; d. Frank E. and Dorothey-Lee (Culver) Pelton; B.A., Smith Coll., 1965; M.A., N.Y. U., 1967; m. Peter Scott Plumb, June 11, 1966; children—Jessica Culver, David Scott. Tchr., Master's Sch., Dobbs Ferry, N.Y., 1967-69; exec. dir. Greater Portland (Maine) Landmarks, 1969-71; engaged in civic and vol. work, 1971-79; mem. Portland City Council, 1979—, mayor, 1981-82; dir. Portland Savs. Bank. Bd. dirs. Maine Devel. Found. Recipient Doric Dames's Bullfinch award for preservation, 1979; Greater Portland Landmark's Preservation award, 1980; Deborah Morton award Westbrook Coll., Portland, 1982; Neal W. Allen award Greater Portland C. of C., 1982; named Portland and Maine Outstanding Young Woman, Jaycees, 1979. Democrat. Office: City Hall 389 Congress St Portland ME 04101

PLUMMER, DEBORAH ANNE, orgn. exec.; b. Ft Walton Beach, Fla., Feb. 9, 1959; d. Curt and Sue (Perry) P.; B.A. in English, Old Dominion U., 1981. Instr. Va. Beach Recreation System, 1978-82; instr. fencing Va. Wesleyan Coll., 1979-82; dir. member relations Norfolk C. of C., 1981—. Mem. Old Dominion Alumnae Assn., Pi Beta Phi. Republican. Methodist. Club: Tidewater Fencing (past sec.). Home: 6314 Richmond Pl Norfolk VA 23508 Office: 420 Bank St Norfolk VA 23501

PLUMMER, EDNA MAE, business ofcl.; b. Conrad, Iowa, May 29, 1921; d. Elmer Leonard and Fern (Haggin) Schultz; diploma in bus. Spencerian Coll., Louisvllle, 1942; 1 son, Jerald D. Plummer. Stenographer, Monarch Equipment Co., Louisville, 1942-45; sec. Army Air Forces, Louisville, 1945-46, L&N R.R., Louisville, 1946; with Chevrolet Motor div. Gen. Motors Corp., Louisville, 1946—, cashier, sec., 1974—. Mem. Am. Bus. Women's Assn. (Woman of Yr. 1979-80, corr. sec. River City chpt. 1976, sec. 1977, v.p. 1978, pres. 1979), Ky. Women's C. of C. (mem. legis. com. 1979-80, exec. bd. 1980—, sec. 1981-82). Democrat. Mem. Christian Ch. Club: Woodson Bend Resort. Office: 4501 Indian Trail Louisville KY 40313

PLUMMER, ELIZABETH MARY, educator; b. Waterbury, Conn., Aug. 3, 1921; d. Thomas F. and Josephine M. (McCarthy) P.; B.A., Hunter Coll., 1944; M. in Nursing, Yale U. Sch. Nursing, 1946; M.A., Columbia U., 1959. Staff nurse Bklyn. Vis. Nurses Assn., 1946-47; sr. dept. head Conn. State Dept. Vocat. Edn., New Haven, 1947-58; field instr. nursing Tchr.'s Coll., Columbia U., N.Y.C., 1959-60; asst. prof. Grad. Sch. Nursing, N.Y. Med. Coll., 1960-62; asst. prof. L.I. U., 1962-64; asso. prof. med. surg. nursing Grad. Sch. Nursing, N.Y. Med. Coll., 1964-65, prof., 1966-73; prof. nursing Grad. Sch. of Nursing, Pace U., Pleasantville, N.Y., 1973—, asst. to dean for clin. affiliations, 1978—, asst. to dean for clin. affairs Sch. Nursing; mem. N.Y.C. Comprehensive Health Planning Com., 1971-74; cons. rehab. nursing Montrose VA Hosp., 1972-73. Mem. Right to Life Com., 1976—, East Harlem Community Health Council, 1970-73. Recipient Outstanding Tchr. award Keenan Trust Fund, 1976; Outstanding Alumna award Yale U. Sch. Nursing, 1982. Mem. Nat. League for Nursing, Am. Public Health Assn., Am. Nurses Assn. (cert. in gerontol. nursing), Am. Heart Assn., Pi Lambda Theta, Kappa Delta Pi, Sigma Theta Tau (charter mem.). Roman Catholic. Contbr. articles on nursing to profl. publs. Home: 317 96th St Brooklyn NY 11209 Office: Pace Univ Elm Rd Briarcliff NY 10510

PLUMMER, ORA BEATRICE, nursing cons; b. Mexia, Tex., May 25, 1940; d. Macie Idella (Echols); B.S. in Nursing, U. N.Mex., 1961; M.S. in Nursing Edn., UCLA, 1966; children—Kimberly, Kevin, Cheryl. Nurses aide Bataan Meml. Meth. Hosp., Albuquerque, 1958-60, staff nurse, 1961-62, 67-68; staff nurse, charge nurse, relief supr. Hollywood (Calif.) Community Hosp., 1962-64; instr. U. N.Mex. Coll. of Nursing, Albuquerque, 1968-69; sr. instr. U. Colo. Sch. Nursing, Denver, 1971-74; asst. prof. U. Colo. Sch. Nursing, Denver, 1974-76; staff asso. III Western Interstate Commn. for Higher Edn., Boulder, Colo., 1976-78; dir. nursing Garden Manor Nursing Home, Lakewood, Colo., 1978-79; nursing cons. Colo. E 11th Ave Denver CO 80013 Health, Denver, 1979—. Active Colo. Cluster of Schs.-faculty devel.; mem. adv. bd. Affiliated Children's and Family Services, 1977; mem. planning com. State Wide Conf. on Black Health Concerns, 1977; mem. staff devel. com. Western Interstate Commn. for Higher Edn., 1978, minority affairs com., 1978, coordinating com. for baccalaureate program, 1971-76; active minority affairs U. Colo. Med. Center, 1971-72; mem. ednl. resources com. public relations com., rev. com. for reappointment, promotion, and tenure U. Colo. Sch. Nursing, 1971-76. Mem. Am. Nurses Assn., Colo. Nurses Assn (affirmative action comm. 1977, 78, 79), Phi Delta Kappa. Contbr. articles in field to profl. jours. Office: 4210 E 11th Ave Denver CO 80013

PLUNKETT, ANNE MARIE CECILIA, banker; b. Rochester, Minn., July 15, 1932; d. Eugene and Anna (Regan) Leddy; B.A., Manhattanville Coll., Purchase, N.Y., 1953; postgrad. Fordham U., 1953-54; m. Richard Harding Plunkett, July 12, 1958; children—Pamela, Patricia, Richard Harding, Julianne, Maureen. Instr. socio-econ. problems St. Marys Sch. Nursing, Rochester, 1957-58, 65-66; chmn. bd. Rochester Bank & Trust Co., 1973—; v.p., sec. Midwest Video Electronics, Inc., Rhinelander, Wis., 1972-79; dir. Medelco, Inc., 1973-78. Pres., Olmsted County Lawyers Wives, 1959-60; leader Girl Scouts U.S.A., 1969-72; vol. tchr. St. Johns Religious Edn., 1972-75; founder Southeastern Minn. Regional Arts Council, 1973; chmn. Minn. Arts Bd., 1974-75; co-chairperson Minn. Bicentennial Commn., 1975-76; v.p., mem. finance com. United Way, Olmsted County, 1978, bd. dirs., 1976-78; chmn. subcom. on elementary edn. Rochester Sch. Dist. 535 Citizens Adv. Com. on Ednl. Facilities, 1976-77; coordinator Minn. Aesthetic Environment Program for Olmsted County, 1977; co-founder condrs. com. Rochester Symphony Orch., 1977; mem. Pres.'s Forum, Minn. Bible Coll., Rochester, 1977-79; mem. exec. com. Rochester Pres.'s Council, Coll. St. Teresa, Winona, Minn., 1977-78; adv. com. Agrl. Interpretative Center, Fairmont, Minn., 1979; 1st Dist. coordinator vol. activities Vice Pres. Walter F. Mondale, 1968; del. State Conv. from Olmsted County, Minn. Democratic Party, 1974, 76, 78; nat. treas. U.S. Sen. Wendell R. Anderson Vol. Com., 1977—; bd. dirs. AAU Rochester Swim Club, Family Consultation Center, Rochester YWCA, 1969-70, Lourdes High Sch. Devel. Fund. Recipient Outstanding Vol. medal St. Marys Hosp., 1967, plaque of appreciation Olmsted County Bicentennial Commn., 1976, medallion and certificate of recognition Minn. Bicentennial Commn., 1976, certificate of appreciation Gov.'s Aesthetic Environmental Program, 1977. AAUW Ednl. Found. grantee, 1976. Mem. AAUW (founder Dayton Benefit for Scholarships 1955, dir. Rochester br. 1955-56, 75-77), Rochester Banks Clearing House Assn. (chairperson 1977-78). Home: 2918 SW 15th Ave Rochester MN 55901 Office: Rochester Bank & Trust Co Box 6478 Rochester MN 55901

PLUNKETT, LAURETTE ALICE, univ. dean; b. Bklyn., Jan. 22, 1920; d. William Douglas and Laura Elizabeth (Roper) Ryan; A.B., Duke U., 1940; m. Jack Plunkett, Apr. 19, 1957; 1 son, Jack. With IBM, 1941-43, 45-47; office mgr. Drs. Lunsford, Terry and Clark, 1948-57; asst. dean research and sponsored programs U. Miami (Fla.), 1960—; dir. Pre-Cast Specialties Corp. Served to lt. USNR, 1943-45. Mem. AAUP, Zeta Tau Alpha. Methodist. Home: 5307 Orduna Dr Coral Gables FL 33146 Office: U Miami PO Box 248293 Coral Gables FL 33124

PLUNKETT, MELBA KATHLEEN, mfg. co. exec.; b. Marietta, Ill., Mar. 20, 1929; d. Lester George and Florence Marie (Hutchins) Bonnett; student public schs.; m. James P. Plunkett, Aug. 18, 1951; children—Julie Marie Plunkett Hayden, Gregory James. Co-founder, 1961, since sec.-treas., dir. Coils, Inc., Huntley, Ill. Mem. U.S. C. of C., Ill. Mfg. Assn., Ill. C. of C., Ill. Notary Assn. Roman Catholic. Home: Route 1 Sleepy Hollow Rd West Dundee IL 60118 Office: 11716 Algonquin Rd Huntley IL 60142

POBANZ, RITA BERNADETTE, nurse; b. Bklyn., Oct. 16, 1941; d. John Daniel and Mary Robert (Simpson) Grady; A.D.N. with honors, Eastern N.Mex. U., 1974; m. Kenneth Walter Pobanz, June 5, 1960; children—Karen, Stephen. Staff nurse Gerald Champion Hosp., Alamogordo, N.Mex., 1974; critical care staff, charge nurse, intensive care instr. Hampton (Va.) Gen. Hosp., 1974-79, patient edn. coordinator, 1978-79, critical care coordinator, 1980—; critical care supr. Holy Cross Hosp., Austin, Tex., 1979-80; head nurse Coliseum Park Nursing Home, Hampton, 1982—. Office chmn. Family Services, USAF, 1961-62, publicity chmn., 1962-64; hosp. vol. ARC, 1967-70; den leader Cub Scouts Am., 1970, C.P.R. instr. Am. Heart Assn., 1979-81. Mem. Am. Assn. Critical Care Nurses (sec. Tidewater chpt. 1981, pres.-elect. Tidewater chpt. 1982), Nat. League Nursing, Carolina-Va. Soc. Critical Care Medicine, Phi Theta Kappa. Home: 1349 Coral Pl Hampton VA 23669 Office: Coliseum Park Nursing Home 305 Marcella Dr Hampton VA 23666

POCOCK, JEANNIE ANN, artist; b. Tokyo, Dec. 1, 1950; came to U.S., 1958; d. Donald Allen and Namiko (Endo) Pocock; ed. U. Mich., 1969-73. Archtl. sec., word-processing ioerator Ayres, Leis, Norris & May, Ann Arbor, Mich., 1972-76; archtl. sec., Prentice & Chan, Olhausen, Architects and Planners, N.Y.C., 1976—; exhibited works group shows, 1977-81; works represented permanent collections. Office: 112 W 14th St New York NY 10011 also 500 Fifth Ave New York NY 10110

PODBIELSKI, ELLEN, educator; b. Tarentum, Pa., July 11, 1928; d. Thomas Paul and Mary (Klaric) Svedi; B.S. Ed., U. Pitts., 1951; M.A. with distinction, Calif. State U., Chico, 1977; m. David J. Podbielski, Apr. 11, 1952; children—Clifford, Ann, Timothy. Tchr. Kindergarten Fall River Joint Unified Sch. Dist., Burney, Calif., 1951—; workshop leader early childhood edn., 1974-77. Vice pres. PTA, 1966-67; elder, Presbyn. Ch., 1964-68; mem. Shasta County Democratic Central Com., 1981-82. Mem. NEA, Calif. Tchrs. Assn., Calif. No. Counties Kindergarten Assn. (pres. 1968-69), Fall River Edn. Assn. (pres. 1981-82), AAUW, Delta Kappa Gamma. Club: Elks Aux. Home: 1616 Ash Ave Burney CA 96013 Office: East Burney Elem Sch Burney CA 96013

PODIUK-KLUFAS, HALYNA IVANNA, physician; b. Ukraine, Oct. 5, 1927; came to U.S., 1949, naturalized, 1963; d. John and Irene (Zaremba) Podiuk; B.A., Syracuse U., 1952; M.D., U. Munich (Ger.), 1958, N.Y.U., 1966; m. Swiatoslau Iosyp Klufas, July 5, 1952; children—Christina, Ulana. Intern, resident Munich and Barbreton, Ohio; pvt. practice, Syracuse, N.Y. Pres. Ukrainian Patriarchal Soc., 1973—. Contbr. articles to women's mags. Home: 613 Cherry Rd Syracuse NY 13219 Office: 210 S Lowell Ave Syracuse NY 13204

PODLES, ELEANOR PAULINE, state senator; b. Dudley, Mass., June 6, 1920; d. Francis and Pauline Magiera; student U. N.H.; m. Francis J. Podles, June 28, 1941; children—L. Patricia Podles Barrett, Elizabeth Lee Podles Keegan. Mem. N.H. Ho. of Reps., 1976-80; selectman City of Manchester, 1976-81; mem. N.H. Senate, 1980—, chmn. public affairs com., mem. banks com., public instns. health and welfare com. Del., N.H. Republican Conv., 1976, 78; pres. Manchester Rep. Women's Club, 1979-80 Mem. Am. Legis. Exchange Council, Orgn. Women Legislators. Club: Manchester Country. Address: 185 Walnut Hill Ave Manchester NH 03104

POE, JOAN BARBARA, wholesale co. exec.; b. Cedar Falls, Iowa, June 9, 1932; d. Stanley Walter and Norma Louise (Blecke) Seroke; student Iowa State Tchrs. Coll., 1950-52; m. Ellsworth Poe, Sept. 15, 1951 (dec. 1971); children—Stanley, David, Thomas, Melinda, Susan, Michael. Pres. Buchanan Wholesale Co., Waterloo, Iowa, 1979—, Crystal Ice & Cold Storage Co., Waterloo, 1980—, Standard Distbg. Co., beer distbrs., Waterloo, 1971—. Bd. dirs. Waterloo Jr. Achievement, 1975-80; mem. Iowa Commn. Status Women, 1974—; mem. athletic policy div. council U. No. Iowa, Cedar Falls, 1978—; pres. Jr. Achievement. Mem. Waterloo C. of C. (dir. 1976-78), Cedar Falls C. of C. (dir. 1978-80), Nat. Beer Wholesalers Assn. (nat. com.), Iowa Wholesale Beer Distbr. Assn. (sec. 1977—, now pres.). Republican. Lutheran. Home: 1310 Lilac Ln Cedar Falls IA 50613 Office: 403 Chestnut St Waterloo IA 50703

POETKER, FRANCES LOUISE, florist; b. Cin., Apr. 16, 1912; d. Charles Benjamin and Louise (Johnston) Jones; B.A., Vassar Coll., 1933; M.A., U. Cin., 1934; m. Joseph G. Poetker, Aug. 10, 1937. Buyer, Mabley & Carew Dept. Store, Cin., 1933-35; owner Jones the Florist, Cin., 1942—; owner flower plant boutique in H. and S. Pogue, Cin., 1982—; dir. Cin. Bell Telephone Co.; co-chmn. flower decorations Winter Olympics, 1980; dir. profl. flower shows, N.Y. and France, commentator wedding shows ; TV appearances. Mem. honors com. U. Cin.; pres.'s com. Xavier U., Cin.; exec. com. Cin. Opera; v.p. Air Pollution Control League Cin.; bd. dirs. Bethesda Hosp., Cin.; mem. Cin. Beautiful Com. Recipient award of appreciation Dept. Agr., 1962, Sylvia award floral excellence, 1976; Tommy Bright award Am. Florist; Appreciation award U. Cin., 1982; Belle Skinner Clark fellow, 1930; named Woman of Year, Cin. Enquirer, 1978; named to Floricultural Hall of Fame. Mem. Am. Hort. Soc. (dir., chmn. nat. conv. Cin. 1982), Soc. Am. Florists (1st Century award 1982, 1st Tommy Bright award 1982), Florists Transworld Delivery Assn. (commentator), Am. Acad. Florists (dir. emeritus), Allied Florists Assn. Cin., Profl. Florist Commentators Internat., MacDowall Soc., McMicken Soc. Lutheran. Clubs: Travel (pres., dir.), Women's, Symphony, Banker's (Cin.); Garden of Am. Co-author: Wild Wealth, 1971; (newspaper column Fun With Flowers, 1949; contbr. articles to mags. Actress, designer 3 syndicated movie shorts for profession. Office: 1037 E McMillan St Cincinnati OH 45206

POETTER, MABLE REECE, nurse; b. Ellijay, Ga., Jan. 11, 1920; d. George W. and Neatie (West) Reece; diploma Sch. Nursing Ga. Baptist Hosp., 1943; m. Louis J. Poetter, Dec. 17, 1943; children—Marcia Ann Poetter Pedigo, Rita Lynn Poetter Evans, Dana Faye. Asst. to dir. nursing Ga. Bapt. Hosp., Atlanta; evening supr., surg. supr., obstet. supr., instr. nursing Mercer (Ga.) U.; co founder with husband Anneewakee Found. and Treatment Center, Douglasville, Ga., also dir. nursing services; pres. Anneewakee Estates Inc.; caterer, wedding cons. Girl Scout leader, also camp nurse; class sponsor Future Nurses Assn.; mem. coms., tchr. Sunday Sch., 1st Bapt. Ch., Douglasville. Mem. Ga. Bapt. Hosp. Alumnae Assn., Emergency Dept. Nurses Assn., Nursing Assn. Ga., 5th Dist. Nurses Assn. Ga., Am., Ga. State nurses assns., Savannah Assn. Garden Clubs, Dougals County Social Services Council. Home: 1946 Tara Circle Douglasville GA 30135 Office: 4771 Anneewakee Rd Douglasville GA 30135

POFFENBERGER, VIRGINIA, lawyer, state legislator; b. Perry, Iowa, Nov. 12, 1934; d. Charles Irving and Loraine (Farr) Joy; B.S., Iowa State U., 1957; J.D., Drake U., 1978; m. Richard Poffenberger, June 23, 1957; children—Elizabeth, Thomas, James. Dietitian, Drake U., Des Moines, 1957-59; admitted to Iowa bar, 1978; asso. firm Joy, Poffenberger & Joy, Perry, 1978—; mem. Iowa Ho. of Reps., 1978—; mem. grievance commn. Iowa Supreme Ct., 1979—. Mem. Perry City Council, 1973-78. Mem. Am. Bar Assn., Iowa Bar Assn., Dallas County Bar Assn., Iowa Trial Lawyers Assn., PEO, Bus. and Profl. Women, Dallas County Women's Polit. Caucus, Dallas County Farm Bur. Republican. Methodist. Home: 1816 Willis Ave Perry IA 50220 Office: 1215 Warford St Perry IA 50220

POGER, RUTH, editor, publisher, former Democratic nat. committeewoman, editor, publisher; b. Bklyn., June 1, 1937; d. Harry L. and Dora (Statsky) Goldberg; student public schs., Bklyn.; m. Sidney Poger, Sept. 13, 1959; children—Julia, Toby Sue. Mcpl. bond trader Fitzpatrick, Sullivan & Co., N.Y.C., 1957-62; exec. dir. Vt. Dem. Com., 1970-74; campaign mgr. Gov. Thomas P. Salmon, Vt., 1974; editor, pub. The Other Paper, South Burlington, Vt., 1977—; Dem. nat. committeewoman for Vt., 1976-78; campaign mgr. Edwin C. Granai, Dem. candidate for gov. Vt., 1978; U.S. census mgr. State of Vt., 1979-80. Justice of Peace, 1974-79; mem. Vt. Water Resource Bd., 1976-79; Chittenden County Dem. state committeewoman, 1975-76. Jewish. Home: 26 Victoria Dr South Burlington VT 05401

POGO, BEATRIZ, cell biologist and virologist; b. Buenos Aires, Argentina, Dec. 24, 1932; d. Dario and Maria Teresa (Vergnory) Garcia-Tunon; came to U.S., 1964, naturalized, 1976; B.S., Lycee No. 1, Buenos Aires, 1950; M.D., Sch. Medicine, Buenos Aires, 1956; D.M.Sci., 1961; m. Angel Oscar Pogo, Jan. 13, 1956; children—Gustav, Gabriela. Asst. prof. cell biology Inst. Cell Biology, Cordoba (Argentina) U., 1962-64; research asso. Rockefeller U., N.Y.C., 1964-67; asst. Public Health Research Inst., N.Y.C., 1967-69, asso., 1969-73, asso. mem., 1973-78; prof. exptl. cell biology and microbiology, Mt. Sinai Sch. Medicine, City U. N.Y., N.Y.C., 1978—. Damon Runyon Fund fellow, 1964-65; Am. Cancer Soc. grantee, 1970-73; NIH grantee, 1975—. Mem. AAAS, Am. Assn. Cancer Research, Am. Soc. Cell Biology, Harvey Soc., Assn. Women in Sci. (v.p. Met. N.Y. chpt. 1981), Am. Microbiol. Soc., N.Y. Acad. Scis. Contbr. articles to profl. jours. Home: 237 Nyac Ave Pelham NY 10803 Office: Mt Sinai Sch Medicine 1 Gustave Levy Pl New York NY 10029

POGODIN, ARLYNE, constrn. co. exec.; b. Chgo., Jan. 21, 1947; d. Arnold M. and Bertha (Erkes) P.; B.A., DePaul U., 1980. Timekeeper Morris Handler Co., Chgo., 1964-70; comptroller, v.p. Lazar & Assos. of Ill., Chgo., 1970-77; corp. sec., comptroller Interior Alterations, Inc., Chgo., 1977—; pres. Rly and Assos. Inc., ins. agts. and cons., Chgo. Office: 646 N Michigan Ave Chicago IL 60611

POGUE, DORIS STROUDE, ins. broker, mfg. co. exec.; b. Chesterfield County, Va., Feb. 26, 1947; d. Guy Stanley and Evelyn (Bradshaw) Trent; student Newark State Coll., 1965-69, 70-72, Profl. Sch. Bus., 1972; m. Stewart W. Pogue, Nov. 24, 1979; 1 son, Nasir Stroude. Ins. broker, pres. Doris Stroude Ins. Agy., East Orange, N.J., 1972—; pres. Doris Hotel Enterprises, Inc., East Orange and Elizabeth, N.J., 1978—. Mem. Nat. Assn. Female Execs., Greater Newark C. of C., Nat. Fedn. Republican Women. Clubs: Club ABC Tours, TWA Ambassador. Office: 396 Central Ave East Orange NJ 07018

POGUE, MARY ELLEN, civic worker; b. Fremont, Nebr., Oct. 27, 1904; d. Frank E. and Mary (Coe) Edgerton; B.F.A., U. Nebr., 1926; studied violin with Harrison Keller, Boston, 1926-28, Kemp Stillings Master Class, N.Y.C., 1939-40; m. L. Welch Pogue, Sept. 8, 1926; children—Richard Welch, William Lloyd, John Marshall. Mem. Potomac String Ensemble, 1948—. Vice chmn. Montgomery County (Md.) Victory Garden Center, 1946-47; pres. Bethesda Community Garden Club, 1946-48; mem. bd. Montgomery County YWCA, 1946-50, 52-55; bd. govs., historian Gov. William Bradford Compact, 1966—; bd. dirs. Ind. Agy. Women, 1983—. Mem. Mayflower Soc. (dir. D.C. 1955—), Nat. Geneal. Soc., Nat. Soc. Women Descs. Ancient and Hon. Arty. Co. Columbia Hist. Soc., Art Group (chmn. 1977-78), Women Descs. Ancient and Honorable Arty. Co. (Va. Ct.), Capital Speaker's, PEO (pres. D.C. chpt. 1957-59), Mortar Bd. (pres. D.C. alumni 1966-67), Delta Omicron Music. Democrat. Methodist. Editor: Favorite Menus and Recipes of Mary Edgerton of Aurora, Nebr. (cookbook), 1963; Edgerton-Coe History, 1965. Home: 5204 Kenwood Ave Chevy Chase MD 20815

POHL, GAIL PIERCE, author, assn. exec.; b. Stigler, Okla., Nov. 18, 1938; d. William James and Kathleen Louise (McConnell) Pierce; B.A., U. Okla., 1960; m. Lee W. Pohl, July 7, 1962; 1 dau., Leslie Kathleen. Reporter, Okla. Bus. News, Oklahoma City, 1960-65, news editor, 1966-72; pub. relations asso. Am. Mut. Ins. Alliance, Chgo., 1972; editor Jour. Am. Ins., 1973-76; dir. publs. Alliance Am. Insurers, Chgo., 1976-78, dir. policy communications, 1978-79; exec. dir. Nat. Self-Service Storage Assn., Eureka Springs, Ark., 1981—. Pres., trustee 1st Montessori Sch. Atlanta Parents Assn., 1980-81. Mem. Women in Communications, Mut. Ins. Communicators (1st place award for editorial excellence 1977, 78), Chgo. Assn. Bus. Communicators (awards for bus. news writing 1978, mag. editing 1978, feature writing 1978; competition judge mag. editing 1979), Ins. Distaff Execs. Assn. Chgo. (legis. com. 1977-78, pub. relations com. 1976-78, exec. bd. 1978-79), Nat. Assn. Ins. Women (ethics com. 1977-79), Soc. Consumer Affairs Profls. in Bus., Am. Soc. Assn. Execs. Home: 270 Spring St Eureka Springs AR 72632

POHLY, SHEILA RIMLAND, ednl. psychologist; b. N.Y.C., Oct. 10, 1946; d. Selig and Anne (Liberman) Rimland; student Russell Sage Coll., 1963-65; B.S. with distinction, Cornell U., 1967, M.S., 1968; permanent cert. sch. psychologist N.Y. State, Columbia U. Tchrs. Coll., 1971; Ph.D. in Psychology, SUNY, Stony Brook, 1979; m. Lawrence M. Pohly, Aug. 20, 1967; children—Michael Brian, Robert Scott. Instr. SUNY, Stony Brook, 1978-79; adj. faculty C.W. Post Coll., L.I. U., 1980—; sch. psychologist, gifted and talented program Northport-East Northport (N.Y.) Union Free Sch. Dist., 1980—; cons. sch. dists. including Pearl River, N.J. Active Citizens-Profl. Adv. Com. on Gifted Edn., Roslyn Public Schs., 1981—; mem. alumni interviewing com. Cornell U., 1981—; mem. sch. bd. local Temple Sch., 1980—. Mem. Am. Psychol. Assn., Nassau County Psychol. Assn., Nat. Assn. Gifted Children, Orton Soc., Cornell U. Alumni Assn., Phi Kappa Phi, Omicron Nu. Contbg. author writings to profl. publs., papers to profl. confs. Home: 70 Rugby Rd Roslyn Heights NY 11577 Office: 110 Elwood Rd Northport NY 11768

POIANI, EILEEN LOUISE, mathematician, educator; b. Newark, Dec. 17, 1943; d. Hugo F. and Eileen Louise (Crecca) Poiani; A.B., Douglass Coll., 1965; M.S., Rutgers U., 1967, Ph.D. in Math., 1971. Teaching asst., instr. math. Rutgers U., 1966-67; asst. counselor Douglass Coll., 1969-70; instr. St. Peter's Coll., Jersey City, 1967-70, asst. prof., 1970-74, assoc. prof., 1974-80, prof., 1980—, asst. to pres. for planning, 1976—; dir. self-study Middle States Assn. rev., 1974-76, 81-83; exec. dir. WAM, nat. program for interesting young women in math., 1975-81, spl. cons., 1981—. Mem. met. adv. bd. Nat. Alliance Bus., 1979-81; discussion leader Nutley (N.J.) Ecumenical Com., 1971-72; trustee Nutley Pub. Library, 1974-77; mem. N.J. Dept. Edn. Adv. Com. on Statewide Higher Edn. Research, 1981—; mem. N.J. Bus.-Industry-Sci. Edn. Consortium, 1981—, Recipient G. Johnson, S.J. Alumni Faculty award, 1976; Danforth asso., 1972—. Mem. AAUP, Math. Assn. Am. (gov., vis. lectr., cons. 1983-84), Nutley Hist. Soc., Douglass Soc., Douglass Coll. Alumnae Assn., Pi Mu Epsilon (nat.

councillor 1972—), Phi Beta Kappa. Home: 49 Carrie Ct Nutley NJ 07110 Office: Dept Math St Peter's Coll Jersey City NJ 07306

POINDEXTER, SHARON FAYE, mgmt. cons.; b. Hope, Ark., Feb. 21, 1944; d. Governor and Minnie Maudell (Littrell) P.; B.S. in Edn. (fellow), Wichita (Kans.) State U., 1967, postgrad. in bus. adminstrn. Lectr. English, Wichita State U., 1969-73, tutorial program dir., 1971-72; dir. tng. Wichita Community Action, 1970-73; communication cons. United Meth. Ministry, 1973-74; pres. Poindexter Assos., Cons., Wichita, 1974—. Cons., nat. bd. dirs. YWCA, pres., 1978-79; cons. fed., state, and city govts., Nat. Assn. Bank Women. Recipient Community Leadership award Wichita State U. Student Leadership Assn., 1979. Mem. Wichita State U. Alumni Assn. (dir. 1979—, mem. fin. com. 1979—), Kans. Assn. Commerce and Industry, Nat. Assn. Women Bus. Owners (pres. local chpt., treas. nat. assn. 1980-81), Am. Soc. Bus. and Mgmt. Cons., Wichita Area C. of C. (chmn. com. 1979-80), Nat. Fedn. Ind. Bus. Contbr. articles to profl. jours. Home: 550 Nims Blvd #317 Wichita KS 67203 Office: 111 W Douglas St #509 Wichita KS 67202

POLAN, NANCY MOORE, artist; b. Newark, Ohio; d. William Tracy and Francis (Flesher) Moore; A.B., Marshall U., 1936; m. Lincoln Milton Polan, Mar. 28, 1934; children—Charles Edwin, William Joseph Marion. One-man shows Charleston Art Gallery, 1961, 67, 73, Greenbrier, 1963, Huntington Galleries, 1963, 66, 71, N.Y. World's Fair, 1965, W.Va. U., 1966, Carroll Reese Mus., 1967; exhibited in group shows Am. Watercolor Soc., Allied Artists of Am., Nat. Arts Club, 1968-74, 76-77, Pa. Acad. Fine Arts, Opening of Creative Arts Center W.Va. U., 1969, Internat. Platform Assn. Art Exhibit, 1968-69, 72, 73, 74, 79, Allied Artists W.Va., 1968-69, Joan Miro Graphic Exhbn., Barcelona, Spain, 1970, XXI Exhibit Contemporary Art, La Scala, Florence, Italy, 1971, Rassegna Internazionale d'Arte Grafica, Siena, Italy, 1973, 79, 82, Opening of Parkersburg (W.Va.) Art Center, 1975, Internat. Platform Assn. Ann. Exhbn., 1979, others. Hon. v.p. Centro Studi e Scambi Internazionale, Rome, Italy, 1977. Recipient Acad. of Italy with Gold medal, 1979; recipient Norton Meml. award 3d Nat. Jury Show Am. Art, Chautauqua, N.Y., 1960; Purchase prize, Jurors award, Watercolor award Huntington Galleries, 1960, 61; Nat. Arts Club for watercolor, 1969; Gold medal Masters of Modern Art exhbn., La Scala Gallery, Florence, 1975, many others. Mem. DAR, Allied Artists W.Va., Internat. Platform Assn. (3d award-painting in ann. art exhbn. 1977), Allied Artists Am. (asso.), Huntington Galleries, Tri-State Arts Assn. (Equal Merit award 1978), Sunrise Found., Pen and Brush (Grumbacher award 1978), Am. Watercolor Soc. (asso.), Am. Fedn. Arts, Nat. Arts Club, Leonardo da Vinci Acad. (Rome), Sigma Kappa. Episcopalian. Address: 2 Prospect Dr Huntington WV 25701 also 2106 Club Dr Vero Beach FL 32960

POLANSKY, GERALDINE FRANCES, automation adviser; b. Kaska, Pa., Nov. 27, 1944; d. Michael and Wanda Frances (Garbish) P.; B.A., Kutztown State Coll., 1966; m. Leo Howard Cairns, May 19, 1974. Computer programmer, analyst Air Products & Chemicals Inc., Pa., 1966-68; data processing cons. Booz, Allen & Hamilton, Inc., Chgo., Raleigh, N.C., San Juan, P.R., Los Angeles, Detroit, Mexico City, 1968-70; programming mgr. Fed. Res. Bank, Chgo., Detroit, 1970-72; mortgage project mgr. Del. Trust Co., Wilmington, 1972-74; info. analyst E.I. duPont de Nemours, Wilmington, 1974-75; internat. banking specialist, project mgr. Western Bancorp Data Processing Co., Los Angeles, London and N.Y.C., 1975-79; asst. v.p. new product devel. United Calif. Bank, Los Angeles, 1979; owner, mgr. G.F. Polansky, automation adv. and cons., Los Angeles, 1980—; sr. partner C/P Industries, retail/wholesale mktg., Thousand Oaks, Calif. Mem. AAUW, Nat. Assn. Female Execs. Club: Sunset Hills Country (Thousand Oaks). Home: 683 Whispering Oaks Pl Thousand Oaks CA 91320

POLASCIK, MARY ANN, ophthalmologist; b. Elkhorn, W.Va., Dec. 28, 1940; d. Michael and Elizabeth (Halko) Polascik; B.A., Rutgers U., 1967; M.D., Pritzker Sch. Medicine, 1971; m. Joseph Elie, Oct. 2, 1973; 1 dau., Laura Elizabeth Polascik. Jr. pharmacologist Ciba Pharm. Co., Summit, N.J., 1961-67; intern Billings Hosp., Chgo., 1971-72; resident in ophthalmology U. Chgo. Hosp., 1972-75; practice medicine specializing in ophthalmology, Dixon, Ill., 1975—; pres. McNichols Clinic, Ltd.; cons. ophthalmology, Dixon Devel. Center; mem. staff Katherine Shaw Bethea Hosp., Dixon, Dixon Developmental Center Hosp. Bd. dirs. Sinissippi Mental Health Center, 1976-81, Winnebago Center for Blind. Mem. AMA, Ill. Med. Soc., Ill., Am. assns. ophthalmology, Alpha Sigma Lambda. Roman Catholic. Clubs: Galena Territory, Dixon Country. Office: 120 S Hennepin Dixon IL 61021

POLATTY, ROSE JACKSON, civic worker; b. Atlanta, Sept. 17, 1922; d. James Wilmot and Esther Ann (Sweeny) Jackson; A.B. in Journalism, U. Ga., 1943; postgrad. Oglethorpe U., 1962-63, Ga. State U., 1963; m. George Junius Polatty, Nov. 27, 1942; children—George Junius, Robert Wilmot, Rose Crystal, Richard James. Active U. Ga. Alumni Soc., pres. Class of 1943 Alumni, 1948-58, bd. mgrs., 1966-69, v.p., 1971-73, chmn. seminar, 1971; exec. sec. Atlanta Boy Choir, 1968-69; bd. dirs. Atlanta Arts Council, 1968-69; advisory com. Kennesaw Coll. on Wheels, 1974-78; bicentennial chmn., City of Roswell, Ga., 1975-76, sec. hist. preservation commn., 1978—; active Ga. Trust for Hist. Preservation, Ga. Conservancy, Roswell Hist. Soc., Women's Assn. Atlanta Symphony Orchestra; adminstrv. bd., chmn. altar guild, Roswell United Meth. Ch. Recipient recognition award Nat. 4-H Alumni, 1959, service award City of Roswell, 1976, community service award Roswell Optimist Club, 1977, Roswell Jaycee Leadership award, 1977, community service award Zion Bapt. Ch., 1977. Mem. Women in Communications, Delta Omicron, Phi Beta Kappa, Phi Kappa Phi, Kappa Delta Pi. Clubs: Kappa Delta, P.E.O. (chpt. AA, Ga., charter 1977), D.A.R. (Joseph Habersham chpt.), Colonial Dames XVII Century (chpt. charter mem., pres. 1982—), Roswell Women's (charter 1948, pres. 1966-68), Roswell Garden (charter 1951, pres. 1975-77), N. Fulton Council Garden Clubs (charter 1975, pres. 1975-77). Home: 889 Mimosa Blvd Roswell GA 30075

POLCAR, GERTRUDE ELIZABETH, judge; b. Cleve., Oct. 10, 1916; d. Martin and Gertrude M. (Jirele) Polcar; student Leland Stanford Jr. U., 1935-36; A.B. in Law, U. Chgo., 1938, J.D., 1940. Admitted to Ohio bar, 1941, U.S. Supreme Ct. bar, 1981; individual practice law, Parma, 1942-44, 50-56, 60-71; asst. atty. gen. of Ohio, 1945-49, 57-59; councilman City of Parma, 1960-68; mem. Ohio Ho. of Reps. from Dist. 51, 1969-71; judge Parma Mcpl. Ct., 1972—, presiding and adminstrv. judge, 1976-77, 82—; v.p.-at-large Greater Cleve. Safety Council. Mem. Republican State Central Com. from 20th Dist., 1954-64; mem. South Ridge Civic Assn.; dir.-at-large Friends of Parma Libraries, 1981—. Recipient superior jud. service awards Supreme Ct. Ohio, 1975, 76, 77, 78, 79, 80, 81. Mem. Ohio, Cuyahoga County, Parma bar assns., Bar Assn. Greater Cleve., Cleve. Women Lawyers' Assn., Ohio Mcpl. Judges Assn. (exec. com.), Greater Cleve. Mcpl. Judges Assn. (pres.), Ohio Jud. Conf., Am. Judges Assn., Parma Area Hist. Soc. Clubs: Order Eastern Star, Ladies Oriental Shrine N.Am. Home: 7060 Ridge Rd Parma OH 44129 Office: 5750 W 54th St Parma OH 44129

POLEVOY, NANCY TALLY, social worker; b. N.Y.C., May 27, 1944; d. Charles H. and Bernice M. (Gang) Tally; student Mt. Holyoke Coll., 1962-64; B.A., Barnard Coll., 1966; M.S. (NIMH Scholar), Columbia U. Sch. Social Work, 1968; m. Martin D. Polevoy, Mar. 19, 1967; children—Jason Tally, John Gerald. Caseworker, unmarried mothers' service Louise Wise Services, N.Y.C., 1967, caseworker, adoption dept., 1969-71; caseworker Youth Consultation Service, N.Y.C., 1968-69; asst. research scientist, psychiat. social worker, dept. child psychiatry N.Y.U. Med. Center, N.Y.C., 1973-81; adv. ct. appointed spl. advs. Manhattan Family Ct., N.Y.C., 1981-82; social work cons., 1981—. Recipient French Govt. prize, 1963. Mem. Nat. Assn. Social Workers, Acad. Cert. Social Workers, Alumni Assn. Columbia U. Sch. Social Work. Contbr. articles on early infantile autism to profl. jours. Home: 1155 Park Ave New York NY 10028 Office: 1155 Park Ave New York NY 10028

POLINSKY, JANET NABOICHECK, state legislator; b. Hartford, Conn., Dec. 6, 1930; d. Louis H. and Lillian S. Naboicheck; B.A., U. Conn., 1953; postgrad. Harvard Bus. Sch., 1954; m. Hubert N. Polinsky, Sept. 21, 1958; children—Gerald, David, Beth. Mem. Waterford (Conn.) 2d Charter Commn., 1967-68, Waterford Conservation Commn., 1968-69; Waterford rep. Town Meeting, 1969-71, S.E. Conn. Regional Planning Agy., 1971-73; mem. Waterford Planning and Zoning Commn., 1970-76, chmn., 1973-76; mem. Waterford Democratic Town Com., 1976—, del. State Dem. Conv., 1976, 78, 80, 82; mem. Conn. Ho. of Reps. from 38th Dist., 1977—, asst. majority leader, 1981—. Trustee Eugene O'Neill Meml. Theatre Center, 1973-76, 81—; mem. New Eng. Bd. Higher Edn., 1981—. Named Woman of Yr., Waterford Jr. Women's Club, 1977, Nehantic Women's Bus. and Profl. Club, 1979, Legislator of Yr., Conn. Library Assn., 1980. Mem. Order Women Legislators, Delta Kappa Gamma (hon.). Home: 19 E Neck Rd Waterford CT 06385 Office: State Capitol Hartford CT 06115

POLIVKA, ANNE T., govt. ofcl.; b. Nesquehoning, Pa., May 2, 1929; d. Michael C. and Margaret M. York; B.S., Pa. State U., 1973; M.Govt. Adminstrn., U. Pa., 1976; m. John Polivka, Nov. 23, 1950; children—Anne L., John M., James J. Med. technician, 1949-72; with Navy Dept., 1973—, supply systems analyst Fleet Materials Support Office, Mechanicsburg, Pa., 1978—. Mem. Federally Employed Women (past chpt. pres.), AAUW, Am. Def. Preparedness Assn. (chpt. officer), Am. Soc. Public Adminstrn., AAUW. Democrat. Roman Catholic. Office: Box 2010 Fleet Material Support Office Mechanicsburg PA 17055

POLK, MARY JO, state legislator; b. Quitaque, Tex.; d. Leon and Lockwood McCracken; B.B.A., U. Tex., El Paso, 1967; m. D. Wade Polk, May 15, 1948; children—Linda, Paul, Laura. Elementary and kindergarten tchr., 1967-78; mem. Tex. Ho. of Reps., 1979—, mem. energy com., jud. affairs com., urban needs com., steering com., mem. ways and means com., chmn. select com. on teenage pregnancy. Bd. dirs. Runaway Center and Sch. for Teen-Age Parents. Mem. Tex. Tchrs. Assn. (life), Tex. Elected Women. Democrat. Methodist. Office: 2267 Trawood B-5 El Paso TX 79935

POLK-REED, SANDRA GAYLE, leasing co. exec.; b. Abilene, Tex., Apr. 22, 1942; d. Charles Mason and Bennie Katherine (Byram) Hubbard; student Abilien public schs.; children—Laurie Gayle, Kristy Lynn. Cosmetician, Univ. Drug., Albuquerque, 1960-61; owner antique store, 1968-70; pharm. sec., 1970-73; gen. mgr., leasing mgr., dir. Village Leasing, Inc., Abilene, 1973—. Active Muscular Dystrophy, 1964; S.W. Abilene Area chmn. March of Dimes, 1978. Mem. Nat. Fedn. Ind. Bus. Research and Edn. Found., Profl. Automobile Salesmans Assn., PTA, Women's Internat. Bowling Congress. Democrat. Baptist. Home: 4301 Bob-o-Link St Abilene TX 79606 Office: 5209 S 1st St Abilene TX 79605

POLLACK, BETTY GILLESPIE, assn. exec.; b. Oak Park, Ill., Apr. 4, 1940; d. Leon H. and Elta F. Gillespie; B.A., Whittier coll., 1962; M.S., Columbia U., 1964; m. David Pollack, Dec. 18, 1971; 1 son, Michael Alan. Community organizer, Boston, 1964-66; faculty mem. Grad. Sch. Social Welfare, U. Calif., Berkeley, 1967-71; exec. dir. Calif. chpt. Nat. Assn. Social Workers, Millbrae, 1971-81, Vis. Nurse Assn., Santa Clara County, Calif., 1981—; chmn. Cert. Assn. Execs. Study Course, 1981. Mem. No. Calif. Soc. Assn. Execs. (sec.-treas. 1980-82, pres.-elect 1982-83), Peninsula Profl. Women's Network (sec. 1981-82, chmn. networking conf. 1981, pres. ednl. fund 1981-82), Bay Area Profl. Women's Network (mem. newsletter com. 1980-81), Am. Soc. Assn. Execs., LWV. Democrat. Club: Comstock. Home: 316 Sycamore St San Carlos CA 94070 Office: 2216 The Alameda Santa Clara CA 95050

POLLACK, CAROL LOUGH, nurse, photojournalist; b. Wheeling, W.Va., Dec. 25, 1924; d. John J. and Mabel L. (Dague) Lough; R.N., Ohio Valley Gen. Hosp., 1945; B.S., Western Res. U., 1955; postgrad. Johns Hopkins U., 1962-63, Catholic U., 1965-66, N.Y. U., 1949-50; m. Ronald Paul Pollack, Jan. 26, 1956; 1 son, John Ronald. Adminstr. charge nursing service Mt. Sinai Hosp., Cleve., 1953-57; instr. public health City of Cleve., 1957-59; instr. surgery Sinai Hosp., Balt., 1961-63; sch. nurse Franklin Sr. High Sch., Reisterstown, Md., 1964—; polit. reporter Times Newspapers, Baltimore County, Md., 1964-71; editor Northwest County News, 1971-75; editor Tribune, Reisterstown, 1976-77; photojournalist, feature writer Times, Reisterstown, 1978—. Sec. Reisterstown Community Corp.; v.p. Historic Reisterstown; chmn. Reisterstown Historic Room; mem. Baltimore County Gen. Hosp. Found. Bd.; mem. exec. bd. Humane Soc., Reisterstown; tchr. Sunday sch. Trinity Lutheran Ch., Reisterstown; mem. Baltimore County Landmarks Preservation Commn., 1982—. Recipient Meritorious Service award Nat. Hdqrs. CAP, 1979; named Woman of Year, Woman's Club Reisterstown, 1979; Outstanding Vol. Service award Baltimore County Public Library, 1982. Mem. Bus. and Profl. Women, Delmarva Press Club, Am. Nurses Assn., Md. State Nurses Assn. Club: Federated Woman's of Glyndon. Author: Reisterstown, 1966, 7th rev. edit., 1976. Home: 303 Cherry Hill Rd Reisterstown MD 21136 Office: 58 Woodley Ave Reisterstown MD 21136

POLLACK, CATHY SUSAN, bus. systems planner; b. N.Y.C., Oct. 25, 1952; d. Herman G. and Ruth R. (Rothenstein) Gelfand; B.A. cum laude, Queens Coll., 1973; Cert. in Bus. Mgmt., N.Y. U., 1976, postgrad. M.B.A. program, 1981—. Sr. programmer Fed. Res. Bank, N.Y.C., 1973-76; sr. systems analyst Depository Trust Co., N.Y.C., 1976-77; sr. tech. writer Bankers Trust Co., N.Y.C., 1977-78; sr. cons. Interactive Data Corp., N.Y.C., 1978-80; bus. systems planner, corp. systems liaison Smith, Barney, Harris, Upham, N.Y.C., 1980—. Mem. Nat. Assn. Female Execs., Women in Data Processing, Mensa, Concert/Theatre Club, Am. Mus. Natural History, Met. Mus. Art, Whitney Mus., Cooper-Hewitt Mus., Mus. of Modern Art. Democrat. Jewish. Club: Hadassah. Home: 900 W End Ave New York NY 10025 Office: 120 Broadway New York NY 10007

POLLACK, ESTHER MRUS, contractor; b. N.Y.C., Oct. 1, 1925; d. Simon and Bella (Nabutowsky) Mrus; B.A., Hunter Coll., N.Y.C., 1944; widow; children—David, Ira, Sharon. Lit. agt. William Morris Agy., N.Y.C., 1945-52; mng. editor True Experience mag., 1952-56; free lance contbr. to Jewish publs.; pres. Prime Decorators Inc., Bayside, N.Y., 1976—. Mem. N. Shore Community Devel. Council, 1977—; v.p. sisterhood Temple Emanuel, Gt. Neck, N.Y., 1975—. Mem. Am. Women's Econ. Devel. Corp. Democrat.

POLLAK, FRANCES ANDERSON, mfg. co. exec.; b. N.Y.C., June 8, 1949; d. Bernard E. and Brenda (Anderson) P.; student Sorbonne, U. Paris, 1969-70; B.A., Hollins Coll., 1971; M.Regulatory Policy, George Washington U. Staff office standards and regulations EPA, Washington, 1971-72; staff Commerce Com. subcom. on aviation U.S. Senate, Washington, 1972-75; asst. dir. govt. relations dept. Nat. Cable TV Assn., Washington, 1975-76; Washington rep. Goodyear Tire & Rubber Co., 1977-81; dep. dir. public affairs Union Camp Corp., 1981—. Mem. Women in Govt. Relations (chmn. regulatory relations com. 1979-80, chmn. congressional relations com. 1980-81, dir. 1980-82, chmn. task force on state chpts. 1981-82), Nat. Council Career Women (dir. 1979-82, chmn. state chpt. com. Women in Govt. Relations 1982-83), Am. League Lobbyists, Women in Housing and Fin., Nat. Energy Resources Orgn., Women's Econ. Roundtables Washington Area State Relations Group, Am. Mgmt. Assn., Washington Soc. Assn. Execs., Nat. Assn. Female Execs., Washington Area State Relations Group, Women in Transp. Clubs: Capital Hill, Nat. Democratic, Republican Women's, City Tavern, Germantown. Office: 1850 K St NW Suite 390 Washington DC 20006

POLLAN, CAROLYN JOAN, state legislator; b. Houston, July 12, 1937; d. Rex and Faith (Basye) Clark; B.S. in Radio and TV, John Brown U., 1959; postgrad. N.Y. U., 1959; m. George A. Pollan, Jan. 6, 1962; children—Cee Cee, Todd, Robert. Mem. Ark. Ho. of Reps., 1974—, now sr. Republican mem.; del. Am. Soviet Seminar, Am. Council Young Polit. Leaders, Exeter, N.H., 1976. Vice chmn. Ark. Rep. Com., 1972-76; del. Rep. Nat. Conv., 1976; bd. dirs. Ark. Cancer Soc., Sebastian County Cancer Soc., Ark. Easter Seals Soc.; adv. bd. Project Compassion; bd. dirs. Greg Kistler Treatment Center for Physically Handicapped, Ark. Found. Assoc. Colls., 4-H Found. for Sebastian County; trustee John Brown U.; mem. So. Regional Edn. Bd. Recipient Conservation Legislator of Yr. award Ark. Wildlife Fedn., Nat. Wildlife Fedn., Sears Roebuck & Co., 1976, Outstanding State Legislator of Yr. award Ark. Pub. Employees Assn., 1979; named 1 of 10 Outstanding Legislators, Assembly of Govtl. Employees, 1980, Legislator of Yr., Ark. Human Service Providers Assn.; voted 1 of Ft. Smith's 10 Most Influential Citizens, S.W. Times Record Readers, 1979. Mem. Ft. Smith (Ark.) Hist. Soc., Inc. (co-editor jour.), Ark. Hist. Soc. (dir., 1st pl. award hist. publs.), Ft. Smith Car Restoration Assn. Baptist. Office: 400 N 8th St Fort Smith AR 72901

POLLARD, DARLENE DAVENPORT, data processing co. sales ofcl.; b. Washington, Feb. 23, 1949; d. Bennett Gibson and Margaret Theresa (Schemmer) Davenport; B.A. in English Lit., Clemson U., 1972; diploma S.C. Bankers Sch., 1979. Teller, First Citizens Bank & Trust, Columbia, S.C., 1972-73, Barnett Bank of Fla., Deland, 1973; utility teller C&S Nat. Bank, Columbia, 1974-75, teller tng. officer, 1975-78, corr. banking asst. ops. officer, 1978-80, ops. officer and corr. banking data processing coordinator, 1980-82; sales rep. Gate City Data Processors Inc., Greensboro, N.C., 1982—. Mem. Am. Inst. Banking, Nat. Assn. Bank Women. Republican. Methodist. Clubs: Civitan (sec. Dutch Fork of Columbia 1980-81, pres.-elect 1981-82, pres. 1982—, named Civitan of Year 1980-81). Office: 311 Pomona Dr PO Box 8149 Greensboro NC 27419

POLLARD, FRANCES MARGUERITE, librarian; b. Florence, Ala., Oct. 7, 1920; d. Lorenzo Marquis and Carrie (Mayfield) Pollard; grad. Selma Jr. Coll., 1938; B.S., Ala. State Coll., 1941; M.S. in L.S., Western Res. U., 1949, Ph.D., 1963; postgrad. Columbia, 1952-54. Tchr. elem. sch., Waterloo, Ala., 1938-39, Marengo County Tng. Sch., Thomaston, Ala., 1941-42, Sterling High Sch., Sheffield, Ala., 1942-43; library asst. Enlisted Men's Library 2, Fort McClellan, Ala., 1943-46, Ala. State Coll., Montgomery, 1946-48; student aide children' room Sterling br. Cleve. Public Library, 1948-49; asst. librarian Ala. State Coll., 1949-61, head librarian, 1961-63; adminstrv. asst. Booth Library, Eastern Ill. U., Charleston, 1963-70, prof. library sci., head library sci. dept., 1970-79, exec. asst. for library services, 1979—; mem. Ill. State Library Adv. Com., 1967-73, subcom. LSCA Title I and Title II, 1967-77. Mem. Am., Ill. library assns., Am. Acad. Polit. and Social Sci., Soc. Applied Anthropology, Am. Sociol. Assn. (asso.), AAUP, AAUW, Alpha Kappa Alpha. Author: (with others) Major Problems in Education of Librarians, 1954, Illinois Literary Reflections of the Bicentennial Year. Editor: Procs. of Personnel Evaluation Inst., 1975. Home: 1330 A St Charleston IL 61920

POLLARD, SHARON MARGARET, state senator; b. Methuen, Mass., Sept. 21, 1950; d. Kenneth H. and Betty I. (Duvall) P.; B.A., Dunbarton Coll.; M.A., Salem Coll., 1974. Legis. aide to U.S. Rep. Les Aspin, 1974-76; mem. Mass. Senate, Boston, 1976—. Del., Democratic Nat. Conv., 1980; Mem. Methuen Bd. Trade. Mem. LWV, Mass. Assn. Legislators, Nat. Trust Hist. Preservation, DAR. Roman Catholic. Office: Room 511 The Statehouse Boston MA 02133

POLLEY, ELIZABETH MARIE, art/photo journalist; b. Hilo, Hawaii, May 9, 1908; d. William Russell and Elizabeth Marie (Menard) Patterson; B.A., U. Calif., 1928; postgrad. Mills Coll., 1949, Calif. Coll. Arts and Crafts, 1951; M.A., U. Guadalajara, 1954; m. Raymond Wheeler Polley, May 30, 1946; 1 son by previous marriage—Russell Earl Jabs. Art editor, critic Gibson Publs., Vallejo, Calif., 1946-74; instr. Vallejo Unified Sch. Dist., 1947-65; art critic Artforum Mag., San Francisco, 1962-66, San Francisco Mag., 1966-68, FM and the Arts, 1965-67, Focus Mag., San Francisco, 1974-76; art commentator KQED-TV, San Francisco, 1974-77; dir., instr. Channel Artists, Vallejo, 1971-80; lectr. art subjects; publicity pub. relations dir. Richmond (Calif.) Art Center, 1967-68; art cons. City of Vallejo, 1977; murals include: Solano County Fair Grounds, U.S. Navy at Mare Island, Taft and Taft Bldg., Vallejo. Pres. Artists League of Vallejo; mem. Vallejo Fine Arts Council, Vallejo Cultural Activities Commn., 1969-71; mem. docent council and accessions com., trustee Vallejo Hist. Mus.; sponsor Vallejo Symphony Assn. Recipient citation Am. Artists Profl. League, 1948, 49, City of Vallejo, 1971, 76. Mem. Calif. Ret. Tchrs. Assn., NEA, Oakland, San Francisco, San Francisco Fine, Asian art mus., Richmond Art Assn., Artists League Vallejo, Univ. Art Mus., Navy League. Democrat. Roman Catholic. Club: Soroptimists Internat. Contbr. articles to nat. art jours. Home: 112 Lain Dr Vallejo CA 94591 Office: 114 Lain Dr Vallejo CA 94590 94591

POLLITT, GERTRUDE STEIN, psychotherapist, clin. social worker; came to U.S., 1949, naturalized, 1951; b. Vienna, Austria; d. Julius and Sidoni (Brauch) Stein; Social Service course Brit. Council, London, 1943-44; B.A., Roosevelt U., 1954; M.A., U. Chgo., 1956; cert. Chgo. Inst. Psychoanalysis, 1963; m. Erwin P. Pollitt, Jan. 13, 1951 (dec. Aug. 1977). Resident social worker Anna Freud Residential Nursery Sch., Essex, Eng., 1944-45; dep. dir. UN, U.S. Zone, Germany, 1945-48; psychiat. social worker Jewish Children's Bur., Chgo., 1955-63; pvt. practice as psychotherapist and/or clin. social worker, Glencoe, Ill., 1961—; cons. Winnetka Community Nursery Sch., 1962-63, North Shore Congregation Israel Nursery Sch., 1966-69, Oakwood Home for Aged, Highland Park High Sch., 1979-80; instr. Chgo. Inst. for Psychoanalysis, 1982. Bd. dirs. Glencoe Youth Service, Menninger Found. Fellow Am. Orthopsychiat. Assn.; mem. Nat. Assn. Social Workers (chmn. pvt. practice com. 1965-70), Ill. Soc. Clin. Social

Workers (dir.), Acad. Cert. Social Workers, Nat. Registry Health Care Providers in Clin. Social Work. Author articles in field. Home and office: 481 Oakdale Ave Glencoe IL 60022

POLLNER, MILDRED BRENNER, film co. exec., educator, psychotherapist; b. N.Y.C., Apr. 6, 1936; d. Harry and Sarah (Bronshuag) Brenner; B.A. cum laude, CCNY, 1957; M.A., Columbia U., 1961, M.Ed., 1973, Ed.D., 1976. Asst. prof. Queens Coll., Flushing, N.Y., 1974-76; psychologist Psychol. Consultation Center, N.Y.C., 1974-76; mem. faculty Miami Dade Community Coll., Miami, Fla., 1976-80, asst. prof. films, psychology, 1976-80; asst. prof. Hunter Coll., 1981—; pres. Cinema Verite, Inc., N.Y.C., 1980—. Bd. dirs. Dance Found., Inc., Ocean Beach Arts Council; juror Am. Film Festival, 1982; mem. Narcotics Guidance Council; mem. Ocean Beach Arts Council. Recipient Gardner Murphy award for outstanding achievement in psychology CCNY, 1957. Mem. Am. Psychol. Assn., N.Y. Soc. Clin. Psychology, Am. Soc. Group Psychotherapists and Psychodramatists, Women in Cable, Edn. Film Library Assn., Am. Humanistic Psychologists, White House Council on Women, Nat. Council Family Relations, CCNY Alumni Assn. (dir.). Producer/dir. Merry X-mas, 1978, Single Parent, 1980, You Can Be, 1980; producer Hispanic and American Women: Adapting to Change, 1980, Women Today: CCEW Cares, 1980. Contbr. articles to profl. publs. Address: 444 E 86th St Apt 21J New York NY 10028

POLLOCK, BEVERLY KING, pub. relations exec., columnist; b. Bessemer, Ala., Jan. 14, 1924; d. Louis and Ella (Baum) King; student Agnes Scott Coll., 1941-43; U. Pitts., 1957; m. Melvin Martin Pollock, May 18, 1944; children—Lawrence Allan, Susan Lynn Pollock Stein, Sally King Pollock Bedrick, Robert Harris. Co-writer, performer Those Two, WPSL, Monroeville, Pa., 1967; columnist Slightly Irreverent, Times Express, Monroeville, 1967—; columnist Quoth the Maven, Am. Jewish press, 1967—; dir. pub. relations United Jewish Fedn. Greater Pitts., 1971—. Recipient Pub. Relations awards Nat. Council Jewish Fedns., 1973, 74, 75, 78, 81, 82; United Way Pub. Relations Thank You award of excellence, 1976. Mem. Women in Communications, Am. Jewish Pub. Relations Soc. Democrat. Jewish. Co-author: Will the Real Economy Size Package Please Stand Up?, 1966. Home: 1898 Brushcliff Rd Pittsburgh PA 15221 Office: 234 McKee Pl Pittsburgh PA 15213

POLLOCK, LOUISE, fin. planner; b. Pitts., Apr. 2, 1919; d. Walter Edward and Anna Katherine (Schoenberger) Brickman; student U. Tex., 1936-37; grad. Coll. Fin. Planning, 1975-77; m. Robert Thomas Pollock, Mar. 10, 1968 (dec.); children by previous marriages, John W. Carlisle, Jr., Noel Griffin, Carol Klippenstein. Branch mgr. Fort Worth (Tex.) Savs. and Loan Assn., 1954-63, Trevost Savs. & Loan Assn., Phila., 1963-68; estate planning specialist Ralph S. Wilford Co., La Mesa, Calif., 1970-77; pres., cert. fin. planner Pvt. Ledger Fin. Services, Inc., San Diego, 1977—; instr. diversified investments div. adult edn. San Diego Community Coll. Mem. Internat. Assn. Fin. Planners, Inst. Cert. Fin. Planners, Nat. Alumni Assn. Coll. of Fin. Planning., Women's Service, Bus. and Profl. Clubs of San Diego (life mem. pres.'s council), Women in Bus. Coll. of the Emeriti (former pres. aux. council). Republican. Swedenborgian. Club: Altrusa (chpt pres.). Home: 9815 Rimpark Way San Diego CA 92124 Office: 2515 Camino del Rio S Suite 204 San Diego CA 92108

POLOVY, MARIAN, lawyer; b. N.Y.C., May 8, 1952; d. Nicholas and Mary (Maksymorch) Polovy; B.A. in English (scholar), Marymount Coll., 1974; J.D., Southwestern U., 1979. U.S. Senate intern, Senator James Buckley, Washington, 1974; admitted to N.Y. State bar, 1980; atty. U.S. Dept. Energy, N.Y.C., 1979-80; asso. firm Martin, Clearwater & Bell, N.Y.C., 1980-81, firm Evans, Orr, Pacelli, Norton & Laffan, N.Y.C., 1981—. Farmer's Ins. Group scholar, 1975; Mabel Wilson Richards scholar, 1978. Mem. N.Y. State Bar Assn., N.Y. Trial Lawyers Assn., N.Y. State Women's Bar Assn., Met. Women's Bar Assn., Internat. Union Advocats, N.Y. County Bar Assn., Cath. Lawyers Guild (fin. sec. 1980—). Mem. Law Rev.; contbr. articles to profl. jours. Home: 2017 Coleman St Brooklyn NY 11234 Office: 15 Park Row New York NY 10038

POLSKY, CYNTHIA HAZEN, artist, art adminstr., publisher; b. N.Y.C., Feb. 28, 1939; d. Joseph and Lita Hazen; student Art Students League and New Sch. Social Research, 1957-60; B.A. in Psychology cum laude, Marymount Manhattan Coll., 1977; M.B.A., Fordham U., 1981; m. Leon B. Polsky, Apr. 19, 1957; children—Alexander M., Nicholas W. Works exhibited in mus. Los Angeles, Houston, East Hampton, N.Y., St. Mary's City, Md., Wichita, Kans., and N.Y.C., 1968-77; represented in public collections: Corcoran Mus., Washington, Herbert F. Johnson Mus., Cornell U., Allentown (Pa.) Mus. Art, Fogg Mus., Cambridge, Mass., Guild Hall, East Hampton, Rockefeller U., 1st Woman's Bank N.Y., Storm King Art Center, Mountainville, N.Y., Israel Mus., Jerusalem; pres. Octagon Communications Internat., N.Y.C.; mem. adv. com. Columbia U.; v.p., trustee Storm King Art Center. Mem. community adv. bd. Sta. WNYC; mem. Far Eastern adv. com. Israel Mus.

POLVAY, JEANNE DONOGHUE, modeling co. exec.; b. Stamford, Conn., May 9, 1941; d. George Edward and Irene Rene (Albert) Donoghue; student Marymount Jr. Coll., 1959, U. Conn., 1972; m. Jerome I. Polvay, July 19, 1981; children by previous marriage—George Gregory, Timothy Joseph. With Conn. Modeling Agy., Stamford, 1960-65; partner Charming Way Boutique, Stamford, 1965-68; tchr. YWCA, Stamford, 1965-73; regional mgr. Community Ambassador, Ridgefield, Conn., 1973-74; instr., dir. admissions Barbizon Schs., Stamford, 1973-75, pres., 1975—, also pres. Barbizon Sch. of Westchester, White Plains, N.Y. Mem. citizens cons. com. J.M. Wright Tech. Sch., Stamford, 1978—. Mem. Better Bus. Bur. (dir. 1979-80). Republican. Roman Catholic. Clubs: Westchester Country, Landmark. Home: 316 Talmadge Hill Rd New Canaan CT 06840 Office: 26 6th St Stamford CT 06905 also 190 E Post Rd White Plains NY 10601

POLVAY, MARINA SCHERBATOFF, food consultant; b. Krasnojars, USSR, July 24, 1928; came to U.S., 1952, naturalized, 1955; d. Konstantine Scherbatoff and Eugenia Szenutovits-Berezsni; B.S., Innsbruck (Austria) U., 1949; m. Murray Polvay, Feb. 26, 1960. Exec. v.p. Slenderella Internat., 1952-60; owner Marina Polvay Assos. Inc., food cons. and public relations, North Miami, Fla., 1968—; author for mags., cookbooks, 1962—; host radio and TV talk shows. Past pres. Miami Ballet Soc., Theatre Arts League, Pearl S Buck Found. Mem. Sommelier Guild, Confrerie de la Chaine des Rotisseurs. Writers Guild and League, Writers Club, Fashion Group, Internat. Assn. Cooking Schs. Republican. Mem. Russian Orthodox Ch. Author: Marina Polvay's Best International Recipies, 1972; Florida Heritage Cookbook, 1976; The Dracula Cookbook, 1978; All Along the Danube, 1979; The Energy Saver's Cookbook, 1980; Slimming and Healthy Cooking of Italy, 1981. Home: 9250 NE 10th Ct Miami Shores FL 33138 Office: 1991 NE 135th St North Miami FL 33181

POLVOGT, ALENE, accountant; b. Dallas, Oct. 5, 1923; d. Carl W. and Bennie (Lowry) P.; B.B.A., So. Meth. U., 1976. Pvt. practice acctg., Dallas, 1974—; mem. faculty U. Tex., Dallas, 1980—. Mem. Am. Inst. C.P.A.s, Tex. Soc. C.P.A.s, Petroleum Accts. Soc. Dallas. Republican. Presbyterian. Office: 2925 LBJ Suite 180 Dallas TX 75234

POLZIN, CONSTANCE ELEANOR MCGREGOR, photojournalist; b. Sault Ste. Marie, Ont., Can., Nov. 6, 1923; came to U.S., 1924, naturalized, 1944; d. Neil Garfield and Mildred (Gibson) McGregor; student public schs., Ishpeming, Mich.; m. Wilmer C. Polzin, Jan. 28, 1947 (div. Nov. 1971); children—Jeff, Cheryl, Lori Beth. Sec.-receptionist Fox Lake (Wis.) Med. Center, 1962-63; sec. John Deere Horicon Works (Wis.), 1963-65; part-time corr. Fond du Lac (Wis.) Reporter, 1962-65, area reporter-photographer, 1965-70; area editor, reporter-photographer Daily Citizen, Beaver Dam, Wis., 1970—. Served with WAVES, 1944-47. Recipient Outstanding Service award Assn. Retarded Citizens in Wis., 1978. Mem. Nat. Fedn. Press Women (1st pl. award, writing contest 1975, 78), Wis. Press Women winner ann. writing contest 1976-79, 81, treas.), Am. Legion, Horicon Hist. Soc., Horicon Jaycettes (hon. life mem.), Horicon C. of C., Mayville C. of C., Juneau C. of C. Home: 316 Rose Ct Horicon WI 53032 Office: Daily Citizen 805 Park Ave Beaver Dam WI 53916

POND, NANCY MCCEARTNEY, social worker; b. Memphis, Dec. 14, 1946; d. John Alden and Nancy (Wood) P.; B.A. in Anthropology, Southwestern at Memphis, 1968; M.S.W., U. Md., 1974. Welfare worker Tenn. Dept. Pub. Welfare, Shelby County, 1969-71; prevention specialist Md. Dept. Juvenile Services, 1972; social worker Md. Dept. Employment and Social Services, Prince George's County, 1974-76; social worker VA Hosp. Memphis, 1976-79, VA Hosp. D.C., 1979—. Mem. adv. com. Montgomery County Long Term Care Ombudsman Program, 1981-82; Montgomery county del. Md. Gov.'s Conf. on Aging, 1980. Bd. dirs. Memphis-Shelby County br. LWV, 1978, 79, mem. state bd., 1979; mem. state bd. Tenn. chpt. Nat. Women's Polit. Caucus, 1978-79, nat. rep. to agenda com. meeting Democratic Nat. Com., 1978, also Memphis Area coordinator ERA fundraiser, 1978; mem. regional steering com. Tenn. Conf. Social Welfare, 1978, 79, regional legis. com., 1978, 79, mem. state legis. com., 1979; mem. Memphis Dist. 5 Ad Hoc Com. for Better Schs., 1979 chairperson platform com.; mem. Mayor's Youth Guidance Commn., 1979, chairperson legis. com.; state conv. del. Tenn. Young Democrats, 1979; county central com. monitor Montgomery County chpt. Alliance for Dem. Reform, 1980, 81; state conv. alt. Md. Young Dems., 1981, 82; co-chairperson social com. Grosvenor Park III Condominium Devel., 1980-81. Mem. Acad. Cert. Social Workers, Nat. Assn. Social Workers (chairperson Memphis Area br. social action com. 1978-79; chairperson social issues subcom. of legis. com. D.C. chpt. 1980-82; chairperson Md. del. Nat. Social Wokers in Politics Conf. 1980; county exec.'s rep. to Montgomery County Health Systems Planning Bd. 1982—). Home: 10401 Grosvenor Pl #1528 Rockvile MD 20852

POND, PHYLLIS JOAN, state legislator; b. Warren, Ind., Oct. 25, 1930; d. Clifford E. and Rosa E. (Hunnicutt) Ruble; B.S., Ball State U., Muncie, Ind., 1951; M.S., Ind. U., 1963; m. George W. Pond, June 10, 1951; children—William, Douglas, Jean Ann. Tchr. home econs., 1951-54; kindergarten tchr., 1961—; mem. Ind. Ho. of Reps. from 15th Dist., 1978—, majority asst. caucus chmn. Del. Ind. Republican Conv., 1976, 80; alt. del. Rep. Nat. Conv., 1980. Mem. NEA, Ind. Tchrs. Assn., AAUW. Lutheran. Club: New Haven Woman's.

PONDER, CATHERINE, clergywoman; b. Hartsville, S.C., Feb. 14, 1927; d. Roy Charles and Kathleen (Parrish) Cook; student U. N.C. Extension, 1946, Worth Bus. Coll., 1948; B.S. in Edn., Unity Ministerial Sch., 1956; D.D. (hon.), Assn. Unity Chs., 1976; m. Robert Stearns, June 19, 1970; 1 son by previous marriage, Richard. Ordained to ministry Unity Sch. Christianity, 1958; minister Unity Ch., Birmingham, Ala., 1956-61; founder, minister Unity Ch., Austin, Tex., 1961-69, San Antonio, 1969-73, Palm Desert, Calif., 1973—. Mem. Assn. Unity Chs., Inc., Internat. New Thought Alliance, Internat. Platform Assn. Clubs: Bermuda Dunes Country, Racquet (Palm Springs, Calif.); Los Angeles. Author: The Dynamic Laws of Prosperity, 1962; The Prosperity Secret of the Ages, 1964; The Dynamic Laws of Healing, 1966; The Healing Secret of the Ages, 1967; Pray and Grow Rich, 1968; The Millionaires of Genesis, 1976; The Millionaire Moses, 1977; The Millionaire Joshua, 1978; The Millionaire from Nazareth, 1979; Secret of Unlimited Prosperity, 1980. Office: 73-669 Hwy 111 Palm Desert CA 92260

PONDER, MARIAN RUTH, educator; b. Waterloo, Iowa, July 12, 1932; d. Lee Roland and Leone Hyacinth (Holdiman) Rigdon; B.A. (Purple and Gold math. scholar), U. No. Iowa, 1952; M.S.E., Drake U., 1960; postgrad. U. Wis., 1961-62, San Diego State U., 1980-81, Carleton Coll., 1980-81, U. No. Ia., 1961-66, Drake U., 1971-75; m. Joseph Glen Ponder, June 28, 1953; children—Dwight Lee, David Glen, Dean Joseph. Tchr. math., sci. Anamosa, Iowa, 1952-53, Monroe, Iowa, 1953-56, Newton, Iowa, 1956-64, 66—, head dept. math. Newton Schs., 1978—. Ch. treas. Community Heights Alliance Ch., 1980-82, Sunday sch. secretariat, 1966-82. Maytag scholar, 1960; Maytag Corp. grantee, 1962; Delta Kappa Gamma scholar, 1960, 81. Mem. Nat. Council Tchrs. Math., NEA, Iowa Edn. Assn., Newton Community Edn. Assn., Iowa Council Tchrs. Math., Jasper County Hist. Soc., Delta Kappa Gamma (state treas. 1978—), Kappa Mu Epsilon, Kappa Delta Pi, Lambda Delta Lambda. Republican. Mem. Christian and Missionary Alliance Ch. Home: 620 E 17 St N Newton IA 50208 Office: E 4th St S Newton IA 50208

PONTIUS, GERALDINE CAROL, architect; b. Greensburg, Pa., Jan. 24, 1947; d. Paul Edward and Doris (Hesselmeyer) Pontius; A.B., Barnard Coll., 1968; M.Arch, Columbia U., 1974. Architect, Urban Deadline Architects, N.Y.C., 1976-77, I. M.Pei and Partners, architects and planners, N.Y.C., 1977-82, Kohn, Pedersen, Fox, Assos., P.C., Architects, N.Y.C., 1982—; vis. faculty Columbia U., summers 1981, 82; faculty Parsons Sch. Design, 1980—; visual artist, 1964—; numerous N.Y.C. exhbns., 1964—. Lic. architect, N.Y. State. Studio: 30 W 26th St New York NY 10010 Office: 111 W 57th St 16th Fl New York NY 10019

POOL, MARY JANE, design and mktg. cons., mag. and book editor; d. Earl Lee and Dorothy (Matthews) Pool Evans; grad. St. de Chantal Acad., 1942; B.A. with honors in Art, Drury Coll., 1946. Staff, Vogue Mag., N.Y.C., 1946-68, asso. merchandising editor, 1948-57, promotion dir., 1958-66, exec. editor, 1966-68; editor, House & Garden mag., 1969, editor-in-chief, 1970-80; design and mktg. cons., 1980—. Mem. com. of friends of environ. design collections Cooper-Hewitt Mus. of Smithsonian Inst.; mem. industry adv. council, interior design dept. Fashion Inst. Tech.; past bd. govs. Fashion Group, Inc., N.Y.C. 1966—; trustee Drury Coll., 1971—; bd. dirs. Isabel O'Neil Found., 1978—; bd. govs. Decorative Arts Trust. Recipient Vogue Prix de Paris, 1946; Drury Disting. Alumni award, 1961; Nat. Soc. Interior Designers award. Mem. Am. Soc. Mag. Editors (bus. com.), Decorative Arts Soc., Women's Forum, N.Y. Zool. Soc. Editor: Billy Baldwin Decorates; House and Garden's 26 Easy Little Gardens; 20th Century Decorating; Architecture. Address: One Sutton Place S New York NY 10022

POOLE, DORIS THEODORE, educator; b. Greenville, S.C., Mar. 9, 1923; d. James V. and Florence Gertrude (Bell) Theodore; B.S., Winthrop Coll., 1944; postgrad. U. Ga., 1946-48; Ph.D., U. N.C., 1962; children—Lucinda Poole de Cabrejas, Sarah Poole Jordan. Chemist, Standard Oil Devel. Co., Bayway, N.J., 1944-46; assoc. prof. Madison Coll., Harrisonburg, Va., 1958-59; instr. to assoc. prof. pharmacology U. N.C. Sch. Medicine, Chapel Hill, 1962—. Mem. Am. Soc. Pharmacology and Exptl. Therapeutics, Soc. for Exptl. Biology and Medicine, AAUP, Sigma Xi. Lutheran. Contbr. articles to profl. jours. Home: Route 4 PO Box 414B Chapel Hill NC 27514 Office: Dept Pharmacology U NC Sch Medicine Chapel Hill NC 27514

POOLE, GERTRUDE MARGARET, investment acctg. exec.; b. N.Y.C., Oct. 26, 1939; d. Robert John and Gertrude Amelia (Toulman) P.; B.B.A., Pace U., 1974; M.B.A., Rutgers U., 1982. Mgr. mdse. acctg. Reader's Digest, N.Y.C., 1965-74; staff acct. Coopers & Lybrand, N.Y.C., 1974-75; sr. acct. SS&O C.P.A.s, Perth Amboy, N.J., 1975-77; tax and internal audit sr. Church & Dwight, Piscataway, N.J., 1977-78; chief acctg. and control div. Fed. Res. Employee Benefits System, N.Y.C., 1978—. C.P.A., N.Y. Mem. NOW (chmn. speaker's bur. Monmouth chpt. 1974-75), Am. Inst. C.P.A.s, Nat. Assn. Female Execs., LINK, Am. Soc. Women Accts. Roman Catholic. Home: 106 Manor Dr Red Bank NJ 07701 Office: Fed Res Employee Benefits System 33 Library St New York NY 10045

POOLE, RACHEL IRENE, coll. adminstr.; b. Uniontown, Pa., Dec. 2, 1924; d. John Jasper and Central A. (Moon) Johnson; B.S. in Nursing, U. Pitts., 1947, M.Letters, 1952, Ph.D., 1977; m. Marion L. Poole, Aug. 4, 1951; children—Andrea Lynell, Adriene Charisse. Staff nurse Western State Psychiat. Inst. and Clinic, Pitts., 1948-49, asst. head nurse, 1949-50, head nurse, 1951-53, asst. dir. nursing service, 1953-54, 56-63, dir. nursing, 1964-67, dir. nursing service, 1967-72; asso. prof. and asso. chmn. Mental Health Nursing Sch. Nursing, U. Pitts., 1967-72, asso. prof., 1972-73, lectr. Inst. for Higher Edn., Sch. Edn., 1974-77; adminstrv. asst. to pres. Community Coll. Allegheny County, Pitts., 1977-79, asst. dean life scis., 1979—; cons. to Southwestern Pa. Higher Edn. Council, 1974-77. Vice pres. Homewood Brushton Community Action Program, 1968-71; organizer and treas. Black Women's Forum, 1969-71. Mem. Am. Nurses Assn., Nat. League for Nursing, Am. Assn. Higher Edn. Democrat. Contbr. articles on nursing edn. to profl. publs. Home: 137 Kilmer St Pittsburgh PA 15221 Office: 808 Ridge Ave Pittsburgh PA 15212

POOR, ANNE, painter; b. N.Y.C., Jan. 2, 1918; d. Henry Varnum and Bessie (Breuer) P.; student Bennington Coll., 1936, 38, Art Students League, 1935. Works exhibited Am. Brit. Art Center, 1944, 45, 48, Maynard Walker Gallery, 1950, Graham Gallery, 1957-59, 62, 68-71; executed murals P.O., Gleason, Tenn., DePew, N.Y.; South Solon (Maine) Free Meeting House, 1957, others; represented permanent collections Whitney Mus., Bklyn. Mus., Wichita Mus., Art Inst. Chgo.; mem. faculty Skowhegan Sch. Painting and Sculpture, 1947-61. Artist corr. WAC, 1943-45. Edwin Austin Abbey Meml. fellow, 1948; grantee Nat. Inst. Arts and Letters, 1957; recipient Benjamin Altman 1st prize landscape painting N.A.D., 1971. Mem. Artists Equity Assn. Illustrator: Greece, 1964. Home: 92 S Mountain Rd New York NY 10956 Office: Graham Gallery 1014 Madison Ave New York City NY 10021

POORE, PATRICIA JOSEPHINE, psychologist, retirement planning cons., educator; b. Jersey City, Jan. 10, 1939; d. Joseph O. and Josephine (Kujalowicz) P.; A.B., Cath. U. Am., 1960; M.A., Fairleigh Dickinson U., 1963, postgrad. Monclair State Coll., 1963-68; m. Jack Cameron McLachlan, Dec. 26, 1972. Personnel asst. Sterns Allied Corp., Paramus, N.J., 1960-61; elementary tchr. Mt. Carmel Sch., Ridgewood, N.J., 1961-62; biology instr., counselor Immaculate Heart Acad., Washington Twp., N.J., 1962-63, dir. guidance, 1963-81; retirement planning cons./asso. Michael Fitzpatrick Assos., Fairfield, N.J., 1981—; psychology instr. Fairleigh Dickinson U., Teaneck, N.J., 1964-67; guest lectr. career edn. William Paterson Coll., Wayne, N.J.; engaged in therapy with teenage narcotics addicts Msgr. Wall Social Service Center, Hackensack, N.J., 1970-71, Valley Center, Ridgewood, N.J., 1972-74; mem. Middle States Evaluation Com., Summit, N.J., 1972, Union City, N.J., 1973; mem. Archdiocese Newark Guidance Council. Lic. Nat. Assn. Security Dealers. Mem. Nat. Vocat. Guidance Assn., Am., N.J. personnel and guidance assns., Assn. for Counselor Edn. and Supervision, Am. Sch. Counselors Assn., Assn. for Measurement and Evaluation in Guidance, N.J. Assn. for Measurement and Evaluation in Guidance, Am., Eastern, N.J. (mem. com. on edn. and standards 1969) psychol. assns., Am. Coll. Personnel Assn., Bergen County Cath., Bergen County (mem. exec. council 1969-70) guidance assns., Dirs. of Guidance of Bergen County, N.J. Mental Health Assn., Cath. U., Fairleigh Dickinson U. alumni assns., Nat. Assn. Life Underwriters, Psi Chi (pres. 1964), Theta Phi Alpha. Home: 15 Partridge Trail Kinnelon NJ 07405 Office: 264 Passaic Ave Fairfield NJ 07006

POPE, ANNEMARIE HENLE, found. adminstr.; b. Dortmund, Germany; came to U.S., 1933; d. Adolf and Tine (Lang) Henle; Ph.D., Heidelberg U., 1932; portgrad. Radcliffe Coll., 1933-34; m. John Alexander Pope, Dec. 10, 1947. Asst. dir. Portland (Oreg.) Art Mus., 1941-42; asst. dir. in charge exhbns. Am. Fedn. Arts, Washington, 1947-51; chief Traveling Exhbns. Service, Smithsonian Instn., Washington, 1951-64; pres. Internat. Exhbns. Found., Washington, 1965—; mem. fine arts adv. panels FRS, Washington and Richmond, Va. Mem. Va. Mus. Fine Arts.; China Trade Mus., Mus. Modern Art, Friends of Kennedy Center, Am. Ballet Theatre. Decorated Order of Merit (W.Ger.); Royal Swedish Order of Polar Star; St. Olaf's medal (Norway); Order of Dannebrog (Denmark); Knight Order of Merit (Italy); Order of Merit 1st class (W.Ger.); chevalier l'Ordre des Arts et des Lettres; officer Order Brit. Empire; Dorothy Whitney Elmhurst travelling fellow, 1934-35. Fellow Frick Collection; mem. Am. Assn. Mus. (trustees com.), Nat. Trust for Historic Preservation, Am. Mus. in Britain (council and chmn. Washington Friends), Master Drawings Assn., Drawing Soc. (nat. council), Asia Soc., Japan Soc., Washington Performing Arts Soc., Chamber Music Soc. of Lincoln Center, Am. Film Inst., Soc. Woman Geographers, Assn. Friends of Mus. Modern Art of Latin Am. (dir.), Victorian Soc. Clubs: Cosmopolitan (N.Y.C.), Radcliffe, 1925 F St (Washington). Home: Shoreham W 617 2700 Calvert St NW Washington DC 20008 Office: Internat Exhibitions Found 1729 H St NW Suite 310 Washington DC 20006

POPE, BARBARA ANN, social worker; b. Raleigh, N.C., Nov. 27, 1926; d. David H. and Sadie (Woodard) P.; grad. St. Mary's Jr. Coll., 1947; B.A. in Sociology, U. N.C., 1949; M.S.W., Coll. of William and Mary, 1953; cert. Harvard Med. Sch., 1968. Caseworker, Edgecomb County (N.C.) Dept. Public Welfare, 1950-51; psychiat. social worker Meml. Guidance Center, Richmond, Va., 1953-55, VA Hosp., Salem, Va., 1955-59; clin. social worker VA Hosp., Houston, 1959-60; personnel cons. The Houston Club, 1960; chief psychiat. social worker Lynchburg (Va.) Guidance Center, 1960-63; field work supr. Richmond (Va.) Sch. of Social Work, 1961-63; instr. psychiat. social work Duke U. Med. Center, Durham, N.C., 1963-67; mental health cons. Fiske Elem. Sch., Wellesley, Mass., 1967-68; pvt. practice social work Duke U. Med. Center, 1964-67, Columbia, S.C., 1978-80, Raleigh, N.C., 1980—; cons. to various ednl. and social work orgns., 1955—; asso. prof. social work U. S.C., Columbia, 1968-80; field reader specialist Bur. of Edn. for the Handicapped, Office Edn., HEW, Washington, 1971-72; teaching cons. Family Service Center, Columbia, 1969. Mem. profl. standards com. Va. Council on Social Welfare, 1956-58, 61-62; mem. devel. com. Lynchburg Comprehensive Community After-Care Program, 1961-63; bd. dirs. Method Day Care Center, Raleigh, N.C., 1981—, chmn. fund raising com.; mem. choir Ch. of Good Shepherd, Raleigh, 1980—. Recipient Outstanding Teaching award S.C. Dept. Social Services, 1972; Ten Year Cert. of Service, State of S.C., 1979. Mem. Nat. Assn. Social Workers, Acad. Cert. Social Workers, Council on Social Work Edn., S.C. Mental Health Assn., AAUW (dir. Lynchburg chpt. 1961-62), N.C. Soc. for Clin. Social Work, Alumni Assn. of Richmond Sch. Social Work (treas. 1953-55), Phi Delta Kappa. Episcopalian. Club: Faculty (U. S.C.). Home: B-3 Raleigh Apts Raleigh NC 27605 Office: Suite 3-B 20 Enterprise St Raleigh NC 27607

POPE, DONNA, govt. ofcl.; b. Cleve., Oct. 15, 1931; d. John Emil and Marie Josephine (Thiel) Kolnik; m. Raymond Pope, Oct. 21, 1950; children—Candace Wooley, Cheryl Ann. Supr. election ofcls. dept. Bd. Elections, Cuyahoga County Bd. Edn., Cleve., 1965-68; mem. Ohio Ho. of Reps., 1972-81, minority whip, 1979-80; dir. U.S. Mint, Washington, 1981—. Vice-chmn. Cuyahoga County Republican Exec. Com. Named Outstanding Woman Legislator, Rutgers U. Inst. Politics, 1972. Mem. Bus. and Profl. Women's Orgn. Roman Catholic. Home: 1101 S Arlington Ridge Rd Arlington VA 22202 Office: 501 13th St NW Room 1010 Washington DC 20220

POPE, KATHLEEN GILLIS, ins. co. exec.; b. Boston, Apr. 27, 1950; d. Joseph Leo and Eileen (Fleming) G.; A.B., Trinity Coll., 1971; postgrad. Boston U., 1972-74; C.P.C.U., U. Conn., 1980. Claims adjuster CG/Aetna Ins. Co., Boston, 1971-72, fire underwriter, 1972-73, comml. fire underwriter, 1973-74, package underwriter, 1974-75; reins. underwriter Gen. Reins. Corp., Hartford, Conn., 1975-77, asst. sec., underwriter, 1977-79, asst. v.p., underwriter, 1979—; speaker in field. Bd. mgrs. YMCA Hartford, 1978—. Mem. Nat. Assn. Ins. Women, Boiler and Machinery Assn., Mut. Underwriters New Eng. Roman Catholic. Home: 6 Diamond Glen Rd Farmington CT 06032 Office: One Financial Plaza Hartford CT 06103

POPE, MARGO COX, newspaperwoman; b. St. Augustine, Fla., Feb. 23, 1947; d. J. Edward and Angela (Mallion) Cox; B.S. in Journalism, U. Fla., Gainesville, 1970; m. Alyn E. Pope, Nov. 27, 1971; 1 son, Edward Neil. Edn. reporter Fla. Times Union, Jacksonville, 1970—. Mem. Cathedral Madrigal Singers, 1980—. Journalism fellow Nat. Inst. Edn.-Inst. Ednl. Leadership, 1979. Mem. Sigma Delta Chi (pres. Greater Jacksonville chpt. 1976-77, nat. chmn. profl. devel. com. 1977-78). Roman Catholic. Clubs: St. Augustine (Fla.) Jr. Women's; U. Fla. Alumni (v.p. 1977) (Jacksonville). Office: Times-Union PO Box 1949-F Jacksonville FL 32231

POPE, SHARON KAY, ednl. adminstr.; b. Kansas City, Mo., Dec. 27, 1944; d. Allen David and Mildred M. (Wilcox) Pope; B.S., U. Mo., 1966, M.Ed., 1967, Ph.D. (Edn. Profession Devel. Act fellow), 1971; m. Robert Callis, Sept. 4, 1971. Adminstrv. asst. Dean Students Office, U. Mo., Columbia, 1967-68, asst. dir. student affairs women, 1968-69, counseling psychologist, asst., prof. edn., 1970-73, coordinator extended services, 1973-74, asst. dir. Center for Student Life, 1974—; mem. staff Edn. Professions Devel. Act Inst., Columbia, 1969-70. Lic. psychologist. Mem. Am. (chmn. Commn. 4 1974-76), Mo. (membership chmn. 1975, pres. 1977-78, Award of Merit 1979) coll. personnel assns., U. Mo. Columbia Edn. Alumni Assn. (dir. 1968-74, chmn. membership 1969-70), Mortar Bd., Delta Gamma. Home: Route 4 Box 205 Columbia MO 65201 Office: 106 Read Hall Univeristy of Missouri Columbia Columbia MO 65201

POPOFF, EDNA SPIELER, psychologist; b. N.Y.C., Jan. 17, 1924; d. Isidor and Rose Spieler; B.A., Hunter Coll., 1945; M.A., Columbia U., 1947; m. William Popoff, Apr. 12, 1946; children—Joshua Julian, Leslie Ellen. Psychologist, VA, Bklyn. Poly. Inst., Vocat. Guidance Center, Bklyn., 1946-48; tchr. emotionally handicapped children Bd. Edn., N.Y.C., 1960-68; sch. psychologist Bur. Child Guidance, N.Y.C., 1969—, dist. sch. psychologist, 1969-73, sch. psychologist with spl. edn. program for emotionally handicapped children, 1974—; cons. Assn. Advancement Blind and Retarded, Inc., Jamaica, N.Y.; resource and vocat. psychologist to reps. community agys. Mem. Am. Psychol. Assn., Nat. Assn. Sch. Psychologists, N.Y.C. Assn. Sch. Psychologists, Am. Jewish Congress. Club: B'nai B'rith. Home: 19 Brook Bridge Rd Great Neck NY 11021 Office: Bur Child Guidance 280 Broadway New York NY 10007

POPRICK, MARY ANN, psychologist; b. Chgo., June 25, 1939; d. Michael and Mary (Mihalcik) Poprick; B.A., De Paul U., 1960, M.A., 1964; Ph.D., Loyola U., Chgo., 1968. Intern psychology Elgin (Ill.) State Hosp., 1961-62; staff psychologist, 1962; staff psychologist Ill. State Tng. Sch. for Girls, Geneva, 1962-63, Mt. Sinai Hosp., Chgo., 1963-64; lectr. psychology Loyola U. at Chgo., 1964-67; asst. prof. Lewis U., Lockport, 1967-70, asso. prof., 1970-75, chmn. dept., 1968-72 (on leave 1972-73); postdoctoral intern in clin. psychology Ill. State Psychiat. Inst., Chgo., 1972-73; pvt. clin. practice David Psychiat. Clinic, Ltd., South Holland Ill., 1973—; asso. sci. staff Riveredge Hosp., Forest Park, Ill., 1975-76. Co-chmn. commn. on personal growth and devel. Congregation of 3d Order St. Francis of Mary Immaculate, Joliet, 1970-71. Mem. Am., Calif., Ill. (sec.-treas. acad. sect. 1975-77, mem. student devel. com. 1975-77, chmn. acad. sect. 1977-78, 78-79, mem. program com. 1977-78, sec. 1979-81, pres.-elect 1981-82, pres. 1982-83, chmn. program com. 1981-82), Midwestern psychol. assns., AAAS, Chgo. Assn. Psychoanalytical Psychology, Kappa Gamma Pi, Psi Chi (sec. 1964-65, pres. 1965-66). Home: 547 Marquette Ave Calumet City IL 60409 Office: 645 E 170th St South Holland IL 60473

POPULIS, POPPY PAULETTE LORRAINE, retail co. exec.; b. New Orleans, June 13, 1949; d. T.C. and Myrtle (Chapman) P.; B.A. in Dramatic Arts/Speech, Southeastern La. U., 1974. Dist. mgr. Worths Stores Corp., New Orleans; owner Pat Mydland, Hammond, La., part-time, 1973—. Founder, Children's Theatre Workshop, Inc.; mem. La. Diocese State happening com. Recipient S.E. Theatre award Southeastern La. U., 1974; Children's Theatre Workshop award, 1976. Mem. NOW, La. Council Music and Performing Arts, Southeastern La. U. Alumni Assn., Hammond Bus. and Profl. Women (pres. 1978-79), Hammond Young Career Woman, Hammond Arts Council, Arabian Horse Assn. La., Columbia Theatre Players. Democrat. Episcopalian. Home: PO Box 992 Hammond LA 70404

PORA, DOROTHY MARGARET, social worker; b. Elizabeth, N.J., June 13, 1953; d. Stanley Joseph and Dorothy Margaret (Koffer) P.; A.A. magna cum laude, Union Coll., Cranford, N.J., 1973; B.A. summa cum laude in Social Work, Kean Coll., 1975; M.S.W., N.Y. U., 1977. Intern in social work J.F.K. Med. Center, Edison, N.J., 1974-75, Kessler Inst. for Rehab., West Orange, N.J., 1975-76; intern in social work J.E. Runnells Hosp., Berkeley Heights, N.J., 1976-77, psychiat. social worker, 1978—. Cert. social worker, N.Y. State. Mem. Nat. Assn. Social Workers, Acad. Cert. Social Workers. Phi Theta Kappa, Lambda Alpha Sigma. Home: 15 Van Buren Ave Cranford NJ 07016 Office: J E Runnells Hosp Berkeley Heights NJ 07922

PORATH, PEARL MARIE BOWMAN, editor; b. Black River Falls, Wis., June 25, 1919; d. Fred J. and Hulda (Emerson) Bowman; student U. Wis., 1937-38, Eau Claire Vocat. Sch., 1939-40, U. Miami (Fla.), 1945-49; m. Herman Porath, Jan. 2, 1965. Buyer, Burdine's Book Dept., Miami, 1944-50; city editor Banner-Jour., Black River Falls, 1956-72; corr. to various newspapers in Wis. area, 1952—; sect. editor Wis. Regional News, 1972—. Alderman, Black River Falls City Council, 1974—; bd. dirs. Black River Meml. Hosp., 1974—, Black River Falls City Library, 1975-80. Home and office: PO Box 243 421 Pierce St Black River Falls WI 54615

PORGES, K(AREN) SHELLY, credit co. exec.; b. Tel Aviv, July 22, 1953; came to U.S., 1958, naturalized, 1963; d. Stefan Eliezer and Inge Yael (Winterfeld) P.; m. Ovidiu Pasternak; B.S. with honors, Cornell U., 1974, M.P.S. in Hotel Adminstrn. (Govt. fellow), 1977; Certificat de Mérite, Institut des Vins de France, 1975. Dir., Cornellcard, Ithaca, N.Y., 1974; mktg. mgr. Hotel Los Monteros, Marbella, Spain, 1975; internat. account exec. Marriott's Essex House, N.Y.C., 1976-77; mgr. service establishment mktg., card div. Am. Express Co., N.Y.C., 1977, mgr. strategic planning and analysis, 1977-79, Gold Card product mgr., 1979-80, dir. corp. strategy, 1980-82, dir. consumer card mktg., 1982—; guest lectr. in mktg. and strategic planning Cornell U. Vice pres. programming Hadassah, Women's Zionist Orgn. Am.; bd. dirs. Cityarts Workshop, Inc. Mem. Internat. Assn. Women in Hospitality Industry (founder, founding pres. 1977-78), Travel Research Assn., Fin. Women's Assn., Cornell Alumni Assn., Cornell Soc. Hotelmen, Hotel Sales Mgmt. Assn. Democrat. Jewish. Editor, writer Los Monteros Quar., 1975.

PORIETIS, LILITA INGRID, food co. exec.; b. Phila., Dec. 24, 1952; d. John and Ludmila Porietis; B.A., Ill. Wesleyan U., 1974; postgrad. U. Ill. Lab. technician, then supr. analytical services Pillsbury Co., Terre Haute, Ind., 1977, mgr. process control, 1981—. Mem. Alpha Gamma Delta. Address: 28 Monroe Blvd Terre Haute IN 47803

PORITSKY, SUSAN, psychiatrist; b. Phila., Apr. 2, 1950; d. Albert L. and Blanche E. (Schwartz) Poritsky; B.A. magna cum laude, U. Pa., 1971; M.D., Hahnemann Med. Coll., 1978. Intern, Pa. Hosp., 1978-79; resident in psychiatry, Inst. Pa. Hosp., Phila., 1979-82; psychology research asst. Am. Inst. Research, 1970; assoc. behavioral analyst The Boeing Co., 1971; employment counselor/employment interviewer Pa. Bur. Employment Security, 1971-74; emergency service psychiatrist N.W. Center Community Mental Health Center, 1979-80; med. staff Northwestern Inst. Psychiatry, 1980; emergency service psychiatrist West Phila. Community Mental Health Consortium, 1980; mgmt. physician Haverford State Hosp., 1980-82; med. staff Eagleville Hosp. and Rehab. Center, 1980-82; faculty U. Pa. Med. Sch., Phila., 1979—. NIMH med. student fellow, 1976; diplomate Nat. Bd. Med. Examiners. Mem. AMA, Am. Med. Women's Assn., Pa. Psychiat. Assn., Am. Psychiat. Assn., Phila. Psychiat. Soc., Del. Valley Group Psychotherapy Soc. Contbr. articles to profl. jours. Office: 111 N 49th St Philadelphia PA 19139

PORT, JANE SUSAN, library adminstr.; b. Bklyn., Sept. 12, 1949; d. Arthur Eugene and Gertrude (Blum) Young; B.A., Queens Coll., City U. N.Y., 1969; M.S.L.S., Columbia U., 1970; m. Mark List Gohen, June 20, 1982. Library assoc. Nat. Library of Medicine, Bethesda, Md., 1970-71; audiovisuals librarian Coll. Medicine and Dentistry N.J., Newark, 1971-75; assoc. librarian, assoc. dir. Gustave L. and Janet W. Levy Library, Mt. Sinai Med. Center, N.Y.C., 1975-79, library dir., 1980—. Mem. Health Scis. Communications Assn., Med. Library Assn., Assn. Acad. Health Scis. Library Dirs. Home: 345 E 93d St New York NY 10028 Office: Mount Sinai Med Center Levy Library Fifth Ave and 100th St New York NY 10029

PORTER, CLARA LOU, mgmt. cons.; b. Tonopah, Nev., Feb. 13, 1940; d. Ernest Clarence and Lois Gail (Titus) Hildebrand; student U. Nev., 1976-77, Clark County Community Coll., 1981—; m. Jimmy O'Neal Porter, Nov. 15, 1957 (div. 1979); children—James Douglas, John Barrett, Barbara Dianne, Robyn Louise, Jeffrey O'Neal. Machine bookkeeper First Nat. Bank, Las Vegas, 1957-58, 63-65; supr. machine bookkeepers Alaska Nat. Bank, Fairbanks, 1960-61; asst. dir. personnel So. Nev. Meml. Hosp., Las Vegas, 1966-77; bus. mgr. Emergency Assocs., Las Vegas, 1978-82; prin. C. Porter Med. Mgmt. Cons., Inc., Las Vegas, 1982—; dir. Exec. Suites of Am. Democrat. Baptist. Home: 127 Victory Rd Henderson NV 89015 Office: 3305 W Spring Mountain Rd Las Vegas NV 89102

PORTER, DIXIE LEE, corp. exec.; b. Bountiful, Utah, June 7, 1931; d. John Lloyd and Ida May (Robinson) Mathis; B.S., U. Calif., Berkeley, 1956, M.B.A., 1957. Personnel aide City of Berkeley, 1957-59; employment supr. Kaiser Health Found., Los Angeles, 1959-60; personnel analyst UCLA, 1961-63; personnel mgr. Reuben H. Donnelley, Santa Monica, Calif., 1963-64, Good Samaritan Hosp., San Jose, Calif., 1965-67; fgn. service officer AID, Saigon, Vietnam, 1967-71; gen. agt. Charter Security Life Ins. Co., Jacksonville, Fla., 1972-82; gen. agt. Kennesaw Life Ins. Co., Atlanta, 1978—, Phila. Life Ins. Co., Phila., 1978—; pres. Women's Ins. Enterprises, Ltd., San Jose, 1979—; cons. in field; dir. Samaritan Home Services, Aegis Health Corp. Family care co-chairperson Comprehensive Health Planning Commn. Santa Clara County, Calif., 1973-76; bd. dirs. U. Calif. Sch. Bus. Adminstrn., Berkeley, 1974-76; mem. Christian Children's Found.; mem. task force on equal access to econ. power U.S. Nat. Women's Agenda, 1977—. Served with USMC, 1950-52. C.L.U. Mem. C.L.U. Soc., U. Calif. Alumni Assn., U. Calif. Sch. Bus. Adminstrn. Alumni Assn., U. Calif. Campanile Assn., Life Ins. Underwriters Assn., AAUW, World Wildlife Fund, Prytanean Alumni, Beta Gamma Sigma. Republican. Episcopalian. Office: PO Box 64 Los Gatos CA 95031

PORTER, ELIZABETH HART, architect; b. Santa Barbara, Calif., June 27, 1938; d. Archibald Murdoch and Elizabeth (Lineberger) Hart; B.A., Radcliffe Coll., 1960; M.Arch., Harvard U., 1960; m. Laurence M. Porter (div.); children—Leon F., Sarah E. Draftsman, Robert Woods Kennedy, Architect, Cambridge, Mass., 1960-63; architect Holmes & Black, Lansing, Mich., 1964-69, 72-75, Lake States Assocs., Lansing, 1977-80, Jewell Downing, Balt., 1980-81, Mark Beck Assocs., Balt., 1981; chief architect, v.p. Upchurch, Davidson & Assocs., Mattoon, Ill., 1981—; mem. East Lansing (Mich.) Bldg. Bd. Appeals, 1976-80, Mich. Bd. Registration for Architects, 1977-80, Mich. Bd. Registration for Land Surveyors, 1979-80. Mem. AIA, Constn. Specifications Inst., Bus. and Profl. Women's Assn. Episcopalian. Home: 203 Harrison Ave Charleston IL 61920 Office: 1811 Broadway Mattoon IL 61938

PORTER, JUDITH DEBORAH REVITCH, sociologist, educator; b. Phila., Mar. 26, 1940; d. Eugene and Esther (Tulchinsky) Revitch; student Vassar Coll., 1958-60; B.A., Cornell U., 1962, M.A., 1963; Ph.D. (NSF fellow), Harvard U., 1967; m. Gerald Joseph Porter, June 26, 1960; children—Daniel, Rebecca, Michael. Lectr., Bryn Mawr (Pa.) Coll., 1966-67, asst. prof., 1967-73, asso. prof. sociology, 1973-79, prof., 1979—. Committeeperson, Haverford Twp. Democratic Party, 1976—. Ford Found. fellow, 1973-74. Mem. Am. Sociol. Assn., Soc. for Psychol. Study Social Issues, Phi Beta Kappa, Phi Kappa Phi. Jewish. Author: Black Child, White Child: The Development of Racial Attitudes, 1971. Contbr. articles to profl. jours. Home: 161 Whitemarsh Rd Ardmore PA 19003 Office: Dept Sociology Bryn Mawr Coll Bryn Mawr PA 19010

PORTER, KATHLEEN, social agy. exec.; b. Sulphur, Okla., Nov. 9, 1942; d. Arthur Phillip and Callie Louise (Hunter) Harris; student Okla. State U., 1960-62; B. Urban Affairs and Community Service magna cum laude, St. Louis U., 1976; m. Ronald Dean Porter, Nov. 11, 1961; children—Kevin, Kelly, Kristi. Adminstrv. asst. Citizens Edn. Task Force, 1977; asst. dir., 1977-78; dir. public relations Mo. Goodwill Industries, St. Louis, 1979—, also dir. community relations and collections; field faculty Coro Found. Co-founder Project BOLD, Inc., 1973-75; plan devel. and implementation com. Greater St. Louis Health Systems Agy., 1981—. Mem. Community Service Public Relations Council St. Louis. Home: 4450 Green Valley Dr Arnold MO 63010 Office: 4140 Forest Park Blvd Saint Louis MO 63108

PORTER, MAXIENE HELEN GREVE (MRS. DALE R. PORTER), civic worker; b. Los Angeles; d. Henry Chris and Meyerl (Dixon) Greve; student U. So. Calif., 1928; m. Wellington Denny Palmer, Nov. 18, 1929 (dec. Mar. 1933); children—Virginia Porter Stanhagen, Wellington Denny; m. 2d, Dale R. Porter, May 17, 1941. Accounting clk. Inglewood (Calif.) Sch. System, 1948-51; dep. tax collector City of San Luis Obispo (Calif.), 1963-65; acctg. clk. San Luis Obispo County Schs., 1965-66; asst. innkeeper Holiday Inn, Darien, Conn., 1967, Alexandria, Va.; innkeeper Holiday Inn, Falls Church, Va., 1973—; asst. gen. mgr. Darien Motor Lodge Assos.; sec.-asst. treas. Seven Fountains Corp.; tax cons. H & R Block, 1975-79, office mgr., 1976; acctg. and sales rep. Frankie Welch of Va. and Am., 1979-81. Officer, Native Daus. Golden West, 1953—, state pres., 1959-60; chmn. various coms. Calif. Fedn. Womens Clubs, 1960-63; v.p. Bus. and Profl. Women, 1936-37; sec. Inglewood Coordinating Council, 1945-47, pres., 1947-48; pres., various other offices West Ebell Club, Los Angeles, 1947, 60-63; mem. public relations com. YWCA, Fairfax County, Va., 1967-68, Fairfax Hosp. Aux., 1967-68, spl. pub. com. Smithsonian Assn., 1967-68; sec.-treas. Pinecrest Citizens Assn., 1968, v.p., 1974; chmn. finance com. Va. Commn. Status of Women, 1973-75; docent vol. chmn. Green Spring Farm Park, Fairfax County, 1979-80; treas. Greater Falls Church Republican Womens Club, 1968-70, v.p., 1973-74, pres., 1975-76; treas. Va. Fedn. Rep. Women, 1968—, parliamentarian, 1976-80; vice-chmn. Va. Nixon Inaugural Com., 1968-69; treas. Va. Women for Nixon, 1968; mem. Fairfax County Nixon for Pres. Com., co-chmn. Fairfax County Ladies for Lin—Gov.'s Campaign, 1969; mem. Fairfax County Rep. Com., 1968—, dist. chmn., 1974—, sec., 1975-76. Mem. Fairfax County C. of C. (legis., edn., polit. activities coms. 1973-74), Nat. Trust for Historic Preservation, Nat. Hist. Soc., Va., Metro (mem. program com., v.p. 1972-73) motel assns., Am. Mgmt. Assn., Fairfax Cultural Assn. (membership com. mem. 1969—). Clubs: Toastmistress (treas. No. Va. 1975, organizer, charter pres. Falls Church 1977-78, regional extension chmn. 1977-78, council treas. 1979-80, council sec. 1980-81, council v.p. 1981-82, council pres. 1982-83, editor council newsletter 1978-79), Annandale Women's, No. Va. Fedn. Women's (registration chmn. 1980, conservation and energy com., scholarship com. 1982-83). Lutheran. Home: PO Box 11464 Alexandria VA 22312

PORTER, NATALIE, clin. psychologist; b. Charlton, Mass., Dec. 14, 1948; d. Philip Edward Porter and Elia Frances (Santilli) Carver; B.A. in Psychology, Duke U., 1970; M.Ed., Glassboro State Coll., 1974; Ph.D. in Clin. Psychology, U. Del., 1981. Fellow in psychology, dept. of psychiatry Harvard Med. Sch., Boston, 1978-79; instr. U. Del., Newark, 1979-80, mem. exec. com. for women's studies, 1977-80, pres.' com. for status of women, 1976-78; asst. prof., dir. Psychol. Consultation Center, U. Nebr., Lincoln, 1980—, mem. exec. com. for women's studies, 1980—; cons. in field. Co-chmn. Citizens for Human Rights, Lincoln. Recipient Am. Psychol. Assn./Psi Chi award, 1979, pres.'s award for research, U. Del., 1980. Mem. Am. Psychol. Assn., Nebr. Psychol. Assn., Women in Sci. (sec. 1982—), Assn. for Women in Psychology, NOW. Condr. research; contbr. chpt. to book, articles to publs. in field. Office: 111 Burnett Univ Nebr Lincoln NE 68588

PORTER, S(YLVIA) F(IELD), writer; b. Patchogue, N.Y., June 18, 1913; d. Louis and Rose (Maisel) Feldman; B.A. magna cum laude, Hunter Coll., 1932; postgrad. Grad. Sch. Bus. Adminstrn., N.Y. U.; 14 hon. degrees; m. Reed R. Porter, 1931; m. 2d, Sumner Collins, 1943; m. 3d, James F. Fox, 1979. Founder weekly news letter Reporting on Govts.; asso. N.Y. Post, 1935-77; with Daily News as financial columnist writing syndicated daily newspaper column, also monthly column Ladies Home Jour. Mem. Phi Beta Kappa. Author: How to Make Money in Government Bonds; If War Comes to the American Home; Sylvia Porter's Annual Income Tax Guide; Sylvia Porter's Money Book; Sylvia Porter's New Money Book for the 1980's, 1979; co-author: How to Live Within Your Income; Managing Your Money. Home: 2 Fifth Ave New York NY 10011 Office: 1271 Ave of Americas New York NY 10020

PORTNER, DOREEN LINDSAY, social worker, educator; b. Oakland, Calif., Apr. 6, 1929; d. Marian Lavon and Elfrieda (Cooper) Lindsay; B.A., U. Calif., Berkeley, 1950, M.A., 1952; M.S.W., U. So. Calif., 1958, D.S.W., 1977; m. Gordon Wallace Portner, July 30, 1965. Sr. psychiat. social worker Met. State Hosp., Norwalk, Calif., 1958-62; pvt. practice clin. social work, Whittier, Calif., 1965-77; asst. prof. social welfare Calif. State U., Long Beach, 1977-82; asso. prof. social work Chapman Coll., Orange, Calif., 1982—; social work cons. to skilled nursing facilities, 1976—. Mem. Pomona Concert Band, 1963—. Fellow Soc. Clin. Social Work; mem. Nat. Assn. Social Workers, Council on Social Work Edn. Contbr. articles to profl. jours. Office: Social Work Dept Chapman College Orange CA 92666

PORTTEUS, ELNORA MARIE MANTHEI, librarian; b. Rosendale, Wis.; d. H. R. and Anna M. (Kentop) Manthei; student Oshkosh State Coll., 1937-39; B.S., U. Wis., 1941; M.A., Kent State U., 1954; m. Paul Portteus, Oct. 19, 1942; children—Carrie Jo (Mrs. J.P. Thomas), Lane Paul, Andre Eugene. Librarian, tchr. Racine-Kenosha Normal Sch., 1942; library asst. Fed. Res. Bank of Cleve., 1943; asst. librarian Indsl. Relations Counselors N.Y., 1947-48; librarian Findlay (O.) City Schs., 1948-58; asst. prof. dept. library sci. Kent State U., 1958-65; dir. ednl. media services Cleve. Bd. Edn., 1965—; cons., Coop. Ednl. Services, Columbus, 1956-65; adv. bd. H.W. Wilson Standard Catalogue Series. Dir. NDEA Inst., 1965; mem. adv. bd. library tech. program Cuyahoga Community Coll.; adj. asso. prof. Sch. Library Sci. Kent State U. Chmn. Findlay Council Youth Serving Agys., 1954-56. Recipient 1st place Ency. Brit. Sch. Library, 1967; Distinguished Alumna award, Kent State U., 1967. Mem. AAUW, Am. (chmn. adv. com. Midwest Program on Airborn TV Instrn. 1964-68; John Cotton Dana Publicity award, 1967, 70, 1st v.p., pres. 1972-74), Ohio (pres. 1957-58) assns. sch. librarians, Ohio Library Assn. (chmn. book examination center com. 1964-65, chmn. scholarship com. 1965-67; Ohio Librarian of Yr. 1972), ALA, Beta Phi Mu, Delta Kappa Gamma. Club: Order Eastern Star. Contbr. articles to profl. jours.; reviewer Library Jour. Home: 7357 West Lake Blvd Kent OH 44240 Office: 10600 Quincy Ave Cleveland OH 44106

PORTWOOD, HAZEL HARRISON, civic worker; b. Miss.; d. Jennie (Puffer) Harrison; B.A., U. Miss.; M.A., So. Meth. U. Pres., Gulfport (Miss.) Opera Assn.; pres. bd. dirs. Gulf Coast Art Council; bd. dirs. Gulfport Symphony Orch.; mem. State of Miss. Bd. Humanities; active Girl Scouts Am., past pres. State of Miss. council; former pres. Gulfport Little Theatre; pres. bd. dirs. Garden Park Hosp., Houston; bd. dirs. Salvation Army. Recipient Laurel Wreath award as most outstanding citizen Miss. Gulf Coast. Mem. DAR (officer). Baptist. Home: 1528 Olive St Gulfport MS 39601

POSEY, IMOGENE ALLEN, acct., educator, b. Concord, Tenn., Nov. 4, 1929; d. Virgil Elmer and Lucy Mae (Stafford) Allen; B.S., U. Tenn., Knoxville, 1956, M.S., 1962; m. John Cassatt Posey, Aug. 23, 1953; children—Thomas A., Robert S. Lab. technician Union Carbide Nuclear Corp., Oak Ridge, 1951-55; asst. prof. acctg. U. Tenn., Knoxville, 1966-72, assoc. prof., 1972—. C.P.A., Tenn. Mem. Tenn. Soc. C.P.A.s (pres. 1982-83), Nat. Assn. Accts. (nat. dir. 1980-82), Am. Acctg. Assn., Am. Womens Soc. C.P.A.s, Phi Kappa Phi, Beta Gamma Sigma, Beta Alpha Psi. Republican. Presbyterian. Club: Concord Yacht (treas. 1976-80). Contbr. articles to profl. jours. Home: 4732 Santala Dr Knoxville TN 37919 Office: Dept Acctg U Tenn Knoxville TN 37996

POSNER, MARY MCCLEARY, public relations exec.; b. Kansas City, Mo., Mar. 21, 1939; d. Glenn Avann and Julia Porter (Quinby) McCleary; student Ohio Wesleyan U., 1957-59; A.B., U. Mo., 1961; M.A., Ind. U., 1962; postgrad. N.Y.U., 1967-69; m. Alan Kent Posner, Dec. 27, 1965. Public relations supr. Am. Telephone & Telegraph Co., N.Y.C., 1962-68; sr. v.p. Harshe-Rotman & Druck, Inc., N.Y.C., 1968-79; pres., owner Posner Public Relations, Inc., N.Y.C., 1979—. Bd. dirs. Empire State Found.; bd. dirs. Ohio Wesleyan U., 1973—, mem. exec. com., 1980—. chmn. student affairs com., 1981—; mem. N.Y. Dist.

Council, U.S. SBA, 1972-76; mem. N.J. Dist. Export Council, 1980-81. Mem. Internat. Public Relations Assn., Assn. Pvt. Enterprise Edn. Republican. Methodist. Office: 275 Madison Ave New York NY 10016

POSNER, RENEE ZWIEBEL, mktg. ofcl.; b. Bronx, N.Y., Dec. 7, 1950; d. Samuel and Faye (Kahn) Zwiebel; student Am. U., Georgetown U.; spl. student Harvard U. Med. Sch.; summer student fellow Albert Einstein Coll. Medicine, N.Y.C., 1970, 71; m. Mitchell Posner, June 14, 1975. With Shriners Burn Inst., Mass. Gen. Hosp., Boston, 1972; research asst. Harvard U. Med. Sch., Boston VA Hosp., 1973-74; research specialist Rockefeller U., N.Y.C., 1974-76; student for instrs. transcendental meditation program, France, Switzerland, 1976-77; research specialist Cornell U. Med. Coll., N.Y.C., 1977-78; condr. research and devel., founder, pres. Kleda, Ltd., U.S. and abroad, 1978-79; mktg. dir. product devel. Commonwealth Toy and Novelty Co., N.Y.C., 1979-82; merchandising and licensing cons. cosmetic and toy industry, 1982—. Office: 200 Fifth Ave Room 526 New York NY 10010

POSS, MARY CANADA, banker; b. Dallas, Oct. 25, 1951; d. William Ralph and Eula Belle (Key) Canada; B.B.A. in Personnel Mgmt., U. Tex., Austin, 1973, B.B.A. in Fin., 1976; m. James Michael Poss, June 16, 1973. Product mgr. ACH services First Nat. Bank, Dallas, 1978-79, research and product devel. analyst, ops. officer, 1979-80, asst. v.p. internat. ops., 1980-81, mgr. money transfer and internat. communications, . 1981-82, v.p., corp. cash mgmt. cons., 1982—. Mem. Am. Inst. Indsl. Engrs., Am. Inst. Banking, Planning Execs. Inst. (v.p. programs). Republican. Mem. Christian Ch. Home: 6405 Mercedes St Dallas TX 75214

POST, EDITH, sch. counselor; b. N.Y.C., Mar. 22, 1920; d. Samuel and Sarah (Bucholtz) Dolitzky; B.S., Boston U., 1941, M.S.W., 1943; m. Milton Macy Post, Sept. 8, 1946; chidlren—Andrea Post Rae, Judith Post Yudkoff. Sch. adjustment counselor South Hadley Public Schs., 1966-72; coordintor community-family resources Mt. Holyoke Coll. Learning Devel. Center, 1972-77; counselor Holyoke (Mass.) Public Schs., 1977—, tchr. support team, 1981—; cons. Incorporator, Holyoke Vis. Nurse Assn., 1962—; bd dirs. Pioneer Devel. Center, 1978—. Lic. ind. clin. social worker, Mass. Mem. Holyoke Tchrs. Club, Mass. Tchrs. Club, NEA, Nat. Assn. Social Workers, Acad. Cert. Social Workers, Mass. Acad. Psychiat. Social Workers, Delta Kappa Gamma. Home: 1319 Northampton St Holyoke MA 01040

POST, JACKIE EDITH, bus. exec.; b. Lakewood, Ohio, Nov. 17, 1928; d. Sidney Walter and Della N. (Korver) Jackson; B.S. cum laude, Miami U., Oxford, Ohio, 1950; 1 dau., Deborah Downs Cottingham Dryer. Sec. (to Henry Laribee), Laribee & Cooper, Lawyers, Medina, Ohio, 1955-69, (to Baya M. Harrison), Harrison, Greene, Mann, Davenport, et al, Lawyers, St. Petersburg, Fla., 1970-72; corp. sec., sec. to chmn. bd. Jack Eckerd Corp., Clearwater, Fla., 1972—. Mem. Beta Gamma Sigma. Republican. Home: 830 Gulfview Blvd S Clearwater Beach FL 33515 Office: PO Box 4689 Clearwater FL 33518

POST, MARGARET MOORE, journalist; b. Plainfield, Ind., Aug. 16, 1909; d. Robert Wans and Sara Virginia (Rupe) Stephenson; A.B., La. State U., 1930; L.H.D. (hon.), Franklin (Ind.) Coll., 1973; m. Everett L. Moore, Dec. 4, 1932 (dec. Mar. 1952); children—Jo Ann Moore Long, Sue Ellen Moore Walker; m. 2d, H. J. Post, 1970 (div. 1977). Reporter, then city editor Logansport (Ind.) Press, 1930-32; editor Mooresville (Ind.) Times, 1933-38; columnist Indpls. Star, 1932-42; head journalism dept. Franklin Coll., 1942-51; copy editor Indpls. News, 1952-53, with public relations dept. Indpls. Star, also Indpls. News, 1953-68, polit. and feature writer Indpls. News, 1968—; tchr. journalism Ind. U., Indpls., also Def. Info. Center, Ft. Harrison, Indpls., 1954-56; mem. faculty Sch. Police Adminstrn., U. Louisville, 1973-75; editorial adv. bd. Franklin Coll. Mem. Ind. Criminal Justice Commn., 1969—, Ind. Juvenile Justice and Deliquency Adv. Bd., 1979—; mem. crime control panel U.S. C. of C., 1959-74; co-chmn. Ind. 1st Child Abuse Conf., 1977; coordinator Indpls. Anti-Crime Crusade, also Women Against Rape, 1962-75; mem. Presdl. Crime Prevention Commn., 1972; bd. dirs. United Cerebral Palsy Indpls.; founding mem. Ind. Assn. Prevention Blindness, Big Sisters Indpls. Recipient Nat. Recognition award Freedoms Found. at Valley Forge, 1968; 1st pl. award Gen. Fedn. Women's Club-Sears Roebuck Found., 1968; award Ind. Council Juvenile Judges, 1980; Casper Community Services award, 1956, 62, 65, 68, 72, 76, 76; name Sagamore of Wabash, 1970, 78, Ind. Mother of Yr., 1965. Mem. Women in Communications (nat. v.p. 1946-52; Headliner award 1968, Clarion award 1975, 75), Nat. Fedn. Press Women, Women's Press Club Ind., Ind. Acad., Gen. Fedn. Women's Clubs, AAUW, Am. Mothers' Com., Ind. Forum, Delta Gamma Mothers' Club. Republican. Quaker. Author: Wives of Indiana Governors, 1982; co-author: The Lawbreakers, 1968. Home: 2805 Barbary Ln Apt E Indianapolis IN 46205 Office: 307 N Pennsylvania St Indianapolis IN 46206

POST, MARY LOUISE, tng. and devel. co. exec.; b. St. Paul, Oct. 7, 1944; d. Edmund A. and Geneva Louise (Leavenworth) P.; B.A., Marymount Coll., N.Y., 1970; m. H. Larry Wilson, Dec. 14, 1977. Intern, Equitable Life Assurance Assn., N.Y.C., 1970; rep. Friesen Kaye and Assos., N.Y.C., Ottawa, Ont., Can. and Mpls., 1970-73; self-employed cons., N.Y.C. and Mpls., 1971-74; dir. affirmative action and human resources Wilson Learning Corp., Mpls., 1974—, also dir.; bd. dirs. Rational Life Center; cons. in field. Mem. Am. Soc. Tng. and Devel., Assn. Humanistic Psychology, Minn. Women's Network (dir.), Inst. Noetic Scis., Congressional Inst. for Future. Home: 27965 Woodside Rd Excelsior MN 55331 Office: 6950 Washington Ave S Eden Prairie MN 55344

POSTA, ELAINE LOUISE, tng., career and image cons.; b. Mt. Pleasant, Pa., May 6, 1938; d. James A. and Frances Barbara (Kukla) P.; B.S. in Edn., Thiel Coll., 1960. Sch. tchr., 1961; with Trans. World Airlines, 1961-70, dir. grooming, dir. flight attendant public relations, public relations liaison with White House; with Erno Laszlo Inst., 1970-74, regional dir.; Eastern regional dir., dir. public relations EPCO div. Glemby Internat., 1975-78; pres., founder Image Inst., Inc., N.Y.C., 1979—; lectr. in field. Mem. Vol. for Children, Fifth Ave. Presbyn. Ch. Mem. Fashion Group, Women's Econ. Roundtable, Am. Soc. Tng. and Devel., N.Y. Assn. Women Bus. Owners, Nat. Speakers Assn., Nat. Assn. Exec. Females. Fifth Ave. Women's Network. Author tng. manuals, books, and articles in field. Office: 4 E 82d St Suite 5F New York NY 10028

POSTELL, CAROLYN MILTON, educator; b. Oliver, Ga., Jan. 22, 1948; d. Ceverio, Jr. and Maude (Bostic) Milton; B.S. in French, Ga. So. Coll., Statesboro, 1970, M.Ed. in English, 1976; m. Curtis Lamar Postell, July 11, 1970; children—Andrea Zenobia, Ashley Olivia. Tchr. pub. schs., Ga., 1970-75, Marvin Pittman Lab. Sch., Ga. So. Coll., 1975—; asst. prof. English and French edn. Ga. So. Coll., 1975—. Mem. NEA, Nat. Assn. Student Activity Advisers, Ga. Edn. Assn., Bullock County Edn. Assn., Pi Delta Phi, Phi Delta Kappa. Democrat. Baptist. Clubs: Black Women of Profession (pres. 1981), Stabucettes Civic (v.p. 1979—). Home: Route 5 Harris Rd Statesboro GA 30458 Office: Marvin Pittman Sch Ga So Coll Statesboro GA 30460

POSTON, ERSA HINES, govt. ofcl.; b. Paducah, Ky., May 3, 1921; d. Robert S. and Adele (Johnson) Hines; A.B., Ky. State Coll., 1942; M.S.W., Atlanta U., 1946; LL.D., Union Coll., 1971, Fordham U., 1978; D.H.L., Mercy Coll., 1980. Community orgn. sec. Hartford (Conn.) Tb and Health Assn., 1946-47; teen-age program dir. W. side br. YWCA, N.Y.C., 1947-48, adult dir., 1948-49; asst. dir. Clinton Community Center, N.Y.C., 1949-50; dir., 1950-53; field sec. N.Y.C. Welfare and Health Council, 1953-55; field project supr. N.Y.C. Youth Bd., 1955, asst. dir. program rev., 1955-57; area dir. N.Y. State Div. for Youth, 1957-62, youth work coordinator, 1962-64; confidential asst. to Gov. Rockefeller, 1964; dir. N.Y. State Office Econ. Opportunity, 1964-67; pres. N.Y. State CSC, 1967-75, commr., 1975-77; commr. U.S. CSC, 1977-79; vice-chmn. U.S. Merit Systems Protection Bd., 1979—; mem. Internat. CSC; mem. adv. council Federally Employed Women. Former mem. Nat. Commn. to Study goals for State Colls. and Univs.; chmn. Pres.'s Adv. Council Intergovtl. Personnel Policy; v.p. Nat. Urban League; U.S. del. UN Gen. Assembly, 1976; vice presiding officer U.S. Commn. on Observance of Internat. Woman's Year Bd. govs. Albany Med. Center Hosp.; bd. dirs. Whitney M. Young Meml. Found. Recipient Achievement awards Bklyn. club Nat. Assn. Negro Bus. and Profl. Women's Clubs; Dutchess of Paducah award; Dau. of Paducah plaque; named Ky. col.; Distinguished Alumni award Ky. State Coll.; Distinguished Service award Greater N.Y. chpt. Links; Woman of Year award Central Jersey club Nat. Assn. Negro Bus. and Profl. Women's Clubs; Achievement award Phi Delta Kappa; Populus Dei award Mercy Coll.; Woman of Year award Utility Club; Outstanding Woman of Year award Iota Phi Lambda; Nat. Achievement award Nat. Assn. Negro BPW Clubs, 1967; Outstanding Service award 26th A.D. Rep. Orgn. Queens County; Trail Blazer award Jamaica Club Nat. Assn. Negro BPW Clubs; Benjamin Potoker Brotherhood award, 1970; named 1970 Woman of Year, BPW Club Albany; Equal Opportunity Day award Nat. Urban League, 1976; Spl. award Psi Nu chpt. Omega Psi Phi, 1977; Disting. Public Servant award Capital Press Club, 1978; Founders' Day award Alpha Kappa Alpha, 1978; First award Nat. Black Personnel Assn., 1978; named to N.Y. State Women's Hall of Fame, 1980; many others. Mem. Nat. Assn. Social Workers, Acad. Cert. Social Workers, Nat. Acad. Public Adminstrn., Am. Soc. Public Adminstrn., Internat. Personnel Mgmt. Assn. (Exec. Bd. award Nat. Capital area 1979, hon. life mem.), Nat. Council Negro Women, Links, Nat. Bus. and Profl. Women, Girlfriends, Inc., Lambda Kappa Mu (hon.; Achievement award Nu chpt.), Alpha Kappa Alpha (outstanding awards Bklyn. chpt. 1960, 65). Club- Zonta. Office: US Merit Systems Protection Bd 1120 Vermont Ave NW Washington DC 20419

POSTON, JO ANN DUDLEY, educator; b. Bloomington, Ill., Apr. 24, 1947; d. Oswald Augustus and Syrene (Dow) Dudley; B.Mus. Edn., Madison Coll., 1968; M.Mus., U. N.C., Greensboro, 1977; postgrad. 1982—; postgrad. Westminster Choir Coll., 1969; m. Paul Wade Poston, Jr., June 22, 1968; 1 dau., Lisa Dow. Choral dir. Lexington (N.C.) City Schs., 1968-70; accompanist N.C. Sch. Arts, Winston-Salem, 1970-71; pvt. paino tchr., Lexington, N.C., 1970—; dir. youth choirs First Presbyn. Ch., Lexington, 1977-82; head music div., instr. Davidson County Community Coll., Lexington, 1973—; founder, co-dir. Lexington Women's Choral Soc., 1972—; counselor Jr. Music Club, 1970—. Mem. exec. bd. Council Creative Arts, 1978-80; bd. dirs. Community Concert Assn. Lexington, 1981—. Grantee Arts Council Davidson County, Council Creative Arts, 1979-82. Mem. Am. Women Composers (state chmn. 1974-77), Nat. Fedn. Music Clubs (life), Nat. Guild Piano Tchrs., Am. Coll. Musicians, Am. Choral Dirs. Assn. (state chmn. two-year and community colls. com.), Community Coll. Humanities Assn., Lexington Music Study Club (pres. 1972-74), Sigma Alpha Iota, Pi Lambda Kappa. Presbyterian. Clubs: Twin City Track. Home: 900 Nottingham Dr Lexington NC 27292 Office: Davidson County Community Coll Box 1287 Lexington NC 27292

POSTON, MARY JANETTE, ednl. adminstr.; b. Malta, Ohio, Mar. 21, 1929; d. Lewis G. and Lela A. (Glidden) Carpenter; B.Ed., Ohio U., 1963, M.Ed., 1966; postgrad. W.Va. U., 1968; m. Willard E. Poston, Feb. 20, 1949; children—Samuel Thomas, Glen Willard. Tchr., St. Clairsville, Ohio, 1959-61, Flushing, Ohio, 1961-63; elem. supr. Belmont County Schs., 1963-68; dir. elem. edn. Union (Ohio) Local Schs., 1968-74; cons. Ohio Dept. Edn., Columbus, 1974-76, asst. dir. elem. sect., 1976-79, dir. div. elem. and secondary edn., 1979—; tchr. Ohio U., Belmont Campus. Mem. Ohio Right To Read Commn., 1969-74; mem. Belmont County Pub. Library Bd., 1969—. Recipient Austin Furbee award Ohio U. Mem. NEA, Assn. Supervision and Curriculum Devel., Buckeye Assn. Sch. Adminstrs., Ohio Sch. Suprs. Assn., Ohio Edn. Assn., Delta Kappa Gamma, Pi Lambda Theta, Phi Delta Kappa. Republican. Methodist. Club: Executive (Columbus). Home: Niemiec's Ln Flushing OH 43977 Office: Room 1005 65 S Front St Columbus OH 43215

POTASH, MARLIN SUE, psychologist; b. Paterson, N.J., Oct. 23, 1951; d. Monroe and Perle (Cohen) P.; B.S. magna cum laude, Tufts U., 1973; M.Ed., Boston U., 1975, Ed.D., 1977; m. Frederick H. Fruitman, Nov. 21, 1981. Research asso. Center for Study of Edn., Yale U., 1976; vis. lectr. Tufts U., 1975-76; instr. Emmanuel Coll., 1975-79; dir. clin. services, resocialization treatment coordinator Columbus Nursing Home, East Boston, 1975-76; asst. prof. behavioral sci., dept. public health and community dentistry Boston U. Sch. Grad. Dentistry, 1977-81, asst. clin. prof., 1981—; courtesy staff psychologist McLean Hosp., Belmont, Mass., 1978—; pvt. practice psychotherapy, 1979—; asso. Levinson Inst., Cambridge, Mass. Trustee, Boston Ballet Soc., 1981—. Mem. Am. Psychol. Assn., Mass. Psychol. Assn. (bd. profl. affairs 1979-82), Assn. Transpersonal Psychology, Northeastern Soc. Group Psychotherapy. Contbr. chpt. to book, articles to profl. jours. Home: 52 Hedge Rd Brookline MA 02146

POTEAT, CAROL MARTIN, ednl. adminstr.; b. Washington, Mar. 29, 1929; d. George William and Hattie Carroll Martin; B.S. magna cum laude, Miner Tchrs. Coll., 1950; M.A., Hunter Coll., 1963; 1 dau., Linda. Tchr. English, Springfield Gardens High Sch., Queens, N.Y., 1961-69, coordinator student affairs, 1969-74; prin. Middle Coll. High Sch., Queens, 1974-76; exec. asst. div. high schs. N.Y.C. Bd. Edn., 1976-79, dir. pupil personnel services, div. of high schs., 1979—. Recipient Builder of Brotherhood award NCCJ, 1973; NDEA grantee, 1966; Nat. Alliance Postal and Fed. Employees scholar, 1978; Adminstrv. Women in Edn. grantee, 1980; Ednl. Leadership Policy fellow, 1981-82. Mem. Nat. Assn. Secondary Sch. Prins., Council Suprs. and Adminstrs., Adminstrv. Women in Edn., Nat. Assn. Female Execs., Kappa Delta Pi. Democrat. Episcopalian. Office: NYC Bd Edn High Sch Div 110 Livingston St Brooklyn NY 11201

POTENZA, DAISY MCKASKLE, newspaper exec.; b. Houston, Mar. 5, 1906; d. George Washington and Dora Amy (Crump) McKaskle; student Sinclair Bus. Coll., 1925, Massey's Bus. Coll., 1924-26, U. Houston; m. Julius Orian Potenza, Sept. 26, 1928; 1 dau., Marjorie Ann (Mrs. William L. Hale) (dec.). With Houston Chronicle, 1926—, adminstrv. asst. to editor-in-chief, 1930—. Exec. sec. Houston Endowment, Inc., 1968-69; bd. dirs. Pin Oak Charity Horse Show, 1978, 79, 80, 81, 82. Recipient award United Fund, 1967—; outstanding ticket sales awardee Pin Oak Charity Horse Show, Tex. Children's Hosp., 1975-82. Mem. Nat., Tex. press women, Women in Communications, Press Club Houston (hon. life). Democrat. Methodist. Club: Farm and Ranch. Home: 2405 San Felipe Rd Houston TX 77019 Office: 801 Texas Ave Houston TX 77002

POTTER, CAROL STEWART, actress; b. N.Y.C.; d. Harry Randolph and Catharine Stewart (Howie) Potter; B.A. cum laude, Radcliffe Coll., 1970. Appeared in plays: Hedda Gabler, Cyrano, Mother Courage, Enemies, The Effect of gamma Rays on Man in the Moon Marigolds, 1972-73, Overnight, 1974, The Last Days of the British Honduras, 1974, The Country Girl, 1974, Gemini, 1977-78; TV appearances include: The Doctors, 1977, One Life to Live, 1979, also numerous commls. Mem. Actors Equity Assn., Screen Actors Guild, AFTRA, NOW, Nat. Women's Polit. Caucus, Nat. Abortion Rights Action League. *

POTTER, DOROTHY WILLIAMS (MRS. J. LEITH POTTER), publisher; b. Chattanooga, Aug. 6, 1937; d. John Malcolm and Eva Lee (McWaters) Williams; ed. U. Tenn.; m. John Leith Potter, Dec. 15, 1957; children—Stephen Leith, Dorothy Anne, Carol Jean. Owner, pub. DWP Publs., Tullahoma, Tenn., 1962—; cons., adviser, lectr. in field. Mem. Tenn. Am. Revolution Bicentennial Commn.; chmn. Tullahoma Bicentennial Commn. Recipient citation Tenn. Hist. Commn., 1973, Spl. Recognition award City of Tullahoma, 1976. Mem. Soc. Am. Archivists, N.C. Lit. and Hist. Assn., Nat. Archives Assn., New Eng. Hist. and Geneal. Soc., Ky., Tenn., Coffee County (Tenn.) (chmn. bd. 1972-74, editor quar. 1969-74) hist. socs., Nat. Trust for Historic Preservation, Tenn. Anthrop. Assn., Tenn. Archaeol. Soc., Nat. Geneal. Soc., Soc. Descs. Washington's Army at Valley Forge, Nat. Soc. Colonial Dames XVII Century (nat. chmn., state pres.), Nat. Soc. Dames of Ct. of Honor, Nat. Soc. Sons and Daus. Pilgrims (state treas.), DAR, Nat. Soc. U.S. Daus. 1812, Nat. Soc. Daus. Colonial Wars. Author: Indian, Spanish and Other Land Passports for the Southeastern U.S., 1770-1823, 1980. Home: 200 Sheffield Place Nashville TN 37215

POTTER, EMMA JOSEPHINE HILL, educator; b. Hackensack, N.J., July 18, 1921; d. James Silas and Martha Loretta (Pyle) Hill; A.B. cum laude with honors, in Classics, Alfred (N.Y.) U., 1943; A.M., Johns Hopkins U., 1946; m. James H. Potter, Mar. 26, 1949. Tchr. Latin, Baltimore County Public Schs., 1943-44; instr. French and Spanish, Balt. Poly. Inst., 1950—; instr. Spanish adult edn. classes, 1946-48; sec.-treas. Bruno-Potter Inc., accts., 1980—. Mem. NEA, Md. Edn. Assn., Johns Hopkins U. Alumni Assn., Alfred U. Alumni Assn. Democrat. Roman Catholic. Club: Johns Hopkins U. Faculty.

POTTER, EVELYN GOODWIN (MRS. NEIL POTTER), exec. recruiter; b. Dumont, N.J.; d. Russell M. and Marie (Hermida) Goodwin; B.A., U. Mich., 1949; m. Neil Potter, June 30, 1950; children—Eugene, Jill. Exec. sec. Office Bd. Trustees, SUNY, N.Y.C., 1950-52; asst. to dir. Profl. Exam. Service, Am. Public Health Assn., 1953-54; dir. public relations SUNY Downstate Med. Center, Bklyn., 1954-75, asst. to pres., 1967-75; v.p. univ. relations Clark U., Worcester, Mass., 1975-77; v.p. The Cantor Concern, N.Y.C., 1977—; cons. health careers N.Y.C. Bd. Edn., 1963-69; mem. com. on health careers Empire State Health Council, 1964—; public relations com. Council Higher Ednl. Instns. in N.Y.C., 1961-69; bd. dirs. N.Y.C. Health Planning Agy., 1974-75, West Midwood Assn., 1964-65. Recipient certificate of merit Acad. Hosp. Public Relations, 1972, Award Community Agys. Public Relations Assn., 1975. Mem. Assn. Am. Med. Colls., Nat. Assn. Sci. Writers, Am. Coll. Public Relations Assn. (citation of merit 1959, 72), Met. Coll. Public Relations Assn., Health and Welfare Public Relations Soc. (charter mem., dir., chmn. publs. com.), Council Advancement and Support Edn. Club: Boston Press. Author: Medical Education in Brooklyn-The First 100 Years, 1960. Home: 270 Bronxville Rd Bronxville NY 10708 Office: The Cantor Concern 39 W 55th St New York NY

POTTER, JACQUELINE RILEY, advt. agy. exec., writer; b. Joplin, Mo., Dec. 8, 1929; d. Perry Cromwell and Lorraine Crystal (Hammons) Riley; A.A., U. Calif., Berkeley, 1949; A.A., U. Ill., 1951; m. Ernest Elliott Potter, Feb. 4, 1951; children—Jamey Neal, Lisa Gail. Tchr. public schs., Ludlow, Ill., 1951-52; jr. copywriter Spiegel's Co., Chgo., 1952-53; continuity editor Sta. KSWM, Joplin, 1953-54; advt. copywriter Carthage Marble Corp. (Mo.), 1953-61, advt. mgr., 1962-67; pres. Jacqueline Potter Advt. Agy., Carthage, 1967—. Bd. dirs. Carthage Public Library, 1971-75; chmn. commn. on edn. Meth. Ch., 1965-67, mem. adminstrv. bd., 1965-67, 80—. Recipient advt. excellence award Archtl. Record, 1965; 1st pl., Joplin Globe award Ozark Creative Writers Conf., 1977. Mem. Carthage Writers Guild (pres. 1977-79), Shakespeare Soc., PEO. Author mass market paperback romances; contbr. poems and articles to mags.

POTTER, JOY HAMBUECHEN, educator; b. Zurich, Mar. 4, 1935; d. Joseph W. and Dorothy Hambuechen; B.A. summa cum laude, Radcliffe U., 1956; cert. Program in Bus. Adminstrn., Harvard-Radcliffe, 1957; M.A., Rutgers U., 1965, Ph.D., 1967; 1 dau., Karen Antonia. Instr., Rutgers U., 1965-67; asst. prof. U. Pa., 1967-71; prof. Italian, U. Tex., Austin, 1971—; mem. Romance langs. adv. screening com. Council Internat. Exchange Scholars, 1980—. Fulbright fellow, 1962-63; NEH fellow, 1977-78. Mem. MLA, Dante Soc., Am. Assn. Tchrs. Italian, Am. Assn. Univ. Profs. Italian. Author: Elio Vittorimi, 1979; Five Frames for the Decameron, 1982. Office: French Italian Dept U Texas Austin TX 78712

POTTER, MARIANNE STADLER, nurse; b. Erie, Pa., Dec. 25, 1935; d. Joseph Lawrence and Jeannette Kathryn (Alberstadt) Stadler; B.S. in Nursing, Barry Coll., Miami, 1957; m. Richard D. Potter, July 14, 1966; children—Kathryn Jean Clark, Cheryl Ann Clark Herrera, Patrick Joseph Clark, Amy Marya; 1 stepdau., Connie Maureen Potter Yaple. Staff nurse, instr., supr., ob-gyn dept. Hamot Hosp., Erie, Pa., 1962-67; obstetrics supr. Meth. Hosp., Indpls., 1967-68; instr. practical nurses Bartow Manpower Devel. Tng. Act programs, Cartersville, Ga., 1969-71; dir. nurses Roberta (Ga.) Intermediate Care Home, 1979—. Mem Ga. Assn. Nurses Long Term Care (sec. W. Central council). Democrat. Roman Catholic. Home: 403 Panorama Pl Box 637 Macon GA 31210 Office: PO Box 146 Roberta GA 31078

POTTER, MARY LEE, nursing adminstr.; b. Jeffersonville, Ind., Dec. 1, 1925; d. Joseph Herman and June Zenobia (Chapman) Beatty; B.S. in Nursing Edn., Ball State U., 1947; children—Lee, Nancy, Duane. Instr., U. Hawaii, 1967-69; exec. dir. Hawaii Nurses Assn., Honolulu, 1969-73; field rep. Am. Nurses Assn., Kansas City, Mo., 1973-77; dir. profl. services Comprehensive Care Corp., St. Louis, 1977—; mem. Hawaii Regional Med. Bd.; mem. Adv. Bd. Practical Nursing, Maui, Hawaii. Mem. Hawaii Status of Women's Commn. Named Nurse of Yr., Hawaii, 1968; recipient cert. appreciation U.S. Army, 1969. Mem. Am. Nurses Assn., Indsl. Relations Research Assn., Nat. Assn. Female Execs., NOW. Author articles in field. Office: 12255 De Paul Dr Bridgeton MO 63044

POTTER, MILDRED JOSEPHINE, educator; b. Davidson, Tenn., Aug. 29, 1920; d. William Joseph and Clara Ellen (Sapp) Hawkins; B.A. in English, Upsala Coll., East Orange, N.J., 1975; cert. Montessor; Internat. Assn., 1975; m. Clarence George Potter, Apr. 14, 1940; children—Joyce, Ronald, Clare, Gerald, Ruth, Loretta, Beth, Daniel, Amy. Dir. Children's House, Verona, N.J., 1973-75, S. Orange (N.J.) Country Day Sch., 1975-77; owner, dir., prin. Independence Montessori Sch., N. Plainfield, N.J., 1977—. Mem. AAUW. Mormon. Home: 30 Coddington Ave North Plainfield NJ 07060 Office: 32 Coddington Ave North Plainfield NJ 07060

POTTER, NANCY DUTTON, psychologist; b. St. Joseph, Mo., Jan. 16, 1946; d. Paul Vernon and Rosa Lee (Hatfield) Dutton; B.A., Pitzer Coll., 1968; M.A., U. Kans., 1971; Ph.D., U. Mo., 1974; postgrad. Georgetown U., 1977-79; m. Caryl Ashby Potter, III, Aug. 24, 1969; 1 dau., Blakeslee Ann. Chief clin. psychology Keesler AFB Med. Center, Miss., 1976-77; clin. psychologist Malcolm Grow Med. Center, Andrews AFB, Md., 1977-78; asso. dir. Georgetown U. Counseling Center,

1978-79, acting dir., 1979-80, dir. internship tng., 1978-81; pvt. practice psychology, Washington, 1978—. Bd. dirs. Family Counseling Agy., Biloxi, Miss. Served to capt. USAF, 1974-78. Lic. psychologist, D.C., Md. Mem. Am. Psychol. Assn., Am. Personnel and Guidance Assn. Club: Altrusa. Home: 7400 Carath Ct Springfield VA 22153 Office: 1301 20th St NW Washington DC 20036

POTTKER, JANICE MARIE, sociologist; b. Lake Forest, Ill., Oct. 22, 1948; d. Ralph Eugene and Olga Norma (Somenzi) P.; B.A., Am. U., 1969; M.A., U. Md., 1971; Ph.D., Columbia U., 1978; m. Andrew Stuart Fishel, Aug. 17, 1969; children—Tracy Lynn, Carrie Gene. Preceptor sociology and edn. Tchrs. Coll., Columbia U., 1971-72; instr. sociology Bklyn. Coll., CCNY, 1972-73; research scientist biometric research N.Y. State Dept. Mental Hygiene, 1973-74; research assoc. Human Scis. Research, McLean, Va., 1974-75; dir. Center for Study of Sex Differences in Edn., Bethesda, Md., 1974-79; cons. Office for Civil Rights, HEW, 1978-79, chief research and evaluation br. Office for Civil Rights, Dept. of Edn., 1979—; project dir. U.S. Office Edn. Women's Ednl. Equity Program, 1976-77; bd. dirs. Internat. Inst. Women Studies, 1970-73; mem. gov.'s roster qualified women to serve on state bds. and commns. on status of women. Mem. Am. Sociol. Assn., Sociologists for Women in Soc., Am. Ednl. Research Assn., Am. Ednl. Studies Assn., Women Educators. Editor: Sex Bias in the Schools: The Research Evidence, 1976; author: National Politics and Eliminating Sex Discrimination in Education, 1977; contbr. articles to profl. jours.

POTTRUFF, BETTY ANN, lawyer; b. Moose Jaw, Sask., Can., Feb. 6, 1950; d. Rupert R. and Annetta (Norman) P.; LL.B., U. Sask., 1977. Crown prosecutor Atty. Gen. Dept., Govt. of Sask., Yorkton, 1978-79, crown solicitor, 1979-82, crown prosecutor, Regina, 1982—. Mem. Can. Bar Assn. Office: 2222 13th Ave Regina SK S4T 1W6 Canada

POTTS, CALLIE ANN, postal exec.; b. Lexington, Ky., Apr. 24, 1945; d. Edward E. and Frances (Logdon) Roberts; student Ind. U.; m. James L. Potts, June 2, 1973; children—Robert Sparks, Paul Sparks, Mark Sparks. With U.S. Postal Service, Louisville, 1969—, opns. analyst, 1978-81, dir. mail processing, 1981—. Recipient Equal Opportunity award U.S. Postal Service, 1978, Meritorious Service citation, 1980. Mem. Nat. Assn. Female Execs., Fed. Employeed Women. Home: 1816 Depauw Ave New Albany IN 47150 Office: 1420 Gardiner Ln Louisville KY 40231

POTTS, TERESA JOYCE, med. technologist; b. Morristown, Tenn., June 9, 1954; d. Clarence Hewton and Teresa Montieze (Fogle) P.; student Knoxville Health Occupations Center, 1972-73. Student technician Oak Ridge (Tenn.) Methodist Hosp., 1972-73; co-chief technologist Hawkins County Meml. Hosp., Rogersville, Tenn., 1973—, supr., 1982—, sec. Candy Stripers, 1971. Mem. Am. Soc. Clin. Pathologists. Methodist. Clubs: Bus. and Profl. Women's, Hawkins County Tennis Assn. (sec. 1981). Home: Route 3 Rogersville TN 37857 Office: Locust St Rogersville TN 37857

POUNDS, AUGUSTINE WRIGHT, univ. ofcl.; b. Wadley, Ala., July 20, 1936; d. Cortelyou T. and Flossie (Wilkes) Busbee; B.A., Oakland U., 1973, M.A., 1974; Ph.D., Iowa State U., 1980; m. Russell G. Pounds, July 4, 1981; children—Georgina Renee Wright; Karen Y. Williams. Asst. dir. commuter services Oakland U., Pontiac, Mich., 1973-75, asst. dir. Student Center, 1972-75; asst. dir. minority affairs Iowa State U., Ames, 1975-76, assoc. dean students, 1978—. Bd. dirs. United Way, Ames; mem. Ames Human Relations Commn.; del. Democratic Precinct Com., 1980. Recipient Outstanding Alumni award Oakland U., 1970. Mem. Am. Personnel and Guidance Assn., Nat. Assn. Women Deans, Adminstrs. and Counselors, Nat. Assn. Student. Personnel Adminstrs. Home: 1941 Paulson Dr Ames IA 50010 Office: Iowa State U Ames IA 50011

POUNDS, JANET LYNN, chemist; b. Dallas, Nov. 29, 1944; d. Truman Edward and Marilynn (Carlton) P.; B.A. in Chemistry, La. State U., 1966, M.S. in Organic Chemistry, 1969; m. Richard Miles Bowen, July 19, 1980; 1 dau., Kristina. Grad. teaching asst. La. State U., 1966-69; tchr. sci. Baker (La.) Jr. High Sch., 1969-70; instr. chemistry So. U., Baton Rouge, 1972-77; research chemist PPG Industries, Corpus Christi, Tex., 1977-80, Barberton, Ohio, 1980—. NIH fellow, 1978. Mem. NOW (La. legis. coordinator 1973-74, ERA coordinator 1974-75), Am. Chem. Soc. Episcopalian. Club: Akron Ski. Home: 3097 Baughman Rd Clinton OH 44216 Office: PO Box 31 Barberton OH 44203

POUSSAINT, ANN ASHMORE, psychologist; b. Atlanta, June 23, 1942; d. Clifford M. and W. Mae (Walker) Ashmore; B.A., Spelman Coll., 1963; M.S. in Social Work, Simmons Coll., 1965; M.A., U. Calif., Berkeley, 1976, Ph.D., 1979; m. Alvin F. Poussaint, Nov. 4, 1973; 1 son, Alan Machel. Psychiat. social worker Child Guidance Clinic, San Mateo, Calif., 1965-68; social work supr. Roxbury Multi-Service Center, Boston, 1968-69; patient coordinator partial hospitalization program, N.Y. Med. Coll., N.Y.C., 1969-70; lectr. dept. nursing State U. Calif. at San Francisco, 1970-72; lectr. dept. psychology San Francisco State U., 1970-72; clinician and cons. Pacific Psychotherapy Associates, San Francisco, 1970-73; private practice clin. psychology, Cambridge, Mass., 1974—; supr. post-doctoral fellows and Ph.D. candidates in clin. psychology Minority Tng. Program in Psychology, Psychology Internship Center, Boston City Hosp. and Boston U. Sch. Medicine, 1978; founder, dir. Urban Psychol. Assos.; dir. Urban Psychol. Assos., Brookline, Mass.; adj. asst. prof. Boston Coll.; cons. in forensic psychology, 1971—; also cons. to industry and employee assistance programs. Bd dirs. PSI Associates, Inc., Washington, 1979—. USPHS fellow, 1971-73. Mem. Am. Psychol. Assn. (mem. nat. com. on media 1979-80), Mass. Psychol. Assn. Contbr. articles in field to mags. and profl. jours. Office: 1152 Beacon St Brookline MA 02146

POUSSAINT, RENEE FRANCINE, TV journalist; b. N.Y.C., Aug. 12, 1944; d. Christopher Wallace and Bobbie Mae (Vance) P.; B.A., Sarah Lawrence Coll., 1966; postgrad. Yale U. Law Sch., 1966-67; M.A., UCLA, 1971; postgrad. Ind. U., 1972-73, Columbia U., 1973; m. Henry Richardson, III, Sept. 10, 1977. Legal researcher NAACP, Washington, 1965-66; adminstrv. asst. Radio Malawi, 1967-68; program dir. AIESEC, fgn. student orgn., N.Y.C., 1968-69; dancer Jean Leon Destine Haitian Dance troup, N.Y.C., 1965; free lance art critic, editor African Arts Mag., Los Angeles, 1969-72; newswriter WBBM-TV, Chgo., 1973-74; reporter, 1974-76; reporter Midwest Bur., Chgo. and Washington Bur., CBS-TV Network, 1976-78; weeknight anchor WJLA-TV, Washington, 1978—; cons. in field; tutor Operation Rescue, Washington. Bd. dirs. Folger Shakespeare Library, Washington, 1979-81, Nat. Kidney Found., (hon. dir.) 1981—; membership chmn. Arthritis Found., Washington, 1981-82; program advisor WETA (PBS) Minority Journalism program, 1980-81. Recipient (2) Emmy awards Nat. Acad. TV Arts and Scis.; 1980 Religion in Media award; Excellence in Broadcasting award AAUW, 1979—; NAACP Broadcast award, 1980; reporting award Nat. Assn. Media Women; community service awards, Operation Push, 1975, Ill. Mental Health Assn., 1976, YMCA, 1976, Am. Firefighters Assn., 1977, Govt. of D.C., 1981, Multiple Sclerosis Soc., 1981, others. Mem. Women in Communications, AFTRA, Writers Guild of Am., NAACP (life), Sigma Delta Chi. Founding editor Ufahamu, UCLA, 1971-72; translator: Les Siecles Obscurs de l'Afrique Noire by R. Mauny, 1972. Office: 4461 Connecticut Ave NW Washington DC 20008

POWELL, ANICE CARPENTER (MRS. ROBERT WAINWRIGHT POWELL), librarian; b. Moorhead, Miss., Dec. 2, 1928; d. Horace Aubrey and Celeste (Brian) Carpenter; student Sunflower Jr. Coll., 1945-47, Miss. State Coll. Women, 1947-48; B.S., Delta State Coll., 1961, M.L.S., 1974; m. Robert Wainwright Powell, July 19, 1948; children—Penelope Elizabeth, Deborah Alma. Librarian, Sunflower (Miss.) Pub. Library, 1958-61; tchr. English, Isola (Miss.) High Sch., 1961-62; dir. Sunflower County Library, Indianola, Miss., 1962—; mem. adv. council State Instl. Library Services, 1967-71; chmn. pub. library category Sunflower County Merit Program, 1973—; mem. adv. bd. library services and constrn. act com. Miss. Library Commn., 1978-80, Miss. Heart Assn., Sunflower, 1963-72; mem, Miss. Gov.'s Library Conf. Mem. ALA, Miss. Library Assn. (exec. dir. Nat. Library Week 1975, steering com. 1976, intellectual freedom com. 1975, chmn. right to read com. 1976, South Delta Dist. chmn. 1978-79, chmn. legis. com. 1979, chmn. intellectual freedom com. 1980, mem. legis. com. 1980, chmn. membership com. 1982, v.p.-pres. elect 1983; Peggy May award 1981), Southeastern Library Assn., Sunflower County Hist. Soc., Kappa Delta Pi. Methodist. Home: Box 310 Sunflower MS 38778 Office: Sunflower County Library 201 Cypress Dr Indianola MS 38751

POWELL, BARBARA, clin. psychologist; b. Dexter, Mo., Apr. 25, 1929; d. Clarence Albert and Ethel (Mohrstadt) P.; B.A., Wellesley Coll., 1950; M.A., Columbia U., 1967; Ph.D., Fordham U., 1975; m. Richard W. O'Neill, Jan. 3, 1953 (div. 1966); children—Richard W., Susan P., Jennifer A., Julia K.; m. 2d, Charles J. McCarthy, May 13, 1967 (div. 1978). Copywriter, Parade mag., 1951-52, McCall's, 1952-53; publicity dir. Silvermine Guild Art, New Canaan, Conn., 1964-66; reporter Bridgeport (Conn.) Post, 1964-69; psychologist Dunlap & Assos., Darien, Conn., 1966-67; dir. Guidance Center for Women, U. Conn., 1968-69; intern N.Y. Hosp., Westchester, 1972-73; psychologist St. Mary's in-the-field, Valhalla, N.Y., 1973-77, Behavior Therapy Inst., White Plains, N.Y., 1975-78; pvt. practice clin. psychology, Rowayton, Conn., 1976—; lectr. U. Conn., 1976-77; co-founder, assertive tng. leader Woman's Place, Darien. USPH grantee, 1970-71. Mem. Am. Psychol. Assn., Am. Assn. Marriage and Family Therapists, Am. Assn. Advancement Behavior Therapy, Soc. Clin. and Exptl. Hypnosis, Phi Beta Kappa, Sigma Xi. Author: Careers for Women after Marriage and Children, 1965; How to Raise a Successful Daughter, 1979; Overcoming Shyness, 1979. Address: 20 Covewood Dr Rowayton CT 06853

POWELL, BARBARA KEY, lawyer; b. Houston, June 26, 1949; d. Norbonne Berkeley and Elizabeth B. Powell; student Mt. Holyoke Coll., 1967-68; B.A., Duke U., 1971; J.D., U. Houston, 1973. Admitted to Tex. bar, 1973, Okla. bar, 1975; atty. Tenneco Oil Co., Houston, 1973-74, Denver, 1974, Oklahoma City, 1974-75, Shell Oil Co., Houston, 1975-79, Marathon Oil Co., Findlay, Ohio, from 1979; now pvt. practice, Houston. Mem. State Bar Tex. (natural resources sect.), Houston Bar Assn. (internat. law sect.), Okla. State Bar, Ohio State Bar, Houston Young Lawyers Assn., AAUW, Mt. Holyoke Alumnae (Houston exec. com.). Presbyterian. Club: Houston World Trade. Office: 2640 Fountain View Suite 204 Houston TX 77057

POWELL, BETTY ANNE, govt. ofcl.; b. Hutchinson, Kans., Apr. 24, 1919; d. James Blaine and Vera Elizabeth (Phillips) P.; student U. Okla., 1935-37, 57—, U. Wis., summer 1963, Oxford U., 1977. Staff writer Okla. Daily, 1937; asst. program dir. Sta. KSWO, Lawton, Okla., 1941; asst. to officer in charge, book dept. Fort Sill, Okla., 1941-44, asst. sec. communications dept. Field Arty. Sch., 1944-48, asst. public info. officer, dep. info. officer, public info. officer, 1948-79, dep. public affairs officer, 1979—. Bd. dirs. Great Plains Country Assn., 1979-82. Mem. Lawton C. of C., Okla. Anthropol. Soc. (past dir.), Okla. Ornithol. Soc., SW Okla. Archeol. Soc. Republican. Mem. Ch. Disciples of Christ. Clubs: Fort Sill Officers, Oklahoma City Press. Home: 725 NW 36th St Lawton OK 73505 Office: Public Affairs Fort Sill OK 73503

POWELL, BEVERLY JOAN BANKSON, accountant; b. Kansas City, Mo., Aug. 5, 1936; d. Floyd Randolph and Eva Lenora (Porter) Bankson; A.A., Indian Hills Community Coll., Centerville, Iowa, 1981; m. Floyd Earl Powell, Aug. 6, 1953; children—Cheryl, Donald, John. Exec. sec., office mgr. Hall Engrng. Co., also corp. sec.-teas. Allerton Gas Co., both Centerville, 1963-77; owner Powell Acctg. and Tax Service, Unionville, Mo., 1977—; cons., speaker in field. Organist, Broadlawn Bapt. Ch., Unionville. Mem. Nat. Soc. Public Accts., Ind. Accts. Soc. Mo., Putnam County C. of C. (dir.), Unionville Bus. and Profl. Women. Republican. Office: 1608 Washington St Unionville MO 63565

POWELL, BIDDIE ANN, communications cons.; b. Oklahoma City, Oct. 6, 1943; d. Walter Alexander and B.B. (McCarley) P.; B.A. in English, U. Tulsa, 1966; teaching certificate U. Ind., Fort Wayne, 1974; M.A., U. Colo., Boulder, 1975; postgrad. U. Iowa, 1981—; m. George Lee Lorenzen, May 27, 1966 (div. 1979); children—Jason George, Susan Stephanie. Public info. specialist GSA, Denver, 1975-81. Recipient Suggestion award GSA, 1976. Mem. Women in Communications, Sigma Delta Xi, Psi Chi, Pi Gamma Mu. Lutheran. Club: Denver Press. Co-author: The Student Guide to Mass Media Internships, 1974, 75, 76; The Student Guide to Business Internships, 1980. Address: Dept Mass Communications U Iowa Iowa City IA 52242

POWELL, CAROL CHRISTINE, social worker; b. Mayberry, W.Va., Nov. 25, 1947; d. Lawrence Edward and Hattie Mae (Price) Brown; B.A., Hampton (Va.) Inst., 1969; police cert., Am. U., 1970; M.S.W. (fellow 1975), Va. Commonwealth U., Richmond, 1975; m. Clarence Powell, July 18, 1970; 1 son, Curtis Eugene. Policewoman, Met. Washington Police Dept., 1969-71; sr. social worker, protective services specialist Hampton Social Services, 1975-76; social work cons. Peninsula Boys Club, Hampton, 1975-76; clin. social work supr. Eastern State Hosp., Williamsburg, Va., 1976-79, patient advocate, 1979-80; asst. prof. sociology and social work Hampton (Va.) Inst., 1980—. Mem. Nat. Assn. Social Workers, Nat. Assn. Black Social Workers (co-founder, past pres. Peninsula chpt.), Va. Council Social Welfare. Office: Dept Sociology Hampton Inst Hampton VA 23668

POWELL, CHARLENE LITTLEJOHN, ednl. adminstr.; b. Marshall County, Ky., June 5, 1911; d. Charles Clyde and Ila Gertrude (Chumbler) Littlejohn; B.S., Murray State U., 1936, M.A., 1960, postgrad., 1961; m. Harry Elmore Powell (dec. 1967). Tchr. pub. schs. Calvert City, Ky., 1932-35, Gilbertsville, Ky., 1939-43; chemist Ky. Ordnance Works, Paducah, 1943-46; prin. Farley Elem. Sch., Paducah, 1947-76; supr. Adult Basic Edn. Program, Night Sch., Paducah, 1967-76. Treas., Reidland Farley Vol. Fire Assn., 1955. Recipient Service award Boy Scouts Am., 1966, Honor award Soil Conservation Dist. Bd. Suprs., 1974, McCrocken County Fiscal Ct. award, 1976, resolution of appreciation McCrocken County Bd. Edn., 1976. Named Citizen of Year, Southside Kiwanis Club, Paducah, 1969, Duchess of Paducah, City of Paducah, 1970, Ky. col., 1976. Mem. McCrocken County Tchrs. Credit Union (clk. 1962—), Murray Alumni Assn. (life), PTA (life), Nat., Ky., McCrocken (past pres.) edn. assns., Ky., Western Ky. suprs. assns., First Dist. Ret. Tchrs. Assn. (sec. i979-80, treas.-elect 1979-80), Paducah-McCrocken County Ret. Tchrs. Assn. (pres.-elect 1979-80, pres. 1980-81). Democrat. Baptist. Home: Route 13 Box 432 Paducah KY 42001

POWELL, DEBORAH ELIZABETH, pathologist; b. Lynn, Mass., Nov. 28, 1939; d. Walter Henry and Elizabeth Christina (Walker) Forbes; A.B., Radcliffe Coll., 1960; M.D., Tufts U., 1965; m. Ralph Dewey Powell, Jr., Feb. 6, 1971; children—Joshua Norris, Nathaniel James; children by previous marriage—Amanda Elizabeth, Adam Forbes. Intern, Georgetown U. Hosp., Washington, 1965-66; resident in pathology Clin. Center, NIH, Bethesda, Md., 1966-69, research pathologist div. Biologies Standards, 1969-70; asst. prof. pathology Georgetown U., Washington, 1970-75; asso. prof. U. Ky., Lexington, 1975-80, prof., vice-chmn. dept., 1980—, dir. diagnostic pathology, 1975—; dir. Cytoscan Labs., Silver Spring, Md., 1973-75. Diplomate Am. Bd. Pathology. Mem. Am. Assn. Pathologists, Am. Soc. Cytology, Arthur Purdy Stout Soc. Surg. Pathologists, Internat. Acad. Pathologists, Internat. Soc. Gynecologic Pathologists. Democrat. Episcopalian. Contbr. articles to profl. jours. Home: 3345 Overbrook Dr Lexington KY 40502 Office: Medical Center U Kentucky Lexington KY 40506

POWELL, DIANA KEARNY, lawyer, poet; b. Washington, Apr. 15, 1910; d. William Glasgow and Alice Van Voorhees (Joline) P.; LL.B., Columbus U., 1940, LL.M., 1942; A.A., George Washington U., 1945; postgrad. Law Sch. Georgetown U., 1957. Admitted to D.C. bar, 1940, U.S. Supreme Ct. bar, 1959; practice law, Washington; contbr. poetry to various mags., 1930—; poetry recitations. Precinct chmn. Republican Party, 1965-68, co-chmn., 1972-75; mem. various campaign coms.; sec. Sodality Holy Name Soc. of St. Matthew's Cathedral, 1978-81, chmn. workshop com., 1975-81, pres., 1981—; mem. Republican Presdl. Task Force, 1982. Recipient various local and nat. poetry awards Nat. League Am. Pen Women; cert. of appreciation Anchor Mental Health Assn., 1975. Mem. Am. Bar Assn., Nat. Assn. Women Lawyers, Internat. Platform Assn, Saintpaulia Internat. Roman Catholic. Asso. editor: Washington Vistas, 1953. Home and Office: 1500 Massachusetts Ave NW Washington DC 20005

POWELL, DOROTHY JEAN, banker; b. Nocona, Tex., Nov. 15, 1927; d. Arthur William and Bertie Belle (McMurtry) McNabb; student Kilgore Coll., 1945-46, Joliet Jr. Coll., 1965-68, Lewis U., 1969-71; m. Robert E. Powell, Apr. 16, 1948; children—Elizabeth Joyce, Patrick Vernon. Clk., First Nat. Bank, Longview, Tex., 1946-47; teller, bookkeeper Cleveland Nat. Bank (Tenn.), 1947-49; sec. to dean students Lewis U., Lockport, Ill., 1965-67; v.p., cashier Heritage First Nat. Bank, Lockport, 1967-82, pres., 1982—, dir., 1978—. Chmn. Vocat. Adv. Com., Sch. Dist. 205, Lockport, 1968-70; dir. Luth. Ch. Women, Bethany Luth. Ch., Lemont, Ill., 1960—. Mem. Nat. Assn. Bank Women (state chmn. Ill. group 1976-77), Zonta Internat., Am. Soc. Profl. and Exec. Women, Lockport Bus. and Profl. Women's Club (pres. 1976-77). Home: 158 135th St Lemont IL 60439 Office: 800 State St Lockport IL 60441

POWELL, ERNESTINE BREISCH, lawyer; b. Moundsville, W.Va., Feb. 16, 1906; d. Ernest Elmer and Belle (Wal-lace) Breisch; student Dayton YMCA Law Sch., 1929; m. Roger K. Powell, Nov. 15, 1935; children—R. Keith (dec.), Diane L.D., Bruce W. Admitted to Ohio bar, 1929; tax analyst tax dept. Wall, Cassell & Groneweg, Dayton, Ohio, 1929-31; pvt. practice law, 1931-40; gen. counsel for Dayton Jobbers amd Mfrs. Assn., 1931-41; mem. firm Powell and Powell, Columbus, Ohio, 1944—. Ohio chmn. Nat. Woman's Party, Washington, 1950-51, nat. chmn., 1953-54, hon. nat. chmn. Pres. vol. activities com. Columbus State Sch., 1960-61, trustee, 1957-59. Mem. Nat. Assn. Women Lawyers, Am., Ohio, Columbus bar assns., Nat. Soc. Arts and Letters (pres. Columbus chpt. 1963-64), Nat. Lawyers Club (charter mem.). Co-author: Tax Ideas, 1955; Estate Tax Techniques, 3 vols., 1955-82. Editor-in-chief: Women Lawyers Jour., 1943-45. Office: 1382 Neil Ave Columbus OH 43201

POWELL, JEAN DELORES, city ofcl.; b. Balt., Oct. 23, 1934; d. Vernon Nickens and Camilla Ann (Briscoe) P.; B.S., Morgan State U., 1958. Tchr. phys. edn. Balt. City Public Schs., 1958-60; recreation leader Balt. City Bur. Recreation, 1960-61, dir. recreation center, 1962-65, supr. girls and women's activities, 1965—; sec. Balt. City Phys. Fitness Commn., 1972—; mem. Tennis Adv. Com., 1971-74. Bd. dirs. Girl Scouts Greater Balt.; mem. day care bd. Union Bapt. Ch.; mem. exec. bd. U.S. Youth Games. Recipient leadership and communications certificate Md. Recreation Assn., 1967; Thomas W. Harrison III Meml. award Md. Tennis Assn., 1972; award Balt. Sandlotters Hall of Fame, 1979; various service plaques. Mem. Nat. Recreation and Park Assn., Md. Recreation and Parks Assn. Baptist. Club: Zonta. Home: 4605 Pall Mall Rd Baltimore MD 21215 Office: Balt City Bur Recreation 1129 N Calvert St Baltimore MD 21202

POWELL, JEANNE ADELE, devel. biologist; b. Los Angeles, Jan. 18, 1933; d. James Robert and Adele (Romer) P.; A.B., Brown U., 1954; M.A., Bryn Mawr Coll., 1959, Ph.D., 1967. Sci. tchr. Baldwin Sch., Bryn Mawr, Pa., 1955-64; instr. Bryn Mawr Coll., 1966-67; asst. prof. biology Smith Coll., Northampton, Mass., 1967-74, assoc. prof., 1974-79, prof., 1979—; vis. sr. scientist Inst. Nat. de la Sante et de la Recherche Medicale, France, 1979. MDA grantee 1974-76, 79-82; NIH grantee, 1969-73, 80—. Mem. AAAS, Internat. Soc. Devel. Neurosci., Soc. Devel. Biology, Soc. Cell Biology, Sigma Xi. Contbr. articles on regeneration and muscle devel. to sci. jours. Home: 46 Winthrop St Northampton MA 01060 Office: Clark Science Center Smith College Northampton MA 01063

POWELL, JOYCE WEBER, pub. co. exec.; b. Winona, Minn., Dec. 4, 1928; d. Arnold W. and Marcella M. (Heuer) Weber; student Buffalo County Normal Sch., 1947, Winona Area Vocat. Sch., 1976-77; m. William G. Powell, July 20, 1947; 1 son, Mark W. Sec. to clk. of ct., Alma, Wis., 1949; tchr. kindergarten St. Michael's Sch., Fountain City, Wis., 1961-62; sec. Hal Leonard Pub. Corp., Winona, Minn., 1962-65, credit mgr., 1965—. Lutheran. Home: 204 Main St Cochrane WI 54622 Office: Hal Leonard Pub Corp 960 E Mark St Winona MN 55987

POWELL, JULIE NEGELE, retail exec.; b. Memphis, Jan. 19, 1939; d. Walter David and Doris Helen (Bade) Negele; B.A., Memphis State U., 1960, postgrad div. continuing studies, 1969; postgrad. Sch. Theology, U. of South, 1980—, State Tech. Inst. Mephis. 1982; m. James Wilbert Powell, Aug. 27, 1960; children—Pamela Shawn, Stacy Ann, Leigh Allison, Kristin Julie. Mgr., Hallmark Shop, Auburn, Ala., 1960-62; mem. wholesale sales staff Cotton States Fashion Exhibitors, Memphis, part time 1964-74; asst. mgr. Merribee Needlecraft Store, Memphis, 1974-75; owner, mgr. Julie's Needle Art Shop, Memphis, 1975-82, Julies Needle Art Shop, Germantown, Tenn., 1981-82; salesman B. Blumenthal & Co., Inc., 1982—; cons., designer needlework mfrs. and pubs.; lectr. civic. orgns. Sec. Episcopal Met. Ministry, 1980-82; chmn. outreach com. St. John's Episcopal Ch., 1980—, vestry, 1980-83. Mem. Memphis C. of C., Nat. Needlework Assn., Danish Handcraft Guild, Am. Profl. Needlework Retailers, Mid-South Embroiderers Guild, Nat. Standards Council Am. Embroiderers, Network. Home: 1490 Goodbar Ave Memphis TN 38104

POWELL, LOUISA ROSE, psychologist; b. Highland Park, Mich., Oct. 10, 1942; d. Albert and Mildred Loraine (Bos) Feldman; B.S., Roosevelt U., 1966; M.S., U. Chgo., 1969, Ph.D., 1973; m. Philip Melancthon Powell, Dec. 29, 1962; children—David, Aaron, Robert. Intern in psychology VA Hosp., Newington, Conn., 1973-75; instr. So. Conn. State Coll., New Haven, 1975-76; psychologist Austin (Tex.) Evaluation Ctr., 1979-80, 81-82; dep. dir. gen. clin. services Austin Child Guidance and Evaluation Ctr., 1982—; sch. psychologist San Rafael (Calif.) Schs., 1980-81; instr. S.W. Tex. State U., San Marcos, 1978-79; pvt. practice psychology. Chmn. Cub Scouts Pack #54, 1977-78. Cert. sch. psychologist, Calif.; lic. psychologist, health services provider, Tex.

Mem. Am. Psychol. Assn. Democrat. Home: 3910 Edgerock Dr Austin TX 78731 Office: 612 W 6th St Austin TX 78701

POWELL, MARIE ELIZABETH, geriatrics home adminstr.; b. Orange, N.J., Feb. 15, 1942; d. Anthony F. and Anna E. (Huggins) Meyer; B.S. in Acctg., Rutgers U.; B.S. in Bus. Adminstrn., Bloomfield Coll.; M.B.A., Manhattan Grad. Coll.; m. William R. Powell; children—Sherri Ann, Toni Lynn, Robin Marie. Corporate controller Meml. Center for Women, West Orange, N.J., 1960-79, asst. adminstr., 1979-81, exec. dir., 1981—; Co-owner Martin & Co. Mem. St. Michael's Parish Council; v.p., past treas. St. Michael's Home Sch. Assn. Mem. Nat. Assn. Female Execs., Lic. Nursing Home Assn., Am. Coll. Nursing Home Adminstrs. Republican. Home: 2247 Alpine Ave Union NJ 07083 Office: 103 Pleasant Valley Way West Orange NJ 07052

POWELL, MARY LOUISE WELLS, psychologist, educator; b. Asheville, N.C., July 7, 1935; d. John Kendall and Beatrice (Rice) Wells; A.B., U. N.C., 1957, M.S., 1964, Ph.D., 1976; m. Elton George Powell, June 21, 1969. Tchr., Myers Park High Sch., Charlotte, N.C., 1957-58; editorial research asst. Time, Inc., N.Y.C., 1959-60; recreation and program dir. Spl. Services U.S. Forces Europe, Germany and France, 1960-62; resident adviser undergrad. women U. N.C., Chapel Hill, 1963-64, research asso. and asst. to project coordinator State/Fed. Inst. for Profl. Devel., 1964-66; prof. organizational indsl. personnel psychology Appalachian State U., Boone, N.C., 1967—. NDEA fellow, 1966; NASA fellow, 1981. Mem. Am., N.C., Southeastern psychol. assns., Am., N.C. personnel and guidance assns., N.C. Coll. Personnel Assn., Nat., N.C. vocat. guidance assns., Am. Soc. Personnel Adminstrn. (accredited personnel diplomate, tng. and devel.), Am. Soc. Tng. and Devel., Organizational Behavior Teaching Soc., AAUW, NOW, Pi Delta Phi. Home: 200 Anne Marie Dr Boone NC 28607 Office: 112-A Smith Wright Hall Appalachian State University Boone NC 28608

POWELL, MAXINE BELL, mgmt. cons., co. exec.; b. Kosciusko, Miss., Feb. 10, 1935; d. Albert W. and Susan (Stuckey) Bell; B.S., Jackson State U., 1956; postgrad (NSF fellow) N.Mex. State U., 1959, Case Western Res., U., 1962, U. Cin., 1966-67; postgrad. Nat. Tng. Labs. courses, 1974-76; m. Lavatus V. Powell, Jr., Nov. 23, 1956 (div. Jan. 1978); children—Robin LaJoyce, Judith LaVonne, Lavatus V. III. Tchr., Lanier High Sch., Jackson, Miss., 1956-59, Walnut Hills High Sch., Cin., 1959-60, 62-64, 65-67; research library mgr. U.S. Indsl. Chemicals div. Nat. Distillers Corp., Cin., 1961; with Procter & Gamble Co., Cin., 1970-81, mgr. tech. info., 1972-75, sect. head research and devel., tech. transfer, 1976—, also sect. head soap and toilet goods services; pres. Greenspaces Inc., 1979—. Chmn. unit United Appeal, 1974; trustee Resident Arts and Humanities Consortium, 1974-76; staff organizer Fannie Lou Hamer Found.; bd. dirs. Planned Parenthood Assn. Mem. AAAS, Am. Soc. Info. Sci., Spl. Libraries Assn., Delta Sigma Theta, NAACP, Alpha Kappa Mu. Home: 2 Revel Ln Cincinnati OH 45217 Office: PO Box 17112 Cincinnati OH 45217

POWELL, ROSALIE, home economist; b. Milw., Oct. 24, 1947; d. William and Daisy P.; B.S., U. Wis., Stout, 1969, M.S. in Home Econs. Edn., 1974. Extension home economist U. Wis. Extension, Langlade County, 1969-74; Waukesha County, 1976—; instr. U. Wis.-Stout, Menomonie, 1975-76; asst. prof. dept. family devel. U. Wis. Extension, 1976-81, asso. prof., 1981—. Mem. Am. Home Econs. Assn., Wis. Home Econs. Assn., Nat. Assn. Extension Home Economists, Wis. Assn. Extension Home Economists, Soc. Nutrition Edn., Epsilon Sigma Phi, Bus. and Profl. Women (chpt. pres. 1970-74), Gamma Sigma Sigma (nat. pres. 1975-77). Club: Waukesha Altrusa. Home: 403 Sheffield Rd Waukesha WI 53186 Office: 515 W Moreland Rd Waukesha WI 53186

POWER, HELEN MARY BLACKBURNE, univ. ofcl.; b. Rochester, N.Y.; d. William Hugh and Kathryn (Maher) Blackburne; A.B., U. Rochester, 1927, Litt.D. (hon.), 1971; Litt.D., Nazareth Coll., 1964; L.H.D., Keuka Coll., 1968; LL.D., Hobart Coll., 1970, St. John Fisher Coll., 1974, Alfred U., 1975; m. Kenneth T. Power, Sept. 29, 1927; children—Kenneth T., William B., Bruce D. Bd. regents State U. N.Y., Albany, 1964-75, regent emeritus, 1975—, chmn. regent's legislative com., 1968—; cons. Susan B. Anthony Meml.; adv. council Bd. Coop. Ednl. Services. Mem. Community Planning Com. on Nursing Edn., Rochester, 1967—; active A.R.C.; mem. N.Y. State Internat. Women's Year Com.; mem. Monroe County Republican Com., 1950; sec. N.Y. State Fedn. Rep. Women's Clubs, 1942-44, chmn. task force edn.; pres. bd. trustees Judy Weis Meml. Ednl. Fund, 1963—; trustee Nazareth Coll. bd. dirs. Monroe County Mental Health. Recipient awards including Helen Power Internat. grant Am. Assn. U. Women, 1958. Mem. Am. Assn. U. Women (br. pres. 1952-53, div. v.p. 1958-69), Fedn. Women's Clubs, (Rochester pres. 1963-64), Delta Kappa Gamma (hon.). Republican. Clubs: Seventh Judicial District Past Presidents (hon.), Monroe County Past Presidents (hon.), Susan B. Anthony (hon.). Home: 16 Southern Pkwy Rochester NY 14618

POWER, JOYCE HAWKINS, business exec.; b. Detroit, Apr. 30, 1946; d. Frederick Bowen and Julia Jane (Oliphant) Hawkins; B.A., No. Ill. U., DeKalb, 1968; M.Ed. (grantee), U. Cin., 1971, Ed.D. (grantee), 1975; 1 dau., Julia Lynne. Ednl. cons., Cin., 1975—; ednl. dir. Adolescent Family Center, Cin., 1978-80; dir. Power Learning Systems, also Project Read Summer Program, Cin., 1977—; pres. Adscience. Mem. Cin. Commn. Human Services, 1980—. Mem. Orton Soc. (dir.), Alpha Lambda Delta, Pi Beta Phi. Home: 7134 Goldengate St Cincinnati OH 45244 Office: PO Box 30139 Cincinnati OH 45230

POWER, MARY ANNE, social worker, rancher; b. N.Y.C., June 20, 1935; d. Monte James and Viola Mary (Murray) Power; B.A., Rosary Coll., 1958; M.S.W., St. Louis U., 1960; children—Michael James, Katie Ann. Supr. intake dept. Women's Christian Alliance, Phila., 1966-69; supr., counselor Cumberland County Comprehensive Community Mental Health Services, Millville, N.J., 1970-72; supr. adoption service, br. office, Spaulding for Children, Westfield, N.J., 1972-74; owner MJK Ranch, Belen, N.Mex., 1974—; feminist counselor Siren Prodns., Inc., Albuquerque, 1978-80, bd. dirs., 1978-81; counselor, coordinator Cottonwood Center, Belen, 1981—; mem. nat. staff Grail. Named Handicapped Profl. Woman of Yr., Pilot Club, Valencia County, N.Mex., 1981, Colo., N.Mex. and El Paso region, 1982. NSF scholar, 1958-60. Mem. Nat. Assn. Social Workers, Acad. Cert. Social Workers, N.Mex. Handicapped Assn., NOW. Democrat. Roman Catholic. Home: Star Route 7 Box 73 Belen NM 87002 Office: Cottonwood Center 1138 River Rd Belen NM 87002

POWER, MARY SUSAN, polit. scientist; b. Hazleton, Pa., May 7, 1935; d. Younger Lovelace and Cleo LaVerne (Boock) P.; B.A., Wells Coll., 1957; M.A., Stanford U., 1959; Ph.D., U. Ill., 1961; 1 dau., Catherine L. Asst. prof. polit. sci. Susquehanna U., Selinsgrove, Pa., 1961-64; assoc. prof. U. Ark., 1964-68; prof. polit. sci. Ark. State U., State University, 1968—; commr. from Ark., Edn. Commn. States, 1981. Sec., Ark. Republican Com., 1978-80. Mem. AAUP (chpt. pres. 1982). Roman Catholic. Author articles in field. Home: 1705 Loberg St Jonesboro AR 72401 Office: Ark State U State University AR

POWERS, ANN RUTLEDGE, educator; b. Wauwatosa, Wis., Feb. 12, 1940; d. Harold and Helen Frances (Hyde) Rutledge; B.S., U. Wis., Milw., 1964; M.A., Northwestern U., 1967; postgrad. Mich. State U., 1969-70; Ed.D., U. Ariz., 1976; m. Louis Edward Powers, Aug. 29, 1971. Tchr. deaf Milw. Public Schs., 1964-66; tchr. aurally handicapped Mt. Diablo Unified Sch. Dist., Concord, Calif., 1967-69; asst. project dir. deaf blind U. Ariz., 1971-72; asst. prof. psychology and spl. edn. Eastern N.Mex. U., Portales, 1972-77; asst. prof. edn. hearing impaired So. Methodist U., Dallas, 1977-80, also dir. programs for edn. of hearing impaired, adj. prof., 1980—; asso. prof. dept. spl. edn. U. Ala., 1980—; instr. continuing edn. U. Ga., 1980; adj. prof. Lenoir Rhyne Coll., Hickory, N.C., 1981; postdoctoral intern Nat. Tech. Inst. for Deaf, Rochester, N.Y., summer 1978; adj. prof. Navajo Indian project U. Ariz., 1976. Charles Stewart Mott Found. fellow, 1969-70; U. Ariz. fellow, 1970-71. Mem. Council Exceptional Children (sec.-treas. div.), Assn. Children with Learning Disabilities, Orton Soc., Internat. Reading Assn., Alexander Graham Bell Assn. for Deaf, Conf. Am. Instrs. Deaf (nominations com.), AAUW, Phi Delta Kappa. Methodist. Contbr. articles to profl. jours. Home: 622 Quail Valley 2501 15th St E Tuscaloosa AL 35404 Office: Dept Spl Edn U Ala University AL 35486

POWERS, EVA AGOSTON, clin. psychologist; b. Budapest, Hungary, Mar. 30, 1938; came to U.S., 1940, naturalized, 1945; d. Tibor and Jeanne Iseult (Watson) Agoston; A.B., Smith Coll., 1960; M.A., Boston U., 1962; Ph.D., 1969; m. James F. Powers, July 4, 1960; children—Wayne, Glenn. Psychologist, Childrens' Hosp. Med. Center Boston, 1964-69, Newton (Mass.) Sch. System, 1969-71, Conway (N.H.) Sch. System, 1972-78; dir. child and youth services Seacoast Regional Counseling Center, Portsmouth, N.H., 1979-80; pvt. practice psychol. counseling, Portsmouth, 1980—, York Harbor, Maine, 1979—; cons. to Maine Sch. System, 1978, Center of Hope, Conway, N.H., 1971-73; supr. tng. program N.H. Dept. Edn., Concord, 1972-74. NIMH grantee, 1961, 62; S. Burt Wolbach Research Fund grantee, 1968. Mem. Am. Psychol. Assn., Maine Psychol. Assn., N.H. Psychol. Assn., N.H. Soc. Psychologists, Mass. Psychol. Assn., Nat. Assn. Psychologists, Am. Orthopsychiat. Assn., Sigma Xi, Phi Beta Kappa. Club: York Golf and Tennis. Contbr. articles to profl. publs. Home: 358 York St York Harbor ME 03911 Office: 127 High St Portsmouth NH 03801

POWERS, GEORGIA MONTGOMERY DAVIS, govt. ofcl., state senator; b. Springfield, Ky., Oct. 29, 1923; d. Ben G. and Frances (Walker) Montgomery; student Louisville Mcpl. Coll., 1940-42; m. James L. Powers, Aug. 17, 1973; 1 son by previous marriage, William F. Davis; stepchildren—Cheryl Campbell, Carlton, Deborah (Mrs. Dan Rattle). Supr., U.S. Census Bur., Jeffersonville, Ind., 1958-61, Louisville, 1969—; asst. hosp. adminstr. Red Cross Hosp., Louisville, 1964-65; mem. Ky. Senate, 1968—, chmn. labor and industry com. Active in civil rights; mem. SCLC, NAACP, Urban League. Mem. Jefferson County Democratic Exec. Com., 1964-66. Recipient King-Kennedy award Young Democrats of Ky., 1968; Achievement award Alpha Kappa Alpha, 1970; Ky. Congress Beauticians and Barbers award, 1971; Woman of Year award Women's Coalition, 1978; Achievement award Zion Baptist Ch., 1973; Recognition award Ky. chpt. NAACP, 1979; Achievement award Watson Meml. Bapt. Ch., 1979. Home: 733 Cecil Ave Louisville KY 40211

POWERS, HELEN, writer; b. Alton, Ill., Jan. 13, 1925; d. Charles Lawrence Rayborn and Ethel (Lowder) Rayborn Howard; self-educated; m. Henry Powers, Mar. 8, 1949; children—Larry, Timothy J. Newspaper journalist, theatre critic, columnist, theatrical feature writer, 1959-70; writer, playwright, 1972-78; books include: Signs of Silence, 1972; The Biggest Little Cat Book in the World (Nat. Assn. Press Women award), 1978; plays include: A Nice Jewish Affair, 1975; Save the Seeds, Darling, 1977; Of Hearts and Hoofers, 1978; publicist, public relations cons. Candlewood Theatre, New Fairfield, Conn., 1974-81, theatrical public relations cons., 1980—, also lectr., tchr., tutor and interpreter for deaf, 1973—, and freelance writer Grolier, Inc., Danbury, Conn., 1979—; tchr. sign lang. Danbury High Sch., 1974-77; vol. deaf mental patients, 1973-75; hostess First Nighter radio show, 1978-80. Recipient Blue ribbon for poetry from Walter Damrosch, 1934; recipient awards for services to community and to deaf. Mem. Nat. Fedn. Press Women (past pres. Conn. chpt.), Hearing and Deaf United, Nat. Fedn. Press Women, Conn. Fedn. Press Women (past pres.), New Fairfield Writers' Workshop. Roman Catholic. Clubs: Quota Internat., Overseas Press. Home and Office: 19 Dogwood Dr Danbury CT 06810

POWERS, JANET NEEDHAM, direct mail and advt. cons. co. exec.; b. West Grove, Pa., May 7, 1943; d. James Walter and Beulah Deane (Wilson) Needham; B.A., Pa. State U., 1965; m. Francis Benjamin Powers, Jr., Dec. 9, 1967. Field rep. Repro Corp., Wilmington, Del., 1965-67; adminstrv. asst. to pres. Mgmt. Cons., Inc., Washington, 1967-69; asst. to pub. Nation's Cities Mag., Washington, 1969-75, advt. sales mgr., 1975-77; dir. membership and mktg. Alexander Graham Bell Assn. for Deaf, Washington, 1977-80; mgr. sales promotion MCI Telecommunications Corp., 1980—. Mem. Women in Advt. and Mktg., Direct Mktg. Club Washington, Scrolls, Zeta Tau Alpha. Address: 1133 19th St NW Washington DC 20036

POWERS, JEANETTE NICOLA, govt. ofcl.; b. Montgomery County, Md., Mar. 19, 1942; d. Jesse and Ruth (Davis) Glover; diploma paralegal specialist, U. Md., 1977; m. Terry Powers, June 12, 1967; children—Joseph, Alan Jerome, Ron Omari. With Dept. Def., 1959-61; with Dept. Labor, 1961—, paralegal specialist employment and tng. legal services div., 1974—. Mem. Oxon Hill Boys/Girls Club. Home: 5006 Winthrop St Oxon Hill MD 20745 Office: 200 Costitution Ave NW Washington DC 20210

POWERS, JEANNE AUDREY, clergywoman; b. Mankato, Minn., July 5, 1932; d. Philip Raymond and Florence Margaret (Jones) P.; B.S., Mankato State U., 1954; postgrad. Princeton Theol. Sem., 1955-56, St. Andrews U., Scotland, 1958-59, S.T.B., Boston U., 1958. Ordained to ministry Meth. Ch., 1958; campus minister Wesley Found. U. Minn., St. Paul, 1959-64; mem. conf. program staff United Meth. Ch., Mpls., 1964-67; minister Univ. United Meth. Ch., Mpls., 1967-69; sec. for missionary personnel Bd. Missions, United Meth. Ch., N.Y.C., 1969-73, asst. gen. sec. ecumenical and interreligious concerns div. Bd. Global Ministries, 1973-80, asso. gen. sec. commn. on Christian unity and interreligious concerns, 1980—; rec. sec. United Meth. Commn. Status and Role of Women, 1972-76; chmn. Commn. Faith and Order Nat. Council Chs. of Christ, 1975-81; exec. com. commn. on faith and order World Council Chs., 1976—; exec. com. N.Am. Acad. Ecumenists, 1978-80; del. World Council Chs., Nairobi, 1975, jurisdictional confs. United Meth. Ch., 1964, 76, 80, gen. conf., 1980. Recipient Disting. Alumni awards Boston U. Sch. Theology, 1970, Tau Kappa Alpha, 1977, Mankato State U., 1977. Danforth Grad. fellow, 1954-55; Lucinda Bidwell Bebee fellow, 1958-59. Home: 501 W 123d St New York NY 10027 Office: 475 Riverside Dr New York NY 10115

POWERS, KATHRYN DOLORES, social adminstr.; b. Chgo., Dec. 17, 1929; B.A., Colgate-Rochester U., 1951; M.S.W., Smith Coll., 1964. Child welfare worker, supr. Cook County Dept. Pub. Aid Children's Div., Chgo., 1953-68; dir. program Central Bapt. Children's Home/Family Services, Lake Villa, Ill., 1968—; chmn. bd. Community Residential Network, Inc.; instr. field work U. Wis., 1975-76. Recipient Spl. Merit Citation, Am. Bapt. Homes and Hosps. Assn., 1979. Mem. Nat. Assn. Social Workers, Acad. Certified Social Workers, Child Care Assn. Ill. Home: 309 Milwaukee St Lake Villa IL 60046 Office: Box 218 Lake Villa IL 60046

POWERS, KAY CARSON, communications exec.; b. Monticello, Ark., Mar. 22, 1947; d. Frank and Vivian Eloise (Groves) Carson; B.A., U. Ark., 1969; m. Lonnie Austin Powers, July 3, 1969. Journalism tchr. Fayetteville (Ark.) High Sch., 1969-70; mng. editor Squire Publs. Inc., Shawnee Mission, Kans., 1970-71; asso. editor Ark. Bankers Assn., Little Rock, 1973-75; info. mgr. Ark. Dept. Local Services, Little Rock, 1975-78; account exec. v.p. Leavitt and Assos., Little Rock, 1978-79; pres. Kay Powers Communications, Little Rock, 1979—. Co-chmn. exhibit Internat. Women's Yr., Ark. Conf. Women in Ark. History, 1977. Recipient Ark. Press Women Communications 1st place award, 1977-78, 81; Nat. Fedn. Press Women 1st place award, 1977; 2d place award, 1978, 81. Fellow Inst. Politics and Govt.; mem. Ark. Assn. Bus. Communicators (pres. 1977), Ark. Press Women (pres. 1979-80, Woman of Achievement 1982), Pub. Relations Soc. Am., Quapaw Quarter Assn. (dir., pres. 1976-79), Women's Edn. and Devel. Inst. (dir. 1978-79, chmn. 1980), Nat. Fedn. Press Women. Democrat. Methodist. Home: 112 Midland St Little Rock AR 72205 Office: 300 Spring Bldg No 620 Little Rock AR 72201

POWERS, (LUCY) LINDLEY, educator; b. Albany, N.Y., Aug. 19, 1926; d. William Tibbits and Winifred (Lispenard) Powers; A.B., Smith Coll., 1948; M.A. in Speech, U. Wis., 1963, M.F.A. in Theater Directing, 1963, Ph.D. in Theatre (E.B. Fred fellow), 1968; postdoctoral Espiscopal Theol. Sch., 1972-74, Weston Coll. Sch. Theology, 1974—; m. Davis Spencer, Mar. 5, 1949 (div. 1961); children—Eleanor Tibbits Spencer Tupper, Joseph Allen Powers Spencer; m. 2d, Gerald E. Fosbroke, Dec. 17, 1976. Children's librarian N.Y.C. Public Library, 1948-49; tchr., Racine, Wis., 1959-61; dir. Wis. 4-H Drama Program, also research asst. U. Wis., 1961-64; instr. U. Wis., 1964-65, 66-67, teaching asst. Sch. Music, 1965-66; asst. prof. drama Bridgewater (Mass.) State Coll., 1968-69; assoc. prof., dir. grad. study theatre edn. Emerson Coll., Boston, 1969-71, assoc. prof. fine arts, 1971-76, prof., 1977-79, adviser creative service interdisciplinary program, 1974-79. Condr. community and conv. workshops in theatre arts; lectr. to clergy and parishes on liturgical experience of myth and symbol; also active in ch. renovation and conducting classes for lay readers. Vice pres. bd. dirs. Ch. Home Soc., Boston; sec. Iona Community New World Found.; founder, bd. dirs. Iona Cornerstone Found., Inc., 1981—, Iona Cornerstone Found. Ltd., 1982—; sec. Diocesan Ecumenical Commn., 1980-82; mem. Mass. Council Chs./Jewish Community Council Dialogues, 1981—. Mem. AAUP, Iona Community (asso. mem.), Soc. St. John the Evangelist (asso.), Dobbs (dir., mem. exec. com. 1949-57, editor Bull., 1949-57), Smith alumnae assns., Shakespeare Club Boston. Author: Proclaim the Word, 1980, also drama ednl. materials. Episcopalian (lay reader). Home: 48 Beacon St Apt 9R Boston MA 02108

POWERS, MALA, actress; b. San Francisco, Dec. 20, 1931; d. George Evart and M. Dell (Thelen) Powers; student U. Calif. at Los Angeles; pupil Michael Chekhov; m. M. Hughes Miller, May 17, 1970; 1 son by previous marriage, Toren Michael Vanton. Motion picture appearances include Cyrano de Bergerac, 1950, Outrage, Edge of Doom, Yellow Mountain, Bengazi, Tammy, Daddy's Gona A'Hunting, Temple of the Ravens, 1975, Six Tickets to Hell, 1975; recs., star RCA records for pre-Christmas, 1977; stage prodns. include Absence of a Cello, 1964-65, Hogan's Goat, Night of the Iguana, Bus Stop, Far Country, The Rivalry; also starred radio and TV prodns. including Lux Radio Theater, This is Your FBI, Cisco Kid, Hazel, Man from Uncle, G.E. Theater, Bonanza, Ironside, Perry Mason, Rookies, Charley's Angels, Med. Story; co-star with Anthony Quinn in The Man and the City, 1971-72; v.p. Book Publishers Project, Inc., 1978—; lectr. in field. Entertainer troops, U.S.O., Korea, 1951-52; chmn. So. Calif. Mother's com. March of Dimes, 1972-82. Mem Acad. Motion Picture Arts and Scis. (mem. fgn. film com.), Nat. Acad. TV Arts and Scis., ANTA (v.p., exec. com. 1974-75). Mem. Unity Sch. Christianity. Author: Follow the Star, Am., Brit., Italian and Spanish edits., 1980. Editor The Secret Seven and the Grim Secret; The Secret Seven and the Old Fort Adventure, 1972. Rec. advent calendar and book Follow the Star, 1977; creator, writer, narrator Children's Story, daily 1-minute telephone broadcast for N.Y. Telephone Co., 1979-81, Cleve. and Detroit Telephone Cos., 1981-82. Home: 4317 Forman Ave North Hollywood CA 91602 Office: 1270 Ave of Americas Suite 2211 New York NY 10020

POYDOCK, MARY EYMARD, coll. ofcl.; b. Sykesville, Pa., Dec. 3, 1910; d. John Andrew and Anna Mary (Dryna) P.; A.B., Mercyhurst Coll., 1943; M.A., U. Pitts., 1946; Ph.D., St. Thomas Research Inst., 1965. Joined Sisters of Mercy, 1932; tchr. elem. schs. Erie (Pa.) Diocese, 1935-41; tchr. high sch., Pitts., 1941-47; with Mercyhurst Coll., Erie, 1947—, dir. cancer research, 1965—. Sec. exec. bd. Erie unit Am. Cancer Soc. Sperti fellow, 1963-65; NSF grantee, summer 1966. Mem. AAAS, Pa. Acad. Sci., Beta Beta Beta. Contbr. in field. Home and office: 501 E 38th St Erie PA 16501

POYNTER, MARION KNAUSS, journalist; b. Poughkeepsie, N.Y., Apr. 17, 1926; d. Louis Eugene and Rose Alvina (Arndt) Knauss; A.B., Vassar Coll., 1946; postgrad. Fla. State U., 1950, Am. U., 1960, U. South Fla., 1971; m. Nelson Paul Poynter, May 4, 1970. Advt. sales rep. R.H. Donnelley Corp., 1946-47; researcher Time-Life, Inc., N.Y.C., 1948-49; researcher CIA, Washington, 1952-60; editorial writer, researcher St. Petersburg (Fla.) Times, 1961-70; v.p. Teleworld Communications, Inc., Phila., 1981—; dir. Times Pub. Co. Bd. dirs. Modern Media Inst., St. Petersburg, 1975—. Mem. Women in Communication, Internat. Press Inst. Address: 629 —A— St SE Washington DC 20003

PRACHT, IRENA, mfg. co. exec.; b. Council Grove, Kans., Dec. 24, 1927; d. Berend Hiram and Amanda (Anderson) Bicker; student Kans. Agrl. Coll., 1945-46; B.S., Kans. State Coll., Emporia, 1949; m. Harold Ray Pracht, Oct. 23, 1948; children—Rae Ann Pracht Lowery, Gregory Ray, Rena Rochelle Pracht Coby, Glen Frederick. Bookkeeper, Eby Constrn. Co., Wichita, 1951-52; partner Bell Sewing Centers, Tex., N.Mex., 1954-62, Tri State Sewing Machine Distbrs., Council Grove, Kans., 1962-68; staff acct. Mize, House & Reed C.P.A.s, Topeka, 1968-69; staff acct., gen. ledger supr., controller Farah Mfg. Co., Inc., El Paso, 1969—; partner Pracht Enterprises, El Paso, 1975—; sec. treas. Vernon Investment Corp., El Paso, 1971—; v.p., dir. Tex. Pure Products, El Paso, 1981—. C.P.A., Tex. Mem. Tex. Soc. C.P.A.s, Theta Sigma Upsilon, Xi Phi. Home: 3110 Dundee St El Paso TX 79925 Office: 8889 Gateway West El Paso TX 79925

PRACHT, PEGGY SUE, sci. lab. adminstr.; b. Oakland, Calif., Dec. 23, 1947; d. Loren Eugene and Frankie Ethelene (Dupree) P.; B.A. in Music, Calif. State U., Hayward, 1970, student in Bus. Adminstrn.; 1 son, John Thomas Yeandle. Computer operator Haskins & Sells, C.P.A.s, San Francisco, 1974-75; staff asst. to dir. Lawrence Berkeley Lab., 1976—. Mem. Nat. Assn. Female Execs. Home: 21033 Redwood Rd Castro Valley CA 94546 Office: Lawrence Berkeley Lab Calif 1 Cyclotron Rd Berkeley CA 94720

PRACKUP, LORRAINE, employee benefits specialist; b. Bklyn., Mar. 25, 1939; d. Michael and Josephine (Parrella) Ferrone; student public schs.; m. George M. Prackup, Sept. 7, 1959; children—George M., Jeffrey, Richard, Michael. Various clerical and secretarial positions, 1957-59; mem. office staff Norwalk (Conn.) Hosp., 1956-62; office mgr., sec. to pres. Bomar Inc., N.H., 1977-78; dir. fin. and adminstrn. Redington, Inc., Stamford, Conn., 1978-80; dir. fin. Allied Elevator Cos. Conn. and N.Y., Bridgeport, Conn., 1980-81; employee benefits specialist Stanley A. Thal Assos., Stamford, Conn., 1981—. Mem. Nat. Assn. Female Execs., Women's Guild, Catholic Daus. Am. Republican. Roman Catholic. Club: Columbiettes. Home: 21 Tannery Ln S Weston CT 06883 Office: 400 Main St Stamford CT 06901

PRADO, MARTA, nurse; b. Havana, Cuba, Apr. 24, 1950; d. Fernando and Beatriz Marta (Leon) P.; R.N., Jackson Meml. Hosp. Sch. Nursing, 1970; nurse practitioner U. Miami, 1974; cert. emergency med. services Fla. Internat. Sch. Bus., 1974; Staff nurse Jackson Meml. Hosp., Miami, 1970-71, head nurse, 1971-75, nurse practitioner, 1975-77; nurse cons. emergency med. services Dade County Fire Dept., Miami, 1976—; nursing adminstrn. cons. Emergency Med. Services Assos., Miami, 1976—, dir. continuing edn., 1977—. Co-chmn. Gov.'s Council on Emergency Med. Services, 1976—. Recipient Jackson Meml. Citizenship award, 1970. Mem. Fla. Emergency Dept. Nurses Assn. (pres. 1974-76), Nat. Emergency Dept. Nurses Assn. (dir.; pres. 1979—), Am. Heart Assn. Greater Miami, Fla. Nurses Assn., Fedn. Splty. Nursing, Nat. Health Council. Contbr. articles to profl. jours. Office: 3900 NW 79th Ave Miami FL 33166

PRAGER, DOROTHY BEATRICE, advt. agy. exec.; b. Chgo., Nov. 10, 1924; d. Samuel L. and Clara (Mite) Prager; B.S., Northwestern U., 1947. Advt. mgr. Mandel Bros. Dept. Store, Chgo., 1947-52, 58-61; group advt. mgr. Aldens Inc., N.Y.C., 1952-55; account supr. and creative supr. State Advt. Agy., Chgo., 1955-57; account exec. Bozell & Jacobs, Inc., Chgo., 1961-63; mgr. info. services, cons. advt. and sales promotion Nat. Home Furnishings Assn., Chgo., 1963-77; pres. Dorothy Prager Advt. Ltd., Chgo., 1977—; cons., lectr. in field. Recipient Award for outstanding contbn. to success of Nat. Home Furnishings Assn., 1977. Mem. Nat. Home Fashions League (v.p.). Asso. editor NHFA Reports, 1965-77; contbr. articles to profl. jours.

PRÄGER-BENETT, NANCY ANN, artist; b. N.Y.C., Mar. 17, 1943; d. Sigmund Godfrey and Eleanor Pauline Prager; student M.A. program Syracuse U., 1961-62, Accademia de Belle Arte, Florence, Italy, 1964-65; A.B., Cooper Union Coll., 1968; m. Barry Lawrence Benett, June 19, 1966; children—Lara Christina, Andrew Bernard, Ariane Alison. Work exhibited in pvt. individual shows, also mus. and univ. group shows, U.S., Italy, France, Can., Turkey; represented pvt. and corp. collections U.S., Italy, Eng., France, Can.; represented by Raymond Duncan Gallery, Paris; tchr. Black Emergency Cultural Coalition, Met. Mus., N.Y. prison systems. Mem. Bd. TV Arts and Scis.; Recipient Prix de Paris, 1975, Grand Prix Humanitaire de France, 1976. Mem. Am.-Scandinavian Found., Les Surindependants Societaire, Graphic Art Assn., Smithsonian Assos., Met. Mus. Presbyterian. Club: Saltaire Yacht (dir. 1972-80, gov.). Work noted in Artist USA Bicentennial, N.Y. Art Yearbook, Nouvelle Littaire, Art News Mag., Arts Mag. Home: New York NY 10021 Office: 545 8th Ave New York NY 10018

PRANCE, JUNE ELIZABETH, writer-illustrator, educator; b. Huddersfield, Eng., June 25, 1929; d. George Herbert and Beatrice (Hill) Shaw; came to U.S., 1946; student Victoria Coll., Toronto, Ont., Can., 1947-48; B.A. in Journalism, Fla. State U., 1972; post grad., U. Fla., 1973—; m. Dewey W. Prance; children—Brian, Marilynn, David, Michael, Nancy, John, Cathryn, Dewey. Promotional artist, columnist Sarasota (Fla.) News, 1957-61, Tampa (Fla.) Tribune Co., 1961-66; instr. comml. art. Tampa Bay Vocat.-Tech. Center, 1966—; freelance writer, illustrator, 1949—; lectr., cons. in field. Bd. dirs. Friends of the Library, Tampa, 1977—. Mem. Women in Communications, Am., Tampa advt. fedns., Soc. Children's Book Writers, Fla. Vocat. Assn., Brit., Am. amateur press assns., Travel Writers Internat., Transatlantic Brides and Parents Assn. Baptist. Author-illustrator: Traditional British Recipes for American Cooks, 1971; The Creative Commercial Art Workbook, 1976; editor, pub. quar. jour. Brit. Digest Illustrated; contbr. articles, illustrations to profl. jours. Home: 10104 Tucker Jones Rd Riverview FL 33569 Office: 6410 Orient Rd Tampa FL 33610

PRANGE, SALLY BOWEN, ceramist; b. Valparaiso, Ind., Aug. 11, 1927; d. Milton Matern and Louise (Mammen) Bowen; B.A., U. Mich., 1950; m. Arthur J. Prange, Jr., Feb. 4, 1950; children—Christine Anne, Martha Louise, Laura Beth, David Elliott. Ceramist and tchr., 1948—; tchr. workshops, 1956—; one-woman exhbns. include: Dupont Gallery of Art, Washington and Lee U., 1975, 1980, San Jose (Calif.) Mus. Art, 1980, Greenwood Gallery, Washington, Marcia Rodell Gallery, Los Angeles, Sumter (S.C.) Gallery Art; group exhbns. include: Butler Inst. Am. Art, Indpls., 1967-69, N.C. Artists Exhbn., 1971, 73, 76-77, 79, Mint Mus., Charlotte, N.C., 1972, 76, 78, 80, Internat. Exhbn. Ceramics, Faenza, Italy, 1976, 78, S.E. Center for Contemporary Art, 1976, Marietta Coll. Crafts Nat., 1975, Ceramic Conjunction '77, Long Beach (Calif.) Mus. Art, 1977, Am. Porcelain, Renwick, Smithsonian, 1980—, Gray Art Gallery, East Carolina U., Greenville, 1982, also in Balt. and Scottsdale, Ariz., 1982; represented in permanent collections Victoria and Albert Mus., London, Pa. State U. Mus. Art, N.C. Mus. Art, Ackland Meml. Art Center at U. N.C., Chapel Hill, J. Patrick Lannon Found., Palm Beach, Fla., Nat. Mus. Am. Art, Smithsonian Instn., Arrowmont Sch. of Art and Craft, Gatlinburg, Tenn., U. Mich. Mus. Art, Ann Arbor. Mem. Piedmont Craftsmen, Am. Crafts Council, World Crafts Council, Nat. Council Edn. Ceramic Arts. Democrat. Address: 1804 Rolling Rd Chapel Hill NC 27514

PRATHER, JOAN JEAN, nurse; b. Longton, Kans., Jan. 3, 1941; d. Lloyd E. and Mary E. (Towner) P.; grad. Wesley Med. Center Sch. Nursing, Wichita, 1962; B.S., Calif. State U., Hayward, 1975; M.B.A. in Health Services Mgmt., Golden Gate U., 1980. Staff nurse Wesley Med. Center, Wichita, Kans., 1962-63; nurse thoracic surgery unit Ohio State U. Hosp., Columbus, 1963-65; commd. 2d lt. Nurses Corps, U.S. Air Force, 1965, advanced through grades to capt., 1969; nurse Kaiser Found. Hosp., San Francisco, 1969-70; nurse CCU, Kaiser Found. Hosp., Oakland, Calif., 1970-80, asst. unit supr. critical care units, 1980-82, unit supr., 1982—, instr. critical care nursing Kaiser No. Calif. Regional Office of Edn. and Tng. Mem. Am. Assn. Critical Care Nurses, Am. Nurses Assn., Am. Heart Assn. Home: 2347 Arf Ave Hayward CA 94545 Office: 280 W MacArthur Blvd Oakland CA 94604

PRATT, ANN B(OGUE), psychologist, educator; b. Austin, Tex., May 6, 1929; d. William John and Gladys Margaret (Bogue) Reilly; A.B., Antioch Coll., 1952; M.A. in Psychology, U. Minn., 1961, Ph.D. in Psychology, 1970; m. Richard F. Pratt, Aug. 13, 1965; children from previous marriage—Douglas Owen Cornog, Clay Ian Cornog. Psychometrist U. Chgo., 1962-63; guidance counselor Michael Reese Hosp. Sch. of Nursing, Chgo., 1963-70; asst. prof. psychology Elmhurst (Ill.) Coll., 1970-72; asst. prof. psychology Capital U., Columbus, Ohio, 1972-77, asso. prof., 1977—; cons. learning, motivation and self-measurement for Chgo. and Columbus area schs. of nursing, 1968—; cons. local sch. dists. Mem. Am. Psychol. Assn., A.A.A.S., Am. Ednl. Research Assn. Contbr. to psychology jours. Home: 477 Delaware Court Westerville OH 43081 Office: 114 Learning Center Capital University Columbus OH 43209

PRATT, E(LLEN) MARCELLA MORIN, designer; b. Trail, B.C., Canada (parents Am. citizens); d. Francis George and Rose Delima (Bousquet) Morin; student extension courses Wash. State Coll.; grad. Normal Coll., Victoria, B.C.; m. George Collins Pratt, Sept. 22, 1946. With art dept. Universal Internat. Pictures 1935-46; now home designer and decorator, Calif., Wash. Mem. Assistance League So. Calif. (life), Canadian Red Cross (life), Navy League of the U.S. (life), Mary and Joseph League (life), Eisenhower Med. Aux., Palm Desert, Calif. (life). Republican. Home: Box 427 Cathedral City CA 92234

PRATT, JUDITH ALLAN, state legislator, educator; b. Albuquerque, May 7, 1941; d. Earl P. and Louise G. Webb; B.A., U. N.Mex., 1964, M.A. in Edn., 1972, postgrad., 1972-78; m. Orville R. Pratt, June 10, 1966; children—Heather Alice, Emily Haven. Secondary English tchr., Albuquerque, 1964-70; English tchr., Shawnee Mission, Kans., 1970-71; tchr. tng. programs, supr. student tchrs. rural, Indian, local programs, Albuquerque and Mescalero, N.Mex., 1971-78; coordinator Labor Edn. Clearinghouse, Albuquerque, 1978—; mem. N.Mex. Ho. of Reps., 1978—, vice chmn. Labor Com. Chmn. bd. Citizens Edn. Clearinghouse; bd. Community Services to the Handicapped, 1978-79; exec. bd. Albuquerque Equal Rights Council, 1976-80; pres. Bandelier PTA, 1979-80; mem. N.Mex. Dem. Women. Recipient hon. award U. Albuquerque, 1979. Mem. Nat. Assn. State Legislatures. Contbr. articles to publs. including El Cuhamil, Coal Field Defender, Clearinghouse News. Office: 5102 Grand NE Albuquerque NM 87108

PRATT, MARGARET WADE, info. sci. corp. exec.; b. Kansas City, Mo., Apr. 5, 1925; d. Walter Wesley and Leone (Smith) P.; B.A., Washburn U., 1945. Dir. maternal and child health studies George Washington U., Washington, 1962-73; dir. maternal and child health studies project Minn. Systems Research, Inc., Washington, 1974-75; pres., project dir. Info. Sciences Research Inst., Washington, 1976—. Mem. Am. Pub. Health Assn., Assn. MCH and CCS Program Dirs. Office: 8720 Georgia Ave Suite 1006 Silver Spring MD 20910

PRATT, MARIANNA BAITSELL, mag. editor; b. Ottumwa, Iowa, Sept. 10, 1923; d. Karl M. and Gladys E. (McKinney) Baitsell; B.A. cum laude, Central Coll., Pella, Iowa 1946; postgrad. Columbia U.; div.; children—Gregory F., Kevin C. Editorial asst. Food Bus. mag. Putman Pub. Co., Chgo., 1956, asst. editor Industry and Power mag., 1958; feature writer Herald Palladium Pub. Co., Benton Harbor, Mich., 1963; mng. editor Agrl. Engring. mag., Am. Soc. Agrl. Engrs., St. Joseph, Mich., 1965—. Mem. Am. Agrl. Editors Assn., Communicators Forum, AAUW, Soc. Tech. Communication (chpt. pres. 1967, nat. sec. 1976), S.W. Mich. Writers (founder 1971). Republican. Mem. United Ch. Christ. Club: Main St. Toastmasters. Home: 2900 Cleveland St Apt 214 St Joseph MI 49085 Office: 2950 Niles Rd St Joseph MI 49085

PRATT, MILDRED INEZ, educator; b. Henderson, Tex., Oct. 15, 1928; d. R. P. and Eula (Thirkill) Sirls; B.A., Jarvis Coll., 1951; M.A., Butler U., 1952; M.A., Ind. U., 1955; Ph.D., U. Pitts., 1969; m. Theodore A. E.C. Pratt, Nov. 24, 1964; children—Awadagin, Menah. Program dir. All Nations Found., Los Angeles, 1956-59, Rouge Ecorse United Center, Ecorse, Mich., 1959-63; asst. prof. U. Pitts., 1963-69; prof. social work Ill. State U., Normal, 1969—; faculty Cath. U., Rio de Janeiro, Brazil, 1972-73, Fed. U., Rio de Janerio, 1972-73. Mem. Council on Social Work Edn. Contbr. articles to profl. jours. Home: 1405 W Hovey Ave Normal IL 61761 Office: Dept of Sociology and Anthropology Ill State U Normal IL 61761

PRAVDER, MARSHA DEBORAH, psychologist; b. N.Y.C., Apr. 14, 1953; d. Sidney and Ann Toby (Goldman) P.; B.A. (Regents scholar 1969-73, Sullivan award 1973), SUNY, Stony Brook, 1973; Ph.D., SUNY, Albany, 1979. Tchr. high sch. English, 1973-74; unit psychologist O.D. Heck Devel. Center, Schenectady, 1976-77; group home supr. Bosco House of St. Catherine's Center Children, Albany, 1977-78; intern Children's Psychiat. Center, Red Bank, N.J., 1978-79; adolescent clin. cons. Charles River Counseling Center, Newton, Mass., 1979-81; coordinator adolescent psychotherapy Charles River Hosp., Wellesley, Mass., 1981, dir. adolescent psychotherapy, 1981—clin. instr. psychiatry Boston U. Med. Sch., 1981—; guest lectr., cons., workshop leader in field. Mem. Am. Psychol. Assn., Am. Orthopsychiat. Assn., Soc. Family Therapy and Research, Union Concerned Scientists (sponsor). Folk Music Soc. Greater Boston. Jewish. Author papers in field. Office: 203 Grove St Wellesley MA 02181

PRECUP, ALICEMARIE VERONICA, editor; b. N.Y.C., Apr. 28, 1945; d. C. Benedict and Alice Isabelle (Fanelli) Mauro; B.A., George Washington U., 1967; m. Ronald G. Precup, Dec. 19, 1964; children—Ronald G., Elizabeth Anne, Margaret Joy. Secondary sch. tchr. D.C. Pub. Schs., 1967-68; references editor Ralph Nader Congress Project, Washington, 1972; prodn. editor Am. Personnel & Guidance Assn., Washington, 1972-75, Am. Inst. Biol. Scis., Washington, 1975-81; editorial cons. Am. Inst. Biol. Scis., Nat. Acad. Scis., Smithsonian Instn. Press, 1982—. Mem. St. Agnes Choir, 1972—, Arlington (Va.) Met. Chorus, 1973—; cantor St. Agnes Parish, 1978—. Mem. Council Biology Editors, Smithsonian Assos., Soc. for Scholarly Pub., Washington Ind. Writers, Nat. Assn. Female Execs., NOW. Democrat. Roman Catholic. Contbr. articles to profl. jours. Address: 4123 N Richmond St Arlington VA 22207

PREDKO, ANNY EMILIE, travel agy. exec.; b. Marburg, West Germany, Apr. 12, 1927; came to U.S., 1953, naturalized, 1958; d. Jakob and Sophie Louise (Ludwig) Lauer; M. Music Edn., State Conservatory of Hesse, 1952; m. William W. Predko, July 20, 1953; children—Peter Daniel, Stephanie Ann. Pvt. music tchr., Schenectady, N.Y., 1953-60; office mgr. Rainbow Car Wash, Inc., 1964-69; co-owner, mgr. Stockade Travel, Inc., 1969—. Fellow Inst. Cert. Travel Cons.; mem. Am. Soc. Travel Agts. Republican. Lutheran. Club: German Am. Home: 2307 Pine Ridge Rd Schenectady NY 12309 Office: Stockade Travel Inc 1421 Erie Blvd Schenectady NY 12305

PREISKEL, BARBARA SCOTT, lawyer, assn. exec.; b. Washington, July 6, 1924; d. James and B. Beatrix Scott; B.A., Wellesley Coll., 1945; LL.B., Yale U., 1947; m. Robert H. Preiskel, Oct. 28, 1950; children—John S., Richard A. Admitted to D.C. bar, 1948, N.Y. bar, 1948, U.S. Supreme Ct. bar, 1960; law clk. U.S. Dist. Ct., Boston, 1948-49; asso. firm Poletti, Diamond, Roosevelt, Freidin & Mackay, N.Y.C., 1949-50; asso. firm Dwight, Royall, Harris, Koegel & Caskey, N.Y.C., 1950-54, cons., N.Y.C., 1954-59; cons. Ford Found. Fund for the Republic, N.Y.C., 1954; dep. atty. Motion Picture Assn. Am., Inc., N.Y.C., 1959-71, v.p., legis. counsel, 1971-77, sr. v.p., gen. atty., 1977—; dir. Jewel Cos., Inc., Amstar Corp., Textron Inc., Levi Strauss & Co., R.H. Macy Corp. Mem. Pres.'s. Commn. on Obscenity and Pornography, 1968-70; bd. dirs. Citizens Com. for Children, 1966-72, Child Adoption Service of State Charities Aid Assn., 1961-68, Hillcrest Center for Children, 1958-61, Fedn. of Protestant Welfare Agys., 1959-61, 64—, N.Y. Philharm. Soc., 1971—; bd. dirs. Wiltwyck Sch., 1950—, chmn. bd., 1969-78; mem. N.Y.C. Bd. Ethics, 1976—; successor trustee Yale Corp., 1977—; mem. distbn. com. N.Y. Community Trust, 1978—; mem. operating corp. N.Y. Conv. Center, 1980—. Mem. Am. Bar Assn., Bar Assn. City of N.Y. (exec. com. 1972-76), ACLU (dir. 1971-79). Home: 300 West End Ave New York NY 10023 Office: 522 Fifth Ave New York NY 10036

PREMINGER, EVE M., judge; b. Vienna, Austria, Sept. 20, 1935; d. Ingo and Kate Maria (Musil) P.; student Antioch Coll.; LL.B., Columbia U., 1960; m. Theodore H. Friedman, Dec. 6, 1962; children—Wendy Kate, Sarah Elizabeth. Admitted to N.Y. State bar, 1961, U.S. Supreme Ct. bar, 1967; asso. firm William G. Mulligan, N.Y.C., 1960-62; trial counsel Marshall & Morris, N.Y.C., 1965-70; dir. legal services bur. Correctional Assn. City of N.Y., 1971-76, pres., 1971-76; legal advisor Columbia U., N.Y.C., 1971-73; mem. faculty Columbia U. Law Sch., 1972-76; spl. asst. atty. gen., State of N.Y.-Inquiry on Attica Prosecution, 1975; judge Criminal Ct., City of N.Y., 1976—; acting justice Supreme Ct. State of N.Y., N.Y.C., from 1978. Mem. Am. Law Inst., Assn. Bar City of N.Y. (chairperson com. on sentencing), N.Y. County Lawyers Assn., Women in Criminal Justice, Am. Bar Assn. Office: Criminal Ct 100 Centre St Room 319 New York NY 10013 *

PREMO, BLANCHE LILLIE, govt. agy. adminstr.; b. Highland Park, Mich., Jan. 20, 1943; d. Charles G. and Anna Catherine (Clair) Kolar; A.B., Marygrove Coll., 1967; M.A., Marquette U., 1969, Ph.D., 1974; children—Mary Katharyn, Bianca Caroline. Assoc. prof. philosophy St. Mary's Coll., 1972-76, v.p. acad. affairs, 1976-79; asst. dir. higher edn. Nat. Endowment Humanities, Washington, 1979—; professorial instr. Cath. U. Am., Georgetown U. NDEA fellow, 1969-71; Alfred J. Schmitt fellow, 1971-72. Mem. Am. Philos. Assn., Am. Cath. Philos. Assn. Contbr. articles in field. Office: 806 15th St NW Washington DC 20506

PRENDERGAST, RUTH, state legislator; b. Wood Lake, Nebr., Dec. 20, 1928; student U. Nebr., 1948-49; m. Frank Prendergast; children—Eileen, Elaine, Patrick. Adminstrv. sec. Election Commn., Denver, 1971-72; sec. to majority leader Colo. Ho. of Reps., 1973-74; real estate sales, 1977-79; Mem. Colo. Ho. of Reps., 1980—; mem. Denver Election Commn., 1979-80; Denver Reagan Chmn., 1976. Active PTA, Girl Scouts U.S.A., YWCA. Mem. Colo. Conservative Union (dir., chmn.). Presbyterian. Clubs: Lincoln (Colo.); Order of Eastern Star. Office: Colorado House of Representatives State Capitol Denver CO 80203 *

PRENTICE, MARY LEA, media ednl. adminstr.; b. Plymouth, Ill., May 16, 1930; d. Clyde J. and Mary R. (Huddleston) Ware; B.S., Western Ill. U., 1958; NDEA scholar Purdue U., summer 1966; M.S. (Delta Kappa Gamma scholar), Ill. State U., 1974; postgrad. U. Mo., 1982; postgrad. (scholar) Photographer's Edn. Workshop, St. Cloud State U., summer 1982; m. Richmond Ellis Prentice, Aug. 4, 1950; children—Rodney Ellis, Gina Luan. Tchr. elem. sch., Hancock County, Ill., 1950-55; library asst. Streator (Ill.) Elem. Schs., 1956-57; media supr. Pikeland Community Unit No. 10 Schs., Pittsfield, Ill., 1961—; mem. North Central Accreditation Visitation Teams, 1965—; cons. Library Book Selection Service, Inc., 1977—. Bd. dirs. Pittsfield Public Library, 1975—, West Central Ill. area Gt. River Library System, 1982—. Mem. NEA, Ill. Assn. Media Educators, Western Ill. Audiovisual Assn., Div. Sch. Media Specialists, Assn. Ednl. Communications and Tech., Ill. Assn. Edn. Communications and Tech. (treas. 1982—), Delta Kappa Gamma. Methodist. Contbr. articles to profl. jours. Office: Pittsfield High Sch Pittsfield IL 62363

PRESCOTT, ETHELIND SOUTHERLAND, educator; b. Arcadia, Fla., Sept. 22, 1930; d. Frederick and Clara (Warlick) Southerland; B.S. in Edn. magna cum laude, Fla. So. Coll., 1969; m. Bedford Prescott, Mar. 18, 1951; children—Donald B., Linda Gail. Tchr., Zolfo Elem. Sch., Zolfo Springs, Fla., 1969-71, migrant child reading tchr., 1971-73, classroom tchr., 1973-74; migrant child lang. arts tchr. Hardee County, Fla., 1974—. Organist, New Hope Bapt. Ch., Wauchula, Fla., 1973—; mem. youth devel. com., Wauchula, 1974. Mem. Hardee County Edn. Assn., Fla. Edn. Assn. Baptist. Clubs: Wauchula Jr. Woman's (sec. 1956-58). Address: PO Box 52 Wauchula FL 33873

PRESCOTT, EVELYN DORA, educator; b. Bogalusa, La., Apr. 8, 1921; s. Robert William and Ollie (Brumfield) P.; A.A., Southwest Miss. Jr. Coll., 1940; postgrad. La. State U., 1940, 46; B.S., U. So. Miss., 1949; M.S., U. N.C., 1952; postgrad. U. Minn., 1958; Ed.D., U. Ark., 1970. Tchr., coach Carter's Creek High Sch., Holmesville, Miss., 1940-41, Johnston Sta. (Miss.) Consol. High Sch., 1941-43, Enterprise High Sch., McComb, Miss., 1946-48; dir. phys. edn. women Perkinston Jr. Coll. Miss., 1949-50; dir. girls' phys. edn., coach High Point (N.C.) High Sch., 1950-53; coordinator women's phys. edn. Ark. State U., 1953—, prof. health and phys. edn., 1970—, student tchr. supr., 1960-73; mem. Ark. com. to review and recommend changes in cert. requirements for phys. edn. Served with WAC, U.S. Army, 1943-45. Mem. AAHPER (v.p. Ark. phys. edn. div. 1982—), Nat. Wildlife Assn., Phi Delta Kappa, Delta Kappa Gamma. Contbr. articles to profl. jours. Home: 208 Scott St Jonesboro AR 72401 Office: PO Box 120 Ark State U State University AR 72467

PRESCOTT, RITA ELIZABETH, judge; b. North Tonawanda, N.Y., June 6, 1921; d. William Waldo and Marie Eleanore (Dreyer) P.; B.S., U. Pa., 1943, M.S., 1944; LL.B., Temple U., 1949. Tchr. comml. subjects Prospect Park (Pa.) High Sch., 1945-51; admitted to Pa. bar, 1952; individual practice law, 1952-75; law clk. to James C. Crumlish, Sr., Phila., 1951-58, to Judges Sweeney and Diggins, Ct. Common Pleas Delaware County, Media, Pa., 1958-60; ct. adminstr. County of Delaware, Media, 1961-75; judge Ct. Common Pleas, 32nd Jud. Dist. Commonwealth Pa., 1976-80, adminstrv. judge civil div., 1980—. Bd. overseers Del. Law Sch., Widener U., Brandywine, 1982—. Mem. Am. Bar Assn., Pa. Bar Assn., Deleware County Bar Assn., Phila. Bar Assn., Am. Judicature Soc., Inst. Jud. Adminstrs., Nat. Assn. Women Lawyers, Nat. Assn. Trial Ct. Adminstrs., Nat. Fedn. Bus. and Profl. Women, Mortar Bd., Pi Lambda Theta, Alpha Xi Delta. Office: Courthouse Media PA 19063

PRESCOTT, SANDRA K., Maine state rep.; b. Portland, Maine, Mar. 11, 1943; d. Preston Clyde and Laura (Trenholm) Kinney; student Wash. State Tchrs. Coll., 1961-62; m. William A. Prescott, Jr., 1961; children—William A., Jo-Marie, Michael M. Mem., Hampden Town Council, Maine, 1975—; mem. Maine Ho. Reps., Dist. 70, 1977—, mem. adv. com. Med. Edn., mem. select com. Rural Health and Med. Edn., ho. chmn. Health Inst. Service Com. Office: Maine Ho Reps State Capitol Augusta ME 04330 *

PRESKA, MARGARET LOUISE ROBINSON, univ. pres.; b. Parma, N.Y., Jan. 23, 1938; d. Ralph Craven and Ellen Elvira (Niemi) Robinson; B.S. summa cum laude, SUNY, Brockport, 1957; M.A., Pa. State U., 1961; Ph.D., Claremont (Calif.) Grad. Sch., 1969; postgrad. Manchester Coll., Oxford (Eng.) U., summer 1973; m. Daniel C. Preska, Jan. 24, 1959; children—Robert, William, Ellen. From instr. to asso. prof. history and govt. U. LaVerne (Calif.), 1968-75, acad. dean, 1972-75; instr. Starr King Sch. Ministry, Berkeley, Calif., summer 1975; v.p. acad. affair, EEO officer Mankato (Minn.) State U., 1975-79, pres., 1979—; trustee Fielding Inst.; bd. dirs. Minn. Council Econ. Edn.; mem. commn. govtl. relations Am. Council Edn.; dir. No. State Power Co., Inc. Sec., Pomona Sign Study Commn., 1965-66; pres. Pomona Valley (Calif.) chpt. UN Assn., 1968-69, Unitarian Soc. Pomona Valley, 1968-69, Pomona (Calif.) chpt. LWV, 1972-74, Lincoln Elem. Sch. PTA, Pomona, 1973-74; mem. Pomona City Charter Revision Commn., 1972; exec. bd. Twin Valley council Boy Scouts Am., 1978; bd. dirs. Mankato Salvation Army, 1979—. Named Outstanding Alumna, Claremont Grad. Sch., 1979, Disting. Educator, 1980; grantee Carnegie Found., 1974. Mem. Am. Assn. Univ. Adminstrs. (dir. found.), Am. Assn. State Colls. and Univs., AAUW, Women's Equity Action League, Mankato C. of C. (dir.), P.E.O., Phi Kappa Phi, Pi Lambda Theta, Delta Kappa Gamma, Kappa Delta Pi. Mem. Democratic-Farmer-Labor Party. Club: Benedicts Dance. Office: Box 24 Mankato State U South Rd and Ellis Ave Mankato MN 56001 *

PRESSLER, MARION JOAN, librarian; b. Hollidaysburg, Pa., June 24, 1925; d. Howard Delo and Alice Elizabeth (Buehler) Pressler; B.S., State Tchrs. Coll., Slippery Rock, Pa., 1946; M.L.S., Carnegie Inst. Tech., 1959; certificate of advanced study U. Chgo., 1969. Tchr. high sch., Sandy Lake, Pa., 1946-47; librarian high sch., Phillipsburg, Pa., 1947-49; staff mem. Altoona Mirror, newspaper, 1950-53; tchr. high sch., East Berlin, Pa., 1953-55, Hollidaysburg, 1955-58; librarian Mt. Lebanon Sch. Dist., Pitts., 1959—. Gen. chmn. Council Sch. Librarians, Pitts., 1967-68. Frick Found. scholar, 1960-63. Mem. Nat., Pa. edn. assns., Mt. Lebanon Edn. Assn., Am., Pa. library assns., Blair County Hist. Soc., Friends of the Library, Altoona Music League, Sigma Tau

Delta, Beta Phi Mu, Pi Lambda Theta, Alpha Psi Omega. Contbr. articles to profl. jours. Home: Chatham Center Pittsburgh PA 15219 Office: Mount Lebanon School District Moffett St Pittsburgh PA 15243

PRESSMAN, BARBARA ELLEN WAPNER, lawyer, educator; b. Phila., Apr. 5, 1933; d. Albert and Esther (Gartzman) Wapner; student Syracuse U., 1951-52, Harvard U., 1953, U. Bordeaux, 1954; A.B., Vassar Coll., 1955; postgrad. U. Mich., 1955-57; J.D., Temple U., 1958; m. Herbert Pressman, Apr. 7, 1957; children—Cynthia Jo, Richard Bradford, Craig Stuart, Andrew Blair. Admitted to Pa. bar, 1959; individual practice law, Phila., 1960-66; partner firm Pressman & Pressman, Phila., 1966-69, 73—; asso. firm Astor & Weiss, Phila., 1969-73; instr. polit. sci., econs. and bus. law Temple U., 1960-68, instr. polit. sci., 1980-81; instr. polit. sci. and law Phila. Coll. Textile and Sci., 1966-72. Dem. com. woman Cheltenham Twp., Pa., 1960-66, ward leader, 1961-66; bd. judges James A. Finnegan Fellowship Found., 1977, 80; chmn. coordinating com. Vital Jewish Issues, 1979—; chmn. polit. action com., solicitor Pa. Fedn. Democratic Women, 1978—. Mem. Kappa Beta Pi, Delta Phi Epsilon. Home: 611 Harriton Rd Bryn Mawr PA 19010 Office: Suite 1215 1420 Walnut St Philadelphia PA 19102

PRESSMAN, HILDA TUCKMAN, speech pathologist; b. N.Y.C., June 16, 1943; d. Sidney and Ida (Puro) Tuckman; B.A., Queens Coll., 1963; M.A. Seton Hall U., 1974; m. Alan Pressman, June 6, 1963; children—Robin, Michael. Tchr. speech New Utrech High Sch., Bklyn., 1963-65; speech and lang. pathologist Mt Carmel Guild, Newark, 1973-80, United Hosps., Newark, 1980-82, supr. speech pathology services, 1982—. Trustee Valerie Fund Childrens Cancer Clinic, Overlook Hosp., Summit, N.J., 1977—, corr. sec., 1981—; mem. bd. edn. Temple B'Nai Abraham, Livingston, N.J., 1975—, co-chmn., 1980—, mem. ritual com., 1977—, trustee, 1980—. Mem. Am. Speech Lang. Hearing Assn., N.J. Speech and Hearing Assn. Home: 59 Edgewood Ave West Orange NJ 07052 Office: 15 S 9th St Newark NJ 07107

PREST, DOROTHY BOYD, microbiologist; b. Manchester, Mass., July 25, 1920; d. John Lee and Gertrude Appelton P.; B.S., Mass. State Coll., 1942; A.M., Boston U., 1957; Ph.D., U. Ariz., 1966. Med. technologist Salem (Mass.) Hosp., 1942-46, N.E. Baptist Hosp., 1946-47; chief technologist Salem Hosp., 1949-59; microbiologist Tucson Med. Center, 1959-65; research asst. U. Ariz., 1965-66; research asst. U. Wis., Madison, 1966-68; prof. biology Keuka Coll., Keuka Park, N.Y., 1978—. Mem. Am. Soc. Microbiology, Mycological Soc. Am., N.Y. Acad. Scis., AAAS, AAUP, Sigma Xi. Republican. Episcopalian. Home: Box 178 Keuka Park NY 14478 Office: Keuka Coll Keuka Park NY 14478

PRESTAGE, JEWEL LIMAR, educator; b. Hutton, La., Aug. 12, 1931; d. Brudis L. and Sallie Bell (Johnson) Limar; B.A., So. U., Baton Rouge, 1951; M.A., U. Iowa, 1952, Ph.D., 1954; m. James J. Prestage, Aug. 12, 1953; children—Terri, James, Eric, Karen, Jay. Asso. prof. polit. sci. Prairie View (Tex.) Coll., 1954-55, 56; asso. prof. polit. sci. So. U., Baton Rouge, 1956-57, 58-62, prof., 1962—, chairperson dept., 1965—. Chairperson, La. State adv. com. U.S. Commn. on Civil Rights, 1975—; mem. Nat. Adv. Council on Women's Ednl. Programs, 1980, chairperson, 1981-82. Rockefeller fellow, 1951-52; NSF fellow, 1964; Ford Found. postdoctoral fellow, 1969-70. Mem. Am. (v.p. 1974-75), So. (pres. 1975-76) polit. sci. assns., Southwestern Social Sci. Assn. (pres. 1973-74), Nat. Conf. Black Polit. Scientists (pres. 1976-77). Author: (with M. Githens) A Portrait of Marginality: Political Behavior of the American Woman, 1976; also articles. Home: 2145-77th Ave Baton Rouge LA 70807 Office: Box 9222 Southern U Baton Rouge LA 70813

PRESTBO, DARLENE PARRISH, psychiat. social worker; b. Ft. Wayne, Ind., May 3, 1941; d. Lake Osborn and Lorena Martha (Ford) Parrish; B.S. in Theatre, Northwestern U., 1963; M.S.W., U. Ill., 1971; postgrad. in psychotherapy Case Western Res. U., 1980; m. John Andrew Prestbo, Aug. 14, 1965; children—Bradford Jonathan, Laura Christine. Tchr. high sch. English and drama, 1963-64; instr. Internat. Bus. Coll., Ft. Wayne, 1964-65; profl. actress Acad. Playhouse, Chgo., 1967; caseworker Chgo. Dept. Public Aid, 1967-69, therapist Bowen Center for Abused Children, 1971-73; pvt. practice psychotherapy, Summit, N.J., 1974-77, Bay Village, Ohio, 1978-82, Skillman, N.J., 1982—; workshop leader, lectr. in field, 1974—. Mem. Acad. Cert. Social Workers, Nat. Assn. Social Workers, Actors Equity, Mortar Board. Presbyterian. Home and Office: 14 Charleston Dr Skillman NJ 08558

PRESTON, FAITH, coll. pres.; b. Boston, Sept. 14, 1921; d. Howard Knowlton and Edith Smith (Wilson) P.; B.A., Boston U., 1944; M.A., 1945; Ed.D., Columbia U. Tchr. Coll., 1964; m. Winthrop Wadleigh, Dec. 19, 1970. Tchr., Georgetown (Mass.) High Sch., 1945-47; tchr. Stoneham (Mass.) High Sch., 1947-50; tchr. Endicott Jr. Coll., Beverly, Mass., 1950-53; dir. research P.R. Jr. Coll., 1953-55; dean adminstrn., 1955-63, v.p., 1963-65; pres. White Pines Coll., 1965—, also trustee. Bd. incorporators Cath. Med. Center, Manchester, N.H., 1978—; bd. dirs. Derry Area Youth Service Bd., So. N.H. Dist. YMCA. Kellogg fellow, 1964. Mem. Am. Assn. Jr. Colls., Phi Lambda Theta, Kappa Delta Pi, Delta Kappa Gamma. Republican. Clubs: Univ. Women's (London); The College (Boston); Fortnightly. Author: David and the Handcar, 1950; Jose's Miracle, 1955; The Silver Box, 1979. Home: PO Box 25 Chester NH 03036 Office: White Pines Coll Chester NH 03036

PRESTON, MARY LEE, educator; b. New Willard, Tex., Nov. 20, 1931; d. Damon and Angeline Fletcher Hunter; B.S., Tex. So. U., 1972, M.A.Ed., 1981; m. Foster Preston, Dec. 5, 1950; children—Angie, Alfred, Annie, Foster, Rosemary, Ava, Sherry, Michael, Mona. Clk., Community Chapel, Funeral Benefit Assn., Houston, 1966-81; instructional coordinator Dunbar Elem. Sch., Houston, 1978-80; 4th grade tchr. Anson Jones Sch., Houston Ind. Sch. Dist., 1980—; tchr. vol. Adult Basic Edn. and Gen. Edn. Diploma, 1980-82; edn. cons. Martin Luther King Jr. Community Center, 1979-82, treas. bd. dirs., 1980-81. Pres., Dunbar Alliance Parents, Tchr. Assos. and Patrons, 1975-81; chmn. bd. Purpose, Inc., 1970-74; Mem. NEA, Nat. Assn. Female Execs., Tex. State Tchrs. Assn., Houston Tchrs. Assn., Tex. So. Reading Club. Baptist. Club: Order Eastern Star. Home: 3401 Oakdale St Houston TX 77004

PRESTON, RUTH PESKIN, editor; b. N.Y.C., July 26, 1906; d. Joseph Michael and Augusta (Stadler) Levin; B.A. cum laude, Syracuse U., 1927; postgrad. Sorbonne, Paris, 1929; M.A., Columbia U., 1931; m. A. Robert Peskin, Nov. 15, 1931; children—Abbey Sara Peskin Klein, Stephen David. Caseworker, Fedn. Jewish Philanthropies, N.Y.C., 1929-30; with advt. dept. Macy's, N.Y.C., 1930; dist. dir. Temp. Emergency Relief Assn., 1932-33; asso. promotion dir. Harper's Bazaar, 1944-45; fashion editor N.Y. Post, 1946-78; partner Airport Plaza, Ltd., 1950-78; contbg. editor Ladies Home Jour., Whitney Communications, 50 Plus, Mode Internat.; cons. N.Y. State U. Fashion Inst. Tech., 1978—. Vice pres. bd. govs. Fashion Group Inc., 1977-78, bd. dirs. Am. Com. Shenkar Coll. for Fashion in Israel, 1975; hon. bd. advs. Costume Mus., Kent State U.; bd. vocat. edn. N.Y.C. Bd. Edn., 1968—. Mem. Newspaper Guild, U. Syracuse Alumni Assn., Phi Beta Kappa, Phi Kappa Phi, Alpha Epsilon Phi.

PRESTON, VERA ALMA, educator; b. Oklahoma City, May 30, 1942; d. Joe Lafayette and Liberty (Bennett) P.; B.S., Okla. State U., 1962; M.A. (grad. asst.), U. Maine, 1969; m. Norman Bruce Callahan, Oct. 4, 1964 (div. 1976); children—Melissa, Mark. With Peace Corps, Banos, Tungarahua, Ecuador, 1962-64; tchr. Gaithersburg (Md.) High Sch., 1964-65, Edgewood (Md.) High Sch., 1965; grad. asst. West Chester (Pa.) State Coll., 1967; part-time math. instr. Berkshire Community Coll., 1973-76; tchr. Zebulon (N.C.) High Sch., 1978-81; tchr. math. Red Rock (Okla.) Public Sch., 1982—. Tchr., Sunday sch. Unity Ch., 1978—; organizer, 1st pres. Family Centered Parents, Inc., Wilmington, Del., 1970; organizer Literacy Vols. Am., Pittsfield, Mass., 1976. Mem. Nat. Council Tchrs. of Math., Okla. Council Tchrs. of Math. (dir. 1982—), Assn. Supervision and Curriculum Devel., Kappa Delta Pi. Republican. Home: 124 Dells Dr Stillwater OK 74074 Office: PO Box 96 Red Rock OK 74651

PRESTON, WINIFRED AINSLEE, public service agy. writer; b. Zanesville, Ohio, Apr. 17, 1927; d. F. Bringle and Kathleen (Girton) Crowder McIntosh; student Randolph-Macon Women's Coll., 1942-43; B.A., Ohio State U., 1947; postgrad. N.Y. U., 1976—; m. James Preston Mar. 5, 1959 (div.); children—Heather Lee. Actress as Winifred Ainslee on Broadway and in road and stock prodns., 1947-63; featured roles include: Brigadoon, Paint Your Wagon, Seventh Heaven, Bus Stop, Cat on a Hot Tin Roof, Invitation to a March, Auntie Mame, others; with Port Authority of N.Y. and N.J., 1963—, staff info. officer public affairs dept., 1979—. Mem. Women in Communications, Port Authority Women's Equity, Mensa. Methodist. Home: 115 W 73d St New York NY 10023 Office: Port Authority of NY and NJ One World Trade Center 68W New York NY 10048

PRIBIS, YOLANDA, psychiatrist; b. Brommov, Czechoslovakia; came to U.S., 1967, naturalized, 1973; M.D. Massaryk U., Czechoslovakia, 1951; 1 dau., Milena. Internist, Czechoslovakia, 1956-66; resident II Policlinic, Bratislava, Czechoslovakia, 1951-66; practice medicine specializing in psychiatry, 1971—; sr. psychiatrist VA Med. Center, Montrose, N.Y., 1979—. Mem. AMA, Am. Psychiat. Assn. Home: PO Box 292 Montrose NY 10548 Office: VA Med Center Montrose NY 10548

PRICE, ALICE WILLIAMS, mgmt. cons., ret. pharm. co. exec., cons.; b. Bloomfield, N.J.; d. Lawrence and Ruth Ellen (Lawson) Williams; diploma in nursing Lincoln Sch. for Nurses, Bronx, 1945; B.S. in Community Nursing (USPHS Scholar), N.Y.U., 1947, M.A. in Teaching, 1957; postgrad. Seton Hall U., 1955-56; m. John Boyson Price III, Feb. 25, 1944; children—Beatrice Valerie Price Floyd, Patricia Alice. Health edn. nurse Assn. for Aid to Crippled Children, N.Y.C., 1944-45; vis. nurse ARC, Bloomfield, N.J., 1950-52, Community Nursing Service, Montclair, N.J., 1952-54; with Mountainside Hosp. Sch. Nursing, Montclair, 1954-59; instr. Fairleigh Dickinson U., Rutherford, N.J., 1959-61; asso. dir. St. Mary's Hosp. Sch. Nursing, Orange, N.J., 1961-65, St. Joseph's Hosp. Sch. of Nursing, Paterson, N.J., 1965-66; with Hoffmann-La Roche Inc., Nutley, N.J., 1966-80, mgr. ednl. services, 1970-79, career devel. profl. programs asso. Roche Labs div., Montclair, 1977-80; ind. cons. AWP Mktg., Mgmt. & Tng. Cons., 1980—; cons. editor nursing publs., 1980—; vis. prof. Black Exec. Exchange Program, 1977, Tchr's. Coll., Columbia U., 1975-77; mem. faculty continuing edn. Am. Nurses Assn., 1977; lectr. numerous univs. including La. State U., U. Wis., U. Ark., U. Colo., U. So. Calif., UCLA. Mem. adv. bd. St. Barnabas Sch. Nursing; pres. PTA, 1957-59; publicity chmn. Nat. Council of Alcoholism Aux., 1978-79; program chmn. evening circle Women's Guild of Central Presbyn. Ch., 1969, now commr. to Newark Presbytery, mem. session and budget com., chmn. for missions, mem. Korean ch. commn., cons. to central ward project, Newark, clk. of session, 1980-82; bd. dirs. Montclair YWCA; trustee Bloomfield Coll., 1980—. Recipient Black Achievers in Industry award, 1971; Internat. Women's Yr. award Essex County Urban League, 1975; Woman of Yr. award in health edn. Montclair chpt. Nat. Council Negro Women, 1976, Montclair chpt. YWCA, 1977; meritorious award Alaska Heart Assn.; registered nurse, N.Y., N.J. Mem. Am. Nurses Assn. (Nat. Com. on Careers), Nat. League for Nursing (past dir. N.J.), Am. Heart Assn. (mem. cardiovascular nursing council), AAUW, Lincoln Sch. for Nurses Alumnae Assn., N.Y.U. Alumnae Assn., N.J. Soc. for Health Edn. and Tng., Nat. Assn. Female Execs., Common Cause. Club: Order of Eastern Star, Coll. Women's Club. Contbr. articles to profl. jours. Home: 5 Gardiner Pl Montclair NJ 07042

PRICE, BARBARA EASTER, lawyer; b. Lafayette, Ind., Oct. 8, 1943; d. George E. and Eleanor E. P.; B.A., Mount Holyoke Coll., 1965; J.D., U. Calif., Davis, 1976; 1 son, Andres Garcia. Legis. aide Senator Birch Bayh, U.S. Senate, Washington, 1965-67; research writer U.S. Commn. on Civil Disorders, Washington, 1967-68; adminstrv. asst. Office Consumer Affairs, Dept. Justice, Washington, 1968-69; adminstrv. asst. Rep. Jon Rotenbug, Mass. Ho. of Reps., Boston, 1972-73; admitted to Calif. bar, 1976; individual practice law, San Francisco, 1977—. Mem. San Francisco Bar Assn., Queens Bench of San Francisco, Calif. Womens Lawyers, Bay Area Lawyers for Arts. Office: 1714 Stockton St San Francisco CA 94133

PRICE, CHERYL AVIS, librarian; b. Oak Park, Ill., Mar. 14, 1944; d. Minor Carr and Malvina D. P.; B.S., Mo. Valley Coll., 1966; M.A., No. Ill. U., 1971; M.A.L.S., Rosary Coll., 1977. Jud. liaison specialist DuPage County Govt., Wheaton, Ill., 1971-73, county law librarian, 1973-79; polit. sci./law librarian No. Ill. U., DeKalb, 1979-81, internat. documents and law librarian, 1981—. Mem. AAUW, Bus. and Profl. Women, Nat. Hist. Soc., Am. Law Librarians Assn. Office: Founders Library No Ill U DeKalb IL 60115

PRICE, CORA LEE BEERS, educator; b. Janesville, Wis., Nov. 28, 1908; d. Clarence Palmer and Cora Bertha (Griffith) Beers; B.A., Beloit Coll., 1932; M.A., Claremont Coll., 1933; Ph.D., Stanford U., 1940; m. Griffith Baley Price, June 18, 1940; children—Cora Lee, Griffith Baley, Lucy Jean, Edwina Clare, Sallie Diane, Doris Joanne. Instr. English, Beloit (Wis.) Coll., 1933-34; asst. in English, Stanford (Calif.) U., 1934-36; instr. English, Cath. U. Am., summer, 1935; tchr. Latin and English, Tulare (Calif.) High Sch., 1936-38; instr. English, Wilson Coll., Chambersburg, Pa., 1938-40; instr. English, U. Kans., Lawrence, 1945-46, 61-65, instr. classics, 1962-67, lectr. classics, 1967-73, asst. prof. classics, 1973-79, emerita, 1979—; instr. English, Baker U., Baldwin, Kans., 1980—; organist Bapt. Ch., Janesville, Wis., 1925-34, Lawrence, 1957-59, 61-62. Sec., City Council PTA, Lawrence; bd. dirs. Am. Bapt. Student Center, U. Kans., 1967-72, Lawrence Civic Choir, 1973-74. Claremont Coll. grad. fellow, 1932-33. Mem. Nat. Council Tchrs. English, Am. Classical League, Classical Assn. Middle East and South, AAUW. Baptist. Clubs: Lawrence Music (pres. 1945-47), Kans. U. Women's, Zodiac. Contbr. articles to profl. jours. Home: 1520 Barker Ave Lawrence KS 66044 Office: Classics Dept U of Kans Lawrence KS 66044

PRICE, EDITH MARTHA, psychotherapist, nurse; b. Detroit, May 18, 1935; d. Rudolph Reinhardt and Erna Hertha (Gerbstadt) Heupel; student U. Mich., 1955; B.S. in Nursing summa cum laude, Mercy Coll., Detroit, 1971; m. Richard J. Price, Jan. 28, 1956 (div. 1971); children—Kim M., Laura L. Psychiat. staff nurse, then head nurse Lafayette Clinic, Detroit, 1971-74; crisis therapist Crisis Clinic, Sinai Hosp., Detroit, 1974-76, psychotherapist sexual marital dysfunction, 1976—; group leader Kinsey Inst.; lectr. Nat. Physicians Workshop on Sexuality, Wayne State U., U. Mich., Oakland U., Mich. Heart Assn.; speaker profl. confs.; cons. Detroit News; TV and radio cons. Campaign worker Oakland County Republican Party; active PTA, Girl Scouts U.S.A. Recipient Catherine McCauley award Mercy Coll., 1971. Mem. Nat. League Nursing. Home: 25250 Greenbrooke St Southfield MI 48034 Office: 14800 McNichols Rd Detroit MI 48235

PRICE, IDA LUTZ JONES, former govt. ofcl.; b. Dickerson, Md., Nov. 4, 1926; d. Samuel Creighton and Constance Beulah (Nicholson) Jones; student Md. schs.; divorced; children—Lawrence, D. Jane Parsley, Michael Creighton, Ida Susan Ricketson, Samuel Darby, John Francis, Mary Elizabeth Lynch, William Nicholson, Harry Edwin, Vincent Andrew; m. 2d, R.P. Brown, Nov. 13, 1981. Postmaster, Barnesville, Md., 1951-79, New Market, Md., 1979-81; ret., 1981. Commr., Barnesville, 1975-79; charter sec. Sugarloaf Citizens Assn., 1972; founder Barnesville Day, 1969. Recipient Bicentennial award U.S. Postal Service, 1976; Editor's award, 1980. Mem. Nat. Assn. Postmasters U.S. (Editor's award 1977, 79). Democrat. Roman Catholic. Club: Soroptomist Internat. (past pres. Upper Montgomery County). Editor: Free State Postmaster, 1977-80. Home: 8009 Clearfield Rd Frederick MD 21701

PRICE, LEONTYNE, concert, opera singer; b. Laurel, Miss., Feb. 10, 1927; d. James A. and Kate (Baker) Price; B.A., Central State Coll., Wilberforce, Ohio, 1949, D.Mus., 1968; student Juilliard Sch. Music, 1949-52; pupil Florence Page Kimball; L.H.D., Dartmouth Coll., 1962; Mus.D., Howard U., 1962; L.H.D., Fordham U., 1969; Dr. Humanities, Rust Coll., 1968; m. William Bess, Vienna, Berlin, Paris, London, under auspices U.S. State Dept., also N.Y.C. and U.S. tour, 1952-54; recitalist, soloist with symphonies, U.S., Can., Australia, Europe, 1954—; appeared concerts in India, auspices State Dept., 1956, 64; soloist Hollywood Bowl, 1955-59, 66, Berlin Festival, 1960; opera debut as Mme. Lidoine in Dialogues des Carmelites, San Francisco Opera, 1957; opera singer NBC-TV, 1955-58, 60, 62, 64, San Francisco Opera Co., 1957-59, 60-61, 63, 65, 67, 68, 71, Vienna Staatsoper, 1958, 59-60, 61, Berlin Opera, 1964, Roman Opera, 1966, Paris Opera, 1968; recital Brussels Internat. Fair, auspices State Dept., 1958, Verona Opera Arena, 1958-59, recitals Yugoslavia for State Dept., 1958; rec. artist RCA-Victor, 1958—; appeared Covent Garden, London, 1958-59, 70, Chgo. Lyric Theatre, 1959, 60, 65, soloist Salzburg Festival, 1959-63, Tetro alla Scala, Milano, 1960-61, 63, 67; appeared Met. Opera, N.Y.C., 1961-62, 63-70, 72, now resident mem.; soloist Salzburg Festival, 1950, 60; debut Teatre Dell'Opera, Rome, 1967, Teatro Colon, Buenos Aires, Argentina, 1969, Hamburg Opera, 1970. Hon. bd. dirs. Campfire Girls; hon. vice-chmn. U.S. com. UNESCO; co-chmn. Rust Coll. Upward Thrust Campaign; trustee-Internat. House. Decorated Order at Ment (Italy), recipient merit award for role of Tosca in NBC-TV Opera; Mademoiselle mag., 1955; 20 Grammy awards for classical vocal recs. Nat. Acad. Rec. Arts and Scis.; citation YWCA, 1961; Spirit of Achievement award Albert Einstein Coll. Medicine, 1962; Presdl. medal of freedom, 1964; Spingarn medal NAACP, 1965; Schwann Catalog award, 1968; named Musician of Year Mus. Am. mag., 1961; others. Fellow Am. Acad. Arts and Scis.; mem. AFTRA, Am. Guild Mus. Artists, Actors Equity Assn., Sigma Alpha Iota, Delta Sigma Theta. Address: care Columbia Artists Mgmt Inc 165 W 57th St New York NY 10019 *

PRICE, LISA ANN, coll. public relations exec.; b. Oklahoma City, Oct. 8, 1955; d. Norris Allen and Betty Ann (Durham) P.; student Oscar Rose Jr. Coll., summers 1974-75; B.S. in Radio/TV/Film, Okla. State U., 1977; postgrad. Okla. U., 1980—. Motor lic. agt. coordinator Okla. Tax Commn., 1977; sec. sales office, producer, dir. Sta. KOCO-TV, Oklahoma City, 1977-78; coordinator for student info./public relations Oscar Rose Jr. Coll., 1978—; mem. home econs. adv. council Del City High Sch. Vol., Aquaticus, Oklahoma City, Ballet Okla., Oklahoma City Arts Festival; mem. Women's Com. Okla. Symphony Orch.; mem. Okla. State Adv. Council for Vocat. Tech. Edn., 1980-83. Recipient Community Service award United Way, 1979, 80, Bronze Derrick runner-up award Public Relations Soc. Am. competition, 1980, Outstanding Participation award Muscular Dystrophy Assn., 1981. Mem. Nat. Assn. Female Execs., Okla. Coll. Public Relations Assn. (dir. 1981-82), Nat. Council Community Relations, Midwest City C. of C., Okla. State U. Alumni Assn., French Heels of Oklahoma City (v.p. 1981-82, pres. 1982-83), Jr. Service League Midwest City, Oscar Rose Jr. Coll. Women's Assn. (chmn. membership), Alpha Chi Omega Alumni Assn. Democrat. Baptist. Editor, chief photographer Oscar Rose Back-to-sch. newspaper supplement, 1978-81; producer multi-media slide/tape presentation on Oscar Rose Jr. Coll., 1981; moderator weekly TV series on edn. Office: 6420 SE 15th St Midwest City OK 73110

PRICE, LUCILE BROWN (MRS. CHARLES EDWARD PRICE), civic worker; b. Decorah, Iowa, May 31, 1902; d. Sidney Eugene and Cora (Drake) Brickner; B.S., Iowa State U., 1925; M.A., Northwestern U., 1940; m. Maynard Wilson Brown, July 2, 1928 (dec. Apr. 1937); m. 2d, Charles Edward Price, Jan. 14, 1961. Asst. dean women Kans. State U., Manhattan, 1925-28; mem. bd. student personnel adminstrn. Northwestern U., 1937-41; personnel research Sears Roebuck & Co., Chgo., 1941-42, overseas club dir. ARC, Eng., Africa, Italy, 1942-45; dir. Child Edn. Found., N.Y.C., 1946-56. Participant 1st and 2d Iowa Humanists Summer Symposiums, 1974, 75. Del. Mid Century White House Conf. on Children and Youth, 1950; mem. com. on program and research of Children's Internat. summer villages, 1952-53; mem. bd. N.E. Iowa Mental Health Center, 1959-62, pres. bd., 1960-61; mem. Iowa State Extension Adv. Com., 1973-75; project chmn. Decorah Hist. Dist. (listed Nat. Register Historic Places); trustee Porter House Mus., Decorah, 1966-78, emeritus bd. dirs., 1982—; participant N. Central Regional Workshop Am. Assn. State and Local History, Mpls., 1975, Midwest Workshop Historic Preservation and Conservation, Iowa State U., 1976, 77; mem. Winneshiek County (Iowa) CSC, 1978—. Recipient Alumni Merit award Iowa State U., 1975. Mem. Am. Coll. Personnel Assn., (life), Am. Overseas Assn. (nat. bd.; life), AAUW (life mem., mem. bd. Decorah; recipient Named Gift award 1977), Nat. Assn. Mental Health (del. nat. conf. 1958), Norwegian-Am. Mus. (life, Vesterheim fellow), Winneshiek County Hist. Soc. (life), DAR, Common Cause, Internat. Platform Assn., Pi Lambda Theta, Chi Omega. Designer, builder house for retirement living. Home: 508 W Broadway Decorah IA 52101

PRICE, LYNN WISENBAKER, interior design co. exec.; b. Dallas, May 7, 1948; d. John D. and Jean Louise (Jones) W.; student U. Colo., 1966-67, U. Tex., Austin, 1967-69, U. Tex., Arlington, 1970-71; B.A. in Painting and Drawing, N. Tex. State U., 1973; m. Charles Wesley Price, Dec. 22, 1969; children—Zachary Wisenbaker, Devin Louise. Owner, operator, designer Wisenbaker Design Group, comml. and residential interior design, Dallas, 1972—. Bd. dirs. Theatre Three, Dallas, 1970-74, Creative Arts Center Dallas, 1974-78; chmn. fund raising com. Tex. Mental Health Assn.; chmn. funds solicitation Dallas unit Am. Cancer Soc., 1978-80, mem. cattle baron's com.; chmn. James K. Wilson Silver Cup Award. Recipient Voertman award N. Tex. State U., 1972. Mem. Kappa Kappa Gamma Alumnae (officer and dir.). Clubs: Jr. League Dallas, Dallas Women's, Brookhollow.

PRICE, MARGARET ANN, civic worker; b. Westfield, Ill., Feb. 16, 1921; d. Harry Albert and Margaret Remington (Madison) Day; student Lincoln Trail Coll., 1972-76; m. William Keith Price, Nov. 11, 1941; children—Richard Keith, Robert Kent. Pres., Jr. Woman's Club, Ill. Fedn. Women's Clubs, 1956-57, pres. Minerva Club, 1962-64, pres. 23d Dist., 1976-78; regent James Halstead, Sr. chpt. DAR, 1976-78, pressbook chmn. for Ill., 1979-80; leader Cub Scouts, Wabash Valley council Boy Scouts Am., 1954-60, v.p. cub scouting, 1980—. Recipient Silver Fawn award Boy Scouts Am., 1972; Community Service award Robinson (Ill.) C. of C., 1981. Mem. Crawford Meml. Hosp. Aux. Republican. Methodist. Club: Crawford County Rep. Women's (pres. 1981-82). Editor: Chimes, quar. publ. United Meth. Women. Home: 307 St Petersburg Robinson IL 62454

PRICE, MARGARET STAFFORD, night club exec.; b. Belleville, Ill., Feb. 12, 1944; d. John and Helen Klich; student Belleville Jr. Coll., 1961; m. Herschel Price, Mar. 27, 1966; children—Dennis, Melissa, Teresa. Bunny, St. Louis Playboy Club, 1962-66 owner, mgr., 1975—. Mem. NOW. Home: 18 Sackston Woods Creve Coeur MO 63141 Office: St Louis Playboy Club 6926 S Lindbergh Saint Louis MO 63125

PRICE, MARILYN JEANNE, fund raising cons; b. N.Y.C., Jan. 24, 1948; d. George Franklin and Mary Anastasia (Barnishin) Lawrence; student Temple Bus. Sch., 1964-66; student U. Md., 1973-74; children—Kimberly Jean. Asst. to sr. printing and paper buyer ARC, Washington 1965-67; conf. planner for classified mil. confs. Nat. Security Indsl. Assn., Washington, 1967-69; fund devel. office asst. Nat. Urban Coalition, Washington, 1970; direct mail/membership coordinator Common Cause, Washington, 1970-72; mgr. direct mail fund raising Epilepsy Found. of Am., Washington, 1973-76; exec. v.p. Bruce W. Eberle & Assocs., Vienna, Va., 1977-81; pres. Response Dynamics, Inc., Vienna, Va., 1981—; v.p. The Best Lists, Inc., Vienna, 1981—, also dir.; cons. in field. Asst. to Young Citizens for Johnson, 1964; vol. George McGovern campaign, 1972; Hubert Humphrey campaign, 1968. Recipient Silver Echo award, Direct Mail/Mktg. Assn. Internat. competition for mktg. excellence, 1980. Mem. Nat. Soc. Fund Raisers, Direct Mail Mktg. Assn., Direct Mktg. Club. Home: 9614 Lindenbrook St Fairfax VA 22031 Office: 8214 Old Courthouse Rd Vienna VA 22180

PRICE, MARY KATHLEEN, law librarian; b. Buffalo, Feb. 28, 1942; d. Donn Dale and Mary Elizabeth P.; B.A., U. Fla., 1963; M.S., Fla. State U., 1967; J.D., U. Ill., 1973. Tchr., Fla. secondary schs., 1963-67; asst. librarian U. Ala. Law Library, 1967-70, U. Ill. Law Library, 1970-73; admitted to Ill. bar, 1973; asso. firm Ross, Hardies, O'Keefe, Babcock & Parsons, Chgo., 1973-75; law librarian, prof. law Duke U. Law Sch., 1975-80; dir. law library, prof. law U. Minn. Law Sch., 1980—; cons. in field. Mem. Am. Assn. Law Libraries (pres. elect 1982-83), Order of Coif, Beta Phi Mu. Democrat. Roman Catholic. Office: 316 Law Bldg 229 19th Ave S Minneapolis MN 55455

PRICE, NORMA LORRAINE, Can. provincial minister cultural affairs; b. Winnipeg, Man., Can., Aug. 19, 1920; d. Clement A. and Aurora (Martel) Killeen; student St. Mary's Acad.; m. James Edward Price, Feb. 1, 1940; children—Linda, Randy, Donna. Mem. Man. Legis. Assembly from Assiniboia, 1977—, minister tourism and cultural affairs, 1978, former minister of labor, minister responsible for Civil Service Act, Public Servants Ins. Act, Pensions Benefits Act, Civil Service Superannuation Act, now minister cultural affairs and hist. resources. Conservative. Roman Catholic. Office: Room 343 Legislative Bldg Winnipeg MB R3C 0V8 Canada *

PRICE, OLIVE MARIE, author; b. Pitts., Sept. 21; d. Harry Wilson and Lydia Barchfeld Price; student U. Pitts., 1922; m. Rosslyn M. Cherryholmes, June 30, 1927. Advt. copywriter dept. stores, Pitts., 1923-27; author books for young people: A Donkey for the King, 1945, Italian edit., 1951; Miracle by the Sea, 1947, Italian edit., 1951, Danish edit., 1950; Three Golden Rivers, 1948; The Valley of the Dragon, 1951, Brit. edit., 1955; The Glass Mountain, 1954; The Blue Harbor, 1956; The Story of Marco Polo, 1953, Portuguese edit., 1962, Norwegian edit., 1955, Hebrew edit., 1972; The Story of Clara Barton, 1954, paperback, 1955; The Call of the Wild (adaptation), 1961; Bob, Son of Battle (adaptation), 1960; Five Little Peppers and How They Grew (adaptation), 1963; Snifty, 1957; The Golden Wheel, 1958; Reindeer Island, 1959; River Boy, 1960; Mystery of the Sunken City, 1962; The Phantom Reindeer, 1961; The Donkey with Diamond Ears, 1962; The Boy with One Shoe, 1963; The Island of the Silver Spoon, 1963; The Island of the Voyageurs, 1964; The Dog That Watched the Mountain, 1967; Kim Walk-In-My-Shoes, 1968; Rosa Bonheur, 1972; plays pub. in: Short Plays from American History and Literature, 1925, 28, 33, 35; Plays of Belles and Beaux, 1937; Debutante Plays, 1936; American History in Masque and Wig, 1931; Plays of Far Places, 1936; plays produced on radio and TV; contbr. articles to Vogue mag., others. Mem. Kappa Delta. Baptist. Address: Box 229 RD 2 Asbury NJ 08802

PRICE, ROSALIE PETTUS, artist; b. Birmingham, Ala.; d. Erle and Ellelee (Chapman) Pettus; A.B., Birmingham-So. Coll., 1935; M.A., U. Ala., Tuscaloosa, 1967; m. William Archer Price, Oct. 3, 1936. Painter in watercolors, casein, oil and acrylic; one man shows include: Samford U., 1964, Birmingham Mus. of Art, 1966, 73, 82, Town Hall Gallery, 1968, 75, South Central Bell, 1977; instr. Birmingham (Ala.) Mus. Art, 1967-70, Samford U., 1969-70. Bd. dirs. Birmingham Mus. of Art, 1950-54, chmn., 1950-51; bd. trustees Birmingham Music Club, 1956-66, rec. sec., 1958-62. Recipient purchase award Watercolor U.S.A., 1972. Mem. Nat. Watercolor Soc., Nat. Soc. Painters in Casein and Acrylic (W.Alden Brown Meml. award 1970), Birmingham Art Assn. (pres. 1947-49, Little House on Linden purchase award 1968), So. Watercolor Soc., Watercolor Soc. Ala. (sec. 1948-49), La. Watercolor Soc., Phi Beta Phi. Episcopalian. Clubs: Jr. League of Birmingham (chmn. art com. 1947-50), Window Box Garden. Home: 300 Windsor Dr Birmingham AL 35209 Office: 2335 20th Ave Birmingham AL 35223

PRICE, RUTH ELLEN, med. technologist, lab. adminstr.; b. Chgo., May 19, 1931; d. Stanley and Kathryn Ellen (Carpenter) P.; B.A. in Biology, Willamette U., 1953; cert. in med. tech. Northwestern, 1954; M.A. in Mgmt., Central Mich. U., 1977. Med. technologist St. Catherine's Hosp., Kenosha, Wis., 1955—, clin. lab. supr., 1966—; product evaluator E. I. DuPont de Nemours, Wilmington, Del. Active Friends of the Museum, Kenosha. Mem. Am. Soc. Clin. Pathology (asso. mem., cert. med. technologist), Nature Conservancy, Am. Soc. Med. Tech. (27 yr. mem.), AAUW, Clin. Lab. Mgmt. Assn. Episcopalian. Club: PEO (30 yr. mem.). Home: 4510 18th St Kenosha WI 53142 Office: St Catherine's Hosp 3556 7th Ave Kenosha WI 53140

PRICE, SAMMIE LEE, banker; b. Athens, Tex., May 14, 1943; d. Porter S. and Minnie (Evans) Lee; grad. Durhams Bus. Coll., 1963; 1 son, Thomas Lee. With First Nat. Bank, Athens, Tex., 1963-68, People's Nat. Bank, Tyler, Tex., 1968-69, Parkdale State Bank, Corpus Christi, 1969-70; with Allied First Bank, Edna, Tex., 1970—, asst. cashier, 1976-79, cashier, 1979-82, v.p., cashier, 1982—. Bd. dirs. Jackson County unit Am. Cancer Soc.; treas. Jackson County Unit Salvation Army; chmn. Miss Jackson County Scholarship Pageant. Mem. Nat. Assn. Bank Women (sec. Mid-Coastal Group), Am. Bus. Women's Assn. Home: 905 Live Oak St Edna TX 77957 Office: Box 310 Edna TX 77957

PRICHARD, ELIZABETH ROBINSON, social worker, civic worker; b. N.Y.C., Oct. 20, 1915; d. Harold Grant and Kathryn Virginia (Robinson) P.; B.A., Adelphi U., 1943; M.S., Columbia U. Sch. Social Work, 1947. Home service worker ARC, Bklyn. and N.Y.C., 1943-45, 47-48; social worker N.Y. U., Bellevue Pilot Home Care Project, N.Y.C., 1948-49; asst. dir. social service Columbia-Presbyn. Med. Center, N.Y.C., 1949-54, dir. social services, 1954-81; asst. prof. clin. social work Coll. Physicians and Surgeons, Columbia U., 1957-81; mem. profl. adv. bd. for social work Found. Thanatology, 1970—, mem. exec. com., 1974—. Trustee, Greater N.Y. chpt., also social work advisor Myasthenia Gravis Found., 1981—; mem. pub. affairs com. Cancer Care N.Y.C., 1981—; participant seminar on death Columbia U.; mem. New York County Democratic Com. Mem. Nat. Assn. Social Workers, Acad. Cert. Social Workers, Nat. Conf. Social Welfare, Internat. Conf. Social Welfare, Am. Pub. Health Assn., AAAS, N.Y. Acad. Scis. Clubs: Womens City (health and governing operating com. 1981—), City (health and quality of life coms. 1981—). Editor 2 books on death and dying; contbr. articles on social work and care of terminally ill to profl. publs. Address: 510 E 86th St New York NY 10028

PRICKETT, MARGARET LENORA, mfg. co. exec.; b. Council Bluffs, Iowa, Apr. 15, 1940; d. Paul Emmit and Pauline Irene (Pierson) Prickett; student pub. schs., El Monte, Calif.; children—Deborah Ann and Sharon Pauline (twins). With Fenton Industries, Inc., Los Angeles, 1960—, exec. v.p., treas., 1974—; owner A to Z Bookkeeping Services, Sylmar, Calif., 1980—; mem. pres. adv. bd. World Opportunities Inc., 1981—. Served with USAF, 1958-59. Democrat. Baptist. Club: Bus. and Profl. Womens. Home: 13790 Oro Grande St Sylmar CA 91342 Office: 5801 S Central Ave Los Angeles CA 90011

PRIDDY, MARJORIE, former hosp. exec., civic worker; b. Cleve.; d. Joseph Patrick and Margaret Haley (Cain) Nealon; R.N., Charity Hosp. Sch. Nursing, 1932; postgrad. Ohio State U.; m. Newton D. Priddy, Dec. 3, 1935 (dec.); children—Marjorie Ann, Dale (foster son). Former owner (with husband) Ravenswood (W.Va.) Hosp. Bd. dirs. Jackson County Humane Soc. Mem. Ohio Heritage Club, Internat. Platform Assn. Clubs: Senior Women's, DeSales Heights Academy Mother's (past pres.). Address: 255 1/2 Washington Ravenswood WV 26164

PRIER, ORVALIN LAJUNE ADAMS, oil and gas co. exec.; b. Antioch, Okla., Nov. 28, 1924; d. Orval Thomas and Beatrice Ellen (Murdock) Adams; student Okla. U., 1955-56; m. Edwin Richard Prier, June 27, 1940; children—Anna June Prier Shursen, Margaret Ellen Prier Schaeffer. Acct., S.W. Bell Telephone Co., 1943-44; sec.-treas. Ed Prier, Inc., Norman, Okla., 1962—; co-owner, mgr. Thunderbird Marine Supply Co., Norman, 1970-73; v.p., sec.-treas. Richoils, Inc., Norman, 1978—; owner, mgr. Party Line Antique Shop, Norman, 1978—. Vice chmn. Republican Party Cleveland County, 1968-70, Rep. Women's Club, 1970; mgr. lt. gov.'s campaign for Cleveland County (Okla.), 1970. Mem. DAR. Mem. Christian Ch.

PRIESAND, SALLY JANE, rabbi; b. Cleve., June 27, 1946; d. Irving T. and Rose E. Priesand; B.A. in English, U. Cin., 1968; B. in Hebrew Letters, Hebrew Union Coll., Jewish Inst. Religion, 1971; M.A.H.L., 1972; D.H.L. (hon.), Fla. Internat. U., 1973. Ordained rabbi, 1972; asst. rabbi Stephen Wise Free Synagogue, N.Y.C., 1972-77; asso. rabbi 1977-79; rabbi Temple Beth El, Elizabeth, N.J., 1979-81, Monmouth Reform Temple, Tinton, Falls, N.J., 1981—. Named Outstanding Young Woman of Yr. of Ohio, 1972; recipient World Gratitude Day award; Eleanor Roosevelt Humanities award State of Israel, 1980. Mem. Am. Jewish Com., Am. Jewish Congress, Central Conf. Am. Rabbis (exec. com., task force on women in the rabbinate), Assn. Reform Zionists Am. (founding mem.), NOW, Religious Leaders for a Free Choice, NCCJ in Manhattan (dir.), Clergy and Laity Concerned (nat. interim steering com.). Clubs: B'nai B'rith, Hadassah. Author: Judaism and the New Woman, 1975; contbr. articles on Judaism to profl. jours. Home: 10 Wedgewood Circle Eatontown NJ 07724 Office: 332 Hance Ave Tinton Falls NJ 07724

PRIME, EUGENIE ELSA, librarian; b. Trinidad, W.Indies; came to U.S., 1972; d. Harold John and Millicent L. Prime; B.A. with honors, U. W.Indies, 1966; M.A. in History, Andrews U., Berrien Springs, Mich., 1974; M.S. in L.S., Drexel U., Phila., 1976; M.B.A., UCLA, 1982. Postgrad. research fellow history U. W.Indies, 1966-69; head dept. history Naparima Girls High Sch., Trinidad, 1969-72; psychiat. social worker N.Y. State Dept. Mental Hygiene, 1974; exec. editor Cumulative Index to Nursing Lit., also med. librarian Glendale (Calif.) Adventist Med. Center, 1976—. Mem. Med. Library Assn., Am. Soc. Indexers, Nat. Assn. Female Execs., Med. Library Group So. Calif. and Ariz. Seventh-day Adventist. Home: 1727 Holly Dr Apt 301 Glendale CA 91206 Office: 1509 E Wilson Terr Glendale CA 91206

PRIMEAUX, ELIZABETH ANN (BETTY), med. technologist, swim instr.; b. Valentine, Nebr., Mar. 9, 1947; d. Edwin M. and Mary Elizabeth (Herdener) Wilson; student U. Nebr., 1965-67; B.S. in Biology, Nebr. Wesleyan U., 1970; grad. med. technologist St. Elizabeth Community Health Center Sch. Med. Tech., 1971; m. Michel E. Primeaux, Nov. 2, 1972; children—Christopher Marc, Michelle Leight Instr., med. technologist, chemistry and hematology depts. St. Elizabeth Community Health Center, Lincoln, Nebr., 1971-72; chief med. technologist Butler County Hosp., David City, Nebr., 1972-73; asst. chief med. technologist, chemistry Guadalupe Med. Center, Carlsbad, N.Mex., 1973-74; office mgr. Ram K. Pai, M.D., Carlsbad, 1976-77; chief med. technologist, chemistry, ins. clk. A.H. Gutierrer, Jr., M.D., Carlsbad, 1980—; swimming instr., exercise instr. Carlsbad, 1978—; instr. med. terminology and physiology for med. assts. N.Mex. State U. and Guadalupe Med. Center, Carlsbad, 1974-76. Sec. precinct 35, Carlsbad, 1976-77, alt. presiding election judge, 1982-83; sec. ward 3A, Democratic party, Carlsbad; del. N.Mex. Central Dem. Com.; adult vol., chaperone Spl. Olympics; active Girl Scouts U.S.A., past troop leader; sec. Eddy Elem. Sch. Parents Council, 1982-83. Mem. Am. Soc. Clin. Pathologists (registered med. technologist), Cath. Daus. Am. Roman Catholic. Club: Elks Wives. Home: 1006 Dearborn St Carlsbad NM 88220

PRIMO, MARIE NASH, mgr. shopping centers; b. Clarksburg, W.Va., Dec. 10, 1928; d. Frank and Josephine (DiMaria) Nash; student pub. schs. Clarksburg; m. Joseph C. Primo, Sept. 27, 1953; 1 dau., Joan E. Sec., Nat. Bank Detroit, 1945-46; exec. sec. Cutting Tool Mfrs. Assn., Detroit, 1946-50; adminstrv. asst. Irwin I. Cohn atty., Detroit, 1950—; mgr. Bloomfield Shopping Plaza, Birmingham, Mich., 1959—; North Hill Center, Avon Twp., Mich., 1957—; Drayton Plains Shopping Center (Mich.), 1958—; South Allen Shopping Center, Allen Park, Mich., 1953-77, Huron-Tel Corner, Pontiac, Mich., 1977—; officer, dir., numerous privately held corps. Mem. steering com., treas. Univ. Liggett Antiques Show, 1971-76, advisory com., 1977-80; mem. parents' com. Wellesley Coll., 1979-1981. Mem. Founders Soc. Detroit Inst. Arts, Women's Econ. Club, Mich. Humane Soc., Detroit Sci. Center, Detroit Zool. Soc., Smithsonian Assos., Hist. Soc. Mich., Grosse Pointe War Meml. Assn., Grosse Pointe Pub. Library Assn., Detroit Grand Opera Assn. Roman Catholic. Home: 1341 N Renaud Rd Grosse Pointe Woods MI 48236 Office: 2290 1st National Bldg Detroit MI 48226

PRIMROSE, BETTE REILLY, city ofcl.; b. Haileyville, Okla., July 31, 1933; d. William James and Thelma Irene (Emberton) Reilly; diploma Hill's Bus. U., Oklahoma City, 1951; m. David Earl Primrose, June 26, 1954; 1 son, Gregory Earl. Instr., Hill's Bus. U., 1952; exec. sec. Townsend Co., Santa Ana, Calif., 1952-57; office mgr. CTL div. Studebaker Corp., Santa Ana, 1958-63; sec. Boyle Engrng. Co., Santa Ana, 1963-64; exec. sec. Garcia/Conolon Corp., Santa Ana, 1965-66; office systems dir. CH2M Hill, Redding, Calif., 1967-82; info. mgr. City of Redding (Calif.), 1982—; cons. in bus. systems; leader seminars; speaker in field. Active local United Way. Mem. Internat. Info./Word Processing Assn. (pres. 1980-81), Phi Epsilon Phi. Democrat. Baptist. Author mag. column. Office: 1313 California St Redding CA 96001

PRIMUS, MARY JANE DAVIS, social worker; b. Marion, Iowa, May 31, 1924; d. Lawrence Henry and Verna Leona (Suman) Davis; B.S., Iowa State U., 1950; m. Paul C. Primus, Aug. 23, 1955; children—Kenneth Roy, Donald Karl. Asst. cashier First State Bank, Greene, Iowa, 1942-46; tchr. Oskaloosa (Iowa) public schs., 1950-52; extension home economist Iowa State U., Oskaloosa-Eldora, 1952-57; homemaker, dist. supr. Iowa Dept. Social Service, Webster City, 1970-77. Substitute tchr. Eldora Pub. Schs., 1966-68; homemaker health aide supr. Mid-Iowa Community Action OEO, Iowa Dept. Social Service, 1968-69. Den mother Boy Scouts Am., Steamboat Rock, Iowa, 1966-71; leader Girl Scouts Am., Steamboat Rock, 1969-72; mem. Iowa State U. Extension Family Living Council, Hardin County, 1961-65; outreach chmn. Iowa Family and Children Services, 1966-72; field days women's program chmn. Iowa Soil Conservation, 1968. Mem. Am. Home Econs. Assn., Nat. Council Homemaker-Home Health Aide Services, Nat. League Am. Pen Women, Nat. Soc. Lit. and the Arts, Soil Conservation Soc. Am., Am. Legion, Internat. Platform Assn., PEO Mem. United Ch. of Christ (pres. 1963-65). Mem. Order Eastern Star. Club: Federated Women's (Steamboat Rock). Author: Through the Window, 1973; Through the Window Twice, 1974; Tracery Windows, 1975; Shuttered Windows, 1977; Wings, 1979; outdoor cooking editor Iowa Wildlife Fedn., 1980; contbr. poems to various publs. Office: Steamboat Rock IA 50672

PRINCE, BARBARA ANN HOFREITER, truck repair co. exec.; b. Pekin, Ill., July 16, 1943; d. Robert Christian Hofreiter and Frances (Rebufoni) Hofreiter Burke; jr. acctg. degree Midstate Coll. of Commerce, 1963; student U. Ariz., 1968, supervisory devel. certificate, 1970; m. Albert William Prince III, Mar. 14, 1970; 1 dau., Roberta Christiana. Bookkeeper, South Side Bank, Peoria, Ill., 1962-63, Pyrofax Gas, Pekin, 1963-64, Farmers Automobile Ins. Assn., Pekin, 1964-65, WEEK-TV, Peoria, 1965-66; bookkeeper Hamilton Equipment Co., Inc., Tucson, 1966-68, sec.-treas., 1968-71; partner, sec.-treas., dir. Pyramid Truck Repair, Silverton, Oreg., 1975—. Water safety instr. ARC. Mem. Oreg. Retriever Trial Club (dir.), Salem Retriever Trial Club (treas.), Common Cause. Home: 5365 Lancers Ct NE Salem OR 97303 Office: Pyramid Truck Repair 827 N Railway NE Silverton OR 97381

PRINCE, BETTY, mktg. exec.; b. Sycamore, Ill., Nov. 29, 1942; d. Bertrand Bradford Prince and Margaret Hammond Safford; B.S., U. N. Mex., 1964, M.S., 1965; M.S. in Physics, U. Calif., Berkeley, 1973; M.B.A., U. Tex., Austin, 1980; children—David Patrick Phelan, Sharon Margaret Phelan. Sr. product engr. Fairchild Semicondr., Mountain View, Calif., 1973-76; tech. staff RCA corp., Findlay, Ohio, 1976-77; mgr. internat. mktg. Motorola I.C. Div., Austin, Tex., 1977-80, mgr. European mktg. Motorola Internat. div., East Kilbride, Scotland, 1980—; community coll. lectr.; gen. mgr. Prince Enterprises. Smithsonian asso., 1976-78; advancement chmn. Boy Scouts Am., 1977-78; mem. ACLU, 1965-75; dist. dir. United Methodist Ch. Calif. Conf., 1972-73. Life certified community coll. tchr., Calif.; Ford Found. fellow, 1963-65. Mem. IEEE, Am. Mgmt. Assn., Soc. Women Engrs. (v.p. S. Tex. sect.), Phi Kappa Phi, Kappa Mu Epsilon. Democrat. Office: Motorola Semiconductors Ltd Colvilles Rd Kelvin Estate East Kilbride Glasgow G75 0tG Scotland

PRINCE, BLANCHE STERN, psychotherapist, social worker; b. Phila., Aug. 11, 1926; d. Solomon and Ida (Kohen) Stern; student (Scholar), Temple U., 1943-44; B.A. magna cum laude, Radcliffe Coll., 1952; M.S.W., Columbia U., 1954; postgrad. U. Calif., Los Angeles, 1969-75; m. Morton B. Prince, June 15, 1947; 1 dau., Judith Ann. Clin. psychiat. researcher U. Calif., Los Angeles, 1963-68; researcher dept. pharmacology Hebrew U., Jerusalem, 1968-69; sr. social worker U. So. Calif.-Los Angeles County Med. Center, Los Angeles, 1970-72; cons. counselor So. Calif. Counseling Center, Los Angeles, 1972-75; pvt. practice psychotherapy, cons., Washington, 1976—. Founding mem. Washington Profl. Women's Coop., 1976. Licensed clin. social worker, Calif., D.C. Mem. Nat. Assn. Social Workers Acad. Certified Social Workers, Soc. for Clin. Social Work, ORT, Hadassah, Gray Panthers, Phi Beta Kappa. Office: 2700 Virginia Ave NW Washington DC 20037

PRINCE, FRANCES ANNE KIELY, civic worker; b. Toledo, Dec. 20, 1923; d. John Thomas and Frances (Pusteoska) Kiely; student U. Louisville, 1947-49; A.B., Berea Coll., 1951; postgrad. Kent Sch. Social Work, 1951, Creighton U., 1969; M.P.A., U. Nebr., Omaha, 1978; m. Richard Edward Prince, Jr., Aug. 17, 1951; children—Anne, Richard III. Instr. flower arranging Western Wyo. Jr. Coll., 1965, 66. Chmn., Lone Troop council Girl Scouts U.S.A., 1954-57, trainer leaders, 1954-68, mem. state camping com., 1959-61, bd. mem. Wyo. state council, 1966-69; chmn. Community Improvement, Green River, Wyo., 1959, 63-65, Wyo. Fedn. Women's Clubs State Library Services, 1966-69; mem. Wyo. State Adv. Bd. on Library Inter-Co-op., 1965-69; bd. mem. Sweetwater County Library System, 1962—, pres. bd., 1967-68; adv. council Sch. Dist. 66, 1970—; bd. dirs. Opera Angels, 1971, fund raising chmn., 1971-72, v.p., 1974—; bd. dirs. Morning Musicale, 1971—; bazaar com. Children's Hosp., 1970-75; docent Joslyn Art Mus., 1970—; mem. Nebr. Forestry Adv. Bd., 1976—; citizens adv. bd. Met. Area Planning Agy., 1979—; mem. Nebr. Tree-Planting Commn., 1980—. Recipient Library Service award Sweetwater County Library, 1968; Girl Scout Services award, 1967; Conservation award U.S. Forest Service, 1981; Plant Two Trees award, 1981. Mem. AAUW, New Neighbors League (dir. 1969-71), Ikebana Internat., Symphony Guild, Omaha Playhouse Guild, ALA, Nebr. Library Assn., Omaha Council Garden Clubs (1st v.p. 1972, pres. 1973-75), Internat. Platform Assn., Nat. Trust for Hist. Preservation, Nebr. Flower Show Judges Council, Nebr. Fedn. Garden Clubs (pres. 1978-81). Mem. United Ch. of Christ. Clubs: Intermountain (dir. 1963-69), Garden (dir. 1970-72, pres. 1972-75). Home: 8909 Broadmoor Dr Omaha NE 68114

PRINCE, MONSITA RAMOS, coatings and plastics co. exec.; b. Aguirre, P.R., Dec. 19, 1934; d. Juan Ramon and Justina (Fernandez) Ramos; student in bus. adminstrn. Interboro Inst., N.Y., 1954; student El Camino Coll., 1961-63, UCLA, 1963-65; m. Floyd J. Prince, Jr., June 4, 1966. Exec. sec. to D. H. Pupo, Ambassador to Canada, 1954; adminstrv. asst. Johns-Manville Corp., N.Y.C., 1955-60, Aerospace Corp., Los Angeles, 1961-65; with F.J. Prince Co., Inc., Torrance, Calif., 1965—, chief fin. officer, 1970—; sec.-treas. Liquid Plastics Co. of Calif. Vol., San Pedro Peninsula Hosp. Aux., 1978. Mem. Am. Builders and Contractors Assn. Republican. Roman Catholic. Clubs: Rotary Ann (pres. 1972), Pan American (pres. 1955). Home: 5 Outrider Rd Rolling Hills CA 90274 Office: 22521 S Normandie Ave Torrance CA 90501

PRINCIPAL, VICTORIA, actress; b. Fukuoka, Japan, Jan. 3; d. Victor and Ree (Veal) P.; student Miami-Dade Community Coll.; studied acting with Max Croft, Al Sacks and Estelle Harman. Worked as model, including TV comml. appearances; film debut in The Life and Times of Judge Roy Bean, 1972; other movie appearances include: The Naked Ape, Earthquake; I Will, I Will. . .For Now; Vigilante Force; TV film appearances include: Fantasy Island, Delancey, The Night They Stole Miss Beautiful; became theatrical agt., 1975; appears on TV series Dallas, 1978—; other TV appearances include: Love Story, Love, American Style, Greatest Heroes of the Bible, Battle of the Network Stars, Ester Queen of Hebrews, Pleasure Palace, Sixty Years of Seduction. Office: care Lorimar Prodns 10202 Washington Blvd Culver City CA

PRINE, HELEN FRANCES, newspaper pub.; b. Calhoun County, Mich., Nov. 13, 1936; d. Henry Woodside and Mildred Martha (Meyer) Hyatt; student Springport (Mich.) public schs.; m. Wesley S. Prine, Aug. 11, 1979; children—Joel, Jeffrey, Anita. Apprentice, Springport Signal, 1953-59, owner, operator, 1977—; linotype and teletype puncher Jackson (Mich.) Citizen Patriot, 1959-67; teletype puncher, layout Lansing (Mich.) State Jour., 1967-77. Vice pres. Springport Bus. Assn. Recipient Public Service awards 4-H, Boy Scouts Am. Mem. Mich. Press

Assn. Home: 11640 Prine Rd Springport MI 49284 Office: 104 Maple St Springport MI 49284

PRINGLE, HANNAH MARGARET, cytology supr.; b. Merrittstown, Pa., Apr. 10, 1925; d. Oscar S. and Estella Mae (Newell) Pringle; B.S. in Edn., Calif. State Coll., 1946; M.T., Uniontown Hosp. Lab., 1947; student Ohio State U., 1963. Sr. med. technologist Uniontown (Pa.) Hosp., 1948-59; med. technologist in histology W.Va. U., Sch. Medicine, Morgantown, 1960-61; chief med. technologist Connellsville (Pa.) State Gen. Hosp., 1961-62; with Johannsmann-Miller Med. Lab., Columbus, Ohio, 1963; cytotechnologist Westmoreland Hosp. Assn., Greensburg, Pa., 1963-67, chief technologist, 1967-74; free lance cytotechnologist, Merrittstown, Pa., 1974—. Vol. emergency med. technician, Republic Vol. Fire Dept. Ambulance Service, 1980. Am. Cancer Soc. scholar, 1963. Mem. Internat. Acad. Cytology, Am. Soc. Med. Technologists (chpt. pres. 1972-73), Pa. Soc. Med. Technologists, Am. Soc. Clin. Pathologists, Am. Soc. Cytology, Ohio Soc. cytology, Buckeye Soc. Cytology. Republican. Presbyterian. Address: PO Box 102 Merrittstown PA 15463

PRIOLEAU, ELIZABETH STEVENS, writer, educator, public affairs exec.; b. Richmond, Va., Nov. 14, 1942; d. Hugo Osterhaus and Adeline (Howle) Stevens; A.A., Bennett Coll., Millbrook, N.Y., 1962; B.S., U. Va., Charlottesville, 1966, M.A., 1972; Ph.D., Duke U., 1980; m. Philip Gendron Prioleau, Apr. 3, 1972. Asst. feature editor Charlottesville Daily Progress, 1963-64; instr. English, Fairleigh Dickinson U., 1980; lit. cons. Am. Jour. Dermatopathology, 1980—, John Barnes Prodns., 1980-81; public affairs dir. Marcel Breuer Assocs., N.Y.C., 1981—; vis. scholar Inst. Research in History, 1981. Recipient Jean Besselievre Boley prize for fiction, 1963. Mem. MLA, Victorian Soc. Am., Lychnos Hon. Soc. Author: Circle of Eros, 1982. Contbr. articles to profl. jours. Home: 122 E 92d St New York NY 10028 Office: 15 E 26th St New York NY 10010

PRIOR, JEAN CUTLER, research geologist; b. Akron, Ohio, Nov. 5, 1940; d. Thomas Edward and Martha Perry (Adams) Cutler; B.A., Purdue U., 1962; M.S., U. Ill., 1964; m. Stanley J. Prior, Jr., Sept. 5, 1964. Research asst. coal petrography Ill. Geol. Survey, part-time 1962-64; research geologist Iowa Geol. Survey, 1965—, sr. research geologist, 1975—. Mem. Geol. Soc. Am., Assn. Am. Geographers, Soil Conservation Soc. Am., Iowa Acad. Sci., Geol. Soc. Iowa, Sigma Xi. Author guide, papers in field. Home: Rural Route 1 Box 166 West Branch IA 52358 Office: 123 N Capitol St Iowa City IA 52242

PRISK, PATRICIA, nurse; b. Troy, N.Y., Nov. 6, 1944; d. Harold George and Mary Alice (Murphy) Connor; student Hudson Valley Community Coll., 1962; R.N., Samaritan Hosp. Sch. Nursing, 1965; m. William Prisk; children—Kimberly, Rebecca. Staff nurse Samaritan Hosp., 1965, Mt. Sinai Hosp., Hartford, Conn., 1966-69, Johnson Meml. Hosp., Stafford Springs, Conn., 1972-74; supr. Riverside Health Care Center, 1974-76; staff Middletown (Conn.) Health Care Center, 1974—, dir. nursing, 1976-81, staff nurse, 1981-82; staff nurse Lorraine Manor, Hartford, 1981-81; computer programmer Aetna Life and Casualty Co., Hartford, 1982—; lectr., cons. in field. Mem. Conn. Assn. Health Care Facilities. Office: Brainerd Rd Hartford CT

PRITCHARD, DONNA JEAN, bus. forms co. exec.; b. Boone, Iowa, June 29, 1930; d. Charles Leonard and Ida Alma (Wills) Ross; student public schs., Boone, Iowa; m. Elmer Lewis Pritchard, June 20, 1948; children—Linda Lee, Patti Kay. Bookkeeper, First Nat. Bank of Council Bluffs, Iowa, 1955-66; prin. Zeph Telpner C.P.A., Council Bluffs, 1966-74; sales rep. S.W. Iowa, Reynolds & Reynolds, Omaha, 1974-76; owner, pres. Asso. Bus. Forms, Council Bluffs, 1976—. Recipient Woman of Yr. Gold Star chpt. Am. Bus. Women's Assn., 1972. Mem. Progressive Bus. Assn. (pres. 1980—), Council Bluffs C. of C. (dir. 1982—Am. Bus. Women's Assn., Nebr. Motor Carriers Assn. (dir. 1982—), Nat. Orgn. Women Bus. Owners (past sec. Omaha chpt.), Nebr. Acctg. and Fin. Council. Republican. Presbyterian. Office: 200 S 1st St Council Bluffs IA 51501

PRITCHARD, YVONNE TUDOR, city ofcl.; b. Calif., Aug. 28, 1953; d. Martin and Barbara L. Tudor; B.A., Calif. State Poly. U., 1976; M.P.A., U. So. Calif., 1979. Personnel analyst County of San Bernardino (Calif.), 1976-79; sr. compensation analyst UCLA, 1979, personnel cons., 1980; personnel analyst City of San Bernardino, 1980—. Mem. Internat. Personnel Mgmt. Assn., Nat. Pub. Employee Relations Assn., Am. Soc. Pub. Adminstrn., Inland Area Personnel Mgmt. Assn. (treas. 1981-83). Office: Dept Personnel City Hall 300 North D St San Bernardino CA 92418

PRITCHETT, CONNIE CHARLENE, apparel mfg. co. exec.; b. Royal Oak, Mich., July 17, 1949; d. Lawrence Joseph and Margaret Mary Bauman; B.S., Eastern Mich. U., 1974; M.B.A., U. Mich., 1977; m. Jeffrey Pritchett, July 31, 1970. Personnel mgr. Dixie Mfg., Inc., Ypsilanti, Mich., 1967-73; dir. public relations Tower, Inc., 1973-75; vocat. instr., coop. edn. coordinator Oxford (Mich.) Sch. System, 1975-78; personnel mgr. Reeves Bros. Inc., Denver, Pa., 1978-80; corp. personnel and tng. dir. V. F. Corp., Reading, Pa., 1980—; cons. Mem. Am. Soc. Personnel Adminstrs., Assn. MBA Execs., Nat. Assn. Female Execs., Am. Soc. Tng. and Devel., Phi Gamma Nu (past pres., internat. rep.). Home: 405 Orchard View Ln Reading PA 19606

PRITCHETT, MATTELYN YVONNE, social worker; b. St. Louis, Aug. 14, 1944; d. Raymond Wesley and Edna (Edwards) P.; B.A., Lane Coll., 1970; M.S.W., St. Louis U., 1974. Dep. juvenile officer St. Louis City Juvenile Ct., 1970-72; social worker Cath. Charities Dept. Children, St. Louis, 1974-76; social worker University City Sch. Dist. 725, 1976—; adj. prof. St. Louis U., 1976-79; abuse-neglect cons. University City Schs. Mem. Nat. Assn. Social Workers, NEA, Nat. Council Negro Women, NAACP, Lane Coll. Alumni Assn. (v.p.), Alpha Kappa Alpha. United Methodist (ch. sch. supt., vacation Bible sch. dir., mem. council on ministries, adminstrv. bd.). Home: 7718 Peach Tree Ln University City MO 63130 Office: 725 Kingsland Ave University City MO 63130

PRITCHETT, PAULETTE SHIREY, pathologist; b. Guin, Ala., Dec. 25, 1943; d. Paul Floyd and Dorothy Lee (Perry) Shirey; B.S., Florence State U., 1965; M.D., U. Ala., 1969; m. Robert Monroe Prichett, Mar. 19, 1972; 1 dau., Nancy Katherine. Intern, U. Ala. Hosps. and Clinics, Birmingham, 1969-70, resident in pathology, 1970-73; resident in pathology Santa Clara Valley Med. Center, San Jose, Calif., 1973-74; instr. pathology Med. Coll. of Va., Richmond, 1973-75; asst. prof. U. Ala., Birmingham, 1975-77, clin. asst. prof., 1977-81, clin. asso. prof., 1981—; asso. pathologist Cooper Green Hosp., Birmingham, 1977—. Recipient Roche award, 1967; Stuart Graves award, 1967; William Boyd Medal, 1969. Mem. Am. Soc. Cytology, Jefferson County Med. Soc., Med. Soc. of Ala., AMA, Am. Acad. Dermatologists, Am. Soc. Clin. Pathologists, Alpha Omega Alpha. Republican. Home: 3336 E Briarcliff Birmingham AL 35223 Office: 1515 6th Ave S Birmingham AL 35233

PRIVITERA, MARIA ANTONIA, mfg. co. ofcl.; b. Cleve., June 30, 1947; d. Santo and Theresa (Romeo) P.; B.S.E., St. John Coll., Cleve., 1969; B.A., Cleve. State U., 1974; postgrad. U. Akron; m. James M. Horejsi, Sept. 2, 1978. Elem. tchr. Holy Redeemer Sch., Cleve., 1969-72; claims adjuster Retail Clks. Ins. Fund, Cleve., 1972-74; assoc. producer instrnl. TV, Los Angeles Community Colls., 1974-76; producer, writer, dir. Babcock & Wilcox TV Center, Barberton, Ohio, 1976-79; audio visual producer B. F. Goodrich Co., Akron, Ohio, 1979—; freelance comml. scriptwriter. Speaker United Way. Recipient award Internat. Film and TV Festival N.Y., 1978. Mem. Internat. TV Assn. (service award), Assn. Multi-Image. Democrat. Roman Catholic. Home: 759 Tollis Pkwy Broadview Heights OH 44147 Office: 500 S Main St Akron OH 44318

PROBERT, CANDY WILSON, home economist; b. Inglewood, Calif., Sept. 13, 1952; d. Richard W. and Dorothy Elaine (Page) Wilson; B.S. in Child Devel. cum laude, U. Utah, 1974, B.S. in Psychology cum laude, 1974; m. Ronald L. Probert, July 10, 1981; 1 dau., Erin McCall. Tchr., Jewish Community Center, Salt Lake City, 1974-75; ballet instr. community edn. Highland High Sch., Salt Lake City, 1970-75; home economist Harmon's Supermarket, Midvale, Utah, 1975—; editor, corr. sec. Food Mktg. Consumer Advs., 1975-76. Apptd. assoc. mem. Kearns (Utah) Town Council, 1982. Recipient Mathew Baird award CIA, Washington, 1973; Ednl. Aid Fund scholar, 1970-73. Mem. Home Economists in Bus., Am. Home Econs. Assn., Food Mktg. Inst., Utah Home Econs. Assn. (co-chmn. spring conv. 1980). Home: 4404 Twilight Dr Kearns UT 84118 Office: 980 E 7200 S Midvale UT 84047

PROBERT, DOROTHY WITTMAN, social worker; b. Ridgeway, Pa., Nov. 17, 1921; d. William Edward and Marie Genevieve (Ticknor) Wittman; B.A., Pa. State U., 1944; M.S.W., Fordham U., 1967, postgrad., 1968; m. Lionel W. Probert, June 15, 1946; children—Susan Zaveruha, Sally Caldarazzo, William L., Marguerite A., Thomas J. Homefinder, Conn. State Welfare, Bridgeport, 1962; psychiat. social worker Cath. Family and Community Services, Bridgeport, 1962-69, supr., 1967-69; sch. social worker Trumbull (Conn.) Bd. Edn., 1969-73, Bridgeport Bd. Edn., 1973—; cons. Trumbull-St. Mary's Convalescent Home, Trumbull, 1977—; liaison psychiat. worker for students under 16, Park City Hosp., 1981—. Cert. sch. social worker, Conn. Mem. Nat. Assn. Social Workers, Acad. Cert. Social Workers, Bridgeport Edn. Assn., Conn. Edn. Assn., NEA. Republican. Roman Catholic. Home: 25 Denton Pl Stratford CT 06497 Office: Kolbe Bldg 389 Kossuth St Bridgeport CT 06608

PROBST, LOUISE GALE, nurse; b. Bethesda, Md., June 3, 1947; d. Thomas Andrew and Louise Gale (Fentress) Ahroon; B.S., U. Va., 1970; M.A., Pepperdine U., 1976; M.Nursing, U. Wash., 1981; m. Frederick William Probst, Oct. 14, 1972. Commd. ensign, Nurse Corps, U.S. Navy, 1969, advanced through grades to lt. comdr., 1979; staff/charge nurse Naval Regional Med. Center, San Diego, 1970-73, instr., Naval Sch. Health Scis., San Diego, 1973-75; supr., charge nurse Naval Regional Med. Center, Guam, 1975-77; charge nurse, supr. Naval Regional Med. Center, Oakland, Calif., 1977-80; quality assurance coordinator Naval Regional Med. Center, San Diego, 1981—. Recipient George Washington Honor medal, Freedoms Found., 1979. Mem. Am. Assn. Critical Care Nurses, Assn. Operating Room Nurses, Emergency Dept. Nurses Assn., Assn. Mil. Surgeons of U.S., Assn. Occupational Hearing Conservationists. Republican. Episcopalian. Home: 950 O Connell St North Bend OR 97459

PROCACCI, DEBRA CATHERINE, utilities co. exec.; b. Camden, N.J., Oct. 20, 1954; d. Louis John and Mary Dolores (D'Anastasio) P.; B.A. in Communications, Glassboro (N.J.) State Coll., 1976, postgrad., 1979. Public info. officer Dept. Community Devel., City of Camden (N.J.), 1977-79; supr. govt. communications, communications dept. S.Jersey Gas Co., Folsom, 1979—. Exec. dir. N.J. Natural Resources Bond Issue Citizens Com., 1980; vice chmn. N.J. Natural Resources Citizens Adv. Com., 1981—. Mem. N.J. Environ. and Econ. Devel. Assn., S.Jersey C. of C., N.J. Employer Legis. Com. (chmn. Atlantic County 1980—), Associated Gas Distbrs. (coordinator legis. com. 1980—), Am. Gas Assn., Nat. Sch. Public Relations Assn. Office: 1 S Jersey Plaza Rt 54 Folsom NJ 08037

PROCTER, CAROL ANN, cellist; b. Oklahoma City, June 26, 1941; d. Leland Herrick and Alice (McElroy) P.; student Eastman Sch. Music, 1958-60; B.Mus., New Eng. Conservatory of Music, 1963; M.Mus. (Fromm fellow), Berkshire Music Center, Tanglewood, Mass., 1965. Cellist, Springfield (Mass.) Symphony Orch., 1961-65, Cambridge (Mass.) Festival Orch., 1961-65, Boston Symphony Orch. and Boston Pops, 1965—; mem. New Eng. Harp Trio, Berkshire String Trio; viola da gambist Curtisville Consortium; soloist viola da gamba Boston Symphony Orch., 1976, 81, cello Boston Pops, 1980. Recipient Fulbright award, 1965. Mem. Mu Phi Epsilon. Office: Boston Symphony Orchestra Symphony Hall Boston MA 02115

PROCTOR, BARBARA GARDNER, advt. agy. exec., writer; b. Asheville, N.C.; d. William and Bernice (Baxter) Gardner; B.A. Talladega Coll., 1954; m. Carl L. Proctor, July 20, 1961 (div. Nov. 1963); 1 son, Morgan Eugene. Music critic, contbg. editor Down Beat Mag., Chgo., 1958—; internat. dir. Vee Jay Records, Chgo., 1961-64; copy supr. Post-Keyes-Gardner Advt., Inc., 1965-68, Gene Taylor Assos., 1968-69, North Advt. Agy., 1969-70; contbr. to gen. periodicals, 1952—; now chmn. bd., pres., creative dir. Proctor & Gardner Advt., Chgo. Mem. Chgo. Urban League, Chgo. Econ. Devel. Corp. Bd. dirs. People United to Save Humanity, Better Bus. Bur. Cons. pub. relations and promotion, record industry. Recipient Armstrong Creative Writing award, 1954; awards Chgo. Fedn. Advt. Clubs, N.Y. Art Dirs. Club. Woman's Day; Frederick Douglas Humanitarian award, 1975; named Chgo. Advt. Woman of Year, 1974. Mem. Chgo. Media Women, Nat. Assn. Radio Arts and Sci., Women's Advt. Club, Cosmopolitan C. of C. (dir.), Female Execs. Assn., Internat. Platform Assn., Smithsonian Instn. Assos. Author TV documentary Blues for a Gardenia, 1963. Office: Proctor and Gardner Advt 111 E Wacker Dr Chicago IL 60601

PROCTOR, DOROTHEA ESCHERICH, social worker, adminstr.; b. Pasadena, Calif., Sept. 30, 1925; d. Carl and Elsa Antonie (Falk) Escherich; A.A., Stephens Coll., 1945; B.A., Stanford U., 1946; M.S.W., Sacramento State U., 1974; m. George Alan Proctor, July 20, 1946; children—G. Alan, Robert Alexander, David Thomas. Social worker Sonoma County (Calif.) Social Service, 1967-72, social service practitioner, Santa Rosa, Calif., 1974-80; psychotherapist Family Service Agy. of Sonoma County, 1974—; dir. Living with Cancer Project, 1979-80; coordinator adolescent and children's case mgmt. Sonoma County Dept. Mental Health, 1981—. Pres., trustee Rincon Valley Union Dist. Sch. Bd., 1959-73. Mem. Soc. Clin. Work, Nat. Assn. Social Workers., AAUW. Office: 1212 4th St Santa Rosa CA 95404

PROCTOR, LINDA NADINE, educator; b. Cass County, Iowa, Dec. 14, 1954; d. Mayo George and Janet Sibyl (Dorsheimer) Proctor; B.S., U. Tenn., 1974, M.S., 1976; Ed.S., U. Ga., Athens, 1981. Tchr., Little Tenn. Ednl. Coop., Alcoa, 1975, Knoxville (Tenn.) City Sch. System, 1975-78; instr. Ga. Retardation Center, U. Ga., Athens, 1978-82; instr. Inst. of Logopedics, Wichita, Kans., 1982—; pvt. tutor; cert. data collector Ga.'s Beginning Tchr. Assessment Program. Mem. Council for Exceptional Children, Athens Area Assn. for Retarded Citizens, Phi Kappa Phi, Kappa Delta Pi. Republican. Home: 2200 S Rock Rd Apt 614 Wichita KS 67207 Office: 2400 Jardine Dr Wichita KS 67219

PROCTOR, PAMELA LYNN, retail stores advt. mgr.; b. McAlester, Okla., July 29, 1944; d. O. P. and Alverna Ray (McAlpine) P.; B.B.A., Tex. Tech. U., 1967. Jr. exec. Foley's, Houston, 1967, asst. dept. mgr., 1968; stewardess Frontier Airlines, Denver, 1968; sec. to v.p. publicity Sanger Harris, Dallas, 1969-71, copywriter, 1969-71, asst. dept. mgr. radio and TV, 1971-75, dept. mgr., 1975-78, ops. group mgr.-broadcast, 1978-81, divisional mgr.-broadcast, 1981—. Vol., Presbyn. Hosp., Dallas, 1969—. Mem. Assn. Broadcast Execs. Tex. (treas. 1977, dir. 1978), Am. Women in Radio and TV. Republican. Methodist. Office: 303 N Akard St Dallas TX 75201

PROCTOR, PATRICIA BROWN, librarian; b. Tallahassee, Oct. 14, 1937; d. Dearen Nathaniel and Frances (Williams) Brown; B.S., Fla. A. & M. U., 1960, M.Ed., 1967; M.L.S., Fla. State U., 1980, now student; m. William Curtis Proctor, July 12, 1958; 1 son, William Curtis. Librarian, Howard Acad., Monticello, Fla., 1960-64, Fla. A. & M. Univ. High Sch., Tallahassee, 1964—. Den mother Suwannee council Boy Scouts Am., 1968-76; committeewoman Democratic Exec. Com., 1974; sec. Capital City Voters League, 1974-75, pres., 1980-81. Mem. NAACP, Fla. Assn. Media in Edn., Kappa Delta Phi. Democrat. Home: 3313 North Ridge Rd Tallahassee FL 32304 Office: Fla A & M Univ High Sch PO Box 19 Tallahassee FL 32307

PROCTOR, RUTH ALICE, county extension agt.; b. Noblesville, Ind., Oct. 14, 1930; d. Leland H. and Lula Mae Carson; B.S., Purdue U., 1953; M.A., Am. U., 1976; m. Frank Baker Proctor, Oct. 5, 1957; children—Gail Lynn, Jennifer Ruth, Suzanne Elaine. Extension agt. Ind. Coop. Extension Service, 1953-55; internat. fellow in Md., Nat. 4-H Council, 1955-56; with nat. sch. lunch program Dept. Agr., Washington, 1956-58; extension agt. 4-H and youth Md. Coop. Extension Service, 1975—; supr. work-study students U. Md. Coordinator childrens edn. programs Marvin Meml. United Meth. Ch., Silver Spring, Md. Recipient Nat. 4-H Alumnae award, 1974, Md. Coop. Extension Service Rookie award, 1977, Montgomery County (Md.) C. of C. Nat. Figure of Yr. award, 1974. Mem. Nat. Assn. Extension 4-H Agts. (Disting. Service award 1980), Md. Assn. 4-H Agts., Internat. 4-H Youth Exchange Alumnae, Purdue U. Alumnae Assn. (Citizenship award 1975), Phi Mu (chpt. pres. 1979-80); life mem. Md. 4-H All Stars, Montgomery County Agrl. Center. Editor papers in field. Home: 11905 Grandview Ave Silver Spring MD 20902 Office: 600 S Frederick Ave Gaithersburg MD 20760

PRODOEHL, PATRICIA ANN, nurse, bus. exec.; b. Oak Park, Ill., Mar. 16, 1938; d. Carl Olaf and Elizabeth Mable (Maas) Larson; R.N., Swedish Am. Hosp., Rockford, Ill., 1959; m. Henry William Prodoehl, June 3, 1961; children—James Carl, Judith Ann; step-children—Lawrence Paul, R. Theresa. Nurse, Swedish Am. Hosp., Rockford, Ill., 1959-60, Johns Hopkins Hosp., Balt., 1960-61, Lutheran Hosp., Balt., 1961-62; sec.-treas. Free State Adjusters, Inc., Balt., 1978—; pres. Office E-Z Move, Balt., 1981—. Active Camp Fire Girls, Inc., 1971-81, recipient numerous awards; active Boy Scouts Am., recipient Merit award, 1974; tchr. Sunday Sch., 1968-71, 80-82, supt., 1981—. Recipient Book of Golden Deeds award Exchange Club of Randallstown (Md.). Mem. Am. Mgmt. Assn., Nat. Fedn. Ind. Bus. Lutheran. Club: Woman's (pres. Randallstown 1980-82). Office: 9621 Reistertown Rd Box 5705 Baltimore MD 21208

PROFIT, LORETHA SPURS, elementary sch. tchr.; b. Monroe, La., Aug. 15, 1947; d. James and Willie Mae (Kiper) Spurs; B.A., N.E. La. U., 1976; m. Simon Profit, Jr., June 6, 1966; children—Anthony Simeon, Adriane Sirena, Simon, III. Asst. mgr. Nelsons Drive In and Motel, Monroe, 1966-68, mgr., 1970-73, co-owner, 1980—; substitute tchr., vol. tutor Ouachita Prish Sch. Bd., Monroe, 1968-69; paraprofl. Swayze Elem. Sch., Monroe, 1973-76; tchr. 2d grade Woodlawn Elem. Sch., W. Monroe, 1976—. Mem. NEA, La. Assn. Educators, Ouachita Assn. Educators (faculty rep.), Industrious Black Bus. Alliance. Club: Order Eastern Star. Home: 4002 Gaston St Monroe LA 71203 Office: Route 3 Box 126-C West Monroe LA 71291

PROKOP, RUTH TIMBERLAKE, lawyer; b. San Saba, Tex., May 30, 1939; d. Harry Carver and Anna Grace (Winslow) Timberlake; B.A., George Washington U., 1961, J.D., 1965; m. John Andrew Prokop, Aug. 29, 1962; 1 dau., Kristina Elizabeth. Admitted to D.C., U.S. Supreme Ct. bars; mem. staff Vice Pres. Lyndon B. Johnson, 1961-62; legis. asst. Pres.'s Commn. on Status of Women, 1962-64; legis. counsel Pres.'s Com. on Consumer Affairs, 1964-66; spl. asst. to sec. HUD, 1966-69; mem. firm Brownstein Zeidman & Schomer, 1970-72; sr. counsel Gen. Telephone & Electronics Corp., 1972-77; gen. counsel HUD, Washington, 1977-79; chmn. U.S. Merit Systems Protection Bd., Washington, 1979-81; partner firm Curtis, Mallet-Prevost, Colt & Mosle, Washington, N.Y.C., 1981—; tax commr. D.C., 1976-77; bd. dirs. Nat. Com. on Household Employment, 1973-77, Fed. Nat. Mortgage Assn., 1977-79. Bd. govs. Women's Nat. Democratic Club, 1972-77. Mem. Am. (council sci. and tech. sect. 1976-77; chmn. privacy com. 1976), Fed., FCC bar assns., D.C. Integrated Bar, George Washington U. Law Sch. Alumni Assn. (pres. 1973). Democrat. Episcopalian. Office: 1735 I St NW Washington DC 20006 also 100 Wall St New York NY 10005

PROM, ELEANOR KLECKNER, bus. exec.; b. Belgium, Wis., May 16, 1933; d. John W. and Catherine M. (Schumacher) Kleckner; B.B.A., Cardinal Stritch Coll., 1979; m. Richard G. Prom (dec.); children—Kay Marie, Mark Earl, Sid Robert, Jill Mary, Lynn Geralee, John Henry, Craig Floyd. Instr., Wis. Sch. Real Estate, Milw., 1976-79, Lakeshore Tech. Inst., Cleveland, Wis., 1976-79; tax cons. H & R Block, Sheboygan, Wis., 1978-79; instr. real estate Cardinal Stritch Coll., Milw., 1978-79; asst. fiscal mgr. Comunidad deAmigo, Belgium, Wis., 1978-79; controller Bergin Corp., Thiensville, Wis., 1979-81; pres. Promel Services, Belgium, Wis., 1981—. Mem. Wis. Bd. Realtors, Nat. Bd. Realtors, Nat. Assn. Accts., Ozaukee County Bd. Realtors, Wis. Assn. Accts. Home: 140 West Ln Belgium WI 53004

PROPES, ALICE IDA, Realtor; b. Gold Beach, Oreg., Aug. 9, 1927; d. Elmer Revis and Helen Violet (Fischer) Costelloe; student public schs., Gold Beach; grad. Realtors Inst.; m. Frank Findley Propes, June 17, 1952; children—Sheri Lue, Michael Frank. Chief operator West Coast Telephone Co., Gold Beach, 1945-52; partner Washington Utilities Constrn. Co., 1952-60, sec.-treas., 1960—; partner Mt. Springs Arabian Ranch, 1962—; owner, Realtor 5 Mt. Springs Realty, Willamina, Oreg., 1973—. Mem. Polk County Planning Commn., 1981-82. Mem. Oreg., Portland, Polk County (Realtor of yr. 1976, pres. 1978) bds. Realtors, Farm and Land Inst. (accredited), Oreg. Assn. Realtors (dist. v.p. 1980—), Dallas Area C. of C. Republican. Presbyterian. Home: 225 SE Walnut Dr Dallas OR 97338 Office: PO Box 899 Willamina OR 97396

PROPHIT, PENNY PAULINE, educator, nurse; b. Monroe, La., Feb. 7, 1939; d. C. Alston and Hortense (Callahan) P.; B.S.N., Marillac Coll., 1966; M.S.N., Catholic U. Am., 1971, D.N.Sc., Ph.D., 1974. Asso. prof. nursing U. So. Miss., 1974-75, La. State U. Med. Center, New Orleans, 1974-75; vis. prof. Cath. U. Louvain, Belgium, 1978-80; prof. Cath. U. Am., Washington, 1975-80, Cath. U. Louvain, 1980—; cons. NIMH, NIH. Mem. AAUP, Council Advanced Practitioners in Psychiat.-Mental Health Nursing, Am. Nurses Assn., Am. Assn. Humanistic Psychology, Nat. League Nursing, D.C. Nurses Assn. (dir. 1978-81), Am. Assn. Suicidology, Am. Assn. Thanatology, Assn. Life and Health Scis., Mental Health Law Project, Delta Epsilon Sigma, Sigma Theta Tau. Democrat. Roman Catholic. Author: Understanding/Responding, 1979. Home: 127 Taussig Pl NE Apt 6 Washington DC 20011 Office: Catholic U Louvain Centrum voor Ziekenhuiswetenschap Vital Decosterstraat 102 3000 Leuven Belgium

PROPST, MARY FRANCES, librarian; b. Skipwith, Va., Oct. 29, 1917; d. John Edwin and Lucy Jane (Woltz) Thomas; B.S. in Edn., Longwood Coll., 1939; A.B. in L.S., Coll. William and Mary, 1946; m. Noel Laurence Propst, Jan. 30, 1948; 1 son, Noel Laurence. Tchr. pub.

schs., Hanover County, Va., 1939-41, Mecklenburg County, Va., 1941-45; librarian hist. research dept. Colonial Williamsburg, Va., 1946-47, Southside Regional Library, Boydton, Va., 1948—. Sunday Sch. tchr. Baptist Ch., 1960—, supt. youth dept., 1961-72; mem. Adult Basic Edn. Participatory Planning Com. for Mecklenburg County, 1980—; trustee Prestwould House Mus., 1968—; chmn. Mecklenburg County Bicentennial Commn., 1975—. Mem. Va. Library Assn. (chmn. regional sect. 1951-52), Bus. and Profl. Womens Club (dist. rec. sec. 1968-69), Va. Farm Bur. (sec. womens com. 1954-55, chmn. dist. womens com. 1956-59), Assn. Preservation Va. Antiquities (chmn. Va. library com. 1955-58), DAR (chaplain Prestwould chpt. 1980—), Delta Kappa Gamma. Clubs: Boydton Womens; Boydton Community Center; Home: Route 2 Box 256 Boydton VA 23917 Office: Southside Regional Library Boydton VA 23917

PROSKOURIAKOFF, TATIANA, archaeologist; b. Tomsk, Russia, Jan. 23, 1909; came to U.S., 1916, naturalized, 1923; d. Avenir and Alla (Nekrassova) P.; B.S. in Architecture, Pa. State Coll., 1930; LL.D. (hon.), Tulane U., 1977. Draftsman, mem. staff div. hist. research, Carnegie Instn. Washington, 1939-58; assoc. Peabody Museum, Harvard U., from 1958, now ret.; mem. U. Pa. expdn., 1936-37, other expdns., 1938-55. Recipient Alfred Vincent Kidder award, 1962; named Pa. State Woman of Yr., 1971. Mem. Peabody Mus. Assn. Author books, including: An Album of Maya Architecture, 1946, A Study of Classic Maya Sculpture, 1950, Jades from Sacrificial Cenote at Chichen Itza, 1974; contbr. numerous articles to profl. jours. Office: Peabody Mus Harvard U Cambridge MA 02138

PROSS, SUSAN HYMES, microbiologist; b. N.Y.C., May 20, 1949; d. Bernard J. and Beatrice (Litvin) Hymes; B.S. with distinction, Cornell U., 1970; Ph.D., U. Pa., 1975; m. Ronald Michael Pross, Aug. 27, 1972. Teaching asst. dept. biology U. Pa., Phila., 1970-74; instr. dept. biology Hillsborough Community Coll., Tampa, Fla., 1975; instr. dept. med. microbiology U. South Fla. Coll. Medicine, Tampa, 1975-76, asst. prof., 1976—. Mem. AAAS, S. Fla. Soc. for Microbiology, Orgn. for Rehab. Through Tng., Mortar Board, Phi Kappa Phi. Democrat. Jewish. Home: 12603 Clendenning Dr Tampa FL 33624 Office: 12901 N 30th St Tampa FL 33612

PROTERO, DODI, soprano; b. Toronto, Can., Mar. 13, 1935; came to U.S., 1965; d. Stewart and Dorothy (Flaherty) McIlraith; ed. in Europe. Soprano with Vienna State Opera, Salzburg Festival, Glyndebourne Festival, Rome Opera, San Carlo Opera, Can. Opera, Vancouver Opera, San Antonio Opera, Pitts. Opera Co.; prof. voice U. Ill., Urbana, 1976—; tchr. pvt. voice students, N.Y.C., 1975—; prof. voice Banff (Alta.) Sch. Fine Arts. Can. Council fellow, 1965, 69, 73. Mem. Nat. Assn. Tchrs. of Singing, Equity, AFTRA, Am. Guild Musical Artists, Screen Actors Guild, Ill. State Music Tchrs. Assn. Recorded for Phillips Records on Epic Label; appeared in movie, Vienna City of My Dream, 1958. Home: 1809D Valley Rd Champaign IL 61820 Office: 257 Central Park W Apt 12H New York NY 10024

PROUDFIT, SHARON LOUISE, ednl. adminstr.; b. Adrian, Mich., Oct. 19, 1938; d. LeRoy and Delores (Happel) Wood; B.A., U. Mich., 1960, M.A., 1961, Ph.D., 1967; postgrad. U. London, 1973-74, Courtauld Inst. Art History; m. June 10, 1961; children—Charles, Kerren. Asst. prof. English, Colo. Women's Coll., Denver, 1967-74, assoc. prof., 1974-78, chmn. English and modern langs., 1977-78; assoc. prof. humanities U. Colo., Boulder, 1978—, dir. Sewall acad. program, 1978-81, dir. Farrand acad. program, 1981—. Trustee, Rocky Mountain Inst., 1977-79; trustee Colo. Music Festival, 1980—, v.p., 1981—. Mem. Boulder Valley U. of Mich. Alumni Assn. (pres. 1977-78, scholarship dir. 1974-77, 79-81), MLA, Rocky Mountain Modern Lang. Assn., AAUP, Virginia Woolf Soc., Colo. Women's Studies Assn. Club: Sierra. Democrat. Contbr. articles to profl. jours. Home: 425 Christmas Tree Dr Boulder CO 80302 Office: Campus Box 180 Univ Colo Boulder CO 80310

PROUTY, BERNADINE MARIE, ret. county ofcl.; b. Browns, Ill., Feb. 12, 1925; d. Chester A. and Mae (Shelby) Hensley; A.A., Diablo Valley Coll., 1978; m. Robert Roy Prouty, June 10, 1951; children—Diane Leigh, Janelle Faye. Owner, mgr. Colusa Circle Hardware, Berkeley, Calif., 1958-65; sec. Contra Costa County, Martinez, Calif., 1970-80. Mem. Apt. and Property Owners Assn. Contra Costa (dir. 1975-79), Nat. Womens Polit. Caucus. Republican. Baptist. Home: 65 Viking Dr Pleasant Hill CA 94523

PROVENZANO, MARIA CELESTE, data processing auditor; b. Boston, July 28, 1954; d. Rosario William and Teresa Maria P.: A.B. with honors, Boston Coll., 1976, M.B.A. with honors, 1978. Mgmt. adv. services, electronic data processing cons. Price Waterhouse & Co., Boston and N.Y.C., 1978-79; sr. electronic data processing auditor Cabot Corp., Boston, 1979—; cons. electronic data processing. Youth mgr. Senator Brooke, Mass., 1973. Mem. Am. Mgmt. Assn., Electronic Data Processing Auditors Assn., Nat. Assn. Women Execs. (dir.), Women in Bus., Internat. Platform Assn. Clubs: Boston Coll. Alumni, Squash. Contbr. to fin. mgmt. textbooks. Office: 125 High St Boston MA 02110

PROVENZANO, SANDRA, pilot; b. Tulsa, Jan. 8, 1938; d. Mansford Allen and Mary Elizabeth (Barnes) Hulme; children—Ross Anthony, David Allen, Mark Andrew. With Cruse Aviation, Inc., Houston, 1970—, chief pilot, chief flight instr., dir. ops., 1979—; pilot examiner, accident prevention counselor FAA, Houston, 1977—; mem. adv. council Houston Aviation, 1980—. Roman Catholic. Mem. Greater Houston Assn. Flight Instrs. (pres. 1982). Club: Bergstrom Aero (chief pilot 1979, mgr. 1979). Contbr. articles to tng. catalogs. Home: 3909 Burke St Pasadena TX 77504 Office: 8501 Telephone Rd Houston TX 77061

PROVUS, BARBARA LEE, mgmt. cons.; b. Washington, Nov. 20, 1949; d. Severn and Birdell (Eck) P.; student N.Y. U., 1969-70; B.A., Russell Sage Coll., 1971; postgrad. Smith Coll., 1971; M.S.I.R., Loyola U., Chgo., 1979. Cons. exec. search and corp. mgmt. devel. Booz, Allen & Hamilton, Inc., Chgo., 1973-80; mgr. mgmt. devel. Federated Dept. Stores, Inc., Cin., 1980-82; v.p. Lamalie Assos., Inc., Chgo., 1982—. Mem. Human Resources Planning Soc., Am. Soc. Tng. and Devel., Am. Soc. Personnel Adminstrn., Assn. Exec. Search Cons. Home: 1660 N LaSalle St Chicago IL 60614 Office: 120 S Riverside Plaza Chicago IL 60606

PROVYN, SUSAN FARMER, life ins. co. exec.; b. Alexandria, Va., June 9, 1949; d. Henry Tudor and Ingeborg Maria (Goletz) Farmer; B.S. with high honors, U. Md., 1971; m. Frank Ronald Provyn, June 10, 1978; 1 son, Frank Hunter. Mem. office audit staff Ernst & Whinney, Washington, 1971-78, audit supr., 1974-78; controller Bankers Security Life Ins. Soc. subs. United Services Life Ins. Co., Washington, 1978—, 2d v.p., 1978-80, v.p., 1980—. Fellow Life Mgmt. Inst.; mem. Am. Soc. Women Accts. (pres. D.C. chpt. 1981-82), Am. Women's Soc. C.P.A.s, Md. Assn. C.P.A.s, U. Md. Bus. Alumni Assn. (dir.), Beta Alpha Psi, Beta Gamma Sigma. Office: 1701 Pennsylvania Ave NW Washington DC 20006

PRUCNAL, PEGGY ANN, home economist; b. Gadsden, Ala., Nov. 24, 1946; d. Walter Joseph and Ethel Mae (Orr) P.; B.S. in Home Econs., Jacksonville State U., 1969; M.A.T., U. Montevallo, 1974. Assoc. county agt., then county agt. 4H, Coop. Extension Service, Shelby County, 1969—. Mem. Ala. Assn. Extension Home Economists (4H Youth Cert. of Achievement 1979, Disting. Service award 1981), Nat. Assn. Extension Home Economists, Ala. Home Econs. Assn., Am. Home Econs. Assn., Ala. Assn. Extension 4H Agts., Epsilon Sigma Phi. Roman Catholic. Home: PO Box 1433 Columbiana AL 35051 Office: PO Box 1606 Columbiana AL 35051

PRUETT, AGNES MURRAY, former tchr., photographer; b. Pelzar, S.C., Nov. 8, 1903; d. John Colley Garrison and Camely (Whitmire) Murray; B.S., George Peabody Coll. Tchrs., 1926; tchr.'s cert. Southwestern Tchrs. Coll., Okla., 1921; m. Haskell Pruett, July 28, 1920; children—Mildred, Dresslar Murray. Grade sch. tchr., Eastview, Okla., 1921-23; high sch. tchr., Jones, Okla., 1924-25; mem. faculty Coll. Inst., Okla. A&M Coll., Stillwater, 1942-45; social photographer Pruett Shutterbugs, Stillwater, 1939-75. Historian, Univeristy Heights Baptist Ch., Stillwater, 1949-79. Mem. AAUW, Nat. Ret. Tchrs. Assn., Okla. Edn. Assn. Democrat. Baptist. Clubs: Round Table (pres. council 1935-37, Unit 2 1939-42), Order Eastern Star, White Shrine Jerusalem. Home: 155 S Redwood Dr Stillwater OK 74074

PRUETT, SHARON HENSON, petroleum landwoman, b. Houston, Jan. 8, 1941; d. V. Earl and Foy Lorene (Morton) Henson; diploma, Durham Bus. Coll., 1965; B.S. with honors, East Tex. State U., 1977, now postgrad.; children—Kevin Wayne, Nancy Caroline, Donna Lorene. Sec., Tex. Dept. Human Resources, Pittsburg, 1972-74; med. eligibility worker Tex. Dept. Human Resources, Quitman, 1974-79, proposal devel. specialist, regional planner, dir. data sect. Paris, 1979-80; ind. petroleum land rep., Tyler, Tex., 1980—; cons. Tex. Child Welfare Bds., 1980, Study of Child Welfare Staffing Issues, 1980—. Wood County Rep. Gov.'s Com. on Aging, 1974; sec. ARC, 1973; active PTA. Mem. East Tex. Assn. Petroleum Landmen, Am. Soc. for Public Adminstrn., Nat. Assn. Female Execs., Acad. Polit. Sci., NOW, East Houston Athletic Assn., Pi Sigma Alpha. Contbr. articles to profl. jours. Address: PO Box 764 Quitman TX 75783

PRUITT, ANNE LORING SMITH, univ. dean; b. Bainbridge, Ga.; d. Loring Alphonzo and Anne Lee (Ward) Smith; B.S. cum laude, Howard U., 1949; M.A., Columbia U., 1950, Ed.D., 1964; D.H. (hon.), Central State U., Ohio, 1982; m. Ralph L. Pruitt; 1 dau., Leslie Anne; stepchildren—Dianne, Pamela, Sharon, Ralph L. Counselor, Howard U., Washington, 1950-52; dir. guidance Hutto High Sch., Bainbridge, 1952-55; dean of students Albany (Ga.) State Coll., 1955-59, Fisk U., Nashville, 1959-61; prof. edn. Case Western Res. U., Cleve., 1963-79; prof. edn., assoc. dean Grad. Sch., Ohio State U., Columbus, 1979—; cons. So. Regional Edn. Bd., So. Edn. Found.; cons. Cuyahoga Community Coll. Mem. Pres. Johnson's War on Poverty Com., Women's Job Corp.; chmn. com. edn. and youth incentives bd. dirs. Cleve. Urban League, 1965-71; chmn. Street Acad.; mem. Com. Fair Housing; vice chmn. bd. dirs. Central State U.; gen. bd. dirs. Cleve. chpt. ARC, 1978-79; adv. com. USCG Acad. 1980—. ACE fellow, 1977-78; EPDA Tng. grantee, 1974-76; Grad. and Profl. Opportunity Program grantee, 1980—; grantee Plans for Progress, So. Edn. Found.; named Alumna of Yr., Howard U., 1975. Mem. Am. Assn. Higher Edn., AAUP, Am. Personnel and Guidance Assn., Am. Coll. Personnel Assn. (sec. 1972-73, pres. 1976-77), Nat. Vocat. Guidance Assn., Pi Lambda Theta, Kappa Delta Pi, Psi Chi, Alpha Kappa Alpha. Congregationalist. Club: Links. Editorial bd. Jour. Coll. Student Personnel, 1971-72, 76-77; contbr. articles to profl. jours., also chpts. in books. Office: 250 University Hall 230 N Oval Mall Ohio State University Columbus OH 43210

PRUITT, JANET MCCRACKEN, ednl. adminstr.; b. Sharpsville, Pa., Nov. 10, 1930; d. Clarence Paul and Hazel Gladys (Palmer) McCracken; B.S., Oreg. Coll. Edn., 1952; M.S., So. Oreg. Coll., 1957; Ed.D., Oreg. State U., 1977; children—Marion, Randall. Tchr. public schs., Roseburg, Oreg., 1952-55, Ashland, Oreg., 1955-56; tchr., supr. student tchrs., asst. prof. Campus Sch., So. Oreg. Coll., Ashland, 1956-63; resource tchr. public schs., Ashland, 1963-68; instr. part time Oreg. State U., Corvallis, 1968-72, instr. div. continuing edn., 1972-73; asst. prof., Lewis and Clark Coll., Portland, Oreg., 1973-74; project coordinator Title I Salem (Oreg.) Public Schs., 1975-81, reading coordinator, 1981—; cons. in field. Mem. Internat. Reading Assn. (pres. Capitol Council br.), Assn. Adminstrv. Personnel, Assn. Supervision and Curriculum Devel., Western Coll. Reading Assn., Oreg. Reading Assn. (dir.), Assn. Student Tchrs., Phi Kappa Phi, Phi Delta Kappa, Delta Kappa Gamma. Democrat. Methodist. Home: 549 Hansen Ave S Salem OR 97302 Office: 2825 Commercial St S Salem OR 97302

PRUITT, JEAN HAMPTON, govt. ofcl.; b. Paris, Ark., Mar. 25, 1935; d. Clyde Roosevelt and Mary Lucille (Hoffman) Hampton; student (state scholar), Ark. Tech. U., 1953-55; B.S., U. Ark., 1957, M.S., 1958; m. Robert Marshall Pruitt, July 9, 1960; children—Jeanne Michele, Anne Tiffany. Tchr., Ark., Fla. and Md., 1957-62; ind. cons., vol., Montgomery County, Md., 1962-74; cons. testing, 1974-75; tchr. Montgomery County Pub. Schs., 1976-77; project officer Dept. of Justice, 1977-78; spl. asst. Dept. Agr. (Outstanding Achievement Award, Dept. of Justice), 1978-79; mgr. nat. communications/consumer edn. maj. appliance labeling program Dept. of Energy, Washington, 1979-81, mgr. energy communications speaker, Common Market, Brussels, Belgium, Internat. Energy Agy, OECD, Agence Pour Les Economics d'Energie, Paris, France; presentations Eng., Can., U.S. and edn., 1981—; on network TV, cable TV and radio, 1979-81; cons. Panasonic Small Appliances; guest lectr. U. No. Ariz. Energy Inst., Am. U. Pres. YWCA Women's Service Orgn., 1968; region II sec. Md. Citizens Consumer Council, 1982; liaison fed. energy communications, 1981-82; D.C. Program chair; mem. task force on world hunger, 1981, 82; Jr. Women's Club Chevy Chase; mem. Fox Hills Civic Assn. Honoree Purdue Old Master's Program, 1981; named Successful Grad., U. Ark. Mag., 1982. Mem. Am. Women in Radio and TV, Women in Energy (Region II sec.), Soc. Consumer Affairs Profls. in Bus. (consumer edn. and instrn. liaison) Ark. Tech. Alumni Assn., Delta Delta Delta. Methodist (fin. com.). Club: Connell Sch. Parents. Editor: Fed. Energy Mgmt. Updates; 1981-82; contbr. articles to nat. periodicals.

PRUNEAU, ANNETTE MARIE, nurse; b. Dearborn, Mich., June 23, 1951; d. Richard Joseph and Hedwig (Janik) P.; B.S.N., U. Mich., 1974. Staff nurse intensive care unit Harper Hosp., Detroit, 1974-77, critical care instr., 1977-78; emergency room staff nurse Wayne County Hosp., Detroit, 1978-79; head nurse open heart ICU, Garfield Hosp., Monterey Park, Calif., 1979-80, critical care supr., 1979-80; emergency room clinician East Los Angeles Dr.'s Hosp., 1980—. R.N., Calif. Mem. Am. Assn. Critical Care Nurses, Emergency Dept. Nurses Assn., NOW, Sigma Theta Tau. Democrat. Roman Catholic.

PRUNIER, JOSEPHINE MARIE RUSSO, nursery sch. dir.; b. Boston, Aug. 21, 1947; d. Alfio and Ida Helen Russo; B.A. in English, Merrimack Coll., North Andover, Mass., 1969; m. Gary George Prunier, Apr. 4, 1971; children—Kathryn Rebecca, Matthew Ryan, Elizabeth Rene. Elementary and jr. high sch. tchr., Mass. and Maine, 1969-76; dir. Living and Learning Ctr., Methuen, Mass., Mary Moppetts Sch., Phoenix, 1978-79; dir., owner Rockinghorse Pre-Sch., Phoenix, 1979—. Mem. Ariz. Assn. Child Devel. and Edn. (publicity chmn., membership chmn. 1980-81), NOW, Women Emerging. Republican. Roman Catholic. Home: 6344 E Fanfol Dr Paradise Valley AZ 85253 Office: 1601 E Maryland Ave Phoenix AZ 85016

PRUZAN, ANN ELAINE, health care exec.; b. Bklyn., Dec. 7, 1929; d. Simon Aaron and Jeannette Powsner; B.S. in Retail Distbn. (Retailing award 1950), L.I. U., 1950; m. Gerald J. Pruzan, June 22, 1952; children—Francine Pruzan Ehmann, Jeffrey Scott. Mdse. trainee Macy's, N.Y.C., 1948-50; dept. mgr. Oppenheim & Collins, Bklyn., 1950-51; asst. buyer Hecht's, N.Y.C., 1951-52; with bus. office West Side Furniture Co., Dayton, Ohio, 1952-54; bus. mgr., sec.-treas. Ednl. Clinic, Inc., psychol. clinic, Columbus, Ohio, 1962—. Vol., Mt. Carmel Hosp. W., Columbus, 1974-75; chmn. world union Temple Israel Sisterhood, Columbus, 1966-67, chmn. youth group liaison, 1968-72, sec. youth activities com., 1968-76; sec. religious sch. com. Temple Israel, 1973-79. Recipient Service award Central Ohio Psychol. Assn., 1980. Mem. Am. Acctg. Women's Assn., Franklin Park Conservatory Vols., L.I.U. Alumni Assn., LWV, Women's Am. Ort, Council Jewish Women, Central Ohio Orchid Soc. Club: B'nai B'rith Women. Home: 79 St Stephens Ct Gahanna OH 43230 Office: 867 S James Rd Columbus OH 43227

PRYOR, MARILYN ANN ZIRK, educator; b. Harrisonburg, Va., Mar. 9, 1936; B.S., Madison Coll., 1956; M.S., U. Tenn., 1958, Ph.D. in Physiology, 1961. Instr. cell physiology and biochemistry Bryn Mawr Coll., 1961-62; research assoc. renal physiology Mt. Holyoke Coll., 1962-64, dean studies, 1974-77, asst. prof. to assoc. prof., 1970-77, prof. biol. sci., 1977—. NSF faculty fellow Inst. Arctic and Alpine Research, U. Colo., 1970-71. Mem. Am. Soc. Zoologists. Office: Dept of Biology Mount Holyoke College South Hadley MA 01075 *

PRYOR, ROSALIE GAIL, mgmt. devel. cons.; b. Seattle, Aug. 10, 1950; d. John and Doris (McClintock) Mack; B.A., U. Wash., 1972; also profl. seminars; m. Lee J. Amate, May 14, 1982. Purchasing mgr. Container Corp. Am., 1973-76; mgmt. cons. VIDA Corp., 1977-79; v.p., dir. ops div. Alamo Cons. Group, 1979—. Mem. Bay Area Human Resource Planners, Am. Soc. Tng. and Devel., Nat. Soc. Performance and Instrn., Am. Assn. Fitness Dirs. Bus. and Industry, Soaring Soc. Am., Nat. Joggers Ann. Club: San Francisco Dolphin. Author mgmt. devel. programs. Office: 47 Quail Ct Suite 300 Walnut Creek CA 94596

PRZEPIS, ROSEMARIE ANN, banker; b. Newark, Nov. 24, 1927; d. Peter and Hilda (Carrer) Zitniak; A.A., Pasco-Hernando Community Coll., New Port Richey, Fla., 1980; postgrad. La. State U.; m. Edward Robert Przepis, Mar. 20, 1949; children—Robert William, Bruce Edward. Office supr, Blue Cross/Blue Shield, Newark, 1957-60; sec., Benjamin Moore & Co., 1960-70; real estate Loan processor First State Bank, Toms River, N.J., 1970-73; with Barnett Bank Pasco County, New Port Richey, 1973—, asst. v.p., 1977—, br. mgr. Holiday office, 1981-82; guest lectr., chmn. banking and fin. adv. bd. Pasco-Hernando Community Coll., 1981-82. Capt., Barnett People for Better Govt., 1979; treas. Tarpon Springs unit Boys Clubs Pinellas County, 1981-82. Mem. Nat. Assn. Bank Women (past edn. chmn. Gulf Central group; Fla. regional scholar 1979; Fla. awards and scholarships chmn. 1982-83), Fla. Bankers Assn., Calusa Bus. and Profl. Women's Club (charter), Pasco Builders Assn. Aux. (charter, past parliamentarian), Am. Bus. Women's Club, Am. Inst. Banking, Phi Theta Kappa. Club: Gulf Harbors Yacht. Office: PO Box 1055 New Port Richey FL 33552

PRZYBYLSKA, MARIA, x-ray crystallographer; b. Warsaw, Poland, Mar. 2, 1923; came to Can., 1949, naturalized, 1956; d. Wladyslaw and Helena (Majewska) Kolasa; B.Sc., Glasgow (Scotland) U., 1946, Ph.D., 1949; m. Waclaw Przybylski, Sept. 19, 1947; children—A. E. Martin, Steven A. Asst. research officer Nat. Research Council of Can., Ottawa, Ont., 1952-56, assoc. research officer, 1956-60, sr. research officer, 1960—. Brit. Council scholar, 1942-44; U. Glasgow scholar, 1947-49; Nat. Research Council Can. fellow, 1950-52. Mem. Am. Crystallographic Assn. Contbr. articles to profl. jours. Office: Div Biol Scis Nat Research Council of Can Ottawa ON K1A 0R6 Canada

PTAK, VIOLET MARIE, recreation dir.; b. Coraopolis, Pa., Feb. 7, 1928; d. Joseph and Rose (Sestak) Klepal; student Coraopolis and Cleve. public schs.; m. Elmer F. Ptak, Sept. 6, 1947; children—Daniel Bruce, Doreen Ann. Various positions to mgr. Franklin Ice Cream Co., Bedford, Ohio, 1953-58; various positions to center dir. Hialeah (Fla.) Recreation Dept., 1959—. Recipient cert. Multiple Sclerosis Soc. Mem. Fla. Recreation and Parks Assn. Home: 950 E 17th St Hialeah FL 33010 Office: 501 Palm Ave City Hall Hialeah FL 33011

PUCHALA, LINDA ANN, labor union ofcl.; b. Norway, Mich., Jan. 25, 1949; d. William John and Elizabeth Cecelia (VanLaere) Peterson; ed. Mich. State U.; m. Roman L. Puchala, Jr., Aug. 7, 1970; children—Jennifer, Jessica. Flight attendant, 1969—; negotiator, local leader Assn. Flight Attendants, 1971-79, nat. pres., 1979—. Mem. Nat. Aviation Club. Office: 1625 Massachusetts Ave NW Washington DC 20036

PUFF, JEAN ELLINGWOOD, civic worker; b. Evanston, Ill., July 25, 1924; d. Lloyd and Margaret (Brown) Ellingwood; B.S. in Nursing, Northwestern U., 1947; m. Henry B. Puff, June 10, 1950; children—James Raymond, Margaret Elizabeth. Nurse, student health service, Northwestern U., Evanston, Ill., 1947-48; Pres. Gov. Wentworth Arts Council, N.H., 1973—; bd. dirs. Wolfeboro (N.H.) Playhouse, 1975—; vol. Delta Gamma vision screening, Buffalo, 1960-65, Buffalo Philharmonic, 1959-69; mem. Republican Women's Club., Huggins Hosp. Aid (Wolfeboro). Mem. Evanston Hosp. Alumni Assn., Northwestern U. Alumni Assn., Delta Gamma. Presbyterian. Clubs: Lakes Region Tennis. Home: Box 743 Springfield Point Wolfeboro NH 03894

PUFF, MARY A. M., editor, cons.; b. Mpls., Jan. 14, 1953; d. Marvin F. and Kathleen M. (Sullivan) P.; B.A., Carleton Coll., 1975; Faculté des Lettres, Univ. de Pau, 1973; postgrad. internat. grad. studies Oxford U., 1975; M.A. (univ. fellow), U. Chgo., 1977; M.B.A., Columbia U., 1983; Sr. editor Resource Planning Assos., Inc., Cambridge, Mass., 1980—; Nat. del. Democratic Nat. Conv., 1980, floor whip Women's Rights Coalition; dir. 5th Congressional Dist. Minn., 1978-80; mgr. Ho. of Reps. campaign for Dee Long, 1980; bd. dirs. Minn. Civil Liberties Union; mem. Amnesty Internat., Communicators for Nuclear Disarmament, Council for a Livable World; sponsor Union of Concerned Scientists. Arts and Letters fellow, Schloss Brunnenburg, Italy, 1977; recipient Creativity award 3M Corp. Editor: The Medical Casebook of Adolf Hitler, 1979; author: A Gathering of the Faithful: The James Joyce Symposium Paris, France, 1975.

PUGH, ANDREA LEE, pharmacist; b. Chambersburg, Pa., May 15, 1952; d. Andrew Richard and Sara Elizabeth (Bert) P.; student Shippensburg State Coll., 1970-72; B.S., Phila. Coll. Pharmacy and Sci., 1975. Staff pharmacist Park Ave. Pharmacy, Chambersburg, Pa., 1975-78; cons. pharmacist Menno Haven nursing home, 1975-78; asst. mgr. Robert T. Henry Pharmacy, Shippensburg, Pa., 1978—. Bd. dirs Health Planning and Resource and Devel., Inc., 1980-83, Franklin County Heart Assn., 1981-83, Shippensburg Community Services, Inc., 1982-83. Mem. Pa. Pharm. Assn. (chmn. public relations 1978-81, public relations adv. 1981-82 legis. day chmn. 1981), Am. Pharm. Assn., Acad. Pharmacy Practice, S. Central Pa. Pharm. Assn. (pres. 1982), Lambda Kappa Sigma, Shippensburg Bus. and Profl. Women's Club. Lutheran (adv. Luther League 1978-80). Home: 12345 Cumberland Hwy Orrstown PA 17244 Office: 54 E King St Shippensburg PA 17257

PUGH, PATRICIA ANNE, educator; b. Astoria, N.Y., July 4, 1941; d. George Francis and Mary Cecelia (Fallon) P.; student Syracuse U.,

1959-60; B.S., N.Y. U., 1963; M.S., Hofstra U., 1973. Tchr., Baldwin (N.Y.) Pub. Schs., 1963-66, tchr. adult edn., 1963-65; tchr. adult edn. Herricks (N.Y.) Pub. Schs., 1965-66; tchr. Bellmore-Merrick Central High Sch. Dist., Merrick, N.Y., 1966—, tchr. adult edn., 1973; 2d v.p. Bellmore-Merrick United Secondary Tchrs. Assn., 1975-77, 1st v.p., 1978-79. Co-chmn. maintenance and use com. Strathmore Ct. Homeowners Assn., 1976—, bd. dirs., 1979—; active Catholic Youth Orgn., 1964-65. Mem. Am. Fedn. Tchrs., N.Y. State United Tchrs., Bellmore-Merrick United Secondary Tchrs. (pub. relations chmn. 1975—, trustee 1975—, Title IX com. 1977—; editor quar. The Observer 1976—), Grand Ave Parent Tchrs. Assn., Assn. Women Phys. Edn. N.Y. State (art editor The Reflector 1964, editor-in-chief 1965-68; sec. Nassau zone 1968-70; state exec. bd. 1965-70), N.Y. State Assn. Health, Phys. Edn. and Recreation (state exec. bd. 1971, Nassau Zone exec. bd. 1970-71, Nassau membership chmn. 1972-74). Democrat. Roman Catholic. Home: 71 Federal Ln Coram NY 11727

PUGLIESE, BARBARA WIERCIOCH, research and analysis co. exec.; b. Lowicz, Poland, Apr. 1, 1941; came to U.S., 1949; naturalized, 1959; d. Henryk and Ludwika (Gostkiewicz) Wiercioch; B.A. cum laude in Math., Conn. Coll. for Women, 1963; m. William Pugliese, Aug. 15, 1973. Programer, mathematician Naval Underwater Systems Center, New London, Conn., 1959-63, ops. research analyst, 1963-67; sr. systems analyst (sonar-tactics) Marine Research Lab., Raytheon Corp., New London, 1967-69; sr. v.p., mgr. effectiveness analysis dept., plank owner Analysis and Tech., Inc., Stonington, Conn., 1969-81; pres. BWP Cons., 1981—; cons., instr., lectr. on mil. ops. research, navy tactics, tactical and strategic measures of effectiveness and performance exercise/operational design and analysis. NSF grantee, 1962-63. Mem. Mil. Ops. Research Soc., Am. Def. Preparedness Assn., Nat. Security Indsl. Assn., U.S. Naval Inst., Am. Mgmt. Assn. Republican. Contbr. articles on naval ops. to profl. jours.

PUHL, CASSANDRA LEE, microbiologist; b. Cleve., May 6, 1950; d. Peter Krist and Marian Elizabeth (Valvoda) P.; B.A. in Microbiology, Miami U., Ohio, 1972; postgrad., Cleve. Clinic Sch. Med. Tech., 1972-73. Med. technician in microbiology Cleve. Clinic Found., 1972-73, med. technologist parasitology, 1973-75, sect. leader parasitology lab., 1975—, mem. admissions com., 1977-80; condr. seminars. Mem. Am. Soc. Clin. Pathologists (med. technologist 1973, specialist in microbiology 1979), Am. Soc. Microbiology, S. Central Assn. Clin. Microbiology. Research in field of microbiology. Office: Cleve Clinic Found 4Z20 Parasitology Lab 9500 Euclid Ave Cleveland OH 44106

PUIG, AMELITA UBALDE, med. technologist; b. Philippines, Apr. 20; came to U.S., 1969, naturalized, 1978; d. Francisco Busil and Angeles (Ubalde) P.; B.S. in Med. Tech., U. San Agustin, Philippines, 1966; curso de lengua y cultura Universidad de Salamanca, 1979. Asst. supr. chemistry Yale New Haven Med. Center, 1970-73; sr. technician hematology dept. Columbia Presbyn. Hosp., N.Y.C., 1973-74; sr. technician chemistry dept. N.Y.U. Med. Center, 1974—. Mem. Am. Soc. Clin. Pathologists (affiliate mem.), Am. Soc. Clin. Pathologists, Kahirup U.S.A. (dir. 1974-81, exec. sec. 1981—). Address: 525 E 14th St Apt 12E New York NY 10009

PUISHES, DENISE SUZANNE, psychologist; b. San Francisco, Aug. 5, 1950; d. Alfons and Claire Gertrude (Heine) P.; Psy.D., Rutgers U., 1979. Pvt. practice psychology, N.Y.C.; cons. psychology, clin. pyschology. Mem. Am. Psychol. Assn., Phi Kappa Phi. Home: 32-33 79th St Jackson Heights NY 11370

PULITANO, CONCETTA NORIGENNA, sch. ofcl.; b. Sicily, Italy, June 16, 1941; came to U.S., 1947, naturalized, 1948; d. Umberto and Benedetta (Triassi) Norigenna; student public schs., North Miami, Fla.; m. Francis Joseph Pulitano, Dec. 29, 1962; children—Maria Anne, Margaret Theresa, Angela Marie. Sec., Ka-Line Pool Products, Hialeah, Fla., 1959-61, Westinghouse, Balt., 1961, Bendix Communications, Balt., 1961-63; student council moderator, sec., learning center coordinator Cathedral Sch., Balt., 1974—, dir. activities, 1981. Recipient Balt.'s Best award. Mem. Internat. Platform Assn. Democrat. Roman Catholic. Club: Valley Country. Office: Cathedral School 111 Amberly Way Baltimore MD 21210

PULITZER, EMILY S. RAUH (MRS. JOSEPH PULITZER, JR.), former museum curator; b. Cin., July 23, 1933; d. Frederick and Harriet (Frank) Rauh; A.B., Bryn Mawr Coll., 1955; student Ecole du Louvre, Paris, France, 1955-56; M.A., Harvard U., 1963. Mem. staff Cin. Art Mus., 1956-57; asst. curator drawings Fogg Art Mus., Harvard, 1957-64, asst. to dir., 1962-63; curator City Art Mus., St. Louis, 1964-73; mem. painting and sculpture com. Mus. Modern Art, 1975; chmn. visual arts com. Mo. Arts Council, 1976-81; co-chmn. fellows Fogg Art Mus.; mem. bd. Inst. Mus. Services, 1979—; commr. St. Louis Art Mus., 1981—; bd. dirs. 1st St. Forum, St. Louis, 1980—. Vice pres. Mark Rothko Found., 1976—. Mem. Am. Fedn. Arts (dir. 1976—). Home: 4903 Pershing Pl Saint Louis MO 63108

PULLEN, ALICE ROSSO, graphics co. exec.; b. Princeton, N.J., Sept. 19, 1919; d. Joseph and Angelina (Pirone) Rosso; student Princeton schs.; m. Cecil David Pullen, Dec. 16, 1950 (dec.); children—David Gary, Michele Lorena. Sec.-bookkeeper Brown's Trucking Co., Trenton, N.J., 1950-60; bus. mgr. Haskins Press, Princeton, 1960-69; pres. Princetonian Graphics, Inc., 1969—. Address: Princetonian Graphics Inc 3490 US Route 1 Princeton NJ 08540

PULLEN, BEVERLY ANN, acct.; b. Sheffield, Ala., Sept. 30, 1954; d. Charles Augustus and Carrie Mae (Speake) P. B.S. with highest honors, U. N. Ala., 1975; M.B.A., U. Miss., 1976. Acct., Fried Rappaport & Co., Jacksonville, Fla., 1977-78; controller Consumers Warehouse, Inc., Jacksonville, 1978-80; acct. Deloitte Haskins & Sells, Jacksonville, 1980-82; asst. controller Edgewater Machine and Fabricating Co., Inc. (Fla.), 1982—. Bd. dirs. Nutrition Network, Jacksonville, 1981; active Project Bus. div. Jr. Achievement. C.P.A. Mem. Am. Inst. C.P.A.s, Fla. Inst. C.P.A.s, Miss. Inst. C.P.A.s, Am. Soc. Women Accts., Phi Kappa Phi, Beta Alpha Psi. Methodist. Club: Volunteer Jacksonville. Home: 8090 Atlantic Blvd Apt H-145 Jacksonville FL 32211 Office: PO Box 358 Edgewater FL 32032

PULLEN, PENNY LYNNE, state legislator; b. Buffalo, Mar. 2, 1947; d. John William and Alice Nettie (McConkey) P.; B.A. in Speech, U. Ill., 1969. TV technician Office Instructional Resources, U. Ill., 1966-68; community newspaper reporter Des Plaines (Ill.) Pub. Co., 1967-72; legislative asst. to Ill. legislators, 1968-77; mem. Ill. Ho. of Reps., 1977—, chmn. ho. exec. com., 1981—. Del., Atlantic Alliance Young Polit. Leaders, Brussels, 1977; active Maine Twp. Mental Health Assn. Recipient George Washington Honor medal Freedoms Found., 1978, Dwight Eisenhower Freedom medal Chgo. Captive Nations Com., 1977, Outstanding Legislator awards Ill. Press Assn., Ill. Podiatry Soc., Ill. Coroners Assn., Ill. County Clks. Assn., Ill. Hosp. Assn., Ill. Health Care Assn.; named Ill. Young Republican, 1968, Outstanding Person, Park Ridge Jaycees, 1981, One of 10 Outstanding Young Persons, Ill. Jaycees, 1981. Mem. Am. Legis. Exchange Council (dir. 1977—, exec. com. 1978—, 2d vice chmn. 1980—), DAR. Republican. Home: 2604 W Sibley St Park Ridge IL 60068 Office: 22 Main St Park Ridge IL 60068

PULLIAM, FREDDA MARGUERITE, banker; b. Lathrop, Mo., Sept. 25, 1926; d. Allison Lee and Reba Maureen (Nicholas) P.; student public schs., Lathrop. Bookkeeper, Robison Elevator, Lathrop, 1944-58; bookkeeper Lathrop Bank, 1958-60, asst. cashier, 1960-64, cashier, 1964-78, v.p., 1978—, dir., 1966—. Treas., City of Lathrop, 1963-67. Mem. Nat. Assn. Female Execs., Sweet Adelines (Sweet Adeline of Yr. 1973, past pres. Century Singers chpt.). Office: Lathrop Bank 606 Oak St Lathrop MO 64465

PULLIG, LOIS KATHRYN, artist, illustrator, writer; b. Homer, La., Feb. 26, 1915; d. Albert and Helen Mae (Sanders) Hicks; grad. Famous Artist Schs., 1962, Decorative Art Inst., 1965, Greeting Craft Sch., 1969; m. Dolan A. Pullig, Sept. 29, 1933; children—Jimmie Eugene, Jackie Neal. Pvt. art instr., 1962-67; operator Magna Studio Gallery, Bossier City, La., 1971-73; chmn. Western Elec. Art Project, 1971-72; freelance artist, illustrator, 1973—; pvt. tchr. art, 1962—; muralist; art demonstrator; solo exhibits include: Minden (La.) Civic Center, Minden Public Library, U. Southwestern La.; group shows include: Hobby Gallery, La. State Mus., Barnwell's Garden and Art Center, Shreveport, La., The Gallery, Hollister, Mo. Active Am. Mothers Com., recipient nat. certificates of honor. Recipient numerous art awards local, regional, state, nat. arts and craft shows. Mem. Nat. League Am. Pen Women (pres. Caddo br. 1980-82), The Fine Arts Group, Shreveport Art Club, Shreveport Hoover Watercolor Soc., Am. Mothers Com. (pres. NW unit. La. chpt., chmn. art and music, gen. chmn. 1979, state exec. bd. Baptist. Clubs: Eastern Star, Shriners, Daus. of Nile, Ladies Aux. Mithra Grotto, White Shrine, Ladies Oriental Shrine Am. Illustrator children's books including The Turtle Who Wanted to Fly, Mr. 88 Plays a Happy Tune, A Collection of Christmas Verse, others. Contbr. poetry, articles on art to newspapers. Home: Route 3 Box 465 Minden LA 71055

PUNCSAK, SANDRA, metal and chem. co. exec.; b. Melbourne, Australia, May 28, 1946; came to U.S., 1946, naturalized, 1960; d. Frank and Thelma May Elizabeth (Maher) Puncsak; A.B., U. Calif., Berkeley, 1968; M.A., San Francisco State U., 1970; M.A. in Counseling and Guidance, Lewis and Clark Coll., 1974; postgrad. Pepperdine U., 1970-73. Edn. therapist schs. in Fullerton, Calif. and Beaverton, Oreg., 1973-76; student coordinator Community Experiences for Career Edn., Tigard (Oreg.) Sch. Dist. 233, 1976-78; dep. center dir. Portland (Oreg.) Job Corps Center, 1978; mktg. mgr. Singer Edn. Div., Santa Clara, Calif., 1978-81; mgr. corp. contbns. and social investment Kaiser Aluminum and Chem. Corp., Oakland, Calif., 1981—; cons. in field; lectr. in field. Mem. Peninsula Republican Women's Task Force, 1980—. Phi Beta Kappa Grad. Sch. fellow, 1969-70. Mem. Am. Mgmt. Assn., Bay Area Exec. Women's Forum West, Bay Area Profl. Women's Network, East Bay Women's Polit. Action Com., Phi Beta Kappa. Republican. Roman Catholic. Club: Commonwealth. Profiled in Professional Women and their Mentors, 1982. Home: 254 Barnett Terr Pleasant Hill CA 94543 Office: 300 Lakeside Dr Oakland CA 94643

PUNTILLO, LISA BETH, devel. co. exec.; b. Manhasset, N.Y., Aug. 12, 1955; d. Michael S. and Helen (Mathias) P.; student N.C. Sch. Arts, 1970-72; B.F.A., Carnegie-Mellon U., 1977; degree in constrn. tech., M.B.A., N.Y.U., 1982. Asst. to account exec. B. T. Grant Advt. Co., N.Y.C., 1977-78; studio mgr. Michael Reinhardt Photography, N.Y.C., 1978-79; devel. officer The Jobco Orgn., pres. KLM & M Developers, Inc., Great Neck, N.Y., 1979—. Mem. Assn. of Bus. and Profl. Women in Constrn. Office: 277 Northern Blvd Great Neck NY 11021

PURCELL, GWENDOLYN, chemist; b. Maysville, Ga., July 5, 1933; d. Thornton and Lou Etta (Rumsey) P.; B.S. in Biology, Ga. State U., 1964. Dept. and shift supr. Linden Labs. Inc. (Upjohn Co.), Atlanta, 1959-74; chemistry supr. Cobb Gen. Hosp., Austell, Ga., 1976-77; chemist, med. technologist Kennestone Hosp., Marietta, Ga., 1977—, safety officer, mem. hosp. safety edn. com., nat. lab. week com., career counselor for hosp. in ref. to allied health. Named Lab. Employee of Yr., 1982. Mem. Nat. Registry Clin. Chemistry, Am. Assn. for Clin. Chemistry, Am. Soc. Clin. Pathologists, Alpha Xi Delta. Baptist. Club: Order Eastern Star. Home: 1135 Corner Rd SW Powder Springs GA 30073 Office: 735 Church St Marietta GA 30060

PURCELL, JOYCE M., congressional staff asst., sci. and natural resources analyst; b. Las Vegas, N. Mex., Apr. 20, 1949; d. John Donald and Helen Marie (Griffin) P.; B.A., U. N.Mex., 1975, M.A., 1978; 1 son, W. Daniel Schneider. Staff asst. Coll. Pharmacy, U. N.Mex., 1970-71; authorizations analyst VA, 1971-73; claims analyst Social Security Adminstrn., 1974-75; staff asst. VA Hosp., Albuquerque, 1977-78; cons. Los Alamos Pub. Schs., 1977-78; now natural resources and space and sci. analyst Senate Budget Com., Washington. Mem. Am. Communication Assn., Am. Soc. Tng. and Devel. Office: Room 203 Carroll Arms Hotel Washington DC 20510 *

PURCELL, MARGARET LOUISE, social work adminstr.; b. Albany, N.Y., July 22, 1920; d. Thomas H. and Mary (McConnell) P.; A.B., Coll. of St. Rose, 1943; M.S., Columbia U., 1956. Dir., N.Y. State Girls Tng. Sch., Wynantskill, 1958-62; dir. admissions Children's Village, Dobbs Ferry, N.Y., 1962-66, dir. clin. services, 1966-70, dir. Revere unit, 1970—. Cert. social worker, N.Y. Mem. Nat. Assn. Social Workers, Acad. Cert. Social Workers, Assn. Cert. Child Care Workers, NOW. Home: Box 43 Valatie NY 12184 Office: Children's Village Dobbs Ferry NY 10522

PURCELL, MARY LOUISE GERLINGER, educator; b. Thief River Falls, Minn., July 17, 1923; d. Charles and Lajla (Dale) Gerlinger; student Yankton Coll., 1941-45, Yale Div. Sch., 1949-50, N.Y. U., summer 1949; M.A. (alumni fellow), Tchrs. Coll. Columbia, 1959, Ed.D., 1963; m. Walter A. Kuyawski, June 9, 1950 (dec. July 1954); children—Amelia Allerton, Jon Allerton; m. 2d, Dale Purcell, Aug. 26, 1962. Teen-age program dir., YWCA, New Haven, 1945-52; dir. program in family relations, asst. prof. sociology and psychology Earlham Coll., Richmond, Ind., 1959-62, conf. co-ordinator undergrad. edn. for women, 1962; chmn. div. home and community Stephens Coll., Columbia, Mo., 1962-73, chmn. family and community studies, 1962-78, dir. Learning Unltd., continuing edn. for women, 1974-78, developer course The Contemporary Am. Woman, 1962, cons., 1962; prof., head dept. family and child devel. Auburn (Ala.) U., 1978—; vis. prof. Ind. U. Summer Sch., 1970. Cons. student personnel services, Trenton (N.J.) State Coll., 1958-59, 61. Recipient Alumni Achievement award Yankton Coll., 1975. Mem. Am. Home Econs. Assn. (chmn. family relations child devel. sect. 1967-69, bd. dirs.), AAUW, Groves Conf. on Family, Nat. Council Family Relations (dir., chmn. elect affiliated councils, 1981-82, chmn., 1982-83, nat. program chmn. 1977, chmn. file awards com., chmn. spl. emphases sect., bd. dirs., Ernest G. Osborne award for excellence in teaching 1979), Kappa Delta Pi, Pi Lambda Theta. Presbyterian. Contbr. articles to coll. bulls, jours. Home: 2408 Heritage Dr Opelika AL 36801

PURDY, NORMA DIANE, nurse; b. Haverhill, N.H., Sept. 9; d. William Joseph and Berenice Hazel (Sibley) Reed; diploma in vocat. nursing Moore Gen. Hosp., 1960; R.N., City Coll. San Francisco, 1970; m. Earl Ray Purdy, Oct. 20, 1966; children by previous marriage—Carol, Robert, William, John, Jean. Vocat. nurse Lakes Region Gen. Hosp., Laconia, N.H., 1959-64, Mound Park Hosp., St. Petersburg, Fla., 1963-65; vocat. nurse San Francisco Gen. Hosp., 1965-68, registered nurse, 1970—, head nurse surg. unit, 1974-78; head nurse jail med. services San Francisco County Jail #3, 1978—. Office: 1 Moreland Dr San Bruno CA 94066

PURDY, VIRGINIA CARDWELL, archivist; b. Columbia, S.C., Aug. 1, 1922; d. Thomas Davant and Nannie Berry (Edmonds) Cardwell; B.A. (Algernon Sidney Sullivan award), U. S.C., 1942; M.A., George Washington U., 1960, Ph.D. (Univ. fellow), 1970; m. Donald R. Purdy, June 4, 1946. Instr., then lectr. Am. history George Washington U., 1961-64; reference librarian Library of Congress, 1964-66; asst. historian, then keeper catalogue Am. portraits Nat. Portrait Gallery, Smithsonian Instn., 1966-69; archivist for exhibits, then dir. edn. div. Nat. Archives, 1969-76, women's history specialist, 1976—; 1st pres. Nat. Archives Assembly, 1980-81; cons. in field. Founding v.p., program chmn. Oak Ridge YWCA, 1955-56. Recipient Commendable Service award GSA, 1971, 73, Outstanding Woman award, 1975. Mem. Soc. Am. Archivists (council 1981—), Am. Hist. Assn., Orgn. Am. Historians, Am. Assn. State and Local History, Mid-Atlantic Regional Archives Conf., Phi Beta Kappa, Alpha Kappa Gamma. Co-author: Presidential Portraits, 1968; editor: Am. Archivist, 1978-81; co-editor: Clio Was a Woman, 1980; contbr. articles to profl. jours. Home: 509 S Irving St Arlington VA 22204 Office: Nat Archives 8th and Pennsylvania Ave NW Washington DC 20408

PURDY, VIRGINIA FLETCHER, advt. public relations cons.; b. San Antonio, Oct. 11, 1926; d. Benjamin Darlington and Mary (Reno) White; B.A., B.S., Tex. Women's U., 1948; m. Robert Hyde Purdy, June 14, 1975; children—Mary, Melissa, Martha; stepchildren—Janet, Alison. Fashion artist, layout, copy, prodn. and advt. mgr. Frank Bros., San Antonio, 1948-54; free lance fashion artist, San Antonio, 1954-67; advt. mgr. Tex., N.Mex. div. Dillard's Dept. Stores, Inc., San Antonio, 1968-75; owner Ginger Purdy Advt. and Public Relations, San Antonio, 1975—. Team capt. Nat. Women's Employment and Edn. Corp., 1981—; mem. Community Video/TV Task Force, 1981-82; mem. Bexar County Women's Polit. Caucus, 1981-82. Recipient Cert. of award Wilford Hall Med. Center Lackland chpt. Federally Employed Women, 1981; Northeast Sch. Dist. Distributive Edn. award, 1974. Mem. Women in Communications, Southwest Found. Forum, San Antonio Symphony League, San Antonio Conservation Soc., Tex. Women's Univ. Nat. Alumnae Assn. Democrat. Episcopalian. Club: San Antonio Press. Home and Office: 1045 Ivy Ln San Antonio TX 78209

PURIM, FLORA, singer; b. Rio de Janeiro, Brazil, Mar. 6, 1942; d. Naum and Rachel (Vaisberg) Purim; came to U.S., 1967; student U. Cal. at Long Beach; 1 dau. by previous marriage, Niura Band; m. Airto Moreira, Mar. 19, 1972; 1 dau., Diana. With RCA Records, Rio de Janeiro, Brazil, 1965-67; with Buddah Records, N.Y.C., 1969-71, CTI Records, N.Y.C., 1971-73, Warner Bros. Records; composer-lyricist: (with Airto Moreira) Seeds on the Ground, 1970, Natural Feelings, 1969, Free, 1971, Fingers, 1972, Identity, 1975, Promises of the Sun, 1976; with Milestone Records, Berkeley, Calif., 1973—; solo albums: Butterfly Dreams, 1973, Stories to Tell, 1974, Open Your Eyes You Can Fly, 1976, 500 Miles High in Montreaux, 1976, Encounter, 1977, Nothing Will Be As It Was Tomorrow, 1977; album (with Airto Moreira) Virgin Land, 1972; albums (with Chick Corea) Return to Forever, 1972, Light as a Feather, 1973; album (with Carlos Santana) Welcome, 1973, Borboletta, 1974; composer/lyricist: (with Stanley Clarke) Light as a Feather, 1972, (with Airto Moreira, Neville Potter) San Francisco River, 1972, (with McCoy Tyner) Search for Peace, 1974, (with George Duke) Love Reborn, 1973, Feel, 1974, (with Airto Moreira) Alue, 1969, (with Hermeto Paschoal) We Love, 1970, (with Ernie Hood) Mountain Train, 1974, (with Duke Pearson) How Insensitive, 1969, It Could Only Happen with You, 1970; (with Airto and Deodato) Deodata/Airto in Concert, 1973; producer (with Moreira) I'm Fine, How Art You, 1977. Named Number 1 Female Singer Deserving Wider Recognition, Down Beat Critics Poll, 1974, Number 1 Established Female Singer, Down Beat Readers' Poll, 1974, 75, 76, 77, Top Female Jazz Artist, Record World, 1974, 76, Top New Female Jazz Artist Cash Box, 1974. Office: care Berkeley Agy 2490 Channing Way Suite 406 Berkeley CA 94704 *

PURNELL, MARJORIE AXFORD, physician; b. North Troy, N.Y., Nov. 13, 1915; d. Oliver James and Grace Lillian (Kite) P.; B.A., Converse Coll., 1936; M.T., Rochester Gen. Hosp., 1938; M.A., Boston U., 1945, M.D., 1949. Chief bacteriologist Rockville (Conn.) Gen. Hosp., 1938-43; intern, Newton Wellesley Hosp., 1949-50; resident in medicine Mass. Meml. Hosp., 1950-51, resident in ob-gyn New Eng. Hosp., 1951-52; mem. med. staff Rockville Gen. Hosp., 1952—, chief of staff, 1967-78; dir. health Town of Tolland (Conn.), 1957-78; co-chmn. med. adv. com. Rockville Public Health Nurses, 1973—; cons. in field; dir. Savs. Bank Rockville. Diplomate Am. Acad. Family Practice. Fellow Am. Acad. Family Physicians (charter, pres. Conn. chpt. 1974-75); mem. AMA, Conn. Med. Assn., Tolland County Med. Assn. (pres. 1960), Conn. Med. Soc. (chmn. com. on public health 1967-77), Am. Med. Women's Assn. Address: 23 Davis Ave Rockville CT 06066

PURSER, JOHN HELEN, style shop propr.; b. Killeen, Tex., July 7, 1935; d. Garland Parker and Essie Elizabeth (Gautier) Levy; student pub. schs.; m. Gary William Purser, Nov. 17, 1951; children—Elizabeth Ann, Gary William, Sue Ellen. Saleslady Adams Shoe Store, 1951-53; saleslady, buyer Levys Tot to Teen Shop, 1953-55; owner, buyer, saleslady, bookkeeper, sec. Style Shop, Killeen, 1962—; owner, bookkeeper, sec. Purser Constrn. Rentals, Killeen, 1967—, Purser & Chafin Constrn. Rentals, Killeen, 1967—, Purser & Chafin Constrn., Killeen, 1962—, Purser, Bay & Assos., Killeen, 1962—. Mem. Beta Sigma Phi. Democrat. Methodist. Home: 405 Roy Reynolds Dr Harker Heights TX 76541 Office: 902-440 Plaza Killeen TX 76541

PURTLE, CAROL JEAN, art historian, educator; b. St. Louis, Feb. 20, 1939; d. Clarence Philipp and Rose Bertha (Kloeppel) P.; B.A. magna cum laude, Maryville Coll., St. Louis, 1960; M.A., Manhattanville Coll., Purchase, N.Y., 1966; Ph.D. (NDEA fellow), Washington U., St. Louis, 1976. Joined Religious of Sacred Heart, Roman Catholic Ch., 1963; tchr. Acad. Sacred Heart, St. Charles, Mo., 1964-66, Grand Coteau, La., 1966-68; lectr. art history Maryville Coll., St. Louis, part time 1969-75; instr. art history Washington U., part time 1970-76; asst. prof. art and coordinator art history Memphis State U., 1977-82, asso. prof., 1982—; coordinator nat. symposium 600 Years Netherlandish Art, Memphis, 1982. Bd. dirs. Acad. Sacred Heart, New Orleans, 1971-73; trustee Acad. Sacred Heart, Grand Coteau, La., 1982—. Recipient M. Spalding Young award Maryville Coll., 1960, Ann. Scholarship award 1960; Advanced Research fellow Belgian-Am. Endl. Found., 1974-75; Faculty Devel. award Memphis State U., 1980; NDEA fellow, 1968-71; Nat. Endowment for Humanities fellow, 1982; Danforth Assos., 1979—. Mem. Coll. Art Assn. Am., Southeastern Coll. Art Conf., Mid-West Art History Soc., Delta Epsilon Sigma. Author: The Marian Paintings of Jan van Eyck, 1982, also articles. Home: 767 Mount Moriah Apt 32 Memphis TN 38117 Office: Dept Art Jones Hall Memphis State U Memphis TN 38152

PURVIS, DOROTHY LA RUE, telephone co. service adminstr.; b. Indpls., Sept. 20, 1934; d. Frank Edward and Alberta Kellem (Jessup) Simko; student Coll. St. Thomas, 1979; children—Dawn P. Jensen, Patricia La Rue Dumond, Wesley J. La Rue, Mark H. La Rue, Diane E. La Rue. Long distance telephone operator, 1951-63; sr. clk. network mgmt. Ind. Bell Telephone, Indpls., 1963-65, traffic engr., 1965-70; separations mgr. Continental Telephone, St. Paul, 1970-73, div. traffic engring. mgr., 1973-77, network services adminstr., 1977-78, network mgmt. center task force, 1979-80, div. network service adminstr., 1980—; active seminars in field. Women in Mgmt. cert. Coll. St. Catherine, 1978. Mem. Nat. Assn. Female Execs., Lake state Telephone Pioneers. Republican. Roman Catholic. Home: 10650 Brunswick St Bloomington MN 55438 Office: 3500 W 80th St Minneapolis MN 55431

PURVIS, NANCI LEE, author, photographer; b. Burlingame, Calif., Aug. 11, 1938; d. Ford Kingsbury and Gladys Louise (Duane) Edwards; B.A., Am. U., 1982; divorced; 1 dau., Monica Lee Zum Felde. Copywriter, Diefenbach-Price Agy., Bethesda, Md., 1967-68; adminstrv. asst. Am. U., 1968-69; dir. continuity Sta. WBBH-TV, Ft. Myers, Fla., 1969-71; dir. customer relations Dunfey Hotel Mgmt., Atlanta, 1971-72; assoc. dir. women's programs Nat. Rifle Assn., 1976-77; freelance wrier/photographer, 1977—; exec. dir. Aura Assos., women in media promotions, 1978—; part-time instr., Barstow Coll., 1973-74. Mem. subcom. on pub. edn. Montgomery County Arson Task Force. Recipient Montgomery Coll. Chancellor's award, 1981, 82; co-recipient Plover Nat. Graphic Design award, 1976; named Hon. Outstanding Citizen, State of Md., 1978. Mem. Nat. Assn. Female Execs., W.Va. Press Assn., Montgomery County Press Assn., Washington Ind. Writers, Am. Women in Radio and TV, Mid-Montgomery Bus. and Profl. Women (founding pres.). Address: 16 Prairie Rose Ct Gaithersburg MD 20760

PUSATERI, EVELYN JOAN, real estate broker; b. St. Louis, Dec. 23, 1929; d. Ernest V. and Louise A. (Gosebrink) Sciaroni; student parochial schs., St. Louis; m. Joseph Pusateri, Jan. 6, 1951; children—Joseh, Michael, Denise, Mary, Debra, Lisa, Larry. Salesman, Montgomery Co., Louisville, 1971-78; sales mgr. Shell & Assos., Louisville, 1979-80; broker Remax Profls., Louisville, 1980—. Pres. Louisville Condominium Council. Master realty asso. Interstate Referral Service. Mem. Realtors Nat. Mktg. Inst. (grad. realtor inst.), Women's Council Realtors, Nat. Home Builders, Ky. Home Builders, Louisville Home Builders (dir. 1979), Nat. Bd. Realtors, Ky. Bd. Realtor (cert. resdl. specialist), Louisville Bd. Realtors. Club: Hurstbourne Country. Home: 703 Nottingham Pkwy Louisville KY 40222 Office: 9117 Leesgate Dr Louisville KY 40222

PUSEY, ELLEN PRATT, home economist; b. Milford, Del., Aug. 27, 1928; d. Algeo Newell and Ruby Newton (Boorman) Pratt; B.S., U. Md., 1950, M.S., 1951; m. William W. Pusey, June 12, 1950; children—William W., Patricia A., Cynthia L., Daniel N. Camp dietitian N.Y. Herald Tribune Fresh Air Fund Camps, 1947; supr. cafeteria Roosevelt Hosp., N.Y.C., 1948; supt. sch. cafeterias, Seaford, Del., 1964; field faculty home economist Md. Coop. Ext. Service, Wicomico County, Md., 1967—. Chmn. lower shore council Am. Lung Assn., Md., 1978-79. Mem. Am. Home Econs. Assn., Md. Home Econs. Assn., Nat. Assn. Extension Home Economists, Md. Assn. Extension Home Economists, Tri-County Home Econs. Assn., U. Md. Coll. Home Econs. Alumni Assn. (dir.), Nutrition Jour. Club of Eastern Shore, Phi Kappa Phi, Alpha Xi Delta. Methodist. Club: Soroptimists (pres. 1978) (Salisbury, Md.). Home: 301 W Federal St Snow Hill MD 21863 Office: PO Box 1836 Salisbury MD 21801

PUSEY, MARY HOPE SMITH, farmer; b. Munday, Tex., Sept. 28, 1914; d. John Robert and Maggie Vernon (Benedict) Smith; B.S., U. San Antonio, 1935; M.S., Columbia U. Tchrs. Coll., 1939; m. William Webb Pusey, III, June 18, 1940; children—Mary Faith Pusey Pankin, Diana Enid Pusey Pickral. Engaged in farming, West Tex., 1931—; vol. worker, 1940—; pres. Rockbridge Mental Health Assn., 1966-68, 70-72; bd. dirs. Va. Assn. Mental Health, 1970-76, regional v.p., 1974-76; chmn. adv. bd. Rockbridge Mental Health Clinic, 1970-74; co-chmn. Va. Commn. Study Mental Health and Mental Retardation, 1962-64; hon. mem. Rockbridge Assn. Retarded Citizens, 1970—; mem. bd. Valley Workshop, 1970-78. Recipient Disting. Service award Va. Assn. Mental Health, 1970, Outstanding Service award, 1973, cert. commendation, 1974; numerous certs. recognition. Mem. Grain Sorghum Producers Assn., Am. Agr. Movement. Presbyterian. Clubs: Garden of Va. (conservation chmn. 1954-56, admissions chmn. 1956-58); Blue Ridge Garden (Lexington). Address: 618 Marshall St Lexington VA 24450

PUSKAR, MITZI SPENCER, fin. exec.; b. Natrona, Pa., Feb. 5, 1940; d. John Joseph Spencer and Louise Ruth (Hensel) Spencer Geer; student Seton Hill Coll., 1958-61; acctg. degree, Strayer Coll., 1971; children—C. James, Melissa. Income tax tchr. Prince George's County Bd. Edn., Crossland Div. Adult Edn., 1971—; income tax cons. MJM Assocs/M&S Assocs., Forestville, Md., 1970—; faculty Community Services Div., P.G. Community Coll., Largo, Md., 1981—; lectr. in field. Mem. Prince Georges County Econ. Devel. Com., 1980—, prime CETA sponsor com., 1980-81; mem. Prince George's County Pvt. Industry Council, 1981—, bd. dirs., 1971-82, pres. 1981-82; bd. dirs. Prince Goerge's County Bd. Trade, 1971—, pres., 1981-82, editor Tradewinds, 1975—; bd. dirs. Prince Georges County Crime Solvers, 1980—. Mem. Nat. Assn. Female Execs. (area network dir. 1980). Democrat. Roman Catholic. Address: 6016 Surrey Sq Forestville MD 20747

PUTCAMP, LUISE, JR., newspaper editor, writer; b. San Diego, Mar. 9, 1924; d. William J. and Luise (Zimmermann) P.; student Phoenix Jr. Coll., 1942-43, So. Meth. U., 1946-47, U. Utah, 1955-56; m. Robert H. Johnson, Feb. 24, 1945; children—Robert H., III, Luise Robin, Jan Leah, Stephanie Neale, Jennifer Anne. Reporter, feature writer Anniston (Ala.) Times, 1939-40; Ariz. Republic, Phoenix, 1941-43; asst. news editor Ariz. Network, Phoenix, 1943-44; night news editor Radio Sta WINX, Washington, 1945; telegraph editor Miami Beach Sun-Tropics, 1944, 46; copy editor Dallas News, 1946-51; book page editor Dallas Times Herald, 1951-52; freelance writer, 1953-59; columnist, feature writer Indpls. News, 1961-62; vol. publicist, 1963-66; book page editor Dallas Times Herald, 1968-69; freelance writer, 1973-75; editor, writer The Advocate, Stamford, Conn., 1976—. Recipient Kaleidograph Press award for Sonnets for the Survivors, 1951; Christopher award for short story in Good Housekeeping, 1955. Mem. Nat. Fedn. Press Women (1st pl. award for personal columns 1980) Tex. Inst. Letters. Author: Sonnets for the Survivors, 1952; The Christmas Carol Miracle, 1971; The Night of the Child, 1972. Home: 15 Cobblers Green New Canaan CT 06840 Office: 75 Tresser Blvd Stamford CT 06901

PUTMAN, MARGARET ELIZABETH, home economist, educator; b. Rutherford County, Tenn., Sept. 11, 1917; d. Ervin T. and Bernice (Jennings) P.; B.A., Tenn. Coll. for Women, 1938; M.S., U. Tenn., 1942; postgrad. Western Mich. State U., 1955, Okla. State U., 1963. Tchr. home econs. Public Schs. Rutherford County (Tenn.), 1939-42; home mgmt. supr. Farmer's Home Adminstrn., 5 Middle Tenn. counties, 1942-45; home econs. extension agt. Dept. Agr., Perry County, Tenn., 1945-47; tchr. vocat. home econs. Public Schs. Columbia (Tenn.), 1947-50, also U. Tenn. student tchr. supr.; dist. supr. Home Econs. Edn. for 41 Middle Tenn. counties, 1950-52, 54-57; head home econs. dept. Austin Peay State U., 1952-54; head home econs. dept. Middle Tenn. State U., 1957-67, prof. home econs., 1957-78; prof. home econs. edn., head dept. home econs. Judson Coll., 1978—; vis. prof. various schs. Com. Mem. Middle Tenn. State U. Devel. Found. Mem. Am. Home Econs. Assn., Nat. Council Adminstrs. Home Econs., Am. Vocat. Assn., NEA (life), AAUW, Future Homemakers Am. (hon.), Future Farmers Am. (hon.), Delta Kappa Gamma, Kappa Omicron Phi, Phi Delta Kappa, Delta Omicron. Baptist. Coordinator and editor Tenn. Home Econs. Secondary Curriculum Guides, 6, 1970. Home: Elmcrest Judson Coll Marion AL 36756 Office: Home Econs Dept Judson Coll Marion AL 36756

PUTNAM, ASHLEY, soprano; b. N.Y.C.; B.A. in Music, U. Mich., M.A. Debut in opera with Va. Opera Assn., in Lucia di Lammermoor, 1976; appearances include Met. Opera, N.Y.C. Opera, Opera Theatre of St. Louis, Santa Fe Opera, Houston Grand Opera, Netherlands Opera, San Francisco Opera, Greater Miami Opera, Portland Opera, Scottish Opera, Opera Co. of Boston, San Diego Opera, Seattle Opera, Tulsa Opera; appearance as Mary Stuart in Mary, Queen of Scots with N.Y.C. Opera; rec. artist for New World Records, MMG, Philips. Recipient 1st prize Met. Opera Auditions, 1976. Office: Colbert Artists Mgmt Inc 111 W 57th St New York NY 10019 *

PUTNAM, BARBARA ELAINE, non-commd. army officer; b. Highland Park, Mich., May 15, 1949; d. Donald Scott and Edna May (Trevena) P.; B.S. in Bus. Adminstrn., SUNY, Albany, 1982; grad. various army schs. Enlisted in U.S. Army, 1967, service in U.S. and Europe; br. chief Combat Service Support Br., St. Louis, 1980—; mem. Office Sec. Def. Armed Forces Rev. Bd., 1979. Decorated Army Commendation medal; life-Study fellow, 1971-78. Mem. Nat. Assn. Female Execs., U.S. Army Res. Benefit Assn. Republican. Methodist. Office: 9700 Page Blvd St Louis MO 63132

PUTNAM, CAROLINE JENKINS, civic worker; b. Glymont, Md., Nov. 16, 1892; d. Thomas Canfield and Eleanor (Compton) Jenkins; student Mt. St. Agnes Acad., 1905-07; LL.D., Newton Coll. Sacred Heart, 1967, St. Mary's Coll., 1959, Regis Coll., 1952, St. Michael's Coll., 1956; L.H.D., Am. Internat. Coll., 1950, Manhattanville Coll., 1959; L.H.D. (hon.), Duquesne U., 1969; m. Roger Lowell Putnam Oct. 9, 1919; children—Caroline Canfield, Roger Lowell, William Lowell, Anna Lowell (Mrs. Everett P. Tomlinson), Mary Compton (Mrs. Charles W. Chatfield), Michael Courtney Jenkins. Mem. Springfield (Mass.) Housing Authority, 1952-62; mem. adv. bd. Mass. Commn. Against Discrimination, Springfield, 1949—; mem. Commn. for Study of De Facto Segregation Public Schs. of Mass., 1964-65; mem. Mass. sub-com. under Nat. Commn. on Civil Rights, 1959-64; pres. Catholic Scholarships for Negroes, Inc., 1946—. Recipient Jefferson award, 1982. Mem. Kappa Gamma Phi (hon.). Democrat. Roman Catholic. Home: 101 Mulberry St Springfield MA 01105

PUTNEY, MARY ENGLER, educator; b. Overland, Mo., May 1, 1933; d. Bernard Joseph and Marie Theresa (Kunkler) Engler; student Fontbonne Coll., 1951-52; A.A., Sacramento City Coll., 1975; B.S. in Bus. Adminstrn., Calif. State U., 1981; m. Patrick J. Putney, Oct. 25, 1952; children—Glennon, Denise, Patrick M., Michelle. Asst. to acct. Mo. Research Labs., Inc., St. Louis, 1953-55, sec. to controller, 1955-56, adminstrv. asst. to pres., 1958-60; sec. to mgr. Western region fin. Gen. Electric Co., St. Louis, 1960-62; sec. to regional v.p. agrl. loans Crocker Nat. Bank, Sacramento, 1962-67, asst. credit analyst No. region, 1967, sec. to v.p. and mgr. capital office, Sacramento, 1967-72; student tchr. Sacramento County Dept. Edn., 1979—. Mem. Sacramento Community Commn. for Women, 1978—, rec. sec., 1980-81, bd. dirs., 1980—; mem. planning bd. Golden Empire Health Systems Agy. Mem. Nat. Assn. Accts., Fontbonne Coll. Alumni Assn., AAUW, Beta Gamma Sigma, Beta Alpha Psi. Roman Catholic. Club: Arden Hills Swim and Tennis. Home: 2616 Point Reyes Way Sacramento CA 95826

PUTTERMAN, FLORENCE, artist; b. N.Y.C., Apr. 14, 1927; d. Nathan and Jean (Feldman) Hirsch; B.S., N.Y.U., 1947; M.F.A., Pa. State U., 1972; m. Saul Putterman, Dec. 19, 1947. Founder, pres. Arts Unlimited, Selinsgrove, Pa., 1969—; curator Milton Shoe Collection, 1970—; artist-in-residence Title III Program, Cultural Enrichment in Schs. Program, 1969-70; instr. Lycoming Coll., Williamsport, Pa., 1972-74; one woman shows Everson Mus., Syracuse, N.Y., 1976, Print Club, Phila., 1977, Mus. Fine Arts, Hagerstown, Md., 1978; exhibited group shows Library Congress, 1977, Soc. Am. Graphic Artists, Ball State Drawing Ann., Muncie, Ind., Arts Club N.Y., Colorprint, U.S.A., Smithsonian Instn., 1980, Potsdam (N.Y.) Drawing Exhbn., 1981; Bd. dirs. Fetherston Found. Recipient award Silvermine Guild, Conn. Appalachian Corridors, Arena, 1976; Gold medal of honor Audubon Artists ann. competition; award Chautauqua (N.Y.) Art Assn.; Nat. Endowment Arts grantee. Mem. Am. Fedn. Arts, Art Alliance Central Pa., Audubon Artists, Colorprint Soc., Soc. Am. Graphic Artists. Home: 3 Fairway Dr Selinsgrove PA 17870

PUZZUOLI, GINA MICHELLE, psychiatrist; b. Lakewood, Ohio, Dec. 20, 1951; d. David Anthony and Jean (Adams) P.; B.A. in Chemistry magna cum laude, W.Va. U., 1972; M.D., W.Va. Sch. Medicine, 1976; m. Edmund Carr Settle, Jr., Jan. 26, 1980. Resident dept. behavioral medicine and psychiatry W.Va. Univ., Charleston, 1976-78; resident U. South Fla., Tampa, 1978-79; practice medicine specializing in psychiatry, Charleston, 1979—; clin. asst. prof. psychiatry W.Va. Univ., 1979—; mem. staffs Charleston Meml. Hosp., Charleston Gen. Hosp., St. Francis Hosp., Kanawha Valley Hosp. Mem. W.Va. State Bd. Health, 1981—. Bd. trustees Goodwill Industries, 1981—, Allergy Rehab. Found., 1981—, Bronco Junction, 1981—. Recipient Scholastic Achievement award, U. South Fla., 1979; diplomate Am. Bd. Psychiatry and Neurology. Mem. AMA, W.Va. State Med. Assn., Am. Psychiatry Assn., Kanawha County Med. Soc. Home: 2116 Kanawha Blvd Charleston WV 25311 Office: 5600 MacCorkle Ave Charleston WV 25301

PYBURN, MARY ETHEL ABERNATHY, educator; b. Greenwood, Miss., Sept. 10, 1921; d. Jim Eddie, Sr., and Bettie Jeneva (Thomas) Abernathy; B.S., Kans. State Coll., 1943; postgrad. U. Chgo., 1944, Pepperdine U.; M.S.W., Atlanta U., 1949; B.S., Macalester Coll., 1955; m. Marion Greg Taylor, June 21, 1953; 1 son, Marion Greg; m. 2d, Leroy Pyburn, July 31, 1972. Tchr. Douglas Sch., Kansas City, Kans., 1943-48; vis. tchr., Atlanta, 1948-49; tchr. Lincoln Sch., Kansas City, Kans., 1949-53; family practice case worker St. Paul Family Service, 1953-54; tchr. Madison Sch., Mpls., 1955-74, Greeley Elementary Sch., 1974; tchr. reading adult edn. Mann Sch., Mpls., summer 1967; tchr. Edina (Minn.) Adult Armchair Edn., 1968-70; mem. Minn. Team Action for the Gifted, 1973; now tchr. ABC Unified Sch. Dist., Cerritos, Calif. Mem. Twin Cities Internat. Program, 1967—; mem. Guidelines for Human Relations Edina Schs., 1972, observor Edina Human Rights Commn. Bd. dirs. Mpls. YWCA, 1953-54, Madison Sch. PTA, 1971-72. Named Minn. Honor Roll Tchr., 1974. Mem. LWV, Kans. Tchrs. Assn (pres. grade tchrs. 1945-47), Am. Assn. Retired Persons, Assn. Retired Tchrs., Luekemia Soc. Am., NEA, Minn. Edn. Assn., Assn. Chilhood Edn. Internat. (state pres. 1974). Women in Edn., AAUW, NAACP, Urban League, Alpha Kappa Alpha. Home: 17128 Stowers Ave Cerritos CA 90701

PYLE, BEATRICE ALZIRA, educator; b. West Chester, Pa., May 21, 1922; d. Norman James and Audrey (Dilks) Pyle; B.S., Gettysburg Coll., 1944; M.S. in Hygiene and Phys. Edn., Wellesley Coll., 1946; certificate U. Oslo, 1960. Instr. Gettysburg Coll., 1938-40, Vassar Coll., 1946-52; tchr. pub. schs., Winnetka, Ill., 1952-57; asso. prof. phys. and health edn. Miami U., Oxford, Ohio, 1957—. Mem. Am. Pub. Health Assn., Royal Soc. Health Can. and Eng., Nat., Ohio edn. assns., AAHPER (coordinator aquatic insts. for aquatic council), Ohio Coll. Assn., Am. Camping Assn., AAUW, Ohio, Midwest assns. health, phys. edn. and recreation. Author: Small Craft: An Instructional Textbook for Teachers; Anatomy Handbook; Kinesiology Laboratory Manual. Home: 119 N Campus Ave Oxford OH 45056

PYLE, BETTY JUNE, educator; b. San Angelo, Tex., Mar. 12, 1938; d. Austin Lamar and Grace Mae (Scott) Casbeer; A.S., Odessa Coll.; B.S. in Edn., Tex. Tech. U.; M.Ed., U. Tex., Permian Basin; m. Josephy N. Pyle, Jan. 18, 1965; 1 son, David. With Lone Star Gas Co., 1957-60, Frontier Pontiac, 1960-62, Nelson's Clothing, 1962-64, Sid Richardson, 1964-65; tchr. First Bapt. Ch. Kindergarten, 1968-70; tchr. earth and life sci. Ector County Ind. Sch. Dist., Odessa, Tex., 1973—; chmn. task force Outdoor Learning Center for Ector County Schs. Reporter, Ector County Democratic Women's Club; del. Dem. state conv., 1968-78, del. nat. Dem. Mini Conv., 1978; bd. dirs. Permian Basin Zool. Soc., Presdl. Mus., YWCA, Ector County Hist. Commn., Ector County Park Bd. Mem. AAAS, Nat. Sci. Tchrs. Assn., Sci. Tchrs. Tex., Tex. Assn. Environ. Edn., Tex. Classroom Tchrs. Assn. 1978-81, pres. 1982-84), Odessa Classroom Tchrs. Assn. (pres. 1977-78), Internat. Platform Assn., Phi Kappa Phi, Beta Beta Beta, Alpha Delta Kappa (pledge chmn. 1981-82). Presbyterian. Home: 801 W 21st Odessa TX 79763 Office: PO Box 3912 Odessa TX 79760

PYLE, JACKIE LOU, educator; b. Lead Hill, Ark., May 4, 1935; d. Alva Francis and Glessie Pauline (Jenkins) Anderson; B.S. in Edn., Ark. State Tchrs. Coll., 1963; M.S., State Coll. Ark., 1967; postgrad. U. Ark., 1969, U. No. Colo., 1970, La. Tech. U., 1969-70; m. Charles Edward Pyle, Jr., Sept. 13, 1953; children—Charles Steven, Larry Douglas. Tchr. Bellfonte Elementary Sch., Valley Springs, Ark., 1959, Hollister (Mo.) Elementary Sch., 1960-63, Hollister Jr. and Sr. High Sch., 1963-64; instr. health and phys. edn. Sch. of Ozarks Coll., Point Lookout, Mo., 1964; asst. prof. health and phys. edn. La. Tech. U., Ruston, 1966—; cons. in field. Mem. La. Tchrs. Assn., Am. Alliance for Health, Phys. Edn. and Recreation, La. Assn. Higher Edn., La. Assn. Health, Phys. Edn. and Recreation. Mem. Ch. of Christ. Home: 1404 St John St Ruston LA 71270 Office: Woodard Hall 113 La Tech U Ruston LA 71270

PYLMAN, DAWN ELAINE, psychiat. social worker; b. Grand Rapids, Mich., Oct. 22, 1949; d. Arnold Thomas and Marian Huizinga; A.B., Calvin Coll., 1971; M.S.W., Western Mich. Sch. Social Work, 1973; m. Gerald J. Pylman, II, Sept. 12, 1975; 1 dau., Elizabeth Leigh. Clin. social worker Cath. Social Services, Grand Rapids, Mich., 1973-74; clin. social worker adult services Pine Rest Christian Hosp., Grand Rapids, 1974—, program asst. adminstrn., 1979—. Mem. Nat. Assn. Social Workers, Acad. Cert. Social Workers.

PYNES, NINA, restaurant exec.; b. Syracuse, N.Y., June 25, 1936; d. Samuel and Palma (Quinto) Collette; student Syracuse U., 1955-60; m. Buddy Pynes, Nov. 9, 1967; children—Patricia, Mitchell. Owner, operator Big M Supermarket, Weedsport, N.Y., 1962-65; owner, pres., acct. Soo Lin Restaurant, Inc., DeWitt, N.Y., 1967—. Mem. N.Y. State Restaurant Assn., N.Y. State Sheriffs Assn., Everson Mus., Central N.Y. Tavern Keepers. Office: Soo Lin Restaurant Erie Blvd E DeWitt NY 13214

PYSZ, JEAN ANN, personnel exec.; b. Taunton, Mass., May 1, 1947; d. Paul J. and Adela (Baran) Ladebauche; student Fisher Jr. Coll., 1982; 1 son, Mark Richard. Sec. to dist. mgr. Prudential Ins. Co., Taunton, 1965-66; sec. to personnel mgr. Raytheon Co., North Dighton, Mass., 1967-75; exec. sec. to mgr. corporate audity Motorola Inc., Phoenix, 1977-79; asst. to corporate dir. employee relations Robertson Factories, Inc., Taunton, 1979-82, now dir. personnel. Team capt. United Way, 1982; co-dir. Miss Taunton Scholarship Pageant, 1980. Mem. Taunton Area C. of C. (personnel com. 1981—). Ballet instr., 1963-65. Home: 8 McSoley Ave Taunton MA 02789 Office: 33 Chandler Ave Taunton MA 02780

QUAINTANCE, MARILYN LOUISE KOCH, indsl. psychologist; b. Washington, Nov. 27, 1948; d. Robert Magoon and Helene Josephine (Radowicz) Koch; B.A., Coll. William and Mary, Williamsburg, Va., 1970; M.A., George Washington U., 1975, Ph.D., 1981; m. John Weston Quaintance, III, Aug. 18, 1973. Summer intern IRS, Washington, 1970, 71; sr. research asso. Am. Insts. Research, Washington, 1973-75; personnel psychologist HUD, Washington, 1975-78; dir. assessment services Internat. Personnel Mgmt. Assn., Washington, 1978—; instr. evaluation of performance and productivity seminars, 1978—. Mem. Am. Psychol. Assn. Personnel Testing Council Met. Washington (program chair), Psi Chi, Kappa Kappa Gamma. Methodist. Home: 1307 Carper's Farm Way Vienna VA 22180 Office: 1850 K St NW Washington DC 20006

QUALLS, MARLENE MARIE, cosmetic co. exec.; b. Providence, Nov. 3, 1938; d. Alfred A. and Ardella F. (Grandy) Walker; A.S., South Central Community Coll., 1971; B.S., U. New Haven, 1973; postgrad. U. Bridgeport; m. Michael Qualls, Sept. 7, 1957; 1 dau., Michelle Y. Corp. accountant Xerox Corp., Stamford, Conn., 1971-73; payroll acctg. supr. Chesebrough Pond's Inc., Clinton, Conn., 1973-75, mgr. domestic and internat. payroll, 1975-77, div. mgr. payrolls and payrolls systems Health-Tex. div., Cumberland, R.I., 1977-81; corporate payroll mgr. Cheseborough Pond's, Inc., Trumbull, Conn., 1981—. Mem. Nat. Assn. Female Execs., Soc. Women Accts., Nat. Assn. Payroll Profls., U. New Haven Alumni Assn. Office: 55 Merritt Blvd Trumbull CT 06611

QUALTERS, MARGARET KATHLEEN, real estate economist and appraiser; b. McKeesport, Pa., May 6, 1946; d. Robert L. and Stella Teresa (Wolf) Q.; B.A., Temple U., 1968; grad. Pa. Realtors Inst., 1972; student Am. Inst. Real Estate Appraisers, 1972-78. Appraisal asst. R.L. Qualters, McKeesport, Pa., 1968-72; propr., mgr. Qualters Realty, McKeesport, 1973-77; asst. v.p. Oliver Realty, Inc., Pitts., 1977-79; v.p. Oliver Evaluation Services, Inc., Pitts., 1979—; instr. Duquesne U., 1976-77, Am. Inst. Real Estate Appraisers, 1980, U. Pitts., 1978-80, Allegheny County Community Coll., 1974; chmn. McKeesport Mcpl. Bldg. Authority, 1974-76. Sec. McKeesport Adv. Council to Pa. Human Relations Commn., 1968-70; sec. Pitts. Drama League, 1973-75; mem. Mayor's Study Com. on Neighborhood Housing, McKeesport, 1977-78; bd. dirs. McKeesport Little Theatre, 1975-80. Mem. Am. Inst. Real Estate Appraisers, Am. Inst. Corp. Asset Mgmt., Nat. Assn. Realtors, Pa. Assn. Realtors (dir. 1974), Greater Pitts. Bd. Realtors, Mon-Yough Mgmt. Assn. (pres. 1977-78). Home: 13 Foster Sq Pittsburgh PA 15212 Office: 2800 Two Oliver Plaza Pittsburgh PA 15222

QUAN, ALICE BROWNE, civic worker, clubwoman; b. Ft. Worth, Apr. 4, 1908; d. Virgil and Maimee Lee (Robinson) Browne; student Christian Coll., Columbia, Mo., 1925-26; grad. Miss Mason's Sch., Tarrytown, N.Y., 1928; A.B., Okla. U., 1930, M.A. in History, life tchr.'s cert., 1939; m. Frank James Quan, Feb. 22, 1966; 1 son, Floyd Davis Raupe. Substitute tchr. history jr. and sr. high schs., Oklahoma City, 1941-45; Okla. state pres. Children Am. Revolution, 1941-45, hon. pres., 1945, nat. v.p., 1945-47, nat. librarian, curator 1947-51, editor 1st and 2d state yearbooks, 1941-47; mem. council Girl Scouts U.S.A., Oklahoma City, 1941-43; organizing regent, hon. regent DAR, Paul's Valley, Okla., 1947, Okla. state chmn. bldg. fund, 1950-52, Okla. state membership chmn., 1946-50, rec. sec. Okla. state officers club, 1960; Okla. state women's com. chmn. savs. bond div. U.S. Treasury Dept., 1950-64; docent Bklyn. Children's Mus., 1940-41; mem. pres.'s council Sch. of Ozarks, Mo., 1973—chmn. UN Day, Oklahoma City, 1981; co-chmn. 3d Ann. Heart Ball, 1978; bd. dirs. Oklahoma City Heritage Assn., 1982-83; pres.'s council Oklahoma City U., 1974-79, mem. bishop's council, 1980—; charter mem. women's com. Okla. Symphony Soc., fund raising chmn., 1950-52; life mem., mem. bd., past v.p. Okla. Art Center, mem. liaison bd., 1973—; decoration chmn. Beaux Arts Ball, 1958; organizing chmn. Musicade, Okla. Fedn. Music Clubs, 1960; hospitality chmn. Town Hall, Oklahoma City, 1967-70; bd. dirs., v.p. Civic Music Assn., 1974-75, 76-82; adv. com. Oklahoma City Sch. Music, 1975-79; asso. mem. nat. council Met. Opera, 1975-79, patron, 1979—; chmn. Phoebe Circle, 1st Presbyterian Ch., 1976-77, Priscilla Circle, 1977-78, program chmn. women's group, 1979-81; bd. dirs. Oklahoma City Opera, Met. Opera Southwestern Hospitality; dir. Glencoe Vacherie Plantation, Franklin, La., 1963—, sec.-treas., 1980—; mem. liaison bd. Art League, 1973—; dir. Ardmore Coca Cola Bottling

Co., Ardmore, Okla., 1976-79. Recipient Outstanding Service award U.S. Treasury Dept. 1962; Spl. Service cert. ARC, 1942-46; life teaching cert. in jr. and sr. high sch. history, Okla. Mem. Okla. Soc. Mayflower Descs. (life), Nat. Soc. Old Plymouth Colony Descs. (life), Jr. League Oklahoma City (sustaining), Okla. Sci. and Arts Found. (life), Sovereign Colonial Soc. Ams. Royal Descent (life), Order of Washington (life), Nat. Soc. Descs. Ancient and Honorable Arty. Co., Plantagenet Soc. (life), Soc. Descs. Knights Most Noble Order Garter (life), English Speaking Union (travel chmn. 1974-76, membership chmn. 1976-78, program chmn. 1979-81), Colonial Order of Crown (life), Okla. Assn. Women Hwy. Leaders, Okla. Zool. Soc. (life mem.), Magna Carta Dames (state pres. 1981-83), Okla. Art League (pres. 1968-69, program chmn. 1981-82), Reviewers Clique (pres. 1978-79), Gamma Phi Beta (Golden 50 Crescent award 1979), Alpha Tau Omega (state wives and mothers club pres. 1953-54). Clubs: Ladies Music (v.p. 1957-64), Redbud Women's (pres. 1968-69, dir. 1969—), Oklahoma City Golf and Country, The Beacon, Lotus, Mayfair, Embassy, Seventy Five, Eagle Nest, Colonial Bridge (trophy 1935). Alice Quan Wing at Sch. of Ozarks dedicated in her honor, 1980. Address: 1304 Huntington Ave Oklahoma City OK 73116

QUAN, LYNDA MARYE, psychiat. social worker; b. New Orleans, July 9, 1945; d. William Evans and Mary (Hom) Q.; B.A., U. Colo., Boulder, 1966; M.A., U. Mo., Columbia, 1971, M.S.W., 1975. Mem. Peace Corps, Brazil, 1967-69; grad. teaching asst. U. Mo., Columbia, 1969-71; substitute tchr. Columbia Public Schs., 1971; psychiat. social worker Fulton (Mo.) State Hosp., 1971-76; dep. juvenile officer St. Louis County Juvenile Ct., 1975; with Farmington (Mo.) State Hosp., 1976—, supr. psychiat. social work, 1981—; cons., speaker in field. Mem. Nat. Assn. Social Workers, Acad. Cert. Social Workers (chmn. nominations and leadership Mo. chpt. 1981—, del. assembly 1981), Bus. and Profl. Women, Women's Sports Found., U. Mo. Alumni Assn. (life). Home: PO Box 366 Farmington MO 63640 Office: Farmington State Hosp Farmington MO 63640

QUANTIUS, FRANCES WELLS, economist; b. Milw., July 21, 1915; d. Frank Bernard and Frances Kent (Wells) Q.; B.A., U. Wis., 1937, M.A., 1938, Ph.D., 1943. Instr. econs. Ohio State U., 1942-45, asst. prof., 1946-53, assoc. prof., 1954-62, prof., 1963—; speaker, TV appearances. Treas., bd. dirs. Summit Chase Condominium Assn. Mem. Am. Fin. Assn., Am. Econs. Assn., Columbus Rock and Mineral Soc., Beta Gamma Sigma, Omicron Delta Epsilon, Phi Alpha Kappa. Clubs: Ohio State U. Faculty, Mus. Art. Author: (with others) Economics: Basic Problems and Analysis, 1951; contbr. articles and book revs. to econ. and fin. jours.; contbr. to Ency. Brit., Lincoln Library Ency. Home: 1000 Urlin Ave Columbus OH 43212 Office: 1775 College Rd Ohio State University Columbus OH 43210

QUARTUCCIO, FRANKLYNNE XAVIER, ins. co. exec.; b. Rockville Center, N.Y., Jan. 1, 1945; d. Frank Antonio and Virginia Caroline (McNally) LaRocca; asso. degree with distinction, Suffolk County Community Coll., 1979; student SUNY, Stony Brook, 1979-81, St. Joseph's Coll., Patchoque, N.Y., 1981—; m. John Quartuccio, Mar. 20, 1962; children—John, Christopher. Adminstrv. asst. Suffolk Community Coll., Selden, N.Y., 1977-79; sr. adminstrn. analyst Equitable Life Assurance Soc. U.S., 1980—. Democratic candidate for town clk. Town of Islip, 1981; dep. zone leader Suffolk County Dem. party, 1982—; mem. Suffolk County Dem. Com., 1981—; Suffolk County chmn. Women's Equal Opportunity Council, 1980—; mem. adv. bd. Paumanok Algonquin Found., 1978—; bd. dirs. Community Programs Center, 1981-82. NSF Grantee, 1979-80. Mem. Women's Equal Rights Congress, Equitable Networks, L.I. Women's Coalition (dir.), NOW, Wider Opportunities For Women. Home: 79 Harp Ln Sayville NY 11782

QUATTLEBAUM, DOROTHY EVELYN CLEWIS (MRS. WALTER EMMETT QUATTLEBAUM, JR.), investment co. exec.; b. Unadilla, Ga., Nov. 1, 1924; d. Otis Clyde and Mabel (DuPree) Clewis; student Puttman Bus. Sch., 1953, Chipola Jr. Coll., 1962-64; m. Walter Emmett Quattlebaum, Jr., Oct. 19, 1946; children—Walter Emmett III, Amalia Ann. Sec.-treas. Sneads Telephone Co., 1948-55, Cottondale Telephone Co., 1954-55, Grand Ridge Telephone Co., 1954-55; sec.-treas., dir. Tri-County Telephone Co., Inc., Bonifay, Fla., 1955-62; asst. to stock analyst Quattlebaum Investments, Bonifay, 1962—. Methodist (pres. Wesleyan service guild 1957, 58). Address: PO Box 36 Bonifay FL 32425

QUEEN, PHILLIS AULD, real estate broker; b. Pasadena, Calif., Dec. 23, 1928; d. Samuel Hayward and Wilda Ballou (Jackson) Auld; student Pasadena Coll., 1946. U. Calif., Berkeley, 1947; m. James Michael Queen, May 11, 1947 (div. 1974); children—James Michael, John Gregory. Salesperson, Alps Realty, Huntington Station, N.Y., 1968-69; broker Babicz Realty, East Islip, N.Y., 1969-72, Quality Real Estate, East Islip, 1972-73; partner-owner Sure Enterprises, Inc., Fire House Five Car Wash; broker Carll S. Burr Real Estate, Sayville, N.Y., 1979—; antique dealer DBA Antiques Internat., doing bus. with Christies, Park Bernet Galleries, 1977-79; interior designer Jeri's Interiors, Chico, Calif., 1980. Pres., PTA, 1958; bd. dirs. Christian Drug Service. Mem. L.I. Bd. Realtors (asso.). Mem. Christian Missionary Alliance Ch. Club: Ind. Order Foresters.

QUELER, EVE, conductor; b. N.Y.C.; student Mannes Coll. Music, Coll. City N.Y. Music staff N.Y.C. Opera, 1958-70; asso. condr. Fort Wayne (Ind.) Philharmonic, 1970-71; founder, music dir. Opera Orch. N.Y., 1968—; condr. Lake George Opera Festival, Glen Falls, N.Y., 1971-72, Oberlin (Ohio) Music Festival, 1972, Romantic Festival, Indpls., 1972, Mostly Mozart Festival, Lincoln Center, 1972, New Philharmonia, London, 1973, Teatro Liceo, Barcelona, 1973, San Antonio Symphony, 1975, Montreal Symphony, 1975. Guest condr. Paris Radio Orch., 1972, P.R. Symphony Orch., 1975, Mich. Chamber Orch., 1975, Phila. Orch., 1976, Cleve. Orch., 1977. Recipient Martha Baird Rockefeller Fund for Music award, 1968; named Musician of Month, Mus. Am. Mag., 1972. Address: care Shaw Concerts 111 W 57th St New York NY 10019

QUERY, GRACE AUSTIN, pest control co. exec.; b. Wingate, N.C., Jan. 7, 1923; d. Daniel Palmer and Lydia Colan (Meigs) Austin; student pub. schs., Wingate; m. Grady Wendell Query, Mar. 30, 1941; children—Oliver Grady, Lydia Jane Query Kessler. Clk., Kerrison's Dept. Store, Charleston, S.C., 1941-43; office sec. So. Pest Control Co. Inc., Charlotte, N.C., 1954-58, office mgr., 1959-74, exec. adminstr., sec., treas., 1974—, also dir.; office sec. Charlotte Exterminators and Chem. Co. (N.C.), 1954-58; office mgr. Charlotte Exterminating Co., 1959-74, exec. adminstr., sec., treas., dir., 1974-80; office mgr. CESSCO, Inc., Charlotte, 1959-74, exec. adminstr., sec., treas., dir., 1974—. Sunday sch. tchr. Matthews United Methodist Ch., 1957-69. Democrat. Home: 1725 Mint Hill Rd Matthews NC 28105 Office: 1109 Central Ave PO Box 18452 Charlotte NC 28218

QUERZE, ELISSA R., graphic designer, art dir., cons.; b. Quincy, Mass., d. Antero and Ida R. Querze; B.F.A. cum laude, Pratt Inst., 1953; postgrad. Art Students League, 1957, New Sch., 1965, Sch. of Visual Arts, 1970, 78. Art dir. Norman Craig & Kummel, N.Y.C., 1960-61, West Weir and Bartel, N.Y.C., 1961-67, L.W. Frohlich Intercon Internat., Inc., N.Y.C., 1968-72, Ted Bates, N.Y.C., 1972-73, William Douglas McAdams, N.Y.C., 1973-74, Wesson and Warhaftig, N.Y.C., 1974-79, Sudler and Hennessey, N.Y.C., 1980—; corp. design dir. Celanese Corp., Korafab, Inc. Active, Sierra Club, Friends of the Earth, Friends of the Animals, Natural Resources and Def. Council, Citizens for Clean Air. Recipient Triangle award McGraw-Hill, 1979, 80; Graphics ann. award, 1967, 68; Ad Gage award, 1970; Andy award for creativity, 1980, others. Mem. Art Dirs. Club (award 1969), Am. Inst. Graphic Arts (award 1965), Art Students League, Type Dirs. Club. Clubs: Westchester Sports, Matterhorn Sports. Speaker profl. group; contbr., author, editor to exploration project Girl Scouts U.S.A., 1979. Office: 1633 Broadway New York NY 10019

QUICK, SHIRLEY ANN, publisher; b. Farina, Ill., Mar. 18, 1943; d. Cecil Edwin and Helen Elsie (Whitt) Q.; student public schs., Farina. With Farina News, 1961—, owner, pub., 1976—. Mem. Ill. Press Assn., So. Ill. Editors Assn., Nat. Newspaper Assn. Baptist. Home: Jefferson and Hickory Sts Farina IL 62838 Office: Farina News Walnut St Farina IL 62838

QUIGGLE, LYNN KAY WUTSCHKE, psychotherapist; b. Northfield, Minn., Dec. 18, 1951; d. Kenneth Earl and Patricia Ruth (Bailey) Wutschke; B.A. magna cum laude, U. Minn., 1973, M.S.W., 1977; m. Scott S. Quiggle, July 28, 1973. Psychiat. social worker No. Community Mental Health Center, Ashland, Wis., 1977-79; psychotherapist Human Devel. Center, Duluth, Minn., 1980—; lectr. on family and individual dynamics, condr. workshops and seminars on personal growth, stress mgmt., and related topics. Mem. Women's Network, Northwoods Women (co-founder), NOW. Home: 2332 Jefferson St Duluth MN 55812 Office: 1401 E 1st St Duluth MN 55805

QUIGLEY, BARBARA WETZLER, hosp. adminstr.; b. Phila., Feb. 28, 1943; d. Frank Michael and Margaret Barbara (Pauli) Wetzler; B.A. in History, Holy Family Coll., Phila., 1964; M.A. in Health Edn., St. Joseph's U., Phila., 1978; m. Robert E. Quigley, Aug. 22, 1964; children—Patrick, Kathryn, Jennifer Rebecca. Counselor, instr., bd. dirs. breastfeeding info. services Childbirth Edn. Assn. Greater Phila., 1965-78; dir. health edn. dept. Lankenau Hosp., Phila., 1978—. Mem. Am. Soc. Health Care Edn. and Tng. (pres.-elect Southeastern Pa. chpt. 1982), AAHEPER, Consumer Health Edn. Assn. Del. Valley (v.p. 1981). Office: Health Edn Dept Lankenau Hosp Lancaster Ave Philadelphia PA 19151

QUIGLEY, BEHNAZ ZOLGHADR, educator; b. Tehran, Iran, Nov. 17, 1944; came to U.S., 1968, naturalized, 1978; d. Hamid and Behjat (Shoaibi) Zolghadr; diploma in edn. Tchrs. Tng. Coll., Tehran, 1964; B.A., (scholar), U. Tehran, 1968; M.B.A., U. D.C., 1975; m. Herbert Gerald Quigley, Aug. 24, 1974; 1 dau., Narda. Tchr. secondary sch. Ministry of Edn., Tehran, 1964-68; instr. in bus. Strayer Coll., Washington, 1975-76, U. D.C., 1975-76, Prince George's Community Coll., Largo, Md., 1976-77; asst. prof. bus. adminstrn. Mt. Vernon Coll., Washington, 1976—, chmn. dept., 1978-79; aide to chief economist Iranian Econ. Mission, 1974; freelance cons. World Trade Assos., summer 1975, Distbn. Systems, summer 1979; co-owner, freelance cons. Univ. Systems Assos., 1978—; instr., curriculum developer Middle East Inst., summers 1976—. Mt. Vernon Coll. faculty devel. grantee, George Washington U., summers 1978, 79, Mt. Vernon Coll. ednl. travel grantee, 1978, 79, 80; grantee Middle East Inst., 1977. Mem. Nat. Assn. Female Execs. (dir. Washington area), Assn. M.B.A. Execs., Am. Acctg. Assn., Acad. Mgmt., U. D.C. Alumni Assn. Democrat. Co-editor: Management Systems: Contemporary Perspectives, 1982; contbr. articles to profl. jours. Home: 5 Canfield Ct Potomac MD 20854 Office: 2100 Foxhall Rd Washington DC 20007

QUIGLEY, PATRICIA JEAN, grants agy. exec.; b. Washington, Feb. 22, 1943; d. James and Helen C. Quigley; B.F.A., U. Iowa, 1975; children—Timothy J. Byler, Christine A. Byler, Therese L. Byler. With Basic Grant Project, Los Angeles, system specialist, 1978-80, mgr., 1980—. Bd. dirs. Woman View, Woman's Film and Photography Festival, Iowa City 1974. Mem. Iowa Orgn. Women Artists (founder 1974-78), Nat. Assn. Female Execs. Home: 4240 Centinela Apt #2 Los Angeles CA 90066 Office: 2500 Colorado Los Angeles CA 90406

QUIGLEY-WOLF, ANNA MARIE HELEN, orgn. devel. cons.; b. Phila., Aug. 15, 1950; d. William Joseph, Jr. and Elizabeth (Harkins) Ailes; B.A., Point Park Coll., Pitts., 1972; postgrad. Temple U., Phila. Ednl. resource specialist Community Coll. Phila., 1972-74; edn. coordinator Penn Mut. Life Ins. Co., Phila., 1974-76, human resource cons., 1976-81; adminstr. orgn. devel. RCA Service Co., Cherry Hill, N.J., 1981—; chmn. Women's Resource Group, Phila., 1980-81; speaker in field. Mem. Orgn. Devel. Network, Am. Soc. Tng. and Devel., Nat. Assn Female Execs., Middle Atlantic Career Counselors Assn. Office: Route 38 Bldg 204-2 Cherry Hill NJ 08358

QUILLIAN, ELAINE MURIEL GROSS, social worker; b. Chgo., Aug. 14, 1933; d. Leonard Morse and Mildred (Dubin) Gross; B.A., Roosevelt U., 1958; M.S.W. (Woods fellow), U. Ill., 1961; student Gestalt Therapy Inst., 1978; 1 dau., Pamela Phoebe. Adoption caseworker Ill. Children's Home and Aid Soc., Chgo., 1961-68; staff devel. coordinator Ill. Dept. Children and Family Services, Chgo., 1968-74; asst. exec. dir. Long Beach (Calif.) Jewish Community Center, 1974-76; dir. family and children's services Bell Gardens (Calif.) Community Center, 1976—; casework therapist Children's Home Soc. Calif., Long Beach. Mem. adv. bd. S.E. dist. Family Service Assn., Downey, Calif., 1977-80. Lic. clin. social worker, Calif. Mem. Acad. Cert. Social Workers, Assn. for Humanistic Psychology (pres. Long Beach/Orange County). Home: 1109 Pacific Ave Long Beach CA 90813 Office: 920 Atlantic Ave Suite D Long Beach CA 90813

QUIMBY, JANE SOUTHWARD, city ofcl.; b. Toledo, Sept. 15, 1926; d. Charles Russell and Emma G. (Smith) Southward; B.S. in Med. Tech., U. Colo., 1948; m. Robert Louis Quimby, June 10, 1947; children—Charles, Steven, Douglas, Richard, Paul, Jane. Mem. city council, City of Grand Junction (Colo.), 1973-79, mayor pro-tem, 1976-77, 78-79, mayor, 1979-81, chmn. City Planning Commn., 1981—. Mem. State Colo. Energy Impact Assistance Adv. Com.; bd. dirs. Grand Junction Mus. Arts Assn., Grand Junction Symphony Guild; mem. State Council on Criminal Justice; v.p. Colo. Mcpl. League, 1980-81, pres., 1981-82; mem. Colo. Energy Coordinating Council. Mem. AAUW, LWV, Women in Mcpl. Govt., Delta Kappa Gamma (hon.). Democrat. Roman Catholic. Office: 250 N 5th St Grand Junction CO 81501

QUIMBY, SALLY CROSBY, nursing adminstr.; b. Washington, Nov. 19, 1946; d. Lowell Horace and Millicent Winn (Childs) Quimby. B.S. in Nursing, La. State U., 1975; M.S. in Nursing, Med. Coll. Ga., 1980. Asst. head nurse E. Jefferson Hosp., Metairie, La., 1976; head CCU St. Joseph Hosp., Savannah, Ga., 1977-78, asst. supr. CCU, 1978-80, supr., 1980; head nurse ICU El Camino Hosp., Mountain View, Calif., 1980—; planner CCU for computer monitoring system, 1978-79; instr. CPR, 1978-80. Task force organizer Save Our Satellite, 1977. Named outstanding Graduating Nursing Student, La. State U., 1975. Mem. Am. Nurses Assn., Calif. Nurses Assn. (dir. region 10 1981-82), Am. Assn. Critical Care Nurses, Calif. Soc. Nursing Service Adminstrs., AAUW. Sigma Theta Tau. Democrat. Methodist. Home: 1315 Miravalle Los Altos CA 94022 Office: 2500 Grant Rd Mountain View CA 94042

QUIN, CAROL LYNELLE, musicologist; b. Yazoo City, Miss., Oct. 12, 1947; d. Carroll Lucius and Rose (Thornberry) Q.; B.A., Millsaps Coll., 1970; M.Mus., U. Ark., Fayetteville, 1974; postgrad. U. Vienna (Austria), summers 1971, 72; Ph.D. (research fellow 1979), U. Ky., 1981. Gen. music tchr., band and choir dir., choreographer S. Mississippi County Sch. Dist. 57, Wilson, Ark., 1970-72; grad. asst. music history, class piano and music appreciation U. Ark., Fayetteville, 1972-74; gen. music tchr., piano instr., adult edn. Calvert County Bd. Edn., Prince Frederick, Md., 1974-77; grad. teaching asso. in music history U. Ky., Lexington, 1977-79; asst. prof. humanities, music theory and piano Lane Coll., Jackson, Tenn., 1979—; music critic-reviewer Lexington (Ky.) Leader, 1978-79. Bd. dirs. Jackson Symphony Orch. Named Outstanding Teaching Asso., U. Ky., 1979. Mem. Am. Musicological Soc., Coll. Music Soc., West Tenn. Music Tchrs. Assn., Music Educator's Nat. Conf., Music Tchrs. Nat. Assn., Pi Kappa Lambda, Sigma Alpha Iota. Home: Route 1 Box 131 Medon TN 38356 Office: Box 332 Lane Coll Jackson TN 38301

QUINN, BARBARA ANN, athletic adminstr.; b. Freehold, N.J., Jan. 13, 1933; d. Walter Stanley and Mary (Craig) Harris; B.S. in Health and Phys. Edn., Ursinus Coll., 1955; M.A., Trenton State Coll., 1968. Dir. phys. edn. for girls Charles Ellis Sch., Newtown Square, Pa., 1956-60; instr. phys. edn. Pennsbury Schs., Yardley, Pa., 1960-63, Exeter Twp. High Sch., Reading, Pa., 1963-66, Hartwick Coll., Oneonta, N.Y., 1966-68; asst. prof. phys. and health edn. Madison Coll., Harrisonburg, Va., 1968-71; instr. phys. edn. Whitemarsh Jr. High Sch., Plymouth Meeting, Pa., 1971-74; dir. women's intercollegiate athletics U. Nev., Las Vegas, 1974-76; dir. women's intercollegiate athletics Simpson Coll., Indianola, Iowa, 1977-78; dir. women's athletics U. N.C., Asheville, 1978-81; dir. women's intercoll. athletics SUNY, Cortland, 1981—; site dir. Western Region, Women's U.S. Olympic Basketball Trials, Las Vegas, 1976, U.S. Volleyball Assn. Coaches Clinic, Simpson Coll., 1977; chmn. selection com. Va. State Lacrosse Tournament, 1970-71; mem. selection com. So. Dist. Lacrosse Tournament, 1970-71; coach So. dist. team U.S. Women's Lacrosse Assn. Nat. Tournament, 1971; mem. Nat. Collegiate Athletic Assn. Women's Soccer Com., 1982; participant 5th Nat. Inst. Girls' Sports Advanced Basketball Coaching, 1969. Mem. AAHPER (sec. coll. div. N.Y. State chpt. 1967), Va. Women's Lacrosse Assn. (chmn. nominations com. 1970-71), Nat. Assn. Coll. Athletic Dirs., N.Y. Assn. Intercollegiate Athletics for Women (ethics and eligibility com. 1982). Address: 14 Lake Rd Dryden NY 13053

QUINN, BETTY NYE, educator; b. Buffalo, Mar. 22, 1921; d. Fritz Arthur and Alma (Svenson) Hedberg; A.B., Mt. Holyoke Coll., 1941; A.M., Bryn Mawr Coll., 1942, Ph.D., 1944; m. John F. Quinn, Sept. 21, 1950. Analyst, U.S. Army, 1944-46, CIA, 1947; instr., asst. prof. Vassar Coll., Poughkeepsie, N.Y., 1948-59, dir. pub. relations, 1952-59, assoc. prof., 1959-68; prof. classics Mt. Holyoke Coll., South Hadley, Mass., 1968—. Am. Acad. Rome fellow, 1942-43; Am. Philos. Soc. grantee, 1952. Mem. Am. Philos. Assn., Mediaeval Acad. Am., Classics Assn. New Eng. (pres. 1970-71) Vergilian Soc. Am. Republican. Lutheran. Home: 27 W Parkview Dr South Hadley MA 01075 Office: Mount Holyoke Coll South Hadley MA 01075

QUINN, CHRISTINE AGNES, radiologist; b. Cleve., Sept. 23, 1946; d. Paul Leo and Estelle Christine Q.; B.A., Marquette U., 1967; M.D., Med. Coll. Pa., 1971; m. Paul C. Janicki, July 11, 1970; 1 dau., Sarah Christine. Intern, St. Luke's Hosp., Cleve., 1971-72; resident in diagnostic radiology Cleve. Clinic Found., 1972-75, radiologist, 1975-81; radiologist Marymount Hosp., Cleve., 1981—. Diplomate Am. Bd. Radiology. Mem. Radiol. Soc. N. Am., Am. Coll. Radiology, Soc. Nuclear Medicine, Ohio, Cuyahoga County med. socs., AMA. Contbr. to CRC Handbook Series, Vol. II, 1977; contbr. articles to profl. jours. Home: 2436 Loyola Rd University Heights OH 44118 Office: 12300 McCracken Rd Cleveland OH 44125

QUINN, HELEN RUSSELL, social worker; b. Los Angeles, Jan. 31, 1927; d. John F. and Helen Ruth (Riddell) Russell; B.A., Stanford U., 1948; M.S.W., U. So. Calif., 1950; m. Noel J. Quinn, Feb. 23, 1952; children—Noel Patrick, Brian Russell, Tara Kathleen, Erin Ann, Terence Davey, Sheila Grace. Social worker Los Angeles County Bur. Adoptions, 1950-52; social worker Adoption Inst., 1960-62; social worker Salvation Army Booth Meml. Hosp., 1962-73, dir. social services, 1973-75; social worker St. Anne's Maternity Home, Los Angeles, 1975-80, asso. dir. social services, 1980—. Lic. clin. social worker, Calif. Mem. Nat. Assn. Social Workers, Acad. Cert. Social Workers, U. So. Calif. Sch. Social Work Alumni Assn. (v.p. bd. dirs.). Democrat. Roman Catholic. Home: 3946 San Rafael Ave Los Angeles CA 90065 Office: 155 N Occidental Blvd Los Angeles CA 90026

QUINN, JANE BRYANT, journalist; b. Niagara Falls, N.Y., Feb. 5, 1939; d. Frank Leonard and Ada (Laurie) Bryant; B.A. magna cum laude, Middlebury Coll., 1960; m. David Conrad Quinn, June 10, 1967; children—Matthew Alexander, Justin Bryant. Asso. editor Insiders Newsletter, N.Y.C., 1962-65, co-editor, 1966-67; sr. editor Cowles Book Co., N.Y.C., 1968; editor-in-chief Bus. Week Letter, N.Y.C., 1969-73, gen. mgr., 1973-74; syndicated fin. columnist Washington Post Writers Group, 1974—; contbr. fin. column Women's Day mag., 1974—; contbr. NBC News and Info. Service, 1976-77; columnist Newsweek, 1978—; bus. corr. WCBS-TV News, 1980-81; spl. corr. CBS-TV Morning News, 1981—. Mem. Phi Beta Kappa. Author: Everyone's Money Book, 1978; Updated Everyone's Money Book, 1980. Office: Newsweek 444 Madison Ave New York NY 10022

QUINN, JULIA PROVINCE, civic worker; b. Franklin, Ind., Feb. 23; d. Oran Arnold and Lillian (Ditmars) Province; B.A., Franklin Coll., 1937; M.S., Smith Coll. Sch. Social Work, 1939; m. Robert William Quinn, Jan. 21, 1942; children—Robert Sean, Judith Ditmars. Caseworker, student supr. Community Service Soc., N.Y.C., 1939-44; caseworker community research Family Service Soc., New Haven, 1946; social worker in research, dept. preventive medicine Yale U. Sch. Medicine, New Haven, 1946-49; research asst. dept. preventive medicine Vanderbilt U. Sch. Medicine, Nashville, 1969-70. Bd. dirs. Tenn. Bot. Gardens and Fine Arts Center, 1976-81, Friends of J. F. Kennedy Center, 1976-81, Family and Children's Service, Nashville, 1977—, Friends of Cheekwood, 1966-81, Nashville Symphony Assn., 1978—, Tenn. Performing Arts Found., 1979—; chmn. public relations Friends of Cheekwood, 1966-68, 72-74, 76-78, Tenn. Performing Arts Found., 1978—, Family and Children's Service, 1978—; mem. adv. bd. Vanderbilt Center for Fertility and Reproductive Research, 1981—. Recipient Nashville Vol. Activist award Cain-Sloan and Germaine Monteil, 1979. Mem. Nat. Assn. Social Workers, Acad. Cert. Social Workers, Ladies Hermitage Assn., Vanderbilt Med. Center Aux., Nashville Area C. of C. (cultural affairs com. 1979—). Democrat. Presbyterian. Clubs: Smith Coll., Centennial (dir.) (Nashville); Vanderbilt Garden, Vanderbilt Woman's. Contbr. articles to social work and med. jours. Home: 508 Park Center Dr Nashville TN 37205

QUINN, KATHLEEN MARY, elec. equipment mfg. co. exec.; b. Troy, N.Y., Apr. 13, 1955; d. Raymond J. and Anne C. Quinn; B.S., Russell Sage Coll., 1977; M.B.A., Rensselaer Poly. Inst., 1978. With Gen. Electric Co., 1978—, lead material specialist Knolls Atomic Power Lab., Windsor, Conn., 1982—. Vol., Meals-on-Wheels program, 1976-77, Ellis Hosp., Schenectady, 1980-81; aide Sr. Citizen Center, Troy, N.Y., 1977-78; adv. Jr. Achievement, Schenectady, 1981-82; active Jr. League of Hartford (Conn.), 1982. Home: Apt 1-H 126 Hopmeadow St Simsbury CT 06089 Office: Knolls Atomic Power Lab Gen Electric Co PO Box 545 Windsor CT 06095

QUINN, LOIS MARIE, nursing mgmt. cons.; b. Boston, Sept. 8, 1933; d. Charles Edward and Grace Marie (Lowder) Seabrook; R.N., Boston City Hosp., 1954; B.A., Glassboro State Coll., 1977; M.A., Central

Mich. U., 1982; m. Richard Edward Quinn, Feb. 2, 1955; children—Deborah Marie, Christopher Edward, Erin Elizabeth, Patrick Richard. Pediatric staff nurse Boston City Hosp., 1954-56; staff nurse, coronary care nurse, supr., patient edn. coordinator, dir. nursing service Rancocas Valley Hosp., Willingboro, N.J., 1967-78; nursing mgmt. cons. Am. Medicorp., Bala Cynwyd, Pa., 1977-78; asst. adminstr. Washington Meml. Hosp., Turnersville, N.J., 1978-80; pres. Lois Quinn Assocs., Nursing Mgmt. Cons., Willingboro, N.J., 1980—. Cert. nursing adminstr. Mem. Common Cause, Am. Nurses Assn., N.J. Nurses Assn. (coordinator So. N.J. nursing adminstrs. and educators 1975-77), So. N.J. Soc. Nursing Service Adminstrs. (sec.-treas. 1976-77), Am. Heart Assn., ARC, Am. Soc. Profl. Cons., Sigma Iota Epsilon. Roman Catholic. Featured in newspaper articles. Address: 130 Club House Dr Willingboro NJ 08046

QUINN, MARION, inst. adminstr.; b. Norfolk, Va., Apr. 25, 1947; d. Thomas Donald and Rosina Anastasia (Grogan) Q.; B.A. in Communication Arts/Sci., Queens Coll., 1973; M.A. in Speech Pathology and Audiology, N.Y. U., 1974; m. Gerald J. Sigler. Substitute remedial tchr. St. Patrick's Sch., Balt., 1968-69; adminstrv. asst. Internat. Com. on English in the Liturgy, Washington, 1970-71; research asst., programmer Woodstock Coll. Center for Program Design, N.Y.C., 1971-74; sr. speech and hearing therapist Willowbrook Devel. Center, S.I., N.Y., 1974-77; dir. programs for devel. disabled Phila. Elwyn Inst., 1978—; mem. task force Health Systems Agy. S.E. Pa. Cert. tchr., Pa., N.Y. State. Mem. Am. Speech Lang. and Hearing Assn. (cert. clin. competence), Am. Assn. Mental Deficiency, Council Exceptional Children, Am. Assn. Edn. of Severely Profoundly Handicapped, Montgomery County Assn. Retarded Citizens. Office: 4017 Ludlow St Philadelphia PA 10194

QUINN, SALLY, journalist; b. Savannah, Ga., July 1, 1941; d. Lt. Gen. and Mrs. William Wilson Quinn; grad. Smith Coll.; m. Benjamin Crowninshield Bradlee, Oct. 20, 1978. Reporter Washington Post, 1969-73, 74—; co-anchorperson CBS Morning News, N.Y.C., 1973-74. Author: We're Going to Make You a Star, 1975. Address: Washington Post 1150 15th St NW Washington DC 20005

QUIRK, BEVERLY JOYE, med. technologist; b. Trempealeau, Wis., July 16, 1938; d. Maurice Eugene and Marian Ruth (Larson) Maxwell; cert. med. tech. Rockford Meml. Hosp. Sch. Med. Tech., 1959; B.A., Western Ill. U., 1980; m. Keith H. Quirk, Aug. 23, 1958; children—Peggy Lynn, Cheryl Ann. Med. technologist John H. McGlothlin, M.D., Pecatonica, Ill., 1959, Riverside Hosp., Kankakee, Ill., 1964-68, Physicians Med. Lab., Appleton, Wis., 1969-70, Clin. Labs. of Nashville, 1970-71; microbiologist Bapt. Hosp., Nashville, 1971-72; med. technologist Charleston (Ill.) Community Meml. Hosp., 1973-75, Mercy Med. Center, Dubuque, Iowa, 1976-77; med. technologist Met. Med. Lab., Quad Cities Pathologists Group, Inc., Moline, Ill., 1977—, supr., 1978-81. Leader Girl Scouts U.S.A., Kankakee, 1967-68, com. mother Appleton, 1969-70; mem. YMCA Aux., Appleton, 1969; v.p. Lutheran Ch. Women, Rock Island, Ill., 1978, active Dubuque, Iowa, Mattoon, Ill.; active social activities for halfway homes, Charleston, 1974-75; active Newcomers Groups, Rockford, 1958-59, Winnebago, Ill., 1959-61, membership chmn., Kankakee, 1962-66, Appleton, 1968-70, Charleston, 1972-75, publicity chmn., 1972-73, membership chmn., 1973-74, treas., 1974, v.p., 1975-76. Mem. Ill. Med. Tech. Assn., Am. Soc. Clin. Pathologists, Nat. Certification Agy. for Med. Lab. Personnel, Am. Soc. for Med. Tech., AAUW. Clubs: Welcome Wagon (Rock Island), Peabody Dames (publicity chmn. 1971-72), U. Dubuque Dames (gourmet group chmn. 1976-77). Home: 3504 12th St Rock Island IL 61201 Office: 1980 1st St A Moline IL 61265

QUIRK, NOREEN, lawyer; b. N.Y.C., Sept. 14, 1953; d. Alfred J. and Rita C. (O'Connor) Quirk; B.A. cum laude, N.Y.U., 1975; J.D., Rutgers U., 1978; m. Peter Lenahan, Oct. 31, 1981. Admitted to N.Y. bar; asso. firm Fragomen, Del Rey & Bernsen, P.C., N.Y.C., 1977—. Supervising atty. No. Manhattan Coalition Immigrant Rights. Mem. Am. Immigration Lawyers Assn. Contbg. author: Immigration Law Report. Office: 525 Madison Ave New York NY 10022

QUISENBERRY, SHARRON SUE, entomologist, educator; b. Kirksville, Mo., Apr. 19, 1945; d. Thomas Leonard and Bonnie P. (Hays) Grogan; B.S. (NSF and Regents scholar), N.E. Mo. State U., 1966; postgrad. Thiel Coll. (NSF scholar), 1972; M.A., Hood Coll., 1975; M.S., U. Mo., 1977, Ph.D., 1980; m. Larry D. Quisenberry, Oct. 10, 1965. Tchr. sci. high schs. Lewis County, Mo., 1966-67, Macon County, Mo., 1968-69, Prince George's County, Md., 1969-74; devel. specialist Research and Devel. Center for Cognitive Learning, U. Wis., Madison, 1974-75; asst. prof. entomology Iowa State U., Ames, 1980-82, La. State U., Baton Rouge, 1982—. Recipient Leonard Haseman Recognition award U. Mo., 1979. Contbr. articles to entomol. jours. Office: Dept Entomology 402 Life Scis Bldg La State U

QUITMAN, CLEO, dancer, singer, educator; b. Edwards, Miss.; d. Cleo Quitman and Eula Mae (Clinton) Hayes; student Wayne State U., 1951; studied dance with Maria Nevelska, 1952-57, with Alfredo Corvino, 1952-54; 1 son, Byian Johnson. Ballerina, N.Y. Negro Ballet, N.Y.C., 1956-58; dancer on tour, Eng., France, Italy, Spain, Switzerland, 1957-59; dancer Town and Country prodn. Apollo Theatre, N.Y.C., 1963, Internat. prodn., 1963; featured dancer Smart Affairs prodn. Club Harlem, Atlantic City, 1964; dancer on tour with Sammy Davis Review, Can., 1969; dancer prodns. Show Boat at N.Y.C. Center, 1962, Fiorello, 1963; actress Black Nativity, 41st St. Theatre, N.Y.C., 1962; ballerina prodn. The Four Marys, Am. Ballet Theater, Lincoln Center, N.Y.C., 1966; dancer Newport (R.I.) Jazz Festival, 1964; mem. tour nat. co. Purlie, U.S., Can., 1971-72; dancer film The Wiz, 1977, All That Jazz, 1979; guest artist City Center Joffrey Ballet, N.Y.C., 1967; soloist Am. Dances prodn. Walter Terry Co., Delacort Theatre, N.Y.C., 1965; dancer TV shows The Strolling Twenties, 1967, Dean Martin Show, 1969, Hollywood Palace, 1969; tchr. ballet jazz and modern dance, drama, N.Y.C., 1964—; tchr. ballet to profls. Showcase Studios, N.Y.C., 1972-76; dir., choreographer, dancer, artistic dir. Cleo Quitman Dance Expedience Co., N.Y.C., 1972—; choreographer Angela, Etc. prodn., N.Y.C., 1972; choreographer, dancer J.C. Penny comml., 1975. Nat. Endowment Arts grantee, 1972, N.Y.C. Dept. Parks and Recreation grantee, 1972-75. Mem. Actors Equity Assn. (dir.), Screen Actors Guild (dancers com., ethnic minorities steering com.), AFTRA, AGVA. Democrat. Mem. Religious Sci. Ch. Home: New York NY

QUITTELL, MURIEL GOLDBERG, social worker; b. Tarrytown, N.Y., Mar. 16, 1916; d. Max and Goldie (Schwartz) Goldberg; B.A. cum laude, SUNY, Albany, 1938; postgrad. Sch. of Social Work, Columbia U., 1938-42; M.S.W., N.Y. U., 1968; m. Jules Quittell, Nov. 15, 1942; children—Glenn, Frederic, Lynne. Social worker Westchester County Dept. Welfare, 1938-42, St. Agnes Hosp. children's unit, White Plains, N.Y., 1968—. Mem. lay adv. com. on continuing edn. New Rochelle (N.Y.) Schs., 1945—. Cert. social worker, N.Y. State. Mem. Nat. Assn. Social Workers. Jewish. Home: 101 Hilary Circle New Rochelle NY 10804 Office: St Agnes Hosp 305 North St White Plains NY 10605

RAABE, HAZEL UDSETH, educator; b. Summit, S.D., Apr. 26, 1917; d. R. and Anna Christina (Lerum) Udseth; B.A., Ellendale (N.D.) Tchrs. U., 1963; M.S., No. State Coll., Aberdeen, S.D., 1970; m. Stanley Raabe, July 24, 1943; children—William, Suzanne Mary. Tchr. rural schs., 1937-43, 55-56, Lake Benton, Minn., 1956-57, Frederick (S.D.) Schs., 1957-63; tchr. reading and English, Wilmot (S.D.) Schs., 1963-66; librarian, tchr., elem. prin. Java (S.D.) Schs., 1966-74; reading specialist Mobridge (S.D.) Ind. Schs., 1974—. Precinct chairperson Democratic party, 1978-80. Mem. AAUW, NEA, S.D. Edn. Assn., Mobridge Edn. Assn., Delta Kappa Gamma. Lutheran. Clubs: Country, Bridge, Golf, Elks Wives, Moose, Sons of Norway, Christian Women's, Naomi Circle, Bridge City Concert, Hosp. Aux. Home: 702 2d Ave W Mobridge SD 57601

RAABE, JANIS ASAD, ednl. writer and cons.; b. Lakewood, Ohio, Apr. 28, 1949; d. Theodore Charles and Jenifer Irene (Snitko) Asad; student St. John Coll. of Cleve., 1967-69; B.S. in Edn., Bowling Green State U., 1971, M.Ed. in Reading, 1972; m. Richard A. Raabe, Aug. 11, 1972; 1 son, Jason Richard. Grad. asst. Bowling Green State U., 1971-72; reading tchr. and cons. Mentor-Ridge Jr. High Sch., Mentor, Ohio, 1972-75; writer ednl. materials Modern Curriculum Press, Cleve., 1972—; freelance editorial cons. Ohio Dept. Edn., 1975-77; ednl. cons. Coronet Instructional Media, Chgo., 1976-79. Mem. Ohio Arts and Crafts Guild, Kappa Delta Pi. Author: MCP Primary Readers, sets 1-4, 1974-78; ednl. cons. Read-Along Beginning Phonics, sets 1 and 2, 1978. Home: 5901 Kerry Circle NW Canton OH 44718

RAACKE, ILSE DORTHEA, biologist, educator; b. Rio de Janeiro, Brazil, Oct. 10, 1925; U.S. citizen; B.A., Parana Sch. Chemistry, Brazil, 1947; M.A., Oreg. State Coll., 1949; Ph.D. in Biochemistry, U. Calif., Berkeley, 1954; div. Teaching asst. in analytical chemistry Oreg. State Coll., 1948-49; vis. research scientist U. Upsala, 1949-51; research asst. in biochemistry U. Calif., Berkeley, 1952-54, asst. research biochemist, 1954-56; Am. Cancer Soc. fellow Cambridge U., 1956-57, Virus Lab., U. Calif., Berkeley, 1957-58; USPHS trainee in virology, 1958-59; assoc. research biochemist Kaiser Found. Research Inst., 1959-64; assoc. prof. biology Boston U., 1965-69, prof., 1969—; assoc. specialist Space Sci. Lab., U. Calif., 1963-65; vis. scientist Max Planck Inst. Molecular Biology, 1971; research assoc. in hist. of sci. U. Calif., Berkeley, 1976-78. Research grantee NIH, NSF, Am. Cancer Soc., Am. Heart Assn., Nat. Endowment Humanities. Mem. AAAS, Am. Soc. Biol. Chemists, Am. Soc. Cell Biology, Endocrine Soc., Hist. Sci. Soc. Office: Dept of Biology Boston University Boston MA 02215 *

RAAD, VIRGINIA, pianist, lectr.; b. Salem, W.Va., Aug. 13, 1925; d. Joseph M. and Martha (Joseph) Raad; B.A., Wellesley Coll., 1947; spl. student New Eng. Conservatory Music, 1947-48; diplome Ecole Normale de Musique, Paris, 1950; Doctorat de l'Universite (French Govt. grantee 1950-52, 54-55), U. Paris, 1955. Artist-in-residence Salem Coll., 1959-70; musician-in-residence N.C. Arts Council, 1971-72; concerts, lectures, master classes at Carleton Coll., Northfield, Minn., Viterbo Coll., Portland State U., Notre Dame U., Mt. Mary Coll., Mundelein Coll., Trinity Coll., Washington, Phillips Gallery, Washington, Norton Gallery, Rollins Coll., Marietta (Ohio) Coll., Huntington (W.Va.) Galleries, W.Va. U., Coll. William and Mary, Channel 13 (WQED), Pitts., Channel 24 (WWVU), Morgantown, W.Va., Lincoln (Pa.) U., U. Pitts., U. Mich., Dearborn, Fordham U., N.Y. Piano Tchrs. Congress, So. Conn. State Coll., Wellesley (Mass.) Coll., Middlebury (Vt.) Coll., Manhattanville (N.Y.) Coll., Elmira (N.Y.) Coll., Ladycliff (N.Y.) Coll., numerous others; Am. rep. Debussy Colloque, Paris, 1962; adjudicator W.Va. Music Tchrs. Assn., W.Va. Fedn. Music Clubs, Nat. Guild Piano Tchrs. Mem. com. Nat. Endowment Arts, 1979; panelist, grant reviewer Nat. Endowment Humanities, 1978—. Named Outstanding W.Va. Woman Educator, Delta Kappa Gamma, 1965; included in Schlesinger Library on History of Women in Am., Radcliffe Coll., 1967; Am. Council Learned Socs. grantee, 1962. Mem. Soc. Francaise de Musicologie, Am. Musicol. Soc. (regional officer 1960-65), Am. Soc. for Aesthetics, Internat. Musicol. Soc., Coll. Music Soc., Music Tchrs. Nat. Assn., Contbg. author Debussy et l'Evolution de la Musique au XXe siècle, 1965; also articles in profl. jours. Address: 60 Terrace Ave Salem WV 26426

RAAPHORST, MADELEINE ROUSSEAU, educator; b. Tours, France, Sept. 20, 1918; d. Eugene Rene and Jeanne Marie (Bergeron) Rousseau; came to U.S., 1954, naturalized, 1959; Licence en Droit, U. Paris, 1942; Ph.D., Rice U., 1959; children—Christine, Beatrice. Instr. Tex. So. U., Houston, 1956, asst. prof., 1957-60; asst. prof. Ohio Wesleyan U., Delaware, 1960-63; asst. prof. French Rice U., Houston, 1963-65, asso. prof., 1965-70, prof. French, 1970—, chmn. dept. French and Italian, 1972-79; vis. prof. U. Houston, 1961, NDEA Insts., 1961-65. Recipient John Gardner award Rice U., 1959, Chevalier des Palmes Academiques, French Govt., 1975. Mem. MLA, Am. Assn. Tchrs. French, Alliance Francaise de Houston, So. Central Modern Lang. Assn., Houston Assn. Tchrs. Fgn. Langs. Author: Colette: Sa vie et son art, 1964; contbr. articles to profl. jours. Office: Dept French and Italian Rice Univ Houston TX 77001

RABBANI, LILLIAN DELARAM, microbiologist; b. Tehran, Iran, Oct. 25, 1943; d. Edward and Miriam (Yadegar) Rabbani; came to U.S., 1955, naturalized, 1962; B.S., CCNY, 1966; Ph.D., Cornell U. Med. Sch., 1974. Microbiologist, 1970; postdoctoral fellow biology N.Y. U., N.Y.C., 1975-76, acting prin. investigator, 1975; postdoctoral asso. virology Yale U. Sch. Medicine, 1976-77, Cornell U. Med. Sch., 1978, fellow, 1980-82; research asso. in molecular biology Columbia U., 1979-80; instr. med. microbiology Cornell Med. Sch., 1971-72. NIH predoctoral grantee, 1970-74. Mem. N.Y. Acad. Scis., Am. Soc. for Microbiology, Am. Chem. Soc., AAAS. Research on protein chemistry, cell regulation, membranes. Home: 539 W 112th St New York NY 10025

RABE, JEAN MARIE, publishing co. exec.; b. Dickinson, N.D., Jan. 11, 1942; d. Arthur William and Marie Agnes (Zielsdorf) R.; B.A. in Elem. Edn., U. Wash., Seattle, 1963; M.Ed., Whitworth Coll., Spokane, 1968. Tchr. schs. in Wash., D.C. and Calif., 1963-72; dist. sales mgr. World Book-Childcraft Internat., Inc., Spokane, 1974-79, career sales person, 1980—; dir. Seven Up Bottling Co., Spokane, 1975-78. Recipient various awards for sales performance. Mem. U. Wash. Alumni Assn. (dist. gov. 1978-80), Whitworth Coll. Alumni Assn., Spokane Coll. Women's Assn., Alpha Phi. Republican. Presbyterian. Office: W 106 Mission St Spokane WA 99201

RABENOLD, KATHRYN TUTTLE, missionary, pianist, public accountant; b. Burlington Boro, Pa., Apr. 21, 1907; d. Clay F. and Mae Elsie (Beach) Tuttle; student public schs., Sayre, Pa., courses Internat. Accts. Soc., Pa. State U.; m. LeRoy M. Cook, Dec. 26, 1929 (dec. June 1953); children—Doris Anne (Mrs. Thomas P. Knapp), William LeRoy; m. 2d, Clarence R. Rabenold, Sept. 19, 1959 (dec. June 1971). Bookkeeper, Merritt Plumbing Shop, Waverly, N.Y., 1923-26; clk.-stenographer Ingersoll-Rand Co., Athens, Pa., 1926-29; payroll clk. Perfection Laundry, Sayre, 1930; partner with husband in acctg. office, Athens, 1937-53; owner, operator Cook Acctg. Service, Athens, 1953-69; public acct. with H. E. Weller, Athens, 1969-77; pianist with Patsy Prescott, gospel singer, 1977—. Telephone counselor Trinity Broadcasting Assn., Phoenix; mem. Glendale Women Aglow Fellowship. Enrolled to practice before IRS. Mem. Nat., Pa. socs. public accts., Nat. Soc. Tax Cons. (life). Mem. Assembly of God Ch. Home: 6500 W Glendale Ave Sp 49 Glendale AZ 85301

RABINOF, SYLVIA, pianist, educator; b. N.Y.C.; d. Morris and Fannie (Edelstein) Smith; student N.Y. U.; Mus.D. (hon.), Lincoln Meml. U., 1947; m. Benno Rabinof, violinist, Sept. 17, 1945. Debut as pianist with Pasdeloup Orch., Paris, 1943, Town Hall, N.Y.C., 1943; appeared with husband as duo, U.S., Can., Europe, Middle East, Bermuda, V.I.; soloist with symphony orchs. in Phila., Ind., Portland (Oreg.), Athens (Greece), Haifa; soloist recordings Decca Records and Paganiniana; mem. piano faculty State U. N.Y., Fredonia, 1970, Bklyn. Coll., 1971, Juilliard Sch. Music, 1971-79, Brevard Music Center, N.C., 1973-79. Mem. ASCAP, Piano Tchrs. Congress N.Y., Am. Music Tchrs. League, Sigma Alpha Iota. Clubs: Musicians of N.Y. (pres.), N.Y., Fed. Music. Author: Musicianship through Improvisation and the Improvisor, 1969. Composer: Three Profiles, piano; The Deluge, cantata. Contbr. articles to music jours. Home: Pump House Rd Brewster NY 10509

RABINOWITZ, MICHELE NANCY, clin. psychologist; b. Phila., Feb. 17, 1947; d. Jacob Morris and Betty (Cohen) R.; B.A., George Washington U., 1969; M.A., Montclair State Coll., 1971; Psy.D. in Psychology, Rutgers U., 1977; m. Joshua Rabinowitz, June 15, 1969; children—Shana, Beth. Sch. psychologist, Bridgewater, N.J., 1971-73, Middletown, N.J., 1973-74, Cranford, N.J., 1974-76; psychol. cons., adj. prof. Kean Coll. Evaluation Clinic, Union, N.J., 1977-79; psychol. cons. Navesink Diagnostic and Treatment Center, Red Bank, N.J., 1977—; pvt. practice psychotherapy, Red Bank, 1979—; sch. psychologist Winfield Park (N.J.) Sch., 1979—; adj. prof. community services Brookdale Community Coll., 1978—. Mem. Community Services Council, 1978-81; v.p. community services Nat. Council Jewish Women, 1978-80, v.p. edn., 1980-82; bd. dirs. Mental Health Assn. Monmouth County, 1978—. active United Way. Mem. Am. Psychol. Assn., N.J. Assn. Sch. Psychologists, Monmouth Ocean County Psychol. Assn. (treas. 1979-81, sec. 1981-83), N.J. Psychol. Assn., Nat. Register Health Service Providers in Psychology, Phi Beta Kappa, Phi Sigma Sigma. Club: Hadassah. Office: 110 Hwy 35 Red Bank NJ 07701

RACANSKY, BARBARA PHILLIPS, psychiat. social worker; b. Ashford, Conn., Mar. 15, 1928; d. Joseph W. and Mary Elizabeth (Baca) Phillips; B.S., U. Conn., 1951; M.S.W., U. So. Calif., 1961. Child welfare worker Ventura County Welfare Dept., 1959-63, sr. social work supr., 1963-65; social work supr. Family Centered Services Project, New Haven, Conn., 1965-66; social worker Children's Center, Hamden, Conn., 1966-67; psychiat. social work supr. Conn. Valley Hosp., Middletown, 1967-74; chief psychiat. social worker Norwich (Conn.) Hosp., 1974-78; dir. psychiat. social work Dept. Mental Health, State of Conn., Hartford, 1978—. Mem. Nat. Assn. Social Workers, Acad. Cert. Social Workers, Soc. Hosp. Social Work Dirs. Office: 90 Washington St Hartford CT 06115

RACHWAL, ESTHER BALDISSEROTTO, savs. and loan exec.; b. Paterson, N.J., Feb. 26, 1924; d. Anthony and Annette (Sella) Baldisserotto; student Sherwood Sch. Bus., Am. Inst. Fin. Edn.; m. Walter J. Rachwal, Oct. 12, 1969. Asst. sec. First Savings and Loan Assn. of Fair Lawn (N.J.), 1942-46; asst. sec., treas. First Fed. Savs. and Loan Assn. of Paterson, 1947-60, 2d v.p., 1960-66, exec. v.p., 1967-81, pres., 1981—, dir., 1966—. Treas. Cedar Cliff Methodist Ch., Haledon, N.J., 1960-69. Mem. Passaic County Savs. and Loan League (pres. 1960-62), Women's Assn. Savs. and Loan Instns. (pres. 1958-60). Clubs: Hamilton, High Mountain Golf, Zonta Internat. (rec. sec. Greater Paterson area chpt. 1965-67, treas. 1979-81). Office: 177 Market St Paterson NJ 07505

RACINE, BARBARA ANN, realtor; b. Dorchester, Wis., Jan. 23, 1949; d. Alvin Frank and Barbara J. Stoiber; student U. Wis., Eau Claire, 1967-68; m. Joseph A. Racine, Sept. 16, 1978; 1 son Greg. With Pratt Agy., Longmont, Colo., 1972-75, Abstract & Title Co., 1975-78; owner, broker Real Estate Exchange, Gillette, Wyo., 1979—. Mem. Women in Bus. (v.p. 1979), Nat. Assn. Realtors, Wyo. Assn. Realtors (Outstanding Service award 1980), Campbell County Bd. Realtors (sec.), Farm and Land Inst., Campbell County C. of C. (sec.). Republican. Roman Catholic. Home: 3103 Foothills Blvd Gillette WY 82716 Office: PO Box 1898 Gillette WY 82716

RACKIN, PHYLLIS ROSALYN, educator; b. Newark, Sept. 15, 1933; d. Milton Philip and Ethel (Shulman) Finkelstein; B.A., Douglass Coll., 1954; M.A., Auburn U., 1957; Ph.D. in English (Univ. fellow), U. Ill., 1962; m. Donald Rackin, Jan. 1, 1954; children—Rebecca Jane, Ethel Elizabeth Gussie. Manuscript editor Modern Romance mag., N.Y.C., 1955; teaching asst. Auburn (Ala.) U., 1956-57, U. Ill., Urbana, 1960-62; asso. prof. Beaver Coll., Glenside, Pa., 1970-71; mem. faculty U. Pa., Phila., 1962—, assoc. prof. English in gen. honors, 1975—, dir. gen. honors program, 1981—. Democratic committeewoman 17th div. Phila. Mem. MLA, Northeast MLA (chmn. Shakespeare sect. 1971), Women for Equal Opportunity U. Pa. (v.p. 1972-74, 82-83). Jewish. Author: Shakespeare's Tragedies, 1978. Contbr. articles to profl. jours. Home: 405 W Price St Philadelphia PA 19144 Office: Box 41 College Hall U Pa Philadelphia PA 19104

RADDATZ, DIANE, savs. and loan exec.; b. Chgo., July 20, 1944; d. William Edward and Mildred R.; student Loyola U., Rome, 1962-63; B.A., Santa Clara U., 1965; M.A., DePaul U., 1969; postgrad. U. Chgo., 1978-79. Asst. to dean Med. Sch. Northwestern U., 1970; with East Side Savs. and Loan Assn., Chgo., 1967—, pres., 1978—. Chmn., fund raising and ednl. com. East Side Cancer Soc., 1981-82. Mem. U.S. Savs. and Loan League, Ill. Savs. and Loan League, East Side C. of C. Roman Catholic. Feature columnist Daily Calumet, 1959-60. Office: 11157 Ewing Ave Chicago IL 60617

RADELOFF, DEANNA JEAN BOLFA, educator; b. Gibsonburg, Ohio, Sept. 18, 1940; d. John and Geraldine F. (Martin) Bolfa; B.S., Bowling Green State U., 1962; M.S., Ohio State U., 1965; Ed.S., U. Toledo, 1973; Ph.D., U. Mich., 1978; m. Roger Radeloff, June 13, 1964; children—Brentley John, Dean Franklin. Tchr. high sch., 1964-68; mem. faculty Bowling Green (Ohio) State U., 1962-64, 73—, asso. prof. home econs., 1978—; propr. Color Charisma; cons. Head Start; sec. Ohio Child Devel. Consortium, 1973-76; chmn. Ohio Early Childhood Tchr. Edn. Cert. Force, 1977-80. Mem. Am. Home Econs. Assn., Nat. Assn. Edn. of Young Children, Assn. Coll. Profs. Textiles and Clothing, Ohio Assn. Edn. Young Children (chmn. communications sect.), Internat. Platform Assn., Pi Lambda Theta, Omicron Nu, Phi Delta Kappa. Lutheran. Author: Experiences In Math for Young Children, 1978; Children in Your Life, 1981. Home: 840 Oak Knoll Dr Perrysburg OH 43551 Office: 310 Johnston Hall Bowling Green State U Bowling Green OH 43402

RADER, MILLICENT CAROLYN, artist; b. Utica, N.Y., May 13, 1936; d. LeRoy Arthur and Irene Anna (Schwenk) R.; B.F.A., Wichita State U., 1958; M.F.A., Cath. U. Am., 1975; postgrad. Trinity Coll., 1980-81; 1 dau., Heather Viola Harris. Sr. tech. illustrator Analytic Services, Inc., Falls Church, Va., 1959-67, cons., 1967-68; co-owner MRRH Studio Gallery, Fairfax, Va., 1970-75; corr. Begonia Soc. Jour., 1966-72, Indoor Light Gardening Soc. Jour., 1967-72, Alexandria (Va.) Gazette, 1972; artist-in-residence, bd. dirs. Trident Found., Washington, 1974-77; instr. art women's bur. D.C. Dept. Corrections, 1974—; instr. Nat. Park Service, Art Barn, Washington, 1976-79; tech. asst. Catholic U., 1974-75; artist in residence St. Anns Ch., Washington, 1976—; adv. bd., art cons., dir. exhbns, Women's Nat. Bank, Washington, 1978—; one-man show Regis Coll., Boston, 1974; exhibited in group shows Wichita (Kans.) Art Mus., 1957, 58, 59, Mulvane Art Inst., Topeka, 1958, Smithsonian Instn., Washington, 1962, 63, Dept. Commerce, Washington, 1966, Salt Palace, Salt Lake City, 1970, Goldman Fine Arts Gallery, Rockville, Md., 1971, 72, Arts Club, Washington, 1973, 74, 75, 76, Art Barn, Washington, 1973, 74, 75, 77, Cath. U. Am., Washington, 1973, 74, FDIC, 1975, 76, 77, 78, Am. Spirit Gallery, Washington, 1974, Salve Regina Gallery, Washington, 1974, Sculpture Garden at Firenze, Washington, 1974, Martin Luther King Library, Washington, 1976, 77,

78, Nat. Geol. Survey, Reston, Va., 1977, Women's Nat. Bank, Washington, 1978, 80, others; represented in permanent collections: The Vatican, Holy Name Coll., Wichita State U. Area chmn. March of Dimes, 1970-74; asst. Stepping Stones, Washington, 1965—; art cons. Office of Worship, Archdiocese of Washington, 1980—; campaign mgr. Congl. candidate, 1972. Mem. exec. bd. No. Va. Conservation Council, 1973. Recipient best in show award, best portrait, state exhibit Nat. League Am. Pen Women, 1970, also 1st prize in nat. yearbook competition, 1971. Mem. Artists Equity Assn. (dir., public relations 1974-75), Stained Glass Assn. Am. (asso.), Washington Watercolor Assn. (exhbns. chmn. 1973, 75, 76, pres. 1974-75, 76-77, bd. mgrs. 1976—), Nat. League Am. Pen Women (br. v.p. 1972-74, state art chmn. 1972-74), Cultural Alliance Washington (asso.), Va. Women's Polit. Caucus (state council 1972), Mortar Bd., Kappa Pi (sec.), Delta Delta Delta (v.p.). Roman Catholic. Mem. 3d Order St. Francis. Illustrator: Artist, Sex and Health, 1982; adv. bd. Outstanding Young Artists in An. Elem. Schs., 1982—; subject of various publs., TV program. Office: 4001 Yuma St Washington DC 20016

RADEWALD, DIANE, ct. reporter; b. Niles, Mich., Apr. 24, 1954; d. Stanley Otto and Barbara Ann (Meyer) R. Supr., Radewald Farms, 1965-74; resident asst. Ferris State Coll., 1973; ct. reporter Holle & White Ct. Reporters, St. Joseph, Mich., 1974-77, Radewald Reporting, Niles, 1977-79; realtor asso. Crest Home Sales, Niles, 1977-79; ofcl. ct. reporter 2d Jud. Circuit, Berrien County, Mich., 1979—; part-time instr. Lake Mich. Coll., Benton Harbor, 1979—; instr. Swiss Valley Ski Resort, Jones, Mich., 1976, 77. Youth-teen advisor YMCA, Niles, 1976, 77. Recipient Mich. 4-H Key Club award, 1971, 4-H I Dare You award, 1972; Mich. State Consumer Edn. Award, 1972; named Berrien County Apple Queen, 1972; YMCA Service award, 1976, 77; certified shorthand reporter, Mich. Mem. Nat. (registered profl. reporter), Mich. shorthand reporters assns., Central Mich. Ski Instrs. Assn., Southwestern Mich. Bd. Realtors. Republican. Lutheran. Home: 4550 M 140 Niles MI 49120 Office: Berrien County Courthouse Saint Joseph MI 49085

RADFORD, KATHERINE CHAMBERLIN HYATT, psychologist; b. Louisville, Feb. 17, 1911; d. Leonard Powell and Laura Talbot (Galt) Hyatt; B.A., Lynchburg Coll., 1953; M.A., Duke U., 1960; M.S., Richmond Profl. Inst., 1961; Ed.D., U. Va., 1967; m. du Val Radford, July 18, 1929; children—Laura Talbot Radford Goley, Anne Waller Radford Barrett. Rural and urban public schs. classroom tchr and adminstr. Central Va., 1948-58; instr. Richmond Profl. Inst., 1959-60, U. Va., 1964-65; mem. faculty Lynchburg (Va.) Coll., 1965-76, emeritus, 1976—; pvt. practice psychology Radford Psychol. Services, Lynchburg, Va., 1976—. Bd. dirs. Camp Child and Learning Bridge Sch., 1975-79; bd. dirs. Central Va. Mental Health and Mental Related Services, 1968-74, chmn., 1974. NIH grantee, 1962, Fla. State sch. psychology trainee, 1962-63. Mem. Am. Psychol. Assn., Nat. Register Health Service Providers, Eastern Psychol. Assn., Va. Psychol. Assn., DAR, Colonial Dames Am. (mem. Va. com.). Episcopalian. Home: Woodbourne Farm Route 1 Forest VA 24551 Office: 1900 Tate Springs Rd Lynchburg VA

RADFORD, MARY GLADYS, psychologist; b. Hot Springs, Ark., Aug. 18, 1927; d. James Edward and Amy (Anderson) R.; B.S., U. Chattanooga, 1962; M.A., George Peabody Coll., 1964, Ph.D., 1970; m. Stanley Wallace Hahn, July 19, 1975; children—Dan, David. Asst. to dir. Inst. Mental Retardation and Intellectual Devel., Peabody Coll., 1970; clin. psychologist Chattanooga Psychiat. Clinic, 1970-74; staff teaching psychologist William S. Hall Psychiat. Inst., Columbia, S.C., 1974-75; acting chief mental health unit VA Outpatient clinic, Chattanooga, 1975-76; psychologist Area Edn. Agy. 15, University Park, Iowa, 1976-81, Knoxville (Iowa) VA Med. Center, 1981—. Grad. fellow, 1964-68. Mem. Am. Psychol. Assn., Nat. Register Health Service Providers in Psychology, Southeastern Psychol. Assn., Iowa Psychol. Assn. Home: 1015 High Ave E Oskaloosa IA 52577 Office: VA Med Center Knoxville IA 50138

RADFORD-ROBINSON, BRENDA JOYCE, mental health agy. exec.; b. Gadsden, Ala., Aug. 2, 1949; d. Calude, Jr. and Ida Mae (Wyatt) R.; B.A. cum laude, Stillman Coll., 1970; M.S.W., U. Ala., 1973; m. Paul Robinson, July 5, 1980. Psychiat. social worker Partlow State Sch. and Hosp., Tuscaloosa, Ala., 1973, Jefferson County Bur. Mental Health, Birmingham, Ala., 1974-76; psychiat. social worker CED Mental Health Center, Gadsden, 1976-77, unit chief parial hosp., 1977—; bd. dirs. CED Fellowship House. Mem. Nat. Assn. Social Workers, Am. Assn. Partial Hospitalization, CED Mental Health Assn., Mission Soc., NAACP, Delta Sigma Theta. Democrat. Methodist. Club: Cosma. Home: 914 N 9th St Gadsden AL 35901 Office: 901 Goodyear Ave Gadsden AL 35903

RADIN, JOAN PAULINE, pharmacist; b. Stratford, Conn., June 6, 1933; d. Joseph Edwin and Anna McNamara; B.S. in Pharmacy, U. Conn., 1955; m. Frank Robert Radin, Aug. 1, 1957; children—Cheryl Ann, Jo-Ann Pauline, Kathleen Ann. Pharmacist, Blake Drug Co., Ansonia, Conn., 1963-67; pharmacist Lear Pharmacy, Ansonia, 1955-57, 68-75, owner, pharmacist, 1975—; cons. nursing homes. Mem. Nat. Assn. Retail Druggists, Conn. Pharm. Assn., Nat. Assn. Female Execs., U.S. C. of C., Ansonia C. of C. Nat. Fedn. Ind. Bus., Lower Naugatuck Valley Ostomy Assn. Office: 198 Wakelee Ave Ansonia CT 06401

RADKE, LOIS DE ORSEY SNYDER, public relations exec.; b. Whitinsville, Mass., Aug. 12, 1929; d. Francis X. and Germaine Gagnon De Orsey; A.B., Lenoir-Rhyne Coll., 1953; postgrad. Duke U., 1953-56; m. Harry M. Snyder, Jr. (dec. 1974); children—Stephen De Orsey, Melissa Anne; m. 2d, Donald N. Radke, Oct. 10, 1981. French tchr. Lenoir-Rhyne Coll., 1952-53; tchr. English, speech and drama Hickory (N.C.) High Sch., 1953-54; dir. public relations Hickory Furniture Mart, 1979-81; pvt. practice public relations, Hickory, 1981—. Pres., Hickory Dyslexia Found., Catawba County Arts Council, Hickory Landmarks Soc., ARC, Catawba County Mental Health Assn., N.C. Cerebral Palsy Assn. Recipient Outstanding Service award N.C. Assn. Cerebral Palsy, 1965. Mem. Catawba County Execs. Club, Catawba County C. of C. (dir.), Lenoir-Rhyne Coll. Alumni Assn. (pres.), Alpha Psi Omega. Republican. Home: 20th Ave Dr NW Hickory NC 28601

RADMACHER, CAMILLE J., librarian; b. Monmouth, Ill., Apr. 14, 1917; d. Harry M. and Esther (Greenleaf) R.; student Monmouth Coll., 1935-37. With adult dept. Warren County Library, Monmouth, 1937-48, head county librarian, 1948—, exec. dir. Western Ill. Library System, 1965—; exec. dir. Nat. Library Week in State of Ill., 1959. Mem. Monmouth Coll. Community Concert Lecture Bd., 1967-72; mem. adv. com. Ill. State Library, 1962-72. Mem. Ill. Library Assn. (Ill. Librarian Citation award 1967), Women's Nat. Book Assn., DAR. Methodist. Clubs: Order Eastern Star, Altrusa (treas. 1968-69, dir. 1978—). Home: 500 N 1st St Monmouth IL 61462 Office: 60-62 Public Sq Monmouth IL 61462

RAFFERTY, CAROL A., publishing co. exec.; b. Wayne, N.J., Sept. 5, 1937; d. William J. and Ella (Suter) R.; B.A., Cornell U., 1959. Employment interviewer Macy's Co., N.Y.C., 1960-63; personnel asst. MacMillan Co., N.Y.C., 1963-64; asst. personnel dir. Scholastic Inc., N.Y.C., 1964-69, personnel mgr., 1969-79, personnel dir., v.p. personnel, 1977—. Mem. N.Y. Personnel Mgmt. Assn., Am. Compensation Assn., Am. Soc. Personnel Adminstrn. Office: 50 W 44th St New York NY 10036

RAFFERTY, GENEVIEVE KENNEDY, social service agy. adminstr.; b. Davenport, Iowa, Jan. 21, 1922; d. Thomas Cyril and Mabel Veronica (Finefield) Kennedy; B.A., St. Ambrose Coll., 1942; postgrad. U. Iowa, 1972; m. Daniel J. Rafferty, Aug. 22, 1942; children—Daniel D., Michele M., Genevieve, Thomas K., Eileen M., Margaret M., Sheila M. Real estate saleswoman Manhard Realty, Moline, Ill., 1950-59; substitute tchr., Rock Island, Ill., 1963-67; head start tchr. Rock Island-Scott County Dept. Social Services, 1966; public welfare worker Scott County Dept. Social Services, Davenport, Iowa, 1967-72; exec. dir. Info., Referral and Assistance Service, Rock Island, 1972—; commr. Rock Island Housing Authority Adv. Bd.; mem. Quad-City Council on Crime and Delinquency, 1977-80; mem. Rock Island County Council on Alcoholism, 1976—; chairperson CETA Adv. Bd., 1982—; dir. Quint-City Drug Abuse. Named Social Worker of Yr. Quad-City, Nat Assn. Social Workers, 1973. Mem. Nat. Assn. Social Workers, Iowa Council Info. and Referral Providers, Nat. Conf. Social Welfare, Ill. Welfare Assn., NOW, Alliance Info. and Referral Services. Republican. Roman Catholic. Office: 2002 3d Ave Rock Island IL 61201

RAFSKY, JEANNE CAROL, physician; b. N.Y.C., July 16, 1925; d. Henry A. and Bertha M. (Fischel) Fafsky; A.B. cum laude, Brown U., 1945; M.D., N.Y. U., 1949; m. Norman Jaspan, Dec. 22, 1946; children—Michael D., Ronald H. Rotating intern Lenox Hill Hosp., N.Y.C., 1949-50, resident in medicine, 1951-53, resident in gastroenterology, 1953-54, asst. adj. gastroenterology, 1954—; asst. in medicine Univ. Hosp., N.Y.C., 1954-58; clin. asst. vis. physician Bellevue Hosp., N.Y.C., 1954-58; gastroscopist Grand Central Hosp., 1956-62; asst. attending radiologist Univ. Hosp., 1958-67; clin. teaching asst. in radiology N.Y. U., 1960-67; physician Sidney Hellman Hosp., 1964—; cons. gastroscopist Wickersham Hosp., 1965—; gastroenterologist, gastrointestinalradiologist Sidney Hillman Health Center, 1966—; adv. council Senate Com. on Health, 1966-70; specialist in internal medicine and gastroenterology N.Y. State Workmen's Compensation Bd. Diplomate Nat. Bd. Med. Examiners. Fellow N.Y. Acad. Medicine; mem. Am. Soc. Gastrointestinal Endoscopy, N.Y. County Med. Soc., Acad. Sci., AMA. Jewish. Club: Brown University (N.Y.C.). Contbr. articles to profl. jours. Office: 79 E 79th St New York NY 10021

RAGAINI, FLORENCE SCHUELE, coll. adminstr.; b. Winston, Mo., July 23, 1931; d. Henry George and Pauline Mary (Wagner) Schuele; A.A., St. Louis Community Coll., 1974; B.A., St. Louis U., 1978; children—Stephen, Daniel (dec.). Sec., Consumers Pub. Power Dist., Columbus, Nebr., 1949-52; stenographer FBI, Washington, 1953-54, Chgo. and Northwestern Ry., Chadron, Nebr., 1956-59; sec. St. Louis Community Coll., 1964-69, office services mgr., 1969-78, asst. dir. bus. services, 1978—, mem. charter alumni bd., 1980. Internal loaned exec. United Way, 1978, 79; lector Sacred Heart Ch., Florissant, Mo., 1981, 82. Mem. Adminstrv. Mgmt. Soc., Mo. Assn. Community and Jr. Colls. (bd. dirs. 1977). Republican. Roman Catholic. Home: 1004 Castello St Florissant MO 63031 Office: 3400 Pershall Rd St Louis MO 63135

RAGAN, ELIZABETH HOFFMAN (MRS. HERBERT TOMLINSON RAGAN), wholesale co. exec.; b. Albemarle, N.C., Nov. 11, 1916; d. Joseph Filson and Lilly Bassett (Carter) Hoffman; cert. bus. adminstrn. High Point Coll., 1937; m. Herbert Tomlinson Ragan, Oct. 14, 1939; 1 son, Herbert Tomlinson. Head bond dept. Sunflower Ordnance Works, Hercules Powder Co., DeSota, Kans., 1942-45; sec.-treas. Ragan-Carmichael, Inc., High Point, N.C., 1956-74, Staple Products, Inc., High Point, 1956-74, R & C Holding Co., Inc., High Point, 1956-74, sec. Ragan Hardware Co., Inc. (merger), High Point, 1974—; trustee Ragan-Carmichael, Inc. Profit Sharing Trust and Pension Trust. Cellist, N.C. Symphony, 1932-35. Mem. adv. bd. Maryfield Nursing Home, 1975-79; bd. visitors High Point Coll., 1979—; mem. exec. bd. Friends of Guilford Coll. Library. Democrat. Mem. Soc. of Friends (organist, choir dir.), High Point Hist. Soc. (dir. 1977-81, pres. 1979-80). Author, compiler: The Lineage of the Amos Ragan Family, 1976. Home: 201 Lake Drive East Thomasville NC 27360 Office: 1116 Ward St High Point NC 27261

RAGINS, NAOMI (MRS. MARK GOLDSMITH), psychiatrist; b. Chgo., Apr. 23, 1926; d. Oscar B. and Ida (Kraus) Ragins; student U. Ariz., 1943-44; Ph.B., U. Chgo., 1946, B.S., 1947, M.D., 1951; postgrad. U. Pitts., 1952-57, Pitts. Psychoanalytic Inst., 1967; m. Mark Goldsmith, July 31, 1955. Intern, U. Chgo. Clinics, 1951-52; resident and teaching fellow Western Psychiat. Inst. and Clinic, U. Pitts. Med. Sch., 1952-55, 56-57; practice medicine specializing in adult and child psychiatry and psychoanalysis, Pitts.; clin. asso. prof. child psychiatry U. Pitts. Med. Sch., 1968—; faculty Pitts. Psychoanalytic Inst., 1968—, tng. and supervising analyst, 1971—; cons. Carlow Coll., 1958-70; staff Western Psychiat. Inst. and Clinic, Pitts., 1957—; sr. supervising psychiatrist, research asso. Pitts. Child Guidance Center, 1957-73; teaching cons. Beaver-Rochester Mental Health Clinics, Warren State Hosp., Arsenal Family and Children's Center, Children's Hosp. Pitts., others. Mem. AMA, Am. Psychoanalytic Assn., Am. Psychiat. Assn., Pitts. Psychiat. Soc., Pitts. Psychoanalytic Soc., Am. Orthopsychiat. Assn., Am. Acad. Child Psychiatry, Assn. for Child Psychoanalysis, Alpha Omega Alpha. Office: 121 University Pl Pittsburgh PA 15213

RAGLAND, ALWINE MULHEARN, lawyer, judge; b. Monroe, La., July 28, 1913; d. Peter Sherlock and Alwine Louise Johanna (Peters) Mulhearn; A.A., Principia Coll., 1932; J.D., Tulane U., 1935; m. LeRoy Smith, 1947 (dec. 1971); children—LeRoy, Caroline Smith Christman; m. 2d, L. Percy Ragland. Admitted to La. bar, 1935; individual practice law, Tallulah, La., 1935-72; partner firm Mulhearn & Smith, Tallulah, 1972-74; spl. asst. atty. gen. La., 1954; atty. for inheritance tax Coll. La., 1965-73; town atty., Delta, La., 1973-74; judge 16th Jud. Dist., Lake Providence, La., 1974—, 2d Circuit Ct. Appeals, Shreveport, 1976; former pres. Smith Abstract Co., Inc. Active Silver Waters council Girl Scouts U.S.A., 1938-64, dist. dir., 1964; den mother Cub Scouts Am., 1956-57; pres. Band Boosters, 1964-65, PTA, 1965-66; mem. jud. bd. Delta Christian Sch., 1967-74. Mem. Am. Bar Assn., 6th Jud. Dist. Bar Assn. (pres. 1945), La. Bar Assn., Am. Judicature Soc., Am. Judges Assn., La. Judges Assn., Nat. Council Juvenile Ct. Judges, La. Council Juvenile Ct. Judges, So. Juvenile Ct. Judges, Assn. Trial Lawyers Am., La. Trial Lawyers Assn., Family Conciliation Cts. and Services, Nat. Juvenile Ct. Service Assn., La. Conf. Social Welfare, Practicing Law Inst. Methodist. Clubs: Lake Providence Ladies Golf and Tennis, Madison Parish Book. Index editor Tulane Law Rev. Bd., 1932-35. Home: PO Box 392 Lake Providence LA 71254 Office: Court House Bldg PO Box 392 Lake Providence LA 71254

RAGLAND, MARTHA RAGSDALE, civic worker; b. Paducah, Ky., May 14, 1906; d. Joseph Senter and Viva (Troutt) Ragsdale; A.B., Vanderbilt U., 1927, M.A., 1928; m. Thomas Ragland, July 27, 1932; children—Thomas, Sandra Ragland Demson. Researcher, Nat. Research Council, Washington, 1929-32; tchr. econs. U. Chattanooga, 1946; mem. Democratic Nat. Com., 1952-56; Tenn. del. Dem. Nat. Conv., 1952; vice chmn. Vol. for Stevenson-Kefauver, 1956; U.S. del. Atlantic Congress of NATO, London, 1959; chmn. Tenn. adv. com. to U.S. Commn. on Civil Rights, 1963-69; mem. Fedn. Adv. Council on Employment Security, 1963-69; pres. Tenn. Women's Polit. Caucus, 1974; mem. steering com. Nat. Womens Polit. Caucus, 1974—; trustee Citizens Research Found., Los Angeles, 1976—. Mem. LWV (nat. dir. 1944, pres. Tenn. chpt. 1945), NOW, AAUW. Episcopalian. Author: After Three Centuries, 1935. Home: 3821 Abbott Martin Rd Nashville TN 37215

RAGOSIN, EDRIA DEANNE MIRMAN, speech pathologist; b. Cleve., May 30, 1938; d. Ben and Millie Mirman; B.S., Kent State U., 1968, M.A., 1971; m. David R. Ragosin, Dec. 21, 1958; children—Tami, Teri, Sam. Resource tchr. hard of hearing classes Stark County Schs., 1968-70; clin. supr. Goodwill Rehab. Center, 1971-78; pvt. practice speech-lang. pathology, Canton, Ohio, 1978—; speech and lang. pathologist Alliance Vis. Nurses Assn.; cons., lang. devel. specialist Carroll County Bd. Mental Retardation, 1979-81; speech pathologist, audiologist VA Outpatient Clinic, Canton, 1980—. Vice pres., chmn. personnel com., trustee Child and Adolescent Service Center, Children's Mental Health Assn.; trustee Temple Israel Sisterhood; chmn. parents group Crate and Canvas Youth Theatre; a team coordinator Jewish Marriage Encounter Northeastern Ohio, sec. treas., Cleve.; prin. Canton Community Hebrew Sch.; sec.-treas. Gov.'s Com. on Employment of the Handicapped, Canton. Mem. Am. Speech and Hearing Assn. (cert. clin. competence), Ohio Speech and Hearing Assn. Democrat. Jewish. Clubs: Quota (pres. Canton 1977-79; chmn. com. 6th Dist., chmn. internat. community service com., mem. internat. speech and hearing com.); Hadassah (co-chmn. edn. com., co-editor newsletter). Home and Office: 2513 Rowland Ave NE Canton OH 44714

RAGOZZINO, JUDITH B., banker; b. N.Y.C., Feb. 8, 1940; d. Harold and Florence (Abrams) Martin; B.A. cum laude, Hunter Coll., 1960; M.A., 1967; postgrad. Columbia U., 1970-72; children—Mara Milrad, Joshua Milrad. Tchr. Latin, Mt. Vernon (N.Y.) High Sch., 1960-64; adj. prof. Hunter Coll., 1967-71, Bklyn. Coll., 1971-72; v.p., team leader, comml. lender Chem. Bank, N.Y.C., 1973—. Bd. dirs. Grace Ch. Sch., 1968-69; sec. Ind. Citizens of 9th Congressional Dist., 1964. Mem. Nat. Assn. U. Women, Hunter Alumni Assn., Phi Beta Kappa. Episcopalian. Office: 633 Third Ave New York NY 10017 *

RAHDERT, ELIZABETH ROSE QUANZ, clin. pharmacist, clin. psychologist; b. Evanston, Ill., May 13, 1935; d. Carl Peter and Josephine Anne (Kirk) Quanz; student Albert Ludwigs Universitat, Freiburg, W.Ger., 1955-56; B.S. in pharmacy, Purdue U., 1958, M.S. in Psychology, 1975, Ph.D. in Psychology (David Ross fellow), 1980; m. June 7, 1958 (div. 1982); children—David A., Diana M. Research pharmacologist asst. in biomed. research Dow Chem. Co., Indpls., 1959-61; asst. dir. spl. edn. Greater Lafayette (Ind.) Area Spl. Services, 1976-77; psychology intern VA Hosp., Danville, Ill., 1979-80; asst. prof. clin. pharmacy Purdue U., 1980—. Bd. dirs. Family Service Agy., Tippecanoe County, Ind., 1971-75; bd. dirs. Tippecanoe County Youth Services Bur., 1973-76, pres. bd., 1974-76. Mem. Am. Psychol. Assn., Ind. Psychol. Assn., Am. Pharm. Assn., Ind. Pharmacists Assn., Am. Soc. Hosp. Pharmacists, Ind. Soc. Hosp. Pharmacists, Am. Assn. Colls. Pharmacy, AAUW, Kappa Epsilon. Office: Clin Pharmacy Purdue U West Lafayette IN 47907

RAHEEL, MASTURA, textile scientist; b. Lahore, Pakistan, Mar. 1, 1938; d. Sultan Mohamad and Firdous Dean; M.S., Punjab U., 1959, Okla. State U., 1962; Ph.D., U. Minn., 1971; m. Akbar Javed Raheel, Jan. 25, 1959; children—Seemal, Salman. Asst. prof., head dept. textiles and clothing Home Econs. Coll., Lahore, Pakistan, 1960-77; lectr. textiles and clothing U. Minn., 1977-78; vis. prof. Ind. U., Bloomington, 1978; asst. prof. textile sci. U. Ill., Urbana, 1978—. Ford. Found. fellow, 1960-62, 68-71, research award grantee, 1979, 80. Mem. Am. Coll. Profs. Textiles and Clothing, Am. Assn. Textile Chemists and Colorists, Am. Home Econs. Assn., Omicron Nu, Sigma Xi. Contbr. research articles to profl. and tech. jours. Home: 1805 Rebecca Dr Champaign IL 61820 Office: 239 Bevier Hall U Ill Urbana IL 61801

RAHIMIAN, BONNIE LOU, educator; b. Lincoln, Kans., Apr. 23, 1947; d. Delbert Leroy and Wanette Mae (Miller) Anderson; B.S. in Spl. and Elem. Edn., Ft. Hays (Kans.) State Coll., 1972; M.A. in Teaching English as 2d Lang., U. Kans., Lawrence, 1977; m. Nasser (John) Rahimian, Feb. 1, 1969; children—Showrh, Chris. Tchr. Vietnam English program, Kansas City, Mo., 1972-75; tchr. adult continuing edn. English program, Lawrence, 1976; sr. English dir., supr., adminstrv. teaching supr. Iran, Am. Soc., Tehran, 1977-79; instr. English as 2d lang. U. Southwestern La., Lafayette. 1979—; cons. in field. Mem. TESOL. Home: 118 Scorates Pl Lafayette LA 70508

RAHM, KAREN ELIZABETH LANE, state ofcl.; b. Bklyn., Apr. 21, 1944; d. Gilbert H. and Joan Elizabeth (Dean) Lane, Jr.; A.A., Packer Collegiate Inst., 1962; B.A. magna cum laude, Allegheny Coll., 1964; M.A., Ind. U., 1966; m. Carl Michael Rahm, Feb. 3, 1968; 1 son, Christopher Michael. Economist, Fed. Res. Bank of N.Y., 1966-70; planning devel. officer Econ. Devel. Adminstrn., Seattle, 1970-71; successively urban economist, asst. dir. econ. devel., dir. econ. devel. Seattle Dept. Community Devel., 1971-77; mgr. planning div. King County, Seattle, 1977-81; dir. Wash. State Planning and Community Affairs Agy., Olympia, 1981—; mem. Wash. Corrections Standards Bd. Mem. Seattle Bd. Freeholders, 1974-75, Wash. Commn. Constl. Alternatives, 1976. Mem. Am. Econ. Assn., Seattle Economists Club, LWV, Lambda Alpha. Club: Mt. Baker Community. Office: MS GH 51 9th and Columbia Sts Olympia WA 98504

RAILSBACK, BERNICE HICKMAN (MRS. JAMES ERNEST RAILSBACK), educator; b. Mountain Home, Ark.; d. Charles Isaac and America Maria (Lewis) Hickman; student Mountain Home Coll., 1927, 29, Ark. State Coll., summers 1930-31; B.S., Tex. Tech U., 1941, M.S., 1951; m. James Ernest Railsback, June 9, 1932; children—Norman Leighton, Charles Hickman, Phyllis Elaine Railsback Carlton. Tchr. pub. schs., Budford, Ark., 1927-28; tchr., girls coach Salem (Ark.) Pub. Schs., 1929-32, McClung Sch., Slaton, Tex., 1933-34; tchr. Hodges Sch., Levelland, Tex., 1939-41; tchr. jr. high sch. math. and reading Levelland Pub. Schs., 1947-54, dir. elementary edn., 1954-70. Mem. exec. com. S. Plains Coll. Found.; state v.p., dir. Tex. affiliate Am. Heart Assn.; chmn. Levelland Bicentennial Assn., 1975-76; bd. dirs. S. Plains Mus.; past bd. dirs. Cook Meml. Hosp. Recipient poetry awards S. Plains Writers Assn., 1964, 65, 76, Writers Assn., 1976; Vol. Recognition award Tex. affiliate Am. Heart Assn., 1980; named Woman of Year, Levelland C. of C., 1969. Mem. Assn. Supervision and Curriculum Devel. (Tex. rep. to nat. bd. 1962-67, state pres. 1966-67, 69-70), Tex., West Tex. (regional pres. 1966-67) assns. supervision and curriculum devel., NEA, Tex. Elementary Prins. and Suprs. Assn., Tex. Assn. Instructional Suprs. (state pres. 1959-60), AAUW, Tex. Congress Parents and Tchrs. (life), Poetry Soc. Tex., South Plains Writers Assn., West Tex. Writers Guild, Tex. Assn. for Improvement of Reading, Internat. Reading Assn., Tex. Assn. Edn. Young Children, Assn. for Gifted, Tex. Edn. Agy. (mem. state certification com.), Nat., Tex. assns. Realtors, Hockley Cochran Bd. Realtors, Delta Kappa Gamma. Clubs: Order Eastern Star (past worthy matron); Levelland Music (past pres.), Maids and Matrons Study (pres. 1975-76). Contbr. to various publs. Home: 307 Sandalwood Ln PO Box 156 Levelland TX 79336

RAINER, LOUISE ELAINE, fin. planning and tax seminar exec.; b. Indpls., Sept. 25, 1942; d. John Francis and Wynona E. (Thonrburg) Byrd; grad. S. Jersey Bus. Machines, 1960; student Purdue U., 1960-61, Cambridge (Ohio) Coll., 1962-63; children—Brenda Louise, Veronica Jean. Pvt. sec. Edmund Sci. Research Co., Barrington, N.J., 1961-62, RCA, Cambridge, Ohio, 1962-64, Prudential Ins. Co., Cheyenne, Wyo., 1964-67, Muncie, Ind., 1967-69, Columbus, Ohio, 1970-72; operator Texaco Service Sta., Winchester, Ind., 1968-70; golden galaxy mgr. Tupperware, Dart Industries, Columbus, 1972-75; with The Merchant Prince (Trading Corp. Am.), Columbus, 1975—, state dir., 1976-79; founder and pres. IDEA, Income Devel. and Econ. Advs., Colorado

Springs, Colo.; planning tax seminar exec., Colorado Springs, 1979—. Fund raiser chmn. Fire Dept., New Albany, Ohio; chmn. ARC, Haddonfield, N.J.; chmn. Heart Fund Dr., Cheyenne; mem. Columbus Schs. PTO; inservice leader, tchr. devel. course, dir. youth orgn., co-chmn. Y.S.I, Mormon Ch., Columbus, Colo. Springs. Recipient Lions Club Citizenship award, 1959. Mem. Nat. Assn. Life Underwriters, Postal Commemorative Soc., Powder Room Guns and Ammo Pistol Club. Republican. Office: 4420 Montebello Dr Suite 405 Colorado Springs CO 80918

RAINES, BETTY ANN BIVENS, broadcasting exec.; b. Hinton, W.Va., May 4, 1928; d. Mastin Harve and Norma Victoria (Deeds) Bivens; student public schs., also specialized courses; m. Lacy G. Raines, Jr., June 6, 1975. Secretary, 1945-62; with sta. WKBA, Roanoke and Vinton, Va., 1962—, program dir., 1972. Democrat. Home: Route 1 Box 357-B Daleville VA 24083 Office: 2043 10th St NE Roanoke VA 24012

RAINES, JOAN BINDER, lit. agt.; b. N.Y.C., July 25, 1931; d. Samuel Lawrence and Shirley (Cooper) Binder; student Columbia U.; m. Theron Raines, July 29, 1971; 1 son, Keith B. Korman. Office mgr. Raines Agy., N.Y.C., 1968, agt., 1969—, partner, 1974—. Mem. Soc. Authors' Reps., Authors Guild (asso.). Jewish. Office: 475 Fifth Ave New York NY 10017 *

RAINEY, IDELLA ANITRA, educator, learning disabilities therapist; b. Athens, Ala., Mar. 1, 1933; d. Tom and Patience Caudle R.; B.S., Ala. A&M U., 1954; M.Ed., Nat. Coll. End., Ill., 1975. Tchr., Einstein Sch., Chgo., 1959-70, head tchr. Title I Summer Headstart Programs, 1965-68, classroom tchr., instrnl. team teaching, 1970-75, programmed instrns. tchr. Title I System 80 Learning Center, 1975; learning disabilities therapist Einstein Sch., 1975-82. Coordinator Einstein Sch. Crusade of Mercy, 1975-82. Mem. Council Exceptional Children, Coordinating Council Handicapped Children, Chgo. Assn. Children with Learning Disabilities, Spl. Edn. Tchrs. Orgn., Nat. Assn. Female Execs., Chgo. Tchrs. Union, PTA. Presbyterian.

RAINEY, PATRICIA ANN, counselor, writer; b. Dover, N.H., Oct. 14, 1937; d. Wilbur Robert and Helen Mary (Keddy) R.; B.A., U. N.H., 1960, M.Ed., 1967, C.A.G.S., 1976; postgrad. U. Maine, 1967, George Peabody Coll., 1968. Grad. asst., Ford Found. grantee U. N.H., Dover, 1960-61, lecture asst., 1973-74, writer, also Centrex office, 1974—; counselor Renew Counseling Center, Rye, N.H., 1977-82; co-founder, clin. dir. Green Pastures Counseling Assos., 1982—; tchr. social studies Colebrook (N.H.) Acad., 1961-65; counselor Exeter (N.H.) High Sch., 1965-66, Newport (N.H.) High Sch., 1966-68; asst. prof. psychology Cleveland (Tenn.) State Community Coll., 1968-72. Recipient creative teaching award A.B. Dick Co., 1970. Author: Illusions: A Journey into Perception, 1973; contbr. articles to profl. publs. Home: 173 Mount Vernon St Dover NH 03820

RAINWATER, NANCY GREGG, clin. psychologist; b. Pensacola, Fla., Dec. 17, 1951; d. Crawford Veazey and Betty (Gregg) R.; B.A., Wellesley Coll., 1973; M.A., Ga. State U., Atlanta, 1975, Ph.D., 1979. Clin. psychology resident U. Miss. Med. Center, Jackson, 1977-78; research asso. VA Med. Center, Jackson, 1978-79; NIH research fellow Nat. Asthma Center, Denver, 1979-80; asst. clin. prof. dept. pediatrics U. Colo. Health Scis. Center, Denver, 1980—, clin. psychologist Barbara Davis Center for Childhood Diabetes. Lic. clin. psychologist. Mem. Am. Psychol. Assn., Assn. Advancement Behavior Therapy, Assn. Advancement Psychology, Assn. Behavior Analysis, Soc. Behavioral Medicine, Colo. Psychol. Assn. Author papers in field. Office: Barbara Davis Center for Childhood Diabetes 4200 E 9th Ave Denver CO 80262

RAITT, JILL, educator; b. Los Angeles, May 1, 1931; d. Arthur Taylor and Lorna Genevieve (Atherton) R.; B.A. in Philosophy, San Francisco Coll. Women, 1953, M.A. in English, 1964; M.A. in Theology (scholarship 1964-65), Marquette U., 1967; M.A., U. Chgo., 1967, Ph.D. (tuition grant 1965-68, Univ. fellow 1968-69), 1970. Mem. Roman Catholic Ch., 1951—; instr., then asst. prof. theology San Francisco Coll. Women, 1963-64; mem. summer faculty Marywood Coll., Scranton, Pa., 1966, Immaculate Heart Coll., Hollywood, Calif., 1967; instr., then asst. prof. St. Xavier Coll., Chgo., 1966-68; asst. prof. program religious studies U. Calif. at Riverside, 1969-73; asso. prof. hist. theology Duke Div. Sch., 1973-81; prof., chmn. dept. religious studies U. Mo., Columbia, 1981—. Mem. Ofcl. Roman Catholic/Lutheran Dialogue in U.S.A. Radcliffe Coll scholar, 1949-51; scholar Goethe Inst., Germany, summer 1965; Jr. fellow Found. Reformation Research, summer 1968; Faculty fellow U. Calif. at Riverside, summer 1970, Humanities Inst. grantee, 1972-73; Nat. Endowment for Humanities fellow, 1975-76; Radcliffe Inst. fellow, 1975-76; Duke Research Council fellow, summer 1975. Mem. Am. Acad. Religion (sec. Western region 1972-73, nat. sec. 1972-75, nat. v.p. 1978-79, pres. 1980-81, asso. dir. 1981—), Friends of Reformation Research (sec.), Am. Soc. Ch. History (council), Soc. Reformation Research, Calvin Soc. (council). Author monographs, articles, revs. Address: Dept Religious Studies 416 GCB U Mo Columbia MO 65211

RAJAGOPAL, SHAKUNTALA, pathologist; b. Kerala, India, Oct. 1, 1940; d. K.V. and Retnamma (Pillai) Sivaraam; grad. Womens Coll., Trivandrum, Kerala, 1956; M.B., B.S., Med. Coll., Trivandrum, 1963; m. K.G. Rajagopal, Jan. 21, 1963; children—Devi, Nimmi. Resident in pathology West Suburban Hosp., Oak Park, Ill., 1964-69; pathologist, dir. labs., Westlake Community Hosp., Melrose Park, Ill., 1970—; demonstrator in pathology Northwestern U. Med. Sch., Chgo., 1967-75; med. dir. Triton Coll., 1972—. Troup leader Girl Scouts U.S.A., 1978-79. Fellow Coll. Am. Pathologists, Am. Soc. Clin. Pathologists (continuing med. edn. award); mem. AMA, Chgo. Med. Soc., Am. Assn. Blood Banks, Am. Cancer Soc., Kerala Assn. Chgo. (pres. women's aux. 1977-79; v.p. 1980-81). Hindu. Club: The Right. Home: 1868 Prestwick Dr Palatine IL 60067 Office: 1225 Superior St Melrose Park IL 60160

RAKAY, DONNA JANE, musician; b. Delray, Mich., Mar. 16, 1943; d. Louis and Delilah Ann (Leadingham) R.; B.Mus.Edn., Eastern Mich. U., Ypsilanti, Mich., 1965, M.A., 1969. Mem. faculty Lincoln Park (Mich.) schs., 1965—, band dir., music supr. Huff Jr. High Sch., Lincoln Park High Sch. bands, 1974—. Recipient various service awards. Mem. NEA, Mich. Edn. Assn., Mich. Parents, Tchrs. and Students Assn., Nat. Assn. Female Execs., Mu Phi Epsilon. Office: 1701 Champaign St Lincoln Park MI 48146

RAKESTRAW, CAROLINE LEIDING, former assn. exec.; b. Atlanta, June 28, 1912; d. Christopher Boone and Caroline Stella (Adkins) Leiding; student U. Ga., 1929-34; D.D. (hon.), U. of South, 1974; m. Emmett Raymond Rakestraw, Sept. 2, 1934; 1 dau., Catherine Leiding. Exec. sec. Diocese of Atlanta, 1945-54; exec. sec. Episcopal Radio-TV Found., Atlanta, 1954-59, exec. dir., from 1959; now cons. Trustee, Protestant Radio and TV Center. Recipient Ohio State U. award, 1969. Mem. Am. Women in Radio and TV. Home: 750 Longwood Dr NW Atlanta GA 30305 Office: 3379 Peachtree Rd NE Atlanta GA 30326

RAKOW, CELE REVA, retail exec.; b. N.Y.C., Sept. 25, 1944; d. Samuel David and Esther (Newman) R.; B.A., Hunter Coll., N.Y.C., 1965. Tng. instr. Gimbels, N.Y.C., 1965-68; tech. writer, systems analyst Allied Stores Corp., N.Y.C., 1968-74; sr. systems analyst Dobbs-Life Savers Co., N.Y.C., 1974-75; mgr. systems Macy's, N.Y.C., 1975-78; systems cons., 1978-79; mgr. retail systems Allied Stores Corp., 1979—; speaker in field. Mem. Assn. Systems Mgmt., Nat. Assn. Female Execs. Clubs: N.Y. Health and Racquet, Single Gourmet. Home: 200 E 33d St New York NY 10016 Office: 1114 Ave Americas New York NY 10036

RAKOWSKI, BARBARA ANN, ednl. adminstr.; b. Flint, Mich., Jan. 24, 1948; d. Casimir Anthony and Harriet Ann (Craft) R.; B.S., Central Mich. U., 1971, M.S., 1978. Tchr. langs. and scis. Sts. Peter and Paul Area High Sch., Saginaw, Mich., 1971-79, chmn. dept. fgn. langs., 1974-79; instr. high sch. program field studies Central Mich. U., Beaver Island, Mich., 1973-81; prin., tchr. Beaver Island Community Schs., 1981—, also career edn. coordinator. Mem. Nat. Assn. Biology Tchrs., Mich. Elem. and Middle Sch. Prins. Assn., Mich. Assn. Secondary Adminstrs. mem. Byzantine Catholic Ch. Home: PO Box 70 Saint James MI 49782 Office: Beaver Island Community Schs Saint James MI 49782

RALABATE, PATRICIA KELLY, speech, lang. pathologist; b. Dubois, Pa., June 4, 1950; d. William Daniel and Mary Jane (Wagner) Kelly; B.S. in Edn., SUNY, Fredonia, 1972; M.A., U. Mass., Amherst, 1977; m. Samuel Patrick Ralabate, Sept. 2, 1972. Speech pathologist Rockland County Speech and Hearing Center, Nanuet, N.Y., 1973-74; adminstrv. asst. Hampshire Ednl. Collaborative, Hadley, Mass., 1975-76; speech, lang. pathologist Hatfield (Mass.) Public Schs., 1976-77, Coop. Ednl. Services, Norwalk, Conn., 1977-78, Hill and Plain Sch., New Milford, Conn., 1978—; cons. Danbury Kiwanis Yr. of Disabled Project, 1980-82. Recipient Easter Seal award, 1972. Mem. Am. Speech-Lang.-Hearing Assn., Conn. Speech-Lang.-Hearing Assn., NEA, Conn. Edn. Assn. (public relations commn.), New Milford Edn. Assn. (bldg. rep., chmn. public relations com., rec. sec.), Fairfield County Early Childhood Spl. Edn. Network Phi Delta Kappa (1st v.p. Western Conn. Coll. chpt.). Contbr. articles to profl. jours. Home: 90 S King St Danbury CT 06810 Office: Hill and Plain Sch Old Town Park Rd New Milford CT 06776

RALSTON, CLARICE MCDUFFIE, nurse; b. Tampa, Fla., Feb. 11, 1932; d. Welbourne Clifton and Louise Teresa (Sellers) McDuffie; R.N. diploma Gordon Keller Sch. Nursing, 1953; m. William Kent Ralston, Mar. 12, 1954; children—Diana Lynn (dec.), Stephen Kent. Staff nurse Jackson Meml. Hosp., Miami, Fla., 1953-54, New Braunfels (Tex.) Gen. Hosp., 1954-55; nurse supr. Wichita Falls (Tex.) State Hosp., 1971—. Mem. Am. Nurses Assn. (cert. gerontol. nurse), Tex. Nurses Assn. (charter mem. continuing edn. program), Fla. State Student Nurses Assn. (charter), Tex. Pub. Employees Assn., Am. Legion Aux. Democrat. Methodist. Club: Order Eastern Star. Research on hygiene for elderly patients. Home: 815 Preston St Burkburnett TX 76354 Office: Wichita Falls State Hosp PO Box 300 Wichita Falls TX 76307

RALSTON, LUCY VIRGINIA GORDON, artist; b. Washington, Sept. 9, 1926; d. Byron Brown and Lucy Virginia (Gordon) R.; grad. Finch Jr. Coll., 1942; pvt. art tng., student Leon Kroll. One-man show Pelham (N.Y.) Meml. High Sch., 1939; pvt. shows in Pelham home, 1939-45; group shows include Manor Club, Pelham, 1945-48, Nat. Arts Club, N.Y.C., 1950-62, Westchester Fedn. Women's Clubs, Bronxville, N.Y., 1954, Mt. Vernon (N.Y.) Art Assn., 1955, Allied Artists Am. ann. exhbn., N.Y.C., 1955; represented in permanent collections Assn. Jr. Leagues Am., N.Y.C. and on tour U.S. and Can.; John Jay and Eliza Jane Watson Found., Elizabeth, N.J., mural called Gay Nineties for Westchester Restaurant, Mamaroneck, N.Y.; freelance artist Tiffany and Co., 1947-48; designer U.S.S. Constn. book plate used by Am. Bible Soc. and John Jay and Eliza Jane Watson Found. for presentation Bibles to grads. U.S. Naval Acad., C.G. Acad., Merchant Marine Acad., 1953—. Recipient Popular prize Manor Club Exhibit, 1947, 48, 2d prize, 1958, 1st prize for graphic art, 1957; Popular prize Westchester Assn. Women's Clubs, 1951, Mt. Vernon Art Assn., 1954; 2d prize Met. Mus., Pelham, 1969. Mem. Jr. League Pelham, Nat. Soc. Colonial Dames in State N.Y., Internat. Garden Club, Bartow-Pell Mansion Mus., Nat. Arts Club, DAR (registrar Knapp chpt. 1961-63), Daus. of the Cincinnati (registrar 1973—), Colonial Soc. Ams. of Royal Descent, Nat. Soc. Magna Charta Dames, Allied Artists Am. (asso.), Colonial Soc. Descs. Knights of Garter, Colonial Order Crown, Huguenot Soc. Am. Commd. by pres. Brit.-Am. Soc. to paint life-size portraits of Princess Anne and Prince Charles, in his investiture robes as Prince of Wales, to be published in London in British-American Chronicle and exhibited at ann. reception of Daus. of the Cincinnati, N.Y.C., 1974. Home and Studio: 37 Quincy St Chevy Chase MD 20815

RAMANAUSKAS-MARCONI, HELENE MARIA APOLLONIA STROECKER, educator; b. Graz, Austria, June 4, 1924; d. Johann and Katharina (Auer) Stroecker; M.A., Tech. U., Munich, Germany, 1945; Ph.D., U. Munich, 1948; M.B.A., Northwestern U., 1955; C.P.A. cert. U. Ill., 1959; m. Giuseppe E. Marconi, Mar. 24, 1976. Faculty, DePaul U., Chgo., 1959—, prof. accountancy, 1966—; mgmt. cons. Speaker 8th Internat. Congress Accountants, N.Y.C., 1962, 9th Congress, Paris, 1967, del. 10th Congress, Sydney, Australia, 1972. C.P.A., Ill. Mem. Am. Women's Soc. C.P.A.'s (Chgo. area pres. 1963-64), Budget Execs. Inst. (chpt. chmn. audit com. 1967-68), Planning Execs. Inst. (nat. chmn. research 1972—), Ill. Soc. C.P.A.'s (com. internat. accounting), Am. Accounting Assn. (research com. internat. accounting), AAUP (pres. Chgo. chpt. 1971-72), Munich Bus. Economists Assn., Am. Inst. Decision Sci. (charter), Delta Mu Delta, Beta Alpha Psi, Epsilon Eta Phi, Beta Gamma Sigma. Contbr. numerous articles to publs. Home: 728 S Norbury Ave Lombard IL 60148 Office: 25 E Jackson Blvd Chicago IL 60604

RAMBO, CYNTHIA ANN, state exec.; b. Shawnee, Okla., June 7, 1944; d. Frank A. and Betty Grall; B.S., Okla. State U., 1966; m. G. Dan Rambo; children—Blake, Grier. Tchr., Norman (Okla.) Pub. Schs., 1969-74; adminstrv. asst. to Gov. of Okla., Oklahoma City, 1978-80; exec. dir. Okla. Dept. Econ. and Community Affairs, Oklahoma City, 1981—; sec. Gov. of Okla.'s Cabinet; mem. nat. task force White House Conf. on Families. Active Women's Leadership Project, Oklahoma City. Mem. Council State Community Affairs Agys. (exec. com.), Council State Planning Agys., Jr. Service League, Cleveland County Democratic Women. Methodist. Office: 4545 N Lincoln Blvd Suite 285 Oklahoma City OK 73105

RAMBO, SYLVIA H., fed. judge; b. Royersford, Pa., Apr. 17, 1936; d. Granville and Hilda (Leonhardt) R.; A.B., Dickinson Coll., 1958; J.D., Dickinson Sch. Law, 1962; LL.D. (hon.), Wilson Coll., 1981; m. George F. Douglas, Jr., Aug. 1, 1970. With trust dept. Bank of Del., Wilmington, 1962-63; admitted to Pa. bar, 1963; pvt. practice law, Carlisle, Pa., 1963-76; pub. defender, Carlisle, 1974-76, chief pub. defender, 1976; judge Ct. Common Pleas, Carlisle, 1976-78; judge U.S. Dist. Ct. Middle Dist. Pa., Harrisburg, 1979—; asst. prof. law Dickinson Sch. Law, 1973-77. Named Alumnus of Yr., Dickinson Sch. Law, 1981. Mem. ABA, Pa. Bar Assn., Nat. Assn. Women Judges, Am. Judicature Soc., Phi Alpha Delta. Democrat. Presbyterian. Home: 13 Shagbark Carlisle PA 17013 Office: PO Box 868 Federal Bldg Walnut St Harrisburg PA 17108

RAMBO, VIRGINIA RISHER, social worker; b. Selma, Ala., Mar. 11, 1919; d. James Oliver and Louise (Beers) Risher; B.A., Ala. Coll., 1941; m. Louise George Rambo, Jr., Sept. 30, 1944; children—Rosemary Rambo Green, Kitty Rambo Reeves, Louis George III. Social worker Dallas County Dept. Public Welfare, Selma, 1941-45; social worker Dallas County Dept. Pensions and Security, Selma, 1968-69; dir. social services Lowndes County Community Health Project, Hayneville, Ala., 1969-71; dir. social services dept. Med. Center Hosp., Selma, 1971—; coordinator West Central Ala. Tumor Clinic, 1975-76. Vol. Am. Cancer Soc., 1972-80; coordinator Reach to Recovery Program, Selma-Dallas County Cancer Soc., 1972-80, pres., 1975, outstanding service award, 1978-79. Recipient Dr. Thomas E. Frist Humanitarian award Hosp. Corp. Am., 1981. Mem. Am. Hosp. Assn., Ala. Soc. Hosp. Social Workers, Ala. Hosp. Assn., Soc. Hosp. Social Work Dirs. Republican. Baptist. Club: Altrusa (Selma, Ala.). Home: Route 1 Box 147 Tyler AL 36785 Office: 1015 Medical Center Parkway Selma AL 36701

RAMELL, GUNILLA CHRISTINA, sr. energy policy analyst; b. Gothenburg, Sweden, Apr. 23, 1946; came to U.S., 1966, naturalized, 1978; d. Victor K. A. and Alice Linnea (Hornberg) Ramell; B.A. summa cum laude, UCLA, 1970; M.A., Harvard U., 1974. Govt. relations analyst Atlantic Richfield Co., Los Angeles, 1974-77; communications program mgr. Internat. Paper Co., N.Y.C., 1977-78; public affairs specialist Indsl. Indemnity Co., San Francisco, 1978-80; sr. analyst Revenue Requirements, Pacific Gas & Electric Co., San Francisco, 1980—; teaching fellow Harvard U., 1971-74. Mem. platform com. No. Calif. Democratic Party, 1981; United Way sponsored exec., 1982. Alfred P. Sloan Found. fellow, 1972; Washington internship fellow office of Sen. Charles E. Goodell. Mem. Assn. Public Policy Analysis and Mgmt., Internat. Assn. Energy Economists, Issues Mgmt. Assn.(founding). Democrat. Club: Harvard of N.Y. Home: 2323 Larkin St San Francisco CA 94109 Office: Pacific Gas and Electric 77 Beale St Room 1054 San Francisco CA 94106

RAMEY, FRANCES KATHLEEN, former city ofcl.; b. Arco, Idaho, May 25, 1917; d. Simon Andrew and Margaret Frances (Coates) R.; B.S., Creighton U., M.A., 1947. Tchr., Sch. Dist. 1, Helena, Mont., 1945-80, tchr. Russian and English, Capital High Sch., also Helena High Sch. Mem. Helena City Commn., 1972-77; mayor City of Helena, 1978-80. Mem. Am. Bus. Women's Assn., Mont. LWV, Alpha Delta Kappa. Roman Catholic. Home: Helena MT 59601

RAMEY, MARY BULLARD, health records cons.; b. Elizabeth, La., May 24, 1928; d. Elijah Bullard and Aszlee Mobbs; A.A.S., Mott Community Coll., 1982; m. William Edward Ramey, Nov. 24, 1963; children—Clarence Arthur, Victor James, James Andrew Thompson, Sherrie Lynn Ramey Harrison. Sec. to dr., Flint, Mich., 1947, to atty., Flint, 1952-53; supr.-mgr. office Clarence B. Kimbrough, M.D., Flint, 1966; supr. admissions dept. Hurley Med. Center, Flint, 1954-72, supr. med. records dept., 1972-75; psro data coordinator Profl. Standards Rev. Orgn. Genesee, Lapeer, Schiawassee Counties, Flint, 1975-78, med. care evaluation mgr., 1979-81; dir. med. records dept. Flint Gen. Hosp., 1981; cons. on quality assurance and health care records to health care orgns., health care practitioners, Otisville, Mich., 1981—; speaker in field. Accredited record technician. Mem. East Central Med. Record Assn., Mich. Med. Record Assn., Nat. Assn. Female Execs., Am. Med. Record Assn. (accredited). Democrat. Baptist. Club: Toastmasters. Home: 7142 N Irish Rd Otisville MI 48463

RAMIREZ, BETTY LOU, mortgage co. exec.; b. Valley Twp., Ark., Sept. 16, 1940; d. John and Lela Venice (Couch) Patrick; children—Greg, Margaret, Mark, Wayman, Tara. Loan officer Loper Mortgage Co., San Antonio; asst. v.p., processing supr. Alamo Savs. Assn., San Antonio, 1976-78; asst. v.p., dist. mgr. Mercantile Mortgage Co., San Antonio, 1978—, area mgr. Citicorp Homeowners, Inc., 1981—; instr. San Antonio Bd. Realtors. Mem. San Antonio Assn. Profl. Mortgage Women (charter pres. 1981), San Antonio Bd. Realtors, Tex. Assn. Realtors, San Antonio Homebuilders Assn., Bexar County Real Estate Assn., San Antonio Mortgage Bankers Assn., Tex. Mortgage Bankers Assn., Women's Council of Realtors. Baptist. Home: 6910 Brookport St San Antonio TX 78230 Office: 6243 IH 10 Suite 845 San Antonio TX 78201

RAMÍREZ, MARJORIE LUCILLE SCOTT, nurse; b. N.Y.C., Jan. 4, 1940; d. Robert and Juanita (Vicens) Scott; R.N., St. Luke's Hosp., 1960; B.S. in Nursing, Hunter Coll., 1967; M.A., Tchrs. Coll., Columbia U., 1980, M.Ed., 1981; postgrad. Adelphi U.; m. Antonio Ramírez, June 6, 1964; children—David Scott, Benjamin John. Nursing instr. St. Luke's Hosp., N.Y.C., 1961-64, various positions nursing service dept., 1965-73, patient care supr., adminstrv. supr. pvt. pavilion, 1973-74; spl. projects supr. Community Hosp., Glen Cove, N.Y., 1975-82; clin. supr. Mt. Sinai Med. Center, N.Y.C., 1982—; adj. clin. instr. Adelphi U., 1981-82, Kingsborough Community Coll., 1981. Mem. L.I. Diabetes Assn., Am. Nurses Assn. Episcopalian. Contbr. article to profl. publ.

RAMIREZ, MIRIAM JEAN, physician; b. Caguas, P.R., June 24, 1941; d. Victor M. and Angela (Garcia) Ramirez; student Marymount Coll. br., Barcelona, Spain, 1958, U. Md. br., Munich, Ger., 1959; pre-med. degree, U. P.R., San Juan, 1960; M.D., U. Madrid (Spain), 1967; m. Tomas Ferrer, Sept. 6, 1974; 1 dau., Lissette Therese; children by previous marriage—Miriam Jean, Tommy, David, Roberto. Intern, Caguas Municipal Hosp., 1968-69; resident in ob-gyn Caguas Sub-Regional Hosp., 1970-73; regional dir. Family Planning Agy., P.R. Dept. Health, Caguas, 1973-74; clin. obstetrician, gynecologist, Mayaguez, P.R., 1974—. Chmn., Bush for Pres. Com. Western P.R.; Republic nat. committeewoman from P.R., 1982—. Mem. Am. Acad. Family Physicians (affiliate), Internat. Photog. Soc. (charter), Assn. Planned Parenthood Physicians (dir.), P.R., Caguas (del.-at-large 1973-74) med. assns., Med. Doctor's Wives Assn. Caguas (pres. 1973-74). Mem. Statehood Polit. Party. Roman Catholic. Club: Altrusa (pres. Caguas 1972-74, pres. Mayaguez 1975-76). Address: Box 3225 Mayaguez PR 00709

RAMO, VIRGINIA M. SMITH (MRS. SIMON RAMO), civic worker; b. Yonkers, N.Y.; d. Abraham Harold and Freda (Kasnetz) Smith; B.S. in Edn., U. So. Calif., D.H.L. (hon.), 1978; m. Simon Ramo; children—James Brian, Alan Martin. Nat. co-chmn. ann. giving U. So. Calif., 1968-70, vice chmn., trustee, 1971—, co-chmn. bd. councilors Sch. Performing Arts, 1975-76, co-chmn. bd. councillors Schs. Med. and Engring.; vice-chmn. bd. overseers Hebrew Union Coll., 1972-75; bd. dirs. The Muses of Calif. Mus. Sci. and industry, UCLA Affiliates, Estelle Doheny Eye Found., U. So. Calif. Sch. Medicine; adv. council Los Angeles County Heart Assn., chmn. com. to endow Chair in cardiology at U. So. Calif.; vice-chmn., bd. dirs. Friends of Library U. So. Calif.; bd. dirs., nat. pres. Achievement Rewards for Coll. Scientists Found., 1975-77; bd. dirs. Les Dames Los Angeles, Community TV So. Calif.; bd. dirs., v.p. Founders Los Angeles Music Center; v.p. Los Angeles Music Center Opera Assn.; v.p. corp. bd. United Way; v.p. Blue Ribbon-400 Performing Arts Council. Recipient Service award Friends of Libraries, 1974; Nat. Community Service award Alpha Epsilon Phi, 1975; Disting. Service award Am. Heart Assn. 1978; Service award U. So. Calif.; Spl. award U. So. Calif. Music Alumni Assn., 1979; Life Achievement award Mannequins of Los Angeles Assistance League, 1979; Woman of Yr. award PanHellenic Assn., 1981; Disting. Service award U. So. Calif. Sch. Medicine, 1981. Mem. UCLA Med. Aux., U. So. Calif. Pres.'s Circle, Commerce Assos. U. So. Calif., Cedars of Lebanon Hosp. Women's Guild (dir. 1967-68).

RAMOS, CARMEN ROSA, psychiatrist; b. Santurce, P.R., Nov. 28, 1948; d. Francisco and Carmen Vega Ramos; student Coll. Notre Dame, Balt., 1966-68; B.A., Boston U., 1970; M.D., SUNY, Buffalo, 1974. Resident in psychiatry Tulane U.-S.E. La. State Hosp., 1974, Charity Hosp., 1975-77, out patient psychiatry clinic Tulane Med. Sch., 1975-77; practice medicine specializing in psychiatry, Metairie, La., 1977-81, New Orleans, 1981—; staff psychiatrist Pontchatrain Mental Health Clinic, New Orleans, 1977-80; mem. staff DePaul Psychiat. Hosp., Coliseum House Psychiat. Hosp.; clin. instr. Tulane U. Med. Sch., 1977—. Mem.

Am., La. psychiat. assns., Am. Med. Women's Assn., AAAS, C. of C., Sociedad Espanola of New Orleans. Office: 3625 Chestnut St New Orleans LA 70115

RAMSBURG, HELEN HARRIS, microbiologist; b. Miami, Fla., Oct. 29, 1925; d. William Henry and Naomi Catharine (Shafer) Harris; A.B. in Biology, Hood Coll., 1947. M.A. in Environ. Biology, 1982; postgrad. U. Md., 1956-60; m. Staley William Ramsburg, Sept. 7, 1946; 1 dau. Cassandra Lee Duncan; foster dau., Angela Andrea Fry. Lab. technician Frederick (Md.) Meml. Hosp., 1947-48; biol. aide NIH, Bethesda, Md., 1948-50; med. biology technician med. unit., Ft. Detrick, Frederick, Md., 1957-59; bacteriologist U.S. Army Research Inst. Infectious Diseases, Ft. Detrick, 1959-62, microbiologist, 1962—. Recipient Spl. Act and Service award, 1964. Lutheran. Co-author profl. articles. Home: 9201 Dublin Rd Walkersville MD 21793 Office: Virology Div US Army Research Inst Infectious Diseases Fort Detrick Frederick MD 21701

RAMSEY, BARBARA JEAN, railway co. mgr.; b. San Jose, Calif., Dec. 18, 1920; d. Dorrace Glenn and Norris (Mickelson) Wallace; A.B., San Jose State U., 1941; M.A., U. Calif., Berkeley, 1953; Certificat D'Etudes Degré Supérieur, U. Paris, Sorbonne, 1972; m. Taufek H. Ramsey, July 12, 1950 (div.); children—Stephanie, Karin. Instr., French, San Jose (Calif.) State U., 1946-50; asst. to dir. Bancroft Library, U. Calif., Berkeley, 1951-53; asst. to pres. Cutter Labs., Berkeley, 1953-56; corp. officer Wescosa, Inc., Calif., 1956-68; tchr. French, Colonial Sch. Dist., Plymouth-Whitemarsh Sr. High Sch., Plymouth Meeting, Pa., 1970-80; supr. mgmt. services Phila. Belt Line R.R. Co., 1980—. Vestry and acctg. warden Episcopal Ch., 1977—, edn. coordinator, 1976. Recipient Hawthorne award Los Gatos High Sch., 1936; French medal French Consulate San Francisco, 1941. Mem. AAUW, Am. Assn. Tchrs. of French, Montgomery County Assn. Tchrs. of Fgn. Langs., Am. Council Teaching of Fgn. Langs., Am. Mensa (local sec.), Nat. Assn. Female Execs., Women's Transp. Seminars, Am. Soc. Profl. and Exec. Women, Nat. Platform Assn., Pi Lambda Theta, Alpha Chi Omega. Office: Phila Belt Line RR Co Philadelphia PA

RAMSEY, BARBARA KAETHER SAND, nurse; b. Madison Wis., Dec. 29, 1949; d. James Edward and Virginia Rose (Parr) Kaether; student No. State Coll., Aberdeen, S.D., 1968-70; R.N., Methodist Sch. Nursing, Mitchell, S.D., 1973; B.A. in Psychology, Dakota Weslyan U., 1977; m. John T. Ramsey, Oct. 14, 1979; 1 dau., Amy Elizabeth; 1 son by previous marriage, Timothy Christopher. Staff nurse St. Joseph Hosp., Mitchell, S.D., 1973-74, evening supr., 1974-77; staff telemetry nurse emergency room St. Therese Hosp., Waukegan, Ill., 1977-78; supr. emergency room Am. Internat. Hosp., Zion, Ill., 1978-80; staff nurse ICU-CCU, Mission Bay Hosp., San Diego, 1980-81; staff triage telemetry nurse emergency room Victory Meml. Hosp., Waukegan, Ill., 1981—; vol. ARC. Registered emergency med. technician; cert. emergency nurse, advance cardiac life support provider. Mem. Emergency Dept. Nurse Assn. Roman Catholic. Club: Rainbow Girls (worthy advisor 1966). Home: 618 Westmoreland Ave Waukegan IL 60085

RAMSEY, DONNA JEAN, banker; b. Anderson, Ind., Mar. 20, 1936; d. Kenneth Lee and Beulah Lavera (Whitlow) May; cert. LaSalle Extension U., 1962; degree Nat. Grad. Trust Sch., Northwestern U., 1974; m. Korlin Benjamin Ramsey, June 17, 1956; children—Gail Ann, Karen Sue, Curtis Allen. Bookkeeper, Poitiers (France) Army Officers Club, 1956-57; teller, proof machine operator, clk. Pendleton (Ind.) Banking Co., 1959-62; bookkeeper, income tax practitioner Baker's Fed. Tax Service, Lafayette, Ind., 1963-66; tax acct. Lafayette Nat. Bank, 1967-76, trust tax officer, head trust ops., 1976—. Vice pres. Harrison High Sch. Booster Club, 1975. Mem. Nat. Assn. Bank Women, Nat. Assn. Accts., Nat. Soc. Pub. Accts., Am. Inst. Banking (basic cert. 1972), Ind. Soc. Pub. Accts., Estate Planning Council Lafayette, Lafayette C. of C. Home: 1305 Palmer Dr Apt 312 West Lafayette IN 47906 Office: Lafayette Nat Bank Trust Dept 337 Columbia St Lafayette IN 47902

RAMSEY, DONNA MOORE, med. technologist, educator; b. Toledo, Jan. 13, 1941; d. Wendle Adolphus and Thelma Grace (Wilson) Moore; B.S. in Zoology, Ohio U., Athens, 1962; diploma med. tech., Mercy Hosp., Toledo, 1963; M.Ed. in Supervision/Coordination Vocat. and Tech. Edn., Rutgers U., 1976; m. James Albert Ramsey, Feb. 9, 1963; children—James Albert, Wendle Scott. Med. technologist, instr. Mercy Hosp., 1963-65, Mt. Carmel Hosp., Columbus, Ohio, 1965-69; med. technologist Doctor's Hosp., Columbus, 1970-71; instr. med. lab. tech. Columbus Tech. Inst., 1972-73; instr. vocat. and tech. edn. Middlesex County (N.J.) Bd. Edn., 1974; med. tech. coordinator Rutgers U. Med. Sch., 1974-75; supr. med. lab. Douglass Coll., Rutgers U., 1976; asst. prof. med. tech. Cuyahoga Community Coll., Cleve., 1976-81, program dir. med. assisting/med. lab. tech., 1981—; panelist med. assisting edn. Ohio Acad. Family Physicians; critiquer, surveyor Nat. Accrediting Agy. for Clin. Lab. Scis. Mem. Am. Soc. Clin. Pathologists, Am. Assn. Med. Assts., Am. Soc. Med. Technologists, Kappa Delta Pi. Office: 2900 Community College Ave Cleveland OH 44115

RAMSEY, JOANNE MARIE, data processing exec.; b. Long Branch, N.J., Oct. 13, 1945; d. Erwin P. and Erna M. (Green) Forrest; B.S., Monmouth Coll., 1967; M.S., Stevens Inst. Tech., 1971; 1 dau., Cheryl. Mem. tech. staff Bell Telephone Labs., Holmdel, N.J., 1967-71; programmer analyst Cooper Electric Supply Co., Middletown, N.J., 1971-73; sr. programmer Insco Systems Corp., Neptune, N.J., 1973-78; programmer analyst Internat. Flavors & Fragrances, Hazlet, N.J., 1978-80; mgmt. systems analyst E.R. Squibb & Sons, Inc., East Brunswick, N.J., 1980—. Mem. Am. Prodn. and Inventory Control Soc., Assn. for Women in Computing. Home: 424 E Highland Ave Atlantic Highlands NJ 07716 Office: 25 Kennedy Blvd East Brunswick NJ 08816

RAMSHAW-REED, JANE, group health ins. broker; b. Albuquerque, Mar. 31, 1949; d. William George and Jean Ramshaw; grad. Trans-World Airlines Flight Hostess Sch., 1969; student U. N.Mex., 1967-71. Sales rep. Clinton P. Anderson, Albuquerque, 1973-74; sales rep. Blue Cross-Blue Shield, Rochester, N.Y., 1974-75; regional dir. mktg. Calif. Pacific Ins. Services, San Diego, 1976-80; owner Jane Ramshaw-Reed, R.H.U., San Diego, 1980—. Registered health underwriter. Mem. San Diego Assn. Life Underwriters (pres. 1981), Calif. Assn. Life Underwriters (state health ins. chmn. 1980-81), Nat. Assn. Health Underwriters, Nat. Assn. Life Underwriters (vice chmn. health com. 1982), Employee Benefit Council, North County Assn. Life Underwriters, Group Health Assn. Am. Republican. Clubs: Soroptimists of Rancho Bernardo, Toastmasters. Home: 3940 Gresham St Apt 142 San Diego CA 92109 Office: 2615 Camino del Rio S Suite 403 San Diego CA 92108

RANCK, SHIRLEY ANN, clergywoman, psychologist; b. Jersey City, Oct. 22, 1930; d. Gilbert Holmes and Ann (West) Bush; B.A., Montclair State Coll., 1953; M. Religious Edn., Drew U., 1958; M.A., CCNY, 1964; Ph.D., Fordham U., 1976; M.Div., Starr King U., 1978; children—Scott Holmes Page, James Philip Page, Christina Ann Ranck Cervantez, Laura Nelle Ranck. Ordained to ministry Unitarian Universalist Ch., 1980; psychologist public schs., Livingston, N.J., 1968-75; clin. psychologist Greystone Park (N.J.) Hosp., 1976; research asso. Grad. Theol. Union, Berkeley, Calif., 1978-79; minister Starr King Unitarian Ch., Hayward, Calif., 1980, No. Hills Fellowship, Cin., 1980—; psychologist Counseling Center, U. Cin., 1982—. Mem. Am. Psychol. Assn., Unitarian Universalist Ministers Assn. Contbr. articles in field to profl. publs. Office: 460 Fleming Rd Cincinnati OH 45231

RANCOUR, JOANN SUE, registered nurse; b. Elyria, Ohio, Nov. 10, 1939; d. Joseph and Ann (Donich) Sokol; diploma M.B. Johnson Sch. Nursing, 1960; B.S. in Profl. Arts, St. Josephs Coll., N. Windham, Maine, 1981; student in psychology Alfred Adler Inst., Chgo., 1976—, Lorain County Community Coll., 1973-75, Ursuline Coll., Cleve., 1976, Baldwin Wallace Coll., 1982; m. Richard Lee Rancour, July 29, 1961; children—Kathleen Ann, Donna Marie. Staff nurse Elyria Meml. Hosp., 1960-62, 72-75, head nurse psychiat. unit, 1975-79; sec.-treas. Alfred Adler Inst. Cleve., 1978-79; nurse Lorain County Juvenile Detention Home, Elyria, 1980; nurse VA Med. Center, Brecksville, Ohio, 1981—. Active PTA, yearbook com., 1969-70, co-chmn. ways and means, 1971; Democratic poll worker, 1971-72; sec. St. Mary's Confrat. Christian Doctrine Program, 1970-71. Mem. Am. Nurses Assn. (cert. generalist practitioner psychiat. and mental health nursing practice), Ohio Nurses Assn., N.Am. Soc. Adlerian Psychology, Nat. League Nursing, Internat. Platform Assn. Roman Catholic. Home: 205 Denison Ave Elyria OH 44035

RAND, AYN, writer, lectr.; b. St. Petersburg (now Leningrad), Russia, 1905; grad. U. Leningrad, 1924; D.H.L. (hon.), Lewis and Clark Coll., 1963; m. Frank O'Connor, 1929. Came to U.S., 1926, naturalized, 1931. Screen writer, 1932-34, 44-49; vis. lectr. Yale, 1960, Princeton, 1960, Columbia, 1960, 62, U. Wis., 1961, Johns Hopkins, 1961. Ford Hall Forum, Boston, 1961—, Harvard, 1962, Mass. Inst. Tech., 1962, U.S. Mil. Acad. at West Point, 1974, other univs. Author: Night of January 16th (play, revived as Penthouse Legend 1973), 1935; We the Living, 1936; Anthem, 1938; The Unconquered (play), 1940; The Fountainhead (also screenplay), 1943; Atlas Shrugged, 1957; For the New Intellectual, 1961; The Virtue of Selfishness, 1965; Capitalism; the Unknown Ideal, 1966; Introduction to Objectivist Epistemology, 1967; The Romantic Manifesto: A Philosophy of Literature, 1969; The New Left: The Anti-Industrial Revolution, 1971. Editor: The Objectivist, 1962-71, The Ayn Rand Letter, 1971-76. Address: Ayn Rand Letter 201 E 34th St New York NY 10016 *

RAND, ELLEN S., writer; b. N.Y.C., Feb. 3, 1948; d. Herbert Jacob and Beatrice (Marx) Kaplow; B.A., Queens Coll., 1968; m. Edward J. Rand, Feb. 2, 1973; 1 son, Matthew Ian. Mng. editor Apt. Constrn. News mag., N.Y.C., 1968-75; v.p./account exec. Howard J. Rubenstein Assos., public relations, N.Y.C., 1975-77; freelance writer, Teaneck, N.J., 1977—; weekly columnist N.J. sect. N.Y. Times, 1978—; contbg. editor bus. publs.; co-author: Successful Vacation Homes. Alt. mem. Teaneck Twp. Planning Bd., 1982—. Recipient Media award One to One Found. Mem. Phi Beta Kappa. Jewish.

RAND, HELEN PIERCE (MRS. ROBERT W. RAND), civic worker, artist; b. Coldwater, Mich., Jan. 31, 1926; d. L. Earl and Marjorie (Treacher) Pierce; A.B., U. Mich., 1949; m. Robert W. Rand, Dec. 17, 1949; children—Carl Wheeler II, Richard Pierce. Instr. dentistry U. Mich., 1948-50, translator of Russian, 1951; one-woman show: Gallery 8, Pasadena, Calif., 1980; group shows: Tower Gallery, Hollywood Park, 1965, Pasadena (Calif.) Pub. Library, 1965, Los Angeles City Hall, 1966, Pacific Art Guild Gallery, Westchester, Calif., 1966, Brand Library Gallery, Glendale, 1966, Occidental Bldg., Los Angeles, 1968, Westwood Art Assn., Los Angeles, 1965-67. Rec. sec. Jr. Philharmonic Com., Los Angeles, 1966—, 1st v.p., liaison rep. to Women for Music Center, 1971-72; rec. sec. Coll. Alumnae Aux. Assistance League, Los Angeles, 1959—. Mem. Women's Aux. Los Angeles County Med. Assn., U. Calif. Los Angeles Med. Faculty Wives (dir., chmn. ways and means 1967-68), Jr. Women Assos. U. Religious Conf., Mother's Club Harvard Sch. (bd. dirs. 1971-72), Town Hall, Blue Ribbon 400. Home: 521 N Bristol Ave Los Angeles CA 90049

RANDALL, CAROLYN DINEEN, U.S. judge; b. Syracuse, N.Y., Jan. 30, 1938; d. Robert E. and Carolyn E. (Bareham) Dineen; A.B. summa cum laude, Smith Coll., 1959; LL.B., Yale U., 1962; m. James D. Randall, Sept. 9, 1961; children—James, Philip, Stephen. Admitted to D.C. bar, 1962, Tex. bar, 1963; individual practice law, Houston, 1962-79; circuit judge U.S. Ct. Appeals 5th Circuit, Houston, 1979—. Trustee, mem. exec. com., treas. Houston Ballet Found., 1967-70; mem. Houston dist. adv. council SBA, 1972-76; mem. Dallas regional panel Pres.' Commn. White House Fellowships, 1972-76, mem. commn., 1977; bd. dirs. Houston chpt. Am. Heart Assn., 1978-79; nat. trustee Palmer Drug Abuse Program, 1978-79; trustee, chmn. audit com. United Way Tex. Gulf Coast, 1979—. Mem. ABA, Fed. Bar Assn., State Bar Tex., Houston Bar Assn., Phi Beta Kappa. Roman Catholic. Office: US Courthouse 515 Rusk St Houston TX 77002 *

RANDALL, JULIA VAN NESS, educator; b. Balt., June 15, 1923; d. Richard Harding and Mary Scott (Buzby) R.; B.A., Bennington Coll., 1945; M.A., Johns Hopkins U., 1950. Asst. prof. English, Towson State U., 1958-62; prof. English, Hollins Coll., Va., 1962-73; lectr. English, Goucher Coll., Towson, Md. NEA grantee, 1966, 82, Nat. Inst. Arts and Letters grantee, 1967; recipient Shelly award Poetry Soc. Am., 1980. Author: (poetry) The Solstice Tree, 1952, Mimic August, 1960, The Puritan Carpenter, 1965, Adam's Dream, 1969, The Farewells, 1981. Home: Hartley Mill Rd Glen Arm MD 21057

RANDALL, LAURA ROSENBAUM, economist; b. N.Y.C., Nov. 18, 1935; d. Bernard and Frances (Friedman) Rosenbaum; B.A., Barnard Coll., 1957; M.A., U. Mass., 1959; Ph.D., Columbia U., 1962; m. Francis B. Randall, June 11, 1957; children—David, Ariane. Economist, Fed. Res. Bank, N.Y.C., 1961-63; instr., then asst. prof. dept. econs. Queens Coll., 1963-67; successively asst. prof., asso. prof., prof. dept. econs. Hunter Coll., N.Y.C., 1968—. Mem. Latin Am. Studies Assn., Am. Econ. Assn. Author: A Comparative Economic History of Latin America, 1500-1914, vol. 1, Mexico, vol. 2, Brazil, vol. 3, Mexico, vol. 4, Peru, 1977—; An Economic History of Argentina in the 20th Century, 1978; editor: Economic Development, Evolution or Revolution, 1964. Contbr. articles to profl. jours. Home: 425 Riverside Dr Apt 10I New York NY 10025

RANDALL, LYNDA RAE, mfg. co. exec.; b. Los Angeles, Apr. 14, 1945; d. Edward Daleand Gwen (McCarl) Worley; B.A., U. Okla., 1981; children—Robin Elizabeth, Richard Dewey. Mgmt. trainee Columbia Savs., Denver, 1972-73; credit mgr. Modern Am. Mortgage, Tulsa, 1973-74; sr. account exec. Southwestern Bell Tel. Co., Tulsa, 1974-80; dist. mktg. mgr. Plantronics Co., Dallas, 1980—. Adv., Jr. Achievement, Tulsa, 1976; bd. dirs. Univision, 1977-80; mem. Dallas Council World Affairs, 1980-81. Unitarian. Home: 901 S Coit St Apt 2046 Richardson TX 75080 Office: 5505 LBJ Freeway Suite 500 Dallas TX 75240

RANDALL, MONICA E., hist. photographer; b. L.I., N.Y., Mar. 14, 1942; student C.W. Post Coll., 1966, New Sch. for Social Research, 1976. Photographer hist. homes and estates, L.I.; pres. Locations Inc., agy. listing hist. homes for comml. film and TV prodns. with fees used for restoration and conservation, Oyster Bay, N.Y.; lectr. in field; exhbn. of hist. photographs Costume Dept., Met. Mus. Art, N.Y.C., 1977; exec. dir. N. Shore Preservation Soc.; costume curator William K. Vanderbilt Mus., Centerport, N.Y. Mem. Internat. Kirlian Research Assn., Soc. Mag. Photographers, Internat. Platform Assn. Author: Mansions of Long Island's Gold Coast, 1979; Winfield, 1982. Home and Office: Timerwood RD Box 75 Oyster Bay NY 11771

RANDALL, RUTH, med. technologist; b. Monticello, Utah, May 7, 1946; d. Harry Smith Randall; A.S., Snow Coll., 1966; B.S., Utah State U., 1968. Supr. microbiology Meth. Hosp. Med. Center, St. Joseph, Mo., 1967-69; microbiologist St. Joseph's Hosp., St. Joseph, Mo., 1972; supr. Scharf Med. Labs. Inc., Fla. and Ga., 1972-75; staff technologist Watson Clinic, Lakeland, Fla., 1976-78; supr. Beta Lab. Inc., Lakeland, 1979-80; med. technologist in chemistry Winter Haven (Fla.) Hosp., 1981—. Mem. Am. Soc. Med. Tech., Am. Soc. Clin. Pathologists. Mormon.

RANDALL, SARAH HAMPTON, auditor; b. Rockingham, N.C., Feb. 22, 1925; d. Booker T. Dogherty and Nezzie A. (Pierce) R.; A.S. (Math. Div. scholar, Atlantic City and County Bd. Realtors scholar), Atlantic Community Coll., 1979; student acctg., Stockton State Coll., 1979—. Bill adjustment clk. John Wanamaker's, Phila., 1967-71; asst. to sales mgr. Consol. Laundries, Atlantic City, 1971-72; ins. clk. Equitable Assurance Soc. U.S., Atlantic City, 1972-76; head night auditor Penthouse Boardwalk Hotel, Atlantic City, 1974—; instr. Atlantic Community Coll., 1980—. Mem. curriculum adv. bd. Hospitality Mgmt. div. Atlantic Community Coll., 1978-80; active NOW. Mem. Phi Theta Kappa. Home: 1921 Blaine Ave PO Box 401 Atlantic City NJ 08401 Office: Penthouse Boardwalk Hotel Atlantic City NJ 08404

RANDEL-COYTE, CAROLINE, writer; b. Panama C.Z., June 9, 1951; d. Hugh Wayne and Gloria (Scott) Randel; student Am. U., 1969-71, George Washington U., 1972-73; B.A. in Polit. Sci., U. Ariz., 1973; m. Michael Alan Coyte, June 26, 1978. Profl. staff/writer U.S. Senate Republican Policy Com., Washington, 1973-77; legis. asst./speechwriter U.S. Senator Cliff Hansen, Washington, 1977-78; dir. legislation Nat. Asphalt Pavement Assn., Washington, 1979-80; with Wickes Cos., San Diego, 1981-82, corp. govt. affairs analyst, 1982. Mem. Nat. Assn. Female Execs. Methodist.

RANDELL, BONNIE JOAN, editor, lawyer; b. Chgo., Feb. 7, 1941; d. Harold Edward and Fannie (Gollay) R.; B.S., Ill. Inst. Tech., 1962; J.D., Calif. Western Sch. Law, 1967; m. Elmer C. Cowley, Jr. Nov., 28, 1975. With Bancroft-Whitney, San Francisco, 1967—, editor, 1969, publ. mgr., 1974-81, mng. editor, 1981—. Mem. Calif. State Bar. Contbr. articles to profl. jours. Office: 301 Brannan St San Francisco CA 94107

RANDISI, ELAINE MARIE, engring. co. exec.; b. Racine, Wis., Dec. 19, 1926; d. John Dewey and Alveta Irene (Raffety) Fehd; A.A., Pasadena Jr. Coll., 1946; B.S. cum laude (Giannini scholar), Golden Gate U., 1978; m. John Paul Randisi, Oct. 12, 1946 (div. July 1972); children—Jeanine Randisi Manson, Martha Randisi Cheney, Joseph, Paula, Catherine Randisi Tateo, George, Anthony. With Kaiser Engrs., Inc., Oakland, Calif., 1969-75, 77—, corp. acct., 1978-79, sr. corp. acct., 1979—; corp. buyer Kaiser Industries Corp., Oakland, 1975-77; lectr. on astrology Theosophical Soc., San Francisco, 1979—; mem. faculty Am. Fedn. Astrologers Internat. Conv., Chgo., 1982. Mem. Speakers Bur., Calif. Assn. for Neurologically Handicapped Children, 1964-70, v.p., 1969; bd. dirs. Ravenwood Homeowners Assn., 1979-82, v.p., 1979-80, sec., 1980-81; mem. organizing com. Minority Bus. Fair, San Francisco, 1976. Mem. Am. Fedn. Astrologers, Calif. Scholarship Fedn. (life), Alpha Gamma Sigma (life). Mem. Ch. of Religious Science. Initiated Minority Vendor Purchasing Program for Kaiser Engrs., Inc., 1975-76. Home: 742 Wesley Way Apt 1-C Oakland CA 94610 Office: PO Box 23210 Oakland CA 94623

RANDOL, JAMIE DANCER, systems engr.; b. Houston, Feb. 16, 1943; d. Ernest and Ada Roseman (Dedman) Dancer; B.A. cum laude, Radcliffe Coll., 1965; m. Burton S. Randol, June 19, 1964. Tchr. math. and sci. Day Prospect Hill Sch., New Haven, 1965-67; instr. data processing So. New Eng. Telephone Co., New Haven, 1968; tech. and mktg. positions IBM, White Plains, N.Y. and N.Y.C., 1969-81, mgr. systems engring. N.Y. banking br. office, N.Y.C., 1982—. Bd. dirs. Longvale Homeowners Assn., 1981—. Recipient br. mgrs. award IBM, 1978, regional mgrs. award, 1980. mem. NOW, N.Y.C. Ballet Guild. Clubs: Radcliffe (N.Y.C. and Westchester). Office: 77 Water St 21st Floor New York NY 10005

RANDOLPH, ANNE ATHERTON, opera dir.; b. Montgomery Ala.; d. James Peyton and Anna Avary (Thomas) Atherton; B.A. in English, Birmingham So. Coll., 1969; M.A., 1972; B.A. in Theatre, U. Ala., Birmingham, 1975; M.F.A., Fla. State U., 1977. Public sch. tchr. music theatre, English, Birmingham, Ala., 1969-75; stage dir. Opera Omaha, 1979, Minn. Opera, 1978-80, Central City Opera, 1978-80; staff producer English Nat. Opera, 1980; exec. dir. Opera Memphis, 1981—; tchr. Western Ill. U., Memphis State U. Recipient award Nat. Opera Inst., 1978-79; Nat. Endowment Arts Bicentennial fellow, 1980. Unitarian. Club: Network, Inc. Home: 11 Riverview Dr 6AW New York NY 10023 Office: Opera Memphis Inc Memphis State U Memphis TN 38152

RANDOLPH, CAROLYN EILEEN, broadcasting exec.; b. Ft. Campbell, Ky., Aug. 20, 1951; d. Leroy N. and Ona V. (Howald) R.; B.S. in Edn., Bowling Green (Ohio) State U., 1972; m. Philip D. Jursek, Aug. 24, 1980. Instr., Ft. Wayne (Ind.) public schs., 1973-75; announcer sta. WLYV, Ft. Wayne, 1975; broadcast journalist stas. WMEE/WMEF, Ft. Wayne, 1976; research supr. Howard Swink Advt., Marion, Ohio, 1977-78; research mgr. sta WNCI/Stereo 98, Columbus, Ohio, 1978—. Mem. Am. Mktg. Assn. (pres. Columbus chpt. 1981-82), Am. Women in Radio and TV, Nat. Abortion Rights Action League. Co-author monograph Living in Columbus, 1979; Living in Columbus II, 1981. Office: 4900 Sinclair Rd Columbus OH 43214

RANDOLPH, ELIZABETH GARLAND SCHMOKE (MRS. JOHN DANIEL RANDOLPH), former ednl. adminstr.; b. Farmville, N.C.; d. John Hagans and Pearl (Johnson) Schmoke; A.B., Shaw U., 1936, H.H.D. (hon.), 1979; M.A., U. Mich., 1945; postgrad. U. N.C., 1964; m. John Daniel Randolph, June 7, 1950 (dec. Dec. 1963). Tchr., English and French, New Hope High Sch., Rutherfordton, N.C., 1936-37; tchr. librarian DuBois High Sch., Wake Forest, N.C., 1937-43, Jordan Sellars High Sch., Burlington, N.C., 1943-44; tchr. English, adminstrv. asst. W. Charlotte (N.C.) High Sch., 1944-58; prin. University Park Elem. Sch., Charlotte, 1958-68; dir. ESEA activities Charlotte-Mecklenburg Schs., 1968-73, adminstrv. asst. for sch. ops., 1973-76, asst. supt., 1976-77, asso. supt., 1977-82. Mem. Charlotte Hosp. Authority, Charlotte-Mecklenburg Arts and Scis. Council, Charlotte Clean City Commn.; bd. dirs. Charlotte-Mecklenburg Public Library; bd. mgrs. Charlotte Meml. Hosp. Mem. AAUW, NEA (life), Assn. Supervision and Curriculum Devel. (pres. 1977-78), Nat. Assn. Adminstrv. Women in Edn., Nat. Council Negro Women, Links, NAACP, Phi Delta Kappa, Delta Kappa Gamma, Alpha Kappa Alpha (Mid-Atlantic regional dir. 1964-68, chmn. standards com., nat. parliamentarian 1974—). Home: 1616 Patton Ave Charlotte NC 28216

RANES, CAROL GULASKY, computer co. exec.; b. Williamsburg, Va., Aug. 12, 1945; d. Joseph and Anne (Grigsby) Gulasky; student U. Richmond, 1963-64; B.S. in Math., E. Carolina U., 1967; postgrad. Am. U., 1974-76, George Washington U., 1981—. Tchr. math. Alexandria (Va.) Sch. System, 1967-68; programmer/systems analyst Dept. Agr., Alexandria, 1968-77; sr. systems analyst/project mgr. Planning Research Corp., McLean, Va., 1977-78; mgr. software services Warrex Computer Corp., Bethesda, Md., 1978-80; dist. systems mgr., fed. dist. Wang Labs., Inc., Arlington, Va., 1980-81; sales support mgr. CLI, Inc., Washington, 1981—. Mem. Nat. Assn. Exec. Women, Women in Info. Processing, Alpha Xi Delta, Chi Beta Phi. Republican. Baptist. Home: 520 N St SW #S-113 Washington DC 20024 Office: 1126 16th St NW #210 Washington DC 20036

RANGEL, IRMA, lawyer, state legislator; b. May 15, 1931; J.D., St. Mary's Law Sch., San Antonio. Admitted to Tex. bar; mem. Tex. Ho. of Reps., 1977—, mem. judiciary com., transp. com. Democrat. Office: Tex Ho of Reps Room 412B Austin TX 78711 *

RANGELL, SYDELLE RAY, advt. agy. exec.; b. Bklyn., July 25, 1931; d. Morris and Pauline (Kaiser) R.; M.A. magna cum laude, Bklyn. Coll., 1954. Former producer Jack Tinker & Partners, Tinker Dodge Delano; v.p., exec. producer Needham Harper & Steers Inc., N.Y.C., 1971—. Recipient numerous awards. Office: 909 3d Ave New York NY 10022

RANGILA, NANCY ARNEVNA, investment counselor; b. Petrozavodsk, Russia, Mar. 28, 1936 (parents Am. citizens); d. Arne and Myrtle Marie (Jacobson) Kujala; B.A., U. S.C., 1958, M.A., 1964; M.B.A., U. So. Calif., 1973; student Reed Coll., 1953-54, Portland State U., 1954-57. Employment counselor Nancy Nolan Agy., Los Angeles, 1960; sec., adminstrv. asst. Bekins Bus. Records Center, Los Angeles, 1961-64; sec., statistician, securities analyst Capital Research & Mgmt. Co., 1964-73; portolio mgr., v.p. Capital Cons., Inc., Portland, Oreg., 1973-82; v.p., mgr. Franklin Securities, subs. Benjamin Franklin Savs. and Loan Assn., Portland. Pres. Planned Parenthood Assn., Portland, 1979-81, dir., 1976-82; bd. dirs. Portland Hosp. Facilities Authority, 1979—; bd. dirs. Portland Civic Theatre, 1977-79, Delaunay Mental Health Clinic, 1979-81. Chartered fin. analyst; cert. employee benefit specialist. Mem. Fin. Analyst Fedn., Western Pension Conf., Internat. Assn. Cert. Employee Benefit Specialists, Portland Soc. Fin. Analysts (past pres., dir.). Republican. Clubs: City of Portland, Multnomah Athletic. Home: 2221 SW 1st Ave 1625 Portland OR 97201

RANKIN, DIANNE MARY, fin. planner; b. Mineola, N.Y., May 27, 1947; d. David Jay and Rose Mary (Ruggerio) Keller; B.A., U. Louisville (Deans scholar), 1969, postgrad., 1976—; m. Eric Lynn Rankin, Nov. 18, 1972. Stewardess, Pan Am. Airways, 1969-72; material controller RCA, Somerville, N.J., 1972-75; pvt. practice acctg., Flemington, N.J., 1975—; investment adv. SEC, 1982; instr. tax preparation, Flemington, 1976-78. Mem. Delaware Twp. Mcpl. Utilities Authority, 1979—. C.P.A., N.J.; cert. fin. planner. Mem. Nat. Soc. Public Accts., Nat. Tax Tng. Inst., Nat. Tax Limitation Com., Female Exec. Address: RD 2 Ferry Rd Flemington NJ 08822

RANKIN, GLORIA BANKS, artist; b. Greenville, S.C., Apr. 23, 1927; d. James Edward and Sonya Jolly Banks; student Miami Inst. Art, U. Oreg., Atlanta Inst. Art, Art Students League N.Y.; m. Gordon Elliott Rankin, Aug. 4, 1944; children—Linda Alyce, Laura Amber, Gordon Earl, Robin Kim. Co-owner, artist Anchorage advt. agy., 1967-69; artist Anchorage Times, 1962-67; owner Art Center Mus., Anchorage, 1972-80; tchr. art to Eskimo children in the Bush, 1979—. Mem. Nat. Fedn. Press Women, Alaska Watercolor Soc. (pres. 1976-79), Alaska Press Women, Portrait Club N.Y. Home: 1776 Forest Park Dr Anchorage AK 99503

RANKIN, JUDITH TORLUEMKE, profl. golfer; b. St. Louis, Feb. 18, 1945; d. Paul W. and Waneta (Clifton) Torluemke; student public schs., Eureka, Mo.; m. Walter Rankin, June 12, 1967; 1 son, Walter. Profl. golfer; pres. Ladies Profl. Golfers Assn., 1976-77. Recipient Vare trophy for lowest scoring average, 1973-76; Victor award for Female golfer, 1976; leading money winner, 1976-77; first woman to win more than $100,000 in one year, 1976. Author: Natural Way to Golf Power. Address: 2405 Culpepper Midland TX 79701

RANKIN, L. HELEN, state legislator; b. Ala., Sept. 12, 1936; d. Curtis Connie (Nelms) Key; ed. U. Cin.; children—Sharron G., James W., Connie L. Mem. Ohio Ho. of Reps., 1978—. Office: Ohio Ho of Reps State Capitol Columbus OH 43215 *

RANNEY, HELEN MARGARET, physician; b. Summer Hill, N.Y., Apr. 12, 1920; d. Arthur C. and Alesia (Toolan) R.; A.B., Barnard Coll., 1941; M.D., Columbia U., 1947; Sc.D., U. So. Calif., 1979. Intern, Presbyn. Hosp., N.Y.C., 1947-48, resident, 1948-50; practice medicine, specializing in internal medicine, hematology, N.Y.C., 1954-70; asst. physician Presbyn. Hosp., 1954-60; instr. Coll. Physicians and Surgeons, Columbia U., 1954-60; asso. prof. medicine Albert Einstein Coll. Medicine, 1960-64, prof. medicine, 1965-70; prof. medicine State U. N.Y., Buffalo, 1970-73; chmn. dept. medicine U. Calif. at San Diego, 1973—. Mem. Am. Soc. Clin. Investigation, Am. Soc. Hematology, Harvey Soc., Am. Assn. Physicians, Nat. Acad. Sci., Inst. Medicine, Phi Beta Kappa, Sigma Xi, Alpha Omega Alpha. Home: 6229 La Jolla Mesa Dr La Jolla CA 92037 Office: Dept Medicine 8110 University Hosp 225 W Dickinson St San Diego CA 92103

RANSOHOFF, PRISCILLA BURNETT, psychologist, educator; b. Pitts., June 16, 1912; d. Levi Herr and Clara Amelia (Brown) Burnett; B.S., U. Pitts., 1941; M.A., Columbia U., 1952, Ed.D., 1954; m. James Hampton Johnston, Aug. 4, 1934; 1 dau., Priscilla Burnett; m. 2d, Nicholas Sigmund Ransohoff, Nov. 27, 1947. Dir. rehab. Monmouth Med. Center, Long Branch, N.J., 1944-54; pres. Cons. Assos., Inc., Long Branch, 1954-64; v.p. Dale-Elliot Mgmt. Cons., N.Y.C., 1958-60; edn. adviser U.S. Army Electronics Command, Ft. Monmouth, N.J., 1964-78; organizational effectiveness staff officer U.S. Army Communications Materiel Readiness Command, Ft. Monmouth, 1978—; coadj. prof. Ocean County Community Coll., Toms River, N.J.; coadj. instr. Monmouth Coll., West Long Branch, N.J., Brookdale Community Coll., Lincroft, N.J. Founder, pres., chmn. bd. Monmouth Rehab. Workshop, Red Bank, N.J., 1954-58; vice chmn. N.J. del. Women's Conf., Houston, 1977. Cert. practitioner neuro linguistic programming. Mem. Orgn. Devel. Network, Internat. Platform Assn., Federally Employed Women (pres. 1973, 74), Assn. U.S. Army (sec.), Def. Preparedness Assn., Assn. U.S. Army (sec.), Pi Lambda Theta, Kappa Delta Pi, Delta Zeta. Clubs: Toastmistress, Order of Eastern Star. Home: 13 River Ave Monmouth Beach NJ 07750 Office: Hdqrs US Army Communication and Electronics Material Readiness Command and Ft Monmouth ATTN DRSEL-OE Fort Monmouth NJ 07703

RANSOM, BURNELLA JACKSON, public relations exec., bus. mgr.; b. Louisburg, N.C., Nov. 16, 1940; d. Burnall J. and Elizabeth Louise (Day) Hayes; B.S., N.C. Coll., 1961; M.S., N.C. Central U., 1970; m. Raymond L. Ransom, Jr., May 13, 1979; children by previous marriage—Elizabeth L. Jackson, Brooke Renee Jackson, Maynard H. Jackson. Grad. asst. in bus. N.C. Coll., Durham, 1961-62; instr. bus. Bennett Coll., Greensboro, N.C., 1962-63; adminstrv. asst. Econ. Opportunity Atlanta (Ga.), 1964, contract specialist, 1966, program coordinator, 1967-68, dir. planning and program devel., 1968-70; public relations exec. and dir. program planning Pvt. Cons. Services, Atlanta, 1971-75; propr., pres. First Class, Inc., Atlanta, 1975—; v.p., co-propr. BJT, Inc., Atlanta, 1979—; bus. mgr. The SOS Band, 1979—. Named Outstanding Young Woman of Ga., 1970; recipient Outstanding Service award U.S. Dept. Justice, Bur. of Prisons, 1973, Woman's Day Service award W.Hunter St. Bapt. Ch., 1974. Mem. Nat. Assn. Media Women (Community Leader award 1975), Nat. Assn. for Female Execs., NOW, Nat. Council for Negro Women, Atlanta C. of C., Black Music Assn., LWV, NAACP, Delta Sigma Theta (cert. of service 1972). Democrat. Baptist.

RANSOM, MARGARET PALMQUIST, food products co. exec.; b. Davenport, Iowa, Aug. 13, 1935; d. Herman Phillip and Margaret (Burchell) Palmquist; B.A. in Speech and English, Augustana Coll., Rock Island, Ill., 1957; m. David D. Ransom, July 16, 1960; 1 son, D. Burke. Tchr. speech and English, Beloit (Wis.) High Sch., 1957-59, Lake Forest (Ill.) High Sch., 1959-60, Warren High Sch., Gurnee, Ill., 1960-62, 64-66; with Kitchens of Sara Lee, Deerfield, Ill., 1972—, mgr. public affairs, 1980—. Mem. Central Lake County Human Relations Council, 1965-66, Workshop on Human Relations, 1968, Libertyville High Sch. Caucus, 1968-70; mem. steering com. YMCA, Libertyville, 1968-69; mem. Youth and Family Counseling Assn., 1966-68. Mem. Grocery Mfrs. Am. (consumer affairs com.), Am. Frozen Food Inst. (legis. and publicity com.), Public Relations Soc. Am., Soc. Consumer Affairs Profls., Mortar Bd. Office: 500 Waukegan Rd Deerfield IL 60015

RANSOM, MARGARET PRISCILLA, govt. ofcl.; b. Jackson, N.C., Sept. 17, 1947; d. Lister and Argentina (Lockhart) R.; B.S., N.C. A&T State U., 1969; M.A., Central Mich. U., 1981. With IRS, various locations, 1969—, exempt orgns. analyst, Washington, 1976-82, group mgr., Balt., 1982—. Recipient Communications and Services to Public award IRS, 1971. Mem. Nat. Assn. Black Accts., Federally Employed Women, Profl. Mgrs. Assn., Delta Sigma Theta. Office: 31 Hopkins Plaza Baltimore MD 21203

RAPIN, LYNN SUZANNE, psychologist, educator; b. Sault Ste. Marie, Mich., Nov. 26, 1946; d. John Floyd and Ruth Antoinette (Martin) R.; B.A., Fla. State U., 1968; M.Ed., U. Ill., 1970, Ph.D., 1973. Asso. and resident dir. Coll. Liberal Arts and Sci. Unit One Living and Learning Center, U. Ill., Urbana, 1971-73; asst. prof. psychology Ill. State U., Normal, 1973-74, asst. prof. edn., 1974-78, asso. prof., 1978-80, staff psychologist Student Counseling Center, 1973-76, center coordinator ednl. programs, 1976-80; adj. asso. prof. counselor edn. U. Cin., 1981—; cons. psychologist, Cin., 1980—; cons. Ill. Wesleyan U., 1975-78. Ill. State U. grantee, 1974-79; registered psychologist, Ill., Ohio. Mem. Am., Midwest psychol. assns., Am. Personnel and Guidance Assn., Am. Coll. Personnel Assn. (Ill. rep. Women's Task Force 1976-80), Assn. Specialists in Group Work, Assn. Counselor Edn. and Supervision, NOW, Am. Soc. for Tng. and Devel. Contbr. articles on group research, program devel., human sexuality, faculty devel. to profl. jours., 1974—; mem. editorial bd. Jour. Specialists in Group Work, 1979-82. Home: 1134 Cryer Ave Cincinnati OH 45208 Office: Suite 550 Carew Tower Cincinnati OH 45202

RAPP, DORRIE LOUISE, clin. psychologist; b. Chgo., Sept. 14, 1949; d. Edward Thomas and Louise Kathryn (Leisten) Tholke; B.A., U. Ill., Chgo., 1970; Ph.D., Cambridge U., Eng., 1977, diploma in clin. psychology, 1981. Psychologist, Spastics Soc., London, 1976-79; clin. and sch. psychologist Delaware Valley Psychol. Clinics, Phila., 1979—; asst. dir. psychol. services Moss Rehab. Hosp., Phila., 1980—. Lic. psychologist, Pa. Fellow Am. Acad. Cerebral Palsy and Devel. Medicine (Richmond Cerebral Palsy Center award 1980); mem. Am. Psychol. Assn., Pa. Psychol. Assn., Phila. Soc. Clin. Psychologists, Brit. Psychol. Soc. Invented drool control electronic device, 1979; contbr. articles in field to profl. publs. Office: Moss Rehab Hosp 12th St and Tabor Rd Philadelphia PA 19141 also Delaware Valley Psychol Clinics 1536 Pratt St Philadelphia PA 19124

RAPP, LA WANDA LEA KELLEY, psychologist; b. McAlester, Okla., July 22, 1935; d. Lealand Lyle and Lenora Wyvette (Swilling) Kelley; B.S. in Edn. (AAUW scholar), U. Oreg., 1957; M.A. in Psychology, Eastern N.Mex. U., 1966; Ed.S., Eastern N.Mex. U., 1969; Ed.D., U. Nev., Reno, 1980; m. Dennis Burton Rapp, Dec. 22, 1955; children—Edward Burton III, Warren Lee. Acctg. and disbursing clk.-typist, naval civil service, 1952-53; classroom tchr., 1955-56, 57-62; tchr., counselor, 1963-64; designer multi-level guidance programs (K-12) for Dora and Melrose (N.Mex.) Public Schs., 1966-69: psychologist, child devel./diagnostic clinics, Montgomery, Ala., 1970-72, Hampton and Falls Church, Va., 1972-74; psychologist Fairfax County Public Schs., Fairfax, Va., 1974-77; psychologist Spl. Children's Clinic, Reno, 1978-80; adminstr.-supr. Washoe High Sch., Reno, 1979—. Named an Outstanding Young Woman in Am., Women's Club of Montgomery (Ala.), 1972. Mem. Internat. Council for Exceptional Children, Phi Delta Kappa. Republican. Methodist. Club: Order of Eastern Star (Hawthorne, Nev.). Home: 4385 Bridle Way Reno NV 89509 Office: Washoe High Sch 395 Booth St Reno NV 89509

RAPP, MARJORIE LENORE (GREEN), fin. planner; b. Elmhurst, Ill., June 5, 1932; d. DeWitt Clinton and Ruth Marion (Mueller) Green; B.A. with honors, U. Chgo., 1951, M.A. with honors, 1954; postgrad. U. Colo.; m. Alan Dean Rapp, June 14, 1953; children—Jeffrey Clinton, Martha Coralynne, David Cyril. Gen. mgr. Sark Aviation, Colorado Springs, Colo., 1961-64; North Union Devel. Co., also LaSalle Devel. Co., Colorado Springs, 1964-76; v.p., chief fin. officer Janus Corp., Colorado Springs, 1964-70; v.p., treas. Med. and Data Services, Inc., Colorado Springs, 1977-78; founder, 1978, owner Pandora Enterprises, Colorado Springs, 1978—; seminar tchr., 1975—. Dir. Candy-Stripe program Meml. Hosp., Colorado Springs, 1967-68; asst. to minister music First Presbyn. Ch., Colorado Springs, 1967-75; genealogy research librarian Penrose Public Library, Colorado Springs, 1971-73; pres. guild Colorado Springs Choral Soc., 1962-63; treas., bd. dirs. Colo. Opera Festival, 1978-81. Mem. Nat. Trust Historic Preservation, New Eng. Hist. and Geneal. Soc., Soc. Preservation New Eng. Antiquities, Colo. Geneal Soc., Pikes Peak Geneal. Soc., AAUW, DAR, Mayflower Soc., Meml. Hosp. Aux. (life), Quadrangler Alumni Assn. (life), El Paso County Med. Aux., Phi Beta Kappa. Republican. Address: 4807 Avondale Circle Colorado Springs CO 80917

RAPPAPORT, PAMELA FLUMMERFELT, nurse; b. Vincennes, Ind., May 21, 1949; d. Mavorette Nadine (McGinnis) F.; B.S. in Nursing, Ind. U., 1972, M.S. in Nursing, 1978; Pediatric Nurse Practitioner, Methodist Hosp., Indpls., 1976; m. June 20, 1982. Staff nurse sch. age unit Riley Hosp. for Children, Indpls., 1972-73, asst. head nurse, 1974-75; clin. nurse specialist, pediatric nurse, 1976-82; asst. head nurse, pediatric nurse hematology-oncology outpatient dept. Cin. Children's Hosp., 1982—; clin. asst. prof. pediatric nursing Ind. U., 1979-82; mem. rehab. com. Ind. service div. Am. Cancer Soc., 1980-82; mem. nat. children's cancer study group A nursing com. Nat. Cancer Inst., 1980-82. Mem. adv. bd. Riley Cancer Research Inc., 1979-82, Compassionate Friends, Inc., 1979-82. Mem. Council Adult and Child Nurse Practitioners, Ind. Nurses Assn., Am. Nurses Assn., Assn. Pediatric Oncolgy Nurses (parlimentarian), Ind. U. Alumni Assn., Sigma Theta Tau, Psi Iota Xi. Methodist. Home: 774 Chipley Ct Cincinnati OH 45240 Office: Children's Hosp Med Center Elland and Bethesda Aves Cincinnati OH

RAPPAPORT, YVONNE KINDINGER, educator, lectr.; b. Crestline, Ohio, Feb. 15, 1928; d. Paul Theodore and Florence Iona (Cover) Kindinger; B.S. summa cum laude, Northwestern U., 1949; M.A., Va. Poly. Inst. and State U., 1973, Ph.D., 1980; m. Norman Lewis Rappaport; children—Michael, Laura, Hilary, Stephen, Jocelyn. Personnel officer, then cons. and mgmt. analyst USAF, 1953-63; cons. mgmt. analysis, personnel and public relations, 1963-67; cons. program devel., instr. U. Va., 1967-70, dir. continuing edn. for women, 1970-75, dir. and faculty continuing edn. for adult, 1975—; dir., performer theatre, children's theatre, radio and TV, 1953—; bd. dirs. Coalition Adult Edn. Orgns. U.S., 1979—, sec.-treas., 1981—; cons. in field. Mem. Va. Legis. Adv. Com. Continuing Edn., 1970-71, No. Va. Adv. Com. Ednl. Telecommunications, 1971—; bd. dirs. Home and Sch. Inst., Washington, 1971—; adv. bd. Service League Va., 1976-78. Recipient Meritorious Service award USAF, 1959; Career Devel. award ASTD/TOC, 1980. Mem. Nat. Assn. Women Deans, Adminstrs. and Counselors (S.E. regional coordinator 1973-76), adult edn. assns. U.S. (Nat. Leadership award 1973, 74, 76, 78, 79; v.p. 1978-79; chmn. commn. status women in edn. 1972-74, dir. 1973—, chmn. council affiliate orgns. 1974-75, chmn. pub. affairs 1975-78), Va. (pres. 1971-73; Recognition of Merit award 1971-73), LWV (state dir. 1968-73, nat. public relations com. 1970-75), AAUW, PTA, Am. Personnel and Guidance Assn., Nat. Univ. Extension Assn., Assn. Continuing Higher Edn., Am. Bus. Women Assn. (award 1960). Club: Order Eastern Star. Author handbooks and work books, also radio, TV scripts. Home: 3225 Atlanta St Fairfax VA 22030 Office: Sch Continuing Edn Univ Va Charlottesville VA 22903

RAPPLEYEA, TOMI JEAN, financial analyst; b. Peoria, Ill., Nov. 14, 1941; d. Donald Denver and Nadine Alice (Burns) Wilkey; B.S. in Quantitative Methods, U. Ill., 1978; M.B.A., U. Chgo., 1979; m. Frederick Arthur Rappleyea, Nov. 9, 1968; children—Christopher David, Catherine Lynn, Frederick Arthur, Jr. Treas. Cougar, Inc., Bensenville, Ill., 1970-76; sr. systems analyst Exxon, U.S.A., Houston, 1979-80; sr. fin. analyst Exxon USA, Houston, 1980-81, refining analyst, Baytown, Tex., 1981-82, fin. and bus. analysis specialist Hdqrs. Computing Services, Houston, 1982—. Head Coach Schiller (Ill.) Park Youth Assn., 1968-74; active Park Ridge Citizens Party, Park Ridge, Ill., 1976-79; dir., treas. Park Ridge Swim Club, 1977-78. C.P.A., Ill., Tex. Mem. Am. Inst. C.P.A.s, Tex. Soc. C.P.A.s (Houston chpt.), Phi Kappa Phi, Beta Gamma Sigma. Clubs: AAU; American Contract Bridge League. Home: 8806 Cedarbrake St Houston TX 77055 Office: PO Box 2180 Houston TX 77001

RAPPS, RHONDA WILKINSON, psychologist; b. Baytown, Tex., Aug. 28, 1947; d. John Meier and Helen Alice (Powers) Wilkinson; B.A. with high honors in Psychology, U. Ark., 1969; M.A. (teaching fellow), cert. sch. psychology, Fairleigh Dickinson U., 1973; Psy.D. (teaching fellow) Rutgers U., 1975; m. Paul E. Rapps, Sept. 11, 1975. Sch. psychologist Newark Public Schs., 1972-73, Westfield (N.J.) Public Schs., 1975-81; pvt. practice psychology Human Potential Inst., Warren, N.J., 1978—; cons. mental health agy., nursing home, sch. emotionally disturbed children, Hunterdon Med. Center; tchr. Middlesex County Coll., Fairleigh Dickinson U., Hackensack Hosp. Profl. adv. com. Somerset County Assn. Retarded Citizens. Lic. psychologist, N.J.; cert. sch. psychologist, dir. student personnel services, N.J.; instr. parent effectiveness tng. Mem. Am. Psychol. Assn., Nat. Assn. Sch. Psychologists, Alpha Epsilon Delta, Psi Chi, Kappa Delta Pi, Alpha Chi Omega. Home and Office: 45 Washington Valley Rd Warren NJ 07060

RASBERRY, SHAROL BARTA, acct., mgmt. co. exec.; b. Red Cloud, Nebr., Oct. 15, 1947; d. Allen James and Orfa Irene (Copley) Barta; B.B.A., U. Nebr., 1969; m. Robert E. Rasberry, Dec. 29, 1968; children—Kimberly, Robert E. Tax prin. Arthur Young & Co., Wichita, Kans., 1969-79; dir. taxes CWG Enterprises, Wichita, Kans., 1979-80; dir. investments Capital Management Co., Wichita, 1980—. Bd. dirs. YWCA, 1978. Mem. Am. Inst. C.P.A.s, Kans. Soc. C.P.A.s. Republican. Home: 220 Post Oak Wichita KS 67206 Office: 300 N Main St Suite 200 Wichita KS 67201

RASDALL, JOYCE OLIVER, home economist, educator; b. Simpson County, Ky., Dec. 10, 1944; d. Thomas Franklin and Ruth A. (Heard) Oliver; B.S., Western Ky. U., 1965; M.S., U. N.C., Greensboro, 1968; Ph.D., Ohio State U., 1973; m. L. D. Rasdall, Jr., Aug. 15, 1965; children—L. Dow, Rebecca Ruth. Consumer service specialist Warren Rural Electric Coop. Corp., Bowling Green, Ky., 1966-68; research asso. Ohio State U., Columbus, 1970-71; instr., then asst. prof. dept. home econs. and family living Western Ky. U., Bowling Green, 1968-78, asso. prof. housing and household equipment, 1978—, sabbatical leave, 1982; TV program Women, Yes, 1966-68; radio program House Call, 1967-68. Trustee, Warren Assn. Bapt. Properties, 1978—, Campbellsville Coll., 1983—; mem. N. Warren Bicentennial Events Com., 1976; assn. dir. Ky. Bapt. Young Women, 1978—; founding benefactor, College Heights Found.; v.p., then pres. N.Warren PTA, 1978-80; cons. and judge electricity projects 4-H Club. Recipient MACAP vol. award, 1974, research award Am. Council on Consumer Interests, 1974, outstanding mem. service award Nat. Rural Electric Coops., 1968, R.C.P. Thomas award Western Ky. U., 1965; faculty research grantee, 1979; Am. Home Econs. Assn. fellow Ohio State U., 1970-71. Mem. Am. Home Econs. Assn., Am. Assn. Housing Educators, Ky. Home Econs. Assn. (various coms.), Elec. Women's Roundtable (nat. chmn. Julia Kiene grad. fellowship and Lyle Marner grad. scholarship), Ky. Elec. Women's Round Table (officer, v.p.), Coll. Educators of Home Equipment (pres. elect, pres., chmn. ann. meeting), Internat. Microwave Power Inst., Ky. Youth Electric Adv. Council, Nat. Trust Hist. Preservation, Phi Upsilon Omicron (sponsor univ. chpt.), Omicron Nu. Clubs: Smiths Grove Woman's (pres.), Ky. Fedn. Women's Clubs (coms.). Author: The Utility of Product Information as a Resource for Consumer Use, 1977; Consumer Competencies in Household Equipment, 1975; Information on Consumer Products: A Study of Factors Affecting its Use by Consumers, 1974; Product Information as a Resource: Factors Affecting its Usefulness to Consumers, 1974; Plan the Light in Your Home, 1970; (with others) Microwave Ovens, 1972; The Energy Dilemma: Some Choices Confronting the American Family, 1978; Energy Productivity and Creativity in the Household (series of slides sets and scripts), 1982, others. Home: PO Box 206 Smiths Grove KY 42171 Office: Dept Home Economics and Family Living Western Ky U Bowling Green KY 42101

RASKIN, EVELYN, psychologist, educator; b. Bklyn.; d. Nathaniel B. and Elizabeth (Herman) R.; B.A., Barnard Coll., 1932; Ph.D., U. Minn., 1937; m. Philip Dawson. Adj. prof. Randolph-Macon Women's Coll. 1937-42; personnel technician Adjutant-Gen. Office Dept. War 1942-45; chief appraiser Veterans' Advisement unit Bklyn. Coll. 1945-48, asst. prof. psychology 1948-53, asso. prof. 1953-67, prof. 1968—; lectr., research assoc. SUNY Downstate Med. Center 1967-71. Registered psycologist, N.Y. Mem. Womens Internat. League for Peace and Freedom, Am. Psychol. Assn., Eastern Psychol. Assn., Soc. Research in Child Devel., Am. Women in Sci., Sigma Xi. Co-author: Differential Aptitude Tests, Group Embedded Figures Test; contbr. articles to profl. jours. Office: Department Psychology Brooklyn College Brooklyn NY 11210

RATEAVER, BARGYLA, horticulturist, educator; b. Ft. Dauphin, Madagascar, Aug. 3, 1916; came to U. S., 1935; d. Eugene Alaric and Margaret (Schaffnit) Rateaver; B.A. in Botany, U. Calif., Berkeley, 1943, M.S. in L.S., 1959, postgrad., 1965-66; M.S. in Botany, U. Mich., 1950, Ph.D. in Botany, 1951; m., 1944; 1 child, Gylver. Plant collector U.S. Dept. Agr., Madagascar, 1930-34; plant collector in U.S. for European collections and herbaria, 1936; gardener for pvt. homes, 1938-43; organizer, preparer herbarium Palm Springs Desert Mus., 1944; research asst. U. Mich., 1945-51; specialist U. Calif., Davis, 1951-52; technician hort. dept. UCLA, 1953-54; partner in experimentation with Dr. Charles Wingle, San Diego County, 1954-55; lit. researcher on tropical plants, 1956-58; lit. researcher for Library Sch., U. Calif., Berkeley, 1958-59; organizer sci. libraries, Calif., 1959-64; lectr. on organic gardening, radio and TV, 1965—; organic gardening instr. U. Calif., Calif. State U., Community Coll. System, 1968—; reorganizer sci. collection Santa Rosa City County Library, 1968-69; organizer sci. symposia; lectr. and cons. in field. Recipient 1st prize Della Sizler Graphic Arts Collection, U. Calif., Berkeley, 1959; Pres.'s scholar, DePauw U., 1935; Price-Pottenger Nutrition Found. fellow, 1980; Longwood Gardens grantee; Chgo. Mus. Natural History grantee, 1955; Am. Acad. Arts and Scis. grantee, 1955. Mem. Internat. Fedn. of Organic Agr. Movements (coordinating com., working group on edn., working group on info.

1978—). Author: Plant Microtechnique Manual, 1964; Organic Method Primer, Condensation of Biodynamic Farming, 1973; Marketing Manual-computerized, N.Am. Aviation, 1963; author, pub. Conservation Gardening and Farming Series, 1972—; columnist, nat. mags., 1972—. Address: 9049 Covina St San Diego CA 92126

RATHBUN, NANCY ANNE, trade assn. exec.; b. Ft. Wayne, Ind., Dec. 26, 1941; d. Robert Howard and Dorothy Anne Rathbun; ed. Internat. Christian U., U. Tex.; m. Randall W. Scott; children—Michael Henry, Jennifer Jane. Trade assn. exec., 1964—; dir. public relations and publs. Internat. Franchise Assn., Washington, 1979—. Mem. Am. Soc. Assn. Execs., George Washington Soc. Assn. Execs., Word Guild, No. Va. Bd. Realtors. Club: Toastmistresses. Editor: Franchising World, 1979—; How to Organize a Franchise Advisory Council, 1979. Home: 3512 Maple Ct Falls Church VA 22041 Office: 1025 Connecticut Ave NW Suite 1005 Washington DC 20036

RATHBUN, ROSE DOLORES, nurse; b. East Chicago, Ind., Feb. 11, 1914; d. George and Rose Magdeline (Yuhacz) Vargo; diploma Kahler Meth. Sch. Nursing, 1936; m. William A. Rathbun, May 28, 1937; children—Phyllis, Ruth, William, Barbara. Nurse, Kahler Hosp., 1936, Meth. Hosp. Gary, Ind., 1937, Bobs Roberts Hosp., U. Chgo., 1937-42; asst. supt. Meth. Hosp., Gary, 1942, part time, 1954-55; pvt. duty, Gary and East Chicago, 1942-49, 50-52, 53-54; staff surg. nurse St. Catherine Hosp., East Chicago, 1949-50; night supr. Patrick Henry Hosp., Newport News, Va., 1962-63; with Eastern State Hosp., Williamsburg, Va., 1956-57, 63—, asst. dir., 1979—, nurse coordinator; pvt. duty nurse, Williamsburg, 1963-69; night supr. part time Williamsburg Community Hosp., part time, 1969-70, staff nurse surgery and med. floor, part time 1970-81, on call, 1981—. Mem. Va. Govt. Employees Assn., Va. Nurses Coalition Action Politics. Roman Catholic. Club: St. Bedes Womans. Home: 119 Stanley Dr Williamsburg VA 23185 Office: Eastern State Hosp Drawer A Williamsburg VA 23185

RATHER, LUCIA JOHNSON, librarian; b. Durham, N.C., Sept. 12, 1934; d. Cecil Slayton and Lucia (Porcher) Johnson; A.B., U. N.C., 1955, M.S. in Library Sci., 1957; m. John Carson Rather, July 11, 1964; children—Susan Wright, Bruce Carson. Mem. staff Library of Congress, 1957—, asst. chief MARC devel. office, 1973-76, dir. cataloging, 1976—. Mem. ALA, Internat. Fedn. Library Assns. and Instns. (chmn. working group corp. headings 1977-79, chmn. standing com. cataloging 1978-81, chmn. internat. standard bibliog. rev. com. 1981—), Phi Beta Kappa. Democrat. Co-author: The MARC II Format, 1968. Office: Library of Congress Washington DC 20540

RATHJE, RHONDA JEAN, telephone co. ofcl.; b. Chgo., Aug. 28, 1958; d. Victor Dean and Rae Jean (Henzen) R.; B.A. in Journalism and Speech (various grants), Iowa State U., 1980. Reporter, Clinton (Iowa) Herald, 1979; editor internal newsletter E.I. duPont Co., Clinton, 1980; pub. affairs rep. Gen. Telephone of S.W., League City, Tex., 1980-81, pub. affairs mgr., Garland, Tex., 1981—. Mem. Women in Communications, Bus. and Profl. Women's Club (publicity chmn. Dickinson), South Tex. Press Assn. Republican. Lutheran. Home: 6300 Round Rock Apt 1207 Plano TX 77523 Office: Gen Telephone SW 3622 N Star St Garland TX 75040

RATNER, LILLIAN GROSS, psychiatrist; b. N.Y.C., Aug. 18, 1932; d. Herman and Sarah (Widelitz) Gross; B.A., Barnard Coll., 1953; postgrad. U. Lausanne (Switzerland), 1954-56; M.D., Duke U., 1959; m. Harold Ratner, Feb. 4, 1961; children—Sanford Miles, Marcia Ellen. Intern, Kings County Hosp., Bklyn., 1959-60, resident, 1967-70, fellow in child psychiatry, 1969-70, psychiatrist devel. evaluation clinic, 1970-72; resident Jewish Hosp. Bklyn., 1960-62, fellow in pediatric psychiatry, 1962-63; physician in charge pediatric psychiat. clinic Greenpoint (N.Y.) Hosp., 1964-67; pvt. practice psychiatry, Great Neck, N.Y., 1970—; clin. instr. psychiatry Downstate Med. Center, Bklyn., 1970-74, clin. asst. prof., 1974—; psychiat. cons. N.Y.C. Bd. Edn., 1972-75, Queens Children's Hosp., 1975—; mem. med. bd. Camp Sussex (N.J.), 1963—, Saras Center, Great Neck, N.Y., 1977—. Diplomate Am. Bd. Pediatrics, Am. Bd. Psychiatry and Neurology, Am. Bd. Child Psychiatry. Fellow Am. Acad. Pediatrics, Am. Acad. Psychiatry, Am. Acad. Child Psychiatry; mem. Am., Nassau, Bklyn. psychiat. assns., Bklyn. (sr. mem.), Nassau pediatric socs., Soc. Adolescent Psychiatry, N.Y. Council Child Psychiatry, Soc. Clin. and Exptl. Hypnosis, AMA, N.Y., Kings County med. socs., Am. Soc. Clin. Hypnosis. Home and Office: 55 Bluebird Dr Great Neck NY 11023

RATNER, SARAH, research biochemist; b. N.Y.C., June 9, 1903; d. Aaron and Hannah Ratner; A.B., Cornell U., 1924; Ph.D., Columbia U. Coll. Physicians and Surgeons, 1937; D.Sc. (hon.), U. N.C., Chapel Hill, 1981, Northwestern U., 1982. Successively instr., asso., asst. prof. biochemistry Columbia U. Coll. Physicians and Surgeons, N.Y.C., 1937-46; asst., then asso. prof. pharmacology N.Y.U. Coll. Medicine, N.Y.C., 1946-54, research prof. biochemistry, 1968—; mem. dept. biochemistry Public Health Research Inst., N.Y.C., 1954—; past mem. NIH Adv. Council. NIH research grantee, 20 yrs; NIH Fogarty scholar-in-residence, 1978, 79. Fellow AAAS, Nat. Acad. Sci., Am. Acad. Arts and Scis.; mem. Am. Soc. Biol. Chemists, Am. Chem. Soc., Harvey Soc. (life), N.Y. Acad. Sci. (life), Sigma Xi. Mem. editorial bd. Jour. Biol. Chemistry, 7 yrs.; contbr. numerous articles to biochem. jours. and books. Home: 70 E 10th St New York NY 10003 Office: Public Health Research Inst of City NY Inc 455 1st Ave New York NY 10016

RATTAN, JOANNE ROBINSON, social worker; b. Beverly, Mass., July 26, 1926; d. Harry George and Kathleen Anderson (Raymond) Robinson; B.S., Mass. Coll. Art, 1948; postgrad U. Wis. Parkside, 1971-73; M.S.W., U. Wis. Milw., 1976; m. Walter Rattan June 8, 1948; children—Neil Whitney, Eric Norman, Mark Walter, Martha Kathleen. Tchr. public schs., Detroit, 1948-49, Kenosha (Wis.) Mus. Art, 1960-61, Kenosha Public Schs., 1965-68; psychiat. social worker Family Counseling Center, Kenosha, 1975-77; psychiat. social worker, owner Kenosha Counseling and Psychiat. Clinic, 1977—; co-founder Women's Horizons, 1976, pres. bd. dirs. 1976-78, staff counseling cons., 1977—; bd. dirs. Childrens Service Soc. Wis., 1960-64, Family Counseling Center, 1964-68, Kenosha Homemakers, 1972-74; v.p. bd. dirs. Planned Parenthood Kenosha, 1977—, Kenosha and Racine ACLU, 1964—, treas. bd. dirs. Wis. ACLU, 1973-77. Mem. Nat. Assn. Social Workers, NOW, Kenosha Art Assn., Kenosha Symphony League Aux., Friends of the Library, Friends of the Mus. Home: 114 68th Pl Kenosha WI 53140 Office: 5910 39th Ave Kenosha WI 53142

RATTRAY, HELEN SELDON, newspaper editor, pub.; b. Bayonne, N.J., Sept. 29, 1934; d. Abraham Harry and Yetta (Spivack) Seldon; B., Douglass Coll., 1956; postgrad. Columbia U., 1958-60; m. Everett T. Rattray, July 22, 1960 (dec.); children—David E., Daniel S., Bess E. Editor, Pub., columnist East Hampton (N.Y.) Star, 1960—; dir. Graphics of Peconic, Peconic Pioneers. Former treas., bd. trustees Hampton Day Sch., 1969-73. Home: 17 Edwards Ln East Hampton NY 11937 Office: 153 Main St East Hampton NY 11937

RAU, ARLENE LOWY, equipment co. exec.; b. Pitts., Dec. 25, 1951; d. Alexander David and Sybil Dorren (Silvert) Lowy; B.Spl. Edn., U. Miami, 1973, M. Learning Disabilities, 1974; m. Timothy Joseph Rau, Dec. 20, 1981. Mfrs. reg. Lawrence J. Rogoff, Leetsdale, Pa., 1977; dist. sales rep. SONY-Bryhar Corp., Pitts., 1977-80; territory mgr. Panasonic Microwaves-Cambria Equipment Co., Pitts., 1980—. Mem. Nat. Female Execs. Assn., Alpha Lamda Delta, Kappa Delta Pi. Home: 5502 Bartlett St Pittsburgh PA 15217 Office: PO Box 610 Johnstown PA 15907

RAU, WANDA LOU, nurse; b. Florence, Mo., July 26, 1941; d. Ernest Edward and Evelyn Maxine (Adams) Homan; A.S., Lincoln U., 1975; B.S.N., St. Louis U., 1979; m. James Victor Rau, May 27, 1960; children—Kathleen Susanne Rau, Victoria Louise Rau, John David Rau. Sec., Co-Mo Electric, Tipton, Mo., 1959-60; sec. U.S. Rents It, Jefferson City, Mo., 1960-61, co-mgr., Sedalia, Mo., 1961-70; staff nurse Charles E. Still Hosp., Jefferson City, 1975-76; head nurse intensive care unit Meml. Hosp., Jefferson City, 1976-79, staff devel. coordinator, 1981—; instr. clin. psychology Trenton (Mo.) Jr. Coll., 1981—; instr. nursing sci. dept. Lincoln U., 1979-81. Mem. Am. Nurses Assn., Critical Care Nurses Assn. Republican. Mem. United Ch. of Christ. Clubs: Nightingals China Painting. Home: 1714 Greenberry Rd Jefferson City MO 65101

RAUCH, KATHLEEN, computer programmer; b. Franklin Square, N.Y., Oct. 30, 1951; d. William C. and Marian (Shull) R.; B.A., U. Rochester, 1973; M.A. in L.S., U. Mich., 1974; postgrad. N.Y. U., 1981-82. Media specialist Sutton (Mass.) Sch., 1974-76; program cons. Advanced Mgmt. Research Internat., N.Y.C., 1976-79; pub. relations cons., N.Y.C., 1979; pres. N.Y. chpt. NOW, N.Y.C., 1979-80; computer programmer Blue Cross/Blue Shield of Greater N.Y., N.Y.C., 1981-82; Federal Reserve Bank of N.Y. Mem. Assn. for Women in Computing, Women's Sports Found., NOW (dir. pub. relations N.Y.C. chpt. 1978, v.p. programs 1978, chmn. bd. 1981, founding mem., sec. Service Fund, N.Y.C. chpt. 1981), N.Y. Caths. for a Free Choice. Office: Federal Reserve Bank of N.Y. Maiden Ln New York NY 10045

RAUDONIS, MARY ANN, govt. ofcl.; b. Chgo., Nov. 23, 1924; d. Mary S.; student DePaul Sch. Music, 1948, Loop Coll., 1973, Northwestern Evening Sch., 1953. With Social Security Adminstrn., Chgo., 1951—, card maintenance clk., 1953-66, direct action examiner, 1978—. Roman Catholic. Cert., Am. Extension Sch. Law, 1952.

RAUFMAN, CECILIA ELIZABETH (LISA), coll. counselor; b. Los Angeles, May 18, 1949; d. Zale and Minna Judith (Davis) R.; A.B., U.C.L.A., 1971; M.S., Calif. State U., Los Angeles, 1973. Grad. student asst. State Dept. Mental Health, Sacramento, Calif., 1971-72, Dean of Students Office, Calif. State U., Los Angeles, 1972-73; profl. asst., community services asst. Los Angeles Valley Coll., Van Nuys, 1973-75; counselor Moorpark (Calif.) Coll., 1975—. Vice-pres. adv. com. Comosi Community Mental Health, 1980-81; mem. Conejo Community Redevel. Adv. Com., 1981. Cert. marriage family and child counselor. Mem. Calif. Personnel and Guidance Assn., Calif. Community Coll. Counselors Assn., Am. Assn. Women in Community and Jr. Colls., Nat. Career and Life Planning Network (contbr. to newsletter). Office: Moorpark Coll 7075 Campus Rd Moorpark CA 93021

RAUNER, THERESE MADELINE, sch. psychologist; b. N.Y.C., Sept. 18, 1925; d. Andrew Joseph and Anna (Kelly) R.; B.A., Trinity Coll., Washington, 1946; M.S., Fordham U., 1951, Ph.D., 1959. Tchr., Moravian Sem., Bethlehem, Pa., 1951-52, Highland Falls (N.Y.) Central Sch., 1952-55; asst. dir. guidance Ladycliff Coll., Highland Falls, N.Y., 1956-58, dir. guidance, 1959-65; dean of students Elizabeth Seton Coll., Yonkers, N.Y., 1965-67; sch. psychologist West Point (N.Y.) Elem. Sch., 1968—. Mem. Am. Psychol. Assn., Eastern Psychol. Assn. Republican. Roman Catholic. Home: Fort Montgomery NY 10922 Office: West Point Elem Sch West Point NY 10996

RAUTIO-MITCHELL, JOYCEANNA, realty saleswoman, writer; b. Astoria, Oreg., Feb. 29, 1948; d. Arni Theodore and Julie Kathryn (Kendzierski) Rautio; A.A., Clatsop Community Coll., 1968; B.A. in Polit. Sci., U. Oreg., 1970; M.A. in Internat. Affairs (Scottish Rite Found. fellow), George Washington U., 1975; m. Timothy Clay Mitchell, Aug. 30, 1980; stepchildren—Timothy Clay, Glenn Christopher, Heidi Laura Nichole. Congl. asst. U.S. Ho. of Reps., Washington and Lexington, Ky., 1971-77; cons. immigration law, Lexington, 1977-80; sr. adminstrv. aide Commr. Public Works Lexington-Fayette Urban County Govt., 1978-80; realtor-asso. Century 21 Golden Shores Realty, Naples, Fla., 1981—; free-lance writer, Naples, 1980—. Legis. liaison Naples chpt. NOW, 1982-83; sec. Willoughby Acres Homeowners Assn., Naples, 1982-83. Recipient Pres.'s Cup, Clatsop Community Coll., 1967. Mem. Naples Area Bd. Realtors, Fla. Assn. Realtors, Nat. Assn. Realtors, Women's Council Realtors, Nat. Assn. Female Execs., LWV, Phi Theta Kappa. Roman Catholic. Clubs: Fla. Extension Homemakers, North Naples. Research on divorced fathers and stepmothers. Home: 142 Willoughby Dr Naples FL 33942 Office: 2641 Airport Rd S A-104 Naples FL 33942

RAVEN, PATRICIA ELAINE (PENNY), real estate broker, fuel alcohol distillery exec. columnist; b. Oakland, Calif., Apr. 27, 1943; d. Allen James and Patricia Elaine (McClure) Nichelini; student U. So. Calif., 1961-62, U. Calif., Fresno, 1962-63, Fresno City Coll., 1973; m. Larry Joseph Raven, June 15, 1963; children—Laurence Tagge Allen, Corbyn Lance. Model, Fresno, Calif., 1960—; owner, operator Del Mar Motel and apts., Fresno, 1963-64; owner R Pantry Markets, 1965-72, v.p., 1968—; owner Holy Cow Meat Markets, Fresno, 1965-72; real estate salesman and developer, 1973; real estate broker, owner Raven Co., Fresno, 1974—; v.p. Raven Devel., Inc., 1980—; owner Raven Alcohol Distillery, 1979—; pres. Am. Gasohol, Inc., 1980—; columnist Party Line, Fresno Bee, 1978—. Democratic candidate for lt. gov. Calif., 1978; Fresno County Dem. central com. alt., 1977; pres. Fresno Cancer League, 1972-73, Jackson Sch. PTA, 1980-82; bd. dirs. Women's Symphony League, 1973-74; hon. mem. Fresno Zool. Soc. Named Nat. Betty Crocker Homemaker of Tomorrow, 1961; recipient Mayor's award, 1976; Hon. Service award Jackson Sch. PTA, 1982; Appreciation award United Cerebral Palsy Assn., 1982, Calif. Solid Waste Mgmt. Bd., 1982, Fresno Zool. Soc., 1982. Roman Catholic. Co-author: National Handbook on Toll Roads, 1977. Home: 3504 E Huntington Blvd Fresno CA 93702

RAVENELL, MILDRED WIGFALL, lawyer, educator; b. Charleston, S.C., Dec. 1, 1944; d. Switzon Samuel and Mildred Gwendolyn (Mance) Wigfall; B.A., Fisk U., 1965; J.D., Howard U., 1968; LL.M., Harvard U., 1971; m. William Hudson Ravenell, Aug. 30, 1969; children—William Samuel II, Teressa Emlynne. Systems engr. IBM, Atlanta, 1968-69; mktg. rep., Cambridge, Mass., 1969-70; admitted to Mass. bar, 1971; asst. dean Sch. Law Boston U., 1971-72; asst. prof. law Fla. State U. Coll. Law, Tallahassee, 1972-76, assoc. prof., 1976—; trustee Law Sch. Admission Council, 1979-81. Mem. ABA (council sect. legal edn. and admission to bar 1980—), Mass. Bar Assn., Soc. Am. Law Tchrs., LWV. Office: Coll Law Fla State U Tallahassee FL 32306

RAVENSCRAFT, GRACE ELENOR, communications cons.; b. Columbia, Mo., June 18, 1941; d. Emmett L. and Bessie L. (Madden) Crane; student Am. Corr. Sch., 1964-66; 1 son, Ralph Dean. Bus. service rep. Gen. Telephone Co. of the Midwest, Columbia, Mo., 1966-70, bus. office supr., 1970-72, communications specialist, 1972-75, communications cons., 1975-78, sr. communications cons., 1978—. Recipient Top Revenue Prodn. award Gen. Telephone of the Midwest, 1975, 76, 77, 78, named Salesperson of the Yr., 1977, 79. Clubs: Altrusa, Gen. Telephone Mgmt. Employees Good Govt. (pres. 1978-80), Women's Internat. Bowling Congress (dir. 1978-82). Home: 144 Columns IV Columbia MO 65201 Office: 625 E Cherry St Columbia MO 65201

RAVIOLA, GIUSEPPINA ENRICA, anatomist, physician, educator; b. Arona, Italy, Aug. 30, 1935; came to U.S., 1970; d. Giovanni and Milena (Di Toma) d'Elia; M.D. summa cum laude, U. Pavia (Italy), 1959; Ph.D. in Anatomy, 1968; m. Elio Raviola, Mar. 24, 1960; 1 child, Giuseppe James. Resident in oncology U. Pavia, 1964-68, asst. prof., 1960-70; asst. in opthalmology Harvard U. Med. Sch., Cambridge, Mass., 1970-71, lectr. opthalmology, 1978—; assoc. prof. anatomy Boston U. Med. Sch., 1972-78, prof., 1979—; cons. in glacoma NIH Eye Inst., 1971—. Fulbright scholar, 1964. Mem. Am. Soc. Cell Biology, Am. Assn. Anatomists, Assn. Research in Vision and Opthalmology, Internat. Soc. Eye Research. Club: Harvard. Office: Dept Anatomy Boston Univ Med Sch Boston MA 02118

RAWLINS, JENNIE BROWN, author, artist; b. Ogden, Utah, Jan. 24, 1910; d. John Alfred and Jeanette (Gatchell) Brown; B.A., Weber Coll., 1930; student Ricks Coll., summer 1931; student Brigham Young U., 1950, Idaho State U., 1951; m. Alma Narvel Rawlins, Dec. 20, 1934; children—Veldon Lane, Barbara Rawlins Matson. Tchr. in public schs., 1930-35; author: Talk Topics, 1959; High Button Shoes, 1962; Exploring Idaho's Past, 1963; Secret in the Cave, 1967; Tame the Wild Wind, 1968; columnist The Deseret News, 1959-63, contbr. articles, stories, poems, 1957-80. Pres., Relief Soc., 1955-58, cultural relations tchr., 1960-70. Mem. Writers League (pres. 1965-70). Mormon. Address: Route 3 Box 62 Blackfoot ID 83221

RAWLS, JANET THOMAS, coll. dean; b. Asheboro, N.C., June 19, 1954; d. William M. and Betty (Thomas) R.; B.F.A., Converse Coll., 1976, M.Ed., 1981. Asst. buyer Shop of John Simmons, Winston-Salem, N.C., 1976-77; buyer's asst. sportswear Thalhimers, Winston-Salem, N.C., 1977-78; admissions counselor Converse Coll., Spartanburg, S.C., 1978-80, asst. dean students/dir. student activities, 1980—. Mem. Nat. Assn. Women Deans, Adminstrs. and Counselors, Nat. Assn. Campus Activities, Assn. Coll. Unions Internat., Southeastern Assn. Housing Ofcls., Carolina Assn. Collegiate Registrars and Admissions Officers, Southeastern Center for Contemporary Art. Methodist. Clubs: Ladies (Spartanburg); Friends of Center (docent 1977-78). Office: Converse Coll Spartanburg SC 29301

RAWSON, LINDA KENNETT, lawyer; b. N.Y.C., Oct. 31, 1954; d. Kennett Longley and Eleanor S. R.; B.A. cum laude, Harvard U., 1976; J.D., N.Y. Law Sch., 1979; m. Charles Maxwell Harrison, Aug. 28, 1982. Admitted to N.Y. bar; asst. N.Y.C. Law Dept., 1977-78; asst. to gen. counsel Harper & Row Pubs., Inc., N.Y.C., 1980—. Capt. Women's C Squash Team, 1978-80; class agt., reunion chmn. for Class of 1972 Phillips Acad. Alumni Council, 1981-82. Recipient cert. for service to law dept. Mayor of N.Y.C., 1978. Mem. N.Y. Women's Bar Assn. Clubs: Harvard, Radcliffe (bd. govs. 1980-82), Met. Squash Recquets Assn. (N.Y.C.). Contbr. chpt. to book. Office: 10 E 53d St 9th Floor New York NY 10022

RAY, DIXY LEE, former gov. State of Wash.; b. Tacoma, Sept. 3, 1914; d. Alvis Marion and Frances (Adams) Ray; B.A., Mills. Coll., 1937, M.A., 1938, LL.D., 1967; Ph.D. (John Switzer fellow, Van Sicklen fellow), Stanford U., 1945; D.Litt., St. Martin's Coll., 1972; D.Sc., Hood Coll., 1973, Ripon Coll., 1974, St. Mary's Coll., 1974, U. Puget Sound, 1974, No. Mich. U., 1974, U. Alaska, 1975; Smith Coll., 1975, Russell Sage U., 1976, Kenyon Coll., 1976, U. Mo., 1976, Rensselear Poly. Inst., 1978; LL.D., Seattle U., 1973, Mich. State U., 1974; D.C.L., Union Coll., 1974; numerous other hon. degrees; Tchr. pub. schs., Oakland, Calif., 1938-42; asso. prof. zoology U. Wash., Seattle, 1945-72; commr. AEC, Washington, 1972-73, chmn., 1973-74; asst. sec. State Dept., 1975-76; gov. State of Wash., 1977-81; writer, lectr., 1981—; nat. lectr. Sigma Xi, 1982—; dir. Kaiser Aluminum and Chem. Corp., Pico-Wave Processors; cons. Lawrence Livermore Lab. (Calif.), Gen. Atomic Co., San Diego, TRW, Inc., Calif., Bio-Mass, Internat., Ogden, Utah, Energy Commercialization Enterprises, Calif.; mem. exec. com. Friday Harbor Labs., 1945-60; spl. cons. biol. oceanography NSF, 1960-62; dir. Pacific Sci. Center, Seattle, 1963-72; chief scientist, vis. prof. Stanford research ship Te Vega in Internat. Indian Ocean Expdn., 1964; mem. Presdl. Task Force on Oceanography, 1969. Recipient William Clapp award in marine biology Am. Soc. Corrosion Engrs., 1959; Seattle Maritime award, 1966; Frances K. Hutchinson medal for service in conservation Garden Club Am., 1973; 1st Citizen award City of Seattle, 1973; Francis Boyer sci. award Widener Coll., 1974; Woman of Year award Ladies Home Jour., 1973; Fellowship award Assn. Sci.-Tech. Centers, 1974; Proctor prize Sigma Xi, 1975; Abram Sacher award Brandeis U., 1976; Man of Yr., State of Israel Bond Orgn., 1977; Nat. Comdr.'s award DAV, 1978; Am. Exemplar Medal Freedoms Found. at Valley Forge, 1978; others; Guggenheim fellow, 1952-53. Fgn. mem. Danish Royal Soc. Natural History; mem. Phi Beta Kappa, Sigma Xi. Author: Marine Boring and Fouling Organisms, 1959; contbr. articles, sci. papers to profl. lit. Office: 600 3d Ave Fox Island WA 98333 *

RAY, HOPE WALKER, b. McConnelsville, Ohio, Oct. 11, 1906; d. S. Carlton and Grace (Wells) Walker; student Malta Normal Sch., 1924-25, Ohio U., 1940-41; B.A. in Edn., George Washington U., 1958; m. Kenneth C. Ray, June 24, 1931; children—John Walker, Beverly Ann Ray Klincko. Tchr., Morgan County (Ohio) Schs., 1925-31. Mem. DAR (past regent), Daus. Colonial Wars, Columbian Women George Washington U., Pi Lambda Theta. Republican. Methodist. Club: Order Eastern Star. Author: (elementary grade workbooks) Number Trails, 1938. Address: 1135 Brandywine Blvd H The Plains Zanesville OH 43701

RAY, JUDITH DIANA, educator; b. St. Louis, Sept. 14, 1946; d. Arthur Charles and Pauline (Malloyd) R.; A.B. in Edn., Harris Tchrs. Coll., 1968; M.A. in Edn., Washington U., St. Louis, 1972; M.S., Wash. State U., 1979. Tchr., St. Louis Bd. Edn., 1968-72; teaching asst. Washington U., 1970-72; lectr. phys. edn. York Coll., City U. N.Y., 1972-75; teaching and research asst Sch. Vet. Medicine, Wash. State U., 1975-78; asst. prof. phys. edn. West Chester (Pa.) State Coll., 1978—; reflexologist; equine researcher Washington U., 1970-72, U. Wash. State U. 1975-79, West Chester State Coll. Equine Lab., 1980-81. Mem. AAHPER, ASTM, Internat. Soc. Biomechanics, Am. Soc. Biomechanics, AAUP, Amateur Fencing League Am., Alpha Kappa Alpha, Phi Delta Kappa. Office: #306 SC West Chester State Coll West Chester PA 19380

RAY, PATRICIA SILVER, ednl. adminstr.; b. Sacramento, Calif., June 3, 1946; d. John Merlin and Hannah Mary (Silver) Porter; B.A., Coll. Notre Dame, Belmont, Calif., 1968; M.A., Calif. Poly. State U., 1978; Ed.D., Brigham Young U., 1983. Tchr., Oakgrove Sch. Dist., San Jose, Calif., 1968; dept. chmn. Lucia Mar Unified Sch. Dist., Arroyo Grande, Calif., 1970-76, orientation tchr., vice-prin. high sch., 1979-81, vice prin., dir. activities, 1981—. Mem. Commn. on Status of Women, 1978—. Mem. AAUW, Am. Home Econs. Assn., Assn. Calif. Sch. Adminstrs., Calif. Tchrs Assn., Calif. Assn. Dir. Activities, Phi Delta Kappa (3d v.p. 1981-82). Democrat. Roman Catholic. Club: Women's (v.p. 1977-79) (Arroyo Grande, Calif.). Office: 495 Valley Rd Arroyo Grande CA 93420

RAY, SHARON KENNEDY, market researcher; b. Evanston, Ill., Apr. 13, 1950; d. Angus John and Ethyl (Kennedy) R.; B.A. in Psychology, Chatham Coll., 1972; m. John Marshall McQueen, Jr., Sept. 29, 1979; 1 son, John Marshall. Qualitative research asst. Market Facts, Inc., Chgo., 1972-74; research asso., research supr. Needham, Harper & Steers Advt., Chgo., 1974-78; v.p. Step 1 Research, Chgo., 1979; pres. Sharon

K. Ray Research, Inc., Chgo., 1979—. Recipient Maurice H. Needham award Needham, Harper & Steers, 1975. Mem. Am. Mktg. Assn., Chgo. Council Fgn. Relations, Jr. League of Chgo. Club: Exec. of Chgo. Office: 625 N Michigan Ave Chicago IL 60611

RAY, VENAH KAY, mfg. co. exec.; b. Allegan, Mich., Nov. 8, 1947; d. Cameron Earl and Marcia Jean (Beery) Baxter; exec. secretarial degree, Parsons Bus. Sch., Kalamazoo, Mich., 1966; student Western Mich. U.; m. Guyton Ray, June 9, 1973; children—Renee Nicole, Melissa Andrea. Legal sec., 1966-67; ct. recorder, 1968-73; dir. Kal-Equip Co., Otsego, Mich., 1973—, corp. asst. sec., 1978—. Mem. Nat. Assn. Accts., Nat. Assn. Female Execs. Home: 6666 West F Ave Kalamazoo MI 49009 Office: 411 Washington St Otsego MI 49078

RAYBURN, GEORGINA HANSON, retail exec.; b. New Sweden, Maine, Mar. 27, 1920; d. Eric Wilhelm and Naemi Victoria (Rodin) Hanson; physical therapist, Boston Evening Clinic, 1939; med. technologist, Wilson Sch., 1941; B.S., Donsback U., 1978; m. J. Gurney Doore, Oct. 1940; 1 son, James Hanson; m. 2d, George B. Rayburn, Oct. 17, 1950; 1 son, Eric Edward. Floor supr., Boston Evening Clinic; supr. photo shop Coop Drug, Fairbanks, Alaska, 1947-49; clk. Alaska Communication System, Fairbanks, 1949-52; pres., mgr. Gina's Corner Health Food Store, Fairbanks, 1970—, chief exec. officer, 1976. Mem. C. of C. Republican. Lutheran. Clubs: Pioneers of Alaska (pres. 1968, trustee 1972-76), Order Eastern Star (past matron). Home: PO Box 1450 Fairbanks AK 99707 Office: 215 Cushman St Fairbanks AK 99707

RAYBURN, LETRICIA GAYLE, acct., educator; b. Murray, Ky., May 4, 1940; d. Harold Ray and Myrtle (Crawford) Douglas; B.S., Murray State U., 1961; M.S., U. Miss., 1962; Ph.D., La. State U., 1966; m. John Michael Rayburn, June 23, 1962; children—Douglass Michael, Beverly Gayle. Systems analyst Humble Oil & Refining Co., Baton Rouge, 1962-63; asst. prof. acctg. Western Ky. U., Bowling Green, 1965-66; prof. accountancy Memphis State U., 1967—. C.P.A., Tenn., Miss., La.; cert. internal auditor; cert. in mgmt. acctg. Mem. Am. Inst. C.P.A.s, Inst. Mgmt. Accts., Am. Acctg. Assn. Methodist. Author: Principles of Cost Accounting with Managerial Applications, 1979; Financial Tools for Effective Marketing Administration, 1976, 82; contbr. articles to profl. jours. Home: 5737 Buxbriar St Memphis TN 38119 Office: Coll Bus Memphis State U Memphis TN 38152

RAYE, MARTHA, actress; b. Butte, Mont., Aug. 27, 1916; d. Pete and Mabel (Hooper) Reed; ed. pub. schs., Mont., Cath. schs., Chgo., Profl. Children's School, N.Y.C. Appeared in vaudeville act with her parents at ages 3-13; then mem. Benny Davis Revue and later with Ben Blue Co.; appeared in Calling All Stars, musical comedy and then returned to clubs and vaudeville; began in motion pictures, Mar. 1936; made personal appearances, 1937, 38, 39, 40; played in pictures Boys from Syracuse, 1940; Navy Blues, Keep 'Em Flying, Helzapoppin, 1942, Double or Nothing, Artists and Models, Pin Up Girl, Four Jills and a Jeep, Monsieur Verdoux, 1947; appeared in numerous stage plays including Hold on to Your Hat, 1940, Annie Get Your Gun, 1952, The Solid Gold Cadillac, 1960, Personal Appearance, 1961, Separate Rooms, 1961, Calamity Jane, 1961, Wildcat, 1962, Call Me Madam, 1963, Everybody Loves Opal, 1965, 77, Hello Dolly, 1967, No, No, Nanette, 1972; radio artist; TV appearances include All Star Revue, Milton Berle shows, Martha Raye Show, 1954-56, Carol Burnett Show, 1968-75, The Bugaloos series, 1970-72, McMillan series, 1976. Recipient Jean Hersholt Humanitarian award Acad. Motion Picture Arts and Sci., 1968. Mem. Screen Actors Guild, Actors Equity Assn., Am. Fedn. Radio Actors. Address: 7500 Devista Dr Los Angeles CA 90024 *

RAYFIELD, RITA VERONICA, distbg. co. exec.; b. N.Y.C., May 10, 1902; d. Elias and Madge (Mylan) Golden; grad. high sch.; m. George Bernard Rayfield, Feb. 8, 1925; children—Dolores Mae Epperheimer, Marilyn Talbott. With Nat. City Co., N.Y.C., 1920-22, Los Angeles Times, 1923-25; pres. Inland Distbrs. Wholesale Wine & Liquor, 1939—. Mem. Nat. Republican Congressional Com. Mem. Exec. Women's Assn. Republican. Roman Catholic. Clubs: Arrowhead Country, Desert Inn Country. Home: 135 E Ralston Apt 19 San Bernardino CA 92404 Office: 785 S Lugo PO Box 5088 San Bernardino CA 92412

RAYLE, KATHLEEN ZIMMERMAN, mfg. co. exec.; b. Hammond, Ind., May 9, 1944; d. Warren Lee and Irene Rose (Glass) Zimmerman; B.S., Purdue U., 1967; M.B.A., U. Chgo., 1970; postgrad. in taxation DePaul U., 1979—. Pharmacist, various cos., Indpls. and Chgo., 1967-70; revenue agt. IRS, Des Moines, 1971-72; tax specialist McGladrey, Hendrickson & Co., Des Moines, 1972-75; tax mgr. Clow Corp., Oak Brook, Ill., 1975-79; tax compliance mgr. U.S. Gypsum Co., Chgo., 1979-82; tax mgr. Global Marine Inc., Houston, 1982—; tax cons., 1976—. Mem women's bd. Chgo. Maternity Center. C.P.A., Iowa, Ill. Mem. Tex. Execs. Inst. (dir.), Am. Inst. C.P.A.s, Iowa Soc. C.P.A.s, Ill. C.P.A. Found., Am. Women's Soc. C.P.A.s, U. Chgo. Women's Bus. Group, Beta Alpha Psi. Office: 10260 Westheimer St Houston TX 77042

RAYMOND, ELIZABETH ROYER, labor relations exec.; b. Balt., Mar. 4, 1938; d. David Lee and Elizabeth Levering (Crane) Royer; student pvt. schs., Balt.; 1 son, Edward Northcroft Trail Mathias. Bus. agt., edn. and polit. dir. for 4 state area upper South dept. Internat. Ladies' Garment Workers Union, AFL-CIO, Balt., 1967-77; asst. to sec. HUD for labor relations, Washington, 1977-81; dir. manpower planning U.S. Synthetic Fuels Corp., Washington, 1981—. Chmn. bd. dirs. Eastpoint Health Center, Balt., 1975-77. Mem. Am. Council Young Polit. Leaders. Home: 1319 33d St NW Washington DC 20007 Office: 2121 K St NW Washington DC 20006

RAYMOND, JUDITH ELLEN, advt. exec.; b. N.Y.C., Oct. 21, 1946; d. Ben and Katherine Rita R.; A.S., Fashion Inst. Tech., N.Y.C., 1967; m. Andrew N. Hadjandreas, Nov. 27, 1977. Account exec. Eleanor Lambert Inc., N.Y.C., 1967-69; public relations exec. Essie Pinsker, Inc., N.Y.C., 1969-71; with Butterick Fashion Mktg. Co., N.Y.C., 1971-73, publicity coordinator, dir. advt. and promotion, 1973-75, v.p. advt., promotion and market services, 1975-80; v.p. advt. and promotional services McCall Pattern Co. subs. Norton Simon, Inc., 1980—. Recipient citation Art Dirs. Club, 1974, Copy Club, N.Y.C., 1974. Mem. Public Relations Soc. Am., Advt. Women N.Y., Publicity Club N.Y. Home: 411 Bronx River Rd Yonkers NY 10704 Office: 230 Park Ave New York NY 10169

RAYMOND, (MYRTLE) ROBY, tire co. exec.; b. Alfred, N.D., May 4, 1920; d. John J. and Myrtle (Robison) Klundt; student Yankton Coll., 1939-40; B.S., Northwestern U., 1944; M.A., Fairfield U., 1974; student U. New Haven, 1972-75, Paier Sch. Art, 1973-74; m. Robert A. Knight, 1945; children—William Atherton, Richard Robison, James Everett; m. 2d Harry C. Raymond, 1962. News writer NBC News Room, Chgo., 1944-45, Milford (Conn.) Citizen, 1950-53; writer, asst. to dir. info. and devel. Yale-New Haven Hosp., 1959-69, dir. publs., 1969-75; public relations cons. U. New Haven, 1976, adj. prof. dept. communication, 1976; dir. communication, public relations The Armstrong Rubber Co., New Haven, 1977—; guest speaker area colls. Dir. public relations com., bd. dirs. South Central chpt. ARC, 1978—; public relations staff Tire Industry Safety Council, 1977—; sec. Orange Bd. Edn., 1954-68; adv. council Cable TV, 1972—; Orange County rep. Health Systems Agy., 1975. Mem. Rubber Mfrs. Assn. (mem. public relations com.), Internat. Assn. Bus. Communicators, Internat. Mgmt. Council, Public Relations Soc. Am., AAUW. Congregationalist. Club: Paugusset Club of Orange (Conn.). Contbr. articles to numerous publs., including Yale Alumni Mag., World Tennis, 1973; Pictorial Rev., 1972; Connecticut mag., 1975, others. Home: 854 Oakwood Rd Orange CT 06477 Office: 500 Sargent Dr New Haven CT 06507

RAYNARD, SHIRLEY M., librarian, corp. exec.; b. Lynn, Mass., Aug. 30, 1942; d. Lyle Austin and Blanche Louise (Tisdell) Paul.; B.A., Boston U., 1964; postgrad. Northeastern U.; m. Edward L. Raynard, Feb. 4, 1961; children—Robert, William. Social worker City of Beverly (Mass.), 1964-67; librarian Town of Middleton (Mass.), 1974—; owner Raynard Assos., Middleton, 1976—. Committeewoman, Democratic State Com., Essex and Middlesex Dist., Mass., 1973—; mem. Middleton Council on Aging., 1972-82, Middleton Charter Commn. Mem. ALA, Mass. Library Assn., New Eng. Library Assn. Congregationalist. Club: Middleton Garden. Home: 53 Boston St Middleton MA 01949 Office: 2 N Main St Middleton MA 01949

RAYNER, MARY ANN (POLLY), editor; b. Bethlehem, Pa.; d. John Joseph and Cecilia M. (Skledar) R.; B.A., Moravian Coll., 1953; postgrad. Lehigh U. Gen. reporter, photographer, feature writer Call-Chronicle, Allentown, Pa., family living sect. editor, 1966—, women's editor Morning Call and Evening Chronicle, 1973—, now exec. women's editor. Bd. dirs. Women's Ednl. Liaison div. United Fund, Allentown, Pa.; chmn. nominating com. for bd. dirs. Moravian Coll., 1966, scholarship com., 1972; bd. dirs. Lehigh Valley Mental Health Assn., 1970; bd. assos. Muhlenberg Coll., Allentown. Recipient citations for outstanding community service, United Fund, Allentown, also numerous other state and nat. awards for writing, Frany award for meritorious and outstanding fashion reporting, 1974; named Pa. News Writer of Yr., 1982. Mem. AAUW, Nat. Fedn. Press Women, Pa. Women's Press Assn., Women Editors Am. Dailies (charter mem.), Pa. Soc. Newspaper Editors, Washington, Overseas, Pa. press clubs, Sigma Delta Chi, Pi Delta Epsilon, Moravian Coll. Alumni Assn. (day com., dir.). Home: 1130 E 3d St Bethlehem PA 18015 Office: 6th and Linden Sts Allentown PA 18105

RAYNOR, MISA BROOKS, med. social worker; b. Greenville, S.C., Jan. 14, 1950; d. Nathan Cohn and Ruby (Hayes) Brooks; student Mars Hill Coll., 1968-70; B.A., U. N.C., 1972; M.R.E., So. Bapt. Theol. Sem., 1974; M.S.W., Kent Sch. Social Work, 1975; m. Harvey W. Raynor, III, May 27, 1972; 1 son, Tolan C. Med., oncology social worker VA Hosp., Durham, N.C., 1975—; field instr. for social work masters students, U. N.C., Chapel Hill, 1979—. Vice pres. Hospice of Wake County, 1979, pres., 1980-81; bd. dirs. Hospice N.C., 1979—, mem. exec. com., 1979—; sec., 1981. Recipient Superior Performance award VA Hosp., Durham, 1978. Mem. Acad. Cert. Social Workers, Nat. Assn. Social Workers. Baptist. Club: Altrusa (corr. sec. 1981-82). Home: 1918 Sunset Dr Raleigh NC 27608 Office: 508 Fulton Rd Durham NC 27705

RAYNOR, VERA A., poet, educator; b. Boston, Nov. 24, 1937; d. Harry and Esther Goldstein; m. Doug Raynor, Nov. 24, 1969; children—Sheri, Craig, Susan Smith, Nicole Smith. Founder, dir. The Environ. Dance Group, 1969-71; editor, pub. Patterns mag., Denville, N.J., 1970-73; poet-in-residence N.J. State Council on the Arts, 1972-74; editorial adv. bd. Stone Country, Madison, N.J., 1974—; teaching asst. Montclair (N.J.) State Coll., 1976-77; writer, dir., producer Whales, Waddies and Other Wonders, Bell & Barter Theatre and Arts Center, 1977, Woman at the Mirror, 1979; writer, dir. The Sculptor, 1978; photog. exhbn. Windows, 1982. Mem. Poets and Writers N.J. (founding mem.), Poetry Soc. Am. Contbr. articles to profl. and popular mags. Home: 2 Whaleback Waddy Denville NJ 07834

REA, HAZEL WHITE, govt. research adminstr.; b. Van Buren, Ark., Feb. 2, 1911; d. James Bernie and Massie (Bedford) White; m. Courts D. Rea, Jan. 7, 1938 (dec.); 1 dau., Ruth Rea Hilken. Adminstrv. asst. intramural research program NIMH, Bethesda, Md., 1949-57, adminstrv officer, 1957-75, asso. dir. program mgmt., intramural research program, 1975—; mem. employee adv. com. on group life ins. U.S. Civil Service Commn., 1971-74. Recipient Superior Service award HEW, 1970; Adminstr.'s award Alcohol, Drug Abuse and Mental Health Adminstrn., 1979. Mem. League Fed. Recreation Assns. (pres. 1961, 62, 64), Found. for Advanced Edn. in Scis. Home: 6700 Melody Ln Bethesda MD 20817 Office: NIH 9000 Rockville Pike Bldg 36 Room 1A-07 Bethesda MD 20205

REA, N. TERESA, urban planner; b. San Francisco, June 24, 1949; d. Frederic Melford and Nancy Hawley (Hubbard) R.; B.A., U. Calif., Berkeley, 1971; M.City Planning, Harvard U., 1975. Urban planner U. Calif., Berkeley, 1976-77; project planner John Blayney Assos., San Francisco, 1976-77; sr. planner, bus. devel. officer Bolles Assos., San Francisco, 1977—, also dir., corp. sect.; sr. asso. EDAW Inc., San Francisco, 1981—. Mem. Am. Planning Assn., Urban Design Inst., San Francisco Planning and Urban Research Assn., U. Calif. Berkeley Alumni Assn., Sierra Club. Clubs: Harvard, Commonwealth Calif. Home: 2745 Octavia St Apt 4 San Francisco CA 94123 Office: 14 Gold St San Francisco CA 94133

READ, DONNA RAE, enamelist; b. Council Bluffs, Iowa, Mar. 11, 1938; d. William and Madge Palmer (Donnelly) R.; B.S., Iowa State U., 1960; M.S., U. Tenn., 1962. With Denware Ceramics, Costa Mesa, Calif., 1961; grad. asst. U. Tenn., 1961-62; art coordinator Judson Coll., Marion, Ala., 1962-66; condr. craft workshops U. Tenn., 1964-65, Lock Haven (Pa.) State Coll., 1976-78; asso. prof. art Tex. Tech. U., Lubbock, 1966—; group exhbns. include Iowa State Coll., 1958-60, Seal Beach (Calif.) Mus., 1961, 62, 67 (mosiac award 1961, stitchery award 1962), Laguna (Calif.) Art Festival, 1961, Orange County (Calif.) Art Assn., 1961 (award), So. Highland Exhbn., Gatlinburg, Tenn., 1962-65, ann. Tex. Tech. U. faculty show, 1966-82, Nelson Gallery, Kansas City, Mo., 1970, others; represented in permanent collections museums, chs., pvt. collections; chmn. fine arts com. Tex. Tech. U. Mus.; mem. women's council Nat. Minature Works Exhbn., 1974-76, coordinator, 1975; mem. nat. com. aesthetic responsibilities Am. Home Econs. Assn., 1973-74; sec. art com. Lubbock YWCA, 1970-71; art festival juror, 1979—. Recipient award Little Rock Art Show, 1975. Mem. Am. Craftsman's Council, Nat. Art Edn. Assn., AAUP, Tex. Tech. U. Mus. Assn., Tex. Designer Craftsmen (pres. 1971-72, exhibitor 1968-79), Lubbock Art Assn., Nat. Enamelist Guild, Delta Zeta (past chpt. pres.). Methodist. Clubs: Lubbock Women's (life), Lubbock Cultural Affairs. Home: 3302 21st St Lubbock TX 79410 Office: Dept Art Tex Tech Univ Lubbock TX 79409

READOUT, ROSALEE JOYCE, educator; b. Urbana, Ohio, Nov. 24, 1936; d. Floyd Emerson and Naomi Helen (Hartzler) King; B.Ed., Colo. State U., 1979; Cert. in Fashion Merchandising, Parks Bus. Sch., 1971; A.A., Aims Community Coll., 1977, 1978; m. David Earl Readout, Oct. 29, 1976; children by previous marriage—Judy Allene Stehman Ziller, Jerry Allen Stehman, Kathy Lynn Stehman Potts. Bookkeeper, Shamrock Truck Stop, Greeley, Colo., 1960-63; underwriting asst. State Farm Ins. Co., Greeley, 1964-66; office mgr. Stehman Distbg. Co., Greeley, 1966-70; buyer, asst. bridal cons. Joslins Dept. Store, Denver, 1971-73, buyer, bridal/fashion cons., dept. mgr. Greeley, 1973-77; office mgr., bus. cons. Montey Roofing Co., Loveland, Colo., 1978-80; adult edn. instr. small bus. mgmt. Larimer County Vocat.-Tech. Center, Ft. Collins, Colo., 1978-79, post-secondary instr. clk.-typist program, 1979-82; instr. bus. and office dept. Eastern Okla. County Area Vocat. Center, Choctaw, Okla., 1982—; lectr. in field; corp. sec. Stehman Distributing Co., 1968-73. Mem. bus. women's panel, Job Opportunities Week, 1981—. Mem. Nat. Assn. Female Execs., Larimer County Vocat.-Tech. Edn. Assn., Am. Vocat. Assn., Colo. Vocat. Assn., Okla. Vocat. Assn., Okla. Bus. Edn. Assn., Alpha Delta Epsilon. Republican. Home: 9908 Larkspur Ln Oklahoma City OK 73139 Office: 4601 N Choctaw Rd Choctaw OK 73020

REAGAN, JANET THOMPSON, psychologist; b. Monticello, Ky., Sept. 15, 1945; d. Virgil Joe and Carrie Mae (Alexander) Thompson; B.A., Berea Coll., 1967; Ph.D., Vanderbilt U., 1972; m. Robert Barry Reagan Jr., Aug. 7, 1977; 1 dau., Natalia Alexandria. Mgr. research and evaluation Nashville Mental Health Center, 1971-72; mgr. evaluation Family Health Found., New Orleans, 1973-74; asst. prof. dept. health systems mgmt. Tulane U., New Orleans, 1974-77; dir. evaluation Project HEAVY West, Los Angeles, 1977-78; asst. prof. health adminstrn. Calif. State U., Northridge, 1978—cons. in field. Mem. Am. Psychol. Assn., Am. Public Health Assn., Western Psychol. Assn., Evaluation Research Soc., Am. Coll. Nursing Home Adminstrs., LWV. Democrat. Home: 10881 White Oak St Granada Hills CA 91344 Office: California State University 18111 Nordhoff St Northridge CA

REAGAN, JOY PARTNEY, child care adminstr.; b. St. Louis, Sept. 25, 1928; d. Donald Richard and Ruth (Barber) Partney; B.S. in Sociology, Lamar U., Beaumont, Tex., 1967; M.A. in Social Rehab., Sam Houston State U., 1971; m. Luther David Reagan, Aug. 26, 1948; children—Cyndy Leigh, Bonnie Ruth, Eric David. Children's counselor and intake worker, then resident dir. Beaumont Children's Home, 1967-70; adminstr. Buckner Children's Village and Family Care Center, Beaumont, Houston and Conroe, Tex., 1970—; instr. Lamar U.; mem. Tex. Legis. Com. Execs. Tex. Homes Children-Tex. Lic. Children's Services; adv. bd. Tex. Center Human Devel.; cons. in field. Mem. Nat. Assn. Homes Children, S.E. Tex. Social Welfare Assn. (Social Work Contbr. of Yr. award 1973), Execs. Tex. Homes Children (sec. 1975-79), S.W. Assn. Homes Children (v.p. 1979), Am. Assn. Psychiat. Services Children, Tex. Assn. Lic. Children's Services, Tex. United Community Services, Tex. Council Families, Beaumont C. of C., Jefferson Theatre Restoration Soc. Baptist. Club: Etudier Lit. Women (founder 1955). Author papers in field. Office: 9055 Manion Dr Beaumont TX 77706

REAGAN, NANCY DAVIS (B. ANNE FRANCIS ROBBINS), wife of Pres. U.S.; b. N.Y.C., July 6, 1923; d. Kenneth and Edith (Luckett) Robbins; stepdau. Loyal Davis; B.A., Smith Coll.; m. Ronald Reagan, Mar. 4, 1952; children—Patricia Ann, Ronald Prescott; stepchildren—Maureen, Michael. Contract actress MGM, 1949-56; films include: The Next Voice You Hear, 1950, Donovan's Brain, 1953, Hellcats of the Navy, 1957; civic worker; visited wounded Viet Nam vets., sr. citizens, hosps. and schs. for physically and emotionally handicapped children; active in furthering foster grandparents for handicapped children program, fighting drug and alcohol abuse; hon. nat. chmn. Aid to Adoption of Spl. Kids, 1977; hon. chmn. U. So. Calif. Panhellenic Council, 46 others; Named one of Ten Most Admired Am. Women, Good Housekeeping mag., 1977, Gallup Poll, 1981; Woman of Yr., Los Angeles Times, 1977; One of 10 Most Influential Women, 1981; permanent mem. Hall of Fame of Ten Best Dressed Women in U.S.; USO Woman of Year, 1982; Author: Nancy, 1980; To Love a Child, 1982; formerly author syndicated column on prisoner-of-war and missing-in-action soldiers and their families. Address: care White House 1600 Pennsylvania Ave Washington DC 20500 *

REAGIN, YNEZ MOREY (MRS. CHARLES EDWARD REAGIN), graphoanalyst, educator; b. Flasher, N.D., Mar. 3, 1913; d. Gideon Earl Morey and Margie (Ozbun) Morey Real; B.S., Colo. State U., 1934, postgrad., 1935; postgrad. U. Colo., 1945, 60, U. No. Colo., 1961-64, Western State Coll., 1967-68, 74; graphoanalysis cert. Internat. Graphoanalysis Soc., Chgo., 1958, resident tng. cert., 1965, advanced seminar cert., 1968, postgrad., 1970-74, 76; m. Charles Edward Reagin, July 10, 1935 (dec. Jan. 1979). Tchr. biology high sch., Sisseton, S.D., 1942-44; tchr. biology, gen. sci., high sch., Pueblo, Colo., 1944-46; tchr. biology Pueblo Jr. Coll., 1946-47; tchr. high sch., Lamar, Colo., 1947-50, tchr. English, 1950-51, sec. to prin., 1952-53; office mgr. Troy Public Acct., Lamar, 1953-55; self-employed tax work, 1955-58; tchr. English high sch., Canon City, Colo., 1958-59, Women's Correctional Instn., 1967; tchr. psychology Adult Edn. Program, Canon City, 1970-74, graphoanalysis, 1974—; instr. psychology Internat. Graphoanalysis Congress, Chgo., 1964-75; tchr. graphoanalysis, Canon City, 1962-74. Organizer Great Books Found. Discussion Group, Canon City, 1961, mem. 1961-66; judge Fremont, Chaffee counties 4-H Talent Festivals; active self-help groups Colo. State Prison, Colo. Women's Prison; organizing sec. Jane Jefferson Democratic Club, Canon City, 1963, precinct com. woman, 1960-64, 1968-75, sec. precinct caucuses, judge on election bds.; bd. dirs. Entertainment, Inc., 1964-68; cert. vol. Suicide Prevention and Crisis Center, Fremont County, Colo., 1972-75. Recipient Pres.'s Merit award Internat. Graphoanalysis Soc., 1969, Gold Pen award Colo. chpt., 1978. Mem. Internat., Colo. (charter mem. 2d v.p. 1971-72), So. Colo. (chmn. 1963-71) graphoanalysis socs., AAUW (pres. 1968-70, treas. 1964-66, state historian 1970-72), Canon City Graphoanalysis Study Group (organizer, chmn. 1962-75), Internat. Platform Assn., Nat. Fedn. Bus. and Profl. Women's Club, Delta Zeta, Beta Beta Beta. Mem. Order Eastern Star (worthy matron 1944-45). Democrat. Methodist. Clubs: Altrusa Internat. (dir. 1970-72, archives chmn., pub. and membership chmn. 1967-72, publicity award Dist. 10, 1972) (Canon City); Internat. Knife and Fork (dir. 1956-67), Toastmistress (charter mem., pres. 1981-82) (Fremont County, Colo.). Contbr. articles to profl. jours. Address: 610 Burrage St Canon City CO 81212 Office: 610 Burrage St Canon City CO 81212

REAME, NANCY ELIZABETH KING, nursing educator; b. Ft. Erie, Ont., Can., May 16, 1947; came to U.S., 1949, naturalized, 1969; d. Marc H. and Irene E. (Rosene) King; B.S. in Nursing, Mich. State U., 1969; M.S., Wayne State U., 1974, Ph.D. in Physiology, 1977; postgrad. (fellow) U. Mich., 1982; m. Ronald D. Reame, Nov. 13, 1971; 2 daus. Staff nurse Sparrow Hosp., Lansing, Mich., summer, 1969; charge nurse St. Joseph Hosp., Mt. Clemens, Mich., 1969-70; part-time pvt. duty nurse Home Care Nursing Agy., Chgo., 1970-71; vol. counselor Planned Parenthood, Detroit, 1972; airline stewardess Pan Am. World Airways, Chgo., 1970-72, Washington, 1972-74; part-time staff nurse Fertility Clinic, Detroit, 1974; cons. to Wayne State U. Coll. Nursing, 1975-77, asst. prof. dept. physiology Sch. Medicine and Coll. Nursing, 1977-80, project dir. health care of disabled women Ctr. for Health Research, Coll. Nursing, 1980; asso. prof. Sch. Nursing, U. Mich., Ann Arbor, 1980—; cons. to div. feminine hygiene research and devel. Kimberly-Clark Corp., Neenah, Wis., 1977-80; health issues cons. to Sta. WXYZ-TV, 1977-81. Mem. Am. Nurses Assn., Am. Fertility Soc., Midwest Nursing Research Soc., Assn. for Women in Sci., Soc. for Menstrual Cycle Research, AAAS, N.Y. Acad. Scis., Sigma Theta Tau, Alpha Lambda Delta. Contbr. chpts. to books on clin. nursing. Office: 400 N Ingalls Bldg Ann Arbor MI 48109

REAMS, ELINOR PAYNE (MRS. ARTHUR A. REAMS), internat. edn. specialist, cons., ret. govt. ofcl.; b. Dothan, Ala., Apr. 17, 1914; d. Alvin A. and Gladys Wise (Fritter) Payne; A.B. cum laude, Fla. State U., 1935; postgrad. George Washington U., 1940; m. Arthur Arnold Reams, Jan. 11, 1941; 1 dau., Anne Emily. Newspaper work, Panama City, Fla., 1935; mgr. Clements Ins. Agy., Miami, Fla., 1935-39; head dept. English, Redland High Sch., Dade County, Fla., 1936-40; writer confidential reports Bur. Contract Information, 1940-41; editorial asst. War Dept., 1941; personnel asst. Co-ordinator Information, 1941-42; personnel officer FSA, 1942-43; mgmt. planning analyst O.W.I., 1945; mgmt. planning officer Dept. State, 1945-48, chief deptl. staff U.S. Adv.

Commn. Ednl. Exchange, 1948-52, cons. internat. information adminstrn., 1952-53, Bur. Internat. Sci. and Tech. Affairs, Dept. State, 1973-75; ind. cons. U.S. govt., also pvt. orgns., 1975—; cons. Am. Council Edn., 1955-56, spl. asso. and cons. commn. edn. and internat. affairs, 1956-61, also liaison officer with UNESCO relation staff Dept. State; sr. personnel mgmt. officer Dept. State, 1961-62, chief program planning and mgmt. staff, 1962-63; fgn. affairs officer Policy Review and Research Staff, Bur. Ednl. and Cultural Affairs, Dept. State, 1963-65, asst. dir. policy review and coordination staff, 1965-67, sr. policy officer and asst. exec. dir. council on internat. ednl. and cultural affairs, 1967-70; ind. research cons., 1970—; mem. asst. sec. states com. reorgn., 1946; mem. survey mission rev. ednl. exchange activities in Europe and Near East, Dept. State, 1949; Am. Council Edn. rep. 3d gen. conf. Internat. Assn. Univs., 1960; trustee Jr. Mus. Bay County, Inc., 1976-77; pres. Friends of Bay County Pub. Libraries, Inc., 1977-78. Recipient Meritorious Service award Dept. State, 1964, Superior Service award, 1966, Superior Service Honor award, 1970. Mem. DAR, Delta Delta Delta, Phi Kappa Phi, Beta Pi Theta. Democrat. Presbyn. Clubs: Washington Golf and Country, St. Andrews Bay Yacht, Diplomatic and Consular Officers Club. Author report profl. jour. Home: 2521 Spanish Moss Ct Reston VA 22091

REBELSKY, FREDA ETHEL GOULD, psychologist; b. N.Y.C., Mar. 11, 1931; d. William and Sarah (Kaplan) Gould; B.A., U. Chgo., 1950, M.A., 1954; Ph.D., Radcliffe Coll., 1961; m. William Rebelsky, Jan. 1, 1956 (dec. 1979); 1 son, Samuel. Counselor, U. Chgo. Orthogenic Sch., 1952-55; research asst. Kenyon & Eckhart, Inc., 1956-58; research asst. lab. human devel. Harvard U., 1959-60, teaching asst. psychology, then instr. edn., 1960-61; research asso. Speech research lab. Children's Hosp., Boston, 1960-61, M.I.T., 1961-62; mem. faculty Boston U., 1962—, prof. psychology, 1972—, dir. doctoral program in devel. psychology, 1969-74; vis. lectr. U. Utrecht (Netherlands), 1965-67; Froman prof. Russell Sage Coll., Troy, N.Y., 1972. Grantee U.S. Office Edn., 1964-65, Boston U. Grad. Sch., 1967-70, OEO, 1967—, NIMH, 1974-76; recipient Distinguished Tchr. Psychology award Am. Psychol. Found., 1970; Harbison award excellence teaching Danforth Found., 1971; Metcalf award Boston U., 1978; Disting. Career in Psychology award Mass. Psychol. Assn., 1982. Mem. AAAS, Soc. Research Child Devel. (sec. Boston 1963-65), AAUP (sec. Boston U. 1964-65), Am., Eastern, Mass. (chmn. program com. 1962-64) psychol. assns., Mass. Children's Lobby (pres. 1977—), Sigma Xi, Psi Chi. Author: Child Behavior and Development: A Reader, 1969; Child Behavior and Development, 2d edit., 1973: Life: The Continuous Process, 1975; Growing Children, 1976. Address: 1 Billings Park Newton MA 02158 Office: 64 Cummington St Boston MA 02215

REBER, MARY KENETTA, lawyer; b. Louisville, Jan. 18, 1941; d. Richard Kenneth and Ruth Keith (Crump) R.; B.A. in Polit. Sci., Calif. State U., Northridge, 1973; J.D., Southwestern U., Los Angeles, 1976; 1 dau., Lisa Robin Jones. Law clk. Community Legal Assistance Center, Los Angeles, 1974-75; research/teaching asst. Southwestern U. Sch. Law, Los Angeles, 1975-76; cert. law clk. Los Angeles Dist. Atty.'s Office, 1975-76; admitted to Calif. bar, 1976, U.S. Supreme Ct. bar, 1980; dep. public defender San Bernardino County, Ontario, Calif., 1977—; instr. law Calif. Community Colls. Recipient Disting. Service award Southwestern U. Sch. Law, 1975. Mem. State Bar Calif., Calif. Women Lawyers Assn., Am. Bar Assn., Calif. Attys. for Criminal Justice, ACLU, Inland Women Lawyers Assn. Democrat. Club: Toastmasters (past officer). Office: 1051 W 6th St Ontario CA 91762

REBHUN, JOYCE ANNE, lawyer, gas co. exec.; b. Pitts., July 21, 1944; d. Charles W. and Margaret F. (Joyce) Rebhun; B.A., Carlow Coll., 1965; J.D., Duquesne U., 1968, M.B.A., 1971; Ph.D., Carnegie-Mellon U., 1982. Admitted to Pa. bar, 1969, Nebr. bar, 1982, U.S. Supreme Ct. bar, 1976; individual practice law, Pitts., 1969-73; tax atty. IRS, Pitts., 1973-78; adj. prof. U. Pitts., Grad Sch. Bus. Adminstrn., 1977-81; internat., corp. tax atty. Westinghouse Electric Corp., Pitts., 1978-80; mgr. tax research PPG Industries, Inc., Pitts., 1980-81; head tax dept. No. Plains Natural Gas Co., Omaha, Nebr., 1981—; mng. partner No. Border Pipeline Co., Omaha, 1981—; cons. in field; Named Outstanding Alumnae of the Yr. in Bus., Carlow Coll., 1980; Carnegie Mellon U. fellow, 1971-72. Mem. Am. Bar Assn., Douglas County Bar Assn., Allegheny County Bar Assn. Republican. Roman Catholic. Address: 224 S 108th Ave PO Box 3330 Omaha NE 68103

RECH, JEAN MAY, mgmt. cons. co. exec., family therapist; b. Des Moines, Jan. 20, 1921; d. George S. and Alice A. May; B.A., Wheaton Coll., 1942; M.A., U. So. Calif., 1963; m. Arthur P. Rech, June 4, 1943; children—Dale Palmer, Daryl Ann Webster. Owner, v.p. George S. May Internat. Co., Park Ridge, Ill., 1940—; pvt. practice marriage and family therapy, 1962—; co-founder Centinella Hosp. Mental Health Clinic, Inglewood, Calif., 1964—; mem. City of Los Angeles Family Service Bd., 1967. Mem. Western Assn. Christians for Psychol. Services (dir.), Am. Sociol. Assn., Am. Assn. Marriage and Family Therapists, Calif. Assn. Marriage and Family Therapists, Alpha Kappa Delta. Home: 2170 Ridge Dr Los Angeles CA 90049

RECK, RUTH ANNETTE, scientist; b. Rolla, Mo.; d. Enoch Peter and Dorothy Ruth (Klammer) Gabriel; B.A., Mankato State U., 1954; Ph.D., U. Minn., 1964; children—Ronald Paul, Cathrine Elizabeth. Analytical chemist Archer-Daniels-Midland Co., 1954; instr. math., Braconne, France, 1955-56; teaching asst. U. Minn., 1956-57, 58-59, 61-64, U. Tex., 1957-58; instr. U. Wis., 1959-61; research asso. Brown U., 1964-65; asso. sr. research physicist Gen. Motors Research Lab., 1965-70, asso. sr. research chemist, 1971-76, sr. research chemist, 1976-78, sr. research scientist, 1978-81, staff research scientist, 1981—; head Climate and Chemistry Center, La Jolla Inst., 1980. Mem. Am. Chem. Soc., Am. Phys. Soc., AAAS, Am. Geophys. Union, Sigma Xi, Sigma Zeta, Sigma Delta Epsilon, Iota Sigma Pi. Contbr. chpts. to books and articles in field. Office: Dept Physics General Motors Research Lab Warren MI 48090

RECKAHN, MARIAN ELIZABETH, nurse; b. Medina, N.Y., June 16, 1944; d. Clinton and Mary Ann (Baker) Smithl grad. E.J. Meyer Sch. Nursing, 1960; m. James Robert Reckahn, June 17, 1961; 1 son, James Robert. Gen. duty nurse E.J. Meyer Hosp., 1960-78; staff nurse, team leader Buffalo VA Med. Center, 1978-80; neurosurg. nurse Erie County Med. Center, Buffalo, 1981—. Cert. neurosurg. nurse, operating room nurse. Mem. N.Y. State Nurses Assn., Am. Nursing Assn., Assn. Operating Room Nurses, Neurosurg. Nurses, Fedn. Splty. Nurses. Home: 2536 W Oakfield Rd Grand Island NY 14072 Office: 463 Grider St Buffalo NY 14214

RECKER, GLENDA JUNE, remfg. co. exec.; b. Mountainair, N.Mex., June 7, 1941; d. Luther Clabourn and Viola Merle (McBee) Jones; grad. in cost acctg. Durham's Sch. Bus., 1964; m. Clifton Simon Recker, July 31, 1958; children—June Michelle Recker Johnson, Brett Steven, Monelle Kathryn, Brent Clifton. Bookkeeper, girl Friday, E & R Shannon, San Antonio, 1964-65; bookkeeper K. J. Smith & Sons, Inc., San Antonio, 1965-69; accts. receivable clk. Ace Brake Co., San Antonio, 1969-70; bookkeeper R & R Auto Parts Co. (name now R & R Auto Electric Rebuilders), San Antonio, 1958-71, also Pleasanton, Tex., 1980—, corp. sec.-treas., comptroller, 1971—. Pres., Wood Valley Acres Home Owners Assn., Adkins, Tex., 1974-76; chmn. entertainment com. La Vernia Jr. Livestock Show, 1979—; youth dir. Glad Tidings Assembly of God Ch., 1981—. Recipient numerous bowling awards, winner numerous championships, including San Antonio Women's Bowling Assn. Local All-Events Champion, 1975, 76, 81 Appreciation trophy United Way, 1975, Girls Softball, 1975; cert. appreciation La Vernia Cystic Fibrosis Breath of Spring Bike-A-Thon, 1979, 80; named Citizen of Month, Tex. Bank, 1976. Mem. S.E. Bus. and Profl. Women's Club (editor bull. 1977-78; state 2d pl. award 1978), Am. Bus. Women's Club, S.E. Devel. Found. (dir.), La Vernia C. of C., Greater San Antonio C. of C., Nat. Write Your Congressman Club, Women's Internat. Bowling Congress (del. nat. convs. 1979, 80, 82), Tex. Women's Bowling Assn. (co-chmn. scrapbook 1981), San Antonio Women's Bowling Assn. (dir.), Nat. Ind. Businesspersons Assn., 600 Bowling Club, Les Dames 700 Bowling Club, PTA, Tex. Farm Bur., Nat. Motor Club. Mem. Assemblies of God Ch. Clubs: Sons of Hermann, Moose Aux., Turner's Bowling, Highland Social. Editor ch. bull., 1969-73; editor periodic column Thinkin' Out Loud, La Vernia News, 1977—; reporter, columnist Commr.'s Ct., Wilson County. Home: Route 2 Box 860 Adkins TX 78101 Office: 2750 Rigsby Ave San Antonio TX 78222

RECORD, ANNA JOYCE, savs. and loan exec.; b. Ogden, Utah, Jan. 5, 1935; d. Lyman Lloyd and Minnie (Buckway) Carter; certs. Inst. of Fin. Edn., 1954, 55, 74; student Weber State Coll., 1956, 76; grad. Savs. Instns. Mktg. Sch., U. Wis., 1977; m. Ocie Clayton Record, Jr., Nov. 21, 1970; children—Colleen Johnstun, Deborah Anthony; stepchildren—Dayle Whitworth, Ocie Clayton Record, Joel Dyar Record. Teller new accounts, sec. Interstate Bldg. and Loan Assn., Washington, 1954-55; proof dept. Comml. Security Bank, Ogden, Utah, 1956; teller, loan sec., collections, sec. to pres. and bd. dirs., corp. sec., v.p., dir. mktg., br. mgr. Ogden 1st Fed. Savs. and Loan Assn., 1956—; mem. adv. bds. Sch. Bus. Weber State Coll. and Weber and Morgan Counties Experienced Based Career Edn. Program. Judge econs. fair Weber County Schs., 1979, 80; del. Weber County Rep. Conv.. 1968; active Utah Heart Assn., 1980; mem. spl. events com. St. Benedicts Found. Recipient award in advt.. Savs. Instns. Mktg. Soc. Am. Mem. Am. Bus. Women's Assn. (rec. sec. Golden Spike chpt. 1979, v.p. 1980, pres. 1981), Ogden C. of C. Mormon. Home: 3743 Eccles Ave Ogden UT 84403 Office: 2425 Washington Blvd Ogden UT 84401

RECTOR, LOIS MARIE, artist, author; b. Okemos, Mich., 1912; d. Ross Alward and Lotta Lura (Baker) Hickok; A.B., Western Mich. U., 1934; postgrad. SUNY, 1963; postgrad. in textiles Arrowmont Arts and Craft Sch., 1981; m. Hilden LaVerne Rector, June 25, 1937; children—Robert L., Richard D. Tchr. schs. in Mich., 1934-41; head Muskegon (Mich.) Day Care Centers, 1942-51; tchr. tng. instr. Poughkeepsie Day Sch. for Vassar Coll., 1952-53; instr. Dunedin Fine (Fla.) Arts Center, 1976—; recreation leader Edgewater Arms, Dunedin; v.p. Rector's Lemon Tree Nursery, 1970—; garden columnist Clearwater (Fla.) Sun Daily, 1975—; one-women shows include Fla. State Capital, Nat. Arboratum, Washington, IBM Corp., U.S. Mil. Acad.; represented IBM Traveling Art Show, 1967, State of Tex. Fine Arts Dept. Traveling Show, 1969; exhibited in group shows Artist Alliance, Tampa, Fla., 1981, Fla. Craftsmen Travelling Show, 1981. Recipient numerous awards including 1st place Gulf Coastal Art Show, Merit award Nat. Sails and Am. Banners Show, 1982, 12 other blue ribbons, other painting awards; named One of 81 for '81, Tampa Bay Life. Mem. Am. League Pen Women in Arts and Letters, Fla. Craftsmen. Contbr. articles to jours. and mags. Address: 711 Sparrow Ave Palm Harbor FL 33563

RECTOR, MICHELLE DAWN, constrn. co. exec., truss and cabinet fabrication co. exec.; b. Eureka, Calif., June 10, 1952; d. Donald Charles Bent and Beverly Mae Rector; student in acctg. Coll. of Redwoods, 1978; m. Thomas Carl Rector, July 11, 1970; children—Shannon Kay, Nathan Thomas. Kitchen helper Gen. Hosp., Eureka, 1968-70; sec. Bayley Suit, Inc., Eureka, 1970-71; co-owner, co-mgr. J.T. Rentals, Eureka, 1971-74; co-owner, sec.-treas. M. T. Builders, Inc., Arcata, Calif., 1974—; co-owner, co-mgr. Thomas Industries, Arcata, 1975—; sec., treas., co-owner Thomas Home Center, 1982—; owner Profl. Bus. Services, 1982—. Mem. Nat. Republican. Congl. Com.; mem. Nat. Right to Work Com.; leader troop Girl Scouts U.S.A., 1982. Mem. Nat. Assn. Female Execs. Lutheran. Club: Humboldt Bay Bus. and Profl. Women's Luncheon (v.p. 1978-79, pres. elect 1979-80, pres. 1980-81, Top Hat award 1980). Office: 1355 Giuntoli Ln Arcata CA 95521

REDDAN-DEWEY, KATHERINE WETZEL, retail store exec.; b. Trenton, N.J., Jan. 12, 1946; d. Martin W. and Alma May (Wetzel) R.; B.A., Rider Coll., 1968; M. Social Work Adminstrn., Rutgers U., 1975; m. Paul Thomas Dewey, Jr.; 1 dau., Kayce Ann. Social worker various instns. and agys., State of N.J., 1968-71, instl. liaison, interstate compact on parole coordinator, 1971-75, supr. residential treatment and ambulatory program devel., youth services, 1975-76; partner Barondorf, Inc., Yardley, Pa., 1971-75; dir. bus. and govt. relations 70001 Ltd., Newark, Del., 1976-78, v.p. bus. and govt. relations, Washington, 1978-79; v.p. Semerad Assos., Washington, 1980-82; owner Me To You, Allison Park, Pa., 1982—. Mem. N.J. Gov.'s Task Force Juvenile Justice Delinquency Prevention Task Force, 1975-76, exec. v.p., 1979. Mem. Del. Adv. Com. on Vocat. Edn., 1977; mem. adv. bd. Joint Center for Polit. Studies, 1980. Mem. Am. Soc. Assn. Execs., Nat. Retail Mchts. Assn., Am. Retail Fedn. Republican. Roman Catholic. Address: 1842 Dolphin Dr Allison Park PA 15101

REDDICK, MARY CLUNAS, assn. exec.; b. Detroit, Mar. 3, 1920; d. James K. and Maybelle Edith (Martin); R.N., Evangelical Deaconess Hosp. Sch. Nursing, Detroit, 1941; student Wayne U., Detroit, 1945. Nurse, Evangelical Deaconess Hosp., 1941-45, Highland Park (Mich.) Gen. Hosp., 1946-48; pvt. surg. nurse Edward M. Vardon, M.D., Highland Park, 1948-69; nat. field dir. Degree of Honor Protective Assn., St. Paul, 1969-73, nat. pres., 1973—. Bd. dirs. St. Paul Winter Carnival. Mem. Nat. Fraternal Congress Am., Fraternal Ins. Counselors Am., Minn. Fraternal Congress (past pres.), St. Paul C. of C. (dir.). Episcopalian. Clubs: Soroptimist (pres.), Amaranth (St. Paul); Women's Rotary (Mpls.); Order Eastern Star. Office: Degree of Honor Protective Assn 325 Cedar St Saint Paul MN 55101

REDGRAVE, LYNN, actress; b. London, Eng., Mar. 8, 1943; d. Michael Scudemore and Rachel (Kempson) Redgrave; ed. Queensgate Sch., London, also Central Sch. Speech and Drama, London; m. John Clark, Apr. 2, 1967; children—Benjamin, Kelly, Annabel. Theatrical appearances include Midsummer Night's Dream, The Tulip Tree, Andorra, Hayfever, Much Ado About Nothing, Mother Courage, Love for Love (all with Nat. Theatre Co. of Gt. Britian, 1963-66), Black Comedy, N.Y.C., 1967, Zoo, Zoo, Widdershins Zoo, Edinburgh Festival, 1969, The Two of Us, London, 1970, Slag, London, 1971, A Better Place, Dublin, 1972, Born Yesterday, Greenwich, 1973; N.Y. appearances include Black Comedy, 1967, My Fat Friend, 1974, Mrs. Warren's Profession, 1975, Knock, Knock, 1976, Hellzapoppin, 1976, California Suite, 1977, St. Joan, 1977; appeared in Twelfth Night, Stratford Conn. Shakespeare Festival, 1978; film appearances include Tom Jones, Girl with the Green Eyes, Georgy Girl, The Deadly Affair, Smashing Time, The Virgin Soldiers, Last of the Mobile Hotshots, Don't Turn the Other Cheek, Every Little Crook and Nanny, Everything You Always Wanted to Know About Sex, The National Health, The Happy Hooker, The Big Bus, Sunday Lovers; TV appearances include Centennial, 1978; The Muppets, Gauguin the Savage, Beggarman Thief, The Seduction of Miss Leona, Housecalls, 1979; co-host Not for Women Only, nat. TV syndication, 1977—; rec. albums include Make Mine Manhattan, 1978, Cole Porter Revisited, 1979. Recipient N.Y. Film Critics award, Golden Globe award, Oscar nomination for best actress, all for Georgy Girl, 1967; named Runner-Up Actress, All Am. Favorites, Box Office Barometer, 1975; Sarah Siddons award as Chgo.'s best stage actress of 1977, 78. Address: Box 1207 Topanga CA 90290

REDGRAVE, VANESSA, actress; b. London, Jan. 30, 1937; d. Michael and Rachel (Kempson) R.; student Central Sch. Speech and Drama, London, 1955-57; m. Tony Richardson, Apr. 28, 1962 (div.); children—Natasha Jane, Joely Kim. Prin. theatrical roles include: Helena in Midsummer Night's Dream, 1959, Stella in The Tiger and the Horse, 1960, Katerina in The Taming of the Shrew, 1961, Rosaline in As You Like It, 1961, Imogene in Cymbeline, 1962, Nina in The Seagull, 1964, Miss Brodie in The Prime of Miss Jean Brodie, 1966; other plays include: Cato Street, 1971, Threepenny Opera, 1972, Twelfth Night, 1972, Anthony and Cleopatra, 1973, Design for Living, 1973, Macbeth, 1975, Lady from the Sea, 1976, 78, 79; film roles include: Leonie in Morgan-A Suitable Case for Treatment (Best Actress award Cannes Film Festival 1966), 1965, Sheila in Sailor from Gibraltar, 1965, Anne-Marie in La Musica, 1965, Jane in Blow Up, 1967, Guinevere in Camelot, 1967, Isadora in Isadora Duncan (Best Actress award Cannes Film Festival), 1968, Cosima in Wagner, 1982. other films include: The Charge of The Light Brigade, 1968, The Seagull, 1968, A Quiet Place in the Country, 1968, Daniel Deronda, 1969, Dropout, 1969, The Trojan Women, 1970, The Devils, 1970, The Holiday, 1971, Mary Queen of Scots, 1971, Murder on the Orient Express, 1974, Winter Rates, 1974, 7% solution, 1975, Julia, 1977, Agatha, 1978, Yanks, 1978, Bear Island, 1979, Playing for Time, 1980; My Body My Child, 1981; bd. govs. Central Sch. Speech and Drama, 1963—. Decorated comdr. Order Brit. Empire; recipient Drama award Evening Standard, 1961, Best Actress award Variety Club Gt. Brit., 1961, 66, Brit. Guild TV Producers and Dirs., 1966; Golden Globe award, 1978, Acad. award for best supporting actress, 1977; Emmy award for Playing for Time, 1980-81. Author: Pussies and Tigers, 1964. Address: 1 Ravenscourt Rd London W6 England *

REDLER, SHERRY PRESS, audiologist; b. N.Y.C., July 3, 1933; d. Martin M. and Elsie (Opin) Press; B.A., Adelphi U., 1954; M.S., So. Conn. State Coll., 1971, postgrad., 1976-79; children—Michael, Steven, Lynda. Speech pathologist Roslyn (N.Y.) Public Schs., 1954-56; tchr. drama Rollins Coll., Winter Park, Fla., 1961-63; personnel counselor Internat. Bus. Assn., Pitts., 1965; speech pathologist Fairfield (Conn.) Public Schs., 1968-75, ednl. audiologist, 1976—; clin. audiologist Rehab. Center, Bridgeport, Conn., 1976-77; sign lang. instr. Bridgeport Rehab. Center, 1976-78, Steeples High Sch., Westport, Conn.; instr. So. Conn. State Coll., New Haven, 1976—; lectr., cons. in field; ind. evaluator of programs for hearing impaired; author, project dir. Title IV Fed. Grant, Conn., 1976-80; mem. Conn. State Task Force to assess services provided to mentally retarded, 1981—; author, project dir. sch. audiology program, Conn., 1981. Mem. Conn. Speech and Hearing Assn. (co-chmn. com. on edn. hearing impaired 1976—), NEA, Conn. Edn. Assn., Fairfield Edn. Assn., Am. Speech and Hearing Assn. Home: 28 Lockwood Circle Fairfield CT 06430 Office: 60 Thompson St Fairfield CT 06430

REDO, DOROTHY MCDERMOTT, city ofcl.; b. Pittsfield, Mass., Aug. 21, 1917; d. Peter and Mary Rose (Lawson) McDermott; student Hunter Coll., City U. N.Y., 1944-50, Fordham U., 1950-51; m. Louis Redo, Dec. 29, 1956. In various clerical, secretarial positions, Pittsfield, 1937-44; sec. Texaco Inc., N.Y., 1944-68, adminstrv. asst. dept. advt., 1968-71; sec.-dir. pub. works City of Boulder City (Nev.), 1973—. Mem. Adv. Commn. to Legislator John Gallagher, N.Y. State Legislature, 1966-70. Mem. The Forum (formerly Texaco Women's Club) (pres. 1967). Republican. Roman Catholic. Home: 1360 Denver St Boulder City NV 89005 Office: 900 Arizona St Boulder City NV 89005

REDO, MARIA ELAINE, gerontologist; b. N.Y.C., Jan. 12, 1925; d. Ernest and Mary C. Lappano; B.S. in Edn., Fordham U., 1945; cert. in gerontology, Brookdale Sch. Social Sci., 1979; m. S. Frank Redo, June 27, 1948; children—Philip L., Martha Maria. Tchr. pvt. sch., N.Y.C., 1946-56; dir. Child Service League, Queens, N.Y., 1949-57; founder, dir. Community Concern for Sr. Citizens, Inc., N.Y.C. Dept. for the Aging, 1971—. Bd. dirs. Escort Service of Yorkville (N.Y.), 1977—, Sr. Citizen Outreach Program for Elderly, N.Y.C., 1970—; mem. Community Planning Bd., N.Y.C., 1970-77; del. Nat. Republican Conv., N.Y.C., 1976, N.Y. State White House Conf. on Aging, 1981, Nat. White House Conf. on Aging, N.Y.C., 1981. Recipient Mayor's Cert. of Appreciation N.Y.C., 1975; Hon. Sec. of State of Mont., 1975; Franny award WPIX-TV, 1974. Mem. LWV, Roman Catholic. Clubs: Met. Rep. (pres. 1975-77), Pamet Harbor Yacht and Tennis. Contbr. tng. manuals, brochures for dept. on aging., 1973—. Home: 435 E 70th St New York NY 10021 Office: 280 Broadway Room 212 New York NY 10007

REECE, CHERI DODSON, nurse, educator; b. Altoona, Pa., Apr. 17, 1946; d. Paul Francis and Evely Pearl (Brown) Dodson; diploma in nursing Western Pa. Hosp. Sch. Nursing, Pitts., 1967; B.S. in Nursing, Cedar Crest Coll., Allentown, Pa., 1969; postgrad. in nursing Kent State U., 1979—; m. David Alan Reece, June 21, 1969; 1 dau., Michelle Lynn. Nurse coll. infirmary, 1967-69; staff nurse Western Pa. Hosp., 1968; pvt. duty nurse, 1969, 78; staff nurse Nason Hosp., Roaring Spring, Pa., 1969; instr. inservice edn. N.D. State Hosp., Jamestown, 1969-71; staff nurse Santa Clara Valley Med. Center, San Jose, Calif., 1971-72; instr. nursing San Jose Hosps. and Health Center, 1972-74; instr. nursing Kent State U., 1974-75, 78—, Ohio Valley Hosp., Steubenville, Ohio, 1975-77; staff nurse Ashtabula (Ohio) Medicare Center, 1977-78; instr. adult edn. Ashtabula Joint Vocat. Sch., 1978-79; phys. exam. nurse Phys. Measurements, Inc., Ashtabula, 1978; continuing edn. instr.; cons. well-baby care; adv. local Student Nurses' Assn. Active in campaign U.S. Rep., Am. Cancer Soc., Am. Heart Fund; patron Straw Hat Theatre; councilmatic aide Ashtabula City Council, 1981—; head Center Shop at Ashtabula Arts Center, also patron. Mem. Nat. League Nursing, AAUW (sec. chpt. 1980-82), Alumni Assn. Claysburg-Kimmel High Sch., Women's Service League. Office: 3325 W 13th St Ashtabula OH 44004

REECE, KELSIE IRENE NIXSON, educator; b. Cullman, Ala., Feb. 5, 1922; d. Willie Green and Ada Jewell Christman Nixson; B.S. in Home Econs., U. Ala., 1945; M.Ed., U. N.C., 1956; m. William T. Reece, June 2, 1946; children—William T., Frank Edward. Tchr. secondary schs., Gibsonville, N.C., 1954-56; sch. lunch supr., Williamsburg, Va., 1963-69; sch. lunch dir. Virginia Beach, Va., 1972-73; mem. faculty Tidewater Community Coll., Virginia Beach, 1973—, prof. hotel, restaurant and instl. mgmt., Mem. Nat. Restaurant Assn., Va. Restaurant Assn., Council Hotel Restaurant Instn. Educators, Internat. Food Service Exec. Assn., AAUW, Tidewater Nutritional Council. Presbyterian. Club: Order Eastern Star.

REED, ANNETTE ZIMMERN, counseling psychotherapist, nurse; b. Exeter, Va., Feb. 7, 1933; d. Samuel C. and Zella Edith (Nelson) Wacks; R.N., Sinai Hosp., Balt., 1954; A.A., Anne Arundel Community Coll., Md., 1967; B.A. magna cum laude, U. Md., 1969, M.Ed., 1971, Ph.D., 1976; m. James Robert Reed, Aug. 11, 1979; children by previous marriage—Kenneth Andrew Zimmern, Ronald Curtis Zimmern. Occupational health nurse Johns Hopkins U. Applied Physics Lab., Silver Spring, Md., 1958; head nurse neurosurgery Univ. Hosp., Balt., 1961-63; commd. officer USPHS, 1976—; with USPHS Hosp., Balt., 1976-80; dir. employee counseling service program Div. Fed. Employee Occupational Health, Rockville, Md., 1980—; mem. Annapolis Mental Health Bd.; mem. scientist career devel. com. USPHS for Surgeon Gen.; officer Md. Bd. Cert. of Alcoholism Counselors. Election judge Anne Arundel County, 1966. Recipient plaque USPHS, 1977, merit award for superior performance, 1980. Mem. Am. Orthopsychiat. Assn., Am. Nurses Assn., Am. Psychol. Assn., Occupational Program Cons., Delta Kappa Phi, Phi Theta Kappa. Club: Bayberry Garden (pres. 1964). Office: 5600 Fishers Ln Room 13A40 Rockville MD 20857

REED, BETTY JO, microbiologist; b. Houston; d. James Henry and Annie M. (Waite) Reed; B.S., Tulane U., 1966, M.S., 1968, postgrad., 1968-71. Instr. infectious diseases Tulane U. Sch. Medicine, New Orleans, 1968-74; chmn. immunology dept. Universidad Del Valle, Cali, Colombia, 1968-74; microbiologist W. Jefferson Hosp., New Orleans, 1974-80, Montelepre Meml. Hosp., New Orleans, 1980—; cons. WHO; infection control instr.; lectr. alcohol and drug abuse program LWV, 1978—. USPHS fellow, 1966-71; HEW cert. in environ. control. Mem. Am. Soc. Med. Technologists, Am. Soc. Microbiologists, Am. Soc. Clin. Pathologists. Republican. Methodist. Author: Manual of Infection Control, 1975. Home: 206 E Maplridge Metairie LA 70001 Office: 3125 Canal St New Orleans LA 70119

REED, BETTY LOU, state legislator; b. Flint, Mich.; student Lake County Community Coll.; m. Richard C. Reed; 2 daus. Chmn., sec. Lake County Republican Central Com.; committeewoman Ill. State Central Com.; exec. dir. Republican Woman Power, Illinois Style; mem. Lake County Bd. Suprs., 1969-72; commnr. Lake County Forest Preserve, 1969-72; mem. exec. and legislative com. Ill. Assn. Suprs., 1969-72; pres. Twp. Ofcls. Assn., 1971-72; presdl. appointee Midwest Regional Adv. Council, SBA; mem. 79th 81st Gen. Assemblies, Ill. Ho. Reps. Mem. West Deerfield Twp. Commn. on Youth, Deerfield Park Dist. Sr. Citizens Adv. Bd. Office: Ill Ho Reps State Capitol Springfield IL 62706 *

REED, BOBBIE LYNN, hosp. adminstr.; b. Neosho, Mo., July 10, 1944; d. Robert Moore and Wilma Dean (Edison) Butler; student Ariz. Bible Coll., 1962-63; A.A., Orange Coast Coll., 1976; M.P.A., Calif. State U., Los Angeles, 1978; Ph.D., U. Central Calif., 1982; m. Jerold Reed, July 5, 1963 (div. Mar. 1973); children—Jonathan Robert, Michael Jay. With Calif. Dept. Health, 1974-75, 79-78, mgr. disabled manpower unit, 1978-79; dir. staff devel. Fairview State Hosp., Costa Mesa, Calif., 1975-78; chief personnel services sect. Calif. Dept. Devel. Services, 1979-82; adminstr. Agnews State Hosp., San Jose, Calif., 1982—; mem. founding faculty, instr. Coastline Community Coll., Fountain Valley, Calif., 1976-78; lectr., cons. single adult ministries, 1976—. Public relations officer Concerned Citizens Coalition, 1974-75. Recipient Single Purpose Internat. Single Adult Ministry award, 1978, Postive Christian Singles Outstanding Service award, 1977. Democrat. Mem. Ind. Fundamental Chs. Am. Author: Developing a Single Adult Ministry, 1979; Single on Sunday, 1979; Making the Most of Single Life, 1980; Stepfamilies, 1980; I Didn't Plan To Be A Single Parent!, 1981; Rx for a Broken Heart, 1982; 12 others; also numerous articles. Home: PO Box 4601 Santa Clara CA 95054 Office: Agnews State Hosp San Jose CA 95134

REED, DORIS I., pub. co. ofcl.; b. Marion County, Iowa, Nov. 27, 1911; d. James Roscoe and Lyde Core McGraw; student public schs., Knoxville, Iowa; m. Ralph G. Reed, Mar. 14, 1936; 1 dau., Judy Lea Ogden. With World Pub. Co., Shenandoah, Iowa, 1938—, office mgr., 1942—, prodn. supr., 1965—. Recipient Outstanding Service awards C. of C., Edn. Assn., Easter Seal Soc., Am. Field Service, United Way, Girl Scouts, Meth. Ch. Mem. Shenandoah C. of C., Bus. and Profl. Women's Club (past pres.), Am. Legion Aux. (past pres.), Nat. Press Women. Republican. Editor, Iowa Bus. Woman, 1964—. Home: 210 W Sheridan Ave Shenandoah IA 51601 Office: 506 W Lowell St Shenandoah IA 51601

REED, DORRIS HULL, TV cons.: b. Phila., Sept. 7, 1924; d. Claude Lewis and Genevieve Marie (Turner) Hull; student Mich. State U., 1942-43, U. Mich., 1943-44; m. Willard James Musson, July 2, 1948 (dec. 1967); children—Willard James Musson, Julie Anne Musson Booth, Scott Hull Musson; m. 2d, John LeRoy Reed, Jr., May 12, 1972. Radio broadcaster Minute Parade, Detroit, 1947-50; TV traffic mgr. Sta. WWJ-TV, Detroit, 1950-54; v.p. adminstrn., corporate sec.-treas. McHugh & Hoffman, Inc., Fairfax, Va., 1969—. Mem. City, Univ. and Bus. Com., City of Fairfax. Mem. Fairfax City C. of C. (pres., dir., co. rep. 1978—), Am. Women in Radio and TV (Washington chpt.), Fairfax Profl. Women's Network. Republican. Office: 3970 Chain Bridge Rd Fairfax VA 22030

REED, ELVIRA ARMAN, owner automobile agy.; b. Italy, Jan. 11, 1921; came to U.S., 1927, naturalized, 1927; d. Louis Victor and Palmira (Machiovecchio) Cacio; grad. high sch.; m. Dallas R. Arman, Sept. 17, 1940 (dec.); children—Donna, Barbara; m. 2d, Clarence C. Reed, Dec. 21, 1973. With Lamerdin Pontiac (name changed to Arman Pontiac Inc. 1969), Compton, Calif., 1949—, gen. mgr., 1950-67, owner, 1967—; owner Compton Toyota (Calif.), 1970—; dir. Community Savs. & Loan, Long Beach. Mem. Pontiac Nat. Dealer Council, 1972-73, 76-77; chairwoman Los Angeles Internat. Automobile Show, 1972; mem. Calif. New Motor Vehicle Bd., 1976—, pres., 1978. Pres., YMCA, 1970-72; mem. UCLA Chancellor's Assos., 1975—. Recipient Import Auto Dealer of Distinction award AI ADA, 1980. Mem. Compton C. of C. (pres. 1978—), So. Calif. Pontiac Dealers Assn. (pres. 1970, treas. 1975-80), Motor Car Dealers Assn. So. Calif. (treas., dir. 1973—), Long Beach Motor Car Dealers Assn., Compton Motor Car Dealers Assn. Club: Friday Morning (Los Angeles). Home: 1300 Oxford Rd San Marino CA 91108 Office: 201 Auto Dr S Compton CA 90221

REED, ENID JANSSEN, clin. psychologist; b. N.Y.C., June 10, 1939; d. Edward F. and Laura Gale Janssen; Ph.D., UCLA, 1974; m. Lewis W. Reed., Dec. 24, 1963 (dec.). Buyer, Sears Roebuck & Co., Los Angeles, 1960-62; psychologist Los Angeles City Schs., 1963-73, VA Hosp., Sepulveda, Calif., 1973-74; pvt. practice clin. psychology, Beverly Hills, Calif., 1975—; dir. Psychologics, Inc., Beverly Hills, 1977—; media psychologist, host Successful Living radio show, 1981-82. Recipient Spl. Commendation U.S. Senate, 1974; grantee UCLA, 1973. Mem. So. Calif. Psychotherapy Affiliation (dir. 1977—), AAAS, Am. Psychol. Assn., Internat. Neuropsychology Soc. Office: 337 S Beverly Dr Suite 107 Beverly Hills CA 90212

REED, JEAN ANN, educator; b. Greensburg, Ind., Jan. 3, 1943; d. Ralph Ellsworth and Mildred Lucille (Johnson) Ponsler; B.S., Purdue U., 1965; M.Ed., Miami U., 1969; postgrad. Ball State U., 1974; m. Norman Maurice Reed, Feb. 13, 1966; children—Kenneth Ralph, Lora Nell. Apprentice extension agt. Coop. Extension Service, Perry County, Ind., 1964, extension agt.-in-tng., Wayne County, Ind., 1965, extension agt. home econ., Franklin County, Ind., 1965-76, Decatur County, Greensburg, Ind., 1976—. Pres., Hoosier Recreation Workshop, 1970-71; solicitor Cancer Fund 1975-76; March food chmn. March of Dimes, 1979; pres. PTO, 1976, 79. Recipient Outstanding Citizen award Franklin County Sr. Citizens, 1975. Mem. Am. Home Econ. Assn., Ind. Home Econ. Assn., Nat. Extension Home Economists Assn., Ind. Extension Home Economists Assn., Ind. Extension Agts. Assn., Epsilon Sigma Phi, Alpha Omicron Alpha. Baptist. Clubs: Tree City Sq. Dance, Order Eastern Star. Home: Route 4 Box 282 Greensburg IN 47240 Office: 766 W Main St Greensburg IN 47240

REED, JEANNETTE C., coll. adminstr.; b. Port Gibson, Miss., Feb. 17, 1935; d. Prince, Sr., and Inez (Smith) Coleman; B.S. in Urban Adminstrn. (career scholar), Washington U., 1980, cert. in bus. adminstrn. 1980; postgrad. in mgmt. and bus. adminstrn. Webster Coll., 1981-82; children—Curtis, Anthony Renard. With St. Louis Public Schs., 1959-72, Monsanto Co., St. Louis, 1972-76, Ralston Purina Co., St. Louis, 1977-81; adminstrv. asst./exec. sec. to pres. and bd. regents Harris-Stowe Coll., St. Louis, 1982—; part time instr. St. Louis Community Coll. Adviser Jr. Achievement, 1980-81; United Way loaned exec., 1981; state chaplain AMVETS Aux., pres. Post 67 Aux.; active Friends of Sherwood Camp, Inc.; bd. dirs. West Side Bapt. Ch. Fed. Credit Union, active Sunday Sch., bd. Christian edn. Recipient Black Writers in Mass Communication award Sigma Gamma Rho, 1981, cert. of recognition West Side Bapt. Ch. Youth Guidance Council, Sunday Sch., Bd. Christian Edn.; O.E.S. Community Service award, 1982. Mem. Black Bus. Women United (founder, organizer, pres.), Black Bus. Women United (founder, organizer, pres.), Nat. Assn. Female Execs., Profl. Secs. Internat., Conf. on Edn. (25th anniversary com.), AAUW, NAACP, Urban League, Zeta Phi Beta Amicaes. Presbyterian. Clubs: Saturday Reading (pres. 1974-76, public relations coordinator 1982), Order Eastern Star (Pride of the West chpt. 99). Religious editor/columnist St. Louis Am. News. Home: 3404C Laclede Ave Saint Louis MO 63103 Office: 3026 Laclede Saint Louis MO 63103

REED, JENENE ARNOLD, mfg. co. mgr.; b. Wheeler, Mich., June 2, 1935; d. Joseph N. and Geneva N. (Jones) A.; B.S., Okla. U., 1957, M.S., 1960; m. William Earnest Reed, Feb. 13, 1971; 1 son by previous marriage, Jess Joseph Reed. High sch. and jr. coll. tchr., 1957-61; owner moving and storage bus., 1961-63; freelance comml. artist, 1964-82; real estate saleswoman, 1977-81; sales mgr., then customer service mgr. D.L. Auld Co., automotive equipment mfrs., Columbus, Ohio, 1979—. Pres. Welcome Wagon, Reynoldsberg, Ohio, 1978. Mem. Nat. Assn. Female Execs. (dir.), Auld Mgmt. Club (dir.), Bus. and Profl. Womens Club (dir.), Females in Action, Nat. Assn. Mfg. Engrs., Am. Mgmt. Assn., AAUW. Lutheran. Clubs: Women's, Order Eastern Star. Office: 1209 N 5th St Columbus OH 43201

REED, JOANNE, telephone co. exec.; b. Olton, Tex., June 22, 1931; d. Willis Eugene and Sally S. (Thetford) Wright; student Tex. Tech. U., 1975; U. Kans., 1978, various mgmt. schs.; children—Dennis, Joni. Service rep., operator Gen. Telephone Co. of S.W., Ralls, Tex., 1950-63, chief operator, 1963-67; operator services mgr. Denton Gen. Telephone (Tex.), 1967-73, area bus. office supr., 1973-74, div. mgr., Sulphur Springs, Tex., 1974-76, div. mgr., Denton, 1976-78; div. mgr. Gen. Telephone Co. S.W., Garland, Tex., 1978-82, gen. mgr. N. Central div., 1982—; dir. Republic Bank, Garland, Tex., 1980—. Precinct chmn. Republican Party, 1980-81; mem. adv. com. Salvation Army, 1980—; bd. dirs. YMCA, 1980-82, Garland Symphony, 1980; chmn. United Way, 1976-80, Am. Cancer Soc., 1978; mem. Garland Indsl. Devel. Bd., 1982. Republican. Clubs: Soroptimists, Bus. and Profl. Women's, Eastern Hills Country. Home: 913 Fair Oaks St Garland TX 75040 Office: PO Box 401308 Garland TX 75040

REED, KARAN WARD, real estate co. exec.; b. Damariscotta, Maine, Sept. 11, 1953; d. Neal Raymond and Virginia (Clark) Ward; B.S. in Spl. Edn., U. Maine, 1975. Dir. edn. programs so. Maine County Jails, 1974-76; crisis worker Counseling Center, Augusta, Maine, 1976-77; mgr. restaurant, Damariscotta, 1978-80; real estate agt. Edward C. Roberts Realty, Albrightsville, Pa., 1980—; owner, mgr. Hanney-Reed Realty, Albrightsville, 1979—. Mem. Nat. Assn. Female Execs. Home: 12 Azalea Ln Lake Harmony PA 18624 Office: Towamensing Trails Albrightsville PA 18210

REED, KATHLYN LOUISE, occupational therapist; b. Detroit, June 2, 1940; d. Herbert Curtis and Jessie Ruth (Krehbiel) R.; student U. Wis., 1958-61; B.S., U. Kans., 1964; M.A., Western Mich. U., 1966; Ph.D., U. Wash., 1973. Temporary supr., occupational therapist Vis. Nurse Assn., Beloit, Wis., 1964; staff occupational therapist Kans. U. Med. Center, Kansas City, 1964-65; instr. U. Wash., Seattle, 1967-70; research asso. Child Devel. Center, Seattle, 1972-73; chmn., prof. dept. occupational therapy U. Okla., Oklahoma City, 1973—; cons. HEW Pub. Health grant to Ohio State U., 1970-71, NIH grant to Am. Occupational Therapy Assn., 1972-73; cons. Okla. Dept. Health, 1976-77, Oklahoma City Pub. Schs., 1979-81; acting instr. U. Puget Sound, Tacoma, 1971. Telephone worker, counselor Open Door Clinic, 1968-72; mem., co-chmn. citizen's bd. Seattle Mental Health Center, 1970-72, mem. exec. bd., 1971-72. Recipient Elmer H. Wilds award Western Mich. U., 1966, Traineeship Dept. HEW-Rehab. Services Adminstrn., 1970-72. Fellow Am. Occupational Therapy Assn. (nominating com. chmn. 1972, bylaws chmn. 1979-81); mem. Am. Assn. Mental Deficiency, Council Exceptional Children (chpt. treas. 1970-72, chpt. v.p. 1976-77), Am. Pub. Health Assn., Okla. Assn. for Severely Handicapped, Okla. (practice chmn. 1973-74, pres. 1974-76, del. 1976-79), Wash. (del. 1968-73) occupational therapy assns., Am. Assn. Higher Edn., Am. Soc. Allied Health Professions, World Fedn. Occupational Therapists, Sigma Kappa, Pi Lambda Theta. Co-author: Concepts of Occupational Therapy, 1980. Home: 8800 Rolling Green Oklahoma City OK 73132

REED, MARLENE MINTS, educator; b. San Antonio, Sept. 25, 1937; d. Woodie John and Heloise (Pittman) Mints; B.B.A., Baylor U., 1959; M.B.A., N.E. La. U., 1977; D.B.A., La. Tech. U., 1981; m. Bill J. Reed, Aug. 29, 1958; children—Lisa Rochelle, William Barclay. Various positions in industry, Houston, Ft. Worth, Monroe, La., and Birmingham, Ala., 1959-73; asst. prof. mgmt. N.E. La. U., 1979-81; asst. prof. mgmt. and econs. Sch. Bus., Samford U., Birmingham, 1981—; cons. small bus. Named Most Disting. Prof. Bus., Alpha Kappa Psi, 1982. Mem. Acad. Mgmt., S.W. Small Bus. Inst. Assn., Nat. Bus. Edn. Assn., Beta Gamma Sigma, Omicron Delta Epsilon, Delta Pi Epsilon, Pi Omega Pi, Kappa Kappa Gamma. Republican. Baptist. Home: 1582 Panorama Dr Birmingham AL 35216 Office: Samford U Sch Bus 800 Lakeshore Dr Birmingham AL 35229

REED, MARTHA ANN, sch. adminstr.; b. Houston, Sept. 8, 1930; d. Emmett Conway and Evelyn Ysleta (Spurlock) Swain; student Tex. Christian U., 1948-50; A.A., U. Houston, 1956; m. Charles G. Reed, Apr. 20, 1974; children by previous marriage—Rebecca Hemphill Sanders, Ann Hemphill Walker, Steven Earl. Tchr., Oakdale, La., 1956-60, Goose Creek, Tex., 1962-64; asso. editor Oakdale Jour., 1959-62; women's editor Baytown (Tex.) Sun, 1963-70; lifestyle editor Beaumont (Tex.) Enterprise & Jour., 1970-77; dir. public info. Lamar u., 1977-79; spl. asst. to supt. Port Arthur (Tex.) Ind. Sch. Dist., 1979—; mem. spl. grand jury, Jefferson County, Tex. Named Ky. Col., 1981, Adm. Nebr. Navy, 1981. Mem. Nat. Fedn. Press Women (past pres.), Tex. Press Women (past pres.), Nat. Sch. Public Relations Assn., Tex. Sch. Public Relations Assn., Southeast Tex. Press Club, Assn. Sch. Adminstrs., Beaumont Art Mus., Beaumont Symphony Assn., Beaumont Heritage Soc., Lamar U. Friends of Arts, Beta Sigma Phi. Contbr. articles in field. Office: PO Box 1388 Port Arthur TX 77640

REED, MARY ELLEN, advt. co. exec.; b. Pitts., Nov. 30, 1942; d. James Fulton and Wilhelmina Bartlebaugh McEwan; B.S., U. Ky., 1967; m. William Richard Reed, Feb. 3, 1962; 1 dau., Julia Catherine. Creative dir., account exec. Abbott Advt., Lexington, Ky., 1969-74; pres., creative dir. M.E.R. & Assos. Advt., Lexington, Ky., 1975—; adv. Communications Sch., Eastern Ky. U.; instr. Morehead State U., 1978-79. Chmn. Fayette County Heart Fund, 1978; trustee, Ky. Ind. Coll. Found., Sayre Sch. Mem. Lexington Advt. Club (dir.). Episcopalian. Home: 3396 Montavesta Dr Lexington KY 40502 Office: 114 Clay Ave Lexington KY 40502

REED, PATRICIA BRIDGES, psychiat. social worker; b. Dallas, Aug. 12, 1927; d. Murphy Foster and Bess Ethel (Jones) Bridges; B.S., La. State U., 1948; M.S.W., Tulane U., 1971; m. Warren Gardner Reed, Oct. 1, 1948 (div.); 1 dau., Tena Patricia. Social worker Caddo Parish Welfare Dept., Shreveport, La., 1965-70; psychiat. social worker Hill Crest Hosp., Birmingham, Ala., 1971—, dir. social work, 1974—; dir. social work Higdon Hill Sch. and Residential Group Home; asso. prof., adj. faculty, field supr. (part-time faculty) U. Ala., Birmingham. Cert. clin. social worker, Ala. Mem. Nat. Assn. Social Workers, Acad. Cert. Social Workers, Soc. Hosp. Social Work Dirs. of Am. Hosp. Assn., Ala. Soc. Hosp. Social Workers, Am. Group Psychotherapy Assn., Am. Assn. Marital Family Therapy, Mental Health Assn. Jefferson County (Ala.), Central Neuropsychiat. Hosp. Assn. (social work sect.), Med. Social Workers Club Ala., Alumnae Club Pi Beta Phi. Democrat. Episcopalian. Home: 4225 Warren Rd Birmingham AL 35213

REED, PATTY LOU, furniture warehouse exec.; b. DuBois, Pa., June 19, 1941; d. Edward A. and Dorothy L. (Welsh) Lundberg; student pub. schs., DuBois; m. Larry Reed, Nov. 23, 1967; children—David, Cherri, Cindy, Lisa. With B.F. Goodrich Co., DuBois, 1958-68; mgr., clk. Auction Service, DuBois, 1968-74; real estate salesperson firm of Larry Reed, DuBois, 1974; owner, mgr. furniture outlet and showroom, DuBois, 1974—. Bd. dirs. DuBois Area United Way. Mem. Profl. Bus. Women, Nat. Home Furnishing Assn., C. of C. of DuBois (dir.). Office: Rustic Acres RD 3 DuBois PA 15801

REED, SUE ASSUNTA NUGENT, sch. prin.; b. Bklyn., Aug. 15, 1933; d. Joseph and Anna (Merola) Montella; B.A., Hunter Coll., 1955; M.S.Ed., 1956; Ph.D., N.Y.U., 1973; m. Scott Gordon Reed, Jan 9, 1974; children—Jessica Lindsay, Scott Gordon. Tchr., public schs., N.Y.C., 1956-65, asst. prin., 1965-73; prin. Congers Elem. Sch. (N.Y.), 1973—; adj. asst. prof. Hunter Coll., 1973, Coll. New Rochelle, 1980—. Mem. Clarkstown Bicentennial Commn., New City, N.Y., 1975-76; counselor Vol. Counseling Service, New City, 1975-76. NDEA grantee, U. PR., 1965; Danforth fellow, 1975; Nat. Humanities Faculty grantee, 1975; Ford Found./Am. Assn. Sch. Adminstrs. grantee, 1977; Inst. for Devel. Ednl. Activities fellow, 1982; Primary Mental Health Project scholar, 1981. Mem. Am. Assn. Sch. Administrs., Assn. Suprs. Curriculum Devel., Internat. Reading Assn., Nat. Council Accreditation Tchr. Edn., Bus. and Profl. Women's Assn. (chmn. young careerist com.) Phi Delta Kappa, Kappa Delta Pi. Club: Soroptimist (pres. 1982-84). Home: 9 Van Houten Fields West Nyack NY 10994 Office: 57 Lake Rd Congers NY 10920

REED, SUZANNE WATTERS, innkeeper; b. Springfield, Vt., Apr. 5, 1933; d. Warren William and Ruth Elizabeth (Lovell) Watters; B.S., U. Mass., 1955; M.Ed., State Coll. Worcester, 1962; cert. advanced grad. study Holy Cross Coll., 1971. Tchr., chmn. sci. dept. Wachusett Regional Sch. Dist., Holden, Mass., 1956-77, dir. summer recreation program, 1958-74; co-owner, The Inn at Princeton (Mass.), 1977—. Recipient Tchrs. award NSF, 1968. Mem. Mass. Tchrs. Assn., NEA, Nat. Sci. Tchrs. Assn., Mass. Assn. Sci. Tchrs., Small Businessmens Assn., Kappa Alpha Theta. Author, editor: Encounters with Science, 1975; co-author: The Metric System, 1975. Home: Mountain Rd Princeton MA 01541 Office: The Inn at Princeton Princeton MA 01541

REED-ROWE, HELEN PATRICIA, mgmt. assistance co. exec.; b. Balt., Oct. 22, 1949; d. John Walter and Gladys Rebecca Reed; B.A., U. Md., 1971; M.B.A. candidate Southeastern U., 1982; children—Nikkia Tenee, Kevin Anthony. Adult edn. instr., Balt., 1971-72; EEO specialist Dept. Agr., 1972-73; personnel mgmt. specialist Md.-Nat. Capital Park and Planning Commn., Silver Spring, Md., 1973-81; pres., chief exec. officer Libscor Assos., Inc., Balt., and Washington, 1981—. Pres. Balt. City Wide Republican Club, 1981; mem. Balt. City Rep. Central Com., 1981, Md. Rep. State Central Com., 1981; co-chmn. membership com. Md. Fedn. Rep. Women; mem. Cherry Hill Devel. Corp. Recipient Community Service award Balt. Police Dept., 1980; Md. Senatorial scholar, 1969-71. Mem. Nat. Assn. Female Execs., Md. Assn. Affirmative Action Officers, NAACP, Am. Soc. Tng. and Devel., Nat. Assn. Human Rights Workers, Internat. Personnel Mgmt. Assn., LWV, Cherry Hill Improvement Assn., Alpha Kappa Mu, Alpha Kappa Alpha. Presbyterian. Club: 4th Dist. Women's Polit. Office: 644 Hillview Rd Baltimore MD 21225

REEDY, VIRGINIA MITCHELL, food co. exec.; b. Quincy, Fla., Jan. 10, 1920; d. Eugene Augustus and Ruby Claire (Smith) Mitchell; certificate Aetna Life & Casualty Agy. Sch., 1944; certificate advanced mgmt. Harvard U., 1973; children—Dorothy Reedy Friedman, Virginia Dianne, John Wesley III. Acctg. clk. Mather Furniture Co., 1939-40; sec. Aetna Life & Casualty Co., 1940, adjuster, 1944-46; benefits clk. foods div. Coca-Cola Co., Minute Maid Corp., Plymouth, Fla., 1954-59, adminstr. employee benefits, Orlando, Fla., 1959-68, mgr. employee benefits, Houston, 1968—; resident asst. corp. sec. Aetna Life & Casualty Co., Jacksonville, Fla., 1942-46; mem., sec. adminstrv. com. Butter-Nut Trust, 1970—. Mem. Am. Mgmt. Assn. Democrat. Presbyterian. Home: 13906 Britoak Ln Houston TX 77079 Office: PO Box 2079 7105 Old Katy Rd Houston TX 77001

REEPMEYER, MARIE CHRISTINA, librarian; b. Cohoes, N.Y., Oct. 4, 1947; d. Herman John and Marion Lula (Debien) Reepmeyer; A.A., Stephens Coll., 1967; B.A., SUNY, Buffalo, 1969; M.L.S., SUNY, Albany, 1974. Caseworker, central intake, Erie County Dept. Social Services, Buffalo, 1969-70; head legal services librarian Upstate N.Y., Legal Aid Soc., Albany, 1977-79; asst. librarian N.Y. State Dept. Law, Albany, 1979—; sr. dir. We Care Mink Oil Products, Albany, 1971—; cons. Legal Aid Soc., Albany, 1979. Chmn., Miss Mo. Young Republicans Queen Contest, 1966-67; bd. dirs. Albany br. YWCA, 1982-83; pres. Young Reps. Club, 1966-67. Recipient Elks Youth Leadership contest award, Colonie, N.Y., 1962-63. Mem. AAUW (nominating com. Albany br. 1982-83 vice chmn. Eastern Area Interbranch Council 1981-82), Nat. Assn. Female Execs. (network dir. 1980-81), Am. Assn. Law Libraries, Alumni Assn. SUNY, Albany. Roman Catholic. Club: Internat. Cath. Alumni. Contbr. articles to profl. jours.; editor Albany br. AAUP Newsletter, 1980-82. Home: 15 MacDonald Circle Menands NY 12204 Office: NY State Dept Law Library The Capitol State St Albany NY 12224

REES, DEIRDRE MARY GOOD, biologist, audiologist, linguist; b. Cambridge, Mass., Feb. 5, 1947; d. John Joseph and Alice M. (McAuliffe) Good; B.A., Tufts U., 1969; M.A., Brown U., 1971, Boston U., 1973; m. Christopher W. Rees, Jan. 15, 1977. Teaching fellow Boston U., 1972-73, adj. instr., 1977-79; clin. and research audiologist Channing Labs. Center, Harvard U., 1974-75; tng. coordinator Mass. Gen. Hosp., Boston, 1977-79; pvt. practice audiology, Burlington, Mass., 1975—; cons. linguist and biologist, 1975—; adj. instr. Emerson Coll., 1977-79. Cert. clin. competence in audiology and speech lang. pathology; registered emergency med. technician. Mem. Am. Speech, Hearing and Lang. Assn., Mass. Speech, Hearing and Lang. Assn., New Eng. Sign Lang. Study Group, Mass. Audubon Soc., New Eng. Sierra Club, Burlington Hist. Soc., Charles River Skating Club (pres.), Colonial Figure Skating Club, Minuteman Samoyed Club (dir.), Concord Dog Tng. Club, Newfoundland Club New Eng. Roman Catholic.

REES, JANE L., home economist; b. Carbondale, Pa.; B.S., Syracuse U., 1945; M.S., Columbia U., 1947; Ph.D., Pa. State U., 1959. Asst. prof. Rutgers U., New Brunswick, N.J., 1953-66; exec. dir. Am. Home Econs. Assn., Washington, 1966-67; prof., chmn. dept. home econs. and consumer scis. Miami U., Oxford, Ohio, 1958—, also dir. Family Child Studies Center; dir. Cin. Gas & Electric Co. Fulbright awardee, 1964; recipient fellowships. Mem. AAUW, PEO, Delta Gamma. Clubs: Miami U. Faculty (pres. 1968-69); Hamilton City. Home: 940 Silvoor Ln Oxford OH 45056 Office: 260 McGuffey Miami U Oxford OH 45056

REESE, CASSANDRA JEAN, food co. exec.; b. Chgo., Aug. 13, 1942; d. Anderson and Iola (Wilkerson) Brown; B.S. in Bus. Adminstrn., Roosevelt U., 1974; M.B.A., Governors State U., Park Forest, Ill., 1977; m. Ronald Reese, Nov. 24, 1961; children—Rodney, Gregory. Registrar, Plano Sch. Optometric Technicians, Chgo., 1972-74; dir. devel. Step, Inc., Chgo., 1974-75; asst. advt. project mgr. Kraft, Inc., Glenview, Ill., 1975—; cons. Max Factor Co. Mem. Nat. Assn. Female Execs., Phi Gamma Nu. Club: Toastmistress. Address: 333 S Taylor St Oak Park IL 60302

REESE, KAREN LOU, nurse; b. Imperial, Nebr., Nov. 17, 1951; d. Harold Lyle and Esther Mae (Vaughn) Ward; B.S. in Sociology/Anthropology, Nebr. Wesleyan U., 1974; diploma Bryan Meml. Hosp. Sch. Nursing, 1974; m. Clark W. Reese, Aug. 25, 1973. Staff nurse Meml. Hosp., Seward, Nebr., 1974; head nurse med./surg. unit Luth. Meml. Hosp., Grand Island, Nebr., 1974-76, supr. intensive/coronary care unit, 1976-82, dir. nursing, 1982—; instr. cardio-pulmonary resuscitation, instr. advanced life support Am. Heart Assn.; nurse adv. Diabetic Assn., 1975-76; mem. profl. adv. planning com. Kearney State B.S. in Nursing program. Recipient Woman of Yr. award Grand Island Bus. and Profl. Women's Assn., 1982-83. Mem. Am. Nurses Assn., Nebr. Nurses Assn., AAUW, Am. Assn. Nursing Service Adminstrs., Nebr. Heart Assn. (nurse edn. com. Central Nebr.), Nebr. Consortium Hosp. Schs. Nursing, Nebr. Soc. Respiratory Therapy, Am. Soc. Nursing Service Adminstrs., Nebr. Nurses Assn. Dist. IV, Am. Nurses Assn., Central Nebr. Critical Care Nurses Assn. (v.p.), PEO. Methodist. Club: Delta Zeta Alumni Assn. Home: 106 W 22nd St Grand Island NE 68801 Office: Lutheran Memorial Hospital Grand Island NE 68801

REESE, MARIE ROMETTA, state govt. ofcl.; b. Scottsboro, Ala., Dec. 24, 1923; d. Samuel H. and Josia M. (Gist) Elrod; grad. Snead State Jr. Coll., 1976; B.S. in Bus. Mgmt., U. Ala., 1978, postgrad., 1979-80; m. Douglas Olan Reese, June 17, 1939 (dec. Apr. 1973); 1 son, Donald W.; m. 2d, Buford S. Durhan, June 22, 1977 (dec. July 1979). Instr., Gadsden (Ala.) Bus. Coll., 1962-64; clk. dept. agr. and industries State of Ala., Guntersville, 1964-75, interviewer dept. indsl. relations, Albertville, Ala., 1975—; exec. editor Reese Publishers, Albertville, 1973-74. Hon. houseparent Omaha Home for Boys, 1960-75; fund raiser March of Dimes, 1970-75, Cancer Crusade, 1960-77; pres. Am. Legion Aux., 1969-72; bd. dirs. Ala. Heart Assn., 1975-78, Am. Cancer Soc., 1970—, pres. Marshall County unit, 1970-75, del. to state meetings, 1970-79, mem. field services com., 1970-76. Recipient cert. of appreciation Am. Legion Aux., 1971, Meritorious Service award Ala. Heart Assn., 1973; named hon. lt. col. City of Albertville, 1975. Mem. Internat. Assn. Personnel in Employment Security (pres. Ala. chpt. 1978-79), Ala. State Employees Assn., Internat. Platform Assn., Albertville C. of C., Sand Mountain Mental Health Assn., Ala. Fedn. Bus. and Profl. Women's Clubs (pres. 1966-67, citation award 1968). Baptist. Club: Order Eastern Star. Home: PO Box 614 Albertville AL 35950 Office: PO Box 800 Albertville AL 35950

REESE, MARY LOUISE, writer, realtor; b. Red Oak, Iowa, Aug. 11, 1938; d. Charles Arthur and Alice (Hayes) Reese; student Grinnell Coll.; B.A., U. Nebr., 1966; postgrad. Augustana Coll., Western Ill. U.; m. Francis Bartly O'Gara, July 7, 1962 (div. 1976). Copy editor Lincoln (Nebr.) Jour., 1960-61; reporter-photographer Ogden (Utah) Standard-Examiner, 1963-64; owner retail bus., Davenport, Iowa, 1968-72; salesman Success Motivation Inst., Davenport, 1971-76; prin. The Word Works, writing, editing, cons.; asso. broker, sales mgr. Rex Realty; free-lance writer contbg. to Family Circle, Lady's Circle, community devel. publs., others. Iowa tax chmn. LWV, 1973. Mem. Women in Communications (legis. com. 1973-74, chmn. S.W. regional mems. at large 1981—), Women's Equity Action League (Iowa pres. 1972-73, 74-75, nat. dir. and publicity chmn. 1975), Nat. Assn. Realtors, N.Mex. Women's Polit. Caucus (state steering com. 1981-82), PEO. Kappa Tau Alpha. Mem. Ch. of Religious Sci. Address: 4401 Montgomery St NE Suite 180 Albuquerque NM 87109

REESE, MILDRED LYONS, social worker, civic worker; b. New Orleans, July 28; d. Colman and Emily Eleanor (Carter) Lyons; B.A., Dillard U., 1942; M.S.W., Atlanta Sch. Social Work, 1952; m. Lorenzo J. Reese, Nov. 11, 1948. Classroom tchr. Orleans Parish Sch. System, 1937-48, sch. social worker, 1948-59, asst. prin. secondary sch., 1960, prin. elem. sch., 1961-77; program dir. New Orleans Council on Aging, part-time, 1978; spl. asst. to adminstrn. Urban League Greater New Orleans, part-time, 1980-81. Vice pres. Ind. Women's Orgn., 1979—; bd. dirs. YWCA, 1970-79; mem. Task Force on Talent Bank of Women, 1977—; co-chmn. Citizens Com. Against Crime, 1979; del. Internat. Women's Year Conf., 1976; bd. dirs., 3d v.p. Family Service Soc., bd. dirs. Bright Pre-Sch. for Deaf; mem. adv. com. Women's Office, City of New Orleans; bd. dirs. Mental Health Assn. Greater New Orleans. Recipient award Orleans Neighborhood Center, 1961; award PTA, 1959, 62, 66, 79; meritorious community service cert., New Orleans, 1979. Mem. Nat. Assn. Elem. Sch. Prins., Nat. Assn. Social Workers, Urban League Greater New Orleans, Nat. Ret. Tchrs. Assn. Democrat. Baptist. Clubs: Les Inseparables.

REEVE, JACQUELINE ANNE, nurse; b. Warren, Ohio, Apr. 10, 1951; d. James Arnold and Thelma Joyce (Trask) R.; A.A. in Nursing, Kent State U., Ashtabula, 1971. Nursing supr. Char-Lotte Nursing Home, Inc., Rock Creek, Ohio, 1971-79; team leader Northeastern Ohio Gen. Hosp., North Madison, 1979-80; dir. nursing Con-Lea Nursing Home, Geneva, Ohio, 1980-81, Good Samaritan Nursing Home Corp., East Peoria, Ill., 1982; dir. nursing service Wickliffe (Ohio) Country Pl., 1982—; pvt. practice cons. for nursing homes; profl. reviewer med. records: mem. Ohio Health Care Assn. peer rev. survey team, 1981-82. Active ACLU, Cleve.; mem. Jefferson Vol. Fire Dept. Rescue Squad, 1978—. Mem. Nat. League Nursing, Nat. Honor Soc., Quill and Scroll. Organizer, condr. inservice courses in field. Home: PO Box 93 Jefferson OH 44047 also 141 Steele Ave Apt 203 Painesville OH 44077

REEVES, BETTY JENE, editor; b. Great Bend, Kans., Dec. 2, 1924; d. George Whitney and Alma Myrtle (Fesser) Bell; student Phillips U., 1943-44. Wichita Bus. Coll., 1944; m. Licurgous F. Reeves, Oct. 21, 1961; 1 stepson, Michael F. Floral designer, Bells Flower & Gift Shop, Great Bend, Kans., 1944-49; owner, operator City Floral, McPherson, 1951-53; owner, operator Betty's Flowers, Salina, 1953-55; designer Hutchinson Floral, (Kans.), 1955-61; lifestyle editor, feature writer Newton (Kans.) Kansan, 1968—. Named hon. Jaycee Jayne, 1974; recipient award Girl Scouts. Mem. Kans. Press Assn., Am. Legion Aux., Epsilon Sigma Alpha. Republican. Mem. Disciples of Christ Ch. Clubs: Soroptimists, Eagles Aux. (past pres.), Ladies Elks (pres.), Axtell Christian Hosp. Aux., VFW Aux. Pochontas (past state pres.). Home: 1206 N Duncan St Newton KS 67114 Office: 121 W 6th St PO Box 268 Newton KS 67114

REEVES, CAROLINE BUCK (MRS. WILLIAM HARVEY REEVES), civic worker, author; b. St. Louis; d. Philo Melvin and Aletheia (Hall) Buck; A.B., Wellesley Coll., U. Wis., 1928; M.A., Columbia, 1934; m. William Harvey Reeves, Aug. 29, 1931; children—Aletheia Nevius, H. Van Kirk. Editorial, coll. depts. Henry Holt & Co., pubs., N.Y.C., 1928-31; indsl. economist U.S. Govt., Washington, 1942-45, Rockefeller U., 1970—. Pres. bd. mgrs. Home for Old Men and Aged Couples (name changed to Isaac H. Tuttle Fund 1981), N.Y.C., 1955-58, bd. dirs., 1951—, sec. bd., 1960-62, trustee, 1969—, mem. com. on aging Fedn. of Protestant Welfare Agys., N.Y.C., 1951-58; mem. hobby show com. Community Council of Greater N.Y., 1955-63; mem. N.Y. Com. Frontier Nursing Service, Inc.; bd. dirs. The Bargain Box, Inc., 1962-69; bd. dirs. Amsterdam Nursing Home Corp., 1974—. Mem. Colonial Dames Am., Delta Delta Delta. Club: Colony. Author: Impact of War on Tri-City Area, 1917-19, 1943; Impact of World War I on Hampton Roads Area, 1944, Disposition of Surplus Machine Tools by the War Department following World War I, 1944, also articles. Home: 273 Harbor Rd PO Box 214 Southport CT 06490

REEVES, FRANCES RHODA CAMPBELL II (CAMPBELL REEVES), poet, art cons.; b. Auckland, N.Z., June 8, 1921; came to U.S., 1946, naturalized, 1961; d. George Alister and Rhoda Mary (McQuarrie) Campbell; student Auckland Bus. Coll. 1938-40, Auckland Sch. Arts, 1940-43; cert. journalism Am. Sch. Journalism, 1960; m. Ralph Bernard Reeves, July 17, 1944; children—Ralph Bernard III, Ross Campbell. Copywriter advt. dept. Sta. WRAL-Radia-TV, Raleigh, N.C., 1953-55; contbr. poetry, book revs. to News and Observer, Raleigh; owner, operator Art Cons., Ltd., Raleigh, 1977—; N.C. chmn. Friends of Kennedy Center; poet in classroom N.C. Public Schs., 1970-77; pres. Raleigh Fine Arts Soc., 1974. Chmn. N.C. Symphony Ball, Gov.'s Mansion, 1964. Recipient First prize N.C. Poetry Council, 1968, 68, N.C. Poetry Soc., 1970, 70. Mem. Nat. Assn. Female Execs., Am. Soc. Appraisers (asso.), N.C. Art Soc. (exec. bd. 1965-72), N.C. Mus. Guild, Am. Assn. Mus. (trustee com.). Democrat. Episcopalian. Clubs: Carolina Country (Raleigh); Nat. Press (Washington). Author: Bane of Jewels, 1968; Coming Out Even, 1973 (Best Book by N.C. Poet award 1974); contbr. poetry to numerous anthologies. Office: 815 Marlowe Rd Raleigh NC 27609

REEVES, GEORGIA LYETH, banker; b. Clayton, N.Mex., May 1, 1930; d. Robert Edward and Ruth Ermina (Lyeth) Hamblen; student Wayland Bapt. Coll., Plainview, Tex.; m. Richard Douglas Reeves, Sept. 15, 1950. Bookkeeper, teller First Nat. Bank, Amarillo, Tex., 1950-53; bookkeeper First State Bank, Dumas, Tex., 1954; loan and discount teller Midland Nat. Bank (Tex.), 1954-57, sec. new accounts, v.p., adminstrn. and ops. mgr., oil dept., 1958—; teller First State Bank, Roswell, N.Mex., 1958. Bd. dirs. Midland chpt. ARC, 1966—; div. chmn. United Way Midland. Mem. Nat. Assn. Bank Women (chmn. Panhandle W. group 1975, vice chmn. Permian Basin group 1980-81 chmn. 1982-83), Desk and Derrick Club (pres. 1966, Deserving Dame award 1972), Am. Inst. Banking. Baptist. Office: PO Box 2097 Midland TX 79702

REEVES, KATHRYN RANDALL, nurse, author; b. Albion, Mich., Nov. 8, 1934; d. Tom R. and Eleanor (Householder) Randall; student Albion Coll., 1952-54; A.D.N., Fullerton Coll., 1964; B.S., Calif. State U., 1969; B.A., Calif. State U., Fullerton, 1982; m. George I. Reeves, June 25, 1954; children—Thomas Charles, Mary Kathryn, Susan Elisabeth. Charge nurse, asst. dir. nursing Childrens Hosp., Orange County, Calif., 1964-73, head nurse adolescent unit, med. surg. supr., 1973-76; dir. emergency nursing, emergency dept. St. Joseph Hosp., Orange, 1976—. Vol. nurse ARC. Cert. emergency nurse. Mem. Am. Assn. Neurosurg. Nurses, Nat. Critical Care Inst., Emergency Dept. Nurses Assn. (pres. Orange County chpt. 1982-83), DAR, Orange County Geneal. Soc., Mensa, Alpha Lambda Delta, Alpha Gamma Sigma, Psi Chi, Delta Gamma. Democrat. Episcopalian. Home: 201 Friar Pl Fullerton CA 92635 Office: 1100 Stewart Ave Orange CA 92668

REEVES, PATRICIA RUTH, constrn. and engring. co. exec.; b. Bklyn., Mar. 26, 1931; d. Maurice G. and Ethel Helen (Kessler) Der Brucke; B.A., Adelphi U., 1952; m. Cedric E. Reeves, June 22, 1952. Chief of records sect. Hydrocarbon Research, Inc., N.Y.C., 1952-65; lead sec. C.F. Braun & Co., Murray Hill, N.J., 1965-69; exec. sec. Wilputte Corp., Murray Hill, N.J., 1969-75, adminstrv. asst., 1975-79, sales coordinator, 1979-81, personnel adminstr., 1981—. Pres., Mountain Jewish Community Center, Warren, N.J., 1976-77, bd. dirs., 1972—. Mem. Nat. Assn. Female Execs., AAUW, Central N.J. Women's Network Group. Jewish. Home: 89 Knollwood Dr Watchung NJ 07060 Office: Wilputte Corp 152 Floral Ave Murray Hill NJ 07974

REEVES, SANDRA LEE, state legislator; b. Lake Charles, La., Oct. 19, 1942; student La. Coll.; B.M.E., Midwestern State U.; m. Clay Jack Reeves, Oct. 20, 1962; 2 daus. Former profl. singer, sch. tchr., free-lance writer, part-time voice instr.; mem. Mo. Ho. of Reps., 1978—. Mem. Tri-County Mental Health Adv. Bd. and Youth Task Force; mem. North Kansas City Bd. Edn.; pres. W. Central Mo. Sch. Bds. Assn. Recipient Outstanding Alumni award Midwestern State U., 1979. Baptist. Democrat. Office: Mo State Ho of Reps Jefferson City MO 65101 *

REFORD, STEPHANIE MCCANDLESS (MRS. ROBERT W. REFORD), educator, cons. exec.; b. St. Louis, Mar. 8, 1934; d. Lee and Mary (Glor) McCandless; B.A. cum laude, Principia Coll., 1956; M.A., U. Wash., 1962; m. Robert W. Reford. Tchr. world history Punahou Acad., Honolulu, 1958-59, 62-63; program specialist Inst. Internat. Edn., N.Y.C., 1960; asst. dean students SUNY, Oswego, 1960-61; exec. dir. Pacific and Asian Affairs Council, Honolulu, 1963-70; project adminstrn. officer UN Inst. Tng. and Research, N.Y.C., 1970-72; pres. Reford-McCandless Internat. Cons.'s Corp., Reford-McCandless Internat. Inst. U.S.A.; v.p. Reford-McCandless Internat. Cons. Corp. Can., Reford-McCandless Internat. Inst. Can. Bd. dirs. Couchiching Inst. Public Affairs. Mem. World Council Curriculum and Instrn., UN Assn. (dir. 1966-70), Internat. Studies Assn., Comparative and Internat. Edn. Soc. Can., Canadian Soc. Asian Studies, Canadian Soc. Studies in Edn., Canadian Inst. Internat. Affairs, Royal Ont. Mus., Theta Sigma Phi. Home and Office: 12 Metcalfe St Toronto ON M4X 1R6 Canada

REGAN, ELLEN FRANCES (MRS. WALSTON SHEPARD BROWN), ophthalmologist; b. Boston, Feb. 1, 1919; d. Edward Francis and Margaret (Moynihan) R.; A.B., Wellesley Coll., 1940; M.D., Yale U., 1943; m. Walston Shepard Brown, Aug. 13, 1955. Intern, Boston City Hosp., 1944; asst. resident, resident Inst. Ophthalmology, Presbyn. Hosp., N.Y.C., 1944-47, asst. ophthalmologist, 1947-56, asst. attending ophthalmologist, 1956—; instr. ophthalmology Columbia Coll. Physicians and Surgeons, 1947-55, asso. ophthalmology, 1955-67, asst. clin. prof., 1967—. Mem. Am. Ophthal. Soc., AMA, Am. Acad. Ophthalmology, Assn. Research Ophthalmology, N.Y. Acad. Medicine, N.Y. State, Mass. med. socs. Clubs: River, Wellesley. Home: Tuxedo Park NY 10987 Office: 2 E 94th St New York NY 10028

REGAN, HELENE, personnel agy. exec.; b. Bklyn., Nov. 12, 1938; d. Abraham Bernard and Yetta (Pepper) Straussman; ed. Baruch Coll.; children—Scott Lawrence, Keith Martin, Andrea Beth. Coordinator display advt. Blaine-Thompson, N.Y.C., 1957-59; owner, mgr. Helene Ltd., N.Y.C., 1967—; owner, mgr. Fabulous Furs by Helene, N.Y.C., 1967-76; 2d v.p. Prescott & James, personnel agy., N.Y.C., 1976—; cons. Kolmar Corp.; fashion coordinator for fur industry. Active in fundraising Cancer Care, NAACP, United Jewish Appeal, and Orgn. Rehab. and Tng., N.Y.C. Recipient 12 medals for achievement Women's Am. Orgn. for Rehab. and Tng., 1969-74. Mem. Nat. Assn. Female Execs. Republican. Home: 4 Lexington Ave New York NY 10010 Office: 170 Broadway New York NY 10038

REGAN, SUZANNE MARIE, food co. mgr.; b. Camden, N.J., May 11, 1950; d. Cornelius Joseph and Jeannette (Way) R.; B.S., U. Conn., 1972; M.B.A., Drexel U., 1978; m. Ronald L. Feldberg, Apr. 10, 1976. Acctg. procedures analyst Campbell Soup Co., Camden, N.J., 1972-74, mktg. research analyst, 1974-77, asst. mktg. mgr. Swanson div., 1977-78, mktg. mgr. Swanson div., 1978-81, mktg. dir. pet foods, 1981—. Mem. Nat. Assn. Female Execs. Home: 59 Woodhurst Dr West Berlin NJ 08091 Office: Campbell Pl Camden NJ 08101

REGARDIE, RENAY NADLER, market research co. exec.; b. Bronx, N.Y., May 30, 1942; d. Samuel and Lillian (Wolfson) Nadler; B.S. magna cum laude in Bus. Adminstrn., Am. U., 1964; m. William Arthur Regardie, May 29, 1965; children—Jon, Marc. Sr. copywriter Robert Kline Advt., Richmond, Va., 1964-65; research analyst Chesapeake and Potomac Telephone Co., Washington, 1965-68; sr. research analyst Am. Research Bur., Beltsville, Md., 1970-72; pres. Housing Data Reports, Inc., Bethesda, Md., 1976—. Mem. Nat. Assn. Home Builders, Urban Land Inst., Washington, Suburban Md. and N.Va. Home Builders. Jewish. Office: 4330 East West Hwy Bethesda MD 20814

REGAZZI, CLOTILDE MARIA, utilities co. exec.; b. N.Y.C., Nov. 11, 1931; d. Joseph and Edvige (Bruni) R.; B.A., Hunter Coll., 1972; M.A., N.Y. U., 1976. Sr. tng. rep. human resourses and devel. dept. Consol. Edison Co., N.Y.C. Mem. Am. Soc. Tng. and Devel., Am. Soc. Personnel Adminstrs., Nat. Bus. Edn. Assn., Delta Pi Epsilon. Roman Catholic. Office: Consol Edison 4 Irving Pl New York NY 10003

REGES, MARIANNA ALICE, pub. co. exec.; b. Budapest, Hungary, Mar. 23, 1947; came to U.S., 1956, naturalized, 1963; d. Otto H. and Alice M. R.; A.A.S. with honors, Fashion Inst. Tech., 1967; B.B.A. with high honors, Baruch Coll., N.Y.C., 1971, M.B.A. in Stats., 1978; m. Charles P. Green, Feb. 15, 1975; 1 dau., Rebecca. Media research analyst Doyle, Dane, Bernbach Advt., N.Y.C., 1967-70; research supr. WCBS-TV, N.Y.C., 1970-71; research mgr. Woman's Day Mag., N.Y.C., 1971-72; asst. media dir. Benton & Bowles Advt., N.Y.C., 1972-75; mgr. research and sales devel. NBC Radio, N.Y.C., 1975-77; group research dir. Ziff Davis Pub. Co., N.Y.C., 1977—. Mem. Vt. Natural Resources Council, 1977—; mem. Nature Conservatory, 1980—; advisor Baruch Coll. Advt. Soc., 1975—. Mem. Am. Mktg. Assn., Am. Advt. Fedn., Media Research Dir. Assn., Radio and TV Research Council, Women in Communications, Advt. Women N.Y., Beta Gamma Sigma, Sigma Alpha Delta. Home: 10 Stuyvesant Oval New York NY 10009 Office: 1 Park Ave New York NY 10016

REGGIE, DORIS BOUSTANY, civic and polit. worker; b. Lafayette, La.; d. Frem F. Sr. and Beatrice (Joseph) Boustany; B.S. in Home Econs., U. Southwestern La., 1950; m. Edmund M. Reggie, June 17, 1951; children—Ed Michael, Vicki Reggie Raclin, Denis, Gregory, Alicia, Ray. Former pres. St. Michael Sch. Parents Club, St. Michael Paris Altar Soc.; adv. bd. U. Southwestern La. Endowment Fund drive; mem. Democratic State Central Com.; del. Dem. Nat. Conv., 1976, 80; mem. Gov.'s Commn. Internat. Yr. of Child; mem. Crowley Preservation and Beautification Coms.; mem. state and nat. Dem. Fin. Councils, Dem. Exec. Council Acadia Parish; del. Dem. Mid-Term Conf., Phila., 1982. Named Disting. Alumna in Home Econs., U. Southwestern La., 1975. Mem. Crowley LWV (past officer), Nat. Trust for Historic Preservation, Lafayette Fine Arts Found., La. Preservation Alliance, Crowley Arts Assn., Acadia Arts Council, Nat. Assn. Smithsonian Instn., Friends of Archives of La., Delta Delta Delta. Club: Crowley Garden (past. v.p.). Address: PO Box Drawer D Crowley LA 70526

REGISTER, ETHEL WILCOX, mcpl. clk.; b. New Bern, N.C., Aug. 15, 1931; d. Herbert Edwin and Annie Lucretia (Sutton) Wilcox; student Harbarger Coll. Sch. Bus., 1951-53; m. Marvin O. Register, July 24, 1954; children—Mia Jeanne, Loucresia Ann, Dell. Exec. sec. Page & Smith Architects, Raleigh, N.C., 1953-54; sec. div. engring. Chemstrand Corp., Pensacola, Fla., 1955-56; sec. to chmn. bd. suprs. Fairfax County (Va.), 1968-69; sec. to dep. county exec. Fairfax County Govt., 1969-70, clk. to planning commn., 1973-74, clk. to Fairfax County Bd. Suprs., 1974—; mem. Fairfax County Com. on Records Mgmt., 1980. Nat. rep., sec. Internat. Mil. Staff Women's Group, 1970-73; organizer French/English Conversation Group, 1971; Mem. Internat. Inst. Mcpl. Clks. (internat. conf. records mgmt. discussion panel 1981, cert. mcpl. clk. 1981), Va. Mcpl. Clks.' Assn. Club: Zonta Internat. (treas. chpt. 1976-78, rep. to UN 1978, v.p. chpt. 1978-80, pres. chpt. 1981-83) (Fairfax). Home: 534 Marshall Rd Vienna VA 22180 Office: 4100 Chain Bridge Rd Fairfax VA 22030

REGNART, CLAUDIA SWANNACK, educator; b. Spokane, Wash., Aug. 11, 1937; d. John William and Leone Estelle (Roth) Swannack; B.A., U. Puget Sound, 1959; postgrad. E. Wash. Coll. Edn., summers 1958, 60, U. Wash., summer 1966, Alaska Pacific U., 1968-69, U. Alaska, summers 1972, 74; m. Ronald I. Regnart, Nov. 21, 1962; children—Jeffrey, Patrick. Tchr., Anchorage Sch. Dist., 1959-63, 64-65, 67, Nome (Alaska) Sch. Dist., 1963-64; tchr., owner Rabbit Creek Pre-Sch., Anchorage, 1972—. Chmn. PTA, Anchorage, 1970—; den mother Boy Scouts Am., 1973-79; vol. worker Cancer Fund, Heart Fund, FISH, Little League. Mem. Alaska Edn. Assn., NEA, Am. Assn. for Edn. of Young Children. Methodist. Club: Order Eastern Star. Home: 4900 Rabbit Creek Rd SRA Book 476A Anchorage AK 99507 Office: PO Box 476A Anchorage AK 99507

REGNIER, CLAIRE NEOMIE, mktg. and bus. cons.; b. Fort Riley, Kans., May 2, 1939; d. Eugene Arthur and Claire Janet (Macfarlane) Regnier; B.S. cum laude in Journalism, Trinity U., San Antonio, 1961. Advt. cons., San Antonio, 1961-68; editor Paseo del Rio Showboat newspaper, San Antonio, 1968-81; exec. dir. San Antonio River Assn., San Antonio, 1968-81; pres. Metro Cons., San Antonio, 1981—. Chmn. Centro 21 Downtown Revitalization Task Force, San Antonio; rep. San Antonio River Corridor Com.; mem. Fiesta San Antonio Commn., San Antonio Parks and Recreation Adv. Bd.; bd. dirs., chmn. public relations com. San Antonio Area council Girl Scouts U.S.A. Recipient awards of excellence for Showboat, Alamo Bus. Communicators, 1970, 71, 73, 74; Headliner award San Antonio chpt. Women in Communications, 1980. Mem. Internat. Assn. Bus. Communicators, Women in Communications (Southwest region banner award 1981), Tex. Public Relations Assn., Alamo Bus. Communicators (Communicator of Yr. 1977), San Antonio Mus. Assn., San Antonio Conservation Soc. Club: San Antonio Press. Home: 7772 Woodridge St San Antonio TX 78209 Office: One Riverwalk Pl 14th Floor San Antonio TX 78205

REHBERG, IRENE LEE, elastic coating exec.; b. Shanghai, China, Feb. 22, 1946; came to U.S., 1969, naturalized, 1982; d. Kam Yee and Chang Hing (Ho) Lee; B.S., Ohio U., 1973; m. John Thomas Rehberg, Aug. 24, 1980; 1 son, Eric Lee. Lab. specialist Fusion, Inc., Willoughby, Ohio, 1973-77; profl. chemist SCM-Gidden Metals, Cleve., 1977-78; sr. chemist Tremco, Cleve., 1978-80; v.p., dir. Elastic Coating Systems, Inc., Medina, Ohio, 1980—; tchr. Chinese culture; soldering and brazing cons. Recipient award for outstanding contbn. to Lakeland Community Coll., 1974. Mem. Delta Phi Alpha. Roman Catholic. Patentee in field. Home: 20735 White Bark St Strongsville OH 44136 Office: 2552 Lester Rd Medina OH 44256

REHFELD, DAWN ARLENE, real estate exec.; b. Sask., Can., Feb. 26, 1940; d. Clinton Lloyd and Thelma (Kirkpatrick) Ward; ed. Niagara Christian Coll., 1959, Fla. Bapt. Coll., 1970, U. LaVerne, 1981; m. Richard Wallace, May 22, 1959; children—Dale Wallace, Dean Robert.

Adminstrv. asst. exec. v.p. Fla. Bapt. Coll., 1967; with music dept. EMC Schs., El Monte, Calif., 1973; asso. Beach & Flaaten, 1978-80, broker asso., 1980—. Mem. Nat. Assn. Realtors, Calif. Assn. Realtors, Women in Real Estate, Arcadia Bd. Realtors. Republican. Mem. Ch. of Nazarene. Club: Republican Women's. Contbr. article to jour. Home: 8417 Vicara Alta Loma CA 91701 Office: 150 Santa Anita Suite 100 Arcadia CA 91006

REHM, NANCY EVANS, nurse; b. Louisville, Sept. 20, 1944; d. Howard Heath and Emily Trimble (Muir) Evans; B.S. in Nursing, U. Pitts., 1973; M.S. in Nursing and Midwifery Tng., U. Ky., Lexington, 1975; postgrad. U. Montpellier (France), 1962, U. Georgetown (Ky.), 1962-63, Norton Meml. Infirmary Sch. Nursing, Louisville, 1965-67, U. Louisville, 1965-67; children—Keith Hayes, Catherine Howard. Staff and charge nurse Norton Meml. Infirmary, Louisville, 1967; staff nurse Magee Women's Hosp., Pitts., 1968-71, charge nurse delivery rooms, 1971-73, staff nurse family center care, 1973-74; nurse midwife Mercy Health Center, Pitts., 1976-77; perinatal nurse dept. Ob-Gyn, U. Louisville, 1977-79; mem. clin. faculty dept. Ob-Gyn, U. Utah, Salt Lake City, 1979—; coordinator outreach edn. and maternal transport system. R.N., Ky., Pa., Utah; lic. nurse midwife Ky., Pa., Utah. Mem. Am. Coll. Nurse Midwives, Am. Coll. Obstetricians and Gynecologists Nurses Assn. (chmn. Utah sect.), Nat. Perinatal Assn., Ky. Perinatal Assn., Utah Perinatal Assn. Baptist. Office: Dept Ob-Gyn U Utah Med Center 50 N Medical Dr Room 5B302 Salt Lake City UT 84132

REIBMAN, JEANETTE FICHMAN (MRS. NATHAN L. REIBMAN), state senator; b. Ft. Wayne, Ind., Aug. 18, 1915; d. Meir and Pearl (Schwartz) Fichman; B.A., Hunter Coll.; LL.B., Ind. U.; LL.D. (hon.), Lafayette Coll., Cedar Crest Coll., Wilson Coll.; m. Nathan L. Reibman; 3 children. Atty. tax amortization br. U.S. War Dept., Washington; atty. U.S. War Prodn. Bd., 1941-44; mem. Pa. Ho. of Reps., 1954-56, 58-66, sec. com. of welfare, chmn. com. on edn., 1959-62, com. on twps., 1965; mem. Pa. Senate, 1966—, chmn. edn. com., 1967-80. Pa. commr., Edn. Commn. of States; mem. Pa. Adv. Com. on Probation. Del. White House Conf. on Problems of Aging, White House Conf. on Children; mem. Gov.'s Citizens Commn. on Basic Edn.; mem. Joint State Govt. Commn. on Decedents' Estates; mem. Pa. Council Arts; mem. Pa. coordinating com. Internat. Women's Yr., 1976, del. nat. conf., 1977; mem. Fed. Citizen's Com. for Dept. Edn., 1977. Trustee, Lafayette Coll., St. Luke's Hosp. of Bethlehem; mem. commonwealth bd. Med. Coll. Pa.; bd. dirs. Pa. Higher Edn. Assistance Agy. Named Disting. Dau. Pa.; elected to Hunter Coll. Alumni Hall of Fame; recipient State of Israel-City of Jerusalem Peace award, 1977. Mem. AAUW, LWV, Delta Kappa Gamma, Sigma Delta Tau, Phi Delta Kappa. Democrat. Home: 514 McCartney St Easton PA 18042

REICH, KATHLEEN JOHANNA, educator; b. Mannheim, Germany, May 1, 1927; came to U.S., 1955, naturalized, 1958; d. Robert and Luise Charlotte Helene (Kurowsky) Weichel; M.A.T. in English, Rollins Coll., 1976, Ed.S., 1981; 1 son, Robert Weichel. With Orlando (Fla.) Pub. Library, 1955-57; cataloguer, instr. U. Detroit, 1957-60, Trinity U., San Antonio, 1960-61; adminstr. Fla. Book Processing Center, Orlando, 1961-68; bur. chief, div. library services Fla. State Dept., Winter Park, 1968-71; assoc. prof. library sci. Rollins Coll., Winter Park, 1971—, asst. dean faculty, 1981—. Mem. AAUP, African Literature Assn., Nat. Assn. Fgn. Student Affairs, Am. Water Ski Assn. Home: 211 Fawsett Rd Winter Park FL 32789 Office: Rollins College Winter Park FL 32789

REICH, PAULINE CAROLE, equal opportunity specialist, Asian specialist; b. Kew Gardens, N.Y., Nov. 13, 1946; d. Stanley Garfield and Elsa (Doctor) R.; B.A. in Polit. Sci., CCNY, 1968, M.A. in Comparative Lit., City U.N.Y. 1972; cert. Critical Langs. Program./Polit. Sci. (Carnegie and Princeton fellow 1966-67), Princeton U., 1967; m. Brian M. K. Poon, May 16, 1978. Tchr., English as second lang., high sch. tchr. N.Y.C. Bd. Edn., 1970-72, 74-76, 77-78; instr. English as a second lang., comparative lit. Tsuda Coll. Sophia U. Internat. div., Tokyo Woman's Christian Coll. Jr. Coll., Chuo U., Tokyo, 1972-74; owner-operator Am. Lang. and Culture Inst., pvt. inst. for Japanese execs., N.Y.C., 1974-76; Title IX coordinator U. Calif., Irvine, 1977; career devel. cons. BABEL/Lau Center, Berkeley, Calif., 1976-77; instr. English as second lang., career skills N.Y.C. Bd. Edn. Adult Indochinese Refugee Program, 1977-81; sr. equal opportunity specialist Office for Civil Rights, Postsecondary Edn. Div., U.S. Dept. Edn., N.Y.C., 1978—; researcher, tchr., cons. Asia, Asian-Am. subjects; Japan Found. fellow, Tokyo, 1973; mem. Nat. Adv. Com. on Japanese Bilingual Edn., 1976; chairperson internat. comparisons com. Council on Mcpl. Performance, N.Y.C., 1981—; participant CORO Found. Pub. Affairs and Leadership Program, 1981; chairperson Cambodian refugee sponsorship com. Community Ch. N.Y., N.Y.C., 1980-81; East Coast dir. Ind. Scholars Asia affiliate Assn. Asian Studies, 1982—, nat. dir., 1983—; mem. edn. com., San Francisco Commn. on Status of Women, 1976-77. Mem. Assn. Asian Studies U.S., Japan Soc., Asia Soc. (ad hoc com. on Cambodian Buddhism 1980), Asian-Pacific Am. Women's Network (hon.), CORO Assos. Contbr. numerous articles on Japan and Asia to Japanese, English publs. Office: Office for Civil Rights US Dept Edn 26 Federal Plaza Room 33-130 New York NY 10278

REICHEL, LEATRICE IDA, banker; b. Erie, Pa., Jan. 31, 1930; d. Jacob Charles and Ida Eva (Bovee) Seib; student public schs.; widow. With Security Bank, Erie, 1948—, asst. sec., 1970-75, personnel officer, 1972—, asst. v.p., 1975—. Mem. personnel com. Erie chpt. ARC, 1980-82. Mem. Nat. Assn. Bank Women (past chmn. N.W. Pa. group), Am. Soc. Personnel Adminstrn., Personnel Assn. N.W. Pa. (pres. 1981-82). Clubs: Aviation Country, Erie Maennerchor Aux., East Erie Turners, Order Eastern Star. Office: 801 State St Erie PA 16501

REICHENBACH, NANCY ELOISE ALFORD, counseling adminstr., b. Warrenton, N.C., Sept. 29, 1939; d. Roy Hines and Margaret Susan (Moss) Alford; B.S. in Home Econs., U. N.C., Greensboro, 1961; m. Carl F. Reichenbach, Jr., July 2, 1961; children—Tracy Marie, Carl Franklin III. Tchr., Wake Forest Baptist Coll. Nursery Sch., Winston-Salem, N.C., 1961-62; presch. tchr. Day Care Center, Portsmouth, Va., 1962-63; with Portsmouth Welfare Dept., 1963-64; co-owner NuTurf Garden Shop, Margate, Fla., 1973—; dir. Thrift Shop Center Group Counseling, Elizabeth H. Faulk Found., Inc., Boca Raton, Fla., 1975-78, program coordinator, 1978-80; exec. dir. Gratitude Guild, Inc., West Palm Beach, Fla., 1980—. Sunday sch. tchr., sec. women of ch. Green Acres Presbyterian Ch., Portsmouth, 1967; pres. Tedder Elem. Sch. PTA, Pompano Beach, Fla., 1973. Recipient plaque Tedder Elem. Sch. PTA, 1973, cert. appreciation Center Group Counseling, 1975. Mem. Omicron Nu. Club: Soroptimists. Home: 3199 NW 120th Ave Coral Springs FL 33065 Office: 317 N Lakeside Ct West Palm Beach FL 33407

REID, AUDREY YVONNE, physician; b. Jamaica, Dec. 4, 1941; d. Harry Uriah and Carmen (Riley) Reid; came to U.S., 1959; B.A., Andrews U., 1961; M.D., Howard U., 1967; M.P.H., U. Calif. Los Angeles, 1978; m. Leon Kruger, Apr. 20, 1975; children—RuthAnne, Leondra. Intern, St. Elizabeth Hosp., Dayton, 1967-68; resident in pediatrics Children's Hosp., Detroit, 1968-70; fellow in infectious disease Los Angeles County/U. So. Calif. Med. Center, 1970-72; pediatrician Calif. Med. Group, Los Angeles, 1972-76; practice medicine specializing in pediatrics, Pasadena, 1976—; sch. physician Pasadena Community Coll., 1976-78; mem. staff Huntington Meml. Hosp., St. Lukes Hosp., Pasadena. Mem. adv. bd. Pan African studies Pasadena City Coll.; bd. dirs. Child Care Info. Services, Pasadena, 1979. Diplomate Am. Bd. Pediatrics. Mem. AMA, Am. Public Health Assn., Nat., Calif. med. assns., Los Angeles Pediatric Soc., AAUP. Author: (with others) New Life Options, The Working Woman's Handbook, 1976. Office: 111 Congress St W Suite A Pasadena CA 91105

REID, CAROL MARCHISOTTO, dental hygienist; b. N.Y.C., Jan. 8, 1950; d. Paul Richard and Louise (Swink) Marchisotto; B.S. in Dental Hygiene, U. N.C., Chapel Hill, 1973; m. Charles Timothy Reid, Mar. 22, 1975; children—Charles Timothy, Robert William, Kristin Reneé. Instr. dental hygiene Guilford Tech. Inst., Jamestown, N.C., summer 1973; substitute dental hygiene cons. N.C. State, 1974-75; public health dental hygienist Rockingham County Health Dept., Mayodan, N.C., 1973—; tchr., tng. coordinator in field. Recipient Outstanding Service award Rockingham County Dental Soc., 1978, Disting. Service award Madison-Mayodan Jaycees, 1979. Mem. Am. Dental Hygienists Assn., N.C. Dental Hygienists Assn., N.C. Public Health Assn., Rockingham County Dental Hygiene Study Club. Democrat. Episcopalian. Clubs: Madison Jr. Service (outstanding new mem. award 1979), Woodmen of World. Office: 215 W Main St Mayodan NC 27027

REID, FAYE PIERCE, educator, rancher; b. Tyler, Tex., Jan. 25, 1918; d. Clifton Louis and Edna Eunice (Price) Pierce; B.Mus., La. State U., 1939; postgrad. Baylor U., 1937-38, also U. N.Mex., U. Colo., U. Madrid, others; m. Charles Arthur Reid, Jr., June 9, 1942; children—Faye Reid Reynolds, Charles Arthur III. Tchr., Edwards Sch., Beaumont, Tex., 1939-41, demonstration sch., Stephen F. Austin U., 1941-42, Colorado Springs Pub. Schs., 1952-61, 64-82, Albuquerque Pub. Schs., 1961-64; owner, operator ranch, Colorado Springs, 1946-66; counselor girls camp; performer with several community symphony orchs. Leader, 4-H Club, El Paso County, Colo., 1958-61. Mem. AAUW, Nat., Colo. edn. assns., Colorado Springs Tchrs. Assn., La. State U. Alumni Assn., Baylor U. Alumni Assn., Colorado Springs Fine Arts Center, Colorado Springs Community Orch., Marine Corps. Aux., Alpha Delta Kappa, Pi Beta Phi Alumnae. Mem. Christian Ch. Author curriculum materials, critiques. Home: 1770 Sawyer Way Colorado Springs CO 80915

REID, GERRI WOLD, artist; b. Portland, Oreg., Apr. 11, 1944; d. Alden Elroy and Verna (Kocinski) Wold; B.A. in Fine Art, Calif. State U., Sacramento, 1972, M.F.A., 1975; postgrad. Ind. U.-Purdue U. Instr. dental aux. edn. U. Minn., 1966-70; anthrop. research asst., 1975-76; asst. prof. dental aux. edn. Ind. U.-Purdue U., 1976-78; mng. editor Nat. Arts Guide, Chgo., 1978-80; freelance artist, Chgo., 1981—; dir. show coordination Circle Fine Art, Chgo., 1981; seminar lectr., 1977; one-woman shows include Artists' Coop. Gallery, Santa Fe, 1976, Artlink, Ft. Wayne, Ind., 1979, D.E.O. Fine Arts, Inc., Chgo., 1982; group exhbns. include Crocker Art Mus., Sacramento, 1975, Ft. Wayne Mus. Art, 1978, Artists Guild Chgo., 1981. Mem. Artists Guild Chgo., Chgo. Artists' Coalition.

REID, JEANNE MARIE, nutritionist; b. Tampa, Fla., Oct. 8, 1923; d. William Clarence and Christine Alicia (Mahoney) Reid; B.S., U. Ala., 1945; M.S., U. Md., 1962; postgrad. U. Minn., 1969. Dietetic intern N.Y. Hosp.-Cornell Med. Center, N.Y.C., 1946; asst. dietitian Charity Hosp., New Orleans, 1946-47, assoc. dir. therapeutic dietetic services, 1947-51; chief therapeutic dietitian Jackson Meml. Hosp., Miami, Fla., 1951-53; research dietitian Clin. Center, NIH, Bethesda, Md., 1953-57, metabolic research dietitian, out-patient clinic dietitian, 1957-67, research nutritionist Nat. Inst. Arthritis, Metabolism and Digestive Diseases, 1967—. Mem. Am. Dietetic Assn., Nat. Assn. Uniformed Services, Am. Inst. Nutrition, Commd. Officers Assn. USPHS, Nutrition Today Soc., D.C. Dietetic Assn., Assn. Mil. Surgeons, Sigma Xi. Contbr. articles in field to profl. jours. Home: 8315 North Brook Ln Apt 901 Bethesda MD 20814 Office: National Institute of Arthritis Metabolism and Digestive Diseases National Institutes of Health 9000 Rockville Pike Bldg 31 Room 4B-58 Bethesda MD 20205

REID, LORINE MAY, lawyer; b. Toledo, Apr. 29, 1932; d. Edwin McKechnie and Eleanor Mary (DeMars) R.; B.A., Wayne State U., 1958; M.S.W., U. Mich., 1965; J.D., U. Toledo, 1969. Social worker, 1958-70; dir. Lucas County Bd. Mental Health, Toledo, 1970-72; planning dir. Pilot Cities Criminal Justice Project, Dayton, Ohio, 1972-75; admitted to Ohio bar, 1973; individual practice law, Dayton, 1975—; legal dir. Children Services Bd. Montgomery County, Dayton, 1977-80. Bd. dirs., citizens adv. bd. Dayton Mental Health Center, 1978—. Mem. Am. Bar Assn., Ohio State Bar Assn., Dayton Bar Assn., LWV, AAUW, Nat. Assn. Women Lawyers. Democrat. Office: 5518 N Main St Dayton OH 45415

REID, LOTA SPENCE, ret. ednl. adminstr.; b. Norfolk, Va., June 10, 1911; d. John Paul and Susan Virginia (Hudgins) Spence; B.A., Coll. William and Mary, 1933; M.Ed., U. Va., 1967; postgrad. St. Mary's of Winchester, Oxford, Eng., summer 1970; m. John J. Reid, June 15, 1938; 1 son, John Spence. Tchr., Norfolk, 1934-38, Suffolk, Va., 1939-41, 50-54, Chgo., 1946-48, Emporia, Va., 1954-69; supr. secondary schs. Emporia, 1969-76; instr. Va. history and freshman English, Southside Community Coll., Alberta, Va., 1975-77. Pres. Suffolk Jr. Women's Club, 1941-43, Riparian Women's Club Emporia, 1958-59; coordinator county schs. bicentennial activities, 1974-76; mem. Emporia-Greensville County Bicentennial Com., 1974-76; bd. dirs. Tri Clubs. Recipient outstanding tchr. award local Civitan Clubs, 1970, tchrs. medal, 1968, Sch. Men's medal Freedoms Found., 1973; NDEA fellow, 1965, Old Dominion Found. fellow 1967; Freedoms Found. scholar Civitan Internat., 1970. Mem. Greensville County, NEA, Va. Edn. Assn., Nat., Va. councils for social studies, Nat., Va. assns. sch. execs., Greensville County Hist. Soc. (historian), UDC (sec.), Gamma Phi Beta, Tau Kappa Alpha, Kappa Delta Pi. Baptist. Contbg. author: Sketches of Greensville County, Virginia, 1650-1967, 1968; author: A Story of the Development of Education in Greensville County, Virginia, 1781-1980, 1981. Home: 409 Laurel St Emporia VA 23847 Office: Greensville County High Sch Emporia VA 23847

REID, LYNNE MCARTHUR, pathologist; b. Melbourne, Australia, Nov. 12, 1923; d. Robert Muir and Violet Annie (McArthur) Reid; M.D., U. Melbourne, 1969; M.D. (hon.), Harvard U., 1976. Pathologist-in-chief The Children's Med. Center, Boston; S. Burt Wolbach prof. pathology Harvard U. Fellow Royal Coll. Physicians, Royal Coll. Pathologists, Royal Australian Coll. Physicians, Can. Thoracic Soc.; mem. Am. Assn. Pathologists, Am. Pediatric Soc., Fleischner Soc., Brit. Thoracic Soc., Am. Thoracic Soc. Clubs: University Women's (London); Harvard (Boston). Office: 300 Longwood Ave Boston MA 02115

REID, MARIANNE D., civic worker; b. Omaha, Apr. 26, 1922; d. Charles LeRoy and Martina Doherty; B.S., Colo. State Coll., 1948; m. Preston Harding Reid, June 21, 1948; 1 dau., Jeralee Susanne (Mrs. Timothy D. Sigley). Head traffic dept. Sta. WRAL-TV, Raleigh, N.C., 1950-60; vol. asst. Norfolk Juvenile Ct., 1970-73, 80—; asst. to editor Peanut Sci. Jour., 1973-76; bd. dirs. Suffolk (Va.) Art League and Va. Mus.; state outreach coordinator for Va., Pilot Internat.; v.p. Obici Hosp. Aux., 1974-80; meml. chmn. Suffolk Heart Assn., 1980—; dir. for Suffolk area Va. Lung Assn. Republican. Roman Catholic. Clubs: Nat. Fedn. Women's, Holland Women's, Council Garden Raleigh. Home: 1204 West Point Dr Suffolk VA 23434

REID-GRANT, MYRNA LOIS, educator, writer; b. Hamilton, Ont., Can.; came to U.S., 1956; d. Harold Claude and Florence Grace (Jackson) Reid; student McMaster U., Hamilton, 1955; B.Sc., Moody Bible Inst., 1969; M.A., Wheaton (Ill.) Grad. Sch., 1971; postgrad. Northwestern U., 1982—; children—Christopher, Drew, Susan, Jennifer. Books: Vanya, 1974; Katya and the Silver Cross, 1982; The Journey, 1978; children's books include: Ivan the Informer, 1974; Ivan and the Hidden Bible, 1975; Ivan and the Daring Escape, 1976; asst. prof. communications Wheaton Grad. Sch., 1977—, coordinator broadcasting, 1978—; freelance voice work for audio prodns.; contbr. articles in field. Bd. dirs. Keston Coll., 1978—. Mem. Fellowship of Christians in the Arts, Nat. Religious Broadcasters, Nat. Assn. Educators in Broadcasting, Speech Communications Assn., Internat. Communication Assn. Office: Wheaton Graduate School Wheaton IL 60187

REIFEL, ROSEMARY HAYES, accountant; b. Houston, Oct. 25, 1937; d. Harry Augusta and Myrtle Florence (Booth) Hayes; B.A., Rice Inst., 1959; m. Michael Dean Reifel, Dec. 26, 1958; children—Alixe Frances, Mitchell Hayes, Ross Booth. Acct., Harris, Kerr, Forster & Co., 1970-73, J.K. Lasser & Co., 1973-77, Touche Ross & Co., 1977-78; tax partner Aaronson & Susman, Houston, 1978—. C.P.A., Tex. Mem. Santa Gertrudis Breeders Internat., Am. Inst. C.P.A.s, Tex. Soc. C.P.A.s, Houston Soc. C.P.A.s. Republican. Office: 2900 Weslayan Suite 550 Houston TX 77027

REIHEL, DOROTHY L., bank officer; b. Portland, Oreg., June 19, 1927; d. Russell and Mary T. (Ellison) Blanchard; grad. Fresno (Calif.) Public Schs.; m. Francis J., June 4, 1960. Clk. lunch counter K-P Drug Store, Fresno, 1943-44; operator Pacific Telephone Co., Fresno, 1944-45; temporary civil servant U.S. Army Telephone, Fresno, 1945-46; sec. Chgo. City Bank & Trust Co., 1952-68; with The State Bank, Lake Havasu, Ariz., 1969—, asst. cashier, 1974—, adminstrv. asst. 1978, personnel and payroll, 1979, now purchasing agt. Bd. dirs. Community Fund, Lake Havasu, 1977-80. Named Club Woman of Yr., Lake Havasu City Bus. and Profl. Women's Club, 1976. Mem. Nat. Assn. Bank Women, Nat. Fed. Bus. and Profl. Women, Nat. Assn. Female Execs., Ariz. Fed. Bus. and Profl. Women's Club. Republican. Roman Catholic. Clubs: Women of Moose, Cath. Women's Soc. Home: 2943 Appaloosa Dr Lake Havasu AZ 86403

REIK, AULETA ARNOLD, music store owner; b. Milw., Oct. 27, 1928; d. John L. and Caroline E. (Weber) Arnold; A.A., West Valley Coll., 1969; BA., San Jose State U., 1971; m. Edward J. Reik, May 30, 1949; children—Paul, Marie, Laura, David. Sec., First Wis. Trust Co., Milw., 1946-47; owner Arnold's Music Store, Milw., 1947-56; tchr., Milw., 1957-62, San Jose, Calif., 1962-71; pres., tchr. Reik Music, Inc., San Jose, 1971—; also lectr. Organist, St. Mary's Ch., Los Gatos, Calif., 1962-80. Mem. Nat. Assn. Music Mchts. (dir.), Santa Clara County Music Mchts. (past pres.), Music Tchrs. Assn. Calif. Republican. Roman Catholic. Clubs: Organists; Lady Lions. Office: 5353 Almaden Expressway San Jose CA 95118

REILLY, CATHERINE REGINA, info. mgr.; b. Cooperstown, N.Y., July 22, 1949; d. John Patrick and Catherine Regina (Dempsey) Reilly; B.A., Coll. of Mt. St. Vincent, 1970; M.L.S. magna cum laude, Pratt Inst., 1972. With Chase Manhattan Bank, N.Y.C., 1972—, research supr., 1975, asst. treas., mgr. research library, 1977, 2nd v.p., mgr. info. center, 1981—. Mem. Nat. Info Conf. (mem. program com. 1980), Spl. Libraries Conf. (coordinator fin. insts. rountable 1979), Spl. Libraries Assn. (program chmn. N.Y. chpt. 1980-81), ALA, Am. Soc. Info. Sci., Assn. Info. Mgrs., Phi Beta Mu. Editor, Biz-dex, 1975-80; editor Bus. and Fin. Newsletter, 1980—. Office: 1 Chase Manhattan Plaza New York City NY 10081

REILLY, HARRIET R., ins. corp. exec.; b. Chgo., Feb. 23, 1941; d. George and Goldie (Berman) Harris; student North Park Coll., 1967-70; m. James Patrick Reilly, Sept. 15, 1961 (dec.); children—Dale Anthony, Renee Marie. Comml. underwriter, mgr. Assurance Agy., Arlington Heights, Ill., 1971-78, comml. account rep., sales, 1978-79; v.p. Columbian Agy., New Lenox, Ill. 1979-82; pres. HRR Cons. Corp., New Lenox, 1979—. Mem. Ind. Ins. Agts., Will Grundy Contractors Assn., Ill. Road Builders, Associated Gen. Contractors (ins. com.), Nat. Assn. Women in Constrn. (pres. O'Hare Suburban #193, 1980-81), Nat. Assn. Women Bus. Owners. Republican. Roman Catholic. Club: Lake Shore Ski (Chgo.). Office: 201 W Maple St Box H New Lenox IL 60451

REILLY, JEANETTE P., clin. psychologist; b. Denver, Oct. 19, 1908; d. George L. and Marie (Bloedorn) Parker; A.B., U. Colo., 1929; M.A., Columbia U., 1951, Ed.D., 1959; m. Peter C. Reilly, Sept. 15, 1932; children—Marie Reilly Heed, Sara Jean Reilly Wilhelm, Patricia Reilly Davis. Lectr. psychology Butler U., Indpls., 1957-58, 60-65; cons. child psychologist Mental Hygiene Clinic, Episcopal Community Services, Indpls., 1959-65; cons. clin. psychologist VA Hosp., Indpls., 1965-66; Christian Theol. Sem., 1968-70; pvt. practice clin. psychology, Indpls., 1967—; cons. clin. psychologist St. Vincent's Hosp., 1973—; adv. cons. middle mgmt. group Indpls. City Council, 1980-81. Mem. women's aux. council U. Notre Dame, 1953—; trustee Hanover (Ind.) Coll., 1975—; bd. dirs. Community Hosp. Found., Indpls., 1978—. Mem. Am. Psychol. Assn., Am. Personnel and Guidance Assn., Am. Vocat. Assn., Ind. Psychol. Assn., Central Ind. Psychol. Assn., Midwestern Psychol. Assn., Ind. Personnel and Guidance Assn., Nat. Registry Psychologists in U.S.A. Office: 1015 Stratford Hall Indianapolis IN 46260

REILLY, PATRICIA KATHRYN, educator; b. Phila., July 5, 1934; d. Patrick John and Marguerite Rita (Rush) R.; A.B. (Coll. scholar), Immaculata Coll., 1956; M.Ed., U. Md., 1971; adminstrv. cert. for elem. and secondary principalship U. Pa., 1979. Tchr. social studies Shaw Jr. High Sch., Phila. 1956-58, Woodrow Wilson Jr. High Sch., Phila., 1958—, chmn. dept. social studies, 1971—, adminstrv. intern, 1978-79, desegregation chairperson, 1978—; tchr. Homework Hotline, 1979—; dist. and city-wide rep. Desegregation Resource Team. Chairperson Sch. Dist. No. 8, United Way, Phila., 1976-80. Recipient Appreciation award Jefferson chpt. Nat. Jr. Honor Soc., 1966; named Outstanding Tchr. Geography in Pa., Phila. Social Studies Council, 1975; Carnegie Fellowship grantee, 1959-60,; Fed. Edn. grantee, 1965. Mem. Phila. Council Adminstrv. Women in Edn., Nat. Council Adminstrv. Women in Edn., Phila. Council Social Studies, Phila. Fedn. Tchrs., Pa. Fedn. Tchrs., Am. Fedn. Tchrs., Pa. Labor History Soc., Emerald Soc., Phi Delta Kappa, Democrat. Roman Catholic. Club: Phila. Theater. Author curriculum guides on Phila. city govt., 1979, Am. history and govt., 1980, world history and govt., 1981. Office: Woodrow Wilson Jr High Sch Cottman and Loretto Sts Philadephia PA 19111

REILLY, SUSAN ELIZABETH, nurse; b. Dubuque, Iowa, Sept. 17, 1939; d. George Norbert and Modesta Lillian (Hoerner) R.; diploma Finley Hosp. Sch. Nursing, Dubuque, 1960; student U. Dubuque, 1957-58, 70-75, U. No. Iowa, 1971, U. Iowa, 1976. Staff nurse Xavier Hosp., Dubuque, 1960-66, head nurse intensive care, 1966-67, dir. nursing, 1967-81; dir. patient care Mercy Health Center, Dubuque, 1981—; mem. Tri State Health Planning Council, 1970-74; mem. adv. bd. nursing program U. Dubuque, 1976-79. Lay distbr. Roman Cath. Ch.; chmn. follies Hosp. Aux., 1978, 80, 82; vol. fund drives Civic Center, Stonehill Nursing Home. Mem. Am. Nurses Assn., Nat. League Nursing, Am. Soc. Nursing Service Adminstrs., Am. Bus. Women's Assn. (Woman of Yr. local chpt. 1978, pres. chpt. 1979-80). Republican. Home: 686 Grandview St S Dubuque IA 52001 Office: Mercy Health Center Dubuque IA 52001

REIMER, LINDA MARY, art dealer, jewelry importer; b. Elgin, Ill., Dec. 4, 1951; d. William C. and Marilyn S. Reimer; B.A., So. Ill. U., Carbondale, 1972; M.P.A., George Washngton U., 1975. Supr. med. programs Pfizer Med. Systems, Inc., Columbia, Md., 1976-78; mgr. med.

ops. Pfizer, Inc., N.Y.C., 1978-81; pres. LMR Enterprises Inc., N.Y.C., 1981—; exec. dir. Art In Sites, N.Y.C., 1981—. Mem. Mcpl. Art Soc., Nat. Assn. Women Bus. Owners. Office: 60 Sutton Pl S New York NY 10022

REIN, FAITH KATHLEEN, assn. exec.; b. Schenectady, Nov. 6, 1934; d. Herbert Dyer and Kathleen Virginia (Drumm) Johnson; student Ohio U., 1953-54; A.A., U. Toledo, 1975; B.S., Bowling Green State U., 1978; m. Don Caris Rein, Dec. 27, 1972; children—Linda Faith (Mrs. Loren Marcee), David Clarence Mackey, Frederick Herbert Mackey, Paul Johnson Mackey, Diane Grace Mackey. Asst. promotion dir. WOHO Radio, Toledo, 1970; program dir. YWCA, Toledo, 1971-76, exec. dir., 1977—. Mem. recreation adv. com. Owens Tech. Coll. Nat. YWCA Edn. grantee, 1973; Bowling Green State U. fellow, 1976. Cert. food service mgr., Ohio. Mem. Women Involved in Toledo. Republican. Clubs: Zonta Internat., Maumee Fedn. Garden Clubs (pres. 1965), Council Toledo Jr. Coterie Clubs (pres. 1966). Home: 3060 Villa Dr Toledo OH 43614 Office: 1018 Jefferson Ave Toledo OH 43624

REINER, ANNE ELIZABETH WALKER, editor; b. Phila., Sept. 3, 1933; d. Harry and Anna Walker; A.B. with honors and distinction in French, Wilson Coll., 1955; M.A., U. Tex., Dallas, 1980, postgrad., 1980—; m. S. Theodore Reiner, Sept. 3, 1955; children—Samuel, David, Theodore, Geoffrey. Editor, Am. Soc. Testing Materials, Phila., 1952-55; fgn. lang. cryptanalyst Nat. Security Agy., Washington, 1956-57; freelance editor, 1969—; research asso. Public Policy Toward Animals research project, U. Tex., Dallas, 1978—, teaching asst., 1979, 80-81. Mem. observer team sent to monitor Alaskan seal harvest, 1979; Southwest coordinator Nat. Coalition for Alternatives to Animal Experimentation, 1979-80. Recipient Sarah Wilson Scholarship award, 1951; Regina B. Frankenberg award, 1978. Author: The Trap, 1978; editor: Doing Business in Puerto Rico, 1974; co-editor: Doing Business in Mexico, 1980, Southern Methodist University Symposia on Federal Taxation, 1979, 80. Home: 315 Quincy Albuquerque NM 87108

REINER, NORMA ANN PEYSER, arts cons.; b. N.Y.C., Apr. 1, 1922; d. Nat J. and Blanche (Levy) Peyser; B.A., Washington Square Coll., N.Y. U., 1944; postgrad. New Sch. Social Research, 1971; m. Jules C. Reiner, Sept. 19, 1942; children—Charles, Elizabeth, Nanette, Barry. Music specialist, group leader, head adminstr. several children's camps, 1938-45; tchr. music various schs., 1940-67; founder, dir. Reiner Sch. Creative Music, Woodstock, N.Y., 1951-55; chmn. music North Shore Community Arts Center, Gt. Neck, 1958-62, exec. bd., 1961-64, exec. dir., 1964-77, 80-81, adminstrv. cons., 1977—; arts cons. Mayor's Task Force, Palace Theater Project, Pittsfield, Mass.; exec. dir. North Shore Community Arts Center, 1980—. Named Woman of Yr., Eleanor Roosevelt chpt. Am. Jewish Congress, 1977. Home: 31 Maple Ave Lenox MA 01240

REINER, PAULA, systems cons.; b. N.Y.C., Apr. 3, 1950; d. Samuel Reiner and Elaine (Klein) Reiner Blau; B.A. cum laude, Bklyn. Coll., 1971; M.B.A., N.Y.U., 1977. Systems engr. ICL Inc., N.Y.C., 1977-78; sr. systems engr. NCR Corp., N.Y.C., 1978-79; sr. mgmt. adv. services cons. Price Waterhouse, N.Y.C., 1979-80; data processing mgr. Rec. for Blind, Inc., N.Y.C., 1980-81; cons. computer systems, N.Y.C., 1981—. Bd. dirs. NOW-N.Y.C., 1980, chairwoman consciousness raising com., 1980, leader consciousness raising group, 1979-80. Mem. Networks Unltd., Nat. Assn. Female Execs., Hewlett-Packard Computer System Users Group. Research in field. Office: 319 E 24th St New York NY 10010

REINERT, KATHLEEN HERRON, analytical chemist; b. Santa Monica, Calif., July 1, 1956; d. Thomas James and Virginia (Owen) Herron; Alumni scholar, Pomona Coll., 1974-78; m. Ted Reinert, Aug. 25, 1979. With Beckman Instruments, 1976, U.S. Borax Research, 1977-78; analytical chemist Burroughs Corp., Carlsbad, Calif., 1978-82, microelectronics complex, San Diego, 1982—. Alumni career adv. Pomona Coll. Mem. Am. Chem. Soc., Am Soc. Profl. Chemists, Southwestern Prospectors, Pomona Coll. Alumni. Home: 4851 Regency Circle Oceanside CA 92056

REINHARDT, CINDY LOU, real estate devel. co. exec.; b. Ft. Worth, Apr. 2, 1950; d. Marvin and Marjeree (Downing) R.; B.A. in Polit. Sci., S.W. Tex. State U., 1971; M. Urban and Regional Planning, Tex. A&M U., 1975. Program dir. South/West Planning Assos., Bryan, Tex., 1973-75; community planner Houston-Galveston Area Council, 1975-76; dir. planning and policy devel. Houston Housing Authority, 1976-79, dep. exec. dir., 1979-80; pres. Creative Transitions Inc., Houston, 1980-81; v.p. Realm Devel. Corp., Houston, 1982—; adj. prof. city planning Tex. So. U., 1979-81. Vice pres. Young Democrats Tex., 1972. Mem. Am. Inst. Cert. Planners (charter), Am. Planning Assn. (chmn. profl. devel. com. Tex. chpt. 1980-82). Home: 1201 McDuffie St #129 Houston TX 77019 Office: 11 Greenway Plaza Suite 2704 Houston TX 77046

REINHERZ, HELEN ZARSKY (MRS. SAMUEL E. REINHERZ), ednl. adminstr.; b. Boston, Aug. 4, 1923; d. Zachary and Anna (Cohen) Zarsky; A.B. magna cum laude, Wheaton Coll., 1944; M.S., Simmons Coll., 1946; S.M., Harvard U., 1963, Sc.D., 1965; m. Samuel E. Reinherz, Aug. 29, 1943; 1 son, Ellis. Social worker Newton (Mass.) Family Service, 1946-49, Mass. Gen. Hosp., Boston, 1949-51; supr. psychiat. social work State Hosp., Waltham, Mass., 1958-61; prof. methods research Simmons Coll., Boston, 1965—, dir. research Sch. Social Work, 1968—, cons. Simmons drug tng. program, 1972-76; research cons. Dept. Mental Health, 1970-73; prin. investigator HEW study to identify children at risk, 1975-83; prin. investigator study of adolescent drug abuse, 1971-73. Chmn. Gov.'s Adv. Council Mental Health and Retardation, 1972. Recipient Maida H. Solomon award Simmons Coll. Alumni, 1961; NIH tng. fellow, 1961-65; Grant Found. grantee, 1963, Med. Found. grantee, 1967-69; NIMH grantee, 1975. Fellow Am. Orthopsychiat. Assn.; mem. Acad. Certified Social Workers, Am. Pub. Health Assn., Council Social Work Edn., LWV (dir. 1951-59), Harvard Sch. Pub. Health Alumni Assn. (sec. treas. 1965-68), Phi Beta Kappa, Delta Omega. Author: (with H. Wechsler, D. Dobbin) Social Work Research in the Human Services, 1976; cons. editor Community Mental Health Jour., 1968-79, Jour. of Prevention, 1979—; contbr. articles on mental health to profl. publs. Home: 17 Corey Rd Malden MA 02148 Office: Simmons Coll Sch Social Work 51 Commonwealth Ave Boston MA 02116

REINIG, ALICE BENITA, clin. psychologist; b. Panama, Iowa, May 23, 1932; d. John G. and Margaret (Schwery) R.; B.A., Mt. St. Scholastica Coll., 1954; M.A., U. Denver, 1969, Psy.D., 1979; children—Deborah Ann Anderson, Jean Marie Muenchrath, Mary Carol Muenchrath. Tchr. Denver Public Schs., 1967-69, St. Mary's Acad., Denver, 1969-71; psychotherapist J.G. Benedict, Ph.D. and Assocs., Denver, 1974-79; instr. Chapman Coll., San Diego, part-time 1979-80, U. of LaVerne, San Diego, 1980—; postdoctoral fellow Mercy Hosp. and Med. Center, San Diego, 1979-80; pvt. practice clin. psychology, San Diego, 1980—; mem. staff Grossmont, Alvarado, Mercy, Mesa Vista hosps.; cons. Interfaith Counseling Inst. Mem. Am. Psychol. Assn. (div. psychotherapy), Calif. Psychol. Assn., Acad. San Diego Psychologists, Am. Assn. Pastoral Counselors and Pacific Region, Am. Assn. Sex Educators, Counselors, and Therapists, San Diego Soc. for Sex Therapy and Edn., Giving and Receiving Orgn. for Women. Club: Internat. Elite. Author: Self-Testing in Clinical Psychology Graduate Training Programs: Practices and Issues. Home: 434 8th St Del Mar CA 92014 Office: 3519 Front St San Diego CA 92103

REINING, BETH LAVERNE (BETTY), public relations cons.; b. Fargo, N.D.; d. George and Grace (Twiford) Reimche; student N.D. State Coll., U. Minn., Glendale Community Coll., Phoenix, Calif. State Coll., Carson; m. 2d, Jack Warren Reining, Oct. 3, 1976; 1 dau., Carolyn Ray Toohey Hiett; stepchildren—Joan, Amy. Originated self-worth seminars, Phoenix, 1970-76; owner Janzik Public Relations, Phoenix, 1971-76; TV talk show reporter-hostess What's Happening in Ariz., 1970-73; writer syndicated column People Want to Know, Today Newspaper, Phoenix, 1973; owner JB Communications, Phoenix, 1976—; a founder Quadroma, Inc., dir., 1980-81, sec.-treas., 1981-82, mktg. dir., 1982—; tchr. self-worth courses Phoenix Coll., Rio Solado Community Coll., Phoenix, 1976—; free-lance writer, 1969—; mural works include 25 figures for med. office, Des Moines. Founder, Ariz. Call-A-Teen Youth Resources, 1975, pres., 1975-76, bd. dirs., 1975—. Recipient Good Citizen award Builders Greater Ariz., 1961. Mem. Nat. Fedn. Press Women (1st place nat. TV writing award 1971), Public Relations Soc. Am., Nat. Acad. TV Arts and Scis., Ariz. Press Women (state journalism awards 1971-76), Phoenix Press Club. Inventor stocking-tension twist footlet. Address: 314 W Orangewood Ave Phoenix AZ 85201

REINKE, LINDA JEANETTE GRABILL, social services adminstr.; b. Harrisburg, Pa., July 18, 1941; d. William Marcus and Gladys A. (Bock) Grabill; B.S., George Williams Coll., Chgo., 1963; M.S.W. with honors, Va. Commonwealth U., 1975; m. Marvin E. Reinke, June 22, 1963. Social worker Wis. State Parole, Milw., 1965-67; caseworker Calhoun County Dept. Pensions and Securities, Anniston, Ala., 1967-68; supr. counseling and evaluations Goodwill Industries, Sioux City, Iowa, 1969-71; social worker child welfare Alexandria (Va.) Dept. Social Services, 1972-73, 75-78; tng. coordinator Fairfax (Va.) Dept. Social Services, 1978-80, social work supr., 1980—; field instr. George Mason U., Va. Commonwealth U., 1979-82; del. Am.-Soviet Youth Conf., Kiev, Ukraine, 1976. Mem. adv. com. Sch. Social Work, Cath. U., 1979-80; chmn. social work adv. council George Mason U., 1980-82; mem. Fairfax Adv. Council on Refugee Affairs, 1980—, Met. D.C. Coalition for Refugee Resettlement, 1980—. Pitts. YMCA scholar, 1959-63; Sears Roebuck scholar, 1960-61. Mem. Va. Council Social Welfare (chmn. No. fall conf. 1979-80, v.p. 1979-80), Acad. Cert. Social Workers, Nat. Assn. Social Workers (mem. Va. state nominations and leadership indentification com. 1979-81), Am. Public Welfare Assn. Office: Fairfax Dept Social Services 4041 University Dr Fairfax VA 22030

REINKER, SHERRY MILLER, publisher; b. Columbus, Ga., July 4, 1945; d. Hugh T. and Elizabeth Y. (Yanko) Miller; student Austin Peay State U., 1963-65; B.A., U. Calif., Irvine, 1970; 1 son, Jeffrey Stephen. Pres., Sherry Reinker Advt., Newport Beach, Calif., 1967-70; editor Bay Window mag., Balboa Bay Club, Newport Beach, 1970-74; pub., founder Winners Circle mag. Jockey Club of Miami (Fla.), 1973-80; pres. SMR Mag. Mktg. Co., Inc., Miami, 1980—, Variety Club Publs., Inc., Miami, 1980—. Mem. Am. Advt. Fedn., Public Relations Soc. Am., Fla. Mag. Assn. Clubs: Jockey, Turnberry Isle Yacht and Racquet, Racquet, Costa Del Sol Golf and Racquet (Miami). Author: White Summers, 1965.

REINTJES, VERNA MARONEY, psychologist; b. Santa Ana, Calif., Apr. 28, 1923; d. Frank Vernon and Belle (Higgins) Maroney; A.B., Stanford U., 1944, M.A., 1945; m. John William Reintjes, Mar. 11, 1950; children—Anne, Christine, Susan, Peter. Psychologist, San Francisco Juvenile Ct., 1945-47; pvt. practice psychology, Honolulu, 1947-52; psychologist N.C. State Bd. Public Welfare, 1962-67; cons. psychologist Camp Lejeune (N.C.) Schs., 1966-68; psychologist N.C. Dept. Social Services, 1973-74, Neuse Mental Health Center, New Bern, N.C., 1967—; pvt. practice clin. psychology, Morehead City, 1962—. Mem. Am. Psychol. Assn., N.C. Psychol. Assn., Assn. Eastern N.C. Psychologists. Home: Route 3 Box 85 Morehead City NC 28557 Office: 1707 Arendell St Morehead City NC 28557

REISER, LYNN WHISNANT, psychiatrist; b. Charlotte, N.C., July 28, 1944; d. Ward William and Susan (Richardson) Whisnant; B.S., Duke U., 1966; M.D., Yale U., 1970; m. Morton F. Reiser, Dec. 19, 1976. Intern, Hosp. of St. Raphael, New Haven, Conn., 1970-71; resident in psychiatry, Yale U., 1971-74, asst. clin. prof., 1975—, asso. dir. undergrad. edn., 1978—. Diplomate Am. Bd. Psychiatry and Neurology. Mem. Am. Psychiat. Assn., Internat. Coll. Psychosomatic Medicine, Am. Psychosomatic Soc., AMA, Am. Psychoanalytic Soc., Western New Eng. Psychoanalytic Soc. Contbr. articles in field to profl. jours. Home: 99 Blake Rd Hamden CT 06517 Office: Yale Medical School Dept Psychiatry New Haven CT 06511

REISLER, HELEN BARBARA, pub.-advt. ofcl.; b. N.Y.C., June 21, 1933; d. George and Elizabeth Lois (Schultz) Gottesman; B.S., in Edn., N.Y. U., 1954; M.S. in Edn. and Reading, L.I. U., 1978; m. Melvin Reisler, June 5, 1955; children—Susan-Jo, Karen-Jane, Keith James. Elem. tchr., N.Y.C., 1954-78; instr. grad. sch., adj. lectr. L.I. U., Bklyn., 1978; account exec. N.Y. Yellow Pages, Inc., N.Y.C., 1979, personnel mgr., 1979, adminstrv. dir., 1980—, also dir. Mem. Sales Execs. Club N.Y., Adminstrv. Mgmt. Soc., Nat. Assn. Female Execs. Home: 47 Plaza St Park Slope Brooklyn NY 11217 Office: New York Yellow Pages Inc 113 University Pl New York NY 10003

REISMAN, FREDRICKA KAUFFMAN, psychologist, educator; b. Rochester, N.Y., Sept. 22, 1930; d. Samuel Hopkins and Rosalind (Lessen) Kauffman; student Barnard Coll., 1951; B.A., Syracuse U., 1952, M.S., 1963, Ph.D., 1968; 1 dau., Lisa Maxine Reisman Halterman. Lectr. math edn. Syracuse U., 1967-69; adj. asso. prof. ednl. psychology Maria Regina Coll., Syracuse, N.Y., 1968; prof. math. edn. and chmn. div. elem. edn. U. Ga., Athens, 1969—; vis. prof. U. Calif., Riverside, 1976, 77, 78, Marianne Frostig Center, Calif., 1974. S.E. Regional Resources Center Network grantee, 1978-80. Mem. Am. Psychol. Assn., Nat. Council Tchrs. Math, Am. Edn. Research Assn., Nat. Assn. Edn. Young Children, Soc. for Research in Child Devel., Council Exceptional Children, Assn. Children with Learning Disabilities. Author: Guide to Diagnostic Teaching of Arithmetic, 3d edit., 1982; Diagnostic Teaching of Elementary School Math, 1977, 2d edit., 1981; (with S.H. Kauffman) Teaching Mathematics to Children With Special Needs, 1980. Home: 130 Cedar Circle Athens GA 30605 Office: Div Elem Edn 427 Aderhold U Ga Athens GA 30602

REISS, DALE ANNE, real estate exec.; b. Chgo., Sept. 3, 1947; d. Max and Nan (Hart) R.; B.S., Ill. Inst. Tech., 1967; M.B.A., U. Chgo., 1970; m. Jerome L. King, Mar. 5, 1978; 1 son, Matthew Reiss King. Cost acct. First Nat. Bank of Chgo., 1967; asst. controller City Colls. Chgo., 1967-70; dir. fin. Chgo. Dept. Public Works, 1970-72; prin. Arthur Young & Co., Chgo., 1972-80; sr. v.p., controller Urban Investment and Devel. Co., Chgo., 1980—; dir. Urban Diversified Properties. Pres., bd. dirs. Streeterville Orgn. Active Residents, 1975-79; mem. Lincoln Park Zool. Soc.; fund raiser Grad. Sch. Bus., U. Chgo. C.P.A., Ill.; cert. mgmt. cons. Mem. Fin. Execs. Inst., Am. Inst. C.P.A.s, Ill. Soc. C.P.A.s, Nat. Assn. Real Estate Cos. (chmn. membership com.), Chgo. Fin. Exchange, Am. Woman's Soc. C.P.A.s. Clubs: Econ. Chgo., Exec. Chgo. Office: 845 N Michigan Ave Chicago IL 60611

REISS, ELAINE SERLIN, lawyer, advt. agy. exec.; b. N.Y.C., Oct. 27, 1940; d. Morris and Dorothy Miriam (Geyer) Serlin; B.A., N.Y. U., 1961, LL.M., 1973; LL.B., Columbia U., 1964; m. Joel A. Reiss, Sept. 1, 1963; children—Joshua Adam, Naomi. Admitted to N.Y. State bar, 1965; legal dept. Doyle Dane Bernbach, N.Y.C., 1965-68; with Ogilvy & Mather, Inc., N.Y.C., 1968—, v.p., mgr. legal dept., 1972-77, sr. v.p., mgr. legal dept., 1977—, mem. council of dirs., 1979—. Mem. Assn. Am. Advt. Agys. (chmn. legal affairs com.), Assn. Bar City of N.Y. Office: Ogilvy & Mather 2 E 48th St New York NY 10017 *

REISS, MARY LORANGER, state ofcl.; b. Superior, Wis., Feb. 19, 1935; d. Egbert Fletcher and Mary Josephine Loranger; B.S., Wayne State U., Detroit, 1961; M.A. in Edn., U. Mich., 1965, Ph.D. in Admistrn., 1971; children—Eric, Merritt. Ednl. cons. Wayne County Intermediate Sch. Dist., 1967-70, Mich. Dept. Edn., 1970-73; dir. allied health occupations Washtenaw Community Coll., Ann Arbor, Mich., 1973-74; dir. continuing edn. N.Y. State Dept. Edn., Albany, 1974-78; dir. service area Mich. Dept. Edn., Lansing, 1978—, dir. adult extended learning service area; assoc. prof. sociology Oakland Community Coll., Dearborn, Mich.; lectr. in field; mem. Mich. Task Force on Policy Analyses, Gov. Mich. Task Force on Volunteerism. Mem. Nat. Council State Dirs. Adult Edn., Adult Edn. Assn. Am., Nat. Assn. Pub. Continuing Adult Edn. Author papers, reports in field.

REISS, RHONA GORSKY, occupational therapist; b. Phila., Sept. 24, 1944; d. Martin and Freda Lillian (Kleinman) Gorsky; B.S. in Occupational Therapy, U. Pa., 1966; M. Occupational Therapy, U. Fla., 1975; m. Theodore Reiss, July 28, 1974 (div.); 1 son, Daniel Paul. Occupational therapist Widener Meml. Sch., Phila., 1967-72; instr. Fuchu Inst. Rehab., Tokyo, 1972-74; asst. prof., community coordinator U. Ill., Chgo., 1975-76; asst. prof., tutor, 1976-77; dir. occupational therapy edn. Rehab. Inst. Chgo., 1977—; asso. Dept. Health Scis. and Arts, Northwestern U. Med. Sch.; mem. adv. bd. Rush Presby. St. Luke's Occupational Therapy Masters Degree Program; regional site and program dir. U. Ky. Teaching Improvement Project system; cons. Chgo. Sch. and Workshop for the Retarded. Mem. World Fedn. Occupational Therapists, Am. Occupational Therapy Assn., Ill. Occupational Therapy Assn., Am. Congress Rehab. Medicine, Phi Kappa Phi, Alpha Eta. Home: 1227 Edmer Ave Oak Park IL 60302 Office: 345 E Superior St Chicago IL 60611

REITER, ELAINE MARY, state. ofcl.; b. Ellsworth, Minn., July 12, 1928; d. Jacob Nicholas and Esther Suzanne (Kappes) R.; B.S. in Bus. Adminstrn., Marquette U., Milw., 1953; M.Ed. in Counseling, U. Mo., Columbia, 1967, M.P.A., 1976. Personnel asst. Square D Co., Milw., 1953-56; exec. asst. Psychol. Service Corp., St. Louis, 1957-63; services mgr. Psychol. Assos., St. Louis, 1963-64; counselor Mo. Employment Service, St. Louis, 1964-68; dep. dir. Mo. Office Aging, Jefferson City, 1968-72; cons. adult services to State of Mo., 1973-76; regional adminstr. Mo. Div. Family Services and Aging, 1977-81, service access mgr. Mo. Div. Aging, 1981—; bd. dirs. Mo. Green Thumb, 1978; mem. nat. protective services task force Adminstrn. Aging, 1982; del. White House Conf. Aging, 1971. Recipient various service awards. Mem. Am. Public Welfare Assn. (chmn. membership Mo. chpt. 1976-77), Mo. Assn. Social Welfare (dir. 1975-82, exec. com. 1976-79, chmn. aging task force 1975-80, chmn. Kansas City div. 1981-82), AAUW, Geront. Soc., Mo. Assn. Prevention Adult Abuse, Mid-Am. Congress Aging. Roman Catholic. Club: Lakewood. Office: Broadway State Office Bldg Jefferson City MO 65102

REITZ, PATRICIA KAY, greeting card co. mgr.; b. St. Louis, Sept. 15, 1945; d. Harry Sayles and Berenice (Laury) Duncan; B.A. in German, S.W. Mo. State U., 1969; m. Roger F. Reitz. Asst. trading dept. Stix Friedman & Co., 1969-72, registered rep. N.Y. Stock Exchange, 1970; with Scherck, Stein & Franc, Inc., St. Louis, 1972-73; registered rep. Sentry Life Ins. Co., Maryland Heights, Mo., 1973-78; account mgr. Ambassadors Cards div. Hallmark Cos., Kansas City, Mo., 1976—. Recipient sales award. Mem. Nat. Assn. Security Dealers, Nat. Assn. Life Underwriters, Nat. Fedn. Bus. and Profl. Women, Mo. Bus. and Profl. Women (fin. chmn. St. Louis chpt.), YWCA, Alumni Assn. S.W. Mo. State Coll., Gamma Theta Upsilon, Alpha Mu Gamma. Home: 8911 Wilma Dr Saint Louis MO 63123 Office: 25th and McGee Sts Kansas City MO 64108

RELKIN, DOLLY DOROTHEA, civic worker; b. N.Y.C., May 29, 1931; d. Jack William and Betty (Uffer) Adler; B.A. cum laude, Queens Coll., 1973; m. Donald B. Relkin, May 9, 1953; children—David, Leslie. Dir., Great Neck Arts Council, 1974-76; trustee Great Neck Library, 1976—, pres., 1977—. Mem. N.Y. State Assn. Library Bds., LWV. Club: B'nai B'rith. Home: 9 Meadow Woods Rd Great Neck NY 11020

RELYEA, MEREDITH EWING, fin. analyst; b. Balt., Aug. 17, 1946; d. Sam Mann and Genevieve (Delfs) Ewing; B.S., Hollins (Va.) Coll., 1968; postgrad. N.Y. U., 1969; m. William Allen Relyea, May 6, 1972; children— Christopher Scott, Melinda Bergen. Security analyst Pershing & Co., N.Y.C., 1968-75, Joseph H. Oliphant Inc., N.Y.C., 1975-76; sr. analyst Norton Simon Inc., N.Y.C., 1976, Paine Webber Jackson & Curtis, N.Y.C., 1976-79. Mem. Fin. Woman Assn. (v.p. 1973-74), N.Y. Soc. Security Analysts, Greenwich Jr. League. Home: 333 Shore Rd Greenwich CT 06830

REMBISZ, LINDA SCULTHORPE, speech pathologist; b. Long Branch, N.J., May 7, 1946; d. Robert Ferris and Geraldine (Garippo) Sculthorpe; B.S., Ithaca Coll., 1968; M.A., Mich. State U., 1969; m. Gerald Rembisz, Dec. 4, 1971; children—Thaddeus, Amanda, Tamara. Speech pathologist Children's Specialized Hosp., Westfield, N.J., 1970-77, dir. dept. speech, 1971-75, part-time speech pathologist, 1975-77, dir. speech therapy services, 1976—; cons. feeding therapy Woodbridge State Sch. for profoundly mentally retarded, 1979—; cons. The Learning Center, Tinton Falls, N.J., 1979—; also 15 nursery and pre-sch. centers. Recipient Cert. of Appreciation, Children's Specialized Hosp., 1976, 77; Outstanding Young Woman, Monmouth County Jaycettes, 1980. Mem. Am. Speech and Hearing Assn. (cert.), N.J. Speech and Hearing Assn., Monmouth County Speech and Hearing Assn. Author: Neuromuscular Facilitation Techniques in Treating the Dysarthric Patient, 1977; Feeding Therapy for the Dysarthric Patient, 1976 (ednl. films). Home: 23 Cypress Neck Rd Lincroft NJ 07738 Office: 4 Swimming River Rd Lincroft NJ 07738

REMICK, LEE, (MRS. WILLIAM RORY GOWANS), actress; b. Quincy, Mass., Dec. 14, 1935; d. Frank E. and Margaret (Waldo) R.; student Barnard Coll., 1953; m. William A. Colleran, Aug. 3, 1957 (div. 1969); children—Kate, Mathew; m. 2d, William Rory Gowans, Dec. 18, 1970. Broadway debut in Be Your Age, 1953, other Broadway plays include Anyone Can Whistle, 1964, Wait Until Dark, 1966; films include A Face in the Crowd, 1956, The Long Hot Summer, 1957, Anatomy of a Murder, 1959, Wild River, 1959, Sanctuary, 1960, Experiment in Terror, 1961, Days of Wine and Roses, 1961, The Wheeler Dealers, 1962, Baby The Rain Must Fall, 1963, Hallelujah Trail, 1965, No Way to Treat a Lady, 1967, The Detective, 1968, Hard Contract, 1969, Loot, 1972, A Delicate Balance, 1973, Hennessy, 1974, The Omen, 1976, Telefon, 1977, The Europeans, 1979, The Competition, 1980, Tribute, 1980; appeared in TV prodn. Jennie, Lady Randolph Churchill, 1975; appeared TV series Wheels, 1978, TV mini-series Haywire, 1980, Torn Between Two Lovers. Address: care Internat Creative Artists 8899 Beverly Blvd Los Angeles CA 90048 *

REMLAND, MARJORIE ELLEN (MRS. KEITH P. REMLAND), communications co. exec.; b. Bklyn., Sept. 13, 1943; d. Murray and Ann Rae (Weisman) Block; B.S., CCNY, 1964; M.B.A., Fairleigh Dickinson

U., 1978; postgrad. Pace U.; m. Keith Peter Remland, Mar. 5, 1967. Researcher, asso. producer CBS News, N.Y.C., 1964-67; pub. relations asso. Am. Lung Assn., N.Y.C., 1968-73, Warner-Lambert Co., Morris Plains, N.J., 1973-77; editor Morris Plains News and Warner Lambert World, until 1977; mgr. employee communications Schering-Plough Corp., Kenilworth, N.J., 1977-79; staff mgr. bus. market ops. AT&T, Basking Ridge, N.J., 1979—. Pub. relations cons. Am. Occupational Therapy Assn., 1968-71, Assn. Children with Learning Disabilities, 1973; mem. Lincoln Park (N.J.) Environ. Control Com., 1970-73; chmn. Morris County (N.J.) Selective Service Bd. 37. Mem. Internat., N.J. assns. bus. communicators. Club: Ramapo Kennel (trustee). Home: 8 Brightwood Rd Lincoln Park NJ 07035 Office: 295 N Maple Ave Basking Ridge NJ 07920

REMLER, HELGA FRIEDERIKE, psychologist; b. Koenigsberg, East Prussia, Ger., June 25, 1937; d. Otto Herman and Elfriede Hermine (Senger) Delitzsch; came to U.S., 1957, naturalized, 1964; B.S., Coll. William and Mary, 1973, M.A. in Psychology, 1980; m. Edward Antoine Remler, Dec. 26, 1961; children—Daniel, Ariel. Vis. scientist Weizmann Inst. Sci., Rehovot, Israel, 1978; staff psychologist Hancock Geriatric Treatment Center, Eastern State Hosp., Williamsburg, 1978-79, dir. psychol. services, 1979—; bd. dirs. Family Counseling Forum, Williamsburg. Mem. Am. Psychol. Assn., Geront. Soc., Va. Agy. Aging, LWV. Democrat. Jewish. Office: Hancock Geriatric Treatment Center Drawer A Williamsburg VA 23187

REMSON, JANE FRANCES, charitable assn. exec.; b. New Orleans, Sept. 15, 1940; d. Marcel and Josephine Marie (Frey) R.; B.S., St. Mary's Dominican Coll., 1964. Intern, Mercy Hosp., New Orleans, 1964-65; chief Blood Bank, St. Joseph Hosp., Thibodaux, La., 1965-67; set up hosp. lab. Holy Child Hosp., Dumaguete City, Philippines, 1967-69, dir., co-founder Mt. Carmel Mobile Clinic, 1978-80; research technologist Tulane U. Med. Center, 1970-77; dir. Bread For the World, New Orleans, 1982—; tchr. hematology, hunger edn. Mem. Am. Soc. Clin. Pathologists, Am. Soc. Med. Technologists. Democrat. Roman Catholic. Home: 420 Robert E Lee St New Orleans LA 70124 Office: Inst of Human Relations PO Box 12 Loyola U New Orleans LA 70124

RENDER, SYLVIA LYONS, Afro-Am. specialist; b. Atlanta, June 8, 1913; d. Lewis Rudolph and Mamie Beatrice (Foster) Lyons; B.S., Tenn. State U., 1934; M.A., Ohio State U., 1952; postgrad. U. Wis., 1954, 56; Ph.D. (scholar, So. Edn. Found. fellow), George Peabody Coll. for Tchrs., 1962; m. Frank Wyatt Render, July 14, 1935; 1 son, Frank Wyatt II. Various clerical and profl. posts state and fed. agys. in Columbus, Ohio, and Tallahassee, Fla., 1939-51; instr. English, Fla. A&M U., 1952-56, asst. prof. to prof., 1956-64; prof. N.C. Central U., 1964-75; specialist in Afro-Am. history and culture manuscript div. Library of Congress, Washington, 1973—; cons. Ford Found., Nat. Endowment Humanities, So. Assn. Colls. and Schs., Macmillan Co., N.C. Dept. Edn.; vis. prof. George Peabody Coll., Black Exec. Exchange Program of Nat. Urban League; adj. faculty Duke U., George Washington U. Vol., Boy Scouts Am., 1943-45, Nat. Urban League, 1947-50, Com. Mgmt. of YWCA, UN, 1946, ARC, 1962-64, Durham Council Human Relations, NAACP; bd. dirs. Hopkins House, 1980-81. Recipient Mary M. Sullivan award George Peabody Coll. Tchrs., 1960, award Am. Philos. Soc., 1964; fellow Coop. Program in Humanities Duke U., 1967-68; Ford Found. research and writing grantee, 1971; Nat. Endowment for Humanities sr. fellow for ind. study and research, 1976; recipient citation Kappa Delta Pi, 1978; named Outstanding Woman of Yr., NAACP, 1981, Outstanding Alumna, Tenn. State U., 1982. Mem. Nat. Council Tchrs. of English, Coll. Lang. Assn., Soc. Study of So. Lit., Assn. Study of Afro-Am. Life and History, Assn. Documentary Editing, Afro-Am. Hist. and Geneal. Soc., Library of Congress Profl. Assn., Alpha Kappa Mu, Kappa Delta Pi, Alpha Kappa Alpha. Author: Charles W. Chesnutt, 1980; editor: The Short Fiction of Charles W. Chesnutt, 1974; contbr. articles to profl. jours., chpts. to books. Home: 6429 Princeton Dr Alexandria VA 22307 Office: Library of Congress Washington DC 20540

RENO, JUDITH MARIE, public health adminstr.; b. Pratt, Kans., Dec. 1, 1937; d. Rhonald Clifford and Mary Ruth (Judy) Hogg; R.N.; m. Wayne Reno, Nov. 26, 1959; children—Troy, Kelly Marie, Michael. Pediatrics charge nurse St. Joseph Hosp., Wichita, Kans., 1958-59, surg. staff nurse, 1960; staff nurse Wichita-Sedgwick County Dept. Community Health, 1959-60, 63-66, nursing supr., 1966-69, chief Model Cities Health Services, 1969-71, asst. personal health services dir., 1971-81, dir., 1981—; tng. cons. Region VII, 1979—; med. staff nurse Trinity Hosp., Amarillo, Tex., 1960; head nurse med. floor Hotel Dieu, El Paso, Tex., 1961-62; adj. faculty Coll. Health Related Professions Wichita State U. Bd. dirs. Health Systems Agency SE Kans., 1978—, Mid-Way (Kans.) chpt. ARC; profl. adv. bd. United Way; mem. Sedgwick County Subarea Council Health Systems Agy. SE Kans., 1977—, chmn., 1979; chmn. Region VII Family Planning Tng. Adv. Com., 1978-80; mem. Inter-Agy. Council on Aging; pres. Wichita Employees Retirement System, 1979-80, 81-82; pres. Sedgwick County Med. Services Bur., 1981-82. Mem. Kans. Public Health Assn. (pres. 1979-80, chmn. public health nursing sect., 1976-77), Assn. Vol. Adminstrs., Kans. Assn. Sch. Health, Kans. Assn. Home Health Agys. (mem.-at-large bd. dirs., 1977-80), Am. Nurses Assn., Nat. Family Planning and Reproductive Health Assn., NOW. Roman Catholic. Office: 1900 E 9th St Wichita KS 67214

RENQUIST, CHRISTINE LARSON, educator; b. Cheyenne, Wyo., June 27, 1950; d. Alfred Eugene and Jean Marilyn (Samuelson) L.; B.A. in Elem. Edn. and Music cum laude, Augustana Coll., Rock Island, Ill., 1972. Elem. tchr. St. Vrian Valley Schs., Longmont, Colo., 1972-74; exec. adminstr. Christian Artists Corp., Thousand Oaks, Calif., 1974-76; youth dir. Augustana Lutheran Ch., Denver, 1976-78; dir. Christian edn. and youth Grace Luth. Ch., Davenport, Iowa, 1978-79; instr., asst. to exec. dir. Twin Cities Opportunities Industrialization Center, Mpls., 1979-80; asst. for personnel services Rochester (Minn.) Public Schs., 1980-82; tng. and edn. coordinator St. Mary's Hosp., Rochester, 1982—. mem. adv. com. Child Devel. Assistance Program; mem. ch. synod coms. and task forces, 1976—; violinist with orchs., 1966—. Mem. Am. Assn. Sch. Personnel Adminstrs. Home: 2824 Pinewood Rd SE Rochester MN 55901 Office: St Mary's Hosp Rochester MN 55901

RENSHAW, DOMEENA CYNTHIA, psychiatrist; b. Douglas, Cape, S.Africa, July 20, 1929; d. Alfred Joseph and Esme Mary (Add) Steir; M.D., U. Capetown; m. Robert Harris Renshaw, June 13, 1965. Intern, Groote Schuur Hosp., U. Cape Town, 1961; resident in pediatrics Harvard U. Children's Hosp., Boston, 1962-63; resident in surgery Livingstone Hosp., Port Elizabeth, S.Africa, 1963-64; med. officer St. Mary's Hosp., S.Africa, 1964-65; mem. faculty Loyola U. Med. Sch., Maywood, Ill., 1968—, prof. psychiatry, 1977—, asst. chmn. dept., dir. Sexual Dysfunction Tng. Clinic. Recipient Aescalupian award teaching U. Ottawa (Ont., Can.), 1978, Spl. Tchr. award Oreg. Acad. Family Physicians, 1978; diplomate Am. Bd. Psychiatry and Neurology. Fellow Am. Psychiat. Assn., Am. Coll. Psychiatry; mem. AMA, Am. Assn. Sex Therapists, Soc. Sex Therapy Research, Ill. Med. Soc., DuPage Med. Soc. Roman Catholic. Author: The Hyperactive Child, 1974; El Ninos Hyperactivo, 1976; also over articles, chpts. in books. Office: 2160 S 1st Ave Maywood IL 60153

RENTER, LOIS IRENE HUTSON, librarian; b. Lowden, Iowa, Oct. 23, 1929; d. Thomas E. and Lulu Mae (Barlean) Hutson; B.A. cum laude, Cornell Coll., Iowa, 1965; M.A., U. Iowa, 1968; m. Karl A. Renter, Jan. 3, 1948; children—Susan Elizabeth, Rebecca Jean, Karl Geoffrey. Tchr. Spanish, Mt. Vernon (Iowa) High Sch., 1965-67; head librarian Am. Coll. Testing Program, Iowa City, Iowa, 1968—; vis. instr. U. Iowa Sch. Library Sci., 1972—. Mem. Am. Soc. Info. Sci., ALA, Spl. Libraries Assn., Phi Beta Kappa. Methodist. Home: 1125 29th St Marion IA 52302 Office: Box 168 Iowa City IA 52243

RENTERIA, ESTHER G., coll. public relations adminstr.; b. East Los Angeles, Calif., May 1, 1939; d. Oliver Jay and Violet Gatfield; A.A., East Los Angeles Coll., 1958; B.A., Calif. State U., Los Angeles, 1974; m. Martin Renteria, Feb. 13, 1971; children—Christopher, David. Reporter, Alhambra (Calif.) Post Advocate, 1959-61; reporter, soc. editor East Los Angeles Tribune & Gazette, 1962-68; desk editor, newswriter Sta. KNX, Los Angeles, 1968; asso. producer, hostess-moderator Ahora! TV Series, Public Broadcasting Sta. KCET, 1969-70; public info dir. East Los Angeles Coll., 1970—; producer Sta. KNXT TV Series: Bienvenidos and The Siesta is Over, 1970-74, ednl. cons. bilingual edn. series Juntos, 1979-82; sec., dir. Future Broadcasting Corp., 1980—; bd. dirs. Plaza de la Raza Cultural Center, Amigos of Sta. KCET TV; mem. East Los Angeles Service Center Adv. Council; bd. dirs. Bilingual Found. of the Arts, Cleland Ho. of Neighborly Service; bd. dirs. East Los Angeles Regional Occupational Center Adv. Bd.; public relations dir. Los Angeles Street Scene Festival, 1978—. Mem. Calif. Community and Jr. Coll. assn. Public Info. Dirs. Democrat. Roman Catholic. Club: Job's Daus. Home: 301 Dochan Circle Montebello CA 90640 Office: East Los Angeles Coll 1301 Brooklyn Ave Monterey Park CA 91754

RENWANZ, GRACE DANIELLE, nurse; b. Bklyn., Aug. 30, 1923; d. Daniel F. and Mary Elizabeth (Madden) Luna; R.N., Somerset Hosp., Somerville, N.J., 1944; m. Roger A. Renwanz, May 10, 1947; children—Andrea G., Marsha E., Ingrid J., Mark R. Staff nurse Somerset Hosp., 1944-45; mem. staff Muhlenberg Hosp., Plainfield, N.J., 1965—, ICU, 1969-79, intravenous therapy specialist, 1980-81, sr. staff nurse emergency room, 1981—; trustee Somerset Valley Vis. Nurses Assn., 1961—, sec., 1968—. Sec., Bound Brook (N.J.) Recreation Commn., 1954-56; v.p. Bound Brook Republican Club, 1962-64. Served to 1st lt., Nurse Corps, AUS, 1945-47; PTO. Recipient various service awards. Mem. Assn. Critical Care Nurses. Presbyterian. Home: 155 Farm Ln Bound Brook NJ 08805 Office: Muhlenberg Hosp Randolph Rd Plainfield NJ 07061

REPASS, NANCY BERNICE, nurse; b. Springfield, Mo., Dec. 21, 1916; d. Hiram Turner and Iva Dell (Putman) Huff; R.N., Stormant Sch. Nursing, Topeka, 1950; postgrad. Med. Coll. Ga., 1959-60; diploma Dominican Herbal Coll., 1980; m. Fred Pierce Repass, Dec. 23, 1948. Lic. practical nurse U.S. Army hosps., 1941—; mem. staff U.S. Army Hosp., Ft. Gordon, Ga., 1957—. Mem. Royal Neighbors Am. Address: 2836 Rocky Creek Rd Augusta GA 30906

REPLOGLE, ROSE ELEANOR, oriental rug restorer expert; b. Omaha, Jan. 14, 1909; d. John Isaiah Taminosian and Ellen Maria (Grant) Taminosian Cook; grad. Omaha Tech., 1927; m. Fahy Norris Replogle, Jan. 10, 1931; children—Ronald, Richard Harold, Charles Martin. Sec. to pres. Nebr.-Iowa Grain Co., Omaha, 1927-31; apprentice to Ellen G. Cook, oriental carpet restorer, 1955-65; owner Replogle Oriental Rug Restoration, Kansas City, Mo., 1968—; cons./appraiser oriental carpets, tapestries; commd. to restore four tapestries U. Kan. Art Mus., Lawrence, 1977; restorer oriental carpets Kan. City Club, 1958—. Mem. Women's C. of C. of Kansas City Mo. (sec., chmn. constitution/by-laws 1982, dir.). Republican. Mem. Christian Ch. Clubs: Soroptimists, P.E.O. (chpt. budget com. 1982), Kings Daus. and Sons Internat., Woman's City, Red Mitten Writers, Adult Friendship. Address: 6821 Brookside Rd Kansas City MO 64113

REPPERT, NANCY LUE, city govt. ofcl., b. Kansas City, Mo., June 17, 1933; d. James Everett and Iris R. (Moomey) Moore; student Central Mo. State U., 1951-52, U. Mo., Kansas City, 1971-75; cert. legal asst., Rockhurst Coll., Kansas City, Mo., 1980; cert. risk mgr., 1979; m. James E. Cassidy, 1952 (div.); children—James E., II, Tracy C. With Kansas City (Mo.) chpt. ARC, 1952-54, N. Central region Boy Scouts Am., 1963-66, Clay County Health Dept., Liberty, Mo., 1966-71, City of Liberty, 1971-80; risk mgr. City of Ames (Iowa), 1980—; mem. faculty William Jewell Coll., Liberty, 1975-80; vis. prof. U. Kans., 1981; seminar leader, cons in field. Lay minister United Meth. Ch., 1965—; dir. youth devel. Hillside United Meth. Ch., Liberty; co-chmn. youth dir. Collegiate United Meth. Ch., mem. Council of Ministries; advancement chmn. Mid-Iowa Council Boy Scouts Am. Recipient Order of Merit, Boy Scouts Am., 1979, Living Sculpture award, 1978,79; Service award Rotary Internat., 1979. Mem. Am. Mgmt. Assns., Internat Platform Assn., Risk and Ins. Mgrs. Soc., Public Risk and Ins. Mgmt. Assn., Am. Soc. Profl. and Exec. Women. Author: Kids Are People, Too, 1975. Pearls of Potentiality, 1980; also articles. Home: 4606 Ontario St Apt 5 Ames IA 50010 Office: 621 Main St Ames IA 50010

REPPKE, KATHY ANN, dir./producer; b. Detroit, June 1, 1951; d. Robert E. and Ann (Kwiatkowski) R.; B.A., Wayne State U., 1973, M.A. summa cum laude (fellow), 1975. Asst. editor/producer Wilding Video, Detroit, 1975-77; writer/producer Mich. Bell, Southfield, 1977-79; exec. producer/dir. Graphic Media Corp., Fairfield, N.J., 1981—. Mem. Internat. TV and Video Assn., Internat. Study and Research Inst., Phi Beta Kappa. Home: 7002 Blvd E 40D Gutenberg NJ 07093 Office: 1275 Bloomfield Ave Fairfield NJ 07006

RERICK, CAROLE A., surety underwriter; b. Syracuse, N.Y., Apr. 1, 1938; d. Lester C. and Loretta C. (Wilkinson) R.; student Syracuse parochial schs. With CNA, Syracuse, 1955—, beginning as jr. record clk. acctg. dept., transmittal clk., gen. clk., operative supr., underwriting clk. surety dept., asst. surety underwriter, field surety underwriter, 1955-78, sr. surety underwriter, 1978—. Mem. Syracuse Ins. Women's Assn. (past pres.), Surety Assn. Syracuse. Democrat. Roman Catholic. Home: 100 Village Dr Syracuse NY 13206 Office: 100 Elwood Davis Rd North Syracuse NY 13212

RESE, GEORGIA MOSS, clin. social worker, child devel. specialist, educator; b. Detroit, Aug. 2, 1929; d. George Pearce and Marianna Marr (Murphy) R.; B.S. in Edn., U. Mich., 1953; M.S., Coll. Medicine, U. Pitts., 1962; Tchr., public and pvt. schs., Mich., N.J., Pa., Vt. and Maine, 1953-59; grad. research asst. U. Pitts., 1959-62; tchr., therapist for autistic children and developmentally disabled, adminstr. Unit Disturbed Children, Neuropsychiat. Inst., Princeton, N.J., 1963-64; therapist Pitts. Public Schs. and various Pa. hosps., 1964-71, Vt. and N.H., 1971—; residential and adminstrv. staff Spring Lake Ranch, 1970-75; cons., field worker for day care, elderly and adolescents, 1975-80; fieldworker cross-disabilities Vt. Center for Ind. Living, 1981—; pvt. practice psychotherapy, 1961—. Mem. Nat. Assn. Social Workers N.H. Mental Health Assn., NEA, AAHPER. Contbr. articles to profl. jours. Home: Box 263 Barton VT 05837

RESNECK-SANNES, HELEN RAE, psychologist; b. Marion, Ind., Dec. 14, 1947; d. William Saul and Charlotte Helen (Mayer) Resneck; B.A., U. Wis., Madison, 1969, M.A., 1972, Ph.D., 1974; postgrad. SUNY, Buffalo, 1969-70; m. L. David Sannes, June 20, 1976; 1 dau., Myrrhia Rae; 1 stepson, Aaron. Psychology intern Kaiser Permanente, Los Angeles, 1973-74; clin. psychologist Monterey County Mental Health, Salinas, Calif., 1974-76; asst. prof. Antioch Coll., Monterey, Calif., 1977; psychodiagnostician Rebekkah Odd Fellows Childrens Home, Gilroy, Calif., 1977; pvt. practice Ben Lomond, Calif., 1977—. Mem. Environ. Council Santa Cruz, 1979; bd. dirs. Women in Transition, Womans Place, 1972-73. Western Interstate Commn. for Higher Edn. grantee. Mem. Am. Psychol. Assn., Assn. Women in Psychology, Assn. Humanistic Psychology, Assn. Transpersonal Psychology, Assn. Behavior Therapy, Western Psychology Assn., Phi Kappa Phi. Home: 10061 Riverside Dr Ben Lomond CA 95005

RESNICK, CYNTHIA BILT, speech and lang. pathologist; b. Bklyn., Mar. 8, 1946; d. Murray and Helen Francis (Rubin) Bilt; B.A. cum laude, Marymount Manhattan Coll., 1976; M.S. in Speech Pathology, Tchrs. Coll., Columbia U., 1978; m. Jerry Resnick, June 17, 1967 (dec. 1972). Trainee in speech and language clin. pathology Marymount Manhattan Coll., N.Y.C., 1975, Columbia U., N.Y.C., 1976-77, Kennedy Child Study Center, N.Y.C., 1977, Beth Abraham Hosp., Bronx, N.Y., 1977; speech and language clinician L.I. Jewish-Hillside Med. Center, New Hyde Park, N.Y., 1977; tchr. speech and hearing handicapped Good Shepherd Sch., Inwood, N.Y., 1977-78; mem. staff Bur. Speech Improvement, N.Y.C. Bd. Edn., 1978; speech/lang. pathologist Lorge Sch., N.Y.C., 1978-80 Summit Sch., N.Y.C., 1980; speech/lang. cons. Forest Hills Nursing Home, 1980—; speech/lang. cons. Arigo Ear, Nose and Throat Center, 1981—; pvt. practice, 1981—. Recipient hon. mention for acad. excellence in speech sci., Marymount Manhattan Coll., N.Y.C., 1976; citizenship award Roosevelt Prep. Sch., Stamford, Conn., 1963. Mem. Am. (cert.), N.Y. State speech and hearing assns., Speech Communication Assn., Internat. Assn. Logopedics and Phoniatrics. Address: 200 E 71st St New York NY 10021

RESNIK, REGINA, operatic singer; b. N.Y.C., Aug. 30, 1924; d. Sam and Ruth Resnick; B.A., Hunter Coll., 1942; m. Harry W. Davis, July 18, 1946; 1 son, Michael Philip; m. 2d Arbit Blatas, 1975. Debut as Lady Macbeth, 1942; mezzo-soprano debut Met. Opera Co., N.Y.C., 1946; regular guest Vienna State Opera, La Scala, Milan, Italy, Covent Garden, Salzburg, Deutsche Opera, Berlin, Teatro Colon, Buenos Aires, Bayreuth, Germany, Munich Saatsoper, Chgo., Phila., San Francisco, others; co-dir., starred in Carmen at Hamburg Opera, 1971, in Electra, 1971, in Falstaff at Nat. Opera Poland, 1975; condr. seminars on opera New Sch. for Social Research; dir. The Medium (Menotti), The Telephone (Menotti), The Rise and Fall of the City Mahagonny (Weill). Decorated comdr. French Acad. Arts, Scis. and Letters; recipient awards including U.S. Pres.'s medal, Kannersängerin (Austria). Office: care Met Opera Co 50 W 56th St New York NY 10019 *

RESSLER, MARY BETH, data processing exec.; b. Pine Bluff, Ark., Nov. 29, 1947; d. Isaac Buchanan and Elizabeth (Cole) Edwards; B.A. in English, U. Ark., 1972; m. Edwin A. Ressler, Jr., July 14, 1972. Programmer, analyst Systematics, Inc., Fayetteville, Ark., 1969-72, dir. communications, 1975-76, data center mgr., 1976—; tchr. English, Am Coop. Sch., La Paz, Bolivia, 1972-75. Mem. Data Processing Mgmt. Assn., Phi Beta Kappa. Contbr. articles to banking publs. Office: 5 Commercial Blvd Novato CA 94947

RETTALIATA, ANTONIO P., state rep.; b. Huntington, N.Y., Oct. 20, 1944; d. Pasquale and Mary (Finello) Bifulco; student public schs., Huntington; m. John B. Rettaliata, Jr. Adminstrv. asst. Suffolk County (N.Y.) Ct. System, 1969-78; mem. N.Y. State Assembly, Albany, 1979—. Pres., Huntington Young Republican Club, 1970-73; committeewoman 8th Assembly Dist. Rep. Party, N.Y., 1974-78; sec. local United Fund; active Am. Cancer Soc.; mem. Italian-Am. Arts and Assistance Council. Named Woman of Yr., South Huntington Rep. Club, 1978-79. Roman Catholic. Office: Room 426 Legis Office Bldg Albany NY 12248 *

RETZER, MARY ELIZABETH HELM (MRS. WILLIAM RAYMOND RETZER), librarian; b. Balt.; d. Francis Leslie C. and Edna (Smith) Helm; B.A., Western Md. Coll., 1940; M.A., Columbia U., 1946; postgrad. George Washington U., Ind. U., U. Ill., Ill. State U., Bradley U.; Ph.D., Western Colo. U., 1972; m. William Raymond Retzer, June 28, 1945; children—Lesley Elizabeth, Apryl Christine. Mem. faculty Rockville (Md.) Bd. Edn., 1940-47, elementary supr., 1945-47; mem. staff Peoria Public Library, 1957-63, homebound librarian, 1961-63; cons. librarian Bergan High Sch., 1964-67; condr. library sci. course in reference Bradley U., 1966—; librarian Hines Elementary Sch., 1963-66, Roosevelt Jr. High Sch., 1966-69; head media center Manual High Sch., Peoria, Ill., 1969—. Instr. water safety courses ARC, summers 1940—; pres. women's bd. Salvation Army, 1952-54; pres. Peoria Nursery Sch. Assn., 1953-54; mem. legis. action com. Ill. Congress PTA, 1955-56; mem. Crippled Children's Adv. Com., Peoria, 1957-60; active various community drives; mem. women's adv. bd. Peoria Jr. Star, 1970-73. Mem. Ill. Valley Librarians Assn. (pres. 1971-72), ALA, Ill. Library Assn., Ill. Assn. Media in Edn. (certification com. 1973—), NEA, Ill., Peoria edn. assns., Ill. Audiovisual Assn., AAUW, Internat. Platform Assn. Republican. Presbyterian. Clubs: Order Eastern Star, Ill. State U. Adminstrs., Willowknolls Country. Home: 1317 W Moss Ave Peoria IL 61606 Office: 811 S Griswold St Peoria IL 61605

REUBEN, LUCY JEANETTE, fin. analyst, educator; b. Sumter, S.C., Dec. 15, 1949; d. Odell Richardson and Anna Mays (Daniels) R.; A.B. in Economics, Oberlin Coll., 1971; M.B.A. in Fin. with distinction, U. Mich., 1974, Ph.D. in Fin., 1981; 1 son, Kwame Odell Oliver. Fin. analyst Ford Motor Co., World Hdqrs., Dearborn, Mich., 1974-75; research asst. U. Mich., Ann Arbor, 1975-77, tchg. fellow Finance, 1977-79, cons. center for cont. edn., 1977-79, mem. search com. for Dean of Bus. Sch., 1977-78, academic caucus for women, coordinator Black Business Students Alumni Assn.; asst. prof. fin. Duke U., Durham, N.C., 1979—. Recipient award for doctoral study Nat. Fellowships Fund, U. Mich., 1977-79, Earhart Found. Fellowship, 1978. Mem. Nat. Black M.B.A. Assn., Nat. Economic Assn., Am. Fin. Assn., Nat. Assn. Female Execs., AAUP, Beta Gamma Sigma. Editor: Black Economic Development: Analysis and Implications, 1975; contbr. research paper in field. Office: Fuqua Sch Bus Duke U Durham NC 27706

REUDER, MARY EILEEN, psychologist, educator; b. Mpls., Mar. 12, 1923; d. Leo Aloysius and Mary Agnes (McGuire) Reuder; B.A., Coll. of St. Catherine, 1944; M.A., Brown U., 1945; Ph.D., U. Pa., 1951; m. Marvin Alvin Iverson, July 11, 1953 (dec.); children—Carol Mary, Kent Gery. Research psychologist personnel research br. Adj. Gen.'s Office, Dept. Army, Washington, 1952-54; dir. research survey of non-acad. functions Queens Coll., City U. N.Y., Flushing, 1955, from instr. to prof. psychology, 1955—, chmn. evening dept. psychology, 1957-75, supr. psychol., summer session, 1964-66, prof., 1971—, mem. grad. faculty, 1977—, chmn. acad. senate, 1982-83; cons. NATO postdoctoral fellowships, NSF, 1978, Brown U. Network Resources Bank, 1979—. Fellow Am. Psychol. Assn. (council of reps. 1979-81, chmn. div. fellows com. 1981—, exec. com. divs. 1 and 36, 1979-81, liaison for div. 36), N.Y. Acad. Sci.; mem. Eastern Psychol. Assn., Psychometric Soc., Biometric Soc., AAAS, Am. Statis. Assn., Sigma Xi (nat. dir. 1972-75, 1977, nat. lecturership com. 1972—), Pi Gamma Mu, Delta Phi Lambda, Kappa Gamma Pi, Alpha pi Epsilon, Psi Chi, Alpha Sigma Lambda. Clubs: Brown U. of L.I., U. Pa. of L.I. (gov. 1980—, sec.-bd. govs. 1982-83). Contbr. articles to profl. jours. Home: 154 Charles St East Williston NY 11596 Office: Psychology Dept Queens Coll of City Univ NY Flushing NY 11367

REUTER, LINDA NEAL, designer, educator; b. Akron, Ohio, Dec. 27, 1947; d. George William and Charlotte Neal (Gray) Reuter Miller; B.S. in Design with honors, U. Cin., 1971; M.F.A. in Design, U. Utah, 1975; m. Allan Harding, Feb. 14, 1981. Spl. projects art dir. May Co., Cleve.,

1972-73; teaching fellow U. Utah, Salt Lake City, 1973-75; asst. prof. No. Ill. U., DeKalb, 1975-77; mgr. graphic design Kimberly-Clark Corp., Neenah, Wis., 1977—. Active Talbert House, Cin., 1971, Bountiful (Utah) Art Center, 1974; mem. Big Sisters Neenah, 1980-81, Future Neenah Com., 1982—. Recipient Golden award Franklin Typographers Competition, N.Y.C., 1970; 4 awards Chgo. Ann. Design Exhbn., 1976. Mem. Am. Inst. Graphic Arts. Episcopalian. Office: Kimberly-Clark Corp 401 N Lake St Neenah WI 54956

REUTHER, ROSANN WHITE, advt. agy. exec.; b. Nashville, Nov. 24, 1943; d. Wiley Butler and Mildred Elizabeth (Little) White; student George Peabody Coll., 1961-64; m. Peter Martin Reuther, Oct. 3, 1964. Advt. copywriter WHMA Radio, Anniston, Ala., 1964-65, Bapt. Sunday Sch. Bd., Nashville, 1965-72, Thomas Nelson Pubs., Nashville, 1972-73; account exec. Holder-Kennedy Pub. Relations, Nashville, 1973-74; pub. relations dir. T. Nelson, Nashville, 1974-75; pension adminstr. Wood, Bateman, Nord, Assos., Nashville, 1975-76; owner, pres. In-Vision Advt. and Pub. Relations, Brentwood, Tenn., 1976—; lectr. Tenn. State U., 1978-79. Worker, Carter for Pres. campaign, Tenn., 1976. Recipient Paul M. Hinkhous award of excellence in advt., 1974. Mem. Religious Pub. Relations Council, Nashville Advt. Fedn., Am. Women in Radio and TV (pres. Nashville chpt. 1981-82, dir. dist. B, 1982—). Baptist. Home: 1315 Haber Dr Brentwood TN 37027 Office: 4107 Hillsboro Circle Nashville TN 37215

REUTHER, RUTH ELIZABETH (MRS. J. R. REUTHER), author, ret. educator b. Gainesville, Tex., Feb. 27, 1917; d. Edwin Jerry and Grace (Patrick) Huffaker; A.A., Gainesville Jr. Coll., 1936; B.S., N. Tex. State Coll., 1938; m. J. R. Reuther, Jan. 26, 1941; 1 dau., Alma Grace. Tchr. English, Valley View (Tex.) Ind. Sch., 1944-46; tchr. Sam Houston Elem. Sch., 1957-58, tchr. reading and lit., Wichita Falls, Tex., 1958-74; ret. Author: Wife of Four Hobbies, 1956; (juvenile) Gray C. Circus Horse, 1970; (poetry) Texas is My Home, 1982; (history) A Century of Faithful Witness, 1983; also short stories, articles on visual tng. profl. jours. Mem. Visual Tng. Assts. Congress, Ft. Worth. Mem. Tex. State Tchrs. Assn., Circus Fans Assn. Am., NEA, Assn. Childhood Edn., Woman's Forum, Wichita Falls (pres.), Tex. poetry socs., Internat. Reading Assn., Delta Kappa Gamma. Baptist. Clubs: Order Eastern Star, Poetry (Wichita Falls). Home: 4450 Phillips Dr Wichita Falls TX 76308

REX, LINDA KAY, retail exec.; b. Ft. Madison, Iowa, Jan. 24, 1949; d. Richard Thomas and Dorothy May Hall; student Indian Hills Community Coll., Ottumwa, Iowa; m. James Wesley Rex, Apr. 2, 1966; 1 dau., Lissa Dawn. With Rider Nursery & Floral Co., Farmington, Iowa, 1971-77, Harmeier Tax Service, 1977-78; clk. Van Buren County Ct. House, Keosauqua, Iowa, 1977-78; pres. R-2, Inc., agrl. and recreation supplies, Bonaparte, Iowa, 1974—; owner R-2 Supply, retail store and tax service, Bonaparte, 1975—; horse trainer and owner, 1965—. Founder, 1975, since leader Trot Right In 4-H Club; bd. dirs. Van Buren Riding Club, 1977, sec-treas., 1978-79; chmn. Bonaparte Pony Express Riders for Easter Seals, 1977-78; treas., tourist promotion dir., mem. budget and legis. coms. Van Buren Devel. Assn., 1980, adminstrv. asst., 1981, exec. dir., 1982—; bd. dirs. Van Buren County Fair, 1981; project dir. Van Buren County Fine Arts Council, 1982—. Mem. Nat. Family Opinion, Internat. Platform Assn. Author articles in field. Address: Farmington IA 52626

REYES, MARCIA STYGLES, med. technologist; b. Winchester, Mass., July 15, 1950; d. Bernard Francis and Eleanore Cecilia (Nicgorska) Stygles; B.S. in Med. Tech., Merrimack Coll., North Andover, Mass., 1972; M.S. in Health Scis. (Kellogg Found. grantee), SUNY, Buffalo, 1977; m. Carlos Reyes, Aug. 5, 1978. Sr. med. technologist Symmes Hosp., Arlington, Mass., 1970-73; sr. microbiologist and serologist Mt. Auburn Hosp., Cambridge, Mass., 1973-75; asst. prof., clin. coordinator Quinnipiac Coll., Hamden, Conn., 1976-81; lab. supr. Canberra Clin. Labs., Meriden, Conn., 1981—; cons. in med. tech. Mem. Am. Soc. Clin. Pathologists, Am. Soc. Med. Tech., Conn. Soc. Med. Tech. (Speaker awards), Am. Soc. Microbiology, Am. Soc. Allied Health Profls. Address: 45 Gracey Ave Meriden CT 06450

REYHER, REBECCA HOURWICH, writer, lectr., educator; b. N.Y.C., Jan. 21, 1897; d. Isaac A. and Lisa (Joffe) Hourwich; student Columbia U., N.Y. Sch. Social Work; B.A., U. Chgo.; m. Ferdinand Reyher, July 13, 1917 (div. 1934); 1 dau., Faith Reyher Jackson. Woman's suffrage worker for Women's Polit. Union, Nat. Woman's Party, N.Y., Boston, Chgo., and 30 states, 1915-23; feature writer Hearst's Internat. mag., Africa, 1923-24; advt. writer, editor J. Walter Thompson & Co., 1927-29; pub. relations asst. Joseph McKee (pres. bd. aldermen, later mayor), N.Y., 1930-31; cons., adviser Sears, Roebuck & Co., 1931-33; regional dir., profl., service, arts projects Fed. Works Progress Adminstrn., N.Y., N.E., 1935-37; asst. to dir., dir. motion pictures Info. Service, W.P.A., 1937-39; exec. sec., mem. bd. dirs. Dominican Rep. Settlement Assn. Inc., 1939-43; weekly broadcast City Fun with Children, Sta. WYNC, N.Y.C., 1945-49, also radio series Behind the Scenes with UN, 1946; mem. faculty New Sch. Social Research, N.Y.C., 1963-70; cons. Internat. Inst. Women's Studies, Washington, 1971—. Mem. flying caravan del. People's Mandate Com. Inter-Am. Peace and Cooperation throughout 17 countries, S. and C.Am., 1937. Author: The Stork Run, 1944; Babies and Puppies are Fun, 1944; My Mother is the Most Beautiful Woman in the World, 1945; Zulu Woman, 1948 (paperback edit. 1972); The Fon and His Hundred Wives, 1953; Search and Struggle for Equality and Independence; editor anthology: Babies Keep Coming, 1947; contbr. articles leading mags. and newspapers. Traveled South and Portuguese East Africa to gather material for books and articles, 1924-25, North Africa, Europe, Russia, Egypt, Greece, Turkey, Near East, 1929. Nigeria, Brit. Cameroons, 1949-50, South Africa, 1950-51, Belgian Congo, Nigeria, Uganda, Kenya, Pakistan, India, Ceylon, Europe, 1957, 13 African countries, 1965, France, 1966; contbr. biography to oral history project on personal experience in suffrage movement and Equal Rights Amendment from its beginning U. Calif. Address: 14 Washington Pl E New York NY 10003 also Robinhood ME 04670

REYNES, WENDY WARNER, pub. co. exec.; b. Boston, Sept. 29, 1944; d. Philip Russell and Elizabeth (Patton) Warner; A.A., Conn. Coll., 1966; m. Jose (Tony) Antonio Reynes, III, Apr. 26, 1969; children—Jose (Tad) Antonio, Gabrielle Elizabeth. With Foote, Cone, Belding, N.Y.C., 1966-68; advt. sales rep. Cosmopolitan Mag., N.Y.C., 1968-69, Co-Ed Mag., N.Y.C., 1969-70; asst. product mgr. Avon Products, N.Y.C., 1970; advt. sales rep. Mag. Networks, N.Y.C. and Chgo., 1970-72; midwest mgr. advt. sales Girl Talk Mag., Chgo., 1972-75; div. mgr. advt. sales Pattis Group, Chgo., 1975-79; pres. Reynes & Assos., Inc., 1979—. Bd. dirs. Multiple Sclerosis, 1974—, St. Joseph's Sch. PTA, 1979—, Marriage Encounter, 1976—; active Jr. League Greenwich, Conn., 1965-67, Jr. League N.Y.C., 1967-75. Mem. Agate Club (dir.), Advt. Assn., Women's Advt. Club Chgo. (co-chmn.). Clubs: Chgo. Advt., Wilmette Tennis, North Shore Country, Court House, East Bank. Home: 1701 Forest Ave Wilmette IL 60091

REYNOLDS, ANNA CHRIST, timber mgmt. cons.; b. New Bedford, Mass., Dec. 25; d. John and Jenny (Teremeke) Christ; student Campbells Sec. Sch., 1937, 20th Century Bus. Coll., 1952; m. Dan H. Lee, May 9, 1949 (dec.); m. 2d, James S. Reynolds, Nov. 24, 1960 (dec.). Sec., Dixon & Tomato Co., Mobile, Ala., 1952-60; exec. sec. Larson & McGowin, Inc., Mobile, 1961—. Chmn., Knights Templar Eye Found., 1978-80; corr. sec. Ala. Legis. Council, 1978-79, auditor Mobile Legis. Council, 1979—. Mem. The Exec. Female, Am. Legion Aux. (pres.), Nat. Trust Hist. Preservation. Democrat. Greek Orthodox. Mem. Order Eastern Star, Order Beauceant Assembly. Home: 2453 N Pineway Dr Mobile AL 36605 Office: 254 N Jackson St Mobile AL 36603

REYNOLDS, BARBARA ANN, journalist; b. Columbus, Ohio, Aug. 17, 1942; d. Harvey and Mae L. (Stewart) R.; B.A. in Journalism, Ohio State U., 1966; L.H.D. (hon.), Daniel Hale Williams U., 1976. Reporter, Cleve. Press, 1967-68; asst. editor Ebony mag., 1968-69; with Chgo. Tribune Co., Chgo., 1969-78, nat. corr. Washington bur., 1978-81, editor Dollars and Sense mag., 1969—; syndicated columnist Intercontinental Press Syndicate, 1981—; weekly commentator Sheridan Broadcasting Co., 1981—; regular commentator Nat. Public Radio, 1982—; columnist Sepia and Essence mags.; vis. lectr. Sch. Journalism, U. Calif., Berkeley, 1977—; lectr. civil rights and social issues. Nieman fellow, 1976-77; recipient Communication Excellence to Black Audiences award for radio commentaries, 1981. Mem. Women in Communications (Headliner award 1976), Media Women, Sigma Delta Chi. Club: Washington Press. Author: Jesse Jackson, the Man, the Movement and the Myth, 1975. Office: Chgo Tribune Co 1707 H St NW Washington DC 20006

REYNOLDS, BETTY JANE, tng. cons.; b. Detroit, Jan. 4, 1925; d. Clifton James and Grace Darling (Mayberry) Hager; B.S., Wayne State U., 1951, M.S.W., 1970, Ph.D., 1979; 1 son, James Dudley. Program adminstr., tng. coordinator Wayne County Juvenile Ct., 1970-73; dir. juvenile justice tng. div. Criminal Justice Inst., 1973-76, orgn. devel. and tng. cons., 1976-79; mem. asso. grad. faculty, dept. criminal justice Wayne State U.; pres. Group Associated Mgmt. Services, Inc., Detroit. Mem. Am. Acad. Criminal Justices Scis., AAUW, Am. Edn. Research Assn., Am. Soc. Tng. and Devel., Nat. Assn. Female Execs., Nat. Assn. Social Workers, Nat. Assn. Correctional Trainers, Nat. Soc. Performance and Instrn. Democrat. Baptist. Office: 3002 Woodward Tower Detroit MI 48226

REYNOLDS, BONNIE LEE, publishing co. mgr.; b. Erie, Pa., Aug. 5, 1943; d. Aubrey Edward and Clara Sybil (Burns) R.; student Coll. of Sch. Ozarks, Point Lookout, Mo., 1963, 64, U. Ark., 1964, 65, 67, Ark. Tech. U., Russellville, 1967, 68. Bookkeeper, Cenla Community Action Com., Alexandria, La., 1966; bookkeeper Wheatley Brothers Auto Supply, Hot Springs, Ark., 1964; prodn. mgr. The Hot Springs News, 1969-79; office mgr., layout mgr. LaVilla Publs., Hot Springs, 1979—. Recipient Ark. Writers Conf. Alice Leight Night 1st prize, 1976; 1st prize Ark. Poetry Day, 1980. Mem. Nat. Fedn. State Poetry Socs., Ark. Authors, Composers and Artists Soc. (1st prize for oil painting 1982), Am. Acad. Poets, Tenn. Poetry Soc., Poets Study Club Terre Haute. Baptist. Author: A Touch of Wonder, 1977. Contbr. poetry to numerous publs. Home: 105 Euclid St Hot Springs AR 71901 Office: Star Route 10 Box 490A Hot Springs AR 71901

REYNOLDS, JACQUELINE ANN, physiologist; b. Los Angeles, Oct. 19, 1930; d. James Richard and Ethel Mary (Tuthill) Harding; B.S. in Chemistry, Pacific U., Forest Grove, Oreg., 1951; Ph.D. in Phys. Chemistry, U. Wash., Seattle, 1963; children—Thomas Burnett, Benjamin James, Deborah Tamsen, Rebecca Brighid. Research chemist IBM, Yorktown Heights, N.Y., 1963-65; research asst. prof. microbiology Washington U., St. Louis, 1966-69; mem. faculty Duke U. Med. Center, Durham, N.C., 1969—, prof. physiology, 1980—; mem. study sects. NIH. Guggenheim fellow, 1977-78. Mem. Am. Soc. Biol. Chemists, Biophys. Soc., AAUP, N.Y. Acad. Scis. Co-author: Multiple Equilibria in Proteins, 1969; mem. editorial bd. Archives of Biochemistry and Biophysics; contbr. articles to profl. jours. Office: Dept Physiology Duke U Med Center Durham NC 27710

REYNOLDS, JOYCE HINSON, physician; b. Durham, N.C., Nov. 13, 1925; d. Thera Earl and Irene (Brown) Hinson; B.S. in Medicine, U. N.C., 1947; M.D., Bowman Gray Sch. Medicine, 1952; m. William Joseph Reynolds, Apr. 2, 1948; 1 son, Richard Joseph. Intern, N.C. Bapt. Hosp., 1952-54; gen. practice medicine, Kernersville, N.C., 1954-64; founder, dir. emergency dept. Forsyth Meml. Hosp., Winston-Salem, N.C., 1964-71, chief of staff, 1970-71; pres. Forsyth Emergency Services, P.A., 1970—; instr. surgery Bowman Gray Sch. Medicine. Recipient Disting. Alumna award Bowman Gray Sch. Medicine, 1972, Excellence in Teaching award, 1981-82. Mem. AMA, Am. Coll. Trauma, Univ. Asso. Emergency Med. Services, Am. Coll. Emergency Physicians, N.C. Bd. Med. Examiners (pres. 1981, 82), N.C., Forsyth County (pres. 1981-82) med. socs., Phi Beta Kappa, Alpha Omega Alpha. Republican. Episcopalian. Home: 9550 Freeman Rd Kernersville NC 27284 Office: Emergency Dept Forsyth Meml Hosp Winston Salem NC 27103

REYNOLDS, JOYCE KEREKES, advt. exec.; b. Rahway, N.J., June 19, 1943; d. John and Elizabeth (Sandor) Kerekes; B.S., Ind. U., 1969. Sales promotion cons. Lincoln Nat. Life Ins. Co. Fort Wayne, Ind., 1969-70; copy chief H.S. Pogue Co., Cin., 1971-72, Stockton-West-Burkhart, Inc., Cin., 1972-74; account exec. Baer, Kemble & Spicer, Cin., 1975-77; v.p., account supr. Kenrick Advt., Inc., St. Louis, 1977-81; v.p. advt. John Wanamaker, Phila., 1981—. Mem. TRAC, Phila.; bd. dirs. Phila. Civic Ballet. Women in Communications, Home: 315 Monroe St Philadelphia PA 19147 Office: John Wanamaker 1300 Market St Philadelphia PA 19101

REYNOLDS, JUDY NELLIE, childbirth educator; b. Kellogg, Idaho, May 27, 1948; d. William J. and Hazel N. Noyen; cert. childbirth educator Childbirth Without Pain Edn. League, Inc., 1978; m. Randy L. Reynolds, June 10, 1967; children—Ryan Stacy, Robin Blake. Sec., U. Idaho, Moscow, 1967-71; various secretarial positions, Olympia, Wash., 1972-77; adult communicator TeeDruNar, drug rehab. program, Olympia, 1972-73; sec. State Bd. Community Colls., Olympia, 1977; chmn. bylaws revision com. Childbirth Without Pain Edn. League, Inc., Riverside, Calif., 1979, nat. tchr. trainer, 1979—, bd. dirs., 1980—. Tumwater (Wash.) coordinator Mother's March, Nat. Found. March of Dimes, 1979-82, Cert. of Achievement, 1980, 81. Mem. Internat. Childbirth Edn. Assn., Nat. Assn. Childbirth Edn. (correspondence tng. coordinator 1981-82. Democrat. Lutheran. Club: Boosters (Tumwater). Home and Office: 520 W Dennis St Tumwater WA 98501

REYNOLDS, LINDA CAROLINE, writer, educator; b. Ft. Worth, Jan. 20; d. James Daniel and Martha Caroline (Valigura) Little; B.B.A., Tex. Christian U., 1965, M.B.A., 1970. Tchr., Ft. Worth Pub. Schs., 1965-73; instr. Tarrant County Jr. Coll., 1974-75, Tex. Christian U., Ft. Worth, 1976—, also self-employed writer, lectr. and cons., Ft. Worth, 1976—. Bd. dirs. Mus. Western Transp.; active Van Cliburn Council, Opera Guild. Mem. Am. Vocat. Assn., Am. Bus. Communication Assn., Tex. Bus. Edn. Assn., Nat. Bus. Edn. Assn. Author: Snow Country Typewriting Practice Set, 1974; Air Country Typewriting Practice Set, 1980; Dimensions in Personal Development, 1976; Dimensions in Professional Development, 1982. Office: Texas Christian University Dan Rogers Hall Fort Worth TX 76129

REYNOLDS, LYNNAE CAROL, marine corps officer; b. Denver, Dec. 2, 1949; d. Mac Maine and Elsie Elizabeth (Fletcher) Ruske; B.A. in Environ. Biology, U. Colo., Boulder, 1971; m. Michael L. Reynolds, Oct. 13, 1973 (separated). Commd. 2d lt. USMC, 1972, advanced through grades to capt., 1977; traffic mgmt. officer Marine Corps Base, Camp Lejeune, N.C., 1978-80; head personal property sect. Transp. br. Hdqrs. Marine Corps, Washington, 1980—. Mem. Am. Philat. Soc., Nat. Def. Transp. Assn., Delta Nu Alpha. Republican. Presbyterian. Office: Personal Property Sect Transp Br Hdqrs Marine Corps Code LFT-4 Washington DC 20380

REYNOLDS, NANCY BRADFORD DUPONT (MRS. WILLIAM GLASGOW REYNOLDS), sculptor; b. Greenville, Del., Dec. 28, 1919; d. Eugene Eleuthere and Catherine Dulcinea (Moxham) duPont; student Goldey-Beacom Coll., Wilmington, Del., 1938; m. William Glasgow Reynolds, May 18, 1940; children—Kathrine Glasgow Reynolds Sturges, William Bradford, Mary Parminter Reynolds Savage, Cynthia duPont Reynolds Farris. Exhibited one-woman shows: Rehoboth (Del.) Art League, 1963, Del. Art Mus., Wilmington, Caldwell, Inc., 1975, Wilmington Art Mus., 1976; exhibited group shows: Corcoran Gallery, Washington, 1943, Soc. Fine Arts, Wilmington, 1937, 38, 40, 41, 48, 50, 62, 65, NAD, N.Y.C., 1964, Pa. Mil. Coll., Chester, 1966, Del. Art Center, 1967, Met. Mus. Art, N.Y.C., 1977, Lever House, N.Y.C., 1979; represented in permanent collections: Wilmington Trust Co., E.I. duPont de Nemours & Co., Children's Home, Inc., Claymont, Del., Goldsbrough Bldg., Wilmington, Children's Bur., Wilmington, Stephenson Sci. Center, Nashville, Luterine Towers Bldg., Travelers Aid and Family Soc. Bldg., Wilmington, Bronze Fountain Head, Longwood Gardens, Kennett Square, Pa. Guide, mem. research staff Henry Francis DuPont Winterthur Mus., 1955-63. Organizer vol. service Del. chpt. ARC, 1938-39; chmn. Com. for Revision Del. Child Adoption Law, 1950-52; pres. bd. dirs. Children Bur. Del.; pres., trustee Children's Home, Inc. Recipient Confrerie des Chevaliers du Tastevin Clos de Vougeot-Bourgogne France, 1960; Hort. award Garden Club Am., 1964, medal of Merit, 1976; Dorothy Platt award Garden Club of Phila., 1980; Alumni medal of merit Westover Sch., Middlebury, Conn. Mem. Pa. Hort. Soc., Wilmington Soc. Fine Arts, Mayflower Descs., Del. Hist. Soc., Colonial Dames, League Am. Pen Women, Nat. Trust Hist. Preservation. Episcopalian. Clubs: Garden of Wilmington (past pres.), Garden of Am. (past asst. zone 4 chmn.), Vicmead Hunt, Greenville Country, Chevy Chase (Washington); Burr Artist, Catherine Lorillard Wolfe Art (N.Y.C.). Contbr. articles to profl. jours. Address: PO Box 3919 Greenville DE 19807

REYNOLDS, NANCY CLARK, corp. exec., lobbyist; b. 1927; B.A., Goucher Coll., 1949. Co-anchorman Sta. KTVB, Boise, Idaho, 1958-62; spl. asst. to Calif. Gov. Ronald Reagan, 1967-74; account exec. Deaver & Hannaford, 1975-76; assoc. dir. nat. affairs Boise Cascade Corp., 1976-77; v.p. nat. affairs Bendix Corp., Southfield, Mich., 1977—. Office: Bendix Corp Bendix Center Southfield MI 48037 *

REYNOLDS, PATRICIA ELLEN, painter; b. Portchester, N.Y., Apr. 6, 1934; d. Edwin and Anna (Pacewicz) Steeg; student SUNY, Plattsburg, 1951-52, Moon Bus. Sch., N.Y.C., 1953; pupil of Robert Whitney, Mario Cooper; m. Carlyle Reynolds, Oct. 4, 1953; children—Clifford, Stephanie. Watercolor painter, Willsboro, N.Y., 1960—; past treas., gallery dir. Adirondack Art Assn.; condr. workshops in field, mem. art juries; one-woman exhbns. include Adirondack Center Mus., 1978, 80, Wood Mus., 1976, U. Vt., 1976, Four Winds Gallery, Ferrisburgh, Vt., 1979, Washington (Conn.) Art Assn., 1977, Gallerie Camille Renaud, Paris, 1979, Hollsworthy Gallery, London, 1980, Melka Assos., Montreal; group exhbns. include Schenectady Mus., SUNY, Plattsburgh, St. Lawrence U., Canton, N.Y., Center for Music, Drama and Arts, Lake Placid, N.Y., 1980, Audubon Artists Ann., 1980, Fleming Mus., Burlington, Vt., Center for Modern Design, Riyadh, Saudi Arabia. Recipient Best of Show award No. Vt. Artists, 1970, 71, 76, 78, 79, Outstanding Woman Artist award Am. Pen Women, 1975, Benedictine Nat. award, 1975, Adirondack Art Exhbn. award, 1973. Mem. Essex County Hist. Soc., Adirondack Art Assn., No. Vt. Artists, Schenectady Mus. Artists, Audubon Artists (asso.), Am. Watercolor Soc. (asso.). Address: Willsboro Point Rd Willsboro NY 12996

REYNOLDS, RUTHIE GRACE, educator; b. Covington, Ga., Dec. 3, 1945; d. Horace Joe and Lucille (Freeman) R.; A.S., Mary Holmes Jr. Coll., 1965; B.S., U. Dubuque, 1967; M. Acctg., U. Ariz., 1970; Ph.D., Ga. State U., 1981; children—Reiko Renee Tate, Thomas Anthony Tate, Jr. Tax tecnician IRS, Atlanta, 1967-68; auditor Touche Ross & Co., San Francisco, 1970-71; auditor U. Calif., Berkeley, 1971-72; instr. Tenn. State U., Nashville, 1972-75; acct. R.G. Reynolds, C.P.A., Nashville, 1973-75; asst. prof. U. Tenn., Nashville 1976-77, Ga. Inst. Tech., Atlanta, 1981—. C.P.A., Tenn.; John Hay Whitney fellow, 1968-69; Arthur Andersen & Co., fellow, 1980. Mem. Am. Inst. C.P.A.s, Am. Acctg. Assn., Tenn. Soc. C.P.A.s. Home: 1419 Hartford Ave SW Atlanta GA 30310 Office: Coll Mgmt Ga Inst Tech Atlanta GA 30332

REYNOLDS, SANDRA LYNN, banker; b. Norwalk., Conn., Oct. 20, 1949; d. Kendall Wright and Norma Louise (Caswell) Reynolds; B.A. with high honors in Sociology, U Conn., 1973; grad. New Eng. Sch. Banking, 1982. With First Bank of New Haven, 1973—, asst. to mgr., Waterford br., 1977, officer, asst. mgr., 1977, asst. trust officer trust dept., 1978, trust officer, 1981—; mem. trust curriculum com. New Eng. Sch. Banking, Williams Coll., 1982. Vol. Library of Congress, Library for Blind and Physically Handicapped, 1979—; treas. Internat. Center, 1982. Recipient YWCA Women in Leadership award, 1979. Mem. Am. Inst. Banking, Nat. Assn. Bank Women (chmn. Conn. group 1980-81, state edn. and tng. chmn. 1981-82, state membership chmn. 1982-83), Phi Beta Kappa. Office: 1 Church St New Haven CT 06509

REYNOLDS, WYNETKA ANN, univ. chancellor; b. Coffeyville, Kans., Nov. 3, 1937; d. John E. and Glennie King; B.S. in Biology and Chemistry, Kans. State Tchrs. Coll., 1958; M.S. in Zoology (NSF fellow), State U. Iowa, 1960, Ph.D., 1962; children—Rachel Rebecca, Rex King. Asst. prof. zoology Ball State U., Muncie, Ind., 1962-65; mem. faculty U. Ill. Med. Center, Chgo., 1965-79, asso. vice chancellor research, dean Grad. Coll., 1977-79; provost Ohio State U., Columbus, 1979-82; chancellor Calif. State System, Long Beach, 1982—; mem., chmn. com. nutrition mother and pre-sch. child Food and Nutrition Bd., Nat. Acad. Scis., 1973—, mem. council Inst. Lab. Animal Resources, 1979—; mem. grad. record exams. com. Advanced Biol. Test, 1974-82; mem., chmn. animal resources rev. com. Primate Research Centers, NIH, 1977—. Recipient award Central Assn. Obstetricians and Gynecologists, 1968, Disting. Alumni award Kans. State Tchrs. Coll., 1972. Assoc. fellow Am. Coll. Obstetricians and Gynecologists; mem. AAAS, Am. Assn. Anatomists, Am. Diabetes Assn., Endocrine Soc., Perinatal Research Soc., Soc. Exptl. Biology and Medicine, Soc. Gynecol. Investigation, Am. Council on Edn. (exec. council chief acad. officers 1981—). Presbyterian. Author papers in field. Home: 620 Stone Canyon Rd Los Angeles CA 90024 Office: 400 Golden Shore Long Beach CA 90802

REZNIKOFF, SHIRLEY CAULKING, educator; b. New Iberia, La.; d. Hiram Henry and Sarah Elizabeth (Riggs) Caulking; B.A. in Art Edn., U. Southwestern La., 1950; M.A. in Design, La. State U., 1960; m. Marvim M. Reznikoff, Nov. 22, 1950; children—Tamara Adena Reznikoff, David Fran Reznikoff. Founder-pres. La Interior Design Inst., Baton Rouge, 1960-72; asso. prof. interior design Coll. Architecture Ariz. State U., Tempe, from 1972, now prof.; adj. faculty Nat. Fire Acad., 1979; free lance artist, 1960—; one-woman exhibits include: Madison Gallery, N.Y.C., 1960; Gallery 1, Baton Rouge, 1962-63; Baton Rouge Gallery, 1966-68; Glade Gallery, New Orleans, 1969; Gallery Extempore, Baton Rouge, 1969-70; 550 Gallery, Baton Rouge, 1970-72; group exhbn.; LA. Profl. State Art Exhibits, 1968-69; founding mem. Baton Rouge Gallery, 1967, 550 Gallery, Baton Rouge, 1970. Environ. Design grantee, Am. Soc. Interior Designers, 1971. Mem. Am. Soc. Interior Designers, Inst. Bus. Designers, Nat. Fire Protection Assn., Constrn. Specifications Inst.,

ASTM, Interior Design Educators Council, AAUP, Women's Image NOW. Jewish. Author: Specifications for Commercial Interiors, Professional Liabilities, Regulations and Performance Criteria, 1979. Office: Coll Architecture Ariz State U Tempe AZ 85281

RHEINER, JUDITH DIANE, publicity cons., editor; b. Pitts., Sept. 25, 1940; d. Maynard and Muriel (Rosenblum) Gross; A.B. in Telecommunications, U. So. Calif., 1962; m. Richard Rheiner, Feb. 26, 1967. Market research and promotion coordinator Sta. KABC-TV, Hollywood, Calif., 1962-66; sales and on-air promotion dir. Sta. KHJ-TV, Hollywood, 1966-68; publicist Warner Bros. Pictures, Hollywood, 1968-72; unit prodn. publicist Metromedia Producers Corp., Hollywood, 1972-73; dir. publicity The Burbank (Calif.) Studios, 1973-75; info. dir. Screen Actors Guild, Hollywood, 1975-79; editor Screen Actor mag., Hollywood, 1975-79; publicity cons. Norman Winter Assocs., Hollywood, 1980—, Pasadena (Calif.) Civic Light Opera, 1980; publicity dir. Huddleston Co., 1980—; film prodn. publicist, 1980—; mem. Lantana Prodns., 1980—. Mem. Alcoholism Council Pub. Info. Com., Motion Picture Industry Program; nat. chairperson citizens' com. Toys for Tots, 1977. Recipient YWCA certificate leadership, 1975, Soroptimist award of merit, 1974. Mem. Western (v.p.), Internat. (v.p.) labor press assns., Publicists Guild Am. (v.p. East Coast), Hollywood Women's Press Club, Acad. TV Arts and Scis., Hollywood Film Council, Md. Filmmakers Group (founding), Internat. Alliance of Theatrical Stage Employees (East Coast Council), Alpha Epsilon Rho.

RHEINGOLD, HARRIET LANGE, psychologist; b. N.Y.C., Feb. 13, 1908; d. Oscar and Lillian (Brown) Lange; A.B., Cornell U., 1928; M.A., Columbia U., 1930; Ph.D., U. Chgo., 1955; m. Don W. Hayne, Oct. 16, 1960; children by previous marriage—Paul D., Arnold L. Psychologist, Ill. Inst. Juvenile Research, Chgo., 1938-45; mem. faculty Rockford (Ill.) Coll., 1945-53; psychologist NIMH, Bethesda, Md., 1955-64; mem. faculty U. N.C., Chapel Hill, 1964—, prof. psychology, 1964—; fellow Ctr. for Advanced Study in Behavioral Scis., 1967-68; mem. President's Biomed. Research Panel, 1975; cons. in field. Recipient Research Career award Inst. Child Health and Human Devel., 1964; Profl. Achievement award U. Chgo., 1979. Fellow Am. Psychol. Assn. (G. Stanley Hall award 1977); mem. AAAS, Internat. Soc. Study Behavior Devel., Soc. Research Child Devel., Phi Beta Kappa, Sigma Xi. Author articles in field; editor: Maternal Behavior in Mammals, 1963; Early Behavior: Comparative and Developmental Approaches, 1967. Home: 312 Azalea Dr Chapel Hill NC 27514 Office: Dept Psychology O13A U NC Chapel Hill NC 27514

RHEINHEIMER, JOYCE SCHULTZ, psychologist; b. Chgo., June 11, 1944; d. Albert Matthew and Bridget (Brown) Schultz; B.A., U. Ill., Chgo., 1970; M.S., Ill. Inst. Tech., 1974, Ph.D., 1976; m. Robert Rheinheimer, Feb. 19, 1966; children—Robert, Kimberly, Scott, Kelly. Ednl. cons. Behavioral Research Labs., Chgo., 1973-75; instr. Chgo. State U., 1975; sch. psychology intern Sch. Dist. 62, Des Plaines, Ill., 1975-76; instr. Little Co. of Mary Hosp., Evergreen Park, Ill., 1976; clin. psychologist Roth Group, Northbrook, Ill., 1975-78; instr. Lewis U., Lockport, Ill., 1978, DePaul U., Chgo., 1979; psychotherapist in pvt. practice, Oak Forest, Orland Park, Ill.; cons. psychologist Libra Sch., Riverside, Ill. Mem. South Subarea Adv. Council, Health Services Agy., 1979—, vice chmn., 1980—; co-chmn. Mental Health Coalition South Cook County, 1979—. Cert. sch. psychologist. Mem. Am. Psychol. Assn., Ill. Psychol. Assn., Chgo. Psychol. Assn. (pres. 1979). Address: 16464 Laura Ln Oak Forest IL 60452

RHEINLANDER, MARY LINDA, assn. exec.; b. Evansville, Ind., Nov. 7, 1941; d. Clarence Joseph and Margaret Lucille (Herron) Behme; student parochial schs., also continuing edn. classes; m. Robert Edward Rheinlander, Jan. 14, 1961; children—Karen Lynn, Kristine Louise, Keith Edward, Kami Jo. Sec., Whirlpool Corp., 1960; asst. Evansville's Future, Inc., 1965-67; interviewer students Evansville Vanderburgh Sch. Corp., 1974; coordinator job placement service Ind. State U., Evansville, 1970-73; exec. sec. Ind. U. Med. Sch., Indpls., 1975-78; exec. dir. Sheet Metal Contractors Assn., Evansville, 1978—; mem. council Evansville Area Labor-Mgmt. Com.; speaker in field. Mem. Nat. Assn. Women in Constrn., Ind. Sheet Metal Council, Nat. Assn. Sheet Metal and Air Conditioning Contractors, Nat. Assn. Female Execs., U.S. C. of C., Evansville C. of C., Ind. Lawyers Wives Assn., Evansville Lawyers Wives Assn., Am. Soc. Assn. Execs. Roman Catholic. Home: 5318 West Haven Dr Evansville IN 47712 Office: PO Box 6201 Evansville IN 47712

RHO, CORRINE MAE CLEMENT, pharmacist; b. New Castle, Pa., Oct. 31, 1935; d. William Roscoe and Sophia Marie (Gardner) Clement; B.S. in Pharmacy, U. Pitts., 1957; M.B.A., Baldwin-Wallace Coll., 1980; m. Richard Euro Rho, Nov. 22, 1958; children—Barbara C., Richard Euro, Steven M. Staff pharmacist Children's Hosp., Akron, Ohio, 1957-62; employed with various retail pharmacies, 1962-72; pharmacist Klein's Pharmacy, Cuyahoga Falls, Ohio, 1969-74; pharmacy rep. Blue Cross of N.E. Ohio, Cleve., 1975-80; owner C. Rho & Assos., pharm. cons.; coordinator continuing med. edn. Area Health Edn. Centers, 1981-82. Corr. sec. Heritage Com., Copley, Ohio, 1979-80; chmn. worship commn., mem. fin. com., trustee Copley Methodist Ch. Fellow Am. Soc. Cons. Pharmacists; mem. Ohio State Pharm. Assn. (HEW com., resolutions com.), Summit County Pharm. Assn. (pres. 1980-81). Home: 4191 Ridgewood Rd Copley OH 44321

RHOADS, CHERYL M. (SHERRY), businesswoman; b. Bklyn., Oct. 28, 1947; d. Alton Norman Greenblatt and Isabel (Leeman) Marcus; student U. Nevada, 1964-67, U. Alaska, 1978-80; m. James Lane Rhoads, Oct. 29, 1965; children—Cedric, Michelle, Matthew. Sec., receptionist Hughes-Nevada Ops., Las Vegas, 1968-69; sec. Samaritan Health Service, Phoenix, 1969-72; info. specialist Trans Alaska Pipeline, Anchorage, 1972-78; account exec. Studio 8 Advt., Anchorage, 1978-79; v.p. mktg. Delta Cos., Anchorage, 1979; owner Serendipity Services, advt. and pub. relations, Serendipity Gifts, Anchorage; exec. dir. The New Anchorage Network. Mem. Women in Bus., Anchorage C. of C., Alaska Press Women (regional dir. 1980-82), Nat. Fedn. Press Women, Advt. Fedn. Alaska, Alaska Press Club (dir.). Jewish. Home: SRA Box 2040-C Anchorage AK 95507 Office: 2600 Denali St Suite 102 Anchorage AK 99507

RHOADS, GERALDINE EMELINE, editor; b. Phila., Jan. 29, 1914; d. Lawrence Dry and Alice Fegley (Rice) R.; A.B., Bryn Mawr Coll., 1935. Publicity asst. Bryn Mawr (Pa.) Coll., 1935-37; asst. Internat. Students House, Phila., 1937-39; mng. editor The Woman mag., N.Y.C., 1939-42; editor Life Story mag., 1942-45; editor Today's Woman mag., N.Y.C., 1945-52, Today's Family mag., 1952-53; lectr. Columbia U., 1954-56; asso. editor Readers Digest, 1954-55; producer NBC, 1955-56; asso. editor Ladies Home Jour., 1956-62; mng. editor, 1962-63; exec. editor McCall's mag., 1963-66; editor-in-chief Woman's Day Mag., 1966-82, editorial dir., 1982—, v.p., 1972-77; dir Anchor Hocking Corp.; v.p. consumer publs. CBS, N.Y.C., 1977—.

RHODEN, JOYETTE MUSSELMAN, city ofcl.; b. New Orleans, Mar. 31, 1947; d. Donald Lee, Sr. and Joy Elise (DuBlanc) Musselman; B.S. in Econs., U. New Orleans, 1969, teaching cert., 1978; m. Robert Conklin Rhoden, Jr., June 6, 1970. Chief budget Adminstrv. Office, City of New Orleans, 1969-70, recruiter civil service dept., 1970-72, chief budget and ops. mgmt. div. Adminstrv. Office, 1972-74, chief personnel mgmt. and gen. services div. Adminstrv. Office, 1974—. Mem. Internat. Personnel Mgmt. Assn., U. New Orleans Alumni Assn., Delta Zeta. Democrat. Roman Catholic.

RHODES, ANN L(OUISE), constrn. co. exec.; b. Ft. Worth, Oct. 17, 1941; d. Jon Knox and Carol Jane (Greene) R.; student Tex. Christian U., 1960-63, 75—. Vice pres. Rhodes Enterprises, Inc., Ft. Worth, 1963-77; owner-mgr. Lucky R Ranch, Ft. Worth, 1969—; pres., chmn. bd. ALR Enterprises, Inc., Ft. Worth, 1977—; owner Ann L. Rhodes Investments, Ft. Worth, 1976—. Bd. dirs. Tarrant County Council on Alcoholism, 1973-78, hon. bd. dirs., 1978—, named Outstanding Vol., 1972, recipient Vol. Service awards, 1970-78; bd. dirs. N.W. Tex. chpt. Arthritis Found., 1977—; mem. exec. com. Tarrant County Republican Com., 1964-69. Mem. Am. Mgmt. Assn., Nat. Fedn. Ind. Bus., Am. Horse Council, Kappa Kappa Gamma. Episcopalian. Office: ALR Enterprises Inc Suite 908 Republic Bank Ridglea Fort Worth TX 76116

RHODES, CYNTHIA STRAHLER, telephone co. ofcl.; b. Allentown, Pa., May 28, 1947; d. George Robert and Janet Gordon Strahler; student Ursinus Coll., 1965-66, U. Md., 1970; m. Robert Wesley Rhodes, Oct. 22, 1966; children—Danielle Renee, Robert Carver. Supr. network engrng. AT&T Long Lines, 1972-75, market adminstr., 1975-78, supr. spl. communications project, 1978-79, supr. service costs, Bedminster, N.J., 1979-81, staff supr. tariff planning and adminstrn., 1981-82, staff mgr. interstate tariff implementation, 1982—. Mem. Nat. Assn. Female Execs. Republican. Moravian. Club: Chrysalis Dancers. Office: 2C210 Bedminster NJ 07921

RHODES, MARY ELIZABETH FRECHTLING (MRS. IRWIN S. RHODES), former editor; b. Madison, Ind., May 3, 1911; d. George William and Laura (Lory) Frechtling; student Butler U., 1928-30, Herron Art Sch., 1925-30; m. Irwin S. Rhodes, Dec. 12, 1941; children—Elana Susan, Irwin Lawrence. With Marx-Flarsheim Advt. Co., Cin., 1930-32; exec. sec. Perfect Mfg. Co., Cin., 1932-36; sales promotion, real estate mgmt. Am. Service Assos., Cin., 1936-40; asst. editor The Papers of John Marshall, U. Okla. Press, 1969, The Papers of Roger B. Taney, 1970-81. Chmn. Cin. Fine Arts Dr., 1947-59, Cin. Summer Opera Women's Com., 1966-67; mem. adv. bd. Air Pollution Control League, 1958-62; adv. com. Cin. Juvenile Ct., 1960—; mem. exec. com. Am. Cancer Soc. Balls, 1966-78; chmn., v.p. Women's Com. Cin. Symphony Orch., 1959-64; sponsor Irwin S. and Elizabeth F. Rhodes Legal History Collection, U. Okla. Mem. Soc. Ind. Pioneers, Cin., Ky., Md., Lancaster County (Pa.) hist. socs., DAR, Nat. Press Club, Cin. Art Mus., Am. Soc. Profl. and Exec. Women, Ky. Soc. Washington. Editor C.A.R. Nat. Mag., 1966-67. Home: 3815 Erie Ave Cincinnati OH 45208

RIAVE, DIANE, lawyer; b. Los Angeles, Aug. 30, 1946; d. Richard and Beatrice (Tucker) R.; B.A., Calif. State U., Northridge, 1969, M.A., 1970; postgrad. U. So. Calif., 1970-71; J.D., San Fernando Coll. Law, 1978; m. Gregory M. Pokorski, Jan. 30, 1971; 1 son, Mark G. Instr. communications U. So. Calif., Los Angeles, 1970-71; admitted to Calif. bar, 1979; law clk. to Judge Vincent Dalsimer, Los Angeles, 1977-78; asso. firm David Negri, San Fernando, Calif., 1979-80; partner firm Miller & Riave, San Fernando, 1980-81; individual practice, 1982—; tchr. law for laymen Pierce Jr. Coll., Mission Coll. Recipient numerous speaking and debate awards. Mem. State Bar Calif., San Fernando Valley Bar Assn., Bus. and Profl. Women's Orgn. San Fernando. Democrat. Office: 563 S Brand Blvd San Fernando CA 91340

RIBBLE, ANNE HOERNER, info. rep.; b. Balt., Oct. 30, 1932; d. Jerold Kiser and Helen Blythe (Miller) Hoerner; B.A., Smith Coll., 1954; M.A., Harvard U., 1955; m. John C. Ribble, July 26, 1974; 1 dau. by previous marriage—Helen Blythe Strate. Tchr. English, Weston (Mass.) High Sch., 1955-57, tech. asst. IBM, N.Y.C., 1958-63, editor, Armonk and White Plains, N.Y., 1969-75, mgr. editorial services data processing div., White Plains, 1976-77, program adminstr. systems communications div., N.Y.C., 1977-78, staff tech. edn., fed. systems div., Houston, 1978-80, info. rep., 1980—. Mem. Manhattan County Com., Democratic party, 1961-62; co-chmn. English Teaching Program, N.Y. Jr. League, 1965-67, honored vol., 1968, bd. dirs. 1968-69; bd. dirs. Stanley Isaacs Community Center, 1968-72; vestry Ch. of Holy Trinity, N.Y.C., 1976-78. Mem. Internat. Assn. Bus. Communicators (pres. Houston chpt. 1982), Women's Profl. Assn. (bd. dirs. 1980-81). Home: 6200 Willers Way Houston TX 77057 Office: IBM 1322 Space Park Dr Houston TX 77058

RIBICOFF, BELLE K., ednl. adminstr.; b. N.Y.C., Nov. 22, 1924; d. Abraham and Mary (Poses) Krasne; B.A., Vassar Coll., 1945; m. Irving S. Ribicoff, 1955; children—Dara, Sarai (dec.). Asst. editor Mag. of Art, 1946-47; asso. editor Art News, 1948-49; editor-in-chief Art Digest, 1949-54, Craft Horizons, 1954-55; summer sch. faculty Radcliffe Coll., 1954, 55. Mem. Hartford (Conn.) Bd. Edn., 1961-67, v.p., 1962-63, 65-67; mem. Conn. Commn. Arts, 1965-71, chmn. edn. com., 1966-67, vice chmn., 1968-70, chmn., 1970; author, chmn. planning bd. Project Create, 1966-70; chmn. bd. Conn. Office Advocacy and Protection for Handicapped and Developmentally Disabled Persons, 1977-79; trustee Hartford Conservatory, 1960-63, incorporator, 1963—; bd. dirs. Hartford Stage Co., 1966-71, 77—; founding co-chmn. Friends of Vassar Coll. Art Gallery, 1973—; Charter mem. Nat. Council for Vassar Coll., 1980-82; bd. incorporators Wadsworth Atheneum, v.p. bd. dirs., chmn. ann. fund dr., mem. exec. com. Watkinson Sch.; bd. dirs. Hartford Art Sch., U. Hartford, 1977-80; bd. regents U. Hartford, 1978-80; dir. devel. Hartford Art Sch., 1980-82; asso. in devel. U. Hartford, 1982—; dir. Mott's Super Markets, Inc. Recipient Frank Jewett Mather award for critical writing Coll. Art Assn., 1954; Charter Oak Leadership medal Greater Hartford C. of C., 1968. Home: 56 Scarborough St Hartford CT 06105

RIBNER, MURIEL SOLOMON, bus exec., lawyer; b. N.Y.C., Mar. 8, 1924; d. Nathan Lewis and Lillian (Titan) Solomon; B.A., N.Y. U., 1945, LL.B., 1951; m. H. J. Coman, Aug. 15, 1945 (div. 1950); m. 2d Lloyd D. Ribner, Jan. 24, 1952 (div. 1978); children—Andrew B., Loyd D. Soc. editor Bronxville Rev.-Press, 1941-42; AP researcher Rockefeller Pl., N.Y.C., 1942-43; admitted to N.Y. State bar, 1951; partner Ribner Bus. Systems, N.Y.C., 1954-58; pres. Estey Corp., Englewood, N.J., 1976-80; v.p. Merry Traders, N.Y.C., 1981—; active trustee family trusts and investments. Democrat. Address: 444 E 57 St New York NY 10022

RICARDO-CAMPBELL, RITA (MRS. WESLEY GLENN CAMPBELL), educator; b. Boston, 1920; d. David and Elizabeth (Jones) Ricardo; B.S., Simmons Coll., 1941; M.A., Radcliffe Coll., 1945, Ph.D., 1946; m. Wesley Glenn Campbell, Sept. 15, 1946; children—Barbara Lee, Diane Rita, Nancy Elizabeth. Instr., Harvard, 1946-48; asst. prof. Tufts, 1948-51; labor economist U.S. Wage Stblzn. Bd., 1951-53; economist ways and means com. U.S. Ho. of Reps., 1953; cons. economist, 1957-60; vis. prof. San Jose State Coll., 1960-61; sr. fellow Hoover Instn. on War, Revolution and Peace, Stanford, 1968—; lectr. Health Services Adminstrn., Stanford Med. Sch., 1973-78; dir. Watkins-Johnson Co., Palo Alto, Calif., Gillette Co., Boston. Commr., Western Interstate Commn. for Higher Edn., Calif., 1967-75, chmn., 1970-71; mem. Pres. Nixon's Adv. Council on Status Women, 1969-76; mem. task force on taxation Pres. Council on Environ. Quality, 1970-72; mem. Pres.'s Com. Health Services Industry, 1971-73, FDA Nat. Adv. Drug Com., 1972-75, Pres.' Econ. Policy Adv. Bd., 1981—, Nat. Council on Humanities, 1982—. Bd. dirs. Ind. Colls. No. Calif., 1971—; mem. com. assessment of safety, benefits, risks Citizens' Commn. Sci., Law and Food Supply, Rockefeller U., 1973-75; mem. adv. com. Center Health Policy Research, Am. Enterprise Inst. Pub. Policy Research, Washington, 1974-80; mem. adv. council on social security HEW, 1974-75; bd. dirs. Simmons Coll. Corp., Boston, 1975-80; mem. adv. council, bd. assos. Stanford Libraries, 1975-78; mem. council SRI Internat., Menlo Park, Calif., 1977—. Mem. Am. Econ. Assn., Mont Pelerin Soc., Phi Beta Kappa. Author: Voluntary Health Insurance in the United States, 1960; Economics of Health and Public Policy, 1971; Food Safety Regulation: Use and Limitations of Cost-Benefit Analysis, 1974; Drug Lag: Federal Government Decision Making, 1976; Social Security: Promise and Reality, 1977; The Economics and Politics of Health, 1982; contbr. articles to profl. jours. Home: 26915 Alejandro Dr Los Altos Hills CA 94022 Office: Hoover Instn Stanford CA 94305

RICCA, LINDA HIGGINS, nurse, hosp. adminstr.; b. Houston, Dec. 16, 1952; d. John Oliver and Doris Louise (Paty) Higgins; student Stephen F. Austin U., 1971-73, U. Houston, 1973-74; B.S. in Nursing, Houston Bapt. U., 1977; postgrad. in bus. adminstrn. U. Houston; m. John Bernard Ricca, Sept. 6, 1980. Staff nurse neonatal ICU, Hermann Hosp., Houston, 1977-79, with computerized info. system (MIS), 1980-82, dir. computerized med. info. system, 1981—; cons. area hosps. on MIS. Active local polit. campaigns. Mem. ARC, Am. Mgmt. Assn., Nat. Assn. Female Execs. Republican. Lutheran. Club: Church Couples. Home: 9907 Sagegate Houston TX 77089 Office: 1203 Ross Sterling St Houston TX 77030

RICE, ALICE MARIE, constrn. co. exec.; b. Cullman, Ala., Sept. 15, 1942; d. Joseph Cycrl and Opal Hazel (Schultz) Lane; student Anderson Bus. Coll., 1961-62, John C. Calhoun Jr. Coll., 1962-63; m. Charles Aubrey Rice, May 25, 1979; children by previous marriage—David Timothy Howell, Tammy Marie Howell. PBX operator Baugh-Wiley-Smith Hosp., Decatur, Ala., 1961-62; exec. sec. Compton Co., Decatur, 1962—; office mgr. Compton Constrn. Co., Inc., Decatur, 1962—; corp. sec. Westmeade, Inc., Decatur, 1979—. Mem. Nat. Secs. Assn., Morgan County Bd. Realtors. Republican. Home: 2265 Westmeade Dr SW Decatur AL 35603 Office: 1540 4th Ave SE Decatur AL 35601

RICE, BETTYE FOUST, phys. therapist; b. Delphi, Ind., Feb. 5, 1922; d. Jay Laurel and Eveth Deane (Hamil) Foust; B.A., Tex. Woman's U., 1942, B.S., 1942; cert. in phys. therapy Walter Reed Gen. Hosp., 1945; postgrad. Baylor U., 1947; children—John A., Ruby. With VA Hosp., Waco, Tex., 1946-47, U. Tex. Med. Br., Galveston, 1948-52; pvt. practice phys. therapy, Clovis, N.Mex., 1952-54; with Physician's Phys. Therapy Service, Houston, 1955-56; founder dept., phys. therapist St. Mary's Infirmary, Galveston, 1956-61; founder phys. therapy dept. Knapp Meml Meth Hosp., Weslaco, Tex., 1961, dept. mgr., 1961—. Served with U.S. Army, 1944-46. Recipient Employee of Yr. award Knapp Meml. Meth. Hosp., 1973. Mem. Am. Phys. Therapy Assn., Tex. Phys. Therapy Assn. (Ruby Decker award 1968), Tex. Woman's U. Alumnae Assn. Republican. Methodist. Clubs: Rebekah, Order of Eastern Star. Home: 330 Granada St San Benito TX 78586 Office: Knapp Meml Meth Hosp Weslaco TX 78596

RICE, BOBBYLYNE, sch. social worker; b. Selma, Ala., Oct. 5, 1936; d. Robert Henry and Pauline (Heade) R.; student Ala. State U., 1953-54, 70; B.A., Calif. State U., San Francisco, 1973; M.S.W., San Francisco State U., 1975; 1 dau., Deirdra. Various positions in industry, 1963-71; tchr. San Francisco Unified Sch. Dist., 1972-76, sch. social worker, 1976—; chmn. alumni community support group, dept. social work edn. San Francisco State U., 1978—; mem. com. child care relative issues, joint legis. task force Nat. Assn. Social Workers-Calif. Assn. Sch. Social Workers, 1978—. Mem. Nat. Assn. Social Workers, Calif. Assn. Sch. Social Workers (treas., dir. 1978-79), San Francisco Black Tchrs. Caucus, San Francisco Classroom Tchrs. Assn. Democrat. Roman Catholic. Home: 1305 Laguna St San Francisco CA 94115 Office: 135 Van Ness Ave Room 34 San Francisco CA 94102

RICE, DOROTHY PECHMAN (MRS. JOHN DONALD), med. economist; b. Bklyn., June 11, 1922; d. Gershon and Lena (Schiff) Pechman; student Bklyn. Coll., 1938-39; B.A., U. Wis., 1941; D.Sc. (hon.), Coll. Medicine and Dentistry N.J., 1979; m. John Donald Rice, Apr. 3, 1943; children—Kenneth D., Donald B., Thomas H. With hosp. and med. facilities USPHS, Washington, 1960-61; med. econs. studies Social Security Adminstrn., 1962-63, health econs. br. Community Health Service, USPHS, 1964-65; chief health ins. research br. Social Security Adminstrn., 1966-72, dep. asst. commr. research and stats., 1972-75; dir. Nat. Center Health Stats., Rockville, Md., 1976-82; regent's lectr. dept. social and behavioral scis. Sch. Nursing, U. Calif., San Francisco, 1982—. Recipient Social Security Adminstrn. citation, 1968, Disting. Service medal HEW, 1974; award Jack C. Massey Found., 1978. Fellow Am. Public Health Assn. (Domestic award for excellence 1978), Am. Statis. Assn.; mem. Inst. Medicine, Am. Econ. Assn., Population Assn. Am., LWV. Developer health ins. research program Social Security Adminstrn. Contbr. articles to profl. jours. Home: 1055 Amito Ave Berkeley CA 94705 Office: Sch Nursing N631 San Francisco CA 94143

RICE, EDGENIE HIGGINS, ednl. and arts cons.; b. Worcester, Mass., Feb. 8, 1942; d. Milton Prince and Alice Lord (Coonley) Higgins; A.A., Bradford Coll., 1962; cert. Ecole du Louvre, France, 1963; B.A., Boston U., 1965; m. Donald Sands Rice, Aug. 27, 1966; children—Alice Higgins, Edgenie Reynolds. Exhibits coordinator Smithsonian Inst. Traveling Exhibition Service, 1966-67; visual arts coordinator N.Y. State Council on the Arts, N.Y.C., 1967-70; asst. dir. Community Environments, N.Y.C., 1970-71; cons. Mus. Collaborative, N.Y.C., 1972; originator, dir. UN-US Mother-Child Workshop, N.Y.C., 1972-81. Bd. dirs. YWCA, N.Y.C., 1972—, chmn. vol. com., 1979-81, exec. com., 1976-77, 78—; mem. program com. World Mut. Service Com., 1972-76, vice chmn. program com., 1982—, chmn. visitors service for nat. bd., 1971-72; mem. jr. council Mus. Modern Art, 1973-76; mem. grants com. Ch. of the Heavenly Rest, 1979-81; mem. benefit com. Cooper-Hewitt Nat. Mus. Design, Legal Aid Soc., YWCA-YMCA Camping Council; parents league rep. Chapin Sch., 1980-81; trustee, mem. arts and student affairs coms. Clark U., Worcester, Mass., 1981—; pres. Civitas, 1982—. Clubs: Cosmopolitan, The River.

RICE, E(UNICE) JEAN, comml. bank exec.; b. Corbin, Ky., Nov. 8, 1933; d. Hiriam and Agnes M. Reynolds; consumer credit cert. Kent State U., 1979; cert. Ohio State U. Sch. Banking, 1981; m. Richard D. Rice, July 31, 1954; Teller, sec. Cardinal Fed. Savs. & Loan Assn., Vermilion, Ohio, 1970-76; sec. Lorain County Savs. & Trust Co., Vermilion, 1976-78, asst. mgr., br. mgr., 1978-82, br. mgr., asst. sec., 1982—. Bd. dirs. Vermilion YMCA, 1980—. Mem. Am. Inst. Banking, Vermilion C. of C. (dir. 1978—), Am. Fedn. Women's Clubs. Republican. Lutheran. Home: 4958 Southview Dr Vermilion OH 44089 Office: Lorain County Savs & Trust Co 4530 Liberty Ave Vermilion OH 44089

RICE, GEORGIA RUTH DOBROVOLNY, supt. schs.; b. N.D., 1936; student U. N.D., 1954; B.A. in Secondary Edn., Eastern Mont. Coll., Billings, 1957; postgrad. U. N.D., Minot Extension, 1962-63, U. Wash., 1967, U. Idaho, 1968, No. Mont. Coll., 1970, Central Mo. State U., 1970, 75, So. Ill. U., 1971, Mont. State U., 1972-75, U. Pa., 1974, Dickinson State Coll., 1975. Tchr., Billings Central High Sch., 1957, Green River (Wyo.) High Sch., 1958, Vallejo (Calif.) High Sch., 1958-59, Minot Jr. High Sch., 1959-60, Ramstad Jr. High Sch., Minot, 1960-62; supr. high sch. and adult traffic edn. program Havre (Mont.) High Sch., 1963-73; faculty Mont. State U., 1973-75; asst. traffic edn. and pupil transp. safety supr. Office Supt. Pub. Instrn., Helena, Mont., 1973-75, pupil transp. safety supr., 1975-76, supt. pub. instrn., 1977—; co-chmn. N.W. Regional Conf. for Am. Driver and Traffic Safety Edn. Assn.; condr. N.W. Conf. for traffic safety edn.; project dir. for devel. Sch. Bus. Driver

Edn. Program for Mont.; mem. Bd. Pub. Edn., Bd. Regents, State Library Commn., Tchrs. Retirement Bd., State Bd. Land Commrs. Recipient Distinguished Service award Mont. Pupil Transp. Conf., 1976, award for outstanding service Mont. Sch. Bus Contractors Assn., 1976. Mem. Nat. Pupil Transp. Assn., Am. Driver and Traffic Safety Edn. Assn. (nat. bd.), Am., Mont., Minot, Havre (charter) fedns. tchrs., League Women Voters (publs. mgr.), Mont. Traffic Edn. Assn. (pub. relations mgr.), Am. Legion Aux., Am., Mont. (v.p.) assns. health, phys. edn. and recreation, Nat., Mont. edn. assns., Burlington No. Credit Union, Am. Bicycle Assn., Nat. Safety Council, N.D. Traffic Edn. Assn. (charter), Mont. Sch. Bus Drivers Assn. Contbr. articles to state and nat. publs. Office: Office Supt Public Instrn Room 106 State Capitol Helena MT 59601 *

RICE, GERI EILEEN, mgmt. cons.; b. Chgo., Apr. 13, 1947; d. Benjamin Louis and Perle Bertha Friedman; student, So. Ill. U., 1966-68, DePaul U., 1978-80; Legal Asst. Cert. with honors, Mallinckrodt Coll., 1975. Legal asst. law dept. Urban Investment and Devel. Co., Chgo., 1972-79; law office mgr. Coffield Ungaretti Harris & Slavin, Chgo., 1979-80; law office adminstr. Dinkelspiel & Dinkelspiel, San Francisco, 1980-82; mgmt. cons., San Francisco, 1982—; mem. faculty Practising Law Inst., N.Y.C., 1978-79; mem. adv. com., lectr. Mallinckrodt Coll., Harper Coll., 1977-79; mem. faculty Paralegal Tng. and Resource Center, San Francisco, 1981—, San Francisco State U., 1982—. Mem. Ill. Paralegal Assn. (dir. 1976-79; pres. 1977-79), Nat. Fedn. Paralegal Assns. (chmn. com.), Assn. Legal Adminstrs. (co-chmn. edn. com., dir. 1981—, treas. 1982—). Office: 55 Sutter St Suite 416 San Francisco CA 94104

RICE, HILDRED ATKINSON, city ofcl.; b. Portland, Oreg., Dec. 30, 1907; d. Thomas and Rose Hilda Atkinson; B.S. in Vocat. Sci., Oreg. State U., 1931; summer postgrad. in dance U. Pacific, 1954-57, 71-77, Lewis and Clark Coll., 1959-60; m. Arthur John Rice, Dec. 16, 1939; With Corvallis (Oreg.) Parks and Recreation Dept., 1952—, dance specialist, 1966—. Mem. Am. Assn. Health, Phys. Edn. and Dance, Northwest Folkdancers (hon.), Folk Dance Fedn. Oreg. Home: 2415 NW 13th St Corvallis OR 97330

RICE, JEAN C., public relations exec.; b. Adairsville, Ga., Sept. 4, 1930; d. Fite H. and Nettie Mae (Adcock) Casey; A.B., U. Ga., 1951; m. Edward J. Rice, Dec. 12, 1952. With Cotton Producers Assn. (name changed to Gold Kist, Inc.), Atlanta, 1951—, v.p. public relations and advt., 1972-81, v.p., 1981—. Trustee, Am. Inst. Cooperation; mem. communications com. Fertilizer Inst.; mem. adv. com. Sunbelt Agrl. Expn., Moultrie, Ga. Mem. Nat. Agri-Mktg. Assn., Nat. Farm-City Council, Nat. Council Farmer Coops., Am. Feed Mfrs. Assn., Advt. Council Coops. Baptist. Gold Kist Inc Atlanta 244 Perimeter Center Pkwy NE Atlanta GA 30346

RICE, JENNIFER SUSAN, devel., public relations exec.; b. Houston, Jan. 18, 1951; d. Myer and Rose (Forrest) R.; B.A. with honors, U. Tex., Austin, 1972, M.A. in Communications, 1974. Dist. exec. dir. Am. Cancer Soc., Austin, Tex., 1974-75, br. dir., Miami, Fla., 1975-76; dir. public info./research Urban League Greater Miami, 1976-77; mental health planning cons., communications coordinator Miami Jewish Home and Hosp. for Aged, 1977-79; dir. public relations and devel. James Archer Smith Hosp., Homestead, Fla., 1979-81; asso. dir. N.J. region Deborah Hosp. Found., Browns Mills, N.J., 1981—. Mem. public edn. com. Am. Cancer Soc.; mem. Child Abuse Task Force, Mental Health Assn. NIMH fellow, 1972. Mem. Public Relations Soc. Am., Nat. Assn. Hosp. Devel., Nat. Soc. Fund Raising Execs., Fla. Hosp. Assn., S. Fla. Hosp. Public Relations Assn., Internat. Assn. Bus. Communicators (pres. S. Fla. chpt.), Phi Kappa Phi. Home: 7 W Central Ave Moorestown NJ 08057 Office: Deborah Hosp Found Browns Mills NJ 08015

RICE, JOY KATHARINE, clin. psychologist, educator; b. Oak Park, Ill., Mar. 26, 1939; d. Joseph Theodore and Margaret Sophia (Bednarik) Straka; student Rosary Coll., 1956-57; B.F.A. with high honors, U. Ill., 1960; M.S., U. Wis., Madison, 1962, M.S. (teaching fellow, Knapp fellow), 1964, Ph.D. (USPHS predoctoral fellow), 1967; m. David Gordon Rice, Sept. 1, 1962; children—Scott Alan, Andrew David. Asst. dir. U. Wis. Counseling Center, Madison, 1966-74, dir. Office of Continuing Edn. Services, 1972-78, prof. ednl. policy studies and women's studies, 1974—; pvt. practice psychology, 1967—; mem. State of Wis. Ednl. Approval Bd., 1972-73, Office of Career Edn. Adult Edn. Commn., Washington, 1978. Office of Edn. instnl. grantee, 1974-77. Mem. Am. Psychol. Assn., Wis. Psychol. Assn., Nat. Register Health Service Providers Psychology, Am. Ednl. Research Assn., Adult Edn. Assn. (merit service award 1978, 79, 80), Am. Assn. Higher Edn., Phi Delta Kappa. Mem. editorial bd. Lifelong Learning, 1979—; contbr. articles to profl. jours. Home: 4230 Waban Hill Madison WI 53711 Office: 243 Education Bldg University of Wisconsin Madison WI 53706

RICE, MARIE WALRATH, credit union exec.; b. Boston Corners, N.Y., Apr. 11, 1917; d. Milton Jane and Charlotte (McDonald) Walrath; grad. Nat. Floral Inst., 1963, Chgo. Sch. Restaurant Mgmt., 1963, Inst. Broadcasting Arts, 1969; m. Seward Nelson Rice, Dec. 26, 1940 (dec.). Acct., Lux Clock Mfg. Co., Waterbury, Conn., 1939-43, 45-51; with Pacific Telephone & Telegraph Co., Pomona, Calif., 1944-45, 51-63; supr. communications Pacific State Hosp., Pomona, 1964-72; treas.-mgr. Los Angeles County Grange Fed. Credit Union, San Dimas, Calif., 1974—. Recipient Commendation of Services, City of San Dimas, 1960, cert. of recognition for contbns. toward promoting the city City of San Dimas, 1963. Mem. Yucaipa Valley Bus. and Profl. Woman's Club, Ret. Public Employees' Assn. Calif., Nat. Assn. Female Execs., Am. Assn. Ret. Persons, Nat. Assn. Deaf, Calif. State Employees' Assn., Good Sam Recreational Vehicle Club, Golden State Mobilehome Owners League. Republican. Lutheran. Clubs: Grange, Yucaipa (Calif.) Women's. Home: 12220 5th St Apt 175 Yucaipa CA 92399 Office: 1123 Wehner Ln PO Box 416 San Dimas CA 91773

RICE, MARTHA B., ins. agy. exec.; b. Vienna, Va., Sept. 15, 1942; d. Clarence D. and Marjorie D. (Durham) Boyd; student So. Meth. U., 1960-61, N.Tex. State U., 1961-62; m. Earl D. Rice, Nov. 26, 1965; 1 dau., Jennifer L. Real estate agt. Henderson Realty, McLean, Va., 1966-69; owner, agt. Martha B. Rice, Ins., Great Falls, Va., 1972—. Mem. No.Va. Life Underwriters Assn., Nationwide Agts. Coop. Assn., Nat. Assn. Female Execs., Nat. Ins. Ind. Contractors Assn., Women Life Underwriters Conf. of Nat. Assn. Life Underwriters. Clubs: Riverbend Golf and Country, Glebe Harbor. Home: 431 Springvale Rd Great Falls VA 22066 Office: 766A Walker Rd Great Falls VA 22066

RICE, MATILDA M., psychiatrist; b. Bucarest, Romania, Sept. 28, 1931; d. Adolph and Fanny Holban; M.D., U. Bucarest, 1955; postgrad. N.Y. Sch. Psychiatry, 1965; m. Robert J. Rice, June 20, 1964; children—Danielle, Kristine. Dir. in-patient services dept. psychiatry Nassau County (N.Y.) Med. Center, 1967-76; med. dir. N.E. Nassau Alcoholism Counseling Services, 1977—; dir. psychiatry Nassau County Dept. Drug and Alcohol Addiction; med. dir. Roosevelt (N.Y.) Counseling Center; asst. clin. prof. psychiatry SUNY, Stony Brook. Recipient Spl. award Women for Sobriety. Fellow Am. Psychiat. Assn. (minority del. women at assembly); mem. Am. Med. Women's Assn., Am. Med. Soc. on Alcoholism, N.Y. State Med. Soc., L.I. Council on Alcoholism, Nassau Psychiat. Soc. (editor dist. br. newsletter). Home: 9 Bridle Path Dr Old Westbury NY 11568

RICE, PATRICIA BRITTINGHAM, real estate exec.; b. Guyton, Ga., July 14, 1941; d. Kenneth L. and Faye (McClelland) Brittingham; student DeKalb Coll., U. Ga.; m. Robert Leroy Rice, Dec. 12, 1969; children—Philip Charles, Debora Faye, Jeffrey Allan. Various corp. sec.-treas. and controller positions, positions, 1970-78; pres. Charles S. Roberts & Co., Atlanta, 1978—; corp. sec. Spalding & Co., Securities Brokers, Atlanta, 1980-81. Democrat. Presbyterian. Home: 155 Teepee Ln Lavonia GA 30553 Office: PO Box 28744 Atlanta GA 30328

RICE, ROMA JEAN, mag. editor; b. Lincoln, Nebr., Sept. 14, 1936; d. Conrad and Elizabeth (Brumm) Leichner; B.S. in Bus. Adminstrn., U. Nebr., 1958. Buyer, Macy's Mo.-Kans., 1958-65; adminstrv. asst. City Mgrs. Office Kansas City (Mo.), 1965-69; editor The Workbasket, Modern Handcraft, Inc., Kansas City, 1977—. Mem. Fashion Group, Independence Young Matrons, Eastern Jackson County Bar Aux., AAUW, Phi Chi Theta. Office: 4251 Pennsylvania St Kansas City MO 64111

RICE, RUTH DIANNE, perinatal psychologist; b. Oklahoma City, Mar. 29, 1924; d. Isaac Benson and Lela (Ward) R.; R.N., St. John's Hosp., Tulsa, 1949; cert. in neuropsychiat. nursing, Inst. Electro-Medizin, Rankweil, Austria, 1957-58; B.A. in Psychology summa cum laude, East Tex. State U., Commerce, 1965, M.A. magna cum laude, 1966; Ph.D., U. Tex., 1975; children—Sheri, Cynthia, Paul. Research dir. Tenn. Sch. Delinquent Girls, Nashville, 1966-67; research asst. Learning Disabilities Research Project, Greeley, Colo., 1967-68; dir. Psychol. Services Center, Harlingen, Tex., 1968-69; dir. Child Study Team, Dallas, 1971-72; asst. prof. U. Tex., Dallas, 1975-76; adj. asso. prof. East Tex. State U., 1976-78; research dir. Cradle Care, Inc., Dallas, 1975—; pvt. practice, 1975—; cons., lectr. in field; mem. profl. bd. Cesarian Awarness, Dallas Assn. Parent Edn., Kwanli Acad., Dallas Family Council. NDEA fellow, 1969. Mem. Am. Psychol. Assn., Am. Assn. Marriage and Family Therapists, Soc. Pediatric Psychology, Council Exceptional Children, Nat. Assn. Parents and Profls. Safe Alternatives in Childbirth, Southwestern Psychol. Assn. (award 1976), Sierra Club. Author teaching manuals, articles in field. Developer infant sensorimotor stimulation technique for premature/high risk infants used in U.S., Can., European hosps. Home: 6455 Meadow Rd Dallas TX 75230 Office: 6455 Meadow Rd Suite A Dallas TX 75230

RICE, SUSAN JOETTE, nurse; b. Topeka, Nov. 15, 1946; d. Claude Harvey and Martha May (McClellan) R.; student Pasadena Nazarene Coll., 1964-66; B.S. in Nursing, Calif. State U., Los Angeles, 1969, M.S.W., 1982. Staff nurse Children's Hosp. Los Angeles, 1969-75, asst. head nurse, 1972-74, nurse mgr., 1974-75; nursing unit coordinator newborn and neonatal intensive care nurseries, perinatal clinician Glendale (Calif.) Adventist Med. Center, 1976-78; neonatal clin. specialist Huntington Meml. Hosp., Pasadena, 1981—. Mem. Am. Assn. Critical Care Nurses, Calif. Perinatal Assn. Republican. Mem. Nazarene Ch. Home: 133 E Pamela Rd Monrovia CA 91016

RICE-AVILA, PATRICIA ANN, fin. planner; b. Aldrich, Mo., Aug. 24, 1946; d. William Wayne and Wilda Mae (Lowery) Rice; A.A., S.W. Baptist U., Bolivar, Mo., 1966; B.A., S.W. Mo. State U.; postgrad. Calif. State U., Fullerton; m. Anthony Avila III; children—Jessica Jean, Clifford Wayne, Jacqueline Marie. Office mgr. Patscheck-Veiga Constrn. Co., Tustin, Calif., 1972-75; asst. to controller Richards West Co., Newport Beach, Calif., 1976-78; acctg. supr. Warner Lambert Co., Anaheim, Calif., 1978-80, supr. fin. analysis and planning, 1980; mgr. fin. control Pepsi Cola, Torrance, Calif., 1980-82; sr. fin. planner Microdata Corp., Newport Beach, Calif., 1982—. Mem. Nat. Assn. Female Execs., Am. Prodn. and Inventory Control Soc., Am. Mgmt. Assn., NOW (chpt. program chmn. 1977), LaLeche League (chpt. publicity chmn. 1972-73). Democrat. Roman Catholic. Home: 24525 Kings Rd Laguna Niguel CA 92677 Office: 4000 MacArthur Blvd Newport Beach CA 92660

RICH, ADRIENNE, writer; b. Balt., May 16, 1929; d. Arnold Rice and Helen Elizabeth (Jones) R.; A.B., Radcliffe Coll., 1951; Litt.D. (hon.), Wheaton Coll., 1967; m. Alfred Conrad (dec. 1970); children—David, Paul, Jacob. Tchr. workshop YM-WHA Poetry Center, N.Y.C., 1966-67; vis. lectr. Swarthmore Coll., 1967-69; adj. prof. writing div. Columbia, 1967-69; lectr. Coll. City N.Y., 1968-70, instr., 1970-71, asst. prof. English, 1971-72, 74-75; Fannie Hurse vis. prof. creative lit. Brandeis U., 1972-73; prof. English Douglass Coll., Rutgers U., 1976—. Adv. bd. The Feminist Press. Recipient Yale Series of Younger Poets award, 1951; Ridgely Torrence Meml. award Poetry Soc. Am., 1955; Nat. Inst. Arts and Letters award poetry, 1961; Bess Hokin prize Poetry mag., 1963, Eunice Tietjens Meml. prize, 1968; Shelley Meml. award, 1971; Nat. Book award, 1974. Guggenheim fellow, 1952, 61; Amy Lowell traveling fellow, 1962; Bollingen Found. translation grantee, 1962; Nat. Translation Center grantee, 1968; Nat. Endowment for Arts grantee, 1970; Ingram Merrill Found. grantee, 1973-74; Lucy Martin Donnelly fellow Bryn Mawr Coll., 1975. Author: A Change of World, 1951; The Diamond Cutters and Other Poems, 1955; Snapshots of a Daughter-in-Law, 1963; Necessities of Life; Poems 1962-65, 1966; Leaflets; Poems 1965-68, 1969; The Will to Change, 1971; Diving into the Wreck, 1973; Poems Selected and New, 1950-74, 1975; Of Woman Born: Motherhood as Experience and Institution, 1976; The Dream of a Common Language: Poems 1974-77, 1978; contbg. editor: Chrysalis: A Magazine of Women's Culture; contbr. to numerous anthologies. Contbr. numerous articles, revs. to Jours. and mags. Address: care WW Norton Co 55 Fifth Ave New York NY 10003 *

RICH, DONNA BONEM, social worker; b. N.Y.C., Feb. 13, 1942; d. Morton and Margaret (Spott) Cohn; B.A. magna cum laude (Univ. scholar) U. R.I., 1963; M.S.W. (NIMH fellow) Hunter Coll., N.Y.C., 1976; Wilson Fund fellow, N.Y.U., 1963-64; m. Martin E. Rich, Oct. 15, 1978; children—Julia Bonem, Jane Bonem. Program asst. OEO, 1964-65; congressional asst., 1966-68; fin. aid coordinator SEEK program John Jay Coll. Criminal Justice, City U. N.Y., also asst. dir. Univ. Year ACTION program, 1972-75; staff mem. Henry St. Settlement, N.Y.C., 1976—, dir. devel., dir. govt. relations, 1980—; mem. faculty Hunter Coll. Sch. Social Work; fundraising cons. to social agys. Mem. N.Y. County Democratic Com., 1972—; trustee William Alanson White Inst. Mem. Acad. Cert. Social Workers, Nat. Assn. Social Workers. Home: 90 Riverside Dr New York NY 10024 Office: 265 Henry St New York NY 10002

RICH, DOROTHY, ednl. adminstr.; b. Monroe, Mich.; B.A. with Distinction in Journalism, Wayne State U., 1954; M.A., Columbia U., 1955; Ed.D., Cath. U. Am., 1976; m. Spencer Rich, 1956; children—Rebecca, Jessica. Designer, instr. writing program U. Va., 1961-73; mem. faculty edn. Cath. U. Am., 1971; founder, dir. Home and Sch. Inst., Trinity Coll., Washington, 1972—, program developer, 1964—, cons. family and community service programs, 1964—; condr. workshops in family based home learning, 1971—. Workshops in basic skills-career devel., 1964—; guest lectr. various schs. and colls., 1971—; mgmt. and tng. cons. U.S. Office Edn. Tchrs. Corps, 1973—; mem. Forum HEW work groups, mem. Smithsonian Forums, 1976-80. Trustee Nat. Child Research Center, Washington, 1966-72. Recipient Nat. Edn. Writers award, 1972, Charles Stewart Mott spl. citation award, 1975, Greater Washington Sch. Bell award, 1970. Mem. Edn. Writer's Assn. Am., Nat. Community Edn. Assn., Assn. for Women in Govt. Contractors. Author: A Family Affair: Education, 1977; The Three R's Plus, 1978; Families as Educators of their Own Children, 1979; Families Learning Together, 1980; Bright Idea, 1981; contbr. articles on edn. to profl. publs. Home: 3301 Newark St NW Washington DC 20008 Office: Home and School Inst Spl Projects Office 1201 16th St NW Washington DC 20036

RICH, HELEN WALL (MRS. ARTHUR L. RICH), educator; b. Chester, S.C., May 4, 1912; d. George Addison and Georgia (Hardin) Wall; student Queen's Coll., 1930-32; B.S. summa cum laude, Catawba Coll., 1934; diploma in piano playing Juilliard Sch. Music, 1938; diplomas Christiansen Choral Sch., 1950, 51; m. Arthur Lowndes Rich, July 26, 1934; children—Arthur Lowndes, Ruth Anne. Instr. music Catawba Coll., Salisbury, N.C., 1934-43; univ. organist Mercer U., Macon, Ga., 1944-50, asst. prof. music, 1950-73, prof. emeritus, 1973—; organ recitalist throughout S.E.; v.p. Tudor Apts., Inc., Atlanta, 1960-73; pres. Biscayne Apts., Atlanta, 1976—. Mem. Federated Music Clubs (hon.; chmn. scholarship contest), Ga. Piano Tchrs. Guild, Nat. Assn. Schs. Music (asso.), Am. Coll. and Univ. Concert Mgrs. Assn. (asso.), Cardinal Key Soc. Mercer U. (hon.), Delta Omicron. Club: Morning Music (Macon, dir.). Home: 369 Candler Dr Macon GA 31204

RICH, JAYNE THOMAS, coll. police ofcl.; b. Washington, Sept. 19, 1927; d. Charles Murdaugh and Lelia Marie (Scott) Thomas; B.S., U. D.C., 1948; postgrad. U. Pa., 1975-76, N.Y. U., 1981—; m. Apr. 23, 1955 (div.); 1 son, John William, IV. Claims analyst Social Security Adminstrn., Wheeling, W.Va. and Washington, 1952-53; police officer Met.Police Dept., Washington, 1953-72, advanced through grades to lt., 1966; adminstrv. asst. Washington Hosp. Center, 1972-74; chief of staff/security specialist Campus Police U. Pa., Phila., 1974-75; sr. asso., cons. Univ. Research Corp., Washington, 1976-77; pres., cons. Jay Rich Assos., Washington, 1977-78; chief of police Montclair State Coll., 1978—; instr. U. D.C., 1972-74; cons., tchr. in field; designer, producer workshops in field. Mem. Montclair Housing Commn., 1979-81; bd. dirs. Women of Montclair State Coll., 1979-81; bd. dirs. LWV, Montclair, 1981-82, chairperson com. adminstrn. justice 1981-82; trustee Montclair YWCA, 1981-82. Recipient Community Service award Iota Phi Lambda, 1972, Merit Performance award Montclair State Coll., 1980; named Unsung Heroine for Excellence in Law, NAACP, 1981, Black Pioneer in N.J. in field of law Delta Sigma Theta, 1980. Mem. Nat. Orgn. Victim Assitance (life; dir. 1967-81), Police Assn. D.C., Internat. Assn. Chiefs of Police, Am. Soc. Indsl. Security, N.J. Assn. Affirmative Action in Higher Edn., Internat. Assn. Campus Law Enforcement Adminstrs., N.E. Assn. Colls. and Univs. Security Dirs., Nat. Assn. Black Law Enforcement Execs., Internat. Assn. Women Police (dir.), N.J./N.Y. Assn. Women Police (pres.), Madison Ave. Civic Group, Alpha Kappa Alpha. Democrat. Presbyterian. Author: Take Care: Common Sense in Self Defense for Today's Woman, 1976; contbr. chpt. to book. Home: 55 Madison Ave Montclair NJ 07042 Montclair State Coll Valley Rd and Normal Ave Upper Montclair NJ 07043

RICH, KAREN ELAINE, quality control, analytical chemist; b. Glendale, W.Va., Nov. 21, 1955; d. Rocco Louis and Helen Elaine (Filter) Rich; B.A. in Chemistry, Seton Hill Coll., 1978; postgrad. John Carroll U. (grad. scholar), 1978-79, Cleve. State U., 1979—. Lab. technician Ohio Valley Med. Center, Wheeling, W.Va., 1977-78; lab instr., teaching asst. John Carroll U., Cleve., 1978-79; lab technician Mangill Chems. Cleve., 1979, quality control/analytical chemist, 1979-82; analytical research chemist Franklin Oil Corp., Bedford, Ohio, 1982—; cons. acquisition of instrumentation. Participant various seminars. Mgr. Girl's Little League Softball Team, 1979—. Mem. Am. Chem. Soc., AAAS. Home: 6501 Marsol Rd

RICH, LYNNE DIANE, psychologist; b. N.Y.C., Nov. 20, 1947; d. Murray Louis and Sally (Neiderbach) R.; B.A., Mich. State U., 1969, Ph.D., 1979. Intern in counseling U. Wis., Oshkosh, 1971-72; grad. teaching and research asst. Mich. State U., East Lansing, 1969-71, 72-75; psychotherapist, diagnostician Psychol. Evaluation and Treatment Center, Lansing, Mich., part-time, 1973-76; clin. psychologist Ingham Community Mental Health Center, Lansing, 1973-75; psychotherapist, diagnostician Genesee Psychiat. Center, Flint, Mich., 1975-79; Mich. Analytic Cons. Outpatient Clinic, Howell, Mich., 1979-81; psychol. cons. McPherson Hosp.; postdoctoral fellow in neuropsychology Inst. Rehab. Medicine, N.Y.C., 1981-82. Mich. State U. fellow, 1975. Mem. Am. Psychol. Assn., Internat. Neuropsychol. Soc., ACLU, NOW. Author booklet: How Psychotherapy Works, 1979. Home: 601A Coraydor Ave Norfolk VA 23507 Office: Inst Rehab Medicine NY U Med Center 400 E 34th St New York NY 10016

RICH, MONICA JANE, architect, artist; b. N.Y.C., Dec. 22, 1953; d. Martin and Maria F. Rich; B.Arch., Cornell U., 1976. Jr. designer Russell Johnson, Acoustician and Theater Cons., 1976-77; designer Janko Rasic Architect, N.Y.C., 1977-80, Ulrich Franzen Architect, N.Y.C., 1980-81; sr. designer Lawrence Horowitz Architect, N.Y.C., 1981—; artist, paintings in collections of Thomas Hoving, SUNY Fredonia and Stefan Zweig Room (Salzburg).

RICHARD, BETTI, sculptor; b. N.Y.C., Mar. 16, 1916; d. Edwin H. and Therese (Schramm) R.; student Art Students League, N.Y.C., 1935-40; pupil of Paul Manship; m. Franz Matsch, July 2, 1953 (dec. July 1973). Exhbns. throughout U.S. and Europe, 1942—; prin. works include bronze doors Ch. Immaculate Conception, N.Y.C.; bronze statue Cardinal Gibbons, Balt.; St. Francis statue St. Francis Assisi Ch., N.Y.C.; marble madonna House Theology, Centerville, Ohio; 3 ornamental panels Bellingrath Gardens, Mobile; marble madonna with child Rosary Hill Coll., Buffalo; St. Francis statue Our Lady Angels Convent, Aston, Pa.; busts of Wagner, Mozart and Rudolf Bing, Met. Opera; bronze St. Francis, St. Francis Interfaith Center, Auraria Higher Edn. Complex, Denver; also works in mus., pvt. collections, U.S. and Europe, including Phoenix Art Mus., San Joachin Pioneer Mus. and Haggin Art Galleries, Stockton, Calif., Eureka (Ill.) Coll., Met. Opera, N.Y.C.; v.p. Archtl. League, N.Y.C., 1961-63; bd. dirs. Fine Arts Fedn. N.Y., 1973-74, chmn. nominating com., 1979—. Recipient Barnett prize Nat. Acad., 1946; Lindsay Morris prize, 1974; decorated Cross of Honor for Sci. and Art (Austria). Fellow Nat. Sculpture Soc. (sec. 1970-73, del. to Fine Arts Fedn. 1978—; rec. sec. 1979—; John Gregory award 1960); mem. Allied Artists Am. (Gold medal sculpture 1956), Artists Equity, Audubon Artists, Austrian Am. Fedn. (hon.). Clubs: Cosmopolitan, Colony (N.Y.C.). Address: 131 E 66th St New York NY 10021

RICHARD, LINDA JEAN GRIFFETH, farmer, former health center adminstr.; b. Beloit, Kans., Feb. 24, 1950; d. Robert Mahlon and Miola Louise (Shane) G.; student Kans. State U., 1968-70; secretarial and data processing cert. North Central Kans. Area Vocat. Tech. Sch., 1971; m. Charles Michael Richard, Apr. 25, 1980; 1 son, Casey Robert. Sec.-bookkeeper, Campbell Distbrs., Manhattan, Kans., 1971-72; exec. sec. St. Joseph Hosp., Concordia, Kans., 1973-76; sec. Sunflower Mental Health Center, Concordia, 1976-77, office mgr., 1977-80; co-mgr. Hog Farm, 1980—. Mem. Women, Inc., (chairperson chpt. 1979-80). Methodist. Clubs: Miltonville Young Farm Wives (sec.-treas. 1982-83), Women of Moose (Concordia, Kans.). Home: Rural Route 2 Box 33 Miltonvale KS 67466

RICHARDS, ARLENE KRAMER, psychologist, psychoanalyst; b. N.Y.C., June 24, 1935; d. Emanuel and Edith (Burstein) Kramer; m. Arnold Richards, Mar. 21, 1954; children—Stephen, Rebecca, Tamar. Mem. faculty Jewish Bd. Child and Family Services, Inst. for Psychoanalytic Tng. and Research; prof. Sch. Social Work, Smith Coll. Mem. Am. Psychol. Assn., Inst. for Psychoanalytic Tng. and Research, N.Y. Freudian Soc. Author: (with Irene Willis) How To Get It Together when your Parents Are Coming Apart, 1975, Boy Friends, Girl Friends, Just Friends, 1978, Leaving Home, 1982. Home: 50 E 89th St New York NY 10023 Office: 40 E 89th St New York NY 10023

RICHARDS, CHRISTINE-LOUISE, artist, music pub. co. exec.; b. Radnor, Pa., Jan. 11, 1910; d. Joseph Ernest and Catherine (Fletcher) R.; student pvt. schs., art schs., N.Y.C., Munich, Ger. One-woman shows: Stockbridge, Mass., 1947, 48, 52, 53, Oneonta, N.Y., 1960, 61; group shows include: Stockbridge Art Assn., 1931-32; represented in collections, Calif., Mass., N.Y.; owner, founder, pres. Blue Star Music Pub. Co., Pittsfield, Mass., 1946—, now Morris, N.Y. Recipient Silver medal Internat. Inst. Community Service, Cambridge, Eng. Fellow Internat. Biog. Assn.; mem. Phila. Art Alliance, Am. Fedn. Musicians, Nightingale-Bamford Alumni Assn., Academia Italia delle arte e del Lavoro (recipient gold medal), Met. Mus. Art, Audubon Soc., Nat. Assn. Composers USA, Emergency Aid of Pa., Pa. Acad. Fine Arts, others. Club: Peale (Phila.). Author: The Blue Star Fairy Book of Stories for Children; The Blue Star Fairy Book of More Stories for Children; The Blue Star Fairy Book of New Stories for Children, 1980. Composer: (song) What Makes Me Dream of You, 1950, numerous others. Contbr. portrait to Artists U.S.A., 1970-71, 76. Address: Blue Star Music PO Box 185 Morris NY 13808

RICHARDS, CORY DANA, mktg. exec.; b. Los Angeles, July 30, 1955; d. Alfred and Meryl Jean (Weinman) R.; B.A. with honors in Advt./Communications (Calif. State scholar 1973-77, Ballet Assn. scholar 1973-77), U. Calif., Santa Cruz, 1977; postgrad. Loyola Marymount U. Account exec. Public Media Center, San Francisco, 1974-77; public affairs adv. Calbe Channel 6, San Francisco, 1976-77; cons. on public affairs to radio stas., Los Angeles, 1977-78; dir. mktg., product mgr. MCA Records, Los Angeles, 1978-80; dir. mktg. Hang Ten Internat., San Diego, after 1980; now asst. to chmn., dir. advt. Carole Little for Saint Tropez West; asso. producer Live from Gilley's radio show; speaker on women in music UCLA Extension. Vol. nutritionist, tchr. slim living program, fund-raising team capt. YMCA, Los Angeles. Recipient spl. recognition award Cowell Health Center, 1976. Mem. Interfaith Council San Fernando Valley, Women in Bus., Nat. Country Music Assn., Sales and Mktg. Execs., Now. Club: N.Y. Publicity. Home: 536 N Sweetzer Ave Los Angeles CA 90048 Office: Los Angeles CA 90048

RICHARDS, ELISABETH MUIR, mfg. co. exec.; b. Worcester, Mass., Nov. 9, 1913; d. Joseph N. and Mabel E. (Robinson) Muir; B.A., Wellesley Coll., 1935; m. Mervyn E. Richards, June 10, 1939; children—Elisabeth, David, John, William (dec.). With Muir's Laundry, Inc., Worcester, 1936-80, treas., 1940-80, dir., 1940—; pres., treas. Cadet Labs., Inc., Worcester, 1974—. Western Mass. rep. Nat. Cathedral Assn., 1979—; class of 1935 reunion chmn. Wellesley Coll., 1980, reunion gift chmn., 1981—. Mem. Internat. Dry Cleaners Congress. Republican. Episcopalian. Club: Soroptimist, Paxton Women's, Worcester Woman's, Cape Cod Wellesley. Home: 205 Pleasant St Paxton MA 01612

RICHARDS, JANET ALICE, high sch. tchr.; b. Honesdale, Pa., Sept. 18, 1936; d. Wesley A. and Dorothy Alice (Robinson) Orth; B.S., East Stroudsburg (Pa.) State Coll., 1958, M.Ed., 1969; M.S., State Univ. Coll. New Paltz, N.Y., 1964; m. Lawrence D. Richards, Aug. 18, 1962. Tchr. schs. in N.J., 1958-59; mem. faculty Minisink Valley High Sch., Slate Hill, N.Y., 1959—, tchr. chemistry, 1964—, head sci. dept., 1967—. Mem. Nat. Sci. Suprs. Assn., N.Y. State Sci. Tchrs. Assn., N.Y. State Sci. Suprs. Assn., Nat. Sci. Tchrs. Assn., Am. Chem. Soc., N.Y. State United Tchrs., Minisink Valley Tchrs. Assn. Home: 110 Hudson St Port Jervis NY 12771 Office: Box 217 Slate Hill NY 10973

RICHARDS, LACLAIRE LISSETTA JONES (MRS. GEORGE A. RICHARDS), social worker; b. Pine Bluff, Ark.; d. Artie William and Geraldine (Adams) Jones; B.A., Nat. Coll. Christian Workers, 1953; M.S.W., U. Kans., 1956; postgrad. Columbia U., 1960; m. George Alvarez Richards, July 26, 1958; children—Leslie Rosario, Lia Mercedes, Jorge Ferguson. Psychiat. supervisory, teaching, community orgn., adminstrv. and consultative duties Hastings Regional Center, Ingleside, Nebr., 1956-60; supervisory, consultative and adminstrv. responsibilities for psychiat. and geriatric patients VA Hosp., Knoxville, Iowa, 1960-74, field instr. for grad. students from U. Mo., EEO counselor, 1969-74, com. chmn., 1969-70, Fed. women's program coordinator, 1972-74; sr. social worker Mental Health Inst., Cherokee, Iowa, 1974-77; adj. asst. prof. dept. social behavior U. S.D.; instr. Augustana Coll.; outpatient social worker VA Med. and Regional Office Center, Sioux Falls, S.D., 1978—; EEO counselor. Mem. Knoxville Juvenile Adv. Com., 1963-65, 68-70, sec., 1965-66, chmn., 1966-68; sec. Urban Renewal Citizens' Adv. Com., Knoxville, 1966-68; mem. United Methodist Ch. Task Force Exptl. Styles Ministry and Leadership, 1973-74; counselor Knoxville Youth Line program; sec. exec. com. Vis. Nurse Assn., 1979-80; canvasser community fund drs., Knoxville; mem. Cherokee Civil Rights Commn. Fellow Royal Soc. Health; mem. Nat. Assn. Social Workers (co-chmn. Nebr. chpt. profl. standards com. 1958-59), Acad. Cert. Social Workers, S.D. Assn. Social Workers (chmn. minority affairs com., v.p. S.E. region 1980, pres. 1980-82), Nebr. Assn. Social Workers (chmn. 1958-59), AAUW (sec. Hastings chpt. 1958-60), AMA Aux., Seventh Dist. S.D. Med. Soc. Aux. Methodist (Sunday sch. tchr. adult div.; mem. commn. on edn.; mem. Core com. for adult edn.). Home: 1701 Ponderosa Dr Sioux Falls SD 57103

RICHARDS, LEORA FRANCES (BROOKS), corporate pilot, flight instr.; b. Louisville, Oct. 9, 1932; d. William Francis and Frances Mary (Nelson) Lucas; student U. Louisville, 1950-52; m. John L. Richards, 1952 (div. 1975); children—John L., Nancy Brooks, William Lucas, Jane McGowan. Flight instr. single and multi-engine planes, instruments Ky. Flying Service, Louisville, 1970—, charter pilot, 1972—; corporate pilot Luckett & Farley, Architects, 1977—; participant Powder Puff Derby, 1976, Angel Derby, 1977, Air Race Classic, 1977. Mem. Jr. League of Louisville, 1963-66; mem. ball group, charities com. Younger Women's Club, Louisville, 1962-68. Named Flight Instr. of Yr. in Ky., FAA, 1973. Mem. Air Craft Owners and Pilots Assn., Ninety Nines. Democrat. Episcopalian. Airline transport rating, 1974. Home: 577 Sunnyside Dr Louisville KY 40206

RICHARDS, MILDRED VERONNEAU, real estate broker; b. Meriden, Conn., Dec. 5, 1918; d. Henry August and Mary Theresa (Wollschlager) Veronneau; student Pequod Bus. Sch., 1936-37; grad. Realtors Inst., 1969; m. Joseph Maurice Richards, Oct. 26, 1940; children—Joseph M., Mark O., Christine M., Deborah R. Owner, mgr. Richards Agency, Meriden, 1961—; v.p. Invesco, Inc., Meriden, 1974-81, pres., 1981-82; sec. People's Mortgage of Meriden, Inc., 1972-73. Treas. Meriden Council Catholic Women, 1950-51; pres. St. Mary's Ch. Aux., 1952-53; bd. dirs. Meriden chpt. ARC, 1979—; bd. dirs. Meriden Public Health and Vis. Nurse Assn., 1950-55, 62-64, sec., 1954-55; mem. Meriden Bd. Edn., 1982—; mem. Conn. Task Force Housing for the Elderly. Cert. real estate brokerage mgr. Mem. Meriden Hosp. Women's Aux., Greater Meriden C. of C. (dir. 1977—), Central Conn. Bd. Realtors (past pres., Realtor of Year award 1973, 76), Conn. Assn. Realtors (dir. 1968—, sec. 1974-78, sr. v.p. 1978, pres.-elect 1978, pres. 1979), Nat. Assn. Realtors, Central Conn. Bd. Realtors (past sec., treas. 1981—) (dir. 1978), Realtors Nat. Mktg. Inst., Nat. Inst. Farm and Land Brokers, Women's Council Realtors (pres. local chpt. 1976—, nat. gov. 1977-78, chmn. by-laws com. 1978), Greater Meriden C. of C. (dir. 1977-80). Clubs: Meriden Women's, Charity. Home: 14 William Ave Meriden CT 06450 Office: 247 S Broad St Meriden CT 06450

RICHARDS, RHODA ROOT WAGNER, civic worker; b. Phila., Oct. 2, 1917; d. Edward Stephen and Rhoda Earley (Root) Wagner; student U. Pa., 1937-39; A.A., Wildcliff Jr. Coll., 1938; m. J. Permar Richards, Jr., May 18, 1940; children—Patricia A.V. Richards Cosgrave, J. Permar III. Profl. artist; founder, chmn. Hosp. Corps, Navy League Service, 1941-43; chmn. ARC Nurses Aide Corps, Jacksonville, Fla., 1944-45, Long Beach, Calif., 1945-46; founder, chmn. Fiesta Benefits, Hahnemann Hosp., 1950-57; former chmn. jr. com. Met. Opera; bd. dirs. Phila. Lyric Opera Co.; chmn. Ring for Freedom Republican Campaign of S.E. Pa., 1960; pres. Emergency Aid of Pa., 1961-64; v.p. bd. dirs. Inglis House, Phila., 1977-82; pres. women's bd. Phila. div. Am. Cancer Soc., 1978-81, hon. life mem.; founder, chmn. Community Activities Calendar, 1970-80; gen. chmn. 1st Ann. Washington Crossing Assembly, 1978; trustee Baldwin Sch.; co-chmn. fundraising com. Ambulatory Service Pavilion, Presbyn.-U. Pa. Med. Center; vice chmn. Women's Commn. for Bicentennial, 1976; bd. dirs., mem. Appleford Commn. Parsons-Banks Arboretum; bd. dirs. St. Johns Settlement House, 1954-81, Vol. Services for Blind, Phila. div. Am. Cancer Soc., 1978-81, Phila. chpt. Lupus Found., 1980-81; mem. Delaware Valley women's bd. Freedoms Found. at Valley Forge; past v.p. women's assn., past chmn. fin. com., chmn. centennial spl. event and gen. com. for the celebration Bryn Mawr Presbyn. Ch.; hon. col. corps of cadets Valley Forge Mil. Acad. and Jr. Coll.; chmn. Rittenhouse Preservation Coalition, 1982—. Recipient Crusade award Am. Cancer Soc., 1976; spl. award for community service St. John's Settlement House, 1977. Mem. Phila. Mus. Art, Pa. Acad. Fine Arts, Woodmere Art Gallery, Hahnemann Hosp. Women's Assn., DAR, Daus. of the Cincinnati, Dames of Loyal Legion, Nat. Soc. Colonial Dames of XVII Centuary (librarian), Dames Sovereign Mil. Order Temple of Jerusalem, Honolulu Mus. Art, Geneal. Soc. Pa., Am. Hist. Soc., Nat. Trust for Historic Preservation, Smithsonian Instn. Clubs: Sedgeley, Cosmopolitan, Peale, Safari, Bald Peak Colony. Home: 1250 Lafayette Rd PO Box 608 Bryn Mawr PA 19010

RICHARDS, RUTH FARNAN, educator, ret. govt. ofcl., educator; b. Worcester, Mass., Apr. 5, 1917; d. Amedee Oliver and Ruth M. (Farnan) R.; B.S., Worcester State Coll., 1938; M.A., Boston U., 1948; M.P.H., U. N.C., 1950. High sch. tchr., counselor, Framingham, Mass., 1938-48; officer naval intelligence USNR, Boston, Pearl Harbor, 1942-46; exchange tchr. Hutcheson's Girls Sch., Glasgow, Scotland, 1947-48; health educator Dist. Health Dept., Chapel Hill, N.C., 1950-51; health edn. cons. USPHS, HEW with rank of health services dir. div. chronic diseases, Oreg., Boston, Washington, regional health edn. cons., edn. officer office of dir., div. hosp. and med. facilities, Washington, 1951-76, dir. consultation br., div. facilities utilization, until 1976, ret., 1976; vis. prof. continuing edn. program U. N.C. Sch. Public Health; mem. Surg. Gen.'s Com. on Health Edn. in USPHS; prof., field work supr. Sch. Public Health, UCLA, 1976—, co-chmn. div. behavioral scis. and health edn., 1977-79. Pres., permanent sec. Coll. Class Worcester State Coll., 1934—; leader Algonquin council Girl Scouts U.S.A., 1940s; co-chmn. class Sch. Public Health U. N.C., 1950—; mem. Civic League, Framingham, 1939-49; mem. edn. com. Arthritis Assn., N.Y.C., 1962-64; mem. edn. com. Community Career Control; Los Angeles; mem. edn. com. March of Dimes. Recipient Commendation medal USPHS, 1969, Meritorious Service medal, 1973. Fellow Am. Public Health Assn., Soc. Public Health Edn. (com. chmn., past sec., v.p., bd. mem.); mem. Am. Hosp. Assn., Am. Heart Assn. (affiliate), Adult Edn. Assn., Am. Soc. Tng. and Devel., USPHS Commd. Officers Assn., Ret. Officers Assn., Kappa Delta Pi, Delta Kappa Gamma. Clubs: Framingham Women's, Framingham Cath. Woman's. Home: 1428 Oak St South Pasadena CA 91030 Office: Sch Public Health UCLA Los Angeles CA 90024

RICHARDS, SUZANNE VIRGINIA, lawyer; b. Columbia, S.C., Sept. 7, 1927; d. Raymond and Elise (Gray) R.; A.B., George Washington U., 1948, J.D. with distinction, 1957, LL.M., 1959. Admitted to D.C. bar, 1958; exec. asst. to pres. United Mine Workers Am., 1947-72; practice law, Washington, 1973—; mem. Jud. Conf. D.C., 1976-82. Recipient John Bell Larner award George Washington U. Law Sch., 1958. Mem. Bar Assn. D.C. (treas. 1979-81, sec. 1981-82, dir. 1982—), Women's Bar Assn. (pres. 1977-78, Woman Lawyer of Yr. 1977), Assn. Plaintiffs Trial Lawyers D.C. (gov. 1979-82, treas. 1982—), Am. Bar Assn., Fed. Bar Assn., Nat. Assn. Women Lawyers, Assn. Immigration and Nationality Lawyers. Home: 530 N St SW Washington DC 20024 Office: 1701 K St NW Washington DC 20006

RICHARDSON, ANNA FRANCES, savs. and loan exec.; b. Victoria, Mich., Aug. 25, 1905; d. Joseph Peter and Anna (Mravinec) Wertin; cert. bus. adminstrn. Platt Comml. Coll., 1925; m. Leo J. Urbanski, Oct. 6, 1945; m. Lloyd E. Richardson, June 23, 1973. Bookkeeper Provident Savs. & Loan Assn., St. Joseph, Mo., 1925-50, mgr.-sec., 1950—, dir., 1962—, sec. bd. dirs., 1972—. Active local charitable orgns. Mem. Mo. Savs. and Loan League (dir. 1944-45, 48-49, 50-52), Kansas City Savs. and Loan Controllers (sec. 1952-68), NOW, St. Joseph Woman's Bowling Assn. (dir. 1940-68, sec. 1940-68), Daus. of Isabella (regent 1945-47), Cath. Order Foresters, St. Ann's Altar Soc., Phi Eta. Clubs: St. Joseph Camera, Elizabeth Prescott (pres. 1972—). Home: 3101 Floral Ave Saint Joseph MO 64506 Office: 513 Francis St Saint Joseph MO 64501

RICHARDSON, BERTHA ANN, brokerage account exec.; b. Columbus, Ohio, June 12, 1928; d. Vernon F. and Helen E. (Hedges) R.; student Columbus public schs. Owner, Bertha Richardson Realty, 1956-77; account exec. Merrill Lynch Pierce Fenner & Smith, Columbus, Ohio, 1977—. Mem. Exec. Club. Home: 2687 St Patrick Rd Columbus OH 43204 Office: 100 E Broad St Columbus OH 43215

RICHARDSON, CONSTANCE COLEMAN, (MRS. EDGAR PRESTON RICHARDSON), artist; b. Indpls., Jan. 18, 1905; d. Christopher Bush and Juliet (Brown) Coleman; student Vassar Coll., 1923-25, Pa. Acad. Fine Arts, 1925-28; m. Edgar Preston Richardson, Sept. 15, 1931. One man shows Macbeth Gallery, N.Y.C., 1944, 46, 50, Wildenstein & Co., N.Y., 1955, Kennedy Galleries, N.Y., 1960, 63, 70; exhibited in group shows at Macbeth Galleries, Wildenstein & Co., Met. Mus. Art, Carnegie Inst., Corcoran Art Gallery, Whitney, Mus.; represented in permanent collections Pa. Acad., Indpls. Mus. Art, Saginaw Mus. Grand Rapids Art Gallery, Detroit Inst. Arts, Art Mus. N.B. Inst., U. Del., Santa Barbara Mus., Columbus Gallery Fine Arts, Whitney Mus. Western Art, Joslyn Art Mus., Omaha, Coll. Mrs. John D. Rockefeller 3d, and others. Address: 285 Locust St Philadelphia PA 19106

RICHARDSON, DOROTHY VIRGINIA, accountant; b. Bennington, Okla., Sept. 26, 1937; d. William Lycurgus and Mittie Mae (Richardson) Ray; student Eastern Okla. A&M, 1955-56; B.B.A., U. Alaska, 1974; m. Charles Howard Richardson, Dec. 28, 1958; children—Charles Timothy, Michael Todd. Asst. acct. Peat, Marwick, Mitchell & Co., Omaha, 1975-76; gen. acct. U. Alaska Statewide System, Fairbanks, 1976; asst. bus. mgr. Geophys. Inst., Fairbanks, 1976-77; dir. grant and contract services U. Alaska, Fairbanks, 1977-80; controller Alaska Legal Services Corp., Anchorage, 1980-81; bus. mgr. div. community colls., rural edn. and extension U. Alaska, Anchorage, 1981—. Active Cub Scouts, Mothers March of Dimes, PTA. Served with USAF, 1957-59. Mem. Assn. Women Accts., Am. Inst. C.P.A.s, Am. Woman's Soc. C.P.A.s, Alaska Soc. C.P.A.s, Soc. Research Adminstrs. Office: 3601 C St Suite 400 Anchorage AK 99503

RICHARDSON, ELLEN, personnel dir.; b. Salt Lake City, Dec. 4, 1947; d. Warren Delos and Evyln (Green) R.; student Utah State U., 1966-68; B.S., Brigham Young U., 1974; postgrad. Weber State Coll. Tchr., Weber County Schs., Ogden, Utah, 1975-77; exec. sec. Wadman Real Estate, Ogden, 1977-78; employment specialist/curriculum analyst Utah Dept. Employment Security, Ogden, 1978-80; personnel dir. Bonneville Prodns., Salt Lake City, 1980—; guest lectr., cons. Vol., March of Dimes Nat. Telerama, 1981, 82; leader 4-H Club; vol. in Gt. Britain for Ch. Jesus Christ of Latter-day Saints, 1969-71. Sperry Hutchison scholar, 1966-67. Mem. Am. Soc. Personnel Adminstrs., Am. Soc. Tng. and Devel., Internat. Assn. Personnel in Employment Security, Nat. Assn. Female Execs., Women in Communications, Utah Edn. Assn., NEA. Club: Spurs. Office: 130 Social Hall Ave Salt Lake City UT 84111

RICHARDSON, EMILIE WHITE, mfg. co. exec.; b. Chattanooga, July 8, 1929; d. Emmett and Mildred Evelyn (Harbin) White; B.A., Wheaton Coll., 1951; 1 dau., Julie Richardson Phinney. With Christy Mfg. Co., Inc., Fayetteville, N.C., 1952—, sec. 1956-66, v.p., 1967-74, exec. v.p., 1975-79, pres., chief exec. officer, 1980—; v.p. E. White Investment Co., 1968—; cons. Aerostatic Industries, 1979—; v.p. Gannon Corp., 1981—; cons. govt. contacts and offshore mfg., 1981—. Vice pres. public relations Ft. Lauderdale Symphony Soc., 1974-76, v.p. membership, 1976-77, adv. bd., 1978—; active Atlantic Found., Ft. Lauderdale Mus. Art, Beaux Arts, Freedoms Found.; mem. E. Broward Women's Republican Club, 1968—, Americanism chmn., 1971-72. Presbytrian. Club: Green Valley Country. Home: 1531 NE 51st St Fort Lauderdale FL 33334 Office: PO Box 35375 Fayetteville NC 28303

RICHARDSON, FRANCES MASON, savs. and loan assn. exec.; b. Russellville, Ky., Sept. 15, 1929; d. Robert Jewell and Anna Belle (Miles) Mason; B.B.A., Bethel Coll., 1950; m. Lewis H. Richardson, Apr. 5, 1958. With First Fed. Savs. & Loan Assn. of Russellville, 1951—, sec.-treas., 1966-75, exec. v.p., 1976-77, pres. 1977—, also dir. Mem. West Ky. Savs. & Loan League (chmn.), Ky. Savs. & Loan League (dir.), Russellville C. of C., U.S. Savs. and Loan League. Democrat. Baptist. Home: Route 3 Russellville KY 42276 Office: 135 W 4th St Russellville KY 42276

RICHARDSON, JACQUELINE LEE (NIERENHAUSEN), tech. recruiter, cons.; b. Paynesville, Minn., July 21, 1951; d. Walter Lowell and Rosemary (Thielen) Dilley; student U. Minn., 1970-73; m. Reginall Richardson, Feb. 14, 1982. Sr. tech. recruiter COMPDATA, subs. CDI), Costa Mesa, Calif., 1978-79; dir. support services Systems Software, Inc., Anaheim, Calif., 1979-81; v.p. mktg., 1981-82; tech. recruiter, pres. J. Richardson Staffing Cons., Inc., 1982—; cons. in field. Mem. Chatsworth C. of C., Nat. Assn. Female Execs. Republican. Roman Catholic. Home: 3359 Bryan Ave Simi Valley CA 93063 Office: 21757 Devonshire St Suite 3 Chatsworth CA 91311

RICHARDSON, JANETTA CAROL, steel co. exec.; b. Neptune, N.J., Dec. 18, 1952; d. Reginald John and Margie Jane (Woolley) R.; B.A., Hood Coll., 1975. Salesman, Jones & Laughlin Steel Corp., Pitts. and Memphis, 1975-79, A. Baldwin & Co., Inc., New Orleans, 1979; dist. mgr. Intercontinental Metals Trading Corp., New Orleans, 1979—. Mem New Orleans chpt. Alliance for Good Govt. Mem. Nat. Assn. Female Execs., NOW, Assn. Steel Distbrs. Clubs: Racquetball One, Order Eastern Star. Home: 913 Washington Ave New Orleans LA 70130 Office: Canal Pl One Suite 2012 New Orleans LA 70130

RICHARDSON, JEAN MCGLENN, civil engr.; b. Everett, Wash., Nov. 15, 1927; d. Clayton Charles and Marie Elizabeth (Mellish) McGlenn; B.S.C.E., Oreg. State U., 1949; m. William York Richardson, II, June 11, 1949; children—William York III, Paul Kress II, Clayton McGlenn. Engr., Walter Schoel Engring. Co., Birmingham, Ala., 1950-54; office engr. G.C. McKinney Engring. Co., San Jose, Calif., 1972-74; civil design leader Harland Bartholomew & Assos., Birmingham, 1974-78, Rust Engring. Co., Birmingham, 1978—; counselor to female students on engring. as a career. Mem. Soc. Women Engrs. (sr. sect. rep. to nat. bd.), Alpha Phi. Republican. Episcopalian. Clubs: Inverness Country, Women's Golf Assn. Office: 1130 22d St S Birmingham AL 35201

RICHARDSON, JULIA HARRISS, nurse, bus. exec.; b. Wilmington, N.C., Apr. 17, 1928; d. Andrew Howell and Mary (Bolles) Harriss; student U. N.C., 1946-47; Jr. Coll. diploma Stratford Coll., 1948; cert. in nursing Johns Hopkins Hosp., 1951; B.S. in Nursing (scholar), Johns Hopkins U., 1953; M.S. in Psychiat. Nursing, U. Md., 1956, postgrad., 1960-63; 1 dau., Julia H. Gen. staff nurse Henry Phipps Psychiat. Clinic, Johns Hopkins Hosp., 1951-52; supr. nurses Psychiat. Inst., U. Md., 1952-55, instr. psychiat. nursing, undergrad. program, 1956-58, asst. prof. psychiat. nursing, grad. program, 1958-60; asst. prof. nursing, grad. program advanced psychiat. nursing Rutgers U., 1963-64; dir. nurses Friends of Psychiat. Research, Inc., 1964-66; asst. dir. nursing St. Elizabeth's Hosp., Washington, 1966-73, chief nurse O'Malley Div., 1973; pvt. practice nursing, 1973—; owner, pres. Rural Delivery Nursing Services, Mechanicsville, Md., 1975—; cons. Bd. dirs. St. Mary's County Dept. Social Services, 1974-77; vice chmn. bd. dirs. St. Mary's Nursing Home, 1973-74, sec. bd. dirs., 1977-78, 78-79, chmn. bd. dirs., 1980-82; bd. dirs. Beach Mgmt. Corp. of Golden Beach, Md., 1974-76, 81—; chmn. Hist. Preservation Com.; mem. St. Mary's County and Md. Hist. Soc., 1973-77, Roads Com. Kellogg Found. fellow, 1955-56; spl. nursing research fellow HEW, 1960-63; recipient Internat. Women's Year award St. Mary's County, Md., 1975. Mem. Md. Nurses Assn. (apptd. com.), Johns Hopkins and U. Md. Nursing Alumnae Assn., Sigma Theta Tau. Democrat. Episcopalian. Contbr. articles to profl. publs. Home and Office: 586 County Oak Rd Route 2 Mechanicsville MD 20659

RICHARDSON, KAREN LEROHL, lawyer; b. Albuquerque, Sept. 15, 1950; d. John Kenneth and Ann (Castleman) Lawrence Lerohl; B.A., Coll. William and Mary, 1972; J.D., Am. U., 1978; postgrad. George Washington U., 1980-82. Admitted to Va. bar, 1979, U.S. Ct. Claims bar, 1980, U.S. Supreme Ct., 1982; supr. law dept. Prudential Ins. Co., Washington, 1972-74; law clk. Arnold and Porter, Washington, 1975-78; atty. Def. Logistics Agy., Alexandria, Va., 1978-80; atty. Office Sec. Def., Washington, 1980—. Recipient Presidential Sports award, 1980; Disting. Youth award Dept. Army, 1976. Mem. Am. Bar Assn. (dep. chmn., mem. subcom. 1980—), Fed. Bar Assn., Va. Bar Assn., Nat. Assn. Female Execs., Nat. Council Career Women. Club: Cameron Station Tennis (pres. 1980). Office: The Pentagon 3D937 Washington DC 20301

RICHARDSON, MARTHA, nutrition analyst; b. Noble, La., Apr. 22, 1917; d. Alexander M. and Olive (Barlow) R.; A.B., U. Mo., 1938, Ph.D., 1953; M.S., Kans. State U., 1939. Dietitian, William Newton Meml. Hosp., Winfield, Kans., 1940-42, Molly Stark Sanatorium, Canton, Ohio, 1942-47; asst. dir. residence halls, instr. home econs. U. Mo., 1947-50, instr. home econs., 1951-53; head of foods and nutrition U. Utah, 1953-55; nutrition analyst Agrl. Research Service, Washington, 1955-80. Named Disting. Alumna, U. Mo., 1968. Fellow AAAS; mem. Am. Dietetic Assn., Am. Home Econs. Assn., Am. Med. Writers Assn., Am. Inst. Food Techologists, Am. Chem. Soc. Am. Assn. Cereal Chemists, Am. Forestry Assn., AAUW, N.Y. Acad. Scis., Sigma Xi, Gamma Sigma Delta, Phi Upsilon Omicron, Sigma Delta Epsilon. Contbr. articles to profl. jours. Home: 403 Russell Ave #309 Gaithersburg MD 20877

RICHARDSON, MIDGE TURK, editor; b. Los Angeles, Mar. 26, 1930; d. Charles Aloyisius and Marie Theresa (Lindekin) Turk; B.A., Immaculate Heart Coll., Los Angeles, 1951, M.A., 1956; postgrad. Pitts. U., 1964, Duquesne U., 1964, U. Calif., Santa Barbara, 1965-66; m. Hamilton Farrar Richardson, Feb. 8, 1974. Mem. Sisters of Immaculate Heart of Mary, 1948-66; tchr., head dept. English and drama Conaty High Sch., Los Angeles, 1950-59; prin. Our Lady Queen of Angels High Sch., Los Angeles, 1959-64, Mercy High Sch., Merced, Calif., 1964-66; asst. to dean Sch. Arts, N.Y. U., 1966-67; coll. editor Glamour mag. Conde Nast Publs., N.Y.C., 1967-74; editor-in-chief Co-Ed mag., editorial dir. Forecast and Co-Ed mags., Scholastic Mag., Inc., N.Y.C., 1974-75; exec. editor Seventeen mag. Triangle Communications, N.Y.C., 1975-79, editor, 1979—; lectr. Tishman Seminars, Hunter Coll., 1975-77; co-hostess Kennedy and Co., ABC, Chgo., 1971, Ask Youth, Channel 10, N.Y.C., 1972; guest appearances on television shows Girl Talk, 1967, Julia Meade, 1970, To Tell The Truth, 1971, Gary Moore, 1971, Arnold Zinker, 1971, Marie Torre, 1971, Dick Cavett, 1971, Today, 1978, radio shows Barry Gray, Sta. WMCA, 1971-73, Monitor, 1967, 69, 71, 72, Caspar Citron, 1970, John Wingate, 1970, 71. Mem. Women's com., nominating com. Girl Scout Council of Greater N.Y., Inc., 1976-82; trustee Internat. House, 1979—; bd. dirs. YMCA, N.Y.C., 1972-73. Recipient Calif. Lifetime Secondary credential, 1956. Mem. Am. Soc. Mag. Editors (exec. com.), Fashion Group, Inc. of New York, Cosmetic, Toiletry and Fragrances Assn., Inc. Democrat. Clubs: Murrayhill Racquet; River. Author: The Buried Life, 1971; Gordon Parks, A Biography for Children, 1971. Office: 850 3d Ave New York NY 10022

RICHARDSON, MOZELLE GRONER, author; b. Hereford, Tex., Jan. 26, 1914; d. Grover Cleveland and Jessie Leah (Head) Groner; student E. Tex. Bapt. Coll., 1930-33, Central State U., Edmond, Okla., 1967-69, Okla. U., 1969-71; m. William T. Richardson, Aug. 25, 1939; children—William T., Judy Richardson Markley, Susan Ann Richardson Gumerson, Rock Grover. Novels include: The Curse of Kalispoint, 1971, Portrait of Fear, 1971, Masks of Thespis, 1973, Candle in the Wind, 1973, The Song of India, 1975, Daughter of the Sacred Mountain, 1977; speaker to writer-related groups, high schs. Recipient Writer's award Okla. U., 1973. Mem. Mystery Writers Am., Authors Guild, PEN. Democrat. Home: 1611 Guilford Ln Oklahoma City OK 73120

RICHARDSON, MYRTLE, abstractor, former judge; b. Jefferson County, Ohio, July 2, 1907; d. Thomas and Blanche (Whitecotton) Heinselman; student Kans. State Tchrs. Coll., 1926; A.A., Dodge City Community Coll., 1978; m. Harold E. Richardson, Mar. 4, 1929 (div.); 1 dau., Nancy Lee Richardson Ridgway. Tchr. public schs., Edwards County, Kans., 1924-28; reporter, advertiser Kinsley (Kans.) Graphic, 1928-35, mgr., 1937-41; editor, advt. mgr. So. Standard, McMinnville, Tenn., 1935-36; abstractor H. F. Thompson, Kinsley, 1943-54; editor Kinsley Mercury, 1954-57; abstractor, Kinsley, 1957—; probate judge, Kinsley, 1958-69; judge Mcpl. Ct. Kinsley, 1958-69. Bd. dirs. United Drive, 1947-57, Edwards County chpt. ARC, 1940-50; community and project leader 4-H Club, 1943-52; community and project leader Edwards County 4-H Who's Who Club, 1943-52; pres. PTA, 1940-44. Vice chmn. Edwards County Democratic Com. 1956—; pres. Edwards County Fedn. Dem. Women's Club, 1970-74, 76—; chmn. Dem. Central Com., Edwards County, 1981; dist. dir. South 1st Dist. Fedn. Dem. Women's Clubs, 1981. Mem. C. of C. (sec.-mgr. 1947-54), Edwards County Hist. Soc. (historian), S. Central Kans. Probate Judges Assn. (pres. 1966). Author: Oft Told Tales-A History of Edwards County, Kansas from 1873 to 1900. Home: 120 N 2d St Kinsley KS 67547 Office: 218 W 8th St Kinsley KS 67547

RICHARDSON, NANCY JORDAN, oilfield equipment mfg. exec.; b. Beaumont, Tex., Mar. 23, 1936; d. Joe Justine and Imogene Melissa (Carter) Jordan; student Chiener Bus. Coll., 1955; m. Reuben S. Richardson, Aug. 16, 1956; children—Cheryl Lynn, Kathryn Kay, Lorraine Susan. Sales mgr. Promotional Specialties, Inc., Houston, 1969-72; partner, mgr. Health Equipment of Tex., Inc., Houston, 1974; exec. sec., office mgr. Ken Wind Co., Inc., Houston, 1976-78, v.p. ops., 1978—. Mem. Am. Soc. Profl. and Exec. Women, Nat. Assn. Female Execs. Democrat. Methodist. Office: PO Box 19056 Houston TX 77024

RICHARDSON, PATRICIA ELLEN, nurse; b. Clark Lake, Mich., Sept. 2, 1941; d. Herbert Goulden and Mary Hilda Kelly; diploma Saginaw Gen. Hosp. Sch. of Nursing, 1965; student Central Mich. U., 1962-64; B.S. in Nursing, U. Va., 1968; M.S., Va. Commonwealth U., 1970; 1 dau., Kelly Lee. Night supr. Prince William Hosp., Manassas, Va., 1965-66; asst. prof. nursing No. Va. Community Coll., Annandale, 1969-72; dir. nursing Warren Meml. Hosp., Front Royal, Va., 1976—; mem. adj. faculty Shenandoah Coll., Winchester, Va., 1976-78. Mem. Am., Va. (pres.-elect dist. 12) nurses assns., Va. League for Nursing (dir.), Assn. Critical Care Nurses, Nursing Service Adminstrs. Home: 486 Hamilton Circle Front Royal VA 22630 Office: 1000 Shenandoah Ave Front Royal VA 22630

RICHARDSON, PEGGY ANN, human resources adminstr.; b. New Albany, Ind., Jan. 20, 1950; d. Nathaniel E. and Mildred Addrienne Phillips; student Morgan State Coll., 1968-69; B.S., Ind. State U., 1972; M.S., U. Louisville, 1980; m. Charles Richardson, May 5, 1979; children—Charles Nathan, Adrian Jamel. Social service coordinator Big Bros. and Big Sisters of Kentuckiana, Louisville, 1973-74; social worker Park DuValle Community Health Center, Louisville, 1974-78; dir. Floyd County Head Start, New Albany, 1978-80; ind. contractor Princess House, Inc., North Dighton, Mass., 1982—. Bd. dirs. So. Ind. Minority Families, Inc., 1980—. Recipient regional award Project Head Start, 1980. Mem. NAACP, Alpha Kappa Alpha. Methodist.

RICHARDSON, ROBBIE ANN, Campus minister; b. Yazoo City, Miss., Aug. 16, 1949; d. John Robert and Annie Louise (Burrough) Cummings, Sr.; student Jefferson Davis Jr. Coll., Gulfport, Miss., 1979, U. So. Miss., 1981; m. Jimmy Gray Richardson, Nov. 21, 1967; children—Joyce Adelli, Ryan Gray. Lab. technician Miss. State U., Starkville, 1968-73; campus minister, asso. dir. Bapt. Student Union, Miss. Gulf Coast Jr. Coll., Gulfport, 1974—; conf. leader, banquet speaker. 4-H Club leader, 1979-82. Mem. Assn. So. Bapt. Campus Ministers, Nat. Assn. Fgn. Student Affairs, So. Farm Bur. Fedn. (bd. dirs.). Address: Route 7 2405 Knox St Gulfport MS 39502

RICHARDSON, ROBERTA NUTTALL, nurse; b. Newport, N.J., Oct. 15, 1941; d. Robert and Ann Elizabeth Haviland Nuttall Slimmer; R.N. Cooper Hosp. Sch. Nursing, Camden, N.J., 1965; student St. Josephs Coll.; m. George Richardson, Jan. 1, 1964; children—Joyce Ann, Stuart, Judy. Nurse, Clinton County (Ind.) Hosp., 1967-69, Rochelle (Ill.) Community Hosp., 1973-76, Americana Healthcare Center, Rochelle, 1974-76; dir. nursing Hacienda Convalescent Hosp., Concord, Calif., 1977-79; dir. nursing Casa San Miguel Rehab. Center, Concord, 1979—. Pres., United Meth. Women, 1974-75, sec., 1975-76; pres. Campfire Girls, Rochelle, 1971-76, Crippled Children, Ind., 1968; leader Cub Scouts, 1970-76. Mem. Beta Sigma Phi. Republican. Clubs: Moose, Order Eastern Star. Home: 4005 Santa Fe Ct Concord CA 94521 Office: 1050 San Miguel Rd Concord CA 94518

RICHARDSON, RUTH GREENE, social worker; b. Washington, Mar. 30, 1926; d. Arthur Alonzo and Ruth Naomi (Conway) Greene; B.S., St. Louis U., 1948; M.S.W., Washington U., St. Louis, 1950; m. Frederick D. Richardson, June 7, 1968; 1 son, Arthur William. Exec. dir. Anna B. Heldman Community Center, Pitts., 1962-64; asso. dir. Hillhouse Assn., Pitts., 1964-67; asso. dir. Dixwell House, also supr. group work services in community schs., New Haven, 1967-69; exec. dir. Three Rivers Youth Inc., Pitts., 1969—; adv. bd. Sch. Social Work, U. Pitts., 1979-80; pres. Assn. Residential Youth Care Agencies, 1973-77; pres., bd. dirs. Pa. Council Vol. Child Care Agys., 1973-78; asst. v.p. Allegheny Children and Youth Services Council, 1974-76; adv. council Booth Home. Recipient Social Assistance award Pitts. region Women's Am. ORT, 1975, Internat. Year of Child award region III, HEW, 1979. Mem. Nat. Assn. Social Workers, Midwest Watercolor Soc., Nat. Assn. Female Execs. Presbyterian. Paintings exhbited in Pitts. region. Home: 641 Robinwood Dr Pittsburgh PA 15216 Office: 2039 Termon Ave Pittsburgh PA 15212

RICHARDSON, SELMA KATHERINE, educator; b. Allison Park, Pa., Oct. 23, 1931; d. John J. and Laura Ingrid (Kuijala) R.; student Suomi Coll., 1948-49, Capital U., 1949-51; Mus.B., St. Olaf Coll., 1953; M.A., U. Mich., 1959, A.M. in L.S., 1962, Ph.D., 1969. Tchr. vocal music and elem. grades, Berkley, Mich., 1953-60; librarian elem. sch., Oak Park, Mich., 1960-68, high sch., 1968-69; asst. prof. Ball State U., Muncie, Ind., 1969-70; dir. media services Oak Park and River Forest High Sch., Ill., 1970-74; asso. prof. Grad. Sch. Library and Info. Sci., U. Ill., Urbana, 1974—; mem. summer faculty Simmons Coll., No. Ill. U., Rosary Coll., U. Chgo. Recipient Disting. Alumnus award Sch. Library Sci., U. Mich., 1978; Library Services and Constrn. Act grantee. Mem. Childrens Lit. Assn., ALA, Assn. Library Service to Children, Am. Assn. Sch. Librarians, Assn. Am. Library Schs., Ill. Library Assn., Ill. Assn. Media in Edn., Friends Internat. Bd. Books for Young People, Phi Kappa Phi, Pi Lambda Theta, Beta Phi Mu. Author: Analytical Survey of Public Library Services to Children, 1978; Childrens Services of Public Libraries, 1978; Study and Collection of Historical Childrens Books, 1979; research on 19th Century children and books, 1980. Home: 814 Phoenix Dr Champaign IL 61820 Office: Grad Sch Library and Info Sci U Ill Urbana IL 61801

RICHARDSON, WINNIFRED STEWART, ret. librarian, ret. educator; b. Montreal, Que., Can., May 3, 1908; d. William McKenzie and Elizabeth Jane (Malcolm) Stewart; came to U.S., 1948, naturalized, 1955; A.B., U. Denver, 1958, M.A., 1960; postgrad. U. N.C., 1960-65; m. Andrew Richardson, Dec. 5, 1928 (dec. Nov. 1979); children—Winnifred Richardson Redman, David William, Andrew James. Tchr., Sunflower Consol. Sch., Nebr., 1954-56; high sch. librarian, Mitchell, Nebr., 1957-59; reference librarian, asso. prof. librarianship U. No. Colo., 1960-73, ret. Bible tchr. Ch. of Christ, 1922-65. Mem. Am., Colo. (life), Mountain Plains library assns., AAUW (chmn. theatre arts study group), Univ. Profs. for Academic Order (charter), AAUP, Stewart Soc. Republican. Author: (with Bryan Cooke) A Bibliography on Drugs, by Subject and Title, 1972. Home: 2935 11th Ave #1-A Evans CO 80620

RICHENS, MURIEL WHITTAKER, counselor, educator; b. Prineville, Oreg.; d. John Reginald and Victoria Cecilia (Pascale) Whittaker; B.S., Oreg. State U.; M.A., San Francisco State U., 1962; cert. in sch. adminstrn. U. Calif., Berkeley; postgrad. U. Birmingham (Eng.), 1973, Center for Human Communications, Los Gatos, Calif., 1974, U. P.R., 1977, U. Ariz.; children—Karen, John, Candice, Stephanie, Rebecca. Instr., counselor, Springfield, Oreg., San Francisco State U., Coll. San Mateo, high sch. dist., Calif., 1961—; marriage, child, and family counselor; guest West Germany/European Acad. seminar, West Berlin, 1975. Lifeguard, ARC. Mem. U. Calif. at Berkeley Alumni, Am. Contract Bridge League (life master, cert. bridge instr., tournament bridge dir.), Women in Communications, Computer-Using Educators, Pi Lambda Theta, Delta Pi Epsilon (sec. 1965, v.p. 1966). Home: 847 N Humboldt St San Mateo CA 94401 Office: 650 N Delaware St San Mateo CA 94401

RICHES, AGNES MARGARET (PEGGY), ins. agt.; b. Toledo, Apr. 2, 1938; d. Vincent Paul and Elsie Mae (Robeson) Slaninka; student public schs.; cert. Life Underwriters Tng. Council, Toledo, 1976; divorced; children—Russell, Kent, Michelle, Karen. Agt., Lutheran Mut. Life Ins. Co., Perrysburg, 1974-76; mgr. Parota Tire Co., Toledo, 1976-77; mgr. Weight Loss Med. Center, Toledo, 1977; self-employed ins. agt., Perrysburg, 1977—; part-time jewelry designer, 1977—. Mem. parent adv. bd. Rossford High Sch., Perrysburg, 1974-75. Lutheran. Address: 9360 Five Point Rd Perrysburg OH 43551

RICHEY, MARY ANNE, fed. judge; b. Shelbyville, Ind., Oct. 24, 1917; d. H. Wallace and Emma (Nading) Reimann; student Purdue U., 1937-40; J.D., U. Ariz., 1951; m. William K. Richey, Oct. 8, 1959; 1 dau., Anne Marie. Admitted to Ariz. bar, 1951; dep. county atty. Pima County (Ariz.), 1952-54; asst. U.S. atty. Dist. Ariz., 1954-59, U.S. atty., 1960; judge Superior Ct. Pima County, 1964-76, asso. presiding judge, 1972-76; U.S. dist. judge Dist. Ariz., 1976—; mem Jud. Qualifications Commn., 1970-76, Criminal Code Revision Commn., 1973-76, Gov.'s Commn. on Status Women, 1971-73; Tucson chmn. Supreme Ct. Com. to Revise Civil Jury Instn., 1971-73; mem. exec. com. 9th Circuit, 1978-81, exec. com. Nat. Conf. Fed. Trial Judges, 1980—. Bd. dirs. YWCA, Tucson, 1963-69, pres., 1968-69; mem. adv. bd. Salvation Army, Tucson, 1968—. Served with WASP, 1944-45. Mem. ABA, Ariz., Pima County bar assns., Am. Arbitration Assn., State Judges Assn. (pres. 1970-71), Kappa Kappa Gamma, Kappa Alpha Phi. Republican. Presbyterian. Office: US Courthouse Tucson AZ 85701

RICHMAN, GERTRUDE GROSS (MRS. BERNARD RICHMAN), civic worker; b. N.Y.C., May 16, 1908; d. Samuel and Sarah Yetta (Seltzer) Gross; B.S., Tchrs. Coll. Columbia U., 1948, M.A., 1949; m. Bernard Richman, Apr. 5, 1930; children—David, Susan. Vol. worker Hackensack Hosp., 1948-70; mem. bd. dirs. YM-YWHA, Bergen County, N.J., 1950-75, bd. mem. emeritus, 1975—; chmn. Leonia Friends of Bergen County Mental Health Consultation Center, 1959; founder, hon. pres. Bergen County Serv-A-Com., affiliated with women orgns. Div. Nat. Jewish Welfare Bd.; v.p. N.J. sect. Nat. Jewish Welfare Bd., 1964-71; hon. trustee women's div. Bergen County United Jewish Community; mem. adv. council Bergen County Office on Aging; mem. Hackensack Bd. Edn., 1946-51; mem. pub. relations com. Leonia Pub. Schs., 1957-58; N.J. del. White House Conf. on Aging, 1971; trustee Mary McLeod Bethune Scholarship Fund; v.p. Bergen County nat. women's com. Brandeis U., 1966-67. Recipient citation Nat. Council Jewish Women and YWCA in Bergen County, 1962; citation Nat. Jewish Welfare Bd., 1964, Harry S. Feller award N.J. Region, 1965; 14th Ann. Good Scout award Bergen council Boy Scouts Am., 1977; Woman Vol. of Distinction, Bergen County council Girl Scouts, 1979; Human Relations award Bergen County sect. Nat. Council Negro Women, 1982. Mem. Kappa Delta Pi. Home: Hackensack NJ 07601

RICHMOND, JANICE DORIS, social worker; b. Boston, Feb. 28, 1926; d. Harry Hyman and Lillian (Cohen) Saltman; B.S., Simmons Coll., 1946; M.S.W., U. Md., 1963; m. Edward Stanley Richmond, Nov. 26, 1950; children—Kenneth Arnold, Michele Dawn. Cheryl Ann. Caseworker protective services Balt. Dept. Social Services, 1961-64; field instr. U. Md., 1965-66, 77-78; with Welfare Unit, Sinai-Druid Comprehensive Pediatric Center, Balt., 1966-68, dist. supr., 1966-70; chief Div. Day Care, Balt. Dept. Social Services, 1970-72, chief Client Rehab. through Ednl. Activities Tng., Manpower Program, 1972-75, chief div. adult services, 1975-80, ret., 1980; field instr. Howard U., 1976-78; lectr. in field; cons. Office of Aging, 1975-80. Recipient citations, Mayor of Balt., 1978, 79, Gov. of Md., 1977. Mem. Nat. Assn. Social Wokers, Am. Public Welfare Assn., Md. Conf. Social Concern, Md. Advocates for Aging. Club: Order Eastern Star (matron 1960-61). Home: 8901 SW 8 St Boca Raton FL 33433

RICHMOND, LEE JOYCE, psychologist, educator; b. Balt., May 31, 1934; d. Alexander J. and Anne M. Blank; B.S., Loyola Coll., 1961; M.Ed., Johns Hopkins U., 1966; Ph.D., U. Md., 1972; m. Alvin Richmond, Aug. 9, 1953; children—Ruth, Stephen, Sharon, Jessica. Tchr., English and history Seton High Sch., Balt., 1964-66; counselor Garrison Jr. High Sch., Balt., 1967-69; asso. prof. psychology Essex Community Coll., Balt., 1969-71; prof. psychology and chairperson social sci. div. Dundalk Community Coll., Balt., 1974-76, assoc. prof., chairperson, 1971-74; asst. prof. edn. in counseling and human devel. Johns Hopkins U., Balt., 1976-78, assoc. prof., 1978—; mem. Md. Adv. Council for Career Edn., 1981-83; Md. Bd. Edn. Task Force on Guidance and Counseling, 1978-79; trustee Hannah Moore Center for Emotionally Disturbed Adolescents, 1974-78; mem. Md. Commn. for Women, 1970-78, chairperson Child Care Commn., chairperson exec. council continuing edn. for women; Bd. dirs. YWCA, 1977-79. Lic. psychologist, Md. Mem. Am. Personnel and Guidance Assn. (chairperson program conv. Washington 1983, com. on women 1978—), Nat. Vocat. Guidance Assn. (co-chairperson com. accreditation, standards and credentialism 1981—, chairperson com. on liaison to Assn. of Counselor Educators and Suprs. 1979—, resource devel. com. 1980-81), Assn. for Counselor Educators and Suprs. (interdivisional collaboration com. 1981—), Am. Psychol. Assn., Internat. Council Psychologists (com. on devel. of children and youth 1980—), Soc. Assn. Counselor Educators and Suprs. (exec. council 1978-79), Md. Personnel and Guidance Assn. (co-editor Jour. 1982, licensure com. 1981—, editor Compass Points 1978-79), Md. Assn. Counselor Educators and Suprs. (pres. 1978-79), Md. Assn. for Non-White Concerns in Personnel and Guidance (research com. chairperson), Md. Vocat. Guidance Assn., Md. Psychol. Assn. (editor Newsletter 1976-77), Balt. Area of Cons. Psychologists (nomination com. 1981, rec. sec. 1979-80), Eastern Psychol. Assn., Soc. for Sci. Study of Religion, Am. Vocat. Assn., Pi Lambda Theta (faculty advisor), Phi Delta Kappa, Phi Delta Gamma, Nat. Register of Health Service Providers in Psychology. Contbr. articles to profl. jours. Home: 8907 Greylock Rd Baltimore MD 21208 Office: Johns Hopkins U 105 Whitehead Hall Baltimore MD 21218

RICHMOND, MARY FRANCES, educator; b. Ft. Scott, Kans., Apr. 12, 1951; d. Herman Abbot and Betty Lee (Armsworthy) Clark; A.A. (scholar), Ft. Scott Community Coll., 1971; B.S. in Home Econs. Edn. (acad. scholar), Pittsburg State U., 1973; M.S. (Elinor Anderson Scholar), Kans. State U., 1979-81; m. Larry Joe Richmond, Aug. 1, 1970. Faculty, Kans. State U./home economist Osage County Extension Service, Lyndon, 1975—; adv. Lyndon High Sch. vocat. programs, 1979—; mem. Kans. State com. for tng. new extension agts., 1977—. Asst. ch. pianist Lyndon United Methodist Ch., 1979—, ch. family edn. coordinator, 1980—, Sunday sch. tchr., 1979—. Named Woman of Yr., Bus. and Profl. Women's Club, 1979; Mary Kern Martin Meml. scholar, 1973; Alumni Merit scholar, 1972; dist. winner Young Career Woman competition Kans. Bus. and Profl. Women's Club, 1978. Mem. Kans. Extension Agts. Assn., Kans. Assn. Extension Home Economists, Nat. Assn. Extension Home Economists, Osage County Home Econ. Assn. (pres. 1976), Phi Upsilon Omicron, Epsilon Sigma Phi, Phi Kappa Phi. Republican. Clubs: Lyndon Bus. and Profl. Women's (corr. sec. 1979—, pres. 1981), Order Eastern Star, Lyndon Saddle (show sec. 1978-79). Home: RFD Lyndon KS 66451 Office: Courthouse PO Box Q Lyndon KS 66451

RICHMOND, NANCY JANE, mfg. co. sales ofcl.; b. Indpls., Aug. 5, 1948; d. William Stanley and Margaret Ruth (Crawford) Scott; student U. Ariz., 1965-68. Ins. agt. Arapahoe Ins. Agy., Englewood, Colo., 1968-69; pvt. practice ins. broker, Denver, 1969-73; owner, propr. Frames Et Cetera, Denver, 1973-77; dist. sales mgr. Rocky Mountain Region, Lightolier, Denver, 1977—; lighting design cons. Rocky Mountain region. Recipient sales awards, Arapahoe Ins. Agy., 1969, Lightolier, 1974. Mem. Ins. Brokers Colo., Profl. Picture Framers Assn., Illuminating Engring. Soc., Coll. Fin. Planners, Beta Sigma Phi (sec.-treas. Alpha Lambda chpt. 1976-77), Nat. Assn. Female Execs. Participant Nat. Picture Framers competition, 1976; first woman dist. sales mgr., lightolier. Address: 1847 S Jasmine Denver CO 80224

RICHMOND, ROSALIND, social service adminstr.; b. Boston, May 18, 1938; d. Leonard Julius and Esther Freda (Greenberg) R.; B.S., Simmons Coll., 1960, M.S., 1962. Clin. social worker, oncology service, handicapped children Mass. Eye and Ear Infirmary, Boston, 1962-65; clin. social worker med.-surg. services VA Med. Center, San Francisco, 1965-75, adminstr. psychiat. outpatient clinic, 1975—. Lic. clin. social worker. Mem. Nat. Assn. Social Workers, Acad. Cert. Social Workers. Home: 2201 Laguna St San Francisco CA 94115 Office: 4150 Clement St San Francisco CA 94121

RICHMOND, SALLY DUVAL, info. scis. co. exec.; b. Orlando, Fla., Aug. 19, 1934; d. Alexander C. and Daphne (Alexander) Duval; B.A., Fisk U., 1955; children—Christopher G., Eric D., Tracy B. Aerospace systems technologist NASA, Goddard Space Flight Center, 1956-63, sect. mgr., 1963-70; mgr. programming Gorman Computer Systems, Bowie, Md., 1970-71; pres. Info. and Edn. Systems, Inc., Lanham, Md., 1972-75; center dir. Computer Scis. Corp., Silver Spring, Md., 1975—. Mem. Women in Info. Processing, Nat. Tech. Assn., Nat. Assn. Female Execs., IEEE, Am. Mgmt. Assn. Office: 8728 Colesville Rd Silver Spring MD 20910

RICHTER, DONNA LORRAINE, ednl. adminstr.; b. Charleston, S.C., Jan. 20, 1951; d. Lawrence Edward and Helen Louise (Reynolds) Richter; B.A., Duke U., 1973, M.A. (Ednl. Professions Devel. Act fellow), 1974; Ed.D., U. S.C., 1982; 1 son, Reynolds Lawrence. Asst. to provost, instr. U. S.C., Columbia, 1974-78, asst. provost, 1978-80; dir. adult advising and non-credit programs Coll. of Charleston (S.C.), 1980-82, assoc. dean for continuing edn., 1982—. Recipient Young Career Woman of Yr. award Bus. and Profl. Women's Club, 1980. Mem. S.C. Assn. Higher Continuing Edn. (program chmn. 1981-82), S.C. Acad. Sci. (v.p. 1981-82), S.C. Women in Higher Edn. Adminstrn. (state planning com. 1978-82), Am. Assn. Higher Edn., Nat. Assn. Women Deans, Adminstrs., Counselors, Assn. for Study of Higher Edn., AAUW (corp. rep. 1981-82), Charleston Women's Network. Office: Coll of Charleston Center for Continuing Edn 25 Saint Philip St Charleston SC 29424

RICHTER, JACKIE WILSON, bus. exec.; b. Hornbeck, La., Oct. 30, 1933; d. Jack Caraway and Marie (Self) Wilson; student Nacogdoches Bus. Coll., 1951; student Victoria Coll., 1951, 72, Del Mar Coll., 1978-80; m. Clyde Joseph Richter, Dec. 12, 1952; children—Lisa Anne, Clyde Joseph, Sara Elizabeth. With R.W. Hill Coll., Victoria, Tex., 1952, So. Pacific R.R., 1953-57; owner, operator Richter's Precision Air Co., Victoria, 1962—, Intra-Coastal Enterprises, Corpus Christi, Tex., 1975—. Alt. del. Republican State Conv., 1982; regional walk coordinator Collins for U.S. Senate, 1982. Mem. C. of C., Tex. Restaurant Assn., Better Bus. Bur., Tex. Retail Grocers Assn., DAR, Colonial Dames XVII Century, Daus. Am. Colonists. Lutheran. Club: Corpus Christi Photo. Office: PO Box 226 909 N Staples Corpus Christi TX 78403 *

RICHTER, KAY, psychiat. social worker; b. Frankfort, Mich., Feb. 15, 1951; d. Arthur L. and Frances G. (Mikesell) R.; B.A. with high honors, Mich. State U., 1973; M.S.W., Ariz. State U., 1975; m. Milton Frank, June 23, 1979; children—Elizabeth Frank, Adam Frank. Clin. social worker St. Joseph Hosp., Tucson, 1975-79; psychiat. social worker Eastside Counseling Center, Tucson, 1975—; asso. faculty Pima Coll., Tucson, 1977-78, Ariz. State U., Tucson, 1978—. Law Enforcement

Adminstrn. Agy. grantee, 1975. Mem. Nat. Assn. Social Workers, Acad. Cert. Social Workers, Registry Clin. Social Workers, Geneal. Soc., NOW, Ariz. Hist. Soc. Clubs: So. Ariz. Roadrunners, Hiking. Office: Eastside Counseling Center 1011 N Craycroft Tucson AZ 85711

RICHTER, MARCIA ILENE, nurse; b. N.Y.C., May 18, 1938; d. Charles and Jacqueline (Burinescu) Richter; R.N., Muhlenberg Hosp., 1965; B.S., Redlands U., 1981. Staff nurse West Essex Gen. Hosp., Livingston, N.J., 1966-68; psychiatric headnurse Greystone Park Hosp., Morris Plains, N.J., 1966; dir. nursing Convalescent Hosp., San Fernando Valley, Calif., 1969-74; tchr. vocat. nursing program Los Angeles Unified Sch. Dist., 1975—; owner Dimar Enterprises, 1979—. Mem. Calif. Assn. Health Educators, NOW. Home: 5651 Buffalo Ave Van Nuys CA 91401 Office: 450 N Grand Ave Los Angeles CA 90012

RICHTER, MARGARET, health facilities cons., author; b. Paterson, N.J., Aug. 5, 1948; d. Joseph and Florence (Zalfeman) R.; L.P.N., Princeton (N.J.) Hosp., 1968; student Fordham U., 1975-78. Staff nurse Princeton Hosp., 1968-70; leadership and staff nurse Mt. Sinai Med. Center, N.Y.C., 1970-76; health care analyst L.I. Coll. Hosp., Bklyn., 1976-77; exec. asst. N.Am. Railco, Inc., N.Y.C., 1977-78; health records analyst Beth Israel Med. Center, N.Y.C., 1978-79; project coordinator, health facilities cons. Duffy, Inc., Planners and Designers, N.Y.C., 1979-81; project dir., health facilities cons. Henry Meltzer Group, Inc., N.Y.C., 1981-82; founder, pres. Margaret Richter & Co., 1982—, freelance writer Contract Mag. Lic. practical nurse, N.Y., N.J. Mem. AIA, Women Bus. Owners N.Y. Home: 1700 York Ave New York NY 10028

RICHTER, MARION MORREY, pianist, composer, educator; b. Columbus, Ohio, Oct. 2, 1900; d. Charles Bradfield and Grace Hamilton (Jones) Morrey; B.A., Ohio State U., 1921; M.A., Columbia U., 1933, Ed.D., 1961; grad. Juilliard Sch., 1928; m. Otto C. Richter, Sept. 12, 1928; children—Lawrence Morrey, Anthony Bradfield. Instr. music/music edn. Tchrs. Coll., Columbia U., N.Y.C., 1929-52; instr. piano Juilliard Sch., 1930-52; concert pianist/lectr., U.S., Eng., Japan, Korea, Mexico, 1962—, around the world Bicentennial Tour of 24 concerts, 1975, others; lectr. series Japan House, 1972-74; N.Y.C. pianist in Premiere of Antheil's Ballet Mecanique, 1927; pianist NBC Symphony, 1934; currently concertizing and working with Nat. Fedn. Music Clubs and U.S. Nat. Music Council. Internat. Music Relations chmn., 1971-75; N.Y. State coordinator Bicentennial Celebration, 1975-76. Recipient citation 8th U.S. Army Korea, 1969, N.J. FMC for Am. Music Concert, 1970; Disting. Alumna award Delta Omicron, 1977; others. Mem. Nat. Fedn. Music Clubs (nat. dir. 1971-73, 81—, nat. chmn. Am. music dept. 1967-71, 1981—), N.Y. Fedn. Music Clubs (pres. 1976-80), Nat. Music Council, Nat. League Am. PEN Women, European Piano Tchrs. Assn., LWV, Am. Women Composers, Westchester Musicians Guild, Delta Omicron (chmn. broadcasts on WNYC 1953-71). Republican. Club: Travel (Greenwich, Conn.). Composer: This Is Our Camp, 1931; Sonata for Trio, 1958; The Waste Land, 1959; Timberjack Overture, 1961; others. Address: 31 Bradford Rd Scarsdale NY 10583

RICHTER, ROBERTA BRANDENBURG (MRS. J. PAUL RICHTER), educator; b. Osborn, Ohio, Dec. 29; d. Warren F. and Mary M. (Davis) Brandenburg; student Miami-Jacobs Coll., 1930, Wittenberg U., 1930-31, Coll. Music, U. Cin., 1931-32, U. Dayton, 1954, 64; B.S., Miami U., Oxford, Ohio, 1958, M.Ed., 1959; postgrad. Wright State U., 1966-70, Ohio State U., 1969—; m. Jean Paul Richter, Oct. 6, 1934; 1 son, James Paul. Bus. mgr. T.D. Peffley, Inc., 1929-32; sec., prodn. mgr. Delco Products div. Gen. Motors, 1932-34; exec. sec. Meth. Union, 1932-38, LWV, 1935-38, Elder & Johnston Dept. Store, 1938-40; ct. reporter Common Pleas Ct. Montgomery County, 1940-46; adminstrv. asst. Ch. Fedn. Greater Dayton, Ohio, 1946-50; audio-visual cons. schs., chs. Twyman Films, 1950-53; legal asst. Nadlin Law Offices, 1953-58; instr. stenotype, office practice Miami-Jacobs Coll., Dayton, 1941-48; tchr. stenotype, guidance counselor Stebbins High Sch., Dayton, 1958-82; vocat. guidance coordinator Mad River Planning Dist., Montgomery County, Ohio, 1968-73. Instr. workshops in stenotype for ct. reporting Wright State U., Dayton, 1970—; 1st cellist youth div. Symphony Orch.; dir. Lang. Unlimited, Inc., Lake Forest, Ill. Supt., tchr., adviser youth div. Grace United Meth. Ch., Dayton, 1942-72, sec. adminstrv. bd., 1940—, council on ministries, 1972-74, past pres. Excel Club, circle leader, hospitality chmn., pres. homebuilders class, program chmn., laywoman chmn. Christian higher edn.; instr., counselor Camp Miniwanca, Am. Youth Found., 1949-68. Mem. Am., Ohio, Miami Valley personnel and guidance assns., Nat., Ohio bus. tchrs. assns., Am., Ohio sch. counselor assns., Nat., Ohio edn. assns., Nat. Vocat. Guidance Assn., Dayton Area Bus. Soc. (v.p. 1969-82), Delphian Soc. (past pres.), Pub. Speaker Bur., Council World Affairs, AAUW, LWV (past pres. and treas.), Internat. Platform Assn., World Trade Club (1st woman), Greater Dayton C. of C., Bus. and Profl. Women, Pi Omega Pi. Clubs: Order Eastern Star, Progressive Mothers (chmn. program Dayton 1969-70). Author ednl. handbooks, pamphlets. Contbr. articles to profl. jours.; lectr. in field. Home: 3865 Seiber Ave Dayton OH 45405

RICHTER, SUSAN ELIZABETH, nurse; b. Salt Lake City, Jan. 12, 1944; d. Joseph Leo and Sara Jane (Bero) Shalvoy; R.N., St. Vincent's Sch. Nursing, 1964; student U. New Haven, 1978—; m. Edward Frederick Richter, Jr., Nov. 6, 1965; children—Meghan, Heidi, Edward, Kathleen, Colin. Staff nurse St. Vincent's Med. Center, Bridgeport, Conn., 1964-71, evening supr., 1972-78, evening adminstrv. dir., 1978-82, dir. community health relations, 1982—. Chmn., Community Projects Com., 1979—; sch. vol. Assn. of Bridgeport, 1977—, bd. dirs. 1977—, chmn., 1979-80; co-leader Jr. Girl Scout Troop, 1974-77; bd. dirs. Fairfield County chpt. Am. Heart Assn., 1980-82; mem. Bridgeport Coalition on Hypertension Control, 1980—. Mem. St. Vincent's Sch. Nursing Alumni Assn., Alpha Sigma Lambda. Republican. Roman Catholic. Clubs: St. Vincent's Med. Center Aux., Home Sch. Assn. of Assumption Sch., Barnum Festival Soc.

RICKARD-RIEGLE, BARBARA KATHERINE, journalist, news broadcaster; b. Los Angeles, May 1, 1931; d. Thomas and Katherine Elizabeth (Blackburn) Rickard; student pvt. schs., Santa Rosa, Calif.; children—Katherine, Karen, Christopher, Melissa, Richard. Editor, Phenix City (Ala.) Herald, 1957-58; news broadcaster, editor WRBL-Radio-TV, Columbus, Ga., 1958-62; polit. reporter Esquire Broadcasting Co., Sta. WQXI, Atlanta, 1962-63; news commentator Sta. WAII-TV, Atlanta, 1962-63; polit. writer, columnist Los Angeles Herald Examiner, 1963-66; Congressional news sec., Washington, 1966-67; news writer, guest broadcaster Stas. KNXT, KABC-TV, Hollywood, Calif., 1964-67; broadcaster, women's news editor Sta. KNX-CBS, 1967-71; news broadcaster, producer, reporter, bur. chief Westinghouse Broadcasting Corp., Sta. KFWB, Hollywood, 1971—; guest broadcaster Pub. Broadcasting System, Sta. KCET, 1975—; propr., pres. Calico Feature Prodns., Anaheim, Calif., 1969—; instr. journalism Calif. State U., Fullerton, 1972-73. Republican candidate for Calif. State Assembly, 1976. Named Journalist of Year, Cypress Coll., 1980; recipient Angel of Distinction award City of Los Angeles, 1973, John Swett award, 1974, 79. Mem. Am. Women in Radio and TV (chpt. pres. 1982-83; chairperson bus. and industry forum Ednl. Found. 1979), Nat. Women's Polit. Caucus, Investigative Reporters and Editors, Orange County Press Club (dir. 1979—), Women in Communications (award 1979), Pioneer Broadcasters W., Sigma Delta Chi. Author: The Long Hot Summer of 1962; Something is Missing: The Majority Sex, 1971; Dinner for One: Soupçon for Singles, 1977. Home and office: 2512 W Chain Ave Anaheim CA 92804

RICKBEIL, CLARA EVELYN SHELLMAN (MRS. RAYMOND E. RICKBEIL), club woman; b. Gibson City, Ill.; d. Kilian and Anna Marie (Johnson) Shellman; grad. Brown's Bus. Coll., Champaign, Ill., 1922; student U. Ill., 1927-28; m. Raymond Earl Rickbeil, May 8, 1930. Office sec. Ford County Farm Bur., Gibson City, 1922-26; secretarial position Raymond E. Rickbeil, C.P.A., Springfield, Ill., 1928-61, Ernst & Ernst, Springfield, 1961-65. Mem. bd. King's Daus.; adv. bd. Am. Security Council; mem. Community Concert Assn., Nat. Fedn. Republican Women, Rep. Women's Club Sangamon County, Sangamon County Farm Bur. Recipient award for work pub. accounting legis. Ill. Soc. C.P.A.'s, 1956. Mem. U. Ill. Alumni Assn., U. Ill. Pres.'s Club, Am. Legion Aux., Meml. Hosp. Aux., Sangamon County Hist. Soc. Republican. Presbyterian. Clubs: Woman's (reception com. 1962-63, social com. 1963-64, corr. sec. 1972-75, dist. program chmn. dist. 21 1968-69, dist. corr. sec. 1969-72), Mariama (vice chmn. chpt. 5 1966-67, chmn. 1967-72), Amateur Musical, Order Eastern Star, Zonta (treas. 1954-57, fin. com. 1965—, fin. chmn. 1957-63, 64, service chmn., mem. service com. 1953-62), Sangamo (asso.). Home: 937 Feldkamp Ave Springfield IL 62704

RICKELL, ANNA SHADOIN, social work psychotherapist; b. Chattanooga, Dec. 22, 1941; d. Thomas Matson and Mary Kathryn (Ailshie) Shadoin; B.A., Meredith Coll., 1962; M.S., Columbia U., 1969 (N.Y.C. scholar); m. C. Eugene Rickell, Oct. 10, 1964; children—Thomas Eugene, David Arthur. Stewardess, United Airlines, 1962-64; caseworker N.Y.C. Dept. Social Services, 1964-66, supr., 1966-67; psychiat. social worker, sch. cons. San Pedro (Calif.) Community Mental Health Dept., 1969-70; asso. staff mem. Family Service Marin, San Rafael, Calif., 1973-80, dir. group therapy, 1979-80; sr. citizens advocate, Pelham, N.Y., 1981—; psychiat. social worker Counseling Center South Westchester, 1981—; cons. Eliza Corwin Frost Child Care Center, 1982; tchr., writer, lectr. parenting and child devel. Bd. dirs. Colburn Meml. Sr. Residence, 1982; v.p. Couples Club Pelham, 1981, pres., 1982. Lic. clin. social worker, marriage, child and family counselor, Calif.; cert. social worker, social work psychotherapist, N.Y. State. Fellow Soc. Clin. Social Workers; mem. Nat. Assn. Social Workers, Acad. Cert. Social Workers, Westchester Assn. Mental Health. Club: N.Y. Athletic (N.Y.C.). Home: 115 Corona Ave Pelham NY 10803 Office: 17 Sagamore Rd Bronxville NY 10708

RICKIN, SHEILA ANNE, mag. pub. co. exec.; b. N.Y.C., Oct. 13, 1945; d. Louis and Ethel (Shmuckler) Bernstein; B.A., CCNY, 1969; postgrad. N.Y.U. Research asst. pre-baccalaureate program CCNY, 1966-68; placement counselor Eleine Revell, Inc., N.Y.C., 1968; adminstr. asso. to chief exec. officer Planned Parenthood Fedn. of Am., N.Y.C., 1968-74; personnel mgr. Family Circle Mag./N.Y. Times Mag. Group, 1974—. Mem. Am. Soc. Personnel Adminstrs., Am. Mgmt. Assn., Met. N.Y. Assn. for Applied Psychology, Mag. Pubs. Assn. (personnel com.). Club: N.Y. Health and Racquet. Office: Family Circle Inc 488 Madison Ave New York NY 10022 *

RICKMAN, REBECCA BLAKEMORE, hosp. purchasing exec.; b. Ft. Smith, Ark., Feb. 14, 1950; d. Hiram J. and Katie Spoon Blakemore; student Ark. Tech. U., 1968-70, Westark Community Coll., 1972-76, U. Ark., 1977-80; m. Phillip E. Rickman, Dec. 30, 1970. Buyer, Sparks Regional Med. Center, Ft. Smith, 1972-78; purchasing agt. Washington Regional Med. Center, Fayetteville, Ark., 1979-81. Mem. Soc. Ark. Hosp. Purchasing, N.W. Ark. Group Purchasing (sec.), Phi Alpha Theta. Republican. Methodist.

RIDDELL, MYRA BEATRICE, psychotherapist; b. San Diego, Nov. 23, 1926; d. Harvey Hosea and Sadie Mina (Mandel) Epstein; A.B., UCLA, 1948, M.W.S., 1952; m. Robert Allen Riddell, Oct. 19, 1946. Pyschiat. social worker VA Hosp., Long Beach, Calif., 1952-56, Calif. State Mental Hygiene Clinic, Los Angeles, 1956-58; adminstrv. social worker Alcoholism Research Clinic, Dept. Psychiatry, UCLA, 1956-59; pvt. practice psychotherapy, Los Angeles, 1959—; cons. Topanga Center for Human Devel., 1968-70; cons. Gay and Lesbian Community Services Center, 1969-74, adv. bd., 1977—; field supr. group therapy U. So. Calif. Sch. Social Work, 1970-71. Co-chmn. New Alliance for Gay Equality, 1978-80; adv. bd. Mcpl. Elections Com. of Los Angeles, 1979—; commr. Los Angeles County Commn. on Status of Women, 1979—; mem. Bd. Concerned Voters of Calif., 1978-79; bd. dirs. Nat. Gay Task Force, 1981—. Los Angeles County scholar, 1949-50; VA scholar, 1951-52. Mem. Nat. Assn. Social Workers, Social Workers in Pvt. Practice (founding bd. dirs. 1956-58), UCLA Sch. Social Wk. Alumni Assn. (pres. 1952-54, So. Calif. Women for Understanding (chmn. bd. dirs. 1976—), So. Calif. Soc. Psychic Research, NOW. Democrat. Jewish. Office: 6736 Laurel Canyon Blvd Suite 221 North Hollywood CA 91606

RIDDER, MARIE WASSERMAN, writer; d. William Stir and Marion (Fleisher) Wasserman; B.A. with honors, Bryn Mawr Coll., 1946; m. Walter T. Ridder, May 22, 1948; children—Cary, Stephanie, Victor, Pamela. Washington corr. Phila. Evening Bull., 1945-48; Europe corr. N. Am. Newspaper Alliance, 1948-52; Washington editor Conde Nast, 1962-65; dep. to dir. Head Start, Washington, 1965-68; corr. Ridder Newspapers, 1968-76; free lance archtl. writer, McLean, Va., 1978—. Bd. dirs. Outdoors Found., Richmond, Va.; vice chmn. Piedmont Environ. Council; Democratic candidate Va. Legislature. Home: 4509 Crest Ln McLean VA 22101

RIDDER, RUTHE B., state legislator; b. Pullman, Wash., June 13, 1929; d. Fred H. and Esther (Johnson) Burmaster; B.S., U. Wash., 1950; m. Robert Carl Ridder, 1950; children—Janet Ridder Blume, Robert (Andy), Susan, David, William. Mem. Wash. State Senate, 1973—, chmn. labor com., 1975-78; mem. urban devel. com. Nat. Conf. State Legislators, 1976—; mem. Edn. Com. of the States, 1977—. Co-pres., South Shore PTA, 1974. Mem. Rainier C. of C. Lutheran. Club: Rainier Beach Women's (co-pres. 1974—). Office: Wash State Senate State Capitol Olympia WA 98504 *

RIDDICK, LAZETTA ANNETTA, radiologic technologist, educator, b. Balt., June 20, 1948; d. Henry Paul and Daisy Helen (Botts) Church; B.S., U. Mass., 1977; M.A., Antioch U., 1981; m. Oliver W. Riddick, Jr., Dec. 18, 1969; children—Le-Titia Jewel, Christopher Dominique. Acting dir., instr. Bunker Hill Community Coll., 1975-76; tng. specialist Pfizer Med. Systems, Columbia, Md., 1977-78; dir. ednl. program devel. Fellows Read and Weber, Hagerstown, Md., 1978; prior learning coordinator Antioch U., Balt., 1980-82; product specialist CGR Med. Corp., Balt., 1981-82. Mem., Dansforth Task Force on Individualized Edn., 1975-76; chairperson intercultural com. Bunker Hill Community Coll., 1976. Mem. Am. Registry of Radiologic Technologists, Nat. Tech. Assn. Republican. Roman Catholic. Home: 835 Shadwell Dr Houston TX 77062

RIDDICK, MILDRED MAVIS, cons.; b. Roanoke Rapids, N.C., Jan. 2, 1954; d. Willie B. and Christine (Mason) High; B.S., Coppin State Coll., 1977; M. Social Service (scholar 1977, 78), Bryn Mawr Coll., 1979; 1 dau., Stacie Christine. Community organizer Phila. Council Neighborhood Orgns., 1977-78; asst. to exec. dir. Big Sisters Phila., 1978-79; staff asst. Congressman Parren J. Mitchell, 7th Congressional Dist. Balt., 1979; research assoc. Mayor's Office Manpower Resources, Balt., 1979-82; adminstrv. research assoc. Joline, Inc., health and edn. systems analysts. Mem. Welfare Advocates, Md. Recipient Pres. Emeritus Human Relations award Coppin State Coll., 1977. Mem. Student Council Exceptional Children (v.p. in charge publs. 1976-77), Nat. Assn. Social Workers (Bryn Mawr Coll. liaison Pa. chpt. 1978-79), Alpha Kappa Mu. Baptist. Dept. editor Edn. and Tng. of Mentally Retarded, 1976-77. Home: 1618 Ashburton St Baltimore MD 21216 Office: Joline Inc 800 4th St SW Suite 602 N Washington DC 20024

RIDENHOUR, NANCY ANN, fin. exec.; b. Cabarrus County, N.C., Jan. 22, 1954; d. Charles Edward and Helen Elizabeth (Rudisill) Ridenhour; B.S. in stats., N.C. State U., 1976. Researcher, N.C. State U., summer, 1974; summer employee N.C. Dept. Revenue, Raleigh, 1975; programmer Cannon Mills, Kannapolis, N.C., 1976-77; programmer/analyst Riegel Textile, Greenwood, S.C., 1978-80; systems developer First Computer Services, Charlotte, 1980—. Mem. First Union Mgmt. Assn., Nat. Assn. Female Execs., AAUW, N.C. Alumni Assn. Lutheran. Club: N.C. State Wolfpact. Office: First Union Plaza FCS 7 Charlotte NC 28292

RIDER, KATHERINE LOVETA THOMPSON, clin. social worker; b. Roswell, N.M., Apr. 18, 1945; d. Donald and Setta Loveta (Jones) Thompson; B.A., U. Tex., 1967, M.S.S.W., 1969; m. Kent Morrison Rider, June 8, 1968; children—Tracy Lyn, Courtney Elizabeth, Kelley Michelle. Social worker adult mental health staff, Austin-Travis County Mental Health-Mental Retardation Center, 1969-77; cons. Model Cities Project, Austin, Tex., 1971-72, community orgn. specialist alcohol-related services, 1974-76; clin. field faculty Sch. Social Work, U. Tex., Austin, 1977-81; pvt. practice social work, 1977—; mem. homemaker services bd. Child & Family Service Austin, 1970-75. Mem. First Baptist Day Sch. Bd., Austin, 1980-82. Lic. Social Psychotherapist, Tex. Mem. Nat. Assn. Social Workers (dir. Tex. chpt. 1980-84), Tau Beta Sigma. Baptist. Home: 6001 Westgate Blvd Austin TX 78745 Office: 812 San Antonio St Suite 502 Austin TX 78701

RIDER, MARILYN ANN, stockbroker; b. Conrad, Mont., Dec. 15, 1941; d. Louis E. and Emmi V. (Markuson) Schroer; diploma acctg., Gt. Falls (Mont.) Comml. Coll., 1960; m. Joe Raunig, Jan. 2, 1960 (div. 1971); children—Christina M., Rodney B., Brett R.; m. 2d, Lloyd D. Keith, Apr. 19, 1972 (dec. July 1973); m. 3d, Bruce A. Rider, Dec. 10, 1977 (div. 1979); 1 son, Marc D. Engaged in acctg., 1960-74, 75-77; owner Keith Enterprises, Chester, Mont., 1974-75; account exec. Merill Lynch, Pierce Fenner and Smith, Spokane, 1977—; tchr. courses in field. C.P.A., Wash. Mem. Wash. Soc. C.P.A.s. Roman Catholic. Club: Spokane Duplicate Bridge (dir. 1976). Home: N 7927 Pine Meadow Nine Mile Falls WA 49026 Office: 1st Ave and Wall St Spokane WA 99201

RIDGE, CLAIRE LILLIAN, gen. contractor; b. Bklyn., Jan. 2, 1936; d. William Carl and Elizabeth Norma (Braun) Edwards; student Palm Beach Jr. Coll., 1981—; m. William J. Ridge, Nov. 6, 1968; children by previous marriage—Glenn A. Simonin, Diane C. Graziano. Real estate saleswoman Provident Properties, Inc., 1965-67; owner, real estate broker Piper Realty, Inc., 1967-73; owner, builder St. Mark's Estates, Inc., Fieldcrest Homes, Inc., 1971—; owner, builder Sunshine Custom Builders, Inc. and Sunshine Builders of Palm Beach, Inc., 1977—; real estate saleswoman Martha A. Gottfried, Inc. Mem. Singer Island Civic Assn. Notary public, Fla.; lic. Realtor-asso., Fla. Mem. North Palm Beach County Bd. Realtors, Nat. Home Builders Assn., Home Builders Assn. Palm Beach County, Nat. Assn. Notaries. Republican. Lutheran. Club: Frenchmen's Creek Country. Home: 1037 Morse Blvd Singer Island Riviera Beach FL 33404 Office: Singer Island Palm Beach County FL 33404

RIDGWAY, ROZANNE LEJEANNE, ambassador; b. St. Paul, Aug. 22, 1935; d. H. Clay and Ethel Rozanne (Cote) R.; B.A., Hamline U., 1957, LL.D. (hon.), 1978. Commd. fgn. service officer Dept. State, 1957; various assignments in Washington, 1957-59, 64-67, 70-73, dep. asst. sec. Dept. State, ambassador for oceans and fisheries, 1975-77; various fgn. assignments in Manila, 1959-61, Palermo, Italy, 1962-64, Oslo, 1967-70; dep. chief of mission, Nassau, 1973-75; ambassador to Finland, Helsinki, 1977-80; counselor Dept. State, Washington, 1980-81, spl. asst. to sec. state, 1981-82; ambassador to German Democratic Republic, 1982—. Recipient citations Dept. State, 1967, 70, 75, 81; Person of Yr. award Nat. Fisheries Inst., 1977; Joseph C. Wilson award for achievement in internat. relations, 1982.

RIDLEY, LANI SUE, sales exec.; b. Altadena, Calif., Mar. 21, 1948; d. Mahuel Joseph and Vera Jean (Van Steenwyk) Pedrini; B.A., UCLA, 1971; M.Bus., U. So. Calif., 1973; 1 son, Jason Michael. Free lance graphic designer/comml. artist, 1966-77; prodn. mgr., comml. artist Lloyd's Fashion Advt., Los Angeles, 1972-73; advt. prodn. mgr. McMahan's Furniture Co., Santa Monica, Calif., 1973-75; media dir./prodn. mgr. Walgers & Assos. Advt., Inc., Hollywood, Calif., 1975-77; account exec./media dir./prodn. mgr. Darryl Lloyd Advt., Inc., Encino, Calif., 1977-78; mktg. rep. Memorex Corp., W. Los Angeles, 1978-79; sales mgr. Prime Computer Inc., Culver City, Calif., 1980—; pres. LRS, Inc.; cond. seminars in field. Recipient Quota Club-Prime Computer Million Club Award, 1980, 81. Rookie of the Yr. award, Prime Computer Inc., 1980, Top Producer in Western Region award, 1981, others. Mem. Nat. Assn. Female Execs., Am. Soc. Profl. and Exec. Women, Working Women Soc., Data Processing Mgmt. Assn., Career Guild, Alpha Phi. Clubs: Data Processing, Personal Profit. Office: 6089 Bristol Pkwy Culver City CA 90230

RIDLON, MARGARET AGNES, social worker; b. Pittsburg, Kans., Feb. 27, 1923; d. Evan Anthony and Agnes Jessie (Staib) Naylor; B.A., B.S., Pittsburg State U., 1943; M.S. in Social Work (fellowship 1969-71, univ. grantee 1971), U. Tenn., 1971; divorced; children—Evan Anthony, William Frank, II. Med. supr. Ark. Social Services, 1967-71, utilization rev. supr., 1971-73; social work supr. Ark. State Hosp., Little Rock, 1973-76; counselor supr. Ark. Mental Retardation Dept., 1976-82, dir child and family social services, developmental disabilities dept., 1982—; mem. Ark. Comprehensive Health Planning Commn., 1972-76, Environ. Barriers Council, 1977—; bd. dirs. N. Central Ark. Mental Health, 1974-76. Mem. Am. Assn. Mental Deficiency (chmn. social work Ark. 1979—), Nat. Assn. Social Workers, Acad. Cert. Social Workers, Sigma Delta Chi, Alpha Sigma Alpha. Democrat. Methodist. Home: 212 Indianhead Dr Sherwood AR 72116 also 602 Halligan Warren AR 71671 Office: Suite 400 Waldron Bldg 7th and Main St Little Rock AR 72201

RIECHEL, ROSEMARIE ADELE, librarian; b. Germany, Nov. 29, 1937; d. Carl and Maria Adele (Kohl) R.; came to U.S., 1938; B.A., Hunter Coll., 1959; M.S., Columbia U., 1965, postgrad. Sch. Library Service, 1977—. Gen. asst. Butler Library, Columbia U., N.Y.C., 1961-65; librarian Queens Borough Pub. Library, Auburndale br., 1965-66, librarian lang. and lit. div. Central Library, 1966-67, asst. head pub. catalog, telephone reference div., 1967, acting head, 1967-68, head, 1968—. Mem. Am., N.Y. library assns., N.Y. Library Club, Queens Hist. Soc., Met. Opera Guild, Cath. Library Assn. Home: 151-31 25th Ave Whitestone NY 11357 Office: 89-11 Merrick Blvd Jamaica NY 11432

RIEGEL, MARILYN RUTH, human resources mgmt. exec.; b. Chgo., Oct. 13, 1944; d. Sam and Reva Levine; B.A., Northeastern Ill. U., 1969; Ed.M., U. Ill., 1977; postgrad Northwestern U., 1977-79. Tchr., Chgo. Bd. Edn., 1970-77; dir. staffing and employee relations Urban Investment & Devel. Co., 1977—. Mem. Am. Soc. Tng. and Devel., Internat. Assn. Personnel Women. Office: 845 N Michigan Ave Chicago IL 60611

RIEGGER, GERI MARIANNE, data processing exec.; b. N.Y.C., Feb. 23, 1939; d. Arthur and Johanna Lina (Schmidt) R.; B.S., Concordia

Tchrs. Coll., River Forest, Ill., 1960; m. Alan L. Krakow, Aug. 22, 1969; 1 son, Jason. Adv. systems engr. IBM Corp., N.Y.C., 1961-69, adminstrv. asst. to group exec., White Plains, N.Y., 1973-77; v.p. computer ops. Mfrs. Hanover Trust Co., N.Y.C., 1969-73; v.p. systems devel. Fed. Res. Bank N.Y., 1977—; mem. computerization bd. Multiple Sclerosis Soc., 1971-73. White House fellow, 1974-75. Mem. Assn. Computing Machinery, Nat. Assn. Bank Women, Computer Execs. Roundtable (exec. com. 1980—), White House Fellows Alumni Assn. (class rep. 1980-81, mem. regional bd. 1978-79), NOW, Nat. Women's Polit. Caucus, Common Cause. Office: 33 Liberty St New York NY 10045

RIEHM, COLLEEN SHARKEY, airline exec.; b. Reno, Nev., Oct. 10, 1948; d. Jack T. and Bernie C. (Vogel) Sharkey Wright; B.S. in Bus. Adminstrn., U. Nev., Reno, 1974; m. Peter R. Riehm, Feb. 4, 1970. Acct., Atlantic City Airlines, 1970-72, Ann Miner, public acct., Reno, 1972-74; v.p. fin., dir. Munz No. Airlines, Inc., Nome, Alaska, 1976—. Home: PO Box 1085 Nome AK 99762 Office: PO Box 790 Nome AK 99762

RIELY, PHYLLIS ELEANOR, microbiologist; b. Welshfield, Ohio, Jan. 25, 1918; d. Clifford James and Ethel (Corliss) Brunton; student Capital U., 1936-39; grad. Sch. Med. Tech. Huron Rd. Hosp., 1941; m. Charles T. Riely, Nov. 28, 1942 (div.); children—Terrence, Patricia, Maura, Shawn. Systems microbiologist Fairchild Hiller Co., Farmingdale, N.Y., 1960-66; life support coordinator Pall Corp., Glen Cove, N.Y., 1966-69; mgr. med. product devel. Internat. Paper Co., Tuxedo, N.Y., 1969-71; dir. med. products East-West Med. Products Co., Hauppage, N.Y., 1973-74; mgr. biomed. regulatory affairs Pall Corp., Glen Cove, 1973-74; mgr. microbiol. devel. Marion Labs., Kansas City, Mo., 1974-81; mgr. tech. edn. Marion Sci. div. Marion Labs., Kansas City, Mo., 1981-82. Mem. Am. Soc. Microbiology, Royal Soc. Health. Republican. Methodist. Patentee in field; author book; contbr. articles to profl. jours. Home: 12818 Maplewood St Sun City West AZ 85375

RIES, BERNADETTE, hosp. adminstr.; b. Conrad, Mont., Aug. 29, 1938; d. Alfred John and Mary Josephine (DeBoo) R.; Radiol. Technologist, Providence Hosp., Seattle, 1959; B.S., Marquette U., 1970; postgrad. Whitworth Coll., 1979-80. Joined Dominican Sisters of Spokane, Roman Catholic Ch., 1955; radiol. technologist Mt. Carmel Hosp., Colville, Wash., 1960-66; radiol. technologist Holy Family Hosp., Spokane, 1966-69, personnel dir., 1973-76; info. systems coordinator Dominican Sisters of Wash., Spokane, 1971-73, corp. mgr., 1976-78; pres. Dominican Health Services, Spokane, 1979—; mem. State Health Coordinating Council, 1981—; trustee Cath. Health Corp., Omaha. Mem. Wash. State Hosp. Assn. (governing bd. com.). Office: E 235 Rowan St Suite 109 Spokane WA 99207

RIES, LYNNRAE MARIE, telemarketing specialist; b. St. Paul, Sept. 18, 1949; d. Herschel M. and Bernice Elsie (Sjogren) Pepin; student Albany Jr. Coll., 1972-73, Mpls. Community Coll., 1978-80, U. Minn., 1981—. Legal sec. Perry Walters, Lippett & Custer, Albany, Ga., 1971-73; paralegal Beauchamp & Howell, Albany, 1973-74; legal sec. Honeywell, Inc., Mpls., 1974-75, exec. sec., 1975-81, telemktg. specialist, 1982—; Mpls. Community Coll. field rep. to Honeywell. Co-chmn. Honeywell, Inc. div. Mpls. United Way, 1976-81, chmn., 1981—; Mpls. Am. Cancer Soc. rep., 1979. Named Young Career Woman of Yr., Highland Park Bus. and Profl. Women's Orgn., 1979. Mem. Nat. Fedn. Bus. and Profl. Women's Clubs (chpt. pres. 1980-81). Club: Toastmasters (chpt. pres. 1979, named Toastmaster of Yr. 1979, asso. area 4 gov. 1979-80, area 4 gov. 1980-81). Office: Honeywell Plaza Minneapolis MN 55408

RIESS, DORIS GAIL, clin. psychologist; b. Bklyn., May 3, 1938; d. Samuel Harold and Natalie (Arbeit) Flowerman; student Barnard Coll., 1955-57; B.A., CCNY, 1959; M.A. (Woodrow Wilson fellow 1959), Columbia U., 1960, postgrad., 1960-61; Ph.D. (USPHS fellow 1963-66), George Washington U., 1966; m. Michael Riess, Apr. 1, 1961; children—Gail Michele, Holly Sue, Adam Guy. Resident in clin. psychology Saint Elizabeths Hosp., Washington, 1965-66; dir. vocat. rehab. George Washington U. Hosp., Washington, 1966-67; dir. research and evaluation, staff psychotherapist Alexandria (Va.) Community Mental Health Center, 1967-70; asso., clin. psychologist Psychol. and Psychiat. Services, P.C., Darien, Conn., 1970-72; staff psychologist Lyons (N.J.) VA Hosp., 1972-73; co-founder, corporate officer, sec., treas., dir. Bistro Internationale, Inc., Warren, N.J., 1973-82; pvt. practice psychotherapy, Bernardsville, N.J., 1977—. Mem. Am. Psychol. Assn., N.J. Psychol. Assn., N.J. Acad. Psychology, N.Y. Acad. Scis., Phi Beta Kappa, Sigma Xi. Office: 50 Morristown Rd Bernardsville NJ 07924

RIFAS, GAYLEN GOLDSTEIN, lawyer; b. Cin., Dec. 28, 1943; d. Leonard Jack and Gratian Dorothy (Block) Goldstein; B.A. (Dean's Merit scholar) U. Miami (Fla.), 1966, J.D., 1969; m. Earle V. Rifas, Sept. 28, 1968; children—Kobi, Eagan, Evan. Admitted to Fla. bar, 1969; individual practice law, Miami, 1969—; partner firm Rifas & Rifas, 1969—. Mem. bd. local PTA, 1975—. Mem. ACLU, Audubon Soc., Izaak Walton League. Democrat. Jewish religion. Home: 13975 SW 73d Ct Miami FL 33158 Office: 19 W Flagler St Miami FL 33130

RIGDON, IMOGENE STEWART, educator; b. St. Joseph, Mo., Apr. 2, 1937; d. George Francis and Mary Elizabeth (Byrne) Stewart; B.S.N., Marillac Coll., 1961; M.S.N., Cath. U., 1973; m. Michael Allen Rigdon, Nov. 1, 1973; 1 dau., Mary Lisa. Pediatric nursing supr. Burn Center, St. Mary's Hosp., Milw., 1965-70; nursing supr. DePaul Hosp., St. Louis, 1970-71; clin. specialist, asst. dir. nursing St. Anthony's Hosp., Oklahoma City, 1974-76; registered teaching nurse III, Shands Teaching Hosp., Gainesville, Fla., 1976-77; asst. prof. Coll. Nursing, U. Fla., Gainesville, 1977-82. Mem. troop com. Girl Scouts U.S.A., 1980—; mem. Citizens for an Alternative to Death Penalty, 1980—. Served to capt. Air Force NG, 1972-73. Recipient Book of Yr. award Am. Jour. Nursing, 1981. Mem. Am. Nurses Assn. (council clin. specialists in psychiat. mental health nursing), Sigma Theta Tau. Home: 329 South 1200 East Salt Lake City MO 84102

RIGER, ELEANOR SANGER, TV producer, writer; b. Hong Kong, Sept. 15, 1929; d. Richard and Lonni (Wernicke) Sanger; B.A. magna cum laude, Smith Coll., 1950; postgrad. Russian Inst., Columbia U., 1951-52; m. Robert Riger, June 10, 1950 (div. July 1981); children—Christopher, Victoria , Robert, Charlotte. Mgr. public affairs Sta. WNBC-TV, N.Y.C., 1957-60; writer ABC news, 1967; mgr. client relations, asso. producer ABC Sports, 1966-69; free lance TV documentary producer, writer, 1969-70; producer, writer Tomorrow Entertainment, N.Y.C., 1971-73; staff producer, writer ABC Sports, N.Y.C., 1973—. Bd. dirs. Women's Sports Found., Wonder Woman Found. Recipient Emmy award for sports, 1976, for summer olympics, 1977, for Wide World of Sports, 1980, for winter olympics NCAA Football, 1981; Smith Coll. medal, 1982. Mem. Acad. TV Arts and Scis., Writers Guild Am., Am. Women in Radio and TV, Women in Communications, Phi Beta Kappa. Democrat. Episcopalian. Office: ABC 1330 Avenue of Americas New York NY 10019

RIGG, DIANA, actress; b. Doncaster, Yorkshire, Eng., July 20, 1938; d. Louis and Beryl (Helliwell) Rigg; attended St. Christopher's Sch., Great Missenden, Buckinghamshire, Eng.; grad. Fulneck Girl's Sch., Pudsey, Yorkshire; studied two years at Royal Acad. Dramatic Art; m. Menahem Gueffen, July 6, 1973 (div. Sept. 1976); 1 dau., Rachael Atlanta Sterling. Made stage debut as Natella Abashwilli in The Caucasian Chalk Circle at the Theatre Royal, York, Eng., summer, 1957; after appearing in repertory in Chesterfield and Scarborough, joined Royal Shakespeare Co., Stratford-on-Avon, 1959; made Stratford debut as Andromache in Troilus and Cressida, summer 1960; made London debut at Aldwych Theatre in Ondine, 1961; other appearances in repertory at Aldwych Theatre include: Phillipe Trincante in The Devils, Gwendolen in Becket, Bianca in The Taming of the Shrew, 1961, Madame de Tourvel in The Art of Seduction, 1962, Monica Stettler in The Physicists, 1963; at the Royal Shakespeare, Stratford-on Avon, played Helena in A Midsummer Night's Dream, Bianca in The Taming of the Shrew, Lady Macduff in Macbeth, Adriana in The Comedy of Errors, Cordelia in King Lear, 1962; toured the provinces, spring, 1963, in A Midsummer Night's Dream, subsequently appearing at The Royal Shakespeare and at the Aldwych in The Comedy of Errors, Dec., 1963; again played Cordelia in King Lear at the Aldwych, Feb., 1964, prior to touring with both plays for the Brit. Council in Europe, USSR, and U.S.; during this tour made first appearance in N.Y.C. at the State Theatre, May, 1964, in the same plays; played Viola in Twelfth Night at Stratford, June, 1966, and Heloise in Abelard and Heloise at Wyndham's, May, 1970, and Brooks Atkinson, N.Y.C., Mar., 1971; joined The Nat. Theatre, 1972; appeared in Jumpers, 'Tis Pity She's a Whore and as Lady Macbeth in Macbeth, 1972; Celimene in The Misanthrope, 1973; Eliza Doolittle in Pygmalion, Albery, 1974; rejoined Nat. Theatre for U.S. tour of The Misanthrope at Kennedy Center, Washington, St. James Theatre, N.Y.C., 1975, at Old Vic, 1975, also Governor's Wife in Phaedra Britannica, 1975; film appearances include: A Midsummer Night's Dream, Assassination Bureau, On Her Majesty's Secret Service, Julius Caesar, The Hospital, Theatre of Blood, A Little Night Music, 1977, The Great Muppet Caper, 1981; first appeared on TV, 1964, as Adriana in The Comedy of Errors, also appeared in The Hothouse, 1964, Women Beware Women, 1965; co-starred as Emma Peel in Brit. TV series The Avengers, 1965-67; appeared in TV movie Married Alive, 1970, then in series Diana, 1973-74, TV movie In This House of Brede, 1975, TV series Three Piece Suite, 1977. Nominated for Tony award as best actress in a dramatic play for Broadway appearance in Abelard ahd Heloise, also for the Misanthrope, Emmy nominations, 1967, 68, 75; recipient Plays and Players award as best performance by actress for Phaedra Britannica. Office: care London Mgmt 235 Regent St London W1A 2JT England *

RIGG, MARGARET RUTH, educator, publisher, graphic designer, calligrapher; b. Pitts., Dec. 14, 1929; d. Carl Hazlett and Ruth Standish (Massey) R.; B.A., Fla. State U., 1951; M.A., Presbyn. Sch. Christian Edn., 1955; postgrad. Carnegie-Mellon U., 1946-50, Sch. Art Inst. Chgo., 1963. Staff artist bd. publs. Fla. State U., Tallahassee, 1950-53; art editor Motive mag., Nashville, 1954-65; asso. prof. visual arts Eckerd Coll., St. Petersburg, Fla., 1981—, dir. Elliott Teaching Gallery; artist-in-residence Fla. Presbyn. Coll., St. Petersburg, 1965-67; owner-pub. Possum Press, 1969—; TV programs: I Need to Hear from You, 1969, Keep in Touch, 1971; Stone lectr. Princeton Sem., 1972. Mem. Com. of Seventy-Five for Higher Edn.-Asian Women. Fulbright-Hays sr. research grantee, 1972. Mem. Soc. Arts, Religion and Contemporary Culture, St. Petersburg Soc. Scribes (pres. 1978-81). Methodist. Exhibited 60 solo visual arts shows; contbr. articles to profl. jours. Office: Eckerd Coll PO Box 12560 Saint Petersburg FL 33733

RIGGINS, ANNA MARGARET, educator; b. Louisville, Apr. 4, 1945; d. Henry Garrison and Nora Lee (Winfrey) Garrison; B.S. Music, Ky. State U., 1967; postgrad D.C. Tchrs. Coll., 1969; M.A.T., Oakland U., 1976; postgrad Wayne State U., 1981; children from previous marriage—William Robert II, Alexis Morann. Tchr. music, Hine Jr. High Sch., Washington, 1967-69; tchr. music C.B. Sabbath Sch., River Rouge, Mich., 1969-80; tchr. elem. sch. River Rouge, Mich., 1980—; tchr. adult edn., evenings River Rouge, 1981—. Dir. youth choir Tabernacle Bapt. Ch.; mem. youth leadership council; mem. exec. bd. PTA Sabbath Sch., 1975-77. Mem. Assn. Supervision and Curriculum Devel., NEA, Mich. Edn. Assn., River Rouge Edn. Assn., NAACP, YWCA, Ky. State U Alumni Assn. Democrat. Home: 2235 Calvert St Detroit MI 48206 Office: 340 Frazier St River Rouge MI 48218

RIGGINS, JOSEPHINE DAWKINS, social worker; b. Hurtsboro, Ala., Feb. 23, 1914; d. Algie and Julia (Borom) Dawkins; student Fisk U., 1932-34; B.A. in History, Ky. State U., 1938; postgrad. U. Chgo., 1939-41; widow; 1 son, Carl III. Jr. visitor Lake County Dept. Public Welfare, Gary, Ind., 1939-42, sr. visitor, 1942-45, supr., 1945-49, asst. div. head, 1949-55, div. head, 1955-67, asst. dir., 1968-70, dir., 1970-71, asst. dir., 1971—; adv. bd. Indsl. Nat. Bank of East Chicago (Ind.). Former dir. christian edn. 3d Episcopal dist., dir. Christian edn. Mich. conf. African Meth. Episcopal Zion Ch.; dir. Christian edn. St. Mark A.M.E. Zion Ch.; former bd. dirs. Twin Community Services, East Chicago Vis. Nurses Assn.; bd. dirs. Referral and Emergency Services, Lake County Community Devel. Com.; former chmn. bd. East Chicago Multi-Service Centers; mem. personnel com. St. Catherine Hosp.; v.p. Community Health Assn.; adv. bd. Gary Manpower; Sec. adv. bd. East Chicago Rehab. Center. Recipient St. Joseph the Worker award Trustees of St. Josephs Coll., East Chicago, Ind., 1970; cert. of appreciation Lake County Econ. Opportunity Council, 1970; award St. Mark A.M.E. Zion Ch., East Chicago, 1970; award Club Reginas, 1972, Ind. Conf. on Social Welfare, 1974; social service award Twin City Community Services, East Chicago, 1975; Outstanding Vol. award Lake Area United Way, 1975; longevity service award Twin City Community Services, 1979. Mem. Nat. Assn. Social Workers, Am. Public Welfare Assn., Nat. Conf. on Social Welfare, Ind. Conf. on Social Concerns, N.W. Ind. Regional Conf. on Social Concerns, NAACP, Alpha Kappa Rho, Delta Sigma Theta (life). Josephine Riggins Service award established in her honor. Home: 4326 Hidalgo Ln East Chicago IN 46312 Office: Lake County Dept Public Welfare 800 Massachusetts St Gary IN 46402

RIGGS, CONSTANCE KAKAVECOS, coll. adminstr.; b. Indpls., Apr. 6, 1928; d. James Eustace and Dorothy Amelia (Boren) Kakavecos; B.A., St. Mary-of-the-Woods Coll., Terre Haute, Ind., 1975; m. Kenneth Wesley Riggs, Dec. 4, 1947 (dec.); children—Ken Roger, Yvonne Denise Riggs Rench, James Cary, Vicki Catherine, Constance Amelia, Jeffrey Allan. Med. edn. coordinator St. Vincent Hosp., Indpls., 1967-72; asst. to pres. Wabash Coll., Crawfordsville, Ind., 1972-78; asst. v.p. for devel. St. Mary-of-the-Woods Coll., 1978-79; asst. to pres. Rollins Coll., Winter Park, Fla., 1979—; lectr. in field. Bd. dirs. Montgomery County (Ind.) United Fund, 1973-75, Terre Haute YWCA, 1978; trustee Ind. Council for Advancement and Support of Edn., 1978. Hon. fellow Ind. Collegiate Press Assn. Mem. Nat. Fedn. Press Women, Fla. Press Women. Greek Orthodox. Club: Altrusa. Author: Sam Shue and the Seven Satchels, 1976. Editor: Montgomery County Remembers, 1976; editorial bd. Vigo County Hist. Soc., 1978. Home: 3503 St Andrews Blvd Winter Park FL 32792 Office: Rollins Coll Winter Park FL 32789

RIGGS, JEAN MIRIAM, dietitian; b. Ralston, Iowa, Jan. 4, 1917; d. Fred Arthur and Lillie May (Repp) R.; B.S., Iowa State U., 1939, M.S., 1956. Dietetic intern Michael Reese Hosp., Chgo., 1940; dietitian McMillan Hosp., Charleston, W.Va., 1940-43; adminstrv. dietitian Michael Reese Hosp., Chgo., 1943-45, asst. dir. dietary dept., 1945-48; dir. sch. lunch Highland Park (Ill.) High Sch., 1949-56; dir. dietary dept. Montefiore Hosp., Pitts., 1948-49; asst. prof. instl. mgmt. Coll. Home Econs., Iowa State U., Ames, 1956-60; asso. prof. instl. mgmt., asso. dir. housing, dir. residence hall food service Kans. State U., Manhattan, 1960-82, emeritus, 1982—. Mem. Nat. Assn. Coll. and Univ. Food Service (Ted Minah award 1981; regional pres.), W.Va. Dietetic Assn. (sec.), Ill. Dietetic Assn. (sec., pres.), Kans. Dietetic Assn. (treas.), Am. Home Econs. Assn., chmn. instl. mgmt. sect.), Nat. Restaurant Assn., Am. Home Econs. Assn., Am. Sch. Food Service Assn., Food Service Systems Mgmt. Edn. Council, Omicron Nu. Methodist. Home: 3436 Southdale Dr Ames IA 50010

RIGGS, JEANETTE TEMPLETON, civic worker; b. Little Rock, Mar. 13, 1933; d. Donald M. and Fay (Templeton) Brewer; student Little Rock U., 1950-51, Tex. Coll. for Women, 1951-52; B.S., U. Ark., 1955; m. Byron Lawrence Riggs, June 1955; children—Byron Kent, Ann Templeton. Founder, Rochester (Minn.) Ballet Guild, 1970, pres., 1974; mem. establishing bd., exec. bd. Rochester Arts Council, 1972, producer, dir. T.S. Elliot's The Rock, 1970; founder, performer So. Minn. Ballet Co., 1974; sponsor Nat. Ballet Cos., Rochester, 1970-75; exec. bd. for restoration 1875 Pattern Book House, Rochester Heritage Assn., 1975-77; exec. bd. Savino Ballet Nat., 1975-78; founder, exec. bd. Citizens Action Com., 1977-79; asso., commentator Women, Cable TV Program for Women, Rochester, 1979; mem. Mayor's Com. on Drug Abuse, 1979-80; mem. Olmsted County Steering Com. for George Bush, 1979-80, a founder, mem. exec. bd. Olmsted County Republican Women's Orgn., 1979—, mem. Olmsted County Rep. Central Com., 1979—, exec. bd. issues com., 1979-80. Home: 432 SW 10th Ave Rochester MN 55901

RIGGS, SALLIE ANN, univ. adminstr.; b. Rochester, N.Y., Jan. 12, 1941; d. Allan Edward and Eleanor Lorraine (Snyder) Kappelman; B.A. in Biology, Brown U., 1962; children—V. Anne, Susan J. Biochemistry researcher Northwestern U., 1962-63; editor alumnae mag. Brown U., Providence, 1968-71, asso. v.p. univ. relations alumni and spl. programs, 1971—. Public relations com., trustee Wheeler Sch., 1978-80; bd. dirs. YWCA, Pro Cap. Mem. Council Advancement and Support of Edn. (writing awards). Contbr. articles travel mags. Office: Box 1920 Brown U Providence RI 02912

RIGNEY, MARY EASTMAN, communications exec.; b. Bonners Ferry, Idaho, July 23, 1930; d. George Washington and Golda (Wilson) Tautfest; B.A., U. Wash., 1950; postgrad. Calif. State U., Fullerton, 1970-71; children—Steven George, R. Bennett, R. Noah. Profl. actress, N.Y. and Hollywood, 1950-60; founder, owner, mgr. Orange (Calif.) Studio Theater, 1964-68; mem. faculty Calif. State U., Fullerton, 1967, Chapman Coll., Orange, Calif., 1968; tchr. Marywood High Sch., Orange, 1965-69; producer, dir., coach, tchr. Profl. Actors Workshop, Orange, 1964-68; owner, writer, account exec. Mary Eastman Rigney, Newport Beach, Calif., 1971—. Recipient Orange County Press Club Headliner, 1967; U. Wash. scholar, 1948-50; U.S. Office Edn. grantee, 1966. Mem. Bldg. Industry Assn. So. Calif., Nat. Assn. Home Builders, Bldg. Industry Assn. (sales and mktg. council, home builders council), Nat. Assn. Real Estate Editors, Women in Communications, Public Relations Soc. Am., Am. Women's Econ. Devel., Women's Referral Service, Sigma Kappa, Pi Kappa Psi. Writer-producer Little Man in Search of His Serious Side, 1964-65. Home: 9971 Center Dr Villa Park CA 92667 Office: 3822 Campus Dr Suite 218 Newport Beach CA 92660

RILEY, BARBARA POLK, librarian; b. Roselle, N.J., Nov. 21, 1928; d. Charles Carrington and Olive Bond P.; A.B., Howard U., 1950; B.S., N.J. Coll. Women, 1951; M.S., Columbia U., 1955; m. George Emerson Riley, Feb. 23, 1957 (dec.); children—George E., Glenn C., Karen O. Asst. librarian, Fla. A&M U., 1951-53; with Morgan State Coll., 1955; with Dept. Def., 1955-57, S.C. State Coll., 1957-59, U.Wis., 1958-59; asst. librarian Atlanta U., 1960-68; asst. dir. Union County Anti Poverty Council, 1968; librarian Union County Tech. Inst., Scotch Plains, N.J., 1968—. Mem. Roselle Bd. Edn., 1976-78; bd. dirs. Union County Anti Poverty Council, 1969-72; mem. Roselle Human Relations Commn., 1971-73, Plainfield Sci. Center, 1974-76, Union County Psychiat. Clinic, 1980—, Pinewood Sr. Citizens Council, 1981—. Mem. N.J. Library Assn., Council Library Tech., ALA (Black caucus), N.J. Black Librarians, Alpha Kappa Alpha. Mem. A.M.E. Ch. Club: Just-A-Mere Lit. Home: 114 E 7th Ave Roselle NJ 07203 Office: 1776 Raritan Rd Scotch Plains NJ 07076

RILEY, CATHERINE I., state senator; b. Balt., Mar. 21, 1947; d. Francis Worth and Catherine (Cain) Riley; B.A., Towson State Coll., 1969. Mem., Md. Ho. Dels., 1975-83, chmn. Joint Energy Com., 1977-83, mem. Environ. Matters Com., 1975-83, mem. adminstrv., exec. and legislative rev. com., 1978-83, mem. Bistate Com. on Chesapeake Bay, 1981-83; mem. Md. State Senate, 1983—. Recipient Young Democrat of Year award, 1975. Mem. Order of Women Legislators. Office: Senate Office Bldg Annapolis MD 21401

RILEY, CHRISTINE BOONE, controller; b. Nash County, N.C., Sept. 18, 1939; d. George Lunis and Eva Christine (Collins) Boone; student Carolina Sch. Commerce, 1958-59; corr. cert. in advanced acctg. U. Tenn., 1973; m. Phillip C. Riley, Nov. 24, 1962; children—Elizabeth Christine, Sheri Lynn. Asst. bookkeeper N.C. Supply, Inc., Rocky Mount, 1960-61, bookkeeper, 1962-63; staff accountant C. Jackson Luper, C.P.A., Rocky Mount, 1963-69; cost acct. Central Builders, Inc., Rocky Mount, 1969-71; staff acct. Biggs, Meadows, Batts, Etheridge & Winberry, Attys., Rocky Mount, 1972-81; controller and asst. treas. Tar River Communications, Inc., Rocky Mount, 1981—; dir. Central Builders, Inc., 1969-71, Arrow, Inc., 1969-79; personal tax cons. numerous individual bus. firms, 1970—. Mem. Nat. Assn. Female Execs. Club: Rocky Mount Evening Pilot (dir. 1976-77). Republican. Baptist. Home: 1224 Tarboro St Rocky Mount NC 27801 Office: 1509 W Mount Dr Rocky Mount NC 27801

RILEY, CLARA MAE, psychologist; b. Kilgore, Tex., July 27, 1931; d. Joseph and Elsie Irene (Richardson) Marion; B.A. in Psychology and Speech, Pepperdine Coll., 1953, M.A. in Psychology, 1956; Ph.D. in Child Devel., Fla. State U., 1963; children—Randall, René. Asst. prof. Pepperdine Coll., 1963-67, 81—; gen. practice clin. psychology, Laguna Beach, Calif., 1970—; asst. clin. prof. med. psychology U. Calif., Irvine, 1970—. Mental health cons. Project Head Start, 1965-71, also vol. award; mem. social needs com. City Laguna Beach (Calif.), 1975-77. Mem. Orange County Soc. Clin. Hypnosis (past pres.), Am. Psychol. Assn. Author: (with Frances Epps) Head Start In Action; writer film: From City Streets to Mountain Ranch: How Children Learn. Diplomate Am. Bd. Profl. Psychology, Am. Bd. Psychol. Hypnosis; cert. clin. psychologist, Calif.; specialist in psychotherapy, biofeedback, psychosomatic disorders, hypnosis, diagnosis. Office: 31542 South Coast Hwy South Laguna CA 92677

RILEY, COLLEEN MARIE, oil co. sales rep.; b. Seattle, Oct. 6, 1950; d. William Lloyd and Eleanor (Schade) R.; student U. Wash., 1968-70, 74, N. Seattle Community Coll., 1975; B.A. in Bus., Central Wash. U., 1976. Receptionist Group Health Hosp., Seattle, 1971-73; with Shell Oil Co., Seattle, 1977—, ter. sales rep. in mgmt. tng., 1979—. Automotive adv. com. Seattle Public Schs. Roman Catholic. Clubs: Wash. Athletic, Women's Univ. Office: 400 108th NE Bellevue WA 98004

RILEY, EILEEN V., librarian; b. Hartford, Conn.; d. Jeremiah and Mary (Garvey) Riley; A.A., Boston U., 1952, B.A., 1954; M.S. in L.S., Columbia U., 1959. Library intern Nat. Library of Medicine, Bethesda, Md., 1959-60, librarian cataloger, 1960-61, librarian acquisitions, 1961-71; chief tech. processes VA Central Office Library, Washington, 1971-73; chief acquisitions br. U.S. Dept. of Labor Library, Washington, 1973—. Mem. ALA, Med. Library Assn., Spl. Library Assn. Home:

6304 Haviland Dr Bethesda MD 20817 Office: US Dept of Labor Library Washington DC 20210

RILEY, ELLA WALKER, home economist; b. Cairo, Miss., Mar. 8, 1937; d. L.T. and Jannie Bell (Johnson) Walker; B.S., Alcorn A. and M. U., 1963; m. Willie George Riley, Aug. 29, 1965; children—Eleana Bell, Enid Louett, Chad Decartes. Asst. home demonstration agt., Decatur, Miss., 1963-65; asso. home demonstration agt., Greenwood, Miss., 1965-66, asso. extension home economist, 1966-76; extension home economist, Macon, Miss., 1976—; nat. conf. del. 4-H, 1959. Cert. applied gerontology. Mem. Am. Home Econs. Assn., Miss. Home Econs. Assn., Epsilon Sigma Phi. Baptist. Home: PO Box 282 Macon MS 39341 Office: PO Box 387 Macon MS 39341

RILEY, JANE ANN, manpower adminstr.; b. Boston, May 19, 1948; d. Leo Alfred and Florence D. R.; B.A. in History, Calif. Lutheran Coll., 1970; M.A. in History, Calif. State U., Los Angeles, 1973. Adminstrv. asst. Pasadena (Calif.) Community Services Commn., 1975-76; program developer Tribal Am. Cons. Corp., Commerce, Calif., 1976-77, asso. dir., 1977-79; planner County of Orange, Santa Ana, Calif., 1979—; cons. adminstrn. Native Am. programs, 1977-78. Mem. museum service council Los Angeles County Mus. Art, 1976—. Mem. Orgn. Am. Historians, Calif. Women in Govt., Am. Assn. State and Local History, Nat. Assn. Female Execs. Democrat. Roman Catholic. Home: 651 Grand-D South Pasadena CA 91030 Office: 623 N Broadway Santa Ana CA 92701

RILEY, MATILDA WHITE, sociologist; b. Boston, Apr. 19, 1911; d. Percival and Mary (Cliff) White; A.B., Radcliffe Coll., 1931, M.A., 1937; D.Sc., Bowdoin Coll., 1972; m. John Winchell Riley, Jr., June 19, 1931; children—John W., III, Lucy Ellen Riley Sallick. Research asst. Harvard U., Cambridge, Mass., 1932; v.p. Mktg. Research Co. Am., N.Y.C., 1938-49; chief cons. economist War Prodn. Bd., 1941-43; research specialist Rutgers U., N.Y.C., 1950, prof., 1951-73, prof. emeritus, 1973—, dir. sociology lab., 1959-73; prof., chmn. dept. sociology and anthropology Bowdoin Coll., Brunswick, Maine, 1973—, D.B. Fayerweather prof. polit. economy and sociology, 1974—; asso. dir. Nat. Inst. on Aging, Bethesda, Md., 1978—; sr. mem. Inst. Medicine, Nat. Acad. Scis., 1978—; faculty Harvard U., summer 1955; asso. and dir. on aging and society Russell Sage Found., N.Y.C., 1964-73, staff sociologist, 1974-77; vis. prof. N.Y. U., 1956-61; cons. Nat. Council on Aging, Acad. Ednl. Devel. Mem. study group NIH, 1971-78, Social Sci. Research Council Com. on Life-course Perspectives, 1973—; trustee Big Sisters Assn. Fellow Center Advanced Study in Behavioral Scis., 1978-79. Recipient Lindback research award Rutgers U., 1970; Social Sci. award Andrus Gerontology Center, U. So. Calif., 1972. Mem. Am. Sociol. Assn. (exec. officer 1949-60, v.p. 1973—), AAAS (chmn. sect. social and econ. scis. 1975-77), Am. Assn. Public Opinion Research (sec.-treas. 1949-51), Eastern Sociol. Soc. (v.p. 1968-69, pres. 1977-78), Sociol. Research Assn., Phi Beta Kappa, Phi Beta Kappa assns. Author: (with P. White) New Product Research, Gliding and Soaring, 1931; (with Riley and Toby) Sociological Studies in Scale Analysis, 1954; Sociological Research, vol. I, II, 1964; (with others) Aging and Society, vol. I, 1968, vol. II, 1969, vol. III, 1972; (with Nelson) Sociological Observation, 1974; Aging from Birth to Death: Interdisciplinary Perspectives, 1978; (with R. Merton) Sociological Traditions from Generation to Generation, 1980; Aging from Birth to Death: Sociotemporal Perspectives, 1982; contbr. articles to profl. jours. Home: 3311 Maud St NW Washington DC 20016 Office: Nat Inst on Aging Bethesda MD

RILEY, MICHELE TRAVERS, clin. social worker; b. Worcester, Mass., Dec. 31, 1942; d. Abraham and Paula (Kleinman) Travers; A.B., Boston U., 1964; M.S.W. (VA trainee 1966-67), Columbia U., 1967; m. Edward Riley, Jan. 27, 1973. Psychiat. social worker Bellevue Psychiat. Hosp., N.Y.C., 1967-69; sr. gen. social worker Maimonides Community Mental Health Center, Bklyn., 1969-73; prin. clin. social worker Tri-City Mental Health Center, Malden, Mass., 1973-81; psychiat. Social worker Cable Hosp., Ipswich, Mass., 1978-80; mem. profl. adv. bd. Malden Community Nurses Orgn., 1977-81; field instr. Boston Coll. Sch. Social Workers, 1975-81; cons. Hegner Center Workshop Retarded, 1977-80; pvt. practice psychotherapy, 1975—; supr./coordinator mental retardation services North Shore Community Mental Health Center, Salem, Mass., 1981—. Recipient Ann. award Hegner Center, 1978. Lic. ind. clin. social worker, Mass. Mem. Nat. Assn. Social Workers, Acad. Cert. Social Workers. Democrat. Jewish. Home: 43 Boxford Rd Ipswich MA 01938 Office: 47 Congress St Salem MA 01970

RILLERA, EVELYN LOUISE, psychiat. nurse; b. Detroit, Jan. 12, 1931; d. Lazaro and Elsie Lucille (Sexton) Pelayo; grad. Santa Rosa Coll. Sch. Nursing, 1962; m. Herbert Rillera, July 28, 1957; children—Lyric April, Heather Lyn, Roman Mark. Psychiat. nurse Napa State Hosp., Imola, Calif., 1962-67; group therapist Napa County Mental Health Services, 1967-70, founder, dir. Phoenix House, day treatment center, 1970-75, staff devel. cons., 1975; psychiat. nurse cons. Howell Johnson Social Rehab. Center, Napa, Calif., 1975-76; counselor, trainer Phoenix House, Napa County Mental Health Services, 1976-78; clin. instr. Napa Community Coll., 1978-79, instr. psychiat. technician program, 1979—; founder, dir. Creative Living Center, Napa, 1967-73. Bd. dirs. Napa Mental Health Assn., 1973-79, pres., 1977. Recipient Outstanding Achievement award Calif. Assn. Mental Health, 1968, 70. Home: 3480 Young Ave Napa CA 94558 Office: Napa Coll Napa CA 94558

RINALDI, MARY LOU THERESA, mgmt. cons.; b. Stamford, Conn., May 21, 1953; d. Dominic Francis and Edith Elizabeth (LaBella) R.; B.A. in English and Communications summa cum laude, U. Bridgeport, 1975; M.A. in Communications, Fairfield U., 1980. With HEI, Inc./Howard Johnson, Stamford, Conn., 1975-80, asst. gen. mgr., 1980—; sr. mgmt. cons. Weatherby Assos., Norwalk, Conn., 1980—; notary public State of Conn., 1979—. Bd. reps. City of Stamford, 1980—. Recipient Baxter award for lit. U. Bridgeport, 1975; named Mgmt. Employee of Yr., Howard Johnson Co., 1978. Mem. Nat. Assn. Female Execs., Conn. Hotel/Motel Assn., Stamford Area Commerce and Industry Assn., Stamford Citizens Action Group. Democrat. Home: 46 Wilson St Stamford CT 06902 Office: 25 Van Zant St Norwalk CT 06855

RINALDI, SANDRA BRUCE, banker; b. Inglewood, Calif., Apr. 27, 1948; d. Robert Glen and Florence Taylor (Fuller) Bruce; student Foothill Coll., 1966-68, Golden Gate U., 1976; m. William Rinaldi, Aug. 17, 1968. Teller, Crocker Nat. Bank, San Rafael, Calif., 1969-71, loan clk., 1971-72, sr. loan clk., 1972-73, installment loan specialist, 1973-75, sr. installment credit specialist, 1975-77, asst. br. mgr., corp. officer, 1977-79, retail banking officer, 1979—. Mem. Am. Inst. Banking, Nat. Assn. Female Execs. Republican. Episcopalian.

RINEHART, LEILA MAE KIRKHOFF, bus. services co. exec.; b. Chester County, Pa., July 16, 1938; d. Chester G. and Elsie Annie (Dahms) Kirkhoff; student Pierce Jr. Coll., Phila., 1955-57, LaSalle Extension U., 1963-64, Northwestern Sch. Taxidermy, Nebr., 1967-69. Exec. sec., Phila., 1957-64; plant security officer Penguin Industries Inc., Parkesburg, Pa., 1964-70; partner F.J. D'Imperior Sales & Internat. Trade Co., Exton, Pa., 1960-65; co-owner, bus. mgr. Rinehart's Inc., Nantmeal Village, Pa., 1967-75; v.p., adminstrv. asst. Woodcrest Mgmt. Corp./Andrew Devel. Corp./Fred Sternberg Wynn Devel. Corp., Fort Lauderdale, Fla., 1972-78; v.p., corp. sec. Standard Mech. Contractors, Inc., Pompano Beach, Fla., 1978-80; owner L. M. Rinehart Bus. Services Co., Pompano Beach, 1978—. Mem. Nat. Rifle Assn. (life), Am. Water Ski Assn. (affiliate). Contbr. articles to World of Taxidermy and Popular Mechanics. Home: Apt 110 Club House Cove 1100 Crystal Lake Dr Pompano Beach FL 33064

RINEHART, PAULA CUMMINGS, nursing educator, ednl. adminstr.; cons.; b. Soda Springs, Idaho, Idaho, May 29, 1927; d. Delbert John and Madge (Butler) Panting; diploma Mont. State Coll. Sch. Nursing, 1947; B.S. in Nursing, Mont. State U., 1970, M.S. in Nursing, 1971, postgrad. adult and higher edn., 1974—; m. Jerry Longeway Cummings, Sept. 22, 1951; children—Mark G., Clifford S., Steven D.; m. 2d, Donald R. Rinehart, July 9, 1982. Supr. emergency room and outpatient dept. Billings (Mont.) Deaconess Hosp., 1947-49, supr. operating room, 1950-51, head med. services, 1966-69; operating room nurse Magic Valley meml. Hosp., Twin Falls, Idaho, 1949-50; head nurse nursery St. Anthony Hosp., Pocatello, Idaho, 1951-52; part-time and relief positions, 1952-63; night nurse Westminister (Colo.) Convalescent Center, 1962-63; night supr. Valley View Hosp., Thornton, Colo., 1963-65; asst. prof. Boise State U., 1972-73, dir. continuing edn. Sch. Health Scis., 1974-77; instr., part-time, dept. nursing Mont. State U., Bozeman, 1974; adj. assoc. prof. continuing edn. Oreg. Health Scis. U., Portland, 1979-80; clin. instr. (adj.) Oreg. Inst. Tech., Klamath Falls, 1979-80; asst. prof. Portland (Oreg.) State U. div. continuing edn., 1977-80; dir., coordinator Oreg. Statewide Continuing Edn. Project for Nurses, Salem, 1977-80; coordinator staff devel. Salem Hosp., 1980—; cons. Closed Circuit TV Ednl. Program for Hosp. Personnel, devel. self learning modules for critical care nursing; cons., liaison Salem Hosp., Chemeketa Community Coll., Clin. Experience for Health Care Personnel; resource to Oreg. legislators on nursing related issues, 1977—. HEW grantee, 1977-80; recipient continuing edn. grants. mem. Nat. League Nurses, Oreg. League Nurses (pres.-elect 1982, dir. 1981—, program chmn. 1981—), Am. Soc. for Healthcare Edn. and Tng. of the Am. Hosp. Assn. (pres. 1982, program chmn. 1982), Oreg. Continuing Nursing Edn. Network (pres. 1982), Willamette Continuing Nursing Edn. Coordinators (chairperson 1981), Phi Kappa Phi, Alpha Tau Delta. Republican. Club: PEO. Developer continuing edn. programs. Home: 3837 Meadowlawn Loop SE #10 Salem OR 97301 Office: 665 Winter St SE Salem OR 97301

RING, BARBARA ANN, mktg. and health care services cons.; b. St. Louis, Mar. 7, 1945; d. Oliver C. and Ann (McCarron) Garleb; A.A. in Nursing, El Camino Coll., 1964; B.A., UCLA, 1967; J.D., Whittier Coll., 1971; B.S. in Mgmt., Pacific Christian Coll., 1978; m. Douglas Ralph Ring; 1 son, Michael Francis. With Harbor Gen. Hosp., Torrance, Calif., 1964-66, Gardena Meml. Hosp., 1967-68, UCLA Med. Center, 1969-70, Brotman Meml. Hosp., Culver City, 1971-73; cardiac specialist Calif. Hosp. Med. Center, Los Angeles, 1974-77; asst. dir. nurses Fountain Valley Community Hosp. (Calif.), 1978-79; cons. Upjohn Health Care Services, City of Industry, Calif., 1980—. Youth camp dir. YMCA, also caravan dir. Bank Am. scholar, 1962; Westment Coll. scholar, 1962. Mem. Am. Mgmt. Assn., Nat. Assn. Female Execs., Critical Care Nurses Assn. Office: PO Box 3543 City Industry CA 91744

RING, BONNIE, psychologist; b. N.Y.C., Apr. 22, 1940; d. Richard I. and Rita A. (Meyer) Kilstein; student Vassar Coll., 1957-59; B.A., N.Y.U., 1962; M.Ed., Boston U., 1964, Ed.D., 1972; postgrad UCLA, 1966-68, U. Calif., San Francisco, 1977-78. Teaching fellow dept. behavioral scis. Sch. Mgmt., Boston U., 1963-65, grad. asst. Human Relations Center, 1964-65, fellow Center for Applied Behavioral Sci., 1963-65; tng. specialist Econ. Youth Opportunities Agy., Los Angeles, 1966; research asst. Center for Study and Evaluation of Instructional programs UCLA, 1966-67; tng. asso. Western Center for Community Edn. and Devel., U. Calif. Statewide Extension, Los Angeles, 1967-68; counseling psychologist U. Calif., Santa Cruz, 1969-73; lectr. Merrill Coll., 1971-72; asso. dir. clin. services Center for Counseling and Spl. Services, U. Calif., Irvine, 1973-75, lectr. Grad. Sch. Adminstrn., clin. instr. dept. psychiatry and human behavior, 1974-75; asso. dean Calif. Coll. Podiatric Medicine, 1975-77, clin. asst. prof., 1975-77; pvt. practice psychotherapy and organizational cons., San Francisco, 1977—; pres. Bonnie Ring, Ed.D., A Psychol. Corp., 1980—; tng. staff Exec. Effectiveness Course, Am. Mgmt. Assn., 1978-81; adj. faculty human relations and orgn. behavior U. San Francisco, 1978-79; host psychol. call in talk show Sta. KSFO, San Francisco, 1980-81; specialist Media Psychology, 1980—. HEW grantee, 1976-77; lic. psychologist, Calif. Mem. AFTRA, Am. Psychol. Assn., Calif. Psychol. Assn., San Francisco Bay Area Psychol. Assn., NOW, Organizational Devel. Network, Nat. Register Health Care Providers in Psychology, Pi Lambda Theta. Democrat. Episcopalian. Office: 450 Sutter St Suite 1634 San Francisco CA 94108

RING, KAREN JENTOFT, travel agy. exec.; b. Mpls., Oct. 8, 1939; d. Albert B. and Else Jentoft (Lindholm); B.A., Colby Coll., 1961; children by previous marriage—Timothy R., Marcie L. Sales agt. Northwest Airlines, Inc., Mpls., 1962; office mgr. Travel Center, Inc., Mankato, Minn., 1963-72, Champions Travel, Inc., Louisville, 1972-73; gen. mgr. Dittmann Tours, Northfield, Minn., 1973; Hennessey Travel Service, Excelsior, Minn., 1973-74; div. mgr. Diamonds Co., Phoenix, 1974-80; instr. SST Travel Schs., Phoenix, 1981-82; mgr. Davidson Travel, Phoenix, 1982—. Bd. dirs. YWCA camps, 1955-57; instr. water safety ARC; mem. Mankato First Bapt. Ch. Bd. Edn., 1968-69; chmn. Republican 5th Precinct Com., 1968-71, Neighbor to Neighbor Fund Drive, 1969-71; alt. del. Rep. State Conv., 1970. Mem. AAUW (state conv. housing chmn. 1966), Am. Soc. Travel Agts. (treas. 1976-80), Inst. Cert. Travel Counselors (cert travel counselor), Ariz. Women in Travel, Pacific Area Travel Assn. Home: 6625 E Granada Rd Scottsdale AZ 85257 Office: 7975 N Hayden Rd Suite B121 Scottsdale AZ 85258

RINGEN, CATHERINE OLESON, linguist, educator; b. Bklyn., June 3, 1943; d. Prince Eric and Geneva Muriel (Leigh) Oleson; B.A., Ind. U., 1970, M.A., 1972, Ph.D., 1975; m. Jon David Ringen, Nov. 22, 1969; 1 son, Kai Mathias. Vis. lectr. U. Minn., Mpls., 1973-74; Fulbright prof. English dept. U. Trondheim (Norway), 1980; asso. prof. linguistics U. Iowa, Iowa City, 1975—. NSF grantee, 1976-77; faculty scholar U. Iowa, 1981-84. Mem. Linguistic Soc. Am., Phi Beta Kappa. Contbr. numerous articles to profl. jours. Office: 564 EPB U Iowa Iowa City IA 52242

RINGLER, NORMA MILLER (MRS. ALBERT RINGLER), educator; b. Cleve.; d. Alex and Dora (Snyder) Miller; B.A., Case Western Res. U., 1945, M.A., 1946, Ph.D. in Speech Pathology, 1973; m. Albert Ringler, Jan. 6, 1944; children—Ann Leslie, Kim Debra, Lisa Joan. Tchr. of deaf, Cleve., 1946-48; mem. faculty speech pathology Case Western Res. U., 1948-54, lectr., part-time 1954—, mem. faculty dept. speech communication, 1975—, also researcher on teaching, practicum coordinator; lang. cons. Cuyahoga County Retarded Children's Program div. Child Welfare, 1964-66; supr. students in tng. speech pathology Ohio U., Cleve. area, 1965—; asst. prof. dir. speech pathology, clin. dir. speech clinic Cleve. State U., 1971-73, sr. researcher, dir. student practicum Cleve. Hearing and Speech Center, 1975—, researcher dept. neonatology Sch. Applied Social Scis., Univ. Hosps., grant project dir. Sch. Applied Social Scis. Sec., New Democratic Coalition, Cleve., 1968; mem. ednl. com. Bellfaire-Residential Treatment Center for Emotionally Disturbed Children, Cleve., 1969—; co-chmn. Coalition To Support Human Services; mem. welfare com. Fedn. for Community Planning and Communications Commn.; mem. Greater Cleve. Interch. Council; mem. Gov.'s Citizens Adv. Com. for Social Services, 1976; mem. adv. bd. state social services, county welfare services, children's services. Mem. Am., Ohio (constl. com. 1964) speech and hearing assns., Am. Assn. Mental Retardation, Learning Disabilities Assn., Council Exceptional Children (dir., legis. chmn.), Mich. Infant Mental Health Assn., Cleve. Civil Liberties Union (chmn. dramatic arts 1965—), LWV (recipient nat. award 1963, state welfare com. 1969—, local v.p. 1964-68, local chmn. welfare 1968—, welfare chmn. Cuyahoga County 1972—, dir. human resources Ohio chpt.), Kappan Hon. Fraternity. Contbr. articles to profl. jours.; internat. bd. Jour. Infant Mental Health, editor communications edits., 1981. Home: 3721 Lytle Rd Shaker Heights OH 44122 Office: Case Western Res Univ Cleveland OH 44106

RINK, SUSAN, coll. pres.; b. Tulsa, Aug. 8, 1927; d. Raymond B. and Helen Frances (McEvoy) R.; B.A. in Biology, Clarke Coll., Dubuque, Iowa, 1948; M.S. in Biology (NSF grantee 1962-63), 1963; M.A. in Counseling Psychology (univ. scholar 1970), Northwestern U., 1971, Ph.D., 1973. Joined Sisters of Charity of the Blessed Virgin, Mary, Roman Catholic Ch., 1948; instr. sci. Holy Angels Acad., Milw., 1951-53 tchr., chmn. sci. dept. Xavier High Sch., St. Louis, 1953-66; asst. prof. biology, chmn. dept. Clarke Coll., 1966-69; mem. staff counseling lab. Sch. Edn., Northwestern U., 1970-71; mem. faculty Mundelein Coll., Chgo., 1969—, dir. continuing edn., 1971-73, asso. prof. edn., 1973-75, acad. dean, 1973-75, pres., 1975—; evaluator N. Central Assn.; mem. commn. leadership devel. edn. Am. Council Edn., 1978—. Bd. dirs. Chgo. Lighthouse for Blind, 1975-78, Analytical Psychology Club Chgo., 1975-76; mem. Health Care Service Corp. Chgo., 1977—. Recipient Disting. Service award Northwestern U., 1975, Leadership award Internat. Orgn. Women Execs., 1978; grantee Atomic Energy Inst., 1965, NSF, 1968. Trustee Marycrest Coll., 1981—. Mem. Econ. Club Chgo., Chgo. Com. Council Fgn. Relations, Assn. Colls. Ill. (v.p.), Assn. Higher Edn., Blessed Virgin Mary Commn. (higher edn. com.), Kappa Gamma Pi, Pi Lambda Theta. Office: 6363 Sheridan Rd Chicago IL 60660 *

RINKE, CARLOTTA MARIE, physician; b. St. Louis, Apr. 23, 1951; d. George F. and Olga M. (Stillnovic) R.; student U. Colo. 1969-71, B.A. in Chemistry, St. Louis U., 1973, m.D., 1977; m. Boyd E. Huffman, July 26, 1980. Intern, Med. Coll. Va., 1977-78, resident, 1978-80; fellow AMA, 1980-81; Morris Fishbein Fellow Highland Park (Ill.) Hosp., 1980-81; emergency physician Louise Obici Hosp., Suffolk, Va., 1980-81, Silver Cross Hosp., Joliet, Ill., 1981—; staff physician Good Samaritan Hosp., Downers Grove, Ill., 1981—. mem. AMA, Am. Soc. Internal Medicine, ACP, Am. Coll. Emergency Physicians, Am. Med. Writers Assn. Contbg. editor: AMA Family Health Guide, Jour. AMA 1981—. Office: 535 N Dearborn St Chicago IL 60610

RINSLEY, JACQUELINE ANN, nurse; b. Chgo., Apr. 5, 1933; d. John Lancelot and Margaret Elizabeth (Zeilinger) Louk; student Washington U., St. Louis, 1951-52; diploma in nursing St. Luke's Hosp. Sch. Nursing, 1955. Psychiat. nurse Topeka State Hosp., 1955-56, sect. head nurse, 1955-56; gen. and pediatric nurse St. John's Hosp., Springfield, Mo., 1956-57, Burge Hosp., 1957-58; head pediatric nurse Stormont-Vail Hosp., Topeka, 1958-60; psychiat. nurse Kans. Neurol. Inst., Topeka, 1960-70, adminstr., 1970-80, dir. nursing edn., 1980-82. Mem. Am., Kans. nurses assns., Am. Assn. Mental Deficiency, Nat. Rehab. Assn., Nat. Audubon Soc., Am. Mus. Nat. History, Smithsonian Assos., Zeta Tau Alpha. Republican. Lutheran. Home: 208 NE 7th St Apt 6 Newport OR 97365

RIORDAN, FRANCIS ELLEN, linguist, educator, nun; b. Solomon, Kans., Oct. 24, 1915; d. Patrick Francis and Ella (Barret) R.; A.B., Marymount Coll., 1936; M.A., Cath. U. Am., 1945, Ph.D., 1952. Joined Sisters St. Joseph, 1937; directress St. Mary Acad., Silver City, N.Mex., 1950-51; prin. Luckey High Sch., Manhattan, Kans., 1951-53, Cathedral High Sch., Salina, Kans., 1953-57; prof. French, chmn. fgn. langs. dept. Marymount Coll., Salina, 1962—, chmn. humanities div., 1980—, dir. interdisciplinary program, 1973-76. Mem. coordinating com. State of Kans. Women's Meeting, 1977. Lang. dept. fellow Cath. U., 1948-49. Mem. Am. Assn. Tchrs. of French, Kappa Gamma Pi. Author: Concept of Love in the French Catholic Literary Revival, 1952; The Brave Walk Single File, pageant, 1959. Home and Office: Marymount Coll Salina KS 67401

RIPIN, MAUREEN CATHERINE, data processor; b. N.Y.C., Oct. 14, 1929; d. Joseph Benedict and Mary (Clarke) Matthews; B.S., C. W. Post Coll., 1970; m. Frederick Ripin, Mar. 15, 1975; children—Colleen, Maureen, Patricia. Sci. programmer Data Master, L.I., N.Y., 1966-69; dir. data processing Harry Winston, Inc., N.Y.C., 1970—; founder Christie Clarke—Beautiful Things for Your Home, Washington Depot, Conn. Mem. Data Processing Mgmt. Assn., Am. Mgmt. Assn., Women in Info. Processing, NOW, Alpha Sigma Lambda. Home: Horseheaven Rd Washington CT 06793

RIPPELMEYER, LYNN JANET, pilot; b. St. Louis, Apr. 3, 1951; d. Robert Walter and Doris Mary (Niebruegge) R.; B.A. in English Edn., U. Ill. 1973, postgrad. Miami Dade Community Coll., 1976. Flight attendant TWA, N.Y.C. 1972-78, second officer, 1978-80; first officer Air Ill., Carbondale, 1977-78, Seaboard World Airlines/Flying Tigers, N.Y.C., 1980-81; pilot People Express, Newark, 1981-82, capt. 1982—, also mgr. personnel. Mem. Internat. Social Affiliation of Women Airline Pilots. First woman to fly B-747; first female capt. People Express. Office: People Express Airline North Terminal Bldg Newark International Airport Newark NJ 07114

RIPPY, FRANCES MARGUERITE MAYHEW (MRS. N. MERRILL RIPPY), educator; b. Ft. Worth, Sept. 16, 1929; d. Henry Grady and Marguerite Christine (O'Neill) Mayhew; B.A., Tex. Christian U., 1949; M.A., Vanderbilt U., 1951, Ph.D., 1957; postgrad. (Fulbright scholar), U. London, 1952-53; m. Noble Merrill Rippy, Aug. 29, 1955 (dec. 1980); children—Felix O'Neill, Conrad Mayhew, Marguerite Hailey. Instr., Tex. Christian U., 1953-55; instr. to asst. prof. Lamar State U., 1955-59; asst. prof. English, Ball State U., Muncie, Ind., 1959-64, asso. prof., 1964-68, prof., 1968—, dir. Ph.D. studies in English, 1966—, editor Ball State U. Forum, 1960—; vis. asst. prof. Sam Houston State U., 1957; vis. lectr., prof. U. P.R., summers 1959, 60, 61; cons.-evaluator N. Central Assn. Colls. and Schs., 1973—. Recipient McClintock award, 1966; Danforth grantee, summer 1964, asso., 1965—; Ball State U. research grantee, 1960, 62, 70, 73; Lilly Library summer research grantee, 1978. Mem. MLA, Coll. English Assn., Johnson Soc. Midwest (sec. 1961-62), AAUP, Nat. Council Tchrs. English, Am. Soc. 18th Century Studies. Contbr. articles to profl. jours., chpt. to anthology. Home: 4709 W Jackson Muncie IN 47304

RISHEIM, WANDA JOAN, educator; b. July 11, 1935; d. Arthur J. and Meta C. Wands; A.B., Lincoln Christian Coll., 1961; M.S., Ft. Hays State Coll., 1963. Tchr. high schs. in Mo., Ill. and Calif., 1963-74; tchr. San Dieguito High Sch. Dist., Encinitas, Calif., 1976—; area dir. mktg. Jim Rohn Prodns., 1981; one-woman exhbn. Clayton Gallery, St. Louis, 1970; group exhbn. Art Inst. San Diego, 1974-75. Mem. Nat. Assn. Female Execs., NEA, Nat. Art Edn. Assn., Women in Sales, Women in Mgmt., Calif. Tchrs. Assn. Club: Toastmasters. Address: 1123 Santa Helena Park Ct Solana Beach CA 92075

RISINGER, DOROTHY EXAAH, social worker, educator; b. Mansfield, La., Sept. 10, 1919; d. Marlin and Mary Iva (McBride) R.; A.B.A., Stephens Coll., 1938; B.A., La. State U., 1940; M.S.W., Tulane U., 1954. Exec. sec. and home service dir. ARC, Mansfield, La., 1940-46; welfare caseworker, Mansfield, 1950-52, New Orleans, 1954-55; clin. social worker, instr. in rehab. and comprehensive care Tulane U. Sch. Medicine, New Orleans, 1955-60, coordinator disability evaluation study, 1960-65, asst. coordinator rehab. teaching program, 1965-66; asst.

prof., asst. coordinator Office of Dean, La. State U. Sch. Medicine, Shreveport, 1966-75, asst. prof., med. social cons., clin. social worker, 1975-80; joint faculty Tulane U. Sch. Public Health, 1957-60, Sch. Social Work, 1955-66; faculty dept. medicine La. State U. Sch. Medicine, 1968-75; cons. N.W. La. Comprehensive Health Planning Council, 1969, N.W. La. Rehab. Center, 1967-75, Mollie E. Webb Regional Speech and Hearing Center, 1972-76; pvt. practice clin. social work, med.-social cons. Bd. dirs. Community Council, Inc., Shreveport, 1968-74, 76—, chairperson agy. conf. com., 1980—. Recipient Service award ARC, 1945, Am. Cancer Soc., 1962, 65, Arthritis Found., 1973. Mem. Nat. Rehab. Assn., Nat. Assn. Social Workers (pres. La. chpt. 1980—), Family Relations Council La. (pres. 1972-74), Mental Health Assn., Soc. Hosp. Social Work Dirs., Am., La. hosp. assns., AMA (spl. affiliate), Nat. Council Family Relations, Nat. Assn. Retarded Citizens, AAUP, Phi Beta Phi. Democrat. Episcopalian. Contbr. articles on rehab. to profl. jours. Home: 957 Monrovia St Shreveport LA 71106 Office: Suite 1118 Fountain Towers Shreveport LA 71101

RISKUS, LINDA PATRICIA, title ins. co. exec.; b. Pitts., Mar. 22, 1951; d. Michael E. and Sophia Z. Riskus; B.A., Fla. State U., Tallahassee, 1974; m. Olen W. Meredith, Nov. 4, 1977; 1 dau., Jessica Leigh. Title researcher Lawyer's Title Ins. Corp., Pitts., 1969-70; abstractor, examiner St. Augustine Land Title Co. (Fla.), 1974-75; title examiner Title Ins. Co. Minn., Jacksonville, Fla., 1975-76; br. mgr., closing officer Am. Title Ins. Co., Orange Park, Fla., 1976-77; free-lance title researcher, 1977; pres. Title Ins. Co. St. Augustine, Inc., 1977—. Sec., Friends St. Johns County Library, 1979. Mem. Am. Land Title Assn., Fla. Land Title Assn., AAUW, NOW (v.p. St. Augustine chpt. 1979), Nat. Assn. Female Execs., St. Augustine and St. Johns County C. of C. Democrat. Club: Matanzas Bay (St. Augustine). Home: 65 1/2 Saragossa St St Augustine FL 32084 Office: 90 Cedar St St Augustine FL 32084

RISLEY, EDYTH C., petroleum geologist; b. Little Rock, Oct. 12, 1928; d. Elmer J. and Lillie L. (McNeill) R.; student Randolph-Macon Woman's Coll., 1945-47; B.S., So. Meth. U., 1949; postgrad. U. Colo., 1949; M.S., Stanford U., 1951. Jr. geologist McAlester Fuel Co., Magnolia, Ark., 1949; geologist Continental Oil, Midland, Tex., 1951-56; sr. geologist, cons. McCord & Assos., Dallas, 1957-63; sr. sci. reference librarian Dallas Public Library, 1963-74; hdqrs. staff geologist Holly Corp., Dallas, 1975-77; cons. geologist, sr. geologist Ray Holifield & Assos., Dallas, 1977—. Mem. Am. Assn. Petroleum Geologists (ho. of dels. 1981—), Dallas Geol. Soc. (sec. 1979-80), W. Tex. Geol. Soc., Nat. Audubon Soc., Pi Beta Phi. Contbr. publs. in field. Home: 4517 Westway Dallas TX 75205 Office: 16800 Dallas N Pkwy Suite 220 Dallas TX 75248

RISTOW, LINDA SUE, city govt. ofcl.; b. Osceola, Iowa, May 17, 1947; d. Robert David and Mary Ellen (Sawyer) Musson; student Calif. State U., Fullerton, 1965-66, Fullerton Jr. Coll., 1966-67; m. Paul Gary Ristow, Sept. 2, 1966. Programmer, Transam. Ins. Co., Los Angeles, 1967-68; programmer/analyst Thom McAn Shoe Co., Worcester, Mass., 1969-70, Hunt Wesson Foods, Inc., Fullerton, 1971-77; project leader Santa Fe Internat., Orange, Calif., 1977-79; mgr. bus. systems Braegen Corp., Anaheim, Calif., 1979-81; data processing mgr. City of Irvine, Calif., 1981—. Chmn., Coalition of Neighborhood Assns., Laguna Beach, Calif., 1978—; pres. Arch Beach Heights Assn., Laguna Beach, 1978—; mem. adv. com. for Laguna Canyon Rd., Orange County Bd. Suprs., 1978-79; exec. v.p. Laguna Greenbelt, 1979—; mem. adv. com. Laguna Beach Gen. Plan, 1979-81; chmn. Orange County Coastal Coalition, 1981. Cert. in prodn. and inventory control mgmt. Mem. Calif. Data Base Mgmt. Assn., Am. Prodn. and Inventory Control Soc., Data Processing Mgmts. Assn. Democrat. Methodist. Home: 917 Quivera Laguna Beach CA 92651 Office: City of Irvine Data Processing Office 17200 Jamboree St Irvine CA 92713

RITCH, KATHLEEN, diversified co. exec.; b. Harbor Beach, Mich., Jan. 23, 1943; d. Eunice (Spry) R.; B.A., Mich. State U., 1965: student Katharine Gibbs Sch., 1965-66. Exec. sec., adminstrv. asst. to pres. Katy Industries, Inc., N.Y.C., 1969-70; exec. sec., adminstrv. asst. to chmn. Kobrand Corp., N.Y.C., 1970-72; adminstrv. asst. to chmn. and pres. Ogden Corp., N.Y.C., 1972-74; asst. sec., adminstr. office services, asst. to chmn. Ogden Corp., N.Y.C., 1974-81, corp. sec., adminstr. office services, 1981—; part-owner Unell Mfg. Co., Port Hope, Mich., 1966—. Mem. Am. Soc. Corp. Secs. Home: 500 E 77th St New York NY 10162 Office: 277 Park Ave New York NY 10172

RITCHESON, BETTY RUTH, med. technologist; b. Maysville, Okla., Dec. 9, 1927; d. Charles F. and Jewell I. (Vaughn) R.; B.A., U. Sci. and Arts of Okla., 1951; M.T., Baylor U. Hosp., 1952. Med. lab. owner, dir. Ritcheson Med. Lab., Woodbury, N.J., 1961—. Mem. Am. Soc. Clin. Pathologists, N.J. Assn. Bioanalysts, Am. Assn. Bioanalysts. Methodist. Home: 163 S Glassboro Rd Woodbury Heights NJ 08097 Office: Westwood Med Bldg Woodbury NJ 08096

RITCHIE, INGRID MARIA, environ. health scientist, educator; b. Munich, W.Ger., May 26, 1949; came to U.S., 1952; d. Curtis Huey and Johanna Leokadia (Kroll) Ritchie; A.S., Murray State Coll., 1969; B.S. summa cum laude, Southwestern State U., 1971; M.S., U. Minn., 1973, Ph.D. (USPHS fellow), 1980. Research scientist Air Quality Minn. Pollution Control Agy., Mpls., 1974-76, Regional Copper-Nickel Study, Mpls., 1976-79, health risk assessment Minn. Dept. Health, Mpls., 1979-82; asst. prof. Sch. Pub. and Environ. Affairs, Ind. U., Indpls., 1982—; vice chmn. Sci. and Tech. Resource Adv. Council to Minn. Joint Legis. Com. on Sci. and Tech. Mem. Upper Midwest Air Pollution Control Assn., Nat. Air Pollution Control Assn. Office: Ind U BS-SPEA Room 4083 801 W Michigan St Indianapolis IN 46223

RITCHIE, MARY MOORE MEACHAM, court reporter, bus. exec.; b. Mecklenburg County, N.C., Oct. 4, 1939; d. James Bess and Christine Neilson (Rosebro) M.; A.A.S., Sullins Coll., 1959; m. Barron L. Ritchie, Jr., Mar. 19, 1960; children—Barron III, James Mark, Virginia Brooke. Sec., tax dept., Belk Stores Services, Charlotte, N.C., 1959-61, legal sec., 1962-63; com. clk. Ho. of Reps., N.C. Gen. Assembly, 1967; owner, mgr., pres. Ct. Reporting Services, Inc., Raleigh, N.C., 1969—; instr. Meredith Coll., 1979-80. Mem. Nat. Stenomask Verbatim Reporters Assn. (past chmn. bus. mgmt. com.), Nat. Assn. Women Bus. Owners (pres.-elect Triangle chpt.), Raleigh C. of C., Nat. Assn. Female Execs. Republican. Presbyterian. Clubs: MacGregor Downs Country, Capital City. Home: 1809 Falls Church Rd Raleigh NC 27609 Office: PO Box 1729 Raleigh NC 27602

RITTENHOUSE, SHIRLEY BASH, univ. ofcl.; b. Champaign, Ill., Nov. 23, 1928; d. Elmer Clarence and Alice Josephine (Lee) Bash; B.S. in Chemistry with honors, U. Ill., Champaign-Urbana, 1950; m. Warren L. Rittenhouse, Nov. 29, 1975; children—Janice L. Woodward, Barbara A. Pfaller. Research asst. phys. chemistry Parke-Davis Co., Detroit, 1950-52; teaching asst. chemistry U. Ill., 1959-60, research asst. biochemistry, 1960-65, staff asst. president's office, 1965-79, staff asso., 1979—. Mem. Phi Beta Kappa, Iota Sigma Pi, Sigma Delta Epsilon, Kappa Alpha Theta. Home: 5 Imperial Ct Champaign IL 61820 Office: 364 Adminstrn Bldg U Ill 506 S Wright St Urbana IL 61801

RITTER, ALMEDA LOUISE, univ. ofcl.; b. Lansing, Mich., Apr. 24, 1923; d. Loren Harvey and Vena Belle (Fitch) Keeney; grad. Bus. U. Lansing, 1943; m. Sept. 12, 1947 (dec.); children—Linda, Nadine. With Mich. Millers Ins. Co., 1941-46, Nat. Biscuit Co., 1946-51, John Bean Mfg. Co., 1951-56; with Mich. State U., East Lansing, 1957—, asst. dean's office, 1957-63, supr. community devel. programs, 1976—. Pres. bd. dirs. Colonial Townhouses, Lansing Mich., 1971-82; pres., v.p. Midwest Assn. Housing Coops., 1973-82. Mem. Community Devel. Soc., Nat. Assn. Housing Coops. Home: 2410 S Wadsworth Dr Lansing MI 48910 Office: Kellogg Center Harrison Rd Mich State U East Lansing MI 48824

RITTER, JOYCE HELEN, educator; b. N.Y.C., Feb. 11, 1941; d. William J. and Emily Ritter; B.A., N.Y. U., 1963, M.A. in Devel. and Remedial Reading, 1966; M.S. in Counseling, Ind. U., 1971, Ed.D., 1974. Dir., Reading Clinic, U. Man., Winnipeg, Ca., 1966-68; reading specialist and counselor Oregon State U., Corvallis, 1968-69; research and teaching asst. spl. edn. Ind. U., Bloomington, 1970-73; asst. prof. spl. edn. Western Ky. U., Bowling Green, 1973-74; asst. prof. ednl. psychology N.Y. U., N.Y.C., 1974-75; reading and math. specialist Bedford (Ind.) North Lawrence High Sch., 1975-76; asst. prof. spl. edn. Chadron (Nebr.) State Coll., 1977—. Mem. Internat. Reading Assn., Council Learning Disabilities, Council Exceptional Children, AAUP, Pi Lambda Theta. Contbr. articles on teaching and edn. to profl. publs. Office: Chadron State College Chadron NE 69337

RITTER, LAURA LEE, ednl. adminstr.; b. Toledo, Ohio, Jan. 7, 1938; d. Ray Thomas and Laura Amelia (Wadsworth) Everly. B.S. in Edn., Ind. U., 1959; M.Ed., Purdue U., 1962; postgrad. U. Md., U. San Francisco, Va. Commonwealth U., Prince George's Community Coll.; m. David Lawrence Ritter, Aug. 22, 1959; 1 dau., Elizabeth Anne. Elem. tchr., West Lafayette, Ind., 1959-62, Pitts., 1962-63, Prince George's County, Md., 1963-73; dir. Grace Christian Sch., Bowie, Md., 1974—; reviewer, writer TV math tchr. manual Md. Ednl. Instructional TV. Com. precinct chmn. Republican Party, 1979—. Mem. Prince George's County Council on Children and Youth, 1981—. Mem. Am. Assn. Christian Schs., Md. Assn. Christian Schs. Republican. Baptist. Club: Capitol Bapt. Chorale. Writer Guidelines for Early Childhood Education, State of Maryland, 1972. Home: 16531 Abbey Dr Mitchellville MD 20716

RITTER, LUCY ELIZABETH, business exec.; b. Shanghai, China, Sept. 10, 1910 (parents Am. citizens); d. Ovid Herbert and Lucy (Corker) R.; A.B., Stanford U., 1930, M.A., 1931. Research sec. Calif. Taxpayers Assn., 1931-34; security analyst Calif. Western States Life Ins. Co., Sacramento, 1935-43, asst. treas., 1943-54, 2d v.p., asst. treas., mgr. securities dept., 1954-68, v.p. securities, 1968-75, now ret. Bd. dirs. Sacramento Community Chest, 1953-56, Sacramento Children's Home, 1949-55; dir. nat. exec. bd. Stanford Alumni Assn., 1955-58; life mem., bd. govs. Mercy Hosps. Found., 1971—, Crocker Art Mus., Sacramento, 1974—; trustee Sacramento Symphony Trust Fund Found.; mem. bd. regents U. Pacific, 1974—; mem. vis. libraries com. Stanford U., 1976-82; mem. Calif. Gov.'s Retirement Bd., 1961-69; alt. del. Democratic Nat. Conv., 1956, 64; chmn. woman's Citizens for Kennedy, 3d congl. dist., 1960. Mem. Inst. Chartered Fin. Analysts, Security Analysts of San Francisco, Crocker Art Mus. Assn. Clubs: Del Paso Country, Sacramento, Metropolitan, San Francisco. Author: Lucy's Twentieth Century, 1974; An Ode to Common Sense, 1977; Lucy Goes to South America, 1979; contbr. articles to profl. jours. Home: Capitol Towers 1500 7th St Sacramento CA 95814

RITTER, MARCELLE FRANCES, container co. exec.; b. N.Y.C., May 28, 1941; d. Marcel George and Frances (North) Bastianello; B.S., LeMoyne Coll., Syracuse, N.Y., 1963; M.S. in Bus., Columbia U., 1980; children—Erich Layden, Alan Kurz, Allison North. Supr. gen. programming Hall & McChesney, Syracuse, N.Y., 1963-64; supr. systems programming, tech. analyst Mut. N.Y., Syracuse, 1964-69; analyst data base Rochester (N.Y.) Telephone Co., 1973-74; analyst data base Xerox Corp., Rochester, 1974-76, mgr. billing ops., 1977; mgr. data adminstrn. and control Am. Can Co., Greenwich, Conn., 1977-79, mgr. bus. systems planning metal packaging, 1979—. Various leadership positions nursery sch., 1971-72; active drs. Meml. Art Gallery, 1972-73; bd. dirs. Clover Montessori Sch., 1973-75; sector leader 3d. dist. Democratic com. Brighton, N.Y., 1976; vol. fundraising Rochester Pub. TV, 1977. Le Moyne Partial scholar, 1959; Regents scholar, 1959-63. Home: 4 Ridge Rd Cos Cob CT 06807 Office: Am Can Co American Ln 1A7 Greenwich CT 06830

RITTER, MARY CATHERINE, biochemist, educator; b. Mpls., May 10, 1943; d. George Michael and Lorraine Maria (Schwappach) R.; B.S. magna cum laude, Coll. St. Francis, Joliet, Ill., 1965; M.S. (NDEA fellow), U. Minn., 1969, Ph.D. (NIH fellow), 1971. USPHS tng. grantee, postdoctoral fellow U. Minn., Mpls., 1971-72; postdoctoral fellow U. Chgo., 1971-75, Chgo. Heart Assn. research fellow, 1972-73, NIH research fellow, 1973-75, research asso., 1975-77, instr., 1977-79, asst. prof., 1979—. Chgo. Heart Assn. grant-in-aid awardee, 1976-78; NIH research grantee, 1979—. Mem. Am. Chem. Soc., AAAS, Am. Oil Chemists Soc., Am. Heart Assn., Chgo. Heart Assn., Sigma Xi, Kappa Gamma Pi, Kappa Mu Epsilon, Iota Sigma Pi (v.p. Mercury chpt. 1971-72), Sigma Delta Epsilon, Phi Lambda Upsilon. Roman Catholic. Contbr. articles to biol. and biol. chemistry jours. Office: McLean Meml Research Inst U Chgo 950 E 59th St Chicago IL 60637

RITTER, NAOMI, educator; b. Boston, Nov. 8, 1937; d. Samuel L. and Eileen (Goodman) Gargill; B.A., Vassar Coll., 1959; Ph.D., Harvard U., 1965; divorced; 1 son, Jonathan. Mem. faculty Harvard U., 1964-65, U. Va., 1965-66, Mary Baldwin Coll., Staunton, Va., 1966-69, Sweet Briar Coll., 1970-71, Ind. U., 1972-75; mem. faculty U. Mo., Columbia, 1975—, asso. prof. German, 1981—; cons. in field. Grantee U. Mo., Columbia. Mem. MLA, Internat. Comparative Lit. Assn., Internat. Arthur Schnitzler Research Assn., Kafka Soc. Am. Author: House and Individual, 1977; also articles. Address: 454 GCB Univ Mo Columbia MO 65211

RITTER, VEDA IRENE, ins. agy. exec., civic worker, pvt. investor; b. Weatherford, Tex., Aug. 11; d. Wesley Marion and Callie Ann (Hudlow) Hill; student Barnes Bus. Sch., 1934-35, Denver U. Sch. Commerce, 1935-36; m. Chauncey Hirsch Ritter, July 16, 1943 (dec., Dec. 1981). Assoc., Ritter Ins. Agy., Denver 1935—, owner, 1966—; pvt. investor stocks and bonds. Bd. dirs. Friends of Pub. Library, 1950; active vol. Vis. Nurse Assn., Denver, 1956—; 1st v.p. Republican Assocs., 1960, mem. Colo. fin. com., 1964, alt. del. Nat. Conv., 1960. Episcopalian. Clubs: Ladies of Rotary (dir. 1950), Denver Press, Cherry Hills Country, Brown Palace, Denver Athletic.

RITVALSKY, NANCY R.K., fin. exec.; b. Hazleton, Pa., June 4, 1952; d. Robert H. and Frances M. (Dvorshock) Krensavage; B.S., Pa. State U., 1973; M.B.A., LaSalle Coll., 1979; m. Joseph B. Ritvalsky, Nov. 29, 1975. Chief evaluator United Cerebral Palsy Assn., Phila., 1973-76; controller United Way of S.E. Delaware County, Chester, Pa., 1976-79; corp. fin. analyst Alco Standard Corp., Valley Forge, Pa., 1979-81, asst. to pres. in charge corp. planning, 1981—; fin. cons. Bd. dirs. ARC, 1980-82, instr. CPR, advanced first aid, 1975—; mem. Republican Nat. Com., 1978-82. Recipient citation ARC, 1981. Mem. Fin. Mgmt. Assn., Eastern Fin. Assn., N. Am. Soc. Corp. Planning (treas. Phila. chpt.), Phila. Fin. Assn., Pa. State U. Alumni Assn. Republican. Roman Catholic. Contbr. articles to profl. jours. Office: PO Box 834 Valley Forge PA 19482

RITVO, MIRIAM MEYERS, state adminstr., educator; b. Lawrence, Mass.; d. Harry and Celia B. (Dworkin) Meyers; A.B. in History and Fine Arts, Smith Coll., 1937; M.S. in Edn. and Communication, Boston U., 1952; postgrad. Harvard U. Med. Sch., 1954-56; m. Meyer Ritvo; children—Roger Alan, James Meyers. Asst. prof. behavioral sci. Boston U., 1956-70, asst. prof. Grad. Sch. Edn., 1965-70, lectr. Sch. Nursing, 1964-69, sr. staff mem. human relations center, 1965-70; assoc. prof. edn., dean students Lesley Coll., Cambridge, Mass., 1970-78; spl. asst. dep. commr. Mass. Dept. Edn., Boston, 1978—; dir. mgmt. devel. Commonwealth of Mass., 1980—; dir. Nat. Tng. Labs. Inst., 1977-80; mem. vis. com., affirmative action com. Mass. Bd. Higher Edn.; lectr. profl. seminars; cons., speaker on organizational devel. and quality of worklife; dir. Cert. Cons. Internat., Rath & Strong, Inc. Mem. Mass. Gov.'s Commn. on Status Women, 1974-78; bd. dirs. Cambridge YWCA, 1974-76, Simons-Gutman Found., Brookline, Mass., 1968-78, Mass. Minimum Wage Commn., 1965-68, Women's Equity Action League, 1970-78, Mass. Com. Children and Youth, 1965-78, New Eng. Regional Bd. Anti-Defamation League, 1965—; mem. adv. com. Mass. Council Pub. Schs., 1955-65; mem. exec. com. Boston Expt. Internat. Living, 1958-65; trustee Center Tech. and Soc., Cambridge, 1976—, Hebrew Coll. HEW grantee, 1967-70; U.S. Office Edn. grantee, 1965-67; USPHS grantee, 1970-78. Fellow Internat. Assn. Applied Social Scientists; mem. Mass. Child Study Assn. (dir. 1963-68), Nat. Assn. Intergroup Relations Ofcls., Adult Edn. Assn. U.S.A., Soc. Psychol. Study Social Issues, Am. Psychol. Assn., Archeol. Inst. Am., AAUW (corp. mem.), Am. Assn. Higher Edn., AAUP, Mass. Assn. Women Deans, Adminstrs. and Counselors, Boston Assn. Women Social Scientists, Eastern Assn. Coll. Deans and Advisors Students, Nat. Assn. Student Personnel Adminstrs., Organizational Devel. Network, Am. Soc. Tng. and Devel. Author: (with Adelma Mooth) Developing Supervisory Skills, 1966; (with others) Diagnosing the Professional Climate of Schools, 1973; Developing the Supervisory Skills of the Nurse, 1974, 2d rev. edit., 1974; author multi-media presentation: A New Look at TLC, 1969; contbr. articles to profl. jours. Home: 63 Bennington St Newton MA 02158 Office: One Ashburton Pl Boston MA 02108

RITZ, HARRIETTE FRANCES SMITH, ednl. adminstr.; b. Terre Haute, Ind., Mar. 8, 1909; d. Harry Franklin and Charlotte Jane (Allen) Smith; B.S., Ind. U., 1934, M.S., 1936; postgrad. Dayton U., U. Mich.; M. Div., Winebrenner Theol. Sem., 1971; m. Gale Ritz, Dec. 22, 1947. Prof. acctg. Beaver Coll., 1936; head dept. bus. Beech Grove High Sch., 1936-41; mem. naval tng. staff Ind. U., 1941-44; chmn. dept. bus. Findlay Coll., 1944-46, prof. acctg., 1963-74, assoc. prof. bus. adminstrn., 1963-74, prof. emeritus bus. adminstrn., 1974—, adminstrv. asst. in community edn., 1974—; faculty bus. Bloomsburg State Tchrs. Coll., 1946-47; chmn. div. bus. Ohio No. U., 1947-63. Auditor, Hancock County (Ohio) United Way, 1963-80; mem. scholarship com. Winebrenner Village Aux., 1974; trustee Winebrenner Theol. Sem., 1972; chmn. bd. elders First Christian Ch., Findlay, Ohio. Recipient Disting. Assoc. award Findlay Coll., 1976, scholarship award established in her name, 1981, Ritz Auditorium named for her and her husband, 1983; named Disting. Alumnus Winebrenner Theol. Sem, 1982. Mem. Ohio Community Edn., Findlay Coll. Assocs., Women Findlay Coll. and Winebrenner Theol. Sem., Faculty Christian Fellowship (dist. pres. 1955-65, state sec. 1955-63, regional rep. 1959-62), Nat. Fedn. Bus. and Profl. Women (past pres. local chpt.), AAUW, Am. Assn. Ret. Persons, Delta Phi Epsilon, Kappa Delta Phi, Zeta Tau Alpha. Clubs: Altrusa, Order Eastern Star. Home: 1500 Tiffin Ave Findlay OH 45840 Office: Findlay Coll Findlay OH 45840

RITZENHOFF, URSULA CHRISTA, fgn. lang. educator; b. Remscheid, Ger., Dec. 18, 1934; d. Rudolf Robert and Helen Aline (Picard) R.; came to U.S., 1969; B.A., Staatl. Inst., Oberhausen, Ger., 1959; M.A., U. Muenster, 1963; M.A., U. Conn., 1974, Ph.D., 1976. Tchr. public schs., Arnsberg, W.Ger., 1963-69; teaching asst. U. N.C., Greensboro, 1969-70, U. Conn., Storrs, 1970-75; sr. lectr. U. Natal, South Africa, 1975-77; asst. prof. German, Colo. State U., Ft. Collins, 1977-78, U. Tenn., Knoxville, 1978—. Grantee U. Conn., U. Natal, U. Tenn. Mem. MLA, Am. Assn. Tchrs. German, Tenn. Fgn. Lang. Assn., Phi Beta Kappa, Phi Kappa Phi. Author: Hermann Brochs Pasenow—Roman Eine Re-Orientierung, 1977; Erläuterungen und Dokumente zu Goethe: Die Wahlverwandtschaften, 1982. Office: Dept German U Tenn Knoxville TN 37916

RIVARD, PHYLLIS KELTGEN, graphic arts co. exec., bus. cons.; b. Mankato, Minn., Aug. 23, 1943; d. Leo M. and Catherine M. (Peters) Keltgen; student Mankato State U., 1961-64, Metro State U., 1978-79; children by previous marriage—Alan, Daniel. With DM Printing, Inc., Mankato, Minn., 1960—, newsletter editor, 1962-80, mgr. art dept., 1962-77, instr. inservice tng., 1977-80, v.p. sales, 1977—, co-propr., 1961—; v.p. mktg. The Press, Inc., Chanhassen, Minn., 1981—. graphic arts broker and cons. Par Cons., Mpls. 1977—. Mem. All-America City Com., 1978; bd. dirs. Jr. Achievement, Mankato chpt., 1980—. Mem. Sales and Mktg. Execs. of Mpls., Graphics Now, Nat. Assn. of Female Execs., Minn. Women's Network, Mankato C. of C. (dir. 1977-80), Mankato State Alumni Assn. (pres. 1978-79, dir. 1976—). Home: 1920 S First St Minneapolis MN 55454 Office: 1609 N Front St PO Box 996 Mankato MN 56001

RIVERA, CHRISTINE RACHAEL, banker; b. Pocatello, Idaho, Aug. 30, 1953; d. Mike F. and Aurelia (Garcia) R.; student Idaho State U., Boise State U., Mundelein Coll., Chgo. With 1st Security Bank of Idaho, N.A., Boise, 1971—, beginning as clk., successively mgmt. trainee, teller, teller supr., ops. officer, affirmative action officer, 1971-81, installment loan officer, asst. br. mgr., 1981—. Bilingual edn. com. Students Econ. Edn. Assn.; former pres. Idaho Assn. Affirmative Action; mem. Minority Bus. Devel. Assn., YWCA. Mem. Am. Inst. Banking, Nat. Assn. Bank Women (N.W. regional scholar). Democrat. Roman Catholic. Club: 300 Main St. Home: 1215 N 22d St Boise ID 83702 Office: PO Box 7069 Boise ID 83730

RIVERA, JO-ANN MAGDALENA, psychologist; b. N.Y.C., Sept. 16, 1948; d. Jorge Modesto and Anna Maria (Lartigaut) R.; B.A., Hunter Coll., 1970; Ph.D., Adelphi U., 1978; m. Edward Anthony Rodriguez, June 14, 1975; 1 dau., Marisol. Tchr. elem. schs. N.Y.C. Bd. Edn., 1970-71, tchr. Spanish, part time, 1971-74; psychologist Bronx Psychiat. Center, Albert Einstein Coll. Medicine, 1975—, mem. faculty, family studies sect., 1978—, supr. clin. psychology internship, 1979—, clin. instr. Coll. Medicine, 1979—. Flower Fifth Ave Hosp. fellow, 1971-73; Bronx VA Hosp. fellow, 1973-74; Albert Einstein fellow Bronx Psychiat. Center, 1974-75. Mem. Am. Psychol. Assn., Am. Orthopsychiat. Assn., Nat. Hispanic Psychol. Assn. (charter), Am. Assn. Family Therapy (charter).

RIVERA, LESLIE ANN, assn. adminstr.; b. Miami, Fla., Mar. 7, 1947; d. Luis and Jean Bancroft (MacIvor) R.; student Gulf Park Jr. Coll., 1965-66, U. Colo., Boulder, 1967-68; B.A. in Ancient History, U. Miami, Coral Gables, Fla., 1970; M.A. in European History, U. R.I., 1977; M.A. in Brit. Lit., Wroxton Coll., Fairleigh Dickinson U., Wroxton-Near Banbury, Eng., 1978. Tchr. history Carrollton Sch. for Girls, Coconut Grove, Fla., 1970-72; tchr. history and English, Our Lady of Lourdes Acad., South Miami, Fla. 1973-74; tchr. social studies West Miami (Fla.) Jr. High, 1974-75; curatorial asst. Hist. Assn. So. Fla., Miami, 1978-79, vol. coordinator, 1981—; instr. English, Miami Dade Community Coll., 1978; dir. spl. events Burdines Dept. Store, Miami, 1980-81. Corr. sec. Friends of Mental Health br. Dade County (Fla.) Mental Health Assn., 1978, Barton Ravlin chpt. Women's Cancer Assn., Miami, 1979; mem. founding com. Fla. Trust for Hist. Preservation, 1978; pres. La Lega dei Viscayani decorative arts museum, Miami, 1981-82; Bd. dirs. Coconut

Grove Republican Women's Club, Miami, 1981. Cert. jr. coll. and secondary edn. tchr., Fla. Mem. S. Fla. Dirs. Vols. in Agys. (corr. sec. 1981). Assn. for Vol. Adminstrn., Nat. Assn. Female Execs., Villagers Preservation, Tequestans of Hist. Assn. So. Fla., Nat. Trust Hist. Preservation, Royal Oak Soc., Lowe Art Mus. of U. Miami, Dade Heritage Trust, Asolo Theater Festival Assn., English Speaking Union, Fairchild Tropical Garden, Mus. Sci. and Space Planetarium. Presbyterian. Club: Bath (Miami Beach, Fla.); Jr. League (Miami). Office: 101 W Flager St Miami FL 33130

RIVERA, RHONDA RAE, lawyer; b. Phila., Mar. 9, 1938; d. Preston Robert and Kathrine Lowe (MacSorley) Rieley; B.A. cum laude, Douglass Coll., 1959; M.P.A., Syracuse U., 1960; J.D. magna cum laude, Wayne State U., 1967; 1 son, Robert Preston Rivera. Research economist Fed. Res. Bank Cleve., 1960-62, instr. public adminstrn., 1962-64; admitted to Mich. bar, 1968, Ohio bar, 1976; prof. econs. Hope Coll., Holland, Mich., 1968-72; asst. dean William James Coll., Grand Valley State Colls., Allendale, Mich., 1972-74; asst. dean Law Sch., U. Mich., Ann Arbor, 1974-76; prof. law Ohio State U. Law Coll., Columbus, 1976—, dir. clin. law programs, 1982—. Bd. govs. Lambda Legal Def. and Edn. Fund; lay reader, mem. vestry St. Stephen's Episcopal Ch., Columbus; mem. diocesan ct. Diocese So. Ohio Episc. Ch. Cert. urban econs. M.I.T., 1973; recipient Uppity Woman of Yr. award NOW, 1973; Susan B. Anthony award Mich. Women Law Students, 1974. Mem. ACLU, NOW, Women's Action Equity League, AAUP, Nat. Lawyers Guild, Nat. Gay Task Force, Soc. Am. Law Tchrs., Ohio Bar Assn., Columbus Bar Assn., Mich. Bar Assn. Contbr. articles to profl. jours. Home: 385 E Schreyer Pl Columbus OH 43214 Office: 1659 N High St Columbus OH 43210

RIVERS, MARIE DAVIDSON, psychologist, educator; b. Selma, Ala.; d. William and Emily (Bradley) Davidson; B.S., N.C. Agrl. Tech. U., 1946; M.A., U. Mich., 1952, Ph.D., 1959. Pub. sch. tchr. High Point, N.C., 1945-51, Dayton (Ohio) city schs., 1951-59; prof. English and ednl. psychology Agrl. and Tech. U., Greensboro, N.C., 1959-61; asst. prof. edn., psychology Ball State U., Muncie, Ind., 1961-64; asst. prof. ednl. and counseling psychology U. Pacific, Stockton, Calif., 1964-65; asst. prof. psychol. founds., then prof. Calif. State U., Northridge, 1965—; pvt. practice clin. psychology Family Health Med. Group, Pasadena, Calif., 1974-76; staff psychologist Pasadena Community Hosp., 1979-80; pres. Rivers Psychol. Group, 1970—; dir. psychol. services McCall Community Mental Health Center, 1977-78; cons. psychologist Aplebaum Psychiat. Med. Group, Pasadena. Lectr. human devel. Pacific Oaks Coll., Pasadena; lectr. early child growth and devel. UCLA; lectr. Calif. Luth. Coll., Thousand Oaks. Founder, pres. Fairwood Convalescent Hosp. Guild, Pasadena, 1965-70; pres. Mental Health Adv. Bd. Head Start Programs Los Angeles County; mem. Altadena Town Council, 1975—. Ford Found. fellow, 1953; Clifford A. Woody award U. Mich., 1955; named Tchr. of Year, Dayton Tchrs. Guild, 1953. Mem. Am. Group Psychotherapy Assn., Am. Orthopsychiat. Assn., Soc. Study Negro History Culture, Am. Psychol. Assn., Soc. Psychol. Study Social Issues, Calif. State Psychologists, Calif. Tchrs. Assn., NEA, Calif. Psychol. Assn., Gamma Phi Delta (chmn. nat. exec. bd. 1960-70, pres. Delta Sigma chpt. 1981—), Zeta Phi Beta, Phi Lambda Theta, Sigma Rho Sigma. Home: 3508 N Marengo Ave Altadena CA 91001

RIVERS, MIRIAM WOODING, guidance counselor; b. Brit. West Indies (parents Am. citizens); d. Isaac Nathaniel and Matilda Clara (Hunt) Wooding; B.A., Hunter Coll., 1944; M.A., Tchrs. Coll., Columbia U., 1948; postgrad. in psychology Ohio State U., 1963-66; grad. Gestalt Inst., Cleve., 1979; m. Frederic Lee Rivers, Dec. 29, 1957 (dec. 1979). Social worker Dept. Public Welfare, N.Y.C., 1948-50; tchr. public schs. Bklyn., 1950-52; intern psychologist Crownsville (Md.) State Hosp., 1952-53; clin. psychologist Manteno (Ill.) State Hosp., 1954-55, Vineland (N.J.) Inst., 1955-58; guidance counselor Charles W. Eliot Jr. High Sch., Cleve., 1966—. Vol. in therapy Cleve. Free Clinic; bd. dirs. Katherine Tyler Center. LaVenburg scholar, 1951-52; Gund Found. scholar, 1964; fed. govt. grantee, 1963-66; lic. clin. psychologist. Mem. Am. Psychol. Assn., Ohio Psychol. Assn., Gestalt Inst., Cleve. Psychol. Assn., Assn. Black Psychologists (profl. vol.), Cleve. Sch. Counselors Assn., Alpha Kappa Alpha. Episcopalian. Office: 15700 Lotus Dr Cleveland OH 44128

RIVLIN, ALICE MITCHELL, economist; b. Phila., Mar. 4, 1931; d. Allan C. G. and Georgianna (Fales) Mitchell; B.A., Bryn Mawr Coll., 1952; M.A., Radcliffe Coll., 1955, Ph.D., 1958; m. Lewis Allen Rivlin, 1955 (div. 1977); children—Catherine Amy, Allan Mitchell, Douglas Gray. Research fellow Brookings Instn., Washington, 1957-58, staff econ. studies div., 1958-66, sr. fellow, 1969-75; dir. Congl. Budget Office, 1975—; dep. asst. sec. program coordination HEW, Washington, 1966-68, asst. sec. planning and evaluation, 1968-69. Staff, Adv. Commn. on Inter-govtl. Relations, 1961-62. Mem. Am. Econ. Assn. Author: The Role of the Federal Government in Financing Higher Education, 1961; (with others) Microanalysis of Socioeconomic Systems, 1961; The U.S. Balance of Payments in 1968, 1963; Systematic Thinking and Social Action, 1971; (with others) Setting National Priorities: The 1974 Budget, 1973. Office: Congl Budget Office House Annex Bldg 2 2d and D Sts SW Washington DC 20515

RIZZO, MARY ANN FRANCES, internat. trade exec., former educator; b. Bryn Mawr, Pa., Jan. 11, 1942; d. Joseph Franklyn and Armella Louise (Grubenhoff) R.; B.A. magna cum laude (N.Y. State scholar), Marymount-Manhattan Coll., 1963; M.A. (fellow), Yale U., 1965, Ph.D. (Lounsbury-Cross fellow), 1969; grad. smaller co. mgmt. program Harvard U. Bus. Sch., 1979. Instr., Romance langs. and lit. Yale U., New Haven, 1966-70; asst. prof. Finch Coll., N.Y.C., 1971-73; v.p. Joseph F. Rizzo Co., N.Y.C.- Fla., 1969—. Mem. Am. Assn. Tchrs. of Italian, MLA, Am. Assn. Univ. Profs. Italian, Am.-Italy Soc., Il Circolo Italian Cultural Club (Palm Beach, Fla.), Fgn. Trade Council Palm Beach County (charter mem.), Ariz. World Trade Council, Scottsdale C. of C., Alpha Chi. Republican. Roman Catholic (community council 1972-74). Clubs: Harvard Bus. Sch. Greater N.Y., Yale (N.Y.C.); Yale of Palm Beaches; Cercle Français de Palm Beach (Fla.). Translator: From Time to Eternity, 1967; bibliographer: Italian Literature-Roots and Branches, 1976. Home: Villa Serein 2170 Ibis Isle Rd Palm Beach FL 33480 also 5665 N 74th Pl Scottsdale AZ 85253 Office: PO Box 1376 Lake Worth FL 33460 also 5111 N Scottsdale Rd Scottsdale AZ 85253

RIZZUTO, LORRAINE ACHÉE, blood bank specialist; b. New Orleans, Jan. 17, 1936; d. Charles A. and Alice C. (Hogan) Achée; B.A. in Humanities, Thomas Edison Coll., 1979; M.B.A., Fairleigh Dickinson U., 1980; m. Anthony B. Rizzuto, Feb. 2, 1957; children—Richard T., Judy A., Joan M., Robert C. Blood bank technologist St. Peters Med. Center, New Brunswick, N.J., 1963-69; chief technologist Sera-Tec Biologics, North Brunswick, N.J., 1969-75, supr. central testing, 1975-77; new products coordinator Ortho Diagnostics, Raritan, N.J., 1977-79, prodn. services coordinator, 1979—; instr. blood banking Mercy Hosp., New Orleans, 1957-58. Active fund raising coms. various socs.; chmn. Raritan Valley YMHA Swim Team, 1968-71; chmn. Twenty-first Ann. Internat. Air Mail Swim Meet, 1970; bd. dirs. Cub Scouts, Troop 68, 1967, J.W.B. Internat. Swim Com., 1967-73, Jersey Masters Swim Team, 1973-75. Mem. Am. Assn. Blood Banks, Am. Soc. Clin. Pathologists, N.J. Blood Bank Assn., Am. Mgmt. Assn., Nat. Fedn. Bus. and Profl. Women's Clubs, Fairleigh Dickinson Alumni Assn. (sec.). Clubs: Lake Naomi; Toastmaster. Home: 61 Goldfinch Glen Hackettstown NJ 07840 Office: Route 202 N Raritan NJ 08879

ROACH, DOROTHY ANNETTE, legal sec.; b. Jasper, Ind., Oct. 18, 1953; d. William George and Eileen Zelma (Seitz) Schaber; A.S., Vincennes U., 1974; m. Jerald Allen Roach, June 17, 1972 (dec. 1981); Sec. credit dept. Gimbel-Bond Dept. Store, Vincennes, Ind., 1972-75; legal sec.,/asst. Kixmiller, Sturm & Smith, Vincennes, 1975—; instr. Vincennes U., 1980—. Mem. Knox County Assn. Legal Secs., Ind. Assn. Legal Secs., Nat. Assn. Legal Secs. (gov. 1979—), Vincennes Fedn. Bus. and Profl. Women, Ind. Fedn. Bus. and Profl. Women (2d v.p. 1982-83), Nat Fedn. Bus. and Profl. Women (dist. dir. 1979-80, state new club expansion chmn. 1980-81). Republican. Lutheran. Club: Bus. and Profl. Women's (editor monthly pub. The Tattler 1976—). Home: Route 6 Box 14 Vincennes IN 47591 Office: PO Box 393 Box 395 Vincennes IN 47591

ROACH, VELORIES ANTOINETTE, fin. brokerage co. co. exec.; b. Meridian, Miss., July 8, 1931; d. Otha Lee and Ester (Mayatte) Ethridge; student public schs., Waco, Tex., Collinsville, Miss.; m. Billy J. Green, May 5, 1979; children—Carl Lowell Roach, Nan Roach Kurth, Mike Roach, Jackie Roach Pilkinton. Ins. and real estate salesperson, 1964-81; pres., owner, operator Lubbock Mortgage Co., Inc. (name now Guaranty Fin. Services, Inc.), Lubbock, Tex., 1976—; pres. Delta Cotton Co., 1977—; pres. Hunter & Roach Advt. Co., Lubbock, 1978—. Mem. Nat. Assn. Fin. Cons., Nat. Assn. Female Execs. Inc., Better Bus. Bur., Sheriff Assn., Internat. Bus. Assn., Am. Alliance Small Bus. Club: Presidents of Tex. Home: 3013 78th St Lubbock TX 79423 Office: 1220 Broadway Suite 1706 Lubbock TX 79401

ROALES, JUDITH M., journalist, pub. co. exec.; b. Vincennes, Ind., Jan. 28, 1942; d. Ralph N. and Pauline F. (Stiegelbauer) R.; B.S., So. Ill. U., 1965; children—N. Gregory Brooks, Jennifer Michelle Brooks. Reporter, The News-Journal Co., Wilmington, Del., 1965-66; asst. pub. affairs officer U.S. Army Chem. Biol. Research Center, Ft. Detrick, Md., 1966; mag. editor The Free Lance-Star, Fredericksburg, Va., 1967; asst. to dir. Sch. Journalism, So. Ill. U., Carbondale, 1968-71; asso. editor Independent Newspapers, Inc., Dover, Del., 1972-75, Washington bur. chief, 1975-76; sr. program analyst Office Tech. Assessment, U.S. Congress, Washington, 1976-78; spl. asst. to dept. adminstr. NOAA, Washington, 1979-81; v.p. Independent Newspapers Inc., Arcadia, Fla., 1981—. Recipient numerous press awards including Washington Region awards Capitol Press Women, 1976, Nat. Sci. Writing award AAAS, 1975, Coastal Zone award Watch Our Waterways, 1974, Spl. citation Am. Oceanic Orgn., 1979. Contbr. articles on marine policy to profl. publs. Home: Nocatee Rd Arcadia FL 33821 Office: 209 W Oak St Arcadia FL 33821

ROBARDS, KAREN P., investment banking exec.; b. New Britain, Conn., Mar. 13, 1950; d. Joseph Richard and Helen (Kulig) Puskarz; A.B. in Econs., Smith Coll., 1972; M.B.A., Harvard U., 1976; m. Thomas F. Robards, June 19, 1976. Analyst, Morgan Stanley & Co. Inc., N.Y.C., 1972-74, asso., 1976-80, v.p., 1981—. Mem. YWCA Acad. Women Achievers. Roman Catholic. Office: 1251 Ave of the Americas New York NY 10020

ROBB, LYNDA JOHNSON, writer; b. Washington, Mar. 19, 1944; d. Lyndon Baines and Claudia Alta (Taylor) Johnson; B.A. with honors, U. Tex., 1966; m. Charles Spittal Robb, Dec. 9, 1967; children—Lucinda Desha, Catherine Lewis, Jennifer Wickliffe. Writer, McCall's mag., 1966-68; contbg. editor Ladies Home Jour., 1968-80; lectr. Bd. dirs. Reading Is Fundamental, 1968—, L.Q.C. Lamar Soc., 1974—, Lyndon B. Johnson Family Found., 1969—; mem. Woodlawn Bd. Historic Trust; chmn. Pres.'s Adv. Com. for Women, 1979-81; bd. dirs. Nat. Home Library Found. Mem. Zeta Tau Alpha. Democrat. Episcopalian. Office: Executive Mansion Capitol Sq Richmond VA 23219

ROBB, ROSE ANN, banker; b. Oak Lawn, Ill., Oct. 12, 1943; d. Ignatius and Lillian Mary (Cerveny) Lichner; student public schs., Oak Lawn and Phoenix; m. Bernard L. Robb, Mar. 13, 1982. With First Nat. Bank of Ariz., Phoenix, 1967—, asst. trust officer, 1975-76, trust officer, 1976-78, corp. trust adminstr., v.p., trust officer, 1978—. Mem. Am. Soc. Corp. Secs. (sec. Phoenix chpt.), Stock Transfer Assn., Nat. Assn. Bank Women. Office: First Interstate Bank of Ariz 100 W Washington St Phoenix AZ 85036

ROBBINS, CARRIE MAE, costume designer; b. Balt., Feb. 7, 1943; d. Sidney W. and Bettye A. (Berman) Fishbeib; B.A., Pa. State U., 1964; M.F.A., Yale U., 1967; m. Richard D. Robbins, Feb. 15, 1959. Costume designer Broadway shows including Grease, Over Here, Agnes of God, The 1st, Yentl, Happy End, Broadway Molly, Secret Affairs of Mildred Wild, also Hamburg (Ger.) State Opera, Sarah Caldwell's Opera Co. of Boston, San Francisco Opera, Lincoln Center, Chelsea Theatre, John Houseman's Acting Co., WNET Theatre in America seres, Popp's Shakespeare in the Park, Circle-in-the-Sq., Guthrie Theater, Mpls., Kennedy Center, Washington Opera Soc., Mark Taper Forum, Los Angeles, Am. Conservatory Theater, San Francisco, others including off-Broadway and summer stock; guest speaker various univs. Mem. hon. bd. steering com. Nat. Center for Women in Performing Arts. Recipient Drama Desk award, 1971-72, 73-74; Maharam Found. award, 1975; work selected for inclusion in U.S. Internat. Theatre Inst. Touring Exhibit, 1974—; Yale U. Drama Sch. award; Tony nominee, 1971-72, 73-74. Mem. League Profl. Theatre Tng. Programs (steering com.), League Profl. Theatre Women, United Scenic Arts Local, Am. Soc. Interior Designers, Scribes, Graphic Arts Guild, Met. Mus., Mus. Contemporary Crafts, Mus. Am. Folk Art, Japan Soc., Phi Beta Kappa. Home and studio: 32 E 36th St New York NY 10016

ROBBINS, DOROTHY ELAINE, sculptor; b. Lakewood, Ohio, Feb. 15, 1920; d. Benjamin Jay and Ella (Schwartz) Schochen; B.A. with distinction, Ohio State U., 1942; student Cranbrook Acad. Art, 1945-47; M.A., Hunter Coll., 1962; student Cin. Art Acad., 1947-49; div.; 1 dau., Dena. Asst. prof. art dept. SUNY, New Paltz, 1966-71; sr. lectr. art dept. U. Haifa (Israel), 1972—; exhibited one-man shows Sculpture Center, N.Y.C., Cober Gallery, N.Y.C., Donnell Library, N.Y.C., Roko Gallery, N.Y.C., Jaffo Gallery, Israel, Beit Rothschild, Haifa, Herzliya Mus., Kibbutz Hazorea; exhibited maj. N.Y.C. exhbns., internat. exhbns.; work represented in numerous mus. collections, pvt. collections. Recipient Cin. Mus. Purchase prize, Audubon Artists Purchase prize; sculpture award City of Haifa, 1982; Yaddo fellow, 1963; SUNY Research Found. grantee, 1967, Faculty Research fellow, 1969. Mem. Israel Painters and Sculptors Assn., Ein-Hod Artists Village. Home: Ein-Hod Artists Village Hof Hacarmel Israel Office: U Haifa Mount Carmel Haifa Israel

ROBBINS, JANE LOUISA, educator; b. Bangor, Maine, Dec. 25, 1944; d. Howard Allen and Rebekah May (Gross) Gray; B.S., Wright State U., 1975; M.B.A., 1981; m. Derek Robbins, Dec. 26, 1963; children—D. Christopher. Mgmt. asst., aero. systems div. Wright Patterson AFB, Ohio, 1971-73; instr. bus. edn., public schs., Bucksport, Maine, 1952-64; fin. specialist, aero. systems div. Wright Patterson AFB, 1977-79, cost analyst, 1979-81, asst. prof. quantitative contract price analysis Air Force Inst. Tech., Sch. Systems and Logistics, 1982—. Mem. drug intervention adv. group Beavercreek High Sch. Mem. Nat. Estimating Soc., Internat. Soc. Parametric Analysis, Nat. Assn. Female Execs., Kappa Delta Pi. Episcopalian. Office: Air Force Inst Tech Sch Systems and Logistics Wright Patterson AFB OH 45431

ROBBINS, JANE TURNEY, devel. banker; b. Santa Barbara, Calif., Apr. 27, 1943; d. Chauncey and Doris (Turney) R.; B.A., Duke U., 1965; M.A. (Univ. fellow), Yale U., 1970; postgrad. Taiwan Normal U., Taipei, 1972. China analyst Dept. State, Washington, 1970-71; mgr. Citibank, N.A., Internat. Banking Group, N.Y.C., Taiwan and Philippines, 1973-76; polit. risk ins. officer Overseas Pvt. Investment Corp., Washington, 1977-80; country officer Asian Devel. Bank, Manila, 1980—. U.S. Govt. Title IV fellow, 1967-68. Mem. Mass. Soc. Mayflower Descs., NOW, Cum Laude Soc., Phi Beta Kappa, Kappa Alpha Theta. Republican. Episcopalian. Home: RFD 4 Houlton ME 04730 Office: PO Box 789 Manila Philippines 2800

ROBBINS, KAREN ANN, financial exec.; b. Putnam, Conn., Sept. 9, 1953; d. Robert Merrill and Mercedes Jaqueline R.; B.S., U. Conn., 1975; M.B.A., Northeastern U., 1977. Fin. analyst bus. forms div. Burroughs Corp., Office Products Group, Rochester, N.Y., 1977-78, cost and fin. acctg. supr., 1978-79, acctg. mgr. office supplies div., Fairport, N.Y., 1979-82, acctg. supr. bus. fin. div., Rochester, 1982—. Mem. Nat. Assn. Female Execs., U. Conn., Northeastern U. alumni assns. Republican. Roman Catholic. Home: 24 Swan Trail Fairport NY 14450 Office: 1150 University Ave Rochester NY 14003

ROBBINS, MARYHILL MAIN, interior designer; b. Maryhill, Wash., Oct. 27, 1915; d. William Wier and Martha Humphrey (McBride) Main; student Wash. State U., 1932-34, Peabody Inst., Balt., 1954-58, Seattle U., 1973-77, U. Wash., 1976-78; grad. interior design Cornish Sch. Allied Arts, 1971; m. Charles A. Robbins, Jr., Sept. 15, 1940 (dec. 1954); children—Charles A. Robbins III, Thomas William Robbins. Legis. liaison in U.S. Senate, Sec. Army, Dept. Def., Washington, 1955-56; exec. sec. Maj. Gen. Paul F. Yount, Chief Transp. of U.S. Army, Washington, 1956-58, also to Lt. Gen. Frank S. Beeson, 1958; interior designer, Seattle, 1971—. Gray lady ARC, 1954-58. Mem. Nat. Soc. Interior Designers, DAR, Kappa Alpha Theta. Episcopalian. Piano concerts in Salzburg, Austria, 1938, Tacoma, 1939, Atlanta, 1951, 52. Home: 1902 2d Ave The Josephinum Seattle WA 98101

ROBBINS, MOLLY KATHRYN, utility info. ofcl.; b. Cin., July 7, 1952; d. Robert William and Elizabeth Jane (Barton) Shannon; B.S., Purdue U., 1974; m. Donald Eston Robbins, June 28, 1975; stepchildren—Michelle Lynn, Thomas Eston. With Public Service of Ind., 1974—, elec. living cons., Shelbyville, 1978-80, info. service coordinator Public Relations Gen. Hdqrs., Plainfield, 1975—. Mem. Am. and Ind. Optometric Assn. Aux. (soc. pres. 1976-78, public info. trustee 1978-79, bull. press trustee and key woman 1980—), Am. Home Econ. Assn., Ind. Home Econ. Assn., Home Economists in Bus., Elec. Womens Roundtable, Nuclear Energy Women, Zeta Tau Alpha, Kappa Kappa Kappa. Republican. Methodist. Home: 102 W McKay Rd Shelbyville IN 46176

ROBBINS, PAULA, psychiat. social worker; b. Bklyn., Jan. 1, 1938; d. Morris and Hannah (Beckman) Star; B.A., Ramapo Coll., 1976; M.S.W., Fordham U., 1979; postgrad. N.Y. Sch. Psychoanalytic Psychotherapy; m. Warren T. Robbins, Jan. 5, 1957; children—Cory Scott, Glenn Curtis, Adam Todd, Russ Evan. Supr. students, tchr.-tng. program Vol. Counselling Service, New City, N.Y., 1975—; dir. coping skills program Pomona-Rockland County (N.Y.) Mental Health Center, 1979-81; mem. faculty Rockland Community Coll.; pvt. practice clin. social work psychotherapy. Vol., Am. Cancer Soc. Mem. Nat. Assn. Social Workers, Soc. Clin. Social Work Psychotherapists, Am. Orthopsychiat. Assn., NOW, Am. Group Psychotherapy Assn., Equal Rights for Fathers, Soc. for Advancement Developmental Psychoanalytic Psychotherapy (dir.), Rockland County Mental Health Assn. (adult rehab. com.), Hadassah (chpt. v.p. 1963). Democrat. Jewish. Home and Office: 9 Beckett Ct Monsey NY 10952

ROBBINS LEET, MILDRED ELOWSKY, consultant; b. N.Y.C., Aug. 9, 1922; d. Samuel Milton and Isabella (Zeitz) Elowsky; B.A., N.Y. U., 1942; m. Louis J. Robbins, Feb. 23, 1941 (dec. 1970); children—Jane, Aileen; m. 2d, Glen Leet, Aug. 9, 1974. Partner, Leet & Leet, cons. on women in devel., N.Y.C., 1978—. Pres. women's div. United Cerebral Palsy, N.Y.C., 1951-52, bd. dirs., 1953—, chmn. bd., 1953-55; rep. Nat. Council Women U.S. at UN, 1957-64, 1st v.p., 1959-64, pres., 1964-68, hon. pres., 1968-70; sec., v.p. conf. group U.S. Nat. Orgns. at UN, 1961-64, 76-78, vice chmn., sec., 1962-64, mem. exec. com., 1961-65, 75-79, chmn. hospitality info. service, 1960-66; vice chmn. exec. com. NGO's with UN Office Pub. Info., 1976-78, chmn. ann. conf., 1977, chmn. com. on water, desertification, habitat and environment Conf. NGO's with consultative status with ECOSOC, 1976—, mem. exec. com. World Conf. of UN Decade for Women, 1980; mem. exec. com. Internat. Council Women, 1960-73, v.p., 1970-73; chmn. program planning com., women's com. OEO, 1967-72; cons. Club of Rome, UNITAR-CEESTEM, Joint Symposium on Regionalism and the NIEO, UN, 1980; chmn. com. on natural disasters N.Am. Com. on Environment, 1973-77; N.Y. State chmn. UN Day, 1976; co-chmn. Vols. for Stevenson, N.Y. State, 1956; vice chmn. task force Nat. Dem. Com., 1969-72; mem. N.Y. State Commn. on Power of Local Govt., 1970-73; vice chmn. Coll. for Human Services; bd. dirs. Am. Arbitration Assn., Save the Children Fedn., Trickle Up Program, N.Y.C., 1979—; v.p. Am. Council Human Services, 1981; mem. presdl. del. to Brazzaville (Congo) Centennial Celebration, 1980; sec. Inst. for Mediation and Conflict Resolution, Spirit of Stockholm, Hotline Internat.; rep. Internat. Peace Acad. at UN, 1974-77, Internat. Soc. Community Devel., 1977—; del. at large 1st Nat. Women's Conf., Houston, 1977; chmn. task force on internat. interdependence N.Y. State Women's Meeting, 1977; bd. dirs. New Directions, 1978-81; mem. Task Force on Poverty, 1977-81; chmn. Task Force on Women, Sci. and Tech. for Devel., 1978—; U.S. del. UN Status of Women Commn., 1978; U.S. del. UN Conf. Sci. and Tech. for Devel., 1979, mem. global adv. bd. Internat. Expn. of Rural Devel.; trustee Internat. Inst. Haiti, 1981—; fellow council internat. fellows U. Bridgeport, 1982—. Editor: UN Calendar and Digest, 1959-64; Measure of Mankind, 1963: bd. editors Peace & Change, 1980; contbr. articles to various publs. Home: 54 Riverside Dr New York NY 10024 also 2 Briar Oak Dr Weston CT 06883 Office: 790 Madison Ave New York NY 10021

ROBE, LUCY BARRY, (MRS. ROBERT S. ROBE, JR.), med. researcher; b. Boston, Jan. 15, 1934; d. Herbert and Lucy Manning (Brown) Barry; B.A., Radcilffe Coll., 1955; postgrad. N.Y. U., 1962-63, 69, L.I. U., 1971-72; cert. Rutgers Inst. Alcohol Studies, 1979; m. Robert S. Robe, Jr., Feb. 6, 1971; 1 dau., Parrish Cameron. Prodn. asst. various Broadway producers and writers, 1956-68, prodns. include Bells Are Ringing, 1958, How to Succeed, 1961, Generation, 1965; librarian Charisma Prodns., N.Y.C., 1968-70; reporter Oyster Bay (N.Y.) Guardian, 1972-74; research asso. N.Y. Med. Coll., 1980—; lectr. for L.I. Council Alcoholism in schs., colls., fetal alcohol syndrome. Bd. dirs. North Nassau Mental Health Center, Friends of Council; v.p. L.I. Council on Alcoholism; mem. Fetal Alcohol Syndrome Task Force N.Y. State and L.I.; mem. N.Y. County Republican Com., 1968-71. Mem. Authors Guild, Am. Med. Writers Assn. Named Woman of Year, L.I. Alliance Women and Alcoholism, 1980. Club: Radcliffe Alumnae of L.I. (dir.). Author: Stagestruck Secretary, 1966; Just So It's Healthy-New Evidence that Drinking and Drugs Can Harm Your Unborn Baby, 1978, rev. edit., 1982; Haunted Inheritance, 1980. Past contbg. editor L.I. Mag.; contbr. articles to mags., books, newspapers, others. Home: 143 Cove Rd Oyster Bay NY 11771

ROBEK, MARY FRANCES, educator; b. Superior, Wis., Jan. 30, 1927; d. Stephen and Mary (Hervert) R.; B.Ed., U. Wis., 1948; M.A., Northwestern U., 1951; M.B.A., U. Mich., 1962, Ph.D., 1967. Tchr., Bergland (Mich.) High Sch., 1948, Tony (Wis.) High Sch., 1948-50, Sch. of Vocat. and Adult Edn., Superior, Wis., 1950-58; prof. adminstrv.

services and bus. edn. Eastern Mich. U., Ypsilanti, 1958—. Mem. Assn. Records Mgrs. and Adminstrs., Internat. Word Processing Assn., Am. Word Processing Assn., Am. Inst. Decision Scis., Inst. Cert. Mgrs. (pres. 1980), Delta Pi Epsilon, Delta Kappa Gamma, Pi Lambda Theta. Democrat. Roman Catholic. Club: Catholic Daughters Am. Author: Information and Records Management, 1980. Home: 1230 W Cross St Ypsilanti MI 48197 Office: Sill Hall Coll Tech Eastern Mich U Ypsilanti MI 48197

ROBERS, MARTHA MARIE, social worker; b. Pueblo, Colo., Aug. 29, 1947; d. Richard Joseph and Rachelle Marie (Mattingly) R.; B.A., U. Santa Clara, 1969; M.S.W., U. Denver, 1971. Social worker Denver Dept. Public Welfare, 1969-70, Denver Head Start Program, 1970-71; community organizer Cath. Youth Orgn., Canoga Park, Calif., 1971-73; social worker II Children's Home Soc. of Calif., Los Angeles, 1973-78; clin. social worker Santa Monica Hosp. Med. Center and Rape Treatment Center, 1978—; field instr. U. So. Calif. Mem. steering com. So. Calif. Cath. Peace Coalition; adv. bd. Santa Monica Catholic Youth Orgn., 1st v.p., 1980-81. Lic. clin. social worker. Mem. Nat. Assn. Social Workers, Nat. Assn. Christians in Social Work (pres. So. Calif. chpt. 1979-80). Democrat. Roman Catholic. Home: 928 10th St Apt 4 Santa Monica CA 90403 Office: 1225 15th St Santa Monica CA 90404

ROBERSON, EDITH PEGRAM, nurse; b. Forsyth County, N.C., Sept. 19, 1933; d. Arnold Wade and Annie Sue (Gravette) Pegram; R.N., City Meml. Hosp. Sch. Nursing, 1954; m. Charles E. Roberson, Sept. 6, 1957; children—Charles David, Robert Joseph. Staff nurse City Meml. Hosp., Winston-Salem, 1960-64; adminstrv. supr. Forsyth Meml. Hosp., 1964-66, clin. specialist, 1964-66, asst. dir. nursing, 1966-81, asso. dir. nursing, 1981—. Registered nurse, N.C. Mem. City Meml. Hosp. Alumni Assn., Forsyth County Heart Assn., Quill and Scroll. Democrat. Baptist. Club: NC. Farm Bur. Contbr. articles to profl. jours. Home: PO Box 1 Walkertown NC 27051 Office: 3333 Silas Creek Pkwy Winston Salem NC 27103

ROBERSON, ELIZABETH WILLOUGHBY, mktg. research exec.; b. Phila., Dec. 15, 1927; d. Jason Theodore and Elizabeth Bell (Sullivan) R.; student Columbia U., 1947-50. Research trainee Young & Rubicam Inc.; mgmt. cons. The Diebold Group; field dir. Market Facts, Inc., Stockton & Ott, Inc., N.Y.C., 1979—. Deacon, Fifth Avenue Presbyn. Ch. Mem. Market Research Assn. (President's award). Home: 52-40 39th Dr Woodside NY 11377 Office: Stockton & Ott Inc 20 E 46th St New York NY 10017

ROBERSTON-SMITH, MARY PATRICIA (PEIRCE) (MRS. JOHN A. SMITH), coll. dean; b. Key West, Fla., Jan. 10, 1942; d. Robert P. and Jemeile (Seamon) Peirce; B.S. magna cum laude (Centennial Honor scholar), La. State U., 1963, M.S., 1964; M.Ed., Southeastern La. U., 1973; Ed.D., Rutgers U., 1982; m. John A. Smith; children—Stephanie Dawn, Debbie, Diane, John. Young adult librarian Enoch Pratt Free Library, Balt., 1964-65, adminstrv. asst., 1965-66; instr. Balt. Jr. Coll., 1966-67; library specialist and tchr. Ednl. Media Center, Covington, La., 1967-70; instr. NASA Miss. Test Facility, 1967-68; field librarian St. Tammany Parish Sch. Bd., Covington, 1967-70; librarian S.E. La. Hosp., Mandeville, 1970-73, coordinator adult edn., 1972-73; asst. prof. library and learning resources Bergen Community Coll., Paramus, N.J., 1973-79, asso. prof., 1979-81, asst. dean instructional services, 1979-81, asso. dean instructional services, 1981-82, dean instructional services, 1982—; tchr., cons. in reading, library work and spl. edn.; prodn. asso. CBS summer semester, 1974-75; mem. Gov.'s Com. Libraries; mem. acad. council Thomas A. Edison State Coll. Staff instr. 1st Army Instr. Tng. Sch., USAR, 1975, 76, 77. Bd. dirs. Bergen County Health and Welfare Council; chmn. fin., bd. dirs. Sherbruke Co-op. Mem. AAUW (v.p.), Mensa, Delta Kappa Gamma, Kappa Delta Pi, Mu Sigma Rho, Beta Phi Mu, Alpha Lambda Delta, Kappa Delta Pi, Tau Kappa Alpha. Contbg. editor: The Special Child, 1976. Home: 125 Prospect Ave Hackensack NJ 07601 Office: Bergen Community Coll 400 Paramus Rd Paramus NJ 07652

ROBERTS, AMELIA SEAWRIGHT (MRS. JAMES F. ROBERTS), educator; b. Sumter, S.C.; d. William and Lavinia (Barnes) Seawright: B.S., S.C. State Coll., 1946; M.A., Columbia U., 1950; Ed.D., U. Okla., 1964; m. James F. Roberts, Mar. 9, 1946 (dec. Oct. 1967); 1 dau., Toni Amelia. Tchr. public schs., Horry County, 1940-43; substitute tchr. N.Y.C. Public Schs., 1946-47; tchr. Orangeburg (S.C.) City Schs., 1947-51; dir. elem. workshop S.C. State Coll., Orangeburg, summers 1949-52, asst. supr. of directed teaching, 1951-63, dir. Felton Lab. Sch., 1964-70, dean Sch. Edn., 1970-81; ret., 1981; del. World Assemby of Internat. Council on Edn. for Teaching, Singapore. Founder, 1st pres. S.C. Assn. of Colls. for Tchr. Edn.; mem. adv. bd. S.C. Children's Bur.; past chmn. Orangeburg Mental Health Bd.; mem. S.C. Com. on Children and Youth; trustee Orangeburg Dist. 5, New Mt. Zion Bapt. Ch. Mem. So. Assn. Colls. and Schs. (past mem. commn. on elem. schs.), AAUP, Am. Assn. Sch. Adminstrs., S.C. Edn. Assn., Am. Assn. of Colls. for Tchr. Edn. (dir. 1978-81), S.C. Council of Edn. Deans (past chmn.), Jack and Jill of Am., Nat. Council of Negro Women, Ladies Aux. VFW (past pres.), Nat. Assn. Lab. Schs., Nat. Assn. Coll. Women (past pres.), AAUW, Ch. Women United, Delta Sigma Theta (past pres.), Kappa Delta Pi, Phi Delta Kappa. Eagle. Mem. Order Eastern Star. Contbr. articles to profl. jours. Home: 2685 Old Cameron Rd Orangeburg SC 29115

ROBERTS, ANITA GAYLE, nurse, adminstr.; b. Stamford, Tex., Nov. 25, 1945; d. Floyd Ray and Robbye Louise (Jeter) Jones; B.S.N., Okla. Bapt. U., 1970; m. Edwin Earl Roberts, Jr., June 1, 1968; 1 dau., Robyn Marie. Staff nurse Okla. U. Hosp., Oklahoma City, 1970-72; dir. nurses Physicians and Surgeons Hosp., Med. Center. Hosp., Duncan, Okla., 1972-74; public health nurse Stephens and Jefferson counties (Okla.) Health Dept., 1974-77; dist nursing supr. North Central and Panhandle Okla., Okla. Health Dept., Oklahoma City, 1977—. Registered nurse, Okla. Mem. Am. Nurses Assn., Okla. Public Health Assn. (chmn. nursing sect. 1980-82), Okla. Nursing Assn. (dist. 4 treas.). Democrat. Baptist. Club: Family Bass. Home: 2804 W Pine St Enid OK 73701 Office: NE 10th and Stonewall Oklahoma City OK 73152

ROBERTS, BARBARA ANN, telephone co. ofcl.; b. Milw., Feb. 21, 1929; d. Andrew Max and Ersilia (Celia) Gertrude (Comparoni) Maglio; student Milw. public schs.; m. Albert Lloyd Roberts, Sept. 3, 1949; children—Marybeth, Bradley J., David L. With Wis. Telephone Co., Milw., 1961—, now group mgr. operator services. Mem. Bus. and Profl. Women Milw. (pres. 1979-81), Wis. Bus. and Profl. Women (dist. dir. Eastern Dist. 8 1981-82). Home: 8411 W Cheyenne St Milwaukee WI 53224 Office: 2140 Davidson Rd Waukesha WI 53186

ROBERTS, BARBARA ELIZABETH, lawyer; b. Kansas City, Mo., Oct. 29, 1946; d. Ralph Thomas and Margaret Naomi (Owen) Henderson, Jr.; B.A., U. Mo., Kansas City, 1969, J.D., 1971. Admitted to Mo. bar, 1971, Fed. bar, 1981; asst. counsel Oppenheimer Industries, Inc., Kansas City, Mo., 1971-72, counsel, sec., 1972-76, counsel, sec., asst. v.p., 1976-81, counsel, 1981—; of counsel Sheridan, Sanders & Simpson, P.C., Kansas City, 1981-82; v.p., dir. Gunsight, Inc., Kansas City, 1978-82; assoc. Henri Watson and Dennis Godden, 1982—; ; dir Christobal Wine Co., Number 1 TV, Inc., Bus. Enterprise Resources, Inc. Pres. N.W. Mo. citizens adv. bd. Vols. in Correction, 1978, bd. dirs., 1977-81; vol. probation officer, 1974-81. Recipient Vol. of Yr. award N.W. Mo. Probation and Parole Office, 1978; citation for meritorious service Am. Bar Assn., 1979. Mem. Am. Bar Assn. (chmn. project adv. 1977-80, criminal editor Barrister, 1978-81), Mo. Bar Assn., Kansas City Bar Assn. (co-chmn. real estate com. 1976-81, chmn. 1982), Phi Alpha Delta. Republican. Home: 3 Janssen Pl Kansas City MO 64109 Office: 2506 Holmes St Kansas City MO 64108

ROBERTS, BARBARA PADGETT, ins. co. exec.; b. Leesburg, Fla.; d. Reubin Donald Padgett and Juanita Padgett Yaps; B.S., George Peabody Coll., Vanderbilt U., 1969; postgrad. U. Ga., 1970; m. James Allen Roberts, July 5, 1969; children—James Allen, John Andrew. With Atlanta Employment and Evaluation Service Center, 1969; instr. in child devel. Atlanta Tech. Sch., 1970-71; career agt. Pan Am. Life Ins. Co., Shreveport, 1979—. Bd. dirs. March of Dimes. Mem. Am. Home Econs. Assn., Nat. Assn. Life Underwriters, La. Assn. Life Underwriters, Shreveport Assn. Life Underwriters, Beta Sigma Phi. Clubs: Home Extension, Mes Amis (pres. 1976-77). Home: 6754 N Club Circle Shreveport LA 71107 Office: 520 Spring St Shreveport LA 71101

ROBERTS, BEVERLY KAY, former air force officer, city ofcl.; b. Swedesboro, N.J., May 6, 1936; d. Harold Smith and Mildred Lamb (Hurlock) Huber; B.A. in Sociology, Temple U., 1959; M.A., Central Mich. U., 1976; m. Edward Hartwell Roberts, Jr., July 5, 1974; 1 son, Mark David. Commd. 2d lt. U.S. Air Force, 1960; advanced through grades to maj., 1970; assigned Vietnam, 1967-68, 72-73; spl. asst. for human resources devel. Air Force Systems Command, 1978-79; exec. officer Electronic Warfare during Close Air Support Joint Test Force, Nellis AFB, Nev. 1979-80; ret., 1980; mem. Nev. Gov.'s Mgmt. Task Force, 1980; dir. Records Bur., Las Vegas Met. Police Dept., 1981—. Founder Wipe-out, Inc., Pedricktown, N.J. Decorated Bronze Star. Mem. Am. Soc. Tng. and Devel., Soc. Advancement of Mgmt., Am. Mgmt. Assn., Air Force Assn., Am. Bus. Womens Assn. Republican. Baptist. Home and office: PO Box 2 Pedricktown NJ 08067

ROBERTS, CAROL ANNETTE WALKER, legal asst.; b. Atlanta, Feb. 27, 1951; d. Charles Wesley and Daisy Beatrice (Key) Walker; student Dekalb Jr. Coll., Atlanta, 1976; m. Donald Roberts, Dec. 9, 1970; children—Donna Dannette, Donald Christopher, Kortnie Le Andra. Various office and secretarial positions, 1969-71, 73-76; adminstrv. asst. firm Thompson and Pace, Atlanta, 1976—; immigration cons., 1978—; with firm Thompson, Mann & Hutson, Atlanta, 1979—. Methodist. Club: Order Eastern Star. Address: 1864 Joseph Ct Decatur GA 30032

ROBERTS, CELIA ANN, librarian; b. Bangor, Maine, Feb. 6, 1935; d. William Lewis and Ruey Pearl (Logan) R.; A.A., U. Hartford, 1957, B.A., 1961; postgrad. So. Conn. State Coll., 1963—. With catalog, acquistion and circulation depts. U. Hartford Library, 1956-65; librarian Simsbury (Conn.) Free Library, 1965; reference librarian Simsbury Public Library, 1969—. Tchr. ballet classes, 1965-66; ballet mistress Ballet Soc. Conn., Inc., 1968-70; with corps de ballet Conn. Opera Assn., 1963-64; active in prodns. Simsbury Light Opera Assn., 1964, 69. Mem. ALA, Conn. Library Assn., Simsbury Hist. Soc., Ont. Geneal. Soc., AAUW (past pres. Greater Hartford br.), Pro Dance, DAR (Abigail Phelps chpt.), Conn. Soc. Genealogists, Soc. Mayflower Descs. Conn., Dance Masters Am. Universalist. Office: 749 Hopmeadow St Simsbury CT 06070

ROBERTS, DOROTHY HYMAN, apparel co. exec.; b. N.Y.C., Dec. 6, 1928; d. Edgar C. and Theresa M. (Marks) Hyman; B.A., Conn. Coll., 1950; m. Paul M. Roberts, June 18, 1950; children—Lynn, Steven. With Echo Scarfs, Inc., N.Y.C., 1950—, pres., 1978—. Mem. The Fashion Group. Office: 10 E 40th St New York City NY 10016

ROBERTS, EVELYN FREEMAN, composer, condr., musician; b. Cleve., Feb. 13, 1919; d. Ernest A. and Gertrude (Richardson) Freeman; B.Mus., Cleve. Inst. Music, 1941; grad. student Calif. State U., Los Angeles, 1964-66, UCLA, U. So. Calif., 1967-70; m. Thomas S. Roberts; children—Anita, Ernest, Claire, Lisa. Tchr. music Karamu Ho., Cleve., 1937-40; performed Cafe Soc., N.Y.C., Town and Country, Club Elegante, Bklyn., Dunes Hotel, Las Vegas, Desert Inn Hotel Hilton, Las Vegas, Harrah's, Reno, Sahara-Tahoe; appeared in movies, including Toys in The Attic, A Clash of Cymbals; TV appearances include Jonathan Winters, Ed Sullivan shows, Andy Griffith Spl., Profiles in Courage, numerous local shows, spls.; staff arranger Leslie Uggams Show; spl. performance at White House, 1970; recorded albums; arranger for numerous rec. stars; co-founder, dir., program coordinator Young Saints Acad. Performing Arts and Skills, Los Angeles, 1971—. Recipient numerous commendations, citations, awards from civic orgns. Mem. Am. Soc. Composers and Pubs., Am. Guild Authors and Composers, Musicians Union (life). Methodist. Home: 2000 Wellington Rd Los Angeles CA 90016 Office: 6216 S Main St Los Angeles CA 90003

ROBERTS, HELEN MARIA, physician; b. Poland, Aug. 19, 1924; came to U.S., 1949, naturalized, 1954; M.D., U. Edinburgh, 1949; M.Sc., U. Minn., 1954; m. Frank D. Mann, Apr. 14, 1956; 1 dau., Roberta F. Fellow in dermatology Mayo Clinic, Rochester, Minn., 1951-54; chief dermatology VA Med. Center, Phoenix, 1955—; adj. asso. prof. internal medicine U. Ariz. Med. Coll., Tucson, 1972—; cons. USPHS Indian Service, 1964-76. Recipient Best Tchr. of Yr. award, Good Samaritan Hosp. Family Practice, 1980. Mem. Am. Med. Soc. Vienna, AAUW, Am. Acad. Dermatology, Pacific Dermatologic Assn., Mayo Alumni Assn. Republican. Roman Catholic. Contbr. articles to profl. jours. Home: 5316 E Roadrunner Rd Scottsdale AZ 85253 Office: VA Med Center Phoenix AZ 85012

ROBERTS, JOAN ILA, psychologist; b. Salt Lake City, June 26, 1935; d. Wallace Byron and Ila (Nelson) R.; B.A. with honors, U. Utah, 1957; M.A. in Social Psychology, 1960, Ph.D., 1970. Cons. psychologist Herold Assos., N.Y.C., 1958-61; mem. research staff Columbia U., also U. London and Makerere Coll., Kampala, Uganda, 1961-63; research asso. Hunter Coll., N.Y.C., 1964-67; asst. prof. U. Wis., Madison, 1968-75; asso. prof. psychology Upstate Med. Center, Syracuse, N.Y., 1976-79, Syracuse U., 1979—; adj. asso. prof. Upstate Med. Center; cons. in field. Vice pres. Center Human Futures, Syracuse, 1979—. Recipient Research award Syracuse U.; Faculty Research fellow U. Wis. Mem. Am. Psychol. Assn., Am. Anthrop. Assn., Am. Sociol. Assn., Nat. Women's Studies Assn., Groves Family Conf., NOW (chpt. dir. 1979-81; Woman of Courage award Central N.Y. chpt.), Assn. Women in Psychology, Assn. Women in Sociology, Council Anthropology and Edn., Nat. Council Family Relations, Soc. Applied Anthropology, Soc. Med. Anthropology. Club: Corinthian. Author: School Children in the Urban Slum, 1967; Scene of the Battle, 1971; Beyond Intellectual Sexism, 1976; Educational Patterns and Cultural Configurations, 1976; Schooling in the Cultural Context, 1975; also articles. Home: 235 Waring Rd Syracuse NY 13224 Office: 100 Walnut Ave Syracuse NY 13210

ROBERTS, JOSIE CALHOUN, med. technologist; b. Bryceland, La., Jan. 29, 1946; d. June Crawford and Zelda (Pecor) Calhoun; student La. Inst. Tech., 1964-66; B.S., So. State Coll., 1968; cert. Confederate Meml. Med. Center, 1968; m. George Hamilton Roberts, Aug. 13, 1966; children—Amy Michelle, Kelley Ruchelle, John Brandon. Phlebotomist, Confederate Meml. Med. Center, Shreveport, La., 1967-68; med. technologist Willis Knighton Hosp., Shreveport, 1968, Assoc. Pathologist Lab., El Dorado, Ark., 1969, U. Miss. Med. Center, 1970, Union Meml. Med. Center, El Dorado, 1971-75, Drs. Beauregard, Irwin, Daniels, Monroe, La., 1980-81; relief med. technologist Dr. Ed Brown, Monroe, 1980-82, St. Francis Med. Center, 1982—. Mem. Am. Soc. Med. Tech., La. Soc. Med. Tech., Lambda Tau. Democrat. Baptist. Home: Route 2 Box 257B West Monroe LA 71291

ROBERTS, JOY, controller; b. Kansas City, Mo., Dec. 12, 1928; d. William and Francis (Swanson) Woods; student St. Teresea's Coll., 1958, UCLA, 1975, 76, 78, 79; 1 dau., Paula. Media supr. Selders, Jones, Covington, Kansas City, Mo., 1958-60; acct. Barickman, Selders Advt., Kansas City, 1960-64; controller Sheldom Marks Assos., Los Angeles, 1965-70; gen. mgr., controller Foster, Gilbert, Rumar, Inc., Santa Monica, Calif., 1970-75; owner, mgr. Joy Assos., Advt., Los Angeles, 1975—; corp. controller Jenkins Covington Newman, Los Angeles, N.Y.C., 1977—. Mem. Women in Bus., Women in Communications, Women in Mgmt. Office: 1007 N Seward St Los Angeles CA 90038

ROBERTS, KATHLEEN, former army officer; b. Glendale, Calif., Nov. 29, 1948; d. Henry and Virginia Dare (Allen) R.; B.A. in Psychology, Calif. State U., Northridge, 1976; postgrad. Life Chiropractic Coll., Marietta, Ga., 1981—. Served with USN, 1967-70, 71-75; commnd. 2d lt. U.S. Army, 1976, advanced through grades to capt., 1980; alcohol and drug control officer, Ft. McPherson, Ga., 1977-81, resigned, 1981; mem. Peachtree/Parkwood Adv. Council Alcoholism, Ga. Occupational Forum on Alcohol and Drugs, Met. Atlanta Council Alcohol and Drugs. Mem. Ga. Mental Health Assn., Nat. Assn. Female Execs.

ROBERTS, KATHLEEN JOY DOTY, educator; b. Jamaica, N.Y., Apr. 19, 1951; d. Alfred Arthur and Helen Caroline (Sohl) Doty; B.A. in Edn., Queens Coll., 1972, M.S. in Spl. Edn., 1974; cert. of advanced study in ednl. adminstrn. Hofstra U., 1982; m. Robert Louis Roberts, Nov. 24, 1974; children— Robert Louis, Michael Sean. Health conservation tchr. Woodside Jr. High Sch., Woodside, N.Y., 1973-77; health conservation tchr. Ridgewood (N.Y.) Jr. High Sch., 1977-78, ednl. cons., 1978-79, tchr. coordinator, 1979-81; resource room tchr. Grover Cleveland High Sch., Ridgewood, 1981—. Cert. N.Y. State Dept. Mental Hygiene; cert. N.Y. State Sch. Dist. Adminstr., Ednl. Adminstr., Ednl. Supr. Mem. NEA, N.Y. State Tchrs. Assn., Nat. Educators Fellowship, Council for Exceptional Children, Soc. Mayflower Descs., Grand Cross of Color State N.Y., AAUW, Phi Delta Kappa. Republican. Baptist. Author: Closed Circuit Television and Other Devices for the Partially Sighted, 1971. Home: 52 Hicksville Rd Massapequa NY 11758 Office: 2127 Himrod St Ridgewood NY 11385

ROBERTS, KATHLEEN MATTMILLER, public relations exec.; b. Barstow, Calif., Apr. 7, 1952; d. d. John Henry and Aileen Jane (O'Mara) Mattmiller; student Pepperdine U., 1970-75, B.A. in Journalism, 1975; M.A. in Communication Arts, Loyola Marymount U., 1982; m. Richard Roberts, Aug. 3, 1974. Missionary trainee, missionary, Cartagena, Colombia, 1975-76; dir. public relations Calif. Center Bible Studies, Culver City, 1977-78; public relations asst., writer Loyola Marymount U., Los Angeles, 1978-80; asst. dir. public relations, 1980—; cons. Media 2, 1980—; spl. advisor for profl. staff to pres. Loyola Marymount U., 1981—. Vol. publicity chmn. Calif. Center Bibl. Studies Library Assos., 1980—. Neighborhood Ch., Culver City, 1974-80, Calif. Center Bibl. Studies Women's Aux., 1979—. Mem. Calif. Women Higher Edn. (v.p.), Women in Communications, Am. Film Inst., Acad. TV Arts and Scis., Univ. and Coll. Designers Assn. Office: Loyola Marymount U Public Relations Dept Loyola Blvd W 80th St Los Angeles CA 90045

ROBERTS, LILLIAN, state ofcl.; b. Chgo., Jan. 2, 1928; d. Henry and Lillian Davis; ed. U. Ill.; Litt.D. (hon.), Coll. New Rochelle, 1973; children—Carl, Ralonzo, Donzel. Nurses aide Chgo. Lying-in Hosp., 1945; labor rep. AFSCME, Chgo. and N.Y.C., 1958-65, dir. hosp. div., 1965-67, assoc. dir. dist. 37, N.Y.C., 1967-81; commr. of labor N.Y. State Dept. Labor, Albany, 1981—. Nat. exec. bd., Jewish labor com. Am. Jewish Congress; adv. bd. Resources for Children with Spl. Needs; mem. Interagy. Inst. Fed. Health Care Execs., Upstate Found. Vietnam Vets., A. Philip Randolph Inst., Ams. Democratic Action, NAACP (Roy Wilkins award N.Y. br.), Alvin Ailey/City Center Dance Theater, Kingston Artists Group, Workers Def. League, NOW; indsl. and labor relations adv. council Cornell U., also trustee; mem. Cornell U. Council. Recipient Benjamin Potoker award N.Y. State Employees Brotherhood Com., Achievement award for industry Westchester Minority Contractors Assn., Humanitarian award Am. Trade Council for Histadrut, Good Govt. award N.Y. State Careerists Soc., Adam Clayton Powell Govt. award Opportunities Industrialization Center N.Y., 1982; Aspen Inst. fellow and grantee. Mem. Internat. Assn. Personnel in Employment Security, Delta Sigma Theta. Office: NY State Dept Labor Bldg 12 State Campus Albany NY 12240 *

ROBERTS, LINDA GAIL, educator; b. Abilene, Tex., May 5, 1940; d. James Harold and Vera Christine (Carlson) Marshall; student McMurry Coll., 1958-59, U. Tex., 1959-60; B.A., U. Mo. at Kansas City, 1967, M.A., 1970; m. Raymond Dean Roberts, Oct. 8, 1960; children—Christina Kay, Gregory Dean. Tchr. speech Paseo High Sch., Kansas City, Mo., 1968-69, Smith-Hale Jr. High Sch., Kansas City, 1969-70, 74—; lectr. speech dept. U. Mo. at Kansas City, 1970-74, Longview Community Coll., 1972-74; research asst. Police Found., 1973-74; communications cons. Response Time Analysis Study, Kansas City, 1974; dist. speech coordinator Consol. Sch. Dist. No. 1, Kansas City, 1980—. Mem. Speech and Theatre Assn. Mo., Central States Speech Assn., NEA, Mo. Edn. Assn., United Tchrs. Assn., Speech Communications Assn. Home: 8213 E 104 St Kansas City MO 64134

ROBERTS, LOUISE KAREN, metals and minerals co. exec.; b. Fairview, Ohio, June 17, 1945; d. Theodore Magnus and Ida Belle R.; B.A., Ohio U., 1967. Traffic control adminstr. Ataka Am., Inc., N.Y.C., 1969-72; asst. v.p. Asso. Metals & Minerals Corp., N.Y.C., 1973—. Mem. Am. Soc. Personnel Adminstrn., Nat. Assn. Female Execs., N.Y. Personnel Mgrs. Assn. Democrat. Home: 330 E 49th St Apt 9-A New York NY 10017

ROBERTS, LOUISE NISBET, philosopher; b. Lexington, Ky., Apr. 21, 1919; d. Benjamin and Helen L. Nisbet; A.B., U. Ky., 1942, M.A., 1944; Ph.D. (univ. scholar 1945-46, Delta Delta Delta fellow 1946-47, AAUW fellow 1947-48), Columbia U., 1952; m. Warren Roberts, June 14, 1952; children—Helen Ward, Valeria Lamar. Instr. philosophy Fairfax Hall, Waynesboro, Va., 1943-44, Fairmount Casements, Ormond Beach, Fla., 1944-45; mem. faculty Newcomb Coll., Tulane U., 1948—, prof. philosophy, 1969—, head dept., 1969. Mem. Am. Philos. Assn., Southwestern Philos. Soc., So. Soc. Philosophy and Psychology, Am. Soc. Aesthetics, AAUP (chpt. sec.-treas. 1966-68), Phi Beta Kappa (chpt. pres. 1956-57), Delta Delta Delta. Democrat. Episcopalian. Author articles in field. Office: Newcomb Coll 1229 Broadway New Orleans LA 70118

ROBERTS, MARGARET (PEG) ANN, secretarial service co. exec.; b. Muskegon, Mich., July 26, 1935; d. Carl Joseph and Bernice C. (Bair) Olsen; grad. Kelsey-Jenney Bus. Coll., 1954; children—David Howard, Julie Anne. Office mgr. U. Humanistic Studies; bus. mgr. Dee Evers & Assos.; owner, mgr. Gal Friday, San Diego, 1979-80; profl. gospel singer, 1962-78, ret., 1979. Active, Mended Hearts, Inc., including founder chpt. 62, 1970, nat. rec. sec., 1977-80. Recipient numerous award from San Diego County Heart Assn., Calif. Heart Assn. and Mended Hearts, including This is your Life award, 1972. Mem. Nat. Assn. Female Execs., Nat. Small Bus. Assn., Mensa. Office: 5797 Chesapeake Ct Suite G San Diego CA 92123

ROBERTS, MARIE DYER, mathematician, computer specialist; b. Statesboro, Ga., Feb. 19, 1943; d. Byron and Marhta (Evans) Dyer; B.S., U. Ga., 1966; student Am. U., 1972; m. Hugh V. Roberts, Jr., Oct. 6, 1973. Mathematician, computer specialist U.S. Naval Oceanographic Office, Washington, 1966-73; systems analyst, programmer Sperry Microwave Electronics, Clearwater, Fla., 1973-75; data processing mgr., asst. bus. mgr. Trenam, Simmons, Kemker et al, Tampa, Fla., 1975-77; mathematician, computer specialist U.S. Army C.E., Savannah, Ga., 1977-81, Frankfurt, W. Ger., 1981—. Mem. Am. Soc. Hist. Preservation, Am. Soc. Info. Scientists, Data Processing Mgmt. Assn., Am. Women in Sci., Nat. Assn. Female Execs., Am. Film Inst., U. Ga. Alumni Assn., Sigma Kappa.

ROBERTS, MARSHA LYNN, cons. social psychologist; b. Balt., Mar. 12, 1944; d. Ford Lee and Elma Lillian (King) Roberts; B.A. magna cum laude, Marshall U., 1972; M.S., Va. Polytech. Inst. and State U., 1974; Ph.D., Pa. State U., 1979; postgrad. George Washington U., 1979; m. Alan Jeffrey Burnes, June 15, 1981; children—James Patrick Harshbarger, Samuel David Harshbarger. Resident instr. Pa. State U., State College, 1976-77; research fellow George Washington U. Med. Center, Washington, 1978-79; asst. prof. child and family studies Wash. State U., Pullman 1979-81; pres. Adience, Inc., Ithaca, N.Y., 1981—; mem. staff Tech. Systems Internat., Ithaca, 1981—; mem. bd. profl. adv. Internat. Council Orgn. and Human Resources, Ithaca, 1981—. Mem. adv. bd. Gifted Children, Arlington, Va., 1978-79; den mother Cub Scouts Am., 1969-71. Mem. Am. Psychol. Assn., Nat. Council on Family Relations, Am. Home Econs. Assn., Pacific Sociol. Assn., Phi Kappa Phi, Phi Kappa Delta, Kappa Omicron Phi, Omicron Nu, Alpha Kappa Delta. Contbr. articles in field to profl. jours. Home: 203 Highgate Rd Ithaca NY 14850 Office: Suite 408 First Bank Ithaca Bldg Ithaca NY 14850

ROBERTS, MARY BELLE, cons. social worker; b. Akron, Ohio, Sept. 27, 1923; d. Joseph Gill and Inez Wilson (Garvey) Roberts; B.S., U. Mich., 1948, M.S.W., 1950. Instr. dept. psychiatry U. Ala. Med. Coll., 1950-53; psychiat. social worker div. mental hygiene Ala. Dept. Pub. Health, 1950-52, acting dir., dir., 1952-53; sr. psychiat. social worker bur. mental health div. community service Pa. Dept. Welfare, 1954-55; cons. psychiat. social work community service br. NIMH, USPHS, HEW, 1955-64; pvt. practice psychiat. social work, 1964-68; caseworker Family Service, Miami, Fla., 1968-70, Family and Childrens Service, Miami, 1971-75; casework cons. United Family and Childrens Services, Miami, 1975—. Cert. social worker, Md.; lic. clin. social worker, Fla. Home: 501 Valencia Ave #2 Coral Gables FL 33134 Office: 2190 NW 7th St Miami FL 33125

ROBERTS, MARY WENDY, state ofcl.; b. Champaign, Ill., Dec. 19, 1944; d. Frank and Mary C. R.; student (Nat. Def. Fgn. Lang. fellow) Chinese Japanese Inst., U. Colo., 1964; B.A. in Polit. Sci., U. Oreg., 1965; M.A., U. Wis., 1971; m. Richard P. Bullock, Nov. 27, 1976; 1 dau., Alexandra Louise McKay Prentice. Social worker Children's Services Div., 1967-71; counselor Juvenile Ct., 1971; mem. Oreg. Ho. of Reps., 1972-74; mem. Oreg. Senate, 1975-78; commr. Oreg. Commn. Labor and Industries, 1978—. Mem. Democratic Nat. Com., del. nat. conv., 1980. Recipient Mary Rieke award, 1978. Mem. Portland Art Assn., Oreg. Hist. Soc., Nat. Assn. Govt. Labor Ofcls., Am. Council Young Polit. Leaders. Office: 240 Cottage St SE Salem OR 97310

ROBERTS, PRISCILLA WARREN, painter; b. Glen Ridge, N.J., June 13, 1916; d. Charles Asaph and Florence Mary R.; student Art Students League, 1936-43, NAD, 1939-43. One-woman shows: Grand Central Art Galleries, N.Y.C., 1961, 81; group shows include: NAD, N.Y.C., ann. 1945—, Carnegie Instn., Pitts., 1946, 47, 48, 49, Rutgers U., New Brunswick, N.J., 1982; represented in permanent collections: Met. Mus. Art, N.Y.C., Butler Inst., Youngstown, Ohio, Dallas Mus., Canton (Ohio) Art Inst., others. Mem. NAD, Catherine Lorillard Wolfe Assn.

ROBERTS, RUTH OLIVE, musician; b. Fryeburg, Maine; d. John Henry and Ellen (Deane) Roberts; A.B., Colby Coll.; pvt. study piano with Heinrich Gebhard, organ with John Hermann Loud; studied in Europe with Alfred Cortot, Switzerland and Zecchi, Austria, and others. Featured on several musical programs in London and Scotland during Coronation Season, 1953, Internat. Congress Organists, London, 1957, Am. Music Nat. Music Week, Nat. Fedn. Music Clubs; concert tour Europe, 1962; local musicales, 1968-71; concert engagements Am. and Europe, 1974. Mem. Am. Guild Organists, AAUW, Leschetizky Assn., Inc., MacDowell Colony, Mus. Guild Boston, Assn. Am. Composers and Arrangers, Nat. Guild Pianoforte Tchrs., Am. Coll. Musicians, Nat. Fedn. Music Club, Victoria Soc. Maine (charter mem., pres. 1960-64), Portland Symphony Orch., Women's Com. Hon. mem. editorial bd. Music and Dance in New Eng. states. Home: 342 Main Saco ME 04072

ROBERTS, SANDRA MAE DEHAVEN, jewelry co. exec.; b. Parkersburg, W.Va., July 14, 1947; d. William Joseph and Evelyn Mae (Jackson) DeH.; A.A., Mountain State Coll., 1969; m. Clifford A. Roberts. Salesman, Franklin & DeHaven Jewelers, Parkersburg, W.Va., 1969—, sec.-treas., buyer, 1971—, bus. mgr., 1972—. Mem. Parkersburg Revitalization Commn. Mem. Downtown Retail Mchts. Assn. (exec. dir. 1976—), Parkersburg C. of C., Nat. Fedn. Ind. Bus., Nat. Retail Mchts. Assn., W.Va. Retail Jewelers Assn. Methodist. Home: 1321 31st St Vienna WV Office: 405 Market St Parkersburg WV 26101

ROBERTS, SHARON KAY, educator; b. Merced, Calif., Dec. 4, 1941; d. Harold Nicholas and Pauline Mae (Osborn) Hansen; B.A. in Biology, Calif. State U., San Jose, 1963; Med. Technology, Santa Clara Valley Med. Center, 1964; M.A. in Health Edn., Central Mich. U., 1976; now postgrad. in allied health adminstrn. Tex. A&M U.; m. Dean Christopher Sheehy, Jan. 13, 1981; children by previous marriage—Scott Nicholas, Laura Ann, James Durant. Med. technologist, immunohematologist various hosps., Los Angeles, Fresno, and San Jose, Calif., 1963-71; adminstrv. technologist Kern Med. Center, Bakersfield, Calif., 1972-73; asst. prof., edn. coordinator Calif. State Coll., Bakersfield, 1973-78, assoc. prof., 1978—, dir. med. tech. program, 1982—; cons. in field. Mem. Am. Assn. Blood Banks, Am. Soc. Allied Health Professions, Am. Soc. Med. Tech., Am. Soc. Clin. Pathologists, Calif. Blood Bank System, Calif. Soc. Med. Tech. (dir. 1978-79, 79-80, editor chpt. newsletter 1979-80), No. Calif. Assn. Med. Tech. Programs, So. Calif. Med. Tech. Educators, Calif. Assn. Med. Lab. Technologists (treas. Kern chpt. 1976-77, pres. 1978-79), NOW. Home: 3404 Belle Terr Bakersfield CA 93309 Office: 9001 Stockdale Hwy Bakersfield CA 93309

ROBERTS, SHELLY, advt. exec.; b. Chgo., Dec. 9, 1943; d. Leonard and Mildred Brown (Uhlman) Rhodes; B.A., U. Calif., Berkeley, 1965; divorced; 1 son, Sean Christopher Ian Patrick. Copy supr. Leo Burnett, Chgo., 1969-70; asso. creative dir. N.W. Ayer, Seattle and Los Angeles, 1972-75, 76-78; sr. writer Keye/Donna/Pearlstein, Los Angeles, 1975; v.p., group head Doremus & Co., N.Y.C., 1978-79; v.p., creative supr. Benton & Bowles, N.Y.C., 1979—; founding pres. Seattle Women in Advt., 1977; guest lectr. YWCA, 1978—. Recipient Best-in-West award Am. Advt. Fedn., 1976; Best Mktg. Campaign award Advt. Age, 1977; also Addy, Andy, Clio, Belding awards, numerous others. Mem. Advt. Women N.Y., Bus. and Profl. Women N.Y., Women in Communications, NOW (communications dir. Los Angeles 1974-75), Nat. Women's Polit. Caucus. Author: What To Do With a Liberated Woman, 1978.

ROBERTS, SONJA JAYNE HILL, interior designer; b. Madison, Wis., Feb. 12, 1949; d. Norman and Margaret Hill; B.S., U. Wis., 1971; m. Benjamin E. Roberts, Dec. 10, 1977; 1 dau., Regan Rebecca. Dir. planning and design Pigott, Inc., Des Moines, 1978-82; interior designer Bussard/Dikis Assos., Ltd., Des Moines, 1982—. Recipient cert. of honor Women in Design Internat., 1981. Mem. Inst. Bus. Designers, AIA (profl. affiliate). Home: 2505 Terrace Rd Des Moines IA 50312 Office: 414 61st St Des Moines IA 50312

ROBERTS, SUSAN BROWNING, editor; b. Summit, N.J., May 27, 1941; d. Roland Browning and Geraldine Harper (Davidson) R.; A.B., Grinnell Coll., 1963; M.A., U. Idaho, 1982; m. Louis A. Hieb, June 8, 1963 (div. June 1975); children—Matthew Alan, John Andrew. Soc. news writer New Haven Register, 1963-64; asst. young adult and teen program dir. New Haven YM-YWCA, 1964-65; reporter, sch. editor The Princeton (N.J.) Packet, 1965-70; corr. Spokane (Wash.) Daily Chronicle, Pullman, 1974-75; editor Forest Wildlife and Range Expt. Sta. U. Idaho, Moscow, 1975—; editorial adv. Jour. Interpretation, 1982. Bd. deacons First Presbyn. Ch., Moscow, 1980-82; den mother Lewis Clark council Boy Scouts Am., 1976-77, 81-83, awards chmn., 1977-79. Mem. Agrl. Communicators in Edn. (awards for excellence 1979, 80), Am. Sociol. Assn. Democrat. Presbyterian. Club: Palouse Promenaders Square Dance. Office: Coll Forestry Wildlife and Range Sci U Idaho Moscow ID 83843

ROBERTS, TERRY JEAN, hosp. adminstr.; b. Dallas, July 17, 1950; d. Billy Edward and Mary Lucille (Whitlow) Byington; student Navarro Jr. Coll., 1969-70; cert. environ. relations Tarrant County Jr. Coll., 1981, cert. fin. analysis, cert. econs. and fin. mgmt., 1981; m. Robert Lynn Roberts, Nov. 19, 1977; children—Shanna Rene, Amber Lynn. Sec. to adminstr. Alexander Hosp., Terrell, Tex., 1969-71; dep. drivers licenses, Dept. Public Safety, Dallas, 1971-73; sec. Blue Cross/Blue Shield Tex., Dallas, 1973-79; adminstrv. asst. Harris Hosp.-Meth., Fort Worth, 1979-80; sr. adminstrv. asst. Harris Meth. Health, Grand Prairie Tex., 1980—. Mem. Nat. Assn. Female Execs. (network dir.), Profl. Secs. Internat., Am. Mgmt. Assn., Am. Soc. Profl. and Exec. Women, Tex. Notary Public Assn., Fort Worth Area Med. Staff Secs. and Adminstrv. Assts. Assn., Profl. Secs. Internat. Episcopalian. Home: 5216 Ruston Ave Fort Worth TX 76133 Office: 1418 W Rosedale Fort Worth TX 76104

ROBERTS, VERDELL MAURICE TAYLOR, educator; b. Mobile, Ala., Jan. 1, 1944; d. William and Rosina (Allen) Taylor; B.A., Knoxville Coll., 1965; postgrad. Yale U., 1968-69; M.S., So. Conn. State Coll., 1971, sixth year cert., 1978; Ph.D., Union Grad. Sch., 1981; m. Lee A. Roberts, Aug. 23, 1969; children—Tarah Renita, Leigh Allendria. Tchr. reading readiness New Haven Public Schs., 1966-72, resource tchr., 1972-73; tchr. coordinator African Am. Resource Center, New Haven, 1973-76; tchr. sci., social studies, house coordinator Jackie Robinson Middle Sch., New Haven, 1977-80; editorial intern Zerox Ednl. Publs., Middletown, Conn., 1981; tchr. New Haven Public Schs., 1980—, bldg. supr. Jackie Robinson Middle Sch., 1979—; cons. Dade County Public Schs., 1980; Sec., bd. dirs. Upper Hill Project Area Com., 1981; bd. dirs. Conn. Afro Hist., Soc., 1979, Alliance Theater, 1981; sec., bd. dirs. Upper Hill Project Area Com., New Haven, 1981. Cert. intermediate adminstrn. and supervision, Conn.; Yale New Haven fellow, 1978. Mem. Adminstrn. and Supervision Assn., Am. Fedn. Tchrs., Assn. Supervision and Curriculum Devel., Black Educators Assn., Greater New Haven Council Adminstrv. Women Edn., NAACP, Nat. Assn. Female Execs., Nat. Council Negro Women, Delta Sigma Theta. Democrat. New Haven CT 06515

ROBERTS, VIRGINIA L., govt. official; b. Parkersburg, W.Va., Apr. 1, 1927; student bus. adminstrn. Morris Harvey Coll.; Belford Roberts. Fiscal and research coordinator for W. Va. Bd. of Regents; budget and research analyst, Legis. Auditor's Office, Charleston, W. Va.; chief clk., asst. state auditor, 1961-71, apptd. commr. Motor Vehicles, 1977—. Mem. Am. Assn. Motor Vehicles Adminstrs. (pres. Region II 1979—). Baptist. Club: Civitan. Office: Dept Motor Vehicles 1800 Washington St E Charleston WV 25305 *

ROBERTSON, BRENDA MARY, Can. govt. ofcl.; b. Sussex, N.B., Can., May 23, 1929; d. John James and Clara (Rothwell) Tubb; B.S., Mt. Allison U., Sackville, N.B., 1950; L.H.D. (hon.), Mt. St. Vincent U., 1973; m. Wilmot W. Robertson, July 23, 1955; children—Douglas, Leslie, Tracy. Home economist N.B. Dept. Agr., 1950-52; engaged in sales and mgmt. family bus., 1967; minister N.B. Dept. Youth, 1970—, minister social services, 1971—. Office: Box 6000 Fredericton NB E3B 5H1 Canada

ROBERTSON, CORGENA EUNICE, nurse; b. Jamaica, B.W.I., Nov. 3, 1945; came to U.S., 1962; d. Augustus and Claris Adina Morgan; A.A.S. in Nursing, Bronx Community Coll., 1969; student Hunter Coll., 1975-77; B.S. in Community Health, St. Joseph Coll., Bklyn., 1977-79; m. Lester Robertson, Aug. 27, 1977; children—Deryck Henry, Sean. Surg. technician Lincoln Hosp., Bronx, N.Y., 1967-69, staff nurse, 1969-73, head nurse surg. unit, 1973—; tchr. adult edn. Evander Child High Sch., Bronx, 1979—. R.N., N.Y. State. Mem. Am. Nurses Assn., N.Y. Nurses Assn.

ROBERTSON, ELIZABETH BRESLIN, educator; b. Milton, Mass., June 28, 1947; d. James Louis and Frances Mary (Doucette) Breslin; B.S., State Coll. Mass., Framingham, 1969; M.S., U. Ill., 1971; m. William B. Robertson, Jr., Oct. 20, 1978. Acad. adv. Coll. Liberal Arts/Sci., U. Ill., Urbana, 1970-72, instr., head tchr., Sch. Human Resources and Family Life, 1972-76; instr., head tchr. Sch. Home Econs., U. Ala., University, 1976-81, asst. dean, 1981—; condr. workshops in field. Mem. LWV, Ala. Conservancy, NOW, Am. Home Econs. Assn., Ala. Home Econs. Assn. (sec.), Nat. Assn. for Edn. Young Children, Ala. Assn. for Young Children (historian), Ala. Council on Family Relations (edn. sect. rep.), So. Assn. Coll. Registrars and Admissions Officers. Episcopalian. Co-author energy curriculum unit for children; contbr. articles to popular mags. Home: 1104 Myrtlewood Dr Tuscaloosa AL 35401 Office: PO Box 1488 University AL 35486

ROBERTSON, GAYLE PRICE, mortician; b. Levelland, Tex., Dec. 22, 1947; d. George Copeland and Ophelia (Eudaly) Price; student Tex. Tech U., 1967-68, Dallas Inst. Mortuary Sci., 1970-71; A.S., South Plains Coll., 1967; m. Jerry D. Robertson, Aug. 23, 1975; 1 dau., Lindsay Riann. With Geo. C. Price Funeral Dirs., Levelland, 1962—, funeral dir., embalmer, 1972—. Mem. Ranching Heritage Assn. (charter), Nat. Assn. Female Execs., Panhandle Funeral Dirs. Assn., Tex. Funeral Dirs. Assn., Nat. Funeral Dirs. Assn., Nat. Tole and Decorative Painters Soc., West Tex. Cotton Pickin' Painters, Democrat. Methodist. Clubs: South Plains Horsemen Assn., Order Eastern Star, Jr. Womens (past pres.). Home: PO Box 657 Levelland TX 79336 Office: PO Box 517 Levelland TX 79336

ROBERTSON, MARGARET ELIZABETH, retirement devel. counselor; b. Aberdeen, Miss., Sept. 8; d. Edgar T. and Mattie Tullula (Coleman) Henson; student Massey Bus. Coll., 1938-40; children—Bonnie Sue, Rogers White. Supr. procurement and cost acctg. Brookly AFB, Mobile, Ala., 1942-44; resident mgr. Snug Harbor Homes, Mobile, 1944-48; v.p., bookkeeper Mountain Brook Realty Co., Birmingham, Ala., 1949-77; gen. mgr. Valley View Apts., Birmingham, 1949-73; dist. insp. La Sands Motel, Shreveport, La., 1953-56; dist. dir., exec. counselor Fairfield Manor Apts., Shreveport, 1953-56; sec., treas. Transo Oil Corp., Shreveport, 1953-56; v.p. B.B. Investment Corp., Birmingham, 1958-70; gen. property mgr. various apts. for So. div. Hillmark Corp., Ltd., Birmingham, 1973-77; v.p., counselor Mt. Royal Towers, retirement devel. Birmingham, 1978-80; counselor Fin. Mgmt. Assos., Kirkwood-By-The-River, retirement devel., Birmingham, 1980—. Mem. Jefferson County Transp. Citizens Adv. Com., 1976-82; adv. counselor Ret. Sr. Vol. Program, Jefferson County, Ala., 1979-82; vol. VA Hosp., Birmingham; 1979-80; Sunday sch. tchr. Pike Ave. Baptist Ch., 1950-70; rep. Homewood Bd. Edn. and Library, 1977-82; mem. Homewood City Council, 1976—. Home: 1503 Valley Ave Birmingham AL 35209 Office: Mount Royal Towers 2099 Medical Center Dr Birmingham AL 35209

ROBERTSON, MARY ELLA, ednl. adminstr., social worker; b. Lake Charles, La., Sept. 5, 1924; d. John and Mildred (Gardner) Robertson; B.A. summa cum laude, Xavier U., 1947; M.S.W., Atlanta U., 1949; advanced cert. in social work, Smith Coll., 1955; research fellow Adminstrv. Sci. Center, U. Pitts., 1959-60; D.Social Work, U. Pitts., 1962. Psychiat. social worker VA, Montrose, N.Y., 1949-53; supr. social services Family Service Assn., Ann Arbor, Mich., 1953-54; asst. prof. Case Western Res. U. Sch. Social Work, Cleve., 1955-57; exec. dir. Cleve. Guidance Center, 1957-59; asst. dean, asso. prof. U. Pitts. Grad. Sch. Social Work, 1962-66; vis. prof., asst. dean curriculum devel. U. Wis., Milw., 1966-67; dean, prof. Howard U. Sch. Social Work, Washington, 1967-69; prof. Boston Coll. Grad. Sch. Social Work, Chestnut Hill, Mass., 1969-72; prof. social service Ind. U.-Purdue U. at Indpls., 1972-74; v.p. for community services at Gov.'s State U., Park Forest South, Ill., 1974-77; prof. social policy Kent Sch. Social Work, U. Louisville, 1977—, dir. continuing edn. and community programs, 1977—; cons. social services various state and govt. agys.; dir. John Hancock Mut. Life Ins. Co. Mem. adminstrv. rev. panel child welfare policies Office of Children and Youth, Harrisburg, Pa., 1964-65; mem. com. on profl. edn. Comprehensive Mental Health Study Com. for Pa., 1964-66; mem. adv. com. to pres. Mt. Mercy Coll., Pitts., 1965-68; mem. adv. com. to sec. labor and industry Commonwealth of Pa., 1965-66; mem. adv. com. on population HEW, 1972-76; mem. adv. com. on youth employment U.S. Dept. Labor, 1978-80; mem. exchange groups in social welfare policy to Kenya, Somalia, Trinidad, People's Republic of China, 1978-81. Bd. dirs. Human Life Found., Washington, Parents and Childrens Services Children's Mission, Boston. Named Pitts. Woman of Year Mayor's Com. on Public Service, 1965; Outstanding Alumna, Atlanta U. Sch. Social Work, 1969; Dau. Commonwealth of Pa. Mem. Nat. Assn. Social Workers, Council on Social Work Edn. (past chmn. nat. com. on admissions, mem. dean's adv. com., mem. Ho. of Dels. 1967-70), Pitts. Commn. Cath. Charities (del. assembly), Kappa Gamma Pi, Alpha Kappa Mu. Contbr. articles to profl. jours. Home: 800 S 4th St Louisville KY 40203 Office: Kent Sch Social Work U Louisville Louisville KY 40208

ROBERTSON, MAY ROSE, ret. librarian; b. Donaldsonville, La., May 17, 1924; d. Clarence J. and Rose (Juneau) Robertson; B.S., La. State U., 1943, B. L.S., 1944, spl. student, 1944-46; student overseas program U. Md., 1960-61. Librarian, La. State U. Library, 1944-46, U.S. Dept. Army, Bayreuth and Coburg, Germany, 1946-48, Ft. Riley (Kans.) Army Library, 1949, Mitchel AFB, N.Y., 1950-51, Hdqrs. 14th Air Force, Warner Robins, Ga., 1951-52, U.S. Dept. Army Library Program, Germany, 1952-62, Nat. Agrl. Library, Washington, 1962-65, FDA Library, Arlington, Va., 1965-67, U.S. Dept. Transp. Library, Washington, 1967-79, ret., 1979. Mem. ALA, Spl. Libraries Assn., Potomac Tech. Processing Librarians, DAR (chpt. regent 1979-82, pres. chpt. regents club Washington 1981-82, state librarian 1982-84), Soc. Desc. Colonial Clergy, Beta Phi Mu, Alpha Lambda Delta, Phi Kappa Phi, Kappa Delta Pi, Phi Sigma Iota. Roman Catholic. Home: 3341 Ardley Ct Falls Church VA 22041

ROBERTSON, SARAH GREENSHIELDS, banker; b. Easterhouse, Scotland, Oct. 30, 1930; came to U.S., 1954, naturalized, 1969; d. George and Mary Walker (Kirkwood) Greenshields; student U. Glasgow, 1947-49, Am. Inst. Banking, 1971-77, U. Wis., Madison, 1978-80; m. William Robertson, Dec. 26, 1952; children—William Duncan, Deborah May. Bookkeeper-teller Bank of Hinsdale (Ill.), 1969-71, note teller, 1971-73, bookkeeping supr., 1973-74, ops. supr., 1974, asst. cashier, 1974-77, asst. v.p., 1977, cashier, 1977-79, v.p., cashier, 1979—. Bd. mem. PTA, 1968-69; vol. art appreciation instr. Hinsdale Grade Sch., 1963-66, library helper, 1965-67. Mem. Bank Adminstrn. Inst., Chgo. Bank Women's Assn. Presbyterian. Club: Junior Women's (Hinsdale). Office: 400 E Ogden Ave Hinsdale IL 60521

ROBEY, KATHLEEN MORAN (MRS. RALPH WEST ROBEY), club woman; b. Boston, Aug. 9, 1909; d. John Joseph and Katherine (Berrigan) Moran; B.A., Trinity Coll., Washington, 1933; m. Ralph West Robey, Jan. 28, 1941. Actress appearing in Pride and Prejudice, Broadway, 1935, Tomorrow is a Holiday, road co., 1935, Death Takes a Holiday, road co., 1936, Left Turn, Broadway, 1936, Come Home to Roost, Boston, 1936; pub. relations N.Y. Fashion Industry, N.Y.C., 1938-43. Mem. Florence Crittenton Home and Hosp., Women's Aux. Salvation Army, Gray Lady, ARC; mem. Seton Guild St. Ann's Infant Home. Mem. Christ Child Soc., Fedn. Republican Women of D.C. English-Speaking Union. Republican. Roman Catholic. Clubs: City Tavern, Cosmos (Washington), Nat. Woman's Republican. Home: 4000 Cathedral Ave NW Washington DC 20016

ROBICHAUD, PHYLLIS IVY ISABEL, artist, educator; b. Jamaica, West Indies, May 16, 1915; came to U.S., 1969, naturalized, 1977; d. Peter C. and Rose Matilda (Rickman) Burnett; grad. Tutorial Coll., 1933, Kingston, Jamaica, Munro Coll., St. Elizabeth, Jamaica, 1946; student Central Tech. Sch., Toronto, Ont., Can., 1960-63, Anderson Coll., Can., 1968-69; m. Roger Robichaud, July 22, 1961; children by previous marriage—George Wilmot Graham, William Henry Heron Graham, Mary Elizabeth Graham Watson, Peter Robert Burnett Graham. Sec. to supr. of Agr., St. Elizabeth, 1940-50; loans officer and cashier Confederation Life Assn., Kingston, 1950-53; tchr. art Jamaica Welfare Ltd., 1963; tchr. art recreation dept. New Port Richey, Fla., 1969-77; tchr. art Pasco Hernando Community Coll., New Port Richey, 1977—; propr., mgr. Band Box Dress Shop, Kingston, Jamaica, 1954-57; numerous one-woman shows of paintings including various banks, libraries, Kingston, 1963-64, 67, Toronto, 1968, New Port Richey, 1969, 70, 73, 76, Tampa, Fla., 1974, 75, 76, Omaha Cattle Company restaurant, Clearwater Fla., 1982; numerous group shows, latest being: Sweden House, Tampa, 1977-78, Chasco Fiesta, New Port Richey, 1977, Magnolia Valley Golf and Country Club, New Port Richey, 1978, W. Pasco Art Guild, New Port Richey, 1978, 79, other cities in Fla.; executed murals, New Port Richey and Kingston; represented in permanent collections: New Port Richey C. of C., Magnolia Valley Golf and Country Club, also pvt. collections. Patron, St. Alban's 4H Club, 1942; sec. Sunday sch. Ch. of Eng., Kingston, 1937-39. Recipient award T. Eaton Co. of Can., 1961, cert. of merit, Mayor of New Port Richey, 1976, appreciation award New Port Richey Recreation Dept., 1977; award Fla. Heart Fund. Mem. Nat. League Am. Pen Women (v.p. Tampa br. 1978-80, dir. 1969—), West Pasco Art Guild (Blue ribbons 1978, 79), Fla. Fine Arts Guild. Republican. Roman Catholic. Club: Holiday (Fla.) Lioness (v.p.). Address: 1053 Lenox Circle New Port Richey FL 33552

ROBIE, KATHLEEN LYNCH (MRS. WILLIAM F. ROBIE), real estate developer, civic worker; b. Knoxville, Tenn., May 27, 1919; d. Abel P. and Jessie (Seabolt) Lynch; m. William F. Robie, May 2, 1936; children—Eileen (Mrs. Norval R. Stephens), Nancy (Mrs. Martin George Hill), William F. Asst. statis. sect. chief U.S. Census Bur., Washington, 1940-41; sec. to powder expert Naval Powder Factory, Indian Head, Md., 1941-43, accot., 1944-46; chief acct. Nat. Housing

Agy., Potomac Heights, Md., 1943-44; sec. to chief So. lumber OPS, Washington, 1952-54; asst. to career devel. officer Bolling AFB, Washington, 1960-61; office mgr. regional office McCormick and Co., 1961-62; now owner, developer Robie Manor subdivision, Charles County, Md. Chmn. high sch. services Md. Congress Parents and Tchrs., 1954-60, pres., 1960-63, sch. edn. chmn., 1963-66, hon. pres., 1973; nat. bd. mgrs. Nat. Congress Parents and Tchrs., 1960-67, mem. exec. com., 1962-63, nat. program service chmn., also hon. life mem.; judge Nat. Safety Patrol Lifesaving Medal, 1960-64; nat. publicity dir. Nat. Home Demonstration Council (now Nat. Extension Homemakers Council), 1958-61, internat. chmn., 1980-83; past pres. Md. State Council Homemakers' Clubs, Charles County Homemakers' Clubs: pres. Prince George's County Extension Homemakers, 1971-73. Mem. Gov.'s Commn. Phys. Fitness, 1961-66, Gov.'s Com. to Keep Md. Beautiful, 1955-63; v.p. Md. Consumers Council, 1962-66; mem. Md. State Bd. Edn., 1963-75, also mem. steering com. legislation and planning com. ann. edn. conf.; adv. com. adoption State Dept. Public Welfare, 1962-65; del. Md. Constl. Conv., 1966-68; mem. Pres.'s Ad Hoc Nat. Vol. Orgns.' Adv. Com. Consumer Interests; mem Nat. Citizens Com. Better Schs., Nat. Com. for Support Public Schs.; 1st v.p. Tb and Respiratory Disease Assn. So. Md., 1972-75; mem. Md. Adv. Bd. for Libraries 1975—; mem. Md. Gov.'s Com. for Employment of Handicapped; pres. Charles County Children's Aid Soc. Trustee, State Tchrs. Coll., Towson, Md., State Tchrs. Coll., Frostburg, Md., Salisbury State Tchrs. Coll., Bowie State Coll., Coppin State Coll., Balt.; exec. dir. Prince George's County Assn. Mental Health; mem. Nat. Assn. Mental Health Staff Council; del. World Food Congress, 1964; dir.-at-large Nat. Assn. State Bds. Edn., 1966-67, v.p. N.E. area, 1969-71; vice chmn. Gov.'s Commn. on Malnutrition, 1969. Recipient Outstanding Leadership award U. Md., 1960; award Prince George's County Tchrs. Assn.; award Phi Delta Kappa, 1966. Mem. Associated Country Women of World (del. internat. conf., 1953, 59, 65, 68, 71, 74, 77, 80, mem. UN com. 1980—), Country Women's Council, Tchrs. Edn. and Profl. Standards, Md. Tchrs. Assn., Delta Kappa Gamma (hon.). Home: Route 1 Box 449E Robie Manor White Plains MD 20695 also (winter) 5980 Shore Blvd Gulfport FL 33707

ROBILLARD, JENNIFER KARZY, lectr., author; b. Ludlow, Mass., May 27; d. Thomas and Julia (Wrobel) Karzy; student langs., U. Mass., 1959, Muskingum Coll., 1962, home econs., Pa. State U., 1964, landscape design, U. Md., 1973; m. Raymond A. Robillard, July 30, 1960; children by previous marriage—Thomas Peter Brodowski, John Michael Brodowski; stepchildren—Philip R. Robillard, Paul F. Robillard. Tech. acct. U.S. Ordnance, Springfield, Mass., 1951-58; asst. comptroller Continental Air Command, L.I., N.Y., 1959-60; exec. dir. mktg. Eastern Shore Arts and Crafts Center, Princess Anne, Md., 1971—; lectr. Federated Garden Clubs of Md., Inc.; author: Herb Culture, 1966; Favorite Recipes, 1967; How About Cooking with Herbs, 1969; Collection of Del Marva Recipes, 1971; Around the Kitchen, 1973; Christmas Cookies, 1974. Bd. dirs. Cylburn Wildflower Preserve & Garden Center, Balt., 1971-72; v.p. ex officio Federated Garden Clubs of Md., 1973-75, state awards chmn., chmn. dist. III flower shows, 1975—, exec. com. adv. 1975-77, dir. dist. III, 1973-75, rec. sec., 1980-83; flower show judges council State of Md., 1971—; landscape design council State of Md., 1971—; founder, organizer Spring Valley, Hampton Garden Clubs, Towson, Md., 1973—, Pinewood Garden Club, 1975; mem. Towson Valley Garden Club, 1966—, pres., 1969-71. Bd. mgrs., sec. exec. com. YMCA, Towson, 1966-69; mem. Council Environ. Quality, Washington, 1973—; trustee Hampton Nat. Hist. Site, Towson, 1973-75. Recipient Gov.'s (Md.) Silver Dish Award for artistic design, 1974; Creativity award Nat. Council State Garden Clubs, 1974; Best of Show, Sweepstakes awards Am. Iris Soc., 1972; Edn. award Conservation Exhibit, 1973; award of distinction Nat. Council State Garden Clubs, 1971. Mem. Internat. Platform Assn., Soc. Preservation Md. Antiquities, Md. Hist. Soc., Ikebana Internat. (2d v.p. Balt. chpt. 1977-79, treas. 1979-80, pres. 1980-83). Clubs: Johns Hopkins, Towson Newcomers (pres. 1965-66), Towson Gourmet (founder, organizer 1967, chmn. 1967-68), Dulaney Valley Federated Woman's (bd. govs. 1975-76, v.p. 1976-78, pres. 1978-79). Home: Hillcreek 1305 Milldam Rd Towson MD 21204

ROBINETT, ELIZABETH ANN, counselor; b. Keene, Tex., June 30, 1936; d. Ted Roy and Ida Mae (Hutson) McClain: B.A., Angelo State U., 1968; M.Ed., Tex. Tech. U., 1972, Ed.D., 1975; children—Lee Marshall, Lisa Marlene. Tchr., Central High Sch., San Angelo, Tex., 1968-69; ednl. specialist Fort Richardson, Alaska, 1969-71; student life adv. Tex. Tech. U., Lubbock, 1972-75; counselor Midland (Tex.) Coll., 1975—; pvt. practice psychotherapy, Midland, 1975—. Mem. Human Relations Council, Midland, 1976—. Mem. Am. Psychol. Assn., Jr. Coll. Student Personnel Assn., Am. Personnel and Guidance Assn. (Tex. chpt.), Mayflower Soc. Mem. Disciples of Christ. Home: 2001 Community Ln Midland TX 79701 Office: 3600 N Garfield St Midland TX 79701

ROBINOW, BEATRIX HENDRIKA, librarian; b. Standerton, S. Africa, Nov. 5, 1915; d. Jan Daniel and Susan Mary Elizabeth (Faul) Minnaar; immigrated to Can., 1964, naturalized, 1969; B.A. (S. Africa Library Assn. fellow), U. Witwatersrand (Johannesburg), 1935; m. Richard F. Robinow, Jan. 1, 1938; children—Carl Philip, Franz Gerd Mesnard, Susan Marianne Robinow Madigan. Lectr., Cape Town Library Sch., 1946; tutor, examiner S. African Library Assn., 1942-50; librarian U. Natal Med. Sch., 1951-62, Fudger Med. Library, Toronto Gen. Hosp., 1964-66; health sci. librarian, assoc. univ. librarian McMaster U., Hamilton, Ont., Can., 1966-82; tchr. Sheridan Coll., Oakville, Ont., 1975; cons. in field. Mem. Assn. Canadian Med. Colls. (chmn. spl. resource com. med. sch. libraries 1974-76), Hamilton Dist. Health Library Network (chmn., organizer 1967-82), Ont. Council Health, Med. Library Assn. (council developing med. libraries 1967—, chmn. certification com. 1973-78, dir. 1978-81). Contbr. articles to profl. jours. Home: 122 Airdrie Rd Toronto ON M4G 1M5 Canada

ROBINS, CAROL LANGFORD, pediatrician; b. Chgo., July 20, 1940; d. Robert Erwin and Beatrice (Hall) Langford; B.A., Stanford U., 1962; M.D., U. Chgo., 1969; m. Arthur G. Robins, June 14, 1969; children—Sebastian, Jeremy. Pediatrician Roxbury Dental and Med. Group Boston, 1977—; instr. psychiat. day hosp., Tufts U, Boston, 1979-81; instr. pediatrics New Eng. Sch. Acupuncture, Boston, 1981—; herbal and acupuncture cons. Whole Health Assos., Watertown, Mass., 1981—; health book reviewer New Age mag. Den mother Boy Scouts Am.; tour leader, vol. Arnold Arboretum. May C. Willett fellow in child neurology, 1975-77. Diplomate Am. Bd. Pediatrics, Mem. Mass. Med. Soc., Mass. Acupuncture Soc., Fla. Native Plant Soc., Boston Mycological Club, Sierra Club, Audubon Soc., Friends of the Farlow. Mem. Assembly of God Ch. Author booklet: Aloe Vera Queen of Medicinal Plants, 1980. Office: 70 Phillips St Watertown MA 02172

ROBINS, JUDY ROSELYN, interior designer, fine art cons.; b. Cleve., Sept. 2, 1948; d. Stanley and Esther (Resnick) Waxman; A.A.S., Fashion Inst. Tech., 1969; B.S., N.Y. U., 1970, M.A., 1972; m. Kenneth M. Robins, Sept. 26, 1971. Fabric coordinator Celanese Corp., N.Y.C. 1970-71; merchandiser Bayly Corp., Denver, 1973-74; free-lance interior designer, 1975—; instr. interior design Met. State Coll., Denver, 1977-81, Judy Robins Interiors, Denver, 1977—. Mem. Young Womens Leadership Cabinet United Jewish Appeal, 1977-82; bd. dirs. Jewish Family and Childrens Service Colo., 1978—, Sec., 1981-82; bd. dirs. Congregation B.M.H., 1981—; bd. dirs. Allied Jewish Fedn., 1977—, Am. Jewish Com., 1980-81; mem. bd. Nat. Jewish Hosp., 1978-80; steering com. Alliance for Contemporary Art, Denver Art Mus. Recipient Young Leadership award Allied Jewish Fedn., 1977. Democrat. Home and Office: 755 Lafayette St Denver CO 80218

ROBINS, MARJORIE MCCARTHY (MRS. GEORGE KENNETH ROBINS), civic worker; b. St. Louis, Oct. 4, 1914; d. Eugene Ross and Louise (Roblee) McCarthy; A.B., Vassar Coll., 1936; diploma St. Louis Sch. Occupational Therapy, 1940; m. George Kenneth Robins, Nov. 9, 1940; children—Carol Robins Von Arx, G. Stephen, Barbara A. Robins Foorman. Mem. Mo. Library Commn., 1937-38; mem. bd. St. Louis Jr. League, 1945, 46; mem. bd. Occupational Therapy Workshop of St. Louis, 1941-46, pres., 1945, 46; mem. bd. Ladue Chapel Nursery Sch., 1957-60, 61-64, pres. bd., 1963, 64; past regional chmn. United Fund; past mem. St. Louis Met. Youth Commn., St. Louis Health and Welfare Council; bd. dirs. Internat. Inst. of St. Louis, 1966-72, 76—82, sec., 1968, v.p., 1981; bd. dirs. Mental Health Assn. St. Louis, 1963-70, Washington U. Child Guidance and Evaluation Clinic, 1968-78; bd. dirs. Central Inst. for Deaf, 1970—, v.p., 1975-76, pres., 1976-78; bd. dirs. Met. St. Louis YWCA, 1954-63, 64—, pres. bd., 1960-63, trustee, 1977—; mem. nat. bd. YWCA, 1967-79, nat. v.p., 1973-76; vol. tchr. remedial reading clinic St. Louis City Schs., 1968-71; trustee John Burr Burroughs Sch., 1960-63, John Burroughs Found., 1965-80, Roblee Found., 1972—, Nat. YWCA Retirement Fund, 1979—; bd. dirs. Gambrill Gardens United Meth. Retirement Home, 1979—, Thompson Retreat and Conf. Center, 1981—; bd. dirs. Springboard to Learning Inc., 1980—, v.p., 1980—. Clubs: Vassar (sec. and pres. 1939-40), Wednesday (dir. 1968-70, 77-79, 80-81) (St. Louis). Home: 45 Loren Woods Saint Louis MO 63124

ROBINSON, AGNES CLAFLIN, civic worker; b. N.Y.C., Oct. 2, 1918; d. Crittenden Hull and Agnes Sanger (Claflin) Adams; student Radcliffe Coll., 1936-39; A.B., Barnard Coll., 1941; M.S., N.Y. U., 1949; m. Albert Lewis Robinson, (div.); children—Nicholas Adams, John Claflin, Hugh Wesley, James Allen, Lewis Stewart. Tech. asst. Bell Telephone Labs., Whippany, N.J., 1943-44; v.p. Family Service Assn., Morristown, N.J., 1946-48; bd. dirs. Adult and child Guidance Clinic, San Jose, Calif., 1955-58; v.p. Palo Alto Mental Health Soc., 1959-63; pres. PTA, Palo Alto, Calif., 1961-63; trustee Palo Alto Unified Sch. Dist., 1963-73, pres., 1965-67; chmn. Drug Abuse Bd., Palo Alto, 1971-74; mem. adv. bd. Nairobi Day Schs., East Palo Alto, 1969-72; mem. adv. bd. Child Care Now, 1972-73; mem. Calif. Post-Secondary Edn. Commn., 1974-80, chmn., 1978-80; advisor to pub. affairs com. YWCA, 1974—; mem. Mid-Peninsula Com. for Integrated Edn., 1974-80; bd. dirs. Addiction Research Found., 1974-78, pres., 1974-77; bd. dirs. Mid-Peninsula Learning Center; pres. New Ways to Work, 1976-79; mem. spl. legis. com. Calif. Student Fin. Aid Study Group, 1979; mem. Palo Alto Human Relations Commn., 1981—; bd. govs. Calif. Community Colls., 1982—. Mem. NAACP (life), PTA (life), Nat. Com. for Citizens in Edn. Democrat. Clubs: Radcliffe of Mid-Peninsula, Palo Alto. Author: (with Ruth McAneny Loud) New York, New York! A Knickerbocker Holiday for You and Your Children, 1946. Home: 1765 Fulton St Palo Alto CA 94303

ROBINSON, ANNE DURRUM (MRS. HAROLD G. ROBINSON), human resources devel. cons.; b. Hugo, Okla., May 14, 1913; d. William Landon and Effie Anne (Lear) Durrum; B.J., Tex. Women's U., 1935; M.A., U. Tex., 1960; m. Harold G. Robinson, June 6, 1945; 1 dau., Marye Lear. Staff writer NBC, Hollywood, Cal., 1945; continuity editor KTBC, Austin, 1942-44, KNOW Radio, Austin, 1946-49; KASE, hostess TV program Sta. KTBC-TV, Austin, 1955-56; editor Sta. KASE, Austin, 1959-61; hostess KLRN-TV, Austin, 1961-63, KHFI-TV, Austin, 1966-67; mng. editor jour., writer Travis County Med. Soc., Travis County Med. Soc. Blood Bank and Med. Exchange, Austin, 1961-63; free-lance writer, lectr., performer, tchr., 1968; copywriter, office mgr. David G. Benjamin, Inc., 1963-68; asst. dir. curriculum devel. Tex. Dept. Public Welfare, Austin, 1973-77, edn. dir. mgmt. tng. div., 1977-78; ind. cons. human resource devel., 1978—. Grantee research Women in Communications, Inc., 1959, 71, nat. one-act play prize Hermit Club, Cleve., 1947, 1948, three-act play prize Houston Little Theatre, 1947, song lyrics award Nat. Five Arts awards, 1947, numerous poetry prizes. Mem. Women in Communications (chpt. pres. 1952, named Outstanding Woman in Continuing Edn., Austin chpt. 1977), Am. Soc. Tng. and Devel., Intergovtl. Tng. Council, Inst. Noetic Scis., World Future Soc., ESP Research Assos. Found., Nat. Assn. Gifted Children, AAAS, Assn. for Understanding of Man, Tex. Public Employees Assn., Women's Symphony League, Center Positive Prayer. Home and Office: 2309 Shoal Creek Blvd Austin TX 78705

ROBINSON, BARBARA LYNN, publishing co. exec.; b. Cleve., Sept. 16, 1951; d. Lennart Uno and Louise Ulla (Borenius) Gunnerfeldt; B.Mus., Mich. State U., 1975; M.Ed., Fla. Atlantic U., 1976, Ed.S., 1980; m. Kenneth H. Robinson, Feb. 7, 1976; stepchildren—Joseph Paul, Sharon Sue. Editor's asst. Mich. State U., 1969-70; instr. flute Lansing Conservatory of Mus., 1970-73; instrumental tchr. Music for Am., Inc., 1974; research asst., editor monthly newsletter Center for Econ. Edn., Fla. Atlantic U., 1976-77; founder, pres. Lynnco Publs., East Lansing, Mich., 1978—. Mem. Nat. Assn. Female Execs., Mensa, Phi Delta Kappa. Democrat. Lutheran. Author: Guidebook to Happiness, Living With the Unknown, 1978; The Art of Talking: A Handbook of Marital Communication, 1979. Office: PO Box 1071 East Lansing MI 48823

ROBINSON, BEATRICE DEL, ins. exec.; b. Wallace, N.C., Apr. 3, 1950; d. Charlie and Willie Mae (Johnson) R.; B.S., Fayetteville State U., N.C., 1972; M.B.A. with honors, Long Island U., 1977; 1 son, Warren. With RCA Service Co.; tchr., cons. U. N.Y., 1974-76; ednl. cons. N.Y.C. Bd. Edn., 1977-78; field underwiter, salesperson N.Y. Life Ins. Co., N.Y.C., 1979-81, network women's leader. Recipient N.Y. Life Top Club award, 1979, 80, Centurion award, 1979, 80, Summer Sizzler award. Mem. Nat. Assn. Female Execs., Am. Mgmt. Assn., Nat. Assn. Life Underwriters (dir. Queens div. 1980-81), Million Dollar Round Table. Home: 114 Taylor Ave Roosevelt NY 11575 Office: 97-77 Queens Blvd Rego Park New York NY 11374

ROBINSON, BRENDA PERRY, metals co. exec.; b. Richlands, Va., June 21, 1946; d. Joseph Franklin and Irene (Jessee) Perry; student public schs., Va. and Md., also various seminars; m. Walter Warren Robinson, Aug. 24, 1977; 1 dau. by previous marriage, Lori Kay White. File clk. Tabb Brockenborough & Ragland, Richmond, Va., 1963-64; acctg. clk. So. states R.H. Donnelley Co., Richmond, 1965; with Reynolds Metals Co., Richmond, 1966—, mgr. employee med. benefits, 1978-81, mgr. adminstrv. services, mgr. office systems instrumentation and automation edn., 1981—; condr. seminars in field. Sec., Miss Softball Am., Richmond; co. rep. United Way, Richmond; substitute rep. Va. Nutrition Com. Named Boss of Yr., Am. Businesswomen's Assn., 1976. Mem. Adminstrv. Mgmt. Soc. (speakers' bur.), Office Automation Roundtable, Richmond Office Automation Roundtable (sec.), Women's Network, Nat. Assn. Female Execs. Baptist. Home: 702 Sleepy Hollow Rd Richmond VA 23229 Office: 6601 W Broad St Richmond VA 23261

ROBINSON, CARLAN MARIE, clin. psychologist; b. Norfolk, Va., Aug. 29, 1944; d. Ralph Carlan and Frances Richards (Fluker) Robinson; A.B. cum laude, N.Y.U., 1972, M.A., 1975, Ph.D., 1977; m. Joseph Lawrence Restivo, June 3, 1964 (div.); 1 dau., Julian Marie. Research asst. N.Y.U., 1971-76, teaching asst., 1972-73; indsl. cons. MABSTOA, N.Y.C., 1974; clin. psychology intern Psychiat. Inst., Columbia-Presbyn. Hosp., N.Y.C., 1975-76; teaching asst. Columbia U., N.Y.C., 1976-77; dir. research, staff mem., supr. Asso. Psychotherapists/Grammercy Park Inst., N.Y.C., 1978-80; teaching asst., postdoctoral fellow dept. psychiatry N.Y.U. Med. Sch., N.Y.C., 1978-80, clin. instr., 1980-81; mgmt. cons. Am. Tel. & Tel., Westinghouse, 1980-81; sr. staff psychologist VA Outpatient Clinic, Los Angeles, 1981—; pvt. practice, Marina del Rey, Calif., 1981—. Lic. psychologist, N.Y., Calif., Mem. Am. Psychol. Assn., Western Psychol. Assn., Los Angeles County Psychol. Assn., Am. Assn. Women in Sci., AAAS, Soc. for Psychol. Study Social Issues, Soc. for Personality Assessment, Psi Chi. Republican. Quaker. Home: 15 1/2 Quarterdeck St Marina del Rey CA 90291 Office: 425 S Hill St Los Angeles CA 90016 also 330 Washington Sq Suite 515 Marina del Rey CA 90291

ROBINSON, CAROL SUSAN, advt. agy. exec.; b. Detroit, Oct. 28, 1938; d. Allen Lawrence and Sally (Cutler) R.; student Mich. State U., 1956-57; B.S., Boston U., 1960; student Soc. Arts and Crafts, Detroit, Calif. Coll. Arts and Crafts, Oakland, Otis Art Inst., Los Angeles; m. Richard Allen Clarke, Mar. 23, 1974; stepchildren—Richard, Janis Clarke Meldahl, William, Robert. Tchr. public schs., Sharon, Mass., 1960, Woodland Hills and Granda Hills, Calif., 1960-61; art buyer, exec. sec. Foote, Cone & Belding, Los Angeles, 1961-65; copy chief, continuity dir. KFOX, Long Beach, Calif., 1966-68; mgr. visual design Mattel, Inc., Los Angeles, 1968-75; pres. Seven Fleet St., Ltd., San Francisco, 1975-77; partner, v.p. King, Robinson & Clarke, San Francisco, 1978; pres., treas. bd. Robinson-Clarke, Inc., Los Angeles and Berkeley, Calif., 1978—. Mem. Nat. Assn. Female Execs., NOW, San Francisco Art Commn., Los Angeles County Mus. Art, Oakland Art Mus., San Francisco Advt. Club. Office: 39 Oakvale Ave Berkeley CA 94706 also 6399 Wilshire Blvd Los Angeles CA 90048

ROBINSON, CHARLOTTE HILL, artist; b. San Antonio, Nov. 28, 1926; d. Lucius Davis and Charlotte (Moore) Hill; student Art Students League, 1948, N.Y. U., 1949, Corcoran Art Sch., 1951; m. Floyd Irvin Robinson, Mar. 7, 1943; children—Floyd Irvin, Laurence H., Elizabeth H. Instr. painting Art League, Alexandria, Va., 1967-75; instr. drawing and rubbing Smithsonian Asso. Program, Washington, 1976; bd. dirs., dir. exhbns., instr. Art World Seminars, Washington Women's Art Center, 1978—; coordinator, dir. The Artist and Quilt Mus., traveling exhbn. funded by Nat. Endowment for Arts, 1980—; one woman shows at Foundry Gallery, Washington, 1977; San Jose (Calif.) State U., 1978; Gallery 4, Alexandria, 1979; Rutgers U., New Brunswick, N.J., 1979; Garden Gallery, Raleigh, N.C., 1980, others; exhibited in group shows at Mint Mus., Charlotte, N.C., 1977; Haslem Gallery, Washington, 1978; Gallery 501, Charlotte, 1978, others; represented in permanent collections at New Sch. for Social Research, N.Y.C., USIS, Nairobi, Kenya, AT&T, N.Y.C. and Chgo., Mobil Oil, Houston, Rainier Bank, Seattle, others. Nat. program dir. Washington Conf. for the Women's Caucus for Art, 1979—; trustee Bronx Mus., 1976-77; Nat. Endowment for Arts grantee, 1977, 79. Mem. Coll. Art Assn., Women's Caucus for Art. Address: 6324 Crosswoods Dr Falls Church VA 22044

ROBINSON, DELIA MAE, mental health adminstr.; b. Nov. 16, 1934, Omaha; d. Robert and Sarah Ethel (Speese) Gardner; B.B.A., Lincoln U., Mo., 1955; M.S.W., U. Nebr., Omaha, 1974; children—Walter George, Waddell Craig. Caseworker, St. Louis County Dept. Public Welfare, Maplewood, Mo., 1957, St. Louis City Dept. Welfare, 1958-59, Douglas County (Nebr.) Dept. Welfare, Omaha, 1959-65; counselor Women's Job Corps Center, Omaha, 1966; child protective service worker Douglas County Social Service, Omaha, 1967-68, casework supr., 1968-73; psychiat. social worker Douglas County Hosp. Community Mental Health Center, Omaha, 1974-75; dir. social service dept. Douglas County Hosp./Annex, 1975-80; cons. Native Am. Alcoholism Program, Omaha, Omaha NAACP, 1981. Mem. adv. bd. Woodson Center, 1968-70, ENCOMH South Clinic, 1977-78. Mem. Nebr. Welfare Assn., Nat. Assn. Social Workers (sec. Nebr. chpt. 1980-82), Nat. Assn. Black Social Workers, Nat. Soc. Hosp. Social Work Dirs., Nebr. Soc. Hosp. Social Work Dirs., Alpha Kappa Alpha. Democrat. Baptist. Office: 4102 Woolworth Ave Omaha NE 68105

ROBINSON, DORRIS REGINA, ednl. adminstr.; b. Little Rock, Oct. 4, 1947; d. James and Eleise (Cox) Brown; B.S., Ark. Bapt. Coll., 1970; M.S.E., Ouachita Bapt. U., 1975; m. Preston D. Robinson, Oct. 2, 1966; 1 dau., Patrina Mechelle. Insp., Timex, Inc., Little Rock, 1966-70; asst. to the registrar Ark. Bapt. Coll., Little Rock, 1970, bus. mgr., dir. fin. aid, 1978-79, dir. bus. and fiscal affairs, 1979—. Sec., Stephen Sch. PTA, Little Rock, 1979—; mem. bd. Christian edn. St. Mark Baptist Ch., 1979-80, chmn. benevolent com., 1978-80. Mem. Nat. Assn. Student Fin. Aid Adminstrs., Nat. Assn. Female Execs., Ark. Assn. Student Fin. Aid Adminstrs., SW Assn. Student Fin. Aid Adminstrs., So. Assn. Coll. and Univ. Bus. Officers, Ark. Student Personnel Assn., Urban League. Clubs: Order Eastern Star, Order Golden Circle. Office: Ark Bapt Coll 1600 High St Little Rock AR 72202

ROBINSON, EDNA LINDSEY, pub. co. exec.; b. Mt. Vernon, Tex., Dec. 21, 1938; d. Thomas Colquitt and Myrtle (McGill) Lindsey; B.A., Baylor U., 1960; m. Raymond R. Robinson, June 3, 1960; 1 son, Randall Ray. Exec. sec. Prescolite Mfg. Corp., El Dorado, Ark., 1960-62; exec. sec. Blanchard, Walker, O'Quin & Roberts, Shreveport, La., 1962-71, office mgr., 1971-76; corp. sec. Shreveport Pub. Corp., 1976—, Beaird Media Corp., Shreveport, 1976—; dir., corp. sec. Lickskillet Plantation, Inc., Shreveport, 1976—. Sec., Charles T. Beaird Found., Shreveport, 1976—. Cert. profl. sec., 1971; named Sec. of Yr., Nat. Secs. Assn., 1973. Mem. Nat. Secs. Assn. (chpt. pres. 1976-77), La. Assn. Cert. Profl. Secs. Democrat. Baptist. Home: 3208 Pines Rd Shreveport LA 71119 Office: 222 Lake St PO Box 31110 Shreveport LA 71130

ROBINSON, FLORA ELEANOR, former data processing exec.; b. Delaware, Ohio, Feb. 12, 1923; d. Ralph Leroy and Blanche Estelle (Kinnard) R.; student public schs., Utica, Ohio. With Licking Rural Electrification, Inc., Utica, 1942-80, asst. billing clk., 1945-50, chief billing clk., 1950-69, mgr. data processing dept., 1969-80. Recipient Service awards Ohio Rural Elec. Coops., 1975, Rural Electrification Adminstrn., 1977, Licking Rural Electrification, Inc., 1977. Democrat. Home: 101 N Main St Utica OH 43080

ROBINSON, FLORENCE CLAIRE CRIM, educator; b. Carbondale, Ill., Oct. 26, 1932; d. Alonzo V. and Doddridge M. (Taylor) Crim; B.A., So. Ill. U., 1950, Ph.D., 1963; M.A., Denver U., 1956; postgrad. U. Colo., Northwestern U.; m. Carl Robinson, Aug. 9, 1951 (div.); children—Carl Emil, Joan Gayle. Tchr., coordinator music Public Schs. Denver, 1953-65; asso. prof. music So. Ill. U., Carbondale, 1965-67; prof., chmn. dept. music Bishop Coll., Dallas, 1967-71; prof., chmn. dept. music, head div. arts and humanities Clark Coll., Atlanta, 1971—, Fuller E. Callaway Disting. prof. music, 1981—; vis. prof. Atlanta U., Emory U., Fisk U., U. Colo.; tchr. music KRMA-TV, Denver; hostess Florence Robinson Radio Show, Sta. WPLO, Atlanta, 1971-73, The Many Sides of Black Music, syndicated, 1974—; also lectr., condr., adjudicator. Trustee, Clark Coll., 1981—. Recipient Atlanta Bronze Jubilee award, 1980; Disting. Alumni award So. Ill. U., 1982. Mem. Human Relations Commn., Denver, 1965. Mem. Music Educators Nat. Conf., Nat. Assn. Negro Musicians (Outstanding Musician award 1973), AAUP, NEA, AFTRA, Kappa Delta Pi, Phi Kappa Phi, Pi Delta Theta, Mu Phi Epsilon, Alpha Kappa Alpha. Contbr. articles to profl. jours. Piano and organ recitals European tour, 1973; also recs. The Many Sides of Black Music. Home: 2885 Pine Needle Dr Atlanta GA 30344 Office: Div Arts and Humanities Clark College Atlanta GA 30341

ROBINSON, GAY ELIZABETH CLARA, clergywoman; b. Stamford, Conn., Aug. 13, 1933; d. Theodore Alfred, Sr. and Elizabeth (Majher) Guilmette; student L.I.F.E. Coll., 1951-52; A.A., Orange Coast Coll., 1966; B.A., Calif. State U., 1968, M.A., 1970; postgrad., Golden State U., 1980—; m. Gary Garth Robinson, Feb. 3, 1952; children—Joy Leah Robinson Thornton, Clayton David. Asst. credit mgr. Phelps-Terkel, 1951-52; exec. adminstrv. asst. Pozzo Constrn. Co., 1952-53; ordained to ministry Internat. Ch. Foursquare Gospel, 1962; asso. pastor Perris, Calif., 1955-58, SW Dist. Conf. rep., 1958-60, Worldwide Mission rep. 48 countries, 1965—; pastoral staff Ch. by the Sea, Huntington Beach, Calif., 1960—; founder Breath of Life, 1975; instr. Irvine Coll., 1976-78; SW dist. sec., 1960-78; broadcaster sta. KYMS, 1979—; tour dir., 1977—; participant exec. mgmt. seminars, 1976—. Mem. Republican Women's Nat. Com. Scholarship Chapman Floating Coll. of the Seas, 1966; scholar Pepperdine U., 1951-55. Mem. Nat. Assn. Evangelicals, Western Psychol. Assn., World Pentecostal Conf., United Foursquare Women (program chmn.), L.I.F.E. Alumni Assn. (past alumni sec.). Club: Temple City Jr. Women's (devotion leader, sec., 1957-60). Author: The Inner Woman, 1978; What is Your God Concept?, 1982; contbr. book revs., articles to publs. in field. Office: 715 Lake St Huntington Beach CA 92648

ROBINSON, JANE ALEXANDER, clin. psychologist; b. Chgo., Jan. 17, 1931; d. C. A. Alexander and Janie Alexander Walton; Ph.D., U. Detroit, 1978; children—David Robinson, Amorie Robinson, Richard Robinson. Tchr. elem. public schs., Detroit, 1957-63; psychologist Southfield (Mich.) Public Schs., 1964-68, Detroit Public Schs., 1968-72; clin. psychologist Tri-County Mental Health Services, P.C., Southfield, Mich., 1977-81, Northwest Counseling and Psychotherapy Center, Southfield, 1981—. Mem. Am. Psychol. Assn., Mich. Psychol. Assn., Nat. Assn. Black Psychologist (award 1977), Mich. Assn. Black Psychologists (pres. 1975-76). Author: Self-Esteem in Black and White Women, 1978. Home: 79 Rhode Island St Highland Park MI 48203 Office: Northwest Counseling and Psychotherapy Center 24555 Southfield Rd Suite 200 Southfield MI 48705

ROBINSON, JEAN RUTH, educator; b. Rockford, Ill., Dec. 9, 1925; d. Albert Eric and Eleanor Cora (Peterson) Anderson; B.A., Beloit Coll., 1947; M.A., Radcliffe Coll., 1952, Ph.D., 1953; m. Kenneth Leon Robinson, July 10, 1954; children—James Carl, Alan Eric. Lectr., Wells Coll., 1954-56; faculty Cornell U., Ithaca, N.Y., 1965—, lectr., sr. lectr., 1965-81, prof. consumer econs. and housing, 1981—, dept. chmn., 1981—. Trustee Village of Cayuga Heights, 1976-79, 80—; bd. dirs. N.Y. State Council Econ. Edn. Lutheran. Office: 121 MVR Cornell Univ Coll Human Ecology Ithaca NY 14853

ROBINSON, JEWEL ALDA, producer, announcer; b. N.Y.C., Sept. 21, 1952; d. Hubert Louis and Cora May (Day) R.; B.A. cum laude (Univ. scholar in music), Central State U., Wilberforce, Ohio; M.S. in Mass Communications (Corp. Pub. Broadcasting scholar), Miami U., Oxford, Ohio. Successively broadcast trainee Sta. WLWD, TV, Dayton, Ohio, floor dir. Sta. WDTN-TV, Dayton, producer, announcer Sta. WMUB-FM, Oxford, Ohio; producer, announcer Sta. KUNI/KHKE-FM, Cedar Falls, Iowa; now news and public affairs reporter Sta. KUOM, Mpls. Mem. Cotton Top Co-op. Address: Station KUOM 330 21st Ave S Minneapolis MN 55455

ROBINSON, LEATRICE CRAIG, educator; b. Cleve., Apr. 16, 1933; d. Lafayette Manual and Lula (Reed) Craig; B.S. in Edn., Bowling Green State U., 1955; m. Emerson Robinson, Sept. 1, 1956; 1 son, Jon. Service rep. Ohio Bell Telephone Co., Cleve., Dayton, 1951-61; tchr. Glenville High Sch., Cleve., 1961-67, Mumford High Sch., Detroit, 1967-79, head fgn. lang. dept., 1978-79; owner, dir. Robinson's Advantage Inst. for Children, Detroit, 1977—; co-founder Mach-Kit Shoppe. Pres., Pinehurst Block Club, 1969-81; active United Negro Coll. Fund dr., 1982. Recipient cert. of award for outstanding Bus. Achievement and Community Service Mich. Dept. Commerce. Mem. Better Bus. Bur., NAACP, Nat. Black Child Devel. Inst., Nat. Assn. for Edn. Young Children, Mich. Assn. Child Care Adminstrs., Detroit-Wayne County Child Care Coordinating Council, Nat. Assn. Women Bus. Owners, Booker T. Washington Bus. Assn., Alpha Kappa Alpha. Roman Catholic. Club: Thursday Luncheon Group. Office: 20503 Washburn St Detroit MI 48221

ROBINSON, LILIEN FILIPOVITCH, educator; b. Ljubljana, Yugoslavia, Feb. 7, 1940; d. Milenko and Branka Filipovitch; B.A. with distinction, George Washington U., 1962, M.A., 1965; Ph.D., Johns Hopkins U., 1978; m. David Robinson, June 8, 1974. Grad. teaching fellow George Washington U., 1962-64, lectr. in art history, 1964-65, asst. prof. art history, 1965-71, asso. prof., 1971-76, prof., 1979—, chmn. dept. art, 1976—. Mem. Coll. Art Assn. Am., Phi Beta Kappa, Omicron Delta Kappa, Delta Gamma. Serbian Orthodox. Office: Art Dept George Washington U Washington DC 20052

ROBINSON, LINDA MAY, tour guide, moving cons., author; b. El Dorado, Kans., Nov. 9, 1937; d. Forrest Edward and Edith May (Heck) Carlson; student U. Kans., 1955-57, Wichita State U., 1958, U. Denver, 1962-64, U. Colo., 1970-71; children—Chris Dale, Carin Dene, Curtis Dean. Wrangler, counselor Skyland Camp, Crested Butte, Colo., 1954-56; tour guide Queen City Tours, Denver, 1976—, tour guide writer, 1979—, trainer, 1979—; moving cons. Kamp Moving & Storage, Denver, 1978—; tour guide Molly Brown House, Hist. Denver, 1975-81, day chmn., 1976-81, vice-chmn. vol. council, 1977-78; vol. chauffeur Christian Fellowship of Blind, 1977—. Named Outstanding Young Woman of Am., 1970; cert. moving cons. Mem. U. Kans. Alumni Assn. (life), Mensa, Nat. Assn. Profl. Saleswomen, Phi Alpha Theta. Mem. Christian Ch. (Disciples of Christ). Club: D.A.R. (Outstanding Jr. Mem. in Colo. 1970, Outstanding Jr. Mem. Western div. 1970). Author: (with Vickie Schroeder) Mile High Denver, A Guide to the Queen City, 1981; columnist Rocky Mountain Christian, 1964-69. Home: 2130 Upham Lakewood CO 80215 Office: 4591 Ivy St Denver CO 80216

ROBINSON, MARGERY LEVERN, sch. psychologist; b. Oklahoma City, Dec. 12, 1924; d. Albert George and Esther Ruby (Walley) LeV.; student Okla. A&M Coll., 1941-43, Tex. Tech. Coll., 1945; B.S., Oklahoma City U., 1951; M.S., Fort Hays (Kans.) State Coll., 1964; D.Ed., Okla. State U., 1973; m. Robert W. Robinson, Apr. 1, 1947; children—Robert W. II, Suzanne, Rand W., Vicki L. Tchr. elem. sch., Malaga, Calif., 1945-46, Oklahoma City, 1949-50, Liberal, Kans., 1962-63; tchr. jr. high sci. Liberal, 1963-64, Oklahoma City, 1964-65; tchr. high sch. chemistry and physiology, Oklahoma City, 1965-66; counselor, sch. psychologist State-Operated-Schs., Elmendorf AFB, Anchorage, 1967-72; sch. psychologist Anchorage Sch. Dist., 1973-77; spl. edn. program specialist, sch. psychologist, Barrow, Alaska, 1977-78; coordinator spl. services North Slope Borough Sch. Dist., Barrow, 1978-80; pvt. practice counseling psychology with New Beginnings, Anchorage, 1980—; dir. Centerpoint, Anchorage, 1974—. County Republican committeewoman, Kans., 1957; sec. Children Have a Potential, 1971-72, recipient Service award, 1972. Mem. Internat. Sch. Psychology Assn. (state coordinator), Nat. Assn. Sch. Psychologists (state del.), Am. Psychol. Assn., Council Exceptional Children, Internat. Council Psychology, Alaska Sch. Psychologists Assn. (past pres.), Alaska Psychol. Assn., Alaska Assn. Dirs. Spl. Edn. Republican. Episcopalian. Home and Office: New Beginnings 4501 Arctic Blvd #1 Anchorage AK 99503

ROBINSON, MARIE J., educator; b. Monaca, Pa., Jan. 21, 1915; B. in Drama/Speech with honors, Emerson Coll., 1935; M.A. with honors, Mich. State U., 1944; Ph.D., Northwestern U., 1960. Dir. of plays Lockport (N.Y.) Sr. High Sch., 1935-43; head dept. speech and drama State Tchrs. Coll., Bemidji, Minn., 1944-45; instr. Sch. Speech, Syracuse (N.Y.) U., 1945-49; prof. speech Ill. Wesleyan U., Bloomington, 1950-82, head dept. speech, 1953-73; vis. lectr. various colls., 1966-80; vis. artist Carthage Coll., Wis., 1966, 68, 70. Recipient Tchr. of Year award Ill. Wesleyan U., 1966. Mem. Speech Communication Assn. (life emeritus 1980), Central States Speech Assn., Am. Theatre Assn., Am. Forensic Assn. (life emeritus), Ill. Speech and Theatre Assn. (pres. 1962-63; Presdl. award and life emeritus 1980), Kappa Delta Pi, Pi Kappa Delta (lt. gov. province of Ill. 1972-74, gov. 1974-76), Alpha Epsilon Rho, Alpha Lambda Delta, Theta Alpha Phi, Phi Kappa Phi (life emeritus 1981). Contbr. articles on speech to profl. publs. Home: 2205 Lamon Dr Bloomington IL 61701

ROBINSON, MARION SWETT, banker; b. Boston, Aug. 3, 1947; d. Albert Hersey and Mary (Stewart) Swett; B.A., Wellesley Coll., 1969; M.B.A., Stanford U., 1979; M.A., Stanford Food Research Inst., 1979; m. Lawrence R. Robinson III, June 30, 1979; 1 son, Albert Hersey. Sr. asst. dir. Morgan Grenfell & Co. Ltd., London, 1970-77; asst. v.p. Mfrs. Hanover Trust, N.Y.C., 1979-80; v.p. Bankers Trust Co., N.Y.C., 1980—. Mem. steering com. Young Profls. for Seymour. Republican. Congregationalist. Club: N.Y. Wellesley. Office: 280 Park Ave New York NY 10017

ROBINSON, MARY LOU, judge; b. Dodge City, Kans., Aug. 25, 1926; d. Gerald J. and Frances Aynn (Pierce) Strueber; student Amarillo Coll., 1946; B.A., U. Tex., 1948, LL.B., 1950; m. A.J. Robinson, Aug. 28, 1949; children—Rebecca Aynn Robinson Gruhlkey, Diana Ceil, Matthew Douglas. Admitted to Tex. bar, 1949; individual practice law, 1950-55; judge County Ct., Potter County, Tex., 1955-59; judge 108th Dist. Ct., 1961-73; asso. justice Ct. Civil Appeals, 7th Supreme Jud. Dist. Tex., 1973-77, chief justice, 1977-79; judge U.S. Dist. Ct. for No. Dist. Tex., 1979—. Elder Westminster Presbyn. Ch. Named Tex. Women of Yr. Tex. Fedn. Bus. and Profl. Women, 1973, one of 10 Outstanding Panhandle Women, W. Tex. State U., 1976. Mem. Nat. Assn. Women Lawyers, Amarillo Bar Assn., Tex. Bar Assn., Am. Bar Assn., Delta Kappa Gamma. Home: 5302 Berget St Amarillo TX 79106 Office: 205 E 5th St Amarillo TX 79101

ROBINSON, MARY LOUISE, mktg. cons.; b. Yonkers, N.Y., Mar. 22, 1942; d. Francis J. and Frances (Sikerzycki) Wazeter; B.A., Wellesley Coll., 1963; M.B.A., Harvard U., 1970. Product devel. mgr. Dansk Designs, Ltd., Mt. Kisco, N.Y., 1970-73; product group mgr. Clairol, Inc., N.Y.C., 1974-76; sr. product mgr. Matchabelli, Cheseborough Ponds, Greenwich, Conn., 1977; exec. v.p. 800 Spirits, Inc., N.Y.C., 1980—; pres. M. Robinson Assos., N.Y.C., 1979—, dir. 1980—. Mem. Women Bus. Owners of N.Y. (bd. dirs. 1979-81), Women in Bus. Clubs: Harvard, Vanderbilt Toastmasters (pres. 1980). Contbr. articles to profl. jours. Address: 160 E 48 St New York NY 10017

ROBINSON, MARY ROWLAND, univ. provost; b. Ashtabula, Ohio, May 23, 1927; d. Russell King and Helen Elizabeth (Price) R.; B.A., Duke U., 1949; M.A., Columbia U., 1957. Dean of women Eastern Wash. State Coll., Cheney, 1959-60, Am. U. Beirut, 1960-69; dean women, then assoc. dean students Western Wash. State Coll., Bellingham, 1969-78, affirmative action officer, 1972-77, vice provost acad. adminstrn., 1979—; bd. dirs. Watcom Ednl. Credit Union, 1978—; participant AAUW/State Dept. African/Am. Educators Program, Sierra Leone, 1981. Bd. dirs. United Way Whatcom County, 1976—, St. Luke's Hosp., Bellingham, 1977—; pres. Bellingham YWCA, 1972-74, trustee, 1977—; trustee Mt. Baker Kidney Center, Bellingham, 1978—, founding pres., 1978-79. Grantee, Carnegie Corp., 1977; Diamond Jubilee honoree Bellingham YWCA, 1982. Mem. Nat. Assn. Women Deans, Admistrs. and Counselors (life), Wash. Assn. Women Deans, Adminstrs. and Counselors (past pres.), AAUW (life, corp. del.; ednl. found. grantee 1979), Delta Gamma. Author papers in field. Office: Western Wash U Bellingham WA 98225

ROBINSON, NAOMI JEAN, tng. systems analyst; b. Storm Lake, Iowa, Oct. 10, 1951; d. Wendell and Norma (Wright) R.; B.A., Buena Vista Coll., 1973; M.A.Ed., George Washington U., 1978. Tchr., elem. schs., Storm Lake, Iowa, 1973-75; edn. specialist intern U.S. Army, Fort Monroe, Va., 1976-78, edn. specialist, Fort Eustis, Va., 1978-79, tng. systems analyst, White Sands Missile Range, N.Mex., 1979—. Vice pres., Young Republicans, 1972-73. Mem. Nat. Assn. Exec. Females, Federally Employed Women, Human Factors Soc., Iowa Edn. Assn. Republican. Presbyterian. Club: Bus. and Profl. Women. Author: Guidelines for Development of Skill Qualification Tests, 1977. Home: 2850 Fairway Dr Apt 4 Las Cruces NM 88001 Office: US Army TRASANA attn ATAA THA WSMR NM 88002

ROBINSON, NELLIE CHAPMAN, govt. ofcl.; b. Washington, Dec. 23, 1923; d. James Spottswood and Nellie (Bowler) Chapman; student Howard U., Am. U., U.S. Dept. Agr. Grad. Sch., La Salle U., also adult edn. courses; m. Raymond A. Sutton, Jr. (dec.); children—Ronald N., Raymond A., III; m. 2d, Elliott R. Robinson, June 27, 1963; 1 dau., Dawn E. With U.S. Govt., 1942—; acctg. clk. U.S. Marshal's Service, 1962-80, disbursing officer, 1976-82, matron dep., 1962-78. Vice pres. Met. Democratic Women, D.C., 1961-62, amenities chmn., 1963-64; transition coordinator Met. Bapt. Ch., 1981—. Recipient Outstanding Service award Dept. Justice, 1977, 78. Mem. Nat. Assn. Female Execs., Howard U. Women's Aux. Baptist. Club: Order Eastern Star (grand lectr. 1981). Office: US Marshals Service US Dist Courthouse 3d and Constitution Ave NW Washington DC 20001

ROBINSON, PATRICIA ISABELL, registered nurse; b. Tucson, May 14, 1947; d. Monroe Leon and Isabell Anne (Tuck) R.; Asso. in Nursing, Mesa Coll., Grand Junction, Colo., 1967. Staff nurse St. Mary's Hosp., Grand Junction, 1967; supr. Fairbanks (Alaska) Community Hosp., 1967-69; charge nurse Laramie (Wyo.) Hosp., 1969-70, Sacred Heart Hosp., Eugene, Oreg., 1970-73; asst. head nurse Providence Med. Center, Portland, Oreg., 1973-76, supr., 1976-77, adminstrv. asst. patient care services, 1977-79; indsl. nurse J.F. Shea Co. Inc., 1980—. Instr. 1st aid and C.P.R., ARC. Mem. Oncology Nursing Soc. Home and Office: PO Box 70 Heber City UT 84032

ROBINSON, PEGGY ELLAIN, pub. relations exec., realtor, writer; b. Slaton, Tex., June 24, 1928; d. John T. and Gladys B.L. (Olson) Whitesides; B.F.A. in Broadcasting, U. Tex., 1951; postgrad. Sch. Journalism, U. Mo., 1967-68; m. Frank Eugene Robinson, June 4, 1952; 1 dau., Lindley Ellain. Asst. writer of advt. and promotion NBC-TV, N.Y.C., 1951-52; asst. pub. relations exec. TV sta. WOAI, San Antonio, 1952-53; writer Mithoff Advt. Co., El Paso, Tex., 1954-56; free lance pub. relations exec. Emcee TV show, KELP-TV, KROD-TV, El Paso, 1956-58; editor, propr. Shop Talk mag., Lawton, Okla., 1958-60; owner, pub. relations dir. Town and Country Real Estate Co., Lawton, 1959-62, 1970—; free lance writer feature stories for newspapers, mags., various TV and radio stations, 1953—; columnist Shop Talk, Ideas in Homes, Lawton, 1959—; dir. pub. relations Lawton Bd. Realtors, 1978—. Mem. Women in Communications, Internat. Communications Assn., Nat., Okla. assns. Realtors, Am. Bus. Women's Assn., AAUW, Honolulu Press Club, Lawton Heritage Assn., Gt. Plains Tourism Assn., Lawton C. of C. (internat. relations com.), Kappa Tau Alpha, Alpha Delta Pi. Democrat. Methodist. Asso. editor Lawton Heritage News, 1978. Clubs: Ft. Sill Officer's Wives Club, Lawton Book and Play Rev. Club. Home: 1614 NW 34 St Lawton OK 73501 Office: 626 D St Suite 6 Lawton OK 73501

ROBINSON, RHETTA FAITH, guidance counselor; b. Preston, Okla., Nov. 26, 1933; d. John Floyd and Essie Amanda Nesbitt; B.S. in Edn. and English, (Luther Brown award 1955), Northeastern Okla. State U., 1955; M.A. in Guidance and Counseling, U. Tulsa, 1970; m. Ronald H. Robinson, Dec. 23, 1955; 1 son, Joey Ronn. Tchr., Tulsa Public Schs., 1955-70, counselor, 1970-82, guidance dean Nimitz Jr. High Sch. and Clinton Middle Sch., 1982—. Mem. Am. Personnel and Guidance Assn., NEA, Nat. Panhellenic Assn., Okla. Personnel and Guidance Assn., Okla. Edn. Assn., Okla. Middle Sch. Assn., Tulsa Personnel and Guidance Assn. (pres. 1980-81). Tulsa Classroom Tchrs. Assn., Tulsa Panhellenic Assn., Alpha Sigma Alpha (nat. pres. 1980-82, 84—), Kappa Kappa Iota, Delta Kappa Gamma. Democrat. Baptist. Home: 5880 S Joplin St Tulsa OK 74135 Office: 2224 W 41st St Tulsa OK 74107

ROBINSON, SALLY WINSTON, artist; b. Detroit, Nov. 2, 1924; d. Harry Lewis and Lydia (Kahn) Winston; B.A., Bennington Coll., 1947; student Cranbrook Acad. Art, 1949; grad. Sch. Social Work, Wayne U., 1948, M.A., 1972; M.F.A., Wayne State U., 1973; m. Eliot F. Robinson, June 28, 1949; children—Peter Eliot, Lydia Winston, Suzanne Finley, Sarah Mitchell. Psychol. tester Detroit Bd. Edn., 1944; pyschol. counselor and tester YMCA, N.Y.C., 1946; social caseworker Family Service, Pontiac, Mich., 1947; instr. printmaking Wayne State U., Detroit, 1973—. One person shows U. Mich., 1973, Wayne State U., 1974, Klein-Vogol Gallery, 1974, Rina Gallery, 1976, Park McCullough House, Vt., 1976, Williams Coll., 1976, Arnold Klein Gallery, 1977; exhibited group shows Bennington Coll., Cranbrook Mus., Detroit Inst. Art, Detroit Artists Market, Soc. Women Painters, Soc. Arts and Crafts, Bloomfield Art Assn., Flint Left Bank Gallery, Balough Gallery, Detroit Soc. Women Painters, U. Mich., U. Ind., U. Wis., U. Pittsburg, Toledo Mus., Krannert Mus.; represented in permanent collections, Detroit, N.Y.C., Birmingham, Bloomfield Hills; tchr. children's art Detroit Inst. Art, 1949-50, now artistic advisor, bd. dirs. drawing and print orgn. Bd. dirs. Planned Parenthood, 1951—, mem. exec. bd., 1963—; bd. dirs. PTA, 1956-60, Roeper City and Country Sch., U. Mich. Mus. Art, 1978; trustee Putnam Hosp. Med. Research Inst., 1978; mem. Gov.'s Commn. Art in State Bldgs., 1978-79. Mem. Detroit Artists Market (dir. 1956—), Bennington Coll. Alumnae Assn. (regional co-chmn. 1954), Detroit Soc. Women Painters, Birmingham Soc. Women Painters (pres. 1974-76), Bloomfield Art Assn. (program co-chmn. 1956), Founders Soc. Detroit Inst. Art. Unitarian (mem. Council 1963—). Clubs: Village Women's (Birmingham, Mich.); Women's City (co-ordinator art shows 1950) (Detroit). Home: 572 Linden Rd Birmingham MI 48009 also 7 Monument Circle Old Bennington VT 05201 also 708 Pine Run Dr Osprey FL 33559

ROBINSON, SHIRLIE LORENE, educator polit. worker; b. Port Townsend, Wash., Mar. 27, 1933; d. Joel Craft and Berniece Ardelle (Ricker) Waddell; B.S. in Edn., Gorham (Maine) State Tchrs. Coll., 1949-53; M.S. in Edn., Calif. State U., Hayward, 1976; postgrad. U. Maine, Orono, 1957-63, Coll. Notre Dame, Belmont, Calif., 1971, U. Calif., Santa Cruz, 1976; m. Frederick Leroy Robinson, Sept. 19, 1953; children—Dana Lee, Dion Jay. Tchr., Emerson Elem. Sch., Portland, Maine, 1954-56; spl. edn. tchr. North Sch., Portland, 1961-62, Brown Elem. Sch., South Portland, Maine, 1962-64; spl. edn. tchr. John F. Kennedy High Sch., Fremont, Calif., 1965-69, 70-71, dep. head spl. edn. dept., 1970-71, work experience coordinator spl. edn. dept., 1970-71; sect. chmn. Fremont United Sch. Dist. Secondary Level Educable Mentally Retarded Com., 1968-69, mem. com. to develop grading philosophy for secondary level educable mentally retarded pupils, 1968, mem. secondary level educable mentally retarded curriculum guide com., 1968; now tutor spl. edn. South Portland Sch. Dist. Publicity chmn. Tri-City, Am. Cancer Soc., 1973; mem. Fremont Democratic Women's Forum, Fremont, Calif., 1975—, sec., 1976-77, chmn., 1977-79, legis. reporter; mem. steering com. South Alameda County Dem. Hdqrs., Hayward, Calif., 1977-79; mem. Calif. State Dem. Central Com., 1978-80, del. Calif. state conv., 1979, secretarial co-asst. Calif. 25th Assembly Dist. Steering Com., Santa Clara County, Calif., 1980. Mem. Nat. Tchrs. Assn., Vols. in Politics.

ROBINSON, SUSAN, bank exec.; b. 1943; B.A., Duke U., 1964. Tchr., Montgomery County Pub. Schs., Rockville, Md., 1964-68; with Wells Fargo Bank, N.A., 1968—, dir. planning, 1978-80, sr. v.p. planning, 1980-81, sr. v.p. bus. div. retail banking group, 1981—. Bd. dirs. Children's Hosp., San Francisco. Office: Wells Fargo and Co 420 Montgomery St San Francisco CA 94104 *

ROBINSON, VIOLET BAN, educator; b. San Francisco, Sept. 23, 1921; d. Samuel and Helen Ban; B.A., San Francisco State Coll., 1953, M.A., 1958; Ed.D., Stanford U., 1970; m. John Taylor Robinson, Sept. 24, 1960 (dec. 1970). Tchr., Millbrae (Calif.) Elem. Sch. Dist., 1953-54; mem. faculty dept. edn. San Francisco State U., 1954—, lab. sch. tchr., kindergarten and primary grades lab. tchr., 1954-71, asst. prof. elem. edn., 1963-65, asso. prof., 1968-74, prof. elem. edn., 1974—, coordinator early childhood edn., 1975—; cons. to various sch. dists. in Calif., 1970—; asst. prof. edn. Sonoma State Coll., 1971-72. Mem. NEA, Nat. Assn. for Edn. of Young Children, Nat. Council Tchrs. English, Am. Ednl. Research Assn., Internat. Reading Assn. (mem. early childhood com. 1974-75), Calif. Ednl. Research Assn., Calif. Profs. of Reading, Calif. Reading Assn., Calif. Tchrs. Assn., Soc. for Research in Child Devel., Assn. for Childhood Edn. Internat., Calif. Profs. Early Childhood Edn. (mem. governing bd. 1974-77), Assn. Tchr. Educators, East Bay Assn. for Childhood Edn., Jean Piaget Soc., Far Western Philosophy of Edn. Soc., AAAS, Peninsula Assn. for Edn. of Young Children, Central Coast Assn. Tchrs. of English, Calif. Curriculum Forum, Phi Delta Kappa. Democrat. Author: (with Leonard Meshover) The World of Language, Book I, 1970, The World of Language, A Guide and Resource Book, 1970; contbr. chpts. to books on edn. Office: 1600 Holloway Ave San Francisco CA 94132 *

ROBINSON, WILLIE MAE, coll. adminstr.; b. Sapelo Island, Ga., July 7, 1937; d. Charlie Sam and Sarah Jane (Gardner) Hall; B.S., Savannah (Ga.) State Coll., 1973; M.A., U. Chgo., 1976; divorced; children—Reginald J., Cheryl Denise. Mem. adminstrv. staff Savannah State Coll., 1966—, counseling coordinator div. student spl. programs, 1976-77, dir. spl. programs, 1977—; part-time social work tchr., 1981—. Coordinator 2d Dist. Voters Assn., Savannah; chmn. Episcopal Ch. Women, Ch. Periodical Club, Diocese of Ga. Mem. Acad. Cert. Social Workers, Nat. Assn. Social Workers, AAUW, Nat. Assn. Black Social Workers, Southeastern Assn. Ednl. Opportunity Programs Personnel, Ga. Assn. Spl. Programs Personnel, NAACP. Episcopalian. Author research papers in field. Home: 203 E 31st St Savannah GA 31401 Office: Savannah State Coll PO Box 20488 Savannah GA 31404

ROBISON, ALICE MERCEDES, publishing co. exec.; b. Chgo., Sept. 26, 1919; d. Howard Edwin and Mary Lenore (Douthart) Carlson; A.B., U. Chgo., 1941; m. Henry E. Robison, June 19, 1954 (dec.). Editor corp. mags., asst. to adv. mgr. Continental Casualty-Assurance Cos., Chgo., 1941-53; editor Safety Edn. mag. Nat. Safety Council, Chgo., 1953-56; freelance editor, 1956-66; with Trailer Life Pub. Co., Agoura, Calif., 1966—, mng. editor, 1968-73, v.p. editorial dept., 1973—, editorial dir., 1975—, editor-in-chief Book div., 1982—; asso. pub. In-Cruise Network, 1980-81; asso. pub., editor RV Dealer, also Manufactured Housing Dealer, 1980—; speaker to Recreation Vehicle Industry Assn., Recreation Vehicle Dealer Assn., B.C. Recreation Vehicle Dealer Assn., others. Mem. Western Publs. Assn., N.J. Campground Owners Assn. Home: 6430 Shirley Ave Apt 27 Reseda CA 91335 Office: 29901 Agoura Rd Agoura CA 91301

ROBISON, ANN GREEN, educator, columnist; b. N.Y.C., Nov. 19, 1904; d. Boris and Mary Green; B.A., U. Maine, 1924, L.H.D. (hon.), 1975; cert. Woman's Inst., Jewish Theol. Sem. of Am., 1959; M.A., Columbia U., 1936; LL.D. (hon.), U. East Asia, 1982; m. Adolf Robison, Aug. 27, 1928; children—Peter Jordan, Michael Douglas. Tchr. of French, English and drama Mattanawcook Acad., Lincoln, Maine, 1924-25; tchr. French, New Rochelle, N.Y., 1925-38; columnist, 1965—; treas. Robison-Anton Textile Co., Inc., Fairview, N.J., 1949—; v.p. Robison Industries, Fairview, 1966—; frequent interview appearances Sta. NCJW-TV; frequent appearances on For Women Only Show; appeared on John Madigan Talk Show, Chgo., 1972; frequent radio appearances in U.S. and abroad; UN observer in U.S., France and Ger., 1947-52; adviser to U.S. UN Mission, Milan, Italy, 1951. Mem. community adv. council Easter Seal Soc., 1977—; sec. Am. Israel Public Affairs Com., 1973-76; mem. United Way of Bergen County (N.J.), 1981—; chmn. Golden Ball, 1981; sec., nat. v.p. Nat. Jewish Community Relations Adv. Council, 1973-76; chmn. State of Israel Bonds, 1978—; bd. dirs. Community Mus. of Bergen County, 1972—; bd. dirs., chmn. edn. com. YM & YWHA, Bergen County; bd. dirs. Easter Seal Soc. of N.J., 1977—; nat bd. dirs. Jewish Nat. Fund of Am., 1982—; bd. dirs. Am. Lung Assn. of N.J., also chmn. pub. relations long-range planning adv. com., 1975—, v.p., 1972; bd. dirs. United Jewish Community, 1982—, mem. recruitment of Soviet Jews, 1980—; trustee Solomon Schechter Jewish Day Sch., 1982—. Elected to Hall of Fame, Am. Lung Assn., 1980; recipient Honoree award Jewish Nat. Fund, 1981, Citation of Honor, Jewish Nat. Fund, 1968, Medal of Merit, Fairleigh Dickinson U., 1966, Cert. of Achievement, YM-YWHA, 1968, Cert. of Merit, United Jewish Appeal, 1970, Brandeis award Zionist Orgn. of Am., 1972, Solidarity award Israel Bonds, 1978, Merit award NCJW, 1978, Maimonedes award Jewish Fedn. of Bergen County, 1977, fellowship award AAUW, 1970. Mem. Internat. Assn. of U. Pres., Hadassah (Lovers of Peace award 1979, Golden Doorway award 1959), Federated Women's Clubs (chmn. internat. relations 10th dist. 1945), Jewish Newspaper Guild, Synogogue Council Am., Nat. Council of Jewish Women (editorial bd. Jour. 1981—, chmn. nat. com. on internat. affairs 1968-74, chmn. Israel affairs com. 1974-80), Internat. Council of Jewish Women (editor mag. 1969, chmn. public relations com. 1970-72, v.p. 1972-79), Brandeis U. Women's Assn. Republican. Club: Teaneck Coll. Columnist for The Jewish Standard, 1965—; contbr. articles to mags. Home: 554 S Forest Dr Teaneck NJ 07666

ROBISON, BERYL POWERS, county ofcl.; b. Washinton, Mar. 9, 1939; d. Ralph Wilson and Penelope (LeClair) Powers; A.B. in Sociology, Hollins (Va.) Coll., 1961; M.S.W., Portland (Oreg.) State U., 1972; m. Horace Clovis Robison, Jr., Aug. 26, 1961; children—Harrison Gunn, Seth Kerr. Clin. social worker, psychotherapist Longview, Wash., 1970-77; Cowlitz County commr., 1977—, chmn., 1979-81; chmn. Cowlitz Emergency Services Council; exec. com. Cowlitz Econ. Devel. Council; vice chmn. Cowlitz-Wahkiakum Govtl. Conf.; pres. bd. dirs. Displaced Homemakers; mem. regional adv. com. Wash. Dept. Social and Health Services, 1979—; vice chmn. Cowlitz-Wahkiakum Bd. Health, 1979—; Mem. Acad. Cert. Social Workers, Nat. Assn. Counties (human services steering com.). Club: Altrusa. Office: 207 4th Ave N Kelso WA 98626

ROBISON, DIXIE RUTH, savs. and loan assn. exec.; b. Livingston, Tex., Aug. 7, 1931; d. Harry Allen and Mary Lula (Lockhart) Lott; student U. Houston, Tex. Tech. U., Fairfield U.; cert. Inst. Certifying Secs., 1973; diploma Savs. and Loan Sch., 1977, 79; m. Donald Robison, June 3, 1978; children—Peggy Ruth Huddle, Thomas Wade Cummings, Gary Reece Cummings. Various secretarial positions, 1956-76; v.p. Cullen Savs. Assn., Houston, 1976—; adv. bd. Sch. Profl. Studies, U. Houston, Clear Lake City; chmn. vocat. edn. adv. bd. Clear Creek Ind. Sch. Dist. Chmn. bd. mgmt. Bay Area YMCA; bd. dirs. Met. Houston chpt. Nat. Found.-March of Dimes; vice chmn. adv. bd. Bay Area Community Service; adv. trustee United Way Tex. Gulf Coast; mem. Bay Area Symphony League. Named Vol. of Year, YMCA Greater Houston Area, 1979; named Sec. of Yr., Clear Lake chpt. Nat. Secs. Assn., 1972. Mem. Nat. Mgmt. Assn., Women's Council Realtors, Nat. Savs. and Loan League, Tex. Savs. and Loan League, Clear Lake Personnel Assn., Clear Lake C. of C. (chmn. subcom. community devel. div. 1980, pres. 1976). Methodist. Clubs: Bay Area Mil. Wives, Clear Lakes Ladies Golf Assn. Home: 15802 Larkfield St Houston TX 77059 Office: 601 Jefferson Houston TX 77002

ROBISON, PAULA JUDITH, flutist; b. Nashville, June 8, 1941; d. David Victor and Naomi Florence R.; student U. So. Calif., 1958-60; B.S., Juilliard Sch. Music, 1963; m. Scott Nickrenz, Dec. 29, 1971; 1 dau., Elizabeth Hadley Nickrenz. Soloist with various maj. orchs., including N.Y. Philharmonic; mem. Orpheus Trio, 1970—; prin. ann. recital series: Paula and . . ., 1976—; co-dir. chamber music Spoleto Festivals, Charleston, S.C. and Spoleto, Italy; mem. faculty Juilliard Sch. Music. Recipient First prize Geneva Internat. Competition, 1966; named Musician of Month, Musical Am., 1979; Martha Baird Rockefeller grantee, 1966. Mem. Cousteau Soc., Chamber Music Soc. Lincoln Center (founding). Address: care Kazuko-Hillyer Internat Inc 250 W 57th St New York NY 10107 *

ROBLIN, GLORIA LANDSMAN, psychologist; b. N.Y.C., Apr. 29, 1925; d. Benjamin F. and Helen E. (Lehman) Landsman; B.A., Barnard Coll., 1945; M.A., Columbia U., 1947; Ph.D., SUNY, Buffalo, 1963; m. Daniel A. Roblin, Jr., Oct. 3, 1918; children—Diane S. Roblin Finlayson, Daniel A. Asst. prof. U. Va., Richmond, 1946-48; instr. Columbia U., 1948-49; instr. Med. Coll., SUNY, Buffalo, 1963-65, asso., 1965-68, asst. prof., 1968-72, asso. prof., 1972-75, clin. prof., 1975—, research psychologist Research Found., 1973—. Mem. Am. Psychol. Assn., Psychol. Assn. Western N.Y., Religion Studies Center of Canisius Coll., Am. Soc. Clin. Hypnosis, Am. Soc. Clin. and Exptl. Hypnosis, Ont. Soc. Clin. Hypnosis, Soc. Sci. Study Sex, Sigma Xi. Republican. Jewish. Clubs: Buffalo, Westwood, Met. Home: 50 Danbern Ln Williamsville NY 14221 Office: Erie County Medical Center Kannex Ceder St Buffalo NY 14215

ROBSON, LINDA SUE, florist; b. Tulsa, Oct. 31, 1946; d. Earl Shannon and Almanita Dodson; student Northeastern Okla. State U., 1971-74; m. Edward Dodge Robson, Dec. 27, 1971; children—Clint Nicholas, Jarrod Lee. With Shell Oil Co., Tulsa, Tulsa Urban Renewal; mgr. Scholars Inn Apts., Tahlequah, Okla., owner, mgr. Day Care Center, Tahlequah, 1974-76; owner, mgr. Mustard Seed Flower Shop, Tahlequah; now dir. Christian Pre-Sch., Tulsa. Lic. real estate agt. Mem. Bus. Women's Assn., Christian Womens Assn., Beta Sigma Phi (local pres. 1976—). Republican. Home: 7755 E 30th Pl Tulsa OK 74129 Office: PO Box 1427 Tahlequah OK 74464

ROBSON, SHERRY, publishing co. exec.; b. Hollywood, Calif., Sept. 3, 1928; d. Charles and Minerva Eva (New) Sherick; A.A., Pierce Coll., 1960; m. John Whitworth Robson, III, Feb. 14, 1948. Pub. relations and exec. sec. Beaute Vues, Hollywood, Calif., 1960-62; exec. sec. Central Vac, Los Angeles, 1962-64, MTI Bus. Colls. Corp., Hollywood, 1964-71; owner Career Pub. Co., Orange, 1972-74; v.p., sec.-treas. Career Pub., Inc., Orange, 1974—; v.p., sec. Career Ednl. Cons., Inc., Orange, 1974—; owner Career Furniture & Equipment Co., Orange, 1972—; v.p. Career Property & Investment Corp., Orange, 1977—. Mem. Assn. Ind. Colls. and Schs. (hon.), Creative Soc. Home: 2132 Pami Circle Orange CA 92667 Office: PO Box 5486 Orange CA 92667

ROBY, SHIRLEY GREY, dancer, educator; b. Staunton, Va.; d. Roy E. and Irene (Sipe) R.; B.S., Longwood Coll., 1954; M.F.A., U. N.C. at Greensboro, 1958; postgrad. Juilliard Sch. Music, N.Y.C., Conn. Coll. for Women, Sch. Dance, Adelphi U., Calif. State U. at Long Beach. Mem. dance faculty U. Mass., 1958-63; prof. dance Coll. of William and Mary, Williamsburg, Va., 1964—; dance artist-in-residence Project Radius, Ga. Commn. on Arts, summers 1970-72; choreographer 18th Century dances for 18th Century Show, Colonial Williamsburg, 1972—; choreographer, performer CBS-TV spl. A Christmas in Williamsburg, Landmarks in Am., 1970; choreographer Pre-Classic Dance Suite for Arts in the South, 1972, 74, Europe in Colonial Art, Nat. Antiques Forums for Colonial Williamsburg. Mem. Twentieth Century Gallery, Williamsburg, Va. Mus. Fine Arts, Richmond.

ROBY, STEPHANIE LOUISE, pub. co. exec.; b. Columbus, Ohio, Aug. 12, 1948; d. L.L. and Shirley Louise (Wilson) R.; B.A. with high honors in History (Durant scholar), Wellesley Coll., 1970; M.A. (Tchrs. Coll. scholar), Columbia U., 1971; postgrad. U. Pa., 1973. Intern, Columbia U. Tchrs. Coll., 1970-71; tchr. Lakeland High Sch., Shrub Oak, N.Y., 1970-71; club adminstr. N.Y. Wellesley Club, N.Y.C., 1971-73, also dir., 1976-80, treas., 1980-82; editorial asst. Harcourt Brace Jovanovich, N.Y.C., 1973-75; asst. editor Am. Book Co., N.Y.C., 1975-76, asso. editor, 1976-77; editor Prentice-Hall, Englewood Cliffs, N.J., 1977-79, sr. editor, 1979—. Vol. tutor, inner-city schs., N.Y.C., 1971-73; vol. counselor N.Y.C. Mayor's Action Center, 1973-76. Mem. Nat. Council Tchrs. English, Assn. Am. Pubs. Home: 65 E 93d St New York NY 10028 Office: Prentice-Hall Englewood Cliffs NJ 07632

ROCHE, KATHLEEN ANNE, nursing adminstr.; b. Washington, Sept. 25, 1943; d. Frank S. and Catherine (Carter) R.; R.N., Bon Secours Sch. Nursing, 1965; M.A. in Thanatology, Goddard Coll., 1979; Ms.T., Potomac Myotherapy Inst., Washington, 1981. Staff nurse med. unit Holy Cross Hosp., Silver Spring, Md., 1965-66; staff nurse Clin. Center, Nat. Inst. Arthritis and Metabolic Diseases, Bethesda, Md., 1966-68, psychiat. nurse Clin. Center, 1968-76; dir. home health/hospice Church Hosp., Balt., 1979—; lectr. Montgomery Coll., Takoma Park, Md., 1977-79; nursing cons. to Com. to Combat Huntington's Disease, Washington, 1974-76; lectr. various radio and TV programs, 1974—; cons. to Sta. WJLA-TV, 1976-77; lectr. edn. and tng. br. nursing dept. NIH, 1973-76; organizer and coordinator Md. chpt. Make Today Count, 1975—, regional dir., 1978-81, pres. nat. bd. dirs., 1980-81. Vol., Am. Cancer Soc. 1974-76; mem. social concerns com. St. Rose of Lima Cath. Ch., Gaithersburg, Md., 1974-81. Recipient Superior Performance in Nursing award USPHS, 1973, Merit award HEW, 1973, 75. Mem. Forum for Death Edn., Am. Cancer Soc. (Outstanding Service award 1976, dir. 1977—), Washington Hospice Soc., Assn. for Advancement of Ret. Persons, Internat. Meditation Soc., Bon Secours Sch. Nursing Alumnae Assn. Democrat. Roman Catholic. Club: Ladies Aux. Order of Hibernians. Contbr. to Hospice: Complete Care of the Dying, 1981, Death Anxiety in Huntington's Disease. Home: 2811 Baneberry Ct Baltimore MD 21209 Office: Home Health Dept Church Hosp Baltimore MD 21231

ROCHETTO, EVELYN MARIE, state ofcl.; b. Chgo.; d. Lucius J. and Clara M. (Jung) Young; Ph.B., Northwestern U., 1952; m. Paul A. Rochetto, June 9, 1937. Profl. musician, 1930-50; membership sec. Internat. Soc. Gen. Semantics, 1950-55, exec. sec., from 1955, dir., from 1952; now counseling specialist State of Ill. Mem. AAUW (pres. Chgo. br. 1956, 58, 64—, mem. bd. 1953—), Chgo. Story League (pres. 1970—), Am. Legion (dir.), Friends Mentally Ill (pres. 1958—), Alpha Sigma Lambda (dir.). Club: Woman's Univ. (pres. 1966—). Home: 5240 N Sheridan Rd Chicago IL 60640

ROCHFORD, DENISE GALLAGHER, journalist; b. Cleve., Feb. 10, 1940; d. John J. and Marian S. Gallagher; A.B., Notre Dame Coll., Cleve.; postgrad. Cleve. Marshall Law Sch.; m. Joseph P. Rochford, Nov. 17, 1962; children—Megan, Kevin, Terence, Eileen. Advt. copywriter Higbee Co., Cleve., 1961-62; with Fairchild Publs. Co., 1962—, corr. N.E. Ohio for Home Furnishings Daily, 1974-78, Ohio corr., glassware specialist, 1978—; freelance reporter McGaw-Hill News Bur., 1971; writer news and feature stories Sun Newspapers, 1967-74. Mem. Nat. Fedn. Press Women, Ohio Press Women (Writing Distinction award 1974-77), Cleve. Press Club, Sigma Delta Chi. Roman Catholic. Office: Room 504 Euclid Ninth Tower Cleveland OH 44115

ROCHON, SANDRA PALMA, banker; b. Laredo, Tex., Sept. 16, 1947; d. Edward Anthony and Ofelia (Dickinson) Palma; A.A., San Antonio Jr. Coll., 1967. Credit dept. mgr. Del Rio Bank & Trust Co. (Tex.), 1964-71; mgmt. trainee Household Fin. Corp., Silver Spring, Md., 1975; asst. v.p., comml. loan officer Dominion Nat. Bank, Vienna, Va., 1975-79; v.p., compliance officer, collections supr., br. mgr. Town & Country Bank & Trust Co., Falls Church, Va., 1979—. Sec. Reflection Homeowners Assn., 1980-81, pres. 1981—.Mem. Nat. Assn. Bank Women (sec. No. Va. chpt.), Nat. Assn. Female Execs. Office: 7787 Leesburg Pike Falls Church VA 22043

ROCKEFELLER, DORI SELENE, educator; b. Norfolk, Va., Oct. 18, 1942; d. Harry Elmo and Mary (Gibson) Liles; A.B., High Point Coll., 1964; M.Div., Union Theol. Sem., 1970; M.A., Columbia U., 1971, Ed.D. candidate; m. Steven C. Rockefeller, July 30, 1977; 1 dau., Laura Selene. Asst. dir. children's work The Riverside Ch., N.Y.C., 1974-75; elem. tchr. public schs., Mass. and N.Y., 1971-74; asst. prof. edn. SUNY, Plattsburgh, 1975-77; lectr. tchr. edn. Middlebury (Vt.) Coll., 1978—. Trustee, Frog Hollow Craft Center, Middlebury, Wendell Gilley Mus. Southwest Harbor, Maine. Mem. AAUP, History Edn. Soc., Am. Acad. Religion. Episcopalian. Office: Middlebury College 119 Munroe Hall Middlebury VT 05753

ROCKER-BROWN, JACQUELINE, child devel. services exec.; b. Atlanta, Dec. 15, 1946; d. Samuel William and Rheba (Craft) Rocker; B.A., Spelman Coll., 1969; M.A., Howard U., 1974; m. Donald Edward Brown, Nov. 21, 1969; children—Kobie Feather, Njeri Dietrich. Curator, Mus. African Art, Washington, 1969-70; mem. art staff devel. D.C. Public Sch. System, 1970-73; prof. art history Community Coll. of Phila., 1974-78; exec. dir. Newark Pre-School Council, Inc., 1980—; edn. cons., mgmt. cons. human service. Recipient Howard U. teaching fellowship, 1973-74. Mem. Head Start Dirs. Assn., Nat. Head Start Dirs. Assn., Nat. Conf. Artists, Spelman Alumni Assn., Nat. Urban League. Baptist. Office: 300 Chancellor Ave Newark NJ 07112

ROCKEY, RUTH, fin. planner; b. N.Y.C., Mar. 5, 1929; d. Robert and Elizabeth (McFadden) Whiteman; student Bklyn. Coll., 1964-68; M.B.A., Pepperdine U., 1971; C.F.P., Coll. Fin. Planning, 1981; m. Edward H. Rockey, Oct. 23, 1948; children—John, Stephen, Paul. Dir. planning Pepperdine U. Sch. Bus. and Mgmt., Los Angeles, 1972-73, dir. program devel., 1973-74; v.p. mktg. Lawrence Co., Encino, Calif., 1975-76; pres. Ruth Rockey Investments, Inc., Encino, 1976-79; v.p. Fin. Planning Cons., Inc., Westlake Village, Calif., 1980; pres. Rockey Fin. Services Corp., Westlake Village, 1981—; dir. USLIFE Savs. and Loan Assn. Chmn. bd. trustees West Park Hosp. Lic. real estate broker, ins. broker; registered prin. Nat. Assn. Securities Dealers. Mem. Inst. Cert. Fin. Planners, Internat. Assn. Fin. Planners, Pepperdine Assos., Women in Bus. Clubs: North Ranch Country, Westlake Yacht. Home: 1212 B Westlake Blvd Westlake Village CA 91361 Office: 2659 Townsgate Rd #109 Westlake Village CA 91361

ROCKHOLD, LYNN ELIZABETH, graphic artist; b. Dayton, Ohio, Jan. 23, 1951; d. Robert L. and Helen E. (Ebright) Kohler; B.S. in Edn. cum laude, Ohio U., Athens, 1973; m. Herbert C. Rockhold, June 30, 1973. Adminstrv. asst. for divs. EG&G Idaho Co., Idaho Falls, 1974-77, prin. illustrator, supr. graphic arts dept., 1978—; freelance graphic and comml. artist. Recipient award excellence, award merit Soc. Tech. Communicators, 1980-81, nat. award achievement, 1980-81; Best of Category award Idaho Advt. Fedn., 1980-81, Julia Anne Davis award Ohio U., 1972. Mem. Internat. Graphics, Inc. (internat. award merit 1981, 2 hon. mention awards 1982), Phi Upsilon Omicron. Home: 806 10th St Idaho Falls ID 83401

RODANO, EDITH MARY, govt. ofcl.; b. Washington, Nov. 5, 1936; d. Joseph Dominick and Virginia Edythe (Scelzi) R.; 1 son, Joseph V. Sec., U.S. Office of Edn., Washington, 1955-61, program asst., 1961-63; exec. asst. to dean U. Pitts. Faculties in Ecuador, Quito, 1963-65; program control clk. FAA, Washington, 1965-67; secretarial positions Office Sec. Transp., Washington, 1967-73, Fed. R.R. Adminstrn., Washington, 1973-74; secretarial positions Urban Mass Transp. Adminstrn., Washington, 1974-77, program asst., 1977-79, program specialist, 1979-81, EEO counselor, 1981—. Treas., White Oak Flag Football League, 1978-79; tchr. Confrat. Christian Doctrine, St. John the Baptist Catholic Ch., Silver Spring, Md., 1974-77, 79-80, minister to handicapped, 1977-81. Recipient Bronze medal for superior achievement U.S. Dept. Transp., 1981. Mem. Nat. Assn. Female Execs. Roman Catholic. Home: 1318 Canyon Rd Silver Spring MD 20904 Office: Urban Mass Transp Adminstrn 400 7th St SW Washington DC 20590

RODDA, LYNN EDITH, pharmacist; b. Spokane, Wash., May 30, 1942; d. Robert Arthur and Lois Helen (Sylvester) Fisher; student Whitman Coll., 1960-62; B.S., Portland State U., 1964; B.Pharm., Wash. State U., 1977; m. Thomas Cook Rodda, July 6, 1974; children—Paula Ruth, Kabrena Eileen. Tchr. jr. high sci. and math., Beaverton, Oreg., 1964-65, St. Louis Park, Minn., 1965-66, Rochester, Minn., 1966-67; pharmacist Drug Fair, Moscow, Idaho, 1976-78, Pay 'n Save Corp., Fairbanks, Alaska, 1978-80, head pharmacist, 1979-80; staff pharmacist Teamster Health Care Corp., Anchorage, 1980, Pay 'n Save Corp., Anchorage, 1980-81; acting interim asst. dir. pharmacy Providence Hosp., Anchorage, 1981—. Active Anchorage Poison Control Center. Mem. Am. Pharm. Assn., Am. Soc. Hosp. Pharmacists, Alaska Pharm. Assn. (chmn. profl. affairs com.). Republican. Episcopalian. Office: Providence Hosp Pharm 3200 Providence Dr Anchorage AK 99502

RODDEN, DONNA STRICKLAND, mayor; b. Albion, N.Y., Aug. 10, 1926; d. Burroughs A. and Mildred C. (MacDuffie) Strickland; B.S., Syracuse U.; M.S., SUNY, Brockport; postgrad. N.Y. U., U. Toronto, SUNY, Geneseo; children—Roberta Ann Rodden Tundermann, Ellen Christine Rodden Capurso. Editor, Lydonville (N.Y.) Enterprise, 1947-48, Middleport (N.Y.) Herald Tribune, 1948-49; TV dir., N.Y.C., 1949-56; free-lance writer, 1956—; mayor Village of Albion (N.Y.), 1973—. Bd. dirs. Theatre of Performing Arts, Northwestern Frontier Assn. Village Ofcls.; pres., bd. dirs. Orleans County Council on Arts, 1975-77; bd. dirs. Cobblestone Soc., 1976-80, Swan Library Bd.; co-chmn. N.Y. State Concerned Citizens for the Arts, 1976-80; mem. N.Y. State Friendship Force, 1978-80; program chmn. N.Y. State Mental Health Assn.; chmn. bd. Orleans County Mental Hygiene, 1974—. Recipient Disting. Service award Girl Scouts Am., 1973; Woman in Govt. award LWV, 1975; Omega Alpha Presdl. award Jaycees, 1975; medal Kennedy Found., 1975; Citizenship award Am. Legion, 1976. Mem. Internat. Platform Assn., Bus. and Profl. Women's Club (past pres.). Republican. Baptist. Clubs: Abeel Rebakkahs, Order Eastern Star (past matron). Author: High Huckleberry, Case History of a Missouri Farm Boy; The Bear House; composer: You Are My Angel, St. Marys of the Snow, From the Top of the Tower. Office: Village Hall East Bank St Albion NY 14411

RODDY, ARDITH JANINE, retail bldg. supply co. exec., educator; b. Cin., May 8, 1942; d. James Leonard and Wilma Mary (Draper) Hollis; B.Mus.Ed., W.Va. Wesleyan Coll., 1964; student U. Md., 1966; B.S., N.C. Wesleyan Coll., 1978; m. Richard Webster Roddy, Sept. 5, 1964; children—Richard Webster, Erika Lynn. Tchr. various schs., N.C., Va., Md., Fla., 1964-68; office mgr. Lake Gaston Supply Co., Littleton, N.C., 1972—, sec.-treas., 1972—; now also high sch. spl. edn. tchr. Chmn. vols. Vaughan Sch. PTA, 1976, chmn. programs, 1977, sch. vol., 1974—; Brownie leader Pines of Carolina council Girl Scouts U.S.A., 1977-78, leader Girl Scout troop, 1978—, troop organizer, 1977—, chmn. service team, 1981—. Mem. Lake Gaston C. of C., Carolina Lumber and Bldg. Materials Dealers Assn., Alpha Gamma Delta. Republican. Baptist. Club: Rocky Mt. Christian Women's (past chmn.). Office: PO Box 160 Littleton NC 27850

RODE, EMMY MARGUERITE, food distbg. co. exec.; b. Semarang, Indonesia, July 26, 1926; came to U.S., 1957, naturalized, 1962; d. Elie Albert and Dorathea Paulina (Bamberg) Nieuveld; acctg. student Franklin U., Columbus, Ohio, 1962-66; m. Carl Bruno Rode, Feb. 15, 1951 (div. 1972, dec. 1974); children—Carl Andre, James Edward. Sec., Dutch Govt., Dept. Justice, The Hague, 1946, office mgr. Dept. Commerce, Djakarta, Indonesia, 1947-51; office mgr. Singer Sewing Machine Co., Djakarta, 1952-55; sec. Algemeen Dagblad, The Hague, Holland, 1955-57; sec. Lumbermen's Mut. Ins. Co., Columbus, Ohio, 1957-60; acct. Dobson, Kinney & Lindblom, Cons. Engrs., Columbus, 1961-63; corp. treas., dir. adminstrv. services Remarks, Inc., Dublin, Ohio, 1964—. Diana Ekonomen scholar Iota Tau Lambda, 1965. Home: 2786 Clifton Rd Columbus OH 43221 Office: 6728 Hyland-Croy Rd Dublin OH 43017

RODEHEAVER, JANET LITTLE, educator; b. Phila., Nov. 29, 1928; d. William Miles and Beatrice (McCouch) Little; B.S., Fla. State U., 1950; M.Ed., U. Fla., 1967; m. John David Rodeheaver Jr., Nov. 25, 1953; children—Karen Elizabeth, Diane Lynn Rodeheaver Griffin. Med. tech. intern St. Vincents Hosp., Jacksonville, Fla., 1950-51, med. technologist, 1951-52; med. technologist Blood Bank of Dade County, Miami, Fla., 1952-54; tech. dir. John Henry Thomas Meml. Blood Bank, Gainesville, Fla., 1954-56; sr. med. technologist dept. pathology U. Fla., Gainesville, 1957-58, instr. med. technology, 1961-67, asst. prof., 1967—; sr. med. technologist J. Hillis Miller Health Center, Gainesville, 1959-61. Mem. Am. Soc. for Med. Tech., Am. Soc. Allied Health Professions, Fla. Soc. Med. Technologists, Lambda Tau, Alpha Eta. Lutheran. Club: Altrusa. Contbr. articles to profl. jours. Office: University of Florida PO Box J-194 Gainesville FL 32610

RODGERS, AUDREY PENN, mcpl. ofcl.; b. Berkeley, Calif., Aug. 8, 1923; d. Lewis and Edith Penn; A.B., U. Calif., Berkeley, 1944; m. David Leigh Rodgers, June 13, 1943; children—Timothy Leigh, Janice Leigh Rodgers Bracken. Research asst. U. Rochester (N.Y.) Sch. Medicine, 1943-46, 49-51, NIH, Bethesda, Md., 1948-49; design/cons. landscaping pvt. homes and gardens, 1960-69; pres. Campaign Data Service, Inc., San Francisco, 1970-80; public info. dir. East Bay Infiltration/Inflow Study, San Francisco, 1980—. Mem. San Francisco Charter Revision Com., 1968-70; chmn. design group Seward St. Park Task Force, Eureka Valley Promotion Assn., 1970-73; chmn. Dolores Hts. Spl. Use Dist. Com., 1978-80; bd. dirs. The Urban Sch., 1968-69, Dolores Hts. Improvement Club, 1962-64, San Francisco Planning and Urban Research Assn., 1968-78. Mem. LWV (dir. San Francisco 1966-67), Acad. Polit. Sci.,

Public Relations Soc. Am. (accredited), Orgn. Women in Landscape, Sierra Club, People for Open Space, Alpha Xi Delta. Democrat. Club: Met. Office: PO Box 24055 care EBMUW Oakland CA 94623

RODGERS, AUDREY TROPAUER, educator; b. N.Y.C., May 21, 1923; d. David and Rebecca Tropauer; B.A., Hunter Coll., 1945; M.A., Pa. State U., 1953, Ph.D., 1967; m. Allan L. Rodgers, May 14, 1944; 1 son, Peter. Corr. VA, N.Y.C., 1945-46; teaching asst. U. Wis.-Madison, 1946-48; instr. Pa. State U., University Park, 1956-67, asso. prof. English, 1974—, coordinator Women's Studies program, 1979—; prof. Associazione per gli Studi Americani, Genoa, 1955-56, Rome, 1960-61. Inst. Arts and Humanistic Studies grantee Pa. State U., 1972-80, Liberal Arts Central Fund for Research grantee, 1970-79. Mem. Pa. State U. Commn. for Women. Democrat. Club: Hadassah. Author: The Universal Drum: Dance Imagery in the Poetry of Eliot, Crane, Roethke & Williams, 1979; contbr. book reviews, chpts. to books and articles to publs. Home: 641 Glenn Rd State College PA 16801 Office: Pa State Univ English Dept University Park PA 16802

RODGERS, NANCY LUCILLE, businesswoman; b. Denver, Aug. 22, 1934; d. Francis Randolph and Irma Lucille (Budy) Baker; student public schs.; m. George J. Rodgers, Feb. 18, 1968; children by previous marriage—Kellie Rae, Joy Lynn, Timothy Francis, Thomas Francis. Mgr., Western Telearm, Inc., San Diego, 1973—; pres. Rodgers Police Patrol, Inc., San Diego, 1973—; br. mgr. Honeywell Inc., Protection Services div., San Diego, 1977-79; pres. Image, Inc., Image Travel Agy., Cairo, Egypt, 1981—, Western Solar Specialties, 1979-80; founder, pres. Internat. Metaphysicians Associated for Growth through Edn., San Diego, 1979; cons., mem. speakers' bur. MOVE, Profl. Women's Center. Bd. dirs. Central City Assn. Mem. Am. Soc. Indsl. Security Assn., Western Burglar and Fire Alarm Assn., Nat. Burglar and Fire Alarm Assn., Calif. Assn. Lic. Investigators, Sales and Mktg. Execs. Internat., Am. Soc. Women Execs., Nat. Assn. for Holistic Health, Profl. Women's Assn., Apt. Rental and Owners Assn., Am. Bus. Women's Assn., Am. Union Metaphysicians, Nat. Assn. Women Contractors. Republican. Clubs: San Diego Yacht, Soroptimist Internat. Home and office: 4734 E Crystal Ln Paradise Valley AZ 85253

RODIGER, GEORGIANA GLENN, psychotherapist; b. Cambridge, Mass., Feb. 11, 1931; d. C. Leslie and Georgiana (Sibley) Glenn; B.A., Pomona Coll., 1952; postgrad. George Washington U., 1951, U. So. Calif., 1953; M.A., Fuller Theol. Sem., 1975; Ph.D., Fuller Grad. Sch. Psychology, 1980; m. William B. Rodiger, Jan. 31, 1953, (div. 1976); children—Georgiana, William B., James, Margaret, John. Field dir. Pasadena Area Girl Scouts U.S.A., 1952-53; developmental disabilities cons., trainer, research asst. Bur. Training and Manpower Devel. Sect., Calif. Dept. Health, Sacramento, 1973-76, psychol. asst., 1977-79; intern psychiat. div. Children's Hosp., 1978-80, trainer hospice vols., 1978-79; psychotherapist in pvt. practice, exec. dir. Georgiana Rodiger Center, Pasadena, 1980—; cons. Pasadena Unified Sch. Dist., 1979-81; faculty Pacific Oaks Coll., 1980—, Fuller Grad. Sch. Psychology, 1975-80. Co-founder, Hospice of Pasadena, 1979, Candlelighters, 1981; adv. for sr. high youth All Saints Ch., Pasadena, 1981; adv. Women in the Middle, 1981, Anorexic Bulemic Group, 1981—; active United Way, PTA, Vis. Nurse Assn., others. Recipient Nat. award, United Community Funds and Councils of Am., 1968; Newton D. Baker Cert. of Recognition. Mem. Am. Psychol. Assn. Episcopalian. Club: Pasadena Jr. League. Home: 1102 Arden Rd Pasadena CA 91101 Office: 54 N Oakland Ave Pasadena CA 91101

RODIN, JUDITH SEITZ, psychologist, educator; b. Phila., Sept. 9, 1944; d. Morris and Sally R. (Winson) Seitz; A.B., U. Pa., 1966; Ph.D., Columbia U., 1970; m. Nicholas Niejelow, Feb. 12, 1978. Asst. prof. psychology N.Y. U., N.Y.C., 1970-72; asso. prof. Yale U., 1973-78, prof., dir. grad. studies, 1979—. Woodrow Wilson fellow, 1966-68; NSF grantee, 1975—. Fellow Am. Psychol. Assn. (mem. bd. sci. affairs 1979-82); mem. AAAS, Soc. Psychol. and Social Issues, Soc. Exptl. Social Psychology, Eastern Psychol. Assn. (exec. bd. 1980—, pres. 1982), Phi Beta Kappa, Sigma Xi. Author: (with S. Schachter) Obese Humans and Rats, 1974; Exploding the Obesity Myths, 1980. Editor: Appetite Jour., 1979—. Contbr. articles to profl. jours. Office: Yale U Box 11A Yale Station New Haven CT 06520

RODINO, ELAINE ANN, psychologist; b. N.Y.C., Apr. 16, 1940; d. Americo Joseph and Rachel (Cafiero) Lamberti; B.S. cum laude, C.W. Post Coll., L.I. U., 1961; M.A., Hofstra U., 1963; Ph.D., Calif. Sch. Profl. Psychology, 1978; m. Robert J. Rodino, July 3, 1965; 1 dau., Michelle Lynn. Sch. psychologist Long Beach (N.Y.) City Sch. Dist., 1964-67, 70-71, Roslyn (N.Y.) Sch. Dist., 1971-76, Gt. Neck (N.Y.) Sch. Dist., 1973-75; mem. supervisory staff Center for Legal Psychiatry, Santa Monica, Calif., 1978—; pvt. practice clin. psychology, Santa Monica, 1978—; psychologist Los Angeles Suicide Prevention Center, 1978—; psychologist, clin. dir., 1982—; mem. Calif. Task Force on Positive Parenting, 1978-79. Mem. Los Angeles County Psychol. Assn. (pres. 1983), Am. Psychol. Assn., Calif. State Psychol. Assn., Western Psychol. Assn., Am. Assn. Suicidology, Pi Gamma Mu, Psi Chi. Office: 233 Wilshire Blvd Suite 910 Santa Monica CA 90401

RODMAN, SANDRA HUDLOW, found. exec., b. Arlington, Tex., Oct. 1, 1942; d. Paul Bennett and Sadie (Reedy) Hudlow; student U. Tex., 1961-67; Baylor U., 1963; m. Thomas J. Rodman, Oct. 7, 1967 (div.). Founding mem. Phoenix House Found., N.Y.C., exec. asst. to sr. v.p., 1973-79, bus. officer, Santa Ana, Calif., 1979-81; dir. adminstrn., officer devel. corp. Phoenix Found., N.Y.C., 1981—; cons. to pres. Strategic Learning Systems, N.Y.C., 1981—; mem. N.Y. State Drug Abuse Task Force Fin. Stability, Albany, 1977; chmn. Nat. Therapeutic Communities Task Force on Program/Planning, 1981—; asst. instr. Phoenix Inst. Fin. Mgmt., 1978. Bd. trustees Potter's Field Theatre Co., N.Y.C., 1981—, chmn. fund raising com., 1981—. Recipient Best Actress Award, U. Tex., 1967. Mem. Nat. Assn. Female Execs., World Fedn. Therapeutic Communities, Phi Kappa Phi, Alpha Lambda Delta. Playwright: The Mullions, 1966; Cosmic Cowboys, 1979. Office: 164 W 74th St New York NY 10023

RODMANN, DOROTHY ELLEN, assn. adminstr.; b. Washington, Feb. 1, 1930; d. Michael Albert and Georgie Rebecca (Stant) Peters; B.A., George Washington U., 1954, postgrad., 1954-55; m. Horst Rodmann, June 7, 1958; children—Leslie Ann, Karen Lynn. Adminstr. asst. Am. Polit. Sci. Assn., Washington, 1954-58; personnel asst. NEA, Washington, 1959-69, personnel asso., 1969-71, employment mgr., 1971-72; personnel mgr. Nat. League Cities-U.S. Conf. of Mayors, Washington, 1972-76; personnel dir. Am. Chem. Soc., 1977—. Mem. Washington Personnel Assn. Conf. Instl. Adminstrs., Alpha Delta Pi. Club: Arminius Social (Washington). Home: 8428 Georgian Way Annandale VA 22003 Office: 1155 16th St NW Washington DC 20036

RODRIGUES, LILLIAN ISABELLE, dental nurse; b. Oakland, Calif., July 7, 1951; d. Sidoro Carvalho and Alvira Angeline (Santiago) Rodrigues; A.A., Chabot Coll., 1972. Clin. asst. Oaknoll Naval Base, Oakland, Calif., 1973-74; clin. surg. nurse Paul B. Menges, D.D.S., Castro Valley, Calif., 1974-75; clin. nurse, adminstrv. mgr. Charles M. Fischer, D.D.S., San Ramon, Calif., 1975-82, dir., coordinator dental arts edn., 1975—. Mem. ADA, Dental Arts Edn. Assn. Democrat. Roman Catholic. Home: 20227 Santa Maria St Castro Valley CA 94546 Office: 9260 Alcosta Blvd San Ramon CA 94583

RODRIGUEZ, ANA MERCEDES, legis. asst.; b. San Juan, P.R., June 29, 1952; d. Isaias Rodriguez-Moreno and Hilda M. Rodriguez; B.A. in History, Trinity Coll., 1973; J.D., George Washington U., 1976. Admitted to D.C. bar, 1978; staff asst. Sen. Edward M. Kennedy, Washington, 1969-76; legis. asst. Congressman Baltasar Corrada, Washington, 1977—. Mem. D.C. Bar, D.C. Bar Assn., Fed. Bar Assn., George Washington Law Alumni Assn. Democrat. Roman Catholic. Office: 1410 Longworth House Office Bldg Washington DC 20515

RODRIGUEZ, BONNIE JEANNE, trade assn. exec.; b. Harlingen, Tex., Oct. 2, 1928; d. Stephen Pruitt and Drue Hazel (Hatfield) Rogers; B.S. in Edn., Wilson Tchrs. Coll., 1951; m. Angelo J. Rodriguez, May 3, 1960; children—Paul M., Kathleen A. Partner, So. Star Constrn. Co., Venezuela, 1952-59; librarian, adminstrv. asst. legis, research dept. Nat. Rural Electric Co-op Assn, Washington, 1960-66; adminstrv. asst., sr. v.p. govt. affairs Direct Mail Mktg. Assn., N.Y.C., 1971-73, adminstr. ethics, 1972-78, dir. info. central, 1973-78, dir. spl. interest councils, 1978-82, v.p. new product devel., 1982—; lectr. in field. Mem. N.Y. Soc. Assn. Execs., Am. Soc. Assn. Execs., Women's Direct Response Group, Product Devel. and Mgmt. Assn. Democrat. Lutheran. Club: 100 Million. Editor, Direct Mail Mktg. Assn. Fact Book on Direct Response Marketing, 1978. Home: 315 E 86th St Apt 4D/E New York City NY 10028 Office: 6 E 43rd St New York City NY 10017

RODRIGUEZ, SALLIE ANN, mfg. co. ofcl.; b. Highland Park, Mich., May 30, 1947; d. Robert Gilbert and Ruth Mary (Brown) Domke; B.S. in Bus. Edn., Central Mich. U., 1970; M.B.A., U. Detroit, 1975; m. Reynel Rodriguez, Nov. 7, 1970; children—Heather, Holly. Instr., Detroit Bus. Inst., 1971-75; staff cons. Learson Assos., Detroit, 1975-76; compensation analyst, employment rep. Diamond Shamrock Corp., Cleve., 1976-78; mgr. salary and benefits J. Ray McDermott, Babcock & Wilcox, Bloomfield Hills, Mich., 1978-81; gen. compensation mgr. Massey-Ferguson, Detroit, 1981—; owner Glouster Gallery, Inc., Farmington Hills, Mich. Mem. Am. Compensation Assn. (cert.), Salary Adminstrn. Council, Am. Soc. Personnel Adminstrn., Am. Soc. Tng. and Devel., Assn. M.B.A. Execs. Home: 31767 Thirteen Mile Rd Farmington Hills MI 48018 Office: PO Box 322 Detroit MI 48232

RODVIEN, CAROLE FRANCES, clin. psychologist; b. N.Y.C., Jan. 31, 1939; d. Abraham and Dorothy (Friedman) Rodvien; M.S., CCNY, 1965; Ph.D., U. Mass., 1968; M.P.H., Johns Hopkins U., 1972. Asst. prof. psychiatry and pediatrics Johns Hopkins Hosp., Balt., 1969-73; coordinator child and adolescent services Shiawassee County Community Mental Health Center, Owosso, Mich., 1973-76; psychologist Taylor Manor Hosp., Ellicott City, Md., 1977-78; sr. psychologist State of Md., 1978-81; pvt. practice psychology, 1969—. Lic. psychologist, Md., Mich.; lic. marriage counselor, Mich., Va. Mem. Am. Psychol. Assn., Md. Psychol. Assn., Am. Orthopsychiat. Assn., Nat. Register Health Care Providers in Psychology, Johns Hopkins U. Alumni Soc. Jewish. Home: 76 Shetland Circle Reisterstorm MD 21136

ROE, DONNA JENSEN, former found. exec.; b. Akron, Ohio, Nov. 22, 1930; d. John Davidson and Helen Graves (Shipley) Miller; student Kent State U., 1949-51; C.P.S., Ariz. State U., 1962; A.A., Phoenix Coll., 1974; postgrad. Grad. Sch. Bus., U. Wis.-Madison, 1980; m. Robert B. Roe, July 5, 1975 (dec.); children—Pamela, Christopher. Community, communication specialist Sperry Flight Systems, Phoenix, 1957-76; appointments sec. Gov. Wesley Bolin, State of Ariz., Phoenix, 1977-78; corr. sec. Gov. Bruce Babbitt, State of Ariz., Phoenix, 1978; asst. to dir. Ariz. Dept. Econ. Security, Phoenix, 1978-79; asst. exec. dir. Samaritan Med. Found., Phoenix, 1979-82. Mem. exec. bd. Theodore Roosevelt Council, Inc. Boy Scouts Am., 1977—; bd. dirs. Phoenix Arts Coming Together, 1981; trustee Camelback Hosp. Found., 1982. Mem. Nat. Assn. Hosp. Devel., Nat. Soc. Fund Raising Execs., Internat. Assn. Bus. Communicators, Women in Communications, Inc., Phoenix Art Mus. League, Phoenix Symphony Guild. Repbulican. Presbyterian. Home: 77 E Missouri Ave Phoenix AZ 85012

ROEBLING, MARY G., banker; b. West Collingwood, N.J.; d. I.D. and Mary W. (Simon) Gindhart; student U. Pa., N.Y. U.; LL.D. (hon.), Ithaca Coll., 1954; D.S. in Bus. Adminstrn. (hon.), Bryant Coll.; D.Sc. (hon.), Muhlenberg Coll.; H.H.D. (hon.), Wilberforce U.; D.F.A. (hon.), Rider Coll.; D.C.S. (hon.), St. John's U.; m. Siegfried Roebling (dec.); children—Elizabeth (Mrs. David J. Hobin), Paul. Chmn. bd. Nat. State Bank, Trenton, N.J., Women's Bank, Denver; dir. Companion Life Ins. Co., Tattersall Co., Trenton. Bd. trustees Center for the Study of the Presidency; founding pres. Mercer County Community Coll. Found.; mem. nat. bd. USO; mem. adv. bd. Nat. Multiple Sclerosis Soc.; hon. mem. nat. council Boy Scouts Am., founding pres. Army War Coll. Found., Inc.; mem. adv. bd. Assn. U.S. Army; life trustee George C. Marshall Research Found., N.J. Dental Service Plan; mem. council on N.J. affairs Woodrow Wilson Sch. Public and Internat. Affairs; mem. Citizens Adv. Com. on Armed Services Tng. Installations, 1950; mem. 4th dist. Adv. Council on Naval Affairs; emeritus mem. Def. Adv. Com. on Women in the Services. Recipient Outstanding Civilian Service medal Dept. Army, 1969; Pres.'s medal Assn. U.S. Army; Disting. Service award U.S. Marine Corps League; Eisenhower Prayer award U.S. Savs. Bond; Brotherhood award N.J. Conf. Christians and Jews; Gen. William Booth Humanitarian award Salvation Army; Jerusalem Holy City of Peace award State of Israel; Americanism award Anti-defamation League B'nai B'rith; George Washington Honor medal Freedoms Found. Valley Forge; Woman of Yr. award Phila. Bus. Club, 1975; Golden Key award N.Y. Fedn. Jewish Charities; Spirit of Achievement award Women's div. Einstein Med. Coll.; Bus. Statesman of Yr. award Sales Exec. Club N.J., 1970; Humanitarian award N.J. chpt. Nat. Arthritis Found., 1970; Citizenship award Allied Citizens Com. Trenton; and numerous other awards. Mem. Internat. C. of C. (trustee U.S. council), Phila. C. of C., Greater Trenton C. of C., Am. Bankers Assn., Am. Inst. Banking, N.J. Bankers Assn., Nat. Assn. Bank Women, LWV, Soc. Mayflower Descendents, DAR, Colonial Daus. 17th Century, New Eng. Women, Pilgrim John Howland Soc., Daus. Colonial Wars, Am. Swedish Hist. Found. Clubs: Seaview Country (Absecon, N.J.); 1925 F Street (Washington); Trenton Country, Contemporary. Office: National State Bank Trenton NJ 08605

ROEBUCK, BETTY JEAN, med. technologist; b. Shreveport, La., Feb. 2, 1937; d. Matthew Mack and Maggie B. (Robinson) Kellum; A.S. in Biology, Wilson Jr. Coll., 1956; B.S., Roosevelt U., 1961; M.T., Mt. Sinai Sch. Med. Tech., 1958; m. Donald Roebuck, June 20, 1980; children by previous marriage—Stephanie E. Woodson, Carter M. Woodson. Med. technologist Mt. Sinai Hosp., Chgo., 1957-58; sr. hematologist technologist Mercy Hosp. and Med. Center, Chgo., 1961-67, supr. hematology sect., 1967-75, dept. head hematology pathologist, 1975—; liaison instr. med. tech. U. Ill., 1980-82; mem. hematology coagulation rev. for med. hematology technologist program Central YMCA Coll., 1981-82; lectr. in field. Sunday sch. tchr. St. James A.M.E. Ch., 1975-80. Acad. Edn1. scholar, So. U., Baton Rouge, 1954-55. Mem. Am. Soc. Clin. Pathologists, Am. Soc. Med. Technologists. Democrat. Club: Nursing-Laboritorium Liaison. Contbr. articles to profl. jours. Home: 9600 S Indiana Ave Chicago IL 60628 Office: 2537 S Indiana Ave Chicago IL 60616

ROEDDER, DEBORAH LYNNE, educator; b. St. Louis, Aug. 24, 1952; d. Charles George and Ruth Helen (Buchanan) R.; B.S.B.A. summa cum laude, St. Louis U., 1974; M.B.A., Kent State U., 1976; Ph.D., Northwestern U., 1980. Teaching fellow Kent (Ohio) State U., 1975-76; instr. Northwestern U., Evanston, Ill., 1979-80; asst. prof. Grad. Sch. Mgmt. UCLA, 1980-82, asst. prof. Grad. Sch. Bus., U. Wis., Madison, 1982—; cons. in field. Recipient doctoral dissertation award, Am. Psychol. Assn., 1981; Am. Mktg. Assn. doctoral dissertation grantee, 1978; Kent State U. grad. fellow, 1974-75; Northwestern U. grad. fellow, 1976-79. Mem. Am. Mktg. Assn., Assn. for Consumer Research, Alpha Sigma Nu, Beta Gamma Sigma. Contbr. articles to profl. jours. Office: 1155 Observatory Dr Madison WI 53706

ROEHM, MARYANNE EVANS, nurse, univ. dean; b. Vigo County, Ind., Nov. 29, 1925; d. Herbert Elmer and Reba Fern Evans; diploma Union Hosp. Sch. Nursing, 1946; B.S., Ind. State U., 1953, M.S., 1957; M.S.N., Ind. U., 1965, Ed.D., 1966; m. Joseph L. Roehm, Aug. 10, 1947. Instr. and asst. dir. Union Hosp. Sch. Nursing, Terre Haute, Ind., 1946-55; asso. dir. edn. St. Anthony Hosp. Sch. Nursing, Terre Haute, 1957-64; asst. prof., then asso. prof. Ind. State U. Sch. Nursing, Terre Haute, 1966-70, dir. continuing edn., 1970-77, interim dean and dir. continuing edn., 1977-78, dean, 1978—; mem. Ind. State Bd. Nurses Registration and Nursing Edn., 1978-81, pres., 1980-81; mem. adv. com. Master's Degree program Ind. U. Sch. Nursing, 1981; mem. adv. com. hypertension project Vigo County Health Dept., 1981; mem. health occupations adv. com. Ind. Vocat. Tech. Coll., 1970—; mem. tech. adv. panel Ind. Commn. Higher Edn., 1979-80; mem. Ind. Council Baccalaureate and Higher Degree Deans and Dirs., Ind. Council Asso. Degree Deans and Dirs.; mem. adv. com. pediatric nurses asso. program Ind. U. Sch. Nursing, 1972-78; numerous workshops and confs. Mem. Vigo County Blood Donor Council, 1980; mem. community adv. council Terre Haute Center for Med. Edn. at Ind. State U., 1977—; mem. Vigo County Home Citizens Com., 1970—; vice-precinct committeeman; active ARC, Baptist Ch., CD, Am. Heart Assn. Named Nurse of Yr., Ind. Citizens League Nursing, 1978; cert. of recognition Ind. State Nurses Assn., 1977. Mem. Am. Nurses Assn. (council continuing edn.), Ind. Nurses Assn., Nat. League Nursing, Ind. League Nursing, AAUP, Am. Assn. Higher Edn., Ind. Health Careers (dir.), Am. Assn. Collegiate Deans, Midwest Alliance Nursing, Ind. U. Alumni Assn., Ind. State U. Alumni Assn., Union Hosp. Sch. Nursing Alumni Assn., Pi Lambda Theta, Sigma Theta Tau, Kappa Delta Pi, Phi Kappa Phi. Club: Altrusa. Republican. Asso. editor Nursing Digest, 1973-75; contbr. articles to profl. jours. Home: Rural Route 22 Box 561 Terre Haute IN 47802 Office: 8th and Chestnut Sts Terre Haute IN 47809

ROELKER, NANCY LYMAN, educator; b. Warwick, R.I., June 15, 1915; d. William Greene and Anna R. (Koues) Roelker; A.B., Radcliffe Coll., 1936; Ph.D., Harvard U., 1953. Tchr. history Winsor Sch., Boston, 1941-63; asst. prof. history Tufts U., 1963-65, asso. prof., 1965-69, prof., 1969-71; prof. European history Boston U., 1971-80; adj. prof. Brown U., 1979—. John Simon Guggenheim fellow, 1965-66; recipient medal for disting. achievement Radcliffe Coll., 1970. Mem. Am. Hist. Assn., (v.p. research div. 1975-78, chmn. internat. activities com., U.S. del. to Internat. Congress Hist. Scis. 1982—), Soc. French Hist. Studies (pres. 1977-78), Am. Soc. Reformation Research, Am. Acad. Arts and Sci. Author: The Paris of Henry of Navarre, 1958; Editor, translator In Search of France, 1963, From Wilson to Roosevelt: American Foreign Policy 1913-1945, 1963; Queen of Navarre, Jeanne d'Albret, 1528-1572, 1968. Contbr. articles to profl. jours. Home: 777 Love Ln East Greenwich RI 02818 Office: 226 Bay State Rd Boston MA 02215

ROESCHLAUB, JEAN (MARIAN) CLINTON, restaurant chain exec.; b. Berkeley, Calif., June 1, 1927; d. Clifford E. and Nelda M. (Patterson) Clinton; A.A., Stephens Coll., 1944; m. David J. Davis III, June 26, 1946 (dec. 1963); children—David J. Davis IV, Diane Davis Clardy, Bruce Clinton Davis; m. 2d, Ronald Curtis Roeschlaub, Jan. 9, 1965; 1 son, Ronald W. Civilian cons. on loan to Q.M. Gen., 1944-45; co-owner, dir. foods, v.p. Clinton's Restaurants, Inc., operators Clinton's Cafeterias, Los Angeles, 1944—; dir. Glendale Fed. Savs. and Loan Assn. Chmn. bd. curators Stephens Coll.; bd. dirs., mem. exec. com. Assistance League of So. Calif.; mem. aux. bd. Braille Inst. Am., Los Angeles. Mem. Nat. Restaurant Assn., Calif. State Restaurant Assn. Republican. Presbyterian. Clubs: Orphanage Guild, Los Angeles Country, Los Angeles Athletic. Home: 5005 Los Feliz Blvd Los Angeles CA 90027 Office: 515 W 7th St Los Angeles CA 90014

ROESKE, MARILYN HATLEY, univ. adminstr.; b. Chgo., Oct. 3, 1949; d. William Martin and Charlotte Lorraine (Hedin) Hatley; student U. Ill., 1967-70; B.F.A., Drake U., 1979. Fashion artist Younker Bros., Des Moines, 1970-71; art dir. Distinctive Packaging Co., Des Moines, 1971-73; graphic designer Graphic Corp., Des Moines, 1974; asso. dir. univ. relations Drake U., Des Moines, 1974—; free-lance graphic design, 1972—. Recipient Silver award Art Dirs. Assn. Iowa, 1974, Spl. Merit award 1977, award of Excellence (2), 1982; 1st pl. award (2) Iowa Advt. Fedn., 1975, 1st pl. award (4), 1976. Mem. Council for Support and Advancement Edn. (dist. award 1976; nat. publs. com. 1980-82), Art Dirs. Assn. Iowa (Outstanding Achievement award 1976), Univ. and Coll. Designers Assn., Pi Beta Phi Alumni Orgn. Republican. Presbyterian. Home: 700 S 32d Ct Des Moines IA 50265 Office: 1166 27th St Des Moines IA 50311

ROGALIN, WILMA CLARE SIVERTSEN (MRS. JOHN A. ROGALIN), ret. personnel services coordinator, polit. worker; b. Mpls., Dec. 7, 1916; d. Ivar and Clare (Wilmes) Sivertsen; B.S., U. Minn., 1937; M.A., Columbia, 1944; m. John A. Rogalin, Apr. 24, 1962. Personnel mgr. Pan Am. World Airways, N.Y.C., 1942-73, sr. mgr. women's opportunities, 1973-78, dir. personnel services, Rockleigh, N.J., 1978-81. Mem. nat. laywomen's com. Nat. Council Chs. of Christ in U.S.A., 1952-55; chmn. employee contbns. Salvation Army, Queens, N.Y., 1961-62; mem. N.Y. State Women's Council; mem. Def. Adv. Com. for Women in Services, chmn., 1974. Chmn. bd. dirs. N.Y. Young Women's Republican Club, 1947-48; pres. Young Women's Rep. Club N.Y.C., 1948-50; v.p. Assn. N.Y. State young Rep. Clubs, 1950-52; treas. Fedn. Women's Rep. Clubs N.Y. State, 1950-52, 1st v.p., 1952-54, pres., 1959-70; v.p. region 2 Nat. Fedn. Young Rep. Clubs, 1950-55; pres. N.Y.C. Rep. Bus. Women, 1953-55; assoc. leader 9th Assembly Dist., N.Y. County Rep. Club, 1953-57, 58-59; vice chmn. N.Y. State Rep. Com., 1959-70; bd. dirs. Women's Nat. Rep. Club, 1959-65, 68-71; del., platform com. Rep. Nat. Conv., 1960, 64, 68. Bd. dirs. Queens YWCA, 1945-48, N.Y.C. Vis. Nurses, 1971—. Mem. N.Y. Personnel Mgmt. Assn., N.Y. Airlines Personnel Mgrs. Assn. (sec. 1958), U. Minn. Alumni of N.Y. (pres. 1953-54), Kappa Alpha Theta. Presbyn. Coauthor: Women's Guide to Management Positions. Home: Cedar Hill Ln Pound Ridge NY 10576

ROGALSKI, ADRIENNE ALICE, cell biologist; b. Chgo., Aug. 2, 1953; d. Edward Joseph and Viola Veronica (Komen) R.; B.A., U. Chgo., 1975; Ph.D., U. Ill., 1981. Sr. research technician U. Chgo., 1975-76; research asst., Univ. fellow U. Ill., 1976-81; NIH fellow U. Calif., San Diego, 1981—. Mem. Am. Soc. Cell Biology, AAAS, Sigma Xi. Office: University of California-San Diego Dept Biology B-022 La Jolla CA 92093

ROGALSKI, LOIS ANN, speech and lang. pathologist; b. Bklyn., Dec. 17, 1947; d. Louis J. and Filomena Evelyn (Maro) Giordano; B.A., Bklyn. Coll., 1968; M.A., U. Mass., 1969; Ph.D., N.Y. U., 1975; m. Stephen James Rogalski, June 27, 1970; children—Keri Anne, Stefan Louis. Speech and lang. pathologist Rehab. Center of So. Fairfield County, Stamford, Conn., 1969, Sch. Health Program-P.A. 481, Stamford, 1969-72; pvt. practice speech and lang. pathology, Scarsdale, N.Y., 1972—; cons. Bd. Coop. Ednl. Services, 1976-79, Handicapped Program for Preschoolers for Alcott Montessori Sch., Ardsley, N.Y., 1978—;

research methodologist Burke Rehab. Center, 1977. Mem. profl. adv. bd. Found. for Children with Learning Disabilities, 1978—. Lic. speech and lang. pathologist, N.Y. State; Rehab. Services Adminstrn. fellow, 1968-69; N.Y. Med. Coll. fellow, 1972-75. Mem. N.Y. Speech and Hearing Assn., Westchester Speech and Hearing Assn., Am. Speech, Hearing and Lang. Assn. (cert. clin. competence), Council for Exceptional Children, Assn. on Mental Deficiency, Am. Acad. Pvt. Practice in Speech Pathology and Audiology, Internat. Assn. Logopedics and Phoniatrics, Sigma Alpha Eta. Contbr. articles to profl. jours. Office: Scarsdale Med Arts Bldg 340 Ardsley Rd Scarsdale NY 10583

ROGEL, CAROLE ROSE, educator; b. Cleve., Jan. 30, 1939; d. John N. and Rose T. Rogel; B.A., Western Res. U., 1960; M.A., Columbia U., 1961, cert. East Central European Inst., 1962, Ph.D., 1966; m. Philip Poirier, June 8, 1968. Instr. history Ohio State U., 1968-71, asst. prof., 1971-82, asso. prof., 1982—. Mem. Am. Hist. Assn., Am. Assn. Advancement Slavic Studies, Am. Southeast European Studies Assn. (v.p. 1980, pres. 1981), Soc. Slovene Studies, Phi Beta Kappa. Author: The Slovenes and Yugoslavism, 1890-1914, 1977; contbr. in field. Office: Dept History Ohio State U Columbus OH 43210

ROGELL, IRMA ROSE, harpsichordist; b. Malden, Mass.; d. M. Edward and Sara (Freedman) Rose; A.B., Radcliffe Coll.; student Wanda Lankowska; m. Bernard C. Rogell (dec. 1964); children—Gerald, Gillian, Michael. Profl. debut Boston Jordan Hall, 1960; N.Y. debut, 1961; soloist with symphony orchs. including: Boston Symphony Orch., Brazil Symphony; European concert tours; radio-TV appearances; rec. artist; mem. faculty CUNY, 1973-78, Ethical Culture Sch. of N.Y.; guest lectr.-recitalist at various colls. and univs. Mem. Coll. Music Soc., Piano Tchrs. Congress N.Y. (sec.). Jewish. Club: Harvard (N.Y.C.). Home and Studio: 165 West End Ave New York NY 10023

ROGERS, AILENE KANE, educator; b. Jamaica, N.Y., Jan. 17, 1938; d. Daniel H. and Helen (Shirkey) Kane; B.A., Middlebury Coll., 1959; M.S., Am. U., 1963; m. Edward Lee Rogers, Nov. 18, 1961; children—Ruth, John, Helen, Daniel. Asst. dir. program Student Conservation Assn., Charlestown, N.H., 1959-60; dir., 1960; teaching asst. Am. U., Washington, 1961-62, naturalist Nat. Park Service 1966-68; tchr. sci. Hauppaugue (N.Y.) Middle Sch., 1972-73; tchr. sci. Oak Grove Coburn Sch., Vassalboro, Maine, 1974-75, head sci. dept., 1976-79; tchr. sci. lower sch. Nat. Cathedral Sch., Washington, 1979-82, tchr. sci. upper sch., 1982—. Founder Setauket Environ. Center, 1970, bd. govs., 1970-72; bd. dirs. Student Conservation Program, 1970-79; cons. Sch. Wide Environ. Edn. Program, N.Y.C., 1978; cons. edn. programs Nat. Geog. Soc., 1980—; founder, chmn. Pittston (Maine) Conservation Commn., 1975-78. NSF grantee, 1962. Mem. Nat. Parks and Conservation Assn., Student Conservation Assn., Nature Conservancy (dir. Maine chpt. 1976-78). Club: The Grange (Pittston, Maine). Home: 6601 Jerry Pl McLean VA 22101 Office: National Cathedral School for Girls Mt St Albans Washington DC 20016

ROGERS, BARBARA JOAN, artist, educator; b. Newcomerstown, Ohio, Apr. 28, 1937; d. Willis A. and Ethel (Keith) Wilson; B.Sc., Ohio State U., 1959; M.A., U. Calif., Berkeley, 1963; 1 son by previous marriage, Christopher. Mem. faculty dept. art U. Calif., Berkeley, 1965-67, 72-73, San Francisco Art Inst., 1974, U. Wash., Seattle, 1975, San Francisco Art Inst., 1975-76, Contra Costa (Calif.) Coll., 1977-78, San Jose (Calif.) State U., 1978—; one-woman shows of paintings include: Michael Walls Gallery, San Francisco, 1968, 69, San Francisco Mus. Art, 1973, Linda Farris Gallery, Seattle, 1976, Hansen Fuller Gallery, San Francisco, 1977, Michael Berger Gallery, Pitts., 1978, 81, Marianne Deson Gallery, Chgo., 1980; numerous group shows, latest being: Oakland (Calif.) Mus., 1975, Ill. Bell Telephone, Chgo., 1975, Linda Farris Gallery, Seattle, 1975, Helen Euphrat Gallery, Cupertino, Calif., 1975, Hansen Fuller Gallery, San Francisco, 1977, Fine Arts Mus. of San Francisco, 1977, Santa Barbara (Calif.) Mus. Art, 1980, U. Pitts., 1981, Judith Christian Gallery, N.Y.C., 1981, San Jose State U., 1982; represented in permanent collections: San Francisco Mus. Modern Art, Oakland Mus., Evergreen Coll., Olympia Wash. Trustee San Francisco Art Inst., mem. artists com. Recipient Eisner prize U. Calif. Mem. Coll. Art Assn. Home: 6387A Colby St Oakland CA 94618 Office: San Jose State Univ San Jose CA 95192

ROGERS, BONNIE LOU, coll. dean; b. Olive Hill, Ky., Apr. 14, 1940; B.A., Morehead State U., 1961; M.L.S., U. Md., 1967; Ed.D., U. So. Calif., 1980. Tchr. social studies, English, Public Schs., Long Beach, Calif., 1961-64, Prince Georges County, Md., 1964-66; cataloging librarian U.S. Naval War Coll., Newport, R.I., 1967-68; reference librarian U.S. Internat. U., Elliot, San Diego, 1968-69; librarian, coordinator library public services Palomar Community Coll., San Marcos, 1969-77, acting dean library services, 1973-74, evening dean, 1976-77, dean library services, 1977-79, dean instructional resources, 1979—. Pres., San Diego Area Community Coll. Learning Resources Coop., 1978—. U.S. Labor Mgmt. Relations Service fellow, 1978. Mem. AAUW, Calif. Library Assn. (pres. community coll. chpt. 1979), ALA, Assn. Calif. Community Coll. Adminstrs., NEA, Beta Phi Mu. Club: Order Eastern Star. Home: 751 Hoska Dr Del Mar CA 92014 Office: Palomar Coll W Mission Rd San Marcos CA 92069

ROGERS, CAROL ANN, hair stylist; b. Huntington, Ind., Feb. 3, 1936; d. Russell F. and Jeanette D. (McClintock) Ade; student Warners Beauty Coll., 1954, Huntington Coll., 1974, Ind. U., 1961, Tri-State U., 1963-65, Purdue U., 1979; m. Charles W. Rogers, Mar. 1, 1957; children—David C., Michael J. Owner, Carols Hair & Skin Care, Inc., Huntington, 1966—. Mem. Nat. Hairdressers and Cosmetology Assn., Ind. Hairdressers and Cosmetology Assn., Ind. Hair Design Guild (past pres.), Huntington Hairdressers Assn. (past pres.), Delta Theta Tau. Democrat. Mem. Ch. of Christ. Club: Eastern Star. Home: 472 W Park Dr Huntington IN 46750 Office: 472 W Park Dr Huntington IN 46750

ROGERS, CAROL JEAN, computer system cons.; b. St. Paul, Oct. 3, 1940; d. John Edward and Luella Grace (Holland) Christensen; grad. Estelle Compton Inst., Mpls., 1964, also specialized courses; children—Wade William, Sue Ann, Roxanne Leigh. Data entry specialist Hennepin County Dept. Ct. Services, Mpls., 1959-63; scheduling coordinator Sta. WTCN-TV, Mpls., 1963-65; coordinator for Minn., Miss Am. Teenager, St. Paul, 1967-69; upper Midwest coordinator Miss Universe, St. Paul, 1967-69; dir., instr. Mary Lowe Modeling Sch., Mpls., 1969-70; mktg. services coordinator Naidas Girl's Modeling Agy., Mpls., 1970-72; system flow tech. analyst Super Valu Stores, Inc., Hopkins, Minn., 1974-78, systems cons., 1980—; ind. systems cons., Edina, Minn., 1979—; adv. council Sawyer Sch. Bus., Mpls.; instr. Minn. public schs. Sunday sch. tchr. Grace Lutheran Ch., Deephaven, 1980-82. Mem. Nat. Assn. Female Execs., Am. Bus. Women's Assn., All the Good Old Girls. Home: 4752 Thomas Ave South Minneapolis MN 55410 Office: 101 Jefferson Ave Hopkins MN 55343

ROGERS, DOROTHY, psychologist, educator; b. Ashburn, Ga., May 31, 1914; d. Edwin Augustus and Ella Mae (Evans) Rogers; A.B., U. Ga., 1934, M.A., 1936; Ph.D., Duke U., 1947. Tchr., Birmingham Public Schs., Ala., 1935-44; instr. State Univ. Coll., Oswego, N.Y., 1946-47, asst. prof., 1947-50, prof., 1950—, disting. service prof., 1977—. Lic. psychologist, N.Y. State. Mem. Am. Psychol. Assn., Eastern Psychol. Assn., Nat. Woman's Party, (nat. council 1953-81, 4th v.p. 1981—), Nat. Council Family Relations, NOW. Republican. Author: Mental Hygiene in Elementary Education, Oswego: Fountainhead of Teacher Education, 1961; Readings in Child Psychology, 1969; Issues in Child Psychology, 1969; Child Psychology, 1969; Highways Across the Horizon, 1966; Psychology of Adolescence, 1969; Issues in Adolescent Psychology, 1969; Adolescence: A Psychological Perpective, 1972; The Adult Years, 1979; Issues in Adult Development, 1981; Adolescence and Youth, 1981; Issues in Life Span Development, 1981; Life Span Human Development, 1982. Home: 5143 Franklin St Oswego NY 13126 Office: State Univ Coll Oswego NY 13126

ROGERS, ELIZABETH RAE, radio exec.; b. Spokane, Wash., Mar. 14, 1948; d. Raymond A. Bendickson and Iris Elizabeth (Henderson) Sparkman; student U. Alaska, 1967-74; m. Dennis Allan Rogers, Aug. 27, 1973. Neurol. historian Sansum Clinic, Santa Barbara, Calif., 1974-75; editor Culinary Workers Local 879, Fairbanks, Alaska, 1976; community affairs dir. KFQD AM Radio, Anchorage, 1977—, producer, dir. Pub. Opinion Hotline, 1978—. Producer radio pub. service announcements Alaska Repertory Theatre; producer, writer, dir. pub. service announcements Greepeace Alaska. Recipient Best Radio Community Affairs Program award Alaska Press Club, 1980; U. Alaska scholar, 1968-69. Mem. Alaska Broadcasters Assn., Alaska World Affairs Council, Anchorage Audubon Soc., Greenpeace Alaska, Cousteau Soc., Oceanic Soc., Alaska Soc. for Prevention of Cruelty to Animals, NOW. Home: SRA Box 1451 W Anchorage AK 99502 Office: KFQD 9200 Lake Otis Parkway Anchorage AK 99507

ROGERS, EUGENIA MARGARET, ednl. adminstr.; b. Suffern, N.Y., Feb. 5, 1947; d. Wesley and Margaret P. (Van Cott) Rogers; B.A. in Speech Pathology and Audiology, U. Conn., 1968, M.A. (Univ. fellow), 1971; postgrad. (Univ. fellow), Boston U., 1975-76. Teaching asst. U. Conn., 1970-71; speech pathologist Wrentham (Mass.) State Sch., 1973-76; program coordinator Greater Lawrence Ednl. Collaborative, Andover, Mass., 1976-77; program mgr. evaluation team liaison project Bur. Instl. Schs., Boston, 1977-79, project coordinator, 1979—; clin. asso. Boston U.; cons. speech therapy; supr. student tchrs. Mem. Am. Speech and Hearing Assn. (cert. clin. competence speech pathology), Am. Assn. Mental Deficiency. Research on Navy underwater communications. Home: 552 Metropolitan Ave Hyde Park MA 02136 Office: 312 Stuart St Boston MA 02116

ROGERS, GINGER (VIRGINIA KATHERINE MCMATH), dancer, actress; b. Independence, Mo., July 16, 1911; d. William Eddins and Lela Emogene (Owens) McMath; ed. pub. schs. Began as a child dancer, 1926; appeared in motion pictures, 1930—; starred in Broadway prodns. Top Speed and Girl Crazy, 1929-30; danced with Fred Astaire in Flying Down to Rio, 1933; has co-starred with Astaire in numerous motion picture prodns., including Top Hat, Gay Divorcee, Follow the Fleet, Swing Time, Roberta Shall We Dance; has also appeared in Twenty Million Sweethearts, Change of Heart, Chance at Heaven, The Sap from Syracuse, Sitting Pretty, Young Man of Manhattan, Star of Midnight, Top Hat, In Person, Golddiggers of 1933, Stage Door, Vivacious Lady, Having a Wonderful Time, Carefree, The Story of Vernon and Irene Castle, Bachelor Mother, Fifth Avenue Girl, Primrose Path, Lucky Partners, Kitty Foyle, Tom Dick and Harry, Roxy Hart, Major and Minor, Tales of Manhattan, Once Upon a Honeymoon, Lady in the Dark, Tender Comrade, I'll Be Seeing You, Week-end at the Waldorf, Heartbeat, Magnificent Doll, It Had to Be You, Barkleys of Broadway, Perfect Strangers, Storm Warning, Groom Wore Spurs, We Are Not Married, Monkey Business, Forever Female, Dreamboat, Twist of Fate, Black Widow, Teenage Rebel, Tight Spot, O Men O Women, Harlow, The Confession; TV appearances include Bob Hope Show, Perry Como Show; star plays Hello Dolly, 1965, Mame, 1969. Recipient Academy award for Kitty Foyle, 1940. *

ROGERS, HELEN EVELYN, newspaperwoman; b. Tacoma, Wash., Jan. 24, 1924; d. John Sigurd and Emma Elina (Carlson) Wahrgren; B.A., U. Wash., Seattle, 1946; m. Charles Dana Rogers, July 24, 1948. Mem. editorial staff Holiday mag., Phila., 1946; civilian public relations writer, Ft. Lewis, Wash., 1946-47; asst. society editor Tacoma News Tribune-Sunday Ledger, 1947-51, radio-TV editor-columnist, 1951—. Mem. Newspaper Guild, Tacoma-Pierce County Geneal. Soc. Democrat. Lutheran. Home: 2906 N 24th St Tacoma WA 98406 Office: 1950 S State St Tacoma WA 98411

ROGERS, IRENE, librarian; b. Yonkers, N.Y., Oct. 12, 1932; d. Franklyn Harold and Mary Margaret (Nealy) R.; B.S. in Edn., New Paltz State Tchrs. Coll., 1954; M.L.S. (N.Y. State Tng. grantee), Columbia U., 1959. Tchr., West Babylon (N.Y.) Sch. System, 1954-57, Yonkers Sch. System, 1957-58; reference librarian Yonkers Pub. Library, 1959-67, adult services coordinator, 1967-73, asst. library dir., 1973—. Mem. Mayor's Adv. Com. Consumer Edn., Yonkers, 1970—; mem. curriculum adv. com., report card revision com. Office Supt. Schs., 1982; mem. Yonkers unit Am. Cancer Soc. West Library System grantee, 1966. Mem. Westchester, N.Y. library assns. Club: Soroptimist (pres. 1978-79, 80-81) (Yonkers). Home: 41 Amackassin Terr Yonkers NY 10703 Office: 7 Main St Yonkers NY 10701

ROGERS, JANET, pay TV programmer; b. N.Y.C., June 24, 1948; d. Eugene and Shirley (Levine) Kornberg; student Syracuse U., 1966-68, Fairleigh Dickinson U., 1968-69; m. Allan H. Rogers, Aug. 15, 1970. Adminstrv. asst./film booker Schoenfeld Film Distributing Corp., N.Y.C., 1968-74; adminstrv. asst./film booker Playboy Enterprises, Inc., N.Y.C., 1974-76; program dir. Hollywood Home Theatre, N.Y.C., 1976—. Mem. Women in Cable, Nat. Assn. Female Execs. Club: Motion Picture Bookers. Home: 185 Prospect Ave Hackensack NJ 07601 Office: 49 W 57 St New York NY 10019

ROGERS, JANET CARLENE SARGENT, county extension agt.; b. Lubbock County, Tex., Jan. 20, 1948; d. Carl Walter and Alice Marie (Killingsworth) Sargent; B.S. in Home Econs. Edn. (Ethel Foster scholar, Elizabeth and Wylie Brisco Found. scholar), Tex. Tech. U., 1969, M.S. in Home Econs. Edn., 1970; postgrad. W. Tex. State U., 1973-74; Specialist cert. in aging, N. Tex. State U., 1982; m. Donald Ray Rogers, Sept. 3, 1977. Nursery sch. aide Cissie's Nursery Sch., Lubbock, 1966, 67-69; waitress Youngblood's Restaurant, Lubbock, 1969; grad. research asst. Home Econs. Instrnl. Materials Center, Tex. Tech. U., 1970; homemaking tchr. Canyon (Tex.) Ind. Sch. Dist., 1970-71, 71-76; county extension agt. home econs. Tex. Agrl. Extension Service, Big Spring, 1976-82; tchr. cons. Tex. Edn. Agy., Home Econs. Instrnl. Materials Center, Tex. Tech. U., 1975. Assoc. dir. Howard County Fair, Big Spring, 1976-82. Named Boss of Yr., Big Spring chpt. Am. Bus. Women's Assn., 1981. Provisionally cert. in vocat. homemaking, cert. in profl. vocat. homemaking, Tex. Mem. Tex. Assn. Extension Home Economists, Am. Home Econs. Assn., Phi Upsilon Omicron. Presbyterian. Author articles and instructional materials. Home: Route 1 Box 144 D-5 Midland TX 79701 Office: PO Box 790 Big Spring TX 79720

ROGERS, JEAN DOROTHY, med. lab. cons.; b. Scranton, Pa., May 1, 1924; d. Leland Curtis and Phoebe (Maddock) R.; B.S. in Med. Tech., Temple U., Phila., 1946; M.A. in Mgmt. and Supervision Health Adminstrn., Central Mich. U., Mt. Pleasant, 1980. Med. lab. technologist, Pa., N.Y., Ind. and Tex., 1946-51; commd. 1st lt. USAF, 1951, advanced through grades to lt. col., 1968; service in Newfoundland, 1953-55, Philippines, 1966-68; ret., 1971; lab. cons. Fla. Dept. Health, 1972-82; pres. J.D. Rogers Assocs., Inc., Med. Lab. Cons., St. Augustine, Fla., 1982—; mem. adv. council N.E. Fla. Area Agy. Aging, 1981—, vice-chmn., 1983—. Decorated USAF Commendation medal with oak leaf cluster. Cert. clin. lab. scientist. Mem. Am. Soc. Med. Tech., Ret. Officers Assn., Air Force Assn., Am. Soc. Profl. Cons., Am. Soc. Clin. Pathologists (assoc. mem., cert. med. technologist), Nat. Assn. Female Execs., Am. Legion, Am. Assn. Ret. Persons. Democrat. Episcopalian (vestryman). Office: 97 Orange St Suite 2A Saint Augustine FL 32084

ROGERS, JENNIFER ENGLES, educator; b. Batesville, Ark., July 28, 1943; d. Jake Raymond and Bess Ermine (Goodin) Engles; B.A., Ark. Coll., 1965; M.A., Memphis State U., 1973; m. Francis Xavier Rogers, Jr., Jan. 26, 1974; 1 son, Joshua Francis. Debate, drama tchr. Malden (Mo.) High Sch., 1965-66; sec. Dan River Mills, N.Y.C., 1966; drama tchr. Bald Knob (Ark.) High Sch., 1966-68; entertainer Silver Dollar City, Branson, Mo., 1967-69; actress Bloody Mama, Mt. Home, Ark., 1969; asst. mgr. Melba Theatre, Batesville, Ark., 1969-70; actress H & H Productions, So. states, 1970; remedial reading tchr. Newark (Ark.) Elem. Sch., 1970-71; producer, dir. Sta. WREG-TV, Memphis, Tenn., 1973-81; asst. prof. broadcasting Okla. State U., Stillwater, 1981—. Named Miss Ark. Coll., 1965. Mem. Batesville Community Theatre (pres.), Alpha Psi Omega. Republican. Mem. Ch. of Christ. Author: The Autobiography of Miss Punkin Jones, 1977. Office: Okla State U Paul Miller Journalism Bldg Stillwater OK 74074

ROGERS, JUDY, social worker; b. Newark, Jan. 29, 1943; d. John Oliver and Grace (Daniels) R.; A.B. with honors in Sociology, Dickinson Coll., 1965; M.S.W., N.Y.U., 1970; 1 child. Kimani. Coordinator social rehab., anti-recidivism project, Jersey City. 1967-68; therapist Bklyn. Psychiat. Centers, 1970-72; abortion counselor VIP Med. Assos., N.Y.C., 1972-73; clin. coordinator Harlem Center for Child Study, Harlem Hosp., N.Y.C., 1973—; field instr. Sch. Social Work, Columbia U.; mem. prof. adv. com. James Weldon Johnson Mental Health Center, 1980—. First v.p. Parents Assn., Hunter Coll. Elem. Sch. 1981-82; active Operation Crossroads Africa, 1963, U.S. Youth Council, 1966-68. Recipient Gaylord H. Patterson Meml. prize for sociology, 1965. Mem. Nat. Assn. Social Workers (bd. dirs. N.Y.C. chpt., chmn. child and family advocacy com.), Nat. Assn. Black Social Workers. Office: 121 W 128th St New York NY 10027

ROGERS, KATE ELLEN, educator; b. Nashville, Dec. 13, 1920; d. Raymond Lewis and Louise (Gruver) R.; M.A. in Fine Arts, George Peabody Coll., 1947; Ed.D. in Fine Arts and Fine Arts Edn., Columbia U., 1956. Instr., Tex. Tech. Coll., Lubbock, 1947-53; co-owner, v.p. Design Today, Inc., Lubbock, 1951-54; student asst. Am. House, N.Y.C., 1953-54; asst. prof. housing and interior design U. Mo., Columbia, 1954-56, assoc. prof., 1956-66, prof., 1966—, chmn. dept. housing and interior design, 1973—; mem. accreditation com. Found. for Interior Design Edn. Research, 1975-76. Nat. Endowment for Arts research grantee, 1981-82. Mem. Interior Design Educators Council (pres. 1971-73, chmn. bd. 1974-76, chmn. research com. 1977-78), Found. for Interior Design Edn. Research (chmn. standards com. 1976-82, dir. research 1982—), Am. Soc. Interior Designers, (hon.), Am. Home Econs. Assn., Environ. Design Research Assn., Soc. Archtl. Historians, Am. Real Estate and Urban Econs. Assn. Democrat. Author: The Modern House, USA, 1962; editor Jour. Interior Design Edn. and Research, 1975-78.

ROGERS, KATHARINE MUNZER, educator; b. N.Y.C., June 6, 1932; d. Martin and Jean (Thompson) Munzer; B.A. summa cum laude, Barnard Coll., 1952; Fulbright scholar, Newnham Coll., Cambridge U., 1952-53; Ph.D., Columbia U., 1957; m. Kenneth C. Rogers, Aug. 4, 1956; children—Margaret, Christopher, Thomas. Instr. English, Skidmore Coll., Saratoga Springs, N.Y., 1954-55, Cornell U., 1955-57; lectr. to prof. English, Bklyn. Coll., 1958—; mem. doctoral faculty City U. N.Y. Mem. MLA. Author: The Troublesome Helpmate: A History of Misogyny in Literature, 1966; William Wycherley, 1972; Feminism in Eighteenth Century England, 1982. Editor anthologies: Before Their Time: Six Women Writers of the Eighteenth Century, 1979; The Signet Classic Book of 18th and 19th Century British Drama; Selected Writings of Samuel Johnson, 1981. Contbr. articles to profl. jours. Home: Hoxie House Stevens Inst Hoboken NJ 07030 Office: Dept English Bklyn Coll Brooklyn NY 11210

ROGERS, LINDA HOWARD, pediatrician; b. Billings, Mont., Mar. 28, 1950; d. Curtis Stephen and DeLois Wiley Howard; B.S. with honors, U. Calif., Santa Barbara, 1972; M.D., Albany Med. Coll., 1976; m. Neal Lawrence Rogers, Jan. 20, 1979. Intern, U. Utah Med. Center, 1976-77; resident Albany (N.Y.) Med. Center, 1977-79; partner Butte (Mont.) Pediatrics, Inc., 1979—; mem. attending staff St. James Community Hosp., Butte, 1979—, chmn. dept. pediatrics, 1980, mem. ad hoc com. for hosp. expansion, 1981—; instr. Mont. State U. Nurses Sch., Butte, 1979—, Emergency Med. Services, Region 1B, 1979—. Mem. Am. Acad. Pediatrics, AMA, Mont. Pediatric Soc., Silver Bow County Med. Soc. Home: 800 W Platinum St Butte MT 59701 Office: 401 S Alabama St Butte MT 59701

ROGERS, LINDA LEE, journalist; b. Detroit, June 17, 1952; d. Henry A. and Nancy A. (Meyer) R.; B.A. in English Lang. and Lit., U. Mich., Ann Arbor, 1974, M.A. in Journalism, 1979. Reporter, intern Grand Rapids (Mich.) Press, 1978; sr. editor World Press Rev., N.Y.C., 1979—. Office: 230 Park Ave Room 1610 New York NY 10169

ROGERS, LORETTA GAIL, mfg. co. exec.; b. Proctorville, Ohio, Mar. 10, 1936; d. Sanford Dale and Beatrice Emily Brumfield; student Huntington (W. Va.) Bus. Coll., 1962-63, Ohio U., Athens, 1975; m. Charles L. Rogers, Dec. 7, 1963; children—Michael, Kimberly, Steven. Various clerical and secretarial positions, 1966-77; with Anchor Hocking Corp., 1977—, indsl. relations mgr., Lancaster, Ohio, 1977—; mem. exec. council hosp. intervention program Nat. Safety Council, 1978. Adv. bd. Lancaster Vis. Nurses Assn., 1981. Recipient Cameron award safety, 1979. Mem. Lancaster-Fairfield County Personnel Assn., Fairfield County Safety Assn. Republican. Club: Lady Lions. Home: 154 E Walnut St Apt 4 Lancaster OH 43130 Office: Anchor Hocking Corp S Ewing St Lancaster OH 43130

ROGERS, LOUISA, educator; b. N.Y.C., May 28, 1945; d. Elmer and Susan (Schaefer) R.; A.A., Borough of Manhattan Community Coll., City U. N.Y., 1967; B.A., Hunter Coll., City U. N.Y., 1969, M.A., 1972; Ed.D., Rutgers U., 1978; 1 dau., Marla. Instr. specialized tng. Consol. Edison of N.Y., 1970-73; instr. S.I. Community Coll., City U. N.Y., 1972-73, Bklyn. Coll., Queensborough Community Coll., City U. N.Y. and Kean Coll., Elizabeth, N.J. 1974-75; asst. prof. Rutgers U., Newark, 1976-81; adj. asst. prof. Borough of Manhattan Community Coll., 1978-81; asst. prof. English, U. Miami, Coral Gables, Fla., 1981—; cons. in field; adminstr. High Sch. Equivalency Testing Center, 1972-73. Mem. Nat. Council Tchrs. English, Coll. Conf. on Composition and Communication, N.Y. English Council, Am. Soc. for Tng. and Devel., Women in Communications. Contbr. articles to profl. jours. Office: Dept English Univ of Miami Coral Gables FL 33124

ROGERS, MARGARET GAY, ins. co. ofcl.; b. Ketona, Ala., Mar. 25, 1937; d. James Elbert and Margaret Louis (Nolde) Haigler, Jr.; student Massey Bus. Coll., 1957; m. Douglas Earl Rogers, June 30, 1975. Tng., inventory clk. Goodwill Industries, Ft. Wayne, Ind., 1959; with Ala. Title Co., Inc., Birmingham, 1963, file clk., asst. bookkeeper, 1965, policy clk., asst. bookkeeper, 1966, asst. bookkeeper, exec. asst. to pres., 1975—. Mem. Nat. Assn. Female Execs., Mem. Nat. Fraternal Soc. of the Deaf. Repbulican. Lutheran. Home: 3024 Forest Dr Fultondale AL 35068 Office: 615 N 21st St Birmingham AL 35203

ROGERS, MARGARET NITA BRABHAM, social worker; b. Clinton, S.C., Aug. 13, 1950; d. Thomas Jefferson and Margaret Emily (Workman) Brabham; B.S., U. S.C., 1971, M.S.W., 1976; m. Francis Drew Rogers, Jan. 23, 1971. Caseworker I, Aid to Families with Dependent Children Services, Dept. Social Services, Beaufort, S.C., 1972-74, asst. to dir., 1975, case mgr. II, Children and Family Services, 1976-78; social worker III, maternal and child care Low Country Dept. Health and Environ. Control, Beaufort, 1978—; mem. Head Start Policy Adv. Council, 1977-80; Child Abuse and Neglect Treatment Team, 1979—; mem. adv. com. S.C. Perinatal Assn., 1978; social work cons. Beaufort Meml. Hosp., 1979-81. Registered social worker, S.C. Mem. Nat. Assn. Social Workers, Acad. Cert. Social Workers, S.C. State Employees Assn., NOW. Democrat. Methodist. Home: 705 Sunset Circle River Reach Burton SC 29902 Office: PO Box 1479 Beaufort SC 29902

ROGERS, MARGARET SHAW, retail exec.; b. Decatur, Ala., Apr. 5, 1950; d. William Reed, Jr. and Lillian Russell (Shaw) R.; student Birmingham So. Coll., 1968-69, U. Hawaii, summer 1971; B.S. in Retail Merchandising, U. Ala., 1972. Buyer and mgr. Miss Ala. Fashions, Tuscaloosa, 1972-74; dept. mgr. Rich's, Birmingham, 1974-75; buyer Blach's, Birmingham, 1975-78; store mgr. County Seat, Charlotte, N.C., 1978-79; buyer Eckerd Apparel (Junction), Charlotte, 1979-81; div. group mdse. mgr. L.S. Ayres & Co., Indpls., 1981—; guest lectr. mktg. U. Ala. Mem. Am. Assn. Legal Adminstrs., AAUW, Jamestowne Soc., Alpha Gamma Delta. Republican. Methodist. Club: Cotillion (Tuscaloosa). Office: L S Ayres & Co 1 W Washington St Indianapolis IN 46204

ROGERS, MERENA MAXINE, personnel cons.; b. Phillipsburg, Kans., Sept. 22, 1947; d. Roy Rich and Luella Agnes (Bretton) Hollingshead; student Phillipsburg schs.; m. David Lee Rogers, Sept. 24, 1965; children—Shari Lynette, Shani Michelle. Receptionist, counselor Dunhill of Topeka, 1974-78; partner, counselor Systems 3, Inc., Topeka, 1978-80; owner, cons. Rogers & Rogers, Inc., Topeka, 1980—. Vol. Tchr. painting Topeka Assn. Retarded Citizens, 1981—; vice chmn. Topekans in Action, 1980; pres. Elmont Sch. PTA, Topeka, 1978-79. Named Office Services Counselor of Yr., 1977. Mem. Am. Business Women's Assn. (pres. Mid-day chpt. 1981, chpt. Woman of Yr. award 1981), Nat. Assn. Personnel Cons. Office: 3601 SW 29th St Topeka KS 66614

ROGERS, MYRTLE BEATRICE, state legislator; b. Haverhill, Mass., Mar. 24, 1925; d. Rufus Cecil and Rose Beatrice (Chabot) Fanjoy; student pub. and pvt. schs., Haverhill; m. Roland I. Rogers, Nov. 30, 1952; children—Richard Newhall, Rebecca; foster children—Mark Swasey, Mary Rogers. Mem. N.H. Ho. of Reps., Concord, 1972—, clk. joint com. on elderly affairs. Chmn. Newton 225th Ann. Com. and Bicentennial Com.; sec.-treas. Newton Conservation Com.; Newton commr. to regional planning; supt. ch. sch., deacon 1st Christian Ch., Newton. Recipient Community Citizen award Eclipse Grange, 1978. Mem. Newton Hist. Soc. Republican. Home: Box 435 Route 2 Newton NH 03858

ROGERS, ROWENA EMERY, state land mgr.; b. Denver, Dec. 8, 1921; d. Roe and Jeanette (Carpenter) Emery; B.A., Vassar Coll., 1943; m. Ranger Rogers, Nov. 1, 1944; children—Susan, Jeanette, Roxanna, Lorna, Robert, Sarah. Pres., mem. Colo. State Bd. Parks and Outdoor Recreation, Denver, 1971-75; mem. Natural Areas Council, Denver, 1978; mem. State Recreational Trails Com., Denver, 1979-82; co-chairperson public lands com. Interstate Oil Compact Commn., Denver, 1980; pres. Colo. Bd. Land Commrs., 1975—. Dist. commr. Platte Valley Pony Club, 1956—; vice chmn. Arapahoe County Republicans, 1966-68, Rep. 2d Dist. Com., 1962-64; bd. dirs. Met. Denver YWCA, 1968-72, Kent Sch., 1960-62; bd. dirs. Greenwood Village Open Space Commn., 1974-76. Mem. Western States Land Commrs. Assn. (pres. 1980-82), Colo. Womens Forum, Profl. Women in Public Sector. Episcopalian. Clubs: Petroleum; Arapahoe Hunt; Vassar of Colorado. Home: 3001 Willamette Ln Littleton CO 80121 Office: 1313 Sherman St Room 620 Denver CO 80203

ROGERS, RUTH, coll. counselor; b. Willich, Ger., Jan. 23, 1926; came to U.S., 1946, naturalized, 1949; d. Albert and Karola (Klein) Lion; m. Alfred A. Rogers, Sept. 8, 1947; children—Jonathan Lion, Daniel Stephen, Miriam Carol. Paraprofl. counselor Coe Coll. Cedar Rapids, Iowa, 1970-76, counselor Center for Acad. and Career Planning, 1976—, co-developer, instr. Jewish Holocaust in history course, 1982. Mem. Jane Boyd Community House Bd.; mem. bd. Temple Judah; mem. Sisterhood Temple Judah; adv. Women Concerned about Women, Shalom, Continuing Edn. for Women; vice chmn. Mayor's Commn. on Human Rights, 1969-76; mem. YWCA bd.; chmn. Women's Resource Center, 1976-79; chmn. Family Service Agy. bd. family life edn., 1963-70; mem. panel Friendship Forum, 1965-70. Mem. Am. Coll. Personnel Assn., Am. Personnel and Guidance Assn., Nat. Assn. Women Deans, Adminstrs. and Counselors, Profl. Women's Network, NOW, Nat. Abortion Rights Action League, Mental Health Assn., Alpha Lambda Delta (advisor). Developer curriculum on Holocaust through lit. and film, 1980. Home: 327-30th St SE Cedar Rapids IA 52403 Office: Center for Acad and Career Planning Coe Coll Cedar Rapids IA 52402

ROGERS, TERI-ELLEN, mfg. co. exec.; b. Chgo., Nov. 18, 1946; d. Frank and Elaine Augusta (Mullan) Naccarato; B.A. in Math., Northwestern U., 1968; M.S. in Math., Western Ill. U., 1971; m. David J. Rogers, Nov. 26, 1971; 1 son, Jeremy. Asst. portfolio mgr. Harris Trust and Savs. Bank, Chgo., 1968-69; tchr. math. J.S. Morton High Sch., Berwyn, Ill., 1969-70, 71-75; retirement plans mgr. Internat. Harvester Co., Chgo., 1975—. Mem. Northwestern U. Alumni Assn., Alpha Gamma Delta. Baptist. Club: DAR (state jr. membership chmn. 1975-76, chpt. regent 1976-78, chpt. vice regent 1975, 79-80). Office: 401 N Michigan Chicago IL 60611

ROGIN, CAROLE MILLER, business exec.; b. Camden, N.J., June 27, 1949; d. Leo and Beatrice (Miller) R.; student Mary Washington Coll., 1967-69; B.S., U. Va., 1971; M.A., George Washington U., 1972; m. Barry L. Grossman, Dec. 29, 1974. Speech lang. pathologist Arlington County (Va.) schs., 1972-77; cons. Info. Spectrum, Inc., Arlington, 1977; project dir. Am. Speech and Hearing Assn., Rockville, Md., 1977-80; account exec. Hauck & Assos., Inc., Washington, 1980—; guest lectr. U. Va., Med. Coll. Va.; cons. in field. U.S. Office Edn. fellow, 1971-72; Bur. Edn. for Handicapped tng. grantee, 1977-80. Mem. Am. Speech Lang.-Hearing Assn., Meeting Planners Internat., Am. Soc. Assn. Execs., Nat. Council Career Women. Author manuals, articles in field. Home: 212 S Royal St Alexandria VA 22314 Office: 1800 M St NW Washington DC 20036

ROGLITZ, CATHERINE ANN, med. social worker; b. Beloit, Wis., June 27, 1943; d. Carl R. and Elizabeth (Stringer) Roglitz; B.S., Mercy Coll. of Detroit, 1966; M.S.W., U. Mich., 1977. Foster care worker Cath. Social Services, Flint, Mich., 1966-68; med. social worker St. Joseph Mercy Hosp., Ann Arbor, Mich., 1968-78, supr. med. social work, 1978-79, asst. dir. social work, 1979-81, mental health specialist emergency room, 1981—; guest lectr. U. Mich. Sch. Social Work, Ann Arbor, 1977-82, Mercy Sch. Nursing, Ann Arbor, 1979; field instr. U. Mich., 1978; cons. VA Hosp., Ann Arbor, 1977-80; curriculum planning cons. Eastern Mich. U., 1981—; presentor workshops to Am. Assn. Neurosurg. Nurses, 1976, 78. Mem. Mayor's Com. for Problems of the Handicapped, Ann Arbor, 1973-75; mem. profl. adv. bd. Vis. Nurse Assn. of Washtenaw County, 1976-80. Cert. social worker, Mich. Mem. Washtenaw County Med. Social Workers, Nat. Assn. Social Workers, Acad. Cert. Social Workers. Contbr. articles to profl. jours. Home: 3301 Burbank Dr Ann Arbor MI 48105 Office: PO Box 995 Ann Arbor MI 48106

ROGNER, BARBARA ANN, banker; b. Frankenmuth, Mich., July 15, 1950; d. Arnold H. and Mildred (Schreiner) R.; grad. Nat. Sch. Real Estate Fin., 1976. With Frankenmuth Bank and Trust (Mich.), 1967—, asst. cashier, 1976—, adminstrv. asst. to pres., 1979-81, asst. v.p., 1981—. Mem. choir St.Lorenz Luth. Ch., treas. real estate fund, 1981—. Designated C.P.S. Mem. Nat. Secs. Assn. (Sec. of Yr. Saginaw Valley 1979; treas. 1979-80), Frankenmuth Devel. Corp. (asst. treas. 1976—), C. of C. (dir. 1981—). Home: 9421 King Rd Frankenmuth MI 48734 Office: 210 S Main St Frankenmuth MI 48734

ROGUS, FRANCES AGNES (MRS. HENRY JOSEPH ROGUS), horse trainer, driver, owner; b. Chgo., Jan. 11, 1922; d. Albert and Agnes (Murzyn) Wojnicki; student Triton Coll., 1968, 74, 78, 80, Chgo. Conservatory of Music, 1950-52; m. Henry Joseph Rogus, June 6, 1942; children—Susan Barbara Rogus Swatek, William Henry, Nancy Rose Rogus Shields, Joseph Guy, Mary Jane Hope Rogus Kucia, Mark Andrew, Margot Ann. Code clk. War Dept., Q.M.C., Transp. Corp., Tracy, Calif., 1943-45; owner, tchr. ballet classes Sch. of Dance, Westchester, Ill., 1958; sec. to personnel dir. Alberto-Culver Co., Melrose Park, Ill., 1962; actress in Music Man, Temple Theatre, Westchester, 1961, Guys and Dolls, 1963, Pajama Game, 1964; sec. Oak Brook Sch. of Horsemanship, Oak Brook Sports Core, Oakbrook, Ill., 1967; owner harness horses, Westchester, 1964—, trainer harness horses, Chgo., 1968—, standardbred horse breeder, Harvard, Ill., 1968—. Patron, DuPage Ballet. Bd. dirs. Divine Infant Guild, 1961-63; ofcl. Ill. Girls High Sch. Assn. Track and Field. Mem. Hinsdale Community Artists, Bus. and Profl. Women's Club, U.S. Trotting Assn., Ill., Ky. harness horseman's assns., Internat. Platform Assn. Clubs: Variety, Polish Am. Cultural (constn. com.), Chgo. Zephers Track (dir.). Address: 1406 Gardner Rd Westchester IL 60153

ROHDE, JEAN CATHERINE, social worker; b. N.Y.C., June 27, 1948; d. John Francis and Nancy Anastasia (Robuck) R.; B.A. cum laude, Fairleigh Dickinson U., 1970; M.S.W., N.Y. U., 1975; Postgrad. Columbia U., 1979—, Psychoanalytic Inst. for Clin. Social Workers, 1978-79. Group leader Manhattan Psychiat. Center, N.Y.C., 1972-73, supr., 1975-77, outpatient program coordinator, 1977-79; program asst. Council on Social Work Edn., N.Y.C., 1980-81; research asso. Columbia U. Sch. Social Work, Indsl. Social Welfare Center, N.Y.C., 1981-82; lectr. dept. sociology Barnard Coll., 1982—; guest speaker on treatment of mentally ill. N.Y. State Dept. Mental Hygiene scholarship awardee, 1973-75; NIMH trainee, 1979-80. Mem. Council on Social Work Edn., Nat. Assn. Social Workers, Acad. Cert. Social Workers. Home: 52 W 56th St Apt 4R New York NY 10019 Office: Columbia Univ Sch Social Work 622 W 113th St New York City NY 10025

ROHDE, MARJORIE SHERRIFF, rehab. psychologist; b. Detroit, July 8, 1927; d. Leslie Major and Edithia Lois (Wilde) Buck; student Barmore Sch., 1947-48, Brenau Coll., 1948-49, Hunter Coll., 1949-50, Stanford U., 1950, U. Calif., Berkeley, 1952; B.A., San Jose State Coll., 1953; postgrad. U. So. Calif., 1957-59, Fullerton Jr. Coll., 1959; Ed.M., Columbia U., 1977; doctoral candidate Boston Coll., 1977—; m. Max Spencer Rohde, June 22, 1946 (dec. Apr. 1973). Employee relations interviewer, counselor Helipot div. Beckman Corp., Newport Beach, Calif., 1956-57; research asst. dept. pharmacology Calif. Coll. Medicine, Los Angeles, 1960; profl. cons. Nat. Council Jewish Women, Long Beach, Calif., 1961; group worker dept. group work and recreation Braille Inst. Am., Los Angeles, 1960-61; caseworker I & II, Bur. Public Assistance, Los Angeles County, 1961-63; arts and crafts supr. Vacation Camp for Blind, Spring Valley. N.Y., 1964; center supr. Cerebral Palsy Pavilion, Brownsville Boys Club, Bklyn., 1964-65; research asst. dept. radiology St. Luke's Hosp. Center, N.Y.C., 1965-66; patient services dir. N.Y. County chpt. Nat. Multiple Sclerosis Soc., N.Y.C., 1966-68; cons. group leader Leadership Resources, Inc., Washington, 1968; sec., research asst. Research and Demonstration Center for Edn. Handicapped Children, Tchrs. Coll., Columbia U., N.Y.C., 1968-70; research asso., supr. counselors Quaker Com. on Social Rehab., N.Y.C., 1970-74; prin. psychologist Dept. Mental Health, Commonwealth of Mass., Taunton and Pocasset, 1975-79; teaching fellow peripatology program Boston Coll., 1979-80; staff psychologist developmental disabilities unit Mass. Mental Health Center, 1980—; mem. Mass. Adv. Council Mental Health and Mental Retardation. Served with USNR, 1953-55. Mem. Am. Psychol. Assn., Am. Assn. Mental Deficiency, Alpha Gamma Delta, Tau Gamma. Republican. Roman Catholic. Home: 43 Tyler St Attleboro MA 02703 Office: 20 Vining St Boston MA 02115

ROHMAN, CAROL ROSE, psychologist; b. Plainfield, N.J., June 15, 1947; d. Matthew Anthony and Genevieve (Bartkowiak) Udzielak; B.A., Douglass Coll., 1969; M.Ed. in Counselor Edn., Boston U., 1970; profl. diploma in sch. psychology Kean Coll., 1977; m. Aug. 11, 1973. Counselor, Mercer County Community Coll., Trenton, N.J., 1970-77; psychologist Pemberton Twp. Schs., Browns Mills, N.J., 1977-78, East Brunswick (N.J.) Pub. Schs., 1978—. Mem. Am. Psychol. Assn., N.J. Psychol. Assn., Am. Personnel and Guidance Assn., Council for Exceptional Children, NEA, N.J. Assn. Sch. Psychologists, Phi Beta Kappa. Home: 2 Riverview Terr Belle Mead NJ 08502

ROHRBAUGH, JOANNA BUNKER, clin. psychologist; b. Washington, Sept. 1, 1943; d. Lewis H. and Ruth (Bunker) R.; B.A., Brown U., 1964; M.A., Harvard U., 1976, Ph.D., 1976; m. Nathan Edward Clark, June 13, 1964 (div. 1970). Copywriter, Houghton Mifflin Co., Boston, 1964-66; dir. publs. and pub. relations Pine Manor Jr. Coll., Chestnut Hill, Mass., 1966-67; social worker children's program Dept. Pub. Welfare, San Diego, 1967-69; teaching fellow Boston U., 1971, instr., summer 1976; teaching fellow dept. psychology and social relations Harvard U., 1974-75, instr., summers 1977-80, 83; instr. psychology of women Boston Center for Adult Edn., 1975-77; instr. Harvard U. Extension, 1980—; research fellow in psychology dept. psychiatry Harvard Med. Sch., 1976-78, instr., 1978—; clin. fellow in psychology dept. psychiatry Mass. Gen. Hosp., 1976-78, asst. in psychology, 1978-79, asso. in psychology, 1980—; pvt. practice psychotherapy, Boston, 1978—. NSF fellow, 1971-74; Danforth fellow, 1971-76. Mem. Assn. Women in Psychology, Am., Mass. psychol. assns., Assn. Advancement of Psychology, NOW, Phi Beta Kappa. Author: Women: Psychology's Puzzle, 1979. Office: 4 Pinckney St Boston MA 02114

ROLANDI, GIANNA, soprano; b. N.Y.C., Aug. 16, 1952; d. Enrico G. and Jane E. (Frazier) R.; Mus.B., artist diploma, opera cert., Curtis Inst. Music, 1975. Operatic debut at N.Y.C. Opera, 1975; Met. Opera debut, 1979, mem. Met. Opera, 1979—; mem. N.Y.C. Opera; appeared with major opera cos., symphonies throughout U.S., P.R., Buenos Aires, Argentina. Met. Opera Auditions winner; Rockefeller grantee; Nat. Opera Inst. grantee. Mem. Am. Guild Musical Artists, Jr. League of N.Y. Office: care Columbia Artist Mgmt Inc 165 W 57th St New York NY 10019 *

ROLFE, MARIA, orgn. exec.; b. Alexandria, Egypt, Jan. 22, 1913; d. Vasilis and Agathi (Loverdos Lusi) Vernicos; ed. Eng.; m. Sidney E. Rolfe, 1960; 1 dau., Constantine Carras. Chmn., Women's Econ. Round Table, 1978—. Decorated gold cross Order of Benevolence (Greece); recipient Greek Dept. Navy medal, 1950, Greek Red Cross, 1949. Mem. Fgn. Policy Assn. Clubs: Nat. Economists; Cosmos. Address: 860 UN Plaza New York NY 10017 *

ROLLÉ, TAMMY EARLENE CLEVELAND, mgmt. cons.; b. Kings Mountain, N.C., Apr. 10, 1946; d. Ephraim Watkins and Nettie Viola (Hunt) C.; B.S., Iowa State U., 1969; postgrad. Roosevelt U., 1978, DeVrey Inst., 1982; 1 son, Eban Anthony. Corp. acct. Balt. News Am., 1973-74; asst. adminstr. child abuse program Sinai Hosp., Balt., 1974-75; corp. sec., adminstr. Druid Elec. Contractors, Balt., 1975-77; self-employed as mgmt. cons. Cleveland Enterprises, Chgo., 1977—; paralegal, office adminstr. Kleinfeld & Assos., Ltd., Chgo., 1977-80; prodn. adv. Johnson Pub. Co., 1981—. Active Girl Scouts Am., Jr. Women's League. Mem. Nat. Assn. Notary Publics, Nat. Assn. Women in Constrn. (dir., nat. conv. del.), Nat. Assn. Female Execs., Nat. Assn. Bus. Women, Ill. Paralegal Assn., Internat. Platform Assn. Democrat. Methodist. Club: Order Eastern Star. Home and Office: 820 S Michigan Ave Chicago IL 60616

ROLLINS, OTTILIE HIRT, librarian; b. Vienna, Austria, Nov. 18, 1915; d. Alfred and Christine (Cepelak) Hirt; came to U.S., 1935, naturalized, 1944; B.S. cum laude, Russell Sage Coll., 1945; M.S. in Library Sci., Western Res. U., 1960; m. John Pletcher Rollins, Sept. 5, 1945; children—Alfred Hirt, Christopher John. Acad. sec., tchr. German, Putney (Vt.) Sch., 1935-42; instr. phys. edn. Russell Sage Coll., Troy, N.Y., 1945-48; sec. Clarkson Coll. Tech., Potsdam, N.Y., 1948-50, cataloger, asst. librarian, acting librarian, 1961-67, asso. prof., head librarian, 1967-80, asso. dir. Ednl. Resources Center/library info. resources, 1980-81, lectr. German, 1958-60, 61-65; cons. Mem. AAUW (past pres.), ALA, N.Y. Library Assn. (legis. com.), Spl. Libraries Assn., Am. Soc. Engring. Edn., North Country Reference and Research Resources Council (chmn. bd. trustees), No. Folk Dancers (leader), Beta Phi Mu. Home: 44 Bay Potsdam NY 13676 Office: Clarkson Coll Tech Potsdam NY 13676

ROLLO, VERA FOSTER, publisher, author; b. Raleigh, N.C., Dec. 24, 1924; d. Joseph Milton and Hilda Alice (Graf von Schilling) Prevette; B.A., U. Md., 1972, M.A., 1965; divorced; children—Michael J. Foster, Sally M. Foster. Publisher, editor Md. Hist. Press, Lanham, 1965—; sr. aviation editor Am. Soc. Aerospace Edn., Washington, 1981—; asst. prof., coordinator aviation mgmt. program Wilmington (Del.) Coll., 1977-78, asst. prof. U.S. history, 1977-78; lightplane editor Am. Aviation and AA Daily, Washington, 1957-58, asso. editor, 1974-75; asst. copy editor Johns Hopkins U. Press, 1973; vol. flight instr., search and rescue flyer; author: Your Maryland, 3d rev. edit., 1976; Ask Me!, 1980; Maryland Personality Parade, I, 1971; Maryland's Constitution and Government, 1968; Henry Harford: Maryland's Last Proprietor, 1976; Aviation Law: An Introduction, 1982; The Black Experience in Maryland: An Illustrated History, 1980; A Geography of Maryland: Ask Me!, 1981. Historian, Lanham United Methodist Ch., 1960—. Mem. Ninety-Nines, Md. Hist. Soc., Washington Book Pubs. Assn., Ednl. Sales Assn. Home: 9205 Tuckerman St Lanham MD 20706 Office: Md Hist Press Lanham MD 20706

ROLLS, JAYME ELIZABETH, advt. exec.; b. Norwalk, Conn., Feb. 1, 1952; d. James Michael and Shirley Elizabeth (Mages) Muro; B.S., U. Bridgeport, 1975, M.S., 1980. Mgr. communications Barnes Engring. Co., Stamford, Conn., 1972-78; sr. communications specialist Service Bur. Co. div. Control Data Corp., Greenwich, Conn., 1978-80; account supr. Shepherd, Tibball & Galog, Fairfield, Conn., 1980-81; pres. Corp. Communicators Advt. Agy., Wilton, Conn., 1981—; vis. asst. prof. advt. U. Bridgeport. Founder, psychotherapist Clarity Counseling Service, 1981—; bd. dirs. Meridian House Alcoholic Rehab. Center, Stamford, Conn. Mem. Internat. Transactional Analysis Assn., Assn. Humanistic Psychology, Am. Psychotherapy Assn., Bus./Profl. Advt. Assn. (past pres. So. Conn. chpt.). Unitarian. Home and Office: 156 Westport Rd Wilton CT 06897

ROLPH, SHARON MURIEL, data processing adminstr.; b. Anacortes, Wash., Nov. 7, 1947; d. Harry Donald and Ruth Marie (Cohrs) R.; student N.W. Coll., 1966-67; cert. Northwestern Sch. Bus., 1967; A.Tech. Arts, Edmonds Community Coll., 1979; B.A., City U., 1982. Acctg. clk. Peoples Bank, Royal City, Wash., 1965; asst. bookkeeper N.W. Coll., Kirkland, Wash., 1966; proof operator People's Bank, Seattle, 1967; computer operator, lead data control clk. Nat. Bank Commerce, Seattle, 1968-72; computer operator GTE Data Services, Everett, Wash., 1972-73, scheduler, 1973-76, data control technician, 1976-78, programmer, 1978-79, programmer analyst, 1979-80; methods analyst Gen. Telephone N.W., Everett, Wash., 1980-82, methods adminstr., 1982—. Emcee, mem. exec. com., co-chmn., chmn. Pacific N.W. Christian Singles Conv., 1980—, drama producer, 1979. Club: Fellowship Christian Adult Singles II. Office: 1800 41st St Everett WA 98201

ROM, JOANNE EVA, govt. ofcl.; b. N.Y.C., Jan. 16, 1952; d. Julius and Rose (Podgor) R.; A.B., Bryn Mawr Coll., 1974; M.B.A., George Washington U., 1981; m. Steven Goldberg, Aug. 11, 1979. Asst. to exec. v.p. Peasant Shop Co., Bryn Mawr, 1974-75; with NSF, 1975—, policy specialist, 1980-81, grants and contracting officer, 1981—. Mem. Nat. Council Univ. Research Adminstrs. (asso.), AAAS, Career Network, NOW, Beta Gamma Sigma. Club: Washington Area Bryn Mawr. Home: 2227 20th St NW Washington DC 20009 Office: 1800 G St NW Washington DC 20550

ROM, MARGUERTIE EUSTIC, editor and publisher; b. Clinton, Iowa; d. William Centennial and Blanche (Neisslie) Eustice; B.A., Knox Coll., Galesburg, Ill., 1927; B.S., U. Chgo., 1930; postgrad. Northwestern U.; m. George Rom, Feb. 11, 1947; children—Quin, Dennis O'Brien. Tchr., Chgo. public high schs., 1930-47; editor and pub. Crystal Lake (Ill.) News, also McHenry County Guide, 1947—; corr. Chgo. Sun Times, UPI. Mem. No. Ill. Editorial Assn., Lambda Phi Delta. Clubs: Crystal Lake Woman's, Country Side Garden (founder). Author: Hong Kong From a Woman's Point of View, 1965; Las Vegas From a Woman's Point of View, 1967; Big Feet in the Orient; ABC's of Travel in the Virgin Isles and Puerto Rico, 1968. Editor Garden Glories, 1950-53. Office: 404 Virginia St Crystal Lake IL 60014

ROMAIN, MARGARET ANN, accountant; b. Mercer, Pa., Jan. 1, 1940; d. Peter Paul and Susie Anne (Murcko) Kutcher; student Youngstown (Ohio) State U., 1957-58, 68-69; cert. LaSalle Extension U., Chgo., 1963, 64, 66, 67; postgrad. Pa. State U., 1974; m. Joseph Romain, Jr., Nov. 23, 1968; children—Lucretia Ann, Kimberly Rose, Annette Marie. Sec., bookkeeper Voytik Constrn. Co., Sharpsville, Pa., 1957-58; bookkeeper Ernst, Inc., Sharon, Pa., 1958-60, Mort-Bohn & Assos., C.P.A.s, Sharon, 1960-62, D.G. Reed & H. Hudson, public accts., Sharon, 1962-64; asst. office mgr. J.V. McNicholas Transfer Co., Youngstown, 1965-66; partner Reed-Romain & Assos., 1966-70; pvt. practice acctg., Sharpsville, 1970-76, 78—; partner Romain-Pendel & Assos., Public Accts., 1976-78; owner, partner RP Computer Services and Romain-Pendel Office Service, 1976-80; mem. Pa. Public Accts. Adv. Com., 1977—. Asst. treas. St. John's Episcopal Ch., Sharon, 1974, 75; exec. bd. Episc. Churchwomen, 1977—; 4H Club leader, 1977—. First runner-up Queens Contest, chairwoman Children's Pet Parade, Sharpsville Centennial, 1974. Mem. Nat. (asso. state dir. 1977—), Pa. (state bd. dirs. 1973—, state sec. 1978—, editor Pa. Acct. 1980, numerous coms., sec.) socs. public accts., Nat. (sec. 1972-73), Pa. (pres. 1972-74, exec. dir. 1975—) assns. enrolled fed. tax accts., Nat., Pa. (exec. dir.) assns. enrolled agts. Republican. Clubs: Baldwin Organ (pres. 1969) (Sharon,

Pa.); Saddlemates Saddle (treas. 1979) (Transfer, Pa.). Home: 125 Koehler Dr Sharpsville PA 16150 Office: 2048 Buckeye Dr Sharpsville PA 16150

ROMAKER, JANET JUNE, newspaper editor; b. Toledo, Nov. 4, 1952; d. Charles Edward and Barbara Ann (Russell) Romaker; B.S., Bowling Green State U., 1974. Reporter, The Blade Newspaper, Toledo, 1974-75, 76-79, asst. regional editor, 1979, regional editor, 1979—; editor Swanton Enterprise Newspaper, Swanton, Ohio, 1976; faculty Sch. Journalism, Bowling Green State U., 1982—. Chmn. fund drive Am. Heart Assn., 1980. Mem. Soc. Profl. Journalists (treas. 1981—), Sigma Delta Chi. United Methodist. Club: Toledo Press. Office: 541 N Superior St Toledo OH 43660

ROMANO, CHRISTINE DOROTHY PROVENZALE (MRS. CHARLES F. ROMANO), businesswoman, civic worker; b. Bklyn.; d. Leonardo and Concetta (Marino) Provencale; student Bklyn. Coll., 1956, Mitchell Coll., 1962; m. Charles F. Romano, Oct. 16, 1938; children—Charles, Katherine. Treas., Red Stack Towing Co., Bklyn., 1956-58, v.p., 1958, pres., 1958-61, dir., 1956-61; sec.-treas. New London Towing Co., Bklyn., 1956-58, v.p., 1958-61, dir., 1956-61; sec. A&R Towing Co. Ltd., Bklyn., 1969—; v.p., sec. Smoke Rise (N.J.) Shipping, S.A. Sec., Bergen Beach Civic Assn., 1950-56, pres. 1956-62, dir., 1950-62; mem. Bklyn. Civic Council, 1956-62, dir., 1958-62; mem. 40th Sch. Dist. Sch. Bd., 1958-62, sec., 1959-62; chmn. ARC, 1956-63, vol. worker, Smoke Rise, 1964-66; vol. Heart Fund, Smoke Rise, 1964-66; chmn. Mothers March of Dimes, N.J. state rep., 1967-68; vice-chmn. No. N.J. chpt. Paterson Gen. Hosp. Aux., 1973—; chmn. Greater Paterson Gen. Hosp. Charity Ball, 1977. Clubs: Women of Smoke Rise, Smoke Rise Garden. Home: 734 Ridge Rd Smoke Rise NJ 07405

ROMANOFF, MARJORIE REINWALD, educator; b. Chgo., Sept. 29, 1923; d. David E. and Gertrude (Rosenfield) Reinwald; student Northwestern U., 1941-42, 43-45, Chgo. Coll. Jewish Studies, 1942-43; Ed.B., U. Toledo, 1947, Ed.M., 1968, Ed.D., 1976; m. Milford M. Romanoff, Nov. 6, 1945; children—Bennett S., Lawrence M., Janet Beth (dec.). Tchr., Old Orchard Elem. Sch., Toledo, 1947-48; substitute tchr. Toledo public schs., 1958-68; tchr. McKinley Sch., Toledo, 1964-65; cons. curriculum revision in lang. arts Toledo public schs., 1966, ethnic studies program, 1976-77; supr. student tchrs. U. Toledo, 1968-73, instr. Am. Lang. Inst., 1978—; adj. asst. prof. Bowling Green State U., 1978, 79—; cons. Toledo Hebrew Acad. Elem. Sch., 1968—; instr. reading Mary Manse Coll., Toledo, 1974; tchr. temple religious sch., Congregation Shomer Emunin, Toledo, 1947-73, bd. dirs. temple sisterhood, 1958-62; bd. dirs. Hadassah, 1952—, pres. Toledo chpt., 1961-64; trustee Lucas County Children's Services Bd., 1974-76; trustee Cummings Treatment Center for Adolescents, 1976-80, pres. 1978-81; trustee Toledo Bd. Jewish Edn., 1975—, v.p., 1975-79, pres., 1982—; trustee Big Sisters, 1978-79; trustee Jewish Family Service, 1978—, v.p., 1982—; bd. dirs. Jewish Welfare Fedn. Budget and Planning Commn., 1977-81, Toledo Community Planning Council, 1980—; mem. allocations com. Mental Health and Retardation Bd., 1980-82. Mem. Nat. Soc. for Study Edn., Assn. for Supervision and Curriculum Devel., Internat. Reading Assn., Am. Ednl. Research Assn., Am. Assn. Colls. Tchr. Edn., Tchrs. English to Speakers of Other Langs., Toledo Assn. Children's Lit., Orgn. for Rehab. Through Tng., Toledo Zool. Soc., Toledo Modern Art Group, Toledo Orch. Aux., ACLU (dir. 1968-78), Women's Internat. League for Peace and Freedom, Common Cause, Northwestern U. Alumni Assn. Phi Kappa Phi, Kappa Delta Pi (past pres.), Phi Delta Kappa, Pi Lambda Theta (pres. 1976-78, nat. membership chmn. 1978—). Contbr. to Children's Lit. Assn. Quar., 1982. Home: 2514 Bexford Pl Toledo OH 43606 Office: Am Lang Inst U Toledo CE C 1006A Toledo OH 43606

ROME, FLORENCE MILES, author; b. Chgo., Sept. 24, 1910; d. Maurice David and Rose Miles; student, U. Ill., 1927-29; m. Harold Rome, Feb. 3, 1939; children—Joshua David, Rachel Miles. Author: The Scarlett Letters, 1971; The Tattooed Men, 1975, Arlene Francis, 1978; contbr. articles and short stories to profl. jours. Home: 1035 Fifth Ave New York NY 10028

ROMER, JEANNE GERALDINE, delivery service exec.; b. Camden, N.J.; d. Clifford G. and Pauline (E'del) Chalfant; B.S. with honors, Rutgers U.; m. Lewis S. Romer, Jr.; children—Stephen, Kenneth, Michael. Founder, pres. LSR Delivery Service, Inc., Haddon Heights, N.J. Democratic committeewoman Haddon Heights; active drama club Village Playbox; trustee Haddon Heights Redevel. Authority; sch. agt. Rutgers U., 1982-83. Mem. Rutgers U. Alumni Assn. (pres. 1980-82), Fedn. Dem. Women, NOW, Alpha Sigma Lambda. Home and Office: 1126 Prospect Ridge Haddon Heights NJ 08035

ROMERO, ALICE JOSEPHINE, photography co. exec.; b. Houston, Jan. 29, 1948; d. Louis Yancey and Pearle Francis (Renfroe) Johnson; m. Luis Romero, Oct. 8, 1967; children—Stephanie, Shelley. Clk.-typist Laughlin AFB, Tex., 1968-70; bus. mgr. Photography by Romero, Huntsville, Tex., 1973—. Neighborhood chmn. Huntsville Girl Scouts, 1974—; campaign chmn. United Fund, 1978; mem. Huntsville Parks Bd., 1980. Recipient Walnut plaque Girl Scouts U.S.A., 1978. Mem. Profl. Photographers Am., Southwestern Photographers, Tex. Profl. Photographer, Houston Photographers, Beta Sigma Phi. Office: 1112 11th St Huntsville TX 77340

ROMERO, HAZEL NINA, state ofcl.; b. Silver City, N.Mex., Sept. 24, 1952; d. Jaime and Benita G.; A.B., N.Mex. State U., 1974; B.B.A. cum laude, Coll. Santa Fe, 1979; m. Edward Romero, June 14, 1975. Group sec. Los Alamos Sci. Lab., 1975-76; clk. Nat. Park Service, Santa Fe, 1976-78; budget analyst N.Mex. Dept. Edn., Santa Fe, 1979; cons. SBA. Mem. Assn. Govt. Accts., Nat. Assn. Female Execs. Democrat. Roman Catholic. Home: Route 1 Box 198 Santa Fe NM 87501 Office: Dept Edn Santa Fe NM 87503

ROMERO, LUISA JOSEFINA, banker; b. San Diego, Oct. 30, 1951; d. Pietro Guido and Anna Hermina (Foradori) Serena; m. Ricardo Javier Romero, Apr. 27, 1974; 1 son, Erik. With Security Pacific Nat. Bank, San Diego, 1972—, internat. ops. officer, 1976-81, asst. v.p. charge overall ops., 1981—, bank rep. Western Council Internat. Banking, 1979—. Home: 10360 Moorpark St Spring Valley CA 92078 Office: 1200 3d Ave Suite 220 San Diego CA 92101

ROMIE, FRANCES, physician and surgeon; b. Pa., Aug. 21, 1921; B.A., UCLA, 1948; M.D., U. Rome, 1954; children—Leonard K., Jerry C. Practice medicine, Canoga Park, Calif., 1959—. Mem. AMA, Am. Women's Med. Assn., Calif. Med. Assn., Los Angeles County Med. Assn. Address: 7525 Topanga Canyon Blvd Canoga Park CA 91303

ROMNESS, SHARON LEE, psychiat. nurse, counselor; b. Chgo., Feb. 6, 1945; d. Naurice Orville and Helen Francis (Olsen) R.; B.S.N., St. Olaf Coll., 1967; M.N., U. Wash., 1970; M.A., Roosevelt U., 1978; postgrad. Northwestern U., 1979—. Instr. psychiat. nursing U. Wis., Eau Claire, 1970-72; psychiat. clin. nurse specialist Lutheran Gen. Hosp., Park Ridge, 1972-73, program coordinator in patient psychiatry, 1973-77, developer Human Resource Center, 1979-80, coordinator employee assistance program Employee Health Center, 1980—, staff asso. to v.p. human relations, 1977-79; psychotherapist to patients with chronic diseases, 1972—. NIMH stipend, 1968-69. Mem. Am. Diabetes Assn., Am. Nurses Assn., Ill. Psychol. Assn. (asso.), Am. Psychol. Assn. (asso.), Sigma Theta Tau, Phi Kappa Delta. Lutheran. Office: 1775 Dempster St Park Ridge IL 60068

ROMZICK, MARGUERITE, automotive co. exec.; b. Detroit, Mar. 20, 1938; d. Domenic and Carina (Faricelli) Novelli; grad. East Commerce High Sch., Detroit, 1955; m. Vernon C. Romzick. Stenographer, Gen. Motors Corp., Detroit, 1956-60, sec., 1960-62, exec. sec., 1962-72, asst. corp. sec., 1972—, also sec., dir. 20 U.S. subs. cos. of Gen. Motors. Mem. stockholders relations task force, mem., sec. corp. interstaff minority affairs com. Gen. Motors Inst., Flint, Mich. Club: Nomads (dir.) (Detroit). Home: 23355 Beechcrest Dearborn Heights MI 48127 Office: Gen Motors Corp 8-217 GM Bldg Detroit MI 48202

RONA, DONNA COOK, coastal engr.; b. Jacksonville, Fla., Oct. 6, 1954; d. Robert Harold and Veneda Louise (Brawner) Cook; A.A., Marymount Coll., 1971; B.S., Fla. Atlantic U., 1973; M.S., U. Miami, 1976; m. Peter A. Rona, Aug. 16, 1974; 1 dau., Jessica Rose. Oceanographer, NOAA, 1973-75; research asst. U. Miami, 1975-76; coastal engr., Dade County, Fla., 1976-77; project engr. Connell, Metcalf & Eddy, Miami, 1977-80; pres. Rona Coastal Cons., Key Biscayne, Fla., 1980—; adj. prof. Nova U., 1980—. Recipient Disting. Authorship Award NOAA-Environ. Research Labs., 1976, Outstanding Paper Award Atlantic Oceanographic and Meteorol. Labs., 1976. Registered profl. engr., Fla., La.; Mem. Nat. Soc. Profl. Engrs., ASCE, Acoustical Soc. Am., Am. Geophys. Union, Marine Tech. Soc., IEEE, Fla. Acad. Scis. Author: Handbook of Environmental Permitting. Office: PO Box 490102 Key Biscayne FL 33149

RONAN, ELENA VINADÉ (MRS. WILLIAM JOHN RONAN), real estate broker; b. Havana, Cuba; d. Ricardo Poblet and Virtudes (Alpérez-Inclán) Vinadé; B.A., N.Y. U., 1943; m. William John Ronan, May 29, 1939; children—Monica Ronan Nourie, Diana Ronan Quasha. Asst. v.p. Douglas, Elliman, Gibbons & Ives, N.Y.C., 1976—. Clubs: Cosmopolitan; Maidstone (East Hampton, L.I.); Knickerbocker; Winged Foot Golf; Creek. Home: 655 Park Ave New York NY 10021 Office: 575 Madison Ave New York NY 10021

RONEY, SHIRLEY FLETCHER, retail co. exec.; b. Atlanta, Dec. 3, 1935; d. Grady Franklin and Grace Ilene (Camp) Fletcher; student public schs., Atlanta; m. Sept. 19, 1953 (div.); 1 son, Joseph Clay. Collection corr. GMAC, Atlanta, 1953-64; sales rep. Washburn Realty, Atlanta, 1964-67; sec.-treas. Frank Jackson Lincoln Mercury, Inc., Sandy Springs, Ga., 1967-79, sec. treas., 1971—, comptroler, 1979—; v.p., dir. J&J Investment Corp., 1975—; v.p., dir. Rivergate Corp., 1979—; sec. treas., dir. Ajax Rent a Car, Sandy Springs Toyota. Div. vice chmn. United Way, 1979. Mem. Am. Bus. Womens Assn., Am. Contract Bridge League. Home: 290 Lakeview Ridge E Roswell GA 30076 Office: 6475 Roswell Rd Atlanta GA 30328

RONHOVDE, VIRGINIA SEDMAN, polit. and civic worker; b. Missoula, Mont., Dec. 17, 1909; d. Oscar Alfred and Harriet Laura (Rankin) Sedman; student U. Mont., 1925-27; B.A., Wellesley Coll., 1929; M.A., Columbia U., 1930; postgrad., 1930-33; postgrad. (Columbia U. fellow) U. Berlin, 1933-35; m. Andreas G. Ronhovde, Apr. 7, 1936; children—Erik Sedman, Andrea Rankin, Nora Montana Ronhovde Hohenlohe, Kent McGregor. Instr. sociology and labor problems Rutgers U., 1935-36; salesman Boss and Phelps, Inc., Simmons Properties, Washington, 1954-76. Sec., League Republican Women, Washington, 1969-71, bd. dirs., 1971-73, 75-77, 1st v.p., 1973-75; del. Nat. Fedn. Rep. Women Conv., Dallas, 1975; del., mem. permanent orgn. com. Rep. Nat. Conv., 1976; mem. central com. D.C. Rep. Com., 1976-80, 80-84, alt. nat. committeewoman, 1980-84. Mem. Kappa Kappa Gamma. Episcopalian. Home: 600 Beverly Ave Missoula MT 59801

RONSTADT, LINDA MARIA, singer; b. Tucson, July 15, 1946; d. Gilbert and Ruthmary (Copman) Ronstadt. Recorded numerous albums, including Evergreen, 1967, Evergreen Vol. 2, 1967, Linda Ronstadt, The Stone Poneys and Friends, Vol. 3, 1968, Hand Sown, Home Grown, 1969, Silk Purse, 1970, Linda Ronstadt, 1972, Don't Cry Now (Gold album), 1973, Heart Like a Wheel (Gold album, Platinum album), 1974, Prisoner In Disguise (Gold album, Platinum album), 1975, Hasten Down the Wind (Gold album, Platinum album), 1976, Greatest Hits (Gold album, Platinum album), 1976, Vol. 2 (Gold album), 1981, Simple Dreams (Gold album, Platinum album), Blue Bayou (Gold single), 1977, Living in the U.S.A. (Gold and Platinum albums), 1978; Mad Love (Gold album, Platinum album), 1980; Greatist Hits, Vol. II (Gold album), 1980. Appeared on Broadway as Mabel in Pirates of Penzance, 1981. Recipient Grammy awards for best country vocal female, 1975, best pop vocal female, 1976, Am. Music award, 1978. Address: care Peter Asher Mgmt Inc 644 N Doheny Dr Los Angeles CA 90069

ROODKOWSKY, TATIANA, lobbyist; b. N.Y.C., Sept. 21, 1951; d. Nikita Dimitri and Alice May (Juenger) R.; B.A., Newton Coll. Sacred Heart, 1973; postgrad. internat. affairs Cath. U., 1978—; m. Donald D. Evans, Jr., Nov. 25, 1977. Research analyst NRA, Washington, 1975-77; Washington rep. Synthetic Organic Chem. Mfrs. Assn., 1977-78; asso. dir. U.S. C. of C., Washington, 1978—. Chmn., Mass. Coll. Young Republicans, 1970-72; mem. Natick (Mass.) Town Meeting, 1973. Mem. Women in Govt. Relations (sec. 1981-82), Nat. Assn. Environ. Profls. Byzantine Rite Catholic. Home: 4006 Thornton St Annandale VA 22003 Office: 1615 H St NW Washington DC 20062

ROOSE, MARY KATHRYN, psychologist; b. Iowa City, Dec. 29, 1927; d. Vernon Elmer and Laura Kathryn (Beard) R.; B.A., U. Iowa, 1950, M.A., 1963, Ph.D., 1965; postgrad. Colo. State U., 1957, U. So. Calif., 1955, 58, Columbia U. Coll. Physicians and Surgeons, 1953, (Lab. Community Psychiatry fellow) Harvard U. Med. Sch., 1969-70. Therapist, Ill. Children's Hosp.-Sch., 1951-56; dir. Gateway Center, Ft. Collins, Colo., 1956-57; occupational therapist Spokane (Wash.) Public Schs., 1957-58, Univ. Hosps., Iowa City, 1958-62; sch. psychologist State Juvenile Home, Toledo, 1965-66, County Spl. Edn. Services, Washington, Iowa, 1966-69; elem. guidance cons. Greenfield (Mass.) Public Schs., 1970-73; coordinator children's services Bluegrass Mental Health, Danville, Ky., 1973-76; asso. prof. Eastern Ky. U., 1976-77; sch. psychologist Jefferson County (Ky.) Public Schs., 1978; lectr. psychology dept. U. Wis., LaCrosse, 1978-81; sch. psychologist Natchitoches Parish, La., 1981—; cons. Head Start; v.p. Downey Side Homes, Springfield, Mass., 1971-73; bd. dirs. Mental Health Assn. LaCrosse County, 1979-81. Mem. social ministry com., mem. library com., mem. ch. council English Lutheran Ch., LaCrosse. Cert. psychologist, Iowa, Mass., Ky., Wis. Fellow Am. Orthopsychiatry Assn.; mem. Nat. Assn. Sch. Psychologists (Ky. del. 1975-76), Am. Psychol. Assn., Am. Occupational Therapy Assn., Council Exceptional Children, AAUW (pres. Danville br. 1974-76), Am. Bd. Profl. Psychology (diplomate sch. psychology). Home: 411A Chris Rd Natchitoches LA 71457 Office: Parish Sch Bd 310 Royal St Natchitoches LA 71457

ROOT, ELEANOR, sculptress; b. Chgo., Mar. 4, 1910; d. Michael and Catherine (Bas) Muszynski; student public schs., Chgo.; m. Herman Root, Sept. 29, 1934; children—Joan Root Ericksen, Randy. Bookkeeper, sec. Mut. Benefit Health & Accident Co., Chgo., 1925-30, Pon & Co., Chgo., 1930-34, Root Bros., Chgo., 1934-44, part-time 1944—; sculptress numerous busts of pub. figures, 1965—; works include Mayor Daley in bronze for Chgo. Heart Assn., Mayor and Mrs. Daley for Chgo. Hist. Soc., Pres. and Mrs. Kennedy, 1965, Pres. and Mrs. Johnson, 1966, John Wayne, Pope John Paul II, John Cardinal Cody, Pres. Jimmy Carter. Pres., Bus. and Profl. Women's Club of Roseland, Chgo., 1971-74; v.p. Merchants of C. of C. in Roseland. Recipient hons. as publicity chmn. District II, Bus. and Profl. Women's Clubs of Ill., 1972-75. Mem. Chgo. Heart Assn., Sun Found., Gastrointestinal Research Found., Am. Legion Aux. Democrat. Roman Catholic. Office: 10317 S Michigan Ave Chicago IL 60628 *

ROOT, JOAN SCHIMPF, civic worker, mus. trustee, b. Phila., Jan. 25, 1926; d. Henry Leonard and Josephine Abbott (Sibson) Schimpf; B.A., Skidmore Coll., 1947; m. Stanley W. Root, Jr., Sept. 3, 1949; children—Henry W., Louise A., Walter W. Chmn. mus. guide program Phila. Mus. Art, 1971-74, exec. com. Friends of Mus., 1975-77, pres. women's com., 1977-80, ex-officio mem. bd. trustees, 1977-80, trustee, mem. exec. com., 1980—; port warden, mem. exec. com. Phila. Maritime Mus., 1979—; bd. dirs. Friends Ind. Nat. Hist. Park, 1975-78, mem. capital projects com., 1980, mem. intern selection com., 1981—; mem. trustee com. Mus. Council Phila., 1981; exec. com. U.S. Assn. Mus. Vols., 1980-82. Mem. Internat. Council Mus., Am. Assn. Mus., Vol. Com. Art Mus., Eastern Nat. Parks and Monuments Assn., Am. Craft Council, Nat. Trust Historic Preservation. Republican. Episcopalian. Clubs: Acorn, Sedgeley. Address: 8037 Seminole Ave Philadelphia PA 19118

ROOT, PHYLLIS ROY, stockbroker; b. Kankakee, Ill., Aug. 17, 1924; d. Edward Joseph and Evelyn Denise (Arseneau) Roy; B.J., U. Ill., 1945; postgrad. U. Chgo., 1957-58, Inst. Fin. N.Y., 1967-68; m. Edmond M. Root, Sept. 18, 1950. With Loeb, Rhoades, Frankfurt, W.Ger., 1967-71; with E.F. Hutton, La Jolla, Calif., 1971-81; 2d v.p. Shearson/Am. Express, La Jolla, 1981—; lectr. in field. Mem. San Diego Art Mus., Fin. Analysts Soc., Salk Inst. Soc., Scripps Oceanographic Inst. Contbr. articles to profl. jours. Office: PO Box 1928 La Jolla CA 92038

ROOTHAAN, JUDITH GRACE COSIN, mgmt. cons. in personnel appraisal and career guidance; b. Bklyn., Oct. 13, 1924; d. Joseph Jesse and Etta Cosin; B.B.A. magna cum laude, Baruch Coll., U. City N.Y., 1944; postgrad. in anthropology and sociology New Sch. for Social Research, Columbia U.; postgrad. in sociology (Eliza Walker scholar 1947-48, Colver Rosenberger fellow 1948, Sigmund Livingston fellow 1948-49) U. Chgo., 1947-49; m. Clemens C. J. Roothaan, Jan. 6, 1950; children—Karen, John, Peter, Charles, Elizabeth. Dir. dept. research Caldwell-Clements, Inc., N.Y.C., 1944-46; instr. sociology U. Ind., 1948; research asst. U. Chgo., 1948-49, patient intake counsellor Counseling Center, 1950-52; exec. dir. Hyde Park-Kenwood Community Conf., Chgo., 1967-68; sr. staff asso. Worthington Hurst and Assos., Chgo., 1969—; free-lance hist. house restoration and interior design, 1972—. Chmn., Lab. Schs. Parent Council, 1962-64; pres. Kozminski PTA, Chgo., 1965-67; chmn. Hyde Park Conf. Parks and Recreation Com., Chgo., 1966-67; charter bd. dirs., spl. cons. Chgo. Civic Disarmament Com., 1972-77. Mem. AAUW, Chgo. Psychol. Club, Am. Personnel and Guidance Assn., Hist. House Assn., Landmark Preservation Council Chgo., Hyde Park Hist. Soc. (charter), Chgo. Acad. Scis., Am. Museum Natural History, Chgo. Natural History Mus. (life), U. City N.Y. Alumni Assn., Art Inst. Chgo., Save Dunes Council, Beta Gamma Sigma. Club: Univ. Colony (exec. bd. and chmn. membership 1976—). Editor: Jour. Econs. and Stats., 1943-44; chief statistician for nat. market analysis: Distribution Areas and Quotas, 1946; testimony before city, state and nat. legis. bodies on air pollution and gun control, 1964-68. Home: 5235 S University Ave Chicago IL 60615

ROOTS, LINDA LEE, lawyer; b. N.Y.C., Apr. 4, 1949; d. Howard S. and Lenora M. (Mitchell) R.; B.A. summa cum laude, Queens Coll., 1973; J.D., St. John's Sch. Law, 1980; 1 dau., Jade L. Sr. tng. specialist N.Y. Community Tng. Inst., N.Y.C., 1974-77; cons. Donchian Mgmt. Services, N.Y.C., 1977-80; admitted to N.Y. Bar; asst. dep. atty. gen. N.Y. State Dept. Law, N.Y.C., 1980-82; assoc. firm Robinson, Silvermen, Pearce, Aronsohn & Berman, N.Y.C., 1982—; co-chmn. Third World Lawyers Caucus, N.Y. State Dept. Law, 1981-82. Co-chmn. PTA Lewis Armstrong Middle Sch., Queens. Recipient plaque Third World Lawyers Caucus. Mem. Macon B. Allen Black Bar Assn., St. Johns Law Sch. Alumni Assn., Black Am. Law Student Assn. Alumni Group. Office: Robinson Silvermen Pearce Aronsohn & Berman 230 Park Ave New York NY 10047

ROOZEN, MARY LOUISE SILVERMAN, bank holding co. exec.; b. Milw., Mar. 31, 1921; d. E. Edward and Margaret (May) Silverman; B.A. in Speech, U. Wis., Madison, 1942; m. Edwin Cramer Roozen, Sept. 18, 1943; children—Mary Katrina, Joanna, Margaret Anne. With conv. bur. Met. Milw. Assn. Commerce, 1942-43; adminstrv. asst. Curative Workshop of Milw., 1968-69; adminstrv. asst. mktg. Marine Corp., bank holding co., Milw., 1969-70, mktg. officer, 1970-73, asst. v.p., 1973-76, v.p. public relations, 1976—; v.p. Nat. Exchange Bank of Milw.; dir. Germantown Marine Bank. Bd. dirs., v.p. Curative Workshop of Milw., 1970-78; bd. dirs., v.p. Neighborhood House of Milw., Inc., 1963-78, now hon. dir.; bd. dirs. Friends of Art, 1980; bd. dirs., v.p. Wis. Humane Soc., 1976—; bd. dirs. Ozaukee Humane Project, 1979—. Recipient vol. activist award Nat. Center for Voluntary Action/Germaine Monteil, 1977. Mem. Public Relations Soc. Am. (exec. com. fin. instns. div., dir. fin. instns. sect.), Nat. Assn. Bank Women (chmn. Milw. group 1976-77), Tempo (v.p. 1979-80, pres. 1980—, dir.), Met. Milw. Assn. Commerce (Downtown Assn. promotion com. chmn. 1979-80), Gamma Phi Beta. Episcopalian. Clubs: Milw. Press; River Tennis; Woman's of Wis. Office: 111 E Wisconsin Ave Milwaukee WI 53202 also PO Box 481 Milwaukee WI 53201

ROPELLA, LORETTA MARIE, educator; b. Stevens Point, Wis., Sept. 2, 1923; d. John Stanley and Caroline Rose (King) Worzalla; B.A., Coll. St. Teresa, 1943; M.S.S.W., Cath. U. Am., 1945; m. Myron E. Ropella, Sept. 30, 1950. Med. social worker, instr. Georgetown U. Hosp., Washington, 1945-47; clin. social worker VA Hosp. and Milw. County Med. Complex, 1948-56; faculty U. Wis., Milw., 1956—, assoc. prof. social work, 1960—. Mem. Nat. Assn. Social Workers, AAUP, Am. Hosp. Assn., Wis. Council Edn. Social Workers, Pi Gamma Mu, Alpha Delta Kappa. Republican. Roman Catholic. Home: 9267 N Lake Dr Milwaukee WI 53217 Office: University of Wisconsin Milw 2400 E Hartford St Milwaukee WI 53211

ROPER, BIRDIE ALEXANDER, educator; b. New Orleans; d. Earl and Ethel (Charmer) Alexander; R.N., Homer G. Phillips Hosp., St. Louis, 1945; B.S., U. Dayton, 1949; M.A., Azusa Pacific Coll., 1971; M.A., Claremont Grad. Sch., 1978, Ph.D., 1980; m. Morris F. Roper, Aug. 9, 1952; 1 dau., Andree Marie. Dir. nurses Flint Goodridge Hosp., New Orleans, 1954-55; instr. sci. Woodrow Wilson High Sch., Camden, N.J., 1957-58; nurse Los Angeles Unified Sch. Dist., 1963-72; extended day instr. sociology Pasadena City Coll., 1972—; tchr. elem. sch. Los Angeles Unified Sch. Dist., 1972—. Mem. Assn. Study Afro Am. Life and History (historian), Assn. Calif. Intergroup Relations Educators, Am. Assn. Study Afro Am. Life and History, NEA, Calif. Tchrs. Assn., Internat. Platform Assn., AAUP, Phi Delta Kappa. Club: Toastmistress. Home: 550 Fernpark Dr Glendora CA 91740

ROPER, RITA MAE, accountant; b. Ashland, Ohio, Oct. 22, 1931; d. John Wilbert and Carrie Naomi (Williams) Farver; student Ashland Coll., 1962-63; m. James D. Roper, Nov. 16, 1963 (dec.); children—William, James, Steven. Asst. mgr. accounts receivable dept. Eagle Rubber Co., Inc., Ashland, 1949-57; bookkeeper, asst. office mgr. Sarver Paving Co., Ashland, 1958-65; chief accountant, co-mgr. divisional offices Raike Assos., Inc., Ashland, 1978—. Mem. Nat. Assn. Profl.

Businesswomen. Republican. Lutheran. Home: 893 St Route 302 RD 3 Ashland OH 44805 Office: 207 E Liberty St Ashland OH 44805

ROPKEY, ANN SAMONIAL, educator, lectr.; b. Vincennes, Ind., Jan. 31, 1917; d. Charles Edward and Martha Ann (Love) Samonial; A.A., Vincennes U., 1936; B.S., Peabody Coll., 1938, M.A., 1941; postgrad. Vanderbilt U.; Litt.D. (hon.), Steed Coll., 1957; m. Stewart Winning McClelland, Aug. 2, 1947 (dec. Feb. 1977); m. 2d, F. Noble Ropkey, Aug. 16, 1980. Tchr., Bogalusa (La.) High Sch., 1938, Holmes High Sch., Covington, Ky., 1939-45; instr. Okla. Coll. Women, 1938-39; dean women Licoln Meml. U., 1945-47; sponsor Dale Carnegie courses, Fla., Ind., 1947—; asso. with Mrs. Dale Carnegie in Dorothy Carnegie Courses Women, 1956—. Pres. Decorative Arts Soc., Indpls. Mus. Art; state chmn. DAR Mus., Washington; mem. adv. bd. Pompeiiana, Inc. Fellow Royal Soc. Arts (London); mem. Indpls. Propylaeum (past pres.), Internat. Platform Assn., AAUW, Wedgwood Internat. Seminar, Wedgwood Soc. (London), English Speaking Union, DAR (chpt. regent), Am Ceramic Circle, Kappa Kappa Kappa, Pi Gamma Chi. Republican. Roman Catholic. Club: Fortnightly (Indpls.). Authority on Coin glass, Lithophanes and Wedgwood. Home: 6360 W 79th St Indianapolis IN 46278

ROQUEMORE, JEAN ELLEN, educator; b. Queen City, Tex., Oct. 24, 1939; d. Walter Morris and Mabel Vernessa (Green) Johnson; B.A., Wiley Coll., 1960; M.Ed., E. Tex. State U., 1970; m. Clayton Roquemore, Jr., Oct. 19, 1979. Sec., dir. admissions Wiley Coll., Marshall, Tex., 1960-61; bus. tchr. Atlanta Ind. Sch. Dist., Booker T. Washington High Sch., 1961-70; now bus. tchr. Atlanta (Tex.) Ind. Sch. Dist., Atlanta High Sch. Mem. Tex. Tchrs. Assn., NEA, Tex. Bus. Edn. Assn., Atlanta Bus. Edn. Assn., Nat. Bus. Edn. Assn., Atlanta Edn. Assn., Zeta Phi Beta. Methodist. Clubs: Order Eastern Star, Daus. of Sphinx. Home: PO Box 1733 Kildare TX 75562 Office: 705 Rabbit Blvd Atlanta TX 75551

RORABAUGH, JOAN FORAKER, pharmacy exec., polit. worker; former educator; b. Marion, Kans., Nov. 13, 1928; d. Clifford Benson and Ethel (Hill) Foraker; A.B., Coll. of Emporia, 1950; M.A., Columbia U., 1958, postgrad., 1958-65; m. Curtis Arthur Rorabaugh, Nov. 18, 1969 (dec.). Tchr. pub. schs., 1950-56; instr. Coll. of Emporia (Kans.), 1956-69; mgr., owner Red X Pharmacy, Emporia, 1979—. Pres. Kans. Fedn. Republican Women; vice dir. 5th Dist. Rep. Women; vice chmn. 5th Dist. Reps.; vice chmn. Lyon County Rep. Central Com.; mem. exec. com. Kans. Rep. Com.; bd. dirs. Hetlinger Devel. Center; vol. ARC; driver Meals on Wheels; bd. dirs., former Sunday Sch. tchr. Methodist Ch. Named Woman of Yr. Beta Sigma Phi, 1975. Mem. DAR, Lyon County Rep. Women, P.E.O., Delta Kappa Gamma. Clubs: Altrusa (past pres.), Emporia Garden (past pres.), Etude (past pres.). Columnist Kitchen Corner, Emporia Gazette. Home: 1707 Yucca Ln Empoira KS 66801 Office: 624 Commercial St Emporia KS 66801

RORKE, MARIE MOORE, financial exec.; b. N.Y.C., Oct. 6, 1933; d. William J. and Cleo (Kascpre) Moore; student Hunter Coll., 1951-52; A.S. in Bus. Mgmt., Adelphi U.; m. Charles Rorke, May 15, 1953; 1 son, C. William. Exec. sec. Avis Car Leasing Co., Plainview, N.Y., 1964-66; bus. office rep. N.Y. Telephone Co., Huntington, 1966-67; corp. sec., asst. treas., corp. controller Geotel, Inc., Amityville, N.Y., 1967—; dir. AFP Industries. Sec., Heatherwood Civic Assn., Huntington, 1965—. Mem. Am. Inst. Corp. Controllers, Am. Soc. Profl. and Bus. Women. Home: 8 Coe Pl Huntington NY 11746 Office: 185 Dixon Ave Amityville NY 11701

ROSADO, ELMA BEATRIZ, chemist; b. Arecibo, P.R., Jan. 31, 1954; d. Rafael and Maria (Barbosa) R.; B.S., U. P.R., 1976; m. Pedro J. Panzardi, July 1, 1979. Research asst. P.R. Nuclear Center, Rio Piedras, 1976; chemist Roche Products, Inc., Manati, P.R., 1976-80; tech. cons. PJP & Assos., San Juan, P.R., 1980—. Mem. Assn. Women in Sci. Home: PO Box 1020 Vega Baja PR 00764

ROSADO, PEGGY MORAN, actress, singer, dancer, educator; b. Canton, Ohio, Apr. 16, 1946; d. Clarence Ellsworth and Mabel Cecilia (Kearns) Moran; student Northwestern U.; B.S., Kent State U.; M.A., Hunter Coll., 1969; student Arthur Mitchell, Dance Theatre of Harlem, 1971, 76— Am. Ballet Theatre, 1972-74; m. Richard Robert Garcia di Magpiong, Apr. 7, 1979. Dir., lead dancer New World Dancers Inc., N.Y.C., 1971—; dancer Dance Theatre of Harlem, 1976—; dance tchr. performing arts program Franklin K. Lane High Sch., Bklyn., 1970-71; dance tchr., choreographer Lincoln Sq. Community Center, N.Y.C., 1971—; student head NBC Theatre Workshop, N.Y.C., 1960-61; film appearances Serpico, Dog Day Afternoon, Nunzio, Prince of the City, So Fine, Ragtime. Mem. Actors Equity Assn., Screen Actors Guild, AFTRA, AGVA, Assn. Am. Dance Cos., Am. Indian Community House. Roman Catholic. Choreographer New World Journey, 1971, The Creation, 1982. Home and Office: 345 W 58th St New York NY 10019

ROSBERGER, ANNE WALDMAN, psychotherapist; b. N.Y.C., Nov. 23, 1932; d. Joseph and Susan (Wagner) Waldman; B.A., Bklyn. Coll., 1953; M.S., Columbia U., 1955; postgrad Yeshiva U., 1977—; m. Henry Rosberger, Oct. 12, 1958; children—Daniel, Richard. Sr. caseworker, supr. Salvation Army Family Service Bur., N.Y.C., 1955-59; field instr., 1968-69; chief cons., supr. Widows Consultation Center, N.Y.C., 1971-76; pvt. practice psychotherapy, N.Y.C., 1958—; exec. dir. Bereavement and Loss Center of N.Y., N.Y.C., 1976—; cons. St. Vincent's Hosp. Hospice, N.Y.C., 1979—; lectr. in field. Mem. Nat. Assn. Social Workers, Acad. Certified Social Workers, Alpha Kappa Delta. Author articles. Office: 170 E 83d St New York NY 10028

ROSCHER, NINA MATHENY, chemist, educator; b. Uniontown, Pa., Dec. 8, 1938; d. Charles K. and Wilma P. Matheny; B.S. in Chemistry (Gen. Motors scholar), U. Del., 1960; Ph.D. (fellow), Purdue U., 1964; m. David Roscher, Dec. 27, 1964. Phys. chemist Nat. Bur. Standards, 1958-61; research asst. dept. chemistry Purdue U., 1960-64, instr., 1964-65; instr. dept. chemistry U. Tex., Austin, 1965-67; sr. staff chemist Coca-Cola Export Corp., 1967-68; asst. prof. dept. chemistry Douglass Coll., Rutgers State U., N.J., 1968-74, asst. dean, 1971-74; dir. acad. adminstrn. Am. U., Washington, 1974-76, asso. prof. chemistry, 1974-79, prof., 1979—, vice provost acad. services, 1979—, dean faculty affairs, 1981—. NSF grantee, 1976-82. Fellow Washington Acad. Scis.; mem. Am. Chem. Soc. (Virgil Payne award 1977, treas. Monmouth county sect. 1970-72, mem. various coms. 1974—), Dist. Inst. Chemists (dir.-at-large 1981—, pres. 1978-79, sec. 1976-77), AAAS (mem. edn. sect. 1976-78), Am. Assn. Univ. Adminstrs., Soc. Applied Spectroscopy, Assn. Women in Sci. (exec. bd. 1975-78), Sigma Xi, Phi Kappa Phi (pres. chpt. 1978). Methodist. Contbr. articles on chemistry to sci. publs. Home: 10400 Hunter Ridge Dr Oakton VA 22124 Office: The American Univ 4400 Massachusetts Ave Washington DC 20016

ROSDOLSKY, CHRISTINE DORA, fashion designer; b. Phila., Dec. 6, 1953; d. John and Mary (Grosseibl) R.; student Drexel U., 1971-73, Parsons Sch. Design, 1973-74. Design asst. Vera Maxwell, N.Y.C., 1974-76; asst. designer Hooper-Bleyle, N.Y.C., 1976-78; designer Talbott-Givenchy, N.Y.C. and Paris, 1978-79, Scott Barrie, N.Y.C., 1979-80; asst. fashion designer Russ Togs, Sportswear, N.Y.C., 1981; designer Dary Sue Fashions/David Strauss Fashions, N.Y.C., 1981—. Mem. Costume Soc. Am. Office: 525 7th Ave New York NY 10018

ROSE, CAROL JO, real estate broker; b. San Francisco, June 13, 1945; d. Arthur Daniel and Irene Pearl (Park) Frye; m. Roy Tsuruda, Nov. 15, 1978; children—Heidi, Kimberly, Tiffany. Salesman, Gary Gillmor and Assos., Santa Clara, Calif., 1972-74; salesman Albers Gallery of Homes, San Jose, Calif., 1974; asso. broker Allstate Realtors, San Jose, 1974-76; broker, owner Omega Phi Investments, Inc., Campbell, Ga., 1978—; owner, mgr. Carol Rose Real Estate, San Jose, 1977-79; dir. edn. Oak Ridge Realty Inc., San Jose, 1976-77; owner, dir. Omega Phi Inst., San Jose, 1978-79; exec. adminstr. Allstate Realtors Acad. Edn., San Jose, 1979-80. Mem. Calif. Assn. Realtors (table leader conv. 1977), San Jose Real Estate Bd., Nat. Assn. Realtors, Calif. Assn. Real Estate Tchrs. Club: Toastmasters Internat. Home: 5985 Vista Loop San Jose CA 95124 Office: Omega Phi Investments Inc 1475 S Bascom Suite 205 Campbell CA 95008

ROSE, CONSTANCE, real estate co. exec.; b. Chgo., June 18, 1935; d. Athony and Adeline LaRosa; student Hunter Coll., 1953-55, Atlanta Sch. Real Estate, 1970, agt. 1970, broker, 1973; 2 children. Founder, owner, agt., broker Connie Rose & Assos., Atlanta, 1973—. Bd. dirs. Jewish Nat. Fund, 1981—. Mem. Million Dollar Club, Atlanta Bd. Realtors (com. mem.), AGREE. Club: B'nai B'rith (v.p. 1969). Office: 1874 Piedmont Rd Suite 320-C Atlanta GA 30324

ROSE, CYNTHIA PEARL, physician; b. Boston, Apr. 26, 1936; d. Irving and Eleanor Lillian (Fox) R.; A.B., Tufts U., 1959; M.D., Boston U., 1963; children—Scott David, Daniel Irving. Intern, U. Calif. Hosps., San Francisco, 1963-64; resident U. Colo. Med. Center, Denver, 1964-69; staff psychiatrist Pikes Peak Mental Health Center, Colorado Springs, Colo., 1969-70, acting dir., 1970; research asso., reading research U. Colo. Med. Center, Denver, 1968-74; med. dir. Pikes Peak Family Counseling Mental Health Center, Colorado Springs, 1970—; asso. clin. prof. psychiatry U. Colo. Med. Center, Denver; psychiat. cons. Colo. Coll., 1970-77. Mem. White House Commn. on Youth, El Paso County, 1970; mem. gov.'s task force on rev. of criminal insanity plea, 1978-80; mem. U.S. Olympic Sports Medicine Council, 1979—. Diplomate Am. Bd. Psychiatry and Neurology. Mem. AMA, Am. Acad. Child Psychiatry, Am. Psychiat. Assn., Colo. Psychiat. Soc. (pres. 1981), Colo. Med. Soc. Office: 875 W Moreno Colorado Springs CO 80905 also 730 N Cascade Ave Colorado Springs CO 80903

ROSE, DENISE BEYE, ins. co. mgr.; b. Portsmouth, Va., Oct. 22, 1953; d. Fred Lewis and Donna Kathleen (Luing) Beye; B.A., U. Ark., 1974; m. Andy Murray Rose, Nov. 23, 1979. With Nationwide Ins., Denver, 1974-75; with Ins. Co. of N.Am., 1975-77, bond underwriter, Dallas, 1976-77; resident mgr. states of Tenn., Ky., Lawyers Surety Corp., Nashville, 1977—. Cert. profl. ins. woman (CPIW). Mem. Nat. Assn. Ins. Women, Tenn. Ins. Assn., Surety Assn. Nashville, Profl. Ins. Agts. Tenn., Nat. Assn. Female Execs., Ark. Alumni Assn. Republican. Baptist. Club: 1752 (v.p. 1980, pres. 1981, sec.-treas. 1982). Home: 4000 Anderson Rd Apt 25 Nashville TN 37217 Office: PO Box 17126 Nashville TN 37217

ROSE, ELAINE, psychotherapist; b. Milw., Apr. 14; d. Harry Carl and Sara Mendelsohn; B.A., Calif. State U., Northridge, 1968, M.S.W., 1970; children—Steven, Susan, Kenneth. Music tchr., music therapist, Sherman Oaks, Calif., 1963-68; social work intern VA Hosp., Sepulveda, Calif., 1968-70; clin. social worker Olive View Med. Center, Sylmar, Calif., 1970-74; crisis clin. coordinator Cedars-Sinai Med. Center, Thalians Community Mental Health Center, Los Angeles, 1974-76; pvt. practice specializing in psychotherapy, Sherman Oaks, 1972—; cons. mental health Los Angeles County Probation Dept., 1974-75, Los Angeles City Schs., 1973—, Los Angeles County Regional Mental Health Services, 1974—; pvt. practice psychotherapy, Beverly Hills, Calif., 1979—; clin. supr. Cedars-Sinai Med. Center, Los Angeles, 1976—, Wright Inst., Los Angeles, 1979—. Mem. United Way Planning Council, 1974-76, South Forum Task Force for Counseling and Community Coordinating Services, 1975-77. Lic. clin. social worker, Calif. Mem. Acad. Cert. Social Workers, Nat. Registry Health Care Providers, Nat. Assn. Social Workers, Calif. Soc. Clin. Social Work, Los Angeles Group Psychotherapy Soc., Los Angeles Inst. Psychoanalytic Studies. Author: Redefining and Preventing Mental Health Emergencies in the Schools., 1976; contbr. articles to profl. publs. Office: 360 N Bedford Dr Suite 312 Beverly Hills CA 90210

ROSE, ELAINE EMMA, pub. co. ofcl.; b. Chgo., Nov. 23, 1933; d. Arthur Otto and Marie Elizabeth (Nicoll) Doyle; A.A.S., Harper Coll., 1975; student Roosevelt Coll., 1975-76; m. Donald E. Rose, June 13, 1964; 1 son, John Edward. Exec. sec. Chgo. Transit Authority, 1951-57; legal sec. Whizz Office Service, Chgo., 1957-64; legal asst. Hobbs, De La Parte, Whigham, Gonzales, Tampa, Fla., 1964-66; asst. to dir. franchises Shakees, Inc., Des Plaines, Ill., 1966-68; exec. asst. to pres. Time Life Libraries, Inc., Palatine, Ill., 1968-79; dir. office of chmn. World Book, Inc., Chgo., 1979—; exec. sec. Howard V. Phalin Found. Mem. Direct Selling Assn. (dir. 1980—), Nat. Assn. Female Execs., Assn. Internat. Execs. Clubs: Arlington Outdoor, Woodfield Racquet, River Trails Tennis, BB Lodge. Home: 318 Braeside Dr Arlington Heights IL 60004 Office: 510 Merchandise Mart Chicago IL 60654

ROSE, GLADYS DORTCH, cytotechnologist; b. Memphis, Sept. 6, 1939; d. William Tell and Lillie (Thompson) Dortch; B.S., LeMoyne Coll., 1959; cert. in cytotech. U. Tenn., 1961; M.S. in Organizational Psychology, So. Ill. U., Edwardsville, 1978; m. Lucius Victor Rose, June 17, 1967; 1 dau., Gladys Ann. Substitute tchr. Memphis Public Schs., 1959, 61; supr. cytology Western Bapt. Hosp., Paducah, Ky., 1961-67; part-time cytotechnologist Cardinal Glennon Hosp., St. Louis, 1979-82; ednl. coordinator profl. edn. in cytology St. Louis U. Sch. Medcine, 1980-81; supr. cytology lab. St. Luke's Hosp., St. Louis, 1967—; cons. in field. Recipient various service awards. Mem. Am. Soc. Clin. Pathology, Am. Cytology Soc., St. Louis Cytology Soc., St. Louis Med. Tech. Soc., Am. Public Health Assn., LWV, Nat. Assn. Univ. Women, Sigma Gamma Rho. Mem. A.M.E. Ch. Club: Order Calanthe. Author articles in field. Home: 7006 Stanford St St Louis MO 63130 Office: 5535 Delmar St St Louis MO 63112

ROSE, JACQUELINE CAROLE, planner, adminstr.; b. Phila., Apr. 2; d. David Morris and Betty Lorraine (Gelb) R.; B.Arch., B.S. Environ. Design, U. Okla., 1978; B.S. in Liberal Studies, SUNY, Albany, 1978; student Rensselaer Poly. Inst. Pvt. practice architecture, Kansas City, Mo.; planner, designer URS/Hewitt & Royer, Inc., Kansas City; cons., chief planner Sci. Mus. Va., Richmond; archtl. cons., Alexandria, Va., 1978-79; architect Office of Sec., Office of Facilities Engrng., U.S. Dept. Health and Human Services, Washington, 1980—; dir. Broadway-Westport Neighborhood Devel. Corp. (Kansas City), 1973-75; vis. lectr. Cornell U., 1977, 78, Washington, 1979, 80, U. Va., 1977, U. Mo. Sch. Law, U. Kans. Sch. Law, Va. Commonwealth U., 1977. Mem. Mo. Adv. Council Hist. Preservation, 1974-75, Landmarks Commn. Kansas City (Mo.), 1970-75; mem. Mid-Am. Regional Council Govts. Citizens Adv. Bd., 1973-75, also total transp. policy com. Registered architect, Mo. Mem. AIA (nat. com. hist. resources, nat. com. regional devel. and natural resources), Citizens Environ. Council Greater Kansas City (adv. bd.), Nelson/Atkins Gallery Art Soc. Fellows. Office: Dept Health and Human Services Room 4613 North Bldg 330 Independence Ave SW Washington DC 20201

ROSE, JOY DIXON, polit. cons.; b. King's Daughters, Miss., Jan. 25, 1953; d. James Lavelle and Eliza Deloris (Hood) Dixon; student Holmes Jr. Coll., 1973; B.A., Miss. State U., 1979; m. Benny J. Rose, Aug. 31, 1974; 1 dau., Lindsay Lane. County chmn. Com. to Re-elect Pres. Ford, coordinator primary coordinatory Yazoo County Republican Com., 1978; hdqrs. chmn., steering com. Thad Cochran for Senate, 1978; exec. dir. telephone bank ops. Miss. Reagan for Pres., 1980; kickoff chmn. Barbour for Senate, 1981, exec. dir. telephone bank ops., 1981—; alt. del. Miss. Rep. Conv., 1975, 79; chmn. Yazoo County Rep. Exec. Com., 1981—; vice chmn., 1976-81; del. So. Rep. Leadership Conf., 1979; polit. cons. Vol. chmn. Easter Seals, 1982; zone capt. March of Dimes, 1979; area coordinator Am. Cancer Soc., 1978. Mem. Nat. Assn. Female Execs., Nat. Assn. Polit. Cons. Baptist. Home and office: Route 1 Box 7A Benton MS 39039

ROSE, KATHERINE CAST (MRS. HORACE CHAPMAN ROSE), civic worker; b. Akron, Ohio; d. John Frederick and Amy (Motz) Cast; A.B., Wellesley Coll., 1929; m. Horace Chapman Rose, Oct. 1, 1938; 1 son, Jonathan Chapman. Actress, Cleve. Play House, Chautauqua Repertory Co., 1929-36; trustee Goodrich Social Settlement, 1936-43, Jr. League Cleve., Nat. Cathedral Assn., Washington, 1948-56, 59-65, Children's Theatre of Washington, 1947-49, Cleve. Internat. Youth Leaders, Cleve. Playhouse; chmn. stage com. Washington Stage Door Canteen, 1943-46; chmn. box com. Nat. Symphony Orch., 1947-48; mem. adv. council Nat. Inst. Mental Health, 1956-59; co-chmn. Ohio Citizens for Eisenhower, 1952, 56; vice chmn. women's div. Nat. Citizens for Eisenhower's Congl. Com., 1954; mem. adv. council Nat. Accident Prevention Bur., 1959-63; chmn. Blueprint for Life, Cleve., 1963; mem. Ohio Arts Council, 1976—. Republican. Episcopalian. Clubs: Intown (Cleve.); Sulgrave (Washington). Home: 12407 Fairhill Rd Cleveland OH 44120 also 2701 31st St NW Washington DC 20008

ROSE, MARIAN JUNE, nurse; b. Wareham, Mass., June 8, 1941; d. Bertram and Mary Agnes (Viera) Rose; A.S., Capecod Community Coll., 1963; B.S. in Nursing, Southeastern Mass. U., 1978; 1 dau., Jennifer Anne. Fashion designer Bob-O's Fashion Shop, Sandwich, Mass., 1959-62; exec. legal sec. Judge Gersham D. Hall, Harwich, Mass., 1963-66; millinery mgr. Zayre Corp., Hyannis, Mass., 1966-68; nursing asst. Roland Thatcher Nursing Home, Wareham, 1970-73; charge nurse Paul Denver State Sch. for Handicapped, Taunton, Mass., 1978; staff nurse, supr. Francis P. Meml. Hosp., New Bedford, Mass., 1978; charge nurse spinal cord injury unit Brockton (Mass.) VA Hosp., 1979-81; staff nurse, asst. head nurse Fresno (Calif.) VA Hosp., 1981—. vol. Tobey Hosp., Wareham, 1975-78, Manomet Fire Dept. Ambulance Service, 1978-79. Mem. Wareham Area Counseling Service, 1977-80, Fresno Community Theatre Group, Big Bros./Big Sisters. Mem. Am. Rifle Assn., Cath. Nurses Assn. Cape Cod, Am. Nurses Assn., Am. Critical Care Nurses Assn., Equal Opportunity in Human Resources Assn., Am. Notary Assn., Mass. Emergency Med. Technicians Assn., Nat. Pacer and Trotting Assn., Roeding Park Zool. Soc. Roman Catholic. Club: Lioness, Our Lady's Rosary Makers. Home: 349 Onset Ave Onset MA 02558

ROSE, MARILYN GADDIS, comparative literature educator, author; b. Fayette, Mo., Apr. 2, 1930; d. Merrill Elmer and Florence Georgia (Lyon) Gaddis; B.A., Central Methodist Coll., 1952; M.A., U. S.C., 1955; Ph.D., U. Mo., 1958; m. James L. Rose, Dec. 23, 1956; m. 2d, Stephen David Ross, Nov. 16, 1968; 1 son, David Gaddis. Instr. Stephens Coll., 1958-68; prof. comparative lit. SUNY, Binghamton, 1968—, dir. Translation Research and Instrn. program, 1973—; vis. asso. prof. Ind. U., 1968. Humanities Research Center Australian Nat. U. fellow, 1977. Mem. MLA, Northeast MLA, Am. Assn. Tchrs. French, Am. Translators Assn., Am. Lit. Translator Assn., Am. Com. Irish Studies. Author: Julian Green, Gallic American Novelist, 1971; Jack B. Yeats, Painter and Poet, 1972; Katharyn Tynan, 1975; Translation Spectrum, 1981; translator: Axel, 1970; Eve of the Future Eden, 1981. Home: 4 Johnson Ave Binghamton NY 13905 Office: SUNY Binghamton NY 13901

ROSE, MARY ANN MCCARTHY, nursing educator; b. Cleve., Jan. 16, 1942; d. John F. and Margaret E. (Heckel) McCarthy; B.S. in Nursing, Georgetown U., 1963; M.S. in Nursing, Case Western Reserve U., 1974; Ed.D., N.C. State U., 1982; m. Walter J. Pories, June 4, 1977; children—Mary Lisa, Michael M.; stepchildren—Susan, Mary Jane, Carolyn, Kathleen. Asso. dir. Cancer Center, Inc., Cleve., 1974-77; asst. prof. nursing E. Carolina U., 1977—, asst. to chancellor, 1981—. Bd. dirs. Am. Cancer Soc., Pitt County, N.C., 1978-79. Am. Cancer Soc. fellow, 1973. Mem. Am. Soc. Clin. Oncology, Oncology Nursing Soc., Sigma Xi, Sigma Theta Tau, Phi Kappa Phi. Contbr. articles to profl. jours. Home: 203 Chowan Rd Greenville NC 27834 Office: East Carolina University Greenville NC 27834

ROSE, MARY ETTA MORRISON, educator; b. Indpls., Oct. 3, 1917; d. Robert and Florence Etta (Brooking) Taylor; B.S., Ball State U., 1937; M.S., Butler U., 1947, postgrad., 1969—. Elem. and Jr. high sch. tchr. music, Indpls., 1942—, now tchr. Mapleton-Fall Creek Sch., 1975—; ch. organist, choir dir. Bethel A.M.E. Ch., 1938-60, Barnes United Meth. Ch., 1977-81, Witherspoon United Presbyn. Ch., 1977-82; pres. Indpls. Music Promoters, 1977—. Semi-finalist for Ind. Tchr. of Yr., 1982; named Tchr. of Yr., Indpls. Pub. Schs., 1982; Lilly Endoment fellow, Indpls. Sch. Bd. fellow Temple U., 1964. Mem. Internat. Soc. Music Edn., Internat. Council Traditional Music, Indpls. Edn. Assn., Ind. Tchrs. Assn., NEA, Music Educators Nat. Conf., Ind. Music Educators Assn., U.S.-China Peoples Friendship Assn., NAACP, Nat. Assn. Negro Musicians, Indpls. Mus. Art, Indpls. Children's Mus., Nat. Council Negro Women, ACLU, Soc. Intensified Edn. (Outstanding Classroom Tchr. award 1982), Phi Delta Kappa (citation 1965). Unitarian. Club: Bridgette (Indpls.).

ROSE, SHIRLEY, publisher; b. Kansas City, Mo., Mar. 12, 1921; d. Harry G. and Esther (Mendelson) Mallin; B.A., U. Mo., 1941; m. Stanley Jay Rose, Oct. 7, 1942; children—Roberta Susan, Stephen Frederick. Co-founder, co-pub. Sun Newspapers, Overland Park, Kans., 1950—; sec., dir. Sun Publs. Inc., 1973—. Mem. exec. com. Kans. div. Am. Cancer Soc.; pres. Johnson County Cancer unit, recipient Bea Johnson Meml. cancer award, 1975, 76, honoree for outstanding achievement in journalism Women in Communication, 1979. Mem. Theta Sigma Phi. Republican. Club: Soroptimist. Home: 7 Navajo Ln W Lake Quivira KS 66106 Office: Sun Publs Bldg 7373 W 107th St Overland Park KS 66212

ROSEBROCK, ELLEN FLETCHER, writer, archtl. historian; b. Pasadena, Tex., Dec. 28, 1947; d. Delbert Van and Juanita (Arrowood) Fletcher; B.A., Pa. State U., 1968; M.A., Columbia U., 1972; Dir. publs. program South Street Seaport Museum, N.Y.C., 1973-77; asso. The Preservation Partnership, Natick, Mass., 1977-79; project historian Inst. Conservation Archaeology, Harvard U., Cambridge, Mass., 1979—. Trustee Roslyn Landmark Soc., 1976-77; v.p. Beacon Hill Civic Assn., Boston; cons. Soc. Preservation L.I. Antiquities; mem. Beacon Hill Archtl. Commn., 1981—. N.Y. State Council on the Arts grantee, 1975-76; Nat. Endowment for Humanities grantee, 1976-77. Mem. Soc. Archtl. Historians, Soc. for Indsl. Archaeology, L.I. Hist. Soc., Soc. L.I. Antiquities, Soc. Preservation New Eng. Antiquities. Author: Walking Around in South Street, 2d edit., 1980; Counting House Days in South Street, 1975; Farewell to Old England; New York in Revolution, 1976; South Street. Dover, 1977; Historic Fall River, 1978. Home: 80 Mount Vernon St Boston MA 02108

ROSEBURY, AMY L., clin. psychologist; b. N.Y.C., Feb. 12, 1918; d. Martin J. and Anna Loeb; M.A. in Psychology, Columbia U., 1939, M.S. in Psychiat. Social Work, 1942; m. Theodor Rosebury, Nov. 21, 1949 (dec.). Numerous positions as supr., cons. to social service agys., hosps. and treatment centers; adminstr., supr., tchr. psychiat. residents Inst.

Juvenile Research, 1966-67; pvt. practice psychol. therapy, Chgo. and Conway, Mass., 1972-81, Amherst, Mass., 1981—. Mem. Am. Group Therapy Assn., Am. Psychol. Assn., Acad. Cert. Social Workers, Nat. Assn. Social Workers. Address: 256 N Pleasant St Apt 4R Amherst MA 01002

ROSELLE, SUE E., health care adminstr.; b. Tarentum, Pa., June 30, 1947; d. William John and Suzanne Esther (Clever) R.; B.S., Pa. State U., 1968; M.S.W., U. Ill., Urbana-Champaign, 1977; m. Kenneth E. Worstell, Sept. 6, 1969; 1 dau., Beth. Adminstrv. asst. Upward Bound, Pa. State U., 1970; social worker Norfolk (Va.) Family Planning Project, 1972-74, Burnham City Hosp., Champaign, Ill., 1976-77; sr. social worker S. Hills Health System Home Health Agy., Homestead, Pa., 1977-78, dir. allied health services, 1978-81; exec. dir. Emergency Med. Service Inst., Pitts., 1981—. Mem. Nat. Assn. Social Workers (state dir.), Acad. Cert. Social Workers, Phi Kappa Phi. Home: 160 Lloyd Ave Pittsburgh PA 15218 Office: 3600 Forbes Ave Suite 206 Pittsburgh PA 15213

ROSELLINI, LYNN CHRISTINE, journalist; b. Seattle, May 23, 1947; d. Albert Dean and Ethel Katherine (McNeil) Rosellini; student Sch. Communications, U. Wash., 1964-68. Reporter, Newsday, Garden City, N.Y., 1968-73, Washington bur., 1974-75; reporter Washington Star, 1975-80, Washington bur. N.Y. Times, 1980—. Recipient Front Page award N.Y. Newswomen's Club, 1973, Human Interest Reporting award Newspaper Guild, 1978. Mem. Newspaper Guild. Contbr. articles to periodicals. Office: Washington Bur NY Times 1000 Connecticut Ave Washington DC 20036

ROSEN, DOROTHY GRANOWITTER, educator; b. N.Y.C., Sept. 5, 1938; d. Albert and Clara Granowitter; B.A., Queens Coll., 1970, M.A., 1972; postgrad. C.W. Post Coll., 1979—; m. Leonard Rosen, Sept. 7, 1957 (dec.); children—Jill Susanne, Glenn Michael. Speech and lang. therapist N.Y.C. Spl. Edn. Center, 1972-76; unit coordinator preplacement unit P.S. 188Q, P.S. 46Q, 1976-78; diagnostician speech/lang./learning disabilities com. on the handicapped Dist. 29 N.Y.C. Office Student Support Services, 1978-79; field coordinator citywide programs, spl. edn. program N.Y.C. Schs., 1979—; tchr. trainer Spl. Edn. Teaching Resource Center, N.Y.C., 1979-80. Cert. speech pathologist, N.Y. State. Mem. Am. Speech and Hearing Assn. (cert. of clin. competence in speech), United Fedn. Tchrs., N.Y. State United Tchrs., Pioneer Women, Phi Beta Kappa. Home: 26 Flower Ln Jericho NY 11753 Office: PS 38 450 Pacific St Brooklyn NY 11217

ROSEN, GAYLE BRODY, state ofcl.; b. Newark, June 6, 1934; d. Harry and Anne (Helfmann) Brody; B.A. magna cum laude, Montclair (N.J.) State Coll., 1975; children—Neil Jared, Hilary Beth. Realtor, South Orange, N.J., 1963-65; dir. Children's Theatre Troupe, Nat. Council Jewish Women, 1965-71; tchr. theatre workshops, 1965-71; asst. dir. N.J. Div. Consumer Affairs, Newark, 1977—; mem. West Orange City Council, 1974—, pres., 1976-79. Ward and com. leader Democratic Party; active LWV, Nat. Council Jewish Women, Am. Jewish Congress, NOW, P.T.A. Recipient Woman Who Broke a Barrier award YWCA, 1974. Mem. Assn. Elected Women Ofcls., Phi Kappa Phi, Phi Sigma Sigma. Jewish. Home: 9 Ridgeway Ct West Orange NJ 07052 Office: 1100 Raymond Blvd Newark NJ 07102

ROSEN, JACQUELINE HELENE, oil trading co. exec.; b. Mineola, N.Y.; d. Georges Jules and Helene Marguerite (Cellar) Moraillon; Bac., L'Institut de L'Assomption, Paris, 1965; Lic. Scis. Politiques, U. Poitiers (France), 1969; coursework Inst. Advanced Traffic, N.Y.C., 1975 World Trade Inst., N.Y.C., 1980; m. Daniel Rosen, June 15, 1975; 1 son, Jason Benjamin. Adminstrv. asst., interpreter to chmn. bd. and chief exec. officer Specilait, S.A., La Mothe-St. Heray, France, 1969-71; spl. asst., interpretor to exec. v.p. Credit Lyonnais, N.Y.C., 1971-72; adminstrv. asst. Carbonit Am., Inc. div. Carbonit Netherlands, N.Y.C., 1972-73, marine traffic mgr., 1973-76; mgr., adminstr., marine traffic mgr. Petromer Am., Ltd. subs. Cargill, Inc., N.Y.C., 1981-82, corp. sec., 1978-82; v.p. ops., sec.-treas. Pegasus Petroleum Corp., N.Y.C., 1982—. Home: 20 W 86th St New York NY 10024 Office: 595 Madison Ave New York NY 10022

ROSEN, PHYLLIS, art dealer, appraiser; b. Boston, May 31, 1937; s. Samuel and Lillian (Smith) Bornstein; student U. Heidelberg, Germany, 1956-58; m. Theodore Rosen. Dir., Obelisk Gallery, Inc., Boston, 1961—, Parker 470 Gallery, Boston, 1971-74, Harcus Krakow Rosen Sonnabend Gallery, Boston, 1972-74, Sculpture to Wear, Inc., N.Y.C., 1973-76; appraiser, cons. 20th Century art, Appraisal Services, 1976—. Office: 90 Commonwealth Ave Boston MA 02116

ROSEN, SANDRA HELEN, ednl. adminstr.; b. Pitts., Dec. 14, 1943; d. Daniel I. and Marcia R. (Robbins) Danovitz; B.S., U. Pitts., 1964, M.Ed., 1978; m. Lawrence J. Rosen, June 12, 1964; children—Amy Lynn, Hilary Beth. Tchr., Churchill Area High Sch., Pitts., 1964-68; instr. Allegheny County Community Coll., 1979-81; instr. bus. edn. Wheeler Sch., Pitts., 1976-81; instr. ICM Sch. Bus. div. Litton Industries, Pitts., 1981, supr., 1981—. Bd. dirs. Rodef Shalom Congregation, 1981—; trustee Jewish Community Center, Zionist Orgn. Am. Mem. Nat. Bus. Edn., Internat./Info. Word Processing, Tri-State Bus. Edn. Assn., Phi Beta Lambda. Democrat. Office: 10 Wood St Pittsburgh PA 15222

ROSEN, VIRGINIA L., state legislator; b. Branford, Fla., Dec. 31, 1938; d. Irvin P. and Mary Evelyn Philpot; B.Ed., U. Miami, 1961, M.Ed., 1967; m. Feb. 7, 1959; children—Alex, Rosen. Positions held include: asst. dean U. Miami Sch. Edn.; asso. dir. Tchr. Tng. Corps.; adj. prof. Fla. Internat. U.; originator, owner, operator S. Fla. Plant Fair; now mem. Fla. Ho. of Reps. Mem. Common Cause, Fla. Wildlife Fedn., Nat. Audubon Soc., LWV, Democratic Club Miami Beach, Democratic Club North Dade County, Tiger Bay Polit. Club, Phi Delta Kappa. Club: Women's. Office: 370 NE 146 Trail North Miami FL 33161

ROSENBAUER, DONNA LOUISE, writer; b. Boston, Oct. 26, 1936; d. Oscar E. and Mary C. R.; B.A., Emmanuel Coll., 1958; M.Ed., State Tchrs. Coll., Boston, 1969; J.D., New Eng. Sch. Law, 1979. Children's librarian Bookmobile Service, Boston Public Library, 1958-60; tchr. 4th grade, public schs., Boston, 1960-63; instr. Hickox Secretarial Sch., Boston, 1965-68, Boston U. Sch. Journalism, 1971-72; editor Allyn & Bacon, Inc., Boston, 1963-66; sr. editor Ginn Pub./Xerox, Lexington, Mass., 1966-75; free-lance writer ednl. and legal materials, Boston, 1975—; guest lectr. journalism Northeastern U.; vol. high sch. tchr. for writing, basic English. Cert. tchr., Mass. Mem. Internat. Reading Assn., Nat. Ret. Tchrs. Assn., Nat. Writers Club. Author books, including: Introduction to Fire Protection Law, 1978; Exploring Language with the Dictionary, 4 book workbook series, 1979; Fire Science Series, 5 books on arson, 1982.

ROSENBAUM, LILIAN, psychotherapist, educator; b. Guatemala City, Guatemala, July 30, 1934; came to U.S., 1952, naturalized, 1959; d. Guillermo Rosenbaum and Rosita Widawer de Rosenbaum; B.A. magna cum laude, Tufts U., 1956; M.S.W. (HEW Vocat. Rehab. trainee fellow, 1966, NIMH research trainee, 1967), U. Md., 1968, Ph.D., 1972; children—Marleen K., Russell R., Denise C., Valerie S. Winer. Psychotherapist, pvt. practice, Rockville, Md., 1968—; clin. assoc. prof. psychiatry Sch. Medicine, Georgetown U., 1970—, dir. Biofeedback Programs, Family Center, 1975—; psychotherapist Community Psychiat. Clinic, 1968-78; cons. in field. Mem. Biofeedback Soc. Am. (pres. local chpt., chmn. various nat. coms.), Soc. for Psychophysiol. Research, Am. Orthopsychiat. Assn., Nat. Assn. Social Workers, Am. Family Therapy Assn. (charter), Biofeedback Certification Inst. Am. (treas., bd. mem., cert.), Psi Chi. Democrat. Jewish. Speaker in field, profl. confs.; contbr. articles to jours. Home: 4 Cumbernauld Ct Rockville MD 20850 Office: 4380 MacArthur Blvd NW Washington DC 20007

ROSENBAUM, POLLY, state rep.; B.A., U. Colo.; M.Ed., U. So. Calif. Mem. Ariz. State Ho. Reps. Mem. Gila County Tuberculosis Control Bd. Clubs: Globe Bus. and Profl. Women's, Zonta, Order Eastern Star (past matron). Office: Capitol Bldg Ho Reps Wing Phoenix AZ 85007 *

ROSENBERG, AUDRAY GOLD, social worker; b. Boston, July 31, 1933; d. Daniel and Ruth (Harris) Gold; B.A., Wheaton Coll., 1954; M.S.W., Simmons Coll., 1956; m. Manuel Rosenberg, Aug. 28, 1955; children—Peter, Beth. Social worker Hebrew Home for the Aged, Boston, 1971-74, Phila. Geriatrics Center, 1974-77, Pa. Hosp., Phila., 1978-79; personnel counselor Woodward and Lothrop, Washington, 1981—. Mem. Acad. Cert. Social Workers. Jewish. Home: 4325 Westover Pl NW Washington DC 20016

ROSENBERG, CECILIA HELENE, export co. exec.; b. Stockholm, Apr. 8, 1947; came to U.S., 1978; d. Bjorn Edgar and Inga Ebba (Bergendal) Oker-Blom; student Stockholm Bus. Coll., 1967-69, U. Stockholm, 1969-71; m. C.F. Peter Rosenberg, Nov. 9, 1973; children—John B., Nicholas A. Mgmt. asst. Sunwing S.A., Palma de Mallorca, Spain, 1971-73; interpreter, W. Ger., 1972-73; mgmt. cons., Antwerp, Belgium, 1975-78; gen. mgr. Trans-Continental Products, Inc., Mpls., 1979—; tchr. Swedish, Montessori Sch., Mpls., 1979. Mem. Swedish Am. C. of C. (gen. mgr. St. Paul chpt. 1979-80), Am. Swedish Inst., Swedish Assn. (master 1974-75). Author: How to Trace Your Swedish Ancestry, 1979. Office: Weaver Lake Osseo MN 55369

ROSENBERG, CLAIRE FREHLING, educator; b. Cin., Aug. 20, 1926; d. Joseph Morris and Lillian Ann (Matz) Frehling; B.S., U. New Orleans, 1967, M.Ed., 1973, Ed.D., 1977; m. Samuel I. Rosenberg, Nov. 1, 1945; children—Ann, Robert. Tchr., Orleans Parish Sch. Bd., 1967-73; lectr. U. New Orleans, 1969-74, instr., 1974-76, asst. prof., 1977-81, asso. prof. bus. communication and office systems, 1981—. Mem. NEA, Nat. Bus. Edn. Assn., AAUP, Am. Vocat. Assn., Am. Records Mgmt. Assn., Nat. Council Jewish Women, La. Assn. Educators, La. Assn. Higher Edn., La. Assn. Supervision and Curriculum Devel., La. Bus. Edn. Assn., La. Vocat. Assn., Assn. Tchr. Educators, So. Bus. Edn. Assn., Office Systems Research Assn., Phi Chi Theta, Phi Delta Kappa, Kappa Delta Pi, Alpha Theta Epsilon, Phi Kappa Phi, Beta Gamma Sigma. Democrat. Jewish. Contbr. articles in field to profl. jours. Home: 4915 Bancroft Dr New Orleans LA 70122 Office: U New Orleans BA 327 New Orleans LA 70148

ROSENBERG, ELIZABETH HARTWELL, direct mail pub. and mktg. co. exec.; b. Rome, N.Y., July 19, 1949; d. Walter H. and Carolyn (Searle) Hartwell; B.A. in Sociology, Elmira Coll., SUNY, Buffalo, 1971; m. Jack A. Rosenberg, May 19, 1979. Account rep. customer service Xerox, Buffalo, 1972-74, sales rep. mktg., 1974-76, sr. sales exec., product specialist mktg., Los Angeles, 1976-78; sales specialist mktg. Compugraphic, Los Angeles, 1979-81; account exec. mktg. Anaconda Ericsson, Santa Ana, Calif., 1981-82; pres. Horizons Internat., Laguna Beach, Calif., 1982—. Office: 1278 Glenneyre Suite 228 Laguna Beach CA 92651

ROSENBERG, JO, psychiat. social worker, psychoanalyst; b. Albany, N.Y., June 12, 1948; d. Irving H. and Madeline P. Rosenberg; B.A., Goucher Coll., Towson, Md., 1970; M.S., Columbia U., 1973; psychoanalysis cert. (fellow 1975-79), Postgrad. Center Mental Health, N.Y.C., 1979; postgrad. N.Y.U., 1981—. With maternal and child health dept. Bronx (N.Y.) Mcpl. Hosp. Center, 1973-76, coordinator emergency services children dept. child psychiatry, 1976-79; field work instr. N.Y.U. Sch. Social Work, 1977-79; sr. psychiat. social worker div. child and adolescent psychiatry N.Y. Hosp.-Cornell Med. Center, Westchester div., White Plains, N.Y., 1979-82, social work coordinator, 1982—; faculty Cornell U. Med. Sch., 1982— pvt. practice psychoanalysis and psychotherapy, N.Y.C. Fellow N.Y. State Soc. Clin. Social Work Psychotherapists; mem. Nat. Assn. Social Workers, Acad. Cert. Social Workers, Am. Orthopsychiat. Assn., Am. Group Psychotherapy Assn. Contbr. articles on group therapy to profl. jours. Home: 25 W 64th St Apt 9D New York NY 10023 Office: 70 E 80th St New York NY 10021

ROSENBERG, PEARL POLLACK, clin. psychologist; b. Boston, June 22, 1923; d. Benjamin Fisher and Gertrude (Sherman) Pollack; B.A., Radcliffe Coll., 1944; M.A., Harvard U., 1948, Ph.D., 1952; m. Murray David, Sept. 7, 1947; children—Carl Elihu, Lois Mae, Sandra Kay. Research asst. Research Center for Group Dynamics, M.I.T., Cambridge, 1945-48; instr. Simmons Coll. and psychologist Wellesley (Mass.) Human Relation Service of Wellesley, 1959, instr. Harvard U. Sch. Public Health, 1959; asst. prof. rehab. medicine Albert Einstein Sch. Medicine, N.Y.C., 1965; lectr., asso. prof. dept. phys. medicine and rehab. and psychiatry U. Minn. Med. Sch., Mpls., 1973—, also asst. dean student affairs; project dir. human relations seminar with nursing students, NIMH; cons. Big Bros., Nat. League Nursing; cons. VA Mental Health Clinic, Mpls.; mem. U. Minn. Com. on Coms., 1978-81; vol. Walk-In Counseling Center, Mpls., 1968-74. Fellow Am. Group Psychotherapy (dir.); mem. Am. Guidance and Personnel Assn. (chmn. ad hoc com. on accreditation), Minn. Guidance and Personnel Assn., Minn. Psychol. Assn., Am. Psychol. Assn., Assn. Am. Med. Colls. (chmn. nominating com. central region), Am. Edn. Research Assn., Assn. Women Psychologists, Minn. Women's Psychologists, Adminstrv. Women in Edn., Minn. Med. Found., Minn. Group Psychotherapy Assn. (chmn.), Nat. Council Jewish Women. Clubs: Radcliffe (pres. Minn. 1973-76, dir. 1979-81), Harvard (exec. bd. Minn. 1975-76). Contbr. articles to profl. jours. Home: 560 Mountain Curve Blvd Saint Paul MN 55116 Office: U Minn Med Sch PO Box 293 Mayo Meml Bldg Minneapolis MN 55455

ROSENBERG, SHELI, lawyer; b. N.Y.C., Feb. 2, 1942; d. Stephen Bernard and Charlotte (Laufer) Zysman; B.A., Tufts U., 1963; LL.B., Northwestern U., 1966; m. Burton X. Rosenberg, Aug. 30, 1964; children—Leonard, Marcy Joy. Admitted to Ill. bar, 1966, U.S. Tax Ct., 1973; asso. Cotton, Watt, Jones, King & Bowlus, Chgo., 1966-71; mem. firm Schiff, Hardin & Waite, Chgo., 1971-73, partner, 1973-81; v.p., gen. counsel Equity Fin. & Mgmt. Co., Chgo., 1981—. Mem. Fed. Judiciary Selection Com., 1970—; mem. hearing bd. Atty. Registration Commn., 1978—. Mem. Am. Bar Assn., Ill. Bar Assn., Chgo. Council Lawyers, Legal Club.

ROSENBERGER, CAROL, concert pianist; b. Detroit, Nov. 1, 1935; d. Maurice Seiberling and Whilamet (Gibson) R.; B.F.A., Carnegie-Mellon U., 1955; postgrad. Acad. Performing Arts, Vienna, 1956-59. Internat. concert career, 1964—; New York debut, 1970; appeared several times at Carnegie Hall; soloist Am. Symphony, Nat. Symphony, Royal Philharmonic, San Diego Symphony, Detroit Symphony, Houston Symphony, St. Louis Symphony, Indpls. Symphony, Los Angeles Chamber Orch.; performed world premiere of Buenaventura piano concert with Philippine Philharmonic, 1977 with Am. Symphony, 1977; recital series in Am., European Asian music capitals; recorded Chopin Preludes, Schubert Sonata Op. 42, Four Impromptus Op. 90, Szymanowski Mazurkas, Hindemith's Four Temperaments with London Royal Philharm., Water Music of the Impressionists; mem. artist faculty U. So. Calif.; vis. artist numerous colls. and univs.; chosen to represent Am. women musicians by Nat. Commn. on Observance Internat. Womens Year, 1976. Recipient Steinway Centennial medal, 1954. Mem. Nat. Acad. Rec. Arts and Scis. Contbr. articles to music publs. Office: care Dorothy Cone Artist Reps 250 W 57th St 2316 New York NY 10019 *

ROSENBLATT, ADYLIN ISABELLE, gerontologist, clin. social worker; b. N.Y.C., Apr. 3, 1926; d. Morris James and Goldie Sylvia (Goldman) Lipson; B.A., Hunter Coll., N.Y.C., 1947; M.S.W., San Diego State U., 1971; m. Murry Rosenblatt, July 17, 1949; children—Karin Ann, Daniel Bernard. Prin. investigator, coordinator volunteerism U. Calif. Extension, La Jolla, 1971, instr., coordinator aging and leisure, 1971, 73; psychiat. social worker Adult Protective Services, San Diego, 1973-75; clin. social worker in pvt. practice, San Diego, 1975—; dir. social services Tri City Hosp., Oceanside, Calif., 1976-77; dir. social services, clin. social worker Green Hosp. of Scripps Clinic, La Jolla, 1977-79; program chmn. San Diego Pvt. Practice Council, 1980—; founding mem. Human Resource Assos., cons., 1981—; condr. workshops on social work 4th Ann. Symposium, European chpt. Nat. Assn. Social Workers, 1977; rec. sec. Health Council of San Diego, 1977-78; mem. Health Systems Agys. N. San Diego City Subarea Adv. Council, 1978-81; guest lectr. Nat. Council Alcoholism, Mental Health Assn. San Diego; bd. dirs. Cedar Sr. Community Center, 1974-76, Diversified Tech., Inc., 1974-75. Mem. service com. Am. Cancer Soc., 1976-81. Mem. Nat. Assn. Social Workers (v.p. San Diego 1973-81), Am. Orthopsychiat. Assn., Acad. Certified Social Workers, Gerontol. Soc., Soc. Dirs. of Hosp. Social Work. Contbr. articles to profl. publs. Address: 7734 Esterel Dr La Jolla CA 92037

ROSENBLATT, LOUISE MICHELLE, educator; b. Atlantic City, Aug. 23, 1904; d. Samuel and Jennie (Berman) R.; B.A. with honors, Barnard Coll., 1925; certificat d'etúdes francaises, U. Grenoble, France, 1926; D.Comparative Literature, U. Paris, 1931; postgrad. in Anthropology, Columbia U., 1932-34; m. Sidney Ratner, June 1932; 1 son, Jonathan. Instr., English, Barnard Coll., 1927-38; asst. prof. English Bklyn. Coll., 1938-48; asso. chief Western European sect., chief central reports sect. Bur. Overseas Intelligence, Office War Info., 1943-45; prof. English edn. N.Y. U., 1948-72, prof. emeritus, 1972—; vis. prof. Rutgers U., 1972-75; cons. in field. Franco-Am. Exchange fellow, 1925-26; Guggenheim fellow, 1942-43; recipient N.Y. U. Great Tchr. award, 1972; Nat. Council Tchr. English Disting. Service award, 1973; Russell award for disting. research, 1980; Leland Jacobs award for Lit., 1981. Mem. MLA, Am. Soc. Aesthetics, AAUP, Nat. Council Tchrs. English, Nat. Conf. Research in English, Am. Comparative Literature, Internat. Comparative Lit. Assn., Phi Beta Kappa. Author: L'Idee de l'Art pour l'Art, 1931; Literature as Exploration, 1938, 3d rev. edit., 1976; (with William S. Gray) Reading in an Age of Mass Communication, 1949; Research Development in the Teaching of English, 1963; The Reader. The Text. The Poem: The Transactional Theory of the Literary Work, 1978; also articles in field. Home: 11 Cleveland Ln Princeton NJ 08540

ROSENBLATT, M. JOY, employment counselor; b. Indpls., Sept. 20, 1946; d. Herman Arthur and Mary (Levy) R.; B.S. with honors, Loyola U., Chgo., 1975; M.A., Northeastern Ill. U., 1978. Office mgr. Chgo. Computer Billing Service, 1964-68; asst. office rep. Union Carbide, Chgo., 1968-70; jr. acct. Kroeschel Engring., Chgo., 1970-72; loan officer Gen. Fin./Local Loan, Chgo., 1975-77; employment counselor Ill. Dept. of Labor, Chgo., 1978—. Mem. Rogers Park Sr. Citizens Coordinating Council, 1972-76. Mem. Phi Beta Kappa (exec. bd.). Jewish. Home: 1134 W Armitage St Apt 3 Chicago IL 60614 Office: 910 S Michigan Ave Chicago IL 60605

ROSENBLOOM, NORMA FRISCH, lawyer; b. N.Y.C., Dec. 2, 1925; d. Jacob Frisch and Anna (Fox) Frisch Schwartz; B.A., New Sch. Social Research, 1951; J.D., Rutgers U., Newark, 1979; m. Philip Rosenbloom, Oct. 31, 1946; children—David, James, Eric. Mem. faculty, head dept. music Ranney Sch., Tinton Falls, N.J., 1962-74; admitted to N.J. bar, 1979, N.Y. State bar, 1980; chief law clk. Monmouth County (N.J.) Prosecutor's Office, 1979-80; assoc. firm Karasic & Karasic, P.C., Oakhurst, N.J., 1980-82, Abrams & Gatta, Ocean Twp., N.J., 1982—. Sec., mem. exec. bd. Temple Beth Miriam, Elberon, N.J., 1969-74; mcpl. leader Monmouth Beach (N.J.) Democratic Com., 1973—; del. Dem. Nat. Conv., 1976; freeholder rep. to Monmouth County Community Action Program, poverty program, 1975-76; bd. dirs. Central Jersey Regional Health Planning Bd., 1973-75, Planned Parenthood Monmouth County, 1981—. Recipient award for community involvement Asbury Park-Neptune Youth Council, 1970. Mem. ABA, Monmouth County Bar Assn., N.J. State Bar Assn., N.Y. State Bar Assn., Women Lawyers Monmouth County. Home: Channel Club Tower Monmouth Beach NJ 07750 Office: 1127 Hwy 35 Ocean NJ 07712

ROSENBLUM, ESTELLE HELENE, nurse educator; b. Davenport, Iowa, Feb. 8, 1933; d. Dan and Cecil (Spiwak) Masters; B.S. in Nursing, Wayne State U., 1956; M.A. in Audiology, U. N.Mex., 1971, Ph.D., 1979; M.S. in Nursing, 1981; m. Sidney Rosenblum, Aug. 30, 1953; children—Jay Douglas, Gail Rae, Paul Mitchell. Nurse, Northville Psychiat. Hosp., Mich., 1956; public health and rehab. nurse, Mich., Colo., 1957-62; adminstrv. nurse Bern County Hosp., Albuquerque, 1963-66; sch. nurse Albuquerque Public Schs., 1967-69; asso. prof. nursing U. N.Mex., Albuquerque, 1972—; dir. continuing nursing edn. Profl. Seminar Cons., Inc., Albuquerque, 1979—. Mem. Amigos of Albuquerque Civic Light Opera, Opera Assn.; chmn. prof. adv. com. Rehab. Center. Recipient Alyce Richards Rehab. award. Mem. N.Mex. Nurses Assn. (dist. officer, pres. 1974-75, del. nat. ho. of dels. 1974, 78), Am. Public Health Assn., Am. Nurses Assn., Council Nurse Researchers, Phi Kappa Phi, Sigma Theta Tau (founder, pres. 1975-78). Democrat. Jewish. Author: Fundamentals of Hearing, 1979; contbr. articles to profl. jours. Home: 1407 Florida NE Albuquerque NM 87110 Office: Coll Nursing U NMex Albuquerque NM 87131

ROSENDAHL, PEARL PHILBROOK, educator; b. Lewiston, Maine, Sept. 16, 1924; d. Lawrence W. and Arlene (Grover) Philbrook; student U. Maine, 1962-64; M.S., Boston U., 1968, Ed.D., 1972; cert., U. Rochester, 1980; m. Winston Rosendahl, Mar. 6, 1945; children—Sonya, Rana, Jinja. Sch. nurse U. Maine, 1962-64; clin. instr. New England Bapt. Hosp., Boston, 1966-68; instr. Boston U., 1968-70, asst. prof., 1970-74, asso. prof., 1974—, acting chairperson grad. med. surg. dept., 1981-82, mem. overseas faculty, Ger., 1982; vis. prof. U. Rochester, 1981; vol. nurse practitioner Brockton (Mass.) VA Med. Center, 1980-82. Robert Wood Johnson Found. fellow, 1969-80. Mem. Adult Edn. Assn. U.S., Am. Nurses Assn., Nat. League Nursing, Sigma Theta Tau. Unitarian-Universalist. Club: Toastmasters. Contbr. articles to profl. jours. Office: Boston University 635 Commonwealth Ave Boston MA 02215

ROSENE, CAROLYN HYDE, educator, sports coach; b. N.Y.C., Feb. 13, 1938; d. William Truslow and Mary (Robertson) Hyde; A.A., Elgin Community Coll., 1972; B.A., Aurora Coll., 1974; m. Robert W. Rosene, Jr., Aug. 24, 1957; children—Stephen, Robert, Donald, Katherine. Tchr. phys. edn. Holy Angels Sch., Aurora, Ill., 1974—; founder Geneva Track Club, 1974; dir., head coach St. Charles Park Dist. Track Club, 1975—; founder, dir., head coach W. Chgo. Park Dist. Track Club, 1979—; head track coach Rosary High Sch.; track ofcl. Ill. High Sch. Assn., 1974—, head high jump ofcl. state meet for girls, track starter, cross country coach for age group; chmn. AAHPER sect. for conv., 1976. Ofcl. local track meets for civic groups, track meet for visually handicapped children, 1973, St. Charles Track Club Invitational track meet, 1973-79. Recipient award for phys. fitness program, state phys. edn. conv., 1976; Gold Ivy Leaf award Aurora Coll., 1974. Mem. Ill. High Sch. Assn., AAU. Roman Catholic. Author track handbook for St. Charles Dist. Track Club and W. Chgo. Park Dist. Track Club. Home: 1414 S 4th St Saint Charles IL 60174 Office: 720 Kensington Pl Aurora IL 60506

ROSENER, JUDY BOGEN, univ. adminstr.; b. Los Angeles, Nov. 9, 1929; d. Robert and Sylvia (Livingston) Bogen; B.A. in Sociology with honors, UCLA, 1951; M.A. in Polit. Sci., Calif. State U., Fullerton, 1968; Ph.D. in Govt., Claremont Grad. Sch., 1979; m. Joseph Rosener, Jr., July 1, 1951; children—Lynn, Doug, Janet. Coordinator, instr. univ. extension U. Calif., Irvine, 1970-72, lectr. program social ecology, dir. extended univ. program planning in social ecology, 1972-75, lectr. Sch. Engring., 1975—, lectr. Grad. Sch. Mgmt., 1972—, asst. dean Grad. Sch. Mgmt., 1982—; rev. panel Sci. for Citizens, NSF, 1977, 80; cons. Los Angeles and Jacksonville (Fla.) dists. Army Corps of Engrs., Calif. Dept. Transp., Orange County (Calif.) Bd. Suprs., Buena Park. Bd. dirs. Sta. KCET Channel 28; mem. Calif. Coastal Commn., 1973-81; chmn. Southcoast Regional Calif. Coastal Commn., 1976-77; mem. Orange County Grand Jury, 1969; adv. bd. Newport Harbor Jr. League, 1981. Named Woman of Yr., Sta. KNXT, 1973; recipient Faculty Community Service award U. Calif. Irvine Alumni Assn., 1976; named Outstanding Woman in Orange County, Orange County YWCA, 1980; recipient Conservation award Sea and Sage Audubon Soc., 1981, Career Devel. award U. Calif., Irvine, 1981, Excellence in Teaching award U. Calif. Irvine Grad. Sch. Mgmt., 1982. Mem. Am. Polit. Sci. Assn., Am. Soc. Pub. Adminstrn. (v.p. Orange County chpt. 1976-77), LWV, AAUW, Pi Sigma Alpha. Contbr. articles to profl. jours., chpts. in books. Office: Graduate School of Management University of California Irvine CA 92712

ROSENFELD, FLORENCE, lawyer, Can. govt. ofcl.; b. Ebenezer, Sask., Can., Oct. 20, 1922; d. Moses Lionel and Sonia (Jampolsky) Margulies; LL.B., U. Man., 1945; m. Gdalyah Ben Zion Rosenfeld, Feb. 6, 1955; children—Anita and Jocelyn (twins). Admitted to B.C. bar, 1947; individual practice law, Vancouver, B.C., 1947-50; labour law editor Commerce Clearing House Can. Ltd., Toronto, Ont., 1950-55; title examiner Land Title Guarantee Trust Co., Cin., 1955-56; editor W. H. Anderson Co., Cin., 1956-58; asst. editor Royal Commn. on Taxation, Ottawa, Ont., 1964-65; chief editor Com. on Election Expenses, Ottawa, 1966-67; sec. Statute Revision Commn. Dept. Justice, Ottawa, 1967-71; editor Fed. Ct. Reports Office of Commr. for Fed. Judicial Affairs, Ottawa, 1971—. Created Queen's Council, 1978. Mem. Bar Assn. B.C., Can. Bar Assn., Govt. Can. Fed. Lawyers Club. Jewish. Office: 66 Slater St Ottawa ON K1A 1E3 Canada

ROSENFELD, LULLA, actress, writer; N.Y.C., Mar. 3, 1919; d. Joseph and Frances (Adler) Schoengold; student drama Eva Le Gallienne, 1934-36, Morris Carnovsky, 1936-38; m. Paul M. Rosenfeld, May 5, 1937; 1 dau., Josie Oppenheim Appeared in Group Theatre prodn., The Gentle People, N.Y.C., 1939, Broadway prodn. Enemy of the People, 1951, also in film Reunion in France, 1942; writer for film Paris Blues, 1960; contbr. book revs. to Saturday Rev. Lit., 1950's; author (biography) Bright Star of Exile: Jacob Adler and the Yiddish Theatre, 1978; (novel) Death and the I Ching, 1981. Nat. Endowment for Humanities fellow, 1975-76. Mem. Authors Guild, Authors League.

ROSENFELD, RUTH COHAN, psychiat. social worker; b. Phila., Oct. 10, 1917; d. Irving Israel and Rose (Switkay) Cohan; B.F.A., Temple U., 1959; M.S.S., Bryn Mawr Coll., 1963; postgrad. Family Inst. Phila., 1975; m. Irvin Rosenfeld, Dec. 24, 1939; 1 dau., Regina Rosenfeld Banks. Social worker, spl. services Pa. Dept. Pub. Welfare, 1961-65; chief psychiat. social worker, adolescent mental health clinics Phila. Div. Mental Health, 1965-68, health programs analyst, drugs, alcohol and geriatric specialist Phila. Office Mental Health and Mental Retardation, 1968-71, adminstr., diagnostic and rehab. center drug program, 1971-72, asso. dir. drug treatment program Phila. Psychiat. Center, 1972—, dir. multi agy. adolescent poly drug program, 1973—, asso. dir. self-employment skills tng. program, 1977—; suicidologist Phila. Suicide Prevention Center, 1967-71. Pa. Dept. Welfare fellow, 1961-63. Mem. Nat. Assn. Social Workers, Acad. Certified Social Workers, Family Inst. Phila., Forum Drug and Alcohol Programs (treas.), Phila. Women's Task Force on Drugs, Cheltenham Twp. Art Center (bd. dirs.), Am. Jewish Congress (past pres. Phila. women's div. past nat. bd. dirs. women's div.). Contbr. articles to profl. jours. Home: 313 Bent Rd Wyncote PA 19095 Office: Philadelphia Psychiatric Center Ford Rd and Monument Ave Philadelphia PA 19131

ROSENHECK, JEAN BIRNBAUM, advt. exec.; b. Monticello, N.Y., Aug. 15, 1930; d. Adolph and Sarah (Haber) Birnbaum; B.A., Syracuse U., 1952; m. Seymour Rosenheck, Dec. 17, 1955; 1 dau., Sari. Asst. personnel dir. Channel Master Corp., Ellenville, N.Y., 1954-58; founder, pres. Princess Advt., Glen Wild, N.Y., 1960—; asst. mgr. Holiday Motor Lodge, Rock Hill, N.Y., 1968—. Mem. Monticello Sch Bd.; past v.p. Jewish Community Center; past bd. dirs. Temple Sholam; bd. dirs. Periwinkle Players; chmn. com. for Recognition of J.C. Johnson. Recipient Pyramid award Splty. Advt. Assn. Internat., 1979. Mem. Advt. Splty. Inst., Sullivan County Sch. Bds. Assn. (pres. 1978—). Republican. Jewish. Home: E Glen Wild Rd Glen Wild NY 12738 Office: Holiday Motor Lodge Rock Hill NY 12775 also Glen Wild NY 12738

ROSENHEIM, MARGARET KEENEY, social welfare educator, lawyer; b. Grand Rapids, Mich., Sept. 5, 1926; d. Morton and Nancy (Billings) Keeney; student Wellesley Coll., 1943-45; J.D., U. Chgo., 1949; m. Edward W. Rosenheim, June 20, 1947; children—Daniel, James, Andrew. Admitted to Ill. bar, 1949; mem. faculty Sch. Social Service Adminstrn., U. Chgo., 1950—, asso. prof., 1961-66, prof., 1966—, Helen Ross prof. social welfare policy, 1975—, dean, 1978—; vis. prof. U. Wash., 1965; acad. visitor London Sch. Econs., 1973; cons. Pres.'s Commn. Law Enforcement and Adminstrn. of Justice, 1966-67, Nat. Adv. Commn. Criminal Justice Standards and Goals, 1972; mem. Juvenile Justice Standards Commn., 1973-76. Bd. trustees Children's Home and Aid Soc. Ill., 1981—, Nat. Inst. Dispute Resolution, 1981—, Carnegie Corp., N.Y.C., 1979—. Ford Found. grantee, 1967-68. Mem. Chgo. Bar Assn. Editor, contbr.: Justice for the Child, 1962; Pursuing Justice for the Child, 1976; contbr. articles and book revs. to profl. jours. Address: 969 E 60th St Chicago IL 60637

ROSENSTIEL, LÉONIE, musicologist; b. N.Y.C., Dec. 28, 1947; d. Raymond and Annette (Bitterman) R.; cert. (scholar) Juilliard Sch., 1964; A.B., Barnard Coll., 1968; M.A., Columbia U., 1970, Ph.D., 1974; diploma Mexican Nat. Inst. Fine Arts, 1975. Asso. editor Current Musicology, N.Y.C., 1969-71; spl. projects editor, 1971-73; founder, dir. Manhasset Chamber Ensemble, 1974-76; cons. editor DaCapo Press, 1976; freelance editorial cons. Fairleigh Dickinson U. Press, W.W. Norton Co., others, 1977—; pres. Research Assos. Internat., 1980—; v.p. Author Aid Assos., 1980—; asso., spl. projects editor Current Musicology, 1969-74, contbr. translations, book revs., articles to profl. jours., 1972—; translator Musica Enchiriadis, 1976; writer record liner notes Gemini Hall and Spectrum records, 1976—; author: The Life and Works of Lili Boulanger, 1978; Nadia Boulanger: A Life in Music, 1982; gen. editor, author: New World sect. Schirmer History of Music, 1982. N.Y. State Regents scholar, fellow, 1964-69; grantee Rockefeller Found., 1978-79, Am. Council Learned Socs., 1978. Mem. Profl. Children's Sch. Alumni Assn. (alumni trustee 1972-74), Authors Guild Am., Authors League Am., Am. Musicol. Soc., Internat. Musicol. Soc., Sonneck Soc., Project for Oral History of Music in Am., Music Library Assn. Address: Research Assos Internat 340 E 52d St New York NY 10022

ROSENTHAL, HATTIE ROTHSCHILD, psychologist; b. Bretten-Baden, Germany, May 21, 1894; student U. Heidelberg, 1915; psychoanalytic tng. with Frieda Fromm-Reichman, 1929; Litt.D. (hon.), Heed U., Hollywood, Fla., 1976. Asst. to Hilde Maas, M.D., 1939; practice psychoanalysis, N.Y.C., 1943-72; founder psychiat. wing Hosp. of Histadrut, Jerusalem, 1973; regional coordinator Nat. Accredition Assn. and Am. Exam. Bd. Psychoanalysis, 1978; lectr. Cert. psychologist, N.Y. Mem. Nat. Assn. Accreditation of Psychoanalysis, Manhattan Center Advanced Psychoanalytic Studies, N.Y. Soc. Clin. Psychology, Nat. Psychol. Assn. Psychoanalysis, Council Psychoanalytic Psychotherapists, Individual Psychology Assn., Am. Acad. Psychotherapists. Contbr. articles profl. jours. *

ROSENTHAL, LAURA SUE, govt. ofcl.; b. N.Y.C., Dec. 1, 1945; d. Sam and Yvette Lorraine (Kopelov) R.; A.B. magna cum laude, Goucher Coll., 1967. Research psychologist NIMH, Bethesda, Md., 1967-71, Nat. Inst. Neurol. Diseases and Stroke, NIH, Bethesda, 1971-73; mgmt. intern HEW, Rockville, Md., 1973-75; mgmt. analyst FDA, Rockville, 1973-74; spl. asst. to adminstr. Alcohol, Drug Abuse and Mental Health Adminstrn., Rockville, 1974-78; dep. asso. dir. research Nat. Inst. Alcohol Abuse and Alcoholism, Rockville, 1978—. Recipient Goucher Coll. Psychology award, 1967; Jessie L. King prize, 1967; Spl. Achievement award HEW, 1975, Performance award, 1980. Hon. fellow NSF; mem. AAAS, Am. Public Health Assn., Phi Beta Kappa. Office: 5600 Fishers Ln Rockville MD 20852

ROSENTHAL, MARILYN SILVER, publishing exec.; b. N.Y.C., Aug. 15, 1940; d. Jack and Isabel (Rosenfeld) Silver; A.B., Boston U., 1961; M.A., Am. U., 1962; Ph.D., Georgetown U., 1973; m. Jacob Rosenthal, Apr. 6, 1963; children—John Nicholas, Anne Wallace. Asst. prof. linguistics York Coll. and Grad. Center, City U. N.Y., 1973-76; mgr. English lang. teaching dept. Oxford U. Press, N.Y.C., 1976—. Mem. TESOL, Nat. Assn. Female Execs. Author: The Magic Boxes: Children and Black English, 1977. Home: 5427 Independence Ave Riverdale NY 10471 Office: 200 Madison Ave New York NY 10016

ROSENTHAL, MARYLYN JOAN, chem. co. exec.; b. N.Y.C., Aug. 31, 1937; d. Dan and Lena (Green) Vogel; B.S. in Edn. magna cum laude, Bklyn. Coll., 1957, M.A. in Edn., 1960; m. Howard Rosenthal, Mar. 29, 1959; children—David, Caryn. Tchr. elem. sch., N.Y.C., Edison, N.J., 1957-72; sales asst. Ball Bros. Research Corp., N.J., 1974-75; chem. trader Parlin Chem., Parlin, N.J., 1975—, sales mgr. Den mother Cub Scouts, 1969-72; chmn. fund raising Temple Emanu-El Sisterhood, 1973-74, 1st v.p., 1974-75, trustee, 1975-78. Certified elem. tchr., K-8, N.Y. State, N.Y. Mem. Northeastern Chem. Assn. (exec. bd., rec. sec., membership chmn.), Phi Beta Kappa, Kappa Delta Pi. Office: 3145 Bordentown Ave Parlin NJ 08859

ROSENTHAL, SHERI JILL, speech pathologist; b. N.Y.C., June 14, 1951; d. Norman I. and Edith (Spitzberg) Schlessberg; B.A., Queens Coll., 1971; M.A., Hofstra U., 1973; m. David Rosenthal, Mar. 28, 1971. Speech pathologist Lakewood (N.J.) Public Schs., 1973-75, Garden State Rehab. Hosp., Toms River, N.J., 1975-78, Monmouth Med. Center, Long Branch, N.J., 1978—; pvt. practice, Jackson, N.J.; cons. Claremont Care Center, Point Pleasant, N.J., Long Branch Public Health Nursing Services (N.J.), Family Resource Assos., Inc., Shrewsbury, N.J. Mem. Am. Speech Lang. and Hearing Assn., N.J. Speech and Hearing Assn., Monmouth County Speech and Hearing Assn. Home: 394 Maple Dr Belford NJ 07718 Office: Monmouth Med Center 3d and Pavillion Aves Long Branch NJ 07740 also 401 W County Line Rd Jackson NJ 08527

ROSENWALD, DOROTHY SHUBART, civic worker; b. Denver, May 15, 1916; d. Benedict and Daisy (Newhouse) Shubart; B.A., Mills Coll., 1936; m. Robert E. Rosenwald, Aug. 9, 1937; 1 son, Richard S. Pres., LWV, Kansas City, 1943-44, state v.p. Mo., 1944-46; state conf. chmn. Mo. Assn. Social Welfare, 1957; pres. Nat. Council Jewish Women, Kansas City, 1953-55, dist. pres., 1963-65, nat. dir., 1963-75, v.p. nat. bd., 1971-75, hon. life dir.; mem. Jackson County Child Welfare Adv. Com., 1966-72, 74-76; mem. Mo. State Day Care Adv. Com., 1971-75, Gov.'s Com. for Children and Youth, 1978-81; chmn. Mo. Adv. Com., White House Conf. Families, 1980; mem. Jackson County Commn. on Children's Services 1964-67. Recipient Outstanding Service award Mo. Assn. Social Welfare, 1981. Mem. AAUW, Phi Beta Kappa. Democrat. Reform Jewish. Home: 111 W 68th St Kansas City MO 64113

ROSEWATER, ANN, congressional aide; b. Phila., July 30, 1945; d. Edward and Maxine (Friedmann) R.; B.A. with distinction, Wellesley Coll., 1967; M.A., Columbia U., 1969. Research, editorial, adminstrv. asst. Tchrs. Coll., Columbia U., N.Y.C., 1969; research asst. Met. Applied Research Center, N.Y.C., 1969-70; program asso. Nat. Urban Coalition, Washington, 1970-73; edn. specialist Children's Def. Fund, Washington, 1973-77; freelance cons. edn., handicapped children, disability rights, child health, 1977-79; lectr. Coll. Gen. Studies, George Washington U., Washington, 1977; asso. producer public TV series Sta. WETA, Washington, 1978; sr. legis. asst. to Congressman George Miller of Calif., Washington, 1979—. Mem. citizens adv. com. for D.C. Bar Assn., 1974-82, exec. com., 1978-82; mem. hearing panel bd. profl. responsibility D.C. Bar Assn., 1979-81. Fellow Soc. Values in Higher Edn. Office: 2422 Rayburn House Office Bldg US Ho of Reps Washington DC 20515

ROSHER, JERELENE, cytotechnologist; b. Safety Harbor, Fla., Jan. 29, 1945; d. John Louis and Alberta (Crockam) R.; A.A., Indian River Community Coll., 1966; student Lincoln Jr. Coll., 1945-65, Bethune-Cookman Coll., 1978—. Cytotechnologist, Halifax Hosp. Med. Center, Daytona Beach, Fla., 1967-78; supr. Asso. Med. Labs., Ormond Beach, Fla., 1979—. Cert. cytotechnologist. Mem. Fla. State Soc. Cytology, Am. Soc. Clin. Pathologists, Nat. Student Nurses Assn. Baptist.

ROSHNOW, KATHERYN ANN CAMENISCH, mfg. co. ofcl.; b. Madison, Ind., May 15, 1950; d. Herman John and Louise Valeska (Aust) Camenisch; student Purdue U., 1968-69; B.S. in Bus. Adminstrn., Ind. U., 1972; M.B.A., U. Mich., 1977; m. George Nickolas Roshnow, Oct. 23, 1973. Sales mgr. Sheraton Motor Inn, Woodhaven, Mich., 1973-75; market research analyst Kerr Mfg. Co., Romulus, Mich., 1976; mktg. rep. IBM, Detroit, 1977-80, account rep., 1980-81, mktg. mgr., Seattle, 1981-82, sr. product planner, Boulder, Colo., 1982—. Adviser Jr. Achievement Southeastern Mich., 1980; mem. founders soc. Detroit Inst. Arts. Mem. Assn. M.B.A. Execs., Ind. U. (life), U. Mich. alumni assns. Presbyterian. Home: 4887 Old Post Rd Boulder CO 80301 Office: IBM Corp Dept 59U/025-2 PO Box 1900 Boulder CO 80302

ROSHONG, DEE ANN DANIELS, educator; b. Kansas City, Mo., Nov. 22, 1936; d. Vernon Edmund and Doradell (Kellogg) Daniels; B.Mus.Ed., U. Kans., 1958; M.A. in Counseling and Guidance, Stanford U., 1960; postgrad. Fresno State U., U. Calif.; Ed.D., U. San Francisco, 1980; m. Richard Lee Roshong, Aug. 27, 1960 (div.). Counselor, psychometrist Fresno City Coll., 1961-65; counselor, instr. psychology Chabot Coll., Hayward, Calif., 1965-75; coordinator counseling services Chabot Coll., Valley Campus, Livermore, Calif., 1975-81, asst. dir. student personnel services, 1981—; writer, coordinator I, a Woman Symposium, 1974, Feeling Free to be You and Me Symposium, 1975, All for the Family Symposium, 1976, I Celebrate Myself Symposium, 1977, Person to Person in Love and Work Symposium, 1978; The Healthy Person in Body, Mind and Spirit Symposium, 1979; Feelin' Good Symposium, 1980, Change Symposium, 1981; Sources of Strength Symposium, 1982; Love and Friendship Symposium, 1983; mem. cast TV prodns. Eve and Co., Best of Our Times, Cowboy; chmn. Calif. Community Coll. Chancellor's Task Force on Counseling; Statewide Conf. on Emotionally Disturbed Student in Calif. Community Colls., 1982—. Mem. Assn. Humanistic Psychologists, Western Psychol. Assn., Nat. Assn. Women Deans and Counselors, Calif. Personnel and Guidance Assn. Alpha Phi. Author: Counseling Needs of Community Coll. Students, 1980. Home: 808 Comet Dr Foster City CA 94404 Office: 3033 Collier Canyon Rd Livermore CA 94550

ROSLANSKY, PRISCILLA FENN, molecular biologist; b. Rochester, N.Y., Nov. 24, 1925; d. Wallace Osgood and Clara Bryce (Comstock) Fenn; B.A., Smith Coll., 1947; M.A., Radcliffe Coll.-Harvard U., 1948; Ph.D., U. Rochester, 1952; m. John Dale Roslansky, June 20, 1953; children—Louise, John Wallace, William Fenn., Clara Ruth. Clin. lab. technician, Calif., N.J., part-time, 1952-59; research asso. U. Calif., Berkeley, 1953-55; NIH fellow, Copenhagen, 1959-60; research asso. U. Ill., Urbana, 1960-63; research asso. Marine Biol. Lab., Woods Hole, Mass., 1964-68, 75-79, now researcher on ultrastructure of nerves; research asso. U. Saarlandes, Homburg-Saar, W.Ger., 1968-69; clin. lab. technician Falmouth Med. Assos., 1969-75, fellow Bunting Inst. of Radcliffe Coll., 1981—. Vice pres. Woods Hole Community Assn., 1976; mem. Woods Hole Civic Assn., 1967-68. Mem. Am. Soc. Microbiology, LWV (observer corps 1979—), Sigma Xi. Club: Woods Hole Women's. Contbr. articles to profl. jours. Home: 57 Buzzards Bay Ave Woods Hole MA 02543 Office: Marine Biol Lab Woods Hole MA 02543

ROSNESS, BETTY JUNE, advt. and public relations agy. exec.; b. Oklahoma City, Mar. 4, 1924; d. Thomas Harrison and Clara Marguerite (Stubblefield) Pyeatt; student Oklahoma City U., 1940-41; m. Joseph H. Rosness, Aug. 5, 1960; children—Melody L. Johnson (dec.), Michael C., Randall L., Melinda Rosness Mason, John C. Continuity dir. Sta. KFBI, Wichita, Kans., 1957-58; sales exec. Sta. KFH, Wichita, 1958-60; U.S. senatorial press sec., 1961-66; dir. advt. and public relations Alaska State Bank, Anchorage, 1966-68; prin. Rosness Advt. Assos., Goleta, Calif., 1968—; dir. Fin. Corp. Santa Barbara (Calif.). Pres., Goleta Valley Girls Club, 1972-75, Ret. Officers Womens Assn., 1970; v.p. Santa Barbara Symphony Assn., 1977-80; bd. dirs. Channel City Womens Forum, 1976—, Goleta Valley Community Hosp.; Chmn. U. Calif. at Santa Barbara Affiliates; bd. dirs. Cancer Found., Santa Barbara, 1978—, chmn. community edn. com., founding mem. Goleta Beautiful, Club West Track and Field; mem. allocations com., bd. dirs. United Way, Santa Barbara; founding mem., bd. dirs. Children's World of Hospice; mem. evangelism com. Good Shepherd Lutheran Ch. Recipient Disting. Sales award Kans. Sales Exec. Assn., 1959, 60; named Woman of Year, Santa Barbara County, 1978. Mem. Greater Santa Barbara Advt. Club. (past v.p.), Goleta Valley C. of C. (past dir.), Santa Barbara C. of C., Goleta Valley C. of C. Address: 7 W Figueroa St Santa Barbara CA 93101

ROSS, BETTY B., communications exec.; b. Hartford, Conn., Nov. 14, 1925; d. Harry Hyman and Frances (Horowitz) Beckanstin; A.B. cum laude, Smith Coll., 1946; m. Richard Stellan Ross, Dec. 2, 1950 (div. Dec. 1958); 1 dau., Elisabeth Hewitt. Writer/public relations cons., 1951-62; dir. public relations Shoreham Hotel, Washington, 1962-71; free-lance writer/cons., 1971-77; spl. asst. to dir. Voice of America, 1977-80; press sec. to Alfred E. Kahn, presdl. adv. on inflation, Washington, 1980-81; pres. Betty Ross Communications, Washington, 1981—. Past mem. bd. govs., sec., ways and means chmn., publicity chmn. Woman's Nat. Democratic Club; alt. del. Dem. Nat. Conv., 1960; past mem. women's bd. Opera Soc. Washington, Prevention of Blindness Soc. Met. Washington. Mem. Soc. Am. Travel Writers (past dir. and treas.), Am. Soc. Authors and Journalists, Washington Ind. Writers. Jewish. Clubs: Woodmont Country; Nat. Press. Author: How to Beat The High Cost of Travel, 1975, rev. edit., 1977. Office: 3516 Albemarle St NW Washington DC 20008

ROSS, BETTY GRACE, med. distbn. co. exec.; b. N.Y.C., July 14, 1931; d. Philip and Nancy Anna (Meredith) Boccella; R.N., Presbyn. Hosp., 1952; student Ariz. State U., 1960-62; m. Robert W. Ross, Mar. 1, 1968 (div. July 1976). Sr. operating room nurse Roosevelt Hosp., N.Y.C., 1953-58; pvt. surg. nurse Neurosurgery Group, Orthopedic Group, Phoenix, 1960-64; sales asso. Zimmer, Inc., Phoenix, 1964-71; distbr., owner Zimmer-Ross Assos., Phoenix, 1971—, Zimmer-Ross-Ltd., 1978—; partner Desert-Star Devel. Co. Mem. ch. bd. Gloria Dei Luth. Ch., also pres. bd., congregation, congregation; charter mem. Center for Living of Paradise Valley. Mem. Assn. Operating Room Nurses of Phoenix (charter), Bloomfield Coll. Alumni Assn. Republican. Home: 5713 N Cattletrack St Scottsdale AZ 85253 Office: 1232 E Missouri St Phoenix AZ 85014

ROSS, BETTY JEAN, jewelry mfg. co. exec.; b. Kansas City, Mo., Aug. 6, 1928; d. George W. and Ida Mae (Wolf) Terry; student Phillips U., 1946-47, LaSalle Extension U., 1954-55, U. N.Mex., 1970-71; m. Bob L. Ross, Feb. 19, 1950; children—Lee, Elizabeth, Eric, Eden. Mem. prodn. and control staff Black, Sivalls & Bryson, Kansas City, Mo., 1946-50; purchasing and credit mgr. Maisel Co., Albuquerque, 1956-72; credit mgr. Sunbell Corp., Albuquerque, 1972—. Block chmn. Am. Heart Assn., Am. Cancer Soc.; funding chmn. Bric Ross Meml. Library. Mem. Am. Mgmt. Assn., Nat. Assn. Credit Mgmt., Nat. Assn. Female Execs., Dun & Bradstreet Credit Roundtable. Republican. Methodist. Home: 1501 Betts St NE Albuquerque NM 87112 Office: Sunbell Corp 7500 Bluewater Rd NW Albuquerque NM 87104

ROSS, CATHERINE LAVERNE, educator; b. Cleve., Nov. 1, 1948; d. Anthony and Essie R.; B.A., Kent State U., 1971; M.Regional Regional Planning, Cornell U., 1973, Ph.D., 1979; m. Thomas D. Boston, June 15, 1974; 1 son, Linje Ross. Grad. researcher Regional Planning Commn. Cleve., 1972; transp. planner Dalton-Dalton-Little-Newport, Cleve., 1973-74; asst. prof. Atlanta U., 1977-79; asst. prof. architecture Ga. Inst. Tech., 1976—; cons. Atlanta Regional Commn., Cleve. Urban League. Bd. dirs. Com. for Open Housing, 1981—. Cornell U. Grad. fellow, 1971-73, 74-76; Rockefeller Found. fellow, 1975-76; Am. Soc. Planning Ofcls. Found. fellow, 1971-73. Mem. Am. Planning Assn. (treas. women's div. 1982—), AAAS, Black Women Academicians. Home: 3689 Calumet Rd Decatur GA 30034 Office: Old Civil Engring Bldg Ga Inst Tech Atlanta GA 30332

ROSS, CLAIRE TUXFORD, home economist; b. Jackson, Miss., July 6, 1916; d. Walter Edward and Anne Noreene (Powell) Tuxford; B.S., Miss. State Coll. Women, 1937; m. John Curlee Ross, July 20, 1940; children—John Curlee, Anne Tuxford. Home service advisor Alcorn County Electric Power Assn., Corinth, Miss., 1937-38, City of Sheffield (Ala.), 1938, Jackson (Tenn.) Electric Dept., 1939-40; home mgmt. supr. Farm Security Adminstrn., Iuka, Miss., 1941-42, Farmers Home Adminstrn., Tupelo, Miss., 1945-46; tchr. sci. and home econs. Corinth Separate Schs., 1955-63; home economist Coop. Extension Service, Booneville, Miss., 1963—. Recipient various service awards. Mem. Nat. Home Econs. Assn., Miss. Home Econs. Assn., Miss. Assn. Extension Home Econs. (dir. 1971, asst. dir. 1980-81, Disting. Service award 1971), Nat. Assn. Extension Home Econs. (Disting. Service award 1981), Prentis County Devel. Assn. (dir. 1978-81, dir. community appearance 1980-81), Epsilon Sigma Phi. Methodist. Club: Booneville Woman's (v.p. 1978-80, pres. 1981-82). Home: 100 6th St Booneville MS 38829 Office: 404 E Church St Booneville MS 38829

ROSS, DIANA, singer, actress, entertainer; b. Detroit; d. Fred Earl and Ernestine Ross; grad. high sch. Lead singer Diana Ross and the Supremes; now soloist; star motion picture Lady Sings the Blues, 1972, Mahogany, 1975, The Wiz, 1978; appeared Broadway An Evening with Diana Ross, 1976; TV spl. Diana, 1981. Recipient citation Vice Pres. Humphrey for efforts on behalf Pres. Johnson's Youth Opportunity Program; citation Mrs. Martin Luther King and Rev. Abernathy for contbn. to So. Christian Leadership Conf. cause; awards Billboard, Cash Box and Record World as worlds outstanding singer; named Female Entertainer Yr., NAACP, 1970; Grammy award as Top Female Singer Yr.; London Musical Express Poll winner as Top Female Singer in World; nominee Acad. award for best actress, 1972; Golden Globe award Hollywood Fgn. Press Assn., 1972; Image award for Best Actress, NAACP, 1972; Entertainer of Yr., Cue mag., 1972; Cesar award French Acad. Cinema Arts and Technique, 1976; Female Entertainer of Century, Billboard mag., 1976; Antoinette Perry award, 1977; star placed in Hollywood's Walk of Fame, 1982. Office: care RTC Action Mgmt 595 Madison Ave Suite 1103 New York NY 10021

ROSS, DONA RUTH, speech pathologist; b. Hot Springs, S.D., June 17, 1930; d. Gordon Richard and Margaret Elizabeth (Emery) Bartell; student Aims Jr. Coll., 1968-69; B.A. (state scholar), U. No. Colo., 1972, M.A., 1973; postgrad. U. S.D., 1975—, Black Hills State Coll., 1974-75, No. State Coll., 1981, U. Eastern N.Mex., 1973; children—Judy, Barbara, Dale, Peggy, Randall. Speech pathologist Shannon County Schs., Pine Ridge Indian Reservation, Batesland, S.D., 1973-76, Yankton (S.D.) Schs., 1976-77; prin. New Underwood (S.D.) Schs., 1977-80, Pierre (S.D.) Indian Learning Center, 1980-81; speech pathologist Office Indian Edn. Programs, Bur. Indian Affairs Schs., Pine Ridge (S.D.) Indian Reservation, 1981—; cons. Oglala Sioux Tribe Early Childhood Programs, 1973-80. Sec. Shannon County Democratic Party, 1975-76. Mem. Am. Speech, Lang. and Hearing Assn., Council for Exceptional Children. Democrat. Congregationalist. Home: 3902 W Saint Louis St Rapid City SD 57701 Office: Office Indian Edn Programs Bur Indian Affairs Pine Ridge Agy Pine Ridge SD 57770

ROSS, DORIS G., civic worker; b. Thompsonville, Conn.; d. Phillip A. and Eva (Saffir) Sisitzky; student Barnard Coll., Max Reinhardt Drama Workshop, N.Y. U. Radio Workshop, Lee Strasberg Theatre Inst., Royal Acad. Dramatic Arts; m. Lewis H. Ross, Jan. 4, 1942; children—Phyllis, Allyne. Dir. New Eng. Zionist Youth Com., 1943-45; dir. theatre arts Manchester Inst. Arts and Scis., 1947-48; pres. Manchester Girls Club, 1950-51, dir., 1949-53, 54-58, 59-69; bd. dirs. Girls Clubs Am., 1954-81, mem. exec. com., 1955-60, 78-80, chmn. nat. adv. bd., 1955-57, v.p., 1956-57, pres., 1957-59, chmn. 15th ann. conf., 1960, 1st pres. past pres. club, 1975-77, chmn. silver jubilee com., 1969-70, chmn. directions and social concerns com., 1978-79, hon. mem., 1981—, developer, 1st chmn. Children's Creative Theatre, 1978-81; mem. exec. com. Girls Clubs N.Y., 1970-73, bd. dirs., 1970-73, sustaining dir., 1973—, co-chmn. long-range planning com., 1970-71; hon. mem. Girls Clubs of Am 1981—; 1st pres. Theatre Art Players, Temple Emanuel, N.Y.C., 1970-71; dir. Manchester Settlement Assn., 1951-54, Manchester Vis. Nurses Assn., 1955-61; del. Nat. Soc. Welfare Assembly, 1957-59, White House Conf. on Children and Youth, 1960, voting del. nat. council state coms., 1960, mem. N.H. state exec. com., 1960, N.H. state sub-com. on Leisure Time Activities chmn., 1960; mem. Pres.'s Citizens Adv. Com. on Fitness of Am. Youth, 1958-60; mem. exec. com. Gov.'s Com. on Children and Youth, 1961-63; gov.'s rep. to Pres.'s Conf. on Youth Fitness, 1962; charter colleague Nat. Assembly Nat. Vol. Health and Social Welfare Orgn., Inc., 1976—; trustee Actors Studio, 1978-82, concerned Actors Studio Achievement Awards Celebration, 1981; pres. Manchester Garden Club, 1963-64; dir. Opera League New Hampshire, Inc., 1964-69. Mem. Hadassah (pres. Manchester chpt. 1943-44, dir. Manchester chpt. 1942-49, New Eng. regional v.p. 1944-46). Address: 985 Fifth Ave New York NY 10021

ROSS, DOROTHY MARIE, assn. exec.; b. Whiteford, Md.; grad. high sch. Floor supr. heel dept. Bata Shoe Factory, Belcamp, Md., 1939-40; with Civil Service Commn., 1940; office clk. George F. Muth Co., Washington, 1941-47; with Am. Automobile Assn., Washington, 1947-62, supr. hotel-motel reservations, 1947-62; pres. Automotive Hall of Fame, Inc. (formerly Automotive Orgn. Team, Inc. and Automotive Old Timers, Inc.), Midland, Mich., 1963-80, pres., 1980—, editor AOT News, 1966—. Hon. bd. dirs. Boys Home of South, Greenville, S.C. Recipient Disting. Women's award Northwood Inst., 1971, Automotive Replacement Edn. award, 1978; Disting. Service citation Automotive Orgn. Team, 1972, Nazarene (Sunday sch. supt. 1956-60, sec. ch. bd. 1955-60, treas. 1954-56). Mem. Soc. Automotive Historians. Home: 5300 Perrine Rd Midland MI 48640 Office: PO Box 1742 Midland MI 48640

ROSS, EVELYN (LOL) KOUTSOS, health care rev. cons.; b. Washington, Nov. 9, 1941; d. James John and Angelina Daniel (Cokinos) Koutsos; B.S. in Edn. cum laude (scholar), U. Md., 1964; postgrad. various specialized courses; m. Philip W. Ross, Sept. 9, 1963; children— Angelle Marie Philip, James John Philip. Tchr., then substitute tchr. schs. in Md. and Pa., 1963-75; biostatistician Montgomery/Bucks Profl. Standards Rev. Orgn., Blue Bell, Pa., 1975-76, dir. data analysis, 1976-77, dir. mgmt. info. systems, 1977-78, asso. exec. dir., 1978-81; cons. Del./Chester Area X Profl. Standards Rev. Orgn., 1981—; speaker, cons., nat. expert in field. Women's vol. chmn. Montgomery County (Md.) Xmas Seals Campaign, 1970; co-chmn. Open Schs. Study Com., Olney, Md., 1972; v.p. bd. dirs. Oxbow Meadows Community Assn., Chalfont, Pa., 1975-76; mem. Equal Edn. for Gifted Bucks County, Pa., 1976-78. Honors scholar, 1960-64. Mem. Soc. Hosp. Info. Systems (chmn. program com. 1977-78), Am. Assn. Profl. Standards Rev. Orgns. (data com. 1979-80), Mensa, Mortar Bd., Phi Kappa Phi, Kappa Delta Pi (pres. 1962-63). Democrat. Greek Orthodox. Co-author HEW assessment reports; also physicians handbook; contbg. editor Peer Rev. Home: 8 Hickory Ln Chalfont PA 18914 Office: 8 Hickory Ln Chalfont PA 18914

ROSS, GAIL SHARON, pediatric psychologist; b. Paterson, N.J., Nov. 19, 1946; d. Samuel Michael and Matilda (Gershon) R.; B.A. magna cum laude with honors in Psychology, Barnard Coll., 1968; M.A., U. Chgo., 1969; Ph.D., Harvard U., 1978; m. Robert Jay Schwartz, Jr.; children—Matthew Alexander, Michael Benjamin. Asso. in research in psychology Yale U., New Haven, 1976-78; research asso. in psychiatry and pediatrics Cornell U. Med. Coll., N.Y.C., 1978-80, instr. psychiatry and pediatrics, 1980, asst. prof. pediatrics, 1982—, staff psychologist Perinatology Center, N.Y. Hosp., N.Y.C., 1978—; dir. Early Childhood Direction Center of Manhattan and Bronx, 1980—. NDEA Title IV fellow, 1968-69; NIMH grantee, 1972-76; N.Y. State Developmental Disabilities grantee, 1979-82. Mem. Am. Psychol. Assn., Am. Acad. Scis., N.Y. Acad. Scis., Soc. Research in Child Devel., Am. Assn. Women in Psychology, Phi Beta Kappa, Phi Delta Kappa. Contbr. articles to profl. jours.; research in devel. of normal and highrisk infants. Office: Perinatology Center 525 E 68th St New York NY 10021

ROSS, GWENDOLYN BLANCHE, social worker; b. Spokane, June 10, 1915; d. Edward Wayland and Faye Blanche (Jamieson) R.; B.A., Linfield Coll., 1937; M.S.S., Smith Coll., 1956. Secondary sch. tchr., Oreg. and Calif., 1937-42; with ARC, Naval Welfare Service, Calif. and Fla., 1943-47; social worker in public welfare Fla. and N.Y., 1947-53; adoption specialist Child Welfare Agy., N.Y., 1953-55; psychiat. social worker Child Guidance Clinic, Washington, 1956-61; pvt. practice psychiat. social work, Washington, 1956-61; social worker overseas schs. Dept. Def., 1961—; cons. in field. Fellow Am. Orthopsychiat. Assn.; mem. Acad. Cert. Social Workers, Nat. Assn. Social Workers, Am. Personnel and Guidance Assn., Internat. Round Table for Advancement of Counseling, Phi Delta Kappa. Home: Karl Christstrasse 19 Heidelberg Germany Office: Heidelberg Elementary School #1 Mark Twain Village APO New York NY 09102

ROSS, HELGOLA GERTRUD, psychologist, researcher, educator; b. Greifswald, Germany, Dec. 5, 1933; came to U.S., 1957, naturalized, 1962; d. Helmuth and Gertrud Stoppelhaar; B.A., U. Calif., Berkeley, 1967, Ph.D., 1975. Sec., U.S. Army, W. Ger., 1954-57; sec., adminstrv. asst. various law firms, Monterey, San Jose, Calif., 1957-64; research and teaching asst. psychology dept. U. Calif., Berkeley, 1968-74; asst. prof. edn. dept. ednl. leadership U. Cin., 1974-80, asso. prof., 1980—. Univ. Research council grantee, 1979—. Mem. Am. Psychol. Assn., Am. Ednl. Research Assn., Assn. Women Faculty, Phi Beta Kappa. Contbr. articles to profl. jours. Home: 6113 Belleaire Pl Cincinnati OH 45224 Office: Dept Ednl Leadership U Cin Cincinnati OH 45221

ROSS, HOPE SNIDER, physician; b. Vonore, Tenn., May 23, 1910; d. Henry Tipton and Iris (Ellis) Snider; B.S., Maryville (Tenn.) Coll., 1931; M.D., U. Okla., 1935; m. George T. Ross, June 4, 1931; children—Julia, Jerry, Mary. Intern, U. Okla. Hosps., 1935-36; resident anesthesiology North Hudson Hosp., Weehauken, N.J., 1936-37; practice medicine specializing in family practice, Enid, Okla., 1937-78, in gynecology, Enid, 1980—; physician Okla. del. Nat. Democratic Conv., 1964-80. Named Woman of Yr. Enid YWCA, 1981. Fellow Am. Acad. Family Practice; life mem. Okla. Med. Assn. Democrat. Methodist. Address: 28 Woodlands St Enid OK 73701

ROSS, JANE DAGMER (HAMILTON), med. technologist; b. Morgatown, W.Va., Apr. 14, 1935; d. Delbert Dewey and Agnes Marie (Anderson) Hamilton; B.S., W.Va. U., 1957, postgrad.; m. Clyde Francis Ross, June 2, 1962; stepchildren—Karen Joyce, Mary Jane. Staff technologist Union Carbide, Institute, W.Va., 1957-69, The Pathology Lab., Metairie La., 1969-70; med. technologist Charleston (W.Va.) Gen. Hosp., 1970-72, chem. sect. head, 1972-77; chem. sect. head Charleston Area Med. Center, 1977-80, asst. lab. mgr., 1980—; clin. instr. med. technologist program U. Charleston. Mem. Am. Soc. Clin. Pathologists, (cert. med. technologist). Democrat. Mem. Christian Ch. (Disciples of Christ). Home: 1505 Grandview Dr Charleston WV 25302 Office: 3200 MacCorkle Ave SE Charleston WV 25304

ROSS, JANET, author; b. Duluth, Minn., Apr. 19, 1914; d. Guy Whittier Chadbourn and Helen (Mason) R.; B.A., U. Minn., 1935, M.A., 1941; Ph.D., U. Iowa, 1960. Tchr. high sch., Carlton, Minn., 1936-40, Rapid City, S.D., 1941-45; personnel asst. U. Hawaii, 1945-46; asst. in student personnel U. Wyo., 1946-49; instr., asst. in student personnel U. Minn., 1940-41, 46-47, 59-60; instr. Fla. State U., 1949-52; instr. U. Iowa, 1952-53, 55-57; asst. prof. Macalester Coll., 1957-60; Fulbright tchr., Heerenveen, Holland, 1953-54; asst. prof. U. N.C., 1960-61; prof. English, Ball State U., Muncie, Ind., 1961-80; vis. prof. Pontificia Universidade Catolica, Porto Alegre, Brazil; cons. U. Panama, 1981; books include: Language and Life in the U.S.A., 4th edit., 1981, Writing English, 2d edit., 1975; Understanding English, 1982. Danforth grantee, 1964; Ball State U. grantee, 1966, 78-79. Mem. TESOL, Nat. Assn. Fgn. Student Affairs, Nat. League Am. Penwomen. Home: 500 Mohawk Dr Apt 606 Boulder CO 80303

ROSS, JANET NIELSEN, market researcher, writer; b. Oakland, Calif., Jan. 4, 1936; d. Gordon Andrew and Sarah Dorothy (Mason) Nielsen; B.A. in Comml. Art with honors, San Jose (Calif.) State U., 1957; m. Richard Ross, May 3, 1958 (div.); children—Lisa Janine, Peter Donovan. Tech. illustrator McClellan AFB, Calif., 1957; layout artist Weinstock-Lubin, Sacramento, 1957-58; substitute tchr., Ill. and Calif., 1970-73; library technician Sparks (Nev.) Br. Library, 1973-76; art dir. Dill & Assos., Reno, 1976-77; media coordinator Capital Advt., Reno, 1977-79; office mgr. Mktg. Systems Internat., Reno, 1979—; columnist, asso. editor Gambling Scene West, Mountain View, Calif., 1973—. Mem. Nat. Fedn. Press Women, Nev. Press Women (1st pl. award personal columns and feature articles 1975-80, pres. 1981), Reno Ad Club, Am. Bus. Women's Assn. Episcopalian. Office: 100 W Grove St Suite 475 Reno NV 89509

ROSS, JUDITH PARIS, life ins. co. exec.; b. Boston, Dec. 23, 1939; d. Max and Ruth P.; ed. Boston U., 1961, UCLA, 1978; grad. Life Underwriting Tng. Council, 1978; 1 son, Adam Stuart. Producer, co-host Checkpoint TV show, Washington, 1967-71; hostess Judi Says TV show, Washington, 1969; brokerage supr., specialist impaired risk underwriting Beneficial Nat. Life Ins. Co., Beverly Hills, Calif., 1973-82; ins. specialist salary savs. plans, v.p., sec. West Los Angeles Life Underwriters, 1981-82, sec., v.p., 1982-83; dir. mktg. Brougher Agy., Beverly Hills, 1982—. Active local PTA, Boy Scouts Am.; mem. early childhood edn. adv. com. Beverly Hills Unified Sch. Dist., 1977. Mem. Nat. Assn. Life Underwriters, Calif. Assn. Life Underwriters (dir. W. Los Angeles 1980—, chmn. public relations). Office: 9300 Wilshire Blvd Beverly Hills CA

ROSS, LEABELLE I. (MRS. CHARLES R. ROSS), ret. psychiatrist; b. Lorain, Ohio, Feb. 11, 1905; d. Charles E. and Harriet (Dobbie) Isaac; A.B., Western Res. U., 1927, M.D., 1930; m. Charles R. Ross, Sept. 23, 1941; children—Charles R., John Edwin. Surg. intern Lakeside Hosp., Cleve., 1931-32; resident obstetrics and gynecology Iowa State U. Hosp., 1932-33; resident obstetrics and surgery N.Y. Infirmary, N.Y.C., 1933-34; pvt. practice, Cleve., 1935-40; staff physician Cleve. State Hosp., 1938-42; dir. student health Bowling Green (Ohio) State U., 1942-45; psychiatrist Bur. Juvenile Research, Columbus, Ohio, 1946-47; psychiat. cons., 1948-51; psychiatrist Mental Hygiene Clinic, Columbus VA, 1951-55; dir. med. services Juvenile Diagnostic Center, 1955-59, acting supt., 1958, 61-62, dir. psychiat. services, 1959-62, clin. dir., 1962-70. Mem. Am. Psychiat. Assn., Ohio Psychiat. Assn., Am. Group Psychotherapy Assn., Tri-State Group Psychotherapy Soc., Neuropsychiat. Assn. Central Ohio, Assn. Physicians Div. Mental Hygiene and Correction (pres. 1963-64), Alpha Sigma Rho, Nu Sigma Phi. Club: Soroptimist. Home: 1289 Gold Ridge Rd Sebastopol CA 95472

ROSS, LINDA MARY, devel. exec.; b. Los Angeles, Aug. 27, 1938; d. William and Virginia (Smith) Ross; B.A., U. Calif., Santa Barbara, 1962; postgrad. Occidental Coll., 1972. Adminstrv. asst. North Am. Rockwell Co., Washington, 1962-63; legis. asst. to Congressman John Moss, Washington, 1963-64; protocol sec. to Mrs. Merriweather Post, Washington, 1964-65; adminstrv. asst. for project devel. U. So. Calif. Gerontology Center, 1967-70, dir devel., 1970-75; owner, pres. Linda M. Ross, devel. cons., 1975-82; exec. dir. devel. Otis/Parsons, Los Angeles, 1982—. Mem. audit com. United Way. Ford Found. Coro fellow, 1962-63. Mem. World Futurist Soc., Gerontology Soc., World Affairs Council, Coro Found. Alumni Assn., Friends of Park Century Sch., Friends of Kritt Found. Clubs: West Hills Hunt, Malibu Racquet. Office: Otis/Parsons 2401 Wilshire Blvd Los Angeles CA 90057

ROSS, MARILYN ANN MARKHAM, author, publisher; b. San Diego, Nov. 3, 1939; d. Glenn James and Dorothy Verna (Scudder) Markham; student San Diego State U., 1977-78; m. Tom M. Ross, May 25, 1977; children—Scott, Steve, Kevin, Laurie. Dir. mktg. South Bay Trade Schs., San Diego, 1969-74; writer, tchr., advt. and pub. cons., 1974-78; pres. Communication Creativity, La Jolla, Calif., 1978—; co-founder, dir. Copy Concepts, Inc., La Jolla, Calif. Trustee Religious Sci. Ch. Recipient 1st place award in non-fiction books Calif. Press Women, 1978-79. Mem. Internat. Platform Assn., Nat. Speakers Assn., Authors Guild, Nat. Fedn. Press Women, Women in Bus. (funding bd. dirs. San Diego chpt.), Profl. Speakers of San Diego. Author: Creative Loafing, 1978; Discover Your Roots, 1977; Finding Your Roots, 1977; The Encyclopedia of Self-Publishing, 1979; The Force of Us, 1980. Office: 5644 La Jolla Blvd La Jolla CA 92037

ROSS, MARY COWELL (MRS. JOHN O. ROSS), lawyer; b. Oklahoma City, Okla., Oct. 1, 1910; d. Sears F. and Elizabeth (Van Zwaluwenburg) Riepma; A.B., Vassar Coll., 1932; LL.B., Memphis State U., 1938; LL.D., U. Nebr., 1973; m. Richard N. Cowell, Mar. 1, 1946 (dec. Jan. 1953); m. 2d, John O. Ross, Mar. 31, 1962 (dec. June 1966). Admitted to Tenn. bar, 1938, D.C. bar, 1944, N.Y. bar, 1947; atty. U.S. Govt., Washington, 1940-44; pvt. practice Cromelin & Townsend, Washington, 1944-46. Royall, Koegel & Rogers and predecessors, N.Y.C., 1946-61; individual practice law, 1961—; treas., dir. 39 E. 79th St. Corp., 1966-73; treas., dir. 795 Fifth Ave. Corp., 1977—; mem. adv. com. N.Y. Commn. on Estates, 1965-67. Bd. dirs. Silver Cross Day Nursery, N.Y.C., 1963-70, Cunningham Dance Found., 1969-72, Central Park Community Fund, 1977-81; trustee U. Nebr. Found., 1966—, bd. dirs., 1974-79; hon. trustee Nebr. Art Assn. Mem. Am. Bar Assn., N.Y. Women's Bar Assn. (pres. 1955-57, dir. 1957-63, 74-80, adv. council 1963—), Bar Assn. City N.Y. (surrogate cts. com. 1961-65, library com. 1965-78, com. on profl. responsibility 1972-75), Nat. Assn. Women Lawyers (assembly del. 1962-64, 73-74, UN observer 1965-67, v.p. 1967, chmn. 1971 ann. conv., distinguished service award 1973), Vassar Coll. Alumnae Assn., Phi Alpha Delta, Delta Gamma. Clubs: Met., Doubles, Vassar (N.Y.C.). Address: 2 E 61st St New York NY 10021

ROSS, MICHELE MARY, editor; b. Salem, Ohio, May 24, 1952; d. Albert Anthony and Helen Jean (Tarcy) R.; B.A. cum laude, Miami U. Ohio, 1974. Customer relations staff, editor Harrison Pub. Co., Atlanta, 1974-76; reporter Atlanta Constitution, 1976-79, book rev. editor, columnist combined Atlanta Jour. and Constitution, 1979—. Mem. Nat. Book Critics Circle, Sigma Delta Chi. Office: Atlanta Jour Box 4689 Atlanta GA 30302

ROSS, NELL TRIPLETT, fin. cons. co. exec.; b. Winterville, Miss., Feb. 14, 1922; d. Ethel Earl and Myrtie (Harrison) Triplett; B.A., Millsaps Coll., 1942; m. William Dee Ross, July 25, 1944; 1 son, William Dee III. Tchr., Consol. Sch. of Chatham (Miss.), 1942-43, Glen Allan (Miss.) Consol. Sch., 1943-46, Durham (N.C.) High Sch., 1947, E.K. Powe Sch., Durham, 1947-48, Lakewood Elem. Sch., Durham, 1948-49; with purchasing dept. La. State U., Baton Rouge, 1949-50; enrollment officer La. Hosp. Service, Inc., Baton Rouge, 1950-51; owner Mentone Plantation, Erwin and Chatham, Miss., 1961—; owner, dir. Fin. Cons. Services, Inc., 1970—. Methodist. Clubs: Baton Rouge Country, Camelot, Bocage, Piedmont. Home: 2738 McConnell Dr Baton Rouge LA 70809

ROSS, PATTI JAYNE, physician; b. Sharon, Pa., Nov. 17, 1946; d. James J. and Mary N. Ross; B.S., DePauw U., 1968; M.D., Tulane, U., 1972; m. Allan Robert Katz, May 23, 1976. Asst. prof. U. Tex. Med. Sch., Houston, 1976-82, asso. prof., 1982—, dir. adolescent obstetrics and gynecology, 1976—, also dir. phys. diagnosis; speaker in field. Bd. dirs. Pituitary Found., 1982—; mem. Rape Council. Diplomate Am. Bd. Ob-Gyn. Mem. Tex. Med. Assn., Harris County Med. Soc. So. Perinatal Assn., Houston Obstetric and Gynecologic Soc., Assn. Profs. Obstetrics and Gynecology, Soc. Adolescent Medicine, AAAS, Am. Women's Med. Assn., Orgn. Women in Sci., Sigma Xi. Roman Catholic. Clubs: River Oak Breakfast, Profl. Women Execs. Contbr. articles to profl. jours. Office: 6431 Fannin St Houston TX 77030 *

ROSS, ROBERTA MAYE, diversified cos. exec.; b. Santa Paula, Calif., Jan. 9, 1928; d. Theodore Arthur and Minnie Thelma Stangland; student Ventura Jr. Coll., 1946; Calif. State U., Los Angeles, 1952-56; B.A., LaVerne U., 1972; m. John Paul Ross, June 20, 1959; children—Theodore David, Victoria Lou. Office mgr. Southport Engrng. Co., Los Angeles, 1949-57; controller Framing Contractors Ltd. also Trent Meredith Inc., Oxnard, Calif., 1957-60; owner Adminstrv. Assts., Oxnard, Calif., 1960-78, sr. partner, 1978-81, sec.-treas., 1981—; sec.-treas. Victoria Land Co. Inc., Oxel Inc., Gard Trucking, Inc. (all Oxnard), C-D Woodworks Inc., Santa Paula, Calif. Cert. profl. sec. Mem. Profl. Secs. Internat., Am. Soc. Women Accts. Clubs: Mediodia Bus. and Profl. Women's Altrusa (2d vice-gov. Dist. 11, 1981—). Address: Administrative Assistants PO Box 2128 Oxnard CA 93030

ROSS, RONNIE JEAN WALITSKY, univ. ofcl.; b. Newark, Feb. 15, 1950; d. Barney and Hannah Myra (Krauss) W.; B.S. in Foods and Nutrition, Drexel U., 1972; M.A. in Bus., Central Mich. U., 1978; certs. mgmt. seminars, 1973, 74; m. Mar. 7, 1982. With Marriott Corp., Washington, 1972-78, relief mgr., 1974-76, unit mgr., 1976-78; unit mgr. Macke Corp., Cheverly, Md., 1978-79; food prodn. mgr. Duke U., 1979-81, mgr. nutrition service, 1981-82, mgr. West Campus dining halls, 1982—; student dean Coll. Home Econs., Drexel U., 1971-72. Fund raiser, party cons. Lechner for Lt. Gov. of Va., 1976; food cons. Morris Udall Campaign, Washington, 1977. Named Outstanding Sr., Drexel U. Office Alumni Affairs, 1972. Mem. Nat. Restaurant Assn., Home Economists in Bus., Am. Home Econs. Assn., Nat. Assn. Coll. and Univ. Food Services Execs., Am. Dietetic Assn., LWV, AAUW. Editor-in-chief Perspective, 1969-72. Home: 301 Carl Dr Chapel Hill NC 27514 Office: Duke U Food Services Durham NC 27706

ROSS, SUSAN JULIA, lawyer; b. Phila., July 24, 1943; d. Herbert Joseph and Susan Eshleman (Reese) R.; B.A., magna cum laude, U. Pa., 1965, J.D. magna cum laude, 1969; postgrad. N.Y. U. Law Sch., 1972-75. Admitted to N.Y. bar, 1971, N.Mex. bar, 1976; asso. firm Dewey, Ballantine, Bushby, Palmer & Wood, N.Y.C., 1969, 71-76; partner firm Natelson & Ross, Taos, N.Mex., 1976—; vis. asso. prof. law U. Oreg., 1978; dir. Beneficial Corp., Wilmington, Del., 1979—. Trustee Millicent Rogers Mus., Taos. Thouron-U. Pa. fellow, Oxford U., 1969-70; Am. Scandinavian Assn. fellow, Stockholm U., 1970. Mem. Phi Beta Kappa, Order Coif. Contbr. in field articles to jours.

ROSS, VIRGINIA R., business exec.; b. Los Angeles; d. Roy Renwick and Olivia Marie (Macbride) Wilson; B.S., U. Redlands; children—Will, Brian, Darrell, Leslie. Writer/designer needlework, crafts, toys, 1965-70; product mgr. A Stitch 'n' Time, San Marino, Calif., 1970-75; product mgr. research and devel. Hazel Pearson Handicrafts, Industry, Calif., 1976-81. Mem. Am. Crafts Council, Soc. Craft Designers. Republican. Presbyterian. Home: 1350 Winston San Marino CA 91108 Office: 7330 N Figueroa St Los Angeles CA 90041

ROSSER, PATRICIA ANNE, orgn. exec.; b. Savannah, Ga., June 29, 1948; d. Hoyt Paul and Annie Alberta (Cobb) Canady; B.A., Ga. So. Coll., 1970; M.Ed., Ga. State U., 1973; m. David Jere Rosser, Jan. 4, 1975; step children—Barbara Lynn, Michael Judson, Jennifer Claire. Personnel and devel. asst. Crawford Long Hosp., Atlanta, 1970-72; tchr. Holy Innocents Episcopal Sch., Atlanta, 1972-76, Harding Acad., Nashville, 1976-77; saleswoman NLT Computer Services Co., Nashville and Clearwater, Fla., 1978-81, Western Res. Fin. Services Co., also Western Res. Life Ins. Co., Clearwater, 1980-81; exec. dir. Channel

Markers for Blind, Clearwater, 1981—; cons., seminar leader in field. Bd. dirs., treas. Found. Mental Health; pres. Mental Health N. Pinellas. Mem. NOW, Fla. Assn. Agys. Serving Blind, Suncoast Network, Clearwater C. of C., Delta Zeta (regional collegiate dir.). Democrat. Episcopalian. Office: 1610 N Myrtle Ave Clearwater FL 33515

ROSSER, RACHELLE KAREN, cable TV exec.; b. Cleve., Jan. 21, 1955; d. Alvin Ramon and Barbara E. (Roth) R.; student (Rotary exchange student) S. Wiltshire Sch. for Girls, Salisbury, Eng., 1972-73, Mt. Holyoke Coll., 1973-75, U. Pa. Wharton Evening Sch., 1978—. Sales rep. Anixter Pruzan, Wharton, N.J., 1976-77, Cable TV Supply Co., Los Angeles, 1977-79, account exec. Jerrold div. Gen. Instrument Corp., Hatboro, Pa., 1979-81; regional sales mgr. Pioneer Communications Am., Columbus, Ohio, 1981—. Recipient Salesman of Yr. award Jerrold Electronics Co., 1981. Mem. Soc. Cable TV Engrs., Phila. Cable Club, Women in Cable, N.J. Cable TV Assn., Pa. Cable TV Assn., Va. Cable TV Assn., Md./Del. Cable TV Assn., New Eng. Cable TV Assn. Home: PO Box 268 Haddonfield NJ 08033 Office: 2200 Dividend Dr Columbus OH 43228

ROSSI, KATHLEEN HEIDTMANN, nurse; b. Mineola, L.I., N.Y., Oct. 22, 1942; d. Henry George and Ruth (Martin) Heidtmann; R.N., Bklyn. Meth. Hosp., 1963; m. Ettore Rossi, June 27, 1981; children by previous marriage—Christyne Kim Mallon, Paul John Mallon, Kevin Sean Mallon, Kathleen Ruth Mallon. Operating rm. nurse L.I. Jewish Med. Center, 1963-65; surg. asst. Exptl. Canine Kidney Transplantation, Downstate Med. Center, Bklyn., 1964-65; nurse in charge patient care during exptl. drug therapy Nassau County Med. Center, East Meadow, N.Y., 1971-79; exec. asst., office mgr., operating room asst. plastic surgery Peter Fries, M.D., N.Y.C., 1979—. Leader, Girl Scouts U.S.A., 1976; pres. United Meth. Women, 1974-75; asst. mgr. Floral Park Little League Baseball, 1978-79; mgr. Floral Park Indians Soccer, 1977-78; active PTA, Boy Scouts Am. Mem. Nat. Assn. Female Execs. Clubs: Church Choir; Italian Cooking; Bi-Lingual Italian-English. Home: 70 Walnut Ave Floral Park NY 11001

ROSSI, MARIE THERESA, mktg. co. exec.; b. N.Y.C., Apr. 19, 1939; d. Dominick and Theresa (Marino) Porco; B.A., Coll. New Rochelle (N.Y.), 1960; m. Louis F. Rossi, June 11, 1960 (dec.); children—Donna, Laura. Dir. alumnae relations Coll. New Rochelle, 1973-75, dir. ann. giving/estate planning, 1975-77; dir. sales and mktg. Aero-Vend, Inc., Portchester, N.Y., 1977-80; pres. Organized Bus. Techniques, Inc., OBT, Inc., Valhalla, N.Y., 1979—. Bd. dirs. Coll. New Rochelle. Mem. Valhalla C. of C. (pres. 1980-81), Women in Sales Assn. (founder 1979), Sales and Mktg. Execs. Westchester (exec. dir. 1980—), Am. Soc. Assn. Execs. Roman Catholic. Author articles in field. Office: 21 Cleveland St Valhalla NY 10595

ROSSKY, JUNE BUNIAK, clin. social worker; b. Albany, N.Y., Sept. 16, 1949; d. Laddie and Virginia (Niebergall) Buniak; B.S., Tufts U., 1971; M.S., Simmons Coll., 1973; m. Peter J. Rossky, Aug. 24, 1974. Child welfare specialist Mass. Div. Family and Children's Services, Boston, 1973-75; social worker program for emotionally disturbed Beverly (Mass.) Public Schs., 1975-77; social worker Cath. Charities, Big Bros.-Big Sisters of Suffolk County, Commack, N.Y., 1977-78; coordinator visual impairment services VA Med. Center, Northport, N.Y., 1978-79; clin. social worker Settlement Club Home, Austin, Tex., 1980-82. Vol. counselor Planned Parenthood, Austin, 1979—. NIMH fellow, 1972-73. Mem. Acad. Cert. Social Workers, Nat. Assn. Social Workers, Phi Beta Kappa, Psi Chi, Delta Zeta. Home: 7505 Pineleaf Pl Austin TX 78757

ROSSMAN, JOANNE WALKER, artist; b. Los Angeles, Aug. 27, 1937; d. Harold Norman and Ruth Mary (McDowell) Walker; student Woodberry Coll., Los Angeles, 1955-57, Cerritos (Calif.) Coll., 1971-72; children—Brenda, Dean, Dan, Daryl. Asst. advt. mgr. Buzza Greeting Card Co., Anaheim, Calif., 1972-75; asst. advt. prodn. mgr. Star Crest Co., Costa Mesa, Calif., 1976; portrait artist Knotts Berry Farm, Buena Park, Calif., 1976—; owner, mgr. Comml. Center, Fullerton, Calif., 1974-78, Med. Center Rossman Med. Plaza, Santa Ana, Calif., 1978—, Tom and Jerri's Dance Studio, Long Beach, Calif., 1977-80; owner Dancin DeLights, mobile sound system, 1978—. Recipient various dance awards. Mem. Nat. Assn. Female Execs. Address: 2932 Cottonwood St Apt 19 Orange CA 92665

ROSSNER, JUDITH, novelist; b. N.Y.C., Mar. 31, 1935; d. Joseph George and Dorothy (Shapiro) Perelman; student City Coll. N.Y., 1952-55; m. Robert Rossner (div.); children—Jean, Daniel; m. 2d, Mordecai Persky. Author: (novels) To the Precipice, 1966; Nine Months in the Life of an Old Maid, 1969; Any Minute I Can Split, 1972; Looking for Mr. Goodbar, 1975; Attachments, 1977; Emmeline, 1980; also short stories. Address: care Julian Bach Agy 747 3d Ave New York NY 10017 *

ROSSO, DAWN COOPER, telephone co. exec.; b. Schenectady, N.Y., Oct. 12, 1952; d. Jack and Jean (Ritchie) Cooper; B.A. in English cum laude, Dickinson Coll., 1974; M.B.A. in Mktg., Rider Coll., 1978; m. Mark F. Rosso, Nov. 30, 1974. Research asso. Response Analysis Corp., Princeton, N.J., 1974-78; market research mgr. United Jersey Banks, Princeton, 1978-80; staff mgr. N.Y. Telephone Co., N.Y.C., 1980—. Mem. Am. Mktg. Assn., Sigma Iota Epsilon. Democrat. Presbyterian. Home: 12 Holly Dr East Windsor NJ 08520 Office: 1095 Ave of the Americas New York NY 10036

ROSTER, LAILA BERGS, artist, mus. dir.; b. Dresden, Ger., Dec. 12, 1944; came to U.S., 1950; d. Hugo Edgar and Valeska Milda (Koshkin) Bergs; B.A., San Jose (Calif.) State U., 1967; 1 son, Cade. Asst. dir. Lytton Center Visual Arts, Palo Alto, Calif., 1967-68, dir., 1968-69; tchr. Hawaii Prep. Acad., 1969-70; instr. art Honolulu Acad. Arts, 1970-80, art specialist dept. edn., 1972-74, 78-80; instr. Coll. Continuing Edn., 1978-79; dir. Contemporary Arts Center Hawaii, 1974—; art reviewer Honolulu Star-Bull., 1973-75; solo exhbns. include: The Foundry; Honolulu, 1974, 76, Gima's Gallery, 1978; group juried shows include: Honolulu Acad. Arts, 1974, 75, 79, Gima's Gallery, 1975, 78, Amfac Plaza, 1975, 76, 78, 79, 80, Downtown Gallery, 1978, 79; juror art exhbns., speaker, cons. in field. Recipient 1st pl. award painting Windward Guild, 1976; purchase award Hawaii Found. Culture and Arts, 1976, 78, 79; Leader award Honolulu YWCA, 1979. Mem. Hawaii Craftsmen (dir. 1971-74), Honolulu Printmakers (dir. 1973-74, 77—; award 1975, 78), Hawaii Artists League (pres. 1976-79), Honolulu Acad. Arts, Honolulu Art Educators Assn., Hawaii Mus. Assn., Pacific Inst. Environ. Art, Pacific Regional Conservation Center (pres. 1979-81), Women in Arts. Office: 605 Kapiolani Blvd Honolulu HI 96813

ROTBERG, IRIS COMENS, research psychologist; b. Phila., Dec. 16, 1932; d. Samuel Nathaniel and Golda (Shuman) Comens; B.A. in Sociology, U. Pa., 1954, M.A. in Psychology, 1955; Ph.D. in Exptl. Psychology (NSF fellow), Johns Hopkins U., 1958; m. Eugene Harvey Rotberg, Aug. 29, 1954; children—Diana Golda, Pamela Lynn. Research asso. Human Resources Research Office, Washington, 1958-63, Johns Hopkins U., Balt., 1963-66; research psychologist Pres.'s Commn. on Income Maintenance Programs, Washington, 1968-69, Office of Planning, Research and Evaluation, OEO, Washington, 1970-73; research psychologist, acting chmn. Early Learning Task Force, Nat. Inst. Edn., Washington, 1973-74, dep. dir. Compensatory Edn. Study, 1974-77, dir. Office of Planning and Program Devel., 1978—. NSF fellow, 1956-58. Mem. Am. Psychol. Assn., AAUP, Sigma Xi. Contbr. articles to profl. jours. Home: 10822 Childs Ct Silver Spring MD 20901 Office: 1200 19th St NW Washington DC 20208

ROTERT, DENISE ANNE, occupational therapist, army officer; b. Sioux Falls, S.D., Nov. 18, 1949; d. Leonard Joseph and Irene Winnifred (Jennings) R.; B.S., U. Puget Sound, 1971; M.A., U. No. Colo., 1975. Commd. 2d lt. Med. Specialist Corps, U.S. Army, 1970, advanced through grades to capt., 1976; staff occupational therapist Tripler Army Med. Center, Honolulu, 1973-76, officer in charge occupational therapy sect. Ireland Army Hosp., Fort Knox, Ky., 1976-77; clin. supr. occupational therapy sect. Letterman Army Med. Center, Presidio of San Francisco, 1977-79; chief instr. occupational therapy asst. course Acad. Health Scis., Ft. Sam Houston, Tex., 1979—. Mem. Am., Tex. occupational therapy assns., World Fedn. Occupational Therapists. Roman Catholic. Home: 5915 Oak Run San Antonio TX 78247 Office: Occupational Therapy Br Acad Health Scis Fort Sam Houston TX 78234

ROTGIN, HELAINE (KAUFMAN), community action exec.; b. Charleston, W.Va., Dec. 26, 1915; d. Lawrence Chester and Clara (Kraus) Kaufman; B.A. in Sociology, U. Wis., 1936; m. Charles M. Rotgin, Apr. 4, 1937; children—Charles M., Carole Jean Rotgin Glasser, Kitty. With social service div. W.Va. Dept. Public Assistance, 1937-41; part-time, then full time sec. Temple Israel, Charleston, 1945-61; rep., area mgr. World Book, Field Enterprises Ednl. Corp., 1960; owner-mgr. Jean's Dress and Gift Shop, Charleston, 1961-77; coordinator Energy Crisis Assistance Program, Charleston, 1979—; mem. Charleston Human Rights Commn., 1970-76; chmn. Area 17, W.Va. Dept. Welfare Citizens Adv. Council, 1975-77, 79-81. Mem. W.Va. Ho. of Dels., 1976-78; organizer, pres. Citizens Recycling Council, 1972-79, 80—; organizer, bd. dirs. Central Child Care Bd., Charleston, 1972—; pres. Temple Israel Sisterhood, 1953-55, W.Va. Fedn. Temple Sisterhoods, 1957-59; exec. bd., chmn. com. interfaith activities Nat. Fedn. Temple Sisterhoods, 1957-61; sec. W.Va. Mental Health Adv. Council, 1978—; bd. dirs. W.Va. Health Coordinating Council, 1978—, Manna Meal, Inc.; sec. Interdenominational Council on Social Concerns, 1980, v.p., 1981—. Recipient Hannah G. Solomon award Charleston sect. Nat. Council Jewish Women, 1974, Light of People award Nat. Fedn. Temple Sisterhoods, 1975; named Environmentalist of Year, Citizens Environ. Protection, 1974. Democrat. Club: Charleston Quota (past pres.). Author manual, brochure, articles in field, chpt. in book. Home: 4800 Virginia Ave SE Charleston WV 25304

ROTH, AUDREY G., state legislator; b. Sept. 12, 1915; student U. Minn. 1935-37, B.A. U. Mont. 1939; m. Arthur H. Roth, 1937. Profl. skier, 1937-67; cattle rancher, 1937-81; mem. Mont. Ho. of Reps. 1977—, chmn. water com. 1981. Named Mont. Water Person of Yr., 1980-81. Mem. Stockgrowers of Mont., Cowbells. Office: Montana House of Representatives Capitol Station Helena MT 59620

ROTH, BRENDA JOYCE KNERR, hotel exec.; b. Harrisburg, Pa., Jan. 2, 1952; d. Lawrence D. and Joyce M. (Shutt) Knerr; student Keystone Jr. Coll., 1969-70; m. Todd Allen, July 11, 1970; 1 dau., Jennifer Allyssa. Sec./receptionist Hershey Estates, Hershey, Pa., 1972-74, expiditor, buyer, 1974-75; asst. food buyer Herco Inc., Hershey, 1975-76, mgr. food buying, 1976-77, mgr. purchasing, 1977—. Mem. Am. Purchasing Soc., Exec. Women Internat. Congregationalist. Home: 879 Sandhill Rd Hershey PA 17033 Office: Herco Inc 200 E Airport Rd Hershey PA 17033

ROTH, SISTER, E. SUE, social work adminstr.; b. Cleve.; d. Walter H. and Adele M. (Schlueter) Roth; Ph.B., Mt. Mary Coll., 1944; M.A. in Social Work, U. Minn., 1949. Supr. case work Mpls. Soc. for Blind, 1946-48, Luth. Children's Bur., Phila., 1950-52; registrar Luth. Deaconess Sch. Ch. Workers, 1952-58, dir. clin. tng., 1952-58; cons. Services to Blind and Partially Sighted with Luth. Synod Eastern Pa. Bd. Social Ministry, Phila., 1958-67, with Luth. Synod Southeastern Pa., Com. on Social Ministry, Phila., 1967-70; dir. social service Center for Blind, Phila., 1970-74; dir. social service Center City Hosp., Phila., 1977—; pvt. clin. practice, 1974—. Guest lectr. Scheie Eye Inst., Phila., 1972. Mem. tech. adv. com. Nat. Aid to Visually Handicapped, 1966-72. Diaconate Luth. Ch. Am. Recipient Madonna medal for profl. achievement Mt. Mary Coll., Milw., 1966; Community Service award Pa. Acad. Ophthalmology and Otolaryngology, 1970. Mem. Acad. Certified Social Workers, Nat. Assn. Social Workers, Nat. Assn. Workers for Blind, Am. Acad. Med. Adminstrs., Luth. Social Welfare Conf. Am. Home and Office: 1810 Rittenhouse Sq Philadelphia PA 19103

ROTH, HELEN COBURN, community action agy. exec.; b. Logan, Utah, July 29, 1927; d. John L. and Alta Merle (Hammond) Coburn; B.A., Utah State U., 1949; M.S., Pa. State U., 1951; postgrad. Radcliffe U., 1951-58; 1 son, Peter. Clin. psychologist VA Mental Hygiene Clinic, Boston, 1953-56; instr. San Francisco State Coll., 1959-61; sr. researcher Oakland (Calif.) Econ. Devel. Council, 1965-66; manpower dir., reporting systems dir., sr. info. analyst San Francisco Econ. Opportunity Council, 1967-69; exec. dir. Bear River Community Action Agy., Logan, Utah, 1975—; cons. Kaiser Hosp., Oakland, Social Dynamics Corp., Berkeley. Mem. Logan Ad Hoc Com. for Better Govt., Cache Citizens Com.; sec. Bear River Women's Work Force Consortium Bd.; Utah Human Resource Council rep. Gov.'s Adv. Council on Community Affairs; exec. com. Region VIII Community Action Assn.; vice chmn., treas. ACLU; vice chmn. Utah Human Resource Council; pres. Utah Community Action Assn., bd. dirs. Title XX, Easter Seals Senate, Utahn's Against Hunger, Utah Manpower Planning Council, Planned Parenthood Assn. Utah, Vol. Action Center; mem. corrections task force Utah Internat. Women's Yr.; sec. Cache Handicap Awareness Council; mem. Utah Rural Labor and Tng. Bd. Joseph Hayes Whitney fellow, 1951-53; NSF grantee, 1956-57; Vol. of Yr. award Vol. Action Center, 1978. Mem. Nat. Community Action Agy. Exec. Dirs. Assn. (dir.), LWV (v.p., dir. rep. govt. portfolio, dir. action portfolio), NOW, Utah Equal Rights Coalition, Mormons for ERA, Phi Kappa Phi (fellow 1950-51), Psi Chi, Phi Gamma Mu, Alpha Chi Omega. Club: Harvard Alumni. Home: 47 N 200 E Logan UT 84321 Office: 170 N Main Logan UT 84321

ROTH, JUNE, author; b. Haverstraw, N.Y., Feb. 16, 1926; d. Harry I. and Ida (Glazer) Spiewak; student Pa. State U., 1942-44; grad. Tobe-Coburn Sch., 1945; B.A., Thomas Edison Coll., 1981; M.S., U. Bridgeport, 1982; m. Frederick Roth, July 7, 1945; children—Nancy, Robert. Author: The Freeze and Please Homefreezer Cookbook, 1963; The Rich and Delicious Low-Calorie Figure Slimming Cookbook, 1964; Thousand Calorie Cookbook, 1967; How to Use Sugar to Lose Weight, 1969; Fast and Fancy Cookbook, 1969; How to Cook Like a Jewish Mother, 1969; The Take Good Care of My Son Cookbook for Brides, 1969; The Indoor/Outdoor Barbecue Book, 1970; The Pick of the Pantry Cookbook, 1970; Let's Have a Brunch Cookbook, 1971; Edith Bunkers' All in the Family Cookbook, 1972; Healthier Jewish Cookery The Unsaturated Fat Way, 1972; Salt Free Cooking with Herbs and Spices (R.T. French Tastemaker award), 1975; The Troubled Tummy Cookbook, 1976; Cooking for Your Hyperactive Child, 1977; The Food/Depression Connection, 1978; (with Don Mannerberg) Aerobic Nutrition, 1981; author Special Diets, nationally syndicated newspaper column, 1979—. Vice pres. evening group Teaneck (N.J.) br. Nat. Council Jewish Women, 1954, pres., 1955, v.p. day group, 1956. Mem. Authors League Am., Tobe Coburn Alumni Assn., Am. Soc. Journalists and Authors (pres. 1982-83), Nat. Fedn. Press Women, Nat. Press Club, Newspaper Food Editors and Writers Assn. Address: 1057 Oakland Ct Teaneck NJ 07666

ROTH, LUCY TARBELL, educator, rancher; b. Colorado Springs, Colo., Aug. 22, 1902; d. Winfield Scott and Grace Elizabeth (Butler) Tarbell; certificate Denver U., 1924; postgrad. U. Mex., 1953; m. Charles B. Roth, July 1, 1924; children—Patricia (Mrs. J.E. Coulter), Meri (Mrs. Merlyn Wheeler). Prin., tchr. Ralston Sch., Arvada, Colo., 1947-48; rancher, breeder of Arabian horses, 1936—. Active March of Dimes, ARC, Community Chest Drives; girl scout leader, 1967-68; pres. Salvation Army Rehab. Aux., 1969-70; pres. Friends of Library, Arvada, 1972. Republican councilwoman in Denver, 1934, 35. Named Hidden Heroine, Girl Scouts U.S.A., 1976, Woman of Year, City of Arvada, 1978. Mem. Photog. Soc. Am., D.A.R., Pikes Peak Cowbell Assn., Pi Beta Phi. Clubs: Arvada Garden (pres. 1950, 65-66, 69-70, 75-76), Woman's (pres. 1951). Home: 7995 Alkire St Arvada CO 80005

ROTH, REGINA DIXON, psychologist; b. Lake Forest, Ill., Mar. 6, 1950; d. Richard James and Shirley (White) R.; A.B. with honors, Conn. Coll., 1972; M.A., N.Y. U., 1974, Ph.D. (NIMH trainee), 1976; postdoctoral student Northwestern U. Med. Hosp. Inst. Psychiatry, 1978-79. Staff cons. clin. div. Worthington Hurst & Assos., Chgo., 1977-78; psychology postdoctoral trainee Hines (Ill.) VA Hosp., 1979; psychology postdoctoral trainee West Side VA Hosp., Chgo., 1979-80; pvt. practice clin. psychology, 1980—. Mem. Am. Psychol. Assn., Ill. Psychol. Assn., Nat. Register Mental Health Service Providers, Chgo. Assn. Psychoanalytic Psychology. Home: 3001 S King Dr #508 Chicago IL 60616 Office: 333 N Michigan Ave Suite 1928 Chicago IL 60616 also 1800 Glenview Rd Glenview IL 60025

ROTHBAUM, VIRGINIA EDEL, therapist, adminstr., artist; b. Savannah, Ga., Jan. 30, 1924; d. Herman Myers and Riette (Levy) Edel; A.A., Armstrong Jr. Coll., 1943; A.B. in Journalism, U. N.C., Chapel Hill, 1945; A.S. in Mental Health, Armstrong State Coll., U. Ga., 1978, pediatric devel. studies, 1979-81; children—Stephen Ira, Peggy Ann, John Edel. Public relations Bell Telephone-System, 1945-48, Savannah, Phila. and Woodbury, N.J., 1952-53; substitute tchr., Phila., 1948-49; owner, br. adminstr. Diners/Fugazy Travel, Savannah, 1970-72; advt. sales Savannah Mag., 1972; reading therapist Royce Reading Center, Savannah, 1971-76, 79—, asso. dir., 1976-78; edn. therapist asst. Ga. PsychoEd Network, 1978-79; participant learning disability seminars Armstrong State Coll., 1972, 74-82; life counselor Am. Cancer Soc., Savannah, 1977—, coordinator Reach to Recovery, 1979-82; counselor Hospice of Savannah, 1978—; mem. ad hoc com. Savannah Alliance for Mentally Ill, 1980—. Active Parent Tchr. Orgn./PTA, Girls Scouts U.S.; mem. community adv. com. World Coll. West, Marin County, Calif., 1977—, Founding sponsor, 1980. Mem. AAUW, Savannah Artists Guild, Savannah Art Assn., Ga. Assn. Children with Learning Disabilities, Orton Soc. Jewish. Watercolor artist; one woman show Newsweek Gallery, N.Y.C., 1967, Heritage Gallery, Savannah, 1982; also illustrator, designer.

ROTHBERG, JOAN O., advt. exec.; b. Newark, Aug. 29, 1942; d. Abraham and Nettie Rasnick Oxman; A.B., Vassar Coll.; M.B.A., Harvard U. Exec. v.p., gen. mgr. Ted Bates Advt., N.Y.C.; dir. The Progressive Corp., Triplar, Inc. Recipient Tribute to Women in Internat. Industry award Nat. YWCA. Office: Ted Bates & Co Inc 1515 Broadway New York NY 10036

ROTHENBERG, ELEANORE, health care adminstr.; b. N.Y.C., Oct. 7, 1934; d. Max and Dorothy (Kaplan) Dubin; B.A. cum laude, Bklyn. Coll., 1955; M. in Public Adminstration. (NIH fellow), N.Y. U., 1969, Ph.D., 1975; m. Stanley Rothenberg, Mar. 17, 1961; children—David, Michael, Seth. Asst. dir. dept. policy analysis N.Y. U. Med. Center, 1970-74; cons. Nat. Inst. Alcoholism and Alcohol Abuse, 1972-73; dep. exec. dir. N.Y. County Health Services Rev. Orgn., N.Y.C., 1974-75, exec. dir., 1975-80, spl. adv. to chmn. bd., 1980-81; adj. asst. prof. Sch. Public Health and Adminstrv. Medicine, Columbia U., N.Y.C., 1976—; dir. health care standards and evaluation N.Y.C. Health and Hosps. Corp., 1981—. Mem. Am. Public Health Assn., Public Health Assn. of N.Y.C., Med. and Health Research Assn. (mem. com. on use of human subjects in research 1976-79), Alliance for Continuing Med. Edn. (mem. governing body 1978—), Met. Health Adminstrs. Assn., N.Y. Assn. for Ambulatory Care, Assn. for Women in Sci., Hermann Biggs Soc. Jewish. Author: Regulation and Expansion of Health Facilities, 1976; contbr. numerous articles on quality assurance, program evaluation and continuing med. edn. to profl. jours. Home: 500 E 77th St New York NY 10021 Office: 125 Worth St New York NY 10013

ROTHENHAUS, CLARICE JACOBS, non-profit mgmt. cons. co. exec.; b. N.Y.C., Jan. 12, 1936; d. Clarence Albert and Daisy Mae (Lawhorne) Jacobs; grad. Katharine Gibbs Sch., N.Y.C., 1955; divorced; children—Todd Curtis, Kurt Joseph. With Elizabeth Kennedy & Assos., N.Y.C., 1973-76, Amherst Group, Ltd., N.Y.C., 1976-78; dir. office adminstrn. Nat. Exec. Service Corps, N.Y.C., 1978—. Treas, Jackson Heights (N.Y.) Community Fedn., 1970-72; bd. dirs. Jackson Heights Civic Assn., 1974-76. Mem. Internat. Wordprocessing Assn., Nat. Assn. Female Execs., Gotham Bus. and Profl. Women's Clubs (pres. 1976). Republican. Home: 531 Main St Roosevelt Island NY 10044 Office: 622 3d Ave New York NY 10017

ROTHMAN, ESTHER POMERANZ, psychologist, author; b. N.Y.C.; d. Max and Annie (Reiner) Pomeranz; B.A., Hunter Coll., 1942; M.A., Columbia, 1946; M.A., Coll. City N.Y., 1951; Ph.D., N.Y. U., 1957; m. Arthur Rothman, Apr. 13, 1946; 1 dau., Amy. Tchr., N.Y.C. schs., 1942-49, Bellevue Psychiat. Hosp., N.Y.C., 1949-55, tchr.-therapist, 1957-58; psychologist Univ. Hosp., 1956-57; research supr. Shield of David, 1958-62; prin. Livingston Sch. for Girls, 1959-80; staff psychologist Girls Service League, 1959-62; guest lectr. Queens Coll., N.Y. U., Hunter Coll.; adj. prof. Fordham U., 1973-74; cons. Center for Urban Edn., 1967-71; project dir. Crisis Intervention by Use of Telephone Therapy, 1972-75; exec. dir. Glie Community Youth Programs. Recipient Am. Educators Medal award Freedoms Found. Valley Forge; elected to Hunter Coll. Hall of Fame. Fellow Am. Orthopsychiat. Assn.; mem. Am., N.Y. State psychol. assns., Council Exceptional Children (chpt. pres.), Pi Lambda Theta, Kappa Delta Pi. Author: (with Pearl Berkowitz) Disturbed Child, 1958; Buttons: Protective Test of Personality, 1963; (with Pearl Berkowitz), Education for Disturbed Children in N.Y.C., 1966; Angel Inside Went Sour, 1971; Troubled Teachers, 1977. Contbr. numerous articles to profl. jours. Home: 200 E 16th St New York NY 10003

ROTHSCHILD, AMALIE RANDOLPH, filmmaker, producer, dir.; b. Balt., June 3, 1945; d. Randolph Schamberg and Amalie Getta (Rosenfeld) R.; B.F.A., R.I. Sch. Design, 1967; M.F.A. in Motion Picture Production, N.Y. U., 1969. Spl. effects staff in film and photography Joshua Light Show, Fillmore E. Theatre, NYC, 1969-71; still photographer TWA Airlines Pub. Relations Dept., Village Voice newspaper Rolling Stone magazine, Newsweek magazine, After Dark, N.Y. Daily News, numerous others, 1968-72; co-founder, partner New Day Films, distbn. coop., 1971—; owner, operator Anomaly Films Co., NYC, 1971—; mem., co-founder Assn. of Independent Video and Filmmakers, Inc., NYC, 1974, bd. dirs., 1974-78; instr. in film and TV, N.Y. U. Inst. of Film and TV, 1976-78; cons. in field to various organizations including Youthgrant Program of Nat. Endowment for Humanities, Washington, 1973-76; motion pictures include: Woo Who? May Wilson, 1969; It Happens to Us, 1972; Nana, Mom and Me, 1974;

Radioimmunoassay of Renin, Radioimmunoassay of Aldosterone, 1973; Conversations with Willard Van Dyke, 1981; editor: Doing It Yourself, Handbook on Independent Film Distribution, 1977. Active mem. Community Planning Bd. 1, Borough of Manhattan, N.Y.C., 1974—. Recipient spl. achievement award Mademoiselle mag., 1972; independent filmmaker grant, Am. Film Inst., 1973; film grantee N.Y. State Council on the Arts, 1977, Nat. Endowment Arts, 1978. Mem. Internat. Film Seminars (bd. trustees 1975-80), Independent Cinema Artists and Producers (bd. dirs. 1976—), Univ. Film Assn., N.Y. Women in Film. Democrat. Address: 135 Hudson St New York NY 10013

ROTHSTEIN, BARBARA JACOBS, fed. judge; b. Bklyn., Feb. 2, 1939; d. Solomon and Pauline Jacobs; B.A., Cornell U., 1960; LL.B. (winning oralist Ames Moot Ct. competition), Harvard U., 1966; m. Ted L. Rothstein, Dec. 28, 1968; 1 son, Daniel Glen. Admitted to Mass. bar, 1966, Wash. bar, 1968; pvt. practice, Boston, 1966-68; asst. atty. gen. Wash. Gen. Consumer Protection Div., 1968-77; mem. faculty U. Wash. Law. Sch., 1975-77; judge Wash. Superior Ct., 1977-80; judge U.S. Dist. Ct. Western Dist. Wash., 1980—. Officer, bd. dirs. Seattle Mental Health Inst., Seattle Treatment Center; trustee Am. Jewish Com. Named Cornell Woman of Year, 1978. Mem. Am. Judicature Soc., Am. Bar Assn., Am. Trial Lawyers Assn., Nat. Assn. Women Judges, Wash. Bar Assn., Seattle-King County Bar Assn. (trustee young lawyers sect. 1971-72), Urban League, Mcpl. League. Club: Cornell (officer, dir.) (Seattle). Address: US Courthouse Seattle WA 98104

ROTHSTEIN, JANET, advt. copywriter; b. Bklyn., Jan. 16, 1945; d. Herman and Nellie (Schwartz) R.; B.A., Bklyn. Coll., 1965. Copywriter, Esquire, Inc., N.Y.C., 1965-67; asst. advt. mgr. Round-the-Clock Hosiery, 1967-71; free-lance copywriter, 1971-73; copy supr. Chem. Bank, 1973-76; dir. sales promotion Sandgren & Murtha, N.Y.C., 1976-77; copywriter Dow Jones & Co., N.Y.C., 1977-78; partner, sr. copywriter TLK Direct Mktg., N.Y.C., 1978-82; copy group head Pubs. Clearing House, Port Washington, N.Y., 1982—. Producer, Dazy, mus. drama. Mem. Direct Mktg. Creative Guild. Office: Publishers Clearing House 382 Channel Dr Port Washington NY 11050

ROTTINGHAUS, (MARY) ANN BALLMAN, optical co. exec.; b. Cin., July 25, 1949; d. Robert John and Marjory Ann (Brennan) Ballman; B.A. in Art Edn., U. Cin., 1972; advanced profl. courses in mgmt. Part-owner Rottinghaus Gallery, Cin., 1972-74; with Whitehall Labs., div. Am. Home Products Co., 1974-79, div. mgr., Atlanta, 1977-79; key account mgr. Bausch & Lomb Inc., 1979, dist. sales mgr., Woodstock, Ga., 1979—. Mem. Nat. Assn. Female Execs. Roman Catholic. Club: Atlanta Ski. Office: 1400 N Goodman St Rochester NY 14602

ROTWEIN, SUZANNE, med. record adminstr.; b. Jackson, Miss., Apr. 9, 1952; d. Abe Arthur and Helene Rose (Ascher) R.; B.S., U. Ala., Birmingham, 1975. Dir. med. record dept. New Vaughan Meml. Hosp., Selma, Ala., 1975-78; dir. med. record dept. Druid City Hosp. Regional Med. Center, Tuscaloosa, Ala., 1978-82; dir. med. record dept. Bexar County Hosp. Dist., San Antonio, 1982—; mem. adj. faculty dept. health services adminstrn. U. Ala., Birmingham; cons. to hosps.; leadership lectr. U. Ala. Capstone Sch. Nursing. Chmn. apt. complex Am. Cancer Soc. Fund Dr., Tuscaloosa. Mem. Am. Med. Records Assn., Ala. Med. Record Assn. (editor newsletter 1977-78), Tex. Med. Records Assn., Tex. Hosp. Assn., AAUW, Am. Hosp. Assn., Assn. Records Mgrs. and Adminstrs., Hadassah (life), Delta Phi Epsilon. Home: 7600 Callaghan Rd Apt 411 San Antonio TX 78229 Office: 4502 Medical Dr San Antonio TX 78284

ROUDYBUSH, ALEXANDRA BROWN (MRS. FRANKLIN ROUDYBUSH), author; b. Hyères, Côte d'Azur, France, Mar. 14, 1911 (parents Am. citizens); d. Constantine and Ethel (Wheeler) Brown; B.A., London Sch. Econs., 1930; m. Franklin Roudybush, May 22, 1941. Corr., London Evening Standard, Washington, 1931; sec. to Drew Pearson, 1932; asst. Agence Havas, 1935; research news analyst Time mag., N.Y.C., 1936; sec. to chief news dept. CBS, 1936; White House corr. MBS, 1940; asst. to sect. head Nat. Acad. Scis., Washington, 1957-60; adminstr., sec. firm Dewey, Ballantine, Bushby, Palmer & Wood, attys., Paris, 1965-80. Mem. Mystery Writers Am. Author: Before the Ball was Over, 1965; Death of a Moral Person, 1967; A Capital Crime, 1969; The House of the Cat, 1970; A Sybaritic Death, 1972; Gastronomic Murder, 1973; Suddenly in Paris, 1975; The Female of the Species, 1978; Blood Ties, 1981. Home: 15 Ave du President Wilson Paris 16e France Office: 45 Ave George V Paris 8e France also Sauveterre de Rouerque 12 Aveyron France

ROUFF, LENORE LYNNE, psychologist; b. Pitts., Oct. 23, 1937; d. Ernest and Agnes Cecelia (Fleishaker) R.; B.A., W.Va. U., 1958, M.A., 1961; Ph.D., Bryn Mawr Coll., 1973. Clin. psychologist, psychiatry dept. Phila. Gen. Hosp., 1961-69, cons. high-risk pediatric clinic, 1970-71; cons. Inter-Ch. Child Care Soc., Phila., 1971-74, Pediatric Clinic, Hahneman Hosp. and Med. Coll., Phila., 1971-74; clin. psychologist People Acting to Help, Phila., 1974-76, S. Central Mental Health, Los Angeles, 1977-78; clin. psychologist, supervising clinician S.E. Mental Health Region, Los Angeles County, Los Angeles, 1978—; asst. prof. dept. psychiatry Martin Luther King Hosp. and Chas. R. Drew Postgrad. Med. Sch., Los Angeles, 1980—; pvt. practice, Beverly Hills, Calif., 1980—clin. asso. dept. psychology U.So. Calif., 1981—. Child devel. and edn. fellow Bryn Mawr Coll., 1969-70. Mem. Am., Los Angeles County psychol. assns., Los Angeles Soc. for Psychoanalytic Psychology, Nat. Audubon Soc., Sierra Club, Phi Beta Kappa. Contbr. articles to profl. jours. Office: SE Mental Health Region Los Angeles County 5850 S Main St Los Angeles CA 90003 also 152 S Lasky Dr Suite 206 Beverly Hills CA 90212

ROUGH, MARIANNE JOHNSON, librarian; b. Long Island, N.Y., June 27, 1941; d. Michael Anthony and Ann Nancy (Kulka) Scarangello; student Pratt Phoenix Sch. Design, 1959-61; A.A.S., SUNY, Farmingdale, 1976; B.S., Empire State Coll., 1977; M.L.S., L.I. U., 1978; postgrad. Columbia U.; m. Allan C. Rough, July 12, 1980; 1 son, William Michael. Art dir. Technamation, Inc., Port Washington, N.Y., 1962-68; dir. new product design Queens Lithography, Inc., Long Island City, N.Y., 1968-70; tech. specialist Media Center, SUNY Coll., Farmingdale, 1970-78; dir. library learning resources center SUNY Coll., Old Westbury, N.Y., 1978—. Mem. Assn. Ednl. Communications and Tech., ALA, N.Y. Library Assn., Nassau County Library Assn., Beta Phi Mu. Home: 6 Sealey Ave Apt 1-K Hempstead NY 11550 Office: Library Learning Resources Center SUNY Old Westbury NY 11568

ROUGHTON, MARJORIE BIDLACK, auditor; b. Oakwood, Ohio, Feb. 23, 1927; d. Guy S. and Cleo Bidlack; student Tiffin Bus. Coll., 1945, LaSalle Coll., 1960, Am. Inst. Banking, 1975, 78, 79, Bank Adminstrn. Inst., 1978; m. Dale L. Roughton, July 12, 1947; children—Sue Annette, Jan Kay. With Oakwood (Ohio) Deposit Bank Co., 1947-53; with State Bank & Trust Co., Defiance, Ohio, 1970—, auditor, 1973—. Auditor, United Meth. Ch., Oakwood, dir. ch. choir, 1957-64; pres. Oakwood Band Booster Assn., 1960; sec. Oakwood PTA, 1960. Mem. Nat. Assn. Bank Women (past chmn. Maumee Valley group), Bank Adminstrn. Inst., (chpt. auditor, dir. auditors conf. N.W. Ohio 1980), Rural Letter Carriers Aux. (pres. 1975-82). Methodist. Home: Rural Route Oakwood OH Office: State Bank & Trust Co 401 Clinton St PO Box 467 Defiance OH 43512

ROUILLARD, MARILEE HACKLER, state legislator; b. Keene, N.H., Jan. 1, 1943; d. George T. and Edna G. (Cole) Hackler; B.Ed., Keene State Coll., 1964; postgrad. U. N.H., 1965-66; M.A., Eastern Mich. U., 1967; m. David Rouillard, Aug. 22, 1967; children—Rachel, Matthew. English tchr. Saugerties (N.Y.) High Sch., 1964; tchr. math. and sci. Hooksett, N.H., 1965-66; instr. Crotched Mt. Rehab. Center, N.H., 1966-67; mem. N.H. Ho. of Reps., 1980—. Chmn. St. Joseph's Parents Assn., 1981—; selectman Ward 1, Keene, 1971-72; active vol., bd. mem. various orgns. Democrat.

ROULETTE, HEDL DRESDNER, newspaper co. exec.; b. Trenton, N.J., Oct. 23, 1930; d. Karl George and Miriam Virginia Dresdner; B.A., Elmira Coll., 1950; postgrad. Wharton Sch., U. Pa.; m. William Roulette, Dec. 28, 1953 (div.); children—Karla Roulette Rauch, William Brooke. With public relations dept. Princeton (N.J.) U., 1950-53; owner Hedl Yuletree Farm, sculpture and design in brass, Coopersburg, Pa., 1965-79; dir. advt. Quakertown (Pa.) Free Press, 1973-79; dir. advt. The Trentonian, Trenton, N.J., 1979—. Active, Jr. League, Delaware Valley United Way; vol. St. Luke's Hosp.; bd. govs. Trenton Symphony; vol. Citizens for Eisenhower; bd. dirs. George Washington council Boy Scouts Am.; active YWCA, Princeton. Mem. N.J. Press Assn., Pa. Newspaper Pub. Assn., Internat. Newspaper Advt. Assn., Interstate Newspaper Advt., Suburban Phila. Newspaper Advt. Assn.. S. Jersey Newspaper Advt., DAR (dir. George Washington chpt.), Nat. Assn. Republican Women, Trenton C. of C. Presbyterian. Club: Soroptimist (dir. Trenton 1980-81). Home: 105 Penn Valley Terr Yardley PA 19067 Office: 600 Perry St Trenton NJ 08602

ROULHAC, ANN BROWN, pharmacist; b. Moultrie, Ga., Sept. 17, 1949; d. Robert and Daisy Mae (Wilson) Brown; B.S. in Pharmacy, Fla. A&M U., 1972; M.S. in Human Resource Mgmt., Nova U., Ft. Lauderdale, Fla., 1983; m. Elmer Henderson Roulhac, July 29, 1972; 1 son, Elmer Henderson. Staff pharmacist Imperial Point Med. Center, Ft. Lauderdale, 1973—. Mem. Am. Bus. Women's Assn. (v.p. 1977; Woman of Year award 1980), Broward County Pharmacy Assn., Fla. A&M Alumni Assn. Democrat. Methodist. Home: 11301 NW 30th Pl Sunrise FL 33322 Office: 6401 N Federal Hwy Fort Lauderdale FL 33308

ROUNTREE, MARY MARTIN, educator; b. Atlanta, Sept. 26, 1931; d. Robert Emory and Mary (Thompson) Martin; A.B., U. Ga., 1952, M.A. in French, 1954; M.A. in English, U. Pitts., 1963, Ph.D. in English, 1965; m. Dec. 18, 1953; children—Ashley Everett, Meredith Martin. Asst. prof. English and Am. studies Mt. Holyoke Coll., South Hadley, Mass., from 1966, then assoc. prof., now prof.; Fulbright prof. U. Toulouse (France), 1970-71, U. Tunis (Tunisia), 1981-82; lectr., Africa. Mem. MLA, South Atlantic MLA, Phi Beta Kappa. Democrat. Research, publs. on fiction Conrad Aiken, poetry of Jean de Boschere. Home: 26 Ashfield Ln South Hadley MA 01075 Office: Dept English Mount Holyoke Coll South Hadley MA 01075

ROURKE, ROSEMARIE FRITSCHI, plastics co. exec.; b. Karlsruhe, W.Ger., Nov. 17, 1942; d. Ernst and Annemarie Fritschi; abitur Lessinggymnasium, Karlsruhe, 1962; m. Lowndes Edward Rourke, Mar. 19, 1966; 1 dau., Loren Lynn. Mgr., Berlitz Sch. Langs., Karlsruhe, 1962-67; chief adminstr. Freedman Bros., Bridgeport, Conn., 1967-72; controller Norfield Corp., Danbury, Conn., 1972-74, v.p., 1974-78, v.p., gen. mgr. Norfield div. Fallek Chem. Co., 1978-82, pres., 1982—; dir., sec. Corp. Devel. Systems, Inc. Mem. Am. Mgmt. Assn. Republican. Roman Catholic. Patentee plastics. Office: 36 Kenosia Ave Danbury CT 06810

ROUSE, DORIS JANE, physiologist; b. Greensboro, N.C., Oct. 3, 1948; d. Welby Corbett and Nadia Elizabeth (Grainger) R.; B.A. in Chemistry, Duke U., 1970, Ph.D. in Physiology and Pharmacology, 1980; m. Blake Shaw Wilson, Jan. 6, 1974. Sci. instr. Peace Corps, Liberia, 1970-71; research scientist Burroughs Wellcome Co., Research Triangle Park, N.C., 1971-76; dir. biomed. applications team NASA, Research Triangle Inst., Research Triangle Park, 1976—; cons. VA. Mem. adv. bd. Assn. Retarded Citizens. Recipient group achievement award NASA, 1979. Mem. Assn. Advancement Med. Instrumentation, Rehab. Engring. Soc. N.Am. Club: Triangle Dive. Contbr. articles profl. jours. Home: 709 Reta Rd Durham NC 27704 Office: PO Box 12194 Research Triangle Park NC 27709

ROUSE, JOHNNIE ANITA, automated data processing adminstr.; b. Liberty, S.C., June 5, 1943; d. John Henry and Bernice (McDowell) R.; B.S., Howard U., 1965; M.A., Am. U., 1967. Computer specialist Dept. Army, Washington, 1966-72, Bur. Labor Stats., Dept. Labor, Washington, 1972-74; chief br. employment service data systems D.C. Dept. Manpower, Washington, 1974-79; chief div. mgmt. data systems D.C. Dept. Employment Services, 1979—; dir. Black Ski, Inc.; pres. Diversified Interiors. Vol. tutor for jr. high and high sch. students; vol. hospitality coms., local hosps. Recipient plaque for outstanding performance D.C. Dept. Manpower, 1976, Performance award, 1978; also numerous commendations for systems designed, 1968-81. Mem. Internat. Assn. Personnel in Employment Security, Automated Data Processing Mgrs. Assn., Nat. Assn. Female Execs., Delta Sigma Theta. Democrat. Baptist. Home: 7730 Burnside Rd Hyattsville MD 20785 Office: Dept Employment Services/OMIDS Room 411 500 C St NW Washington DC 20785

ROUSE, SUE THOMPSON, educator; b. Ulman, Mo., Aug. 28, 1920; d. Clyde Waldo and Retta (Darr) Thompson; A.B., Harris Tchrs. Coll., St. Louis, 1942; M.A., U. N.C., Chapel Hill, 1950; Ed.D. (fellow 1960), George Peabody Coll., Nashville, 1963; postgrad. U. Minn.; m. Linwood I. Rouse, Aug. 29, 1945 (div.). Elem. sch. tchr., Mo. and N.C., 1947-59; mem. faculty U. S.C., Columbia, 1961—, prof. edn., 1974—; cons. infield. Chmn., S.C. Commn. Ministry for Christian Ch. (Disciples of Christ), 1973-80; mem. regional bd. Christian Chs. in S.C., 1979-83, moderator, 1980-82; pres. Regional Assembly Christian Chs. in S.C., 1977-78; mem. nat. adv. com. ministry Christian Ch., 1978-82, nat. bd. dirs. Div. Homeland Ministries, 1981—. Served with USCGR, 1943-46. Fellow Am. Assn. Mental Defiency; mem. NEA (life), S.C. Edn. Assn., Council Exceptional Children, S.C. Psychol. Assn., S.C. Mental Health Assn., Nat. Audubon Soc., Delta Kappa Gamma, Phi Delta Kappa. Democrat. Author articles in field, chpts. in books. Office: Coll Edn U SC Columbia SC 29208

ROUSEK, SISTER, MARIE, librarian; b. East Orange, N.J., July 12, 1925; d. Charles Elmer and Bertha Marie (Everett) R.; A.B., Coll. St. Elizabeth, 1947; A.M., Seton Hall U., 1955; M.L.S., St. John's U., 1958. Joined Sisters of Charity, 1947; tchr. English Bayley-Ellard High Sch., Madison, N.J., 1949-55, St. Michael High Sch., Union City, N.J., 1955-56; asst. librarian Mahoney Library, Coll. St. Elizabeth, Convent Station., N.J., 1956-63; librarian, 1963—; mem. N.J. Task Force on Libraries, 1978-79. Mem. Am., N.J., Cath. library assns., Met. Cath. Coll. Librarians (exec. com. 1970-75, 79-81, chmn. 1977-79), Kappa Gamma Pi. Address: Mahoney Library Coll of St Elizabeth Convent Station NJ 07961

ROUSH, ANNE FRANCES, adminstrv. social worker; b. Carroll, Iowa, Nov. 20, 1930; d. Lawrence James and Frances Xavier (Whalen) Lane; R.N., Mercy Hosp. Sch. Nursing, Des Moines, 1951; B.S., St. Louis U., 1953; M.S.W., U. Hawaii, 1968; m. Howard Patrick Roush, Aug. 6, 1955; children—Mary Frances, Louise Catherine, Jenny Elizabeth, Frederick Lawrence, Martin Louis. Head nurse Barnes Hosp., asst. in nursing Washington U., St. Louis, 1953-54; instr. St. Marys Hosp. Sch. Nursing, Tucson, 1955-56; psychiat. social worker So. Ariz. Mental Health Center, Tucson, 1968—, unit dir., 1977—; field instr. Sch. Social Work Ariz. State U., Tempe; cons., co-founder, mem. bd. COPE, 1975-81. Mem. Nat. Assn. Social Workers (steering com. Ariz. chpt. 1976-78), Acad. Cert. Social Workers. Research in manpower in social work, 1968. Home: 6260 N Oasis St Tucson AZ 85704 Office: 1930 E 6th St Tucson AZ 85719

ROUSSEAU, SANDRA MAHLER, med. technologist; b. Beacon, N.Y., July 2, 1950; d. Joseph P. and Irma M. (Franke) Mahler; B.S. in Med. Tech., U. Vt., 1972; m. William A. Rousseau, Oct. 7, 1972; children—Benjamin F., Laura A. Clin. med. technologist VA Hosp., White River Junction, Vt., 1972-75, research med. technologist Dr. Leo R. Zacharski Coagulation Lab., Va Hosp., White River Junction, 1975—; bookkeeper, acct. Rousseau Lumber Co., 1972—. Bd. dirs. The Childrens Place Nursery and Daycare, South Royalton, Vt. Mem. Am. Soc. Clin. Pathologists, Nat. Abortion Rights League Vt. Republican. Lutheran. Club: Woodstock (Vt.) Country. Home: RD 2 Bethel VT 05032 Office: VA Hospital White River Junction VT 05001

ROVELSTAD, MATHILDE VERNER, educator; b. Kempten, Ger., Aug. 12, 1920; d. George and Therese (Hohl) Hotter; came to U.S., 1951, naturalized, 1953; Ph.D., U. Tübingen, 1953; M.S. in L.S., Catholic U. Am., 1960; m. Howard Rovelstad, Nov. 23, 1970. Cataloger, Mt. St. Mary's Coll., Los Angeles, 1953; sch. librarian Yoyogi Elementary Sch., Tokyo, 1954-56; mem. faculty Cath. U. Am., 1960—, prof. library sci., 1975—; vis. prof. U. Montreal, 1969. Research grantee German Acad. Exchange Service, 1969. Mem. ALA (internat. relations com. 1977-79), Internat. Fedn. Library Assns. and Instns. (standing adv. com. library schs. 1975-81), Am. Assn. Library Schs. Contbr. profl. jours. Home: 11 Banbury Rd Gibson Island MD 21056 Office: Dept Library Sci Catholic Univ Am Washington DC 20064

ROVET, JOANNE FRANCES, psychologist; b. Montreal, Que., Can., Feb. 24, 1946; d. David George and Jane (Adelman) Rigler; B.Sc. magna cum laude, York U., 1968; Ph.D., U. Toronto, 1974; m. Ernest Rovet, Dec. 26, 1967; children—Benjamin, Heather, Jennifer. Asst. prof. Ont. Inst. Studies in Edn., Toronto, 1974-75; postdoctoral fellow Hosp. Sick Children, Toronto, 1975-78, research asso., 1978—. Exec. mem. PTA, 1978-80. Recipient Lionel Charles Worth prize York U., 1965; York U. scholar, 1964, Can. Council doctoral fellow, 1971-73, Med. Research Council postdoctoral fellow, 1975-78, Ont. Mental Health Found. fellow, 1981-82. Mem. Soc. Research Child Devel., Behavior Genetics Soc., Am. Psychol. Assn., Ont. Bd. Examiners Psychology. Club: Cedar Highlands Ski. Contbr. articles to profl. jours. Home: 399 Glengrove Ave Toronto ON M5N 1W8 Canada Office: 555 University Ave Toronto ON M5G 1X8 Canada

ROVIN, ADRIENNE LEE, social worker; b. Cleve., Dec. 16, 1947; d. Morris and Violet (Neer) Sirkin; B.A., Kent State U., 1970; M.S.S.A., Case Western Reserve U., 1972; m. Ronald Rovin, June 13, 1971; 1 son, Eric. Social worker Cuyahoga County (Ohio) Welfare Dept., Cleve., 1970-71, Center for Human Services, Cleve., 1971-72, Jewish Family Service Assn., Cleve., 1972-73; social worker Sch. Dist. #54, Schaumburg, Ill., 1977—; pvt. practice marriage and family counseling, Schaumburg, 1977—. Vice chmn. Schaumburg Twp. Mental Health Bd., 1976-77, chmn., 1977-79. Mem. Nat. Assn. Social Workers, Ill. Assn. Sch. Social Workers, Acad. Cert. Social Workers (cert.). Office: 524 E Schaumburg Rd Schaumburg IL 60194

ROVNER, ILANA DIAMOND, lawyer; b. Riga, Latvia, Aug. 21, 1938; came to U.S., 1939, naturalized, 1954; d. Stanley and Ronny Diamond; A.B., Bryn Mawr Coll., 1960; postgrad. King's Coll., U. London, 1960-61, Georgetown Law Sch., 1961-64; J.D., Ill. Inst. Tech., 1966; m. Richard N. Rovner, Mar. 9, 1963; 1 son, Maxwell. Admitted to Ill. bar, 1972; law clk. to Judge James B. Parsons, U.S. Dist. Ct., No. Dist. Ill., 1972-73; chief, public protection unit, U.S. Atty.'s Office, No. Dist. Ill., 1973-77; dep., legal counsel to Gov. James R. Thompson, Chgo., 1977—. Bd. dirs. Anti-Defamation League; trustee Anshe Emet Synagogue. Recipient spl. commendation awards Dept. of Justice, 1975, 76, ann. nat. law and social justice leadership award League to Improve the Community, 1975, ann. guardian police award, 1977. Mem. Am. Bar Assn., Fed. Bar Assn. (2d v.p. No. Dist. Ill.), Ill. State Bar Assn., Chgo. Bar Assn., Women's Bar Assn., Chgo. Council of Lawyers, Decalogue Soc. of Lawyers, Kappa Beta Pi. Office: 160 N La Salle St Chicago IL 60601

ROWAN, BETTY LOU, ins. and real estate agt.; b. Cin., Jan. 22, 1927; d. Harry Thomas and Lula (Kraft) Snell; student U. Ariz., 1944-45; m. Blaine J. Rowan, June 1, 1946; children—Roger M., Camille Rowan Freeman, Cynthia Rowan Smith; stepchildren—Shirley, Ralph, Ronald R. Co-owner, sec. Rowen Agy. Ins. and Real Estate, Rigby, Idaho, 1961—, co-owner, mgr., agt., Rexburg, Idaho, 1971-76; sec. Upper Valley Bd. Realtors, 1971-77. Vol. Reach to Recovery Am. Cancer Soc., 1974—. Named Woman of Year Rigby Jay-Cee-Ettes, 1964. Mem. Ins. Women Snake River Valley (pres. 1972-74), Upper Valley Bd. Realtors (sec. 1971-73), Nat. Assn. Ins. Women, Idaho Assn. Realtors, Nat. Bd. Realtors, Idaho Falls Panhellenic Assn., Gamma Phi Beta. Club: Soroptomist (pres. 1976-77, sec. Rexburg 1978-80, chmn. devel. and edn. Rocky Mountain area 1978-80). Home: 270 N 3d West Rigby ID 83442 Office: 205 E Fremont Rigby IA 83442

ROWE, DOROTHY LEE, educator; b. Huntington, W.Va., Oct. 30, 1920; d. McKinley Leander and Mabel Mae (Ferris) Rowe; B.S. in Edn., Ohio U., 1941; postgrad. Harvard Grad. Sch. Edn., 1953, Purdue U., summer, 1956; M.A., U. Chgo., 1958; postgrad. Bowdoin Coll., summer, 1962. Tchr. math. Chesapeake, Ohio, 1941-43, Ironton (Ohio) High Sch., 1943-46, Gallia Acad. High Sch., Gallipolis, Ohio, 1946-58; instr. math. Miami U., Oxford, Ohio, 1958-73, sr. instr., 1973-78, prof. emeritus math. and stats., 1978—. Nat. adv. bd. Am. Security Council, 1978-82; sustaining mem. Republican Nat. Com., 1971-82; active McCullough-Hyde Hosp. Aux., Friends of Lane Public Library. Ford Found. fellow, 1952-53; Gen. Electric fellow, summer, 1956; NSF fellow, 1957, 58, summer 1962. Mem. AAUW, AAUP, Math. Assn. Am., NEA, Nat. Ret. Tchrs. Assn., Ohio Ret. Tchrs. Assn., Pi Lambda Theta, Pi Mu Epsilon, Delta Kappa Gamma, Kappa Delta Pi. Republican. Presbyterian. Address: 6192 Vereker Dr Oxford OH 45056

ROWE, MARY HELEN, educator; b. Ogden, Ark., Sept. 4; d. Alexander and Norvell (Moore) Thurston; B.A., Calif. State Coll., San Bernardino, 1970, M.A. in Bus. Adminstrn., 1975, adminstrv. credential, 1976, M.A. in Edn., 1977; m. Jesse Leroy Rowe, Oct. 20, 1953 (div. 1961); 1 adopted son, James Raymond Joseph. Psychiat. technician Patton State Hosp., 1961-72; tchr. high sch. Riverside (Calif.) City Sch. Dist., 1972-78; tchr. bus. edn. Barstow (Calif.) Community Coll., 1978—. Sec. to trustee bd. St. Paul A.M.E. Ch., San Bernardino, Calif., 1977-79; tchr. San Bernardino High Sch., 1979—. Mem. Calif. Bus. Edn. Assn., AAUW, Delta Sigma Theta. Home: 1584 N Massaro Ln San Bernardino CA 92411

ROWE, SANDRA MIMS, editor; b. Charlotte, N.C., May 26, 1948; d. David Lathan and Shirley Lurlene (Stovall) Mims; B.A. in English, E. Carolina U., 1970; m. Gerard Paul Rowe, June 5, 1971; children—Mims Elizabeth, Sarah Stovall. Reporter, The Ledger-Star, Norfolk, Va., 1971-75, asst. city editor, 1975, editor The Daily Break, 1976-78, asst. mng. editor, 1978-80, mng. editor, 1980—. Recipient Outstanding Profl. Woman in Tidewater award, 1982. Mem. AP Mng. Editors Assn., Nat.

Fedn. Press Women, Kappa Tau Alpha, Chi Omega. Roman Catholic. Office: 150 W Brambleton Ave Norfolk VA 23501

ROWEN, RUTH HALLE, musicologist, educator; b. N.Y.C., Apr. 5, 1918; d. Louis and Ethel (Fried) Halle; B.A., Barnard Coll., 1939; M.A., Columbia U., 1941, Ph.D., 1948; m. Seymour M. Rowen, Oct. 13, 1940; children—Mary Helen Rowen Obelkevich, Louis Halle. Mgr. ednl. dept. Carl Fischer, Inc., N.Y.C., 1954-63; asso. prof. musicology CCNY, 1967-72, prof., 1972—; mem. doctoral faculty in musicology City U. N.Y., 1967—. Mem. ASCAP, Am. Musicological Soc., Music Library Assn., Coll. Music Soc., Nat. Fedn. Music Clubs (nat. musicianship chmn. 1962-74, nat. young artist auditions com. 1964-74, N.Y. state chmn. Young Artist Auditions 1981), Phi Beta Kappa. Author: Early Chamber Music, 1948, reprinted, 1974; (with Adele T. Katz) Hearing—Gateway to Music, 1959; (with William Simon) Jolly Come Sing and Play, 1956; Music Through Sources and Documents, 1979. Home: 115 Central Park W New York NY 10023

ROWER, MARGARETTA FRANCISCA, audiologist, speech pathologist, educator; b. N.Y.C; d. Alfred H. and Katherine (Messmer) R.; B.S., SUNY, New Paltz, 1964; M.S., Ithaca Coll., 1972; postgrad. (Noyes Found. fellow), Cornell U., 1972-74; 1 dau., Nancy. Tchr. pub. schs., N.Y. State, 1964-72; audiologist, mobile audiology clinic Ithaca (N.Y.) Coll., 1972-73, instr., clin. supr., dept. speech pathology and audiology, 1973-75, grad. instr., part-time, 1975—; chief of speech pathology and audiology Broome Devel. Services, N.Y. State Dept. Mental Hygiene, Binghamton, N.Y., 1975—; tchr. Dept. Def., Okinawa (Japan) and Würzburg (Germany), 1981-82. adj. prof. Broome Community Coll. Fruehauff Found. grantee, summer 1971; lic. audiologist, N.Y. State; lic. tchr., N.Y. State. Mem. Am. Assn. Mental Deficiency, Am. Speech and Hearing Assn. (cert. of clin. competency), Assn. Speech Pathologists and Audiologists of Mental Hygiene. Contbr. articles to profl. jours. Home: 1005 Baylor Dr Binghamton NY 13903 Office: Würzburg American Schools DODDS Germany APO 09801

ROWLAND, BARBARA JANE, businesswoman; b. Cin., Nov. 1, 1949; d. Robert Charles and Jane Mildred (Minor) R.; student Miami-Dade Jr. Coll., 1967; grad. Ga. Inst. Real Estate, 1970, Eastern Airlines Mktg. Sch., 1972, Realtors Inst., Atlanta, 1973; diploma in mgmt. Rochester Inst. Tech., 1981; student Coll. Advanced Traffic, 1979-80. Asst. tennis pro Cherokee Town Club, Atlanta, 1971; with dept. mktg. and sales Eastern Airlines, Atlanta, 1972; passenger rep. passenger dept. So. Ry. System, Atlanta, 1974-79, officer mgr. freight sales dept., Rochester, N.Y., 1979-80, sales rep., 1981-82; sales rep. Norfolk So. Corp., Atlanta, 1982—. Western N.Y. Coca-Cola Women's Doubles Tennis Tournament winner, 1979. Mem. Nat. Ry. Bus. Women's Assn., Women's Transp. Club of Atlanta, Transp. Club of Atlanta, Am. Soc. Traffic and Transp., Women's Transp. Seminar, Nat. Assn. Female Execs., U.S. Lawn Tennis Assn. Office: Norfolk Southern Corp Sales Dept 185 Spring St SW Atlanta GA 30303

ROWLAND, JADA, actress; b. N.Y.C., Feb. 23, 1943; d. Richard and Anna Caroline (Bissell) Rowland; student New Sch. Social Research, Columbia U., Art Students League; m. David John Helfand; 1 son, Sparks Blue Grassly. Appeared in broadway plays: That Lady, 1949, Crimes on Crimes, 1950, Season in the Sun, Sunday Breakfast, Mrs. McThing, Remarkable Mr. Pennypacker, Cold Wind and the Warm; appeared on numerous shows including Kraft Theatre, Philco, Armstrong, Sesame Street, As the World Turns, Secret Storm, Mystery Theatre; actress The Doctors, NBC TV, N.Y.C. Recipient Afternoon TV Daytime TV award, 1974. Mem. Actors Equity Assn., AFTRA, Screen Actors Guild, Nat. Acad. Arts and Scis. *

ROWLAND, JEFFIE LANDERS, artist; b. Murray Cross, Ala., July 10, 1924; d. Eli Jefferson and Pearl Dorsey (Baskin) Landers; B.S., Jacksonville (Ala.) State Tchrs. Coll., 1945; postgrad. U. Ga., Athens; pupil of Lamar Dodd; m. Jack Lamb Rowland, Dec. 23, 1947; children—Mary Jane, Nancy Eugenia, Alice Alden. Elem. sch. tchr., Athens, 1947-48, 1st schs. art supr., 1948-52; 1st schs. art supr. Clarke County schs., Athens, 1952-62; art cons. North Ga. elem. schs., 1962-80; chmn. docents U. Ga. Mus. Art, Athens, 1978—, sch. coordinator for docents program, 1981—, also mem. bd. Friends of Mus.; one-woman show Jacksonville State Tchrs. Coll., 1948; group exhbns. include High Mus. Art, Atlanta, S.E. Art Assn. Mem. show com. Renfrew Hunter-Jumper Shows. Recipient Belle Meade Fox Hunt Hammerhead award, 1982, other art awards. Mem. Arts Alliance, Greater Atlanta Dressage Assn. (coordinator Pony club). Republican. Presbyterian. Club: Belle Meade Fox Hunt (Thomson, Ga.). Author articles in field. Address: Beech Haven Athens GA 30606

ROWLAND, POLLY ROBERTS, state legislator; b. Rutland, Vt., June 16, 1942; student U. Vt.; widowed; 1 dau. Mem., Burlington Democratic Com., Chittenden County Democratic Com., Ward IV Democratic Com.; mem. Bd. Bread and Law Task Force; mem. Vt. Ho. Reps., 1979-80, 81—. Office: Vt Ho Reps State Ho Montpelier VT 05602 *

ROWLEY, MAXINE LEWIS, educator, writer; b. Provo, Utah, Sept. 23, 1938; d. Max Thomas Lewis and Illa Lewis Sanford; B.A. (Ford Found. scholar, merit scholar), Brigham Young U., 1960; B.S., U. Utah, 1974; M.A., Utah State U., 1979; m. Arthur William Rowley, Sept. 23, 1960; children—Anne, Jenefer. Promotion writer sta. KCPX-TV, 1960; extension home economist USDA, 1961; grad. asst. Brigham Young U., Provo, 1965; mgmt. trainee Desserett Book Co., Salt Lake City, 1967; chmn. dept. Patricia Stevens Career Coll., Salt Lake City, 1969; chmn. consumer and homemaking dept. Weber Sch. Dist., Ogden, Utah, 1974, learning experience designer, 1975-78; consumer and homemaking staff Utah State U., Logan, 1978-79, spl. appointee to Utah State U. by Utah State Bd. Edn., 1978-79, cons. Utah State Bd. Edn., instrumental writer Utah State U. Found., 1979; author texts and teachers guide CHECS, 1979; author curriculum guide Operation: Free Enterprise, 1977; author filmstrips on consumer econs. and career exploration, 1977. Active ward, stake and region positions Mormon Ch., primary pres., 1969, relief soc. counselor, 1978, tchr. devel. leader, 1976, cons. region library, 1972, stake librarian, 1971; leader 4-H Club, mem. councils and adv. bds.; leader Girl Scouts U.S.A., Young Homemakers; mem. State Text Book Evaluation Com., 1978-80, U. Utah Evaluation Com., 1979. Named Outstanding Woman Student, Brigham Young U., 1960, Nat. Tchr. of Yr., 1977. Mem. Nat. Assn. Vocat. Home Econs. Tchrs., Am. Home Econs. Assn. (cons.), Am. Vocat. Assn., NEA, Utah Home Econs. Assn., Utah Vocat. Assn., Utah Council for Improvement of Edn., Utah Edn. Assn. (award for womens' awareness task force project 1976), County Welfare Com., Home Econs. Edn. Assn., Vocat. Home Econs. Tchrs. (nat. chmn. public relations and legis. coms. 1978), Mortarboard (pres. 1960), Omicron Nu, Phi Kappa Phi, Spurs, Gamma Phi Omicron. Mem. Republican Party. Home: 1419 W L750 N Layton UT 84041 Office: Smith Family Life Bldg Brigham Young U Provo UT 84321

ROY, BARBARA JEAN, marine corps officer; b. Webster County, W.Va., Sept. 16, 1938; d. Ross Edward and Kathleen Louise (Aggleson) R.; B.S. in Recreation, Fairmont State Coll., 1960; postgrad. U. Va., 1961, Am. U., 1972-73. Commd. 2d lt. U.S. Marine Corps, 1960, advanced through grades to col., 1980; asst. public officer Marine Corps Schs., Quantico, Va., 1960-63; head, asst. head public affairs br. Hdqrs. 8th Marine Corps Dist., New Orleans, 1963-67; projects coordinator Def. Adv. Com. on Women in the Services, Office of Asst. Sec. Def., 1967-69, exec. sec., 1978-79; asst. G-1, Office of Asst. Chief of Staff G-1, Camp S.D. Butler, Okinawa, 1970-71; community relations officer, spl. projects officer, spl. asst. for women marine affairs div. info., Hdqrs. U.S. Marine Corps, Washington, 1971-74; dep. dir. Woman Officer Sch. Edn. Center, Quantico, 1974-75, asst. test and evaluation officer acad. dept., 1975, protocol officer Marine Corps Devel. and Edn. Commn., Quantico, 1975-77; mil. asst. to asst. sec. def. for manpower, res. affairs and logistics Dept. Def., 1977-79; asst. dir., dir. Marine Corps Extension Sch., Hdqrs. Edn. Center, Quantico, 1979-81, asst. chief of staff for leadership instrn., 1980-81, asst. chief staff personnel and services, 1981-82; recorder Naval Discharge Rev. Bd., Naval Council Personnel Bds., Washington, 1982—; mem. Commd. Officers Mess Adv. Bd., Council of Advs. on Profl. Edn., Family Assistance Adv. Council, Gen. Ct.-Martial Bd. and numerous other bds. Mem. Quantico Mil-Civilian Community Relations Council; mem. Sleepy Hollow Citizens Assn.; active Young Republicans; life mem. Girl Scouts U.S.A. Mem. Nat. Assn. Female Execs., Nat. C. of C. for Women, Wolf Trap Farm Park (asso.), Smithsonian Instn. (resident asso.), Nat. Zoo (asso.), U.S. Naval Acad. Athletic Assn., Fairfax County Police Dept. Neighborhood Watch Assn., Marine Corps Combat Corrs. Assn., Ret. Officers Assn., Marine Corps Assn., Woman Marines Assn. (life), Nat. Thespians Soc., Sigma Sigma Sigma. Editorial bd. Marine Corps Gazette. Home: 6426 Eppard St Falls Church VA 22044 Office: Naval Council Personnel Bds Washington DC 22203

ROY, ELSIJANE TRIMBLE (MRS. JAMES M. ROY), judge; b. Lonoke, Ark., Apr. 2, 1916; d. Thomas Clark and Elsie Jane (Walls) Trimble; J.D., U. Ark., 1939; m. James M. Roy, Nov. 23, 1943; 1 son, James Morrison. Admitted to Ark. bar, 1939; mem. firm Reid, Evrard & Roy, Blytheville, Ark., 1947-54, Roy & Roy, Blytheville, 1954-63; atty. Ark. Revenue Dept., Little Rock, 1939-64; law clk. Ark. Supreme Ct., Little Rock, 1963-65; judge Pulaski County Circuit Ct., Little Rock, 1966; asst. atty. gen. State of Ark. Little Rock, 1967; sr. law clk. U.S. Dist. Ct., Little Rock and Ft. Smith, 1968-74; asso. justice Ark. Supreme Ct., Little Rock, 1975-77; U.S. dist. judge East and West Dists. of Ark., Little Rock, 1977—. Mem. med. adv. com. U. Ark. Med. Center, 1952-54; mem. chmn. com. Ark. Constnl. Commn., 1967-68. Committeewoman Democratic party 16th Jud. Dist., 1940-42; vice-chmn. Ark. Dem. State Com., 1946-48. Named Woman of Yr. for Ark., 1976; recipient Disting. Alumna award U. Ark., 1977. Mem. Nat. Assn. Women Lawyers, Ark. Bar Assn., Am. Assn. U. Women, Little Rock Women Lawyers (pres. 1939, 42), U. Ark. Alumni Assn. (dir. 1946-48), Ark. Women Lawyers (pres. 1940-1941), Mortar Bd., P.E.O., Chi Omega. Home: 1101 Riviera Apts Little Rock AR 72202 Office: US Post Office and Courthouse Little Rock AR 72201

ROY, JOYCE ELIZABETH ENSLIN, educator; b. N.Y.C., Apr. 28, 1923; d. Eugene and Elizabeth Enslin; student Duke U., 1941-43; B.S. in Early Childhood Edn., Tchrs. Coll., Columbia U., 1945; M.A. in Spl. Edn. (Elks Scholar), Calif. State U., Los Angeles, 1967; m. Harold E. Roy, Oct. 4, 1946 (div. Dec. 1975); children—Glenn E., Barbara Anne and Suzanne Elizabeth (twins). Tchr. elem. schs., 1945-80, including Byron Thompson Orthopedic Sch., El Monte, Calif., 1964-67; instr. LaVerne (Calif.) U., 1968-70, Pepperdine U., Los Angeles, 1970-79; resource specialist in learning handicap, 1980—; free-lance work with local schs. in greater Capistrano Valley, 1979—; tchr. courses for parents of emotionally and learning handicapped children; tchr. parents of handicapped children Tri-Community Adult Sch., Covina, Calif., 1967-70; adviser, lectr. Hope House for Multiple Handicapped Children; condr. art insts. for tchrs. of physically handicapped. Mem. AAUW, NEA, Calif. Assn. for Neurologically Handicapped Children (dir., lectr.), Calif. Assn. Profs. Spl. Edn., Calif. Tchrs. Assn., Allied Artists, Glendora, Kappa Delta Pi (regional alumni dir. 1967-69). Republican. Episcopalian. Contbr. articles to local newspapers.

ROY, LOIS D., govt. ofcl.; adminstr.; b. Graniteville, Vt., Aug. 17, 1932; d. John K. and Blanche Morrison Campbell; student U. Vt., 1973-74; m. Donald G. Roy, Feb. 1, 1968 (dec.); children—Debra Jane, Gregory Scott. Clk., U.S. Post Office, 1951-52; sec., clerical supr. Immigration and Naturalization Service, U.S. Dept. Justice, 1955-69, personnel staffing specialist, 1973-75, personnel mgmt. specialist, 1976-77, employee relations specialist, Burlington, Vt., 1977-82; sec. IRS, 1969-73; pres., dir. Personal Devel. Assn., Inc., Burlington, Vt.; dir. U.S. Govt. Employees Credit Union, 1973-79. Fund raiser Public Broadcasting System, Burlington. Mem. Nat. Assn. Female Exec., Vt.-N.H. Field Fed. Safety and Health Council (founding), Burlington Bus. & Profl. Womens Club (past pres., recipient Women award 1975). Republican. Clubs: Altrusa Internat. (v.p. 1979-80, pres. 1981-82), Christian Women's Council (co-chmn.). Home: 101 Dale Rd Burlington VT 05401

ROY, SUSAN JANE, spl. edn. adminstr.; b. Bklyn., May 21, 1942; d. Emanuel and Nettie (Reinstein) R.; B.A., Bklyn. Coll., 1964; M.S. in Edn. of Deaf and Physically Handicapped, Hunter Coll., 1967, advanced cert. in ednl. supervision, 1973. Classroom tchr. of deaf Sch. for Lang. and Hearing Impaired Children, N.Y.C., 1964-67; head tchr. classes for lang. and hearing impaired children, N.Y.C. Public Schs., 1967-68, coordinator classes lang. and hearing impaired, 1970-74, asst. prin., 1975-77; lectr. Bklyn. Coll., 1968-70; coordinator evaluation and placement City-Wide Center for Visually and Hearing Impaired Children, N.Y.C., 1977-78; asst. prin. Sch. Lang. and Hearing Impaired Children, N.Y.C., 1978—. Mem. Am. Speech and Hearing Assn. (cert.), Council Exceptional Children, Council Suprs. and Adminstrs. N.Y.C., Alexander Graham Bell Assn. for Deaf, Assn. Spl. Sch. Prins. and Asst. Prins., Kappa Delta Pi. Office: 421 E 88 St New York NY 10028

ROYALL, MARY SUE SMYTH, med. sec.; b. Rosedale, Va.; d. Blythe Deems and Mary (Douglas) Smyth; m. Samuel Henry Royall, 1948; 1 dau., Susan Blythe. Supr. med. records Clinch Valley Clinic Hosp., Richlands, Va., 1938-78, Clinch Valley Physicians, Richlands, 1978—; mem. secretarial and clerical curriculum adv. com. S.W. Va. Community Coll., Richlands, 1977-80; tchr. med. terminology; supr. med. records Coop. Office Edn., 1970-79. Tchr. Sunday Sch., Main St. Meth. Ch., 1954-68; vol. ARC. Club: Womans. Home: Route 1 Box 662 Tazewell VA 24651 Office: 2949 W Front St Richlands VA 24641

ROYBAL, JUDITH JEAN GROSSWILER, keypunch operator; b. Dayton, Ohio, Sept. 11, 1944; d. Ralph Edward and Margaret Coletta (Woods) Grosswiler; student Beaux Arts, Orleans, France, 1963-65, Adams State Coll., Alamosa, Colo., 1965-67; m. Orlando T. Roybal, Oct. 1, 1966; children—Donald Thomas, Kelly Sue, Karen Lynne. Cashier, Maison Fort, Orleans, 1963-65; file clk. art dept. Adams State Coll., 1965-67; clk. So. San Luis R.R., Blanca, Colo., 1975; sec., bookkeeper, keypunch operator Colo. Aggregate Co., Inc., Blanca, 1975-82; trustee Town of Blanca, 1975-81; keypunch operator, bus. office San Luis Valley Med., P.C., Alamosa, Colo., 1982—; oil painter; works exhibited Rio Grande Art Shows, 1976-78. Mem. Bilingual Parent Adv. Com., 1975-79; pres. Mt. Blanca Extension Club, 1974-78; bd. dirs. Blanca-Ft. Garland Community Center, 1980—. Democrat. Roman Catholic. Office: 1847 2d St Alamosa CO 81101

ROYER, MARLENE MILDRED, nurse; b. Sun Prairie, Wis., Mar. 21, 1941; d. Floyd Gerald and Sylvia Inga (Halverson) Gallagher; L.P.N., N.H. Vocat. Tech. Coll., 1975; m. Raymond Arthur Royer, June 4, 1960; children—Daniel R., William Raymond. Seamstress, Jack Winter Garment Co., Colubus, Wis., 1958-60; factoryworker Clarostat Mfg. Co. and United Tanners, Inc., Dover, N.H., 1960-68; nurses aide Riverside Rest Home, Dover, 1969-74; nurse Wentworth Douglass Hosp., Dover, 1975-76; nurse, charge nurse Mapleshade Nursing Home, East Lebanon, Maine, 1976; nurse, charge and med. nurse Riverside Rest Home, Dover, 1976—. Denmother Boy Scouts Am. N.H. nursing grantee, 1974-75. Lutheran. Home: Box 254 County Farm Cross Rd Dover NH 03820

ROYSE, V. ANN, transp. exec. b. Chgo., May 11, 1939; d. Glenn Phillip and Mary Bertha (Miles) McAtee; student St. Mary-of-the-Woods Coll., West Terre Haute, Ind., 1966-67, Ind. State U., Terre Haute, 1968, Ind. Vocat. Inst. Tech., Terre Haute, 1971; 1 dau., Christine Mary. Casualty broker McAtee Ins. Agy., Chgo., 1958-62; analyst trust dept. Mchts. Nat. Bank, Terre Haute, 1963-68; gen. mgr. Artco Press-Collector Prints & Gallery, Terre Haute, 1968-75; with Americana Graphics Inc., Nashville, 1975-80, sec.-treas., 1976-77, pres., 1977-80, also dir.; sec.-treas. O&J Trucking Inc., Auburn, Ind., 1981—; cons. in field. Bd. dirs., sgt.-at-arms Cook County (Ill.) Young Republicans, 1961-62; pres. Children's Theatre, Terre Haute, 1964-65; pres. United Way Wabash Valley (Ind.), 1974, chmn. bd., 1975. Recipient various certs. appreciation. Mem. Profl. Picture Framers Assn., Cable Club Nashville.

ROYSTER HORN, JUANA RACQUEL, home economist; b. Detroit, Jan. 12, 1942; d. James Roquell and Florence Mylette (Youree) Royster; B.A., Wayne State U., 1968, M.A., 1969, teaching cert., 1970; Ph.D., U. Wash., 1980. Extension home economist Rutgers U., 1970-73; asst. prof. food and nutrition Central Wash. U., Ellensburg, 1973-76; researcher, asst. prof. Fla. A&M U., Tallahassee, 1981—; mem. nutrition com. Camden County (N.J.) Heart Assn., 1971-73; mem. Health and Welfare Council Camden County, 1971-73, Camden County Nutrition Council, 1971-73. Mem. Center Sci. in Public Interest, 1973-76, Planned Parenthood Greater Camden, 1971-73, Wash. Gov.'s Long-Range Planning Com., 1974. Recipient Gold Star award Cook Coll., Rutgers U., 1972; W.W. Stout fellow, 1979. Mem. Agrl. Edn. Assn., Am. Home Econs. Assn., Am. Soc. Tng. and Devel., Soc. Nutrition Edn. Home: 2023 S Martin Luther King Jr Blvd Tallahassee FL 32301 Office: 305-A Perry-Paige Fla A&M U Tallahassee FL 32307

ROZELL, JUDITH ALMA, acctg. officer, fin. system exec.; b. Lansing, Mich., Dec. 1, 1940; d. Andrew Melancthon and Mary Gladys (Brown) Rozell; student Mich. State U., 1958-59, Lansing Community Coll., 1978-79; 1 son, Andrew Wayne. Mgr. F.W. Woolworths Restaurant, Lansing, Mich., 1961-65; raw steel schedular Diamond Reo Trucks, Lansing, 1965-68; accrual acct. Am. Bank & Trust, Lansing, 1968-73, acctg. supr., Lansing, 1973-78, acctg. officer, fin. system mgr., 1978—. Mem. Community div. Lansing Safety Council, 1981-82; safety chmn. Mt. Hope Sch., 1981-82; den mother Cub Scouts Am., 1978-81, cubmaster, 1981-82; treas. CIC Allen Sch., 1978-79. Mem. Am. Inst. Banking, Parents Without Partners. Republican. Methodist. Home: 512 N Francis St Lansing MI 48912 Office: PO Box 30120 Lansing MI 48909

ROZICH, ILEENE SHAFFER, clubwoman; b. Greenville, Pa., Jan. 5, 1932; d. Charles Tennyson and Elizabeth Irene (McClimans) Welk; student Youngstown State U., 1950-51; m. John Henry Shaffer, Dec. 1, 1951 (dec.); children—Kathy Charlene Spadin, Marybeth Dawn Lang, Jon Mark; m. 2d, William Steve Rozich, Feb. 14, 1975; stepchildren—Ken Shaffer, Karen Allen. With G.M. McKelvey, Youngstown, Ohio, 1948-51; with Livingston's, Youngstown, 1951-53; with Tippecanoe Country Club, Canfield, Ohio, 1965-73; pres. Girard Republican Club, 1979—; precinct committee person, Girard City, Ohio, 1965—; mem. exec. com. Trumbull County, Ohio, 1968—; mem. Dames of Malta, 1955—, Queen Esther, 1961; mem. Protectors Club, pres., 1971-75; mem. Mahoning chpt. DAR; Charter mem. Tjaatje De Witt Chpt. Colonial Dames XVII Century, 1982. Republican. Lutheran. Mem. Ohio Geneal. Soc. (First Families Ohio), Mercer County Geneal. Soc. (pres. 1980, VFW Aux. Author: Welk Family History. Home: 362 Iowa Ave Girard OH 44420

RUAN, JUDITH SUELLEN, library dir.; b. Orillia, Ont., Can., July 21, 1944; d. Verdun Arnott and Jessie Ellen (Rumball) Adamson; B.A., U. Toronto, 1965, B.L.S., 1966; m. John Jardine Ruan, Mar. 10, 1972; children—Colin, Tyler. Children's librarian Leaside Public Library, Toronto, Ont., 1966-67; dir. Twp. Chinguacousy (Ont.) Public Library, 1967-74, Brampton (Ont.) Public Library, 1974—. Mem. Ont. Library Assn., ALA, Can. Library Assn., Personnel Assn. Toronto. Anglican. Office: 65 Queen St E Brampton ON L6W 3L6 Canada

RUANE, BARBARA ANN, nurse; b. Scranton, Pa., Jan. 9, 1937; d. Edward W. and Mildred E. (Lally) Mullarkey; B.Health Sci., Jersey City Coll., 1973; M.P.A., L.I. U., 1982; children—Maureen, Ellen, Tara, Denis. Head nurse East Orange (N.J.) Gen. Hosp., 1958-63, adminstrv. supr., 1963-75, quality assurance coordinator, 1975-80, dir. nursing/asst. adminstr., 1981—; quality assurance cons. Recipient Soroptomist award, 1981. Mem. East Orange Gen. Nurses Alumni (pres. 1979-82), Am. Nurses Assn., N.J. Nurses Assn., Quality Assurance Profls., N.J. Soc. Nursing Service Adminstrs., Nat. Soc. Nursing Service Adminstrs., Nat. League for Nursing, Nat. Forum Nursing Services. Club: Ladies Aux. KC (pres. 1969-71). Home: 15 Gould Pl Caldwell NJ 07006 Office: 300 Central Ave East Orange NJ 07019

RUARK, ELEANOR ROSE, banker; b. Athens, Ga., June 25, 1924; d. Elwood and Zora Mae (Williams) Kirk; student U. Ga. Banking Sch., 1968; m. Rexford G. Ruark, Oct. 23, 1944; children—Elaine, Stanley, Karen. With Farmers Bank, Union Point, Ga., 1956—, asst. v.p. Greensboro br., 1980—; sec. to supt. Greene County Bd. Edn., 1976-77. Mem. Nat. Assn. Bank Women (charter, chmn. N.E. Ga. group 1970-71), Bank Adminstrn. Inst. (chpt. treas. 1962), Ga. Bankers Assn. (women's com.). Baptist (treas. ladies aux. 1975-78). Club: Greene County Country. Home: RFD 1 Box 161 Union Point GA 30669 Office: 202-A S Main St Greensboro GA 30642

RUARK, THEODORA WILMA, health care exec.; b. Flandreau, S.D., Jan. 22, 1935; d. Theodore and Louella Lenora (Paul) Lathrop; B.B.A., U. Houston, Clear Lake, 1981; m. Vernon R. Ruark, May 16, 1976; children—Julie, Dwain, Darrell, Kenneth, Patrick. From credit mgr. to dir. hosp. bus. services U. Nebr. Med. Center, Omaha, 1962-80; mgr. hosp. bus. systems Lifemark Corp., Houston, 1980—. Mem. Internat. Comsumer Credit Soc., Am. Guild Patient Account Mgrs. (treas. elect 1981; award individual achievement, 1979, 80), Hosp. Fin. Mgmt. Assn., Am. Hosp. Assn., Am. Mgmt. Assn., Mensa. Republican. Methodist. Contbr. column to jour., 1979—. Home: 543 Pompano Dr Hitchock TX 77563 Office: Park Plaza Hosp 1313 Hermann St Houston TX 77001

RUBEN, IDA GASS, state legislator; b. Washington, Jan. 7, 1929; d. Sol and Sonia Esther (Darman) Gass; m. L. Leonard Ruben, Aug. 29, 1948; children—Garry Dennis, Michael Keith, Scott Kevin, Stephen Derek. Mem. Md. Ho. of Dels., 1974—, chairperson Montgomery County del.; active in local, state and nat. polit. campaigns, 1964—. Pres., Md. Women's Legis. Caucus, 1982—. Recipient Woman of Commitment award Md.-D.C. Anti-Defamation League, 1982. Mem. B'nai Brith Women (pres. Independence chpt. 1959-60, pres. dist. 5, 1971-72, internat. bd. 1974-78, internat. treas. 1978-80, internat. v.p. 1980—), Nat. Order Women Legislators, Nat. Assn. Jewish Legislators, Council of State Govts. (com. proposed legis.), Md. Women Legislators' Caucus (v.p.). Democrat. Jewish. Office: 222 Lowe House Office Bldg Annapolis MD 21404

RUBENAK, MARTHA OLIVIA VAZQUEZ, architect; b. Mexico City, Dec. 10, 1931; came to U.S., 1977; d. Jose and Lila (Alarid) Vazquez Santaella; B.Arch., Nat. U. Mex., 1953; m. Joseph A. Rubenak, Mar. 12, 1971; children—Joseph C.H., Cynthia N., William G., Thomas

A. Tchr., Nat. U. Mex., 1959-63; project architect Sanborns, Mex., 1966-68; mng. archtl. designer, San Francisco Xonacatlan, Mex., 1968-71; prof. Nat. U. Mex., 1971-77; freelance architect for home builder, San Antonio, 1977-78; intern architect Kinnison & Assos., San Antonio, 1978—. Mem. AIA (asso. dir. San Antonio), Colegio Nacional de Arquitectos Mex. Office: 342 W Woodlawn St Suite 200 San Antonio TX 78212

RUBENDALL, ELIZABETH, librarian; b. Omaha, Oct. 30, 1913; d. Clarence and Elizabeth (Shortliff) Rubendall; A.B., U. Nebr., 1936; diploma library sci., U. Wis., 1937. Mem. staff U. Nebr. Libraries, 1937-50, 61—, asst. serials librarian, asso. prof. library sci., 1976-79, prof. emeritus, 1979—; chief med. librarian VA Hosp., Topeka, 1950-60. Mem. ALA, Med., Nebr., Lincoln library assns., Spl. Libraries Assn. (chpt. treas. 1960), AAUP, AAAS, AAUW, Nebr. Acad. Sci. (life), Nebr. Ornithol. Union, Nebr. Art Assn., Alpha Phi, Chi Delta Phi. Republican. Presbyterian. Clubs: Lincoln Univ., U. Nebr. Faculty, U. Nebr. Faculty Women's. Home: 4547 Hill Dr Lincoln NE 68510 Office: Love Meml Library Univ Nebr Lincoln NE 68588

RUBENSTEIN, ALICE K(LEINBERG), psychologist; b. N.Y.C., Oct. 23, 1946; d. Paul and Gertrude (Voron) Kleinberg; B.A. in Psychology, SUNY, Stonybrook, 1966; M.A. in Psychology, St. Lawrence U., 1968; Ed.D. in Counselling, U. Rochester, 1972; m. Gerald Rubenstein, Jan. 22, 1967; children—Jennifer Cyd, Heather Kaye. Psychologist, Rush-Henrietta Central Schs., Henrietta, N.Y., 1968-70, 71-72; psychologist Convalescent Hosp. for Children, Rochester, N.Y., 1972-77, supervising psychologist, 1977-79; sr. asso. Monroe Psychotherapy and Consultation Center, Pittsford, N.Y., 1979—; cons. on mental health to schs., agys., bus., especially on power and sexual differences; individual, group and family psychotherapist; co-chairperson Rochester Conf. Mental Health for Women Challenges and Choices, 1977. Cert. ind. practice psychology, sch. psychology, N.Y. State. Fellow Am. Orthopsychiat. Assn.; mem. Am. Psychol. Assn. (program chair div. psychotherapy), Genesee Valley Psychol. Assn., N.Y. State Psychol. Assn., Western Monroe Task Force on Adolescent Services. Home: 38 Modelane Rochester NY 14618 Office: 4 Tobey Village Office Park Pittsford NY 14534

RUBENSTEIN, ELIZABETH SUAREZ, cosmetic mfg. exec.; b. Lucena City, P.I., Dec. 28, 1942; d. Inocencio Bolos Suarez and Eufrocina Laceste Quinsaat; came to U.S., 1969, naturalized, 1975; B.S. in Chem. Engring., U. Santo Tomas, Manila, 1964; m. Leslie Ronald Rubenstein, July 2, 1976; 1 dau., Lisa Anne. Chemist, H. Kohnstamm, N.Y.C., 1969; analytical chemist Allied Testing & Research, Hillsdale, N.J., 1970; research dir. Chromex Chem. Corp., Bklyn., 1970-75; tech. dir. Chem. Spray (A.T.I.), Totowa, N.J., 1975, Krueger (Cosmetic) Corp., Bklyn., 1975-78, Paramount Cosmetics, Union City, N.J., 1978—. Mem. Am. Inst. Chem. Engrs., Am. Chem. Soc., Soc. Cosmetic Chemists, Cosmetic Toiletry and Fragrance Assn. Home: 153 Freeman St Brooklyn NY 11222 Office: 3710 Hudson Ave Union City NJ 07087

RUBENSTEIN, JUDITH LOUISE, psychologist; b. N.Y.C., Aug. 13, 1940; d. Martin and Frances (Hoffs) Goldstein; A.B., Radcliffe Coll., 1961; M.A., Boston U., 1962, Ph.D., 1967; B.J.Ed., Hebrew Coll., 1959; m. Joel Rubenstein, June 24, 1962; children—Mark Howard, Lauren Elizabeth. Staff fellow NIH, Bethesda, Md., 1966-68, cons. psychologist, 1968-72; research psychologist Tufts New Eng. Med. Center, Boston, 1972—; asst. prof. psychiatry Tufts U. Sch. Medicine, Boston, 1972-78, asso. clin. prof., 1978—. William T. Grant Found. grantee, 1975-80; Spencer Found. grantee, 1977-79. Mem. Am. Psychol. Assn., Soc. Research in Child Devel., Eastern Psychol. Assn. Jewish. Author: (with L. Yarrow and F. Pedersen) Infant and Environment: Early Cognitive and Motivational Development, 1975; also articles, book chpts.

RUBIN, ALICE FISHER, state ofcl.; b. Bklyn., June 8, 1940; d. Harold L. and Betty Fisher; B.A., St. John's U., 1964, M.A. (Ford Found. scholar), 1968; m. Lowell M. Rubin, Dec. 7, 1972; children—David Fisher, Emily Claire. Research asst. N.Y. State Conf. Mayors, Albany, 1966; spl. asst. Nassau County (N.Y.), 1967; research and liaison coordinator N.Y.C. Comptroller's Office, 1970-74; asst. commr. Agy. for Child Devel., N.Y.C., 1974-78; asst. sec. to Gov. N.Y. State for intergovtl. relations Exec. Chamber N.Y. State, N.Y.C., 1978—; adj. lectr. City U. N.Y., 1971-82. Bd. trustees Bklyn. Public Library, 1975—; chmn. adv. bd. Prep. Center, Bklyn. Coll., 1979—; bd. dirs. Bklyn. chpt. ARC, 1977—, Coll. Community Services, Inc., Bklyn., 1979—, Bus. Game at L.I. U., 1981—; founder Jewish Women's Leadership Caucus, Bklyn., 1981. Mem. Jr. League Bklyn., AAUW. Home: 141 Argyle Rd Brooklyn NY 11218

RUBIN, CAROL ANN, mech. engr.; b. N.Y.C., Apr. 2, 1945; d. Herman and Molly (Cooper) Shames; B.S. in Mech. Engring., Columbia U., 1966; M.S., Kans. State U., 1969, Ph.D. (NDEA fellow), 1971; m. Abba Rubin, June 9, 1963; children—Aviel David, Rachel, Tova, Yaacov. Asst. machine design engr. Gibbs & Cox, Inc., N.Y.C., 1967; instr. Kans. State U., 1967-71; lectr. Technion, Haifa, Israel, 1971-76; asst., asso. prof. mech. engring. U. Ala., Birmingham, 1976-80; asso. prof. Vanderbilt U., Nashville, 1980—; cons., industry. Registered profl. engr., Ala. Mem. ASME, Sigma Xi. Jewish. Contbr. articles to profl. jours. Office: PO Box 1670B Nashville TN 37235

RUBIN, DOROTHY MOLLY, educator; b. N.Y.C., Feb. 11, 1932; d. Harry and Clara Schleimer; student Hunter Coll., 1949-51; B.A. in English, Rutgers U., 1959, M.Ed., 1961; Ph.D. in Ednl. Psychology, Johns Hopkins U., 1968; m. Arthur I. Rubin, Aug. 24, 1950; children—Carol, Sharon. Tchr., N.J. Sch. System, 1959-62; asst. prof. edn. Coppin State Coll., 1962-63; asst. prof. Towson State Coll., 1963-66; grad. research asst. Johns Hopkins U., 1966-67; adj. prof. Rollins Coll., 1968-69; asso. prof. Trenton State Coll., 1969-73, prof., 1973—; cons. Mem. Nat. Council Tchrs. English, Internat. Reading Assn., Kappa Delta Pi, Pi Lambda Theta. Author textbooks including: Teaching Elementary Language Arts, 1975, 80; Gaining Word Power, 1978; The Vital Arts-Reading and Writing, 1979; The Intermediate-Grade Teacher's Language Arts Handbook, 1980; Reading and Leaning Power, 1980; The Primary-Grade Teacher's Language Arts Handbook, 1980; The Teacher's Handbook of Reading-Thinking Exercises, 1980; The Teacher's Handbook of Writing-Thinking Exercises, 1980; Gaining Sentence Power, 1981; The Teacher's Handbook of Primary-Grade Reading/Thinking Exercises, 1982; A Practical Approach to Teaching Reading, 1982; Diagnosis and Correction in Reading Instructions, 1982; Vocabulary Expansion I, 1982; Vocabulary Expansion II, 1982; cons. Harper & Row English K-8, 1983; syndicated columnist Gannet News Service; contbr. articles to profl. jours. Home: 917 Stuart Rd Princeton NJ 08540 Office: PO Box 940 Trenton NJ 08625

RUBIN, IDA ELY, art cons., writer; b. N.Y.C., Nov. 27, 1923; d. Thurston Van Vechten and Elizabeth Boomer (Scheffer) Ely; B.A. with high honors, Wells Coll., Aurora, N.Y., 1944; postgrad. Inst. Fine Arts, N.Y.U., 1944-49; m. Jerome Sanford Rubin, Mar. 1, 1957; children—Richard Ely, Alicia Mirella. Exec. dir. XX Internat. Congress Art History, N.Y.C., 1959-61; dir. devel. Inst. Fine Arts, 1962-63; dir. visual arts Inter-Am. Found. Arts, N.Y.C., 1963-64; spl. cons. Art Gallery Center Inter-Am. Relations, N.Y.C., 1965-68; dir. visual arts Inst. Contemporary Hispanic Art, N.Y.C., 1973-77; art cons., curator pvt. collections, 1970-80; fgn. corr. Arte en Colombia; mem. selection com., mem. Jury Contemporary Painting, Drawing, Sculpture and Photog. Exhbns., 1960—; mem. faculty Manhattanville Coll., Purchase, N.Y., 1970-71; lectr. in field. Fellow Belgium-Am. Edn. Found., Brussels, 1951; vice chmn. visual arts com. N.Y. Cultural Council, 1969-72; chmn. mus. acquisitions com. Council Arts, M.I.T., 1972-82; active U. Andes Found., 1981-82; mem. exec. com. Drawing Soc. N.Y.C., 1961-82; mem. profl. adv. com. on arts Am.-Scandinavian Found., 1979-82. Clubs: Nat. Arts (gov.), Cosmopolitan (N.Y.C.). Editor: Acts of XX Internat. Congress of Art History, 4 vols., 1963; Drawings of Morris Graves, 1974; Catalogue of the Guennol Collection, 1976. Author articles, books, catalogues. Address: 158 Indian Head Rd Riverside CT 06878

RUBIN, JANE ELLEN, state ofcl.; b. N.Y.C., Aug. 22, 1945; d. Benjamin J. and Ann R.; B.A. cum laude, Adelphi U., 1966; M.A., U. Fla., 1968. Lectr. psychology Housatonic Community Coll., Stratford, Conn., 1968-70; with N.Y. State Dept. Labor, 1970—, sr. counseling cons., 1979-81, asso. mgr. unemployment ins. div., 1981—. NDEA fellow, 1966-68. Mem. Internt. Assn. Personnel in Employment Security, N.Y.C. Women's Task Force of N.Y. State Dept. Labor, Orgn. Mgmt. Confidential Employees, Nat. Assn. Female Execs. Home: 345 W 21st St New York NY 10011 Office: 2 World Trade Center New York NY 10047

RUBIN, JANICE ANN, lawyer; b. Newark, Nov. 12, 1941; d. Carl and Helen Edith (Baletin) Edelstein; A.B. cum laude, Smith Coll., 1964; J.D., George Washington U., 1973; m. Burton Jay Rubin, Feb. 17, 1974; 1 dau., Jennifer Sidell. Admitted to Va. bar, 1974, U.S. Supreme Ct. bar, 1979; editor McKinsey & Co., Washington, 1971-72; editor Bur. Nat. Affairs, Inc. Patent, Trademark & Copyright Jour., Washington, 1972-74; legis. atty. Am. Law div. Congressional Research Service, Library of Congress, Washington, 1974—. Mem. Fed. Bar Assn. (sec. Capitol Hill chpt. 1980—), Am. Bar Assn. Club: Smith Coll. Washington. Contbr. in field. Office: 101 Independence Ave SE Washington DC 20540

RUBIN, JOYCE, psychiat. social worker; b. N.Y.C., May 29, 1928; d. Isaac and Jennie Tractenberg; B.A., Hofstra U.; M.S.W., Adelphi U., 1975; m. Harris E. Rubin, Mar. 18, 1951; children—Jeffrey, Ira. Psychotherapist, Long Beach Meml. Hosp., 1975-77, program coordinator, 1977-79; adminstr. Long Beach Mental Health Clinic, 1979-80; dir. community services Peninsula Counseling Center, Woodmere, N.Y., 1980—; field instr. Adelphi U. Bd. dirs. S.E.R.V.E. Mem. Assn. Mental Health Adminstrs., Nat. Assn. Social Workers, N.Y. State Soc. Clin. Psychotherapists, Am. Orthopsychiat. Assn., Am. Assn. Marriage and Family Therapists. Home: 136 Lefferts Rd Woodmere NY 11598 Office: 124 Franklin Pl Woodmere NY 11598

RUBIN, NANCY PAULA, social services adminstr.; b. Chgo., Apr. 17, 1950; d. Ben and Betty (Edwin) Rubin; A.A., Los Angeles Valley Jr. Coll., 1971; B.A., Calif. State U., 1973; M.S. (acad. scholar), Pepperdine U., 1979. Eligibility worker County of Los Angeles, 1973-74; dir. social service Lavina Respiratory Hosp., Altadena, Calif., 1974-77; med. social worker public relations Intercity Home Health, Los Angeles, 1977-79; dir. social service Glendora (Calif.) Community Hosp., 1979-80, community educator, 1980—; dir. social service Greater El Monte (Calif.) Community Hosp., 1980—; tchr. assertive tng. W.P. Assos., Los Angeles, 1979—; instr. on death and dying Nursing Edn. Assos., 1980—; coordinator child abuse and neglect teams San Gabriel Valley (Calif.); mem. Child Abuse Council. Tae Les Savants scholar, 1968. Mem. Nat. Assn. Social Workers, Nephrology Social Workers, Hosp. Social Work Dirs. Democrat. Jewish. Home: 6001 Greenbush Ave Van Nuys CA 91401 Office: 1701 Santa Anita Ave South El Monte CA 91733

RUBIN, ROBERTA IRIS, educator; b. Bklyn., Sept. 22, 1951; d. Philip and Edna (Goldstein) R.; B.A. with honors, U. Fla., 1973, M.Ed., 1974, Ph.D., 1976; m. Samuel Mark Streit, Dec. 11, 1971. Statis. cons. U. Fla., Gainesville, 1973-75, grad. research asst. and data coordinator Inst. Devel. Human Resources, 1974-77; clin. asst. prof. Sch. Edn., U. N.C., Chapel Hill, 1977-82, clin. asso. prof., 1982—, supr. grad. students, 1977—; manuscript reviewer Children and Youth Services Rev., 1980—; cons. to various public sch. systems and sch. dists., 1976—. Del., N.C. Gov.'s Conf. on Mental Health, 1979—; bd. dirs. N.C. Advocates for Children, Inc., 1979—. Recipient Outstanding Research award Phi Delta Kappa. Mem. Am. Psychol. Assn., Am. Ednl. Research Assn., Eastern Ednl. Research Assn., Assn. Supervision and Curriculum Devel., N.C. Assn. Research in Edn., Nat. Council Measurement in Edn., Phi Delta Kappa, Pi Lambda Theta, Phi Kappa Phi, Kappa Delta Pi. Jewish. Contbr. articles on ednl. research to profl. publs. Home: Route 1 105 Leslie Dr Chapel Hill NC 27514 Office: U NC 105 Peabody Hall Chapel Hill NC 27514

RUBIN, ROSALYN AARON, psychologist; b. Mpls., Sept. 29, 1933; d. Meyer and Mary (Resnick) Aaron; B.A. magna cum laude, U. Minn., 1954, B.S., 1955, M.A., 1957, Ph.D., 1961; m. Edmond H. Rubin, Dec. 18, 1960; children—Ellen Judith, Beth Joanne. Sch. psychologist, dir. research Robbinsdale (Minn.) Public Schs., 1960-63; asst. prof. psychology Macalester Coll., St. Paul, 1964-66; research asso. ednl. psychology U. Minn., Mpls., 1966—, interim dir. Research and Devel. Center Edn. Handicapped Children, 1971, asso. prof. ednl. psychology, 1971—, dir. ednl. follow-up study, 1971-80; cons. in field. Grantee Nat. Inst. Edn., Bur. Edn. Handicapped. Mem. Am. Ednl. Research Assn., Am. Psychol. Assn., Council Exceptional Children, U. Minn. Edn. Assn. (v.p.). Author articles in field. Home: 681 Woodlawn Ave Saint Paul MN 55116 Office: Pattee Hall U Minn Minneapolis MN 55455

RUBIN, SONYA, advt. exec.; b. Newburgh, N.Y., July 13, 1940; d. Abram and Dorothy (Harris) R.; student Barnard Coll., 1957-59; m. C. Julian Fish, Oct. 17, 1967. Copywriter, asst. account exec. Resley Advt., N.Y.C., 1960-69; account exec. Mfrs. Advt., N.Y.C., 1969-76; pres. Rubin-Walter Advt., N.Y.C., 1976—. Mem. Knitted Textile Assn., Fathers Day Council (v.p., dir.), Young Menswear Assn. (bd. govs.), Fashion Group. Office: 341 Madison Ave New York NY 10017

RUBINSTEIN, SHIRLEY JOY, nursing service exec.; b. Toronto, Ont., Can., Nov. 19, 1927; came to U. S., 1928, naturalized, 1948; d. Harry Hyman and Ida Ruth (Albert) Adel; m. Philip F. Rubinstein, Aug. 17, 1947; children—David Brian, Wendy Sue, Hope Terri. With Jewish Agy. for Palestine, Washington, 1947-49; coordinator Nursing Staff, Inc., 1975-78; co-founder, pres. Nursing Services, Inc., Silver Spring, Md., 1978—. Democrat. Jewish. Club: B'nai Birth. Office: PO Box 4133 Silver Spring MD 20904

RUBY, BERTHA M., rehab. services adminstr.; b. Ont., Can., July 9, 1937; d. Aaron and Laura (Schwartzentruber) R.; B.S. in Sociology, Ariz. State U., 1969; M.Rehab. Adminstrn., U. San Francisco, 1978. Correctional program officer Adobe Mountain Reform Sch., Phoenix, 1971-74; dir. adult services Glenhaven, Inc., Glendale, Ariz., 1974-76, adminstrv. asst., 1976-78; dir. program services United Cerebral Palsy Central Ariz., Phoenix, 1978—. Mem. Nat. Rehab. Assn.

RUBY, RUTH JANET, govt. ofcl.; b. Detroit, June 19, 1931; d. George and Janet Elizabeth (Taylor) R.; B.S. in Edn., Wayne State U., 1953; postgrad. (fellow), Stanford U., 1970-71. With Social Security Adminstrn., 1954—, asso. regional rep. Midwest, 1974-76, regional dir. div. mgmt. and adminstrn., 1976-78, asst. regional commr. supplemental security income, 1978-80, asst. regional commr. mgmt. and budget N.W. region, 1980—. Mem. Fgn. Relations Council, Alpha Sigma Tau. Address: 2901 3d Ave Kirkland WA 98033

RUBY, SALLY ANNE, city ofcl.; b. Hershey, Pa., Sept. 25, 1944; d. Edward Mark and Sarah Ellen (Tobias) Keeney; B.S., Labanon Valley Coll., Annville, Pa., 1973; M.Ed., Millersville (Pa.) State Coll., 1974; m. Herbert L. Weed. Counselor, Fla. Div. Corrections, 1974-76; compliance coordinator City of Clearwater (Fla.), 1976—. Bd. dirs. Counsumer Credit Counseling Service, Clearwater, 1981-82; mem. Tampa Bay Open Housing Coalition, 1980-81; mem. human rights com. Pinellas Opportunity Council, 1979-81; sec. Clearwater Urban League Guild, 1980-81; mem. loan com. Neighborhoood Housing Service, Clearwater; mem. bi-racial com. Pinellas County (Fla.) Sch. Bd.; mem. cons. Council FACE. Mem. Nat. Assn. Human Rights Workers, Fla. Assn. Community Relations Profls. (sec. 1981-82), NOW, Nat. Abortion Rights League, Nat. Assn. Female Execs., LWV, Millersville State Coll. Alumni Assn. Unitarian-Universalist. Home: 416 N Lincoln Ave Clearwater FL 33515 Office: PO Box 4748 Clearwater FL 33518

RUCINSKI, CAROLE ANN, restaurant chain exec.; b. Moundsville, W.Va., Sept. 6, 1942; d. Harold William Brown and Annabelle (Heflin) Brown Theiss; student Capitol U. Without Walls, 1978-79; m. Kenneth J. Rucinski, July 20, 1963. Sec., Richman Brothers Co., Cleve., 1960-68; exec. sec. Columbia Gas System, Charleston, W.Va., and Columbus, Ohio, 1969-72; with McDonald's Corp., Columbus, 1972-78, regional licensing mgr., 1974-76, zone licensing mgr., Atlanta, 1978—; pres. Out of the Woods, Inc., 1982—. Mem. Nat. Assn. Female Execs., Am. Soc. Profl. and Exec. Women, Cobb County C. of C. Roman Catholic. Clubs: Providence Corners Civic Assn., Providence Corners Swim and Tennis, Fairfield Country. Partner, Big Red Q Quickprint Center, Atlanta, 1979—. Home: 1140 Gray Squirrel Crossing Marietta GA 30062 Office: 5775 Peachtree Dunwoody Rd Suite 200-A Atlanta GA 30342

RUCKER, HELEN BORNSTEIN (MRS. B. WALLACE RUCKER), author; b. Seattle; d. Maurice Sello and Julia (Gyle) Bornstein; grad. Nat. Park Coll., 1923; student Cornish Sch. Allied Arts, 1934-35, 46-47, 55-56, U. Wash.; m. B. Wallace Rucker, Jan. 30, 1932; children—B. Wallace, Stephen Morley. Author: Cargo of Brides, 1956, 69; The Wolf Tree, 1960; also short stories. Unit chmn. ARC, 1940-45; trustee, membership chmn., sec., corrs. sec., chmn. programs spastic children Seattle Jr. Programs, 1941-56; trustee Cornish Sch. Allied Arts, 1935-38, Friends Seattle Public Library, 1957-60, Franklin Guild Children's Orthopedic Hosp.; chmn. N.W. Authors Bookshelf, Seattle Public Library, 1964-66; bd. dirs. Wash. State Jewish Hist. Soc., 1980. Mem. Nat. League Am. Pen Women (sponsoring com. Spirit of Seattle 1949 for Mus. History and Industry), Seattle Free-Lance Writers, N.W. Internat. Writers Conf., Pioneer Assn. State Wash., Friends of Crafts, Phi Delta Nu. Clubs: Soroptimist (Seattle; co-chmn. student loan fund 1968-69, Achievement award Past Pres. Assembly 1960), Seattle Tennis, Wash. Athletic. Editor: The Bull., Friends Seattle Public Library, 1958-60. Home: 1620 43d Ave E Seattle WA 98112

RUCKER, SUZANNE JUNE, fin. specialist; b. Coral Gables, Fla., June 27, 1945; d. Thomas John, Jr. and June Ethel Agusta (Stones) R.; B.B.A., Fla. Atlantic U., 1971, M.B.A., 1975. Asso. dir. Am. Soc. Cons. Pharmacists, 1971-73; chpt. specialist Epilepsy Found. Am., 1973-74; asso. dir. devel. Fairfax Hosp. Assn. Found., Springfield, Va., 1974-81; treas./adminstr. Phoenix Corp., McLean, Va., 1981—; seminar speaker in field. Lic. real estate agt. Mem. Am. Mgmt. Assns. Republican. Club: Jr. Woman's Fairfax County (treas., chmn. health com., chmn. sr. citizens activity com.). Office: 1700 Old Meadow Rd McLean VA 22102

RUCKER-HUGES, WAUDIUR ELIZABETH, educator; b. Washington, July 30, 1947; d. Jeter and Jeannette Belle (Toomer) Rucker; B.S., D.C. Tchrs. Coll., 1969; M.A. in Edn., U. Redlands, 1974; 1 child, Teliece E.M. Tchr. history J.W. North High Sch., Riverside, Calif., 1969-76, dean students, 1976-79; lectr. Afro-Am. history Riverside City Coll., 1972-74; exec. dir. Inland Area Opportunities Industrialization Center, Riverside, 1979—; cons. in field. Commr. Community relations City of Riverside, 1972-76; sec. State Inter-Group Relations Educators, 1976-77; pres. Coalition of Urban Peoples, 1978-80; lay mem. Riverside County Jud. Selection Com., 1978—; Calif. State Bar ct. referee, 1979—. NSF fellow, 1970-71; Center for Leadership Edn. grantee, 1978. Mem. NAACP, Urban League, Riverside Women's Polit. Caucus, Nat. Women's Polit. Caucus, Exec. Dirs. Assn., Nat. Council Negro Women, Delta Kappa Gamma. Mem. C.M.E. Ch. Club: The Thurs. Group. Author: Canine Capers, 1976; A Book to Match our Diversity, 1980. Home: 8907 Delano Dr Riverside CA 92503 Office: 2222 Kansas Ave Riverside CA 92507

RUDACILLE, SHARON VICTORIA, med. technologist; b. Ranson, W. Va., Sept. 11, 1950; d. Albert William and Roberta Mae (Anderson) R.; B.S. cum laude, Shepherd Coll., 1972. Med. technologist VA Center, Martinsburg, W. Va., 1972—, instr. Sch. Med. Tech., 1972-76, asso. coordinator edn., 1976-77, edn. coordinator, 1977-78, quality assurance officer clin. chemistry, 1978-80, lab. service quality assurance and edn. officer, 1980—; adj. faculty mem. Shippensburg (Pa.) State Coll., 1977-78. Mem. Am. Soc. Med. Tech., Am. Soc. Clin. Pathologists, W.Va. Soc. Med. Technologists, Shepherd Coll. Alumni Assn., Sigma Pi Epsilon. Baptist. Home: PO Box 14 Ranson WV 25438 Office: Route 9 Martinsburg WV 25401

RUDD, AMANDA SULLIVAN, library ofcl.; b. Greenville, S.C., Apr. 9, 1923; d. Wesley and Delarion Sullivan; B.S., Fla. A&M U., 1955; M.L.S., Western Res. U., 1962. Tchr., librarian schs., S.C., Alaska, Fla. and Ohio; asst. supr. sch. libraries, Cleve. Public Schs., 1965-70; cons. ednl. services dept. Field Enterprises Ednl. Corp., Chgo., 1970-75; asst. chief librarian community relations and spl. program of service Chgo. Public Library, 1975, dept. commr., 1975-81, commr., 1981—. Bd. overseers Sch. Library Sci. Case Western Res. U.; mem. Chgo. dist. bd. ARC; mem. adv. council Chgo. Urban Skills Inst.; mem. adv. com. Ill. State Library. Mem. ALA, Public Library Assn., Ill. Library Assn., Case Western Res. U. Alumni Assn. Home: 601 E 32d St Chicago IL 60616 Office: 425 N Michigan Ave Chicago IL 60611

RUDD, PENNY SUE, corp. exec.; b. Mpls., Nov. 6, 1947; d. John Byron and Marion Lydia (Campbell) Watschke; student schs. Bloomington, Minn.; m. Thomas Rudd, Sept. 10, 1966 (div.); children—Jesse, Zak. Cancellation clk., underwriter Gen. Motors Ins. Co., Mpls. 1965-71; payroll clk., accounts payable and receivable, salesperson, personnel div., shipping, fin. officer, computer program design Drag Specialties, Inc., Hopkins, Minn., 1971—, now pres.; pres. Pine Plating, Inc.; corp. dir., officer Ty's Metal Finishing, Inc. Mem. Am. Mgmt. Assn., Better Bus. Bur. Republican. Office: Drag Specialties Inc 5401 Smetana Dr Hopkins MN 55343

RUDD, SARA DEE MCARTHUR, psychologist; b. Atlanta, Mar. 23, 1948; d. Robert Stuart and Ernestine Rose (Adams) McArthur; B.A., Mercer U., 1970; M.A., U. Kans., 1971; Ph.D., 1973; m. Gerald Patrick Rudd, Dec. 24, 1972; 1 son, Samuel Patrick McArthur. Asst. prof. N.E. Mo. State U., Kirksville, 1973-74; reading cons., psychologist Mary Immaculate Sch., Kirksville, Mo., 1974-76; staff psychologist Community Counseling Center, Inc., Winslow, Ariz., 1977—. Bd. dirs. Four County Conf. Developmentally Disabled, 1979-80, Winslow Headstart, 1979-80. HEW Bur. Child Research trainee, 1972-73. Mem. Am. Psychol. Assn., Mich. Psychol. Assn., Ariz. Psychol. Assn. Baptist. Home: 1016 N Prairie St Winslow AZ 86047 Office: 1015 E 2d St Community Counseling Center Winslow AZ 86047

RUDDY, BARBARA FORTUNE, psychiat. social worker; b. N.Y.C., May 25, 1945; d. John Francis and Margaret Mary (O'Connor) Fortune; B.A., Queens Coll., 1974; M.S.W., N.Y. U., 1977; m. Michael Bernard Ruddy, Oct. 17, 1970. Psychiat. social worker Jewish Bd. Guardians, N.Y.C., 1977; psychiat. social worker, supr. Project Contact/Ednl. Alliance, N.Y.C., 1977-80; asst. dir. day treatment program Project Contact/Ednl. Alliance, 1980—; field instr., supr. Rutgers U. Sch. Social Work. Mem. Nat. Assn. Social Workers, Nat. Council Crime and Juvenile Delinquency, Am. Orthopsychiat. Assn., Acad. Cert. Social Workers, N.Y. U. Alumni Assn. Home: 459 W Broadway New York NY 10012 Office: 380 Lafayette St New York NY 10003

RUDERMAN, ANNE TULLY, hypnoanalyst; b. Wilmington, Del., June 26, 1927; d. James Joseph and Adeline (Van Buren) Tully; B.A., Antioch Coll., 1948; postgrad. Yale U., 1949-50; M.S.W., Smith Coll., 1952; m. S.G. Ruderman, July 23, 1947; children—James Michael, Dan Tully. Clin. social work psychotherapist Westchester County Div. Mental Hygiene, 1952-54; pvt. practice psychotherapy, 1954—; sr. staff therapist, practicum supr. Morton Prince Center, Inst. Research in Hypnosis, N.Y.C., 1970-77; co-founder, co-dir. Cancer Counseling and Tng. Center of Westchester, Scarsdale, N.Y., 1977—; disting. lectr., guest lectr. orgns., colls. and univs. Cert. in hypnotherapy and hypnoanalysis Inst. Research in Hypnosis; cert. social worker N.Y.; cert. in Neuro-Linguistic Programming; cert. Acad. Cert. Social Workers. Mem. Nat. Assn. Social Workers, Soc. Clin. Social Work Psychotherapists. Soc. Clin. and Exptl. Hypnosis, Internat. Hypnosis. Home and Office: 29 Quentin Rd Scarsdale NY 10583

RUDMAN, FRANCES ZIMMERMAN (MRS. JACK RUDMAN), pub. co. exec.; b. N.Y.C., June 26, 1912; d. Isadore and Dora (Deutsch) Zimmerman; m. Jack Rudman; children—Gerald J., Stephanie R. (Mrs. William K. Joseph), Michael P. Vice pres., treas., sec., dir. Coll. Pub. Corp., Bklyn., 1954-66; v.p., sec., dir. Nat. Learning Corp., Bklyn., 1967—, v.p., treas., dir. subs. Delaney Books Inc., Frank Merriwell Inc., 1967—. Mem. Assn. Am. Pubs. Office: 212 Michael Dr Syosset NY 11791

RUDMAN, ILENE HILLMAN, cons. co. exec.; b. Balt., July 6, 1945; d. Isadore and Lillian Rosalyn (Barmack) Hillman; B.A., U. Md., 1966; M.P.A. (fellow), Harvard U., 1978; m. Bernard Joel Rudman, June 13, 1971; 1 son, Jonah Louis. Personnel mgmt. asst. U.S. IRS, Washington, 1966-67; manpower devel. specialist U.S. Dept. Labor, Washington, 1967-71; evaluation cons. Abt Assos., Cambridge, Mass., 1971-72; manpower and civil service specialist Commonwealth of Mass., Boston, 1972-74; cons. U.S. Commn. on Civil Rights, Boston, 1974-75; fed. women's program mgr. U.S. Dept. HEW, Boston, 1975-80; regional fed. women's program mgr. U.S. Office Personnel Mgmt., Boston, 1980-81; incorporator, dir. Govt. Center Child Care Corp., 1979; prin. Rodgers and Rudman Cons. Services, Inc., 1980—. Mem. Mass. State adv. com. U.S. Commn. on Civil Rights, 1973-75; pres. Mass. Civil Service Modernization Com., Inc., 1973-74; bd. dirs. Wider Opportunities for Women, Boston, 1975-78. Recipient HEW Outstanding Performance award, 1976. Mem. Boston Network of Women in Politics and Govt., Federally Employed Women. Home: 56 Florence Ave Arlington MA 02174 Office: 93 Abbottsford Rd Brookline MA 02146

RUDNICK, IRENE KRUGMAN, lawyer, state legislator; b. Columbia, S.C., Dec. 27, 1929; d. Jack and Jean (Getter) Krugman; A.B. cum laude, U. S.C., 1949, LL.B., 1952; m. Harold Rudnick, Nov. 7, 1954; children—Morris, Helen Gail. Admitted to S.C. bar, 1952; individual practice law, Aiken, S.C., 1952—; instr. bus. law U. S.C., Aiken, 1962—; tchr. Warrenville Elem. Sch., 1965-70; supt. edn. Aiken County, 1970-72; mem. S.C. Ho. of Reps., 1972-78, 80—. Active, Aiken County Democratic Party, S.C. Dem. Party. Recipient Citizen of Yr. award, 1976-77, Bus. and Profl. Women's Career Woman of Yr., 1978, Aiken County Friend of Edn. award. Mem. NEA, S.C. Tchrs. Assn., Aiken County Tchrs. Assn., Am. Bar Assn., Aiken County Bar Assn., Nat. Order Women Legislators, AAUW, Alpha Delta Kappa. Jewish. Clubs: Order Eastern Star, Hadassah, Am. Legion Aux. Office: Box 544 224 Park Ave Aiken SC 29801

RUDNIK, SISTER, MARY CHRYSANTHA, librarian; b. Winona, Minn., Dec. 2, 1929; d. Basil John and Sarah (Knopick) Rudnik; student Loyola U., 1951-52, Felician Coll., 1952-54, Cardinal Stritch Coll., 1954-57, Coll. St. Francis, 1957; Ph.B., DePaul U., 1958; postgrad. Mundelein Coll., 1959-60; M.A., Rosary Coll., 1962; postgrad. Northeastern Ill. State Coll., 1964. Page, clk. Hill Reference Library, St. Paul, 1946-48; tchr. Holy Innocents Sch., Chgo., 1948-49, 50-54, St. Bruno Sch., Chgo., 1954-55, Holy Family Sch., Cudahy, Wis., 1955-57, Good Counsel High Sch., Chgo., 1958-67; instr. Felician Coll., Chgo., 1963—, librarian, 1957—, also dir. devel. and public relations. Organizer, coordinator Felician Library Service, 1966-74, coordinator instl. self-study for accreditation North Central Assn.; mem. task force for study of instl. research for Ill. Assn. Community and Jr. Colls., 1968; library cons. St. Clement Sch., 1969; Ill. del. White House Conf. on Library and Info. Services, 1978; mem. exec. bd. Council for Advancement and Support of Edn., 1981—. Rev. Andrew Bowhuis, meml. scholar Cath. Library Assn., 1960. Mem. ALA, Ill. Library Assn., Cath. Library Assn. (life, chmn. No. Ill. unit 1968-69), Art Inst. Chgo. (life), Council on Library Tech. (v.p. 1970, pres. 1971), Nat. Soc. Fund Raising Execs. (cert). Address: 3800 Peterson Ave Chicago IL 60659

RUDOLPH, ANNE FAGAN, sexuality and family therapist; b. N.Y.C., Mar. 23, 1937; d. James A. and Anne (Bohan) Fagan; diploma Bellevue Hosp. Sch. Nursing, N.Y.C., 1957; B.S. in Edn., Columbia U., 1959; M.S., Russell Sage Coll., 1971; Ph.D., Walden U., 1977; m. Donald J. Rudolph, Oct. 17, 1959; children—Anne, Donald, Lisa. Staff nurse Bellevue Hosp., 1959; head nurse St. Clares Hosp., Schenectady, 1962-65, Albany (N.Y.) Manpower Program, 1965-68; lectr. State U. N.Y. at Albany Sch. Nursing, 1968-70, instr., 1970-73, asst. prof. nursing, 1973-77; pvt. practice sexuality and family counseling, 1977—. Active Tri County on Human Sexuality, Marriage Bd. Albany Roman Cath. Diocese. Mem. AAUP, Nurses Assn. Am. Coll. Obstetrics, Gynecology, Am., N.Y. State nurses assns., Council Human Sexuality, Albany County Mental Assn., Bellevue Alumnae, Columbia U. Alumnae, Russell Sage Alumnae. Roman Catholic. Author: Priorities in Preparation for Nursing Practice, 1973; Pre-Coma Instruction Manual, 1976; Role Perceptions of Post Partum Patients and the Corollary Role of the Nurse in Health Teaching, Guidance and Counseling, 1977. Home: 14 Thunderbird Dr Ballston Lake NY 12019 Office: 3010 Troy Rd Schenectady NY 12309

RUDULPH, MIMI, journalist, civic worker; b. Boston, Oct. 29, 1923; d. Frank Newell and Frederica (Lord) Terhune; B.A., U. N.H., 1944; postgrad. Juilliard Sch. Music, 1944-45, Columbia U., 1945, Boston U., 1948; m. Burwell Blount Rudulph, Dec. 30, 1948; 1 dau., Frederica Lord Rudulph. Founder Sunday Afternoon Concerts, Palm Springs (Calif.) Desert Mus., 1963, mem. performing arts and women's coms.; founder Palm Springs Friends of the Los Angeles Philharmonic, Met. Opera Showcase Concert, 1977; co-founder Palm Springs Opera Guild; producer-host weekly radio interview program: Window to the Arts, 1977—; coordinator Festival of the Desert, 1980—; music critic Desert Sun, 1962—; arts columnist Sand to Sea mag., 1977—; mem. first community adv. bd. sta. KCET (PBS), 1979—; arts advisor Coll. of the Desert, coordinator MGM lecture series, author People to People Day Proclamation, 1971; founder Walk for Devel., 1968, Freedom From Hunger, 1969, Internat. Friendship Fiesta, 1967-72; pres. Desert Chpt., People to People, 1972-77; chmn. Books and Authors Luncheon, 1973; mem. regional bd. Western Opera Theater, 1973-77; co-chmn. Welcome N.Z., 1972, Welcome Israel, for Conv. and Visitors Bur., 1973; mem. adv. panel Valley Solar Environ. Grant. Named Mother of Yr., recipient C. of C. award, 1961; honored testimonial luncheon, various civic groups, 1967; recipient vol. award Patton Hosp. various yrs., Betty Ford award, Coll. of the Desert, 1981, B'nai B'rith award, 1975, Am. Soc. Interior Designers award, 1977, 20th Year Outstanding Citizen award, Coll. of the Desert, 1982. Mem. Music Critics Assn., World Affairs Council (bd.), Met. Opera Nat. Council. Clubs: Palm Springs Pathfinders. Writer on the arts; sonnet Two Silent Watchers used by composer Ernst Krenek for his Opus 200, 1975. Home and Office: 729 High Rd Palm Springs CA 92262

RUDY, DOROTHY LUCILLE, educator, poet; b. Hamilton, Ohio, June 27, 1924; d. William Herman and Marjorie Delma (Rammel) Richardson; B.A. in English, Queens Coll., 1945; A.M. in Philosophy, Columbia U., 1948; postgrad. Radcliffe Coll., 1949-50; m. Willis Rudy, Jan. 31, 1948; children—Dee Dee, Willis Philip (dec.), Willa Catherine. Jr. trust adminstr. Bankers Trust Co., N.Y.C., 1945; tchrs. various schs., N.Y. State, Mass., 1945-61; mem. faculty Worcester (Mass.) Jr. Coll., 1961-63, Tenafly (N.J.) High Sch., 1963-64, Rutgers U. Evening div., New Brunswick, N.J., 1963-64; prof. English and creative writing Montclair (N.J.) State Coll., 1964—. Recipient Scimitar and Song Poetry award, 1950. Mem. N.Y. Poetry Forum, N.J. Pen Women, Bergen Poets, Composers, Artists and Authors Am., Coll. English Assn., Eleanor Gay Lee Gallery Found., Poets and Writers, Inc. Author: (poetry) Quality of Small, 1971; Psyche Afoot, 1978; Grace Notes to the Measure of the Heart, 1979; essay editor Composers, Artists and Authors Am.; editor: N.Y. Poetry Forum Books. Home: 161 W Clinton Ave Tenafly NJ 07670 Office: Montclair State Coll Upper Montclair NJ 07043

RUE, WENDY, assn. exec.; b. Detroit; d. Harry and Sally (Gilbert) Fox; student schs. Los Angeles; children—Dennis Shafer, Harlan Rue. Designer, mfg. jr. sportswear, Los Angeles, 1956; owner N.Y. Exec. Recruiting Co., N.Y.C., 1970; founder pres., exec. dir. Nat. Assn. Female Execs., N.Y.C., 1972—; founder Exec. Female mag., N.Y.C., 1977—; cons. interagency com. SBA. Address: 160 E 56th St New York NY 10022

RUETENIK, SAMMY JEAN, educator; b. Monroe, Mich., June 23, 1929; d. Samuel Jether and Alta Ruth Rubley; B.A., U. Mich., 1950; M.A., Oakland U., 1971; m. David Gibbons Ruetenik, Aug. 25, 1950; children—Katheryn, Christopher, Heidi, Daniel, Bennett. Tchr., Lansing (Mich.) Schs., 1950-51, Lakewood (Ohio) Schs., 1963-67; tchr. Bloomfield Hills (Mich.) Schs., 1967-78, 79-82, asst. prin., coordinator early entrance program Bloomfield High Sch., 1978-79; owner MSSAM, West Bloomfield, Mich., 1979—. Vice-pres. Lakewood Safety Council, 1959; regional dir., bd. dirs. Mich. Reproductive Freedom Council, 1981—; bd. dirs. Mich. Women's Hall of Fame. Cleve. Council Human Relations grantee, 1963. Mem. Mich. Edn. Assn. (women's task force, pres. women's caucus), NEA (regional coordinator, v.p. women's caucus), Mich. Women's Studies Assn., Coalition for Non-Sexist Edn., NOW, Nat. Women's Polit. Caucus, Mich. Women's Polit. Caucus, Mich. Social Studies Council, Mich. Bus. and Profl. Women's Network, Mich. Council Women in Adminstrn. Democrat. Presbyterian. Author: The Family, 1979. Address: 6505 Alden Dr West Bloomfield MI 48033

RUFF, LORRAINE MARION, travel agy. exec.; b. Chgo. Apr. 17, 1926; d. Walter M. and Hazel B. (Reed) Bogen; student Internat. Travel Sch., 1971; m. Aaron Eugene Ruff, Feb. 16, 1946; children—Jeri Lynn Ruff Lotts, Darlene Mae Ruff Baier. Ticket checker Warner Bros. Theatres, 1943-47, acct., 1947; bookkeeper Itasca State Bank (Ill.), 1968-70; comml. salesperson Around the World Travel Agy., Palatine, Ill., 1971-73; asst. mgr. First State Travel, Chgo., 1973-75; co-owner, mgr. Ruff Travel Inc., Schaumburg, Ill., 1975—. Supt. sch., lay tchr. 1st Presbyn. Ch., Itasca; tchr. Christian edn. Monmouth Coll., 1960-64. Mem. Internat. Travel Alumni Assn., N.W. Suburban Assn. Commerce and Industry, Schaumburg C. of C. Clubs: Make Today Count, Republican Woman's (treas. 1962). Home: 606 Country Club Ln Itasca IL 60143 Office: 1732 W Wise Rd Schaumburg IL 60193

RUFFALO, SIBYL WINIFRED MASQUELIER, mgmt. cons.; b. Canonsburg, Pa., July 8, 1946; d. David Jules Grace (Strickland) Masquelier; A.B., U. Pitts., 1967; M.Ed., U. Miami, 1969; 1 dau., Phaedra Danielle. Teaching asst. U. Miami, Coral Gables, Fla., 1967-69; personnel mgr. Div. Family Services, State of Fla., Miami, 1970-73; employment mgr. Miami Herald, Knight Ridder Newspapers, 1974-76; search cons. Gordon Wahls Co., Media, Pa., 1976—. Active, March of Dimes. Mem. Assn. for Learning Disabled Children, Am. Soc. Personnel Adminstrn., Am. Soc. Profl. and Exec. Women (adv. bd.), Am. Soc. Tng. Dirs. Republican. Unitarian. Home: 120 Pennock Pl Media PA 19063 Office: Gordon Wahls Co 610 E Baltimore Pike Media PA 19063

RUGGLES, BEULAH MAE, nurse; b. Jamestown, N.D., Aug. 10, 1931; d. Arthur Virgil Wood and Ella Irene (Gallea) Wood Clemens; R.N., Denver U. Sch. Nursing at Presbyn. Hosp., 1953; m. Richard Gene Ruggles, Aug. 15, 1954; children—Jaylene, Andrea. Staff nurse East Morgan County Hosp., Brush, Colo., 1954, supr. operating room, 1954-67, dir. nurses, 1967—; affiliate faculty U. No. Colo. Sch. Nursing, 1981, 82; mem. vocat.-agrl. adv. council Brush High Sch.; mem. nurse aide adv. council Morgan Community Coll.; mem. adv. bd. Home Health Care, 1980—. Active 4-H, Morgan County, 1969-76, horse supt. Jr. Fair, 1975, 76; mem. Morgan County Fair Bd., 1977—; mem. Dist. Sch. Bd., 1977—; sec.-treas. meml. com. Bethlehem Lutheran Ch., Brush, 1974-77, chmn. com., 1977—. Recipient 20-Year Service award Luth. Hosp. and Homes Soc., 1974; named Morgan County Woman of Yr., 1980-82. Mem. Colo. Soc. Healthcare Nursing Service Adminstrs. (N.E. Colo. dir. 1977-81). Republican. Home: 28253 Rd Z Snyder CO 80750

RUH, LORI ANN, educator; b. Sandusky, Ohio, Apr, 23, 1954; d. William E. and Helen (Worosher) Walton; A.A., 1974; B.A. in Edn. (K.C. scholar), Bowling Green (Ohio) State U., 1976; m. Richard David Ruh, June 21, 1974. Elem. sch. tchr., Ohio, 1976—; tchr. 2d grade St. Albert The Gt. Sch., North Royalton, 1977—, head primary dept., 1979-82. Sec., Sandusky Jaycettes, 1976-77; pres. North Royalton Jaycee Women, 1978-79; mem. Brook Park Recreation Dept., 1979; vol. Am. Cancer Soc., March of Dimes. Mem. Nat. Catholic Edn. Assn. Home: 26060 Redwood Dr Olmsted Falls OH 44138 Office: 6667 Wallings Rd North Royalton OH 44133

RUHE, SHIRLEY LOUISE, govt. ofcl.; b. Des Moines, Mar. 20, 1943; d. Merritt Elton and Grace Alberta (Crabtree) Bailey; B.S., Iowa State U., 1965, M.S., 1969; m. Jonathan Mills Ruhe, Feb. 28, 1970; children—Alix-Nicole, Jonathan G. B. Wire editor, photographer Ames (Iowa) Daily Tribune, 1968-69; legis. asst. Congressman John Culver, 1969-72; staff asst. Congressman John Blatnik, 1973-75; asso. dir. budget com. U.S. Ho. of Reps., Washington, 1976—; spl. asst. Budget Process Task Force, 1976-77, chief budget process, 1978-79, dir., 1980—; mem. Congl. Reconciliation Task Force, 1981-82. Ford Found. grantee, 1969. Mem. Delta Sigma Phi, Phi Kappa Phi. Democrat. Presbyterian. Home: 6426 Patience Ct Alexandria VA 22310 Office: 203 House Annex 1 Washington DC 20010

RUKEYSER, MURIEL, poet; b. N.Y.C., Dec. 15, 1913; d. Lawrence and Myra (Lyons) R.; student Vassar Coll., Columbia U., 1930-32; Litt.D., 1961; 1 son, William L. Author poems, biographies, motion pictures, TV; lectr., tchr.; faculty Sarah Lawrence Coll., 1956-67; bd. dirs. Tchrs.-Writers Collaborative, 1967—. Pres. PEN Am. Center, 1975-76. Recipient Nat. Inst. award, 1942; Swedish Acad. Trans. award, 1968; Copernicus award, 1977; Shelley award, 1977; Guggenheim fellow, 1943; Am. Council Learned Socs. fellow, 1963. Mem. Nat. Inst. Arts and Letters, Soc. Am. Historians. Author: Theory of Flight, 1935; U.S. 1, 1938; A Turning Wind, 1939; Soul and Body of John Brown, 1941; Willard Gibbs, 1942; Beast in View, 1944; The Green Wave, 1948; Orpheus, 1949; The Life of Poetry, 1949; Selected Poems, 1951; One Life, 1957; Body of Waking, 1958; Waterlily Fire, 1962; The Orgy, 1965; The Speed of Darkness, 1968; The Traces of Thomas Hariot, 1971; Breaking Open, 1973; The Gates, 1976; Collected Poems, 1979; (children's books) Come Back Paul, 1955; I Go Out, 1959; Bubbles, 1967; Mazes, 1970; translator: Sun Stone, 1963; Selected Poems of Octavio Paz, 1963; (with Leif Sjoberg) Selected Poems of Gunnar Ekelof, 1967; Brecht's Uncle Eddie's Moustache, 1974. Address: care McGraw Publishers 1221 Ave of Americas New York NY 10020

RULE, VETA FRANKLIN TURNER (MRS. EDGAR WRIGHT RULE, JR.), writer, civic worker; b. Montgomery, Ala.; d. William Prescott and Lucy Houston (Reynolds) Turner; student U. Denver, 1927-31; m. Edgar Wright Rule, Jr., May 18, 1932; children—Lucie (Mrs. Gordon Lee Kidd, Jr.), James Randolph. Free lance writer, 1927—; pres. Denver Press Council, 1968—; writer, promoter original steering com. for Channel 6, Denver Ednl. TV, 1951-53; publicity dir. Colo. br. Am. Ch. Union, 1963-65; mem. Denver Civic Theater; mem. pub. relations staff, Presbyn. Hosp. Aux., 1951-55. Mem. Nat. League Am. Pen Women (pres. Denver br. 1956-58), Poetry Soc. Colo. (pres. 1969-70, asst. in compilation Golden Anniversary anthology), Nat. Assn. Parliamentarians, Nat. Fedn. State Poetry Socs. (conv. del. 1973-75), Denver Press Council (hon.), Alpha Gamma Delta. Anglican. Contbr. articles to profl. jours. Home: 2467 S Milwaukee St Denver CO 80210

RUMAN, MARILYN MAGIDA, psychologist; b. El Paso, Tex., Nov. 27, 1943; d. John Martin and Esther Magida; B.A. in Polit. Sci. and Psychology, UCLA, 1965, M.S.W., 1968; Ph.D. in Clin. Psychology, U.S. Internat. U., San Diego, 1977; m. Ian Richard Ruman, July 7, 1963; children—Angela Danielle, Andrea Denise. Psychotherapist Los Angeles Child Achievement Center, 1968-71; dir. Westside Center Edn. Devel., Sherman Oaks, Calif., 1971-80; co-dir. Synergetics, mgmt. cons., Encino, Calif., 1978; founder, 1980, since dir. Marilyn Ruman Clin. and Cons. Assocs., Encino, Calif.; assoc. prof. feminine psychology U.S. Internat. U.; mem. San Fernando Valley Rape Crisis Council; founder, dir. Am. Assn. Mediated Divorce; cons. in field. Mem. citizens adv. com. Los Angeles Olympics. Grantee HEW, NIMH. Mem. Am. Psychol. Assn., Calif. Psychol. Assn. Author: Beyond Sanity and Survival-A Personal Guide to Stress Management, 1980; also articles. Office: 5435 Balboa Blvd Encino CA 91316

RUMMEL, SUE ANN, hematologist; b. Nampa, Ida., Dec. 3, 1949; d. Talma Henry and B. Jeanne (Mitchell) Rummel; B.S. cum laude in biology, Bethany Nazarene Coll., 1971; M.S., U. Mo., 1981. Med. technologist Bapt. Meml. Hosp. Clin. Lab., Kansas City, Mo., 1972-75, asst. supr. hematology lab., 1975-81; instr. Affiliated Sch. Med. Tech., Kansas City, Mo., 1981—, dir. Research/Devel. Dept. for Clin. Labs., 1982—; lectr. in field. Certified med. technologist, specialist in hematology. Mem. Am. Soc. Clin. Pathologists. Office: 6601 Rockhill Rd Kansas City MO 64131

RUMSEY, F. M. CLAIRE, painter, sculptor, poet; b. N.Y.C., May 11, 1916; d. David and Frances (Davidge) Rumsey; grad. N.Y. Sch. Applied Design for Women, 1937, Degree in Advanced Window Display, 1939. One-woman shows: Warner Pub. Library, 1974, 75, Greenburgh Pub. Library, 1975, County Ct. House, White Plains, N.Y., 1977; group shows include: Guild Hall, E. Hampton, N.Y., 1960, Expn. Intercontinentale, Monaco, 1965, 66, Katonah (N.Y.) Gallery, 1958-69; represented in pvt. collections; creator painted poems; contbr. poems to numerous mags. Mem. NOW. Home: 3 Byram Brook Pl Armonk NY 10504

RUMSEY, MARY CORNELIA, med. social worker; b. Batavia, N.Y., Jan. 18, 1915; d. Matshall Canfield and Elizabeth Wallace (Van de Carr) R.; A.B., U. N.C., Chapel Hill, 1937; M.S.W., U. Calif., Berkeley, 1948; 1 dau., Ellen E. V. R. Bellenot. Med. social worker, 1943—; mem. faculty U. Tenn. Med. Coll., 1952—; dir. social services Memphis and Shelby County Health Dept., 1962—. Mem. Acad. Cert. Social Workers, Nat. Assn. Social Workers. Republican. Anglican. Home: 684 S White Station Rd Memphis TN 38117 Office: 815 Jefferson St Memphis TN 38105

RUNDEN, CHARITY EVA WILLIAMS (MRS. JOHN PAUL RUNDEN), psychologist, educator; b. Lake City, Minn., Oct. 1, 1910; d. Harley Albert and Edith (Burchard) Williams; A.B., Ball State U., 1933, M.A., 1940; M.S. in Pub. Health (USPHS fellow), U. N.C., 1944; Ph.D., Ind. U., 1951; m. John Paul Runden, Aug. 23, 1944; children—John Paul, Ingrid Eve. Tchr. high schs., Ind., 1937-43; health educator, N.C. and Ind., 1944-46; faculty Ind. U., 1950-52, U. Ky., 1952-54; instr. Western Ill. U., Macomb, 1954-57, acting dean grad. div., 1957-59; asst. prof. psychology and edn. Montclair State Coll., Upper Montclair, N.J., 1959-63, dean of women, 1963-65, asso. chmn. grad. studies, 1965-67, prof. psychology and edn., 1966-79, exec. dir. Ednl. Found. for Human Sexuality, 1967-79; dir. Runden Inst., 1979—. Fellow Am. Pub. Health Assn.; mem. Modern Lang. Assn., N.J. Health Edn. Council, N.J. Assn. Health, Phys. Edn. and Recreation, Nat. Council on Family Relations, Am. Assn. Sex Educators and Counselors, Sex Information and Ednl. Council U.S. (asso.), Soc. Sci. Study Sex. Author: Twentieth Century Educators, 1965; Selected Readings in Sex Education, 1968. Contbr. articles to profl. jours. Home: Glen Rock Rd Little Falls NJ 07424 Office: Runden Inst Valley at Cooper Ave Upper Montclair NJ 07043

RUNDEN, LOIS, communications exec.; b. Covington, Ky.; d. Edgar Lee and Verna Mae (Henthorn) Shryock; B.A. with high distinction, U. Ky.; M.A., New Sch., N.Y.C., 1981. Agt. selection cons. Francis L. Merritt Sales Cons., Montclair, N.J.; staff writer Prudential Ins. Co., South Plainfield, N.J., 1966-67, asst. editor, 1967-70, editor, sales promotion cons., 1970-72, mgr. pub. relations and advt., 1972-75, sr. communications cons., 1975-81, mgr. communications and tng., 1982—. Trustee N.J. Oratorio Soc., 1963-72, publicity chmn., 1963-72; publicity chmn. Newark (N.J.) Fresh Air Fund, 1971—; trustee Newark Day Center, 1973—; publicity chmn. Friends of the Earth, 1975-77. Recipient award of excellence Life Ins. Advertisers Assn., 1979. Mem. Communicators Assn., Internat. Assn. Bus. Communicators (award of merit 1976), South Plainfield C. of C. (bd. dirs.), Kappa Delta Pi. Home: 150 Lenox Ct Piscataway NJ 08854 Office: Box 750 South Plainfield NJ 07080

RUNDHAUG, JANIE ESTELLE, trucking and water blasting co. exec.; b. Greenville, Tex., Jan. 19, 1936; d. Forrest Donald and Millie Angeline (Thomason) Moore; student U. Kans., 1963, U. Md., 1965; m. Neal C. Rohrig, Feb. 13, 1951; 1 son, Neal C.; m. 2d, Philip M. Rundhaug, Feb. 8, 1953; children—Dianna L., Phyllis J., James P., Brenda K. With acctg. office USAF AFBs, 1963-65; acct. Alexander Grant, C.P.A.s, San Antonio, 1965-68; owner, chmn. bd. Wilco Delivery Services, Inc., Houston, 1970—, JERCO Waterblasting, Inc., Houston, 1978—; partner New Leaf, Ltd., 1980—. Mem. Am. Bus. Women's Assn. (past chpt. treas.), Houston Cartage Assn. (past treas.). Republican. Lutheran. Club: Order Eastern Star. Home: Route 2 Box 543 New Caney TX 77357 Office: 3215 McKinney St Houston TX 77002

RUNKEL, JANE ELIZABETH, coll. adminstr.; b. Port Washington, Wis., Aug. 27, 1952; d. Paul David and Jean (Goettmann) R.; A.B., Ripon Coll., 1974; M.Ed., U. Wis., Oshkosh, 1979. Admissions counselor Ripon Coll., 1974-77, asst. dean admissions, 1977-78, asst. dean admissions, asst. career planning, 1978-79, asst. dean admissions, asst. dir. career planning and placement, 1979-80, asst. dean students, dir. career planning, 1980-82, dir. career planning and placement, 1982—. Chmn. nominating com. WauBun council Girl Scouts Am., 1981—. Mem. Am. Coll. Personnel Assn. (coordinator com. status and concerns of women 1981-82), Nat. Assn. Women Deans, Adminstrs. and Counselors, Ripon Soc. Scholars, Wis. Career Planning and Placement Assn., Wis. Soc. Higher Edn. (coordinator), New Eng. Historic and Geneal. Soc., DAR, Soc. Colonial Dames (state scholarship chmn.), Alpha Delta Pi. Clubs: Bowne House Restoration, Ripon Study (sec.). Office: 300 Seward St Box 248 Ripon WI 54971

RUNTE, ROSEANN, educator; b. Kingston, N.Y., Jan. 31, 1948; d. Robert Benedict and Anna Loretta (Schorkopf) O'Reilly; B.A. summa cum laude, SUNY, New Paltz, 1968; M.A., U. Kans., 1969, M.Ph., 1971, Ph.D. (NDEA fellow), 1974; m. Hans-Rainer Runte, Aug. 9, 1969. Instr., lang. lab. dir. Bethany (W.Va.) Coll., 1970-71; lectr. adult studies St. Mary's U., Halifax, N.S., Can., 1971-72; lectr. Dalhousie U., Halifax, 1972-73, asst. prof., 1973-79, asso. prof., 1979—, asst. dean faculty arts and scis., 1980-82, chairperson French dept., 1980—. Mem. Can. Fedn. Humanities (v.p. 1981-82, pres. 1982-83), Can. Soc. 18th Century Studies (pres. 1976, exec. bd. 1976—), Internat. Soc. 18th Century Studies (exec. bd. 1976-80), Atlantic Soc. 18th Century Studies (pres. 1972-76), MLA (regional del. eastern Can., New Eng. 1979-81). Contbr. numerous articles to profl. jours.; editor: Studies in Eighteenth Century Culture, vols. VII, VIII, IX; co-editor: Of Nature and of Man, 1982; author: Brumes Bleues (poetry), 1982. Office: French Dept Dalhousie U Halifax NS B3H 3J5 Canada

RUNYAN, DEBORAH ANN, computer systems cons.; b. Denver, Apr. 3, 1949; d. William Neill and Dorothy Belle (Tuttle) Miner; B.A. in Chemistry (Nat. Merit scholar, Jackling scholar), U. N.Mex., 1970, postgrad. in math., 1971-73; postgrad. in elec. engring. San Jose State U., 1975-77; m. Noel Howard Runyan, June 7, 1969; children—Tamala Dawn, Arthur Jeremy. Chemist, Air Force Weapons Lab., Kirtland AFB, N.Mex., 1971-72, mathematician, 1972-73; programmer Internat. Data Applications, San Jose, Calif., 1977-78; pvt. practice cons. microprocessor systems, San Jose, 1978—. Mem. No. Calif. Solar Energy Assn. Club: Flying Aces (dir. 1974-77, communications officer 1974-75, 76-77, v.p. ops. 1975-76, meritorious service award 1978). Home: 638 Sobrato Ln Campbell CA 95008

RUNYON, ALICE LOUISE MINNERLY (MRS. JAMES G. RUNYON), restoration research, educator, musician; b. North Tarrytown, N.Y., June 12, 1902; d. Percy Charles and Phernetta Elizabeth (Miller) Minnerly; B.S., N.Y. U., 1943, M.A., 1947; grad. Guilmant Organ Sch., 1940; m. James Garfield Runyon, June 30, 1928 (dec. 1955). Tchr. pub. sch., 1921-46; asst. dir. Philipse Castle restoration, 1943-47; head research for restoration Sunnyside, Washington Irving's home, 1945-47; asso. dir. Philipse Castle and Sunnyside, 1947-51, Sleepy Hollow Restorations, Inc., 1951-55, corp. sec., trustee, 1951-55; dir. Specialized Research, 1956—. Curator Horace Greeley Mus., 1958-68; genealogist Dutch Colonial of Del., 1967-71. Organist and choir master Christ Evang. and Ref. Ch., N.Y.C., 1942-52; lectr. sec., v.p. USO, The Tarrytowns, World War II. Mem. Am. Guild Organists, Hist. Soc. Tarrytowns (dir., sec.), Sons and Daus. Pilgrims (organizing pres. past nat. officers club, 1st dep. gov. gen., N.Y. State gov., dep. gov., treas., sec., nat. bd. mem.), Am. Hist. Soc., Patriotic Women Am., Daus. Am. Colonists, Colonial Daus. 17th Century, DAR (chmn. Jr. Am. Citizens, registrar, historian), Daus. Founders and Patriots Am. (life; N.Y. pres., v.p., nat. councillor, nat. chmn. hist. edn., nat. corr. sec.), Daus. Colonial Wars (pres. N.Y. State, nat. historian, mem. nat. exec. bd., rec. sec., 2d v.p. Nat. Officers Club), Ams. Armorial Ancestry (nat. councillor, nat. pres., nat. treas., nat. registrar, genealogist), Manuscript Soc., Soc. Holland Dames, Ames. Royal Descent (past nat. councillor), Colonial Dames Am., Huguenot Soc. Am. (nat. registrar, council), Descs. Knights of Garter, Women's Nat. Republican Club, Am. Friends Lafayette, Daus. Union 1861-1865, Order of Washington, Order Three Crusades, Descs. William the Conqueror, Women Descs. Ancient and Honorable Arty. Co., N.Y. State Hist. Assn. (organizer 1st jr. chpt.), Westchester County, Chappaqua (trustee), Somers (hon.) hist. socs., Kappa Delta Pi. Author: Minne Johannes and Some of his Descendants; Frederick Miller of Colchester and Some of His Kin; others. Contbr. articles in field. Historian village of N. Tarrytown, N.Y., 1947-81; past archivist Order of Crown of Charlemagne in Am. Home: 483 Munroe Ave North Tarrytown NY 10591 Office: Specialized Research PO Box 187 North Tarrytown NY 10591

RUNYON, NORMA LEE, banker; b. Seminole, Okla., Nov. 7, 1940; d. James Wilford and Opal Allene (Alexander) Osborn; A.A. with high honors, Tarrant County Jr. Coll., Hurst, Tex., 1978; postgrad. U. Tex., Arlington; grad. Southwestern Grad. Sch. Banking, So. Meth. U., 1981; m. Stephen C. Runyon, Sept. 5, 1981; children by previous marriage—Terri, James W.; stepchildren—Stephanie, David. Sec. to pres. First Nat. Bank Grapevine (Tex.), 1959-62; sec. to pres. First Nat. Bank Euless (Tex., 1963-64, v.p., 1965—; asst. city sec. City of Euless, 1964-65; tchr. cons. local high schs. Vice pres. Hurst Euless Bedford unit Am. Cancer Soc., 1981-82; bd. dirs. Northeast YMCA, Euless, 1980-83, mem. 1000 Club, 1981; treas. Miss Hurst-Euless-Bedford Scholarship Found. Pageant, 1980—; sec. Euless Planning and Zoning Commn., 1981-82. Recipient various service awards. Mem. Hurst-Euless-Bedford C. of C. (pres. 1981-82). Home: 710 Marlene Ct Euless TX 76039 Office: 1010 W Euless Blvd PO Box 608 Euless TX 76039

RUPERT, ELIZABETH ANASTASIA, ednl. adminstr.; b. Emlenton, Pa., July 12, 1918; d. John Hamilton and Eva Blanche (Elliott) R.; B.S., Clarion State Coll., 1959; M.S. in Library Sci., Syracuse U., 1962; Ph.D., U. Pitts., 1970. Sec., Quaker State Oil Refining Corp., 1939-56; tchr., librarian Oil City (Pa.) Public Schs., 1959-61; librarian Clarion State Coll., Venango, Pa., 1961-62, prof. sch. library sci., 1962-70, dean sch. library sci., 1970—, acting pres., 1977. Recipient Disting. Faculty award Clarion State Coll. Alumni Assn., 1976. Mem. ALA, Pa. Library Assn., Pa. Sch. Librarians Assn., Assn. Am. Library Schs., Am. Assn. Sch. Librarians. Republican. Author: Pennsylvania Practicum Program for School Librarians: An Appraisal, 1970; contbr. writings to ency. in field. Office: Sch Library Sci Clarion State Coll Clarion PA 16214

RUPRECHT, MARY MARGARET WYANT, word processing, mgmt. cons.; b. O'Neill, Neb., Oct. 20, 1934; d. Charles Ellsworth and Mary Loretto (Cuddy) Wyant; student Coll. St. Benedict, 1952-54; cert. Am. Inst. Banking, 1970; m. Gregory Earl Ruprecht, Sept. 24, 1955; children—Mary Debra, Sharie Marie. Dist. clk. U.S. Soil Conservation, Aitkin, Minn., 1956-68; comml. loan sec. No. City Nat. Bank, Duluth, Minn., 1965-71; office mgr. Fryberger, Buchanan Law Firm, Duluth, 1971-72; pvt. practice word processing and mgmt. cons., Duluth, 1972-76; v.p., prin. Altman & Weil, Inc., mgmt. cons., 1976-79; pres. Mary M. Ruprecht & Assos., 1979—; tchr. Am. Inst. Banking. Mem. adv. council Minn. State Bd. Edn., Duluth Office Edn. Assn., Coll. Applied Scis. at Miami U., Oxford, Ohio, Ball State U., Muncie, Ind. Fin. dir. 8th Congressional Dist. Dem.-Farm Labor Party, 1972-73. Cert. mgmt. cons. Mem. Internat. Word Processing Assn. (internat. pres. 1974-75), Am. Inst. Banking (nat. chmn. women's com. 1970-71), Adminstrv. Mgmt. Soc., Am. Mgmt. Assn., Bus. and Profl. Women's Assn., Internat. Platform Assn. Co-Author: Managing Office Automation; Office Automation: Concepts and Principles; Office Automation: A Management Approach. contbr. articles to profl. jours. Home: 140 W Myrtle St Duluth MN 55811

RUSCH, ROSEMARIE ANN, distbg. co. exec.; b. Buffalo, Aug. 30, 1943; d. Richard G. and Clara M. (Jankowski) Rusch; A.O.S. in Bus. Adminstrn., Bryant & Stratton Bus. Inst., 1977; B.S., Medaille Coll., 1979. With Hy-Grade Distributors, Inc., Tonawanda, N.Y., 1961—, office mgr., purchasing agt. janitorial products, 1972-77, purchasing mgr. Janitorial Products Div., 1978—. Recipient Profl. Devel. Person of the Yr. award, 1978-79, 8th Dist. Nat. Assn. Purchasing Mgmt., 1979, cert. purchasing mgr. Mem. Nat. Assn. Purchasing Mgmt., Purchasing Mgmt. Assn. Buffalo, Am. Bus. Women's Assn., Center for Women in Mgmt. Republican. Roman Catholic. Club: Interclub Council of Western N.Y. Home: 245 Garland Ave Cheektowaga NY 14206 Office: 574 Main St Tonawanda NY 14150

RUSH, ANNE KENT, pub. co. exec.; b. Mobile, Ala., July 28, 1945; d. George LeGrand and Cynthia (Williams) R.; B.A., Wayne State U., 1967; D.D., Crown of Life Fellowship, 1974. Comml. writer Little Brown Pubs., Boston, 1968; teaching staff Esalen Inst. Psychology, San Francisco and Big Sur, Calif., 1970-74; comml. artist The Book Works Pubs., Berkeley, Calif., 1970-71; co-dir. Alyssum Inst. Feminist Consciousness, San Francisco, 1974-75; co-dir. Moon Books Pubs., Berkeley, 1976—, exec. dir., 1975—. Bd. dirs. Bay Area Women's Philharm., 1982—, Berkeley Women's Health Collective, 1981. Mem. Authors Guild, Feminist Writers Guild. Author: The Massage Book, 1971; Getting Clear, 1972; Feminism as Therapy, 1974; Moon, Moon, 1976; The Basic Back Book, 1979; AK Rush, 1972. Address: PO Box 9223 Berkeley CA 94709

RUSH, BARBARA, actress; b. Denver, Jan. 4, 1930; d. Roy L. and Marguerite Rush; student U. Calif., Santa Barbara; m. James Gruzalski, Sept. 24, 1970; children—Christopher, Claudia. First stage appearance at age of ten, Loberto Theatre, Santa Barbara, in fantasy Golden Ball; won acting award in coll. for characterization of Birdie (The Little Foxes); scholarship Pasadena Playhouse Theatre Arts Coll.; motion pictures include The First Legion, 1951, Quebec, 1951, Molly, 1950, When Worlds Collide, 1951, Flaming Feather, 1952, Prince of Pirates, 1953, It Came from Outer Space, 1953, Taza Son of Cochise, 1954, Magnificent Obsession, 1956, Black Shield of Falworth, 1957, Captain Lightfoot, 1955, Kiss of Fire, 1955, World in My Corner, 1956, Bigger Than Life, 1957, Oh Men! Oh Women!, 1960, Harry Black and the Tiger, 1958, The Young Philadelphians, 1959, Bramble Bush, 1960, Strangers When We Meet, 1960, Come Blow Your Horn, 1963, Robin and the Seven Hoods, 1964, Hombre, 1967, Airport, 1970, The Man, 1972, Superdad, 1974, Can't Stop the Music; numerous theatrical appearances; appeared in TV films Crime Club, 1973, The Last Day, 1975; TV series Flamingo Road, 1980—; numerous other TV appearances including Love Boat, Medical Center, Police Story, Streets of San Francisco, Ironside. Office: care Internat Creative Mgmt 40 W 57th St New York NY 10019 *

RUSH, JEAN COCHRAN, artist, researcher, educator; b. Bloomington, Ill., Nov. 21, 1933; d. Gilbert Emlyn and Florence Margaret (Scott) Cochran; B.F.A., Ill. Wesleyan U., 1955; M.F.A., U. Iowa, 1958; Ph.D., U. Ariz., 1974; m. Andrew Rush, Apr. 18, 1957 (div.); children—Benjamin Emlyn, Samuel Charles, Joseph Harvey, Margaret Ruth. Free-lance artist, 1958-70; ednl. researcher U. Ariz., Tucson, 1970-71, lectr., 1971-75, asst. prof., 1975-80, asso. prof. dept. art, coordinator art edn. program, 1978—. Mem. Oracle (Ariz.) Sch. Bd., 1971-73. Recipient First prize in Oil Painting, Ariz. State Fair, 1960. Mem. Nat. Art Edn. Assn. (Pacific Regional V.P. award 1981), Council Policy Studies in Art Edn., Ariz. Art Edn. Assn., Am. Psychol. Assn., Am. Ednl. Research Assn., Coll. Art Assn., AAUP, Ariz. Assn. Supervision and Curriculum Devel. Contbr. articles to profl. jours.; co-editor Studies in Art Edn., 1981—. Office: Dept Art U Ariz Tucson AZ 85721

RUSHEN, RUTH L., state agy. ofcl.; b. Laurel, Miss., Dec. 19, 1924; d. Samuel and Violet P. Harris; B.A. in Social Studies, Clark Coll., Atlanta, 1945; M.P.A., U. So. Calif., 1971; m. Allen R. Rushen, Feb. 7, 1953; children—Patrice, Angela. With Los Angeles Probation Dept., 1956-75, div. chief, 1974-75; vice chmn. bd. Calif. Bd. Prison Terms, 1975-80; mem. Calif. Bd. Corrections, 1977—, dir., 1980—; mem. panel on sentencing research Nat. Acad. Sci., 1980-82; instr., guest lectr. in field. Named Disting. Am., Sta. KABC, 1971; recipient corrections award Pepperdine U., 1972, Trail Blazers award Nat. Assn. Negro Bus. and Profl. Women, 1975. Mem. Calif. Probation, Parole and Correctional Assn., Black Probation Officers Assn., Calif. Black Coorections Coalition, So. Calif. Alumni Public Adminstrn. Assn. (dir.), NAACP. Author reports in field. Address: 630 K St Sacramento CA 95814

RUSHING, CONSTANCE FORDE, computer mfg. co. exec.; b. N.Y.C., Jan. 28, 1944; d. William Kenneth and Roslyn Helen (Morrison) Forde; B.A. in Math., Queens Coll., 1964; M.S. in Ops. Research, N.Y. U., 1973; grad. exec. mgmt. seminar Ga. State U., 1976. With IBM, 1964—, mgr. mgmt. devel., Atlanta, 1975-77, mgr. cross industry programs, 1977—. Vice pres. bd. dirs. Atlanta Women's Network, 1980-82; pres. Council on Battered Women, 1981-82; mem. adv. bd. Ga. Alliance for Children, 1981; mem. budget and fin. com. YWCA, 1982. Recipient Dist. and Regional Mgrs. awards IBM, 1966-71, named to One Hundred Percent club, 1973; award for service to Bur. Police Services, City of Atlanta, 1976; named Outstanding Young Women Am., U.S. Jaycees, 1977. Mem. Feminist Action Alliance. Home: 3302 Pinestream Rd Atlanta GA 30327 Office: PO Box 2150 Atlanta GA 30055

RUSKELL, VIRGINIA ANN, librarian, educator; b. Nashville, June 4, 1948; d. George Channing Ruskell and Douglass (McFerrin) Rudkoff; A.A., Reinhardt Coll., 1967; B.A. in history, Emory U., 1969; M.L.S., George Peabody Coll., 1970; M.A. in English, West Ga. U., 1975. Library asst. George Peabody Coll. Library Sch., 1969-70; interlibrary loan librarian West Ga. Coll., Carrollton, 1970-76, bibliog. instrn. librarian, 1977-80, reference coordinator, 1980—, assoc. prof., 1980—. Treas., LWV, Carrollton, 1975-77; chmn. social concerns St. Andrew United Meth. Ch., Carrollton, 1981-82, fin. sec., 1980-81, chmn. fin. com., 1982. Council Library Resources Library Services Enhancement grantee, 1976-77. Mem. Southeastern Library Assn., AAUP (sec. 1974-75, v.p. 1975-76), AAUW (v.p. programs 1982—), Beta Phi Mu, Phi Kappa Phi. Democrat. Home: PO Box 844 Carrollton GA 30117 Office: W Ga Coll Library Carrollton GA 30118

RUSS, DEBORAH JAROW, psychotherapist; b. Oceanside, N.Y., Apr. 14, 1952; d. Harold and Harriet Ann (Goodstein) Jarow; B.A. magna cum laude, Boston U., 1973; M.S. in Social Work, Columbia U. 1975; m. George M. Russ, Oct. 6, 1979. Pvt. practice psychotherapy, N.Y.C., 1977—, Upper Montclair, N.J. 1980—; adj. prof. Montclair State Coll., Upper Montclair, N.J., 1981—. Cert. social worker N.Y. State. Mem. Nat. Assn. Social Workers, Acad. Cert. Social Workers. Home: 61 W 89th St New York NY 10024 Office: 209 Cooper Ave Upper Montclair NJ 07043

RUSSELL, ANNE V., govt. ofcl.; b. Archie, Mo., Nov. 9, 1926; d. John D. and D. Muriel (Gilbert) R.; student Rizer Sch. Music, Cranston Sch. Music, 1943-45, Kans. City Jr. Coll., 1946, West Tex. State U., 1958. Advt. and public relations dir. numerous pvt. industries, Kansas City, Mo., Denver and Amarillo, Tex., 1946-61; field editor Horse Lover's Mag., Richmond, Calif. and Amarillo, 1956-59; public info. specialist The White House, Washington, 1962-64; editor USPHS, Washington, 1965-70, HEW Newsletter, Washington, 1971-74; bicentennial dir. HEW (now Dept. Health and Human Services), 1975-76, mgr. visitors info. and edn. center, 1977-78, exhibits mgr., 1979-80; on leave as dir. spl. affairs 1982 World's Fair, City of Knoxville (Tenn.), 1980—. Mem. adv. council Capital Childrens Mus., 1976—; spl. advisor Hugh O'Brian Youth Found., 1976—. Republican. Home: 1431 Cherokee Trail Apt 103 Knoxville TN 37920 Office: Dept Health and Human Services 200 Independence Ave Washington DC 20201

RUSSELL, DESI RAKICH, mgmt. cons.; b. Ljubovo, Yugoslavia, Feb. 16, 1949; came to U.S., 1953; d. Milan S. and Milka M. Rakich; B.A., De Paul U., 1972; postgrad. Inst. Indsl. Relations, Loyola U., Chgo., 1973; m. John F. Russell, Dec. 18, 1976. Systems analyst, instr. Bowne Info. Systems, Chgo., 1971-74; mktg. rep., 1974-76, product mgr., N.Y.C., 1976-77; cons. Data Processing Staff Cons., Chgo., 1979-80; pres. SysteMethods, Inc., Arlington Heights, Ill., 1980—. Mem. Mensa, Intertel, Chgo. Sales Tng. Assn. (past pres.). Home: 1314 S Fernandez Ct Arlington Heights IL 60005

RUSSELL, DIANA ELIZABETH HAMILTON, sociologist; b. Cape Town, South Africa, Nov. 6, 1938; d. James Hamilton and Kathleen Mary (Gibson) Russell; came to U.S., 1963; B.A., U. Cape Town, 1958; grad. diploma with distinction, London Sch. Econs., 1961; M.A., Harvard U., 1967, Ph.D., 1970. Research assoc. Center Internat. Studies, Princeton, N.J., 1967-68; asst. prof. sociology Mills Coll., Oakland, Calif., 1969-75, asso. prof., 1975—; an organizer 1st Internat. Tribunal on Crimes Against Women, Brussels, 1976; prin. investigator, study of rape and sexual assault NIMH, 1977-79; prin. investigator study of intrafamilial childhood sexual abuse Nat. Center on Child Abuse and Neglect, 1980-82. Mem. Women Against Violence in Pornography and Media (co-founder, bd. dirs.), Bay Area Women Against Rape (bd. dirs.), Sociologists Women in Soc. Author: Rebellion, Revolution and Armed Force, 1974; The Politics of Rape, 1975; Crime Against Women, 1976; Rape in Marriage, 1982. Editor: (with others) Sadomasochism: A Radical Feminist Analysis, 1982. Office: Div Social Sci Mills Coll Oakland CA 94613

RUSSELL, ELEANOR, musicologist; b. Denver, Aug. 19, 1931; d. J. Stephen and Eleanor Russell; A.A., Stephens Coll., 1951; B.Mus., U. Colo., 1953; M.A. (Marshall fellow), U. So. Calif., 1960, Ph.D. (Fulbright-Hays fellow), 1970; m. George Truett Hollis, June 30, 1971. Tchr., Hamilton Jr. High Sch., Long Beach, Calif., 1954-57; instr. Long Beach City Coll., 1957-61; asst. prof. Long Beach State Coll., 1961-62, San Fernando Valley State Coll., 1962-77; prof. music Calif. State U., Northridge, 1977—. Mem. state bd. Calif. Congress Parents and Tchrs. Orgn., 1975-76. Faculty fellow Calif. State U., Northridge, 1970; Faculty research grantee, 1975, 81. Colaborador honrado Instituto Espanol de Musicologia, Consejo Superior de Investigaciones Cientificas, 1974. Mem. Am. Musicol. Soc. (faculty rep.), Soc. Netherlandish Music History, Music Tchrs. Nat. Assn., Sigma Alpha Iota. Asso. editor, Festival Essays for Pauline Alderman, 1976. Contbr. articles to profl. jours.; contbr. to New Grove's Dictionary. Office: Calif State U 18111 Nordhoff St Northridge CA 91330

RUSSELL, GRACE JARRELL WILLIAMS, journalist, writer, artist, ch. and civic worker; b. Memphis, July 4, 1924; d. Aubrey Hamilton and Lill (Jarrell) Williams; student Lambuth Coll., 1942-43; B.A., So. Meth. U., 1946; m. Henry Ewell Russell, Apr. 7, 1945; children—Margaret Lill Russell Rudolph, Rose Ellen Russell Weiner, Henry Ewell, Stephen A., Betty Grace Russell Houser. Tchr. English, art Dyersburg (Tenn.) High Sch., 1964-65; pvt. tchr. art Dyersburg and Brownsville, Tenn., Paducah, Ky., Memphis; columnist Gracelines newspapers, Tenn. and Ky., 1976—; one-woman shows at People's Bank, Paducah, 1971, Famous French Galleries, Memphis, 1978; exhibited in group shows: Carnegie Library, Brownsville, 1966, 67, Dyersburg Art Show, 1964, 65, Nat. League Am. Pen Women State Show, Memphis, 1979, also numerous local ch. and city shows; represented in numerous pvt. collections. Active various charitable orgns.; del. Memphis Ann. Conf. United Meth. Ch., City Rd. Chapel, London, 1978; del. World Meth. Conf., Honolulu, 1981, Christian Heritage in Govt. Conf., London, 1981. Named Duchess of Paducah, 1972; recipient prize for short story Tenn. chpt. Nat. League Am. Pen Women. Mem. Nat. League Am. Penwomen (state pres. 1980-82), Susanna Wesley Fellowship, Memphis Ann. Conf. Susannas (pres. 1973), Ch. Women United, Delta Delta Delta. Democrat. Methodist. Clubs: Am. Mothers' Com., Woman's. Author: Rings and Things, 1970; Hope in My Heart, 1978; How I See England, 1981; contbr. articles to denominational mags. Home: 709 Wade Hampton Rd Dyersburg TN 38024 Office: PO Box 277 Dyersburg TN 38024

RUSSELL, HARRIET VIRGINIA HEIT, mental health adminstr.; b. Ossining, N.Y., Dec. 31, 1936; d. George and Ruth Virginia (Miller) Heit; student Barnard Coll., 1954-55; B.S., Ohio U., 1958; M.A., U. Mich., 1959; postgrad. SUNY, New Paltz; m. J. Thomas Russell, Oct. 24, 1959 (div. 1979); children—Elizabeth, Margaret, Gregory. Tchr. public schs., Buena Vista, Va., 1959-61; counselor Newburgh (N.Y.) City Sch. Dist., 1967-70, dir. guidance, 1970-74; dir. profl. services Family Counseling Service of Orange County, Inc., Newburgh, 1974-75, exec. dir., 1975—. Mem. planning bd. Village of Cornwall, N.Y., 1972-80, chairperson, 1977; mem. Hudson Valley Health Systems Agy., mem. regional project rev., mental health com., chmn. mental health task force; mem. Orange County Health Adv. Council, 1978—, chmn. project rev.; mem. exec. bd. Vol. Community Agys. N.Y. State. visitors Letchworth Village Devel. Center; trustee Washington's Hdqrs., Newburgh.; pres. Greater Cornwall Assn.; mem. choir, trustee Cornwall Presbyn. Ch. Mem. N.Y. State Assn. Family Service Agys. (pres.), Assn. Mental Health Adminstrs., Greater Newburgh Council Community Agys. (pres. 1976-77), Mental Health Action Network/State Communities Aid Assn. (project com.), Eastern Orange County C. of C. (edn. com. 1974-80), Kappa Delta. Home: Wilson Rd Cornwall-on-Hudson NY 12520 Office: 21 Grand St Newburgh NY 12550

RUSSELL, JEANNE VINE, educator; b. Alton, Ill., Nov. 21, 1940; d. Paul and Gladys (Wentz) Vine; B.A. in Math., So. Ill., U., 1962; Ph.D. in Chemistry, U. Colo., 1966; m. Thomas Webb Russell, July 18, 1964. Vis. asst. prof. La. State U., 1966-67; tchr. math. and sci. Floyd (N.Mex.) High Sch., 1968-69; instr. math. and chemistry Eastern N.Mex. U., 1969-70, 73-81, dir. coll. opportunity program, 1976-78, dir. Learning Center, 1978-81, temporary asst. prof. chemistry, 1977-78; asso. prof. chemistry Odessa (Tex.) Coll., 1981—. Leader, camp counselor Mile High council Girl Scouts U.S.A., Denver, 1959-64; active Roosevelt County (N.Mex.) chpt. ARC, 1974-81, Sierra Blanca Nat. Ski Patrol, Ruidoso, N.Mex., 1973-80; Campus Girl Scout leader, 1980-81. Recipient cert. of appreciation Roosevelt County chpt. ARC, 1976; Nat. Ski Patrol System, 1976; Service to Youth award Kiwanis Internat. Club, 1976; medal Roadrunner chpt. ARC, 1978. Mem. NEA (dir. chpt. 1979), Am. Chem. Soc., N.Mex. Network Women in Sci. and Engring. (membership chmn. 1981-82), Quantum Chemistry Program Exchange. Home: Route 1 Box 340 AX Odessa TX 79763 Office: Odessa Coll Odessa TX 79762

RUSSELL, LAO COOK (MRS. WALTER RUSSELL), philosopher, author, educator; b. Ivinghoe, Buckinghamshire, Eng., Nov. 6; naturalized U.S. citizen, 1947; d. Alfred William and Florence (Hills) Cook; ed. pvt. tutors; m. Walter Russell, July 29, 1948. Founder Walter Russell Found. (now known as U. of Sci. and Philosophy), 1948, mng. dir., 1948—, pres., 1949—; lectr. numerous cities in U.S., 1947—; founded Shrine of Beauty at Swannanoa Palace, nr. Waynesboro, Va., 1948. Founder Man-Woman Equalization League, 1955, Internat. Age of Character, Arts and Cultural Centers, 1966, Internat. Age of Character Clubs, 1966. Author: God Will Work With You But Not For You, 1955 (named one of 6 best books of year N.Y. Herald-Tribune, 1955); An Eternal Message of Light and Love, 1964; My Love I Extend to You, 1966; Love-A Scientific and Living Philosophy of Love and Sex, 1966; Why You Cannot Die!-The Continuity of Life, Reincarnation Explained, 1972; (with Walter Russell) One Year Home Study Course in Universal Law, Natural Science and Living Philosophy, 1950, Scientific Answer to Human Relations, 1951, Atomic Suicide?, 1957; The World Crisis—Its Explanation and Solution, 1958; The One-World Purpose—A Plan to Dissolve War by a Power More Mighty than War, 1960. Executed 5-foot statue (with husband) The Christ of the Blue Ridge, 1948, also colossal model, 1950 presented colossal bronze bust of George Washington (sculpted by Walter Russell) to Fredericksburg Bicentennial Commn., 1976. Address: Univ Sci and Philosophy Swannanoa Palace Waynesboro VA 22980

RUSSELL, MATTIE UNDERWOOD, librarian; b. Randolph, Miss., May 14, 1915; d. William Vance and Mattie Pearl (Underwood) R.; B.A., U. Miss., 1937, M.A., 1940; Ph.D., Duke U., 1956. Tchr. social studies high schs., Miss. 1937-43; asst. prof. history Mars Hill (N.C.) Coll., 1943-46; asst. curator manuscripts Duke U., Durham, N.C., 1948-52, curator 1952—; vis. assoc. prof. library sci. U. N.C., Chapel Hill 1969-78. Bd. dirs. Tobacco History Corp., Inc., Durham. Fellow Soc. Am. Archivists; mem. Durham Historic Preservation Soc., So. Hist. Assn. (rep. to Nat. Archives Adv. Council), ALA, Am. Assn. State and Local History, Manuscript Soc., Nat. Trust Historic Preservation, Hist. Soc. N.C., N.C. Lit. and Hist. Assn., Assocs. Nat. Archives. Democrat. Contbr. in field. Office: 344 Perkins Library Duke Univ Durham NC 27706

RUSSELL, NORMA CALDWELL, state senator; b. Joanna, S.C., Aug. 23, 1937; d. Torrence E. and Julia (Dominick) Caldwell; student U. S.C., 1955-56; m. Rodney Jennings Russell, Apr. 21, 1957; children—Robin Leigh, Rodney Jennings, Jr. Mem. S.C. Ho. of Reps., 1973-80, S.C. Senate, 1981—. Mem. Seven Oaks Community Improvement Assn.; S.C. Senate attache, 1964-68; commr. Lexington County Rural Recreation Commn., 1968-69; sec. Woodland Hills Republican precinct, 1970-71, vice-chmn., 1972-75, exec. committeeman, 1976; chmn. March of Dimes, Woodland Hills, 1968; reporter St. Andrews News, Woodland Hills Community, 1967; bd. dirs. S.C. Lung Assn., 1973-76; mem. Consumer Credit Counseling Service Midlands, 1974-76; bd. dirs. Nat. Com. Status of Women; mem. Citizens for Advancement Physically Handicapped, 1973—; mem. Citizens to Save Lake Murray from Pollution, 1975-76; mem. adv. bd. Midlands Tech. Coll. Ct. Reporting Sch.; mgr. Congressman Spence's Campaign Office, 1970; bd. dirs. Am. Legis. Exchange Council, 1980; mem. Nat. Edn. Task Force, 1981. Named Outstanding State Legislator in Am., Am. Legis. Exchange Council, 1980. Mem. Nat. Order Women Legislators (regional dir. 1979, 81).

RUSSELL, PEGGY TAYLOR, soprano, educator; b. Newton, N.C., Apr. 5, 1927; d. William G. and Sue B. (Cordell) Taylor; Mus.B. in Voice, Salem Coll., 1948; Mus.M., Columbia U., 1950; postgrad. U. N.C., Greensboro, 1977; student Am. Inst. Mus. Studies, Austria, 1972, 78; student of Clifford Bair, Nell Starr, Salem Coll., Winston-Salem, N.C., Edgar Schofield, Chloe Owen, N.Y.C.; student opera-dramatics Boris Goldovsky, U. N.C., Greensboro, Ande Andersen, Max Lehner, Graz, Austria; m. John B. Russell, Feb. 23, 1952; children—John Spotswood, Susan Bryce. Mem. faculty dept. voice Guilford Coll., Greensboro, 1952-53, Greensboro Coll., 1971-72; pvt. tchr. of voice, Greensboro, 1963—; vis. instr. in voice U. N.C., Chapel Hill, 1973-77; lectr. on music history and opera; condr. recital, master classes Mars Hill (N.C.) Coll., 1981; debut in light opera as Gretchen in The Red Mill, Winston-Salem Opera Assn., 1947; debuts include: Rosalinda in Die Fledermaus, Piedmont Festival Opera Assn., 1949, Lola in Cavalleria Rusticana, Greensboro Opera Assn., 1951, Violetta in La Traviata, Greensboro Opera Assn., 1953, Fiordiligi in Cosi fan tutte, Piedmont Opera Co., 1956; appeared as Marguerite in Faust, Brevard Music Center Resident Opera Co., 1967, First Lady in The Magic Flute, Am. Inst. Mus. Studies, Graz, Austria, 1972; mem. Greensboro Oratorio Soc., 1955-59, soprano soloist in The Messiah, 1952, 58, The Creation, 1955, Solomon, 1958; soprano soloist Presbyterian Ch. of the Covenant, Greensboro, 1958-71; guest appearances Sta. WFMY-TV, Greensboro, 1958-62; soprano soloist with Greensboro Symphony Orch., 1964, 80, Eastern Music Festival Orch. 1965, St. Marguerite in Jeanne d'Arc (Honegger), 1980, Greensboro Chamber Orch., 1980; soloist in numerous recitals including: Wesleyan Coll., 1964, Roanoke Symphony Guild, 1967, Am. Inst. Mus. Studies, Austria, 1972, 78, U. N.C., Chapel Hill, 1974, 75, 76, 77, N.C. Mus. Art, 1978; dir. N.C. Lyric Opera Co., 1979; adjudicator N.C. High Sch. Honors Chorus Auditions, 1979. Bd. dirs. Music Theater Assos., Greensboro Friends of Music. Mem. Nat. Assn. Tchrs. of Singing (state gov. 1976-82, coordinator Mid-Atlantic regional artist award 1981, 82), Music Educators Nat. Conf., N.C. Fedn. Music Clubs (dir. 1956-58), Greensboro Music Tchrs. Assn. (pres. 1966-67), Symphony Guild (dir. 1977-78), Broadway Theater League (chmn. 1961-63), Civic Music Assn. (chmn. 1963-64). Presbyterian. Home: 3012 W Cornwallis Dr Greensboro NC 27408

RUSSELL, VICKI ROSEANN, educator; b. Houston, Sept. 15; d. Harry Chesson and Bennice (Vick) R.; B.A.T., Sam Houston State U., 1976. Tchr. lang. arts Kingwood (Tex.) Middle Sch., 1979—, head dept. history, 1979-80. Mem. Tex. Tchrs. Assn., NEA, Phi Mu. Baptist. Home: PO Box 411 Humble TX 77338

RUSSELL, VICKI SUE, newspaper pub.; b. Dodge City, Kans., Sept. 12, 1950; d. C. L. and Ellen Joyce R.; B.J., U. Mo., 1972, postgrad., 1972-75. Asst. instr. journalism U. Mo., 1974-76, asst. prof. communications and info. specialist, 1976-77; pub. Kingdom Daily Sun-Gazette, Fulton, Mo., 1977—; instr. journalism Westminster Coll., 1981. Pres. bd. dirs. Callaway County United Way, 1980-82; bd. dirs. Arrow Rock (Mo.) Lyceum Theater, Fulton Art League, Mid-Mo. chpt. Friends of Winston Churchill Meml. Recipient 1st place award for newsletters Am. Assn. Agr. Coll. Editors, 1977. Office: 115 5th St Fulton MO 65251

RUSSELL, VIRGINIA ADALINE, newspaper editor; b, Union, Iowa, June 2, 1918; d. Ernest and Clara (Whinery) Hauser; student Central Iowa Bus. Coll., 1938-39; m. Charles L. Russell, Oct. 12, 1961 (dec.). Sec. agy. dept. Modern Woodmen of Am., Rock Island, Ill., 1941-51, editor Agy. mag., 1945-61, asst. public relations dir., editor, 1951-61; with Farmer City (Ill.) Jour., 1961—, co-owner, 1961-77, editor, mgr., 1978—; co-owner DeWitt County Observer, Clinton, Ill., 1961-77. Mem. Farmer City C. of C. (pres. 1980), Am. Bus. Women's Assn., Ill. Press Assn. Republican. Christian Scientist. Home: 702 N John St Farmer City IL 61842 Office: 115 W Green St Farmer City IL 61842

RUSSELL, VIRGINIA DEGANAHL, public relations exec.; b. N.Y.C., Apr. 2, 1931; d. Joe and Josephine (Coombs) deGanahl; student Mt. Vernon Sem. and Coll., 1949-52, U. Calif. extension, George Washington U., 1951; m. Thomas Hale Russell, June 21, 1952; children—George, Sarah, Edward, Josephine, Charles, Michael, Kenneth. Mem. bd. Vt. Symphony Orch., Burlington, 1970-81; v.p. Dvorak Internat. Fedn., Brandon, Vt., 1976-79, pres., 1981—; art historian on Jacob van Ruisdael and 17th century Holland. Mem. Otter Valley (Vt.) Sch. Bd., 1976-77; bd. dirs. Girl Scouts U.S.A., 1967-69, Brandon chpt. Am. Cancer Soc., 1967-70, Hockey League, 1979-80. Mem. Am. Nat. Standards Inst. (chmn. com.) Democrat. Episcopalian. Clubs: Arts (Washington); Dutch-Am. Acad. Soc. (Boston). Home: 11 Pearl St Brandon VT 05733

RUSSELL, WILMA HAIL, elem. sch. prin.; b. Somerset, Ky., June 9, 1915; d. Robert L. and Amanda E. (Sears) Hail; B.S., Miami U., Oxford, Ohio, 1955, M.Ed., 1961; m. Virgil M. Russell, June 19, 1936; children—Betty Russell Zellner, Ben. Elem. sch. tchr., Ky. and Ohio, 1944-62; counselor, then dean of students George Washington Jr. High Sch., Hamilton, Ohio, 1962-73; prin. Pierce Elem. Sch., Hamilton, 1973—; vis. tchr., supr. student tchrs. Miami U., summers 1958-61; pres. Hamilton Tchrs. Club, 1955; sec. Hamilton Classroom Tchrs. Assn., 1964. Exec. dir. Butler County Easter Seal Soc. Crippled Children and Adults, 1979. Mem. Nat. Assn. Elem. Sch. Prins., Ohio Assn. Elem. Prins., Hamilton Elem. Prins. Assn., AAUP, PTA, Delta Kappa Gamma (chpt. pres. 1958-60). Republican. Methodist. Office: Pierce Elem Sch Hamilton OH 45015

RUSSO, IRMA HAYDEE ALVAREZ DE, pathologist; b. San Rafael, Mendoza, Argentina, Feb. 28, 1942; came to U. S., 1972, naturalized, 1982; d. Jose Maria and Maria Carmen (Martinez) de Alvarez; B.A., Escuela Normal M.T.S.M. de Balcarce, 1959; M.D., U. Nat. of Cuyo, Mendoza, 1970; m. Jose Russo, Feb. 8, 1969; 1 dau., Patricia Alexandra. Intern, Sch. of Medicine Hosps., Argentina, 1969-70; resident in pathology Wayne State U. Sch. Medicine, Detroit, 1976-80; research asst. and instr. Inst. of Histology and Embryology Sch. Medicine U. Nat. of Cuyo, 1963-71, assoc. prof. histology Faculty of Phys., Chem. and Math. Scis., 1970-72; research asso. Inst. for Molecular and Cellular Evolution, U. Miami, Fla., 1972-73; research asso. exptl. pathology lab. div. biol. scis., Mich. Cancer Found., Detroit, 1973-75, research scientist, 1975-76, vis. research scientist, 1976-82, pathologist, 1982—; chief resident physician dept. pathology Wayne State U. Sch. Medicine, 1978-80, asst. prof., 1980—; mem. staff Harper-Grace Hosps., Detroit, 1980-82; Rockefeller grantee, 1972-73; Nat. Cancer Inst. grantee, 1978-81; guest lectr. dept. obstetrics Sch. Medicine U. Nat. of Cuyo, 1965-71. Diplomate Am. Bd. Pathology. Mem. Am. Soc. Clin. Pathologists, Am. Assn. for Cancer Research, Mich. Soc. Pathologists, AMA, Electron Microscopy Soc. Am., Mich. Electron Microscopy Forum, Sigma Xi. Roman Catholic. Contbr. numerous articles on pathology to profl. jours. Office: 110 E Warren Ave Detroit MI 48201

RUSSO, KAREN SORLIE, lawyer; b. Grand Forks, N.D., Oct. 2, 1943; d. George Esterly and Elphie (Langen) Sorlie; B.A., U. N.D., 1963, postgrad., 1963-66; postgrad. Nat. U. Mexico, 1963-64; J.D., U. San Francisco, 1967; m. Salvatore B. Russo, Nov. 8, 1969; children—Peter Sorlie, Jacquelyn Joy. Fashion model, 1961-64; state chmn. N.D. Coll. Republicans, 1962; mem. N.D. exec. com. Rep. Party, 1962; regional v.p. Nat. Young Reps., 1963; research dir. Calif. Rep. Party, 1968; admitted to N.D. bar, 1968, Calif. bar, 1968; adminstrv. asst. to Calif. State Senator George Deukmejian, 1968-70; legal affairs analyst Calif. OEO, 1970; dep. atty. gen. for criminal appeals State of Calif., Sacramento, 1970-79; individual practice law, Sacramento, 1979-82; atty. U.S. Dept. Interior, Sacramento, 1982—; appellate justice McGeorge Sch. Law for moot ct. work; judge Calif. Hwy. Patrol moot ct. Chmn., Sacramento Libertarian Party, 1980-81; mem. Cathedral of Blessed Sacrament. Mem. Am. Trial Lawyers Assn., Am. Bar Assn., Women Lawyers Sacramento, Alpha Phi. Mem. Order Rainbow Girls. Clubs: Encorps, Ancil Hoffman Golf, Sacramento Ski. Author: California Fact Book, 1968; Budding Portia, 1975; recognized authority on fed. elections campaign act. Home: 6330 Palm Dr Carmichael CA 95608 Office: 1225 8th St Sacramento CA 95814

RUSSO, PATRICIA ANN, govt. adminstr.; b. Chgo., Oct. 19, 1951; d. Joseph and Louise Ann (Chiodo) Russo Broz; B.A., N. Ill. U., 1972; M.B.A., U. Ill., 1974. Contract adminstr. AEC, Argonne, Ill., 1974-75, ERDA, Argonne, 1975-77; contract specialist Dept. Energy, Argonne, 1977—. Bd. dirs. Lady Luck Prodns. Mem. Soc. Logistics Engrs. (program/membership chairperson), Assn. M.B.A. Execs., Am. Mgmt. Assn., Nat. Assn. Female Execs., Chgo. Phi Alpha Theta, Sigma Iota Epsilon, Alpha Xi Delta. Democrat. Roman Catholic. Club: Chgo. Cinema. Home: 6425 S Clarendon Hills Rd Willowbrook IL 60514 Office: 9800 S Cass Ave Argonne IL 60439

RUST, LIBBY KAREN, social services orgn. adminstr.; b. York, Maine, Feb. 8, 1951; d. Myron Davis and Meta Mildred (Libby) R.; B.A., Wheaton Coll., 1973; M.S., Columbia U., 1977. Day care field asst. Childhood Ednl. Enrichment Program, Waterville, Maine, 1974-75; cons. Center for Community Planning and Cons., N.Y.C., 1975-76; intern Morgan Guaranty Trust Co., N.Y.C., 1976; staff asst. subcom. on mental health Task Force on N.Y.C. Fiscal Crisis, 1976-77; auditor AT&T, N.Y.C., 1977; budget examiner Legis. Office of Budget Rev., N.Y.C., 1977-78; exec. dir. Strafford County Human Services, Dover, N.H., 1978-79; dir. allocations and agy. relations United Way, Inc., Portland, Maine, 1979-82, planning and allocations div. dir., 1982—. Mem. budget com. Town of York, 1979-80. Republican. Clubs: Portland Wheaton; N.Y. Golf and Tennis; York Golf and Tennis. Home: 102 Eastern Promenade Portland ME 04101

RUTAN, MARTY (MARTHA SOULLES), writer-photographer; b. Los Angeles, Feb. 22, 1921; d. Nicholas and Florence (Bond) Souleles; grad. Met. Sch. Bus., Los Angeles, 1939; grad. Sherwood Music Sch. Chgo., 1939; B.A., U. Minn., 1949; m. Bertram Harvey Rutan, Feb. 9, 1946; children—Marcia Ellen Rutan Drogin, Leslie Jean. Asso., Inst. Musical Art, Los Angeles, 1935-40; sec. to exec. in premium acctg. Pacific Mut. Life Ins. Co., Los Angeles, 1940-41; exec. sec. to pres. Universal Engring., Los Angeles, 1941-42; exec. sec. to dirs. Christian Servicemen's Center, Los Angeles, 1942-44; freelance writer, photographer, 1969—; contbns. include Clavier; scripts for TV's Laugh-In; Ladies Home Jour.; Seattle Post Intelligencer; The Oregonian; The Aberdeen Daily World; Laubach Literacy; Monday Morning mag.; Reader's Digest; The Congregationalist; public relations photography Gray's Harbor Coll., Aberdeen, Wash., 1974-77. Mem. Washington Press Women, Nat. Fedn. Press Women. Presbyterian-United Ch. of Christ. Address: 6546 18th NE Seattle WA 98115

RUTENBERG, BILLY BERMAN, civic worker; b. Chgo., Aug. 13, 1927; d. Kuafman Carl and Edna (Margolis) Berman; R.N., Mt. Sinai Hosp. Sch. Nursing, 1948; m. Feb. 24, 1947; children—Barry, Sharon, Jan. Vol., Clearwater (Fla.) Free Clinic, 1975-77, Morton Plant Hospital, Clearwater, 1971-78; bd. dirs. Clearwater YWCA, 1979—, council Girl Scouts, 1977-79; pres. Pinellas County Council P.T.A's, 1973-75; Region IX pres. Fla. PTA Bd., 1976-78; mem. adv. com. Pinellas County Bd. Public Instrn., 1970-78; pres. Temple B'nai Israel Sisterhood, 1977-79; chmn. social action Southeast Fedn. Temple Sisterhoods, 1978—. Mem. Suncoast C. of C. (edn. com. 1975-77), Dist. Nursing Assn., Women's Am. ORT, B'Nai B'rith Women, Hadassah. Democrat. Home: 18 S Pine Circle Clearwater Belleair FL 33516

RUTENBERG-ROSENBERG, SHARON LESLIE, journalist; b. Chgo., May 23, 1951; d. Arthur and Bernice (Berman) R.; student Harvard U. Summer Sch., 1972; B.A., Northwestern U., 1973, M.S.J., Medill Grad. Sch. Journalism, 1975; m. Michael J. Rosenberg, Feb. 3, 1980. Bus. mgr. Northwestern U. Yearbook, 1971-72; reporter-photographer Lerner Home Newspapers, Chgo., 1973-74; corr. Medill News Service, Washington, 1975; reporter-newsperson UPI, Chgo., 1975—; mem. exec. bd. Northwestern U. Student Adv. Council, 1972-73. Vol. worker Chgo.-Read Mental Health Center. Recipient Peter Lisagor award for exemplary journalism (Chgo. feature), 1980, 81; Golden Key award Nat. Adv. Bd. Children's Oncology Services Inc., 1981; hon. Ky. Col., 1982. Mem. Hadassah, Sigma Delta Chi, Sigma Delta Tau. Exclusive interviews include White House chief of staff, nation's only mother and son on death row. Home: 745 Marion Ave Highland Park IL 60035 Office: 360 N Michigan Ave Chicago IL 60601

RUTGERS, KATHARINE PHILLIPS (MRS. FREDERIK LODEWIJK RUTGERS), dancer; b. Butler, Pa., Sept. 2, 1910; d. Thomas Wharton and Alma (Sherman) Phillips; diploma Briarcliff Coll., 1928; student L'Hermitage, Versailles, France, 1929-30; pupil ballet Vera Trefilova, Paris, Carl Raimund, Vienna, Varga Troyanoff, Budapest; pupil modern dance with Iris Barbura, Bucharest Ballet, Vincenzo Celli, N.Y.C., Igor Schwezoff, N.Y.C., Mme Huapola, Hawaii, Jean Yazvinsky, N.Y.C.; m. Frederik Lodewijk Rutgers, Feb. 2, 1942; children—Alma Rutgers Bulazel, Corinne Rutgers Tolles. Performed dance concerts Bucharest, 1937-40, U.S., 1941—; repertoire includes religious, patriotic, dramatic, poetical dances; dance therapist St. Barnabas Hosp., N.Y.C., 1965-70. Chmn. ethnol. dance dept. Bruce Museum Assos., Greenwich, Conn., 1970—. Bd. dirs. Bruce Museum. Recipient citation for promoting culture with dance programs Nat. Fedn. Music Clubs, 1973. Mem. N.Y. Fedn. Music Clubs (chmn. dance dept. 1979-80), Nat. League Am. Pen Women (local pres. 1980—), Alliance Francaise, Sacred Dance Guild, Colonial Dames Am., D.A.R., Internat. Biog. Soc. Clubs: Regency (N.Y.C.), Indian Harbor (Greenwich, Conn.). Author numerous pamphlets on the dance, also verses for choreographies; styled nat. dances for stage. Home: La Cova Pecks Land Rd Greenwich CT 06830 Studio: 211 W 58th St New York NY 10023

RUTH, CAROL ANN, public relations exec.; b. N.Y.C., June 19, 1942; d. Edward B. and Dorothea (Beauman) McDonald; B.B.A. cum laude, CUNY, 1977; postgrad. N.Y.U. Corp. lending ofcl. Chase Manhattan Bank, 1965-68; with Hill & Knowlton, Inc., N.Y.C., 1968—, fin. relations v.p., 1975-78, sr. v.p., 1978—, dir. banking div., 1982—; lectr. Pace U., Marymount Coll., Syracuse U. Mem. Nat. Investor Relations Inst. (dir.), Fin. Communications Soc. (pres. N.Y. chpt., dir.). Home: 170 Rowayton Woods Rowayton CT 06853 Office: 420 Lexington Ave New York NY 10017

RUTH, DORIS MAY, savs. and loan co. exec.; b. Merchantville, N.J., June 2, 1928; d. Howard P. and C. Araeta (Longacre) Ruth; student Phila. Mus. Acad., 1946-53. Title search clerk Land Title Bank & Trust Co., Phila., 1946-50; acctg. clk. Bell Tel., Phila., 1950-53; teller Cheltenham Fed. Savs. & Loan Assn., Phila., 1953-55, bookeeper, 1955-57, head teller, 1957-73, comptroller, 1973-76, asst. v.p., personnel mgr., 1976—. Mem. Internat. Personnel Mgrs. Assn., Nat. Assn. Female Execs., Savs. Assn. Women's Soc. Office: 6425 Rising Sun Ave Philadelphia PA 19111

RUTKOWSKI, BARBARA LANG CONWAY, nurse; b. Hays, Kans., Aug. 12, 1945; d. Donald Robert and Hilda Mary (Rathke) Lang; B.S.N., U. Fla., 1966, M.N., 1968; m. Arthur Donald Rutkowski, July 8, 1968; children—Laura Mary, Michele Patrice, Cheryl Lynn. Team leader Shands Teaching Hosp. Coll. Nursing, U. Fla., Gainesville, 1966-67, service team leader, 1968-69, instr., clin. specialist, 1969-70; asst. dir. nursing, patient care coordinator Variety Children's Hosp., Miami, 1970-76; asst. prof., clin. specialist U. Evansville (Ind.), 1976-78; owner Nurse Consultation Services, Evansville, 1978—. Chmn. learning resources South Fla. Allied Health Manpower Consortium, 1971-74; mem. edn. com. Vanderburgh Mental Health Assn., 1977—; bd. dirs. Evansville Mus., 1979—, Legal Wives, 1978—, Plaza Park PTA, 1978—; active Jr. League Evansville. Recipient award U. Fla., 1968; Book of Yr. award Am. Jour. Nursing, 1978; NIMH trainee, 1965-66, USPHS trainee, 1967-68. Mem. Am. Nurses Assn., Nat. League Nursing, Mental Health Assn., Sigma Theta Tau, Phi Kappa Phi, Phi Kappa Theta, Alpha Lambda Delta. Author: Pediatric Neurological Nursing, 1977; Carini's and Owens Neurological and Neurosurgical Nursing, 1982; contbr. articles to profl. jours. Home and Office: 206 Charmwood Ct Evansville IN 47715

RUTLEDGE, PRISCILLA, tech. inst. ofcl.; b. White Oak, Ga.; d. Joe Robinson and Mary (Nelson) Smart; cert. Central State U. Garfield Tng. Center, 1959; student Miami Jacobs Jr. Coll., 1961-62; grad. Capital U., 1970; children—Tyrus Carter, Maurice Rutledge. Machine operator, timer Kurz-Kasch, Inc., Dayton, Ohio, 1955-69; clk. typist Chemineer, Inc., Dayton, 1970-71; placement dir. ITT Tech. Inst., Dayton, 1971—. Recipient 6 awards for outstanding placement performances. Mem. Miami Valley Personnel Assn., 2-Yr. Coll. Placement Assn., Nat. Assn. for Female Execs., Human Relations Council. Baptist. Club: Toastmistress. Address: 1904 Litchfield Ave Dayton OH 45406

RUTT, MELANIE GAY, educator; b. Gordonville, Pa., July 12, 1943; B.A., Millersville State Coll., 1970; m. Jan C. Rutt, June 21, 1966; children—Bryan Edward, Marcus Ian. Resource room aide Manheim Twp. Schs., 1980-81; project coordinator, asst. to dir. program for devel. intellectual potential Franklin and Marshall Coll., Lancaster, Pa., 1980-82; tutor Center for Academic Devel., Millersville State Coll., 1982; tchr. Jenkins Early Childhood Center, 1982—. Exhibited group shows, Lancaster Open Award Art Shows, 1979-81, Lancaster County Art Assn. Shows, 1979-81; represented in pvt. collections, U.S. Mem. Pa. Assn. Gifted Edn., Assos. Sisters of the Holy Cross, Lancaster County Art Assn., Holy Cross Alumnae of Sacred Heart Acad. (dir. 1980-81, corr. sec. 1978-80). Address: 80 Knollwood Dr Lancaster PA 17601

RUTTY, BRIDGET, systems analyst; b. Elmira, N.Y., Dec. 20, 1944; d. John Francis and Anna Mae (Sprague) R.; student public schs., Syracuse, N.Y. Computer operator Rae Oil Co., Rochester, N.Y., 1966-67; programmer Security Trust Co., Rochester, 1967-68; systems analyst SCM Corp., Syracuse, 1968—. Recipient Service award Data Processing Mgmt. Assn., 1977. Mem. U.S. Dressage Fedn., Data Processing Mgmt. Assn. (pres. chpt. 1975-76), Am. Assn. Individual Investors. Republican. Office: 3695 Erie Blvd E Syracuse NY 13159

RUYLE, ELIZABETH SMITH (BETH), assn. exec.; b. Atlanta, Oct. 26, 1946; d. Daniel Lester and Mae (Coley) Smith; B.A., U. Fla., 1968; M.P.A., U. Ga., 1975; 1 dau., Leigh Ann. Health planner Met. Council for Health, Atlanta, 1970-72; govtl. services coordinator Atlanta Regional Commn., 1972-75, govtl. relations coordinator, 1975-78; exec. dir. South Suburban Mayors' and Mgrs. Assn., Oak Forest, Ill., 1978—; interim dir. South Towns Agy. for Risk Mgmt., 1980—, South Suburban Cable Council, 1980—. Bd. dirs. Work Edn. Council for South Suburbs, FOCUS Council on South Suburbs; v.p. Work Edn. Council; mem. Cook County Housing Adv. Com. Mem. Internat. City Mgmt. Assn., Ill. City Mgmt. Assn., Met. Mgrs. Assn., Ill. Public Employer Labor Relations Assn., Public Risk and Ins. Mgmt. Assn., Chgo. Council on Fgn. Relations, Chgo. Assn. Commerce and Industry. Contbr. articles to profl. and devel. mags. Office: South Suburban Mayors and Mgrs Assn 15440 S Central Ave Oak Forest IL 60452

RYALL, JO-ELLYN M., psychiatrist; b. Newark, May 25, 1949; d. Joseph P. and Tekla (Paraszczuk) R.; B.A. in Chemistry with gen. honors, Douglass Coll., Rutgers U., 1971; M.D., Washington U., St. Louis, 1975. Resident in psychiatry Washington U., 1975-78, psychiatrist Student Health, 1980—, clin. instr. psychiatry, 1978—; impatient supr. Malcolm Bliss Mental Health Center, St. Louis, 1978-80, psychiatrist outpatient clinic, 1980-82; pvt. practice medicine specializing in psychiatry, St. Louis, 1980—. Bd. dirs. Women's Self Help Center, St. Louis, 1980—. Diplomate Am. Bd. Psychiatry and Neurology. Mem. Am. Psychiat. Soc. (pres. Eastern Mo. Dist. Br. 1983—), Am. Med. Women's Assn. (pres. St. Louis Dist. br. 1981-82), AMA, St. Louis Met. Med. Soc. (del. to state conv. 1981—). Roman Catholic. Club: Washington U. Faculty. Office: 1034 S Brentwood Suite 1160 Saint Louis MO 63117

RYALS, MARY JOHNSTON, assn. exec.; b. Pampa, Tex., Oct. 29, 1934; d. James Wayne and Olive Jo (Miller) Johnston; student Baylor U., 1953-54, Colo. Coll., 1956; m. Carthy R. Ryals, Sept. 5, 1953 (div.); children—R. Dawne, C. Ronway, Carthy R. Owner, mgr. Amarillo Travelodge, 1965-70; adminstrv. coordinator of continuing edn. U. Tex. Southwestern Med. Sch., Dallas, 1972-78; dir. postgrad. edn. San Diego Radiology Research & Edn. Found., 1978-82; pres. Ryals and Assos., 1982—; v.p. J2R Computer Software, 1979-82; v.p. Savvy Spouse, 1980-82. Recipient Merit award, Travelodge, 1965. Mem. Meeting Planners Internat. (dir. San Diego chpt. 1981-82), Nat. Assn. Female Execs., Inc., Profl. Conv. Mgmt. Assn., Am. Soc. Assn. Execs. Republican. Baptist. Club: Winners Circle. Office: PO Box 401336 Spring Valley Sta 13770 Noel Rd Dallas TX 75240

RYAN, ADRIANA FRIDA, accountant; b. Santiago, Chile, Mar. 22, 1949; came to U.S., 1964, naturalized, 1970; d. Hans Wolfgang and Ursula Maria (Zondek) Philippi; B.A. in Acctg., San Francisco State U., 1970; divorced. Staff acct. Richard T. Dwyer & Co., Daly City, Calif., 1970-72; staff acct., then mgr. Good & Fowler, C.P.A.s, South San Francisco, 1972-79, partner, 1979—, mng. partner, 1982—. Chmn. accts. div. Jewish Community Fedn. San Francisco, 1980-82. C.P.A., Calif. Mem. Am. Inst. C.P.A.s, Calif. Soc. C.P.A.s. Office: 262 Grand Ave South San Francisco CA 94080

RYAN, DOROTHY BARGER, writer; b. Lancaster, Pa., Oct. 24, 1942; d. Clay Miller and Dorothy Esther (Barger) R.; B.A. magna cum laude, Pa. State U., 1964, postgrad., 1964-65; postgrad. U. Del., 1980—; children by previous marriage—Lisa, Jon, Craig Miller. Freelance writer, 1970—; editor Subject Guide to Books in Print, R.R. Bowker & Co., Lancaster, Pa., 1961-65, Gotham Book Mart Monograph Series, 1977—; instr. English, Goldey Beacom Coll., Wilmington, Del., 1979-80; instr. English U. Del., 1980—, intern Office of Devel., 1981-82; exhibited rare Am. postcards Gotham Book Mart Gallery, 1976, Valentine postcards Rockwood Mus., Wilmington, Del., 1978. Named Woman of Yr., Postcard History Soc., 1979. Mem. Hist. Soc. Del., Chester County (Pa.) Hist. Soc., Lancaster County Hist. Soc., Del. Art Mus., Met. Postcard Collectors Club, S. Jersey Postcard Club, Deltiologists of Am., Phi Beta Kappa, Phi Kappa Phi, Sigma Tau Delta, Alpha Lambda Delta. Episcopalian. Author: Picture Postcards in the United States, 1893-1918, 1976, 2d edit., 1982; Philip Boileau Painter of Fair Women, 1980; contbr. numerous articles on postcards as hist. data to various mags.; contbr. revs. to publs. on antiques. Home: 91 Ritter Ln Newark DE 19711 Office: Dept English 204 Memorial Hall U Del Newark DE 19711

RYAN, ELEANORE A., clin. psychologist; b. Chgo.; B.S. with honors in Chemistry, Mundelein Coll.; Ph.D. in Clin. Psychology, Northwestern U., 1978; children—Robert, James, Mark, John, Christopher, Marynel. Staff psychologist Porter-Starke Services, Valparaiso, Ind., 1978-80; psychol. cons. Gary (Ind.) Community Mental Health Center, 1980-81; pvt. practice clin. and cons. psychology, Clarendon Hills, Ill., 1981—; mem. faculty Ill. Benedictine Coll., Elmhurst Coll. Cert. psychologist, Ill., Ind. Mem. Am. Psychol. Assn., Ill. Psychol. Assn., Midwest Psychol. Assn., Assn. DuPage Psychologists (sec.), Nat. Register Health Service Providers in Psychology. Roman Catholic. Home and office: 215 Coe Rd Clarendon Hills IL 60514

RYAN, ELLEN BOUCHARD, psycholinguist; b. Holyoke, Mass., Jan. 11, 1947; d. Raoul Rosaire and Etiennette Marie (Morin) Bouchard; B.A. in Math. and Linguistics, Brown U., 1968, M.A. in Linguists, 1968; Ph.D. in Psycholinguists, U. Mich., 1970; m. Patrick J. Ryan, July 12, 1969; children—Lorraine Yvette, Dennis Patrick, Kevin Myles. Asst. prof. psychology U. Notre Dame (Ind.), 1970-76, asso. prof., 1976-81, prof., 1981—, chmn. psychology dept., 1978—. Danforth fellow, 1968-70; Woodrow Wilson Hon. fellow, 1968-70; NSF fellow, 1968-70; NSF Research grantee, 1976-79; Nat. Inst. Child Health and Human Devel. grantee, 1972-75; Nat. Inst. Edn. grantee, 1979-82. Mem. Am. Psychol. Assn., Psychonomic Soc., Soc. Research in Child Devel., Am. Ednl. Research Assn. Roman Catholic. Editor: Attitudes Toward Language Variation: Social and Applied Contexts, 1982—; contbr. articles to profl. publs. Office: Dept Psychology Univ Notre Dame Notre Dame IN 46556

RYAN, GABRIELLE CONRAD, instrument co. exec.; b. Houston, Sept. 18, 1942; d. Prentice Gabrielle and Frederica Margaret (Moore) Conrad. Owner, Animal Kingdom Pet Shop, Houston, 1968-69; computer programmer Houston Instrument, Austin, Tex., 1971-74, software mgr., 1974-78, eastern regional sales mgr., 1978-81, product mgr., 1981—. Mem. Nat. Assn. Women Execs. (chmn. Austin chpt.), Tex. Women's Polit. Caucus, Nat. Computer Graphics Assn., Am. Congress Surveying and Mapping. Republican. Roman Catholic. Home: 6900 Columbia St Austin TX 78723 Office: 8500 Cameron St Austin TX 78723

RYAN, GRETCHEN MARGARETE FRIEDA, artist; b. Niederschoena, Saxon, Germany, Nov. 2, 1929; came to U.S., 1952, naturalized, 1957; d. Paul Robert and Frieda Gertrud (Kupsch) Luetzner; A.A., Hoehre Handelsschule, 1948; student Berlin Art Acad., 1970, Mich. Coll., 1960-61, Cerro Coso, 1972-74, Am. River Coll., 1975; pvt. art studies in Germany; m. Raymond A. Ryan, May 12, 1952; children—Michael D., Ralph T., Robert Ph., Ronald J., Rex W., Renee G. Art instr. McClellan AFB, 1967, Am. Women's Club Berlin, 1969-72, AYA Berlin, 1969-72, Edwards AFB, 1972-74; art instr. Am. River Coll. and San Juan Sch. Dist., 1975—; art instr. Sr. Citizens Centers, Fair Oaks Park Dist; vol. tchr. sr. citizens; operator art workshop retreats; works exhibited Cunningham Meml. Art Gallery traveling art exhibit, 1973-74; works rep. maj. shows in No. Calif., 1974-78; sr. signature artist No. Calif. Arts, Inc. Named Air Force Wife of Year for Berlin, 1971; recipient Community Service award U.S. Comdr. in Berlin, 1972, Air Force Purchase award, 1976. Mem. Highlands Artists Guild (v.p. 1969), Desert Art Assn. (v.p.), No. Calif. Art Assn. (pres.). Democrat. Roman Catholic. Club: Am. Women's (Berlin). Home and Office: 6225 Luna Ln Carmichael CA 95608

RYAN, JOYCE EUGENIA, govt. ofcl.; b. Hattiesburg, Miss., Oct. 22, 1926; d. Lamont M. and Lillie Mae (Chambliss) Lacy; student Miss. State U., 1978, U. So. Miss., 1980—; m. John S. Ryan, Sr., July 4, 1951; 1 dau. by previous marriage, Judy Gayle Ladner; 1 stepson, John S. Ryan. Sec. asst. Brandon & Long Ins. Agy., Gulfport, Miss., 1943-44; credit mgr. Bradley Jewelry, Gulfport, 1944-50, Peacock Jewelry, Biloxi, Miss., 1950-53; partner Stop & Shop Grocery, Biloxi, 1953-56; with U.S. Air Force, 1956—, mil. family housing project mgr., Keesler AFB, Miss., 1981—. Am. Cancer Soc. dr. chmn., 1953; mem. Biloxi Civic Council, 1953-56, pres., 1955; sec. lay adv. com. Biloxi Sch. Bd., 1957; mem. Harry S. Truman Library Com., 1977-79. Recipient Outstanding Performance award U.S. Air Force, 1960, Superior Performance award, 1975, Outstanding Achievement award, 1981. Mem. Hotel, Motel, Restaurant Assn., Nat. Geog. Soc., Nat. Pest Control Assn., Miss. Pest Control Assn., Am. Assn. Ret. Persons, Smithsonian Inst., Fed. Mgrs. Assn., Profl. Housing Mgmt. Assn., Nat. Assn. Female Execs. Clubs: Trade and Indsl. (pres. 1945), Bus. and Profl. Women's, Les Donsuers Carninal Assn., Les Femmes Carninal Assn., Elks. Home: 1672 Lopez Pl Biloxi MS 39530 Office: 3380 CES/DEHH Keesler AFB MS 39534

RYAN, JUDITH LYNDAL, educator; b. Sydney, Australia, Apr. 6, 1943; d. William Matthew and Kathleen (Ferris) O'Neil; B.A. with honors, U. Sydney, 1964; Dr.Phil., U. Muenster (W.Ger.), 1970; m. Lawrence Ryan, Feb. 24, J964; children—Antony Lawrence, Vanessa Lyndal. Mem. faculty Smith Coll., 1967—, prof., 1980—, now Doris Silbert prof. humanities; vis. asso. prof. Brown U., 1979-80. Mem. MLA, Am. Assn. Tchrs. German, New Eng. MLA, AAUP. Author: Umschlag and Verwandlung: Rilkes Lyrik dermittleren Periode, 1972; also articles. Office: Dept German Smith Coll Northampton MA 01063

RYAN, LAVONNE BLINDERMAN, speech pathologist; b. Southampton, N.Y., Aug. 2, 1932; d. Leo M. and Gwen (Smith) Blinderman; B.S., SUNY, Buffalo, 1954; M.A., Coll. St. Rose, 1963; postgrad. SUNY, Albany, 1963; m. F. Paul Ryan, July 4, 1955; children—Kathleen Ryan Goodwin, Laura Marie, Scott Paul. Speech therapist Buffalo Public Schs., 1954; speech lang. therapist Norfolk (Va.) Cerebral Palsy Center, 1955, 56, Bethlehem Central Sch. Dist., Delmar, N.Y., 1969-74; supr. clin. practicum, dept. speech pathology and audiology SUNY, Albany, 1975-76; chief ednl. therapist VA Hosp., Albany, N.Y., 1977; speech lang. pathologist South Colonie Sch. Dist., Albany, 1978—; pvt. practice speech pathology, 1958-69. Bd. dirs. YWCA, 1962-70. Mem. 3d Dist. Dental Soc. Aux. (dir. 1959-69), Am. Speech and Hearing Assn., N.Y. State Speech Lang. Hearing Assn., Kappa Delta Pi. Home: 49 Thorndale Rd Slingerlands NY 12159 Office: 100 Hackett St Albany NY 12205

RYAN, LOYE MARIE, psychologist; b. Flandreau, S.D., Jan. 16, 1941; d. William F. and Catherine (Gage) Johnson; B.A., Moorhead State U., 1971, M.A., 1973; Ed.D., U. S.D., 1976; m. Robert A Ryan, Dec. 15, 1963; children—Catherine, Carolyn, Robert, Jennifer. Counselor, Am. Indian students Moorhead (Minn.) State U., 1971-73, U. S.D., 1975-76; research asso. U. Wash., 1976-77; scholar in residence Nat. Center Am. Indian and Alaska Native Mental Health, Portland, Oreg., 1977-79; profl. tng. and devel. cons., exec. dir. Personal, Ednl. and Profl. Services, Inc., Portland, 1978-80; supr. Urban Indian Mental Health Clinic; counseling psychology, 1980—. Pres. swim team parent club Mittleman Jewish Community Center, also mem. aquatics bd.; pres. bd. dirs. Mental Health Services West. Ford. Found. fellow, 1973-76. Mem. Soc. Indian Psychologists (v.p.), Am. Psychol. Assn., Mental Health Counselors Assn. Home: 3365 SW Miles St Portland OR 97219

RYAN, MARILYN GRAMS, state legislator; b. Milbank, S.D., Dec. 10, 1932; d. Theodore G. and Harriet Evelyn (Johnson) Grams; student Los Angeles Community Coll., 1950-52, Calif. State U., Dominguez Hills, 1966-67; children—Cynthia Ryan Brickner, Stephanie Kristine. Mem. Calif. Assembly, 1976—; mayor Rancho Palos Verdes, Calif., 1973-76. Mem. LWV (state dir. 1971-73), Calif. Elected Women's Assn. (pres. 1978-79). Office: State Capitol Sacramento CA 95814

RYAN, MARLEIGH GRAYER, ednl. adminstr.; b. N.Y.C., May 1, 1930; d. Harry and Betty (Hurwick) Grayer; B.A., N.Y. U., 1951; M.A., Columbia U., 1956, cert. E. Asian Inst., 1956, Ph.D. (Ford fellow), 1965; m. Edward Ryan, June 3, 1950; 1 son, David Patrick. Lectr., asst. prof., asso. prof. Japanese, Columbia U., N.Y.C., 1960-72; chmn. dept. Asian langs. and lit. U. Iowa, Iowa City, 1972-81, asso. prof., 1972-75, prof., 1975-81; dean Liberal Arts and Scis., prof. Japanese, SUNY, New Paltz, 1981—. Japan Found. fellow, 1973. Mem. Assn. Asian Studies (dir. 1975-78), Assn. Tchrs. of Japanese (sec. 1962-71), AAUP, MLA (del. assembly 1979-81, exec. com. Asian lit. 1981—). Author: Japan's First Modern Novel, 1965; The Development of Realism in the Fiction of Tsubouchi Shoyo, 1975; editor Jour. Assn. Tchrs. of Japanese, 1971-75. Office: FT614 SUNY New Paltz NY 12561

RYAN, MARTHA JANE, nurse; b. Corning, N.Y., Oct. 5, 1950; d. George Alvin and Barbara Jane (Miller) Haar; B.S., D'Youville Coll., 1973; m. Pierce John Ryan, Sept. 1, 1973; children—Briget Moira, Patrick Alvin. Staff nurse VA Hosp., Syracuse, N.Y., 1973-75; nursing instr. Loretto Geriatric Center, Syracuse, 1975-76, asst. dir. nursing, 1976-79, acting dir. nursing, 1979-81; infection control practitioner Center for Disease Control, Atlanta, 1981; endoscopy nurse Community Gen. Hosp., Syracuse, 1982—. Mem. Am. Gerontologic Soc. Democrat. Roman Catholic. Home: 127 Bennington Dr Syracuse NY 13205

RYAN, MARY JANE MARIE, clin. psychologist; b. Summit, N.J., Nov. 20, 1955; d. Paul Benedict and Thelma Racie (McCardle) R.; B.A. in Psychology/Sociology, Allegheny Coll., 1977; M.A. in Clin. Psychology, Radford U., 1979. Clin intern Meadville (Pa.) Mental Health Clinic, 1976-77; intern Devereux Found., Devon, Pa., 1979-80, clin. psychologist, 1980—, supr. pre and post-doctoral psychology interns, 1980—, developer/coordinator staff inservice tng. program Edward L. French div., 1981—. Mem. Am. Psychol. Assn., Soc. for Personality Assessment, Psi Chi, Kappa Alpha Theta. Office: 119 Old Lancaster Rd Devon PA 19333

RYAN, MARY JO, mass communications exec.; b. Lodi, Wis., Sept. 12, 1940; d. Herold Eugene and Lois Josephine (Carncross) R.; B.A., U. Wis., Madison, 1962; postgrad. in pub. relations U. Wis., 1971; 1 son, Rodney Alan. News editor Sun Prairie (Wis.) Star Countryman, 1962; in pub. relations Miller Brewing Co., Milw., 1963; pub. info. officer U. Wis., Madison, 1964-71; advt. mgr. Blue Shield, Madison, 1972-74; market communications mgr. Borg Warner Chems. Internat. Center, Parkersburg, W.Va., 1975-79; dir. communications Ohio Med. Products, Madison, 1979—. Mem. Bus. and Profl. Advt. Assn., Sales and Mktg. Execs., Women in Communications, Pi Kappa Delta, Mu Kappa Tau. Home: 7214 Colony Dr Madison WI 53717 Office: 3030 Airco Dr Madison WI 53707

RYAN, MARY PATRICIA, historian; b. Prairie du Chien, Wis., Jan. 12, 1945; d. Patrick H. and Marguerite H. R.; B.A., U. Wis., 1967, M.A., 1968; Ph.D., U. Calif., Santa Barbara, 1971. Asst. prof. Pitzer Coll., Claremont, Calif., 1971-72; asst. prof. to asso. prof. SUNY, Binghamton, 1972-79; prof. history U. Calif., Irvine, 1980—. Recipient Bancroft prize for book in Am. history, Am. Hist. Assn., 1982; Berkshire prize, 1982; award for best article Am. Quar., 1979; Rockefeller Found. fellow, 1974-75; Am. Council Learned Socs. fellow, 1982; Nat. Endowment Humanities fellow, 1973. Mem. Am. Hist. Assn., Orgn. Am. Historians, Berkshire Conf. Women Historians. Author: Womanhood in America from Colonial Times to the Present, 1975; Cradle of the Middle Class: The Families of Oneida County, New York 1790-1865, 1981; The Empire of the Mother: American Writing About Domesticity 1830-1860, 1982; editor Feminist Studies, 1974-82. Office: Dept History U Calif Irvine CA 92717

RYAN, NANCY JEAN, hotel exec.; b. Chgo., Nov. 25, 1952; d. Edward Charles Ryan and Mary (Simpson) Ryan Townsend; student John Carroll U., 1970-72, Rome Center of Loyola U. of Chgo., 1972-73; B.S. in Mktg./Bus. Adminstrn., Bradley U., 1974. Reservations mgr. Ambassador West Hotel, Chgo., 1975-78, asst. exec. mgr., 1978-79; front office mgr. Tremont Hotel, Chgo., 1979-80; front office mgr. Mayfair Regent Hotel, Chgo., 1980-81, sales rep./corp. accounts, 1981-82; sales mgr. Grand Met. and Forum hotels, 1982—. Active Stritch Sch. Medicine Jr. Service League, 1969—, Presentation Ball Jr. Aux., Chgo., 1970, Northwestern Meml. Hosp. Service Bd., 1978—, Presbyterian-St. Luke's Hosp. Vol. Services, Chgo., 1981—; mem. Landmarks Preservation Council Ill., 1982—; mem. Gov. James R. Thompson Re-election Com., 1979, 82. Named to Outstanding Young Women Am., 1982. Mem. Hotel Front Office Execs. Assn. (sec.-treas. 1979-80), Nat. Assn. Female Execs., Ill. Opera Guild, Chgo. Drama League, Hotel Sales Mgmt. Assn., Midwest Passenger Traffic Assn. Clubs: Jr. League Chgo., Chgo. Travel Women's. Home: 1550 N Lake Shore Dr Chicago IL 60610

RYAN, NANCY TATE, accountant; b. Atascadero, Calif., Apr. 18, 1940; d. Henry Webb and Marjorie (Phillips) Tate; B.A., U. Calif., Berkeley, 1963; M. Acctg., U. Denver, 1978; m. J. Mack Ryan, Nov. 29, 1963; children—Steven Ryan, Kirk Ryan. Tax auditor IRS, San Francisco and Bakersfield, Calif., 1963-67, 70-74; staff acct. Meeks, Eyherabide & Albert Accts., Inc., Bakersfield, 1975-77; gen. acctg. mgr. Tosco, Bakersfield, Calif., 1979-81; prin. Nancy T. Ryan, C.P.A., 1981—. NIMH fellow, 1978. Mem. Am. Inst. C.P.A.s, Calif. Soc. C.P.A.s, Am. Women's Soc. C.P.A.s, Am. Soc. Women Accts., Nat. Assn. Accts. Home: 6024 Friant Dr Bakersfield CA 93309

RYAN, SONJA LEE, med. social worker; b. Orange City, Iowa, Aug. 2, 1937; d. Albert Lee Gerard and Clarice Victoria (Brown) deBey; B.A., Western Md. Coll., 1959; M.S.W., U. Md., 1973; m. Richard J. Gebhardt, June 6, 1959; children—Russell, Cheryl, Kurt; m. 2d, George W. Ryan, Dec. 28, 1968; 1 dau., Alanna (dec.). Caseworker, Springfield State Hosp., Sykesville, Md., 1959-61; dir. social work dept. Hanover (Pa.) Gen. Hosp., 1966—; cons. Golden Age Nursing Home, Hanover, 1973-76, Carlisle (Pa.) Hosp., 1974-78, Hanover Vis. Nurse Assn., 1977—; mem. social work adv. council Western Md. Coll., 1979—. Bd. dirs. Hospice of York, 1980—, Hanover chpt. ARC, 1976-79, Adams-Hanover Mental Health, 1973-76; pres. Human Services Orgn., 1980; treas. Hanover Community Progress Com., 1976-80; mem. Adams-Hanover Sheltered Workshop Com., 1968-70; bd. dirs. Hanover Community Players, 1974-77, sec., 1982; organizer local chpt. Make Today Count and Preemie Parent Support Group, 1979—; initiator Children's Cardiac Fund, 1979; mem. Hanover Oratorio Soc., 1964—; active YWCA, 1979—; mem. vestry All Saints Episcopal Ch., 1973-74, 76-79, vestry sec., 1975, diocesan del. Central Pa., 1978, 80, 81, 82. mem. alter guild, 1968—, treas. ch. women, 1979—. Recipient York Daily Record Exceptional Citizen award, 1979, Spl. Recognition cert. Col. Richard McAllister chpt. DAR, 1980. Mem. Nat. Assn. Social Workers, Acad. Cert. Social Workers, Soc. Hosp. Social Work Dirs., Central Pa. Hosp. Social Workers. Clubs: Order Eastern Star, YMCA Jr. Women's. Home: 109 Frederick St Hanover PA 17331 Office: Hanover Gen Hosp 300 Highland Ave Hanover PA 17331

RYCHECK, JAYNE BOGUS (MRS. R. RICHARD RYCHECK), ret. ednl. adminstr.; b. Schenectady; d. Peter and Sylvia (Cywinski) Bogus; M.A., N.Y. U., 1953; B.S., State U. N.Y., Albany, 1941; postgrad. Syracuse U., 1957-66; m. R. Richard Rycheck, July 26, 1942. Tchr. various schs., 1935-43; elementary sch. tchr. Schenectady (N.Y.) City Schs., 1943-51, leadership intern, 1951-52, elementary sch. prin., 1952-61, dir. spl. edn., 1961-72. Instr. Russell Sage Coll., 1955-58, State U. N.Y., Oneonta, 1956; cons. bur. handicapped children N.Y. Edn. Dept., 1966-76, mem. commrs. and hoc coms., 1964-72, State Planning Com. Insts. for In-Service Edn., 1964-67; rep. to Community Welfare Council Schenectady County, 1961-62; adv. council N.Y. State Joint Legislative Com. Mental and Phys. Handicapped, 1970-72; mem. adv. com. Schenectady County Office for Aging, 1976—, vice chmn., 1977-78, chmn., 1978-80; advisory com. Older Ams. Act program N.Y. State Office of Aging, 1977-80. Trustee, chmn. edn. Schenectady Mus., 1974-77. Recipient Humanitarian service awards United Cerebral Palsy Schenectady County, 1966, 67, Capital dist. Assn. for Brain-Injured Children, 1967; Meritorious Alumni award State U. N.Y. Coll. at Oneonta, 1972; Capitol Dist. Speech and Hearing award, 1972; Distinguished Service award N.Y. Fedn. chpts. Council for Exceptional Children, 1972; Joseph P. Kennedy, Jr. Found. award for outstanding activity for the mentally retarded, 1972, achievement award for contbns. to quality of life for sr. citizens N.Y. State Legislature, 1979; Disting. Service award Council Adminstrs. Spl. Edn., 1980. Mem. N.Y. State (sec. 1967-68), Nat. councils adminstrs. spl. edn., Assn. Childhood Edn. (state sec. 1952-55, state exec. bd. 1951-59), Council Exceptional Children (mem. chpt. regional and state bds. 1966-78, state regional dir. 1966-68, state adv. bd. 1966-72, v.p. 1968-69, state pres. 1970), Schenectady County Assn. Childhood Edn. (treas. and v.p. 1952), N.Y. State Assn. Childhood Edn. Internat. (sec., v.p. 1962-65), Am. Assn. Mental Deficiency, N.Y. State Assn. Brain-Injured Children (state adv. bd. 1963-67, dist. adv. bd. 1966-72), Nat. Soc. Autistic Children, Assn. Retarded Children (adv. bd.), Gifted Children Soc. (adv. com.), Schenectady C. of C. (edn. com.), Schenectady County Ret. Tchrs. Assn. (v.p. 1973, pres. 1974-76), Am. Assn. Ret. People (program com. chpt. 1973-76), AAUW (topic chmn. 1977-79), N.Y. Assn. Elementary Prins. (hon. life), N.Y. State Ret. Tchrs. Assn. (county dir. Eastern zone, del. state conv. 1974-76), Delta Kappa Gamma (chmn. chpt. profl. affairs com. 1972-76, del. state legis. forum 1974-79, mem. state com. profl. affairs 1974-75). Contbr. articles to publs. Home: 1537 Kingston Ave Schenectady NY 12308

RYDER, GEORGIA ATKINS, educator; b. Newport News, Va., Jan. 30, 1924; d. Benjamin Franklin and Mary Lou (Carter) Atkins; B.S., Hampton (Va.) Inst., 1944; Mus.M., U. Mich., 1946; Ph.D., N.Y. U., 1970; m. Noah Francis Ryder, Sept. 16, 1947; children—Olive Diana, Malcolm Eliot, Aleta Renee. Resource music tchr., Alexandria, Va., 1945-48; faculty music dept. Norfolk State U., 1948—, prof., 1970—, head dept., 1969-79, dean Sch. Arts and Letters, 1979—; mem. music panel Nat. Endowment for Arts. Bd. dirs. Va. Orch. Group, Inst. Research in Black Am. Music, Norfolk Commn. Arts and Humanities; mem. advisory com. Norfolk chpt. Young Audiences. Grantee So. Fellowship Fund, 1967-69, Consortium Research Tng., 1973; recipient award Norfolk Com. Improvement Edn., 1974. Mem. Music Educators Nat. Conf., Nat. Assn. Tchrs. Singing, Coll. Music Soc. (council), Intercoll. Music Assn., Va. Music Educators Assn., Assn. Study Afro-Am. Life and History, Delta Sigma Theta. Contbr. articles to profl. jours. Office: Norfolk State U Norfolk VA 23504

RYERSON, MARGERY A., artist; b. Morristown, N.J., Sept. 15, 1886; A.B., Vassar Coll.; student Art Students League, with Robert Henri, also with Charles Hawthorne, Provincetown, Mass. Dealer, Grand Central Art Galleries, N.Y.C., Chapellier Galleries, N.Y.C.; exhibited group shows Vassar Coll. Gallery, French Mus., Seattle, Met. Mus. Art, N.Y.C., Philbrook Art Center, Tulsa, Bibliot Nat., Paris, Allied Artists Am., N.Y.C., 1971, 77, N.J. Watercolor Soc., Morristown, 1971, Am. Watercolor Soc., 1972, 76, NAD and Audubon Artists, 1972, 74. Recipient Maynard prize, NAD, 1959, Hook prize, Am. Watercolor Soc., 1962, Silver Medal, Nat. Arts Club, 1971. Mem. Audubon Artists (corr. sec. 1958-59, recording sec.), Am. Soc. Graphic Artists (recording sec.), Allied Artists Am. (v.p. 1952-53), NAD, Am. Watercolor Soc., Allied Artists Am., N.J. Watercolor Soc., Nat. Arts Club. Illustrator: Winkie boo, 1948. Address: 15 Gramercy Park S New York City NY 10003 *

RYLAND, CHACHI PAGANO, business ofcl.; b. Camagüey, Cuba, Jan. 9, 1938; came to U.S., 1938; d. Nicholas and Pearl (Norman) Pagano; B.A. (Altrusca Club scholar), U. Fla., 1959; M.S., U. So. Calif., 1979; m. Walter Moncure Ryland, III, Aug. 27, 1961; children—William Norman, Robert Walter, Ada Virginia. Mathematician, RCA, Cape Canaveral, Fla., 1960-62; supervisory acct., Verdun, France, 1963-64; programmer/analyst Macro Services Corp., Boston, 1968-69; computer specialist U.S. Army Computer Systems Command, Ft. Eustis, Va., 1970-71; programmer/analyst Nev. Power Co., Las Vegas, 1974-75; cons. data processing, Yuba City, Calif., 1976-79; systems engr. Electronic Data Systems Corp., Dallas, 1979-81, system mgr., 1981—. Mem. Yuba City Ad Hoc Com. on Status of Women, 1977; mem. Sutter County (Calif.) Welfare Adv. Bd., 1977; bd. dirs. Women's Issues Network, Dallas, 1980—. Recipient cert. of achievement U.S. Army Computer Systems Command, 1971. Mem. Data Processing Mgmt. Assn., Am. Mgmt. Assns. Democrat. Developed program to facilitate locating data on magnetic disks, 1975. Home: 4024 Fechin Circle Plano TX 75023 Office: 7171 Forest Ln Dallas TX 75230

RYLES, NANCY, Oreg. state rep.; b. Portland, Oreg., Dec. 18, 1937; d. William Dunn and Madlyn (Nutting) Wyly; student Willamette U., Oreg., 1955-56, Portland State U., 1969-72; m. Vernon B. Ryles, Jr., 1957; children—Scott, Ashley. Mem., Beaverton Dist. 48 Sch. Bd., Oreg., 1972-78; mem. Gov.'s Commn. Status Women, 1973-75; mem. state adv. council Career & Vocat. Edn., 1975-78; mem. Oreg. Ho. Reps., 1979—. Recipient Oreg. Edn. Assn. Human Rights award, 1974; Excellence in Action award, Delta Kappa Gamma, 1976; First Citizen award, Beaverton, 1977; Disting. Service award Oreg. Vocat. Assn., 1978. Mem. Beaverton C. of C. (dir.), Washington County Pub. Affairs Forum, Oreg. Women's Polit. Caucus. Office: Oreg Ho Reps State Capitol Salem OR 97310 *

RYMER, GRACE MCNUTT, floral design cons.; b. Knoxville, Tenn., Nov. 20, 1915; d. George Edgar and Daisy (Fox) McNutt; student Brailey Music Studio, U. Tenn., 1930-35, Tenn. Wesleyan Art Dept., 1942-45, Chadek Conservatory, U. Chattanooga, 1942-46, N.Y. Sch. Interior Design, 1965, Ohara Sch. Floral Design (Tokyo), 1965, Rob Thomas Abstract Design, 1966; m. Marvin Joseph Rymer, Oct. 29, 1947 (dec. Sept. 1968); children—Edwin Frank, Christopher Joseph. Freelance floral designer, cons., 1950—; exhibited Internat. Flower Show, N.Y., 1957-70; assisted in decorations for Pres. Nixon's Inaugural Balls, Rose Bowl Parade, 1965, Miss Am. Pageant, 1962-63; mem. Everette Conklin Design team, 1957—; lectr. in U.S., Can., 1970, Japan, 1973, 77, Lisbon, Portugal, 1973; artist, commentator design sch. programs throughout U.S. Pres., Am. Cancer Soc., 1969-70. Bd. dirs., chmn. Bradley County Nursing Home; bd. dirs. Tenn. Cancer Soc. Recipient Silver trophy Nat. Flower Show, Washington, 1958, Purple award Federated Garden Club, 1959, 74, Silver trophy Internat. Flower Show, 1962-78, 1st award Nat. Orchid Growers, 1966, Sylvia award Expose, Balt., 1967, Disting. Service award Nat. Council State Garden Clubs, 1979, Tenn. State Florists Assn. Mem. Am. Act Florists (nat. bd. 1972—), Am. Inst. Floral Designers, Profl. Floral Commentators Internat., Cleveland Garden Club (nat. life and state life mem., pres. 1971-72), 3d Dist Garden Club (dir. 1957-58, 71-72). Author: Floral Design Art, 1963; (booklet) Drying Flowers in Microwave, 1978; contbr. articles to trade jours. Home: 1755 N Ocoee St Cleveland TN 37311

RYNIEWICZ, W. SHERRY RINEHART, cons.; b. Weehawken, N.J., Aug. 5, 1931; d. Warren Andrew and Marion Wilhelmina (Jonghaus) Rinehart; student U. Hartford, 1973—; children—Douglas, Dwight, Desiree, Debra-Lee. With Saks Fifth Ave, N.Y.C., 1955-56, Witco Chem. Co., Paramus, N.J., 1960-62, Gen. Motors Co., Englewood Cliffs, N.J., 1963-64, Green Manor Constrn. Co., Manchester, Conn., 1967-68, Sears, Roebuck & Co., Manchester, 1968-72; dir. payroll U. Hartford, 1972-82; cons., 1982—. Asst. chmn. publicity Guild of Our Lady of St. Bartholomew, 1969-70; chmn. scholarship fund U. Hartford Women's League; bd. dirs. Central Conn. Tchrs. Credit Union, chmn. credit com. Democrat. Roman Catholic. Club: U. Hartford Faculty. Home and Office: 40 Bloomfield Ave Windsor CT 06095

RYTTING, EMMA NAVAJAS, govt. ofcl.; b. Ponce, P.R., Mar. 26, 1947; d. Cesar Francisco and Emma Mercedes (Souffront) Navajas; B.A. magna cum laude (scholar 1964-67), Catholic U. P.R., 1967, J.D. magna cum laude (scholar 1968-71), 1971; m. Arthur James Rytting, Jan. 26, 1973. Asst. prof. history Cath. U. P.R., 1967-68, 69; admitted to P.R. bar, 1971, U.S. Supreme Ct. bar, 1977, D.C. bar, 1978; trial atty. criminal div. Dept. Justice, 1971-73; law enforcement program lectr. I, Harford Community Coll., Athens, Greece, 1973-74; atty.-adv., then gen. counsel P.R. Fed. Affairs Adminstrn., Washington, 1977-79, dep. dir., 1979-81, dir., 1981—; speaker in field. Mem. Am. Bar Assn., Fed. Bar Assn., P.R. Bar Assn., Phi Alpha Theta, Alpha Mu Gamma, Phi Alpha Delta. Republican. Roman Catholic. Home: 7615 Carissa Ln Laurel MD 20810 Office: 734 15th St NW Washington DC 20005

SAARI, DOROTHY REYNOLDS, mfg. co. exec.; b. Bedford, Va., Aug. 1, 1937; d. Royston Hamilton and Elsie Vivian (Burch) Reynolds; student Phillips Bus. Coll., 1955; m. Harold James Saari, Nov. 14, 1958; 1 dau., Conya Jean. With Owens-Ill., Inc., Jasper, Tex., 1955—, personnel dir., 1976—. Methodist. Club: Pilot (gov. 1979-80, dir. 1982—). Home: Route 5 111 Lakewood Dr Jasper TX 75951

SABA, ALEXANDRA A., psychologist; b. B.S. with honors, No. Ariz. U., 1970, M.A. in Psycholinguistics, 1972; M.C. Counseling Psychology, Ariz. State U., 1978; Ph.D., Psychol. Studies Inst., 1980. Linguist, Bur. of Indian Affairs, Kayenta, Ariz., 1969-70; chmn. English dept. Paradise Valley Sch. Dist., Ariz., 1971-78; sch. psychologist Phoenix South Mental Health Clinic, 1977-78; adolescent program supr. Ariz. State U., Tempe, 1976-78; instr. Maricopa County (Ariz.) Community Coll., 1975-78; v.p., psychologist Drake-Beam-Morin, Inc., San Francisco, 1979—; founder Mountain Bell Pioneer's Adult Edn. Fgn. Lang. Program, 1971. Mem. Republican Womens Caucus, 1976—; bd. dirs. Planned Parenthood, Tempe, Tempe Women's Center, South Mountain Free Clinic. Mem. Am. Psychol. Assn., Nat. Assn. Female Execs., Bay Area Exec. Women's Forum (edn. dir.), Bus. and Profl. Womens Club, San Francisco Symphony Guild, San Francisco Ballet, Phi Kappa Phi, Pi Beta Phi. Contbr. articles to profl. jours. Office: 417 Montgomery St Suite 502 San Francisco CA 94104

SABATINI, MARIA THERESA, pathologist; b. Argentina, Feb. 10, 1939; d. David and Delphina E. Sabatini; m. Meldonado-Calfon, Aug. 8, 1967; children—Thomas, Theresa, Marcelle. Resident in pathology N.Y. U. and Bellevue Hosp., N.Y.C., 1969-72, attending physician in pathology, 1972-75; surg. pathologist Cabrini Med. Center, N.Y.C., 1975—; clin. asst. prof. pathology N.Y. U., N.Y. Med. Coll. Diplomate Am. Bd. Pathology; cert. clin. lab. dir., N.Y. State. Fellow Coll. Am. Pathologists, N.Y. Acad. Medicine. Club: Wykagyl Country (New Rochelle, N.Y.). Office: 227 E 19th St New York NY 10003

SABIO, MORADA AQUIAS, physician; b. Philippines, Apr. 21, 1934; d. Juan Tadeo and Mercedes (Balbuena) Aquias; student Manila Central U., 1950; M.D., U. Santo Tomas, 1957; m. Andres R. Sabio, June 4, 1959; children—John, Marguerite, Elaine, Andrew, Christine, Neysa, Morada, Victoria. Intern, Kanawha Valley Hosp., Charleston, W.Va.; resident in anesthesiology Marymount Hosp., Cleve., 1961-64; staff anesthesiologist Forest City Hosp., Cleve., 1964-75; chief anesthesia dept. Shaker Med. Center, Hosp., Cleve., 1976-77, now mem. staff; staff anesthesiologist Marymount Hosp., Garfield Heights, Ohio, 1978—; pres. Parkwood Anesthesia Group, Cleve., 1978—. Mem. Assn. Philippine Physicians Ohio (bd. govs. 1976—), Womens Aux. Assn. Philippine Practicing Physicians Am. (treas. 1977-78), Philippine Am. Soc. Ohio Womens Aux. (treas., 1976-78, pres. 1978-80), Am., Ohio, Cleve. socs. anesthesiologists, AMA, Assn. Philippine Physicians in Ohio (treas. 1980-82), Ohio Med. Assn., Cleve. Acad. Medicine, Internat. Anesthesia Research Soc. Republican. Roman Catholic. Home: 6900 Norvale Circle W Gates Mills OH 44040 Office: 11710 Shaker Blvd Cleveland OH 44120

SABLE, BARBARA KINSEY, educator; b. Astoria, L.I., N.Y., Oct. 6, 1927; d. Albert and Verna Rowe Kinsey; B.A., Coll. Wooster, 1949; M.A., Tchrs. Coll. Columbia U., N.Y.C., 1950; D.Mus., U. Ind., 1966; m. Arthur J. Sable, Nov. 3, 1973. Office mgr., music dir. sta. WCAX, Burlington, Vt., 1954; instr. Cottey Coll., 1959-60; asst. prof. N.E. Mo. State U., Kirksville, 1962-64; asst. prof. U. Calif., Santa Barbara, 1964-69; now prof. music U. Colo., Boulder, Mem. Nat. Assn. Tchrs. Singing (state gov., asso. editor bull.), AAUP, Colo. State Music Tchrs. Assn. Democrat. Author: The Vocal Sound, 1982. Home: 3430 Ash Ave Boulder CO 80303 Office: Coll Music Campus Box 301 U Colo Boulder CO 80309

SABOE, ELENA PROTA, hosp. info. systems mgr.; b. Phila., July 6, 1943; d. Joseph Thomas and Elena (Perri) Prota; B.A., Cabrini Coll., Radnor, Pa., 1965; m. Jon Saboe, Mar. 29, 1969; 1 dau., Kirsten Elyn. Tchr. English, Bishop McDevitt High Sch., Wyncote, Pa., 1966-72; mng. editor Franklin Inst. Research Labs., Phila., 1975-79; mgr. documentation SMS, Malvern, Pa., 1979—. Mem. Soc. Tech. Communications, Network Women in Computer Tech., Nat. Assn. Female Execs. Office: 51 Valley Stream Pkwy Malvern PA 19355

SABOYA, MARIA ELENA, bank exec.; b. Palma Soriano-Oriente, Cuba, May 27, 1951; came to U.S., 1960, naturalized, 1970; d. Casimiro and Irma (Gross) S.; student in data processing mgmt. Automated Bus. Coll., Harvard U., 1971-72; A.A. in Acctg., Miami Dade Jr. Coll., 1981. Computer clk. Sears Roebuck, Chgo., 1972-74; tax clk. Met. Dade County (Fla.), 1974; with Capital Bank, 1974—, v.p. North Miami Beach office, 1980-81, v.p., br. mgr. North Bay Village office, 1981—; notary public; mem. faculty Am. Inst. Banking 1982. Mem. North Dade C. of C., North Miami Beach C. of C. Democrat. Roman Catholic. Home: 1329 71 St Miami Beach FL 33141 Office: 1666 Kennedy Causeway North Bay Village FL 33141

SACCA, HARRIET WANDS, music educator; b. Pittsfield, Mass, July 21, 1919; d. Harry J. and Anna F. (Mara) Wands; B.S., Coll. St. Rose, 1939, M.A., 1962; student SUNY, Albany, Oneonta. Tchr. public schs., Albany, N.Y., 1942-66; instr. Coll. St. Rose, 1962-63; dir. music edn. Albany (N.Y.) Bd. Edn., 1966—; bur. assoc. examiner personnel N.Y. State Dept. Edn. Past pres. Soroptimist Internat., 1969-70, City Club Albany, Inc., 1974-75; active Albany County Democratic Com., 1962—; jud. del. 3d Jud. area N.Y. State, 1975-81; mem. Albany Local Devel. Corp.; bd. dirs. St. Joseph's Housing Corp., Youth Emergency Shelter, Albany Tulip Festival. Recipient Citizen of Yr. award Ford Motor Co., 1971; Women Helping Women award Soroptimist, 1975. Fellow Harry Truman Library; mem. Music Educators Nat. Conf., N.Y. State Sch. Music Assn., Capitol Hill Choral Soc. (dir.), Albany Adminstrs. Assn., Albany Civic Auditorium (dir.), Delta Kappa Gamma, Delta Epsilon. Democrat. Roman Catholic. Clubs: Bus. and Profl. Women's, Soroptimist, Club of Albany, Cath. Women's Service League, Monday Musical, Coll. St. Rose Alumni, Pres.'s Soc. Home: 226 Morris St Albany NY 12208 Office: Albany Bd Edn Academy Park Albany NY 12207

SACHSE, ELINOR YUDIN, economist; b. N.Y.C., Sept. 10, 1940; d. Lazarus Simon and Genevive (Goldberg) Yudin; B.A. with honors in Econs., Barnard Coll., 1962; M.A., Columbia U., 1964, Ph.D., 1968; m. Harry R. Sachse, Nov. 30, 1975; children—Michael Judah, Marianna Victoria. Mem. faculty dept. econs. N.Y. U., N.Y.C., 1966-69; various positions World Bank, Washington, 1969-79, chief internat. economy div., 1974-78; sr. staff economist internat. trade Council Econ. Advs., White House, 1980—. Ford Found. fellow, 1965-66; Internat. Econs. Workshop fellow, 1963-64, 64-65; Francis M. Dibblee scholar, 1962-63. Author: Human Capital Migration, Direct Investment and the Transfer of Technology, 1976; also articles. Mem. Am. Econs. Assn. Jewish. Home: 2934 Newark St NW Washington DC 20008 Office: Old Executive Office Bldg Washington DC 20500

SACHSE, JANICE RUBENSTEIN (MRS. VICTOR A. SACHSE, JR.), artist; b. New Orleans, May 6, 1908; d. Isaac Harry and Madeleine (Phillips) Rubenstein; student art La. State U., 1927-29; Newcomb Coll., 1928, Corcoran Gallery Art Sch.; m. Victor A. Sachse, Jr., Jan. 2, 1929; children—Victor Alphonse III, Harry Rubenstein. One-man shows at La. State U. Union Gallery Invitational, Sally Jackson Gallery, Hong Kong, New Orleans profl. galleries, others; exhibited in group shows at La Boetie, N.Y.C., N.Y. World's Fair, 1965, Berlin, Germany Volkfest, Joslyn Art Mus., Omaha, New Orleans Mus. Art, Witherspoon Gallery, U.N.C., also others. Represented in permanent collections: Anglo Am. Mus. Art at La. State U., New Orleans Mus. Art, Lauren Rogers Mus., Laurel, Miss., others. Adv. bd. New Orleans Mus. Art; bd. dirs. Vols. Am., now hon. mem. Recipient Purchase award Bi-Centennial Art Exhbn., 1974; recognized regional painter of La. landscapes. Home and Home and Studio: 370 S Lakeshore Dr Baton Rouge LA 70808

SACHTLEBEN, BETTY JUNE, social services adminstr.; b. Centralia, Ill., Oct. 29, 1929; d. William Charles and Nellie Josephine (Winstead) Sissom; B.S., Washington U., 1962, M.S.W., 1966; m. Roland Sachtleben, Feb. 9, 1951; children—Stewart Gary, Cynthia Barbara, Sherwood Roland, Sanford Stanley, Kristin Charles. Psychiat. social worker Malcolm Bliss Mental Health Center, St. Louis, 1966-67; with div. pupil personnel St. Louis Public Schs., 1967-68; supr. social service dept. Parkway Sch. Dist., Chesterfield, Mo., 1969-72; social worker Family and Children's Service, St. Louis, 1972-73; pvt. practice psychiat. social work, St. Louis, 1973-75; exec. dir. Mo. Counseling Service, Bridgeton, Mo., 1975-81, REACH Internat. Communications Horizons, Creve Coeur, Mo., 1981—; adj. asst. prof. St. Louis U.; instr. Washington U. Bd. dirs. New Hope Found. for Retarded Children, 1972-73; dir., sec. Sunshine Found., 1973—; dir. Parents Without Partners, 1975—. Mem. Nat. Assn. Social Workers, Am. Assn. Marriage and Family Therapists. Lutheran. Home: 12669 Northwinds Dr Creve Coeur MO 63141 Office: Creve Coeur MO 63141

SACKETT, DONNA CHRISTINE, personnel exec.; b. Bklyn., Nov. 26, 1947; d. Benjamin R. and Florence M. (Bender) Gurdison; A.A. with high honors, Brookdale Community Coll., 1975; B.A. with high honors, Douglass Coll., 1977; M.S., Rutgers U., 1981; m. Raymond A. Sackett, July 28, 1973. Adminstrv. sec. Bell Telephone Labs., Holmdel, N.J., 1965-75; student intern employee devel. dept. Johnson & Johnson, Skillman, N.J., 1977; personnel cons. Prudential Property & Casualty Ins. Co., Holmdel, 1977—; cons. U.S. Army Res., 1981—; instr. Brookdale Community Coll., Lincroft, N.J., 1978—. Mem. mgmt. and personnel adminstrn. com. Women's Ctr., Brookdale Community Coll. Mem. Am. Soc. Tng. and Devel., Nat. Soc. Performance and Instrn., Eastern Communication Assn. (chmn. applied communication div. 1980). Office: 23 Main St Holmdel NJ 07733

SACKETT, MARY LOU, chiropractor; b. Ann Arbor, Mich., May 12, 1949; d. Lester Walter and Helen Beeken (Miller) S.; A.S., Monroe County Community Coll., 1975; D.Chiropractic, Palmer Coll. Chiropractic, Davenport, Iowa, 1979. Chiropractor, Hillsdale (Mich.) Family Chiropractic Life Center, 1980—. Diplomate Am. Bd. Chiropractic Examiners. Mem. Internat. Chiropractic Assn., Mich. Chiropractic Council. Mem. Unity Ch. Office: 502 W Carleton St Hillsdale MI 49242

SACKS, NORMA ISABEL, psychotherapist; b. Chgo., July 27, 1928; d. Lionel and Anna (Nagdeman) Dyck; B.A., U. Ill., 1951; M.S.W., N.Y. U., 1955; m. Leonard Sacks, Dec. 2, 1962; children—Glenn, Valerie. Clin. social worker Community Service Soc. Clinic, Jewish Community Service of L.I. Community Service, N.Y.C.; 1960-63; psychotherapist Morningside Psychiat. Clinic, N.Y.C., 1960; pvt. practice psychotherapy, Los Angles, 1968—; psychotherapist Santa Clarita Valley Counseling Center, 1976—, Grenada Hills Hospice, 1979—. Mem. Acad. Cert. Social Workers, Lic. Clin. Social Workers Calif., Soc. Clin. Social Work, Nat. Assn. Social Workers, AAUW. Jewish. Office: 8949 Reseda Blvd Suite 203 Northridge CA 91324

SACKS, PAULINE, securities corp. exec.; b. Phila., Apr. 5, 1935; d. Emanuel and Florence (Lomazoff) Levy; B.S., W. Chester (Pa.) State U., 1956; postgrad. Temple U., 1957-60; P.H.T. in Bus. Adminstrn., LaSalle Coll., Phila., 1961; m. Marvin Sacks, July 3, 1957; children—Sharon Ann, Emanuel Ellick. Pub. sch. tchr., Bristol Twp., Pa., 1957-60, Phila., 1961-65, San Diego, 1967, Alexandria, Va., 1967-70; real estate salesman, Phila., 1962-64; registered rep. Walston & Co., Washington, 1971-73, Reynolds Securities, Inc., Arlington Va., 1973-75; v.p. Loeb Rhoades & Co., Inc., Washington, 1975-77; v.p. Thomson McKinnon Securities, Arlington, 1978-79, Smith Barney Harris Upham, 1979-80, Moseley Hallgarten Estabrook & Weeden, 1980-82; br. office mgr. Richardson Securities, Inc., 1982—; ins. salesman TransAm. Occidental Ins., Traveler's Ins. Co., Capital Life Ins. Co., 1973—; lectr. investing to various groups; mem. Chgo. Bd. Trade, Mercantile Exchange, Chgo. Bd. Option Exchange, N.Y. Stock Exchange, Am., Midwest, Phila.-Balt. stock exchanges. Sunday sch. tchr. Hebrew Sunday Sch. Soc. Phila., 1951-64, Alexandria, 1968-71, Arlington, Va., 1973-75; pvt. tutor, 1951-65; nat. committeewoman Republican Party, Phila., 1964-65, del. Va. Rep. Orgn., 1980; bd. dirs. YMHA, Phila., 1952-54; pres. Women's Am. ORT, 1968-72; vol. CAP, 1968-72; mgr. Pa. CD Shelter 1962-63; sponsor Campfire Girls Am., Alexandria, 1970-72; mem. Nat. PTA, 1957—, chmn. curriculum com. 1972-73; founder, pres. Levi Sacks, Rothberg Charitable Found. Recipient ARC Tchr.-Leadership Area award, 1959, sales awards, 1972-82. Mem. Westchester Coll. Alumni Assn. (life). Jewish. Clubs: Temple Beth El Couples, ORT (life), Hadassah (life), Brandeis (life), Technion (life). Home: 3835 N Woodrow St Arlington VA 22207

SACKSTEDER, MARY ELLEN, educator; b. Sandusky, Ohio, May 22, 1914; d. Leo Anthony and Antoinette Frances (Riedy) Sacksteder; B.S., Heidelberg Coll., 1936; M.A., Ohio State U., 1937; certificate Mayo Clinic Sch. Phys. Therapy, 1944. Tchr. biology Port Clinton (Ohio) High Sch., 1938-42; social worker Catholic Charities, Dayton, 1942-43; phys. therapist Army Med. Specialist Corp, 1944-64; instr. phys. therapy State U. N.Y., Buffalo, 1965-66, asst. prof., acting chmn. dept. 1966-69; dir. div. phys. therapy edn., asso. prof. Sch. Allied Health Professions U. Nebr. Coll. Medicine, Omaha, 1969-79, interim dir., asso. prof., 1979-80. Served to maj. Army Med. Specialists Corps, 1944-64. Mem. Am. Phys. Therapy Assn., Ret. Officers Assn., Res. Officers Assn., Women's Overseas Service League, Altrusa, Ohio State U. Alumni Assn. Democrat. Roman Catholic. Home: 1320 S 93d Ave Omaha NE 68124

SADDLEMYER, (ELEANOR) ANN, educator; b. Prince Albert, Sask., Can., Nov. 28, 1932; d. Orrin Angus and Elsie Sarah (Ellis) S.; B.A., U. Sask., 1953; M.A., Queen's U., 1956, LL.D., 1977; Ph.D., U. London, 1961. Lectr., Victoria (B.C.) Coll., 1956-57, instr., 1960-62, asst. prof., 1962-65; asso. prof. U. Victoria, 1965-68, prof. English, 1968-71; prof. English, Victoria Coll., U. Toronto, 1971—, dir. Grad. Centre for Study of Drama, 1972-77, sr. fellow Massey Coll., 1975—; Berg prof. N.Y.U., 1975; dir. Theatre Plus, Colin Smythe Pubs. Can. Council scholar, 1958-59, fellow, 1968; Guggenheim fellow, 1968, 77. Fellow Royal Soc. Can.; mem. Internat. Assn. Study Anglo-Irish Lit. (chmn. 1973-76), Assn. Can. Theatre History (pres. 1976-77), Can. Assn. Irish Studies, Humanities Assn., Assn. Can. Univ. Tchrs. English, Can. Assn. Univ. Tchrs., Assn. Can. and Que. Lit. Author: The World of W.B. Yeats, 1965; In Defence of Lady Gregory, Playwright, 1966; Synge and Modern Comedy, 1968; J.M. Synge Plays Books One and Two, 1968; Lady Gregory Plays, 4 vols., 1970; Letters to Molly: Synge to Maire O'Neill, 1971; Letters from Synge to W.B. Yeats and Lady Gregory, 1971; Theatre Business, The Correspondence of the First Abbey Theatre Director, 1982; Collected Letters of J.M. Synge, Vol. I, 1983; co-editor: Theatre History in Canada; editorial bds. Modern Drama, 1972, English Studies in Can., 1973, Themes in Drama, 1974, Shaw Rev., 1977, Research in the Humanities, 1976, Irish Univ. Rev., 1970; contbr. articles to profl. jours. Home: 297 Watson Ave Oakville ON L6J 3V3 Canada Office: Dept English Victoria Coll U Toronto Toronto ON M5S 1K7 Canada

SADKER, MYRA POLLACK, educator; b. Portland, Maine, Mar. 3, 1943; d. Louis Robert and Shirley (Schilling) Pollack; B.A., Boston U., 1964; M.A.T., Harvard U., 1965; Ed.D., U. Mass., 1971; m. David Sadker, July 4, 1965; children—Robin, Jacqueline. Tchr. secondary schs., various locations; asst. prof. edn. U. Wis., Parkside; prof. Am. U., 1979—, also dean Sch. Edn. Recipient Am. Ednl. Research Assn. Women Educators award; U. Mass. William Cosby Alumni award. Mem. Am. Ednl. Research Assn., NOW. Author: (with others) Sexism in School and Society, 1973, Now Upon a Time: a Contemporary View of Children's Literature, 1977, Teachers Make the Difference, 1980, Sex Equity Handbook for Schools, 1982. Home: 8608 Carlynn Dr Bethesda MD 20817 Office: Roper Hall Sch Edn Am U Washington DC 20034

SADLER, ELVA ELIZABETH, ret. English-teaching specialist; b. Birmingham, Ala., Feb. 22, 1905; d. James Reed and Mary Christine (Craig) Sadler; B.A., Howard Coll., 1927; M.A., U. Ala., 1941; postgrad. U. N.C., 1929, U. Bonn, 1955, U. Mexico, 1961. Tchr. pub. schs., O'Hatchee, Ala., 1927-28, Birmingham, Ala., 1928-43; instr. Ward-Belmont Coll., 1943-44; asst. prof. English No. Mont. Coll., 1947-48; editor Abingdon-Cokesbury Press, Nashville, 1944-47, fgn. service officer, English-speaking specialist USIA, Japan, 1950, Thailand, 1950-51, Phillipines, 1951-53, Ger., 1953-58, Washington, 1958-62, El Salvador, Peru, 1962, Costa Rica, Haiti, Dominican Republic, Bolivia, Brazil, 1963, Washington, 1964; editor USIA English Teaching Forum, 1965-75, also writer; English teaching cons., 1961-75. Bd. dirs. Parkfairfax Citizens Assn., 1968—, treas., 1968-71. Mem. Nat. Council Tchrs. English, N.E.A., Delta Zeta. Presbyn. Club: Parkfairfax Garden (pres. 1969-70). Author articles New Eng. Quarterly, Link, Chaplain, Pacific Stars and Stripes, also English teaching articles and books. Home: 3114 Wellington Rd Alexandria VA 22302

SADOCK, VIRGINIA ALCOTT, psychiatrist; b. Sofia, Bulgaria, Nov. 25, 1938; came to U.S., 1941, naturalized, 1947; d. Fred and Rica (Boni) Alcott; A.B., Bennington Coll., 1960; M.D., N.Y. Med. Coll., 1970; m. Benjamin J. Sadock, Oct. 20, 1963; children—James, Victoria. Intern, N.Y. Med. Coll.-Met. Hosp. Center, N.Y.C., 1970-71, resident, 1971-73; dir. human sexuality program, asst. prof. clin. psychiatry N.Y. Med. Coll., 1973-81; practice medicine specializing in psychiatry, N.Y.C., 1973—; mem. staff N.Y.U. Hosp., Bellevue Hosp.; assoc. prof. clin. psychiatry, dir. grad. edn. in human sexuality N.Y.U. Med. Center, 1980—. Diplomate Am. Bd. Psychiatry and Neurology. Fellow Am. Psychiat. Assn.; mem. AMA, Am. Med. Women's Assn., N.Y. State

Med. Soc., N.Y. County Med. Soc. Contbr., asst. to editors: Comprehensive Textbook of Psychiatry, 2d edit., 1975, 3d edit., 1980. Office: 4 E 89th St New York NY 10028

SAENT-JOHNS, GERALDINE MCCORMICK, painter, miniaturist, sculptor; b. Montreal, Que., Can., Sept. 12, 1930; d. Alexander Gerald Makohoniac and Anne (Lubkowski) McCormick; came to U.S., 1952, naturalized, 1965; student McGill U., 1948-49. Artist, Ohio Bell Telephone Co., 1962-65; comml. tech. artist Jayme Orgn., 1965-69; freelance artist, 1969—; owner, operator Eden Mood Studio Galleries, 1973—; lectr. animals in art; miniature painting on gemstone rep. in collection of Pres. and Mrs. Gerald Ford, 8th Duke of Wellington. Mem. Audubon Soc., East African Wild Life Soc. (pres. Ohio area chpt.), Nat. Wildlife Fedn., Aircraft Owners and Pilots Assn., Canadian Nature Fedn. Republican. Home: 4800 Lander Rd Orange Village OH 44022

SAFAYAN, ZINAT S., nurse, educator; b. Shiraz, Iran, Sept. 23, 1934; came to U.S., 1965, naturalized, 1974; d. Morad and Bibi Soleimani; B.S. in Nursing, Nemazi Sch. Nursing, Iran, 1957; B.S. in Nursing, Utah State U., 1961; M.S. in Nursing, U. Evansville, 1974; m. Esfandiar Safayan, Nov. 3, 1956; children—Ali, Elham, Amir. Asst. dir. nursing Sadi Hosp., Pahlavi U., Shiraz, Iran, 1963-65; med.-surg. nursing faculty Gilfoy Sch. Nursing, Jackson, Miss., 1966; instr. med.-surg. nursing Capital City Sch. Nursing, Washington, 1967-68; nursing coordinator cancer research Va. Hosp., Washington, 1969-70; asst. prof. nursing Ind. State U., 1971—. Chmn. hospitality Terre Haute Symphony, 1976-78. Mem. Vigo County Med. Aux. (pres. 1975, chmn. scholarship com.), Terre Haute Regional Hosp. Guild (pres. 1980), Am. Nurses Assn., Ind. Nurses Assn., Brit. Nurses Assn. Moslem. Home: 21 Longridge Rd Terre Haute IN 47802 Office: Sch Nursing Ind State Univ 8th and Chestnut Sts Terre Haute IN 47809

SAFER, RENA, social worker; b. Jerusalem, Israel, Dec. 22, 1936 (parents Am. citizens); d. Milton Lyon and Shirley (Solomon) Scheingarten; B.A. in Psychology, Boston U., 1958; M.S.W., U. Wis.-Milw., 1964; m. Fredrick James Safer, June 15, 1958; children—Hershel Meir, Dena Tamar. Dir., Milw. Young Judaea, 1962-64; social worker Devel. Tng. Center, Milw., 1966-67; caseworker Milw. County Dept. Social Services, 1967-68, unit. supr., 1968-72, sect. supr., 1972—. Chmn, Gov.'s Com. on Day Treatment, 1977-78; del. Gov.'s Conf. Children and Families, 1980; bd. dirs., sec. Milw. Bd. Jewish Edn., 1979-80. Mem. Nat. Assn. Social Workers, Acad. Cert. Social Workers, Assn. Wis. Child Care Instns., Assn. Public Profl. Social Service Employees (v.p.), Am. Soc. Public Adminstrn., Mental Health Assn. Milwaukee County, Milw. Area Soc. Public Adminstrn. (dir. 1980-82). Jewish. Clubs: Kalaniot Dance Group, Atzmaut Labor Zionist Orgn., Hadassah (life). Home: 2510 W Brantwood Ave Glendale WI 53209 Office: 1220 W Vliet St Milwaukee WI 53205

SAFIAN, JOYCE LYNN, family nurse practitioner; b. Porterville, Calif., July 3, 1948; d. Lee Gum and Soo (Gong) Quock; R.N. diploma O'Connor Hosp. Sch. Nursing, San Jose, Calif., 1969; family nurse practioner cert. U. Calif., Davis, 1977; M.A. in Health Services Adminstrn., Antioch U. West, 1979; m. Michael Safian, Apr. 17, 1971 (div. 1978); 1 son, Christian. Asst. dir. nurses Arroyo Vista Hosp., Santa Rosa, Calif., 1971; clin. nurse cons. Sonoma State Hosp., Elderidge, Calif., 1973-77; cons. phys. assessment, Santa Rosa, 1977-82; dir. employee/employer health services Santa Rosa Meml. Hosp., 1977—; pres., chmn. Corp. Health Services, Inc., Santa Rosa, 1982—; tchr. phys. assessment. Sec., Sonoma County (Calif.) Bd. on Alcoholism, 1977-80. Mem. Assn. Hosp. Employee Health Profls. (founder, exec. pres. 1981), Am. Public Health Assn., (governing council), Sonoma County Forum, Nat. Assn. Female Execs. Democrat. Roman Catholic. Author articles. Home: 123 Hidden Valley Ct Santa Rosa CA 95404 Office: 95 Montgomery Dr Suite 114 Santa Rosa CA 95404

SAFRIT, MARGARET JOANNE, educator; b. Salisbury, N.C., June 16, 1935; d. Ernest Crawford and Margaret Cannon (Cline) S.; B.S., U. N.C., Greensboro, 1957; M.S., U. Wis., Madison, 1962, Ph.D., 1967. Instr. phys. edn. U. Tex., Austin, 1957-60; asst. prof., then assoc. prof. U. Wis., Milw., 1965-70; prof. phys. edn. and dance U. Wis., Madison, 1970—, chmn. dept., 1980—; cons. in field. Grantee, U. Wis., 1978. Mem. AAHPER, Am. Acad. Phys. Edn., Nat. Council Measurement in Edn., Am. Ednl. Research Assn., Nat. Assn. Phys. Edn. in Higher Edn., Wis. Assn. Health, Phys. Edn. and Recreation, Bus. and Profl. Women's Club. Author articles in field. Editor, Research Quar., 1977-80. Office: 200 Observatory Dr Madison WI 53706

SAGAFI-NEJAD, NANCY GAIL BLACK, lawyer; b. Park Falls, Wis., Dec. 29, 1937; d. Crawford Harold and Adaline Clara (Gropp) Black; B.A., Northwestern U., 1959; M.A., U. Hawaii, 1965; J.D., U. Tex., 1982; m. Tagi Sagafi-Nejad, Nov. 22, 1967; children—Jahan, David. Curatorial asst. Isabella Stewart Gardner Mus., Boston, 1961-63; univ. tchr. U.S. Peace Corps, Shiraz, Iran, 1966-68; tchr. Rosemont (Pa.) Coll., 1969-71; lectr. Phila. Mus. Art, 1969-71. Mem. ABA, Tex. State Bar Assn. Democrat. Quaker.

SAGER, RUTH, geneticist; b. Chgo., Feb. 7, 1918; B.S., U. Chgo., 1938; Ph.D., Columbia U., 1948; m. Arthur B. Pardee. Merck fellow NRC, Rockefeller Inst., N.Y.C., 1949-51, mem. staff, 1951-55; research scientist Columbia U., 1955-65; prof. molecular biology Hunter Coll., N.Y.C., 1966-75; prof. cellular genetics Sidney Farber Cancer Inst., Harvard Med. Sch., 1975—. Guggenheim fellow, 1972-73. Mem. Nat. Acad. Scis., Genetics Soc. Am., Am. Soc. Naturalists, Am. Soc. Biol. Chemists, Am. Soc. Cell Biology. Author: Cytoplasmic Genes and Organelles, 1972; co-author; Cell Heredity, 1961. Contbr. articles to profl. jours. *

SAHAGIAN, LUCILLE BEDROSIAN, businesswoman; b. Chgo., Mar. 27, 1927; d. Kesrow and Rebecca (Babian) Bedrosian; m. John Sahagian, Jan. 10, 1953; 1 dau., Rebecca Jan. Exec. sec. William Morris Theatrical Agy., Chgo., 1944-46; exec. sec. Goldblatt's Dept. Stores, Chgo., 1946-53; exec. sec. Ross Roy Advt. Agy., Chgo., 1953-54; partner, dealer John Sahagian Service Sta., Fairfield, Conn., 1958-64; owner partner John Sahagian Service Stas., Conn. Turnpike, Darien, Conn., 1972—; treas. John Sahagian, Inc., Fairfield; owner, partner N.Y. State Thruway Sahagian Stas., Ramapo, 1968—, Palisades Interstate Pkwy. Sahagian Stas., Englewood Cliffs, N.J., 1981—. Dir., Fairfield County Charity for Autistic Children, 1961-64. Mem. Gasoline Retailers Assn., Armenian Relief Soc. Mem. Armenian Apostolic Ch. (Ladies Guild of Armenian Prelacy. Congregationalist. Home: 168 Spring Hill Rd Fairfield CT 06430 Office: Conn Turnpike Westbound PO Box 3243 Darien CT 06820

SAIBARA, MARJORIE LYNN, accountant; b. Houston, Sept. 20, 1950; d. Robert and Rola Saibara; B.B.A., U. Houston, 1972. Joint venture acct. Union Oil of Calif., Houston, 1973-74; joint interest, revenue accountant Coastal States Gas Corp., Houston, 1974-78; Dept. Energy liaison for controller's dept. revenue crude oil and gas processing supr., spl. projects acct., asst. mgr. revenue acctg., project leader for revenue acctg. software installation Cabot Corp., Houston, 1978—; counselor U. Houston Career Day. Chmn. worship ministry Presbyn. Ch. of Covenant, 1980—; Presbytery del., 1980; ruling elder Presbyn. Ch., mem. pulpit nominating com., 1982. Mem. Am. Soc. Women Accts. (dir., membership chmn.), Petroleum Accts. Soc. of Houston (membership chmn.), Phi Mu (treas., v.p.). Office: 921 Main St Suite 900 Houston TX 77002

SAIKI, PATRICIA (MRS. STANLEY MITSUO SAIKI), state senator; b. Hilo, Hawaii, May 28, 1930; d. Kazuo and Shizue (Inoue) Fukuda; B.S., U. Hawaii; m. Stanley Mitsuo Saiki, June 19, 1954; children—Stanley Mitsuo, Sandra S., Margaret C., Stuart K., Laura H. Tchr., Dept. Edn. Hawaii, 1959-66; research asst. Hawaii State Senate, 1966-68; mem. Hawaii Ho. of Reps., 1968-74, Hawaii State Senate, 1974—. Dir. Amfac, Inc., Hawaiian Airlines. Mem. Pres.'s Adv. Council on Status of Women, 1969-76; mem. Nat. Commn. Internat. Women's Year, 1969-70; commr. Western Interstate Commn. on Higher Edn.; fellow Eagleton Inst., Rutgers U., 1970. Mem. Kapiolani Hosp. Aux. Sec. Hawaii Republican party, 1964-66, vice chmn., 1966-68; del. Hawaii Constl. Conv., 1968; alt. del. Rep. Nat. Conv., 1968; mem. Fedn. Republican Women. Bd. dirs. Aloha council Boy Scouts Am.; trustee Hawaii Pacific Coll. Episcopalian. Address: 784 Elepaio St Honolulu HI 96816

SAILOR, DOROTHY HOLIN, educator; b. Evanston, Ill., Jan. 30, 1929; d. Arnold Bernard and Edith Mae (Yearsley) Holin; A.A., Stephens Coll., 1948; B.S., U. Ill., 1950, M.S., 1952, postgrad., 1952-56; postgrad. Calif. State U., 1967-68, Chapman Coll., 1979; m. Danton Bridgford Sailor, June 9, 1956; children—Kevin, Timothy, Dorton. Tchr., Sidney (Ill.) Jr. High Sch., 1952-53; teaching asst. U. Ill., 1953-54; tchr. DeKalb (Ill.) Jr. High Sch., 1956-58; dir. Child Study Center, Chapman Coll., 1963-65; instr., asst. prof. child devel. and family life Fullerton Coll., 1966-78, asso. prof., 1978—; lectr. in field. Mem. edn. adv. bd. Child Devel. Inst., Calif. State U., Fullerton, 1973—; mem. Nat. Council Chs. Child and Family Justice Project, 1978-80; mem. Coalition for Children and Families, Inc., 1980—, pres., 1981—; Fullerton Coll. Innovation grantee, 1973. Mem. DeKalb Classroom Tchrs. Assn. (sec. 1957), Calif. Tchrs. Assn. (advisor 1978, dir. Fullerton-Cypress chpt. 1979—), World Orgn. for Edn. Young Children, Citizens for Responsible Orgn. Assn. Childhood Edn. Internat., Calif. Assn. Childhood Edn., Nat. Assn. Edn. Young Children, Calif. Assn. Edn. Young Children, So. Calif. Assn. Edn. Young Children, Calif. Advocacy Network. Congregationalist. Author research articles; mem. publs. com. for research Jour. Childhood Edn., 1980—. Home: 2255 Skyline Dr Fullerton CA 92631 Office: 321 E Chapman Ave Fullerton CA 92634

SAINT, CANDACE ANN, mental health exec.; b. St. Louis, Nov. 14, 1946; d. Richard George and Ann Marie (Felt) Milford; B.A., U. Denver, 1968; M.A., U. Chgo., 1973; m. William Saint. Aug. 2, 1969; children—Amari, Correll. Vol., Peace Corps, Paraguay, 1968-71; clin. social worker Family and Children's Service, Ithaca, N.Y., 1973-75; researcher Instituto de Psiciatria U. Rio De Janeiro, Brazil, 1978-80; coordinator Lima (Peru) Mental Health Project, 1981—; instr. U. of the Andes, 1981—. Mem. Nat. Assn. Social Workers, NOW. Home: 130 Calle V Lima Peru Office: 320 43d St New York NY 10017

ST. ANGELO, BELINDA FRANCES, psychotherapist; b. Providence, Feb. 13, 1950; d. Frank E. and Louise Eliza (Narducci) St. A.; B.A. (Goulet scholar), Salve Regina Coll., Newport, R.I., 1968; M.S.W. (grantee Vocat. Rehab. Adminstrn.), Boston Coll., 1970; diploma (NIMH grantee, found. scholar), Menninger Found. Sch. Psychiatry, 1972; postgrad. Cleve. Center for Research in Child Devel., 1976. Child psychotherapist Lakeside Children's Center, Milw., 1971-73; child psychotherapist Wis. Psychiat. Services Ltd., Milw., 1973-75; child therapist, supr. and cons. to staff members Catholic Counseling Center, Cleve., 1975—; field work instr. Sch. Applied Social Scis., Case Western Res. U., Cleve., 1980. Mem. Nat. Assn. Social Workers, English Speaking Union, Sigma Phi Sigma. Home: 2575 Kemper Rd Shaker Heights OH 44120 Office: 1001 Huron Rd Cleveland OH 44115

ST. AUBIN, PHYLLIS ANN, agri bus. exec.; b. Camden, Mo., Dec. 24, 1938; d. Charles Dan and Alberta (Archer) Feeney; student (Lion Oil Co. scholar) Memphis State U., 1956-57; m. Forrest Edmund St. Aubin, Nov. 26, 1971; 1 dau., Pamela DeAnn Gooch Schultz; stepchildren—Mark Randall, Leslie Alexandra St. Aubin Brown. Advt. asst. Mobay Chem. Corp., Kansas City, Mo., 1968-80; mgr. coop. sales devel. Farmland Industries, Kansas City, Mo., 1980—. Recipient Voice of Democracy award Lion Oil Co., 1955. Mem. Nat. Agri Mktg. Assn. (dir. Mo.-Kans. chpt.), Nat. Assn. Female Execs., Kansas City Ad Club. Republican. Baptist. Home: 1 Wycklow Overland Park KS 66207 Office: Farmland Industries 3315 N Oak Hwy Kansas City MO 64116

ST. AUBREY, BARBARA J., self-help therapist; b. Yonkers, N.Y., Oct. 13, 1934; d. Arthur and Edna (Miller) Fink; B.A., CCNY, 1955; B.A. in Counseling, Northwestern U.; postgrad. Columbia U.; divorced. Counsciousness-raising counselor, assertiveness trainer, self-help group therapist, 1970—; speaker for ERA. Mem. Am. Personnel and Guidance Assn., Suffolk Personel and Guidance Assn., Self-Help U.S.A., Women's Polit. Caucus, NOW (pres. Huntginton, N.Y.), Freedom of Choice. Democrat. Episcopalian. Address: 5 Leeward Ln Commack NY 11725

ST. CLAIR, GLORIANA STRANGE, librarian; b. Tonkawa, Okla., Dec. 13, 1939; d. Glen L. and Doris Mildred (Furber) Strange; B.A., U. Okla., 1961; M.L.S., U. Calif., Berkeley, 1962; Ph.D., U. Okla., 1970; M.B.A., U. Tex., 1980; m. Nicholas Grimes, Jr., Aug. 29, 1977. Asst. librarian Water Resourses Center Archives, U. Calif., Berkeley, 1963-65; cataloguer U. Okla., Norman, 1965-68; asst. prof. Western Carolina U., Cullowhee, 1969-71; asst. prof. Coll. of Charleston, S.C., 1971-76; adj. prof. Walsh Coll., 1976-78; supervising librarian for tech. services San Antonio Public Library, 1980—; adj. mgmt. faculty U. Tex., San Antonio, 1979—; communications cons. Mem. Tech. Services Interest Group (pres. 1981-82), Tex. Library Assn. (chmn. elect dist. 10 1982), S.W. Library Assn., Bexar County Library Assn., ALA, Mythopoeic Soc., Nat. Assn. Female Execs. Episcopalian. Club: Zonta (dir. 1982—). Editor, Working Papers, U. Tex., San Antonio, Coll. of Bus., 1980—; editor Ga.-S.C. Coll. English Assn. Newsletter, 1974-75. Home: PO Box 29000 Apt 271 San Antonio TX 78229 Office: 203 S Saint Marys St San Antonio TX 78205

ST. CLAIR, HELEN ALLISON, assn. exec.; b. Stevenson, Ala., July 23, 1932; d. George Milton and Frances Carolyn (Grider) Allison; student U. Ala., 1949-52, U. Va., 1961-62; m. Fred Weems St. Clair, Aug. 4, 1950; children—Loyce Anne, Fred Weems, Thomas Reid. Supr., Camp LeJeune (N.C.) Sitting Service, 1956-60; tchr. pub. schs., Prince William County, Va., 1960-64, substitute tchr., 1967-69; mem. spl. activities staff Miss. Optometric Assn., 1974-76, exec. dir., 1976—; cons. internat. assn./interprfl. com. Am. Optometric Assn. Mem. Miss. Council on Aging, 1976-80, mem. Inst. on Aging, 1976-82; trustee So. Coll. Optometry, Memphis, 1979-82; bd. dirs. Central Miss. chpt. ARC, vice chmn. community vol. service com., 1981-82, chmn., 1982-83; chmn. Central Miss. Sub Area council Miss. Health Systems Agy., 1981-83, vice chmn., 1980-81. Mem. Am. Soc. Assn. Execs., Internat. Assn. Optometric Execs. (v.p., pres. 1980), So. Council Optometric Execs., Am. Public Health Assn., Miss. Public Health Assn. (vision care sect.), Miss. Soc. Assn. Execs. (dir. 1982-83), Am. Soc. Assn. Execs. (membership devel. com. 1981-83), LWV. Methodist. Club: Miss. Women's (ofcl.). Contbg. editor Miss. Optometrist, So. Jour. Optometry, 1976—. Home: 102 Meadow Ln Lake Cavalier Route 3 Jackson MS 39213 Office: 5420 I-55 N Suite D Jackson MS 39236

ST. CLAIR, MARY JACQUELINE, light center exec.; b. Washington, Apr. 3, 1943; d. Michael Joseph and Josephine Mary (Banis) Smith; diploma in nursing Capitol City Sch. Nursing, Washington, 1964; m. Eugene Nelson St. Clair, July 10, 1964; children—Michelle, Stephanie, Jeannine, Eugene Nelson II. Staff nurse D.C. Gen. Hosp., 1964-66; head nurse and night supr. Jr. Village, Washington, 1966-70; staff nurse Cafritz Hosp., Washington, 1970-71; office nurse, Ft. Washington and Oxon Hill, Md., 1972-75; v.p. Taylor Plumbing & Electric Inc., Hollywood, Md., 1975-77; owner, gen. mgr. Hollywood Light Center (Md.), 1975—; part time staff nurse pediatrics dept. Calvert Meml. Hosp., Prince Frederick, Md., 1981—. Troop leader D.C. council Girl Scouts U.S.A., 1977-78. R.N., Washington, Md. Roman Catholic. Home: Coombs Creek Compton MD 20627 Office: PO Box 166 Hollywood MD 20636

ST. JOHN, ARLEN KELLY, contractor; b. Balt., Apr. 6, 1937; d. Hugh and Ruth Marie (Grothaus) Kelly; B.S. in Acctg., U. Md., 1959; children—Edward, Kellay, Julianne. Acct., McArdle & Walsh, Inc., Timonium, Md., 1959-63, Balt. Wholesalers, Inc., 1963-68; gen. mgr. Sin-Jin Industries, Inc., Balt., 1968-73; owner, mgr. Arlen, Ltd., Riderwood, Md., 1978—; real estate salesperson O'Conor & Flyns, Inc., 1978—. Prin. St. Thomas More Presch. Confraternity of Christian Doctrine, 1967-73; ann. giving chmn. McDonogh Sch.; asso. Balt. Symphony, 1977—. Mem. Home Builders Assn. Md. (chmn. builders mart, bd. dirs.), U. Md. Alumni Assn., Md. Hist. Soc., Balt. Opera Guild (pub crawl chmn., opera ball chmn.), Mortar Bd., Delta Gamma (Cable award 1970), Beta Alpha Psi. Republican. Lutheran. Home and Office: 1812 Landrake Rd Towson MD 21204

ST. JOHN, DOROTHY GARNER, social work adminstr.; b. Ft. Sam Houston, July 11, 1933; d. Gervais Justin and Willie Anna (Porter) Garner; B.A. in Anthropology, U. Tex., Austin, 1954; M.S. in Social Work, U. Tex., Arlington, 1975; m. Gene St. John, July 24, 1954 (div. July 1975); children—Dana Louise, Scott Alan. Pvt. practice psychotherapy, Ft. Worth, 1975—; therapist Human Resource Center, U. Tex., Arlington, 1975, trainer, 1975-78; asst. dir. Parenting Guidance Center, Ft. Worth, 1975-76, exec. dir., 1976—. Mem. Benbrook Park and Recreation Bd., 1974-76; bd. dirs. Circle T council Girl Scouts U.S.A., 1958-68, 72-75, 79—, mem. nat. council, 1963-66; ruling elder Presbyterian Ch. Mem. Nat. Assn. Social Workers, LWV (dir. 1960-64), Chi Omega. Home: 7232 Martha Ln Fort Worth TX 76112 Office: Parenting Guidance Center 1409 Summit St Fort Worth TX 76102

ST. MARIE, DIANE LAURA, writer; b. Granite City, Ill., Mar. 4, 1939; d. Ernest Eugene and Alta Marie Fauser; B.S., Baldwin-Wallace Coll., 1960; M.S.W., U. Hawaii, 1976; children—Richard, Robert, Ann Marie. Tchr. public schs., Pa., Ohio, 1960-64; asso. dir. Akron Forum, 1973-74; pvt. practice psychiat. social work, Honolulu, 1978-80; therapist Women's Counseling Clinic, Honolulu, 1977; script and prodn. asst. Ednl. TV, Honolulu, 1978-79; owner St. Marie Unltd., Seattle, 1980—, Video Presentations, 1981—; batik artist 1978—. Mem. Internat. Transactional Analysis Assn., Internat. TV Assn., Nat. Assn. TV Arts and Scis., Internat. Platform Assn., Wise Women Unltd., NOW. Address: 17816 3d NE Seattle WA 98155 painter, printmaker; b. Navahradak, Byelorussia; came to U.S., 1950, naturalized, 1956; d. Alexander and Maria (Boris) Stahanovich; B.A., Western Coll., Oxford, Ohio, 1954; M.F.A., Columbia U., 1956; m. Alexander Kolba, Feb. 22, 1958. Free-lance printmaker, artist, 1956—; one-woman shows include: Western Coll., 1955, Aenle Gallery, N.Y.C., 1956, Avanti Galleries, N.Y.C., 1968, Asbury Park (N.J.) Art Mus., 1973, Free Pub. Library of Woodbridge (N.J.), 1975, Guild of Creative Art, Shrewsbury, N.J., 1975, 77, West Long Branch (N.J.) Library, 1979; exhibited in group shows Young Printmakers traveling exhbn., 1967-69, Herron Sch. Art, Indpls., Nat. Print and Drawing Exhbn., DeKalb, Ill., 1968, UNICEF, N.Y.C., 1969, 74, 76, 79, Audubon Artists, N.Y.C., 1971, 79, Davidson (N.C.) Nat. Print and Drawing Competition, 1972, 73, First Miami (Fla.) Graphics Biennial, 1973, G.W.V. Smith Mus., Springfield, Mass., 1973, 74, 76, 77, 3d Hawaii Nat. Print. Exhbn., Honolulu, 1975, 65th Ann. Exhbn., Wadsworth Atheneum, Hartford, Conn., 1975, Va. Highlands Festival, Abington, Va., Salmagundi Club, N.Y.C., 1979, 11th Ann. Biennial Nat. Art Exhbn., Valley City, N.D., 1979, 81, Printmaking Council of N.J., Somerville, 1981, Charlotte (N.C.) Printmakers Soc., 1981, 1st Ann. Juried Show, Southport, N.C., 1981, Nat. Miniature Show, Cuyahoga Falls, Ohio, 1982, 14th Nat. Art Show, La Junta, Colo., 1982, Lever House, N.Y.C., 1982. Mem. Met. Mus. and Art Center, Hunterdon Art Center, Printmaking Council N.J., Guild Creative Art, Byelorussian Inst. Arts and Scis., Catherine Lorillard Wolfe Art Club, Print Club of Albany. Illustrator: Biography of a Polar Bear, 1972; Come Visit a Prairie Dog Town, 1976; Animal Games, 1976; Save that Raccoon, 1978; author, illustrator: Asian Crafts, 1970; Chickaree—A Red Squirrel, 1980. Home: 235 Hockhockson Rd Tinton Falls NJ 07724

SAINTE-MARIE, BUFFY, singer, composer; b. Piapot Reserve, Craven, Sask., Can., Feb. 20, 1941; adopted d. Albert C. and Winifred (Kenrick) Saint-M.; B.A. in Philosophy, U. Mass., 1962; m. Dewain Kamaikalani Bugbee, Sept. 16, 1967 (div. 1972); m. 2d, Sheldon Peters Wolfchild, 1975; 1 son, Dakota Starblanket. Appearances at Saladin, Gaslight, Village Gate, Troubedour, also various coffeehouse theatres; concert appearances at Carnegie Hall, 1965, Royal Albert Hall, London, Eng., 1965, N.Y. Philharmonic, 1967, Queen Elizabeth Theatre, Vancouver, Can., 1967, Newport Folk Festival, 1965, 67, Helsinki (Finland) Music Festival, 1967; founder, owner, pres. Gypsy Boy Music Inc. and Caleb Music Inc.; appeared TV shows The Virginian, Bronson; recording artist for Vanguard Recording Soc., MCA and RCA. Adviser Upward Bound. Recipient Billboard award, 1965, Outstanding Artist of the Year award Nat. Assn. of FM Broadcasters, 1975, Premio Roma award from Italy for performance at Sistina Theatre. Founder and major contbr. NIHEWAN Found. for Native Am. Scholarships, founder Native N.American Women's Assn., Creative Native, Inc. mem. AFTRA, Am. Fedn. Musicians. Author, composer, illustrator-The Buffy Sainte-Marie Songbook. Composer of over 300 published songs including It's My Way, Many a Mile, Little Wheel Spin and Spin, Fire and Fleet and Candlelight, I'm Gonna Be a Country Girl Again, Until It's Time for You to Go (ASCAP award), Universal Soldier, Piney Wood Hills, My Country 'Tis of The People You're Dying, Now That the Buffalo's Gone. Address: care Magna Artists Corp 595 Madison Ave Suite 901 New York NY 10022 *

SAIZAN, PAULA THERESA, oil co. exec.; b. New Orleans, Sept. 12, 1947; d. Paul Morine and Hattie Mae (Hayes) Saizan; B.S. in acctg. maxima cum laude, Xavier U., 1969; m. George H. Smith, May 26, 1973 (div. July 1976). Systems engr. IBM, New Orleans, 1969-71; acct., then sr. acct. Shell Oil Co., Houston, Tex., 1971-76, sr. fin. analyst, 1976-77, fin. rep., 1977-79, corp. auditor, 1979-81, treasury rep., 1981—. Treas., Inwood Forest Civic Club. C.P.A.; notary public. Mem. Am. Inst. C.P.A.s, Tex. Soc. C.P.A.s, Nat. Assn. Accts., Inwood Forest Improvement Assn., LWV of Houston, Xavier U. Alumni Assn. (membership dir.), Phi Gamma Nu. Roman Catholic. Home: 5426 Long Creek Ln Houston TX 77088 Office: 4095 One Shell Plaza PO Box 2463 Houston TX 77001

SAKS, JUDITH-ANN, artist; b. Anniston, Ala., Dec. 20, 1943; d. Julien David and Lucy-Jane (Watson) S.; student Tex. Acad. Art, 1957-58, Mus. Fine Arts, Houston, 1962, Rice U., 1962; B.F.A., Tulane U., 1966; postgrad. U. Houston, 1967; m. Haskell Irvin Rosenthal, Dec. 22, 1974; 1 son, Brian Julien. One-man shows include: Alley Gallery, Houston, 1969, 2131 Gallery, Houston, 1969; group shows include: Birmingham (Ala.) Mus., 1967, Meinhard Galleries, Houston, 1977; Galerie Barbizon, Houston, 1980, Park Crest Gallery, Austin, 1981; represented in permanent collections including: L.B. Johnson Manned Space Mus., Clear Lake City, Tex., Harris County Heritage Mus., Windsor Castle, London, Smithsonian Instn., Washington: commns. include: Pin Oak Charity Horse Show Assn., Roberts S.S. Agy., New Orleans; curator student art collection U. Houston, 1968-72; artist Am. Revolution Bicentennial project Port of Houston Authority, 1975-76. Recipient art awards including: 1st prize for water color Art League Houston, 1969, 1st prize for graphics, 1969, 1st prize for sculpture, 1968. Mem. Art League Houston, Artists Equity. Home: care Mrs S B Weiner 434 Hunterwood St Houston TX 77024

SALAVERRIA, HELENA CLARA, educator; b. San Francisco, May 19, 1923; d. Blas Saturnino and Eugenia Irene (Loyarte) Salaverria; A.B., U. Calif., Berkeley, 1945, secondary teaching certificate, 1946; M.A., Stanford U., 1962. High sch. tchr., 1946-57; asst. prof. Luther Coll., Decorah, Iowa, 1959-60; prof. Spanish, Bakersfield (Calif.) Coll., 1961—, chmn. dept., 1973-80. Mem. Calif. (dir. 1976-77), Kern County (pres. 1975-77) fgn. lang. tchrs. assns., NEA, Union Concerned Scientists, Natural Resources Def. Council, Calif. Tchrs. Assn. (chpt. sec. 1951-52), Yolo County Council Retarded, Amnesty Internat., Common Cause, Sierra Club, Prytanean Alumnae, U. Calif. Alumni Assn., Bakersfield Coll. Faculty Assn., Internat. Lang. Club Bakersfield, Kern County Basque Club, Am. Farmland Trust. Democrat. Presbyn. Address: PO Box 63 Cambria CA 93428 Also: 1801 Panorama Dr Bakersfield CA 93305

SALAZAR, ADELA NORA, med. technologist; b. Pueblo, Colo., Nov. 14, 1953; d. Petronillo and Sarah (Madrid) S.; B.S. in Med. Tech., N.Mex. Highlands U., 1975. Intern, Meml. Gen. Hosp., Las Cruces, N.Mex., 1974-75; med. technologist St. Vincent Hosp., Santa Fe, 1975—. Mem. Am. Soc. Clin. Pathologists, N.Mex. Soc. Med. Tech. Democrat. Roman Catholic. Office: 455 St Michael's Dr Santa Fe NM 87501

SALAZAR, CONSTANCIA SILVA, publs. specialist; b. Corpus Christi, Tex., July 16, 1945; d. Leonard Lozano and Lily (Sanchez) Silva; student public schs., Brownsville, Tex.; m. Andrew G. Salazar, Mar. 20, 1981; 1 son, Steven; 1 son from previous marriage, Edward Garcia. Office mgr. Read A Rama, 1963-64; editorial asst. Brownsville Herald, 1964-70; purchasing expeditor Marathon LeTourneau, 1970-73; asso. editor Hughes News mag. Hughes Tool Co., Houston, 1982—. Sec.-treas., East End Little League, exec. bd., booster chmn.; mem. publs. com. Fiestas Patrias Assn. Mem. Internat. Assn. Bus. Communicators, Beta Sigma Phi. Democrat. Roman Catholic. Home: 2231 Des Jardines Houston TX 77023 Office: 5425 Polk Ave Houston TX 77023

SALAZAR, ROSALIE MAE, county ofcl.; b. Los Angeles, Mar. 18, 1937; d. Alfonso and Carmen (Fajardo) Robles; student Rio Hondo Coll., 1976—; children—Laura Lynn, Sandra Marie. With Bank of Am., Los Angeles, 1955-59, Security Pacific Nat. Bank, Los Angeles, 1959-69; with County of Los Angeles, 1969—, community dept. analyst I, spl. investigator, program rep., 1979—; cons. in field. Tchr., C.C.D. classes St. Mary's Ch., Whittier, 1961. Recipient award Chicana Action Service Center, 1978. Mem. The Exec. Female, Nat. Assn. Female Execs., Am. Soc. Profl. and Exec. Women. Democrat. Roman Catholic. Home: 7221-B Comstock Ave Whittier CA 90602 Office: 3175 W 6th St Los Angeles CA 90020

SALE, DEBORAH MARY, entertainment co. exec.; b. Piggott, Ark., May 6, 1948; d. Gerald and Ora Dean (Williams) Sale; B.A. in History, Southwestern U. at Memphis, 1970. Exec. dir. Com. of Interns and Residents, N.Y.C., 1971-72; dir. career edn. Office of Mayor, City of N.Y., 1972-76; spl. asst to Vice pres. Walter F. Mondale, 1977-79; dep. chmn., dir. staff and ops. Fed. Council on Arts and Humanities, Washington, 1979-81; dir. corp. services Columbia Pictures Industries, Inc., N.Y.C., 1981—; lectr. in field; dir. Dance Theatre Workshop, The Second Stage; cons. Am. Women's Econ. Devel. Corp., 1976; mem. N.Y.C. Manpower Planning Council Youth Com., 1974-76; dir. Reel to Reel Video Corp., 1971-72; dir. Washington Visual Artists Slide Registry, 1980-81, Millennium Chamber Ensemble, 1982—; mem. adv. council on Hist. Preservation, 1981—; cons. Mayor's Office on the Film Industry, 1973. Mem. staff Congressman Bob Eckhardt, Tex., 1971, Senator Albert Gore, Tenn., 1971; mem. Muskie presdl. campaign staff 1972; mem. Presdl. Inaugural Com., 1976-77; active Dem. presdl. campaign, 1976; active Big Sister program, 1970-71. Mem. Arts and Artifacts Indemnity Council (exec. com. 1979-81), Nat. Student Assn. (dir., chmn. steering com. 1969-70). Democrat. Office: 711 Fifth Ave New York NY 10022

SALERNO, EVELYN, cons. pharmacist; b. Passaic, N.J., Dec. 14, 1936; d. John C. and Elvira (Infante) S.; B.S., Rutgers U., 1958; D.Pharmacy, Mercer U., 1975. From clk. to part-time registered pharmacist Martini's Pharmacy, Hackensack, N.J., 1956-60; chief pharmacist Pascack Valley Hosp., Westwood, N.J., 1960; pharmacist Prescription Pharmacy, Hialeah, Fla., 1961-63; registered pharmacist, asst. mgr., dir. pharmacy South Fla. State Hosp., Hollywood, 1963-74, dir. profl. services, asst. dir. hosp. pharmacies, 1975—; with RCW Cons., Inc., 1975-82; dir. clin. services Nursing Home Assos., Inc., 1981-82; vis. lectr. U. Miami Sch. Nursing, asso. prof., 1977—; cons. Hospice S. Fla., Sunrise, community for retarded. Mem. Am. Pharm. Assn., Am. Soc. Hosp. Pharmacists, Am. Inst. History Pharmacy, Southeastern Soc. Hosp. Pharmacists, S. Fla. Soc. Hosp. Pharmacists, Fla. Pharm. Assn., Fla. Soc. Hosp. Pharmacists, Rutgers U. Alumni Assn., Mercer U. Alumni Assn., Am. Pharm. Assn. Acad. Pharmacy Practice, Heart Assn. Greater Miami. Democrat. Roman Catholic. Author papers in field, profl. reviewer. Office: 8768 SW 131st St Miami FL 33176

SALERNO, SUSAN CORINE, mfg. co. ofcl.; b. Burlington, Wis., Sept. 22, 1950; d. Richard L. and Ardine B. Haugen Hebron; B.S., U. Wis., 1971; M.B.A., Roosevelt U., 1982; m. F. Robert Salerno, Sept. 6, 1975. Office mgr., adminstrv. asst., Hertz Corp., Milw., 1972-75; fleet adminstr. Digital Equipment Corp., Maynard, Mass., 1975-78; adminstrv. mgr. The Trane Co., Chgo., 1978-81; fin. analyst-metals Anaconda Industries, Rolling Meadows, Ill., 1981—; workshop panelist, cons. in field. Mem. Women in Communications, Nat. Assn. Fleet Adminstrs., Nat. Assn. Van Pool Operators (co-editor newsletter; mem. internat. communications com., dir. 1978—), Nat. Safety Council (cert. instr. def. driving course). Author brochure, booklet in field. Home: 4542 Gettysburg Dr Rolling Meadows IL 60008 Office: 1701 Golf Rd Rolling Meadows IL 60008

SALHANICK, BRENDA CRANE, pension cons.; b. Keene, N.H., Aug. 2, 1951; d. Clayton Howard and Anita (Barry) Crane; B.A. cum laude, St. Anselm's Coll., 1974; student paralegal and para-actuarial dept. Bentley Coll. 1977, C.L.U. Northeastern U. 1978; m. Joel Alan Salhanick, Sept. 16, 1978. With Jules Meyers Assocs., Chestnut Hill, Mass. 1975—, dir. pension dept. 1977—, v.p. Employee Benefit Plan Services 1979—. Instr. first aid ARC 1972-81. Mem. Nat. Assn. Security Dealers. Republican. Clubs: New England Aquarium Dive (newsletter editor), St. Anselm's Coll. Century. Office: 1330 Boylston St Chestnut Hill MA 02167

SALINAS, MARIE RUTH ORTIZ, educator; b. Kenedy, Tex., Dec. 3, 1935; d. Dionel R. and Conseulo R. Ortiz; A.A., Bee County Coll., 1976; B.S. cum laude, U. Houston Victoria Campus, 1979; m. Rosalio F. Salinas, Apr. 26, 1952; children—Rose Marie, Lydia Jane, Aurora Diane, Debra Renee, Helen Virginia, John Dionel, Rosalio, Joseph Emilio, Consuelo Yvonne, Ruth Anne. Bilingual kindergarten and adult basic edn. tchr Houston Pub. Schs. Clk., treas., tchr. 1st Mexican Baptist Ch.; sec., tchr., dir. tchrs. Gambrell Bapt. Assn.; pres. Bapt. Women's Missionary Union. Cert. tchr. bilingual, kindergarten, gen. and Spanish, Tex. Mem. Tex. Tchrs. Assn., NEA, Tex. Coll. Tchrs. Assn. Democrat. Office: University of Houston 523 E Houston St Kenedy TX 78119

SALING, STELLA MARIA, clin. psychologist; b. Wildflecken, Germany, Feb. 1, 1948; d. Louise Saling; B.A., U. Calif., Riverside, 1970; M.A., U.S. Internat. U., 1975, Ph.D., 1978. Psychologist, Grosse Pointe (Mich.) Psychol. Center, 1978-79; staff New Alternatives, San Diego, 1980-81; pvt. practice psychotherapy and psychodiagnosis, 1981—; cons. residential assessment and treatment child abuse victims. U. Calif. Pres.' scholar, 1967-68. Mem. Am. Psychol. Assn., San Diego Psychology and Law Soc., San Diego Mental Health Assn. Club: Sierra. Contbr. to Sr. Life Newspaper, 1980-81. Office: 7290 Navajo Rd Suite 209 San Diego CA 92119

SALINGER, JOAN MARIE, data processor; b. New Rochelle, N.Y., Mar. 14, 1949; d. John Gerard and Dorothea Eleanor (Lucy) Kelleher; B.A. in Math., Coll. New Rochelle, 1970; M.S. in Computer Sci., Poly. Inst. N.Y., 1978. With AT&T Co., White Plains, N.Y., 1971—, tng. mgr. long lines, 1978-80, data processing mgr. long lines, 1980—; lectr. Coll. New Rochelle. Mem. Ursuline Alumnae Assn. (class agt.). Democrat. Roman Catholic. Office: 99 Church St White Plains NY 10601

SALISBURY, GRETCHEN M., editor, pub. co. exec.; b. Berkeley, Calif., Mar. 16, 1949; d. Yale and Audrey Nell (Kittel) Meyer; student Barnard Coll., 1966-70; m. Stephen P. Salisbury (div.). Editorial asst. Farrar, Straus & Giroux, N.Y.C., 1975-76; asst. editor Am. Rev. mag. and Bantam Books, N.Y.C., 1976-78; assoc. editor Thomas Congdon Books, E.P. Dutton, N.Y.C., 1978-79; sr. editor Congdon & Lattes, N.Y.C., 1979-82; v.p., sr. editor Congdon & Weed, N.Y.C., 1982—. Home: 200 W 90th St New York NY 10024 Office: 298 Fifth Ave New York NY 10001

SALITERMAN, LAURA SHRAGER, pediatrician; b. N.Y.C., June 26, 1946; d. Arthur M. and Ida Shrager; A.B. magna cum laude, Brandeis U., 1967; M.D., N.Y. U., 1971; m. Richard Arlen Saliterman, June 15, 1975. Intern, resident in pediatrics Montefiore Hosp. and Med. Center, Bronx, N.Y., 1971-74; pediatrician Morrisania Family Care Center, Bronx, 1974-75, Share Health Plan, St. Paul, 1975—, dir. pediatrics, 1976-82; clin. instr. pediatrics U. Minn., 1975—. Mem. nat. women's com. Brandeis U., 1975—, Sherwood Forest Neighborhood Assn., 1977—. Recipient Greenberg Meml. Sci. award Brandeis U., 1967; diplomate Am. Bd. Pediatrics. Mem. Am. Acad. Pediatrics, N.Y. U. Sch. Medicine Alumni Assn., Phi Beta Kappa. Club: Oak Ridge Country (Hopkins, Minn.). Home: 11911 Live Oak Dr Minnetonka MN 55343 Office: 555 Simpson Saint Paul MN 55104

SALKIN, GERALDINE (JERI) FAUBION, dancer, dance therapist, educator; b. Denver, Mar. 18, 1916; d. George Everett and Hanna Viola (Harvey) Faubion; student Lester Horton Dance Theater, Carmelita Maracci, Trudi Schoop, Los Angeles, 1937-47, Doris Humphrey, N.Y.C., 1952-53, Rudolf Von Laban, London, 1956-57, Hanna Fenichel, Ph.D., 1965-70, UCLA, 1959-60; Ph.D., 1978; m. Leo Salkin, June 29, 1936; 1 dau., Lynn Salkin Sbiroli. Concert dancer Lester Horton Dance Group, Los Angeles, 1937-47, tchr. creative modern dance, 1939-47; tchr. creative modern dance Dance Assos., Hollywood, Calif., 1949-53, Am. Sch. of London (Eng.), 1956-57, Jeri Salkin Studio and Center for Child Study, Hollywood, 1968-73; developer body ego technique Camarillo (Calif.) State Hosp., 1957-64; movement specialist Nat. Endowment Arts grantee, 1973—; dir., body ego technique dept. Cedars-Sinai Thalians Community Mental Health Center, Los Angeles, 1965—; dance cons., tchr. Nat. Head Start Program, Calif., 1964; dir. workshops, mem. aux. faculty Goddard Coll., Antioch Coll., various hosps. and univs. Calif. Dept. Mental Hygiene grantee, 1960-63. Mem. Am. Dance Therapy Assn., AAHPER, Calif. Dance Educators Assn., Calif. Assn. Health, Phys. Edn. and Recreation, Nat. Assn. Edn. Young Children, Child Devel. Specialists, Com. Research in Dance. Democrat. Author: Body Ego Technique, an Educational and Therapeutic Approach to Body Image and Self-Identity, 1973; author, choreographer film (with Leo Salkin and Trudi Schoop) Body Ego Technique, 1962 (U.S. Golden Eagle Council on Internat. Nontheatrical Events award 1963). Home: 3584 Multiview Dr Hollywood CA 90068 Office: 8730 Alden Dr Los Angeles CA 90048

SALLEY, VIRGINIA SUTTON, bus. exec.; b. Miami, Fla.; d. Durward Belmont and Sarabelle (Burns) Sutton; student Sullins Coll., Rollins Coll.; m. George H. Salley, Aug. 28, 1961. Asso., jr. partner D.B. Sutton Jewelry Co., Miami, 1948-50; singer (Gloria Manning, profl. name) with Vincent Lopez Orch., Ben Ribble Orch., 1951-60; owner, operator Wiscasset Antiques, 1960-62; owner, mgr., pres. Sutton Manning Corp., 1962—. Mem Met. Dade County Zoning Apls. Bd., 1966-70, vice-chairperson, 1970-71; bd. dirs. Big Bros., 1971-72; founder, pres. Theatre Arts League, 1959, Jr. Theatre Guild of Miami, 1961. Mem. Nat. League Am. Pen Women, Am. Guild Variety Artists, Screen Actors Guild. Mem. Christian Ch. Clubs: Miami Yacht, Key Largo, Indian Creek, Boothbay Harbour Yacht. Contbr. articles in field to profl. jours. Office: Sutton Manning Corp 100 N Biscayne Blvd Suite 700 Miami FL 33132

SALMON, ALICE SULLIVAN, nurse; b. N.Y.C., July 22, 1949; d. James Stephen and Ellen Hanna (Smith) Sullivan; B.S. in Nursing, Molloy Coll., 1971; M.A. in Nurse Edn., N.Y. U., 1975; m. Francis W. Salmon, Oct. 12, 1975. Staff nurse Hosp. Albert Einstein Coll. Medicine, 1971-72, asst. head nurse, 1972-74, asst. dir. II, 1975-80, asst. dir. nursing, 1980—. Mem. Am. Nurses Assn., Sigma Theta Tau. Office: 1825 Eastchester Rd Bronx NY 10461

SALMONS, JOANNA, nursing adminstr.; b. Smiths Grove, Ky., Nov. 7, 1933; d. Walter Scott and Birdie Wilma (Jackson) Parker; R.N., Fla. Hosp. Sch. Nursing, 1954; student So. Missionary Coll., 1979; cert. in health systems mgmt. Harvard U., 1980; B.S.N. SUNY, 1982; postgrad. Trinity Coll.; m. William L. Salmons, June 6, 1970; children by previous marriage—Robert B., Scott Alan. Dir. nursing Larkin Gen. Hosp., Miami, Fla.; adminstr., Ft. Walton Beach (Fla.) Hosp., 1974-75; dir. surg. nursing Fla. Hosp., Orlando, 1976-78; dir. nursing Adventist Health Systems/Sunbelt Corp., Orlando, 1978-79; sr. v.p. nursing adminstrn. Fla Hosp. Orlando, 1979—; cons. in field. Mem. A Thousand Plus com. Am. Cancer Soc. Recipient Outstanding Achievement award, Larkin Gen. Hosp., Miami, 1969 Mem. Fla. Nurses Assn. (bd. dirs. 1980-81), Am. Heart Assn., Retarded Children's Assn. Orange County, Fla. Hosp. Assn., Am. Nurses Assn. (cert. nurse adminstr.), Fla. Soc. Nursing Adminstrs., Am. Soc. Nursing Adminstrs., Assn. Seventh-Day Adventist Nursing Club: Buena Ventura Lakes Golf and Tennis. Home: 341 Beach St Longwood FL 32750 Office: 601 Rollins St Orlando FL 32803

SALOMON, JANET LYNN, profl. figure skater; b. Chgo., Apr. 6, 1953; d. Florian W. and Ethelyne L. (Gerhke) Nowicki; m. Richard Marc Salomon, Oct. 18, 1975; children—Dustin Patrick, Nicolas Ajax, Benjamin Misha. Nat. ladies figure skating champion, 1969-73; Ladies figure skating bronze medalist, 1972 Olympics; bronze medalist World Figure Skating Championship, 1972, silver medalist, 1973; star Ice Follies, 1973-75; appeared in TV commercials, 1973-75. Bd. dirs. Sinnissippi Lung Assn. Author: Peace & Love, 1973.

SALOMON, SUZANNE EVAN, real estate broker, securities rep.; b. Chgo., Mar. 15, 1947; d. Joseph Klee and Jane Evonne (Rovee) Salomon; B.A. (Durant scholar), Wellesley Coll., 1969; M.P.A. (Woodrow Wilson Sch. fellow) Princeton U., 1971; certificate lit. Oxford (Eng.) U., 1967. Asso. real estate cons. Gladstone Assos., Washington, 1971-74; pres. Susal Assos., econ. cons., Washington, 1974-76; real estate market analyst Internat. Paper Co., N.Y.C., 1976-77, mgr. strategic planning, 1977-78; v.p. corporate devel. dept. Chase Manhattan Bank, 1978-79, pres. Internat. Corp. Strategies, 1979-81; v.p. Sybedon Equities Corp., N.Y.C., 1981—; lectr. in field. Vice pres. bd. dirs. N.Y. Com. for Young Audiences; trustee McBurney Sch. Registered securities rep.; lic. real estate broker. Mem. Fin. Women's Assn., Assn. Real Estate Women, Real Estate Securities and Syndication Inst. Home: 320 E 57th St New York NY 10022 Office: 121 Ave of Americas New York NY 10036

SALSBURY, GLENNA RUTH, speaker, cons.; b. Peoria, Ill., Sept. 13, 1937; d. Glenn Albert and Helen Bethia (Lake) Arnold; B.S., Northwestern U., 1959; M.A., UCLA, 1961; M.A., Fuller Theol. Sem., Pasadena, Calif., 1977; m. James W. Salsbury, Feb. 10, 1979; children by previous marriage—Monica Osborn, Melissa Osborn, Michelle Osborn. Pres., Cameo Tapes and Books, Santa Ana, Calif., 1972-77; v.p. human resources Tarbell Realtors, Tustin, Calif., 1977-80; pres. Salsbury Enterprises, El Toro, Calif., 1980—; mgmt. and sales tng. cons. Mem. Nat. Speakers Assn., Sales and Mktg. Execs. Republican. Mem. Christian Ch. Author: Reflections, 1977; The Bible: Fact or Fiction?, 1968; Can Humans Be Christians?, 1972; Have You Considered Job?, 1972. Home and office: 22135 Debra El Toro CA 92630

SALSE, ELIZABETH LANDON, cross-cultural communication cons. co. exec.; b. Rio de Janeiro, Aug. 19, 1929; d. Archie Blake and Ambrosina (Salse) Landon; B.A., Andrews U., 1949; M.S., No. Ill. U., 1978; m. Eduardo A.B. Salse, Dec. 25, 1956; children—Elise Landon Johnson, Victoria Lynne Switzer, John Blake, Angela Marie. Instr., Harper Coll., Palatine, Ill., 1971-77; developed high sch. English as 2d lang. program Joliet (Ill.) Jr. Coll., 1977; coordinator English as 2d lang. program Mundelein Coll., Chgo., 1977-78; pres., owner Sales Cross-Cultural Communication; Arlington Heights, Ill., 1978—. Mem. Soc. Intercultural Edn., Tng. and Research, TESOL. Home and Office: 306 N Carlyle Pl Arlington Heights IL 60004

SALSTROM, SARA-JANE, med. technologist; b. Youngstown, Ohio, May 19, 1946; d. Martin and Edna Hazel (Theis) Mueller; B.S., Kent State U., 1971; 1 dau., Valerie Jean. Intern in med. tech. Akron (Ohio) City Hosp., 1970-71, staff med. technologist, 1971-74, research med. technologist specializing in infectious disease research, 1974—. Mem. Am. Soc. Clin. Pathologists (cert. med. technologist), Am. Soc. Microbiology. Republican. Lutheran. Club: Zeppelin Rifle. Contbr. articles to profl. jours. Office: Akron City Hosp 75 Arch St Suite 204 Akron OH 44304

SALTA, WENDY ANN KEHL, public relations fund raising exec.; b. Akron, Ohio, Mar. 16, 1942; d. James Howard and Alice Jayne (Hilbish) Ake; B.A., Pacific Northwestern U., 1961, M.B.A., 1963; 1 son, John Thomas. Spl. survey technician Dept. Commerce, Bur. Census, N.Y.C., 1970-71; dir. devel. Queensboro Soc. Prevention Cruelty to Children, N.Y.C., 1971-73; regional coordinator Muscular Dystrophy Assn., N.Y.C., 1973-77; dir. mktg. Greater Jamaica Devel. Corp., N.Y.C., 1977-80; dir. devel. Myasthenia Gravis Found., N.Y.C., 1980—; founder, owner Service Bur. for Lawyers, N.Y.C., 1970. Campaign mgr. state senator, 1967, state assemblyman, 1978. Mem. Am. Arbitration Assn., Nat. Soc. Fund Raising Execs., Archaeol. Soc. Presbyterian. Home: 35-20 Leverich St Jackson Heights NY 11372 Office: 15 E 26th St New York NY 10010

SALTER, DIANNE SHARON, clin. psychologist; b. Trenton, Sept. 1, 1950; d. Richard Lee and Ruby Lee (Reed) S.; B.A., Antioch Coll., 1972; M.A., Adelphi U., 1974, Ph.D., 1977. Cons. psychologist Williamsburg Child Devel. Centers, Bklyn., 1973-75; psychology intern Eastern Pa. Psychiat. Inst., Phila., 1975-76; clin. sch. psychologist Trenton Bd. Edn., 1976-78; psychol. cons. Atlantic Human Resources, Inc., Atlantic City, 1979—; supervising psychologist Irving Schwartz Inst., Phila., 1978-81, dir. psychol. services, 1981—; pvt. practice psychology, Phila., 1979—. Bd. dirs. Family Services Assn. Bucks County (Pa.), 1978—. NIMH fellow, 1972-75. Mem. Am. Psychol. Assn., Am. Personnel and Guidance Assn., Assn. Black Psychologists, Delaware Valley Assn. Black Psychologists (pres.), Phila. Soc. Clin. Psychology. Baptist. Home: 357 W Johnson St W-311 Philadelphia PA 19144 Office: 5555 Wissahickon Ave Philadelphia PA 19144

SALTZER, ELEANOR BUCKMAN, psychologist; b. Los Angeles, May 31, 1945; d. Alfred Leonard and Gertrude Ann (Papermaster) Buckman; B.S., UCLA, 1966, M.Nursing, 1968; Ph.D., U. Calif., Irvine, 1979; m. Eugene I. Saltzer, July 10, 1965; children—Karen Rebecca, David Paul. Instr., UCLA Sch. Nursing, 1968-69; corp. v.p., sec. Med. office mgr. Nurse-Eugene I. Saltzer, M.D., Inc., Orange, Calif., 1972-79; lectr. program in social ecology U. Calif., Irvine, 1978-79. asso. dir. research and clin. asst. prof. dept. family medicine, 1979-81, dir. nursing research, Irvine Med. Center and asst. clin. prof. dept. pediatrics, 1981—; corp. v.p., sec. Eugene I. Saltzer, M.D., Inc., 1974—. Sec., mem. bd. dirs. Opera Soc. Orange County, 1980-82; den leader, parent com. chmn. Cub Scouts 850, Canyons Dist., Orange County Council, Boy Scouts Am., 1979-82. U. Calif. Regents scholar, 1965, 66; USPHS Nurse traineeship, 1967-68; named Grad. Student of the Yr., UCLA Sch. Nursing, 1968; U. Calif. Regents Patent Fund grantee, 1978-79. Mem. Am. Nurses Assn. (council on nurse researchers), Am. Psychol. Assn., Am. Public Health Assn., Orange County-Long Beach Nursing Consortium, Am. Sociol. Assn., Western Council on Higher Edn. in Nursing, Soc. Behavioral Medicine, Western Soc. Research in Nursing, UCLA Sch. Nursing Alumni Assn., Sigma Theta Tau. Contbr. articles to profl. jours. Office: 101 City Dr S Orange CA 92668

SALTZMAN, ESTELLE GOODMAN, advt. co. exec.; b. Eureka, Calif., Apr. 24, 1942; d. Max John and Bernice (Feldman) Goodman; student UCLA, 1959-61; B.A., U. Calif., Berkeley, 1963; m. Morton L. Saltzman, Aug. 29, 1965. Reporter, Humboldt (Calif.) Times, 1964-66, Reno Evening Gazette, 1966-69, Van Nuys (Calif.) News, 1969-71; freelance writer, Sacramento, 1971-72; writer Dannenfelser, Runyon, Craig, Inc., Sacramento, 1972-75; owner, mng. partner Runyon/Saltzman, Inc., Sacramento, 1976—. Bd. dirs. Friends of State Fair; Jr. Statesmen Found., Community Interaction Program, women's council Sacramento C. of C. Golden ERA Handicrafts. Mem. Public Relations Roundtable Sacramento. Home: 2505 Los Feliz Way Carmichael CA 95608 Office: 2131 L St Sacramento Ca 95816

SALYARDS, DENISE ANN, bank ofcl.; b. Providence, Feb. 10, 1954; d. William Bradford and Dorothy Mary (Thibodeau) Smith; student Providence Coll., 1975-79; m. Michael Jeffrey Salyards, Dec. 29, 1979; children—Michael Jeffrey, II, Kristina Alaine. Clk.-typist money market dept. Indsl. Nat. Bank, Providence, 1972, bookkeeper, 1972-75, asst. fin. analyst, 1975-76, market research asst., 1976-78, market research analyst, 1978-79; dir. market research Hamilton Bank, Lancaster, Pa., 1979-82; mgr. market research 1st Nat. Exchange Bank, Roanoke, Va., 1982; asst. v.p., dir. market research Dominion Bankshares Corp., 1982—; cons. Strategic Planning Task Force, 1981, Hamilton Bank, 1982—. Mem. Am. Mktg. Assn. (chpt. pres. 1981-82), Bank Mktg. Assn., Nat. Assn. Bank Women, Market Research Assn., Nat. Assn. Female Execs., Roanoke Network Profl. and Managerial Women. Roman Catholic. Home: Route 1 Box 200-B Goodview VA 24095 Office: PO Box 13327 Roanoke VA 24040

SALYER, PAULINE A., artist, author, editor, real estate broker; b. Minco, Okla., Sept. 30, 1912; d. Leslie E. and Nora Dell (Thompson) Johnson; student Hills Business Coll. 1934-35, Okla City U. 1944-45, 1967, U. of Okla. 1965-66; m. B.M. Salyer, Jr., Jan. 18, 1931; children—Jerry J., Mona Sue Salyer Lambird, Christopher M. Vice pres. Salyer Refining Co., Oklahoma City, 1948-57; sec.-treas. Salyer Stay Ready Filter Co., Oklahoma City, 1957-69; pres. Salyer Publishing Co., Oklahoma City, 1964—; real estate broker Pauline Salyer Realty, Oklahoma City, 1964—; founder World Orgn. of China Painters, Oklahoma City, 1967—, pres., 1967-77, chmn. bd. dirs. 1977-79, also life trustee; one-man shows Patrician Room, Oklahoma City, 1972, juried show Art Gallery, Calif. State U., Fullerton, 1977, Stovall Mus., 1977, San Francisco Mus. Art, 1979, State Capitol Okla., 1979. Recipient Byliners award Women in Communications, 1979. Mem. Okla. State Fedn. China Decorators (life, founder), Internat. Porcelain Art Tchrs., Okla. Art League. Methodist. Author china-painting textbook: Great Artists of China Decoration, 1964. Address: 3111 NW 19th St Oklahoma City OK 73107

SAMARA, BRENDA MARY, psychologist; b. Cambridge, Mass., Dec. 8, 1941; d. Edward and Helen (Maloof) S.; B.A., Bennington Coll., 1963; M.A., U. New Hampshire, 1965; Ph.D., Temple U., 1974. Staff psychologist Phila. State Hosp., 1965-67, Phila. Gen. Hosp., 1967-69, Jefferson Hosp., Phila., 1969-70; pvt. practice clin. psychology, Phila., 1970—. Mem. Am. Psychol. Assn., Assn. Humanistic Psychology, Internat. Inst. for Bioenergetic Analysis, NOW. Democrat.

SAMBOLD, MARGIE LOU, banker; b. McKees Rocks, Pa., Nov. 22, 1935; d. Fred and Ann Louise (Gernandt) Enghardt; student Am. Inst. Banking; m. Albert James Sambold, May 1, 1956; children—Albert James, Sylvia Ann, Angela Janine. Bookkeeper, proof operator Commonwealth Trust, McKees Rocks, Pa., 1952-56; teller First Nat. Bank Topeka, 1956-59, Bank of Bellevue (Nebr.), 1962-66; teller, credit analyst, loan officer, br. mgr., asst. cashier Hampton (N.H.) Nat. Bank, 1971—, also banking services officer, br. adminstr. Active Boy Scouts Am., Friends of Library; Hampton Housing Authority, 1977-78. Mem. Am. Inst. Banking (dir. eastern N.H. chpt.), Bus. and Profl. Women's Club, (pres.). Republican. Clubs: Catholic Women's, Officers Wives, Band Boosters. Home: 35 Milbern Ave Hampton NH 03842 Office: 100 Winnacunnet Rd Hampton NH 03842

SAMMARTINO, SYLVIA (MRS. PETER SAMMARTINO), univ. ofcl.; b. Boston, Dec. 5, 1903; d. Louis J. and Anna E. (Bianchi) Scaramelli; A.B., Smith Coll., 1925; M.A., Columbia U., 1926; LL.D., Kyung Hee U., Seoul, Korea, 1964; D.H.L., Fairleigh Dickinson U., 1966; m. Peter Sammartino, Dec. 5, 1933. Tchr. pub. high sch., N.Y.C., 1927-28, 1933-35; treas. Scaramelli and Co., Inc., N.Y.C., 1928-33; ednl. editor Atlantica 1933-35; circulation mgr. La Voix de France, N.Y.C., 1935-37; registrar Fairleigh Dickinson U., 1942-50, dir. admissions, 1950-59, dean of admissions, 1959—. Chmn. statewide conf. N.J. Commn. on Women, 1971. Bd. govs. N.Y. Cultural Center; chmn. bd. trustees Integrity Inc.; pres. Garden State Ballet; mem. Restore Ellis Island Com.; trustee Newark Symphony Hall, William Carlos Williams Center for Performing Arts. Recipient Amita award, 1960; medal Smith Coll., 1967; Pres.'s medal Mercy Coll.; decorated officer Ordre National (Ivory Coast); Order of Star of Africa (Liberia); officer Order of Merit (Italy). Mem. Am. Assn. Coll. Registrars and Officers of Admission. Home: 140 Ridge Rd Rutherford NJ 07070

SAMMON, PEGGY LOUISE, water pollution abatement co. exec.; b. Toronto, Ont., Can., Jan. 21, 1954; came to U.S., 1969; d. Roger Breen and Mary Bridget Sammon; B.A. in Design, Bucknell U., Lewisburg, Pa., 1975. Freelance artist, 1976-78; co-dir., owner Pendragon Inc., theatre and art prodn. co., Santa Fe, 1978—; pres. Am. Digital Systems, Inc., Huntsville, Ala., 1978—; designer ADS Field Mgmt. Program, 1977. Mem. Water Pollution Control Fedn., Am. Mgmt. Assn., Alpha Chi. Roman Catholic. Home: 2021 Highridge Dr Apt 5A Huntsville AL 35802 Office: 2227 Drake Ave SW Huntsville AL 35804

SAMPLE, CAROL BERNIECE, educator; b. Watertown, S.D., Aug. 2, 1924; d. Carl M. and Gertrude (Larson) Kvinge; B.A., Union Coll., Lincoln, Nebr., 1947; M.A., East Tenn. State U., 1962; Ph.D., Tex. Christian U., 1975; m. Melvin Leon Sample, Aug. 20, 1945; children—Terry Lee, Robert Lynn. Secondary sch. tchr., 1946-50; sec. S.D. Conf. Seventh-day Adventist Ch., 1954-60; instr. in English, Columbia Union Coll., 1963-67; asst. prof. English, Southwestern Adventist Coll., Keene, Tex., 1967-68, asso. prof., 1969-74, prof., 1975—; supt. Keene Seventh-day Adventist Sabbath Sch., 1968-71. Mem. Modern Lang. Assn., AAUP, Assn. Adventist Forums (sec.-treas. Keene chpt.). Home: PO Box 167 Keene TX 76059 Office: Southwestern Adventist Coll Keene TX 76509

SAMPLE, DOROTHY EATON, state legislator, civic worker; b. Nyack, N.Y., May 1, 1911; d. Samuel Edward and Olive Bowers (Eddy) Eaton; B.A., Duke U., 1933, postgrad. Law Sch.; m. Richard Lardner Sample, Dec. 28, 1939; children—Dianne, Dee, Dicky. Sec., firm Edwards & Leatherwood, Bryson City, N.C.; atty. Home Owners Loan Corp., Salisbury, N.C.; sec. and atty. firm Whitlock, Dockery & Shaw, Charlotte, N.C.; mem. Fla. Ho. of Reps., 1976—. Pres. Save Our Bays, PTA, Pasadena Property Owners Assn., Band Boosters; v.p., regional dir. Fla. Wildlife Fedn.; v.p. West St. Petersburg Property Owners Assn.; chmn. Gerontology Council; VIP chmn., bd. dirs. Mothers March of Dimes; chmn. Coastal Coordinating Council; founder Alliance for Conservation of Natural Resources; sponsor Jr. Coll. Service Club; legis. chmn. LWV; bd. dirs. Gulf Coast and Fla. Tb Assn., Council Neighborhood Assns., Community Welfare Council, St. Petersburg Hist. Soc., Suncoast Active Vols. for Ecology; Fla. state chmn. Am. Legis. Exchange Council; bd. trustees Gulf Coast chpt. Nat. Multiple Sclerosis Soc.; mem. adv. council on conservation and the environ. Fla. Dept. Natural Resources; mem. state adv. com. on coastal zone mgmt. Fla. Dept. Environ. Regulations; mem. Pinellas County Edn. Study Com.; mem. Citizens Council on Crime; chmn. Coastal Coordinating Council; mem. Pinellas Pkwy. Adv. Bd.; mem. St. Petersburg Bicentennial Com. Recipient Outstanding Conservationist award Rod and Gun Club, 1967, Ecology award Suncoast Gem and Mineral Soc., 1973, Outstanding Service to Mankind award Sertoma Club, 1974, Spl. Service award Fla. Wildlife Fedn., 1977, Good Govt. award Conservative Union, 1981, Freedom award Tampa Women for Responsible Legislation, 1982. St. Petersburg Beach Homeowners Assn. Outstanding Public Ofcl. award, 1982. Mem. Duke U. Alumni Assn. (chmn.), AAUW (legis. chmn.), Pan Hellenic Assn., Chi Phi, Delta Phi Rho Alpha. Republican. Episcopalian. Club: Sinawik (pres.), St. Petersburg Yacht. Office: 3110 1st Ave N Saint Petersburg FL 33713

SAMPLE, DOROTHY ELLIOTT, psychol. counselor, educator; b. Winfield, Ala., Nov. 1, 1938; d. John Belton and Annie Earl (Franks) Elliott; B.A., F.W. Bapt. Coll., 1961; A.B., U. Mich., 1966, M.A., 1967, Ph.D., 1976; Th.D., Toledo Sem., 1973; m. Richard Howard Sample, Aug. 27, 1961; children—Richard Howard, Scott Elliott, Lisa Deanne. Tchr., Linden (Mich.) Community Schs., 1963-65, Flint (Mich.) Community Schs., 1967-82; faculty John Wesley Coll., Owasso, Mich., 1973-75, adj. prof. psychology, 1973-75; tchr. Center for Christian Studies, Flint, 1979-80; tchr. piloted jr. high gifted edn. program Flint Schs., 1977; profl. counselor Personality Dynamics, Flint and Southfield, 1977—; lectr. Pres., Women's Missionary Union, So. Bapt. Conv., 1981; mem. exec. bd. Bapt. State Conv. Mich., 1977-80, mem. exec. com., 1978-80, mem. com. bds., 1979-80; vol. counselor County Jail, Flint, 1978-80. Recipient Delta Epsilon Chi Outstanding Student Merit award, 1961; Lit. Soc. award, 1961. Mem. U. Mich. Alumni Assn., AAUW, Christian Assn. Psychol. Studies, Mich. Edn. Assn., Delta Kappa Gamma, Phi Kappa Phi, Delta Epsilon Chi. Baptist. Contbr. articles to profl. jours. Home: 3119 Prospect St Flint MI 48504 Office: 600 N 20th St Birmingham AL 35203

SAMPLE, LEE MARLLENE, univ. ofcl.; b. Tuscaloosa, Ala., Sept. 26, 1955; d. Steve O. Sample and Joe Ann M. Slact; B.A., U. Ala., 1977, postgrad., 1977—. Asst. grad. registrar U. Ala., University, 1977-81, registrar Coll. Edn., 1981—. Mem. Am. Assn. Coll. Registrars and Admission Officers, Ala. Assn. Coll. Registrars and Admissions Officers, So. Assn. Coll. Registrars and Admissions Officers, Kappa Delta Pi. Presbyterian. Home: 10 Abrams Ct Tuscaloosa AL 35401 Office: University of Alabama Drawer R Room 109 Graves Hall University AL 35486

SAMPLE, MIRIAM TYLER, planning cons.; b. Balt., Mar. 1, 1920; d. Harold Norwood and Lucyle (Palmalary) Tyler; A.A., Stephens Coll., 1940; m. Joseph S. Sample, Nov. 19, 1965. With Donohue-Cooke, Chgo., 1962-63, Chgo. Sun-Times, 1963-65; vol. exec. dir. Midland Empire Council for Arts and Humanities, Billings, Mont., 1976—. Campaign dir. Citizens for Charter Govt. Home: 606 Highland Park Dr Billings MT 59102

SAMPSON, EVA BREWINGTON, nurse; b. Robeson County, N.C., July 31, 1932; d. Clyde and Lillie Mae (Jones) Brewington; R.N., Southeastern Community Coll., 1968; B.S., B.A., Pembroke State U., 1973; m. John W. Sampson, Feb. 6, 1954; children—Ursula Kaye, Kelvin Dale, Karen Gale, Suzanne. Office nurse for gen. practitioner, Pembroke, N.C., 1956-66; staff nurse Southeastern Gen. Hosp., Lumberton, N.C., 1968-70; nursing dir. student health service Pembroke State U., 1970—; vol. home vis. nurse. Mem., inservice edn. instr. Pembroke Vol. Rescue Squad; trustee N.C. Cancer Inst.; chpt. bd. dirs. nursing and bloodmobile programs ARC; mem. N.C. Health Study Commn., Dept. Public Instrn. Mem. Am. Nurses Assn., N.C. Nurses Assn., Sigma Sigma Sigma. Baptist. Home: PO Box 626 Pembroke NC 28372 Office: Student Health Service Pembroke State U Box 75 Pembroke NC 28372

SAMPSON, JUNE ELISABETH, hist. mus. adminstr.; b. Phila., May 31, 1946; d. William Herbert and Helen Elizabeth (Whitall) Stafford; B.A. in History, Earlham Coll., Richmond, Ind., 1968; M.A. in History Mus. Tng., SUNY, Oneonta, 1972; m. Earl Sampson, Jan. 22, 1972; stepchildren—Earl Brett, Daniel C., Shawn, Indira. Mus. curator S.D. State Hist. Soc., Pierre, 1969-72; asst. dir. W.H. Over Mus., U. S.D., Vermillion, 1972-73, dir., 1973-79; dir. Western Heritage Center, Billings, Mont., 1980—; instr. dept. anthropology U. S.D., 1973-79. Mem. Landmarks, Inc., Billings, 1980—. Mem. Mountain Plains Mus. Assn., Mont. Archaeology Soc., AAUW. Quaker. Office: 2822 Montana Ave Billings MT 59101

SAMS, DORIS LAVERNE, coll. counselor; b. Youngwood, Pa., Apr. 26, 1926; d. Benjamin F. and Lucinda (Myers) S.; B.A., Seton Hill Coll., 1950; M.Ed., U. Pitts., 1959. Employment interviewer Conn. State Employment Service, Thompsonville, 1950-53; tchr. Hempfield Area Schs., Greensburg, Pa., 1953-58, sch. psychologist, 1958-66; counselor Broward Community Coll., Ft. Lauderdale, Fla., 1966—; human potential seminar leader Rational Behavior Therapy Workshops. Mem. Gov.'s Com. on Handicapped. Frick scholar. Mem. Profl. Counselors Assn., Am. Personnel and Guidance Assn. Republican. Clubs: Ft. Lauderdale Dog, Samoyed Club Am. Home: 1400 SW 19th St Fort Lauderdale FL 33315 Office: Broward Community Coll Fort Lauderdale FL 33314

SAMUEL, JO ANN, newspaper sales and advt. exec.; b. Cushing, Okla., Nov. 26, 1929; d. Carlton Earl and Elsie Faye (Brown) De Graw; student Internat. Corr. Sch., 1958-60, UCLA, 1970-79, Pierce Coll., 1971, Valley Jr. Coll., 1975, Center for Degrees Study, Scranton, Pa., 1981—; m. Thomas Joseph Hess, July 16, 1949; children—Sherrie Lynne, Thomas Joseph III; m. 2d, Jean Samuel Clothier, May 11, 1956; 1 son, Geoffrey Vaughan; m. 3d, John William Samuel, Mar. 2, 1967 (div.). Billing clk. typist Swift & Co., South San Francisco, Calif., 1947-49; comptroller's sec. Farmers Ins. Co., Des Moines, 1953-55; with Valley News (now Daily News), Los Angeles, 1958—, mktg. analyst, 1973-76, advt. sales account exec., 1976-82, mgr. inside sales dept., retail advt. account expc., supr., 1982—; owner, operator Jo Ann Clothier Press Clipping Service, 1962-72. Mem. com. Marathon Run of Press, Pierce Coll., 1979. Mem. Adventures in Achievement (life). Republican. Mem. Christian Ch. (Disciples of Christ). Club: Grand Squares Square Dance (Sepulveda, Calif.). Home: 6545 Wilbur Ave Space 45 Reseda CA 91335 Office: Daily News 14539 Sylvan St Los Angeles CA 91411

SAMUELS, SHIRLEY CHASINS, psychotherapist; b. Bronx, N.Y., Dec. 6, 1930; d. Rubin and Clara (Traub) Chasins; B.S., Syracuse U., 1952, M.S., 1957; Ed.D., Columbia U., 1969; postgrad. Child Psychoanalysis, Center for Preventive Psychiatry, 1974; m. Stanley Samuels, Sept. 9, 1951; children—Jeffrey, Nita, Mark. Tchr., Syracuse (N.Y.) U. Nursery Sch., 1955-57, Maywood Nursery Sch., Hartsdale, N.Y., 1961-63; dir. Mt. Vernon (N.Y.) YM-YWHA Nursery Sch., 1963-65; dir. early childhood program Conservative Synagogue of Riverdale, Bronx, N.Y., 1966-68; adj. asst. prof. Hunter Coll., N.Y.C., 1968-74; asso. prof. edn. Manhattan Coll., Purchase, N.Y., 1969-80; child psychotherapist Center for Preventive Psychiatry, White Plains, N.Y., 1974-80, clin. supr. 1980—; adj. prof. Coll. New Rochelle (N.Y.), 1978—; pvt. practice psychotherapy, White Plains, 1977—; cons., lectr. in field. Bd. dirs. Union Day Care, Greenburgh, N.Y., 1981—, Westchester Assn. Young Children, White Plains, 1974—, Early Childhood Resource and Info. Center, N.Y.C. Libraries, 1981—; pres. Youth Bd. Westchester County, 1981-82; mem. adv. bd. therapeutic activity program Grasslands Hosp., Valhalla, N.Y., 1981—. Recipient award Youth Bd. Westchester County, 1981, Proclamation Service award, 1981. Mem. Assn. Child Psychoanalysis, Am. Psychol. Assn., Am. Orthopsychiat. Assn., Assn. Marriage and Family Therapy. Democrat. Jewish. Author: Enhancing Self-Concept in Early Childhood, 1977, Disturbed Exceptional Children: An Integrated Approach, 1981; editorial bd. Jour. Preventive Psychiatry, 1981—. Home: 10 Crest Dr White Plains NY 10607 Office: 19 Greenridge Ave White Plains NY 10601

SANAELLA, IRMA VIDAL, lawyer, state govt. ofcl.; b. N.Y.C., Oct. 4, 1924; d. Rafael and Sixta (Thillet) Vidal; acctg. degree Modern Bus. Coll., 1942; B.A., Hunter Coll., 1959; LL.B., Bklyn. Law Sch., 1961, J.D., 1967; children—Anthony, Ivette. Public acct., N.Y. state, 1957—; admitted to N.Y. bar, 1961; individual practice law, N.Y., 1961-63, with partner, 1966-68; dep. commr. N.Y.C. Dept. Correction, 1963-66; mem. N.Y. State Human Rights Appeal Bd., N.Y.C., 1968—, chmn., 1975—. Mem. N.Y.C. Adv. Council on Minority Affairs, 1982—, N.Y.C. Commn. on Status of Women, 1975-77; founder, chmn. Legion of Voters, 1962-68; nat. del. Presdl. Democratic Convs., 1968, 72, 76, 80, vice chmn. N.Y. State del. 1976 Conv.; founder Nat. Assn. for Puerto Rican Civil Rights, 1962, Hispanic Community Chest Am., 1972; chmn. bd. dirs. Puerto Rican Parade, 1962-67; bd. dirs. Catholic Interracial Council, 1968-81; nat. co-chmn. Coalition Hispanic People, 1970; fund raiser Boy Scouts Am., 1962-63; chmn. Children's Camp, South Bronx (N.Y.) 41st Police Precinct, 1967; active City-Wide Steering Com. for Quality Edn., 1962-64, Community Service Soc., 1972-74. Talbott Perkins Children's Services, 1973-75, Planned Parenthood Assn., 1968-69, Puerto Rican Crippled Children's Fund, 1965-69; founder N.Y. chpt. Clinica Grillasca, P.R. Cancer Assn., 1974—. Recipient citations for civic work Gov. Rockefeller, 1972, Gov. Carey, 1982; citations for work on voting and human rights N.Y. State Assembly, 1982, P.R. Senate, 1982, others. Mem. Am. Judicature Soc. Roman Catholic. Home: 800 Fifth Ave New York NY 10021 also 869 Concourse Village W Bronx NY 10451 Office: NY State Human Rights Appeal Bd 2 World Trade Center New York NY 10047

SANBORN, ANNA LUCILLE, pension and ins. cons.; b. Bklyn., Mar. 29, 1924; d. Peter Francis and Matilda M. (Stumpp) Galligen; B.A., Bklyn. Coll., 1945; 1 son, Dean Sanborn. Head dept. benefit and estate planning Union Central Life Ins. Co., N.Y.C., 1949-51; adminstr. employee benefits Seaboard Oil Co., N.Y.C., 1952-56; with Frank J. Walters Assocs., Inc., N.Y.C., 1957—, pres., 1970—. Bd. dirs. Archdiocesan Service Corp. Mem. Am. Acad. Actuaries, Republican. Roman Catholic. Home: 58-11 Seabury St Elmhurst NY 11373 Office: 509 Madison Ave New York NY 10022

SANCHEZ, BEATRICE MARY ALIRE, savs. and loan exec.; b. Denver, Nov. 16, 1943; d. Willie and Bertila Alire; student Savs. and Loan Inst., U. Houston, 1976; m. Paul F. Sanchez, Apr. 4, 1964; children—Alden, Michael. Secretarial position Pioneer Investment Co., 1962-63; receptionist Vodian Optometrist, 1965-66; teller Am. Fed. Savs., Pueblo, Colo., 1966-71, teller supr., 1971-73, br. mgr., 1974-76, br. mgr. 2 offices, 1976-80, regional savs. mgr., 1980-81, regional savs. mgr. 3, 1981—. Mem. Credit Womens Internat., U.S. League of Savs. and Loan Assns., Belmont Mchts. Assn., Sunset Plaza Mchts. Assn., Pueblo C. of C., Savs. and Loan Inst. (bd. dirs.). Home: 2002 Northmoor Terr Pueblo CO 81008 Office: Am Fed Savs 601 N Main St Pueblo CO 81002

SANCHEZ, CORDELIA CHAVEZ, educator; b. Albuquerque, Mar. 22, 1926; d. Elfido and Gregorita M. Chavez; B.A., U. N.Mex., 1946; postgrad. U. Albuquerque, 1964-78; children—Kenneth John, Margaret Marie. Tchr., Albuquerque Public Schs., 1946-51, 65—, Prince George's County, Md., 1959-60, Washington Schs., 1958-59; Mem. juvenile parole bd. N.Mex., 1978, chmn. Com. Children and Youth, 1976-78; mem. adv. council N.Mex. Employment Security Commn., 1977-78; vice chmn. N.Mex. Dem. Party, 1978-82; del. Nat. Dem. Party Conf., Kansas City, Mo., 1974, Memphis, 1978; del. Nat. Dem. Conv., 1976, 80. Recipient Disting. Woman of N.Mex. award N.Mex. Women's Polit. Caucus, 1976. Mem. NEA. Roman Catholic. Home: 6500 Rio Grande NW Albuquerque NM 87107

SANCHEZ, JUANITA, nurse; b. Harlingen, Tex., Aug. 10, 1953; d. Pablo and Vicenta (Zapata) Rios; Diploma in Nursing, Mercy Hosp. Sch. Nursing, 1974; 1 son, Antonio. Nurse, E. Morgan County Hosp., Bruch, Colo., 1974—; charge nurse Sunset Manor Nursing Home, Brush, 1977-80, in service dir., 1980, dir. nurses, 1980—. Williams Family Found. scholar, 1971-74; Stephen Bufton Meml. Edn. Fund grantee, 1982. Mem. Am. Bus. Women's Assn. (rec. sec. 1979; Woman of Yr. 1980), N.E. Colo. Profl. Nurse Registry, Colo. Soc. Health Care Nursing Service Adminstrs., Nurse Conf. Group of Colo. Health Care Assn. Office: 2200 Edison St Brush CO 80723

SANCHEZ, LYDIA MARIA, devel. corp. exec., acct.; b. Bronx, N.Y., Sept. 23, 1935; d. Blas Candelario and Ana (Rivera) S.; B.A., Pace U., 1982; m. Armando Ramos, Jan. 28, 1958 (dec.); 1 son, Rafael C. Bookkeeper, Internat. House, N.Y.C., 1965-73; office mgr. Internat. Center Photography, N.Y.C., 1976-77; comptroller Union Theol. Sem., N.Y.C., 1977-80; staff accountant Sotheby Parke Bernet, N.Y.C., 1975-76; dir. fin. and adminstrn. South Bronx 2000 Local Devel. Corp., N.Y.C., 1980—. Served with USAF, 1956-58. Mem. Network Bronx Woman Orgn., Inc., Nat. Coll. and Univ. Bus. Officers. Home: 2265 Gleason Ave Bronx NY 10462 Office: 800 E Tremont Ave Bronx NY 10460

SANCHEZ, SARA MARIA, librarian; b. Havana; d. Ramiro Jesus and Sara Maria (Rodriguez-Baz) S.; B.A., U. Villanova, 1959; B.L.S., U. Havana, 1960; M.L.S., SUNY, Geneseo, 1974. Librarian, Merici Acad., Havana, 1959-61; librarian Cuban Nat. Library, 1960-67; asst. prof. library sci. U. Miami, 1970—. Mem. Met. Mus. Miami, Coalition Hispanic Am. Women, Dade County Library Assn. (sec. 1979-81), Fla. Library Assn., Assn. Caribbean Univ. and Research Libraries, Cuban Mus. Arts. Democrat. Roman Catholic. Home: 1860 SW 22d St #8 Miami FL 33145 Office: Library Univ Miami Coral Gables FL 33124

SANDA, KRISTA LINNEA GANDRUD, state ofcl.; b. Detroit Lakes, Minn., Dec. 26, 1937; d. K. I. and Luella Elizabeth (Meyer) Gandrud; student St. Cloud State U., 1955-57; m. Donald James Sanda, Dec. 28, 1956; children—John Howard, Karin Marie, Steven Emil, Timothy James, Paul George, David Christopher Gandrud. Substitute tchr., Staples (Minn.) Public Schs., 1958-65; with C. of C., Staples, Minn., 1965-66; reporter, columnist Staples World newspaper, 1967-68; exec. sec., customer service rep. Benson Optical Co., Inc. Lab., Staples, 1968-79; dir. Office Consumer Services, Dept. Commerce, State Minn., St. Paul, 1979—. Pres., Todd County Cancer Soc., 1975-77; chmn. Staples (Minn.) Bicentennial Commn., 1976; mem. Todd County (Minn.) Bicentennial Commn., 1976; del. nat. convs. Republican party, 1972, 76, del. state convs., 1966-82; state vice-chmn. Minn. Ind.-Rep. party, 1973-79, chmn. 7th Congressional dist., 1969-73, chmn. Todd County, 1965-69. Recipient Alpha Psi Omega Speech Scholarship, St. Cloud State U., 1955. Mem. Nat. Assn. Consumer Affairs Adminstrs., Minn. Hist. Soc., Minn. Soc. Consumer Affairs Profls., Minn. Women for Agr. (treas. Met. chpt.). Republican. Lutheran. Club: F & F Network (co-chmn.) (St. Paul). Contbr. articles in field to weekly and daily newspapers. Office: 128 Metro Square Bldg St Paul MN 55101

SANDAGE, ELIZABETH ANTHEA, educator; b. Larned, Kans., Oct. 13, 1930; d. Curtis Carl and Beulah Pauline (Knupp) Smith; student Okla. State U., 1963-65; B.S., U. Colo., 1967; M.A., 1970; postgrad. in communication U. Ill., 1970-71, 77—; m. Charles Harold Sandage, July 18, 1971; children by previous marriage—Diana Louise Danner (Mrs. Vern White), David Alan Danner. Public relations rep., editor Martin News, Martin Marietta Corp., Denver, 1960-63, 65-67; retail advt. salesperson Denver Post, 1967-70; instr. advt. U. Ill., 1970-71, vis. lectr. advt., 1977—. Mem. Women in Communications, Sigma Delta Chi, Kappa Tau Alpha. Republican. Presbyterian. Editor: Occasional Papers in Advertising, 1971; The Sandage Family Cookbook, 1976; The Inkling, Carle Hosp. Aux. Newsletter, 1975-76. Home: 106 The Meadows Urbana IL 61801

SANDAGE, SHIRLEY MARIE, social scientist; b. Mason City, Iowa, May 5, 1927; d. Jack D. and Flossie M. (Reynolds) Farrer; ed. Cornell Coll., Mt. Vernon, Iowa, 1949; m. Richard Sandage, Feb. 10, 1946; children—Richard, John, Scott. Exec. dir. Migrant Action Program, Iowa and Minn., 1965-69; dep. dir. Migrant Research Project, Washington, 1969-72; cons. welfare reform Office Sec. Labor, 1972-73; leader spl. task force U.S. Employment Service, Washington, 1972-74; dir. hazardous waste project study in Iowa, Garrity-Sandage Assos., 1974-76; exec. dir. The Door Opener, center for women, Mason City, 1976—; pres. bd. Displaced Homemaker Network, 1981-82; mem. nat. bd. dirs. Older Women's League; mem. Iowa Health Care Commn. Recipient Achievement award Mason City YWCA, 1978; Spl. Recognition award for significant contbn. to welfare of Iowa, Gov. of Iowa, 1982. Mem. Nat. Assn. Female Execs., Rural Am. Women, Bus. and Profl. Women, Iowa Women's Polit. Caucus, Older Women's League. Democrat. Mem.

Christian Ch. (Disciples of Christ). Author: Child of Hope, 1964; also articles. Home: 842 6th Pl SE Mason City IA 50401 Office: 124 N Federal Ave Mason City IA 50401

SANDELIN, MARGARET HELEN JENKINS GASKILL, lawyer; b. Phila., Sept. 18, 1921; d. Frederick John and Margaret (Swarz) Jenkins; B.S. in Law, U. Wash., 1946, J.D., 1947; m. Herbert Leo Gaskill, Mar. 1, 1944; children—Margaret Vesta, Herbert Leo; m. 2d, D. Scott Sandelin, July 9, 1977. Admitted to Wash. bar, 1947, since practiced in Seattle; partner Hardy & Gaskill, 1952-54, Holland & Gaskill, 1954-57; individual practice law, 1958-64; partner Weyer, Sandelin, Sterne & Gaskill, 1964-66, Weyer, Sterne & Gaskill, 1966-69, Sandelin & Sandelin, Seattle, 1977—; individual practice, 1969-77; judge protem superior ct.; 1961. Mem. Citizens' Adv. Com. Senate Interim Com. Financial Instns., 1973-74. Docent, Seattle Art Mus., 1961-72, now mem. Mem. Am., Wash. State, King County Seattle King County (sec. 1963) bar assns., Am. Trial Lawyers Assn., Wash. Women Lawyers, Phi Alpha Delta. Democrat. Home: 4022 E Mercer Way Mercer Island WA 98040 Office: Suite 480 Colman Bldg Seattle WA 98104

SANDER, FAYE, psychotherapist; b. N.Y.C., Apr. 8, 1923; d. Harry Wolf and Kate Brauner Schnee; B.R.E., Philathea Coll., Toronto, 1967, M.A., 1969; cert. art therapy Turtle Bay Sch., 1971; M.S.W., Rutgers U., 1974; children—Ellen Jane, Kenneth, Karen Victoria. Encounter group therapy leader Inst. Applied Psychology, 1969-70, N.Y.C., group therapy co-leader, 1970-72; individual and group art therapist Inst. Emotional Edn., 1970-73; med. social worker Jersey City Med. Center, 1974; generic social worker Jewish Assn. Services for Aged, N.Y.C., 1975-76; pvt. practice psychotherapy, N.Y.C., 1976—; dir. social service long term care facilities Haym Solomon Home for Aged, Bklyn., 1977-80; lectr. Rutgers Grad. Sch. Social Work, 1976-79; cons. Task Force Sr. Citizens, Addiction Service Agy., Flushing Manor Care Center. N.Y.C. Democratic Mayoral campaign worker, 1976-77; mem. Community Services Com., Tilden Dem. Club, 1976—. Mem. Nat. Assn. Social Workers, Am. Assn. Art Therapist, Social Work Vocat. Bur., Coalition Profl. Social Workers, Long Term Care Facilities, Central Bur. Jewish Aged, N.Y. State Soc. Clin. Social Work Psychotherapists. Jewish. Home and Office: 300 E 34th St New York NY 10016

SANDERLIN, OWENITA HARRAH, author, educator; b. Los Angeles, June 2, 1916; d. Owen Melville and Marigold (Whitford) H.; B.A. summa cum laude, Am. U., 1937; postgrad. U. Maine, U. Calif., San Diego State U.; m. George William Sanderlin, May 30, 1936; children—Frea Elizabeth, Sheila Mary, David George, John Owen. Freelance writer, speaker, 1940—; tchr. English, U. Maine, 1942, 46; head dept. speech and drama Acad. of Our Lady of Peace, San Diego, 1961-68; cons. gifted programs San Diego city schs., 1971-73, 80—; author: Jeanie O'Brien, 1965; Johnny, 1968. Pyramid, 1969; Creative Teaching, 1971; Teaching Gifted Children, 1973; Tennis Rebel, 1978; Match Point, 1979; co-author: Gifted Children: How to Identify and Teach Them, 1979. Recipient Poetry award Alpha Chi Omega, 1936. Mem. Nat. Assn. Gifted Children, Assn. San Diego Educators of Gifted, Mortar Bd. Clubs: San Diego State U. Women's; Singing Hills Tennis. Address: 997 Vista Grande Rd El Cajon CA 92021

SANDERS, BEATRICE EDNA THOMASON, real estate broker, realtor; b. Haskell, Tex., Mar. 24, 1914; d. Young Lytle and Edna (Ham) Thomason; B.A., N. Tex. State U., 1934; M.A., E. Tex. State U., 1958; m. Gale Draper, June 1935 (div.); 1 son, Billy George; m. 2d, Leonard Sanders, April 1946; children—Robert Michael, Wanda Elaine, Gary Lynn. Clk., asst. supr. Bur. Ships, Navy Dept., Washington, 1940-47; bus. tchr. Central High Sch., Ashland City, Tenn., 1953-55, Detroit (Tex.) High Sch., 1955-56, Bogata (Tex.) High Sch., 1956-57; tchr. English and journalism Espanola (N.Mex.) High Sch., 1957-59, Belen (N.Mex.) Consol. Schs., 1960-76; owner, broker Colonial Realty, Los Lunas, N.Mex., 1972—. Mem. NEA, N.Mex. Edn. Assn., Nat. Assn. Realtors, Realtors Assn. N.Mex., Los Lunas Bus. Assn. (bd. dirs.), Nat. Writers Club. Democrat. Presbyterian. Home and office: 927 Hwy 85 SW Los Lunas NM 87031

SANDERS, CHRISTINE CULP, microbiologist; b. Tampa, Fla., Sept. 3, 1948; d. Edward R. and Lois (Holder) Culp; B.S., U. Fla., 1970, Ph.D., 1973; m. W. Eugene Sanders, Jr., Feb. 22, 1974. Microbiologist, Shands Teaching Hosp., Gainesville, Fla., 1969-70, Alachua Gen. Hosp., Gainesville, 1970; asst. prof. microbiology Creighton U. Sch. Medicine, Omaha, 1973-79, asso. prof., 1979—; reviewer jours. in microbiology and antibiotics, 1979—; cons. research microbiology, 1973—. Grantee in field. Mem. Am. Soc. Microbiology, Am. Chem. Soc., Am. Fedn. Clin. Research, Infectious Disease Soc. Am., Am. Venereal Disease Assn., Internat. Assn. Dental Research, N.Y. Acad. Scis., Sigma Xi. Contbr. articles on research in microbiology and antibiotic therapy to profl. jours. Office: 2500 California St Omaha NE 68178

SANDERS, ESTHER JEANNETTE, aerospace co. exec., b. Ogden, Utah, Feb. 19, 1926; d. Warren Lynn and Esther Marguerite (Harris) Garner; B.A., U. Colo., 1948; m. Thomas Wesley Sanders, Jan. 10, 1946. With Calif., Inst., Tech. Coop. Wind Tunnel, Pasadena, 1948; with Sperry Gyroscope Co., Point Mugu, Calif., 1949-55; with Propulsion Research Corp., Santa Monica, Calif., 1957-59; with TRW, Redondo Beach, Calif., 1957—, now head engring. test data analysis sect. Home: 2424 Burritt St Redondo Beach CA 90278 Office: 1 Space Park Redondo Beach CA 90278

SANDERS, FRANCES BEYER, ct. reporter; b. Iowa City, Iowa, June 11, 1923; d. Henry Frederick and Wilma Carolina (Beckjorden) Beyer; student Mason City Jr. Coll., 1942-43, Mcht. Marine Ct. Reporting Sch., 1944, Tampa U., 1945-46; m. James Chesley Sanders, Apr. 27, 1946; children—James Chesley, Gary H., Kari Mayre. Ct. reporter USCG, Tampa, Fla., 1944-46; freelance ct. reporter, Tampa, 1947-48; high sch. and adult edn. tchr. typing, shorthand and bookkeeping, Southport, N.C., 1953-54; office mgr. Yaupon Beach, Southport, 1954-59; legal sec., Juneau, Alaska, 1959-62; asst. sec. Alaska Senate, Juneau, 1962; freelance ct. reporter, operatior Taku Reporters, Juneau, 1962—; co-owner, operator S & S Ceramics, 1978—. Bd. dirs. Juneau Receiving Home, 1970-73, Greater Juneau Arts and Humanities Council, 1968-71, 75—. Served with USCG, 1943-45. Decorated citation for outstanding performance of duty. Mem. Nat. Shorthand Reporters Assn. Democrat. Presbyterian. Clubs: Eastern Star; Women of Moose. Home: 9358 Lee Smith Dr Juneau AK 99803 Office: PO Box 2340 Juneau AK 99803

SANDERS, GLORIA JEAN, court reporter; b. Gainesville, Fla., Oct. 7, 1948; d. Clarence Richard and Betty Ellen (Lamb) S.; student U. S.C., 1978-82. Stenographer, FBI, Columbia, S.C., 1966-67; legal sec. Atty. Harvey L. Golden, Columbia, 1967-73; freelance typist, Columbia, 1971-75; court reporter S.C. Public Service Commn., Columbia, 1973-82; freelance court reporter, Columbia, 1974-82; pres. Sanders Stenographics, Orange, Tex., 1982—. Mem. Nat. Assn. Female Execs. (network dir.), Women in Sales and Mgmt. (pres.), Nat. Stenomask Verbatim Reporters Assn. (pres., instr., cert. examiner, Cert. of Merit 1978, 3d place Nat. Speed Contest 1980, 1st place 1981, 82), DAR, Interesting Women in S.C. (founder, dir.). Club: Met. Jr. Women's (Columbia). Office: PO Drawer 7 Orange TX 77630

SANDERS, JANE FRANCES, state legislator; b. N.Y.C., July 26, 1948; d. Jack and Theresia (Plechner) Taylor; B.A. cum laude in History, Jackson Coll., Tufts U., 1970; grad. Eastman Sch. Music, Rochester, N.Y., 1966; postrad. Franklin Pierce Law Center, Concord, N.H.; m. Harvey L. Sanders, Mar. 25, 1973; children— Seth James, Judd Matthew. Mem. editorial staff Nashua (N.H.) Telegraph, 1970-72; writer, producer/dir. C-I-E Films, Inc., Dover, N.H., 1972—; mem. N.H. Ho. of Reps. from Belknapp Dist. 4, 1976—, vice chmn. exec. com. county del., 1978—, mem. com. on resources, recreation and devel., 1978—, ad-hoc com. on water pollution regulation standards, 1979-80. Mem. State Song Selection Bd., 1976-77; del. Republican State Conv., 1976, 78, 80, mem. platform com., 1978; bd. dirs. Belknap-Merrimack Community Action Program, 1977-81, Lakes Region Mental Health Center, 1978-82, sec. Alton Conservation Commn., 1977-80, chmn., 1981—; mem. Alton Sch. Study Com., 1980, Alton Hydro-Electric Study Com., 1980—; mem. water quality grant adv. bd. NSF. Recipient ann. award Lakes Region Planning Commn., 1981. Office: 104 Washington St Dover NH 03820

SANDERS, JANET LYNN, public relations exec.; b. Louisville, June 25, 1948; d. Lloyd Thomas and Willie Mae (Guinee) S.; B.A. with honors, Trinity Coll., Washington, 1970; M.A., U. Colo., Boulder, 1972. Writer/reporter Edn. Commn. States, Denver, 1972-73; copywriter/pub. relations asst. Mefford Weir Advt., Denver, 1973-77; writer/asst. account exec. Francis X. Kohler Pub. Relations, Marina del Rey, Calif., 1978-79; account exec. Reeds & Farris, Los Angeles, 1979; corp. pub. relations mgr. Allstate Savs. & Loan Assn., Glendale, Calif., 1979-81; nat. mktg. services mgr. Ticor Title Insurers, Los Angeles, 1981—; teaching asso. U. Colo., Boulder, 1972; instr. English, Community Coll. Denver, 1973. Mem. Women in Communications, Publicity Club Los Angeles. Office: 6300 Wilshire Blvd Los Angeles CA 90048

SANDERS, MARLENE, television corr., producer; b. Cleve., Jan. 10, 1931; d. Mac and Evelyn R. (Menitoff) Sanders; student Ohio State U., 1948-50; m. Jerome Toobin, May 27, 1958; children—Jeff, Mark. Writer, producer various programs on WNEW-TV, N.Y.C., 1955-60, P.M. program Westinghouse Broadcasting Corp., N.Y.C., 1961-62; asst. dir. news and pub. affairs Radio Sta. WNEW, N.Y.C., 1962-64; news corr. ABC, 1964-72, producer numerous documentaries; writer, producer documentaries Children in Peril, 1972, Population: Boom or Doom, 1973, hour-long spl. Woman's Place (Golden Eagle certificate CINE, Clarion award), 1973, Womens Health: A Question of Survival, 1975, The Right to Die (Ohio State award, Front Page award, Writers Guild of Am. award), 1974; v.p., dir. television documentaries ABC News, 1976-78; corr., producer CBS Reports, CBS News, N.Y.C., 1978—; anchor woman Saturday Edition Newsbreak, 1981—. Recipient Headliner award Nat. Press Club award for Lawyers: Guilty as Charged?: documentary, 1976, Matrix award N.Y. Women in Communications for outstanding achievement in broadcast industry, 1976, N.Y. State Broadcasters Assn. award, 1976, Deadline award Deadline Club of N.Y. chpt. Soc. Profl. Journalists, Sigma Delta Chi, 1977, others. Mem. Women in Communications (past pres.), Am. Women in Radio and Television, Womens Forum, Assn. Radio and Television Analysts, Sigma Delta Chi. Office: CBS News 524 W 57th St New York NY 10019 *

SANDERS, MICHELE GARSIDE HENSILL, ednl. adminstr.; b. Richmond, Calif., Nov. 10, 1942; d. John R. and Inez Sophia (Lonquist) Garside; B.A., Chico State U., 1964; M.A., San Francisco State U., 1973; postgrad. U. Calif., Berkeley; m. Steven Neil Sanders, Apr. 3, 1979. Tchr., Belmont and Richmond, Calif., 1964-76; adminstrv. asst. to supt. Belmont Sch. Dist., 1976-78, prin. Ralston Intermediate Sch., 1978-82, also dist. adminstr. communications; asst. supt. Portola Valley (Calif.) Sch. Dist., 1982—; instr. U. Calif., Berkeley Extension, U. San Francisco, Dominican Coll., 1974—; instr. art therapy Coll. Notre Dame; cons. theatre arts, motivation, communications, mgmt. Co. mem. Lamplighters, San Jose Civic Light Opera, 1975—; bd. mgrs. Carlmont YMCA, 1978-80; pres. bd. dirs. Homeowners Assn., 1977-78; auctioneer Sta. KQED, 1976—; chmn. fin. Belmont Faculty Assn., 1975-76. Bank of Am. grantee, 1979. Mem. Assn. Calif. Sch. Adminstrs. (achievement award 1978), Assn. for Humanistic Psychology, Assn. Supervision and Curriculum Devel., Calif. Assn. Gifted, PTA (Service award 1981), Sierra Club, Alpha Delta Kappa, Phi Delta Kappa. Pub. Belmont Reports, 1976-78. Office: 200 Shawnee Pass Portola Valley CA 94107

SANDERS, PEGGY JO W., ednl. coordinator; b. Laramie, Wyo., Apr. 25, 1948; d. John and Mae Helen White; B.A. in English, U. Wyo., 1966, Edn. Specialist in Adminstrn., 1980-81; M.A. in Guidance and Counseling, Eastern Mont. Coll., 1975; m. Jerry D. Sanders, Sept. 6, 1969; children—Dallas R., Kassahn, Spenser J. Tchr. reading and English, McClave, Colo., 1970-73; diagnostician, psychologist Johnson County Schs., Buffalo, Wyo., 1975-79, coordinator gifted edn., 1980—; cons. devel. of gifted program. Johnson County rep. Wyo. Commn. on Status of Women, treas., 1977—; mem. Johnson County Democratic Com., chmn., 1981—; pres. LWV, 1978-80; bd. dirs., pres. Buffalo Day Care, 1979-80. Mem. NEA, Council of Exceptional Children, Wyo. Assn. for Gifted Edn., Child Protection Team of Johnson County, Internat. Reading Assn. Home: PO Box 451 705 Klondike Buffalo WY 82834 Office: 550 S Burritt Buffalo WY 82834

SANDERS, PHYLLIS ADEN, radio/TV broadcaster; b. Buenos Aires, Argentina, June 27, 1919; d. Fred and Anna Almeda (Pettit) Aden; B.A., Occidental Coll., 1941; M.A., Scarritt Coll., 1943; m. Olcutt Sanders, Apr. 8, 1947; children—Lynn Edwin, Marta Almeda, Jay Olcutt, Fred Aden, R. Elizabeth. Formerly tchr.; lectr., workshop leader on changing roles of women, 1973-75; producer/host weekly radio interview show Changing World of Women, Sta. WNYC, N.Y.C., 1972-79; TV reporter/host/commentator on women's issues Sta. WNYC-TV, N.Y.C., 1975-78; regular weekly commentator Prime of Your Life, NBC-TV, N.Y.C., 1979—; reporter Age Whys, AM Phila., Sta. WPVI-TV, 1981—. Community relations dir. Town of New Castle (N.Y.), 1972-73, originator, coordinator Community Day, New Castle, 1971; coordinator N.Y.C. women's adv. com. on meeting with network mgmt., 1976-77. Recipient award N.Y. chpt. NOW, 1973, N.J. Women, 1976. Mem. AFTRA, Nat. Acad. TV Arts and Scis., Women's Inst. for Freedom of Press, ACLU, Friends Com. on Nat. Legis., NOW, Older Women's League. Mem. Soc. of Friends.

SANDERS, SCOTT SHANKLIN, arts adminstr.; b. Eglin Field AFB, Fla., June 10, 1944; d. Edward Henry and Ferryle (Yeager) Shanklin; B.A., Columbia (S.C.) Coll., 1966; grad. Arts Adminstrn. Inst., Harvard U.; children—Buck Henry, Stacie Aaron. Jr. profl. asst. S.C. Employment Security Commn., 1966-70; dir. arts edn. div., then dep. dir. S.C. Arts Commn., 1972-80, exec. dir., 1980—; bd. dirs. So. Arts Fedn. Office: 1800 Gervais St Columbia SC 29201

SANDERS, SUNNY MINA, optometrist; b. Chgo., Aug. 16, 1952; d. Harvey Eugene and Pauline W. (Fleischmann) S.; B.S. with honors and distinction in Biol. Scis. (James scholar 1970-73, Ill. State scholar 1970-74), U. Ill., Chgo. Circle, 1974; B.S. in Visual Scis., Ill. Coll. Optometry, 1977, D. Optometry, 1978; m. Anthony Nizza, Jr., June 20, 1980. Optometric technician and asst. Eye Care Center, Chgo., 1976-77; research asst. research div. Wesley-Jessen Contact Lens Co., Chgo., 1977-78; clin. fellow Ill. Coll. Optometry, 1978-79, instr., dir. gen. clinic, 1979-81; asst. prof. optometry, 1981-82, dir. ocular prosthetics clinic, 1981-82; practice optometry, San Diego and Escondido Calif., 1982—; mem. com. for pub. relations and pub. info. Am. Optometric Student Assn., 1977-78; com. mem. Bd. Admissions, Ill. Coll. Optometry, 1977-78, adviser to in-coming students, 1977-78. Fellow Am. Acad. Optometry; mem. Am., Ill. optometric assns., Council on Ethics, Optometric Extension Program Found., Better Vision Inst., Field Mus. Natural History, Smithsonian Assos., Internat. Fund for Animal Welfare, Animal Protection Inst. Am., Gold Key, Phi Theta Upsilon (pres. local chpt. 1977-78, Alumnus of Yr. 1978-79). Clubs: Am. Turners, N.W. (Chgo.). Home: 818 Centennial Dr Vista CA 92083 Office: 4225 Balboa Ave San Diego CA 92117 also 1711 East Valley Pkwy Escondido CA 92027

SANDERS, SUZANNE NANNETTE, nurse, health co. exec.; b. Tacoma, Mar. 17, 1945; d. Thomas Benton and Eleanor Nannette (Vaughan) Wilson; B.S. in Nursing with high honors, U. Tex., 1975; M.S., Tex. Woman's U., Houston, 1982; m. James L. Sanders, Jan. 25, 1974; children—Jeanene Cooper, Charlotte Cooper, Marilyn Cooper, Lindsey Sanders. Research asst. zoology dept. U. Tex., 1969-71, M.D. Anderson Hosp., Tex. Med. Center, Houston, 1971; nurse St. Joseph's Hosp., Houston, 1975; dir. nursing Richmond (Tex.) State Sch., 1979; pres., owner Liftercise Inc., Sugar Land, Tex., 1980—; mem. bd. Office of Early Childhood Devel., 1977, chmn. bd., 1980-81. Vice pres. Mcpl. Utility Dist. No. 13, 1980, bd. mem., 1977-81; mem. Mus. Natural Scis. Mem. Sigma Theta Tau. Democrat. Club: Sugar Land Lioness (charter mem.). Various radio and TV appearances: author: Liftercise: A Program for Women Using Weights with Exercise, 1980. Office: PO Box 304 Sugar Land TX 77478

SANDERS, SYLVIA ANNE, polit. activist; b. Butler, Pa., Feb. 4, 1948; d. Howard Earl and Jeanette Leonard (Link) S.; B.A. cum laude in Social Relations, Radcliffe Coll., 1970; m. Ben L. Olson, Dec. 31, 1977. Tchr. sci. and math. Nashoba Coutry Day Sch., Cocord, Mass., 1970-74; saleswoman, 1975; journalist Port Towsend (Wash.) Leader, 1976; engaged in farming, Pocohontas, Iowa; sec. Libertarian Nat. Com., 1978-81; campaign mgr. various polit. campaigns; Libertarian candidate for sec. of state, Iowa, 1982. Mem. Amnesty Internat., Nature Conservancy, ACLU, Assn. Libertarian Feminists, Libertarian Futurist Soc., Free Press Assn. Address: RR 1 Box 114 Pocahontas IA 50574

SANDERSON, CAROL JEAN, newspaper editor; b. Wichita, June 2, 1932; d. Willis Kenneth and Ruth Anna (Bryant) Hill; student Wichita State U., 1950-52; children—Mark Douglas Brinton, Bambi Lynn Brinton Bird, Mike Douglas Brinton, Todd Douglas Brinton. Sec., bookkeeper United Sch. Dist. 426, Howard, Kans., 1975-77; freelance writer Howard Courant-Citizen, 1975-77, Salina (Kans.) Jour., 1978-80, Scandia (Kans.) Jour., 1978-80; owner, editor Courtland (Kans.) Jour., 1980—; founder Prairie Valley Empire Newspaper, Belleville, Kans., 1982—. Mem. steering com. Courtland PRIDE, 1980-82. Cert. elem. tchr.; recipient PRIDE award Gov. Kans., 1982. Mem. Kans. Press Assn., Kans. Press Women Assn., Nat. Fedn. Press Women. Lutheran. Home: RR 1 Courtland KS 66939 Office: 1913 M St Belleville KS 66935

SANDERSON, GLENDA JOYCE, histotechnologist; b. Chickasha, Okla., Feb. 2, 1947; d. Parley Ohlow and Christine Tula (Cornelius) Sanderson; cert. histology Wesley Med. Center, 1971; student Labette County Community Jr. Coll., 1974-75. Staff histologic technician Associated Labs., Wichita, Kans., 1971-74; head histology dept. Labette County Med. Center, Parsons, Kans., 1974-76; chief histotechnologist Hertzler Clinic, Halstead, Kans., 1976—. Mem. Nat. Soc. for Histotech., Inc. (charter mem., region V sec., health, safety, membership coms., chmn. nomination and election com., Kans. del. to ho. of dels., past mem. awards com.), Kans. Soc. for Histotech., Inc. (pres. 1982—, past pres., sec., chairperson of membership com., charter mem.), Am. Soc. Clin. Pathologists (affiliate mem., cert. histologic technician and histotechnologist). Baptist. Home: 725 Spruce Apt #4 Halstead KS 67056 Office: 327 Chestnut St Halstead KS 67056

SANDFORD, JUANITA DADISMAN, sociologist, educator; b. Wichita, Kans., June 20, 1926; s. Carl Orville and Mabel Bernice (Stearman) Dadisman; B.A., Baylor U., Waco, Tex., 1947, M.A., 1948; m. Herman Prestridge Sandford, Dec. 22, 1946; children—Susan Jane, Linda Ann, Mary Kay. Instr. sociology Wayland Bapt. Coll., Plainview, Tex., 1948-49, Ft. Smith (Ark.) Jr. Coll., 1959, Ouachita Bapt. U., Arkadelphia, Ark., 1960-68; asst. prof. sociology, coordinator women's studies Henderson State U., Arkadelphia, 1968—; chmn. bd. Coll. Community Action, Inc.; bd. dirs. Central Ark. Devel. Council; cons. human relations Ark. Tech. Assistance and Consultative Center; mem. Arkadelphia Council Aging, Gov. Ark. Commn. Status of Women, Ark. Atty. Gen.'s Adv. Bd. Mem. Am., So., Southwestern sociol. assns., AAUW, Ark. Council Women in Higher Edn., NOW, Nat. Assn. Women's Studies, Ark. Women's Polit. Caucus (named Ark. Women of Achievement 1975). Democrat. Author: I Didn't Get A Lot Done Today, 1974—; Poverty in the Land of Opportunity, 1978; contbg. author: Women and Religion: Images of Women in the Bible, 1977; Arkansas: State in Transition, 1981; Arkadelphia, 2000 AD, 1982; contbg. editor: Women's Studies Newsletter. Home: Ouachita Hills Arkadelphia AR 71923 Office: Henderson State Univ Arkadelphia AR 71923

SANDLAN, BRENDA CHAMBERLIN, nurse; b. Brattleboro, Vt., Sept. 1, 1948; d. Thomas and Bernice (Fairbanks) Chamberlin; A.L.A., Pensacola Jr. Coll., 1973, A.S. in Nursing, 1973; B.S., St. Joseph's Coll., Maine, 1980. Nursing asst. Brattleboro (Vt.) Meml. Hosp., 1965-66, practical nurse, 1967-69; nurse Extended Care Facility, Tallahassee, 1969-71, Univ. Hosp., Pensacola, Fla., 1971-73; nurse Reconstrn. Home, Ithaca, 1974-75; relief indsl. nurse Nat. Cash Register Co., Ithaca, 1975-76 Ithaca Gun Co., 1976; charge nurse, relief supr. Oak Hill Manor Nursing Home, Ithaca, 1976-77, asst. dir. nursing services, 1977-81, dir. nursing services, 1981—, nurse coordinator, 1981—. Health cons. Tompkins County Agrl. and Hort. Soc.; mem. adv. com. profl. nursing program Tompkins-Cortland Community Coll.; religious edn. instr. Roman Cath. Ch.; vol. ARC, 1967, nurse, 1974, chpt. chairperson, 1979-81; mem. Vt. State 4-H Hon. Soc. Mem. Nurses United for a Respectfully Supportive Environ., Cath. Daus. Am. Home: 908 Danby Rd Ithaca NY 14850 Office: 602 Hudson St Ithaca NY 14850

SANDLER, LUCY FREEMAN, educator; b. N.Y.C., June 7, 1930; d. Otto and Frances (Glass) Freeman; B.A., Queens Coll., 1951; M.A., Columbia U., 1957; Ph.D., N.Y.U., 1964; m. Irving Sandler, Sept. 4, 1958; 1 dau., Catherine. Asst. prof. fine arts N.Y.U., N.Y.C., 1964-70, asso. prof., 1970-75, prof., 1975—. Trustee, Godwin-Ternbach Mus., Queens Coll., 1982—. AAUW fellow, 1959; Nat. Endowment Humanities fellow, 1967, 76. Mem. AAUP, Internat. Center Medieval Art, Coll. Art Assn. Am. (pres. 1982—), Medieval Acad. Am. Office: NYU Fine Arts Dept New York NY 10003

SANDMAN, SUSAN GOERTZEL, musician; b. N.Y.C., July 9, 1945; d. Gerald H. and Martha (Bendheim) Goertzel; B.A. summa cum laude, Vassar Coll., 1967; M.A., Stanford (fellow), 1968, Ph.D., 1974; m. 1967 (div. 1977); children—Alison, Jennifer. Instr., U. Mich., Ann Arbor, part-time 1974; asst. prof. music Wells Coll., Aurora, N.Y., 1975-81, asso. prof., 1981—. co-dir. Sine Nomine Players, Ann Arbor, 1972-75; dir. Wells Consort, 1975—; mem. Baroque Music for Two, 1979—; lutist. N.Y. State fellow, 1967; Nat. Endowment Arts fellow, summer 1981. Mem. Am. Musicol. Soc. (sec.-treas. chpt. 1980-82), Phi Beta Kappa, Lute Soc. Am., NOW. Jewish. Contbr. articles to profl. jours. Home: Box 148 Main St Aurora NY 13026 Office: Dept Music Wells Coll Aurora NY 13026

SANDMANN, LORILEE ANN RASKOB, home economist; b. Mpls., Apr. 18, 1951; d. Lester Bernard and LaVergne Marie (Dahlheimer) Raskob; B.S. in Home Econs. Edn., U. Minn., St. Paul, 1973; M.A. in

Adult Edn., U. Minn., Mpls., 1980; m. Douglas A. Sandmann, Nov. 10, 1973; children—Michael Douglas, Leah Ann. Research asst. agrl. econs. U. Minn., 1970; with Minn. Agrl. Extension Service, 1971—, extension agt., Yellow Medicine County, 1973-75, Washington County, 1975-81; dist. program leader home econs./family living U. Minn. Agrl. Extension Service, 1981—; mem. faculty Met. State U., St. Paul, 1979—; grad. asst. staff devel. Agrl. Extension Service, U. Minn., 1980—; adv. com. Vol. Action Center St. Croix Valley, 1975—, Washington County Aging Adv. Com., 1975-79, S. Washington County Parent Adv. Com., 1978—, Canby Community Edn. Adv. Com., 1973-74. Mem. Am. Home Econs. Assn., Nat. Assn. Extension Home Economists, Minn. Home Econs. Assn., Minn. Assn. Extension Home Economists, Minn. Assn. Continuing Adult Educators, Mortar Board, Phi Upsilon Omicron, Phi Lambda Theta, Phi Delta Kappa, Gamma Sigma Delta, Epsilon Sigma Phi. Author papers in field. Home: 2329 Legion Ave N Lake Elmo MN 55042 Office: U Minn Saint Paul MN 55042

SANDS, ADELE GOODWYN GRIFFIN (MRS. JAMES SANDS), educator; b. Swarthmore, Pa., June 25, 1920; d. Frank Hastings and Priscilla (Goodwyn) Griffin; A.B. cum laude, Vassar Coll., 1941; M.A., Villanova U., 1970; m. William Logan MacCoy, Jr., Dec. 28, 1942 (dec. June 1944); 1 dau., Marguerite L. (Mrs. James Pinckney Borden); m. 2d, James Sands, Jan. 18, 1947; children—Priscilla G. (Mrs. Robert Ernest Watson III), James, William Franklin, Elizabeth Keating, Adele Griffin, Geoffrey Keating. Tchr. English, Agnes Irwin Sch., 1941-43; head middle sch. Agnes Irwin Sch., Rosemont, Pa., 1964-67, asso. headmistress, 1967-81, headmistress, 1981—. With Red Cross Valley Forge Gen. Hosp., 1950-62. Bd. dirs. Country Day Sch. Sacred Heart, West Hill Sch., Montgomery Country Day Sch.; pres. bd. dirs. Sleighton Sch. Mem. Headmistresses Assn. of East, Pa. Assn. Women Deans and Counselors, Nat. Assn. Prins. Girls Schs. (council). Home: Sunnyside Wawa PA 19063 Office: Ithan Ave Rosemont PA 19010

SANDS, BARBARA LEE, golf co. exec.; b. N.Y.C., June 28, 1932; d. Jack D. and Hylda A. (Aptheker) Levine; student Hunter Coll., 1949-52; m. Lawrence Sands, Apr. 6, 1968; children—David, Lori, Doria. Mng. editor True Experience Mag., 1968-70; outdoor editor Sporting Guide mag., 1970-71; N.Y. State editor, columnist Outdoor Jour., 1970—; pres. Par-Mate Golf Gloves, 1972—; corp. dir. Jack D. Levine Inc.; freelance writer various nat. outdoor mags. Mem. Outdoor Writers Assn. Am., N.Y. State Outdoor Writers Assn., Nassau County Outdoor Writers Assn., Mensa. Home: 1415 Holiday Park Dr Wantagh NY 11793 Office: 10 W 33d St New York NY 10001

SANDS, BRENDA FAYE, home economist, educator; b. Warsaw, Ind., May 13, 1949; d. Dale Minear and Delta Dean (Jones) Sands; B.S., Manchester Coll., 1970; M.A., Ball State U., 1973, vocat. edn. cert., 1975, postgrad., summers 1976-78. Librarian, Whitko Sch. Corp., Pierceton, Ind., 1971; tchr. home econs. Maconaquah Sch. Corp., Bunker Hill, Ind., 1971-75; asst. prof. home econs. Manchester Coll., North Manchester, Ind., 1975—, chmn. dept., 1975—; mem. study com. on aging Nutrition Hearing Summary for Wabash (Ind.), 1976; nutrition cons. RFD Wabash, Inc., 1976—. Mem. Am. Home Econs. Assn., Ind. Home Econs. Assn. (student adv. 1976), Assn. Tchr. Educators Ind. (program chmn. 1982), Ind. Council on Family Relations, Am. Vocat. Assn., Soc. for Nutrition Edn., Nutrition Today Soc., Nat. Council Adminstrs. Home Econs. Contbr. to nutrition series Wabash Plain Dealer, 1979. Home: Rural Route 2 Claypool IN 46510 Office: Box 114 North Manchester IN 46962

SANDSTROM, ALICE WILHELMINA, accountant; b. Seattle, Jan. 6, 1914; d. Andrew William and Agatha Mathilda (Sundius) S.; B.A., U. Wash., 1934. Office mgr. Star Machinery Co., Seattle, 1935-43, Howe & Co., Seattle, 1943-46; practice as C.P.A., Seattle, 1945—; controller Children's Orthopedic Hosp. and Med. Center, Seattle, 1948-75, asso. adminstr. fin., 1975-81; lectr. U. Wash., Seattle, 1957-72. Mem. Wash. State Title XIX Adv. Com., 1975-82; mem. Wash. State Vendors Rate Adv. Com., 1980—; mem. Mayor's Task Force for Small Bus., 1981—; bd. dirs. YWCA, Seattle, 1981—, Children's Orthopedic Hosp. Found., 1982—. C.P.A., Wash. Fellow Hosp. Fin. Mgmt. Assn. (charter; state pres. 1956-57, nat. treas. 1963-65, Robert H. Reeves merit award 1970), Wash. State Hosp. Assn. (treas. 1956-70), Am. Soc. Women Accts. (pres. Seattle 1946-48), Am. Soc. Women C.P.A.s. Club: Women's Univ. (Seattle). Home and office: 5725 NE 77th St Seattle WA 98115

SANDSTROM, BODEN (BARBARA) C., sound engr.; b. Rochester, N.Y., Sept. 19, 1945; d. Louis Charles and Marion (Gridley) S.; B.A. (N.Y. State Regents scholar 1963-67, Univ. trustee scholar 1963-67), St. Lawrence U., 1967; A.M.L.S. (Work-Study scholar), U. Mich., 1968; grad. in Synergetic Audio Concepts, Washington, 1977, grad. in advanced rec. Omega Rec. Studio, Silver Spring, Md., 1977. Librarian, San Jose State Coll., 1968-69; head circulation dept. Northeastern U. Library, 1969-72; librarian lit. div. Martin Luther King Library, Washington, 1972-75; owner, operator Woman Sound, Washington, 1975—; sound engr. Mich. Women's Music Festival, 1977-78, 81-82, Nat. Women's Writers Conf., 1977, 3d, 4th, 5th and 7th Nat. Women's Music Festivals, West Coast Women's Music Festival, 1981, 82, Am. Folk Life Festival, 1981, Lilly Tomlin tour, 1982, Chris Williamson tour, 1980, Casse Culver tour, 1976, 77; tchr. sound engring. privately and at Am. U.; office mgr. Female Liberation, Boston, 1970-72; grad. asst. audio tech. program Am. U., Washington, 1980—. Mem. Audio Engring. Soc., Acoustical Soc. Am., Mortar Bd. Home: 19 Logan Circle A NW Washington DC 20005 Office: PO Box 1932 Washington DC 20013

SANDVEN, JUANITA SANDRA, record systems mgr.; b. Rome, N.Y., Apr. 28, 1940; d. Albert Roy and Dollie Mae (Tingle) Meiss; grad. Central City Bus. Inst., 1959; student Ariz. State U., 1977-78, Ottawa U., 1980. Legal sec., Shaffer & Leverton, Syracuse, N.Y., 1959-60; inside sales rep., sec. Brown-Thompson Sales, DeWitt, N.Y., 1960-63; with various mfr. reps., inside sales electronic components and test equipment, 1963-71; with The Greyhound Corp. Phoenix, 1971—, legal asst., 1978-80, mgr. record systems, 1980—; dir. Greyhound|Armour F.C.U., 1974-77. Pres., Inter-Club Council of Ariz., 1979-80, recipient Cert. of Achievement, 1979. Mem. Am. Bus. Women's Assn., DAR, Republican. Episcopalian. Clubs: Phoenix Emblem (pres. 1972-73), Supreme Emblem (nat. officer 1973-79, 81—), Order Eastern Star. Editor: Emblegram, 1971-72, Saguaro, 1973-74, Squaw Talk, 1975-76. Home: 5749 N 8th Pl Apt 1 Phoenix AZ 85014 Office: Greyhound Tower Phoenix AZ 85077

SANDY, CATHERINE ELLEN, librarian; b. Italy; d. Felice Antonio and Guglielma Elena Santaniello; student Rosary Coll., 1933-34, U. Florence, Italy, 1951; B.S., Columbia U., 1953. Librarian, Port Washington (N.Y.) Pub. Library, 1926-73. Bd. dirs. Art Adv. Council, Port Washington Pub. Library; trustee, charter mem. Cow Neck Peninsula Hist. Soc. Recipient Alumni medal Columbia, 1970. Mem. Am., N.Y., N.C. library assns., UN Assn., Gen. Studies Alumni Assn. Columbia. Roman Catholic. Editor: Cow Neck Peninsula Hist. Jour. Home: 35 Davis Rd Port Washington NY 11050

SANFORD, FAYE ARCHER, Realtor; b. Stratford, Okla., July 26, 1932; d. Benjamin Harrison and Ada Lee (Hart) Archer; student Okla. State U., 1954, Okla. U., 1956-58; m. Paul Ray Sanford, June 20, 1951; children—Patricia Ann, Buddy Sanford. Advt. writer Lindsay (Okla.) News, 1953-56; asst. adminstr. Lindsay Meml. Hosp., 1956-63; extension sec. Okla. State U., 1963-64; organizer, instr. Dale Carnegie Courses, 1964-73; pres. Faye Enterprises, Inc., Oklahoma City, 1973—. Publicity chairperson Democratic Women, 1980; active work for Chickasaw Indians. Mem. Nat. Assn. Realtors, Okla. Assn. Realtors, Nat. Farm and Land Inst. (sec.), Okla. Farm and Land Inst. (pres. 1981-82), Nat. Grad. Real Estate Inst., Nat. Speakers Am., Oklahoma City Farm Club (treas.), Bus. and Profl. Women (v.p. 1973-74), Oklahoma City C. of C., UDC. Democrat. Baptist. Clubs: Lake Texoma Lodge, Chickasaw Nation Sales and Service. Home: 3025 NW 10th St Oklahoma City OK 73107 Office: 3021 NW 10th St Oklahoma City OK 73107

SANFORD, MARILOU K., assn. exec.; b. Cleve., Oct. 29, 1948; d. Edward L. and Eileen M. (Murray) Green; student in bus. and mktg., Ball State U., Muncie, Ind., 1966-70; m. Bruce W. Sanford; 1 dau., Lisa Marie. Client services dir. Newspaper Enterprise Assn., Cleve., 1972-76, mktg. mgr., N.Y.C., 1975-80; dir. pub. promotion and research U.S. C. of C./Nation's Bus., Washington, 1980—. Mem. Women in Communications, Women in Advt. and Mktg., Friends of Kennedy Center, Ad Club Washington, Smithsonian Assos. Office: 1615 H St NW Washington DC 20062

SANFORD, RUTH BOSTROM, tabulating co. exec.; b. Two Harbors, Minn., Mar. 15, 1925; d. John Arvid and Helene (Lind) Bostrom; diploma Cable's Secretarial Coll., St. Paul, 1944; student Northwestern U., 1966; m. Keith N. Sanford, Sept. 21, 1950 (div. Sept. 1960). Various exec. secretarial and adminstrv. asst. positions, 1952-66; corp. sec., adminstrv. asst. to pres. Statis. Tabulating Corp., Chgo., 1966—. Mem. Nat. Assn. Exec. Secs. Lutheran. Club: Women of Moose. Home: 400 E Randolph St Chicago IL 60601 Office: 2 N Riverside Plaza Chicago IL 60606

SANFORD, RUTH COOPER, educator, counselor; b. North Warren, Pa., Dec. 26, 1906; d. Elden Oscar and Elma Miretta (Dorn) Cooper; B.A., Lebanon Valley Coll., 1930; M.A., Columbia U., 1938; postgrad. N.Y. U., Rutgers U., Columbia U.; m. Daniel Seymour Sanford, Aug. 7, 1940; 1 dau., Mei-Mei Elma Cooper. Tchr., head dept. English, Lakewood (N.Y.) High Sch., 1930-37; asst. to sec. Tchrs. Coll., Columbia U., 1937-40; guidance officer, assoc. prof. We. Md. Coll., Westminster, Md., 1944-49; dir. guidance Lakewood (N.J.) High Sch., 1952-55; chmn. guidance and counseling services, West Hempstead, N.Y., 1955-72; co-dir. Center Interpersonal Growth, Port Jefferson, N.Y., 1977—; adj. prof. L.I. U., 1972—, Hofstra U., 1980—; facilitator person-centered internat. workshops with Dr. Carl R. Rogers, 1978—. Recipient Peter Zenger award in pub. service and journalism, 1976, award for outstanding contbn. to edn. Lebanon Valley Coll., 1975; named Counselor of Yr., N.Y. State Personnel Assn., 1976. Mem. Am. Personnel and Guidance Assn., Assn. Humanistic Psychology. Democrat. Author: Creativity and Intelligence: Implications for Counselors, 1965; Intimacy in a Person-Centered Way of Being: Paradigm for Change, 1982; co-author (with Dr. Carl Rogers) Journey to the Heart of Africa, 1982; contbr. to Freedom to Learn by Carl R. Rogers, 1983; weekly columnist As I See It, 1975-81. Home and Office: 2023 Cecilla Pl Seaford NY 11783

SANGER, MARIANNE ELIZABETH, mfg. co. exec.; b. Monroe, Mich., Nov. 19, 1941; d. George Phillip and Marie Lucille (Mills) S.; A.A., Henry Ford Community Coll., 1977; B.B.A. in Acctg., U. Detroit, 1979, postgrad., 1980—. Shipping/traffic clk. Calgon Corp., Rockwood, Mich., 1960-69; sec. HUD, Rockwood, 1970-73; exec. dir. Rockwood Housing Commn., 1972-73; stenographer, sec. Ford Motor Co., Allen Park, Mich., 1973-77, fin. analyst, 1977—, also mem. motor assembly employee involvement com. Recipient cert. of appreciation for serving as exec. dir. Rockwood Housing Commn., Rockwood City Council, 1973. Mem. Nat. Assn. Female Execs., Assn. M.B.A. Execs., AAUW, Ford B.&A. Women's Bowling League (treas. 1982-83), Beta Gamma Sigma, Phi Gamma Nu. Roman Catholic. Clubs: William Penn, Silhouette-Am. Health, Ford Motor Women's. Office: Ford Motor Co Body and Assembly Gen Office PO Box 1586 17000 Oakwood Blvd Allen Park MI 48121

SAN GIOVANNI, FRANCINE ELISA, psychiatrist; b. Newark, Oct. 12, 1945; d. Ralph and Frances (Papandrea) SanGiovanni; B.A. cum laude, Seton Hall U., 1967; M.D., Georgetown U., 1971. Intern, Monmouth (N.J.) Med. Center, 1971-72; resident in psychiatry Met. Hosp., N.Y.C., 1972-75; practice medicine specializing in psychiatry, N.Y.C., 1975—; instr. dept. clin. psychiatry Met. Hosp., 1977-78; attending staff psychiatrist Gracie Sq. Hosp., N.Y.C., 1978—; cons. Diet Control Center, S.I. Community Coll. Sponsor, United Vailsburg Softball Team, Big Bass Lake Softball; vol. St. Gerard's Feast. Mem. Am. Psychiat. Assn., Am. Med. Women's Assn., AMA (recipient Physician's Recognition award 1979). Office: 250 E 87 St 2B New York NY 10028

SANGREY, DAWN, author; b. Lancaster, Pa., Feb. 11, 1942; d. Abram Warfel and Dorothy Lorraine (Herr) S.; A.B., Mt. Holyoke Coll., 1963; M.A.T., Johns Hopkins U., 1964; m. Paul McKenna Fargis, Apr. 23, 1977; 1 son, Christopher Sangrey. Tchr., public schs. Pelham, N.Y., 1964-66, Scarsdale, N.Y., 1966-72; textbook editor D. VanNostrand Co., N.Y.C., 1972-74, Latham Pub. Co., N.Y.C., 1974-77; free lance writer, editor, N.Y.C., 1977—; adj. lectr. Borough of Manhattan Community Coll., City U. N.Y., 1974; author: (with Morton Bard) The Crime Victim's Book, 1979. Home and Office: 200 Haines Rd Bedford Hills NY 10507

SANJENKO, GRACE LORETTA, health adminstr.; b. Saskatoon, Can., Jan. 9, 1943; d. Fred and Ruth SanJ.; came to U.S., 1963; B.S., Calif. State U., Northridge, 1971, M.S.P.H., 1973; postgrad. U. So. Calif. Sch. Pub. Adminstrn., 1974—; m. Malcolm David Cobb, May 21, 1978. Tech. editor Children's Hosp. Los Angeles, 1972-73; adminstrv. asst. Central Los Angeles Health Project, 1973; dist. dir. community health edn. Los Angeles County Dept. Health Services, 1973-75; mem. faculty dept. health sci. Calif. State U., Northridge, 1974—, faculty supr. grad. resident and intern program, 1974—; risk mgr. Los Angeles County Dept. Health Services, 1975-78; assoc. prof. Chapman Coll., 1978—; dir. Office Quality Assurance, Children's Hosp. Los Angeles, 1980-81. Mem. Am. Public Health Assn., Soc. Profl. Health Educators (nat. chpt. rep. 1976-78), Los Angeles County Health Assn. (v.p. 1974-75), Am. Mgmt. Assn., Am. Hosp. Assn. Risk Mgrs. Author: Implementation of Risk Management for Reduction of Malpractice Costs in Public Hospitals, 1977. Home: 13212 Schoenborn St Sun Valley CA 91352 Office: Chapman Coll Regional Edn Center WLA 8740 La Tijera Blvd Los Angeles CA 90045

SANNA, LUCY JEAN, writer; b. Menomonie, Wis., Apr. 20, 1948; d. Charles Albert and Margaret Sheila (McGee) S.; B.A., St. Norbert Coll., 1969; postgrad. U. Wis., Madison, 1970-74; m. Peter Lawrence Frisch, Jan. 2, 1971; 1 dau., Katherine Sanna. Asst. editor Scott Foresman & Co., Glenview, Ill., 1970-73; freelance editor, Palo Alto, Calif., 1973-75; editor FMC Corp., San Jose, Calif., 1975-78; supr. corp. advt. Memorex Corp., Santa Clara, Calif., 1978-79, exec. presentations adminstr., 1979; mgr. communications services Electric Power Research Inst., Palo Alto, 1980—. Mem. adv. council Energy Source Edn. Program; mem. Calif. Energy Edn. Forum. Mem. Nat. Assn. Female Execs., Internat. Assn. Bus. Communicators. Club: Toastmasters Internat. (v.p.). Home: Los Altos CA 94022 Office: EPRI PO Box 10412 Palo Alto CA 94303

SANNER, ALICE MATHILDA, machine tool co. exec.; b. Dubuque, Iowa, Oct. 31, 1913; d. Louis A. and Emma (Gross) Sanner; grad. high sch., Dubuque. With Rockford Machine Tool Co. (Ill.) subs. Greenlee Bros. & Co., 1942—, advt. mgr., 1946-75, ret., 1975, editor Hot Chips mag., 1951-80, also advt. mgr. Machine Tool Products-Greenlee Group, 1972-75; editor publ. Greenleaves, 1972-75. Mem. Rockford Art Assn., Chgo. Art Inst., Orch. Guild of Rockford Symphony Orch., Inc., Rockford Mus. Assn., Friends of Rockford Mus., Cath. Woman's League, St. James Altar and Rosary Soc., No. Ill. Communicators. Roman Catholic. Contbr. short stories coll. and popular publs. Home: 122 N Chicago Ave Rockford IL 61107

SANTA-MARIA, MARIA LOURDES, psychotherapist; b. Havana, Cuba, Sept. 13, 1947; d. Rafael R. and Lillian Alvarez S.-M.; came to U.S., 1960, naturalized, 1970; student U. Dayton, 1965-68; B.A., Ohio Dominican Coll., 1970; M.A., Ohio State U., 1972; D.Min., San Francisco Theol. Sem., 1981. Asst. dir. residence hall complex Ohio State U., Columbus, 1970-72; asso. dir., coll. psychologist Career and Personal Counseling Center, Eckerd Coll., St. Petersburg, Fla., 1972-75, acting dir., coll. psychologist, 1975-76; dean of students St. Andrews Presbyterian Coll., Laurinburg, N.C., 1976-77; pvt. practice individual and family counseling, St. Petersburg, 1978—; mgmt. cons. to physicians, ednl. cons. to tchrs. Mem. Am. Psychol. Assn. (asso.), Am. Personnel and Guidance Assn., Am. Mental Health Counselors Assn., Assn. for Religious Values in Counseling, Assn. for Clin. Pastoral Edn. Presbyterian. Home: 5282B Beach Dr SE Saint Petersburg FL 33705

SANTELL, ROBERTA (RICKIE), polit. worker; b. Los Angeles, July 23, 1937; d. Hyman and Sue (Fields) Thompson; student Los Angeles City Coll., 1955-56; m. Richard Alfred Santell, June 17, 1956; children—Mitchell James, Lisa Gaye. Sec. criminal div. Office of Los Angeles County Clk., 1955, CBS-TV, Los Angeles, 1956. Exec. bd. Covina Valley Fair Housing Council, 1969-70; co-organizer Police Community Relations Bd., La Puente area, 1970; mem. Los Angeles County Democratic Central Com., 1976—; assembly dist. chmn., regional vice-chmn. Calif. State Central Com., 1978—, co-chmn. credentials com.; del. Dem. Nat. Conv., 1980, 82, also mem. credentials com. Recipient Dem. Women of Year award, 1971-72, Los Angeles County Central Com. Dem. of Year award, 1980. Jewish. Home: 336 S Barranca St West Covina CA 91791

SANTIAGO, GLADYS, govt. librarian; b. Guaynabo, P.R., Jan. 12, 1929; d. Pedro and Julia (Rodríguez) S.; B.A., U. P.R., 1955, M.L.S., 1971; m. Ángel Meléndez, July 20, 1974. Asst. librarian P.R. Dept. Health, Bayamón Dist. Hosp., 1949-60, P.R. Bur. of Budget, Office of Gov., 1960-72; chief librarian reference dept. Inter-Am. U., Met. Br., P.R., 1972-75; dir. library P.R. Office of Mgmt. and Budget, San Juan, 1975—; del. White House Conf. Libraries and Info. Services, 1981. Recipient merit certs. for disting. public service Govt. of P.R., 1968, 71, 79, 81; P.R. Govt. grantee, 1970-71. Mem. NEA, P.R. Tchrs. Assn., Sociedad de Bibliotecarios de P.R. Home: Urb Monte Verde H25 No 4 Toa Alta PR 00758 Office: 254 Cruz y Tetuan San Juan PR 00904

SANTILLO, JOSEPHINE LOUISE, state ofcl.; b. Passaic, N.J., June 11, 1943; d. Richard Lawrence and Minnie Theresa Santillo; B.A., Fairleigh Dickinson U., Rutherford, N.J., 1965; M.S.W., Va. Commonwealth U., Richmond, 1977. With N.J. Employment Service, Hackensack, 1965-66; counselor N.J. Rehab. Service, Newark, 1967; psychiat. social worker Essex County Hosp. Center, Cedar Grove, N.J., Greystone Hosp., Morris Plains, N.J., 1968-74, N.J. Bur. Local Ops., Wayne and Trenton, 1968-77; fair hearing officer N.J. Bur. Adminstrv. Rev. and Appeals, Trenton, 1977-79; tng. officer N.J. Office Staff Devel., Trenton, 1979—, supr. div. youth and family services, 1981—; pvt. practice psychotherapy, 1977—. Mem. Nat. Assn. Social Workers, Soc. for Clin. Social Work, Am. Public Welfare Assn., Acad. Cert. Social Workers, AAUW, Nat. Council Family Relations, Huxley Inst., N.J. Council Tng., LWV, Willowbrook Ministries. Home: 14 West End Ave Pompton Plains NJ 07444 Office: 3535 Quakerbridge Rd Trenton NJ 08619

SANTINI, SANDRA, psychiat. social worker; b. St. Paul, Oct. 15, 1930; d. Harold and Ida Millunchiok; B.A., Calif. State U., Northridge, 1961; M.S.W., U. So. Calif., 1963; m. Orlando L. Santini, Oct. 20, 1951; children—Kim, Nikola. Psychiat. social worker Pasadena Child Guidance Clinic (Calif.), 1963-66, Adult Psychiat. Clinic, U. So. Calif. Med. Center, Los Angeles, 1966—; pvt. practice psychiat. social work, Marina del Rey, Calif., 1970—. Exam. commr. Calif. Bd. Behavioral Sci. Examiners, Los Angeles, 1972-74. Mem. Nat. Assn. Social Workers, Acad. Cert. Social Workers. Contbr. articles in field to profl. publs. Home: 306 Bora Bora Way Marina Del Rey CA 90291 Office: 1937 Hospital Pl Los Angeles CA 90033

SANTOS, FRANCES AFLAGUE, acct.; b. Agana, Guam, Nov. 15, 1935; d. Francisco and Pilar San Miguel (Aflague) Santos; student Dunbarton Jr. Coll., 1955-57; B.B.A. in Acctg., George Washington U., 1959; children—Roderic Lee, Stephanie Rose, Kendric Francis. Exec. sec. Father Duenas Meml. Sch., Guam, 1959-60; law clk. Guam Legis., 1960-62; asst. public info. officer Guam Legis., 1962-64, pub. relations/info. officer, 1964-70; records mgmt. officer Dept. Adminstrn., Govt. Guam, 1970-74; spl. asst. for fed. programs, U.S. Hos. of Reps., Washington, 1976-80; pvt. practice acctg., Gwinn, Mich. Pres., Young Democratic Party, 1960-64; sec. Dem. Party Guam, 1968-69; 1st v.p., mem. exec. bd. Big Sis., 1969-72; del. nat. and mini convs. Dem. Party, 1972, 74; mem. Dem. Nat. Com. Mem. Am. Mgmt. Assn., Nat. Assn. Female Execs., Nat. Assn. Real Estate Brokers, NOW. Roman Catholic. Clubs: Franklin Mint Collectors Soc., Guam Women's.

SANTSCHI, JEAN ANDERSON, mgmt. cons.; b. Chgo., May 2, 1927; d. Alfred and Celia (Gronek) Anderson; student Northwestern Bus. Coll., Chgo., 1944; m. Roger Santschi, Feb. 29, 1944; children—Karen, Cheryl. Contractor, Santschi Builders, No. suburbs of Chgo., 1946-62; v.p. Smith Assos., Lake Forest, Ill., 1977-79; owner, mgr. Condominium Mgmt. Cons., Lake Forest, 1975—. Treas., Condell Hosp. Aux., 1977; v.p. Am. Legion Aux., 1949-50. Mem. Community Assn. Inst. Presbyterian. Home: 1507 Bull Creek Dr Libertyville IL 60048 Office: 680 N Western Ave Lake Forest IL 60045

SANTY, JEANNE-LOIS MARSCHALL, nurse; b. Stamford, Conn., June 26, 1931; d. Frederick and Louise (Ritchie) Marschall; R.N., Stamford Hosp., 1952; cert. occupational health nurse, 1975; m. May 9, 1953; children—Robyn Kimberlee Santy Richar. Head nurse polio unit Stamford Hosp., 1952-53, asst. supr. aux. personnel, 1953-55; supr. nursing services Am. Cyanamid Co., Stamford, 1955—. Mem. Bd. Reps. Stamford, 1975—, pres., 1981—, dep. mayor, 1981—; vice chmn. Stamford Republican Town Com., 1973-75; pres. Young Republicans; mem. Conn. Republican Central Com., 1976—; justice of peace, 1970—; asst. minority leader Stamford Bd. Reps., 1979-81, chmn. health and protection com.. 1979-81; chmn. diaconate Bapt. Ch., Stamford. Mem. Stamford Alumnae Assn. (past pres.), Am. Assn. Occupational Health Nurses, New Eng. Assn. Occupational Health Nurses, Conn. Assn. Occupational Health Nurses (past v.p.), Stamford Assn. Occupational Health Nurses (past pres.). Home: 133 Thornridge Dr Stamford CT 06903 Office: 1937 W Main St Stamford CT 06901

SAPHAR, AUDREY WOLLENBERG, advt. agy. exec.; b. Balt., Dec. 24, 1940; d. Thomas Spedden and Naomi Owings (Crooks) Wollenberg; A.B. cum laude, Bryn Mawr Coll., 1961; M.S. with honors, Columbia U., 1962; m. Edwin George Saphar, Jr., Sept. 21, 1963. Asso. editor Suburbia Today mag., N.Y.C., 1962-63; researcher ABC Network, N.Y.C., 1963-64; dir. pub. info. Tchrs. Coll., Columbia U., N.Y.C., 1964-66; mng. partner Saphar & Assos., Inc., advt. and public relations,

Rochester, N.Y., 1966—. Bd. dirs. Rochester Bus. Com. for Arts, Rochester Center for Govtl. Research, Margaret Woodbury Strong Mus., Rochester; past bd. dirs. Rochester Midtown br. YMCA. Mem. Women in Communications (Matrix award 1974), Advt. Council Rochester (Lantern award 1979, dir., mem. exec. com.), Rochester C. of C. (dir.). Presbyterian. Office: Saphar & Assos Inc 175 Gibbs St Rochester NY 14605

SAPINSLEY, LILA MANFIELD, state legislator; b. Chgo., Sept. 9, 1922; d. Jacob and Doris (Silverman) Manfield; B.A., Wellesley Coll., 1944; D. Pub. Service, U. R.I., 1971; D.Pedagogy, R.I. Coll., 1973; m. John M. Sapinsley, Dec. 23, 1942; children—Jill Sapinsley Mooney, Carol Sapinsley Rubenstein, Joan, Patricia. Mem. R.I. senate, 1972—, minority leader, 1974—. Mem. R.I. Gov.'s Commn. on Women; commr. Edn. Commn. of States; pres. bd. trustees Butler Hosp., 1978—; trustee R.I. State Colls., 1965-70, chmn., 1967-70; trustee U. R.I., R.I. Coll. Found.; bd. dirs. Miriam Hosp., Hamilton House, Trinity Repertory Co., Lincoln Sch., Wellesley Center for Research on Women, 1980. Recipient Alumnae Achievement award Wellesley Coll., 1974. Republican. Jewish. Home: 25 Cooke St Providence RI 02906

SAPONE, MARY LOU, health edn./adminstrn. specialist; b. New Castle, Pa., Mar. 20, 1946. Pres., World Health Devel. Inst., Danbury, Conn., 1979—; past exec. dir. Childbirth and Family Devel. Inst., Danbury; bd. dirs., mem. med. adv. com. Fairfield County (Conn.) chpt. March of Dimes Birth Defects Found.; mem. anesthetic and life support drugs adv. com. FDA; cons. fertility and maternal health adv. com. FDA. Recipient Jefferson award Am. Assn. Public Service, 1981; Disting. Service award Danbury Jaycees, 1981. Fellow Internat. Council; mem. Am. Soc. Psychoprophylaxis in Obstetrics (cert. childbirth educator), Am. Soc. Sex Educators, Counselors, and Therapists (cert. sex therapist). Office: 57 North St Suite 403 Danbury CT 06810

SAPP, PHYLLIS WOODRUFF, author, lectr., real estate co. exec.; b. Oklahoma City, Oct. 21, 1908; d. John A. and Maude (Laws) Woodruff; student Oklahoma City U., 1926-27; B.A., Okla. U., 1930; m. J. D. Sapp, June 5, 1930; children—Kathryn Sapp Malthaner, John Davis, Phillip Woodruff. Organizer, dir. Oklahoma City's first children's theatre, 1930-35; dir. Oklahoma City Theatre Guild, 1940-42; jr. high sch. tchr. drama Oklahoma City pub. schs., 1946-49; writer curriculum materials Women's Missionary Union of So. Bapt. Conv., 1969—; real estate broker; co-dir. J. D. Sapp Sch. Real Estate, 1972—. Mem. exec. bd. Oklahoma City YWCA, 1973-81, 1st v.p., 1976-77, pres., 1977-79; nat. bd. YWCA, 1979—, v.p. Mid States region; mem. Oklahoma City Human Rights Commn., 1980—, chmn., 1982-84. Recipient $4,000 first prize Zondervan's Christian Fiction Contest, 1957. Mem. Nat. League Am. Pen Women (br. v.p. 1963, pres. 1968-70, 76-78, treas. 1973-75, 4th nat. v.p. 1970-72, chmn. nat. letters bd. 1972-74, nat. chaplain 1974-76), Internat. Platform Assn., Mortar Bd., Alpha Phi (disting. alumnae award of honor 1972), Pi Kappa Delta. Baptist (writer Jr. Pupil and Jr. Tchr. for So. Bapt. Sunday Sch. Bd. 1952-71). Author: Accidental Hero (3-act play), 1949; The Ice Cutter, 1948; Whisper Out of the Dust, 1951; For Such a Time, 1954; The Long Bridge, 1957; God of All the Earth, 1960; Gifts from God, 1962; Small Giant, 1957; Life at Its Best, 1963; Living for Jesus, 1961; Working Together in Our Church, 1963; Lighthouse on the Corner, 1964; Creative Teaching in the Church School, 1967; Children of Men, 1968; Fifty Nine Programs For Pre-Teens, 1969; Teaching Guide for Youth Sunday School Work, 1970; Jeff the Baptist, 1972; Real Estate Workbook, 1972; Very Best Friend, 1976; Whose Plan Is This?, 1978; House of God, a History of Olivet Baptist Church, 1980. Address: 7100 S Kentucky Ave Oklahoma City OK 73159

SAPPENFIELD, DIANE HASTINGS, devel. co. exec., civic worker; b. Marion, Ohio, Apr. 22, 1940; d. Edgar Dean and Marguerite Elizabeth (Alexander) Hastings; B.A. in Sociology and Econs., Mills Coll., 1962; tchr.'s cert. Calif. State U., Los Angeles, 1963; m. Ronald Eugene Sappenfield, July 6, 1962; children—Derek Ronald, Ann Elizabeth. Tchr. elem. sch., El Segundo, Calif., 1963-66; asst. dir. admissions Mills Coll., 1972-74; v.p., dir. DDA Assos., Inc., McLean, Va., 1978—; asst. to chmn. bd. Watergate Complex, Washington, 1979-81; dir. corp. mktg. Watergate Devel. Inc., McLean, 1981—. Vol. tchr. Saugatuck Elem. Sch., Westport, Conn., 1976-79; active benefits for Corcoran Sch. Art, Nat. Symphony Orch., Washington; bd. dirs. Westport-Weston Arts Council, 1973-79; mem. Levitt Pavilion Governing Com., 1974-79; pres. Friends of Levitt Pavilion, 1977; trustee Stauffer-Westport Fund, 1976-79; mem. Westport Young Woman's League, 1969-79, pres., 1975-76; bd. dirs. Stamford-Norwalk br. Jr. League, 1977-78; exec. com. Hope Ball, Washington, 1980—, Health and Homemaker Aid Services of Greater Washington, 1981—. Mem. Mills Coll. Club N.Y., Washington Jr. League. Office: 6833 Beverly Rd McLean VA 22101

SARAFIAN, SYLVIA ANNETTE, computer systems specialist; b. Newton, Mass., June 16, 1931; d. Antranig Arakel and Elizabeth (Zorian) S.; B.A., Mt. Holyoke Coll., 1953. Chemist, Mass. Meml. Hosps., Boston, 1953-56; programmer, Honeywell Inc., Newton, Mass., 1956-58, System Devel. Corp., Santa Monica, Calif., 1958-61, Bedford, Mass., 1961-64, computer systems specialist, Santa Monica, 1966-71; programmer Bolt, Benarek & Newman, Cambridge, Mass., 1964-66; owner COMPUFARM and The Aurora, Marina Del Rey, Calif., 1971—, Advanced Bus. Microsystems, Marina Del Rey, 1981—; speaker symposium on computers in agr.; participant programs in field. Asso. mem. Calif. Republican State Central Com., 1975-76, 78; bd. dirs. Marina Rep. Club, 1982; mem. Dornan for Congress campaign, 1976, 78, 80; active Calif. Women for Agr., 1977-79. Mem. Armenian Apostolic Church. Club: Appalachian Mountain. Author CompuFARM, computer system for agr., written for time-sharing, 1971, for microcomputers, 1981; author: The Aurora, written for time-sharing, 1977, for microcomputers, 1982; prodn. asst. for TV show Face to Face, 1976. Home: 13856 Bora Bora Way #105C Marina Del Rey CA 90291 Office: PO Box 9352 Marina Del Rey CA 90291

SARBO, WANDA DIXON, educator; b. Advance, Mo., Aug. 19, 1924; d. Clifford Martin and Ruth (Copman) Dixon; diploma Central Bible Coll., Springfield, Mo., 1944; student S.W. Mo. U., 1944-46; B.A., Spalding Coll., 1956; postgrad. U. Louisville, intermittently 1958-77, Murray U., summer 1966; M.A., U. de las Americas, Puebla, Mex., 1978; m. Alfred William Sarbo, June 24, 1946; children—Adela Ruth, Anita Jeanette. Ordained to ministry, 1947; minister various chs., 1946-55; tchr. music and math. Gottschalk Jr. High Sch., Louisville, 1956-64; tchr. Spanish, English and humanities Iroquois Sr. High Sch., Louisville, 1965—, chmn. langs. dept., 1976—. Sec., dir. Louisville-Jefferson County Youth Orch., 1962-64. Named Best Student of Mex., 1981. NDEA grantee, 1966, 67. Mem. Am. Assn. Tchrs. Spanish and Portuguese (pres. Ky. 1982—), Ky. Council on Teaching of Fgn. Langs. (dir.), Sigma Delta Pi, Alpha Mu Gamma. Home: 1290 Willow Ave Louisville KY 40204 Office: Iroquois Sr High Sch 4615 Taylor Blvd Louisville KY 40215

SARDINA, MARTA ISABEL, engr.; b. Havana, Cuba, June 28, 1952; came to U.S., 1972, naturalized, 1981; d. Alberto and Guadalupe (Zuniga) S.; B.S. in Math. UCLA, 1977; M.S. in Program Mgmt., West Coast U., 1981. Sr. tracking system analyst Bendix Field Engring. Corp., Pasadena, Calif., 1978-80, project leader, sr. engr., 1980-82; sr. engr. system definition and requirements group Convair div. Gen. Dynamics, San Diego, 1982—. Recipient Cert. of Achievement, Bendix-Jet Propulsion Lab., 1979; NASA-Group Achievement award, 1981. Mem. Nat. Assn. Female Execs., Bendix Mgmt. Club. Home: 5402 Balboa Arms Dr Apt 322 San Diego CA 92117 Office: Convair Div Gen Dynamics PO Box 80847 Mail Zone 35-6470 San Diego CA 92138

SARETSKY, LORELLE ELAINE, psychoanalyst, univ. adminstr.; b. N.Y.C.; d. Jerome and Shirley June (Sokoloff) Bunkin; B.A., Bklyn. Coll., U. N.Y., 1969; Ph.D. in Clin. Psychology (NIMH fellow), Adelphi U., 1973, certificate in psychoanalysis, 1977; m. Theodore Saretsky, June 21, 1963; children—Meri, Robin. Pres., Mercury Uniform Supply Corp., Bklyn., 1967-73; asst. dir. clin. services Postdoctoral Psychotherapy Center, Adelphi U., 1973—, asso. clin. prof. psychology, sr. supervising psychologist Inst. Advanced Psychol. Studies, 1973—; pvt. practice psychoanalysis, Hewlett Neck, N.Y., 1973—; cons. South Oaks Hosp., Amityville, N.Y., 1975—. Mem. Am. Psychol. Assn., Nassau County (N.Y.) Psychol. Assn., Adelphi Soc. Psychoanalysis (pres. 1977). Home: 1 Madison St Newlett Neck NY 11598 Office: Postdoctoral Psychotherapy Center Adelphi U Garden City NY 11530

SARGEANT, NANCY REARDON, editor; b. Providence, Oct. 30, 1933; d. Vincent T. and Margaret M. (Mackenzie) Reardon; B.Ed., R.I. Coll., 1955; M.A., Boston U., 1958. Tchr., Warwick, R.I., 1955-57, Denver, 1957-58, Warwick, 1958-60, Burlington, Mass., 1960-63; editor Houghton Mifflin Co., Boston, 1963-67, supervising editor, 1967-74, exec. editor sch. reading dept., 1974—; reading cons. Sec., social chmn. R.I. Young Democrats, 1958-60. Mem. Internat., New Eng. reading assns., Bookbuilders, Kappa Delta Pi. Roman Catholic. Contbr. to anthologies. Office: One Beacon St Boston MA 02107

SARGENT, ALICE GOLDSTEIN, cons., author; b. Cin., Feb. 5, 1939; d. Harold D. and Adele (Linch) Goldstein; B.A. in English Lit., Oberlin Coll., 1960; M.A., Brandeis U., 1963; M.Ed. in Group Dynamics, Temple U., 1966; Ed.D., U. Mass., Amherst, 1974; m. G. Dann Sargent, June 2, 1963 (dec. 1976); 1 dau., Elizabeth. Orgn. and affirmative action cons., Washington, current clients include E.I. Dupont de Nemours, INA Corp., Fed. Exec. Inst., Nat. Tng. Labs.; mem. mgmt. faculty Sch. Bus. Adminstrn. San Diego State U., 1974; project coordinator Nat. Conf. on Women in Edn., Office of Asst. Sec. Edn., HEW, Washington, 1975-76; dir. M.B.A. program Trinity Coll., Washington 1976-77; mem. faculty Am. U. Sch. Govt. and Pub. Adminstrn.; seminar leader Australian Inst. Mgmt. Mem. Acad. Mgmt., Am. Psychol. Assn., Organizational Devel. Network (dir.). Author: Beyond Sex Roles, 1976; The Androgynous Manager, 1981. Home: 4819 Dexter Terr NW Washington DC 20007

SARGENT, CAROLINE LOUISE, ednl. adminstr.; b. Richmond, Ind., Nov. 7; d. George Andrew and Margaret (Kromer) S.; Mus.B., Wittenberg U., 1972; postgrad. Cath. U. Am., 1972-74, N.Y.U., 1979. Asst. adminstr. Sch. Engring. and Arch., Cath. U. Am., Washington, 1973-76; nat. program clk. Foster Grandparent Program Hdqrs., Washington, 1977-78; coordinator public relations and vols. Montclair (N.J.) Community Hosp., 1979; public relations asst. Bloomfield (N.J.) Coll., 1979-80, asst. dir. devel., 1980-82; dir. devel. and pub. relations Far Brook Sch., Short Hills, N.J., 1982—. Alida Attwell scholar, 1968. Mem. Council Advancement and Support Edn., Nat. Assn. Female Execs., N.J. Press Women. Office: Far Brook Sch 52 Great Hills Rd Short Hills NJ 07078

SARGENT, DIANA RHEA, bookkeeper; b. Cheyenne, Wyo., Feb. 20, 1939; d. Clarence and Edith (de Castro) Hayes; grad. high sch.; m. Charles Sargent, Apr. 17, 1975; children—Rene A. Coburn, Rochelle A. Weldy, Clayton R. Weldy, Christopher J.; stepchildren—Laurie E. Sargent, Leslie E. Sargent. IBM proof operator Bank Am., Stockton, Calif., 1956-58, gen. ledger bookkeeper, Modesto, Calif., 1963-66; office mgr., head bookkeeper Central Drug Store, Modesto, 1966-76, Sargent & Sargent, Modesto, 1976—. Bd. dirs. Haven Stanislaus Women's Refuge Center. Mem. NOW, San Francisco Mus. Soc., Nat. Soc. Public Accts., Merced Accts. Soc. Republican. Roman Catholic. Address: PO Box 919 Modesto CA 95353

SARGENT, MARGARET HOLLAND, artist; b. Hollywood, Calif., Dec. 30, 1927; d. Cecil Claude and Norma Mary Holland; student U. Calif., Los Angeles, 1946-4 , 54-55; studied with Herbert Abrams, N.Y.C., John Howard Sanden, N.Y.C.; m. Howard Leroy Sargent, June 22, 1947; children—Christopher Lee, Kenneth Dean. One women shows: Frye Art Mus., Seattle, 1977, Woodside Gallery, Seattle, 1972, Excelsior, N.Y., 1975, Turkish-Am. Assn., Ankara, 1963, Art League No. Va., 1968; group shows include: Salmagundi, N.Y.C., 1974, 75, 76, Overseas Press Club, N.Y.C., 1975, Frye Art Mus., Seattle, 1972; represented in permanent collections: West Point Mus., Pentagon, Washington; commd. by Time, Inc. for covers of Gerald Ford, Margaret Thatcher, Karen Quinlan; staff lectr. Nat. Portrait seminar, N.Y.C. Recipient numerous awards. Home: 2750 Glendower Ave Los Angeles CA 90027

SARIS, ELEANOR MARIE, ednl. adminstr.; b. New Brunswick, N.J., Oct. 29, 1930; d. James J. and Ann Marie (Scandone) Tumulty; student Immaculate Heart Coll., 1971-72; Ed.M., U. Beverly Hills, 1978; children—A. Jamie, Jason, Elena, Elnora. Trainer for various workshops tchr. tng.; cons. San Carlos Apache Indian Reservation, Ariz., 1978, Wichita Falls, Tex. Sch. Dist., 1978; instr. tng. programs in parent effectiveness and youth effectiveness tng., Burbank, Calif., Glendale, Calif., Pasadena, Calif., 1970-74; guest lectr. Glendale Community Coll., 1974, Whittier Coll., Calif., Los Angeles Valley Coll., 1974-76; trainer Interpersonal Communication, Inc., Whittier, 1974-78, v.p., 1977-78; cons. for exec. dir. Inst. for Adolescent Studies, Pasadena, Calif., 1979—; cons. for adminstrn., curriculum of family communication programs, 1979—; curriculum dir. Project Info, Inc., Whittier, 1978. Mem. Nat. Assn. Female Execs., Book Publicists of So. Calif. Republican. Author: (curriculum) (with J.L. Woodard) Living Skills, 1978; (with Peter H. Buntman) How to Live with Your Teenager, 1979. Home: 315 S San Gabriel Blvd Pasadena CA 91107 Office: 311 S San Gabriel Blvd Pasadena CA 91107

SARNOFF, DOROTHY, speech cons., former actress and singer; b. N.Y.C.; d. Jacob and Belle (Roossin) S.; B.A., Cornell U.; m. Milton Harold Raymond, Mar. 15, 1957. Appeared in Broadway plays: Rosalinda, 1942; Magdalena, 1948, The King and I, 1951, My Darling Aida, 1953; debut in opera as Marguerite in Faust, Phila. Opera, 1942; leading roles with N.Y.C. and Phila. operas include La Bohème, Tosca, Tales of Hoffmann, Carmen; soprano soloist with various orchs.; soloist and guest on numerous TV programs, 1951—; founder, chmn. Dorothy Sarnoff Speech Dynamics and Communications Services Inc. subs. Ogilvy & Mather, N.Y.C., 1975; cons. speech and image, 1963—; cons. Dept. State, 1974—; lectr. in U.S. and abroad, 1975—. Mem. Authors Guild. Author: Speech Can Change Your Life, 1970; Make the Most of Your Best, 1981; contbr. numerous articles to mags. Office: 111 W 57th St New York NY 10019

SARNOFF, LILI-CHARLOTTE DREYFUS (LOLO SARNOFF), artist, business exec.; b. Frankfurt, Germany (Swiss citizen), Jan. 9, 1916; d. Willy and Martha (Koch von Hirsch) Dreyfus; grad. Reimann Art Sch. (Germany), 1934, U. Berlin, 1935; student U. Florence (Italy), 1936-37; m. Stanley Jay Sarnoff, Sept. 11, 1948; children—Daniela Martha, Robert B.L. Came to U.S., 1941, naturalized, 1944. Research asst. Harvard Sch. Public Health, 1948-54; research asso. cardiac physiology Nat. Heart Inst., Bethesda, Md., 1954-59; pres. Rodana Research Corp., Bethesda, 1958-61; v.p. Catrix Corp., Bethesda, 1958-61; inventor FloLite light sculptures under name Lolo Sarnoff, 1968; one-woman shows: Agra Gallery, Washington, 1969, Corning Glass Center Mus., Corning, N.Y., 1970, Gallery Two, Woodstock, Vt., 1970, Gallery Marc, Washington, 1971, Hood Coll., Frederick, Md., 1972, Internat. Art Mart, Basel, Switzerland, 1972, Franz Bader Gallery, Washington, 1976, Art Barn, Washington, 1976, Art Fair, Washington, 1976, Gallery K, Washington, 1978, 81, Washington Project for Arts, 1980; Alwin Gallery, London, 1981, Galerie von Bartha, Basel, Switzerland, 1982, Gallery K, Washington, 1982, La Galerie L'Hotel de Ville, Geneva, Switzerland, 1982; represented in collections: Fed. Nat. Mortgage Assn., Washington, Corning Glass Center Mus., Nat. Air and Space Museum, Washington, David Lloyd Kreeger Collection, Washington, Kennedy Center, Washington, Nat. Acad. Sci., Chase Manhattan Bank, N.Y.C., others. Past trustee Nat. Ballet, Mt. Vernon Coll., Washington; trustee Art Barn; bd. dirs. Fgn. Student Service Council, Washington Performing Arts Soc. Mem. women's com., trustee Corcoran Gallery of Art. Recipient Gold medal Accademia Italia delle Arti e del Lavoro, 1980. Club: City Tavern (Washington). Democrat. Co-inventor electrophrenic respirator; inventor flowmeter. Home: 7507 Hampden Ln Bethesda MD 20814 also Barnard VT 05031

SARRIS, SHIRLEY CORNELIA KOPATZ, publishing co. exec.; b. N.Y.C., July 25, 1938; d. Reuben Alexander and Sara (Kahan) Kopatz; B.A. in English, City Coll. N.Y., 1966; M.A., U. Chgo., 1967; m. George Sarris, June 27, 1959 (dec.). Library mktg. dir. John Wiley & Sons, N.Y.C., 1970-74; mktg. dir. Arno Press, 1974; mktg. services mgr. Franklin Watts, 1974-75; mktg. dir. R.R. Bowker Co., N.Y.C., 1975-78; pres. Sarris Bookmktg. Service, N.Y.C., 1978—. Woodrow Wilson fellow, 1966. Mem. ALA, N.Y. Library Assn., Am. Assn. Pubs., Spl. Libraries Assn., Womens Nat. Book Assn., Book League, N.Y. Library Club. Democrat. Jewish. Address: 218 E 19th St New York NY 10003

SARTON, MAY, author, poet; b. Wondelgem, Belgium, May 3, 1912; brought to U.S., 1916, naturalized, 1924; d. George Alfred Leon and Eleanor Mabel (Elwes) Sarton; student Shady Hill Sch., Cambridge, Mass., Inst. Belge de Culture Francaise, Brussels, Belgium, 1924-25; grad. Cambridge High and Latin Sch., 1929; Litt.D. (hon.), Russell Sage Coll., 1959, Clark U., 1975, U. N.H., 1976, Bates Coll., 1976, Colby Coll., 1976, Thomas Starr King Sch. Ministry, 1976. Lectr. poetry U. Chgo., Harvard U., U. Iowa, Colo. Coll., Wellesley Coll., Beloit Coll., U. Kans., Denison U., others; Briggs-Copeland instr. composition Harvard U., 1950-52. Awarded Golden Rose for poetry, 1945; Edward Bland Meml. prize Poetry Mag., 1945; Alexandrine medal Coll. St. Catherine, 1975. Bryn Mawr fellow in poetry, 1953-54. Guggenheim Found. fellow, 1954-55. Fellow Am. Acad. Arts and Scis.; mem. N.E. Poetry Soc., Poetry Soc. Am. (Reynolds lyric award 1953). Author: Encounter in April, 1937; The Single Hound, 1938; Inner Landscape (poems), 1939; The Bridge of Years, 1946, The Lion and The Rose (poems), 1948; Shadow of a Man, 1950; A Shower of Summer Days, 1952; The Land of Silence (poems), 1953; Faithful Are the Wounds, 1954; The Birth of a Grandfather, 1957; In Time Like Air, 1957; The Fur Person (fiction), 1957; I Knew a Phoenix, 1959; The Small Room, 1961; Cloud, Stone, Sun, Vine, 1961; Joanna and Ulysses, 1963; Mrs. Stevens Hears the Mermaids Singing, 1965; A Private Mythology (poems), 1966; Miss Pickthorn and Mr. Hare, 1966; As Does New Hampshire (poems), 1967; Plant Dreaming Deep (autobiography), 1968; The Poet and the Donkey, 1969; Kinds of Love, 1970; A Grain of Mustard Seed (poems), 1971; A Durable Fire (poems), 1972; Journal of a Solitude, 1973; As We Are Now, 1973; Collected Poems, 1974; Crucial Converstaions (novel), 1975; A World of Light (autobiography), 1976; The House by the Sea (a journal), 1977; A Reckoning (novel), 1978; Halfway to Silence (poems), 1980; Recovering (a journal), 1980; Writings on Writing (essays), 1981. *

SARTOR, CYNTHIA MARIE, social worker; b. Battle Creek, Mich., Nov. 23, 1948; d. Ambrogio and Domenica Theresa (Conto) S.; B.A. Mercy Coll., Detroit, 1971; M.S.S.W., U. Louisville, 1979. Patient advocate St. Lawrence Community Mental Health Center, Lansing, Mich., 1971-74; devel. disabilities specialist, social work outpatient therapist Mountain Comprehensive Care Center, Prestonburg, Ky., 1974-78; dir. econ. devel. Ctr. for Housing Alternatives and Socio-Econ. Options, David, Ky., 1977-79; instr. social work, sociology Pikeville (Ky.) Coll., 1979-80; asst. prof. social work Ind. State U., Terre Haute, 1981—. Bd. dirs., chmn. policy com. David Community Devel. Corp. (Ky.), 1975-77; mem. Christian Service Ministry, Prestonsburg, 1975-78. Mem. Vigo County Assn. Retarded Citizens, Nat. Assn. Social Workers, Ind. Assn. Social Work Educators, Council on Social Work Edn., Phi Kappa Phi. Home: 4232 S 15th St Terre Haute IN 47802 Office: Dept Sociology and Social Work Ind State U Terre Haute IN 47802

SASAKI, PATRICIA ANN, state ofcl.; b. Honolulu, Feb. 19, 1950; d. Chester H. and Barbara M. (Takata) Akamine; B.A., U. Hawaii, 1973; m. Randall M. Sasaki, Apr. 5, 1980. Asst., U. Hawaii InterArts Festival and Hawaii Dance Theatre, 1976-77, U. Hawaii Multicultural Curriculum Project, 1977; info. specialist State Manpower Commn., Honolulu, 1978-80; payroll clk. Lola of Hawaii, Honolulu, 1978-82; program specialist Office Gov., Exec. Office Aging, Honolulu, 1980-82; v.p., partner Peppovision, Honolulu, 1980—. Pres., 2M Community Council, 1978-80; vol. Moiliili Community Center, 1972—. Mem. Women in Communications, Inc. (sec. Hawaii profl. chpt. 1980).

SASEK, GLORIA BURNS, educator; b. Springfield, Mass., Jan. 20, 1926; d. Frederick Charles and Minnie Delia (White) Burns; B.A., Mary Washington Coll. of U. Va., 1947; Ed.M., Springfield (Mass.) Coll., 1955; postgrad. Sorbonne, summer 1953; A.M., Radcliffe Coll., 1954; postgrad. Universitá per Stranieri, Perugia, Italy, summer 1955; m. Lawrence Anton Sasek, Sept. 5, 1960. Tchr. high sch. English in Conn. and Mass., 1947-60; mem. faculty La. State U., Baton Rouge, 1961—, asst. prof. English, 1971—, chmn. freshman English, 1969-70. Recipient George H. Deer Distinguished Tchr. award La. State U., 1977. Mem. Modern Lang. Assn., AAUP, South Central Modern Lang. Assn., South Central Renaissance Soc., NEA. Roman Catholic. Home: 1458 Kenilworth Pkwy Baton Rouge LA 70808 Office: Dept English 219 Allen Hall La State U Baton Rouge LA 70803

SASSIN, CAROL PAMELA, bank exec.; b. N.Y.C., July 22, 1947; d. Jerry A. and Estelle Sassin; B.A. in Fine Arts, Rutgers U., 1970. Sports feature writer Newark Star Ledger, 1970-73; public relations dir. N.J. Soccer Coaches Assn., 1970-73, Schaefer Soccer League, 1970-73; client services rep. Reddy Communications, Inc., Greenwich, Conn., 1973-76; client services coordinator Central Survey Inc., Shenandoah, Iowa, 1976-79; dir. communications QUESTER div. GMI, Ltd., Des Moines, 1979-81; market research mgr. Iowa-Des Moines Nat. Bank, 1981—. Named Outstanding Young Woman of Am., 1978. Mem. Am. Mktg. Assn. Exhibited painting in statewide exhibition, N.J. Office: 7th and Walnut St Des Moines IA 50304

SASSO, ELEANOR C., state senator; b. Fall River, Mass., Dec. 9, 1934; grad. Immaculata Coll., 1957; m. Louis Sasso. Legis. researcher Bur. Nat. Affairs; mem. R.I. Senate, 1978—. Pres. LWV of R.I., LWV of Cranston; dist. chmn., group leader Camp Fire Girls; co-chmn. Cranston Heart Fund; mem. Cranston Area Vocat.-Tech. Facility Adv. Com., U. R.I. Women in Polit. and Govtl. Careers Program Adv. Com.; class instr. St. Mark's Ch. Confraternity of Christian Doctrine; mem. Mental Health Assn., Vols. in Action, Cranston Vols. in Cranston Schs., Vis. Nurses Assn., Cranston Hist. Soc., Audubon Soc. R.I., Save the Bay, Common Cause. Democrat. Office: Rhode Island State House Providence RI 02903 *

SASSO, RUTH MARYANN, educator; b. Bridgeport, Conn., Dec. 9, 1928; d. Angelo Nicholas and Mildred Rita (Hayes) Sasso; B.S. in Edn., St. Joseph Coll., 1957, M.A., 1968. Tchr., Catholic Schs. of Conn., 1950-68; founder, dir. Berkeley Primary Sch., Waterbury, Conn., 1969-71; prof. early childhood edn., coordinator child care program Mattatuck Community Coll., Waterbury, 1971—, dir. early childhood edn., coordinator child care program Mattatuck Community Coll., Waterbury, 1971—, dir. early childhood edn. lab. sch., 1976—; cons. in field. Bd. dirs Child Care Center Abused Children, Waterbury, 1971—, dir. early childhood edn. lab. sch., 1976—; cons. in field. Bd. dirs. Child Care Center Abused Children, Waterbury, 1972-73. Recipient Service award Head Start Policy Com., Danbury, Con., 1973. Mem. Nat. Assn. Edn. Young Children, Soc. Nutrition Edn., Action Children's TV, Nat. Council Campus Child Care Centers, Day Care and Child Devel. Council Am., Conn. Council Community Coll. Coordinators Early Childhood Edn. Democrat. Roman Catholic. Author: Field Placement Manual for Student Teachers, 1971; Field Manual for E.C.E. Observation Skills; Field Manual for Student Teaching in Early Childhood Education. Home: 75 New St Naugatuck CT 06770 Office: Mattatuck Community Coll Harvester Rd Waterbury CT 06708

SASSONE, ROSEMARY STANFORD, extension home economist; b. Mobile, Ala., Sept. 13, 1946; d. John N. and Geraldine Stanford; B.S., Belhaven Coll., 1968; M.A., Miss. State U., 1977; 1 son, Paul Ashley. Asst. extension home economist, Magnolia, Miss., 1968-71, extension home economist, from 1971; now area consumer mgmt. specialist Coop. Extension Service, Tupelo, Miss.; adv. com., dept. home econs. Miss. State U., 1979, state planning com. extension home economists, 1979; mem. Pike County Rural Health Adv. Council, 1977-80. Adv. com. Pike County Arts Council, 1979-80. Mem. Miss. State U. Alumni Assn. (pres. Pike County), Miss. Home Econs. Assn. (sec. S.W. dist. 1979-80, state hospitality chmn. 1978-79, public relations chmn. 1979-80, 1st v.p. 1981—), Am. Home Econs. Assn., Nat. Assn. Extension Home Economists, Miss. Assn. Extension Home Economists, Miss. Council on Family Relations, Epsilon Sigma Phi, Gamma Sigma Delta. Presbyterian. Home: 1321 Ida St Tupelo MS 38801 Office: 2604 W Main St Suite C Tupelo MS 38801

SASSOWER, DORIS LIPSON (MRS. GEORGE SASSOWER), lawyer; b. N.Y.C., Sept. 25, 1932; d. Abraham and Rose (Weitz) Lipson; B.A. summa cum laude, Bklyn. Coll., 1954; LL.B. cum laude (Florence Allen scholar), N.Y. U., 1955, J.D., 1968; m. George Sassower, Aug. 24, 1952; children—Elena Ruth, Carey Adina, Lizbeth Avery. Admitted to N.Y. bar, 1955; law asst. chief justice N.J. Supreme Ct., 1956-57; partner firm Sassower & Sassower, N.Y.C., 1955-72; individual practice, N.Y.C., 1972-80; pres. Doris L. Sassower, P.C., 1980—; author, lectr. in field; counsel Bus. Council UN Decade for Women, 1977—, Outlook . . . Personal Motivation, Inc., N.Y.C., 1977 Women's Sports Assn., 1978, Daily Plan-It, 1980. Trustee, Supreme Ct. Library 9th Jud. Dist., White Plains, N.Y., 1977—, chmn., 1982—. Recipient Disting. Alumna award of honor Bklyn. Coll., 1973; Disting. Woman award Northwood Inst., 1976; Spl. award for outstanding achievements in family law N.Y. State chpt. NOW, 1981; named Outstanding Young Woman of Am., State of N.Y., 1969. Fellow Am. Acad. Matrimonial Lawyers, N.Y. Bar Found.; mem. Internat., Am. (steering com. women's rights com., sect. individual rights and responsibilities, family law, litigation), Fed., N.Y. Women's (pres. 1968-69), N.Y. State (jud. selection com. 1972—, legis. com. family law sect. 1974—), Westchester County bar assns., Consular Law Soc., Bklyn. Coll. Alumni Assn. (pres. lawyers group 1963-65, spl. citation for disting. service 1965, dir. 1965-71), N.Y. U. Law Alumni Assn. (dir. 1974-75), Assn. Bar City N.Y. (chairperson subcom. women in legal profession, subcom. matrimonial law reform), Assn. Trial Lawyers Am., N.Y. State Trial Lawyers Assn. (matrimonial law com.), Nat. Conf. Lawyers and Social Workers (ABA chmn. 1973-74), Profl. Women's Caucus (co-founder, spl. cons. 1970), Profls. Organized for Women's Equal Rights (founder 1970), Nat. Conf. Profl. and Acad. Women (co-organizer 1970), Human Rights for Women, Women's Equity Action League (Women's Econ. Equity award 1978), Am. Judicature Soc., Nat. Assn. Women Lawyers (ofcl. observer to UN 1969-70, legis. com. 1976—), Nat. Council Women U.S. (chmn. com. law and status of women 1977—), Am. Arbitration Assn. (nat. panel arbitrators), Am. Friends of Hebrew U., N.Y. Civil Liberties Union, Assn. Feminist Cons.'s, Women United for UN, Women's Forum, Women's Econ. Roundtable, Exec. Women (adv. bd.), Nat. Women's Polit. Caucus, Women's Sports Assn. (award as champion of equal rights N.Y. assn. 1981), Phi Beta Kappa (pres. N.Y. alumnae 1970-71), Iota Tau Tau (dean N.Y. alumnae chpt. 1956-57). Columnist, mem. editorial adv. bd. Woman's Life Mag., 1981. Contbr. numerous articles to profl. jours. Home: 283 Soundview Ave White Plains NY 10606 Office: Pan Am Bldg 200 Park Ave New York NY 10017 also 283 Soundview Ave White Plains NY 10606

SATINOVER, TERRY KLIEMAN, lawyer; b. Chgo., Apr. 25, 1936; d. Charles D. and Mary (Klieman) S.; student Shimer Coll., 1952-54; B.A. cum laude, U. Chgo., 1955, J.D. magna cum laude (Weymouth Kirkland scholar), 1958; m. Richard Rees Fagen, June 15, 1958 (div. June 1970); children—Sharon, Ruth, Elizabeth, Michael. Admitted to Ill. bar, 1970; practice in Chgo., 1971—; partner firm Pope, Ballard, Shepard & Fowle, Ltd., Chgo., 1971-78; mem. inquiry panel Ill. Disciplinary and Registration Com. Bd. dirs. Charles Satinover Fund, Akiba-Schechter Day Sch., Chgo. chpt. Am. Friends of Hebrew U. Mem. Am., Ill., Chgo. (sec. exec. and real taxation subcoms. of real property com. 1972-73, mem. exec. subcom. 1973-74, co-chmn. newsletter) bar assns., Order of Coif, Phi Beta Kappa. Jewish (officer, trustee congregation). Home: 155 N. Harbor Dr Apt 4207 Chicago IL 60601 Office: 69 W Washington St Suite 3200 Chicago IL 60602

SATO, EUNICE NODA, city ofcl.; b. Livingston, Calif., June 8, 1921; d. Bunsaku and Sawa (Maeda) Noda; A.A., Modesto Jr. Coll., 1941; B.A., Colo. State Coll. Edn., 1944; M.A., Columbia U., 1948; m. Thomas Takashi Sato, Dec. 9, 1950; children—Charlotte Patricia, Daniel Ryuichi, Douglas Ryuji. Tchr. public schs., Alpha, Mich., 1944-47; ednl. missionary, Yokohama, Japan, 1948-50; community vol., Long Beach, Calif., 1958-75; mem. Long Beach City Council, 1975—, mayor, Long Beach, 1980-82; corp. sec. Health Systems Agy. Los Angeles County, 1978-79. Bd. dirs. ARC, 1974—, United Way Region III, 1975-80, Goodwill Industries, 1978—, Sr. Care Action Network, 1978-80, Women's Council of Long Beach C. of C., 1977—; trustee St. Mary's Hosp., 1977—; pres. Long Beach Council of Chs., 1973-75, Long Beach PTA Council, 1973-75. Recipient Outstanding Lay Woman of Yr. award Long Beach Area Council of Chs., 1976; Outstanding Woman of Yr. award Women's Council of State C. of C., Calif., 1979; Community Service award Long Beach Coordinating Council, 1969; Medal of Honor, DAR, 1981; Woman of Yr. award Los Altos YMCA, 1982, Long Beach Internat. Bus. and Profl. Women's Club, 1982. Mem. Calif. State PTA (hon. life), Nat. PTA (hon. life), Calif. Assn. Elected Women in Edn. and Research, AAUW. Republican. Methodist. Contbr. monthly articles for neighborhood papers. Home: 2895 Easy Ave Long Beach CA 90810 Office: 333 W Ocean Blvd Long Beach CA 90802

SATTERFIELD, MARY (YARBROUGH) MCADEN, ret. educator, civic worker; b. Semora, N.C., Mar. 15, 1911; d. John H. and Ella T. (Yarbrough) McAden; A.B., Meredith Coll., 1931; postgrad. N.C. State U., 1965, U. Va. Extension, 1965, U. N.C., summer, 1963; m. Lynn Banks Satterfield, Nov. 29, 1933; children—Lynn Banks, John De Berniere. Tchr. Caswell County (N.C.) elem. schs., 1931-34; tchr. sci. Caswell County high schs., 1934-36; postmaster U.S. Post Office, Milton, N.C., 1936-41; tchr. elem. grades Caswell County Pub. Schs., 1962-71. Clk., Town of Milton, 1959-61, sec. bd. of elections, 1976, registrar bd. of elections, 1979-81; mem. Caswell County Transp. Efficiency Council, 1981-83. Named Caswell County Mother of Yr., 1980. Mem. N.C., Caswell County (pres. 1962-64, sec. 1977—) hist. assns., N.C. Assn. Educators, Nat. Ret. Tchrs. Assn., Semora Homemakers Extension, Mus. Assos. of N.C., UDC. Democrat. Baptist. Clubs: Milton Woman's (pres. 1961-62, v.p. 1962-64, sec. 1965—), Milton Community (sec. 1937-44, pres. 1965-67), Order Eastern Star.

SATTERFIELD, ROCHELLE KRILL, clin. social worker; b. Cleve., Dec. 22, 1938; d. Harold J. and Hilda (Davis) Krill; B.A., U. Calif., San Diego, 1964; M.S.W., Calif. State U., San Diego, 1969; m. Ben Satterfield, June 22, 1958 (div.); 1 son, Jeffrey Mark. Psychiat. social worker Brown Schs., Oaks Treatment Center, Austin, Tex., 1969-79; pvt. practice clin. social work, Austin, 1974—; cons. Transitional Treatment Center, Austin, 1978-81. Mem. Austin Group Therapy Assn. (pres., exec. com.), Southwestern Group Psychotherapy Assn. (exec. com., sec.), Am. Group Psychotherapy Assn., Nat. Assn. Social Workers. Home: 5500 Windward Dr Austin TX 78723 Office: 2813 Rio Grande Austin TX 78705

SATTERTHWAITE, HELEN FOSTER, state legislator; b. Blawnox, Pa., July 8, 1928; d. Samuel J. and Lillian (Schreiber) Foster; B.S. in Chemistry, Duquesne U., 1949; m. Cameron B. Satterthwaite, Dec. 23, 1950 (div. July 1979); children—Mark Cameron, Tod Foster, Tracy Lynn, Keith Alan, Craig Evan. Biol. technician U.S. Dept. Agr., 1967-68; research asst. Iowa State U. Coll. Agr., 1971; lab. technician U. Ill. Coll. Agr., 1968-70; research chemist E.I. duPont de Nemours & Co., Wilmington, Del., 1951-53; research asst. Gulf Research and Devel., Harmarville, Pa., 1950; natural sci. lab. technician U. Ill. Coll. Vet. Medicine, 1971-74; rep. Gen. Assembly Ill., 1974—, chairperson sub-com. on spl. edn. 1978; mem. Commn. on Mental Health and Devel. Disabilities, 1975—, mem. exec. com., 1977—, vice chairperson, 1979—; mem. Commn. to Visit and Examine State Instns., 1977—. Bd. dirs. East Central Ill. Health Systems Agy., 1977-79; bd. dirs. Champaign County (Ill.) United Way, 1970-74, mem. budget com., 1973-74, mem. joint rev. com. on funding Champaign County Mental Health Programs, 1973; co-chairperson Task Force on Mental Retardation for Champaign County Mental Health Bd., 1973; mem. Ill. Developmental Disability Advocacy Authority, 1977—, vice chmn., 1979-80; chairperson Ill. House Democratic Study Group, 1979-81. Recipient Freshman Legislator of Yr. award Ill. Edn. Assn., 1975; commendation Ill. State's Attys. Assn., 1975; Best Legislator award Ind. Votors Ill., 1976, 78, 80, 82; cert. honor Assn. Students Govts., 1977; Disting. Service cert. Am. Vets. World War II, Korea and Viet Nam, 1977; Environ. Legis. of Yr. award Ill. Environ. Council, 1977, 79, 81; Meritorious Service award Champaign County Council on Alcoholism, 1978; Perfect Voting Record award Ill. Credit Union League, 1979, Ill. Wildlife Fedn., 1979; cert. spl. recognition Ill. Women's Polit. Caucus, 1979, 80, Public Service award Izaak Walton League, 1980; named Person of Yr., Champaign County Mental Health Assn., 1981, Public Citizen of Yr., Illini Dist. and Ill. chpt. Nat. Assn. Social Workers, 1981. Mem. Ill. Conf. Women Legislators (co-convenor 1981—), Nat. Order Women Legislators (dir. Region IV 1982), Delta Kappa Gamma. Quaker. Office: 2137 Stratton Office Bldg Springfield IL 62706 also 118 E University Ave Champaign IL 61820

SATTERWHITE, JOAN HATCH, precast concrete co. exec.; b. Birmingham, Ala., Nov. 27, 1933; d. Charles Edward and Virginia Hazel (Saddler) Hatch; student U. Ga., LaGrange (Ga.) Coll., LaGrange Bus. Coll.; 1 son, William Lewis, III. With Callaway Mills, LaGrange, 1958-63; with Harris Concrete Products Co., Inc., Pensacola, Fla., 1963—, pres., 1970—. Mem. W.Fa. Regional Planning Council, 1980-82, Consol. Youth Employment Program Escambia County, 1981. Mem. Asso. Gen. Contractors, Nat. Assn. Women in Constrn. (Woman of Constrn. of Yr. 1976, Boss of Yr. 1981), Fla. Septic Tank Assn. (treas., dir.), Brownsville C. of C. (past sec., treas. dir.; Profl. Bus. Woman of Yr. 1977), Democrat. Presbyterian. Club: Greater Pennsacola Pilot. Home: 580 Meander Farms Cantonment FL 32533 Office: Mobile Hwy Pensacola FL 32523

SAUCHIN, LORRAINE FRANCES, mgmt. cons.; b. Pitts., Nov. 22, 1954; d. Walter and Sophie Sauchin; B.S. in Math., Indiana U. Pa., 1976. Systems analyst Applied Systems Assos., Inc., Monroeville, Pa., 1976-78; cons. Arthur Young & Co., Pitts., 1978-81, mgr. data processing consulting, 1981—. Cert. data processor. Mem. Assn. Women in Computing (public relations v.p.), Data Processing Mgmt. Assn., World Affairs Council Pitts., Earthwatch. Contbr. articles to profl. jours. Office: 2400 Koppers Bldg Pittsburgh PA 15219

SAUER, MARY LOUISE, civic worker; b. Chillicothe, Ohio, June 26, 1923; d. Maurice Eichholtz and Sarah Katherine (Kieffer) Steinhilber; B.M.E., Northwestern U., 1945; postgrad. U. Mo., Kansas City, 1962, 71-78; m. Gordon Chenoweth Sauer, Dec. 28, 1944; children—Elisabeth-Ruth, Gordon Chenoweth, Margaret Louise, Amy Kieffer Sauer Doyle. Substitute tchr. Kansas City Public Schs., 1978-79; music dir. Shepherd Center, Kansas City, Mo., 1980—; pres., Philharm. League, 1959-60; membership chmn. Lyric Opera Women's Guild, 1960—; pres. women's com. Conservatory Music, U. Mo., Kansas City, 1962, trustee, 1980—; bd. mgrs. George H. Nettleton Home, 1975-80; bd. dirs. women's council U. Mo., Kansas City, 1978-81; co-chmn. Kansas City Chamber Choir, 1972-75; co-chmn. Assos. of Kansas City Mus. Club, 1980—; trustee Kansas City Conservatory of Music. Mem. DAR, AAUW, Am. Guild Organists, Univ. Assos., Jackson County Med. Aux., Calvary Bible Coll. Aux., Mu Phi Epsilon (patrons com. 1981-82), Kappa Delta. Republican. Presbyterian. Clubs: Rockhill Tennis, Woman's City. Home: 830 W 58th Terr Kansas City MO 64113

SAUER, SHARON KAY, accountant; b. Montrose, S.D., Apr. 2, 1938; d. George Leland and Oleta Marie (Baade) Johnson; B.A. in Bus. Adminstrn., U. S.D., 1973; M.B.A., U. Minn., 1981; m. Harold A. Sauer, Dec. 30, 1974; children—Elizabeth, Clifford, Richard. From semi-sr. auditor to mgr. adminstrn. IDS, Mpls., 1973-81, mgr. payments and office service, 1981—; owner Sauer Acctg. Service, Mpls., 1978—. Mem. Nat. Assn. Accts., Nat. Assn. Female Execs., Am. Mgmt. Assn. Home: 6495 Valley View Rd Hamel MN 55340 Office: 5702 W Broadway Minneapolis MN 55428 also IDS Center 9/524 Minneapolis MN 55402

SAUER, SUSAN MARIE, mfg. co. ofcl.; b. Geneva, Ill., Nov. 21, 1952; d. Walter Francis and Margaret Marie Sauer; B.S., Ill. State U., 1974; postgrad. in bus. adminstrn. No. Ill. U. With Container Corp. Am., Chgo., 1974—, casualty mgr., 1979-80, mgr. workers compensation and regional claims coordinator, internat. ins. coordinator, 1980—. Mem. Nat. Council Self-Insurers. Lutheran. Office: 33 W Monroe St 6th Fl Chicago IL 60603

SAUERBREY, ELLEN ELAINE RICHMOND, state legislator; b. Balt., Sept. 9, 1937; d. Edgar Arthur and Ethel Frederika (Landgraf) Richmond; A.B. summa cum laude in Biology and English, Western Md. Coll., 1959; m. Wilmer John Emil Sauerbrey, June 27, 1959. Biology instr., chmn. sci. dept. Baltimore County Sch. System, 1959-64; Baltimore County dist. mgr. U.S. Census, 1970; mem. Md. Ho. of Dels. from 5th Legis. Dist., 1978—. Del., Rep. nat. convs., 1968, 76; vice chmn. Rep. State Central Com. of Balt. County, 1966-71. Mem. Md. Fedn. Rep. Women, Am. Legis. Exchange Council (Md. chmn.), Women Legislators of Md., So. Legis. Conf. (consumer protection com.), Md. Conservative Union, Nat. Tax Limitation Com., Beta Beta Beta. Presbyterian. Office: House Office Bldg Annapolis MD 21401

SAUERBRUNN, KATHLEEN HANDLEY, lawyer, govt. ofcl.; b. Little Silver, N.J., Oct. 18, 1917; B.A., Douglass Coll., 1939; LL.B., So. Meth. U., 1962; m. Bertram J.L. Sauerbrunn; children—Randa Meredith, Sharon Doyle, Jennifer Harper. Admitted to Tex. bar, 1962, U.S. Supreme Ct. bar, 1965, D.C. bar, 1979; asst. dist. atty., 1962-63; asso. counsel firm Boyd, Veigel and Gay, McKinney, Tex., 1963-65; atty.-adv. higher edn. br., Office Gen. Counsel, HEW, Washington, 1965-67; atty.-adv., adminstrv. law br., Office Gen. Counsel, HUD, Washington, 1967-70, dir. adminstrn., mng. partner functions for gen. counsel, 1971-72, asst. gen. counsel for land sales, ins. and disaster assistance, 1972-77, asso. gen. counsel for regulatory programs, 1977—. Recipient Disting. Alumna award Douglass Coll., 1978; charter mem. Sr. Exec. Service, 1979. Mem. Am. Bar Assn., Tex. Bar Assn., D.C. Bar Assn., Exec. Women in Govt., Fed. Bar Assn. Clubs: Tantallon Golf and Country, Laconia Country, Women's Golf Assn. Home: 1315 Swan Harbour Rd Fort Washington MD 20744

SAUL, SHURA, gerontologist; b. N.Y.C., July 8, 1920; d. Froim Camenir and Rose (Lisenco) Rudin; B.A., Hunter Coll., 1940; M.S.W., Columbia U., 1963, Ed.D., 1972; m. Sidney R. Saul, Dec. 14, 1941; children—Mark, Jonathan, Jennifer. Tchr. kindergarten N.Y.C. Bd. Edn., 1943-48; dir. Bronx River Child Care Center, 1948-49; group worker Jewish Guild for Blind, N.Y.C., 1954-61; cons. social worker United Hosp. Fund, N.Y.C., 1964-67; mem. faculty Sch. Social Work, N.Y.U., N.Y.C., 1967-69; mem. faculty Brookdale gerontology program Adelphi U., Garden City, N.Y., 1975—, Wurzweiler Sch., N.Y.C., 1981—; dir. student unit Self Help Community Services, N.Y.C., 1969-71; coordinator profl. services Kingsbridge Heights Nursing Home, Bronx, 1971-78, ednl. coordinator, 1978—; cons. psychogeriatrics and edn. Borders Health Bd., others, Scotland, 1974—. Chmn. bd. dirs. Bronx-North Manhattan Coalition for Elderly and Long Term Care, 1981-82; observer, del. White House Conf. on Aging, 1981. Recipient Woman of Yr. award Jewish Welfare Bd., Bronx, 1954. Mem. Goldens Bridge Community Assn. (history com. 1978—), Nat. Assn. Social Workers, Nat. Council on Aging, Am. Group Psychotherapy Assn. Author: The Right To Be Different, 1962, Aging: An Album of People Growing Old, 1974, Sophia Moses Robison, Woman of the Twentieth Century, 1981; editor: Social Group Work for Frail Elderly, 1982; producer, editor: (videotape series) Enhancing the Quality of Life for Institutionalized Elderly, Scotland, 1980, other videotapes on aging, 1976, 82; contbr. articles to profl. publs. Home: Box 281 Goldens Bridge NY 10526

SAUNDERS, ALMA ANNETTE, educator; b. Brunswick, Ga., Sept. 24, 1930; d. William Van and Cora Mae (Young) Gunter; B.Bus.Edn., Ga. State U., 1971, M.Bus. Edn., 1978; m. William J. Saunders, Dec. 11, 1948 (dec. 1977); children—Amanda Lou Robertson, Michael William. Sec., United Electric Co., Jacksonville, Fla., 1957-58; bookkeeper Blue Marlin Co., Key West, Fla., 1959-60; billing clk. Hoffmann-La Roche, Inc., Decatur, Ga., 1965-66; statis. asst. Tb program Center for Disease Control, Atlanta, 1966-68; tchr. Blayton Bus. Coll., Atlanta, 1971-72; tchr. bus. edn. Fulton County Sch. System, Atlanta, 1972—; cons., lectr. in field. Mem. exec. bd. North Springs United Methodist Ch., Atlanta, 1979, adult Sunday sch. tchr., 1979. Recipient Educator of Yr. award 5th congl. dist. Ga. Vocat. Assn., 1977, 81; Outstanding Service award Ga. Dept. Edn., Bus. and Office Edn., 1979, 81. Mem. Internat. Soc. Bus. Edn., Nat. Bus. Ednl. Assn., Ga. Bus. Edn. Assn., Am. Vocat. Assn., Ga. Vocat. Assn., Am. Soc. for Tng. and Devel., North Fulton C. of C., Am. Council on Consumer Interests, Delta Pi Epsilon. Home: 6987 J Roswell Rd Atlanta GA 30328 Office: 1131 Alpharetta St Roswell GA 30075

SAUNDERS, BEATRICE NAIR (MRS. DERO AMES SAUNDERS), editor, assn. exec.; b. New Britain, Conn., Dec. 26, 1915; d. Frank and Sophie (Adler) Nair; B.A., Smith Coll., 1936; m. Dero Ames Saunders, May 23, 1936; children—David Nair, Richard Ames. Tchr. pub. schs., New Britain, 1936; editorial asst. Cordon Co., N.Y.C., 1937-39, Family Welfare Assn. Am., N.Y.C., 1939-42; supr. editorial div. publs. div. ARC, Washington, 1943-46; free-lance editor various publs. N.Y.C., 1946-50; editor-in-chief, publs. dept. Girl Scouts U.S.A., N.Y.C., 1950-55; dir. publs. dept., editor Social Work, Nat. Assn. Social Workers, N.Y.C., 1955-82, publs. cons., 1982—; mem. adj. faculty Grad. Sch. Social Services, Fordham U., Lincoln Center, N.Y.C., 1982—. Vol., ARC, Freeport, L.I., 1946-47, Child Care Center, Freeport, 1946-47; chmn. parents assn. Downtown Community Sch., 1948-50; chmn. 22d-21st St. Community Council, 1954-58, 62-63; chmn. com. on existing housing Chelsea Community Council, 1957-60; vice chmn. Chelsea Com. for Neighborhood Devel., 1960-63, chmn., 1963-65. Clubs: Smith Coll., Heights Casino. Home: 446 W 22d St New York NY 10011 Office: Nat Assn Social Workers 257 Park Ave S New York NY 10010

SAUNDERS, BETH PENN, advt. exec.; b. Asher, Okla., Dec. 9, 1932; d. Floyd Glenn and Florence E. (Seckinger) Embry' B.F.A., Art Center, 1952; m. Robert D. Saunders, Dec. 13, 1975; children from previous marriage—Kathryn Elizabeth, Wesley Alan, David Embry. Art dir. Gottschalks, Fresno, Calif., 1952, Scope Advt., 1965-67; advt. dir. BuildMart Corp., 1967-75; head AD-Vantage Advt., Chino, Calif., 1975—; pres. Embryline Inc. Pres., Republican Women of Long Beach (Calif.). Mem. Bus. and Profl. Women. Home: 8441 Wilson Ct Alta Loma CA 91701 Office: 13364 Central Ave Chino CA 91710

SAUNDERS, BETTY HUEY (MRS. AULUS WARD SAUNDERS), writer; b. St. Louis, July 11, 1909; d. Leslie and Kathryn Artimissia (Hyer) Huey; A.A., Stephens Coll., 1929; B.J., U. Mo., 1931; m. Aulus Ward Saunders, June 12, 1931; children—Alan Ward, Susan Beth Saunders Cook. Staff writer, corr., columnist, advt. salesman News-Champion, St. Louis County, Mo., 1937; playwright, one-act plays and radio plays, 1930—; free-lance writer pub. in newspapers and mags. including Reader's Digest, New Yorker, St. Louis Post-Dispatch, Wall St. Jour., People, Columbia Pictorial, Modern Maturity, numerous others. Public relations chmn., playwright, v.p. Oswego (N.Y.) Players, 1941-69; cons. public relations N.Y. community theatres, 1949-69; lit. critic Nat. Writers Club, 1964—; playwrighting cons. Oswego (N.Y.) Chancel Theatre Group, 1973-78. Former mem. exec. bd., chmn. public relations Oswego County chpt. ARC, also Community Chest. Recipient poetry and short story writing prizes Nat. Writers Club Contests, 1959, 64; prize N.Y. State Drummond One-Act Playwrighting Contest, 1956. Mem. Bus. and Profl. Women's Club (sect. cons. public relations). Congregationalist. Author: (play) Don't Argue With a Ghost, 1977. Editor The Grail, weekly religious mag., 1928-30. Editor-agt.-collaborator (with Dan Saunders) non-fiction books on Alaska. Model for Miss America on St. Louis Gold medal for Charles Lindbergh, 1927. Address: 165 E 3d St Oswego NY 13126

SAUNDERS, CLARA IRENE, publisher, writer; b. Entiat, Wash., Aug. 20, 1917; d. Leroy and Laura Marie (Murdock) Foote; ed. public schs., spl. courses; children—Dianne, Donna, Nancy, Eugene, David. Practical nurse, World War II; mgr. South Kitsap C. of C., 1964-69; pub. Who, 1974-75; freelance writer; poetry includes: This Is Me, 1975; Remembering You, 1980; Very Personal, 1982; children's books include: The David Stories, 1982; David and His Friends, The Once in Awhile, 1974. Coordinator Kitsap Mental Health Group; organizer crisis clinic and office Kitsap County Council on Aging, 1962-65. Named Citizen of

Day, Sta. KIXI, Seattle, 1981. Mem. Grey Panthers. Republican. Episcopalian. 2440 Snyder Ave Bremerton WA 98312

SAUNDERS, FRANCES MILLER, mfg. co. exec.; b. Brownville, Junction, Maine, Sept. 11, 1916; d. Hugh and Isabella Victoria (Young) Miller; student Farmington Tchrs. Coll., 1937, U. Maine, 1940; m. Wallace Saunders, Aug. 22, 1944; children—Robert, Patricia Saunders Cook. Tchr., Brownville Junction public schs., 1937-42, Houlton. Maine, 1942-47; treas. Hanover Dowel Corp., Bethel, Maine, 1966—. Mem. Democratic Town Com., 1956-70; bd. dirs. Rumford (Maine) Community Concert Assn., 1977—; pres. United Meth. Women, 1975-79; mem. Rumford Hosp. Aux.; chaplain Order Eastern Star, 1972-76; pres. PTA, Bethel, Maine, 1950-52. Mem. Wood Products Mfg. Assn. Home: 7 Elm St Bethel ME 04217 Office: 7 Cross St Bethel ME 04217

SAUNDERS, KATHERINE (KIT), univ. athletics adminstr.; b. Teaneck, N.J., Sept. 25, 1940; d. Alfred Roberts and Katherine Margaret (Krall) S.; B.A., Trenton State Coll., 1962; M.S., U. Wis., Madison, 1966, Ph.D., 1977. Phys. edn. tchr. and coach Teaneck High Sch., 1962-64; instr., lectr. and coach U. Wis., Madison, 1966-74, dir. athletics for women, 1974-82, assoc. dir. non-income sports, 1982—; commr. Midwest Assn. Intercollegiate Athletics for Women; mem. Wis. Gov.'s Commn. on Sport and Fitness, 1974, Wis. Gov.'s Commn. on Prevention and Wellness, 1978. Bd. dirs. Madison YMCA. Mem. AAHPER, Wis. Assn. Health, Phys. Edn. and Recreation, Nat. Assn. Collegiate Athletic Dirs., Assn. Intercollegiate Athletics for Women (nat. v.p. div. 1 colls.), Wis. Women's Intercollegiate Athletic Conf. (pres. 1979-80, dir.), NOW, Nat. Women's Polit. Caucus. Club: Altrusa (pres. 1982). Author: Development of Women's Athletics at University of Wisconsin, 1978. Home: 1701 Prairie Rd Madison WI 53711 Office: 1440 Monroe St Madison WI 53706

SAUNDERS, LENORE MCCALL, coll. adminstr.; b. Florence, S.C., Mar. 7, 1922; d. Lemuel Allsobrook, II and Irene (French) McCall; A.B., Queens Coll., Charlotte, S.C., 1943; m. M. H. Saunders, Oct. 13, 1944; children—Lenore, Manford H., Leslie McCall. Bookkeeper, teller Guaranty Bank, Florence, S.C., 1943-45; tchr., dir. girls schs., Belgian Congo, 1951-60; tchr., Tenn. and N.C., 1963; registrar, dir. instl. research, dir. internat. student affairs Montreat (N.C.)-Anderson Coll., 1970—. Pres. Women of Ch., Darlington (S.C.) U.S. Presbyn. Ch., 1949; chmn. fgn. missions Appalachian Synod, 1964. Mem. Am. Assn. Collegiate Registrars, So. Assn. Collegiate Registrars, Carolinas Assn. Collegiate Registrars (sec. 1979-82), Delta Kappa Gamma, Gamma Delta, Alpha Gamma Delta. Home: Box 188 Mississippi Rd Montreat NC 28757 Office: Montreat-Anderson Coll Montreat NC 28757

SAUNDERS, LYNNE KAY, mktg. exec.; b. Manitowoc, Wis., June 25, 1944; d. Robert Charles and Betty Jean (Woodland) Ginke; student Purdue U., 1962-64, U. Wis., 1964-65; m. Sterling H. Saunders, July 15, 1974 (div. Aug. 1981); children by previous marriage—Rayenna Marie Durfee, Benjamin Richard Durfee. Sales and fin. mgr. Sta. WAGO, Oshkosh, Wis., 1969-71; partner Newsmaking Internat., San Francisco, 1972-74; dist. mgr. Network Courier Service, San Francisco, 1974-79; dir. mktg. Sky Courier Network West Coast div., 1979-80; regional mgr. No. Calif. and Nev. Purolator Courier Corp., San Bruno, 1980—; mktg. cons. Saunders Assos., 1971—. Mem. Sales and Mktg. Execs. Assn., Nat. Def. Transp. Assn., Am. Mgmt. Assn., Embarcadero Forum, Todos Santos Bus. and Prof. Women, Nat. Assn. Female Execs. Republican. Club: Mt. Diablo Women's. Home: 363 Horizon Way Pacifica CA 94044 Office: 1198 Cherry Ave San Bruno CA 94066

SAUNDERS, MAUDERIE HANCOCK, psychologist, educator; b. Bartlesville, Okla., June 13, 1929; d. Allen Alonzo and Maude (Giddings) Hancock; B.A., Langston (Okla.) U., 1947; postgrad. George Peabody Coll., 1956; M.Ed., U. Okla., 1950, Ph.D., 1961; postgrad. U. Chgo., 1964-65; m. Leonard I. Saunders, July 4, 1959; children—Cheryle Saunders Crawford, Leonard Anthony. Vis. counselor Oklahoma City Public Schs., 1951-60; asso. prof. edn. So. U., Baton Rouge, 1960-62; prof. psychology Minot (N.D.) State Coll., 1963-66; prof., coordinator devel. studies W.Va. State Coll., 1966-70; psychologist Dept. Mental Health State of W.Va., 1966-70; prof. psychology Eastern Ill. U., 1970-73; asst. dir. Center for Study of Handicapped Children Howard U., 1973-74, prof. edn., coordinator spl. edn., 1974-76, chairperson psychoeducational studies, 1976-79, prof., dir. spl. edn., 1979—; research asso. Pres.'s Com. on Mental Retardation, Washington, 1981—. Pres. NuVista Club, Oklahoma City, 1956. Mem. Am. Psychol. Assn., Council Exceptional Children, Am. Council Edn., Delta Kappa Gamma, Alpha Kappa Alpha. Methodist. Club: Florigian. Contbr. articles in field to profl. jours. Office: Howard University 2400 6th St NW Washington DC 20059

SAUNDERS, RUTH LYNCH, psychiat. social worker; b. Longview, Wash., Nov. 4, 1927; d. Harry Hudson and Marion Lucille (Gibson) Lynch; B.S., UCLA, 1949; M.S.W., Columbia U., 1976; cert. Psychoanalytic Tng., Inst. for Contemporary Psychotherapy, 1979; m. Frank A. Saunders, May 24, 1958; 1 son, Anthony David. Projects editor The Sat. Rev. of Lit., N.Y.C., 1960-65; asst. med. editor McCall's, N.Y.C., 1965-67; editor Warner Bros., N.Y.C., 1967-69, Roche Med. Image, 1969-73; psychotherapist Inst. for Contemporary Psychotherapy, N.Y.C., 1976—; mem. staff Center for the Study of Anorexia, N.Y.C., N.Y., 1979—; pvt. practice, N.Y.C. Mem. Manhattan adv. bd. N.Y. Urban League, 1962-74, pres. Lucy Stone League, 1972-74. Cert. social worker. Fellow Am. Acad. Arts and Scis.; mem. Nat. Assn. Social Workers, N.Y. Soc. Clin. Social Workers, Phi Beta Kappa, Alpha Mu Gamma. Clubs: Union League (N.Y.C.); Sankaty Head Golf, Siasconset Casino (Nantucket, Mass.). Home: 680 West End Ave New York NY 10025 also Box 248 Slasconset MA 02564 Office: 940 Park Ave New York NY 10028

SAUNDERS, SALLY LOVE, poet; b. Bryn Mawr, Pa., Jan. 15, 1940; d. Lawrence and Dorothy (Love) S.; student Temple U., Phila., 1962-63; B.S., George Williams Coll., Downers Grove, Ill., 1965; postgrad. The New Sch. of Social Research, N.Y.C., 1968-69. Group worker Univ. House, Phila., 1961-63, Young Men's Jewish Youth Center, Chgo., 1965-66; author: Pauses, 1978; contbr. poems to publs. including the N.Y. Times, London Times Lit. Supplement, Mark Twain Jour., Golden mag., Seventeen mag. City of Phila Recreation Dept. grantee, 1969; U.S. Dept. State grantee, 1969. Mem. The Author's Guild, Inc., Pen Women, Pen and Brush, Poetry Forge, Acad. Am. Poets, Am. Poetry League, Nat. Fedn. State Poetry Socs., Nat. Writers Club, Poetry Soc. of N.H., Pa. Poetry Soc., Phila. Regional Writers Assn., Cath. Poetry Soc. Am., Fla. State Poetry Soc., Poets and Writers Guild of N.Y.C. Address: Academy House-36C 1420 Locust St Philadelphia PA 19102

SAUNDERS-CARR, JUDITH ANN, social worker; b. Charleston, W.Va., Apr. 26, 1942; d. James Allen and Grace Ann (Revels) Saunders; B.S. in Social Work, Eastern Mich. U., 1975, M.Guidance and Counseling, 1979; M.S.W., U. Mich., 1977, cert. specialist in gerontology, 1979; children—Marcia Arlene, Martin Anthony. With Ann Arbor (Mich.) Community Center, Inc., 1966—, dir. sr. citizen program, 1977—; field instr. U. Mich.; dir. Washtenaw County Area Agy. on Aging. Mem. Nat. Assn. Social Workers, Huron Valley Assn. Social Workers, Nat. Council on Aging. Home: 2918 Verle Ave Ann Arbor MI 48104 Office: 625 N Main St Ann Arbor MI 48104

SAVAGE, ADRIENNE ELIZABETH, mfg. co. exec.; b. Bedford, Ind., Nov. 3, 1928; d. Ben A. and Edith E. (Still) Hitchcock; B.S. in Acctg., Ind. U., 1951; m. Orville M. Savage, Apr. 26, 1952; children—Craig McKinley, Leigh Ann. With Cummins Engine Co., Inc., Columbus, Ind., 1951—, asst. corp. controller, 1974-76, v.p. corp. auditing, 1976-82, v.p. investor relations, 1982—. Treas., exec. com. United Way Columbus, 1980—; treas. Region XI, Retirement Found., Columbus, 1980; treas., bd. dirs. Presbyn. Found., Columbus; mem. dean's assos. Ind. U. Mem. Inst. Internal Auditors (bd. govs. Indpls. chpt.), Beta Gamma Sigma. Republican. Presbyterian. Office: Cummins Engine Co Inc Box 3005 Columbus IN 47201

SAVAGE, BERNICE, nurse; b. Luxora, Ark., Oct. 31, 1932; d. James Ottman and Elvelor (Venzant) S.; R.N., St. Louise Mcpl. Sch. Nursing, 1974; m. Albert Jones, Dec. 25, 1965 (div. 1978); children—Darla Celeste, Wallace, Deborah Elaine. Staff nurse, Max C. Starkloff Hosp., St. Louis, 1974-80, charge nurse family planning clinic, 1975-80; project dir. Madison County Urban League, Inc., Madison, Ill., 1980—. Mem. Mental Health Adv. Bd., Madison County, 1980—. Lic. cosmetologist, Ill. Mem. Pentecostal Ch. Club: Ladies Aux. Madison. Home: 313 Allen St Madision IL 62060 Office: 500 Madison Ave Madison IL 62060

SAVAGE, DEBORAH LOUISE, electronics co. exec.; b. Altoona, Pa., July 2, 1953; d. William G. and V. Cleona (Anderson) Mitchell; B.S. with honors, Shippensburg State Coll., Pa., 1975. Sales and prodn. control NL Industries, Inc., Hightstown, N.J., 1975-79; sales supr. Fry Metals, Inc., Altoona, 1979-81; prodn. and materials mgr. Youngwood Electronic Metals, Inc., Murrysville, Pa., 1981—. Mem. Nat. Assn. Female Execs., NOW.

SAVAGE, E. LYNN, sedimentologist; b. N.Y.C.; B.S., Bklyn. Coll.; M.S., N.Y. U.; Ph.D. in Sedimentology, Rutgers U., 1967. Mem. faculty Bklyn. Coll., City U. N.Y., 1954—, assoc. prof. geology, sedimentology and med. geology, 1973—; instr. Hunter Coll., 1954-55, adj. asso. prof., 1978—. Fellow Geol. Soc. Am.; mem. Soc. Econ. Palentontologists and Mineralogists, Soc. Sedimentology, N.Y. Acad. Sci., Bklyn. Coll. Geology Alumni Assn. (founder, pres. 1980—), Sigma Xi. Address: Dept Geology Bklyn Coll Brooklyn NY 11210

SAVAGE, JOAN LEONHARDT, oil shale devel. co. exec.; b. Milw., Aug. 18, 1924; d. Lawrence Edwin and Lucille Eva (Brandeis) Leonhardt; R.N., Columbia Sch. Nursing, 1945; m. John William Savage, Aug. 6, 1950; children—John, Roy Edward, Marshall Thomas, Daniel. Partner, Savage Oil Shale Devel. Co., Rifle, Colo., 1950—, Savage Ranches, 1957—; pres., 1978-80; pres. Shale Inc., 1981—; gen. partner JOJO Oil Shale Devel., 1953—, Buffalo Basin Ltd., 1963—; sec.-treas. Rifle Ski Corp., 1963—. Active Tb Assn., 1960-75; Colo. Mental Health Assn., 1972-75; mem. citizens adv. council Mesa Coll., 1974-75, also Rifle High Sch.; mem. Grand Valley Sch. Bd., 1959-62. Served with Cadet Nurse Corps, 1942-45. Mem. Arabian Horse Assn., Colo. Assn. Housing and Bldg. (dir.), Rifle C. of C., Colo. Woman's Forum. Clubs: Colo. W. Arabian Horse, 20. Home: 1122 293 Rd Rifle CO 81650 Office: 0873-293 Rd Rifle CO 81650

SAVAGE, MARGARET, microbiologist; b. Jamaica, W.I., Apr. 15, 1935; d. Felix and Anneta (Smith) Thomas; B.S., L.I. U., 1968, M.S., 1971; Ph.D., Otag Mesa Coll., 1975; Ph.D., Sussex Coll. Tech., 1975; Ed.D., Anca Dunbar U., 1980; M.T., St. Mary Hosp., Bklyn., 1960; m. June 15, 1960; children—George Savage, Geraldine and Jacqueline. Microbiologist, Mary Imaculate Hosp., Jamaica, N.Y., 1969—, med. technologist, 1969—; adminstr., dir. Franklin Med. Lab. Sch., N.Y.C., 1960—, regional overseer for World Bible Way fellowship, 1980-82; pastor World Bible Way Fellowship Ch., Westbury, N.Y., 1976-82. Mem. Am. Public Health Assn., Better Bus. Bur., Am. Soc. Clin. Pathologists. Club: PTL. Contbr. articles to profl. jours. Home: 740 Franklin St Westbury NY 11590

SAVAGE, PATRICIA WERNER, social worker; b. Reading, Pa., Nov. 17, 1949; d. Carl Clenroy and Margaret Eveline (Harris) Werner; B.A., Alvernia Coll., 1971; postgrad. Kutztown State Coll., 1971-74; M.S.W., Marywood Coll., 1976; m. John William Savage, Jr., Aug. 16, 1975. Social worker Telespond, Scranton, Pa., 1975-76, sr. companion program dir., 1976-78; geriatric specialist Northeast Tri-County Mental Health-Mental Retardation Center, Carbondale, Pa., 1978-80, coordinator geriatrics and aftercare services, 1980—. Sec., Lackawanna County Aging Task Force, 1978-79; chairperson recognition com. Ret. Sr. Vol. Program, 1979-80, chmn. evaluation com., 1981—, chairperson adv. council, 1979-80; rep. adv. council Telespond Sr. Companion Program, 1978, chmn. project appraisal com., 1979-80; vol. tutor Scranton Council Literacy Advance, 1979—, chmn. bd., 1981—; mem. Health Systems Agy. Adv. Council No. Lackawanna County, 1981—; mem. adv. council Allied Community Access Network, 1981—; mem. exec. com., sec. bd. dirs. Women's Resource Center, 1981—; mem. council St. John's Lutheran Ch., 1982—, chmn. social ministry com., 1982—; bd. dirs. Luth. Welfare Service N.E. Pa., 1981—; mem. adv. council Luth. Welfare Service Hospice St. John, 1981—. Mem. Nat. Assn. Social Workers (mem. women's task force Pa.; chpt. exec. com. 1981—), Acad. Cert. Social Workers, Alvernia Coll. Alumnae Assn., AAUW, Marywood Coll. Alumnae, Women's Resource Center. Home: Parkland Village Apt H-5 Blakely PA 18447 Office: 141 Salem Ave Carbondale PA 18407

SAVAGE, VERNITA LOUISE, civic worker; b. Malvern, Ark., Sept. 5, 1942; d. Vern and Waunita Elizabeth (Snider) Sherwin; student Waynesburg (Pa.) Coll., 1960-64; m. Sam Charles Savage, Sept. 3, 1966; children—Mark Matthew, Rachel Louise, Sam Charles. Clk., Mentor-on-the-Lake (Ohio) City Council, 1972-75, mem. at large, 1976-79, v.p., 1976-77; mem. City Records Commn. 1975—; Republican precinct committeemen City of Mentor-on-the-Lake, 1978—; legis. chmn. PTA, Mentor-on-the-Lake, 1978-81; mem. exec. bd., chmn. legis. com. Lake County Adoptive Parents Orgn. Mem. Lake County Hist. Soc. (library com.), Ohio Archaeol. Soc., Ohio Fed. Republican Women's Assn., Right to Life Soc. Club: DAV Aux. Republican Women's. Home: 7707 Fern Dr Mentor-on-the-Lake OH 44060

SAVARD, LORENA BERUBE, bus. exec.; b. Putnam, Conn., Aug. 30, 1942; d. J. Alfred and Florence H. (Dumas) Berube; bookkeeping cert. Dudley Hall Bus. Coll., 1968; A.S. in Acctg., Quinebaug Valley Community Coll., 1976, A.S. in Mgmt., 1978; student Thames Valley State Tech. Coll., 1979; m. Roger D. Savard, June 2, 1962; 1 son, Dean R. Calculator clk. Phoenix Mut. Life Ins. Co., Hartford, Conn., 1961-63; teller Citizen's Nat. Bank, Putnam, 1966-67; invoice records clk. Montgomery Ward and Co., Putnam, 1968-70; mgr. D.K.H. Credit Union, Inc., Putnam, 1974-80; office mgr. Waters Bros. Oil Co., Putnam, 1980-82; sales rep. Robert K. Mann Investments, div. SW Telephone Co., Naples, Fla., 1981-82. Bd. dirs. Quinebaug Valley Youth Services Bur., 1981—; mem. steering com. Career Planning Support System, 1980-81; vol. tchr. aide Putnam Elem. Sch., 1968; vol., bus. office Quinebaug Valley Community Coll., 1974; treas. N.E. Conn. Assn. for Children with Learning Disabilities, 1978-82. Roman Catholic. Mem. Volkswagen Club Central New Eng. (past treas.), Internat. Platform Assn., Nat. Assn. Female Execs., Aspinock Hist. Soc. Home: RFD 1 Putnam CT 06260 Putnam CT 06260

SAVARY, SUZANNE JOYCE, publishing co. exec.; b. N.Y.C., July 5, 1947; d. Richard and Edith Joyce; B.A., SUNY, Oswego, 1969; M.A., Hunter Coll., N.Y.C., 1972; Ph.D., N.Y.U., 1978; m. Kenneth Savary, Aug. 24, 1969; children—Scott, Jennifer, Mem. communications faculty Pace U., 1976-78; mgmt. cons. Beverly Hyman Assos., 1978; seminar leader Am. Mgmt. Assn., 1978; v.p. mktg. Cosmos Store, Montrose, Calif., 1980—; cons. in field. Sociables chmn. Newcomers Club La Canada (Calif.), 1979. Mem. Internat. Communications Soc., AAUP, Speech Communications Assn., AAUW, Eastern Communciations Assn., Am. Soc. Tng. and Devel., Western Communications Assn. Democrat. Roman Catholic. Asso. producer planetarium series Cosmos, The Ancestors. Office: 2409 Honolulu Ave Montrose CA 91020

SAVASTANO, PATRICIA JOAN, mgmt. cons.; b. Paterson, N.J., June 18, 1946; d. Patsy Joseph and Edith (DiPetrillo) S.; B.A. in Psychology (scholar), Rutgers U., 1968; M.A. in Indsl. Psychology, Clayton U., St. Louis, 1980. Sr. mgr. tng. Blue Cross N.J., Newark, 1968-74; corp. tng. dir. Nat. Convenience Stores, Inc., Houston, 1974-79; mgmt. cons., propr. Patt Savastano & Assos., Belmont, Calif., 1976-81; mgr. mgmt. devel. Lawrence Livermore (Calif.) Lab., 1979-80; mgr. tng. and program devel. Levi Strauss & Co., San Francisco, 1980—; partner Porter & Savastano Assos., 1982—; mem. faculty N. Harris County Coll., Houston, 1976-79, U. Houston, 1976-79, Trinity Coll., San Antonio, 1978-79; speaker in field; dir. Houston Transactional Analysis Tng. Center. Cert. transactional analyst. Mem. Am. Soc. Tng. and Devel. (v.p. N.J. chpt. 1974; award 1978), Internat. Transactional Analysis Assn., Nat. Assn. Female Execs., Orgn. Devel. Network, AAUW. Address: 130 Belvedere San Francisco CA 94117

SAVINO, PAULA MARY, psychiat. social worker; b. Fresno, Calif.; d. Elia and Grace Elizabeth Savino; A.A., Fresno City Coll., 1967; B.A., Calif. State U., Fresno, 1969; M.S.W., 1972. Psychiat. social worker Calif. Dept. Social Welfare, Fresno, 1972; counselor Central Valley Regional Center, Fresno, 1973-74; psychiat. social worker Porterville (Calif.) State Hosp., 1975—. Lic. clin. social worker. Mem. Nat. Assn. Social Workers, Acad. Cert. Social Workers. Roman Catholic. Office: PO Box 2000 Porterville CA 93258

SAVINO-BACHNER, NANCY PATRICIA, pet products co. ofcl.; b. Jersey City, Mar. 16, 1949; d. Vincent Joseph and Ann Rosaria (Salvatore) Massa; grad. Dale Carnegie Course, 1980; m. Ronald J. Bachner, Feb. 14, 1981; 1 dau. by previous marriage, Leslie Ann Savino. Eastern zone personnel coordinator Admiral group Rockwell Internat., East Rutherford, N.J., 1966-71, 76-79; asst. personnel dir. Deloitte, Haskins & Sells, Hackensack, N.J., 1979-80; mgmt. recruiter Blue Cross/Blue Shield N.J., 1980-81; personnel mgr. Hartz Mountain Corp., Bloomfield, N.J., 1981—. Recipient cert. of appreciation Dale Carnegie Courses. Mem. Am. Soc. Personnel Adminstrs., Nat. Assn. Female Execs. Democrat. Roman Catholic. Home: 1106 Danvers Ct Schaumburg IL 60193 Office: 192 Bloomfield Ave Bloomfield NJ 07071

SAVIT, CHRISTINA ERIKA, diversified corp. exec.; b. Syracuse, N.Y., Nov. 13, 1953; d. Irving James and Erika Margaret (Engelhardt) June; B.S., Cornell U., 1975; m. Jeffrey Bruce Savit, May 8, 1977. Research technician Cornell U., Ithaca, N.Y., 1975-77; product mgr. Informatics, Inc., Fairfield, N.J., 1977-78, mktg. mgr., 1978-79; teleprocessing group leader Exxon Corp., Florham Park, N.J., 1980—; v.p. Savvy Comp., Inc., Upper Montclair, N.J., 1981-82. Sponsor, Futures for Children, Albuquerque, 1974-82. Mem. Assn. Computing Machinery, AAAS, Nat. Wildlife Fedn. (life), NOW, Nat. Audubon Soc., Animal Protection Inst., Greenpeace. Office: Exxon Corp PO Box 153 Florham Park NJ 07932

SAVITCH, JESSICA, television news corr.; b. Kennett Square, Pa.; B.S., Ithaca Coll., 1968; m. Donald Rollie Payne, Mar. 1981. Researcher, Sta. WCBS-Newsradio, N.Y.C., 1969-70; with Sta. KHOU-TV, Houston, 1970-72; gen. assignment reporter, anchor Sta. KYW-TV, Phila., 1972-73, weekend anchor, 1973-74, co-anchor Eyewitness News, 1976-77; corr. NBC News, N.Y.C., 1977—, anchor NBC Nightly News, Saturday/Sunday edit., also anchor nightly updates, polit. corr. Recipient Clarion award for documentary, 1974; Broadcast Media Conf. award, Woman in Communications award, 1977. Office: care NBC News 30 Rockefeller Plaza New York NY 10020 *

SAVITSKY, DOLORES JOSEPHINE, banker; b. Bklyn., Nov. 14, 1932; d. Joseph and Anna Maria Demarchi; A.A. in Bus. Adminstrn., Suffolk County Community Coll., Selden, N.Y., 1981; m. John Thomas Savitsky, Jan. 16, 1954; children—JoAnn, Stephanie. Bookkeeping mgr., then office asst. mgr., Reuben H. Donnelley Corp., N.Y.C., 1950-57; fin. aide Sayville (N.Y.) Sch. Dist., 1964-69; sec. to librarian Sachem (N.Y.) Sch. Dist., 1969; bookkeeping mgr. Oystermen's Bank and Trust Co., Oakdale, N.Y., 1969-71, bank mgr., 1971—. Active local Girl Scouts Am.; pres. Sayville Schs. PTA, 1973; religious edn. tchr. St. Lawrence the Martyr Roman Catholic Ch., Sayville, 1964-69. Mem. Nat. Assn. Bank Women, Oakdale Mchts. Assn., Oakdale C. of C. (charter; dir. 1980-81, sec. 1981-82, 1st v.p. 1982-83), VFW Ladies Aux. (post treas. 1956-57), Pi Alpha Sigma, Alpha Beta Gamma Home: 32 High St Sayville NY 11782 Office: 951 Montauk Hwy Oakdale NY 11769

SAVITZ, HARRIET MAY, author; b. Newark, N.J., May 19, 1933; d. Samuel and Susan (Trulick) Blatstein; student Rutgers U.; m. Ephraim Savitz, Oct. 27, 1957; children—Beth Sharon, Steven Wayne. Staff, Wheelchair Sports Programs; lectr. on problems of the physically disabled to various local schs. and civic groups, 1968—; author novels: Fly, Wheels, Fly, 1970; On the Move, 1973; The Lionhearted, 1975; Wheelchair Champions, 1978; Run, Don't Walk, 1979; Wait Until Tomorrow, 1981; If You Can't Be The Sun, Be a Star, 1982. contbr. numerous articles on the disabled to various mags. and newspapers. Co-founder Children's Reading Round Table, 1968. Recipient Outstanding Pa. Author award Pa. Sch. Library Assn., 1981. Mem. Pen Women. Address: PO Box 181 Plymouth Meeting PA 19462

SAWYER, CORINNE HOLT, educator; b. Chisholm, Minn., Mar. 4, 1924; d. Grover Justine and Grace Margaret (Ueland) Holt; B.A. summa cum laude, U. Minn., 1945, M.A., 1947; Ph.D., Birmingham (Eng.) U., 1954; postgrad. U. Fla., 1950-52; m. Hugh Alton Sawyer, Jr., Aug. 25, 1965 (dec.). Continuity dir. sta. WCCO-CBS, Mpls., 1945-46; asso. instr. speech U. Minn., 1946-47; instr., then asst. prof. radio and TV, U. Miami (Fla.), 1947-50; instr. U. Md. Overseas, Eng., 1954-58; asst. prof., then asso. prof. English, coordinator closed circuit TV, E. Carolina U., Greenville, N.C., 1958-65; asso. prof. English, head honors program, dir. minority workshops Clemson (S.C.) U., 1965—; women's editor, TV show personality WNCT-TV, Greenville, 1960-64. Sec., Clemson Area Arts Council, 1972-75. Mem. Nat. Council Tchrs. English, AAUP, Malone Soc., S.E. Renaissance Soc., Phi Beta Kappa, Phi Kappa Phi, Alpha Lambda Delta (hon.). Author: John Darrell: Minister and Exorcist, 1962; co-author: Huckleberry Finn, adapted for children's theatre, 1947. Home: 105 Hunnicutt Ln Clemson SC 29631 Office: 209 Sikes Hall Clemson Coll Clemson SC 29631

SAWYER, GENE, journalist; b. Danvers, Mass., Sept. 9, 1910; d. Morse Leon and Harriet Elizabeth (Adams) Lewis; student Syracuse U., 1928-30; m. W.P. Sawyer, Sept. 9, 1930. Radio announcer, writer, producer, Honolulu, N.Y.C., China, 1937-49; officer U.S. Fgn. Service, Burma, Cambodia, Indonesia, Washington, 1950-65; corr. in Honolulu, Voice of Am., Washington, 1966-71; student interviewer manuscripts Hawaii Pacific Coll. and East West Center, Honolulu, 1972-79; editor original material on Burma and Cambodia, U. Hawaii, 1980-81. Vice-pres., Hawaii div. U.N. Assn., 1971-73, bd. dirs., 1975—. Recipient cert. of Merit, Sr. Achievement, 1980. Mem. Women in Communications, Honolulu Acad. Arts, Theta Sigma Phi. Author: Celebrations, Asia and the Pacific, 1978. Home: 1465 Aala St Apt 802 Honolulu HI 96817

SAWYER, HELEN ALTON, painter; b. Washington; d. Wells Moses and Kathleen Alton (Bailey) Sawyer; student at Master's School, Dobbs Ferry, 1914-18; studied art with Johansen and Hawthorne; m. Jerry Farnsworth, Aug. 26, 1925. Painter, artist in oil and water color, lithographer; exhibited at principal galleries and museums of U.S. Represented permanent collections numerous museums including Whitney Mus. Am. Art, Pa. Acad., Toledo Mus., Syracuse U. Mus., John Herron Mus., Indpls., Atlanta Mus., Amherst Coll. Mus., Williams Coll. Mus. Art, Chrysler Mus., others, IBM collection, Library of Congress, C. & O. R.R. collections; oil painting Clown Still Life owned Norfolk Mus. Recipient numerous awards, honors. Mem. N.A.D., Nat. Arts Club, Provincetown, Yonkers, Sarasota art assns., Audubon Artists, Nat. Assn. Women Artists. Contbr. articles and verse to jours. Has painted in U.S., Spain, France, Mexico. Home: 3482 Flamingo Sarasota FL 33581

SAWYER, KATHERINE H. (MRS. CHARLES BALDWIN SAWYER), librarian; b. Cleve., July 11, 1908; d. Willard and Martha (Beaumont) Hirsh; A.B., Smith Coll., 1930; M.S. in Library Sci., Western Res. U., 1956; m. Charles Baldwin Sawyer, Aug. 19, 1933; children—Samuel Prentiss, Charles Brush, William Beaumont. With Cleve. Pub. Library, profl. librarian hosps., instns. dept., 1956-61; med. librarian St. Luke's Hosp., Pittsfield, Mass., 1965-66; library cons. Ministry of Health, Guyana, S.Am., 1966-68; curator Sophia Smith Collection, Smith Coll., 1970-71; parish librarian St. Paul's Episcopal Ch., Cleveland Heights, Ohio, 1971-79, mem. vestry, 1974-77. Library chmn. exec. com. Garden Center of Greater Cleve., 1959-65; chmn. Friends of Western Res. Hist. Library, 1972-77. Bd. mgrs. Episcopal Ch. Home, 1954-64, pres., 1961-64, trustee, 1965—; bd. govs. Western Res. U., 1957-66, bd. visitors Sch. Library Sci., 1958-68, 69—; trustee Friends of Cleve. Pub. Library, 1962-67, Christian Residences Found., 1976-82. Mem. Western Res. Hist. Soc. (trustee 1979—), Archeol. Inst., Spl. Libraries Assn. Clubs: Union, Intown. Co-author (talking books for blind) Gardening for Blind Persons, 1962; Beauty, Glamour and Style, 1963. Home: 525 Paseo del Oro Green Valley AZ 85614

SAWYER, SANDRA MC COMMAS, judge; b. Tulsa, Sept. 1, 1937; d. Franklin Delmar and Irene (Adams) McCommas; student Tex. Tech. Coll., Draughon Bus. Sch., LL.B., Oklahoma City U., 1967; m. L.L. Sawyer, Mar. 6, 1981; children—Lise Dyann, Richard Owen, Whitney Michelle. Legal sec., 1956-64; admitted to Okla. bar, 1967; legal asst. to U.S. Ct. Appeals judge, 1964-67, law clk., 1967-68; bill drafter Okla. Legislature, 1969-70; chief traffic ct. project Okla. Supreme Ct., 1970-75; individual practice law, Oklahoma City, from 1967; partner firm Moran & Johnson, Oklahoma City; referee juvenile div. Okla. County Dist. Ct., 1977-78, spl. dist. judge, 1978—; lectr. Okla. Center Continuing Legal Edn., 1969-75, Okla. Bar Found. Legal Secs. Ednl. Series, 1974; mem. Okla. Legislature Interim. Com. Municipal Cts. Revision, 1973-74. Sunday Sch. tchr., supt. Resurrection Episcopal Ch., Oklahoma City. Recipient Outstanding Civic Contbn. award Modern Woodmen Am., 1977. Mem. Am. (nat. v.p. law student div. 1966; Gold Key award 1965, 66), Okla. (Outstanding Grad. Law Student award 1967, grievance com. 1977-78), Okla. County bar assns., Oklahoma City U. Law Sch. Alumni Assn. (sec. 1971), Iota Tau Tau, Zeta Tau Alpha. Author, editor in field; spl. cts. reporter Am. Judicature Soc., 1974-78. Home: 300 White Oak St Medford OR 97501

SAWYERS, ELIZABETH JOAN, library adminstr.; b. San Diego, Dec. 2, 1936; d. William Henry and Elizabeth Georgianna (Price) S.; A.A., Glendale Jr. Coll., 1957; B.A. in Bacteriology, UCLA, 1959, M.L.S., 1961. Intern, Nat. Library Medicine, 1961-62, asst. head acquisition sect., 1962-63, head, 1963-66, spl. asst. to chief tech. services div., 1966-69, spl. asst. to asso. dir. for library ops., 1969-73; asst. dir. Univ. Libraries for Tech. Services SUNY, Stony Brook, 1973-75; dir. Health Scis. Library Ohio State U., 1975—. Mem. Med. Library Assn., Am. Soc. Info. Sci., Spl. Libraries Assn., Ohio Library Assn., Acad. Library Assn. Ohio. Home: 135 W Kenworth Rd Columbus OH 43214 Office: 376 W 10th Ave Columbus OH 43210

SAXION, SANDRA LEE, communications exec.; b. Cleve., Sept. 6, 1947; d. Robert and Louise A. (Schotsch) Dangel; B.A. in Social Sci. and Edn., Heidelberg Coll., Tiffin, Ohio, 1969; m. Barry Dean Saxion, May 10, 1980. Sales rep. N.J., Gillette Co., 1973-76; mktg. mgr. Warner-Amex Cable Co., N.Y.C., 1977-79; dir. mktg. Teleprompter Manhattan Cable TV, N.Y.C., 1979-80; dir. mktg. UTV Cable Network, Fair Lawn, N.J., 1981—; speaker in field. Mem. Women in Cable, LWV, Bus. and Profl. Women. Republican. Methodist. Home: 137 Rockaway Valley Rd Boonton NJ 07005

SAXON, CORA BETTY JO, restaurant and candy stores exec.; b. Clay County, Ala., Mar. 17, 1908; d. Felix H. and Caroline (Rice) Watwood; student public schs., Lineville, Ala.; m. Henry Elbert Saxon, Feb. 26, 1932; 1 dau., Peggy Ann Saxon Wright. Founder, owner with husband Saxon's Candy Kitchen, 15 stores in Ala., Tenn., Ga. and Fla., pres., 1968—. Vol. worker Am. Assn. Ret. Persons, Miss. NE Ala. Pageant. Saxon Talent scholarship of Miss NE Ala. Pageant named in her honor. Mem. Nat. Candy Assn., Alpha Tau Omega, Alpha Xi Delta (hall of Fame 1972). Baptist. Home: Wellington AL

SAXON, JANET DUNHAM, adminstrv. law judge; b. N.Y.C., Apr. 15, 1927; d. O. Glenn and Catherine M. (Dunham) S.; A.B., Vassar Coll., 1948; M.A., Harvard U., 1949; LL.B., U. Mich., 1952. Admitted to D.C. bar, 1954; adminstrv. law judge U.S. Internat. Trade Commn., Washington, 1978—. Mem. Am. Bar Assn. Address: 1418 Kirby Rd McLean VA 22101

SAXON, SUE VIRGINIA, educator; b. Brooksville, Fla., Feb. 13, 1932; d. Eston Lewis and Mildred Blanche (Zoller) S.; B.S., Fla. State U., 1953, M.S., 1954, Ph.D., 1963. Research psychologist NIH, Bethesda, Md., 1958-60; research asso. Yerkes Lab. Primate Biology, Orange Park, Fla., 1960-61; with U. South Fla., Tampa, 1963—, now prof. gerontology and developmental psychology. Mem. Am. Psychol. Assn., Gerontol. Soc., Am. Personnel and Guidance Assn., So. Gerontol. Soc., Fla. Council Aging. Methodist. Author: (with M. J. Etten) Physical Change and Aging, 1978. Home: 1253 Griffin Rd Brooksville FL 33512 Office: U South Florida Dept Gerontology Tampa FL 33620

SAY, CANDACE JANE HADLEY, nurse; b. Plainfield, N.J., Apr. 4, 1948; d. Charles Russell and Amelia Elizabeth (Brandt) Hadley; B.S.N., W.Va. Wesleyan Coll., 1970; postgrad. Trinity Evang. Sch. Div., 1970-71; m. Ronald Say, June 20, 1971; children—Christin, Paul, Adam. Office nurse, 1971-72; instr. Germanna Community Coll., Lignum, Va., 1972-74; coordinator inservice edn. Fauquier Hosp., Warrenton, Va., 1974-75, Mary Washington Hosp., Fredericksburg, Va., 1977-80; staff nurse St. Francis Hosp., Evanston, 1980-81. Active adult edn. Manassas Bapt. Ch., 1971-75, Mt. Carmel Bapt. Ch., 1974-75, Oakland Bapt. Ch., 1976—. Mem. Phi Beta Kappa. Address: RD2 Box 241-A King George VA 22485

SAYRE, ANNE BODZANY, editor, writer; b. Perth Amboy, N.J., Oct. 18, 1930; d. Ferenc and Ilona (Bodzany) Cserr; B.A., Douglas Coll., 1952; postgrad. in Am. lit. N.Y.U., 1955; postgrad. in creative writing New Sch. of Social Research, 1956-57. Mng. editor Paperbound Books in Print, NYC, 1960-66; coll. textbook editor Allyn & Bacon, Boston, 1966-69; dir. publicity M.I.T. Press, Cambridge, 1969-77; freelance writer, editor, specialist in women'-oriented books, holistic writing, publicity, pub. relations, Boston, 1977—. Recipient Northeastern Poetry award, Millay Colony for Arts, 1977. Mem. Women's Inst. for Freedom of Press, Writers' Guild. Contbr. poetry to Univ. Rev., 1969, Voices, 1980, Sojourner, Womanspirit, 1981; contbr. news and arts articles for Equal Times, Boston. Address: 162 H St S Boston MA 02127

SCALETTA, MARION WITTE, travel co. exec.; b. Fargo, N.D., Apr. 20, 1948; d. Alvin Glenn and Wilma Marion (Serum) Witte; B.S. summa cum laude in Bus. Adminstrn. U. N.D., 1969; m. Paul John Scaletta, Apr. 4, 1981. Mgr., Touche Ross & Co., C.P.A.s, Mpls., 1969-76; v.p. Internat. Travel Arrangers, St. Paul, 1977—. Bd. dirs. Minn. Acctg. Aid soc., 1979—; treas. Breconwood Homeowners Assn., 1980—. C.P.A., Minn., N.D. Mem. Nat. Assn. Accts. (past pres. Mpls. Viking chpt.), Am. Soc. Women Accts. (past pres. Mpls./St. Paul chpt.), Am. Inst. C.P.A.s, Am. Women's Soc. C.P.A.s, Minn. Soc. C.P.A.s, Beta Alpha Psi, Alpha Lambda Delta. Home: 17910 Tioga Trail Wayzata MN 55391 Office: 666 Transfer Rd Saint Paul MN 55114

SCALIA, CONSTANCE ANNE, fin. services co. exec.; b. Lakewood, N.J., Sept. 7, 1932; d. Frank and Jean (Pulcrano) Vasapoli; R.M.A., Eastern Sch. for Physician's Aides, 1950; B.A., Monmouth Coll., 1952; postgrad. U. So. Calif., 1960-61; children—Joseph, Jeanne Scalia Jannicelli. With Travelers Ins., Los Angeles, 1960-64; life, accident, health supr.; controller Internat. Computer Scis., Oakhurst, N.J., 1965-70; bus. mgr., controller Chrysler Corp., Toms River, N.J., 1970-78; gen. mgr. Pierson-Vergilio & Assocs., Reno, Nev., 1979—; fin. cons.; lectr. in field. Republican county committeewoman, 1955-60. Recipient Project T award, Travelers Ins., Los Angeles, 1964, Employee Suggestion award, 1963. Mem. Am. Quarterhorse Assn., Nev. Horseman's Assn., Nat. Assn. Female Execs. Contbr. articles to profl. jours. Home: 1265 Farm Dist Rd Fernley NV 89408 Office: PO Box 7015 3388 Lakeside Dr Reno NV 89509

SCANLON, DOROTHY THERESE, educator; b. Bridgeport, Conn., Oct. 7, 1928; d. George F. and Mazie (Reardon) S.; A.B., U. Pa., 1948, M.A., 1949; M.A., Boston Coll., 1953; Ph.D., Boston U., 1956; postdoctoral scholar Harvard U., 1962-64, 72. Tchr. history and Latin Marycliff Acad., Winchester, Mass., 1950-52; tchr. history Girls Latin Sch., Boston, 1952-57; prof. Boston State Coll., 1957—. Recipient Disting. Service award Boston State Coll., 1979. Mem. Pan-Am. Soc., Latin Am. Studies Assn., Am. Hist. Assn., Orgn. Am. Historians, Am. Studies Assn., Am. Assn. History of Medicine AAUP, AAUW, Phi Alpha Theta, Delta Kappa Gamma. Author: Instructor's Manual to Accompany Lewis Hanke, Latin America: A Historical Reader, 1974. Home: 140 Thornton Rd Chestnut Hill MA 02167 Office: Boston State Coll Dept History 651 Huntington Ave Boston MA 02115

SCANLON, JOAN PATRICIA, psychologist; b. Washington, Aug. 16, 1952; d. James Patrick and Katherine Dillon Scanlon; B.S., Newcomb Coll., Tulane U., 1974; M.A., U. So. Miss., 1975, Ph.D., (fellow), 1978. Intern psychology Gulf Coast Mental Health Center, Gulfport, Miss., 1976-77, Western Mo. Mental Health Center, Kansas City, 1977-78; dir. mental health Whittier St. Health Center, Roxbury, Mass., 1979—; psychologist Gateway Counselling Services, Framingham, Mass., 1978—; staff Mass. Mental Health Center, Boston, 1979—; cons. Natick Schs., Mass. Rehab. Com. Lic. psychologist, Mass. Mem. Am. Psychol. Assn. Roman Catholic. Home: 390 Riverway #17 Boston MA 02115 Office: 20 Whittier St Health Center Roxbury MA 02120

SCANZONI, LETHA DAWSON, writer, lectr.; b. Pitts., Oct. 9, 1935; d. James Jackson and Hildegard Elizabeth-Emma (Koch) Dawson; student Eastman Sch. Music, Rochester, N.Y., 1952-54, Moody Bible Inst., Chgo., 1954-56; A.B. with high distinction, Ind. U., Bloomington, 1972; m. John H. Scanzoni, July 7, 1956; children—Stephen James, David John. Rural religious worker Village Missions Southwestern Oreg., 1958-61; freelance writer, lectr. religion, social issues, 1961—; weekly columnist Sunday Sch. Times, Phila., 1964-67; editorial asso. The Other Side, Phila., 1975-79, columnist, 1978; contbg. editor Radix, Berkeley, Calif., 1976—; guest speaker various colls., univs., theol. sems., regional and nat. confs. including Minn. Gov.'s Conf. on Battered Women, 1980, Nat. Council on Family Relations, 1981; cons. on sex roles, sexuality, family and feminism for Protestant denominations. Nat. officer Evang. Women's Caucus, program chmn. nat. conf., 1980. Mem. NOW, Phi Beta Kappa. Democrat. Presbyterian. Author: Youth Looks at Love, 1964; Why Am I Here? Where Am I Going?, 1966; Sex and the Single Eye, 1968 (reissued as Why Wait?, 1975); Sex Is a Parent Affair, 1973, rev. edit., 1982; (with Nancy Hardesty) All We're Meant To Be, 1974; (with John Scanzoni) Men, Women, and Change: A Sociology of Marriage and Family, 1976, 2d rev. edit., 1981; (with Virginia Ramey Mollenkott) Is the Homosexual My Neighbor?, 1978; contbr. articles to profl. and religious publs. Home and Office: 4512 Grendel Rd Greensboro NC 27410

SCARBOROUGH, MARY JOANNA, scholarship program adminstr.; b. Dalton, Ga., June 22, 1932; d. William Arthur and Jewell Thomas (Turman) Clark; B.Mus., Shorter Coll., 1953; M.Mus. in Applied Music, M.Mus. in Music Edn., U. Ky., Lexington, 1956; m. George Francis Scarborough, Aug. 14, 1955; children—Carol Elizabeth, George Clark, Charles Joseph. Music tchr. public schs., Ky., Ga., Miss., 1955-63; organist, choirmaster Episcopal Chs., Ky., Ga., N.Y. also organist Baptist Chs., Ky., Ga., La., Miss., 1950-78; state dir. Nat. Teen-Ager Pageant, N.Y., N.J., Md., Del., D.C., Mich., Pa., 1972—; pres., chmn. bd. dirs. Outstanding Young Americans, Inc., 1978—; judge Nat. Guild of Piano Tchrs. Bd. dirs. Pensacola Community Concerts; scholarship and social coms. Little Theatre-Miss. Mem. Am. Guild Organists, Nat. Music Tchrs. Assn., Matinee Music Club, Symphony Guild. Republican. Baptist. Club: Fortnightly. Editor, pub. Encyclopedia of Outstanding Young Americans, 1979. Address: 3415 Brookshire Dr Pensacola FL 32503

SCARBOROUGH, RUTHANN, educator; b. Marion, Ill., July 30, 1936; d. Floyd and Aretha (Stilley) Jent; B.A., So. Ill. U., Carbondale, 1956; M.R.E., Southwestern Bapt. Theol. Sem., Ft. Worth, 1958; m. Curtiss C. Scarborough, Nov. 23, 1955; children—Karol Ruth, Keith Curtiss. Tchr., Odessa (Tex.) Public Schs., 1958-59, St. Mark's Mini Sch., Florissant, Mo., 1966-72; early childhood edn. dir. North Side Baptist Ch., 1972-82; organizer North Side Day Care Center, 1972, dir. programs, 1972-82; dir. Preschool Edn. Center, 3d Bapt. Ch., St. Louis, 1982—; leader tchr. tng. workshops Mo. Bapt. Conv. and So. Bapt. Conv., presch. skill workshops, Taiwan, 1982, parenting groups Christian Civic Found.; tchr. Drug, Alcohol, Tobacco and Edn. Inc. Mem. Nat. Assn. Edn. of Young Children, Metro St. Louis Weekday Early Edn. Dirs. (pres.). Baptist. Contbr. to Ounce of Prevention, 1979; contbr. articles to Bapt. Sunday Sch. Bd. Home: 2476 Buttonwood Ct Florrisant MO 63031 Office: 3rd Baptist Ch Grand & Washington Sts Saint Louis MO 63103

SCARBROUGH, BARBARA JEAN, social welfare adminstr., educator; b. Kansas City, Mo., Jan. 18, 1932; d. Emmett Theodore and Gladys (Brown) Streeter; B.A., Philander Smith Coll., 1953; M.S.W., U. Nebr., 1974; m. George Scarbrough, Nov. 3, 1956. Caseworker, Douglas County Social Services, 1956-66, casework supr., 1966-74; supr. adoption and foster care unit Nebr. Dept. Public Welfare, Omaha, 1974—; instr. Sch. Social Work, U. Nebr., Omaha. Mem. adv. bd. Immanuel Mental Health and Alcoholism Center, 1979—; deacon United Presbyn. Ch. U.S.A. Recipient award Omaha chpt. Adoptive and Foster Parents Assn., 1976. Mem. Nat. Assn. Social Workers, U.P. Women Assn. Republican. Club: Altrusa. Home: 5738 Tucker St Omaha NE 68152 Office: Nebr Dept Public Welfare 1313 Farnam Omaha NE 68102

SCARFF, MAVIS SEWARD, ednl. adminstr.; b. Portland, Oreg., Mar. 8, 1924; d. Paul Domby and Dorothy Ann (Painter) Seward; B.A. in Elem. Edn., UCLA, 1951; M.A. in Secondary Adminstrn., Calif. State U., 1961; m. Howard Darell Scarff, May 28, 1949; children—Lynn, Larry. Clerical positions Lockheed Aircraft, Los Angeles, 1953-55, Sta. KFAC, Los Angeles, 1946-48, Gen. Telephone, Los Angeles, 1948-49; tchr. Longfellow Elem. Sch., Long Beach, Calif., 1951-53, John Muir Jr. High Sch., Burbank, Calif., 1955-67; asst. prin. Luther Burbank Jr. High Sch., Burbank, Calif., 1967-76; prin., 1976—. Mem. Assn. Supervision and Curriculum Devel., Assn. Calif. Sch. Adminstrs., Burbank Assn. Sch. Adminstrs., Nat. Math. Council, Calif. Math. Council, Nat. Assn. Secondary Sch. Prins. Home: 5155 Beeman Ave North Hollywood CA 91607

SCATES, ALICE YEOMANS, govt. ofcl.; b. Pitts., Jan. 21, 1915; d. William E. and Georgiana L. (Lloyd) Yeomans; B.S., State Tchrs. Coll., Glassboro, N.J., 1936; M.Ed., Duke U., 1949; Ed.D., George Washington U., 1963. Tchr. elem. sch., Haddon Heights, N.J., 1937-43; civilian personnel officer Sedalia Army Airfield, Mo., Greenville Army Air Field, S.C., 1944-46; tng. officer VA Center, Dayton, Ohio, 1947-48; research asso., dir. Am. Council on Edn. Staff for Office Naval Research Projects, 1949-53; asst. dir. Nat. Home Study Council, 1954; editor, research asst. Office of Edn., HEW, 1955, research analyst and coordinator coop. research program, 1956-64, program planning officer occupational research program, 1965-66, dir. basic research br. secondary edn., 1967-69, program planning and evaluation officer Nat. Center Ednl. Research and Devel., 1969-71, evaluation specialist Office Program Evaluation, 1971-80; evaluation officer Office of Mgmt., U.S. Dept. Edn., 1980—. Served to capt. U.S. Army, 1943-46. Fellow AAAS; mem. Am. Sociol. Assn., Am. Anthrop. Assn., Am. Acad. Polit. and Social Sci., Am. Ednl. Research Assn. Adult Edn. Assn., Kappa Delta Pi, Phi Delta Gamma. Author research reports, articles in field. Home: 560 N St SW Washington DC 20024 Office: Performance Mgmt Systems US Dept Edn Washington DC 20202

SCHAAL, JEANNE ELIZABETH, assn. ofcl.; b. Springfield, Ohio, Sept. 13, 1920; d. Raymond E. and Leona (Hall) McCoy; student public schs., Columbus, Ohio; m. Erwin L. Purnhagen, Sept. 13, 1940 (div. 1948); children—William L.; stepchildren—Gary M. Schaal, Patrick J. Fleming; m. 2d, H. Mansfield Schaal, Oct. 19, 1975. Service rep. Ohio Bell Telephone Co., Columbus, 1938-43; sec. to pres. and dir. Battelle Meml. Inst., Columbus, 1948-57; corp. sec., asst. treas. Clyde Williams & Co., Columbus, 1958-70; region adminstrv. mgr. Gt. Lakes region YMCA, Columbus, 1970—. Mem. fin. com. Maple Grove United Methodist Ch., mem. pastor-parish relations com. Mem. Assn. Profl. Dirs., Columbus Council World Affairs; cert. Profl. Dirs. Am. Bus. Women's Assn. (Named Woman of Yr. Rose Capital chpt. 1961). Republican. Methodist. Clubs: Toastmistress, Columbus Met. Home: 2972 Welsford Rd Columbus OH 43221 Office: 40 W Long St Columbus OH 43215

SCHAAR, JACQUELINE KAY COUCH (MRS. ROBERT L. SCHAAR), pub. relations exec.; b. San Diego, Apr. 2, 1933; d. Edwin Newton and Nina Mae (Sweetwood) Couch; grad. pub. schs., 1951; m. Robert L. Schaar, May 11, 1962; children—Robert, Denise. Exec. sec. various firms, 1951-57; asst. to community relations dir. Convair-Astronautics, San Diego, 1957-59; advt., pub. relations exec. Frederick C. Whitney & Assocs., San Diego, 1959-62, J. Jessop & Sons, San Diego, 1962-64; regional dir. pub. relations United Way, Arcadia, Calif., 1964-73; dir. pub. relations Orange County United Way, 1973-77; assoc. exec. dir. Bldg. Industry Assn. Calif., 1977-80; pres. Jacqueline Schaar Assocs., Inc., 1980—. Vice pres. Girl Scout council Orange County; adv. council Orange County Music Center. Mem. Pub. Relations Soc. Am. (accredited mem., nat. bd. dirs., past pres. Orange County chpt.), Orange County Press Club, Charter 100, Orange County Performing Arts Center, Public Relations Council U. Calif., Irvine. Home: 23282 Morobe Circle Laguna Niguel CA 92677 Office: 151 Dove St Suite 290 Newport Beach CA 92660

SCHAEFER, KATHLEEN ANN, lab. adminstr.; b. Racine, Wis., Aug. 12, 1948; d. Victor Louis and Mary Claire Weinfurter; B.S., U. Wis.-Whitewater, 1970; M.B.A., Lake Forest Sch. Mgmt., 1982. Staff technologist St. Luke's Meml. Hosp., Racine, Wis., 1970-72, Presbyn. Hosp. Center, Albuquerque, 1972-75; control analyst Hyland Diagnostics, div. Travenol Labs., Inc., Round Lake, Ill., 1976, sr. control analyst, 1976-78, supr. quality labs., 1978, supr. stability assurance, 1978-80, sect. mgr. quality assurance services, 1980-81, mgr. quality assurance labs., 1981—; adv. bd. Lake County Coll. Med. Technician Program. Mem. Am. Assn. for Clin. Chemistry, Am. Soc. Clin. Pathologists (asso. mem.), Nat. Assn. Female Execs. and Women in Healthcare. Office: Rt 120 Wilson Rd Round Lake IL 60073

SCHAEFER, MARGIE VIOLA, ins. agy. exec.; b. Racine, Wis., Oct. 8, 1938; d. William H. and Julia E. (Christiansen) Uggerby; B.A. (Alice Bemis Taylor scholar), Colo. Coll., 1960; postgrad. in bus. Drake U., 1973-74; C.L.U., Am. Coll., Bryn Mawr, Pa., 1982; m. Terry Bard Moore, 1977; children by previous marriage—Barton Evan, Todd Michael, Matthew Peter. Tchr., Ames (Iowa) Public Schs., 1960-62; owner, partner Les Cuisineres Catering Service, Des Moines, 1972-75; spl. agt. Lincoln Nat. Life Ins. Co., Des Moines, 1975-79, mem. Lincoln Nat. Sales Corp. Emancipator Club, 1976-79; brokerage sales mgr. Lincoln McGoldrick & Assos., Des Moines, 1979-80; v.p. Iowa Bankers Ins. & Service, Inc., Des Moines, 1980—; v.p., annuity specialist Interstate Banking Ins. Services, Inc.; tax deferred annuity specialist, lectr. Iowa Bankers Assn., Bd. dirs. Des Moines Zoo, 1980—; mem. coms. LWV, Des Moines, 1972—; mem. Des Moines Zoo Docents.; pres. Des Moines Jr. Women's Club, 1970, Byron Rice Elem. Sch. PTA, 1974; state internat. affairs chmn. Iowa Fedn. Women's Clubs, 1970-72; vice chmn. Iowa Jr. Fedn. Women's Clubs, 1972-74; chmn. Project Concern, Iowa, 1970-72; chmn. Iowa CARE, 1970-72; mem. Women Leaders Round Table, 1976-78. Named Des Moines Jr. Woman of Yr., 1970; recipient John Karnes award Lincoln Nat. Life Ins. Co., 1975, 76; registered SEC; lic. ins. agt. Iowa. Mem. Nat. Assn. Security Dealers (registered rep.), Des Moines Assn. Life Underwriters, Nat. Assn. Life Underwriters, Women Life Underwriters Conf., Life Underwriters Polit. Action Com., Nat. Assn. Female Execs., Nat. Assn. Bank Women, Am. Bus. Women's Assn., Bankpak Iowa Bankers Polit. Action Com., Des Moines Women Estate Planners Council (charter), Phi Beta Kappa, Delta Gamma. Lutheran. Club: Lawrenceville Parents. Home: 2805

SCHAEFER, PATRICIA, librarian; b. Ft. Wayne, Ind., Apr. 23, 1930; d. Edward John and Hildegarde Hartman (Hormel) S.; B.Mus., Northwestern U., 1951; M.Mus., U. Ill., 1958; Asso.M. L.S., U. Mich., 1963. Typist U.S. Rubber Co., Ft. Wayne, Ind., 1951-52; sec. to promotion mgr. sta. WOWO, Ft. Wayne, 1952, sec. to program mgr., 1953-55; coordinator publicity and promotion Home Telephone Co., Ft. Wayne, 1955-56; sec. Fine Arts Found., Ft. Wayne, 1956-57; library asst. Columbus (Ohio) Public Library, 1958-59; audio-visual librarian Muncie (Ind.) Public Library, 1959—, asst. library dir., 1981—; chmn. Ind. Library Film Circuit, 1962-63; sec. Ind. Library Film Service, 1969-70, exec. bd., 1981—; exec. bd. Ind. Film Council, 1981—; mem. Ind. State Library Audio-Visual Task Force, 1979-80; cons., adv. two-yr. technicians program library sci. dept. Ball State U. Bd. dirs. Muncie Symphony Assn., 1964-74; adv. com., bookshop dir. Midwest Writers' Workshop, 1976-77; pres. Del. County Council for Arts, 1979-81; bd. dirs. Muncie YWCA, 1977—, treas., 1980—; gen. chmn. Ind. Renaissance Fair, 1978, 79; vice chmn. Sta. WBST Community Adv. Com.; mem. Del. County History Task Force. Mem. ALA, Ind. Library Assn. (dist. chmn. 1972-73, chmn. Ind. Library Assn.-Ind. Library Trustee Assn. library planning com. 1969-73, treas. 1973-75, chmn. awards and hons. com. 1977-80), Dist. Library Assn. (sec.-treas. 1971-72), Nat. League Am. Pen Women (pres. Muncie Br. 1974-78), Delta Zeta. Republican. Roman Catholic. Clubs: Am. Recorder Soc., Northeastern Ind. Recorder Soc., Muncie Matinee Musicale (pres. 1965-67), Ind. Fedn. Music Clubs (dist. sec.-treas. 1967-68), Riley-Jones (charter mem.), Altrusa (rec. sec., Muncie). Program annotator E.Central Ind. Community Singers, 1980—, Muncie Symphony Orch., 1963—. Home: 405 S Tara Ln Muncie IN 47304 Office: 200 E Main St Muncie IN 47305

SCHAEFER, PATRICIA ANN, librarian; b. Lebanon, Ohio, Jan. 22, 1933; d. Riley Ray and Louise Collette (Fraher) Freeze; B.S., Miami U., Oxford, Ohio, 1954; m. William H. Schaefer, Aug. 11, 1956; children—Susan P., Nancy A., William H. III (dec.). Med. technologist Mercy Hosp., Hamilton, Ohio, 1954-58, Middletown (Ohio) Hosp., 1958-62; librarian Middletown City Schs., 1979—, intermediate librarian McKinley Sch., 1982—. Active, YMCA, pres., 1977-79; bd. dirs. Middletown Symphony, 1974-78; hon. bd. dirs. Am. Cancer Soc., 1961—; chmn. legis. City Charter Rev. Com., 1970; residential chmn. United Way, 1976; chmn. Sch. Tax Levy, 1978. Recipient Stuart Ives Service to Youth award, 1980. Mem. Am. Soc. Clin. Pathologists, Registry Med. Technologists, Am. Bus. Women's Assn. (pres. 1961-62), LWV (pres. 1962-63), PEO, Sigma Sigma Sigma. Methodist. Club: Browns Run Country. Home: 1909 Antrim Ct Middletown OH 45042

SCHAEFFER, LORRAINE DEY, librarian; b. Phila., Dec. 14, 1946; d. Joseph William and Hilda Lorraine (Ritchey) Dey; B.A., Fla. State U., 1968, M.S., 1969. Extension dir. Santa Fe Regional Library, Gainesville, 1969-71; pub. library cons. State Library of Fla., Tallahassee, 1971-78, asst. state librarian, 1978—; cons. in field. Del. Pres.'s Com. on Mental Retardation Regional Forum, Atlanta. 1975; del. Fla. Gov.'s Conf. on Library and Info. Services, 1978. Mem. ALA (orgn. com. 1979—, council 1982—), Assn. Specialized and Coop. Library Agys. (dir. 1976-82, chmn. planning and orgn. com. 1976-80, chmn. nominating com., 1980-81), Southeastern Library Assn. (exec. bd. 1976-80), Fla. Library Assn. (sec. 1978-79, dir., 1976-80), Am. Soc. Pub. Adminstrn. Democrat. Methodist. Contbr. articles in field. Office: State Library of Florida R A Gray Bldg Tallahassee FL 32301

SCHAEFFER, RUTH MARY, psychotherapist; b. Sunbury, Pa., May 1, 1951; d. Jason E. and Alice K. (Fargo) S.; B.A., Ill. Wesleyan U., 1973; M.S., So. Ill. U., 1977; postgrad. City Coll., City U. N.Y., 1978—. Therapist, Chester (Ill.) Mental Health Center, 1975-76; project dir. Anna (Ill.) Mental Health Center, 1974-75; staff tng. dir. Dept. Treatment Devel., Anna, 1975-76; counselor Center Human Devel., Carbondale, Ill., 1976-77; psychotherapist Biofeedback and Behavior Therapy Centers Conn., Greenwich, 1977-78; pvt. practice psychotherapy, Stamford, Conn., 1978—; domestic violence service coordinator Stamford Community Anti-Crime, 1979—; Agent Orange victim coordinator VA, 1980—; outreach counselor VA Vet. Center, Queens, N.Y., 1981—; instr. CUNY, 1978-80. Bd. dirs. Stamford Rape Crisis Service, 1978—, sec., 1978, treas., 1979. Mem. AAAS, Am. Psychol. Assn., Am. Personnel and Guidance Assn., Eastern Psychol. Assn., Biofeedback Soc. New Eng., Biofeedback Soc. Am., Stamford Bus. and Profl. Women's Club (Career Devel. award 1979). Democrat. Unitarian. Home: Apt #041 3451 Giles Place Bronx NY 10463 Office: 148-43 Hillside Ave Jamaica NY 11435

SCHAEFFER, SUSAN FROMBERG, educator, writer; b. Bklyn., Mar. 25, 1941; d. Irving and Edith (Levine) Fromberg; B.A., U. Chgo., 1961, M.A. with honors, 1963, Ph.D. with honors, 1966; m. Neil J. Schaeffer, Oct. 11, 1970; children—Benjamin Adam, May Anna. Instr. English, Wright Jr. Coll., Chgo., 1964-65; asst. prof. Ill. Inst. Tech., Chgo., 1965-67; successively asst. prof., asso. prof., prof. Bklyn. Coll., 1967—; guest lectr. U. Chgo., Cornell U., U. Ariz., U. Maine. Recipient E.L. Wallant award, Friends of Lit. award. Mem. PEN, Authors Guild, Poetry Soc. Am. Democrat. Jewish. Author novels: Falling, 1973; Anya (nominee Nat. Book award), 1974; Time In Its Flight, 1978; Love, 1981; The Madness of a Seduced Woman, in press; poetry: The Witch and the Weather Report, 1972; Alphabet For the Lost Years, 1976; Granite Lady, 1974; Rhymes and Runes of the Toad, 1975; The Bible of the Beasts of the Little Field, 1980; short stories: The Queen of Egypt and Other Stories, 1980. Address: 783 E 21st St Brooklyn NY 11210

SCHAFER, BETTY ELAINE KEEL, social worker; b. Lucedale, Miss., Dec. 16, 1952; d. Riley E. and Ethel Mae (Holliman) Keel; A.A., Southeastern Bapt. Jr. Coll., 1971; B.S., William Carey Coll., 1972; M.S. in Counseling, U. So. Miss., 1974, M.S.W., 1977; m. Rodney Lee Schafer, Jan. 4, 1974; Psychology technician Ellisville (Miss.) State Sch., 1973; tchr. aide W. H. Jones Elem. Sch., Hattiesburg, 1974-74; ins. investigator Equifax, Hattiesburg, 1974; social worker Pine Belt Work Activity Center, Hattiesburg, 1974-77, program dir., 1978—. Mem. Human Rights Adv. Bd. for Group Home Living, Ellisville State Sch. Mem. Nat. Assn. Social Workers, Am. Pub. Welfare Assn., Miss. Council Mental Health and Retardation, Miss. Council Social Welfare, Forrest County Assn. Retarded Citizens. Baptist. Home: 305 Weathersby Rd Hattiesburg MS 39401 Office: PO Box 1030 Hattiesburg MS 39401

SCHAFER, MARVEL VIRGINIA, ambassador; b. Iowa City, Mar. 26, 1931; d. Mark Minter and Margaret Lucille (Nicholson) S.; B.A., Wash. State U., Pullman, 1952; postgrad. Indsl. Coll. Armed Forces, 1978. With Gen. Electric Co., 1953-54; commd. fgn. service officer Dept. State, 1954; overseas assignments, Manila, Moscow, Vienna, Bucharest, Conakry, Sydney, Beijing, 1954-74; program officer Bur. Ednl. and Cultural Affairs, Dept. State, Washington, 1975, dep. exec. dir. Bur. Near Eastern Affairs, 1976-77, dep. asst. sec. state Bur. Adminstrn., 1979-81; ambassador to Papua New Guinea, 1981—. Office: Port Moresby Dept State Washington DC 20520

SCHAFER, SUSAN VAUGHN, ednl. adminstr.; b. Richmond, Va., June 12, 1946; d. Eddie Raymond and Hazel Isabelle (Axselle) Vaughn; B.Mus. Edn., Tex. Tech. U., 1968; M.A. in Ednl. Adminstrn., U. Tex., El Paso, 1982. Music tchr., Ralls, Tex., 1968-69; elem. tchr., Grants, N.Mex., 1969-70; social studies tchr., Hatch, N.Mex., 1970-72; pastor's sec., El Paso, Tex. and Tampa, Fla., 1972-74; sec. Tarrant Bapt. Assn., Ft. Worth, 1974-75; substitute tchr. Ft. Worth Schs., 1975-76; social studies tchr., Pine Hill, N.Mex., 1976-79; cons. U. N.Mex., Albuquerque, 1980; tchr., El Paso, 1980-81; prin. Immanuel Bapt. Christian Sch., El Paso, 1981—; bd. mem. Tchr. Center, rural N.Mex., also travel rep. Mem. NEA, Tex. Classroom Tchrs. Assn., Assn. Individually Guided Edn. (facilitator), Assn. Supervision and Curriculum Devel., Nat. Assn. Female Execs. Baptist. Office: 1201 Hawkins El Paso TX 79925

SCHAFFER, GLORIA WILINSKI, govt. ofcl.; b. New London, Conn., Oct. 3, 1930; d. Arthur and Charlotte (Reiner) Wilinski; m. Eugene Schaffer, 1949; children—Susan, Stephen. Mem. Conn. State Senate, 1959-71; sec. of state, Conn., 1971-73; del. Democratic Nat. Conv., 1972; mem. Civil Aeronautics Bd., Washington. Recipient Nat. Merit award Council Crime and Delinquency; Nat. Cystic Fibrosis Soc. award; Conn. Assn. Hearing Impaired Children and Conn. Assn. Vocat. Inst. award; Jewish War Veterans citation; Nat. Human Relations award; NCCJ Disting. Service award. Mem. New Haven Community Council (dir.), Urban League, Conn. Hosp. Planning Çommn., Order Women Legislators, White Ho. Conf. Edn. (rep. conf., mem. nat. edn. com.). Office: Civil Aeronautics Bd 1825 Connecticut Ave NW Washington DC 20428 *

SCHAFFER, KATHLEEN THOMSON, cons. urban edn.; b. Los Angeles, Mar. 18, 1922; d. H. Britton and Edith Thomson; B.A., Rutgers U., 1969; M.Edn. Adminstrn., Villanova U., 1971; Ph.D., N.Tex. State U., 1978; m. Robert K. Schaffer, Sept. 30, 1944; children—Kathleen Patricia, Ann Schaffer Lackey, Deborah K. Tchr. high sch. English, Kinnelon, N.J., 1967-69, reading specialist, 1969-71; spl. edn. tchr., reading cons. Dallas Public Schs., 1971-78, ednl. cons., 1980—; pres. DABKO Assos., pub. co. Mem. adv. bd. community relations Dallas Public Sch. N.W. Subdist., 1978-80; mem. adv. bd. Creative Arts for Children, 1979—. U. Pitts. grantee, 1967-68. Mem. Internat. Reading Assn., Assn. Tex. Educators, N. Tex. State U. Adminstrv. and Supervisory Council, Assn. Jr. Leagues Am. Republican. Presbyterian. Author: Children's Books, 1980. Home: 5940 Meadow Crest Dr Dallas TX 75230

SCHAFFER, MERYL IVY, personnel exec.; b. Bklyn., May 17, 1954; s. Nathaniel and Harriet Phyllis Schaffer; B.S., Am. U., 1976, M.S. (fellow), 1978. Auditor, Regardie, Brooks, & Lewis, Inc., Washington, 1978-79; acct. Pepco, Washington, 1979-81; sr. personnel cons. Atlas Personnel Agy., 1981—; tchr. acctg. Am. U., Washington. Home: 1111 Army Navy Dr A 705 Arlington VA 22202 Office: 1900 Penn Ave 417 Washington DC 20068

SCHAFFRAN, SUSAN DELL STANTON, aerospace co. ofcl.; b. Atlanta, Mar. 25, 1948; d. James Lee and Mary Dell (Garner) Stanton; A.B. in Journalism, U. Ga., 1970. Copywriter WKTM-WNCG Radio Stas., Charleston, S.C., 1970-71; pub. relations news editor Meridian (Miss.) Pub. Sch. System, 1971-72; advt. account exec. Whidbey News-Times, Whidbey Island, Oak Harbor, Wash., 1973; commd. ensign U.S. Navy, 1974; public affairs officer Whidby Island Naval Air Sta., Oak Harbor, 1974-75; public info. specialist 13th Naval Dist., Seattle, 1975-79; customer relations rep. Boeing Aerospace Co., Seattle, 1979—. Mem. AAUW, Women in Communications, Alpha Chi Omega. Methodist. Address: Boeing Aerospace Co PO Box 3999 (MS 85-11) Seattle WA 98124

SCHAG, CYNDIE COSCARELLI, psychologist; b. Phoenix, Aug. 1, 1955; d. Donald Anthony and Shirley (Tyer) Coscarelli; A.B. in Psychology with honors, U. Calif., Santa Cruz, 1976; M.A., Calif. Sch. Profl. Psychology, 1978, Ph.D., 1980; m. Daniel Steven Schag, Aug. 20, 1976. Clin. intern Open Door Clinic, Los Angeles, 1976-77, Youth Services Center, Los Angeles, 1977-78, UCLA Med. Center, 1978-79, Orange Coast Coll. Student Health Center, 1979-80; clin. research psychologist, dir. cancer research project VA, Sepulveda, Calif., 1980—; asst. research psychologist dept. psychiatry and biobehavioral sci. UCLA, 1980—; assoc. mem. UCLA Jonsson Comprehensive Cancer Center. UCLA grantee, 1982-83; lic. psychologist, Calif. Mem. Am. Psychol. Assn., Assn. for Women in Psychology. Contbr. chpt., articles to profl. publs.; research on women in ednl. instns. and psychosocial impact of cancer. Office: VA Behavioral Rehab Research Lab (151P) 16111 Plummer St Sepulveda CA 91343

SCHALLER, GLORIA JEAN, mktg. exec.; b. Chgo., Aug. 2, 1953; d. George Joseph and Dolores (Riley) Schaller; B.S., Western Ill. U., 1975; M.B.A., Keller Grad. Sch. Mgmt., 1982. Market research analyst Allied Van Lines, Broadview, Ill., 1975-77, sr. market research analyst, 1977-78; mktg. mgr. Allied Air Freight, Broadview, 1978-81; mktg. specialist Continental Bondware, Rolling Meadows, Ill., 1981—. Mem. Am. Mktg. Assn. Office: 1701 Golf Rd Tower Two Rolling Meadows IL 60008

SCHAPER, CHERYL ANN, steel tank mfg. co. exec.; b. Fairview, Ohio, Feb. 20, 1945; d. Alvin J. and Eleanor Scigay) Palack; B.S., Bowling Green State U., 1967; m. Richard P. Schaper, Aug. 6, 1967 (div. 1979); m. 2d, Ralph E. Ennis, Jr., Apr. 24, 1982. Office mgr., Rink's Bargain City, Bowling Green, Ohio, 1968-70; tchr. bus. edn. Liberty Benton High Sch., Findlay, Ohio, 1967-70; tchr. vocat. edn. North Olmsted High Sch. (Ohio), 1970-71; asst. controller Vacuform Corp., Columbus, Ohio, 1971-77; controller Airmark Corp., Kansas City, Mo., 1977-78, v.p. fin., 1978—; sec.-treas. Kansas City Spray Foam Inc., Grandview, Mo., 1978-79. Mem. Nat. Assn. Accts., Am. Soc. Women Accts., Womens C. of C., Bowling Green State U. Alumni Assn., Kappa Delta. Home: 7005 Hallet St Shawnee KS 66216 Office: 1700 29th St W Kansas City MO 64108

SCHAPIRO, EDITH IRENE, journalist; b. Newark, Dec. 22, 1929; d. Lewis A. and Bertha (Ellins) Kravet; B.A., Douglass Coll., Rutgers U., 1951; M.S. in Journalism, Columbia U., 1953; m. Jerome B. Schapiro, Dec. 27, 1953; children—Lois Schapiro Thom, Robert, Kenneth. With CBS Radio, 1952, Newark News, 1953-55; freelance writer, 1955-75; with Jewish News, East Orange, N.J., 1975-78, founder, editor Spectrum of Young Jewry, 1979—; columnist Jewish Telegraphic Agy., N.Y.C., 1978-79; asso. editor Advt. and Publishing News, Montclair, N.J., 1980-81; editor Morris-Sussex Jewish News, Ledgewood, N.J., 1981—. Mem. charter change com. Town of Montclair, 1979. Mem. Nat. Fedn. Press Women, World Fedn. Jewish Journalists, Phi Beta Kappa; life mem. Nat. Council Jewish Women, Hadassah. Home: 197 N Mountain Ave Montclair NJ 07042 Office: 51 Upper Montclair Plaza Upper Montclair NJ 07043

SCHAPIRO, MIRIAM, artist; b. Toronto, Ont., Can., Nov. 15, 1923 (parents Am. citizens); d. Theodore and Fannie (Cohen) S.; B.A., U. Iowa, 1945, M.A., 1946, M.F.A., 1949; m. Paul Brach, 1946; 1 son, Peter. Exhibited in one man shows at Andre Emmerich Gallery, N.Y.C., 1958, 60, 61, 63, 67, 69, 71, 73, 76, 77, Franklin Siden Gallery, Detroit, 1965, Lyman Allen Mus., New London, Conn., 1966, Comsky Gallery, Los Angeles, 1974, 75, Benson Gallery, Bridgehampton, N.Y., 1975, A.R.C. Gallery, Chgo., 1976, Douglas Drake Gallery, Kansas City, Mo., 1976, Mitzi Landau Gallery, Los Angeles, 1976, 77, also numerous colls.; exhibited in numerous group shows, 1947—, latest at Bronx Mus. Art, 1975, Womens Interart Center, N.Y.C., 1975, Ashwagh Hall, Springs, N.Y., 1975, Guild Hall, East Hampton, N.Y., 1975, 76, Marion Koogler McNay Art Inst., San Antonio, 1976, Alessandra Gallery, N.Y.C., 1976, 77, Landmark Gallery, N.Y.C., 1976, Mulvane Art Center, Topeka, 1977, Bklyn. Mus. Art Sch., 1977; represented in numerous permanent collections; instr. Parsons Sch. Design, N.Y.C., 1966-67; lectr. dept. art U. Calif., San Diego, 1967-69, asst. prof., 1969-70; faculty Art Sch., Calif. Inst. Arts, Valencia, Calif., 1970-75, co-dir. Feminist Art Program, 1971-73, dir., 1973-75; guest prof. Bryn Mawr (Pa.) Coll., 1977—, Tyler Sch. Art, Phila., 1977—; producer Womanhouse, 1972; artist in residence U. Minn., Coll. St. Catherine, St. Paul, 1976. Nat. Endowment Visual Arts fellow, 1976; Ford Found. grantee, 1964. Mem. Los Angeles Inst. Contemporary Art (founding bd. mem. 1974), Coll. Art Assn. (dir. 1974-77), Womens Caucus for Art (bd. advisers 1974—), Heresies Collective N.Y.C. (founding mem. 1976—). Editor: Anonymous Was A Woman; Art, A Woman's Sensibility, 1977. Contbr. articles to profl. jours. Home: 393 W Broadway New York NY 10012

SCHAPIRO, RAYA CZERNER, psychiatrist; b. Prague, Czechoslovakia, May 1, 1934; d. Max and Irma (Froehlich) Czerner; student U. Wis., 1951-53; M.D., U. Ill., 1958; m. Joseph S. Schapiro, Mar. 2, 1957; children—Andrew, Tamar. Practice medicine specializing in psychiatry, Chgo., 1963—; mem. vol. staff and attending staff Michael Reese Hosp., Chgo.; instr. Northwestern U. Med. Sch., 1970-76. Mem. Am. Psychiat. Assn. Office: 111 N Wabash Chicago IL 60602

SCHAPIRO, RUTH GOLDMAN (MRS. DONALD SCHAPIRO), lawyer; b. N.Y.C., Oct. 31, 1926; d. Louis Albert and Sarah (Shapiro) Goldman; A.B., Wellesley Coll., 1947; LL.B., Columbia, 1950; m. Donald Schapiro, June 29, 1952; children—Jane Goldman, Robert Andrew. Admitted to N.Y. bar, 1950; asst. to reporters Am. Law Inst. Fed. Income Tax Statute, N.Y.C., 1950-51; asso., then mem. Proskauer Rose Goetz & Mendelsohn, 1955—; nominating commn. U.S. Tax Ct., 1978-81. Mem. adv. com. N.Y. U. Inst. on Fed. Taxation, 1972—. Mem. Am. Bar Assn., N.Y. State Bar Assn. (chmn. com. partners and partnerships tax sect. 1974-76, chmn. com. incentives tax sect. 1977-78, exec. com. tax sect. 1974—, sec. 1978-79, 2d vice chmn. 1979-80, 1st vice chmn. 1980-81, exec. com. 1982—), Assn. Bar City N.Y. (taxation com. 1972-75, 78-79), N.Y. County Lawyers Assn., Am. Judicature Soc. Jewish. Club: N.Y. Wellesley (N.Y.C.). Notes editor Columbia Law Rev., 1949-50; editor Tax Shelters, 1980; contbr. articles to legal jours. Home: 1035 Fifth Ave New York NY 10028 Office: 300 Park Ave New York NY 10022

SCHARETT, CAROL MARIE, personnel cons.; b. Corning, N.Y., Jan. 9, 1949; d. Theodore and Elizabeth Reed; grad. pub. schs.; m. Joseph L. Scharett, Sept. 1, 1967; children—Annette Mareie, Patricia Lynn, Jessica Elizabeth. Mem. customer service dept. Dunn & Bradstreet, N.Y.C., 1968-70; mem. customer billing dept. Clifton Springs (N.Y.) Hosp., 1971-73; br. mgr. Kelly Services, Geneva, N.Y., 1973-75; pres., owner Additional Personnel Services Inc., Geneva, N.Y., 1975—. Pres., owner 42 Seneca Street Devel. Corp. Mem. Nat. Assn. Female Execs. Inc., Adminstrv. Mgmt. Soc. (pres. Finger Lakes chpt. 1977-78), Bus. and Profl. Women, Internat. Mgmt. Council (edn. chmn. Finger Lakes chpt. 1981-82). Republican. Home: Route 1 Box 38A Serven Rd Waterloo NY 13165 Office: 29 Linden St Geneva NY 14456

SCHARY, SUSAN, artist; b. Phila., Aug. 7, 1936; d. S. Stanley and Fay M. Schary; student Phila. Sch. Fine Arts; with honors, Temple U., 1960; children—Jennifer Lyn, Karima Ann. Instr. art Fleisher Art Meml., Phila., 1967-68, Harcum Jr. Coll., Bryn Mawr, Pa., 1960-62; profl. artist, 1960—. Mem. Artists' Equity Assn., Internat. Platform Assn. Home: 228 St Albans Ave South Pasadena CA 91030

SCHATZ, CECIL RUSKAY (MRS. ARTHUR H. SCHATZ), civic worker; b. Far Rockaway, N.Y., Jan. 9, 1923; d. Cecil Benjamin and Sophie (Liebovitz) Ruskay; A.B., Cornell U., 1943; M.S. in Social Work, Columbia, 1945; m. Arthur H. Schatz, Feb. 11, 1945; children—Ellen L., Robert F., Daniel N. Placement worker specializing in handicapped children Children's Services Conn., Hartford, 1946-51, 62-71. Life mem. women's div. Am. Soc. Technion, N.Y.C., 1961—; life mem. women's div. Brandeis U., Waltham, Mass., 1960—; life mem. Hadassah, 1961—, Mt. Sinai Hosp. Assn., Hartford, 1970—; bd. dirs. Hartford div. Nat. Council Jewish Women, 1958—, v.p., 1966-68, pres., 1968-71; mem. Nat. Com. on Problems of Aging, Nat. Com. on Internat. Affairs; mem. bd. Beth El Temple Sisterhood, 1964-74; chmn. Artists in Residence Scholarship Program, 1969-73; co-chmn. Beth El Art Show, Hartford, 1964-66; mem. Jewish Theol. Sem.; counselor Sr. Citizens Jobs Bank, West Hartford, 1973-74; bd. dirs. Hartford Women's Aux. Brandeis U., 1968-75; bd. dirs. Hartford Jewish Community Center, 1974—, chmn. older adult program com., 1976-78; bd. dirs. Planned Parenthood League Conn., 1977—; com. for older adult Hartford Jewish Fedn., 1976—. Mem. Am. Assn. Social Workers. Clubs: Cliffside Country (Simsbury, Conn.); Bloomfield (Conn.) Indoor Tennis; Eastlakes Country (Palm Beach Gardens, Fla.). Author: Placement of Handicapped Children, 1945. Donor, Celia Pessin Scholarship Technion, Haifa, Israel, 1962. Home: 33 Juniper Rd Bloomfield CT 06002 also 13267 Touchstone Pl Palm Beach Gardens FL 33410

SCHATZ, PAULINE, dietitian; b. Sioux City, Iowa, Sept. 25, 1923; d. Isaac and Haya (Kaplan) Epstein; B.S., UCLA, 1945, M.S., 1950, M.S. in Public Health, 1963; doctoral candidate U. So. Calif.; m. Hyman Schatz, Sept. 2, 1951; children—Barbara, Larry. Head dietitian VA, 1946-54; asso. prof. Los Angeles City Coll., 1958-68; prof. home econs. Calif. State U., Los Angeles, 1968—, dir. center dietetic edn., 1979—. Grantee VA, Kellogg Found., HEW. Mem. Am. Dietetic Assn., Am. Public Health Assn., Am. Home Econs. Assn., Calif. Dietetic Assn., Los Angeles Dietetic Assn. Author: Manuel for Clinical Dietetics, 1978. Office: Dept Home Econs Calif State Univ Los Angeles CA 90032

SCHATZLE, DOROTHY CATHERINE, nurse; b. Oswego, N.Y., July 28, 1924; d. William Francis and Anna Louise (Hourigan) Doyle; R.N., St. Francis Hosp., 1945; m. Robert Lawrence Schatzle, Nov. 9, 1946; 1 dau., Barbara Jean Schatzle Tozzi. Staff nurse Leonard Hosp., Troy, N.Y., 1945-67, asst. supr. 1953-57, supr., 1963-67; emergency rm./evening supr. Samaritan Hosp., Troy, 1968-75; staff St. Mary's Hosp., Troy, 1976—, dir. central services, 1980—. Mem. Hosp. Central Service Personnel Assn. (chpt. v.p. 1981—), Assn. Operating Rm. Nurses, Emergency Dept. Nurse Assn., others. Club: Mother's (v.p. 1967). Address: 1003 9 Ave Troy NY 12182

SCHAUB, MARILYN MCNAMARA, educator; b. Chgo., Mar. 24, 1928; d. Bernard Francis and Helen Katherine (Skehan) McNamara; B.A., Rosary Coll., 1953; Ph.D., U. Fribourg, Switzerland, 1957; diploma Ecole Biblique, Jerusalem, 1967; m. R. Thomas Schaub, Oct. 25, 1969; 1 dau., Helen Ann. Asst. prof. classics and bibl. studies Rosary Coll., River Forest, Ill., 1957-69; prof. bibl. studies Duquesne U., Pitts., 1969-70, 73—; participant 7 archeol. excavations in Middle East; administrv. dir. expdn. to Dead Sea, Jordan, 1977—. Hon. asso. Am. Schs. Oriental Research, 1966-67; Danforth asso., 1972—. Mem. Soc. Bibl. Lit., Cath. Bibl. Assn., Am. Acad. Religion, Eastern Gt. Lakes Bibl. Assn. (pres. 1981-82). Democrat. Author: Friends and Friendship for St. Augustine, 1964. Translator: (with H. Richter) Agape in the New Testament, 3 vols., 1963-65. Home: 25 McKelvey Ave Pittsburgh PA 15218 Office: Theology Dept Duquesne U Pittsburgh PA 15219

SCHAUBERT, LAUREL VIRGINIA, med. illustrator; b. Portland Oreg., Aug. 3, 1923; d. John and Mildred (Hall) Karg; student Reed Coll., 1940-43, U. Calif., 1947-49, Art League San Francisco, 1950-53, U. Calif. San Francisco Med. Center, 1953-55; m. Arvid D. Schaubert, Nov. 10, 1962; children—Gay Lee Schaubert Giannini, Leslie May (dec.). Med. illustrator Ft. Miley VA Hosp., 1955; sr. illustrator dept. surgery U. Calif., San Francisco, 1955-69; prin. illustrator Lange Med. Publs., Los Altos, Calif., 1961—; now also co-owner, pres. Biomed Arts Assocs., Inc., San Francisco; instr. U. Calif., 1959-61, 74-78. Recipient cert. of commendation Calif. Dist. Attys. Assn., 1977; Merit award Fedn. Biocommunication Socs., 1979. Mem. Assn. Med. Illustrators (Outstanding Service award 1972; chmn. bd. govs. 1971-72, v.p. 1975-76, pres. 1976-77), Graphic Artists Guild. Co-author: Scientific Illustration: Standards for Publication; contbr. articles to profl. jours. Office: 350 Parnassus Ave Suite 905 San Francisco CA 94117

SCHAUPP, JOAN POMPROWITZ, author, lectr.; b. Green Bay, Wis., Sept. 29, 1932; d. Joseph and Helen Elizabeth (Vander Linden) Pomprowitz; B.S. with honors, U. Wis., 1954; Cert. in Theology, Norbert

Coll., 1979; postgrad. U. Wis., Green Bay; m. Robert J. Schaupp, Sept. 4, 1956; children—Margaret A., Frederick J., John R., Elizabeth T. Research asst. Calif. Inst. Tech., 1954; staff writer, women's editor Green Bay Press-Gazette, 1955-57; free-lance writer, author, lectr., 1957—; author: Jesus Was a Teenager, 1972; Woman: Image of the Holy Spirit, 1975; contbr. articles to Parent Educator, Marriage, Franciscan Message, others. Publicity chmn. Republican Party of Brown County, 1964-66; public relations chmn. Fedn. Wis. Rep. Women's Clubs, 1967-68; bd. govs. U. Wis. Green Bay Founders Assn. Recipient Wis. Press Women award, 1975. Mem. Nat. Press Club, Nat. Fedn. Press Women, Wis. Press Women, Wis. Regional Writers, Wis. Council Writers, Authors Guild, Internat. Platform Assn., Altrusa Internat., AAUW. Roman Catholic. Master gardener, 1981, 82. Home: 836 White Pine Ave De Pere WI 54115

SCHECK, ROSANNE A., educator; b. N.Y.C., Sept. 19, 1949; d. Joseph Dominick and Theresa Marie Leone; B.A. magna cum laude, Fairleigh Dickinson U., 1971; M.A., Dartmouth Coll., 1981; m. Donald Gordon Scheck, July 30, 1972; 1 dau., Anne Catherine. Tchr. Robert Erskine Sch., Ringwood, N.J., 1972-75, Cornish (N.H.) Elem. Sch., 1975-77, J.M. Hill Sch., East Stroudsburg, Pa., 1977-82. Grantee State N.J. Dept. Edn., 1974. Mem. NEA, Pa. Edn. Assn., Childbirth Edn. Assn. Poconos, La Leche League. Home: East Dogwood Ln Mountainhome PA 18342

SCHEELE, ADELE MARCUS, career cons., author, columnist; b. Phila., Dec. 18, 1938; d. Sol and Lillian (Katz) Marcus; B.S., U. Pa., 1960; M.A., Calif. State U., 1968; Ph.D. with honors (Change Mgmt. fellow), UCLA, 1976. Tchr. English, Grant High Sch., Los Angeles, 1968-69, Coronado High Sch., El Paso, Tex., 1962-63, Cheyenne, Mont. Colorado Springs, Colo., 1964-65, Overbrook Sch., Phila. 1960-62; instr. English, Santa Monica (Calif.) Coll., part-time 1968-71; researcher, negotiator Joint Council AFL-CIO, Los Angeles, 1969-71; v.p. Social Engring. Tech., Inc., Los Angeles, 1971-77; cons. career strategist, Los Angeles, 1977—; speaker, cons. to bus., profl. assns., colls., univs.; talk show host Sta. KABC, 1981—; career expert Today Show, PM Magazine, Hour Magazine. Recipient Best Presenters award Am. Soc. Tng. and Devel., 1980. Mem. Women in Bus. (dir. 1978-81), Center Communication Ministry (dir. 1980-82). Author: Skills for Success: A Guide to the Top for Men and Women, 1979; syndicated columnist Using College, 1982. Office: 1722 Westwood Blvd Los Angeles CA 90024

SCHEELE, MARY ALICE HAHN, advt. agy. account exec.; b. Milw., Mar. 25, 1947; d. Elmer Paul and Marguarite Cecilia (Hitchings) Hahn; student U. Wis., Whitewater, 1964, Wash. State U., 1970-71, Eastern Mich. U., 1977-78; A.B. with honors, U. Mich., 1979; m. Robert F. Scheele, Sept. 6, 1964; children—Michael, Jonathan, Jeffrey. Dir., producer news, public affairs WEMU-Radio, Ypsilanti, WCBN-Radio, Ann Arbor, 1974-77; asst. producer WXYZ-TV, Southfield, Mich., 1978; public relations women's athletics U. Mich., 1979; promotion specialist Univ. Microfilms Internat., 1979-81; account exec. Widerschein Strandberg Assos., Toledo, 1981—; announcer women's basketball games Crisler Arena, 1978. Asst. dir. Sex Info. Clinic, Pullman, Wash., 1971; den leader Cub Scouts Am., 1975-77; publicity vol. presdl. campaign, 1976; participant public auction KQED, San Francisco, 1980, KGO-TV Cystic Fibrosis Telethon, 1980; chmn. sch. fund-raising activities, 1978. Mem. Women in Communications, Profl. Women in Communications, Kappa Tau Alpha. Democrat. Lutheran. Club: Toledo Advt. Home: 1128 Olivia St Ann Arbor MI 48104 Office: Widerschein Strandberg Assos 3035 Moffat Dr Toledo OH 43615

SCHEERER, ANNE ELIZABETH, univ. dean; b. Phila., Aug. 7, 1924; d. Frederick Hyacinth and Anna Elizabeth (Kenny) S.; B.S., U. Pa., 1946, M.S., 1947, Ph.D., 1953; postgrad. U. Chgo., 1948, Inst. Henri Poincare, Paris, 1963-64. Instr. math. Temple U., Phila., 1948-51, Washington U., St. Louis, 1953-55; asst. prof. Georgetown U., Washington, 1955-60, asso. prof., 1960-66; asst. dean Coll. Engring., Boston U., 1966-67; higher edn. specialist Md. Council Higher Edn., Balt., 1967-68; dean summer sessions and Lifelong Learning Center, Creighton U., Omaha, 1968—; cons. math. Ops. Adv. Group, USN, 1962-64, David Taylor Model Basin, 1959-61. Active United Way of Midlands, 1974—; editor newsletter Omaha Opera Angels, 1978-79; mem. Mayor's Com. on Urban U., Omaha, 1970-71, Riverfront Edn. Task Force, 1973-76; bd. dirs. Landmarks Inc., Omaha, 1977-80, Opera/Omaha, 1978—, Douglas-Sarpy Counties chpt. ARC, 1978-79. Ellis L. Phillips Found. intern in acad. adminstrn., 1965-66. Mem. N.Am. Assn. Summer Sessions (pres. 1978-79), N.Central Conf. Summer Schs. (pres. 1977-78), Am. Assn. Higher Edn., Math. Assn. Am., Am. Math. Soc., Sigma Xi. Roman Catholic. Author: (with McCoart and Oliphant) Elementary Analysis, 1964; Probability on Discrete Sample Spaces with Applications, 1969. Contbr. articles to profl. jours. Home: 2037 N 53d St Omaha NE 68104 Office: Creighton U 2500 California St Omaha NE 68178

SCHEETZ, MARY JOELLEN, coll. pres.; b. Lafayette, Ind., May 20, 1926; d. Joseph Albert and Ellen Isabelle (Fitzgerald) S.; A.B., St. Francis Coll., Ft. Wayne, Ind., 1956; M.A., U. Notre Dame, 1964; Ph.D., U. Mich., 1970. Joined Sisters of St. Francis of Perpetual Adoration, Roman Cath. Ch., 1946; high sch. tchr., 1956-67; dean of girls Bishop Luers High Sch., Ft. Wayne, 1967; acad. dean St. Francis Coll., 1967-68, pres., 1970—. Bd. dirs. Ind. Colls. and Univs. Ind., Ft. Wayne Public TV, Cath. Charities Diocese Ft. Wayne-South Bend. Mem. Assn. Cath. Colls. and Univs., Conf. Small Colls. Address: 2701 Spring St Fort Wayne IN 46808

SCHEIBNER, RUTH MARTIN (MRS. LAWRENCE F. SCHEIBNER, JR.), psychologist educator; b. Phila., Aug. 24, 1921; d. James Frederick and Rebecca Bamford (Carmen) Martin; A.B., Temple U., 1960, M.A., 1962, Ph.D., 1969; m. Lawrence Frederick Scheibner, Jr., May 27, 1950; 1 dau., Judith (Mrs. John Joseph Massaro). Psychology intern VA Hosp., Coatesville, Pa., 1961-62, VA Hosp., Phila., 1962-63; instr., counseling psychologist, acad. adviser Temple U., 1963-69; sch. psychologist, Marlton, N.J., 1966-67; lectr. Thomas Jefferson U., 1968-69; asst. prof. Phila. Coll. Pharmacy and Sci., 1968-70, asso. prof., 1971-75, prof., 1976—, chmn. dept. humanities and social scis., 1980—; individual practice psychotherapy, 1968—; counsellor family relations com. Phila. Soc. Friends, 1969-75. Bd. dirs. Phila. br. human engring. lab. Johnson O'Connor Research Found., 1954-56. Recipient award for excellence in psychology Psi Chi, 1962. Mem. Am., Eastern, Pa. psychol. assns., AAUP, AAAS, Phila. Soc. Clin. Psychologists (chmn. continuing edn. com., dir. Human Services Center 1977-80), Kappa Epsilon. Home: 1654 E Butler Pike Ambler PA 19002 Office: Phila Coll of Pharmacy and Sci 43d St and Woodland Ave Philadelphia PA 19104

SCHEIDING, JANET ELIZABETH, coll. adminstr.; b. California, Mo., Jan. 18, 1942; d. Herman U. and Mary Elizabeth (Reichel) Dearixon; B.S., Iowa State U., Ames, 1964; M.Ed., Eastern N.Mex. U., Portales, 1980; m. David Oscar Scheiding, Nov. 25, 1962; children—Douglas Scot, Randall Scott. Tchr. high sch. English, Del Rio (Tex.) Ind. Sch. Dist., 1966-67, 68-70, 71-72; tchr. high sch. English, biology and health Northside Ind. Sch. Dist., San Antonio, 1975-77; tchr. secondary English and speech St. James Sch., Montgomery, Ala., 1977-78; tchr. adult basic edn. Eastern N.Mex. U., Clovis, 1980-81, tchr. psychology, Portales, Clovis, 1980-82, acad. counselor, Clovis, 1981-82, dir. counseling, testing and advising, 1982—. Mem. Am. Personnel and Guidance Assn., Am. Psychol. Assn., N.Mex. Personnel and Guidance Assn., N.Mex. Sch. Counselor's Assn., N.Mex. Student Personnel Assn., N.Mex. Placement Council, Phi Delta Kappa, Phi Kappa Phi, Psi Chi, Kappa Delta. Baptist. Office: 417 Schepps Blvd Suite 136 Clovis NM 88101

SCHEIN, VIRGINIA ELLEN, organizational psychologist, educator; b. Rahway, N.J., June 23, 1943; d. Jacob Charles and Anne Schein; B.A. cum laude, Cornell U., 1965; Ph.D., N.Y.U., 1969; m. Peter Bulterman, May 10, 1977; 1 son, Alexander Nikos. Sr. research asso. Am. Mgmt. Assn., N.Y.C., 1969-70; mgr. personnel research Life Office Mgmt. Assn., N.Y.C., 1970-72; dir. personnel research Met. Life Ins. Co., N.Y.C., 1972-75; asso. prof. Case Western Res. U., Cleve., 1975-76; vis. asso. prof. Yale U., New Haven, 1976-77; asso. prof. mgmt. U. Pa., Phila., 1977-80; cons., pvt. practice organizational psychology, Stamford, Conn., 1980-82; assoc. prof. psychology Baruch Coll., CUNY, 1982—. Mem. Internat. Assn. Applied Psychology, Am. Psychol. Assn., Met. N.Y. Assn. Applied Psychology (pres. 1973-74), Acad. of Mgmt. (dir.), Organizational Dynamics, Acad. Mgmt. Rev. Psi Chi. Contbr. articles to profl. jours. Office: Psychology Dept Baruch Coll 17 Lexington Ave Box 512 New York NY 10010

SCHELCHER, CYNTHIA EYRE, rehab. adminstr.; b. Cedar Rapids, Iowa, July 15, 1948; d. Harlan Ainsworth and Helenruth (Becker) Eyre; B.A., Calif. State U., Fresno, 1972; cert. in human services, U. Calif., Santa Cruz, 1978; M.R.A., U. San Francisco, 1979; m. George James Schelcher, Aug. 12, 1972; 1 dau., Erin Nicole. Youth and community service coordinator Broadway-Hale (Weinstocks), 1970-72; devel. dir. Kentuckian Center Health and Research, 1972; exec. dir. Crippled Children's Soc. Santa Clara County, Calif., 1973—; pvt. cons., lectr.; mem. adj. faculty U. San Francisco; field cons. depts. of health. Named Woman of Year, San Jose Jaycees, 1977, Miss Monterey County, 1967, Miss Calif. finalist, 1967; recipient Bonne Bell Nat. Community Service award, 1972, Environ. Leadership award Seventeen Mag., 1972. Mem. Am. Camping Assn. (dist. pres. 1976-77), Nat. Council Handicapped, Assn. Recreational Services for Handicapped (v.p. 1976-77), Cousteau Soc. Democrat. Roman Catholic. Clubs: Sierra, Soroptimist. Author: Self-Sufficiency Seminars for Non-Profit Organizations, 1977—; Fundraising Survival Handbook for Non-Profit Agencies, 1980. Office: 2581 Park Ave Santa Clara CA 95050

SCHELL, EILEEN, Mass. state govt. ofcl.; b. Chgo., July 1, 1934; d. Paul R. And Magdaline E. (Mooney) Conaghan; B.A., Stanford U., 1956; postgrad. Internat. Tng. Center for Aerial Survey, 1957; M.A., Boston U., 1958, Ph.D., 1964; m. Allan Schell, May 25, 1957; children—Alice Rosalind, Cynthia. Owner, prin. Eileen Schell Market Research, Winchester, Mass., 1964-79; cabinet sec. Commonwealth of Mass., Boston, 1979—, sec., exec. Office of Consumer Affairs; dir. Mt. Vernon Coop. Bank, United Mortgage Co., Workingmen's Coop. Bank, Union Mut. Asset Mgmt. Co.; vis. lectr. Boston U. Grad. Sch., 1966-68, Harvard U. Grad. Sch. Bus. Adminstrn., Cambridge, Mass., 1971-74; Corporator ABC of Winchester, bd. dirs. Winchester Scholarship Fund; mem. Suffold U. Adv. Bd. Fulbright Scholar, 1956-57; Am. Council of Learned Socs. grantee, 1957; U.S. Ednl. Found. grantee, 1965; Retail Research Inst. fellow, 1964; cert. mgmt. cons.; real estate broker, Mass. Democrat. Conglist. Contbr. articles in field to profl. jours. Office: One Ashburton Pl Boston MA 02108

SCHELL, KAREN ANNE, art dir.; b. Allentown, Pa., Feb. 8, 1949; d. Robert George and Margaret Rebecca (Hoehle) S.; cert. Sch. Visual Arts, N.Y.C., 1970. Art dir. McGraw-Hill, N.Y.C., 1971-74; studio mgr., art dir. Stewart Seidman & Assos., Inc., N.Y.C., 1974-75; asst. art dir. Bus. Week Mag., N.Y.C., 1976-78; art dir. Rodale Press, Inc., Emmaus, Pa., 1979—. Recipient Best Art Dir. award McGraw-Hill, Inc., N.Y.C., 1972; Am. Mgmt. Assn. award for Continuing Edn. Rodale Press Inc., 1980. Mem. Old Allentown Preservation Assn., Nat. Rifle Assn., Rural Sportsmen's Assn. Office: 33 E Minor St Emmaus PA 18049

SCHELL, MERLE, advt. exec.; b. Boston, Jan. 31, 1948; d. Jules J. and Thelma (Klass) Smolker; B.S. magna cum laude, Simmons Coll., 1968; postgrad. Hunter Coll., 1971, 72. Singer, actress, N.Y.C., 1969-71; account exec. Gaynor & Ducas Advt. Co., N.Y.C., 1971-72; sr. account exec. Needham, Harper & Steers, N.Y.C., 1972-73; account supr. Foote, Cone & Belding, N.Y.C., 1973-75; sr. account exec. Norman, Craig & Kummel, N.Y.C., 1976; mktg. dir. Faberge Corp., N.Y.C., 1977-78; sr. brand mgr. Bristol Myers Co., N.Y.C., 1978-81; sr. v.p. mgmt. supr. Rosenfeld, Sirowitz & Lawson Advt., Inc., N.Y.C., 1981—; sr. v.p. pres. Healthy Kitchens, Inc., N.Y.C., 1978—. Mem. Cosmetic Career Women, Fragrance Found., Authors Guild, Advt. Women of N.Y., Am. AGVA, Coop. for Am. Policy Everywhere, N. Shore Animal League, Sierra Club. Author: Tasting Good, The International Salt Free Diet Cookbook, 1981. Home: 225 E 57th St #15K New York NY 10022 Office: 1370 Ave of Americas 20th Floor New York NY 10019

SCHENCK, ROSEMAE MURPHY, hosp. exec.; b. Hannibal, Mo., Apr. 17, 1923; d. Raina and Mallie Elizabeth (Dickerson) Murphy; m. Albert F. Schenck, July 26, 1942 (dec.); children—Loretta Schenck Grunden, Elizabeth Schenck Murphy. Instr. airplanes Curtiss Wright Aircraft Co., 1942-45; bookkeeper Internat. Shoe Co., Hannibal, Mo., 1951-65; purchasing agt. Levering Hosp., Hannibal, 1967—. Mem. Am. Legion Aux. (past post pres.); Assn. Hosp. Purchasing Materials Mgmt. Greater St. Louis, N.E. Mo. Med. and Dental Soc. (past pres.), Bus. and Profl. Women (past pres.), Epsilon Sigma Alpha (past pres. Loveland, Colo.). Club: Bowling Assn. Monday Night Hannibal Ladies League (pres. 1969-81). Home: 1500 Paris Ave Hannibal MO 64301 Office: 1734 Market St Hannibal MO 63401

SCHENK, KATHRYN LOUISE, computer programmer; b. New Orleans, Sept. 29, 1951; d. Theodore Michael and Shirley Victory (Begault) S.; B.A. in Math., U. New Orleans, 1973; M.S. in Computer Sci., U. Tenn., 1976; m. James Robert Pinkert, Dec. 19, 1974. Programmer Center for Bus. and Econ. Research U. New Orleans, 1972-73, U. Tenn., 1973-75; computer cons. Oak Ridge Nat. Labs., 1974; instr. Tech. Inst., Knoxville, Tenn., 1976-77; instr. Calif. State U., Chico, 1977-78, programmer, 1979—; programmer County of Butte, Calif., 1978-79. Mem. Assn. Computing Machinery, Nat. Assn. Female Execs. Contbr. articles to profl. jours. Office: Computer Center California State U Chico CA 95929

SCHENK, LYNN ALICE, state cabinet ofcl.; b. N.Y.C., Jan. 5, 1945; d. Sidney and Elsa (Roth) S.; B.A., UCLA, 1967; J.D., U. San Diego, 1970; postgrad. London Sch. Econs., 1971; m. C. Hugh Friedman, Nov. 25, 1972. Admitted to Calif. bar, 1971, U.S. Supreme Ct. bar, 1976, D.C. bar, 1978; dep. atty. gen. criminal div. Office of Atty. Gen. State of Calif., San Diego, 1971-72; atty. San Diego Gas and Electric Co., 1972-77; dep. sec. Calif. Bus. and Transp. Agy., Sacramento, 1978-80; sec. Calif. Bus., Transp. and Housing Agy., Sacramento, 1980—; adj. prof. U. San Diego Law Sch., 1974-78; White House fellow, spl. asst. to Vice-pres. Rockefeller and Vice-pres. Mondale, 1976-77; mem. state atty. gen.'s Consumer Protection Task Force, 1972-74, San Diego Adv. Bd. on Status of Women, 1973-76, state atty. gen.'s Women's Rights Task Force, 1975, Calif. Commn. on Indsl. Innovation, 1981; ex officio mem. Calif. Coastal Commn., 1978; bd. dirs. Calif. Housing Fin. Agy., 1980; interim chmn., dir. State of Calif. Safe-Bidco 1981; chmn. State of Calif. Small Bus. Adv. Bd., 1981; mem. BiNational Adv. Com. of S.W. Border Regional Conf., 1982; co-founder, bd. dirs., v.p. Equal Rights Advisors, Inc., 1973-75. Bd. trustees United Way Sacramento Area, 1978; mem. community relations com. United Jewish Fedn., 1976-77; bd. dirs., v.p. San Diego Democratic Profl. Club, 1975-76; Calif. del. to Dem. Nat. Conv., 1976; bd. dirs. Legal Aid Soc. San Diego, 1973-76, exec. com., 1975-76; bd. visitors U. San Diego Law Sch., 1974—; co-founder, chmn. organizational exec. com. Women's Bank (Calif. Coastal Bank), San Diego. Named Woman of Achievement, pres.'s council Women's Service Bus. and Profl. Club San Diego, 1974, Bus. and Profl. Women's Club, Calif. So. Dist., 1974, Woman of Yr., San Diego, 1975, Headliner of Yr., San Diego Press Club, 1977, Women of Dedication, San Diego Salvation Army, 1978, one of 82 people to watch, San Diego Mag. and the Reader, 1982, Outstanding Lawyer in Govt. San Diego Trial Lawyers Assn., 1982; recipient awards B'nai B'rith Women, 1981, Calif. Women in Govt., 1981, State of Israel Peace Medal, 1981. Mem. Calif. State Bar (adminstrv. com. dist. 9 1974-76), San Diego County Bar Assn. (del. to state bar conv., 1973-77, del. whip 1977, vice chmn. land use planning com. 1977, subcom. chmn. future planning com. 1976, chmn. public relations com. 1973-75), Calif. Women Lawyers (co-founder, dist. gov., 1st v.p. 1975-76), Lawyers Club San Diego (co-founder, pres. 1974-75, woman of achievement 1974), U. San Diego Law Sch. Alumni Assn. (pres., 1975-76, bd. dirs., v.p. 1972-74, co-chmn. trust fund 1972-73, disting. alumni of yr. 1979), San Diego Bus. and Profl. Women's Club (program chmn. 1974-75). Office: 1120 N St #2101 Sacramento CA 95814

SCHENKEL, SUSI, psychologist; b. Wroctaw, Poland, Apr. 21, 1946; came to U.S., 1949, naturalized, 1953; d. Leon and Siddi S.; B.A., U. Wis., 1967; M.A., SUNY, Buffalo, 1970, Ph.D. in Clin. Psychology, 1973. Psychologist, Fitchburg (Mass.) State Coll., 1972-75; staff psychologist div. alcoholism Boston City Hosp., 1975-76; chief psychologist Cambridge (Mass.) Ct. Clinic, 1976-80; instr. psychology dept. psychiatry Harvard U. Med. Sch., Cambridge Hosp., 1976-80; pvt. practice psychology, Cambridge, 1976—; therapist Boston Psychol. Center for Women, 1976—; tchr. Fitchburg State U., 1973-74, U. Mass., Boston, 1978. SUNY Research Found. grantee, 1971-72, N.Y. State scholar, 1968-70, USPHS fellow, 1967-70. Mem. Am. Psychol. Assn., Am. Soc. Tng. and Devel., Mass. Psychol. Assn. Home and office: 417 Concord Ave Cambridge MA 02138

SCHENKMAN, ANNE WOERNER, psychologist, educator; b. Indpls., July 7, 1930; d. Clarence Julius and Velma Mary (Murphy) Woerner; A.B., Ind. U., 1952, M.S. (NDEA fellow), 1966, Ed.D., 1967; postgrad. Coll. William and Mary, 1963-65; m. Walter Allen Schenkman, Feb. 7, 1970; children—by previous marriage—Linda Bergmann Chambreau, Robert Bergmann. Cost acct. Nurre Glass Co., Bloomington, Ind., 1951-52; tchr. art Thorpe Jr. High Sch., Hampton, Va., 1961-65; research asso., Ind. U., Bloomington, 1966-67; asst. prof. U. No. Colo., Greeley, 1967-70, asso. prof., 1970-75, prof., 1975—, dir. div. counseling dept. psychology, 1980—. Mem. Greeley Philharm. Guild. Mem. Am. Psychol. Assn., Am. Personnel and Guidance Assn., Assn. Counselor Edn. and Supervision, Colo. Assn. Counselor Edn. and Supervision, Rocky Mountain Assn. Counselor Edn. and Supervision (editor newsletter), Phi Beta Kappa, Phi Delta Kappa. Office: U No Colo Greeley CO 80639

SCHENSTED, ELIZABETH MALONEY, editor; b. Yakima, Wash., June 30, 1929; d. Thomas Gleason and Eunice Elizabeth (Montague) Maloney; B.A., Wash. State U., 1951; m. Warren Curtis Schensted, Sept. 25, 1954; children—David, Robert. Asst. dist. public info. officer, 6th Naval Dist. Hdqrs., Charleston, S.C., 1952-55; editor Mercer Island (Wash.) Reporter, 1972-79; Seattle news bur. chief, regional editor Soundings, monthly, 1979-81; editor-in-chief Argus Pub., Seattle, 1981—. Bd. dirs. Wash./Alaska chpt. Cystic Fibrosis Found., 1977. Served as lt. (j.g.) USN, 1951-54. Recipient 1st place award Nat. Newspaper Assn., 1977, Nat. Press Women, 1977, 78; Superior Performance award Wash. Press Women, 1976. Mem. Mercer Island C. of C. (dir. 1977-79), Wash. Press Women, Wash. Newspaper Pubs. Assn., N.W. Marine Trade Assn., Mortar Bd., Sigma Delta Chi, Delta Gamma. Democrat. Roman Catholic. Home: 7500 Mercer Terrace Dr Mercer Island WA 98040

SCHEPERS, JEAN, adminstrv. judge; b. McGregor, Tex., Feb. 15, 1938; d. Joseph William and Ella Beeson (Bruce) S.; B.S. with honors, Tex. Technol. U., 1960; M.A., U. Tex., Austin, 1963, LL.B., 1967; postgrad. So. Conn. State Tchrs. Coll., 1960-61, N.Y. U., 1961-62. Asst. to personnel mgr., regional office Nationwide Ins. Co., Hamden, Conn., 1960-61; asst. to dir. food services N.Y. U., N.Y.C., 1961-62; tchr. English, Brazosport Ind. Sch. Dist., Lake Jackson, Tex., 1963-64; admitted to Tex. bar, 1967, U.S. Supreme Ct. bar, 1973; asso. firm Fulbright & Jaworski, Houston, 1967-72; trial atty. comml. litigation sect., civil div. U.S. Dept. Justice, Washington, 1972-80; adminstrv. judge Armed Services Bd. Contract Appeals, Alexandria, Va., 1980—. Mem. Am. Bar Assn., Exec. Women in Govt., Nat. Assn. Women Judges, State Bar Tex. Episcopalian. Home: 2700 Virginia Ave NW Apt 509 Washington DC 20037 Office: Armed Services Bd Contract Appeals 200 Stovall St Alexandria VA 22332

SCHER, HELENE LENZ, educator; b. N.Y.C., Dec. 26, 1935; d. Harold and Emma Lenz; student Oberlin Coll., 1952-54; A.B., U. Mich., 1956; M.A., Yale U., 1959, Ph.D., 1967. Instr. German, Yale U., 1962-63, So. Conn. State Coll., 1963-64, CCNY, 1965-67; asst. prof. German, Fairfield (Conn.) U., 1967-75; assoc. prof. Amherst (Mass.) Coll., 1975—; mem. rev. panel for summer stipends Nat. Endowment for Humanities; participant summer seminar Nat. Endowment for Humanities, 1979. Fulbright summer seminar grantee, 1981. Mem. MLA, N.E. MLA, Am. Assn. Tchrs. German, Internat. Brecht Soc., Aircraft Owners and Pilots Assn., Phi Beta Kappa. Author introduction, translator: Four Romantic Tales, 1975; contbr. articles on 20th century German writers, revs. to profl. publs. Office: Dept German Amherst Coll Amherst MA 01002

SCHERER, MARITA ROSE, repertory theatre adminstr.; b. Indpls., July 30, 1947; d. John Edward and Patricia Marie (Spragg) S.; B.S., Ind. U., 1971; 1 dau., Heather Patricia Schneider. Editor Sportlite newspaper, Louisville, 1975; asst. mgr. Scherer Market, Morristown, Ind., 1976-78; supr., tchr. Thrift Shop, Shelby County Assn. Retarded Citizens, Shelbyville, Ind., 1978-79; community affairs dir. Fairbanks Hosp., 1979-80; exec. asst. Ind. Repertory Theatre, Indpls., 1980-81, dir. devel., 1981—. Pres., Morristown Dodds Hall Players, 1977; pres. Shelby Arts Council, Shelbyville, 1979. Mem. Public Relations Soc. Am., Ind. Bus. Communicators, Ind. Council Fund Raising Execs. Inc., Shelby Arts Council. Roman Catholic. Club: Dodds Hall Players (pres.). Home: RR 1 Box 499 Morristown IN 46161 Office: 140 W Washington St Indianapolis IN 46204

SCHERGER, MOZELLE SPAINHOUR (MRS. GEORGE RICHARD SCHERGER), librarian; b. Forsyth County, N.C., Dec. 17, 1916; d. Earnest Sidney and Mertie Blanche (Hauser) Spainhour; B.S., Appalachian State Tchrs. Coll., Boone, N.C., 1937; B.S. in L.S., U. N.C., 1943; m. George Richard Scherger, Feb. 23, 1946; children—Teresa Ann (Mrs. Richard Martin), George Richard, Joseph John, Daniel M. Tchr. English and French, sch. librarian Cramerton (N.C.) High Sch., 1937-42; librarian Laurinburg-Maxton AFB, 1943, Piedmont Jr. High Sch., 1944, Pope Field AFB, 1945-46, Charlotte (N.C.) Coll., 1957-64; documents and serials librarian U. N.C. at Charlotte, 1965-69, asst. reference librarian, 1969-78, reference librarian, 1979-80. Mem. AAUP. Home: 701 St Julien St Charlotte NC 28205

SCHERICH, ESTHER ANNE, editor; b. New Haven, Dec. 15, 1943; d. Millard and Esther (Petersen) Scherich; B.A., Oreg. State U., 1966; M.A., U. Oreg., 1970, D.Arts, 1973, Ph.D., 1975. Sec. dept. English, U. Oreg., Eugene, 1966-69; research asst., 1969-70, teaching fellow English, 1970-75; manuscript editor Moody Bible Inst., Chgo. Mem. Women in Communications, MLA, Am. Soc. for 18th Century Studies, Am. Bus. Women's Assn., Conf. on Christianity and Lit., Kappa Delta. Episcopalian. Home: 821 N Washington Wheaton IL 60187 Office: Moody Bible Inst 820 N LaSalle St Chicago IL 60610

SCHERLING, BEV, state legislator, real estate agt.; b. Ottumwa, Iowa, May 22, 1930; B.S., Augustana Coll., Rock Island, Ill.; m. Richard Scherling; children—Doug, Pam, Barb. Former tchr., real estate agt.; mem. Colo. Ho. of Reps., vice chmn. house services, mem. judiciary com., edn. com. Adv. bd. Children in Need of Supervision; mem. Child Protection Team for Arapahoe County, Aurora Parks and Recreation Bd., Human Services Council Arapahoe County. Named Women of Yr., Aurora C. of C., 1976. Republican. Presbyterian. Office: Colorado House of Representatives State Capitol Denver CO 80203 *

SCHERM, THERESA ANNE, mktg. exec., consumer products mfr.; lawn and garden equipment; b. Los Angeles, Nov. 27, 1949; d. John Edward and Betty Noreen (Sinette) Tate; student Compton Jr. Coll., 1972-73, Advanced Mgmt. Research, 1980, Mgmt. Action Program, 1982; m. Jack Rogers Scherm, Mar. 25, 1972; 1 son, Michael Jared. Exec. sec. Bateman Eichler, Hill Richards, Woodland Hills, Calif., 1976-77; exec. sec. NMB America, Chatsworth, Calif., 1971-75; mktg. exec. Allegretti & Co., Chatsworth, 1977—. Democrat. Home: 13532 Polk St Sylmar CA 91342 Office: 9200 Mason Ave Chatsworth CA 91311

SCHETLIN, ELEANOR M., univ. adminstr.; b. N.Y.C., July 15, 1920; d. Henry Frank and Elsie (Chew) Schetlin; B.A., Hunter Coll., 1940; M.A., Tchrs. Coll., Columbia, 1942, D.Edn., 1967. Playground dir. Dept. of Parks, N.Y.C., 1940-42; librarian Met. Hosp. Sch. Nursing, N.Y.C., 1943-44, dir. recreation, 1944-48, dir. recreation and guidance, 1948-59; coordinator student activities State U. N.Y., Plattsburgh, 1959-63, asst. dean students, 1963-64; asst. prof., coordinator student personnel services City U. N.Y., Hunter Coll., 1967-68; asst. dir. student personnel Columbia U., Coll. Pharm. Scis., N.Y.C., 1968-69, dir. student personnel, 1969-71; asso. dean for students, health scis. center State U. N.Y. at Stony Brook, 1971-73, asst. v.p. student services, 1973-74, asso. dean for students, dir. student services, 1974—. Mem. So. N.Y. League Nursing (dir. 1954-56, 64-66), Student Nurse Assn. N.Y. State (adviser 1955-59), NEA, Am. Personnel and Guidance Assn., Nat. Assn. Women Deans, Adminstrs. and Counselors, Am. Coll. Personnel Assn. Contbr. articles to profl. jours. Home: 20 Barberry Ln Sea Cliff NY 11579 Office: Health Scis Center State U Stony Brook NY 11794

SCHEUERMANN, MONA, educator; b. N.Y.C., June 6, 1946; d. Philip and Irene Rifkin; B.A., Queens Coll., 1967; M.A., Hunter Coll., 1969; Ph.D., SUNY-Stony Brook, 1974; m. Peter Scheuermann, Dec. 28, 1973. Asst. prof. English, York Coll., 1974-75; asst. prof. J.S. Reynolds Community Coll. 1974-76; asst. prof. Oakton Community Coll., Des Plaines, Ill., 1976-79, assoc. prof. 1979—; vis. prof. U. Utrecht. NDEA fellow. Mem. MLA, Am. Assn. Eighteenth-Century Studies, Keats-Shelley Assn., Wordsworth Soc., Phi Beta Kappa. Author: The Novels of William Godwin, 1980; Contbr. in field. Office: 1600 E Golf Rd Des Plaines IL 60016

SCHEUNEMAN, JANICE DOWD, psychometrician; b. Seattle, Aug. 24, 1940; d. Lionel and Vivian (Jacobson) Dowd; B.S., U. Wash., 1962; M.S., Purdue U., 1965; Ph.D., Ind. U., 1973; children—David Matthew, Joel Eric. Research asst. instructional media research unit Purdue U., Ind., 1963-65; research asst. The Psychol. Corp., N.Y.C., 1965-66; research psychologist Harcourt Brace Jovanovich, 1973-76, sr. research psychologist, 1976-78; statis. asso. Ednl. Testing Service, Princeton, N.J., 1978-79, dir. statis. analysis elem. and secondary sch. programs, 1979—. Mem. Am. Psychol. Assn., Am. Ednl. Research Assn., Nat. Council Measurement in Edn., Northeastern Ednl. Research Assn., Eastern Ednl. Research Assn. Democrat. Unitarian. Contbg. author to books on measurement; contbr. articles to profl. jours. Home: 159 Marlboro Rd Lawrenceville NJ 08648 Office: Ednl Testing Service Princeton NJ 08541

SCHEWE, LOLA M. (LEE), telephone co. ofcl.; b. Mt. Vernon, Ohio, Feb. 4, 1936; d. John Malcolm and Leona Marie (Opre) A'Hearn; student Mt. Vernon Bus. Coll., 1955, Ill. Benedictine Coll., 1980—; m. Howard William Schewe, June 5, 1981; children by a previous marriage —David Lee Taggart, Theresa Lynn Bergandi, Thomas Lew Taggart. Sec., Continental Can Co., Mt. Vernon, 1955-56; dept. mgr. Madigans, Yorktown, Ill., 1968-69; with Bell System Center for Tech. Edn., Lisle, Ill., 1969—, mgr. student adminstrn., 1981—. Sec., Bennington Homeowners Assn., 1982—. Home: 583 Windham Ln Naperville IL 60540 Office: Bell System Center 6200 Route 53 Lisle IL 60532

SCHEXNAYDER, CHARLOTTE TILLAR, editor, pub.; b. Tillar, Ark., Dec. 25, 1923; d. Jewell Stephen and Bertha Elizabeth (Terry) Tillar; B.S., La. State U., 1944, postgrad., 1946-47; student Ark. A&M Coll., 1940-41, U. Chgo., 1942; m. Melvin John Schexnayder, Aug. 18, 1946; children—Melvin John, Sarah, Stephen. Asst. editor La. Agr. Extension, 1944; editor McGehee (Ark.) Times, 1945-46, 48-53; editor, co-pub. Dumas (Ark.) Clarion, 1954—; seminar chmn. Nat. Newspaper Found., 1980. Del., Ark. Democratic Conv., 1972-76; 1st woman appointee Ark. Bd. Pardons and Parole, 1975-80; bd. dirs. Desha County (Ark.) Mus., Jodie Partridge Center, Dumas; bd. dirs. Winthrop Rockefeller Found., 1982—, charter mem. Ark. Humanities Council, 1974; mem. dean's adv. bd. on journalism U. Ark.; past mem. Dumas Library Bd., Meml. Park Commn., Dumas. Recipient. 25-yr. vol. award Easter Seal Soc., 1975; Outstanding Service award Ark. Extension Homemakers Council, 1960; Service award Ark. Rice Council, 1974; Pub. Interest award Nat. Safety Council, 1955-60; George Washington honor medal for column Am. Freedoms Found., 1973; numerous state and nat. press awards; named Outstanding Arkansan, Ark. C. of C., 1971. Mem. Nat. Newspaper Assn. (Emma McKinney award 1980, dir. 1982—), Ark. Press Assn. (1st v.p. 1980, pres. 1981), Nat. Fedn. Press Women (pres. 1977-79, edn. fund dir. 1982), Ark. Press Women (past pres., Woman of Yr. 1969), Women in Communications, Dumas C. of C. (dir. 1980, 1st v.p. 1982), Desha County Mus. Soc. (v.p. 1980), Sigma Delta Chi (1st woman pres. Little Rock profl. chpt. 1973). Roman Catholic. Home: 322 Court St Dumas AR 71639 Office: Box C Dumas AR 71639

SCHICK, CONSTANCE JOYCE, educator; b. Abilene, Tex., Apr. 11, 1939; d. M.F. Wilson; B.B.A. in Accounting, Angelo State U., 1969; Ph.D. in Exptl. Psychology, Tex. Tech U., 1973; m. William Brewster Schick; 1 dau., Jana Kaye Hamrick. Mgr., partner Hamrick Photog. Studio, Graham, Tex., 1958-60; treas. Concho Camera Corp., San Angelo, Tex., 1961-63; research asst., instr. psychology Tex. Tech U., 1971-73; asst. prof. Bloomsburg State Coll., 1973-78, asso. prof., 1978—; mem. coordinating com. for human relations Affirmative Action Commn., 1974—, also com. on human research, 1978—. Mem. Am., Eastern, Rocky Mountain psychol. assns., Soc. Psychol. Study Social Issues, World Future Soc., Alpha Chi, Phi Kappa Phi (pres. 1977-78, treas. 1979-82), Psi Chi. Recipient Acad. Achievement awards Angelo State U., 1968, 69, Tex. Tech U., 1970, 71; contbr. articles on familiarity, social facilitation, risk taking, problem solving and counseling to profl. jours.; research on teaching of problem solving and health psychology. Home: 827 Lightstreet Rd Bloomsburg PA 17815 Office: Dept of Psychology Bloomsburg State Coll Bloomsburg PA 17815

SCHIEMEL, JOAN MARIE, aerospace engr.; b. N.Y.C., June 19, 1936; d. Frank and Florence Marie (MacDowell) S.; A.A., Concordia Collegiate Inst., 1955; B.A., Queens Coll., 1957; postgrad. Columbia U., 1957-58; M.S., L.I. U., 1971; postgrad. Adelphi U., 1973-79. Student social worker Luth. Social Services, N.Y.C., 1957-58; with Fairchild Republic Co. (and predecessor cos.), 1958—, flight test engr., 1958-63, sci. programmer, 1963-65, sr. sci. programmer/analyst, 1965-69, flight dynamics analyst, 1969-78, flight simulation engr., 1978-80, sr. sect. chief digital flight simulation, Farmingdale, N.Y., 1980—. Mem. AIAA (council 1979-81, exec. sec. 1981—). Contbr. articles to profl. jours. Office: Route 110 and Conklin St Farmingdale NY 11735

SCHIER, MARY JANE, newspaper reporter; b. Houston, Mar. 10, 1939; d. James F. and Jerry Mae (Crisp) McDonald; B.S. in Journalism, Tex. Woman's U., 1961; m. John Christian Schier, Aug. 26, 1961; children—John Christian, II, Mark Edward. Reporter, San Antonio Express and News, 1962-64; med. writer Daily Oklahoman, also Oklahoma City Times, 1965-66; reporter, med. writer Houston Post, 1966—. Recipient award Tex. Headliners Club, 1969, Tex. Med. Assn., 1972-74, 76, 78, 79, 80, 82 Tex. Hosp. Assn., 1974, 82, Tex. Public Health Assn., 1976, 77, 78, others. Lutheran. Club: Houston Press (pres. 1974-75). Home: 9742 Tappenbeck St Houston TX 77055 Office: 4747 Southwest Freeway Houston TX 77001

SCHIESS, BETTY BONE, priest; b. Cin., Apr. 2, 1923; d. Evan Paul and Leah (Mitchell) Bone; B.A., U. Cin., 1945; M.A., Syracuse U., 1947; M.Div., Crozer Sem., 1972; m. William A. Schiess, Aug. 28, 1947; children—William A. (dec.), Richard Corwine, Sarah. Ordained priest Episcopal Ch., 1974; priest asso. Grace Episc. Ch., Syracuse, N.Y., 1975; chaplain Syracuse U., 1976-78, Cornell U., Ithaca, N.Y., 1978-79; writer, lectr., cons. religion and feminism, 1979—. Bd. dirs. People for Public TV in N.Y., 1978; trustee Elizabeth Cady Stanton Found., 1979; mem. policy com. Council Adolescent Pregnancy. NOW (pres. Syracuse), Internat. Assn. Women Ministers (dir. 1978), Theta Chi Beta. Democrat. Contbr. article to religious jour. Home: 107 Bradford Ln Syracuse NY 13224

SCHIFF, HELEN D., clothes designer; b. Bklyn., May 17, 1947; d. Harry Bale and Esther Genin; student Fashion Inst. Tech., SUNY, 1964-67, County Coll., Morris, N.J., 1981—; m. Stuart B. Schiff, Oct. 22, 1972. Designer infantswear Playmore Knits, 1971-72, Little Topsy, 1972-73, Catton Bros., 1973-76; dir. design Mayfair Infantswear, N.Y.C. and Tawil Assos., Avenel, N.J., 1976—. Pres. Par-Troy chpt. Cancer Care, Inc., 1980-82, v.p. regional fundraising, N.J., 1979-80, fundraising co-chmn., chpts. coordinating com., 1982-83. Recipient various awards Cancer Care, Inc. Office: Tawil Assocs 1414 Randolph Ave Avenel NJ 07001

SCHIFF, NANCY JUSTER, med. social worker; b. N.Y.C., June 29, 1952; d. Julian J. and Barbara L. (Wallach) Juster; B.A. (teaching fellow 1972-74), Ithaca (N.Y.) Coll., 1974; M.S.W., Washington U., St. Louis, 1976; m. Marshall S. Schiff, May 7, 1978; 1 dau., Ariel Naomi. Social worker Planned Parenthood St. Louis, 1975; med. social worker St. Louis Children's Hosp., 1976-78; social worker family care Bronx (N.Y.) Devel. Center, 1978; med. social worker pediatrics Montefiore Hosp., N.Y.C., 1978—. Mem. Nat. Assn. Social Workers. Democrat. Home: 2727 Palisade Ave Riverdale NY 10463 Office: 111 E 21oth St Bronx NY 10467

SCHILKE, SHIRLEY PLATT, corp. exec.; b. Berlin, Pa., July 23, 1925; d. Frank I. and Matilda H. (Baughman) Platt; student Strayers Bus. Coll., Washington, 1943, High Mus. Sch. Art, Atlanta, 1948; m. Carl Richard Schilke, Dec. 3, 1944; children—Kristie Lee, Wendy Lee, Richard Frank. Civilian sec., fin. officer Ft. Belvoir, Va., 1942-46; with Harcar Aluminum Products Co., Sanford, Fla., 1957—, now treas.; co-owner, v.p. Schilke Enterprises, Inc., Sanford, Fla., 1975-78, pres., 1978—. Past pres. Seminole Meml. Hosp. Aux., Women of First Presbyn. Ch., Sanford; mem. chmn.'s com. U.S. Senatorial Bus. Adv. Bd., 1981, 82; past sec. Seminole County PTA Council, Seminole-DeBary Heart Council. Mem. Home Builders Assn. Mid/Fla., Nat. Home Builders Assn., Sanford C. of C., C. of C. U.S., Nat. Fedn. Ind. Bus., Internat. Platform Assn., Smithsonian Assos., Nat. Soc. Lit. and Arts. Author: (poetry) The Many Facets of Love, 1976. Home: 100 Cove Lake Ct Sweetwater Cove Longwood FL 32750 Office: Silver Lake Dr PO Box 1148 Sanford FL 32771

SCHILLER, ANITA ROSENBAUM, librarian; b. N.Y.C., June 16, 1926; d. Aaron and Helen (Camnitz) Rosenbaum; B.A. in Econs, N.Y. U., 1949; M.L.S., Pratt Inst., 1959; m. Herbert I. Schiller, Nov. 5, 1946; children—Daniel T., P. Zachary. Reference librarian Nat. Indsl. Conf. Bd., 1960-61; instr. U. Ill. Grad. Sch. Bus. Adminstrn., 1961-62; reference librarian Pratt Inst., 1962-63; successively research asst., research asso., research asst. prof. U. Ill. Library Research Center, 1964-70; reference librarian, bibliographer U. Calif., San Diego, 1970—; Ralph R. Shaw vis. scholar Rutgers U., 1978. Fellow, Council Library Resources, 1976-77. Mem. ALA (councillor 1972-76, sec.-treas. library research round table 1978-80, mem. council com. on status of women in librarianship 1980). Contbr. articles to profl. publs.; editor Aware column Am. Libraries, 1971-72; mem. editorial bds. profl. jours. Home: 7109 Monte Vista St La Jolla CA 92037 Office: Central U Library U Calif San Diego La Jolla CA 92093

SCHILLER, ARDITH MARLENE, secretarial/bookkeeping service exec.; b. Jackson, Minn., Oct. 12, 1939; d. Thomas William and Maxine Dorothy Raine; A.A. in Bus. Adminstrn. and Office Occupations, U. Alaska, 1979, A.A.S. in Bus. Adminstrn., 1980; m. Jerome J. Schiller, Oct. 11, 1968; 1 dau., Gretchen Susan. Stenographer, Prudential Ins. Co., Winona, Minn., 1957-57, First Nat. Bank, Winona, 1959; sec., stenographer Monarch Marking System Co., Garden Grove, Calif., 1960-62; exec. sec. Acoustica Assos., Inc., Los Angeles, 1962-65; adminstrv. sec. Fgn. Services, Dept. State, Washington, 1965-67; sec., office mgr. U.S. Army Europe Hdqrs. Polit. Adv.'s Office, Dept. Army, Heidelberg, W.Ger., 1967-68, Hamilton Bros. Oil Co., Anchorage, 1969-70; owner, mgr. Bus. Cache, Anchorage, 1971—; dir., sec. C.C. Hawley and Assos., Inc., 1974-81. Cert. profl. sec. Mem. Nat. Assn. Female Exec., Am. Entrepreneurs Assn. Catholic. Research on mgmt. techniques for small bus. Home: Star Route A Box 79B Anchorage AK 99507 Office: 8536 Hartzell Rd Anchorage AK 99507

SCHILLER, BEATRICE B., artist; b. Chgo.; d. Julius J. and Alice S. (Schlosser) Brody; student Inst. of Design, Chgo., 1946-47, Art Inst. Chgo., 1962; m. Maurice A. Schiller, Feb. 27, 1938; 1 son, James D. One-woman exhbns. include: Commonwealth Art Center and Gallery, Chgo., 1965, Chgo. Public Library, 1967, 77, Covenant Club of Chgo., 1971, Garland Bldg. Gallery, Chgo., 1978; group exhbns. include: Union League Club Art Show, Chgo., 1965, 67, 72, Butler Inst. of Am. Art, Youngstown, Ohio, 1967, Art Inst. Chgo., 1967, Catherine Lorillard Wolfe Art Club, Nat. Acad. of Design, N.Y.C., 1971, Municipal Art League of Chgo., 1972, 73, 76, 79, Renaissance Soc., U. Chgo., 1979, Artists Guild of Chgo., 1977, 80, 81, others; represented in permanent collections: Standard Oil Co., Chgo., Michael Reese Hosp., Chgo., Excello, Ltd., Chgo., Zarco Industries, Inc., Chgo., Excel Packing Co., Wichita, Kans.; pvt. collections: Palm Springs, Fla., N.Y.C., Wichita, others. Mem. Chgo. Soc. Artists (dir.), Municipal Art League Chgo., North Shore Art League, Arts Club of Chgo. (profl. mem.). Jewish. Address: 3150 N Lake Shore Dr 14F Chicago IL 60657

SCHILLER, MARY ROSITA, dietitian; b. Mich., June 14, 1936; d. Edmund Martin and Julia Catherine (Greiner) S.; B.S., Mercy Coll., Detroit, 1959; M.S., Mich. State U., 1966; Ph.D. (Hattie Margaret Anthony fellow, Mich. Home Econs. Assn. scholar, Mary Swartz Rose fellow, Hazel Williams Lapp fellow, provisional univ. dissertation yr. fellow), Ohio State U., Columbus, 1972. Joined Sisters of Mercy, Roman Cath. Ch., 1952; dietetic intern Henry Ford Hosp., Detroit, 1959-60; hosp. dietitian Mercy Community Hosp., Manistee, Mich., 1960-62; adminstrv. dietitian St. Lawrence Hosp., Lansing, Mich., 1962-66; from instr. to asso. prof. Mercy Coll., 1966-78, program dir. dietetics, 1972-78; asso. prof. dietetics, dir. med. dietetics div. Ohio State U., Columbus, 1978—; pres. Detroit Dietetic Assn., 1969-70; chmn. nutrition com. Mich. Heart Assn., 1975-76; mem. task force dietetic edn. VA, 1975-77. Mem. Am. Dietetic Assn. (chmn. commn. accreditation 1978-79, program chmn. region IV council edn. 1975-76, editorial reviewer jour. 1975—; Mary Zahasky Meml. scholar 1977), Nutrition Today Soc., Am. Soc. Allied Health Professions, Soc. Nutrition Edn., Am. Soc. Health Manpower Edn. and Tng., Ohio Dietetic Assn. (chmn. 1980-81), Ohio Home Econs. Assn., Columbus Dietetics Assn. Author articles in field. Office: 1583 Perry St Columbus OH 43210

SCHILLING, DEANNA EVANS, psychologist, educator; b. Anacortes, Wash., July 1, 1943; d. Roy Alfred and Lois Meryl (Porter) Evans; B.A., U. Md., 1967; M.A., U. Calif., Davis, 1976, Ph.D., 1977; m. Lee Howard, Sept. 22, 1962. Office mgr. Clara T. Landay Ins. Co., Balt., 1965-67; elem. tchr. Balt., 1964-65, Stockton, Calif., 1967-68, Sanger, Calif., 1968-69; tchr. Fresno (Calif.) Unified Sch. Dist., 1970-74; mem. faculty Calif. State U., Fresno, 1976—, asso. prof. dept. edn., 1977—. Mem. Am. Ednl. Research Assn., Am. Psychol. Assn., Nat. Assn. for Edn. Young Children, Calif. Assn. for Neurologically Handicapped Children, Calif. Profs. Early Childhood Edn., Kappa Delta Pi. Producer, writer, dir. TV series Just for You, 1978—. Home: 440 E Acacia Dr Fresno CA 93704 Office: Calif State U Sch Edn Fresno CA 93740

SCHILLING, KATHERINE LEE TRACY, educator; b. Mitchell, S.D., May 31, 1925; d. Ernest Benjamin and Mary Alice (Courier) Tracy; B.A., Dakota Wesleyan U., 1947; M.A., U. S.D., 1957; postgrad. U. Wyo., U. Nebr., Kearney State Coll.; m. Clarence R. Schilling, Oct. 14, 1951; 1 dau., Keigh Leigh. Tchr. elementary and secondary schs., also colls., S.D. and Nebr.; now with specially funded project for disadvantaged children Winnebago Indian reservation, Nebr. Mem. staff S.D. Girls' State, 1950-51; mem. S.D. Gov.'s Com. on Library, Nebr. Gov.'s Com. on Right to Read. Recipient Outstanding Tchr. award S.D. High Sch. Speech Tchrs., 1966. Mem. NEA, Nebr., Thurston County (pres.) edn. assns., Winnebago Tchrs. Assn., Delta Kappa Gamma. Mem. Order Eastern Star. Club: Internat. Toastmistress (internat. dir. 1963-65, Mitchell Toastmistress of Year 1959). Contbr. articles to profl. jours., also poetry. Home: 39 S Harmon Dr Box 578 Mitchell SD 57301 Office: Winnebago Public Sch or Nebraska Indian Community Coll Winnebago NE 68071

SCHILLINGER, ELISABETH HUPP, editor, author, graphic designer; b. Springfield, Ill., Mar. 28, 1943; d. Walter Wayne and Joyce Dayle (Hartwig) Hupp; B.S. in Journalism, U. Ill., 1965; m. John A. Schillinger, Aug. 28, 1965; children—Liesl Katharine, Justin Hupp, Nathaniel Hartwig. Tech. editor U. Ill. Coll. Engring., 1965-67; writer, editor U. Wis. Office Publs., 1967-70; asst. dir. info. Saginaw (Mich.) Valley State Coll., 1970-73; tech. writing, design cons., 1973-75; engring. editor Purdue U. Schs. Engring., 1975-82; adminstrv. asso. Okla. State U. Sch. Indsl. Engring. and Mgmt., 1982—. Co-author: Men and Ideas in Engineering, 1967. Contbr. articles to profl. publns. Home: 2015 N Husband St Stillwater OK 74074 Office: 301 Engring N Okla State U Stillwater OK 74078

SCHILZ, MARGARET EILEEN HUNT, writer; b. Apple Valley, Calif., Dec. 16, 1917; d. Foy Francis and Minerva Ellen (Smyser) Hunt; student Southwestern U., 1937; m. Herbert John Schilz, Feb. 19, 1938; children—Margaret Cecilia, Allan John. Writer, Sunday Driver column Herald Am., Compton, Calif., 1954, On Location Hollywood column San Gabriel Valley Free Press, Alhambra, Calif., 1964-69; contbg. editor Club and Sports Mag., 1968-72; TV writer Madison Prodns., Hollywood, Calif., 1968; TV editor Writers' Guide, 1968, Calif. Writers Mag., 1969; cartoonist San Gabriel Valley Free Press, 1969; motion picture reviewer Aquarian Times, 1970; lectr. on TV writing; one woman shows of sculpture. Recipient Ten Top medal Calif. Fedn. Mineral. Socs., 1977; Thomas Alva Edison medal, 1978. Mem. Nat. League Am. Pen Women (br. pres. 1976-78), Writers Guild Am., San Gabriel Valley Lapidary Soc. (pres. 1983), San Gabriel Fine Arts Assn., Las Artistas. Congregationalist. Contbr. articles in field of instructional TV to profl. jours., hist. pieces to regional mags. Address: 604 N Almansor St Alhambra CA 91801

SCHIMMEL, NANCY ROTH, social worker; b. Denver, Nov. 1, 1951; d. Leo and Joan Mildred (Taylor) Roth; B.A., U. Denver, 1973, M.S.W., 1976; m. Ronald G. Schimmel, Mar. 8, 1980. Nursing asst. adolescent treatment program Mt. Airy Psychiat. Center, Denver, 1974-76, psychiat. social worker, 1976-80, sr. psychiat. worker, 1980-82, worker, dir. social work services, 1982—; field instr. Denver U. Lic. social worker II, Colo. Mem. Acad. Cert. Social Workers, Nat. Assn. Social Workers, Colo. Soc. Clin. Social Workers, Am. Orthopsychiat. Assn., Pi Gamma Mu. Office: 4455 E 12th Ave Denver CO 80220

SCHIRA, NORMA JEAN MCNABB, educator; b. Youngstown, Ohio, Jan. 12, 1930; d. Dennis Manis and Gean (Duncan) McNabb; diploma, Youngstown Hosp. Assn. Sch. Nursing, 1951; B.S., Youngstown State U., 1955; M.Ed., Kent State U., 1967; Ed.D., U. Ill., 1973; postgrad. Western Ky. U. Grad. Sch., 1981-82; m. Leonard T. Schira, Aug. 30, 1955. Staff nurse Youngstown (Ohio) Hosp. Assn., 1951-55; instr. Choffin Sch. Practical Nursing, Youngstown, Ohio, 1955-62; coordinator, dir. Akron (Ohio) Sch. Practical Nursing, 1962-70; asso. prof. health, safety and occupational edn. Western Ky. U., Bowling Green, 1973—; research asst. U. Ill., 1971-72; curriculum cons. Recipient Edn. Professions Devel. Act fellow, 1970-73. Mem. Am. Vocat. Assn., Assn. Health Occupations Tchrs. Educators, Ky. Vocat. Assn., Council Vocat. Educators, AAHPER, Ky. Sch. Health Assn., Health Occupations Students Am. Home: 2618 Utah Dr Bowling Green KY 42101 Office: Dept Health and Safety Sci and Tech Hall Western Ky U Bowling Green KY 42101

SCHITTONE, MARILYN THERESE, physician; b. N.Y.C., Jan. 19, 1920; d. Vincent Enrico and Clara Helen (von Schmidt) Schittone; M.D., N.Y. U., 1943; m. Thomas D. Reale, Nov. 25, 1942; Intern, Bellevue Hosp., N.Y.C., 1943-44, resident, 1944-45; fellow in hematology New Eng. Med. Center, 1945, 47; practice medicine specializing in internal medicine and hematology, N.Y.C., 1947-69, specializing in hematology and oncology, Setauket, N.Y., 1968—; chief of lab. service Hosp. for Spl. Surgery, N.Y.C., 1950-60, cons. in hematology, 1950-60; chief lab. service, chief hematology sect. Manhattan (N.Y.) VA Hosp., 1961-69; hematologist and oncologist Northport (N.Y.) VA Hosp., 1969-75, chief of Tumor Clinic, 1974—; chief sect. oncology Mather Meml. Hosp., Port Jefferson, N.Y., 1975—; asso. prof. clin. medicine State U. N.Y., Stony Brook, 1973—. Bd. dirs. N.Y. U. Sch. of Medicine, 1963-75. Diplomate Am. Bd. Internal Medicine. Fellow Internat. Am. socs. of hematology;

mem. Women's Am. Med. Assn., AMA, Nat. Acad. Scis., L.I. Cancer Council (v.p. 1977-78), Am. Cancer Soc. (exec. dir. L.I. div. 1975—). Roman Catholic. Home: 2 Split Rail Ln Setauket NY 11733 Office: 4 Split Rail Ln Setauket NY 11733

SCHLAFLY, PHYLLIS STEWART, author, lawyer; b. St. Louis, Aug. 15, 1924; d. John Bruce and Odile (Dodge) Stewart; B.A., Washington U., St. Louis, 1944, J.D., 1978; M.A., Radcliffe Coll., 1945; LL.D., Niagara U., 1976; m. Fred Schlafly, Oct. 20, 1949; children—John F., Bruce S., Roger S., Liza S. Forshaw, Andrew L., Anne V. Admitted to Ill. bar, 1979; author, pub. Phyllis Schlafly Report, 1967—; broadcaster Spectrum, CBS Radio Network, 1973-78; commentator Matters of Opinion Sta. WBBM, Chgo., 1973-76; syndicated columnist Copley News Service, 1976— ; TV commentator Cable News Network, 1980—. Del. Republican Nat. Conv., 1956, 64, 68, alt., 1960, 80; pres. Ill. Fedn. Rep. Women, 1960-64; 1st v.p. Nat. Fedn. Rep. Women, 1964-67; mem. Ill. Commn. on Status of Women, 1975—; nat. chmn. Stop ERA, 1972—; pres. Eagle Forum, 1975—; mem. Pres. Reagan's Def. Policy Adv. Group, 1980. Recipient 10 Honor medals Freedoms Found.; Brotherhood award Nat. Conf. Christians and Jews, 1975; named Woman of Achievement in Public Affairs, St. Louis Globe-Democrat. 1963; named most influential woman in U.S. in social action World Almanac, 1982. Mem. Am., Ill. bar assns., DAR (nat. chmn. Am. history 1965-68, nat. chmn. bicentennial com. 1967-70, nat. chmn. nat. def. com. 1977-80), Phi Beta Kappa, Pi Sigma Alpha. Author: A Choice Not an Echo, 1964; The Gravediggers, 1964; Strike From Space, 1965; Safe Not Sorry, 1967; The Betrayers, 1968; Mindszenty The Man, 1972; Kissinger on the Couch, 1975, Ambush at Vladivostok, 1976; The Power of the Positive Woman, 1977. Address: 68 Fairmount Alton IL 62002

SCHLAMME, MARTHA, singer, actress; b. Vienna, Austria; d. Meier and Gisa Haftel; ed. Vienna public schs.; studied piano with Ferdinand Rauter, voice with Emmy Heim, Olga Ryss, Marinka Gurewich, Hans Heinz, drama with Ludwig Donath; m. Hans Schlamme (div.), Mark Lane (div.). Performer internat. repertoire of folk songs, 1948—; appearances include: Player's Theater, London, BBC Radio, N.Y. Town Hall and Kaufmann Auditorium, Hancock Hall, Boston, Wilshire-Ebell Theater, Los Angeles; nightclub appearances include: Village Gate, N.Y.C., Gate of Horn, Chgo., Ash Grove, Hollywood, Howff, Edinburgh; appeared R.I. folk festivals, benefit concerts for USO, NAACP; stage appearances include: The World of Kurt Weill in Song, N.Y.C., 1963, 80, A Month of Sundays, N.Y.C., 1968, Long Wharf Theater, New Haven, 1969-70, 71-72, Pitts. Playhouse, 1971-72, Solitaire/Double Solitaire, N.Y.C., 1971, Kurt Weill Cabaret, 1979; one woman show off-Broadway A Woman Without a Man Is..., 1978; dir. Threepenny Opera, Aspen, Colo., 1980, Stephen Sondheim Rev., 1981, 2 operas San Francisco Opera, 1982; tchr. musical theater class MB Studio, 1973-75; tchr. acting for opera singers Mannes Coll., Aspen Music Festival, 1977-78; recs. include: Folk Songs of Many Lands, Jewish Folk Songs, Martha Schlamme Sings Israeli Folk Songs, Chansons de Noel, (with Pete Seeger) German Folk Songs, The World of Kurt Weill in Song. Address: care Arthur Shafman Internat Ltd 1560 Broadway New York NY 10036 *

SCHLAUD, MARGARET SUE SCHULTZ, dental asst.; b. Lapeer, Mich., Jan. 27, 1960; d. Bruce Earl and Dorothy Marcella (Mantus) Schultz; diploma Lapeer County Vocat.-Tech. Sch.; student C.S. Mott Coll.; m. Patrick William Schlaud, Mar. 28, 1980. Dental asst., Lapeer, 1978—.

SCHLEIF, RUTH MARIE, educator; b. Superior, Nebr., Dec. 20, 1920; d. Edward August and Mathilda Louise (Brennfoerder) S.; B.A., Kearney State Coll., 1958; M.A. in Edn., U. Nebr., 1967. Tchr., Nuckolls County (Nebr.) Schs., 1941-45, public schs., Hardy, Nebr., 1945-46, Ruskin, Nebr., 1946-47, Gresham, Nebr., 1947-52, Beatrice, Nebr., 1952—; tchr. history Beatrice Jr. High Sch., 1960—. Co-chmn. Beatrice Bicentennial Com., 1974-76. Mem. Beatrice Bus. and Profl. Women (pres. 1961-63, 77-79, mem. state bd.), NEA, Nebr. State Edn. Assn., Beatrice Edn. Assn. (pres. 1965-66, 82-83), AAUW (pres. 1974-78, 80-82, mem. state bd.), Nebr. Council Social Studies, Nebr. State Hist. Soc., Gage County Hist. Soc. (historian), Nebr. Coll. Alumni Assn., U. Nebr. Alumni Assn., Alpha Delta Kappa (past pres. chpt.). Republican. Lutheran. Home: 415 N 6th Beatrice NE 68310 Office: 510 Elk Beatrice NE 68310

SCHLEIFER, ALISON PEDICORD, ednl. cons.; b. Norristown, Pa., Nov. 6, 1942; d. Harry William and Adah (Alison) Pedicord; A.B., Mt. Holyoke Coll., 1964; certs. U. Paris, 1962, 63; M.S., So. Conn. State Coll., 1975; m. James Thomas Schleifer, Aug. 15, 1964; children—Katharine Alison, Margaret Elizabeth. Tchr., Amity Regional Sch. Dist., Woodbridge, Conn., 1964-71, dept. chmn. fgn. langs., 1968-71, tchr. French, part-time, 1976-77; ednl. cons., New Haven, 1976—. Bd. dirs. YWCA, 1971-76, v.p. bd. dirs., 1976; bd. dirs., pres. Downtown Comparative Ministry, 1973-75, v.p., 1976-82; del. gen. synod United Ch. of Christ, 1975, 77. Mem. Ind. Ednl. Counselors Assn. (dir.), New Eng. Assn. Schs. and Colls., New Eng. Assn. Coll. Admissions Counselors, Nat. Assn. Ind. Schs. Mem. United Ch. of Christ. Club: Mt. Holyoke. Contbr. articles to profl. jours. Address: 220 Alston Ave New Haven CT 06515

SCHLEIMER, SHIRLEY BRASSAW, acct.; b. Saginaw, Mich., Sept. 2, 1926; d. Guy Edward and Helen (Siller) Brassaw; student Walton Sch. Commerce, 1947-51; m. Edward C. Schleimer, Dec. 22, 1951 (dec. 1975); 1 dau., Jane Elizabeth. Pvt. practice acctg. Shirley B. Schleimer, C.P.A., Saginaw, 1954-75; partner Rehmann, Robson, Osburn & Co., Saginaw, 1976—. Treas., Saginaw YWCA, 1980-82, Salvation Army, 1981—. C.P.A., Mich. Mem. Am. Inst. C.P.A.s, Am. Women's Soc. C.P.A.s (Nat. Public Service award 1980), Am. Soc. Women Accts. (chpt. pres. 1952-54, 76-78), Mich. Soc. C.P.A.s. Lutheran. Club: Zonta (state treas. 1980-82, internat. treas. 1982—, Saginaw Woman of Yr. 1982). Office: PO Box 2025 Saginaw MI 48605

SCHLEIN, MIRIAM, author; b. N.Y.C.; d. William and Sophie (Bigleisen) S.; B.A. in Psychology, Bklyn. Coll., 1947; children—Elizabeth Weiss, John Weiss. Author over 60 books for children, natural sci. books, concept books, story books, picture books, including: Shapes, 1952, It's About Time, 1955, The Way Mothers Are, 1963, I, Tut: The Boy Who Became Pharaoh, 1978, Antarctica, the Great White Continent, 1980; author adult fiction and non-fiction in publs. including Redbook, McCall's, Ladies Home Jour., Good Housekeeping, Colorado Quar.; included in anthologies; transl. into Danish, Swedish, Italian, French, Dutch, Norwegian, German, Braille. Awards include: Outstanding Sci. Trade Book for Children, Nat. Sci. Tchrs. Assn./Children's Book Council Joint Com. for: Giraffe: The Silent Giant, 1976, Snake Fights, Rabbit Fights, and More, 1979, Lucky Porcupine, 1980; Virginia Kirkus 100 Best Books and Westchester Library Best Children's Books 1974-75 for What's Wrong with Being a Skunk?, 1974; Children's Book Showcase Title/Children's Book Council for Giraffe: The Silent Giant, 1976; Jr. Lit. Guild selections for: The Four Little Foxes, 1952, Elephant Herd, 1954, City Boy, Country Boy, 1955, The Big Cheese, 1957, The Pile of Junk, 1962; Herald Tribune Honor Book award for Elephant Herd, 1954; Boys' Clubs Am. Jr. Book Award for Fast Is Not a Ladybug, 1953; Children's Books of Yr. award Child Study Assn. for Giraffe, The Silent Giant, 1976. Mem. Authors Guild, PEN Am. Center, Forum of Writers for Young People (pres. 1975-76). Author filmstrip materials Guidance Assocs. Home and Office: 19 E 95th St New York NY 10028

SCHLENOFF, MARJORIE LITWIN, psychotherapist; b. Atlantic City, Feb. 27, 1948; d. Theodore S. and Julia T. Litwin; B.A. in Psychology summa cum laude, U. Md., 1969; M.S.W., Columbia U., 1973; m. Larry B. Schlenoff, June 8, 1969; children—Lauren, Jessica. Psychiat. social worker No. Westchester Guidance Center, Mt. Kisco, N.Y., 1973-75; supervising social worker Rockland County Mental Health Clinic, Pomona, N.Y., 1973-77; co-founder Family Service Group of Putnam Community Center, Carmel, N.Y., 1977-78; clin. intern, sexual treatment and edn., dept. psychiatry Cornell U. Med. Center, N.Y.C., 1978-79; faculty mem., field work coordinator Inst. Counseling and Therapy, Found. Religion and Mental Health, Briarcliff Manor, N.Y., 1979—; pvt. practice psychoanalytic psychotherapy and treatment of sexual dysfunctions, 1974—; cons. N.E. Counseling Center; adj. clin. instr. Wurzweiler Sch. Social Work, Sch. Social Work Hunter Coll.; psychoanlytic candidate Westchester Center Study of Psychoanalysis and Psychotherapy, 1980—; developer, host weekly program Let's Talk about Sex, Sta. WVIP, 1982—. Mem. Soc. Clin. Social Work Psychotherapist, Psychoanalytic Assn. of Westchester Center for Psychoanalysis and Psychotherapy, Sex Info. and Edn. Council U.S., Phi Beta Kappa, Alpha Epsilon Phi (outstanding nat. mem. 1969). Democrat. Jewish. Contbr. article to profl. jour. Home: Jean Way Somers NY 10589 Office: 16 Dakin Ave Mount Kisco NY 10549

SCHLESINGER, SUZANNE ROSE, rehab. counselor, cons.; b. Trani, Italy, Jan. 16, 1948; came to U.S., 1960; d. Morris and Rachel (Lederman) Zeif; B.A. in Psychology, Queens Coll., 1971; M.A. in Rehab. Counseling, N.Y.U., 1976. Rehab. counselor VA Hosp., N.Y.C., 1976, City U. N.Y., 1977-78, South Beach Psychiat. Center, Bklyn., 1978-79; mgmt. analyst County of Westchester, White Plains, N.Y., 1979—; vocat. counselor, job devel. coordinator, project dir. Westchester Office for Aging, Office of County Exec., White Plains, 1980—; dir. Inst. for Personal and Profl. Devel., Rockland County, N.Y., 1981—; mem. services and rehab. com. Westchester div. Am. Cancer Soc.; numerous guest appearances on Sta. WFAS, Sta. WWYD-FM, Westchester, 1980-82. Mem. Am. Psychol. Assn., Nat. Rehab. Assn. (exec. com. Westchester-Rockland div.), Nat. Rehab. Counselors Assn. Office: 148 Martine Ave White Plains NY 10601

SCHLESS, PHYLLIS ROSS, packaging co. exec.; b. N.Y.C., Apr. 16, 1943; d. Lewis H. and Doris G. Ross; B.A., Wellesley Coll., 1964; M.B.A., Stanford U., 1966; m. Aaron B. Schless, July 7, 1970; 1 son, Daniel Lewis Ross. Asso. internat. finance Kuhn Loeb & Co., N.Y.C., 1966-70; mgmt. cons., 1971-73; sr. fin. analyst Trans World Airlines, N.Y.C., 1974-75; asso. corporate fin. Lazard Freres & Co., N.Y.C., 1976-79; dir. mergers and acquisitions Am. Can Co., Greenwich, Conn., 1979—; dir. E.M. Chase Co., Manchester, N.Y., 1960-65, L & D Ross, Inc., 1965-72; registered rep. N.Y. Stock Exchange and Nat. Assn. Securities Dealers, 1968-75. Mem. nat. fin. com. Girls Clubs Am., 1978-80, bd. dirs., 1979—; bd. dirs. Pauline Koner Dance Consort, 1979-81; bd. dirs. New Canaan (Conn.) United Way, 1981—, Child Guidance Clinic Greater Stanford (Conn.), 1981—, Nat. Child Labor Com., 1981—; pres. Greater Bridgeport sect., Nat. Council Jewish Women, 1973-74, bd. dirs., 1974-75; fin. adv. Children's Theatre, N.Y.C. Parks Dept., 1969. Recipient certs. Neighborhood Playhouse Sch. Theatre, N.Y.C., 1962, N.Y. Sch. Interior Design, 1964, corp. Bravo award, 1980. Mem. Fin. Women's Assn., Common Cause (mem. Conn. state fin. com. 1973-75), ACLU, Audubon Soc., Fortune Soc., Womens Econ. Roundtable. Clubs: Wellesley of N.Y., Grolier (N.Y.C.). Home: 214 Sunset Hill Rd New Canaan CT 06840 Office: Am Can Co Am Ln Greenwich CT 06830

SCHLICHTING, CATHERINE FLETCHER NICHOLSON, librarian; b. Huntsville, Ala., Nov. 18, 1923; d. William Parsons and Ethel Louise (Breitling) Nicholson; B.S., U. Ala., 1944; M.L.S., U. Chgo., 1950; m. Harry Fredrick Schlichting, July 1, 1950 (dec. Aug. 1964); children—James Dean, Richard Dale, Barbara Lynn. Asst. librarian U. Ala. Edn. Library, Tuscaloosa, summers 1944-45; librarian Sylacauga (Ala.) High Sch., 1944-45, Hinsdale (Ill.) High Sch., 1945-49; asst. librarian Centre for Childrens Books, U. Chgo., 1950-52; instr. reference dept. library Ohio Wesleyan U., Delaware, 1965-69, asst. prof., 1969-79, asso. prof., 1979—, student personnel librarian, 1966-72, adviser Mortar Bd., 1969-72, mem. exec. com., 1973-79, sec. com., 1973-74, 76-77. Mem. adminstrv. bd. Methodist Ch., 1963-81, mem. Council on Ministries, 1975-81, chmn., 1975-77. Recipient Algernon Sidney Sullivan award U. Ala., 1944. Ohio Wesleyan U.-Mellon Found. grantee, 1972-73; GLCA Teaching fellow, 1976-77. Mem. ALA, Ohio Library Assn., Midwest Acad. Librarian Conf., AAUP (chpt. sec. 1967-68, chpt. exec. com. 1973-78), Kappa Delta Pi, Alpha Lambda Delta. Democrat. Clubs: Ohio Wesleyan U. Womans (exec. bd. 1969-72, 77-79, 81—, pres. 1969-70, sec. 1977-78), History (pres. 1971-72, v.p. 1978-79), Fortnightly (pres. 1975-76), Am. Field Service (pres. Delaware chpt. 1975-76) (Delaware). Author: Introduction to Bibliographic Research: Basic Sources, 2d edit., 1978; Checklist of Biographical Reference Sources, 1977; Audio-Visual Aids in Bibliographic Instruction, 1976; Introduction to Bibliographic Research: Slide Catalog and Script, 1980; also articles. Home: 414 N Liberty St Delaware OH 43015 Office: LA Beeghly Library Ohio Wesleyan U Delaware OH 43015

SCHLIPF, CAROLYN BARBARA, temporary service exec.; b. Newport News, Va., Aug. 14, 1947; d. Harold Anton and Estelle Catherine (Brazaitis) S.; B.A. in History, St. Mary's Coll., U. Notre Dame, 1969. Travel planner Travel Wholesalers, Internat., Washington, 1969-71; sales supr. AAA World Wide Travel, Falls Church, Va., 1971-74; gasoline delivery supr. Exxon Co. U.S.A., Newington, Va., 1974-77; v.p., mgr. Temporaries Inc. of Va., McLean, 1977-80, owner, pres., 1980—; pres. bd. dirs. Temporaries Fed. Credit Union. Mem. Pvt. Industry Council of No. Va. Recipient Silver Spur award Temporaries, Inc., 1978. Mem. Nat. Assn. Temporary Services, Fairfax County C. of C. Office: 7900 Westpark Dr McLean VA 22102

SCHLITT, ANNELIES JEANNE, software engr.; b. New Rochelle, N.Y., May 27, 1943; d. Matthew Marcellus and Aukje Hillegonde (Hoogeveen) Dorenbosch; B.S., Columbia U., 1967; m. Gerd Herbert Schlitt, Feb. 27, 1974; 1 son, Alexander Paul. Systems programmer Ciba-Geigy Corp., Ardsley, N.Y., 1968-70, Basel, Switzerland, 1970-71, Wehr, W. Ger., 1971-73; self-employed systems cons., Wehr, 1973-78; software engr. Intel Corp., Santa Clara, Calif., 1979—. Home: 10914 Dryden Ave Cupertino CA 95014 Office: 3065 Bowers Ave Santa Clara CA 95051

SCHLOETEL, CAROLYN STRONG, electronics co. mgr.; b. Pasadena, Calif., Jan. 9, 1951; d. Albert Charles and Juliana (Ray) Strong; B.A. in Math., Whitworth Coll., 1973; postgrad. DeVry Inst. Tech., 1975-77. Math. and aerospace demonstrator Pacific Sci. Center, Seattle, 1970, 71; component info. specialist Tektronix, Inc., Beaverton, Oreg., 1973-75, tech. writer, 1975-76, tech. publs. group mgr., 1976-79, tech. communications mgr., 1979—; cons. Portland Community Coll., Chemeketa Community Coll. Mem. Soc. Tech. Communications (sec. Willamette Valley chpt. 1978, treas. 1979, pres. 1979-80). Home: 1325 NW 92d St Portland OR 97229 Office: PO Box 500 Beaverton OR 97077

SCHLOFF, KAY DAVID, lawyer; b. Wyandotte, Mich., Mar. 18, 1937; d. Harold Charles and Agatha Florence (David) S.; Ph.B. cum laude, U. Detroit, 1959, J.D. magna cum laude, 1962. Admitted to Mich. bar, 1963; mem. firm Raymond, Chirco, Fletcher & Donaldson, Detroit, 1962-64; law clk. U.S. Dist. Judge Talbot Smith, 1965-71; dep. fed. defender Fed. Defender Office, Detroit, 1972-74, dir. legal tng., dir. Criminal Justice Inst., 1974-76, supr. asst. corp. counsel, 1977—; mem. Mich. Bd. Law Examiners, 1974-79. Mem. Mich. Bar Assn., Detroit Bar Assn., Women Lawyers Assn., Pub. Corp. Law Council, Mich. Assn. of Professions (dir. 1979-81). Democrat. Roman Catholic. Home: 9000 E Jefferson St Apt 21-14 Detroit MI 48214 Office: City of Detroit Law Dept 1010 City County Bldg Detroit MI 48226

SCHLOSNAGLE, CAROL ANN, public relations exec.; b. Carlisle, Pa., Dec. 23, 1950; d. Eugene Stanley and Ethel Mae (Smeltzer) S.; B.A. in English Lit., Hood Coll., 1972. Photojournalist, feature writer Carlisle Evening Sentinel, Carlisle, 1968-71, Frederick (Md.) News-Post, 1971-72; v.p. public relations Cole & Weber, Inc., Seattle, 1974-82; v.p. communications Group Health Coop., Seattle, 1982—; speaker at career workshops for coll. students. Public relations vol. Jr. Achievement, Seattle, Spl. Olympics State Wash.; publicity dir., fund raiser Am. Expdn. to K2, Pakistan, 1978. Mem. Bus. Vols. for Arts, Seattle Advt. Fedn., Public Relations Soc. Am. (Wash. State chpt. award of Merit, 1978), Am. Hosp. Assn. Republican. Presbyterian. Clubs: Washington Athletic, Seattle Press. Publicity and travel writer and photographer for consumer and trade mags., newspapers. Home: 612 Prospect St Seattle WA 98109 Office: 300 Elliott Ave West Seattle WA 98119

SCHLOSS, JO ANN BOCK, banker; b. Denver, Aug. 9, 1932; d. Samuel and Rose Bock; B.A. in Communications, U. Colo., 1972, M.A. in Orgnl. Behavior and Communications (grad. fellow 1975), 1975; m. Charles M. Schloss, Jr., Dec. 19, 1948; children—Charles M., III, Sindi Jo, Kristy Anne. Mem. staff, community relations cons. Denver Commn. Community Relations, 1972-75, project dir. commn. youth, 1973-75; with Central Bank of Denver, 1976—, v.p. staff relations and devel., 1979-81, v.p. human resources planning and devel., 1981—; dir. Schloss & Shubart, Inc. Bd. dirs. U. Colo. Alumni and Friends, 1979-80, Center for Women and Work, 1980-81. Mem. Nat. Assn. Bank Women, Am. Soc. Tng. and Devel., Internat. Assn. Bus. Communicators, Human Resources Planning Soc., Internat. Assn. Quality Circles, Am. Soc. Personnel Adminstrs., NOW, Leadership Denver, Women's Forum Colo., Phi Beta Kappa. Home: 801 E Radcliffe St Englewood CO 80110 Office: 1515 Arapahoe St PO Box 5548 TA Denver CO 80292

SCHLOSSER, ANNE GRIFFIN, librarian; b. N.Y.C., Dec. 28, 1939; d. Charles Russell and Gertrude (Taylor) Griffin; Completion Cert., U. Edinburgh, 1961; B.A., Wheaton Coll., 1962; M.L.S., Simmons Coll., 1963; m. Gary Joseph Schlosser, Dec. 28, 1965. Head Theater Arts Library, UCLA, 1964-69; dir. Louis B. Mayer Library, librarian Charles K. Feldman Library, Am. Film Inst., Los Angeles, 1969—, dir. film-TV documentation workshop, 1977—. Mem. Soc. Am. Archivists, Soc. Calif. Archivists, Theater Library Assn. Democrat. Episcopalian. Club: Windjammers Yacht. Project dir. Motion Pictures, Television, and Radio: A Union Catalogue of Manuscript and Special Collections in the Western United States, 1977. Home: 8777 Skyline Dr Los Angeles CA 90046 Office: 2021 N Western Ave Los Angeles CA 90027

SCHLOSSER, THEA SUSSANNE, retail exec.; b. Hasenfeld, Ger., June 1, 1937; d. Theodor and Anna (Poppe) Hermesmeyer; ed. in home econs., Austria; m. Karl Schlosser, June 9, 1956; children—Ingrid, Evelyn. Owner, operator Santa Barbara (Calif.) Camera. Mem. Republican Nat. Com. Mem. Photog. Soc. Am., Western Photog. Collectors Assn., N.Y. Inst. Photography, Internat. Sr. Olympics Assn., Santa Barbara C. of C., Profl. Photo Mktg. Assn. Inventor game show Challenge Your I Qu. Home: 327 Cinderella Ln Santa Barbara CA 93111 Office: 4141 State St B-2 Santa Barbara CA 93110

SCHMALL, VICKI LOUISE, gerontologist; b. Spokane, Wash., Mar. 14, 1947; d. Grant Louis and Iona Grace (Taylor) Flagan; student U. Wash., 1965-68; B.S., Mont. State U., 1969; Ph.D., Oreg. State U., 1977; m. Rodney August Schmall, July 11, 1970. Instr., Wilsall (Mont.) Consol. Schs., 1969-70; research asst., trainer Nat. Nutrition Program for Elderly, Oreg. State U., Corvallis, 1972-73, gerontology field supr., instr., 1973-75, dir. program on gerontology, 1975-78, gerontology specialist, asst. prof. extension service, 1978—; research asso. applied research and devel., Wilsonville, Oreg., 1977-78; gerontol. cons.; condr. workshops for public service agys.; mem. Gov.'s Com. of Oreg. White House Conf. on Families, Mayor's Com. Interim Care for Elderly, Adv. Com. of Area Agy. on Aging, Hospice Devel. Com., Gov.'s Tech. Adv. Com. on Aging; del. White House Conf. on Aging, 1981. Active Nat. Multiple Sclerosis Soc. Recipient Outstanding Performance award Oreg. State U. Extension Service. Mem. Nat. Council on Aging, Nat. Council Family Relations, Oreg. Council Family Relations, Gerontol. Soc., Western Gerontol. Soc., Oreg. Gerontol. Assn. (dir.), Am. Home Econs. Assn., Oreg. Home Econs. Assn., Oreg. Extension Assn., Phi Kappa Phi, Omicron Nu. Contbr. articles profl. jours; creator ednl. game with videotape, Sexuality and Aging: A Game of Awareness and Interaction, 1980; Families and Aging: Dilemmas and Decisions, 1981; mem. editorial bd. Generations, Family Relations: Jour. Family and Child Studies. Home: 835 S Marylhurst Circle West Linn OR 97068 Office: Milam Hall 151 Extension Service Oregon State U Corvallis OR 97331

SCHMATZ-D'AMICO, KATHLEEN, pub. co. exec.; b. Buffalo, Apr. 11, 1950; d. Edward Thomas and Bernadine Elizabeth Schmatz; B.A. in English and Journalism, Kent State U., 1972; M.A., U. Akron, 1976; m. Michael Francis d'Amico, Aug. 31, 1974; 1 dau., Alyse. Staff writer Babcox Publs., Akron, Ohio, 1972, mng. editor automotive publs., 1974-76, dir. mktg., 1976-80, v.p. mktg., 1980—; guest lectr. journalism dept. Kent State U. Guest speaker YWCA careers program, 1981; role model Akton Girl Scouts U.S.A. career opportunities, 1981. Mem. Women in Communications, Inc. (past pres., dir., v.p.), Am. Mktg. Assn., Akron Women's Network, Susan B. Anthony Soc. Club: Akron Press. Home: 734 Mentor Rd Akron OH 44303 Office: Babcox Publs 11 S Forge St Akron OH 44304

SCHMEES, HAZEL KOEHNE, med. technologist; b. Hamilton County, Ohio, June 20, 1934; d. Arthur and Ethel (Poertner) Koehne; B.S., Ohio U., 1956; M.T., Mt. Carmel Hosp. Sch. Med. Tech., 1956; m. William B. Schmees, June 6, 1959; 1 son, Douglas Benard. Lab. technician Jack Kirschner, M.D., Cin., 1961; night supr. EPP Meml. Hosp., 1961-63; dept. head St. Francis Hosp., Cin., 1963-65; lab. supr. Drs. Clin. Lab., Cin., 1965-78; acting lab. dir. Biederman Allergy Clinic, Cin., 1978—. Republican precinct exec., 1966-69. Cert. med. technologist. Mem. Am. Soc. Clin. Pathologists, Ohio Soc. Med. Technologists (membership chmn. dist. 8 1957-61), Am. Assn. Bioanalysis, Internat. Soc. for Lab. Tech., Am. Bd. Bioanalysis, S. Central Assn. Microbiologists. Republican. United Ch. of Christ. Clubs: Ohio U. Alumni (dir. 1982—), St. Peter's Women's Guild (pres. 1970-78, treas. 1979—). Home: 4133 O'Leary Ave Cincinnati OH 45236 Office: 24 W 3 St Cincinnati OH 45202

SCHMERTZ, PHYLLIS KANE, publisher; b. Amittyville, N.Y., Mar. 2, 1949; d. Martin and Rhoda Kane; B.S., N.Y. U., 1971; m. Robert J. Schmertz, June 7, 1975 (dec.). Mem. fund raising staff State of Israel Bonds, 1971-72, bd. dirs. women's div., 1972-75, mem. speakers bur., 1972—; dir. vol. ops. Democratic Nat. Conv., 1976; dep. campaign mgr. Mayor Abe Beame Re-election Com., N.Y.C., 1977; spl. rep., co-founder 1st ann. World Banking Congress, 1977; pres. Embassy News Publs., Washington, 1977—. Co-chmn. Robert J. Schmertz Meml. Games, 1976—; com. mem. Robert F. Kennedy Pro-Celebrity Tournament, 1978—; mem. Democratic House and Senate Council, 1978—. Mem. Internat. Platform Assn. Jewish. Club: New York Univ. Home: 820 Fifth Ave New York NY 10021

SCHMID, ANNE MARIE, med. writer, editor; b. Columbus, Ohio, Aug. 10; d. Casimir J. and Petrona M. (Klimas) Mattsewecz; student U. San Francisco, 1932-35; m. Frank H. Schmid, Aug. 19, 1936; children—Frank R., Monica, Gregory, Elena. Editor, UN Charter, San Francisco, 1945; editor dept. pediatrics U. Calif. Sch. Medicine, San Francisco, 1949-77, prin. editor, 1971-78; freelance book editor, 1971—, thesis rewriter, 1973—; mng. editor Jour. Parenteral and Enteral Nutrition, 1977—. Bd. dirs. San Francsico Chamber Music Soc., 1966—, pres., 1980-82; bd. dirs. Calif. Christians for Israel; bd. dirs. Henry Harris Library Fund, 1975—; mem. health clin. adv. com. Telegraph Hill Neighborhood Assn., 1962-66, Dist. V Health and Mental Health Services, 1981—. Fellow Am. Med. Writers Assn. (past pres. No. Calif. chpt., nat. dir. 1975-76); mem. AAAS, MLA. Republican. Roman Catholic. Club: San Francisco Press. Home and Office: 1820 16th Ave San Francisco CA 94122

SCHMIDT, ANN DOWNING, columnist; b. Denver, Aug. 7, 1926; d. Richard and Dorothy (Simpson) Downing; B.A., Carleton Coll., 1947; m. Richard M. Schmidt, Jr., Jan. 2, 1948; children—Eric Downing, Gregory Marten, Rolf Warwick (dec.), Heidi. Columnist, University Park (Colo.) News, 1962-65; columnist The Denver Post, 1968—, Washington corr., 1971—; columnist Longmont (Colo.) Times-Call, 1968—, Loveland (Colo.) Reporter-Herald, 1968—, Canon City (Colo.) Courier, 1968—. Mem. Washington Press Club, Am. Women's Newspaper Club. Episcopalian. Home: 115 5th St SE Washington DC 20003 Office: 245 2d St NE Washington DC 20002

SCHMIDT, BETTY JO, motel and trailer ct. exec.; b. Kearney, Nebr., Sept. 3, 1938; d. LaVerne Ivan and Vivian Jane (Johnson) Banks; student U. Wyo., U. San Diego; m. Aug. 25, 1954; children—LaVerne, Dennis, Linda. Owner, mgr. Blue Ribbon Cafe & Lounge, Meeteetse, Wyo., 1976-78; mgr. Schmidt Ranch and Limousin Cattle Co., Meeteetse, 1965-78, Don Neet Limousin Cattle Co., Meeteetse, 1970-76; head bookkeeper First State Bank, Cody, Wyo., 1968-71; bookkeeper Barling Constrn. Co., Meeteetse, 1971-73; owner, mgr. Sagebrush Motel and Trailer Ct., Wamsutter, Wyo., 1978—. Mem. Wyo. Limousin Assn., Nat. Assn. Limousin Breeders, Wyo. Stockgrowers Assn., Beta Alpha Psi. Republican. Lutheran. Home and office: 8110 Stadler La Mesa CA 92041

SCHMIDT, CAROL, writer, communications cons.; b. Dearborn, Mich., Sept. 10, 1942; d. Emmett R. and Lorraine G. Schmidt; B.A. magna cum laude, Marygrove Coll., 1964; postgrad. U. N.C., 1964-65, UCLA extension, U. So. Calif.; m. Michael J. Arnoldy, June 21, 1970 (div. June 28, 1977). City editor Mich. Chronicle Newspaper, Detroit, 1965-68; communications cons. Chrysler Corp., Detroit, 1968; edn. editor Macomb Daily Newspaper, Mt. Clemens, Mich., 1969-70; feature editor, sales promotion mgr. Brentwood Pub. Co., Los Angeles, 1971-78; communications dir. Research and Edn. Inst., Inc., Harbor-UCLA Med. Center, Torrance, Calif., 1978—; free-lance writer, polit. speech writer, cons.; part-time instr. Wayne County Community Coll., Detroit, 1969-70. Pub. relations dir. Sunset Junction Neighborhood Alliance and St. Fairs; state del. Democratic Party, Mich., 1968-69; mem. Los Angeles Women's Community Chorus. Recipient First prize Nat. Newspaper Pubs. Assn., 1969. Mem. Am. Soc. Assn. Execs., Am. Hosp. Assn. (communications sect.), Soc. for Hosp. Public Relations, Nat. Mgmt. Assn. (v.p. Harbor-UCLA chpt.), Women in Communications, Am. Med. Writers Assn., Feminist Women's Writers Guild, White Women Against Racism, CORE, NOW (pres. Beach Cities 1979-80, state bd. dir. 1977-81). Contbr. numerous articles to newspapers. Office: 1124 W Carson St Torrance CA 90502

SCHMIDT, ELISABETH BODROG, dietitian; b. Rankin, Pa., Mar. 27, 1932; d. John and Anna S. (Fuga) Bodrog; B.S., Carlow Coll., Pitts., 1954; M.Ed., U. Pitts., 1967; postgrad. Pa. State U., 1982; m. Lawrence Lichti Schmidt, Nov. 11, 1959; 1 son, Lawrence Paul. Menu planning dir. Sky-Chefs, Inc., N.Y.C., 1958-60; dist. dietitian Inter-State United, Pitts., 1961-63; adminstrv. dietitian Johns Hopkins Hosp., Balt., 1965-67; asso. prof., chmn. dept. food sci. mgmt. Indiana (Pa.) U., 1967-71; asso. prof. food and nutrition East Carolina U., Greenville, N.C., 1971-74; dir. ops. services health care div. Macke Co., Cheverly, Md., 1975-76; asst. prof. Coll. Bus., Hotel and Restaurant Mgmt., Fla. State U., Tallahassee, 1976—; treas., dir. Pita Taxi, Inc.; past mem. adv. com. Pa. Nutrition Steering Com.; mem. Nat. Com. Serving Size Standards for Nutritional Labeling, Steering Com. Geriatric Feeding Programs; condr. workshops, cons. in field. Mem. Nat. Restaurant Assn. (exec. dir. 1968-69; found. fellow 1970), Am. Dietetics Assn., Am. Mgmt. Assn., Council Hotel, Restaurant and Indsl. Edn., Soc. Hosts (hon.). Mem. Russian Orthodox Ch. Club: Toastmistress. Author papers in field. Home: 3038 Stillwood Ct Tallahassee FL 32312 Office: 204 DIN Fla State Univ Tallahassee FL 32306

SCHMIDT, HEIDI-ELKE, finishing sch. pres.; b. Magdeburg, Ger., July 12, 1943; came to U.S., 1972, naturalized, 1976; d. Wilhelm Adolf and Elli Elfriede (Heinzer) S.; B., Ballet Acad. Satzky, Wuppertal, Ger., 1961; M., Dance Acad. Cologne, 1963; 1 son, Bryan Earl Tash. Prima ballerina, Oberhausen, W.Ger., 1963-65, Kaiserslautern, 1967-69; owner, mgr. Ecole de Dance, Washington, 1969—; dir. Newport News Ballet Co., 1973-75; freelance high fashion model; pres. Cappa Chell Finishing Sch., Washington, 1980—; sales cons. Andrews AFB. Attache chmn. Officers Club, Bolling AFB, 1978-79; ofcl. hostess diplomatic reception Inauguration of Pres. Carter, 1977; judge Miss Md. Preteen Beauty Contest. Mem. U.S. Amateur Ballroom Assn., Am. Model Assn., Nat. Assn. Female Execs. Republican. Roman Catholic. U.S. amateur champion in dance, 1978, New Eng. champion, 1978; runner-up as Miss Germany, 1966. Office: 1409 Juliana Pl Alexandria VA 22304

SCHMIDT, KAREN ANNE, state legislator, travel agy. exec.; b. Los Angeles, Nov. 27, 1945; d. Ernest Potter and Anne Ruth (Cieslar) Jacobi; student Ariz. State U., 1963-65; m. Gary M. Schmidt, Jan. 30, 1970; children—Geoffrey Alan, Gavin Andrew. Stewardess, TWA, 1965, Western Airlines, 1966-67; agt. Doug Fox Travel, Seattle, 1967-68; sales agt. Delta Air Lines, Seattle, 1968-70; owner, mgr. Go Travel Services, Bainbridge Island, Wash., 1971—; mem. Wash. Ho. of Reps., 1980—. Named Woman of Yr. Bainbridge Island Rotary, 1979. Mem. Bainbridge Island C. of C. (dir. 1971-82, pres. 1976). Republican. Episcopalian. Office: 122 Madrone Ln Bainbridge Island WA 98110

SCHMIDT, MARILYNN JO, speech pathologist; b. Fostoria, Ohio, July 11, 1931; d. George William and Dorothy (Fry) S.; B.S. in Secondary Edn., Bob Jones U., 1954; M.A. in Speech Pathology, Denver U., 1960, Ph.D. in Speech Pathology, 1972. Tchr., Russellville (Mo.) High Sch., 1954-56, Boonville (Mo.) High Sch., 1956-59; tchr. Denver U., 1960-62; asst. prof. speech pathology Central Mo. State U., Warrensburg, 1962-73, asso. prof., 1973-78, prof., 1978—; cons. in field. Office Vocat. Rehab. fellow, 1959-60; VA grantee, 1971-72. Mem.Am. Speech-Lang.-Hearing Assn., Mo. Speech-Lang.-Hearing Assn. Methodist. Home: 409 10th St Warrensburg MO 64093 Office: Speech and Hearing Clinic Central Mo State U Warrensburg MO 64093

SCHMIDT, MARJORIE MINA, banker; b. Chgo., Aug. 5, 1936; d. John Edward and Ada E. (Schipplock) S.; B.A., Valparaiso (Ind.) U., 1957; J.D., Loyola U., Chgo., 1979. Tng. rep. Mandel Bros., Chgo., 1957-61; personnel asst. Am. Nat. Bank, Chgo., 1961-62, Continental Nat. Am. Group, Chgo., 1962-66; personnel adminstr. Booz-Allen & Hamilton, Chgo., 1966-67; with Madison Fin. Corp., also Madison Bank & Trust, Chgo., 1967—, sr. v.p., sec.-treas., chief fin. officer, 1979—. Bd. dirs. 200 E. Delaware Condominium Assn., 1975-78. Named Woman of Year, Woman's Share in Public Service, 1979. Mem. Bus. and Profl. Women's Club. Republican. Lutheran. Home: 200 E Delaware Pl Chicago IL 60611 Office: 400 W Madison St Chicago IL 60606

SCHMIDT, MELBA IRENE, (MRS. MARQUIS RIGHTMIRE SCHMIDT), real estate exec.; b. Grand Junction, Colo., Jan. 14, 1908; d. Claud DeNel and Gertrude Beatrice (Cartmel) Smith; student UCLA, 1926-27; grad. pianoforte pedagogy, New Eng. Conservatory of Music, 1930; m. Marquis Rightmire Schmidt, Aug. 2, 1932; children—Mark Ronald, Ralph Normand, Beatrice Jane Schmidt Garsh. Pvt. tchr. piano and musical readings, Grand Junction, 1930-40; tchr. harmony and music theory Mesa Jr. Coll., Grand Junction, 1943; dir. publicity and pub. relations C.D. Smith Co., drug and sundries wholesalers, Grand Junction, 1951-73, v.p., dir. 1970-73; partner Smith Assos., real estate and investments, 1948—; chmn. bd. Sterling Co., real estate, 1976—; dir. Walsh Enterprises, Inc., Anaheim, Calif., Hy Grade Labs., Inc. Gen. chmn., an organizer Mesa County Community Concert Assn., 1944-60. Bd. dirs. Grand Junction Art Center, 1951-54. Mem. Music Assos., of Aspen (regional dir. 1962-66), Nat. Fedn. Music Clubs (chmn. Aspen music sch. scholar 1964-79, Young Artists adminstrv. com. 1979—), Colo. Fedn. Music Clubs (pres. 1962-64, state bd. mem. 1959-74), P.E.O., Pi Kappa Lambda, Alpha Chi Omega. Republican. Presbyterian. Club: Wednesday Music (pres. 1952-55). Home: 536 N 7th St Grand Junction CO 81501 Office: PO Box 756 Grand Junction CO 81501

SCHMIDT, NORMA GAYLE, educator; b. Altus, Okla., Feb. 18, 1936; d. Allen Everett and Josephine M. (Mitchell) Jackman; B.S. in Nursing, Okla. Baptist U., 1957; M.Ed. in Health Edn., U. Ark., 1969; Ph.D. in Health and Phys. Edn., Tex A&M U., 1974; m. Henry Mack Schmidt, Mar. 8, 1964; children—Andrew, Laura, Amy, Patricia. Various positions in nursing; mem. faculty Tex. A&M U., 1969—, asso. prof. health edn., 1978—, coordinator community health program, 1980—. Elder First Christian Ch. (Disciples of Christ), Bryan, Tex., 1979-81, chmn., 1981; mem. United Campus Ministry, 1977—, pres., 1978-80, treas., 1981-82; co-chmn. public relations A&M Consol. High Sch. Choir Props, 1981-82. Mem. AAHPER, Am. Sch. Health Assn., Tex. Assn. Health, Phys. Edn. and Recreation, Tex. Sch. Health Assn., Eta Sigma Gamma. Author articles in field. Home: 1102 Village Dr College Station TX 77840 Office: Dept Health and Phys Edn Tex A&M U College Station TX 77843

SCHMIDT, RINA JACOBY, physician; b. Danzig, Oct. 14, 1929; d. Kurt and Kate (Becker) Jacoby; came to U.S., 1972; M.D., Hadassah Med. Sch., 1958; m. Moshe Schmidt, Jan. 14, 1951; children—Ehud, Joel. Intern in pediatrics Ramban Hosp., Haifa, Israel, 1956-57; resident Poriah Hosp., Tel-Hashomen Hosp., Israel, 1958-62; fellow in genetics N.Y. Psychiat. Inst., 1963-64, research scientist, 1964-66; dir. genetic unit Assa Harofe Hosp., Zrifin, Israel, 1967-72; co-dir. genetic counseling program Albert Einstein Coll. of Medicine, Bronx, N.Y., 1973—, asst. prof. pediatrics, 1972-78, asso. prof., 1978-81; dir. cytogenetics Met. Pathology, Inc., 1981—; adv. bd. Parents' Assn. Children with Down's Syndrome, L.I., N.Y., 1973—. Served with Army of Israel, 1948-49. Mem. Am., Israeli med. assns., Am. Soc. for Human Genetics, AAAS. Jewish. Contbr. numerous articles in fields to profl. jours. Home: 65-21 Cromwell Crescent Rego Park NY 11374

SCHMIDT, SYBIL MARIE, nurse; b. Fairfield, Ala., Oct. 22, 1924; d. Edward Alexis and Blanche (Gunter) Fredendall; diploma Hosp. Protestant Episcopal Ch. Sch. Nursing, Phila., 1948; m. John Raymond Schmidt, Feb. 14, 1955; 1 son, John Raymond. Head nurse orthopedics, floor night supr. Charity Hosp., New Orleans, 1948-52; pvt. duty nurse, New Orleans, 1952; staff night nurse Mercy Hosp., New Orleans, 1953; staff nurse Grand Canyon (Ariz.) Hosp., 1954; asst. night supr., head nurse pediatrics, asst. to dir. nursing Tulare County (Calif.) Gen. Hosp., 1954-63; staff nurse, night supr. Tulare (Calif.) Dist. Hosp., 1964—. Mem. Nat. League Nursing, Oblate Missionaries Internat., Nat. Critical Care Inst. Democrat. Episcopalian. Clubs: VFW Aux. Home: 741 Auburn Tulare CA 93274 Office: 869 Cherry St Tulare CA 93274

SCHMIDT, SYBIL PARKER, congl. asst.; b. Atlanta, Mar. 19, 1936; d. Claud Reed Burnett and Mattie Lou Parker; student Greenleaf Sch. Bus., 1954-56; m. John Winfield Schmidt, June 7, 1958; children—John Michael, Mark Winfield. Exec. sec. to dean physics Ga. Inst. Tech., Atlanta, 1954-58; staff asst. to Congressman Richard C. White, El Paso, 1979—. Mem. Goals for El Paso Govt. Com., 1977-79; mem. community devel. commn. Mission Heritage Assn., 1977, v.p., 1980, pres., 1981; bd. dirs. Insights, 1979; mem. El Paso County Hist. Commn., 1979-80, treas., 1981, vice chmn., 1982; 29th Senatorial dist. coordinator Jimmy Carter, nat. del., 1976; Carter-Mondale chmn., El Paso County, 1976; mem. state steering com. Jimmy Carter, 1979; active Tex. Sch. Vol. Assn., PTA. Named Ambassador of Goodwill, State Tex., 1976; recipient citation for disting. service Tex. Hist. Commn. and Hist. Found., 1979. Mem. El Paso Hist. Soc., Tex. PTA (hon. life), Nat. Dem. Women. Democrat. Roman Catholic. Clubs: El Paso Corral of the Westerners (sheriff 1978), El Paso Symphony Chorus (pres. 1979). Author: Color Me Sunshine, 1975; book reviewer El Paso Times, 1977-79, El Paso Herald Post, 1977—. Home: 717 Waltham Ct El Paso TX 79922 Office: US Court House Room 146 El Paso TX 79901

SCHMIDTMANN, NANCY DOROTHY, educator; b. N.Y.C., Apr. 13, 1940; d. Charles Bernard and Anna Mary (Gorman) Koonmen; A.B. cum laude, Chestnut Hill Coll., 1961; M.A., St. John's U., 1962, M.L.S., 1982; m. Otto S. Schmidtmann, Dec. 26, 1962; children—Lucie Ann, Mary Catherine, Peter, Emily Jean, Charles. Research asst. St. John's U., Jamaica, N.Y., 1961-62, 80-81; tchr. English Francis Lewis High Sch., Flushing, N.Y., 1962-63; copywriter Barth-Spencer Corp., Valley Stream, N.Y., 1968-70; editor/copywriter Barron's Ednl. Series, Woodbury, N.Y., 1970-72; sch. media specialist Our Lady of Mercy Sch., Hicksville, N.Y., 1973—; panelist Nassau Suffolk Library Inst., 1980; audio-visual reviewer Sch. Library Jours., 1980—; cons. in field. Mem. exec. bd. PTA, Plainview Old-Bethpage pub. schs., 1967-70; 4-H leader, Nassau County, N.Y., 1970—; vol. Roman Cath. Diocese of Rockville Centre, 1965—. Recipient Freedoms Found. award, 1957; Ancient Order of Hibernians award, 1956; N.Y. State Coll. Teaching fellow, 1961-62; St. John's U. grad. assistantship, 1961-62, 80-81. Mem. Cath. Library Assn., Nat. Cath. Edn. Assn., Nassau County Library Assn., ALA, Delta Epsilon Sigma, Beta Phi Mu. Contbr. articles to profl. jours. Home: 149 Orchard St Plainview NY 11803 Office: 520 S Oyster Bay Rd Hicksville NY 11801

SCHMITT, LISA LINNELL, speech pathologist; b. Indpls., May 30, 1952; d. Frederick Francis and Elizabeth Linnell (Briggs) S.; B.A., SUNY, Buffalo, 1974; M.A., N.Y. U., 1976. Speech pathologist Suffolk Devel. Center, Melville, N.Y., 1977-78; sr. speech pathologist, 1979-80; speech pathologist Inst. Rehab. Medicine, N.Y. U. Med. Center, N.Y.C., 1980—; instr. edn. Suffolk Devel. Center. Mem. Am. Speech and Hearing Assn. Office: Inst Rehab Medicine NY U Med Center 34th St and 1st Ave New York NY 10016

SCHMITZ, EUGENIA EVANGELINE, librarian, educator; b. Grand Rapids, Mich.; d. Joseph A. and Eugenia (Newhouse) S.; A.B., Western Mich. U.; B.S., Coll. St. Catherine; A.M., U. Mich., Ph.D., 1966. Br. librarian Grand Rapids Public Library; librarian, Creston High Sch., Grand Rapids, Sr. High Sch., Benton Harbor, Mich.; lectr. dept. library sci. U. Mich., 1963-67, asst. prof., 1967-68; asst. prof. library sci. U. Wis. at Oshkosh, 1968-70, asso. prof., 1970-75, prof., 1975—, chmn. dept. library sci., 1968-81. Mem. ALA, Wis. Library Assn., Phi Beta Kappa, Phi Kappa Phi, Beta Phi Mu, Pi Lambda Theta, Sigma Pi Epsilon. Contbr. book revs. to Best Sellers, Jour. Acad. Librarianship, others.

SCHMITZ-CASTRO, ERIKA, taxicab co. exec.; b. Marktbreit, Germany, Dec. 26, 1944; came to U.S., 1970; d. Johann and Wilhelmine (Bruscher) Schmitz; student Marymount Manhattan Coll., 1979—; 1 son, Dario. Film editor apprentice Saarlandischer Rundfunk, Germany, 1964-66; bi-lingual sec. Swiss embassy, Costa Rica, 1967-69; bi-lingual exec. sec. Bank of Boston Internat., N.Y.C., 1974-77; sales and service coordinator Am. M.A.N. Corp., N.Y.C., from 1977; now owner N.Y.C. Medallion Taxi Cab. Cert. N.Y. Vets. Police, Nat. Assn. Underwater Instrs.

SCHMUCKER, RUBY ELVA, educator; b. Sugarcreek, Ohio, Nov. 17, 1923; d. Walter F. and Carrie M. (Mizer) Ladrach; R.N., Aultman Hosp. Sch. Nursing, 1945; B.S.N. magna cum laude, U. Akron, 1970, M.S., 1973; m. Nelson Schmucker, Oct. 20, 1945; children—Gary, David, Barbara, Steven. Staff nurse, head nurse, instr. Aultman Hosp., Canton, Ohio, 1942-74; instr. Coll. Nursing, U. Akron (Ohio), 1974-76; instr. Div. Nursing Edn., Akron Children's Hosp., 1976-77; psychiat. nurse, ward mgr. and supr. Massillon (Ohio) State Hosp., 1977-80, cons. to nursing service 1980-81, dir. nursing edn. 1981—; cons. Student Nurse Assn., 1972-74. Active ARC. Mem. Ohio League Nursing (steering com.), Nat. League Nursing, Am. Nurses Assn., Am. Personnel and Guidance Assn., Am. Coll. Personnel Assn., Aultman Hosp. Alumni Assn., Alpha Sigma Lambda, U. Akron Alumni Assn. Mem. United Ch. of Christ. Home: 4214 Bellwood Dr NW Canton OH 44708 Office: 3000 Erie St Massillon OH 44646

SCHMUTZ, DANA MAY, accountant; b. St. George, Utah, Nov. 17, 1938; d. David Marshall and Verna (Burgess) S.; B.S., So. Utah State Coll., 1977; children—David, Douglas, Jan, John. Staff acct. Huskinson, Savage & Co., C.P.A.s, St. George, 1977-81, partner, 1981—. Mem. Utah Soc. C.P.A.s (chpt. tng. coordinator 1981-82), Am. Women's Soc. C.P.A.s, St. George Bus. and Profl. Women's Club (treas. 1979, pres. 1981-82; Woman of Yr. award 1980), AAUW (charter mem. St. George br. 1982). Republican. Mormon. Home: 1725 East 800 North St George UT 84770 Office: 435 E Tabernacle St Saint George UT 84770

SCHNACK, GAYLE HEMINGWAY JEPSON (MRS. HAROLD CLIFFORD SCHNACK), corp. exec.; b. Mpls., Aug. 14, 1926; d. Jasper Jay and Ursula (Hemingway) Jepson; student U. Hawaii, 1946; m. Harold Clifford Schnack, Mar. 22, 1947; children—Jerrald Jay, Georgina, Roberta, Michael Clifford. Skater, Shipstead & Johnson Ice Follies, 1944-46; v.p. Harcliff Corp., Honolulu, 1964—, Schnack Indsl. Corp., Honolulu, 1969—, Nutmeg Corp., Cedar Corp.; ltd. partner Koa Corp. Mem. Beta Sigma Phi (chpt. pres. 1955-56, pres. city council 1956-57). Established Ursula Hemingway Jepson art award, Carlton Coll., Ernest Hemingway creative writing award, U. Hawaii. Office: PO Box 3077 Honolulu HI 96802 also 1200 Riverside Dr Reno NV 89503

SCHNALL, EDITH LEA (MRS. HERBERT SCHNALL), mycologist, educator; b. N.Y.C., Apr. 11, 1922; d. Irving and Sadie (Raab) Spitzer; A.B., Hunter Coll., 1942; A.M., Columbia U., 1947, Ph.D., 1967; m. Herbert Schnall, Aug. 21, 1949; children—Neil David, Carolyn Beth. Clin. pathologist Roosevelt Hosp., N.Y.C., 1942-44; instr. Adelphi Coll., Garden City, N.Y., 1944-46; asst. med. mycologist Columbia Coll. Physicians and Surgeons, N.Y.C., 1946-47, 49-50; instr. Bklyn. Coll., 1947; faculty Sarah Lawrence Coll., Bronxville, N.Y., 1947-48; lectr. Hunter Coll., N.Y.C., 1947-67; adj. asso. prof. Lehman Coll., City U. N.Y., 1968; asst. prof. Queensborough Community Coll., City U. N.Y., 1967, asso. prof. microbiology, 1968-75, prof., 1975—; vis. prof. Coll. Physicians and Surgeons, Columbia U., N.Y.C., 1974; advanced biology examiner U. London, 1970—. Mem. Alley Restoration Com., N.Y.C., 1971—; mem. legis. adv. com. Assembly of the State of N.Y., 1972. Mem. Community Bd. 11, Queens, N.Y., 1974—; public dir. of bd. dirs. Inst. Continuing Dental Edn. Queens County, Dental Soc. N.Y. State and ADA, 1973—. Research fellow NIH, 1948-49; faculty research fellow, grantee-in-aid Research Found. of SUNY, 1968-70; faculty research grant Research Found. City U. N.Y., 1971-74. Mem. Internat. Soc. Human and Animal Mycology, AAAS, Am. Soc. Microbiology (council, co-chair ann. meeting com., chair program com., co-chairperson career guidance and continuing edn. com. N.Y.C. br. 1979—), Med. Mycology Soc. N.Y. (sec.-treas. 1967-68, v.p. 1968-69, 78-79, archivist 1974—pres. 1969-70, 79-80, 81-82), Bot. Soc. Am., Med. Mycology Soc. Americas, Mycology Soc. Am., N.Y. Acad. Scis., Sigma Xi, Phi Sigma. Clubs: Torrey Botanical (N.Y. State); Queensborough Community Coll. Women's (pres. 1971-73) (N.Y.C.). Editor: Newsletter of Med. Mycology Soc. N.Y., 1969—; founder, editor Female Perspective newsletter of Queensborough Community Coll. Women's Club, 1971-73. Home: 214-06 29th Ave Bayside NY 11360

SCHNATHORST, WILMA STEVENS, secretary; b. Dolliver, Iowa, Aug. 1, 1924; d. George Alfred and Anna Edith (Hundertmark) Stevens; student pub. schs., Cedar Falls, Iowa; m. Ralph Carlton Schnathorst, June 14, 1974; children—James K., Rodney F., Paige A. Sec., Viking Pump Co., Cedar Falls, 1942, John Deere Co., Waterloo, Iowa, 1943-44, sec. service dept. Tractor Works, Waterloo, 1979—; sec. Clay Equipment Corp., Cedar Falls, 1947-48; exec. sec. Ranking Mfg. Co., Cedar Falls, 1948-49; dept. asst. Rath Packing Co., Waterloo, 1960-75; exec. sec. Blunt, Ellis & Loewi, Inc., Waterloo, 1975-79; mem. adv. bd. Hawkeye Inst. Tech. Judge, Jr. Achievement, Black Hawk Land. Served with WAVES, 1944-45. Mem. Profl. Secs. Internat. (treas. Iowa div. 1979-80, sec. 1980-81, v.p. 1981-82, pres. elec. 1982-83, named Sec. of Yr. local chpt. 1975). Presbyterian (deacon). Home: 1611 Williston Ave Waterloo IA 50702 Office: John Deere Tractor Works Dept 416 Waterloo IA 50701

SCHNECKLOTH, HELEN MAY, mfg. co. exec.; b. Huron, S.D., Sept. 12, 1929; d. Dale Henry and Gladys Elva (Smith) Packard; B.A., Nat. Coll. Edn., Evanston, Ill., 1981; m. Donald Hunt Schneckloth, Aug. 21, 1949; children—Peter Dale, Jeri Lee, Sue Ann, Cynthia Jean. Exec. sec.-treas. Com. for Interdist. Coop., Highland Park and Deerfield, Ill., 1967-68; sec. to prin. Wilmont Jr. High Sch., Deerfield, 1968-70; document coordinator, then document analyst internat. quality control Travenol Labs., Deerfield, 1970-80, document specialist, 1980—; seminar leader, 1976—. Mem. Nat. Assn. Female Execs., PEO. Republican. Presbyterian. Home: 822 Cedar Terr Deerfield IL 60015 Office: 1 Baxter Pkwy Deerfield IL 60015

SCHNEIDER, ADELE GOLDBERG, librarian; b. N.Y.C., May 13, 1924; d. Abraham and Anna (Levy) Goldberg; B.A., Bklyn. Coll., 1945; M.L.S., Pratt Inst., 1965; M.A., Long Island U., 1971; m. Noel Schneider, Jan. 1, 1950; children—Adam Matthew, Tracy Lynn. Field interviewer Gallup Poll, N.Y.C., 1941-48; social worker N.Y.C. Dept. Social Services, 1949-52; editor Bklyn. Coll. Alumni Quarterly, 1961-65; instr. Kingsborough Community Coll. City U. N.Y., 1965-70, asst. prof. dept. library, 1970-72, asso. prof., 1972—. Mem. ALA, Library Assn. City U. N.Y., N.Y. Tech. Services Librarians. Home: 124 Oxford St Brooklyn NY 11235 Office: 2001 Oriental Blvd Brooklyn NY 11235

SCHNEIDER, BRENDA LOUISE, banking exec.; b. Eau Claire, Wis., Feb. 26, 1946; d. Melvin and Joyce Brenizer; B.A., U. Wis., 1968; m. Thomas Schneider, Aug. 24, 1968; 1 dau., Jennifer. Tech. editor Money mgmt. series Waterford (Mich.) Sch. dist., 1975-76; consumer edn. specialist Credit Counseling Centers, Southfield, Mich., 1977-78; now 2d v.p., dir. consumer and urban affairs Mfrs. Nat. Corp., Detroit; lectr. Wayne State U. Mem. Soc. Consumer Affairs Profls. in Bus. (pres. Great Lakes chpt.), Bank Mktg. Assn. Contbr. articles to banking jours. Office: Manufacturers Bank Tower 100 Renaissance Center Detroit MI 48243

SCHNEIDER, CAROLYN BRAUCH, educator; b. N.Y.C., Dec. 15, 1946; d. Elliott David and Marie Alice (Giroux) Brauch; B.S., U. Bridgeport, 1968; m. Thomas J. Schneider, Aug. 3, 1978. Tchr., Westview Elem. Sch., Northglenn, Colo., 1968-72, McElwain Elem. Sch., Thornton, Colo., 1972-75; with Northglenn Recreation Dept., part-time, 1969—; tchr. phys. edn., health Northglenn Jr. High Sch., 1975—, cheerleading sponsor, coach gymnastics, volleyball, track. Mem. NEA, Colo. Edn. Assn., AAHPER. Home: 5316 E 113 Pl Northglenn CO 80233 Office: 1123 Muriel Dr Northglenn CO 80233

SCHNEIDER, CLAUDINE, congresswoman; b. Clairton, Pa., Mar. 25, 1947; B.A., Windham Coll., 1969; m. Eric D. Schneider, 1973. Exec. adminstr. Concern, Inc., Washington, 1969; founder R.I. Com. on Energy, 1973; exec. dir. Conservation Law Found., 1974; fed. coordinator R.I. Coastal Zone Mgmt. Program, 1978; producer, hostess public affairs program Sta. WJAR-TV, Providence, 1978-79; mem. 97th Congress from 2d R.I. Dist., 1979—. State chmn. spl. events Am. Cancer Soc., 1979. Named Outstanding Young Person of Year, South County Jaycees, 1979; Woman of Year, R.I. Women's Polit. Caucus, 1978. Office: Room 1431 Longworth House Office Bldg Washington DC 20515

SCHNEIDER, DOROTHY, educator; b. St. Louis, May 19, 1921; d. Edward P. and Leona (Koerner) S.; B.A., Washington U., St. Louis, 1942, M.A. in English, 1952; postgrad. U. Zurich (Switzerland), 1947-48, Columbia U., 1957, U. Calif., Santa Barbara, 1967-69; Ph.D., Anthony U., 1980. Tchr. elem. schs., St. Louis, 1942-44, 48-50, 58-65, Santa Barbara, Calif., 1965-69; tchr. English to fgn.-born adults, St. Louis, 1950-52; mem. faculty dept. English Lindenwood Coll., St. Charles, Mo., 1956-58; overseas staff ARC, 1945-47, 54-55; mem. faculty Piney Woods (Miss.) Sch., 1973-74; mem. faculty English and bus. Grossmont Coll., San Diego, 1975—. Initiator, UN Day world holiday, proclaimed in 1971. Recipient Diploma of Honor Internat. Order of Vols. for Peace (Italy), 1981. Mem. World Union Internat. (India) (mem. world council), Consortium on Peace Research, Edn. and Devel., NAACP, U. Calif. Santa Barbara Alumni Assn., Internat. House at Columbia U., Gamma Phi Beta. Author: A World Holiday for Peace: United Nations Day, 1980; World Unification Plans and Analyses, 1980. Address: 4452 Caminito Fuente San Diego CA 92116

SCHNEIDER, ELAINE FOGEL, speech, lang. pathologist; b. Bklyn., Mar. 6, 1947; d. Maurice and Lillian Fogel; student Hunter Coll. CUNY, 1963-67, Queens Coll. CUNY, 1967-69; M.A., N.Y.U., 1977; m. Jack Schneider, June 12, 1977; children—Cynthia, Madalyn. Speech, lang. pathologist N.Y.C. Bur. Speech Improvement, 1969-72; co. dir. Cocunit Grove (Fla.) Danse Theatre, 1971-75; chmn. lang/speech dept. Lancaster (Calif.) Sch. Dist., 1978-81; dir. Antelope Valley Lang. Movement, Speech Therapy Center, Lancaster, 1981—; cons. in field. Cert. clin. competency. Mem. Am. Acad. Speech Pathologists, Audiologists in Pvt. Practice, Am. Speech, Langu. and Hearing Assn., Calif. Speech, Lang. and Hearing Assn., Am. Dance Therapy Assn. Contbr. articles to profl. jours; inventor —Slam— technique. Home: 44157 Planet Circle Lancaster CA 93534 Office: 442 N 10th St W Suite L Lancaster CA 93534

SCHNEIDER, FRIEDA, sch. social worker; b. N.Y.C., July 9, 1921; d. David and Fannie (Ethstein) Lippenholtz; B.S., Coll. City N.Y., 1947, M.S., 1959; M.S.W., Columbia U., 1954; postgrad. N.Y. U., 1951; m. Nathan Schneider, Nov. 22, 1951; children—Cathy, Lauren, David. Social worker Central Islip State Hosp., 1950-53, Westchester County Mental Health, 1954-55, St. Dominick's Home for Dependent Children, 1960-63; tchr. Rockland Community Coll., 1966-67; therapist Mental Health Cons. Center, 1966-68; pvt. practice social work, 1968-73; sch. social worker N.Y.C. Bd. Edn., 1973—; speaker's bur. Rockland County Mental Health Assn.; vol. counselor; parent counselor. Voters service chmn. LWV, 1960-65; v.p. New City Civic Assn., 1965-70; v.p. PTA, 1968-69; polit. action chmn. New City Jewish Center, 1965-66. Mem. Nat. Assn. Social Workers, AAUW. Democrat. Jewish. Clubs: B'nai B'rith, Hadassah. Home: 23 Scott Dr New City NY 10956

SCHNEIDER, ILENE ANNE, public relations rep.; b. Cleve., Nov. 15, 1949; d. Jules E. and Sylvia G. (Schaffer) Spector; B.A. in Polit. Sci., U. Pa., 1971; m. Bruce J. Schneider, July 12, 1975. Editor, Cleve. edit. TV Guide mag., 1971-72; asso. editor Sch. Product News mag., Penton/IPC, Cleve., 1972-78; contbg. editor, 1978—; sr. staff writer public relations dept. Beckman Instruments, Inc., Fullerton, Calif., 1978—; propr. Schneider the Writer Communications Service, Irvine, Calif., 1980—. Media coordinator-Rothschild for Mayor Campaign, University Heights, Ohio, 1977; sec. 22d Congressional Dist. Caucus, Cleve., 1973-75; asst. coordinator seminar series Youth in Politics, Dyke Coll., Cleve., 1974. Recipient Clarion award Women in Communications, 1978. Mem. Women in Communications, Public Relations Soc. Am., Am. Soc. Bus. Press Editors, Council Exceptional Children, Assn. Children with Learning Disabilities. Jewish. Contbr. articles to various publs. Home: 4421 Sandburg Way Irvine CA 92715 Office: 2500 Harbor Blvd Fullerton CA 92634

SCHNEIDER, JEAN JOSEPH, social worker; b. Dubuque, Iowa, Oct. 23, 1941; d. Jean Francis and Ann Jayne (Bieler) S.; B.A., Loras Coll., 1963; M.S.S.W., U. Wis., Milw., 1967; m. Patricia Jane Brockmeyer, Aug. 10, 1968; children—Stephanie Ann, Jay Francis. Probation and parole agt. State of Wis., Racine, 1963-66; social worker Ethan Allan Sch., State of Wis., Wales, 1966-67; dist. supr. Bur. Community Corrections, State of Wis., 1967-71; exec. dir. Del. Council on Crime and Justice, Wilmington, 1971-75; social worker for adolescent females Lincoln Hills Sch., State of Wis., Irma, 1975—. Mem. Mayor's Commn. on Status of Women, Merrill, Wis., 1979-80. Mem. Nat. Assn. Social Workers (v.p. Del. chpt.), Acad. Cert. Social Workers. Roman Catholic. Home: 209 N Park St Merrill WI 54452 Office: PO Box 96 Irma WI 54442

SCHNEIDER, LISA DAWN, art dealer; b. Brookline, Mass., Nov. 16, 1954; d. Joseph and Eunice Schneider; B.A., Marymount Coll., 1977. Asst. to dir. Denise Rene Gallery, N.Y.C., 1976-77; co-dir. Rourke Gallery, N.Y.C., 1977; dir. Robert Freidus Gallery, N.Y.C., 1977-78; asso. dir. Bertha Urdang Gallery, N.Y.C., 1979; art editor, art critic Women's Week, Inc., 1977-79; exec. dir. Curatorial Cons. & Galleries, N.Y.C., 1980—.

SCHNEIDER, MARJORIE KLITSNER, ednl. adminstr.; b. Madison, Wis., Aug. 22, 1924; d. Saul and Sara Klitsner; B.A., U. Wis., 1946; m. Alan M. Schneider, June 20, 1948; children—David, Mitchell, Howard, Sara. Program coordinator U. Calif., San Diego Extension, La Jolla, 1969-73, dir. biol. phys. and social scis., mental health and re-entry programs, 1973-81; exec. dir. La Jolla Inst. Continuing Edn., 1981—. Bd. dirs. Clear Air Council, San Diego, 1975. Mem. Nat. Univ. Extension Assn., Charter 100, Western Gerontol. Assn., AAUP.

SCHNEIDER, MARLENE ROBERTA, psychotherapist; b. N.Y.C., June 8, 1940; d. Abraham and Rose Jackman; B.A. in Elem. Edn. and Psychology, SUNY, Stony Brook, 1969, M.A., 1972, M.S.W., 1975; m. Richard Mould, Mar. 20, 1976; children—Cynthia, Madalyn; stepchildren—Jeffrey Daniels, Nancy. Head tchr. Point of Woods Lab. Sch., SUNY, Stony Brook, 1969-79, asst. dir., 1979-81, lectr. in psychology, 1979-81, cons. Sex Therapy Clinic, 1981—, supr., 1982—, extern in strategic family therapy, 1981-82; pvt. practice psychotherapy, 1975—; co-dir. Suffolk (N.Y.) Growth Center, 1977-79; cons. to instns. and schs.; condr. workshops on Gestalt therapy and behavior modification; condr. workshops for industry. Mem. Nat. Assn. Social Workers, Council Exceptional Children. Writer and producer (with Dr. K.D. O'Leary) film: Catch 'em Being Good; contbr. articles to profl. jours.; originator technique to help impulsive children manage their behavior. Home: 11 Kennedy Rd Port Jefferson Station NY 11776

SCHNEIDER, MARY JO, educator; b. Warrensburg, Mo., Nov. 7, 1944; d. Noel Bryan and Alice Berne (Heberling) Grinstead; B.S. in Edn., Central Mo. State U., 1965; Ph.D., U. Mo., Columbia, 1971; postgrad. U. Colo., Boulder, 1963-65; m. William Martin Schneider, Feb. 20, 1975; children—Anne, Rebekah, Jacob. Instr. U. Ark., 1969-73, asst. prof., 1973-76, asso. prof., 1976-82, prof., 1982—, sr. research scientist Rehab. Research and Tng. Center, 1980—. NDEA fellow, 1965-68; grantee in field. Mem. Am. Anthrop. Assn., So. Anthrop. Assn., Soc. Applied Anthropology, Sigma Xi, Alpha Lambda Delta, Kappa Delta Pi. Contbr. in field. Home: 1744 Greenvalley Ave Fayetteville AR 72701 Office: 426 Hotz Hall U Ark Fayetteville AR 72701

SCHNEIDER, VALERIE LOIS, educator; b. Chgo., Feb. 12, 1941; d. Ralph Joseph and Gertrude Blanche (Gaffron) Schneider; B.A., Carroll Coll., 1963; M.A., U. Wis., 1966; Ph.D., U. Fla., 1969; cert. advanced study Appalachian State U., 1981. Tchr. English and history Montello (Wis.) High Sch., 1963-64; dir. forensics and drama Montello High Sch., 1963-64; instr. speech U. Fla., Gainesville, 1966-68, asst. prof. speech, 1969-70; asst. prof. speech Edinboro (Pa.) State Coll., 1970-71; asso. prof. speech East Tenn. State U., Johnson City, 1971-76, prof. speech, 1976—; instr. newspaper course Johnson City Press Chronicle, 1979. Chmn. AAUW Mass Media Study Group Com., Johnson City, 1973-74. Recipient Creative Writing award Va. Highlands Arts Festival, 1973. Danforth asso., 1977. Mem. Speech Communication Assn. (Tenn. rep. to states adv. council 1974-75), So., Tenn. (exec. bd. 1974-77, publs. bd. 1974-78, pres. 1977-78), Religious Speech Communication Assn. (Best article award 1976), Tenn. Basic Skills Council (exec. bd. 1979-80, v.p. 1980-81, pres. 1981-82), AAUW (v.p. chpt. 1974-75, pres. 1975-76, corp. rep. for East Tenn. State U. 1974-76), Nat. Assn. Public Continuing and Adult Edn., Am. Assn. Continuing Higher Edn., Bus. and Profl. Women's Club (chpt. exec. bd. 1972-73, v.p. 1976-77), Nat. Assn. Remedial Developmental Studies in Post Secondary Edn., Western Coll. Reading Assn., Mensa, Delta Sigma Rho-Tau Kappa Alpha, Phi Delta Kappa, Delta Kappa Gamma, Pi Gamma Mu. Presbyterian. Asso. editor: Homiletic, 1974-76. Contbr. articles on speech to profl. jours. Home: C-5 Greenwood Apts 1409 Colony Park Dr Johnson City TN 37601

SCHNEIDERS, LOLITA, state legislator; b. Chhgo., Mar. 3, 1931; d. Albert R. and Eve M. (Lis) Krell; B.Ed., Wis. State U., Stevens Point, 1952; m. Don A. Schneiders, June 12, 1954; children—Nancy Lee, Donna Eve, Lita Sue. Elem. sch. tchr., 1952-56; saleswoman Employers Ins. Wis., 1975-77; indsl. and comml. saleswoman, 1977-80; mem. Wis. Ho. of Reps. from 97th Dist., 1980—. Mem. AAUW, Met. Builders Assn., Bus. and Profl. Women. Republican. Roman Catholic. Address: 314 N State Capitol Madison WI 55702

SCHNEIER, DONNA FRANCES, retail exec.; b. St. Louis, Mar. 30, 1938; d. Irwin H. and Bertha (Gershbock) Makovsky; B.S. summa cum laude, Brandeis U., 1959; M.F.A., N.Y. U., 1964; m. Arthur Schneier, Jan. 12, 1958; children—Marc Steven, Karen Anne. Pres., Gallery 6M, N.Y.C., 1966-73, Donna Schneier, Inc., N.Y.C., 1973-80, B&D Jewelry Corp., N.Y.C., 1977-80, Una Donna Ltd., N.Y.C., 1980—, Donna Schneier Fine Arts, 1980—. Bd. dirs. Yeshiva U., 1973—, Park East Synangogue, 1962—. Mem. Photog. Dealers Am., Nat. Assn. Catalog Showroom Merchandisers, Jewelers Bd. Trade. Office: 251 E 71st St New York NY 10021

SCHNELL, SHIRLEY LUKE, painter, educator; b. Mpls., Jan. 17, 1937; d. Hjalmar and Dorothy Ruth (Ledwein) Luke; B.F.A., Mpls. Coll. Art and Design, 1958; M.F.A., U. Iowa, 1963; m. Lloyd William Schnell, Aug. 26, 1961. Artist, Northwestern Bell Telephone Co., Mpls., 1957-58, Fed. Res. Bank, Mpls., 1958-60; instr. Mpls. Coll. Art and Design, 1962-65, U. Minn., Mpls., 1962-63; prof. Kansas City Art Inst., 1966—; exhibited in one-woman shows at Mpls. Art Inst., 1967, Hildreth Gallery, Nasson Coll., Springvale, Maine, 1971, Charlotte Crosby Kemper Gallery, Kansas City, 1968, 74, Galveston (Tex.) Art Center, 1977, Mulvane Art Center, Topeka, 1982; exhibited in group shows at Time-Life Bldg., N.Y.C., 1965, Walker Art Center, Mpls., Galerie L'Archange, Brussels, Belgium, 1970, Yale U. Summer Show, Norfolk, Conn., 1972, Central Wash. State Coll., Ellensburg, 1975, Nelson Gallery-Atkins Mus., Kansas City, 1975, Krannert Art Mus., U. Ill., Urbana, 1976, 1708 E. Main Gallery, Richmond, Va., 1980, William Crespo Gallery, New Bedford, Mass., 1982, others; represented in permanent collections at Mo. Hist. Soc., Fordham U. Grantee Union Ind. Colls. Art, 1969, 81; fellow MacDowell Colony, 1976, Mo. State Arts Council grantee, 1977. Mem. Nat. Woman's Caucus for Art, Kansas City Artist's Coalition, ACLU, Internat. Meditation Soc., Sierra Club. Roman Catholic. Home: 3917 SW Hidden Cove Circle Raintree Lake Lees Summit MO 64063 Office: Kansas City Art Inst 4415 Warwick St Kansas City MO 64111

SCHNEPF, LAURIE MARIE, pub. co. exec.; b. Nyack, N.Y., Dec. 24, 1956; d. William Albert Schnepf and Ruth Dorothy (Brinkmann) Pieper; B.S. cum laude, Fairleigh Dickinson U., 1978; m. Stephen Lester, May 24, 1981. Research asst. Drexel Burnham Lambert, N.Y.C., 1978-79; asst. research dir. Tech. Pub. Co., N.Y.C., 1979-80, market research mgr., 1981—; asst. account exec. McGraw-Hill Pubs., N.Y.C., 1980-81. Mem. Am. Mktg. Assn., Advt. Women of N.Y. Home: 111 4th Ave Apt 10-B New York NY 10003 Office: Tech Pub Co 875 3d Ave New York NY 10022

SCHNURMANN, ERIKA, librarian; b. Paterson, N.J.; d. Karl and Martha (Buegen) S.; A.B., Pembroke Coll., 1937; postgrad. Simmons Coll., 1938; M.L.S., Columbia U., 1947. Head public relations and order dept. Paterson Public Library, 1940-65; dir. Hawthorne (N.J.) Public Library, 1966-68; librarian-cons. Wayne (N.J.) Public Library, 1960-64, West Paterson Public Library, 1961-62, Nursing Edn. Library Paterson Gen. Hosp., 1963-69; dir. Little Falls (N.J.) Public Library, 1968-69; dir. Kearny (N.J.) Public Library, 1969—. Sec., program chmn. Council Service Clubs, 1960-62; sec. Kearny Safety Council, 1975-80; sec. Hudson County Bicentennial Com., 1973-76. Mem. AAUW, N.J. Press Womens Club, Nat. League Am. Pen Women (past state pres.), N.J. Library Assn. (treas. 1956), Bergen Passaic County Library Club (past pres.), Hudson County Library Club (pres. 1972-74), N. Jersey Libraries Round Table (past chmn.), Library Public Relations Council N.Y., West Hudson C. of C., Passaic County Health Edn. and Welfare Assn. (past pres.). Editor N.J. Library Assn. Newsletter, 1955-56; contbr. articles to profl. jours. Home: 335 Sylvan St Rutherford NJ 07070 Office: Public Library 318 Kearny Ave Kearny NJ 07032

SCHNURPEL, HELEN MAMIE PERSELL (MRS. HANS KARL SCHNURPEL), ret. realtor; b. Omaha, Aug. 25, 1902; d. John Alva and Mamie Ethel (Davis) Persell; student U. Nebr., 1930; certificate in real estate, U. Calif. at Los Angeles, 1959; m. Hans Karl Schnurpel, May 10, 1937. Co-owner Lynwood Realty Co. (Calif.), 1945-81, Real Estate Sch. So. Calif., Lynwood, 1951-81. Mem. Compton-Lynwood Bd. Realtors (hon. life mem., sec.-treas. 1966-67, dir.; pres. 1970), Nat. Assn. Realtors (hon. life), Calif. Assn. Realtors (hon. life), Lynwood C. of C. (treas. 1978-80), Internat. Platform Assn. Republican. Club: Lynwood Womens (pres. 1975-76). Home: 14143 Dunrobin Ave Bellflower CA 90706

SCHOBER, DOROTHY FLORENCE, former educator; b. Green Bay, Wis., Sept. 19, 1910; d. Max William and Addie (Stone) Schober; B.A., U. Wis., 1932; M.P.H., Yale U., 1948; m. Ralph E. Hoffmeyer, Sept. 3, 1982. Visitor, dist. supr., dist. dir. Fla. Welfare Bd., Jacksonville, 1932-37; dir. Public Welfare Dept., Green Bay, 1937-42; cons. Div. Public Assistance, Wis. Dept. Pub. Welfare, Madison, 1942-44; counselor USPHS, 1944-45; health edn. cons. Council Social Agys., New Haven, 1946-49; heart work cons. State Com. on Tb and Public Health, N.Y., 1949-52; program cons., exec. asst. Am. Heart Assn., 1952-64, asst. dir. affiliate relations and services, 1964-65, asst. dir. dept. councils and internat. program, 1965-70, asso. dir., 1970-73, asso. dir. div. sci. affairs, chief sci. councils, 1973-75. Recipient Gold Heart Bracelet in appreciation 10 yr. service Staff Conf. Heart Assn., 1962. Fellow Am. Public Health Assn.; mem. Phi Kappa Phi, Alpha Kappa Delta. Home: 58-B Calle Cadiz Laguna Hills CA 92653

SCHOCH, JACQUELINE LOUISE, educator; b. DuBois, Pa., July 17, 1929; d. Horace Gordon and Cora (Wineberg) S.; B.Sc. in Health and Phys. Edn., Pa. State U., 1951, M.Ed. in Counseling and Psychology, 1960, D.Ed. in Counseling and Psychology, 1965; cert. Inst. Ednl. Mgmt., Harvard U., 1979. Tchr. girls' phys. edn. Jr.-Sr. High Sch., Ford City, Pa., 1951-52; tchr. girl's phys. edn., acad. U.S. history DuBois Area Sr. High Sch., 1952-53, girls' guidance counselor, 1956-65; dir. guidance DuBois Area Sch. Dist., 1965-67, dir. instrn., 1967-70; asst. dir. for resident instrn. DuBois campus Pa. State U., 1970-76, asso. dir. acad. affairs, 1976—, dir. DuBois campus, 1978—, also mem., chmn. univ. coms., faculty senate. Instr. polit. action courses local C. of C., 1963; instr. adult swimming classes local YMCA, 1953-55; instr. continuing edn. program Pa. State U., 1967-70, also asst. prof. edn., 1970—. Cons. Appalachia project, W.Va., 1967-68; mem. evaluating teams for evaluating secondary schs. Middle States Evaluation Com., 1960-62. Bd. dirs. DuBois area United Fund, co-chmn. fund raising campaign, 1967-68, 2d v.p., 1970—; bd. dirs. DuBois council Girl Scouts, 1954-56, Family Life Center-Luth. Services, 1972-76; treas. DuBois Ednl. Found.; bd. dirs. DuBois Area YMCA. Named Boss of Yr., Internat. Secs. Assn., 1977. Mem. Assn. for Higher Edn., Delta Mu Sigma, Delta Psi Omega, Iota Alpha Delta, Delta Kappa Gamma, Pi Lambda Theta, Phi Delta Kappa. Office: DuBois Campus Pa State U DuBois PA 15801

SCHOEDEL, VICKI L., telephone co. exec.; b. Fort Worth, Aug. 20, 1949; d. Lawrence B. and Floyce L. (Haney) Vaughn; B.A. in Psychology, Tex. Christian U., 1971; m. John F. Schoedel, Apr. 3, 1976. With Southwestern Bell Telephone Co., St. Louis, 1967—, supr. course devel., 1974-77, asst. staff mgr. gen. marketing dept., 1977-79, staff specialist staffing, 1979-81, career counselor, 1981—; cons. career mgmt./devel. activities and programs. Vice pres. Aid Assn. for Luths., 1979-81; bd. chmn. adult nurture bd. Concordia Luth. Ch., 1979—, mem. ch. council, 1979—; vol. Arthritis Found. Mem. Tex. Christian U. Alumni Assn., AAUW. Club: Tex. Christian U. Century. Home: 678 Dougherty Estates Dr Manchester MO 63011 Office: 112 N 4th St Room 400 Saint Louis MO 63102

SCHOENBERG, PATRICIA ANN, electronics co. exec.; b. Salisbury, N.C., Apr. 16, 1943; d. Eugene V. and Joyce Q. (Nance) Osborne; m. Charles W. Schoenberg, Dec. 3, 1960 (div. 1972); children—Charles W., Bruce A. Exec. sec., Argus, Inc., Chgo., 1963; office mgr. A.R. Bernard Corp., Chgo., 1963-65, gen. mgr., 1965-68; cons. Mayfair Electronics, Chgo., 1968; asst. to pres. Ross Electronics, Chgo., 1969; v.p., partner IMA, Chgo., 1970-73, exec. v.p., 1973-78, pres., 1979-81; founder, pres. Spectra Merchandising Internat., Inc., Chgo., 1981—; co-founder, pres. Contec Electronics Inc., 1982—. Office: 1150 N State St Suite 305 Chicago IL 60610

SCHOETTLIN, SHIRLEY ANN, Realtor; b. Piggott, Ark., May 3, 1938; d. Raymond Andrew and Sylvia Virginia (Hughes) Wright; student public schs., Piggott; children—Melissa Leigh, Phillip Andrew. Property mgr. Charles F. Curry Co., Kansas City, Mo., 1970-73, project mgr., sales asso., 1973-77; sales asso. TMI Realtors, Lee's Summit, Mo., 1977-78, broker, 1978—, v.p., 1978—; owner Schoettlin Real Estate Co., 1981—; chmn. real estate coms. Mem. bd. dirs. Met. March of Dimes. Mem. Real Estate Bd. Lee's Summit (dir.), Real Estate Bd. Kansas City, Nat. Assn. Realtors, Mo. Assn. Realtors (dir.), Women's Council Realtors (governing bd.). Club: Million Dollar. Contbr. articles to profl. jours. Home: 3741 Woodland Ct Lakewood Lee's Summit MO 64063 Office: 606 B W Third St Lee's Summit MO 64063

SCHOLL, PRISCILLA IRENE, nursing adminstr.; b. Amherst, Wis., Mar. 17, 1925; d. Charles Gerald and Lydia Francis (Schrader) Shanklin; grad. Deaconess Hosp. Sch. Nursing, 1946; student Milw. Tech. Coll., 1957-58, U. Wis., Milw., 1958-71; B.S. in Health Arts, Coll. of St. Francis, 1981; m. Robert Philip Scholl, May 22, 1948; children—Judith Ann, Susan. Staff nurse Deaconess Hosp., Milw., 1946-49, staff nurse circulating evenings, 1956-57, asst. clin. instr. and nursing service supr., 1957-64, inservice supr., 1964-67, supr. and instr. of renal program, 1966—; guest lectr. on renal failure to various nursing orgns. 1970-78. Bd. dirs. Kidney Found. of Wis., 1973—, mem. med. and sci. com., 1973—, patient services com., 1971-75, chmn., 1974-75. Mem. Am. Nurses Assn., Am. Assn. Nephrology Nurses and Technicians (organizer Wis. chpt. 1978). Office: Deaconess Hosp 620 N 19th St Milwaukee WI 53233

SCHOLTZ, ELIZABETH, bot. garden adminstr.; b. Pretoria, South Africa, Apr. 29, 1921; came to U.S., 1960, naturalized, 1978; d. Tielman Johannes and Vera Vogel (Roux) Roos-Scholtz; B.Sc., Witwatersrand U., 1941; D.H.L., Pace U., 1974. Technician, South African Inst. Med. Research, Johannesburg, 1942-44; technician dept. medicine, Johannesburg and Pretoria gen. hosps., 1944-46; with Groote Schuur Hosp., Capetown, as technician charge student labs., 1948-52, technician charge hematology lab., 1952-60; mem. staff Bklyn. Bot. Garden, 1960—, asso. curator instrn., 1964-71, acting dir., 1972-73, dir., 1973-80, v.p., 1980—; trustee Independence Savs. Bank. Recipient Arthur Hoyt Scott Garden and Horticulture award, 1981. Mem. Am. Hort. Soc., Am. Assn. Bot. Gardens and Arboreta (dir. 1976-79), Am. Bonsai Soc. (dir. 1972-79). Clubs: Brooklyn Heights Casino, Cosmopolitan. Office: 1000 Washington Ave Brooklyn NY 11225 *

SCHOLTZ, EVELYN, med. technologist, educator; b. Paterson, N.J., Aug. 17, 1943; d. Frank and Stephanie (Malinkiewicz) S.; A.S. in Chem. Technology, Fairleigh Dickinson U., 1963, B.S. in Med. Technology, 1965; M.A. in Biology, St. Joseph Coll., 1970; M.S. in Health Care Mgmt., Hartford Grad. Center, 1983. Med. technologist bacteriology lab. Hartford (Conn.) Hosp., 1965-67, supr. serology-microscopy lab., 1967-68; edn. coordinator med. lab. asst. program 1968-71, program dir. lab. edn. Sch. Allied Health, 1979—; adj. faculty mem. U. Conn., Storrs, West Conn. State Coll., Danbury, U. Bridgeport (Conn.), St. Joseph Coll., West Hartford, Conn. Bd. dirs. Cromwell Hills Assn., 1974-77. T. Stewart Hamilton fellow, 1976. Mem. Conn. Soc. Med. Tech., Am. Soc. Med. Tech., AAUW. Contbr. articles in field to profl. publs. Home: 29 Margo Ct Cromwell CT 06416 Office: 80 Seymour St Hartford CT 06115

SCHOMER, ELSIE PAULINE, social worker; b. Colorado Springs, Colo., July 21, 1919; d. Paul Olaf and Ellen Arveda (Nelson) Swenson; A.B., Colo. Coll., 1940; postgrad. Chgo. Theol. Sem., 1940-41, U. Chgo. Sch. Social Service Adminstrn., 1941-42; M.S.W., Rutgers U., 1972; m. Howard Schomer, Mar. 23, 1942; children—Karine, Mark, Paul, Ellen. Group worker Firman Settlement House, Chgo., 1941; dir. summer recreational program Black Mountain, N.C., 1942; sec. Conn. State Hosp., 1943; sec. Com. to Oppose Conscription of Women, 1944; organizer of relief supplies Congl. Christian Mission of Fellowship, Chambon-sur-Lignon, France, 1946-48; co-founder, dir. Chambon Internat. Conf. Center, 1952-55, Chgo. Women for Peace, 1960-65; social worker Met. region N.J. Div. of Mental Retardation, Montclair, 1967-81, coordinator home assistance program, 1979-81; coordinator Social Responsibility Adv. Service, 1982—. Mem. staff N.J. Gov.'s Task Force on Welafre Mgmt., 1971; mem. Clergy Del. to Vietnam, 1965; mem. Jesse Jackson Peace Mission to Middle East, 1979. Mem. N.J. Assn. Retarded Citizens, Women's Internat. League for Peace and Freedom (pres. Chgo. br. 1964, nat. dir. 1967-68), Phi Beta Kappa. Mem. United Ch. Christ. Home: 13 Fairmount Ave Upper Montclair NJ 07043

SCHONHOLTZ, JOAN SONDRA HIRSCH (MRS. GEORGE J. SCHONHOLTZ), banker, civic worker; b. N.Y.C., Sept. 8, 1933; d. Joseph G. and Mildred (Klebanoff) Hirsch; student Vassar Coll., 1950-52; B.A., Barnard Coll., 1954; postgrad. Am. U., 1963; m. George J. Schonholtz, Aug. 21, 1951; children—Margot Beth, Steven Robert, Barbara Ellen. With Meml. Hosp., N.Y.C., 1954. Pres., Fort Benning (Ga.) Med. Wives, 1962-63; sec. Montgomery County (Md.) Women's Med. Aux., 1968; sec. Service Guild of Washington, 1969-70, bd. dirs., 1968-78, pres., 1975-77; organizer, chmn. bd. First Women's Bank of Md., Rockville, 1977—. mem. Washington Adv. Council on Deaf-Blind Children, 1972-74; bd. dirs. Pilot Sch. for Blind Multiple Handicapped Children, Washington, 1968-78, Jewish Social Service Agy., 1977-79. spl. gifts chmn. Cancer Soc., Montgomery County, Md., 1968, 69. Recipient Outstanding Service award Service Guild of Washington, 1969. Republican. Jewish. Clubs: Vassar, Barnard. Home: 11310 Old Club Rd Rockville MD 20852

SCHOOLEY, DOLORES HARTER, artist mgr.; b. Nora Springs, Iowa, May 2, 1905; d. Amil A. and Elizabeth (Sefert) Zemke; B.E., B.A., U. Colo., 1927; M.A., Northwestern U., 1931; m. Leslie J. Harter, June 5, 1934 (dec. 1963); m. 2d, Charles Earl Schooley, Apr. 1, 1966. Tchr. high sch. Consol. Schs., Johnstown, Colo., 1927-28, Byers, Colo., 1928-29, Clayton, Mo., 1931-34; theatrical makeup, 1937—; instr. theatrical makeup, dramatic clubs, N.J. Theatre League; lectr., demonstrator theatrical makeup, dramatic and women's clubs, high schs., N.J. and N.Y. area, 1937-53; dir., entertainer mil. posts First Army, 1951-53; dir. mil. project Phi Beta, 1951-61, nat. officer, mem. nat. council, 1956-61, cons. radio broadcast series WNYC, 1962-65; dir. community relations Wingspread Summer Theatre, Colon, Mich., 1955; co-chmn. Valley Shore Community Concerts, Conn., 1958-61; artist mgr., 1959—; chmn. benefit ball Sharon Hosp., 1970; founder, pres. Berkshire Hills Music and Dance Assn., 1970-78; mem. Music Mountain Corp., Falls Village, Conn., 1975-81. Trustee Sharon Creative Arts Found., 1970-73; hon. trustee Bar Harbor Festival, 1968—; founder, pres. Wingspread Found., 1977—. Mem. Alpha Omicron Pi, Phi Beta. Conglist. Clubs: Montclair (N.J.) Dramatic (chmn. makeup, instr. makeup); Rehearsal (program chmn.); Women's (dir. plays, chmn. drama dept.) (Glen Ridge, N.J.); Sharon Women's, Sharon Country (Conn.). Address: Wingspread PO Box 36 Sharon CT 06069

SCHOONOVER, THELMA IRENE, psychologist; b. Columbus, Ohio; d. Harry Orestus and Nellie Maude (Patrick) S.; B.Sc. in Edn., Ohio State U., Ph.D., 1955. Chief psychologist Akron (Ohio) Bd. Edn., 1950-54; prof. U. Akron, 1951-54; prof., chmn. dept. psychology Capital U., Columbus, 1954-72; pvt. practice psychology, Columbus, 1972—; vis. prof. Ohio State U., Miami U., Oreg. State Coll.; cons. Ohio Pardon and Parole Bd. Pres. Columbus CSC, 1974—. Mem. Am. Psychol. Assn., Ohio Psychol. Assn., Central Ohio Cons. Psychologists, Central Ohio Psychol. Assn., Psi Chi, Phi Delta Gamma, Delta Kappa Gamma, Pi Lambda Theta, AAUW. Republican. Episcopalian. Club: Clintonville Woman's. Author: Measurement for Teachers; contbr. in field. Home: 355 Clinton Heights Ave Columbus OH 43202 Office: 236 E Town St Suite 306 Columbus OH 43215

SCHOPP, BARBARA DREW, nursing services adminstr.; b. Pontiac, Ill., Feb. 12, 1941; d. David and Clara (Goff) Durham; student Elgin Community Coll., 1973-74, 76-78; m. John F. Schopp, Jan. 17, 1958; 1 son, Richard. Personnel cons. S-H-S Internat., Elgin, Ill., 1968-69, staff mgr., 1969-71; staff mgr. Carlton Assos., Geneva, Ill., 1971-73; personnel cons. and staff mgr. Van Matre & Assos., Palatine, Ill., 1973-75; pres. Drew Personnel Inc., Elgin, 1975-81; office mgr./mktg. mgr. Quality Care Nursing Services, Elgin, 1981—; tchr. (part-time) Elgin Community Coll., 1977-78; guest lectr. Xavier Coll., 1977-78. Mem. public relations bd. Elgin YWCA, 1977—; v.p. Upper Kane County Heart Assn., 1980—; active vol. Cancer Fund Drive, Carpentersville, Ill., 1967—; mem. prodn. com. Miss Elgin Pageant, 1980—. Mem. Nat. Assn. Female Execs., Nat. Assn. Personnel Cons., Ill. Assn. Personnel Cons. (dir. 1976-79, cert. of appreciation 1976, 77), N.W. Suburban C. of C., Elgin C. of C., Omicron Tau. Club: Order Eastern Star. Home: 1920 Bristol Circle Carpentersville IL 60110 Office: 75 Market St Elgin IL 60120

SCHOR, MARY ANN MCCARTHY (MRS. WARREN SCHOR), public relations exec.; b. Washington; d. Jeremiah John and Ann (Horstkamp) McCarthy; grad. George Washington U., 1962, grad. publ. specialist program, 1977; EPS Program, Trinity Coll., 1982; m. Warren Schor, May 2, 1964; 1 dau., Elizabeth Ann. Public relations, various accounts, Washington, 1962-66; dir. public relations program Met. Police Dept., Washington, 1966-69; public relations D.C. Dept. Public Health, Washington, 1979-70, D.C. Police Dept., Washington, 1970-75; public relations cons., 1976—. Mem. public relations com. D.C. Tb and Respiratory Disease Assn., 1969—. Mem. Am. Newspaper Women's Club (treas. 1982-83), Advt. Club Washington, Zonta. Roman Catholic. Editor: Rambling thru Georgetown, 1978-80; Rambling thru Alexandria, 1978-80. Home: 6206 Wedgewood Rd Bethesda MD 20034

SCHORR, BEVERLY HELEN, ednl. adminstr.; b. Phila., Aug. 23, 1934; d. Isadore and Anne (Greber) Rubin; B.A., Villanova U., 1975, M.A., 1977; m. David Jay Schorr, Aug. 31, 1952; children—Alan, Michael, Steven, Devra. Dir. adult programs Villanova (Pa.) U., 1976—. Chmn. Lower Southampton Commn., Trevose, Pa., 1978—. Mem. Am. Conf. Higher Edn., Am. Edn. Assn., AAUW, Am. Personnel and Guidance Assn., Nat. Assn. Women Deans, Adminstrs., Counselors (nat. directorate for continuing edn. 1981—), Phila. Women's Network, Bus. and Profl. Women's Assn. Jewish.

SCHORR, JULIE ANDERSON, nurse, educator; b. Marquette, Mich., Mar. 22, 1949; d. Robert E. and Phyllis M. (Sundberg) Anderson; B.S.N. cum laude, No. Mich. U., 1972; M.S.N. (Profl. Nurse trainee), Wayne State U., 1977, Ph.D. (Profl. Nurse trainee 1978-79, Univ. scholar 1979-80, 81-82), 1982; m. Robert L. Schorr, May 17, 1975. Charge nurse CCU, Marquette (Mich.) Gen. Hosp., 1972-75; instr. St. Luke's Sch. Nursing, Marquette, 1975-76; asst. prof. nursing, coordinator cardiac rehab. pilot project No. Mich. U., 1976-77; asst. prof. Wayne State U., 1977-78, U. Mich., 1980-81, U. Nev. at Reno Orvis Sch. Nursing, 1981—; bd. dirs. Mich. Heart Assn., Marquette, 1976-77. Mem. Am. Nurse's Assn., Nev. Nurses's Assn., Western Soc. for Research in Nursing, Sigma Theta Tau. Office: Orvis Sch Nursing U Nev Reno NV 89557

SCHORSCH, (MARY) DOLORES (ALMA FRANCES), nun, edn. cons.; b. Morris, Ill., June 16, 1896; d. Anthony and Maria (Czagany) S.; A.B., De Paul U., Chgo., 1920, A.M., 1921, B.S., 1922; Ed.D., Loyola U., Chgo., 1953. Joined Benedictine Sisters Chgo., Roman Catholic Ch., 1922; supr. instruction various parochial schs., Ill. and Colo., 1928-68; prin. St. Scholastica High Sch., 1942-44; instr. De Paul U., Chgo., 1921-69, dir. theses, examiner, 1942-57; guest lectr. Catholic Summer Sch. Am., 1938-39, Mount St. Scholastica Coll., 1937, Marymount Coll., 1937, Coll. at Salina (Kans.), 1936, Ursuline Coll., Louisville, 1936; mem. council, community sec. Benedictine Sisters of Chgo., 1928-51; Confraternity Christian Doctrine coordinator Our Lady of Snows Parish, Chgo., 1977-78. Recipient certs. service and achievement DePaul U., 1969, other honors. Mem. Am. Assn. Higher Edn., Am. Psychol. Assn., Am. Benedictine Acad., Am. Cath. Philos. Assn., Nat. Cath. Edn. Assn., Cath. Audio-Visual Educators, N.E. Council Interfaith Ministry (chmn.), St. Hilary Parish Council. Author: (with A.P. Schorsch) Jesu-Maria Course in Religion, 1934—; Our Lord and Our Lady, 1957; author script Life of Our Lord in Art, 1956, 8 filmstrips on Early History of Church, 1962. Home: St Scholastica Priory 7430 N Ridge Ave Chicago IL 60645

SCHOTZKO, JUDITH GILBERT, nurse, lawyer; b. Rosiclare, Ill., Nov. 19, 1938; d. Maurice Clement and Naomi (Kibler) Gilbert; R.N., St. Luke's Sch. Nursing, 1959; B.A., Met. State U., 1977; J.D., U. Minn., 1980; m. John Rudolph Schotzko, July 16, 1963; children—Clay John, Jonna Marie, Molly Ann, Lee Gilbert. Surg. and psychiat. nurse, U. Minn. Hosp., Mpls., 1959-65; research asst. U. Minn. Law Sch., Mpls., 1979-80; admitted to Minn. bar, 1981; asso. firm Frundt, Frundt & Johnson, Blue Earth, Minn., 1980-82; pvt. practice law, Blue Earth, 1982—; mem. Minn. Ethical Practice bd., 1980-82, chmn., 1982—. Pres., Minn., Mental Health Assn., 1975-76, nat. bd. dirs. 1976-82, nat. regional v.p., 1981-82; chmn. Faribault County Rep. Party, 1972-77, alt. del. nat. conv., 1976. Recipient Blue Earth Women of Achievement award, 1973; Vol. of Yr. award Minn. Mental Health Assn., 1976. Mem. Minn. Student Nurses Assn. (v.p. 1958), Minn. Student Bar Assn., Minn. Bar Assn. Clubs: Med. Aux. Minn. Med. Student Wives (pres. 1966-67), Blue Earth Valley Med. Aux., Nat. Med. Student Wives (sec. 1967-68), Am. Legion Aux., Mitchell Chautaqua Circle. Home: Route 1 PO Box 42 Blue Earth MN 56013 Office: 223 S Main St Blue Earth MN 56013

SCHRAIBMAN, SANDRA MILNER, lawyer; b. Charleston, S.C., Aug. 18, 1947; d. Edward Hampton and Sybil Jeannette (Karesh) Milner; B.A. in Polit. Sci., U. S.C., 1969, J.D., 1973; LL.M. (Prettyman fellow 1973-75), Georgetown U., 1978; m. Julian Stanley Schraibman, July 1, 1969. Admitted to S.C. bar, 1973, Fla. bar, 1975, D.C. bar, 1974; supr. law sch. clinic Georgetown U. Law Center, Washington, 1973-75; asst. prof. law, Holland Law Center, U. Fla., Gainesville, 1975-76; trial atty. Fed. Programs Br. Civil Div., Dept. Justice, Washington, 1976-80, asst. dir., 1980—. Recipient spl. commendation award, Civil Div., 1980. Mem. Am. Bar Assn., S.C. Bar, D.C. Bar, Fla. Bar. Jewish. Office: Dept Justice 10th and Constitution Ave NW Washington DC 20530

SCHRAM, SUSAN GALE, home economist; b. Grand Rapids, Mich., June 19, 1948; d. Paul Gerard and Dorothy Maxine S.; B.S., Mich. State U., East Lansing, 1970, M.A., 1973. Tchr., Lansing City Schs., 1970; mem. child care staff Hawthorn Center Psychiat. Facility, Northville, Mich., 1971-72; research asst. U. Mich., 1973; research asst. Mich. State U., 1972-73, extension home economist, Grand Haven, 1974-76, state program leader Coop. Extension Service, East Lansing, 1976-80; exec. sec. Joint Council on Food and Agrl. Sci., U.S. Dept. Agr., Washington, 1980—; with Food and Nutrition Info. Center, Nat. Agrl. Library, Beltsville, Md., 1977. Named Mich. Regional Young Career Woman of Year, Bus. and Profl. Women, 1976; grantee rural devel. Title V, 1977. Mem. Am. Home Econs. Assn., Exec. Female Assn., Mich. Extension Home Econs. Assn. (Communication award 1976), Washington Women's Network, Phi Kappa Phi, Omicron Nu, Kappa Alpha Theta. Mem. United Ch. of Christ. Author handbooks, papers in field. Office: Room 351-A Adminstrn Bldg USDA 14th and Independence Washington DC 20250

SCHRAMM, PATRICIA CAIN, state ofcl.; b. Kansas City, Kans., Mar. 25, 1937; d. William Howard and Helen (Pospisil) Cain; B.A., Bryn Mawr Coll., 1959, Ph.D., 1971; M.A., U. Chgo., 1963; m. Richard E. Schramm, June 4, 1960. Reporter, Chgo. Sun Times, 1959-61, Phila. Bull., 1961-63; research dir. Greater Wilmington (Del.) Devel. Council, 1963-67; dir. social planning City of Wilmington, 1970-73, dir. planning and devel., 1973-77; sec. health and social services State of Del., Wilmington, 1977—. Office: Adminstrn Bldg Del State Hosp Wilmington DE 19720

SCHREIBER, EILEEN SHER, artist; b. Denver; d. Michael Herschel and Sarah Deborah (Tannenbaum) Sher; student U. Utah, 1942-45, N.Y.U. extension, 1966-68, Montclair (N.J.) State Coll., 1975-79; also pvt. art study; m. Jonas Schreiber, Mar. 27, 1945; children—Jeffrey, Barbara, Michael. Exhibited Morris Mus. Arts and Scis., Morristown, N.J., 1965-73, N.J. State Mus., 1969, Lever House, N.Y.C., 1971, Paramus (N.J.) Mus., 1973, Newark Mus., 1978, Am. Water Color Soc., Audubon Artists, N.A.D. Gallery, N.Y.C., Pallazzo Vecchio Florence (Italy); represented in permanent collections Morris Mus., Seton Hall U., Bloomfield (N.J.) Coll., Barclay Bank of Eng., N.J., Somerset Coll., Morris County State Coll., Broad Nat. Bank, Newark, IBM, Am. Telephone Co., RCA, Johnson & Johnson, Champion Internat. Paper Co., Ga. Pacific Co., Public Service Co. N.J., others; also pvt. collections. Recipient awards N.J. Watercolor Soc., 1969, 72, Nat. Assn. Women Artists, 1970; 1st award in watercolor Hunterdon Art Center, 1972, Best in Show award Short Hills State Show, 1976, Tri-State Purchase award Somerset Coll., 1977, numerous others. Mem. Nat. Assn. Women Artists (chmn. watercolor jury), Nat., N.J. artists equity, Nat. Painter and Sculptors Assn., Hunterdon Art Center. Home: 22 Powell Dr West Orange NJ 07052 also Reece Galleries 39 W 32d St New York NY 10001 also Pason-Weisberg Gallery 822 Madison Ave New York NY 10021

SCHREIBER, JOAN EMELIA, educator; b. La Porte City, Iowa, Feb. 24, 1928; d. Louie and Dorathea Magdalena (Lange) Schreiber; student U. Iowa, 1945-46; B.A., Iowa State Tchrs. Coll., 1949; M.A., State Coll. Iowa, 1960; Specialist in Edn., U. No. Iowa, 1963; Ph.D., U. Iowa, 1967. Tchr. Cedar Rapids (Iowa) pub. schs., 1949-59; ednl. cons. Cass County, Atlantic, Iowa, 1961-63; asst. prof. Edn. Augustana Coll., Rock Island, Ill., 1963-65; asst. prof. history Ball State U., Muncie, Ind., 1966-69, asso. prof., 1969-74, prof., 1974—, coordinator social studies methods, 1968—, pres. senate, 1979-80; program developer (with others) Scott, Foresman Social Studies, Kindergarten through Grade 7. Mem. Ind. State Social Studies Adv. Com., 1974—, Ind. State Tchr. Edn. Adv. Council, 1974-75. Mem. Nat., Ind. (pres. 1974-75) councils social studies, AAUP, Ind. Acad. Social Scis., AAUW, Del. County (Ind.) Hist. Soc., Pi Lambda Theta, Phi Delta Kappa. Author: (with Lloyd L. Smith) Social Studies K-6: A Guide for Curriculum Revision, 1971; Scott, Foresman Social Studies Program Texts for Kindergarten, Grades 1 and 2, 1979; contbr. articles to profl. jours. Office: Dept of History Ball State U Muncie IN 47306 •

SCHREYER-THOMSON, CAMELLA JOY, artist, editor; b. Lawrence, Kans., July 17, 1949; d. George Maurice and Camella Inez (Burnette) Schreyer; B.A. cum laude, Pfeiffer Coll., 1971; M.A., East Carolina U., 1974; research studies Europe and Gt. Britain; m. Douglas Arthur Thomson, May 6, 1973. One-woman shows: Allas Art Galleries, Charlotte, N.C., 1971, Pfeiffer Coll. Gallery, 1975, 79; group shows include: Durham (N.C.) Art Guild, Fayetteville (N.C.) Mus. Art, Shooren's, Rockport, Mass., East Carolina U.; represented in permanent collection Pfeiffer Coll., also pvt. collections; editor-in-chief Am. Biog. Inst., Raleigh, N.C., 1973—; class agt. Pfeiffer Coll. Alumni Assn., 1976—. Cert. tchr. kindergarten through 9th grades, N.C. Mem. Am. Fedn. Arts, Nat. League Am. Pen Women, Stanly County Art Guild, Durham Arts Council, Phi Delta Sigma. Methodist. Contbr. poems to lit. jours.; art editor The Phoenix of Pfeiffer Coll., also various annuals. Address: 5436 Pine Top Circle Raleigh NC 27612

SCHROCK, JANET MARIE MOREHOUSE, interior designer; b. Carlisle, Pa., June 30, 1942; d. Harley Francis and Helen Elizabeth (Kitzmiller) Morehouse; B.S., Indiana U. of Pa., 1964; M.Ed., Pa. State U., 1971; M.S., Okla. State U., 1973; Ph.D., U. Mo., 1978; m. Jay Rupert Schrock, Aug. 3, 1968. Elem. art tchr., Leighton, Pa., 1964-66; art tchr., Chitose, Japan, 1969-70; instr. interior design. Kans. State U., 1974-76; instr. housing and interior design U. Mo., 1976-78; asst. prof. housing and interior design Tex. Tech. U., Lubbock, 1978—. Teaching Devel. grantee Tx. Tech. U., 1982. Mem. Am. Assn. Housing Educators (exec. com., rec. sec.), Interior Design Educators Council, Am. Assn. Home Econs. Contbr. articles profl. jours. Office: 265 Home Economics Dept Family Man and Consumer Science Texas Tech University Lubbock TX 79509

SCHROEDER, KATHLEEN MARY, social worker; b. Dubuque, Iowa, Mar. 11, 1947; d. John Francis and Kathleen Irma (Brahm) S.; B.A., Clarke Coll., 1969; M.S.W., U. Iowa, 1971. Social worker Area Residential Care, Inc., Dubuque, 1971-73; foster care worker Scott County Dept. Social Services, Davenport, Iowa, 1973-74; psychiat. social worker State of Nebr., Hastings Regional Center, 1974—. Cert. alcoholism counselor. Mem. Acad. Cert. Social Workers, Nat. Assn. Social Workers. Home: 1722 W 3rd Hastings NE 68901 Office: Hastings Regional Center Hastings NE 68901

SCHROEDER, LAURA MAY, city mgr.; b. Greenville, Maine, July 2, 1932; d. Ralph Herbert and Bertha Rowe (Wintle) Given; grad. high sch.; m. Roscoe Schroeder, Nov. 26, 1971 (dec.); children—Linda, Ellen, Malcolm, Ann, Rodney, Helen, James, Roscoe. Co-owner, Folsomi's Air Service, Greenville, 1950-65; auditor Dept. Army Finance, Ft. Knox, Ky., 1969-71; adminstrv. asst. USPHS Hosp., Kanakanak, Alaska, 1971-74; fin. dir. City of Dillingham (Alaska), 1975-78; city mgr., 1978—. Payroll worker Native Villages, 1973-82; tech. adv. com. Bristol Bay Area Hosp., 1980-81; ex-officio mem. Dillingham Planning Commn., 1978-82; mem. Dillingham Sch. Bd., 1977, Bristol Bay Area Econ. Devel. Bd., 1978-81. Recipient various award including letter of appreciation City of Dillingham, 1978, USPHS, 1972. Mem. Alaska Mgmt. Assn., Am. Mgmt. Assn. Methodist. Home: Main St Dillingham AK 99576 Office: D St Dillingham AK 99576

SCHROEDER, MARY MURPHY, judge; b. Boulder, Colo., Dec. 4, 1940; d. Richard and Theresa (Kahn) Murphy; B.A., Swarthmore Coll., 1962; J.D., U. Chgo., 1965; m. Milton R. Schroeder, Oct. 15, 1965; children—Caroline Theresa, Katherine Emily. Admitted to Ill. bar, 1966, D.C. bar, 1966, Ariz. bar, 1970; trial atty. Dept. Justice, Washington, 1965-69; law clk. Hon. Jesse Udall, Ariz. Supreme Ct., 1970; mem. firm Lewis and Roca, Phoenix, 1971-75, partner, 1973-75; judge Ariz. Ct. Appeals, Phoenix, 1975-79; judge U.S. Ct. Appeals, 9th Circuits, Phoenix, 1979—; vis. instr. Ariz. State U. Coll. Law, 1976, 77, 78. Mem. Am. Bar Assn., Ariz. Bar Assn., Fed. Bar Assn., Am. Law Inst., Am. Judicature Soc. Democrat. Club: Soroptimists. Contbr. articles to profl. jours. Office: 6421 Federal Bldg 230 N 1st Ave Phoenix AZ 85025

SCHROEDER, PATRICIA FINKE (MRS. EDWARD F. SCHROEDER), former educator and guidance counselor; b. Sheboygan, Wis., July 21, 1927; d. Almore H. and Valeda Marie (Hansen) Finke; B.S. with honors, U. Wis., 1949; M.Ed., Fla. Atlantic U., 1971; postgrad. Broward Community Coll., 1962-63, Fla. State U., 1967-69, Nova U., 1979—; m. Edward F. Schroeder, June 24, 1950; children—Kathleen L. Schroeder Pearson, Walter William. Tchr., Janesville (Wis.) High Sch., 1949-50, Fern Hall Pvt. Sch., Ft. Lauderdale, Fla., 1950-51, Ft. Lauderdale High Sch., 1951-54, Sunrise Jr. High Sch., Ft. Lauderdale, 1964-69; sr. counselor Ft. Lauderdale High Sch., 1971-82. Mem. Delta Kappa Gamma, Phi Kappa Phi, Omicron Nu, Pi Lambda Theta, Phi Upsilon Omicron, Gamma Phi Beta, Sigma Epsilon Sigma.

SCHROEDER, PATRICIA SCOTT (MRS. JAMES WHITE SCHROEDER), congresswoman, educator, lawyer; b. Portland, Oreg., July 30, 1940; d. Lee Combs and Bernice (Scott) Scott; B.A., magna cum laude, U. Minn., 1961; J.D., Harvard, 1964; m. James White Schroeder, Aug. 18, 1962; children—Scott William, Jamie Christine. Admitted to Colo. bar, 1964; field atty. NLRB, Denver, 1964-66; pvt. practice law, Denver, 1966—; mem. faculty U. Colo., Denver, 1969—, Community Coll., Denver, 1969-70, Regis Coll., Denver, 1970—; mem. 93d-95th Congresses from 1st dist. Colo. Dir. Century Casualty Co., Denver. Bd. dirs. Jefferson County Human Relations Council, 1966—, Denver Young Dems., 1968—; Dem. precinct committeewoman, 1968—. Mem. Denver Bar Assn., League Women Voters (unit leader 1967-68), Internat. House, Fair Housing Center. Conglist. Office: 2437 Rayburn House Office Bldg Washington DC 20515 also 1767 High St Denver CO 80218

SCHROEDER, RITA MOLTHEN, chiropractor; b. Savanna, Ill., Oct. 25, 1922; d. Frank Joseph and Ruth Jessie (McKenzie) Molthen; student in chem. engrng. Immaculate Heart Coll., 1940-41, UCLA, 1941; D.C., Palmer Sch. Chiropractic, 1949, Cleve. Coll. Chiropractic, 1961; m. Richard Henry Schroeder, Apr. 23, 1948; children—Richard, Andrew, Barbara, Thomas, Paul, Madeline. Engrng.-tooling design data coordinator Douglas Aircraft Co., El Segundo, Santa Monica and Long Beach, Calif., 1941-47; practice chiropractic, Bklyn., N.Y., 1949-59, Fresno, Calif., 1961—; pres. Schroeder Chiropractic, Inc., Fresno, 1982—. Bd. dirs. Pacific States Chiropractic Coll., 1978-80, pres., 1980-81. Recipient awards Pacific States Chiropractic Coll., others. Mem. Internat. Chiropractic Assn., Calif. Chiropractic Assn., Assn. Am. Chiropractic Coll. Pres. Republican. Roman Catholic. Office: 2535 N Fresno St Fresno CA 93703

SCHROEDER, SANDI JANE, editor; b. Concord, N.C., June 24, 1945; d. Joseph Alexander and Thelma Aline (Fisher) Brantley; B.A., U. N.C., Charlotte, 1968; postgrad. U. Chgo.; m. Kenneth W. Schroeder, May 23, 1970; children—Amber Monite, Donald Kendrick. Asst. news editor Vance Publishing Co., Chgo., 1968; asst. editor Jour. Med. Edn., Evanston, Ill., 1968-69; asst. editor health dept. Scott Foresman Co., Glenview, Ill., 1969-72; editor-in-chief Schroeder Editorial Services, Lombard, Ill., 1972—. Chmn. hist. com. Bicentennial Commn., Villa Park, Ill., 1975. Chgo. Book Clinic Scholar, 1978, 79. Mem. AAUW (editor newsletter Lombard-Villa Park br. 1972-73, chmn. public info. com. 1974-76), Chgo. Women in Pub., Chgo. Book Clinic (mem. book show com. 1979, 80, 81), Am. Soc. Indexers (chmn. Chgo. chpt. 1981-82). Republican. Lutheran. Contbr. articles to profl. jours. Office: 1076 S Edgewood St Lombard IL 60148

SCHROER, ANNE CHRISTINE PARTCHEY, counseling psychologist; b. Kane, Pa., Dec. 13, 1944; d. Charles Howard and Lucille Grace (Painter) Partchey; B.A., Defiance Coll., 1967; diploma U. Strasbourg, France, 1966; M.A., Wash. State U., 1971; Ph.D., U. No. Colo., 1977; m. Nathan Albert Schroer, July 23, 1966; children—Jonathan Peter, Matthew Charles. Tchr. French, Washington Irving High Sch., Clarksburg, W.Va., 1967-68; counselor Houghton (N.Y.) Coll., 1974-76, dir. counseling services, 1976-81; counseling psychologist Tex. A&M U., College Station, 1981—; life asso. Danforth Found. Mem. Am. Personnel and Guidance Assn., Am. Coll. Personnel Assn., Nat. Vocat. Guidance Assn., Nat. Assn. Women Deans, Adminstrs. and Counselors, Nat. Assn. for Christians in Student Devel. Office: Acad Bldg Tex A&M U College Station TX 77843

SCHROERING, ALICE CATHERINE, educator; b. Jasper, Ind., Mar. 5, 1930; d. Martin Fred and Frances May (Seger) S.; student St. Benedict's Coll., 1948-50, summers 1951-59; B.A. in Edn., Ind. U., 1970, also M.S. in Edn.; postgrad., Loyola U., 1972-82; courses Nat. Coll. Edn., Xavier U., Cin., St. John's, Collegeville, St. Frances, Ft. Wayne. Elementary tchr. pvt. schs. Evansville, Ind., 1950-60, Indpls. area, 1960-68; tchr. jr. high sch. math., Niles, Ill., primary math., Chgo. area, 1970-74; learning disabilities cons. Cicero (Ill.) Schs., 1974-78; primary learning disabilities tchr. Burnham Sch., Cicero, 1978-81, kindergarten, Cicero, 1981-82; part time rental agt. Des Plaines, Ill., 1971-73, 76-79; receptionist, typist Temporary Office Service, summers 1972-77; participant profl. workshops, confs. Mem. Ind. U. Alumni Assn. Democrat. Home: 835 Pearson St #303 Des Plaines IL 60016 Office: Dist 99 5110 W 24th St Cicero IL 60650

SCHROTH, EVELYN MARY, educator; b. Ellington, Wis., Aug. 5, 1919; d. Henry A. and Clara M. (Komp) Schroth; B.S., U. Wis., 1940; M.S., U. Ill., 1948, A.M., 1955; Ph.D., Pacific Western U., 1979. Tchr., Rhinelander (Wis.) High Sch., 1940-42; chmn. English dept. Waupun (Wis.) High Sch., 1942-44; tchr. Chgo. pub. schs., 1953-63, chmn. dept. English, Lindblom High Sch., 1956-62; instr. dept. English, U. Ill., Urbana, 1948-50; lectr. Northeastern U., Chgo., 1962-63; asso. prof. English, Western Ill. U., Macomb, 1963—. Program dir. U.S.O., 1946-48. John Hay fellow, 1961. Mem. Linguistic Soc. Am., Nat. Council Tchrs. English, Ill. Tchrs. English, AAUP, Phi Beta, Phi Kappa Phi. Home: 139 Kurlene Dr Macomb IL 61455 Office: 226 I Simpkins Hall Western Ill U Macomb IL 61455

SCHUCHMAN, BETTY JANE, educator; b. New Albany, Ind., Dec. 2, 1931; d. Chester Everett and G. Marion (May) Englaman; B.S. in Elem. Edn., Ind. U., 1953, M.S. in Student Personnel, 1963, Ed.D. in Higher Edn., 1967; m. John Stanley Schuchman, July 4, 1965. Tchr., Ft. Wayne (Ind.) Public Schs. 1953-57, USAF Dependents' Schs., Eng., Ger., Japan, 1957-61, Lafayette (Ind.) Public Schs. 1961-62; resident asst. Ind. U., Bloomington, 1962-63, assoc. head counselor Teter Quad, 1963-64, head counselor Wells Quad, 1964-65, counselor Inst. Internat. Edn. Orientation program, summers 1963, 64, asst. fgn. student adv., 1965-66, instr. higher edn., summer 1966; research psychologist U.S. Dept. Navy, Washington, 1968-69; staff scientist Matrix Corp., Alexandria, Va., 1969-70; asst. prof. George Mason U., Fairfax, Va., 1970-73, asso. prof., 1973—, coordinator grad. program guidance and counseling, 1977-81, asst. dean Coll. Profl. Studies 1982. Recipient Superior Achievement award Office Naval Research, 1969; Ind. U. research grantee, 1966. Mem. AAUP (state pres. 1976-77), Assn. Higher Edn., NEA, Am. Personnel and Guidance Assn., Am. Coll. Personnel Assn., Faculty Senate Va. (rep. George Mason U. 1973-76), Va. Counselor Assn., Va. Coll. Personnel Assn. (state pres. 1982-83), No. Va. Counselor Assn., Phi Delta Kappa, Kappa Delta Pi. Club: Quota. Author: (with Edward C. Merrill, Jr.) Professional Student Teaching Programs, 1973. Home: 2412 N Monroe St Arlington VA 22207 Office: Coll Profl Studies George Mason University Fairfax VA 22030

SCHUCHMAN, MARIAN CAROLYN, sch. psychologist; b. N.Y.C., Nov. 12, 1938; d. Mortimer G. and Deborah (Werner) Jacobs; R.N., Kings County Hosp., 1959; B.A., Adelphi U., 1972; M.A., Hofstra U., 1975, Ph.D., 1977; children—Ilene, Donna. Pres., L.I. Testing & Advisement Services, Baldwin, N.Y., 1976-79; sch. psychologist Garden City (N.Y.) Public Schs., 1979—; adj. prof. psychology Hofstra U., 1975—. Committeewoman, Nassau County Republican Com., 1977—. Cert. sch. psychologist, lic. psychologist, N.Y. Mem. Am. Psychol. Assn., Nassau County Psychol. Assn. Jewish. Research on reduction of test anxiety. Home: 3176 Ann St Baldwin NY 11510

SCHUCHMAN-MCCOY, DOROTHY, educator; b. Pitts., June 28, 1922; d. Walter Roth and Agnes Lavinia (Cowper) Schuchman; student Carnegie Inst., 1942, 44; B.A., Allegheny Coll., Meadeville, Pa., 1944; postgrad. U. Minn., 1952, Cornell U., 1949-50; Ph.D., U. Pitts., 1962; M.A. in French, Middlebury Coll., 1979; m. Paul W. McCoy, 1946; children—Kathleen Couper, Christiane Roth. Instr. English, Geneva Coll., 1946-48, Carleton Coll., 1948-49; chmn. dept. English, Point Park Jr. Coll., Pitts., 1962-65, asst. prof., 1965-66, asso. prof., 1966-76, prof., 1977—; lectr. U. Pitts., 1965-66. Mem. AAUP, MLA, Internat. Arthurian Soc., Medieval Acad., Phi Beta Kappa. Methodist. Author: Tradition and Convention, 1965; December: A Christmas Poem, 1981; contbr. poems and articles to mags. Home: 208 Breading Ave Ben Avon Pittsburgh PA 15202 Office: Lawrence Hall Point Park College Wood St Pittsburgh PA 15222

SCHUCHMANN, BERTHA HELEN, journalist; b. Osage, Iowa, Mar. 23, 1929; d. Leonard Herman and Gertrude Harriett (Wilcox) Cordes; student U. No. Iowa; B.S., Upper Iowa U., Fayette, 1950; m. Paul Schuchmann, Jr., July 16, 1951; children—Randy (dec.), Kevin, Steven, Darla, Sue. Tchr. high sch., Volga, Iowa, 1950-52, Strawberry Point, Iowa, 1952-55; corr. Oelwein Daily Register, Strawberry Point, 1975—, Press Jour., Strawberry Point, 1975—, Fayette County Union, West Union, 1976— Clayton County Register, Elkader, 1977—, Waterloo Courier, 1979—, Cedar Rapids Gazette, 1979—. Democrat. Methodist. Address: Route 2 Arlington IA 50606

SCHUCK, VICTORIA, coll. pres.; b. Oklahoma City, Mar. 16, 1909; d. Anthony B. and Anna (Priebe) S.; A.B. with great distinction, Stanford U., 1930, M.A., 1931, Ph.D., 1937. Fellow, Stanford U., 1931-33, teaching asst., 1934-35, acting instr., 1935-36, instr., 1936-37; asst. prof. Fla. State Coll. for Women, 1937-40; asst. prof. Mt. Holyoke Coll., South Hadley, Mass., 1940-44, asso. prof., 1944-50, prof. polit. sci., 1950-75; pres. Mt. Vernon Coll., Washington, 1977—; prin. program analyst OPA, Washington, 1942-44; vis. lectr. Smith Coll., 1948-49; vis. prof. Stanford U., summer 1952; guest scholar Brookings Instn., 1967, 68; regional editor Ency. Brit., 1958-61; mem. Mass. Bd. Higher Edn., 1976-77. Mem. Secretariat, UN Conf., San Francisco, 1945; mem. Mass. Commn. on Interstate Cooperation, 1957-60; mem. Mass. adv. com. to U.S. Commn. on Civil Rights, 1962-78; mem. Berkshire Community Coll. Planning Com., 1964-68, Greenfield Community Coll. Planning Com., 1965-67, D.C. Commn. Postsecondary Edn., 1979-80; mem. council Nat. Mcpl. League, N.Y.C., 1977—; mem. Planning Bd. South Hadley, 1959-67, chmn., 1961-67; mem. Pres.'s Commn. on Registration and Voting Participation, 1963; trustee U. Mass., 1958-65, mem. bldg. authority, 1960-68; mem. Commn. on Adminstrv. Rev. of U.S. Ho. of Reps., 1977. Haynes Found. grantee, 1951-52; Asia Soc. S.E. Asia Devel. Group grantee, 1971-72. Mem. Am. Soc. Pub. Adminstrn., AAUP (pres. Mt. Holyoke 1962-64), AAUW (state pres. 1946-50, nat. dir. 1965-69), New Eng. (pres. 1950-51), Am. (sec. 1959-60, v.p. 1970-71), Northeastern (v.p. 1971-72), Internat. polit. sci. assns., Assn. Asian Studies, Mortar Bd., Chi Omega, Phi Beta Kappa. Club: Cosmopolitan (N.Y.C.). Contbr. articles to profl. jours.; co-editor: Women Organizing: An Anthology, 1979. Address: Mt Vernon Coll Washington DC 20007

SCHUH, JANICE SUE, mfg. co. exec.; b. Marysville, Kans., Dec. 14, 1942; d. Frederick John William and Violet Clara (Yaussi) Millenbruch; B.S. in Home Econs. and Journalism, Kans. State U., 1966; m. Dec. 31, 1970; children—Jeffrey, Scott. Successively women's reporter Racine (Wis.) Jour.-Times, asst. women's editor Pioneer Press, Wilmette, Ill., food and feature reporter Chgo. Daily News, public relations asso., editorial home economist Kitchens of Sara Lee, Deerfield, Ill.; with Ekco Products, Inc., Wheeling, Ill., 1972—, mgr. advt. promotion and design, 1974-81, mgr. mktg. communications, 1981—. Hearst scholar. Mem. Nat. Restaurant Assn. (adv. com.), Women in Mgmt. (editor newsletter), Aluminum Foil Container Mfrs. Assn., Chgo. Advt. Club. Address: 1013 Duxbury St Schaumburg IL 60193

SCHULDT, JANE ELIZABETH, tour operator exec.; b. Waverly, Iowa, Dec. 16, 1953; d. Minor W. and Margaret (Brandenburg) S.; student U. Minn., 1976—. Secretarial position Centura Inc., 1973-76; registered rep. Centura Securities Corp., 1976-79; v.p. mktg. L.T. Nelson Assos., mgmt. cons., St. Paul, 1979; nat. sales mgr. Venture Tours subs. Dynimex-Pacifex Co., Mpls., 1979-80; sales mgr. N.Am., Pacific World, Ltd. of Hong Kong, Mpls., 1980—. Home: 4444 W Lake Harriet Pkwy Minneapolis MN 55410 Office: Pacific World Ltd of Hong Kong 4444 W Lake Harriet Pkwy Suite 3 Minneapolis MN 55410

SCHULLER, DIANE ETHEL, immunologist, pediatric allergist; b. Bklyn., Nov. 27, 1943; d. Charles William and Dorothy Schuller; A.B. cum laude with honors in Biology, Bryn Mawr Coll., 1965; M.D., SUNY, Downstate Med. Sch., 1970. Intern, then resident in pediatrics Roosevelt Hosp., N.Y.C., 1970-72, resident in allergy Cooke Inst. Allergy, 1972-74; assoc. in pediatrics Geisinger Med. Center, Danville, Pa., 1974-78, dir. dept. cardio-pulmonary and allergic diseases, 1978—; assoc. clin. prof. pediatrics Hershey Med. Coll., Pa. State U., 1974—; mem. Columbia-Montour Home Health Services Adv. Group of Profl. Personnel, 1975—. Mem. scholarship com. Bryn Mawr Club, N.Y., 1970-75. Recipient Physicians Recognition award AMA, yearly, 1973-82. Diplomate Am. Bd. Pediatrics, Am. Bd. Allergy and Immunology. Fellow Am. Acad. Pediatrics, Am. Coll. Allergy, Am. Acad. Allergy, Am. Assn. for Clin. Immunology and Allergy; mem. Pa., N.Y. State allergy socs., N.Y. State, N.Y. County med. socs., Am. Lung Assn. of Pa. (dir. 1981), Central Pa. Lung and Health Service Assn. (dir. 1979). Contbr. articles to med. jours. Home: Box 50 Heather Hills Dr RD 4 Danville PA 17821 Office: Geisinger Med Center Danville PA 17821

SCHULMAN, ELAINE MARJORIE, ophthalmologist; b. N.Y.C.; d. Harold and Bessie (Brimberg) Levin; B.A., Bklyn. Coll.; M.D., N.Y. Med. Coll., 1965. Intern, Maimonides Hosp., 1966; resident in ophthalmology Beth Israel Hosp., N.Y.C., 1967-70; fellow in ophthal. surgery Manhattan Eye and Ear Hosp., 1971; chmn. dept. opthalmology Central Bklyn. Med. Group, 1970-71; practice medicine specializing in ophthal. surgery, Bklyn.; mem. faculty Mt. Sinai Hosp. Diplomate Am. Bd. Ophthalmology. Fellow Am. Acad. Ophthalmology, ACS. Office: 345 Shermerhorn St Brooklyn NY 11217

SCHULMAN, EVELINE DOLIN, psychologist, author, cons.; b. N.Y.C.; d. George and Fannie (Simon) Dolin; B.S., CCNY, 1939, postgrad., 1940-42; postgrad. State U. Iowa, 1939-40, Am. U., 1947; M.Ed., U. Md., 1954, Ed.D., 1957, postgrad., 1979-81; m. Sol Schulman, June 3, 1941; children—Mark H., Ken S. Tchr., Children's Colony, N.Y.C., 1941-42; registrar-tchr. Rockwood Nursery Sch., N.Y.C., 1942-43; asst. dir. Settlement House, Juanita Kauman Nye Council House, dir./tchr. nursery sch., Washington, 1943-44; dir.-tchr. Greenway Co-op. Nursery Sch., Washington, 1947-48, Fairfax Co-op. Nursery Sch., Washington, 1948-50, Community Nursery Sch., Silver Spring, Md., 1952-54; grad. asst. U. Md., 1954-55; psychologist, cons. Prince Georges County Council of Kindergarten and Nursery Schs., 1955-57; psychologist lectr. Am. U., Washington, 1957; instr. psychology Community Coll. of Balt., 1958-62, chmn. dept., 1962-73, prof. psychology, 1964-73, dir. mental health tech. program, 1967-73; lectr. human devel. Inst. for Child Study, U. Md., 1967-68, 69-71; prof. mental health Morgan State Coll., Towson, 1971-77; dir. evaluation and tng. Md. Mental Retardation Adminstrn., Balt., 1974-76, asst. dir. adminstrn., 1976-77; dir., cons. human services Center for Devel. Inter-Personal Skills, Silver Spring, 1977—; cons. Pres.'s Com. on Employment of Handicapped, 1980. Mem. Clifton T. Perkins Adv. Bd., 1972-80, chmn., 1974-80; mem. Mental Health Assn. Montgomery County, 1972, Montgomery County Assn. for Retarded Citizens, 1977; chmn. Disabled Persons Rev. Bd., 1978—, Wheaton Community Mental Health Adv. Com., 1978—; mem. Montgomery County Com. for Community Edn. about Mentally Ill, 1982—. U. Md. fellow, 1954-55. Mem. Am. Psychol. Assn., Eastern Psychol. Assn., Md. Psychol. Assn., Am. Assn. Mental Deficiency, Am. Personnel and Guidance Assn., Am. Mental Health Counselors Assn., Women Educators, Gerontol. Soc., Nat. Council on Aging, Rehab. Internat.-U.S.A., Md. Assn. Jr. Colls. (pres. 1967-69). Author: Intervention in Human Services - A Guide to Skills and Knowledge, 1974, 3d edit., 1982, Focus on the Retarded Adult, 1980, Rehabilitation of the Mentally Ill - An International Perspective, 1981. Contbr. articles in field to profl. jours. Office: Center for Devel Inter-Personal Skills 1103 Caddington Ave Silver Spring MD 20901

SCHULMAN, MARTHA SCHIER, editor; b. N.Y.C., Aug. 18, 1943; d. Alfred Adolf and Josephine Schier; student Hunter Coll., 1961-63; m. Harold L. Schulman, Apr. 3, 1977. Sec., office mgr. to v.p. mdse. R.H. Macy & Co., N.Y.C., 1963-67; asst. in assessories fashion office Bloomingdales, N.Y.C., 1967-68; assessories editor McCalls mag., N.Y.C., 1968-70, sr. fashion, sewing and crafts editor, 1970—. Mem. Fashion Group. Office: 230 Park Ave New York NY 10017

SCHULTE, JOSEPHINE HELEN, historian; b. Foley, Ala., May 9, 1929; d. Mathias Anthony and Theresa Bertha (Honner) S.; A.A., Sacred Heart Jr. Coll., Cullman, Ala., 1949; B.S., Spring Hill Coll., Mobile, 1957; M.A., U. So. Miss., 1961; Ph.D., Loyola U., Chgo., 1969; M.A., Trinity U., 1976. Steamship agt., Mobile, Ala., 1949-58; chief research asso. So. Inst. Mgmt., Mobile, 1959-60; teaching asst. Loyola U., Chgo., 1962-66; mem. faculty dept. history U. of Americas, Mexico City, 1967-70; mem. faculty dept. history St. Mary's U., San Antonio, 1970—, asso. prof., 1970-79, prof., 1979—, dir. Latin Am. studies program, 1974—. Grantee, Govt. of Spain/OAS, 1981-82. Mem. Tex. Hist. Assn., Cath. Hist. Assn., Southwestern Conf. Latin Am. Studies (dir.), Latin Am. Studies Assn., Tex. Assn. German Students, Phi Alpha Theta, Delta Phi Alpha. Roman Catholic. Contbr. articles to profl. jours. Translator books from Spanish and German to English. Home: 6623 Callaghan Rd Apt 1703 San Antonio TX 78229 Office: Dept History St Mary's Univ 1 Camino Santa Maria San Antonio TX 78284

SCHULTE, TINA STALLONE, public relations exec.; b. St. Louis, May 26, 1950; d. Phillip Kenneth and Erna Agnes (Strutman) Stallone; B.A., St. Louis U., 1972; m. Emmerich Carl Schulte, Nov. 12, 1977. Mgr. mktg. and operations F. N. Storey & Asso., Inc., St. Louis, 1972-77; staff asso. Dale Carnegie & Asso., Inc., Garden City, N.Y., 1977-78; pub. relations dir. Dale Carnegie & Asso., Inc., St. Louis, 1978—. Recipient award for outstanding instrn. Dale Carnegie Course, 1978. Mem. Nat. Assn. Female Execs., Art Inst. Chgo. Editor, Comments mag., 1978—. Home: 106 S Waverly Pl Mount Prospect IL 60056 Office: 10880 Baur Blvd Saint Louis MO 63132

SCHULTER-ELLIS, FRANCES PIERCE, anatomist, educator; b. Chilton County, Ala., Sept. 22, 1923; d. William Mack and Lena Roberta (Varden) Pierce; B.S., Birmingham So. Coll., 1952; M.S., Emory U., 1965; Ph.D., George Washington U., 1972; m. Spencer P. Ellis, Apr. 1, 1977; children by previous marriage—Jenny Schulter Varden, Peter Alan Schulter. Instr. biology Chamblee (Ga.) High Sch., 1960-61; instr. biology Marjorie Webster Jr. Coll., Washington, 1961-65; teaching fellow in anatomy George Washington U., 1966-71; asst. prof. anatomy U. Md., Balt., 1972—; research collaborator div. phys. anthropology Smithsonian Instn.; vis. prof. anatomy St. George U., Grenada, W.I.; cons. forensic sci. Md. Med. Examiners Office; book reviewer sci. books and films AAAS. Vol. worker Balt. Symphony Orch., 1973-76, Center Stage Theatre, Balt., 1973-75, George Washington U. Alumni Assn., 1975—, Anne Arundel County (Md.) Mental Health Assn., 1977—, Am. Cancer Soc., 1977—. Recipient Faculty of Yr. award U. Md. Sch. of Medicine, 1974, 78, award for outstanding service and contbn. Student Nat. Med. Assn. of U. Md., 1978, Grad. Sch. Research award U. Md., 1974, 76, 78. Fellow Human Biology Council; mem. Am. Assn. Anatomists, Am. Assn. Phys. Anthropologists, Am. Acad. Forensic Scis., Am. Anthrop. Assn., Md. Soc. Med. Research, So. Soc. Anatomists, AAUP, Phi Sigma, Beta Beta Beta, Theta Chi Delta. Clubs: Bay Hills (Md.) Golf, Annapolis Yacht, U.S. Naval Acad. Officers and Faculty. Contbr. articles to profl. jours. Home: 570 Foxpaw Trail Annapolis MD 21401 Office: 655 W Baltimore St Baltimore MD 21201

SCHULTZ, CLARA CATHERINE PECK, educator, writer; b. Daupin County, Pa., May 21, 1921; d. Maurice Emanuel and Catherine Edna (Buseck) Peck; B.S., U. Pa., 1950, cert. in Dental Hygiene, 1948; M.A., Chapman Coll., 1965; Ph.D. in Lang. Arts Edn., Walden U., 1980; m. John Edward Schultz, Sept. 8, 1951; children—John Edward, Pamela Kay, Catherine Mae. Dental hygienist, Spokane, Wash., 1950-51; tchr. Centralia Sch. Dist., Calif., 1961-66, Fountain Valley (Calif.) Elem. Sch. Dist., 1966-81; adminstr. Faith Chapel Christian Sch., Westminster, Calif., 1981—; vis. lectr. Chapman Coll., Orange, Calif., 1969, 70, Rocky Mountain Coll., 1977; condr. adult and juvenile workshops in creative writing, poetry and prose, 1977-80; with Quills for Kids at Open House at Hollywood Bowl, 1976, 77, 78, 79, 81. Mem. Fountain Valley Bicentennial Com., 1974-76; mem. bd. govs. Lit. Hall of Fame, Huntington Beach, Calif., 1977—. Recipient Fountain Valley City Plaque award, 1977, WHO award, 1976; numerous poetry awards. Mem. Nat. League Am. Pen Women (pres. Orange county br. 1974-76, founding pres. Fountain Valley br. 1977—, historian 1970-74; Woman of Achievement 1980), Fountain Valley Ednl. Assn., NEA, Calif. Tchrs. Assn., Fountain Valley Hist. Soc. (chmn. local hist. sites com. 1975-76). Republican. Episcopalian. Club: Order Eastern Star. Author: A History of the Centralia School District, 1965; Poetry Is a State of Mind; Eop's Corner; Return to Eop's Corner; contbr. numerous poems, articles and children's stories to various mags. and newspapers. Home: 8815 Hummingbird Ave Fountain Valley CA 92708

SCHULTZ, EILEEN HEDY, graphic designer; b. N.Y.C.; d. Harry A. and Hedy E. (Morchel) S.; B.F.A., Sch. Visual Arts, N.Y.C., 1957; postgrad. Columbia U., Art Students League, New Sch., Acad. des Beaux Arts. Comml. artist C.A. Parshall Studios, N.Y.C., 1957-58; editorial art dir. Paradise of the Pacific mag., Honolulu, 1958-59; art dir. Good Housekeeping mag., N.Y.C., 1959—; graphic designer Hearts mags., 1959—; instr. graphic design Sch. Visual Arts; vis. prof. Syracuse (N.Y.) U. Recipient Outstanding Achievement award Sch. Visual Arts Alumni Soc., 1976, Youth award Art Students League, 1976. Mem. Soc. Illustrators (chmn. ann. exhbn. 1978), Art Dirs. Club N.Y.C. (pres. 1975-77), Joint Ethics Com. N.Y.C. (chmn. 1980-82), Am. Inst. Graphic Arts, Soc. Publ. Designers. Author monthly column Art Direction mag., 1970—; art dir., designer, editor 50th Ann. Advt., Editorial and TV Art and Design, 1971. Home: 450 E 63d St Apt 4M W New York NY 10021 Office: 959 8th Ave Suite 457 New York NY 10019

SCHULTZ, ELIZABETH ANNE CRIMMINS, educator; b. Guelph, Ont., Can., Apr. 28, 1922; came to U.S., 1957, naturalized, 1969; d. Daniel and Elizabeth (Roth) Crimmins; diploma St. Joseph's Sch. Nursing, 1943; cert. teaching and supr. psychiat. nursing U. Toronto, 1954; B.S. in Nursing, U. Pitts., 1963, M. Nursing Edn., 1966; Ph.D., Walden U., Fla., 1981; m. Joseph Anthony Schultz, Nov. 25, 1972. Staff nurse St. Joseph's Hosp., Guelph, Ont., Can., 1943-44; pvt. duty nurse, Guelph, 1944-46; staff nurse King Edward Meml. Hosp., Bermuda, 1946-47, asst. head nurse, 1947-48, head nurse, 1948-49; staff nurse Vancouver Gen. Hosp., 1949-51; staff nurse, supr. Homewood Sanitarium, Guelph, 1951-53; head nurse, clin. tchr. Toronto Psychiat. Hosp., 1954-57; staff nurse, head nurse Western Psychiat. Inst., Pitts., 1957-62, asst. dir. nursing, affiliate edn., 1962-64; dir. nursing Western Restoration Center, 1966-69; asst. prof. psychiat. nursing Allegheny Community Coll., Pitts., 1969-71; asst. prof. dept. nursing Duquesne U., Pitts., 1971-75, assoc. prof., 1975-78; assoc. prof. dept. nursing Slippery Rock (Pa.) State Coll., 1978—; cons. psychiat., mental health nursing McKeesport Hosp., 1970-71; cons., lectr. psychiat., mental health nursing Slippery Rock State Coll., 1975. Mem. AAUP, Advanced Practitioners Psychiat. Nursing, Am. Assn. Sex Edn. and Counselors, Am., Pa. nurses Assn., Nat., Pa. leagues nursing, U. Toronto Alumni Assn., U. Pitts. Alumni Assn. Home: 3 Shannopin Dr Pittsburgh PA 15202 Office: Slippery Rock State College Slippery Rock PA 16057

SCHULTZ, ELIZABETH MARY, probation agt.; b. Midland, Mich., July 22, 1953; d. Eugene George and Dolores May (Froeck) S.; B.A., Alma Coll., 1975. Typesetter, McKay Press, Midland, Mich., 1976-77; probation agt. Dept. Corrections, Midland, Mich., 1977—. Bd. dirs. Alcohol Services Midland County, chmn., 1981, sec., 1982; bd. dirs. Youth Devel. Programs, sec., 1980—. Mem. Nat. Assn. Social Workers, Mich. State Employees Assn., Mich. Corrections Assn. Lutheran. Home: 6127 Eastman Rd Apt 11A Midland MI 48640 Office: Courthouse Midland MI 48640

SCHULTZ, HELEN MARY, instrument co. pres.; b. Duncan, Okla., Sept. 10, 1923; d. Paul Joseph and Martha Jane (Melton) Kelly; student U. Iowa, 1939-41; m. Charles J. Schultz, Sept. 29, 1944 (div. Feb. 1973); children—Cathryn Jane, Christy Jean, Charles David. Sales sec. G.T. Collatz Co., Inc., Wellesley, Mass., 1964-68; sales office mgr. Amicon Corp., Lexington, Mass., 1968-73; sales mgr. Tensitron, Inc., Harvard, Mass., 1973-75, mktg. dir., 1975-77, v.p., 1977-81, pres., gen. mgr., dir., 1981—. Home: 20 Joanne Dr Apt 10 Ashland MA 01721 Office: Depot Rd Harvard MA 01451

SCHULTZ, JANET KAY, health care exec.; b. Rochester, N.Y., Jan. 23, 1944; d. Charles Theodore and Madelyn Lenore (Daley) Schultz; student Harpur Coll., 1961-63; B.S. in Nursing with distinction, Ind. U., 1968, M.S., 1980. Staff nurse intensive care unit Ind. Univ. Hosps., Indpls., 1968-69, staff nurse operating room, 1969-70, head nurse, 1970; asst. dir. operating room nursing service, 1971-72, chmn. operating room and allied areas nursing, 1972-76; dir. operating room Kansas City (Mo.) Coll. Osteo. Medicine, 1971; asst. dir. edn. for operating room consultation, Assn. Operating Room Nurses, Inc., Denver, 1976-81; operating room systems mgr. Am. V. Mueller div. Am. Hosp. Supply Corp., McGaw Park, Ill., 1981—; nursing mgmt. cons.; guest lectr. Ind. U. Sch. Nursing, Indpls., 1975, U. Colo. Sch. Nursing, Denver, 1979; seminar leader Assn. Operating Room Nurses, 1976-81; tech. cons. Assn. Operating Room Nurses-Davis & Geck Ednl. films, 1976-81.

Mem. Assn. Operating Room Nurses (chpt. pres. 1975-76), Am. Nurses Assn., Nurse Cons. Assn., Assn. for Advancement of Med. Instrumentation, Hosp. Mgmt. Systems Soc., Am. Soc. Hosp. Central Service Personnel, Ind. U. Sch. Nursing Alumni Assn., Sigma Theta Tau. Democrat. Contbr. to Care of Cardiac Surgical Patient, 1976, Hospital Special Care Facilities, 1981; author (monthly column) Experts Research: Q & A, Assn. Operating Room Nurses Jour., 1976—; contbr. articles to profl. jours. Home: 4200 W Lake St Glenview IL 60025 Office: 1500 Waukegan Rd McGaw Park IL 60085

SCHULTZ, JERELYN BOEHMKE, home economist; b. Cedar Rapids, Iowa, Aug. 25, 1945; d. Walter Eldo and Guinnever Alice (Hoffman) Boehmke; B.A., U. Iowa, 1967, M.A., 1969; Ph.D., Iowa State U., 1975; m. Hugh M. Schultz, June 10, 1967; 1 dau., Kirstin Renee. Instr., Parks Sch. Bus., Denver, 1972, Denver Woman's Coll., 1969-70; asst. prof. home econs. Iowa State U., Ames, 1976-80, asso. prof., 1980—; cons. sexuality edn. and handicapped. Iowa Dept. Public Instrn. grantee, 1978—; recipient Helen L. Hilton Outstanding Young Educator award Iowa State U., 1980. Mem. Am. Home Econs. Assn., Iowa Home Econs. Assn. (dist. rep.), Am. Vocat. Assn., Iowa Vocat. Assn., Am. Vocat. Edn. Research Assn., Am. Ednl. Research Assn., Iowa Ednl. Research and Evaluation Assn. (pres., past sec.-treas.), Nat. Assn. Tchr. Educators of Home Econs. (past sec.), Zeta Tau Alpha, Phi Kappa Phi, Phi Delta Kappa, Phi Upsilon Omicron, Omicron Nu. Democrat. Unitarian. Author: The Decision to Parent, 1980; Sexuality and the Adolescent, 1981; contbr. articles to profl. jours. Home: 3112 Eisenhower St Ames IA 50010 Office: Dept Home Econs Ia State U Ames IA 50011

SCHULTZ, JOYCE ELIZABETH, fin. exec.; b. Sioux City, Ia., May 22, 1942; d. Merl Hansel Scheel and Laila Ardith (Fenster) Scheel Riley; student Concordia Tchrs. Coll., 1960-61, Wartburg Coll., 1967-68; B.S. in B.A. with high distinction, U. Nebr., 1975; M.B.A., Columbia U., 1977; children—Leigh Jeanette, Amy Lynne, Loren Scott. Loan processor State Fed. Savings & Loan, Lincoln, Nebr., 1971-75; fin. analyst Exxon Chem. Co., Linden, N.J., 1977-78, plant analyst, 1978-79; sr. fin. analyst Ethicon Inc., Somerville, N.J., 1979, sect. mgr., mktg. fin. analysis, 1979-80, mgr. mktg. fin. ser⁻ice, 1980—. Jr. achievement adv., 1978-79. Recipient Amena Elliott Webster award for outstanding woman grad. in mktg., Columbia U., 1977; Tribute to Women and Industry award YWCA, 1981; Leta Stettler Hollingsworth fellow, 1976; Mobil Oil Disting. scholar, 1976. Mem. Nat. Assn. Female Execs., PTA. Home: 114 Pacific St Edison NJ 08817 Office: Route 22 Somerville NJ 08876

SCHULTZ, LORRAINE HELENE, assn. exec.; b. North Tonawanda, N.Y., Oct. 23, 1930; d. Francis and Michalina Sofia (Jok) Szemraj; student Alma Coll., 1948-50; m. Arthur Henry Schultz, June 18, 1955; children—Brian, Tracey. Stewardess, Eastern Airlines, 1953-55; v.p. Slenderella Internat., 1955-64; pres., owner Detroit Model Bur., 1964-69; dir. Am. Express Travel Club, Mich., 1969-73; pres., owner LHS Assos., Birmingham, Mich., 1975—; dir. AutoLeather Guild, Birmingham, 1975—. Mem. bd. Juvenile Diabetes Assn. Com. Mem. Nat. Assn. Female Execs., Fashion Group (dir.), Am. Soc. Profl. and Exec. Women, Nat. Council Career Women, Birmingham/Bloomington Bd. Realtors, Publicity Club N.Y. Roman Catholic. Clubs: Village Players, Rolls Royce Owners (newsletter editor region), Ferrari Owners. Home: 776 Waddington St Birmingham MI 48009 Office: 2501 M St NW Washington DC 20037

SCHULTZ, MARILYN F., state legislator; b. Alexandria, La., Jan. 7, 1944; d. Frank William and Catherine (Smith) S.; B.A., U. Tex., 1964, M.A., 1968; postgrad. Laval U., Que., Can., U. Madrid, Ind. U.; m. Alfred I. Towell, June 14, 1972. Mem. Ind. Ho. of Reps., 1972—; co-owner Goods, Inc., 1973—. Mem. Bloomington Bus. Com. for Arts. Recipient Leadership award Ind. Council Chs., 1983; Eagleton Inst. Politics fellow, 1974. Mem. Nat. Women's Polit. Caucus, C. of C., Bloomington Downtown Mchts. Assn., Pi Lambda Theta. Democrat.

SCHULTZ, PAMELA KAY, supermarket ofcl.; b. Madison, Wis., Oct. 21, 1947; d. Charles Floyd and Delores Marie (Rector) Duane; student Madison Area Tech. Coll., 1975; m. James Mallory Schultz, Jan. 22, 1966; children—Julie Katherine, Jennifer Kay, Karen Elizabeth. Sec. to v.p. Nat. Mut. Benefit Life Ins. Co., Madison, 1965-66; sec., bookkeeper Family Market Enterprises, Inc., DeForest, Wis., 1966—; real estate broker, DeForest; founder Win-Fore Women's Investment Club. Leader, Blackhawk council Girl Scouts U.S.A., 1974, 75, 77, 79-80; a founder DeForest Area Hist. Soc., 1975, active membership dr., 1975-79, sec.-treas., 1975-79, bd. dirs., 1975-81; treas. DeForest Moravian Ch., 1977—. Home: 305 Meadow Ln DeForest WI 53532 Office: 302 N Main St DeForest WI 53532

SCHULTZ, REGINA MARY, spirits co. exec.; b. Worcester, Mass., Apr. 18, 1937; d. Joseph Henry and Regina Mary (Dowgielewicz) S.; A.A., Worcester Jr. Coll., 1960; student in acctg. LaSalle Coll., 1972-73; student Conn. Sch. Art, 1976. Comptometer operator, sr. statis. typist Melville Shoe Co., Worcester, Mass., 1954-60; sec. to chief acct. Wyman-Gordon, Grafton, Mass., 1960-64; asst. to mgrs. cost acctg., internal audit, fin. Chandler Evans div. Colt Industries, W.Hartford, Conn., 1964-71; with Heublein Inc., Hartford, Conn., 1971—, sec. to purchasing mgr., raw materials and adminstrn., 1971-72, asst. to purchasing mgr., merchandising materials, 1972-75, merchandising prodn. asst., 1975-77, asst. prodn. mgr., 1977-81, mgr. mktg. budgets, 1981—. Bus. adv., judge officer awards Jr. Achievement, 1971—. Recipient service award sta. WRCH, 1974, Mem. Nat. Assn. Accts. (dir. 1968-72, sec., treas., v.p. Hartford chpt. 1972-76, pres. N.Eng. council, 1973-75, v.p. edn., membership and adminstrn. Springfield chpt. and N.Eng. council 1976-79, pres. chpt. 1979-80, chmn. publicity, public relations, hospitality 1974—, cons., chmn. spl. projects nat. conv. 1979). Author: Subject: It's Reggie's Business World, 1973 (award); writer, editor newsletter N. Eng. council Nat. Assn. Accts., 1975-79, now cons., contbr. Office: Office: Heublein Inc 330 New park Ave Hartford CT 06101

SCHULTZ, RHONDA VANN, newspaper publisher; b. McMinnville, Tenn., Jan. 8, 1943; d. Perry W. and Mary A. Dunham; student public schs.; children—Debra Kay, Tracy Lee. From office mgr. to gen. mgr., corp. v.p. Citizens-News, San Antonio, 1971-79; editor, pub. News Bull., Castroville, Tex., 1979—; pres. Footnotes, Inc., 1979—. Mem. Castroville Planning and Zoning Bd., 1979-82; bd. dirs. Medina County Fair, 1980-82. Mem. Tex. Press Assn. Mem. Ch. of Christ. Club: San Antonio Women's Breakfast. Address: PO Drawer D Castroville TX 78009

SCHULTZ, SUSAN JILL, assn. exec.; b. Flint, Mich., Jan. 16, 1949; d. Robert Malcolm and Justine Ann (Grout) McWilliams; B.S.N. (Mich. Higher Edn. scholar, Mich. Regents Alumni scholar), U. Mich., 1971, M.S. in Health Services Adminstrn., 1979; m. Martin J. Schultz, Aug. 8, 1970; children—Jason Robert, Rachel Rose. With VA Hosp., Ann Arbor, Mich., 1971; dept. head Saginaw County (Mich.) Public Health Dept., 1971-74, asst. dir., 1978-80; supr. Vis. Nurse Assn. Saginaw, 1975-78, exec. dir., 1980—; accreditation visitor Nat. League Nursing, 1980, 82. Vol. Voluntary Action. Kellogg Found. grantee, 1977; recipient E.C. Malcolm Scholarship award, 1978. Mem. Saginaw Dist. Nurse Assn. (dir. 1980), Am. Nurses Assn., Mich. Nurses Assn., Saginaw Nurses Assn. (past sec., dir.), Mich. Public Health Assn., Saginaw Valley Public Health Assn., Mich. League Nurses, Saginaw Child Abuse and Neglect Council. Club: Altrusa (dir.). Home: 7240 Ronald Dr Saginaw MI 48603 Office: 3037 Davenport St Saginaw MI 48602

SCHULTZ-SMITH, BARBARA J., business exec.; b. Oneida, N.Y., Jan. 12, 1934; d. Joseph J. and Nila M. Lomery; B.S. in Bus. Adminstrn., Redlands U., 1979; M.B.A., Loyola Marymount U., 1982; children—Gary Schultz, Geri Schultz, Kathryn Schultz, Glen Schultz. Mgr., Cox, Castle, Nicholson, Los Angeles, 1971-73, Slavitt, King & Foonberg, Los Angeles, 1973-79, Breidenboch, Swainston, Yokaitis & Crispo, Los Angeles, 1979-80, Tosco Corp., Los Angeles, 1980—; cons. on automation bus. systems. Mem. Am. Mgmt. Assn., Internat. Assn. Personnel Women, Assn. Legal Adminstrs., Am. Bar Assn., Women in Bus., Bus. Vols. for Arts. Presbyterian. Home: 311 14th St Santa Monica CA 90402

SCHULZ, DOROTHY MOSES, police officer; b. N.Y.C., July 18, 1946; d. Henry and Marion (Turner) Moses; B.A., N.Y. U., 1966, postgrad., 1973—; M.A. in Criminal Justice, John Jay Coll., 1973; m. David P. Schulz, Aug. 13, 1966. Writer, copy editor Charleston (W.Va.) Gazette, 1966-68, Newark Star Ledger, 1968-70, also other papers; dir. security and police ops. N.Y.C. Human Resources Adminstrn., 1972-78; capt. Conrail Police Dept., N.Y.C., 1978—, comdg. officer Grand Central Terminal, 1979—. Mem. Am. Acad. Indsl. Security, Am. Acad. Profl. Law Enforcement, Am. Soc. Criminology, Am. Studies Assn., Internat. Assn. Chiefs of Police, Internat. Assn. Women Police, N.Y. Women in Criminal Justice, John Jay Coll. Alumni Club. Jewish. Office: Grand Central Terminal Room 1750 New York NY 10017

SCHULZ, PATRICIA ANN, govt. adminstr.; b. Mexico, Mo., Aug. 22, 1926; d. Jack Leroy and Louise Aline (Kircher) Paul; student Tulane U., 1945-46; m. Robert L. Gauchat (dec.); m. 2d, Robert D. Schulz, Dec. 26, 1949 (dec.); children—Carol Davis, Duane, Gary. Supervisory chmn. Orange County Republican Com., Santa Ana, Calif., 1958-62; scheduling chmn. Charles B. Wilkinson, Oklahoma City, 1963-65; office mgr. Ariz. Rep. State Com., Phoenix, 1965-66; office mgr. Senator Paul Fannin, Phoenix, 1966-76; supr. Office of Revenue Sharing, Washington, 1976—; mem. adv. bd. Women's Nat. Bank, Washington. Recipient U.S. Dept. Treasury Spl. Achievement awards, 1978, 79, 1980. Mem. Ariz. State Soc. (treas. 1979-80). Methodist.

SCHULZ, SARA INGABORG SMITH, health facility adminstr.; b. Los Angeles, July 23, 1946; d. Harley Wright and Mary Ingaborg (Stewart) Smith; A.A., Stephens Coll., 1966; B.A., Calif. State U., Dominguez Hills, 1976; m. Kenneth Daniel Schulz, July 19, 1977. Dep. clk. 11th Dist. Magistrate Ct., St. Louis, 1971-72; asst. supr. contracts and grants acctg. UCLA, 1972-76, asst. bus. mgr. Sch. of Engring. and Applied Sci., 1976-79; asst. dir., adminstrv. services supr. Women's Health Care Clinic and Programs, Harbor-UCLA Med. Center, 1979—. Vice pres. Nat. Charity League San Fernando Valley, 1963-64; supt. Sunday sch., mem. covenant choir Neighborhood Ch., 1979—. Mem. Soc. of Research Adminstrs., Adminstrv. and Suprs. Assn., Nat. Assn. Coll. and Univ. Bus. Officers, Nat. Mgmt. Assn., DAR, Stephens Coll. Alumnae Orgn. (pres. San Fernando Valley 1969-70). Republican. Home: 905 Via Mirola Palos Verdes Estates CA 90274 Office: Women's Health Care Clinic and Programs Harbor-UCLA Med Center 1000 W Carson St Torrance CA 90509

SCHULZE, THEODORA ECONOMOU, music dir., educator, investment firm exec.; b. Hammond, Ind., Sept. 19, 1930; d. Xenophon and Emilie (Mueller) Economou; oboist protegee of Alfred Barthel and Kenneth Gekeler, 1943-53; m. Richard Schulze, Apr. 16, 1950; 1 son, Otto. Music dir., soloist The Telemann Soc., N.Y.C. and Ft. Lauderdale, Fla., 1955—; appearances at Carnegie Hall, Town Hall, N.Y. and other world centers, 1955—; dir. and soloist over 45 recs. on Vox, Nonesuch, Everest, Amphion, other U.S. and overseas labels, 1959—; taught at Carnegie Hall, 1954-63; pedagogical work published by Associated Music Pub., N.Y.C., 1970; sec. Philharm. Standard Corp., Acton, Mass., 1969-74; producer nat. syndicated radio show —The Age of Telemann—, 1961—; featured soloist Fla. Pops Orch.; appeared with Robert Goulet, Leonard Pennario, other major soloists, 1977—; treas. Atlantic Futures Inc., commodity investment firm, 1981—. Office: 2500 Hollywood Blvd Hollywood FL 33020

SCHUMACHER, PAULA RUTH, public relations, advt. exec.; b. Hays, Kans., Dec. 17, 1938; d. Henry Andrew and Pauline (Dreiling) Schumacher; B.A., Fort Hays State Coll., 1960; M.S., Kans. State U., 1974; 1 son by previous marriage, Mitchell Roy. Tchr., Stockton (Kans.) Jr. High Sch., 1960-61, Valley Center (Kans.) High Sch., 1961-68, Campus High Sch., Wichita, Kans., 1968-72, pub. schs., Wichita, 1972-75, pub. schs., Leavenworth, Kans., 1975-77; arts and entertainment, design editor Sun Publs., Overland Park, Kans., 1977-79; owner, pres. Paula Schumacher & Assos., public relations and advt., 1979—; instr. Summer Sch. Journalism, Blair Acad., Blairstown, N.J., 1977. Recipient Disting. Journalism Tchr. of Yr. award, 1968. Mem. Kans. Orgn. Publs. Advs. (sec. treas. 1963-65, pres. 1968-72), Journalism Edn. Assn. (pres. 1977—), Women in Communications, Press Women, Kansas City Press Club, Sigma Delta Chi. Roman Catholic. Contbr. articles to profl. jours. Home: 10833 State Line #5 Kansas City MO 64114 Office: 5930 Barton St Shawnee KS 66203

SCHUMACKER, BETSY, educator; b. Phila., Apr. 2, 1938; d. Lloyd John and Elizabeth Wagner (Dolman) S.; S.B., M.I.T., 1960. Applied sci. rep. IBM, Phila., 1960-63, systems engr., White Plains, N.Y., 1963-65, project adminstr., 1965-67; lectr. M.I.T., Cambridge, 1967-81, sr. lectr. civil engring., 1981—. Mem. Soc. Indsl. and Applied Math., IEEE, Assn. Computing Machinery. Club: Greater Lowell Road Runners. Home: 16 Maplewood Rd North Tewksbury MA 01876 Office: 77 Massachusetts Ave Cambridge MA 02139

SCHUMAN, MIRIAM DEROSA, mfg. co. exec.; b. N.Y.C., May 21, 1925; d. Leopold A. and Sara (Harris) DeRosa; student Monmouth Coll., 1943-44, Essex County Coll., 1975-76, Bergen Community Coll., 1978-79; m. Arnold Schuman, Mar. 31, 1946; children—Stephen L., David, Mindy Schuman-Vye, Jill. Secretarial position U.S. Army, Ft. Monmouth, N.J., 1941-46; sales coordinator Minn. Mining & Mfg. Co., Paramus, N.J., 1967-74, coordinator remote facsimile networks, 1974-75, credit mgr., 1975-81. Club: B'nai B'rith Women. Editor local B'nai Brith publ., 1955-59, local ORT publ., 1961-63. Office: Minn Mining & Mfg Co 70 Eisenhower Dr Paramus NJ 07652

SCHUMANN, CLARA (MRS. FREDERICK JOHN SCHUMANN), civic worker; b. Detroit, Dec. 21, 1905; d. Otto Henry and Clara (Schultz) Helm; cert. Detroit Tchrs. Coll., 1926; B.S., Wayne State U., 1932; m. Frederick John Schumann, June 29, 1931; 1 dau., Linda Diane. Bd. dirs. LWV, Grosse Pointe, Mich., 1952-54; v.p. Keep Detroit Beautiful, 1958; Mayor's Com. Keep Grosse Pointe Park Beautiful; bd. dirs. Women's City Club of Detroit, 1941-43; pres. Coll. Women's Club of Detroit, 1936-37; Detroit pres. Women's Nat. Farm and Garden Assn., 1938-40; pres. Federated Garden Clubs of Mich., Inc., 1955-57, bd. dirs., 1970—; bd. dirs. Nat. Council State Garden Clubs, 1955-57; pres. Detroit Garden Center, 1943-44, bd. dirs., 1970—, pres., 1975, 78; sec. Grosse Pointe (Mich.) War Meml. Assn., 1956-58; pres. YWCA of Met. Detroit, 1959, now trustee; mem. world service council of nat. bd. YWCA, 1964; mem. council Internat. Inst. Met. Detroit, v.p., 1970—; pres. Mich. Questers; mem. adv. panel Sta. WTVS, Detroit, 1981—, Sta. WTVS-TV; bd. dirs. Adult Service Centers, 1982—. Mem. Alpha Sigma Tau. Unitarian. Home: 836 Harcourt Rd Grosse Pointe MI 48230

SCHUR, SUSAN DORFMAN, state legislator; b. Newark, Feb. 27, 1940; d. Norman and Jeanette (Handelman) Dorfman; B.A., Goucher Coll., 1961; m. Peter H. Schur, Sept. 8, 1963; children—Diana Elisabeth, Erica Marlene. Adminstr. fed. housing, fgn. aid, anti-poverty programs, 1961-67; mem. Mass. Housing Appeals Com., 1977-81; mem., v.p. Bd. of Alderman, Newton, Mass., 1974—; mem. Mass. Ho. of Reps., 1981—. Bd. dirs. Mass. Assn. Mental Health. Mem. Newton Democratic City Com., 1970—. Mem. LWV, Boston Network Women in Politics and Govt., Mass. Mcpl. Assn., Mass. Legislators Assn., Mass. Caucus Women Legislators. Jewish. Office: State House Boston MA 02133

SCHURKENS, NELL CAHILL, mgmt. cons.; b. Bassett, Va., Dec. 6, 1937; d. George Everette and Lillian (Helms) Cahill; B.A., U. Tulsa, 1963; M.P.A., U. Okla., 1974; m. Bill Schurkens, June 1, 1963. Dir. planning and research San Juan County, Aztec, N.Mex., 1975-77; dir. govt. affairs Builders Assn. Tulsa, 1977-78; from br. mgr. to v.p. MAPCO Engring. Corp., Tulsa, 1978-81; pres. Amber Cons., Inc., Tulsa, 1981—; mem. faculty Langston U., Tulsa. Chmn., Tulsa Growth Guidance Com., 1978; vice chmn. Tulsa Citizens 201 Com.; chmn. Okla. Data Base Com., 1980; treas. Sungate Neighbors, 1981. Mem. Am. Soc. Pub. Adminstrn. (dir. publicity 1981, nat. program evaluator 1982, pres. elect NE Okla. chpt. 1982—), Am. Planning Assn., ASCE, Downtown Tulsa Unlimited. Author articles in field. Home: 6629 E 54th St Tulsa OK 74145 Office: PO Box 33236 Tulsa OK 74135

SCHURZ, RUTH DEAN, clin. social worker, sculptor; b. Elizabeth, N.J., Apr. 14, 1912; d. James Riddle and Marjorie Nott (Thatcher) S.; student Parson's N.Y. Sch. Fine and Applied Arts, 1930-32; sculpture student of Renzo Fenci, 1945-48; B.A. in Psychology, U. Calif., Santa Barbara, 1960; postgrad. U. Vienna, summer 1960; M.S.W., UCLA, 1962. Social worker Children's Home Soc. of Calif., Santa Barbara, 1962-67, Internat. Social Service, Athens, Greece, 1968-69, Family Service Agy. Santa Barbara, 1969-77; pvt. practice psychotherapy, Santa Barbara, 1977—; sculptor specializing in portrait busts, bronze, terra cotta, cast stone, Santa Barbara, 1948—, commns. include Maurice Abravanel, in Abravanel Hall, Music Acad., Santa Barbara, and Herbert P. Broida, in Broida Hall, U. Calif., Santa Barbara. Served with USN, 1943-44. Cert. social worker. Mem. Acad. Cert. Social Workers, Sculptors' Guild Santa Barbara. Episcopalian. Home and Office: 519 Peregrina Rd Santa Barbara CA 93105

SCHUSLER, MARIAN LUCILLE MARTIN (MRS. HERBERT HENRY SCHUSLER), educator; b. Woodcliff, N.J., Oct. 14, 1926; d. Theodore and Marian (Rover) Martin; B.S., Bucknell U., 1946; M.Litt., U. Pitts., 1950, Ph.D., 1964; m. Herbert Henry Schusler, Mar. 3, 1955; 1 dau., Dawn Lucille. Tchr., Reno Sr. High Sch., 1953-55; analytical statistician Census Bur., Washington, 1951-52, Navy Dept., Washington, 1952-53; tchr., chmn. dept. math. Wilkinsburg (Pa.) Sr. High Sch., 1955-66; lectr. U. Pitts., 1964-66; asso. prof. math. Slippery Rock State Coll., Pa., 1966-70; tchr. Shady Side Acad., Fox Chapel, Pa., 1970-80, also dir. testing, middle sch.; tchr. Hempfield Area Sch. Dist., 1980—. Mem. Am. Host Program, Vols. Internat. Tech. Assistance, Box Project; vol. Children's Hosp., Pitts. Recipient NSF award, summer 1961. Mem. Nat. Council Tchrs. Math., Math. Council Western Pa., Am. Ednl. Research Assn., Mensa, Pi Mu Epsilon, Kappa Delta Epsilon. Presbyterian. Author book; contbr. articles to profl. jours. Home: 900 E Pittsburgh St B-24 Greensburg PA 15601

SCHUSTER, ALICE LOUISE GEYER (MRS. WILLIAM T. SCHUSTER), editor; b. Pitts., Feb. 4, 1917; s. Edward Frederick and Anna Grace (Collins) Geyer; B.S. with honors, Carnegie-Mellon U., 1939; postgrad. Pa. State U., 1940, U. Pitts., 1940-41, U. Mich., 1941, Okla. State U., 1950, 69, 71, 73, 75; m. William T. Schuster, July 11, 1959. Tchr. bus. edn. Scottdale (Pa.) schs., 1939-43; sec. U.S. Steel Corp., 1943-44; asst. to editor U.S. Steel News, 1944-59; pres. Geyer Co., retail furniture, Wiesbaden, Germany, 1961-63; sec.-treas. Williamsburg Corp., land devel., Denver, 1965-70; reporter Edn. Colo., publ. Colo. Dept. Edn., Denver, 1966-67, asst. editor, 1967-71, editor, 1971-79; editor Colo. Edn. Directory, 1972-79, EDFO, internal newsletter, 1970-79; Colo. coordinator Internat. Tchr. Exchange Fellowship Program, 1974-79; cons. in journalism and publs., 1979; v.p. Williamsburg Devel. Co., 1972—; cons. in field. Recipient 2d prize, George Washington medal Freedoms Found. at Valley Forge, 1953. Cert. tchr., Pa., Colo. Mem. Ednl. Press Assn. Am. (various awards excellence), Nat. Sch. Public Relations Assn. Home: 690 S Alton Way Denver CO 80231

SCHUSTER, EULA ELAINE, lawyer; b. Oklahoma City, June 8, 1936; d. John Otto and Eula Delone (Campbell) Schuster; A.B., Sweet Briar Coll., 1958; M.A., U. Okla., 1961, J.D., 1968. Prof. econs. Southeastern State U., Durant, Okla., 1961-65; admitted to Okla. bar, 1968; pvt. practice law Whitten & Whitten, Attys., Oklahoma City, 1968-71; asst. dist. atty. Oklahoma County, 7th Dist., 1972-78; partner firm Jones, Schuster & Flaugher, Oklahoma City, 1978—; lectr. in field. Mem. Oklahoma County Bd. Adjustment, 1978—; citizen mem. profl. liaison com. City of Oklahoma City, 1980—; mem. Bd. Edn., Oklahoma City Area Vocat. Tech. Sch., Dist. 22, 1982—. Gen. Electric grantee, 1963. Mem. AAUW (br. pres. 1978-80, Okla. div. bd. 1969-75), Oklahoma County Bar Assn., Okla. Bar Assn., Am. Bar Assn., Kappa Beta Pi, Delta Kappa Gamma. Christian Ch. Office: 515 NW 13th St Oklahoma City OK 73103

SCHUTE, MELROSE MARY, ins. exec.; b. Dubuque, Iowa, Nov. 21, 1924; d. Walter Howard and Viola Margaret (Sweeney) Beresford; ed. public schs., short courses Drake U., Iowa U.; m. Marvin Andrew Schute, Aug. 8, 1953; children—Debra Lee, Michael Marvin. With statis. dept. Interstate Power Co., 1943-45, public relations dept., 1945-53; bookkeeper Lange Ins. Co., Dubuque, 1954-70, treas., 1970-78, sec.-treas., office mgr., 1978—; tchr. ins. courses. Former 2d dist. pres. Am. Legion Aux.; pres. Farley Aux. Unit, 1968-70, 78—; bd. dirs., sec. Farley Bowling Center, 1975—; bd. dirs. Western Dubuque Bobcat Band, 1979-81, Jr. Bowlers, 1974-79; pres. Western Dubuque Bobcat Boosters. Mem. Dubuque Ins. Women, Iowa Women's Bowling Assn., Iowa Ind. Ins. Agts. Roman Catholic. Home: 408 2d St NE Farley IA 52046 Office: 830 Dubuque Bldg Dubuque IA 52201

SCHUYLER, JANE, educator; b. Flushing, N.Y., Nov. 2, 1943; d. Frank James and Helen (Oberhofer) S.; B.A., Queens Coll., 1965; M.A., Hunter Coll., 1967; Ph.D., Columbia U., 1972. Asst. prof. art history Montclair State Coll., Upper Montclair, N.J., 1970; coordinator fine arts, asst. prof. York Coll., City U. N.Y., Jamaica, 1973-77, 78—, C.W. Post Coll., L.I. U., Greenvale, N.Y., 1971-73, adj. asso. prof., 1977—. Mem. Fine Arts Com. Internat. Women's Arts Festival, 1974-76. Columbia U. Summer Travel and Research grantee, 1969. Mem. Coll. Art Assn. Am., Women's Caucus for Art, AAUP, Nat. Trust Hist. Preservation, Renaissance Soc. Am. Democrat. Roman Catholic. Contbr. articles on occult and art to Cakes and Ale, 1978. Author: Florentine Busts: Sculpted Portraiture in the Fifteenth Century, 1976. Home: 35 37 78th St Jackson Heights NY 11372

SCHUYTEMA, EUNICE CHAMBERS, ednl. adminstr.; b. Rochester, N.Y., Feb. 4, 1929; d. Grant Earl and Dorothea Amelia (Fisher) Chambers; B.S., Cornell U., 1951, M.S., 1954; Ph.D., U. Iowa, 1956; m. Carl Guy Schuytema, June 14, 1954; 1 son, Paul. Research scientist Abbott Labs., North Chgo., 1956-67; asst. prof. biochemistry U. Ill. Coll. Medicine, Chgo., 1967-71; asst. prof. microbiology Rush Med. Coll., Chgo., 1971—, asst. dean preclin. curriculum, 1979—. Mem. Am. Soc. Microbiology, Am. Chem. Soc., AAAS, Sigma Xi, Iota Sigma Pi. Home: 600 S Cumberland St Park Ridge IL 60068 Office: 600 S Paulina St Chicago IL 60612

SCHWAB, LOIS OPPER (MRS. KENDALL DREISBACH SCHWAB), educator; b. Lincoln, Nebr., Jan. 26, 1925; d. Raymond Theodore and Lena Dorothea (Schroeder) Opper; student Westmar Coll., 1942-43; B.S., U. Nebr., 1946, M.A., 1947, Ed.D., 1966; m. Kendall Dreisbach Schwab, Aug. 6, 1949; children—Ronald Opper, Brian Edward, Kendra Joan. Am. Home Econs. Assn.-Rehab. Services Adminstrn. traineeship U. Nebr., 1964-66, instr., 1947-53, asso. prof. home econs., dir. programs for home economists in rehab., 1966-75, prof., 1975—. Co-dir. Easter Seal Found. research grant, 1970-71; cons. to home economists in rehab. U. Ala., 1971, N.D. State U., 1972, Iowa State U. Mem. Nebr. Gov's. Com. on Employment Handicapped, 1969—, Pres.'s Com. on Employment of Handicapped, 1977—, Lincoln Mayor's Com. on Employment Handicapped, 1967—; mem. com. on community programs Am. Heart Assn., 1872-74; mem. exec. com. Nebr. Heart Assn., 1968-80, chmn. pub. edn. com., 1969-70, chmn. bd. dirs., 1976-78, sec., 1971-72, mem., 1972-81; mem. task force on ind. living Am. Found. Blind, 1972-74; chmn. bd. dirs. Lincoln Heart Assn., 1967; trustee Nebr. Wesleyan U., 1970-77; chmn. program coordination com. Gt. Plains Heart Assn., 1974-76; mem. Nebr. Regional Med. Program Adv. Bd., 1972-77; treas. Nat. Congress in Homebound and Institutionalized Person, 1974-80; mem. SE Nebr. Health Service Agency Council. Recipient Disting. Alumnae award Westmar Coll., 1974; named to Old Masters, Purdue U., 1981. Mem. Am., Nebr. psychol. assns., Am. (chmn. human services sect. 1977-80), Nebr. home econ. assns., Nat., Nebr. (exec. com. 1967-72) rehab. coms., Mortar Bd., Phi Upsilon Omicron, Omicron Nu. Methodist. Home: 6721 Everett St Lincoln NE 68506

SCHWAB, THERESE ANNE, nurse; b. Detroit, Sept. 18, 1935; d. Charles Joseph and Wilhelmina Josephine (Kengel) Mathes; B.S.N., Barry Coll., 1957; M.P.H., U. Minn., 1965; M.S. in Edn., No. State Coll., 1975; Ph.D., Walden U., 1981; m. Francis Schwab, Aug. 29, 1964; children—Mary, Karen, Jodie, Charles. Staff nurse Univ. Med. Center, Ann Arbor, Mich., 1957-58; office nurse to internist, Birmingham, Mich., 1958-59; public health nurse Washtenaw County Health Dept., Ann Arbor, 1959-62, Tri County Health Dept., Aurora, Colo., 1962-63; nursing instr. Coll. St. Catherine, St. Paul, 1964-65; inservice dir. St. Luke's Hosp., Aberdeen, S.D., 1966-67; coordinator nursing Nebr.-S.D. Regional Med. Program, 1968-73; coordinator extended degree program U. Wyo., Laramie, 1975—; public speaker; cons. N.D. State Sch. Sci., 1972-73; coordinator S.D. Planning Council for Nursing, 1968-70. Vice pres. Laramie br. AAUW, 1977-80; polit. observer LWV of Laramie, 1980—. Named Outstanding Nursing Faculty Mem., U. Wyo., 1980. Mem. Am. Nurses Assn., Wyo. Nurses Assn., Laramie Nurses Assn., Am. Ednl. Research Assn., Sigma Theta Tau. Republican. Roman Catholic. Home: 1212 Custer St Laramie WY 82070 Office: 207 Sch Nursing U Wyo Laramie WY 82071

SCHWABE, CLARA GONZALEZ, lawyer; b. Queens, N.Y., Apr. 15, 1947; d. Gustavo Jaime and Lila (Gonzalez) Schwabe; B.A., Syracuse U., 1968; J.D., Bklyn. Law Sch., 1973; Admitted to N.Y. bar, 1974; asso. firm Stanley E. Kooper, Bklyn., 1973-80; partner firm Kooper and Schwabe, Bklyn., 1980—. Mem. Community Bd. 2, Bklyn., 1973-80, chmn. by-laws com., 1977—. Mem. N.Y. State Trial Lawyers Assn. (editor Notes and Decisions 1980—), Bklyn. Bar. Assn. (co-editor-in-chief Bklyn. Barrister, 1981—), Bklyn. Council of Women Lawyers (founder, 1981, pres. 1981-82), N.Y. State Bar Assn., Puerto Rican Bar Assn., Bklyn. Law Sch. Alumni Assn. (exec. sec. 1980—, editor Veritas 1977—). Home: 175 Adams St Brooklyn NY 11201 Office: 16 Court St Suite 1704 Brooklyn NY 11241

SCHWABEL, MARY JANE, microbiologist; b. Buffalo, Oct. 9, 1946; d. Albert Thomas and Doris Katherine (Schottin) S.; B.S. in Biology, Daemen Coll., 1968; M.S. in Biology Edn., Canisius Coll., 1975. Research asst. Erie County Virology Lab., SUNY, Buffalo, 1968-74; sr. serology techinican, supr. Erie County Lab., Buffalo, 1974-79; chief virologist dept. clin. microbiology and immunology Erie County Med. Center, Buffalo, 1979—. Mem. ASPCA, Nat. Wildlife Fedn., Internat. Wildlife Fedn., Am. Forestry Assn., Nat. Antivivisection Soc., North Shore Animal League, Western N.Y. Infection Control Soc., Nat. Am. Soc. Microbiology, Am. Public Health Assn., N.Y. State Assn. Public Health Labs., N.y. State Public Health Assn., AAAS, Beta Beta Beta, Republican. Roman Catholic. Office: 462 Grider St Buffalo NY 14215

SCHWAETZ, BARBARA CAROL, ins. exec.; b. N.Y.C., June 3, 1952; d. Sigmund and Miriam Schwartz; B.A., Herbert H. Lehman Coll., 1973. Group sales rep. Conn. Gen., N.Y.C., 1974-78; asst. v.p. The Kaye Group, 1978-82; asst. v.p. Robbins Orgn., N.Y.C., 1982—. C.L.U. Mem. Group Ins. Assn. (sec.-treas.). Office: 708 3d Ave New York NY 10017 *

SCHWAGER, EDITH COHEN, editor; b. Trenton, N.J., Dec. 16, 1916; d. Michael and Clara (Panitch) Cohen; children—Michael J., Karen S. Adj. lectr., exec. editor, adminstrv. dir. alcoholism clinic Hahnemann Med. Coll. (now Hahnemann U.), Phila., 1966-75; editor Med. Communications, 1977-81. Fellow Am. Med. Writers Assn. (pres. chpt. 1973-77; John P. McGovern Honor lectr. and award S.W. chpt. 1963). Columnist, Dear Edie. Home: 4404 Sherwood Rd Philadelphia PA 19131

SCHWAGER, ELAINE SUSAN, psychologist; b. Pitts., Aug. 3, 1949; d. Carl and Inge Susi (Weihl) S.; B.A. cum laude in English Lit., CCNY, 1969; M.A. in English Lit., SUNY, Stony Brook, 1971; Ph.D. in Clin. Psychology, L.I.U., 1977; postdoctoral student N.Y.U., 1980—; m. Marvin Hurvich, Nov. 1, 1981. Intern, then postdoctoral fellow N.Y. Hosp. Cornell U. Med. Center, White Plains, 1975-79; asst. prof. psychology Downstate Med. Center, Bklyn., 1979—; staff psychologist Blueberry Treatment Center, Bklyn, 1980-81; ind. practice psychoanalytic psychotherapy, 1978—. Mem. Am. Psychol. Assn., Soc. Personality Assessment, N.Y. Psychol. Assn. Home: 79 W 12th St New York NY 10011 Office: 49 W 12th St New York NY 10011

SCHWALBE, MARY ANNE, sch. adminstr.; b. N.Y.C., Mar. 31, 1934; d. James Alfred, Jr. and Emily Goldsmith; B.A. cum laude, Radcliffe Coll., 1955; postgrad. London Acad. Music and Dramatic Arts, 1956; m. Douglas Schwalbe, Dec. 5, 1959; children—Douglas, William, Nina. Asst. in theatre Barnard Coll., 1957, Irene Mayer Selznick, 1958; prodn. asst. Playwrights Co. and Frederick Brisson Prodns., 1959-62; adminstr. theatre communications group Ford Found., 1962-65; asst. dir., then dir. admissions Radcliffe Coll., 1965-75, asso. dean admissions and fin. aids Harvard U. and Radcliffe Coll., Cambridge, Mass., 1975-79; dir. adminstrn. and coll. counseling The Dalton Sch., N.Y.C., 1979—. Trustee Radcliffe Coll., The Hotchkiss Sch. Mem. Nat. Assn. Coll. Admissions Counselors, Nat. Assn. Prins. Schs. for Girls. Club: Harvard (dir.) (Boston). Office: Dalton School 108 E 89th St New York NY 10028

SCHWANDT, GERMAINE ANNE, social worker; b. Los Angeles, Dec. 30, 1936; d. Earle Kenneth and Leora Lona (Nitz) Vaag; B.A. (grantee), Valparaiso U., 1958; M.S.W., Howard U., 1965; children—Sonia S., Jennifer Joy. Social worker, various agys., Ill., 1957-60, Ohio, 1958-59, Md., 1963-68, Washington, 1968-69; adminstr. social work Montgomery County Pub. Schs., Rocville, Md., 1969—; asso. Mid Atlantic Learning Assos., 1979—; designer, implementer secondary alt. high sch. program Tahoma, 1978; presenter Met. Assn. Social Workers Workshops, 1972, Internat. Assn. Pupil Personnel Workers, 1975, Nat. Assn. for Young Children, 1976, Am. Personnel and Guidance Assn., 1976. Chmn. Community Involvement, Washington, 1962-68. Wheatridge Found. fellow, Howard U., 1961-63. Certified clin. social worker. Mem. Nat. Assn. Social Workers (sec. Washington 1961), Acad. Cert. Social Workers, NEA, local ednl. assns. Democrat. Home: 10100 New Orchard Dr Upper Marlboro MD 20772 Office: 850 Hungerford Dr Rockville MD 20850

SCHWANER, ANNIE MAE GINN (MRS. NELSON MARSHALL SCHWANER), state legislator; b. Carnesville, Ga., Apr. 24, 1912; d. Charles Holman and Mary Elizabeth (Terrell) Ginn; m. Nelson Marshall Schwaner (dec. 1967); children—Gordon Wesley, Audrey Mae, Susan Anne, Marsha Mae, Nelson Marshall II. Sec., Tubize Corp., Hopewell, Va., 1934-35; former reporter Hopewell News; former columnist Progress Index, Petersburg, Va.; mem. N.H. Ho. of Reps., 1963—, mem. mcpl. and county govt. com., 1963, constl. conv., 1964, resources, recreation, and devel. com.; mem. exec. bd. Rockingham County Legis. Del., 1973—. Mem. State Security Task Force, also Price Stblzn. Bd., 1964—; founder, 1st pres. Plaistow (N.H.) Civic Orgn., 1959-60; chmn. vols. Greater Haverhill (Mass.) chpt. ARC, 1954-57, nat. del., 1955, exec. bd., 1954-57; com. chmn. PTA council, Worcester, 1947-48; exec. bd. Sea Coast Regional Plan, 1965-67; v.p. Seacoast Regional Devel. Assn.; mem. Diocesan Sch. Bd., 1965-71; chmn. various fund-raising drs.; mem. nat. fund raising and adv. bd. Am. Heart Assn.; mem. Rockingham County Selective System Draft Bd.; pres. Plaistow Women's Republican Club, 1964-66; mem. N.H. State Constl. Conv., 1964, 74; bd. dirs. N.H. Heart Assn., state heart fund chmn., 1973; bd. dirs. Greater Salem Mental Health Clinic, 1976, So. Rockingham Mental Health Assn., 1975—; mem. N.H. Commn. on Status of Women. Recipient Bronze medal N.H. Heart Assn, 1959, cert. of merit Am. Mothers Com., 1960, cert. of honor N.H. DAV, 1965; citation White House, ARC. Mem. Cath. Daus. Am., Cath. Women's Guild (past pres.), Am. Judicature Soc., Nat. Order Women Legislators (state pres. 1973). Roman Catholic (ch. adv. bd.).

SCHWARTZ, AHLEEN HAAS, judge; b. June 14, 1928; d. Emanuel and Gussie (Silberfarb) Haas; B.S., N.Y. U., 1949, LL.B., 1952; m. Bernard Schwartz, Apr. 18, 1950; 1 son, Brian Michael. Admitted to N.Y. State bar, 1956; sr. law asst. N.Y. State Supreme Ct., 1962-66, N.Y. State Appellate div., 1966-75; judge N.Y.C. Civil Ct., 1973; judge N.Y. State Family Ct., 1975—; mem. Interagy. Council on Child Welfare, 1972-73; mem. N.Y. State Family Court Adv. and Rules Com., 1976—, chairperson forms subcom., 1976-77, rules subcom., 1977—. Mem. adv. council Harold A. Stevens Youth Devel. Center. Mem. Am. Bar Assn., Assn. Bar City N.Y., N.Y. Women's Bar Assn., N.Y. U. Law Sch. Alumni Assn. (dir. 1969-72), N.Y. U. Law Rev. Alumni Assn. (bd. govs. 1980—). Home: 60 Sutton Pl S New York NY 10022 Office: 60 Lafayette St New York NY 10007

SCHWARTZ, ANNE COHN, social work agency exec.; b. Cleve., July 17, 1913; d. Karl and Ida (Farbman) Kohn; B.A., Case Western Reserve U., 1933; M.S.W., Smith Coll., 1938; m. Edward D. Schwartz, Sept. 12, 1940. With Jewish Family Service Assn. of Cleve., 1940-79, asso. exec. dir., 1975-79; lectr. applied social sciences Case Western Reserve U., 1962-66, adj. instr., 1977—; clin. asst. prof. field work Smith Coll.; instr. and leader for numerous insts. and seminars. Trustee, Montefiore Home for Aged, 1979—, Crisis Intervention Team, 1979—. Mem. Family Service Assn. Am., Nat. Assn. Social Workers (social work merit award 1968), Nat. Conf. Jewish Communal Service, Nat. Assn. Jewish Family, Children's and Health Services, Nat. Conf. Social Welfare, Ohio Soc. Clin. Social Workers, Acad. Certified Social Workers. Contbr. articles in field to profl. jours. Mem. editorial bd. Journal Jewish Communal Services, 1967-69. Home: 2543 S Green Rd Beachwood OH 44122 Office: 2060 S Taylor Rd Cleveland Heights OH 44118

SCHWARTZ, CAROL ANN, optometrist; b. Alton, Ill., Dec. 19, 1953; d. Andrew C. and Joyce L. Schwartz; student Ill. State U., 1972-74; O.D., Ill. Coll. Optometry, 1978; postgrad. in bus. adminstrn. U. Chgo. Optometrist/cons. Wesley-Jessen Co., Chgo., 1978-80, mgr. clin. and profl. services, 1980—; adj. asso. prof., preceptor Ind. U., So. Coll. Optometry. Contbr. articles to profl. jours. Home: 900 N Lake Shore Dr Chicago IL 60611 Office: 37 S Wabash St Chicago IL 60603

SCHWARTZ, DEBBIE GALIA, social worker; b. Bklyn., June 16, 1925; d. Israel Noah and Celia (Hendlin) Neiman; B.A., Bklyn. Coll., 1945; M.S.W., Columbia U., 1956; m. Sam Schwartz, Jan. 20, 1957; 1 son, Noah. Asst. dir. Bklyn. Jewish Youth Council, 1946-48; adminstr. public relations Youth Alyah, Jerusalem, 1951-52; group worker-health educator Hadassah Med. Orgn., 1952-54; hostess, moderator Fourth R, Sta. WCRA-TV, 1954-56; day camp dir., Hirschman YMHA of Coney Island, 1961-65, asst. exec. dir., 1965-68; exec. dir. Assn. Jewish Center Workers, N.Y.C., 1976—; field work instr. Hunter Coll., 1961-68. Mem. Assn. Jewish Center Workers, Internat. Conf. of Jewish Communal Services, Columbia U. Sch. Social Work Alumni Assn., Jewish Public Soc.

SCHWARTZ, ELEANOR RACHEL, orgn. exec.; b. Chgo., Dec. 5, 1923; d. Michael and Gertrude (Fagen) S.; B.A., U. Chgo., 1941. With CSC, 1941-48; dir. young people's div. Jewish Fedn. and Welfare Fund of Chgo., 1948-50; dir. youth N.Y. Fedn. Reform Synagogues, 1950-51; assoc. dir. Nat. Fedn. Temple Youth, 1951-59; assoc. dir. Nat. Fedn. Temple Sisterhoods, N.Y.C., 1959-76, exec. dir., 1976—; rep. Union Am. Hebrew Congregations, Rabbinical Placement Commn., 1975-77, mem. exec. com., 1975-77. Bd. dirs. Nat. Interfaith Commn. on Aging, 1980—. Office: 838 Fifth Ave New York NY 10021

SCHWARTZ, FELICE N., sociologist; b. N.Y.C., Jan. 16, 1925; d. Albert and Rose Nierenberg; B.A., Smith Coll., 1945, L.H.D., 1981; L.H.D., Pace U., 1980; m. Irving L. Schwartz, Jan. 12, 1946; children—Cornelia Ann, Tony, James Oliver. Founder, exec. dir. Nat. Scholarship Service and Fund for Negro Students, 1945-51; v.p. for prodn. Etched Products Corp., N.Y.C., 1952-54; founder, pres. Catalyst, N.Y.C., 1962—; dir. Planned Parenthood Fedn. Am. Bd. visitors Grad. Sch. and Univ. Center, CUNY; mem. vis. com. Gen. Motors Inst. Recipient Susan B. Anthony award NOW; Disting. Alumnae medal Smith Coll., 1976; Mademoiselle medal for singular achievement in edn., 1949. Mem. Women's Forum N.Y. Author: How to Go to Work When Your Husband Is Against It, Your Children Aren't Old Enough and There's Nothing You Can Do Anyhow. Home: 1120 Fifth Ave New York NY 10028 Office: 14 E 60th St New York NY 10022

SCHWARTZ, JOYCE GENSBERG, pathologist; b. San Antonio, July 24, 1950; d. Frank and Sara Gensberg; B.A., U. Tex., Austin, 1971, M.A., 1972; M.D., U. Tex., San Antonio, 1980; m. Alan R. Schwartz, July 17, 1977. Speech pathologist Northeastern Ind. Sch. Dist., San Antonio, 1971-73; vet. asst., 1973-74; resident in pathology Audie Murphy VA Hosp., San Antonio. Mem. AMA, Bexar County Med. Assn., Phi Kappa Phi. Jewish.

SCHWARTZ, LITA LINZER, psychologist, educator; b. N.Y.C., Jan. 14, 1930; d. Aaron Jerome and Dorothy Claire (Linzer) Linzer; A.B., Vassar Coll., 1950; Ed.M., Temple U., 1956; Ph.D., Bryn Mawr Coll., 1964; m. Melvin Jay Schwartz, June 18, 1950; children—Arthur Lee, Joshua David, Frederic Seth. Part-time instr., counselor Pa. State U., Ogontz, Campus, Abington, 1961-66, asst. prof. ednl. psychology, 1966-71, assoc. prof., 1971-76, prof., 1976—; cons. in field. Recipient Humanitarian Award N.Y. Philanthropic League, 1973, Christian R. and Mary F. Lindback award for disting. teaching, 1982, Outstanding Tchr. award for 1981-82 Pa. State U. Coll. Edn. Alumni, 1982. Mem. Am. Psychol. Assn., Internat. Council of Psychologists, Am. Ednl. Research Assn., Council for Exceptional Children, Creative Edn. Found., Nat. Assn. for Gifted Children. Author: American Education, 1969, 74, 78; Educational Psychology, 1972, 77; The Exceptional Child: A Primer, 1975, 79; contbr. articles to profl. jours. Office: Pa State U Ogontz Campus Abington PA 19001

SCHWARTZ, MARILYN, artist, interior designer; b. Detroit, Feb. 20, 1947; d. Irving and Belle Kersh; student Wayne State U., 1964-67, Ariz. State U., 1972-74. Owner, mgr. Indomiss-T-Corp., Glendale, Ariz., 1970—; pvt. instr. painting, sculpting, graphics, interior design and furniture design; one woman shows: C. Mann Theater, Rochester, Minn., 1959, RJK Gallery, Atlanta, 1970, 71, Fireside Gallery, Phoenix, 1975; group shows include: Internat. Art Exhbn., Tokyo, 1961, Fellow Wives Art Display, Detroit, 1968, An Art Gallery, Atlanta, 1970, 2d Ann. Easter Seal Show, Phoenix, 1972, Ariz. Artists Guild, Phoenix, 1973, Brandeis 1st Ann. Expression Expn., Phoenix, 1973, 13th Ann. Arts Festival, Glendale, Ariz., 1973-75. Mem. Ariz. Artists Guild, Phoenix Art Mus. Home and Office: 4554 W Echo Ln Glendale AZ 85302

SCHWARTZ, PAULA RUTH, psychotherapist; b. Chgo., d. Martin and Dorothy Oboler; B.A., U. N.M., 19—; M.S.W., Adelphi U., 1968; m. Gerald Gordon Schwartz, Jr.; children—Stephen, Roy. Tng. asso. Nat. Council on Aging, N.Y.C., 1968-70; coordinator social services Town of Islip (N.Y.) Dept. Community Affairs, 1970-71; social work therapist Luther E. Woodward Sch. Emotionally Disturbed Children, Freeport, N.Y., 1971-72; asst. prof., program dir. Adelphi U. Sch. Social Work; 1972-76; pvt. practice psychotherapy, N.Y.C., 1972—; asst. prof. Yeshiva U. Gerontol. Inst., 1977-78; dir. N.Y. Geriatric Consultants, N.Y.C.; past dir. Psychotherapy Assos. of Manhattan; cons. Action Council for Community Services on L.I., 1981—; conf. coordinator, Eighth Ann. Interdisciplinary Ednl. Conf. on Bereavement and Grief, Yeshiva U., N.Y., 1982. Bd. dirs. Found. for Community Living. Mem. Nat. Assn. Social Workers. Club: N. Y. Roadrunners. Home: 141 E 88th St New York City NY 10028 Office: 1311 Lexington Ave New York City NY 10028

SCHWARTZ, RHEA S., lawyer; b. Miami Beach, Fla., Sept. 27, 1950; d. Walter and Linda (Rosenthal) S.; B.A., Pa. State U., 1971; student U. Strasbourg, France, 1970; J.D., Georgetown U., 1974; m. Paul Martin Wolff, Oct. 9, 1976. Admitted to Ill. bar, 1974, D.C. bar, 1976; asso. firm Schiff, Hardin & Waite, Chgo., 1974-75; atty. Office of Solicitor, Dept. Labor, Washington, 1975-77; labor counsel U.S. Air, Inc., Washington, 1977-79; spl. asst. to Sec. Edn., Washington, 1979-80, asst. gen. counsel Dept. Edn., Washington, 1980—; lectr. continuing legal edn. program Georgetown U. Law Center. Recipient Spl. Achievement award U.S. Govt., 1980. Mem. Am. Bar Assn., Ill. Bar Assn., D.C. Bar Assn., U.S. Figure Skating Assn. Author: Women and Credit, 1974. Office: 400 Maryland Ave SW Washington DC 20202

SCHWARTZ, SANDY EICHELBAUM, lobbyist; b. Bronx, N.Y., May 14, 1945; d. Milton and Pauline Yetta (Rosen) Eichelbaum; A.A., San Antonio Jr. Coll., 1965; B.A., U. Tex., Austin, 1967; m. Leonard Jay Schwartz, July 4, 1965; 1 dau., Michele Fay. Tchr. Public Schs. Austin, 1967-68, San Antonio, 1969-71; curriculum coordinator Edgewood Ind. Sch. Dist., San Antonio, 1971-72; govtl. services asso. Ohio Edn. Assn., Columbus, 1972-80; lobbyist Tex. State Tchrs. Assn., Austin, 1980—. Mem. exec. com. Franklin County Democratic party, 1978-80; mem. Internat. Women's Yr. Continuing Com., 1978-79, del.-at-large Nat. Women's Polit. Caucus, 1979-81; del. Dem. Nat. Conv., 1980. Mem. Nat. Assn. Legis. and Polit. Specialists in Edn. (pres. 1982—). Jewish. Club: U. Tex. Century. Home: 5800 Back Ct Austin TX 78731 Office: 316 W 12th St Austin TX 78701

SCHWARTZ, SUSAN STAFFIN, coll. adminstr.; b. Perth Amboy, N.J., Feb. 2, 1954; d. H. Kenneth and Laura (Valk) Staffin; B.A. in Psychology, Boston, U., 1976; M.A. in Individual and Group Counseling, Seton Hall U., 1978; m. Michael Eric Schwartz, Nov. 20, 1976; 1 dau., Merly Staffin. Admissions and fin. aid counselor Stevens Inst. Tech., 1978, asst. dir. fin. aid, 1979, dir. spl. programs for women, 1980—, mem. adv. bd. tech. enrichment program, 1980—. Recipient Merit award for creative and innovative programs N.Am. Assn. Summer Sessions, 1981. Mem. AAUW, Am. Soc. Engring. Edn., Assn. Am. Colls., Nat. Assn. Women Deans, Adminstrs. and Counselors, N.J. Coll. and Univ. Coalition on Women's Edn. Office: Stevens Inst Tech Castle Point Hoboken NJ 07030

SCHWARTZTOL, HOLLY WECHSLER, psychologist; b. Washington, Dec. 20, 1946; d. James Arthur and Nancy (Fraenkel) Wechsler; B.A., Finch Coll., 1968; M.A., C. W. Post Coll., 1971; Ph.D., U. Miami, 1981; m. Robert Ira Schwartztol, Nov. 16, 1975; children—Laurence, Andrew. Instr. psychology C. W. Post Coll., Greenvale, N.Y., 1971, Yorktown High Sch., Yorktown Heights, N.Y., 1971-73; sch. psychologist Dade County Schs., Miami, Fla., 1973—; pvt. practice psychology, Miami, 1982—. Mem. Dade Assn. Sch. Psychologists, Southeastern Psychol. Assn., Am. Psychol. Assn., Am. Personnel and Guidance Assn. Democrat. Author: (with James A. and Nancy F. Wechsler) In a Darkness, 1972. Office: 2201 SW 4th St Miami FL

SCHWARZ, ESTHER DORIS, state and city ofcl.; b. Newark, Mar. 29, 1933; d. Benjamin and Ida (Margolis) Epstein; cert. in bus. adminstrn. Rutgers U., 1955; m. John Schwarz, Sept. 20, 1959; children—Bonnie, Michael, Perry. Office mgr., controller Manson Printers, Hillside, N.J., 1969-73, Classic Distbg. Co., Union, N.J., 1974-76; agt. N.J. Motor Vehicle Dept., 1978—; councilman Town of Irvington, N.J., 1976—. Instl. rep. Robert Treat council Boy Scouts Am., 1972-78; pres. Union Ave. Sch., Irvington, 1968-70, Frank H. Morrell High Sch., Irvington, 1975-76; crusade chmn. Irvington chpt. Am. Cancer Soc., 1980; bd. mgrs. Irvington Gen. Hosp., 1972-74; mem. Irvington Alcoholic Commn., 1976—, chmn., 1977-78; trustee mem. Irvington Adult Sch., 1976—; tchr. Congregation Oheb Shalom, South Orange, N.J., 1969—; mem. Citizens Commn. of Mental Health, 1973—. Recipient Disting. Service award Town of Irvington, 1974, Outstanding Citizenship award Jewish Civic League, 1977, Disting. CD Service award City of Newark, 1951, cert. of honor Congregation Oheb Shalom, 1979. Mem. N.J. Motor Vehicle Agts. Assn. (1st. v.p. 1979—), Essex County Council PTA (pres. 1978-80), Nat. PTA (life), Police Athletic League, Nat. Council Jewish Women (legis. liaison chmn., v.p. adminstrn.), N.J. Elected Women Orgn. (charter), NAACP (charter). Democrat. Home: 117 Webster St Irvington NJ 07111 Office: 1295 Springfield Ave Irvington NJ 07111

SCHWARZE, ESTELLA GERALDINE, social work adminstr.; b. New Orleans; d. William J. and Mary (Reynolds) Schwarze; B.S. in Social Sci., Loyola U., New Orleans, 1957, postgrad., 1958-59, 61-62; M.S.W., Tulane U., 1962. With Asso. Cath. Charities, 1946-59; exec. dir.

Assn. for Retarded Children, 1956-57; with social service dept. Charity Hosp. of La., New Orleans, 1958—, supr., 1965—; dir. social services La. Rehab. Inst., New Orleans, 1979—; field work instr. Atlanta U. Grad. Sch. Social Work, 1967—, Wharton Grad. Sch. Social Work, 1976—, Tulane U. Grad. Sch. Social Work, 1979; lectr. community medicine La. State U. Sch. Medicine, Tulane U. Sch. Medicine. Cons. social work to Treme Neighborhood Improvement Assn. Organizer Project Aquarius; del. White House Conf. on Children and Youth, 1970, White House Conf. on Aging, 1971; founder Irish Channel Action Found., New Orleans, 1964, charter mem.; organizer Parent's Inst., New Orleans, 1962; coordinator symposium Socialization of the Am. So. Teenager, 1973. Adv. bd. health consumer edn. program Urban League. Cert. social worker, La. Fellow La. Soc. Clin. Social Workers; mem. Nat. Assn. Social Workers (social worker of year S.E. La. chpt. 1965), Acad. Cert. Social Workers, La. Consumers League, Mercy Acad. Alumnae (pres. 1956-58), Am. Pub. Health Assn., Bus. and Profl. Women's Club, League Women Voters. Democrat. Home: 915 Jefferson Ave New Orleans LA 70115 Office: Social Service Dept L-M Bldg 1542 Tulane Ave New Orleans LA 70130

SCHWARZROCK, SHIRLEY LORRAINE PRATT, author, lectr., educator; b. Mpls., Feb. 27, 1914; d. Theodore Ray and Myrtle Pearl (Westphal) Pratt; B.S., U. Minn., 1935, M.A., 1942, Ph.D., 1974; m. Loren H. Schwarzrock, Oct. 19, 1945 (dec. 1966); children—Kay Linda, Ted Kenneth, Lorraine V. Sec. to chmn. speech dept., U. Minn., Mpls., 1935, instr. in speech, 1946, team tchr. in creative arts workshops for tchrs., 1955-56, guest lectr. Dental Sch., 1967-72, asst. prof. (part-time) practice adminstrn. Sch. Dentistry, 1972-80; tchr. speech, drama and English, Preston (Minn.) High Sch., 1935-37; tchr. speech, drama and English, Owatonna (Minn.) High Sch., 1937-39, also dir. dramatics, 1937-39; tchr. creative dramatics and English, tchr.-counselor Webster Groves (Mo.) Jr. High Sch., 1939-40; dir. dramatics and tchr.-counselor Webster Groves Sr. High Sch., 1940-43; exec. sec. bus. and profl. dept. YWCA, Mpls., 1943-45; tchr. speech and drama Convent of the Visitation, St. Paul, 1958; editor pro-tem Am. Acad. Dental Practice Adminstrn., 1966-68; guest tchr. Coll. St. Catherine, St. Paul, 1969; cons. for dental med. programs Normandale Community Coll., Bloomington, Minn., 1968; cons. on public relations to dentists, 1954—; guest lectr. to various dental groups, 1966—. Author Effective Dental Assisting, 1954, 59, 67, (with J.R. Jensen), 1973, 78, 82; (with Lorraine Schwarzrock) Workbook for Effective Dental Assisting, 1979, 82, Manual for Effective Dental Assisting, 1978; (with Donovan F. Ward) Effective Medical Assisting, 1969, 76; Workbook for Effective Medical Assisting, 1969, 76; Manual for Effective Med. Assisting, 1969, 76; (with C.G. Wrenn) Facts and Fantasies about Drugs, Facts and Fantasies about Alcohol, Facts and Fantasies about Smoking, Some Common Crutches, The Mind Benders, Alcohol as a Crutch, Food as a Crutch, Can You Talk with Someone Else?, Easing the Scene, In Front of the Table and Behind It, To Like and Be Liked, Changing Roles of Men and Women, What It Means to Youth, Coping with Cliques, I'd Rather Do It Myself, If Your Don't Mind, Living with Loneliness, Parents Can Be a Problem, Grades, What's So Important about Them, Anyway?, 1970, Living with Differences, You Always Communicate Something, Understanding the Law of Our Land, My Life, What Shall I Do with It?, Do I Know the Me Others See?, Crises Youth Face Today, 1973, The Coping With Series Manual, 1973; Contemporary Concerns of Youth, 1979. Pres., University Elem. Sch. PTA, 1955-56; vol. mgr. Eitel Hosp. Gift Shop, 1981—. Mem. Minn. (hon. mem.) Acad. Dental Practice Adminstrn., Zeta Phi Eta (pres. 1948-49), Eta Sigma Upsilon. Home: 7448 W Shore Dr Minneapolis MN 55435

SCHWASS, NORMA ELIZABETH, exec. sec.; b. Phila., Nov. 17, 1932; d. George Russell and Margaret Calhoun Droll; m. H. B. Schwass, Feb. 18, 1956; children—Linda, David, Jeanette. Clk., Farm Jour., 1950-51; typist Leeds & Northrup Co., 1951-55; sec. patent dept. Philco Corp., 1955-58; sec. to corp. atty. Sandura Co., Jenkintown, Pa., 1961-62; sec. to pres. A-O, Ltd., Sellersville, Pa., 1964-70; exec. sec. to pres., corp. sec. Bux-Mont Constrn. Ltd., Southampton, Pa., 1970-75; corp. sec., office mgr., exec. sec. to pres. Best Environ. Service & Tech. Ltd., Southhampton, 1975—; partner, corp. sec. Anaerobic Energy, Inc., Southampton, 1975—. Club: Choraliers. Home: Box 282 Hatboro PA 19040 Office: 630 2d St Pike Southhampton PA 18966

SCHWEBEL, BERNICE LOIS, educator, exec.; b. Hartford, Conn., Sept. 27, 1916; d. Joseph and Sara (Brewer) Davison; B.A., Russell Sage Coll., 1938; teaching cert. SUNY, 1949; M.A., N.Y.U., 1963; m. Milton Schwebel, Sept. 3, 1939; children—Andrew, Robert. Co-founder, dir. Counseling and Placement Services for Refugees, Jewish Community Center, Troy, N.Y., 1936; social case worker Troy Orphan Asylum, 1938-39; cottage mother Pleasantville (N.Y.) Cottage Sch., 1939-40; head tchr. Birnby Nursery Sch., N.Y.C., 1945-46; tchr. kindergarten, primary grades, Valley Stream, N.Y., 1950-67; supr. student tchrs. edn. dept. Douglass Coll., Rutgers U., New Brunswick, N.J., 1973-76; v.p. ednl. programs and materials Univ. Assocs., Columbus, Ohio, 1976—. Trustee, Rutgers-Livingston Day Care Center, 1977-80; chmn. Rutgers-Old Queens Visitation Com., New Brunswick Tercentenary, 1979-80. Mem. Authors Guild, LWV, NOW, Women's League of Rutgers U., Russell Sage Alumnae Assn., N.Y.U. Alumni Assn. Co-author film script Resistance to Learning, 1962; author: Student Teachers Handbook, 1979; contbr. articles to various publs. Home: 1050 George St New Brunswick NJ 08901 Office: Univ Assos 899 Kendale Rd S Columbus OH 43220

SCHWEDER, JEANNE ANN, editor; b. Elyria, Ohio, Jan. 2, 1947; d. Lawrence Allen and Dorothy Mae (Linden) Kuhl; student Calif. State U., Northridge, 1965-66, SUNY, Brockport, 1973-74; m. Doyle L. Schweder, Feb. 25, 1967; children—John Doyle, Jennifer Louise. With Empire State Weeklies, Webster, N.Y., 1967-82, reporter, editor, 1968-79, mng. editor, 1979-82; mgr. editorial services Nat. Alliance Bus., Washington, 1982—. Office: 1015 15th St NW Washington DC 20005

SCHWEINHAUT, MARGARET C., state senator; b. Washington; ed. George Washington U., Nat. U. Law Sch.; LL.D., St. Joseph Coll. Mem. Md. Ho. of Dels., 1955-61; mem. Md. Senate, 1961-63, 67—, chmn. exec. nominations com. Chmn. Md. Commn. on Problems of the Aging. Bd. dirs. Nat. Council of Aging. Recipient Certificate of Merit, Nat. Council of Sr. Citizens. Mem. Internat. Gerontological Soc., Montgomery Retarded Children's Assn. Office: Maryland Senate State Capitol Annapolis MD 21401 *

SCHWEITZER, GERTRUDE, artist; b. N.Y.C. One-woman shows: Montclair (N.J.) Art Mus., Washington Water Color Club, Cayuga Mus. History and Art, Auburn, N.Y., Potsdam Gallery Art, Currier Gallery of Art, Manchester, N.H., Bevier Gallery, Rochester (N.Y.) Inst. Tech., Erie (Pa.) Pub. Mus., Cortland Library, N.Y., Norton Gallery and Sch. Art, West Palm Beach, Fla., Galerie Charpentier, Paris (1st Am. one-man show), Hanover Gallery, London, Worth Ave. Gallery, Palm Beach, Fla., Galleria Al Cavallino, Venice, Italy, Galleria Il Naviglio, Milan, Italy, Galleria L'Obelisco, Rome, High Mus., Atlanta, Witte Meml. Mus., San Antonio, Phila. Art Alliance, Hokin Gallery, Palm Beach, Pratt Manhattan Center, N.Y.C., New Britain (Conn.) Mus. Am. Art, Fla. So. Coll., Lakeland, many others; exhibited in Washington, Chgo., Phila., Denver, Sarasota, Fla., N.Y.C., Los Angeles, Bklyn., Minn., Ill., Santa Fe, Newark; represented in permanent collections: Bklyn. Mus., Toledo Mus., Hackley Art Gallery, Muskegon, Mich., Davenport (Iowa) Mcpl. Gallery, Canajoharie (N.Y.) Library and Art Gallery, Norton Gallery and Sch. of Art, W. Palm Beach, Witte Meml. Mus. San Antonio, Mus. Modern Art, Paris, Albi Mus., France, Rochester (N.Y.) Meml. Art Gallery, Met. Mus. Art, N.Y.C., Columbia U., NAD, Whitney Am. Art, N.Y.C., Walker Art Mus. Bowdoin Coll., Brunswick, Maine, Atlanta Art Assn. Galleries, Montclair (N.J.) Art Mus., Chgo. Art Inst., N.A.D., New Britain (Conn.) Mus. Am. Art, State U. N.Y., Purchase, Soc. Four Arts, Mus. Art, Santa Fe, Palm Beach, others, also numerous pvt. collections, U.S., Eng., France, Denmark. Served as chmn. arts and skills corps, N.Y. chpt. ARC, Ft. Jay Regional Hosp., Governor's Island, N.Y., World War II. Recipient Am. Water Color Soc. medal; Am. Artists Profl. League medal for water color, State of N.J., Pauline Wick award (oil); Phila. Water Color prize, Pa. Acad. of Fine Arts; First prize Norton Gallery of Art, West Palm Beach, Fla.; First prize Soc. Four Arts; oil and watercolor awards; Grand Nat. Exhbn., Miami, Fla.; 1st prize, best woman painter N.J. State Exhbn.; N.Y. State award Am. Artists Profl. League, Nat. Arts Club; First prize Am. Artists Profl. League, Seton Hall U.; First Grumbacher Purchase award Audubon 17th Am. Exhbn., N.Y.C.; others. Mem. Am. Water Color Soc., Nat. Acad., Audubon Soc., N.J. Water Color and Sculpture Soc. Home: Colts Neck NJ 07722 also Palm Beach FL 33480

SCHWEITZER, MARY-ELIOT SMITH (MRS. ROBERT SCHWEITZER, JR.), civic worker, electronics co. exec.; b. San Jose, Calif., July 7, 1927; d. Julius Avery and Elise (Peyton) Smith; A.A., Marymount Coll., 1948; Engring. Tech. degree Normandale Community Coll., 1981 m. Robert Schweitzer, Jr., Sept. 18, 1952; children—Mary-Eliot, James-Peyton, Mary-Neale. Sec., Teen-age Jr's, Stanford Convalescent Home, Palo Alto, Calif., 1944-45; receptionist, driver A.R.C., Palo Alto, 1947-51; mem. Jr. League, San Francisco, 1950-54; mem. Jr. League, N.Y.C., 1956-58; mem. Jr. League, Mpls., 1963—, bd. dirs., 1966-67. Leader, Girl Scouts U.S.A., Mpls., 1966-69; mem. Citizens Com. for Pub. Edn., Mpls., 1968-76, Citizens League, Mpls., 1968-80; docent Mpls. Inst. Arts, 1965-66, Hennepin County Hist. Soc., 1965-66; pres. Douglas Elementary Sch. P.T.A., 1968-70; v.p. West High Sch. P.T.A., 1970-71, pres., 1971-73; bd. dirs. Womens UN Rally, 1966-72; bd. dirs. Assos. James Ford Bell Library, 1968—, pres., 1972-75; bd. dirs. Friends Mpls. Inst. Arts, 1968-73; bd. dirs. Mpls. Council P.T.A.'s, 1969-76, treas., 1974-76; bd. dirs. Minn. World Affairs Center, 1969-76, UN Assn. of Minn., 1970-76; adv. bd. Childrens Theatre Co., Mpls., 1969-72, house mgr., 1971-72; vice chmn. Hennepin Lowry Council, 1972-74; chmn. bd. Jr. League Thrift Shop, 1966-67; mem. citywide adv. com. for ednl. facilities and plant planning Mpls. Pub. Schs., 1975-76; unit mgr. Control Data Corp., Magnetic Peripherals, Inc., 1981—. Named Beautiful Activist, 1973. Mem. D.A.R., Mpls. Soc. Fine Arts, Womens Assn. Minn. Symphony Orch., Mpls. League Catholic Women (dir. 1974-80), League Women Voters, English Speaking Union, Univ. Hosps. Vol. Assn., West Dist. Schs. Assn. (vice-chmn. 1972-73, chmn. 1974-75), Peyton Soc. Va., Minn. Zool. Soc. Republican. Home: 5140 W 102d St Bloomington MN 55437

SCHWEITZER, SHIRLEY KARNES, civic worker; b. Streator, Ill., May 14, 1927; d. Carman Ulric and Lavone Alice (Webster) Karnes; B.S. in Home Econs., U. Cin., 1950; m. William Kenmore Schweitzer, Sept. 2, 1950; children—William Kurt, James Scott (dec.). Lab. technician E.I. duPont Chem. Co., Belle, W.Va., 1947-48; supr. testing laundry Procter & Gamble, Cin., 1951-53; textile chemist Dow Chem. Co., Midland, Mich., 1954-57; del. Republican Midland County (Mich.) Conv., 1964—; mem. Midland Beautification Adv. Commn., 1971-78; bd. mgrs. United Community Fund, Midland, 1972-79, treas., 1974-77, sec., 1977-79; trustee, mem. adminstrv. bd., mem. fin. com., bd. dirs. United Meth. Women, First United Meth. Ch., Midland; mem. Midland County bd. Ch. Women United; docent Midland Art Council. Recipient Keep Mich. Beautiful 1st Pl. award Bicentennial Forest Commn., 1977; AAUW Fellowship Name Grant honoree, 1971-72. Mem. AAUW (Midland br. dir. 1960-70, state dir. 1964-66), Federated Garden Clubs Am. (state dir. 1979—, dist. 6 dir. 1981—), Nat. Assn. Investment Clubs (Saginaw Valley council), Midland County Geneal. Soc. (dir.). Clubs: Seed and Sod Garden, Dow Janes Investors Stock, Midland Country. Home: 516 Crescent Dr Midland MI 48640

SCHWEN, MARCIA GRANN, editor, former newspaper pub.; b. Providence, Nov. 27, 1940; d. Carl Herbert and Olga Charlotte (Josephson) Grann; B.A. cum laude, Gustavus Adolphus Coll., St. Peter, Minn., 1962; m. LeRoy Lewellyn Schwen, June 29, 1963; children—Colin Jeffrey, Gavin Daniel, Vanessa Leah. Asst. to dir. public relations dept., text and film div. McGraw-Hill, Inc., N.Y.C., 1962-63; tchr. English and journalism L.I. Lutheran High Sch., Glen Head, N.Y., 1963-66, Stony Brook (N.Y.) Sch. for Girls, 1966-67; reporter, asso. editor, then mng. editor Three Village Herald, Stony Brook, 1970-76; founder, sec.-treas., pub., editor The Village Times, Inc., East Setauket, N.Y., 1976-79; editor publs. Amnesty Internat./USA, 1980—; weekly columnist Three Village Herald, 1981—; free-lance writer, 1979—; adj. prof. journalism C.W. Post Coll., 1980. Mem. council St. James (N.Y.) Luth. Ch., 1972-76; bd. dirs. Luth. New Yorker, 1975-76, Three Village Community Youth Services, Inc., 1979; co-mng. editor Labor News, Amnesty Internat., 1979; lay asst. Luth. Ch., 1976—; pres. Justice for All, Inc., 1982—. Carnegie Found. grantee for study in Mexico, 1960; recipient 1st pl. award investigative reporting Nat. Newspaper Assn., 1980, N.Y. Press Assn., 1980; 1st pl. award humor N.Y. Press Assn., 1982; Best Column award L.I. Press Club, 1982. Mem. Nat., N.Y. State (Stuart C. Dorman award 1979) press assns., Three Village C. of C. (dir. 1977-79). Home and Office: 22 Stratton Ln Stony Brook NY 11790

SCHWOPE, MARY KATHRYN, state legislator; b. Rock Springs, Wyo., July 21, 1917; d. Charles Alfred and Mary Frances (Moriarty) Viox; student public schs., Green River, Wyo., 1923-35; m. Eldridge Lawson Schwope, July 15, 1940; children—Michael Lawson, Fachon J. Schwope Wilson, Patricia K. Schwope Murphy, Madalaine M. Schwope Connolly. With Union Pacific R.R., 1936-46; mem. Wyo. Ho. of Reps., 1975-76, 79—. Mem. Democratic Precinct Com., Cheyenne, 1957-67; vice chmn., dist. capt. County Dem. Com.; sec. City-County CD Council, 1962-63, Laramie County Fair Bd., 1966-76; mem. State Adv. Council Vocat. Edn., 1976-81; mem. Silver-Haired Legis. Adv. Com., 1982—. Recipient nat. merit cert. Am. Revolutionary Bicentennial Adminstrn., 1976; Four Chaplains Legion of Honor, 1979. Mem. Am. Legion Aux. (state pres. 1968-69, nat. exec. com. 1969-70), Am. Assn. Ret. Persons, Cheyenne Sr. Citizens. Roman Catholic. Clubs: Zonta, Exec.

SCOFIELD, TOMIE ELIZABETH, civic leader, columnist; b. Jacksonville, Fla., Aug. 19; d. William Henry Riggs and Laliah Elizabeth (Riggs) Henry; student McFarland Sch. Floristry, 1961; m. George W. Scofield (dec.); children—Kylene (Mrs. R.L. Wing), Norma Faye (Mrs. R. Ericson). Founder Citrus County (Fla.) unit Am. Cancer Soc., Inverness, 1950, pres., 1953—, also bd. dirs. Fla. div.; chmn. ARC, Citrus County, 1954; dir. publicity, pres. emeritus Am. Cancer Soc. Fla. Div. Inc.; mem. Citrus County Bicentennial Com., 1976; pres. Citrus County Meml. Hosp. Aux., 1967, now life mem.; mem. com. of Whispering Pines Park Devel., Inverness, 1971-76; columnist Citrus County Chronicle, Inverness, 1964—. Mem. Gov.'s Com. on Aging; pres. Woman's Missionary Union Bapt. Ch., Inverness, 1964-67. Recipient Civic Leadership citation Kiwanis Club, 1965, plaque Am. Legion, 1965, 67, H.C. Barnes award, 1967, Sword of Hope award Am. Cancer Soc. unit, 1975, 80, also letters of commendation; 32 yr. pin Am. Cancer Soc. Fla. Div., 1982; cert. appreciation Citrus County Meml. Hosp.; patriotism citation Floral City (Fla.) Am. Legion Mem. Citrus County C. of C. (chmn. bd. 1967-68, service awards 1979, 80), Freedom Found. Valley Forge, Fedn. of Garden Clubs of Fla. (life), Citrus County Art League, Freedom Found. of Valley Forge. Clubs: Withlacoochee Press (historian), Ind. Order of Odd Fellows (dist. dept. 1950, founder Rebekah lodge 1948), Order of the Amaranth, Daughters of the Nile, Inverness Garden Club (founder 1961), Greater Los Angeles Press. Address: PO Box 362 Inverness FL 32650

SCOTHORN, CAROL JUNE ELLER, choreographer, dance educator; b. Chgo., June 18, 1929; d. Harry E. and Alyce (Robers) Eller; B.A., Stanford U., 1950; M.A., Mills Coll., 1951; m. Robert A. Scothorn, July 1, 1951; 1 dau., Hilary. Choreographer Oreg. Shakespeare Festival, 1949, 50; actress, dancer, lighting technician Virginia City (Mont.) Players, 1951-52; mem. faculty UCLA, 1952—, prof. dance, 1972—, chmn. dept., 1980—. Doris Humphrey fellow Am. Dance Festival, 1962. Mem. Nat. Assn. Schs. Dance (bd. dirs. 1982), Am. Coll. Dance Festival Assn. (bd. dirs. 1981), Dance Notation Bur. Choreographer: The Hazarite, 1962; Events and Reverberations, 1973, Volo, En Route, Canti, 1977, Continuing, 1976, Mirror, Mirror, 1981.

SCOTT, ANN BESSER, musicologist; b. Newark, June 8, 1933; d. Hyman and Fannie (Bear) Besser; A.B., Radcliffe Coll., 1955; M.F.A., Brandeis U., 1957; Ph.D., U. Chgo., 1969; m. Gordon H.S. Scott, May 3, 1958; children—Ellen, Melinda. Instr., then asst. prof. music U. Chgo., 1968-73; mem. faculty Bates Coll., Auburn, Maine, 1973—, prof. music, 1979—, chmn. dept., 1974—, chmn. div. humanities, 1976-80; mem. Maine Humanities Council, 1975—; mem. music panel Maine Commn. Arts and Humanities, 1981—. Fellow Nat. Endowment Humanities, 1981. Mem. Am. Musicol. Soc. (sec. council 1974-79, editorial bd. jour. 1975-80), Coll. Music Soc., Phi Beta Kappa. Jewish. Author articles in field. Home: 94 Shepley St Auburn ME 04210 Office: Music Dept Bates Coll Lewiston ME 04240

SCOTT, ANNE BYRD FIROR, historian, educator; b. Montezuma, Ga., Apr. 24, 1921; d. John William and Mary Valentine (Moss) Firor; A.B., U. Ga., 1941; M.A., Northwestern U., 1944; Ph.D., Radcliffe Coll., 1958; L.H.D., Lindenwood Coll., 1968; m. Andrew Mackay Scott, June 2, 1947; children—Rebecca, David MacKay, Donald MacKay. Congl. rep., editor LWV of U.S., 1944-53; lectr. history Haverford Coll., 1957-58, U. N.C., Chapel Hill, 1959-60; asst. prof. history Duke U., Durham, N.C., 1961-67, asso. prof., 1968-70, prof., 1971-80, W.K. Boyd prof., 1980—; vis. prof. Johns Hopkins U., 1972-73, Stanford U., 1974; bd. dirs. Carnegie Corp. N.Y., Woodrow Wilson Internat. Center; adv. com. Bunting Inst. Chmn. Gov.'s Commn. on Status of Women, 1963-64; mem. Citizens Adv. Council on Status of Women U.S., 1964-68. AAUW fellow, 1956-57; grantee Nat. Endowment for Humanities, 1967-68, 76-77, Nat. Humanities Center, 1980—. Mem. Am. Antiquarian Soc., Orgn. Am. Historians (mem. exec. bd. 1973-76, pres. elect), So. Hist. Assn. (mem. exec. bd. 1976-79). Democrat. Author: The Southern Lady, 1970; (with Andrew MacKay Scott) One Half the People, 1974; editor: Jane Addams, Democracy and Social Ethics, 1964; The American Woman, 1970; Women in American Life, 1970; Women and Men in American Life, 1976; mem. editorial bd. Am. Quar., 1974-78, Jour. So. History, 1978—; contbr. articles to profl. jours. Office: Dept History Duke U Durham NC 27706

SCOTT, AUDREY EBBA, city ofcl.; b. Boston, Nov. 25, 1935; d. Carl Arthur and Vera (Bisbee) Hallberg; A.B., Tufts U., 1957; m. John Joseph Scott, May 5, 1962; children—Lawrence, Bryan, Kenneth, Edward. Tchr., North Haven, Conn., La Rochelle, France, Sagamihara, Japan, 1957-62; city councilwoman, Bowie, Md., 1974-75; mayor, Bowie, 1976—; dir. community relations Prince Georges Gen. Hosp. and Med. Center, 1980-81; Spl. asst. HUD, 1981—; pres. Md. Mcpl. League, 1979-80. Pres., chmn. bd. Bowie Health Center, 1973-75; bd. dirs. Council of Govts., Washington, 1976—; chmn. Bowie chpt. Multiple Sclerosis Soc., 1976—, bd. dirs. Nat. Capital Area chpt., 1978—. Named Outstanding Mayor of Yr., VFW, 1979. Mem. Nat. League Cities, Md. Mcpl. League, Republican Mayors Assn., Prince Georges Mcpl. Assn. (Outstanding Mcpl. Ofcl. 1976-77) AAUW, Tufts Alumni Assn., Washington Women's Network, Alpha Omicron Pi, Beta Sigma Phi. Republican. Presbyterian. Clubs: Woman's (pres. 1972-73) (Bowie), Bowie-Crofton Bus. and Profl. Women's, Soroptomists. Office: City Hall Bowie MD 20715

SCOTT, BARBARA JEAN, personnel exec.; b. Miami, Fla., Sept. 28, 1947; d. John Peter and Bertha Ann (Rutkowski) Nace; A.A., Broward Community Coll., 1970; B.A., U. Fla., 1972; M.Ed., U. S.C., 1980; m. Thomas William Scott, Dec. 18, 1971; 1 dau., Amanda Kristin. Adminstrv. asst. Am. Acad., Hollywood, Fla., 1972-73; instr. English, coordinator Am. Heritage Sch., Hollywood, 1973-77; statistician Greenville (S.C.) Tech., 1978-80, coordinator developmental edn., 1980; personnel asst. Builder Marts Am., Greenville, 1981—; cons. Publicity com. mem. Warehouse Theatre, Greenville, 1981, Greenville Library, Friends of the Zoo, 1981. Mem. AAUW, Nat. Assn. Female Execs., Women's Network, Delta Kappa Gamma (pres.). Roman Catholic. Club: Greenville Bus./Profl. Women's. Home: 230 Barrett Dr Maudlin SC 29662

SCOTT, BARBARA MAY ATTEBERY, educator, psychologist; b. Hillsboro, Ill., Dec. 6, 1929; d. Homer Franklin and Edith May (Rolf) Attebery; B.S., U. Ill., 1950; M.S., Iowa State U., 1963, Ph.D., 1967; m. John Thackeray Scott, Jr., Feb. 7, 1953; children—John Roderick, Anne Marlene, Carl Attebery. Home adviser U. Ill. Extension Service, Kankakee, 1950-51, Carmi, 1951-53; asst. prof. child devel. and family relations U. Ill., Urbana, 1965-67; sch. psychologist Champaign County (Ill.) Rural Coop., 1968-77, Vermillion County Assn. Spl. Edn., Danville, Ill., 1978-80, Tri-County Spl. Edn. Coop., Bloomington, Ill., 1980-82; presch. tchr., 1982—. Dist. 7 dir. Sch. Human Resources and Family Studies U. Ill. Alumni Bd., 1979—. Mem. Ill. Sch. Psychologists Assn., East Central Ill. Sch. Psychologists Assn. (pres. 1977-78), Am. Psychol. Assn., Soc. Research in Child Devel., Ill. Psychologists Assn., Krannert Art Mus. Assos., Montgomery County hist. and geneal. socs., Gamma Sigma Delta. Democrat. Methodist. Club: U. Ill. Women's. Home: 5 Bellamy Ct Champaign IL 61820

SCOTT, CHARLOTTE HANLEY, educator; b. Yonkers, N.Y., Mar. 18, 1925; d. Edgar B. and Charlotte Agnes (Palmer) Hanley; A.B., Barnard Coll., 1947; postgrad. Am. U., 1949-53; M.B.A., U. Chgo., 1964; LL.D., Allegheny Coll., 1981; m. Nathan Alexander Scott, Jr., Dec. 21, 1946; children—Nathan Alexander, Leslie Kristin Scott Ashamu. Research assoc. Nat. Bur. Econ. Research, N.Y.C., 1947-48; economist R.W. Goldsmith Assocs., Washington, 1948-55; economist U. Chgo., 1955-56; economist Fed. Res. Bank, Chgo., 1956-71, asst. v.p., 1971-76; prof. bus. adminstrn. and commerce U. Va., Charlottesville, 1976—, fellow Tayloe Murphy Inst., 1976—; mem. consumer adv. council FRS, 1980—, chmn., 1982—; dir. Charlottesville bd. Va. Nat. Bank. Mem. Internat. Assn. Personnel Women (editorial bd. Jour. 1981—, v.p., 1980—), Am. Fin. Assn., Acad. Mgmt., Va. Assn. Economists, Am. Soc. Personnel Adminstrn., Human Resource Planning Soc. Episcopalian. Contbr. in field. Home: 1419 Hilltop Rd Charlottesville VA 22903 Office: PO Box 6550 Charlottesville VA 22906

SCOTT, CHRISTINA MARIE, geologist; b. Seattle, June 24, 1952; d. Theodore James and Sarah Jane (McGalliard) Cross; B.S., U. Puget Sound, 1972; postgrad. Ariz. State U., 1972-75; m. Richard B. Scott, July 11, 1976; 1 son, Austin Michael. Hydrologic field asst. U.S. Geol. Survey, water resources div., Tacoma, Wash., 1975; petroleum geophysicist sr. grade Amoco Prodn. Co., Houston, 1977-80; staff geologist Woodward-Clyde Cons., Houston, 1980—. Mem. Soc. Exploration

Geophysicists nat. com. Women in Geophysics, 1980 Am. Geophys. Union, Am. Assn. Petroleum Geologists, Geophys. Soc. Houston, Houston Geol. Soc., Assn. Women Geoscientists, Delta Delta Delta. Home: 10122 Brinwood St Houston TX 77043 Office: 7330 Westview St Houston TX 77055

SCOTT, DIANA B., newspaper editor; b. N.Y.C., Apr. 17, 1943; d. Joseph C. and Florence R. (Daniel) Strauch; B.A., Bennington Coll., 1963; grad. student Boston U., 1965-66; 1 dau., Kimberley C. Scott. Art supr. public sch. systems, Whitman, Mass., 1966-68, Acton, Mass., 1968-69; staff columnist, feature writer Enterprise-Sun newspapers, Marlboro, Mass., 1972-75; editorial researcher, staff writer The Missoulian newspaper, Missoula, Mont., 1975-76; columnist, feature writer, editor Family Living, Marlboro Enterprise, Hudson Daily Sun, The Free Enterprise, Marlboro, Mass., 1976-80; food editor Worcester (Mass.) Telegram, 1980-82, accent dept. editor, 1982—; guest speaker. Mem. Marlboro Arts Assn., 1974; juror regional art exhibition, 1974, 75; mem. City of Marlboro Occupational Edn. Adv. Com., 1978-79; program chmn. Friends of Marlboro Public Library, 1977—; publicity chmn. fund-raising, Children's Hosp., Boston, 1979-80. Recipient Vesta award for food writing, 1978; Journalism award Progressive Grocer Mag. and Food Mktg. Inst., 1978; 2d pl. edn. writing award New Eng. Press Assn., 1977, 1st pl. bus. writing award, 1978; runner-up nat. Carnation awards for nutrition writing, 1981. Office: 20 Franklin St Worcester MA 01613

SCOTT, DORA HOEFLICH, educator; b. Houston, Aug. 1, 1927; d. Carl M. and Dora Matilda (Werner) Hoeflich; B.S. in Home Economs., U. Tex., 1949; M.Ed., U. Houston, 1952; m. William Howard Scott, Jr., Dec. 28, 1948; children—William Howard, III, Carl Werner, Susan D., Stefanie L. Tchr., Houston Ind. Sch. Dist., 1950—, tchr. 2d grade, 1963—; mem. Tex. Curriculum Adv. Com., 1981—. Active Boy Scouts Am., 4-H, Am. Cancer Soc. Recipient numerous disting. service awards from tchrs. assns. Mem. NEA (dir. 1982-85), AAUW, Assn. Supervision and Curriculum Devel., Tex. State Tchrs. Assn. (pres. 1980-81; TATE-Ben Coody award Dist. XII, 1981, Sch. Bell award 1981), Tex. Assn. Tchr. Educators (1st v.p.), Tex. Women's Polit. Caucus, Harris County Heritage Soc., Delta Kappa Gamma, Alpha Delta Kappa. Roman Catholic. Club: Sons of Herman. Author articles in field. Home: 4043 Greenoch Ln Houston TX 77025 Office: 7402 Albacore St Houston TX 77074

SCOTT, DOROTHY CARNINE, artist; b. Hannaford, N.D., Jan. 30, 1903; d. John Newton and Oma Josella (Langellier) Carnine; A.B. magna cum laude, Colo. Coll., 1925; M.A., U. Chgo., 1935; B.S. summa cum laude in L.S., Syracuse U., 1948; m. Ewing Carruth Scott, June 24, 1926; children—Dorothy, Betty Ruth, Peter (dec.). One man shows: Museu Nacional, Rio de Janeiro, 1942, Va. Mus. Fine Arts, Richmond, 1948, Tunghai U., Taiwan, 1961, Internat. Christian U., Japan, 1962, Sweet Briar Coll., 1965, U. Va., 1966, U. Colo, 1974, SUNY, Alfred, 1976, Cayuga (N.Y.) Mus., 1980, others; group shows include: Acad. Artists Assn., Springfield, Mass., 1965—, Salmagundi Club, 1978, 80, Am. Artists Profl. League, 1978, 80; represented in permanent collections including: Va. Mus. Fine Arts, Richmond, Sandzen Meml. Gallery, Lindsborg, Kans., Farnsworth Mus., Rockland, Maine; owner Dorothy Scott Gallery, Estes Park, Colo.; tchr. lithography. Recipient numerous prizes for lithographs and paintings, including Salmagundi Club award, 1980. Mem. Am. Artists Profl. League (award 1980), Acad. Artists Assn., Estes Park Fine Arts Guild, Phi Beta Kappa, Kappa Kappa Gamma, Beta Phi Mu. Republican. Lutheran. Illustrator: 8 Small Trees (B.R. Scott Taylor), 1965. Home and Gallery: 1240 Devil's Gulch Rd Estes Park CO 80517 also 5709 W Lazy S St Tucson AZ 85713

SCOTT, DRU, author, edn. group exec.; b. Burney, Calif., Apr. 22, 1942; d. Emil and Phyllis (Reece) Anderson; B.A., Calif. State U., Chico, 1963; Ph.D., Calif. Western U., 1977. Tng. dir. West Coast Regional Tng. Center, San Francisco, 1966-74; pres. Dru Scott Assos., Inc., San Francisco, 1974—; dir. Pay Less Drug Stores, 1979-80. Mem. Am. Soc. Tng. and Devel., Nat. Speakers Assn. Club: Commonwealth of Calif. Author: (with Dorothy Jongeward) Affirmative Action for Women, 1974, Women as Winners, 1976; How To Put More Time In Your Life, 1980. Office: 106 Point Lobos San Francisco CA 94121

SCOTT, EDITH NAN, microbiologist; b. Clinton, Okla., Mar. 23, 1943; d. Howard Milton and Lena Corinne (Hopper) S.; B.S., Okla. State U., 1965; M.S., U. Okla. Health Scis. Center, 1973, Ph.D., 1979. Med. technologist Univ. Hosps., Oklahoma City, 1965-67; med. technologist VA Hosp., Oklahoma City, 1967-70, microbiology technologist, 1970-72; research microbiologist VA Med. Center, Oklahoma City, 1972—; adj. asst. prof. 1979—; sr. research scientist Okla. Med. Research Found., 1980—; postdoctoral fellow in microbiology dept. microbiology and immunology U. Okla. Health Scis. Center, 1979-82. Recipient Antarctic Service medal. Mem. Am. Soc. Clin. Pathologists, Am. Soc. Med. Technologists, Internat. Soc. Human and Animal Mycology, Med. Mycology Soc. Ams., Am. Soc. Microbiologists, AAAS, Okla. Zool. Soc., Sigma Xi. Research, publs. on immunity in systemic mycoses and during bio-isolation at South Pole. Office: VA Med Center 111D 921 NE 13th St Oklahoma City OK 73104

SCOTT, GAIL CHARLOTTE, psychologist, educator; b. Berwyn, Ill., May 28, 1945; d. Benjamin J. and Ann E. (Krasnick) Stebor; Asso. in Sci. Palm Beach Jr. Coll., 1965; B.A. in Edn., U. Fla., 1967, M.A. with honors, 1969, Ed.D., 1976; m. Jerry Silliman Scott, Dec. 12, 1967; children—Natalie DeNeise, KeriAnn DeNeise. Instr. dance U. Fla., Gainesville, 1969-71; prof. psychology and counselor Santa Fe Community Coll., Gainesville, 1969-73; interim prof. child devel. Syracuse (N.Y.) U., 1973-74; psychologist Family Behavioral Scis. Clinic, Gainesville, 1975-76; dir. Vocat. Assessment Center, Sioux City, Iowa, 1976-77; counselor and asst. prof. psychology Briar Cliff Coll., Sioux City, 1978—; cons. Native Am. Indian Program, Fed. Region IV, 1976—; cons., tchr. ballet Gainesville Dance and Gymnastics Co., 1975-79; ballet directing cons., Sioux City, 1978—; cons. child abuse Iowa State Social Service Workshop, 1980. Mem. Mayor's Task Force on Econ. and Cultural Devel., Sioux City, 1978-79; vice chmn. Democratic Women's Council, Sioux City, 1979—; bd. dirs. Florence Crittenton Home, 1979—; v.p. bd. dirs. Siouxland Repertory Dance Co., 1979—; bd. dirs., v.p. Sioux City Arts Council; pres. Sioux City Dance Co.; mem. state bd. dirs. Spl. Olympics. Named Tchr. of Year, Santa Fe Community Coll., 1970, 71, 72. Mem. Am. Psychol. Assn., Am. Assn. Supervision and Curriculum Devel., Iowa Psychol. Assn., Fla. Research Assn., Am. Ednl. Research Assn., Iowa Assn. Edn. of Retarded Citizens, Cath. Women's Soc., AAUP, Jr. Women's League, Phi Delta Kappa (cons. 2d World Congress on Comparative Edn.). Democrat. Roman Catholic. Home: 4619 Clinton Ct Sioux City IA 51106 Office: Dept Psychology Briar Cliff College 3303 Rebecca St Sioux City IA 51104

SCOTT, GERALDINE BAIRD, tax analyst; b. Besoco, W.Va., Jan. 16, 1929; d. Gibson and Flossie Fay (Cooper) Baird; diploma in accounting with honors Nat. Bus. Coll., 1947; m. Basil Henry Scott, Apr. 16, 1949; d. Junella White, Basil, Robert. Bookkeeper, Pocahontas Fuel Co. (name now changed to Cnsol. Coal Co.), Amonate, Va., 1947-48, head bookkeeper, McComas, W.Va., 1948-49; tax cons. and instr. H. & R. Block Corp., Roanoke, Va., 1967; pvt. practice tax analysis, Roanoke, 1968—; asso. Berry, Dail & Co., C.P.A.'s, Roanoke, 1977-79; cons. to A-1 Tax Service, Roanoke, 1977—; trustee AFCO Investment Corp. Pension Fund, Roanoke, 1971-76. Commr. of Internal Revenue Service grantee, 1971—. Mem. Nat. Soc. of Public Accountants, Methodist. Home: Route 1 Box 46 Draper VA 24324 Office: 6334 Peters Creek Rd Roanoke VA 24019

SCOTT, GERTRUDE ROSE, metals co. exec.; b. Pitts., Oct. 12, 1932; d. Leroy Lewis and Dorothea Margaret King; B.A. magna cum laude, U. Pitts., 1969, M.A., 1971. Public relations supr. Allegheny Gen. Hosp., Pitts., 1971-73; mgr. communications Jones & Laughlin Steel Corp., Pitts., 1973-76; v.p. corp. communication Meldrum & Fewsmith, Cleve., 1976-81; v.p. Steel Service Center Inst., Cleve., 1981—. Mem. Public Relations Soc. Am. (chpt. pres. 1982—). Office: Steel Service Center Inst 1600 Terminal Tower Cleveland OH 44113

SCOTT, JACQUELINE YVONNE, mfg. co. exec.; b. Kingston, Jamaica, Feb. 15, 1944; came to U.S., 1977; d. Henry Holland and Gertrude Buddington (Preston) Cox; S.R.N., Farnborough Hosp., Kent, Eng., 1965; m. Kenneth Ralph Scott, Dec. 18, 1965; children—Kenneth Mark, Damien Sean, Sherille Arlena. Staff nurse operating room, Kingston, 1965-69; health edn. officer personal products Johnson & Johnson, Kingston, 1969-71, sales rep. Hosp. div., 1971-73, mgr. Hosp. div., 1973-75, hosp. div. mgr. Caribbean, 1975-77, product dir. Patient Care div., New Brunswick, N.J., 1977—. Recipient Silver medal Farnborough Hosp., 1965; named Disting. Sales Rep., Sales and Mktg. Execs., 1974. Mem. Nurses Assn. Jamaica (v.p. 1974), St. Andrew Old Girls Assn. Office: 501 George St New Brunswick NJ 07726

SCOTT, JANE CLAIRE, educator, musician; b. Lake County, Calif., June 18, 1923; d. Joseph Buryl and Lola Scanlan Scott; B.Mus., Conservatory of Music, Coll. Pacific, 1944, B.A., 1947, M. Music, 1951; postgrad. U. of Pacific. Tchr. Stockton (Calif.) High Sch., 1944-48; instr. Stockton Jr. Coll., 1948-56; asst. prof. music W.Va. U., Morgantown, 1958-64; asst. prof., dir. orch. N. Mex. Highlands U., Las Vegas, 1964-68; string specialist, orch. dir. South Orangetown Sch. Dist., Orangeburg, N.Y., 1968—. Recipient Outstanding Secondary Educator award, Washington, 1974. Mem. Music Educators Nat. Conf., AAUP, N.Y. State Tchrs. Assn., Mu Phi Epsilon. Author: Pre-Harmony Theory, 1951.

SCOTT, JOAN WALLACH, historian; b. Bklyn., Dec. 18, 1941; d. Samuel and Lottie (Tanenbaum) Wallach; B.A., Brandeis U., 1962; M.A., U. Wis., Madison, 1964, Ph.D., 1969; m. Donald M. Scott, Jan. 30, 1965; children—Anthony Oliver, Elizabeth Rose. Asst. prof. history U. Ill., Chgo. Circle campus, 1970-72; asst. prof. Northwestern U., 1972-74; asso. prof. U. N.C., Chapel Hill, 1974-77, prof., 1977-80; Nancy Duke Lewis prof., prof. history Brown U., Providence, 1980—; dir. Summer Seminar for Coll. Tchrs., Nat. Endowment for Humanities, 1977, dir. Seminar for Coll. Tchrs., 1980-81; mem. Inst. for Advanced Study, Princeton, N.J., 1978-79. Social Sci. Research Council research tng. fellow, 1966-68; Nat. Endowment for Humanities fellow, 1975-76; Am. Council Learned Socs. grantee, 1978. Mem. Am. Hist. Assn. (chmn. com. on women historians 1978-80), Social Sci. History Assn., Soc. French Hist. Studies. Author: The Glassworkers of Carmaux, 1974 (Am. Hist. Assn. Herbert Baxter Adams prize 1974), (with Louise Tilly) Women Work and Family, 1978. Office: Dept History Brown U Providence RI 02912

SCOTT, JOANN SULLIVAN, educator; b. Tyler, Tex., Aug. 20, 1932; d. Vernon Reid and Gladys Mabell (Turner) Sullivan; B.S. in Edn., U. Houston, 1963; postgrad. Houston Community Coll., 1980; bus. practices cert. Lockheed Tech. Inst., 1967, 70; 1 dau., Debra Ann Bloch. Asso. scientist Lockheed Electronics, Johnson Space Center, NASA, Houston, 1966-70; career edn. cons., Houston Ind. Sch. Dist., 1970-74; pvt. practice, owner contract drafting service, Houston, 1974-75; coordinator tng. and graphics Internat. Field Data, Houston, 1975-76; geol./geophys. tech. asst. Mich. Wis. Pipe Line, Houston, 1976-81; instr., tng. coordinator, Women in Bus., Tex. Engring. Extension Service, Tex. A&M U. System, Houston, 1981—; bus. developer, adult leisure learning, Free U., 1977-82. Officer Civic Club, 1974-77. Mem. Am. Soc. Tng. and Devel., Nat. Soc. for Performance and Instrn., Houston Geol. Soc., Project Mgmt. Inst. Unitarian. Clubs: Am. Mensa (service award, 1978), Gulf Coast Mensa (v.p. 1975-78, proctor, newsletter editor). Author various curriculum bulletins, career devel. programs; researcher, author adult leisure courses. Home: 2501 Yupon St Houston TX 77006 Office: 1200 S Post Oak Blvd Houston TX 77056

SCOTT, JOYCE ELIZABETH, electronics technician; b. Mobile, Ala., Sept. 26, 1950; d. Johnnie and Levia Odell (Watts) Williams; A.A., Am. River Coll., 1974; B.A., San Francisco State U., 1979; M.A., U. Calif., Davis, 1981; m. Russell Alan Scott, July 5, 1980; children—Veronica, Jason. Exec. sec. constrn. br. U.S. Army C.E., San Francisco, 1970-73; adminstrv. asst. Calif. Office Mgmt. and Budget, Sacramento, 1974-75; sales mgr. Jocelyne Starr Accessories, Oakland, Calif., 1977-78; electronics technician Dept. Navy, Naval Air Rework Facility, Naval Air Sta., Alameda, Calif., 1978—, participant electronics apprentice program, 1978-82; tchr., vocat. counselor in field. Recipient Superior Performance award State of Calif., 1975. Mem. Federally Employed Women, Adminstrv. Assn., Assn. Mgrs. Democrat. Club: Order Eastern Star.

SCOTT, KAREN MICHELE, TV sta. exec.; b. Saratoga Springs, N.Y., July 3, 1949; d. Alfred and Rosalie (Martin) Silberman; B.A. in Journalism, Ohio State U., 1971; m. Guy Brannon Scott III, Aug. 20, 1973. News reporter, broadcaster Sta. WRFD-WNCI-AM-FM, Columbus, Ohio, 1971-72; writer, researcher, asst. producer Lou Gordon program Kaiser Broadcasting, Sta. WKBD-TV, Detroit, 1975; TV news writer, producer Sta. WXYZ-TV, ABC, Detroit, 1976-78; TV news producer Sta. WFSB-TV, CBS, Hartford, Conn., 1979—. Ohio State U. broadcasting scholar, 1971. Mem. Women in Communications, Women's Econ. Club Detroit, Radio and TV News Dirs. Assn., Detroit Press Club. Jewish. Office: Broadcast House 3 Constitution Plaza Hartford CT 06115

SCOTT, LUCILLE ELAINE, journalist, educator; b. Brush, Colo., May 22, 1944; d. Arthur Alan and Ruth Fanny (Greenwood) Scott; B.S., Colo. State U., 1965; M.A. in Journalism and Communications, U. Fla., 1976; m. J.T. Midcap III, Aug. 1, 1965 (div. 1977). Writer, Lincoln (Nebr.) Jour., 1967-68; staff writer Manhattan (Kans.) Mercury, 1969-71; dir. public relations, div. continuing edn., Kans. State U., Manhattan, 1971-75; grad. teaching asst., Coll. Journalism and Communications, U. Fla., Gainesville, 1975-76, vis. asst. prof., 1976-77, asst. prof., 1977-78; editor E. Hillsborough Tribune, Tampa (Fla.) Tribune, summer 1977; reviewer editing text, 1978; newswoman AP, Newark, 1978—; adj. prof. dept. journalism and mass communications N.Y.U., N.Y.C., 1980—. Chmn., U. Fla. Journalism Day, 1978, mem. curriculum com. Recipient writing awards Kans. Press Women, 1970; winner photo contest sponsored by Ind. Fla. Alligator, 1976. Mem. Assn. for Edn. in Journalism, Women in Communications (public relations chmn. 1969), Alpha Lambda Delta, Phi Kappa Phi, Kappa Tau Alpha, Gamma Sigma Delta, Spurs, Sigma Delta Chi. Office: Airport Internat Plaza Newark NJ 07102

SCOTT, LUCY, psychologist, consultant; b. Chgo., June 11, 1928; d. Amos H. and Fern (Irvin) Hoff; B.A., Ariz. State U., 1960, M.A., 1969; Ph.D., Fielding Inst., Santa Barbara, Calif., 1979; divorced; children—Cynthia, Susan. Tchr. jr. high sch., Phoenix, 1961-66; dir., tchr., counselor Cyesis Center Phoenix Union High Sch. Dist., 1967-71; tchr., counselor, cons., trainer Family Life Edn. Project, Calif. Youth Authority, San Francisco, 1977-80; mem. faculty dept. health scis. San Jose State U., 1974-80; adj. faculty U. San Francisco, 1980—; dir. Parenthood After Thirty, Berkeley, Calif., 1980—; pvt. practice psychotherapy, Berkeley, 1974—; cons. in field; bd. dirs., adv. Nat. Alliance for Optional Parenthood, Calif. Youth Authority Task Force, Calif. Dept. Health Task Force, Calif. Family Life Edn. Program Devel. Project; lectr. in field. Mem. Assn. Women in Psychology, Internat. Assn. Applied Psychology, Am. Assn. Sex Educators, Counselors and Therapists, Am. Psychol. Assn., Am. Orthopsychiat. Assn., Nat. Family Planning and Reproductive Health Assn. Author: Parenthood After Thirty; Resource Manual, 1981.

SCOTT, MAE RANKIN, fin. exec.; b. Birmingham, Ala., Jan. 1, 1940; d. William Roscoe and Annie Mae (Dobbs) Rankin Johnson; student U. Ala., 1959-61; children—Leslie Ann Scott Garris, William Eugene Scott. With The Heritage Corp. of N.Y., Miami, Fla., 1962-67; v.p. King's Way Mortgage Co., Coral Gables, Fla., 1967-73, sr. v.p., 1973-78, exec. v.p., 1978-81; corp. sec. Veritas Ins. Co., 1970—, Alpha, Inc., 1970—; v.p. Pan Am Mortgage Corp., 1981—. Active, Soc. Prevention of Blindness, S. Fla., 1973—. Mem. Mortgage Bankers Assn. S. Fla., Mortgage Bankers Assn. Am., S. Fla. Home Builders Assn., Nat. Assn. Rev. Appraisers. Democrat. Baptist. Contbr. articles to profl. jours. Mailing Address: Kings Way Mortgage Co PO Box 158 265 Sevilla Ave Coral Gables FL 33134 Office: Pan Am Mortgage Corp 150 SE 3d Ave Rm 325 Miami FL 33131

SCOTT, MARGARET HOFFMAN, biomed. research co. exec.; b. Youngstown, Ohio, May 11, 1941; d. Leonard Frederick and Barbara Jane (Reebel) Hoffman; B.S. in Bus. Adminstrn., Thomas A. Edison Coll., Princeton, N.J., 1978; cert. mgmt., U. Balt., 1978; children—Michael, Barbara, Kevin, Brian. Asst. mdse. mgr. J.B. White Co., Augusta, Ga., 1967-71; office mgr. Med. Coll. Ga., Augusta, 1971-72, sr. sci. buyer, 1972-74; sr. buyer Frederick (Md.) Cancer Research Center, Litton Bionetics, Inc., 1974-75, mgr. purchasing, 1975-79, mgr. purchasing and logistics, 1979—. Mem. Nat. Assn. Purchasing Mgrs., Nat. Contract Mgmt. Assn., Am. Soc. Profl. and Exec. Women, Internat. Mgmt. Council, Assn. Women in Sci., Mensa. Republican. Home: 1464 W Key Pkwy #102 Frederick MD 21701 Office: PO Box B Frederick MD 21701

SCOTT, MARGARET LOUISE, aerospace co. exec.; b. Santa Monica, Calif., June 21, 1925; d. Earl Joseph and Stella May (Miller) Scott; student Los Angeles City Coll., 1947-51, El Camino Coll., 1973. Flight test analyst N.Am. Aviation, Los Angeles, 1943-51; graphics artist N.Am. Rockwell, Los Angeles, 1951-74; illustrations project coordinator Rockwell Internat., Los Angeles, 1974-75, dept. head graphics art dept., Los Angeles div., El Segundo, Calif., 1975—. Mem. trade advisory com. El Camino Coll., Glendale Community Coll., West Los Angeles Coll., 1975—. Home: 1601 Sunset Plaza Dr Los Angeles CA 90069 Office: 815 Lapham St El Segundo CA 90245

SCOTT, MARTIN-ANN, business consultant; b. Washington, Dec. 25, 1928; d. Martin Theodore and Saralla Myers; B.A., Mt. Union Coll., 1951; postgrad. Lake Erie Coll., 1965-66, Kent State U., 1978—; children—Michael J., Christopher. With Higbee Co., Cleve., 1951-52, Thompson Products, Cleve., 1952-54: asst. John M. Scott, M.D., Canton, Ohio, 1954-56; tchr. Warren (Ohio) public schs., 1962-64; guidance counselor Mentor (Ohio) public schs., 1965-68; freelance human resources cons., 1973-79; personnel cons. Office Services, Inc., 1973-79; personnel mgr. Career Planning Inst., Aurora, Ohio, 1979-80; pvt. practice bus. cons., 1980—. Mem. adv. bd. Kent (Ohio) State U., 1974—, Aurora High Sch., 1974-79, Streetsboro High Sch., 1975—; mem. Aurora Sch. Bd., 1974-78, Aurora Parks and Recreation Dept., 1974-76; mem. State of Ohio-State Sch. Bd. Communication Network, 1977-78; bd. dirs. Portage County Cancer Soc., 1973-77; active Speakers Bur. - WVIZ (ednl. TV); pres. Women's Republican Club, 1963-64. Mem. Am. Soc. Personnel Adminstrs., Nat. Assn. Female Execs. Episcopalian. Clubs: Aurora Community Theater, Valley Y. Home and Office: 10267 Spinnaker Run Aurora OH 44202

SCOTT, MERRYL E., wine mktg. co. ofcl.; b. N.Y.C., June 6, 1950; d. Louis A. and Sylvia Mintz; B.A. summa cum laude in Interpersonal Communications, SUNY, Buffalo, 1971. Market research supr. Gen. Foods Corp., White Plains, N.Y., 1974-78; research asso. Batten, Barton, Durstine, and Osborn Advt. Agy., N.Y.C., 1978-79; mgr. market research The Wine Spectrum div. Cola-Cola, Atlanta, 1979-81, brand mgr. Gt. Western Champagne, The Wine Spectrum, 1981-82, Taylor N.Y. State Wines and Champagnes, 1982—. Active Atlanta Arts Festival; mem. High Mus. Art, Atlanta. Mem. Am. Mktg. Assn., Les Amis du Vin, Phi Beta Kappa. Home: 1422 Twin Branches Circle Marietta GA 30067 Office: PO Drawer 1734 Atlanta GA 30301

SCOTT, PATRICIA ANN, public relations exec.; b. Balt., Apr. 12, 1935; d. Charles Andrew and Madeline Margaret (Toomey) Mettee; B.S. in Bus. Mgmt., U. Balt., 1956; postgrad. in public relations Am. U.; m. Charles Edmund Scott, Oct. 20, 1956; children—Richard, Brian Allen. Sec. to v.p. Miller Metal Research Lab., 1956-57; asst. to import mgr. Bata Shoe Co., 1957-59; div. sec. Westinghouse Electric Corp., 1960-62; publs. writer State of Md., 1963-65; pres., owner Scott Assos., Bel Air, Md., 1972—. Pres. Harford County Republican Women, 1979; pres. Long Bar Harbor Community Assn., 1972-73; mem. ladies aux. Abingdon Fire Co. Mem. Harford County C. of C. (sec. 1979), Balt. Public Relations Council, Public Relations Soc. Am. (award for public relations campaign Md. chpt. 1978, 81). Methodist. Office: 23 S Main St Bel Air MD 21014

SCOTT, PATRICIA ANNE, nurse, educator; b. Miami, Fla., July 3, 1938; d. Francis Royal and Catherine Delores (Dunham) Scott; B.S., Columbia Union Coll., 1961; M.S. in Nursing, U. Pa., 1970; postgrad. U. Calif., San Francisco, 1980—; children—David Marc Freedman, Lesli Anne Freedman. Staff and charge nurse, various hosps., Washington, 1961-64; instr. Capital City Sch. Nursing, Washington, 1964-66; nurse Internat. Red Cross, London, 1966-68; asst. prof. Wesley Coll., Dover, Del., 1970-72; Loma Linda (Calif.) U., 1972-73; dir. nursing service SDA Hosp., Karachi, Pakistan, 1973-75; asst. prof., coordinator, So. Missionary Coll., Madison, Tenn., 1975-78, dir. sch. nursing Am. Hosp., Istanbul, Turkey, 1978-80. Mem. Am. Nurses Assn., Calif. Nurses Assn. (region 12), ARC, Profl. Traveling Nurses Assn., AAUP., Sigma Theta Tau. Episcopalian. Address: 1457 Willard St San Francisco CA 94117

SCOTT, PHEBE MARTHA, educator; b. Boston, Sept. 27, 1922; d. Harold Guy and Phebe Scott; B.S., U. Mich., 1944; M.A., Columbia U., 1946; Ph.D., U. Iowa, 1952. Tchr. pub. schs., Detroit, 1944-45, N.Y.C., 1945-46; instr. phys. edn. U. No. Iowa, 1946-49; grad. asst., research asst., instr. phys. edn. U. Iowa, 1949-52; chmn. dept. phys. edn. Bradley U., 1952-55; chairperson dept. health and phys. edn. U. N.D., 1955-59; prof. phys. edn. Ohio State U., 1959-66; prof., chairperson dept. phys. edn. Ill. State U., 1966-76, prof. phys. edn., 1976—. Mem. Am. Acad. Phys. Edn., AAHPER, Nat. Assn. Phys. Edn. Coll. Women (pres. 1971-73), Am. Assn. Higher Edn., AAUP, Assn. Anthrop. Study Play, Pi Lambda Theta, Delta Psi Kappa, Delta Kappa Gamma. Democrat. Unitarian. Author: Track and Field for Girls and Women, 1963. Home: 512 Florence Bloomington IL 61701 Office: Horton Field Ill State U Normal IL 61761

SCOTT, WILLODENE ALEXANDER (MRS. RAY DONALD SCOTT), library adminstr.; b. Ethridge, Tenn., Sept. 4, 1922; d. Jesse Cary and Maud (Goff) Alexander; B.A., George Peabody Coll. for

Tchrs., 1946, B.S. in L.S., 1947, M.A., 1949, Ed.S., 1972, now Ph.D. candidate; m. Ray Donald Scott, Nov. 27, 1959; 1 dau., Pamela Dean. Librarian, Sylvan Park Elem. Sch., Nashville, 1947-51, Waverly Belmont Jr. High Sch., Nashville, 1951-54, Howard High Sch., Nashville, 1954-62, Peabody Demonstration Sch., Nashville, 1962-63; librarian McCann Elem. Sch., Nashville, 1963-66; supr. instructional materials, library div. Metro Nashville-Davidson County Schs., Nashville, 1966-73, dir. instructional materials and library services, 1973—; lectr. Peabody Coll. Library Sch., Nashville, summers, 1950-66, 71-72, 76, U. Tenn., Nashville Center, 1970; Tenn. rep. White House Conf., 1970. Chmn. nat. alumni fund-raising George Peabody Coll. for Tchrs., 1975-76, nat. alumni pres., 1977-78, trustee, 1976-78; bd. dirs. Friends of Music, 1977—; mem. vis. com. bd. trustees Vanderbilt U., 1979—. Mem. ALA, Southeastern Library Assn. (scholarship com. 1968-70), Tenn. Library Assn. (membership chmn. 1955, 64, treas. 1977-78), Tenn. Edn. Assn. (library sect. pres. 1954), Met. Nashville Edn. Assn., NEA (life), Children's Internat. Edn. Center of Nashville (charter mem.-at-large), AAUW, Woman's Nat. Book Assn. (charter mem.), DAR (organizing treas. Buffalo River chpt. 1967-69). Baptist. Clubs: Order Eastern Star; Nashville Library (pres. 1952-53). Home: 525 Clematis Dr Nashville TN 37205 Office: 2601 Bransford Ave Nashville TN 37204

SCOTTO, RENATA, soprano; b. Savona, Italy, Feb. 24, 1935; studied under Ghirardini, Merlino and Mercedes Llopart, Accademia Musicale Savonese, Conservatory Guiseppe Verdi, Milan; m. Lorenzo Anselmi. Debut in La Traviata, Teatro Nuevo, Milan, 1954, then joined La Scala Opera Co.; appeared with Met. Opera, N.Y.C., 1965, Concert Garden, Hamburg State Opera, Vienna State Opera, Nat. Theatre Munich, San Francisco Opera, Chgo. Lyric Opera; roles include La Sonnambula, I Puritani, L'Elisir d'amore, Lucia di Lammermoor, La Boheme, Turandot, Otello (Verdi), Travatore, Vespri Siciliani, Le Prophete, Madama Butterfly, Adriana Lecouvreur, Norma, Tosca, Manon Lescaut, Ballo in Maschera. Address: care Robert J Lombardo 30 W 60th St New York NY 10023 *

SCOVILL, RUTH ALATHEA, TV facility exec.; b. Hudson, N.Y., Nov. 26, 1950; d. Robert Barnard and Janet Patricia (Goodman) S.; B.F.A., San Francisco Art Inst., 1972; M.A., Calif. State U., 1976. Scheduler, One Pass Video, San Francisco, 1977-78, ops. supr., 1978-79; prodn. supr. Reeves Teletape, N.Y.C., 1979-80, mgr. studio facilities, 1980-82, gen. mgr. studio facilities, 1982—; cons. radio, concert and TV prodn. Mem. Nat. Assn. Exec. Women.

SCOZZARI, NINA, communications co. exec.; b. N.Y.C., Oct. 16, 1943; d. Ciro and Mary (Monteleone) S.; ed. U. Americas, Mexico City, Hunter Coll., N.Y.C.; diploma Am. Inst. Banking. Producer radio and TV commls., bus. mgr. Norman, Craig & Kummell Advt., 1965-72; mgmt. cons. Syn-Cronamics, Inc., 1977-78; sr. analyst, mgmt. cons. Marine Midland Bank, N.Y.C., 1978-79; project mgr. mktg. ITT World Communications, Inc., N.Y.C., 1979—; bus. mgr. Nuestros Pequeños Orphanage, Mexico City, 1974-76.

SCRANTON, ANDREA ABBOTT, state legislator; b. Cambridge, Mass., Nov. 7, 1919; d. William G. and Andrea M. Abbott; A.B., Smith Coll., 1941; m. William Maxell Scranton; children—Nancy and John (twins), James, Sarah. Mem. Keene (N.H.) Bd. Edn., 1970-73; mem. N.H. Ho. of Reps., 1973—, chmn. Cheshire County Republican Del., 1978-80. Served with USCGR, 1943-47. Episcopalian. Address: Hurricane Rd Box 506 Keene NH 03431

SCREEN-BERRY, AUDREY BERNITA, nurse; b. Bklyn., May 1, 1955; d. Herbert and Helen Caroline (Moore) Screen; B.S. in Nursing, Russell Sage Coll., 1977; cert. in public adminstrn., Dyke Coll., 1982; m. Tommie Berry, Jr., May 12, 1978. Staff nurse Univ. Hosps. Cleve., 1977-78; public health nurse Vis. Nurses Assn., Cleve., 1978-79, Maternity and Infant Care Project, Cleve., 1979-80; nurse, med. team mgr. Kenneth W. Clement Center Family Health Care, Cleve., 1980—. Registered nurse, Ohio. Mem. Cleve. Council Black Nurses, Am. Nurses Assn., Greater Cleve. Nurses Assn., Nat. Assn. Female Execs., YWCA. Lutheran. Office: 2500 E 79th St Cleveland OH 44104

SCRIBNER, NANCY CAROLYN, holding co. exec.; b. Randleman, N.C., Aug. 10, 1937; d. Roy Leon and Maude Lee (Teasley) Whitson; ed. U. Md.; m. Thomas Scribner, Dec. 14, 1956. Asst. acctg. mgr. Pacific Architects and Engrs., Los Angeles, 1967-70; corp. sec. Exec. Mktg. Corp., Silver Spring, Md., 1971-74; corp. controller-sec. Chesapeake Industries Inc., Newport Beach, Calif., 1974—. Democrat. Roman Catholic. Home: 21432 Dockside Circle Huntington Beach CA 92646 Office: 500 Newport Center Dr Suite 415 Newport Beach CA 92660

SCRIBNER, OLIVE HILLER, investment counselor; b. Corry, Pa., Apr. 21, 1926; d. Richard Carpenter and Genevieve Lucy (Hollister) Hiller; student Jamestown Community Coll., 1962; m. Robert E. Everett, Aug. 31, 1946 (dec. Sept. 1949); m. Henry O. Fox, Oct. 14, 1950 (div. Oct. 1961); children—Kathryn Louise, Nancy Joanne; m. Donald E. Scribner, May 30, 1965. Investment analyst, sec. Karl Smith Investment Counsel, Rochester, N.Y., 1959-68; trust investment officer Canandaigua Nat. Bank & Trust Co. (N.Y.), 1968-75; instr. investments Lock Haven (Pa.) State Coll., 1976—; pvt. practice investment counseling, Lock Haven, 1977—. Mem. Lock Haven Hosp. Aux., Pa. Council Republican Women; mem., sec. Friends of Ross Library, 1977-81, treas., 1981—; bd. dirs. Community Nursing Service, 1981—. Mem. Fin. Analysts Fedn., Rochester Soc. Security Analysts, DAR, Clinton County Hist. Soc. Republican. Methodist. Clubs: Millbrook Playhouse; Woman's (Rochester, N.Y.). Home: 1135 W 4th St Flemington PA 17745 Office: 326 North Grove St PO Box 687 Lock Haven PA 17745

SCRIVNER, BARBARA E., piano tchr.; b. Oreg., May 25, 1931; student (piano student of Lawrence Morton), Bob Jones U., 1962-66; corr. student Inst. Children's Lit., Redding Ridge, Conn., 1974-76; children—R. Dick. Lawrence C., Barbara Ann, Betty Jo. Part time sec., Oreg., 1948-50, 60-62, Census Bur., S.C., 1980; piano tchr., Greenville, S.C., 1963—. Active Republican Nat. Com., Nat. Rep. Senatorial Com., Nat. Rep. Congressional Com., S.C. Rep. Party. Cert. Lanier word processing operator, 1981. Mem. S.C. Music Assn., Music Tchrs. Nat. Assn., Moral Majority. Contbr. articles, letters to newspapers and columns; editor, pub. Golden Nuggets of Truth, 1982—.

SCRIVNER, DOROTHYE LUCILLE, nurse; b. Amoret, Mo., Jan. 20, 1915; d. Frederick William and Nora Agnes (Dale) Allman; R.N., Jane C. Stormont Hosp., 1939; m. Marvin J. Scrivner, Aug. 31, 1941; children—Lee Ann, William Nelson. Staff nurse U.S. Vets. Facility, Chilicothe, Ohio, 1940-41; operating room staff nurse Permanente Found. Hosp., Oakland, Calif., 1942-44; office nurse, operating room nurse Colorado Springs (Colo.) Med. Center, 1956-58, 61-65; asst. supr. med. floor Guadelupe Valley Hosp., Seguin, Tex., 1966; dir. nursing services Guadelupe Valley Nursing Home, Seguin, 1967-68; dir. nursing services Medalion Retirement Residence, Colorado Springs, 1970-75; dir. nursing Medalion W. Retirement Residence, Colorado Springs, 1976—; nurse cons. Sunny Acres Villa, 1976-77. Mem. Colo. Nurses Assn. Home: 2211 N Bonfoy Ave Colorado Springs CO 80909 Office: 417 E Kiowa St Colorado Springs CO 80903

SCRIVNER, JOYCE KAY, computer programmer/analyst; b. Denver, June 12, 1950; d. Mansil Wayne and Harriet Lorraine (Webster) S.; S.S.T.P., Colo. Sch. Mines, 1967; student U. Colo., 1968-72; student Mich. State U., Clarion, 1974; B.S.C.S., Purdue U., 1976. Clk., U.S. Book Exchange, Washington, 1972-73, Govt. Printing Office, Washington, 1973-74; programmer SCADA group Leeds & Northrup Corp., North Wales, Pa., 1976-78; programmer/analyst Energy Mgmt. Systems div. Control Data Corp., Mpls., 1979—; adminstr. Down Under Fan Fund, 1981—. Mem. World Sci. Fiction Conv. Staff, 1977, 78, 80, 81; chairperson art show Minicon, Mpls., 1980-81. Down Under Fan Fund grantee, 1981. Mem. Assn. Women in Computing, Minn. Sci. Fiction Assn. Editor mags.: Gypsy, 1979—, Of Such Are Legends Made, 1978—. Office: 2300 Berkshire Ln Minneapolis MN 55441

SCROGGIE, LOIS JEAN, writer, educator; b. Denver, Nov. 28, 1940; d. John and Ann Allison (Forsyth) Scroggie; B.A., U. Colo., 1964, M.A., 1966, postgrad., 1968, 73; m. Jan Whitinger, Dec. 25, 1975 (div.). Instr. English, Trinidad (Colo.) State Jr. Coll., 1966-82. Mem. AAUP, Modern Lang. Assn., Rocky Mountain Modern Lang. Assn., Women's Caucus for Modern Langs., Nat. Council Tchrs. English, English-Speaking Union, Am. Film Inst., Nat. Writer's Club, Soc. Children's Book Writers, City News Service. Author articles, poems. Home and Office: 777 Monaco Pwky Denver CO 80220

SCROGGS, JANE ASHLEY, former assn. exec.; b. Blanchard, Okla., Apr. 11, 1937; d. Charles E. and Gertrude (Moore) Lowry; B.A. with distinction, U. Okla., 1973, M.S.W., 1975; doctoral candidate in higher edn. adminstrn. U. Okla., 1982—; m. James E. Scroggs, Dec. 22, 1979; children by previous marriage—Charles Russell Ashley, Anita Ann Ashley; stepchildren—Marylin, James, Jeff. Grad. asst. Sch. Social Work, U. Okla., Norman, 1973-75, grad. asst. Center for Studies in Higher Edn., 1976-77; exec. dir. Okla. chpt. Nat. Assn. Social Workers, Norman, 1977-81; lectr. English, Cuttington U. Coll., Liberia, 1980-81. State Regents intern in state govt., 1975. Mem. Assn. Social Workers, Am. Soc. Public Adminstrn., Am. Ednl. Research Assn., Am. Soc. Anthropology and Edn., ACLU, LWV. Democrat. Presbyterian.

SCROGGS, MARIE FRAZIER, educator; b. Tonopah, Nev., June 21, 1923; d. Thomas Arthur and Rose (Craig) Frazier; B.A., UCLA, 1945; M.A., Calif. State U., Los Angeles, 1963; 1 dau., Linda. Tchr., Garfield Elem. Sch., Pasadena (Calif.) Unified Sch. Dist., 1950, tchr. Don Benito Elem. Sch., 1952-65, tchr.-cons. reading for dist., 1965-73, dist. reading cons., 1973-78; tchr. Linda Vista Primary Sch., 1978—. Active Women's Civic League. Mem. NEA, Calif. Tchrs. Assn., Los Angeles Reading Assn., Pasadena Edn. Assn., Women's Civic League, Delta Kappa Gamma. Republican. Episcopalian. Home: 316 W California Blvd Pasadena CA 91105 Office: Linda Vista Primary Sch 1259 Linda Vista Ave Pasadena CA 91103

SCROGGS, MARILEE MUNGER, clergywoman; b. Washington, June 14, 1945; d. Bernard Vernon and Elizabeth (Cuthrell) Munger; B.A., Austin Coll., 1967; B.D., Chgo. Theol. Sem., 1970; m. Robin J. Scroggs, May 29, 1971; 1 son, Jonathan Paul. Ordained to ministry Presbyterian Ch., 1970; minister to youth Presbytery of Northeast Tex., Dallas, 1970-71; pastor Marquette Park Presbyn. Ch., Chgo., 1971-74, interim pastor First Presbyn. Ch., Chgo., 1975-76; pastor Bethany Presbyn. Ch., Chgo., 1976—; moderator Presbytery of Chgo., 1978; mem. gen. assembly Mission Council, United Presbyn. Ch. U.S.A., 1980—. Bd. dirs. Northwest Community Orgn., 1979. Mem. Chicago Network. Home: 4525 N Sacramento St Chicago IL 60625 Office: 1847 N Humboldt Blvd Chicago IL 60647

SCRUGGS, KAREN LAFRANCE, pediatrician; b. May 14, 1947; d. Samuel Hiley and Fannetta (McLean) S.; B.A. with honors, Macalester Coll., St. Paul, 1968; M.D., Washington U., St. Louis, 1973. Pediatric resident Mass. Gen. Hosp., Boston, 1973-75; pediatric endocrinology and metabolism fellow St. Louis Children's Hosp. (Washington U.), 1976-77; dir. community pediatrics St. Louis City Health Div., 1976-77; dep. asst. dir. child health services St. Louis County Dept. Community Health and Med. Care, 1977-81, program mgr. disease prevention services, 1981—; clin. instr. pediatrics Washington U. Med. Sch. Mem. leadership group St. Louis Metro Forum; elder, trustee Berea Presbyn. Ch., St. Louis. Fellow Nat. Endowment Humanities, 1977, Danforth Found., 1979-80; recipient Disting. Alumni citation Macalester Coll., 1982. Mem. Am. Public Health Assn., Mo. Med. Assn., Mo. Public Health Assn., St. Louis Pediatric Soc., St. Louis Public Health Assn., St. Louis Met. Med. Soc. Home: 5554 Waterman Blvd 1 West Saint Louis MO 63112 Office: 801 S Brentwood Blvd Saint Louis MO 63105

SCRUGGS, MELVA CATHERINE HERNANDEZ, state social services adminstr.; b. Victoria, Tex., May 7, 1949; d. Marion and Catherine (Moraida) Hernandez; A.A., Victoria Coll., 1969; M.A., U. Houston, 1976; m. William Franklin Scruggs, Jr., Jan. 26, 1973; 1 son, William Franklin, III. Tchr., Children's Univ. Center, U. Houston, 1972; sales clk., cashier Foley's Dept. Store, Houston, 1972-73; welfare service technician II, Tex. Dept. Public Welfare, Houston, 1973-74, day care lic. rep., 1974—. Exec. com., vice chmn. fin. com. Harris County Democrats, 1981-82. Recipient Public Service award Tex. Dept. Human Resources, 1978. Mem. Nat. Assn. Edn. Young Children, Assn. Regulatory Adminstrn., Houston Area Assn. Young Children, Harris County Women's Polit. Caucus, Houston Dem. Forum, Harris County Heritage Soc., N. Woodland Hills Civic Assn. Roman Catholic. Club: Kingwood Civic.

SCUDDER, PATRICIA DUNHAM, advt. exec.; b. Bishops Stortford, Eng., Nov. 23, 1945; d. Edgar Whitfield and Jean Veronica (Gunson) Dunham (parents U.S. citizens); B.J. with honors, U. Mo., 1966; m. Michael E. Scudder, Apr. 4, 1982. Copywriter, copy supr. Rosenfeld, Sirowitz & Lawson, Los Angeles, 1974-75; copy supr. William Esty Advt., Inc., 1975-76; creative mgr. cosmetics and fragrance Avon Products, Inc., 1976-78; v.p., asso. creative dir. SSC & B Advt., Inc., N.Y.C., 1978—. Active, The Center's Network, 1976-81. Recipient Gold medal Internat. Film and TV Soc., 1976; Effie finalist for TV commls., 1980. Mem. Friends of Shawangunks, Met. Mus. Art, Mus. Natural History. Office: 1 Dag Hammarskjold Plaza New York NY 10017

SCUDIERI, LORRAINE MARY, educator; b. Montclair, N.J., Apr. 25, 1940; d. Harry and Evelyn C. (Palmerie) Alberto; B.A., Montclair State Coll., 1962; M.A., Rutgers U., 1966, now doctoral student; m. Bart Scudieri, Aug. 14, 1965; children—Laura, Matt, Chris, Tim, Patrick. Tchr., Pascack Valley High Sch., Hillsdale, N.J., 1962-65, Pascack Hills High Sch., Montvale, N.J., 1976-77, Montclair State Coll., Upper Montclair, N.J., 1966-68, 69-70, 71, 74, 79—; instr. Fairleigh Dickinson U., 1969-72, 79-81, William Paterson Coll., Wayne, N.J., 1974-76, 82—, Wyckoff (N.J.) Community Learning Center, 1979, Upsala Coll., East Orange, N.J., 1979-81. Den mother Boy Scouts Am. NSF grantee, 1962-66. Mem. Nat. Council Tchrs. Math., Assn. Math. Tchrs. N.J.

SCULL, ANNA (NANCY) CORREY, market research cons.; b. Bryn Mawr, Pa., Oct. 16, 1941; d. Edward Bettle and Anna Correy (Keen) S.; A.B. in Econs., Brown U., 1963; postgrad. in econs. Am. U., 1963-64. Econ. research analyst U.S. Govt., 1963-65; sales analyst/forecaster Polaroid, Cambridge, Mass., 1965-67; mktg. support mgr. Bolt Beranek & Newman, Cambridge, 1967-71; dir. IDC Cons. Group div. Internat. Data Corp., Framingham, Mass., 1971—. Bd. dirs. Cecilia Soc., choral group, Boston, 1965-77, v.p., 1967-68, pres., 1968-69. Mem. Am. Mktg. Assn. (sec. Boston chpt. 1969), Asso. Alumni Brown U. (dir., mem. exec. com. 1976-78, 81-82, chmn. nominating com. 1981-82). Club: Brown U. of Boston (dir. 1974—, pres. 1979-81). Office: 5 Speen St Framingham MA 01701

SCULLY, CELIA GEOGHEGAN, writer; B.A. in English Lit., Trinity Coll., Washington, 1954; M.A. in Journalism, U. Nev., Reno, 1980, postgrad., 1981—. Staff writer Center for Religion and Life, U. Nev., 1972-73; dir. mktg. Sierra Arts Found., Reno, part-time, 1979-82; free-lance writer articles in travel, bus., antique, religious and women's publs. including Travel & Leisure, Travel Holiday, Odyssey, Chevron USA, Writer's Digest, Antique Monthly, Lady's Circle, Marriage and Family Living, Today's Family, Am. Collector; contbg. editor Travel Agt. mag., N.Y.C., 1976-79; instr. non-fiction mag. writing Western Nev. Community Coll., Reno, 1977-78; print media dir. Randolph Schweigert & Co., Reno, 1980-81; editorial cons., 1976—. Bd. dirs. Internat. Visitors Council No. Nev., 1980-81. Recipient 1st place award Nev. State Communications competition Press Women, 1973, 74, 76, 79, 80, 2d place awards, 1977, 78, 80. Mem. Am. Mktg. Assn., Internat. Assn. Bus. Communicators, Authors Guild, Soc. Profl. Journalists, Nat. Fedn. Press Women, Kappa Tau Alpha. Home: 1400 Ferris Ln Reno NV 89509

SCULLY, FRANCES ANNE, mktg. exec.; b. Abington, Pa., Dec. 4, 1956; d. Francis Joseph and Mary Eileen (O'Connor) S.; B.S.B.A., LaSalle Coll., 1981; postgrad. U. Fribourg (Switzerland), 1981. Mgr., Plants 'n Posies Florist, 1973-78; intern to dir. Soc. Advancement Mgmt., Am. Mgmt. Assn., N.Y.C., 1980, 81, campus coordinator, 1981, internat. dir. campus ops., 1981—. Active campaign N.Y. County Republican Com., 1980. Mem. Am. Production and Inventory Control Soc., Alpha Epsilon. Author: SAM Campus Operations Manual, 1980; SAM Campus News, 1982. Office: 135 W 50th St New York NY 10020 *

SCULLY, JULIA, editor; b. Seattle, Feb. 9, 1929; d. Julius and Rose (Hohenstein) Silverman; B.A., Stanford U., 1951; M.A., N.Y. U., 1970; m. Edward Charles Scully, Aug. 3, 1963 (div. Jan. 1980). Asso. editor U.S. Camera, 1956-61; editor Camera 35, 1961-66; editor Modern Photography, N.Y.C., 1966—. Tchr., New Sch. for Social Research, N.Y.C., Ramapo Coll. of N.J., Mahway. Author: Disfarmer: The Heber Springs Portraits, 1939-1946, 1976; editor: The Family of Woman, 1979. Office: 825 7th Ave New York NY 10019

SEA, REBECCA ANN, nurse; b. East Chicago, Ind., June 28, 1953; Paul Eustantious Babbitt and Bonnie Jean (Zaky) Belgau; A.S., Broward Community Coll., 1975; B.S. in Nursing candidate William Carey Coll., 1981—; m. Charles Perry Sea, June 14, 1975; children—David Michael, Brian Scott. Sales clk. Three Sisters, Ft. Lauderdale, Fla., 1970—; nursing asst. Margate Gen. Hosp., Ft. Lauderdale, 1971-73; nursing asst., unit clk. N. Broward Gen. Hosp., Pompano Beach, Fla., 1973-75; staff nurse Park Plaza Hosp., Houston, 1975; staff, relief charge nurse St. Luke's Hosp., Houston, 1975-76; staff nurse coronary care Ochsner Found., New Orleans, 1976-78, unit instr., 1978-80, unit dir., 1980, weekend staff nurse, 1982; nursing supr., then patient services coordinator West Jefferson Gen. Hosp., New Orleans, 1982—. Mem. Emergency Medicine Ednl. Assistance Fund, 1979—, Harahan Oaks Civic Assn., 1980—. Mem. Am. Heart Assn. (CPR instr. 1978—), Am. Assn. Critical Care Nurses. Office: 4500 11th St Marrero LA 70072

SEABROOK, MELISSE GILPIN, telephone co. ofcl.; b. Newark, July 7, 1948; d. Richard Bond and Claire Brownell (Treat) Gilpin; student public schs. With So. Bell Telephone Co., 1966—, 1st level electronic switching foreman, 1972-78, mgr. network adminstrn., Riviera Beach, Fla., 1980-82, mgr. toll and spl. services, 1982—. Mem. Women's Exec. Workshop. Republican. Presbyterian. Club: Zonta (Lake Worth, Fla.). Home: 4024C Palm Bay Circle West Palm Beach FL 33406 Office: 3640 Ave E Riviera Beach FL 33404

SEABROOKS, CAROL TYRANCE, consumer products co. ofcl.; b. Attleboro, Mass., May 2, 1946; d. Herman James and Marian Elizabeth (Taylor) Tyrance; B.A. in Econs., Howard U., 1967; postgrad. N.Y. U., 1969-73. Manpower analyst Dept. Labor, Washington, 1967-68; economist FPC, Washington, 1969; market research analyst Philip Morris, Inc., N.Y.C., 1971-74; campaign planner Avon Products, Inc., N.Y.C., 1974-77, new markets planning adminstr., 1977-78, sales estimator, 1978-80, sr. sales estimator, 1980-81, mgr. gift and decorative, 1981—. Bldg. capt. Fort Lee (N.J.) Tenants Assn., 1974-78, rec. sec., 1974-76. Martin Luther King fellow, 1968-70. Mem. Am. Mgmt. Assn., Alpha Kappa Alpha (chpt. v.p. 1977, 79, 80). Home: 408 W 57th St Apt 10I New York NY 10019 Office: 9 W 57th St New York NY 10019

SEAGEARS, MARGARET JACQUELINE, educator; b. Balt.; d. Robert and Louise (West) Oliver; B.S., N.J. State Tchrs. Coll., 1950; M.A. cum laude, Columbia U., 1953; M.S. cum laude, U. P.R., 1967; postgrad. Harvard U., 1969; Montessori tchr. tng. certificate, Cornell U., 1974; m. Malcolm Thomas Seagears, Sept. 10, 1976; children—George J. Ward, Gary K. Ward. Kingarten primary specialist N.J. Bd. Edn., 1950-59; tchr., asst. prin. V.I. Bd. Edn., 1959-61; reading specialist Davis Clinic, P.R., 1962-65; prin., reading specialist Escuela Las Nereidas, P.R., 1962-73; coordinator curriculum and instrn. P.R., 1964-70; dir. Escuelas Montessori Center, P.R., 1973-77; pres., founder Montessori Tchr. Tng. Coll., P.R., 1973-77; cons., lectr., dir. internship tng. in P.R., 1974-77; cons. Office Edn., HEW, Washington, 1977-78; spl. asst. internat. and territorial affairs U.S. Interior Dept., Washington, 1979-80; lectr., cons. in field; exec. dir. Commn. for Laws on North Mariana Islands, 1979-80. Founder, P.R. Children's Theatre, 1967, P.R. Festival Arts, 1969; dir. C.A.R.E., P.R. 1971-75; bd. dirs. Am. Cancer Soc., 1975; chmn. P.R. Bicentennial Com. Pvt. and Pub. Edn., 1975. Fellow Passaic (N.J.) Bd. Edn., 1951, 52; recipient various certificates appreciation, distinguished service awards; named Woman of Yr., P.R., 1975. Mem. Nat. Women's Polit. Caucus, Women's Equity Action League, Nat. Assn. Ind. Schs., Am. Montessori Soc., AAUW, NEA, Women's Coll. Club, Am. Montessori Internat., Nat. Assn. Child Devel., Nat. Assn. Secondary Prins., Internat. Sch. Assn. Home: 1300 Army Navy Dr Apt 226 Arlington VA 22202 Office: US Dept Interior 18th and C Sts NW Washington DC 20240

SEAL, JUNE, banker; b. Hancock County, Tenn., Feb. 23, 1929; d. James Alonzo and Alice Trecie (Turner) S.; student public schs., Hancock County. Clk. cashier Seal Drug Store, Sneedville, Tenn., 1943-59; with Citizens Bank of Sneedville, 1959—, asst. cashier, 1973—. Sec.-treas., Baptist. Ch. Club: Sneedville Women's (sec.). Home: Rt 1 Box 126 Sneedville TN 37869 Office: PO Box 126 Sneedville TN 37869

SEALS, CLAIRE ELIZABETH, telecommunications co. exec.; b. Memphis, Sept. 13, 1940; d. Julius Otto and Martha Eugene (Chambliss) Leuenberger; B.S. in Bus. Adminstrn., U. San Francisco, 1978. Mgr. adminstrv. services and telecommunications Four Phase Systems Co., Cupertino, Calif., 1969-77; mgr. offices systems and telecommunications Syntex Corp., Palo Alto, Calif., 1977-82, mgr. tech. planning, 1982—; cons. in word processing. Mem. Internat. Word Processing Assn., Telecommunications Assn., No. Calif. Telecommunications Assn. (chmn. telecommunications com., past dir.), Santa Clara Word Processing Assn., Women in Telecommunications (charter). Home: 15500 Madrone Hill Rd Box 451 Saratoga CA 95070 Office: 3401 Hillview Ave Palo Alto CA 94304

SEAMAN, CATHERINE HAWES COLEMAN, anthropologist, educator; b. Nelson County, Va., Aug. 28, 1923; s. William Irby and Bertha Davis (Hughes) Coleman; B.A., U. Va., 1965, M.A., 1967, Ph.D. (NIMH fellow), 1969; m. John Anthony Seaman, Jr., Jan. 19, 1946; children—Catherine Seaman Fisher, Gwendolyn Seaman Whipp, John

Anthony III, Andrew. Mem. faculty Sweet Briar (Va.) Coll., 1967—, prof. dept. anthropology and sociology, 1974—, chmn. dept., 1970—, chmn. div. social studies, 1974-77; chmn. undergrad. research Sch. Nursing, U. Va., 1974-77; participant White House Conf. on Families, 1980. Mem. Nelson County Sch. Bd., 1954—, sometime chmn.; trustee Nelson County Garden Center; bd. dirs. Va. Bapt. Hosp. Served with Nurse Corps, U.S. Army, 1945-46. Ford grantee, 1974-75; Mellon grantee, 1974-75; Sweet Briar Coll. grantee, 1974-75; Ho-Mah grantee, 1976-77; Lily scholar, Fulbright scholar, India, 1980. Fellow Am. Anthrop. Assn.; mem. Ethnological Soc., Soc. Anthrop. Soc., So. Sociol. Soc., Va. Folklore Soc. Democrat. Baptist. Author: Introduction to Research, 1977; (with Verhonick) Research for Undergraduate, 1978; Research Methods, 1982; editor: Environment Studies, 1977. Home: Bicentennial Farm Rockford Faber VA 22938 Office: Sweet Briar Coll Sweet Briar VA 24595

SEARCY, NITA JANE, histotechnologist; b. San Francisco, Dec. 4, 1942; d. Johnnie Allison and Janie Juanita (Weaver) Wilkerson; student Tex. A&I U., 1961-63; m. John Victor Searcy, II, Aug. 29, 1963; children—John Victor, Mary Erin. Chief technician histology Bapt. Meml. Hosp., San Antonio, 1967-70; supr. histology Severance Reference Lab., San Antonio, 1973—. Recipient Cert. of Profl. Excellence, U. Tex. Health Sci. Center, 1981. Mem. Tex. Soc. Histotechnology (founding mem., dir. 1978-81, 1st v.p. 1979-81), Am. Soc. Clin. Pathologists, Nat. Soc. Histotechnology. Home: 4134 Barrington St San Antonio TX 78217 Office: 311 Camden St San Antonio TX 78215

SEARING, HELEN, archtl. historian, educator; b. N.Y.C., Mar. 12, 1933; d. Throckmorton Victor and Grace (Schou) Searing; B.A., Vassar Coll., 1954; Ph.D., Yale U., 1972; m. David Burres, Dec. 31, 1975. Mem. pub. relations dept Near East Coll. Assn., N.Y.C., 1954-56; editorial asst. Newsweek Mag., N.Y.C., 1957-59; nem. faculty Smith Coll., Northampton, Mass., 1967—, prof. art, 1980—. Mem. design rev. com. Northampton Hist. Commn., 1981—. Fulbright fellow, 1956-57; Woodrow Wilson fellow, 1962-63; Sterling fellow, 1965-67. Mem. Soc. Archtl. Historians (dir. 1982—). Contbr. articles to profl. jours. Office: Art Dept Smith College Northampton MA 01063

SEARLES, ANNA MAE HOWARD, educator, civic worker; b. Osage Nation Indian Terr., Okla., Nov. 22, 1906; d. Frank David and Clara (Bowman) Howard; A.A., Odessa (Tex.) Coll., 1961; B.A., U. Ark., 1964; M.Ed., 1970; postgrad. (Herman L. Donovan fellow), U. Ky., 1972—; m. Isaac Adams Searles, May 26, 1933; 1 dau., Mary Ann Rogers (Mrs. Herman Lloyd Hoppe). Compiler news, broadcaster sta. KJBC, 1950-60; corr. Tulsa Daily World, 1961-64; tchr. Rogers (Ark.) High Sch., 1964-72; tchr. adult class rapid reading, 1965, 80; tchr. adult edn. Learning Center Benton County (Ark.), Bentonville, 1973-77, supr. adult edn., 1977-79; tchr. North Ark. Community Coll., Rogers, 1979—, CETA, Bentonville, 1979—. Sec. Tulsa Safety Council, 1935-37; leader, bd. dirs. Girl Scouts U.S.A., Kilgore, Tex., 1941-44, leader, Midland, Tex., 1944-52, counselor, 1950-61; exec. sec. Midland Community Chest, 1955-60; gray lady Midland A.R.C., 1958-59; organizer Midland YMCA, Salvation Army; dir. women's div. Savings Bond Program, Midland; mem. citizens com. Rogers Hough Meml. Library, women's aux. Rogers Meml. Hosp.; sec. Beaver Lake Literacy Council, Rogers, 1973-77, Little Flock Planning Commn., 1975—, Benton County Hist. Soc., 1981—; public relations chmn. South Central region Nat. Affiliation for Literacy Advance, 1977-79; bd. dirs. Globe Theatre, Odessa, Tex., Midland Community Theatre, Tri-County Foster Home, Guadalupe, Midland youth centers, DeZavala Day Nursery, PTA, Adult Devel. Center, Rogers CETA, 1979-81. Recipient Thanks badge Midland Girl Scout Assn., 1948. Mem. NEA (del. conv. 1965), Ark. Assn. Public Continuing and Adult Edn. (pres. 1979-80), South Central Assn. for Lifelong Learning (sec. 1980-81), PTA (life), Future Homemakers Am. (life; sec. 1980—), Delta Kappa Gamma. Episcopalian. Clubs: Altrusa (pres. 1979—), Apple Spur Community (Rogers). Home: Route 2 Rogers AR 72756 Office: 610 SW A St Bentonville AR 72712

SEARLS, EILEEN HAUGHEY, lawyer, educator; b. Madison, Wis., Apr. 27, 1925; d. Edward M. and Anna Mary (Haughey) S.; B.A., U. Wis., 1948, J.D., 1950, M.S. in L.S., 1951. Admitted to Wis. bar, 1950; cataloger Yale U., 1951-52; instr. law St. Louis U., 1952-52, asst. prof., 1953-56, asso. prof., 1956-64, prof., 1964—, law librarian, 1952—. Mem. Wis. Bar Assn., Bar Assn. Met. St. Louis, Am. Assn. Law Librarians, Mid-Am. Assn. Law Libraries, Southwestern Assn. Law Libraries. Roman Catholic. Club: Altrusa. Office: 3700 Lindell Blvd Saint Louis MO 63108

SEARS, MARY ELLEN, telephone co. exec.; b. Oak Park, Ill., Nov. 11, 1924; d. Thomas Henry and Marietta (Hastings) Spencer; student Wright State U., Dayton, Ohio, U. Cin.; divorced; children—Sharon Anne, Kent Thomas, Larry Steven. Staff asst. to chief engr. Consol. Aircraft Corp., San Diego, 1942; with Ohio Bell Telephone Co., 1956—, area coordinator speakers bur., 1973-78, asst. mgr. public relations dept., Dayton, 1982—; speaker, workshop leader in field; adv. com. Coll. Continuing Edn., Wright State U., 1977-82; mem. adv. council Prudential Life Ins. Co., 1980-82. Bd. dirs. Dayton Sr. Citizens Center, 1982; pres.-elect Presidents Club, 1982. Mem. Dayton Exec. Club (pres. 1976-77), LWV, Dayton Council World Affairs, Dayton C. of C. Republican. Mem. Christian Ch. (Disciples of Christ). Office: 369 W 1st St Dayton OH 45402

SEARS, SARAH, mfg. co. ofcl.; b. Montclair, N.J., Jan. 23, 1950; d. William F. and Sarah L. (Booker) S.; B.A. in English with gen. honors, Douglass Coll., New Brunswick, N.J., 1972; M.B.A., Columbia U., 1976. Asst. brand mgr. Quaker Oats Co., Chgo., 1976-78; asst. product dir. Johnson & Johnson, New Brunswick, N.J., 1979-81, product dir., 1981—. Home: 2020 Pheasant Hollow Dr Plainsboro NJ 08536 Office: 501 George St New Brunswick NJ 08903

SEARS, SARAH ANN, nurse; b. Rochester, Minn., June 11, 1929; d. William Amos and Blanche Estelle (Douthirt) Raines; R.N., Coon Meml. Sch. Nursing, 1970; student Inst. Sci. Graphotherapy, 1972, Coronary Care, NW Tex. Hosp., 1972, U. Tex., Austin, 1974, Amarillo Coll., 1976; m. Joe Anthony Welling, Sept. 3, 1946 (dec. 1965); children—Jimmie Leslie, Kenneth Eugene, Jack Weslie, Joe Alan, Randall, Anthony, William Martin; m. 2d, Marvin Gillis Sears, July 9, 1972. Nurse, Coon Meml. Hosp., Dalhart, Tex., 1959-70; med. office nurse, Dalhart, 1970—. Organizer free Blood Pressure Clinics, 1972-78, Cardio Pulmonary Resuscitation Classes, 1977; active Am. Heart Assn., 1972-77, pres., 1977. Lic. vocat. nurse. Mem. Am. Assn. Med. Assts. Democrat. Roman Catholic. Clubs: United Transp. Union Aux., Elkettes, VFW Aux. (pres. 1968, dist. sr. v.p. 1968), Pilots Internat. Home: 510 Olive Ave Box 425 Dalhart TX 79022

SEATON, BEVERLY, educator; b. Penn Yan, N.Y., May 1, 1934; d. Bruce Alfred and Alice (Cooper) Tyrell; B.A., Keuka Coll., 1956; M.A., Ohio State U., 1959, Ph.D., 1968; m. John A. Seaton, June 13, 1958. Mem. faculty Ohio State U., Newark Campus, 1964—, asst. prof. English, 1968—. Mem. AAUP, Popular Culture Assn., Council Bot. and Hort. Libraries, Garden History Soc. Democrat. Baptist. Contbr. articles especially on garden history to profl. jours. Home: 3433 Corner Rd Alexandria OH 43001 Office: Dept English Ohio State U Newark OH 43055

SEAVER, CAROLYN HILDA, nurse; b. Ft. Kent, Maine, Dec. 29, 1954; d. Donald and Laurie (Blier) Deschaine; A.A., Springfield Tech. Community Coll., 1975; student Western New England Coll., 1979; m. John Seaver, Aug. 9, 1974. Dispatcher, Consol. Rail Corp., Springfield, Mass., 1978-80; neonatal intensive care nurse Baystate Med. Center, Springfield, 1975-77; med.-surg. nurse Mt. Sinai Hosp., Hartford, Conn., 1981—. Public relations dir. U.S. Jaycess, Springfield, 1978-80, treas., 1980-81. Recipient Jaycee Rookie of Yr. award, 1979-80, Woman of Yr. award, 1980-81. Mem. Am. Nursing Assn. Home: 36 Wilmont St Springfield MA 01108 Office: Mount Sinai Hosp Blue Hills Ave Hartford CT

SEAY, MIRIAM TYE, social worker; b. Edison, Ga., Oct. 31, 1918; d. Thomas O. and Leta Cowart Tye; A.A., Abraham Baldwin Agr. Coll., 1938; B.S. in Home Econs., U. Ga., 1940; m. Mathew Seay, Aug. 21, 1943; 1 dau., Carol Tye Seay Nichols; 1 stepson, Raymond. Home mgmt. supr. Farm and Home Adminstrn., 1940-43; social worker Fla. Dept. Health and Rehab. Services, Lakeland, 1945-64, social work supr., 1964-80; social dir. Lakeland Convalescent Center, 1981—. Sec., Community Service Council, 1972. Recipient Merit award Health and Rehab. Service, 1973, 80. Mem. AAUW. Democrat. Home: 811 Lafayette Ln Lakeland FL 33805 Office: 1124 N Lake Parker Ave Lakeland FL 33805

SEBELIUS, KATHLEEN GILLIGAN, assn. exec.; b. Cin., May 15, 1948; d. John Joyce and Mary Kathryn (Dixon) Gilligan; B.A., Trinity Coll., 1970; M.P.A., U. Kans., 1980; m. K. Gary Sebelius, Dec. 31, 1974; 1 son, Edward Keith. Community resource specialist Kans. Dept. Corrections, 1976-77, correctional planning specialist, 1975-76; exec. dir. D.C. Citizens Council Criminal Justice, 1971-73; dir. planning Center Community Justice, Washington, 1973-75; exec. dir. Kans. Trial Lawyers Assn., Topeka, 1977—. Nat. governing bd. Common Cause, 1977—; legis. v.p. Kans. Women's Polit. Caucus, 1979—; mem. Govtl. Ethics Commn., 1977-78. Mem. Am. Soc. Assn. Execs., Kans. Soc. Assn. Execs., Nat. Assn. Bar Execs., Nat. Assn. Trial Lawyer Execs. (pres. 1981-82). Democrat. Roman Catholic. Office: 112 W 6th St Suite 300 Topeka KS 66603

SEBRING, MARJORIE MARIE ALLISON, home furnishings exec.; Burnsville, N.C., Oct. 8, 1924; d. James William and Mary Will (Ramsey) Allison Shockey; student Mars Hill Coll., 1943, Home Decorators Sch. Design, N.Y.C., 1948, Wayne State U., 1953; 1 dau.. Patricia Louise Banner Krohn. Dir. decorating div. Robinson Furniture, Detroit, 1949-57; head buyer Tyner Hi-Way House, Ypsilanti, Mich., 1957-63; head buyer Town and Country, Dearborn, Mich., 1963-66; instr. Nat. Carpet Inst., 1963-65; owner Adams House, Inc., Plymouth, Mich., 1966-72; exec. v.p. mktg. and sales, regional sales and mktg. mgr. Triangle Industries, Los Angeles, 1972—. Recipient nat. sales awards, recognition for work with youth and aged. Mem. Internat. Home Furnishings Assn., Fla. Home Furnishings Rep. Assn. (officer), Fla. Furniture Dealers Assn., USCG Aux., Nat. Audubon Soc. Republican. Contbr. creative display to Better Homes and Gardens, 1957-64. Address: 2601-3 Grist Mill Circle New Port Richey FL 33552

SECHZER, JERI ALTNEU, psychologist; b. N.Y.C., Nov. 1, 1930; d. Max M. and Sarah (Lefkowitz) Altneu; B.S., N.Y.U., 1956; M.A., U. Pa., 1961, Ph.D., 1962; m. Philip H. Sechzer, Aug. 20, 1948; children—Ellen Kitty, Inda Marie, Selig Laurence. Predoctoral fellow Inst. Neurol. Scis., U. Pa., Phila., 1958-61, research fellow dept. physiology, 1962-63, mem. Medico Mission to Algeria, 1962, USPHS postdoctoral fellow, 1963-64; asst. prof. anatomy Baylor U. Coll. Medicine, Houston, 1964-66; research scientist rehab. medicine and anatomy N.Y.U., N.Y.C., 1966-70; asst. prof. psychiatry Cornell U. Med. Coll., N.Y.C., 1970-71, assoc. prof., 1971—; asst. attending psychologist N.Y. Hosp.-Cornell U. Med. Center, White Plains, N.Y., 1970-71, assoc. attending psychologist, 1971-76. Active Am. Profs. for Peace in Middle East, 1974—, Asphalt Green project, N.Y.C., 1975—. Recipient Creative Talent award Am. Inst. Research, 1963; NIH grantee, 1964—; NSF grantee, 1973-75; Exxon Edn. Found. grantee, 1979-80. Fellow N.Y. Acad. Scis. (chmn. psychology sect. 1982-84, chmn. animal research com. 1977—); mem. Assn. Women in Sci. in N.Y. (co-chmn. program com. 1978-82), Am. Psychol. Assn. (chmn. com. animal research and experimentation 1982-83), AAAS, Am. Assn. Anatomists, AAUP, Am. Physiol. Soc., Psychonomics Soc., Soc. Neurosci., Sigma Xi. Contbr. articles to profl. publs. Home: 180 East End Ave New York NY 10028 Office: Bourne Lab Dept Psychiatry NY Hosp-Cornell Univ Med Center 21 Bloomingdale Rd White Plains NY 10605

SECRIST, DOLLY ALVAREZ, translator; b. Bucaramanga, Colombia, June 24; d. Justo Jose and Elvira Maria (Rodriguez) Alvarez; grad. John Robert Powers, 1966; A.A., El Camino Coll., 1971; student UCLA, 1971-73; B.S., U. Beverly Hills, 1982; postgrad. SUNY, 1983; m. Harold B. Secrist, Aug. 30, 1975. Varitypist, Biddle Publ. Co., Los Angeles, 1963-67; exec. sec. Alfred M. Lewis Co., Riverside, Calif., 1967-69; multilingual exec. sec. Gen. Electric TEMPO, Santa Barbara, Calif., 1969-71; multilingual exec. sec. UCLA, Westwood, Calif, 1971-73; adminstrv. asst., translator, expediter Bechtel Power Corp., Los Angeles, 1973—. Mem. Nat. Assn. Female Execs. Roman Catholic. Club: Toastmasters (officer). Home: 17341 Chicago Ave Yorba Linda CA 92686 Office: 12400 E Imperial Hwy Norwalk CA 90650

SECUNDA, LENORE, retail store exec.; b. Bklyn., Aug. 27, 1938; d. Borah and Sylvia (Farrowitz) Wydra; student Am. Inst. Antiques, 1967, Adelphi Bus. Sch., 1972, Kingsboro Community Coll., 1973-74; m. Allan Secunda, Mar. 4, 1961; children—Roy, Margo, Darcie. Owner, mgr. Lenore's Antique Jewelry, N.Y.C., 1967-72; store mgr. Brancusi Furniture, Los Angeles, 1976-78; pvt. practice interior designing, Los Angeles, 1976—; dir. showrooms Corsican Furniture Co., Los Angeles, 1978—. Democrat. Jewish. Home: 6561 Wystone Ave #3 Reseda CA 91335 Office: 130 S Robertson Blvd Los Angeles CA 90048

SEDGWICK, DEBORAH COULTER, broadcasting co. sales exec.; b. Bakersfield, Calif., June 22, 1943; d. Frederick Paul and Allison (Coulter) S.; A.A. in Journalism, Stephens Coll., 1963; B.A. in Sociology, U. Colo., 1971; A.A., Sci. of Mind, Inc., Los Angeles, 1979; m. Kent Lawrence Brittan, Oct. 6, 1979. Office mgr. Town & Country Rev., Boulder, Colo., 1967, 69: editor environ. and transp. mag. Elancer Corp., Boulder, 1971-73; founder, v.p. sales Falkenberg & Sedgwick Prodns., Inc., Studio City, Calif., 1975-78; account exec. Sta. KPMC, Bakersfield, 1979—, now dir. sales; free lance producer and writer commls. and sci. fiction. Bd. dirs. First Ch. of Religious Sci., Bakersfield. AAUW grantee. Mem. Nat. Assn. Profl. Saleswomen, NOW, Network, Profl. Women's Group. Clubs: Winners Circle Breakfast (chmn.), Toastmasters (pres.). Home: 1721 Camino Primavera Bakersfield CA 93306 Office: 307 E 21st St Bakersfield CA 93302

SEDGWICK, RAE, psychologist, nurse; b. Kansas City, Kans., Apr. 7, 1944; d. Chalres Rezin and Helen Hanway (Timmons) Sedgwick; student Bethany Sch. Nursing, 1965; B.S. in Nursing, U. Iowa, 1967; M.A., U. Kans., 1970, Ph.D. in Psychology, 1972. Nurse, Mercy Hosp., Iowa City, 1965-67, Community Mental Health, Kansas City, Kans., 1967-68; specialist Lab. Edn., Washington, 1971-72; coordinator Health C.A.R.E. Clinic, Pa. State U., University Park, 1974-76; clin. asso. Community Psychiatry, Altoona (Pa.) Mental Health Center, 1973-76; asst. prof. human devel. Pa. State U., University Park, 1972-76; resident psychologist Family Consulation Program, United Meth. Ch., Bonner Springs, Kans., 1976-80; pvt. practice psychology Sedgwick-Hildebrand Health Asso., Bonner Springs, 1976—; cons. in field; staff Bethany Med. Center, Kansas City, Kans., 1976—, Mid-Continent Psychiat. Hosp., Olathe, Kans., 1976-81, Cushing's Meml. Hosp., Leavenworth, Kans., 1976—, St. John Hosp., Leavenworth, 1976—. Mem. adminstr. bd. United Meth. Ch., Bonner Springs, Kans., 1976—. Recipient Outstanding Young Woman award U. Kans., 1971; Bus. and Profl. Women's Clubs award, 1962; Nurse Scientist fellow and grantee, 1968-72; Bus. and Profl. Women's Club scholar, 1962; lic. psychologist, Kans.; registered nurse, Kans.; cert. clin. specialist in adult psychiat. and mental health nursing, in child and adolescent psychiat. and mental health nursing. Mem. Am. Nurses Assn., Am. Psychol. Assn., Council of Advanced Practitioners in Psychiatric-Mental Health Nursing, Council of Nurse Researchers, Ocean, Inc., Assn. Humanistic Psychologists, Kans. Psychol. Assn., Am. Heart Assn., Am. Orthopsychiat. Assn., AAAS, U. Kans. Alumni Assn., Intercollegiate Assn. Women Students (nat. resource bd. mem. 1972-73), Am. Assn. Psychiat. Services for Children, Am. Group Psychotherapy Assn. (del. to China 1982), Kans. Internat. Womens Yr. Commn., Bonner Springs C. of C. (dir.), Sigma Theta Tau. Club: Bus. and Profl. Women's. Author: Family Mental Health: Theory and Practice, 1980; White Frame House, 1980; asso. editor Jour. Corrective and Social Psychiatry, 1979-82; writer weekly column, An Ounce of Prevention, Bonner Springs Chieftain, 1977—; contbr. articles to profl. jours. Home: Box 377 Bonner Springs KS 66012 Office: PO Box 377 216 E 2d St Bonner Springs KS 66012

SEDWICK, LINDA JEAN, advt. exec., artist; b. Imperial, Pa., Mar. 30, 1947; d. Christopher and Irene A. (Podsiadly) Junker; student Art Inst. Pitts., 1971-73. Art dir. Suburban Gazette, McKees Rocks, Pa., 1974-76; advt. mgr. Coraopolis (Pa.) Record, 1976-80; account exec. Pitts. Press, Post Gazette, 1980—; group exhbns.: Am. Artist Bicentennial Exhbn., 1975-76, Sewickley (Pa.) Library, 1976; instr. Community Coll. Allegheny County; dir., pres. Art/Design, Ideas by Nina. Home: RD 1 Box 333 Coraopolis PA 15108 Office: 926 5th Ave Coraopolis PA 15108 also PO Box 74 Sewickley PA 15143

SEEGAR, CHARLON IONE, hosp. social worker, educator; b. Denver, May 13, 1936; d. Wilner Hopson and Cordelia Ione (Lipman) S.; A.B., LaGrange Coll., 1959; M.S.W., U. N.C., Chapel Hill, 1964. Social worker Am. Nat. Red Cross Service to Mil. Hosps., Ft. Jackson, S.C., 1959-61, Maxwell AFB Hosp., Ala., 1962-63, Ft. Bragg Army Hosp., N.C., 1964-65, U.S. Army Hosp., Frankfurt Am Main, Germany, 1965-67, Charleston (S.C.) Naval Hosp., 1967; family planning cons. Dept. Family and Children Services, State of Ga., 1967-69; chief social worker maternal and infant care project, family planning project dept. ob-gyn Med. Coll. Ga., 1969-80, asst. prof., 1980—, social scientist, 1980—, coordinator outpatient div., 1980—. Treas., SCLC, Augusta, Ga., 1969-73. Mem. Nat. Assn. Social Workers (dir. 1969-75), Planned Parenthood E. Central Ga. (dir. 1975-80), Mental Health Assn. Ga., Mental Health Assn. Augusta, Ga. Conf. Social Welfare, Nat. Assn. Female Execs., Epilepsy Assn. Ga. Home: 5 Lakeshore Loop August GA 30904 Office: 1515 Pope Ave Dept Psychiatry Med Coll Ga Augusta GA 30912

SEEGER, MELINDA WAYNE, occupational therapist; b. Albert Lea, Minn., Dec. 31, 1940; d. Oscar Earnest and Evelyn Josephine (Pihl) Wayne; B.S., U. Minn., 1963; m. Robert Charles Seeger, Mar. 16, 1964; 1 son, Jeffrey Wayne. Chief occupational therapy Rehab. Inst. Oreg., Portland, 1964-66; supr. phys. disabilities and gen. medicine and surgery occupational therapy Mpls. VA Hosp., 1966-68; supr. phys. disabilities occupational therapy Nat. Naval Med. Center, Bethesda, Md., 1968-71; assoc. chief rehab. services, dir. occupational therapy UCLA Med. Center, 1974—. Mem. utilization rev. com. Vis. Nurse Assn. Los Angeles, 1975—, mem. profl. adv. com., 1979-80; mem. exec. com. Allied Health Professions sect. Arthritis Found., 1980—. Recipient Spl. Achievement award Nat. Naval Med. Center, 1971, Outstanding Performance award, 1971; Spl. Performance award UCLA, 1980. Mem. Am. Occupational Therapy Assn., Occupational Therapy Assn. Calif. Author, editor articles in field. Office: UCLA Center for Health Scis LeConte Ave Los Angeles CA 90024

SEELEY, BARBARA GAIL, human services exec.; b. Grand Forks, N.D., June 7, 1936; d. Alfred Thomas and Florence Micken S.; B.S., UCLA, 1957; M.S.W., U. So. Calif., 1970; children—John Mark Doss, Timothy Stephen Doss, Elizabeth Gail Doss. Psychiat. social worker State of Calif., Pomona and Santa Ana, 1970-73; sr. clin. social worker Orange County Mental Health Dept., 1973-79, dep. dir. mental health, 1979-80, dep. regional mgr. human services agy., 1980-82, program mgr. mental health dept. Health Care Agy., 1982—; field educator San Diego State U. Sch. Social Work. Lic. marriage, family and child counselor; lic. clin. social worker. Mem. Acad. Cert. Social Workers, Nat. Assn. Social Workers, DAR. Methodist. Home: 3310 Seashore Dr Newport Beach CA 92663 Office: 1617 Westcliff Dr Newport Beach CA 92660

SEEMANN-BEAUMONT, ROSALIE MARY, logistics cons.; b. St. Louis, July 30, 1942; d. Ulysses Sylvester and Helen Marie (Hootselle) Simon; student Lindenwood Colls., St. Charles, Mo., 1973-76, Harris Tchrs. Coll., St. Louis, 1961; U. Fla., Gainesville, 1964; m. Richard Vaughn, Jan 20, 1968 (dec.); 1 dau., Heather Elizabeth; m. 2d, Dennis Jon Beaumont, May 28, 1982. Records clk. McDonnell Aircraft Corp., St. Louis, 1962-64; vol. U.S. Peace Corps, Brazil, 1964-66; tech. analyst, group leader Conductron-Mo., St. Charles, 1966-71; self-employed, 1971-77; tech. analyst, maintenance engr. McDonnell Douglas Astronautics, St. Louis, 1977-78; mgr. supply support Northrop Def. Systems Div., Rolling Meadows, Ill., 1978-80; logistics cons., Spring Grove, Ill., 1980—. Adv. council Conductron-Mo. Affirmative Action Program; mem. ch. council, commr. ways and means St. John the Bapt. Cath. Ch.; troop leader Sybaquay council Girl Scouts U.S.A. Recipient commendation Conductron-Mo., 1967. Mem. Soc. Logistics Engrs. (Mem. of Yr. award, sr. mem.), Assn. Old Crows, Lindenwood Colls. Assos. Fine Arts, Nat. Assn. Female Execs., Northside Art Assn. Republican. Bus. mgr. Northside Art Assn. News, 1968-70. Home and Office: 3303 Route 12 Spring Grove IL 60081

SEFFER, YVONNE KATHRYN, fin. cons., import/export co. exec.; b. Chgo., Oct. 4, 1950; d. Urosh Lazar and Helen (Musulin) S.; B.A., Ohio U., 1972. Pres., Ivanka Internat. Imports, Chgo., 1973—; realtor asso. Coldwell Banker Co., Oak Brook, Ill., 1979—; internat. fin. cons., 1980—. Mem. Nat. Assn. Exec. Women, Nat. Assn. Realtors, Ill. Assn. Realtors, DuPage Bd. Realtors, La Grange Bd. Realtors, Internat. Sports Core, Internat. Order St. John of Jerusalem Hospitallers-Knights of Malta, Augustan Soc. Office: 1225 W 22d St Suite 110 Oak Brook IL 60521

SEGAL, ALETHEA BIGHAM, med. technologist; b. Rock Hill, S.C., Oct. 2, 1921; d. Boyce Hyatt and Sarah Dorcas (Whiteside) Bigham; B.S. in Chemistry and Zoology, Winthrop Coll., Rock Hill, 1942; M.T., Duke U., 1944; m. William Segal, July 28, 1950; children—Janet Cheryl Segal Fixel, Alethea Gail. Med, technician, office mgr. Dr. Louie Limbaugh and Dr. Karl Hanson, Jacksonville, Fla., 1944-60; med. technician The Clinic for Digestive Diseases, Jacksonville, Fla., 1960-62, clinic mgr., 1963-75, dir. patients accts., 1976—. Mem. Am. Soc. Clin. Pathologists, Fla. Soc. Med. Technologists, Credit Women Internat., Winthrop Coll. Alumni Assn., AAUW. Democrat. Baptist. Club: Ponte Vedra. Home: 5138 Rosebay Terr Jacksonville FL 32207 Office: 1610 Barrs St Jacksonville FL 32204

SEGAL, MARIE SOLDANO, psychologist; b. Bklyn., July 7, 1948; d. A. Frank and Katherine (Saladino) Soldano; B.A., Elmira Coll., 1969; profl. psychology cert. (scholar), Queens Coll., City U. N.Y., 1972;

Ed.D., Lehigh U., 1980; m. Steven Alan Segal, July 5, 1970. Sch. psychologist Glassboro (N.J.) public schs., 1972-74; chmn. child study, sch. psychologist Camden County Vo-Tech Sch., Sicklerville, N.J., 1974-78; documentor/evaluator Tchr. Corps Project, Lehigh U., Bethlehem, Pa., 1978-80, grad. asst., 1979; pvt. practice psychol. cons., Glassboro, 1980—; asst. prof. spl. edn. Kean Coll., Union, N.J., 1981—. Mem. Am. Psychol. Assn., Camden County Psychol. Assn., Council of Exceptional Children. Home: 42 Cricket Ln Turnersville NJ 08012

SEGARRA-MCDERMOTT, DONNA LOUISE, osteo. physician; b. Bayonne, N.J., Oct. 22, 1943; d. Pedro Jose and Alice Antonia (Bosch) S.; B.A., Caldwell Coll. for Women, 1965; D.O., Kirksville Coll. Osteo. Medicine, 1970; m. Mark E. McDermott, Mar. 11, 1982. Intern, Doctor's Hosp., Columbus, Ohio, 1970-71; practice medicine specializing in family practice, Albuqerque, 1971-74, Succasunna, N.J., 1974-77, Thornton, Colo., 1977-78, Wharton, N.J., 1979—; emergency room physician St. Clare's Hosp., Denville, N.J., 1978-79, also mem. staff; mem. staff Dover (N.J.) Gen. Hosp. Recipient award Kirksville Coll. Osteo. Medicine, 1970. Mem. AMA, Morris County Med. Soc., N.J. State Med. Soc., Am. Runners Assn. Roman Catholic. Club: Olympic Racquetball and Health. Home: 4 Mountain View Trail Wharton NJ 07885 Office: 117 S Main Wharton NJ 07885

SEGERSTROM, JANE ARCHER, image specialist; b. Los Angeles, Feb. 1, 1930; d. Francis Gaden and Lyda Mary (Comer) Archer; B.S., George Pepperdine U., 1951; m. Clifford Charles Segerstrom, Feb. 1, 1951; children—John Archer, Carol Anne. Tchr., Lakewood Jr. High Sch., Long Beach, Calif., 1951-53; instr., adult program Long Beach City Coll., 1956-64; pres. Triad Interests, Inc., Houston, 1974—; pub. Triad Press, 1980—. Mem. Home Economists in Bus. (S.W. regional adv. on nat. bd. 1979-81), Tex. Home Econ. Assn. (Home Economists in Bus. chmn. 1977-79), Greater Houston Home Economists in Bus. (chmn., 1977-78), Houston Profl. Writers, Women in Communications, Am. Soc. Profl. and Exec. Women. Republican. Presbyterian. Author: Look Like Yourself and Love It, 1980. Home: 10811 Riverview Dr Houston TX 77042 Office: PO Box 42006-12 Houston TX 77042

SEGGERMAN, ANNE CRELLIN, bio-med. research adminstr.; b. Los Angeles, May 13, 1931; d. Curtin Vergil and Yvonne Madeleine (LaGrave) Crellin; student Sch. of Decorative Arts, Paris, France, 1949-50; student of piano with Albert Levesque, 1948-50, l'Ecole du Louvre, Paris, 1949-50; student Albertus Magnus Coll., Conn., 1949-51; hon. degree Sacred Heart U., 1980; m. Harry G.A. Seggerman, Apr. 14, 1951; children—Patricia, Henry, Marianne, Yvonne, Suzanne, John. Tchr., French, Beverly Hills, Calif., 1958-60; ofcl. translator Los Angeles World Affairs Council, 1958-60; founder, chmn. bd. Fairfield County chpt. Huxley Inst. for Bio-Social Research, Westport, Conn., 1972—, trustee, 1971—; founder Guadalupe Research Inc.; founder, pres. Steiner Prodns. Inc.; trustee, mem. hon. bd. ANUK, Inc., 1980. Mem. Westport com. Am. Shakespeare Festival, Stratford, Conn., 1972; mem. Fairfield County Organic Gardeners; founding mem. West Side Sch. for Gifted Children, Beverly Hills, Calif., 1958-60; bd. dirs. Easter Seal Rehab. Center, Fairfield; mem. Pres.'s Com. on Mental Retardation; precinct capt. Republican Com., West Los Angeles, 1960; founder, pres. 4th World Found. for Interfaith Media Action, 1977—. Mem. Nat. Health Fedn., Am. Soc. for Psychical Research, Am. Fedn. of Homemakers, New Eng. Inst., Natural Food Assn. Roman Catholic. Clubs: Fairfield County Hunt, Country of N.Y., York. Home: 5060 Congress St Fairfield CT 06430 Office: The Huxley Institute 328 Park Ave Bridgeport CT 06604

SEGGEV, LYDIA, psychoanalyst; b. Bucharest, Roumania, Apr. 11, 1937; came to U.S., 1963, naturalized, 1976; d. Jehoshua and Henriette (Kandel) Nadler; B.A. in Sociology, Hebrew U., Israel, 1963; M.A. in Ednl. Psychology, U. Mich., 1965; Ph.D. in Psychology, Syracuse U., 1971; diploma psychotherapy and psychoanalysis Adelphi U., 1979; 1 son, Michael. Intern, Children Psychiat. Hosp., Ann Arbor, Mich., 1965; research asst. dept. psychology Syracuse (N.Y.) U., 1970-71; asst. prof. St. John's U., 1971-72; lectr. Sch. of Edn., Tel-Aviv (Israel) U., 1971-72; lectr. dept. psychology Hebrew U., Jerusalem, Israel, 1971-72; dir. evaluation title 1 programs, Dist. 9, Bronx, N.Y., 1974-75; psychotherapist Jamaica Center for Psychotherapy, 1973-75, L.I. Consultation Center, 1975-77; pvt. practice psychotherapy and psychoanalysis, 1974—. Mem. Am. Psychol. Assn., Nassau Psychol. Assn., N.Y. Psychol. Assn., Soc. for Research in Child Devel., Adelphi Soc. for Psychotherapy and Psychoanalysis, N.Y. Soc. Clin. Psychologists. Address: 24 Pine Dr N Roslyn NY 11576

SEGNER, VENICE CHANDLER, psychologist; b. Sand Springs, Okla., Nov. 7, 1914; d. John Beverly and Beulah Virginia (Sewell) Chandler; B.A., U. Tulsa, 1962; Ph.D., U. Ga., 1968; m. O.E. Segner, Jan. 15, 1934 (dec. 1962); m. 2d Gilbert L. Stewart, Aug. 25, 1972; children—Jane (dec.), Leslie, Eugene (dec.), James. Staff psychologist Long Beach (Calif.) VA Med. Center, 1968-76, supervisory psychologist, 1976-80, ret., 1980; founder, pres. bd. dirs. The Middle Way, Inc., non-profit service orgn. for develop. disabled adults, including tng. in agrl. and related skills, Sebastopol, Calif., 1979—; clin. asso. U. So. Calif., 1973-80, Fuller Theol. Sem., 1977-80. Mem. Am. Psychol. Assn., Western Psychol. Assn. Democrat. Episcopalian. Home: 2759 Dyer Ave Sebastopol CA 95472 Office: 486 S Main Sebastopol CA 95472

SEGO, ARLENE FRONTROTH (MRS. MICHAEL A. SEGO), educator; b. Cleve., Mar. 13, 1938; d. Henry John and Hazel Elizabeth (Kunkle) Frontroth; B.S., Indiana U. of Pa., 1959; M.Natural Scis., Ariz. State U., 1962. Tchr., West High Sch., Cleve., 1959-61, head dept. math., 1962-66; asst. prof. math. Cuyahoga Community Coll., Parma, Ohio, 1966-69, asso. prof., 1969-72, prof., 1972—, also head dept., faculty marshall, 1972; pres. Typographics Group, Inc. Program coordinator, dir. adult programs West High, Cleve., 1966-67, coordinator Head Start Program, 1966. Leader, Girl Scouts U.S.A., Cleve., 1962-64. Shell Merit fellow, 1965; Martha Holden Jennings scholar, 1963-64. Mem. Nat., Ohio, Greater Cleve. (pres. 1966-67) councils tchrs. math., Math. Assn. Am., AAUP, Brunswick C. of C. (dir., pres.), Ohio Assn. Community Jr. Colls. (sec. 1969-70), Assn. Women in Math., AAUW, Alpha Sigma Alpha, Delta Kappa Gamma (treas.). Club: Zonta. (dir., treas.). Author: Good Buddy. Home: 938 Penny's Dr Brunswick OH 44212 Office: 590 Pearl Rd Brunswick OH 44212

SEGREST, JULIA GAINES, public accountant; b. Atlanta, Sept. 20, 1942; d. James Arthur and Mary Moina (Few) Gaines; student Huntingdon Coll., 1959-62; B.S., Auburn U., 1973; m. Paul Benton Turner, Dec. 21, 1960; children—James Edwin, Susan Moina, Catherine Benton; m. 2d, Douglas Broward Segrest, Sept. 8, 1979. Public relations adminstr., sec. YWCO Camp Grandview, Montgomery, Ala., 1966-69; mgr. Cavanaugh Gray & Co., Inc., Montgomery, 1969-71; tax auditor U.S. Treasury Dept., Montgomery, 1973-75, internal revenue agt., 1975-79, supervisory agt., 1979-81; acct. Barganier, Segrest & Assos., C.P.A.s, Montgomery, 1981—. Mem. Am. Soc. Women Accts. (treas. Montgomery chpt. 1974-75, sec. 1975-76, chpt. pres. 1982-83), Am. Inst. C.P.A.s, Ala. Soc. C.P.A.s, Am. Women's Soc. C.P.A.s, Ala. Soc. C.P.A.s. Presbyterian. Home: 2364 Wildwood Dr Montgomery AL 36111 Office: 2640 Zelda Rd Montgomery AL 36107

SEGURA, PEARL MARY, former librarian, educator; b. Lafayette, La., June 12, 1909; d. Joseph Sidney and Celestine (Gutierrez) Segura; B.A., U. Southwestern La., 1930, postgrad., summer 1932, 42-43, 46-48, 51-52; B.S. in L.S., La. State U., 1941; postgrad. summers Tulane U., 1931, Columbia, 1939, U. Ill., 1948, U. Houston, 1954. Tchr., librarian Indian Bayou (La.) High Sch., 1930-31; tchr. Maurice (La.) High Sch., 1931-33, tchr., librarian, 1933-41; asst. circulation librarian Stephens Meml. Library U. Southwestern La., Lafayette, 1941-44, acting reference librarian, 1944-46, reference librarian, 1946-62, librarian Jefferson Caffery La. room Dupre Library, 1962-75, asso. prof. library sci., 1953-75, ret., 1975. Mem. Bicentennial Com., Lafayette. Mem. La. Library Assn., AAUW, Nat. Trust for Historic Preservation, La., Attakapas hist. assns., La. Geneal. and Hist. Soc., La. Folklore Soc., La. Tchrs. Assn., Met. Opera Guild, Lafayette Community Concerts Assn., Lafayette Art Assn., Am. Camellia Soc., La. State U., U. Southwestern La. alumni assns., D.A.R. (1st chpt. vice regent 1968-71, state chmn. U.S.A. bicentennial com. 1967-71, chpt. chmn. 1968-77), U.S. Daus. of 1812, Attakapas Hist. Assn., U.D.C., Cath. Daus. Am., S.W. La. Poetry Soc., France Amerique de la Louisiane Acadienne, Nat. Ret. Tchrs. Assn., La. Ret. Tchrs. Assn., LaFayette Parish Ret. Tchrs. Assn., Am. Assn. Ret. Persons, Phi Kappa Phi (pub. relations officer USL chpt. 1958-75), Beta Phi Mu, Delta Kappa Gamma (pres. Alpha chpt. 1947-49) Kappa Kappa Iota (state handbook chmn. 1969-61, pres. Lambda conclave 1957-60). Democrat. Roman Catholic, Author: Acadians in Fact and Fiction: A. Classified Bibliography, 1955. Contbr. articles to profl. jours. Home: 140 S Magnolia St Lafayette LA 70501

SEIB, ELIZABETH JUNE, advt. agy. exec.; b. St. Louis, Oct. 23, 1936; d. Vincent John and Mary Elizabeth (Harper) S.; cert. in bus. adminstrn. Washington U., St. Louis, 1978. Posting machine operator Union Electric Co., St. Louis, 1954-57; sec., office asst. Miller & Rhodes, Inc., Richmond, Va., 1957-62; with D'Arcy-MacManus & Masius, St. Louis, 1962—, now v.p., assoc. media dir. Mem. St. Louis Advt. Club. Republican. Baptist. Club: Town & Country Racquet. Office: 1 Memorial Dr Saint Louis MO 63102

SEIBERT-NEWBERRY, LINDA SUE, home economist, kitchen designer; b. Albuquerque, Apr. 27, 1952; d. Wayne and Jean (Riche) Seibert; B.S. in Home Econs. Edn. (scholar), U. N.Mex., 1977; m. John Phillip Newberry, Mar. 10, 1979. Receptionist, Public Service Co., Albuquerque, 1970-72; kitchen designer order dept. Creative Kitchens, Albuquerque, 1972-77; kitchen designer, saleswoman Konvert-A-Kitchen, Albuquerque, 1977, T Bird Home Centers Spltys., Artesia, N.Mex., 1979—; sales rep. Designer Kitchens, Albuquerque, 1977-78; cons. for home econs. and kitchen design, Albuquerque, 1977-79; tchr. adult microwave cooking classes, 1972—; condr. workshops on kitchen planning and redecorating, 1973—. Mem. Am. Home Econs. Assn., Nat. Home Economists in Bus., Albuquerque Home Economists in Bus. (public relations com. 1977-79, nominating com. 1977-80), N.Mex. Home Econs. Assn. Republican. Roman Catholic. Home: 1114 S 4th St Space 20 Artesia NM 88210 Office: 310 W Texas St Artesia NM 88210

SEIDE, DIANI JUNE, writer; b. N.Y.C., June 15, 1930; d. Alvin C. and Sylvia V. (Kessler) S.; B.S., Adelphi U., 1953; student creative writer New Sch. for Social Research; children—Michael David, Sabrina Jennifer. Head nurse, supr., instr. nursing Mt. Sinai Hosp., St. Vincent's Hosp. and St. Luke's Hosp., N.Y.C., 1950's; editor RN mag., 1960's; asso. editor Parents' Mag., 1970's; author young adult fiction and non-fiction, various med. articles; author books: Young Nurse in New York, 1967; (with Mark Traynor) New York Beauty Book, 1980. Mem. Authors Guild. Address: 345 E 93d St New York NY 10028

SEIFERT, ELIZABETH (GASPAROTTI), author; b. Washington, Mo., June 19, 1897; d. Richard Chester and Anna (Sanford) S.; B.A., Washington U., St. Louis, 1918; widow; children—John Joseph, Richard, Paul Anthony, Anna Catherine Seifert Felter. Author 81 novels, 1938—, including Young Doctor Galahad (Redbook-Dodd Mead first novel award 1938), 1938; 7 Bayard Books including Substitute Doctor, 1957, The Doctor's Desperate Hour, 1975; Two Doctors, One Love, 1982. Mem. vestry St. James Episcopal Ch., Macon, Mo. Republican. Address: 511 Fort St Moberly MO 65270

SEIFERT, MARGARET FRANCIS, ednl. adminstr.; b. Brownwood, Tex., Nov. 17, 1944; d. Cabell Denny and Helen (Carroll) Francis; B.A., Transylvania Coll., 1966; M.A., Mankato State Coll., 1968; postgrad. Ind. U.; m. Ralph Louis Seifert, July 14, 1979; Adv., Mankato (Minn.) State Coll., 1966-68, head resident, 1967-68, ednl. coordinator, 1968-69, asst. dir. housing, 1969-70, dir. orientation, 1969-70; residence hall dir. Ball State U., Muncie, Ind., 1970-76, instr. directed admissions program, 1971-72, higher edn., 1972-74; asso. dean students, dir. housing Hanover (Ind.) Coll., 1976-82; coordinator Learning Resource Center, Ind. Vocat./Tech. Coll., Madison, 1982—; cons., adv. numerous univ. orgns., coms., bds. Mem. Nat. Assn. Student Personnel Adminstrs. (rep. to Allerton conf. 1979), Nat. Assn. Women Deans, Adminstrs. and Counselors (sec. local arrangements com. for nat. com. 1980-82), Madison Hist. Soc., Assn. of Coll. and Univ. Housing Officers (program com. 1975—), Am. Coll. Personnel Assn. (mem. nat. conv. local arrangements com. 1974-76), Ind. Coll. Personnel Assn. (program presenter 1972—), Ind. Assn. Women Deans, Adminstrs. and Counselors (spring workshop com. 1974-75, membership chmn. 1977-78, v.p. 1978-79, pres. 1980-81, exec. bd., nominations chmn. 1981-82, hon. members chmn. 1982-83), Am. Personnel and Guidance Assn., AAUW (exec. council 1978-79, v.p. for program 1980-82, chmn. book fair 1982-83), LWV, Muncie City Panhellenic (del. 1973-75), Pi Sigma Alpha, Alpha Lambda Delta (adminstrv. liaison Hanover Coll. 1981-82), Phi Eta Sigma, Delta Delta Delta (pres. alumni assn. 1974-75). Democrat. Home: PO Box 365 Hanover IN 47243 Office: Hanover Coll Hanover IN 47243

SEIFFERTT, CARLA LYNN, nurse; b. Belleville, Ill., Mar. 14, 1948; d. Carl William and Charlotte Margaret (Kaysing) S.; B.S. in Nursing, So. Ill. U., Edwardsville, 1971. Mem. nursing staff Christian Welfare Hosp., East St. Louis, Ill., 1971-76; mem. nursing staff Lutheran Med. Center, St. Louis, 1976-81, charge nurse med./surg. div., 1976-81; head nurse intensive care unit Normandy Osteo. Hosp., St. Louis, 1981—; tchr. CPR. Mem. Am. Assn. Critical Care Nurses, Ill. Heart Assn. (lectr.), St. Clair County Heart Assn. (pres. 1977-80), Sweet Adelines (pres. Clin-Clair chpt. 1979-80, asst. dir. chpt. 1981—). Mem. United Ch. Christ. Home: 524 Gilbert St Belleville IL 62221 Office: 7840 Natural Bridge Rd Saint Louis MO 63121

SEIGER, MARILYN SANDRA, hotel co. ofcl.; b. Washington, Jan. 20, 1945; d. Harry R. and Claire D. Seiger; B.S., Ohio State U., 1966; M.A., U. Pitts, 1967; M.B.A., Baruch Coll., 1982; m. Stan Amatucci, June 15, 1979. Editor, Holt, Rinehart & Winston, Inc., N.Y.C., 1969-73; editor/writer Redbook mag., N.Y.C., 1973-77; mng. editor 1,001 Decorating Ideas, N.Y.C., 1978-79; dir. public relations, promotion, advt. Brit. Consulate, N.Y.C., 1979-80; account supr. Peter Martin Assos., N.Y.C., 1980-82; public relations mgr. Marriott Hotels, N.Y.C., 1982—; cons., writer Singer Co., Reader's Digest, Formica, Martex. Lic. tchr., N.Y., Pa. Mem. Public Relations Soc. Am. (chmn. public relations workshops 1982). Office: 1540 Broadway New York NY 10036

SEILER, CHARLOTTE WOODY, ret. educator; b. Thorntown, Ind., Jan. 20, 1915; d. Clark and Lois Merle (Long) Woody; A.A., Ind. State U., 1933; A.B., U. Mich., 1941; M.A., Central Mich. U., 1968; m. Wallace Urban Seiler, Oct. 10, 1942; children—Patricia Anne Bootzin, Janet Alice Seiler. Tchr. elementary schs., Whitestown, Ind., 1933-34, Thorntown, Ind., 1934-37, Kokomo, Ind., 1937-40, Ann Arbor, Mich., 1941-44, Willow Run, Mich., 1944-46; instr. English div. Delta Coll., University Center, Mich., 1964-69, asst. prof., 1969-77, ret., 1977; organizer, dir. Delta Coll. Puppeteers, 1972-77. Treas. Friends of Grace A. Dow Meml. Library, 1974-75, 77-79, corr. sec., 1975-77; bd. dirs. Salvation Army; leader self-discovery through humanities Sr. Center Humanities Program, Midland Community Center, 1977—. Mem. Midland Art Assn., Midland Symphony League, Mich. Library Assn., AAUW, Pi Lambda Theta, Chi Omega, Midland Panhellenic. Presbyterian. Clubs: Tuesday Review (pres. 1979-80), Seed and Sod Garden. Home: 5002 Sturgeon Creek Pkwy Midland MI 48640

SEITTELMAN, ELIZABETH EDITH, educator; b. N.Y.C., Dec. 22, 1922; d. Isidore A. and Jennie (Schorr) Seittelman; A.B. cum laude, Hunter Coll., N.Y.C., 1943; A.M., Fordham U., 1944, Ph.D. (Hugh Grant grad. asst.), 1952. Tchr., Acad. Mt. St. Ursula, N.Y.C., 1947-49, James Monroe High Sch., N.Y.C., 1949-50, Nathan Hale Sch., N.Y.C., 1950-59; asst. prin., then acting prin. Simon Baruch Jr. High Sch., N.Y.C., 1959-69; adj. lectr. English, Bronx Community Coll., 1961-68; adj. lectr. classical and comparative langs. Bklyn. Coll., 1967-69; prof. classical langs. York Coll., CUNY, 1969—, chmn. dept. tchr. preparation, 1972—; resource cons. Airlie House Conf., 1964. Recipient Earle prize Hunter Coll., 1943, Builder of Brotherhood award Queens chpt. NCCJ, 1973. Mem. Am. Ednl. Research Assn., Medieval Acad. Am., Am. Philol. Assn., Classical Assn. Atlantic States, Am. Classical League (chmn. com. for study classical humanities in elementary schs. 1977-81), N.Y. Acad. Public Edn., N.Y. Classical Club, Phi Beta Kappa (Nu chpt.), Kappa Delta Pi (Xi Lambda chpt.). Author numerous articles in field. Editor-in-chief Epitome, 1972—, Dicta, 1973—; audio visual editor Classical World, 1961—. Home: 150 Parkway N Yonkers NY 10704 Office: York Coll 150-14 Jamaica Ave Jamaica NY 11451

SEITZ, CHARMAINE YVONNE GROVE, radio sta. exec.; b. York County, Pa., Oct. 17, 1932; d. Clayton Samuel and Priscilla Margaret (Deller) Grove; asso. in bus. adminstrn. Luzerne County Community Coll., 1981; married; 1 son, Michael Lee. Artist, Guy Hobbs, Inc., Dallastown, Pa., 1949-57; with Sta. WGCB-AM-FM, Red Lion, Pa., 1957-59; co-owner Sta. WBYO-FM, Boyertown, Pa., 1959-67; comptroller Sta. WNAK, Nanticoke, Pa., 1967—, sta. mgr., 1972—; co-owner, sec.-treas. Seven-Thirty Broadcasters, Inc., 1967—. Mem. Nat. Assn. Broadcasters, Pa. Assn. Broadcasters, Radio Advt. Bur., Am. Women in Radio and TV, Advt. Club Am., Nat. Fedn. Ind. Bus., C. of C. Republican. Office: Sta WNAK 84 S Prospect St Nanticoke PA 18634

SEITZER, MARIANNE LOUISE, real estate broker; b. Ellsworth, Kans., June 3, 1940; d. Louis Anthony and Wilma Ann (Novak) Hirt; B.S., Kans. State U., 1962; m. Robert James Seitzer, Aug. 24, 1964; children—Joan Elizabeth, John David. Supr. new product devel. consumer service center Pillsbury Co., Mpls., 1962-65; dir. consumer services Milgram Food Stores and Meyer Dairy, Kansas City, Mo., 1970-75; dir. consumer affairs Colonial Stores, Inc., Atlanta, 1975-77; realtor asso. Kroh Bros. Realty, Overland Park, Kans., 1977-78; broker, sales asso. Re/Max Overland Park Real Estate, Inc. (Kans.), 1978—. Mem. Nat. Assn. Realtors, Kans. Assn. Realtors, Johnson County Bd. Realtors. Home: 9124 Grandview Overland Park KS 66212 Office: 7399 W 97th Overland Park KS 66212

SEIZ, ALICE JEAN, oil co. ofcl.; b. New Brunswick, N.J., Jan. 8, 1954; B.A., Rutgers U., 1976, M.B.A., 1980. Sr. office adminstr. Siemens Corp., Union, N.J., 1976-78; tng. analyst Equitable Life, N.Y.C., 1978-79; mktg. analyst Exxon Co. U.S.A., Dallas, 1980-81, store supr., 1982—. Mem. Assn. M.B.A. Execs., Nat. Assn. Female Execs. Office: Exxon Company USA Western Region Mktg Prestonwood Tower Dallas TX 75240

SELAME, ELINOR, graphic design co. exec.; b. Bklyn., Feb. 25, 1936; d. David and Nettie (Husney) Leventer; student Bklyn. Coll., 1952-54, Boston U., 1965, Harvard U., 1966, Boston Coll., 1967; m. Joseph Selame, June 27, 1953; children—Theodore, Robert, Nadine. With Selame Design Group, Newton Lower Falls, Mass., 1967—, v.p., 1974-80, pres., 1981—; lectr. in field. Pres. Newton Arts Center, 1981-82. Recipient Am. Inst. Graphic Arts Learning Materials Award, 1972. Mem. Smaller Bus. Assn. New England (dir. 1970-72, chmn. speakers bur. 1977), Am. Mktg. Assn., Nat. Speakers Assn., Sales and Mktg. Execs., New England Bus. Owners. Author: So We Spin, 1970; Developing a Corporate Identity: How to Stand Out in the Crowd, 1975; Packaging Power, 1982; contbr. articles in field. Office: 2330 Washington St Newton Lower Falls MA 02162

SELANDER, CAROLYN WHITESIDE, Democratic nat. committeewoman, organist; b. Houston, Oct. 7, 1938; d. Hugh Langhorne and Josie May (Downs) Whiteside; student Southwestern U., Georgetown, Tex., 1956-58; B.A., Boise (Idaho) State U., 1976; m. Glenn Edward Selander, Aug. 30, 1958; children—James Timothy, Andrew Christopher. Organist, Whitney United Methodist Ch., Boise, 1968—, also bd. mem.; pvt. piano tchr., 1973-77; substitute tchr. Boise High Schs., 1976-82; Democratic nat. committeewoman for Idaho, 1972—. Cochmn. Gov. Evans Dinner, 1977; mem. exec. com. Idaho Dem. Party, 1972—, chmn. affirmative action com., 1979-80; mem. rules com. Dem. Nat. Conv., 1972; mem. nat. jud. council Dem. Party, 1977-81; bd. dirs. North End Neighborhood Assn., 1977-79. Danforth asso. Boise State U., 1972—. Mem. Idaho Polit. Sci. Assn. Home: 1814 N 8th St Boise ID 83702

SELANDER, LORRAINE FYDA, univ. ofcl.; b. Chgo., July 2, 1927; d. Michael F. and Marie T. (Ziemba) Fyda; B.A., U. Ill., 1967, M.S., 1976, postgrad., 1981—; m. Richard B. Selander, Nov. 4, 1960; children—John Michael, Donna Marie, Timothy Charles, Steven Richard. Sec., audit and tax dept. Purity Bakeries Corp., Chgo., 1944-48; sec. budget dept. Internat. Mineral & Chem. Corp., Chgo., 1948-50; sec. dept. vocat. agrl. U. Ill., Urbana, 1950-52, sec. dept. entomology, 1957-60, sec. Inst. Communications Research, 1969-75, asst. to head, dept. sociology, 1975-80, asst. to dir. Coordinated Sci. Lab., 1980—. Treas., Central Ill. Opera Theatre Guild, 1980—. NSF fellow, 1966-67. Mem. Soc. Research Adminstrs., Phi Beta Kappa, Phi Kappa Phi. Office: University of Illinois Coordinated Science Lab 1101 W Springfield Ave Urbana IL 61801

SELBY, CECILY CANNAN, educator, scientist, exec.; b. London, Feb. 4, 1927; d. Keith and Catherine Anne Cannan; A.B. cum laude, Radcliffe Coll., 1946; Ph.D. in Phys. Biology, M.I.T., 1950; m. Henry M. Selby, Aug. 11, 1951 (div. 1978); children—Norman, William, Russell; m. 2d., James Stacy Coles, Feb. 21, 1981. Teaching asst. in biology M.I.T., 1948-49; adminstrv. head virus study sect. Sloan-Kettering Inst., N.Y.C., 1949-50, asst. mem. instr., 1950-55; research asso. Sloan-Kettering div. Cornell U. Med. Coll., N.Y.C., 1953-55, also instr. microscopic anatomy, 1955-57; tchr. sci. Lenox Sch., N.Y.C., 1957-58, headmistress, 1959-72; nat. exec. dir. Girl Scouts U.S.A., N.Y.C., 1972-75; acad. dean N.C. Sch. Sci. and Math., Durham, 1980-81; chmn. bd. advs., 1981—; adv. com. Simmons Coll. Grad. Mgmt. Program, 1977-80; mem. Com. for Corp. Support of Pvt. Univs., 1977—; cons. U.S. Dept. Commerce, 1976-77; dir. Avon Products Inc., RCA, NBC, Loehmanns Inc., 1978—; pres. Am. Energy Ind. Founder, chmn. N.Y. Ind. Schs. Opportunity Project, 1968-72; trustee M.I.T., Bklyn. Law Sch., Radcliffe Coll.; mem. corp. Woods Hole Oceanographic Inst., 1981—; mem. council Rockefeller U., 1982—; co-chmn. commn. Nat. Sci. Bd., 1982—. Mem. Headmistresses of East (hon. mem.; pres. 1970-72), Cum Laude Soc. (past chpt. pres., dist. regent), Sigma Xi. Contbr. articles to profl. jours., chpt. to book. Clubs: Cosmopolitan

(N.Y.C.); Women's Forum N.Y. Home and Office: 45 Sutton Pl S New York NY 10022

SELDNER, BETTY JANE, mfg. co. exec.; b. Balt., Dec. 11, 1925; d. David D. and Miriam M. (Mendes) Miller; B.A., Calif. State U., Northridge, 1975, M.A., 1976; m. Alvin A. Seldner, Nov. 15, 1965; children—Jack Seldner, Pat Gray Brown, Barbara Seldner Noone, Deborah Gray Weitzberg. Dir. edn. United Way of Los Angeles County, 1960-66; dir. pub. relations and fin. San Fernando Valley council Girl Scouts U.S.A., Reseda, Calif., 1966-73; asst. dir. pub. affairs Calif. State U., Northridge, 1973-75; dir. performance improvement programs and energy mgmt. hydraulic research Textron Corp., Valenica, Calif., 1975—. Mem. Nat. Assn. Suggestions Systems (pres. So. Calif. chpt.), Nat. Mgmt. Assn., Valley Press Club, Aerospace Writers Assn., Pub. Info. Radio & TV Ednl. Soc., Pub. Relations Soc. Am. (accredited), Energy Mgrs. Soc. Republican. Jewish. Home: 21434 Peggy Joyce Ln Saugus CA 91350 Office: 25200 W Rye Canyon St Valencia CA 91355

SELIG, MARTHA KEISER, social work cons.; b. N.Y.C., Dec. 25, 1912; d. Jacob H. and Sadie (Hammer) Keiser; B.A., Hunter Coll., N.Y.C., 1932; M.S., CCNY, 1933; postgrad. Columbia U., 1933-38; diploma N.Y. Sch. Social Work, 1939; m. Kalman Selig, Mar. 23, 1935; children—Judith Selig Rubenstein, Elaine Selig Gould. Clin. psychologist Edn. Clinic, CCNY, 1932-44; exec. dir. Jewish Community Services L.I., 1944-46; exec. dir. community services Fedn. Jewish Philanthropies N.Y., 1946-74; vis. prof. Adelphia U., Garden City, N.Y., also Jewish Theol. Sem., N.Y.C., 1974—; cons. health and welfare agys. and founds., 1974—; guest lectr. Columbia U., Wurzweiler Sch. Social Work, Hunter Coll. Sch. Social Work; exec. bd. Am. Jewish Com.; bd. dirs. Council Vol. Child Care Agys. N.Y.C., Henry Kaufman Campgrounds, Hebrew Arts Sch., Nat. Found. for Jewish Culture; mem. Mayor's Commn. on Child Care, N.Y. State Adv. Commn. on Welfare. Recipient Naomi Lehman Meml. award, 1960, Samuel W. and Rose Hurowitz award Fedn. Jewish Philanthropies N.Y., 1975; named to Hunter Coll. Hall of Fame, 1976; hon. mem. psychol. assn., also ednl. assn. CCNY. Mem. Nat. Assn. Social Workers, Acad. Cert. Social Workers, Nat. Conf. Jewish Communal Service (past pres.). Author papers in field. Home: 22 E 88th St New York NY 10028 Office: 120 W 57th St New York NY 10019

SELINE-SAPER, SHARON, dept. store exec.; b. Houston, Nov. 14, 1952; d. Ross Stuart and Deloras Anita (Lewis) Seline; B.A. in Journalism, U. Okla., 1973, postgrad., 1974; m. A.J. Saper, Sept. 2, 1979. Buyer/mgr. Rose Jewelers, Norman, Okla., 1973-74; buyer/mgr. fine jewelry Federated Dept. Stores, Houston, 1974-79; fine jewelry buyer/mgr. Marshall Field & Co., Houston, 1979—; jewelry wardrobe cons. to profl. women, 1979—. Dir. charity cookoffs Braeswood Assn., 1979-80; bd. dirs. Braes Village Civic Club, 1980—; active O.R.T., 1980—. Jewish. Office: Marshall Field & Co PO Box 20826 Houston TX 77025

SELK, ELEANOR HUTTON, artist; b. Duboise, Nebr., Oct. 21, 1918; d. Anderson Henry and Florence (Young) Hutton; R.N., St. Elizabeth Hosp., Lincoln, Nebr., 1938; m. Harold Frederick Selk, Aug. 3, 1940; children—Honey Lou, Katherine Florence. Nurse, Lincoln, 1938-40, Denver, 1940-50; owner, mgr. The Pen Point, graphic art studio, Colorado Springs, 1974—; one-woman shows: Colo. Coll., 1970, 72, Nazarene Bible Coll., 1973, 1st Meth. Ch., 1971 (all Colorado Springs); exhibited in group shows: U. So. Colo., 1969, 70, 71, 72, Colorado Springs Art Guild, 1969-72, Pike's Peak Artists Assn., 1969-73, Mozart Art Festival, Pueblo, Colo., 1969-74, numerous others; represented in permanent collection U.S. Postal Service, Pen-Arts Bldg., Washington Rec. sec. Colo. chpt. Medic Alert Found. Internat., 1980-81, chairperson El Paso County and Colorado Springs chpt., 1980-82. Recipient 3d pl. award Nat. Tb and Respiratory Disease and Christmas Seal Art Competition, 1969, finalist award Benedictine Art competition Hanover Trust Bank, N.Y.C., 1970, plaque Medic Alert Found. Internat., 1980. Mem. Nat. League Am. Pen Women (rec. sec. 1972-74; travelling art slide collection 1974—). Contbr. med. articles, short stories, poetry to newspapers. Home: 518 Warren Ave Colorado Springs CO 80906 Office: 333 N Tejon St Agora Mall Colorado Springs CO 80903

SELKREGG, LIDIA LIPPI, geologist, mcpl. ofcl.; b. Florence, Italy, July 24, 1920; came to U.S., 1947, naturalized, 1951; d. Otello and Ida (Chiasserini) Lippi; B.S., Sci. Licee, Tunis, Tunisia, 1938; Dr. Natural Sci., U. Florence, 1942; m. Frederick Mills Selkregg, Sept. 15, 1945; children—Alicia L. (Mrs. R.E. Iden), Sheila (Mrs. J.E. O'Malley), Leif L. Geologist, Ill. State Geol. Survey, Urbana, 1952-58; geologist, engr. U.S. Army C.E., Anchorage, 1959-61; capital improvement coordinator City of Anchorage, 1968-70; planning officer Fed. Field Com. Devel. and Planning, Alaska, 1970-71; sr. scientist Arctic Environ. Info. and Data Center, U. Alaska, 1970-77, prof. resource econs. and planning, 1977—; founder, dir. Alaska Home Fed. Loan Assn. Mem. Greater Anchorage Area Borough Planning and Zoning Commn., 1965-75; mem. Alaska Growth Policy Council, Office of Gov., 1975-80; sci. com. Outer Continental Shelf adv. bd. Dept. Interior, 1979-81; mem. Alaska Coastal Zone Mgmt. Council, 1977—; mem. Anchorage Mcpl. Assembly, 1975—; adv. com. White House Conf. Balanced Nat. Growth and Econ. Devel., 1977-78. Recipient Spl. Achievement award for superior performance Dept. Commerce, 1970; lic. geologist, Alaska; cert. profl. geologist Am. Inst. Profl. Geologists. Mem. Alaska Planning Assn. (pres. 1974), Geol. Soc. Am., Alaska Press Club, AAAS, NEA-Alaska United Teaching Profession, Sigma Xi, Nat. Fedn. Bus. and Profl. Women's Clubs, NAACP. Democrat. Unitarian. Club: Anchorage Dem. Author: (with others) Urban Planning and the Reconstruction-Human Ecology vol. The Great Alaska Earthquake of 1964, 1972; Alaska Regional Profiles, 6 vols., 1974-77; editor: Environmental Atlas of Greater Anchorage Area Borough, 1972. Home: 5811 Radcliffe Dr Anchorage AK 99504 Office: University of Alaska 3210 Providence Dr Anchorage AK 99508

SELLENRAAD, JULIA LILLA PIPPIN, graphometrist, ednl. adminstr.; b. Tulsa, Apr. 15, 1934; d. Frank Johnson and Anne Ozelle (Weems) Pippin; student Phillips U., 1951-53, U. Mo., 1954; Mus.B., So. Meth. U., 1956; postgrad U. Kans., 1957, Calif. State U., Hayward, 1970, Chabot Coll., 1975; Ph.D. in Psychology, Columbia Pacific U., 1978; m. Carel Sellenraad, Mar. 1, 1958; children—Laura Susanne, Paul Frederik Johan, Jennifer Anne. Tchr. music, Corinth Sch., Leawood, Kans., 1956-58; sec. Midwest Research Inst., Kansas City, Mo., 1960; tchr. Headstart, Stanton Sch., Castro Valley, Calif., 1968, tchr. kindergarten, 1968-69; mem. staff Family Service Agy. Alameda County, 1969-70; pvt. instr. piano and voice, Castro Valley, 1968-75; advocate Mental Health Assn., Alameda County, 1975-76; co-founder San Francisco Acad. Handwriting Analysis (now Acad. Psychol. Testing), 1976, dir. edn., 1976—. Mem. Assn. Profl. Graphometrists (v.p.), AAUW, Women Entrepreneurs, Gamma Phi Beta. Author: (with C.A. Stahl) Graphometry I-The Pictorial Aspects of Handwriting, 1976, Graphometry Survey-Graphometry Basics for Classroom Instruction, 1977, Graphometry II and III-Formations and Word Shapes: Mental Functions as Expressed in Handwriting; Graphometry IV-The Structure of Personality, 1978; Graphometry V-Theory of Handwriting, 1979; Graphometry VI-Advanced Stroke Analysis; contbr. articles to profl. jours.; editor, co-publisher The Profl. Handwriting Analyst, quar. forum Assn. Profl. Graphometrists, 1977—. Office: 760 Market St Suite 315 San Francisco CA 94102

SELLERS, CAROL, lawyer; b. Durham, N.C., Mar. 2, 1943; d. George Grover and Mae (Savage) S.; B.A., Duke U., 1964; J.D. cum laude, Whittier Sch. Law, 1976; m. James K. Herbert, Nov. 13, 1980; children—John, Kathie, Paul, Barry. Tchr. high sch. English, Heber, Utah, 1964-67; founder, exec. dir. Fremont Scholastic Inst., Salt Lake City, 1967-71; adminstr., Office of the Dean Whittier Sch. Law, Los Angeles, 1973-76; admitted to Calif. bar, 1976; asso. firm Katz, Granof, Palarz, Beverly Hills, Calif., 1976-78; dir. Western div. Harcourt Brace Jovanovich Legal and Profl. Publs., 1977-81, pres., exec. dir. Harcourt Brace Jovanovich Multistate Workshop, 1981—; dean San Joaquin Coll. Law, 1982—; lectr. women in legal and bus. professions, Calif. Angier B. Duke scholar, 1961-64; Beverly Rubens Gordon scholar, 1972-76. Mem. Beverly Hills Bar Assn., Fresno County Bar Assn. Assn. Women and Law Com. (1st chmn. 1977), Am. Bar Assn. Home: 4412 N Wilson St Fresno CA 93704 Office: 11801 W Olympic St #7 Los Angeles CA 93704

SELLERS, JEANNE ALBERT, word processing services co. exec.; b. N.Y.C., Sept. 27, 1933; d. David and Sarah (Fried) Albert; B.A., CCNY, 1956; children—Naomi Jamie, Jacob Arthur, III. Asst. to pres. AMA, N.Y.C., 1956-60; bus. mgr. Atlanta Profl. Services, 1966-71; pres. M.L.&M. Services, Inc., Atlanta, 1972—, also dir. Mem. Nat. Assn. Female Execs., U.S. C. of C., Women's C. of C. Republican. Mem. Unity Ch. Club: Atlanta Commerce. Author articles in field. Home: 15 Iron Bound Pl NW Atlanta GA 30318 Office: 1938 Peachtree Rd NW Atlanta GA 30309

SELLERS, MARJORIE SCOTT, librarian; b. Decatur, Ala., Apr. 18, 1925; d. Clyde R. and Eula W. (Lewis) Scott; student Kansas City Met. Jr. Coll., Park Coll.; m. Leonard S. Sellers, Nov. 25, 1943; children—Carol, Steve, Mark. Substitute and library asst. Oak Park Sr. High Sch., North Kansas City, Mo., 1968-71; periodicals bank coordinator Kansas City Regional Council for Higher Edn., 1971-74; co-founder, dir. Mid-Am. inter-library services, interlibrary loans librarian Park Coll., Parkville, Mo., 1974-81; founder Access to Info. Services Assos., 1981—; owner, operator Bell Rd. Barn Book, rare and out-of-print books, 1981—; mem. N. Central Evaluation Com. Mem. ALA, Mo. Library Assn., Kans. Library Assn., Mo. Assn. Coll. and Research Libraries, Mountain Plains Library Assn., Am. Assn. for Higher Edn., Oral History Assn., Kansas City Women's C. of C. Methodist. Editor: The Loaner newsletter, 1974-80, Mid Am. Shelflist newsletter, 1981—. Office: PO Box 12265 Parkville MO 64152

SELLERS, PEGGY JEAN, telephone co. exec.; b. Round Hill, Va., Nov. 11, 1932; d. Earl Franklin and Elsie May (Creamer) Cooper; A.A. in Bus. Mgmt., LaSalle Extension U., 1981; m. Gerald Lynn Sellers, Nov. 3, 1951; children—Brian Lynn, Renda Kay, Darwin Alan. With Chesapeake and Potomac Telephone Co. Md., 1949—, sales/adminstrv. mgr., 1974-78, staff mgr. tng. and devel., personnel, 1978—; chmn. Community Relations Team, Balt. Mem. Am. Legion Ladies Aux. (v.p.). Republican. Episcopalian. Home: 7316 Carl Ave Sykesville MD 21784 Office: 930 H St NW Washington DC 20001

SELLERS-MEANS, REGINA TERESA, educator; b. Pitts., Oct. 15, 1934; d. Herman Anthony and Gertrude Anne (Engel) Schwartz; A.A., San Antonio Jr. Coll., 1970; B.A., Incarnate Word Coll., 1973; postgrad. Our Lady of the Lake U., 1976, U. Sci. and Philosophy, 1976; m. Steven P. Means; children—John, Larry, Jerry, Joni, Jesse. Staff, Alcoholic Rehab. Center, San Antonio, 1972-73, San Antonio Children's Center, 1978; tchr. adutl edn. San Antonio Jr. Coll., 1976—; cons. to nursing homes, San Antonio, 1976—; pvt. practice clin. social work and hypnosis, San Antonio, 1976—. Served with USN, 1953-54. Recipient Better Life award in Edn., Tex. Nursing Home Assn., 1976; Public Welfare Dept. grantee, 1974-76. Mem. Acad. Cert. Social Workers, Nat. Assn. Social Workers, Tex. Psychotherapy Assn. Contbr. articles to profl. jours. Address: 427 Byrnes Dr San Antonio TX 78209

SELSAM, MILICENT ELLIS (MRS. HOWARD SELSAM), author; b. Bklyn.; d. Israel and Ida (Abrams) Ellis; B.A., Bklyn. Coll., 1932; M.A., Columbia U., 1934; m. Howard Selsam, Sept. 1, 1936; 1 son, Robert. Recipient Eva L. Gordon award, Am. Nature Study Soc., 1964; Four-Leaf Clover award Lucky Book Club, 1973; non-fiction award Washington Children's Book Guild, 1978. Mem. Am. Nature Study Soc., Authors Guild. Author, editor numerous books, including editor Stars, Mosquitoes and Crocodiles, The American Travels of Alexander von Humboldt (Gold Medal award Boys Club Am. 1962), 1962; Lets Get Turtles, 1965; (with J. Bronowski) Biography of an Atom, 1965 (Thomas A. Edison award 1965); Animals as Parents, 1965; Benny's Animals and How He Put Them In Order (Boys Club Am. jr. book award), 1966; How to be a Nature Detective, 1966; When An Animal Grows, 1966; Bug That Laid the Golden Eggs, 1967; How Animals Tell Time, 1967; Milkweed, 1967; Questions and Answers About Ants, 1967; Maple Tree, 1968; The Tiger, 1969; Peanut, 1969; Hidden Animals, 1969; The Tomato and Other Fruit Vegetables, 1970; Egg to Chick, 1970; The Carrot and Other Root Vegetables, 1971; Vegetables from Stems and Leaves, 1972; More Potatoes, 1972; How Puppies Grow, 1972; Is This a Baby Dinosaur, 1972; A First Look at Leaves, 1972; A First Look at Fish, 1972; A First Look at Mammals, 1973; The Apple and Other Fruits, 1973; Questions and Answers about Horses, 1973; A First Look at Birds, 1974; Bulbs, Corms and Such, 1974; A First Look at Insects, 1975; A First Look at Snakes, Lizards and Other Reptiles, 1975; Harlequin Mother, 1975; How Kittens Grow, 1975; Animals of the Sea, 1975; A First Look at Frogs, Toads and Salamanders, 1976; Popcorn, 1976; A First Look at Animals Without Backbones, 1976; The Amazing Dandelion, 1977; A First Look at Flowers, 1977; Land of the Giant Tortoise, 1977; Up, Down and Around, 1977; Sea Monsters of Long Ago, 1978; (with Deborah Peterson) Don't Throw It, Grow It, 1977; A First Look at the World of Plants, 1978; Tyrranosaurus Rex, 1978; A First Look at the Animals with Backbones, 1978; Mimosa—The Sensitive Plant, 1978; A First Look at Monkeys and Apes, 1979; A First Look at Sharks, 1979; How Animals Live Together, rev. edit., 1979; Night Animals, 1979; A First Look at Whales, 1980; A First Look at Cats, 1981; A First Look at Dogs, 1981; A First Look at Horses, 1981; The Plants We Eat, 1981; juvenile sci. editor Walker & Co. Pubs. Home: 100 W 94th St New York NY 10025 Office: 720 Fifth Ave New York NY 10019

SELTZ, NANCY CLOSSON, univ. adminstr.; b. Logansport, Ind., July 3, 1931; d. Dwight E. and Ruth (Richards) Closson; B.A., Denison U., 1953; B.S., Ind. U., 1955; m. Herbert Seltz, Nov. 3, 1954; children—Julia Richards, Catherine Arnold. Dir. Hoosier Courts Pre-Sch., Ind. U., Bloomington, 1955-59; asso. dir. Bur. Public Discussion, 1967-71, dir. continuing edn. for women, 1971-80, dir. resource devel. Sch. Continuing Studies, 1980—, asst. prof. continuing edn., 1975—. Mem. Nat. Univ. Extension Assn. (chmn. women's div., Creative Program award), Adult Edn. Assn., Nat. Assn. Women Deans, Adminstrs. and Counselors, LWV, Ind. Women's Polit. Caucus, Phi Delta Kappa. Author: Meeting the Educational and Occupational Planning Needs of Adults, 1976; Understanding the Multiple Responsibilities of Working Women, 1979; Adult Learning Services, 1979. Office: Ind U Sch Continuing Studies Bloomington IN 47405

SELTZER, RONNI LEE, physician; b. N.Y.C., Apr. 24, 1952; d. Herbert Melvin and Marian Elaine (Willinger) S.; B.A., Syracuse U., 1973; M.D., Chgo. Med. Sch., 1977; m. Gary Broder, Jan. 20, 1980. Resident in psychiatry N.Y.U. Med. Center, Bellevue Hosp., 1977-81; pvt. practice medicine specializing in psychiatry, Englewood, N.J., 1981—; mem. med. staff Englewood Hosp., 1981—; teaching asst. in psychiatry N.Y.U. Med. Center, 1980—. Mem. Am. Psychiat. Assn., N.J. Psychiat. Assn., Eastern Psychiat. Research Assn., AMA, Bergen County Med. Soc., Am. Med. Women's Assn., North Jersey Psychiat. Assn., Chgo. Med. Sch. Alumni Assn. Home: 245 E 63d St New York NY 10021 Office: 200 Engle St Englewood NJ 07631

SELZ, HARRIET MARION, plastics co. exec.; b. N.Y.C., Jan. 23, 1939; d. Phillip Charles and Muriel (Greenbaum) Gold; student Oneonta State Coll., 1956-58, Bloomfield Coll., 1975-78; m. Jay Selz, Oct. 20, 1957; children—Philip Charles, Bart Michael, Mark Lawrence, Pamela Carol. With Titan Plastics, Inc., East Rutherford, N.J., 1968—, prodn. mgr., 1974-75, purchasing mgr., 1975-79, asst. gen. mgr., 1979—, v.p., 1981—. Mem. legis. com. Montville (N.J.) Bd. Edn. Mem. Soc. Plastics Engrs. (voting rep. to blow molding div. of Soc. of Plastics Industry), Hadassah, Women's Am. Orgn. for Rehab. and Tng. Home: 142 Change Bridge Rd Montville NJ 07045 Office: 433 Murray Hill Pkwy East Rutherford NJ 07073

SEMEGEN, DARIA WOLODYMYRA, composer; b. Bamberg, W. Ger., June 27, 1946; came to U.S., 1951, naturalized, 1958; d. Wolodymyr and Olga (Solocha) S.; Mus.B., Eastman Sch. Music, Rochester, N.Y., 1968; Fulbright vis. scholar, Warsaw (Poland) Conservatory Music, 1968-69; Mus.M., Yale U., 1971; postgrad. Columbia U., 1971-76. Instr., adminstr. Columbia-Princeton Electronic Music Center, 1971-75; sound engr. Columbia U. World Music Collection, 1971-73; asst. prof. to asso. prof., asso. dir. electronic music studios SUNY, Stony Brook, 1974—; nat. adv. bd. 1st conf. on women in music Columbia U.; composer: Lieder auf der Flucht, 1967, Dans la Nuit, 1969, Jeux des Quatres, 1970, Electronic Composition 1, 1971, Electronic Composition 2, 1979, Music for Viola and Tape, 1982, others; rec. on Odyssey, Finnadar, Opus One, CRI records. Recipient prize Internat. Electronic Music Competition, 1975; grantee Nat. Endowment Arts, 1974, 78, 80, 81, SUNY 1979, 80. Mem. Am. Women Composers (nat. adv. electronic music), Broadcast Music Inc. (award 1967, 69), League Women Composers, Internat. Audio Engring. Soc., Am. Soc. Univ. Composers, Coll. Music Soc., Am. Composers Alliance, Mu Phi Epsilon. Office: Dept Music SUNY Stony Brook NY 11794

SEMEL, ELEANOR MESSING MINTZ, speech pathologist, educator; b. N.Y.C., Apr. 10, 1930; B.S., N.Y. U., 1950, M.A., 1953; Ed.D., Boston U., 1973. Speech and lang. pathologist Bellevue Hosp., N.Y.C., 1948-50; dir. speech, hearing and lang. clinic St. Vincent's Hosp., N.Y.C., 1950-52; asst. prof. speech L.I. U., 1952-54; asst. prof. N.J. State Coll., 1954-60; asst. prof. So. Conn. State Coll., 1965-69; asso. prof. speech pathology and audiology dept. Sargent Coll. Allied Health Professions, Boston U., 1973—, mem. faculty Sch. Edn., 1969-73. Mem. Am. Speech and Hearing Assn., Council Exceptional Children, Orton Soc., Assn. Children with Learning Disabilities. Author: Sound-Order Sense: A Developmental Program in Auditory Perception, 1970; Language Disabilities in Children and Adolescents, 1976; Semel Auditory Processing Program, 1978; Language Assessment and Intervention for Learning Disabled, 1980; co-author: Clinical Evaluation of Language Functions, 1980; contbr. articles to profl. jours. Office: Dept Speech Pathology and Audiology Boston U Boston MA 02215

SEMERJIAN, MADELLE LYONS HEGELER, art broker; b. Danville, Ill.; d. Edward C. and Madelle (Lyons) Hegeler; student Northwestern U., 1948; B.A., Vassar Coll., 1952; M.A., Sorbonne, Paris, 1954; postgrad. Ecole du Louvre, Paris, 1955; m. Luigi A. Grassi, Nov. 29, 1962 (div. Oct., 1969); children—Cornelia Maria, Giovanna Camilla; m. 2d, George G. Semerjian, Feb. 19, 1977. Dir. public relations, saleswoman French & Co., N.Y.C., 1956-58, fgn. rep., 1959-60; self-employed art broker, Paris, N.Y.C., 1960—; pres. Meadowmere Interiors & Gallery, Southampton, N.Y. Bd. dirs. Southampton Village Improvement Assn., Stonybrook Found. Mem. Southampton Rose Soc. (pres.), DAR, Delta Delta Delta. Republican. Episcopalian. Home: Brigadune Gin Ln PO Box 214 Southampton NY 11968 also 35 E 76th St New York NY 10021 also 1 Bis Rue Buenos Aires Paris 7 France Office: 25 Main st Southampton NY 11968

SEMINARA, ELEANOR FRANCES, coll. adminstr.; b. Bklyn., Mar. 14, 1931; d. Luigi and Vincenzia (De Stefano) Seminara; B.S., Montevallo U., 1952; M.S., Columbia U., 1958; postgrad. So. Ill. U., 1976-80. Tech. librarian Olin Mathieson Chem. Corp., Niagara Falls, N.Y., 1958-60, Thiokol Chem. Corp., Huntsville, Ala., 1960-61; librarian Niagara Falls public schs., 1961-63; dir. Library Learning Center, Niagara County Community Coll., 1963—; cons. in field. HEW grantee, 1968-69; Delta Kappa Gamma fellow, 1975-76. Mem. ALA, Nat. Assn. Ednl. Broadcasters, Assn. Ednl. Communications and Tech., Nat. Assn. Female Execs., Internat. Platform Assn., Delta Kappa Gamma, Pi Lambda Theta, Phi Delta Kappa. Republican. Roman Catholic. Club: Quota. Contbr. articles to profl. jours. Home: 5105 Dana Dr Lewiston NY 14092 Office: Niagara County Community Coll Library Learning Center Sanborn NY 14132

SEMPLE, MARLENE COCKER, journalist; b. Sarasota, Fla., Feb. 10, 1932; d. Oswald McKellar and Mary (Branch) Cocker; student U. Miami, Fla., 1950-53; B.A., George Washington U., 1958; M.Ed., Loyola U., Chgo., 1983; m. William R. Cotton, Sept. 4, 1954; children—William R., David M., Lynn C.; m. 2d, Dale D. Semple, May 19, 1973. Reporter, Washington Post, 1964-67; editor Croft Ednl. Services, New London, Conn., 1967-69; sr. editor Follett Ednl. Corp., Chgo., 1969-70; ptnr. Other Words Writing and Editing Service, Chgo., 1971-75; editor Sci. Research Assocs., Chgo., 1975-78, text mktg. coordinator, 1979-81, project editor test devel., 1981-82, project adminstr., 1982—. Mem. Chgo. Women in Pub. (pres. 1976), Am. Ednl. Research Assn., Nat. Council Measurement in Edn. Club: Chgo. Press. Author: Introductory Guide to Midwest Antiques, 1976. Office: 155 N Wacker Dr Chicago IL 60606

SEMPLE, MARY ANGELA, pub. co. exec.; b. N.Y.C.; d. Henry Gordon and Mary Agnes (Flanagan) S.; A.B. in French, Coll. New Rochelle, 1961; cert. lang. study Laval U., Que., 1960. Asst. personnel mgr. Sci. Am., N.Y.C., 1965-70; personnel mgr. Psychol. Corp. subs. Harcourt, Brace, Jovanovich, N.Y.C., 1970-74; v.p., dir. of personnel Scribner Book Cos., N.Y.C., 1974—; lectr., cons. U. Denver Publ. Inst., 1978—. Mem. N.Y. Personnel Mgmt. Assn. (dir. 1982—), Assn. Am. Publs. (trustee ins. com. 1978—). Club: N.Y. Jr. League. Home: 1365 York Ave New York NY 10021 Office: 597 Fifth Ave New York NY 10017

SENECHAL, MARJORIE LEE, educator; b. St. Louis, July 18, 1939; d. Abraham and Ada Faye (Fischer) Wikler; B.S., U. Chgo., 1960; M.S., Ill. Inst. Tech., 1962, Ph.D., 1965; m. Lester John Senechal, May 31, 1963; children—Diana, Jennifer. Lectr. math. dept. Smith Coll., 1966-67, asst. prof., 1967-73, asso. prof., 1973-78, prof., 1978—; vis. guest researcher U. Groningen (Netherlands); exchange scientist Acad. Scis. USSR, 1978-79; mem. adv. com. on USSR and Eastern Europe Nat. Acad. Scis., 1982. Recipient Carl B. Allendoerfer award Math. Assn. Am., 1982. Mem. Am. Math. Soc., Sigma Xi. Editor: (with G. Fleck) Patterns of Symmetry, 1977; Structures of Matter and Patterns in Science, 1980. Office: Smith Coll Northampton MA 01063

SENG, MINNIE ANNA, librarian, editor; b. Muskegon, Mich., Nov. 30, 1909; d. Edward and Ella Barbara (Pattie) Seng; student Muskegon Community Coll., 1927-29; A.B., U. Mich., 1932, A.B. in Library Sci., 1935, M.A. in Library Sci., 1943. Asst. med. librarian U. Iowa, 1935-39; cataloger Bay City (Mich.) Pub. Library, 1939-40; order librarian Mich.

Technol. U., Houghton, 1940-42; continuations cataloger U. Ark., 1943-44; head cataloger Calif. State U., Fresno, 1944-59; editor Edn. Index, H.W. Wilson Co., Pubs., Bronx, N.Y., 1959-66; head cataloger St. Ambrose Coll., Davenport, Iowa, 1967-72; periodicals librarian Frostburg (Md.) State Coll., 1972-74; ret., 1974. Mem. AAUW, Smithsonian Assos., Am. Hort. Soc. Republican. Mem. Christian Ch. Home: 110 S Broadway Apt Q Frostburg MD 21532

SENNET, DIANE CAROL, travel agent; b. N.Y.C., Mar. 28, 1948; d. Bernard and Marjorie Jean Sennet; B.A., U. Tenn., 1965-69; student Grace Downs Sch., 1969-70. Supr., Trans World Airlines, N.Y.C., 1970-75; owner, pres. Sennet Service Travel, N.Y.C., 1975—. Recipient awards TWA, Am. Airlines, Eastern Airlines. Mem. Internat. Air Traffic Assn., Air Traffic Conf. Am., Internat. Passenger S.S. Assn., N.Y. Assn. Women Bus. Owners. Office: 34 W 32d St 5th Floor New York NY 10001

SENNHAUSER, SHIRLEY ANN, nurse, educator; b. Los Angeles, Apr. 22, 1942; d. Samuel Edward Hinds and Violet (Manoukian) Lowther; diploma with honors Kings County Hosp. Center, 1968; B.S. summa cum laude in Nursing, Ohio U., 1976; M.S. in Nursing, Boston U., 1978; 1 son, Andrew; Staff nurse obstetrical unit Mt. Sinai Hosp., N.Y.C., 1968-69; nursing cons. Skill Advancement Inc., N.Y.C., 1968-69; staff nurse-cons. Athens (Ohio) Mental Health Center, 1969-70, instr. inservice edn., 1970-72, asst. dir. inservice edn., 1972-73; instr. psychiat. nursing Holzer Med. Center, Gallipolis, Ohio, 1974-77; asst. prof. psychiat. mental health nursing Ohio U., 1978—; diabetes nurse-educator Hocking Tech. Coll., Nelsonville, Ohio, summer 1982; cons. in field. Mem. vestry Ch. of the Good Shepherd, Athens, 1980-82. NIMH trainee, 1977-78; Ohio U. Coll. Health and Human Service grantee, 1980. Mem. Nat. League Nursing, Sigma Theta Tau. Democrat. Episcopalian. Home: 60 Elmwood Pl Athens OH 45701 Office: 312 McCracken Hall Ohio U Athens OH 45701

SENSENICH, ILA JEANNE, lawyer, magistrate; b. Pitts., Mar. 6, 1939; d. Louis E. and Evelyn Margaret (Harbourt) S.; B.A., Westminster Coll., 1961; J.D., Dickinson Sch. Law, 1964. Asso. firm Stewart, Belden, Sensenich and Herrington, Greensburg, Pa., 1964-70; asst. public defender Westmoreland (Pa.) County, 1970-71; U.S. magistrate for Western Dist. Pa., Pitts., 1971—; adj. prof. law Duquesne U., 1982. Mem. Nat. Council U.S. Magistrates (sec. 1979-81, rec. sec. 1981-82), Fed. Bar Assn., Am. Bar Assn., Pa. Bar Assn., Allegheny County Bar Assn., Westmoreland Bar Assn. Contbr. in field. Office: 1026 US Post Office and Courthouse Pittsburgh PA 15219

SENTER, DOROTHY FRANCES, educator, musician; b. Carrolton, Ala., Oct. 14, 1923; d. Samuel Wesley and Gertie Ethel (Smith) Kilpatrick; B.S., Miss. State U., 1950; postgrad. U. Ky., 1965, Southwestern U., Memphis, 1967, U. S. Fla., Ft. Myers, 1975-76; m. Alfred Patrick Senter, Feb. 22, 1942; children—Alfred Patrick, Sandra Camille, Kathy Kilpatrick, Wesley Richard, Al Shane. Tchr., Fulton (Miss.) Public Schs., 1945-71; owner, mgr. Apsco Acctg. Service, 1971-74, The Chalet, 1976-77, Dot's and Pat's Frozen Foods, 1978; office mgr. Tenn-Tom Corp. of Engrs., 1976-77; tchr. voice and piano, 1950-70; tchr. Cypress and Alva middle schs., Ft. Myers, Fla., 1974; dir. Chi Omega Sorority, U. Miss., 1978; tchr. lang. arts Mantachie (Miss.) Sch. System, 1979—; concert recitalist piano and voice; former mem. Memphis Opera Theater. Soloist, Fulton Community Concerts; soloist Meth. Chancel Choir; dir. Meth. Youth Choir, 1949-52; mem. Tupelo Community Concerts. Cert. tchr. in English, elem. edn. and bus. mgmt.; reading specialist. Mem. Nat. Tchrs. Assn., Miss. Tchrs. Assn., Itawamba Tchrs. Assn., Mantachie PTA. Democrat. Methodist. Club: Contract Bridge. Artist, sculptor, designer. Home: Maison de la Coeur Box 365 Route 5 Fulton MS 38843

SENTER, SYLVIA, psychologist; b. N.J., Mar. 3, 1921; d. Samuel and Gertrude (Raphael) Kapralik; Ph.D., Goddard Coll.; m. Jonas Senter, Sept. 30, 1941; children—Leigh Senter Saul, Jill. Intern, Temple U.; dir. Behavior Assos., Greenwich, Conn. Vol., Bellevue Hosp., Univ. Hosp. Author: Women at Work, 1982. Office: 27 Alden Rd Greenwich CT *

SEPE, BARBARA C., speech and lang. pathologist; b. N.Y., Aug. 1, 1936; d. Edward A. and Anne M. (Coleman) Beaver; A.A. cum laude, Nassau Community Coll., 1972; B.A. cum laude, Hofstra U., 1974, M.A., 1976; m. Christopher Sepe, Sept. 15, 1956; children—Patricia Lee, Janice Lynn, Christopher John. Supr. speech and elem. spl. edn. Massapequa (N.Y.) Public Schs., 1974—; pvt. practice speech pathology, Farmingdale, N.Y., 1976—. Lic. speech and lang. pathologist N.Y. State. Mem. L.I. Speech and Lang. Hearing Assn. (pres. 1980-81, 1st v.p. 1979-80, exec. sec. 1976-79), N.Y. State Speech and Hearing Assn., Am. Speech and Hearing Assn. (cert. clin. competency in speech pathology). Address: 92 Woodward Pkwy Farmingdale NY 11735

SEPPALA, KATHERINE SEAMAN (MRS. LESLIE W. SEPPALA), bus. exec., clubwoman, b. Detroit, Aug. 22, 1919; d. Willard D. and Elizabeth (Miller) Seaman; B.A., Wayne State U., 1941; m. Leslie W. Seppala, Aug. 15, 1941; children—Sandra Kay, William Leslie. Mgr. women's bldg. and student activities adviser Wayne State U., 1941-43; pres. Harper Sports Shops, Inc., 1947—; partner Seppala Bldg. Co., 1971—. Mich. service chmn. women grads. Wayne State U., 1962—, 1st v.p., fund bd., active Mich. Assn. Community Health Services, Inc., Girl and Cub Scouts; mem. Citizen's adv. com. on sch. needs Detroit Bd. Edn., 1957—, mem. high sch. study com., 1966—; chmn., mem. loan fund bd. Denby High Sch. Parents Scholarship; bd. dirs., sec. Wayne State U. Fund; precinct del. Rep. Party, 14th dist., 1956—, del. convs. Recipient Ann. Women's Service award Wayne State U., 1963. Recipient Alumni award Wayne State U., 1971. Mem. Intercollegiate Assn. Women Students (regional rep. 1941-45), Women Wayne State U. Alumni (past pres.), Wayne State U. Alumni Assn. (dir., past v.p.), AAUW (dir. past officer), Council Women as Public Policy Makers (editor High lights) Denby Community Ednl. Orgn. (sec.), Met. Detroit Program Planning Inst. (pres.), Internat. Platform Assn., Detroit Met. Book and Author Soc. (treas.), Mortar Bd. (past pres.), Karyatides (past pres.), Anthony Wayne Soc., Alpha Chi Alpha, Alpha Kappa Delta, Delta Gamma Chi, Kappa Delta (chmn. chpt. alumnae adv. bd.). Baptist. Clubs: Zonta (v.p., dir.); Detroit Boat; Les Cheneaux. Home: 22771 Worthington Saint Clair Shores MI 48081 Office: 17157 Harper Detroit MI 48224

SERACUSE, LINDA KAY, archtl. co. ofcl.; b. Denver, Jan. 29, 1945; d. Frebert Otto and Addie Mae (Mosena) Wangerin; B.A. (Boettcher scholar), Colo. Coll., 1966; postgrad. U. Denver; m. Jerome M. Seracuse, May 23, 1981; 1 dau., Jennifer Lyn; children by previous marriage—Todd and Heather Carroll. Tchr. history, co-developer Afro-Am. history studies Denver Public Schs. and S.W. Minn. State Coll., 1968-71; adminstrv. asst. Colo. Commn. Status of Women and Women's Center, 1971-72; pres. Flowers a la Carte, concessionaire nat. airports, 1973-76; community relations dir. Ken-Caryl Ranch Corp., Denver, 1976-77; corp. treas., bus. mgr. Seracuse Lawler & Partners, Inc., Denver, 1977—. Bd. dirs. Chatfield YMCA. Mem. Colo. Hist. Soc., Historic Denver, Nat. Assn. Female Execs., Profl. Services Mgmt. Assn., Phi Beta Kappa. Democrat. Episcopalian. Home: 8105 E Phillips Circle Englewood CO 80112 Office: 730 17th St Suite 714 Denver CO 80202

SERGE-QUIGLEY, GLORIA LOUISE, educator; b. Bklyn., July 19, 1924; d. Anthony and Concetta (Sibilla) Serge; R.N., Kings County Hosp., 1946; B.S., St. John's U., N.Y.C., 1952, M.S., 1961, Ph.D., 1972; m. Walter P. Quigley, Nov. 20, 1954; children—Jean Margaret Quigley-Tully and Elizabeth Ann (twins). Biol. and phys. sci. instr. Bklyn. Hosp., 1951-52, Bklyn. State Hosp., 1952-54; asso. prof. psychology Suffolk County Community Coll., Selden, N.Y., 1972—. Mem. AAUP, Am. Psychol. Assn., Internat. Soc. Psychoneuroendocrinology, St. John's U. Alumni Assn., Disstaff Am. Med. Assn. Home: 136 Monroe Ave Patchogue NY 11772 Office: Suffolk County Community Coll Selden NY 11784

SERKESS, SANDI, counselor, psychologist; b. Boston, July 18, 1952; d. Leonard and Janice (Levinson) Serkess; M.Ed., Boston State Coll., 1977. Pvt. counselor for anorexics and others, Allston, Mass.; public relations writer Am. Geriatric Facilities; free-lance writer; lectr. on Am. history through humor; cons. Polaroid Corp., Productivity Resource Cons.; journalist Last Chance Book Rev.; poet Writer's Corner; stand-up comedienne. Mem. Am. Psychol. Assn., Mass. Psychol. Assn., Internat. Soc. Gen. Semantics, Am. Personnel and Guidance Assn. Author: No Strings Attached: The Lazy Person's Guide to Better Memory and Study Skills. Address: 47 Linden St Apt 15 Allston MA 02134

SERSTOCK, DORIS SHAY, microbiologist, educator; civic worker; b. Mitchell, S.D., June 13, 1926; d. Elmer Howard and Hattie (Christopher) Shay; B.A., Augustana Coll., 1947; postgrad. U. Minn., 1966-67, Duke U., summer 1969, Communicable Disease Center, Atlanta, 1972; m. Ellsworth I. Serstock, Aug. 30, 1952; children—Barbara Anne, Robert Ellsworth, Mark Douglas. Bacteriologist, Civil Service, S.D., Colo., Mo., 1947-52; research bacteriologist U. Minn., 1952-53; clin. bacteriologist Dr. Lufkin's Lab., 1954-55; chief technologist St. Paul Blood Bank of ARC, 1959-65; microbiologist in charge mycology lab. VA Hosp., Mpls., 1968—; instr. Coll. Med. Scis., U. Minn., 1970-79, asst. prof. Coll. Lab. Medicine and Pathology, 1979—. Mem. Richfield Planning Commn., 1965-71, sec., 1968-71. Fellow Augusta Coll.; named to Exec. and Profl. Hall of Fame; recipient Alumni Achievement award Augustana Coll., 1977, Superior Performance award VA Hosp., 1978, 82. Mem. Am. Soc. Microbiology, Minn. Planning Assn. Republican. Lutheran. Clubs: Richfield Women's Garden (pres. 1959), Wild Flower Garden (chmn. 1961). Author articles in field. Home: 7201 Portland Ave Richfield MN 55423 Office: VA Hosp Minneapolis MN 55417

SERTO, MICHELLE JEAN, accountant; b. Kenosha, Wis., Apr. 1, 1949; d. Ferdinand Nathan and Minnie Caroline (Johnson) S.; B.S. magna cum laude, Georgetown U., 1971. Staff acct. Price Waterhouse & Co., Milw., 1971-72; asst. controller, mgr. inventory evaluation Tri-Clover div. Ladish Co., Kenosha, Wis., 1972-74, 75-78; internat. staff acct. Fiat-Allis Corp., Deerfield, Ill., 1974-75; C.P.A., Kenosha, Wis., 1978—. Active Kenosha County council Girl Scouts Am., 1977-79. C.P.A., Wis. Mem. Am. Inst. C.P.A.s, Wis. Inst. C.P.A.s, Racine-Kenosha Estate Planners Council, Nat. Assn. Female Execs. Roman Catholic. Club: Quota (sec. 1981-82). Home: 6623 43d Ave Kenosha WI 53142 Office: 3916 67th St Kenosha WI 53142

SERUGA, SUSAN ANN, chem. engr.; b. Bethlehem, Pa., Feb. 10, 1955; d. Louis and Jeanne Benner (Clause) S.; B.S. in Chem. Engring., Lehigh U., 1977; postgrad. in bus. Lehigh U., 1978-79. Engring. asst. Homer Research Labs., Bethlehem (Pa.) Steel Corp., summer 1976; plant process engr. MPM div. Pfizer, Inc., Easton, Pa., 1977-80; project engr. div. Engring. Scott Paper Co., Phila., 1980—. Mem. Delaware County Assn. Retarded Citizens, 1980-81. Mem. Am. Inst. Chem. Engrs. Democrat. Club: Lehigh U. of Phila. Home: 2402 Aspen Circle Springfield PA 19064 Office: Scott Paper Co Scott Plaza II Philadelphia PA 19113

SESSIONS, JUDITH ANN, librarian; b. Lubbock, Tex., Dec. 16, 1947; d. Earl Alva and Mary (Mayer) S.; B.A. cum laude, Fla. Tech. U., 1970; M.S., Fla. State U., 1971. Asst. librarian, charge public services U. S.C., Spartanburg, 1971-74; head librarian, Salkehatchie campus, Allendale, 1974-77; dir. library and learning resource center Mt. Vernon Coll., Washington, 1977—, asst. prof. children's lit., 1978—; coll. rep. Library Council, Washington Met. Council Govts., 1979-80. Vol., White House Conf. Library and Info. Services, 1979. Fla. fellow, 1970; Mem. ALA (pres. jr. mems. round table 1981-82, councilor-at-large 1982—; Shirley Olafson Meml. award 1978), Library and Info. Tech. Assn. (sec. video and cable communications sect. 1979-81), Freedom to Read Found. (bd. rep. 1978-79), D.C. Library Assn. (sec. 1979-81, v.p., pres.-elect 1981-82). Home: 2100 Foxhall Rd NW Washington DC 20007

SETHALER, ALTA OPAL, electric supply co. exec.; b. Winside, Nebr., May 16, 1917; d. William and Sophia (Dreager) Petersen; student U. Denver, 1936-38, U. Colo., 1938-40; m. K.J. Sethaler, May 14, 1939 (dec.). Sec., bookkeeper Flex Tip Valve Co., Denver, 1936; cashier Comml. Savs. Bank, Sterling, Colo., 1937-40; enrolling clk. Colo. Legislature, 1940; acct. Parker Co., Denver, 1940-43; acctg. asst. Isadore Greenblatt Auditing Firm, Denver, 1943-45; with Central Electric Supply Co., Denver, 1945—, v.p., 1975-76, exec. asst. to chmn. bd., 1977—. Info. clk., asst. Human Services, Travelers Aid, 1977-79; v.p., bd. dirs. Windsor Gardens Assn., 1982 Mem. Nat. Assn. Credit Mgmt. (dir. 1964-65, dir. adv. Rocky Mountain affiliate 1962-68, pres. Nat. Credit Women's Groups 1960-61), Credit Women's Group of Denver (dir. adv. 1962—, pres. 1951-52, Alta Sethaler Scholarship Fund established 1978, award 1979), Woman in Constrn. (charter, com. chmn. 1967-68). Democrat. Lutheran. Clubs: Women's Golf of Windsor Gardens (pres. 1980-81), Park Hill Golf. Home: 625 S Alton Way Denver CO 80231 Office: PO Box 267 500 Quivas St Denver CO 80201

SETON, ANYA, author; b. N.Y.C.; d. Ernest Thompson and Grace (Gallatin) Seton; ed. pvt. tutors in Eng., France, Spence Sch., N.Y.C. Author: My Theodosia, 1941; Dragonwyck, 1944; The Turquoise, 1946; The Hearth and Eagle, 1948; Foxfire, 1950; Katherine, 1954; The Mistletoe and Sword (juvenile), 1955; The Winthrop Woman, 1958; Washington Irving (juvenile), 1960; Devil Water, 1962; Avalon, 1965; Green Darkness, 1973; Smouldering Fires (juvenile), 1975; (all translated into many langs.); also short stories mags. Recipient Medal of Honor, Soc. Colonial Wars, 1958. Mem. League Am. Penwomen, Pen and Brush Club (hon.), P.E.N. Home: Old Greenwich CT 06870

SETSER, CAROLE SUE, food scientist; b. Warrenton, Mo., Aug. 26, 1940; d. Wesley August and Mary Elizabeth (Meine) Schulze; B.S., U. Mo., Columbia, 1962; M.S., Cornell U., 1964; Ph.D., Kans. State U., Manhattan, 1971; m. Donald Wayne Setser, June 2, 1969; children—Bradley Wayne, Kirk Wesley, Brett Donald. Mem. faculty Kans. State U., 1964—, assoc. prof. foods and nutrition, 1981—, asst. to dean Coll. Home Econs., 1966-68. Mem. Inst. Food Technologists, Am. Assn. Cereal Chemists, Am. Meat Sci. Assn., Am. Home Econs. Assn., Common Cause, Sigma Xi, Phi Upsilon Omicron (Founders fellow 1969-70), Omicron Nu, Gamma Sigma Delta. Methodist. Home: 414 Wickham Rd Manhattan KS 66502 Office: Justin Hall Kans State U Manhattan KS 66506

SETTELL, ANGELA LOYOLA, govt. ofcl.; b. New Orleans, Sept. 4, 1944; d. Angel Mina and Carmelite Amelia (Richter) Loyola; B.S., La. State U., 1966; m. Bruce Allen Settell, June 22, 1973; 1 dau., Sommer Hunt. With IRS, 1967—, regional analyst central region, Cin., 1977-79, mgr. internat. examiners and computer audit specialists, 1979—. Mem. Profl. Frat. Assn. (nat. pres. 1981—), Phi Chi Theta (nat. pres. 1974-78; Key award 1966, v.p., trustee found. 1976—), Alpha Xi Delta. Democrat. Roman Catholic. Home: 8656 Totempole Dr Cincinnati OH 45242 Office: 550 Main St PO Box 476 Cincinnati OH 45201

SETTERINGTON, JERI LYNN, credit life ins. co. exec.; b. Lansing, Mich., Oct. 9, 1942; d. Melvin Andrew and Frances Marie (Rockette) Underwood; student Ferris State Coll., 1960-61, Mich. State U., 1963-64; children—Stefanie Lynn, Mark Thomas, Peter Charles. With Redmond Motor Div., Owosso, Mich., 1962-63; personnel asst., 1964-65; trainee Mid-Am. Life Assurance Co., Saginaw, Mich., 1974-77, supr., 1977-78, mgr., asst. sec., 1978-79, adminstrv. v.p. 1979—. Home: 17700 S Sharon Rd Chesaning MI 48616 Office: 4901 Towne Centre Rd Saginaw MI 48604

SETTLE, MARY LEE, author; b. Charleston, W.Va., July 29, 1918; d. Joseph Edward and Rachel (Tompkins) S.; student Sweet Briar Coll., 1936-38; m. William Littleton Tazewell, Sept. 2, 1978; 1 son, Christopher Weathersbee. Asso. prof. Bard Coll., Annandale-on-Hudson, N.Y., 1965-76; vis. lectr. U. Va., 1978, U. Iowa, 1976. Served with Womens Aux., RAF, 1942-43. Recipient Merrill Found. award, 1974, Nat. Book award, 1978. John Simon Guggenheim fellow, 1958, 60. Democrat. Author: The Love Eaters, 1954; The Kiss of Kin, 1955; O Beulah Land, 1956; Know Nothing, 1960; Fight Night on a Sweet Saturday, 1964; All The Brave Promises, 1966; The Clam Shell, 1971; Prisons, 1973; Blood Tie, 1977; The Scapegoat, 1981. Office: care Roberta Pryor Internat Creative Mgmt 40 W 57th St New York NY 10019 *

SETTLEMIRE, BEVERLY MAE, nursing home adminstr.; b. Allen County, Ohio, Jan. 3, 1933; d. Harry Franklin and Margurite (Brothers) Holden; R.N., Lima (Ohio) Meml. Hosp., 1954; B.S. in Nursing Arts, Findlay (Ohio) Coll., 1969; m. Robert Eugene Settlemire, June 11, 1955; children—Edward Eugene, Larry Franklin. Part-time staff nurse Defiance (Ohio) City Hosp., 1958-64, Blanchard Valley Hosp., Findlay, 1964-69; dir. nurses Manley Manor, Findlay, 1972-75; adminstr. Fox Run Nursing Home, Findlay, 1976; dir. nursing Heritage Manor, Findlay, 1978-79; adminstr. Blakely Care Center, North Baltimore, Ohio, 1979—; pres. Definace and Hancock Counties Soc. Crippled Children and Adults, 1960—; bd. dirs. Ohio Soc. Crippled Children and Adults, 1978—. Mem. Phi Beta Lambda, Beta Sigma Phi. Episcopalian. Club: Findlay Country. Home: 610 W Circle Dr Findlay OH 45840

SETZER, DORIS WILLS, fashion, retail mgmt. lectr., cons.; b. Portland, Oreg., Mar. 15, 1917; d. Ralph Edward and Maude (Anderson) Wills; student Portland Bus. Sch., 1935-36; m. James Dallas Setzer, Mar. 15, 1946; 1 dau., Suzan Wendy Setzer Berry. With Charles F. Berg Inc., Portland, 1936-76, v.p., 1956-75, chief exec., 1975-76; cons. fashion retail mgmt., Portland, 1976—; fashion cons. travel wardrobe planning Ellis-Ranian Travel, Inc. Bd. dirs. Portland YWCA, 1978-81, 2d v.p., 1980; mktg. adv. Jr. League of Portland. Mem. Fashion Group, Inc. (charter mem. Portland chpt., 2d regional dir. 1950-52), DAR. Republican. Episcopalian. Home: Portland OR 97225

SETZMAN, EILEEN JUDITH, psychoanalyst; b. Phila., Nov. 26, 1942; d. Bernard and Eleanor (Cohen) S.; B.A., U. Pa., 1964; postgrad. Temple U., 1964-67; Ph.D., N.Y.U., 1973, cert. in psychoanalysis, 1979; m. Gary Wankoff. NIMH grantee Phila. State Hosp., 1965-66; staff psychologist, therapist, ward adminstr. Bronx (N.Y.) Psychiat. Center, 1967-73; counselor, therapist Bklyn. Coll., 1973-74; pvt. practice individual and group psychotherapy, N.Y.C., 1974—; asst. prof. Bklyn. Coll., 1973-74, Bloomfield Coll., 1975-77; adj. prof. Marymount-Manhattan Coll., 1973-75; mem. faculty L.I. Inst. for Mental Health, 1977-79, Met. Inst. for Tng. in Psychoanalytic Psychotherapy, 1979-80; mem. faculty postdoctoral program in continuing edn. N.Y.U., 1981—; cons. women's counseling project Barnard Coll., 1980-81; presenter workshops on sex role stereotypes, peer supervision and use of group modalities with coll. students to psychol. convs., 1972-78. Cert. sch. psychologist, N.Y. State; lic. psychologist, N.J. Mem. Am. Psychol. Assn., Psychoanalytic Soc. N.Y.U. Home: 320 W 86th St Apt 6A New York NY 10024 Office: 100 Riverside Dr Suite D New York NY 10024

SEVER, SYBIL ELSA-MARIA, public relations exec.; b. N.Y.C., Feb. 11, 1951; d. Joseph Paul and Elfriede Elsa-Anna (von Feuerstack) S.; B.A., UCLA, 1974; student Am. Film Inst., 1972. Asst. casting dir. 20th Century Fox Film Corp., Beverly Hills, Calif., 1970-71; asso. dir. public relations Operation Sail 1976, Inc., N.Y.C., 1976; dir. public relations Finnair, N.Y.C., 1977-79; sr. program publicist Showtime Entertainment, N.Y.C., 1980; dir. public relations and advt. St. James Enterprises, Inc., N.Y.C., 1981—. Chmn. public relations com. N.Y. Young Republican Club, 1979-80, editor newsletter, 1979-80; vol. Internat. Primate Protection League. Recipient Disting. Public Service award U.S. Coast Guard; cert. of appreciation Bd. Dirs. Operation Sail, Am. Revolution Bicentennial Adminstrn. Mem. Nat. Acad. TV Arts and Scis. (2 citations), Filmex Soc., Am. Film Inst. Home: 223 E 50th St 4B New York NY 10022

SEVERANCE, DIANNE SYLVIA RUSCOE, author, journalist; b. Bridgeport, Conn., Aug. 31, 1939; d. Garnet William and Pearl Frances (DeForest) Ruscoe; A.A., U. Bridgeport, 1959, student, 1974—; m. Edwin J. Severance, Sept. 5, 1959; children—Steven O., Renee L. Gallo. Reporter, copy editor Post Pub. Co. newspapers, Bridgeport, Conn., 1959-60, 64-73; reporter, editor Conn. Sunday Herald, Norwalk, 1973-74; editor spl. sects. and weekly publs. Brooks Community Newspapers, Westport, Conn., 1975-77; copy editor New Haven Jour.-Courier, 1977-80; freelance writer UPI, 1981; sr. communications specialist Raymark Corp., Trumbull, Conn., 1982—; author novels: Witness to the Light, 1979; Continuo, 1981; collection of short stories; part-time instr. journalism lab. U. Bridgeport, 1970-71; editorial cons., 1981—. Mem. adv. council Bridgeport Sch. Systems Sch. for Unwed Mothers, 1974; publicity dir. fund drives Kidney Found. Conn., 1972-73. Mem. Women in Communications (a founder Fairfield County chpt., pres. 1977). Lutheran. Home: 247 Wade St Bridgeport CT 06604

SEVERANCE, JENNIFER LYNN, geophysicist; b. Dallas, Oct. 25, 1954; d. James Craig and Mary Elizabeth (Nayes) S.; student Am. Inst. Banking, S. Tex. Jr. Coll., U. St. Thomas. Secretary, 1974-76; oil and gas cons., 1976-77; geophys. technician II, Energy Reserves Group, Denver, 1977-79; sr. geophys. technician Tex. Pacific Oil Co., 1979; data cons. Kary Data Inc., Denver, 1979-81; mktg. rep. Neo-Tech, Denver, 1981—. Mem. Soc. Exploration Geophysicists, Denver Geophys. Soc. Republican. Roman Catholic. Clubs: Petroleum Ski, Internat. Athletic. Home: 41 Perry St Denver CO 80219 Office: 1616 Glenarm Pl Suite 1900 Denver CO 80202

SEVERTSON, SUSAN MARGARET QUENEMOEN, pub. co. exec.; b. Eau Claire, Wis., Aug. 29, 1943; d. Marven Harold and Margaret (Sorlie) Quenemoen; student U. Minn., 1962-64, U. Chgo. Grad. Library Sch., 1966-67; m. Johan Severtson, June 13, 1964; children—Severin Trygve, Jörn Anders, Törsten Johan. Peace Corps vol., Sierra Leone, West Africa, 1964-66; asst. library dir. Hampshire Coll., Amherst, Mass., 1967-68; dir. library Franconia (N.H.) Coll., 1968-71; asst. librarian tech. services Middlebury (Vt.) Coll., 1971-74; exec. editor Research Publs., Inc., Woodbridge, Conn., 1974-81; v.p. mktg. Carrollton Press, Inc., Arlington, Va., 1982—; mem. Nat. Adv. Bd. Study Bibliographic Control Materials in Microform, 1979-80; cons. in field. Mem. ALA, Am. Soc. Info. Sci. Contbr. articles to profl. jours. Office: 1911 N Fort Meyer Dr Suite 905 Arlington VA 22209

SEVIER, HELEN BOGAN, publishing exec., assn. exec.; b. Enterprise, Miss., Apr. 21, 1941; d. Charles B. and Lucile B. S.; B.S., U. So. Miss., 1962; M.A., U. Ala., 1966. Buyer, Rich's, Atlanta, 1963-64; consumer mktg. dir. Fuller & Dees, Montgomery, Ala., 1966-70; exec. v.p. Bass

Anglers Sportsman Soc., Montgomery, 1970—; pres. Coll. and Univ. Press, Montgomery, 1980—. Mem. Direct Mail Mktg. Assn. (dir. 1975-81), Sales and Mktg., Mag. Pubs. Assn., Soc. Advancement Mgmt., Assn. Execs., Council Advancement and Support Edn. Republican. Presbyterian. Club: Capital. Home: 5731 Carriage Hills Dr Montgomery AL 36116 Office: 1 Bell Rd Montgomery AL 36141

SEVIGNY, CORINNE ALICE ROSEMARY KERNAN, Realtor; b. Montreal, Que., Can., May 26, 1924; d. Robert Peebles and Alice Louise (Fitzpatrick) Kernan; student pvt. schs.; m. Pierre Sevigny, June 22, 1946; children—Pierrette McConomy, J. Pierre Albert, Robert Kernan. Mng. sec. Colonial Constrn. Co., Montreal, 1950-56, Associated Constrn. Co., Montreal, 1956-65; pres. Horizon Realties Inc., Westmount, Que., 1965—. Pres., Conservative Women of the Province of Que., 1956-63; v.p. com. for Canadian unity Order St. Lazarus of Jerusalem, 1977-81. Served as lt. Can. Women's Army Corps, 1941-45. Decorated dame grand cross Order of St. Lazarus of Jerusalem, 1960, also Silver Service medal, 1980. Mem. La Ligue de la Jeunesse Feminie (pres. Montreal chpt. 1950-52), Nat. Ballet Assn. (pres. 1956). Roman Catholic. Club: Punta Vedra (Fla.). Home and office: 370 Wood Ave Westmount PQ H3Z 1Z2 Canada

SEWALL, CHARLOTTE ZAHN, state legislator; b. Damariscotta, Maine, Nov. 28, 1947; d. Bernard Tucker and Anna (Bartlett) Zahn; grad. New Eng. Coll., 1969; postgrad. U. Maine; m. Loyall Farragut Seawall, May 21, 1977. With William L. Buyers, Inc., 1968-75, security partner, 1973-75; v.p. Electronic Countermeasures Maine, 1971-75; mem. Maine Ho. of Reps., 1974-80; mem. Maine Senate, 1980—. Owner Steamers Restaurant; v.p. Twin Village Mgmt. Corp. Town chmn. Newcastle Republican Com.; trustee Miles Found., New Eng. Coll.; bd. dirs. Mid-Coast Route One Assn. Mem. Nat. Rep. Legislators Assn., Bus. and Profl. Women's Club. Office: Senate Chamber State House Augusta ME 04333

SEWARD, IRENE CHARLOTTE, librarian; b. Duluth, Minn., Aug. 27, 1923; d. Frank A. and Tena A. Miller; B.A., U. Minn., 1944; M.S., 1945; m. Henry V. Seward, Sept. 22, 1943. Librarian, Evanston Public Library, 1944; librarian Spl. Services, Dept. Army, 1947-52; librarian Wilbur Jr. High Sch., Palo Alto, Calif., 1952-55, Cubberley Sr. High Sch., Palo Alto, 1956-79; head librarian Henry M. Gunn Sr. High Sch., Palo Alto, 1979—. Mem. NEA, La. Episcopalian. Home: 555 Center Dr Palo Alto CA 94301 Office: 780 Arastradero Rd Palo Alto CA 94306

SEWELL, PHYLLIS SHAPIRO (MRS. MARTIN A. SEWELL), corp. exec.; b., 1930; B.A. with honors, Wellesley Coll., 1952; 1 son, Charles Steven. With Federated Dept. Stores, Inc., Cin., 1952—, asst. research dir., 1958-61, research dir. store ops., 1961-65, sr. research dir., 1965-70, operating v.p. research, 1970-75, corp. v.p., 1975-79, sr. v.p. research and planning, 1979—; dir., mem. audit, exec. compensation coms. Lee Enterprises, Inc., Davenport, Iowa, 1977—; dir., mem. nominating and audit coms. Huffy Corp., Dayton, Ohio, 1981—. Bd. dirs., past pres. and treas. Cin. chpt. Nat. Cystic Fibrosis Found., 1963—; mem. cabinet, chmn. maj. firms div. Cin. United Appeal, 1982; mem. bus. adv. council Sch. Bus. Adminstrn., Miami U. of Ohio, 1982—. Recipient Outstanding Alumnae award Wellesley Coll., 1979; Disting. Cin. Bus. and Profl. Woman award, 1981; inducted into Ohio Women's Hall of Fame, 1982. Office: Federated Dept Stores Inc 7 W 7th St Cincinnati OH 45202

SEXAUER, ARWIN F.B. GARELLICK, librarian, poet, editor; b. Richford, Vt., Aug. 18, 1921; hon. diploma in arts and letters, Athens, Greece, 1979; D.Litt. (hon.), World U., World Acad. Arts and Letters, 1982; hon. diploma arts and letters Accademia Internazionale, Italy, 1982; m. Charles D. Bashaw, 1942 (dec.); children—Dawn Bashaw Mennucci, Alson C. Bashaw; m. 2d, Jack L. Garellick, 1963 (dec.); m. 3d, Howard T. Sexauer, 1979 (dec.). Asst. librarian Kellogg-Hubbard Library, Montpelier, Vt., 1966-73, head librarian, 1974-76; editor Vt. Odd Fellow mag., 1959-70; author: (book of poetry) Remembered Winds, 1963; poems in numerous anthologies; lyricist, monologist. Co-founder Music Mission Inc., 1963; past pres. United Meth. Ch. Women, Franklin County Pomona Grange, PTA; past v.p. Vt. 4-H Council; youth leader 4-H. Recipient numerous awards, including George Washington Honor medals, 1957, 59, 73, ASCAP Popular Panel awards (13), 1967-78, 82, citation, 1982; Richard Rodgers Music Found. award, Grand Ole Opry Trust Fund award, Dr. Arthur Hewitt Meml. award religious poetry, Virgilio-Mantegna medal, 1982; 2 spl. merit citations for poetry, 1982; spl. citation for poetry Internat. Congress Poets, 1982, numerous others. Fellow Internat. Acad. Poets (life), Anglo-Am. Acad. (hon.); mem. Accademia Leonardo da Vinci (diploma di benemerenza, diploma of honor The Glory, poet award, hon. rep.), World Poetry Soc. Intercontinental (disting. service citation, Vt. state rep.), Hellenic Writer's Club (life), Dr. Stella Woodall Poetry Soc. Internat., Calif. Fedn. Chaparral Poets, Poetry Soc. Vt., Gospel Music Assn., ASCAP, Vt. Library Assn., Internat. Press Assn., numerous others. Club: Rebekah (past noble grand). Poems, songs, other artifacts at Gleeson Library, U. San Francisco. Address: Cherry Tree Hill East Montpelier VT 05651 also Idle Tide Cottage Box 303 Sanibel FL 33957

SEXTON, BARBARA ROYSTER, urban transp. cons.; b. Lafayette, Ind., Feb. 9, 1923; d. Paul F. and Nina E. (Pease) Royster; student Purdue U., 1940-41, Ind. U., 1942-45; m. Burton H. Sexton, Sept. 3, 1946; children—Paul R., Ann Sexton Larson, Mary A. Ind. cons. pub. transp., 1952, 75—; partner Sexton & Sexton Assocs., 1952-73; assoc. Wilbur Smith & Assos., 1973-75; pub. transp. cons., 1975—. Mem. Chi Omega. Address: 7028 Heather Hill Rd Washington DC 20034

SEXTON, DOROTHY LOUISE, nurse, educator; b. Derby, Conn., Dec. 6, 1936; d. Edward James and Dorothy Louise (Burleigh) S.; diploma Hosp. of St. Raphael, 1957; B.S., Boston Coll., 1960; M.S.N., Boston U., 1963, Ed.D., 1974. Staff nurse Hosp. of St. Raphael, New Haven, 1957-58; staff nurse New Eng. Bapt. Hosp., Boston, 1958-60; instr., 1960-62, 63-64; instr. U. Mass., 1964-66, asst. prof., 1966-68; asst. prof. Sch. Nursing, Boston U., 1968-71; asst. prof. nursing Yale U., New Haven, 1974-77, asso. prof., 1977—; cons. in field. Bd. dirs. Conn. Lung Assn., 1977—. Mem. Am. Nurses Assn. (mem. cert. test com. 1977-79, cons. to cert. com. 1979—), Nat. League Nursing, Am. Thoracic Soc., Conn. Thoracic Soc., AAUP, Sigma Theta Tau. Roman Catholic. Author: Chronic Obstructive Pulmonary Disease: Care of the Child and Adult, 1981; contbr. articles to profl. jours. Office: 855 Howard Ave Box 3333 New Haven CT 06510

SEXTON, PATRICIA JOANNE, sporting goods mfg. co. exec.; b. Turlock, Calif., Aug. 24, 1943; d. Kennith Paul and Velma Faye (Rash) Herring; student Modesto Jr. Coll., 1962-68; children—Scott, Jill. Office mgr. various cos., 1971-75; mgr. retail fishing tackle store and saltwater fishing lure mfg., San Diego, 1982—. Mem. Dental Assts. Orgn., Women in Constrn. Republican. Home: 3606 Florida St San Diego CA 92104 Office: PO Box 4875 San Diego CA 92104-0875

SEYBOLD, ADELE NEELY, former Democratic nat. committeewoman, civic worker; b. Comanche, Tex., Nov. 11, 1919; d. Eugene Gentry and Nell (Orand) Neely; B.A., U. Tex., 1940; tchrs. certificate U. Tex., 1940; m. Eugene Murphy Locke, Oct. 27, 1941; children—Aimee Locke Jacoble, John, Tom; m. 2d, William Dempsey Seybold, 1977. State chmn. women's activities Tex. gov.'s primary campaign, 1964; mem. Democratic Nat. Com., 1964-66, exec. com., 1964-66. Mem. hospitality bd. Met. Opera, Dallas, 1962-66, 69-70; mem. exec. com. Greater Dallas Council Chs., 1964-66; area chmn. Dallas Mental Health Assn., 1964; bd. dirs. women's group Dallas Council of World Affairs, 1970—, Bishop Mason Retreat and Conf. Center; hon. chmn. pub. edn. Tex. div. Am. Cancer Soc., also bd. dirs.; bd. dirs., sec. to bd. visitors U. Tex. System Cancer Center, M.D. Anderson Hosp. and Tumor Inst.; mem. found. adv. council Coll. Liberal Arts, U. Tex., Austin; mem. exec. com. chancellor's council U. Tex. Timberlawn Found.; mem. Fine Arts Commn., U.S. Dept. State. Mem. Daus. Republic Tex. (asso.), Ashbel Lit. Soc., Jr. League, Mus. Fine Arts, Young Women of the Arts, Dallas County Heritage Soc. (dir.), Dallas Jr. Assembly (dir. 1961-64). Soc. for Abandoned and Neglected Children, Mortar Bd., Phi Beta Kappa, Alpha Lambda Delta, Sigma Delta Pi, Phi Eta Sigma, Pi Lambda Theta, Pi Beta Phi. Episcopalian (edn. guild leader). Clubs: Dallas Country, Dallas Woman's; River Oaks Country; Houston, Houston City. Home: 3805 McFarlin Blvd Dallas TX 75205

SEYMORE, PEARL, interior design cons.; b. Bklyn., Aug. 15, 1927; d. Joe and Tania Bard; student Bklyn. Coll., 1945-47, Pratt Inst., 1952-56, New Sch. Social Research, N.Y. U.; m. Lutzker Seymore, Mar. 2, 1947 (div. July 1960); children—Rochelle Diane Lewis, Amy Sharon Gottlieb. Salesperson, Charles S. Nathan, Inc., N.Y.C., 1956-60, dir. design, 1960-65, v.p. in charge design and sales coordination, 1965-69; dir. design Brenner Desk & Design Co., Newark, 1969-75; design, sales coordinator Gen. Office Equipment Co., Saddlebrook, N.J., 1975-79; owner Pearl Seymore Design Assos., Hackensack, N.J., 1979—. Recipient Design awards Mcpl. Bldg., City Long Beach, N.Y., 1964, Berlitz Sch. Lang, Rockefeller Center, N.Y., 1965, Internat. Flavors and Fragrances, N.Y.C., 1967. Mem. Am. Soc. Interior Designers, Inst. Bus. Designers, Designers Lighting Forum, Nat. Trust for Historic Preservation, Meadowlands C. of C., N.J. Soc. Architects, Commerce and Industry Assn. No. N.J. Home: 200 Winston Dr Cliffside Park NJ 07010 Office: 479 Main St Hackensack NJ

SEYMOUR, CATHERINE ANN, child and house sitting service exec.; b. Nadeau, Mich., Mar. 6, 1920; d. Adolph and Delphine Leanore (Gauthier) S.; B.A., St. Norbert Coll., 1950; M.A., Medaille Coll., 1957; M.S.W., U. Mich., 1974. Tchr., high sch., Green Bay, Wis., 1941-57; child care worker Our Lady of Charity Sch. for Girls, Green Bay, 1958-65, adminstr., 1965-68; founder, dir. Norlake Home for Girls, Marquette, Mich., 1970-73; asst. prof. social work Coll. St. Teresa, Winona, Minn., 1974-77; salesperson Forest Olson-Coldwell Banker Inc., Fullerton, Calif., 1979-82; founder, dir. Best Sitters Agy., Los Angeles, 1982—. Mem. Nat. Assn. Social Workers, Acad. Cert Social Workers. Democrat. Roman Catholic. Home and Office: 2389 Nichols Canyon Rd Los Angeles CA 90046

SEYMOUR, CATRYNA TEN EYCK, artist; b. N.Y.C., June 30, 1931; d. Barent and Leslie (Van Ness) Ten Eyck; student Smith Coll., 1949-51, Art Students League, 1971, Parsons Sch. Design, 1974; m. Whitney North Seymour, Jr., Nov. 16, 1951; children—Tryntje, Gabriel. One-woman shows include: New Sch. Social Research, N.Y.C., 1973; So. Vt. Art Center, Manchester, 1974; group shows include: Art Assn. Newport (R.I.), 1972, Ogunquit (Maine) Art Center, 1972, Sharon (Conn.) Creative Arts Found., 1973-78, Phila. Print Club, 1976; represented in permanent collections Smithsonian Instn., Nat. Collection Fine Arts, Calif. Palace of Legion of Honor, Achenbach Found., Denver Art Mus., Albany Inst. Arts and Letters, Roswell Mus. and Art Center; designer ofcl. posters Mus. Am. Indian, South Street Seaport, Natural Resources Def. Council; pres. Am. Graphics Gallery, Inc.; sec.-treas. Lime Rock Press, Inc. Bd. dirs. Greater N.Y. council Girl Scouts U.S.A., 1965-79, sec., 1977-79; bd. dirs. YWCA, N.Y.C., 1967-68. Recipient 1st prize graphics Springfield Art League, 1971, 1st prize Tanglewood poster competition Berkshire Art Assn., 1975. Mem. Cooperstown Art Assn. Club: Cosmopolitan. Author: Enjoying the Southwest, 1973. Home: 290 W 4th St New York NY 10014 Studio: Box 363 Salisbury CT 06068

SEYMOUR, MARY POWELL, state legislator; b. Raleigh, N.C., Apr. 12, 1922; d. Robert C. and Annie Rebecca (Seymour) Powell; A.B., Peace Coll., 1941; spl. courses Harvard U., 1947-48, U. Mich., 1949-50, Center Creative Leadership, 1978; m. Hubert E. Seymour, Jr., Feb. 3, 1945; children—Hubert E. III, Robert J. Claims clk. Social Security Adminstrn., Washington, 1941, Goldsboro, N.C., 1941-42; adminstrv. asst. med. supply Overseas Replacement Depot, Greensboro, N.C., 1943-45; sec. to dean Grad. Sch. Bus. Adminstrn., Harvard U., 1946-47; legal sec., ct. reporter, 1951-67; mem. Greensboro City Council, 1967-75, mayor pro-tem, 1973-75; mem. N.C. Ho. of Reps., 1976—; speaker, lectr; cons., participant Center for Creative Leadership. Former pres. Greensboro Legal Aux.; bd. dirs. Tarheel Triad council Girl Scouts U.S.A., Hayes Taylor YMCA, United Arts Council, C. of C. Community Devel. Council, Ea. Music Festival Adv. Council. Recipient Eleanor Roosevelt award, Woman of Yr. award for city beautification, Bryan Citizenship award Nat. Council Federated Women's Clubs, Dolley Madison award Greensboro C. of C., Woman of Yr. award, Quota Club; Disting. Service award YWCA, recognition N.C. Bar Assn.; named Disting. Alumna, Peace Coll. Mem. Bus. and Profl. Women (hon.), Women's Profl. Forum, Nat. Conf. Ins. Legislators (exec. bd.), Nat. Conf. State Legislatures, Legis. Services Commn., N.C. Arts Council, N.C. Parks and Recreation Commn., N.C. Transp. Efficiency Council, State Law Focused Edn. Council, Nat. Order Women Legislators, U.S. Power Squadron. Democrat. Baptist. Clubs: Council Garden Clubs, O. Henry Women's. Home: 1105 Pender Ln Greensboro NC 27408 Office: State Legislative Bldg Raleigh NC 27611

SEYMOUR, PATTI FOX, contract engring. co. exec.; b. N.Y.C., Mar. 14, 1953; d. Arthur T. Fox and Helen Fried; student Pratt Inst., 1970-72; B.F.A., Tufts U. and Sch. Mus. Fine Arts, 1974; m. Terry L. Seymour, Dec. 16, 1979. Personnel dir. Internat. Weekends, Boston, 1974-76, Career Devel. Team, N.Y.C., 1976-78; asst. to pres., corp. adminstrv. mgr. Interglobal, N.Y.C., 1979—; cons. Nat. Assn. Female Execs. Contbg. author: Guerilla Tactics, 1978. Office: 31 W 34th St New York NY 10001

SEYMOUR, STEPHANIE KULP, U.S. judge; b. Battle Creek, Mich., Oct. 16, 1940; d. Francis Bruce and Frances Cecelia (Bria) Kulp; B.A. magna cum laude (Ford Found. grantee), Smith Coll., 1962; J.D., Harvard U., 1965; m. R. Thomas Seymour, June 10, 1972; children—Bart, Bria, Sara, Anna. Admitted to Okla. bar, 1965; asso. firms in Boston, Tulsa and Houston, 1965-71; asso. firm Doerner, Stuart, Saunders, Daniel & Anderson, Tulsa, 1971-79, partner, 1975-79; circuit judge U.S. Ct. Appeals for 10th Circuit, Tulsa, 1979—. Mem. legal adv. panel Tulsa Task Force Battered Women, 1971-77; mem. various task forces Tulsa Human Rights Commn., 1972-76; mem. speakers bur. Oklahomans for ERA. Mem. Am. Bar Assn., Okla. Bar Assn. (asso. bar examiner 1973-79), Tulsa County Bar Assn., Phi Beta Kappa. Office: US Courthouse 333 W 4th St Tulsa OK 74103 *

SFREDDO, CAROLYN JANE JACOBS, univ. ofcl.; b. Indpls., Mar. 18, 1936; d. Samuel J. and Opal (Priest) Jacobs; B.S., Ind. State U., 1958; postgrad. Ind. U., 1966-68, U. Ky., 1969-71; m. Basil A. Sfreddo, July 26, 1958; children—Robert, David, Susan. Tchr., various locations Ill., Ind., 1958-63; asst. to mng. editor Saturday Evening Post, Indpls., 1970-75; with Sta. WTHI, Terre Haute, Ind., 1958-60, Terre Haute Tribune Star, 1958-61; tchr. Perry Meridian High Sch., Indpls., 1976-79; supr. Ind. Research Assn. for Learning Disabilities, 1974-79; public relations dir. Ind. Central U., 1979—. Mem. adv. bd. Plainfield Sch. Bd., 1960-75; dir. St. Michael's Youth Council. Mem. Women in Communications, Ind. Bus. Communicators, Religious Public Relations Council, Nat. Assn. Collegiate Press Advs., Council Advancement Secondary Edn. Republican. Christian. Clubs: Plainfield Garden, Indiana Garden. Office: 1400 E Hanna Ave Indianapolis IN 46227

SHACK, JUDY, data processing trainer; b. N.Y.C., May 6, 1949; d. Arthur and Estelle (Reich) S.; B.A. in Bus. Mgmt. and Econs., Hunter Coll., 1971; cert. in tng. and devel. N.Y.U. Sch. Continuing Edn., 1978. With Standard Security Life Ins. Co. N.Y., N.Y.C., 1971-79, dir. pension adminstrn., 1976-78, dir. pension ops., pension dept., 1978-79; cons. Modular Pension Systems, Metuchen, N.J., 1979-80; edn. coordinator computer/communications dept. Paine, Webber, Jackson, & Curtis, Inc., N.Y.C., 1980-81; edn. cons. computer ops. group Irving Trust Co., N.Y.C., 1981—. Vol., United Cerebral Palsy Telethon, N.Y.C. Mem. Am. Soc. Tng. and Devel. (past N.Y. Met. chpt. treas.), Tri-State Info. Mgmt. Educators. Author articles. Home: 66-01 Burns St Forest Hills NY 11374 Office: 61 Broadway New York NY 10015

SHADDIX, ELIZABETH CADY STANTON, accountant; b. Los Angeles, Oct. 30, 1941; d. Julius and Zelda Eva (Rabinowitz) Gladstein; A.A. in Engring., Santa Monica (Calif.) City Coll., 1964; diploma in computer programming Control Data Inst., 1968; diploma in acctg. Los Angeles Bus. Coll., 1974; m. James William Shaddix, Jan. 14, 1979. Social service coordinator Evolving Door Inc., San Francisco, 1973-74; owner Thomason's Novelty Co., Los Angeles, 1974-76; v.p., partner S & S Draperies, Los Angeles, 1976-78; pvt. practice acctg., Los Angeles, 1974-80; acct. Saul Jackman, C.P.A., Los Angeles, 1980—; v.p. So. Calif. Gender Identity Group, Inc., 1975—. Active Center of Spl. Problems, 1973—; historian Republican Club, 1963. Mem. NOW, Nat. Assn. Female Execs., Am. Entrepreneurs Assn., Harry Benjamin Internat. Gender Dysphoris Assn. Editor: Jour. on Gender Dysphoris, 1972-73.

SHADE, BARBARA JEAN, ednl. psychologist; b. Armstrong, Mo., Oct. 30, 1933; d. Murray Kenneth and Edna Rose (Bowman) Robinson; B.S., Kans. State Tchrs. Coll., 1955; M.S., U. Wis., Milw., 1967; Ph.D., U. Wis., Madison, 1973; m. Oscar DePriest Shade, Mar. 22, 1954; children—Christina Marie Shade Jones, Kenneth Eugene, Patricia Louise. Tchr. pub. schs., Milw., 1960-68; exec. dir. Dane County Head Start, Madison, 1969-71; asst. prof. Afro-Am. studies U. Wis., Madison, 1974-81; assoc. prof. edn. U. Wis.-Parkside, Kenosha, 1981—; cons. Office of Child Devel., HEW, Wis. Dept. Pub. Instrn., 1974-75. Mem. Wis. Humanities Commn.; vice chmn., chmn. St. Mary's Hosp. Med. Center, 1973-81; v.p. Dane County United Way, 1978-81; mem. Equal Opportunities Commn., Gov.'s Health and Policy Task Force, Affirmative Action Commn.,, Wis. Legal Services Bd. Nat. Endowment for Humanities fellow, 1973-74. Mem. Am. Psychol. Assn., Am. Ednl. Research Assn., Pi Lambda Theta, Pi Omega Pi, Delta Sigma Theta. Contbr. articles to profl. jours. Home: 3110 Pelham Rd Madison WI 53713 Office: U Wis-Parkside PO Box 2000 Kenosha WI 53141

SHAEVITZ, MARJORIE HANSEN, psychotherapist, author, cons.; b. Fresno, Calif., May 22, 1943; d. Robert Vedsted and Evelyn (Eskelsen-Beck) Hansen; M.A., Stanford U., 1967; m. Morton H. Shaevitz, Mar. 11, 1972; children—Geoffrey Hansen, Marejka Ann Hansen. Orientation officer East West Center, Honolulu, 1967-68; mem. dean's staff Stanford U., 1968-69; dir. counseling and registration services, Univ. extension U. Calif., San Diego, 1970-73, dir. programs for mental health and edn. profls., 1973-78, cons. to human devel. programs, 1978—; co-dir. Inst. for Family and Work Relationships, La Jolla, Calif., 1978—. Bd. dirs. Imperial council Girl Scouts U.S.A.; co-pres. La Jolla Farms Community Assn., 1978-79. Recipient Outstanding Young Citizen award San Diego Jaycees, 1978. Mem. Am. Psychol. Assn., Nat. Council on Family Relations, Calif. Assn. Marriage and Family Counselors, Calif. Psychol. Assn. Author: So You Want to Go Back to School: Facing the Realities of Re-entry, 1977; Making It Together As A Two-Career Couple, 1980; contbr. articles to profl. jours. Office: 1020 Prospect St Suite 400 La Jolla CA 92037

SHAFER, NORMA RUTH, accountant; financial planner; b. Mt. Carmel, Pa., May 31, 1938; d. Daniel and Pearl Eleanor Smigel; B.S., Temple U., Phila., 1962; divorced; children—Lawrence J., Adele D., Dina M. Inventory control clk. Dept. Def., Phila., 1962-67; individual income tax return checker H & R Block, Phoenix, 1975; staff acct. Seely Mullins & Assos., C.P.A.s, Phoenix, 1976-81; head tax dept. Price & Weider, P.C., C.P.A.s, Phoenix, 1981-82; self-employed acct.; fin. planner, 1982—. Mem. Inst. Cert. Fin. Planners, Am. Soc. Profl. and Exec. Women, Jewish Bus. and Profl. Women, Internat. Assn. Fin. Planners, Am. Soc. Women Accts., Nat. Assn. Female Execs., Hadassah, Women Emerging. Democrat. Office: 5547 N 2d St Phoenix AZ 85012

SHAFER, PAQUITA MIGNON MORTON, journalist; b. Hopewell, Va., Aug. 23, 1918; d. Clarence Littleton Morton and Mignon Reed Osborne Bissell; student U. N.C.; m. Robert G. Shafer, June 27, 1981; children—Paquita Robin, Robert Edward, Deborah Mignon. Free-lance writer, 1950-57; asst. to state editor News and Observer, Raleigh, N.C., 1957-60; living trends editor Chapel Hill Newspaper, Chapel Hill, N.C., 1962—; lectr.; judge journalism contests; cons. Recipient numerous awards from various orgns., including Asso. Press, N.C. Press Women, Girl Scouts U.S.A., Lawyers of N.C., Jr. Service League, Nat. Newspapers Assn. Mem. N.C. Press Women's Assn. (pres. 1969-70), N.C. Press Assn., Sigma Delta Chi. Club: U. N.C. Woman's.

SHAFF, PEGGY FRANK, pub. relations exec.; b. Bronx, N.Y., Mar. 18, 1955; d. Julius and Rita (Namanworth) Frank; A.A. in Gen. Edn., Los Angeles Valley Coll., 1974; B.A. in Journalism, Calif. State U., 1976; m. Vernon Shaff, Feb. 11, 1978; 1 dau., Rachel Sara. Public relations asst. Saint John's Hosp. and Health Center, Santa Monica, Calif., 1976-78; dir. public relations Med. Center Encino (Calif.), 1978-79; dir. public relations and advt. Weight Watchers Greater Los Angeles and Ventura County, 1980-82; owner/pres. Peggy Shaff Pub. Relations, Simi Valley, Calif., 1982—. Mem. Women in Communications (chpt. v.p. career services 1979-80), San Fernando Valley Regional C. of C. (com. 1978-79). Office: 3400 Alameda St Burbank CA 91505

SHAFFER, ANNE PATRICIA, hosp. adminstr.; b. Odessa, Tex., May 24, 1952; d. Paul D. and Thelma M. S.; B.S. in Biology, Tex. Christian U., 1974; B.S. in Nursing, U. Pa., 1975; M.H.A., Ga. State U., 1981. Staff nurse med.-surg. unit Pa. Hosp., Phila., 1976-77, Hosp. Med. Coll. Pa., 1977-79, Shallowford Community Hosp., Chamblee, Ga., 1980-81; adminstrv. resident, asst. to adminstr. Goddard Meml. Hosp., Stoughton, Mass., 1981-82; v.p. ancillary services Meml. Osteo. Hosp., York, Pa., 1982—. Mem. Am. Assn. Critical Care Nurses, Am. Hosp. Assn., Am. Coll. Hosp. Adminstrs., Sigma Theta Tau. Home: PO Box 9 Glen Rock PA 17327 Office: 325 S Belmont St York PA

SHAFFER, DOROTHY BROWNE, educator, mathematician; b. Vienna, Austria, Feb. 12, 1923; d. Hermann and Steffy (Hermann) Browne; arrived U.S., 1940; naturalized, 1944; A.B., Bryn Mawr Coll., 1943; M.A., Harvard U., 1945, Ph.D., 1962; m. Lloyd Hamilton Shaffer, July 25, 1943 (dec. 1978); children—Deborah Lee, Diana Louise, Dorothy Leslie. Mathematician, Mass. Inst. of Tech., Cambridge, 1945-47; tchg. fellow, research asso., Harvard U., Cambridge, 1947-48; asso. mathematician Cornell Aeronautical Lab, Buffalo, N.Y., 1948-58; mathematician Dunlap & Assoc., Stamford, Conn., 1958-60; lectr. grad. engring. U. of Conn. at Stamford, 1962; prof. math Fairfield (Conn.) U., 1963—; vis. prof. Imperial Coll. Sci. and Tech., London, fall 1978, U. Md., College Park, spring 1981, U. Calif., San Diego, summer 1981; NSF faculty fellow IBM-T.J. Watson Research Center, Yorktown Heights,

N.Y., 1979. Mem. Am. Math. Soc., Math. Assn. of Am., Assn. for Women in Math. Contbr. numerous papers in math. analysis. Home: 156 Intervale Rd Stamford CT 06905 Office: Dept of Math Fairfield U Fairfield CT 06430

SHAFFER, GAIL SUSAN, state legislator; b. Kingston, N.Y., Aug. 1, 1948; d. Robert Edwin and Marion Gertrude (Gallagher) S.; B.A. summa cum laude in Polit. Sci., Elmira U., 1970; student U. Paris, 1968-69. Editor, Sam Har Press, 1972-76; supr. Town of Blenheim, N.Y., 1975-77; spl. asst. to N.Y. State Commr. Environ. Conservation, 1977-79; exec. dir. N.Y. State Rural Affairs Council, 1979-80; mem. N.Y. State Assembly, 1980—. Mem. N.Y. State Democratic Com., 1976—. Mem. Phi Beta Kappa. Presbyterian. Club: DAR. Office: Legislative Office Bldg Albany NY 12248

SHAFFER, GRACE DEEELLEN DUFFIELD, educator; b. Des Moines, Sept. 24, 1917; d. John Calvin and Mary Olive (Bennett) Duffield; B.S., Union Coll., 1949; M.A., Ariz. State U., 1963; Ed. Specialist, Peabody Coll., 1969; m. Edward Charles Shaffer, Oct. 23, 1960 (dec. 1981); children—Edward Charles, James Lee. Tchr., Seventh-day Adventist schs., Kans., Colo., 1939-47; sec. ednl. supt. Colo. Conf. Seventh-Day Adventists, Denver, 1949-51; elem. supervisory tchr. Helderberg Coll., Cape Town, South Africa, 1951-54; asst. ednl. supt. Ariz. Seventh-day Adventist Schs., Phoenix, 1955-59; ednl. supr. Fla. Seventh-day Adventist schs., Orlando, 1959-62; dir. student teaching So. Missionary Coll., Collegedale, Tenn., 1962-66; dir. reading center U. Tenn., Chattanooga, 1966-67; grad. asst. Peabody Coll., 1967-68; reading cons., psychometrist Catoosa County Schs., Ringgold, Ga., 1969-72, curriculum dir., 1972—. Mem. sch. bd. Greater Collegedale Sch. System, Tenn., 1980-82; pres. Spaulding Elem. Sch. PTA, Collegedale, 1966-67. Mem. Internat. Reading Assn. (sec. 1973-74, pres. Chattanooga chpt. 1975-76, award 1976), Ga. Assn. for Curriculum and Instructional Supervision, Assn. for Childhood Edn. Internat., Ga. Assn. Educators, Assn. for Supervision and Curriculum Devel., NEA, Ga. Assn. Ednl. Leadership, Union Coll. Alumni Assn. (chpt. pres. 1974-75). Adventist. Author: Africa's Floating Logs, 1972; contbr. articles to profl. jours. Home: PO Box 491 Collegedale TN 37315 Office: PO Box 130 Ringgold GA 30736

SHAFFER, JANE GLORIA, retail food co. mgr.; b. Ithaca, N.Y., Sept. 8, 1944; d. Adrian Gordon and Dorothy Gould; B.S. with honors, UCLA, 1966; m. Homer Edward Shaffer, June 29, 1973; 1 dau., Kelly. Acctg. supr. Pacific Tel., Los Angeles, 1966-67; tech. rep. Burroughs Corp., Los Angeles, 1970-78; sales rep. Tymshare, Inc., Los Angeles, 1978-79; data processing mgr. So. Foods div. Lucky Stores, Buena Park, Calif., 1979—. Job's Daus. scholar, 1962. Home: 15855 Del Prado Dr Hacienda Heights CA 91745 Office: 6565 Knott Ave Buena Park CA 90620

SHAFFER, JANE REGINA, assn. exec.; b. Peoria, Ill., June 4, 1933; d. Archie Henry and Ethel Ruth (Pedreyra) Hall; student Bradley U., Peoria, 1951-53; m. Roy Alvin Shaffer, Jan. 31, 1955; children—Jamie, Roy, Shawn. Sec.-treas., Diverco Corp., Winter Haven, Fla., 1957-70, Mansysco Corp., Peoria, 1970-72; divs. adminstr. Profl. Photographers Am., Inc., Des Plaines, Ill., 1972—. Chmn., Beautification Com. Winter Haven, 1968-69. Mem. Am. Photog. Artistans Guild, Nat. Assn. Female Execs., Nat. Soc. Assn. Execs., Nat. Mgmt. Assn. Democrat. Roman Catholic. Club: St. Mary's Women's. Home: 530 Springside Ln Buffalo Grove IL 60090 Office: 1090 Executive Way Des Plaines IL 60018

SHAFFER, JUNE ANNE, land devel. co. mgr.; b. Tampa, Fla., June 18, 1953; d. Robert J. and Irene (Way) S.; A.A., Manatee Jr. Coll., 1973; B.A., U. South Fla., 1975; postgrad. Miami-Dade Community Coll., 1980. With El Molino Mills, Los Angeles, 1976-78; office mgr. J. R. Schwalbach, Inc., Sarasota, Fla., 1978-79; with Deltona Corp., Miami, Fla., 1979—, corp. property services mgr., 1982—; lectr. Mem. Am. Bus. Women's Assn., Nat. Assn. Female Execs. Prebyterian. Columnist, Prosser (Wash.) Record-Bull., 1970-71; contbr. poetry to anthologies. Home: 114 Menores Ave Apt 6 Coral Gables FL 33134 Office: 3250 SW Third Ave Miami FL 33129

SHAFFER, SUSAN E., ins. co. claim mgr.; b. Nashville, Apr. 14, 1947; d. James G. and Esther W. Shaffer; B.A. in English, Elmhurst (Ill.) Coll., 1969. Mem. claim dept. Allstate Ins. Co., 1971-76, unit mgr., Springfield, Pa., 1976-77, regional life claim mgr., Basking Ridge, N.J., 1977-79, dist. claim mgr., Latham, N.Y., 1979—. Mem. Albany Claim Mgrs. Council, Colonie C. of C., Life Office Mgmt. Assn., Ins. Inst. Am. (asso. in mgmt.). Office: 700 Troy Schenectady Rd Latham NY 12110

SHAFFER, SYBIL SNYDER, teen-ager pageant exec.; b. Greenville, S.C., Sept. 21, 1922; d. William Oscar and Nancy Louise (Walker) Snyder; student Jacksonville U., 1961; m. Edwin Gray Shaffer, May 28, 1966; 1 son, Richard Clyde. Chief clk. So. Rwy. Co., Greenville, S.C., 1943-53; mgr., fire, casualty agt. Spiers Ins. Agy., Columbia, S.C., 1960-66; traveling ins. auditor Agts. Acceptance Corp., Dallas, 1960-66, ins. auditor, Ponte Vedra Beach, Fla., 1966-71; founder, pres., nat. dir. Miss Nat. Teen-ager Pageant, 1971—; tchr. charm and improvement courses, 1959—. Bd. dirs. Cancer Assn., Crippled Children's Soc., Vets. Hosp., Cystic Fibrosis. Mem. Nat. Acad. TV Arts and Scis., Women in Film, Atlanta C. of C., Better Bus. Bur., Beta Sigma Phi (chpt. pres.). Methodist. Club: Ponte Vedra (Ponte Vedra Beach); Atlanta Press, Women's Commerce (founder). Writer Miss Nat. Teen-ager Mini-Modeling charm course Six Parts, 1972.

SHAGER, MERRIE CAROLYN, indsl. psychologist; b. Eau Claire, Wis., Aug. 4, 1946; d. Robert Herman and Irene Lillian (Jevne) Shager; B.A. in Psychology, Wis. State U., 1969; M.A., George Mason U., 1978. Test devel. specialist State of Minn. Employment Service, St. Paul, 1969-72; personnel research psychologist Employment Service Nat. Office, U.S. Dept. Labor, Washington, 1972-75, psychologist Office Fed. Contract Compliance Programs, 1975-79; personnel psychologist U.S. GAO, Washington, 1979; staff psychologist Office of Personnel, Office of Sec. of Treasury, Washington, 1979—. Mem. Personnel Testing Council Met. Washington (pres. 1981-82), Am. Psychol. Assn. (div. indsl./organizational psychology), Internat. Personnel Mgmt. Assn. (assessment council 1979—), NOW. Office: Room 2409 Main Treasury Dept of Treasury Washington DC 20220

SHALALA, DONNA EDNA, asst. sec. HUD; b. Cleve., Feb. 14, 1942; d. James Abraham and Edna (Smith) S.; A.B., Western Coll., 1962; M.S.Sc., Syracuse U., 1968, Ph.D., 1970. Peace Corps. vol., Iran, 1962-64; asst. to dir. met. studies program Syracuse (N.Y.) U., 1965-69, instr. asst. to dean Maxwell Grad. Sch., 1969-70; asst. prof. dept. polit. sci. Bernard M. Baruch Coll., City U. N.Y., 1970-72; asso. prof. politics and edn. Tchrs. Coll., Columbia, 1972-77; asst. sec. for policy devel. and research HUD, Washington, 1977-80; prof. polit. sci. Asst. to chmn. com. on local govt. N.Y. State Constl. Conv., 1967. Vice chmn. New Dem. Coalition of N.Y. State, 1970-72. Trustee Western Coll., Oxford, Ohio; bd. dirs. N.Y. Citizens Union. Recipient Ohio Newspaper Women's scholarship, 1958, trustee scholarship Western Coll., 1958-62, Carnegie fellowship, 1966-68; Spencer fellow Nat. Acad. Edn., 1972—. Mem. Am. N.Y. polit. sci. assns. Author: Neighborhood Governance, 1971; The City and the Constitution, 1972; The Property Tax and the Voters, 1973; The Decentralization Approach, 1974. Office: 695 Park Ave New York NY 10021 *

SHALOWITZ, ADRIEN CAROLE, psychiat. social worker; b. Chgo., Nov. 15, 1939; d. Samuel and Faye (Tish) Wallerstein; B.S., Northwestern U., 1972; M.S.W., Loyola U., 1976; m. Herbert B. Shalowitz, Mar. 29, 1959; children—Lisa, Ronald, Stuart. Social worker Ill. Dept. Public Aid, 1974-75; social worker Jewish Children's Bur., Chgo., 1975-78; social worker Ill. Sch. Dist. #64, Park Ridge, Ill., 1978-80, Jewish Family and Children's Services, Phoenix. Mem. Nat. Assn. Social Workers, Ariz. Assn. Clin. Social Workers and Psychotherapists, Nat. Council Jewish Women. Jewish. Home: 13410 N 82d St Scottsdale AZ 85260

SHANBLUM, MATILDA AMSTATER, club woman; b. El Paso, Mar. 23, 1906; d. John and Molly Amstater; student El Paso Jr. Coll., 1923-24, U. Mich., 1925-27; B.A., Tex. Western Coll., 1934; adminstrv. cert. U. Tex., El Paso, 1960; m. Ben Al Shanblum, Jan. 24, 1937; children—John H., Frances Shanblum Kahn. Tchr., Alamo Sch., El Paso, 1927-37; real estate broker McFall-Turley & Co., Ft. Worth, 1950-52; tchr. White Sch., El Paso, 1953-61, adminstr., 1961-71. Vol. worker Providence Hosp., 1953-55, March of Dimes, 1974-79; edn. dir. Temple Mt. Sinai, El Paso, 1958-70; organizer scholarship program for future tchrs. U. Tex., El Paso, 1960; pres. Sisterhood Temple Beth El, Ft. Worth, 1940-41; pres. El Paso Tchrs. Assn., 1960-61; sec. Trans-Pecos Tchrs. Assn., 1971; pres. Zeta Pi, Delta Kappa Gamma, 1970-71; treas. Nat. Council Jewish Women, Ft. Worth, 1938-39, parliamentarian, El Paso, 1979—. Recipient cert. of appreciation Tex. Classroom Tchrs. Assn., 1961; named Tchr. of Yr., Zach White Sch., El Paso, 1961; Career Woman of Yr., Zeta Pi chpt. Delta Kappa Gamma, 1968. Mem. Nat. Ret. Tchrs. Assn., Tex. Ret. Tchrs. Assn., Tex. Tchrs. Assn., El Paso Ret. Tchrs. Assn. (pres. 1977-79), AAUW, Woman's Aux. U. Tex. El Paso, Nat. Council Jewish Women, Delta Kappa Gamma. Democrat. Home: 4114 N Stanton St El Paso TX 79902

SHANDERA, DOROTHY FRANCES, educator; b. Sardis, Miss., Nov. 8, 1929; d. George Monroe and Mary Browning (Chamblin) Hammitt; B.S., Miss. Women's U., 1951; postgrad. in Criminal Justice, U. Houston, 1971; M.Correctional Edn., Sam Houston State U., 1980; m. Charles Garland Shandera, Apr. 22, 1964; children—Deborah, Cindi. Tchr. high sch. and coll. All Saints Episcopal Coll., Vicksburg, Miss., 1951-52; high sch. tchr. Tyler (Tex.) Ind. Sch. Dist., 1955-59; Harris County probation officer, Houston, 1963-65; tchr. speech and drama Alvin (Tex.) Sch. Dist., 1965-68, Friendswood (Tex.) Sch. Dist., 1968-71; tchr. Spanish and English Round Rock (Tex.) Sch. Dist., 1973-76; bi-lingual instr. Windham Sch. Dist., Tex. Dept. Corrections, Huntsville, 1976-77, life skills instr., 1977-79, bi-lingual specialist, life skills coordinator, 1979—, participant Adkins Life Skills workshop, 1977; guest lectr. Sam Houston State U., 1979-80. Del., Tex. Women's Meeting, 1977; state del. Nat. Women's Conf., Internat. Women's Yr., Houston, 1977; del. Tex. Democratic Conv., 1980; state steering com. Texans for ERA; bd. dirs. Walker County Bd. Human Resources; mem. Tex. Women's Polit. Caucus; legis. aide for Sarah Weddington, 1973; vol. Green Acres Nursing Home; active PTA. Named one of outstanding career women Huntsville, 1978; recipient service cert. Windham Sch. Dist., 1979. Mem. AAUW (nat. del. 1975, travel grantee to conf. 1972, chpt. pres. 1974-76, coordinator state legis. conf.), Tex. Corrections Assn. (pres.-elect state orgn. 1981-82), NEA, Tex. State Tchrs. Assn. (state exec. com., pres.-elect), Windham North Assn. (pres., dist. VI legis. chmn.), Correctional Edn. Assn., Tex. State Ofcl. Ladies, Phi Delta Kappa. Democrat. Presbyterian (elder). Club: Bus. and Profl. Women. Contbr. articles to profl. publs. Home: 205 Royal Oaks Huntsville TX 77340 Office: Windham School District Texas Dept Corrections PO Box 99 Huntsville TX 77340

SHANGE, NTOZAKE, poet, playwright; b. Trenton, N.J., Oct. 18, 1948; d. Paul T. and Eloise Williams; B.A. in Am. Studies cum laude, Barnard Coll., 1970; M.A. in Am. Studies (NDEA fellow), U. So. Calif., 1973. Plays: for colored girls who have considered suicide/when the rainbow is enuf, 1976; negress, 1977; a photograph: lovers in motion, 1977; where the mississippi meets the amazon, 1977; from okra to greens, 1978; magic spell #7, 1979; boogie woogie landscapes, 1980; Mother Courage, 1980; Mouths, 1981; Carrie (operetta), 1981; author books: for colored girls..., 1975; sassafrass, 1976; nappy edges, 1978; 3 Pieces, 1980; dir. Mighty Gents, 1979; contbr. poetry, essays and short stories to numerous mags. and anthologies, including: Black Scholar, Yardbird, Indigine, Ms., Third World Women, Sojourner, Bopp, Essence, Heresies, The Little Mag., Chgo. Rev., Am. Rag, Womansports; performing mem. Sounds in Motion Dance Co.; performed in various jazz/poetry collaborations; mem. faculty Sonoma State U., 1973-75, Mills Coll., 1975, CCNY, 1975, Douglass Coll., 1978; lectr. in field. Recipient award Outer Critics Circle, 1977; OBIE award, 1977, 80; Audelco award, 1977; Frank Silvera Writer's Workshop award, 1978; poetry award Los Angeles Times book prizes, 1981. Guggenheim fellow, 1981. Mem. Actors Equity, Nat. Acad. TV Arts and Scis., Acad. Am. Poets, Dramatist's Guild, PEN Am. Center, Poets and Writer's, Inc., N.Y. Feminist Art Guild. Office: care D Franklin Suite 1290S Omni Internat Atlanta GA 30305 *

SHANK, ORELIA W. HIGH, educator; b. Zebulon, N.C., May 12; d. Windric Clarence and Ada Blanche (Cox) High; student Hampton Inst., 1936-38; A.B., N.C. State Coll., 1942; certificate Chgo. Tchrs. Coll., 1960; postgrad. Columbia, 1953-60; M.A. in Teaching, Speech and Performing Arts, Northeastern Ill. U., 1968; m. Grady O'Neal Shank, May 5, 1945. Riveter, Eastern Aircraft Corp., Tarrytown, N.Y., 1942-45; tchr. Laurinburg (N.C.) Inst., 1945; clk. City Tax Office, Los Angeles, 1948-50; bd. clk. SSS, Chgo., 1951-52; tchr. Chgo. Bd. Edn., 1952-73; clk. med. records Greenburgh Neighborhood Health Center, White Plains, N.Y., from 1973; supr. Westchester County (N.Y.) Dept. Health and Med. Records, until 1979; now tchr. EduCage, spl. high sch. facility, White Plains; tchr. adult edn., White Plains, 1974; English tchr. Alexander Hamilton High Sch., Elmsford, N.Y., 1975; Mem. Chgo. Tchrs. Union, Speech Assn. Am., Internat. Platform Assn., Phi Delta Kappa, Zeta Phi Beta (recipient Finer Womanhood award 1968). Author: Who Am I?, 1975. Home: 155 Ferris Ave White Plains NY 10603 Office: 5 New St White Plains NY 10603

SHANKLES, JEANIE THARPE, therapist; b. Puunene, Maui, Hawaii, Feb. 26, 1953; d. Edgar Jefferson and Gertrude (Addis) Tharpe; student Furman U., Greenville, S.C., 1970-74; B.A. in Psychology, U. Ala., Birmingham, 1974, M.A. in Urban Planning, 1976; postgrad. U. Ga., Athens, 1976, Ga. State U., Atlanta, 1977; m. Glenn Harding Shankles, Aug. 7, 1980. Mem. interview panel weekly public interest TV Kowloon, Hong Kong, 1969-70; librarian Balch, Bingham, Banker et al, Birmingham, 1974-75; dir. human resources Bapt. Med. Center, Ft. Payne, Ala., 1979-80; home visitor outreach program Coosa Valley Area Planning and Devel. Commn., Rome, Ga., 1981; ednl. therapist adolescent program N.W. Psychoednl. Center, Rome, Ga., 1981—. Mem. AAUW, Kappa Delta Epsilon. Home: 2833 Thornhill Rd Apt 151A Birmingham AL 35213 Office: 200 Reece St Rome GA 30161

SHANKS, MARIE JEANETTE, fin. exec.; b. Bloomington, Calif., Aug. 17, 1943; d. Marie Jeanette (Brodeur) Benedict; A.Acctg. and Bus. Mgmt., Central Ariz. Coll., 1972; m. Robert Shanks, Feb. 17, 1965; 1 son, Oscar Lee. Office mgr., med. asst. Dr. Linda Martin D.O., Apache Junction, Ariz., 1974-77; owner-operator Acctg. Dynamics, Tax Service, Apache Junction, 1975—. Citizen response teaching coordinator Paramedics Unltd., Apache Junction, 1978—; emergency med. technician II, Ariz. Disaster Unit #1, 1978—; mem. Apache Junction City Council, 1978—; chmn. Human Resources Devel. Commn., 1979—; sr. health service coordinator, area chmn., 1979—; polit. subdiv. coordinator Apache Junction Area Community Found., 1982; coordinator Reach Out Emergency Food Bank, 1982; mem. Gov.'s Behavioral Health Adv. Council, 1980—; swim instr. ARC, 1978-79. Recipient Vol. Service award Sr. Health Fair, 1979, Civic Service award Eagles, 1980, Jaycees, 1980; cert. of recognition Mayor of Apache Junction, 1981. Mem. Nat. Assn. Female Execs., Ariz. Small Bus. Assn., League Ariz. Towns-Cities, Nat. League Towns-Cities, Am. Soc. Profl. and Exec. Women (area network coordinator). Democrat. Mem. Ch. Jesus Christ of Latter-Day Saints. Clubs: Oddfellows, Rebekas, DAV Aux. Address: 472 S Goldfield Rd Apache Junction AZ 85220

SHANNON, MARGARET RITA, educator; b. Cambridge, Mass.; d. James J. and Catherine M. (McDonough) Shannon; B.S., Mass. State Coll., 1936; M.Ed., Harvard U., 1947, Ed.D., 1959. Tchr. pub. schs., Cambridge, 1936-51; asst. prof. Mass. State Coll., Lowell, 1951-59, asso. prof. 1959-65, prof., 1965-74, chmn. dept. edn., 1969-74; dean Coll. Edn. U. Lowell, 1974-79, dean, prof. emerita, 1979—; sometime lectr. Mem. Internat. Reading Assn. (cons. nat. conf.), Am. Ednl. Research Assn., Nat. Council Tchrs. English (com. on linguistics and reading), Delta Kappa Gamma, Pi Lambda Theta (chpt. pres. 1958-61). Author textbooks; contbr. articles to profl. jours. Office: Coll Edn U Lowell S Campus Lowell MA 01854

SHANNON, MARILYN, state senator; b. Providence, Jan. 3, 1953; student U. R.I., 1975, Boston Coll. Law Sch., 1978. Admitted to R.I. bar; individual practice law, Providence; mem. R.I. Senate, 1980—. Democrat. Office: Rhode Island State House Providence RI 02903 *

SHANNON, MARY FRANCES, med. adminstr.; b. Lowell, Mass., Dec. 8, 1932; d. Francis Michael and Caroline (Khristyniak) McCaughey; R.N., St. John's Hosp. Sch. Nursing, 1953; m. Richard T. Shannon, Sept. 11, 1982; 1 dau. from previous marriage, Karen McDonough. Mem. staff St. John's Hosp., Lowell, 1953—, head nurse, 1975, coordinator emergency dept., 1976—; mem. Greater Lowell Hosp. Emergency Med. Service Com., 1976—; chmn. New Eng. Symposium Emergency Medicine, 1976; instr., trainer Am. Heart Assn., 1975—, affiliate faculty mem. basic life support, 1980—, instr. advanced cardiac life support, 1981—; mem. emergency med. services task planning force Merrimack Valley Health Planning Council, 1977; mem. Commonwealth of Mass. Emergency Med. Care Adv. Bd., 1978—, chmn. nursing continuing edn. com., 1980; chmn. tng. com. Merrimack Valley Emergency Med. Services Corp., 1982, sec. nursing services com., 1982. Recipient Improvement Emergency Med. Services award Commonwealth Mass., 1976. Mem. Nat. Emergency Dept. Nurses Assn. (state chmn. 1977-78, pres. state coordinating council 1977, nat. membership and credentials com. 1977, pres. Beacon chpt. 1976), Nat. Assn. Emergency Med. Technicians (founding mem.), Merrimack Valley Emergency Med. Technicians Assn. (Dedication award), Am. Heart Assn. (emergency cardiac care cardio pulmonary resuscitation com. N.E. chpt. 1978). Democrat. Roman Catholic. Home: 25 Georgia Ave Lowell MA 01851 Office: 1 Hosp Dr Lowell MA 01852

SHANNON, RUTH ILENE, ins. co. claims staff; b. Green Valley, Ill., June 28, 1926; d. Ceasar Lavel and Martha Agnes (Parkins) Dean; grad. public schs.; m. Jack Willard Shannon, Apr. 5, 1947; children—Dennis Dean, Mallory Kay (Mrs. Jack E. Follis). Br. clk. Skelly Oil Co., Mt. Pleasant, Mich., 1962-65; clk.-typist mgmt. analysts U.S. Army, Mannheim, Ger., 1965-67; sec. to dean of faculty Saginaw Valley Coll., 1967-68; sr. claim examiner Pekin Life Ins. Co. (Ill.), 1969—. Pres., Tazewell County Democratic Women's Club, 1978-79. Mem. Am. Bus. Women's Assn. (v.p. 1978). Methodist. Club: Pekin Emblem (1st v.p. 1980-81). Home: 2005 Westgate Dr Pekin IL 61554 Office: 2505 Court St Pekin IL 61558

SHANNON, SARA BELLE MERRITT, genealogist, club woman; b. Balt. County, Md., Dec. 9, 1917; d. Stephen Stewart and Anna Kate (Hopkins) Merritt; student Western Md. Coll., 1934-36; B.S., Johns Hopkins U., 1939; m. William Gilmore Shannon, Dec. 23, 1944 (dec. Feb. 1977); 1 dau., Betty Ann Shannon Evans. Researcher, Johns Hopkins Hosp., Balt., 1937-40, Mass. Meml. Hosp., Boston, 1940-42; with Md. Lab., State Dept. Health, 1942-43, McCormick & Co., Balt., 1943-47; tchr. aide Montgomery County (Md.) Sch. System, 1965-70. Sunday sch. tchr., nursery and primary dept.; chmn. Ch. Circle; chmn. library com., elem. sch. PTA. Mem. DAR (vice regent Capt. Molly Pitcher chpt. 1967-70, regent Columbia, S.C., chpt. 1975-77, dir. dist. III S.C. 1979-81, nat. vice chmn. lineage research Southeastern div. 1976-79, chmn. bd. trustees Tamasee DAR Sch., Inc.), Robert Burns Soc., S.C. Geneal. Soc., Md. Geneal. Soc., Daus. of War of 1812, UDC, Daus. Am. Colonists, Colonial Dames XVII Century. Author: (with William Gilmore Shannon), Smarr Family, 1971, Shannon Family and Connections, 1973, Gilmore Family, 1976; Merritt, Lynch and Allied Families, 1979.

SHANNON, VIRGINIA JEANNE, nurse educator; b. Bayonne, N.J., Mar. 31, 1921; d. Constantine Joseph and Bertha Martha (Mierziewski) Grabowski; R.N., St. James Hosp. Sch. Nursing, Newark, N.J., 1942; B.S. in Nursing, Seton Hall U., 1954; M.S., Ariz. State U., Tempe, 1975; student Columbia U., 1946-47, U. Calif., San Francisco, 1967-69, U. Ariz., 1976-77, No. Ariz. U., 1976, 78; m. Wilfred Raymond Shannon, Mar. 28, 1946; children—Jeanne Constance (Mrs. Harry C. Parham), Carol Ann, David Thomas, Christopher Robert. Staff nurse Mountainside Hosp., Montclair, N.J., 1942; asst. head nurse U.S. VA Psychiat. Hosp., Lyons, N.J., 1946-47; staff nurse, pvt. duty nurse Muhlenberg Hosp., Plainfield, N.J., 1948-53; part-time instr., trainer home nursing ARC, Plainfield, 1949-54; public health nurse Vis. Nurse Service, Plainfield, N.J., 1954-55; sch. nurse Phoenix Union High Sch., 1956-66, area vocat. center psychiat. nursing clin. instr., 1966-73, dir. practical nursing program, 1973—. Committeewoman, Phoenix Democratic Com., 1960-65, precinct capt., 1965-67; active Girl Scouts U.S.; vol. ARC, 1957-65. Served with AUS, 1943-46. Mem. Nat. Assn. Practical Nurse Edn. and Services (bd. dirs.), Assn. Children with Learning Disabilities, Nat. League Nursing, Am. Nurses Assn., Nat. Assn. Practical Nurse Edn. and Services, Nat. Assn. Health Occupations Tchrs., Am. Edn. Assn., Am. Vocat. Assn., Ariz. State Vocat. Assn., Ariz. Mental Health Assn., Women's Overseas Service League (5th area dir.) credentials chmn. 1983 nat. conv.). Democrat. Roman Catholic. Home: 5223 N 22d Ave Phoenix AZ 85015 Office: 315 N 5th St Phoenix AZ 85004

SHAPIRO, BERNICE B., human resources ofcl.; b. Bklyn., July 24, 1954; d. Elias and Nancy (Schlimmer) Berenblit; B.A. in Sociology and Social Work, Bklyn. Coll., CUNY, 1974; M.B.A., M.A. in Human Resources, Labor Relations and Bus., New Sch. for Social Research, 1978; m. Shane Nevin Shapiro, Aug. 24, 1980. Employee benefits adminstr. Reynolds Securities, N.Y.C., 1974; personnel rep. Bonwit Teller, N.Y.C., 1974-75; human resources adminstr. Continental Grain Co., N.Y.C., 1975-79; supr. human resources Continental Can Internat. Corp., Stamford, 1979-80, mgr. human resources, 1980-81; mgr. human resources Continental Can Co., Stamford, 1981, internal cons. quality of work life programs, 1981—; cons., career counselor various placement firms, Stamford. Chmn., United Way campaign, Continental Grain Co., 1977-78, Continental Can Co. Internat., 1980-81. Recipient United Way award, 1980-81, Bronze merit award, 1977, Silver merit award, 1978. Mem. Assn. M.B.A. Execs., Internat. Assn. Personnel Women, Nat. Assn. Female Execs. Office: 51 Harbor Plaza Stamford CT 06904

SHAPIRO, CAROL SADIE, plastic surgeon; b. Pitts., Sept. 24, 1939; d. Leo I. and Charlotte H. (Heller) Shapiro; B.S., U. Pitts., 1961; M.D. Woman's Med. Coll. Pa., 1965; m. Donald E. Morgan, May 1974; stepchildren—Donald E., Leslie Marie. Intern, Phila. Gen. Hosp., 1965-66; resident gen. surgery Georgetown U. Hosp., Washington, 1966-69, resident plastic surgery, 1969-71, post tng. fellow, 1971-72; practice medicine specializing in plastic surgery, Woodbridge, Va., 1972—; mem. staff Potomac Hosp., Woodbridge, Va., chief of staff, 1981-83; mem staff Prince William Hosp., Manassas, Va., Commonwealth Hosp., Fairfax, Va.; clin. instr. Georgetown U. Sch. Medicine, 1972—. Mem. Prince William County Med. Soc. (pres. 1980-81). Home: 7822 Gingerbread Ln Fairfax Station VA 22039 Office: PO Box 431 Opitz Blvd Woodbridge VA 22191

SHAPIRO, DEBORAH, social worker, educator; b. Detroit, Sept. 1, 1923; d. Israel Moses and Bertha (Lightstone) S.; B.A., Wayne State U., 1944; M.A., U. Chgo., 1948; D.S.W., Columbia U., 1966; 1 adopted dau., Sharon Sarah. Research asso. Columbia U. Sch. Social Work, N.Y.C., 1962-73; study dir., dir. research Child Welfare League Am., N.Y.C., 1973-79; asso. prof., chairperson social work dept., dir. M.S.W. program Rutgers U., Camden, N.J., 1979—; research cons., lectr. N.Y. U., 1979—. NIMH fellow, 1960-61; Russell Sage Found. fellow, 1961-62. Mem. AAUP, Nat. Assn. Social Workers, Evaluation Research Soc. Democrat. Jewish. Author: Agencies and Foster Children, 1976; Parents and Protectors, 1979; also articles, book revs. Office: 327 Cooper St Camden NJ 08102

SHAPIRO, EVA, fashion designer; b. Bucharest, Rumania, June 9, 1931; d. Abraham and Yolan (Fried) Baumzweig; ed. Acad. Ronsard, Bucharest, Esvuela de Bellas Artes (Chile); m. Oscar Shapiro, Oct. 7, 1957 (div.); 1 dau., Jacqueline. Founder, Robert Janan Ltd., N.Y.C., 1972, now pres. Address: 530 7th Ave New York NY 10018 *

SHAPIRO, HELEN, public relations specialist; b. Boston; d. Harry and Clara (Tabak) S.; spl. student U. Mass., N.Y. U. Account exec. Harshe-Rotman & Druck Inc., N.Y.C., 1953-61, v.p., 1961-75; cons. Padilla & Speer, Public Relations, Multiple Sclerosis, Mind Movers, Ltd., 1975-77; public relations dir. Catalyst, career guidance orgn., N.Y.C., 1977-78; ind. contractor Doremus & Co., also cons. Charlotte C. Klein, Public Relations, 1978-81; owner, mgr. Helen Shapiro Public Relations, N.Y.C., 1978-81; exec. asst. IntraMed Communications, Inc. div. Sudler & Hennessey, Advt., N.Y.C., 1981—. Mem. Am. Women in Radio and TV, Publicity Club N.Y., Women in Communications. Club: B'nai B'rith.

SHAPIRO, JOHANNA FREEDMAN, psychologist; b. Los Angeles, May 26, 1949; d. Benedict and Nancy Mars Freedman; B.A., Stanford U., 1971, M.A., 1973, Ph.D., 1975; m. Deane H. Shapiro, Jr., Apr. 26, 1970; children—Shauna Lin, Jena Ann. Cons., Center for Research on Women, Stanford (Calif.) U., 1976-77; social scientist Family Focus project, dept. phys. therapy Stanford Med. Sch., 1976-77; asst. prof., dir. behavioral sci., dept. family medicine U. Calif. Irvine Med. Center, 1978—. Recipient faculty devel. award U. Calif. Irvine, 1978, Calif. Coll. Medicine, 1979; March of Dimes Social and Behavioral award, 1980 Mem. Am. Psychol. Assn., Assn. for Advancement of Behavior Therapy, Am. Assn. Marriage, Family Child Therapists, Soc. of Tchrs. of Family Medicine, Soc. Behavioral Medicine, Phi Beta Kappa. Contbr. articles to profl. jours. Home: 1009 Canyon View Dr Laguna Beach CA 92651 Office: 101 City Drive S Orange CA 92668

SHAPIRO, JUDITH DEE, pharm. co. exec.; b. Bklyn., Mar. 11, 1947; d. Leo and Sarah (Schneck) S.; B.A., Douglass Coll., 1967; M.S., Rutgers U., 1972. Various programming and systems analyst positions Johnson & Johnson, New Brunswick, N.J., 1967-68, Services Bur. Corp., IBM, N.Y.C., 1969, Rutgers U., New Brunswick, 1970-71; info. services staff mem.-instr. Western Electric Co., Princeton, N.J., 1971-74; asso. dir. info. services Mathematica Inc., Princeton, N.J., 1974-77; systems engring. mgr. Ortho Pharm. Co., Raritan, N.J., 1977-78, project mgr., 1978-79, mgr. tech. devel., 1979-81, dir. systems and programming, 1981-82, sales rep., 1982—; instr. data processing Somerset County Coll. Dist. committeewoman Democratic Party Somerset County (N.J.), 1971-76; co. vice chmn. United Way Campaign, 1979, co. chmn., 1980; tutor sch.-release program Clinton (N.J.) State Prison, 1974. Cert. in data processing. Mem. Am. Statis. Assn., Assn. for Computing Machinery. Home: 11 Webb Rd Westport CT 06880 Office: Ortho Pharm Corp Route 202 Raritan NJ 08869

SHAPIRO, NORMA SONDRA LEVY, fed. judge; b. Phila., July 27, 1928; d. Bert and Jane (Kotkin) Levy; B.A. in Polit. Theory with honors, U. Mich., 1948; J.D. magna cum laude, U. Pa., 1951; m. Bernard Shapiro, Aug. 21, 1949; children—Finley, Neil, Aaron. Admitted to Pa. bar, 1952, U.S. Supreme Ct. bar, 1978; law clk. to judge Pa. Supreme Ct., 1951-52; instr. U. Pa. Law Sch., 1951-52, 55-56; asso. firm Dechert Price & Rhoads, Phila., 1956-58, 67-73, partner, 1973-78; judge U.S. Dist. Ct. for Eastern Pa., 1978—; asso. trustee U. Pa. Law Sch., 1978—; trustee Women's Law Project, 1978—; mem. lawyer's adv. panel Pa. Gov.'s Commn. on Status of Women, 1974; legal adv. Regional Council Child Psychiatry. Pres., Lower Merion County (Pa.) Bd. Sch. Dirs., 1968-77, 77, v.p., 1976; v.p. Jewish Community Relations Council of Greater Phila., 1975-77; chmn. legal affairs com., 1978; pres. Belmont Hills Home and Sch. Assn., Lower Merion Twp.; legis. chmn. Lower Merion Sch. Dist. Intersch. Council; mem. Task Force on Mental Health of Children and Youth of Pa.; treas., chmn. edn. com. Human Relations Council Lower Merion; v.p., parliamentarian, Nes Ami Penn Valley Congregation, Lower Merion Twp. Named Woman of Yr., Oxford Circle Jewish Community Center, 1979, Woman of Distinction, Golden Slipper Club, 1979; Gowen fellow, 1954-55. Mem. Am. Law Inst., Am. Bar Found., Am. Bar Assn. (vice chmn. com. on law and mental health sect. family law). Pa. Bar Assn. (ho. of dels. 1979—), Phila. Bar Assn. (chmn. com. women's rights 1972, 74-75, chmn. bd. govs. 1977—, chmn. public relations com. 1978), Fed. Bar Assn., Nat. Assn. Women Lawyers, Phila. Trial Lawyers Assn., Am. Judicature Soc., Phila. Fellowship Commn., Order of Coif (chpt. pres. 1973-75), Tau Epsilon Rho. Guest editor Shingle, 1972. Office: US Courthouse Room 10614 601 Market St Philadelphia PA 19106 *

SHAPIRO, PHYLLIS (MRS. ABRAHAM SHAPIRO), hotel adminstr.; b. Montreal, Que., Can., Mar. 12, 1922; d. Isadore and Sadie (Novack) Hochmitz; student Sullivan Bus. Coll., Montreal, 1939-41; m. Abraham Shapiro, Aug. 22, 1961; children—Gerri and Jewel (twins). Asst. mgr. Nat. Food Store Ltd., Montreal, 1942-45; office comptroller Dixon Watch Importing Co., 1945-48, adminstr. Bernard Schaeffer & Sons, importing agy., 1948-51; exec. sec. William Rosenberg, architect, 1951-57; exec. sec. Eugene Meth Assos., financier, 1957-61; adminstr. Twin City Motel, Brewer, Maine, 1968—; pres. The Carriage Inn, Pittsfield, Maine, 1978—. Jewish. Mem. B'nai Brith, Hadassah. Home: 58 Broadway Bangor ME 04401 Office: 453 Wilson St Brewer ME 04412

SHAPIRO, SANDRA M., psychologist; b. N.Y.C., May 23, 1938; d. Jacob and Vera (Gordon) Milstein; A.B. magna cum laude, Hunter Coll., 1957; M.A., Bryn Mawr Coll., 1960, Ph.D. (NSF fellow), 1964; m. Robert Shapiro, Apr. 5, 1964; 1 son, Michael Gordon. Research assoc. Queens Coll., City U. N.Y., Flushing, 1963-65, instr. psychology, 1965-67, asst. prof., 1967-75, assoc. prof., 1975—; pvt. practice psychotherapy, N.Y.C. and Gt. Neck, N.Y.; bd. dirs. Nat. Inst. for Psychotherapies, dir. biofeedback and stress mgmt. service. Lic. psychologist, N.Y. State. Mem. Am. Psychol. Assn., AAUP, Nat. Registry for Health Service Providers in Psychology. Contbr. articles to profl. jours. Home: 23 Ridge Dr E Great Neck NY 11021 Office: Psychology Dept Queens Coll Flushing NY 11367

SHAPIRO, SHARON, hosp. supply corp. exec.; b. Chgo., Jan. 15, 1950; d. Harry H. and Miriam G. Shapiro; B.S. in Bus. Adminstrn. and Mktg., So. Ill. U., 1972; M.B.A. in Mktg., Roosevelt U., 1982. With Warren-Teed Pharms., Columbus, Ohio, 1972-74, Eli Lilly & Co., Indpls., 1974-76; therapeutic systems rep. Alza Corp., Palo Alto, Calif., 1976-78; hyperalimentation specialist Am. McGaw div. Am. Hosp. Supply Corp., Evanston, Ill., 1978-81, nutrition ter. mgr., 1981-82; mktg. cons. Video Intro, 1980-82; account exec. Vicom Assocs., San Francisco, 1982—; guest lectr. Rancho La Puerta, Tecate, Mex. Mem. Med. Mktg. Assn. Office: Vicom Assocs 901 Battery San Francisco CA 94111

SHAPIRO, SUSAN HOLLY, interior designer; b. N.Y.C., Aug. 27, 1943; d. Murray and Roslyn Jeanette Benjamin (Polsky) Chalkin; B.A. in Fine Arts, Syracuse U., 1964; M.A., N.Y.U., 1965; cert. in appraisal, Post Coll., 1981; divorced; 1 son by previous marriage—Christopher A. Morrow. Tchr., N.Y.C. Pub. Schs., 1965-69; interior designer Bagatelle Assos., Roslyn, N.Y., 1971-74, The Wallpaper Place, Unltd., 1974-75; pres. Apricot Designs, Ltd., Roslyn, 1974-79, Trio Design I and Trio Designs II, Inc., Huntington, N.Y., 1975-80, SHS Design Assocs., Ctd., Great Neck, N.Y., 1980—; lectr. interior design adult evening programs. Vice pres. Roslyn LWV, Civic Assn., Norgate; co-chmn. budget adv. com. Roslyn Pub. Schs.; v.p. The Village Sch. Mem. Am. Soc. Interior Designers, Allied Bd. Trade, Internat. Soc. Interior Designers, Assn. Environ. Designers. Club: Roslyn Hadassah (v.p., Woman of Yr.). Editor in chief Hadassah Jour., 1981-82. Office: 98 Cutter Mill Rd Great Neck NY 11521

SHAROFF, GWENDOLYN IDELL ANDERSON, educator; b. Houston, July 16, 1940; d. Leroy Lawrence and Harriett Idell (Galbreath) Anderson; B.A., Baylor U., 1962, M.A., 1963; Ph.D., U. So. Calif., 1981; m. Michael Sharoff, June 20, 1970. Tchr., Victoria (Tex.) High Sch., 1963-64; dir. Galveston (Tex.) Teen-Children's Theatre, 1964-66; asst. prof. speech and drama, dir. theatre Culver-Stockton Coll., Canton, Mo., 1966-69; instr. speech and drama, costumer Bradley U., Peoria, Ill., 1969-70; prodn. supr. studio co. Acad. Dramatic Art, Oakland U., Rochester, Mich., 1970-71; instr. theatre Fullerton (Calif.) Jr. Coll., 1971-72, Cypress Coll., 1972-73; instr. theatre Calif. State Coll., San Bernardino, 1972-73, lectr. speech and drama, 1976-78; asst. prof. communications Chapman Coll., Orange, Calif., 1973-76; lectr. theatre Saddleback Coll., Mission Viejo, Calif., 1978-79; lectr. theatre Fullerton (Calif.) Coll., 1980—, dir. Fullerton Coll. Children's Theatre, 1981—. Recipient Dissertation award Univ.-Coll. Theatre Assn., 1982. Mem. Speech Communication Assn., ANTA, Am. Theatre Assn. (chmn. Region VIII Network for Women), So. Calif. Ednl. Theatre Assn. (adv. council), Alpha Lambda Delta, Alpha Chi, Tau Beta Sigma, Alpha Psi Omega, Pi Alpha Lambda (parliamentarian, historian), Theta Alpha Phi, Mu Phi Epsilon (pres. 1981-83). Contbr. book revs. to profl. jours. Home: 2032 Victoria Dr Fullerton CA 92631

SHARP, ANNE CATHERINE, artist; b. Red Bank, N.J., Nov. 1, 1943; d. Elmer Eugene and Ethel Violet (Hunter) S.; B.F.A., Pratt Inst., 1965; M.F.A., Bklyn. Coll., 1973. One woman shows: Pace Editions, N.Y.C., 1974, Contemporary Gallery, Dallas, 1975, Eatontown (N.J.) Hist. Mus., 1980; group shows include: Mus. Modern Art, N.Y.C., 1975, 76, Arnot Art Mus., Elmira, N.Y., 1975, Bronx (N.Y.) Mus., 1975; represented in permanent collections: Smithsonian Instn., Nat. Air and Space Mus., Albright-Knox Gallery, Buffalo, Philip Morris, Inc.; owner, mgr. Anne Sharp Studio, N.Y.C., 1982—; art tchr. Sch. Visual Arts, 1978—. Mem. Artists Equity, Women in the Arts. Home: 20 Waterside Plaza New York NY 10010

SHARP, DAWN, educator; b. Bradenton, Fla., Oct. 1, 1935; d. Robert Frances Sharp and Helen (Caldwell) Sharp Mooers; B.A. cum laude (Fla. scholar), Fla. State U., 1957, M.A. (Fla. State U. fellow), 1962, postgrad. (NDEA fellow), 1971—. Tchr. English, Miami (Fla.) Sr. High Sch., 1957-59, Druid Hills (Ga.) High Sch., 1960-61, Fla. State U. Bootstrap, Turner AFB, Albany, Ga., 1963; instr. English, St. Petersburg (Fla.) Jr. Coll., 1963-73; asso. project dir. First Nat. Survey Allied Health Occupations Programs in Jr. Colls., USPHS, Am. Assn. Jr. Colls., Washington, 1969-70, program chmn. Southeastern Conf. on English in Two-Yr. Coll.; adminstrv. intern office of v.p. for academic affairs Fla. State U., office of pres. Fla. Senate. Recipient various radio speaking and oratory awards; recipient Panhellenic and Sigma Kappa scholarship medals. Mem. Am. Assn. Higher Edn., Assn. for Study Higher Edn., Am. Polit. Sci. Assn., AAUW, Fla. State U. Found., Nat. Assn. Women Deans, Adminstrs., and Counselors, Internat. Platform Assn., Phi Delta Kappa, Kappa Delta Pi, Phi Kappa Phi, Sigma Kappa, Sigma Tau Delta (past. chpt. pres.). Democrat. Episcopalian. Editor: The Link, 1966-67. Home: 242 Dalton Ct Tallahassee FL 32304 Office: Dept Ednl Leadership College of Education Florida State Univ Tallahassee FL 32306

SHARP, GUN ANITA, public relations exec.; b. Gothenburg, Sweden, Aug. 16, 1943; came to U.S., 1970; d. Andre Olof and Elsa Viola (Henrikson) B.A. in Advt. and Public Relations, Annonsbyra Foren Skola for Advt. and Public Relations, 1962; m. Roger Sharp, June 5, 1976; 1 son, Adam Mikael. Model, Europe, 1957-69; model Wilhelmina Model Agy., N.Y.C., 1970-72; free-lance broadcaster, newspaper journalist, Europe, 1966-69, U.S., 1970-74; with Bonnier Mag. Group Swedish Broadcasting, N.Y.C., 1970-74; head TV dept. R. Marston & Assos., N.Y.C., 1974-78; pres. GRS Communications, Inc., N.Y.C., 1978—. Mem. Am. Women Radio and TV, Women in Communications. Clubs: Englewood (N.J.); Marstrand Yacht; Stamford Yacht. Office: 200 W 57th St New York NY 10019

SHARP, KARLA KAY, farm trailer mfg. co. exec.; b. Duncan, Okla., May 21, 1943; d. Sam and Ethel Geneva (Cody) Willis; m. Edmond E. Sharp, May 30, 1961; children—Tammy, Steve, Joy. Co-founder, 1972, since pres., office mgr. Sharp Mfg. & Distbg. Co., Inc., Butte, Nebr. Republican. Office: Sharp Mfg Distbg Co S Hwy 12 PO Box 137 Butte NE 68722

SHARP, MARY LEE, banker; b. Lancaster, Ky., Dec. 18, 1934; d. William and Jessamine (Burdine) Sharp; ed. high sch.; m. Horace Sharp, Feb. 13, 1952. Gen. bookkeeper Citizens Nat. Bank, Danville, Ky., 1953-58; with Garrard Bank & Trust Co., Lancaster, 1958—, trust officer, 1972—, cashier, 1973-80, asst. v.p., 1980—, also dir. Pianist, Pleasant Grove Christian Ch., 1953—; past treas. Arthritis Found., Cancer Soc. Mem. Nat. Assn. Bank Women (treas. Lexington group 1981-82). Club: Lancaster Women's (compiled cookbook 1973). Home: 123 Hagan Ct Lancaster KY 40444 Office: Garrard Bank & Trust Co PO Box 242 Lancaster KY 40444

SHARP, MELODY ANN, editor; b. East Providence, R.I., Aug. 13, 1948; d. Edward L. and Elsie Mary (Mello) S.; B.A., Fullerton State U., 1973, M.A. in Communications, 1981. . Editorial asst. True mag., Los Angeles, 1974-76; asso. editor East/West Network, Los Angeles, 1976-78; mng. editor, acting editor Playgirl mag., Santa Monica, Calif., 1978-79, v.p., editor spl. publs., 1979-81; editor Couples mag., Santa Monica, Calif., 1980-81; editor mag. series: Diet and Exercise, 1980, Fashion '80, 1980, Fashion and Beauty for Working Women, 1980, Running for Health and Beauty, 1980; dir. communications Cambridge Plan Internat., Monterey, Calif., 1981—. Mem. Women in Communications, Woman Can Win. Democrat. Office: Cambridge Plan Internat Garden Rd Monterey CA 93940

SHARP, PATTY ANN, educator; b. Sikeston, Mo., Dec. 26, 1946; d. John Sam and Pauline (Blagg) Varnon; B.S. in Edn., S.E. Mo. State U., 1968; m. Stephen Rhodes Sharp, June 23, 1967. Tchr., Memphis City Schs., 1969-71; curriculum developer Adult Edn. Center, Memphis, 1971-72; dir. Mo. Delta Community Corp., Hayti, Mo., 1972-73; tchr. Kennett (Mo.) High Sch., 1973—. Committeewoman 25th Senatorial Dist. State Democratic Com. Kennett, 1980—. Mem. S.E. Mo. Scholastic Publs. Assn., Kennett Community Tchrs. Assn., S.E. Mo. Tchrs. Assn., Mo. State Tchrs. Assn., Mo. Interscholastic Publs. Assn., Journalism Edn. Assn., PEO, Delta Delta Delta. Contbr. articles in field to profl. publs. Home: 807 College St Kennett MO 63857 Office: 1400 W Washington St Kennett MO 63857

SHARP, SARAH SONYA, newspaper reporter; b. Quakertown, Pa., Sept. 26, 1933; d. Stanley Evan and Sarah Sigrid (Ostrom) Grant; student Bucks County Community Coll., 1975-76, San Antonio Coll., 1978; m. Robert Sharp, Dec. 25, 1951 (dec.); children—Gregory Robert, Jan. Linnea. Corr., Daily Intelligencer, Doylestown, Pa. and Bethlehem (Pa.) Globe Times, 1957-58; gen. news reporter Morning Call Newspaper, Allentown, Pa., 1959—. Mem. internat. news media adv. com. Nat. Coalition for Children's Justice, 1978—. Mem. Nat. Fedn. Press Women (nat. conv. chmn. 1981, ex-oficio nat. bd. mem.), Pa. Press Club (past pres.). Home: 16 S 11th St Quakertown PA 18951

SHARP, SHARON BARTS, state ofcl.; b. Mishawaka, Ind., Oct. 7, 1939; d. Edwin J. and Gertrude E. (Maculski) Barts; student Holy Cross Central Sch. Nursing, South Bend, Ind., 1957-59; A.A.S., William Rainy Harper Coll., 1975; m. Donald L. Sharp, Sept. 12, 1959; children—Laura Sue, Christopher Barts. Free-lance writer, 1973-77; editor Elk Grove Twp. (Ill.) News, 1975-76; clk. Elk Grove Twp., 1975-79; spl. asst. on women to gov. State of Ill., Chgo., 1979—. Hon. co-chairwoman ERA Ill.; mem. Ill. Displaced Homemaker Adv. Bd.; mem. Cook County Republican Exec. Com., 1975—; co-chmn. Cook County Rep. Central Com., 1975—; Rep. nominee Ill. sec. of state, 1978; pres. Woman's Nat. Rep. Club, 1980—; bd. dirs. Ill. Fedn. Rep. Women; mem. Rep. Women's Task Force of Ill.; mem. Ill. Community Coll. Bd., 1976-79; mem. women's bd. William Rainy Harper Coll. Mem. Chgo. Area Public Affairs Group, Women in Mgmt., Support Chgo., Rep. Women for ERA, Lifespan, LWV. Methodist. Clubs: Altrusa, City, Executive (Chgo.). Home: 1306 W Cedar Ln Arlington Heights IL 60005 Office: 160 N LaSalle St Suite 2010 Chicago IL 60601

SHARPLES, VIRGINIA MITCHELL, copywriter; b. Indpls., July 3, 1942; d. James Sutherin and Ruth (Kennedy) Mitchell; B.A. (Operation Outstanding award 1974), Butler U., Indpls., 1964, M.S., 1970; m. Richard J. Sharples, Dec. 24, 1973; children—Scott Brydson, Greg Black, Glen Black. Tutor high sch. students, Indpls., 1964-70, Phoenix, 1971; high sch. tchr., Phoenix, 1971-74, Tucson, 1974-75; customer services rep. Advanced Computer Techniques, Tucson, 1976-77; tchr. Aldine High Sch. Dist., Houston, 1977-78; tech. services engr. SWACO div. Dresser Industries, 1978-81, engring. writer Atlas div., Houston, 1981-82; copywriter Ogilvy & Mather, 1982—; seminar leader, cons. and speaker. Bd. dirs. Braes Forest Maintenance Fund, 1978-79; mem. women's aux. Casa de los Ninos Crisis Nursery, Tucson, 1975-76. Mem. Soc. Women Engrs. (exec. bd. 1982—), Soc. Petroleum Engrs. Methodist. Club: Dresser Toastmasters (pres. 1981). Author papers in field. Home: 2318 Binley Dr Houston TX 77077 Office: One Allen Center Houston TX 77002

SHARPLESS, ELIZABETH ANN, psychologist; b. N.YC., Jan. 18, 1943; d. Joseph and Katerine (Dwyer) Appledorf; B.A., Bryn Mawr Coll., 1963; M.A., Columbia U., 1967, Ph.D., 1974; advanced cert. CCNY, 1979; m. Thomas K. Sharpless, Mar. 30 1964 (div.); 1 son, Charles M.; m. 2d, Louis J. Gerstman, Sept. 11, 1981. Research asso. N.Y. Hosp-Cornell Med. Center, 1976-77; psychol. intern Coler Meml. Hosp., 1978-79; psychologist children's unit St. Agnes Hosp., White Plains, N.Y., 1979-81; asst. attending psychologist L.I. Jewish Hillside Med. Center, Queens Hosp. affiliation, 1981—; pvt. practice, 1980—. Staff, Family Center West Side YMCA. Lic. psychologist. Mem. Am. Psychol. Assn., N.Y. Psychol. Assn/. N.Y. Soc. Clin. Psychology, Nat. Assn. Sch. Psychologists, Sigma Xi, Kappa Delta. Contbr. articles to profl. jours. Home and Office: 11 Riverside Dr New York NY 10023

SHASSERE, JUNE KNIGHT, public relations and fund raising cons.; b. Chgo., Apr. 22, 1940; d. John and Mary Alice (Rudisel) Knight; B.S., Ind. State U., 1962; M.A., Ball State U., 1976; m. William Glenn Shassere, July 27, 1963. Tchr. high sch. journalism and English in Ind., 1962-64; newspaper reporter, Plymouth, Ind., 1964-66; editor U. Notre Dame, 1966-68; dir. public relations and devel. Culver Mil. Acad., St. Mary's Acad., also Ladywood-St. Agnes Sch., 1968-76; dir. public info. Ind. Office Manpower Devel., 1974-76; ind. public relations cons., 1972—; staff asso. Ind. U., 1977-80, dir. women in politics project, 1977—; vis. lectr. communications Purdue U., 1978-80; mem. Ind. Gov.'s Commn. Status Women, 1973-75; program leader, tng. cons. in field. Active fund raising local Am. Cancer Soc.; bd. dirs. Indpls. YWCA, 1982—. Named Outstanding Woman, Ind. Women's Polit. Caucus, 1979. Mem. Public Relations Soc. Am., Nat. Assn. Govt. Communicators, LWV, Ind. Soc. Public Adminstrn. (chmn. conf. 1979), Soc. Profl. Journalists-Sigma Delta Chi (dir., officer 1975—). Author tng. guides in field; editor: Women in Politics: Practical Hints for Candidates and Campaigners, 1978, Development of Downtown Terre Haute, Indiana: A Feasible Strategy, 1977, The Role of Women on Indiana Newspapers 1876-1976, 1977, Running Winning Leading: Public Leadership Development for Women, 1980. Home: 4491 Washington Blvd Indianapolis IN 46205

SHATAN, NORMA ALTSTEDTER, painter; b. N.Y.C., July 18, 1932; d. Irving Charles and Renee Rose (Green) Altstedter; student Academie de la Grande Chaumiere, Ecole du Louvre and Sorbonne, 1950-51; B.A., Goucher Coll., 1952; postgrad. Columbia U., 1955-58; m. Chaim F. Shatan, May 29, 1955; children—Gregory, Gabrielle, Jessica, Jeremy. One-person exhbns. include: Prince St. Gallery, 1970, 72, 73, 76, 77, 82, Paddlewicker Gallery, Lenox, Mass., 1977, 79; group shows include: Prince St. Gallery, Bklyn. Mus., Berkshire Mus; treas. Prince St. Gallery, 1970-80. Mem. Women in the Arts, Women's Caucus for Art, Found. Community of Artists. Translator: (with Alice Muehsam) The Sense of Form in Art (Heinrich Wolfflin), 1958. Home and Office: 415 Central Park W New York NY 10025

SHATTUCK, CATHIE ANN, lawyer, govt. adminstr.; b. Salt Lake City, July 18, 1945; d. Robert Ashley and Lillian Francis (Culp) S.; B.A., U. Nebr., 1967, J.D., 1970. Vice pres. Shattuck Farms, Inc., Hastings, Nebr., 1966-69, pres., 1969-70; admitted to Nebr. bar, 1970, Colo. bar, 1971, U.S. Supreme Ct. bar, 1975; atty., asst. project dir. Colo. Civil Rights Commn., Denver, 1971-73; trial atty. EEO Commn., Denver, 1973-77; partner firm Roybal & Shattuck, Denver, 1977-82; vice chmn. EEO Commn., Washington, 1982—; trainer, speaker in field. Patron Denver Art Mus. Mem. Fed. Bar Assn., Am. Bar Assn., Nebr. Bar Assn., Colo. Bar Assn., Denver Bar Assn., Am. Judicature Soc., Nat. Assn. Women Lawyers, Alpha Xi Delta, Delta Sigma Rho, Tau Kappa Alpha (pres. 1966-67), Pi Sigma Alpha (v.p. 1966-67). Office: Equal Employment Opportunity Commission 2401 E St NW Washington DC 20506

SHATZ, MARILYN JOYCE, psychologist, educator; b. N.Y.C., Mar. 4, 1939; d. Morris and Frieda Reva (Levinthal) Karpman; student Radcliffe Coll., 1957-59; A.B., U. Pa., 1971, M.A., 1973, Ph.D., 1975; children—Geoffrey, Adria. Asst. prof. CUNY, 1975-77; asst. prof. U. Mich., Ann Arbor, 1977-79, assoc. prof. psychology, 1979—; vis. scholar Harvard U., 1980-81, Wis. Center for Edn., Madison, 1981. NIMH grantee, 1976-80; Guggenheim fellow, 1980-81. Mem. Soc. Research in Child Devel., Linguistic Soc. Am., Psychonomic Soc., Cognitive Sci. Soc. Office: 330 Packard Rd Ann Arbor MI 48104

SHAUBERGER, MARY LOUISE FRANKLIN, home economist; b. Grand Cane, La., Mar. 1, 1930; d. Bernard Arvil and Corrie Lee (Abington) Franklin; B.S., La. Tech. U., 1951; postgrad. N.E. La. U., summers 1963-65; M.S., La. State U., 1973; m. Mial Jennings Shauberger, June 15, 1952; children—Rebecca Louise Shauberger Turner, Mial Jennings III, Gale Franklin (dec.), Sally Elaine Shauberger Rivers. Asst. home demonstration agt. La. Coop. Extension Service, Donaldsonville, 1951-52, asst. home economist, Tallulah, 1966-69, home economist, Coushatta, 1969—; elem. tchr. Madison Parish Schs., Tallulah, La., 1962-66; dietary cons. Red River Parish Council on Aging; adviser Red River Parish Fair Assn., Red River Parish Extension Homemakers Council. Dress chmn. Red River Parish Centennial Com., 1971; vol. worker Cystic Fibrosis Bike-a-thon, 1976-78, Red River Parish Blood Drive, 1977-81; mem. Red River Parish Emergency Med. Services Com., 1980. Recipient La. Extension Communication award, 1977, 81. Mem. Nat. Assn. Extension Home Economists (Disting. Service award 1981), La. Assn. Extension Home Economists (Disting. Service award 1981), Am. Home Econs. La. Tech. U. Home Econs. Found., Nat. Assn. Female Execs., DeSoto Parish Hist. Soc., Epsilon Sigma Phi. Democrat. Mem. Ch. of Christ. Home: PO Box 616 1120 Ashland Rd Coushatta LA 71019 Office: Adminstrn Bldg PO Drawer E Red Oak Rd Coushatta LA 71019

SHAUL, EILEEN ELIZABETH, beverage co. ofcl.; b. Ashtabula, Ohio, Mar. 6, 1952; d. Arthur B. and Mary Frances (Hinds) S. Public relations exec., performer Up With People, Inc., music touring corp., 1976-77; elem. sch. tchr., 1974-76; ter. sales mgr. Coca-Cola USA, Atlanta, 1977-80, account exec., 1980—. Mem. United Ch. Christ. Home: 275 Barrington Dr E Roswell GA 30076 Office: 8601 Dunwoody Pl Atlanta GA 30338

SHAULIS, ANNETTE ELAINE, hypnosis cons., real estate mgmt. exec.; b. Somerset, Pa., Oct. 18, 1948; d. Norman Albert and Janice Lorraine (Robbins) S.; B.A., Dickinson Coll., 1969; M.A., Indiana U. of Pa., 1975. Psychol. services asso. II Bedford/Somerset Mental Health Clinic, Somerset, 1972-78, Somerset State Hosp., 1978-79; pvt. practice hypnosis cons., Somerset, 1976—; pres. Habitability, Inc., real estate mgmt., Somerset, 1978—; exec. mgr. Gt. N.E. Land & Cattle Co., Somerset, 1980-82; owner, mgr. Somerset Credit and Collection Bur., 1981—; cons. Somerset County Headstart Program, 1977, 78. Squadron comdr. CAP, Somerset, 1977-78, recipient Meritorious Service award, 1977. Mem. Somerset Welfare League, Chi Omega. Home: 647 E Main St Somerset PA 15501 Office: 118 N Center Ave Somerset PA 15501

SHAVER, DEBORAH KAY, research lab. exec.; b. Omaha, May 31, 1950; d. Warren Eugene and Ida Charmaine (Ratcliff) Pizinger; B.S. in Chemistry magna cum laude, Creighton U., 1971, M.S. in Chemistry (Univ. fellow), 1973; m. Robert Gale Shaver, Jan. 1, 1980; 1 son, Benjamin. Environ. chemist Versar Inc., Springfield, Va., 1974-78; mgr. environ. services Bur. Explosives, Assn. Am. R.R.s, Washington, 1978-80; mgr. hazardous materials programs Systems Tech. Lab., Arlington, Va., 1980-82, dir. Transp. System div., 1982—. Mem. ASTM (chmn. exec. subcom.), Am. Chem. Soc. (environ. chemistry div.), Gamma Pi Epsilon. Home: 7526 Murillo St Springfield VA 22151

SHAW, ARACELIS GOBERNA, educator; b. Pinar del Rio, Cuba, June 22, 1922; came to U.S., 1948, naturalized, 1955; d. Jose B. and Eloisa (Santiuste) Goberna; B.S., B.L., Inst. Pinar del Rio, 1941; Ph.D. and Letters, U. Havana, 1948; M.A., U. Fla., 1957; m. Steven J. Shaw, June 8, 1952. Instr., Berlitz Sch. Langs., Miami, Fla., 1949-52, N.Y.C., 1952-54; research asst. U. Fla., 1955-57; mem. faculty Columbia (S.C.) Coll., 1957—, prof. Spanish, 1963—, chmn. dept. fgn. langs., 1962—, head Intercultural and Lang. Center, 1977—; dir. lang. workshops, cons. in field. Pres. S.C. chpt. Partners of Americas, 1975-78, 81—. Recipient Cervantes award, 1976, S.C. Bicentennial award, 1976. Mem. Am. Assn. Tchrs. Spanish and Portuguese (pres. S.C. chpt. 1973-74), MLA, Southeastern Conf. Fgn. Lang. Tchrs. (adv. bd.), Nat. Council Fgn. Lang. Teaching, Southeastern Conf. Latin Am. Studies, Sigma Delta Pi. Roman Catholic. Club: Columbia Coll. Internat. Author: (for TV) El Espanol Paso a Pso, 1969; also workbooks, lab. manuals. Home: 4832 Forest Ridge Ln Columbia SC 29206 Office: Intercultural and Lang Center Columbia Coll Columbia SC 29203

SHAW, BETTY LOU, cosmetics co. ofcl.; b. Indpls., Nov. 26, 1936; d. Harry William and Nora Elaine (Bailey) Brooks; student Ind. U., 1974—; children—LaNita Brown, Nikki Smith, Anthony, Tami, Richard. Sec. real estate and ins., Indpls., 1953-59; dist. sales mgr. Avon Products Inc., Indpls., 1967-81; owner, operator Chez Avant et Apres, Inc., 1982—. Treas. SHARP Neighborhood Assn., 1975-78; active NAACP. Mem. Nat. Panel of Am. Women (treas. local chpt. 1973—). Home: Chez Avant et Apres Inc Indianapolis IN 46220

SHAW, DAISY K. (MRS. FREDERICK SHAW), ednl. administr.; b. N.Y.C., Sept. 26, 1913; d. Littman and Lena (Kaplan) Katz; B.A., Hunter Coll., 1933; M.A., N.Y. U., 1955; postgrad. Columbia, 1933-35, 44, Cornell U., 1940, 61, Hunter Coll., 1950-52; m. Frederick Shaw, Nov. 21, 1940; children—Richard, Ellen. Tchr. French, N.Y.C. High Schs., 1935-43; tchr.-in charge L.I. City Evening High Sch., 1944-47; gen. asst. in charge guidance Washington Irving Evening High Sch., N.Y.C., 1950-58, coordinator citywide evening guidance center, 1951-62, asst. prin. Washington Irving High Sch., 1958-62; asst. prin. Simon Baruch Jr. High Sch., N.Y.C., 1955-58; dir. Bur. Ednl. and Vocat. Guidance of N.Y.C. Schs., 1962—; adj. asst. prof. dept. guidance and counseling Hunter Coll., 1964-71. Recipient Bourse Bargy traveling fellowship to France, 1936, Ford Found. fellowship, 1954-55; elected to Hunter Coll. Hall of Fame, 1972; recipient award Council Adminstrs. and Suprs. Mem. Assn. Adminstrv. Women in Edn., N.Y. Acad. Pub. Edn., Am., N.Y. State (counselor of yr. award 1975), N.Y.C. (pres. 1974-75) personnel and guidance assns., Assn. Counselor Edn. and Supervision, Nat. Vocat. Guidance Assn., Am. Sch. Counselors Assn., Council of Dirs. N.Y.C. Bd. Edn., Large City Dirs. Guidance (pres. 1969-70), Phi Beta Kappa. Contbr. articles to encys., textbook, profl. jours. Home: 41 Henry St Brooklyn NY 11201

SHAW, DEBORAH L., educator, spl. edn. cons.; b. Tulsa, July 8, 1950; d. Donald Lawrence and Virginia Sharon (Herron) Shaw; B.S. in Elem. and Spl. Edn. (Spl. edn. fellow 1971), U. Tex., Austin, 1972; M.Ed. (grad. trainee 1973-74, Atlanta Braves Wives Club scholar, summer 1974), Ga. State U., 1974; postgrad. Stephen F. Austin State U., 1978; m. Frank Allen Hertzog, July 28, 1979. Spl. edn. tchr. Spring Br. Ind. Sch. Dist., Houston, 1972-73; learning disabilities tchr. DeKalb County Schs., Atlanta, 1974-75, Dept. Def. Dependent Schs., Fulda (Germany) Am. Sch., 1975-78; spl. edn. tchr. Humble Ind. Sch. Dist., Houston, 1978-79; itinerant learning disabilities tchr., elem. schs. Lawton (Okla.) public schs., 1979—; organizer, condr. workshops; participant confs. in field. Supr. Spl. Olympics, Houston, 1973; active community theater. Recipient Outstanding Performance award Dept. Def. Dependent Schs., 1978. Mem. Council Exceptional Children (div. of children with learning disabilities), Assn. Children with Learning Disabilities, Library of Spl. Edn., Okla. Edn. Assn., Kappa Delta Pi. Republican. Lutheran. Home: 4835 NE Winfield Circle Lawton OK 73501 Office: 2211 NW 25th St Lawton OK 73505

SHAW, DOROTHY WEDGWORTH, home economist; b. Lauderdale, Miss., Jan. 7, 1922; d. Williw Langford and Sally Willis (Peel) Wedgworth; B.S., Miss. U. for Women, 1943; postgrad. U. Ala., 1951-52, Miss. State U., 1972, 77; m. B.E. Shaw, June 21, 1945 (dec. 1964); children—Bennie Ronald, Lowry Wedgworth, Patty Elizabeth. Tchr. Lauderdale County (Miss.) sch. system, 1943-47, 51-60, 62-68; extension home economist Kemper County, Miss., DeKalb, 1968—; cons. in field. Mem. Nat. Assn. Extension Home Economists, Miss. Assn. Extension Home Economists (State Disting. Service award 1979), Epsilon Sigma Phi. Baptist. Home and office: Box 37 DeKalb MS 39328

SHAW, ELEANOR JANE, newspaper editor; b. Columbus, Ohio, Mar. 23, 1949; d. Joseph Cannon and Wanda Jane (Campbell) S.; B.A., U. Del., 1971; m. John M. Flanagan, Sept. 1, 1974. With News-Jour. newspapers, Wilmington, Del., 1970—, acting bus. editor, 1976-77, editor HEW desk, asst. met. editor, 1977-80, bus. editor, 1980—. Bd. dirs. Del. 4-H Found., 1978—. Mem. Sigma Delta Chi. Office: 831 Orange St PO Box 1111 Wilmington DE 19899

SHAW, GRACE GOODFRIEND (MRS. HERBERT FRANKLIN SHAW), publisher; b. N.Y.C.; d. Henry Bernheim and Jane Elizabeth (Stone) Goodfriend; student Bennington Coll.; B.A. magna cum laude, Fordham U., 1976; m. Herbert Franklin Shaw; 1 son, Brandon Hibbs. Reporter, Port Chester (N.Y.) Daily Item, 1942-45; editorial coordinator World Scope Ency., N.Y.C., 1946-50; asso. editor Clarence L. Barnhart, Inc., Bronxville, N.Y., 1950; free-lance writer for reference books, 1951-61; sr. editor, coll. dept. Bobbs-Merrill, N.Y.C., 1961-62, mng. editor, 1963-65; editing supr. World Pub Co., N.Y.C., 1965-68, mng. editor, 1968-69, sr. editor, 1969; mng. editor Peter H. Wyden Co., N.Y.C., 1969-70; asso. editor Dial Press, N.Y.C., 1971-72, sr. editor, 1972; sr. editor David McKay Co., N.Y.C., 1972-75; sr. editor Grosset & Dunlap, 1975-79, chief editor Today Press, 1977-79; exec. editor trade dept. Bobbs-Merrill Co., N.Y.C., 1979, pub., 1980—. Mem. Overseas Press Club Am. Office: 630 3d Ave New York NY 10017

SHAW, JO AN, assn. exec.; b. Coshocton, Ohio, Feb. 3, 1929; d. Cleon K. and Daisy L. Shaw; student Bowling Green State U., 1947, 48, Kent State U., 1949-51. Recreational therapist Massillon (Ohio) State Hosp., 1952-60; recreational therapist Sunny Acres Hosp., Cleve., 1960-63; teen program specialist YWCA of Met. Detroit, 1964-69, creative and performing arts dir., 1969-71, public relations dir., 1971—. Coordinator, initiator Believe in Detroit Coalition, 1976-80; mem. community adv. bd. Channel 56, 1978-82. Mem. Detroit Women's Advt. Club (dir.), Detroit Press Club. Methodist. Home: 38768 Chartier St Mount Clemens MI 48045 Office: 2230 Witherell St Detroit MI 48201

SHAW, JOANN JANE (JOHNSON), computer specialist, cons.; b. Washington, Apr. 17, 1932; d. George Phillip and Ruby Jane (Babcock) Johnson; B.S., Towson State U., 1954; postgrad. U. Md., 1957-62, George Washington U., 1962-63. Elem. tchr., Carroll County, Westminster, Md., 1954-56, Prince Georges County, Upper Marlboro, Md., 1956-59; mgmt. asst., statis. asst. Nat. Center Social Stats., HEW, Washington, 1959-74; computer programmer FDA, Washington, 1974-77; computer specialist Naval Telecommunications Systems Integration Center, Dept. Navy, Washington, 1977—; propr. Women's Consultation Service, Springfield, Va., 1978—. Mem. Am. Statis. Assn., Nat. Council Career Women, Nat. Assn. Female Execs., Am. Soc. Profl. and Exec. Women, Sierra Club. Clubs: Matterhorn, Hostess, Discovery, Open Door, Women's, Washington Apple Pi. Author: Speech Exercise Manual for Elementary Teachers, 1953; Current Outlook on the Aged in America, 1952; Physical Therapy as a Profession, 1973; Standards and Guidelines for Documentation Preparation, 1981; contbr. statis. reports to publs. Home: 5414 Juliet St Springfield VA 22151 Office: Naval Telecommunications Systems Integration Center NAVCOMM Unit Washington DC 20390

SHAW, L. JEANETTE, fin. planner; b. Nashville, Dec. 3, 1942; d. Donald Bourke and Dorothy Corinne (Taylor) S.; B.S. in Microbiology and Chemistry, U. Tenn., 1965; M.S. in Mgmt., U. Utah, 1979. Biochemist, Vanderbilt U., 1965-72; microbiologist VA, Nashville, Tampa, Fla. and Salt Lake City, 1972-77; exec. dir. Utah Nurses Assn., 1978; fin. planner Fin. Estate Planners, Salt Lake City, 1979—; account exec. Wall St. West, Salt Lake City, 1981—; gen. agt. E.F. Hutton Life Ins. Co., Salt Lake City, 1981—. Founder Legacy Unltd., Women's orgn. Recipient various sales awards. Mem. Am. Assn. M.B.A. Execs., Internat. Assn. Fin. Planners, Beta Gamma Sigma, Phi Kappa Phi, Beta Sigma Alpha. Mormon. Author papers in field. Home: 4228 South 4900 West Salt Lake City UT 84120 Office: Huntsman Goodson Plaza 3760 Highland Dr Suite 505 Salt Lake City UT 84106

SHAW, MARGARET HUNTER, civic worker; b. Charlotte, N.C., Dec. 28, 1923; d. Lawrence Gilmore and Sadie Wilder (Manning) Hunter; ed. public schs.; m. Edward David Shaw, Aug. 4, 1945; children—Alan Hunter, David Lawrence, Peggy Shaw. Hagreen. Pres., Grand Strand Aux., Inc., Myrtle Beach, S.C., 1976-80; trustee Grand Strand Gen. Hosp., Myrtle Beach, 1980—, chmn. bd. trustees, 1982; bd. dirs. United Way of Horry County (S.C.), 1977-79, 80—, chmn. agy. ops., 1979-80, v.p. agys., 1980—, mem. exec. bd., 1980—; mem. adv. bd. Waccamaw Dist. Home Health Services; sec. Horry County Heart Unit, 1979, bd. dirs., spl. gift co-chmn., 1980. Methodist. Home: 5701 Country Club Dr Myrtle Beach SC 29577

SHAW, MARY ANN, psychologist; b. Dallas, July 5, 1937; d. Leon V. and Mabel (Bartlett) S.; B.S., U. Tex., 1959; M.Ed., U. Houston, 1966, Ed.D., 1973. Tchr. educable mentally retarded Spring Branch, Tex., 1959-64; vocat. counselor, Houston, 1964-66; psychometrist pvt. psychol. clinic, Houston, 1966-70; coordinator research Tex. Edn. Agency grant project, 1970-72; dir. psychol. services Tex. Scottish Rite Hosp. for Crippled Children, Dallas, 1972—; mem. clin. faculty U. Tex. Health Sci. Center; cons. pvt. and public schs. Mem. Am. Psychol. Assn., Dallas Psychol. Assn., Assn. Pediatric Psychologists. Researcher in field; contbr. article to profl. jour. Office: 2222 Welborn Dallas TX 75219

SHAW, MAURETTA LUCIENNE, med. technologist; b. Omaha, Dec. 17, 1941; d. Vernis Lee and Olive Kathryn (Novinger) Bigley; student San Antonio Jr. Coll., 1960-62; B.A. in Microbiology, U. Tex., Austin, 1966, B.S. in Med. Tech., 1970; postgrad. Baylor U., 1968-69; m. James Bedford Shaw, Aug. 1, 1973; children—Paul Allen Knight, Penny Elaine Shaw. Med. technologist virology lab. Baylor Med. Center, 1966-69; co-chief med. technologist Henderson County Meml. Hosp., Athens, Tex., 1969-71; chief med. technologist, lab. mgr./supr. Kaufman (Tex.) Hosp., 1972-77, Presbyn. Hosp. of Kaufman, 1977—. Recipient Disting. Service award Kaufman Pub. Schs., 1980; cert. of merit Ortho Diagnostics, 1973, others. Mem. Clin. Lab. Mgrs. Assn., Am. Soc. Clin. Pathologists, Am. Soc. Med. Technologists, Am. Legion Aux., U.S. Olympic Soc., Nat. Assn. Female Execs., U. Tex. Ex-Students Assn., Beta Sigma Phi. Methodist. Club: Pilot. Home: 154 Circle Dr PO Box 614 Kaufman TX 75142 Office: Hwy 243 West at Hwy 175 Kaufman TX 75142

SHAW, MAXINE ADELLE CHURCHMAN, home economist; b. Sheridan, Oreg., Jan. 30, 1920; d. Bernie Joseph Churchman and Dora (Savage) Churchman Cornell; B.S., Oreg. State U., 1945; M.S., Mankato State U., 1960; postgrad. Iowa State U., 1966-67, U. Iowa, 1970-72; m. Robert C. Shaw, Oct. 21, 1939; children—Elizabeth Adele, Robert Scott, Cecelia. Homemaking tchr. Marshfield Sr. High Sch., Coos Bay, Oreg., 1945-46; sch. lunch dir. North Bend (Oreg.) public schs., 1950-51; partner Shaw's Home of Ins., Coos Bay, 1952-54; asst. instr. home econs. unit Mankato (Minn.) State U., 1956-60, instr., 1960-66, asst. prof., 1967-70, asso. prof., program leader, 1972-75, asso. prof. design and human environ., home econs. dept., 1975—; housing cons. Recipient Service award Mankato Area C. of C., 1979; Am. Home Econs. Assn. Found. fellow, 1966-67, 70-71, 71-72; Am. Home Econs. Assn. Found. Inner-City grantee, 1969. Mem. NEA, Adult Edn. Assn. U.S.A., Am. Assn. Housing Educators, Minn. Home Econs. Assn. (chmn. art and housing sect. 1965-66, chmn. univ. sect. 1977-78), Am. Home Econs. Assn., Minn. Assn. Continuing Adult Edn. (sec. 1977-78), Missouri Valley Adult Edn. Assn. (pres. 1979-80), Minn. Edn. Assn., Assn. Faculty Women Mankato State U., Kappa Delta Pi, Pi Lambda Theta, Phi Upsilon Omicron, Alpha Gamma Delta Alumni. Episcopalian. Office: Box 44 Mankato State U Mankato MN 56001

SHAW, ROSE MARIE, social worker; b. Apache, Okla., Oct. 3, 1934; d. Edward Lee and Marie (Myers) Inman; A.A.S., Cameron U., 1954; student Okla. State U., 1954-55; B.A., Okla. Coll. Women, 1956; M.S.W., U. Okla., 1967; 1 son, Jeffrey Lee. Caseworker, Okla. Dept. Human Services, Caddo County, 1957-58, Jefferson County, 1958, Grady County, 1960-62, Caddo County, 1962-63, social services supr., Caddo County, 1964-66, McIntosh County 1967-68, county adminstr., McIntosh County, 1968; social worker Anadarko (Okla.) Agy., Bur. Indian Affairs, 1968-78, supervisory social worker, 1978—. Bd. dirs., sec. bd. Apache Rotary Recreation Found., 1972-74; sec. Area Nine Juvenile Delinquency Council, 1970-71, subcom. chmn., 1971-72; mem. Area Nine Council Juvenile Delinquency, 1970-71. Recipient Cert. of Spl. Achievement, U.S. Dept. Interior, Bur. Indian Affairs, 1976, 81, Cert. of Spl. Recognition, S.W. Area Okla. Health and Welfare Assn., 1976, 77. Lic. social worker, Okla. Mem. Nat. Assn. Social Workers, Acad. Cert. Social Workers, Okla. Health and Welfare Assn. (state bd. dirs. 1978-84), Apache Alumni Assn. (treas. 1976), Apache Hist. Soc. Baptist. Club: Order Eastern Star. Home: PO Box 342 Apache OK 73006

SHAW, SHARRILYN WHITING, perfume co. exec.; b. Mobile, Ala., Oct. 6, 1946; d. James Allen and Virginia G. (Hearn) Whiting; student U. Ala., 1965-67, U. South Ala., 1968-70, Sterling Inst., 1979, Tex. Tech. Profl. Devel. Center, 1981; m. Edwin Parker Shaw, Jr., Oct. 20, 1976; 1 son, Ivey. Writer, Nashville Tennessean, 1970, Mobile (Ala.) Press Register, 1968-69; account exec. The Pitluk Group, San Antonio, 1976-77; advt./promotion mgr. Sta. KSAT-TV, San Antonio, 1977-79; advt. mgr. Lone Star Brewing Co., San Antonio, 1979-80, mgr. mktg., 1980-82; v.p. mktg. Swiss Watch Distbn. Center, Inc., San Antonio, 1982; pres., chief exec. officer Dans Un Jardin Tex., Inc., Dallas, 1982—. Chmn., ABC-TV Network Promotion Adv. Bd., 1978-79, San Antonio Women's Edn. and Employment, Inc., 1981-82; commr. San Antonio Conv. and Visitors Bur., 1981-82; mem. steering com. Leadership San Antonio, 1981—; v.p. bd. dirs. Children's Hosp. Found., 1979—; bd. dirs. Monte Vista Hist. Assn., Tex. Women's Employment and Edn., Inc., others; mem. jr. com. San Antonio Symphony. Recipient Pro-Liner awards Women in Communications, 1980; award AP Ala., 1969; Addy awards, 1977, 78, 79; Internat. Assn. Bus. Communicators - Dallas award, 1981; Mem. Am. Mktg. Assn., Tex. Public Relations Assn., Women in Communications, (v.p. 1979-80), Alpha Chi Omega. Clubs: Bright Shawl, St. Anthony, Mills County Hunting & Fishing, First Wednesday Breakfast. Home: 303 W Gramercy Pl San Antonio TX 78212 Office: The Galleria Dallas TX

SHAW, SHIRLEY, real estate devel. co. exec.; b. Dallas, Jan. 28, 1935; d. Lovard E. and Vivian (Hargrave) Ferguson; B.S., Southeastern State U., Okla., 1955; postgrad. U. Okla., 1980; children—John E., Amy Ann. Owner, Shaw Personnel Services, Austin, Tex., 1971-75; mgmt. technician support adminstrn. Tex. Indsl. Commn., Austin, 1975-76, mgr. urban revitalization and urban econ. devel. 1977-79, mgr. small minority and community bus. devel., 1979-82; project mgr. Waller Creek, Ltd., Austin, 1982—. Charter bd. dirs., v.p. Austin Area Urban League, 1977—; bd. dirs. KAZI Austin Community Radio, 1978—. Mem. Tex. Indsl. Devel. Council, So. Indsl. Devel. Council, Nat. Council Urban Econ. Devel. Methodist. Home: 6501 E Hill Dr #116 Austin TX 78731 Office: Waller Creek Ltd 119 Old Pecan St #501 Austin TX 78701

SHAW, SUSAN JEAN, orgn. exec.; b. N.Y.C., Sept. 30, 1943; d. Noah and Sylvia Charlotte (Troy) S.; B.Mus.Edn., Syracuse (N.Y.) U., 1965; postgrad. Hunter Coll., Columbia U. Tchrs. Coll., Alliance Theol. Sem.; divorced; children—Scott Lewis, Tamra Eileen. Tchr. music edn. public and pvt. schs., Westchester County, N.Y., 1966-73; placement counselor Fanning Personnel, N.Y.C., 1974-75; pres. Communiscope, Inc., Miami, Fla., 1976-77; exec. dir. Dental Health Services, Miami, 1977-79; propr. Shaw Enterprizes, Inc., Miami and N.Y.C., 1979-81; communications specialist World Relief Corp., Nyack, N.Y., 1981—; seminar leader, 1978—. Trustee, sec. Bryant Gardens Corp., 1981. Ridgeway Alliance Ch. scholar, 1980; William H. Nelson scholar, 1981. Mem. Profl. Bus. Women's Assn., Profl. Christian Women's Assn., Women in Ministry, Christian Singles Fellowship, AAUW, Pi Lambda Theta, Sigma Alpha Iota. Author articles, revs. in field. Home: 5 Bryant Crescent White Plains NY 10605 Office: PO Box WRC Nyack NY 10960

SHAWCROFT, BARBARA MAVIS JONES, sculptor; b. Lancashire, Eng., Jan. 10, 1930; came to U.S., 1960, naturalized, 1965; d. Arthur Percival and May (Morris) Jones; student Alma Coll., St. Thomas, Ont., Can., 1940-45; M.F.A., Calif. Coll. Arts and Crafts, Oakland, 1973; m. Brian Shawcroft; Mar. 25, 1955 (div.); m. 2d, Richard Kamler, June 24, 1965 (div.); m. 3d, Ugo Guarino, June 10, 1982. Sculptor, 1969—; tchr. San Francisco State U., 1972-74, San Jose (Calif.) State U., 1974-76, Calif. Coll. Arts and Crafts, 1973-74; assoc. prof. program artisanry Boston U., 1979-82; prof. design U. Calif., Davis, 1982—; lectr., condr. workshops in U.S., Japan, Hawaii, Alaska and Eng.; commns. at Bart Embarcadero Sta.-East End Wall, San Francisco, 3 Embarcadero Center, San Francisco, New State Bldg., Sacramento; represented in permanent collections Smithsonian Instn., Sch. Design at N.C. State U., Raleigh, Lannan Found., West Palm Beach, Fla. Fellow Nat. Endowment Art, 1975 (2), 77. Mem. Soc. Arts and Crafts (adv. bd.), Am. Crafts Council, AAUP, Calif. Design. Home: 4 Anchor Dr Apt 243 Emeryville CA 94608 Office: Design Dept U Calif Davis CA 95616 Studio: 2547 8th St Berkeley CA 94710

SHAWCROFT, BETTY LINGER, ednl. adminstr., cattle rancher; b. Colorado Springs, Colo., Feb. 31, 1924; d. Howard K. and Doris (Haynes) Linger; B.A., U. Colo., 1945; M.A., Adams State Coll., 1974; postgrad. Western State U., 1979-81; m. John B. Shawcroft, Nov. 17, 1945; children—Nancy, David, Connie, Donald. Partner, Shawcroft Ranches, Ltd., Alamosa, Colo., 1945—; tchr. English, journalism, Centauri High Sch., La Jara, Colo., 1968-76, prin., 1976—. Pres., San Luis Valley Cowbelles, 1972; sec. So. Peaks Activity League, 1976—. Named Woman of Yr., Conejos County Farm Bur., 1977. Mem. Nat. Assn. Secondary Sch. Prins., Colo. Cattlemen's Assn., Phi Delta Kappa. Republican. Mem. Ch. of Jesus Christ of Latterday Saints. Home: Route 2 Box 290 Alamosa CO 81101 Office: Box 72 LaJara CO 81140

SHAYNE, DOROTHY ANN, hotel co. exec.; b. Evansville, Ind., July 25, 1914; d. Adam and Mary Elizabeth Ziemer; ed. public schs.; m. Nathan Shayne, Nov. 1, 1930; 1 dau., Audrey Ann. Sec., Chippewa Hotel Co., Mackinac Island, Mich., 1946—, sr. v.p., 1960—, chmn. fin. com., 1970—, also dir. Asst. dir. advt. City of Mackinac Island, 1950-65. Roman Catholic. Clubs: Mackinac Island Yacht, Paradise Valley Country (dir. entertainment 1974-77) (Scottsdale, Ariz.); Turf Paradise. Home and Office: Chippewa Hotel Main St Mackinac Island MI 49757

SHEA, CHARLENE RIOPELLE, personal motivation speaker, cons.; b. Lawrence, Mass., Sept. 3, 1934; d. George Andrew and Ruth Knowlton (Pickard) Riopelle; B.S., U. Maine, 1957; m. Thomas Everett, Mar. 30, 1956; children—Valerie Ruth, Thomas Leon, Gwendolyn Beryl. Tchr. 1st grade, Okinawa, Japan, 1958-60, El Paso, Tex., 1961-65, Highland, N.J., 1965-68, Frankfurt, Germany, 1969-72; dir. Mary Kay Cosmetics, Inc., Manchester, N.H., 1972-80; pres. Charlene Shea., Inc., motivational speaking and cons. firm, Manchester, 1980—; instr. U. N.H., Manchester, 1979—. Mem. fin. com. YWCA, 1981, bd. dirs., 1982-84; bd. dirs. WON, 1981. Recipient N.H. Woman in Bus. adv. award SBA, 1982. Mem. Internat. Platform Assn., Manchester C. of C., Nat. Speakers Assn., N.H. Women's Forum. Home and Office: 121 Allied St Manchester NH 03103

SHEA, ELAINE EVANS, civic assn. exec.; b. Ithaca, N.Y., Aug. 1, 1935; d. William Arthur and Genevieve (Covert) Evans; A.A., Stephens Coll., 1955; m. Michael Henry Shea, June 28, 1956; children—Elizabeth Ann, Linda Evans, William Michael. Writer, film previewer Sta. KWTV, Oklahoma City, 1955-56; exec. dir. Save the Tallgrass Prairie, Inc., Shawnee Mission, Kans., 1974—. Bd. dirs. Kans. Natural Resource Council; registered lobbyist; pres. Porter Sch. PTA, 1969; leader Girl Scouts; tchr. Sunday Sch., deacon Village United Presbyn. Ch.; tract chmn. Am. Cancer Soc., 1982; interim dir. Grassland Heritage Found., 1982. Recipient Environ. Quality award EPA, 1978. Clubs: Stephens Coll. Dinner (pres. 1966), Prairie Planters Garden (pres. 1972), Kansas City Country. Editor: Tallgrass Prairie News, 1974—. Home: 6025 Cherokee Dr Shawnee Mission KS 66205 Office: 4101 W 54th Terr Shawnee Mission KS 66205

SHEA, JULIA VAHEY, banker; b. N.Y.C., Oct. 23, 1946; d. John and Delis (Hennelly) S.; B.A., St. Joseph's Coll., 1967; J.D., Fordham U., 1965; m. Martin F. Shea, Sept. 13, 1980. Social worker, 1967-70; investment asst., 1970-72; with Morgan Bank, N.Y.C., staff atty. trust div. legal group, 1979-80, v.p. trust and estate admistrn., 1980—. Bd. dirs. Cath. Home Bur. Mem. N.Y. State Bankers Assn., N.Y. State Bar Assn. Office: 9 W 57th St New York NY 10019

SHEA, KATHLEEN VIRGINIA, counseling psychologist; b. Waukegan, Ill., Mar. 18, 1944; d. George W. and Eleanor M. Shea; B.A., So. Ill. U., 1967; M.A., Northwestern U., 1972, Ph.D., 1979. Grad. instr. Chgo. Consortium Colls., 1977-80; counselor Highland Park-Deerfield Dist. 113 (Ill.), 1979-82; pvt. practice counseling psychologist, Winnetka and Libertyville, Ill., 1979—. Judge, City Chgo. Exec. Leadership Award, Office Mayor. Mem. Am. Psychol. Assn., Internat. Orgn. Women Execs., Phi Delta Kappa. Republican. Author: Psychological Health of High-Achieving Women Executives. Office: 1111 W Park St Libertyville IL 60048

SHEA, NORMA JEAN, speech pathologist; b. Dobbs Ferry, N.Y., May 31, 1955; d. Caleb Harold and Joan (Rooney) Ward; student Rockland Community Coll., 1973-74; B.S., Mercy Coll., 1977; M.A., Hofstra U., 1978; m. David Richard Shea, July 22, 1978. Speech and lang. therapist Headstart program Yonkers Day Care Center, 1976; student tchr., North Salem, Mt. Kisco and Katonah Schs., 1976; intern in speech and lang. pathology Queens Children's Psychiat. Center, 1977; intern Bernard Fineson Developmental Center, Corona, N.Y., 1978; speech therapist Bd. Coop. Ednl. Services, Woodside Elem. Sch., Peekskill, N.Y., 1978-79; customer service rep. Citibank, Huntington Station, N.Y., 1979-81; VISA collector Nat. Bank N.Am., Huntington Station, N.Y., 1981—. Mem. Am. Speech and Hearing Assn. Home: 124 Ketridge St W Babylon NY 11704

SHEA, RUTHMARIE SHEA, health facility adminstr.; b. Detroit, Dec. 13, 1949; d. Ralph George and Marilyn Margaret (Mangan) Shea; A.A. with honors, Oakland Community Coll., 1970, A.A.S. with honors, 1971; B.S. cum laude, U. Detroit, 1974, M.A., 1974; m. Pierre C. Atallah, Sept. 3, 1976. Charge nurse Lakeside Gen. Hosp., Detroit, 1971-72; staff nurse William Beaumont Hosp., Royal Oak, Mich., 1972-73; dir. inservice edn. Sherwood Hall Convalescent Center, Royal Oak, 1973-74; dir. nursing edn. NW Gen. Hosp., Detroit, 1974-75, dir. nursing services, 1975-76; adminstr., dir. clin. services, Cardiac Diagnostic and Rehab. Center, Rochester, Mich., 1976—; med. mktg. cons. Dyanmic Data Systems, Rochester, 1978-81. R.N., Mich.; cert. in advanced cardiac life support Am. Heart Assn. Mem. Am. Nurses Assn., Mich. Nurses Assn., Mich. Nurses United, Detroit Dist. Nurses Assn., AAUW, Fedn. Internat. Univ. Women, Mich. Heart Assn., Birmingham-Bloomfield Art Assn. Roman Catholic. Home: 5105 Provincial Dr Bloomfield Hills MI 48013 Office: 2370 Walton Blvd Rochester MI 48063

SHEAIN, JOANNE CARMELLA, ins. brokerage co. exec.; b. N.Y.C., July 16, 1939; d. Amedeo D. and Diomira (Lemma) Ricciardi; A.A., West Los Angeles Coll., 1975; B.B.A., Calif. State U., Los Angeles, 1978. Sec., Office of the Messrs. Rockefeller, N.Y.C., 1962-65; tng. specialist Revlon, Inc., N.Y.C. and Los Angeles, 1965-71; adminstrv. asst. Global Marine, Inc., Los Angeles, 1973-77; adminstrv. mgr. Harris Kerr Forster & Co., Los Angeles, 1977-78; controller Western Ins. Assos., Los Angeles, 1979—. Mem. investment oversight com. YWCA of Los Angeles. Mem. Calif. State Bus. Assn., Beta Gamma Sigma. Republican. Home: 1386 Calle Gallante San Dimas CA 91773 Office: 1010 S Flower St Los Angeles CA 90015

SHEAR, MAXINE BERNARD, clin. social worker; b. St. Louis, Nov. 5, 1926; d. Abe and Anna (Lipschutz) S.; B.S. in Social Work (scholar), Washington U., St. Louis, 1947; M.S. in Edn., Bank St. Coll. Edn., N.Y.C., 1951; M.S.W., UCLA, 1966; children—Claudia Lynn, Nancy Dale. Child welfare worker Los Angeles County Dept. Adoptions, Panorama City, Calif., 1966-67; clin. social worker Mental Health Devel. Center, Hollywood, Calif., 1967-70; clin. social worker Mental Hygiene Clinic, Brentwood VA Hosp., Los Angeles, 1971-76; dir. group counseling project Los Angeles Coastal Cities unit Am. Cancer Soc., 1976—, cons. group counseling Calif. div., 1980—; pvt. practice psychotherapy, guest lectr., cons. in field. Recipient Service award Am. Cancer Soc., 1976, cert. of spl. recognition, 1979; Women Helping Women honoree, Los Angeles Club, Soroptimist Internat., 1979. Mem. Assn. Humanistic Psychology, Nat. Assn. Social Workers, Soc. Clin. Social Work. Office: 10921 Wilshire Blvd Suite 605 Los Angeles CA 90024

SHEARER, GEORGIA BACKUS, biologist; b. Wichita Falls, Tex., Aug. 13, 1929; d. William Bryan and Elsa K. (Webb) Backus; B.A., U. Tex., 1949, M.A., 1951. Research assoc. Tulane U. Med. Sch., New Orleans, 1951-53; research assoc. dept. botany Washington U., St. Louis, 1953-65, Center for Biology of Natural Systems, 1965-80, dept. biology, 1977—. Mem. Phi Beta Kappa, Iota Sigma Pi. Contbr. articles on plant physiology to sci. jours. Office: Box 1137 Washington Univ Saint Louis MO 63130

SHEARIN, ROBERTA BROOKS (MRS. WILLIAM GASTON SHEARIN), ret. librarian; b. Washington, Oct. 2, 1924; d. Ulysses Simpson and Marzette I. (Tate) Brooks; student Spelman Coll., 1940-42; A.B. cum laude, Johnson C. Smith U., 1944; B.S. in Library Sci., Atlanta U., 1945; m. William Gaston Shearin, July 21, 1947; children—Moneta Marzette (Mrs. Dennis W. Howland), William Gaston. Asst. librarian Talladega Coll., Ala., 1945-47; library asst. Army Library Pentagon, 1952-54, reference librarian, 1955-66, acting chief periodicals, 1967-70, chief periodicals, 1970-81. Editor, Tots and Teens, Inc. Recipient Sustained Superior Performance award Dept. Army, 1963, Outstanding Performance award Dept. Army, 1971. Mem. A.L.A., Nat. Council of Negro Women, N.A.A.C.P., Delta Sigma Theta. Home: 7305 Hilton Ave Takoma Park MD 20012 Office: The Army Library Room 1A522 The Pentagon Washington DC 20310

SHEBAR, ELINOR, wallcovering distbn. co. exec.; b. N.Y.C., June 24, 1936; d. David T. and Dorothy (Levine) Jacobson; A.A., Bklyn. Coll., 1956; m. Arthur Shebar, June 17, 1955; children—Eric, Mathew. Sales rep. Columbus Coated Fabrics, Rockville Centre, N.Y., 1971-74, W.R. Grace, Clifton, N.J., 1974-76; sales rep. Bayview Wall Coverings, Inc., Lindenhurst, N.Y., 1976-78, sales mgr., 1978—. Bd. dirs. Sterns Park, Freeport, N.Y., Union Reform Temple, Freeport, Republican Club, Freeport and Merrick, N.Y. Mem. Bus. and Profl. Woman's Assn., Wall Paper Distbrs. Assn., Paint and Wall Paper Dealers Assn., Color Mktg. Group, L.I. Computer Club, S100 Users Group. Clubs: B'nai B'rith, Hadassah. Home: 2788 Harbor Rd Merrick NY 11566 Office: 41 E Sunrise Hwy Lindenhurst NY 11757

SHEBESTER LOHMANN, NORMA KAYE, oil field exec.; b. Centralia, Ill., Feb. 24, 1940; d. Ralph William and Mildred Marie (Lansford) Shebester; student Okla. U., 1957-58; m. Philip J. Lohmann, June 7, 1959 (div. 1972); children—Jeffrey Jay, Tammy Kaye. Exec. sec. Lohmann Oilwell Service Co., Hobbs, N.Mex., 1962-69; with Shebester, Inc., Maysville, Okla., 1974-80, treas., comptroller, landwoman, 1979-80, also dir.; treas. Marx, Inc.; self-employed investor in oil and gas ventures, 1980—. Mem. Gamma Phi Beta. Republican. Baptist. Home and Office: 1701 Brookhaven St Norman OK 73069

SHEDD, LEMERLE (CHAVERS), comml. banker; b. Prattville, Ala., Jan. 19, 1938; d. Philip Cecil and Flossie (Newman) Chavers; cert. (2) Am. Inst. Banking; grad. U. South Ala.; m. Otis James Shedd, June 23, 1956; children—James Harold, Michael Eugene, Carolyn Denise. With customer service dept. Bank of Prattville, 1966-68, proof operator, 1968-72, teller, 1972-77, proof supr., 1977-81, asst. ops. officer, asst. v.p., 1982—. Active United Way. Mem. Nat. Assn. Bank Women (chmn. year-book), Am. Inst. Banking (bd. govs. Montgomery chpt.). Methodist. Home: Rt 1 Box 260 Prattville AL 36067 Office: PO Drawer 400 Prattville AL 36067

SHEDLOCK, ELIZABETH ANN, city ofcl.; b. Pompey, N.Y., Apr. 29, 1925; d. Frank X. and Mary Agnes (Lane) Costello; student public schs., Manlius, N.Y.; m. Thomas Shedlock, Aug. 13, 1948; children—Ronald, Donald, Ann, Mary. Payroll clk. S. Cheney & Son, Manlius, 1942-45; office mgr., bookkeeper GLF, Syracuse, N.Y., 1945-47, Western Auto Supply Co., Syracuse, N.Y., 1947-48; town clk. Town of Pompey, 1964-70, registrar of vital stats., 1964-70, councilman, 1964—, dep. supr., 1964-70; sec. Pompey Planning Bd., 1971-73, Pompey Zoning Bd., 1967-70. Formerly active Brownies, community council, ch. clubs, fund drive, schs. Mem. Pompey Hist. Soc., Pompey Hill Fire Aux. Democrat. Roman Catholic. Home: 7889 US Route 20 Manlius NY 13104

SHEEDY, KATHLEEN CROWLEY, med. technologist; b. Bridgeport, Conn., Mar. 23, 1950; d. Edward V. and Jeanne (Duhamel) Crowley; B.S., Western Conn. State Coll., 1972; student Danbury (Conn.) Hosp. Sch. Med. Technology, 1971-72, SUNY Upstate Med Center, Syracuse, 1973-74; m. Mark E. Sheedy; children—Paul C., John E. Lab. technologist, Danbury Hosp., 1972-73; instr. med. technology SUNY Upstate Med. Center, 1975-81, supr. blood bank, 1974-81; blood bank supr. Vassar Brothers Hosp., Poughkeepsie, N.Y., 1982—. Barlow House Council scholar, 1968. Mem. Am. Soc. Clin. Pathologists, Am. Assn. Blood Banks. Roman Catholic. Contbr. articles to profl. jours. Home: 24 Horseshoe Dr Hyde Park NY 12538 Office: Vassar Bros Hosp Poughkeepsie NY 12601

SHEEHAN, CAROLE DIANE, ednl. adminstr.; b. Los Angeles, June 1, 1939; d. Andrew Louis and Aletha Enid (Clifford) Barta; B.A., UCLA, 1961; children—Shannon Lee, Brian Patrick. Founder, owner Childs World Schs., Encino and Tarzana, Calif., 1965—; co-leader parenting workshops Gestalt Therapy Center Los Angeles. Mem. Los Angeles Citizens Adv. Com. on Zoning Mayor's Task Force on Child Abuse. Mem. Nat. Assn. Edn. Young Child., Pvt. Sch. Assn. (Calif.). Office: 5465 White Oak St Encino CA 91316 also 6100 Lindley Ave Tarzana CA 91335

SHEEHAN, LORRAINE M., state legislator; b. Manchester, N.H., May 2, 1937. Mem. Md. Ho. of Dels., 1974—, vice chmn. Prince George's County del., mem. ways and means com., subcom. on edn. of task force to study state/local fiscal relationships, humane practices commn., chmn. health care subcom., mem. Med. Assistance Program. Bd. trustees Greater Southeast Community Hosp. Found.; bd. dirs. Suitland Local Devel. Corp. Mem. LWV, PTA, Marlboro Democratic Club, Kettering Civic Fedn., Greater Southeast Center for Aging. Club: Bus. and Profl. Women's. Office: 205 Lowe Bldg Annapolis MD 21401 *

SHEEHAN, PATRICIA JEAN, advt. agy. exec.; b. Oak Park, Ill., Mar. 4, 1953; d. John Raymond and Terese Ann (Bargen) Cagney; B.A., in Journalism, U. Mont., 1975; m. Patrick Kevin Sheehan, May 22, 1976. Creative asst. Kayser Communications, Northfield, Ill., 1975-76; account service coordinator Sieber & McIntyre Advt., Chgo., 1976-77; account exec. Garfield-Linn & Co., Chgo., 1977-78; account mgr. Garfield-Linn & Co., Chgo., 1978-81, account supr., 1981—. Mem. Nat. Assn. Female Execs., Sigma Kappa. Club: Chgo. Advt.

SHEEHAN, SUSAN (MRS. NEIL SHEEHAN), writer; b. Vienna, Austria, Aug. 24, 1937; d. Charles and Kitty C. (Herrmann) Sachsel; came to U.S., 1941, naturalized, 1946; B.A. (Durant scholar), Wellesley Coll., 1958; m. Neil Sheehan, Mar. 30, 1965; children—Maria Gregory, Catherine Fair. Editorial researcher Esquire-Coronet, N.Y.C., 1959-60; free-lance writer, N.Y.C., 1960-62; staff writer New Yorker mag., N.Y.C., 1962—. Mem. adv. com. on employment and crime Vera Inst. of Justice, 1978—; mem. lit. panel D.C. Commn. on Arts and Humanities, 1979—; mem. public info. and edn. com. Nat. Mental Health Assn., 1982—. Guggenheim fellow, 1975-76; Woodrow Wilson Center for Internat. Scholars fellow, 1981; recipient Sidney Hillman Found. award, 1976; Gavel award Am. Bar Assn., 1978; Individual Reporting award Nat. Mental Health Assn., 1981. Mem. Phi Beta Kappa. Author: Ten Vietnamese, 1967; A Welfare Mother, 1976; A Prison and a Prisoner, 1978; Is There No Place on Earth for Me?, 1982. Contbr. articles to various mags. including N.Y. Times Sunday Mag., Harper's, Atlantic, New Republic, McCall's, Holiday. Home: 4505 Klingle St NW Washington DC 20016 Office: New Yorker Mag 25 W 43d St New York NY 10036

SHEEHE, LILLIAN CAROLYN, painter; b. Conemaugh, Pa., Oct. 16, 1915; d. John Jacob and Julia (Bartol) Kukovitz; B.S. in Art, Indiana U. Pa.; student Sheldone Grumbling, Hugh Geise, George Ream; m., June 1, 1938. Art. supr. East Conemaugh Schs., 1936-42; tchr. art and world history, Westmont High Sch., 1944-45, 53-54; art tchr. and supr. Ferndale-Dale Grade and High Schs., 1955-59; instr. arts and crafts Pa. Vocat. Rehab. Center, Johnstown, 1959-72; designer, coordinator Around About Now in Johnstown, 1971-72, Around the County, 1975; designer, printer Christmas cards, Pa. Rehab. Center and Bur. Vocat. Rehab., 1959-71; works include: Ct. of Gabrielle (serigraph), David Glosser Library, Trees at Christmastime in Calif. (serigraph), Flood Mus., 130 glass-fired paintings and sagged bottle collection C. of C. Johnstown; commd. works include: golf mural, J. Cover, Johnstown, 1944, emblem design Lee Hosp. Rehab. Med. Dept., 1966, art calendar Allied Artists Am., 1971, landscape mosaic Mrs. Lyn Hoffman, 1970; one-woman show: Champion Lakes, 1978; exhbns. include: All Allied Artists Shows, 1936—, Pittsylvania Ceramic Guild All-Pa. Competition, 1964-71, Three Rivers Arts Festival, 1965, 66, Allied-Artists Graphic Arts Show, 1970, Sheraton, 1975. Recipient purchase award Allied Artists, 1961, best of show, 1970, U.S. Bank show, David Glosser Library Craft award, 1973; A.B. Crichton award (first prize) Allied Artists Ann. Show, 1979; Sweepstakes award Chrysanthamum Soc. Ann. Show, 1979. Mem. Allied Artists (dir., pres., 1970-72), Pittsylvania Ceramic Guild (Phoebe Jerema award, 1971), Area Arts Council (pres., 1975), Johnstown C. of C. (chmn. cultural affairs com. 1972-82). Author: Dreams in Glass, 1977. Participant TV shows on glass work, 1969; condr. research fired glass, oil, copper enameling; author, illustrator catalogues, Textbook on Photo-Tinting-Color-Oils, 1965; contbr. writings in field to crafts publs. Address: 1333 Christopher St Johnstown PA 15905

SHEEHEY, SHEILA CELESTE, mfg. co. exec.; b. Boston, May 13, 1924; d. Thommas Joseph and Charlotte Mary (Cronin) S.; B.A., N.Y.U., 1975. Asst. to social editor Newark News, 1947-56; asst. to advt. mgr. Handy & Harman, precious metal fabricator and refiner, N.Y.C., 1957-76, adv. mgr., 1976—. Mem. Nat. Assn. Press Women, Bus. and Profl. Advt. Assn. Office: 850 3d Ave New York NY 10022

SHEER, JANE EVANS, mktg. exec.; b. Hannibal, Mo., July 26, 1944; d. L. Terrell and C. M. (Pierce) Evans; B.A., Vanderbilt U., 1965; postgrad. U. d'Aix-Marseills, France, 1962, Fashion Inst. Tech., N.Y.C., 1965, 66; m. George Sheer, July 19, 1970; 1 son, Jonathan. Pres., I. Miller, N.Y.C., 1970-74, Butterick Fashion Mktg. Corp., N.Y.C., 1974-77; v.p. adminstrn. and corp. devel. Fingerhut Corp., Mpls., 1977-79; exec. v.p. Gen. Mills Fashion Group, N.Y.C., 1980—; dir. Philip Morris, Inc., Catalyst. Mem. adv. bd. Vanderbilt U. Grad. Sch. Mgmt., Lab. Inst. Merchandising; alumni bd. dirs. Vanderbilt U.; bd. dirs. Fashion Inst. Tech. Recipient 1981 Entrepreneurial Woman award Women Bus. Owners N.Y. Mem. Com. of 200 (founding), Young Pres.'s Orgn. (chpt. exec. com.), Fashion Group N.Y. Home: 507 Trinity Pass Rd New Canaan CT 06840 Office: 1411 Broadway New York NY 10018

SHEETS, BARBARA JANE CAMPBELL, educator, computer cons.; b. Webster Groves, Mo., Sept. 20, 1948; d. Kenneth O. and Jane Louise (Isaacks) Campbell; B.S. in Math., Purdue U., 1970, M.S. in Math., 1981; children—Roger Wesley, James Kenneth. Programmer, Lincoln Life Ins., Ft. Wayne, Ind., 1970-71; instr. Purdue U., Ft. Wayne, 1975, research, teaching asst. computer tech. dept., 1979-80, instr. computer tech. dept., 1980—; substitute tchr. East Allen County Schs., 1979; partner Triple S and T Software Co., 1981-82; pres. Software Profls., 1982—. Mem. Reorganized Ch. of Jesus Christ of Latter-day Saints. Office: 2101 Coliseum Blvd Fort Wayne IN 46805

SHEETS, JANET ELIZABETH, librarian; b. Winston-Salem, N.C., Jan. 25, 1943; d. John McKaughan and Madge Elizabeth (Burton) S.; A.B., Coll. William and Mary, 1965; M.L.S., U. N.C., Chapel Hill, 1967. Librarian, Free Library of Phila., 1967-68, Duke U., Durham, N.C., 1968-72, Joint Univ. Libraries, Nashville, 1973-75, N.E. La. U., Monroe, 1975-77, Baylor U., Waco, Tex., 1977—; historian Zeta of Tex., Phi Beta Kappa, 1981-83. Vol. worker Brazos River Festival, 1980, Christmas on the Brazos, 1980. Mem. ALA, Tex. Library Assn., AAUW (chmn. awareness study group 1980-81). Baptist. Office: Moody Library Baylor U Waco TX 76706

SHEETS, SUE LAURA, newspaper ofcl.; b. Dayton, Ohio, Nov. 15, 1929; d. Charles LeRoy and Dorothy Ethel (Leis) Schaaf; student Ohio State U., 1947-48, hon. degree Nat. Cash Register Posting Sch., Denver, 1952; student YMCA Coll. of Commerce, Newark, Ohio, 1968; grad. Inst. Children's Lit., Redding Ridge, Conn., 1982; m. R.E. Walters; children—Steven Mitchell, Douglas Charles, Gregg Joseph; m. 2d, Ralph D. Sheets, June 21, 1969. Sec. with Ohio Fin. Co., Dayton, 1948-50, Goulds Pumps, Seneca Falls, N.Y., 1950-52, 53-54; poster, Colo. Nat. Bank, Denver, 1952-53; reporter Ace News, Heath, Ohio, 1966-68; founding dir. LEADS, Buckeye Lake, Ohio, 1968-72; sec. with Garwood Industries, Heath, 1973-74; columnist, editor, editor bus. and farm page, The Advocate, Newark, Ohio, 1978-82, entertainment and TV editor, 1982—; tchr. painting oils and acrylics, owner, operator arts and crafts shop, Hebron, Ohio, 1968-77. Organizer sr. citizens group, Buckeye Lake, 1968. Mem. Licking County Art Assn. Democrat. Methodist. Club: Order Eastern Star (Hebron). Home: 180 S 5th St Newark OH 43055 Office: 25 W Main St Newark OH 43055

SHEFF, TINA YU HENG, art co. exec.; b. Nanking, China, Nov. 22, 1939; d. Chieh and C.H. (Tai) Teng; M.S.W., N.Y. U., 1961; student Art Students League, 1969-71. Supr. psychiat. social work dept. Creedmore State and Meyer Psychiat. Hosp., N.Y.C., 1961-71; pres. Yu Heng Art Co., N.Y.C., 1971—; one person shows China Art Atelier, N.Y.C., 1969; The Way Gallery, N.Y.C., 1970; Jordan Marsh Co., Miami, 1971. Mem. Acad. Cert. Social Workers. Home: 303 E 57th St New York NY 10022 Office: 880 3d Ave New York NY 10022

SHEH, VIOLET MAE, journalist; b. Prince Rupert, B.C., Can., June 3, 1919; d. Mah Bon and Edith (Gee) Quen; student Mun Yew Sch. Chinese Studies, Toishan, Kwangtung, China, 1935-39; m. Kenneth Sheh, Feb. 19, 1948; children—Cheryl Irene Sheh DeHaan, Douglas Wayne, Kenneth Warren. Fgn. corr. Chinatown News, Vancouver, B.C., 1957-58; social and consumer columnist, gen. reporter, Richmond (B.C.) Rev., 1967-72, vol. writer, 1981—; writer travel articles from Fiji, Peru and Argentina, 1967-72; roving reporter Street Scene, 1981—. Home: 10251 Aintree Crescent Richmond BC V7A 3T9 Canada Office: 8271 Westminster Hwy Richmond BC V6X 3B8 Canada

SHEHEE, VIRGINIA KILPATRICK, former state senator; b. Houston; B.A., Centenary Coll., 1943; postgrad. So. Methodist U.; m. W. Peyton Shehee, Jr.; children—Shane, Andrew, Nell, Margaret. Pres., Kilpatrick Life Ins. Co., Shreveport, La., 1971—, Rose-Neath Funeral Homes, Inc., Shreveport, 1971—; chmn. bd. Central State Life Ins. Co., Strand Theatre of Shreveport Corp.; dir. Bank of Commerce; mem. La. Senate from Dist. 38, 1976-80. Bd. dirs. La. State Fair, La. Expo, Inc., Employ-Ex; trustee Centenary Coll., Chamber Legal Centers; mem. Nat. Com. Symphony Orch. Support; mem. adv. com. Shreveport-Bossier Vocat. Tech. Center, Caddo Parish Spl. Edn. Com., State Exhibit Mus. Shreveport; mem. adv. council Magnet Sch., New Orleans Mus. Art; adv. bd. Shreveport chpt. Odyssey House La.; hon. chmn. bd. dirs. Shreveport Symphony; bd. dirs. La. Environ. Soc., La. Youth Concerts, Bus. Com. for Arts, Bus. Com. for Arts, Community Found.; mem. panel of judges Bus. Com. for Arts Bus. in Arts Awards; mem. com. 100, Corps./Founds com. Willis-Knighton Hosp. Devel. Council; mem. planning com. McNeil Pump Sta. and Park; mem. citizens adv. com. La.

State U., Shreveport; former sr. warden of vestry St. Paul's Episcopal Ch., Shreveport. Recipient Clyde F. Fant Meml. award Shreveport Community Council, 1977, also Spl. Humanitarian award, 1977; named to Alumni Hall of Fame, Centenary Coll. Fellow Royal Soc. Arts; mem. La. Funeral Dirs. Assn. (1st v.p. 1977), Nat. Assn. Life Underwriters (life mem. women leaders round table), Zeta Tau Alpha, Omicron Delta Kappa. Democrat. Club: University (bd. govs. 1978—). Address: 1818 Marshall St Shreveport LA 71101

SHEIN, JANET LINDA, accountant; b. San Francisco, Apr. 10, 1948; d. Harold and Rheba (Levine) Shein; student UCLA, 1966-68; B.A., U. Calif., Berkeley, 1973; m. Stephen Chappell, Feb. 12, 1983. Copywriter, statistician Brown, Clark & Elkus, 1973-75; acct. Harold Shein Accountancy Corp., San Francisco, 1976—. Office: 214 Herst Bldg San Francisco CA 94103

SHEININ, ROSE, biochemist, educator; b. Toronto, Ont., Can., May 18, 1930; d. Harry and Anne (Szyber) Shuber; B.A., U. Toronto, 1951, M.A. (scholar), 1953, Ph.D. in Biochemistry, 1956; m. Joseph Sheinin, July 15, 1951; children—David Matthew Khazanov, Lisa Basya Judith, Rachel Sarah Rebecca. Demonstrator in biochemistry U. Toronto (Ont., Can.), 1951-53, asst. prof. microbiology, 1964-75, asst. prof. med. biophysics, 1967-75, prof. microbiology, 1975—, prof. med. biophysics, 1978—, asso. prof. med. biophysics, 1975-78, chmn. microbiology and parasitology, 1975-82, mem. Health Scis. Com.; vis. research asso. chem. microbiology, Cambridge U., 1956-57, Nat. Inst. Med. Research, London, 1957-58; research asso. fellow div. biol. research Ont. Cancer Inst., 1958-67; sci. officer cancer grants panel Med. Research Council Can.; mem. Can. Sci. Del. to People's Republic of China, 1973; mem. adv. com. Provincial Lottery Health Research Awards; vis. prof. biochemistry U. Alta., 1971. Nat. Cancer Inst. Can. fellow, 1953-56, 58-61; Brit. Empire Cancer Campaign fellow, 1956-58; recipient Queen's Silver Jubilee medal, 1978; Josiah Macy Jr. Faculty scholar, 1981-82; fellow Ligue Contre le Cancer, France, 1981-82. Fellow Am. Acad. Microbiology; mem. Can. Biochem. Soc. (v.p. 1974-75), Can. Soc. Cell Biology (pres. 1975-76), Am. Soc. Microbiologists, Assn. Women in Sci., Scitech, Soc. Complex Carbohydrates, Toronto Biochem. and Biophys. Soc. (pres. 1960-70, council 1970-74). Asso. editor Can. Jour. Biochemistry, 1968-71, Virology, 1969-72, Intervirology, 1974—; editorial bd. Microbiol. Revs., 1977-80; author, co-author various publs. Office: Dept Microbiology Univ Toronto 150 College St Toronto ON M5S 1A1 Canada

SHEIRR, OLGA, artist; b. N.Y.C., June 7, 1931; d. Edward E. and Lillian (Tobias) S.; B.A., Bklyn. Coll., 1953; postgrad. Art Students League, Pratt Graphic Center, N.Y.U., Itaglio Workshop, N.Y. Inst. Fine Arts; m. Maurice Krolik, Jan. 28, 1973. One-woman exhbns. include: Internat. Art Exchange, N.Y.C., 1962-63, Noho Gallery, N.Y.C., 1975-76, 78-80, 82, Cicchinelli Gallery, N.Y.C., 1982; bd. dirs. Noho Gallery, 1975—, treas., 1982—; exhbn. organizer Noho for the Arts, 1975-78; v.p., sec. Assn. Artists Run Galleries, N.Y.C., 1976-80, reviewer Artists View Art, 1976-80; group exhbns. include: A.A.A. Gallery, N.Y.C., 1965, 71, Silvermine Guild Artists, New Canaan, Conn., 1966, 76, Landmark Gallery, N.Y.C., 1976, The Arsenal, N.Y.C., 1978, Community Gallery, N.Y.C., 1980-81, Springfield (Utah) Mus. Art, 1981, Riyadh, Saudi Arabia, 1982. Mem. Women's Caucus for Art, N.Y. Artists Equity, Coalition Women's Art Orgns., Women in the Arts. Home: 360 1st Ave 11 G New York NY 10010

SHELBY, JANICE MARIE, state edn. ofcl.; b. Sept. 6, 1945; d. Seamon and Ruth (Greenway) Falls; B.S., Bethel Coll., 1967; M.S., Murray State U., 1971; m. Bill C. Shelby, Oct. 19, 1963; children—Tracye Leigh, Mary Allison. Remedial reading tchr. Lincoln Elem. Sch., Lake County, Schs., 1966-68; remedial reading tchr. Henderson County Sch. System, 1968-72, supr. instrn. kindergarten through 12th grades, 1972-74; kindergarten through 5th grade specialist Tenn. Dept. Edn., Jackson, 1974-79, compensatory edn. specialist, dir. spl. projects, 1979-80, asst. commr. div. curriculum and instruction, Nashville, 1980—. Col. a.d.c. Tenn. Gov.'s Staff, Nashville. Recipient award Tenn. Assn. Pub. and Continuing Edn., cert. of appreciation Tenn. Gov. Lamar Alexander. Mem. Internat. Reading Assn., Tenn. Assn. Curriculum and Devel., Delta Kappa Gamma. Republican. Methodist. Home: Route 3 Montpier Farms Franklin TN 37064 Office: Cordell Hull Bldg Room 112 Nashville TN 37219

SHELBY, JOYCE LYNN, ch. ofcl.; b. Salina, Kans., June 23, 1935; d. Rolan Ivan and Hilda Hennrietta (Holl) Pierce; student Okla. Bapt. U., 1953-55, Central State U., Okla., 1953-55; m. Coy Edward Shelby, Jan. 9, 1953; children—Kimberly, Corky. Minister of youth Dickson Bapt. Ch., Oklahoma City, 1955-65, Rancho Village Bapt. Ch., Oklahoma City, 1965-67, Capitol Hill Bapt. Ch., 1967-68, First Bapt. Ch., Oklahoma City, 1968-74; dir. ch. relations Okla. Bapt. U., Shawnee, 1974-77, dir. placement and career counseling, 1977-78; minister of edn. and adminstrn. Capitol Hill Bapt. Ch., Oklahoma City, 1978—; youth cons. Bapt. Gen. Conv. of Okla., 1968—. Mem. Nat. Assn. Dirs. Christian Edn., Southwest Bapt. Religious Edn. Assn., Okla. Bapt. Religious Edn. Assn. (v.p. 1979-80), Nat. Assn. for Female Execs., Religious Edn. Assn., Capitol Bapt. Assn. (pres. 1979-80). Democrat. Baptist. Home: 9801 NE 30 Spencer OK 73084 Office: 301SW 25 Oklahoma City OK 73109

SHELDON, BEATRICE EVERETT (MRS. ANSON H. SHELDON), polit. worker; b. Gunn, Miss., May 16, 1915; d. John Broadus and Pency Ann (Wooley) Everett; R.N., Dr. Willis Walley Sch. Nursing, Jackson, Miss., 1937; m. Anson H. Sheldon, Feb. 5, 1939; children—Patricia Ann Sheldon Strauss, Anson H., Lawson. Nurse, Kings Daus. Hosp., Canton, Miss., 1937, Greenville, Miss., 1937, Helena (Ark.) Hosp., 1938-39; sec.-treas. Machinery Inc., 1966—; County com. Miss. Republican Party, 1944-60; alternate del. to Rep. State Conv., 1948, 52, 56, 60. Trustee South Washington County Hosp., Hollandle, Miss., chmn. bd., 1978-80. Mem. Miss. Registered Nurse Assn. Episcopalian. Clubs: Longwood Community Culture (pres. 1975-78), Federated Women's. Home: Keystone Plantation Avon MS 38723

SHELDON, BETTY HELENE, retail co. mgr.; co. exec.; b. Chgo., Oct. 16, 1928; d. Jack and Jeannette (Sacks) Reichman; m. Richard Sheldon, Sept. 27, 1973; children—David Rhein, Andrea Freudenthal, Cynthia Anderson. Asst. adminstr. Fox River Pavilion, Chgo., 1968; v.p. mktg. Imperial Camera Corp., Chgo., 1969-80; v.p., chief operating officer Ansco Photo-Optical, Elk Grove, Ill., 1980-81; premium sales mgr. Realook Jewelry Corp., N.Y.C., 1981—. Mem. Internat. Orgn. Women Execs. (named Chgo. Woman of Leadership 1979), Nat. Assn. Camera Mfrs., Nat. Assn. Catalog Showrooms (adv. bd.), Photo Mktg. Assn. Address: 6427 N Kimball Lincolnwood IL 60645

SHELDON, ELEANOR HARRIET BERNERT, sociologist; b. Hartford, Conn., Mar. 19, 1920; d. M.G. and Fannie (Myers) Bernert; A.A., Colby Jr. Coll., 1940; A.B., U. N.C., 1942; Ph.D., U. Chgo., 1949; m. James Sheldon, Mar. 19, 1950 (div. 1960); children—James, John Anthony. Asst. demographer Office Population Research, Washington, 1942-43; social scientist U.S. Dept Agr., Washington, 1943-45; asso. dir. Chgo. Community Inventory, U. Chgo., 1947-50; social scientist Social Sci. Research Council, N.Y.C., 1950-51, research grantee, 1953-55, pres., 1972-79; research asso. Bur. Applied Social Research, Columbia, 1950-51; social scientist UN, N.Y.C., 1951-52; lectr. sociology Columbia U., 1951-52, vis. prof., 1969-71; research asso., lectr. sociology UCLA, 1955-61, asso. research sociologist, lectr. Sch. Nursing, 1957-61; sociologist, exec. asso. Russell Sage Found., N.Y.C., 1961-72; vis. prof. U. Calif. at Santa Barbara, 1971; dir. Rand Corp., Santa Monica, Equitable Life Assurance Soc., Citicorp, Citibank, Mobil Corp. Bd. dirs. Colby-Sawyer Coll., UN Research Inst. for Social Devel., 1973-79; trustee Rockefeller Found, 1978—. William Rainey Harper fellow U. Chgo., 1945-47. Fellow Am. Acad. Arts and Scis., Am. Sociol. Assn., Am. Statis. Assn. mem. U. Chgo. Alumni Assn. (Profl. Achievement award), Sociol. Research Assn. (pres. 1971-72), Council on Fgn. Relations, AAAS, Am. Assn. Public Opinion Research, Eastern Sociol. Soc., Internat. Sociol. Assn., Internat. Union. Sci. Study of Population, Population Assn. Am. (2d v.p. 1970-71), Inst. of Medicine (chmn. program com. 1976-77). Club: Cosmopolitan. Author: (with L. Wirth) Chicago Community Fact Book, 1949; America's Children, 1958; (with R.A. Glazier) Pupils and Schools in N.Y.C., 1965. Editor: (with W.E. Moore) Indicators of Social Change; Concepts and Measurements, 1968. Editor Family Economic Behavior, 1973. Contbr. articles to profl. jours. Home: 630 Park Ave New York NY 10021

SHELDON, GEORGIANA HORTENSE, govt. ofcl.; b. Lawrenceville, Pa., Dec. 2, 1923; d. William Franklin and Georgiana (Root) Sheldon; B.A., Keuka Coll., 1945; M.S., Cornell U., 1949; m. James R. Sharp, May 18, 1979. Dir. admissions Stetson U. Coll. Law, 1954-56; exec. asst. Republican Nat. Com., 1956-61; exec. sec. Hon. Rogers Morton (rep., Md.), 1962-69; dep. dir. Def. Civil Preparedness Agy., Washington, 1969-75; dir. Office Fgn. Disaster Assistance, dep. dir. internat. disaster assistance AID, 1975-76; vice chmn. CSC, 1976-77; mem. Fed. Power Commn., 1977—; mem. Fed. Energy Regulatory Commn., 1977—. Recipient Alumni award for profl. advancement Keuka Coll., 1966. Republican. Presbyterian. Office: 825 N Capitol St NE Washington DC 20426 *

SHELDON, NANCY WAY, mgmt. cons.; b. Bryn Mawr, Pa., Nov. 10, 1944; d. John Harold and Elizabeth (Hoff) Way; B.A. Wellesley Coll., 1966; M.A., Columbia U., 1968, M. Phil., 1972; m. Robert Charles Sheldon, June 15, 1968. Mgmt. cons. ABT Assos., Cambridge, Mass., 1968-70; mgmt. cons. Horbridge House, Inc., Boston, 1970-73, sr. asso., prin., N.Y.C., 1973-77, v.p., Los Angeles, 1977-79; mgmt. cons., pres. Resource Assessment, Inc., Los Angeles, 1979—; partner, real estate developer Resource Devel. Assos., Los Angeles, 1980—; partner Anubis Group Ltd., Los Angeles, 1980—. Registered, lic. pvt. investigator, Calif. Recipient achievement award Nat. Assn. Women Geographers. Mem. Am. Mining Congress, Am. Inst. Mining, Metall. and Petroleum Engrs. Contbr. articles to profl. jours. Address: 2261 Stradella Rd Bel Air CA 90077

SHELL, BARBARA PAMPLIN, civic worker; b. Colonial Heights, Va., Sept. 3, 1928; d. Jennings Cornile and Blanche B. (Temple) Pamplin; B.S., Madison Coll., 1949; m. Louis Calvin Shell, Aug. 5, 1950; children—Pamela, Patricia. Tchr. chemistry, physics Chesterfield County Schs., 1949-51; chemist Brown and Williamson Tobacco Co., Petersburg, Va., 1951-52. Vice-mayor, Petersburg, 1976-78, mem. City Council, 1974-78; mem. Gov. Godwin's Local Govt. Adv. Council, 1977-78; pres. PTA Council, Petersburg, 1967-68; sec. State Va., Student Council Assns. Adv. Bd., 1968-70; chmn. dist. adv. com. Petersburg Public Schs., Emergency Sch. Assistance Act, 1974-75; pres. Women's Soc. Christian Service, St. Mark's United Meth. Ch., 1969-71, mem. adminstrv. bd., 1969-71, treas. United Meth. Women, 1980-81; mem. adv. bd. Salvation Army, 1972-75; mem. Va. Mcpl. League's Community Devel. Policy Com., 1975-78; mem. Nation's League of Cities Community Devel. Policy Com., 1976-78; mem. Interstate 95 Adv. Coms., 1974—; mem. Crater Planning Dist. Commns. Legis. Com., 1976-78; mem. exec. bd. Va. Citizens Planning Assn., Inc., 1978—, chmn. com. on regional work-shops for planning commrs., 1981—; mem. state ethnic minority task force Va. ann. conf. United Meth. Ch., 1980—; v.p. govt. affairs Petersburg C. of C., 1980-81, bd. dirs., 1980-82; co-chmn. public employees div. United Way of Southside Va., 1981-82. Recipient Hon. Life Membership award Va. Congress Parents and Tchrs., 1966; Life Membership Award Women's Soc. Christian Service, 1967; named Petersburg Woman of Yr., Beta Sigma Phi, 1975.

SHELL, MARY KATHERINE JAYNES HOSKING (MRS. JOSEPH C. SHELL), mayor; b. Bakersfield, Calif., Feb. 9, 1927; d. Walter Charles and Mary Ellen (Young) Jaynes; student Bakersfield Coll., 1946-48; m. Richard Hosking, Aug. 21, 1948 (div. 1968); children—Geoffrey Richard, Timothy William (dec.), Meredith Katherine (dec.); m. 2d, Joseph C. Shell, Jan. 8, 1970. Mem. editorial staff Bakersfield Californian, 1944-45; mem. editorial staff Bakersfield News Bull., 1965-68, mng. editor, 1969; polit. columnist Bakersfield Californian, 1971-80; mayor, City of Bakersfield, 1980—. Founding pres. Bakersfield Jr. Woman's Club, 1954-55. Mem. Kern County Republican Central Com., 1956-60; founder, state sec. United Reps. Calif., 1963; mem. Calif. del. Rep. Nat. Conv., 1964. Club: Kern Press (founder 1967). Home: 2930 21st St Bakersfield CA 93301 Office: City Hall 1501 Truxton Ave Bakersfield CA 93301

SHELLER, MARILYN JO, med. technologist; b. Clinton, Iowa, July 30, 1932; d. Wilson Milton and Doris Opal (McQue) S.; A.A., Med. Tech. Sch., 1955; A.A., U. Colo., Pueblo, 1959. Med. technologist Parkview Hosp., Pueblo, Colo., 1955-59, U. Colo., Boulder, 1960-63; biol. technologist Center for Disease Control, USPHS, Phoenix, 1964—. Served with WAC, 1951-54; ETO. Recipient Merit award USPHS, 1979. Mem. Am. Med. Technologists (Disting. Achievement award 1975, pres. 1976-79), Am. Soc. Microbiology, Am. Soc. Med. Technologists, Ariz. Med. Lab. Assn. (pres. 1978), Federally Employed Women, Amvets, VFW. Republican. Congregationalist. Home: 8102 N 7th Ave Phoenix AZ 85021 Office: 4402 N 7th St Phoenix AZ 85014

SHELLEY, CAROLE AUGUSTA, actress; b. London, Aug. 16, 1939; came to U.S., 1964; d. Curtis and Deborah (Bloomstein) S.; studied ballet at Arts Ednl. Sch., 1943-56, Prep. acad. R.A.D.A., 1956-57; studied voice with Iris Warren; m. Albert G. Woods, July 26, 1967 (dec.). Child actress, beginning at age 3; later appeared in revues, films, West End comedies, including New Cranks and Mary Mary at the Globe Theatre; appeared as Gwendolyn Pigeon in stage, film and TV versions of The Odd Couple; Broadway appearances include: The Astrakhan Coat, Loot, Sweet Potato, Hay Fever, The Norman Conquests (Los Angeles Drama Critics Circle award 1975); appeared as Rosalind in As You Like It, King Lear and She Stoops to Conquer at Stratford, Ont., Can., 1972, and their European and Russian tours; appeared as Mrs. Margery Pinchwife in The Country Wife at Am. Shakespeare Festival, Stratford, Conn., 1973, as Nora in A Doll's House, Goodman Theatre, Chgo.; appeared in Man and Superman and as Epifania in The Millionairess, Shaw Festival, 1977; appeared in The Play's The Thing and The Devil's Disciple, Bklyn. Acad. Music, 1978; other stage appearances include The Royal Family (Los Angeles Drama Citics Circle award 1977), The Elephant Man (Outer Critics Circle award for 1978-79 season, Tony award for best actress 1978-79 season); appeared in film The Boston Strangler; created voice characters in Walt Disney films The Aristocats and Robin Hood. Jewish. Office: care Lionel Larner 850 7th Ave New York NY 10019

SHELLEY, GERALDINE CLAIRE, coop. library system adminstr.; b. San Jose, Calif., Dec. 9, 1928; d. William Edward and Clara Agnes (Lopez) Quadros; B.A. with distinction, San Jose State U., 1954; M.S. in L.S., Cath. U. Am., 1967; M.Public Adminstrn (scholar), Pepperdine U., 1974; m. Frank L. Shelley, Aug. 13, 1949; children—Ann, Francis, William, Clare, Catherine, Matthew. Vol. civic worker, 1949-67; various profl. positions Santa Cruz (Calif.) Public Library, 1967-77; dir. 49-99 Coop. Library System, Stockton, Calif., 1977—; free lance indexer, condr. workshops, cons. in field. Mem. Am. Soc. Indexers, Nat. Librarians Assn., Calif. Library Assn., Continuing Library Edn. Network and Exchange. Democrat. Roman Catholic. Office: 605 N El Dorado St Stockton CA 95202

SHELLEY, ROSE ANN, govt. ofcl.; b. McClellandtown, Pa., Sept. 23, 1941; d. John Andrew and Mary Elizabeth (Sluchak) Bellish; student George Washington U., 1972-74; m. Edward Halley Shelley, Sept. 22, 1961. Clk./stenographer Office Internat. Resourses, Fuels and Energy Div., Dept State, Washington, 1959-62, sec. Visa Office, 1962-63; sec. Gulf Oil Corp., Washington, 1963-64; sec. Office of Real Property, GSA, Washington, 1964-66, Procedures and Regulations Staff, 1966-67, Office of Mgmt. Investigations and Rev., 1967-68, Office of Audits and Compliance, 1968-70; program aide Legis. Div, Office of Congl. Affairs, 1970, Office of Telecommunications, 1970-76; exec. sec. Office of the Commr., Automated Data and Telecommunications, GSA, 1976—; EEO counselor, 1972; lectr. in field. Recipient Community Service award Combined Fed. Campaign of the Nat. Capital Area, 1979; Outstanding Performance Appraisal and award GSA, 1974, Spl. Achievement award, 1980, Outstanding Performance Appraisal, 1980. Mem. Montgomery County Hist. Soc., Md. Hist. Soc. Clubs: Slovak Social and Cultural, Linden Hill Tennis, Capital Cotillion Dance. Home: 12333 Dalewood Dr Wheaton MD 20902 Office: GSA 18 and F Sts NW Washington DC 20405

SHELP, JUNE PENO, state ofcl.; b. Dallas, Sept. 21, 1948; d. Michael and Ruth (Russell) Mueller; B.A., U. Tex., Austin, 1970; M.A., Mich. State U., 1972; m. Ronald Kent Shelp, Feb. 14, 1982. Economist, Bur. Labor Stats., U.S. Dept. Labor, N.Y.C., 1971-76; vis. prof. dept. econs. N.C. Central U., Durham, 1978-79; cons. Econs. & Internat. Bus., N.Y.C., 1977-80; exec. dir. N.Y. State Gov.'s Council on Internat. Bus., N.Y.C., 1980—; instr. dept. econs. Baruch Coll. City U. N.Y., 1974-75. Mem. Nat. Assn. Bus. Economists, Am. Econs. Assn. Democrat. Club: Bklyn. Botanic Garden. Home: 32 Washington Sq West New York NY 10011 Office: 230 Park Ave Suite 2240 New York NY 10169

SHELTON, BESSIE ELIZABETH, educator; b. Lynchburg, Va.; d. Robert and Bessie Ann (Plenty) Shelton; B.A. (scholar), W.Va. State Coll., 1958; student Northwestern U., 1953-55, Ind. U., 1956; M.S., SUNY, 1960. Young adult librarian Bklyn. Pub. Library, 1960-62; asst. head central reference div. Queens Borough Pub. Library, Jamaica, N.Y., 1962-65; instructional media specialist Lynchburg (Va.) Bd. Edn., 1966—; ednl. research specialist, 1974-77; ednl. media specialist Allegany County Bd. Edn., Cumberland, Md., 1977—. Guest singer Sta. WLVA, 1966—, WLVA-TV Christmas concerts, 1966—; cons. music and market research. Mem. YWCA, Lynchburg, 1966—, Fine Arts Center, Lynchburg, 1966—; nat. bd. advisers Am. Biog. Inst. Mem. NEA, Md. Tchrs. Assn., Allegany County Tchrs. Assn., Va. Edn. Assn., State Dept. Sch. Librarians, Internat. Entertainers Guild, Music City Songwriters Assn., Vocal Artists Am., Internat. Clover Poetry Assn., Intercontinental Biog. Assn., World Mail Dealers Assn., North Am. Mailers Exchange, AAUW, Am. Assn. Creative Artists, Am. Biog. Inst. Research Assn., Tri-State Community Concert Assn. Pi Delta Phi, Sigma Delta Pi. Contbr. poems to various publs. Democrat. Baptist. Clubs: National Travel, Gulf Travel. Home: PO Box 187 Cumberland MD 21502

SHELTON, BETSY CAMPBELL, fin. exec.; b. Redlands, Calif., May 1, 1949; d. Richard Bailey and Priscilla Alden (Simonds) Cook; student U. Calif., Santa Barbara, 1967-69; B.A. in Econs., U. Redlands, 1969; m. Robert Maurice Shelton, Feb. 8, 1975; 1 stepson, Scott Maurice. Adminstrv. asst. trust dept. Bank of Am., Los Angeles, 1971-72; sales asst./money market desk Goldman Sachs & Co., Los Angeles, 1972-74; sales liaison Bateman Eichles, Los Angeles, 1974-77; investment officer trust investment dept. Security Pacific Nat. Bank, Los Angeles, 1977-80; v.p., mcpl. bond trader Bateman Eichler, Los Angeles, 1980-82, v.p. instnl. sales, 1982—; outside instr. for securities test passing firm, 1981—. Mem. Los Angeles Mcpl. Bond Club. Office: 700 S Flower St Los Angeles CA 90014

SHELTON, LORAINE, bus. services co. exec.; b. Washington, Apr. 13, 1941; d. Wendell Wilfred Shelton and Belle (Steele) Shelton Screen; B.A., U. Md., 1964; children—Shelley, David, Donna. Pres., TLC Bus. Services, Inc., Washington. Active various civic assns.; coach boys' and girls' basketball. Mem. Nat. Assn. Female Execs., Am. Mgmt. Assn. Democrat. Roman Catholic. Home: 1643 Park Rd NW Washington DC 20010

SHELTON, LUCY, soprano; B.A., Pomona Coll., 1965; Mus. M. in Voice, New Eng. Conservatory Music, 1968. Asst. prof. voice Eastman Sch. Music, U. Rochester, 1979; appeared at Chamber Music N.W., Bethlehem Bach and Aspen music festivals, Casals Festival with Baroque ensemble; appeared as soloist with orchs., including Denver Symphony, Rochester Philharm., Buffalo Philharm., Los Angeles Chamber Orch., St. Paul Chamber Orch., and the Pro Arte Chorale and Orch. at Carnegie Hall; 1982-83 appearances with Houston, Balt. and Eugene (Oreg.) symphonies, performance world premiere of Schwantner work with St. Louis Symphony, and nationwide tour as soloist with Helmuth Rilling and Los Angeles Chamber Orch.; also recitals, guest appearances with various groups, including Calliope and Twentieth Century Consort; recs. with Nonesuch Records, Vox, Vanguard, Grenadilla, Sonory, and Smithsonian Instn.; winner Walter W. Naumburg prize, 1977 (with Jubal trio) and 1980 (solo). Office: care Hamlen Mgmt 140 W 79th St New York NY 10024

SHELTON, MILDRED LORINE HUEBNER, truck leasing exec.; b. Shiner, Tex., Mar. 20, 1921; d. Alfred J. and Edna L. (Shulak) Huebner; bus. degree Baldwins Bus. Coll., 1939; m. John R. Shelton, Nov. 17, 1958; children—Cynthia S. Ledford, Stephen W., Sylvia L. Sec., Shell Oil Co., Houston, 1941-42; office mgr. Naylor Oil Co., Houston, 1942-43; asst. cafeteria mgr. McCloskey & Co., Tampa, Fla., 1943-44; bookkeeper, partner Mitchell, H.J., Houston, 1945-50; office mgr. Ryder Truck Rental, Inc., Miami, Fla., 1950-53, asst. to gen. mgr., 1953-60, supr. contracts, 1960-68, mgr. contracts, 1968-74, dir. contracts, 1974—. Bd. dirs. Ryder System Fed. Credit Union, 1961-70, 75-79, pres., 1966-70. Mem. Nat. Secs. Assn., Internat. Word Processing Assn. Democrat. Methodist. Clubs: Daus. of Nile, Women's Shrine, Women's Traffic (v.p. 1957-58). Office: 3600 NW 82d Ave Miami FL 33166

SHELTON, NICOLINA SYLVESTER, public relations exec., journalist; b. New Rochelle, N.Y.; d. Angelo and Filomena (Loungo) Sylvester; student journalism Columbia U., 1946-47, Westchester Comml. Bus. Sch., 1948, Ellery Queen, 1953-56, public relations seminars Iona Coll., 1950, 66-67, 75, Am. Soc. Travel Agts. counselor tng. course, 1974. Public relations specialist House of Seagram, 1946-57, dir. women's market home services, 1957-61; account exec. Fletcher Richards Calkins & Holden Advt., N.Y.C., 1962-64, dep. public relations dir. U.S. Pavilion Dept. Commerce, N.Y. World's Fair, N.Y.C., 1964-65; account exec. Harry W. Graff Advt./Public Relations, 1967-69; dir. public relations Loewy Stempel Zabin Advt./Publicity, N.Y.C., 1969-70; news and info. specialist GAF Corp., N.Y.C., 1971-73; public relations and press relations officer Paul Andrews Assos., 1973-80. Mem. Holy Name Church Choir, 1968—. Recipient The Server's Serverette award, 1956; Cert. of Merit, Publicity Club of N.Y., 1974, 75; contest award Writer's Digest, 1970. Clubs: Huguenot, YMCA, Freelance Writers', Publicity of

N.Y. (hospitality chmn. 1973-74); Scuba Sport Rites (Rye, N.Y.). Editorial asst. spl. issues Aviation News, 1964-65; contbg. editor: Travel Agent mag., 1975—; Travel Age East, Travel Age SE, 1980—, Travel Holiday, 1979—, Airfare Interline mag., 1981—, Cath. N.Y., 1981—, R'gl Evo-Network mag., 1981—;writer lifestyle column Gannett-Westchester Newspapers, Westchester County, N.Y., 1975—; contbr. numerous articles to profl. and popular mags. and newspapers. Home: 21 Rhodes St New Rochelle NY 10801

SHELTON, SALLY ANGELA, bus. cons., former ambassador; b. San Antonio, Aug. 29, 1944; d. Harlan Bryan and Edith Angela (Pratka) S.; B.A., U. Mo., 1966; M.A. (Univ. fellow), Johns Hopkins U., 1968; postgrad. (Fulbright scholar) Institut de Sciences Politiques, Paris, 1968, Georgetown U., 1969. Research asst. Brookings Instn., 1969; prof. internat. relations Iberomerican U. and Nat. Autonomous U. Mex., Mexico City, 1969-71; legis. asst. for fgn. policy to Sen. Lloyd Bentsen, 1971-77; dep. asst. sec. State for Latin Am., Washington, 1977-78; ambassador to Barbados, Grenada, Dominica, St. Lucia, and St. Vincent, 1979-81; spl. rep. to Antigua, St. Kitts-Nevis, Montserrat and Brit. V.I., 1979-81; v.p. Internat. Bus.-Govt. Counsellors, Inc., Washington, 1982—; fellow Center Internat. Affairs, Harvard U., 1981-82. Italian Fgn. Ministry fellow; NDEA fellow. Mem. NOW, Nat. Women's Polit. Caucus, Fulbright Alumni Assn., Caribbean Studies Assn., Phi Beta Kappa. Democrat. Address: 1625 I St NW #719 Washington DC 20006

SHEMORRY, CORINNE JOYNES, mktg. exec.; b. Rolla, N.D., Jan. 24, 1920; d. William H. and Edna Ruth (Conn) Joynes; children—Gay, Jan. Publisher, Williston (N.D.) Plains Reporter, 1953-78; mktg. dir. Williston Credit Union, 1979—; journalist, lectr., cons., author, reporter. Recipient numerous awards in journalism on state and nat. level, including being named Outstanding Woman in Journalism in N.D., 1975. Mem. N.D. Press Assn., N.D. Press Women (past pres.), Nat. Press Women, Williston C. of C., Sigma Delta Chi. Mem. United Ch. Club: Bus. and Profl. Women's (past pres.). Home: 210 E 14th St Williston ND 58801

SHENK, PATRICIA WOOTEN, adult care facility adminstr.; b. Chapmansville, W.Va., Apr. 17, 1935; d. Jasper W. and Hatha (Bays) Wooten; m. Raymond R. Shenk, May 23, 1959; children—Roanne Shenk Mazzucco, Ellen Shenk Perrotto, Mark Greenlee, Raymond Shenk, Timothy Shenk, Zachary Shenk. Rev. clk., mailroom supr. FBI, Washington, 1953-55; registration clk. Santa Clara Jr. Coll., part-time 1966; inventory control clk. Preiser Sci., Charleston, W.Va., 1967-69; owner, adminstr. Summit House, Alton, N.Y., 1973—; pres. Shenk Properties, Inc. Mem. Nat. Assn. Female Execs., Nat. Fedn. Ind. Bus., U.S. C. of C., Sodus C. of C., Empire State Assn. Adult Care Homes. Republican. Methodist. Office: PO Box 194 Alton NY 14413

SHEPANEK, HELENE ANNA, educator; b. Regensburg, Germany, July 26, 1929; came to U.S., 1948, naturalized, 1950; d. Alfons and Alicia (Heidecker) Heiss; diploma Prinzessin von Arnheim Sch., Munich, 1947; B.A. summa cum laude, Am. U., 1972, M.A. with distinction, 1973; children—Marc Allen, Bruce Albert. Instr. German and French, C.I.A., Washington, 1965-66; teaching asst. Am. U., Washington, 1971-72, instr. German, 1972-78, professorial lectr., lang. specialist German studies, 1978—. Mem. AAUP, Am. Assn. Tchrs. of German, Am. Goethe Soc., Delta Phi Alpha, Phi Kappa Phi. Roman Catholic. Home: 2226 Pimmit Run Ln Apt 101 Falls Church VA 22043 Office: Dept of Languages and Foreign Studies American University Washington DC 20016

SHEPARD, JEAN HECK HASTINGS, author; b. N.Y.C., Feb. 2, 1930; d. Chester Reed and Anna S. (Charig) Heck; B.A., Barnard Coll., 1950; m. Lawrence V. Hastings, Mar. 29, 1950; 1 son, Lance Clifford; m. 2d, Daniel A. Shepard, July 26, 1954; 1 son, Bradley Reed. With sch. and library dept. Viking Press, N.Y.C., 1956-57; asst. dir. sch. and library promotion E.P. Dutton Co., N.Y.C., 1957-58; dir. publicity, advt. and promotion Thomas Y. Crowell Co., N.Y.C., 1958-62; dir. advt. Charles Scribner's Sons, N.Y.C., 1962-67; cons. Stephen Greene Press, Brattleboro, Vt., 1970-72; dir. publicity, advt. and promotion A&W Pubs., Inc., N.Y.C., 1979-80; dir. publicity, advt. and promotion Franklin Watts, Inc., N.Y.C., 1980—; author: Simple Family Favorites, 1971, Herb and Spice Cooking, 1972, Cook With Wine!, 1973, The Harvest Home Steak Cookbook, 1974, Earth Watch: Notes on a Restless Planet, 1974, The Fresh Fruits and Vegetables Cookbook, 1975, A Survival Handbook for Women, 1978. Mem. Author Guild, Authors League Am. Methodist.

SHEPARD, VIOLET KATHERINE, home economist; b. Bend, Oreg., May 14, 1935; d. Peter Paul and Anna Rose (Bradetich) Klobas; B.S. in Home Econs. Edn., Oreg. State U., 1956, postgrad., 1959-65; m. Jerome Shepard, Nov. 26, 1958; children—Raymond, Philip. Tchr. home econs. Westfir (Oreg.) High Sch., 1956-57; tchr. home econs., social studies Salem (Oreg.) public schs., 1959-63; extension home economist Oreg. State U. Extension Service, 1958-59, 65-73; instr. Chemeketa Community Coll., 1963—; free-lance home economist in bus., Salem, 1973-78; home economist-cons. Oreg. Trawl Commn., Astoria, 1978-81; home economist Nat. Marine Fisheries, 1981—; mem. Agri-Bus. Council. Vice pres. women's assn. First Presbyn. Ch., Salem, 1971; mem. ad-hoc adv. com. 4-H program, Salem; county and state judge, including 4-H and open class, 1965—. Mem. Oreg. Home Econs. Assn. (2d v.p. 1980-82), Am. Home Econs. Assn., Home Economists in Bus., Internat. Farm Youth Assn., NEA, Oreg. Edn. Assn., Oreg. Nutrition Council, AAUW, Grad. Home Economists. Democrat. Club: Home Extension Homemakers. Author: Holiday Potpourri, 1978; Oregon Trawland Shrimp Story; Microwave Potpourri; Mealtime Potpourri. Home: 1355 Mitzur St S Salem OR 97302 Office: 250-36th St Astoria OR 97103

SHEPHERD, ELSBETH WEICHSEL, ops. engr.; b. Youngstown, Ohio, Dec. 5, 1952; d. Richard Henry and Lesley Frances (Lynn) Weichsel; B.S. in Math., Carnegie-Mellon U., 1974; M.B.A., U. Cin., 1978; m. Gordon Ray Shepherd, Aug. 28, 1976. Asst. indsl. engr. Armco, Inc., Middletown, Ohio, 1974-76, asso. indsl. engr., 1976-78, indsl. engr., 1978-82, sr. ops. engr., 1982—. Mem. news mag. staff Jr. League Cin., 1980-81; vol. Miami Purchase Assn. Am. Iron and Steel Inst. fellow, 1978-81. Mem. Soc. Women Engrs. (pres. sect. 1981-82), Assn. Computing Machinery, Am. Inst. Indsl. Engrs. Home: 9518 E Brook Dr West Chester OH 45069 Office: 1801 Crawford St Middletown OH 45043

SHEPHERD, JUDY CARLILE, govt. ofcl.; b. Kansas City, Mo.; d. John Mercer and Mary Almeda (Chapin) Ellis; student Okla. State U., Tulsa U.; B.A., Am. U., Washington, 1960; m. Joseph Elbert Shepherd; 1 son from previous marriage, John Philip Carlile. Chief probation officer Tulsa County Ct., 1947-50; real estate broker United Farm Agy., 1952-58; bldg. fund campaign mgr. AAUW, Washington, 1958-59; govt. and public relations ofcl. Nat. Counsel Assos., Washington, 1959-61; congressional liaison Dept. Agr., Washington, 1961-65; public info. officer OEO, 1965-70, spl. asst. to dep. dir. ops. Head Start, elderly, Indian and migrant programs, 1970-73; dir. public relations Nat. Assn. Social Workers, Washington, 1973-74; social sci. analyst Congressional Research Service, Library Congress, Washington, 1976—. Pres. bd. govs. Agr. Symphony Orch., 1961-64; bd. dirs. ARC, Boy Scouts Am., 1948-50; bd. dirs. Little Theatre, 1956-57. Recipient 1st place Fed. Editors Blue Pencil award, 1967; cert. humanist counselor. Mem. Nat. Press Club, Public Relations Soc. Am., Nat. Assn. Govt. Communicators, Am. Humanist Assn., Assn. Humanistic Psychology, Am. U. Alumni Assn., Okla. State Soc., Ark. State Soc., Library Congress Profl. Assn., Humanist Assn. Nat. Capital Area (pres. 1977-78), Nat. Congress Am. Indians, DAR. Club: Woman's Nat Democratic. Coordinator, Am. Discovers Indian Art exhibit, Smithsonian Instn., 1967. Home: 2365 N Oakland St Arlington VA 22207 Office: Congressional Research Service Library Congress Washington DC 20540

SHEPLEY, LELA LOCKWOOD, banker; b. St. Louis, Jan. 17, 1952; d. Ethan Allen Hitchcock and Virginia (Hill) S.; B.A., Yale U., 1974. Comml. banking trainee Bankers Trust Co., N.Y.C., 1974-75, account officer eastern Europe, 1975-78, tng. dir. comml. banking program, 1978-80, sr. human resources cons. internat. dept., 1980—. Office: 280 Park Ave New York NY 10017

SHEPPARD, JOCELYN FORTIER, educator; b. Woonsocket, R.I., Nov. 9, 1941; d. Conrad U. and Marie-Jeanne (Dube) Fortier; A.B., Coll. New Rochelle, 1962; M.A. summa cum laude, U. Laval, Que., Can., 1963; postgrad. Providence Coll., 1963-65, U. Calif., Berkeley, 1967-69, UCLA, 1968, U. Calif., San Diego, 1970-71, 79-80, 82, San Diego State U., 1979. Mem. faculty modern fgn. lang. dept. R.I. Coll., 1963-66; mem. faculty evening div. modern fgn. lang. dept. San Jose City Coll., 1966-67; head French program Buchser High Sch., 1966-68; prof., head French dept. Southwestern Coll., Chula Vista, Calif., 1969—. Vol. in pediatrics Bellevue Hosp., N.Y.C., 1960, UCLA Med. Center, 1968, U. Hosp., San Diego, 1973. Recipient award in French, Laval U., 1962. Mem. AAUP, MLA, Faculty Assn. Calif. Community Colls., San Diego Opera Assn.

SHEPPARD, MARLENE M., city ofcl.; b. Phila., Sept. 22, 1940; d. Benjamin I. and Josephine (Della Selva) Avellino; B.A. cum laude, St. Joseph's U., 1974, postgrad., 1975-76; children—Lisa Marie, Mark, Susan. Elem. tchr., Phila. and Charleston, S.C., 1958-61; public housing caseworker, Phila., 1974-75, site dir. multi-service sr. citizens center, 1975-77, adminstr. daycare and elderly programs in public housing, 1977-79; dir. community services Phila. Housing Authority, 1979—; cons. elderly housing and supportive services. Exec. com. Lansdowne Democratic Party, 1972; mem. World Affairs Council, Elderly Housing Task Force. Mem. Southeastern Region Profls. in Aging, Pa. Daycare Adminstrs., Pa. Assn. Housing and Redevel. Authorities, Nat. Assn. Female Execs. Designer model programs HUD, Congregate Housing Services, 1980, Urban Initiatives, 1979, Youth/Ednl./Recreational Program, Gov.'s Justice Commn., 1980. Office: 2012 Chestnut St Philadelphia PA 19103

SHEPPARD, POSY (MRS. JOHN WADE SHEPPARD), vol. social worker; b. New Haven, Aug. 23, 1916; d. John Day and Rose Marie (Herrick) Jackson; student Vassar Coll., 1938; m. John W. Sheppard, May 16, 1936; children—Sandra (Mrs. Allan Gray Rodgers), Gail (Mrs. J. Truman Bidwell, Jr.), Lynn (Mrs. William M. Manger), John W. Vol. field cons. for Conn. ARC, 1955-61, nat. bd. govs., 1960-66, vice chmn. bd. govs., 1962-66; rep. League Red Cross Socs. to UN, 1957-81; rep. Am. Nat. Red Cross to com. internat. social welfare Nat. Social Welfare Assembly, 1957-62; chmn. NGO Com. UNICEF, 1962-64, 71-73; social welfare com. White House Conf. Internat. Coop. Year.; chmn. exec. com. NGO/OPI Conf., UN, 1963-65; pres. conf. ECOSOC, 1966-69. Mem. Nat. Soc. Colonial Dames, Jr. League Greenwich (vice chmn.), Nat. Inst. Social Scis., Am. Soc. Polit. and Social Sci., Internat. Platform Assn., Soc. Internat. Devel. Club: Cosmopolitan (N.Y.C.). Home: 535 Lake Ave Greenwich CT 06830

SHEPPERD, CLARETA LADELL, histologist; b. Houston, Feb. 26, 1931; d. Charles Bozman and Marietta Janette (Robinson) Shepperd; ed. Sam Houston State U. Intern, Hermann Hosp., Houston, 1951-52, staff Dept. Histology, 1952-59; supr. Dept. Histology, Brown & Assos. Med. Lab., Houston, 1959-71; supr. Dept. Histology Park Plaza Hosp., Houston, 1975—. Sponsor, Theater Under the Stars, World Vison Internat., Christian Children's Fund. Mem. Am. Soc. Clin. Pathologists, Tex. Histology Soc. (founding mem.), Nat. Histology Soc. Med. illustrator, Tex. Jour. Medicine, 1958-59. Home: 717 W 30 St Houston TX 77018

SHER, ALICE LEONORE GROSSMAN, med. social work cons.; b. N.Y.C., Jan. 16, 1912; d. Charles and Alice Marion (Weisels) Grossman; B.A., Brown U., 1933; student Inst. Musical Art of Juilliard Sch., N.Y., 1933-34; M.S., N.Y. Sch. Social Work, Columbia U., 1942; m. Philip Sher, Mar. 29, 1961. Med. social worker-supr. Presbyn. Hosp., N.Y.C., 1942-45; asst. prof. med. social work Western Res. U., Cleve., 1945-47; acting dir. social service Lenox Hill Hosp., N.Y.C., 1947-48; dir. social service Univ. Hosp., N.Y. U.-Bellevue Med. Center, N.Y.C., 1948-51; asst. dir. social service Meml. Hosp., N.Y.C., 1951-54; med. social cons. N.Y. Heart Assn., 1954-57; casework specialist N.Y. State Dept. Social Welfare, 1957-59; social work cons. Health Ins. Plan of N.Y., 1959-77; instr. med. students, dept. preventive medicine N.Y. U.-Bellevue Med. Center; lectr. Univ. Hosp., Lenox Hill Hosp. Cert. social worker, N.Y. Mem. Nat. Assn. Social Workers, Acad. Cert. Social Workers, Strathmore Assn. Scarsdale, Met. Opera Guild N.Y. Home: 31 Whistler Rd Scarsdale NY 10583

SHER, JOANN GIFFUNI, lawyer, ins. co. exec.; b. N.Y.C., May 30, 1942; d. Joseph and Flora (Baldini) Giffuni; B.A., Jackson Coll., Tufts U., 1963; LL.B., Fordham U., 1966; postgrad. U. Va., 1977; m. Michael L. Sher, Feb. 2, 1970 (div. 1977). With Mfrs. Hanover Trust Co., N.Y.C., 1966-71; admitted to N.Y. bar, 1968; atty. Tchrs. Ins. and Annuity Assn., Coll. Retirement Edn. Fund., N.Y.C., 1972-73, asst. counsel, 1973-74, asso. counsel, 1974-76, counsel, 1976-78, v.p., 1978—; lectr. in field. Mem. Family Edn. Com., Community Service Soc., 1970-72, mem. com. on edn., 1972-77; bd. dirs. Women's Prison Assn., 1972-74, Turtle Bay Music Sch., 1982—, Pastel Soc. Am., 1977—, Turtle Bay Music Sch., 1982—. Mem. Am. Bar Assn., Assn. Bar City N.Y., Nat. Assn. Coll. and Univ. Attys. Clubs: Cosmopolitan, Nat. Arts. Office: 730 3d Ave New York NY 10017

SHER, JOANNA RUTH, physician; b. Winnipeg, Man., Can., May 23, 1933; came to U.S., 1949, naturalized, 1958; d. Joseph and Dorothy Hellenberg; A.B., U. Chgo., 1952, B.S., 1956, M.D., 1956; m. Norman Sher, Dec. 28, 1955; children—Jonathan Aaron, Katherine Amy. Rotating intern Kings County Hosp., Bklyn., 1956-57, resident pathology, 1957-58; fellow pathology Kings County Hosp., SUNY Downstate Med. Center, Bklyn., 1960-62; Nat. Inst. Neurol. Diseases spl. fellow in neuropath. SUNY Downstate Med. Center, 1962-64; asst. neuropathologist Kings County Hosp., Bklyn., 1964-70, dir. neuropath. lab., 1970—; prof. clin. pathology, asst. dean Downstate Med. Center, Bklyn., 1977—; cons. depts. pathology Brookdale Hosp. and Med. Center, Bklyn., Maimonides Hosp. and Med. Center, Bklyn., Bklyn.-Cumberland Med. Center, L.I. Coll. Hosp. Diplomate Am. Bd. Pathology. Fellow Am. Soc. Clin. Pathologists; mem. Internat. Acad. Pathology, Am. Acad. Neurology, Am. Assn. Neuropathologists, Phi Beta Kappa, Sigma Xi, Alpha Omega Alpha. Editor: (with D. Ford) Primary Intracranial Neoplasms, 1979; contbr. articles in field to profl. jours. Home: 2347 E 63d St Brooklyn NY 11234 Office: Box 25 Downstate Med Center 450 Clarkson Ave Brooklyn NY 11203

SHER, LINDA ROSENBERG, lawyer; b. Chgo., May 16, 1938; d. Sidney and Rebecca Rosenberg; B.A., U. Chgo., 1959; LL.B., Yale U., 1962; m. Stanley O. Sher, Aug. 11, 1963; children—Jeremy Jay, Hellyn Sue. Admitted to D.C. bar, 1962; counsel constl. rights subcom. Senate Judiciary Com., 1962-64; atty. NLRB, 1964-77, asst. gen. counsel supreme ct. br., 1977—. Office: 1717 Pennsylvania Ave NW Washington DC 20570

SHER, PATRICIA RUTH, state legislator; b. Washington, June 19, 1931; d. Harry Eugene and Beatrice Ruth (Whitcomb) Hesse; student U. Md., 1967-71; m. William Sher, Feb. 13, 1955; children—Mark Stephen, Hunter Neal, Valerie Lynn, Tod David. Mem. Md. Ho. of Dels., 1978—, mem. com. econ. matters, joint com. mgmt. of public funds, plain lang. task force; mem. Gov.'s Anti-Arson Council. Montgomery County coordinator Com. to Repeal of Blue Laws, 1976; pres. Eastern Montgomery Kensington Wheaton Democratic Club, 1977-78; v.p. Tifereth Israel Sisterhood; founder, sec. Friends of RAP, 1971; Hornbook award Montgomery County Edn. Assn., 1982.

SHERBY, LINDA BARBARA, psychologist; b. N.Y.C., Mar. 21, 1946; d. Edward and Rose W. S.; B.S., Bklyn. Coll., 1965; M.A., U. Kans., 1967, Ph.D. (NIMH fellow), 1970; m. George E. Brandeberry, June 20, 1981. Supervising psychologist Wyandotte Mental Health Center, Kansas City, Kans., 1970-73; dir. psychology Forensic Center, Ann Arbor, Mich., 1973-76; psychologist in pvt. practice, Ann Arbor, 1976—; cons. to agys. concerned with geriatics and criminal justice system; instr. Eastern Mich. U. Vol., trainer, cons. Women's Crisis Center, Ann Arbor, 1973-77. Mem. Am. Psychol. Assn., Mich. Psychol. Assn., Am. Assn. Psychologists in Pvt. Practice, Mich. Soc. Lic. Psychologists, Nat. Register in Psychology, NOW, ACLU, Common Cause. Author: (with others) Getting Free: Women and Psychotherapy, 1982. Office: 122 1/2 E Liberty Ann Arbor MI 48104

SHERIDAN, JANE ELIZABETH, oil co. exec.; b. Boston, Apr. 17, 1949; d. Michael Joseph and Mary Gertrude Sheridan; B.A. in German, U. Mass., Boston, 1970; M.B.A. in Fin., Suffolk U., 1975. Teller, head teller N.Eng. Mchts. Nat. Bank, Boston, 1970-75; banking specialist Caltex Petroleum Corp., N.Y.C., 1975-76, fgn. banking/credit analyst, 1976-78, internat. auditor, 1978-80, sr. fgn. tax analyst, 1980—. Mem. Am. Mgmt. Assn., Assn. M.B.A. Execs., Nat. Assn. Female Execs. Home: 45 W 10th St New York NY 10011 Office: Caltex Petroleum Corp 380 Madison Ave New York NY 10017

SHERK, LORRAINE MARTHA, nurse, educator; b. Washington, Mo., Nov. 1, 1922; d. William Frederick and Martha Wilhelmina (Dierking) Meyer; student Central Mo. State U., 1940-42; R.N., St. Luke's Hosp. Sch. Nursing, 1945; B.S. in Nursing, Washington U., 1947, M.Ed., 1963; m. George W. Sherk, Sept. 13, 1947; 1 son, George W. Office and pvt. duty nurse, Washington, Mo., 1946-57; instr. Deaconess Sch. Nursing, 1950; instr. St. Luke's Sch. Nursing, 1957-62, assoc. dir., 1962-71, dir. nursing edn., 1971—; accreditation visitor Ind. State Bd. Nursing. Mem. Kirkwood Hist. Soc., Mo. Hosp. Assn., Hosp. Assn. Met. St. Louis (edn. com.), Mo. Citizens for Life, Humane Soc. Mo., Am. Heart Assn., Nat. League Nursing (past chmn. bd. rev. diploma programs), Mo. League Nursing, Assembly Hosp. Schs. Nursing (past mem. governing council, program com.), Show-Me State Diploma Nurse Educators (past chmn.), Deans and Dirs. St. Louis Sch. Nursing (past chmn.), St. Luke's Alumni Assn., Kappa Delta Pi. Presbyterian (deacon). Home: 643 E Jefferson Ave Kirkwood MO 63122 Office: 5535 Delmar Blvd Saint Louis MO 63112

SHERMAN, ANITA GERALDINE, budget analyst; b. Chgo., Nov. 8, 1925; d. Frank George and Dorothy (Derdiger) LeVine; grad. high sch.; m. July 7, 1946 (div.); children—Barry Wynn, Jeffrey Michael. Exec. sec. Navy Regional Fin. Center, San Diego, 1964-72, budget analyst Fleet Acctg. & Disbursing Center, San Diego, 1972-80, budget analyst Navy Acctg. and Fin. Center, Washington, 1980—. Mem. Am. Soc. Mil. Comptrollers (chpt. treas. 1976). Republican. Jewish. Home: 2301 S Jefferson Davis Hwy Arlington VA 22202 Office: Navy Acctg and Fin Center Washington DC 20376

SHERMAN, ANITA SUSAN, barber; b. San Angelo, Tex., Aug. 17, 1950; d. John Henry and Johnnye V. (Anderson) Routa; diploma Colo. Barber Coll., 1970; student Community Coll. Denver, 1969-71, 73-74. Barber/stylist Danny's Hairstyling, Denver, 1969, The Don, Denver, 1970-74; sales rep., then dist. mgr. Redken Labs., Canoga Park, Calif., 1974-76; mgr. Gentleman's Choice, Ladies Preference, San Mateo, Calif., 1976-78; owner Hair Friends, San Carlos, Calif., 1978—; tchr. various hair dressing classes. Winner 1st place Women's Freestyle Competition, Colo., 1970. Mem. Nat. Assn. Hairdressers and Cosmetologists, Nat. Assn. Female Execs. Office: 1750 Laurel St San Carlos CA 94070

SHERMAN, BENNA ZIMMERMAN, psychologist; b. Easton, Pa., June 10, 1952; d. Leonard ElayneDoris (Whitman) Zimmerman; B.A., U. Pa., 1973, M.S., 1974, Ph.D., 1978; m. Steven Hugh Sherman, Nov. 28, 1975; 1 son, Michael Alan. Psychoednl. counselor Counseling or Referral Assistance, Phila., 1975-76; instr. U. Pa., Phila., 1976-78; cons. Research for Better Schs., Phila., 1979. Grad. Sch. Edn. fellow, 1977-78, Grad. Faculty fellow, 1976-77. Mem. Am. Psychol. Assn., Assn. Advancement Psychology, NOW, Nat. Womens Polit. Caucus, Phi Delta Kappa, Pi Lambda Theta. Address: 253 Lamp Post Lane Hershey PA 17033

SHERMAN, ELEANOR B., social worker; b. Chgo., Apr. 23, 1926; d. Alonzo and Sylvia (Burney) Barksdale; B.A., Howard U. 1954; M.S.W., Jane Addams Sch. Social Work, 1975; 1 child, Sylvia Ann Sherman Evans. Caseworker, Ill. Dept. Public Aid, Chgo., 1960-65, supr., 1965-66, intake supr., 1966-73, service supr., 1975—; lectr. in child abuse prevention Speakers Bur., Inc., 1979—, bd. dirs., 1970—. Contact person hunger task force Episcopal Diocese Chgo.; dir./coordinator Meals on Wheels program Bread for the World. Mem. Nat. Assn. Univ. Women (fin. sec. 1976-80), Acad. Social Workers, Am. Public Welfare Assn., Ill. Welfare Assn., Nat. Assn. Social Workers, Internat. Social Welfare Assn., Howard U. Alumni Assn., U. Ill. Alumni Assn., Bread for the World, Episcopal Ch. Women. Office: 8001 S Cottage Grove Ave Chicago IL 60619

SHERMAN, FRANCES BUCK, artist, photographer; b. Barabona, Santo Domingo; d. Harry Catlett and Elizabeth F. Buck (parents Am. citizens); student Sophie Newcomb Coll., New Orleans, 1936-37, St. Mary's Jr. Coll., Raleigh N.C., 1937, New Orleans Acad. Art, 1947-48, Atlanta Sch. Art., 1967-68, Jacksonville Mus. Art, 1976, N.Y. Inst. Photography, 1981; m. Walter Scott Sherman, Jr., Nov. 9, 1950; children—G. Scott, F. Carolyn; children by previous marriage—Thomas M. Frasier, Harry B. Frasier. Pvt. art tchr., New Orleans, 1947; pvt. practice modeling, New Orleans, 1947-48; staff fashion model Burdines Dept. Store, Miami, 1949-50, asst. fashion coordinator, 1951-52; fashion cons. Coronet Sch. Modeling, Miami, 1953-54; instr. art Tampa (Fla.) Realistic Artists Gallery, 1969-70; one-woman shows: Tampa Realistic Art Gallery, 1970, St. Marys Episcopal Ch., Tampa, 1971, Britton Theatre Corp., Tampa, 1970, Royal Trust Bank, Jacksonville, Fla., 1980, 81; group shows include: Va. Mus. Fine Arts, Richmond, Mint Mus. Art, Charlotte, N.C., Isaac Delgado Mus. Art, New Orleans, Swan Coach House Gallery, Atlanta, Jacksonville (Fla.) Art Mus., 1979, St. Augustine (Fla.) Art Assn., 1979, St. Augustine Art Assn., 1980, 81; represented in permanent collections: Jacksonville Shipyards Corp., Robinson-Humphrey Investors, Atlanta, Jacksonville (Fla.) U.; hostess Jacksonville Art Assembly Art Festival, 1977. Active fund raising Pub. Broadcasting TV Sta., Tampa, 1970-71, Jacksonville, 1972-78; active Republican Campaign Hdqrs., Jacksonville, 1976; mem. Nat. Rep. Congl. Com., Duval County Rep. Women's Club. Recipient Certificate of Recognition, The Bicentennial Commn. Jacksonville, 1976; named

Outstanding Patriot, The Patriots of the Am. Bicentennial, 1976. Mem. Am. Artists Profl. League, Inc., Nat. League Am. Pen Women, Inc. (pres. Jacksonville br. 1974-76; Fla. v.p. 1974-76), St. Augustine Art Assn., Fla. Poetry Soc., Arts Assembly Jacksonville, Jacksonville Art Mus., Nat. Writers Club. Episcopalian. Contbr. poetry to books and mags. Home: 4331 San Jose Ln Jacksonville FL 32207

SHERMAN, ISADORA, social work adminstr.; b. N.Y.C., May 28, 1923; d. Louis R. and Ann (Milner) Ruffine; B.A., Queens Coll., 1944; M.A., U. Wis., 1945; M.S.W., U. Chgo., 1950; m. Carlton R. Sherman, Sept. 4, 1949 (dec. 1981); children—Barnard, Steven, Amy. With Jewish Family & Community Service, Chgo., 1950-52; with Irene Jesselyn Clinic, Northfield, Ill., 1955-57; with Jewish Family & Community Service, Highland Park, Ill., 1961—, dist. adminstr. North Suburban dist., 1978—. Cert. social worker. Mem. Nat. Assn. Social Work, Assn. Cert. Social Workers. Jewish. Office: 210 Skokie Hwy Highland Park IL 60035

SHERMAN, KATHLEEN LOUISE, social worker; b. Findley Twp., Pa., Nov. 10, 1941; d. Edward Rudolfus and Mary Belle Louise (Bloomster) S.; B.S., United Wesleyan Coll., 1963; M.S.W., W.Va. U., 1975. Lic. to ministry Ch. of Nazarene, 1974; part time pastor Harmons Creek Ch. of Nazarene, Putnam County, W.Va., 1976-78; caseworker Lycoming County Children's Services, Williamsport, Pa., 1966-70; dir. Spring Garden Day Care Center, Easton, Pa., 1971-73; dir. child abuse and neglect detection ops. Salvation Army, Charleston, W.Va., 1975-79; asst. prof. social work Concord Coll., Athens, W.Va., 1979—; cons. 1st Christian Day Care Center, Beckley Child Care Center. Mem. W.Va. Parents Anonymous State Adv. Com., 1977—, Mercer County Adolescent Health Care Adv. Bd., 1980—, W.Va. Task Force on Child Abuse and Neglect, 1978-80, Charleston Comprehensive Emergency Services for Children Com., 1976-80, bd. dirs. Charleston Domestic Violence Center, Inc., 1979; mem. adv. com. dept. social work and sociology W.Va. State Coll., 1978-79. Mem. Acad. Cert. Social Workers, Nat. Assn. Social Work, Nat. Assn. Christians in Social Work, Am. Humane Assn. Club: Quota. Home: Box 98 Athens WV 24712 Office: Concord Coll Athens WV 24712

SHERMAN, MARY KENNEDY, bus. exec.; b. Chgo., June 17, 1919; d. Robert Thomas and Mary Cecelia (Hammond) Kennedy; A.A., Los Angeles Valley Coll., 1966; B.S., Pepperdine U., 1973; M.B.A., 1974; AEP, Personnel Accreditation Inst., 1977; m. Lloyd McBean Sherman, Dec. 1, 1967; children—Tom D. Akins, Mary Patricia Kraakevik. Indsl. relations supr. Douglas Aircraft Co., Inc., Santa Monica, Calif., 1942-61; dir. personnel Helene Curtis Industries, Studio Girl, Glendale, Calif., 1961-65; dir. personnel Semtech Corp., Newbury Park, Calif., 1965-73, v.p., 1973—; lectr., cons. in field. Mem. Am. Mgmt. Assn., Internat. Assn. for Personnel Women, Am. Soc. Personnel Adminstrn., Personnel and Indsl. Relations Assn., Am. Bus. Women's Assn., Personnel Women of Los Angeles. Republican. Roman Catholic. Club: Zonta Internat. Office: 652 Mitchell Rd Newbury Park CA 91320

SHERMAN, MELINDA ANNE, advt. exec.; b. Chgo., Sept. 17, 1946; d. Gerald Wilfred and Dorothy Anne S.; B.A., U. Colo., 1968; M.S.J., Northwestern U., 1973. High Sch. tchr. English, journalism and drama, Albion and Reading, Mich., 1968-70; account rep. Equitable Life Assurance Soc., Chgo., 1970-72, Young & Rubicam N.Y. Advt., 1973-76; account supr. Leo Burnett USA Advt., Chgo., 1976—. Recipient Spl. Performance award Young & Rubicam Advt., 1975, 76. Mem. Nat. Assn. Female Execs., Am. Mktg. Assn., Gamma Phi Beta. Clubs: Women's Athletic, Plaza (Chgo.). Home: 1560 N Sandburg Terr Chicago IL 60610 Office: Prudential Plaza Chicago IL 60601

SHERMAN, PATRICIA MARIE, nurse; b. Amsterdam, N.Y., Feb. 25, 1940; d. Percy Edward and Marie Louisa (Knost) S.; student Russell Sage Coll., Troy, N.Y., 1957-58; R.N., Albany (N.Y.) Med. Center, 1961; divorced; children—Michael Ruth, Matthew Ruth. Pvt. duty nurse, 1962-74; staff nurse Albany VA Hosp., 1961-62; nurse adminstr. O.D. Heck Devel. Center, Schenectady, 1974-81; sr. investigator N.Y. State Commn. Quality of Care Mentally Disabled, Albany, 1981—. Mem. N.Y. State Nurses Assn. (chmn. pvt. duty sect. 1967-69), Albany Med. Center Alumni Assn. Home: 3 Juniper Ct Schenectady NY 12309 Office: 99 Washington Ave Suite 730 Albany NY 12210

SHERMAN, Z. CHARLOTTE, artist; b. Los Angeles, June 18, 1924; d. Jacob and Celia (Knopow) Pynoos; student UCLA, 1945-47, Otis Art Inst., 1947-50, Kann Art Inst., 1950-52; m. Lawrence James Sherman, Dec. 17, 1943; children—Susan (Mrs. Howard Meyers), Daniel Michael. Exhibited group shows, São Paulo (Brazil) Biennial, 1961; Heritage Gallery, Los Angeles, 1963—; D'Allesio Gallery, N.Y.C., 1965, 66; Grand Prix Internat. de Deauville, Paris, 1972; Prix de Rome, Palais des Beaux Artes, Rome, 1973; represented by Heritage Gallery, Los Angeles; tchr. video films Z. Charlotte Sherman, Portrait of an Artist, 1977, 78; tchr. Los Angeles City Cultural Arts Center, 1970—. Recipient Phelan Found. award, 1961; Pasadena Mus. Art award, 1961; All City Exhbn. award, Barnsdale, Los Angeles, 1963, 65. Mem. Nat. Watercolor Soc., Los Angeles Art Assn. Address: 1300 Chautauqua Blvd Pacific Palisades CA 90272

SHERRY, CANDICE ELAINE, nuclear planner; b. East Liverpool, Ohio, Aug. 1, 1950; d. Donal Irwin and Phyllis Elaine (Reed) Burcham; B.S. in Physics, Journalism with honors, Kent State U., 1972; postgrad. Baylor U., 1973, Ohio State U., 1975; 1 dau., Alexandra. Public relations officer U.S. Army, Ohio, 1976-80, nuclear planner Adj. Gen., 1980—. Served with U.S. Army, 1973-76. Recipient Ohio C. of C. award for art, 1969, Colo. Council Arts award, 1974. Mem. Nat. Orgn. Profl. Planners (founder pres.), Mensa, Internat. Fortean Soc., Fedn. Bus. and Profl. Women, Mystery Writers Guild, Nat. Archery Assn., LWV (ward chmn.). Democrat. Roman Catholic. Club: V.F.W. Editor: Nuclear Newsletter; contbr. to various publs. Office: 2825 W Granville Rd Worthington OH 43085

SHERRY, MARILYN MORIN, psychiat. social worker; b. Worcester, Mass., Mar. 25, 1935; d. Jacob and Gertrude (Greenberg) Morin; A.B., Clark U., 1956; M.S., Simmons Coll., 1958; m. Gerald B. Sherry, Jan. 3, 1960; children—Samuel, Trudy. Social worker Child and Family Services of Conn., Manchester, 1958-61, Hartford, Conn., 1966-71, Dept. Human Services, New Britain, Conn., 1977-79, social worker palliative care and geriatrics Mt. Sinai Hosp., Hartford, 1979-81; psychiat. social worker U. Conn. Health Center, Farmington, 1981—; pvt. practice social work, 1981—. Adv. bd. Encore, YWCA Postmastectomy Program, 1980-81. Mem. Registry of Clin. Social Workers, Acad. Cert. Social Workers, Nat. Soc. Clin. Social Workers, Coalition Social Work Orgns. Conn. (founding mem., sec.-treas. 1981—), Nat. Assn. Advancement Group Psychotherapy, Am. Assn. for Marriage and Family Therapy. Home: West Hartford CT Office: Univ Conn Health Center H 1015 Farmington CT 06032

SHERWIN, JUDITH ANN, health care exec.; b. Strabane, Pa., Sept. 19, 1945; d. Carl and Anna (Gomber) Subrick; B.A., Carlow Coll., 1967. Staff med. technologist Mercy Hosp., Pitts., 1967-69; staff med. technologist Central Blood Bank, Pitts., 1969-72, lab. supr., adminstrv. asst., 1972-77, ednl. coordinator, asst. tech. dir., 1977, tech. dir., 1978-81; exec. dir. Blood Product Devel. Programs, SBB Program instr., clin. asst. prof. U. Pitts., 1981—. Recipient Ned G. Maxwell award for disting. performance, Central Blood Bank, 1981. Mem. Am. Assn. Blood Banks, Pa. Assn. Blood Banks, Am. Soc. Clin. Pathologists, Pa. Soc. Med. Technology. Home: 328 Woodbridge Dr Pittsburgh PA 15237 Office: 812 5th Ave Pittsburgh PA 15219

SHERWIN, JUDITH JOHNSON, author, educator; b. N.Y.C., Oct. 3, 1936; d. Edgar and Eleanor (Kraus) Johnson; B.A. cum laude, Barnard Coll., 1958; m. James T. Sherwin, June 21, 1955; children—Miranda, Alison Dale, Galen Leigh. Author: Uranium Poems (Yale Series of Younger Poets prize 1968), 1969; (short stories) The Life of Riot, 1970; (poems) Impossible Buildings, 1973, The Town Scold, 1977, How the Dead Count, 1978, Transparencies, 1978, Dead's Good Company, 1978; (play) En Avant, Coco, 1962; bd. advisers BOA Editions, Brockport, N.Y., 1976; tech. adviser N.Y. State Council Arts, 1975-76; adviser to poetry and fiction panels Poets and Writers, Inc., 1975-76; tchr. poetry workshop Poetry Center, N.Y.C., 1975, 78, 81; vis. poet Wake Forest U., 1980, SUNY, Albany, 1980-81. Recipient Poetry prize St. Andrews Rev., 1975; prize Acad. Am. Poets, 1958; Amy Loveman Poetry prize Barnard Coll., 1958; Playboy prize for best fiction by new contbr., 1977. Yaddo fellow, 1964; Aspen Writers Workshop fellow, 1967; Woodrow Wilson fellow, 1958-59. Fellow Poetry Soc. Am. (pres. 1975-78, chmn. exec. com. 1979-80); mem. PEN, Authors Guild, Women's Ink, Phi Beta Kappa. Address: care Charlotte Sheedy Lit Agts 145 W 86th St New York NY 10024

SHERWOOD, COLLEEN GAIL, govt. ofcl.; b. Middleboro, Mass., Oct. 22, 1944; d. Robert Bridge and Jeanette Louise (Letendre) Sargent; student Montgomery Coll., 1977—; children—Stephen, Suzanne, Richard. Personnel asst. Nat. Cancer Inst., Bethesda, Md., 1974-76, adminstrv. asst., 1976-79, adminstrv. officer, 1979-81; spl. asst. program planning and evaluation Nat. Inst. Arthritis, Diabetes and Digestive and Kidney Diseases, Bethesda, Md., 1981-82, spl. asst. program analysis, 1982—. Recipient Superior Performance awards Dept. Health and Human Services, 1970, 72, 77, 79. Mem. Nat. Assn. Female Execs., Phi Theta Kappa. Democrat. Roman Catholic. Home: 10259 Arizona Circle Bethesda MD 20817 Office: Nat Inst Arthritis Diabetes and Digestive and Kidney Diseases Bldg 31 Room 9A-07 Bethesda MD 20205

SHERWOOD, PHYLLIS ETHEL, mfg. co. exec.; b. Syracuse, N.Y., Nov. 23, 1931; d. Lawrence David and Ethel Adeline (Harris) S.; student Data Processing Tech. Center, Syracuse, 1966-67. Statis. coder Kemper Ins. Co., Syracuse, 1949-52, key punch operator, 1952-54, key punch supr., 1954-59; with Central Packaging Supply, Inc., Syracuse, 1959—, asst. treas., 1963-73, exec. v.p., 1973—. Methodist. Mem. Order Eastern Star.

SHERWOOD, STEPHANIE JAN WANNER, banker; b. Berwyn, Ill., July 7, 1944; d. Thomas Lewis and Janet Mae (Grissinger) Wanner; B.J., U. Mo., 1967; children—Leslie Christine, Jennifer Lynn, Stuart Miles. Staff writer Springfield (Mo.) Newspapers, Inc., 1974-78; exec. dir. Downtown Springfield Assn., 1978-79; exec. editor Springfield mag., 1979; mktg.-communications officer Boatmen's Union Nat. Bank, Springfield, 1979—. Bd. dirs. Downtown Springfield Assn.; mem. Citizens Adv. Com. for Fed. Community Devel. Funding, 1979-80; charter mem. Springfield Council of Arts; mem. Springfield Sesquicentennial Com., 1979; judge Springfield Sesquicentennial Parade, 1979; bd. dirs., chmn. public relations Dogwood Trails council Girl Scouts U.S.A., 1978—. mem. Springfield Traffic Adv. Bd. Mem. Nat. Assn. Bank Women, Bank Mktg. Assn., Nat. Fedn. Press Women, Mo. Press Women, LWV, C. of C. (dir. women's div.). Home: 910 E University Springfield MO 65807 Office: Boatmen's Union Nat Bank 117 Park Central Square Springfield MO 65805

SHEVLIN, KATHLEEN MARY, social worker; b. Woonsocket, R.I., July 2, 1922; d. Archibald Thomas and Mary Elizabeth (Dwyer) Shevlin; B.A., Emmanuel Coll., 1943; M.S. in Social Work, Cath. U., 1945, Ph.D., 1978. Med. social worker ARC, U.S. Naval Hosp., Bklyn., 1945-47; dir. med. social service St. Mary's Hosp., Bklyn., 1947-59; cons. N.Y.C. Health Dept., 1959-60; dir. social service St. Catherine's Hosp., Bklyn., 1960-61; dir. Dept. Social Work, St. Vincent's Hosp., Worcester, Mass., 1961-63; cons., project coordinator R.I. Hosp., Providence, 1963-66; dir. dept. social work Georgetown U., Washington, 1967—, asst. prof. Sch. Medicine, 1968—; adj. asst. prof. Nat. Catholic Sch. Social Service, Cath. U., Washington, 1978—; clin. asst. prof. Smith Coll. Sch. Social Work, 1971—. Lic. social worker, Md., R.I. Mem. Nat. Assn. Social Workers, Acad. Cert. Social Workers, Am. Public Health Assn., Tchrs. Preventive Medicine, Council on Social Work Edn., Soc. for Hosp. Social Work Dirs., Am. Hosp. Assn., Hastings Inst., Nat. Conf. Cath. Charities. Contbr. articles to profl. jours. Home: 4301 Massachusetts Ave NW Washington DC 20016 Office: 3800 Reservoir Rd NW Washington DC 20007

SHIBER, SUSAN IRENE, public relations agy. exec.; b. Johnstown, Pa., Jan. 3, 1942; d. John H. and Alma L. (Wendle) S.; B.A., Lycoming (Pa.) Coll., 1964. Retail exec. trainee Allied Stores, 1964-66; various advt. positions, 1966-72; public relations dir. Foltz-Wessinger, Lancaster, Pa., 1972-75, Tyson & Partners, Phila., 1976-77; pres. Shiber & Assos., Blue Bell, Pa., 1977—; partner The Sight & Sound People, 1981—; speaker in field. Adv. bd. Corp. Veritas, 1980-81; bd. dirs. Phila. Co., 1981—; chmn. public relations com. Pa. Ballet, 1980-81, chmn. public relations com., 1981; bd. dirs. active public relations com. local Am. Heart Assn., Am. Cancer Soc. Recipient 1st and 2d pl. Public Relations awards for Berks TV Cable, Nat. Cable TV Assn., 1972, award of excellence (2) Art Dirs. Club Phila., 1979, Neographic silver award (3), 1981, also various service awards. Mem, Public Relations Soc. Am. (accredited; chpt. publicity chmn. 1979), Mktg. Communications Execs. Internat. (dir. 1977-78, editor newsletter 1977-78, publicity chmn. 1978, Communicator of Yr. award 1978), Nat. Assn. Female Execs. Address: 41 Winston Ct Blue Bell PA 19422

SHIDELER, ANN MARIE, speech-lang. pathologist; b. Oklahoma City, Aug. 23, 1951; d. Alfred Max and Joy Ann (Austin) S.; B.A., U. Okla., 1973; M.S. (Rehab. Services Adminstrn. trainee), Purdue U., 1975. Speech-lang. pathologist, originator speech and hearing services program Ind. State Soldiers Home, Lafayette, 1973-74; speech-lang. pathologist Wise (Va.) Speech and Hearing Center, 1976-77; speech-lang. pathologist, inservice dir. Hearing and Speech Center Rochester (N.Y.), 1978-80, Rochester Gen. Hosp., 1980—; head community stroke group Am. Heart Assn., 1978-80, mem. stroke com. Genesee Valley chpt., 1978-81. Initiator, co-dir. 1st ann. U. Rochester Summer Carillon Recital Series, 1979; flutist Brighton Symphony Orch., Rochester, 1980; mem. Golden Link Folk Orch. Mem. Am. Speech, Lang. and Hearing Assn., Guild Carillonneurs N.Am., Genesee Valley Speech and Hearing Assn., (v.p. 1981-82), N.Y. State Speech and Hearing Assn. (bd. regional pres. 1981-82), 14621 Assn., Golden Link Folk Singing Soc. Home: 99 Jackson St Rochester NY 14621 Office: 1425 Portland Ave Rochester NY 14621

SHIELDS, IVA ANN NIELSEN, photo-journalist; b. Salt Lake City, Nov. 9, 1933; d. Andrew Alma Ivie Eleanora (Olson) Nielsen; student Latter Day Saints Bus. Coll., 1951-52, Brigham Young U., 1975; m. Romulus Doyle Shields, Sept. 16, 1954; children—Craig Doyle, Gleanne. Sec., Tooele County Sheriff's Office, Tooele, Utah, 1951-55; area corr. Salt Lake Tribune, Salt Lake City, 1956—; free-lance photo-journalist, 1956—. Mem. public relations com. Utah Peageant of Arts; pub. relations dir. and/or com. mem. American Fork Steel Days Celebration, 1965—. Recipient Outstanding Fire Prevention award U.S. Forest Service, 1969, Woodsey Owl award, 1973; award for news coverage American Fork Hosp., 1975; award Cub Scouts, 1966. Mem. Utah Press Women (writing awards 1975, 76, 77, 79, 80, treas.). Mormon.

SHIELDS, LAURA AULL, public relations counselor; b. Taylorville, Ill., Oct. 24, 1917 d. Leo Franklin (dec.) and Gladys Aull (Montgomery) (dec.) Aull; student Ill. Normanl U., 1935, UCLA, 1938; children—Deborah, Beth, Roger, Clark, Constance. Feature writer San Gabriel Valley Tribune, Covina, Calif., 1969—; owner Shields Communications, Santa Monica, Calif., 1976—. Mem. Counselors Acad., Public Relations Soc. Am., Women in Bus., Nat. Assn. Women Bus. Owners. Democrat. Home and Office: 159 Wadsworth Ave Santa Monica CA 90405

SHIFFER, MABEL CROSS, assn. exec.; b. Gibson City, Ill., Jan. 24, 1921; d. Thurman Albert and Lena Isabel (Wagonseller) Cross; R.N., B.S.N., Pediatric Affiliation, Med. Sch. Nursing, Ind. U., 1940; postgrad. Mennonite Nursing Sch., affiliated with Ill. Wesleyan U., 1941; postgrad. in community health Oreg. State U., 1968; m. Maynard Carlisle Shiffer, Oct. 5, 1941; children—Julie, Alan. Public health nurse, Miss., 1942-44; exec. dir. Oreg. Lung Assn., Wilamette Region, 1969-77; exec. dir. Marion-Polk County Med. Soc., Salem, Oreg., 1977—; dir. Blue Cross of Oreg. Vol. coordinator Salem Public Schs., 1965-69; bd. dirs. YWCA, 1960-70, pres. bd. dirs., 1960-61, trustee, 1970—; pres. Salem Hosp. Aux., 1952-53; mem. Marion-Polk Med. Aux., 1949—, pres., 1950-51; ruling elder Presbyn. Ch., 1955—, supr. Christian Edn., 1955-61; bd. dirs. ARC, vol. worker Blood Bank, 1955-60; Camp Fire leader, 1958-65; worker, speaker United Way, 1960-63; adv. bd. Sr. Center; mem. Marion County Bd. of Health, 1969—; bd. dirs. Capital Health Care, 1972—; pres. Tel Med. Inc., 1978—. Mem. Am. Nurses Assn., Oreg. Nurses Assn., Oreg. Public Health Assn. (dir. 1970-77), Alpha Phi (pres. bd., 1966). Republican. Office: 750 Front St NE Salem OR 97308 also PO Box 2291 Salem OR 97308

SHIFFERD, MARILYN LOUISE, assn. exec.; b. Detroit, Sept. 14, 1928; d. Charles and Irene (Edmunds) Hines; R.N., Henry Ford Hosp., Detroit, 1949; B.A., U. Detroit, 1972, M.A., 1972, D. Public Adminstrn.; m. Warren D. Shifferd, Aug. 27, 1949; children—Warren David, Michael John. Dir. health services Oakland Community Coll., 1969-73; mktg. relations rep. Blue Cross/Blue Shield of Mich., 1973-75, profl. cons., 1976, mgr. communications, 1976-77, v.p., exec. dir. Health Saving Services, 1978-80; regional exec. dir. Palm Beach (Fla.) Regional Vis. Nurse Assn., 1980—; tour dir., Iran, Kenya, Russia and other countries, 1975-76. Bd. dirs. Crippled Children's Soc. of Palm Beach, Mid-County Med. Center, Am. Heart Assn., Am. Cancer Soc.; cons. Oakland U., Rochester, Mich.; mem. Interagy. Council on Alcoholism Oakland County (Mich.). Lic. nursing home adminstr., social worker; approved pvt. counselor workers compensation, Mich. Mem. Am. Nurses Assn., Nat. League Nursing, Women in Communications, Am. Personnel and Guidance Assn., Internat. Assn., Bus. Communicators, Women's Econ. Club, Adcraft Club. Club: Soroptimists. Book reviewer Nat. League Nursing Jour. Office: 5601 Corporate Way Suite 400 West Palm Beach FL 33407

SHILLING, NANCY ADAMS, pub. co. exec.; b. Milw., Oct. 24, 1932; B.A., Coll. of St. Catherine, 1954; M.A., U. Minn., 1956; postgrad. Arab studies Am. U., Beirut, Lebanon, 1959-61; cert. in Arabic, Johns Hopkins U., summer, 1960; Ph.D. in Islamic Studies and Polit. Sci., McGill U., 1966. Tchr. secondary sch., Minn., Montreal, Que., Can., Beirut, 1954-58; asst. fgn. student adv. U. Minn., Mpls., 1955-56; dir. race relations program Am. Friends Com. for New Eng., 1961-63; research assoc. Georgetown Research Project, Washington, 1966-67; asst. prof. Briarcliff Coll., Briarcliff Manor, N.Y., 1969-70; asst. prof. polit. sci. Hunter Coll., N.Y.C., 1967-73; owner, mgr. Inter-Crescent Pub. Co., Inc. formerly of N.Y.C., Beirut, Sharjah, United Arab Republic, 1972-77, Dallas, 1979—; speaker, lectr. in field to numerous assns. and orgns. Rockefeller grantee, 1954-56. Mem. Am. Polit. Sci. Assn., Middle East Studies Assn., Acad. of Internat. Bus. Author: Doing Business in Saudi Arabia and Arab Gulf States, 1975; A Practical Guide to Living and Travel in the Arab World, 1978; co-author numerous other books; contbr. articles on politics and Arab women, bus. and econs. to profl. jours.; vis. prof. Grad. Sch. Bus., Baylor U., Waco, Tex., U. Tex., Dallas, 1979-81. Address: PO Box 31413 Dallas TX 75231

SHILLING, SHIRLEY ROMAINE, ins. agt.; b. Butler, Pa., Jan. 19, 1936; d. Arthur W. and Georgia Alberta (Hutzley) Percy; 1 dau., Pamela Kay Shilling Ebert. Underwriter, Nationwide Ins., Butler, 1953-59, Borgal Ins. Agy., Inglewood, Calif., 1961-69; office mgr. Fred E Cimino Ins. Agy., Inglewood, 1969-74; sec.-treas., partner Fred E. Cimino & Assocs., Inc., Los Angeles, 1974—; mem. producer council Mercury Ins. Group, 1979—. Named Ins. Woman of Yr., Calif. Ins. Assn., 1972, Woman of Yr., Torrance YWCA, 1979. Mem. Nat. Assn. Ins. Women (past nat. pres., nat. bldg. chmn., Region VIII Ins. Woman of Yr. 1973), S. Bay Assn. Ins. Women, Ins. Inst. Am. (exam. com.), Soc. CPCU (nat. candidate devel. comm., dir. chpt.), Profl. Ins. Agts., Ind. Ins. Agts. Am., Profl. Ins. Agts. Calif./New., Ind. Ins. Agts. Calif., Ind. Ins. Agts and Brokers Assn. Inglewood/Centinela Valley (dir., Ins. Woman of Yr. 1971, edn. chmn.), Ins. Women of Ingelwood-South Bay (past pres., dir.). Republican. Presbyterian. Contbr. articles to ins. trade jours. Office: Fred E Cimino Assocs Inc Box 45056 Los Angeles CA 90045

SHILLINGSBURG, MIRIAM JONES, educator; b. Balt., Oct. 5, 1943; d. W. Elvin and Miriam (Reeves) Jones; B.A., Mars Hill Coll., 1964; M.A., U. S.C., 1966, Ph.D., 1969; m. Peter L. Shillingsburg, Nov. 21, 1967; children—Robert, George, John, Alice, Anne Carol. Asst. prof. Limestone Coll., Gaffney, S.C., 1967; asst. prof. Mississippi State (Miss.) U., 1970-75, asso. prof., 1975-80, prof., 1980—. Nat. Endowment Humanities fellow in residence, Columbia U., 1976-77. Mem. MLA, Soc. Study So. Lit., Am. Studies Assn., Southeastern Soc. Eighteenth Century Studies. Mem. Editorial bd. Works of W.M. Thackeray; contbr. articles to profl. jours. and mags.

SHILLIS, JOAN LOUISE, microbiologist; b. Easton, Pa., Sept. 13, 1932; d. Justin Joseph and Jennie Pauline (Weber) S.; B.S., Pa. State U., 1954; M.S., Ohio State U., 1959, Ph.D., 1963. Jr. biologist polio research Parke, Davis & Co., 1955-56; grad. asst. Ohio State U., 1956-63; research microbiologist, then sr. research microbiologist Parke, Davis & Co., 1963-72, research scientist, 1972—. Am. Cancer Soc. grantee, 1962. Mem. Am. Soc. Microbiology, Tissue Culture Assn., AAAS. Home: 2092 Yorktown St Ann Arbor MI 48105 Office: 2800 Plymouth Rd Ann Arbor MI 48105

SHIM, KATHYLEEN (KIM) SHERROD, public relations exec.; b. Uniontown, Ala., Feb. 14, 1948; d. Benjamin Herndon and Kathyleen S.; B.S., U. Fla., 1975; M.A., George Washington U., 1980; m. Kye Taik Shim, Dec. 12, 1980. Film prodn. asst. Barton Film Co., Jacksonville, Fla., 1969-70; writer Sta. WTLV-TV, NBC affiliate, Jacksonville, 1970-71; studio prodn. crew Sta. WUFT-TV, PBS affiliate, Gainesville, Fla., 1973-75; reporter, photographer Vero Beach (Fla.) Press Jour., 1975-78; writer press dept. U.S. Senator Bill Roth, 1978-80; press sec. U.S. Rep. Larry J. Hopkins, Washington, 1981—. Recipient 3 2d pl. awards Nat. Better Newspaper Contest, 1977; 1st pl. award Fla. Press Assn., 1979, 2d pl. award, 1979, Claudia Ross Meml. award, 1977. Mem. Republican Communications Assn. Home: 212 N Howard St Apt 303 Alexandria VA 22304 Office: US House of Reps Washington DC 20515

SHIMAHARA, BONNIE KAY, accountant; b. Poston, Ariz., Sept. 30, 1944; d. Hiroshi and Helen Shimahara; B.S. cum laude, Calif. State Coll. at Long Beach, 1967; J.D., Loyola U. Los Angeles, 1975. With Hurdman and Cranstoun, C.P.A.s, Los Angeles and Palo Alto, 1967-76, tax mgr., 1973-76; owner, mgr. Bonnie K. Shimahara, C.P.A., Palo Alto, 1977—; lectr. legal accounting Lincoln U., The Law Sch., 1976-79; admitted to Calif. bar. C.P.A., Calif. Mem. Am. Inst. C.P.A.s, Calif. Soc. C.P.A.s (chmn. tax com. Peninsula chpt. 1978-79, dir. 1979-80), Am. Bar Assn. Buddhist. Club: Zonta Internat. Office: 2450 El Camino Real Palo Alto CA 94306

SHIMANEK, NANCY J., state legislator; b. Monticello, Iowa, Dec. 1, 1947; B.A., Clarke Coll., 1970; J.D., U. Iowa, 1973. Admitted to Iowa bar; law clk. Iowa Supreme Ct., 1973-74; asst. atty. gen., 1974-76; individual practice law, Monticello; mem. Iowa Ho. of Reps. Active Iowa Fedn. Republican Women., Am. Legion Aux. Mem. ABA, Iowa State Bar Assn., Jones County Bar Assn., Iowa Women's Polit. Caucus, Bus. and Profl. Women. Roman Catholic. Office: Iowa State House Des Moines IA 50319 *

SHIMBERG, ELAINE FANTLE, writer; b. Yankton, S.D., Feb. 26, 1937; d. Karl S. and Alfreda (Edelson) Fantle; B.S., Northwestern U., 1958; m. Mandell Shimberg, Oct. 1, 1961; children—Karen, Scott, Betsy, Andrew, Michael. Continuity dir. WALT Radio, Tampa, Fla., 1959-60, WFLA Radio, 1960-61; freelance writer, 1961—; co-hostess WFLA-TV talk show Women's Point of View, Tampa, Fla., 1976-81; tchr. Writing for Publication and Profit, Hillsborough Community Coll., Tampa 1980—. Mem. public info. com. Fla. div. Am. Cancer Soc., 1974—, mem. childhood cancer com. 1975-79; mem. met. bd. YMCA, 1981—; mem. devel. council St. Joseph Hosp., 1982—. Mem. Am. Soc. Journalists and Authors, Authors Guild, Women in Communication, Women's Ink, Athena Soc. Author: How to be A Successful Housewife/Writer, 1979; Two for the Money: A Woman's Guide to a Double Career Marriage, 1981. Contbr. articles to various mags.

SHIMMIN, KATHLEEN GRACE, microbiologist; b. Santa Rosa, Calif., Mar. 7, 1939; d. Melvin Raleigh and Helen Marguerite (Grace) Shimmin; B.S., U. Calif., Berkeley, 1960, M.A., 1963, postgrad., 1963-69; m. Donald P. Harvey, June 27, 1980. Adminstr., dir. regional lab. EPA, Alameda, Calif., 1969-78, adminstr., chief compliance and response br., San Francisco, 1978—; instr. John F. Kennedy U., Martinez, Calif., 1970-71; spl. cons. State Calif., WHO. Area capt. Heart Fund. Calif. Alumni scholar, 1956; USPHS trainee, 1967-68. Mem. AAAS. Clubs: Women's Faculty, Officers (Presidio, San Francisco). Republican. Home: 1074 Cragmont Ave Berkeley CA 94708 Office: 215 Fremont St San Francisco CA 94105

SHINEHOUSE, ELFREDA JANE, biologist; b. Chestnut Hill, Pa., Apr. 13, 1931; d. Arthur Dewey and Elfreda Frances (Ross) Perreten; B.S., Ursinus Coll., 1952; postgrad. U. Pa., 1953; m. Robert R. Shinehouse, Apr. 5, 1952; children—Linda Anne, Patricia G., James P., Lisa Susan. Phys. therapist Montgomery County Hosp., Norristown, Pa., part time 1953, Phoenixville (Pa.) Hosp., part time 1958-60; instr. biology Ursinus Coll., Collegeville, Pa., part time 1960-77, asst. prof., 1977—, asst. premed. adviser, 1981—. Sec., Home and Sch. Assn., 1961-62; tchr. aide Oaks Elem. Sch., 1977-78; Sunday Sch. tchr. St. James Episcopal Ch., 1978-79, chmn. Christian Women in Soc., 1979-80. Recipient Lindback award for disting. teaching Ursinus Coll., 1981; March of Dimes Found. grantee, 1952. Mem. Registry Am. Phys. Therapists, Beta Beta Beta, Pi Nu Epsilon. Republican. Home: 1747 S Collegeville Rd Collegeville PA 19426 Office: 209 LSB Ursinus Coll Collegeville PA 19426

SHINNAMON, MARGARET (MARGOT) LEE, editor; b. Seattle, Dec. 3, 1946; d. Charles Wesley and Lydia Culbertson S.; B.A., Calif. State U., Sacramento, 1970; M.A., Stanford U., 1973. 1973. Sr. editor U. Calif., Davis, 1973-76; graphic designer Lin Litho, San Francisco, 1976-77; publs. writer Lockheed Missiles & Space Co., Sunnyvale, Calif., 1977-78, tng. specialist, 1978-79, corp. editor, 1979—; bd. dirs. Lockheed Employees Recreation Assn., 1979—. Mem. Internat. Assn. Bus. Communicators, Nat. Mgmt. Assn. (v.p. communications Bay Area 1982-83), Women in Communication Internat. Editor, Guide to Basic Language, 1979-80. Office: 1111 Lockheed Way Sunnyvale CA 94086

SHIPLEY, SHIRLEY DAHL, oil co. exec.; b. Orange, N.J., Oct. 17, 1932; d. Conrad George and Sylvia Marion (Gronquist) D.; B.S., Cedar Crest Coll. Allentown, Pa., 1954; m. William Stewart Shipley II, July 2, 1955; children—William Stewart III, Linda Ann, Elizabeth Marion. Tchr., Radnor Twp. (Pa.) Schs., 1954-55, Sarasota County (Fla.) Schs., 1955-56; adminstrv. asst. Shipley-Humble, Inc., York, Pa., 1977—. Pres., York Suburban Sch. Dist. Bd., 1973-79; bd. dirs. York Country Day Sch., Children's Home, York County Mental Health Center, Greater York, Inc., United Community Services, York County Literacy Council, ARC, Women's Assn. York Symphony Orch.; past mem. York, Franklin and Adams County Intermediate Unit Sch. Bd. pres. Jr. League York, 1967-69; nat. bd. dirs. Assn. Jr. Leagues, 1970-72; mem. Pa. adv. council U.S. Commn. Civil Rights; trustee York Coll. Pa. Mem. Pa. Petroleum Assn., Nat. Oil Jobbers Council. Republican. Presbyterian. Home: 1000 Clubhouse Rd York PA 17403 Office: 550 E King St PO Box 946 York PA 17405

SHIPMAN, JEAN AGATHE, home economist, journalist; b. Pitts., Apr. 23, 1921; d. Abram L. and Agathe (Grondahl) S.; B.S., Oreg. State U., 1956; M.S., U. Wis., 1964; postgrad. Colo. State U., 1957, 66, Cornell U., 1960. Successively operator, supr., asst. chief operator Kittanning Telephone Co., Leechburg, Pa., 1939-52; extension home economist Coos County, Oreg., 1956-61; consumer mktg. specialist Oreg. State U., 1961-62; grad. project asst. U. Wis., 1962-64; asst. extension editor Okla. State U., Stillwater, 1964-70, asso. extension editor, 1970, public info. officer home econs., 1975—; dir. numerous workshops on news and feature writing, direct mail, radio broadcasting, TV prodn. Recipient Agrl. Communications award Am. Assn. Agrl. Coll. Editors and Nat. Plant Food Inst., 1968; Profl. award Okla. Home Econs. Assn., 1975. Mem. AAAS, Agrl. Com. in Edn., Assn. Edn. in Journalism, Am. Home Econs. Assn. (past chmn. home econs. communications sect., past chmn. Center for the Family Council 1981-82), Am. Bus. Women, AAUW, Patrons of Husbandry, Okla. Press Women, Omicron Nu, Phi Upsilon Omicron (reporter). Republican. Lutheran. Contbr. articles to home econs., agrl. jours. Home: 508 N Bellis St Stillwater OK 74074 Office: 118 Pub Info Bldg Okla State U Stillwater OK 74078

SHIPP, MAURINE SARAH HARSTON (MRS. LEVI ARNOLD SHIPP), realtor; b. Holiday, Mo., Mar. 6, 1913; d. Paul Edward and Sarah Isabel (Mitchell) Harston; grad. Ill. Bus. Coll., 1945; student real estate Springfield Jr. Coll., 1962; student law LaSalle Extension U., 1959-62; m. Levi Arnold Shipp, Jan. 30, 1941; children—Jerome Reynolds, Patricia (Mrs. Rodney W. England). With Ill. Dept. Agr., Springfield, 1941-65, supr. livestock industry Brucellosis sect.; saleswoman Morgan-Hamilton Real Estate Co., Springfield, 1962-64; owner, mgr. Shipp Real Estate Agy., Springfield, 1965—. Prin. appraiser urban renewal HUD, 1971-72; mem. Public Bldg. Commn. Springfield. Bd. dirs. Springfield Travelers Aid, 1971—. Mem. Springfield Bd. Realtors, Nat., Ill. assns. real estate bds., NAACP, Urban League, Iota Phi Lambda. Episcopalian. Mem. Order Eastern Star. Club: Bridge. Home: 31 Bellerive Rd Springfield IL 62704 Office: 2200 E Cook St Springfield IL 62703

SHIRAS, VIRGINIA ECHOLS, state health agy. ofcl.; b. Monticello, Ark.; d. James R. and Eva L. (Peterson) Echols; B.A., S.E. Mo. State U., 1940; B.S. in Nursing, U. Central Ark., 1972; M.A., Scarritt and George Peabody Coll., 1943; cert. Calif. Coll. in China, 1945; Ms.D., D.D., Am. Bible Inst., 1975; m. Charles Peter Shiras, Dec. 22, 1945 (dec. 1978); children—Ginger Shiras, Kathleen Shiras Hickey. Missionary, Meth. Ch., 1943-45; mem. faculty U. Calif., Berkeley, 1944-45; faculty Mountain Home (Ark.) Public Sch., 1950-69; staff nurse USPHS Indian Hosp., Mescalero, N.Mex., 1972, VA Hosp., Little Rock, 1972-73; registered nurse dir. MERCI Mobile Med. unit, Ark. Dept. Health, 1973-74; med. self-help instr., Baxter County, Ark., 1958-69; vol. worker Salvation Army Adult Rehab. Center, Little Rock, 1969—, adv. council, 1982—; home health nursing coordinator Dept. Health, State of Ark., 1974—; dir. Albert Pike Hotel. Named Ark. Tchr. of Yr., 1958. Mem. Nat., Ark. public, health assns., NEA, Ark. Edn. Assn., Nat., Ark. leagues for nursing, Internat. Transactional Analysis Assn., Am., Ark. nurses assns., Tau Gamma Gamma (pres. 1950), Epsilon Sigma Omicron, Delta Kappa Gamma. Democrat. Author: Influences of Prevailing Religions on Chinese Family Life, 1943; Comparisons of School Systems around the World, 1967; The Bible-Genesis to Revelations - Analogous to the Life of a Man, 1973. Home: 3 Rosemont Little Rock AR 72204 Office: Ark Dept Health 4815 W Markham Little Rock AR 72201

SHIREMAN, JOAN FOSTER, educator; b. Cleve., Oct. 28, 1933; d. Louis Omar and Genevieve (Duguid) Foster; B.A., Radcliffe Coll., 1956; M.A., U. Chgo., 1959, Ph.D., 1968; m. Charles Howard Shireman, Mar. 18, 1967; 1 son, David Louis. Caseworker, N.H. Children's Aid Soc., 1959-61; caseworker Chgo. Child Care Soc., 1961-63, dir. research, 1968-74; research asso., lectr. U. Chgo., 1964-68; asso. prof. Jane Addams Coll. Social Work, U. Ill., Chgo., 1974—, acting asso. dean, 1979-80. Mem. Nat. Assn. Social Workers, Ill. Child Care Assn., Phi Beta Kappa. Co-author monographs; contbr. articles to profl. jours. Home: 2058 Maple St Homewood IL 60430 Office: Box 4343 Chicago IL 60680

SHIRLEY, ROSEMARY HILL, investor; b. Kansas City, Mo., Aug. 15, 1926; d. James Henry and Ethel Briscoe (Hill) H.; student U. Calif., Berkeley; div.; children—Marvin E., Richard Dennis. Royalty holder Middle East Am. Oil Co., 1959—; pres. Gambit VII Investments, Vacaville, Calif., 1975—. Mem. Nat. Assn. Female Execs. (network dir.), Desert Hosp. Assn., St. Patricks Home Guild. Republican. Roman Catholic. Club: Canyon Country (Palm Springs, Calif.). Home: 309 Creekview Ct Vacaville CA 95688 Office: PO Box 4317 Palm Springs CA 92262 Office: PO Box 282 Vacaville CA 95688

SHIRREFFS, JANET HELEN, educator; b. Jersey City, May 16, 1945; d. Thomas Aiken and Jessie S.; B.S., Ithaca Coll., 1967; M.S., Syracuse U., 1969; Ph.D., Tex. Womans U., 1973. Tchr., Jamesville (N.Y.) Dewitt High Sch., 1968-69; instr., coach North Tex. State U., Denton, 1969-72; instr. health edn. Tex. Womans U., Denton, 1972-73; asst. prof. health sci. Ball State U., Muncie, Ind., 1973-77; assoc. prof. health sci. Ariz. State U., Tempe, 1977—; cons. Ariz. Dept. Health Services, Planned Parenthood, Random House, Inc., Ariz. Perinatal Program. Recipient Community Service award Central Ariz. Health Systems Agy., 1979. Mem. chmn. Pub. Health Assn. (vice chmn. health edn. sect. 1980-81), Assn. Advancement Health Edn., Am. Pub. Health Assn., Eta Sigma Gamma. Author: (with B. Corder and R. A. Althaus) Health Science: Current Perspectives, 1981; Community Health: Contemporary Perspectives, 1982; contbr. articles to profl. jours. Home: 10222 S 45th St Phoenix AZ 85044 Office: Dept Phys Edn Health Ariz State U Tempe AZ 85281

SHISHKOFF, MURIEL MENDELSOHN, ednl. adminstr.; b. Chgo., Mar. 5, 1917; d. Henry Robert and Anita (Arnow) Mendelsohn; B.A., U. Chgo., 1936; M.A., Northwestern U., 1940; m. Nicholas Shishkoff, Aug. 26, 1946; children—Andrew, Debra. Elem. tchr., Fond du Lac, Wis., 1936-41; personnel mgr. Twentieth Century Glove Co., 1946; tchr. Newport-Mesa (Calif.) Unified Sch. Dist., 1963-69; founding dir. Women's Opportunities Center, U. Extension, U. Calif., Irvine, 1970-72, asst. dir. ednl. opportunity program Office Relations with Schs. and Colls., 1974-82. Vice pres. LWV, Palos Verdes Peninsula, Calif., 1963. Served to lt. USNR (W-VS), 1942-45. Recipient grant award Reachout, Dept. Mental Hygiene, Sacramento, 1972. Mem. Nat. Assn. Women Deans, Adminstrs. and Counselors. Home: 19542 Sandcastle Ln Huntington Beach CA 92648

SHISLER, ALICE HAFLING, dancer; b. Richmond, Va., Nov. 23, 1923; d. Jacob Mathew and Elise (Atkinson) Hafling; B.A. in French with distinction, U. Va., 1972, postgrad., 1972-75; m. James Douglas Shisler, Apr. 17, 1965; children by previous marriage—Elise Amory Crosswy, Otis Taylor Amory, III, Marcie Tuck Amory. Student, asst. Elinor Frye Dance Sch., Richmond, 1940-44; editorial sec. Commonwealth mag., 1944-46; owner dance sch. Acad. Dance Arts, Charlottesville, Va., 1947—; dir., choreographer Charlottesville Dance Co., 1973—; cons. in field. Recipient Appreciation award Charlottesville Lions Club Minstrel Shows, 1981. Mem. Dance Masters Am. Republican. Episcopalian. Club: Farmington Country. Author syllabi on dance. Address: 901 Rugby Rd Charlottesville VA 22903

SHIVANANDAN, MARY, author, media cons.; b. Rangoon, Burma, Jan. 6, 1932; d. John Francis and Jean Newton (Simpson) Sheehy; came to U.S., 1960, naturalized, 1970; B.A. with honours, Newnham Coll., Cambridge (Eng.) U., 1954, M.A. in Classics, 1967; m. Kandiah Shivanandan, Sept. 17, 1960; children—John Uthya-Surian, Marianne Gauri. Press librarian BBC, 1954-56; asst. producer radio CBC, 1956-58; freelance writer, editor, lectr., 1960-68, 72—; asso. editor Mid East mag., 1968-69; asso. research scientist fgn. area studies Am. U., 1967-70; asso. editor-in-chief New Am. Ency., 1971-72; founder, 1979, thereafter pres. K.M. Assos., media cons., Glen Echo, Md.; contbg. editor Marriage and Family Living; cons. Office Family Planning, HEW; author: Bobtail and Bubtail, 1945; Gamal Abdul Nasser, 1973; Natural Sex, 1979; When Your Wife Wants to Work, 1979; also articles, chpts. in books, columns. Mem. Nat. Council Family Relations, Human Life and Natural Family Planning Found. Democrat. Roman Catholic.

SHOEMAKER, DOROTHY KAY, civic worker; b. Lanerch, Pa., May 5, 1897; d. Robert Gillespie and Mary (Scott) Kay; grad. Goucher Coll., 1920; m. Benjamin H. Shoemaker III, June 30, 1938; children—Robert Kay. Sec. Class 1915 Westtown Sch.; mem. Nat. Soc. Colonial Dames; bd. dirs. Germantown Settlement; mem. women's bd. Germantown Dispensary Hosp., 1930-60; bd. dirs. Ralston House, 1935—. Mem. Pi Beta Phi. Republican. Episcopalian. Home: 515 Locust Ave Germantown Philadelphia PA 19144

SHOEMAKER, HELEN E. MARTIN ACHOR, civic worker; b. Houston, Mar. 24, 1915; d. Earl L. and Blanche L. (Williams) Martin; A.B., Anderson (Ind.) Coll., 1960, LL.D., 1978; m. Harold E. Achor, Oct. 11, 1935; children—Dianne (Mrs. Robert Johnston), Lana (Mrs. Winston Dean); m. 2d, Robert N. Shoemaker, May 19, 1972. Resident dir. Anderson Coll., 1967-69, dir. alumni services, 1969-72; legis. counsel Ind. Colls. and Univ. Ind., 1970-72; spl. asst. Center Public Service, Anderson, 1973-77, spl. asst. to dean for acad. devel., 1977-78. Sec.-treas. Ind. State Library and Hist. Bldg. Expansion Commn., 1973—; mem. com. region VII, Girl Scouts U.S.A., 1958-66; adv. council fin. aid to students Office Edn. HEW, 1976-78. Mem. Ind. Ho. of Reps. from Madison County, 1968-70; v.p. Ind. Fedn. Women's Republican Clubs, 1945-46; treas. Nat. Fedn. Women's Rep. Clubs, 1947-51; Rep. precinct vice chmn. Madison County, 1946-68, vice chmn., Anderson, 1967-68; bd. dirs. Urban League Madison County, 1969-76; adv. com. Georgetown U. Grad. Sch. Acad. in Public Service, 1976—; mem. adv. com. on sex discrimination Ind. Civil Rights Commn., 1978—; trustee Anderson Coll., 1978—; bd. dirs. Opportunities Industrialization Center, Inc., Madison County, 1980—, Ind. Acad. Public Service, 1981—; mem. devel. bd. St. John's Med. Center, Anderson, 1981—. Recipient William B. Harper award Urban League Madison County, 1975; named Sagamore of Wabash, State of Ind., 1979. Hon. mem. Anderson Symphony Orch. Guild; mem. LWV (dir. Madison County 1973-76, 78—), Anderson Council Women, Anderson Fine Arts Center. Mem. Ch. of God. Home: 707 Dresser Dr Anderson IN 46011

SHOENIGHT, PAULINE ALOISE SOUERS (MRS. HURLEY SHOENIGHT), author; b. Bridgeport, Ill., Nov. 20, 1914; d. William Fitch and Carrie (Milhouse) Souers; B.Ed., Eastern Ill. U., 1937; m. James Richard Tracy, Sept. 18, 1946 (dec. Aug. 1972); m. 2d, Hurley F. Shoenight, June 25, 1976. Mem. hon. bd. advs. Am. Biog. Inst., Mem. Nat. Ret. Tchrs. Assn., Eastern Ill. Alumni Assn. (life), PEO Sisterhood, Performing Arts Assn., Am. Poets Fellowship Soc. (hon. life mem.), The Pensters, Pleasure Island Sr. Citizens Club (charter), Am. Poetry League, Foley Extension Club, Ill. Poetry Soc. (charter), Book Club for Poetry, Ala. State Poetry Soc., Acad. Am. Poets. Republican. Baptist. Club: Baldwin Sr. Travelers. Author: His Handiwork, 1954; Memory is a Poet, 1964; The Silken Web, 1965; A Merry Heart, 1966; In Two or Three Tomorrows, 1968; All Flesh Is Grass, 1971; Beyond The Edge, 1973. Address: Route 3 Box 1107 W Riverwood Dr Foley AL 36535

SHOGREN, RUTH ELINOR, computer specialist; b. West Bend, Wis., June 8, 1935; d. William and Lula Elinor (Klipsch) S.; A.B., DePauw U., 1958; student Sophia U., Tokyo, 1955-56; M.A., Duke U., 1961. Computer programmer Gentile Air Force Sta., Dayton, Ohio, 1961-66; computer programmer, analyst Price Waterhouse & Co., N.Y.C., 1966-68; cons. analyst, N.Y.C., 1969-70; computer programmer Systems Automation Center, Def. Logistics Agy., Columbus, Ohio, 1970-75, computer specialist, 1975-79, supervisory computer specialist, 1979—. Mem. adminstrv. bd. Reynoldsburg (Ohio) Meth. Ch., 1980—. Albert J. Beveridge fellow 1958-59. Mem. Mensa, Nat. Assn. Female Execs. Office: PO Box 1605 Columbus OH 43216

SHOLLENBERGER, SYDNI (SYDNEY) ANN CRAWFORD, author, publicist; b. Cleve., June 23, 1940; d. Charles Burger and Carolyn Louise (Hull) Crawford; B.A., Allegheny Coll., 1962; m. Lewis W. Shollenberger, Jr., Aug. 18, 1962. Public info. officer and editor Space News Roundup, NASA, Houston, 1970-72. mng., editor Travel Publs., Am. Automobile Assn., Washington, 1972-74; free lance journalist, publicist, 1974—. Publicity dir. Falls Church Bicentennial Commn., 1976-81; bd. dirs. Falls Church Village Preservation and Improvement Soc.; publicity co-chmn. Falls Church Citizens for a Better City, 1978, fin. chmn., 1982 docent Cherry Hill Farm; pres. Broadmont Citizens Assn., 1978-79; press cons. Fisher for Congress campaign, 1978, 80; chmn. Falls Church Adv. Bd. on Parks and Recreation; community relations coordinator Fairfax County Reentry Women's Employment Center; sec. Welcome to Washington Internat. Club, 1978-80. Mem. Capital Press Women (v.p. 1976-78), No. Va. Press Club. Clubs: Zonta, Woman's Nat. Democratic, Capital Speakers (class pres. 1977, chpt. 3 pres. 1980-81).

SHOLTZOW, ROCHELLE, mfg. co. exec.; b. Bklyn., Mar. 22, 1943; d. Maurice Nathaniel and Irene (Yoselowitz) S.; B.S., CCNY, 1960-64; M.A. in Psychology, U. Hawaii, 1969. Research analyst Eric Marder Assos., N.Y.C., 1969; with Internat. Playtex, Inc., Stamford, Conn., 1970-78, 79—, group market research mgr., 1979—; market research mgr. Bali Co., 1978-79. Office: 700 Fairfield Ave Stamford CT 06902

SHONTZ, PATRICIA JANE, restauranteur; b. Mercer, Pa., Mar. 29, 1933; d. Thomas Cloyd and Glaydes Evelyn (Pease) Buckley; student pub. schools, Grove City, Pa.; m. George Edward Shontz, July 22, 1962; 1 dau. by previous marriage, Sandra Lee McCandless. Clerical asst. Am. News Co., Washington, 1950-51; acct., office mgr. Mundt Motors Chevrolet & Buick, Grove City, 1953-62; sec.-treas. Cajun Corp., Madeira Beach, Fla., 1972—; pres. John's Pass Seafood Festival Corp., 1981—. Madeira Beach City commr., 1973-79, vice mayor, 1977-79, co-chmn. planning bd., 1979-82; chmn. Bicentennial Com., Madeira Beach, 1975-76; mem. John's Pass Village Assn., 1970—, Pinellas County Tourist Devel. Council, 1978-79, Madeira Beach Taxpayers Assn., 1964—. Named Madeira Beach Citizen of the Yr., 1974, 79. Mem. Nat. Restaurant Assn., Madeira Beach C. of C. (dir. 1965, 81-82, pres. 1967-69). Republican. Presbyterian. Clubs: Bus. and Profl. Women, Soroptimist, Order Eastern Star, Order White Shrine. Office: 100 Madeira Way Madeira Beach FL 33708

SHOPE, ALICE MARIE DAVIS, accountant; b. Coral Gables, Fla., May 13, 1955; d. Earl Hubert and Alice Catherine (Mercadante) Davis; B.S., Mesa Coll., 1977; m. Galen Arthur Shope, July 4, 1980. Treas., acct. Daco Constrn. Co., Inc., Grand Junction, 1976—; dir. C&P Wiping Supply Inc. Mem. Nat. Assn. Women in Constrn. (pres.), Grand Junction Area C. of C. (treas. women's div.; dir.), Mesa Coll. Alumni Assn. Roman Catholic. Home: PO Box 427 Palisade CO 81526 Office: PO Box 2783 Grand Junction CO 81502

SHOPE, ELIZABETH ANNE SCHNEIDER, educator, soc. exec.; b. Cin., Dec. 31, 1921; d. Matthew Simpson and Vivian (Walton) Schneider; B.A., Guilford Coll., 1944; M.A., U. N.C., 1955; Ed.S., Appalachian State U., 1975; m. Nathaniel H. Shope, Sept. 1, 1946; children—Patricia Anne, Matthew Walton. Tchr., Tar Heel (N.C.) Schs., 1946-47, Elizabethtown Schs., N.C., 1947-50, Walnut Street Sch., Goldsboro, N.C., 1959-60, Protestant Kindergarten, 1961-66, Appalachian State U., Boone, 1971-73; tchr. English, newspaper adv. Watauga High Sch., Boone, N.C., 1967-78; co-exec. sec. Friends Assn. Higher Edn., 1980—; pres. United Soc. Friends Women, Internat., Richmond, Ind., 1974-80. Co-chmn. com. scouting for handicapped, Old Hickory council Boy Scouts Am., 1979—; pres. bd. dirs. Girls Club Elizabeth City, N.C., 1957-58; bd. mgrs. Ch. Women United, 1974-80. N.C. State div. AAUW fellow, 1978. Mem. AAUW (pres. Boone 1972-74), N.C. Assn. Educators, NEA, Assn. Classroom Tchrs. Nat. Council Tchrs. English, N.C. English Tchrs. Assn., Phi Delta Kappa, Delta Kappa Gamma. Quaker. Club: Women's (1st v.p.) (Elizabeth City, N.C.). Editor: Sketches of Early Watauga, 1974—.

SHOPIRO, ELEANOR MARCHIGIANI, orch. exec.; b. Bedford Hills, N.Y.; d. Angelo and Francis Marchigiani; B.S., Cornell U.; m. Aug. 27, 1966; 1 dau., Suzanne. Buyer, Dey Brothers Dept. Store, 1952-56; owner, mgr. Suburban Hardware & Paint Co., Syracuse, N.Y., 1956-68; dir. devel. Syracuse (N.Y.) Symphony Orch., 1977-79, gen. mgr., 1979—, also former 3d v.p./sec. bd. dirs. Vice pres. Better Bus. Bur., 1978-79; chmn., pres. Lemoyne Coll. Assn., 1978—; former pres. Syracuse Symphony Guild; former charter pres. Syracuse Area Landmark Theater. Office: 411 Montgomery St Syracuse NY 13202

SHORE, DINAH (FRANCES ROSE SHORE), singer; b. Winchester, Tenn., Mar. 1, 1921; d. S.A. and Anna (Stein) S.; B.A., Vanderbilt U., 1939; m. George Montgomery, Dec. 5, 1943 (div. 1962); children—Melissa Ann, John David; m. 2d, Maurice F. Smith, May 26, 1963 (div. 1964). Became singer WNEW, N.Y., 1938; joined NBC as sustaining singer 1938; started contract RCA-Victor, 1940; star Chamber Music Soc. of Lower Basin St. program, 1940; joined Eddie Cantor radio program, 1941; star own radio program for Gen. Foods, 1943; entertained Allied Troops ETO, 1944; radio program Proctor & Gamble;

star TV show for Chevrolet, 1951-61; star show Dinah's Place, NBC-TV, 1970-74, Dinah!, CBS-TV, 1974—. Awarded New Star of Radio Motion Picture Daily Poll and World Telegram-Scripts Howard Poll, 1940; Best Popular Female Vocalist Motion Picture Daily Fame's Ann. Radio Poll, 1941-61; Michael award Best Female Vocalist, Radio and TV, 1950, 51, 52; Billboard award Favorite Female Vocalist on Records, 1947; Billboard award favorite popular female singer in radio, 1949; Gallup poll, America's best known and favorite female vocalist, 1950, 51; Emmy award, Acad. TV Arts and Sciences, 1954, 55, 56, 57, 58, 59, 72, 73; Peabody Award for 1958; Sylvania Award for 1958. Author: Someone's in the Kitchen with Dinah, 1971. Address: care CBS-TV 7800 Beverly Blvd Los Angeles CA 90036 *

SHORE, MIRIAM, psychologist; b. Phila., Dec. 26, 1933; d. Irvin and Anne (Liebowitz) Sklar; B.S., magna cum laude, Temple U., 1970, M.A. in Psychology, 1973, M.A. in English, 1973; m. Arthur Edson Shore, May 24, 1953; children—George Bennett, Anthony David, Joanna Carl. Family therapy tng. supr. E. Pa. Psychiat. Inst., Phila., 1974-77; asso. dir. dept. psychology and human behavior Am. Oncologic Hosp., Fox Chase Cancer Center, Phila., 1973-77; sr. psychologist cons. program for seriously ill and dying Jefferson Med. Coll., Phila., 1978-80; faculty Hahnemann Med. Coll., 1978-79; cons., faculty Jefferson Med. Coll., 1980—; pvt. practice psychology, Phila., 1977—; lectr. in field; cons. Montgomery County Sch., 1980—, St. Luke's Hosp. Bd. dirs. Inst. for Care of Seriously Ill and Dying, 1977-80; mem. task force Rabbi's commn. on Human Needs, Adath Jeshurun Synagogue, 1980-81; bd. dirs. Ars Moriendi, 1977-79; exec. com. Found. Thanatology. Temple U. Pres.'s scholar, 1977; In-Course scholar, 1966-70; lic. psychologist, Pa. Mem. Phila. Women's Network, Am. Psychol. Assn., Pa. Psychol. Assn., Am. Family Therapy Assn., Family Inst. Phila., Phila. Coop. Career Study Group. Contbr. articles to profl. jours. Home: 533 Elkins Ave Elkins Park PA 19117 Office: 1601 Church Rd Glenside PA 19038 also Jefferson Med Coll Philadelphia PA

SHORES, JANIE LEDLOW, justice Ala. Supreme Ct; b. nr. Georgiana, Ala., Apr. 10, 1932; d. John Wesley and Willie (Scott) Ledlow; LL.B., U. Ala., 1959; m. James L. Shores, Jr., May 12, 1962; 1 dau., Laura Scott. Practiced in Selma, 1959; legal dept. Liberty Nat. Life Ins. Co. Birmingham, Ala., 1962-66; prof. law Cumberland Sch. Law, Samford U., 1966-74; asso. justice Ala. Supreme Ct., Montgomery, 1974—. Former legal adviser Ala. Constn. Revision Commn., mem. Nat. Adv. Council on State Ct. Planning. Mem. Am. Judicature Soc., Am. Bar Assn. Democrat. Episcopalian. Contbr. legal articles to profl. jours. Home: 3544 Altamont Rd Birmingham AL 35213 Office: Judicial Bldg Montgomery AL 36104 *

SHORR, MIRIAM KRONFELDT, artist; b. N.Y.C.; student Hunter Coll., Yale U.; m. Eli Yale Shorr, 1931. Exhibited in ann. shows Audbon Artists, City Center Gallery, Bklyn. Mus., Nat. Soc. Painters in Casein, Norfolk Mus., Riverside Mus.; one man shows Brandeis U., Bklyn. Coll., U. Maine, Rutgers U., So. Ill. U., LaSalle Coll., Hillsdale U., Gettysburg Coll., others; group shows U. Houston, N.D. State U., Colo. Mountain Coll., Ottawa (Kans.) U., Washington and Jefferson Coll., others; traveling one-man shows throughout U.S. Recipient 1st prize for drawing Nat. Assn. Women Artists, 1962; Lena Newcastle award, 1961, 65; Aileen O. Webb prize, 1974; 1st prize Fibers and Fabrics Exhbn., 1975; 1st prize enamels Venice (Fla.) Art League, 1982. Mem. Artists Equity Assn. (dir. 1958-64), Nat. Assn. Women Artists (dir. 1970-72), Sarasota Art Assn. (chmn. exhbns. 1976-78, editor The Bull. 1979-81), Art League Manatee County, Fla. Artists Group. Home: 8139 Broughton St Sarasota FL 33580

SHORT, BARBARA JOAN, emergency mgmt. exec.; b. St. Clair County, Mich., Aug. 8, 1934; d. Herman M. and Beulah (Lashbrook) S.; B.S. cum laude, Mich. State U., 1956; postgrad. Central Mich. U., 1973—; children—Richard, Katrina, Graydon, Melissa. With U.S. Dept. Agr., 1956-57, 64-66; tchr. public schs., Capac, Mich., 1958-62, New Haven, Mich., 1962-63, Grand Ledge, Mich., 1963-64, Reese, Mich., 1966-67, Caro, Mich., 1967-71, 77-79; womens editor WKYO, Caro, 1968-69; instr. Mich. Tech. U., 1968-71; mgr. Indianfields Park, Caro, 1977-78; disaster mgmt. cons. Fed. Emergency Mgmt. Agy., Battle Creek, Mich., 1978-81; owner/mgr. RESPONSE, Martin, Mich., 1981— . Chmn. bd. Creative Child Care, 1972; bd. dirs. Thumb Area Econ. Opportunity Commn., 1965-67. Named Woman of Yr., Tuscola County Bus. and Profl. Women, 1965. Mem. Nat. Assn. Female Execs. Contbr. articles to Better Homes and Gardens, Parents, Sci. News, Farm Jour., others. Home: 1222 111th Ave Martin MI 49070

SHORT, IDA CAROL, coll. ofcl.; b. Rome, Ga., Nov. 24, 1949; d. David Benjamin and Frances Eugene (Plummer) Simmons; B.A., U. Mich., 1971, M.A., 1973; m. Roger Short, June 6, 1973; children—Amir, Sonya Abia'de. Tchr., Shaw Coll., Detroit, 1973-74; counselor U. Mich., Ann Arbor, 1970-73, lectr., 1973-76; dir. Met. Detroit Youth Found., 1977-79; dir. Upward Bound program Marygrove Coll., Detroit, 1979-82; dir. learning enrichment and resource center Lewis Coll. Bus., Detroit, 1982—. Mem. Detroit Inter-Agy. Collaborative Bd. Nat. Endowment for Humanities grantee, 1978. Mem. Mid Am. Assn. Ednl. Opportunity Program Personnel, Nat. Council Tchrs. English, Nat. Assn. Devel. and Remedial Edn. in Post Secondary Instns. Office: 17370 Meyers Rd Detroit MI 48221

SHORT, JULIA ANNE (JULEE), communications cons.; b. Duncan, Okla., Oct. 17, 1927; d. Robert Ezekiel and Ima Gay (Jones) Jones; student Okla. Coll. Women, 1944-46, U. Okla., 1947-48; B.A. in Journalism, Tex. Tech Coll., 1949; M.A. in History, U. Okla., 1972; m. Jack M. Short, Feb. 7, 1948 (div. 1974); children—Stephanie Lucinda, Sharon Gayle, Sabrina Jeanette. Asst. dir. public info. Oklahoma City U., 1964-67; asst. dir. info. Okla. Farm Bur., Oklahoma City, 1974; tech. writer, sec. U. Okla. Health Scis. Center, Oklahoma City, 1974-75; instr. English Okla. State U. Tech. Inst., Oklahoma City, 1976; editor The Sage Age, Oklahoma City, 1977-78; owner Words, etc., Norman, Okla., 1979—; cons. Areawide Aging Agy., Wichita State U., Nat. Assn. Royalty Owners, 1979—; book reviewer The Daily Oklahoman, 1956-60. Vice chmn. Stephens County Rupublican Com., Duncan, Okla., 1959-61; leader Great Books, 1954 61; vol. tchr. Salvation Army Home and Hosp., Sand Springs, Okla., 1971; chmn. publicity com. Search for Selves, 1978- . Recipient First Place awared local chpt. Theta Sigma Phi, 1953; Hon. Mention, Am. Assn. Coll. Public Relations, 1966. Mem. Internat. Assn. Bus. Communicators (named up and Comer Central Okla. chpt. 1978), Okla. City Writers Club. Republican. Unitarian. Contbr. articles to various jours. Home and Office: 322 Reed St Norman OK 73071

SHORT, ROSE MARIE, programmer, analyst; b. Buffalo, Dec. 18, 1955; d. Robert and Bertha Beatrice (Everett) Short; B.S. cum laude in Computer Sci., SUNY, Coll. at Brockport, 1973-76; postgrad. Columbia U., 1978, now CCNY; m. John Edward Saxton, Dec. 12, 1980. Programmer, Acad. Computing Center, SUNY, Coll. at Brockport, 1974-76, N.Y. Telephone Co., N.Y.C., 1977—. Mem. Am. Soc. Profl. and Exec. Women, Soc. Career Oriented Profls. in EDP (co-founder 1979; 1st vice chmn. 1980). Home: PO Box 641 Church St Station New York NY 10008 Office: New York Telephone Co 1166 Ave of Americas Room 8-C3 New York NY 10036

SHORT, RUTH PATRICIA, public health adminstr.; b. Brownsville, Tenn.; d. Namon and Ella (Bond) S.; Ph.B., Loyola U., 1943, M.S.W., 1947; M.S. in Hygiene, Harvard U., 1957. Staff social worker Cook County Bur. Public Assistance, 1944-45; staff social worker med. social services dept. Cook County Hosp., Chgo., 1946-49; staff psychiat. social worker West Los Angeles VA Center, 1949-54; chief social worker Marian Davies Children's Clinic, UCLA Sch. of Medicine, Los Angeles, 1954-56; field instr. Sch. Social Work, Boston U., 1957-60; head psychiat. social service div. mental hygiene Mass. Dept. Mental Health, 1957-60; field instr. UCLA Sch. Social Welfare, 1966-71; guest lectr. UCLA Sch. Public Health, Div. Community Mental Health, Sch. Social Welfare, 1971-72, U. So. Calif. Sch. Medicine, Div. Community Psychiatry, 1971-72; community program analyst III Calif. State Dept. Mental Hygiene, Div. Local Programs, Los Angeles, 1960-72; exec. dir. Golden State Community Mental Health Center, Pacoima, Calif., 1972-73; sr. psychiat. social worker Dept. Health Services, County Los Angeles, Central Health Services Region, Substance Abuse Program, 1974-77, program mgr. II, 1977—. Bd. dirs., 1st v.p. Exceptional Children's Found., 1979-80; pres. Mental Retardation Services Bd. Los Angeles County, 1967-68; bd. dirs. Met. YWCA, 1965-70; mem. dist. com. Camp Fire Girls Los Angeles; mem. nat. program com. Health Div., Nat. Conf. Jewish Communal Services; bd. dirs. Anytown U.S.A., Inc., 1964-69; chmn. center com. Angeles Mesa YWCA, 1962-65; com. mem. Kishland Awards, 1965-67; chmn. public forums Concerned Women So. Calif., Inc., 1977—; trustee Holman Meth. Ch., 1979-80; mem. Promotional Bd. for Fgn. Service, 1970. Polio Found. scholar, 1946-47, NIH stipend, 1956-57. Mem. Nat. Assn. Social Workers, NAACP (life), Acad. Cert. Social Workers, Assn. Study Community Orgns., Nat. Conf. Social Welfare, Internat. Conf. Social Work, Inc., Am. Public Health Assn., Concerned Women So. Calif., Harvard Sch. Public Health Alumni Assn. Democrat. Home: 5720 Shenandoah Ave Ladera Heights CA 90056

SHOTWELL, MARY KATHERINE, health care exec.; b. Balt., Feb. 6, 1937; d. William George and Rose Ellen (Martin) Williamson; R.N., St. Agnes Hosp., 1957; B.A., Loyola Coll., Balt., 1976; M.B.A., 1978; m. Larry Shotwell, Nov. 10, 1978; children—Robert E. Cranley III, William Patrick Cranley, Mary Elizabeth Cranley. Asst. to exec. dir. Met. Balt. Health Corp., 1978, ops. dir., 1979, fin. dir., 1980; exec. dir. South County Health Care Corp., West River, Md., 1981-82; dir. program devel./mktg. staff Builders Health Services, Balt., 1982—. Mem. Med. Group Mgmt. Assn., Group Health Assn. Am. Democrat. Club: L'Hirondelle Country. Home: 6638 Walnutwood Circle Baltimore MD 21212 Office: 9 W Saratoga St Baltimore MD 21201

SHOURDS, MARY ELIZABETH, exec. search firm exec.; b. Braddock, Pa., Nov. 7, 1942; d. Hugh Vincent and Mary Caroline (Denne) Gallagher; B.S. magna cum laude in Bus., Pepperdine U., 1973; postgrad. UCLA, 1982. Dir. personnel Rockwell Internat., El Segundo, Calif., 1964-75; co-founder, partner, v.p. Houze, Shourds & Montgomery, Inc., Los Angeles, 1977—; advisor UCLA Grad. Sch. Mgmt., 1979—. Bd. dirs. UCLA Exec. Program Assn., 1975—. Mem. Assn. Exec. Recruiting Cons., Orgn. Women Execs. Club: Univ. Office: 2029 Century Park E Suite 1118 Los Angeles CA 90067

SHOWALTER, IDA, archtl. firm exec.; b. Niota, Ill., Dec. 26, 1919; d. Roy C. and Ivy May (Hubbard) Sparrow; M.Accts., Gem City Bus. Coll., 1937; student Butler U., 1957; m. Russell W. Showalter, Feb. 23, 1945; children—Karen, Linda. Acct., Blessing Hosp., Quincy, Ill., 1937-46, The Gilfillan Clinic, Bloomfield, Iowa, 1946-48; med. sec. Eli Lilly & Co., Indpls., 1949; corp. sec./treas. Woollen Assocs., Inc., Indpls., 1960-80, corp. sec., 1980—; pvt. practice acctg., Indpls., 1950-60; partner The Majestic Partnership, Indpls., 1980—. Treas., missions chmn. Ch. of the Nazarene; v.p. P.T.O. C.P.A., Ind. Mem. Cert. Profl. Sec. Soc., Ind. Tax Practitioners Assn. Republican. Home: 6062 East St Joseph St Indianapolis IN 46219 Office: The Majestic Bldg 10th Floor 47 S Pennsylvania St Indianapolis IN 46204

SHOWSTEAD, JOAN ROSE, jour. editor; b. Clifton, N.J., July 22, 1936; d. Casper Charles and Elizabeth (Molnar) Miller; student Brookdale Community Coll.; children—Julia, William, Steven. Staff reporter Trenton (N.J.) Times, 1968-70; assoc. editor Oil Buyers Guide, 1973-74; asst. editor Platt's Oilgram Report, 1974-75, assoc. editor, 1975-77, editor, 1977-79, mng. editor, 1979-81, editor-in-chief, 1981—. Mem. Greater Paterson Devel. Corp. Mem. Assn. Energy Profls. (founder, dir. 1982), Fgn. Policy Assn., Assn. Petroleum Writers, Am. Bus. Press Assn. Office: 1221 Ave of Americas New York NY 10020

SHREEVE, JEAN'NE MARIE, chemist; b. Deer Lodge, Mont., July 2, 1933; d. Charles William and Maryfrances (Briggeman) Shreeve; B.A., U. Mont., 1953, D.Sc. (hon.), 1982; M.S., U. Minn., 1956; Ph.D., U. Wash., 1961; postgrad. U. Cambridge, Eng. Asst. prof. chemistry U. Idaho, Moscow, 1961-65, assoc. prof., 1965-67, prof., 1967—, head dept., 1973—; mem. proposal evaluation panel U.S. Air Force Office of Sci. Research; mem. adv. com. for chemistry NSF; vis. prof. U. Bristol (Eng.), 1977; mem. Nat. Com. Standards in Higher Edn., 1965-67, 69-73; mem. Internat. Fellowships Com., 1982-83. Recipient Disting. Alumni award U. Mont., 1970, Outstanding Achievement award U. Minn., 1975; Alexander von Humboldt sr. scientist award, Göttingen, W.Ger., 1978, award for excellence in coll. chemistry teaching Mfg. Chemists Assn., 1979; Ramsay fellow, 1967-68; Alfred P. Sloan fellow, 1970-72. Fellow AAAS; mem. AAUW (officer Moscow br. 1962-69), Am. Chem. Soc. (Garvan Medal 1972, award for outstanding contbns. to fluorine chemistry 1978), Am. Inst. Chemists, Assn. Women Scientists, Chem. Soc. (London), Idaho Acad. Sci., Phi Beta Kappa, Sigma Xi. Iota Sigma Pi, Phi Kappa Phi, Sigma Delta Epsilon. Contbr. numerous articles to profl. jours.; mem. editorial adv. bds. Jour. Fluorine Chemistry, 1970—, Accounts of Chem. Research, 1973-75, Inorganic Syntheses, 1976—. Office: Dept Chemistry U Idaho Moscow ID 83843

SHREIBMAN, S. JUNE SNYDER, accountant; b. Asbury Park, N.J.; d. Herman and Anna (Flaxer) Snyder; ed. Coll. City N.Y., N.Y. U., Temple U.; m. Oscar Shreibman (dec.); 1 son, Henry Maynard. Ind. public acct. N.Y.C., also cost acct., N.Y.C.; cost acct. with various firms, various cities; public accts. partner Shreibman, Baron & Schwartz, Phila., dir. small bus. div., 1960-67; ind. public acct. in estate planning, mgmt., Phila., 1967—; ind. public acct., also fin. cons. to women in professions, also cons. in personal fin., estate planning and mgmt., Phila., 1972—; vol. cons. Small Bus. Opportunities Corp., Phila., 1967; designer workshops in fin. mgmt., fin. thanatology, course in personal fin. Inst. Awareness, Phila., 1972-76; 1st woman mem. Pa. Bd. Examiners Public Accts. 1977—; undersec. Pa. CPA Bd. 1979, now sec.; guest lectr. Hebrew U., Jerusalem, Addington Soc., London; lectr. in field. Bd. dirs., project designer, developer Women for Bicentennial, a Commonwealth of Pa. Bicentennial Corp., Phila.; mem. Germantown Jewish Center, Phila., coordinator youth services, mem. sch. bd., 1964-68; treas. Eastern Pa. Women's Polit. Caucus, 1969-71; mem. Hadassah, Phila., past chmn. public relations and nat. affairs; v.p. Women for Greater Phila. Named to Women's Hall of Fame, Bus. and Profl. Women Phila., Seneca Falls, N.Y., 1979. Mem. Nat. Assn. State Bds. Accountancy (com. on continuing profl. edn.), Nat. Soc. Public Accts. (accredited, com. on legislation 1979), Pa. Soc. Public Accts. (chmn. Phila. chpt. 1970-72, pres. Phila. chpt., state dir., mem. IRS liaison com. 1970-72, mem. assistance com. 1969-74, mem. publs. and public relations com. 1961-74), Assn. for Tng. and Devel., Greater Phila. C. of C. (rep. Phila. chpt. Pa. Soc. Public Accts. 1973—, mem. all tax coms. 1974—, mem. Phila. tax. adv. group to Penjerdel Corp. 1975—). Address: 1900 John F Kennedy Blvd Suite 512 Philadelphia PA 19103

SHREVE, IRENE M. (MRS. R. NORRIS SHREVE), librarian; b. Converse, Ind., Sept. 6, 1894; d. Milton D. and Mary O. (Hunt) Macy; A.B., Brenau Coll., Gainesville, Ga., 1912-16; cert. U. Wis. Library Sch., 1930; B.S. in L.S., U. N.C., 1933; m. A. Wright Strieby, Dec. 25, 1917 (dec. 1927); 1 son, Robert Milton; m. 2d, R. Norris Shreve, June 1, 1968. Tchr. high sch., Shreveport, La., 1916-17, Anderson, Ind., 1917-18; librarian and publicity dir. Riverside Mil. Acad., Gainesville, Ga. and Hollywood, Fla., 1929-32, Inst. Research Social Science, Chapel Hill, N.C., 1933-34; publicity dir. Ind. State Com. Govtl. Economy, 1934; librarian, archivist Eli Lilly and Co., 1934-59; mem. faculty Sch. Library Service, Columbia U., summer 1957; cons. indsl. libraries and archives, 1960—; faculty mem. Purdue U. Extension, 1969; v.p. U.S. Book Exchange, Inc. 1948-50, dir., 1950-52; mem. council Nat. Library Assn., 1947-49, joint com. library edn., 1949-61; mem. Com. Econ. Devel. Library Services Com., 1944-50; mem. com. spl. libraries Internat. Fedn. Library Assns., 1947-48. Trustee, Brenau Coll., Gainesville, Ga., 1963-66; life trustee Indpls. Mus. Art, 1971—. Mem. Spl. Libraries Assn. (chmn. biol. sci. div. 1938-39, conv. chmn. 1939-40, 1st v.p. 1940-41, pub. relations com. 1942-43, 1st v.p., pres. elect 1946-47, pres. 1947-48, dir. 1948-49; Profl. award 1956, Hall of Fame 1959); fellow Med. Library Assn. (com. gifts and grants 1949-51); mem. ALA (com. relations with bus. groups 1944-46, subcom. curricula and degrees Bd. Edn. for Librarianship 1950-51, com. library service to aging 1959-63), Ind. Library Assn. (chmn. War Bond Dr. 1943, hon. mem., exec. dir. Nat. Library Week in Ind. 1959-60), Am. Assn. Colls. Pharmacy (joint com. library 1953-58), Ind. Adult Edn. Assn. (treas., dir. 1945-47), Ind. Assn. History Medicine (sec.-treas. 1940-43), Nat. Soc. U.S. Daus. 1812, Ind. State Hist. Soc. (genealogy com. 1944—), DAR, Colonial Dames 17th Century, Soc. Descs. Washington's Army at Valley Forge, Delta Delta Delta. Co-author: Strieby Genealogy and History, 1726-1967, 1969; Scientific and Technical Libraries, 1964, rev. edit., 1972. Asst. editor: Practice of Pharmacy (Remington), 12th edit., 1961. Contbr. articles to profl. jours. Home: Westminster Village Apt 3216 2741 N Salisbury West Lafayette IN 47906

SHREVE, PEGGY ADAMS, state legislator; b. Spencer, W.Va., July 23, 1927; d. Hubert Smith and Pearl (Looney) Adams; A.B., W.Va. U., 1948; postgrad. Western N.Mex. U., U. Wyo.; m. Don Franklin Shreve, June 17, 1950; children—Donna June, Jennifer Adams, John Clyde, II, Don Franklin. Tchr. schs. in W.Va. and Va., 1948-52; tchr. Cody, Wyo., 1971—; now mem. Wyo. Ho. of Reps. Bd. dirs. Girl Scouts U.S.A., 1962-65; pres. Mothers for Better Schs., 1965; chmn. local chpt. ARC, 1966; elder First Presbyn. Ch., Cody, 1976-79; bd. dirs. Cody chpt. Am. Cancer Soc., 1980; chmn. fin. com. Park County Republican Com., 1979. Mem. NEA, Nat. Order Women Legislators, Wyo. Edn. Assn., Cody Edn. Assn., PEO, Delta Kappa Gamma.

SHREVE, SANDRA DIANE, ednl. adminstr.; b. Detroit, May 25, 1941; d. William Orlo and Gladys Lucille (Struthers) S.; B.S., Wayne State U., 1963, M.Ed., 1971; Ph.D. candidate U. Colo., 1978—. Tchr., Detroit Public Schs., 1963-70, career counselor, 1970-74; counselor Aurora (Colo.) Public Schs., 1975-81, adminstrv. intern., 1980-81, asst. prin., 1981-82, prin. Montview Elem. Sch., 1982—. Mem. Colo. Black Women for Polit. Action, Nat. Council Negro Women, LWV, Am. Personnel and Guidance Assn., Assn. Curriculum Devel., Colo. Assn. Curriculum Devel., AAUW, Pi Lambda Theta, Delta Sigma Theta. Democrat.

SHRIER, DIANE KESLER, psychiatrist; b. N.Y.C., Mar. 23, 1941; d. Benjamin Arthur and Mollie (Wortman) Kesler; B.S. in Chemistry and Biology magna cum laude (Regents scholar 1957-61), Queen's Coll., City U. N.Y., 1961; student Washington U. Sch. Medicine, St. Louis, 1960-61; M.D., Yale U., 1964; m. Adam Louis Shrier, June 10, 1961; children—Jonathan Laurence, Lydia Anne, Catherine Jane, David Leopold. Pediatric intern Bellevue Hosp., N.Y.C., 1964-65; psychiat. resident Albert Einstein Coll. Medicine-Bronx (N.Y.) Municipal Hosp. Center, 1966-68, child psychiatry fellow, 1968-70; staff cons. Family Service and Child Guidance Center of the Oranges, Maplewood, Milburn-Orange, N.J., 1970-73, cons., 1973-79; pvt. practice, Montclair, N.J., 1970—; clin. asst. prof. Coll. Medicine and Dentistry N.J., 1978-82, clin. asso. prof., 1982—; cons. Community Day Nursery, E. Orange, 1970-79; psychiat. cons. Bloomfield (N.J.) Public Schs., 1974-75; clin. instr. Albert Einstein Coll. Medicine, 1970-73; psychiat. cons. Montclair (N.J.) Coll., 1976-78. Trustee Montessori Learning Center, Montclair, 1973-75. Diplomate Am. Bd. Psychiatry and Neurology. Fellow Am. Psychiat. Assn., Am. Orthopsychiat. Assn., Acad. Child Psychiatry; mem. N.J. Psychiat. Assn. (councilor 1981—), Tricounty Psychiat. Assn. (Essex County rep. 1976-77, rec. sec. 1977-78, 2d v.p. 1978-79, 1st v.p. 1979-80, pres. 1980-81), Phi Beta Kappa. Contbr. med. jours. Address: 543 Park St Upper Montclair NJ 07043

SHRIVER, DORIS, (MRS. ELLSWORTH H. SHRIVER II), librarian; b. Cleve., Mar. 10, 1921; d. Harry A. and Vada M. (Custer) Ludasher; B.S., Ohio State U., 1943; m. Ellsworth Harold Shriver, II, Feb. 24, 1944; children—Deborah Lane, Ellsworth Harold, III, Keith Robinson. Wage adminstr. Thompson Products Co., Cleve., 1943-44; instr. Miss. So. Coll., 1944; reporter Hattiesburg (Miss.) Am. Newspaper, 1944-45; lab. technician Western Condensing Co., Appleton, Wis., 1945-48; pub. relations Shillito Kenwood Mall Store, Cin., 1966-68; music librarian Jacksonville (Fla.) U., 1971-76; mem. staff Cin. Suburban Newspapers, Inc., 1966; music librarian U. N.Fla. Audio-Visual-Music Library, 1976—. Dir., instr. ARC swimming program Ross County Council Girl Scouts U.S.A., 1954-62; Ohio promotion chmn. Inter-League Survey Com. Ohio River Basin, 1964-66; mem. Gov. Ohio Com. UN Week, 1964-66; sec. Cin. Joint Com. UN Info., 1965-67; sec. League Women Voters, Chillicothe, 1955-57, 59-60, pres., 1960-63; Ohio Tri-Y adviser YWCA, Chillicothe, 1950-54, dir. Ross County, 1956-57; chmn. pub. relations Chillicothe Garden Club, 1961, pres., 1963-64; sec. Ross County PTA, 1956-58; chmn. pub. relations Flagler Coll. Beaux Arts Festival, St. Augustine, Fla., 1970. Mem. AAUW (pres. Jacksonville 1975-76), Ross County Hist. Soc., Am. Assn. UN (sec. Ohio 1962-64), Ohio State U. Alumni Assn. (county treas. 1955, county sec. 1956), Chioana Library Assn. (publicity chmn. 1968), Cin. Ceramic Guild (treas. 1967-68), Fla. Craftsman Guild, Delta Delta Delta (alumnae pres. 1949-50, 76-77), Phi Beta Psi. Christian Scientist. Clubs: Four Season Yacht; Century (Chillicothe); Beaches Woman's (editor 1969-70, 2d v.p. 1970-71); Compass Rose Internat. Toastmistress (council sec. 1979-80). Address: 13919 Shipwreck Circle N Jacksonville FL 32224

SHRIVER, EUNICE MARY KENNEDY (MRS. ROBERT SARGENT SHRIVER, JR.), civic worker; b. Brookline, Mass.; d. Joseph P. and Rose (Fitzgerald) Kennedy; student Manhattanville Coll. of Sacred Heart, L.H.D., 1963; B.S. in Sociology, Stanford U., 1943; Litt.D., U. Santa Clara, 1962; L.H.D., D'Youville Coll., 1962; LL.D., Regis Coll., 1963; m. Robert Sargent Shriver, Jr., May 23, 1953; children—Robert Sargent, Maria Owings, Timothy Perry, Mark, Anthony. With spl. war problems div. U.S. State Dept., Washington, 1943-45; adviser on prevention and control juvenile delinquency Dept. Justice, Washington, 1947-48; social worker Fed. Penitentiary for Women, Alderson, W.Va., 1950; exec. v.p. Joseph P. Kennedy, Jr. Found., 1956—, pres. Spl. Olympics, 1968—; founder Flame of Hope, Inc.; social worker House of Good Shepherd, Chgo., also Juvenile Ct., Chgo., 1951-54; regional chmn. women's div. Community Fund-Red Cross Joint Appeal, Chgo., 1958; cons. to Pres. John F. Kennedy's Panel on Mental Retardation, 1961. Active congl. and presdl. campaigns of John F. Kennedy, 1948-60; co-chmn. women's com. Democratic Nat. Conv., Chgo., 1956. Recipient (with husband) Philip Murray-William Green award, 1966, Albert

Lasker Pub. Service award in health, 1966; decorated Order of Legion of Honor, French Govt., 1974. Home: 2500 Foxhall Rd NW Washington DC 20007 Office: care Joseph P Kennedy Jr Found 1701 K St NW Washington DC 20006

SHROYER, JESSICA LOUISE, fin. exec.; b. Ketchikan, Alaska, May 21, 1946; d. William Edward and Evelyn E. (Dick) Cogo; student Edmonds Community Coll., 1979-80; children—Angelica, Jennifer. Model, Bon Marche, Seattle, 1964-65; with Boeing Comml. Airplane Div., Seattle, Everett, Wash., 1965-69; with J.P. Wilder Co., Inc., Portland, Oreg., 1972-74; accounts payable clk. Sky Chief div. Am. Airlines, Portland, 1974-76; N.W. regional mgr. Sealaska Corp., Seattle, 1976—. Mem. Seattle Mayor Royer's campaign fin. com., 1981—; notary public, 1976—; mem. adv. bd. Seattle Center, 1982—. Mem. Nat. Assn. Female Execs., Alaska Native Sisterhood, N.W. Mining Assn., Seattle C. of C., China Relations Council Washington. Democrat. Club: Alaska Airlines Bd. Room. Home: 14727 60 Ave W Edmonds WA 98020 Office: 3600 15th Ave W Suite 203 Seattle WA 98119

SHUBERT, BETH COHEN, social worker; b. Greencastle, Ind., Aug. 5, 1941; d. Louis David and Tina (Simon) Cohen; A.B., Oberlin Coll., 1962; M.S.W., U. Pitts., 1964; children—Nina, Jeffrey, Adam. Social worker Dorothea Dix Hosp., 1965, N.C. Correctional Center for Women, 1965-67; supr. Durham County Dept. Social Services, 1968-69; chief social worker Durham Rehab. Center, 1970-71; supr. field placements U. N.C. Sch. Social Work, Chapel Hill, 1970-71; dir. Child Abuse Prevention Program, Durham, N.C., 1976-79; family therapist Vance, Warren, Franklin, Granville Mental Health Program, Henderson, N.C., 1979—; cons. N.C. Justice Acad., 1977-79. Mem. legis. task force Child Abuse and Neglect, State N.C., 1977-79; mem. bd. Triangle N.C. Multiple Sclerosis Found., 1970-74. Mem. Acad. Cert. Social Workers, Nat. Assn. Social Workers. Democrat. Jewish. Home: 1012 Wells St Durham NC 27707 Office: C-10 Ruin Creek Rd Henderson NC 27536

SHULKO, PATSY LEE, educator; b. Indpls., Sept. 24, 1934; B.S., Mich. State U., 1956, M.A., 1970; m. Richard M. Shulko, Aug. 4, 1973; 1 son, Gregory. Asst. prof. Med. Coll. Ga., Augusta, 1972—. Mem. Am. Dietetic Assn., Ga. Dietetic Assn., Augusta Dietetic Assn., Am. Home Econ. Assn., Ga. Heart Assn., Ga. Nutrition Council, Soc. Nutrition Edn., Nutrition Today Soc. (charter), AAUP, AAUW, Omicron Nu, Pi Beta Phi. Clubs: Houndslake Country, Racquet. Home: 425 Waverly Dr Augusta GA 30909 Office: Med Coll Ga Sch Nursing Augusta GA 30902

SHULL, SHARRYL LEIGH, clin. psychologist; b. Chgo., May 13, 1950; d. Tarvis Morgan Iversen and Barbara Louise Light; A.A. with honors, Southwestern Mich. Jr. Coll., 1970; B.A. in Psychology cum laude, Western Mich. U., 1972, M.A. in Psychology with honors, 1974; m. Charles Alden Shull, Aug. 25, 1979. Clin. psychologist Kalamazoo Child Guidance Clinic, 1974—; cons. Mich. Disability Determination Service. Lic. psychologist, Mich. Mem. Am. Psychol. Assn. (asso.), Kalamazoo/Battle Creek Tng. and Devel. Assn. Democrat. Home: 2628 Wellington Rd Kalamazoo MI 49008 Office: 2615 Stadium Dr Kalamazoo MI 49008

SHULLER, MARILYN HUNDLEY, mktg. exec.; b. Jenks, Okla., Sept. 18, 1936; d. Charles Virgil and Anna Lee (Wood) Hundley; B.A. in Humanities, Okla. State U., 1957; M.A. in Speech and Drama, U. Ark., 1966; 1 dau., Rebecca Lynn Shuller. Tchr. speech and English, Farmington (Ark.) High Sch., 1957-58; broadcast dir. Hundley, Williams Advt. Agy., Ft. Smith, Ark., 1961-66; instr. speech and drama Jefferson County (Mo.) Jr. Coll., Hillsboro, 1966-69; creative dir. Hundley, Williams Advt., Ft. Smith, 1969-75; account adminstr. Jordan Assn., advt., Oklahoma City, 1975-78; freelance radio and TV prodn., after 1978; now pres. Contemporary Concepts in Mktg., Inc., Edmond, Okla.; instr. creative dramatics workshops, St. Louis, Ft. Smith. Bd. dirs. Children's Theatre, Ft. Smith, 1972-75, Broadway Theatre League, 1971-74. Mem. Ft. Smith, Am. advt. fedns. Republican. Methodist. Home: 1300 S Timberlake Circle Edmond OK 73034 Office: 1603 SE 19th St Suite 207 Canyon Park Edmond OK 73034

SHULMAN, CLAIRE LUCILLE, devel. co. adminstr.; b. N.Y.C., Mar. 27, 1941; d. Jacob Morris and Beatrice Irene (Krieger) Epstein; B.A. in English, Hofstra U., 1961, M.S. in Secondary Edn., 1964; children—Scott, Brian, Russell. Tchr. English, social studies, pvt. and public schs., Westbury and Lawrence, N.Y., 1969-77; owner, operator Metro Hobby Shop, needlework design shop, Woodmere, N.Y. and Miami, Fla., 1969-77; dir. mktg. Ethnic Crafts, Miami, 1977-78; exec. dir. Fla. Regional Minority Purchasing Council, Miami, 1978-79; dir. exchange and travel Interval Internat., South Miami, Fla., 1979-80; exec. adminstrv. asst. Island Developers, Ltd., South Miami, 1980—; pres. Claire Shulman and Assos., fin. services, 1981—; del. White House Conf. on Small Bus., 1979-80. Mem. Dade County (Fla.) Commn. for Status of Women; mem. steering com. Common Cause; mem. planning com. YWCA Women in Mgmt. Program, Miami; mem. women's concern com. Mental Health Bd., Miami, 1979. Recipient recognition for outstanding community service from Pres. Carter. Mem. Mensa, Phi Delta Epsilon, Epsilon Tau Lambda. Democrat. Jewish. Author: How to Build a Successful Needlepoint Business, 1977; editor: Briarlake Newsletter. Home: 9184 SW 132d Ln Miami FL 33176

SHULMAN, LEE CAROL, public relations exec.; b. Boston, June 26, 1954; d. Michael and Sally (Reichert) S.; student Simmons Coll., 1972-74, U. Granada (Spain), 1975; B.A., Colgate U., 1976; M.Ed., Antioch Coll., 1979; cert. advanced study Internat. Mktg. Inst., 1980; Bilingual legal asst., Boston, 1976; archtl./mktg. research asst. Skidmore, Owings & Merrill, Boston, 1976-78; tchr., career edn. coordinator Action for Boston Community Devel., 1978; project dir. cross-cultural tchr. tng. program Proyecto Amistad, Arequipa, Peru, 1979; bilingual career edn. curriculum developer Boston Public Schs., 1978-80; account exec. Shulman & Assos., Public Relations, Boston, 1979—; publicity dir. Boston Harborfest, 1982; lectr. Radcliffe Coll., Boston Pub. Library, Sch. Vols. of Boston. Club: Boston Ski and Sport. Home: 42 Commonwealth Ave Boston MA 02116 Office: 296 Boylston St Boston MA 02116

SHULTZ, DEBORAH SUSAN, sales/mktg. cons.; b. Kansas City, Mo., July 11, 1953; d. James Herbert and Barbara Phyllis (Sharp) Shultz; B.A., U. Kans. Founder, pres. Sentry Control Systems, Lawrence, Kans., 1972-75; product engr. N. Supply Co., Lenexa, Kans., 1975-79; sales/design security cons. Sentry Protective Alarms, Overland Park, Kans., 1979-81; founder, pres. Security Cons. Group, Overland, 1980-81; security mktg. cons. ADT Security, San Francisco, 1982—. Active Jewish Fedn. San Francisco, 1982—, Am. Israel Public Action Com., San Francisco, 1981—, Anti-Defamation League, San Francisco, 1982—. Mem. Nat. Burgler and Fire Alarm Assn., Mid-Am. Alarm Assn. Republican. Clubs: Le Amis de Vin, Mensa. Contbr. articles to profl. jours.

SHULTZ, SUSAN FRIED, exec. search cons.; b. N.Y.C., Mar. 25, 1943; d. L. Richard and Jane (Kent) Fried; B.A. in Govt. and Econs., U. Ariz., 1964; postgrad. in internat. affairs George Washington U., 1967. Congl. legis. asst., 1964-68; campaign and press dir. various polit. campaigns, 1968-78; public relations cons., 1974-81; contbr. editor Phoenix mag., 1973—; pres. Susan Shultz and Assos., exec. search cons., Paradise Valley, Ariz., 1981—; writer Beverly Hills Diet and sequel, 1981-82. Mem. staff Republic Nat. Conv., 1964, 68, 80; charter mem. Charter 100, 1980; charter class mem. Valley Leadership, 1980; membership chmn. Village 5 Phoenix Planning Com., 1980. Mem. Phoenix Com. Fgn. Relations, Ariz. Dist. Export Council Jr. League of Phoenix. Episcopalian. Address: 6001 E Cactus Wren Rd Paradise Valley AZ 85253

SHUMAN, PAMELA SUE, state legislator; b. New Martinsville, W.Va., June 11, d. Leslie W. and Violet (Wright) S.; student W. Liberty State Coll. Apptd. to W.Va. Ho. of Reps., 1974, elected, 1974—, chmn. govt. orgn. com., mem. constl. revision, polit. subdivisions, redistricting coms. Active Brooke County Easter Seal Soc., hon. bd. mem.; adv. bd. W.Va. Commn. on Status of Women; pres. Brooke County Fedn. Democratic Women; mem. exec. com. State Young Dems.; mem. State Dem. Platform Com. Methodist. Club: Women of Moose. Office: West Virginia House of Reps Charleston WV 25305 *

SHUMOFSKY, IRENE, public sch. tchr.; b. Bronx, N.Y., Sept. 24, 1942; d. Milton and Anna (Schneider) S.; B.S., SUNY, Potsdam, 1964; M.S., Hunter Coll., N.Y.C., 1969. Tchr., N.Y. schs., 1964—; tchr. Limekiln Sch., Suffern, 1967—; del. N.Y. State Retirement System, 1979-80; trustee Leland R. Meyer Scholarship Fund, 1978—. Librarian, Pomona Jewish Center, 1981—, social action chmn., 1981—. Mem. NEA (del 1980—), N.Y. Educators Assn. (del. 1978—), East Ramapo Tchrs. Assn. (v.p. 1977—), PTA (life). Jewish. Club: B'nai B'rith (v.p. membership educators unit 1981-82, program chmn. 1982-83). Home: 172C Kearsing Pkwy Monsey NY 10952 Office: Limekiln Sch Limekiln Rd Suffern NY 10901

SHURE, MYRNA BETH, psychologist, educator; b. Chgo., Sept. 11, 1937; d. Sidney Natkin and Frances (Laufman) S.; student U. Colo., 1955; B.S., U. Ill., 1959; M.S., Cornell U., 1961, Ph.D., 1966. Asst. prof. U. R.I., head tchr. Nursery Sch., Kingston, 1961-62; asst. prof. Temple U., Phila., 1966-67, asso. prof., 1967-68; instr. Hahneman Med. Coll., Phila., 1968-69, sr. instr. psychology, 1969-70, asst. prof., 1970-73, asso. prof., 1973-80, prof., 1980—. NIMH research grantee, 1971-75, 77-79, 82—. Lic. psychologist, Pa. Fellow Am. Psychol. Assn.; mem. Eastern Psychol. Assn., Soc. Research in Child Devel., Phila. Soc. Clin. Psychologists. Author: (with George Spivack) Social Adjustment of Young Children, 1974; (with George Spivack and Jerome Platt) The Problem Solving Approach to Adjustment, 1976; (with George Spivack) Problem Solving Techniques in Childrearing, 1978. Editorial bd. Am. Jour. Community Psychology, Jour. Applied Developmental Psychology. Office: 112 N Broad St Philadelphia PA 19102

SHURTLEFF, SUE, health assn. ofcl.; b. N.Y.C., July 9, 1942; d. Jack Amos and Ann (Loncheck) Pierce; student Keuka Coll., 1960, Rochester Bus. Inst., 1961, Rochester Inst. Tech., 1962, Empire State Coll., 1978; m. Ron Shurtleff, Dec. 1, 1961; children—Kelly, Greg, Jeff. Prodn. coordinator Taylor Instruments, Rochester, N.Y., 1960-62, sales rep., 1962-65; sales rep. Fanny Farmer, Rochester, 1965-76; program dir. Monroe County Assn. for Hearing Impaired, Rochester Health Assn., 1976—, program dir. eye conservation com., 1980—. Bd. dirs. Substance Abuse Intervention Services for Hearing Impaired; mem. council Mental Health Services for Hearing Impaired; mem. Rochester Mental Health Services for Hearing Impaired Com.; sec. Rochester Transit Assn. Services to Handicapped and Elderly; mem. N.Y. State Assembly Task Force on Disabled, Mental Health Legis. Com.; bd. dirs., v.p. Pop Warner League. Fed. grantee to establish third-party relay service for deaf, 1981. Mem. Nat. Assn. for Deaf. Editor monthly newsletter for hearing impaired, 1978—, Pop Warner Football Action, 1979-82. Home: 14 Log Cabin Circle Fairport NY 14450 Office: 973 East Ave Rochester NY 14607

SHUTTS, SHARON E., clin. psychologist; b. Macon, Mo., July 11, 1940; d. Clarence Miller and Margaret Jane (Burke) Cox; B.S. in Psychology, Mo. Western State Coll., 1975; M.A. in Psychology, U. Mo., Kansas City, 1977; m. William A. Bowlin, Jr., June 12, 1960 (div., 1973); children—Lori Christine, Billy Alan; m. 2d. Ellis L. Shutts, Sept. 3, 1976 (dec. 1978). Mental health dir. Head Start of Greater St. Joseph (Mo.) Area, 1973-79; psychologist in tng. Clin. Counseling and Consultation Service, St. Joseph, 1975—; clin. psychologist St. Joseph State Hosp., 1979—; vol. adv. council for Head Start; cons. Noyes Home for Children. Bd. dirs. Mental Health Assn., St. Joseph. Mem. Am. Psychol. Assn., Mo. Psychol. Assn., Assn. Women in Psychology, NW Regional Council Comprehensive Psychiat. Services (children and youth task force). Developer color blindness test for young children; researcher early detection of visual perception dysfunction and autism. Home: 1716 S 20th Saint Joseph MO 64507 Office: 34th & Frederick Saint Joseph MO 64502 also 322 Kirkpatrick Bldg Saint Joseph MO 64501

SHWARTZ, SHEILA ALPERT, designer; b. New Bedford, Mass., Mar. 22, 1931; d. Simon and Della (Davidson) Alpert; A.B.A., Curry Coll., Boston, 1950; children—Peter D., Patti Diane. Sportswear buyer Lloyds, New Bedford, 1951-52; founder, 1965, since pres. Faces of Time, Ltd., Inc., jewelry, personal and home accessories, N.Y.C. Pres. New Bedford chpt. Hadassah, 1958-60. Mem. Exec. Female, LWV. Republican. Office: 32 W 40th St New York NY 10018

SIBLEY, CAROL MORSE, med. communications cons.; b. San Antonio, Jan. 11, 1944; d. Edison Spencer and Cecile (Bernard) Morse; student U. Del., 1962-64; B.S., Hahnemann Med. Coll., 1966; m. Frederick Drake Sibley, Mar. 15, 1975; 1 dau., Janet Bernard. Med. writer internat. div. Bristol-Myers, N.Y.C., 1968-72; asso. biomed. communications Turner Assos., Greenwich, Conn., 1972-73; clin. research asso. Pfizer Pharms., N.Y.C., 1974-76, mgr. sci. communications, 1976; cons. pharm. industry, Montclair, N.J., 1976—; asso. biomed. communications J. L. Shapiro Assos., Metuchen, N.J., 1979—. Committeeman, Republican party, Phila., 1965-66. Mem. Am. Soc. Microbiology, Am. Assn. Women in Sci., Am. Soc. Clin. Pathologists. Republican. Episcopalian. Editor Prekindergarten Newsletter, 1979-80. Home and Office: 196 Christopher St Montclair NJ 07042

SIBLEY, DOROTHY FARRAR, county adminstr.; b. Bklyn., June 28, 1922; d. Guy Wilbur and Laurette Miscella (Morris) Farrar; B.S., Simmons Coll., 1943; m. Peter L. Sibley, Apr. 22, 1944; children—Peter L., David Farrar. Mem. adminstrv. staff U. Miami (Fla.) Div. Continuing Edn., 1950-64; adminstrv. asst. to mgr. Dade County, Fla., 1964—; exec. dir. Dade County Commn. on Status of Women, 1975—; pres. Women's Com. of 100, 1979-81; dir. Hemispheric Congress for Women, 1978—; mem. supervisory com. Dade County Employees' Credit Union. Mem. child advocacy com.; mem. Fairchild Tropical Gardens, 1978—, Met. Mus. and Art Centers, 1978—. Mem. Internat. City Mgmt. Assn., Am. Soc. Public Adminstrn., Exec. Dirs. Assn., Nat. Assns. Commns. for Women, Women in Criminal Justice, Fla. Women's Network, AAUW (dir. Miami br. 1974—, pres. 1981—), YWCA. Democrat. Methodist. Home: 13125 SW 81st Ave Miami FL 33156 Office: 73 W Flagler St Room 911 Courthouse Miami FL 33130

SICILIANO, ANN P., cytologist; b. Neptune, N.J., Dec. 20, 1930; d. Gavino and Theresa Siciliano; asso. degree in med. tech. Wilson Jr. Coll., 1948; cert. in cytology Parkway Hosp., 1949; B.S., Northwestern U., 1962. With Parkway Hosp., Brookline, Mass., 1949-53; supr. cytology and isotopes labs. Highland Park (Ill.) Hosp., 1954-60; cytologist U. Ill. Med. Sch., Chgo., 1960-61; cytologist supr. Edgewater Hosp., Chgo., 1961-68, North Suburban Clinic, Skokie, Ill., 1964—. Mem. Internat. Acad. Cytology, Am. Soc. Cytotechnologists, Am. Soc. Clin. Pathology (assoc.), Am. Soc. Cytology (assoc.), Ill. Soc. Cytology (treas.). Roman Catholic.

SICKAFOOSE, JEANNETTE CAROL, pharmacist; b. Coshocton, Ohio, Aug. 6, 1924; d. Guy Russell and Grace Flora (Groene) Tarney; B.Sc., Ohio State U., 1947; postgrad. Akron U., 1962-64; m. Wayne W. Sickafoose, Jan. 20, 1951. Dir. pharmacy Aultman Hosp., Canton, Ohio, 1948—; clin. instr. Ohio State U., Ohio No. U. Mem. Am. Soc. Hosp. Pharmacists, Am. Pharm. Assn., Ohio Soc. Hosp. Pharmacists, Ohio Pharm. Assn., Akron Soc. Hosp. Pharmacists, Stark County Pharm. Acad., Rho Chi, Kappa Epsilon. Episcopalian. Home: 6091 Cleveland Ave East Sparta OH 44626 Office: Aultman Hospital 2600 6th St Canton OH 44710

SICOTTE, GRACE DARLENE DEMENT, assn. exec.; b. Livingston, Mont., Nov. 17, 1922; d. Randolf and Dollie Mae Butler (Clauson) Dement; student U. Portland, 1973; m. Albert Edward Sicotte, Jan. 24, 1939 (div. 1973); children—Joseph Edward, Nancy Darlene Sicotte Cassidy, Charles David. Reporter Butte (Mont.) Credit, 1953; asst. mgr. Nat. Loan Co., Butte, 1954; credit mgr. Phil Judd Sporting Goods Store, Butte, 1954-61; sec. Operating Engrs. Union #378, Butte, 1961-67; credit mgr., office personnel Buttreys Dept. Store, Butte, 1968-69; dir. of spa, YMCA, Butte, 1969-77, also dir. women's referral center; dir. Community Resource Center; civil def. dep. Butte-Silver Bow Sheriff's Dept. Fitness Finders instr., Butte, 1972-74; phys. fitness examiner; Red Cross and emergency med. tech.; chmn. Butte chpt. ARC, 1981-82; exec. chpt. chmn., 1983; bd. dirs. Mont. Friendship Forces, Safe Space for Abused Women and Children; Mont. rep. People-to-People Internat., 1980—. Mem. Nat. Secs. Assn. (pres. 1969-71, Sec. of Year 1971), Bus. and Profl. Women's Club (corr. sec. 1971-72, pres. 1981-83, Woman of Year award 1975, 77, Woman of Achievement award 1976), Am. Ambulance Assn., Christian Women's Assn. Clubs: Soroptomist, (pres. 1983), Toastmistress, Order Eastern Star. Home: 2825 Farragut St Apt 201A Butte MT 59701 Office: Butte Silver Bow Sheriffs Office Butte MT 59701

SIDAMON-ERISTOFF, ANNE PHIPPS, mus. trustee, found. dir.; b. N.Y.C., Sept. 12, 1932; d. Howard and Harriet Dyer (Price) Phipps; B.A., Bryn Mawr Coll., 1954; m. Constantine Sidamon-Eristoff, June 29, 1957; children—Simon, Elizabeth, Andrew. Trustee, Am. Mus. Natural History, N.Y.C., Mus. Modern Art, N.Y.C., Greenacre Found., N.Y.C., Mus. of Hudson Highlands, Cornwall, N.Y.; bd. dirs., sec. The Conservation Found., Washington; bd. dirs. Highland Falls (N.Y.) Public Library.

SIDEBOTTOM, BETTY LOU, nurse; b. Spring Hill, W.Va., Feb. 13, 1926; d. Gay Robert and Emma Vere (Groves) Newell; R.N., St. Francis Hosp., Charleston, W.Va., 1947; B.A., W.Va. State Coll., 1980; m. Homer W. Sidebottom, Aug. 23, 1948 (dec.); 1 son, James Steven. Nurse with Dr. Eugene Holcomb, Charleston, 1947, Thomas Meml. Hosp., 1948; sch. nurse Kanawha County Bd. Edn., Charleston, 1948—. Mem. W.Va. Sch. Health Assn. (Am. award for outstanding contbn. to sch. health). Democrat. Episcopalian. Home: 1333 Pennsylvania Ave Saint Albans WV 25177 Office: 200 Elizabeth St Charleston WV 25311

SIEBERT, EVELYN MARIE KANNEL (MRS. VIRGIL J. SIEBERT), ret. librarian b. Akron, Ohio, Aug. 7, 1916; d. Emmet Franklyn and Julia Veronica (McGuigan) Kannel; B.A., Akron State U., 1939; M.L.S., Western Res. U., 1940; m. Virgil J. Siebert, Sept. 8, 1939; children—John, Thomas, Keith and Craig (twins). Children's librarian Cleve. Public Library, 1940-43, sch. librarian curriculum center, 1941-42; sch. librarian Lakewood (Ohio) Public Library, 1961-62, Vermilion (Ohio) Public Schs., 1962-72; librarian head Vermilion Public Library, 1973-81. Mem. ALA, Ohio Library Assn. Club: College of Vermilion. Home: 5331 Portage Dr Vermilion OH 44089

SIEBERT, MURIEL, former state banking ofcl.; b. Cleve.; d. Irwin J. and Margaret Eunice (Roseman) S.; student Western Res. U., 1949-52; D.C.S. (hon.), St. John's U., St. Bonaventure U. Security analyst Bache & Co., 1954-57; analyst Utilities & Industries Mgmt. Corp., 1958, Shields & Co., 1959-60; partner Stearns & Co., 1961, Finkle & Co., 1962-65, Brimberg & Co., N.Y.C., 1965-67; pres. Muriel Siebert & Co., Inc., mems. N.Y. Stock Exchange, 1968-77; individual mem. (1st woman mem.) N.Y. Stock Exchange, 1967; trustee Manhattan Savs. Bank, 1975-77; supt. banks State of N.Y., N.Y.C., 1977-82; asso. in mgmt. Simmons Coll. Trustee, Manhattan Coll.; v.p., mem. exec. com. Greater N.Y. Area council Boy Scouts Am.; Rep. candidate for U.S. Senate from N.Y., 1982 primary; mem. N.Y. State Econ. Devel. Bd.; dir. Urban Devel. Corp., State N.Y. Mortgage Agy., Job Devel. Authority. Mem. N.Y. Soc. Security Analysts, Money Marketeers N.Y.U. (gov.), Sales Execs. Club (past v.p. dir.). Clubs: Wings (past dir., v.p.), Westchester County, El Morrocco. Office: Two World Trade Center New York NY 10047

SIEBERT, WENDY LOEBBAKA, software co. exec.; b. Chgo., Dec. 14, 1942; d. Harold J. and Beatrice M. (Jebavy) Loebbaka; student, Ill. Inst. Tech., 1960-62; student, Bradley U., 1963-65. Programmer, Western Electric Corp., Chgo., 1965-67; system analyst Westinghouse Electric, Chgo., 1969-71; sr. systems analyst Midas Internat. Corp., Chgo., 1971-74; mgr. installation support Wang Labs., Lowell, Mass., 1974-81; area mgr. Genesys Software Systems, Houston, 1981—. Mem. Data Processing Mgmt. Assn. (pres. 1974-75), Nat. Assn. Female Execs., Nat. Assn. Profl. Saleswomen. Office: 6610 Harwin Dr Suite 274 Houston TX 77036

SIEFERT, SUSAN ELIZABETH, ins. co. exec.; b. Norwalk, Conn., June 22, 1947; d. Robert Ernest and Rosemary Frances (Balla) S.; B.A., Marquette U., Milw., 1969; M.A., 1970, Ph.D. (AAUW fellow 1974), 1974. Instr., Marquette U., 1974-75; asst. prof. English, Concordia Coll., Milw., 1975-76, Alverno Coll., Milw., 1976-78; editor corp. ann. report, then spl. personnel programs cons. Prudential Ins. Co. Am., 1978-80, group mgr., Mpls., 1980—; cons. in field. Recipient award Life Ins. Advertisers Assn., 1978; NDEA fellow, 1969-73. Mem. Am. Com. Irish Studies, AAUW, MLA, Phi Beta Kappa. Author: The Dilemma of the Talented Heroine: A Study in Nineteenth Century Fiction, 1978. Office: 5402 S Cedar Lake Rd Minneapolis MN 55416

SIEGAL, RITA GORAN, engring. co. exec.; b. Chgo., July 16, 1934; d. Leonard and Anabelle (Soloway) Goran; student U. Ill., 1951-53, Roosevelt U., 1953-54; B.A., DePaul U., 1956; m. Burton L. Siegal, Apr. 11, 1954; children—Norman, Laurence Scott. Tchr. elem. schs. Chgo. Public Schs., 1956-58; v.p. Easy Living Products Co., Chgo., 1960-62, pres., 1980—; freelance interior designer, Chgo., 1968-73; dist. sales mgr. Super Girls, Chgo., 1976; v.p. Budd Engring., Skokie, Ill., 1974—. Mem. adv. council Skokie High Schs., 1975-79; adv. Cub Scouts Skokie council Boy Scouts Am.; bus. mgr. Nutrition for Optimal Health Assn., 1980-82, pres., 1982—. Recipient Cub Scout awards Boy Scouts Am., 1971-72; Sales award Super Girls, 1976. Mem. Buten Mus., Women in Mgmt., North Shore Art League. Club: Profit Plus Investment (founder 1970). Office: 8707 Skokie Blvd Skokie IL 60077

SIEGEL, ALBERTA ENGVALL (MRS. SIDNEY SIEGEL), psychologist, educator; b. Pasadena, Calif., Feb. 24, 1931; d. Albert and Portia (Powers) Engvall; B.A., Stanford U., 1951, M.A., 1954, Ph.D., 1955; m. Sidney Siegel, July 31, 1954 (dec. 1961). Faculty, Pa. State U., 1955-63; faculty Stanford (Calif.) U., 1963—, prof. psychology in psychiatry, 1969—, asso. dean undergrad. studies, 1971. Fellow Center

Advanced Study Behavioral Scis., 1961-63; mem. research scientist devel. com. NIMH, 1965-69, mem. panel research consultants to dir., research task force, 1973; mem. sci. adv. com. on TV and social behavior U.S. Surgeon Gen., 1969-71; mem. growth and devel. research and tng. com. Nat. Inst. Child Health and Human Devel., 1972-76; mem. adv. com. on ethical and human value implications of sci. and tech. NSF, 1973-76; dir. Gt. Western Fin. Corp.; mem. developmental problems research rev. com. NIMH, 1977—. Bd. dirs. Population Edn., 1974-79; bd. visitors Learning Research and Devel. Center, U. Pitts., 1975-80. Fellow Am. Psychol. Assn. (pres. div. developmental psychology 1973-74); mem. Soc. Research Child Devel. (governing council), AAAS, Phi Beta Kappa, Sigma Xi. Democrat. Club: Stanford Faculty (pres., 1973-74). Editor: Child Development, 1964-68. Contbr. articles to profl. jours. Office: Dept Psychiatry and Behavioral Scis Stanford U Sch Medicine Stanford CA 94305

SIEGEL, B(ARBARA) JANE RANDALL, counselor; b. Plainfield, N.J., Nov. 6, 1941; d. George Lewis and Edith Ramsing Randall; B.A., U. N.H., 1963; M.Ed., Coll. William and Mary, 1974; children—Randall John, Marc Alan, David Ross. Tchr., Newmarket (N.H.) Public Schs., 1963-65; tchr. Gen. Ednl. Devel., Gen. Tng. program U.S. Army, Ft. Bragg, N.C., 1967-70; instr. continuing edn. programs Coll. William and Mary, 1974-76; instr. continuing edn. program, adminstr. coll. level exam. program, counselor Christopher Newport Coll., Newport News, Va., 1975-77; owner, pres. Counseling Assos., Inc., psychol. and counseling services, Yorktown, Va., 1977—; adj. prof. Thomas Nelson Community Coll., Hampton, Va., 1979—; cons. and trainer in field of counseling psychology and human relations. Bd. dirs. Voluntary Action Center, a United Way orgn. Mem. Assn. of Specialists in Group Work, Am. Psychol. Assn. (asso.), Am. Personnel and Guidance Assn., Peninsula Personnel and Guidance Assn., Am. Mental Health Counselors Assn., AAUW, Phi Mu. Office: 1949 George Washington Memorial Hwy Yorktown VA 23692

SIEGEL, BEATRICE KRONGELB, coll. adminstr.; b. N.Y.C., Jan. 6, 1923; d. Louis and Kate (Miller) Krongelb; B.A., Hunter Coll., 1943; Ed.M., UCLA, 1957, Ed.D., 1973; m. Sol Siegel, June 9, 1946; children—Shelby, Diana. Standards specialist Burndy Engring. Co., N.Y.C., 1943-45; elem. tchr. public schs., N.Y.C. and Los Angeles, 1947-62; instr. adult edn. UCLA, 1970-73; head, div. courses and spl. programs U. Calif. Extension, Santa Cruz, 1973-75; dir. older adult and spl. programs Monterey (Calif.) Peninsula Coll., 1975—. Pres., Congregation Beth Israel, 1982-83. Mem. Nat. Council Sr. Citizens, Assn. Calif. Community Coll. Adminstrs., Older Women's League (chpt. chmn.), Community Coll. Educators Older Adults. Office: Monterey Peninsula College Monterey CA 93940

SIEGEL, BETTY LENTZ, coll. pres.; b. Cumberland, Ky., Jan. 24, 1931; d. Carl N. and Vera (Hogg) Lentz; B.A., Wake Forest Coll., 1952; M.Ed., U. N.C., 1953; Ph.D., Fla. State U., 1961; postgrad. Ind. U., 1964-66; m. Joel H. Siegel, June 6; children—David Jonathan, Michael Jeremy. Asst. prof. Lenoir Rhyne Coll., Hickory, N.C., 1956-59, asso. prof., 1961-64; asst. prof. U. Fla., Gainesville, 1967-70, asso. prof., 1970-72, prof., 1973-76, dean acad. affairs for continuing edn., 1972-76; dean Sch. of Edn. and Psychology, Western Carolina U., Cullowhee, N.C., 1976-81; pres. Kennesaw Coll., Marietta, Ga., 1981—; cons. to numerous sch. systems. Recipient Outstanding Tchr. award U. Fla., 1969; Mortar Bd. Woman of Yr. award U. Fla., 1973. Mem. Am. Psychol. Assn., Am. Ednl. Research Assn., Assn. for Supervision and Curriculum Devel., Am. Assn. Colls. of Tchr. Edn., Nat. Univ. Extension Assn., Adult Edn. Assn., Nat. Assn. State Univs. and Land Grant Colls., Phi Alpha Theta, Pi Kappa Delta, Alpha Psi Omega, Kappa Delta Pi, Pi Lambda Theta, Phi Delta Kappa, Delta Kappa Gamma. Republican. Baptist. Author: Problem Situations in Teaching, 1971; contbr. articles to profl. jours. Office: Kennesaw College Marietta GA 30061

SIEGEL, CLARA, pianist, educator; b. Chgo., 1911; m. Arthur A. Ehrlich, Oct. 30, 1936; children—Linn M., Kayla R. Founder, pianist Siegel Chamber Music Players, 1945-54; dir. performer U. Chgo. Downtown Coll., 1958-59, Cosmopolitan Sch. Music, Chgo., 1962-63; dir. chamber music workshop DePaul U., Chgo., 1976—; dir. chamber music dept. Chautauqua (N.Y.) Instn., 1973—; numerous appearances with Chgo. Symphony String Quartet, Fine Arts Quartet, Chgo. Symphony Woodwind Quartet, Berkshire Quartet; soloist with Mpls. Symphony, Milw. Symphony, Rochester Symphony, Portland Symphony, Buffalo Symphony, Chautauqua Symphony. Home: 30 E Huron St Apt 1204 Chicago IL 60611 Office: DePaul Sch Music 804 W Belden Ave Chicago IL 60614

SIEGEL, DORIS, author; b. N.Y.C.; d. Russell E. and Cora G. (Davis) Taylor; B.A., U. Calif. at Los Angeles; m. William E. Siegel, Dec. 31, 1932; 1 son, Richard Taylor. Author: (under pen name Susan Wells) Murder Is Not Enough, Footsteps in the Air, Death Is My Name, The Witches Pond; (under own name) How Still My Love, 1957. Charter mem., docent, patron, costume council Los Angeles County Mus. Art; women's com. So. Calif. Symphony Assn.; mem. dean's council Coll. Fine Arts, UCLA; trustee UCLA Found. Mem. Colonial Order Crown, Nat. Soc. Magna Charta Dames, Colonial Dames 17th Century (past pres. Plymouth chpt.; nat. chmn. def. programs 1969-72), Los Angeles World Affairs Council, Friends Huntington Library, Soc. Fellows of the Huntington, Sovereign Colonial Soc. Ams. Royal Descent, Le Salon Français, Los Angeles County Natural History Mus. Alliance, UCLA Alumni Assn., Nat. Audubon Soc., Smithsonian Assos., Affiliates UCLA, Pepperdine U. Assos., Occidental Coll. President's Circle, William Stuart Young Soc., Town Hall Assn. of Calif., Las Hermanas Guild Childrens Hosp. Soc., Chi Omega, Chi Delta Phi. Clubs: Internat. PEN, Founders (UCLA), Los Angeles Country. Home: 1520 San Remo Dr Pacific Palisades CA 90272

SIEGEL, LAURA ASCHER-APPEL, orthodontist; b. N.Y.C., Nov. 16, 1912; d. Jay and Fannie Ascher; B.S., N.Y. U., 1933, D.D.S., 1937; cert. orthodontia, Columbia U. Dental Coll., 1962; m. Sidney J. Appel, 1941; children—John Philip, Marjorie Appel Scherer; m. 2d, David Siegel. Intern in pedodontics Guggenheim Dental div., N.Y.C., 1938-39; extern Grassland Hosp., Valhalla, N.Y., 1956; pvt. practice orthodontics, Cedarhurst, 1962-82; tchr. residents Peninsula Hosp. Centre, Far Rockaway, N.Y. Fellow Royal Soc. Health; mem. ADA, Am. Assn. Orthodontists, N.Y. State Dental Assn., 10th Dist. Dental Soc., Northeastern Assn. Orthodontists, 10th Dist. Assn. Orthodontists (pres. 1978-80), Middle Atlantic Assn. Orthodontists, Assn. Women Dentists N.Y. (v.p. 1977-80), Nassau County Dental Assn., Columbia U. Dental Alumni Assn., N.Y. U. Alumni Assn. Home: 9283 Vista del Lago Boca Raton FL 33433

SIEGEL, NORMA P., ednl. adminstr. Prin., Public Sch. 279, Bklyn.; leader workshops and seminars in field. Mem. N.Y. State Tchrs. Assn. (Educator of Yr. 1980), N.Y.C. Prins. Assn. (pres. elect, v.p. council suprs. and adminstrs.). Program for mainstreaming handicapped students used as model N.Y.C. schs. Address: 1070 E 104th St Brooklyn NY 11234

SIEGNER, JANET BOWEN, occupational therapist, social worker; b. New Haven, Apr. 18, 1923; d. William Cary and Elma Logie Bowen; student Coll. Wooster, 1941-43; B.S., U. Pa., 1945; M.S.W., SUNY, Buffalo, 1981; m. Allan Wesp Siegner, Dec. 28, 1946; children—Betty, Cary, Allan Wesp, Hugh R. Chief occupational therapy cerebral palsy unit Children's Hosp., Buffalo, 1946-48; psychol. counselor East Side Counseling Center, Buffalo, 1969-72; head occupational therapist Vis. Nursing Assn., Buffalo, 1972-76; dir., founder Ind. Living Project, research asst. prof. dept. occupational therapy SUNY, Buffalo, 1977-79. Chpt. pres. Am. Field Service, 1967-68; mem. med. com. Planned Parenthood, Buffalo, 1978—; pvt. practice psychotherapy specializing in sexual disfunction and marital therapy, 1981—; mem. Vis. Nursing Assn., Buffalo, 1978-79. Lic. occupational therapist. Mem. Am. Assn. Sex Educators, Counselors and Therapists (certified sex educator 1979), Western N.Y. Assn. Profls. Working in Human Sexuality (co-founder, v.p. 1979-82), Nat. Assn. Social Workers, Am. Occupational Therapy Assn., Assn. Couples for Marriage Enrichment, Center Study Sensory Integrative Dysfunction, World Fedn. Occupational Therapists, LWV, N.Y. State Occupational Therapy Assn. (cert. of merit 1979, chmn. ad hoc com. on ethics 1978-81), N.Y. Geriatric Assn. (mem. program com. 1978-79), Gerontol. Soc. Western N.Y., Niagara Frontier Occupational Therapy Assn. (chmn. nominating com. 1978). Club: U. Pa. Western N.Y. (bd. mem. 1973-77) (Buffalo). Lectr., author in field of sexuality and aging.

SIEGRIST, ALICE PATRICIA, retail exec.; b. Santa Clara, Calif., Apr. 10, 1924; d. John and Mary (Aguiar) Rodrigues; student San Jose State Coll., 1948-50; m. Howard Baker, 1944 (div. 1954); 1 son, John (dec. 1960); m. 2d Kieth Siegrist, 1955 (dec. 1965); m. 3d Boris Stanley, 1969 (div. 1970). Owner, mgr. Town & Country Bottle Shop, Cupertino, Calif., 1950-70, Cupertino Liquors, Inc., 1958-70; owner, mgr. Alicia's Boutique, Cupertino, Calif., 1978—. Bd. dirs. San Jose Symphony, 1972-76, San Jose Light Opera, 1973-77, Cath. Social Service of Santa Clara County, 1974-77, YMCA of San Jose, 1974-76; pres. Crippled Children's Soc. of Santa Clara County, 1975-77; bd. dirs. Performing Arts League, 1975-80; active various polit. campaigns. Mem. Retail Liquor Dealers Assn. Roman Catholic. Club: Saratoga Country, La Rinconada Country. Home: PO Box 2824 Saratoga CA 95070 Office: PO Box 2824 Saratoga CA 95070

SIEGRIST, EDITH BARBARA, librarian; b. McIntosh, S.D., May 9, 1925; d. Bert and Nellie Siegrist; B.A. magna cum laude, Huron (S.D.) Coll., 1950; M.A., U. Denver, 1954. Elem. tchr. S.D. Public Schs., 1945-48, 50-53; asst. librarian No. State Coll., Aberdeen, S.D., 1954-55; librarian Everett High Sch., Lansing, Mich., 1955-61; asso. prof. library U. S.D., Vermillion, 1961—. Recipient Disting. Alumni award Huron Coll., 1973. Mem. ALA, Mountain Plains Library Assn., S.D. Library Assn., Delta Kappa Gamma (notable achievement award Eta chpt. 1982), Phi Delta Kappa. Republican. Presbyterian. Editor: Good Words: Notable Books on the American Indian, 1973; South Dakota editor, Great Plains Bibliography, 1979. Home: 854 Eastgate Dr Vermillion SD 57069 Office: I D Weeks Library U SD Vermillion SD 57069

SIEH, MAURINE KAY, nurse; b. Leon, Iowa, Sept. 28, 1950; d. Vernon Charles and Dorothy Maxine (Akes) Dobson; B.S. in Nursing, N.E. Mo. State U., 1972; m. Robert Hans Sieh, Nov. 18, 1972; children—Robert Carter, Jennifer Clarissa. Charge nurse psychiat. unit St. John's Hosp., Springfield, Mo., 1972-74; public health nurse Will County Health Dept., Joliet, Ill., 1974-75; unit nurse Mental Health Inst. Mentally Retarded Children, Park Forest, Ill., 1977-79; instr. Lamaze method childbirth, Park Forest, 1977-81; psychiat. nurse, chmn. nurse practice and standards com. Menninger Found., Topeka, 1981; nurse neuro-neurosurg. unit Univ. Med. Center, Jackson, Miss., 1981—. Fund raiser local chpts. Am. Cancer Soc., Mental Health Assn. Mem. Nat. Assn. Female Execs., Am. Soc. Psychoprophylaxis in Obstetrics. Mem. Brethren Ch. Home: 4953 Oak Leaf Dr Jackson MS 39212

SIEKIERSKI, KAMILLA MALGORZATA, dental lab. technician; b. Warsaw, Poland, Aug. 4, 1938; came to U.S., 1963, naturalized, 1970; d. Tomasz and Janina W. (Sendzimir) Piotrowski; cert. dental technician Sch. Dental Technicians, Krakow, Poland, 1957; m. Kazimierz Siekierski, Nov. 25, 1959; children—Marzanna, Eva. Owner, operator Kama's Dental Lab., Krakow, 1963; dental technician Dan's Dental Lab., Waterbury, Conn., 1963-65, Wilcox Dental Lab., Wethersfield, Conn., 1965-68; pres. Dentek, Inc., Milford, Conn., 1980—. Mem. Conn. Dental Lab. Assn. (pres. 1977-79), Nat. Assn. Dental Labs., Conf. Dental Labs. Home: 350 Gulf St Milford CT 06460 Office: 158 Cherry St Milford CT 06460

SIEKMANN, SHIRLEY JEANNE, arts adminstr.; b. South Bend, Ind., Aug. 31, 1928; d. George F. and Clarice B. (Rapp) Burdick; student St. Mary's Coll., 1946-47; B.A., DePauw U., 1950; postgrad. Ind. U., South Bend, 1951; m. Max R. Siekmann, June 23, 1951; children—Sheryl, Pamela, David. Tchr. public schs., St. Joseph County, Ind., 1950-51, Greencastle, Ind., 1951-52, Ft. Lauderdale, Fla., 1952-53; exec. dir. Michiana Arts and Scis. Council, Inc., South Bend, Ind., 1973—; tech. asst. cons., adv. panelist Ind. Arts Commn.; treas. Ind. Alliance Arts Councils, 1982—. Mem. St. Joseph County Parks and Recreation Bd., 1971-81; pres. Mental Health Assn. of St. Joseph County, 1972; bd. dirs. Century Center Found., South Bend, 1974-81, St. Joseph County Scholarship Found., 1977-82; pres., bd. dirs. United Way St. Joseph County. Recipient Community Service award Michiana Arts and Scis. Council, 1968. Mem. Ind. Arts Advs., Ind. Alliance Arts Councils, Nat. Assn. Arts Councils. Club: Jr. League South Bend (pres.). Producer 13 week TV series: Inside Our Schools (Jr. League of South Bend Outstanding Community Service award 1964), 1963. Office: 120 S St Joseph St South Bend IN 46601

SIEMENS, BARBARA WOLFE, architect; b. Fremont, Ohio, June 20, 1922; d. Stanley and Margaret (Bowlus) Wolfe; student Kent State U., 1940-41; B.Arch., Ohio State U., 1945; m. Miros Siemens, Oct. 26, 1947; children—Craig, Lucinda, Teresa, Nicholas, Clarissa, Mark, Claudia, Eugenia. Draftsman, Ohio State U., 1944-45; apprentice architect Huszagh & Demuth, Chgo., 1945-47; chief draftsman Herman Charles Light, 1947-48; architect Huszagh & Demuth, 1948-50; pvt. practice architecture, West Lafayette, Ind., 1953-70; chief architect H. Stewart Kline & Assos., Inc., West Lafayette, 1970—; career cons. Tippecanoe Sch. Corp., Lafayette, Ind. Vice pres. Tippecanoe Assn. Retarded Citizens, 1977-78, sec., 1979-80, dir., 1976-82; bd. dirs. Wabash Center, Inc., 1977-82, sec., 1979-80. Registered architect, Ohio, Ind. Mem. AIA (treas. Central So. Ind. chpt. 1977-78), Ind. Soc. Architects (dir. 1982), Nat. Assn. Women in Constrn. (founding pres. Lafayette chpt. 1977-78). Roman Catholic. Project architect Ind. Vocat. Tech. Coll., 1980. Home: 3233 State Rd 43 N West Lafayette IN 47906

SIETMAN, ANNETTE MARIE, enrolled tax agt.; b. Akron, Ohio, Mar. 13, 1944; d. Orville George and Ann Marie (Kloskowski) Seaver; B.S.Ed., Ohio State U., 1966; m. William Howard Ashcraft, Nov. 4, 1966 (dec. Dec. 1972); children—Julie, Joel; m. 2d, J. David Sietman, Mar. 22, 1974. Music tchr. Atherton Community Schs., Flint, Mich., 1966-67; music and math. tchr. Field Schs., Brimfield, Ohio, 1967-68; adminstrv. asst. H & R Block, Akron, 1970-72; bookkeeper Town & Country Interiors, Tallmadge, Ohio, 1972-75; owner Ashcraft-Sietman Tax & Acctg. Service, Kent, Ohio, 1976—; income tax instr., 1971-72. Treas., St. Patrick Home and Sch. Assn., 1977-80. Mem. Ohio Soc. Enrolled Agts. (pres. 1977-78, 78-79, dir. 1979-81), Nat. Assn. Enrolled Agts. (sec. 1979-80, dir. 1980—). Democrat. Roman Catholic. Home: 724 Grove Ave Kent OH 44240

SIFF, MARLENE IDA, artist, designer; b. N.Y.C., Sept. 20, 1936; d. Irving Louis and Dorothy Gertrude (Lahn) Marmer; B.A., Hunter Coll., 1957; m. Elliott Justin Siff, July 11, 1959; children—Bradford Evan, Brian Douglas. Tchr., Stewart Manor (N.Y.) Sch. System, 1957-59, Teaneck (N.J.) Sch. System, 1959-60; free lance interior designer Marlene Siff Interior Design Cons., Westport, Conn., 1966-70; interior designer indsl. plant Varo Inertial Products, Trumbull, Conn., 1970; corp. sec., treas., dir. Belmar Corp., Westport, 1972—; chmn. bd. Marlene Designs, Inc., Bridgeport, Conn., 1973-77; owner Marlene Siff Design Studio, Westport, 1978—; design cons. Conn. Digestive Disease Soc. Active fund raising coms. Levitt Pavillion of Performing Arts, Westport PTA, Temple Israel, Westport; bd. dirs. Westport United Jewish Appeal. Recipient Lower Conn. Mfrs. Assn. award for creating most beautiful working environment in lower Conn., 1970. Mem. Westport-Weston Arts Council, Nat. Council Jewish Women, Kappa Pi. Designer exterior, interior and grounds of her home and studio, 1965, decorative arts designs for wall hangings; designer signature pattern Tailored Elegance under name Marlene for nat. mass market distbn. J.P. Stevens Co., Inc.; designer signature collections Summer Fantasy, Windflowers, Glorious Morning for J.P. Stevens, It's the Berries Kitchen-dining-gift products coordinate program for J.C. Penney Co., 1978; La Salade Kitchen/desk accessories collection for C.R. Gibson Co., 1980; design work chosen by Easter Seal Home Service to decorate Grand Ballroom of Plaza Hotel, N.Y.C. for ann. charity ball, also designer invitation for ball, 1976. Studio: 125 Main St Westport CT 06880

SIGERSON, MARJORIE LORRAINE, librarian; b. Pitts., June 11, 1923; d. Roy Allen and Myrtle Mae (Bering) Parke; student Carnegie Inst. Tech., 1941-42, U. Pitts., 1942-43; m. David Kinley Sigerson, Apr. 9, 1943; children—Diane Parke, David Kinley. Librarian, Mus. Arts and Scis., Daytona Beach, Fla., 1963—, trustee, 1978—, pres. Guild, 1978-79. Mem. com. Halifax Art Festival, 1963—; mem. council Garden Clubs of Halifax Dist., 1965-67; charter mem. Ormond Beach (Fla.) Meml. Hosp. Aux., 1967-76; pres. Street Sch. P.T.A., New City, N.Y., 1958-59; leader Girl Scouts U.S.A., 1956-58; den mother Cub Scouts, 1959-60. Recipient award for disting. service, Mus. Arts and Scis., 1977, 79, 80, 81. Presbyterian. Clubs: Harvard Dames (sec. 1946-47), Atty.'s Wives of Halifax Area, Cherry Laurel Garden (pres. 1966-67), Oceanside Country (v.p. 9-Hole Golf Group). Home: 410 John Anderson Dr Ormond Beach FL 32074 Office: Museum of Arts and Sciences 1040 Museum Blvd Daytona Beach FL 32014

SIGLER, LOIS OLIVER, educator; b. Piney Flats, Tenn., Sept. 8, 1923; d. Willie Campbell and Lillie (Brown) Oliver; B.S. with 1st class honors, E. Tenn. State U., 1944; M.S., U. Tenn., 1952; m. William Virgil Sigler, Jr., Aug. 25, 1962; 1 son, William Oliver. Tchr. home econs. in Va., 1944-46; dist. supr. home econs. edn. Va. State Dept. Edn., 1946-54; asst. nat. adv. Future Homemakers Am. and New Homemakers Assn., 1954-56, nat. adv., 1956-63; coordinator Family Living Pilot Program, Columbus, Ohio, 1963; tchr. home econs., Millington, Tenn., 1966—; pres. Va. Sch. Food Service Assn., 1952-54, U.S. Adv. Com. on Youth Fitness, 1956-57, Food for Peace Council, 1961, Millington Central Elem. PTA, 1974-76; mem. Keep Am. Beautiful Com., 1962; adv. council Lab. Experiences Student Tchrs., Memphis State U., 1972-75. Named hon. mem. Future Homemakers Am.; Tenn. Home Econs. Tchr. of Yr., 1975. Mem. Am. Home Econs. Assn., Am. Vocat. Assn., Nat. Vocat. Home Econs. Tchrs. Assn., NEA, Tenn. Home Econs. Assn., Tenn. Vocat. Assn., Tenn. Vocat. Home Econs. Tchrs. Assn. (sec.-treas. 1974-75), Tenn. Edn. Assn. (dir. 1977-80), W. Tenn. Home Econs. Edn. Assn. (sec. 1972-73), W. Tenn. Edn. Assn., Shelby County Edn. Assn. (exec. com. 1976), Omicron Nu, Pi Lambda Theta. Methodist. Home: Route 3 Box 851 Millington TN 38053 Office: 8057 Wilkinsville Rd Millington TN 38053

SIGWARD, ANGELA COSUMANO, social work cons.; b. N.Y.C., Dec. 28, 1908; d. Vincent and Maria (Armato) Cosumano; B.A., Hunter Coll., 1930; M.A., Columbia U., 1934, M.S.W., N.Y. Sch. Social Work, 1939; postgrad. William Alanson White Inst., 1959; m. Roderick Sigward, Feb. 4, 1942; children—Ellen, Eric. Dir., Family Service of Jersey City, 1944-46; supr. med. social work Maimonides Hosp., Bklyn., 1958-60; with N.Y.C. Youth Bd., 1960-73, asst. dir. youth guidance, until 1973; sr. service adminstr. Group Health, Inc., N.Y.C., 1973-79, cons. social services, 1980—; pvt. practice social work, N.Y.C. Mem. Nat. Assn. Social Workers, Acad. Cert. Social Workers. Club: Women's City (N.Y.C.). Home: 350 Central Park W New York NY 10025 Office: Group Health Inc 326 W 42d St New York NY 10036

SIKORSKI, BERNADINE CAROL, coll. ofcl.; b. Amsterdam, N.Y., Feb. 21, 1951; d. Casimer Frank and Albina Stella (Krupa) S.; student Daemen Coll., Buffalo, 1969-71; B.S., No. Ariz. U., 1973, M.A., 1975; Ph.D., St. Louis U., 1978. Intern fin. aid office, admissions and records, security, career planning and placement center, Counseling Center, No. Ariz. U., Flagstaff, 1973-75, residence hall dir., 1973-75; residence hall coordinator Griesedieck Hall, St. Louis U., 1975-76, grad. asst. Project Cove, 1976-77, asst. dir. housing, acting dir. housing, 1976-78, coordinator student work, 1977-78, coordinator peer-counseling program, 1976-78, instr., 1976-77; dir. ednl. planning St. Edward's U., Austin, Tex., 1978-79; dean students Buena Vista Coll., Storm Lake, Iowa, 1978-81, v.p. for human resources, 1981—. Recipient Pres.'s Leadership and Service award, 1973, Hera award, 1973. Mem. Nat. Assn. Student Personnel Adminstrs., Nat. Assn. Women Deans, Adminstrs. and Counselors, Mortar Bd., Alpha Sigma Nu. Author: A Guide to Residence Hall Living, 1978. Home: 918 W 6th St Storm Lake IA 50588 Office: Buena Vista College Dixon Eilers 123 Storm Lake IA 50588

SILA, JOAN LEE, social worker; b. Benton Harbor, Mich., Sept. 4, 1949; d. Frank T. and Viola D. Sila; A.A., Lake Mich. Coll., 1970; B.A., John Carroll U., 1974; M.S.S.A., Case Western Res. U., 1977; postgrad. John Marshall Law Sch., Cleve. State U., 1979—. Asst. dir. social services Salvation Army, Cleve., 1977-79, coordinator home group for boys, 1979-81, dir. child conservation council, 1981-82; social service supr. Youth Devel. Center, Hudson, Ohio, 1982—. Mem. Nat. Assn. Social Workers, Acad. Cert. Social Workers, Nat. Council Crime and Delinquency, Am. Psychiat. Assn. Democrat. Roman Catholic. Home: 788 Babbitt Rd Euclid OH 44123 Office: 966 Hines Hill Rd Hudson OH

SILBER, DIANE BERMAN, psychologist; b. N.Y.C., Mar. 3, 1944; d. Nathan and Gertrude (Cohen) Berman; B.A., Bklyn. Coll., 1965; M.A., Temple U., 1967; Ph.D., Washington U., St. Louis, 1971; m. Igal Silber, Jan. 6, 1968. Staff psychologist Malcolm Bliss Mental Health Center, St. Louis, 1968; clin. psychology intern VA Hosp., St. Louis, 1968-71; staff psychologist St. Michael's Hosp., Toronto, Ont., Can., 1971-72; pvt. practice psychology, Orange, Calif., 1972—; cons. in field. Mem. Am. Psychol. Assn., Calif. Psychol. Assn., Orange County Psychol. Assn., Mo. Psychol. Assn., Am. Orthopsychiat. Assn. Office: 725 W La Veta St Suite 230 Orange CA 92668

SILBERBERG, KAYLA JUDITH, ednl. cons.; b. Bklyn., Jan. 28, 1932; d. David and Gussie Goldreich; B.A., N.Y.U., 1953; M.A., Columbia U., 1954; m. Martin Y. Silberberg, Nov. 28, 1957; children—Mina, Eve. Head coll. guidance, Tokyo, 1973-76; ednl. cons., prin., owner Chappaqua Coll. Counseling Service, 1976—; lectr. in field. Mem. Coll. Bd. Assn., Westchester Talent and Gifted Edn. Com., Westchester Assn. Women Bus. Owners, Women Working Home Assn. Jewish. Address: 83 Old Lyme Rd Chappaqua NY 10514

SILBOR-DAMASO, MARIA ERLINDA, med. technologist; b. Iloilo, Philippines, Mar. 28, 1954; came to U.S., 1976; d. Andrew and Inocencia (Argenal) Silbor; B.S., U. Santo Tomas, Manila, 1973; diploma med. tech., Central Philippine U., 1975. Med. technologist Sacred Heart

Hosp., Richwood, W.Va., 1976-77, Greenbrier Valley Hosp., Ronceverte, W.Va., 1977-78, W.Va. Sch. Osteo. Medicine, Lewisburg, 1978; phlebotomist Riverside Hosp., North Hollywood, Calif., 1981—. Mem. Am. Med. Technologists Assn. Roman Catholic. Home: 812 N Dillon St Los Angeles CA 90026 Office: 12629 Riverside Dr North Hollywood CA 91607

SILGE, JUDITH RAYNEE, acoustical contracting co, exec; b. Atwater, Minn., Jan. 11, 1941; d. Homer Richard and Ruth Alice (Helpenstein) Curtiss; acctg. degree LaSalle Extention U., 1972; postgrad. Mankato (Minn.) State U.; m. Norman Hans Silge, Feb. 26, 1970; children—Kristine Mary, Douglas James. Office mgr. Kato Entertainment Center, Mankato, Minn., 1965-70, Hendley's, Inc., Mankato, 1968-69, Scheels Hardware and Sporting Goods, Inc., Mankato, 1969-80; office mgr., sec.-tres. Midwest Sound Control, Inc., Eagle Lake, Minn., 1970—. Mem. Bus. And Profl. Women, Women in Constrn., Mankato Better Bus. Bur., Indian Lake Area Preservation Assn. Rupublican. Roman Catholic. Club: Zonta. Home: 166 Terrace View E Mankato MN 56001 Office: Lohr Indsl Park Eagle Lake MN 56024

SILKO, LESLIE MARON, playwright, author, poet, educator; b. N. Mex., 1949; B.A. summa cum laude, U. N. Mex. Writer-in-residence U. Mont., Vassar Coll.; vis. prof. fiction U. Wash.; now asst. prof. English, U. Ariz., Tucson; author: Laguna Woman (poetry), 1974, Ceremony (novel), 1978, Storyteller (short stories), 1981; playwright one act play for Am. Bicentennial Theater Project, San Francisco, 1976. Recipient Poetry award Chgo. Rev., 1974, Pushcart prize for poetry, 1977, MacArthur prize, 1982; Nat. Endowment for Arts writer's fellow, 1974; Woodrow Wilson fellow. Office: Dept English U Ariz Tucson AZ 85721 *

SILLARS, PATRICIA ANN, social worker; b. Columbus, Ga., Nov. 30, 1942; d. Arthur Harold Hale and Martha Ellen (Yates) Barnard; student Bethany Coll., 1961-63; A.B., U. Mich., 1968, M.S.W., 1972; 1 son, Rosh Ian. Therapist, Grand Blanc (Mich.) Mental Health Services, 1972-73; field coordinator Big Bros. Greater Flint (Mich.), 1974-80; eligibility technician Park County Dept. Pub. Welfare, 1981—. Precinct del. Democratic party, Genesee County, Mich., 1970-78; treas. Genesee County campaign Shirley Chisholm for Pres., 1972; bd. mem. Peace Watch of Flint, 1971-72; mem. Housing Opportunities Made Equal, 1966-69. Mem. Acad. Cert. Social Workers, Nat. Assn. Social Workers, NOW (v.p. Flint chpt. 1970), Profl. Assn. Flint Community Schs., Cousteau Soc. Unitarian. Home: PO Box 114 Pray MT 59065

SILLIMAN, ELAINE JOYCE RUBENSTEIN, speech pathologist, educator; b. Buffalo, June 16, 1938; d. Joseph and Dorothy Fineberg Rubenstein; B.S., Syracuse U., 1960; Ph.D. (NDEA fellow), CUNY, 1976; m. Paul Harris Silliman, Jan. 28, 1961; children—Scott L., Dawn R. Speech-lang. clinician Bronx Mcpl. Hosp. Center, 1960-62; supr. speech-lang. services USPHS community health project Albert Einstein Coll. Medicine, Bronx, 1966-68; clin. supr. Center for Communication Disorders, Hunter Coll., CUNY, 1973-76, asso. prof. Sch. Health Scis., 1976—, dir. communication scis. program, 1981—. Mem. Am. Speech-Lang.-Hearing Assn. (cert. of clin. competence), New Eng. Child Lang. Assn., N.Y. Acad. Scis., N.Y. State Speech-Lang.-Hearing Assn. (pres. 1982-84), Westchester Speech-Lang.-Hearing Assn., Sigma Xi. Office: Sch of Health Scis Hunter Coll City U NY 425 E 25th St New York NY 10010

SILLS, BEVERLY (MRS. PETER B. GREENOUGH), coloratura soprano; b. Bklyn., 1929; grad. public schs.; student voice Estelle Leibling, piano Paolo Gallico, stagecraft Desire Defrere; hon. doctorates Harvard U., N.Y.U., New Eng. Conservatory, Temple U.; m. Peter B. Greenough, 1956; stepchildren—Lindley, Nancy, Diana; children—Meredith, Peter B. Radio debut as Bubbles Silverman on Uncle Bob's Rainbow House, 1933; appeared on Maj. Bowes Capitol Family Hour, 1938-41, Our Gal Sunday; operatic debut Phila. Civic Opera, 1947; toured with Shubert Tours, Charles Wagner Opera Co., 1950, 51; debut with N.Y.C. Opera Co., 1955, as Rosalinda in Die Fledermaus; debut San Francisco Opera, 1953, La Scala, Milan, 1969, Royal Opera, Covent Garden, London, 1971, Met. Opera, N.Y.C., 1975; debut, Paris, 1971; appeared throughout U.S., Europe, S.Am., including Vienna State Opera, Teatro Fenice, Venice, Teatro Colon, Buenos Aires, Deutsche Oper, West Berlin, Teatro San Carlo, Naples, 1966; guest appearances with Boston Symphony, Tanglewood Festival, 1968, 69, Robin Hood Dell, Phila., 1969, N.Y. Philharm., San Francisco Symphony, Cleve. Orch., Phila. Orch.; star roles in Handel's Julius Caesar, Manon, La Traviata, Tales of Hoffman, Lucia di Lammermoor, Roberto Deveraux, Anna Bolena, Maria Stuarda, Siege of Corinth, Thaïs, Don Pasquale; gen. dir. N.Y.C. Opera, 1979—; ret. from opera and concert stage, 1980. Named One of America's 25 Most Influential Women in 1977, World Almanac, 1978; recipient Handel medallion, 1973; Pearl S. Buck Women's award, 1979; Medal of Freedom, 1980. Author: Bubbles-A Self-Portrait, 1976. Office: care Edgar Vincent Assos 124 E 40th St New York NY 10016

SILLS-LEVY, ELLEN, bank exec.; b. N.Y.C., Mar. 14, 1942; d. Lewis M. and Diana B. Sills; B.A. cum laude with honors in Econs., Bklyn. Coll., 1963; M.B.A., Columbia U., 1965. Market research analyst Gen. Foods Corp., White Plains, N.Y., 1965-67; v.p., sr. asso. research dir. BBDO, Inc., N.Y.C., 1967-77, etat dir. TEAM/BBDO, Dusseldorf, W. Ger., 1977-78; v.p., mgr. research and bus. devel. Needham, Harper & Steers, Inc., N.Y.C., 1979; v.p., dir. research TBWA, N.Y.C., 1979-80; v.p., dir. communications Citibank, N.Y.C., 1980—; guest speaker Am. Mgmt. Assn., Bank Mktg. Assn. N.Y.U., Columbia U.; mem. faculty New Sch. Social Research. Assoc. bd. dirs. Hosp. Joint Diseases. Mem. Am. Mktg. Assn., Women in Communications, Fin. Women's Assn. (bd. dirs. Fin. Research Council), Public Assn., Soc. Am., Bank Mktg. Assn., Advt. Women N.Y. Club: Columbia Bus. Sch. Office: Citibank 399 Park Ave New York NY 10043

SILTON, BARBARA J., ednl. center adminstr.; b. Fresno, Calif.; d. Joe and Leota S.; B.A., Calif. State U., 1972; M.A., U. San Francisco, 1980, Ph.D. in Psychology, 1983. Counselor, tchr. Yakima Indian Center, Santa Rosa, Calif., 1974-75; hosp.-home instrn. multi-handicapped Los Angeles Unified Sch. Dist., Berenece Carlson Sch., 1974-80; dir. Noble Ednl. Center, Inc., Woodland Hills, Calif., 1975—, dir. Ednl. Therapy Center and Clinic, 1975—, pres. Noble Ednl. Therapy Found.; cons. pvt. schs., including Montessori Sch. Santa Monica. Mem. Council Exceptional Children, Calif. Assn. Ednl. Therapists. Co-founder Noble Method, remediation system for learning disabilities. Office: 22008 Del Valle St Woodland Hills CA 91364

SILVA, MACEL LAVERNE, educator; b. Sayre, Okla., Nov. 18, 1933; d. Lathan Ross and Cullie Mae (Mathews) Ford; B.S., San Jose State U., 1973, M.B.A., 1974; Ph.D., Calif. Western U., 1977; m. Abel Joseph Silva, July 17, 1954; children—William, Steven, James, David, Diane, Christopher. With Gen. Electric Co., San Jose, Calif., 1956-57, Santa Clara (Calif.) Police Dept., 1968, GTE Sylvania Co., Mountain View, Calif., 1959-60, Santa Clara Police Dept., 1961-62; library asst. James Lick High Sch., San Jose, 1964; with Lockheed Co., Sunnyvale, Calif., 1966-67; owner, mgr. Hobby Shop, San Jose, 1967-69; instr. Mountain View (Calif.) Adult Edn., 1971-74, San Jose State U., 1974-78; instr. San Jose City Coll., 1976-79, Ohlone Coll., Fremont, Calif., part time 1979-80; mgr. adminstrv. services U.S. Fleet Leasing, San Mateo, Calif., 1979-80; data processing systems coordinator Santa Clara County Dept. Edn., Santa Clara, Calif., 1980—; pres. Profl. Solutions, Inc., San Jose, 1981—. Treas. troop Boy Scouts Am., 1978-80; Mem. No. Calif. Hobby Assn. (sec. 1968-69), Adminstrv. Mgmt. Soc. (v.p. 1978), Adult Edn. Assn. (pres. 1973), Calif. Tchrs. Assn. Roman Catholic. Author: Modern Office Management, 1974; Records Management, 1975; Modern Office Duplicating, 1976. Office: 51 Pala Ave San Jose CA 95127

SILVA, MARUJA RODRIGUEZ, social worker; b. Santiago, Chile, Apr. 18, 1928; came to U.S., 1958, naturalized, 1964; d. Juan Rodriguez Nieto and Dionisia (Pelaez) Rodriguez; B.A., U. Miami, 1971; M.S.W., Barry Coll., 1973; Ed.D., Nova U., 1980; m. Sergio Silva, Oct. 3, 1948; 1 son, Vincente A. Social worker bilingual and bicultural program spl. edn. Cath. Service Bur., Archdiocese of Miami (Fla.), 1973-74; cons. Probate Ct. for Involuntary Admission to State Instn., 1974-76; cons. Diagnostic Evaluation Regional Div. Mental Retardation, Miami, 1974-75; counselor young epileptics and families Epilepsy Found., Miami, 1975-78; asst. prof. pediatrics, coordinator bilingual program U. Miami Mailman Center, 1974—. Mem. adv. bd. Marian Center Services for Developmentally Handicapped and Mentally Retarded, 1977—; group leader parents and teenage siblings retarded children N. Dade Children's Center, 1975-77; family counselor devel. Disabled Mailman Center, 1972-73. Mem. Acad. Cert. Social Workers, Nat. Assn. Social Workers, Am. Assn. Sex Educators, Counselors and Therapists, Fla. Assn. Clin. Social Workers, Dade County Assn. Retarded Citizens, Psi Chi, Epsilon Tau Lambda, Phi Lambda Pi, Mortar Bd. Home: 27 Hunting Lodge Dr Miami Springs FL 33166 Office: 1601 NW 12th Ave Miami FL 33136

SILVER, BELLA WOLFSON, day care center exec.; b. N.Y.C., Mar. 10, 1937; d. David Michael and Edith (Bienenstock) Wolfson; B.S., Adelphi U., 1958; postgrad. Bank St. Coll., 1958-59; m. Kenneth A. Silver, Oct. 19, 1958; children—James, Daniel. Kindergarten tchr., N.Y.C., 1958, Madison (Wis.) Public Schs., 1959-61, White Fish Bay (Wis.) Public Schs., 1961-65; nursery sch. tchr., Deerfield, Ill., 1975-77; substitute tchr. Deerfield Public Schs., 1975-77; founder., dir., pres. Deerfield Day Care Center, 1978—. Mem. Deerfield Caucus; active Cub Scouts, Deerfield, Outstanding Service award 1973-77; mem. exec. bd. Jewish United Fund; sec. Parents-Tchrs. Orgn. Recipient award Bahais of Deerfield, 1981; teaching cert., Wis., Ill.; lic. tchr., N.Y.C. Mem. AAUW, Assn. Childhood Edn. Internat., Nat. Assn. Edn. Young Children, Chgo. Assn. Edn. Young Children, Nat. Assn. Female Execs., Deerfield C. of C., Phi Sigma Sigma (Pyramid award 1965). Jewish. Home: 309 Willow Ave Deerfield IL 60015 Office: 445 Pine St Deerfield IL 60015

SILVER, HELENE MARCIA, health educator; b. Oakland, Calif., Apr. 2, 1947; d. Sam and Shirley Betty (Kerns) Silver; B.A., UCLA, 1968; postgrad. San Francisco State Coll., 1970-72, Holistic Life U., 1978-79, Antioch U., 1979-80. Tchr. public schs., Oakland, 1968-76; nutritional counselor, Mill Valley, Calif., 1976-79; creator Women's Health Intensive, Mill Valley, 1977-79; project dir. nutrition edn. project Calif. Dept. Edn., San Rafael, Calif., 1979-80; founder, dir. Inst. of Colon Hygiene, San Rafael, 1980—; health edn. cons., 1976—; mem. Health Task Force in Marin County, 1978—. Mem. Soc. Nutrition Edn., AAUW, Prison Reform Assn. Author: Inner Beauty/Outer Beauty. Home: PO Box 348 San Quentin CA 94964 Office: 807 4th St San Rafael CA 94901

SILVER, JOAN MICKLIN, film dir., screenwriter; b. Omaha, Nebr., May 24, 1935; d. Maurice David and Doris (Shoshone) M.; B.A., Sarah Lawrence Coll., 1956; m. Raphael D. Silver, June 28, 1956; children—Dina, Marisa, Claudia. Dir., screenwriter films including Hester Street, 1975, Bernice Bobs Her Hair, 1976; dir. Between the Lines, 1977; producer On the Yard, 1978; dir., screenwriter Head Over Heels, 1979. Mem. Women in Films, Dirs. Guild Am., Writers Guild Am. Democrat. Jewish. Office: 600 Madison Ave New York NY 10022

SILVER, JOYCE ALAINE, banker, pharm. mfg. co. exec.; b. N.Y.C., Dec. 2, 1942; d. Leo and Ida Vera Silver; B.A., Simmons Coll., Adelphi U., 1962; M.S., L.I. U., 1973; Ph.D. candidate Cornell U. Med. Center, N.Y. U. Med. Center, 1973-76; div.; children—Edward Erik, Lisa Sheryl. Research fellow Cornell U.-N.Y. U. Med. Center, 1973-76; supervising engr., plant trouble shooter Ford Motor Co., Dearborn, Mich., 1976-79; with Pfizer, Inc., Bklyn., 1979-82, sr. mfg. supr. diagnostics and sterile products, 1981-82, mgr. materials resource planning, mgr. pharm. warehousing, distbn. ops., 1981-82; v.p. customer service Bankers Trust Co., N.Y.C., 1982—. Lobbyist, Continuation of NSF Funds, 1974; mem. Com. to Re-Elect Carol Berman, Senator, 1979. NIH Fellowship, 1973-76; L.I. U. Teaching Fellowship and Scholarship award, 1971-73. Mem. AAAS, Fedn. Am. Scientists, Engring. Soc. Detroit, N.Y. Acad. Sci., Women's Economic Club Detroit, N.Y. Women's Bus. and Profl. Group, N.Y. Networking. Office: One Bankers Trust Plaza New York NY 10015

SILVER, JUDITH L., artist; b. N.Y.C., Nov. 30, 1950; d. Henry A. and Shiprah Silber; B.F.A., Phila. Coll Art, 1972; M.F.A., Md. Inst.Coll. 1974; m. Richard Thorp, Nov. 20, 1970. Instr. painting Md. Inst. Coll. Art, 1973-74, No. Va. Community Coll., 1974-75; instr. color and design Community Coll. Balt., 1976; Rome prize fellow Am. Acad. in Rome, 1976-78; instr. Canberra, (Australia), Sch. Art, 1981—; one-man shows Hardart Gallery, Washington, 1975, Am. Acad. Rome, 1977, 78, Gallery Huntley, Australis, 1981, Gallery A, Sydney, Australis, 1981. Mem. exec. com. Canberra Opera, 1982—; exec. com. A.C.T. Crafts Council, 1983. Mem. Soc. Fellows Am. Acad. in Rome. Clubs: Univ., House, Nat. Press (Canberra). Home: 26 Arthur Circle Forrest ACT 2603 Australia Office: care Mitchell/Giurgola 170 W 97th St New York NY 10025

SILVER, LILLIAN WEBER, arts adminstr.; b. N.Y.C., Mar. 30, 1942; d. Simon and Sylvia (Lehrer) Weber; A.B. magna cum laude, Syracuse U., 1962; cert. in arts adminstrn. Harvard U., 1976; m. Philip M. Silver, Dec. 30, 1962; children—Daniel David, Elise Beth. Tchr., French and Italian, Benjamin Franklin High Sch., Rochester, N.Y., 1963-65; owner, mgr. Stern/Weber Art Gallery, Rochester, 1969-71; asst. arts dir. Jewish Community Center, Rochester, 1972-75; exhibit cons. Xerox Corp., Rochester, 1972-75, Ont. Sci. Center, Toronto, 1976-77; exec. dir. Rochester Bus. Com. for the Arts, 1976-80; project dir. planning study for proposed performing arts theater, Rochester Cultural Center, 1981; cons. arts and community programs. Mem. Women in Communications (Clarion award hon. mention 1975), Am. Councils Arts, Phi Beta Kappa. Jewish. Creator, producer participatory exhbns. and catalogue on curiosities and deceptions in art and other disciplines.

SILVER, LYNDA JOYCE, educator; b. Many, La., Sept. 14, 1947; d. Marvin and Evelyn Annabelle (Willecke) S.; B.S., Ind. U., 1970, M.S. 1971; student U. Ala., 1972. Grad. asst. audio visual motion picture dept. Ind. U., Bloomington, 1970-71; asst. dir., curriculum design specialist, Russellville, Ala., 1971-72; asst. prof. sch. edn. Ala. A. & M. U., Huntsville, 1972-73; dir. dept. media resources Huntsville Hosp., 1973-75; edn. specialist Staff and Faculty Tng. div. U.S. Army Armor Sch., Ft. Knox, Ky., 1975-77, chief staff and faculty tng. div., supervisory edn. specialist, 1978—; media cons. Mem. Assn. Ednl. Communications Tech., Am. Soc. Tng. and Devel., Assn. U.S. Army, Ind. U. Alumni Assn. Author articles in field. Office: Staff and Faculty Tng Div US Army Armor Center and Fort Knox Fort Knox KY 40121

SILVER, PAULA FRANKL, educator; b. Poughkeepsie, N.Y., Dec. 2, 1934; d. William and Frances (Lerner) F.; B.A., Hunter Coll., 1957; M.A., N.Y.U., 1971, Ph.D., 1973; Tchr. English, N.Y.C. Sch. System, 1957-71; assoc. dir. Univ. Council Ednl. Adminstrn., Columbus, Ohio, 1973-76; assoc. prof. ednl. leadership U. Tulsa, 1976-81; assoc. prof. ednl. adminstrn. U. Ill., Urbana, 1981—; cons. Inst. Ednl. Adminstrn., Victoria, Australia, 1980, 82. NDEA fellow Russian Lang. Inst., 1964; Walter E. Anderson fellow, N.Y.U., 1971-73. Mem. Am. Ednl. Research Assn., Nat. Soc. Study Edn., Phi Delta Kappa. Contbr. articles to profl. jours. Home: 2910B W John St Champaign IL 61820 Office: Coll Edn U Ill Urbana IL 61801

SILVER, RUTH STANLIE SMITH (MRS. HAROLD F. SILVER), civic and ch. worker; b. Salt Lake City, Nov. 1, 1930; d. Joseph F. and Ruth (Pingree) Smith; B.S., U. Utah, 1952; M.A., U. Hawaii, 1955; m. Harold F. Silver, Sept. 16, 1964. Missionary, Ch. of Jesus Christ of Latter-day Saints, 1955-56; grad. asst. speech dept. U. Hawaii, Honolulu, 1952-54; instr. dept. speech Ch. Coll. Hawaii, Laie, Oahu, 1957-60; instr. dept. speech Brigham Young U., Provo, Utah, 1960-62, 63-64; instr. dept. speech Colo. Womens Coll., Denver, 1966, 77. Mem. Sec.'s Com. on Automated Personal Data Systems for HEW, 1972-73; treas. Hilltop Area unit Denver Symphony Guild, 1969-73, sec. exec. bd., 1969-71, asst. sec., 1971-73, membership chmn., 1972-73, mem. young artists' competition com. 1972-73, pres. elect, 1973-74, pres., 1974-75; sec. Colo. Women's Coll. Library Assocs., 1968-70, pres., 1970-72, membership v.p., 1972-74; bd. dirs. Denver Lyric Opera, 1967-70, guild dir., 1968-69, asst. sec. guild, 1971-72; bd. dirs. Denver Civic Ballet, 1967-74, pres. guild, 1977-78, now mem. guild; bd. dirs. Passages, 1982, Young Artists' Orch. of Denver, 1982 trustee Colo. Womens Coll., 1976—; mem. Children's Hosp. Aux.; sec. Central City Opera Guild, 1979-80, chmn. edn., 1980-81. Mem. Nat. Soc. Gen. Semantics, Nat., Colo. (pres. Gamma Gavaliers Unit 1981-82) assns. parliamentarians, Denver U. Women's Library Assn., Chi Omega, Phi Kappa Phi. Mormon. Clubs: Jane Herrick Literary (pres. 1967-68, treas. 1972-73), Zonta (hon.); U. Denver Women's (bd. dirs. 1982-83). Home: 315 Clermont St Denver CO 80220

SILVERA, MARJA MARKETTA, computer services co. exec.; b. Helsinki, Finland, Mar. 17, 1943; came to U.S., 1965, naturalized, 1982; d. Esko Erkko and Kirsti Elina Pammo; B.S. in Econs., Turun Kauppakorkeakoulu, Turku, Finland, 1964; m. Ron Silvera, Sept. 10, 1966. Asst. to econ. attaché Am. Embassy, Bern, Switzerland, 1964-65; asst. editor Ann. Revs., Palo Alto, Calif., 1965-66; programmer Computer Control, Syracuse, N.Y., 1967-69; programmer analyst Computer Synergy, Oakland, Calif., 1969-73; with Xerox Computer Services, South San Francisco, Calif., 1973—, mktg. rep., 1976-78, mktg. mgr., 1978-79, br. mgr., 1979-82, region mgr., 1982—. Named PAR Club pres. Xerox Computer Services, 1977. Mem. Am. Prodn. and Inventory Control Soc. (pres. Golden Gate chpt. 1979-80), Sales and Mktg. Execs. Assn. Home: 99 Tappan Ln Orinda CA 94563 Office: 343 Allerton Ave South San Francisco CA 94080

SILVERBERG, HARRIET ANNE, publicist; b. Washington, Mar. 2, 1937; d. David Eleck and Sophie (Taetle) Snyder; student George Washington U., 1954-55; m. Stanley M. Silverberg, Aug. 28, 1955; children—Denise, Marc. Free-lance public relations work, Washington, 1955-80; advance public relations person Ladybird Johnson Train, 1964; with Smithfield Ham Products (Va.), 1962-75; part-time public relations asst. George Reedy, Lyndon Johnson Adminstrn., 1964-65; with L.N. Hill Co., Rockville, Md., 1968-70; dir. promotion WAVA FM radio, Arlington, Va., 1977-80; pres. Harriet Silverberg Assos. Potomac, Md., 1980—. Bd. dirs. Washington chpt. Am. Diabetes Assn., 1959—, pres.-elect, nat. bd. dirs., 1975-81, vice chmn. communications com., 1976-77; chmn. publicity Montgomery County Youth Orch., 1975; treas. Congregation Beth El Sisterhood, 1965-70; bd. dirs. United Jewish Appeal Women's Div., 1980-82, Am.-Israeli Cultural Found., 1982—, Nat. Health Council, Washington, 1978-82. Recipient Maurice Protas award Am. Diabetes Assn., 1976. Mem. Public Relations Soc. Am. Democrat. Jewish. Club: Advt. of Washington. Address: 8401 Pittsfield Ct Potomac MD 20854

SILVERMAN, BERNICE GRACE ABEL, steel products co. exec.; b. Chgo., Apr. 19, 1932; d. Jacob Israel and Celia (Surkin) Abel; student U. Ill., U. Chgo., De Paul U., m. William J. Silverman, Mar. 14, 1959; children—Robin Lee, Jaci Lynn. Owner, operator Best Locker Service, Washington, 1968—; pres., chief operating officer, dir. Best Steel Products, Inc., Washington, 1975—. Active Multiple Sclerosis Soc., Am. Cancer Soc. Mem. Nat. Automatic Merchandising Assn., Internat. Assn. Amusement Parks and Attractions, Internat. Council Shopping Centers, NOW. Clubs: Hadassah (life), B'nai B'rith (life). Office: 5540 Connecticut Ave NW Washington DC

SILVERMAN, CAROL R., social worker; b. Bklyn., Sept. 11, 1942; d. Ben L. and Sylvia G. Gardner; B.S., U. Bridgeport, 1964; postgrad. Grad. Sch. Social Work, Hunter Coll. 1964-66; m. Gerard Silverman, Aug. 21, 1966; children—Adam, Daniel. Social worker Kings County Psychiat. Hosp., Bklyn., 1966-68, Bklyn. Bur. Community Service, 1968-70, Bklyn. VA Hosp., 1970—; pvt. practice psychotherapy, 1980—; faculty adv. Adelphi Sch. Social Work, 1977—; adv. bd. Women to Women (breast cancer hotline), 1982—. NIMH grantee, 1966-68. Mem. Nat. Assn. Social Workers, Acad. Cert. Social Workers, Nat. Kidney Found. Council Social Work. Home: 11 Brevoort Pl Rockville Centre NY 11570 Office: 800 Poly Pl Brooklyn NY

SILVERMAN, FRANCES R., lawyer; b. Warsaw, Poland, Apr. 1, 1912; d. Morris and Esther G. (Goldberg) Rosenfeld; came to U.S. 1920, derivative citizen; student N.Y. U., 1930, Hunter Coll., 1930-35; LL.B., Bklyn. Law Sch., St. Lawrence U., 1937, LL.M., 1938; m. S. Robert Silverman, June 9, 1937; children—Janet Lee Silverman Galison, Marsha Gail Silverman Firestone. Admitted to N.Y. bar, 1938; law clk. Rappaport Bros., 1937-38; asst. adminstr. records women's div. United Jewish Appeal, 1939; exec. sec. L.I. and Queens women's div. Am. Jewish Congress, 1946-49; partner firm Silverman, Silverman & Seligman, Schenectady, 1949—. Chmn. legis. com. Schenectady chpt. Nat. Council Jewish Women, 1949-50; publicity chmn. Schenectady chpt. Hadassah, 1951-52, v.p. program, 1956; pres. Sisterhood of Nott Terr. Synagogue, 1960; dir. clubs Jewish Community House of Bensonhurst, 1939-41. Mem. N.Y. State (exec. com. workers compensation div. negligence, ins. and compensation law sect.), Schenectady County, N.Y. Workers Compensation bar assns., Assn. Trial Lawyers Am., Women's Bar Assn. State N.Y., N.Y. State Trial Lawyers Assn., Nat. Orgn. Social Security Claimants' Reps. Home: RD 2 Box 432 Rexford NY 12148 Office: 650 Franklin St Schenectady NY 12305

SILVERMAN, HELEN, psychologist; b. N.Y.C., Dec. 11, 1937; d. Hyman and Jeanne Worthman; B.A. cum laude, CCNY, 1957, M.S., 1961; Ph.D., Columbia U., 1968; postdoctoral cert. in psychanalysis, N.Y. U., 1973. Asst. prof. S.E.E.K. Program, psychol. counselor CUNY, 1968-71; asst. prof., psychol. counselor Baruch Coll., CUNY, 1971-76; pvt. practice psychotherapy and psychoanalysis, N.Y.C., 1968—. NIMH postdoctoral fellow, 1970-71. Mem. Am. Psychol. Assn., N.Y. State Psychol. Assn., N.Y.U. Postdoctoral Program Psychoanalytic Soc. (sec.), Sigma Xi, Psi Chi. Office: 100 Riverside Dr New York NY 10024

SILVERMAN, SANDRA THERESE, police officer; b. Atlantic City, Dec. 20, 1949; d. Sebet and Lillian B. Silverman; student Douglass Coll., Rutgers U., 1967-69; grad. New Haven Police Acad., 1976; m. Paul Allen Souder, Dec. 14, 1974. Officer, New Haven Police Dept., 1976—, investigator sexual assault investigation team, 1977—, victim service specialist, 1978, juvenile diversion screener, 1979-81, investigator detective div., 1981-82; co-coordinator nat. rape task force NOW, 1976-77; asso. Jennifer Macleod Assos., Princeton Junction, N.J., 1972-75; feminine cons., lectr. in field. Recipient cert. of commendation New Haven Police Dept. Mem. Conn. Assn. Women Police. Author: You Won't Do: What Textbooks on U.S. Government Teach High School Girls, 1973; also articles. Address: 115 Bishop St New Haven CT 06511

SILVERMAN, SHERLEY, artist; b. Maywood, Ill., Jan. 20, 1909; d. Adam and Elizabeth (Portnoy) Sher; student U. Ill., 1927-28, Chgo. Acad. Fine Arts, 1932-35, pvt. studies; m. I.J. Silverman, Oct. 27, 1928; 1 son, Bernard W. Exhibited in one-man shows in Thor Gallery, Louisville, 1967, Covenant Club, Chgo., 1968, B'nai B'rith Exhbn. Hall, Washington, 1969; exhibited in group shows Salon Internat. de Charleroi, Belgium 1968, Dibuix Premi Internat. Joan Miro, Barcelona, Spain, 1970-73, Galleria D'Arte La Scala, Di Firenze, 1971, Gallery Benhur Sánchez, Bogotá, Columbia, Barry Cleaving, New Zealand; represented in permanent collection B'nai B'rith Hdqrs., Washington, pvt. collections. Recipient Internat. Medal of Honor, Internat. Centro Studi E. Scambi, 1971; Acad. Internat. Leonardo Da Vinci, 1971; Silver medal (hon.) Acad. Internat., Campanella, 1972; Gold medal Recognition and Bronze plaque La Scala Gallery, Florence, Italy, 1972; Cert. of Merit, Internat. Dictionary, 1973. Mem. N. Shore Art League, Internat. Arts Guild (comdr. 1965—), Suburban Fine Art League, Com. Gold Coast Art Fair, U.S. Com. Internat. Centro Studi E, Scambi, Acad. Internat. Leonardo De Vinci, Mid-Am. Art Assn. (pres. 1969-71, recipient award Recognition), Acad. Internat. Home: 9240 W Bay Harbor Dr Bay Harbor Island FL 33154 Studio: 1045 NE 125th St North Miami FL 33161

SILVERSTEIN, MIRA, needlepoint designer, writer; b. Rumania, May 31, 1923; came to U.S., 1940, naturalized, 1945; d. Morris and Sara (Racenberg) Magaziner; m. Irwin M. Silverstein, Mar. 14, 1948; children—Shari, Dean, Elise, Joshua. Tchr., designer needlework; author books include: Fun with Bargello, 1971; Fun with Applique, 1973; Bargello Plus (recipient Nat. Graphics award 1974), 1973; Needlepoint on a Shoestring, 1974; Guide to Slanted Stitches, Guide to Upright Stitches, Guide to Looped and Knotted Stitches, Guide to Combination Stitches, 1977; International Needlework Designs, 1978. Mem. N.Y. State Craftsmen, Inc., Embroiderers Guild, Nat. Assn. Artists in Fiber Media (founding dir.).

SILVERSTEIN, SUSAN SOLOMON, human service cons.; b. Bklyn. Dec. 15, 1951; d. Herbert and Gerry (Bloom) Solomon; B.A. in Psychology, Hofstra U., 1973; M.S.W., Adelphi U., 1977; m. Clifford Silverstein, Mar. 15, 1980. Intake coordinator Woodward Sch. for Emotionally Disturbed, Freeport, N.Y., 1972-73; clin. coordinator Nassau House, Inc., Mineola, N.Y., 1976-78; dir. Women's Center of Central Nassau, Franklin Square, 1974-76; human service cons. Eli Silverstein Inc./Feetstreet Ltd., Huntington, N.Y., 1978—; founder, dir. Littlefolks Learning Center, 1982—. Recipient award for spl. achievement in personel motivation and communication Women's Center of Central Nassau, 1980. Mem. Nat. Assn. Female Execs., Nat. Retail Mchts. Assn. Democrat. Home: Wooley Ln E Great Neck NY 11021 Office: 276 Main St Huntington NY 11743

SILVESTRI, SUSAN MARIE COWLES, speech/lang. pathologist; b. Cleve., June 20, 1950; d. Clifford L. and Julia M. (Peters) Cowles; B.S. in Speech Pathology and Audiology, Kent State U., 1972; M.S. in Communication Disorders, William Paterson Coll. of N.J., 1974; m. Richard Silvestri, Apr. 8, 1972; 1 dau., Kate. Pvt. practice speech therapy, Glen Rock, N.J., 1976—; speech/lang. pathologist Pequannock (N.J.) Twp. Schs., 1974-79; dir. speech and lang. services Comprehensive Counseling Center, North Haledon, N.J., 1976—; speech/lang. cons. Human Services Center, Fair Lawn, N.J. Active non-profit counseling centers, vol. cons. and tester; mem. PTO. Mem. Am. Speech, Lang. and Hearing Assn., N.J. Speech and Hearing Assn., Morris County Speech and Hearing Assn., N.J. Edn. Assn., NEA. Contbr. articles to profl. publs. Home: 590 Doremus Ave Glen Rock NJ 07452 Office: 5 Sicomac Rd North Haledon NJ 07508

SIMMONDS, MARY ANNE, oncologist; b. Danville, Pa., Nov. 16, 1949; d. Henry T. and Harriet Anne Lynn S.; A.B., Smith Coll., 1971; M.D., Med. Coll. Pa., 1975; m. Richard W. Stewart, June 7, 1975. Resident in internal medicine Geisinger Med. Center, Danville, Pa. 1975-78; fellow in hematology Thomas Jefferson U., Phila., 1978-80; fellow in oncology Hershey Med. Center (Pa.), 1980-81; asst. prof. oncology Pa. State U. Med. Coll., Hershey, 1981—. Bd. dirs. Pa. div. Am. Cancer Soc., 1981—. Am. Cancer Soc. jr. faculty fellow, 1981—; Kate Hurd Mead fellow, 1982—; diplomate Am. Bd. Internal Medicine. Mem. AMA, ACP, Am. Fedn. Clin. Research, Central Pa. Oncology Group, Sigma Xi, Alpha Omega Alpha. Republican. Presbyterian. Club: Jr. League Harrisburg. Home: 1811 Warren St New Cumberland PA 17070 Office: Hershey Med Center Hershey PA 17033

SIMMONS, ANITA RUTH, ednl. adminstr.; b. Jersey City, Apr. 20, 1943; d. Lawrence Ambrose and Ruby Mae (Reid) Dorsey; B.S. in Biology, Stillman Coll. 1965; M.Ed. in Ednl. Adminstrn. and Supervision, U. Ga., 1973; m. Craig Edward Simmons, Aug. 5, 1981; children—Melanie Robinson, Danys Robinson. Tchr. biology Peter G. Appling High Sch., Macon, Ga., 1965-67; tchr. adult edn. Bibb County Adult Edn. Program, Macon, 1965—; profl. actress Kaleidoscope Players, Raton, N. Mex., 1967-68; tchr. advanced biology Dudley Hughes High Sch., Macon, 1968-70; asst. prin. Southwest High Sch., Macon, 1970-79; prin. Ballard A. Jr. High Sch., Macon, 1979—. Mem. ad hoc com. Gov.'s Task Force on Adult Edn.; pres. PTA Winship Sch., 1976, 77; chmn. bd. St. Agnes Day Care Center, 1979—. Woodrow Wilson fellow, 1964. Mem. Ga. Assn. Public Sch. Adult Educators, Bibb Assn. Educators, Nat. Assn. Public Sch. Adult Educators, Nat. Assn. Educators, Ga. Assn. Secondary Sch. Prins. Roman Catholic. Home: 1578 N Atwood Dr Macon GA 31204 Office: 1780 Anthony Rd Macon GA 31204

SIMMONS, BARBARA ANN, tech. editing services co. exec.; b. Indpls., May 8, 1941; d. Robert Donald and Mary Elizabeth (Fitzpatrick) Munro; B.A., Purdue U., 1963; m. Edward Earl Simmons, Jr., Aug. 8, 1964; 1 dau., Kathryn Mary. Tech. editor Research Inst., Ill. Inst. Tech., Chgo., 1963-67; operational services supr. Booz, Allen Applied Research, Chgo., 1968-69; editor Warren King & Assos., Chgo., 1969-70; staff editor Hosps., Am. Hosp. Assn., Chgo., 1970-73; tech. editor Inst. Gas Tech., Chgo., 1973-76; mng. editor Mktg. Digests, Northfield, Ill., 1976-79; owner Tech. Editing Services, Skokie, Ill., 1975—. Recipient awards Soc. Tech. Communications, 1974, 77, 78, 82. Mem. Soc. Tech. Communication (chmn. Chgo. chpt., sec. Standards Council), Women in Communications, AAAS, Phi Mu. Roman Catholic. Home and Office: 4943 Fairview Ln Skokie IL 60077

SIMMONS, BETTE RUTH, educator; b. Bison, Okla., Aug. 11, 1926; d. Thomas Harvey and Wilma Ivy (Tuggle) Reeder; B.S. in Secondary Edn., Okla. Bapt. U., 1948; M.A. in Edn., Ariz. State U., 1966; m. Donald G. Simmons, Dec. 19, 1952; children—Timothy D., Stephen E. Instr., Hitchcock (Okla.) High Sch., 1948-50, Capital Secretarial Coll., Oklahoma City, 1956-58, Walker AFB, Roswell, N.Mex., 1961-62, Lamson Bus. Coll., Tucson, 1962-64; mem. faculty Phoenix Coll., 1966—, now prof. dept. bus., coordinator specialized programs in court reporting, legal sec., and word processing, chmn. evening div., dept. bus.; mem. office edn. instrn. council Maricopa Community Coll. Dist. Mem. Nat. Bus. Edn. Assn. (named Postsecondary Tchr. of Yr. 1978), Western Bus. Edn. Assn., Ariz. Bus. Edn. Assn., Nat. Shorthand Reporters Assn., Internat. Word/Info. Processing Assn., Profl. Secs. Internat., Delta Pi Epsilon, Delta Kappa Gamma. Home: 3802 N 15th Dr Phoenix AZ 85015 Office: Phoenix Coll 1202 W Thomas Rd Phoenix AZ 85013

SIMMONS, BRENDA JILIENNE, nurse; b. N.Y.C., Nov. 2, 1947; d. Alphonso and Lucinda (Simmons) Wright; B.S. in Nursing, Adelphi U., Garden City, N.Y., 1969; M.S. (NIMH grantee), N.Y.U., 1975; m. Lawford M. Campbell, June 20, 1976; 1 son, Jonathan Alphonzo Campbell. Psychiat. staff nurse Montifiore Med. Hosp. Center, N.Y.C., 1969-73; pre-kindergarten nurse, 1973-74; geriatric supr. Morningside House, Bronx, N.Y., 1974-75; adult psychiat. supr. Albert Einstein Coll. Medicine, Bronx, 1975—. Cert. nursing adminstr. Mem. Am. Nurses Assn., N.Y. State Nurses Assn. (chmn. grievance com. 1977-78), N.Y. Black Nurses Assn. (dir. 1976-78, chmn. fund raising com. 1977-78), Sigma Theta Tau. Democrat. Baptist. Home: 140 16 Asch Loop Bronx NY 10475 Office: Bronx Mcpl Hosp Center Bronx NY 10461

SIMMONS, CAROL VIVIAN, nursing home adminstr.; b. Toledo, Feb. 27, 1942; d. Cledith H. and Aretta J. (Burnette) Jump; cert. nursing Ind. Vocat. Tech. Coll., 1962; cert. long term care adminstrn., Ind. U., 1975; m. Paul D. Simmons, May 28, 1960; children—Donald, Jonathon, David. Head nurse, supr. Fountainview Place, Elkhart, Ind., 1972-78; adminstr. Fountainview Place, Goshen, Ind., 1978-80, Fountainview Place, Mishawaka, Ind., 1980—; preceptor/adminstr. Nat. Assn. Bds. Examiners for Nursing Home Adminstrs. Mem. Ind. Citizens League of Nurses, Ind. Assn. Quality Assurance Profls., Bus. and Profl. Women, Nat. Assn. Female Execs., Ind. Health Care Assn. (edn. com.), Ind. Fedn. Lic. Practical Nurses (pres.. 1975-78), Am. Legion Aux. Mem. Missionary Ch. (sec.). Club: Altrusa (dir.). Home: 23685 Arlene St Elkart IN 46517 Office: Tangelwood Dr Mishawaka IN 46544

SIMMONS, CAROLINE THOMPSON, civic worker; b. Denver, Aug. 22, 1910; d. Huston and Caroline Margaret (Cordes) Thompson; A.B., Bryn Mawr Coll., 1931; m. John Farr Simmons, Nov. 11, 1936; children—John Farr (dec.), Huston T., Malcolm M. Chmn. women's com. Corcoran Gallery Art, 1965-66; vice chmn. women's com. Smithsonian Assos., 1969-71; pres. Decatur House Council, 1963-71; mem. bd. Nat. Theatre, 1979-80; trustee Washington Opera, 1955-65; bd. dirs. Fgn. Student Service Council, 1956-79; mem. Washington Home Bd., 1955-60; bd. dirs. Smithsonian Friends of Music, 1977-79; commr. Nat. Mus. Am. Art, 1979-81; mem. Folger com. Folger Shakespeare Library, 1979—; mem. Washington bd. Am. Mus. in Britain, 1970—; bd. dirs. Found. Preservation of Historic Georgetown, 1975—; trustee Amherst Coll., 1979-81, Bacon House Found.; v.p. internat. council Mus. Modern Art, N.Y.C., 1978—; mem. council Phillips Collection, 1982—; bd. dirs. Alliance Francaise. Mem. Soc. Women Geographers. Presbyterian. Clubs: Sulgrave, Chevy Chase, 1925 F Street. Address: 1508 Dumbarton Rock Ct Washington DC 20007

SIMMONS, DIANE EILEEN, profl. soc. exec.; b. New Smyrna Beach, Fla., Jan. 28, 1950; d. George Andrew and Carolyn Margaret (Cross) Naser; A.A., Daytona Beach Community Coll., 1971; student U. N.C., 1978, Stanton U., 1978; B.S., U. S. Fla., 1980; m. Paul L. Simmons, June 2, 1973; children—Thomas David (dec.), Paula Kay. Pres., Fla. Trade Publ., Daytona Beach, Fla., 1971-74; project engr. Pollak & Skan Inc., Rosemont, Ill., 1977-78; mgr. S.E. region, 1978-79; exec. dir. Internat. Soc. Pharm. Engrs., Tampa, Fla., 1979—; exec. dir. Seminars, Inc., Tampa, Fla., 1978—. Mem. Parenteral Drug Assn., ASME, Nat. Assn. Female Execs. Republican. So. Baptist. Pub., FACT mag., 1971-74; editor Pharm. Engring. Jour., 1979—. Office: 15943 N Florida Ave PO Box 17758 Tampa FL 33682

SIMMONS, ELLAMAE, allergist; b. Mt. Vernon, Ohio, Mar. 26, 1919; d. Augustus Lawrence and Ella Sophia (Cooper) Simmons; R.N., Hampton Inst., 1940; B.S., Ohio State U., 1948, M.A., 1950; postgrad. Meharry Med. Coll., 1954-55; M.D., Howard U., 1959. Intern, Wayne County (Mich.) Gen. Hosp., Eloise, 1959-60, resident, 1960-62; resident U. Colo. Med. Center, 1962-63, resident in chest medicine Nat. Jewish Hosp., 1964, resident in allergy, 1965; psychiat. nurse Central State Hosp., Petersburg, Va., 1940-41; allergist Permanente Med. Group Kaiser Found. Hosp., San Francisco, 1966—; mem. admissions com. U. Calif. at San Francisco Sch. Medicine, 1974-78. Chmn. No. Calif. Mut. Real Estate Investment Trust, 1967-68. Served with nurses corps U.S. Army, 1942-46. Mem. Am. Acad. Allergy, Am. Coll. Allergy, Am. Assn. Clin. Allergy and Immunology, John Hale Med. Assn., AMA, Nat., Calif., San Francisco med. assns., Am. Med. Womens Assn., Am. Lung Assn., Am. Thoracic Soc. Unitarian. Home: 3711 Clay St San Francisco CA 94118 Office: 2200 O'Farrell St San Francisco CA 94115

SIMMONS, FLORENCE FENELLA WHIPPLE, author; b. Ledyard, Conn., Dec. 22, 1902; d. Thomas Geer and Lillian (Phillips) Whipple; student U. Okla., U. Colo.; m. Hiram Irving Simmons, Apr. 9, 1927; 1 dau., Joyce Simmons Kuhn. Bookkeeper, collections mgr. Conn. Power Co., New London, 1922-27; asst. mgr. sch. savs. dept. Savs. Bank New London, 1931-36; free-lance writer; author: (novel) The Boundless Quest, 1962; Book of Verse: For Lovers, 1982; contbr. articles, book revs., poems to mags., newspapers, anthologies; lectr. Ikebana Internat., Denver, 1960-70, UN Assn., 1965-69. Mem. Poetry Soc. Colo., Nat. League Am. Pen Women, Acad. Am. Poets (assoc.). Address: 615 N Delaware St Independence MO 64050

SIMMONS, GWENDOLYN PATIENCE, personnel mgr.; b. New Brunswick, N.J., Jan. 11, 1945; d. James Weldon and Deborah Gwendolyn S.; A.B., Syracuse U., 1967; M.B.A., Fordham U., 1973. Personnel asst. United Parcel Service, N.Y.C., 1967-69; asst. to dir. housing N.Y. Urban Coalition, N.Y.C., 1969-72; office mgr. Webb, Brooks & Booker, N.Y.C., 1972; asst. to exec. dir. Harlem Teams for Self-Help, Inc., N.Y.C., 1973-75; exec. dir. CETA/OJT Uptown C. of C., N.Y.C., 1975-76; personnel mgr. ARA Services, Inc., White Plains, N.Y., 1976-79; mgr. employment Xerox Learning Systems, Stamford, Conn., 1979—. Mem. Nat. Assn. Female Execs., Employment Mgrs. Assn. Office: 1600 Summer St Stamford CT 06940

SIMMONS, HELEN MARIE, govt. ofcl.; b. Beaver City, Nebr., Aug. 22, 1920; diploma Lincoln (Nebr.) Sch. Commerce, 1938; m. Robert Owen Simmons, Oct. 5, 1947 (dec. Jan. 1979). Various secretarial positions, 1941-42; with Dept. Agr., 1942—, adminstrv. asst. Office Gen. Counsel, Shawnee Mission, Kans. and Kansas City, Mo., 1966—. Recipient Superior Service award Dept. Agr., 1964. Mem. Assn. Legal Adminstrs., Mem. Christian Ch. (Disciples of Christ). Home: 12021 W 66th St Shawnee KS 66216 Office: 9435 Holmes Kansas City MO 64141

SIMMONS, JEAN, actress; b. London, Eng., Jan. 31, 1929; d. Charles and Winifred Ada (Loveland) Simmons; ed. Orange Hill Sch., Burnt Oak, London; m. Stewart Granger, Dec. 20, 1950 (div. June 1960); 1 dau. Tracy; m. 2d, Richard Brooks, Nov. 1, 1960; 1 dau., Kate. Motion picture actress, appearing in English and Am. films, including Great Expectations, Black Narcissus, Hamlet, The Actress, Guys and Dolls, Young Bess, Adam and Evelyn, Big Country, 1958; Home Before Dark, 1958; Spartacus, Elmer Gantry, 1959; The Grass Is Greener, 1960; All the Way Home, 1963; Rough Night in Jericho; Divorce American Style; The Happy Ending; also theatre appearance A Little Night Music, Phila. and on tour, 1974; appeared in TV mini-series The Dain Curse, 1978, A Small Killing, 1981, Valley of the Dolls, 1981. Office: Care William Morris Agy Inc 151 El Camino Beverly Hills CA 90212 *

SIMMONS, MARY RUTH, computer specialist; b. Waldorf, Md., Apr. 7, 1925; d. Henry Dyer and Bertha Evelyn (Cooke) Middleton; student Am. U., 1967, Auburn U., 1977—; m. David Martin Simmons, June 26, 1943; children—David Martin, Robert Michael, Thomas Wayne, Carol Ann, Frank Paul, John Edward. Sec., Dept. Treasury, CSC, Washington, 1942-51; with Middleton & Middleton, Waldorf, Md., 1951-59; with Tri County Fed. Savs. & Loan Assn., Waldorf, 1959-65, asst. mng. officer, 1964-65; programmer, systems analyst USAF, Bolling AFB, Washington, 1966-70; computer specialist, Air Force Data Systems Design Center, Gunter AFS, Montgomery, Ala., 1970—, team leader, 1979—. Mem. Assn. Computing Machinery, Data Processing Mgmt. Assn., Federally Employed Women (charter pres.). Republican. Roman Catholic. Clubs: Ballroom Dance (charter pres.), Toastmistress. Home: 2761 Knollwood Dr Montgomery AL 36116 Office: AFDSDC/LGS Bldg 888 Gunter AFS AL 36114

SIMMONS, NOLA ANN, religious orgn. adminstr.; b. Knoxville, Iowa, Aug. 7, 1937; d. Harley Hanford and Edna Pearl (Wynn) Cox; student State U. Iowa, 1955-57; m. Jerry Laird Simmons, May 27, 1957; children—Christopher Laird, David Harley. Office mgr. Red Ball Engring. and Constrn. Co., Inc., Iowa City, 1957-61; owner, artist Fertile Earth Boutique, San Francisco, 1967-68; ordained to ministry Ch. of Scientology, San Francisco Acad., 1968; sec.-treas. Ch. of Scientology Mission of Davis (Calif.), 1969-71; co-dir. Ch. of Scientology Mission of South Bay, Redondo Beach, Calif., 1972—; pres. bd. dirs., exec. dir. Ch. of Scientology Mission of Long Beach (Calif.); hon. pub. relations officer for L. Ron Hubbard, founder Scientology; pastrol counsellor; chaplain; Hubbard profl. auditor. Mem. Citizen's Commn. for Human Rights, Los Angeles; mem. Nat. Commn. on Law Enforcement, Social Justice; mem. Ministry Pub. Relations, Los Angeles. Recipient Spl. Power award Office of Guardian, 19—, Tech. Upstat award Auditor's Assn., 1976, Triple Grades award Ch. of Scientology, San Francisco, 1969. Mem. Hubbard Assn. Scientologists Internat., Ch. of Scientology Mission Network Worldwide, Am. Citizens for Honesty in Govt., NOW, Internat. Soc. Artists, Met. Museum Art (asso.), Auditor's Assn., Abilities Research Assos. (asso.). Club: Foresters. Office: 1261 Long Beach Blvd Long Beach CA 90813

SIMMONS, PEGGI FRANCES, public relations exec.; b. Mpls., Nov. 23, 1944; d. Arthur Frederick and Marion Rose (Mousseau) S.; B.S., Hofstra U., 1966; m. Craig A. Altschul, Dec. 7, 1974. Tchr., Am. Sch. System, W.Ger., 1966-69; media buyer J. Walter Thompson Advt. Co., N.Y.C., 1969-72; adminstrv. asst. Nat. Council YMCAs, N.Y.C., 1972-74; partner, v.p. Craig Altschul & Assos., New Haven, 1974—. Bd. dirs. Camp Hazen YMCA, Women in Leadership honoree, 1979; vol. Planned Parenthood; docent Peabody Mus. of Yale U. Mem. Internat. Assn. Bus. Communicators.

SIMMONS, SUZANNE ISABELLE, public sch. tchr.; b. Akron, Ohio, Nov. 3, 1941; d. Willie Fate and Virgin Hazel (Varner) S.; B.A., Ohio U., Athens, 1963; M.A. in Teaching, Antioch Coll., Yellow Springs, Ohio, 1968. Tchr., Morgan Community Sch., Washington, 1967-69; counselor Project Crossroads, Washington, 1969-70; edn. dir. Council Econ. Opportunities, Cleve., 1972-74; tng. dir. Martin L. King Hosp., Los Angeles, 1974; exam. asst. Los Angeles Sch. Dist., 1974-75, summer 1976-77; tchr. Inglewood (Calif.) Sch. Dist., 1975—; mem. home econs. adv. council Cleve. Bd. Edn., 1973; bd. dirs Johnnie Tillmon Child Devel. Center, Los Angeles, 1974; cons. in field, rep. numerous ednl. coms. Chmn., Friends of the Avalon-Carver Community Center, Los Angeles, 1982. Recipient Service award Nat. Com. Children and Youth, 1970; grantee Nat. Tchr. Corps, 1966-78. Mem. Am. Fedn. Tchrs., Nat. Assn. Female Execs., Media Forum, Black Women's Forum, Women's Network, Alpha Kappa Alpha. Republican. Mem. A.M.E. Zion Ch. Home: 4335 Don Tomaso Dr Apt 3 Los Angeles CA 90008 Office: 3200 W 104th St Inglewood CA 90303

SIMMONS, SYLVIA, advt. agy. exec.; b. N.Y.C.; d. Noah and Lena Simmons; B.A., Bklyn. Coll.; M.A. in English Lit., Columbia U.; m. Hans H. Neumann, 1962. Dir. sales promotion dept. McCann Erickson, Inc., N.Y.C., 1957-62; v.p., asst. to pres. Young & Rubicam, Inc., N.Y.C., 1962-73; sr. v.p. spl. projects Kenyon & Eckhardt, Inc., N.Y.C., 1975—. Recipient Medal of Freedom, 1946. Author: New Speakers Handbook, 1972; The Great Garage Sale, 1982; How To Be The Life of the Podium, 1982; co-author: The Straight Story on VD, 1974. Office: Kenyon & Eckhardt 200 Park Ave New York NY 10166

SIMMONS, SYLVIA JEANNE QUARLES (MRS. HERBERT G. SIMMONS, JR.), coll. adminstr.; b. Boston, May 8, 1935; d. Lorenzo Christopher and Margaret Mary (Thomas) Quarles; B.A., Manhattanville Coll., 1957; M.Ed., Boston Coll., 1962; m. Herbert G. Simmons, Jr., Oct. 26, 1957; children—Stephen, Alison, Lisa. Montessori tchr. Charles River Park Nursery Sch., Boston, 1965-66; registrar Boston Coll. Sch. Mgmt., Chestnut Hill, Mass., 1966-70; dir. fin. aid Radcliffe Coll., Cambridge, Mass., 1970-75, asso. dean admissions and fin. aid, 1972-75, asso. dean admissions, fin. aid and women's edn., 1975; asso. dean admissions and fin. aid Harvard and Radcliffe, from 1975; asso. v.p. for acad. affairs, central adminstrn. U. Mass., Boston, 1976—, spl. asst. to chancellor, 1979—; v.p. field services Mass. Higher Edn. Assistance Corp., 1982—; mem. faculty Harvard U.; cons. Mass. Bd. Higher Edn., 1973—. Bd. dirs. Rivers Country Day Sch., Weston, Mass., Simon's Rock Coll., Great Barrington, Mass., Wayland (Mass.) Fair Housing, Cambridge Mental Health Assn., Family Service Greater Boston, Concerts in Black and White, Mass. Higher Edn. Assistance Corp.; trustee and alumnae bd. dirs. Manhattanville Coll. Mem. adv. com. Upward Bound, Chestnut Hill Boston Coll., 1972-74; Camp Chimvey Corners, Becket, Mass., 1971-77. Named One of Ten Outstanding Young Leaders, Boston Jr. C. of C., 1971; recipient Bicentennial medal Boston Coll., 1976; Achievement award Greater Boston YMCA, 1977. Mem. Women in Politics, Nat. (exec. council 1973-75), Eastern (1st v.p. 1973) assns. financial aid officers, Coll. Scholarship Service Council, Links, (pres. local chpt. 1967-69), Nat. Inst. Fin. Aid Adminstrs. (dir. 1975—), Jack and Jill Am. (pres. Newton chpt. 1972-74, Delta Sigma Theta, Delta Kappa Gamma. Club: Manhattanville (pres. Boston 1966-68). Home: 3 Dean Rd Wayland MA 01778 Office: 330 Stuart St Boston MA 02116

SIMMONS, THELMA JOHNSON, social worker; b. Watonga, Okla., Jan. 6, 1937; d. Edward Eli Johnson; B.S.W., U. Kans., 1975; M.S.W., 1976; divorced; children—Lawrence, Gerald, Pamela, Andrea, Sheila, Rhonda. Office mgr. North Shore Unitarian Ch., Deerfield, Ill., 1969-71; adminstrv. asst. Med. Center Women, Kansas City (Kans.), 1972-73; sch. social worker spl. service Kansas City (Kans.) Public Schs., 1976-77; sch. social worker diagnostic services Shawnee Mission (Kans.) Public Schs., 1977—; cons. in field. Del., Nat. Women's Polit. Caucus, 1973; adv. bd. Johnson County Mental Health Assn., 1979, Cedar House, Inc., Olathe, Kans, 1979—; citizens adv. bd. Johnson County Community Coll., 1982—. Recipient various service awards. Mem. Jack and Jills (chpt. pres. 1981—), NAACP (br. v.p. 1977—). Home: 13010 Piccadilly Circle Apt 1 Shawnee Mission KS 66215 Office: 4900 Parish Dr Shawnee Mission KS 66205

SIMMONS, VIRGINIA LEE COWAN, ednl. adminstr.; b. Ft. Wayne, Ind., May 17, 1921; d. James Clarence and Julia (Webster) Cowan; A.B., Ind. U., 1942, Ed.S., 1970; M.S., Butler U., 1957; postgrad. U. Wis., 1964-67; m. Eric L. Simmons, Apr. 25, 1943 (div. 1948); children—Nancy Lee (Mrs. Roy Green), Eric Leslie. Market research analyst McCann-Erickson, Chgo., 1944-48; retail mcht. Aquatic Galleries, Cin.,

1949-52; sales, alvt. Empire Tropical Fish Import Co., N.Y.C., 1952-53; Direct Mail Advt., Halvin Products, Bklyn., 1953-55; tchr. Indpls. Sch. 76, 1955-60; asst. prin. Sch. 61, 1960-61, asst. prin. Sch. 101, 1962-63; prin. Lew Wallace Sch. 107, Indpls., 1964-72, Frances Bellamy Sch. 102, Indpls., 1972-74, William H. Evans Sch. 95, Indpls., 1974-80, G.B. Loomis Sch. 85, Indpls., 1980-82; cons. prin., Indpls., 1982—; program supr. audio-visual center Ind. U., Bloomington, 1961-62; lectr. Butler U., summer 1965; cons. Ind. U., summer 1969. Contbg. mem. Childrens Mus.; mem. Indpls. Mus. Art, Indpls. chpt. Project HOPE; sponsoring mem. Met. Indpls. TV Assn., Inc., 1969-73; coordinator Christmas gift and hobby show Indpls. Public Schs., 1969-75. Bd. dirs. Young Audiences of Ind., 1969-80, co-chmn., 1976-78, chmn., 1977-78; bd. dirs. Indpls. chpt. Freedoms Found. at Valley Forge, 1st v.p., 1971-73, 75-77, pres., 1973-75, v.p., 1977—, also awards, 1977—. Recipient Am. Educators medal Freedoms Found., 1972. Mem. NEA (life), Ind. U. Alumni Assn. (life), Indpls. Zool. Soc. (charter), Ind. Tchrs. Assn., Bus. and Profl. Women's Clubs, Inc., Indpls. Council Adminstrv. Women Edn., (dir.), Nat. Soc. Study Edn., Nat. Congress Parents and Tchrs., Butler U. Alumni Assn., Nat. Elem. Prin. Assn., Ind. Edn. Art Assn., Hoosier Salon, Assn. Supervision and Curriculum Devel., Internat. Reading Assn., Indpls. Art League, Brown County Art Gallery Assn., AAUW, Izaak Walton League Am., DAR, Alpha Chi Omega, Delta Kappa Gamma, Phi Delta Kappa (hon.), Pi Lambda Theta. Methodist. Clubs: Ind. Schoolwomens; Century, Indpls. Propylaeum, Indpls. Athletic, Women's Dept. Author monographs. Home: 5715 N Meridian St Box 689005 Indianapolis IN 46268

SIMMONS-WILLIS, BEVERLEY, social worker; b. Chgo., Sept. 30, 1941; d. Ward and Louise (Baskin) Simmons; A.A., Wilson Jr. Coll., 1962; B.A., Roosevelt U., Chgo., 1964; A.M., U. Chgo., 1970; m. Johnnie E. Willis, Oct. 8, 1966. Caseworker, supervising caseworker Cook County (Ill.) Dept. Public Aid, Chgo., 1964-72; caseworker, program coordinator Family Service Bur., United Charities Chgo., 1972-78; coordinator children and adolescent services Chgo. Health Dept., Mental Health Div., 1978—; family therapist, cons. parent effectiveness tng. Cert. social worker, Ill. Mem. Acad. Cert. Social Workers, Nat. Assn. Social Workers, Nat. Assn. Black Social Workers. Office: 1971 W 111 St Chicago IL 60643

SIMMS, MARY MARGARET, physician; b. San Antonio, Aug. 7, 1951; d. Arthur and Helen Anna (Heme) Simank; B.A., Trinity U., 1973; M.D., U. Tex. at San Antonio, 1977; m. Ronald Alan, July 20, 1973; children—Jenny Anne, Adam Bardley. Rotating intern, gen. med. officer, 1977-79; practice medicine specializing in family medicine, San Antonio, 1979-81; staff physician VA Out-Patient Clinic, Lubbock, Tex., 1981-82, also Southcross Minor Emergency Center, San Antonio. Served with U.S. Army, 1977-79. Mem. Tex. Med. Assn., Bexar County Med. Soc., Nat. Assn. VA Physicians, Am. Coll. Gen. Practice. Lutheran. Home: 326 Lorene San Antonio TX 78209 Office: 3930 E Southcross San Antonio TX 78222

SIMON, ALYCE, artist; b. N.Y.C.; d. Irving and Sophie Rothlein; student Pratt Inst., 1939-40, Bklyn. Mus. Art Sch., 1941-42, Art Students League, 1942-43, Syracuse U., 1943-44; children—Michael Scott, Russell Roy. Pres., Alyce Simon Art and Design, N.Y.C., 1974—; partner, art cons. Fred Kolber & Co., N.Y.C., 1981—; numerous one-man shows of paintings and/or sculpture including: Hunter Coll., N.Y.C., 1966-67, Smithsonian Instn., Washington, 1969-70, Ont. (Can.) Mus. Centennial Centre, 1970, Washburn Gallery, Hayden Planetarium, Boston, 1970-71, Palais de Exhibition, Geneva, 1971, Petit Palais Musee, Geneva, 1971, Marcus Jewelry, N.Y.C., 1972, Benson Gallery, Bridgehampton, N.Y., 1972, Weiner Gallery, N.Y.C., 1977, Crickett Club Gallery, Miami, Fla., 1976-79, UN Plaza, N.Y.C., 1980-81; numerous group shows Fine Arts Galleries, Carnegie Inst. Pa., 1942-45, Bklyn. Mus., 1946-50, 68-69, Jersey City Mus., 1964, Nat. Acad. Fine Arts, N.Y.C., 1967-68, 72, Audubon Artists, N.Y.C., 1967, Galerie Internationale, N.Y.C., 1972; represented in permanent collections: Chitose Corp., Tokyo, Albert Knox Mus., Buffalo, numerous pvt. collections. Dir. fin. Internat. Women's Arts Festival, Internat. Women's Yr., 1975-76. Recipient numerous art awards including Carnegie Inst., 1941-44, Bklyn. Mus., 1945, 46, 47, 49, 50, Citta di Reggio award Centro Internazionale di Arte e Cultura, 1982. Mem. Carmel Hist. Soc., Pacific Asian Soc., Womens Econ. Round Table, U.S. Trotting Assn., Women Bus. Owners of N.Y., Experiments in Art and Tech. Republican. Developer technique of using atomic energy art form using high voltage electron energy sources. Address: 860 United Nations Plaza New York NY 10017

SIMON, CARLY, singer, composer; b. June 25; d. Richard Simon; studied with Pete Seeger; m. James Taylor, 1972; children—Sarah Maria, Benjamin Simon. Singer, composer, rec. artist, 1971—. Recipient Grammy award as best new artist, 1971. Albums include Carly Simon, 1971, Anticipation, 1972, No Secrets, 1973, Hotcakes 1974, Playing Possum, 1975, The Best of Carly Simon, 1975, Another Passenger, 1976 Boys in the Trees, 1978, Spy, 1979, Come Upstairs, 1980; single records include Nobody Does it Better, 1977, Torch, 1981. Address: care Arlyne Rothberg Inc 145 Central Park W New York NY 10023 *

SIMON, CHERYL ANN, communications exec.; b. Pottsville, Pa., Dec. 23, 1950; d. Andrew George and Eleanor Helen (Pomian) Hauslyak; student Union County Coll., 1975-77; programming diploma Chubb Inst., 1982; m. Leo Simon, Dec. 11, 1971; 1 dau., Eleanor Louise, Stenographer, Bell Telephone Labs., Piscataway, N.J., 1969-70; with Merck Sharp & Dohme Research Labs., Rahway, N.J., 1970—, group leader Vydec Machines, Med. Affairs Internat., 1975-79, supr. word processing/communications center, 1979—; lectr. Named Sec. of Yr., Union County chpt. Profl. Secs. Internat., 1979-80, N.J. Div., 1980-81; Young Career Woman, Bus. and Profl. Women's Club, 1979; cert. profl. sec. Mem. Profl. Secs. Internat., Internat. Info./Word Processing, Nat. Assn. Female Execs. Contbr. articles to profl. jours. Office: 126 E Lincoln Ave Rahway NJ 07065

SIMON, CHRISTINE COPLEY, state ofcl.; b. Trenton, N.J., Dec. 18, 1948; d. George Dewey and Veronica Helene (Mislan) Simon; student Bucks County Community Coll.; B.A., Lehigh U., 1976, M.A., 1978; children—Stacey, Jack. With Proctor & Gamble, Trenton, N.J., 1969-72; summer cities youth counselor, Bethelehem, Pa., 1975; hist. interpretor U.S. Park Service, Ind. Nat. Park, Phila., 1976; research asst. Sch. Edn., Lehigh U., and Law Enforcement Assistance Agy., Bethelehem, Pa., 1976-77; teaching asst. Lehigh U., 1977-78; field housing service coordinator N.J. Dept. Community Affairs, Toms River, 1978-81, sr. project specialist, 1981—; cons. if field. Vol. researcher N.J. Network TV, Trenton, 1981. Univ. Trustee scholar, 1974-76. Mem. Internat. Reading Council, Ocean County Women's Network, Assn. for Female Execs., NEA, Ocean County Council Social Services. Club: Toms River High Booster's. Contbr. articles to profl. jours. Office: 240 Main St Toms River NJ 08753

SIMON, COSETTE RENEE, assn. exec.; b. Ft. Wayne, Ind., June 18, 1953; d. William Arthur and Lucretia Ann (Hunt) Blanchard; B.A. magna cum laude, Ball State U., 1974; m. James Allen Simon, July 12, 1970. Feature writer Kokomo (Ind.) Tribune, 1974-75; public relations dir. Knightridge Mgmt. Co., Ft. Wayne, 1975-77; editor publs. Indiana and Mich. Electric Co., Ft. Wayne, 1977-80; exec. dir. Ft. Wayne YWCA, 1980—. Mem. adv. bd. Big Brothers-Big Sisters; bd. dirs. Ft. Wayne Flood 82, Inc. Mem. Ft. Wayne Women's Bur. (dir.), Women in Communications Inc. (past pres.), Internat. Assn. Bus. Communicators, NOW, Ft. Wayne Feminists. Democrat. Methodist. Home: 234 Indianola St Fort Wayne IN 46825 Office: 2000 Wells St Fort Wayne IN 46808

SIMON, DOROTHY MARTIN, chemist, bus. exec.; b. Harwood, Mo., Sept. 18, 1919; d. Robert William and Laudell (Flynn) Martin; A.B., S.W. Mo. State U., 1940; Ph.D., U. Ill., 1945; postdoctoral work Cambridge (Eng.) U., 1953-54; Sc.D. (hon.), Worcester Poly. Inst., 1971; D.Eng. (hon.), Lehigh U., 1978; m. Sidney L. Simon, Dec. 6, 1946 (dec. Nov. 1975). Grad. teaching asst. U. Ill., 1941-45; research chemist rayon div. E.I. Du Pont de Nemours & Co., Inc., Buffalo, 1945-47; chemist Oak Ridge Nat. Lab., 1947; asso. chemist Argonne (Ill.) Nat. Lab., 1948-49; aero. research scientist, group leader NACA, Cleve., 1949-53, asst. br. chief chemistry, 1954-55; group leader combustion fundamentals Magnolia Petroleum Co., Dallas, 1955-56; prin. scientist, tech. asst. to pres. research and advanced devel. div. Avco Corp., Greenwich, Conn., 1956-62, dir. corp. research def. and indsl. products group, 1962-64, group v.p. Avco Corp., 1964-68, corp. v.p. research, 1968—; Marie Curie lectr. State U. Pa., 1962; dir. Conn. Nat. Bank, Crown Zellerbach Corp., Warner Lambert Co. Mem. NSF panel sci. and tech., 1973—; trustee Worcester Poly. Inst., Northeastern U.; bd. dirs. Draper Lab.; mem. vis. com. sponsored research M.I.T.; mem. overseers' com. for applied research Harvard U.; mem. nat. materials adv. bd. Nat. Acad. Scis./NRC; mem. Pres.'s Com. for Nat. Medal of Sci.; chmn. Daniel Guggenheim award bd., 1982; mem. com. on fgn. trade Dept. Def., 1978—, chmn., 1982; mem. vis. com. Nat. Bur. Standards, 1981. Recipient Rockefeller Public Service award, 1953; Outstanding Alumnus award S.W. Mo. State U., 1957; Outstanding Profl. Woman award Bus., Profl. Women's Club N.Y., 1966; Disting. Service in Engring. medal U. Mo., Columbia, 1980. Fellow AIAA (nat. dir.), Am. Inst. Chemists; mem. Am. Chem. Soc., Internat. Combustion Inst., Soc. Woman Engrs. (Achievement award 1966), N.Y. Acad. Scis., Conn. Acad. Scis. and Engring., Sigma Xi. Contbr. articles to profl. jours. and collected symposia books. Home: 69 Londonderry Dr Greenwich CT 06830 Office: 1275 King St Greenwich CT 06830

SIMON, ELIZABETH ANN, social worker; b. Kaplan, La., Mar. 21, 1949; d. Luke and Lucy (Marceaux) S.; B.A., St. Mary's Dominican Coll., 1971; M.S.W., Tulane U., 1972. Coordinator Satellite Clinics, Charters Mental Health Center, New Orleans, 1973-74, clin. social worker, 1974-77; field instr. Tulane U. Sch. Social Work, New Orleans, 1975-76; clin. cons., community edn. facilitator Family & Child Services, New Orleans, 1977-79; pvt. practice psychotherapy, New Orleans, 1977—; cons. YWCA Battered Women's Program, New Orleans, 1978-79, bd. dirs., 1979-80. Clin. fellow Tulane U., 1973. Mem. New Orleans Feminist Counseling Collective (founding mem. 1976), Women Against Violence Against Women (chmn. interium com. 1978-79, dir. 1981), Acad. Cert. Social Workers, Nat. Assn. Social Workers, NOW, Feminist Writers Guild. Home: 340 S Jefferson Davis Pkwy New Orleans LA 70119 Office: 3706 Prytania St New Orleans LA 70115

SIMON, ELLEN SHATTUCK, editor; b. Ashland, Kans., Dec. 19, 1921; d. Willis Henry and Ethel Grace (Luther) Shattuck; diploma Cottey Coll. Women, Nevada, Mo., 1941; student U. Mo. Sch. Journalism, 1941-42: m. Alfred Philip Simon, Apr. 5, 1948; children—James Michael, Nancy Ellen. Del. County reporter, feature writer for Phila. Evening Bull., 1961-74; editor-in-chief Springfield (Pa.) Press, 1975—. Mem. ch. and community com. Phila. Presbytery, 1977—; past mem. bd. Del. County Community Nursing Services; vol. chmn. Del. County Christmas Seal Campaign; ruling elder First Presbyn. Ch., Springfield; sec. Springfield Historic Bicentennial Commn. Recipient Keystone Press award Pa. Newspaper Pubs. Assn.-Pa. Soc. Newspaper Editors, 1976, 78; Golden Dozen award Internat. Soc. Weekly Newspaper Editors, 1981. Mem. Women in Communications, Pa. Soc. Newspaper Editors (dir.), PEO, Colonial Dames Am. Democrat. Clubs: Poor Richard (Phila.), Delaware County Press. Address: 331 Spring Valley Rd Springfield PA 19064

SIMON, HONORA GLORIA, clin. psychologist; b. Chgo., Mar. 10, 1932; d. Harry and Annie Simon; student U. Ill., 1949-51; B.S., Northwestern U., 1953, M.A., 1969, Ph.D., 1971; m. Richard I. Scher, Aug. 3, 1953 (div. 1971); children—Amy Diane, Daniel Andrew (twins). Group work supr. Jewish Community Centers, St. Louis, 1962-64; pre-sch. dir. Rhodes Terrace Presch., Dallas, 1964-66; Headstart cons., Tex. and Ill., 1965-70; community resource specialist and bldg. asst. Evanston (Ill.) Sch. Dist. 65, 1966-68; sr. psychologist Michael Reese Hosp., Chgo., 1970-73, Cook County Hosp., Chgo., 1973-82; sch. psychologist Cicero (Ill.) Public Sch. Dist., 1982-83; chief psychologist obesity program Edgewater Hosp., 1982—; pvt. practice clin. psychology, Chgo., 1972—; dir. Biofeedback Cons., 1978—; chmn. Inst. Post-grad. Studies, Ill. Psychol. Assn., 1977-80; mem. staff Edgewater, Barclay, Old Orchard hosps.; tchr., cons. Bd. dirs. Evanston Vol. Bur., 1968-70, Chgo. Council Fgn. Relations, 1972-74; mem. exec. bd. Internat. Visitors Center, 1975-77, fgn. student chmn., 1975-78; v.p. 3800 Lake Shore Assn., 1979. Diplomate, Am. Bd. Profl. Psychology. Mem. Nat. Register Health Care Providers in Psychology, Ill. Group Psychotherapy Assn. (treas. 1976-78), Ill. Psychol. Assn. (profl. affairs and continuing edn. coms. 1977—), Am. Psychol. Assn., Am. Soc. Clin. Hypnosis, Biofeedback Soc. Am. (chmn. employment bur. 1980-82), Ill. Biofeedback Soc. (bd. dirs. 1980-82), Acad. Psychologists of Marital and Family Therapy, Transpersonal Psychology. Home and Office: Biofeedback Cons 3800 Lake Shore Dr Chicago IL 60613 also Stillwaters Galena IL 61036

SIMON, LAURA LEE, human services planner; b. Syracuse, N.Y., Oct. 27, 1929; d. Leon and Jean Reeder; B.A., Syracuse U., 1950; M.A., Columbia U., 1951; m. June 17, 1950; children—Terri Ellen, James John, Andrew David. Pres., Westport (Conn.) PTA Council, 1965-67; mem. exec. bd. Westport Community Council, 1968-76; chmn. CABLE (Community Action for Better Living Environ., 1968-73; bd. dirs. Conn. Assn. Human Services, 1974-76; mem. Southwestern Conn. Health Planning Agy., 1975-77; pres. Southwestern Conn. Funds and Councils, 1974-77; founder, bd. dirs. Westport Weston Counseling Service, 1973-77; mem. adv. council community services div. Conn. Dept. Children and Youth Services, 1973-75, chmn. regional adv. council, 1975-79; mem. exec. bd. Conn. Child Welfare Assn., 1971-81; chmn. Stauffer Westport Fund, 1971-78, exec. dir., 1978—; chmn. Conn. Consortium for White House Conf. on Families, 1977-81; state coordinator White House Conf. on Families, 1979-81. Democrat. Jewish. Home: 3 Hathorne Ln Westport CT 06880

SIMON, LORENA COTTS, music tchr., composer, poet; b. Sherman, Tex., Jan. 16, 1897; d. George Godfrey and Willie (Jones) Cotts; student Am. Conservatory, summer 1938, Juilliard Music Sch., summer 1939; diploma Sherwood Music Sch., 1941; Litt.D. (hon.), Internat. Acad. Leadership, Quezon City, Philippines; L.H.D. (hon.), No. Pontificial Acad., Malmo, Sweden, 1969; Mus.D. (hon.), St. Olav's Acad., Sweden, 1969; m. Samuel C. Simon, Nov. 6, 1918 (dec.). Tchr. violin, piano, theory and harmony, Port Arthur, Tex., 1919—. Organizer, dir. Schubert's Violin Choir, Port Arthur, 1919-55. Named Poet Laureate of Tex. 1961; Poet Laureate of Magnolia Dist., 1962-64; Poet Laureate of Port Arthur, 1962—; recipient gold plaque Tex. Fedn. Women's Club, 1962, spl. award 1st place in poetry and music Tex. heritage dept., 1963; medal of merit and diploma of merit Centro Studi Scambi Internat., Rome, Italy, 1965; Gold medal award, and hon. poet laureate-musician United Poets Laureate Internat., 1966, named Cath. Lady of Humanity, 1977; decorated Equestrian Order of Holy Sepulchre, 1981; recipient Greatness and Leadership award U. Manila, 1967; Silver medal, Gold medal, Diploma Centro Studi E Scambi—Internazionali, 1967; Gold Laurel Wreath, Gold medal, Karte of Award, 1966; named to International Poets' Hall of Fame, 1969, named most outstanding woman internationally Congress of Doctors, Quezon City, Philippines, 1969. Mem. Nat., Tex. press women's assns., Nat. Council Cath. Women, Nat. Guild Piano Tchrs. (charter mem.; adjudicator), Am. Coll. Musicians (adjudicator), Internat. Guild Library, Am. Poetry League, Poets Soc. Tex. (critic judge), Am. Poets Fellowship Soc. Corp., UN Assn. U.S.A., Alpha Delta Kappa. Clubs: Writers' (pres. 1963-64), Symphony. Author: The Golden Kay, 1958; From My Heart (1st place award Ann. Poetry Writers Contest of Tex. Press Women's Assn. 1961), 1959; Children's Story Hour (1st place award Nat. Fedn. Press Women's Ann. Writers' Contest 1962), 1960. Songs pub. include: Live Expectantly, 1962, In Search for Growth, 1963, Freedom's Light, 1963, What Can I Do for Jesus, 1963, I Was a Star, I Was a Lamb, I Was a Donkey; organ piece Mediation, 1967. Chmn. spl. editorial com. World Poets Laureate Anthology, 1969-70. Donor funds for constrn. of 9 churches in Africa. Home: 411 5th Ave Port Arthur TX 77640

SIMONDS, MARY ELIZABETH MINARD (MRS. STUART SWIFT SIMONDS), artists, ret. educator; b. Westminster, Vt., Mar. 27, 1910; d. Seymour Henry and Elizabeth Frances (Frazer) Minard; diploma Vt. Acad., 1927; diploma Springfield Kindergarten-Primary Normal Sch., 1929; student Columbia Tchrs. Coll., 1937, Springfield Coll., 1943, U. Conn., 1944-45, U. Vt., 1949-50, 71, Oreg. Coll. Edn. (NDEA fellow), 1967; studied art with Hubert Rogers, Robert Frick, Deus La Vallé; now studying oil painting with Richard W. Whitney; m. Stuart Swift Simonds, Aug. 21, 1941. Asst. mng. dir. Springfield Girls Club, Mass., 1929-30; tchr. rural schs. Vt., 1931-38; dir. pvt. kindergarten, Saxtons River, Vt., 1939-41; tchr. kindergarten Israel Putnam Sch., Putnam, Conn., 1942-45, Brattleboro (Vt.) Public Schs., 1945-73. Chmn. kindergarten study com. New Eng. Sch. Devel. Council, 1953-58; steering com. New Eng. Kindergarten Ann. Conf., 1960-80. Instigator and chmn. Westminster Devel. Com., 1953-63; chmn. Airport Planning Com. of Windham Regional Planning and Devel. Commn., 1967—; chmn. analysis com. Westminster Planning and Devel. Commn., 1970-80. Pres. Vt. Fedn. Republican Women, 1961-63, county vice-chmn., 1973-75; active state, county and local Republican coms.; trustee Westminster Public Funds, 1956-62; treas. Vt. Acad. Alumni Fund, 1940—; bd. dirs. Fletcher Farm Craft Sch. Mem. Vt. Soc. Colonial Dames (pres. 1970-74, bd. mgmt. 1974—), Vt. Assn. Childhood Edn. (pres. 1950-55), Windham-Southeast Edn. Assn. (pres. 1971-72), Vt. Ret. Tchrs. Assn. (exec. bd.), Vt. Geneal. Soc. (charter), Saxtons River Art Guild, So. Vt. Artists, Inc., Soc. Vt. Craftsmen (exec. bd.), Arts Council Windham County (trustee). Episcopalian. Mem. Rockingham Meetinghouse Assn. (sec. 1980—). Club: Order Eastern Star (past matron council). Author: History of Westminster, 1941. Home: Route 3 Westminster West Putney VT 05346 Office: Pleasant St Saxtons River VT 05154

SIMONETTI, JOAN ESTHER, consumer goods and health products mfg. co. exec.; b. San Antonio, Aug. 17, 1952; d. Lino D. and Florence (Arida) S.; B.S. in Biology (scholar), Bethany (W.Va.) Coll., 1974; postgrad., in indsl. relations Rutgers U., 1977—. Partner, Elizabeth T. Lyons & Assos., New Brunswick, N.J., 1975-79; supr. needle mfg. Ethicon, Inc., Somerville, N.J., 1979-80, mgr. suture mfg., 1980-81, chmn. give cheer program, 1981; mgr. fibre finishing mfg. Johnson & Johnson Products, Sherman, Tex., 1981—. Participant, Women in N.J. bus. com. Kean for Gov. campaign, 1981; bd. dirs. YWCA Central Jersey, 1976-78. Recipient cert. Women in Bus. and Industry, 1981. Mem. Nat. Assn. Female Execs., Am. Soc. Personnel Adminstrs., Indsl. Relations Research Assn., Link. Republican. Roman Catholic. Home: 1903 W Taylor St Apt 210 Sherman TX 75090

SIMONS, CAROLYN LUJAN, ins. exec.; b. Alamosa, Colo., Jan. 16, 1947; d. Alvino Genero and Stella (Mondragon) Lujan; student Adams State Coll., Alamosa, 1965-67; student U. de las Americas, Mexico City, 1967-69; student Sch. Interior Design, Internat. Corr. Schs., 1974-75, N.Y. Sch. Interior Design, 1975-76; grad. U. Colo., Colorado Springs, 1978; m. Frank Statton Simons, Dec. 16, 1978. Dist. ct. div. clk. to Hon. Judge John F. Gallagher, Colorado Springs, 1969-76; dir. resdl. design Innerscape Assocs., Colorado Springs, 1976-77; owner Carolyn Simons Design Studio, Colorado Springs, 1977—; acting job devel. dir. Pikes Peak Community Coll., 1977-78; contract adminstrn. specialist Colo. Interstate Gas Corp., Colorado Springs, 1978-79; mgr. corp. and bus. compensation planning, small estate planning Conn. Mut Life Ins. Co., Colorado Springs, 1980—. State caucus rep. and active in campaign Senator Gary Hart, 1974, El Paso County dist. atty. campaign, 1980, state atty. gen. campaign, 1982. Recipient various profl. awards Conn. Mut. Life Ins. Mem. Million Dollar Roundtable, Nat. Assn. Female Execs., Nat. Assn. Life Underwriters, Life Underwriters Tng. Council, Nat. Assn. Women Underwriters, Women Bus. Owners Orgn., Colorado Springs C. of C., Pikes Peak YMCA. Home: 1725 N Tejon Colorado Springs CO 80907 Office: Conn Mut Life Ins Co 720 N Tejon St Colorado Springs CO 80903

SIMONS, ELIZABETH R., biochemist, educator; b. Vienna, Austria, Sept. 1, 1929; came to U.S., 1941, naturalized, 1948; d. William and Erna Engle (Weisselberg) Reiman; B.Ch.E., Cooper Union, N.Y.C., 1950; M.S., Yale U., 1951, Ph.D., 1954; m. Harold Lee Simons, Aug. 12, 1951; children—Leslie Ann Mulert, Robert David. Research chemist Tech. Operations, Arlington, Mass., 1953-54; instr. chemistry Wellesley (Mass.) Coll., 1954-57; research asst. Children's Hosp. Med. Center and Cancer Research Found., Boston, 1957-59, research asso. pathology, 1959-62; research asso. Harvard Med. Sch., 1962-66, lectr. biol. chemistry, 1966-72; tutor biochemical scis. Harvard Coll., 1971—; asso. prof. biochemistry Boston U., 1972-78, prof., 1978—. Grantee in field. Mem. AAAS, Am. Chem. Soc., Am. Heart Assn., Am. Soc. Biol. Chemists, Am. Soc. Hematology, Am. Fedn. Clin. Research, Assn. Women in Sci., Biophys. Soc., Internat. Soc. Thrombosis and Hemostasis, N.Y. Acad. Sci., Sigma Xi. Contbr. in field. Office: Boston University Sch Medicine 80 E Concord St Boston MA 02118

SIMONS, GAIL M., publishing co. exec.; b. N.Y.C., Jan. 18, 1950; d. Edward Irving and Sylvia (Estrin) Madonick; B.A. in Econs., N.Y.U., 1971; M.B.A., City U. N.Y., 1977; m. A. James Simons, June 10, 1972; 1 dau. Jessica Lauren. Market and advt. research asso. Conde Nast Publs., N.Y.C., 1971-73; credit and fin. analyst European Am. Bank & Trust Co., N.Y.C., 1973-74; dist. lending rep. Nat. Bank of N.Am., N.Y.C., 1974-75; corp. budget analysis mgr. Readers Digest Assn., Inc., Pleasantville, N.Y., 1975-78, fin. mgr., 1979—. Mem. Nat. Assn. Female Execs. Home: 290 Birch St Irvington NY 10533 Office: Readers Digest Assn Pleasantville NY 10570

SIMONS, HELEN, psychologist; b. Chgo., Feb. 13, 1930; d. Leo and Sarah (Prohov) Pomper; student U. Ill., 1947-50; B.A. in Biology, Lake Forest Coll., 1951; M.A. in Clin. Psychology, Roosevelt U., 1972; Psy.D., Ill. Sch. Profl. Psychology, 1980; children—Larry, Sheri. Sch. psychologist Chgo. Bd. Edn., 1974—; intern in clin. psychology Cook County (Ill.) Hosp., Chgo., 1979-80. Mem. Am. Psychol. Assn., Ill. Psychol. Assn., Chgo. Psychol. Assn., Ill. Sch. Psychologists Assn., Chgo. Assn. Sch. Psychologists, Am. Mental Health Assos. for Israel. Jewish. Club: Haddasah. Home: 6145 N Sheridan Rd Chicago IL 60660 Office: 211 S Kildare Chicago IL 60624

SIMONS, MAELENE J., state legislator; b. Deadwood, S.D., July 1, 1935; d. Royal B. and Elsie M. Mills; ed. public schs.; m. Frank Simons, Sept. 27, 1951; children—Linda, Sully; 1 stepson, Frank. Partner, cook, Windy Acres Ranch, Beulah, Wyo., 1952—; mem. Wyo. Ho. of Reps.; pres. Outdoors Unlimited, Inc., 1979—; mem. State Forestry Adv. Bd.; vice chmn. public lands com. Western Council State Govt.; mem. Nat. Public Lands Adv. Bd.; prime sponsor Wyo. Sage Brush Rebellion Bill; mem. Multiple Use of Public Lands Group; pres. Outdoors Unltd. Inc. Leader 4-H Clubs; chmn. county rodeo queen contest, 1970-75; active county, state, nat. Rep. Women, Farm. Bur., Stockgrowers. Mem. Western States Legis. Task Force for Forestry. Methodist. Clubs: Cow-Belles (county, state, nat.), Owls.

SIMONS, NANCY ANN, ins. agt.; b. Pekin, Ill., Oct. 14, 1929; d. Nelson H. and Frances L. (Worley) Mineer; student schs., Pasco and Richland, Wash.; m. Byron D. Simons, May 10, 1946 (dec. 1973); children—Sharon D., Steven H., Lynn A., Sandra L., Judith A. Ins. agt. Mutual of Omaha, United of Omaha, Omaha Indemnity, Kennewick, Wash., 1976—; grad., instr. Life Underwriters Tng. Council. Co-city chmn. March of Dimes, 1965-66; youth leader Blue Mountain council Boy Scouts Am., Girl Scouts U.S.A., Wash. Grange, YMCA, 1950-70. Recipient various co. awards, Nat. Quality Award, 1978. Mem. Woman Leaders Round Table, Nat. Assn. Life Underwriters, Women Life Underwriters Conf. (chmn. polit. action com. 1978-80, edn. chmn. 1980-81, dir. 1980—), Tri City Life Underwriters Assn. (pres.-elect, membership chmn. 1981-82), Tri-Cities Estate Planning Council, Women's Polit. Caucus, Beta Sigma Phi (Order of the Rose 1968). Clubs: Bus. and Profl. Women (pres. 1979-81; Woman of Achievement 1979), Toastmasters Internat., Country, Lady of Moose. Office: 303 1/2 W Kennewick Ave Suite 1 Box 24 Kennewick WA 99336

SIMONSON, DONNA MARIE, govt. ofcl.; b. Decatur, Ill., Jan. 25, 1948; d. Howard Joseph and Geneva Darlene Gleespen; student Alverno Coll., 1966-68; B.A., U. Ill., 1971, M.S.W., 1974. Mental health specialist Ill. Dept. Mental Health, Danville, 1971-74; student asso. Com. on Women in Social Welfare, Nat. Assn. Social Workers, Washington, 1974; children's cons. Ill. Commn. Children, Springfield, 1975, exec. dir., 1977—; mem. Title XX Adv. Council, Dangerous Drugs Adv. Council; nominating chmn. Nat. Council State Coms. on Children and Youth. Mem. Juvenile Justice Del., Citizen ambassador, People to People, USSR and Western Europe, 1982. Mem. Nat. Assn. Social Workers (various offices), Child Care Assn. Editor: Report of Com. on Youth and the Law, 1978; Report of Task Force on Drugs and Alcohol, 1979; Ill. Report White House Conf. on Children, 1980; Ill. Report Conf. on Children's Priorities for 80s, 1982. Office: 3 W Old State Capitol Plaza Room 206 Springfield IL 62701

SIMPKINS, FRANCENA HOWELL, ins. fin. planner; b. Wilson, N.C., Apr. 25, 1952; d. Frank and Ernestine H. Howell; B.S. in Bus. Adminstrn., Ga. State U., 1975; m. Rene L. Simpkins, Aug. 22, 1981. Jr. acct. Case-Hoyt, Atlanta, 1972-76; fin. planner Met. Life Ins. Co., Atlanta, 1977-82; fin. planner, gen. agt. Integon Life Ins. Co., Atlanta, 1982—. Recipient ins. sales awards; mem. Million Dollar Round Table. Mem. Nat. Assn. Life Underwriters, Life Underwriters Tng. Council, Am. Business Women's Assn., Women Leaders Round Table. Address: 1999 Yorktowne Ct College Park GA 30349

SIMPKINS, MARY ELIZA, nurse; b. Edgefield, S.C., Nov. 13, 1933; d. Cornelous and Minnie Bella (Johnson) Chinn; diploma Phila. Gen. Hosp. Sch. Nursing, 1973; m. Albert Simpkins, July 8, 1953; children—Albert, David, Anthony, Mary. Nurse, Phila. Gen. Hosp., 1973-74; charge nurse in orthopedics Temple U., 1974-76; primary nurse, psychiat. group patients Hahneman Med. Coll. and Hosp., 1976-79; shift supr. Kelloggs Psychiat. Hosp., Corona, Calif., 1979-80; shift charge nurse, orthopedics, med.-surg. nurse Parkview Community Hosp., Riverside, Calif., 1980—. Republican. Adventist. Home: 4655 Minier Ave Apt 36B Riverside CA 92505

SIMPSON, ADELE, costume designer; b. N.Y.C., Dec. 8, 1908; d. Jacob and Ella (Bloch) Smithline; grad. Pratt Inst., Bklyn.; m. Wesley William Simpson, Oct. 8, 1930; children—Jeffrey R., Joan Ellen. Pres., dir. Adele Simpson, Inc. Work displayed in Met. Costume Inst., Bklyn. Mus., Dallas Library. Recipient Neiman-Marcus Fashion award, 1946, Coty Fashion award, 1947, First Nat. Cotton Council award, 1953. Mem. Fashion Group, Inc., N.Y.C. Office: 530 7th Ave New York NY 10018 *

SIMPSON, ANDREA, energy co. exec.; b. Pasadena, Calif., Feb. 10, 1948; d. Kenneth James and Barbara Lois (Faries) Simpson; B.A., U. So. Calif., 1969; grad. U. Colo. Sch. Bank Mktg., 1977; M.S., U. So. Calif., 1983. Asst. cashier mktg. First Interstate Bank of Calif., Los Angeles, 1969-73; asst. v.p. mktg. First Hawaiian Bank, Honolulu, 1973-78; dir. corp. communications Pacific Resources, Inc., Honolulu, 1978—; guest lectr. U. Hawaii, 1974-82, Chaminade U., 1975-81. Dir. Hawaii Heart Assn., 1977—; dir. Girl Scouts Pacific, 1982—; publicity chmn. Hawaii YWCA, 1982. Recipient Ursa Major Nat. Award Alpha Phi Internat., 1978; named Panhellenic Hawaii Woman of Yr., 1979; Outstanding Young Person of Hawaii Hawaii Jaycees, 1978. Mem. Am. Mktg. Assn. (dir., v.p.), Public Relations Soc. Am., Honolulu Advt. Fedn., Honolulu Press Club, Public Utilities Communicators Assn. Club: Outrigger Canoe. Office: 733 Bishop St #2800 Honolulu HI 96842

SIMPSON, BARBARA JEAN, state ofcl.; b. Morehead City, N.C., Apr. 2, 1944; A.A., Chowan Coll., 1964; student Atlantic Christian Coll., 1965, N.C. Criminal Justice Acad., 1979. Dept. mgr. Carteret Gen. Hosp., Morehead City, N.C., 1976-78, claims adminstr., 1969-78; sec., bookkeeper Alford's Office Supplies and Gift Store, Morehead City, 1965-69; office clk. acctg. dept. U.S. Civil Service, Cherry Point, N.C., summer, 1965; ct. intake officer dept. adult probation and parole N.C. Dept. Corrections, Beaufort, 1979—; profl. interpreter for the deaf, 1975—. Dir. public relations First Bapt. Ch., Beaufort, 1978-79, mem. fin. com., 1979—; mem. Carteret County Adv. Bd. N.C. Dept. Corrections; mem. Prison Adv. Bd. N.C., 1982-84. Mem. Nat. Assn. Female Execs., Internat. Platform Assn., Carteret County Hist. Research Assn. Club: Miriam Rebekah Lodge. Home: 210 Belle Air St Beaufort NC 28516 Office: Office Adult Probation and Parole Turner St Beaufort NC 28516

SIMPSON, CAROLE JEAN, social worker; b. Portsmouth, Va., Nov. 3, 1934; d. Pretlow Green and Maybell (Burke) Green Melton; B.A., U. Mo., 1960, M.S.W., 1970; cert. youth counseling for U.S., U. Calif., Berkeley, 1964; children by previous marriage—Ansel Patillo, Gayle Yvonne, Jean Gina caSandra Patrice. Social work cons. Los Angeles County Dept. Public Social Services, 1966—, now vol. services coordinator. Recipient awards for vol. services City of Inglewood (Calif.), 1977-79; cert. community coll. counselor, tchr., social workers for grades 1-12, Calif. Mem. Assn. Black Social Workers (life), Los Angeles Public Speakers Bur., Nat. Assn. Social Workers, Black Employees Assn., Internat. Platform Assn., PTA, ACLU, U. Calif. Alumnus, U. Mo. Alumnus, Democrat. Baptist (ch. choir, pres. missionary soc.). Club: Order Eastern Star. Author poem: A Black Man Sleeps (6th prize Clover Collection of Verse) pub. in anthology, 1974. Office: 1326 W Imperial Hwy Gold Room Los Angeles CA 90044

SIMPSON, CLAIRE RITTMEYER, speech-lang. pathologist; b. Cin., May 31, 1923; d. Harry Michael and Clara Elizabeth (Koenig-Wenning) Rittmeyer; student Seton Hill Coll., 1940-42; B.A., U. Cin., 1945; M.S., U. Vt., 1973; m. Lawrence A. Simpson, June 27, 1945; children—Michael Weir, Elizabeth Hay, Deborah Witt, John Gerard, Paula Wenning, Hilary Anne. Remedial reading specialist St. Albans-Fairfield Supervisory Union, St. Albans City Elem. Sch. System, Vt., 1966-68, adult basic edn. tchr., 1967-68, speech-lang. pathologist, 1968—, coordinator communication services, 1976—; adj. prof. dept. communication sci. and disorders U. Vt., 1979—; cons. Franklin County Home Health Agy., 1974—, St. Mary's Parish Lectors Assn., 1974—, Franklin County Vocat. Rehab. Div., State Agy. for Human Services, 1974—. ARC Gray Lady, 1951-61; den mother Cub Scouts, Boy Scouts Am., 1955-56, 61-62; county ways and means chmn. Kerbs Meml. Hosp. Aux., 1957-58; counselor Jr. Cath. Daus. of Am., 1960-65; active various charitable orgns.; music chmn. St. Mary's Parish, 1975-79. Vt. Dept. Spl. Edn. fellow, 1969, 70, 71. Mem. Am. Speech-Lang.-Hearing Assn., Vt. Speech-Lang.-Hearing Assn., Nat. Council for Exceptional Children, Vt. Council for Exceptional Children, NEA, Vt. Edn. Assn., St. Albans City Edn. Assn., Vt. Assn. Mental Health, Nat. Assn. Retarded Citizens, Vt. Children's Aid Soc., Nat. Fedn. Bus. and Profl. Women, AAUW, Seton Hill Coll. Alumni Assn., U. Cin. Alumni Assn., U. Vt. Alumni Assn., Delta Kappa Gamma, Zeta Tau Alpha. Republican. Roman Catholic. Clubs: Cath. Daus. Am., Autonöe. Author: Let's Talk Speech! A Handbook for Parents, 1969; Desensitization With and Without Biofeedback, 1973. Home: 57 Ferris St Saint Albans VT 05478 Office: St Albans City Elem Sch Bldg Bellows St Saint Albans VT 05478

SIMPSON, EVELYN SHIPE, home economist; b. Corryton, Tenn., Dec. 2, 1917; d. Theron William and Theo Aurora (Dunsmore) Shipe; B.S., U. Tenn., 1940, M.S., 1947, Ed.D. (Gen. Foods fellow), 1961; postgrad. Columbia U., 1942; m. Edward B. Simpson, June 10, 1947; 1 son, Edward B. III. Tchr. elem. sch., Knox County, Tenn., 1938-39, tchr. home econs., 1940-46, 47-49, Knoxville, Tenn., 1962-65; crafts dir. Vocat. Rehab., East Tenn., 1949-50; jewelry and metalwork craftsman, 1951-53; designer Tenn. Craftsman, Knoxville, 1953-55; prof. Auburn U., summers 1961-63; prof. home econs. Carson-Newman Coll., Jefferson City, Tenn., 1965-80, coordinator dept. home econs., 1965-80; ret., 1980; freelance writer, 1980—; Mem. Jefferson County Nutrition Com.; mem. Tenn. Textbook Com. for Home Econs.; nat. commr. Gen. Assembly, United Presbyn. Ch.; vol. local Heart Fund, March of Dimes Girls Club. Nat. Tchr. winner Kroger-Westinghouse Cook Off, 1958. Mem. Am. Home Econs. Assn., Tenn. Home Econs. Assn., Nat. Council Adminstrs. Home Econs., Tenn. Council Adminstrs. Home Econs., Am. Vocat Assn., Tenn. Vocat. Assn., NEA, Tenn. Edn. Assn., Farm Bur., Livestock Producers, Tenn. Future Homemakers Am. (hon.), Alpha Lambda Delta, Phi Kappa Phi, Omicron Nu, Pi Lambda Theta, Kappa Omicron Phi, Delta Kappa Gamma. Republican. Clubs: Carson-Newman Faculty Women, Order Eastern Star. Monthly columnist Washington Presbyn. Post, 1978—. Evelyn Simpson Home Econs. scholar established in her honor at Carson-Newman Coll. Home: 5920 Clearbrook Dr Knoxville TN 37918

SIMPSON, LAURA EVELYN, accountant; b. Herrin, Ill., July 19, 1917; d. Roy and Mary (Trout) Wilson; student public schs., Ill.; diploma acctg., income tax and C.P.A. coaching LaSalle Extension U., 1952; m. Levi C. Simpson, Oct. 16, 1936; children—Doris I. Simpson Hill, Suzanne Simpson Barnett, Troy E., Joy. Bookkeeper, Atlas Powder Co., 1932-48; self-employed, 1934-41; with acctg. div. Sherwin Williams Def. Corp., 1942-45, Roy Barger Acctg. Service, Marion, Ill., 1945-52; propr. acctg. service, Marion and Harrisburg, Ill., 1953-79. Treas., Sunday sch. tchr. Cedar Grove United Methodist Ch., Marion, 1946-79; pres. women's div. Holiday United Meth. Ch., New Port Richey, Fla.; leader 4-H Club, 1951, 52. Card holder IRS. Mem. Nat. Fedn. Ind. Bus. (chmn. Saline and Williamson County 1966, nat. adv. council 1971), Nat. Soc. Public Accts., Internat. Platform Assn. Republican. Home: 3634 Claremont New Port Richey FL 33552

SIMPSON, MARILYN JEAN, artist; b. Birmingham, Ala., Aug. 24, 1929; d. Homer Kyle and Ellen (Allan) Parker; student U. Ala., Art Students League N.Y., San Miguel, Mex., Robert Brackman Sch., Conn., Am. U., Avignon, France, Rome and Florence, Italy; children—Carol Leann, Charles Boyd. Dir., Acad. Fine Arts, Ft. Walton Beach, Fla., 1974-77; Marilyn Simpson Sch. Fine Art, Ft. Walton Beach, 1962-73, Artists Workshop, Ft. Walton Beach, 1982—; exhbns. include: Kotter Gallery, Nat. Arts Club, Lever House, Paula Insel Gallery (all N.Y.C.). Recipient award Am. Artist Profl. League, 1975; Gold medal, hon. degree Academia Italia, Rome, 1979, Golden Centaur award, 1982. Mem. Am. Artists Profl. League, Profl. Artists Guild. Address: Route 1 Box 43C Mary Esther FL 32569

SIMPSON, MARY MICHAEL, priest, psychotherapist; b. Evansville, Ind., Dec. 1, 1925; d. Link Wilson and Mary Garrett (Price) Simpson; B.A.B.S., Tex. Women's U., 1946; grad. N.Y. Tng. Sch. Deaconesses, 1949; grad. Westchester Int. Tng. Counseling and Psychotherapy, 1976; S.T.M., Gen. Theol. Sem., 1982. Missionary, Liberia, 1950-52; mem. Order St. Helena, 1952—; acad. head Margaret Hall Sch., Versailles, Ky., 1958-61; sister-in-charge convent, Liberia, 1962-67; dir. novices, 1968-74; pastoral counselor Cathedral St. John Divine, N.Y.C., 1974—, canon residentiary, conan counselor, 1977—; ordained priest Episcopal Ch., 1977; pvt. practice psychotherapy. Mem. Assn. Women in Psychology, Am. Assn. Pastoral Counselors, Feminist Therapy Collective. Contbg. author: Yes to Women Priests, 1978; author: The Ordination of Women in the American Episcopal Church, 1981. Address: 1047 Amsterdam Ave New York NY 10025

SIMS, BETTY KELLETT, educator; b. Greenville County, S.C., July 10, 1937; d. John Henry and Emma Grace (Lathem) Kellett; A.B., Lander Coll., 1958; postgrad. Furman U., 1970; M.Ed., Clemson U., 1973; m. Abner Bruce Sims, Mar. 31, 1961; children—John Bruce, Donald Brian, William Thomas. Gen. music tchr. Davenport Jr. High Sch., Greer, S.C., 1958-60; choral dir. Piedmont Sch., Ellen Woodside Sch., Piedmont, S.C., 1960-62; elem. tchr. Sanoma Sch., Ellen Woodside Sch., Piedmont, 1962-65; choral dir. Wren High Sch., Piedmont, 1965-67; lang. arts tchr. Ellen Woodside Sch., Piedmont, 1967-70; elem. music cons. Sch. Dist. 1 of Anderson County, Williamston, S.C., 1970—; cons. Bd. dirs. South Greenville Youth Assn., 1974—, treas., 1974-76; mem. Lander Coll. Alumni Bd., 1958-60, 77—; bd. dirs. Lander Alumni House, 1979-80; dir. Miss Woodmont pageant, 1976—. Recipient vol. award Woodmont High Sch., Piedmont, 1977; named Tchr. of Yr., Sch. Dist. One of Anderson County, 1979; elected to S.C. State Honor Roll Tchrs. of Yr., 1979; NDEA grantee, 1963; S.C. Dept. Edn. grantee, 1969-70. Mem. NEA, S.C. Edn. Assn., Dist. One Edn. Assn., Music Educators Nat. Conf., S.C. Music Educators Assn., DAR (chpt. regent 1976-79), Alpha Delta Kappa. Home: Route 2 Box 134 Pelzer SC 29669 Office: PO Box 98 Hamilton St Williamston SC 29627

SIMS, BLANCHE PAULINE, orgn. exec.; b. Frederick Hall, Va., Sept. 7, 1914; d. Howard Charles and Eleanor (Carr) Sims; student Washington Bible Inst., 1948-52, Univ. Coll., Richmond, Va., 1964-68, also Eastern Pa. Sch. Alcohol Studies, Southeastern Sch. Alcohol Studies. Various clerical and secretarial positions, 1942-68; acting dir. Alcohol-Narcotics Edn. Council Va. Chs., 1968—, asso. editor Info. Bull. sec.-treas. Middle Atlantic Inst. Alcohol and Other Drug Studies, 1968—; dir. Alcholism Info. Center, coordinator Va. Inst. Alcohol and Other Drug Abuse Studies. Bd. dirs Greater Richmond Council Alcohol and Drug Abuse. Mem. Nat. Assn. Alcoholism Counselors, Va. Assn. Alcoholism Counselors, Christian Bus. and Profl. Women Am. (chmn. chpt.). Republican. Baptist. Home: 4108 Cary St Rd Apt 6 Richmond VA 23221 Office: 3202 W Cary St Richmond VA 23221

SIMS, LORETTA JAMES, employment counselor; b. Holly Springs, Miss., Feb. 7, 1948; d. Sylvester and Elmer (Greer) James; B.S. in Bus. Edn. cum laude, Miss. Indsl. Coll., Holly Springs, 1971; 1 dau., Chyreese Tawana. Personnel mgmt. specialist, then personnel staffing specialist U.S. CSC, Jackson, Miss., 1971-78; equal opportunity specialist Office Fed. Contract Compliance Programs, Kansas City, Mo., 1978—. Mem. Nat. Assn. Female Execs. Urban Leaque, NAACP. Baptist. Home: 6102 E 126th St Apt 305 Grandview MO 64030 Office: DOL/OFCCP 1103 Grand St Room 1400 Kansas City MO 64106

SIMS, LYDIA THERESA, city affirmative action exec.; b. Pennsgrove, N.J., Nov. 18, 1920; d. Clifton and Helen Elvira (Hoskins) Williams; student Wash. State U., 1971, Eastern Wash. State U., 1974-77; m. James M. Sims, Aug. 2, 1941; children—James M., Ronald C., Donald C. Stenographer, sec. YWCA, Spokane, Wash., 1951-63, Spokesman Rev., Spokane, 1964-66, Spokane Neighborhood Centers, 1966-68; dep. dir. Eastside Neighborhood Center, Spokane, 1968-70; manpower tng. specialist, personnel and affirmative action officer Community Action Council, Spokane, 1970-73; affirmative action dir. City of Spokane, 1975—. Precinct com. person Spokane County Central Democratic Com.; mem. Wash. state adv. com. U.S. Commn. Civil Rights; mem., sec. Spokane Hometown Plan.; bd. dirs., chmn. world mut. services com. Spokane YWCA; mem. citizens adv. com. Pine Lodge Correctional Center; bd. dirs. N.W. Women's Law Center; chmn. affirmative action com. Spokane County Central Democratic Com.; mem. Spokane Human Rights Coalition; v.p., Spokane Human Rights Task Force; chmn. Eastern Wash. Agy. on Aging Minority Task Force. Recipient Human Relations award Fairchild AFB, 1977, award of appreciation Kiwanis, 1979. Mem. Am. Assn. Affirmative Action NAACP (pres. N.W. area; exec. com. Spokane br., pres. Spokane br. 1976-80, merit award), LWV, Personnel Mgmt. Assn. Baptist. Club: Links (treas.). Dir. research and devel. Black history slide show, 1979. Home: E 1218 5th Ave Spokane WA 99202 Office: W 808 Spokane Falls Blvd Spokane WA 99201-3333

SIMS, NELROSE ANDERSON, stockbroker; b. Monroe, La., June 8, 1947; d. Guy Armand and Nelrose Barton (Boykin) Anderson; B.A. in Humanities, Centenary Coll., 1969; m. Hoytt DeSha Sims, Nov. 24, 1971; children—Hoytt DeSha, Nelrose Chandler. Tchr., Richland Parish Sch. Bd., Rayville, La., 1969-72; commodities broker Schneider, Bernet & Hickman, Inc., Rayville, 1977—, stockbroker, 1980—; v.p., 1981—; rice buyer Boeuf River Rice Co., 1981—; cotton buyer Cotton Sales, Inc., 1981—. Mem. Richland Parish Library Bd., 1976—; mem. Rayville Town Council, 1978—; bd. dirs. Humpty Dumpty Pre-Sch., Inc., Rayville, 1978—; parish chmn. Silver Waters council Girl Scouts U.S.A. Mem. Nat. Assn. Registered Reps., Nat. Assn. Female Execs., Nat. Women's Polit. Caucus, NOW, DAR Chi Omega. Democrat. Episcopalian. Clubs: Rayville Art and Civic, Bayou DeSiard Country. Author weekly newspaper fin. column. Home: PO Box 398 Rayville LA 71269 Office: Hwy 80 W Rayville LA 71269

SIMSES, DENISE GIROUARD, med. technologist; b. Fitchburg, Mass., Oct. 7, 1921; d. Romeo and Blanche Bella (St. Jacque) Girouard; B.A., Emmanuel Coll., 1943; m. Richard J. Simses, June 19, 1948 (dec. 1971); children—Kathleen, Richard, James, Thomas. Med. tech. intern Lawrence Hosp., Ft. Devons, Mass., 1943-44, Bridgeport (Conn.) Hosp., 1944-47; staff Lawrence Hosp., Bronxville, N.Y., 1947-51, Dr. Kroll's Office, Bronxville, 1951-53; med. technologist Dr. Copper, Burd and Sacks, Fairfield, Conn., 1970—. Mem. Am. Soc. Clin. Pathology, AAUW. Republican. Roman Catholic. Club: Shakespeare Guild. Home: Fairfield CT 06430 Office: 1304 Post Rd Fairfield CT 06430

SIMSON, VERONICA BYRNES CINELLI, civic worker, health services adminstr.; b. Birmingham, Ala.; d. Andrew Louis and Gladys (Foushee) Byrnes; student parochial schs., Atlanta; advanced studies in music and langs., N.Y.C.; m. Albert A. Cinelli (dec. 1972); m. 2d A.A.R. Simson, June 24, 1978. Bd. dirs. Gen. Health Info. Service, Inc., N.Y.C.; adminstrv. coordinator Med. and Surg. Specialists Plan, N.Y.C.; health adminstr. Health Counseling Service, N.Y.C.; founder Med. and Health Services, N.Y.C.; gen. chmn. scholarship fund benefits Italian Charities Am., Inc.; mem. Met. Opera Guild, Inc., ARC, Operatic Group. Home: 47 E 88th St New York NY 10028 Office: 1021 Park Ave New York NY 10028

SIMUNICH, MARY ELIZABETH HEDRICK (MRS. WILLIAM A. SIMUNICH), pub. relations exec.; b. Chgo.; d. Tubman Keene and Mary (McCamish) Hedrick; student Phoenix Coll., 1967-69, Met. Bus. Coll., 1938-40; m. William A. Simunich, Dec. 6, 1941. Exec. sec. sales mgr. KPHO radio, 1950-53; exec. sec. mgr. KPHO-TV, 1953-54; account exec. Tom Rippey & Assos., 1955-56; pub. relations dir. Phoenix Symphony, 1956-62; co-founder, v.p. Paul J. Hughes Pub. Relations, Inc., 1960-65; owner Mary Simunich Pub. Relations, Phoenix, 1966-77. Pub. relations dir. Walter O. Boswell Meml. Hosp., Sun City, Ariz., 1969—; instr. pub. relations Phoenix Coll. Evening Sch., 1973-78. Bd. dirs. Anytown, Ariz., 1969-72; founder, sec. Friends Am. Geriatrics, 1977—. Named Phoenix Advt. Woman of Year, Phoenix Jr. Advt. Club, 1962; recipient award Blue Cross, 1963; 1st Pl. award Ariz. Press Women, 1966. Mem. Internat. Assn. Bus. Communicators (pres. Ariz. chpt. 1970-71, dir.), Pub. Relations Soc. Am. (sec., dir. 1976-78), Am. Soc. Hosp. Pub. Relations (dir. Ariz. chpt. 1976-78), Nat., Ariz. press women. Club: Phoenix Press. Home: 4133 N 34th Pl Phoenix AZ 85018 Office: PO Box 15178 Phoenix AZ 85060

SINANOGLU, PAULA ARMBRUSTER, social work educator; b. N.Y.C., June 30, 1935; d. William and Anna Bertha Armbruster; B.A., U. Conn., 1956, M.S.W., 1974; M.A., Yale U., 1964; children—K. Levni, Elif-Lale A., Murat H. Intelligence analyst Nat. Security Agy., Washington, 1956-62; clin. instr. social work Yale Child Study Center, Sch. Medicine, Yale U., New Haven, 1974-80, clin. asst. prof., 1980—; asso. project dir. HEW tng. grant, asst. prof. residence U. Conn. Sch. Social Work, West Hartford, 1979-80. Fellow, Pierson Coll., Yale Coll. Mem. Nat. Acad. Social Work (sec. Conn. chpt.), Nat. Assn. Social Workers, Acad. Cert. Social Workers, Council Social Work Edn., AAUP, The Mory's Assn. Author, editor works in field. Office: Yale Child Study Center 230 S Frontage Rd New Haven CT 06510

SINAY, RUTH DORIS, psychologist; b. Bklyn., Feb. 5, 1920; d. Maurice Howard and Marion Gertrude (Heller) Milman; A.A., Santa Monica City Coll., 1953; B.A. cum laude in Psychology, U. So. Calif., 1956, Ph.D. (NIMH fellow), 1967; m. Joseph Sinay, Mar. 7, 1961; 1 son, Frederick Allen Schiff. Tchr. pub. schs., Hawthorne, Calif., 1957-58; instr. psychology U. So. Calif. Sch. Medicine, Los Angeles, 1967-71, dir. child and adolescent psychol. tng. program, 1969—, acting dir. child and adolescent psychol. services, 1969-70, dir., 1971—, asst. clin. prof., 1971-79, asso. clin. prof., 1979—; asso. clin. prof. psychology Fuller Theol. Sem., Pasadena, Calif., 1969—; cons. in field. Mem. Los Angeles Mayor's Com. on Youth and Aging, 1974-75; chmn. Take A Giant Step, Los Angeles, 1977; active United Jewish Fund drives; alt. del. Muskie for Pres., 1972. Recipient Judas Magnos award Hebrew U., Jerusalem, Israel, 1977. Mem. Am., Western, Calif. State (sec. 1975-78), Los Angeles County psychol. assns., Psychologists in Pub. Service (sec. 1969-70), Pi Lambda Theta. Club: Los Angeles Variety. Author: (with H. Slucki and N. Tiber) The Really Easy Reader Game, 1974; contbr. articles to profl. jours. Home: 1025 Carolyn Beverly Hills CA 90210 Office: 1934 Hospital Pl Los Angeles CA 90033

SINCLAIR, BEVERLEY ANN, radio exec.; b. Saskatoon, Sask., Can., Jan. 22, 1955; d. Don Smith and Betty Elena S.; student B.C. Inst. Tech.,

1973-75. Reporter, editor CBC Radio, Vancouver, 1973-75; reporter, editor CKIQ Radio, Kelowna, B.C., 1975-77, public affairs, news dir. CJOV-FM, Kelowna, 1977-78; public affairs dir. C-FAX, Victoria, B.C., Can., 1978—; guest lectr. B.C. Inst. Tech. Office: C-FAX Radio 825 Broughton St Victoria BC V8W 1E5 Canada

SINCLEAIR, IRENE CATHERINE, nursing adminstr.; b. Somerville, Mass., Sept. 25, 1940; d. William Joseph and Irene Catherine (Flanagan) Ryan; R.N. Catherine LaBoure Sch. Nursing, 1961; postgrad. Salem State Coll.; m. Forrest Steven, Jan. 13, 1967; children—Katie, Kevin, Kenny. Staff nurse Glenwood Nursing Home, Minn., 1976-80; asst. dir. nursing Lakeview Care Center, Glenwood, 1980-81; dir. nursing Hoffman (Minn.) Care Center, 1981—; instr. nurses aide community edn. classes. Chmn., Circle, vol. instr. Sacred Heart Ch.; Glenwood; chmn. Pope County Research Group, Am. Cancer Soc. Served to lt. USN, 1962-67. Mem. Minnewaska Hockey Assn. (dir.), Minn. Assn. Health Care Facilities, Central Minn. Inservice Educators, Lake Area Dirs. Assn., VFW, Am. Legion. Democrat. Roman Catholic. Home: RR 3 PO Box 115 Glenwood MN 56334 104 6th St Hoffman MN 56339

SINDT, CAROL ANNE WOLD, cable communications franchising rep.; b. Mpls., Nov. 26, 1949; d. Melvin Theodore and Mary Clare (Dalton) W.; B.S. in Polit. Sci. and Social Studies Edn., U. Minn., 1971; m. Michael Alan Sindt, June 27, 1981. Mem. staff Minn. Senate, 1973-74; adminstrv. asst. Mpls. City Council, 1974-78; polit. cons., 1978-80; franchising rep. Storer Cable Communications, Mpls., 1980—. Democratic nat. committeewoman for Minn., 1976-80; mem. State Bd. Med. Examiners, 1976-80; mem. bd. edn. Minn. Cath. Conf., 1981—. Roman Catholic. Home: 1323 Bayard Ave Saint Paul MN 55116

SINES, PAULINE LULU, nurse; b. Seattle, May 2, 1934; d. James Paul and Glow C. (Sackman) O'Connor; student San Diego Jr. Coll., 1952-53; B.S. in Nursing, San Diego State U., 1957; children—Shawn, Tim. Staff nurse County Hosp., San Diego, 1957-59; staff nurse Grossmont Hosp., LaMesa, Calif., 1962-70, supervising head nurse, 1970-78, unit mgr., 1978—; organizer recovery room seminars U. Calif., LaJolla. Recipient cert. for recovery rm. seminars for U.S. nurses U. Calif., LaJolla, 1973; cert. advanced CPR, 1978. Mem. Am. Nurses Assn., Am. Hosp. Assn., Recovery Room Nurses, United Nurses Calif., Crippled Children's Hosp. Aux. San Diego. Republican. Baptist. Club: Duwamish Tribe. Home: 1292 Exeter St El Cajon CA 92021

SINGER, ANNE STAUFFER, clin. psychologist; b. Calcutta, India, Oct. 11, 1928; came to U.S., 1930; d. Samuel Earle and Marthedith (Furnas) Stauffer; A.B., Syracuse U., 1949, M.A., 1959; Ph.D., Stanford U., 1971; children—Elizabeth Josephine, Susan Esther. Lectr., U. Calif., Riverside, 1969-71; asst. dir. Riverside County Mental Health Dept., Indio, Calif., 1971-77; chief psychologist Kaiser Permanente Hosp., Vallejo, Calif., 1977—; pvt. practice clin. psychology, Berkeley, Calif., 1977—. Mem. Am. Psychol. Assn., Am. Orthopsychiat. Assn., Nat. Register of Health Providers Psychology. Author: (with R.D. Singer) Psychological Development in Children, 1969. Home: 33 Beverly Rd Kensington CA 94707 Office: 975 Sereno Dr Vallejo CA 94560

SINGER, CARLA SUSAN, TV exec.; b. Winnipeg, Man., Can., Mar. 4, 1945; d. Martin Samuel and Betty Singer; B.A., Brandeis U., 1966; M.A., Hebrew U., Jerusalem, 1968; postgrad. UCLA Grad. Sch. Mgmt., 1979-80. Producer/writer/dir. PM Mag. Everyday, BBC-TV, London, CTV Network and City TV, Toronto, 1974-76; exec. producer programming KDKA-TV, Pitts., 1978-79; dir. program devel. Group W TV, Los Angeles, 1979-80; dir. dramatic devel. CBS-TV, Los Angeles, 1980—. Bd. mem. Breast Center, Los Angeles, 1979—. Recipient Western Pa. Journalism Soc. award 1978, Gabriel award 1977. Mem. Nat. Assn. Female Execs., Women in Film, NOW. Office: CBS-TV 7800 Beverly Blvd Los Angeles CA 90036

SINGER, GLADYS MONTGOMERY, writer; b. Natick, Mass.; d. Charles Norton and Myrtle (Cates) Taylor; B.A., Wellesley Coll.; m. Alexander John Montgomery (dec. 1955); m. 2d, Russell E. Singer, 1975. Writer, McGraw-Hill mags. in Washington office, 1942-61, Washington editor Textile World, 1943-46, Washington corr. Electronics, 1943-44, Washington editor same, 1944-57, Washington corr. Nucleonics, 1947-52, mem. Washington staff Bus. Week, 1952-61; past sci. and tech. writer Washington News bur. McGraw-Hill; then freelance; ret. Mem. Pres.'s Adv. Com. on Arts, Kennedy Center, 1970-76. Recipient citation Armed Forces Communications and Electronics Assn., 1970. Mem. AAAS, Nat. Assn. Sci. Writers, Washington Press Club (pres. 1957-58), Am. Newspaper Women's Club, English-Speaking Union. Clubs: Sulgrave, Chevy Chase, Wellesley College (Washington). Home: 2725 29th St NW Washington DC 20008

SINGER, JEANNE (WALSH), composer, concert pianist; b. N.Y.C., Aug. 4, 1924; d. Harold Vandervoort and Helen (Loucks) Walsh; B.A. magna cum laude, Barnard Coll., 1944; artist diploma Nat. Guild Piano Tchrs., 1954; student in piano Nadia Reisenberg, 1945-60, composition, Douglas Moore, 1942-44; m. Richard G. Singer, Feb. 24, 1945, dec.; 1 son, Richard V. Composer, concert pianist solo chamber ensembles N.Y., 1947—; tchr. piano Manhasset, N.Y., 1960—; lectr. in field. Recipient spl. award merit Nat. Fedn. Music Clubs, 1st prize in nat. competition Composers Guild, 1979, also various nat. awards; honored at all-Singer concert, Bogotá, Colombia, 1980; N.Y. Council Arts grantee. Fellow Internat. Biog. Assn.; mem. ASCAP (award 1978, 79, 80, 81), Am. Music Center, League Women Composers, Nat. League Am. Pen Women (nat. music chmn.), Composers, Authors and Artists Am. (v.p. N.Y.C., music mag. editor 1972-80, nat. award 1981), Am. Women Composers, Internat. Platform Assn., Phi Beta Kappa. Clubs: Barnard Coll. of L.I., Tuesday Morning Music Douglaston; Bohemians (N.Y.C.). Composed numerous instrumental, vocal works including: Summons (baritone), 1975, A Cycle of Love (4 songs with piano), 1976, Suite in Harpsichord Style, 1976, From The Green Mountains (trio), 1977, (choral work) Composers' Prayer, Nocturne for Clarinet, 1980, Suite for Horn and Harp, 1980, From Petrarch (voice, horn, piano), 1981, Come Greet the Spring (choral), 1981; performed Lincoln Center, radio, TV. Home and office: 64 Stuart Place Manhasset NY 11030

SINGER, JOY DANIELS, writer, advt. cons.; b. N.Y.C., Feb. 22, 1928; d. Maurice Blumberg and Anna (Kleegman) Daniels; B.A., Cornell U., 1948; postgrad. Sorbonne, 1949; m. Jack Singer, July 30, 1955; children—Merianne B., Daniel C., Richard K. Advt. copywriter Franklin Spier, George Knoerr & Assocs., Parents mag., Diener & Dorskind, March Advt., 1950-68; chief exec. officer J.D. Singer Uninc., N.Y.C., 1968—; scriptwriter Magistrate's Court, 1968-69; syndicated columnist (with Marlies Wolf) Women At Work, 1979—. Democratic county committeewoman, from 1960. Mem. Direct Mktg. Creative Guild (chmn. new membership com.), Nat. Acad. TV Arts and Scis. Author: My Mother, the Doctor, 1970. Home: 49 W 87th St New York NY 10024 Office: 79 Madison Ave Suite 1004 New York NY 10016

SINGER, LEA S., lawyer; b. N.Y.C.; d. Herbert F. and Eleanor (Wertheim) Schwartz; B.A., Bklyn. Coll., 1942; J.D., Bklyn. Law Sch., 1942; m. Thomas D. Conway; children—David H., Robert M. Admitted to N.Y. bar, 1942; clk. U.S. Dist Ct. So. Dist. N.Y., 1949-51, sec. to judge, 1951-57; practice law, N.Y.C., 1957-62; asst. corp. counsel City of N.Y., 1962-68, sr. atty. Model Cities program, 1968-72, asst. corp. counsel consumer protection div., 1972-78, spl. asst. atty. gen. Medicaid frauds, 1978-81. Mem. community bd. Goldwater Meml. Hosp., N.Y.C. Recipient numerous citations. Mem. N.Y. State, N.Y. County, Bklyn. (trustee), N.Y. Women's, Bklyn. Women's (pres. 1964-65) bar assns., Med. Jurisprudence Soc., Nat. Assn. Ret. Fed. Employees (1st v.p. N.Y. State, pres. chpt.). Club: Order Eastern Star. Home: PO Box 1304 New York NY 10008

SINGER, LYNN BUCHHOLZ, cons. co. exec.; b. Chgo., June 18, 1948; d. Alexander and Jean (Ross) Buchholz; B.A. cum laude, U. Mich., 1970, M.P.H., 1972; m. Steven M. Singer, Nov. 26, 1976; children—David Benjamin, Michael Lawrence. Program analyst USPHS, Chgo., 1972-73, regional program cons. migrant health, 1973-77, chief profl. consultation services, 1977-79; intergovtl. affairs specialist Dept. Health and Human Services, Chgo., 1980-81; v.p. Community Health Found., Skokie, Ill., 1981—; chairperson adv. com. HEW Fed. Women's Program, 1978, 79. USPHS trainee, 1970, recipient cert. outstanding performance, 1973, 76; citation Dept. Health and Human Services, 1980. Office: 9933 Lawler Skokie IL 60077

SINGER, MARCIA BOSNIAK, educator; b. N.Y.C., d. Meyer and Sadie (Brosterman) Bosniak; B.A., N.Y. U., 1943, M.A. in Edn., 1959; profl. diploma in guidance and counseling, Columbia Tchrs. Coll., 1971; m. Jules Singer, June 12, 1943; children—Barbara Singer Thomas, Nancy, Michael. Tchr. salesmanship for women, Port Washington and New Hyde Park, N.Y., 1959-60; tchr. course for women returning to labor market, Rockville Center (N.Y.) and Sewanaka Sch. Dist., 1963-65, White Plains (N.Y.) Center and Nassau County, auspices N.Y. U., 1963-65; counselor Manpower Devel. and Tng., 1965-67; guidance counselor Port Washington Sr. High Sch., 1967-68; asst. dean students N.Y. Inst. Tech., Old Westbury, N.Y., 1968—, coordinator coll.-wide cultural com.; vocat. counselor for mature women, also pvt. practice and lectr. in field; founder Nassau County Coll. Vol. Consortium. Chmn. task force vol. services L.I. Regional Adv. Council Higher Edn.; adv. bd. Vol. Services Bur. Westchester County, New Sch. Social Research; mem. Nassau Forum for Arts; trustee Village of Saddle Rock, 1978-80; bd. dirs. Nassua council Girl Scouts U.S.A.; adv. bd. Town of Oyster Bay Council on the Arts; mem. Roslyn Bicentennial Commn. Named Greek Faculty Woman of Year, Greek Soc., N.Y. Inst. Tech. Mem. Nat. Assn. Women Deans, Adminstrs. and Counselors, Am., L.I. personnel and guidance assns., Nat. County Bus. and Profl. Women's Assn., Eta Mu Phi, Alpha Phi Epsilon. Author courses in field. Home: 269-27 N Grand Central Pkwy Floral Park NY 11005 Office: NY Inst Tech Old Westbury NY 11568

SINGER, MARGARET THALER, educator; b. Denver, July 29, 1921; d. Raymond Willard and Margaret Burke Coleman (McDonough) Thaler; B.A., U. Denver, 1943, M.A., 1945, Ph.D., 1952; m. Jerome Ralph Singer, June 28, 1956; children—Samuel Robert, Martha Rachel. Med. psychologist U. Colo., 1945-52; sr. psychologist Walter Reed Army Inst. of Research, 1952-58; spl. cons. research asso NIMH, 1958-73; prof. U. Rochester, U. Calif., Berkeley; prof. dept. psychiatry U. Calif., San Francisco, 1973—. Recipient Hofheimer prize Am. Psychiat. Assn., 1966; Stanley R. Dean award, Am. Coll. Psychiatrists, 1976; McAlpin award for achievement in research, Mental Health Assn. U.S., 1977. Mem. Am. Psychosomatic Soc. (pres. 1972-73), Am. Psychol. Assn., Internat. Soc. Polit. Psychology. Mem. editorial bd. Psychosomatic Medicine, Family Process, Familiendynamk, Therapie, Froschung, Entwicklung, Research Communications in Psychology, Psychiatry and Behavior; contbr. articles in field to profl. jours. Home: 17 El Camino Real Berkeley CA 94705

SINGER, MARSHA ANN, sales exec.; b. San Francisco, Sept. 24, 1954; d. Edgar Georg and Jane Eda (Collins) Singer; grad. high sch. From sales to partner firm The Good Guys, San Francisco, 1978-81; partner, sales mgr. audio/video Cordless Phone Center, San Francisco, 1981—. Mem. Nat. Assn. Female Execs., NOW. Democrat. Jewish. Home: 296 Juanita Pacifica CA 94044 Office: 1850 Union St San Francisco CA 94123

SINGER, MAXINE FRANK, biochemist; b. N.Y.C., Feb. 15, 1931; d. Hyman S. and Henrietta (Perlowitz) Frank; A.B., Swarthmore Coll., 1952, D.Sc. (hon.), 1978; Ph.D., Yale U., 1957; D.Sc., Wesleyan U., 1977; m. Daniel Morris Singer, June 15, 1952; children—Amy Elizabeth, Ellen Ruth, David Byrd, Stephanie Frank. USPHS postdoctoral fellow NIH, Bethesda, Md., 1956-58, research chemist (biochemistry), 1958-74, head sect. on nucleic acid enzymology Nat. Cancer Inst., 1974-79; chief Lab. of Biochemistry, Nat. Cancer Inst., 1979—; Regents vis. lectr. U. Calif., Berkeley, 1981. Bd. dirs. Found. for Advanced Edn. in Scis., 1972-78; trustee Wesleyan U., Middletown, Conn., 1972-75, Yale Corp., New Haven, 1975—; bd. govs. Weizman Inst. Sci., Israel, 1979—. Recipient award for achievement in biol. scis. Washington Acad. Scis., 1969, award for research in biol. scis. Yale Sci. and Engring. Assn., 1974, Superior Service Honor award HEW, 1975, Dirs. award NIH, 1977. Fellow Am. Acad. Arts and Scis.; mem. AAAS, Am. Soc. Biol. Chemists, Am. Soc. Microbiologists, Am. Chem. Soc., Inst. Medicine (Nat. Acad. Scis.), Nat. Acad. Scis. Editor: Jour. Biol. Chemistry, 1968-74; Sci. mag., 1972—. Contbr. articles to scholarly jours. Home: 5410 39th St NW Washington DC 20015 Office: Bldg 37 4E-28 Bethesda MD 20205

SINGER, VIVIAN SUSAN, social worker; b. N.Y.C.; d. Joseph I. and Rebecca Singer; B.A. Stern Coll. for Women, 1969; M.S. (NIMH fellow), Columbia U. Sch. Social Work, 1973. Social worker Hadassah Hosp., Jerusalem, 1973; social worker med. clinic Brookdale Hosp., Bklyn., 1974—. Cert. social worker, N.Y. Fellow Orthopsychiat. Assn.; mem. Nat. Assn. Social Workers (cert.), N.Y. State Soc. Clin. Soical Work Psychotherapists, Oncology Network Social Workers Bklyn. and S.I. Home: 185 West End Ave Apt 28E New York NY 10023 Office: Social Service Dept Brookdale Hosp Brookdale Plaza Brooklyn NY 11212

SINGH, SUSHILA, artist; b. Fatehgarh, India, Aug. 29, 1940; d. Ramlal and Ramkumari Katiyar; came to U.S., 1969; B.A., Agra U., 1964, M.A., 1968; diploma advt. and illustrating art Art Instruction Schs., Mpls., 1977, Diploma in Painting, 1978; m. Ramchandra Sitaram Singh, Dec. 12, 1964; children—Rajiv, Sanjay. One-woman exhbns. include: Dharam Samaj Coll., Aligarh, India, 1968. Indian Inst. Tech., Kanpur, India, 1968, U. Ill. Art Gallery, Urbana, 1969, 70, Zigler Mus., Jennings, La., 1977; represented in permanent collection: Spindletop Mus., Beaumont, Tex., Art Instrn. Schs., Mpls.; portrait of Prince Charles, accepted by same as gift; commd. to paint Dr. Denton A. Cooley, Houston; lectr. art classes in community centers, 1977—; tchr. painting leisure-learning program McNeese State U., 1979—. Recipient 3 Gold medals Agra U; 1st prize for painting Rhythm, Art Instrn. Schs., 1972. Mem. Art Assos. Lake Charles. Address: 4801 Orleans St Lake Charles LA 70605

SINGLETARY, LESLIE ELIZABETH, oil co. exec.; b. Tulsa, Nov. 12, 1954; d. Heston Leroy Singletary and Margaret Corbett (Hewgley) Singletary James; student Scripps Coll., 1972-73; B.A. in Communications, U. Tulsa, 1977. Vice pres., dir. Heston Oil Co., Tulsa, 1977—; dir. Welt Drilling Co. Mem. Nat. Assn. Female Execs., Nat. Soc. Colonial Dames, Nat. Trust Hist. Preservation, Jr. League Tulsa. Office: Heston Oil Co 9 E 4th St Suite 200 Tulsa OK 74103

SINGLETON, JANE GURLINE PACE, real estate co. exec.; b. Homestead, Fla., Jan. 6, 1928; d. Leander James and Julia (Laughter) Pace; B.A., Flora McDonald Coll., 1948; student U. Fla., 1952-53, Stetson U., Deland, Fla., 1955-56; children—Robert Maginnis, Nancy Maginnis, Joseph. Tchr. public schs., Orange County, Fla., 1954-59; mem. Bd. Edn., Sequatchie County, Tenn., 1970; county judge, Sequatchie County, 1970-72; ofcl. OEO, Washington, 1972; personal sec. Jeanne Dixon, Washington, 1973-74, Congressman John Duncan, Washington, 1973-74; legis. asst. White House, Washington, 1975-76; pres., mgr. Singleton Properties, Inc., Manalapan, Fla., 1977—; pres. Gold Coast Electric, Inc., Lantana, Fla. Precinct chmn. home precinct, 1976. Recipient Beautification and Renovation award Town of Lantana, 1981. Mem. Nat. Juvenile Judges Assn., Oceanfront Property Owners Assn. (pres. 1982), Manalapan Property Owners Assn. (dir. 1981-82). Republican. Presbyterian. Columnist: Signal Mountain (Tenn.) News, 1970. Home and Office: 1000 S Ocean Blvd Manalapan FL 33462

SINGLETON, JOYCE HARVEY, social service exec.; exec.; b. Melrose, Mass., June 29, 1945; d. Robert Willis and Amy Sheppard (Wood) Harvey; B.A., U. Mass., Amherst, 1967, diploma grad. journalism program, 1969; 1 dau., Joanne Harvey. Sr. tech. writer Itek Corp., Lexington, Mass., 1967-70; dir. public info. Walla Walla (Wash.) Community Coll., 1970; profl. interviewer McGraw Hill Pubs., N.Y.C., 1971-73; coordinator public relations James B. Rendle Assos., Malden, Mass., 1973-76; exec. dir. ARC, Melrose, Mass., 1976-80, regional mgr. Eastern Middlesex, 1980—. Chmn. adv. bd. Mass. Dept. Public Welfare Community Service Area; mem. Melrose Mayor's Energy Commn.; civic adv. bd. Met. Bank & Trust; instr. 1st aid and CPR, ARC, cert. of merit, 1981; clk. of vestry Trinity Episcopal Ch., Melrose, 1972—; merit badge counselor Boy Scouts Am. New Eng. Newspaper fellow, 1969; notary public, lic. cert. social worker, Mass. Mem. AAUW, DAR, Alpha Phi Gamma. Episcopalian. Home: 39 Boardman Ave Melrose MA 02176 Office: 786 Main St Melrose MA 02176

SINGLETON, KATHRYN TRISHAY, med. record adminstr.; b. Orange, Tex., May 15, 1951; d. Lester B. and Gertie (Hodge) Singleton; B.S., Incarnate Word Coll., 1973; M.S., SUNY, 1977. Dir. med. record dept. Highsmith-Rainey Meml. Hosp., Fayetteville, N.C., 1973-76; asst. prof. Sch. Allied Health Professions, U. Wis., Milw., 1977-79; asst. dir. Med. Record Dept., Henry Ford Hosp., Detroit, 1979-80; dir. med. record dept. Holy Cross Hosp., Silver Spring, Md., 1980—; lectr. in field. Recipient Outstanding Performance as Student Tchr. award SUNY, 1977; Kellogg Found. grantee, 1976. Mem. D.C. (exec. bd.), Am. med. records assns., Med. Record Dirs. Div. Nat. Capital Area (chmn.). Home: 14229 Pear Tree Ln Apt 24 Silver Spring MD 20906 Office: 1500 Forest Glen Rd Silver Spring MD 20910

SINGLETON, NAN CHACHERE, educator; b. Prescott, Ark., July 2, 1930; d. Otis A. and Olivia (Dixon) Wells; B.S., La. Tech. U., 1950; M.A., U. Southwestern La., 1962; Ph.D., La. State U., 1974; m. Howard A. Singleton, June 28, 1970; children—Larry Ike Chachere, Barbara Chachere Martin, Jon Scott Chachere. Tchr. home econs. St. Landry Parish (La.) Schs., 1950-73; asst. prof. home econs. La. State U., Baton Rouge, 1974-79, asso. prof., 1979—, asso. dean Univ. Coll., 1977-82, head dept. community edn., 1982—. Mem. La. Home Econs. Assn. (pres. 1981), VFW (dist. pres. aux. 1973), Bus. and Profl. Women Club, Assn. Continuing Higher Edn., Am. Dietetic Assn., La. Dietetic Assn., Am. Home Econs. Assn., Inst. Food Technologists, Soc. Nutrition Edn., Phi Upsilon Omicron, Phi Delta Kappa, Gamma Sigma Delta, Delta Kappa Gamma. Democrat. Episcopalian. Contbr. articles to profl. jours. Home: 2206 Broussard St Baton Rouge LA 70808 Office: Gen Coll La State U Baton Rouge LA 70803

SINGLEY, DORIS MAE, nursing home adminstr.; b. Newberry, S.C., Oct. 21, 1936; d. James Boyd and Eula Mae (Leopard) Robertson; R.N., Greenville Gen. Hosp., 1957; m. Willie Ernest Singley, Aug. 18, 1957; children—Mary Louise, Kathy, Annette. Charge nurse Mobile (Ala.) Infirmary, 1957-58; asst. night supr. Dorchester County Hosp., Summerville, S.C., 1961-62; head nurse, float nurse in charge pediatric clinic Charleston AFB, S.C., 1962-67; charge nurse, asst. head nurse Alaska Native Hosp., Anchorage, 1967-72; substitute sch. nurse Alamogordo, N.Mex., 1972-73; floornurse Nursing Home, Newberry, 1973-76; nursing home adminstr. J.F. Hawkins Nursing Home, Newberry, 1976—. Mem. Midland Human Resource Com. Mem. S.C. Health Care Assn. (sec. dist. adminstrs. 1980—), Bus. and Profl. Women. Presbyterian. Club: Order Eastern Star. Home: 1316 Dave Dr Newberry SC 29108 Office: 1330 Kinard St Newberry SC 29108

SINGREEN, SHIRLEY ANN BASILE (MRS. HARRY VOSS SINGREEN), lawyer; b. New Orleans, Apr. 10, 1941; d. Dominick Joseph and Rose Aile (O'Reilly) Basile; A.B., Loyola U., New Orleans, 1962, J.D., 1964; m. Harry Voss Singreen, May 12, 1979; children—Michael Harry, Elizabeth Alexandra. Admitted to La. bar, 1964; law clk. Civil Dist. Ct., 1964-65; asso. firm Doyle, Smith & Doyle, New Orleans, 1965-66; staff counsel U.S. Fifth Circuit Ct. of Appeals, New Orleans, 1966-68; asso. firm Plotkin & Bradley, 1968-71; spl. research cons. Henican, James & Cleveland, 1972-73; sr. law clk. 24th Jud. Dist. Ct., Jefferson Parish, La., 1973-76; legal cons., trial analyst, New Orleans. Mem. La. State Bar Assn., New Orleans Notaries Assn., Phi Alpha Delta. Republican. Roman Catholic. Office: Suite 1110 First Nat Bank Commerce Bldg New Orleans LA 70112

SINK, ALVA GORDON (MRS. CHARLES A. SINK), clubwoman; b. Rose Twp., Mich.; d. Nathaniel J. and Ella M. (Highfield) Gordon; student Eastern Mich. U., summers 1914, 18; A.B., U. Mich., 1923; m. Charles A. Sink, June 18, 1923 (dec.). Tchr. pub. schs., Rose Center, Mich., 1914-17, Hickory Ridge, Mich., 1917-18, Holly, Mich., 1918-19, Canfield Pvt. Sch., Ann Arbor, Mich., 1919-22. Mem. Women's Republic Club, Ann Arbor. Dir. Washtenaw County chpt. ARC, 1943-48, 53-59, in charge First Aid and Accident Prevention, 1941-61; pres. Mich. House and Senate Club, 1929-30, U. Mich. Alumnae Club, 1931-33, Sara Browne Smith Group Alumnae Club, 1957-59, Women's Soc. Congl. Ch., 1946-48; regent Sarah Caswell Angell chpt. DAR, 1955-57. Recipient Red Cross citation, 1959, Alumnae Council award U. Mich., 1971, Disting. Alumni Service award U. Mich., 1978; Alva Gordon Sink Group of U. Mich. Alumnae named in her honor. Mem. Hist. Soc. Mich., Alumni Assn. U. Mich., French Huguenots, AAUW, Ann Arbor Art Assn., Henry P. Tappan Soc., P.E.O. Clubs: Art Study, Garden, Faculty Women, Presidents of U. Mich. (pres. emeritus 1975-76), Ann Arbor Women's City. Home: 1325 Olivia Ave Ann Arbor MI 48104

SINKEVICH, VALENTINA, librarian; b. Kiev, USSR, Sept. 29, 1926; came to U.S., 1950, naturalized, 1961; d. Aleksei Nikolaevich and Vera Petrovna (Matkovsky) S.; m. Michael Kaczurowski, May 29, 1946; 1 dau., Anna. Bibliog. asst. Union Library Catalogue, Phila., 1960-74; coordinator, 1974—; staff writer Novoye Russkoye Slovo, N.Y.C., 1970—, Phila. Inquirer, 1981—. Mem. Russian Acad. Assn. U.S.A., Phila. Literary Fellowship, Phila. Literary Group, N.Y. Poetry Forum. Author: Ogni, 1973; The Coming of Day, 1978; editor Russian Poetry and Art Almanac Perekrestki, 1978—; contbr. poetry and essays to Russian and Am. jours. Home: 7738 Woodbine Ave Philadelphia PA 19151 Office: 3420 Walnut St Philadelphia PA 19104

SINKFORD, JEANNE CRAIG, dental educator; b. Washington, Jan. 30, 1933; d. Richard E. and Geneva (Jefferson) Craig; B.S., Howard U., 1953, M.S., 1962, D.D.S., 1958, Ph.D., 1963; D.Sc. (hon.), Georgetown U., 1978; m. Stanley M. Sinkford, Dec. 8, 2, children—Dianne Sylvia, Janet Lynn, Stanley M. Ill. Instr. prosthodontics Howard U. Sch. Dentistry, Washington 1958-60, mem. faculty Dentistry, 1964—, asso. dean research coordinator, co-chmn. dept. restorative dentistry, 1968—, dean Coll. Dentistry, 1975; instr. research and crown and bridge Northwestern U. Sch. Dentistry, 1963-64; cons. prosthodontics and research VA Hosp., Washington, 1965—; cons. St. Elizabeth's Hosp.; mem. attending staff Howard U., Washington, 1964—, Children's Hosp. Nat. Med. Center, Washington; Mem. Nat. Adv. Dental Research Council, Nat. Bd. Dental Examiners; mem. ad hoc advisory panel Tuskegee Syphilis Study, HEW; mem. spl. med. advisory group VA; mem. dental devices classification com. FDA; sponsor D.C. Pub. Health Apprentice Program; mem. council Inst. Medicine, Nat. Acad. Sci.; mem. President's Panel for Promotion Child Health. Bd. overseers U. Pa.; contbr. Nat. Symphony Orch. Louise C. Ball fellow grad. tng., 1960-63. Recipient Alumni Achievement award Northwestern U., 1970; Distinguished Alumnus award Howard U. Alumni Fedn., 1971. Fellow Am. Coll. Dentists; mem. Internat. Assn. Dental Research, Dist. Dental Soc., Am. Inst. Oral Biology, North Portal Civic League, ADA (council on dental edn., appeal bd. commn. on accreditation), AAAS, AAUP, Internat. Coll. Dentists, Am. Prosthodonic Soc., Inst. Grad. Dentists (trustee), Wash. Council Adminstrv. Women, Assn. Am. Women Dentists, Am. Assn. Dental Schs., So. Conf. Dental Deans, Sigma Xi, Phi Beta Kappa, Omicron Kappa Upsilon, Psi Chi, Beta Kappa Chi. Office: Howard U Coll Dentistry 600 W St NW Washington DC 20059 *

SINKS, NANCY CLARK, edn. assn. exec.; b. Kansas City, Mo., Jan. 2, 1940; d. John Carol and Willa Minton Clark; B.S. in Edn., Miami U., Oxford, Ohio, 1969; M.A. in Edn., Ohio State U., 1979; children—Mark Frazer Sinks, Kenan Clark, Melanie Minton, Michelle Schubert. Tchr. public schs., Cin. and Columbus, Ohio, 1969-75; Uni-Serv cons. Ohio Edn. Assn., 1975-78; asst. dir. instrn. and profl. devel. Minn. Edn. Assn., St. Paul, 1978—. Recipient longevity service award ARC, 1968; Black Caucus appreciation award, 1978. Mem. Nat. Assn. Expn. Mgrs., NEA, ACLU, Nat. Assn. Female Execs., Minn. Coalition of Orgns. for Sex Equity in Minn., Common Cause, Minn. Interchange. Democrat. Methodist. Home: 1155 Benton Way Saint Paul MN 55112 Office: Minn Edn Assn 41 Sherburne Ave Saint Paul MN 55103

SINNAR, JOAN MARIE, govt. program analyst; b. San Diego, Calif., May 14, 1950; d. Donald John and Dolores Anne (Keating) Sinnar; B.A., St. Mary's Coll. Md., 1973; M.P.A., Am. U., 1978. Mgmt. analyst, dir. adminstrv. procs. staff FDA, Rockville, Md., 1975-79; asst. to dir. for policy analysis office of Asst. Sec. Enforcement and Ops., Dept. Treasury, Washington, 1979—. Founder, chmn. Treasury Women's Network, 1979-82; co-chmn. Young Profl. Forum, 1981-82. Recipient award merit FDA, 1978, Commendable Service award, 1979; Performance award Dept. Treasury, 1981. Mem. Am. Assn. Budget and Program Analysis, Am. Soc. Pub. Adminstrn., Nat. Young Profl. Forum, Treasury's Women Network, Women's Equity Action League, Nat. Assn. Female Execs. Democrat. Roman Catholic. Clubs: Young Professional Forum; Treasury Women Network. Home: 29 Dunsinane Ct Silver Spring MD 20906 Office: 15th and Pennsylvania Ave NW Washington DC 20220

SINNARD, ELAINE JANICE, painter, sculptor; b. Fort Collins, Colo., Feb. 14, 1926; d. Elven Orestes and Catherine (Bennet) S.; student Art Students League, 1948, N.Y. U., 1953, Sculpture Center, N.Y.C., 1954, Academie de la Grande Chaumiere, Paris, 1956. Painter, sculptor; works exhibited Riverside Mus., N.Y.C., 1955, City Center, N.Y.C., 1954-56, Nat. Arts Club, N.Y.C., 1959-82, Lord & Taylor, N.Y.C., 1963-78, Bergdorf Goodman, N.Y.C., 1980-82, Zantman Art Galleries, Carmel-by-the-Sea, Calif., 1970-73, Chevy Chase Gallery, Washington, 1981-82; one woman shows and group exhbns. include: Bergdorf Goodman Nena's Choice Gallery, Chevy Chase Gallery, Bjorn Lindgren Gallery; tchr. open workshop for artists. Mem. Nat. Arts Club N.Y.C. Home and Studio: Box 304 New Hampton NY 10958

SINNOTT, ROSE MARIE YUPPA, county ofcl.; b. Cliffside Park, N.J., Oct. 4, 1936; d. Maurice P. and Jeannette Frances (Cincotta) Yuppa; B.A., Marymount Coll., Tarrytown, N.Y., 1958; postgrad. U. London, Columbia U.; m. John P. Sinnott, May 30, 1959; children—James, Jessica. Tchr. jr. high sch. English, N.Y.C., 1959; freelance writer, 1967—; mem. New Providence (N.J.) Zoning Bd. Adjustment, 1966-70, vice chmn., 1970-73; pres. Sinnott & Bournique, Inc., public relations, New Providence, 1973—; mem. Bd. Chosen Freeholders Union County (N.J.), 1974—, chmn. 1981; trustee Union County Econ. Devel. Corp., 1976-81; mem. Union County Regional Health Council. Chmn. New Providence Heart Fund, 1967, Union County Heart Fund, 1974-80, Union County Mother's March of Dimes, 1978—; Republican mcpl. committeewoman, 1972. Mem. LWV (N.J. moderator 1966—), N.J. Assn. Counties, AAUW, Bus. and Profl. Women's Club, Catholic Daus. Am. (past grand regent). Author monthly newspaper column, also articles. Home: 2 Blackburn Pl Summit NJ 07901 Office: Courthouse Elizabeth NJ 07207

SINRICH, PHYLLIS, public relations cons.; b. N.Y.C., Mar. 22, 1931; d. George and Rose (Warshaw) Roizman; A.A.S., Fashion Inst. Tech., N.Y.C., 1950; m. Norman Sinrich, Dec. 21, 1952; children—William Douglas, Irene Leslie. Asst. fashion coordinator, then fashion coordinator Kirby, Block and Co., N.Y.C., 1950-56; program coordinator continuing edn. U. Conn., Stamford, 1973-75; owner Phyllis Sinrich Communications, Stamford, 1975—; Conn. rep. Dudley-Anderson-Yutzy Public Relations, Inc., N.Y.C., 1976—; incorporator, dir. Conn. Women's Bank, Greenwich. Chmn. Stamford Downtown Enhancement Commn., 1979—; mem. Stamford Planning Bd., 1974—; rep. Southwestern Regional Planning Agy., 1976-78. Recipient award feature story writing Conn. Press Women, 1977, multi-media public relations award, 1980. Mem. Nat. Fedn. Press Women, Nat. League Am. Pen Women, Women in Communications, Fairfield County Public Relations Assn., LWV (past officer), Woman's Place. Club: Midday (past v.p.). Address: 12 Fernwood Dr Stamford CT 06903

SINZER, CLAUDIA, engring. and constrn. co. exec.; b. Bklyn., May 25, 1952; d. Arthur J. and Ann M. Salerno; B.S. in Math., Dumbarton Coll., Washington, 1974; m. Joseph F. Sinzer, Jr., Apr. 30, 1977. With C-E Lummus Co., Bloomfield, N.J., 1975—, supr. procurement computer services, 1978-80, project procurement coordinator, 1980—. Mem. Nat. Assn. Exec. Women. Roman Catholic. Home: 168 Cedar St Cedar Grove NJ 07009 Office: 1515 Broad St Bloomfield NJ 07003

SIOU, LILY, acupuncture physician; b. China, Ot. 18, 1946; came to U.S., 1970, naturalized 1976; d. Pai Hwa and Hui Jeng (Hsu) S.; grad. Tai Hsuan Taoist Monastery, 1965; M.D., Soochoo Coll., 1969; Ph.D., Chinese U. Hong Kong. Resident physician Soochow Hosp., 1966; acupuncture physician Cheng and Siou Chinic Natural Medicine, Hong Kong, 1967, Sch. Six Chinese Arts, Honolulu, 1970—; mem. faculty ind. study program U. Hawaii, 1970-76; mem. Hawaii Bd. Acupuncture, 1975-79; cons. in field. Mem Acupuncture Herbalist Assn. Am. (pres. 1973), Hawaii Assn. Cert. Acupuncturists (dir.) Hawaii Assn. Art and Lit. (dir.), Soc. Chinese Art and Lit. Writers Assn. (dir). Taoist. Clubs: Writers of Am.; Mandarin Hawaii. Author: Chi Kung-The Art of Mastering the Unseen Life Force, 1973, 75, 80; Diary of the Way, 1976; I Ching-The Book of Changes, 1968; Chinese Palmistry and Phrenology, 1967; Dictionary of Chinese Medicine, 1968. Office: 2600 S King St Suite 206 Honolulu HI 96826

SIPE, DORIS ELAINE, coll. dean; b. Hickory, N.C., Aug. 20, 1942; d. Elmer E. and Beulah (Herman) S.; B.S., Concordia Coll., River Forest, Ill., 1964; M.A., Appalachian State U., Boone, N.C., 1970; D.Ed., Pa. State U., 1976. Tchr., Peace Corps, Malaysia, 1964-66, Concordia Christian Sch., Conover, N.C., 1967-69; asst. prof. geography Sacred Heart Coll., Belmont, N.C., 1970-76, dean night coll., dir. continuing edn., 1980—; regional chmn. Gov. N.C. Conf. Leadership Devel. Women, 1978; chmn. Gaston County Commn. Status Women, 1978-79; condr. workshops in field. Pres., Gaston (N.C.) Fine Arts Council, 1981-82. Mem. AAUW (chpt. corr. sec. 1972-75), Am. Assn. Higher Edn., Am. Soc. Tng. and Devel., World Future Soc. Democrat. Lutheran. Club: Altrusa (chmn. community services Gastonia chpt. 1981—). Home: 482 Lincoln St Cramerton NC 28032 Office: 414 N Main St Belmont NC 28012

SIPORIN, RAE LEE, univ. ofcl.; b. Detroit, Apr. 12, 1940; d. Morris and Zelda (Brown) Siporin; B.A., Wayne State U., 1962; M.S., UCLA, 1964, Ph.D. (Emma Wilson Richards fellow), 1968; cert. Inst. Ednl. Mgmt., Harvard U., 1977. Asst. prof. English, U. Pitts., 1968-72, asst. dean Coll. Arts and Scis., 1970-72, exec. asst. to vice chancellor planning and budget, 1973-75, dir. program planning, 1975-76; dean acad. affairs, prof. English Franklin Pierce Coll., Rindge, N.H., 1976-78; dean gen. studies Stockton State Coll., Pomona, N.J., 1978-79; dir. undergrad. admissions and relations with schs., UCLA, 1979—. Mem. adv. bd. Santa Monica (Calif.) YWCA, 1981—. Mem. Am. Assn. Higher Edn., Phi Beta Kappa. Democrat. Author: Women and Education: The Conference as Catalyst, 1972; editor: Female Studies V, 1972. Office: 405 Hilgard Ave Los Angeles CA 90024

SIRENA, ANTONIA MASTROCRISTINO, artist; b. White Plains, N.Y.; d. John and Lucrezia S.; self taught. One woman shows include: Galleria D'URSO, Rome, 1966, Bristol Palace, Ischia, Italy, 1967, Park Sheraton Hotel, N.Y.C., 1968, State Gallery, Opera House Massimo, Palermo, 1970, Galerie de Sfinx, Amsterdam, 1971, Galleria d'Arte, L'Albatross, Rome, 1973; represented in permanent collection Vatican Mus. Rome, Mus. Modern Art, Rome, Mus. Castello Sforzesco, Milan, State of Sicily, Am. consulate, Trieste, Italian line Michelangelo, C.W. Post U., L.I. N.Y., St. Jude's Children Hosp., Memphis, State Mus. Rome. Decorated St. Constantine Gold medal as dame Gran Cross, Rome; named Artist of Yr., Am. Com. Italian Migration, 1981, also Nat. Woman in Arts award; recipient Internat. Gold medal of Nice, Acad. Fine Hundred award, Cultural Internat. Com. Gold medal, 1st prize Gold Cup, Quadrennale of Europe, award Apollo 11, Gold medal Merit Nat. award France, Gold medal Legion d'Oro award, Paris, Silver cup Belgium Cultural Center, Brussels, Michelangelo Gold medal award, Italy, and numerous others. Roman Catholic.

SIROTNAK, VIRGINIA LEO, lawyer; b. Scranton, Pa., Sept. 29, 1935; d. Joseph A. and Theresa (Sebilia) Leo; B.A., Marywood Coll., Scranton, 1957, M.S. in Edn., 1959; J.D., U. Detroit, 1970; m. Joseph M. Sirotnak, Dec. 24, 1974. Tchr. Latin, Scranton public schs., 1957-67; legal clk. orphans ct. Lackawanna County (Pa.), 1970-71; admitted to Pa. bar, 1971; spl. asst. atty. gen. Office Chief Counsel, Pa. Dept. Transp., 1973-79; pvt. practice, Scranton, 1971—; asst. city solicitor City of Scranton, 1982—; mem. pre-law adv. bd. Marywood Coll., also mem. faculty Grad. Sch. Public Adminstrn. Bd. dirs. Scranton YWCA. Fulbright scholar, 1960. Mem. Pa. Bar Assn., Lackawanna County Bar Assn. (exec. com. of bd. dirs.), Lackawanna County Hist. Soc., AAUW (past chpt. pres.), Marywood Coll. Alumnae Assn. (past chpt. pres.), Scranton Bus. and Profl. Women's Club. Democrat. Roman Catholic. Office: 612 Connell Bldg Scranton PA 18503

SIRUSAS, VIRGINIA PAULIS, ins. co. exec.; b. Vilnius, Lithuania, Aug. 21, 1943; came to U.S., 1949, naturalized, 1959; d. Vladas and Mikalina (Zolynas) Paulis; B.A. in Econs., Rutgers U., 1965; m. Peter V. Sirusas, Sept. 6, 1966. Vice pres. Employee Benefit Trust div. Bankers Trust Co., N.Y.C., 1965-80; v.p. charge group pension dept. Equitable Life Assurance Soc., N.Y.C., 1980-82; v.p. charge N.Y.C. Office, Frank Russell Truse Co., 1982—. Home: Old Albany Post Rd Garrison NY 10524 Office: 575 Madison Ave New York NY

SISCA, NANCY LEONA, sch. adminstr.; b. N.Y.C., July 16, 1934; d. Stephan Dimitri and Mary Ann (Styga) Bondarenko; A.B., Coll. Mount St. Vincent, 1956; M.S., U. So. Calif., 1963; Ed.D., Brigham Young U., 1975; m. Marshall F. Sisca, Apr. 12, 1958. Prin., Fernald Sch., UCLA, 1971-72, 15th St. Sch., San Pedro, Calif., 1973-74; prin. Gulf Ave. Elem. Sch., Wilmington, Calif., 1974—. Vice pres. Wilmington Coordinating Council, 1975—. Mem. Assn. Adminstrs. of Los Angeles, Assn. Calif. Sch. Adminstrs., Nat. Assn. Female Execs., Town Hall, Women in Ednl. Leadership, Delta Kappa Gamma, Phi Delta Kappa. Democrat. Roman Catholic. Home: 749 Via Somonte Palos Verdes Estates CA 90274 Office: Gulf Ave Elementary School 828 W L St Wilmington CA 90744

SISKO, MARIE FERRARIS, assn. exec.; b. N.Y.C., Feb. 3, 1928; d. Joseph and Jean (Boaro) F.; B.A., Queens Coll., 1975; postgrad. Adelphi U., 1976; m. Taisto Edward Sisko, Dec. 26, 1948; children—Warren Joseph, Robert Edward. Asst. acct. N.Y.C. Bd. Edn., 1968-69; dir. personnel Daypac Inc., 1969-70; exec. asst. Ponder & Best, 1971-73; sales adminstr. Ampacet Corp., 1973-75; mktg. rep. Better Bus. Bur., 1975-77; asst. exec. dir. Leukemia Soc. Am., 1978—; v.p. Sisko Enterprises, N.Y. World's Fair, 1964-65; editor, salesperson Malba (N.Y.) News & Views Newspaper, 1969-80. Del. White House Conf. on Small Bus., N.Y.C., 1978. Mem. Direct Mail Fund Raisers Assn., N.Y. Assn. Women Bus. Owners (founding 1976, edn. com.), Queens Coll. Alumni Assn. (trustee 1976-82, pres. Ace chpt. 1977-79), Nat. Soc. Fund Raising Execs. (active fund raising day in N.Y. 1980, 81, 82, membership, edn. and research coms.), AAUW. Lutheran. Home: 32 Center Dr Malba NY 11357 Office: 205 Lexington Ave New York NY 10016

SISSON, KATHRYN LOUISE, heat supply co. exec.; b. Zion, Ill., July 18, 1947; d. W. Grant and Barbara J. (Baughman) S.; B.A. in Speech, Wheaton Coll., 1969; M.S. with distinction Lake Forest Sch. Mgmt., 1979; foster 1 son, Michael Twomey. Research asst. Northwest Regional Ednl. Lab., Portland, Oreg., 1969-72; mgr. data processing and adminstrn. Mid-Way Supply, Inc., Zion, Ill., 1974—. Bd. advisers Young Execs., 1981—. Mem. Nat. Assn. Wholesale Distbrs., Ill. Wholesale Distbrs. Assn., Women in Mgmt., Chgo. Land Wang VS Users Group (v.p. 1979—).

SISSON, N. VICTORIA, orgn. exec.; b. St. Louis, Apr. 21, 1938; d. Walter Chester and Dorothy Ruth (McVicar) Andereck; student Northeast Mo. U., 1955-57, Richland Coll., 1975-77; m. John Scogin Sisson, Jr., Apr. 7, 1958; children—John Scogin, Michael Christopher. Office mgr. N.Y. Life Ins. Co., N.Y.C., 1958-60; exec. asst. Consul to Guatemala, Dallas, 1975-76; project bus. mgr. Jr. Achievement, Dallas, 1977-78, divisional dir. project bus., 1979—; mem. women investors roundtable So. Meth. U. Recipient Exceptional Performance award Jr. Achievement, Inc., 1979. Mem. Internat. Assn. Bus. Communicators, Sales and Mktg. Execs. of Dallas, Nat. Assn. Female Execs. (network dir.), Richardson C. of C., Delta Zeta. Club: Zonta (chmn. Amelia Erhart com.) (Dallas). Contbr. articles to various mags. Home: 804 Woodland Way Richardson TX 75080 Office: 1201 Executive Dr W Richardson TX 75081

SISTERSON, JANET MARGOT, physicist; b. Edinburgh, Scotland, July 7, 1940; came to U.S. 1968; d. Thomas James and Lucy Margaret (Smith) Brownlee; B.Sc., U. Durham, 1961; Ph.D., Imperial Coll. Sci. and Tech., U. London, 1965; m. L. Keith Sisterson, Oct. 23, 1965; children—James, Mark. Basic grade physicist London Hosp., 1964-66; sr. physicist Chelsea Hosp. for Women, London, 1966-68; research fellow Cambridge (Mass.) Electron Acceleator, 1968-73; research assoc. Harvard Cyclotron Lab., 1973—. Mem. exec. bd. Harrington Sch. PTA 1977—. Mem. Am. Phys. Soc., Am. Assn. Physicists in Medicine, Am. Women in Sci. Contbr. articles to profl. jours. Office: 44 Oxford St Cambridge MA 02138

SITKO-QUEMORE, CLAUDIA MARIE, petrochem. co. mktg. exec.; b. Detroit, Oct. 30, 1953; d. Stanley Irving and Lucille Magdoline (Pawlowski) Sitko; B.S. in Mktg., No. Mich. U., 1975; m. Kurt Schuster Quemore, June 28, 1980. Salesperson polypropylene and polyvinyl chloride Diamond Shamrock Co., Cherry Hill, N.J., 1976-77; salesperson polypropylene and low density polyethylene No. Petrochem. Co., Chgo., 1977-79, product devel. specialist, research and devel., Omaha, 1979-81, on spl. assignment as product, market and sales specialist for biaxually oriented polypropylene films NPC Film div., Chgo., 1981—. Club: Toastmasters. Home: 208 Hillcrest Dr Strafford PA

SITZMAN, CATHI-JANE, psychologist; b. N.Y.C., June 25, 1952; d. Seymour Sidney and Shirley Terry (Cohen) S.; A.B., Washington U., 1972; M.A., Cath. U., 1975, Ph.D., 1979; m. Michael McDermott, Aug. 5, 1979; 1 dau., Mara Beverly. Research asst. Med. Center George Washington U., Washington, 1973; counseling extern Counseling Center, Cath. U. Am., Washington, 1974-76; counseling intern U. Md. Counseling Center, 1976-77; staff psychologist D.C. Inst. Mental Hygiene, 1977-79; dir. mental health clinic Womens Med. Center Washington, 1977-81; individual practice as psychologist, 1981—; staff asso. U. Md. Counseling Center, 1977—; cons. Wasserman Assos., Mem. Am. Psychol. Assn. Home: 306 Mississippi Ave Silver Spring MD 20910 Office: 2430 Pennsylvania Ave NW Washington DC 20037

SIVERIO, ELIZABETH, auditor; b. Bklyn., Nov. 19, 1955; d. Elias B. and Alice (Graulau) S.; student Am. U., 1973, Ocean County Coll., 1974-75; B.S. in Commerce cum laude, Rider Coll., 1977. Staff auditor United Jersey Banks, Princeton, N.J., 1977-78; EDP staff auditor, Hackensack, N.J., 1979; fin. and mgmt. trainee Navy Fin. Center, Lakehurst, N.J., 1979-80; staff auditor Fedders Corp., Edison, N.J., 1980-81; auditor Solid State div. RCA, Somerville, N.J., 1981—. Mem. Nat. Assn. Female Execs. Democrat. Roman Catholic. Clubs: Central Jersey Ski, Kangaroo Cts. Home: 36 New Prospect Rd Jackson NJ 08527 Office: Route 202 Somerville NJ 08876

SIVERSON, JUDITH BUNT, clin. psychologist; b. Phila., June 27, 1935; d. Michael and Katherine (Lemon) Bunt; A.B. magna cum laude, Temple U., Phila., 1968; M.A., 1969, Ph.D. in Clin. Psychology, 1974; 1 dau., Michele Lyn. Staff psychologist rehab. medicine dept. Temple U. Hosp., 1971-72; staff psychologist alcoholism unit Diagnostic and Rehab. Center, Phila., 1972-73; staff psychologist Community Mental Health Center Gloucester County, Woodbury, N.J., 1973-75; chief psychologist rehab. medicine dept. Rolling Hill Hosp., Elkins Park, Pa., 1975-77; chief psychol. services rehab. medicine dept. Temple U. Hosp., 1977-80; pvt. practice psychology, cons., Glassboro, N.J., and Phila., 1980—; adj. assoc. prof. Temple U. Served with WAC, U.S. Army, 1955-57. Lic. psychologist Pa., N.J. Mem. Nat. Acad. Neuropsychologists, Am. Psychol. Assn., Pa. Psychol. Assn., Phila. Soc. Clin. Psychologists. Address: 22 Dickinson Rd Glassboro NJ 08028

SIWEK, GERALDINE MARY, voluntary health agy. exec.; b. Davenport, Iowa, Apr. 10, 1924; d. Gervase Thomas and Marjorie Sarah (Wilcox) Creeden; B.S., Siena Coll., 1948; postgrad. in elec. engring. Rensselaer Poly. Inst., 1948; m. Erwin Siwek, Apr. 28, 1949; children—Susan, Gretchen, Erwin, Cynthia, Sarah, Eric, Amy. Engr. asst. Gen. Electric Co., Schenectady, 1942-49; sr. citizen cons., Waterford, N.Y., 1965-67; exec. dir. March of Dimes, Saratoga Springs, 1967—; cons. to prenatal clinics, health systems agys. Mem. exec. bd. Mohawk-Pathways council Girl Scouts U.S.A., 1958-65; mem. exec. bd. Capital Dist. LWV, 1969-72. Recipient Outstanding Program award Nat. Found. March of Dimes, 1970, 73, 78, Outstanding Chpt. award, 1975, 77. Mem. N.Y. State Public Health Assn., Eta Gamma Sigma. Home: 20 Excelsior Springs Ave Saratoga NY 12866 Office: 26 Excelsior Springs Ave Saratoga NY 12866

SIWEK, LORRAINE, mfg. co. ofcl.; b. Mpls.; d. Joseph Theodore and Frances Marcella S.; B.S. in Edn., U. Minn., 1967. Elem. tchr., Mpls., 1967-73; sales rep. Hudson's Contract Div., Detroit, 1974-76; account mgr. E.F. Hauserman Co., Detroit, 1976—. Mem. Detroit Women's Econ. Club, Travelers Aid Soc. (dir.), Founders Soc.-Detroit Inst. Arts. Home: 7371 Laurel Ct West Bloomfield MI 48033 Office: 4000 Town Center Suite 1070 Southfield MI 48075

SIXTA, JANE ANNE WATERS, security services co. exec.; b. Bklyn., May 13, 1951; d. Frank Theodore and Irene Regina (Huyck) Waters; B.A., Aurora Coll., 1973; m. Lorrin Lee Sixta, Aug. 19, 1977. Chief of security Fermilab, Batavia, Ill., 1975-77; br. mgr. Advance Security, Inc. div. Figgie Internat., Inc., Kansas City, Mo., 1978—, chmn. mgmt. steering com. corp. hdqrs., Atlanta. Mem. Am. Soc. Indsl. Security (cert. protection profl., chmn. membership com. Greater Kansas City chpt. 1981-82, treas. 1982-83), Nat. Assn. Female Execs., AAUW, Humane Soc. Greater Kansas City (pres. bd. dirs.). Home: 9813 Aberdeen Leawood KS 66206 Office: 3515 Broadway Kansas City MO 64111

SIZEMORE, DOROTHY JOHNSON, coll. dean; b. Kansas City, Kans., Sept. 19, 1932; d. Lloyd Edmund and Lorene Ernie (Walker) Johnson; B.A., William Jewell Coll., Liberty, Mo., 1955; M.A., Georgetown (Ky.) Coll., 1963; m. Burlan Arthur Sizemore, Jr., June 5, 1954 (dec.); children—Sherry Lee, Cynthia Gayle, Burlan Arthur, Rebecca Lorene. Public sch. tchr., Mo., Ky. and Ind., 1952-58; ednl. dir. Head Start, Clay-Platte-Eastern Jackson Counties, Kansas City, Mo., 1970-73; kindergarten tchr., Taipei, Taiwan, 1973-74; dir. family ministries Englewood Baptist Ch., Kansas City, Mo., 1974-79; dean women Wingate (N.C.) Coll., 1979-80; dean students Meredith Coll., Raleigh, N.C., 1980—; cons. in field. Mem. Nat. Assn. Women Deans, Adminstrs. and Counselors, Am. Coll. Personnel Assn., Am. Personnel and Guidance Assn., Nat. Assn. Student Personnel Adminstrs., Nat. Acad. Advising Assn., So. Coll. Personnel Assn., Southeastern Assn. Housing Officers. Baptist. Office: Meredith Coll 3800 Hillsborough St Raleigh NC 27607

SIZEMORE, EARLEEN WILKERSON, state legislator; b. Worth County, Ga., July 29, 1938; d. Joseph Earl and Mamie Eloise (Roberts) Wilkerson; B.S. in Bus. Edn., Ga. So. Coll., 1959; M.Ed. in Bus. Edn., Ga. Coll., 1964; Ed.Sp., U. Ga., 1970; postgrad. in Adminstrn., Valdosta (Ga.) State U., 1976; m. Cortez B. Sizemore, Nov. 8, 1957; children—Vicki Eloise, Staci Barnett, Robby Barnett (dec.). Bus. edn. tchr., 1959-76; mem. Ga. Ho. of Reps., Dist. 136, 1975-82, mem. agr., edn., ways and means coms., Mem. Ga. Assn. Educators, Worth Assn. Educators. Democrat. Baptist. Club: Sylvester Jr. Woman's (2d. v.p. 1974). Contbr. articles to ednl. publs. Office: PO Box 539 Sylvester GA 31791

SIZEMORE, LINDA CAROL, psychologist; b. Boston, July 24, 1943; d. Harry and Ruth (Goldstein) Freeman; B.A., U. Wis., 1965, M.S., 1968; Ph.D., Northwestern U., 1975; m. John A. Sizemore, July 15, 1972; children—John A., Hilary. Pvt. practice psychology, Highland Park, Ill., 1975—; indsl. cons. on alcoholism and drug abuse; leader group on child rearing Abe and Sadie Becker Nursery Sch., Highland Park, 1979-80; lectr. Barat Coll., 1975; program coordinator mental health com. Congregation Solel, Highland Park, 1977-79. NIMH fellow, 1967-68; NIH fellow, 1968-69; Walter Scott Dill fellow, 1974; Northwestern U.

fellow, 1974-75. Mem. Am. Psychol. Assn., Women in Mgmt. (dir. chpt. 1981-82). Jewish. Address: 3360 Brook Rd Highland Park IL 60035

SIZER, JUANITA SINCLAIR, writer, editor; b. Ahoskie, N.C., Feb. 6, 1924; d. Thomas Huntley and Nita Mae (Futrell) Sinclair; student U. N.C., 1941-42, Coker Coll., 1958-59; children—Sharon Sizer Finucane, Walter H., R.E. Editor, Northampton (N.C.) Times-News, 1960-63; news editor Suffolk (Va.) News-Herald, 1963-66; staff writer Virginian-Pilot, 1966-79; sr. analyst, program mgr. mil. electronic tech. manuals ManTech Internat. Corp., Arlington, Va., 1979-81; tech. manual program mgr. Naval Electronics Systems Command, Washington, 1981—. Recipient various Va. and N.C. press awards. Mem. Va. Press Women, Sigma Delta Chi. Home: 5918 Kingsford Rd Springfield VA 22152 Office: Crystal City Arlington VA

SKALICKY, MARY ELIZABETH, organist, music tchr.; b. Greenville, Tex., Dec. 6, 1931; d. James Leslie and Mary Elizabeth (Webb) Moore; Mus.B. in Piano, So. Meth. U., 1952, Mus.B. in Organ, 1952; Mus.M. in Organ, U. Mich., 1955; postgrad. Amsterdam Conservatory, 1958, Netherlands Carillon Sch., 1958, Yale U., 1966, U. Tex., summer 1969, Tex. Tech U., summer 1973; cert. in organ Acad. of Music, Prague, Czechoslovakia, summers 1973, 76; cert. in organ Internat. Mastercourse in Music, Zurich, Switzerland, summer 1976; m. Miloslav Skalicky, Aug. 11, 1970; 1 dau., Celeste Grenier Dale. Teaching asst. U. Mich., 1954-55; tchr. piano Miss Porter's Sch., Farmington, Conn., 1956-58; tchr. piano and organ Julius Hartt Sch. Music, Hartford, Conn., 1956-57; tchr. piano Cleve. Music Sch. Settlement, 1965; instr. music Howard Coll., Big Spring, Tex., 1968-76, head music dept., 1972-73, head fine arts dept., 1973-75; pvt. music tchr., 1982—; organist Lovers Lane Meth. Ch., Dallas, 1950-53, Heights Christian Ch., Shaker Heights, Ohio, 1963-65, First Bapt. Ch., Big Spring, Tex., 1968-69, First United Meth. Ch., Big Spring, 1970-73; organist, dir. Congl. Ch., Ypsilanti, Mich., 1954-56, Trinity Epis. Ch., Wethersfield, Conn., 1955-56, All Saints' Epis. Ch., Meriden, Conn., 1960-62; organist-dir. Ch. of St. Mary the Virgin, Episcopal, Big Spring, 1982—; organ and carillon recitalist in churches throughout East, Midwest and Southwest; judge piano contests, Midland and Abilene, Tex. Mem. bd. Big Spring Community Concert Assn., 1970. Internat. Research and Exchange Bd. travel grantee, Czechoslovakia, 1983. Mem. DAR (rec. sec.), Nat. Soc. Colonial Dames of XVII Century, Czechoslovak Soc. Arts and Scis. in N.Am., Big Spring Piano Tchrs. Forum (v.p. 1971). Republican. Episcopalian. Club: Big Spring Music Study (past pres.). Home and Studio: 2700 Apache Dr Big Spring TX 79720

SKALLE, MAVIS SCHUBERT, corp. exec.; b. Milw., May 6, 1924; d. Gilbert J. and Gertrude S. (Miller) Schubert; B.B.A. summa cum laude, Marquette U., 1945; m. Hans J. Skalle, May 29, 1954; children—Hans J., Heidi Mavis. Controller, Crucible Steel Casting Co., Milw., 1945-54; v.p., treas. Foundry Supply Corp., Milw., 1950-54; asst. sec., treas. Ebaloy, Inc., Rockton, Ill., 1951-54; treas., asst. sec. Foundry Equipment Corp., Chgo., 1950-54; asst. sec., treas. Iowa-Mich. Corp., Chgo., also Whitehall Co., Chgo., 1953-54; exec. sec. Interlachen Country Club, Mpls., 1955-65; v.p., sec., co-owner Camelot, Inc., Bloomington, Minn., 1965-81, Skalco Corp., Edina, Minn., 1975—. Named to Hospitality Hall of Fame, 1966; recipient Ivy award, 1975. Mem. Bus. Adminstrn. Alumni Assn. Marquette U. (steering com. 1955), Am. Bus. Women's Assn., PEO, AAUW, Phi Chi Theta (nat. adv. 1954-56, nat. pres. 1952-54, nat. v.p. 1950-52 nat. scholarship trustee 1973-75), Beta Gamma Sigma, Gamma Pi Epsilon, Alpha Sigma Nu. Lutheran. Clubs: Edina Woman's (treas. 1966-67, pres. 1968-69), Woman's of Mpls. Home: 5021 Ridge Rd Edina MN 55436

SKED, DOROTHY ANNA, librarian; b. West New York, N.J., July 6; d. William Stephen and Lillian May (Loeffel) Busch; B.S., State Tchrs. Coll., Newark, N.J., 1950; B.L.S., State Tchrs. Coll., Trenton, N.J., 1953; m. Harold A. Sked, May 30, 1934; children—Joycelyn Duane Sked Quick, Sandra Jean Sked Lima. Head librarian Pennington (N.J.) Sch. Boys, 1949-51, Thomas Jefferson Jr. High Sch., Fair Lawn, N.J., 1951-54, Coll. High Sch., Montclair, N.J., 1954-58, Hoffman LaRoche, Nutley, N.J., 1958-62; asst. librarian ITT Fed. Labs., Nutley, 1962-64; research and info. scientist E.R. Squibb, New Brunswick, N.J., 1964-65; librarian Kean Coll. N.J., Union, 1965—, instr. library sci., 1965—, asst. prof., edn. librarian, 1977—. Mem. Spl. Libraries Assn., NEA, N.J. Edn. Assn. Home: 32C Molly Pitcher Blvd Whiting NJ 08759 Office: Kean Coll of NJ Nancy Thompson Library Union NJ 07083

SKEELS, NATALIE MAUD, control systems co. exec.; b. Seattle, Aug. 15, 1921; d. Norman Edward and Frances (DeLong) Coles; B.A. summa cum laude, UCLA, 1945; postgrad. U. Wash., Seattle; M. Dell R. Skeels, June 28, 1953; 1 son, Norman Louis. Instr. humanistic social studies dept. U. Wash., 1947-52; with Honeywell Marine Systems, Seattle, 1955—, mktg. services supr., 1972-76, communications mgr., 1977-81, gainsharing mgr., 1982—; dir. Washington Feminist Fed. Credit Union, 1981-82; speaker, panelist in field. Past mem. King County donor council Puget Sound Blood Center; mem. Wash. Balance of State Pvt. Industry Council, 1981—. Mem. Bus. and Profl. Women (past chpt. pres. Woman of Year award 1981), Women and Bus. (pres. 1982-83, chmn. directory publishing com. 1981), Network Exec. Women (past pres.), Inst. Managerial and Profl. Women, Women's Mgmt. and Profl. Network, Internat. Assn. Quality Circles, Urban League, Seattle C. of C., Phi Beta Kappa, Kappa Kappa Gamma. Democrat. Roman Catholic. Clubs: Olympic Racquet and Health, City. Author articles in field. Office: 5303 Shilshole Ave NW Seattle WA 98107

SKELLENGER, SHIRLEY ANN, devel. cons.; b. Cashmere, Wash., Mar. 24, 1938; d. Everett Fred and Sena Louise (Nelson) Vandusen; student Wash. State U., 1956-59; Nat. Urban League fellow U. Wash., 1969; children—Richard Blonden, Kirstin Blonden. Adminstrv. asst. Seattle Urban League, 1966-69; press sec. to Congressman Brock Adams, Seattle and Washington, D.C., 1969-73; dir. devel. Sta. KCTS-TV, Seattle, 1973-74; dir. fiscal planning and devel. King County YWCA, Seattle, 1976-77; dir. devel. Lakeside Sch., Seattle, 1977-80; cons. devel., 1981—. Sec.-treas. Met. Democratic Club, Seattle, 1973-77; mem. Seattle Women's Commn., 1976-80, pres., 1978-80; bd. dirs. World Without War Council, 1977-80; trustee Wash. State Ind. Sch. Fund; mem. adv. council Pacific NW Assn. Ind. Schs. Mem. NW Devel. Officer Assn. (officer), Pacific NW Writers Conf., Kappa Alpha Theta. Office: Cornish Inst 710 E Ray St Seattle WA 98102

SKELTON, DOROTHY GENEVA SIMMONS (MRS. JOHN WILLIAM SKELTON), educator; b. Woodland, Calif.; d. Jack Elijah and Helen Anna (Siebe) Simmons; B.A., U. Calif., 1940, M.A., 1943; m. John William Skelton, July 16, 1941. Sr. research analyst War Dept., Gen. Staff, M.I. Div. G-2, Pentagon, Washington, 1944-45; vol. researcher, monuments, fine arts and archives sect. Restitution Br., Office Mil. Govt. for Hesse, Wiesbaden, German, 1947-48; vol. art tchr. German children in Bad Nauheim, Germany, 1947-48; art educator, lectr. Dayton (Ohio) Art Inst., 1955; art educator Lincoln Sch., Dayton, 1956-60; instr. art and art edn. U. Va. Sch. Continuing Edn., Charlottesville, 1962-75; researcher genealogy, exhibited in group shows, Calif., Colo., Ohio, Washington and Va.; represented in permanent collections Madison Hall, Charlottesville, Madison (Va.) Center. Mem. Nat. League Am. Pen Women, AAUW, Am. Assn. Museums, Coll. Art Assn. Am., Inst. for Study of Art in Edn., Dayton Soc. Painters and Sculptors, Nat. Soc. Arts and Letters (life), Va. Mus. Fine Arts, Cal. Alumni Assn., Air Force Officers Wives Club. Republican. Methodist. Clubs: Army Navy Country; Lake of the Woods (Va.) Golf and Country. Chief collaborator: John Skelton of Georgia, 1969. Address: Lotos Lakes Brightwood VA 22715

SKENDER, LAVERNE JANET, electric motor services co. exec.; b. Oak Park, Ill., Aug. 28, 1935; d. Edward Louis and Philamina Tillie (Baumruk) Stedron; A.A., Morton Jr. Coll., 1955; m. George Joseph Skender, June 9, 1956; children—Jeffrey Scott, Patricia Diane, Edward George, Jacalyn Louise, Amy Lynn. Sec., Sears Roebuck, 1952-58; asst. purchasing agt. Prater Industries, 1967-69; sec. Dykema & Dykema, 1970-71; outside salesman DeBar Electric Motors, Chgo., from 1971, now pres.; dir. Burnex Corp., Stedcor Corp., Ash Manor, Inc. Pres. U.S. Navy League, Forest Park, 1976, 77, 79, 81, 82; active NOW. Named to scroll of honor U.S. Navy League. Mem. Elec. Apparatus Service Assn. (mem. mgmt.), Elec. Motor Distbrs., Assn. Elec. Machinery Trades, World Chpt. Elec. Assn., Am. Soc. Profl. and Exec. Women, Nat. Assn. Female Execs. Clubs: West Suburban Exec., West Suburban Breakfast (dir. 1980-82), Bus. and Profl. Women (legis. chmn. Cicero, 1976-77, 80-81, pres. 1974-75, 79-71, Nike award, dist. dir. 1976, state expansion chmn., 1980-81). First woman in outside motor sales, first woman shop foreman, first woman pres. of motor shop, first woman pres. U.S. Navy League Council. Home: 2211 W Clifton Pl Hoffman Estates IL 60195 Office: 2740 N Pulaski Rd Chicago IL 60639

SKIBINE, MARJORIE LOUISE TALLCHIEF (MRS. GEORGE SKIBINE), ballerina; b. Denver; d. Alexander and Ruth (Porter) Tallchief; ballet tng. with Bronislava Nijinska, David Lichine; m. George Skibine (dec.). Became soloist Am. Ballet Theater while in 'teens; became ballerina Grand Ballet du Marquid de Cuevas, at age 19; later 1st American to become premiere danseuse etoile Paris Opera; now dir. Chgo. Ballet Sch.; former dir. Dallas Ballet Acad. Decorated chevalier du Nisham Iftikar for artistic achievement (Tunisia).

SKINNER, ANGELA KAREN, med. technologist; b. Spartanburg County, S.C., June 20, 1954; d. Harold Eugene and Allie Lillie (Pettit) Skinner; student North Greenville Coll., 1972-73; A.M.T., Spartanburg Tech. Coll., 1976; B. Interdisciplinary Studies, U. S.C., 1979. Med. lab. technologist Spartanburg (S.C.) Gen. Hosp., 1976—, phlebotomy technician supr., 1976—. Mem. Am. Soc. Clin. Pathologists, Palmetto Blood Bank Assn. Democrat. Baptist. Home: Route 1 PO Box 341 Ellenboro NC 28040 Office: 101 E Wood St Spartanburg SC 29303

SKINNER, DOROTHY JEANETTE, pageant adminstr.; b. Atlanta, Jan. 6, 1939; d. Herman Glenn and Lona Ann (Chapman) Smith; student DeKalb Coll., 1968-70; m. William L. Skinner, Mar. 30, 1967; children—Susan, Anthony, Janet, Rodney. Legal sec. Atlanta Legal Aid Soc., 1958-67, Peek & Whaley, Atlanta, 1973-79; state dir. Miss Teen USA, Inc., Stone Mountain, Ga., 1978—, pres., exec. dir., Atlanta, 1979-80. Mem. Nat. Fedn. Bus. and Profl. Women, Nat. Assn. Female Execs. Baptist. Home: 766 Corundum Ct Stone Mountain GA 30083 Office: 2250 N Druid Hills Rd NE Atlanta GA 30329

SKINNER, ELSA MARGARETHE, sand and gravel, contracting exec.; b. Sternau, Kreis Konitz, Ger., Feb. 15, 1918; came to U.S., 1923, naturalized, 1945; d. Leo Leopold and Maria Anna (Inder Rieden) Look; student parochial schs., Cin.; m. Albert George Skinner, Apr. 15, 1944; children—Ray Albert, Maria Elsa Skinner Roy. With Consol. Sash & Door Co., St. Bernard, Ohio, 1936-44, Voice of Am., Mason, Ohio, 1944-46, King Powder Co., Mason, 1944—; with Skinner Sand & Gravel Co., West Chester, Ohio, 1969—, pres., owner, 1975—. Named hon. Ky. col., 1966. Mem. Our Lady of Angels Alumnae Assn., Assn. Miraculous Medal, St. John's Altar Soc. Roman Catholic. Address: 8750 Cincinnati-Dayton Rd West Chester OH 45069

SKINNER, MARY JUST, Vt. state senator; b. South Bend, Ind., July 7, 1946; A.B., cum laude, Barnard Coll., 1968; J.D., Columbia U., 1971; m. Scott Skinner; 1 son. Admitted to Vt. bar, N.Y. bar, Pa. bar; mem. U.S. Commn. on Civil Rights; vice chair Vt. Adv. Com.; mem. Washington County Democratic Com.; mem. Vt. State Senate, 1979-80, 81—. Mem. Montpelier Merchants' Bur., Montpelier on the Move, Building a Better Barre, Inc. Mem. Women in Bus. in the Mad River Valley, Vt. Bar Assn. Office: Vt Ho of Reps State House Montpelier VT 05602 *

SKINNER, PATRICIA MORAG, state legislator; b. Glasgow, Soctland, Dec. 3, 1932; d. John Stuart and Frances Charlotte (Swann) Robertson; A.B., N.Y. U., 1953; m. Robert A. Skinner, Dec. 28, 1957; children—Robin Ann, Pamela. Mdse. trainee Lord & Taylor, N.Y.C., 1955-59; adminstrv. asst. Atlantic Products, N.Y.C., 1954-59; newspaper corr. Salem (N.H.) Observer, 1964—; mem. N.H. Ho. of Reps., 1973—, chmn. labor, human resources and rehab. com., 1975—. Bd. dirs. Castle Jr. Coll., 1975; mem. adv. council N.H. Voc-Tech. Coll., Nashua, 1978. Mem. N.H. Fedn. Women's Clubs (parliamentarian). Republican. Christian Scientist. Clubs: Order of Eastern Star, Windham Woman's (pres. 1981—). Office: 306 Legislative Office Bldg Concord NH 03301

SKIRVIN, ELAINE LOUISE, social worker; b. Akron, Ohio, Aug. 1, 1945; d. Delmar L. and Elizabeth (Neidert) S.; B.A.; Kent State U., 1968; M.S. in Social Adminstrn., Case Western Res. U., 1977. Protective services caseworker Cuyahoga County (Ohio) Child Welfare, Cleve., 1968-69; tchr., counselor Amerikan Kiz Koleji, Izmir, Turkey, 1969-70; social worker Parmadale Children's Village, Parma, Ohio, 1972-75; family and child therapist Child Parent Help Center West Side Community Mental Health Center, Cleve., 1977—; cons. in field. Vice chmn. Kaiser Consumer Council, 1976-77, chairperson, 1978-82; mem. citizens adv. com. for children's services Cuyahoga County Welfare Dept., 1979-82. Mem. Nat. Assn. Social Workers. Club: Handy-Cap Horizons (dir. 1982). Home: 1502 Hillcrest Rd East Cleveland OH 44118 Office: 2031 W 30th St Cleveland OH 44113

SKOLDBERG, PHYLLIS LINNEA, violinist, educator; b. Bremerton, Wash.; d. August Theodore and Esther Amanda Skoldberg; B.M. with honors, New Eng. Conservatory, 1955, M.M., 1957; M. with high distinction in Music Edn., Ind. U., 1964, D.M., 1967. Violinist, Houston Symphony Orch., 1957-59, Cin. Symphony Orch., 1959-62; prof. music SUNY, Oswego, 1964-77; asst. dean, prof. music Coll. Fine Arts, Ariz. State U., Tempe, 1977—; recitals in U.S., Can., France, Scandinavia; appearances at Reston Music Festival, Charles Ives Festival, Western Arts Festival. Recipient Pacific NW Artists Award, 1953, Boston Civic Music Award, 1953. Mem. Ariz. Alliance for Arts in Edn., Nat. Assn. Schs. of Music, Music Educator's Nat. Conf., Am. String Tchrs. Assn., Coll. Music Soc., Arizonians for Cultural Devel. Author: The Strings: A Comparative View, 1982; contbr. articles to profl. jours. Office: Coll Fine Arts 132 Dixie Gammage Hall Ariz State U Tempe AZ 85287

SKONBERG, MADELON BAENZIGER (MRS. JOSEPH E. SKONBERG), educator; b. Chgo., Sept. 8, 1906; d. Rudolph Solomon and Olga Mathilde (Schiska) Baenziger; student Bush Conservatory, 1927-28, Ill. State Normal U., 1932, Chgo. Mus. Coll., 1935-37, North Park Coll., 1940-42, Tchrs. Coll., 1957-58; Mus.B. In Piano, Mus.B. In Theory, Cosmopolitan Sch. Music; postgrad. Northwestern Sch. Music Grad. Sch., 1963—; m. Joseph Emil Skonberg, Apr. 20, 1935; children—Kristin, Karen. Music reviewer Mus. Leader, Chgo., 1950-67; adjudicator Nat. Guild Piano Tchrs., Austin, Tex., 1955—; tchr. piano, organ Cosmopolitan Sch. Music, Chgo., 1956-62. Mem. Art Inst. Chgo., Soc. Am. Musicians, Nat. League Am. Pen Women, Nat., Ill. State music tchrs. assns., Nat. Fedn. Music Clubs, Nat. Soc. Sci. Study Edn., Nat. Fedn. Women Clubs, Mu Phi Epsilon. Club: Women's Literary. Home: 2601 W Sunnyside Ave Chicago IL 60625

SKOOG, ANNE CATHERINE, librarian; b. Rochester, Pa., Jan. 21, 1917; d. Carl Albert and Catherine Gertrude (Elm) S.; B.S., Carnegie Inst. Inst. Tech., 1939, B.S. in L.S., 1940. Cataloger, Westminster Coll. Library, New Wilmington, Pa., 1940-44; asst. bus. br. Carnegie Library, Pitts., 1944-46; social relations br. librarian Carnegie Inst. Tech., 1946-50, asst. cataloger, 1950-66; asso. cataloger Carnegie-Mellon U., 1966-76, fine and rare books librarian, 1966-82; curator Archetype Press, 1973-82. Mem. ALA, Pa. Library Assn. (editor bull. 1957-60), Tri-State Assn. Coll. and Research Libraries, Bibliog. Soc. Am., Pitts. Bibliophiles, Hist. Soc. Western Pa., Pitts. History and Landmarks Found., Nat. Fedn. Bus. and Profl. Women's Clubs (pres. Oakland club 1966-68), Phi Kappa Phi. Methodist. Club: College (Pitts.). Contbr. articles to publs. Home: 5604 5th Ave Apt 206 Pittsburgh PA 15232

SKOV, IVA LEE MARIE, educator; b. Havelock, Iowa, Feb. 23, 1934; d. Reamer H. and Nellie A. Aden; B.S., S.D. State U., 1958, M.S., 1959; Ph.D., U. So. Calif., 1976; m. John V.B. Skov, 1954; m. 2d, Roger Coleman, Jan. 1, 1978; 1 son, James B. V. Skov. Head spl. surveys, mktg. research dept. Los Angeles Times, 1959-62; instr. E. Los Angeles Coll., 1963-65; asst. prof. Harbor Coll., Wilmington, Calif., 1965-72; asso. prof., dir. center for econ. edn. Calif. State U., Long Beach, 1972—; program dir. Calif. Council Econ. Edn. and asso. dir. Calif. State Univs. and Colls. Project for Econ. Literacy, 1976-77; Counselor New Hope Telephone Line; speaker consumer affairs various community groups. Mem. Am., Western econ. assns., Western Regional Sci. Assn., Calif. Council and Joint Council Econ. Edn., Am. Council Consumer Interests, Omicron Delta Epsilon. Lutheran. Author: Outstanding Materials or Projects for Exceptional Students of High School Economics Classes, 1978; (with others) Scope and Content Statement for Social Sciences, 1977; contbr. articles to profl. publs.

SKOV-GORDON, ANDRÉA RIIS, bus. machine exec.; b. Zurich, Switzerland, Sept. 10, 1952; d. Niels Aage and Camille Emery (Burleigh) Skov; B.S. in Physics, Northeastern U., 1973, M.S. in Physics, 1974; m. Michael Franklin Gordon, Aug. 30, 1980. Project engr. aerospace div. Gen. Electric Co., Hanscom AFB, Bedford, Mass., 1975-77; N.E. dist. salesman Ramtek Corp., Lexington, Mass., 1977-78, product mktg. mgr. color graphic terminals, Santa Clara, Calif., 1978-81; dir. product mgmt. Logical Bus. Machines, Sunnyvale, Calif., 1981-82, v.p., 1982—. Mem. Soc. Women Engrs., Tech. Mktg. Soc. Am., NOW, Nat. Dance Tchrs. Assn. Republican. Unitarian. Home: 14970 Sobey Rd Saratoga CA 95070 Office: 1294 Hammerwood Ave Sunnyvale CA 94086

SKREL, SYLVIA MARGARET, state legislator; b. Detroit, Aug. 29, 1928; d. Boleslaw Felix and Veronica (Holota) Kompoltowicz; student Oakland U., 1974, Madonna Coll., 1977; children—Jerome, Gary. Constituent service rep., sr. citizen coordinator Congressman Carl Pursell, 1977-80; mem. Mich. Ho. of Reps., 1980—. Mem. Nat. Order Women Legislators, Livonia C. of C., Westland C. of C. Republican. Roman Catholic. Office: 220 State Capitol Bldg Lansing MI 48909

SKRETTING, RUTH B., ret. educator; b. Milw., Jan. 26, 1926; d. Paul Walter and Minnie (Tapp) Bartelt; B.S., B.A. with honors, U. Wis., Milw., 1943; M.A. cum laude, Northwestern U., 1946; m. John Richard Skretting, June 14, 1947, (dec. Oct. 1972); m. 2, Hans Bertschi, 1980. Tchr., Milw. Schs., 1943-46; tchr. English, Janesville (Wis.) Schs., 1947-48; asst. dir. ednl. placement U. Iowa, 1948-52; Welcome Wagon hostess, Chapel Hill, N.C., 1953-54; acting dean of women U. N.C., Chapel Hill, 1955; tchr. German, English, dean of girls Leon High Sch., Tallahassee, 1957-71; dir. guidance Amos P. Godby High Sch., Tallahassee, 1971-73, tchr. English, 1973-81, ret., 1981. Bd. dirs., del. to Washington, LWV Freedom Conf., 1953-55; del. to White House Conf. on Children and Youth, 1959-60; mem. Fla. White House Com., 1959-60. Named Star Tchr., Leon High Sch., 1969. Mem. Leon County English Tchrs. (chmn. 1957-58), AAUW (pres. Chapel Hill br. 1955, Tallahassee br. 1958-60), LWV, Fla. Edn. Assn., NEA, Nat. Council Tchrs. English, Friends of the Library (pres. 1981—), Kappa Delta Pi, Delta Kappa Gamma (chpt. pres. 1976-78, state sec. 1979-81), Beta Theta Pi Little Sisters, Delta Lambda. Democrat. Christian Scientist. Clubs: Gourmet Cooking, Book Club, Anchor Clubs (coordinator), Pilot (pres. Tallahassee 1965-66), Fla. State U. Women. Home: 1822 Sharon Rd Tallahassee FL 32303

SKRINAK, LORRAINE BARBARA, advt. agy. exec.; b. Wilkes-Barre, Pa., Mar. 18, 1928; d. Louis Phillip and Helen Cecilia (Axomaitis) Kubik; student Wilkes Coll., Kings Coll.; m. William E. Skrinak, Apr. 28, 1951 (dec.); children—Kim, Karen (dec.), William K., Kyle. With Salzburg Advt., Wilkes-Barre, 1947-48, Pomeroy's, Inc., Wilkes-Barre, 1948-50, Bergman's Dept. Store, Wilkes-Barre, 1951-55; owner, mgr. Wes Advt., Wyoming, Pa., 1957—. Bd. dirs. Spark of Life. Mem. N.E. Pa. Advt. Club (dir.). Democrat. Roman Catholic. Club: Fox Hill Country (Exeter, Pa.). Address: 103 Wyoming Ave Wyoming PA 18644

SKROBELA, KATHERINE CREELMAN, data processor; b. N.Y.C., Jan. 18, 1941; d. George Douglas and Marjorie Ethel (Broer) Creelman; A.B., Vassar Coll., 1961; M.L.S., Columbia U., 1964; m. Paul John Skrobela, May 23, 1970. Music cataloger Bklyn. Coll., 1964-71; music librarian Middlebury (Vt.) Coll., 1971-80; programmer ADT Co., N.Y.C., 1981—. Treas., bd. dirs. Middlebury Farmers Market, 1979; bd. dirs. St. Stephen's Motet Choir, Middlebury, 1975-78. Mem. Am. Soc. Info. Sci., ALA, Music Library Assn. (chmn. com. on cataloging, rep. to ALA catalog code revision com.), Country Dance and Song Soc. Am. Editor Music Cataloging Bull., 1970-75. Home: 70 Prospect Park W Brooklyn NY 11215 Office: 2 World Trade Center New York NY 10048

SKYDELL, RUTH HERSKOWITZ, psychologist, educator; b. N.Y.C., Mar. 8, 1922; d. Harry and Etta (Nadelman) Herskowitz; B.A., Hunter Coll., 1941; Ph.D., City U. N.Y., 1972; m. Adrian Skydell, June 1, 1947; children—Laurie Skydell Goldberg, Bernard, Harry. Editor, Liquor Publs., Inc., N.Y.C., 1942-48; lectr. dept. psychology Hunter Coll., 1968-72; asst. prof. dept. guidance and counseling L.I. U., Bklyn., 1972-76, asso. prof., 1976—. Pres., Manhattan chpt. Mizrachi Women's Orgn., 1951-53, Manhattan Day Sch. PTA, N.Y.C., 1958-61. Mem. Am. Psychol. Assn., Eastern Psychol. Assn., Soc. Psychol. Study of Social Issues, Phi Beta Kappa, Psi Chi. Author: (with Gary S. Belkin) Foundations of Psychology, 1979. Office: LI U Brooklyn Center New York NY 11201

SLACK, KAREN KERSHNER, advt. agy. exec.; b. Port Arthur, Tex., Aug. 28, 1951; d. High Cleveland and Eleanor Lucille (Beaty) Kershner; B.J., U. Tex., Austin, 1973; m. Jim Slack, Jr., May 12, 1979. Public relations dir. Lakeway Co., Austin, 1973-74; account coordinator, copywriter Point Communications, Inc., Houston, 1974-76; account exec., then v.p. Rochelle Mktg. Co., Inc., Houston, 1976-80; pres., owner Communications Plus, Houston, 1980—; mem. communications adv. com. Houston United Way, 1980—; chmn. steering com. Houston Festival, 1979—. Mem. Internat. Assn. Bus. Communicators. Home: 204 Old Bridge Lake Houston TX 77069 Office: 2990 Richmond St Suite 405 Houston TX 77098

SLACK, VALDA LEE, univ. dean; b. Toledo, Sept. 27, 1953; d. David L. and Velma (Wilson) Slack; B.A., Dillard U., 1975; postgrad. Calif. State U., 1975-77. Program asst. Westview Mental Hosp., Fresno, Calif., 1975-77; project coordinator Fresno County Econ. Opportunities

Commn., 1977-78; psychologist/evaluator W. Fresno Sch. Dist., 1978-79; asso. dean student affairs Dillard U., New Orleans, 1979—. Vol. chemotherapy asst. in patient —New Life— program DePaul Mental Hosp., 1973-74. Recipient citation Dillard U. Student Govt. Assn., 1980. Mem. Nat. Assn. Women Deans, Adminstrs. and Counselors, AAUW, Nat. Assn. Female Execs., Delta Sigma Theta. Ch. of God in Christ. Office: 2601 Gentilly Blvd New Orleans LA 70122

SLACKE, SALLY ANN, contracting co. exec.; b. S.I., N.Y., Apr. 16, 1933; d. Patrick and Mary G. (Granito) Magdalen; student Drake Bus. Sch., 1951, Adelphi U., 1968, Suffolk County (N.Y.) Community Coll., 1969; m. Felix P. Slacke, Oct. 8, 1955 (dec. 1975); children—Barbara, Diane, Carole Lynn. Sec., Netherland Trading Soc., N.Y.C., 1951-58; v.p. Slacke Drilling Co., Kings Park, N.Y., 1963-73; pres. Slacke Test Boring, Inc., Smithtown, N.Y., 1973—; del. White House Conf. Small Bus., Washington. Coordinator sr. citizen activities Town of Smithtown, 1968-69; trustee L.I. Loves Bus., Inc. Recipient L.I. Bus. Leadership award, 1980; Clara Barton Humanitarian award Suffolk County chpt. ARC, 1981. Mem. Nat. Assn. Female Execs. Inc., 110 Center for Bus. and Profl. Women, L.I. Assn. Commerce and Industry. Republican. Roman Catholic. Club: Zonta Internat. Office: 4 Main St Kings Park NY 11754

SLADE, CYNTHIA RITTENBERG, prodn. co. exec.; b. Chgo., June 22, 1947; d. George and Irene Rittenberg; student, U. Okla., 1965-66; m. Michael Slade, Dec. 1, 1980; children by previous marriage—Alan, Geoff, Jeremy; 1 stepson, Ilia. Office mgr. Feyline, Inc., Denver, 1968-70; exec. v.p., dir. Feyline Presents, Inc., Englewood, Colo., 1972—; guest lectr. Colo. Women's Coll., U. Colo. Candidate for Colo. State Legislature, 1978. Mem. Denver C. of C., Nat. Council Jewish Women, Assn. Am. and Can. in Israel. Democrat. Jewish. Club: Hadassah. Home: Moshav Hamra Beqat Hayarden Israel Office: 2175 S Cherry Denver CO 80222

SLADE, MARY GERTRUDE, ins. co. exec.; b. Syracuse, N.Y., Mar. 9, 1919; student Syracuse U., 1940, Excelsior Sch. of Bus., Utica, N.Y., 1941. Policyholder service rep. Liberty Mut. Ins. Co., 1941-44; asst. sec., mgr. ins. div. Eagan Real Estate, Inc., 1944-60; mgr. Caryl & Murray Ins. Agy., Syracuse, 1960-65; joined Agway companies, 1965, sec. Agway Ins. Co., Agway Life Ins. Co., Agway Gen. Agys., Inc., East Syracuse, N.Y., 1976—. Account exec. United Way Central N.Y., 1978-80. Mem. Nat. Secs. Assn., Syracuse Ins. Women's Assn., Syracuse U. Alumni Assn. Club: Bellevue Country. Office: 5814 Bridge St East Syracuse NY 13057

SLAGLE, PATTI LYNN, broadcasting co. exec.; b. Harlan, Ky., June 5, 1959; d. Jack and Ruby Howard; student Cumberland Coll., 1976, Southeast Community Coll., Cumberland, 1977, Morehead State U., 1978-79. Legal sec. Rice and Huff, attys., Harlan, 1978; continuity dir. Radio Harlan, Inc., Sta. WHLN, 1979—, dir. women's programs, 1979—, sales rep., 1981—. Bd. dirs. Kings Kids Choral Group, 1976—; vol. Harlan County Community Hospice. Democrat. Southern Baptist. Home: PO Box 575 Harlan KY 40831 Office: Box 898 Harlan KY 40831

SLAGLE, ROBERTA ANN, social worker; b. Fayette, Mo., Sept. 27, 1953; d. Robert Lewis and Ann Elizabeth (Keller) S.; B.S.W., U. Kans., 1976, M.S.W., 1979. Protective service worker Social and Rehabilitation Services, Osawatomie, Kans., 1976-78; counselor Neutral Ground, Kansas City, Kans., 1979-80; supr. Live and Learn, Inc., Shawnee, Kans., 1981—. Sec. Miami County Child Protection Team, 1977-79. Mem. Am. Humane Assn., Nat. Assn. Social Workers. Office: 21435 Midland Dr Shawnee KS 66218

SLATER, BARBARA RUTH, psychologist; b. Potsdam, N.Y., Feb. 18, 1934; d. Gilson M. and Eleanor (Robinson) S.; B.A., St. Lawrence U., Canton, N.Y., 1955, M.Ed., 1959; Ph.D. in Sch. Psychology, Tchrs. Coll., Columbia U., 1966. Secondary sch. tchr. Port Dickinson (N.Y.) Schs., 1956-62; sch. psychologist, Pelham, N.Y., 1966-68; asst. prof. psychology Hofstra U., Hempstead, N.Y. 1968-71; prof. psychology, coordinator sch. psychology Towson (Md.) State U., 1971—; ind. practice psychology, 1966—. Diplomate in sch. psychology Am. Bd. Profl. Psychology. Mem. Am. Psychol. Assn., Nat. Assn. Sch. Psychologists, AAUP, Eastern Psychol. Assn., Md. Psychol. Assn. Home: 322 Jodyway Timonium MD 21093 Office: Dept Psychology Towson State U Towson MD 21204

SLATER, LINDA FRANCES, market analyst; b. Denver, May 21, 1947; d. Robert E. and Bernice Hall; A.S., Belleville Area Coll., 1975; B.S. in Bus. Adminstrn., So. Ill. U., 1977, M.B.A., 1978; m. John E. Slater, Sept. 4, 1971; 1 son, Daniel Donovan. Acct., Riverside Supply Co., Evansville, Ind., 1967-71; asst. mgr. Freeburg (Ill.) Recreation Park, 1974-78; market analyst Prell Orgn., St. Louis, 1977-78, Mo.-Kans.-Tex. R.R. Co., St. Louis, 1978-81, mgr. pricing analysis, 1982—. Mem. Freeburg Bicentennial Commn., 1975-76. Mem. Audubon Soc., Phi Theta Kappa, Beta Gamma Sigma.

SLATON, JOYCELYN THERESA DUGAS, accountant; b. Donaldsonville, La., Aug. 18, 1951; d. Henri J. Dugas and Joyce (Falcon) Dugas Cooley; student public schs., La.; m. Hershel B. Slaton, Apr. 28, 1972. Office mgr. Tri-City Fin. Services, Morgan City, La., 1969-70; sec. Comml. Securities, Morgan City, 1970-74; bookkeeper Avco Fin. Services, Morgan City, 1974-77; head bookkeeper Cooley's Tax and Bookkeeping Service, Morgan City, 1977—. Mem. La. Shrimp and Petroleum Assn. (sec. 1978—, co-chmn. Doubloon com.), Am. Legion Aux. Baptist. Home: PO Box 2681 Morgan City LA 70380 Office: 7043 Railroad Ave Morgan City LA 70380

SLATTERY, SISTER, MARGARET PATRICE, coll. pres.; b. St. Louis, June 19, 1926; d. Patrick Joseph and Margaret Mary (Harris) S.; B.A., Incarnate Word Coll., San Antonio, 1952; M.A., Marquette U., 1955; Ph.D., Cath. U. Am., 1966. Prof., English, Incarnate Word Coll., San Antonio, 1955-69, acad. dean, 1969-72, pres., 1972—. Mem. Assn. Tex. Colls. and Univs. (past pres.), Ind. Colls. and Univs. of Tex. (dir.), Higher Edn. Council San Antonio. Roman Catholic.

SLAUGHTER, DIANA TERESA, educator; b. Chgo., Oct. 28, 1941; d. John Ison and Gwendolyn Malva (Armstead) Slaughter; B.A., U. Chgo., 1962, M.A., 1964, Ph.D., 1968. Instr. dept. psychiatry Howard U., Washington, 1967-68; research asso., asst. prof. Yale U. Child Study Center, New Haven, 1968-70; asst. prof. dept. behavioral scis. and edn. U. Chgo., 1970-77; asso. prof. edn. and African Am. studies Northwestern U., Evanston, Ill., 1977—; mem. nat. adv. bd. Fed. Center for Child Abuse and Neglect, 1979-82, Ednl. Research and Devel. Center, U. Tex., Austin; chmn. public policy program com. Chgo. Black Child Devel. Inst., 1982—; dir. Ill. Infant Mental Health Com., 1982—. Mem. Am. Psychol. Assn., Soc. for Research in Child Devel. (governing council 1981-87), Am. Ednl. Research Assn., Assn. Black Psychologists, Nat. Council Black Studies, Delta Sigma Theta. Contbr. articles to profl. jours. Home: 835 Ridge Ave Evanston IL 60202 Office: 2003 Sheridan Rd Evanston IL 60201

SLAUGHTER, EDITH LOUISE, ins. co. exec.; b. Kennett, Mo., Aug. 27, 1941; d. Lloyd James and Carrie Hazel (Shryock) Mulford; student Kent State U., 1968-72, Youngstown State U., 1972-73; 1 son, Gregory Allen. Credit mgr. Spiegel Catalog, Coshocton, Ohio, 1963-64; with Warren (Ohio) City Schs., 1967-73; unit mgr. claim dept. Allstate Ins. Co., Coconut Creek, Fla., 1973—. Vol. Am. Cancer Soc., Ft. Lauderdale, Fla., 1977-80, Am. Heart Assn., Ft. Lauderdale, 1976-80. Mem. Claimsmen's Assn. Republican. Home: 352 Sunshine Dr Coconut Creek FL 33066 Office: 3700 Coconut Creek Pkwy Coconut Creek FL 33066

SLAUGHTER, JACQUELINE G., accountant; b. N.Y.C., Oct. 9, 1923; d. John Thorne and Eleanor Maude (Quigley) de Congo; student R.I. State Coll., 1942-43, N.Y. U., 1942-43, Massey Bus. Coll., Jacksonville, Fla., 1949, Fla. State U., 1954; m. Coaell E. Slaughter, Jan. 3, 1946; 1 dau., Carrie Jane Cederholm. With State of Fla., Tallahassee, 1954—, sr. accountant, supr. records/control sect. Bur. Fin. and Acctg., Fla. Dept. Natural Resources. Pres., PTA, Demonstration Sch. Fla. State U., 1961; leader Apalachee Bend council Girl Scouts U.S.A., 1957-60. Mem. Nat. Assn. Outdoor Recreation Fiscal and Project Officers (dir., 1977-79, pres., 1976-77), Fla. Govt. Acctg. Mgmt. Assn. Democrat. Episcopalian. Office: Marjory Stoneman Douglas Bldg 3900 Commonwealth Blvd Tallahassee FL 32303

SLAUGHTER, JANE MUNDY, author; b. Buchanan, Va., Oct. 2, 1905; d. Luther Thomas and Pearl Carnce (Karnes) Mundy; R.N., Jefferson Hosp., Roanoke, Va., 1926; m. Frank G. Slaughter, June 10, 1933; children—Frank G., Ramdolph M. Operating Room supr. Jefferson Hosp., 1923-24; pvt. duty nurse, 1924-33; freelance author, 1970—; author: Espy and the Catnappers, 1975; also 1st history of Fla. Med. Assn. Aux. Bd. dirs. Jacksonville (Fla.) YWCA, 1960-65. Mem. Fla. Hist. Soc., Jacksonville Hist. Soc., Fla. Fedn. Garden Clubs (life mem. Jacksonville), Fla. Med. Assn. Aux. (historian 1950). Democrat. Presbyterian. Club: Timuquana Country. Address: 5051 Yacht Club Rd Jacksonville FL 32210

SLAUGHTER, LURLINE EDDY, artist; b. Heidelberg, Miss., June 19, 1919; d. Gilbert Emmings and Lurline Elizabeth (Heidelberg) Eddy; B.S., Miss. U. for Women, 1939; m. James Fant Slaughter, Jan. 27, 1946; children—Beverly Lowery, Anne Towles. Tchr. high sch., Silver City, Miss., 1939-41; clk. VA, Washington, 1941-42; one-woman shows Ahda Artzt Gallery, N.Y.C., 1967, Nat. Center, N.Y.C., 1967, 68, Delta State U., Cleveland, Miss., 1973, Gulf States Gallery, Greenville, Miss., 1973, Southeastern La. U., Hammond, 1977, Cheekwood Fine Arts Center, Nashville, 1978, San Pedro Theatre, San Antonio, 1981; exhibited in group shows U. Fla., 1969, Brooks Art Mus., Memphis, 1970, Miss. State U., 1970, Delta State U., 1971; represented in permanent collection Miss. U. for Women, Miss. State U., Delta State U., Pine Bluff (Ark.) Art Mus., Southeastern La. U., U. of South, Recipient Best in Show award Acapulco Ann., Hilton Hotel, 1979. Tchr. Sunday Sch., Meth. Ch., 1953-67; pres. PTA; bd. dirs. Miss. Art Colony, 1965—. Served as lt. USNR, 1942-45. Mem. Miss. Art Assn. Republican. Club: Humphreys Country. Address: Seldom Seen Plantation Silver City MS 39166

SLAUGHTER, SUSAN LEE BRUNDIGE, graphic design co. exec.; b. Cin., Feb. 24, 1947; d. Jerry A. and Betty L. (Thorp) Brundige; B.F.A., Ohio State U., 1969; postgrad. U. Cin., evenings 1971-72; m. James L. Slaughter III, Sept. 16, 1972. Instr. painting Cin. Art Mus., part-time 1969-76; graphic designer Cin. Time Recorder Co., 1969-71, Hank Marowitz Advt. Agy., Cin., 1971-72; pres., graphic designer, cons. Slaughter & Slaughter, Inc., Cin., 1972—; part-time instr. graphics Xavier U., 1982—; painter. Chmn. spl. advt. project, designer posters, folder Radio Reading Services, 1981-82, Appreciation cert., 1981; designer posters, folder Arthritis Found. campaign, 1980—, Appreciation cert., 1979, Disting. Public Service award, 1981; designer Christmas card for fundraising Cancer Family Care, 1981; designer, dir. interior mus., permanent exhbn. African, Latin Am., S.Am. art, artifacts Comboni Fathers Missionary Mus., 1980—. Recipient awards Art Dirs. Club Cin., 1972-82, Am. Advt. Fedn., 1974, 80, Internat. Typographic Composition award, 1980, Bus. and Profl. Advt. Assn., 1981. Mem. Women in Communications (spl. project v.p., dir. 1981-82, recognition cert. 1981), Cin. Indsl. Advertisers (dir. 1979-81, Person of Distinction 1980, 81), Cin. Women's Network, Internat. Assn. Profl. Artists, Alliance Profl. Artists of Ohio, Ky. and Ind. Office: Slaughter & Slaughter Inc 4307 Erie Ave Cincinnati OH 45227

SLAVENS, SHIRLEY ANN (MRS. DONALD SLAVENS), precision machine co. exec.; b. Bend, Oreg., May 19, 1927; d. Harris Gordon and Winifred Beatrice (Webb) Meagher; student Northwestern Sch. Commerce, Oreg., 1946; m. Donald Slavens, Oct. 7, 1946; children—Denise Ann (Mrs. Richard Landreth), William Donald. Sec., Santiseptic Co., cosmetics, Portland, Oreg., 1946; with purchasing dept. Compton (Calif.) Jr. Coll., 1948-50; sec.-treas. S & S Industries, Paramount, Calif., 1962—. Pres. PTA, LaMirada, Calif., 1963-64; bd. dirs. Fullerton Neighborhood Watch, 1979-80. Mem. Calif. Fedn. Women's Club (leadership devel. chmn. 1976-80), Alpha Iota. Club: Ebell (rec. sec. Fullerton 1971-72, 2d v.p. 1973-74, 1st v.p. 1974-75, pres. 1975-76, dean fedn. extension). Home: 3020 Terraza Pl Fullerton CA 92635 Office: 7322 E Madison St Paramount CA 90723

SLAVIN, ROSANNE SINGER, textile converter; b. N.Y.C., Mar. 24, 1930; d. Lee H. and Rose (Winkler) Singer; student U. Ill.; divorced; children—Laurie Jo, Sharon Lee. Prodn. converter Doucet Fabrics, silk prints, N.Y.C., 1953-57; sales mgr., mdse. mgr. print div. Crown Fabrics, N.Y.C., 1957-65; owner Matisse Fabrics Inc., printed fabrics, N.Y.C., 1965—. Recipient Tommy award, 1978. Office: 1457 Broadway New York NY 10036

SLAVIN, SARAH, polit. scientist; b. Salt Lake City, Mar. 26, 1942; d. Hale Burgher and Ruth Martin Slavin; B.A., U. Iowa, 1962; M.A.T., Webster Coll., 1972; Ph.D., George Washington U., 1981; children—Heidi Ruth, Beth, Victor Hale. Religious edn. dir. St. Louis Ethical Soc., 1972-73; lectr. Webster Coll., 1973; research asst. Law Enforcement Assistance Agy., Dept. Justice, 1974; teaching fellow George Washington U., 1974-76; lectr. Mt. Vernon Coll., 1977, 78, La Roche Coll., 1979, Hamilton Coll., 1980, Chatham Coll., 1980, Carlow Coll., 1980, U. Del., 1981, SUNY, Buffalo, 1981—. Mem. Am. Polit. Sci. Assn., Women's Caucus for Polit. Sci. (pres. 1979-80, exec. council 1974—), Midwest Polit. Sci. Assn., Nat. Women's Studies Assn., So. Polit. Sci. Assn., Policy Studies Orgn. Democrat. Editor: Women and Politics: Quar. Jour. Research and Policy Studies, 1979—. Author: Plow Women Rather than Reapers: An Intellectual History of Feminism in the United States, 1979. Contbr. articles to profl. jours. Address: 41 Highland Ave Buffalo NY 14222

SLAYMAKER, (CAROLYN) JANE HOYT, occupational therapist, educator; b. Detroit, Nov. 25, 1930; d. Douglas Granger and Elizabeth Carola (Wyker) Hoyt; B.A. in Art History, Wellesley Coll., 1953; cert. in interior decoration N.Y. Sch. Interior Design, 1954; cert. in occupational therapy (N.Y. State Dept. Mental Health and Hygiene scholar) N.Y.U., 1962, M.A. in Edn. (Am. Occupation Therapy Assn. scholar), 1966; postgrad. in guidance and counseling U. Ill., Urbana, 1969-70, in social change Walden U. West, 1980—; also various seminars, workshops, insts., short courses. Recreational therapist Montefiore Hosp., Bronx, N.Y., 1958-60; staff occupational therapist Manhattan State Hosp., N.Y.C., 1962-65, Manhattan VA Hosp., N.Y.C., 1965-66; asst. prof. occupational therapy U. Fla., 1966-68, assoc. prof., 1970—, activity therapist IV, Ill. Dept. Mental Health and Hygiene, Champaign, 1968-70; cons. gerontology, mental health; bd. dirs. North Central Fla. Community Mental Health Center, Inc., Gainesville, 1979—, sec., 1981-82; bd. dirs. Mental Health Assn. Alachua County (Fla.), 1975-81, treas., 1976, 79, 80, 81, pres., 1978. Bd. dirs. United Way Alachua County, 1976-80, Alachua County Council Child Abuse, 1978-81. Recipient Cert. of Appreciation, Mental Health Assn. Alachua County, 1975, Cert. of Commendation, 1977; Gold award United Way, 1978; Faculty Devel. award Coll. Health Related Professions, summer 1980; assoc. Center Gerontol. Studies and Programs, 1977—. Fellow Am. Occupational Therapy Assn.; mem. World Fedn. Occupational Therapy, Fla. Occupational Therapy Assn. (pres. 1971-73, rep. to Occupational Therapy Council, Bd. Med. Examiners State of Fla., 1975—, assn. alt. rep. 1973-75, 79-82, Award of Excellence 1977), Am. Gerontol. Soc., So. Gerontol. Assn., Pi Lambda Theta, Eta Rho Pi. Episcopalian. Contbr. articles to profl. jours. Office: Box J-164 JH Miller Health Center Gainesville FL 32610

SLEEMAN, MARY (MRS. JOHN PAUL SLEEMAN), librarian; b. Cleve., June 28, 1928; d. John and Mary Lillian (Jakub) Gerba; B.S., Kent State U., 1965; m. John Paul Sleeman, Apr. 27, 1946; children—Sandra Sleeman Swyrydenko, Robert, Gary, Linda. Supervising librarian elementary schs. Nordonia Hills Bd. Edn., Northfield, Ohio, 1965—; children's librarian Twinsburg (Ohio) Pub. Library, 1965-66. Mem. ALA, Ohio Sch. Librarians Assn., NEA, Summit County Librarians Assn., Storytellers Assn., North Eastern Ohio Tchrs. Assn. Methodist. Home: 18171 Logan Dr Walton Hills OH 44146 Office: 115 Ledge Rd Northfield OH 44067

SLEET, CAMMIE LEE KENT (MRS. JAMES TURNER SLEET), coll. adminstr.; b. Itta Bena, Miss., Sept. 25, 1927; d. Phillip Henry and Carrie Lee (Butler) Kent; B.S., Lewis Bus. Coll., 1948; B.A., Wayne State U., 1963, M.A., 1972; postgrad. U. Mich.; m. James Turner Sleet, Nov. 11, 1951; 1 son, Craig Collins. Social research supr. aged study U. Mich., Ann Arbor, 1964-65, research field supr. travel survey, 1965-67; registrar, dir. admissions, fgn. students adviser Mich. Luth. Coll. (name changed to Shaw Coll. 1972), Detroit, 1968-73; asst. dir. admissions, fgn. student adviser U. Mich.-Dearborn, 1973-79, dir. admissions, fgn. student adv., 1979—, also mem. pre-prof. counselor staff; mem. New Detroit Edn. Com.; participant West African Higher Edn. Workshop, 1973. Am. Assn. Collegiate Registrars and Admissions Officers Nat. Assn. Fgn. Student Affairs edn. grantee, summer 1973; recipient Distinguished Alumnus award Lewis Bus. Coll., 1978. Mem. Nat. Assn. Fgn. Student Affairs, Am., Mich. assns. collegiate registrars and admissions officers, Nat. Assn. Coll. Admissions Counselors, Guidance Assn. Met. Detroit (publicity chmn.). Office: 4901 Evergreen St Dearborn MI 48128

SLEITH, BARBARA ANN BALKO, educator; b. Elizabeth Twp., Pa., Jan. 29, 1946; d. Andrew and Elizabeth (Kurutz) Balko; A.A., Robert Morris Jr. Coll., 1966; B.S., Calif. State Coll., 1968, M.Ed., 1970; postgrad. U. Pitts., 1976, U. Indiana (Pa.); m. Melvin R. Sleith, Dec. 18, 1971; 1 dau., Melynda Sue. Tchr., Elizabeth (Pa.) Forward Sch. Dist., 1968-70; learning disabilities tchr. Allegheny Intermediate Unit 3, 1970-77, I.E.P. specialist, 1977-80; cons. in field. Neighborhood chmn. Girl Scouts U.S.A., 1978-80; adult cons. ch. youth group, 1975-78; program rep., mem. liaison bd. Allegheny Intermediate Unit Spl. Services Edn. Assn., 1970-74, 72-74; active PTA, William Penn Sch. Mem. Assn. Children with Learning Disabilities, Phi Delta Gamma (chpt. exec. officer). Democrat. Roman Catholic. Club: Confraternity of Christian Mothers. Address: RD 2 Box 115 West Newton PA 15089

SLESINSKI, JUDITH PAULA, writer; b. Bridgeport, Conn., Sept. 19, 1945; d. Robert E. and Bernice H. (Burstein) Turner; student spl. writer's course Wesleyan U., Middletown, Conn., 1976, Housatonic Community Coll., 1980—; children—John, Robert, Jaimie. Editor, Spl. Song jour., 1970-74; exec. sec. to v.p. mfg. Jenkins Bros., Bridgeport, 1980—; Sunday features corr. Milford (Conn.) Citizen, 1982—; writer poetry and non-fiction for various publs. including: Woman's Circle, Jour. of Univ. English, Harper's Weekly, Shoppers Weekly, Westside Shopper. Vol. Milford Hosp., 1973; mem. letters com. Milford Fine Arts Council, 1982—. Recipient Haiku award Tweed jour., 1973. Mem. Profl. Secs. Internat. Home: 84 Dunbar Rd Milford CT 06460

SLICK, GRACE WING, singer, songwriter; b. Chgo., Oct. 30, 1939; d. Ivan W. and Virginia (Barnett) Wing; student Finch Coll., 1957-58, U. Miami (Fla.), 1958-59; m. Gerald Robert Slick, Aug. 26, 1961 (div. 1970); 1 dau., China; m. 2d, Skip Johnson, Nov. 29, 1976. Singer with Great Society, 1965-66, Jefferson Airplane, 1966-72, Jefferson Starship, 1974—; solo albums Manhole, 1974, Dreams, 1980, Welcome to the Wrecking Ball, 1981. Composer: Somebody to Love, White Rabbit. Address: 44 Montgomery St San Francisco CA 94104 *

SLICK, JEWEL CHERIE, nurse; b. Poplar, Mont., June 13, 1934; d. Ralph and Charity Ruth (Reddoor) Wing; R.N., St. Luke's Hosp., Kansas City, Mo., 1955; m. Virgil Slick, May 31, 1970; 1 dau., Cherie Ann. Pvt. duty nurse, 1958—; advocate for Am. Indians, 1969—; owner Am. Indian Cons. Service, Des Moines, 1980—; dir. Am. Indian Center, 1973-77, 80-81; mem. Des Moines Human Rights Commn., 1974-77, Gov. Iowa Interstate Indian Council, 1975-77, Nat. Indian Bd. Alcoholism, 1975-78; bd. dirs. Des Moines YWCA. Mem. Iowa Nursing Assn., NOW, Nat. Assn. Female Execs. Democrat. Address: 3610 Columbia St Des Moines IA 50313

SLIMMER, VIRGINIA MCKINLEY, home economist; b. Mullinville, Kans., June 21, 1932; d. John W. and Virga (Pridy) McKinley; B.S., Fort Hays State U., 1969; M.S., Kans. State U., 1970; Ed.S., Fort Hays State U., 1977; Ph.D., Iowa State U., 1981; m. Myrl D. Slimmer, Nov. 26, 1950; children—Jackie Slimmer Langholz, Kathy, Bruce. Co owner, mgr. ranch, Plainville, Kans., 1962—; instr. Fort Hays State U., 1970-71; tchr. vocat. home econs. Plainville (Kans.) High Sch., 1972-74; tchr. Hays (Kans.) Sr. High Sch., 1975-79; asst. alumni dir. Fort Hays State U., 1977-79; adminstrv. asst. to dean Coll. Home Econs., asst. prof. clothing, textiles and interior design Kans. State U., Manhattan, 1981-82; asso. prof., chairperson dept. home econs. Murray (Ky.) State U., 1982—. Mem. Ellis County Exec. Bd., 1954-75; sec. bd. Ellis County Fair, 1974-75; leader 4-H Club, 1962-79; bd. dirs. Ellis County Cancer Soc., 1955-73. Kans. Home Econs. Assn. scholar, 1971-72. Mem. Nat. Assn. Women Deans, Adminstrs. and Counselors, Am. Ednl. Research Assn., Higher Edn. Resource Services/West, Am. Assn. Higher Edn., Iowa Ednl. Research and Evaluation Assn., Nat. Council Family Relations, Kans. State U. Alumni Assn., Iowa State U. Alumni Assn., Am. Home Econs. Assn., AAUW, Kappa Omicron Phi, Phi Delta Gamma, Phi Kappa Phi, Phi Delta Kappa. Republican. Methodist. Club: Sunflower Sisters. Contbr. articles to profl. jours. Office: Dept Home Econs Murray State U Murray KY

SLIPHER, MARY ISABEL (BECKY), educator; b. Dunkirk, Ind., Nov. 7, 1921; d. George Cosby and Aletha Mildred (Steele) Thompson; A.B., Fla. State U., Tallahassee, 1943; M.S., Butler U., 1964; m. Charles O. Slipher, Dec. 17, 1943; children—Jean Slipher Wilson, Carol Slipher Zinn, David. Tchr., Dade County (Fla.) Schs., 1943-45; tchr. first grade Carmel-Clay (Ind.) Schs., 1957-80. Recipient Outstanding Elem. Educator award Carmel-Clay Ednl. Found., 1978. Mem. NEA, Ins. State Tchrs. Assn., Carmel Tchrs. Assn., Internat. Reading Assn., Alpha Delta Kappa (historian 1972-73). Republican. Methodist (pres. United Meth. Women, Cape Coral, Fla.). Clubs: Internat. Order Job's Daus. (grand guardian of Ind., 1979-80, com. for supreme council), Order Eastern Star (matron North Park chpt. 1967-68), Ladies Oriental Shrine N. Am., Daus. of the Nile.

SLIVKO, JACQUELINE SUSAN, food co. exec.; b. N.Y.C., Dec. 17, 1950; d. Saul and Seena (Dickman) S.; B.A. magna cum laude, Hunter Coll., 1971; M.S. with honors, CCNY, 1974; M.B.A. with distinction,

Pace U., 1978. Editor-in-chief, Grad. Perspective, Pace U., N.Y.C., 1976-77; fin. analyst J. Walter Thompson Co., N.Y.C., 1977-78; distbn. plan analyst Pepsi Cola Co., Purchase, N.Y., 1978-80, asso. plan mgr., 1980-81, mgr. sales ops., 1981—; fin. cons. small bus. Vice-pres., mgr. Westgate Park Condominium, 1980—. Mellon scholar, 1976-78. Club: Aquamariners Scuba. Home: 119 Dehaven Dr Yonkers NY 10703 Office: Pepsi Cola Anderson Hill Rd Purchase NY 10577

SLOAN, ANNE ELIZABETH, food scientist, nutritionist, journalist; b. Hackensack, N.J., Sept. 1, 1951; B.S., Rutgers U., 1973; Ph.D., U. Minn., 1976. Research asst. Rutgers U., 1973, U. Minn., 1973-76; communication specialist in nutrition Gen. Mills., Inc., Mpls., 1976-77, mgr. nutrition edn. and community services, 1977-79, mgr. nutrition communication and tech. services, 1979-80; dir. sci. services Am. Assn. Cereal Chemists, St. Paul, 1980-81; dir. Good Housekeeping Inst., N.Y.C., 1981—; mem. ad hoc adv. com. Wheat Industry Council, Dept. Agr., 1978-79; mem. food and nutrition adv. council Sugar Assn., 1978-80; mem. sci. adv. com. Am. Inst. Baking, 1979-81; mem. nutrition edn. adv. bd. Nutrition Edn. for Older Ams. Program, ITT Continental Baking Co., 1981; cons., lectr. in field; radio-TV appearances. Recipient numerous awards including Scholastic Excellence award Inst. Food Technologists, 1976. Mem. Am. Assn. Cereal Chemists, Am. Coll. Nutrition, Am. Dietetic Assn., Twin City Dietetic Assn., Assn. Ofcl. Analytical Chemists, Inst. Food Technologists, Minn. Nutrition Council, Sigma Xi, Phi Tau Sigma, Gamma Sigma Delta, Alpha Zeta. Author numerous books, reports including Contemporary Nutrition Controversies, 1979; Food for Thought; contbr. numerous articles to profl. jours. Episcopalian. Home: 1870 Stowe Ave Arden Hills MN 55112 Office: 959 8th Ave New York NY 10069

SLOAN, CHARLOTTE PARKS, data and word processing mktg. rep.; b. Tuscumbia, Ala., Dec. 24, 1948; d. Snethen Neil and Charlotte Elizabeth (Porter) Parks; B.S. in Botany and Art, U. North Ala., 1971; student Johnson County Community Coll., 1976-77; div. Biology aide TVA, Muscle Shoals, Ala., 1968-73; asst. buyer Jones Store Co., Overland Park, Kans., 1973-74; data coordinator EPA, Kansas City, Mo., 1974-77; computer programmer Global Data Systems, Tulsa, 1977-79; mktg. support rep. Wordstream Corp., Atlanta, 1979-80; office automation specialist Prime Computer Inc., Atlanta, 1980—. Pres., Region VII Fed. Women's Adv. Com., EPA, 1976-77. Mem. Internat. Word Processing Assn., U. North Ala. Alumni Assn. Methodist. Home: 4452 Old Mabry Pl Rosewell GA 30075 Office: 5801 Peachtree-Dunwoody Rd Atlanta GA 30342

SLOAN, EVA LAMB (MRS. ROBERT G. SLOAN), lawyer; b. nr. Martin County, N.C., July 20, 1910; d. John Grey and Mattie Ann (Rawls) Lamb; A.B., Eureka Coll., Ayden, N.C., 1925; postgrad. U. N.C., 1926; m. Robert G. Sloan, Jan. 19, 1928; children—Robert A., Charles H., Elizabeth Ann (Mrs. George F. Powers), Toni (Mrs. Forrest Brown). Admitted to Ga. bar, 1952, since practiced in Milledgeville. County chmn. Girl Scouts, 1962, United Fund, 1950-52, Cancer Dr., 1960. Mem. Baldwin County Democratic Com. Mem. Am. Bar Assn., Ga. Bar Assn., Ocmulgee Bar Assn., Am. Trial Lawyers Assn., Ga. Trial Lawyers Assn., Ga. Assn. Women Lawyers, Am. Judicature Soc., Ga. Assn. Women Voters. Baptist. Clubs: Milledgeville Quota, Milledgeville Bus. and Profl. Women's. Home: 1663 Pine Valley Rd Milledgeville GA 31061 Office: Campus Theatre Bldg Milledgeville GA 31061

SLOAN, MADELYN ANN, educator; b. Los Angeles, Jan. 28, 1940; d. Frank Joseph and Mary Frances (Cerkez) Petrovich; B.A., Whittier (Calif.) Coll., 1960, teaching cert., 1961; m. Bill R. Sloan, June 16, 1962; children—Georgianne, Morgan. High sch. tchr. Pacific Grove (Calif.) Unified Sch. Dist., 1961-64, substitute tchr., 1964—, advanced placement coordinator, 1977—; mem. Pacific Grove City Council, 1976—. Planning commnr., Pacific Grove, 1973-76; mem. community devel. com. Calif. League Cities, 1979—; mem. Regional Criminal Justice Planning Bd., Calif. Council Criminal Justice, 1977—; bd. dirs. Monterey Peninsula Youth Project, 1977-80; vice chmn. Monterey Peninsula Recreational Trail Agy., 1979—; chmn. Pacific Grove City Charter Rev. Com., 1974. Mem. Calif. Elected Women's Assn. Edn. and Research, LWV, Am. Field Service, Pi Sigma Alpha. Home: 822 Laurel Ave Pacific Grove CA 93950 Office: 300 Forest Ave Pacific Grove CA 93950

SLOAN, RUTH HELEN, ins. agt.; b. Clarion, Pa., June 24, 1910; d. Edward H. and Clara A. S.; student schs., Clarion. Ins. agt., agy. owner Clarion, Pa., 1946—; sec.-treas., gen. agt. Clarion County Mut. Fire Ins. Co., 1946—; notary public. Mem. adv. com., zoning com. Clarion Borough Council, active hist. soc. Immaculate Conception Roman Cath. Ch. Guild. Mem. Pa. Life Ins. Assn., Clarion Agts. Assn. (pres.), C. of C. Home: 23 E 8th Ave Clarion PA 16214 Office: 1-2 Hahne Bldg 501 Main St Clarion PA 16214

SLOAN, STARKEY ANN, nurse; b. Peoria, Ill., Dec. 27, 1934; d. Robert and Ola Mae (Cunningham) Evans; R.N., Alton (Ill.) Meml. Hosp., 1956; B.A., Stephens Coll., Columbia, Mo., 1975; m. James E. Sloan, Aug. 5, 1978; children—Barbara, Susan, Edward. Staff nurse Alton Meml. Hosp., 1956-60; mem. nursing staff Edward A. Utlaut Meml. Hosp., Greenville, Ill., 1960-80, dir. nursing, 1965-80; dir. spl. care area Richland Meml. Hosp., Olney, Ill., 1981—; CPR instr., 1977—; adv. com. Kaskaskia Jr. Coll., Centralia, Ill., 1974-80; bd. dirs., disaster chmn. Greenville chpt. ARC, 1965-80; chmn. fund drive Mental Health Assn., 1980; bd. dirs. Greensville chpt. Am. Cancer Soc., 1974-80; sec. Southwestern Area Dirs. Nursing Assn., 1978-80. Mem. Ill. Soc. Nurse Adminstrs. Republican. Methodist. Home: PO Box 688 Olney IL 62450 Office: 800 E Locust St Olney IL 62450

SLOANE, ANN BROWNELL, found. cons.; b. New York County, N.Y., Nov. 1, 1938; d. Herbert and Doris McCarter Brownell; B.A. with distinction, Swarthmore Coll., 1960; postgrad. Nat. U. Venezuela, 1960-61; m. Robert Benedict Sloane, Aug. 29, 1969; children—Margaret, Robert Douglas. Community devel. specialist AID, Washington, 1962-64; with Internat. Devel. Found., N.Y.C., 1964-73, v.p., 1968-71, exec. v.p., 1971-73, dir., 1973-77; owner, pres. Sloane & Hinshaw, Inc., N.Y.C., 1979—. Vol. local, state and nat. polit. campaigns, 1958-69; bd. dirs., treas. Block Communities, Inc., 1966-70; trustee Swarthmore Coll., 1973—, chmn. fin. com., mem. investment com., 1975—, treas., 1978—. Mem. Council on Fgn. Relations, Center for Interam. Relations, Women's Econ. Roundtable, Fin. Women's Assn., N.Y., Mortar Bd., Phi Beta Kappa. Club: Cosmopolitan. Office: Sloane & Hinshaw Inc 145 E 74th St New York NY 10021

SLOANE, BEVERLY LEBOV, writer; b. N.Y.C., May 26, 1936; d. Benjamin S. and Anne (Weinberg) LeBov; A.B., Vassar Coll., 1958; M.A., Claremont Grad. Sch., 1975, postgrad., 1975-76; grad. exec. program. Sch. Mgmt., UCLA, 1982; postgrad. Stanford U., 1982; m. Robert Malcolm Sloane, Sept. 27, 1959; 1 dau., Alison Lori. Circulation librarian Harvard Med. Library, Boston, 1958-59; social worker Conn. State Welfare, New Haven, 1960-61; tchr. English, Hebrew Day Sch., New Haven, 1961-64; instr. creative writing and English lit. Monmouth Coll., West Long Branch, N.J., 1967-69; freelance writer, Arcadia, Calif., 1970—. Mem. public relations bd. Monmouth County Mental Health Assn., 1968-69; mem. Town Hall of Calif., Los Angeles, 1976—, vice chmn. community affairs, 1982—; adv. council tech. and profl. writing dept. English, Calif. State U., Long Beach, 1980—; v.p. Council of Grad. Students, Claremont Grad. Sch., 1971-72; trustee Center for Improvement of Child Caring, 1981—; mem. League Crippled Children, 1982—. Coro Found. fellow, 1979. Mem. Women in Communications (dir. 1980—, v.p. community affairs 1981-82, Northeast area rep. 1980-81, chmn. awards banquet 1982), Am. Assn. for Higher Edn., AAUW (legis. chmn. Arcadia br. 1976-77, books and plays chmn. Arcadia br. 1973-74, creative writing chmn. 1969-70, 1st v.p. 1975-76, networking chmn. 1981-82), Coll. English Assn., Am. Med. Writers Assn. (dir. 1980—, Pacific Southwest del. to nat. bd. 1980—), Am. Public Health Assn., Calif. Press Women (v.p. programs Los Angeles chpt. 1982—), AAUP, Internat. Communication Assn., Soc. for Tech. Communication. Clubs: Ex-Rotary of Duarte; Vassar of So. Calif., Calif. Inst. Tech. Women's, Internat. of Los Angeles. Author: From Vassar to Kitchen, 1967; A Guide to Health Facilities-Personnel and Management, 1971, 2d edit., 1977; A Guide to Health Facilities—Personnel and Management, 1971, 2d edit., 1977. Home: 1301 N Santa Anita Ave Arcadia CA 91006 Office: 1301 N Santa Anita Ave Arcadia CA 91006

SLOANE, FAY BETH, stockbroker; b. Yonkers, N.Y., May 22, 1946; d. Morris and Helen (Kaner) Sloane; student Miami (Fla.) Dade Community Coll., 1974-75. Supr. graphic art preparation dept., Miami, 1970-80; photographer, Miami, 1974-78; account exec. G.S. Omni, Denver, 1980-82, Dean Witter Reynolds, Denver, 1982—; fin. cons. Center for Coop. Advt. Mem. pediatric devel. com. N.Y. Hosp., Cornell Med. Center; active Friends of Colo. State Ballet. Mem. Nat. Assn. for Women in Bus., Nat. Assn. for Female Execs. Jewish. Home: 3586 E 124th Ave Thornton CO 80241 Office: 1125 17th St Denver CO 80202

SLOANE, PHYLLIS LESTER, printmaker, painter; b. Worcester, Mass., Sept. 27, 1921; d. Nathan and Goldie (Pollock) Lester; B.F.A., Carnegie Mellon U., 1943; m. David Sloane, Nov. 25, 1943; children—Ginna, Nathaniel, Lisa. Visual aide dept. architecture Okla. A. & M. U., Stillwater, 1943-44; freelance product designer, N.Y.C., 1944-45; partner P.D.A., Cleve., 1946-48; one woman shows at Ross Widen Gallery, Cleve., 1960, 69, Cleve. Play House Gallery, 1972, 74, 76, 81, Sloane O'Sickey Gallery, Cleve., 1973, Gallery 200, Columbus, Ohio, 1974, 78, JohnNorman Roberts Gallery, Albuquerque, 1974, Washington Gallery of Art, 1975, Mansfield (Ohio) Art Center, 1977, Wooster (Ohio) Coll. Art Mus., 1978, Massillon (Ohio) Mus., 1979, Janus Gallery, Santa Fe; exhibited in group shows at Allegheny Coll., 1975, Lake Erie Coll., 1975, Jewish Community Center, Cleve., 1976, Butler Inst. Am. Art, 1976, Malton Gallery, Cin., 1977, Beechwood Mus., Ohio, 1980; represented in permanent collections Cleve. Mus. Art, Cleve. Art Assn., Park Synagogue, Temple, Case Western Reserve U., Cleve., Ohio Edison Co., Akron, Murray State U., Ky., Ky. Hunterdon Art Center, Phila. Art Mus., Massillon Mus., Canton Art Inst., Cleve. Public Library, Bancohio; commd. Convalescent for Addressograph-Multigraph Corp., 1973; mural design for downtown Cleve. for Cleve. Area Arts Council, others. Recipient Graphics award Nova Print and Drawing Exhibition, 1976; Graphics award Jewish Community Center, 1974; Purchase award, Hunterdon Nat. Print Exhbn., 1977; purchase award Print Club of Phila., 1977; Cleve. Mus. Art May Show award, 1978, 79; Okla. Nat. Print Exhbn. award, 1981. Mem. New Orgn. for Visual Arts (trustee 1973, 78). Club: Cleve. Print. Author: 4 prints edits. for Transworld Art Corp., 1979; print edit. U. Print Club, Cleve., 1977; print edit. Nova Printmakers Portfolio, 1973. Home: 2558 Fairmount Blvd Cleveland OH 44106 Office: 12400 Mayfield Rd Cleveland OH 44106

SLOCUM, ELEANOR ENGLISH, nursing home adminstr.; b. Ridge Mills, N.Y., Sept. 5, 1922; d. William Anthony and Hazel Marion (Furney) English; student Atlantic Union Coll., 1942-45; diploma in nursing Union Coll., Lincoln, Nebr., 1948; student, 1945-49; B.S. in Nursing, Colo. U., 1950; m. Floyd O. Slocum, June 17, 1951 (div.); children—Ronald Allen, Rebecca Lynn. Supr., Boulder (Colo.) Meml. Hosp., 1949-50; supr. Alex Nursing Home, Syracuse, N.Y., 1950-51; charge nurse Syracuse U. Hosp., 1951-56; adminstr. Sunnyside Nursing Home, East Syracuse, 1956-58; nursing supr. Scott Nursing Home, Syracuse, 1959; founder, adminstr. Maple Lawn Nursing Home, Manlius, N.Y., 1958-81, Maple Lawn Residential Care Facility, Manlius, N.Y., 1981—. Lic. nursing home adminstrn., N.Y. Fellow Am. Coll. Nursing Home Adminstrs.; mem. Am. Acad. Med. Adminstrs., Nat. Fire Protection Assn., Am. Health Care Assn., N.Y. State Health Care Assn., Nat. Fedn. Ind. Bus., U.S. C. of C., N.Y. State Nursing Home Assn. Republican. Seventh-day Adventist. Home: PO Box 237 Farley Ln Manlius NY 13104 Office: 15 Pleasant St Manlius NY 13104

SLOGGETT, STEPHANIE LYNN, airline co. exec.; b. Inglewood, Calif., Dec. 22, 1949; d. Bruce Carroll and Mildred May (Lynn) Sloggett; student Wichita State U., 1970-71, San Diego State U., 1971-74; B.S.L., Western State U. Coll. Law, San Diego, 1980; student Flight Attendant Safety Sch., U. So. Calif., 1979—. With Pacific Southwest Airlines, San Diego, 1973—, flight attendant, 1973-79, group supr. flight attendant dept., 1979, spl. projects supr., 1979-80, labor relations specialist legal dept., 1980, mgr. union contract adminstrn., legal dept., 1980, dir. labor relations, 1982—; instr. So. Ill. U., 1982—. Mem. Southwest Flight Attendants Assn. (accident investigation team party coordinator 1978-79, sec.-treas. 1977-79, negotiating team 1976-77, chairperson scheduling com. 1975-79), Gamma Phi Beta. Republican. Episcopalian. Home: 5245 Edgepark Way San Diego CA 92124 Office: Pacific Southwest Airlines 3225 N Harbor Dr San Diego CA 92101

SLOHM, NATALIE FIRSTENBERG, producer, publisher; b. Bklyn., May 20, 1929; d. Fred Robert and Helen (Cranzler) Firstenberg; B.A., Goddard Coll., 1950; postgrad. in media New Sch. Social Research, 1973—; m. David B. Slohm, Jan. 29, 1949; children—James, Susan, Douglas. Research asst. Hudson Inst., Harmon, N.Y., 1962; dir. prodn. and ednl. services Spoken Arts, Inc., New Rochelle, N.Y., 1963-75; owner, v.p. Natalie Slohm Assos., Inc., Cambridge, N.Y., 1975—. Trustee Hubbard Hall Assn., Inc., Cambridge, N.Y., 1977—; bd. dirs. Barnard Sch. PTA, New Rochelle, N.Y., 1962-66; leader Troop 21, Girl Scouts of U.S., 1963-70. Mem. Assn. for Ednl. Communications and Tech. (media design and prodn. div.), Nat. Audio-Visual Assn. (ednl. materials producers council 1973-75, tech. standards com. 1974). Editor: Your Own World, 1974; editor-pub. I Am A Woman, 1976; book of Lyn Lifshin poems, 1978; pub. The Women's Audio Exchange Catalogue, 1980, 82. Home: Hickory Hill Rd Shushan NY 12873 Office: 49 W Main St Cambridge NY 12816

SLONIM, ROBERTE RAYMOND, physician; b. Baghdad, Iraq, Mar. 4, 1933; d. Gabriel and Bahija Daoud (Hanna) Raymond; came to U.S., 1949, naturalized, 1961; student Coll. Mt. St. Vincent, N.Y.C., 1949-52; B.S. in Chemistry cum laude, Scranton U., 1953; M.D., George Washington U., 1957; m. Ralph Slonim, Aug. 2, 1958; children—Lloyd Robert, Suzanne M. Intern, Jackson Meml. Hosp., Miami, Fla., 1957; research fellow in rheumatology NIH, Bethesda, Md., 1958-60; NIH research fellow in infectious diseases U. MIami, 1960-61; physician dept. internal medicine VA Hosp., Coral Gables, Fla., 1961-62; clin. instr. arthritis Med. Sch., U. Miami, 1962-64; practice medicine specializing in rheumatology, Miami, 1963-72, in internal medicine, bariatrics and nutrition, Miami, 1972—; active staff Bapt. Hosp. Mem. Dade County, Fla. med. assns., Arthritis Found., Geriatrics Assn., So. Fla. Psychiat. Assn., Nat. China Painting Club, Internat. China Painting Teachers Orgn., Orchid Growers Assn., S.Fla. Avocado and Lime Growers Assn., Nutrition Today Soc. Roman Catholic. Contbr. research articles on arthritis, gout, and treatment of gonorrheal infections to med. jours; letter of commendation from White House, 1962; speaker Am. Rheumatism Assn., 1959, 60, 61; certified in advanced med. hypnotherapy. Office: 9000 SW 87th Ct Miami FL 33176

SLOSHBERG, LEAH PHYFER, mus. dir.; b. New Albany, Miss., Feb. 21, 1937; d. S. K. and M. R. (Sandlin) Phyfer; B.F.A., Miss. State Coll. Women, 1959; M.A., Tulane U., 1961; m. Willard Sloshberg, Dec. 8, 1961; 1 son, Simeon Knox. Asst. curator fine arts N.J. State Mus., Trenton, 1964-66, acting curator arts, 1966-67, curator arts, 1968, acting asst. dir., 1968-69, asst. dir., 1969-71, dir., 1971—. Mem. exec. com. Conservation Center Art and Hist. Artifacts, 1979—. Woodrow Wilson fellow, 1959. Mem. Am. Assn. Mus., N.E. Mus., Conf. (dir. 1977—), N.J. Alliance Arts in Edn. (dir. 1976—) Jewish. Office: 205 W State St Trenton NJ 08625

SLOVITER, DOLORES KORMAN, fed. judge; b. Phila., Sept. 5, 1932; d. David and Tillie Korman; A.B. with distinction in Econs., Temple U., 1953; LL.B. magna cum laude, U. Pa., 1956; m. Henry A. Sloviter, Apr. 3, 1969; 1 dau., Vikki Amanda. Admitted to Pa. bar, 1957; asso. firm Dilworth, Paxson, Kalish Kohn & Levy, Phila., 1956-64, partner, 1965-69; mem. firm Harold E. Kohn, P.A., Phila., 1969-72; asso. prof. law Temple U., Phila., 1972-74, prof., 1974-79; judge U.S. Ct. Appeals, 3d Circuit, Phila., 1979—; mem. Com. of 70, 1976-79; mem. hearing panel Disciplinary Bd. Supreme Ct. Pa., 1978-79. Mem. SE region Pa. Gov.'s Council on Aging, 1976-79. Mem. Phila. Bar Assn. (gov. 1976-78), Fed. Bar Assn., Am. Bar Assn., Am. Law Inst., Order of Coif (pres. U. Pa. chpt. 1975-77), Phi Beta Kappa. Office: US Courthouse Rm 18614 601 Market St Philadelphia PA 19106

SLOWIKOWSKI, MARY KAY, mgmt. cons.; b. Chgo., Sept. 13, 1940; d. John Francis and Mary Katherine (Brennan) Brennan; student Mundelein Coll., 1958-60; Asso. Tchrs. degree Ill. State U., 1963; m. Norbert Slowikowski, Oct. 14, 1961; children—Annemarie, Eileen, Edward, Timothy John. Tchr. parochial sch., Wis., St. Louis and Chgo., 1963-73; relocation cons. McDonald's Corp., Oak Brook, Ill., 1973-75; chmn. bd. Slowikowski & Assos., Darien, Ill., 1975—; tchr. workshops Triton Community Coll., Harper Community Coll., Oakton Community Coll., 1977—; author Future Women Seminars, 1980—; speaker Nat. Assn. Women Bus. Owners. Exec. dir. evangelization com. Community Ch., 1979-80; adv. com. Ill. Benedictine Coll., 1980; advisor Coll. DuPage, Wheaton, Ill., 1979-80; sec. New Theatre Co., Du Page County, 1979-80. Recipient Speakers award No. Ill. Indsl. Assn., 1977-80. Mem. Bus. and Profl. Women Oak Brook, Nat. Assn. Women Bus. Owners, Women in Mgmt. (chpt. pres.), Nat. Bd. Women Mgmt. (v.p.), Chgo. Assn. Commerce and Industry, Nat. Assn. Future Women (founder 1981). Office: 805 Plainfield Rd Suite 216 Darien IL 60559

SLURZBERG, LUCY HELEN, psychotherapist; b. Jersey City, Oct. 3, 1946; d. Benjamin and Ruth (Wasserman) S.; B.A., Boston U., 1968; M.A., Columbia U., 1969; M.S.W., SUNY, Stony Brook, 1976. Psychotherapist, instr. Richmond Coll., Staten Island, N.Y., 1969-76; co-founder Onawa-a growth center for women, Staten Island, 1973-78; pvt. practice psychotherapy, N.Y.C., 1975—; mem. staff Inst. for Contemporary Psychotherapy, 1978—. Mem. Nat. Assn. Social Workers, Soc. Inst. for Contemporary Psychotherapy. Address: 127 W 86th St New York NY 10024

SMAGLICK, PATRICIA ANN NEWCOMB, drywall contractor; b. Neenah, Wis., May 31, 1934; d. Harold George and Kathryn Rose (Aupperle) Newcomb; B.S. in Nursing Edn., Marquette U., 1955; m. James G. Smaglick, 1955 (dec. 1977); children—James Jr., Michael, Christopher, Maria, Shannon. Vice pres., sec. State Drywall Inc., Wauwatosa, Wis., 1963-77, pres., treas., 1977—. Mem. Painting-Decorating Inst. (dir.), Painter and Drywall Contractor's Assn., Allied Constrn. Employers Assn. Roman Catholic. Office: State Drywall Inc 3695 N 126 PO Box 13574 Wauwatosa WI 53213

SMALL, HAZEL CHRISTINE, ednl. adminstr.; b. Russell, Ky., Jan. 20, 1919; d. Carl Leonard and Hazel May (Lynd) Halpin; B.S., U. Mich., 1940, M.S., 1953; postgrad. U. Toledo, 1962; Ed.D., N.C. State U., 1970; m. D. James Payne, Sept. 14, 1940 (dec.); children—Douglas J., John L., Nancy Elizabeth; m. 2d, Howard A. Small, Mar. 15, 1966 (dec.). Asso. dean students Dutchess Community Coll., Poughkeepsie, N.Y., 1962-65; asst. prof. psychology and edn. Shaw U., Raleigh, N.C., 1966-68; asst. prof. adult edn. Elizabeth City (N.C.) State U., 1971-72; asst. dir. staff devel. N.C. Dept. Community Colls., Raleigh, 1972-78, asso. v.p. policy and planning, 1978-80; dean of instrn. Gaston Coll., Dallas, N.C., 1980—. Mem. Am. Assn. Higher Edn., Am. Personnel and Guidance Assn., Nat. Assn. Public Continuing and Adult Edn., Am. Council Edn., Adult Edn. Assn., N.C. Assn. Instl. Research, Phi Delta Kappa, Alpha Delta Pi. Democrat. Unitarian. Clubs: Zonta. Contbr. articles to profl. jours. Office: Box 1 Gaston Coll Dallas NC 28034

SMALL, LORAIN GOULD, educator, assn. exec.; b. Alma, Wash., Oct. 10, 1909; d. James Michael and Pearl Yolo (Winkleman) Gould; A.B., Western Wash. U., 1942; M.A., Eastern Wash. U., 1958; m. James Savage Montgomery, 1927; m. 2d, Frederick Charles Small, 1953; children—Doris Lorain Montgomery (Mrs. Daniel R. Northcutt), Helen Kathleen Montgomery. Tchr., Burlington (Wash.) Schs., 1942-44; tchr. Mt. Vernon (Wash.) Schs., 1944-46, art supr., 1946-48; drama supr. Spokane Park Bd., summers, 1952-58; chmn. art dept. Sacajawea Jr. High Sch., Spokane, 1960-72; chmn. student loan com. Ret. Tchrs. Assn., Spokane, 1972, 73, pres., 1978-80; chmn. adv. bd. Senior Times, 1977-78; mem. planning com. Spokane City Charter Study, 1968-69; audit com. Credit Union, 1980—. Mem. Assn. for a Better Community, Eastern Wash. State Hist. Soc. (treas. art com. 1976-78), Wash. Art Assn. (past pres.). Home: W 2952 Grandview Ave Spokane WA 99204

SMALL, MARY ELEANOR, state legislator; b. Bath, Maine, Sept. 12, 1954; d. Donald Nichols and Marguerite (Brown) Small; student Green Mountain Coll., 1972-73; M.A., U. So. Maine, 1976. Campaign coordinator re-election U.S. Rep. David Emery, 1976; mem. Maine Ho. Reps., 1979—. Mem. Delta Zeta. Episcopalian. Office: Main Ho Reps State Capitol Augusta ME 04330 *

SMALL, MILLIE, state legislator; b. South Portland, Maine, July 13, 1924; grad. pub. schs., South Portland; m. Richard H. Small; two children. Mem., Upper Valley-Lake Sunapee Council Regional Planning Commn.; mem. exec. com. Vt. Republican State Com.; chmn. Windsor County Republican Com.; mem. Hartford Town Republican Com., Hartford Charter Study Com., Quechee Parking and Traffic Com.; mem. Gov.'s Commn. on Status of Women; alt. del. Republican Nat. Convs.; mem. Vt. Ho. Reps., 1981—. Trustee, New Eng. Aquarium. Mem. Quechee C. of C., Vt. Fedn. Republican Women. Congregationalist. Office: Vt Ho of Reps State House Montpelier VT 05602 *

SMALLING, CHERYL LEE, lawyer; b. Chgo., Dec. 15, 1952; d. Wendell O. and Josephine A. (Banjavcic) S.; B.A., DePaul U., 1974; J.D., John Marshall Law Sch., Chgo., 1979. Research analyst Continental Ill. Nat. Bank, Chgo., 1974-79; admitted to Ill. bar, 1979; asst. corp. counsel appeals and rev. div. City of Chgo., 1979—. Mem. ABA, Ill. Bar Assn., Chgo. Bar. Assn., Appellate Lawyers Assn. Home: 55 W Chestnut St Apt 2101 Chicago IL 60610 Office: 511 City Hall Chicago IL 60602

SMALLWOOD, GENEVIEVE CHARLENE, ins. co. exec.; b. Gauley Bridge, W.Va., Jan. 6, 1942; d. Charles Walker and Genevieve (Jones) S.; B.S. in Math and Biology, W.Va. Inst. Tech., 1964; diploma in mgmt. studies Ins. Inst. Am., 1971; postgrad. U. Hartford, 1976-77. Trainee program Ins. Co. N.Am., Phila., 1964-65, computer programmer, 1965-67, sr. systems engr., 1967-69, asst. dir., project mgr., 1969-73; sr. programming specialist Xerox Corp., Rochester, N.Y., 1973-74, mgr.

applications programming, 1974-76; systems cons. Hartford (Conn.) Ins. Group, 1976-77, asst. sec., asst. dir. data processing strategic planning div., 1977-78, asst. sec., dir. human resources devel., 1978-80; asst. sec., personnel mgr. Griffin office, Windsor, Conn., 1980-81, asst. sec., dir. orgn. planning 1981—; lectr. career devel., affirmative action profl. orgns. Bd. dirs., v.p. Greater Hartford Better Bus. Bur.; bd. dirs. W.Va. Tech. Alumni Assn., Minority Profl. Community Support Program; mem. adv. com. on continuing edn. Urban League; active Literacy Vols. Am. Cert. in data processing Data Processing Mgmt. Assn. Mem. Nat. Assn. Female Execs. Baptist. Home: 4 Forest Hill Dr Simsbury CT 06070 Office: Hartford Plaza Hartford CT 06115

SMALLWOOD, JANIS, decal mfg. co. exec.; b. Balt., Aug. 26, 1943; d. Lawrence Albert and Sarah (Carey) S.; B.S. in Advt., U. Md., 1967. Art dir. Stromberg Pubs., Balt., 1967, also Belsinger Fleetmark Inc., Ellicott City, Md.; gen. mgr. pressure sensitive decal co., Balt., 1967-72; founder, pres., owner Md. Decal Ltd., Balt., 1973—. Mem. Screen Printing Assn. Internat., Md. C. of C., NOW, U. Md. Alumni Assn. (life). Democrat. Office: 2900 Whittington Ave Baltimore MD 21230

SMARIGA, LILLIAN ALLEN, accountant; b. Waco, Tex., Sept. 2, 1927; d. Homer Eugene and Lillian Louise (Smith) Allen; student U. Houston, 1964-65; m. Stanley Edward Smariga, Apr. 21, 1950; children—Robert, Melanie, Mary Hope, Russell. Bookkeeper, sec. Houston Carbide Corp., 1951-55; div. sec., bookkeeper, office mgr. Houston Carbide div. Firth Sterling, Inc., 1955-68; asst. to acctg. mgr. F. W. Gartner Co., Houston, 1968-70, asst. to acctg. mgr., office mgr., 1970-75, acctg. mgr., asst. sec.-treas., 1975-77, controller, asst. sec.-treas., 1977—. Mem. Nat. Assn. Accts., Am. Soc. Women Accts. Republican. Episcopalian. Home: 1605 Alabama St Pasadena TX 77503 Office: 3805 Lamar St Houston TX 77001

SMART, DOROTHY CAROLINE, ret. social worker; b. Osborn, Mo.; d. Allen A. and Caroline (Totzke) Smart; student U. Mo., 1929-30; A.B., U. Kans., 1937, M.S.W., 1950; postgrad. U. Chgo., 1963, 65. Advt. copy writer Emery Bird Thayer, Kansas City, Mo., 1937-38; case worker Dept. Pub. Welfare, Kansas City, 1938-44, Jackson County chpt. ARC, Kansas City, 1944-49; disaster rep. Am. Nat. Red Cross, St. Louis, 1950-59, home service rep. area office, 1959-65, regional dir. service mil. families, 1965-70, asst. area dir. service to mil. families, 1970-76. Mem. Group Action Council. Mem. Nat. Assn. Social Workers, Acad. Certified Social Workers, Nat. Conf. Social Welfare, Women in Communications (pres. Kansas City alumni chpt. 1943). Club: Pilot (pres. 1975-77) (St. Louis). Home: 4475 W Pine St Saint Louis MO 63108

SMART, EDITH MERRILL, civic worker; b. N.Y.C., Sept. 10, 1929; d. Edwin Katte and Helen Phelps (Stokes) Merrill; student Smith Coll., 1947-49, Barnard Coll., 1949-50; m. S. Bruce Smart, Jr., Sept. 10, 1949; children—Edith Minturn, William Candler, Charlotte Merrill, Priscilla. Tchr. elementary schs., Gibson Island, Md., 1959-60; guide, instr. Mill River Wetlands Com., Fairfield, Conn., 1967—; treas. Near and Far Aid Assn., Fairfield, 1970-75, v.p., 1975-77, pres., 1977-79; pres. Nature Center of Environ. Activities, Westport, Conn. Leader No. Cook County council Girl Scouts U.S.A., Kenilworth, Ill., 1962-64; chmn. Southport-Westport Antiques Show, 1974-76; vestryman St. Timothy's Ch., Fairfield, 1976-79; trustee Conn. chpt. Nature Conservancy, 1981—. Republican. Episcopalian. Clubs: Sasqua Garden (Fairfield), River (N.Y.C.). Home: 4375 Congress St Fairfield CT 06430 Office: Nature Center for Environ Activities 10 Woodside Ln Westport CT 06880

SMART, MARY-LEIGH CALL (MRS. J. SCOTT SMART), farm operator, civic worker; b. Springfield, Ill., Feb. 27, 1917; d. S(amuel) Leigh and Mary (Bradish) Call; jr. coll. diploma Monticello Coll., 1934; student Oxford U., 1935; B.A., Wellesley Coll., 1937; M.A., Columbia, 1939, postgrad., 1940-41; postgrad. N.Y.U., 1940-41; painting student with Bernard Karfiol, 1937-38; m. J. Scott Smart, Sept. 11, 1951 (dec. 1960). Dir. mgmt. Central Ill. grain farms, Logan County, Ill., 1939—; art collector, patron, cons., 1954—; program dir. sec. 82— Barn Gallery Assos., Inc., Ogunquit, Maine, 1958-69, pres., 1969-70, 82—, hon. dir., 1970-78; curator Hamilton Easter Field Art Found. Collection, 1978-79, curator exhbns., 1979—; owner Lowtrek Kennel, Ogunquit, 1957-73, Cove Studio Art Gallery, Ogunquit, 1961-68. Mem. acquisition com. DeCordova Mus., Lincoln, Mass., 1966-78. Mem. chancellor's council U. Tex., 1972—, U. N.H., 1977—. Chmn. Outdoor-Display Bd. Perkins Cove Assn., Ogunquit, 1972. Bd. dirs. Ogunquit C. of C., 1966, treas. 1966-67, hon. life mem., 1968—; bd. overseers Strawbery Banke, Inc., Portsmouth, N.H., 1971-74, 3d vice-chmn., 1972-73, 2d vice-chmn., 1973-74; bd. advisers Univ. Art Galleries, U. N.H., 1973—, v.p., 1974-81, pres., 1981—; mem. adv. com. Maine 75, Bowdoin Coll. Art Mus. Exhbn., 1975; cons. Bicentennial Exhbn. '76, Maine Artists, Maine State Mus., 1976; mem. adv. com. All Maine Biennial, Bowdoin Coll. Mus. Art, 1979; mem. York Hist. Dist. Com., 1981—; bd. dirs. Old York Hist. and Improvement Soc., 1979-81, v.p., 1981-82. Served to lt. (j.g.) WAVES, 1942-45. Mem. Am. Fedn. Arts, Am. Assn. Museums, Mus. Modern Art, Springfield Art Assn., Solomon R. Guggenheim Mus., Portland Soc. Art, Jr. League of Springfield, Inst. Contemporary Art Boston (corporator 1965-73), Friends of Art Colby Coll., Patrons Fine Arts U. Maine, Maine Coast Artists Rockport (adv. com. 1976-78), Whitney Mus. Am. Art. Republican. Episcopalian. Club: Western Maine Wellesley. Editor: Hamilton Easter Field Art Found. Collection Catalog, 1966; originator, dir. show, compiler of catalog Art: Ogunquit, 1967; originator exhbn. Peggy Bacon—A Celebration, Ogunquit, 1979. Address: Rural Route 2 Box 381 York ME 03909

SMEAL, ELEANOR CUTRI, orgn. exec.; b. Ashtabula, Ohio, July 30, 1939; d. Peter Anthony and Josephine E. (Agresti) Cutri; B.A., Duke U., 1961; M.A., U. Fla., 1963; m. Charles R. Smeal, Apr. 27, 1963; children—Tod, Lori. Mem. bd. Upper St. Clair (Pa.) chpt. League Women Voters, 1968-72, sec.-treas. Allegheny County Council, 1971-72; mem. NOW, 1971—, convenor, 1st pres. S. Hills (Pa.) chpt., 1971-73, 1st pres., state coordinator Pa., 1972-75, nat. bd. dirs., 1973-75, chairwoman bd., 1975-77, pres., 1977—, mem. bd. Legal Def. and Edn. Fund, 1975—; mem. 1st nominating com., founding conf. Nat. Women's Polit. Caucus, 1971; bd. dirs. Allegheny County Women's Polit. Caucus, 1971-72; co-founder, bd. dirs. S. Hills NOW Day Nursery Sch., 1972—; mem. Nat. Commn., Observance of Internat. Women's Year, 1977; chairwoman ERA Strike Force, 1977—; mem. Nat. Adv. Com. Women, 1978, exec. com. Leadership Conf. Civil Rights, 1979. Named One of Twenty-five Most Influential Women in U.S., World Almanac, 1978. Office: 425 13th St NW Suite 1048 Washington DC 20004 *

SMEDRESMAN, INGEBORG FREUNDLICH, artist; b. Germany; came to U.S., 1937, naturalized, 1943; d. Paul and Erna Betty (Simon) Freundich; B.S., U. Frankfurt, Germany, 1934; postgrad. in chemistry U. Zurich, Switzerland, 1934-37, art edn. Nat. Acad. Art Students League, Queens Coll; m. Sidney Smedresman, Aug. 10, 1937; children—Ingrid Braslow, Leonard C., Paulette Mehta, Suzanne van Oers. Art lectr. Forest Hills Jewish Center, 1966-68, Guggenheim Mus., 1973-76; art tchr. Queensboro Art Soc., 1969; art dir. Temple Beth El, Great Neck, L.I., 1969-75, YM-YWHA, Little Neck, 1975; exhibited in one woman shows at Fine Arts Gallery, N.Y.C., 1970, Queens Coll., N.Y.C., summer 1975, Dec. 1978, summer 1981, Harrison (N.Y.) Library, 1979, 80. Exhibited in group shows at ACA Gallery, 1959, Contemporary Art Gallery, 1965-66, Raymond Duncan Gallery, Paris, France, 1965-66, Ahda Arzt Gallery, N.Y.C., 1970, Ten Voorde Gallery, Amsterdam, 1973, Carrol Condit Gallery, White Plains N.Y., 1973, Westchester Art Soc., 1970-75; represented in permanent collections Godwin-Ternbach Mus. of Queens Coll., City Hall, Moncton, N.B., Can., Israel Mus., Jerusalem; art instr. YM-YWHA, Flushing; lectr. Cooper-Hewitt Mus. Recipient art awards Paris Water Colors, 1965, 66, Suffolk County Artists, 1966, Queensboro Art Soc., 1975, 1st prize Westchester Art Soc., 1975. Mem. Art Students League N.Y., Artists Equity Assn., Am. Chem. Soc. Home: 147-43 77th Rd Kew Garden Hills NY 11367

SMELTZER, SUSAN, pianist, composer; b. Sapulpa, Okla., Sept. 13, 1941; d. Frank Cecil and Mary Margaret (Robertson) S.; Mus.B. (scholar), Oklahoma City U., 1964; Mus.M. magna cum laude, U. So. Calif., 1969; postgrad. (Fulbright scholar) Akademie fur Musik, Vienna, 1969-70; master class with Gregor Piatigorsky, Los Angeles, Rosina Lhevinne, Los Angeles; m. Philip S. Snyder, June 14, 1973. Pvt. tchr. music, Sapulpa, Okla., 1956-62, Los Angeles, 1964-72; instr. piano Oklahoma City U., 1961-64, Holy Name Convent, Los Angeles, 1964-65, Valley Conservatory Music, Studio City, Calif., 1965-66, First Congl. Ch., Los Angeles, 1966-67, Mt. St. Mary's Coll., Los Angeles, 1966-69, 70-72; vis. piano faculty mem. Rice U., Houston, 1972-73; profl. accompanist U. Houston, 1972-73; artist-in-residence, instr. humanities Coll. of Mainland, Texas City, Tex., 1972-79; organist various chs., Okla., Calif., intermittently, 1957-71; profl. accompanist throughout midwest, 1961-64, Los Angeles area, 1964-72, Houston, 1972—; performed with chamber groups, Los Angeles area, 1964-69, 70-72; Carnegie Hall debut, 1975; European debut Brahmssaal, Vienna; numerous orchestral appearances; compositions include: Reverie, 1962, Kaleidescope, 1968, Twelve Mood Pictures (variations for piano on theme of Yankee Doodle and the interval sets 1-9-7-6:1-7-7-6), 1975, The Bald Eagle March, 1979, Psalm 121 (for choir and orch.), 1979, An American Tribue For A Royal Marriage, 1982. Recipient numerous awards including: Bloch Young Artist award Ladies Music Club, 1962; award Nat. Fedn. Music Clubs, 1962, Okla. Music Tchrs. Assn., 1962. Mem. Internat. League Women Composers, Am. Women Composers, Nat. Guild Piano Tchrs. (judging staff), Chamber Music Am., Broadcast Music Inc., Pi Kappa Lambda, Sigma Alpha Iota. Club: Tuesday Musica. Author: Selected Orchestrations of Poetic Expressions (book of poetry), 1982. Home and office: 8102 Tavenor St Houston TX 77075

SMID, MARCELYN JOANNE, librarian; b. George, Iowa, Oct. 24, 1932; d. John Eden and Theresa Siebenna (Sudenga) S.; B.Mus., St. Paul Bible Coll., 1954; B.A., Westmar Coll., LeMars, Iowa, 1957; M.A., U. Minn., 1961. Tchr. English, Harris (Iowa) Consol. Sch. Dist., 1957-59; librarian Monroe Jr. High Sch., Mason City (Iowa) Sch. Dist., 1961-66; dir. library St. Paul Bible Coll., 1966—. Mem. Assn. Christian Librarians (exec. sec. 1976—), ALA, Music Library Assn., Minn. Library Assn. Republican. Mem. Christian and Missionary Alliance. Indexer: Christian Periodical Index. Home: 104 Riverside Terr Watertown MN 55388 Office: St Paul Bible Coll Bible College MN 55375

SMILEY, CLEERETTA HENDERSON, ednl. adminstr., home economist; b. Whatley, Ala., June 20, 1930; d. Edward and Rebecca Ann (Odom) Henderson; B.S., Miles Coll., 1954; M.S., U. Md., 1971, postgrad., 1972-73; diploma esoteric sci. and psychology Am. U., 1976; children—Consuela Angelia, Robert Edward, Lisa Kay, Joan Alyssa. Correctional officer Fed. Reformatory for Women, Alderson, W.Va., 1954-55, culinary officer, 1955-56, tchr. home econs., 1956-61, asst. vocat. ednl. dir., 1959-61; tchr. gen. home econs. edn. D.C. Public Schs., 1963-80, asst. supervising dir. home econs., 1980—, dir. Model HERO Youth Employment Tng. Program, Coolidge Sr. High Sch., 1975-80; state adv. for D.C., Future Homemakers Am./HERO, 1980—; condr. fashion shows, model; tchr. coordinator Show Prodns. Tng. Program, 1967-80; mem. Home Econs. Adv. Council, D.C. Public Schs. and Logan Community Sch. Adv. Council; practitioner esoteric sci. Minority affairs adv. to bd. dirs. Social Services Agy., Eastern region Ch. Jesus Christ of Latter-day Saints, 1979—, stake missionary, edn. counselor Relief Soc.; mem. hosting com. Public Communications Council, Kensington, Md., 1979-81; co-chairperson Health Commn., D.C. PUSH, 1979-80; bd. dirs. Aum Spiritual Sci. Center, Washington, 1980—; mem. First Spiritual Leadership Conf. Network Leaders, McLean, Va., 1981. Named Mrs. D.C., Mrs. America Pageant, 1968, Mrs. D.C. Savs. Bonds, 1968; Harambee Mother of Yr., Sta. WDVM-TV, 1969. Mem. Am. Vocat. Edn. Assn., D.C. Vocat. Edn. Assn., Future Homemakers Am. Home Econs. Related Occupations Youth Orgn., Nat. Assn. Black Am. Vocat. Educators (life), Nat. Collaboration of Youth Orgns., Nat. Assn. Female Execs., World Modeling Assn., Afro Am. Jubilee Commn., Am. Meta-Phys. Inst. Network Soc., Iota Phi Lambda. Democrat. Club: Circle I Am, Order Eastern Star. Home: 2209 Ross Rd Silver Spring MD 20910 Office: Macfarland Jr High Sch 4400 Iowa Ave NW Washington DC 20011

SMILEY, KATHRYN ANNE, advt. agy. exec.; b. Richmond, Va., Oct. 6, 1946; d. Cabel Earl and Anne Conway (Baugh) S.; B.A., Va. Commonwealth U., 1964-69; tchr.'s cert. Montessori Internat., 1975. Tchr. public schs., Richmond, 1968; asso. dir. Va. Council on Health and Med. Care, Richmond, 1968-71; v.p. Yolton/Brown Direct Response Advt., Bethesda, Md., 1972—, also dir.; dir. Guy L. Yolton Advt., Inc., Falls Church, Va.; cons., lectr. on media buying. Tutor, Head Start Program, Richmond. Mem. Direct Mktg. Assn. of Washington (dir., v.p.), Direct Mail Mktg. Assn., Sierra Club, NOW. Democrat. Methodist. Office: 4733 Bethesda Ave Bethesda MD 20814

SMILEY, MARILYNN JEAN, musicologist, educator; b. Columbia City, Ind., June 5, 1932; d. Orla Raymond and Mary Jane (Bailey) S.; B.S. in Music (Ind. scholar), Ball State U., 1954; postgrad. Ind. U., 1956-60; Mus.M. in Music History and Lit., Northwestern U., 1958; cert. Ecoles d'Art Americaines, Fontainebleau, France, 1959; postgrad. U. Colo., summer 1960; Ph.D. in Musicology (Delta Kappa Gamma Soc. Internat. scholar 1964-65, Univ. fellow 1964-65), U. Ill., 1970. Tchr. music public schs., Logansport, Ind., 1954-61; instr. dept. music SUNY Coll. Arts and Sci., Oswego, 1961-64, asst. prof. music, 1964-67, asso. prof., 1967-72, prof., 1972-74, Disting. Teaching prof., 1974—, chairperson dept. music, 1976-81. Mem. Oswego County Council on Arts; bd. dirs. Oswego Opera Theatre, 1978—, Oswego Orch. Soc., 1978—. Recipient Outstanding Alumni award Music Div. Ball State U., 1969, Chancellor's award for excellence in teaching SUNY, 1973; SUNY Research Found. fellow, summers 1971, 72, 74. Mem. Am. Musicological Soc. (chairperson N.Y. State chpt. 1975-77), Medieval Acad. Am., Renaissance Soc. Am., Sonneck Soc. Am., Inst. Renaissance Studies, Music Educators Nat. Conf., AAUW (v.p. Oswego br. 1981-83), Renaissance Soc. Am., Oswego County Hist. Soc., Heritage Soc., Delta Kappa Gamma, Phi Delta Kappa, Pi Kappa Lambda, Sigma Alpha Iota, Sigma Tau Delta, Kappa Delta Pi, Delta Phi Alpha. Methodist. Contbr. articles on Am. music, medieval music, local music history, chpts. to various publs.; research on Am. music, Renaissance keybd. music and theory. Home: 77 W Fifth St Oswego NY 13126 Office: Dept Music SUNY Oswego NY 13126

SMITH, ALEXIS, actress; b. Penticton, B.C., Can., June 8, 1921; ed. Los Angeles City Coll.; m. Craig Stevens, 1944. Actress numerous films, stage plays, 1941—; films include The Lady With Red Hair, 1940, Dive Bomber, 1941, The Smiling Ghost, 1941, Gentleman Jim, 1942, The Constant Nymph, 1942, The Doughgirls, 1944, Conflict, 1945, Rhapsody in Blue, 1945, San Antonio, 1945, Nigh and Day, 1946, Of Human Bondage, 1946, Stallion Road, 1947, The Woman in White, 1947, The Decision of Christopher Blake, 1948, Any Number Can Play, 1950, Undercover Girl, 1952, Split Second, 1953, The Sleeping Tiger, 1955, The Eternal Sea, 1956, The Young Philadelphians, 1959, Once is Not Enough, 1975, Casey's Shadow, 1977; stage appearances include Follies (Tony award 1972), 1971, 72, The Women, 1973, Summer Brave, 1975, Lila Halliday in Sunset, 1978. Address: care International Creative Mgmt 8899 Beverly Blvd Los Angeles CA 90048 *

SMITH, ALICE MARIE DROEN, banker; b. Clarkfield, Minn., Dec. 12, 1916; d. Lewis O. and Alma Helmina (Anderson) Droen; student pub. schs., Clarkfield; m. Harold Eugene Smith, June 20, 1942; children—Richard Eugene, Harold Duane, Mary Alice Smith Hegna. Sec., Clarkfield Sch., 1936-37; sec. Farmers & Mchts. State Bank, Clarkfield, Minn., 1937-48, asst. cashier, 1959-68, cashier, 1968-78, v.p., 1972-78, exec. v.p., 1978—, dir., 1968—; dir. F & Agy., Inc., 1972—. Mem. Nat. Assn. Bank Women. Republican. Lutheran. Home: RFD 1 Clarkfield MN 56223 Office: Farmers & Mchts State Bank 940 10th Ave Clarkfield MN 56223

SMITH, ANITA LAIN (MRS. JAMES EDWIN SMITH), educator; b. Macon, Ga., Mar. 21, 1916; A.B., Spelman Coll., 1936; M.Ed., N. Tex. State U., 1959; m. James Edwin Smith, June 27, 1940; children—James Edwin III, Adrien Yvonne (Mrs. Larkin Arnold), Lee Stanley, Annette Louise (Mrs. Jesse Washington). Tchr., Am. Missionary Assn., Fessenden Acad., Martin, Fla., 1936-39, Washington High Sch., El Reno, Okla., 1939-40; supr. U.S.O. Servicemen's Lounge, Dallas, 1944-45; acting mgr. Frazier Cts., Dallas, 1945-46; tchr. art edn. Dallas Ind. Schs., 1959-62; counselor Lincoln High Sch., Dallas, 1962-65; acting counselor Phillips High Sch., Chgo., 1965-66; coordinator-counselor Sealantic program Loyola U. Sch. Nursing, Chgo., 1966-69; student counselor U. Ill. Med. Center, Coll. Nursing, Chgo., 1969-80. Mem. Chgo. Council Community Nursing, dir. 1969-72; mem. standing com. Chgo. Area Coll. Assistance Project, 1968-70; mem. rev. panel, com. Community Fund, Chgo., 1969-75. Mem. Am. Personnel and Guidance Assn., Nat. Vocational Guidance Assn., Am. Coll. Personnel Assn., Delta Sigma Theta. Episcopalian. Home: 6325 Autumn Woods Trail Dallas TX 75232

SMITH, ANN CATHERINE, mfg. co. exec.; b. S. Bend, Ind., Jan. 20, 1947; d. Robert Joseph and Geraldine Frances (Hagerty) Haley; A.B., Ind. U., 1972; m. Philip Neal Smith, Oct. 21, 1967. Asst. mng. editor Bloomington (Ind.) Courier-Tribune, 1969-73; dir. news and public affairs Sta. WTTS/WGTC, Bloomington, 1974-76; mgr. pub. info. Cummins Engine Co., Inc., Columbus, Ind., 1976—. Bd. dirs. Columbus chpt. LWV, 1977-79, AAUW, 1977-78, Columbus Mental Health Assn., 1977-79; v.p. Columbus Disting. Visitors Series, 1981—. Recipient Communications award of merit Ind. Trial Lawyers Assn., 1972; Ann Smith Day proclaimed by Bloomington City Council, 1974. Mem. Pub. Relations Soc. Am. Home: 2805 Whipporwill Dr Columbus IN 47201 Office: Box 3005 Columbus IN 47201

SMITH, ANNA ROBERTS, planning cons. co. exec.; b. Worth, Mo., Mar. 3, 1936; d. Walter Edwin and Esther (Batt) Roberts; B.S., N.W. Mo. State U., 1957; M.Music Edn., U. Kans., 1963; m. Delbert Ely Smith, May 28, 1958; children—Catharine Dianne Almquist, Michael William Delbert. Tchr. pub. schs., Mo., 1957-61; part-time tchr. Iowa Western Community Coll., Council Bluffs, 1966-75; exec. dir. Clarinda (Iowa): Town of Tomorrow, 1976-78; mem. Clarinda City Council, 1974-78; pres., sr. planner Community Devel. Assocs., Inc., Clarinda, 1978—; exec. dir. Des Moines Housing Council, 1978—. Pres. Clarinda Nursery Sch., 1974-75, Clarinda Community Betterment, 1972-73; mem. Iowa Gov.'s Commn. on Compensation, 1974—. Mem. Clarinda Concert Assn. (pres. 1969-70). Methodist. Contbr. articles to profl. publs. Home: 601 S 16th St Clarinda IA 51632 also 930 School St Apt 65 Des Moines IA 50309 Office: Community Devel Assocs Inc 601 S 16th St Clarinda IA 51632 also Des Moines Housing Council Inc 1041 8th St Des Moines IA 50314

SMITH, ANNE MARIE, real estate broker/appraiser; b. Bridgeport, Conn., Oct. 21, 1924; d. John and Louise (Mormile) Oligino; student U. Bridgeport, 1946, U. Conn., 1951, 71-73; m. Joseph I. Smith, Aug. 30, 1947; children—Bradford J., Marilyn M. With IRS, N.Y.C., 1947; real estate broker/appraiser Anne M. Smith Real Estate, Fairfield, Conn., 1949—; owner Pandora's Linens, Fairfield, 1976—. Mem. housing com. Town of Fairfield, 1975; mem. Republican Town com., 1980—; chmn. Fairfield Sidewalk Art Show, 1974. Served with USN, 1944-46. Named Realtor of the Yr., Fairfield Bd. Realtors, 1978. Mem. Fairfield Real Estate Bd. (pres. 1980, dir. 1978-81), C. of C. (v.p. 1973-75, dir. 1970-71), Conn. Assn. Realtors, Nat. Assn. Realtors. Home: 696 Hillside Rd Fairfield CT 06430 Office: 1596 Post Rd Fairfield CT 06430

SMITH, ANNE MOLLEGEN, mag. editor; b. Meridian, Miss., July 28, 1940; d. Albert Theodore and Harriet Ione (Rush) Mollegen; B.A., Smith Coll., 1961; m. David Fay Smith, Nov. 3, 1962; 1 dau., Amanda Wetherbee. Staff corr., asst. editor Ladies Home Jour., N.Y.C., 1961-62; advt. copywriter Hutzler's, Balt., 1962-64; feature editor China Post newspaper, Taipei, Taiwan, 1965-66; staff writer Penney News, J.C. Penney Co., 1966; asso. editor Redbook mag., 1967-72, fiction editor, 1973-77, editor Redbook's Famous Fiction, 1977; mng. editor Your Place mag., McCall Pub. Co., N.Y.C., 1977-78, Redbook, 1978—; staff lectr. numerous writers confs. Mem. NOW, Women's Media Group (pres. 1978-79), Am. Soc. Mag. Editors, Women's Nat. Book Assn. Club: Smith (N.Y.C.). Office: Redbook 230 Park Ave New York NY 10017

SMITH, ANNELLEN PRIM, advt. counselor; b. St. Louis, May 18, 1925; student Dept. Def. schs., 1956-62. Systems analyst Dept. Army, St. Louis, 1944-56, 64-76, Washington, 1956-63, Detroit, 1963-64; advt. counselor Directions Unltd., Fairview Heights, Ill., 1977—. Pres., Ill. Fedn. Bus. and Profl. Women's Clubs, 1982-83. Mem. United Ch. of Christ. Home: 2810 Yale Dr Granite City IL 62040 Office: 10334 Lincoln Trail Fairview Heights IL 62208

SMITH, BANNA ISAACS, high sch. prin.; b. St. Paul, Va., May 18, 1926; d. Blaine George and Lydia Maxie (Lawson) Isaacs; B.S., Lincoln Meml. U., Harrogate, Tenn., 1948; M.A., George Peabody Coll., Nashville, 1960, Ed.S., 1964; m. Ernest Elijah Smith, Aug. 23, 1946; 1 son, William Ernest. Tchr., Ky. and Ohio, 1946-64; mem. staff Troy (Ohio) City Schs., 1964—, prin. Troy Jr. High Sch., 1976—; reading cons., workshop coordinator. Youth leader Lynch (Ky.) Bapt. Ch., 1960-63, adult tng. union leader, 1960-62. Mem. NEA, Ohio Edn. Assn., Troy City Edn. Assn., Delta Kappa Gamma. Home: 192 Carrousel Dr Troy OH 45373 Office: 556 N Market St Troy OH 45373

SMITH, BARBARA ANN, psychologist; b. Boston; d. James M. and Florene S.; student Universidad de las Americas, Cholulu, Puebla, Mexico, summer 1970; B.A. in Psychology, U. Mass., 1971; M.A. in Psychology, Goddard Coll., 1974. Cons., Lena Park Community Devel. Corp., Dorchester, Mass., 1975-77; family psychologist Martha Elliot Health Center Children's Hosp. Affiliate, Jamaica Plain, Mass., 1976; adult day program dir. Solomon C. Fuller Mental Health Center, Boston, 1977-79; psychologist Boston Public Schs., 1979—; adv. bd. Lang. and Cognitive Devel. Center, Jamaica Plain, 1976. Chairwoman recruitment com., debutante cotillion com. Union United Methodist Ch., Boston, 1972. Recipient Sunday Sch. Tchr. Recognition award Union Meth. Ch., 1979. Mem. Am. Psychol. Assn., Mass. Psychol. Assn., Am. Soc. Profl. and Exec. Women. Research in non-discriminatory assessment. Home: Dorchester MA 02124 Office: 26 Court St Boston MA 02108

SMITH, BARBARA ANN, acct., tax cons.; b. Dallas, May 6, 1935; d. George Jefferson and Ina Pearl (Nowlin) Gardner; Asso. Mid. Mgmt., Mountain View Jr. Coll., 1975; 1 dau., Cynthia Marie Dixon. Asst. cashier U.S. Rubber Co., Dallas, 1954-57; sec.-treas. Am. Graphics Co., Dallas, 1974-79; pres. Am. Way Credit Union, Dallas, 1974-76; sec.-treas. Am. Legal Printing Co., Dallas, 1964-79, Abco Inc., Dallas, 1964-79, Am. Poster & Printing Co., Dallas, 1964-79; asst. sec.-treas. Am. Equity Press Inc., Dallas, 1974-79; co-owner MS Services, Dallas and Chgo., 1979—. Republican. Adventist. Home: 3515 Brown St Apt 109 Dallas TX 75219 Office: Oak Lawn Plaza Dallas TX 75207 also Mdse Mart Chicago IL 60654

SMITH, BARBARA GORDON, state ofcl.; b. Los Angeles, Oct. 13, 1927; d. Frank and Anna Louisa (Weidauer) Belcher; B.A., Occidental Coll., 1949; M.P.A., U. So. Calif., 1976; m. Kenneth H. Smith, Aug. 29, 1980; children—Edward Kermit, Parker, Stephen Frank Parker. Tchr., Calif. Public Schs., 1949-72; adminstrv. intern Sacramento (Calif.) Superior Ct., 1975-77; legis. aide, sr. adminstr. Calif. Assembly, Office Speaker Pro Tempore, Sacramento, 1977-80; exec. dir. Calif. Health Facilities Authority, Sacramento, 1980—. Chmn., Contra Costa County Natural Resource Commn., 1965-68. Named Citizen of Year, Orinda, Calif., 1968. Mem. Nature Conservancy, Audubon Soc. Office: 915 Capitol Mall Room 280 Sacramento CA 94814

SMITH, BETTE BELLE, banker, civic worker; b. Modesto, Calif., Jan. 17, 1921; d. James Alfred and Maysel Elizabeth (Hughes) Anderson; A.A., Modesto Jr. Coll., 1939; B.A., UCLA, 1941; m. Jean T. Smith, May 4, 1945; children—Talbott Anderson, Timothy Melton and Mary Margaret (twins). Vice pres., bank relations officer, asst. corp. sec. Modesto Banking Co., 1979—. Mem. Modesto Culture Commn., 1979—, former bd. dirs.; mem. Greater Modesto Found.; mem. Muir Trail council Girl Scouts U.S.A.; former v.p. Stanislaus County Drug Abuse Coordinating Council; bd. dirs. United Crusade, 1969-72; organizing bd., v.p. McHenry Mus. Soc.; organizing bd. pres. McHenry Mus. Guild, 1979; mem. Calif. Republican Central Com., 1970-74; v.p. Modesto Rep. Women; pres. Modesto Jr. Coll. Alumni Found., 1977-80; organizing bd. Gt. Valley Mus.; mem. Stanislaus County Hist. Soc.; past pres. PTAs, hon. service award; former leader Cub Scouts, Brownies, Jr. Girl Scouts U.S.A.; grand pres. Omega Nu, 1954; pres. 50 Plus Club of Stanislaus County; bd. dirs. Downtown Mchts. Assn., Modesto Symphony Orch., Friends of Music, Modesto Arts Adv. Council; mem. Modesto City Beautification Com.; chmn. May Clean Up Month; mem. Charter Rev. Com., 1970; chmn. sr. citizen sect. Progress Greater Modesto Com.; parade chmn. All Am. City Com.; dist. rep. Stanislaus County internat. intercultural scholarship program Am. Field Service, 1961—. Named Women of Yr., Soroptimist Internat., 1958; recipient Loyalty Day award VFW, 1979, Liberty Bell award Stanislaus County Bar Assn., 1980. Club: Soroptimist (hon.). Home: 415 Sycamore St Modesto CA 95354 Office: 1120 11th St Modesto CA 95354

SMITH, BETTY DENNY, county ofcl., fashion exec., civic worker; b. Centralia, Ill., Nov. 12, 1932; d. Otto and Ferne Elizabeth (Beier) Hasenfuss; student U. Ill., 1950-52, Los Angeles City Coll., 1953-57, UCLA, 1965; m. Peter S. Smith, Dec. 5, 1964; children—Carla Kip, Bruce Kimball. Free-lance fashion coordinator Los Angeles and N.Y.C., 1953-58; instr. fashion Rita LeRoy Internat. Studios, 1959-60; mgr. Mo Nadler Fashions, Los Angeles, 1961-64; free-lance polit. book reviewer community newspapers, 1961-62; staff writer Valley Citizen News, 1963; showroom dir. Jean of Calif. Fashions, Los Angeles, 1966—; dir. animal care and control Los Angeles County, 1976—. Bd. dirs. Pet Assistance Found., 1969-76; ind. legis. adv. for human causes, 1969-75; founder, pres., dir. Vol. Services to Animals of Los Angeles, 1972-76; mem. County Com. to Discuss Animals in Research, 1973-74; mem. blue ribbon com. on animal control Los Angeles County, 1973-74; mem. animal health tech. examining com. State of Calif., 1975-79; mem. Calif. Republican Central Com., 1964-72, mem. exec. com., 1971-72; mem. Rep. Central Com. Los Angeles County, 1964-70, mem. exec. com., 1966-70; active polit. campaigns Rep. candidates. Mem. Lawyers Wives San Gabriel Valley (dir. 1971-74, pres. 1972-73), Mannequins Assn. (dir. 1967-68), Internat. Platform Assn., Delta Gamma, Phi Phi Theta. Club: Los Angeles Athletic.

SMITH, BETTY LORETTA, art gallery ofcl.; b. Trinidad, Colo., Oct. 17, 1932; d. Howard Melvin and Anna Belle (Eastwood) Wade; student public schs.; m. Earl Gilbert Smith, Nov. 26, 1950; children—Wayne David, Christine Ella, Clifford Todd. Owner, operator Gilbert's Gallery and Frame Shop, Santa Rosa, Calif., 1964—; condr. seminars, cons., speaker in field. Former mem. Santa Rosa Civic Art Commn. Recipient Liberal Arts award Bank of Am., 1950. Mem. Profl. Picture Framers Assn. Republican. Presbyterian. Author papers, materials in field. Office: 865 3d St Santa Rosa CA 95404

SMITH, BETTY MURNAN, educator; b. Indpls., Sept. 11, 1921; d. Carl J. and Helene Alice (Stephens) Murnan; B.A. cum laude in English, Butler U., 1944; M.A. in English, State U. Iowa, 1950; m. Richard Norman Smith, Oct. 21, 1951; children—Allegra Louise Smith Jrolf, Timothy and Michael (twins). Tchr. Kingsford (Mich.) High Sch., 1944-46, Bosse High Sch. Evansville, Ind., 1946-48; instr. English, Ely (Minn.) Jr. Coll., 1950-51; acting instr. English, U. Wis., Milw., 1961-66; instr. English, U. Wis. Center-Waukesha County, 1966-70, asst. prof., 1970-81, asso. prof., 1981—, senator U. Wis. Center System, 1980-81; lectr. in field. Co-prin. Hdqrs. Freedom Sch. Mil. Sch. Boycott, 1963; bd. dirs. Waukesha Symphony Orch., 1969-72; sec. Waukesha Equal Opportunity Commn., 1970-73; bd. dirs. Waukesha Civic Theatre, 1973-74; mem. Com. for Women's Issues Forum, 1979-80. Recipient award for outstanding achievement in community services U. Wis., Waukesha, 1979. Mem. AAUP (pres. chpt. 1969-70), MLA, Midwest MLA, Nat., Wis. councils tchrs. English, Am. Fedn. Tchrs. (treas. Milw. chpt. 1962-66), Assn. U. Wis. Faculties, Kappa Delta Pi, Sigma Tau Delta. Presbyterian (ruling elder). Contbr. poetry to mags. Home: 1128 Oxford Rd Waukesha WI 53186 Office: Univ Wis Waukesha County 1500 University Dr Waukesha WI 53186

SMITH, BETTYE L. SEBREE, bus. coll. exec.; b. Owensmouth, Calif., Feb. 25, 1926; d. Roy Albert and Thelma Hattie (Alexander) Sebree; student Brigham Young U., 1944-45, Links Sch. Bus., Boise, Idaho, 1946, Nampa (Idaho) Bus. Coll. 1956; B.S., Alaska Meth. U., 1972; m. George R. Motschman, Feb. 26, 1948 (div. June 1959); children—Jerye Lou, Marie Louise; m. 2d, Leroy I. Smith, Mar. 13, 1961 (div. 1968). Office mgr. Intermountain Surg. Supply Co., Boise, 1945-48; sec. payroll, cost acct. Morrison-Knudsen Co., Fairbanks, Alaska and Boise, 1948-52; payroll, cost acct. Lytle, Green, Birch Contractors, Fairbanks, 1952-54; owner Fairbanks Secretarial Sch., 1956-58, Anchorage Secretarial Sch., 1958-59; pres. Alaska Bus. Coll., Inc., Anchorage, 1959—; owner City Employment Center, Anchorage, 1962-68, Western Girl Temps., Inc., 1962-68, Manpower, Inc. Bus. Services, 1969-72, Alaska Employment Agy., Anchorage, 1970-72; franchise holder Speedwriting Shorthand, 1957-76, Nancy Taylor Finishing Sch., 1960-76, ITT-Nat. Data Processing, 1968-76, Taylor Airline Careers, 1968-76; pres. Arctic Tech. Industries, 1972-76, KAVIR, Inc., Sebree, Ltd., Mr. Mixology. Mem. Alaska Gov.'s Task Force on Employment Needs for Alaskans, Anchorage Manpower Planning Council, Accrediting Commn. Assn. of Ind. Colls. and Schs.; mem. bus. and office adv. com. Anchorage Sch. Dist.; mem. adv. com. Ednl. Opportunity Center; mem. Alaska Pvt. Industry Council, Commonwealth North; past pres. Horizons Unltd. Cert. adminstrv. mgr., accredited personnel diplomat. Mem. Nat. Secs. Assn. (chpt. v.p. 1962, seminar chmn. 1961, 67, 73-77, 80), Profl. secs. Internat. (Exec. of Yr. award Billikin chpt.), Credit Women Internat., Alaska Vocat. Assn., Alaska Bus. Edn. Assn., Internat. Platform Assn., Nat. Assn. student Fin. Aid Officer, Nat. Bus. Edn. Assn., Adminstrv. Mgmt. Assn. Office: 5159 Old Seward Hwy Anchorage AK 99503

SMITH, BILLIE NELL BRYSON, nurse; b. Linden, Tenn., May 29, 1933; d. Barney Lee and Julia Mae (Hufstedler) Bryson; grad. St. Thomas Sch. Nursing, Nashville, 1955; m. Lee Garry Smith, Aug. 20, 1960; children—Lee Garry. Office nurse for Drs. G.H. Turner and B.L. Holladay, Linden, Tenn., 1955-56; dir. nursing Perry County Hosp., Linden, 1956-80, inservice dir., 1956-80; staff nurse, charge nurse Perry Meml. Hosp., Linden, Tenn., 1980—. Vol. nurse for mass polio vaccination Pub. Health Dept., 1963, 64; vol. nurse Am. Nat. Red Cross, 1955—. Licensed Tenn. Bd. Nursing. Mem. Tenn. Hosp. Assn., St. Thomas Sch. of Nursing Alumni Assn. Home: Route 4 Box 197 Linden TN 37096 Office: Perry Meml Hosp Squirrel Hollow Dr Linden TN 37096

SMITH, BRENDA JOYCE, social service adminstr.; b. Atlantic City, Feb. 16, 1949; d. Abraham and Margaret Ann (Simmons) S.; B.A., Monmouth Coll., 1971; M.A., Mich. State U., 1974; M.S., Columbia U., 1979; postgrad. Fairleigh Dickinson U., 1979—. Mental health aide Children's Psychiat. Center, Eatontown, N.J., 1970-71; case-aide Monmouth County Welfare Bd., Freehold, N.J., 1971-72; research asst. Mich. State U., East Lansing, 1972-73; rehab. counselor Harlem Hosp., N.Y.C., 1974; social worker East Orange (N.J.) VA Hosp., 1974-80; chief family and community services Newark Redevel. and Housing Authority, 1980—; cons. C. Williams, N.Y.C.; field instr. undergrad. level Kean Coll., Union, N.J. Rutgers U., New Brunswick, N.J. Active Kenneth A. Gibson Civic Assn., Carnegie Ave Tenant Assn., LWV; bd. dirs. United Cerebral Palsy No. N.J. Recipient Superior award VA, East Orange, 1978. Mem. Nat. Assn. Social Workers, Nat. Assn. Black Social Workers (chairperson Essex County chpt., nat. com. nominations and leadership identification), Nat. Council Negro Woman, NAACP, Accts. for Public Interest, Interracial Council for Bus. Opportunities, Minority Women Conf. of Concerns (sec. 1980—). Monmouth Coll. Alumni, Mich. State Alumni, Columbia U. Alumni. Democrat. Baptist. Home: 10 Nassau Pl E Orange NJ 07018 Office: 560 Broad St Newark NJ 07102

SMITH, CARLOTA SHIPMAN, educator; b. N.Y.C., May 21, 1934; d. Charles and Sylvia Shipman; B.A., Radcliffe Coll., 1955; M.A., U. Pa., 1964, Ph.D., 1967; children—Alison, Joel. Asst. prof. U. Pa., 1967; mem. faculty U. Tex., Austin, 1970—, prof. linguistics, 1981—, chmn. dept., 1981—; vis. prof. U. Paris à Vincennes, Brown U.; mem. linguistics panel NSF; mem. Fulbright Selection Com. Bd. dirs., exec. com. Planned Parenthood Austin. NSF grantee, 1979-81. Mem. Linguistic Soc. Am. (exec. com.), U. Tex. Educators for Social Responsibility (a founder), Ground Zero, Union Concerned Scientists. Democrat. Author articles in field. Office: Dept Linguistics U Tex Austin TX 78712

SMITH, CAROL ANN, nurse, univ. dean b. Waterbury, Conn., Dec. 22, 1941; d. Prosper Mark and Emma Edna (Dumschott) Zailskas; B.S. in Nursing, Boston Coll., 1965; Ph.D., 1977; M.S. in Nursing, Boston U., 1971; m. David Dennis Smith, June 19, 1965; children—Amy, Christian, Meghan. Ob-gyn assoc. Chelsea (Mass.) Naval Hosp., 1970-71; coordinator clin. nurse specialist program Boston Coll.-Harvard U. Med. Sch. 1975-78; chmn. grad. program Coll. of Our Lady of Elms, Chicopee, Mass., 1976-78, dir. B.S.N. Program, 1978-80; dean Sch. Nursing, Duquesne U., Pitts., 1980—, dissertation chmn. preceptor adminstrn. intern. Mem. Am. Nurses Assn., Nat. League for Nursing, Am. Assn. Colls. of Nursing, Nat. Assn. Women Deans, Adminstrs. and Counselors, Pa. Nurses Assn. (dir. 1982—), Western Pa. Coalition for Nurse Advancement (Pres. 1981—), Holyoke-Chicopee Mental Health Assn. (dir. 1978-80), Boston Coll. Alumnae Assn., Boston U. Alumnae Assn. Roman Catholic. Club: Boston Coll. (Pitts.). Home: 215 Lytton Ave Pittsburgh PA 15213 Office: Duquesne U 600 Forbes Ave Pittsburgh PA 15282

SMITH, CAROL ANN, music therapist, psychologist; b. Montgomery County, Tenn., Apr. 19, 1951; d. Carl and Ruth (Gettinger) S.; B.M.E. in Music Therapy, U. Kans., 1974; M.A. in Clin. Psychology, Middle Tenn. State U., 1977; Ed.S. in Human Service Mgmt.; Vanderbilt U., 1979. Gen. therapeutic recreation specialist VA Med. Center, Murfreesboro, Tenn., 1973-79; music therapist VA Med. Center, Marion, Ind., 1979; chief, recreation therapy service VA Med. Center, Tucson, 1979—; adj. instr. Middle Tenn. State U., part-time 1978—; vol. Head Start, 1976-77; guest speaker on music therapy to students and Head Start tchrs., 1975—; Mem. Am. Psychol. Assn. (asso.), Nat. Therapeutic Recreation Soc., Nat. Assn. Music Therapy (cert.), AAUW, Women of Moose, Pi Lambda Theta. Democrat. Methodist. Contbr. articles to profl. jours. Home: 2801 W Sheryl Dr Tucson AZ 85713 Office: VA Med Center 3601 S 6th Ave Tucson AZ 85723

SMITH, CAROL ELAINE, social work adminstr.; b. Washington, Apr. 17, 1945; d. William E. and Mary L. Smith; student Wilmington Coll., 1963-65; B.A., U. N.C., 1967, M.S.W., 1969. Sr. med. social worker Balt. City Hosps., 1969-70; program-project coordinator follow through program U. Ga., 1971-72, project adv., 1972-73, sch.-home coordinator, 1973-74, asso. dir. adoption tng. project Sch. Social Work, 1978-79; tng. cons. to local and state welfare depts. various states, 1974-79; dir. high support counseling program Econ. Opportunity Atlanta, 1975, dir. edn. dept., 1975-76; tng. coordinator N. Am. Center on Adoption, Child Welfare League Am., N.Y.C., 1979-80, dir. Developmental Disability Adoptions Project, Permanent Families for Children unit, 1980-81, project dir. State Action Plan Project, 1981—; mem. vocat. edn. adv. com. Smith High, Atlanta, 1975-79. Mem. Nat. Assn. Social Workers, Council on Social Work Edn., Am. Soc. for Tng. and Devel., Sierra Club. Democrat. Episcopalian. Author, contbg. author tng. manuals and video tapes for social workers. Office: care Child Welfare League Am 67 Irving Pl New York NY 10003

SMITH, CAROLYN LORETTA, D.C. govt. ofcl.; b. Lakewood, N.J., Nov. 14, 1942; d. Davis and Arline Loretta (Erwin) Lee; B.A. in Acctg., Howard U., 1965; m. Vernon X. Smith, Oct. 16, 1965; children—Sonia Delores, Angela Maliaka. Vice pres. fin. mgmt. Nat. Inst. Community Devel., 1972-73; audit supr. Coopers & Lybrand, 1973-76, audit mgr., 1976-77; treas. Govt. D.C., 1977-79, dir. dept. fin. and revenue, 1979—. Chmn. D.C. Real Estate Commn., Mayor's Revenue Policy Com. C.P.A.; recipient Outstanding Service award Nat. Assn. Minority C.P.A. Firms, 1979. Mem. Am. Inst. C.P.A.s, D.C. Inst. C.P.A.s, Nat. Assn. Black Accts. (pres., Achievement award 1978), Nat. Assn. Tax Adminstrs., Internat. Assn. Assessing Officers. Office: 300 Indiana Ave NW Washington DC 20001

SMITH, CAROLYNE CIBART, public relations/advt. exec.; b. Calgary, Alta., Can., Apr. 14, 1939; came to U.S., 1954, naturalized, 1977; d. Lloyd Nygaard and Gerda (Johnson) Cibart; student U. B.C., 1957-58, Univ. Center of Harrisburg, 1960-67; m. Dudley Smith, Jr., Nov. 28, 1970; stepchildren—Richard D., C. Robert. Bookkeeper, office mgr. N.W. Tires, Ltd., Prince George, B.C., Can., 1958; bookkeeper, then account exec. Hood, Light & Geise, Inc., Harrisburg, Pa., 1958-80; partner Herbert M. Packer, Jr. & Assos., Harrisburg, 1980—, Packer, Previc, Oesterling & Smith, Inc., Harrisburg, 1980—; lectr. in field. Pres., Girls Club of Harrisburg, 1978-80; mem. Urban League Guild of Harrisburg, 1980-82. Mem. Central Pa. Advt. Fedn. (pres. 1970-71), Am. Advt. Fedn. (sec. 2nd dist. 1971-73, Crystal Prism award 1973), Pa. Soc. Assn. Execs., Cable TV Assn. Marketers, Women in Cable. Club: Monday (Woman of Yr. award 1981). Home: 608 Race St Harrisburg PA 17104 Office: 124 State St Harrisburg PA 17101

SMITH, CARRIE-MERLE, TV prodn. co. exec.; b. Chgo., Feb. 25, 1951; d. Daniel Brown and Frances (Ellington) Green; B.S. in Edn., Drake U., 1972; 1 son, Paul Bradford. High sch. English tchr., girls varsity basketball coach Chgo. Bd. Edn., 1975-80; owner CMG Creative Studio, Bridgeview, Ill., 1981—; TV studio instr. Omega Sch. Communications, Chgo., 1981-82; owner C.M.G. Video Prodns. Studio, Inc., Bridgeview, 1981—. Sr. mng. editor Burbank Cultural Art Center, 1981-82; polit. photographer Bridgeview Active party, 1980—; active Viet Nam Outreach Program, 1980-82. Served with N.G., 1975-80. Democrat. Presbyterian. Club: Burbank Art League. Home: 7730 S Thomas Ave Bridgeview IL 60455 Office: CMG Video Productions Inc 7730 S Thomas Ave Bridgeview IL 60455

SMITH, CATHERINE FARSONS, flutist; b. Rochester, N.Y., Nov. 4, 1933; d. Judson A. and Frances Q. (Holsopple) Parsons; A.B. magna cum laude, Smith Coll., 1954; Mus.M. in Flute, Northwestern U., 1957; D.Mus. Arts (Danforth fellow), Stanford U., 1969; m. Ross Wilbert Smith; children—Walter, Anne, Courtney. Asso. prof. faculty dept. music U. Nev., Reno, 1969—; performer flute and Baroque flute various community ensembles and orchs., Chgo., Denver, Rapid City, S.D., Stanford, Calif., Reno, Boston, Springfield, Mass.; performer with Theatre of Musicke, Reno, Tahoe and Berkeley, Calif.; organizer Black Hills Chamber Music Soc., 1966; contbr. music criticism to Reno Evening Gazette, Nev. State Jour., other newspapers. NEH fellow. Mem. Nat. Flute Assn., Am. Mus. Instrument Soc., Coll. Music Soc., Am. Musicological Soc., Phi Beta Kappa, Mu Phi Epsilon, Delta Kappa Gamma. Contbr. articles to Woodwind World-Brass and Percussion, Am. Recorder, NACWPI Jour., also articles on women in Am. mus. life; editor, translator: Treatise for Oboe, Recorder, Flageolet (Freillon-Poncein). Office: Dept Music Univ Nevada Reno NV 89557

SMITH, CECILIA, educator; b. Johannesburg, South Africa, Mar. 19, 1929; immigrated to Can., 1956, naturalized, 1961; d. Gedaliah and Sophia (Stern) Unterhalter; cert. Joint Matriculation Bd., Univs. South Africa, 1946; letter of credit for tng. in nursery edn., 1950; m. Gerald H.M. Smith, June 29, 1950; children—Janine, Melanie, David, Juliette. Tchr., L.K. Hurwutz Nursery Sch., Johannesburg, 1952; supr. Salisbury Hebrew Nursery Sch., S. Rhodesia, 1953; tchr. Beth Hayazed Nursery Sch., Toronto, Ont., Can., 1967; nursery therapist West End Creche, Toronto, 1961-62; supr. Flemingdon Park Coop. Nursery Sch., Toronto, 1963, Bayview Glen Day Camp, Toronto, summer 1964, Temple Sinai Coop. Nursery Sch., Toronto, 1964-65; tchr., conf. rep. Toy Town, Toronto, 1965-66; research asst. Ont. Inst. Studies in Edn., 1967-68; dir. Cecilia Smith Remedial Nursery Sch. Toronto, 1968—; lectr., cons. in field. Active, Canadian Opera Guild, Nat. Ballet of Can., Art Gallery of Ont.; com. mem. Mental Health Council Toronto, 1975—, sec., 1975-76. Mem. Assn. Childhood Edn. Internat., Canadian Assn. for Young Children, Am. Orthopsychiat. Assn., Orgn. Mondialede l'Education Prescolaire, Nat. Ednl. Council Creative Therapies, Inc., Community Forum on Shared Responsibility, World Fedn. for Mental Health, Canadian Mental Health Assn., Social Planning Council of Met. Toronto; People and Orgns. in North Toronto, Assn. Couples for Marriage Enrichment, Assn. Canadian TV and Radio Artists, Canadian Wildlife Fedn. Unitarian. Author papers. Address: 31 Oriole Rd Toronto ON M4V 2E6 Canada

SMITH, CHARLENE (CHARLI) A., trust co. exec.; b. San Antonio, Oct. 20, 1942; d. Sydney Herbert and Pauline Mae (Rickliff) Biggs; A.A., Eastfield Coll., 1981; m. Billy R. Smith, June 7, 1958; children—Victor Lee, Sandra Lynne, Robin Rene, Charles Matthew. Adminstrv. sec. Coed, Inc., Dallas, 1975-79; sec. to indsl. relations dir. U.S. Industries, Dallas, 1979-80; adminstr. Sponsored Benefit Services, Inc., Dallas, 1979-80; asst. v.p. corp. adminstrn. and ops. Fiduciary Trust Co. of S.W., Dallas, 1980—. Notary public, lic. ins. agt., Tex. Mem. Nat. Assn. Female Execs., Phi Theta Kappa. Methodist. Home: 3829 Plymouth Dr Garland TX 75043 Office: 12700 Hillcrest Rd Suite 209 Dallas TX 75230

SMITH, CHARLOTTE GEORGE, physiologist; b. Cin., Aug. 26, 1938; d. Karl Franklin and Thelma Alena Smith; B.S. in Zoology, U. Ill., Urbana, 1960, M.S. in Physiology, 1961. Physiologist, NASA-Johnson Space Center, 1962—; dir. Independence Inst., 1980—; cons. in field. Recipient NASA Apollo Achievement award, 1969, Petticoat Pilot Achievement award, 1967; lic. pilot. Asso. fellow Aerospace Med. Assn.; mem. Ninety-Nines, AAAS, Found. Sci. and Handicapped, Assn. Women Sci., Philosophy of Sci. Assn., Nat. Assn. Female Execs. Office: NASA-Johnson Space Center Houston TX 77058

SMITH, CHARMAINE (SHERRY) P., nurse, univ. ofcl.; b. Hanover, Pa., Jan. 16, 1936; d. Laverne N. and Myrtle I. (Wentz) Palmer; student Hood Coll., 1952-54; B.S. in Nursing, Johns Hopkins U., 1957; M.S. in Nursing, U. Cin., 1973; Ed.D., Ind. U., 1978; m. Edwin J. Smith, Oct. 24, 1958; children—Sharon, Stephanie, H. David. Staff nurse Johns Hopkins Hosp., 1957-58; clin. instr. York Hosp. Sch. Nursing, 1958-60; instr. Delaware Hosp. Sch. Nursing, 1960-62; asst. prof. Coll. Mount St. Joseph (Ohio), 1973-75; asst. prof. nursing Ind. U., 1975-78; assoc. prof. nursing DePauw U., 1978-79, dir. Sch. Nursing, 1979—; CPR instr. Am. Heart Assn. Capt. diabetic detection Indpls. Diabetes Assn. Recipient Excellence in Teaching award Ind. U. Sch. Nursing, 1978, Am. Heart Assn. award, 1981. Mem. AAUP, Am. Nurses Assn., Sigma Theta Tau. Office: School Nursing DePauw University Greencastle IN 46135

SMITH, CHRISTINE CHEW, painter, collagist, art educator; b. Bryn Mawr, Pa., Sept. 10, 1935; d. David S. B. and Eileen T. (Petchell) Chew; B.A., U. Colo., 1958; part-time student Art Students League, 1958, 59, Columbia U., 1961, N.Y. U., 1977, 78; m. 1960 (div. 1977); children—Jeffrey, Bradford, Randy. Pvt. tchr., founder Heron Studio, N.Y.C.; one-woman shows: Galerie 64, N.Y.C., 1972, South St. Seaport Mus. Gallery, N.Y.C., 1972, Caravan House Galleries, N.Y.C., 1973, 76, Women in the Arts Gallery, N.Y.C., 1979, New Eng. Center for Arts, Conn., 1979, Watermill Mus., L.I., 1980; group shows include: Hudson River Mus., Yonkers, N.Y., 1972, Audubon Artists, 1974, Nat. Arts Club, N.Y.C., (honorable mention), 1975, Va. Poly. Inst. and State U., 1976, CCNY, 1976, N.Y.C. Commn. on Status of Women, 1979, Simon Mayer Gallery, N.Y.C., 1980, M. Greene Gallery, Bridgehampton, N.Y., 1981, Rather Art Center, Sag Harbor, N.Y., 1982; represented by Sandra Bertsch Fine Arts, Inc., Oyster Bay, N.Y.; represented in permanent collections: Colo. Sch. Mines, Golden, HEW, Browning Sch., N.Y. Hosp., IBM, also pvt. collections. Mem. East End Arts Council, Guild Hall, Artists Equity N.Y., Women in the Arts, Artists Studios Center, Phila. Art Alliance. Republican. Studio: 525 E 86 St New York NY 10028 also Bridgehampton NY 11932

SMITH, CLARA JEAN, nursing home adminstr.; b. Berwick, Pa., Aug. 31, 1932; d. Barton Fredrick and Evelyn Miriam (Bomboy) Hough; R.N., Williamsport (Pa.) Hosp., 1953; B.S. in Nursing Edn., Wilkes Coll., Wilkes-Barre, Pa., 1960; M.S. in Edn., Temple U., Phila., 1969; m. Robert W. Smith, June 7, 1958. From staff nurse to dir. nursing Retreat State Hosp., Hunlock Creek, Pa., 1953-80; dir. long term care facility Danville (Pa.) State Hosp., 1980—; dir. accrediatation coordination and quality assurance Nursing Home Adminstrs., 1980—; speaker, instr. in field. Mem. Am. Nurses Assn., Pa. Nurses Assn., Luzerne County Dist. Nurses Assn. Methodist. Club: Sunshine. Author tng. and ednl.

programs. Home: Lake Pinecrest PO Box 5 Huntington Mills PA 18622 Office: Danville State Hosp PO Box 219 Danville PA 17821

SMITH, CLARA MAE, mktg. exec.; b. Algona, Iowa., Jan. 3, 1947; d. Thees and Rachel Bernice (Becker) Schnakenberg; B.S.-A.A., Iowa State U., 1969; postgrad. in profl. selling and computers U. Wis., 1978; 1 dau., Tami Lynn. Interior designer Bank Bldg. Corp., St. Louis and Atlanta, 1969-74, Fin. Bldg. Cons., Atlanta, 1974-75, R.L. Bryan Co., Columbia, S.C., 1975-76, HBE Corp., St. Louis, 1976-79; sr. design mgr. Gresham & Smith, Nashville, 1979-80; mktg. designer McQuiddy Office Designers, Nashville, 1980—; propr. C.S. Designs Ltd., 1975—. Alumna advisor Iowa State U. Coll. Design, 1981—. Recipient awards for outstanding design Bank Bldg. Corp., 1973; Appreciation of Service award Inst. Bus. Designers, 1974. Mem. Nat. Assn. Female Execs., Inst. Bus. Designers (chpt. pres. 1981—, trustee 1974-81), NOW, Delta Zeta Alumnae (province collegiate dir.). Lutheran. Home: 605 Netherlands Dr Hermitage TN 37076 Office: 110 7th Ave N PO Box 25290 Nashville TN 37202

SMITH, CLARA MAE, educator; b. Norfolk, Va.; d. Willie J. and Willie Ann (Smallwood) Walton; B.S., Norfolk State Coll., 1963; postgrad. Chgo. State U., Governors State U.; m. Emile Smith, Apr. 20, 1974; 1 son, Emile Christopher. Sec., Norfolk State Coll., 1960-63; tchr. South East End High Sch., South Hill, Va., 1963-67, J.P. Altgeld Elem. Sch., Chgo., 1967-70, tchr. Louis Wirth Exptl. Sch., Chgo., 1970—. Mem. Nat. Assn. Female Execs., Chgo. Area Alliance of Black Sch. Educators. Home: 8040 S Paulina St Chicago IL 60620

SMITH, CYNTHIA JOY, social worker, computer programmer; b. Glen Ridge, N.J., Dec. 25, 1951; d. Herbert James and Frances Jane (VanNess) Smith; B.A., Springfield Coll., 1973; M.S.W., U. Hawaii, 1976; M.B.A., Pepperdine U., 1981; Asst. program dir. Essex County Heart Assn., East Orange, N.J., 1974; dir. children's music First Presbyn. Ch., 1975—; singer/dancer Maile Aloha Singers, Honolulu, 1975—; med. social worker Upjohns Health Care Services, Honolulu, 1976—, service coordinator, 1976-79, Pacific allied health tech. coordinator, 1979-80; exec. dir. Hale Ho'ola Hou, Honolulu, 1977-81; pvt. instr. piano, guitar; practicum instr. U. Hawaii Sch. Social Work, Honolulu, 1978-81; Computer programmer Computals, Inc., 1981—. Chmn. edn. and outreach com. State Policy Adv. Council for Family Planning Services, 1978—; chmn. State Policy Adv. Group on Family Planning, 1980—; bd. dirs. adv. council Hawaii Center on Deafness, 1979—; chmn. public affairs com. Hawaii Planned Parenthood, 1981—. HEW trainee, 1974-76. Mem. Acad. Cert. Social Workers, Nat. Assn. Social Workers, Nat. Assn. Hosp. Social Work Dirs., Women Entrepreneurs, Nat. Assn. Christians in Social Work, Nat. Assn. Music Therapists, Am. Bus. Women's Assn. Democrat. Presbyterian. Composer: The Upward Way (rec.), 1974. Home: 1802 Keeaumoku St Honolulu HI 96822 Office: 700 Bishop St Suite 302 Honolulu HI 96813

SMITH, CYNTHIA S., editor, publisher, advt. exec., educator, author; b. N.Y.C., Dec. 29, 1924; d. Harry and Sarah Sharfin; B.A., Hunter Coll., 1944; postgrad. Columbia U., 1944-45; m. David Smith, May 21, 1950; 1 dau., Hillary Beth. Advt. dir. Joshua Meier div. W.R. Grace Co., N.Y.C., 1950-63; pres. C/D Smith Advt., Inc., Rye, N.Y., 1964—; pres. Hillbart Publs., Inc., Rye, 1977—; editor, pub. Medical/Mrs. mag., Rye, 1977—; faculty lectr. N.Y. U., 1970-72; faculty instr. U. Conn., Stamford, 1976-77; vis. instr. Marquette U., Vanderbilt U., Temple U., U. Pitts., Drake U., Boston Coll., Baldwin-Wallace Coll., Wayne State U., Butler U., NW Mich. Coll., U. Miami, Am. U. Author: How to Get Big Results from a Small Advertising Budget, 1972; Doctors' Wives: The Truth About Medical Marriages, 1981.

SMITH, DIANE LAVERNA, educator; b. Blackfoot, Ida., Nov. 5, 1937; d. Thomas Bernard and Doris (Andersen) Smith; B.S., U. Ida., 1960; M.S., Stanford U., 1965. Tchr., Monterey (Calif.) Unified Sch. Dist., 1960-61; dance instr. Pebble Beach (Calif.) Club, 1971-75; recreation specialist Monterey Parks and Recreation Dept., 1966—; instr. Monterey Peninsula Coll., 1961—; pres. Focus Unltd., Carmel, Calif., 1979—. Active Boy Scouts Am., Am. Cancer Soc., Am. Heart Assn.; bd. dirs. Armed Service YMCA. Joseph P. Kennedy Jr. Found. grantee, 1969-70; recipient Award of Achievement, Calif. Parks and Recreation Soc., 1970. Mem. Western Soc. Coll. Women, Calif. Assn. Health, Phys. Edn. and Recreation, Nat. Park and Recreation Assn., Monterey C. of C., Stanford U. Alumni Assn., Pi Beta Phi. Republican. Mem. Ch. of Jesus Christ of Latter Day Saints. Clubs: Monterey Mus. Art, Stanford Singles, Pebble Beach Swim and Tennis. Author: Dance at a Glance, 1974, 2d edit., 1979. Home: PO Box 6024 Carmel CA 93921 Office: 980 Fremont St Monterey CA 93940

SMITH, DONNA LILIAN, seminar co. exec.; b. Phila., Oct. 8, 1944; d. Joseph Patrick and Mary Elizabeth (Veronica) Burke; student Calif. State U., Northridge, 1962-64; Asso. degree, Fashion Inst. Calif., 1969; divorced. Fashion coordinator, 1963-68; dir. Fashion Mdsg. Inst., 1968-69; v.p. Fashion Inst. Design and Mdsg., 1969-78; pres., owner Seminars Internat., Los Angeles, 1979—; producer fashion shows, cons. in field; mem. costume council Los Angeles County Mus. Art. Mem. Costume Soc. Am., Fashion Group. Roman Catholic. Office: 15910 Ventura Blvd Suite 800 Encino CA 91436

SMITH, DONNA MAE, nurse, businesswoman; b. Indianola, Iowa, Oct. 15, 1926; d. Donald Roger and Bessie Laura (Merriam) Squire; grad. Iowa Luth. Hosp. Sch. Nursing, 1948; m. Roy Alvin Smith, Apr. 5, 1950; children—Bonita Elaine, Leslie Rae. Nurse, U.S. Indian Health Service, 1947-50; partner Smith Amusement Co., 1956—; partner Stateline Wholesale Co., Whiteclay, Nebr., 1963—; part time nurse USPHS, Pine Ridge, S.D., 1976—. Mem. Nat. Automatic Merchandise Assn., Nat. Assn. Female Execs., Midwest Amusement Assn. Republican. Address: PO Box 85 Whiteclay NE 69365

SMITH, DORIS ANITA, entertainment co. exec.; b. Elizabeth, N.J., Mar. 17, 1935; d. Arthur Thomas and Mildred (Traina) S.; B.A., Douglass Coll., Rutgers U., 1956; postgrad. U. So. Calif., 1960-61, UCLA, 1961-62, 75-76. Asst. corp. sec. Sunkist Growers, Inc., Los Angeles, 1959-63; adminstrv. asst. Lockheed Electronics Co., Plainfield, N.J., 1964-68; with Walt Disney Prodns., Burbank, Calif., 1969—, credit mgr., 1975-80, corp. sec., 1978—. Mem. Republican County Com. N.J., Linden, 1964-68, Mayor's Adv. Com., Linden, 1964-66; bd. dirs. Linden Library, 1964-68. Mem. Nat. Inst. Credit, Am. Soc. Corp. Secs., Soc. Profl. Credit Mgrs. Office: 500 S Buena Vista St Burbank CA 91521

SMITH, DORIS WILMA DUNN, educator, writer, speaker; b. Greensboro, N.C., Aug. 21, 1933; d. David Harry and Wilma Gertrude (Kerns) Dunn; B.S. in Biology, Flora Macdonald Coll., 1955; M.A. in Biol. Sci., U. Calif. Irvine, 1973; Ph.D. in Edn., U. Beverly Hills, 1980; m. Ralph Ray Smith, June 1, 1957; children—Glenn, Harriet, Marcus. Tchr. sci. St Pauls (N.C.) City Schs., 1955-57; tchr. math. Belmont (N.C.) City Schs., 1962-64, Charlotte-Mecklenburg City Schs., Charlotte, N.C., 1964-65, Newport Mesa Unified Schs., Newport Beach, Calif., 1965-67; tchr. math., sci. Anaheim (Calif.) Union High Sch., 1967-81, Carden Christian Sch., Costa Mesa, Calif., 1982—; freelance writer, poet, 1978—; speaker various religious and civic orgns., 1979—. Mgr. Far West Anaheim Bobby Sox Softball, 1969-71, all-star mgr., 1970, all-star coach, 1969-71; leader Girl Scouts Am., 1970. E. I. du Pont de Nemours fellow, 1956. Mem. NEA, Calif. Tchrs. Assn., Anaheim Secondary Tchrs. Assn., Internat. Women's Writers Guild, Woman's World Internat. Democrat. Presbyterian. Club: Toastmasters. Author: A Limb of Your Tree, 1981. Home and Office: 912 Hayward St Anaheim CA 92804

SMITH, DOROTHY MADELAINE, motel chain ofcl.; b. Monroe, Wis., Feb. 21, 1922; d. Anthon J. and Mabel L. (Wollenzien) Opstedal; B.S. magna cum laude, U. Wis., 1941; m. William L. Smith, Jan. 20, 1945 (dec.); children—Anthony, Martin, Christopher. Office mgr. Pauly Realty, St. Louis, 1973-76; dining room mgr. Concourse Hotel, Madison, Wis., 1976-77; reservations mgr. Edgewater Hotel, Madison, 1977-78; front desk supr. Holiday Inn, St. Louis, 1978-81, asst. gen. mgr., Middletown, N.Y., 1981—. Bd. dirs. New Hope Found., St. Louis; dispatcher Law Enforcement K-9 Search and Rescue, St. Louis, 1973-76; hosp. vol. Served to lt. comdr. USNR, 1942-44. Named Wis. Am. Bus. Woman of Yr., 1978. Mem. Ret. Officers Assn., Am. Bus. Women's Assn. (pres. Badger chpt. 1978, pres. Louis IX chpt. St. Louis 1980), Wis. Alumni Assn., Phi Beta Kappa, Theta Sigma Upsilon, Kappa Alpha Theta. Lutheran. Club: West Point Officers. Home: 10150 Cabana Club Dr 1-F Saint Ann MO 63074

SMITH, DOROTHY OTTINGER, jewelry designer, civic leader; b. Indpls.; d. Albert Ellsworth and Leona Aurelia (Waller) Ottinger; student Herron Art Sch. of Purdue U. and Ind. U., 1941-42; m. James Emory Smith, June 25, 1943; children—Michael Ottinger, Sarah Anne, Theodore Arnold, Lisa Marie. Comml. artist William H. Block Co., Indpls., 1942-43, H.P. Wasson Co., 1943-44; dir. Riverside (Calif.) Art Center, 1963-64; jewelry designer, Riverside, 1970—. Adviser Riverside chpt. Freedom's Found. of Valley Forge; co-chmn. fund raising com. Riverside Art Center and Mus., 1966-67, bd. dirs. Art Alliance, 1980-81; mem. Riverside City Hall sculpture selection panel Nat. Endowment Arts, 1974-75; chmn. fund raising benefit Riverside Art Center and Mus., 1973-74, trustee, 1980—, chmn. permanent collection, 1981—, co-chmn. fund drive, 1982—; chmn. Riverside Mcpl. Arts Commn., 1974-76; juror Riverside Civic Center Purchase Prize Art Show, 1975; mem. pub. bldgs. and grounds subcom., gen. plan citizens com. City of Riverside, 1965-66; mem. Mayor's Commn. on Civic Beauty, Mayor's Commn. on Sister City Sendai, 1965-66; bd. dirs., chmn. spl. events Children's League of Riverside Community Hosp., 1952-53; bd. dirs. Crippled Children's Soc. of Riverside, spl. events chmn., 1952-53; bd. dirs. Jr. League of Riverside, rec. sec., 1960-61; bd. dirs. Nat. Charity League, pres. Riverside chpt., 1965-66; mem. exec. com. of bd. trustees Riverside Arts Found., 1977—, fund dr. chmn., 1978-79, project rev. chmn., 1978-79; juror Gemco Charitable and Scholarship Found., 1977—; mem. bd. women deacons Calvary Presbyn. Ch., 1978-80; mem. incorporating bd. Inland Empire United Fund for Arts, 1980-81; bd. dirs. Hospice Orgn. Riverside County, 1982—. Recipient cert. Riverside City Council, 1977, plaque Mayor of Riverside, 1977. Mem. Riverside Art Assn. (pres. 1961-63, 1st v.p. 1964-65, 67-68, trustee 1959-70), Art Alliance of Riverside Art Center and Museum (founder 1964, pres. 1969-70). Address: 3979 Chapman Pl Riverside CA 92506

SMITH, EDNA LANETTE, nurse; b. Birmingham, Nov. 13, 1931; d. John Henderson and Roxie Lee Sanders; B.R.E., Chgo. Bapt. Inst., 1974; A.A., R.N., Malcolm X Coll., 1975; B.A., Governor State U., 1976, M.Health Sci., 1978; 1 dau., Melody Gail. Tchr., Chgo Baptist Inst., 1971—; R.N., Grant Hosp., Chgo., 1978-80; supr. adminstrv. asst., nursing Convalescent Home, 1st Ch. of Deliverance, Chgo., 1980-81; asst. adminstr. Kluwozon Retreat Center, Chgo., 1981; program dir. Somerset Sr. Citizens, Chgo., 1975—; nutrition cons. Stars of Scorpion Health Soc., 1970—. Lic. nursing home adminstr., Ill.; cert. cosmetologist, Ala.; lic. gospel minister. Mem. Am. Nurses Assn., AMA, NAACP. Baptist. Contbr. to Outstanding Black Sermons, Vol. 2, 1980. Home: 7465 South Shore Dr Chicago IL 60649 Office: 417 S Dearborn Ave Chicago IL 60602

SMITH, EILEEN VERONICA, histology technician; b. Needham, Mass., June 23, 1953; d. Anthony Augustine and Margaret Mary (MacLean) Delaney; student Newton-Wellesley Hosp., 1972; m. Philip E. Smith, Dec. 19, 1980. Staff, Newton-Wellesley Hosp., Newton Lower Falls, Mass., 1972-79, New Eng. Deaconess Hosp. Boston, 1979, Norwood (Mass.) Hosp., 1980, 81-82, Md. Med. Labs., Balt., 1981; cons. Wing Meml. Hosp., Palmer, Mass., 1976. Mem. Am. Soc. Clin. Pathologists, Nat. Certification Agy. for Med. Lab. Personnel.

SMITH, ELEANOR JANE, educator, univ. ofcl.; b. Circleville, Ohio, Jan. 10, 1933; d. John Allen and Elenora Jane (Dade) Lewis; B.S., Capital U., 1955; Ph.D., Union Grad. Sch. for Exptl. Colls. and Univs., 1972; m. Paul Milton Smith, Dec. 27, 1972; 1 dau., Teresa Marie Banner. Tchr. elem. sch. Columbus (Ohio) Bd. Edn., 1956-64; tchr. jr. high sch. Worthington (Ohio) Bd. Edn., 1964-72; prof. Afro-Am. studies U. Cin., 1972—, asst. sr. v.p., asst. provost, 1982—; cons. in field. Mem. Assn. for Study Afro-Am. Life and History (dir.), Nat. Council Black Studies (dir.), Am. Hist. Assn., Orgn. Am. Historians, Assn. Black Women Historians (co-founder, dir.), Nat. Women Studies Assn. (dir.), Nat. Assn. Women Deans, Adminstrs. and Counselors, Inst. Black World, Assn. of Women Adminstrs., Assn. for Women Faculty (pres.). Club: Woman's City (dir.). Contbr. articles to profl. jours. Home: 727 Dixmyth Ave Apt 804 Cincinnati OH 45220 Office: 105 Adminstrn Univ Cin Clifton Ave Cincinnati OH 45221

SMITH, ELISE FIBER, found. exec.; b. Detroit, June 14, 1932; d. Guy and Mildred Geneva (Johnson) Fiber; B.A., U. Mich., 1954; postgrad. (Rotary Internat. fellow) U. Strasbourg (France), 1954-55; M.A., Western Res. U., 1956; m. James Frederick Smith, Aug. 11, 1956; children—Gregory Douglas, Guy Charles. Tchr., U.S. Binat. Center, Caracas, Venezuela, 1964-66; instr. English, Am. U., 1966-68; prof. lang. faculty, Cath. U., Lima, Peru, 1968-70; coordinator English lang. and culture program lang. faculty, El Rosario U., Bogota, Colombia, 1971-73; lang. specialist, mem. faculty Am. U. English Lang. Inst., 1975-78; exec. dir. Overseas Edn. Fund, Washington, 1978—. Sec., bd. dirs. U.S. Bi-Nat. Sch., Bogota, 1971-73; ofcl. observer UN Conf. Status Women, 1980; mem. mental health adv. com. Dept. State, 1974-76; U.S. del. planning seminar integration women in devel. OAS, 1978. Dept. State grantee, 1975, Nat. Assn. Fgn. Student Affairs grantee, 1975. Mem. Soc. Intercultural Edn., Tng. and Research, Soc. Internat. Devel., Women in Devel., Washington Soc. Assn. Execs., Coalition Women in Internat. Devel. (founder 1977), Pvt. Agys. in Internat. Devel. (co-chmn. 1980-82, pres. 1982-83), Nat. Assn. Fgn. Student Affairs, U. Mich. Alumnae Assn., Fgn. Service Wives Assn. Unitarian. Co-editor: Toward Internationalism: Readings in Cross-cultural Communication, 1979. Home: 9904 Marquette Dr Bethesda MD 20817 Office: 2101 L St Suite 916 Washington DC 20037

SMITH, ELIZABETH ALICE, psychologist; b. Crossfield, Alta., Can., Apr. 7, 1936; came to U.S., 1957, naturalized, 1967; d. Francis Walter and Florence Ellen (McIntyre) Landymore; B.A. in Psychology, U. Alta., 1956, M.A. in Psychology, U. Wyo., 1963, Ph.D. in Psychology, 1968; m. Charles Robert Smith, Sept. 7, 1957; children—Karen Anne, Julie Kathleen. Librarian, Mobil Oil Co., 1956-57; research asst. U. Tex., Austin, 1960-62; asst. prof. U. Tex., Houston, 1970-75; lab. asst. psychology dept. U. Wyo., 1963-66, asst. prof., 1969-70; asst. prof. Air Force Inst. Tech., F.E. Warren AFB, Cheyenne, 1969-70; evaluator Nat. Cancer Inst. teaching programs sponsored by M.D. Anderson Hosp., U. Tex. Systems Cancer Center, Houston, 1973-76; dir. ednl. programs dept. family practice U. Tex. Med. Sch., Houston, 1979-80; asso. prof. Houston Bapt. U., 1977-79; instr. Oil and Gas Cons. Internat., Inc., Tulsa, 1980—. Pres. Houston Sigma Kappa Found. for Gerontology. HEW grantee, 1969-70, 74-75. Mem. Am. Psychol. Assn., S.W. Psychol. Assn., Tex. Psychol. Assn., Houston Psychol. Assn., Spring Branch-Meml. C. of C. AAUW, Sigma Xi, Sigma Kappa (gerontology com.), Psi Chi. Presbyterian. Author: Psychosocial Aspects of Cancer Patient Care, 1976; Comprehensive Approach to Rehabilitation of the Cancer Patient, 1976; contbr. articles to profl. jours. Home: 1015 Ashford Pkwy Houston TX 77077 Office: Dept Family Practice Med Edn U Tex Med Sch Suite 405 Memorial Hosp 7777 SW Freeway Houston TX 77074

SMITH, ELIZABETH BLOXOM, real estate broker; b. Newport News, Va., Aug. 9; d. Dennis Joseph and Elizabeth Veronica (Carter) Antinori; student Golden Gate U., 1973-74; m. Blair Eldred Smith, Aug. 30, 1968; children—Robert E., Dennis L. Salesman, half owner Bloxom Realty Co., Newport News, Va., 1962-66, broker, 1963—; owner, pres. Libby Bloxom, Inc., Newport News, 1966—. Mem. Nat. Assn. Realtors, Realtor's Nat. Mktg. Inst. (cert. residential broker), Women's Council Realtors, Nat. Assn. Parliamentarians (local treas. 1978, 79, pres. local unit 1981-83), Va. Assn. Realtors (past regional v.p., Cert. of Appreciation 1979), Peninsula Retail Merchants Assn. (dir.), Newport News-Hampton Bd. Realtors (pres. 1975, plaque of appreciation 1975, Realtor of Yr. 1976). Republican. Presbyterian. Clubs: Soroptimists (past sec.); Pioneer Toastmistress. Home: 924 Etna Dr Newport News VA 23602 Office: 14801 Warwick Blvd Newport News VA 23602

SMITH, ELIZABETH MARY, social worker; b. McCook, Nebr., Dec. 15, 1940; d. Fred Clarence and Edith Elizabeth (McKeown) Smith; B.A., U. Nebr., 1960, M.S.W., 1962; Ph.D., Washington U., St. Louis, 1978. Chief social worker Psychiatry Clinic, Barnes Hosp., St. Louis, 1963-67; instr. dept. psychiatry Washington U. Sch. Medicine, 1967-74, asst. prof., 1974—, adj. asst. prof. George Warren Brown Sch. Social Work, 1978—. Mem. Med. Com. for Human Rights, 1968-74; bd. dirs. Abortion Rights Alliance of Mo., 1972—, pres., 1977-78. Nat. Inst. Alcohol Abuse and Alcoholism grantee, 1977-81. Mem. Acad. Cert. Social Workers, Nat. Assn. Social Workers (pres. Mo. chpt. 1979-81, sec. 1980-82), Council on Social Work Edn., World Population Soc., AAUP, Nat. Conf. on Social Welfare, Mo. Assn. for Social Welfare, Am. Public Health Assn. Contbr. chpts. to Love, Marriage and Family, 1975, Abortion: The Emotional Implications, 1977. Office: Dept Psychiatry Washington U Sch Medicine 4940 Audubon Ave Saint Louis MO 63110

SMITH, ELIZABETH REICHERT, health scientist adminstr.; b. South Bend, Ind., May 7, 1923; d. Joseph S. and Irene Margaret (Foley) Reichert; A.B., Radcliffe Coll., 1943; M.N., Yale U., 1945; M.S.N.E., Cath. U. Am., 1949, Ph.D., 1952; m. Donald Eugene Smith, June 17, 1950; children—Gregory, Cecily, Andrea, Veronica, Mark, Teresa, Valerie, Jeffrey, Stephanie. Staff nurse, instr. Boston Psychopathic Hosp., 1945-47; grad. asst. Cath. U. Am., 1948-49, lectr., research asso., 1952-55; instr. Sch. nursing Georgetown U., 1949-51, asst. prof., 1951-52, vis. asst. prof., 1957-60, adj. asso. prof., 1960-63; sr. mental health planner Div. Planning, Research and Stats. D.C. Dept. Public Health, 1963-65, chief Office of Community Mental Health Program Devel., 1965-70; lectr. preventive medicine and public health Howard U., 1966-72; chief new careers br. div. intramural tng. NIMH, HEW, Washington, 1970-71; health scientist adminstr. exptl. and spl. tng. br., div. manpower and tng., NIMH, HEW, Rockville, Md., 1971-74, acting br. chief psychiat. nursing edn. br., 1974-75, chief continuing edn. br., div. manpower and tng. programs, 1975-78, chief Center for State Mental Health Manpower Devel., 1978—. Recipient Yale U. Sch. Nursing Disting. Alumni award, 1975. Mem. D.C. Mental Health Assn., D.C. Sociol. Soc., Am. Public Health Assn., Met. Washington Public Health Assn., D.C. Mental Hygiene Inst. (trustee 1975—), Sigma Theta Tau, Pi Gamma Mu. Contbr. in field. Office: 5600 Fishers Ln Rockville MD 20857

SMITH, ELIZABETH S., state legislator; b. Balt., Mar. 18, 1934; student schs. Ohio, Wis., Calif. Adminstrv. asst. to Senate Minority Leader, 1971-74; mem. Md. Ho. of Dels., 1975—, mem. Gov.'s Com. to Promote Employment of Handicapped, Joint Md.-Va. Legis. Adv. Com. on Chesapeake Bar, State Tourism Adv. Com., Md. State Commn. for Performing Arts. Pres. Md. Clam Festival, bd. dirs. Davidsonville Athletic Assn., Ladies Aux. of Anne Arundel Gen. Hosp.; alt. del Republican Nat. Conv., 1972, 76, del., 1980; mem. 5th Dist. Rep. Club, Severna Park Rep. Women's Club, Crofton Rep. Women's Club, Anne Arundel Community Coll. Adv. Bd. Mem. Md. State C. of C. (dir.), Greater Annapolis C. of C. (past pres.), Annapolis C. of C. (hon. life). Club: Zonta (dir. Annapolis). Office: 215 Lowe Bldg Annapolis MD 21401 *

SMITH, ELSKE VAN PANHUYS, astronomer, univ. dean; b. Monaco, Nov. 9, 1929; came to U.S., 1943, naturalized, 1952; d. Johan Abraham and Vera (Craven) van Panhuys; B.A., Radcliffe Coll., 1950, M.A., 1951, Ph.D., 1955; m. Henry Joseph Smith, Sept. 10, 1950; children—Ralph Andrew, Kenneth Alan. Research assoc. Harvard Coll. Obs., Sacramento Peak, Sunspot, N.Mex., 1955-62; vis. fellow Joint Inst. for Lab. Astrophysics, Boulder, Colo., 1962-63; assoc., prof. astronomy U. Md., College Park, 1963-80, asst. provost, 1973-78, asst. vice chancellor, 1978-80; dean Coll. Humanities and Scis., Va. Commonwealth U., Richmond, 1980—; cons. NASA. Mem. Internat. Astron. Union (chmn. U.S. nat. com. 1979), Am. Astron. Soc. (counselor 1977-80), Phi Beta Kappa, Sigma Xi, Phi Kappa Phi; fellow AAAS. Author: (with H. J. Smith) Solar Flares, 1963; (with K. C. Jacobs) Introductory Astronomy and Astrophysics, 1973; contbr. articles to profl. jours. Home: 8 Waterfall Rd Richmond VA 23229 Office: Coll Humanities and Scis 900 Park Ave Richmond VA 23284

SMITH, ESTHER THOMAS, editor, writer; b. Jesup, Ga., Mar. 13, 1939; d. Joseph H. and Leslie Elizabeth (McCarthy) Thomas; B.A., Agnes Scott Coll., 1962; m. James D. Smith, June 2, 1962; children—Leslie, Amy, James Thomas. Staff writer, Sunday women's editor Atlanta Jour.-Constn., 1961-62; mng. editor Bull. of U. Miami Sch. Medicine, 1965-66; corr. Atlanta Jour.-Constn. and Jacksonville Fla. Times-Union, 1964, 67-68; founding editor Bus. Rev. of Washington, 1978-81; ind. bus. writer, communications cons. Peat, Marwick, Mitchell & Co., Washington, 1981-82; editor Washington Bus. Jour., a Cordovan publ., 1982—; lectr. Pres., Episcopal Young Churchmen, Diocese of Ga., 1955-57; dir. public relations Army Community Service, Ft. Bragg, N.C., 1969-71; co-founder Army Family Symposium, 1979-80; adv. bd. bus. edn. Fairfax County Pub. Schs., 1981—; bd. dirs. MIT Enterprise Forum of Washington/Balt., 1981—, Women's Forum, Washington, 1981—. Republican. Episcopalian. Home: 1335 Timberly Ln McLean VA 22102 Office: 6862 Elm St McLean VA 22101

SMITH, EVANGELINE CHRISMAN DAVEY (MRS. ALEXANDER MUNRO SMITH), civic worker; b. Kent, Ohio, May 30, 1911; d. Martin Luther and Berenice Murl (Chrisman) Davey; A.B. (Scholar), Wellesley Coll., 1933; postgrad. Akron U., 1933-34; m. Alexander Munro Smith, Oct. 5, 1935; children—Berenice Jessie Smith Hardy, Diantha Barret Smith Harris, Letitia Amy Smith Manley. Sec., Davey Tree Expert Co., Kent, 1934, dir., 1962-73, mem. dirs. adv. com., 1973-76. Trustee, Kent Free Library, 1957-77, pres., 1961-63; trustee Patton House, 1966-68, 79—; mem. women's assn. Robinson Meml. Hosp., 1947—, mem. women's assn. governing bd., 1947-68; co-founder Kent council Girl Scouts U.S.A., sec., 1941-45; mem. Kent State U. Pres's. Club, 1976—, Kent State U. Chestnut Soc., 1977—. Mem. Am. Legion Aux., D.A.R. (chpt. regent, 1966-68, registrar, 1973—), Daus. Am. Colonists (regent, 1978-80, registrar 1980—), Colonial Dames XVII Century (1st v.p.), Kappa Kappa Gamma, Phi Sigma Soc.

Congregationalist. Clubs: Akron Area Wellesley, Akron Woman's City. Home: 260 Whittier Ave Kent OH 44240

SMITH, FRAN KELLOGG, lighting designer; b. Chgo., Oct. 28, 1940; d. James Hull and Jean (Defrees) Kellogg; B.A., Pomona Coll., 1966; postgrad. Claremont Grad. Sch., 1966-68; B.S. in Interior Design, Woodbury Coll., 1973; m. Frederick J. Bertolone, July 3, 1976; children—Wayne E. McConnell, Scott Kellogg McConnell, Carol Jean McConnell, Christina Louise Smith. Jr. asso. Omnia Lighting Cons., Los Angeles, 1971-72; lighting cons. Black Swarens Okada, Los Angeles, 1972-73; lighting cons./founder Luminae Inc., Los Angeles and San Francisco, 1973—; instr. U. Calif., Berkeley, 1980—, UCLA, 1982; lectr. in field. Bd. dirs. Villa Esperanza Sch. Retarded, 1970-72; judge Nat. Council Interior Design Quals., 1977, 81; mem. jury Halo/Am. Soc. Interior Designers Lighting competition, 1977. Recipient Designers Lighting Forum Commemorative award, 1978; Pacifica award, 1980; Halo/ASID award, 1980. Mem. Am. Soc. Interior Designers, AIA (affiliate mem.), Illuminating Engring. Soc., Designers Lighting Forum (chpt. pres. 1973-75, chpt. v.p. 1976-77, dir. 1973-77, mem. nat. com. 1973-76); Interior Design Educators Council, Mensa. Republican. Clubs: Calif. State Coll. Faculty Wives (v.p. 1972), Indoor Light Gardening Soc. Am. Home: 315 Orange St San Gabriel CA 91776 Office: 2015 17th St San Francisco CA 94103

SMITH, FRANCES SCOTT, speech pathologist, audiologist; b. Crystal Springs, Miss., Nov. 15, 1932; d. John William and Birdie Estel (Parkinson) Scott; B.A., U. Miss., 1954, M.A., 1956; Ph.D., Purdue U., 1961; m. S. Allen Smith, June 5, 1955; children—Leonard, Lywin, Carl. Speech therapist Laurel (Miss.) City Schs., 1954-55; grad. asst. U. Miss., 1955-56, Purdue U., 1956-59; pvt. practice speech pathology, Hammond, La., 1960-63; speech pathologist Speech and Hearing Clinic, Jacksonville, Fla., 1963-65, chief speech pathologist, 1965-69, acting dir., 1969-70; continuing edn. instr. U. Fla., 1964-66; pvt. practice speech pathology and audiology, Jacksonville, 1970—. Mem. Fla. Speech and Hearing Assn., Fla. State Adv. Council Speech Pathology and Audiology (chmn. council 1974-75), Fla. Cleft Palate Assn. (pres. 1979-80), Am. Speech and Hearing Assn., N.E. Fla. Lang. Speech and Hearing Assn. (pres. 1973-74), Am. Acad. Pvt. Practice for Speech Pathology-Audiology (dir.), Jacksonville Assn. Children with Learning Disabilities (mem. adv. council 1976-78). Home: 308 Brooks Circle Jacksonville FL 32211 Office: 230 Arlington Rd N Jacksonville FL 32211

SMITH, GLORIA EVANS (FINCHER), dietitian; b. Crawfordville, Ga., Apr. 6, 1929; d. John Robert and Ruby Mae (Rainey) Evans; B.S. in Home Economics, Ga. Coll., 1969, M.S. in Adminstrn. in Home Economics, 1976; m. Edward Stanley Smith, Aug. 24, 1968; children by a previous marriage—Cheryl Fincher Wheat, Elizabeth Fincher Humphrey, Jennifer Fincher Shull; stepchildren—Edward Stanley, Robert Jackson, Jeanne Marie, Julia Ann. Asst. dietitian Ga. Coll., Milledgeville, 1963-69; vocat. instr. Vocat. Rehab., Milledgeville, 1969-72; dietitian food service Central State Hosp., Milledgeville, 1972-75; grad. asst. home econs. dept. Ga. Coll., Milledgeville, 1975-76; tng. coordinator Athens Community Council on Aging and Ga. Southwestern Coll., Milledgeville, 1977—; dietary cons. nursing homes; dir. Mary Kay Cosmetics, 1981—; nutritionist for Women, Infant, Children program Dept. Phys. Health. Dir. Milledgeville Community Concert Assn., 1975-78, membership drive chmn., 1976-77, 77-78. Registered dietitian. Mem. Am. Dietetics Assn., Am. Home Economics Assn., Ga. Dietetics Assn., Ga. Nutrition Council, Phi Upsilon Omicron. Roman Catholic. Home: 121 Vinson Hwy Millegeville GA 31061

SMITH, HELEN CATHARINE, author; b. Chgo., June 7, 1903; d. J. A.; B.A., U. Calif. at Los Angeles, 1926; postgrad. U. Wis., 1954-56; M.Sc., Christian Coll., 1962, Ph.D., 1965, Psy.D., 1966; Ph.D. (hon.) Free U., hon. doctorate Gt. China Arts Coll., 1969, St. Olav's Acad., Sweden, 1969, Internat. Acad. Soverign Order Alfred Gt., Eng., 1969; J.D., Ohio Christian Coll., 1969; Ph.D., U. Reno (Nigeria), 1975; m. H. C. Smith, June 7, 1932; children—Glen Dean, DeEtta Ellen (Mrs. Gerald L. Amdahl), George Dale. Tchr. 2d grade Maple Lawn Sch., Clinton, Wis.; legal sec., Janesville, Wis., Office of City Atty., Evansville, Wis., 1933—; v.p., dir. Blue Moon poetry mag., 1952-57. Recipient 1st pl. award for article Herdman Meml. Competition Brit. Press, 1957; John Francis Sims Meml. award for poetry, 1955; award of honor UN Day, Philippines, 1967; laurel wreath, gold medal Pres. Philippines, 1967; certificate recognition Nat. Poetry Day Com., 1972; Distinguished Service award Wis. Jaycees, 1975, certificate Am. Bicentennial Research Inst., 1975; named Hon. Poet Laureate (Am.-Visayan), 1967; Internat. Woman of 1975 with laureate honors by Imelda R. Marcos. Fellow Intercontinental Biog. Assn.; mem. AAUW (awards poetry, short stories 1972), Wis. Regional Writers Assn. (sec. 1949-55, 61—, hon. life dir., leadership citation 1956, Jade Ring winner for short story 1957), Nat. League Am. Pen Women, Am. Poetry League, Wis. Fellowship Poets, Wis. Acad. Scis. Arts and Letters, Brit. Press Assn., United Poets Laureate Internat. (Karta award), Wis. Council for Writers (life, 2d pl. award for short story 1980), Centro Studie Scambi Internazionali Roma (medal of honor 1966-67, internat. exec. bd.), Wis. Edn. Assn., Wis. Regional Artists, State Hist. Soc. Wis., Accademia Internazionale Leonardo Da Vinci (Rome; gold medallion 1972), Accademia Internaziale Di Pontzen, Am. Lit. Assn. (life), World Poetry Soc. (hon. life), UN Assn., Phi Beta Kappa (sustaining), Alpha Psi Omega, Sigma Iota Xi. Author: Laughing Child, books I, II, III, 1945, 46, 47; Off the Record, 1949; From the Countryside, 1952; Stars in My Eyes, 1954; Wind-Falls, 1955; Chiaroscura, 1964; But Not Yet, 1973; You Can't Cry All the Time, 1975. Editor: Evansville Anthology of Verse, 1952, No. Spring, anthology, 1956; Chiaroscura, 1964; Helen's Sketch Book, 1978; contbr. articles, stories to numerous mags., newspapers, anthologies. Home: 455 S 1st St Apt 19 Evansville WI 53536 Office: 14 W Main St Evansville WI 53536

SMITH, HELEN CREEGER, journalist; b. Attleboro, Mass., Apr. 8, 1924; d. Marion James and Florence Elizabeth (Rader) Creeger; B.A. magna cum laude, Alleghency Coll., Meadville, Pa., 1946; M.Ed. (scholarship), Syracuse (N.Y.) U., 1948; m. Kenneth Franklin Smith, July 9, 1949; children—Douglas, Gregory, Bradley, Steven. Women's editor Caracas (Venezuela) Daily Jour., English daily, 1961-65; staff writer U. Miami (Fla.) News Bur., 1966; English tchr. Am. Sch., San Salvador, El Salvador, 1967-78; asst. editor The Progress, Caldwell, N.J., also freelance feature writer Newark Star Ledger, 1969-71; family editor Conroe (Tex.) Daily Courier, 1971-73; drama and dance writer, gen. feature writer Atlanta Constn., 1973—; critic fellow Dance Critics Inst., 1975, O'Neill Theatre Critics Inst., 1977; freelance writer for nat. mags. including Dance mag., Ballet News, Am. Crafts, So. World, Delta Sky. Recipient numerous press assn. awards. Mem. Atlanta Circle Drama Critics (charter mem., co-founder), Am. Theatre Critics Assn., Phi Beta Kappa, Sigma Delta Chi. Office: 72 Marietta St Atlanta GA 30303

SMITH, INNES ADAMS COMER (MRS. EDWARD SAMUEL SMITH), civic worker; b. Birmingham, Ala., May 10, 1920; d. Robert Thornton and May (Adams) Comer; student Birmingham So. Coll., 1937-38; A.B., Randolph-Macon Woman's Coll., 1940; m. Edward Samuel Smith, May 5, 1942; children—Edward Samuel, Innes Smith Cameron Richards. Proof clk. First Nat. Bank, 1940-41; proof trainer Birmingham Trust Nat. Bank, 1941-43; censor U.S. Postal Censorship, 1943; receptionist Textron, Inc., 1943-44; teller Union Trust Co., 1961-62; new accounts clk. Chevy Chase br. Nat. Bank Washington, 1962-64; exec. v.p., dir. Logical Products, Inc., Balt., 1968-78. Active vol. work hosps., Birmingham, Washington and Balt., various fund drives; leader Cub Scouts, Boy Scouts Am., 1952-55. Mem. Jr. League Washington (fin. bd. 1956-57; dir. 1957-58), Jr. League Balt., Nat. Soc. Colonial Dames Am. in D.C., Nat. Soc. Daus. Barons of Runnymede, Descs. of Lords of Md. Manors, Order of Crown in Am., Kappa Delta. Democrat. Episcopalian. Clubs: Homesteaders Garden. Home: 3708 Taylor St Chevy Chase MD 20815

SMITH, IOLA RAGINS (MRS. JAMES ALEXANDER SMITH), ednl. psychologist; b. Phila.; d. Edward and Callie (Watkins) Ragins; B.A., Pa. State U., 1956; M.A., Am. U., 1960; Ph.D., Cath. U. Am., 1966; m. James Alexander Smith, Sept. 1, 1956; children—Staci Gabrielle, Shanon Gervaise. Lectr., Cath. U. Am., 1963-67; asso. prof. edn. Morgan State U., Balt., 1966-69, prof. edn., 1969—, acting chmn. dept., 1972, 78; lectr. Howard U., 1969—; cons., evaluation in-service tchr. workshop on desegregation Washington Pub. Schs., 1967; cons. workshop on sch. desegregation U. Md., 1967; cons. spl. planning Inst. for Center on Urban Studies, Morgan State Coll., 1968, Calvert County (Md.) Pub. Schs., 1969; alt. del. in ednl. adminstrn. Am. Council on Edn., 1977; speaker Md. Reading Assn., 1977. Recipient Distinguished Tchr. of Year award Morgan State Coll., 1969. Mem. LWV, Citizens Planning and Housing Assn., Delta Sigma Theta, Pi Lambda Theta, Pi Gamma Mu, Phi Sigma Iota. Clubs: Jack and Jill, Links, Epicureans. Co-editor: Educational Psychology and Teaching, 1968—; contbr. articles to profl. publs. Home: 11216 Green Dragon Ct Hobbits Glen Columbia MD 21044 Office: Morgan State U Coldspring Ln and Hillen Rd Baltimore MD 21239

SMITH, IRENE E. MACKEY, mayor; b. Belvidere, N.J., Apr. 9, 1910; d. Winfield Scott and Ruth (Hayes) Mackey; grad. East Stroudsburg Coll., 1929; m. Harold J. Smith, July 2, 1932; children—Gary W., Julianne Smith Tieff (dec.); 1 adopted dau., Dona Lynn Tieff. Tchr. Lower Mt. Bethel Twp., Pa., 1929-34; supr. N.J. Div. Motor Vehicles, Trenton, 1954-70, N.J. Dept. Labor, Trenton, 1971-73; aide to Congresswoman Meyner, 1975-79; mayor Town of Belvidere (N.J.), 1978—, council pres., 1977; cons. N.J. Div. Travel and Tourism. Chmn. Pequest River Mcpl. Utilities Authority; Democratic candidate for N.J. Senate, 1965; candidate for Warren County Bd. Freeholders; del. Dem. Nat. Conv., 1968; state committeewoman N.J. Dem. Com. Served with ARC, 1942-45. Mem. N.J. Conf. of Mayors (dir.), N.J. State League of Municipalities (dir.), Warren County League of Municipalities (v.p.), DAR (past regent), Daus. Am. Colonists, East Stroudsburg Coll. Alumni Assn., Belvidere High Sch. Alumni Assn. (past pres.). Clubs: Order of Eastern Star, White Shrine of Jerusalem (past officer); Soroptimist (charter pres.) (Belvidere). Episcopalian. Home: 628 3d St Belvidere NJ 07823

SMITH, IRENE PATRICIA, state senator, ednl. cons.; b. Whitinsville, Mass., May 2, 1935; d. James E. L. and Irene Patricia (Dion) Smith; A.B., Regis Coll., Weston, Mass., 1956; M.A., Columbia U., 1964; Profl. diploma, U. Conn., 1972. Tchr., Burrillville Sch. System, 1957-62; asst. prof., dir. admissions Quinsigamond Community Coll., Worcester, Mass., 1964-69; exec. asst. to Gov. R.I., 1969-72; cons. R.I. Dept. Edn., Providence, 1972—; cons. IBM Corp.; mem. R.I. Senate, 1976—, dep. majority leader. Mem. Burrillville Bd. Adminstrn., 1971—; town moderator, 1974-76; chmn. Town Govt. Study Commn., 1975-77; bd. dirs. Sr. Services, Inc. Mem. Nat. Bus. Edn. Assn., North Providence Bus. and Profl. Womens Club (named Woman of Year 1977), Burrillville C. of C., Delta Pi Epsilon, Kappa Delta Pi, Delta Kappa Gamma. Democrat. Roman Catholic. Home: 61 Chapel St Harrisville RI 02830 Office: 22 Hayes St Providence RI 02908

SMITH, ISABEL FRANCIS, fin. planning exec.; b. Detroit, May 21, 1935; d. Edward Hugh and Isabel Francis (Winegar); student Newton Coll., 1953-54; B.A., U. Mich., 1957, M.A., 1958, postgrad., 1975-76; m. Lawrence Smith, June 8, 1958; children—Mark, Hugh, Claire. Tchr. counselor Edison Sch., Hazel Park, Mich. and Warren Valley Sch., Dearborn, Mich., 1958-62; registered rep., dist. mgr. Investors Diversified Services, Oak Park, Mich., 1980—; instr. Henry Ford Community Coll., 1979—; cons. to women's orgns., 1977—; lectr. Trustee Bloomfield Twp. Library; founder Interlochen Friends, Vol. Network for Women. Recipient Heart of Gold award United Found., 1976; Outstanding New Rep. award Investors Diversified Services, 1979. Lic. rep. Nat. Assn. Securities Dealers. Mem. AAUW, LWV, Nat. Assn. Women Execs. Network, Internat. Assn. Fin. Planners, Inst. Cert. Fin. Planners, Interlochen Alumni Assn. (award, past pres.), U. Mich. Alumni Assn., Phi Beta Kappa (nat. chmn., past pres. Detroit assns., mem. exec. com. Detroit Assn., Pres.'s award), Pi Lambda Theta. Clubs: Women's Econ., Village Women's; U. Mich. (Birmingham, Mich.). Home: 7110 Paterese St Birmingham MI 48010 Office: 30200 Telegraph Suite 466 Birmingham MI 48010

SMITH, JACKIE, social worker; b. Chgo., Apr. 18, 1939; d. Jack Thomas and Stella Katherine (Magiera) S.; B.A., U. Wis., Madison, 1972, M.S.S.W., 1974; m. Samuel C. Wood, Aug. 30, 1975. Dairy farmer, Saxon, Wis., 1963-69; alcoholism specialist Okanogan (Wash.) County, 1975; social worker care unit Silverbow Hosp., Butte, Mont., 1976-78; social worker chem. dependency treatment care unit St. Anthony Hosp., Pendelton, Oreg., 1978-80, dir. unit, 1980—; bd. dirs. Oreg. Council Alcoholism, 1981—; mem. regional adv. task force Nat. Council on Alcoholism, 1982—; pres. Pendelton Interagy. Council, 1980—; cons. in field. Mem. Nat. Assn. Social Workers (dist. chmn. 1980—), AAUW, Nat. Assn. Female Execs., Alcoholism Profl. Staff Soc., Assn. Labor-Mgmt. Adminstrs. and Cons., Council Columbia Basin Hosp. Social Workers, Soc. for Hosp. Social Work Dirs. Club: Altrusa. Home: 219 NW 13th St Pendleton OR 97801 Office: 1601 SE Court Ave Pendleton OR 97801

SMITH, JACQUELINE SARAH, television exec.; b. Phila., May 24, 1933; d. Percy and Gertrude (Elman) Feldenkreis; student Antioch Coll., 1950-54; children—David Anthony, Elinor Sara. Producer, writer childrens program KPIX, San Francisco, 1956-58; dir. on-air-promotion WPIX, N.Y.C., 1960-63; exec. producer childrens program CBS-TV Network, 1964-69, dir. spl. programs, 1973-77; dir. spl. projects Warner Bros. TV, 1969-73; v.p. daytime programs ABC Entertainment, N.Y.C., 1977—. Inducted into YWCA Acad. of Women Achievers, 1981. Author TV-The New Teacher. Office: ABC Entertainment 1330 Ave of Americas New York NY 10019 *

SMITH, JANET SUE, assn. exec.; b. Chgo., Jan. 15, 1945; d. Curtis Edwin and Margaret Louise (Yost) Smith; B.A., Ind. U., 1967. Sales mgr. Marshall Field & Co., Chgo., 1968-70, programmer, 1970-72; sr. programmer, analyst Trailer Train Co., Chgo., 1972-75; data base spl. studies and systems devel. mgr. Railinc-Assn. Am. R.R.s, Washington, 1975—. Nat. student v.p. YWCA, 1966-67; dir. fin. Guide Internat., Friends of the Nat. Zoo; advisor Jr. Achievement. Mem. Ind. U. Alumni Assn. (life), Am. Council R.R. Women, Women's Transp. Seminar. Home: 2000 N St NW Washington DC 20036 Office: 1920 L St NW Washington DC 20036

SMITH, JANIE WILKINS, chem. co. info. specialist; b. Columbia, La., Apr. 5, 1930; d. James Climent and Hester (Bibb) Wilkins; B.A., La. Tech. U., 1951; postgrad. Fla. State U., 1962-70, U. Fla., 1962-63, U. South Fla., 1963-64; m. Thomas L. Smith, Nov. 3, 1950 (div.); children—Linda Karen, Thomas, Jr., Eric Andrew. English librarian Morehouse Parish Sch. Bd., Bastrop, La., 1951-52, Union Parish Sch. Bd., Farmerville, La., 1952-56, East Carroll Parish Sch. Bd., Lake Providence, La., 1957-60, Union Parish Schs., Farmerville, 1970-75, Ouachita Parish Schs., Monroe, La., 1976-79; ref. librarian Ouachita Parish Public Library, 1960-62; librarian lang. arts Brevard County Bd. Public Instrn., Titusville, Fla., 1962-70; info. specialist Columbian Chems. Co., Swartz, La., 1980—. Mem. AAUW (membership com.), Spl. Library Assn., Nat. Library Assn. Methodist. Home: 409 Birchwood Dr Monroe LA 71203 Office: PO Box 96 Swartz LA 71203

SMITH, JANIS ELIZABETH, lab. adminstr.; b. Friendship, Wis., Mar. 27, 1925; d. Percifer Franklin and Bertha Elizabeth (Pierce) Smith; B.S. in Med. Tech., U. Colo., 1955, M.P.A., 1980. Med. technologist Met. Pathologist P.C., Denver, 1955-64, chief med. technologist, 1964-70; chief chemist Longmont (Colo.) Community Hosp., 1970-72; chief med. technologist Longmont United Hosp., 1972-75, adminstrv. technologist, 1975—. Mem. Am. Soc. for Med. Tech., Am. Soc. Clin. Pathologists (affiliate mem.), Colo. Soc. Med. Technologists, Denver Soc. Med. Technologists, Colo. Assn. for Continuing Med. Lab. Edn. Republican. Roman Catholic. Home: 1438 Stuart St Apt #3 Longmont CO 80501

SMITH, JEAN WEBB (MRS. WILLIAM FRENCH SMITH), civic worker; b. Los Angeles; d. James Ellwood and Violet (Hughes) Webb; B.A. summa cum laude, Stanford U., 1940; m. George William Vaughan, Mar. 14, 1942 (dec. Sept. 1963); children—George William, Merry; m. 2d, William French Smith, Nov. 6, 1964. Mem. Nat. Vol. Service Adv. Council (ACTION), 1973-76, vice chmn., 1974-76; dir. Beneficial Standard Corp., 1976—. Vol., Nat Center for Citizen Involvement, 1977—; bd. councillors U. So. Calif. Sch. Performing Arts, 1976—; bd. dirs. Los Angeles chpt. ARC, 1979—, Community TV So. Calif. (KCET); mem. Calif. Arts Commn., 1971-74, vice chmn., 1973-74; bd. dirs. The Founders, Music Center, Los Angeles, 1971-74; bd. dirs. costume council Los Angeles County Mus. Art, 1971-73; bd. dirs. United Way, Inc., 1973-80; trustee Calif. Hist. Soc., 1970-71; bd. dirs. Hosp. Good Samaritan, 1973-80; mem. exec. com., 1975-80; mem. nat. bd. dirs. Boys' Clubs Am., 1977-80; bd. dirs. Los Angeles chpt. NCCJ, 1977-80, Nat. Symphony Orch., 1980—; mem. adv. bd. Salvation Army, 1979—; mem. President's Commn. on White House Fellowships, 1980—. Named Woman of Yr. for community service Los Angeles Times, 1958. Mem. Jr. League of Los Angeles (pres. 1954-55), Assn. Jr. Leagues of Am. (dir. Region XII, 1956-58, pres. 1958-60), Phi Beta Kappa, Kappa Kappa Gamma. Home: The Jefferson 1200 16th St NW Washington DC 20036

SMITH, JENNIFER C., ins. ofcl.; b. Boston, Nov. 3, 1952; d. Herman J. and Margaree L. S.; B.A. in English, Union Coll., 1974; M.A., Fairfield U., 1982. Claim rep. Travelers Ins. Co., Boston, 1974-75, supr., N.J., 1976-78, regional asst., account exec., Hartford, Conn., 1979-81, tng. adminstr., 1981, asst. dir. Casualty and property depts., 1981—; claim rep. Sentry Ins. Co., N.J., 1975-76. Chmn. Nat. Alliance Bus. Youth Motivational Task Force. Mem. Am. Soc. Tng. and Devel., Nat. Assn. Female Execs., Project to Increase Mastery of Math., Hartford Women's Network, Travelers Forum. Contbr. articles to Conn. Bus. Times. Office: 1 Tower Sq Hartford CT 06115

SMITH, JESSIE MAE, educator; b. Madisonville, Tex., May 7, 1937; d. David and Irene Turner Fant; B.A. in Social Studies, Tex. Coll., Tyler, 1960; M.Ed., A&M Coll., 1967; postgrad. U. Ariz., 1973-75, So. Methodist U., 1976; m. Joe Louis Smith, Dec. 22, 1962. Spl. edn. tchr. public schs., Tex., 1967-82, Zavala Elem. Sch., Odessa, 1981-82. Youth dir. YMCA, Tyler, 1961; del., Nat. Dem. Conv., N.Y.C., 1980. Mem. Ector County Tchrs. Assn. (newspaper editor 1979-80, v.p. 1979-80), Odessa Classroom Tchrs. Assn., Tex. State Tchrs. Assn. (dist. newsletter editor), NEA, Presdl. Mus. Baptist. Clubs: Dem. Women 100. Editor: Zavala Bluejay Newspaper, 1973-82. Home: 1635 E Everglade St Odessa TX 79762 Office: Pine and Clifford Sts Odessa TX 79762

SMITH, JILL DENISE, interior designer, educator; b. Chicago Heights, Ill., June 13, 1943; d. Dennis Stanley and Alice Wanda (Adler) Siwicki; B.S. in Home Econs., So. Ill. U., 1966; postgrad. U. Central Fla., 1978—; m. Thomas Zan Smith, Mar. 29, 1969; 1 dau., Alison Denee. Dir. interior design dept. George Stuart, Orlando, Fla., 1966-73; instr. interior design Orange County Sch., Orlando, 1966-79, Seminole Community Coll., Sanford, Fla., 1973-76, head interior design dept., 1973—; owner Jill Smith Interiors, Orlando, 1973—; design interiors for firms receiving Orlando Beautification award, 1970, 79. Recipient cert. of appreciation Maitland Arts Center, 1979. Mem. Am. Soc. Interior Designers (area bd. mem., co-chmn. STEP/NCIDQ 1981, 82). Roman Catholic. Home: 4401 Almark Dr Orlando FL 32809 Office: Seminole Community College Sanford FL 32771 also 4640 S Orange Blossom Trail Suite 306 Orlando FL 32809

SMITH, JO ANNE, journalist; b. Mpls., Mar. 18, 1930; d. Robert Bradburn and Virginia Mae S.; B.A., U. Minn., 1951, M.A., 1957. Wire and sports editor Rhinelander (Wis.) Daily News, 1951-52; staff corr., night mgr. UP, Mpls., 1952-56; interim instr. U. N.C., Chapel Hill, 1957-58; instr. U. Fla., Gainesville, 1959-65, asst. prof. journalism, communications, 1965-68, asso. prof., 1968-76, prof., 1976—, Disting. lectr., 1977; dir. Fla. Freedom of Info. Clearing House. Active, Friends of Library, Alachua County Humane Soc. Named Tchr. of Yr., U. Fla. Coll. Journalism, 1973, 74, 75, 76, 81, Outstanding Tchr. Journalism Dept. U. Fla., 1973, 74, 75, 76; recipient Outstanding Prof. award Fla. Blue Key, 1976; Danforth asso.,1976-82. Mem. Women in Communication, Soc. Profl. Journalists, Assn. Edn. in Journalism, Phi Beta Kappa, Kappa Tau Alpha. Democrat. Unitarian. Author: JM409 Casebook and Study Guide, 1976; Mass Communications Law Casebook, 1980, 2d edit., 1982. Home: 208 NW 21 Terr Gainesville FL 32603 Office: 2082 Weimer Hall U Fla Gainesville FL 32611

SMITH, JOAN MAE, acct.; b. Cin., May 28, 1928; d. Joseph H. and Edna M. (Robinson) Baumgartner; B.S. in Bus. Adminstrn., Wright State U., 1969; m. Alvin C. Smith, July 1, 1960; children—Deborah Ann, Joseph Gregory. Staff acct. Robert E. Stratis, Dayton, Ohio, 1966-74; partner Stratis and Smith, C.P.A.s, Dayton, 1974-81; owner, acct. Joan M. Smith C.P.A., Dayton, 1981—; faculty Wright State U., Dayton, 1973-76. Recipient Outstanding Citizen award Ohio Ho. of Reps., 1978. Mem. Am. Soc. Woman Accts. (nat. pres. 1977-78), Am. Women's Soc. C.P.A.s, Nat. Assn. Accts. (pres. Dayton chpt. 1977-78), Ohio Soc. C.P.A.s, Am. Inst. C.P.A.s, Wright State U. Alumni Assn. (dir. 1980-83). Republican. Methodist. Clubs: Altrusa, Dayton Bus. and Profl. Women. Office: 2590 Shiloh Springs Rd Dayton OH 45426

SMITH, JOAN TRUEHILL, public health program dir.; b. New Orleans, Sept. 21, 1941; d. Marshall and Elizabeth (May) Truehill; B.S., La. State U., 1964; postgrad. IBM, 1968, Tulane U., 1969, Upjohn Inst., 1970, Delgado Coll., 1970; M.P.H., Tulane U., 1978; m. William O. Smith, June 8, 1963; children—Frank, Angela, Treena, Crystal. Tchr. Orleans Parish Sch. Bd., New Orleans, 1964; nurse's asst. Total Community Action, New Orleans, 1966, recreational supr., 1966-67; clk. Family Planning, Inc., New Orleans, 1967, asst. records analyst, 1967-68, data processing supr., 1968-71, mgr. computer ops., 1971-72; asst. to dep. dir. Family Health Found., New Orleans, 1972-73, grants mgr., 1973-74, program coordinator, 1974; exec. asst. La. Family Planning Program, La. State Dept. Health and Human Resources, New Orleans, 1974-76, dir. family planning Office Health Services and Environ. Quality Family Planning Program, New Orleans, 1976—. Recipient Family Planning award Fed. Women's Program New Orleans, 1970. Mem. Nat. Assn. Exec. Females, Am. Public Health Assn., La. Public Health Assn., NAACP, Nat. Family Planning and Reproductive

Health Assn., Nat. Council Negro Women, Epsilon Sigma. Baptist. Home: 153 Louisiana St Westwego LA 70094 Office: 325 Loyola Ave New Orleans LA 70112

SMITH, JOYCE CAROL, nurse, educator; b. Mitchell, S.D., Nov. 24, 1926; d. Arthur Gordon and Alberta Darlene (Patterson) Smith; R.N., Presentation Sch. Nursing, St. Joseph Hosp., Mitchell, S.D., 1948; B.S., U. Colo., 1953; M.S. in Nursing, Ariz. State U., 1971. Staff nurse Boulder (Colo.) Community Hosp., 1948; pediatric staff nurse St. Anthony Hosp., Denver, 1949-52; head pediatric nurse Denver Gen. Hosp., 1953-57; instr. St. Joseph Hosp., Mitchell, S.D., 1957-60; dir. Redfield (S.D.) Community Hosp., 1960-63; instr. St. Joseph Hosp., Phoenix, 1963-69; asst. prof. Intercollegiate Center for Nursing Edn., Spokane, Wash., 1971-77; instr. San Diego State U., 1978—. Mem. Am. Nurses Assn., Assn. for Care of Children in Hosps., Phi Kappa Phi. Republican. Episcopalian. Home: 8754 Rae Jean Ave San Diego CA 92123

SMITH, JUANITA FRANCES, social worker; b. Lee County, Miss., Dec. 31, 1927; d. L.E. and Rose (Haddon) Parton; B.A., U. Miss., 1975, M.A., 1978; m. Carl Thomas Smith, Mar. 2, 1947; children—Ronald Carl, Gregory Thomas. Supr. social work Lee County Extension Service, Tupelo, Miss., 1975-78, counselor social work, 1975—; cons., social worker Miss. Nursing Homes, 1976—; dist. med. social worker Miss. State Bd. Health, 1981—. Mem. Nat. Assn. Social Workers, Miss. Conf. Social Welfare, Lee County (Miss.) Heart Assn. (pres. 1982), NE Miss. Art Assn. Mem. Christian Ch. Home: Route 8 Box 17 Tupelo MS 38801 Office: PO Box 1668 Tupelo MS 38801

SMITH, JUDITH BROOKS, mktg. exec.; b. Shreveport, Sept. 10, 1947; d. Louis Andrew and Hazel L. (Veuleman) Brooks; B.B.A. magna cum laude, Baylor U., Waco, Tex., 1969. Advt. asst. Shell Chem. Co., Houston, 1970-71; new bus. devel. asst. Golemon & Rolfe Architects, Houston, 1973; product mgr. Drawing Board Greeting Cards, Inc., Dallas, 1976-80; retail mktg. mgr. Parker-Garrick Inc., Dallas, 1980-82; divisional mgr. planning and analysis Heublein, Inc., Chgo., 1982—. Mem. Am. Mktg. Assn. (pres. Dallas/Ft. Worth 1982), Bus. and Profl. Women Dallas (dir. individual devel. program 1979). Club: Dallas Fourth Session. Office: 2400 E Devon Ave Des Plaines IL 60018

SMITH, JUDY YAPSUGA, stockbroker; b. Hazleton, Pa., Sept. 13, 1951; d. Leo Michael and Irene (Kanapka) Y.; B.S., Bloomsburg State Coll., 1972; M.S., U. Scranton, 1975; m. James J. Smith, Jr., Sept. 13, 1980. Tchr., Hazleton Area Sch. Dist., 1972-77; account exec. Merrill Lynch Pierce Fenner & Smith, Phila., 1977-80, coordinator estate and legal services, also money mgmt. and planning div., 1979-80; stockbroker E.F. Hutton, Strafford, Pa., 1980-81, Janney, Montgomery, Scott, Cherry Hill, N.J., 1981—; instr. Ogontz and Delaware County campuses Pa. State U., 1981—; speaker investment seminars, Phila. Bar Assn., Jewish Women's League, Paralegal Assn. Mem. NEA, PA. State (pres.-elect. dist. 5 1976-77), Hazleton Area (pres. elect 1976-77) edn. assns., Internat. Fedn. Bus. and Profl. Women (2d v.p. 1975-76, 1st v.p. 1976-77; treas. Camden County, N.J. chpt. 1982—, named Young Career Woman of Yr.), Nat. Assn. Securities Dealers Assn., Internat. Assn. Cert. Fin. Planners, N.J. Assn. Women Bus. Owners, Internat. Platform Assn. Home: 302 Roberts Ln Marlton NJ 08053 Office: 1909 E Marlton Pike Cherry Hill NJ 08053

SMITH, KATHLEEN ANN, med. technologist; b. Buffalo, Mar. 13, 1935; d. Joseph John and Rose Ann (Starke) S.; B.A., Mercyhurst Coll., 1956. From chemist to supr. hemostasis lab. Hamot Hosp., Erie, Pa., 1956-69; with Warner Lambert Co., 1969—, supr. hemostasis ednl. services, 1972—; adv. bd. Morris County Coll.; presentor seminars in field. Named Med. Technologist of Yr. in N.J., 1982. Mem. Am. Soc. Med. Tech. (chmn. hemotology-hemostasis sect.), Am. Soc. Clin. Pathology, N.J. Soc. Med. Tech. (pres. 1975), AAUW, Alpha Mu Tau. Republican. Roman Catholic. Club: Morristown (N.J.) Woman's. Co-author Hemostasis Manual. Assoc. editor Clotters Corner Hema-Topics, 1980—. Office: 201 Tabor Rd Morris Plains NJ 07950

SMITH, KATHLEEN TENER, banker; b. Pitts., Oct. 19, 1943; d. Edward Harrison, Jr. and Barbara Elizabeth (McCormick) Tener; B.A. summa cum laude, Vassar Coll., 1965; M.A., Harvard U., 1968; m. Roger Davis Smith, May 30, 1970; children—Silas Wheelock, Jocelyn Tener, Luke Ewing Taft. Research asst. Harvard Grad. Sch. Bus. Adminstrn., 1967-69; with Chase Manhattan Bank, N.Y.C., 1969—, 2d v.p., 1972-73, v.p., 1973—. Trustee Vassar Coll., 1979—. Mem. Am. Econ. Assn., Am. Fin. Assn., Phi Beta Kappa. Episcopalian. Club: Vassar (N.Y.C.). Home: 454 Route 32 N New Paltz NY 12561 Office: Fin Planning and Budgeting Dept Chase Manhattan Bank 1 Chase Manhattan Plaza New York NY 10015

SMITH, LEAH JOHNSON, economist; b. Ft. Worth, Feb. 1, 1943; d. Francis Bonneau and Leah Townsend (Zeigler) Johnson; B.A., Stanford U., 1964; Ph.D., Johns Hopkins U., 1972; m. Woolcott Keston Smith, Feb. 3, 1968; children—Amelia, Keston. Instr. econs. N.C. State U., 1969-72; economist First Nat. Bank Boston, 1972-73; with Woods Hole Oceanographic Instn., 1973-82, policy asso. marine policy and ocean mgmt., 1982; asst. prof. econs. Haverford Coll., 1981-82; asst. prof. Swarthmore Coll., 1982—; mem. sci. and statis. com. New Eng. Fishery Mgmt. Council; mem. adv. bd. Dept Interior; cons. in field. Trustee, Woods Hole Library, 1976-81, pres., 1978-80. Research grantee Nat. Marine Fisheries Service. Mem. Am. Econ. Assn., AAAS, World Mariculture Soc. Episcopalian. Contbr. articles to profl. jours. Home: 210 Garrett Ave Swarthmore PA 19081 Office: Dept Econs Swarthmore Coll Swarthmore PA 19081

SMITH, LILY MORELINE, govt. ofcl.; b. Boykin, Ala., Feb. 23, 1948; d. Robert Paul Pettway and Bethenia Calhoun; A.A. in Bus., Oscar Rose Jr. Coll., 1980; m. Ralph Smith, Jr., Oct. 26, 1968. Clk. stenographer HUD, Oklahoma City, 1975-76; with FAA, Oklahoma City, 1976—, documentation specialist, 1978-80, lead documentation specialist, 1980—. Served with USAF, 1966-74. Mem. Alpha Chi. Home: 4912 Washington Sq Oklahoma City OK 73135 Office: FAA PO Box 25082 6500 S MacArthur Blvd Oklahoma City OK 73125

SMITH, LINDA DARLENE, journalist; b. Mattoon, Ill., Aug. 1, 1954; d. Donald Wayne and Mary Kathryn (Mooday) Smith; B.J., Eastern Ill. U., 1975. Women's editor Mattoon (Ill.) Jour. Gazette, 1975-76; city reporter Mattoon Jour. Gazette, 1976-80; lifestyle editor Colorado Springs (Colo.) Gazette Telegraph, 1980-81, features writer, 1981—. Named Young Career Woman, Mattoon Bus. and Profl. Women, 1977. Mem. Mattoon LWV (pres. 1978). Home: 4550 LaCresta Dr Colorado Springs CO 80918 Office: PO Box 1779 Colorado Springs CO 80901

SMITH, LOIS CONLEY, educator; b. Montgomery, Ala., Oct. 8; d. Prince Edward and Fannie Fostene (Thompson) Conley; B.S., Ala. State U., 1939; M.A., U. Mich., 1944; m. Lovett Smith, June 14, 1943. Tchr., Montgomery public schs., 1940—, also mem. curriculum com.; vis. prof. Ala. A&M U., 1966; counselor adults night sch. Carver High Sch. Active Landsmark Found. of Montgomery; bd. dirs. Montgomery chpt. Multiple Sclerosis Soc.; trustee Day St. Bapt. Ch., Montgomery. Recipient Proclamation for Outstanding Civic and Community Work, Mayor of Montgomery; grants Fulbright, NDEA, East West, Phelp Stoke, Robert A. Taft; named outstanding woman of So. Region, 1974; grantee to study in India and S.E. Asia, 1977. Mem. Overseas Educators, Nat. Council for Social Studies (dir.), Ala. Council for Social Studies (pres.), Am. Acad. Polit. and Social Sci., NEA, Montgomery Hist. Soc. (dir.), AAUW, Pi Lambda Theta, Iota Phi Lambda, Phi Delta Kappa. Baptist. Clubs: Les Savantes Civic (pres. 1970-74), Eastern Star. Home: 3321 Cleveland Ave Montgomery AL 36105 Office: 2001 Fairview Ave Montgomery AL 36108

SMITH, LUCILLE OLIVIA, social worker; b. Du Quoin, Ill., Aug. 9, 1949; d. Virgil Lee and Isabel Ruth (Farquhar) S.; B.A., U. Ill., 1971, M.S.W., 1973. Intern, Peoria (Ill.) Public Schs., 1972-73; social worker II ARC, Chgo., 1973-75, Harvey, Ill., 1975-76, service to mil. families and vets. specialist, ARC Nat. Hdqrs., Washington, 1976-80, mgr. ARC SE Service Center, 1980—. NIMH fellow, 1971-73. Mem. Nat. Assn. Social Workers, Nat. Assn. Black Social Workers. Democrat. Mem. A.M.E. Ch. Home: 2140 Brooks Dr Forestville MD 20747 Office: ARC SE Service Center 2041 Martin Luther King Jr Ave SE Washington DC 20020

SMITH, LYNNE SANDERS, counselor; b. Charleston, W.Va., May 23, 1951; d. Walter Lee and Laura (Kirkpatrick) Sanders; A.A., N.E. Miss. Jr. Coll., 1971; B.S., U. Miss., 1973; M.Ed., Memphis State U., 1975; m. Kenneth M. Smith, Aug. 4, 1975. Sec., Stenographic Services, Memphis State U., 1973-77, placement counselor, 1978—; counselor Memphis Probation and Diversion Dept., 1977, sr. counselor, 1977; condr. coll. campus interview tng. sessions for corp. recruiters. Active, Memphis Jaycettes, 1974-79, internal. v.p., 1977-78, external v.p., 1978-79; area chmn. March of Dimes, Memphis, 1980, Memphis Heart Assn., 1981; hon. mem. Memphis City Council, 1979, Shelby County (Tenn.) Commn., 1979. Recipient Cert. of Appreciation, Dallas Police Dept., 1979, Memphis Vol. Placement Program, 1980, Memphis State U. Coalition Rehab. Advs., 1980; named Jaycette of Yr., Memphis Jaycettes, 1978, Jaycette of Quarter, 1978. Mem. Memphis Vol. Placement, Memphis Area Coll. Counselors' Assn. (treas.), Memphis State U. Career Women (chmn. membership), Alumni Assn. Memphis State U., U. Miss., N.E. Miss. Jr. Coll., Colonial Acres Neighborhood Assn. Mem. Ch. of Christ. Clubs: Stonebridge Country, Rebel Memphis. Author: Resume-Writing Workshop Manual, 1978; Techniques of Interviewing Workshop Manual, 1978. Office: Memphis State U Placement 315 Scates Hall Memphis TN 38152

SMITH, MADELINE AMELIA MUCCIE, sculptor; b. Trenton, Jan. 10, 1920; d. Frank and Josephine (Tummillo) Muccie; student Famous Artists Schs., Westport, Conn.; m. William J. Smith, Oct. 11, 1941; 1 son, William D. One-man shows including: Phila. Mus. Art, 1974, Pennridge Art Gallery, 1979, Internat. Platform Assn., 1979, Woodmere Art Gallery, 1979, Phillips Mill, 1979, Gentle Winds Gallery, 1980; 2-man show Western Electric Corp. Edn. Center Gallery, 1981; exhibited in group shows including: Arts Alliance, 1978-79, Regional Council Community Art Centers Phila., 1978-79, Rodman House, 1980, World Trade Center-Custom House Mus., N.Y.C., 1981; represented in permanent collections including: Fred Clark Mus., Carversville, Pa. Forest Ackerman Mus., Los Angeles, Pennridge High Sch., Wrightstown Twp. Bldg., also pvt. collections; creator Pearl S. Buck Women's award Pearl S. Buck Found., 1979; executed portraits of Congressman Peter Kostmayer, Dr. Selma Burke, George Trivellini, bas-relief of Pres. Ronald Reagan; writer Straight Talk column Fantasy Artists Network mag., 1979-80. Recipient gold medal Academia Italia della Arti e del Sadoro Italy, 1980; Effective Action award, history and arts com. Central Bucks C. of C., 1978; Golden Centaur for art achievements Accademia Italia, 1982. Mem. Internat. Soc. Artists (charter), Doylestown Art League (pres. 1974-76), Allied Artists Am., Women's Caucus for Art, Yardley Art Assn. (hon. mem.), Central Bucks C. of C. Club: Earhart Noonan Aviation (founder, pres. 1937). Home and Studio: Dogwood Acres Box 91 Penns Park PA 18943

SMITH, MAGGIE, actress; b. Ilford, Eng., Dec. 28, 1934; d. Nathaniel and Margaret (Hutton) Smith; ed. Oxford High Sch. Girls; m. Robert Stephens, 1967 (div. 1974); 2 sons; m. 2d, Beverly Cross, 1974. Stage and film actress, 1952—; stage appearances include New Face, N.Y.C., 1956, Share My Lettuce, 1957, The Stepmother, 1958, Rhinoceros, 1960, Strip The Willow, 1960, The Rehearsal, 1961, The Private Ear and The Public Eye, 1962, Mary, Mary, 1961; mem. Old Vic, 1959-60, Nat. Theatre, London, 1963—; productions at Nat. Theatre include The Recruiting Officer, Othello, The Master Builder, Hay Fever, Much Ado About Nothing, Miss Julie, A Bond Honoured, The Beaux Strategem, Hedda Gabler, Private Lives, 1972, Snap, 1973; participant Stratford Festival (Ont., Can.), 1976, 77, 78, 80; Night and Day, London and N.Y.C., 1979-80; Virginia, London, 1981; films include Othello, 1966, The Honey Pot, 1967, Oh What a Lovely War, 1968, Hot Millions, 1968, The Prime of Miss Jean Brodie (Oscar award), 1968, Love and Pain and The Whole Damn Thing, 1971, Travels With My Aunt, 1972, Murder by Death, 1976, Death on the Nile, 1977, California Suite (Oscar award), 1978, Quartet, 1978 Clash of the Titans, 1981, Evil under the Sun, 1981. Recipient Best Actress award Eve. Standard, 1962, 70; Best Film Actress award Soc. Film and TV Arts U.K., 1968, Film Critics Guild, 1968; named Actress of Year, Variety Club, 1963, 72; decorated comdr. Brit. Empire. Address: care Creative Artists Agy Inc 1888 Century Park E Suite 1400 Los Angeles CA 90067 *

SMITH, MARA KIRK, librarian; b. N.Y.C., Dec. 25, 1933; d. George W. and Lucile D. (Dvorak) Kirk; B.A., Miami U., Oxford, Ohio, 1955; M.A., N.Y. U., 1957; M.A., U. Minn., 1973; m. Ray Smith, Feb. 23, 1969; children by previous marriage—Steve Bauer, Jenny Bauer. Teenage dir. Central Br. YWCA, N.Y.C., 1957-58; tchr. English, Cleve., Mpls., 1958-61; dir. bibliography rm. U. Minn. Library, Mpls., 1964-65, Portuguese, Latin Am., Spanish bibliographer, 1965-69, acquisitions librarian, Duluth campus, 1973—; humanities bibliographer Claremont Colls., 1969-71; pub., editor Kirk Press Books. Manor Club scholar, 1956-57; Wis. Arts Bd. awardee, 1979. Democrat. Unitarian. Editor: Corn Village, 1971; poetry editor Plainsong, 1967-69, N. Country Anvil, 1971-77; translator various books from Spanish; author: (poetry) Some Yellow Flowers, 1979; pub.: Second Pond, 1980; Till Hope Creates, 1981. Home: 1811 Hammond Ave Superior WI 54880 Office: Univ Minn Duluth Library Duluth MN 55812

SMITH, MARCIA JEAN, tax specialist; b. Kansas City, Mo., Oct. 19, 1947; d. Eugene Hubert and Marcella Juanita (Greene) S.; student U. Nebr., 1965-67; B.A.(Coll. Ednl. Opportunity grantee), Jersey City State Coll., 1971; M.B.A. in Taxation, Golden Gate U., 1976, postgrad., 1976-77; M.S. in Acctg., Pace U., 1982; postgrad. Canadian Tax Sch., Queen's U., Can., 1979. Resident adviser Women's Job Corps, Moses Lake, Wash., 1967-68, Jersey City, 1968-71; legal intern Port Authority N.Y., N.J., N.Y.C., 1972; legis. aide to Harrison A. Williams, U.S. Senator, Washington, 1973; internat. tax accountant Bechtel Corp., San Francisco, 1974-77; sr. tax accountant Equitable Life Assurance Soc. U.S., N.Y.C., 1977; asst. sec. Equitable Life Holding Corp., N.Y.C., 1977-79, Equico Lessors, Inc., Mpls., 1978-79, Equitable Gen. Ins. Group, Ft. Worth, 1977-79, Heritage Life Assurance Co., Toronto, Ont., Can., 1978-79, Informatics, Inc., Los Angeles, 1978-79; sec. Equico Capital Corp., N.Y.C., 1977-79, Equico Personal Credit, Inc., Colorado Springs, Colo., 1978-79, Equico Securities, Inc., N.Y.C., 1977-79, Equitable Environ. Health, Inc., Woodbury, N.Y., 1977-79; tax sr. Arthur Andersen & Co., N.Y.C., 1979—; tax cons.; real estate salesperson. Human rights chmn. YWCA, Lincoln, Nebr., 1966-67. Recipient Certificate of Recognition, Central Mo. State Coll., 1965, St. Peter's Coll., 1971; Unicameral award State Neb., 1967, Mary McLeod Bethune award Jersey City State Coll., 1971. Mem. Am. Mgmt. Assn., Am. Assn. Individual Investors, Postal Commemorative Soc., Internat. Platform Assn., Smithsonian Assos., Am. Mus. Natural History Assos., Nat. Trust Hist. Preservation, Internat. Tax Inst., Am. Bus. Assn., Am. Econ. Assn., Nat. Assn. Female Execs. Club: U.S. Senatorial. Home: 300 Mercer St 23C New York NY 10003

SMITH, MARCIA SUE, govt. ofcl.; b. Greenfield, Mass., Feb. 22, 1951; d. Sherman K. and Shirley Fay (Schafer) S.; B.A., Syracuse U., 1972. Adminstrv. asst., corr. AIAA, Washington, 1973-75; sci. and tech. analyst Congressional Research Service, Sci. Policy Research div. Library of Congress, Washington, 1975-80, aerospace and energy tech. specialist, 1980—. Asso. fellow Brit. Interplanetary Soc.; mem. AAAS, Am. Astronautical Soc., AIAA, N.Y. Acad. Scis., Washington Acad. Scis., Sigma Xi. Contbr. articles to profl. publs. Office: CRS/SPRD Library of Congress Washington DC 20540

SMITH, MARGARET, nurse; b. Bklyn., July 21, 1936; d. Terence and Jane (Maloney) S.; R.N., Mary Immaculate Hosp., Jamaica, N.Y., 1962; B.S. in Nursing, Adelphi U., 1969; postgrad. Hofstra U., 1970-72; M.A., Wayne State U., 1974; postgrad. St. Johns U., 1976; M.A., N.Y. U., 1982. Staff nurse Mercy Hosp. Rockville Centre, N.Y., 1962-63, asst. head nurse, 1963-64, head nurse, 1964-65; staff pub. health nurse Nursing Sisters Home-Vis. Service, Nassau County, N.Y., 1965-66; Staff nurse Nassau County Med. Center, East Meadow, N.Y., 1969, instr. div. nursing edn., 1969-72; clin. specialist Adult Diabetic Out-Patient Clinic, Detroit Gen. Hosp., 1972-73; nurse clinician dept. nursing staff devel. Sinai Hosp., Detroit, 1974; asst. dir. nursing Nassau County Med. Center, East Meadow, 1975-77; oncology nurse clinician Catholic Med. Center Bklyn. and Queens Cancer Inst., 1977-79; health services coordinator L.I. Cancer Council, 1979-80; clin. prof. dept. nursing, L.I. U.; adj. instr. clin. nursing Molloy Coll., Rockville Center, N.Y., 1982—; cons. in field. Mem. Am. Nurse Assn., Oncology Nursing Soc., Adelphi U. Alumnae Assn., Wayne State U. Alumnae Assn. Republican. Roman Catholic. Home: 984 N Village Ave Rockville Center NY 11570

SMITH, MARGARET CHASE, former U.S. senator; b. Skowhegan, Maine, Dec. 14, 1897; d. George Emery and Carrie (Murray) Chase; student Skowhegan High Sch., 1912-16; 85 hon. degrees; m. Clyde H. Smith, May 14, 1930 (dec. 1940). Began as tchr., Skowhegan, 1916; office exec. Independent Reporter, 1919-28, Daniel E. Cummings Co., 1928-30; treas. New Eng. Process Co., Skowhegan, 1928-30; mem. 76th to 80th Congresses from 2d Maine Dist., mem. U.S. Senate from Maine, 1949-73; vis. prof. Woodrow Wilson Nat. Fellowship Found., 1973-76; lectr. various univs. including U. Notre Dame, U. Ala. Law Sch. Chmn., Freedom House, 1970-77. Bd. dirs. Lilly Endowment, 1976—; chmn. Northwood Nat. Women's Bd., 1978—; trustee U.S. Supreme Ct. Hist. Soc., 1979—. Name placed in nomination for Pres. of U.S., 1964. Mem. Am. Acad. Arts and Scis. Republican. Address: Norridgewock Ave Skowhegan ME 04976

SMITH, MARGARET LOIS, employment agy. exec.; b. Pinetta, Fla., Feb. 26, 1933; d. John Grambling and Vera Leon (Henderson) Schackleford; student public schs., Tampa, Fla.; m. Robert C. Smith, Nov. 4, 1951 (div. June 1965); children—Robert M., Stephen D., Cindy C., Lisa E. Saleswoman, Amana Food Plan, Honolulu, 1961-63; billing clk. Towers Hardware Co., Jacksonville, Fla., 1963-65; sales mgr. for northeast Fla., Wall St. Jour., Jacksonville, 1965-66; sales mgr. tech. northeast Fla., 3M Co., Jacksonville, 1966-67; mgr. Norrell Temporary Service, Jacksonville, 1967-69; pres., owner Tempo Talent, Inc., Jacksonville, 1969—. Mem. Am. Bus. Women's Assn., Com. 100, Assn. Gen. Contractors. Democrat. Baptist. Home: 3012 Kline Rd Jacksonville FL 32216 Office: 4161 Carmichael Ave Suite 156 Jacksonville FL 32207

SMITH, MARGARET MOORE BONNER, educator; b. Richmond, Va., Sept. 17, 1930; d. John Bryan Havens and Margaret Susan (Moore) Bonner; A.B., Salem Coll., 1952; m. Clarence James Smith, Oct. 8, 1955; children—Clarence James, III, Margaret Bonner, Edward Curtis. Tchr. public schs. Virginia Beach, Va., 1973—. Mem. Internat. Order King's Daus. and Sons, Va. Soc. Children of Am. Revolution (sr. state pres. 1976-80, sr. nat. v.p. Mid-So. region 1980-82), DAR (regent Princess Anne County chpt. 1977-80, dir. Va. dist. I 1980—), Daus. Colonial Wars, Daus. Am. Colonists. Presbyterian. Home: 201 55th St Virginia Beach VA 23451

SMITH, MARILYN CHAPNIK, psychologist, educator; b. Toronto, Ont., Can., Mar. 15, 1942; d. Hyman and Lily (Sugar) Chapnik; B.A., U. Toronto, 1963; Ph.D., M.I.T., 1966; m. Lawrence Berk Smith, June 11, 1963; children—Cynthia, Ilyse, Natalie. Prof. psychology U. Toronto, 1966—; vis. asst. prof. Carleton U., Ottawa, Ont., 1967-68; vis. scholar UCLA, 1973-74, Stanford (Calif.) U., 1981-82. Nat. Research Council of Can. grantee, 1966—. Mem. Can. Psychol. Assn., Am. Psychol. Assn., Psychonomic Soc., Am. Soc. Law and Psychology. Contbr. articles to profl. publs. Home: 69 Old Forest Hill Rd Toronto ON M5P 2R3 Canada Office: Life Sciences Scarborough Coll Univ Toronto West Hill ON M1C 1A4 Canada

SMITH, MARILYN LEWIS, ednl. aminstr.; b. Pitts., May 29, 1938; d. Joseph Edwards and Mary Elizabeth (Dolan) Lewis; B.S., U. Houston, 1959, M.A., 1962; M.S., U. Tex., Dallas, 1979; children—Joseph Lewis, Jefferson Lee, Robert Christopher. Therapist, Houston Speech and Hearing Center, 1960-62; dir. Spl. Care Sch., Dallas, 1964-68; dir. edn. and day care service Dallas County Mental Health and Mental Retardation Center, 1968-70; program dir. Children, Inc., Dallas, 1970-72, Angels, Inc., Dallas, 1971-76; pres. Package Deal, Inc., Richardson, Tex., 1977—; exec. dir. Creative Children's Center, 1977—; instr. community service div. El Centro Jr. Coll., Dallas, 1968-76; faculty Richland Community Coll., 1975-78. Mem. adv. bd. Helping Hand Sch., Irving, Tex., 1969-79. Mem. Am. Assn. Mental Deficiency, Council for Exceptional Children, Gamma Phi Beta. Home: 3950 Clubway Dallas TX 75234 Office: 1015 Newberry St Richardson TX 75080

SMITH, MARION BRADLEY, clin. social worker; b. Charleston, S.C., Oct. 23, 1929; d. Francis Edward and Mary Loretto (Hennesy) Bradley; B.A., Seton Hill Coll., Greensburg, Pa., 1951; M.S.W. (NIMH trainee 1960-61), Va. Commonwealth U., Richmond, 1961. With VA, 1961-64, 66—, clin. social worker VA Med. Center, Charleston, S.C., 1970—; supr. Social Service Bur., Richmond, 1964-66; mem. field faculty Coll. Social Work, U. S.C., Columbia, 1971—; guest lectr. Trident Tech. Coll., Charleston, Med. U. S.C., Charleston. Recipient Service award VA, 1978, cert. appreciation, 1979, summer scholarship award, 1967; Spl. Contbn. award VA Med. Center, Charleston, 1981. Mem. Nat. Assn. Social Workers, Acad. Cert. Social Workers, S.C. Hist. Soc., Berkeley County Hist. Soc., Am. Legion Aux. Roman Catholic. Home: 1620 Oak Island Dr Charleston SC 29412 Office: VA Med Center 109 Bee St Charleston SC 29403

SMITH, MARION CECELIA, educator, former health care exec.; b. Catskill, N.Y., Oct. 23, 1922; d. Nathaniel and Agatha Marie (Delanoy) Smith; B.A., Coll. of St. Rose, 1952; M.A., Siena Coll., 1964. Entered Order of Sisters of Mercy, Roman Catholic Ch., 1940; tchr. elem. and high schs., Albany, Troy, Cuhoes and Oneonta, N.Y., 1943-65; chmn. journalism dept. Cath. Central High Sch., Troy, 1961-65; prin. St. Mary's Sch., Oneonta, 1965-67; asso. dir. Oneonta Newman Found., 1967-76; adminstrv. asst. Stephen Smith Geriatric Center, Phila., 1977-82; faculty SUNY, Oneonta, 1976. Co-founder, chmn. Campus Ministry Com. of Oneonta, 1968-70, 74-75; co-founder, cons., counselor City Drug Crisis Center, —85—, Oneonta, 1971-75; active Human Relations Task Force, 1974-75, Family Service Com. of Oneonta, 1972-76; counselor Planned Parenthood Clinic of Otsego County,

1972-75; campus ministry com. Oneonta, 1968-76, others. Fellow Am. Coll. Nursing Home Adminstrs.; mem. Nat. Council for Basic Edn., Nat. Cath. Campus Ministry Assn., Nat. Inst. Campus Ministry, Religious Edn. Assn., Am. Acad. Religion, Hastings Center Inst. Soc., Ethics and Life Scis., Fellowship of Reconciliation, AAUW, Siena Coll. Alumni Assn., Nat. Assn. Female Execs., Nat. Assn. Profl. and Exec. Women. Contbr. articles to profl. jours.; lit. editor profl. papers and book reviews for non-English speaking profs. in higher edn.; asst. to editor Asian Thought and Soc., 1976. Home: 6119 Ellsworth St Philadelphia PA 19143

SMITH, MARJORIE HAGANS, librarian; b. Atlanta, Nov. 24, 1936; d. Simon Peter and Erma Ruth (Miller) Hagans; B.A., Clark Coll., 1959; M.S. in L.S., Atlanta U., 1969, Ed.S. in L.S., 1980; m. Jimmie L. Smith, Dec. 26, 1959; children—Jimmie Marquette, Jocelyn Marcella, Jevon Marcel. Cataloger, Livingstone Coll., Salisbury, N.C., 1961-62; tchr., librarian Berean Jr. Acad., Atlanta, 1965-68; media specialist, librarian Atlanta Bd. Edn., 1968—. Sec. W. Manor PTA, Atlanta, 1976-77, corr. sec., 1977-78; sec. SW High Sch. Band Parents Club. Mem. Am., Ga. library assns., Am. Assn. Sch. Librarians, NEA, Ga., Atlanta assns. educators. Seventh-Day Adventist (leader hostess com., mem. chancel choir). Co-author: Ethnic Book Bibliography. Home: 3176 Kingsdale Dr SW Atlanta GA 30311 Office: 660 McWilliams Rd SE Atlanta GA 30315

SMITH, MARJORIE WALKER, social worker; b. Huron, S.D., Aug. 16, 1918; d. Clarence George and Zaola Blanche (Pennington) Walker; B.A. magna cum laude, Huron Coll., 1942; M.S.W., U. So. Calif., 1965; postgrad. UCLA, Calif. State U., Long Beach; m. Stanley L. Smith, Dec. 29, 1951 (div. 1965); children—Denver Kennedy, Craig Walker. Tchr., Bryant (S.D.) High Sch., 1942-43; research analyst Army Security Agy., Arlington, Va., 1943-46; recreation therapist VA hosps., Hines, Ill., Van Nuys and Long Beach, Calif., 1946-57; child welfare worker and supr. Los Angeles County Dept. Public Social Service, 1966-77; dir. social services Saddleback Community Hosp., Laguna Hills, Calif., 1977-81; pvt. practice social work cons., 1981—; field instr. Calif. State U. Sch. Social Work, San Diego. Mem. social work subcom. Orange County unit Am. Cancer Soc.; mem. Saddleback Valley Mental Health Adv. Com.; county liaison worker Los Angeles County Foster Parents Assn., 1972-77; mem. Mayor's Adv. Com. on Edn., Long Beach, 1971-72. Mem. Nat. Assn. Social Workers, Acad. Cert. Social Workers, Western Gerontol. Soc., So. Calif. Assn. Social Workers in Oncology, Soc. for Hosp. Social Work Dirs., LWV. Democrat. Mem. United Ch. of Christ. Home: PO Box 4358 San Clemente CA 92672 Office: Saddleback Community Hosp 24451 Via Estrada Laguna Hills CA 92653

SMITH, MARSHA ELAINE, accountant, educator; b. Portsmouth, Ohio, Apr. 21, 1949; d. A. Mac and A. Mary (Delabar) Wamsley; B.B.A. in Acctg. cum laude, Ohio U., Athens, 1974; m. Brent C. Smith, Nov. 16, 1974; children—David Alan, Trisha Jabrina. Asst. ops. mgr. Chase Manhattan Bank, N.A., Agana, Guam, 1971-73; dorm and dining acct. Ohio U., 1974; organized research acct. U. Akron (Ohio), 1975; owner, operator public acctg. firm, McConnelsville, Ohio, 1976, Bath, Ohio, 1978—; staff acct. Dorsey L. Arnold, C.P.A., Bath, 1977; supr., office mgr. Dwite A. Polos, C.P.A., Cuyahoga Falls, Ohio, 1978; instr. acctg. Washington Tech. Coll., 1976, U. Akron, 1982—; dir. Taco Ed's, Inc., 1978—; Treas. ladies aux. Bath Fire Dept., 1979—; Democratic precinct woman Bath Twp., 1980—. C.P.A., Ohio. Mem. Am. Women's Soc. C.P.A.s, Assn. M.B.A. Execs., Nat. Assn. Accts. (dir. profl. devel. Ohio council 1981—), Am. Inst. C.P.A.s, Ohio Soc. C.P.A.s. Home: 2944 Shade Rd Bath OH 44210 Office: 843 N Cleveland-Massillon Rd Bath OH 44210

SMITH, MARTHA HARCROW, acct.; b. Childress, Tex., Feb. 17, 1940; d. James Joseph and Martha Mae (Greenhill) Harcrow; B.B.A., Midwestern U., 1967. Acct., Davis, Mathis, West & Huffines, C.P.A.s, 1969-73, Rariden, Moore, Miller & Elam, C.P.A.s, Wichita Falls, Tex., 1973-76; pvt. practice acctg., Garland, Tex., 1976-78; partner Gustafson & Smith, C.P.A.s, Garland, 1978-81; pvt. practice, Dallas, 1981—. Bd. dirs., treas. The Galaxy Center, Garland, 1978-79, sec., 1979-80. C.P.A., Tex. Mem. Tex. Soc. C.P.A.s, Am. Inst. C.P.A.s, Women's Practice Mgmt. Group Tex., Intercity Study Group, Farmers Branch C. of C., Farmers Branch Bus. Chamber. Clubs: Garland Bus. and Profl. Women's (pres. 1979-80), White Rock Toastmistress, Soroptimist Internat. Garland (asst. treas. 1978-79, treas., 1979-80). Home: 3820 Spring Valley Rd Dallas TX 75234 Office: 4560 Belt Line Rd Suite 214 Dallas TX 75234

SMITH, MARTHA KATHLEEN, mathematician, educator; b. Detroit, Mar. 14, 1944; d. Norman Victor and Alice Margaret (Gullen) S.; B.A., U. Mich., 1965; M.S., U. Chgo., 1967, Ph.D., 1970. G.C. Evans instr. Rice U., Houston, 1970-72; asst. prof. math. Wash. U., St. Louis, 1972-73; asst. prof. U. Tex., Austin, 1973-76, asso. prof., 1976—. Mem. Am. Math. Soc., Math. Assn. Am., Assn. Women in Math. Contbr. articles to profl. jours. Office: U Texas Dept Math Austin TX 78712

SMITH, MARY ALBERTA HAMPTON, physician asst. b. Hopkinsville, Ky., July 18, 1950; d. Richard H. and Bessie M. (Clardy) Hampton; B.S., Austin Peay State U., 1972; B.S., physician asst. cert., Baylor U. Coll. Medicine, 1977; m. Tommy R. Smith, July 19, 1981. Nursing asst. Gen. Care Convalescent Center, Clarksville, Tenn., 1971; substitute tchr. Clarksville-Montgomery County Sch. System, 1972-74; dir. nursery St. John Missionary Bapt. Ch., Clarksville, 1972-74; nursing asst. cardiovascular/ICU units St. Luke Episcopal Hosp., Houston, 1975; child care attendant for autistic children First Presbyn. Ch., Houston, 1976-77; emergency room clk. Med. Center Del Oro Hosp., Houston, 1977-81; cert. physician asst. C. R. Higgins Jr., M.D. and Assos., Houston, 1977-81; with Iowa Vets. Home, Marshalltown, 1981—. Resource person Concord Elem. Sch., Houston Ind. Sch. Dist., 1979-81; active ARC. Mem. Am. Acad. Physician Assts., Am. Assn. Female Exec., Nat. Council Negro Women, Eta Phi Beta. Baptist. Home: 1702 Edgebrook #1 Marshalltown IA 50158

SMITH, MARY ANN BARTHOLOMEW, speech pathologist; b. Cleve., June 22, 1943; B.F.A. in Speech and Hearing Therapy, Ohio U., 1965; M. Communicative Disorders, Calif. State U., Long Beach, 1978; 4 children. Speech pathologist Willoughby (Ohio)-East Lake Schs., 1965-66, Huron County (Ohio) Schs., 1967-68, Princeton City Schs., Cin., 1968-70; aphasia tchr. Whittier City (Calif.) Schs., 1971—. Cert. in spl. edn., Ohio, Oreg., Calif.; specialist in speech and hearing. Home: 220 S Norma St La Habra CA 90631

SMITH, MARY ARDENE THRELFALL, social worker; b. Sharon, Kans.; d. Alfred A. and Cora Ellen (O'Shea) Threlfall; B.A., Wichita State U., 1935, postgrad., 1942-45; m. Bill Eugene Smith, May 27, 1944. Social worker crime prevention div. Wichita Police Dept., 1936-39; referee Juvenile Ct., Sedgwick County, Wichita, 1939-51, chief social worker, 1951-64; social worker Wichita Children's Home, 1965-67, bd. dirs., 1947—; mem. staff adult edn. Wichita Bd. Edn., 1937-43. Vol., chmn. Craft Days, Extension Homemakers Units, Kans. State U., Manhattan, Sedgwick County, 1977—; family council mem. Kans. Christian Home for Elderly, Newton. Mem. Friends of Wichita Art Mus., Women's Aux. Profl. Engrs. (pres. 1965-66), DAR (public relations state chmn. 1963-75), Daus. Colonial Wars, Children Am. Revolution (state pres. 1966-68, nat. v.p. northwestern region 1968-71), Sunflower Soc., Delta Gamma. Republican. Clubs: 20th Century (social chmn. 1976-77, 80—), Newman Book (pres. 1974-75), Woman's Kans. Day (sec. 1982).

SMITH, MARY DIANNE, nurse, dental hygienist; b. Washington, Nov. 10, 1940; d. William Greenwood and Helen Ray (Orme) Yeatman; B.S., U. Md., 1973; R.N., Howard Community Coll., 1980; Instr. dept. dental hygiene U. Md. Sch. Dentistry, Balt., 1973-76, asst. prof. dept. oral and maxillofacial surgery, 1976—; cons. dental hygiene and nursing Perry Point VA Hosp., dept. of oral and maxillofacial surgery, Johns Hopkins Hosp., Balt. Mem. Am. Dental Hygienists Assn. Sigma Phi Alpha. Baptist.

SMITH, MARY ELINOR, univ. dean; b. Louisville, Dec. 18, 1913; d. Harry Robert and Susan (Corrigan) Smith; A.B., Catherine Spalding Coll., 1935; M.A., Cath. U. Am., 1950; student Nat. Def. Edn. Inst., Mich. State U., 1967-68. Tchr. math. public schs., Jefferson County, Ky., 1935-36, Louisville, 1936-44; social worker Louisville, Jefferson County Children's Home, 1946-48; grad. asst. Cath. U. Am., Washington, 1948-50; lectr., 1952-60, dean women, 1952-69, asso. dean students, 1969-79, ret., 1979, now active various coms.; dean women Quincy Coll., 1950-52; lectr. Ursuline Coll., 1953. Hosp. staff aide ARC, Pearl Harbor Naval Hosp., 1944-45; mem. inter sch. com. for Center for Study Pre-Retirement and Aging, Nat. Cath. Sch. Social Service; chmn. Phonathon, Office of Devel., 1980; vol. Office Pastoral Ministry, Providence Hosp., 1978—. Mem. Internat. Fedn. Cath. Alumnae (vice-gov. Ky. 1938-42, vice regent D.C. 1956), Am. Psychol. Assn., Nat. Assn. Women Deans and Counselors (chmn. task force on devel. internships 1974-76), Regional Assn. Women Deans and Counselors (pres. 1966-68), AAUW, Sigma Alpha Iota (patron), Theta Phi Alpha (hon.).

SMITH, MARY JO, govt. space flight program adminstr.; b. Ft. Worth, Mar. 5, 1938; d. Ed and Maggie Mae (Burkes) S.; B.A. in Physics and Math., Tex. Christian U., 1960; postgrad. U. Ala., Huntsville, 1961-67. Discipline scientist Lunar Programs, Hdqrs., NASA, Washington, 1974-75, program mgr. Lunar Polar Orbiter, 1975-78, program engr. Galileo, 1978-80, program mgr. Spacelab Missions 1 and 4, 1980—. Mem. Am. Geophys. Union. Office: NASA Hdqrs EM-8 Washington DC 20546

SMITH, MARY JO, med. technologist, blood bank specialist; b. Muskegon, Mich., Mar. 17, 1936; d. Alvin V. and Bernice (Price) Martin; B.S., Nazareth Coll., 1958; m. Gregory Smith, June 20, 1959; (div.). Med. technologist Borgess Hosp., Kalamazoo, 1958-60, Blodgett Hosp., Grand Rapids, Mich., 1960-61, Mercy Hosp., Muskegon, Mich., 1961-64; chief technologist blood bank dept. hemotherapy Parkland Meml. Hosp., Dallas, 1964—. Mem. Am. Assn. Blood Banks (tech. workshop com., 1976-81, faculty mem. 1968-76), S. Central Assn. Blood Banks (chmn. workshop com. 1973-75, sec. 1971-73). Contbr. articles on med. tech. to profl. jours. Home: 2005 Via Sevilla Carrollton TX 75006 Office: 5201 Harry Hines Dallas TX 75235

SMITH, MARY LOUISE, federal ofcl.; b. Eddyville, Iowa, Oct. 6, 1914; d. Frank and Louise Anna (Jager) Epperson; B.A., U. Iowa, 1935; L.H.D. (hon.), Drake U., 1980; m. Elmer Milton Smith, Oct. 7, 1934; children—Robert C., Margaret L., James E. Mem. Eagle Grove (Iowa) Bd. Edn., 1955-60; Republican precinct committeewoman, Eagle Grove, 1960-62, vice-chairwoman, Wright County, Iowa, 1962-63; mem. Rep. Nat. Com., 1964—, mem. exec. com., 1969—, mem. conv. reforms com., 1966, vice-chairwoman Steiger com. on conv. reform, 1973, co-chmn. nat. com., 1974, chmn. Com., 1974-77; vice-chairwoman U.S. Commn. on Civil Rights, 1982—; vice-chairwoman Midwest region Rep. Conf., 1969-71; del. Rep. Nat. Conv., 1968, 72, 76, 80, alt. del., 1964; vice-chairwoman Iowa Presdl. campaign, 1964; nat. co-chmn. Physicians Com. for Presdl. Campaign, 1972; co-chairwoman Iowa Com. to Reelect the Pres., 1972; mem. Nat. Commn. on Observance Internat. Women's Year, 1975-77; vis. fellow Woodrow Wilson Fellowship Found., 1979; dir. Dial Corp. Mem. U.S. del. to Extraordinary Session of UNESCO Gen. Conf., Paris, 1973; mem. U.S. del. 15th session population commn. UN Econ. and Social Council, Geneva, 1969; mem. Pres.'s Commn. for Observance of 25th Anniversary of UN, 1970-71; mem. Iowa Commn. for Blind, 1961-63, chairwoman, 1963; mem. Iowa Gov.'s Commn. on Aging, 1962; trustee Robert A. Taft Inst. Govt., 1975—, Herbert Hoover Presdl. Library Assn., Inc., 1979—. Active Planned Parenthood, YWCA; pres. Eagle Grove Community Chest; bd. dirs. Mental Health Center N. Iowa, 1962-63. Named hon. col., mil. staff Gov. Iowa, 1973; Iowa Women's Hall of Fame, 1977. Mem. Women's Aux. AMA, UN Assn., Nat. Women's Polit. Caucus (adv. bd. 1978—), PEO, Kappa Alpha Theta. Address: 654 59th St Des Moines IA 50312

SMITH, MILDRED BIRGE, med. records adminstr.; b. Shreveport, La., Nov. 8, 1930; d. Harry James and Mary Leola (A'Brantes) Birge; B.S. in Med. Records Adminstrn. cum laude, La. Tech. U., 1975, M.A. in Human Relations, 1982; m. Robert Lewis Smith, Aug. 21, 1948; children—Charlotte Ann, Marilyn Jean, Ruth Ellen, Robert Lewis, Charles Wayne. Med. records clk. Schumpert Med. Center, Shreveport, 1969; bank teller First Nat. Bank, Shreveport, 1970; med. records clk. Willis-Knighton Hosp., Shreveport, 1971-72; substitute sec./tchr. Caddo Parish Sc., Shreveport, 1973-75; instr. med. terminology Vo-Tech Center, Shreveport, 1976-77; med. records adminstr. Bossier City (La.) Gen. Hosp., 1975-78; med. records cons. Physicians and Surgeons Hosp., Shreveport, 1976; Mid-La. Health Systems Agy., Inc., Baton Rouge, 1978, North La. Health Systems Agy., Shreveport, 1978; med. records adminstr. N.W. La. State Sch., Bossier City, 1978-80; med. records cons., 1980—; clin. site instr. La. Tech. U., Ruston, 1975—; exec. bd. adv. council N. La. Health Systems Agy., 1979-82; instr./model Pamelia's Models, Bossier City, 1980—. Mem. La. Talent Bank of Women. Mem. Am. Soc. Law and Medicine, Am. Soc. Hosp. Risk Mgmt., Am. Med. Records Assn. (registered), La. Med. Records Assn. (exec. bd. 1977—, consultants com. 1980—), Southeastern Med. Records Conf., NW La. Med. Records Assn. (exec. bd. 1976—, v.p. 1976, pres. 1977, 78; rep. to state assn. 1977-81), Am. Bus. Women's Assn., La. Tech. U. Alumni Assn. (hon. faculty 1975—), Phi Kappa Phi. Democrat. Clubs: Elks Ladies Aux., Toastmasters. Home and office: 4003 Santa Monica Ct Shreveport LA 71119

SMITH, MILDRED FREE, educator; b. Altha, Fla., Aug. 4, 1942; d. Leonard Lawrence and Susan Mary (Chason) Free; A.A., Chipola Jr. Coll., 1962; B.S., Miss. State U., 1964; M.Ed. (NDEA fellow), U. Fla., 1967; Ph.D., U. Md., 1978; m. Wayne H. Smith, June 16, 1962. Tchr., public schs., Gainesville, Fla., 1967-69; dir. grant project U. Fla., 1969-73; coordinator evaluation U. Fla. Health Center, 1977-79, asst. prof. extension edn., program evaluation specialist U. Fla. Coop. Extension Service, 1979—; cons. evaluation, 1973-75. Chmn. publs. Univ. Women's Club, U. Fla., 1973-75; campaign asst. to local judges' election, Gainesville, 1978. Mem. Am. Ednl. Research Assn., Evaluation Research Soc., Evaluation Network, U. Fla. Assn. Women Faculty. Contbr. articles to profl. jours.; author, project dir. The Valuing Approach to Career Edn., 1973, 74; editor, contbg. author: Current Issues/Problems in Evaluating Cooperative Extension Programs, 1981. Home: 2903 SW 4 Ct Gainesville FL 32601 Office: 311 Rolfs Hall U Fla Gainesville FL 32611

SMITH, NANCY MURRAY, clin. social worker; b. Washington, Feb. 21, 1936; d. Kenneth A. and Marjorie F. (Travis) Murray; B.S., N.Y. Inst. Tech., 1974; M.S.W., Barry Coll., Miami, Fla., 1977; postgrad. Fla. State U., Tallahassee; m. William F. Smith, Dec. 6, 1957; children—Brian William, Kevin Michael. Clin. social worker, then social work supr. adolescent unit S. Fla. State Hosp., Hollywood, 1977-79; clin. social worker children's assessment and treatment program Nova U., Coral Springs, Fla., 1979-80; pvt. practice marriage and family therapy, 1980—. field instr. Barry Coll. Sch. Social Work. Mem. Nat. Council on Family Relations. Robert Chastain scholar, 1972. Mem. Acad. Cert. Social Workers, Am. Assn. Marriage and Family Therapy, Nat. Assn. Social Workers, AAUW, Broward County Mental Health Assn., Delta Tau Kappa, Omicron Nu. Republican. Methodist. Home: 2965 Shamrock N 32 Tallahassee FL 32308

SMITH, NELLE CREWS, nursing educator; b. Oxford, N.C., Apr. 12, 1925; d. Roy W. and Florence Ruby (Adcock) Crews; student Mars Hill Coll., 1943-44; R.N., Columbia Hosp. Sch. Nursing, 1947; B.S. in Nursing, U. S.C., 1976, M.S. in Nursing, 1981; m. William Clyde Smith, Jr., Nov. 8, 1947; children—William Clyde, Roy Crews, Margie Merrinelle. Head nurse med. disease unit Columbia (S.C.) Hosp., 1947-49, head nurse surg. disease unit, 1949-51; health room supr. A.C. Moore Sch., Columbia, 1957-61; pvt. duty nurse Columbia, 1961-66; R.N. instr. Coronary Care Unit, Columbia Hosp., 1966-68; head nurse CCU, Providence, Hosp., Columbia, 1968-69; instr. Richland Dist. 1 Practical Nursing Program, Columbia, 1969-76, instr./coordinator, 1977-81; med./surg. instr. R.N. Nursing Program, Midlands Tech. Coll., Columbia, 1981—. Active various charitable orgns.; den mother Boy Scouts Am., Columbia, 1957-62. Mem. Nat. League for Nursing (agy. council mem. 1977-81), S.C. Nurses Assn., Richland County Nurses Assn., Am. Vocat. Edn. Assn., S.C. Vocat. Assn., S.C. Tech. Edn. Assn., Am. Heart Assn., S.C. Heart Assn., Sigma Theta Tau. Baptist. Home: 1706 Hollywood Dr Columbia SC 29205 Office: PO Box 2408 Columbia SC 29201

SMITH, NIKKI LEE, computer applications mgr.; b. Lansing, Mich., June 18, 1951; d. William Frederick and Thelma Margaret (Spencer) Knapp; ed. Coll. Mainland, 1980—; children—Michelle Lee Hooter, Brian Edward Hooter, Melinda Lee Smith. Programmer trainee Am. Nat. Ins. Co., Galveston, Tex., 1972-74; data analyst U.S. Auto Assn., San Antonio, 1974; with Am. Indemnity Group, Galveston, 1978—, computer applications mgr., 1981—; cons. Rollerland Skating Center, Texas City. Mem. Christian Ch. (Disciples of Christ). Home: 2815 22d Ave N Texas City TX 77590 Office: 2115 Winnie St Galveston TX 77553

SMITH, OLIVE IRENE PERRY, realty co. exec.; b. nr. Shelbyville, Ill., Dec. 13; d. Joseph Luther and Pearl (Bushart) Perry; grad. Sparks Coll., 1928; student Milligan U., 1929, Northwestern U., 1934-36, UCLA, 1959-60; m. William Smith, May 11, 1942. Hosp. librarian, registrar Chgo. State Hosp., Cook County, 1929-40; dep. assessor San Diego County, Calif., 1951-52; real estate broker O.I. Smith, Hemet, Calif., 1953—; real estate investment and loan counselor. Local rep. Nat. Inst. Real Estate Bds. Active Southland Water Com., 1960-68. Mem. adv. bd. San Jacinto (Calif.) Jr. Coll., 1967-68. Mem. Nat. Inst. Real Estate Brokers, Nat. Traders, Comml., and Investment Brokers Div. (pres. 1961), Hemet-San Jacinto Bd. Realtors (sec. 1960), Calif. Real Estate Assn. (regional v.p. 1964-65), Riverside Art Assn. Republican. Club: Soroptimist (San Jacinto-Hemet, Calif.). Home: 10381 N Lynn Circle PO Box 76 Mira Loma CA 91752 Office: PO Box 331 Hemet CA 92343

SMITH, PAMELA JOAN, govt. ofcl.; b. Newark, Sept. 27, 1952; d. William B. and Ida M. Smith; B.A., Rutgers U., 1974; M.P.A., N.Y. U., 1977; aslo spl. courses; 1 dau., Tiffany. Public service employment specialist Union County Dept. Employment and Tng., Elizabeth, N.J., 1975-76, planner, 1976-77; local coordinator Neighborhood Reinvestment Corp., Washington, 1977-78, asst. field rep., 1978-79, field rep., 1978-80; spl. asst. Office of Under Sec., HUD, Washington, 1980-81, spl. asst. to regional adminstr., 1981—. Chair, Neighborhood Block Assn., Irvington, N.J. Recipient cert. of merit HUD, 1981; Nat. Urban fellow, 1980. Mem. Am. Soc. Public Adminstrn., Am. Soc. Profl. and Exec. Women. Home: 890 De Belle Ct Clarkston GA 30021 Office: 75 Spring St Atlanta GA 30303

SMITH, PATRICIA ALICE, clin. psychologist; b. N.Y.C., Mar. 17, 1949; d. Gregory Arnold and Jeanne G. (Arsenault) S.; student SUNY, Plattsburgh, 1967-69; B.A., SUNY, Brockport, 1971; M.A., Xavier U., 1975; Ph.D. (teaching fellow), U. Detroit, 1980. Clin. psychology intern Ohio Dept. Mental Health and Mental Retardation, Longview State Hosp., Cin., 1973-74, psychol. asst. dir. token economy program female adolescents and young adult women, 1974-76; clin. psychology intern Ingham Community Mental Health Center and Ingham Med. Center, Lansing, Mich., 1979-80; clin. psychologist psychiat. services Lynn Hosp., Lincoln Park, Mich., 1980-81; pvt. practice clin. psychology, Dearborn, Mich., 1980-82; cons. psychologist Raleigh Hills Alcohol Treatment Hosp., Salt Lake City, 1982—; pvt. practice clin. psychology, Salt Lake City, 1982—; cons. Forensic Psychology Inst., 1979, Macomb Counseling Clinic, Warren, Mich., 1978, Tri-County Mental Health Services, Southfield, Mich., 1978, Therapeutic Day Clinic, Inkster, Mich., 1977; instr. Wayne County Community Coll., 1977-79, So. Ohio Community Coll., Cin., 1976, Sinclair Community Coll., Dayton, Ohio, 1975-76. Mem. Community Task Force Project on Child Sexual Abuse Treatment, 1980. Mem. Am. Psychol. Assn., Mich. Psychol. Assn. (cert. acad. credit 1977), Midwestern Psychol. Assn., Assn. women in Psychology, Psi Chi. Democrat. Roman Catholic. Contbr. articles to profl. jours. Home: 5193 Cobble Creek Rd Apt 5A Salt Lake City UT 84117 Office: 1580 East 3900 South Suite 102 Salt Lake City UT 84117

SMITH, PATRICIA LILIAN, librarian; b. Otley, Yorkshire, Eng., Oct. 10, 1931; d. Frank Arthur and Ida Jane (Eagles) S.; A.L.A., Leeds Sch. Librarianship, Yorkshire, 1951-52; B.A. in Gen. Arts, U. Toronto, 1959. Jr. asst. Ipswich public libraries, Suffolk, Eng., 1949-50; gen. asst. West Riding County Library, 1950-51; sr. asst. South Yorkshire regional libraries, 1952-55; intern gen. librarian Toronto Public Libraries, 55-57; br. librarian B.C. Public Library Commn., East Kootenay, B.C., 1959-65; dir. N.W.T. Public Library Services, 1965—. Mem. Library Assn. U.K., Can. Library Assn. Contbr. articles to profl. jours. Address: PO Box 1100 Hay River NT X0E 0R0 Canada

SMITH, PATRICIA SPAFFORD, state legislator; b. Shell Lake, Wis., Aug. 17, 1925; student Superior State Tchrs. Coll.; B.B.A., U. Minn., 1946; postgrad. U. Wis., Eau Claire and Barron County Campus; 6 children. Mem. Wis. Assembly, 1978—. Bd. dirs. Wis. Citizens Concerned for Life, Wis. Sch. Bus Assn.; sec. Barron County Sports Center; dir. Barron County Health Forum; active Boy Scouts Am., Girl Scouts U.S.A.; sec. Barron County Democratic Party; leader Barron County Adult 4-H Leaders Assn.; mem. Wis. Assn. Women Highway Safety Leaders. Office: Room 6 West State Capitol Madison WI 53702 *

SMITH, RAMONA LOUISE, word processing service co. exec.; b. Dayton, Ohio, Oct. 11, 1954; d. Frank Ray and Patricia (Mattingly) S.; B.S., U. Mo., Columbia, 1976. Sales rep. St. Louis Mktg. Surveys, 1976-77; retail salesman Sears Roebuck & Co., Chesterfield, Mo., 1977-78; word processing composition specialist Harris Data Communication, Dallas, 1978-79; v.p. W.P. Services, Plano, Tex., 1979-81; pres., owner, Words Plus, Dallas, 1981—. Mem. state bd. Women's Polit. Caucus, 1975-76; Mo. chmn. 18-year-old voter registration drive, Parkway West High, 1972. Mem. Nat. Assn. Female Execs., Network Career Women, Sales and Mktg. Execs. Dallas (Rookie Mem. of Yr. 1981, bd. dirs. 1982—). Club: Toastmasters (sec. 1981, treas. 1982) (Dallas). Home: 13352 Maham Rd Apt 183 Dallas TX 75240

SMITH, REBECCA MCCULLOCH, educator; b. Greensboro, N.C., Feb. 29, 1928; d. David Martin and Virginia Pearl (Woodburn) McCulloch; B.S., Woman's Coll., U. N.C., 1947, M.S., 1952; Ph.D., U. N.C., Greensboro, 1967; m. George Clarence Smith, Jr., Mar. 30, 1945; 1 son, John Randolph. Tchr. public schs., N.C. and S.C., 1947-57; instr. U. N.C., Greensboro, 1958-66, asst. prof. child devel. and family relations, 1967-72, asso. prof., 1973-78, prof., 1979—, dir. grad. program, 1975—; ednl. cons. depts. edn. N.C., S.C., Ont.; vis. prof. N.W. La. State U., 1965, 67, U. Wash., 1970, Hood Coll., 1976. Recipient Teaching Excellence award U. N.C., Greensboro, 1972, named Outstanding Alumna Sch. Home Econs., 1976; recipient Sperry award for service to families N.C. Family Life Council, 1979. Mem. Am. Home Econs. Assn., Nat. Council Family Relations (exec. com. 1974-76, Osborne award 1973), Soc. Psychol. Study of Social Issues, Omicron Nu. Author: Teaching About Family Relationships, 1975; Klemer's Marriage and Family Relationships, 2d edit., 1975; Resources for Teaching About Family Life Education, 1976; Family Matters: Concepts in Marriage and Personal Relationships, 1982; asso. editor Family Relations (Jour. Applied Family and Child Studies), 1980—; ednl. cons. Current Life Studies, 1977—. Home: 1212 E Ritters Lake Rd Greensboro NC 27406 Office: Dept Child Devel and Family Relations Sch Home Economics U NC Greensboro NC 27412

SMITH, ROBBIE, oil co. ofcl.; b. Monroe, La., June 3, 1948; B.S. in English and Journalism, Roosevelt U., Chgo., 1977. With Standard Oil Co. (Ind.), Chgo., 1967—, urban affairs rep., 1977-80, coordinator urban affairs, 1980—. Chmn. Chgo. City Wide Coll. Adv. Council, 1979—; exec. v.p. Chgo. Urban Affairs Council, 1978, now mem.; mem. task force tng. and employment Neighborhood Inst., 1978-80; bus. adv. council Westside Cluster High Schs., 1978—; mem. adv. bd. United Career Action Now, 1979-82; mem. minority profl. services com. Chgo. United; bd. dirs. Chgo. Old Town Boys Club, 1978-81, vice chmn., 1980-82. Recipient various recognition awards. Mem. League Black Women, Cosmopolitan C. of C. (1st v.p. 1980-82), Nat. Assn. Female Execs., Nat. Assn. Media Women, Assn. Blacks in Energy, Westside Assn. Community Action. Club: Chgo. City. Office: 200 E Randolph Dr Room MC 4308 Chicago IL 60601

SMITH, ROSALYN KAY, mfg. co. exec.; b. Louisville, June 21, 1950; d. Charles Edward and Katherine Estelle (Taylor) S.; M.S.W., U. Louisville, 1981. Mgr. corp. recruiting Lincoln Nat. Life, 1976-78; sr. partner Smith Hires Assos., Wilmington, Del., 1978-80; personnel cons. Control Data Corp., Phila., 1980-81; affirmative action cons. Digital, Maynard, Mass., 1981, mgr. human resources, 1981—; lectr. Mem. Black Exec. Exchange Program, Nat. Assn. Female Execs., Am. Mgmt. Assn., Alpha Kappa Alpha. Democrat. Episcopalian. Office: 14 Walkup Dr Westboro MA 01581

SMITH, ROSE MARIE, writer, photographer; b. Fayette County, Ala., Aug. 18, 1941; d. Horace Everett and Mary Thelma (Bryan) Gardner; student U. Ala., 1959-60; m. Charles Elden Smith, June 12, 1960; children—Roselyn Elizabeth, Charles Elden. Mem. Vernon (Ala.) City Council, 1976—; area newspaper corr. Comml. Dispatch, Columbus, Miss., 1978—; free-lance photographer, Vernon, 1979—. Trustee, Lamar County High Sch., 1971-79; youth leader First United Methodist Ch., Vernon, 1965-79; mem. Vernon Water Works and Sewer Bd., 1976—; tchr. Sunday sch. First United Meth. Ch., Vernon, 1962-80, chmn. communications, 1977—. Democrat. Clubs: Vernon Study, Lamar County High Sch. Band Boosters, Athletic Boosters. Contbr. photos and articles to newspapers. Address: 405 2nd Ave SW Vernon AL 35592

SMITH, RUTH MARION HALL, editor, publisher; b. Chgo., May 31, 1918; d. Albert Neely and Bertha Esther (Cassidy) Hall; student U. Ill., 1937-40, Northwestern U., 1947; m. Robert James Smith, Feb. 8, 1942; children—Gregory Hall, Gerald Edward, Marilyn Emily Smith Lovett, Brian Woodley. Editor, Craft Cos., St. Charles, Ill., 1959—; partner Craft Patterns Co.; sec.-treas. Craft Products Corp.; co-owner Craft Clocks & Gifts, Craft Products Miniatures, Elmhurst, Ill. Sec., Elmhurst Safety Council, 1965-66; active local Camp Fire Girls, Cub Scouts. Mem. Women in Communications, Chgo. Hort. Soc., Am. Rose Soc., Audubon Soc., Ill. Beekeepers Assn., Nat. Assn. Watch and Clock Collectors, Chgo. Press, Alpha Xi Delta. Republican. Methodist. Club: Pottawatomie Garden. Author: Home Handicrafts for Girls, 1942. Home: 6N091 Denker Rd St Charles IL 60174 Office: 2200 Dean St St Charles IL 60174 also Route 83 and North Ave Elmhurst IL

SMITH, SANDRA BATES, mgmt. co. exec.; b. Douglas, Ga., May 16, 1950; d. Jimmy and Jeanette B. Wheeler; B.A., Manhattanville Coll., 1972; postgrad. Tex. So. U. Sch. Law, 1972-74; M.A., Calif. State Coll., Hayward, 1977, Market research asst. Judson B. Branch Research Co., Menlo Park, Calif., 1973-74; project dir. for edn. and tng. Golden State Bus. League, Oakland, Calif., 1974-78; dir. employment and tng. City of Oakland, 1978-81; pres., chief exec. officer S.B.S. Assocs., Inc., Oakland, 1981—; sr. v.p. Pacific Cal Airlines; pres., dir. Builders Mut. Surety Co., 1979—. Chmn., Charities Commn., Oakland, 1975-76; mem. exec. com. Manpower Adv. Bd., Oakland, 1976-78. Recipient Jurisprudence award Bancorft Whitney, 1972, Outstanding Community Work award N.G., 1980; named Woman of Yr., Allen Temple Baptist Ch., 1979, Outstanding Young Woman Am., U.S. Jaycees, 1980; subject of resolution/commendation Oakland City Council, 1981. Mem. Nat. Assn. Female Execs., NAACP, Am. Mgmt. Assn., U.S. Conf. Mayors, Nat. Bus. League, Nat. Assn. Minority Contractors, Black Women Organized for Polit. Action, U.S. Black C. of C., No. U.S. Black Chamber, Alpha Kappa Alpha. Home: 8160 Hansom Dr Oakland CA 94605 Office: 364 14th St Oakland CA 94612

SMITH, SANDRA RUTH, U.S. fgn. service officer; b. St. Louis, Sept. 14, 1947; d. John Henry and Ruth Kathryn Louise (Ehlen) S.; B.A., Valparaiso U., 1970; postgrad. U. Mo., St. Louis, summer 1971; M.S.W. (Mo. Div. Family Services Ednl. Leave grantee), Washington U., St. Louis, 1975; postgrad. Fgn. Service Inst., 1979-80, 82. Dir. youth ministry Evergreen Park (Ill.) Luth. Ch., 1968-69; child welfare worker Mo. Div. Family Services, St. Louis, 1972-75, social service supr., 1975-76, staff devel. specialist, 1976-79; commd. fgn. service officer Dept. State, 1979; 2d sec., vice-consul Am. embassy, Mexico City, 1980-82, 2d sec., vice consul Am. embassy, Lomé, Togo, 1982—. Bd. advs. Univ. City Sch. for Continuing Edn., 1977-79. Mem. Am. Fgn. Service Assn., Nat. Acad. Cert. Social Workers, NOW, Amnesty Internat., Common Cause, ACLU. Home: 128 Central Ave Webster Groves MO 63119 Office: Am Embassy Lomé Togo Dept State Washington DC 20520

SMITH, SARA ELIZABETH WORSLEY, freight co. exec.; b. Youngstown, Ohio, Sept. 17, 1938; d. Wilfred W. and Mildred Worsley; Asso. in Bus. Adminstrn., Kent State U., 1974; m. Thomas Smith, July 8, 1961; children—Thomas Elizabeth, Dale. Acctg. sr. clk. Jones & Laughlin Steel Co., Youngstown, Ohio, 1958-67; corp. sec. Smith Bros. Trucking Co., Girard, Ohio, 1965—; secretarial positions Packard Electric div. Gen. Motors Corp., Warren, Ohio, 1976—. Clairol Nat. scholar, 1975; Kent State U. grantee, 1975. Mem. Dayton Women Working, Nat. Action Forum for Older Women, Nat. Assn. Female Execs., Alpha Gamma Delta (life). Club: Girard Garden (sec.-treas. 1970-74). Home: 1636 Squaw Creek Dr Girard OH 44420 Office: PO Box 431 Warren OH 44486

SMITH, SARA ELLEN, learning cons.; b. Haverhill, Mass., Sept. 26, 1939; d. John D. and Ruth Rosalind (Gould) Shinberg; student Vassar Coll., 1957-58; A.A., Bradford Coll., 1959; B.S., Boston U., 1960; M.A., Montclair State Coll., 1971; m. Fredric Marshall Smith, Apr. 3, 1960; children—Deborah Sue, Faith Joy. Substitute tchr., Chgo., 1962-65, Livingston, N.J., 1966-67; instr. reading Montclair State Coll., 1970-71; learning disabilities tchr., cons. public schs., Parsippany-Troy Hills, N.J., 1972-73; learning cons. Verona (N.J.) Bd. Edn., 1973—. Mem. adult youth adv. bd., worship com. Congregation B'nai Jeshurun. Mem. Verona Ednl. Assn., N.J. Edn. Assn., NEA, Orton Soc. (dir. N.J.), Nat. Assn. Children with Learning Disabilities, N.J. Assn. Learning Cons., Nat. Council Jewish Women (life), Hadassah (life). Author: (with N. Miele) Help!! A Handbook to Enhance Learning Potential, 1974; Keys: Keys to Educating Your Students, 1979. Contbr. articles to profl. jours. Home: 3 Tabor Ct Livingston NJ 07039 Office: Dept Spl Services 118 Forest Ave Verona NJ 07044

SMITH, SARAH JANE (SALLY), state legislator; b. Pekin, Ill., Jan. 23, 1945; d. Claude P. and Jane (Prettyman) S.; B.S. in Music Edn., U. Ill.; postgrad. U. Alaska. Tchr. jr. high sch. Los Angeles City Schs., 1968-69; adminstrv. asst. Office of Gov. of Alaska, 1971-74; project field rep Alaska Dept. Community and Regional Affairs, 1974-76; expeditor H.W. Blackstock, Inc., 1979-82; mem. Alaska Ho. of Reps. from 20th Dist., 1977—, majority whip, 1977-79, chmn. rules chmn., 1981. Dir. choir Juneau Meth. Ch., Fairbanks Presbyn. Ch., 1972-75; historian Fairbanks Drama Assn., 1974-76; adv. bd. Assn. Children with Learning Disabilities, 1978-80. Named Outstanding Freshman Legislator, 1976. Mem. Fairbanks Assn. Arts. Democrat. Club: PEO. Office: Pouch V Junau AK 99811

SMITH, SELMA MOLDEL, lawyer, composer; b. Warren, Ohio, Apr. 3, 1919; d. Louis and Mary (Oyer) Moldel; student Los Angeles City Coll., 1936-37, U. Calif., 1937-39, U. So. Calif., 1939-41; J.D., Pacific Coast U., 1942; 1 son, Mark Lee. Admitted to Calif. bar, 1943, U.S. Dist. Ct. bar, 1943, U.S. Supreme Ct. bar, 1958; gen. practice law; mem. firm Moldel, Moldel, Moldel & Smith. Field dir. civilian adv. com. WAC, 1943; mem. nat. bd. Med. Coll. Pa. (formerly Woman's Med. Coll. Pa.), 1953—, exec. bd., 1976-80, pres.-elect, 1980, pres., 19 . Decorated La Order del Merito Juan Pablo Duerta (Dominican Republic). Mem. Am. Bar Assn., Calif. Bar Assn. (servicemen's legal com.), Los Angeles Bar Assn. (psychopathic ct. com.), Los Angeles Lawyers Club (public defenders com.), Nat. Assn. Women Lawyers (chmn. com. unauthorized practice of law, social commn. UN, regional dir. western states, Hawaii 1949-50, mem. jud. adminstrn. com. 1960, nat. chmn. world peace through law com. 1966-67), League of Ams. (dir.), Inter-Am. Bar Assn., So. Calif. Women Lawyers Assn. (pres. 1947, 48), Women Lawyers Assn. (chmn. Law Day com. 1966), State Bar Conf. Com., Council Bar Assns. Los Angeles County (charter sec. 1950), Calif. Bus. Women's Council (dir. 1951), Los Angeles Bus. Women's Council (pres. 1952), Calif. Pres.'s Council (1st v.p.), Nat. Assn. for Composers U.S. (dir. 1974-79, ann. luncheon chmn. 1975), Nat. Fedn. Music Clubs (nat. vice chmn. for Western region 1973-78), Calif. Fedn. Music Clubs (state chmn. Am. music 1971-75, state conv. chmn. 1972), Docents of Los Angeles Philharmonic (v.p. 1973—, chmn. Latin Am. community relations 1972-75, press and public relations 1972-75, cons. coordinator 1973-75), Euterpe Opera Club (v.p. 1974-75, chmn. auditions 1972, chmn. awards 1973-75), Iota Tau Tau (dean Los Angeles, supreme treas.). Composer: Espressivo Four Piano Pieces. Home: 5272 Lindley Ave Encino CA 91316

SMITH, SHERRY ANN, govt. ofcl.; b. Washington, Apr. 26, 1937; d. Joseph Willard and Mildred Kathleen (Newton) Bradley; B.S., George Washington U., 1974; Pub. Affairs fellow, Princeton U., 1974-75. Adminstrv. asst. Parkins, Rogers & Assos., Detroit, 1960-61; personnel specialist AID, Dept. of State, 1961-66, recruitment specialist, 1965-66, chief East Asia personnel br., 1966-68; chief grantee personnel mgmt. OEO, 1968-73; chief personnel mgmt. Group II, NASA, 1973-74, asst. exec. officer, 1975-76, dir. adminstrn. and mgmt. support Dryden Flight Research Center, mgr. resident office, Pasadena, Calif., 1979-80, dep. assoc. adminstr. for mgmt., Washington, 1980—; cluster leader presdl. mgmt. interns, 1980-82. Served with USAF, 1957-60. Office: NASA Headquarters Washington DC 20546

SMITH, SHIRLEY ANN O'BRYAN, broadcasting exec.; b. Louisville, July 28, 1949; d. Bernard Burch and Shirley Hull (Hardesty) O'Bryan; B.A. in Journalism, English and Speech, Murray (Ky.) State U., 1971; m. Larry James Smith, Aug. 23, 1969. Writer, reporter, copy editor Enterprise Newspaper, Lexington Park, Md., 1969-70; writer Sta. WKCT, Bowling Green, Ky., 1971-74; announcer, writer Sta. WLBJ, Bowling Green, 1974; announcer, public service dir. Sta. WHEL, New Albany, Ind., 1974-75; assignment editor, newscaster, reporter, writer Sta. WKLO, Louisville, 1974-77; news dir., program dir. Sta. WNUU, Louisville, 1977-78; news dir. Ky. Network, Louisville, 1978-82; pres. Ky. UPI Internat. Adv. Bd., 1981-82; nat. correspondent, anchorperson Mut. Broadcasting System, Washington, 1982—; speaker, tchr. in field. Recipient Louie award public affairs programming, 1979, UPI Broadcast awards, 1981; named Ky. col., 1979. Mem. Nat. Assn. Female Execs., Women in Radio and TV, Radio TV News Dirs. Assn., Nat. Assn. State Radio Network News Dirs., Murray State U. Alumni Assn., Sigma Delta Chi. Roman Catholic. Author articles, features in mags. Home: 125 S Reynolds St Apt J-206 Alexandria VA 22304 Office: Mut Broadcasting System 1755 S Jefferson Davis Hwy Arlington VA 22202

SMITH, SUELLEN FANDT, communications co. ofcl.; b. Newton, N.J., June 9, 1943; d. Edward Lloyd and Mary (Boitano) Fandt; B.Mus., Westminster Coll., New Wilmington, Pa., 1965; postgrad. Trenton (N.J.) State Coll., Pace U.; m. Gary Thomas Smith, Aug. 3, 1968. Tchr. elem. sch. music and reading, N.J., 1965-81; with E-Systems Co., Tampa, Fla., 1981; ops. staff mem. Dart Center, GTE Co., Tampa, 1981—; cons. in field. Recipient John Phillip Sousa award, 1961. Mem. NEA, Music Educators Nat. Conf., N.J. Edn. Assn., Mu Phi Epsilon. Author curriculum materials. Home: 17836 Morninghigh Dr Lutz FL 33549 Office: GTE PO Box 110 Tampa FL 33601

SMITH, SUSAN CARAS, TV producer; b. Washington, Sept. 22, 1948; d. Gus S. and Rena Caras; B.A., Ind. U., 1970; M.A., Am. U., 1971; m. Sterling T. W. Smith, Oct. 11, 1975. Formerly producer, hostess talent, news co-anchor, feature news editor Sta. WGHP-TV, High Point-Greensboro-Winston-Salem, N.C.; dir. on-air promotion Sta. WDCA-TV, Washington, 1973-75; dir. broadcast prodn. Ehrlich-Manes & Assos. Advt., Washington, 1975-77; now pres. CaraSmith, Inc., Rockville, Md. Mem. Com. Arts and the Handicapped, Model Secondary Sch. for Deaf, Rockville City Dept. Recreation; com. chmn. Ind. U. Found., 1969-70; trustee Leukemia Soc. Am., Washington, 1973-75; mem. telethon com. Easter Seal Soc., Soc. Crippled Children, telethon asst. dir., 1979—. Recipient Golden Eagle award; Electra High Honors, Birmingham Internat. Film Festival; Spl. award Easter Seal Soc.; HEW grantee. Mem. Nat. Assn. Female Execs., Nat. Acad. TV Arts and Scis., Nat. Bd. Realtors, Montgomery County Bd. Realtors, Kappa Delta. Clubs: Amateur Radio Relay League, Radio Amateur Civil Emergency Service, Montgomery County Amateur Radio, Job's Daus. Author, producer Singing Signs, workbook and video tape to teach music and song to deaf teenagers, 1979; composer: Sing a Sign, 1978. Office: 330 Broadwood Dr Rockville MD 20851

SMITH, SUSAN JOYCE, educator; b. Phila., Aug. 27, 1950; d. William and Joyce Laura (Moyer) Kodad; B.S. cum laude, Lock Haven State U., 1972; M.S., Bloomsburg State Coll., 1974; postgrad. U. S.C., 1983—; m. Jeffrey W. Smith, Aug. 5, 1972; children—Jeffrey W. II, Siri Suzanne. Tchr. severly retarded Central Susquehanna Area Intermediate Unit, Lewisburg, Pa., 1972-74; tchr. of trainable retarded Capital Area Intermediate Unit, Harrisburg, Pa., 1974-78, instructional adv. of the trainable program, 1978-79; ednl. evaluator, coordinator tutoring program Winthrop Coll., Rock Hill, S.C., 1979, asst. prof. spl. edn., 1979—. Mem. AAUW, Council Exceptional Children. Democrat. Roman Catholic. Home: 3811 High Ridge Rd Matthews NC 28105 Office: Winthrop College Withers Bldg Rock Hill SC 29733

SMITH, SUSAN SCHUYLER, interior designer, space planner; b. Newburgh, N.Y., Mar. 28, 1945; d. Robert Warren and Edith May (Thomas) S.; student Wheaton Coll., Norton, Mass., 1963-64; B. Design with honors, U. Fla., 1970. Interior designer Hasco, West Palm Beach, Fla., 1970-72, Robert Shaw & Assos., Palm Beach, Fla., 1972-74; partner Interior Assos., West Palm Beach and Chgo., 1974-76, Michalaros & Smith, Palm Beach and Chgo., 1976-78; pres., owner Spectrum, Interior Design, West Palm Beach, 1978—; mem. interior design adv. com. Palm Beach Jr. Coll., 1976—. Mem. West Palm Beach Downtown Devel. Authority, 1981—, sec.-treas., 1981-83; bd. dirs. West Palm Beach Downtown Assn., 1980—, pres., 1981—; bd. dirs. Palm Beach County Jr. Achievement, 1981—; bd. dirs. Big Bros./Big Sisters of Palm Beach County, 1979—, pres. 1980-81, nat. bd. dirs. 1982—; bd. dirs. United Way Palm Beach County, 1982—. Mem. Am. Soc. Interior Designers, Inst. Bus. Design, AIA (affiliate), West Palm Beach C. of C. (dir. 1981—, v.p. 1981-83). Palm Beach C. of C. Presbyterian. Home: 3701 S Flagler Dr West Palm Beach FL 33401 Office: 501 S Flagler Dr Suite 507 West Palm Beach FL 33401

SMITH, SUSIE IRENE, histotechnologist; b. Columbus, Ohio, Oct. 10, 1942; d. Taft and Evelyn (Samuels) Woodford; student Boston State Coll., 1975-80; m. Eugene Smith, Dec. 2, 1960; children—Regina Marie, Kimberly Denise, Teresa Yvette, Stacia Ann. Med. worker Boston City Hosp., 1970; lab. asst. Boston City Hosp., 1970-75, lab. technician hematopathology lab. Mallory Inst. Pathology, 1975-80, chief med. technologist, 1982—; lectr. and cons. in field. Sec., Com. to Elect Jesse L. Corbin for State Rep., 1981—. Mem. Am. Soc. Clin. Pathologists. Roman Catholic. Office: 784 Massachusetts Ave Boston MA 02118

SMITH, SYLVIA MAE, med. technologist; b. San Bernardino, Calif., Sept. 25, 1947; d. Jesse Clifford and Ieleen Mae (Basham) Stone; B.A., Calif. State Coll., San Bernardino, 1969; cert. med. technician VA Hosp. Sch. Med. Tech., Long Beach, Calif., 1970; m. Peter J. Smith, Feb. 14, 1970. Staff med. technologist, instr. chemistry VA Hosp., Long Beach, 1970-71; supr. automated chemistry and serology, instr. chemistry, immunology, serology, urinalysis Community Hosp., San Bernardino, 1971-75; chief technologist Clin. Lab. of San Bernardino, 1975-76, Calif. Med. Surg. Service, Apple Valley, Calif., 1976; staff med. technologist St. Mary's Desert Valley Hosp., Apple Valley, Calif., 1982—. Mem. Calif. Assn. Med. Lab. Technologists, Am. Soc. Clin. Pathologists. Republican. Methodist. Address: 1290 W 24th St San Bernardino CA 92405

SMITH, VANITA RAE, producer, dir.; b. Lebanon, Mo., Feb. 1, 1944; d. Ray and Esther Asilee (Chastain) S.; B.A., Anderson (Ind.) Coll., 1967. Civilian asst. post entertainment dir. Ft. Leonard Wood, Mo., 1967-69, dinner theatre dir., 1972-75; asst. command entertain dir. U.S. Army, Hawaii, 1969-72; chief army music and theatre, Ft. Knox, Ky., 1975-79; freelance producer, dir., 1979—. Recipient 4 commendations Dept. Army, 3 comdr.'s certs. Ft. Knox, 1 spl. award Air Force, Hawaii. Mem. Am. Theatre Assn., Southeastern Theatre Conf., Army Theatre Arts Assn. (4 spl. awards), Ky. Theatre Assn. Mem. Ch. of God. Address: 94-1039 Upai Pl Waipahu HI 96797

SMITH, VERA GAY, educator; b. Bessemer, Ala., Aug. 9, 1932; d. Floyd G. and Angilee (Streeter) Hearns; B.S. (scholar), Miles Coll., 1952; M.Ed., Bridgewater State Coll., 1967; m. Louis A. Smith, Jr., June 4, 1955; children—Angela, Yolanda, Valencia. Tchr., Choctaw County Tng. Sch., Lisman, Ala., 1952-53, Peoria (Arix.) Child Care Center, 1965-67, Pipe Shop Jr. High Sch., Bessemer, Ala., 1953-56, Dysart High Sch., Peoria, Ariz., 1967-71, Edward C. Stone Elem. Sch., Bourne, Mass., 1962-65, Mesa (Ariz.) High Sch./Kino Jr. Sch., 1971-76; faculty Harris Jr. Coll., Meridian, Miss., 1961-62; tchr./coordinator Westwood High Sch., Mesa, 1971—; dir. Mary Kay Cons., Phoenix, 1982—; mem. Ariz. adv. bd. J.C. Penney's, 1973-75. Founder, pres. Afro-Am. Assn. Concerned People, 1981—. Mem. Am. Vocat. Assn., NEA, Ariz. End. Assn., Mesa Edn. Assn., Home Econs. Educators, Ariz. Assn. Vocat. Educators, Sigma Gamma Rho. Democrat. Baptist. Club: Elks Home: 5401 W Thomas Rd Phoenix AZ 85031 Office: 945 W 8 St Mesa AZ 85201

SMITH, VERNA GREEN, corp. editor; b. Oklee, Minn., Aug. 23, 1919; d. Roy Alva and Sarah Mathilda (Lindberg) Green; B.A. in Journalism (scholar), U. Mont., 1940; M.A. in Edn. Washington U., St. Louis, 1961; Ph.D. in Edn., St. Louis U., 1970; m. Alfred Nelson Smith, II, July 8, 1942 (dec.); children—Philip Roger, Alfred Nelson III, Stuart Thomas. Advt. mgr., columnist Glasgow (Mont.) Courier, 1940-41; reporter Gt. Falls (Mont.) Tribune, 1941-42; editor staff communication U.S. C.E., Ft. Peck, Mont., 1942; news editor Community News of Overland (Mo.), 1953-56; dir. public relations, tchr. English, Ritenour Sch. Dist., St. Louis County, Mo., 1956-66, adv. com. vocat. edn., 1979-80; tchr. sch. public relations St. Louis U., 1976; dir. communication services, editor CEMREL Reports, CEMREL, Inc., St. Louis, 1966—. Pres. PTA, 1953-54; adminstrv. bd. Stephan Meml. Meth. Ch.; bd. dirs. The Learning Center, 1978—. NDEA fellow St. Louis U., 1965; recipient ann. awards for publs. Mo. Press Women, 1967-80; 1st prize award(2), Nat. Fedn. Press Women, 1969, 2d prize, 1970; Disting. Alumnus award U. Mont. Alumni Assn., 1982. Mem. Nat. Sch. Public Relations Assn. (pres., founder Greater St. Louis chpt. 1965-66, citation of appreciation, 1973), Conf. Edn. St. Louis (charter), Met. St. Louis Press Club, Nat. Fedn. Press Women, Mo. Press Women, Ednl. Press Assn. Am., Ednl. Writers Assn., Women in Communications (pres. St. Louis chpt. 1956-57), Council Ednl. Devel. and Research (exec. com. communications group 1969-73, chmn. 1981-82), Hist. Soc. Mont., U. Mont. Alumni Assn. (life), Mortar Bd., Kappa Delta Pi, Delta Kappa Gamma, Pi Lambda Theta. Alpha Chi Omega, Contbr. articles profl. jours. Home: 10311 Pineview Ct Saint Louis MO 63114 Office: 3120 59th St Saint Louis MO 63139

SMITH, VIRGINIA, Congresswoman; b. Randolph, Iowa; B.A., U. Nebr. Mem. Nebr. State Normal Bd., 1950-60; nat. chmn. Am. Farm Bur. Women, 1955-74; dep. pres. Asso. Country Women of World, 1962-68; mem. Gov.'s Commn. on Status of Women, 1964-68; mem. Presdl. Task Force on Rural Devel., 1971-72; mem. 94th-97th Congresses from 3d Nebr. Dist., 1975—; mem. Appropriations Com., Com. on Coms. Home: Chappell NE 69129 Office: Room 2002 Rayburn House Office Bldg Washington DC 20515

SMITH, VIRGINIA BEATRICE, coll. pres., lawyer, economist; b. Seattle, June 24, 1923; d. Frank B. and Myrtle M. (Partridge) S.; B.A., U. Wash., 1944, J.D., 1946, M.A. in Labor and Econs., 1950; postgrad. in Econs. and Law, Columbia U., 1947; D.H.L. (hon.), R.I. Coll., 1978; L.H.D. (hon.), Hood Coll., 1977, Alverno Coll., DePaul U., 1982; LL.D., Ottawa U., 1974. Admitted to Wash. bar, 1947, Calif. bar, 1958; price economist Seattle dist. OPA, 1944-46; instr. econs. and bus. Coll. Puget Sound, Tacoma, 1947-48; instr. Seattle Pacific Coll., 1949-50, asst.

prof., chmn. dept. econs. and bus., 1950-51, asso. prof., acting registrar and dir. admissions, 1951-52; coordinator public programs Inst. Indsl. Relations, U. Calif., Berkeley, 1952-58, instr. extension, 1952-60, adminstrv. analyst, 1958-60, asst. to v.p., 1962-65, coordinator adminstrv. policy unit, 1963-65, asst. v.p., 1965-67; asst. dir. Carnegie Commn. Higher Edn., Berkeley, 1967-71, asso. dir., 1971-73; dir. Fund for Improvement of Postsecondary Edn., HEW, Washington, 1973-77; pres. Vassar Coll., Poughkeepsie, N.Y., 1977—; asso. law offices Sam Kagel, San Francisco, 1958-67; asso. counsel to trustee Yuba Consol. Industries, San Francisco, 1963-64; commr. Edn. Commn. of States, 1976; mem. faculty Salzburg (Austria) Seminar Am. Studies, summer 1976; mem. Am.-USSR Seminar Higher Edn., 1976, Am.-German Study Group on Access to Higher Edn., 1975; mem. commn. scholars Ill. Bd. Higher Edn., 1975; head U.S. observer del. Bucharest UNESCO Conf. Higher Edn., 1974; mem. U.S. del. OECD Conf. Innovation in Higher Edn., Paris, 1973; trustee Ednl. Testing Service, 1977—, chmn. bd., 1981; dir. Marine Midland Banks, Inc. Mem. Berkeley Personnel Bd., 1968-73, chmn., 1970-73; mem. women's adv. council Calif. Fair Employment Practices Commn., 1964-69; chmn. Calif. State Wage Bd. #4, 1962-66; labor-mgmt. arbitrator, 1960-63; trustee Carnegie Found. Advancement of Teaching; mem. adv. com. women in the services Dept. Def., 1979-81; trustee Culinary Inst. Am., 1980—. Inst. Labor Econs. research fellow U. Wash., 1946; Fulbright fellow, Eng., 1956-57. Mem. Assn. Am. Colls. (dir. 1977—, vice-chairperson 1981, chairperson 1982), Soc. Values in Higher Edn. (pres. 1981—), MLA (adv. bd. commn. on future of the profession 1981—), Am. Assn. Higher Edn., Am. Ednl. Research Assn., Calif. Bar Assn., Am. Council Edn. (nat. commn. higher edn. issues). Author: (with A. R. Bernstein) The Impersonal Campus, 1979; contbg. author: Universal Higher Education: Costs and Benefits, 1972; Recurrent Education, 1973; Education and the State, 1975; others. Address: Vassar College Poughkeepsie NY 12601

SMITH, VIRGINIA DODD, Congresswoman; b. Randolph, Iowa, June 30, 1930; d. Clifton Clark and Erville (Reeves) S.; A.B., U. Nebr., 1936; m. Haven N. Smith, Aug. 27, 1931. Nat. pres. Am. Country Life Assn., 1951-54; nat. chmn. Am. Farm Bur. Women, 1954-74; dir. Am. Farm Bur. Fedn., 1954-74, Country Women's Council; world dep. pres. Associated Country Women of World, 1962-68; mem. nat. home econs. research adv. com. U.S. Dept. Agr., 1960-65; mem. European inspection tour Crusade for Freedom, 1958; del. Republican Nat. Conv., 1956, 72; mem. 94th-97th congresses from 3d Nebr. Dist., mem. appropriations com., agr., energy and water subcoms., ranking mem. minority agr. appropriations com.; mem. Nat. Livestock and Meat Bd., 1955-58, Nat. Commn. Community Health Services, 1963-66, Nebr. Territorial Centennial Commn., 1953, Gov.'s Commn. on Status of Women, 1964-66; chmn. Presdl. Task Force on Rural Devel., 1969-70. Bd. govs. Agrl. Hall of Fame; v.p. Farm Film Found., 1964-74; Goodwill ambassador to Switzerland, 1950. Recipient Merit award DAR, 1956; Disting. Service award U. Nebr., 1956, 60; award Freedom Found., 1966; Eyes on Nebr. award Nebr. Optometric Assn., 1970; Internat. Service award Midwest Conf. World Affairs, 1973; Woman of Achievement award Nebr. Bus. and Profl. Women, 1971; selected as 1 of 6 U.S. women for 3-week goodwill mission to France, 1969; Outstanding 4-H Alumni award Iowa State U., 1973, 74. Mem. AAUW, PEO (past pres.), Delta Kappa Gamma (state hon. mem.), Beta Sigma Phi (internat. hon. mem.), Chi Omega. Methodist. Clubs: Order Eastern Star, Bus. and Profl. Women. Office: 2202 Rayburn House Office Bldg Washington DC 20515

SMITH, VIRGINIA DOROTHY, state legislator; b. Haviland, Kans., June 28, 1912; student pub. schs. Nampa, Idaho; m. Willard L. Smith, 1931; children—Patricia Virginia Smith Brown, Karen Lee Smith Strosehein, Molly Lou Smith, Eugene Spencer. Former Senate hostess Idaho State Senate; mem. Idaho Ho. of Reps., 1977—. Mem., vice chmn. Idaho Republican State Central Com.; now mem. Canyon County Rep. Central Com.; campaign mgr. Canyon County Reps.; Idaho chmn. Women for Nixon, 1978; mem. State Com. to Re-elect the Pres., 1972; past sec. Rep. Booster Club. Recipient plaque State of Idaho; named Mrs. Republican, Canyon County Reps., 1972. Office: Idaho Ho of Reps Boise ID 83720 *

SMITH-BRADY, REBECCA ANN, nursing adminstr.; b. Evansville, Ind., Dec. 31, 1953; d. Vernon Ernest and Barbara Jean (Hinkle) Barnes; B.S. in Nursing, U. Evansville, 1975; M.S. in Nursing, 1977, M.A., 1979; 1 dau., Erin Rebecca. Staff nurse Deaconess Hosp., Evansville, 1975; instr. nursing U. Evansville, 1975-78; asst. dir. edn. Welborn Baptist Hosp., Evansville, 1978-79, asst. dir. nursing, 1979—; guest lectr. U. Evansville Sch. Nursing; appointee Ind. State Bd. Nurses. Mem. Am. Nurses Assn., Ind. Nurses Assn. (sec.), Nat. League Nurses, Ind. Citizens League Nurses, Assn. Operating Room Nurses, Nat. Assn. Quality Assurance Profls., Alpha Tau Delta. Republican. Methodist. Contbr. articles to profl. jours. Home: RR 4 Box 209B Boonville IN 47601 Office: 401 SE 6th St Evansville IN 47713

SMITH COLVIN, CHERYL ANN (CHERYL ANN SMITH), broadcasting co. staff; b. New Kensington, Pa., July 28, 1948; d. Charles Louis and Lois Smith (Garner) Smith; student Kennedy King Jr. Coll., Chgo., 1972, Columbia Coll., Chgo., 1973-75; B.A., Roosevelt U., 1976; m. Leon M. Colvin, June 12, 1976. Reservationist, TWA, Pitts., 1967-68, stewardess, Chgo., 1968-70; reservationist Pan Am., Chgo., 1970-77; stewardess United Airlines, Chgo., 1978; public affairs dir. CBS Radio, Chgo, 1979-80; public affairs dir., talk show host Radio Sta. WBMX, Chgo., 1980; account exec., talk show host WBEE Jazz Radio, Chgo., 1980—; reader on air CRIS Radio, Chgo., 1981; stewardess Midway Airlines, Chgo., 1981; tchr. Columbia Coll. Bd. dirs. Christian Action Ministry, Boys Club Old Town, LaHarry Scholarship Found. Mem. Nat. Assn. Media Women, Operation Push, NAACP, Am. Women in Radio and TV, League Black Women. Home: 400 E 33d St Apt 409 Chicago IL 60616 Office: 35 E Wacker Dr Chicago IL 60602

SMITHER, DIANA MARIE, food co. mgr.; b. Indpls.; d. Edward H. and Laverne G. (Graham) Diegel; B.S., Purdue U., 1969. Dept. mgr. Turnstyle Dept. Stores, 1970-72; sales mgr. asst. Sound Classics, Indpls., 1972-76; territorial sales mgr. Kraft Foods, Columbus, Ohio, 1976-77; mktg. mgr. refrigerated products Borden Foods, Columbus, 1977-81; mktg. mgr. food service potatoes Carnation Co., Los Angeles, 1981-82; mktg. mgr. frozen burritos Butcher Boy Food Products, Riverside, Calif., 1982—. Mem. Am. Home Econs. Assn., Home Economists in Bus., Purdue U. Alumni Assn., Beta Sigma Phi. Home: 23629 Real Ct Valencia CA 91355 Office: PO Box 5647 Riverside CA 92517

SMITHERS, JANE BRAITMAYER, mfg. co. exec.; b. Washington, May 25, 1915; d. Otto Ernest and Kathleen (Ketcham) Braitmayer; B.A., Vassar Coll., 1937; m. William Henry Howell, Aug. 7, 1937 (dec. 1961); children—Kathleen, William David, Marian Braitmayer; m. 2d, John Abram Smithers, June 13, 1964; stepchildren—Margaret Smithers, John A., Eleanor B., James P. Rec. sec. Children's Home, Inc., Poughkeepsie, N.Y., 1942, Dutchess County Planned Parenthood, 1941; corp. sec., dir. Smithers Tools and Machine Products, Inc., Rhinebeck, N.Y., 1965—. Chmn. com. on detention Dutchess County Social Planning Council, 1949; pres. Dutchess County Soc. Mental Health, 1958-59; mem. Dutchess County Youth Bd., 1968-70; founder, pres. No. Dutchess Community Services, 1969; founder, pres. No. Dutchess Day Care Center, Inc., 1971-73, now mem. adv. bd. Republican. Episcopalian. Clubs: Sippican Tennis, Beverly Yacht (Marion, Mass.); Jr. League, Vassar (Poughkeepsie); Windermere Island (Bahamas). Home: RD 2 Box 151 Red Hook NY 12571

SMITHGALL, ELIZABETH, educator; b. Lancaster, Pa.; d. James B. and Edith (Mowrer) Smithgall; B.S., Columbia U., 1929, M.A., 1934; postgrad. summers U. Calif. at Berkeley, 1939, N.Y. U., 1940, Temple U., 1954, U. Hawaii, 1962, Pa. State U., 1965, U. Pitts., 1967, U. London, 1970. Tchr., Lancaster Pub. Schs., 1923-50; supr. student teaching Dakota State Coll., 1950-52, Wis. State Coll., 1952-53, Plymouth State Coll., 1955-56; tchr. Thomas Jefferson Sch., Levittown, Pa., 1957-69, St. Michael Sch., Levittown, 1969—. Nathan C. Schaeffer Meml. scholar, 1947; Hilda Maehling Fellowship award, 1970; AAUW grantee, 1978; recipient 1st prize S.F. & Co. contest, 1961. Recipient Freedoms Found. Tchrs. medal, 1962. Mem. Daus. Am. Colonists, D.A.R., Nat. League Am. Pen Women, AAUW, NEA, Pa. Poetry Soc., Nat. Trust for Historic Preservation, Kappa Delta Pi. Author: Lancaster and Children's Literature, 1950; compiler Developing World Understanding in Elementary Schools, 1954; Children's Books for Christmas Gifts, 1957; Human Relations in Education, 1962; Books for Beginning Readers, 1972. Contbr. articles to profl. jours.; contbr. poems to mags., anthologies. Home: 66 Huckleberry Ln Levittown PA 19055

SMITH-GARY, KRICKET NIEMI, design co. exec.; b. Boston, May 1, 1946; d. Walter V. and Beatrice I. (Neal) Niemi; B.A., Mt. Holyoke Coll., 1967; M.L.A., M.R.P., U. Mass., 1969; M.B.A., Plymouth State Coll.; m. Benjamin W. Gary, Feb. 14, 1972; stepchildren—Melaney and Brian (twins), Heather. With drafting, research, project design Moriece and Gary, Inc., Cambridge, Mass., 1967-69, prin., 1970, pres., 1971-79; with Perry Dean and Stewart, Boston, 1969-70; founder, owner, pres. Remarc Inc., Campton, N.H., 1972—. Mem. HUD site plan rev. commn., 1970-74; breeder Palamino Arab horses. Mem. Am. Soc. Landscape Architects (author publs.). Contbr. chpt. to Handbook of Profl. Practice, 1973. Home: Sandwich Notch Rd Campton NH 03223 Office: PO Box 308 Campton NH 03223

SMITHSON, ROSEMARY LEITZ, journalist; b. Kansas City, Mo.; d. Frank Bantley and Marie Van Erkel Leitz; B.A., Mo. U., 1952; m. Lowell L. Smithson, Oct. 30, 1960; children—Carol, Lee. Writer, Hallmark Cards, 1952-59; free lance writer, 1959-64; staff dir. fund raising Planned Parenthood, Kansas City, Mo., 1972-73; feature writer Kansas City Times-Star, 1979—. Pres., bd. dirs. Planned Parenthood, 1970-71; pres. Women's Polit. Caucus, Greater Kansas City, 1974-75; pres. Mo. State Equal Rights Amendment Coalition, 1975-76. Unitarian. Home: 6415 Valley Kansas City MO 64113 Office: 1729 Grand Kansas City MO 64108

SMOGER, MARCI-ELLEN, real estate developer, designer, builder; b. Phila., Feb. 13, 1953; d. Joseph B. and Tremayne A. (Gershenfeld) Selig; B.S. in Psychology Trinity Coll., Hartford, Conn. and U. Pa., Phila., 1974; M. Interior Design, Drexel U., Phila., 1977; m. Barry Richard Smoger, July 7, 1974; 1 son, Julian Selig. Pres., Marci-ellen Smoger Assos., Penn-Valley, Pa., 1977—; lectr. U. Pa., Nat. Assn. Women in Constrn. Mem. Pa. Builders Assn., Nat. Assn. Home Builders, Home Builders Assn. Phila. and Suburban Counties. Home and Office: 1434 Flat Rock Rd Penn-Valley PA 19072

SMOLENS, ALICE PATCHIN AKE HOLMES, assn. exec.; b. Phila., Nov. 12; d. John Williams and Alice Patchin (Ake) Holmes; student Randolph-Macon Woman's Coll., 1931-33; A.B., U. Pa., 1935; postgrad. Columbia U., 1939; m. Stanley Rosenman Smolens, June 22, 1940; children—John Holmes, Sheila Joan. Reporter, Madison (N.J.) Eagle, also Chatham (N.J.) Courier, 1959-60; dir. public relations Fairleigh Dickinson U., Madison, N.J., 1960-65; dir. community relations Camp Fire Girls, Inc., N.Y.C., 1965-69; with Lic. Beverage Assn., N.Y.C., 1970-74; dir. women's activities Distilled Spirit Council U.S., Inc., Washington, 1974—; exec. dir. Nat. Women's Assn. Allied Beverage Industries, 1970—. Mem. Am. Soc. Assn. Execs., Washington Soc. Assn. Execs., Advt. Women N.Y., Nat. Assn. Women Hwy. Safety Leaders (hon. mem., chmn. bd. consultants), Phi Beta Kappa. Clubs: Publicity (N.Y.C.); Nat. Press, Soroptimist (Washington). Home: Alexandria VA 22312 Office: Distilled Spirits Council US 425 13th St NW Washington DC 20004

SMOLINSKI, IRENE KELLEY, psychiat. social worker; b. Cambridge, Mass., Sept. 14, 1945; d. Vincent and Edith (Butcher) Kelley; diploma Hannah Harrison Sch. Nursing, Washington, 1965; B.A. cum laude, Northeastern U., 1972; M.S., Grad. Sch. Social Work, Simmons Coll., 1974; m. Leon Smolinski, May 24, 1974. Coronary care/ICU nurse New Eng. Deaconess Hosp., Boston, 1967-69; infirmary nurse Graham Jr. Coll., Boston, 1969-72; clinician West-Ros-Park Mental Health Center, Boston, 1973-74; instr. family therapy Boston State Hosp. Family Tng. Inst., 1977-78; asso. dir. treatment and tng. Mass. Transition, Roslindale, 1974-78, dir., 1978—; individual practice psychiat. social work, 1976—; instr. psychiatry Tufts U. Sch. Medcine, Boston, 1979-80; clin. instr. social work Boston Coll. Grad. Sch. Social Work, 1979-80. Charles H. Bond scholar, 1970-72; Nat. Inst. Drug Abuse fellow, 1972-74. Mem. Nat. Asn. Social Workers, Acad. Cert. Social Workers, Mass. Acad. Psychiat. Social Workers, Acad. Honor Soc. Home: 60 Old Colony Rd Chestnut Hill MA 02167

SMOOT, CAROLYN ELIZABETH, mgmt. cons.; b. Logan, W.Va., Sept. 24, 1945; d. Edward and Mary Hickman; B.S., W.Va. State Coll., 1967; M.P.A., W.Va. Coll. Grad. Study, 1975; m. Douglas Bruce Smoot, Jan. 27, 1967; 1 dau., Caroline Trucia. Residential advisor Packard Bell Elec. Corp., Charleston, W.Va., 1967-68, sr. instr., 1968-72; dept. head placement service Teledyne Econ. Devel. Corp., Charleston, 1972-76; instr. W.Va. State Coll., 1975-77; mgr. dept. placement and records Thiokol Corp., Charleston, 1976-77; commr. W.Va. Employment Security, Charleston, 1977; corp. cons. Nemederoloc/Medlock Co. Inc., Washington, 1978-80. Mem. Charleston Metro Adv. Bd., 1977; mem. legis. com. Interstate Conf. Employment Security Agys., 1977; bd. dirs. Mountain State Econ. Assn., 1977, Shawnee Community Center; apptd. W.Va. goodwill ambassador by Sec. State; mem. adv. bd. Human Resources Devel. Found., Charleston, 1977, Regional Tng. Center, Charleston, 1977; co-chmn. Vet. Employment and Tng. Adv. Council, Charleston, 1977; co-chmn. W.Va. Gov.'s Com. on Employment of Handicapped. Mem. Nat. Women's Polit. Caucus, W.Va. Polit. Caucus, Bus. and Profl. Women's Club (1st v.p.), Assn. Community Edn. W.Va., Multi-Cap (dir.), NAACP, Delta Sigma Theta, Phi Delta Kappa. Democrat. Baptist. Home and Office: PO Box 222 Institute WV 25112

SMRCINA, CATHERINE MARIE, nurse; b. Chgo., June 27, 1952; d. Edward Francis and Helen Marie (Smalarz) S.; B.S. in Nursing, U. Ill., 1974. Nursing asst. Columbus Hosp., Chgo., 1972-74, staff nurse, 1974-77, head nurse orthopedics, 1977-81, clin. supr., 1981—. Mem. Nat. Assn. Orthopedic Nurses (pres. Chgo. chpt.), U. Ill. Alumni Assn., Chgo. Nurses Assn., Ill. Nurses Assn. (ethics com.), Am. Nurses Assn., Council Cath. Nurses Archdiocese Chgo. Club: Catholic Order Foresters. Home: 2335 S Westover Ave North Riverside IL 60546 Office: 2520 N Lakeview Ave Chicago IL 60614

SMUTZ, DOROTHY DRING, pianist, music educator; b. Kansas City, Mo.; d. Johnson and Emma L. (Mack) Dring; studied with Walter Goff, Sterling, Colo., Dr. Ernest R. Kroeger, St. Louis, E. Robert Schmitz, Paul Badura-Skoda; postgrad. Kroeger Sch. Music, 1926-28; m. Harold Turk Smutz, Oct. 27, 1930; 1 son, Robert Allen. Radio, TV appearances, also concerts, recitals; soloist St. Louis Philharmonic, St. Louis Little Symphony, St. Louis Symphony orchestras; harpsichordist St. Louis Bach Soc., 1940-44; piano, clavichord, seminars for tchrs., 1946—; debut Town Hall, N.Y.C., 1949; guest artist, forum leader Okla. Music Tchrs. Assn., 1950; lecture recital Mo. Music Tchrs. Assn.; mem. faculty, adjudicator Nat. Guild Piano Tchrs.; lectr., guest artist various assns. convs.; dir. tchrs. clinic and workshop So. Ill. U., 1963; guest artist, condr. workshop Coll. William and Mary, 1973, So. Ill. U., Edwardsville, fall 1977; piano faculty St. Louis Conservatory Music, 1974—, lectr., recitalist 48 Bach Preludes and Fugues, 1979-80; solo recitalist, condr. master classes Concordia Coll., Bronxville, N.Y., 1979; lectr. Bach Well Tempered Clavier Seminars, 1974-77; vis. artist in piano Webster Coll., St. Louis, 1981-83; adjudicator state and dist. piano auditions sponsored by Music Tchrs. Nat. Assn. Mem. Nat. (recipient Recognition award 1971), Mo. (exec. bd.) music tchrs. assns., Am. Piano Tchrs. Assn., St. Louis Piano Tchrs. Round Table, Mu Phi Epsilon (past pres. St. Louis alumnae). Presbyn. Home: 619 Hollywood Pl Webster Groves MO 63119

SMYTH, FRAN(CES) DALE, ins. co. exec.; b. N.Y.C., Sept. 6, 1941; d. Max and Aida (Heimerdinger) Goldfarb; B.S., Poly. Inst. N.Y., 1963; M.B.A., Baruch Coll. City U. N.Y., 1973; 1 son, Kevin Jeffrey. Programmer, CIT Fin., N.Y.C., 1965-66; programmer analyst Saks Fifth Ave., N.Y.C., 1966-67; sr. programmer Sealtest Co., N.Y.C., 1967-68; mgr. Kennecott Copper Corp., N.Y.C., 1968-74; asst. v.p. Met. Life Co., N.Y.C., 1974—; asst. adj. prof. mgmt. N.Y.U., 1969—; chmn. industry adv. bd. dept. EDP, Borough of Manhattan Community Coll., 1974—. Bd. dirs. CSC Repertory; mem. Top of the Village; chmn. 15th St. Blck Assn. Home: 40 W 15th St Apt 1C New York NY 10011 Office: Met Life Ins Co 1 Madison Ave New York NY 10010

SMYTH, MARY ELLEN, med. mgmt. cons. firm exec.; b. Lander, Wyo., July 2, 1935; d. Fred and Mary (Kosanovich) Savage; B.A. with honors, U. Wyo., 1956, M.A., 1960; m. W. Patrick Smyth, June 20, 1964; children—Timothy Murphy and Kevin Anthony (twins). Tchr. secondary schs., Colo., 1956-59; instr. U. Wyo., 1959-60, 63-64; instr. speech Pa. State U., 1960-63; tchr. high sch., Ill., 1964-70; bus. mgr. Orthopaedics Corp., River Forest, Ill., 1973-80; owner, mgr. K-T Med. Services, Smyth-Lutz Profl./Med. Bldg. Summer theatre stock appearances, 1959-70; TV show hostess, 1962; speech cons., 1974—. Mem. Ill. Com. on Media; v.p. aux. MacNeal Hosp., 1973-74; program dir. Oak Park Hosp. Aux., 1973-74, pres., 1976-78; mem. Ill. AAUW-League Women Voters del. to China, 1976; mem. governing bd. Chgo. Symphony Orch., Chgo. Zool. Soc.; bd. dirs. Oak Park-River Forest Community Chest. Mem. Speech Communication Assn., Ill. Speech Assn., Chgo. Council Fgn. Relations, Common Cause, AAUW (dir. Ill. div., pres. Riverside br. 1972-74, del. nat. conv. 1973, 75, 77, 81), Phi Beta Kappa, Pi Beta Phi (pres. Chgo. West Suburban chpt. 1973-74), Phi Kappa Phi, Kappa Delta Pi, Theta Alpha Phi. Contbr. articles to publs. Address: 7600 Augusta St River Forest IL 60305

SMYTHE, MABEL M. (MRS. HUGH H. SMYTHE), educator, former fgn. service officer; b. Montgomery, Ala., Apr. 3, 1918; d. Harry S. and Josephine (Dibble) Murphy; student Spelman Coll., 1933-36, LL.D. (hon.), 1980; A.B., Mt. Holyoke Coll., 1937, L.H.D. (hon.), 1977; M.A., Northwestern U., 1940; Ph.D. (Nat. fellow, Harriet Remington Laird fellow, Julius Rosenwald fellow), U. Wis., 1942; postgrad. N.Y. U., 1949; L.H.D. (hon.), U. Mass., 1979; m. Hugh H. Smythe, July 26, 1939 (dec. June 1977); 1 dau., Karen Pamela. Tchr., Fort Valley Normal and Indsl. Inst., 1937-39; asst. prof., asso. prof., acting head dept. econs., bus. adminstrn. Lincoln (Mo.) U., 1942-45; prof. econs. Tenn. A. and I. U., 1945-46; lectr. econs. Bklyn. Coll., 1946-47; vis. prof. econs. Shiga U., Japan, 1951-53; dep. dir. non-legal research NAACP Legal Def. and Ednl. Fund, 1953; core tchr. New Lincoln Sch., N.Y.C., 1954-59, coordinator secondary edn., 1959-69; dir. research and publs. Phelps-Stokes Fund, N.Y.C., 1970-77, v.p., 1972—, on leave, 1977—; ambassador to Cameroon, Yaounde, 1977-80, to Equatorial Guinea, 1979-80; dep. asst. sec. state for African affairs, Washington, 1980-81; Melville J. Herskovits prof. African studies Northwestern U., Evanston, Ill., 1982—; Woodrow Wilson guest scholar The Wilson Center, Smithsonian Instn.; Washington, 1982; lectr. econs. CCNY, 1959-60; asso. prof. Queens Coll., Flushing, N.Y., summer 1962; cons. Carnegie Corp., AID, 1964-66, Urban Coalition, 1968—, Ency. Brit. Ednl. Corp., 1969-73; scholar-in-residence U.S. Commn. Civil Rights, 1973-74. Mem. U.S. Adv. Commn. on Edn. Exchange, 1961-62, on Internat. Edn. and Cultural Affairs, 1962-65, del. UNESCO Gen. Conf. Paris, 1964; mem. U.S. Nat. Commn. UNESCO, 1965-70; mem. adv. council African affairs U.S. Dept. State, 1962-69; cons. mem. adv. com. Operation Crossroads Africa, 1958-65; mem. public affairs com. Nat. YWCA, 1959-65, mem. nat. resources com., 1963-65; mem. Women's Africa Com., 1959-64; mem., incorporator Com. Assessing Progress of Edn. 1964-69; mem. panel bd. examiners N.Y. State CSC, 1960-65; mem. Com. on Research Devel. Internat. Instns., 1965-67, Internat. Cooperation Year Com., 1965; mem. adv. com. Nat. Assessment Ednl. Progress, 1969-76; mem. exec. com. L.A.W.S. div. Atlantic Found., 1968-77; mem. Nat. Advt. Rev. Bd., 1975-77; U.S. del. Internat. Conf. Assistance to Refugees in Africa, Geneva, 1981, So. Africa Devel. Coordination Conf. II, Maputo, 1980. Bd. dirs. African-Am. Inst., 1964-65, N.Y. Center Internat. Visitors, Internat. Schs. Services, 1964-71 (vice chmn. bd. 1970-71), Nat. Corp. for Housing Partnerships; trustee Cottonwood Found., 1965-77, Conn. Coll., 1964-65, 68-77, Hampshire Coll., 1971-77 (vice chmn. 1975-77), Mt. Holyoke Coll., 1971-76 (vice chmn. 1975-76), Spelman Coll., 1980—. Decorated gran dame d'Inore, Order Royal Crown of Crete (Malta), grand officer Order of Valor (Cameroon); recipient Disting. Service award Greater N.Y. chpt. Links, Inc., 1965; Top Hat award Pitts. Courier, 1979; Mary McLeod Bethune Woman of Achievement award Nat. Council Negro Women, 1981; Ella T. Grasso award Mt. Holyoke Coll., 1982. Fellow Holyoke Coll., 1982; Decade of Service award Phelps Stoke Fund, Washington, 1982. Fellow African Studies Assn.; mem. Nat. Council Women U.S., Am. Acad. Polit. and Social Sci., Acad. World Econs., Am., Met. econ. assns., AAUP, Am. Soc. African Culture, Public Edn. Assn. (coordinating com.), N.Y. Urban League (chmn. edn. com.), Nat. Assn. African-Am. Edn. Clubs: Cosmopolitan, Mt. Holyoke. Author: (with Alan B. Howes) Intensive English Conversation, 2 vols., 1953, 54; (with Hugh H. Smythe) The New Nigerian Elite, 1960. Editor: (with Edgar Bley) Curriculum For Understanding, 1965; Black American Reference Book, 1976; Introduction to A Slaver's Log Book, 1976. Office: 630 Dartmouth St Evanston IL 60201

SNAPP, BETTIE LOU, ednl. adminstr.; b. Las Cruces, N.Mex., Jan. 4, 1929; d. Alonzo Perry and Ollie Alma (Beaty) Grogan; B.S., U. N.Mex., 1950; M.Ed., Colo. State U., 1958; m. Wendell Lawrence Snapp, Oct. 19, 1957; children—Stacy Gynel, Wendell Mark. Tchr. home econs., public schs., Carrizozo, N.Mex., 1950-53, Albuquerque, 1953-67; home econs. specialist public schs. Albuquerque, 1967-77, coordinator vocat. edn., 1977—; mem. nat. adv. com. consumer edn. Inservice Program for Changing Times, Ednl. Service, 1970—; mem. Gov.'s Conf. on Food, Nutrition and Health. Vice pres. Alvarado Sch. Parent Tchr. Council, 1971-72. Ives Meml. scholar, 1946-50; named N.Mex. Home Economist of Yr. N.Mex. Home Econs. Assn., 1973. Mem. Am. Home Econs. Assn., N.Mex. Home Econs. Assn., Am. Vocat. Assn., N.Mex. Vocat. Assn., Nat. Assn. Local Suprs. Home Econs., N.Mex. Adv. Council Home Econs. Episcopalian. Clubs: Daughters of Nile, Mothers, Order DeMolay (v.p. 1980), Order Jobs Daughters (parent council). Home: 838 Fairway Rd NW Albuquerque NM 86107 Office: 725 University St SE Albuquerque NM 87106

SNAPP, ELIZABETH, librarian, educator; b. Lubbock, Tex., Mar. 31, 1937; d. William James and Louise (Lanham) Mitchell; B.A. magna cum laude, North Tex. State U., Denton, 1968, M.L.S., 1969, M.A., 1977; m.

Harry Franklin Snapp, June 1, 1956. Asst. to archivist Archive of New Orleans Jazz, Tulane U., 1960-63; catalog librarian Tex. Woman's U., Denton, 1969-71, head acquisitions dept., 1971-74, coordinator readers services, 1974-77, asst. to dean Grad. Sch., 1977-79, instr. library sci., 1977—, acting Univ. librarian, 1979-82, dir. libraries, 1982—, mem. adv. com. on library formula Coordinating Bd. Tex. Coll. and Univ. System, 1981—; project dir. Nat. Endowment for Humanities consultancy grant on devel. core curriculum for women's studies, 1981-82. Co-sponsor Irish Lecture Series, Denton, 1968, 70, 73, 78. Sec. Denton County Democratic Caucus, 1970. Mem. ALA, Southwestern, Tex. (program com. 1978) library assns., AAUW (legis. br. chmn. 1973-74, br. v.p. 1975-76, br. pres. 1979—), So. Conf. Brit. Studies, AAUP, Tex. Assn. Coll. Tchrs. (pres. Tex. Woman's U. chpt. 1976-77), Woman's Shakespeare Club (pres. 1967-69), Beta Phi Mu (pres. chpt. 1976-78; sec. nat. adv. assembly 1978-79, pres. 1979-80, nat. dir. 1981—), Alpha Chi, Alpha Lambda Sigma (pres. 1970-71), Pi Delta Phi. Episcopalian (directress altar guild 1966-68, 73-76). Asst. editor Tex. Academe, 1973-76; book reviewer Library Resources and Tech. Services, 1973—. Contbr. articles to profl. jours. Home: 612 Grove St Denton TX 76201 Office: PO Box 24093 TWU Station Denton TX 76204

SNAVELY, SUSAN LUCY, social worker; b. Middletown, Conn., Oct. 17, 1948; d. Stanley and Lucy Badrick; B.A., St. Joseph Coll., 1971; M.S.W., U. Conn., 1974; m. William P. Snavely, May 11, 1974. Resident social worker, coordinator admissions and discharge com. Holly Center, Salisbury, Md., 1974—; adj. faculty Salisbury State Coll., 1975-80; adj. faculty, field supr. U. Md. Sch. Social Work, 1980-82. Acting sec. Dept. Health and Hygiene Social Workers Orgn., 1980. Mem. Eastern Shore Assn. Profl. Social Workers, Wicomico Council Social Services, Nat. Assn. Social Workers, Nat. Assn. Devel. Disabilities Mgrs. Roman Catholic. Home: Route 6 Box 527 Jeffrey St Salisbury MD 21801 Office: Holly Center PO Box 2358 Snow Hill Rd Salisbury MD 21801

SNEDAKER, CATHERINE RAUPAGH (KIT), editor; b. Fargo, N.D., Apr. 2; d. Paul and Charity (Primmer) Raupagh; B.A., Duke U., 1943; m. William Brooks, 1943; children—Eleanor Brooks Schonfeld, Peter William; m. 2d, Weldon Snedaker, Sept. 17, 1950. Public relations exec. United Seamen's Service, 1950-57; promotion mgr. sta. WINR-TV and WNBF-TV, Binghamton, N.Y., 1957-60; TV editor, feature writer Binghamton Sun, 1960-68; mem. staff Los Angeles Herald Examiner, 1968—, food editor, 1978—, restaurant critic, 1978-80, food and travel editor, 1980—; guest editor Mademoiselle mag., 1942. Recipient 3 awards Los Angeles Press Club. Mem. Newspaper Food Editors and Writers Assn. Democrat. Home: 140 San Vicente Blvd Apt C Santa Monica CA 90402 Office: 1111 S Broadway Los Angeles CA 90015

SNEED, ANNE-MARIE, ct. reporter; b. Worcester, Mass., July 24, 1948; d. Alfred Alderic and Juliette Theresa (LaPlante) DuPont; A.A., Johnson and Wales Jr. Coll., Providence, 1968; grad. Stenotype Inst., Boston, 1969; m. William D. Sneed, Jan. 9, 1972; children—Christopher William, Shannon Marie, Samantha Ann. Ct. reporter for sheriff of Dade County, Miami, Fla., 1969; ct. reporter McCarthy Reporting Service, Worcester, 1969—; tutor in field. Registered profl. reporter, Mass. Mem. Nat., Mass. shorthand reporters assns. Democrat. Roman Catholic. Home: 16 Sherwood Dr Oxford MA 01540 Office: 37 Harvard St Suite 105 Worcester MA 01608

SNEED, MARIE ELEANOR WILKEY, ret. educator; b. Dahlgren, Ill., June 12, 1915; d. Charles N. and Hazel (Miller) Wilkey; student U. Ill., 1933-35; B.S., Northwestern U., 1937; postgrad. Wayne State U., 1954-60, U. Mich., 1967; m. John Sneed, Jr., Sept. 18, 1937; children—Suzanne (Mrs. Geoffrey B. Newton), John Corwin. Tchr. English, drama, creative writing Berkley (Mich.) Sch. Dist., 1952-76. Mem. Mich. Statewide Tchr. Edn. Preparation, 1968-72, regional sec. 1969-70; mem. Pleasant Ridge Arts Council, 1982—, Pleasant Ridge Parks and Recreation Commn., 1982—. Mem. NEA, Mich., Berkley (pres. 1961-62) edn. assns., Oakland Tchr. Edn. Council (exec. bd. 1973-76), Student Tchr. Planning Com. Berkley (chmn. 1971-72), Phi Alpha Chi, Pi Lambda Theta, Alpha Delta Kappa, Alpha Omicron Pi. Club: Pleasant Ridge Woman's (pres. 1980-83). Home: 21 Norwich Rd Pleasant Ridge MI 48069

SNELL, BELINDA RAE, trade assn. exec.; b. Island Falls, Maine, Apr. 24, 1949; d. Keith Huggard and Madeline (Kennedy) Ingraham; B.A., U. Maine, Orono, 1971; M.Ed., U. Portland, 1974; m. Christopher D. Snell, July 31, 1977. Team leader Maine Concentrated Employment, Portland, 1972-73; coordinator Women's Reentry Ednl. Program, Bangor, Maine, 1974-76; personnel mgr. K Mart Corp., Augusta, Maine, 1977; coop. vocat. edn. coordinator Maranacook Sch., Readfield, Maine, 1978; v.p. Maine Oil Dealers Assn., Yarmouth, 1979—; mgr. Maine Energy Trade Show; mem. Gov.'s. Adv. Council on Fuel Assistance. Mem. Cumberland County Energy Coalition; mem. Ft. Williams Adv. Com., Cape Elizabeth, Maine. Club: Garden. Home: 16 Orchard Rd Cape Elizabeth ME 04107 Office: PO Box 536 Yarmouth ME 04096

SNELLS, VERNELLE MARIE MACK, ins. agt.; b. Durham, N.C., Feb. 21, 1950; d. James and Magdaline (Cates) Mack; m. Howard Snells III, Feb. 20, 1977 (div.); Vocalist, USO, S.E. Asia, 1968-74; clk. N.C. Meml. Hosp., 1974-76; vocalist Dynamic Upsetters Bank, Cary, N.C., 1976-78; ins. claim adjuster Blue Cross/Blue Shield, Durham, N.C., 1978-80; ins. agt. Ind. Life & Agy., Durham, 1978—; ins. agt., area coordinator Winston Mut. Life Ins. Co., Winston Salem, N.C., 1980-82, dist. mgr., Raleigh, N.C., 1982—. Named Agt. of Yr., Ind. Life Ins. Co., 1978. Democrat. Baptist. Home: 2217 Watkins St Raleigh NC 27604 Office: Durham NC 27703 also PO Box 998 Winston Salem NC 27102

SNIBBE, PATRICIA MISCALL, advt. co. exec.; b. Hackensack, N.J., June 1, 1932; d. Jack and Margaret Lois (Drake) Miscall; B.F.A., R.I. Sch. Design, 1954; postgrad. New Sch. for Social Research, 1975-80; m. Richard Wilson Snibbe, Sept. 8, 1962; stepsons—John Robinson, Paul Clor. Art dir., film producer Peckham Productions, N.Y.C., 1960-64; art dir., partner Stallman and Snibbe, N.Y.C., 1964-66; art dir. Shevlo Advt., N.Y.C., 1966-72, Bernard Hodes Advt., N.Y.C., 1972-77; owner, creative dir. Designstuff, N.Y.C., 1978—; v.p., creative dir Archtl. Film Library, N.Y.C., 1980—. Recipient Golden Circle award Affiliated Advt. Agys. Internat., 1975-77, Creativity '78 award, 1978. Mem. NOW, ACLU, Nat. Trust for Hist. Preservation, Graphic Artists Guild, Cartoonists Guild, Nat. Acad TV and Scis. Author cartoon: Feminist Funnies, 1981—. Home: 139 E 18th St New York NY 10003

SNIDER, CLAIRE ADABELLE, real estate broker; b. Fortuna, Calif., Feb. 23, 1923; d. Alexander Marion and Lucile Elizabeth (Obarr) Sappingfield; B.A. cum laude, San Francisco State U., 1960; grad. Internat. Acad. Real Estate Mgmt., Newport Beach, Calif., 1979; m. George Paul Snider, July 25, 1944; children—Sandra Paula, Carol JoAnn, Paul Cody. Elem. tchr. Rio Lindo Acad., Headlsburg, Calif., 1965-68, Redwood Jr. Acad., Santa Rosa, Calif., 1968-75; real estate sales rep. All Am. Realty, McCall, Idaho, 1975-78, asso. broker, 1978-79; real estate broker Century 21 Brundage Mountain Real Estate, Inc., McCall, 1979—, also pres., founder, owner; chmn. multiple listing com.; cert. instr. real estate Boise State U. Lifetime teaching credential, Calif.; designated G.R.I., 1978. Mem. McCall Bd. Realtors (v.p. 1979), Nat. Assn. Realtors, Idaho Assn. Realtors (state bd. dirs. 1978-81), Mountain Central Bd. Realtors, Realtors Nat. Mktg. Inst., S.W. Idaho Brokers Council, Century 21 Investment Soc., McCall C. of C. Seventh-day Adventist (organist; ch. treas.). Home: Route 1 Box 115B McCall ID 83638 Office: 317 E Lake St PO Box 932 McCall ID 83638

SNIDER, DONNA KAY, retail co. ofcl.; b. Cin., Aug. 24, 1945; d. James Benjamen and Ruby (Crowley) Battles; A.A., Coll. Mt. St. Joseph of Ohio, 1979, B.A. magna cum laude, 1980; postgrad. Coll. Law No. Ky. U., 1980—; m. Clifford L. Snider, Oct. 10, 1964; children—Michelle Lynn, Lorrie Danielle. With Kroger Co., Cin., 1970—, legal adminstr. and asst. corp. sec. law dept., 1975—, asst. corp. sec., 1982—. Mem. Am. Bar Assn., Greater Cin. Women Lawyers, Assn. Legal Adminstrs., Assn. Legal Adminstrs., Christian Bus. and Profl. Women's Club, Salmon P. Chase Coll. Law Women's Law Caucus, Alpha Chi, Kappa Gamma Pi. Republican. Methodist. Home: 2920 Pond Run Ln New Richmond OH 45157 Office: Kroger Co 1014 Vine St Cincinnati OH 45201

SNIDER, GERI TEREZAS, ednl. cons. co. exec.; b. Canton, Ohio, Feb. 23, 1939; d. Sam and Mary M. (Kopp) Terezas; R.N. Aultman Hosp. Sch. Nursing, Canton, 1960; B.S. in Nursing, U. San Francisco, 1974; M.S. in Nursing Adminstrn., U. Calif., San Francisco, 1975; M.A., Calif. Inst. Transpersonal Psychology, 1982. Staff nurse med. surg. unit Massillon (Ohio) City Hosp., 1960, Timken Mercy Hosp., Canton, Ohio, 1960-61; charge nurse Mt. Agustine Infirmary, West Richfield, Ohio, 1961-62; supr. intern St. Vincent Charity Hosp., Cleve., 1963-64; supr. pediatrics, med.-surg. unit, St. John's Hosp., Cleve., 1964-66; supr. intensive care and neurosurgery unit St. Vincent Charity Hosp., Cleve., 1966-67; asst. clin. instr. Aultman Hosp., Sch. Nursing, Canton, 1967-68) staff nurse U. Hosps., Cleve., 1968-69; head nurse post-anesthesia recovery room Stanford (Calif.) U. Hosp., 1969-72; asso. dir. nurses St. Mary's Hosp., Reno, Nev., 1975-77; founder owner dir. Delta Associates, Carson City, Nev., 1978-80; dir. Delphic Assos., Menlo Park, Calif., 1980—. Founder pres. Council of Post Anesthesia Nurses, 1973-77, chmn., 1973-77. Western Hosps. Assn. scholar, 1972. Mem. Nat. League for Nurses, Am. Assn. of Critical Care Nurses, Am., Nev. nurses assns., Internat. Flying Nurses Assn., Assn. Transpersonal Psychology, Am. Mgmt. Assn., U. Calif. at San Francisco Alumni Assn., Aultman Alumni Assn., U. San Francisco Alumni Assn. (dir. No. Nev.), Sigma Theta Tau. Contbr. articles on nursing edn. to profl. jours.; conf. organizer and leader. Address: PO Box 177 Menlo Park CA 94025

SNIDER, PATRICIA JOANNE, demographer; b. Tiffin, Ohio, Mar. 24, 1946; d. Robert and Margery Doris (Gier) Clingo; B.A. in Sociology, Ohio State U., 1970, M.A., 1973; m. Thomas V. Snider, Sept. 16, 1967 (div. 1975); children—Elizabeth Anne, Christopher Leigh. Teaching asso., research asso. Ohio State U., Columbus, 1971-73; research sociologist Battelle Columbus Labs., Columbus, 1973-75; mgr. forward planning Gen. Motors Corp, Detroit, 1975—; mem. Task force on Employment and Edn., Nat. Acad. Edn., 1977-78; mem. statis. com. Equal Employment Adv. Council, 1976-80, availability monograph task force, 1977-78; mem. affirmative action practices com. Equal Employment Adv. Council, 1980—; mem. availability consortium steering com. Orgn. Resources Counselors, Inc. Mem. World Future Soc., Population Assn. Am. Contbr. articles to profl. jours. Home: 1008 Abbey Birmingham MI 48008 Office: 9-113 General Motors Bldg 3044 W Grand Blvd Detroit MI 48202

SNIEDERMAN, LOUISE ANNE, banker; b. Worcester, Mass., July 5, 1949; d. Nathan and Ruth (Feingold) S.; B.S., Emerson Coll., 1972; M.S., U. So. Calif., 1975. Instructional designer Postgrad. Ednl. Network, U. So. Calif., 1974-75; dir. mktg. Consumers Savs. Bank, Worcester, 1975-78; v.p. E. N.Y. Savs. Bank, 1978-80; v.p. global pvt. banking Chase Manhattan Bank, N.Y.C., 1980—; pres., Radical Chic Enterprises, Inc., 1981—. Mem. Nat. Assn. Mut. Savs. Banks (mem. mktg. com.), Savs. Instns. Mktg. Soc. Am. (mem. public relations com.), Mut. Instns. Nat. Transfer Service, Bank Mktg. Assn. (dir. Met. N.Y. 1980—), Savs. Bank Women N.Y. State. Office: 400 Park Ave New York NY 10022

SNIPES, VALERIE LAWRENCE, petrochem. instrumentation co. exec.; b. Phila., Mar. 21, 1942; d. Maurice A. and Dorothy F. (Rodia) McGuckin; student Immaculate Heart Coll., Calif., Glassboro (N.J.) State Coll., Rutgers U., N.J.; m. David Snipes, July 19, 1980; children from previous marriage—Danita, Nicholas. Tchr. public schs., Los Angeles, Marlton, N.J., P.R., 1961; exec. v.p. Sinco, Inc., Webster, Tex., 1977—. Mem. Houston C. of C., Am. Soc. Profl. and Exec. Women, Instrument Soc. Am. Office: 15502 Old Galveston Rd Webster TX 77598

SNODDERLY, KAREN WEBSTER, univ. ofcl.; b. Knoxville, Tenn., July 16, 1951; d. John Arthur and Martha Elizabeth (Armstrong) Webster; B.S. in Bus. Adminstrn., Carson-Newman Coll., 1971; postgrad. U. Tenn., 1977; m. Lynn J. Snodderly, June 5, 1971. Data control clk. U. Tenn., Knoxville, 1974, research asst., 1974-75, mgr. student info., 1975-79, dir. data analysis, 1979—, mem. fin. aid and admission system design team, 1979-80. Vice chairperson Friends of Strawberry Plains (Tenn.) Library, 1978; vice chmn. bd. dirs. Knoxville Rape Crisis Center, 1982. Mem. Am. Bus. Women's Assn. (Mem. of Month award 1981), Coll. and Univ. Machine Records Conf., Phi Chi Theta. Compiler-editor U. Tenn. Ann. Report Info. Requests, 1979-81. Home: Route 3 Box 421 Strawberry Plains TN 37871

SNOOK, JUDITH MARIE, social worker; b. Morganfield, Ky., May 6, 1943; d. Howard Boyd and Estella Marie (Todd) Skelly; B.A. in Sociology, Wittenberg U., 1966; postgrad. Colo. State U., 1977-78. Caseworker I, Adams County Dept. Social Services, Commerce City, Colo., 1967-69, caseworker II, 1969-77, caseworker III, 1977—; cons. Mem. Nat. Assn. Social Workers. Democrat. Lutheran. Clubs: Boulder Civic Opera, Boulder Chorale. Home: 3395 Aurora St Boulder CO 80303 Office: 4200 E 72nd St Commerce City CO 80022

SNOW, CAROL BULL, banker; b. Middletown, Conn., Apr. 14, 1950; d. Clifford Eugene and Judith Gertrude (Cote) Bull; A.A., Bay Path Jr. Coll., 1969; B.A., U. Conn., 1971; postgrad. Conn. Sch. Savs. Banking, 1976-78; m. Richard Edward Snow, Oct. 12, 1975; 1 dau., Karen Marie. Asst. treas. ops. Laurel Bank and Trust Co., Meriden, Conn., 1971-75; asst v.p., mgr. credit cards, IRA specialist City Savs. Bank of Middletown, Conn., 1975—. Mem. Nat. Assn. Bank Women. Office: 211 S Main St Middletown CT 06457

SNOW, EDWINA FEIGENSPAN (MRS. MACVICKER SNOW), editor, pub.; b. N.Y.C., July 14, 1927; d. Edwin Christian and Flora Marie (Russ) Feigenspan; student Barnard Coll., 1945-46, Columbia, 1946, Juilliard Sch. Music, 1943; m. David Dodge Osborn, June 1946 (div. 1951); children—Dana Dodge Osborn, Christopher Fairfield Osborn; m. 2d, MacVicker Snow, Dec. 19, 1964; children—Marina, Michael Snow. Model, John Robert Powers, N.Y.C., 1947-48, pub. relations dir. Powers cosmetics, 1948-50; model Ford Agy., N.Y.C., 1950-53, Jacques Heim, Paris, France, 1957; bilingual sec. Cofinindus, Brufina, Electrobel Belgian holding cos., 1960; co-editor, pub. Locust Valley (N.Y.) Leader, 1961-67; editor, pub. Oyster Bay (N.Y.) Guardian, 1967—; partner Locust Valley Pub. Co., Inc., 1965—; founder, pub. Glen Cove (N.Y.) Guardian, 1976—; pres. Oyster Bay Pub. Co., Inc. Bd. dirs. Nassau chpt. A.R.C.; benefit dir. Boys Town Italy, 1952-54. Mem. A.S.C.A.P., Am. Horse Protection Assn. Kiwanian (hon.). Home: Centre Island Oyster Bay NY 11771 Office: W Main St Oyster Bay NY 11771

SNOW, JUDITH ROHLETTER, jewelry store exec., gemologist, jewelry designer; b. Miami, Fla., May 6, 1948; d. Guy Eugene and Mary Evelyn (York) Rohletter; student Miami-Dade Community Coll., 1966-67; cert. in diamond evaluation Gemological Inst. Am., 1979, cert. in colored stones and gem indentification, 1980; student Berlitz Sch. Langs., Coral Gables, Fla., 1979—; also grad. various profl. seminars; m. Edward Hugh Snow, May 11, 1974; children—Judith Diane, Kelly Michelle, Mary Alice. Office mgr. Ross Printing Corp., Miami, 1965-74; corp. exec., gemologist Snow's Jewelers, Inc., Coral Gables, 1974—, also dir. Active Scott Kelly for Gov. of Fla. Campaign, 1965. Mem. Retail Jewelers Am., Jewelers Security Alliance, Coral Gables C. of C., Miracle Mile Mchts. Assn., Exec. Women Internat., Coral Bay Property Owner's Assn., Ferrari Club Am., Ferrari Owners Club. Democrat. Clubs: Ocean Reef, Coral Bay Yacht, Coral Reef Yacht, Fla. Philharm. Prelude, Noteworthy, Progress, Bimini (Bahamas) Big Game. Office: 219 Miracle Mile Coral Gables FL 33134

SNUTTJER, ANN MARIE CHAMBERS, nurse; b. Harlan, Iowa, Sept. 11, 1941; d. Floyd V. and Phyllis Maureen (Carstensen) Chambers; R.N., Jennie Edmundson Hosp., Council Bluffs, Iowa, 1962; B.S. in Nursing, U. Nebr. Omaha, 1970; m. Norman Snuttjer, June 8, 1963; children—Deborah, Thomas. Mem. nursing staff Jennie Edmundson Hosp., 1964-65, staff devel. instr., 1977-80, dir. community and personnel edn., 1980-82, mem. faculty Sch. Nursing, 1965-70; tchr. adult health edn. Iowa Western Community Coll., 1974-77; mem. faculty div. nursing Coll. of St. Mary, Omaha, 1982—; bd. dirs. Pottawattamie County chpt. Am. Cancer Soc., 1974—, pres., 1976-79, mem. Iowa edn. com., 1976-77; bd. dirs. Vis. Nurses Assn. Council Bluffs, 1981-82. Mem. S.W. Iowa Health Educators (pres. 1981), Iowa Soc. Health Manpower, Edn. and Tng. Home: 3 Nall Rd Council Bluffs IA 51501 Office: Div Nursing College of St Mary Omaha NE

SNYDER, AUDREY JEAN, author, photographer; b. York, Pa., May 11, 1929; d. John Henry and Bessie Alice (Shermeyer) Kann; m. Edward J. Snyder, July 6, 1956. Freelance photographer, 1969—; feature columnist, sports columnist, horseracing reporter, handicapper Frederick (Md.) Post, also The News, Frederick, 1974-79; sports columnist, harness racing handicapper, reporter Washington Star, 1980—; press cons. Freestate Raceway, Laurel, Md., 1980—; contbr. to Harness Horse; exibited wildlife photography Adelphi and New Carrollton (Md.) libraries, 1969; lectr. public service orgns. Mem. Nat. Fedn. Press Women (1st place award spl. sports article 1977), Nat. Splty. Merchandisers Assn., Md. Press Women (awards 1976-78), Md.-Del.-D.C. Press Assn. (awards 1974-76). Address: PO Box 178 Jefferson MD 21755

SNYDER, BARBARA JEAN, journalist; b. Phila., July 20, 1950; d. Bernard Benjamin and Rose (Cohen) S.; B.J., Pa. State U., 1972; M.A., U. Wis., 1974. Summer intern Buffalo Evening News, 1972-73, reporter, 1974—, reporter Living sect., 1980—; teaching asst., photojournalist U. Wis., 1972-74. Active, Jewish Center Greater Buffalo, Inc., founder Singles Havurah. Mpls. Tribune fellow in consumer reporting, 1973. Mem. Buffalo Newspaper Guild (Rookie-of-Year award 1976). Democrat. Jewish. Weekly columnist Living the Single Life, 1977—, fashion editor, 1982—. Home: 547 Potomac Ave Apt 2 Buffalo NY 14222 Office: Buffalo Evening News One News Plaza PO Box 100 Buffalo NY 14240

SNYDER, ELAYNE, speech cons.; b. Atlantic City, N.J., Mar. 2, 1931; d. Samuel and Bella Diana (Lewis) S.; B.A., U. Miami, 1952. Women's dir. Radio Sta. WOND, Pleasantville, N.J., 1952-53; co-owner Et Cetera Advt., Atlantic City, N.J., 1953-56; asst. to broadcast exec. Kenyon & Eckhardt Advt., N.Y.C., 1956-59; asst. to mktg. v.p. Colgate-Palmolive, N.Y.C., 1959-69; research dir. The Young Group, N.Y.C., 1969-74; dir. Elayne Snyder Speech Cons., N.Y.C., 1974—; cons. N.Y.U., 1979-80; Mem. NOW (past pres. N.Y. chpt., mem. adv. council N.Y., Achievement award 1977), Soc. Tng. and Devel., N.Y. Assn. Women Bus. Owners. Home and Office: 333 E 49th St New York NY 10017 also Harbor Close Bridge St 3F Sag Harbor NY 11963

SNYDER, JANE LOIS, former educator; b. Greensburg, Pa., Dec. 19, 1916; d. Harry John and Alice (Keech) S.; B.Ed., Frick Tng. Sch., U. Pitts., 1937, M.Ed., U. Pitts., 1948, postgrad., 1957-58; postgrad. (scholar) Pa. State Coll., summers 1946-47; postgrad. in communications (scholar) U. Wis., summer 1955; postgrad. in communications U. Mich., summer 1948. Elem. tchr. Avonworth, Pa., 1937-47; specialist speech and lang. therapy, Pitts. Schs., 1947-79, ret., 1979. Chmn. programs for Better Films and TV Guild, 1964; speaker Kindergarten Inst., 1964; judge Optimist Oratorical Contest, 1969; mem. Allegheny County LWV, 1980-81; mem. Vets. Hosp. Radio and TV Guild, 1960-82, program dir., 1977-82; mem. YWCA; founding mem. Ft. Pitt Mus. Assos. Cert. supr. spl. edn. Mem. Am. Speech and Hearing Assn. (life, award, 1981), Pa. Speech and Hearing Assn. (life, co-founder), Nat. Ret. Tchrs. Assn., Frick Scholarship Alumnae Assn. (bd., 1970), Am. Assn. Ret. Persons (editor monthly newsletter), Smithsonian Assos., Carnegie Inst., AAUW (sec. 1963-64, chmn. ednl. funding 1979-80). Republican. Episcopalian. Clubs: Swiss-Am. Soc. of Pitts., Welsh Women's, St. David's Soc. Condr. first survey on Non-English speaking students, 1969; author, participant 36 ednl. TV programs, questionnaire in field; contbr. poems to anthology. Home: 2010 La Cross St Pittsburgh PA 15218

SNYDER, JANE PETERS, public relations exec.; b. Manassas, Va., July 23, 1925; d. James Walker and Alma Dorothy (Cross) Peters; student George Washington U., 1943-45, Columbia U. Sch. Public Health, 1962; children—Susan Leland, James Peters. Reporter, Montgomery County (Md.) Sentinel, 1952-54, Chatham (N.J.) Courier, 1956-59, Morris County (N.J.) Daily Record, 1959-61; public relations asst. East Orange (N.J.) Gen. Hosp., 1962-64, United Hosp., Newark, 1964-65; dir. community relations Georgetown U. Hosp., Washington, 1966-68; dir. public relations Hosp. Council and Met. Regional Med. Program, Washington, 1968-70, Washington Hosp. Center, Washington, 1970—; lectr. George Washington U. Sch. Health Care Adminstrn., 1973, 78, 79, 80, 82. Recipient award Assn. Am. Med. Colls., 1981. Mem. Am. Soc. Hosp. Public Relations (dir. 1973-75), Acad. Hosp. Public Relations (treas. 1973, dir. 1973-78, MacEachern awards 1963, 72-81). Home: 5235 Elliott Rd Bethesda MD 20816 Office: 110 Irving St NW Washington DC 20010

SNYDER, JOAN, painter; b. Highland Park, N.J., Apr. 16, 1940; d. Leon D. and Edythe A. (Cohen) Snyder; A.B. in Sociology, Douglass Coll., 1962; M.F.A., Rutgers U., 1966; m. Laurence Fink, Oct. 12, 1969. One-woman exhbns. include Paley and Lowe, New Brunswick, N.J., 1971, 73, Michael Walls Gallery, San Francisco, 1971, Parker 470, Boston, 1972, Los Angeles Inst. Contemporary Art, 1976, Portland (Oreg.) Center Visual Arts, 1976, Carl Solway Gallery, N.Y.C., 1976, Neuberger Mus., Purchase, N.Y., 1978, Hamilton Gallery Contemporary Art, 1978, 79; travelling one-woman show San Francisco Art Inst. Grand Rapids Art Mus., Renaissance Soc., U. Chgo., Anderson Gallery, Va. Commonwealth U., Richmond, 1979-80; group exhbns. include Whitney Ann., 1972, Whitney Bienniel, 1974, 80, Corcoran Bienniel, 1975, Mus. Modern Art, N.Y.C.; mem. faculty SUNY, Stony Brook, 1967-69, Yale U., 1974, U. Calif., Irvine, 1975, San Francisco Art Inst., 1976, Princeton U., 1975-77. Grantee Nat. Endowment Art, 1974. Address: PO Box 295 Martins Creek PA 18063

SNYDER, LAURA LEE, advt. agy. exec.; b. Oklahoma City, Aug. 24, 1936; d. Cothburn and Frances M. (Boosman) Lemon; student Okla. U., 1954-56; m. Ralph H. Snyder, Oct. 12, 1963; children—Cynthia, Harry, Scott, Chris, Janice. With Sta. KSWO-Radio and TV, Lawton, Okla., 1956-58; account exec. Tom P. Gordon Co., advt., Oklahoma City, 1958-61, Maury Ferguson Assos., Oklahoma City, 1961-64; pres. Associates, Inc., Oklahoma City, 1964-68; account exec. Richard Roby Assos., Oklahoma City, 1970-74; v.p. United Concepts, Inc., Oklahoma

City, 1974-78; pres. Snyder & Co., Oklahoma City, 1978—, Adsociates, Inc. Active local United Fund, Boy Scouts Am., Jr. Achievement; bd. dirs. Dale Rogers Ctr., Kidney Found., Better Bus. Bur. Recipient various Addy awards, others; named Advt. Person of Yr., 1981-82. Mem. Am. Women Radio and TV, Sales and Mktg. Execs. Internat., Women Execs. Network, Advt. Agy. Council, Am. Advt. Fedn., C. of C. (bd. dirs.), Oklahoma City Advt. Club. Democrat. Methodist. Home: 7505 NW 28th St Bethany OK 73008 Office: 4211 NW 23d St Oklahoma City OK 73107

SNYDER, MARGARET MARY LEARY (MRS. GUY SNYDER), found. exec.; b. Pittsfield, Mass.; d. John Joseph and Lola (Winchell) Leary; R.N., St. Luke's Hosp., Pittsfield, 1934; student Leland Stanford U., 1944; m. Guy Snyder, Oct. 18, 1944 (dec. 1966). Pvt. duty nursing, 1934-43; phys. therapist Richmond Field Hosp., Kaiser Shipbldg. Co., Richmond, Calif., 1944-45; head phys. therapy dept. Children's Hosp. Home, Utica, N.Y., 1945-47, Moses Taylor Hosp., Scranton, Pa., 1947-48, emergency polio Santa Clara County Hosp., San Jose, Calif., 1948; head. phys. therapy dept. Bishop and Swenson Orthopedic Clinic, Phoenix, 1949-51; exec. dir. Cerebral Palsy Found., Beaumont, Tex., 1951—. Mem. Tex. Crippled Children Soc., Tex. Welfare Assn., Am. Phys. Therapy Assn. Home: 3660 Bryan Dr Beaumont TX 77707 Office: 855 S 8th St Beaumont TX 77701

SNYDER, MARIAH, nursing educator; b. Austin, Minn., Nov. 28, 1935; d. Peter J. and Agnes Julia (Guiney) S.; B.S.N., Coll. of St. Teresa, 1959; M.S.N., U. Pa., 1972; Ph.D., U. Minn., 1978. Head nurse St. Marys Hosp., Rochester, Minn., 1960-70; cons. Neurol. Inst. Colombia, Bogota, 1972; instr., clin. specialist Vanderbilt U., Nashville, 1972-73; instr. U. Wis., Eau Claire, 1973-75; asso. prof. U. Minn., Mpls., 1975—; cons. Coll. of St. Scholastica, Dalhousie U. Mem. Southeastern Mpls. Community Edn. Planning Group, 1981—. Irene G. Ramey research grantee, 1981, U. Minn. grantee, 1980. Mem. Midwest Research Assn., Am. Nurses Assn., Am. Assn. Neurosurg. Nurses (edit. bd. 1981—), AAUP, Minn. Nurses Assn., 3d Dist. Nurses Assn. (1st v.p. 1980-82), Am. Assn. Tension Control, Sigma Theta Tau. Republican. Roman Catholic. Author: Neurologic Problems: A Critical Care Nursing Focus, 1981; mem. editorial bd. Jour. Neurosurg. Nursing, 1982—; contbr. articles to prof. jours. Home: 626 3d Ave SE Minneapolis MN 55415 Office: 308 Harvard St SE 5-140 HSF U Minn Minneapolis MN 55455

SNYDER, MARLENE RUTH, ednl. adminstr.; b. Chgo., Sept. 23, 1937; d. William S. and Maryellen J. Riegler; B.E.D., U. Miami, 1959; M.S., U. No. Colo., 1974; 1 dau., Kimbery Kelli. Tchr. phys. edn., coach Miami Beach (Fla.) Sr. High Sch., 1959-74; adminstrv. asst., 1974-76; dir. intervention program Nautilus Jr. High Sch., Miami Beach, 1976-82; cons. intervention program Dade County (Fla.) Public Schs; asst. prin. Miami (Fla.) Edison Middle Sch., 1982—; bicentennial chmn. Dade County Schs., 1976. Chmn. City of Miami Beach 50th Birthday, 1975; civic affairs chmn. Dade County PTA, 1975; adv. Rainbow Girls, Hialeah, Fla. Recipient Outstanding Service award Miami Beach PTA, 1974, Miami Beach Sr. High Sch., 1976. Mem. United Tchrs. Dade County, Fla. Assn. Curriculum Devel., Bus. and Profl. Women's Assn., Phi Delta Kappa, Phi Delta Pi. Democrat. Methodist. Clubs; Women of Moose (Outstanding Service award 1978), Order Eastern Star (Hialeah, Fla.). Home: 272 E 35th St Hialeah FL 33012 Office: Miami Edison Middle Sch 6101 NW 2d Ave Miami FL 33127

SNYDER, MARY JOHN, data entry service bur. exec; b. New Orleans, Jan. 1, 1947; d. John Young and Marie Nora (Kelly) S.; B.A., Mt. St. Agnes Coll., 1969. Caseworker, Cath. Social Services, Balt., 1969-74; data entry analyst Sperry Univac, Balt., 1974-76, systems analyst, 1976-78, sales rep., 1978-81; v.p. Data Prep Services, Inc., Balt., 1981—; dir. Snyder Ventures, Inc. Republican. Roman Catholic. Home: 38 Somers Ct Cockeysville MD 21030 Office: 5205 East Dr Baltimore MD 21227

SNYDER, PHYLLIS BOPP, pub. co. exec.; b. Houston, May 1, 1945; d. Otto and Elsie Helene (Grau) Bopp; B.A., Tex. Tech U., 1967; m. Terry Eugene Snyder, June 12, 1965. Prodn. editor John Wiley & Sons, N.Y.C., 1968-71, asst. prodn. mgr., 1971-73; with Grune & Stratton, Inc., N.Y.C., 1973—, dir. editorial prodn., 1974—, v.p., 1980—. Home: 200 E 33rd St Apt 10-J New York NY 10016 Office: 111 Fifth Ave New York NY 10003

SNYDER, RACHEL FRANCES, editor; b. Topeka, Kans., Feb. 12, 1924; d. Otis F. and Lela Gertrude (Retter) S.; A.B., Washburn U., 1945. Reporter, Topeka (Kans.) Daily Capital, 1943-45; writer Kans. Indsl. Devel. Commn., Topeka, 1946-47; asst. WTOP and Washington Post, Washington, 1948; writer FAO, Washington, 1949; reporter, mgr. Emporia (Kans.) Times, 1950-52; asst. editor Workbasket mag., Kansas City, 1952-56; editor Flower and Garden mag., Kansas City, 1957—. Recipient Profl. Writers award Am. Seed Trade Assn., 1967; Garden Writers award Am. Assn. Nurserymen, 1975. Mem. Women in Communications, Garden Writers Assn. Am., Am. Hort. Soc., Nature Conservancy, Wilderness Soc. Unitarian. Club: Sierra. Author: The Complete Book for Gardeners, 1964. Office: 4251 Pennsylvania St Kansas City MO 64111

SNYDER, RUTH COZEN, painter, sculptor; b. Montreal, Can.; d. Harry and Rachel Cozen; student UCLA, Otis Art Inst.; m. Paul Snyder; children—Harry M., Robert Lewis, Douglas M., Nancy J. One-woman shows include: Coos Art Mus., Coos Bay, Oreg., Riverside (Calif.) Art Center and Mus., Galerie Arcadia, Paris, Brigham Young U., Provo, Utah; represented in permanent collections: Frederick S. Wight Gallery of UCLA, Textron Corp., Washington, Clorox Corp., San Francisco, Intercontinental, Singapore, Hyatt-Watertower, Chgo., U.S. Embassy Lisbon, Coos Art Mus., juror art exhibits San Diego, Long Beach and Los Angeles, Calif.; lectr., demonstrator. Recipient 6 awards Nat. Watercolor Soc.; award Scottsdale Watercolor Biennial, 1978, San Bernardino Mus. Art. Mem. Nat. Watercolor Soc., Artists Equity, Watercolor West, Women Painters West, Santa Monica C. of C. Home: 550 Hanley Ave Los Angeles CA 90049

SNYDER, SUSAN BROOKE, educator; b. Yonkers, N.Y., July 12, 1934; d. John Warren and Virginia Grace (Hartung) Snyder; B.A., Hunter Coll., City U.N.Y., 1955; M.A., Columbia U., 1958, Ph.D., 1963. Lectr. English, Queens Coll., City U.N.Y., 1961-63; mem. faculty Swarthmore (Pa.) Coll., 1963—, prof. English, 1975—. Nat. Endowment for Humanities fellow, 1967-68; Folger Library fellow, 1972-73; Guggenheim fellow, 1980-81. Mem. MLA, Renaissance Soc. Am., Shakespeare Assn. Am. (trustee 1980-83), Spenser Soc. Mem. editorial bd. Shakespeare Quar., 1972—. Office: Dept English Swarthmore College Swarthmore PA 19081

SNYDERS, CAROL JOY, sewing patterns co. fin. exec.; b. N.Y.C., Sept. 6, 1955; d. Isaac and Sylvia (Cohen) Golden; B.A. in Polit. Sci., Douglass Coll., Rutgers U., 1977; M.B.A., Wharton Sch., U. Pa., 1979; m. Ron Snyders, July 31, 1982. Student intern Dept. Commerce, Washington, 1976, N.J. Office Internat. Trade, Newark, 1977, N.J. Office Fin. and Budget, Montclair, N.J., 1977, Citibank, N.Y.C., 1978; assoc. acct. Commonwealth Edison, N.Y.C., 1979-81; mgr. forecasts and ops. control Butterick Fashion Mktg. Co., N.Y.C., 1981—; undergrad. assoc. Eagelton Inst. Politics, 1976-77. Mem. exec. bd. N.Y. County (N.Y.) Young Democrats, 1981—. Mem. Am. Mgmt. Assn. Jewish. Clubs: Wharton of N.Y., Jefferson Democratic. Office: 161 Sixth Ave New York NY 10013

SOAMES, CYNTHIA ELIZABETH, percussionist; b. Peru, Ind., Oct. 6, 1946; d. Charles Bertrand and Elizabeth (Lee) S.; B.Mus., U. Cin., 1969; M.Mus., U. Miami (Fla.), 1973; student in acctg. Ind. U., Kokomo. Mem. Nashville Symphony, also mem. faculty Western Ky. U., 1969-70; mem. faculty St. Joseph's Coll., Rensselaer, Ind., 1970; mem. N.C. Symphony Orch., 1970-72; instr. U. N.C., Chapel Hill, 1971-72; grad. teaching asst. U. Miami, 1972-73; instr. U. Wis., River Falls, 1974-75; percussionist Richmond (Ind.) Symphony, Cin. Percussion Ensemble, Indpls. Chamber Ensemble, Indpls. Symphony Orch.; pvt. tchr. percussion, 1975—; clinician, freelance tchr. band camps and music programs. Mem. Percussive Arts Soc. (historian 1977-81, editor newsletter, treas. Ind. chpt. 1977-80), Bus. and Profl. Women's Club. Roman Catholic. Club: Altrusa. Author articles in field of music. Address: 115 N Miami St Peru IN 46970

SOBCZAK, JO ANN, savs. and loan exec.; b. Louisville, Aug. 30, 1931; d. Norman Fletcher and Thelma May (Hillen) Cardwell; standard diploma Inst. Fin. Edn., 1965; m. Richard Raymond Sobczak, Dec. 19, 1969; stepchildren—Roslyn Sobczak Roman, Wayne J., Patricia Sobczak Savilonis, Michael P. Secretarial position R.E. LaPorte, Realtor, 1950-53; with Hollywood Fed. Savs. & Loan Assn. (Fla.), 1953—, asst. corp. sec., 1962-69, asst. v.p., 1969-74, v.p. savs., 1974-76, v.p. retirement systems, 1976—; instr. Inst. Fin. Edn. Mem. Inst. Fin. Edn. (pres. Suncoast chpt. 202 1969-70), Greater Hollywood C. of C. Roman Catholic. Club: Zonta (charter mem., sec. Hollywood area 1979). Office: Hollywood Fed Savs & Loan Assn 1909 Tyler St Hollywood FL 33020

SOBEL, SUZANNE BARBARA, clin. psychologist; b. Bklyn.; d. Albert E. and Jeannette (Schneider) S.; student Clark U., 1960-62; B.A., Adelphi U., 1964, M.A., 1966; Ph.D., U. Tenn., 1971. Psychologist, Orleans (La.) Parish Sch. Bd., 1971-72; asst. prof. Dillard U., 1972-73; clin. psychologist D.C. Children's Center, 1973-75; research clin. psychologist Mental Health Study Center, Nat. Inst. Mental Health, Adelphi, Md., 1975-79; lectr. Univ. Coll., U. Md., 1975-79; pvt. practice clin. psychology, Washington, 1975-80, Indian Harbor Beach, 1980-82, Satellite Beach, Fla., 1982—; asso. dean acad. affairs, prof. psychology Sch. Profl. Psychology, Fla. Inst. Tech., 1980-82; civil rights coordinator Alcohol, Drug Abuse and Mental Health Adminstrn., HEW, Rockville, Md., 1979—; cons. clin. psychologist Children's Brain Research Center, 1976—. Public mem. D.C. Criminal Justice Coordinating Bd., 1977-78; mem. President's Commn. on Mental Health, 1977-78; mem. female offender and female juvenile offender coms. D.C. Commn. on Women, 1976. Fellow Am. Orthopsychiat. Assn., Am. Psychol. Assn. (pres. div. child and youth services 1980-81); mem. Southeastern Psychol. Assn., Soc. Pediatric Psychology, Am. Psychology Law Soc., Am. Soc. Correctional Psychologists, NOW, Nat. Assn. Female Execs., ORT. Mem. editorial bd. Jour. Clin. Child Psychology, 1976—; cons. editor Prof. Psychology, 1979—; editorial cons. Am. Psychologist, 1976—; cons. editor Psychotherapy: Theory, Research and Practice, 1980—. Contbr. articles to profl. jours. Home: 238 Harbor Dr East Indian Harbor Beach FL 32937 Office: 1290 Hwy A1A Suite 103B Satellite Beach FL 32937

SOBELL, LINDA CARTER, research scientist; b. Reno, May 8, 1948; d. Harold Abraham and Betty Anne (Tallman) Carter; B.A. with honors, U. Calif., Riverside, 1970; M.A., U. Calif., Irvine, 1974, Ph.D., 1976; m. Mark Barry Sobell, Aug. 30, 1969; children—Stacey Lianne, Kimberly Allison. Research asst. Patton (Calif.) State Hosp., 1969-71; mental health worker II alcohol services dept. Mental Health Orange County, Calif., 1971-74; dir. alcohol programs Dede Wallace Center, Nashville, 1974-80, adj. assoc. prof. psychology Vanderbilt U., 1974-80; head behavioral intervention research Clin. Inst. Addiction Research Found., Toronto, Ont., Can., 1980—; asst. prof. psychology U. Toronto, 1980—; cons. Nat. Inst. on Alcohol Abuse and Alcoholism; grantee, 1972-74, 1975, 1977-78; project dir. Tenn. Dept. Mental Health and Mental Retardation, 1976, 77-79. Mem. Am. Psychol. Assn., Assn. for Advancement Behavior Therapy. Mem. editorial bd. Addictive Behaviors, 1974—, Behavior Modification, 1976—, Behavioral Assessment, 1979—, Behavior Therapy, 1980—; author: (with M. B. Sobell) Behavioral Treatment of Alcohol Problems: Individualized Therapy and Controlled Drinking, 1978; contbr. numerous articles to profl. jours. Home: 25 Robaldon Rd Etobicoke ON M9A 5A8 Canada Office: Addiction Research Found 33 Russell St Toronto ON M5S 2S1 Canada

SOBOL, LILLIAN, constrn. co. exec., coll. registrar; b. Balt., May 10, 1934; d. Joseph and Celia Dunner; m. Norman Sobol, Oct. 4, 1952 (dec.); children—Pamala Lynne, Tina Ellen, Robyn Gayle. Fatality analyst Md. State Police, 1963-76; pres. Nu-View Contractors, Balt., 1973—; supr. records and transcript office U. Balt., 1976—; condr. seminars. Mem. Covenant Guild, Mildred Mindell Cancer Assn. active fund raising Am. Cancer Soc., Balt. County Gen. Hosp. Democrat. Jewish. Home: 4408D Old Court Rd Baltimore MD 21208 Office: 1420 N Charles St Baltimore MD 21201

SOCHEN, JUNE, historian; b. Chgo., Nov. 26, 1937; d. Sam and Ruth (Finkelstein) S.; B.A., U. Chgo., 1958; M.A., Northwestern U., 1960, Ph.D., 1967. High sch. tchr. English and history North Shore Country Day Sch., Winnetka, Ill., 1961-64; instr. history Northeastern Ill U, 1964-67, asst. prof., 1967-69, asso. prof., 1969-72, prof., 1972—. Nat. Endowment for Humanities grantee, 1971-72. Mem. Am. Studies Assn. Author books including: The New Woman, 1971; Movers and Shakers, 1973; Herstory: A Womans View of American History, 1975, 2d edit., 1981; Consecrate Every Day: The Public Lives of Jewish American Women 1880-1980, 1981; contbr. articles on U.S. cultural and women's history to profl. jours. Office: Northeastern Ill U 5500 N Saint Louis St Chicago IL 60625

SOCHET, MARY ALLEN, psychotherapist, educator, community organizer; b. Plattsburgh, N.Y., Feb. 10, 1938; d. Edwin Elisha and Mary Elizabeth (Thomson) Allen; B.S., SUNY, Plattsburgh, 1958; M.A., N.Y.U., 1961, Ph.D., 1963; postdoctoral student psychotherapy insts.; m. Marvin J. Sochet, 1963; children—Melorra, David. Tchr. kindergarten L.I. Pub. Schs., 1958-62, N.Y.C. Pub. Schs., 1962-64; prof. early childhood edn., child devel. and psychology Bklyn. Coll., 1964-71; program dir., acting exec. dir. Newark Pre-Sch. Council, 1965-66; psychotherapist N.Y.C. Community Guidance Service, 1966-78; staff cons. Human Resources Inst., 1966—; writer, lectr., ednl. cons., editorial cons.; pvt. practice psychotherapy, N.Y.C., 1978—. Founding mem. Community Loft, 1971-74; organizing mem. Children's Free Sch., 1969-81; founding mem. Neighbor's Network, 1979—. NCCJ fellow, 1961-62; recipient Founder's Day award N.Y.U., 1963. Mem. Am. Psychol. Assn., Soc. Psychol. Study of Social Issues, Kappa Delta Pi. Author: (with Robert Allen) Toward a Caring Community, 1980; contbr. articles on edn., community orgn. and mental health to various jours. Home and office: 380 Riverside Dr New York NY 10025

SOCO, PROFITA R., accountant; b. Mactan, Cebu, Philippines, Apr. 10, 1936; d. Lucas G. and Roberta Rosolada (Mejias) S.; came to U.S., 1971, naturalized, 1976; B.S. in Commerce, Far Eastern U., Manila, 1964. Clk. II Div. Sch. Supt.'s Office, Dept. Public Sch. Edn., Marawi City, Philippines, 1962-70; budget officer I, Philippines Sugar Inst., 1970-71; brokerage clk. Overseas Consol. Co., N.Y.C., 1971-72, bookkeeper, 1972-73; jr. acct. J.K. Lasser Co., N.Y.C., 1973-74; asst. voyage acctg. mgr. Overseas Consol. Co., N.Y.C., 1974-76; acctg. mgr. Costa Line Cargo Services, Inc., N.Y.C., 1976-80; voyage acctg. mgr. Kerr Steamship Co., Cranford, N.J., 1981—. Mem. Nat. Assn. Female Execs. Roman Catholic. Home: 25 Clark St Colonia NJ 07067 Office: 505 South Ave Cranford NJ 07016

SOLA, CANDIDA, mfg. co. exec.; b. Yabucoa, P.R., June 6, 1940; d. Tomas and Sandilia (Garcia) Rosario; B.S., Mercy Coll., 1979; postgrad. L.I. U., 1982—; m. Ramon Sola, Dec. 21, 1962; children—Ramon, Samuel. Engring. clk. Ward Leonard Electric Co., Mt. Vernon, N.Y., 1972-74, cost acct., 1975-78; pres. C and C Sportswear, Yonkers, N.Y., 1978-80; owner Top Fashions, Yonkers, 1980—. Mem. Puerto Rican Assn. Community Affairs, Yonkers; treas. Puerto Rican Community Council Westchester; past pres. Puerto Rican and Hispanic Voters Westchester. Recipient P.R. Community Council of West award, 1979. Mem. Nat. Assn. Female Execs., Nat. Assn. Republican Women. Home: 118 McLean Ave Yonkers NY 10705

SOLANO, SISTER, FRANCES, educator; b. Phila., June 27, 1928; d. James and Mary (McCrory) Carmody; B.S., St. John's U., Jamaica, N.Y., 1970; M.S. (grantee N.Y. State), SUNY, Buffalo, 1962; Ph.D. (HEW fellow 1972-74), Syracuse (N.Y.) U., 1974. Joined Sisters of St. Joseph, Roman Cath. Ch., 1949; asst. supt. instrn. St. Francis de Sales Sch. Deaf, Bklyn., 1974—. Mem. Am. Instrs. Deaf (pres.-elect 1979—), N.Y. State Assn. Educators of Deaf (pres. 1970-72), Am. Speech and Hearing Assn., Council on Edn. of Deaf, Assns. for Edn. of Deaf, Assn. Curriculum Devel., Phi Lambda Theta. Mem. editorial bd. Gallaudet Press, Directions mag. Home: 31 Sidney Pl Brooklyn NY 11201 Office: 260 Eastern Pkwy Brooklyn NY 11225

SOLANTO, DIANE HELEN, human services exec.; b. N.Y.C., Jan. 6, 1950; d. Hugo A. and Helen (Alfreo) Bert; B.S., R.I. Coll., 1971; M.A., Columbia U., 1974; M.S.W., N.Y. U., 1979; m. Joseph R. Solanto, Aug. 12, 1979; stepchildren—Paul, Jeanette, Cheryl. Tchr. Cardinal Spellman High Sch., Bronx, N.Y., 1971-74; health educator, co-chmn. peer counseling North Salem (N.Y.) Public Schs., 1974-75; acting chmn. Coll. Mt. St. Vincent, Riverdale, N.Y., 1974-76; asso. prof. Western Conn. State Coll., Danbury, 1976-80; asst. dir. Opengate, Inc., Somers, N.Y., 1980—; cons. in field. Mem. Am. Assn. Sex Educators, Counselors and Therapists, Nat. Assn. Social Workers, Am. Public Health Assn. Democrat. Roman Catholic. Office: 65 Warren St Somers NY 10589

SOLAZZO, ELIZABETH QUINN, brokerage exec.; b. S.I., N.Y., June 14, 1948; d. Joseph Paul and Josephine (Amodeo) Quinn; B.A., George Mason Coll., U. Va., 1970; student Hunter Coll., 1966-69; m. Anthony Solazzo, July 10, 1976. Asst. v.p. Seiden & deCuevas, N.Y.C., 1972-73, v.p., asst. sec. successor firm Furman Selz Mager Dietz & Birney, N.Y.C., 1973—. Home: 90 Rolling Hill Green Staten Island NY 10312 Office: 110 Wall St New York NY 10005

SOLBRIG, INGEBORG HILDEGARD, educator; b. Weissenfels, Germany, July 31, 1923; came to U.S., 1961, naturalized, 1966; d. Reinhold Johannes and Hildegard Marianne Adelheid Ferchland-Solbrig; diploma in chemistry, W.Ger., 1948; B.A. summa cum lade, San Francisco State U., 1964; M.A. (univ. fellow), Stanford U., 1966, Ph.D. (univ. dissertation fellow), 1969. Chem. engr. Schoeller Co., Osnabrück, W.Ger. and Naples, Italy, 1951-61; asst. prof. German, U. R.I., 1969-70, U. Tenn., Chattanooga, 1970-72, U. Ky., Lexington, 1972-75; mem. faculty U. Iowa, Iowa City, 1975—, prof. German lit. and philology, 1981—. Recipient Gold medal pro orientalibus, Austria, 1974; fellow Austrian Ministry Edn., 1968-69; Old Gold fellow, 1977; grantee Am. Council Learned Socs., German Acad. Exchange Service. Mem. Internat. Assn. German Studies, Am. Assn. 18th Century Studies, MLA, Am. Assn. Tchrs. German, Am. Council Study Austrian Lit., Arthur Schnitzler Research Assn., Nat. Assn. Female Execs. Author: Hammer-Purgstall und Goethe, 1973; Rilke heute, 1975; Reinhard Goering: Seabattle/Seeschlacht, 1977; also numerous articles, revs., chpts. to books. Home: 1126 Pine St Iowa City IA 52240 Office: Dept German U Iowa Iowa City IA 52242

SOLDANO, CONNIE LEE, health center adminstr.; b. Connellsville, Pa., May 25, 1934; d. Edward James and Mary Elizabeth (Clark) Hampton; B.S., Calif. State Coll., 1980; postgrad. U. Pitts., 1980-82; m. Nick J. Soldano, May 13, 1967; children—Ken N., Terry J., Cynthia A. Sec., asst. treas. Charles F. Eggers Co., Uniontown, Pa., 1962-72; adminstrv. asst. Bauer Lumber Co., Uniontown, 1972-74; fiscal, statis. asst. Fayette County Mental Health/Mental Retardation Clinic, Inc., Uniontown, 1974-76; fiscal officer Fayette County Health Center, Uniontown, 1979-81, adminstr., 1982—. Asst. leader Girl Scouts U.S., 1949-52; pres. Dunbar Boro PTA 1961-1962; mem. Heart Fund Telethon, 1982—. Mem. Nat. Assn. Accts., Nat. Assn. Female Execs., Soc. Advancement Mgmt., AAUW (legis. chmn.), Calif. State Coll. Alumni Assn. Democrat. Home: 708 S Arch St Connellsville PA 15425 Office: 100 New Salem Rd Uniontown PA 15401

SOLDWEDEL, BETTE JEAN, coll. dean; b. Pekin, Ill., Jan. 2, 1929; B.S., Ill. State U., 1951, M.S., 1953, LL.D. (hon.), 1975; Ed.D., N.Y.U., 1960. Dean women, instr. English, Eureka (Ill.) Coll., 1952-53; dir. women's residence halls Ill. State U., 1953-57; teaching fellow N.Y.U., 1957-58; assoc. prof., assoc. dean students Trenton State Coll., 1958-60; prof. edn. chmn. dept. personnel and guidance N.Y.U., 1960-67; dir. Office Program Devel., Job Corps, Dept. Labor, 1967-73; prof. edn., chmn. dept. U. North Fla., Jacksonville, 1973—, interim dean Coll. Edn., 1980—; cons. in field. Mem. Jacksonville Women's Pub. Leadership Consortium, 1979—, chmn., 1980-81; pres. Kathryn Sisson Phillips Trust, 1981—. Recipient Meritorious Achievement award Dept. Labor, 1971, Disting. Alumni Achievement award N.Y.U. Sch. Edn., 1978, 1st Disting. Faculty award U. North Fla., 1979. Mem. Nat. Assn. Women Deans, Adminstrs. and Counselors (pres. 1977-79, editor jour. 1969-72), Am. Coll. Personnel Assn. Author: Mastering the College Challenge, 1964; Preparing for College, 1966; also monographs, handbooks. Office: U North Fla St John's Bluff Rd Jacksonville FL 32216

SOLE, SELMA, speech pathologist, psychotherapist; b. Newark, Aug. 7, 1915; d. George and Mary (Heidt) Fuhrer; B.A. cum laude, Bklyn. Coll., 1952; M.A. cum laude, N.Y. U., 1954; Ed.D. cum laude, 1957; m. David Sole, Aug. 12, 1934; children—Myra Burstein, Kenneth. Dir. speech clinic Jewish Hosp. Bklyn., 1962-79, cons. Catch program, 1968-79; dir. speech clinic Greenpoint Hosp. Bklyn., 1972-79; pvt. practice speech pathology, psychotherapy, Stamford, Conn. Recipient Founder's Day award N.Y. U., 1958. Mem. Am. Speech, Lang. and Hearing Assn. Address: 51 Irongate Rd Stamford CT 06903

SOLES, ADA LEIGH, Del. state rep.; b. Jacksonville, Fla., May 19, 1937; d. Albert Thomas and Dorothy (Winter) Wall; B.A., Fla. State U., 1959; m. James Ralph Soles, 1959; children—Nancy Beth, Catherine. Mem. New Castle County Library Adv. Bd., 1975-80, chmn., 1975-77; chmn. Del. State Library Adv. Bd., 1975-78; mem. Del. State Ho. Reps., 1980—. Adminstrv. asst. U. Del. Commn. on Status of Women, 1976-77; academic adv. com. U. Del. Coll. Arts and Scis., 1977—. Mem. LWV (state pres. 1978-80), Phi Beta Kappa, Phi Kappa Phi, Mortar Bd., Alpha Chi Omega. Episcopalian. Office: Del Ho of Reps State Capitol Dover DE 19901 *

SOLFRONK, JACQUELINE ANN, psychologist; b. Chgo., Jan. 13, 1943; d. Louis Joseph and Ludmilla Joan (Kuvicek) S.; B.S.Ed., No. Ill. U., 1964; Ed.M., U. Ill., 1965, Ph.D., 1971. Elem. tchr. Chgo. Public Schs., 1965, Villa Park (Ill.) Schs., 1965-66; guidance dir. Plano (Ill.) Public Schs., 1966-68; residence hall asst. U. Ill., 1968-79; counselor St. Joseph-Odgen (Ill.) Public Schs., 1969-70, Morris (Ill.) Public Schs.,

1970-71; mem. faculty psychology and spl. edn. Joliet (Ill.) Jr. Coll., 1971-82; pvt. practice clin. psychology, Joliet, 1976—. Mem. Ill. Gov.'s Commn. for Handicapped, 1973-76. Recipient Bausch & Lomb Sci. award, 1961; Ill. State Tchrs. scholar, 1961-65; cert. spl. kindergarten-14 tchr., supr., guidance counselor, elem. tchr., sch. service personnel-guidance counselor, Ill.; registered clin. psychologist, Ill. Mem. Am. Psychol. Assn., Ill. Psychol. Assn., Nat. Acad. Neuropsychology, Am. Fedn. Tchrs., Internat. Council Psychologists, Sigma Lambda Sigma (a founder). Exhibited paintings in group shows. Office: #23 1520 N Rock Run Joliet IL 60435

SOLIMAN, PATRICIA KATHLEEN BREHAUT, (MRS. ANWAR EL SAYED I. SOLIMAN), publishing exec.; b. New Rochelle, N.Y., Oct. 11, 1937; d. Ernest Henry and Winnifred (Gatehouse) Brehaut; B.A., Tufts U., 1959; M.A., Stanford U., 1962; m. Anwar el Sayed I. Soliman, Sept. 26, 1964. Editorial asst. Harper & Row, Pubs., Inc., 1962-65; asso. editor Coward, McCann & Geoghegan, Inc., N.Y.C., 1965-68, sr. editor, 1968-71, exec. editor, 1971-72, exec. editor, v.p., 1972-74, v.p., editor-in-chief, 1974-79, pres., pub., 1980-81; asso. pub., v.p. Simon & Schuster, 1981—. Woodrow Wilson fellow, 1959. Mem. Women's Media Group, Phi Beta Kappa. Club: Balboa Bay. Address: Simon and Schuster Bldg 1230 Ave of the Americas New York NY 10020

SOLL, HARRIET PREMACK (LUCILLE), govt. communications, bus. and industry specialist; b. Mpls., Apr. 7, 1914; d. J. D. and Ida Rita (Amdur) Premack; B.A., U. Minn., 1934; postgrad. Cath. U. Am., 1973-74; m. Arthur Soll, Aug. 23, 1936 (dec. 1963); children—Elinor Soll Priesman, Sherna. Tchr. creative writing Mpls. Women's Club, Mpls., 1962-63; host talk show Sta.-KRSI, Mpls., 1964-65; cons. Systems Devel. Corp., Washington, 1970-72, Dept. Labor, Washington, 1972-73; cons. SBA, Washington, 1973-75, communications specialist, Washington, 1975—. Mem. Women in Communications, Inc., Nat. Assn. Govt. Communicators, Small Bus. Inst. Dirs. Assn., Internat. Council Small Bus. Mgmt., AAUW, Hadassah (life; regional v.p. 1954-55), Fairfax Symphony Assn., Washington Women's Forum, Common Cause, World Affairs Council D.C., Sierra Club, No. Va. Jewish Community Center. Author: Holiday Readings, Philosophies of Religion, 1965; The Vital Majority, 1973; contbr. articles on bus. and office-related subjects to mags.; editor Insight, 1972-81, SBI Rev., 1973-83, Best of the SBI, 1982. Home: 3404 Hemlock Dr Falls Church VA 22042 Office: SBA 1441 L St NW Washington DC 20416

SOLLISH, ROCHELLE, mktg. exec.; b. N.Y.C.; d. Al and Helen (Sherman) Sollish; B.S., N.Y. U., 1968, M.B.A., 1970. Research analyst Avon Products, N.Y.C., 1965-71; mktg. asso. Selling Areas Mktg., Inc., N.Y.C., 1971-73; dir. market research Am. Express, N.Y.C., 1973-76, dir. mktg. card div., 1976-82; v.p. Citicorp Diners Club, N.Y.C., 1982—. Recipient Founder's Day award N.Y. U., 1964. Mem. Am. Mktg. Assn., Travel Research Assn., Delta Pi Sigma. Club: Lawyers. Home: 400 E 54th St New York City NY 10022 Office: 575 Lexington Ave New York NY 10043

SOLLITTO, ANDREA LYNN, psychologist; b. Aberdeen, Md., Jan. 9, 1948; d. Basil Joseph and Amelia Marie (Portizo) S.; B.A. in Elem. Edn., Georgian Ct. Coll., 1969; M.Ed., Boston U., 1971, Ed.D., 1977; m. Harry J. Hawtin, July 19, 1981. Tchr., Mt. Horeb Sch., Watchung, N.J., 1969-70; psychology intern Framingham (Mass.) Public Sch. System, 1970-71, Paul A. Dever State Sch., Taunton, Mass., 1971-72; research asst. Boston U., 1971-72, asst. prof. psychology and counseling, 1979—; psychology intern Dorchester Mental Health Clinic Boston State Hosp., Mattapan, Mass., 1972-73; title I home-sch. liaison specialist Westford (Mass.) Public Schs., 1973-75, title I coordinator, 1975-76; cons. psychologist Boston Public Schs., 1977; staff psychologist Regional Ednl. Assessment & Diagnostic Services, Inc., Lakeville, Mass., 1977-79, cons. psychologist, 1979; pvt. practice psychol. counseling, 1981—; vis. lectr. Fitchburg (Mass.) State Coll., 1976. Lic. psychologist N.J., Mass. Mem. Am. Psychol. Assn., Mass. Psychol. Assn., Parent Counseling Assn. New Eng. (dir. 1975-78), Am. Personnel and Guidance Assn., Phi Delta Kappa, Pi Lambda Theta. Home: 24 Pleasant Valley Rd Morganville NJ 07751

SOLNICK, LESLIE ILENE, artist, educator; b. N.Y.C., June 29, 1946; d. Jack and Edith (Litowitz) Berkowitz; A.A., Nassau Community Coll., 1966; B.S., Hofstra U., 1968; M.S., C.W. Post Coll., 1972. One-woman show: Tchr.'s Fed. Credit Union, Great River, L.I., N.Y., 1975, Half Hollow Hills Library, 1979; group shows include: (woodcuts) C.W. Post Coll., Greenvale, L.I., 1972, Hofstra U., Hempstead, N.Y., 1974, 75, 77, 78, Firehouse Gallery, Nassau Community Coll., Garden City, N.Y., 1973, 74, W. Islip Library, 1974-75, Woodmere Library, 1974, Heckscher Mus., Huntington, N.Y., 1975, N. Babylon Library, 1977, Bank of Smithtown, 1975; tchr. art elementary and secondary schs., North Babylon, N.Y., 1968—. Recipient 2d prize in graphics Hofstra U. Alumni Art Exhibit, 1975. Mem. Huntington Town Art League, N.Y. State United Tchrs., North Babylon Tchrs. Assn. Home: 26 Balsam Dr Dix Hills NY 11746 Office: Deer Park Ave Elem Sch UFSD 3 5 Jardine Pl North Babylon NY 11703

SOLODOVNICK, SARA LEAH, health services exec.; b. Bklyn., Mar. 28, 1948; d. Theodore J. and Florence B. Solodovnick; A.A., Queensborough Community Coll., City U. N.Y., 1968; B.S., Hunter Coll., City U. N.Y., 1971; M.S.M., Fla. Internat. U., 1974. Sr. clk. dept. med. records N. Shore U. Hosp., Cornell Med. Center, Port Washington, N.Y., 1968-69; med. sec. to neurosurgeons, Great Neck, N.Y., 1969; med. asst., sec. to cardiologist, N.Y.C., 1970; clk., house staff research asst. Roosevelt Hosp., N.Y.C., 1970-71; asst. dir. med. record dept. Mercy Hosp., Miami, Fla., 1971-73; adj. faculty Miami-Dade Community Coll., 1973-74; dir. med. record services Coral Reef Gen. Hosp., Miami, 1973-75; cons. to project coordinator Miami-Dade Community Coll., 1975-76; med. record adminstrv. cons. Westchester Gen. Hosp., Miami, 1975-78; prin. med. investigator Nat. Crash Severity Study, U.S. Dept. Transp., Nat. Hwy. Traffic Safety Adminstrn., U. Miami, 1976-80; records adminstr. Metro. Dade County, Fla. Dept. Human Resources, Office of Health Services, Miami, 1975—; med. record adminstrn. program splty. externship supr. Fla. Internat. U., 1979—; med. record tech. program externship supr. Miami-Dade Community Coll., 1974—; cons. Mem. Dade-Monroe Profl. Standards Rev. Orgn. (adv. council 1978-80), S. Fla. Med. Record Assn. (pres. 1976, 77), Fla. Med. Record Assn. (v.p. 1978-79), Am. Med. Record Assn. (ho. of dels. staff aide 1976), Am. Soc. Public Adminstrn. (dir. 1977—, sec. 1979—), Am. Hosp. Assn., Fla. Assn. Primary Care Centers, Fla. Med. Record Assn. Cons. Listing, Greater N.Y. Med. Record Assn., Med. Record Assn. N.Y. State, S. Fla. Hosp. Assn. Jewish. Contbr. articles to profl. jours. Home: 8335 SW 72nd Ave Miami FL 33143 Office: 140 W Flagler St Suite 1502 Miami FL 33130

SOLOMON, H. ANNE, health care adminstr.; b. N.Y.C., Jan. 22, 1924; d. Jacob S. and Rose (Weiser) Golub; B.A., Antioch Coll., 1945; M.S.W., U. Pa., 1947; M.B.A., Western Wash. U., 1981; m. Arthur L. Solomon, Dec. 13, 1943; children—Louise, David, Jonathan, Roslyn. Project OEO, Springfield, Ohio, 1965-67; mental health counselor Family Service Agy., Springfield, 1967-69; social worker Children's Med. Center, Dayton, Ohio, 1969-70; dir. patient services Island Hosp., Anacortes, Wash., 1970-73; health planning intern Puget Sound Health Systems Agy., Seattle, 1980; dir. dept. patient services St. Luke's Hosp., Bellingham, Wash., 1970-82; adminstrv. asst. Western State Hosp., 1982—; nursing home cons.; instr. Western Wash. U., 1972, Whatcom Community Coll., 1973; bd. dirs. various social agys. County chmn. Wash. State Heart Assn. drive, 1977. Recipient presdl. citation for achievements OEO project, 1968. Mem. Am. Coll. Hosp. Adminstrn., Am. Hosp. Assn., Wash. State Hosp. Assn., Assn. western Hosps., Nat. Assn. Social Workers, Acad. Cert. Social Workers, Soc. Hosp. Social Work Dirs., LWV (dir. Calif. 1959-62). Clubs: AAUW (bd., Calif., 1959-62), Hadassah. Author articles, grant proposals. Office: Ft Steilacoom WA 98494

SOLOMON, LINDA ZENER, psychologist, educator; b. Toronto, Ont., Can., Jan. 11, 1943; came to U.S., 1967; d. Harry and Celia (Sloskin) Zener; B.A., U. Toronto, 1965, M.A., 1966, Ph.D., 1970; m. Henry Solomon, Oct. 16, 1969; children—Miriam, Naomi. Asst. prof. psychology Baruch Coll., N.Y.C., 1971-76; asso. prof. psychology Marymount Manhattan Coll., N.Y.C., 1976—. NIMH grantee, 1975-76. Mem. Am. Psychol. Assn., Soc. for Psychol. Study Social Issues. Editor: (with H. Kaufmann) Readings in Social Psychology, 1974. Office: Marymount Manhattan College 221 E 71st St New York NY 10021

SOLOMON, SHARON FISHEL (SHARRY), civic worker; b. Cairo, Ill., June 30, 1943; d. Ben and Dorothy Lee (Solomon) Fishel; student U. Okla., 1961-62; A.B., Washington U., St. Louis, 1965; m. Michael J. Yatkeman, Feb. 28, 1965; children—Beth, Brent; m. 2d, Steve Solomon, May 23, 1982. Primary tchr. Ritenour Sch. Dist., St. Louis, 1965-68; real estate agt. Kenstan Realty Corp., St. Louis, part-time, 1978—. Bd. dirs. PTA; membership chmn. United Order of True Sisters, 1976, program chmn., 1977, 78, gourmet cooking chmn., 1977; grad. Young Women's Council for Edn., 1978-80; chmn. checkpoints Walk With Israel, 1978, co-chmn. community involvement, 1980. Life cert. elem. edn., Mo.; brokers real estate lic., Mo. Mem. Nat. Assn. Realtors, Mo. Assn. Realtors, Real Estate Bd. Met. St. Louis, Nat. Council Jewish Women, Women's Am. ORT, Shaare Zedek Sisterhood (corr. sec. 1976, dir.), Jewish Hosp. Aux. Clubs: Shaare Zedek Sisterhood, United Order True Sisters. Home: 133 Idlewild Paducah KY 42001

SOLOOK, BARBARA A. STRYKER (MRS. MICHAEL J. SOLOOK), social worker; b. Bound Brook, N.J., Feb. 22, 1928; d. Gysbert O. and Beatrice (Porter) Stryker; B.A., Keuka Coll., 1950; M.S., Columbia, 1953; m. Michael J. Solook, June 11, 1966; 1 dau., Nancy Ann. Staff psychiat. social worker Union County Psychiat. Clinic, Plainfield, N.J., 1953-56, 57-60, dir. psychiat. social work, 1960-72, adminstr. br. office, 1972-80; psychiat. social worker Rochester (N.Y.) Guidance Center, 1956-57; pvt. practice social work, 1970—. Cons. Union County Commn. Sch., Westfield, N.J., 1971-80; clin. social worker, 1980—. Co-chmn. Bound Brook Bi-Centennial Celebration, 1974-76; mem. Bound Brook Bd. Edn., 1974—. Lic. marriage counselor, cert. sch. social worker, N.J. Fellow Am. Orthopsychiat. Assn.; mem. AAUW (1st v.p. br. 1968-70, pres. br. 1970-72), Am. Assn. Psychiat. Services for Children, Nat. Assn. Social Workers, Zonta. Office: 18 E Union Ave Bound Brook NJ 08805

SOMA, ROSE SMERALDI, broadcaster, writer, women's rights activist, TV-radio producer, reporter; b. Bronx, N.Y., Feb. 17, 1940) d. Albert and Jeanette (DiCostanzo) Smeraldi; attended NYC public schs. until 1955; m. Fraser Soma, Sept. 13, 1967; children—Michael, Carl, Paul, Steven, Nancy, Errol. Producer, interviewer, reporter WALK radio, L.I., N.Y., 1976—, producer weekly feminist radio program, 1976—; lectr., condr. workshops on women's rights; media public relations cons. feminist issues for radio and TV, 1978. Chmn. reprodn./abortion rights task force Suffolk (N.Y.) chpt. NOW, 1975—, chmn. media task force, 1975—; producer/host Women Speak Out and People Speak Out, Brookhaven Cable TV, Port Jefferson Sta., N.Y., 1979—, Women Speak Out, Sta. WYFA, Medford, N.Y., 1979—, Suffolk Cablevision, 1979—, Sta. WBLI-FM, 1980—; media coordinator, personal mgr. entertainment acts, 1981—; bd. dirs. Planned Parenthood of East Suffolk, 1977—; coordinator L.I. chpt. Nat. Coalition to Defend the Bill of Rights, 1978—; coordinator public relations and media for L.I. chpt. Internat. Women's Yr. Meeting for N.Y. State, 1977; exec. dir., co-founder Americans United to Save Legal Abortion, 1977—; founder Women Speak Out Internat., 1978; adv. bd. Women's Health Alliance L.I., 1978; chmn. abortion rights task force N.Y. State orgn. NOW, 1978; coordinator L.I. Coalition for Reproductive Rights; asso. Women's Inst. for Freedom of Press, 1976—. Mem. Am. Women in Radio and TV, Nat. Fedn. Press Women. Author: Women Speak Out About Abortion, 1978; contbr. numerous articles to profl. jours.; author monthly column for NOW newsletter, 1974—. Home: PO Box AW Miller Place NY 11764 Office: UACC Brookhaven Cable TV Industrial Rd Port Jefferson Station NY 11776 also Sta WBLI 106 FM Long Island NY 11763

SOMAN, SHIRLEY CAMPER ISENBERG (MRS. ROBERT O. SOMAN), author, social worker; b. Boston; d. David and Fannie (Apteker) Isenberg; B.A., U. Wis.; M.S.S., Smith Coll. Sch. Social Work; m. Frederic R. Camper (div. 1961); children—Frederic Douglas, Frances Ann; m. 2d, Robert O. Soman, Nov. 10, 1962 (dec. 1975). Asso. editor My Baby Mag. and Shaw's Market News, 1952-53; sch. social worker Bur. Child Guidance, N.Y.C. Bd. Edn., 1956-57; family life cons., editor, public info. cons. Family Service Assn. Am., 1957-64; v.p. Asso. Film Cons. and Mercury News Film, 1967-72; adj. asso. prof. CUNY, 1976-77; cons., lectr. social agys. and community groups, 1960-70; chairwoman 1st Nat. Symposium on Child Advocacy, 1974; former mem. bd. Creative Arts Rehab. Center; vice chairperson Public Action Coalition for Toys. Cert. social worker, N.Y. State. Mem. Authors League Am. (chmn. program adv. com. 1972-73), Nat. Assn. Sci. Writers, Soc. Mag. Writers (chmn. non-fiction writers' conf. 1975), Acad. Cert. Social Workers, Nat. Assn. Social Workers, Oral History Assn., Am. Soc. Journalists and Authors (chmn. crafts sessions 1977-78), Nat. Council Family Relations, Nat. Acad. Television Arts and Scis. (producer Forum on Effect TV on Children 1979), Nat. Orgn. Women, Women's Internat. League for Peace and Freedom, Am. Public Welfare Assn., Am. Med. Writers Assn., Writers Guild East. Author: How to Get Along With Your Child, 1962, Brazil edit., 1974; Let's Stop Destroying our Children, 1974; Preparing for Your New Baby; editor: Forging Tools for Mental Health (Jewish Bd. Guardians), 1955; editor Family Service Highlights-Jour., 1957-61. Home: 40 W 77th St New York NY 10024

SOMAYAJI, VIJAYALAKSHMI VISHWANATHA, chemist; b. Saragur, India, June 10, 1952; d. Krishnamurthy and Nagalakshmi (Krishnamurthy) Saragur; came to U.S., 1978; Ph.D. in Chemistry, Indian Inst. Sci., 1977; m. Oct. 17, 1977; 1 child, Ranjani. Postdoctoral research asso. U. Idaho, Moscow, 1978; pool officer, metallurgy dept. Indian Inst. Sci., Bangalore, India, 1979-81; research asso. dept. chemistry Purdue U., West Lafayette, Ind., 1982—. Contbr. articles to profl. jours. Home: 414 1/2 N Salisbury St West Lafayette IN 47906 Office: Dept Chemistry Purdue U West Lafayette IN 47906

SOMERS, CARIN ALMA, librarian; b. Frankfurt, W.Ger., Mar. 18, 1934; d. Josef and Helen Josephine (Badham) Stein; B.A., Newton (Mass.) Coll. Sacred Heart, 1955; M.A., Dalhousie U., Halifax, N.S., Can., 1956; B.L.S., U. Toronto (Ont., Can.), 1961; m. Frank George Somers, Aug. 23, 1958. Registrar, lectr. French St. Mary's U., Halifax, 1956-60; with Halifax City Regional Library, 1958-64; with Halifax County Regional Library, 1964-73; with N.S. Provincial Library, Halifax, 1973—, dir. libraries, 1974—; lectr. Sch. Library Sci. Dalhousie U. Recipient Gov. Gen. medal, 1953, Queens Silver Jubilee medal, 1977. Mem. Can. Library Assn. (2d v.p. 1974-75), Atlantic Provinces Library Assn. (pres. 1969-70), N.S. Library Assn., Can. Nature Fedn., N.S. Bird Soc. Roman Catholic. Club: Royal N.S. Yacht Squadron. Contbr. articles in field. Home: Box 772 Armdale PO Halifax NS B3L 4K5 Canada Office: 5250 Spring Garden Rd Halifax NS B3J 1E8 Canada

SOMERVILLE, EARNESTINE, retail co. ofcl.; b. Sawyerville, Ala., Oct. 18, 1955; d. Earnest Lee and Ella Ruth (Mims) S.; B.B.A. in Bus., Ohio U., 1978, B.S., 1978. Sales asso. May Co., Cleveland, 1977-78, sales mgr., 1978-81, asst. mgr., 1981—; student life intern Ohio Univ., Athens, 1977-78. Mem. Delta Sigma Theta (chpt. pres. 1977-78), Phi Gamma Nu. Democrat. Baptist. Home: 3929 E 120th St Cleveland OH 44105

SOMMERHOF, GRACEMARIE MARY GIUMENTO, nurse, educator, civic worker; b. Dunmore, Pa., Nov. 14, 1928; d. Cataldo and Michelle (Sberne) Giumento; student Keystone Jr. Coll., 1947; diploma Scranton (Pa.) State Gen. Hosp. Nursing Sch., 1949; cert. Skidmore Coll., 1951; student U. Scranton, 1956; teaching cert. U. Md., 1975; m. Roy Andrew Sommerhof, Jr., Feb. 11, 1956; children—Michele-Marie Skelly, Roy Andrew III. Pvt. duty nurse, Balt., N.Y.C., Lackawanna County, Pa., 1951-55; head nurse, supr., instr. Johns Hopkins Hosp., Balt., 1956-63; clinic dir., dir. vols., dir. profl. edn. Planned Parenthood of Md., 1964-69; Mem. Baltimore County Bd. Health, 1976—; vice chmn. Bur. Home Health Services, Balt. Nurse-educator, Dept. Edn., Balt. City, 1969-78; County, 1977, chmn., 1971—; chmn. bd. trustees Spring Grove Hosp. Center, Catonsville, Md., 1977—; mem. adv. bd. ARC, 1971—; mem. child devel., parenting, and family living adv. bd. Balt. Dept. Edn.; mem. women's bd. Johns Hopkins Med. Inst. Recipient Outstanding Service award ARC, 1971; Clara Barton medal ARC, 1972; Robert Woods Johnson Found. grantee, 1974. Mem. Am. Nurses Assn., Md. Nurses Assn., NEA. Am. Vocat. Assn., Nat. Ret. Tchrs. Assn., Md. Ret. Tchrs. Assn., Balt. City Ret. Tchrs. Assn., Md. Council for Social Concern, Md. Council for Family Relations, Balt. Council for Internat. Visitors. Republican. Roman Catholic. Clubs: Johns Hopkins; Univ. (Towson); Greenspring Valley Inn. Home: 622 Coventry Rd Towson MD 21204

SOMMERS, ESTELLE JOAN, retail exec.; b. Balt.; d. David Isaac and Mary Agnes (Curland) Goldstein; grad. high sch.; m. Ben Sommers, Dec. 2, 1962; children—Gayle Jean, Cathy Harriet, Debbie Jane. Stylist, owner Loshins, Cin., 1948-62; mgr., owner Capezio Fashion Shop., N.Y.C., 1964-79; stylist, owner Estar Ltd., N.Y.C., 1969-79; head adminstr., joint owner Capezio Dance-Theatre Shop, N.Y.C., 1970—. U.S. chmn. Dance Library of Israel, 1979—; bd. dirs. Dance Notation Bd., 1980—; mem. Am.-Israel Cultural Fedn., 1979-82; co-chmn. nat. adv. com. Internat Ballet Competition U.S.A., 1979-82. Office: 755 7th Ave New York NY 10019

SOMMERS, HELEN ELIZABETH, Wash. state rep.; b. Woodbury, N.J., Mar. 29, 1932; d. Roy and Christine (Eliasson) S.; B.A., U. Wash., 1969, M.A., 1970; div. Research analyst King County Council, Wash.; mem. Wash. Ho. of Reps. from 36th Dist., 1973—, chairwoman State Govt. Com., 1975-76, Revenue Com., 1977—; personnel research asst. Mobil Oil Co. de Venezuela, Caracas, 1964-68; instr. econs. Edmonds Community Coll., Wash., 1971-72. Mem. NOW, Easter Seal Soc. (dir.), LWV of Seattle, Phi Beta Kappa, Omicron Delta Epsilon. Office: Wash State Ho of Reps State Capitol Olympia WA 98504 *

SONDGEROTH, LILLIAN JO, lawyer; b. Carroll, Iowa, Jan. 5, 1948; d. John Charles and Arlene Mary (Grossman) S.; B.A., U. Nev., 1969, M.A. in Psychology, 1971; J.D. (grantee), Calif. Western Sch. Law, 1976. Admitted to Nev. bar, 1976, D.C. bar, 1979; cert. intern San Diego County Dist. Atty., 1975-76; staff atty. Clark County Legal Services Program, Las Vegas, Nev., 1977; psychologist Clark County Sch. Dist., Las Vegas, 1972-73; instr. sociology, psychology Clark County Community Coll., Las Vegas, 1972-73; pvt. practice law, Las Vegas, 1977—; instr. continuing edn. U. Nev., Las Vegas, 1979—; atty. Community Action Against Rape; community lectr. on fed. and Nev. legis. affecting women, 1978—; commentator on govt. regulations Las Vegas Business-women's Resource Network. Bd. dirs. March of Dimes, 1977-79; mem. panel Clark County Lawyer's Referral Services, 1978-80; del. Republican State Conv., 1978. Fed. Public Defenders intern, 1975; Daus. of Erin scholar, 1975-76. Mem. Am. Bar Assn., Nev. Bar Assn., Clark County Bar Assn., Nat. Assn. Women Attys., NOW, Am. Trial Lawyers Assn., Nev. Trial Lawyers Assn., Psi Chi (v.p.). Roman Catholic. Office: 101 Convention Center Dr Suite 900 Las Vegas NV 89109

SONIES, BARBARA CAROL, speech/lang. pathologist; b. Gloversville, N.Y., Aug. 25, 1939; d. George and Eleanor S. (Kall) Myzal; B.S. with distinction, U. Minn., 1961; M.A., Stanford U., 1963; Ph.D., U. Md., 1981; m. Harvey J. Kupferberg, Jan. 5, 1975; 1 son, Mitchel H. Sonies. Speech therapist Alhambra (Calif.) Schs., 1963-65; speech pathologist U. Minn. Hosps., Mpls., 1965-67; coordinator speech diagnostic clinic Mpls. Public Schs., 1967-68; supr. speech pathology U. Minn. Health Scis. Center, Mpls., 1968-72; instr. communication disorders U. Minn., 1969-72; coordinator speech program Robbinsdale (Minn.) Public Schs., summer 1970; project mgr. sch. programs Am. Speech, Lang. and Hearing Assn., 1972-73; instr., clinic supr. dept. hearing and speech sci. U. Md., College Park, 1974-77; chief Speech-Lang. Pathology Clin. Center, NIH, Bethesda, Md., 1977—; instr. continuing edn. U. Va., Falls Church, 1975-82; research asso. prof. U. Md., College Park, 1981—; cons. Montgomery County Health Dept., Rockville, Md., 1974-79; lectr. in field. Hunt scholar, 1957-61; Rehab. Services Adminstrn. grantee, 1961-63. Mem. Am. Speech-Lang.-Hearing Assn., Md. Speech-Lang.-Hearing Assn. (sec. 1977-79, editor jour. 1981-83), Internat. Neuropsychol. Soc., Mortar Bd., Phi Beta Kappa, Order of Ski-U-Mah. Contbr. articles to profl. jours. Home: 8826 Tuckerman Ln Potomac MD 20854 Office: NIH Clin Center Speech Pathology Rm 5D37 Bethesda MD 20205

SONNENFELD, GRACIELA DIANA, bank mgr.; b. Buenos Aires, Argentina, Oct. 31, 1949; came to U.S., 1978; d. Egon Manfredo and Beatriz (Kamil) Horn; B.S., St. Catherine's Inst., 1971, London Cultural Inst., 1973; m. Peter Sonnenfeld, Oct. 28, 1978. Asst. to pres. OKS KNOS Y CIA, S.A., Buenos Aires, 1970-75; asst. to pres. Aurora S.A., Buenos Aires, 1975-78; personnel mgr. Chgo. br. Banco de la Nacion Argentina, 1979—. Pres., Gradia S.R.L., Chgo. and Buenos Aires; partner Regente S.R.L. Argentina. Mem. Women in Internat. Trade, Soc. Personnel Adminstrs. Jewish. Club: Italian Circle Buenos Aires. Home: 333 E Ontario St Apt 2301B Chicago IL 60611 Office: 135 S LaSalle Room 2240 Chicago IL 60603

SONNENFELD, JANET MARLOFF, lawyer; b. Long Branch, N.J., Feb. 9, 1948; d. Raymond James and Muriel (Goodkin) Marloff; B.A., George Washington U., 1970; J.D. cum laude, Howard U., 1973; m. Marc J. Sonnenfeld, Apr. 27, 1975. Admitted to Pa. bar, 1973, U.S. Supreme Ct., 1981; asso. firm Drinker Biddle & Reath, Phila., 1973-76; asso. counsel consumer banking Fidelity Bank, Phila., 1976-77; individual practice law, Phila., 1977—; partner firm Sonnenfeld & McHugh, personal bankruptcy practice, Phila., 1980—. Committee-woman, Phila. Democratic Party, 1974-76, 78—, mem. policy com., 1978—. Mem. Pa. Bar Assn., Phila. Bar Assn. (Lawyer Referral Service). Home: 322 S Juniper St Philadelphia PA 19107 Office: Two Girard Plaza Suite 2000 Philadelphia PA 19102

SONNENFELD, MARION, educator; b. Berlin, Feb. 13, 1928; came to U.S., 1939, naturalized, 1944; d. Kurt and Sibylla (Lemke) S.; B.A. with honors, Swarthmore Coll., 1950; M.A., Yale U., 1961, Ph.D., 1956.

Instr., Smith Coll., Northampton, Mass., 1954-59, asst. prof., 1959-62; assoc. prof. Wells Coll., Aurora, N.Y., 1962-67, chmn. dept. German, 1962-63, 65-67, dir. German Sch., 1965-67; assoc. prof. SUNY, Fredonia, 1967-74, prof., 1974-77, disting. teaching prof., 1977—, acting dean arts and humanities, 1980-81. Jr. Sterling fellow, 1951-53; NEH fellow, 1977. Mem. AAUP, MLA, Am. Assn. Tchrs. German, Internationale Germanisten-Vereinigung. Club: Zonta (1st v.p. 1981—Fredonia). Translator: Kleist's Amphitryon, 1962, Three Plays by Hebbel, 1974; (with Folkers, Dickens) The Complete Narrative Prose of C. F. Meyer, 1976; editor: Wert und Wort, 1965; Geprägte Form, 1974; Proc. of Zweig Symposium, 1981. Office: State University of New York Fredonia NY 14063

SONNESYN, PATRICIA PITTIS, missionary; b. N.Y., Oct. 29, 1952; d. Robert Eugene and Marie-Calire (Martin du Pan) Pittis; B.A., St. John's Coll., 1974; M. Divinity. Union Theol. Sem., 1979; m. Roger Earl Sonnesyn, Feb. 3, 1979. Prof., Ecumenical Theol. Sch., Butare, Rwanda, 1981-82; adminstrv. asst. to Archbishop of Anglican Francophone Province of Burundi, Rwanda and Zaire, 1982—. Fund for Theol. Edn. fellow, 1976-78. Episcopalian. Home: Boite Postale 227 Butare Rwanda also care Mrs M C Pittis 342 Cove Neck Rd Oyster Bay NY 11771 *

SONS, LINDA RUTH, educator; b. Chicago Heights, Ill., Oct. 31, 1939; d. Robert and Ruth (Diekelman) Sons; A.B., Ind. U., 1961; M.S., Cornell U., Ithaca, 1963, Ph.D. in Math., 1966. Asst. prof. math. No. Ill. U., DeKalb, 1965-70, NSF grantee, 1970-72, 1974-75, assoc. prof., 1970-78, prof., 1978—. Mem. Am. Math. Soc., London Math. Soc., Math. Assn. Am., Nat. Council Tchrs. Math., Ill. Council of Tchrs. Math., AAUP, Assn. for Women in Math., Phi Beta Kappa, Sigma Xi, Pi Lambda Theta, Omicron Delta Kappa. Lutheran. Contbr. articles to profl. jours. Office: Dept Math Scis No Ill U DeKalb IL 60115

SONTAG, SUSAN, film dir., author. Dir. film Duet for Cannibals, 1969, Brother Carl, 1971, Promised Lands, 1974. Guggenheim fellow, 1966, 75; Rockefeller Found. fellow, 1965, 74; recipient George Polk Meml. award for contbns. toward better appreciation of theatre, motion pictures and lit., 1966; Ingram Merrill Found. award in lit. in field of Am. Letters, 1976; Creative Arts award Brandeis U., 1976; Arts and Letters award Am. Acad. Arts and Letters, 1976; prize Nat. Book Critics Circle, 1978. Author: (novels) The Benefactor, 1963; Death Kit, 1967; (stories) I, etcetera, 1978; (essays) Against Interpretation, 1966; Trip to Hanoi, 1968; Styles of Radical Will, 1969; On Photography, 1977; Illness as Metaphor, 1978; Under the Sign of Saturn, 1980; A Susan Sontag Reader, 1981; (film scripts) Duet for Cannibals, 1970, Brother Carl, 1974; editor, author introduction: Antonin Artaud: Selected Writings, 1976. Address: care Farrar Straus & Giroux Inc 19 Union Sq W New York NY 10003 *

SOO, DORIS, univ. adminstr.; b. N.Y.C., May 22, 1953; d. Frank Edward and Ngook Ho (Tow) S.; B.A. in Math., CCNY, 1977; postgrad. Baruch Coll., 1980—. Adj. lectr. Hunter Coll., N.Y.C., 1978-79, grant adminstr. to coordinator of field work Research Found., 1980-81, adminstrv. asst. to dean Sch. Social Work, 1981—; tchr. math. William Alexander Jr. High Sch., Bklyn., 1979; adj. lectr. N.Y. City Tech. Coll., 1979-80; researcher women's bur. U.S. Dept. Labor. NSF grantee, 1979-80. Mem. Nat. Assn. Remedial Devel. Studies in Post Secondary Edn., Assn. Tchrs. Math. N.Y.C., Coalition Asian Am. Profl. Women, Asian Women United, Phi Theta Kappa. Office: Dean's office Hunter Coll Sch Social Work 129 E 79th St New York NY 10021

SOREL, CLAUDETTE, pianist; b. Paris; d. Michel Maximilian and Elizabeth S.; came to U.S., 1940, naturalized, 1947; B.S., Juilliard Sch. Music, 1947; student of Sigismund Stojowski, Sari Biro, Olga Samaroff Stokowski, Mieczyslaw Horszowski, Rudolf Serkin, ensemble with Felix Salmond, musicology with Dr. Robert Tangeman, music history with Marian Bauer; spl. scholar Juilliard Grad. Sch. Music, 1943; grad. Curtis Inst. Music, 1953; B.S. cum laude, Columbia U., 1954. Debut at Town Hall, N.Y.C., 1943, since appeared in leading cities U.S.; performed with N.Y. Philharmonic, N.Y. Little Symphony, Boston Symphony Orch., R.I., Reading symphony orchs., Little Orchestral Soc., NBC, Phila., New Orleans and Cin., Am. Youth Orch.; appeared at Aspen, Berkshire, Chautauqua festivals; European concert tours, 1956, 57, 58, to Eng., Sweden, Holland, Germany, Switzerland, France; appeared on various radio and TV programs; made recs. for R.C.A. Victor Rec. Co., Monitor Records, Musical Heritage; music faculty, vis. prof. Kans. U., 1961-62; asso. prof. music Ohio State U., 1962-64; prof. music, head piano dept. State U. N.Y., Fredonia, 1964—, Distinguished Univ. prof., 1969—; mem. internat. jury Van Cliburn Internat. Piano Competition, Tex., 1966, Que. and Ont. Music Festivals, 1967, 75, 81; solo appearances with 200 orchs. U.S., Europe. Fulbright scholar, 1951; Ford Found. Concert grantee, 1962; recipient Harry Rosenberg Meml., Frank Damrosch prizes, 1947; winner Phila. Orch. Youth Auditions, 1950, to appear with orch. under direction Eugene Ormandy; Nat. Fedn. Music Clubs Young Artist award, 1951; citation for service to Am. music Nat. Fedn. Music Clubs, 1966; named Outstanding Young Woman in U.S.A., 1965; citation Nat. Assn. Composers and Condrs., 1967, Mu Phi Epsilon, 1968, 80. Bd. dirs. Olga Samaroff Found., jr. com. aux. bd. N.Y. Philharmonic Symphony Orch., N.Y. State Nat. Fedn. Music Clubs; mem. adv. bd. Univ. Library Soc.; chmn. music panel Presdl. Scholars in the Arts, program of Ednl. Testing Service, 1979-82. Mem. Nat. Music Council (dir. 1973—), Pi Kappa Lambda, Mu Phi Epsilon (dir. Meml. Found., nat. chmn. Sterling Staff Concert Series, citation 1968). Author: Compendium of Piano Technique, 1970; Mind Your Musical Manners-Off and On Stage, 1972, 2d edit., 1975; The 24 Magic Keys, 3 vols., 1974; The Three Nocturnes of Rachmaninoff, 1974, 2d edit., 1975; Fifteen Smorgasbord Studies for The Piano, 1975, Arensky-Etudes, 1976; spl. editor Music Insider, 1981—; linguist, painter of oil portraits; contbr. articles to profl. mags.; compiler: The Modern Music of Today, 1947; Serge Prokofleff--His Life and Works, 1947; The Ornamentations in Mozart's Music, 1948. Home: 333 West End Ave New York NY 10023

SORENSEN, JOY O'NEAL, motion picture equipment co. exec.; b. Perkinston, Miss., May 9, 1933; d. Eugene Byron and Melissa Louvenia (Bond) O'Neal; student public schs.; m. Charles Edward Sorensen, Oct. 14, 1954; children—James Andres, Cheryl Ann. Legal sec., 1951-54, 56-65; with Brenner Cine Sound, and predecessor, Washington, 1966—, asst. v.p., 1974, exec. bus. mgr., 1974—; sales mgr. Ritz Audio-Visual & Cine div. Ritz Camera Center, Inc., Beltsville, Md., 1981—; lectr. in field. Mem. Profl. Motion Picture Equipment Assn. Democrat. Club: Soroptimist (v.p. internat. 1980-81, dir. 1982-83). Office: 11710 Baltimore Ave Beltsville MD 20705

SORENSON, ALICE MARIE, social worker, family therapist; b. Pettibone, N.D., Oct. 7, 1928; d. Arthur Martin and Louise Esther (Hoffman) Kolberg; A.B. cum laude, Jamestown Coll., 1949; M.A., Ohio State U., 1961; M.S.W., Our Lady of Lake U., 1966; student U. Tex., Austin, 1976—; m. Bruce D. Sorenson, Aug. 29, 1948; children—Jody, Jan, LeAnne, Alisa, Christine. Tchr. public schs., Chgo., 1958-59, Columbus, Ohio, 1959-61, San Antonio, 1961-63; social worker Methodist Mission Home, San Antonio, 1966-67, Salvation Army Home and Hosp., San Antonio, 1967-69; dir. Ret. Sr. Vol. Program San Antonio, 1972-74; dir. counselling Planned Parenthood San Antonio, 1974-80; pvt. practice specialing in adolescent and family counselling, San Antonio, 1979—; dir. Inst. Adolescent Studies, San Antonio, 1979—; instr. English and bus. Jamestown (N.D.) Coll., 1953-56; sociology instr. Tex. Luth. Coll., Seguin, 1979-80. Bd. dirs. YWCA San Antonio, 1978—, interim exec. dir., 1981-82; bd. dirs. Women's Shelter San Antonio, 1977—, Nat. Fedn. Blind, San Antonio, 1974-80. Named Outstanding Woman award Express-News, 1981. Mem. Nat. Assn. Social Workers, Nat. Conf. Social Welfare, Phi Lambda Theta. Home: 535 Cloudcroft San Antonio TX 78228 Office: 1603 Babcock Rd Suite 130G San Antonio TX 78229

SORGENFRIE, BARBARA BASTIAN, bleacher mfg. co. exec.; b. Hudson, Mich., May 20, 1948; d. Forrest Wilson and Willoween Elizabeth (Warner) Bastian; student Parkland Coll., 1979-82; B.A., Eastern Ill., U., 1982. Computer operator Bohn Aluminum & Brass Co., Adrian, Mich., 1968-69, computer programmer, 1969-71; computer programmer Second Nat. Bank, Danville, Ill., 1971-72; exec. sec., treas. Danville (Ill.) Sanitary Dist., 1972-77; personnel mgr. Universal Bleacher Co., Champaign, Ill., 1977—. Mem. Am. Soc. Personnel Adminstrn., Nat. Assn. Female Execs., Nat. Sec. Assn. (cert.), Associated Photographers Internat. Home: 2404 Leeper Dr Champaign IL 61820

SORLIEN, BARBARA JEAN, violinist; b. Fargo, N.D., June 19; d. Leon Cornelius and Norma Barbara (Devol) S.; student U. Minn. 1949-51, Coll. William and Mary 1954; B.M., Curtis Inst. Music, 1955; postgrad. Marlboro Sch. Music, Vt. 1958; Fulbright scholar Mozarteum, Salzburg, Austria, 1958-59. Mem. 1st violin sect. Nat. Symphony Washington 1955-58, Camerata Academica Des Mozarteums, Salzburg 1958-59, New Orleans Philharm., 1959-63; mem. mus. arts string quartet Players for Young Audiences, Inc., 1959-63; mem. 1st violin sect. Santa Fe Opera 1961; founding mem. Bowdoin Coll. Chamber Players 1962, 63; mem. 1st violin sect. Phila. Orch. 1963—. Recipient Heifetz award Berkshire Music Center at Tanglewood 1963. Mem. Sigma Alpha Iota. Club: Plays and Players (Phila). Office: 1420 Locust St Philadelphia PA 19102

SORMANE, STEPHANIE CHARLOTTE, ballet co. exec.; b. Indpls., Aug. 20, 1938; d. Walter and Stephanie Louise (Modersohn) S.; student Northwestern U., 1959-61. Dancer, Ruth Page's Chgo. Opera Ballet, 1957-58; legal sec., Chgo. and San Francisco, 1959-71; dir. ticket sales, then asst. to pres. Ballet Theatre Found. (Am. Ballet Theatre), N.Y.C., 1971-74; adminstrv. asst. Chgo. Ballet, 1975; acad. adminstr. Houston Ballet, 1976-77, co. mgr., 1977—. Mem. Cultural Arts Council Houston, Am. Arts Alliance. Office: Houston Ballet 2615 Colquitt St Houston TX 77098

SOROKA, MARGERY, artist; b. N.Y.C., May 30, 1920; d. Sam and Henrietta (Shindel) Soroka; student Hunter Coll., 1936-38, Art Students League, 1952-53, Sch. Visual Arts, N.Y.C., 1954-55, 62, Pratt Inst., 1960-61. Exhibited group shows Am. Watercolor Soc., 1964-82, Audubon Artists, 1963, 66, 68, 69, 72, 79, Nat. Arts Club, 1960-68, 70-72, Am. Artists Profl. League, 1960-66, Nat. Assn. Women Artists, 1966-70, Catherine Lorillard Wolfe Club, 1962-76 (all N.Y.C.), Hudson Valley Art Assn., White Plains, N.Y., 1964, 78, Watercolor U.S.A., Springfield, Mo., 1968, Wichita (Kans.) Centennial, 1970; exhibited traveling exhibits through mus., colls., various cities in U.S.; represented in permanent collections Forbes, Inc., N.Y.C., Va. State Coll., Columbus (Ga.) Mus. Arts and Crafts; instr. watercolors Salmagundi Club. N.Y.C. Recipient Forbes Indsl. award and Travel Exhibit, Anna G. Morse Meml. award Gwen McClung Meml. award, Grumbacher award, Nat. Arts Club Artists Material award William B. Connor travel grant, Lena Newcastle Meml. award Am. Watercolor Soc., 1968, Winsor Newton award Catherine Lorillard Wolfe Art Club, 1968; Lena Newcastle Meml. award Nat. Assn. Women Artists, 1969; Nat. Spl. award Nat. Arts Club, 1970; Samuel Mann Meml. prize, 1972; 1st prize Nat. Art League, 1976; Best in Show award Midwest Watercolor Soc., 1978; Zinn's award Audubon Artists, 1979; Herb Boston Meml. award Ga. Watercolor Soc., 1979. Mem. Am. Watercolor Soc., Knickerbocker Artists, Salmagundi Club. Featured in Am. Artist mag., Feb. 1971.

SORRELL, ESTHER HARTIGAN, Vt. state senator; b. Burlington, Vt., Apr. 24, 1920; B.S., Trinity Coll., 1942; m. Thomas Sorrell; five children. Mem. Vt. State Senate, 1973-74, 75-76, 77-78, 79-80, 81—. Roman Catholic. Office: Vt State Senate State House Montpelier VT 05602 *

SOSNICK, NIKKI ALBERTA, credit services co. exec.; b. West Islip, N.Y., Oct. 5, 1946; d. Nicholas A. Sosnicki and Lillian L. (Pack) Marshall; student Pratt Inst., 1964-65, SUNY, Farmingdale, 1974, Suffolk County Community Coll., 1977-81, St. Joseph's Coll., 1982—; m. Robert DiSalvo, Aug. 28, 1965 (div. 1974); children—Stephanie, Robert, Stacey. Credit mgr. Sherry Pharm. Co., Ronkonkoma, N.Y., 1974-76, ILC Data Device Corp., Bohemia, N.Y., 1977—; tax preparer Sosnick & Co., Holtsville, N.Y., 1978—. Bd. dirs., asst. treas. ILC Employees Fed. Credit Union, 1980-82. Mem. Nat. Credit Office (aerospace group), Nat. Assn. Credit Mgrs., Network L.I. Businesswomen (co-founder, exec. dir.), N.Y. Credit and Fin. Mgmt. Women's Group of L.I. (pres.), Electronics Industry Assn. (credit com.), NOW (treas. Mid-Suffolk 1980-82). Democrat. Roman Catholic. Office: 315 Walt Whitman Rd Huntington Station NY 11746

SOSPENSO, ELIZABETH T., stockbroker; b. Nuremberg, Ger., Nov. 22, 1936; d. Otto and Ida (Meyer) Laubvogel; grad. Hoehere Handelsschule, Nurnberg, 1955; student U. Erlangen (W.Ger.), 1955-56; m. Joseph P. Sospenso, Jan. 3, 1965. Sec. to pres. Deltec Securities Corp., N.Y.C., 1959-67; account exec. Loeb Rhoades & Co., N.Y.C., 1967-77; stockbroker, v.p. Thomson McKinnon Securities, Inc., N.Y.C., 1977—, mem. pres.'s council, 1979-81. Chairperson, Women in Bus. Chpt. Voice of the Electorate, N.Y. State, 1979—. Mem. Women's Stockbrokers Assn. Lutheran. Office: 1 State St Plaza New York NY 10004

SOTIS, SHIRLEY BURCH, cons. co. exec.; b. Dixon, Iowa, Apr. 17, 1934; d. George William and Norma Marie (Hesse) Burch; A.A., Harbor Jr. Coll., 1972; B.S., UCLA, 1975; m. Franc A. Sotis, Jan. 10, 1953; children—Frank Joseph, Clifford Orlando. Tchr., So. Calif. Regional Occupational Center, El Camino Coll., 1973-75; fin. adminstr. Minn. Inst., Mpls., 1975-78; bus. adminstr. Control Data Corp., Mpls., 1978-80; exec. dir. Working Women's Seminar, Chaska, Minn., 1980-81; adminstr. Cons. Internal Medicine, P.A., Edina, Minn., 1981—; guest lectr. Normandale Coll. Mem. edn. panel LWV, 1976. Mem. Nat. Assn. Credit Mgrs., Minn. Med. Group Mgmt. Assn., North Central Credit and Fin. Mgmt. Assn. (edn. com.). Lutheran. Home: 3733 Towndale Dr Bloomington MN 55431 Office: 3625 W 65th St Edina MN 55435

SOTRES, JOANNE LINK, advt. and public relations exec.; b. York, Pa., July 26, 1934; d. Fred M. and Mildred K. (Coover) Link; grad. Dwight Sch. for Girls, Englewood, N.J., 1952; m. Armando Sotres, 1955 (div. 1963); 1 son, Craig. Founder, La Fiesta Resort Wear Co., Acapulco, Mex., 1954-62; founder, mgr. Restaurant Armando's, Acapulco, 1954-62; adminstrv. asst. to Mr. and Mrs. Johhny Carson, 1962-66; mktg. cons., 1967-69; dir. mktg. Telegeneral Corp., N.Y.C., 1970, v.p., 1970-71; advt. dir. Fabric-News, N.Y.C., 1971-72; founder and partner Sotres-White Assos., N.Y.C., 1972-73; founder, pres., chmn. bd. Sotres-Link Ltd., N.Y.C., 1973—; pres., chmn. bd. Sotres-Link Mgmt., Inc., N.Y.C., 1975—. v.p., dir. mktg. Quali-Tech Telecommunications Group, Inc., 1981—. Adv. council N.Y. regional office SBA, 1976—. Recipient numerous equestrian trophies, 1947-52; named to Ofcl. Horse Show Blue Book Hall of Fame, 1948-50. Republican.

SOULE, SALLIE THOMPSON, state senator; b. Detroit, May 13, 1928; d. Hayward Stone and Elizabeth Robinson Thompson; A.B., Smith Coll., 1950; M.A., U. Vt., Burlington, 1952; m. Gardner Northup Soule, July 26, 1958; children—Gardner Northup, Nancy Soule Brown; stepchildren—Sarah Goodwin, Trumbull Dickson. Sec. trade sales dept. Macmillan Pub. Co., N.Y.C., 1952-57; tech. writer sales service div. Eastman Kodak Co., Rochester, N.Y., 1957-58; feature writer Brighton-Pittsford Post, Pittsford, N.Y., 1958-68; v.p., gen. mgr. F. H. Horsford Nursery, Inc., Charlotte, Vt., 1968-76; partner, v.p. Bygone Books, Inc., Burlington, Vt., 1978—; mem. Vt. Ho. of Reps., 1976-80, mem. ways and means com., 1976-80; mem. Vt. Senate, 1980—, mem. appropriation com., energy and natural resources com. 1980—. Mem. Champlain Civic Center Com.; mem. children's task force Vt. Dept. Social and Rehab. Services; mem. Chittenden County Democratic Com.; mem. Econ. Task Force, Council State Govts.; mem. Gov's. Commn. on Health Care Costs; mem. joint truancy task force Vt. Depts. Edn. and Social Rehab. Services; mem. adv. bd. Lake Champlain Com.; mem. project rev. com. Vt. Health Policy Corp.; mem. Vt. Jud. Nominating Bd.; mem. governing bd. Vt. Ednl. TV. Mem. Vt. Antiquarian Booksellers Assn.

SOURS, WILDA THOMAS, assn. exec.; b. Dayton, Ohio, Nov. 12, 1930; d. Malcolm W. and Christeen B. (Conyers) Thomas; student public schs.; m. Joseph Dale Sours, Jan. 6, 1950; children—Dalynn Kaye, Joyce Elaine. Sec., 1948-54; adminstrv. asst. Accredited Theol. Schs. Ohio and Ind., Dayton, 1969-77, exec. dir., 1977—; vice chmn. bd. dirs. Dayton Yokefellow Acad. Pres., Vandalia Butler Schs. PTA, 1954-77; chmn. bd. mgrs. univ. workshop Ohio PTA, 1972-73. Mem. Nat. Assn. Female Execs. Mem. Ch. of God. Home: 3840 Reinwood Dr Dayton OH 45414 Office: 1714 Harvard Blvd Dayton OH 45406

SOUSA, THERESA ELLEN MALONE, govt. ofcl.; b. Frederick County, Va., Mar. 17, 1927; d. Joseph Harrison and Lillie May (Lehigh) Malone; student Strayer Bus. Coll., Columbia Tech. Inst., Washington, Oceanside-Carlsbad (Calif.) Jr. Coll., Am. U.; m. Joseph Earl Sousa, III, Oct. 20, 1946. Various adminstrv./community relations positions, 1945-50; with U.S. Geol. Survey, 1952—, visual info. specialist, Reston, Va., 1975-80, exhibits and visual info. officer, 1980—. Served with USMCR, 1950-52. Recipient various achievement and service awards. Mem. Fed. Design Council, Nat. Assn. Govt. Communicators, Geol. Soc. Washington, Am. News Women's Club, Federally Employed Women, Women Marines Assn. Presbyterian. Author papers in field. Home: 1415 Springvale Ave McLean VA 22101 Office: US Geol Survey Nat Center MS 790 Reston VA 22092

SOUTH, LINDA LEE PIKE, broadcasting co. exec.; b. St. Joseph, Mo., Apr. 29, 1952; d. Jewel William and Eunice Maxine (Sybert) Pike; ed. public schs., St. Joseph. With Sta. KQTV, St. Joseph, 1970—, asst. controller, 1980-82, controller, 1982—. Adv., Jr. Achievement, 1975-77, 79-81. Baptist. Home: 2713 Maurice Dr Saint Joseph MO 64503 Office: Sta KQTV 40th and Faraon St Saint Joseph MO 64506

SOUTH, LYNDA JOYCE, public relations exec. b. Memphis, Feb. 21, 1948; d. William E. and Katherine (South) S.; B.A., U. Miss., 1970; M.B.A., Marymount Coll., 1981. Dir. publs., exec. editor Miss. State Hwy. Dept., Jackson, 1970-75; press sec. Senator Thad Cochran, U.S. Senate, Washington, 1975-80; editor employee publs. Potomac Electric Power Co., 1980-82, ednl. program coordinator, 1982—. Mem. Nat. Press Women's Assn., Miss Press Women's Assn., Women in Energy Internat. Assn. Bus. Communicators. Republican. Baptist. Home: 1028 S Edison St Arlington VA 22204 Office: 1900 Pennsylvania Ave NW Washington DC 20068

SOUTHARD, HELEN ELIZABETH FAIRBAIRN, psychologist; b. Buffalo, July 4, 1906; d. Robert Weatherston and Lorena May Fairbairn; B.A. cum laude, SUNY, Buffalo, 1927, M.A., 1929; postgrad. Columbia U., 1934; m. Paul John Southard, Feb. 24, 1934; children—John Brelsford, Robert Fairbairn. Personnel adv. SUNY, Buffalo, 1929-37; tchr. psychology, cons. family life Nat. YWCA, N.Y.C., 1941-43, dir. Resource Center on Women, 1970-72, dir. program, 1974-76, cons. personnel, 1978; dir. YWCA Bur. Research and Program, N.Y.C., 1961-70; mgmt. cons., Englewood, N.J., 1978—; mem. adv. bd. Sex Info. Edn. Council U.S., Panhellenic grantee, 1932-33; lic. psychologist, N.Y. State. Mem. Am. Psychol. Assn., N.Y. State Psychol. Assn., Am. Orthopsychiat. Assn., Sigma Kappa. Author: Sex Before 20, 1970; Handbook For Administrative Volunteers, 1981; co-author Sex Education series of AMA and NEA, 1955. Home and office: 100 E Palisade Ave Englewood NJ 07631

SOUTHERN, EILEEN (MRS. JOSEPH SOUTHERN), educator; b. Mpls., Feb. 19, 1920; d. Walter Wade and Lilla (Gibson) Jackson; B.A., U. Chgo., 1940, M.A., 1941; Ph.D., N.Y.U., 1961; M.A. (hon.), Harvard U., 1976; m. Joseph Southern, Aug. 22, 1942; children—April, Edward. Concert pianist, 1940—; instr. Prairie View U., Hempstead, Tex., 1941-42; asst. prof. So. U., Baton Rouge, 1943-45, 49-51; tchr. N.Y.C. Bd. Edn., 1954-60; instr. Bklyn. Coll., CUNY, 1960-64, asst. prof., 1964-69; assoc. prof. York Coll., CUNY, 1969-71, prof., 1972-75; prof. music Harvard U., Cambridge, Mass., 1976—, chmn. dept. Afro-Am. studies, 1976-79. Active Girl Scouts U.S.A., 1954-63; chmn. mgmt. com. Queens Area YWCA, 1970-73. Recipient Alumni Profl. Achievement award U. Chgo., 1970, Deems Taylor award ASCAP, 1973; Nat. Endowment for Humanities grantee, 1979—. Mem. Internat., Am. (dir. 1974-76) musicol. socs., Renaissance Soc., Assn. for Study Afro-Am. Life and History, NAACP, Phi Beta Kappa (hon.), Alpha Kappa Alpha. Author: The Buxheim Organ Book, 1963; The Music of Black Americans: A History, 1971; Readings in Black American Music, 1971; Anonymous Pieces in the Manuscript El Escorial, 1981; Biographical Dictionary of Afro-American and African Musicians, 1982; editor, pub. The Black Perspective in Music, 1973—; contbr. articles to profl. jours., encys. Office: Harvard U Cambridge MA 02138

SOUTHWELL, HELEN, mental health clinic exec.; b. Gary, Ind., Mar. 9, 1933; d. Louis and Evangeline (Christos) Kremizes; A.B. in English, Ind. U., 1981; m. Eugene A. Southwell; children—Jeffrey, Patricia, Evangeline. Sec., The Anderson Co., Gary, 1951-52, Allied Ins. Agy. Gary, 1952-56; exec. sec. Ind. U., Gary, 1963-69; exec. dir. Southwell Inst., Olympia Field, Ill., 1969—. Vice precinct committeewoman, Gary, 1960-64. Mem. St. Helen's Philoptochos Soc. (dir., membership com. 1975-77), Sigma Kappa Pi (pres. 1951). Mem. Greek Orthodox Ch. Home: 5330 Delaware St Merrillville IN 46410 Office: 2555 W Lincoln Hwy Olympia Fields IL 60461

SOUTHWICK, PHYLLIS CLAYTON, social worker; b. Salt Lake City, Nov. 2, 1926; d. David Hyrum and Margaret (Cannon) Clayton; B.S., U. Utah, 1949, M.S.W., 1967, D.S.W., 1976; m. A.J. Southwick, Jr., Apr. 1, 1950; children—Carolyn, Elaine, Portia Marie. Group worker, dir. Salt Lake Neighborhood House and Day Care Center, 1954-67; asso. prof. Grad. Sch. Social Work, U. Utah, 1967—, dir. continuing edn. Grad. Sch. Social Work, 1972—; chmn. Utah Social Workers Lic. Bd. Mem. bd. govs. Utah Health Systems Agy. Mem. adminstrv. bd., adv. com. Utah Juvenile Ct.; mem. Bountiful City Council, 1974—; mem. Utah Constn. Revision Com. NIMH grantee, 1974—. Mem. Nat. Assn. Social Workers (chmn. nat. com. 1976-78, pres. Utah, pres. womens state legis. council 1976-78), Acad. Certified Social Workers, Council Social Work Edn., Phi Kappa Phi, Delta Kappa Gamma. Republican. Mormon. Club: Soroptimist. Contbr. articles to profl. jours. Home: 1314 E Millbrook Way Bountiful UT 84010 Office: Grad Sch Social Work U Utah Salt Lake City UT 84112

SOUTHWORTH, LOIS GILL, educator, psychologist; b. Atoka, Okla., July 21, 1915; d. James Hugh and Lois Elizabeth (McCuiston)

Gill; B.S., NE Okla. State U., 1934; Ed.S., U. Tenn., 1973; m. James Larry Southworth, Feb. 29, 1936 (dec.); children—John Scott, Bruce Alan. Tchr., Strayer Coll., Washington, 1938-39, Ballard Sch., N.Y.C., 1939-45; pvt. practice psychology, Knoxville, Tenn., 1964-68; asst. prof. dept. child and family studies, U. Tenn., Knoxville, 1967—, researcher Appalachian Children and Families. Active Knoxville Symphony Assn., Dulin Art Gallery Assn., Women's Center of Knoxville, Children's Internat. Village, Common Cause. Lic. psychol. examiner, Tenn. Mem. AAUP, AAUW, Am. Psychol. Assn., Nat. Assn. Psychology in the Schs., Nat. Assn. of Disability Examiners, Nat. Assn. of Children with Learning Disabilities, LWV, NOW, Pi Lambda Theta, Phi Delta Kappa. Democrat. Unitarian. Club: Women's Aux. of Knoxville Acad. Medicine. Author: Screening and Evaluating the Young Child—A Handbook of Instruments to Use from Infancy to Six Years, 1980; contbr. articles in field to profl. jours. Home: 921 Kenesaw Ave Knoxville TN 37919 Office: Dept Child and Family Studies U Tenn Knoxville TN 37916

SOVA, DAWN BEVERLY, research cons. firm exec., writer; b. Passaic, N.J., Oct. 6, 1949; d. Emil Jack and Violet Alice (Tomczyk) S.; B.A., Montclair State Coll., 1971; M.A. (grantee 1971-72), Ball State U., 1972; 1 son, Robert. Instr., Tri-State U., Angola, Ind., 1972-74, U. W.Fla., Pensacola, 1975-76, East Carolina U., Greenville, N.C., 1977-78; owner, dir. Pro-Write Cons. Garfield, N.J., 1978—, cons. bus. and acad. Notary Public. AAUP, MLA, AAUW, Nat. Assn. Female Execs. Roman Catholic. Contbr. articles to popular mags. including Times Mag. Home and Office; 126 Banta Ave Garfield NJ 07026

SOVIERO, DIANA BARBARA, soprano; b. Jersey City, Mar. 19, 1946; d. Amerigo and Angelina Catani; student Juilliard Sch. Music, Hunter Coll. Opera Workshop. m. Louis Soviero, May 20, 1967. Appearances with opera cos. including Tulsa Opera, Houston Grand Opera, San Diego Opera, Ottawa (Ont., Can.) Opera, Zurich Opera, Goldovsky Opera Theatre, Lake George Opera, New Orleans Opera, Hamburg (W.Ger.) Opera, Dallas Opera, Chgo. Opera, San Francisco Opera, Montreal (Que., Can.) Opera, Toulouse, France, Caracas, Venezuela; now leading soprano N.Y.C. Opera; instr. master classes The Faculty, sch. for actors, Los Angeles. Recipient Richard Tucker award. Mem. AFTRA, Am. Guild Musical Artists, SAG. Office: Columbia Artists 165 W 57th St New York NY 10019

SOWELL, HAZEL WRIGHT, nurse; b. Rosevine, Tex., Dec. 8, 1913; d. Thomas Mack and Mary Bell (Drawhorn) Wright; diploma Parkland Hosp. Sch. Nursing, Dallas, 1936; student Stephen F. Austin State U., intermittently, 1959-64; m. Curtis Lowe Sowell, Oct. 23, 1938; children—Amy Ann, Patricia Gayle, John Thomas. Staff nurse Hogan-Malone Hosp., Big Spring, Tex., 1936, Meml. Hosp., Nacogdoches, Tex., 1936-39, relief nurse, 1943-44; office nurse A.L. Nelson, M.D., Nacogdoches, 1973-80; Am. Nat. Red Cross nurse, 1969—. Mem. Nacogdoches Bus. and Profl. Women's Club (Nike award 1980, awards chmn. 1979), UDC (v.p. local chpt. 1981-82), Daus. of Republic of Tex., UDC, Nacogdoches Geneal. Soc., Nacogdoches Art League, Alpha Chi. Home: 3609 N Pecan Nacogdoches TX 75962 Office: SFA Sta Box 4624 Nacogdoches TX 75962

SOWELL, KATYE MARIE OLIVER, mathematician; b. Winston Salem, N.C., Apr. 6, 1934; d. William Manton and Katye Mae (Price) Oliver; B.A. cum laude, Flora Macdonald Coll. (name now St. Andrews Presbyn. Coll., Laurinburg N.C.), Red Springs, N.C., 1956; M.S., U. S.C., 1958; Ph.D., Fla. State U., 1965; vis. scholar U. Mich., summers 1980, 81; m. Jesse Clarence Sowell, Sept. 7, 1957 (dec. Feb. 1961); 1 son, David Clarence. Asst. prof. math. Elon (N.C.) Coll., 1958-60; instr. U. So. Miss., 1960-63; research assoc., instr. Fla. State U., 1965; mem. faculty East Carolina U., Greenville, N.C., 1965—, prof. math., 1972—, dir. student teaching program math., 1966-79; cons. in field. Grantee NSF, 1968-75, U.S. Office Edn., 1965, 78, East Carolina U., 1979-81. Mem. Math. Assn. Am., Am. Math. Soc., Nat. Council Tchrs. Math., Internat. Council Computers in Edn., N.C. Council Tchrs. Math. (pres. 1975-77), English Speaking Union. Democrat. Presbyterian. Co-author: Hands-on Mathematics, 1979; Experiencing Mathematics, 1982. Home: 103 College Court Dr Greenville NC 27834 Office: Math Dept East Carolina U Greenville NC 27834

SOWELL, VIRGINIA MURRAY, educator; b. Presidio, Tex., Mar. 23, 1931; d. Marshall Bishop and Mary Alice (Daniel) Murray; B.A., Sam Houston State U., 1951; M.A., Trinity U., 1957; Ph.D., U. Tex., 1975; children—John Houston, III, Paul Orin. Tchr. San Antonio (Tex.) Ind. Sch. Dist., 1951-52, 1955-58; asst. prof. San Antonio Coll., 1969-75, asso. prof., 1976—; asso. prof. spl. edn. Tex. Tech. U., Lubbock, 1976—. Bd. govs. Tex. Sch. for Blind; dir. vols. Witte Mus.; mem. research adv. com. Tex. Tech. U., 1981-82, pres. faculty senate, 1982-83, mem. acad. affairs com. faculty senate, 1978-80; bd. dirs. Developmental Edn., Birth through Two, 1977—. HEW grantee, 1977-84. Mem. Council for Exceptional Children, Tex. Council Exceptional Children (treas. 1981-83), Tex. Div. Children with Learning Disabilities, Internat. Reading Assn., Western Coll. Reading Assn., Assn. for Edn. of Visually Handicapped (pres. elect S. Central region 1982-83), Am. Ednl. Research Assn., Assn. Supervision and Curriculum Devel. (chpt. dir. 1980-83), Tex. Assn. Coll. Tchrs., AAUP, Phi Delta Kappa, Delta Kappa Gamma. Republican. Episcopalian. Home: 4610 28th St Lubbock TX 79410 Office: 164 AD Bldg Box 4560 Tex Tech U Lubbock TX 79409

SOZA, SHARON ELIZABETH, micro-computer cons.; b. Port Arthur, Tex., June 21, 1945; d. Francis Theodore and Mary Elizabeth (Grubbs) Newton; B.S., 1968; m. Albert Rudolph Soza, July 21, 1976; dau., Ravi Narayan Seth. Newspaper proofreader, tech. writer, computer cons., 1968-75; self-employed, 1975—. Mem. central steering com. Libertarian party, Siskiyou County, 1981. Address: 349N Oregon St PO Box 81 Yreka CA 96097

SPACEK, SISSY (MARY ELIZABETH), actress; b. Quitman, Tex., Dec. 25, 1949; d. Edwin S. and Virginia S.; student Lee Strasberg Theat. Inst.; m. Jack Fisk. Appeared in films: Prime Cut, 1972, Badlands, 1974, Carrie (Acad. award nominee Best Actress), 1976, Three Women, 1977, Welcome to L.A., 1977, Heartbeat, 1980, Coal Miner's Daughter; TV movies Katherine, 1975, Verna: USO Girl, 1978; guest host Saturday Night Live, 1977. Named Best Actress by Nat. Soc. Film Critics for Carrie, 1976; Best Supporting Actress, N.Y. Film Critics, 1977. Office: care William Morris Agy 1350 Ave of Americas New York NY 10019

SPADARO, CHARLOTTE, lawyer; b. N.Y.C., June 29, 1941; d. Sol and Eva (Malach) Rubinfeld; student U. Calif. at Los Angeles, 1958-60; B.A., Calif. State U., 1962; J.D., U. So. Calif., 1969; m. George Spadaro, Apr. 8, 1960; children—Michele, Jonathan. Tchr. English, Portola Jr. High Sch., Orange, Calif., 1962-63; substitute tchr. English and French, Santa Ana (Calif.) Unified and Orange (Calif.) Unified Sch. Dists., 1963-64; admitted to Calif. bar, 1970; law clk. Dist. Ct. of Appeals, Los Angeles, 1969; mem. firm Eliot B. Feldman, Los Angeles, 1970—. Chmn., Beverly Hills Gen. Plan Update Study, 1979-80; mem. Nat. Com. for Citizens in Edn.; safety chmn. Beverly Hills PTA Council, 1978-79; mem. early childhood edn. adv. com., sch. improvement site council Beverly Vista Sch.; mem. Beverly Hills Unified Sch. Dist. Bd. Edn., 1979. Mem. Women Lawyers Assn., Ephebian Soc., LWV (fin. chmn. Santa Ana 1965), U. So. Calif. Alumni Assn., World Affairs Council. Home: 221 S El Camino Dr Beverly Hills CA 90212 Office: 9465 Wilshire Blvd Beverly Hills CA 90212

SPAHN, LOIS GENE, corp. exec.; b. Houston, Oct. 10, 1930; d. Samuel L. and Maybelle D. (Pfeffer) Bloomberg; B.S. in Bus. Adminstrn., Wayne State U., 1970; M.B.A., U. Detroit, 1973; J.D., Southwestern U., Los Angeles, 1982; m. John Constantine Spahn, Jr., Mar. 24, 1979. Project task leader, supr. internal profit analysis, J.L. Hudson Co., Detroit, 1970-73; mgr. div. fin. systems Xerox Corp., Ann Arbor, Mich., 1973-74, mgr. gen. acctg. and systems, pub. div., 1974-75, mgr. planning and budgets, El Segundo, Calif., 1975-77, Western regional mgr. adminstrn. printing systems div., Los Angeles, 1977-80, mgr. customer account services, El Segundo, 1980—; instr. introductory acctg. Wayne County Community Coll., Detroit, 1970. Key person Xerox Community Involvement Program. Mem. Am. Bar Assn. (student div.), Assn. M.B.A. Execs., Xerox Mgmt. Assn., Nat. Assn. Female Execs., Beta Gamma Sigma. Republican. Supervising editor Southwestern U. Law Rev., 1981-82. Home: 6176 Rockcliff Dr Hollywood CA 90068 Office: 880 Apollo El Segundo CA 90245

SPAHR, PAMELA CLAIRE, mfg. co. mgr.; b. Iron Mountain, Mich., Sept. 26, 1945; d. John David and Lois (Druse) Harvey; B.A., U. Wis., 1967; postgrad. U. South Wales, 1965-66; m. Robert C. Spahr, June 7, 1969. Cons. dept. clin. onocology U. Wis., 1967-70; programmer analyst mfg. systems Control Data Corp., Mpls., 1970-75; supr., mgmt. applications Electric Machinery, Mpls., 1976-77, Champion Internat. Mpls., 1978-79; mgr. fin. systems Measurex Corp., Cupertino, Calif., 1979-80; mgr. MIS, Fairchild Camera & Instrument Corp., San Jose, Calif., 1980-82; mgr. MIS, Am. Micro Systems, Inc., Santa Clara, Calif., 1982—. Mem. Assn. Systems Mgmt., Assn. Systems Mgrs. (pres.), Peninsula Profl. Women's Assn. Home: 1660 McGregor Way San Jose CA 95129 Office: 3800 Homestead Rd Santa Clara CA 95051

SPAIN, JAYNE BAKER (MRS. JOHN A. SPAIN), businesswoman, educator; b. San Francisco; d. Lawrence Ian and Marguerite (Buchanan) Baker; student U. Calif. at Berkeley, 1944-47, Music U. Cin., 1947-50; LL.D., Edgecliff Coll., Cin., 1969; Dr. Pub. Service, George Washington U., 1970; LL.D., U. Cin., 1971, Dumbarton Coll., 1972, Springfield (Mass.) Coll., 1973, Gallaudet Coll., Washington, 1973; L.H.D. Bryant Coll., 1972, Russell Sage Coll., Troy, N.Y., 1973, Loyola Coll., Balt., 1975; m. John A. Spain, July 14, 1952; children—Jeffry Alan, Jon Kimberly. Pres., Alvey-Ferguson Co., Cin., 1952-66, pres. Alvey-Ferguson Operations div. Litton Industries, Inc., 1966-70, also dir. parent co., 1970—; vice chmn. CSC, 1971—; sr. v.p. Gulf Oil Corp., Pitts., from 1975; Disting. vis. prof. and exec.-in-residence George Washington U., Washington, 1979—; dir. Beatrice Foods, Chgo., Ohio Nat. Life Ins., Cin. Vice chmn. Pres.'s Com. on Employment Handicapped, 1966—; participant internat. trade fairs U.S. Depts. State, Commerce, Europe, North Africa, 1961-66, mem. trade and investment mission, India, 1965; mem. U.S. com. Internat. Council Social Welfare; mem. Internat. Soc. Rehab. Disabled; mem. adv. com. sheltered workshops U.S. sec. labor; mem. Ohio Gov.'s Commn. on Status of Women; mem. bldg. com. Children's Med. Center, Cin. Bd. dirs., past pres. Convalescent Hosp. Children, Cin., Greater Cin. Hosp. Council, Children's Neuromuscular Diagnostic Center, Cin., Cin. Sci. Center; bd. dirs. President's Commn. on Personnel Interchange; chmn. bd. trustees Fed. Women's Award. Recipient Distinguished Service award for work overseas blind People Com., Washington, 1965; Migel medal Am. Found. Blind, N.Y., 1966; Golden Plate award industry Acad. Achievement, Dallas, 1967; Top Hat award Bus. and Profl. Women's Clubs. Am., N.Y., 1967. Mem. Conveyor Equipment Mfrs. Assn. (sec., treas., dir. 1960-63), Machinery and Allied Products Inst., Am. Mgmt. Assn. (dir.) Internat. Platform Assn. Episcopalian. Contbr. articles to profl. jours. Home: 700 New Hampshire Ave NW Washington DC 20037 Office: Sch of Govt and Bus George Washington U Washington DC 20052

SPAIN, NETTIE EDWARDS (MRS. FRANK E. SPAIN), civic worker; b. Alexandria, La., Oct. 9, 1918; d. John Henry and Sallie Tamson (Donald) Edwards; student Alexandria Bus. Coll., 1936-37, Birmingham-So. Coll., 1958-59, Nat. Tng. Inst., United Community Funds and Councils Am., 1965-66; m. Frank E. Spain, May 18, 1974. Reporter, Alexandria Daily Town Talk, 1942-45; staff writer Brimingham (Ala.) Post, 1945-49; pub. relations dir. Community Chest, Birmingham, 1949-53; dir. info. services Pa. United Fund, Phila., 1953-55; asst. exec. dir. Ala. Assn. Mental Health, Birmingham, 1956-57; pub. relations dir. United Appeal, Birmingham, 1958-68, asst. exec. dir., 1968-71; asst. to pres. for devel. U. Ala., Birmingham, 1971-74, acting dir., 1975. Mem. public relations com. Ala. Heart Assn., Birmingham, 1972-75; bd. dirs. Kate Duncan Smith DAR Sch., Grant, Ala., 1981-82; bd. dirs. Children's Aid Soc., 1971-77, 79, v.p., 1976-77; bd. dirs. Jefferson-Shelby Lung Assn., 1972-75, Vol. Bur. Greater Birmingham, 1973-77, Hale County chpt. ARC; adv. com. Jr. League, 1974-75; exec. com. Historic Hale County Preservation Soc.; hon. mem. president's council U. Ala., Birmingham; bd. dirs. Norton Center Continuing Edn., Birmingham-So. Coll.; charter mem. bd. Birmingham Children's Theater. Recipient 1st Place awards Nat. Photos for Fedn., 1966-67; citation Pa. United Fund, 1955, citation for service Jefferson-Shelby Lung Assn., 1975, citation Ala. Heart Assn., 1974, Vol. Bur. Greater Birmingham, 1977; award of Merit, Ala. Hist. Commn., 1977; Rotary Found. Paul Harris fellow; Benjamin Franklin fellow Royal Soc. Arts, London, U.S.A. Mem. Nat. Public Relations Council of Health and Welfare Services (dir. 1967-69), Birmingham Women's Com. of 100, Public Relations Council Ala. (hon. life), Order of Crown in Am., Ala. Hist. Soc., Nat. Soc. Colonial Dames Am., Nat. Trust for Historic Preservation, Met. Opera Guild, Guy E. Snavely Soc. (Birmingham-So. Coll.), Colonial Dames Am., DAR, First Families of Va., Birmingham Astron. Soc. (hon.). Episcopalian. Clubs: Lakeview Country (Greensboro, Ala.); Mountain Brook Country, Relay House, The Club; Northriver Yacht (Tuscaloosa); Crepe Myrtle Garden; Progress Study; Cauldron. Home: 3100 Overhill Rd Birmingham AL 35223 also Medley Greensboro AL 36744

SPALDING, ELAINE R., sales exec.; b. Elmhurst, N.Y., June 26, 1940; d. John Arpod and Thelma (Smith) Rado; student Coll. Wooster, 1958-60; m. Larry Spalding, Dec. 24, 1966; children—Timothy A., Linda L., Med. sec. Duke U. Med. Center, Durham, N.C., 1967-70; adminstrv. sec. Tampa Heights Hosp., Tampa, Fla., 1973-74; lead distributor Seyforth Labs., Inc., Dallas, 1975-79; lead distbr. Futuron Industries, Inc., Dallas, 1979—, dir. Futuron Industries Distbr. Orgn., 1979—. Recipient Distbr. of Year award, 1980, Spirit of Futuron award, 1981. Republican. Address: 1211 Brookside Dr Clearwater FL 33516

SPANDORFER, MERLE SUE, artist; b. Balt., Sept. 4, 1934; d. Simon Louis and Bernice Phyllis (Jacobson) Bank; student Syracuse U., 1952-54; B.S., U. Md., 1956; m. Lester M. Spandorfer, June 17, 1956; children—Cathy, John. One-woman exhbns. include: Phila. Print Club, 1969, Richard Feigen Gallery, N.Y.C., 1970, Marian Locks Gallery, 1973, 78, 82, U. Pa., 1974, Louis Meisel Gallery, N.Y.C., 1976, Beaver Coll., 1976, Phila. Coll. Textiles and Sci., 1977, Ericson Gallery, N.Y.C., 1978, 79, R.I. Sch. Design, 1980, Yoseido Gallery, Tokyo, 1981; works exhibited in 100 group shows U.S., Europe, Japan; represented in permanent collections: Met. Mus. Art, Mus. Modern Art, Phila. Mus. Art, Balt. Mus. Art, Library of Congress, Israel Mus., Toyoh Art Inst., Tokyo; instr. Tyler Sch. Art of Temple U., 1980—, Phila. Coll. Textiles and Sci., 1978; instr., dir. edn. Cheltenham Art Center, 1975—; lectr., workshop condr. Named Outstanding Art Educator, Pa. Art Edn. Assn., 1982; recipient Balt. Mus. Art Gov.'s prize, 1970, award Md. Inst. Art, 1971. Mem. Artists Equity, Am. Color Print Soc. Jewish. Home: 8012 Ellen Ln Cheltenham PA 19012 Office: 307 E Gowen Ave Philadelphia PA 19119

SPANGLER, DAISY KIRCHOFF, (MRS. FRANCIS R. COSGROVE SPANGLER), educator; b. Lancaster, Pa., Jan. 27, 1913; d. Frank Augustus and Lida Flaharty (Forewood) Kirchoff; B.S., Millersville State Coll., 1963; M.Ed., Pa. State U., 1966, Ed.D., 1972; Ph.D., Stanton U., 1974; m. Francis R. Cosgrove Spangler, June 3, 1939 (dec.); children—Stephen Russell, Michael Denis. Tchr. rural sch., Providence, Pa., 1933-35, Rapho Twp., Pa., 1935-42, Mastersonville, Pa., 1942-51; elem. sch. prin. Manheim Central, Pa., 1952-66; tchr., Manheim, Pa., 1967-68; asso. prof. elem. edn. Millersville (Pa.) State Coll., 1968-78, prof. emeritus, 1978—; ednl. cons., 1978—. Dist. chmn. ARC, 1965-66; mem. Hempfield PTA, 1966-67. Mem. Pa. Edn. Assn., Pa. Elem. Prins. Assn., Assn. Pa. State Coll. and Univ. Profs., Am. Assn. Ret. Persons (pres. 1982-84), Nat., Lancaster (pres. 1963-64) prins. assns., Pa. Outdoor Edn. and Conservation Assn., Nat., Pa. councils social studies, Am. Ednl. Research Assn., Manheim Tchrs. Assn. (pres. 1964-65), Hempfield Profl. Women, Pi Lambda Theta (nat. com. 1980—), Delta Kappa Gamma (pres. 1976-78). Lutheran (pres. Lutheran women 1966-67, 79-80, 80-81). Club: Order Eastern Star. Home and Office: Route 7 Box 238 Manheim PA 17545

SPANGLER, NANCY LEE, sch. psychologist; b. Peoria, Ill., Apr. 4, 1949; d. Robert L. and Lerose (Hejda) S.; student Fla. So. Coll., Lakeland, 1967-68, We. Ill. U., Macomb, 1968-71; B.S. in Psychology, Bradley U., Peoria, Ill., 1972, M.A. in Psychology, 1974. Sch. psychology intern Spl. Edn. Coop. South Cook County, Chicago Heights, Ill., 1974-75; sch. psychologist Joliet (Ill.) Pub. Schs. Dist. 86, 1975—; supr. sch. psychology interns Joliet Pub. Schs.; dist. cons. Guardian Angel Home Residential Treatment for Emotionally Disburbed Boys, self-contained behavior disorders programs. Cert. sch. psychologist, Ill. Mem. Ill. Sch. Psychology Assn., Nat. Assn. Sch. Psychologists. Methodist. Research on effectiveness of social and cognitive skills tng. with adolescent behavior disordered boys. Office: 420 N Raynor St Joliet IL 60435

SPANN, CARRIE B., univ. adminstr.; b. Cross, S.C.; d. George William and Mary P. Prioleau; B.S., U. Pa., 1978, now postgrad.; m. Steve Spann; children—George, Steve, Jeffrey, Mary, Anthony. Mktg., sales rep. Avon, 1962-68; mktg., sales rep. Field Enterprise Edn. Corp., 1967-71; office mgr., exec. sec. Minority Enterprise Small Bus. Investment Co., 1972-74; asst. dir. Community-Wharton Edn. Program, U. Pa., Phila., 1977-78, dir., 1978—. Sec., Wharton-Wesley United Meth. Women, 1977—; dir. Work/Learn, Inc.; treas. Sansom St. 49ers, 1979—. Democrat. Office: 111 Centenary Hall/CC Philadelphia PA 19104

SPARACIO, DORINDA ANN, chem. engr.; b. Newark, June 29, 1955; d. Robert Anthony and Helen Marie (Mancuso) Minnefor; B.S.Ch.E., Rutgers U., 1977, postgrad. in material sci. and packaging engring., 1981—; m. Nicholas John Sparacio, Nov. 19, 1978. Research chem. engr. Process Research and Devel. div. Colgate Palmolive Co. Jersey City, 1977-78, chem. engr., spray products/detergents, 1978-81, research chem. engr., specialty products, 1981—; sponsor Colgate Summer Student Program, 1980, 81. Mem. Am. Inst. Chem. Engrs., Am. Chem. Soc., Soc. Women Engrs., Rutgers Alumni Assn., Rutgers Rowing Alumni Assn. Home: 13 Edgemont Rd Edison NJ 08817

SPARBERG, ESTHER, chemist, educator; b. N.Y.C., June 17, 1922; d. Abraham and Sarah (Kurnick) Braun; B.S. in Chemistry, U. N.C., 1943; M.A., Columbia U. Tchrs. Coll., 1945, Ed.D., 1958; m. Lester S. Sparberg, Dec. 31, 1944; children—Andrew, Alice. Chemist, Interchem. Corp., 1943; technician Rockefeller Inst. Med. Research, 1943-44; tchr. chemistry Julia Richman High Sch., N.Y.C., 1946-47; mem. faculty Hofstra U., Hempstead, N.Y., 1959—, prof. chemistry, 1977—, also dir. NSF projects for tchrs. Sci. Manpower fellow, Columbia U., 1956-57. Mem. Am. Chem. Soc., Am. Assn. Physics Tchrs., History Sci. Soc., Am. Sci. Tchrs. Assn., Kappa Delta Pi. Democrat. Jewish. Co-author: A Laboratory Manual of Concepts in Chemistry, 1968; Chemical Quantitative Analysis: A New Approach, 1972; Ideas, Investigation, Thought, A General Chemistry Laboratory Manual, 1980. Contbr. profl. jours. Home: 25 Emerson Dr Great Neck NY 11023 Office: Hofstra Univ Hempstead NY 11550

SPARK, MURIEL SARAH, writer; b. Edinburgh, Scotland; d. Bernard and Sarah Elizabeth Maud (Uezzell) Gamberg; student James Gillespie's Sch. for Girls, Edinburgh; marriage dissolved; 1 son. Gen. sec. Poetry Soc., also editor Poetry Rev., 1947-49. Author: (critical and biographical) Child of Light, a Reassessement of Mary Shelley, 1951, John Masefield, 1953, (With D. Stanford) Emily Bronte: Her Life and Work, 1953; (poems) The Fanfarlo and Other Verse, 1952, Collected Poems, 1967; (fiction) The Comforters, 1957, Robinson, 1958, The Go-Away Bird, 1958, Memento Mori (adapted for stage 1964), 1959, The Ballad of Peckham Rye (Italian prize for dramatic radio 1962), 1960, The Bachelors, 1960, Voices at Play, 1961, The Prime of Miss Jean Brodie, 1961 (adapted for stage 1966, for film 1969, for TV 1978), The Girls of Slender Means, 1963 (adapted for TV 1974), The Mandelbaum Gate, 1965 (James Tait Black Meml. Prize 1965), The Public Image, 1968, The Driver's Seat, 1970 (adapted for film 1972), Not to Disturb, 1971, The Hothouse by the East River, 1973, The Abbess of Crew, 1974 (adapted as film Nasty Habits 1976), The Takeover, 1976, Territorial Rights, 1979; Loitering with Intent, 1981; Collected Stories I, 1967; (play) Doctors of Philosophy, 1963; (children's books) The Very Fine Clock, 1969. Editor: (with D. Stanford) Tribute to Wordsworth, 1950; Selected Poems of Emily Bronte, 1952; My Best Mary, Selected Letters of Mary Shelley, 1953; The Bronte Letters, 1954; (with D. Stanford) Letters of John Henry Newman, 1957. Decorated Order Brit. Empire. Hon. mem. AAAL. Address: care Harold Ober Assos 40 E 49th St New York NY 10017

SPARKS, ELIZABETH HEDGECOCK, dietitian, columnist; b. Kernesville, N.C.; B.S. in Home Econs., Salem Coll., 1939; postgrad. U. Md., Syracuse U. Dietetic intern Phila. Gen. Hosp., 1940-41; adminstrv. dietitian U. Md. Hosp., 1941-44; head dept. home econs. Salem Coll., Winston-Salem; daily newspaper food columnist under byline of Beth Tartan, Winston-Salem Jour. and Sentinel, 1947—; weekly food page writer Newsday, from 1952; cons. R.J. Reynolds Tobacco Co., 1968-70; practitioner in residence, instr. dept. home econs. Appalachian State U., Bonne, N.C., 1976; guest lectr. numerous cooking schs. Recipient numerous press awards; press award of yr. Forsyth County Heart Assn., 1976. Mem. Am. Home Econs. Assn., Home Economists in Bus., N.C. Home Econs. Assn., Am. Dietetic Assn., Assn. Cooking Schs., Internat. Wine and Food Soc., Compagnons de Bordeaux, Confrerie de la Chaine des Rotisseurs, Connoisseurs International, N.C. Consumers Council (dir.), LWV, Hist. Preservation Soc. N.C., Nat. Trust Hist. Preservation. Clubs: Pinehurst Country, Forsyth Country. Author: The Successful Hostess, 1949; Beth Tartan's Cook Book, 1952; North Carolina and Old Salem Cookery, 1955; Menu Maker and Party Planner, 1957; The Good Old Days Cook Book, 1971; The Korner's Folly Cook Book, 1976; (with Rudy Hayes) Miss Lillian and Friends; other books in field. Office: Winston-Salem Jour and Sentinel Winston-Salem NC

SPARKS, MARY ANN, nurse; b. Gray County, Tex., Jan. 4, 1936; d. Albert Houston and M. Evelyn (Wakefield) McPeau; grad. Meth. Hosp. Sch. Nursing, 1957; student Tex. Tech. U., 1973-74, Southwestern Bapt. Theol. Sem., 1973-76; m. Joe D. Sparks, Aug. 31, 1957; children—James Earl, Jack Dwaine. Nurse, various hosps., Lubbock, Tex., 1957-75, Cook

Children's Hosp., Ft. Worth, 1976-77, Valley Bapt. Med. Center, 1976-77; asst. dir. nursing Knapp Meml. Meth. Hosp., Weslaco, Tex., 1977—. Bd. dirs. Weslaco Cancer Soc. Bd., 1980-82. So. Baptist. Home: Route 3 Box 385 Harlingen TX 78550 Office: 1330 E 6th St Weslaco TX 78596

SPARKS, MEREDITH PLEASANT (MRS. WILLIAM J. SPARKS), lawyer; b. Palestine, Ill.; d. John L. and Laura (Bicknell) Pleasant; A.B. with distinction, A.M., Ind. U.; Ph.D., U. Ill., 1936; J.D., Rutgers U., 1958; m. William J. Sparks, Dec. 31, 1930 (dec.); children—Ruth Sparks Foster, Katherine Sparks Crowl, Charles, John. Tchr. chemistry Rochester (Ind.) High Sch., 1928-29; chemist DuPont Co., Niagara Falls, N.Y., 1929-34, Northam Warren Co., N.Y.C., 1939; chem. patent agt. Am. Cyanamid Co., Bound Brook N.J., 1941-46; admitted to Fla. bar, 1958, also U.S. Ct. Customs and Patent Appeals, U.S. Ct. Claims, U.S. Supreme Ct. bars; patent agt., 1946-58; patent atty., 1958—; pres. Sparks Innovators, Inc., 1979—. Mem. nat. bd. Med. Coll. Pa. Mem. Assn. Ind. U. Chemists (pres. 1950-51), Internat., Am., Fla., Coral Gables bar assns., Am., N.J. patent law assns., Internat. Patent and Trademark Assn., Am. Chem. Soc., Nat. Assn. Women Lawyers (pres.), AAUW, Phi Beta Kappa, Sigma Xi, Kappa Delta. Club: Zonta. Contbr. articles to profl. jours. Patentee in field. Address: 5129 Granada Blvd Coral Gables FL 33146 Office: The Law Center 370 Minorca Ave Coral Gables FL 33134

SPARKS, TOMMIELU LAMBETH, nurse, hosp. adminstr.; b. High Point, N.C., Mar. 12, 1939; d. William Bryant and Margaret (Waits) Lambeth; R.N. diploma Charity Hosp. Sch. Nursing, New Orleans, 1960; student Sante Fe Community Coll., 1980—; m. Philip Oliver Sparks, Sept. 1, 1961; children—Steven Philip, Franklin William. Staff nurse Alachua Gen. Hosp., Gainesville, Fla., 1960-62, head nurse, 1963-64, nursing supr., 1970-72, nurse epidemiologist, 1973-76, emergency room supr., 1976-78, asst. dir. nursing service, 1978—. Mem. Nat. League Nursing, Am. Heart Assn., Am. Nurses Assn. (co-chmn. br. infection control 1975), N.E. Fla. Practitioners Infection Control (pres. 1975-76). Baptist. Home: 2016 NW 36th Dr Gainesville FL 32605 Office: 801 SW 2d Ave Gainesville FL 32602

SPARLING, ELAINE HELEN COLE, photog. equipment co. exec.; b. Rochester, N.Y., June 12, 1946; d. Harvey Barrett and Dorothy (Starke) Cole; grad. Rochester Bus. Inst., 1965, Monroe Community Coll., 1975; m. Rodney R. Sparling. With Eastman Kodak Co., Rochester, N.Y., 1965—, exec. sec. sales planning. Cert. profl. sec. Mem. Profl. Secs. Assn. Internat. (mem. exec. bd. Flower City chpt. 1977-79, corr. sec. 1979-80). Home: 1183 State Rd Webster NY 14580 Office: Eastman Kodak CO 343 State St Rochester NY 14650

SPAULDER, JOAN ROISTACHER, broadcasting co. ofcl.; b. N.Y.C., Jan. 5, 1939; d. Charles and Ina (Zirinsky) Roistacher; B.A., Brandeis U., 1959; M.S., Queens Coll., 1963; children—Debra Val, Mara Jill. Tchr., N.Y.C., Westfield, N.J., Scotch Plains, N.J., 1959-69; account exec. Consumer Mktg. Research Services, Inc., Hackensack, N.J., 1969-70; dir. research and edn. Allen Levis Orgn., Inc., Northfield, Ill., 1971-73; dir. mktg. research Food Fair, Inc., Phila., 1974-78; dir. advt. W. B. Saunders div. CBS, Phila., 1978—. Pres., Women's Am. ORT, Westfield, N.J., 1968; v.p. PTA, Scotch Plains, N.J., 1969; mem. Brandeis U. Alumni Admissions Council, 1975—. Mem. Forum Exec. Women (dir. 1978-80), Am. Mktg. Assn. (dir. 1977-79), Assn. Am. Pubs. (dir. mktg. com. 1981—), Direct Mail Mktg. Assn., Phila. Direct Mail Mktg. Club, Phila. Postal Customers Council (chmn. 1981-82), Brandeis U. Alumni Assn. (steering com. Greater Phila. chpt. 1980—). Home: 729 Oak Springs Rd Rosemont PA 19010 Office: W Washington Sq Philadelphia PA 19105

SPAULDING, JEAN MARIE, educator; b. Newberg, Oreg., Sept. 29, 1918; d. H. Clifford and Mary E. (Baker) Spaulding; B.S., Oreg. Coll. Edn., 1941; M.A., Colo. State Coll., 1949, postgrad., 1960; postgrad. Stanford, summer 1955, U. Oreg., 1966. Tchr. elementary schs., Springfield, Oreg., 1939-42, Salem, Oreg., 1942-45, 46-48, 49-50, Seattle, 1945-46, Colo. State Lab. Sch., 1947-49; Eastern Wash. Coll. Lab. Sch., 1950-51; coordinator presch.-primary projects State Dept. Edn., Salem, 1951—. Mem. Nat. Assn. Edn. Young Children (task force 1970), Am. Assn. U. Women, Assn. Childhood Edn. Internat. (chmn. pub. affairs com. 1966-68), Nat. Council State Cons. in Elementary Edn. (treas. 1972-74), Ore. Assn. Sch. Suprs. (pres. 1956), Assn. for Supervision and Curriculum Devel., Ore. Dept. Elementary Sch. Prins., Delta Kappa Gamma (chpt. pres. 1964-66, state 2d v.p. 1969-71, 1st v.p., 1971-73, pres. 1973-75), Phi Lambda Theta. Republican. Presbyterian. Home: 767 Chruch St NE Salem OR 97301 Office: 700 Pringle Pkwy Salem OR 97310

SPAULDING, ROMA ALMA, state legislator; b. Woodstock, Vt., Oct. 16, 1914; d. John Wilhelm and Eveline Victoria (Bourdon) Magnusson; grad. high sch.; m. Bedford T. Spaulding, Dec. 24, 1937; children—Diane, Cynthia (Mrs. Douglas Dutilley). Mem. N.H. Ho. of Reps. from 4th Dist., 1967—, chmn. public health and welfare com., 1971—. Mem. N.H. Comprehensive Health Planning Council, 1971-75; mem. governing bd. Health Systems Agy., 1976-81; mem. State Health Coordinating Council, 1976-81; trustee Valley Regional Hosp., 1982—. Bd. dirs. N.H. Found. for Med. Care. Mem. Claremont Hist. Soc. Republican.

SPEAKER, MARY MARGARET, real estate broker; b. Meadville, Pa.; d. John T. and Rosetta Speaker; student U. Pitts., U. Calif., San Diego; grad. real estate schs.; 1 dau., Karen Lee Holt. Pres., Frankly Speaking Inc., speakers bur.-promotional agy., San Diego, 1977—, Multi-Nat. Properties, Inc., La Jolla, Calif., 1979—, S.W. Advs. Group, Inc., Beverly Hills, Calif., 1979—; owner Gallery d'Art, Beverly Hills, 1973—, Merry Mary Ranch, 1975—; dir. Multi-Vu Resource Center, Inc., La Jolla, Speaker Publs., Inc., La Jolla; mem. Calif. Horse Racing Bd. Mem. Nat. Assn. Realtors, Assn. Women Realtors (sec. 1977), Nat. Assn. Bus. and Profl. Women, NOW, LWV, Nat. Speakers Assn., San Diego C. of C., Women's Council Realtors (chpt. sec. 1978), Women in Sales, Beverly Hills Women's Golf Assn., N. County Exchangers Assn., League Women Bowlers. Republican. Clubs: Soroptimist, Toastmistress. Author papers in field. Office: 7855 Herschel Ave Suite 203 La Jolla CA 93037

SPEAKMAN, GENTA SHARP, home economist; b. Birmingham, Ala., Dec. 20, 1937; d. Fred Hall and Imogene (Murphree) Sharp; B.S., Auburn U., 1960, M.S., 1966, Ed.S. (Mary E. Coleman scholar), 1980; m. Bobby Lee Speakman, Nov. 11, 1961; children—Michael Sharp, Steven Todd. County extension agt. Etowah County, Ala., 1960-61; tchr. Jefferson County, Ala., 1961-62, Galena, Ill., 1962-63, Calhoun County, Ala., 1963-64; specialist in housing, equipment and energy Ala. Coop. Extension Service, Auburn, 1964—. Mem. Am. Home Econs. Assn., Ala. Home Econs. Assn., Auburn U. Home Econs. Alumni Assn., Omicron Nu, Phi Kappa Phi. Baptist. Recipient Alma award Assn. Home Appliance Mfrs., 1973. Home: 1042 Old Mill St Auburn AL 36830 Office: 208 Duncan Hall Mell Auburn AL 36830

SPEAKMAN, MARCIA LOUISE, educator; b. Columbus, Ohio, Feb. 20, 1943; d. Terence R.H. and Martha Elizabeth (Elson) Heffernan; B.S. in Edn., Ohio State U., 1965, M.A., 1968, postgrad.; m. Norman L. Speakman, Apr. 3, 1965. Tchr., Ross County (Ohio) Schs., 1965-67, Columbus Public Schs., 1967-71, Bexley Public Schs., 1971-72; tchr. Florence Crittenton Home, Adult High Sch. (Columbus Public Schs.), 1972—. Mem. Columbus Symphony Orch. Women's Assn., chmn. staccato unit, mem. German village unit; mem. nat. bd. Hospitalized Vets. Writing Project. Mem. Women in Communications (chmn. Matrix Table), Ohio Council Tchrs. English Lang. Arts, NEA, Central Ohio Tchrs. Assn., Columbus Edn. Assn., English Speaking Union, AAUW, Phi Delta Kappa, Delta Kappa Gamma (2d v.p.). Episcopalian. Home: 733 College Ave Columbus OH 43209 Office: 1229 Sunbury Rd Columbus OH 43219

SPEAR, ELLEN MAUD, food co. exec.; b. West Medway, Mass., Oct. 24, 1937; d. Reginald Lloyd and Thelma Annette (Nutting) Briggs; B.S. in Dairy Tech., U. Mass., 1959; m. Jack Spear, May 31, 1968. Technologist, Chr. Hansen's Lab., Milw., 1959-61; mgr. chemistry lab. State of Conn., Hartford, 1961-62; dairy chemist Drew Chem. Co., Boonton, N.J., 1962-67, Durkee Foods Co., Chgo., 1967-68; with Beatrice Foods Co., Chgo., 1968—, mgr. dairy product research, 1976—. Mem. Rollins Meadows (Ill.) Bd. Health, 1969-79, pres., 1976-79. Mem. Am. Dairy Sci. Assn., Inst. Food Technologists, Soc. Nutrition Edn. Office: 1526 S State St Chicago IL 60605

SPEAR, PAULA READING, bus. research exec., cons.; b. Cambridge, Mass., Dec. 7, 1940; d. Thomas James and Katherine Lee Reading; B.A., U. Nebr., 1963; M.A., U. Denver, 1964; m. James Howard Spear, Nov. 28, 1970. Research specialist U.S. Dept. Def., Saigon, Vietnam, 1967-69; bibliographer/researcher/writer Nat. War Coll., Washington, 1969-71; staff cons. Arya-Mehr U. Sci. and Tech., Tehran, Iran, 1975; staff cons. pvt. cabinet Empress of Iran, 1976-77; project writer Applied Mgmt. Scis., Silver Spring, Md., 1977; co-owner, v.p. Central Research Systems, bus. research/cons., Indpls., 1978—; Editor: Indiana Foundations: A Directory, 1981; Europe's Leading Corporate Contenders for Investments in the U.S., 1980; pub. newsletter. Office: 320 N Meridian Suite 1011 Indianapolis IN 46204

SPEARS, CAROLYN HARTMANN, judge; b. Brenham, Tex., Sept. 16, 1941; d. Kurt C. and Frances Marie (Duderstadt) Hartmann; B.S. in Bus. Edn., Tex. Luth. Coll., 1962; postgrad. St. Mary's U., 1965-69; 1 son, Roman Nathaniel. Law clk., sec. George F. Manning, Atty. at Law, San Antonio, 1962-69; atty. The Delevan Trust, San Antonio, 1969-71; dist. atty. Bexar County (Tex.), 1971-73; pvt. practice law, San Antonio, 1973-75; admitted to Tex. bar, 1969; judge Bexar County Ct., San Antonio, 1975—. Mem. profl. adv. bd. Bexar County Mental Health Assn., 1981—; active Arthritis Found., San Antonio Conservation Soc., others; adv. bd. San Antonio Spina Bifida Assn., 1981—. Mem. Nat. Assn. Women Judges, San Antonio Bar Assn., State Bar Tex., Am. Bar Assn., Greater San Antonio C. of C., San Antonio Mus. Assn., N. San Antonio C. of C., Tex. Cradle Soc., Am. Judicature Soc., AAUW. Lutheran. Clubs: Anglers, YMCA, YWCA, Soccer League. Office: Bexar County Courthouse San Antonio TX 78205

SPEARS, GILDA FAYE, mfg. co. exec.; b. Knoxville, Tenn., July 27, 1948; d. James William and Erma (Lee) Gillespie; B.A., Cleve. State U., 1971; J.D., Case Western Res. U., 1976; m. Wilmer L. Spears, June 29, 1968; 1 dau., Katrionne Teresa. Tchr., Cleve. Bd. Edn., 1971-73; admitted to Ohio bar, 1976; atty. firm Arter & Hadden, Cleve., 1976-79; corp. atty. Eaton Corp., Cleve., 1979—; sec., trustee Hough Area Devel. Corp., 1980-81. Trustee, Forest Hills Ch. Housing Corp., 1976—, v.p., 1977; trustee Hill House, 1977-80; mem. candidate rev. bd. Citizens League Greater Cleve., 1979-81; bd. overseers vis. com. Case Western Res. U., 1981—. Mem. Am. Bar Assn., Ohio Bar Assn., Bar Assn. Greater Cleve., Norman S. Minor Bar Assn., Order of Coif, Alpha Kappa Alpha. Home: 2248 Stillman Rd Cleveland Heights OH 44118 Office: Eaton Corp 100 Erieview Plaza Cleveland OH 44114

SPEARS, JAE, state senator; b. Latonia, Ky.; d. James and Sylvia Roxanna (Fox) Marshall; student U. Ky.; m. Lawrence E. Spears; children—Katherine Spears Cooper, Marsha Spears, Larry M., James W. Researcher sta. WLW-WSAI, Cin.; reporter Cin. Post and Cin. Enquirer; tchr. Jiya Gakuen Sch., Japan; lectr. U.S. mil. installations, East Anglia, U.K., 1960-64; rep. W.Va. Legislature, 1974-80, W.Va. Senate, 1980—. Vis. com. extension and continuing edn. W.Va. U., 1977—; mem. Citizens Tech. Adv. Bd. Mental Health Region VII, 1977—; bd. dirs. Potomac Highlands Travel Council, 1978—; adv. bd. W.Va. Women's Commn., 1976—, W.Va. Children's Home, 1977—; bd. dirs. Women's Aid in Crisis, Elkins, W.Va., 1978—; adv. bd. Randolph County Welfare, 1976—; steering com. Community Retardation Center, Romney, W.Va., 1977-78; bd. dirs. Elkins YMCA, 1968—; mem. W.Va. Autistic Task Force, 1982—. Recipient Susan B. Anthony award Nat. Women's History Week, 1982—. Admiral, N.C. Navy. Mem. Nat. Order Women Legislators, DAR, Am. Legion Aux., VFW Aux., Nat. League Am. Pen Women, Delta Kappa Gamma, Theta Sigma Phi. Democrat. Mem. Christian Ch. Clubs: Officers Open Mess, Elks, Elkins Women's, Emma Scott Garden, White Shrine, Bus. and Profl. Women's (Woman of Year 1978), Quota. Home and Office: Drawer 2088 Elkins WV 26241

SPEARS, JANET E., educator; b. Chambersburg, Ill., Sept. 5, 1933; d. Enoch E. and Marguerite Irene (Riley) Downey; A.A., Black Hawk Coll., 1978; B.S. (Chris Hoerr scholar), Bradley U., 1980; postgrad., St. Ambrose Coll., 1981—; m. Keith A. Spears, July 6, 1952; children—Bruce, Roger, Darci, Paul. Secretarial positions Kewanee Machinery Conveyor (Ill.), 1951-52, William E. Trinke, atty., Lake Geneva, Wis., 1952-53, Walworth Co., Kewanee, 1968-72; adminstrv. asst. Kewanee Pub. Hosp., 1972-75; asst. personnel dir. Davenport (Iowa) Osteo. Hosp., 1980-81; bus. mgr. Franciscan Med. Center, Rock Island, Ill., 1981; bus. prof. Black Hawk Coll., Kewanee, 1981—. Mem. Am. Mgmt. Assn., Soc. Advancement Mgrs., Am. Soc. Hosp. Personnel Adminstrn., Kewanee Pub. Hosp. Assn., Kewanee Art League, Phi Chi Theta. Republican. Methodist (ch. liturgist and Sunday sch. tchr., mem. adminstrv. council). Clubs: Henry County Republic Women, Annawan Jr. Women's (pres. 1964-65), United Fairview Women. Home: Rural Route 1 Sheffield IL 61361 Office: Black Hawk Coll East Campus PO Box 489 Kewanee IL 61443

SPEARS, MARY ELLEN, psychologist, educator; b. Decatur, Ala., July 14, 1922; d. Andrew D. and Minnie Lucille (Dodson) Wiley; B.S., Eastern Ky. U., 1944; M.S., Miss. State U., 1960; Ed.D., Auburn U., 1971; m. William D. Spears, June 8, 1974; children—Rebecca, William Dodson, Robert Andrew. Teaching asst. Auburn U., 1968-70, instr. founds. of edn., 1970-72; asso. prof. behavioral scis. Pensacola (Fla.) Jr. Coll., 1972-78, prof. psychology and behavioral scis., head dept. behavioral scis., 1978—. Mem. Southeastern Psychol. Assn., Am. Psychol. Assn., Northwestern Fla. Psychol. Assn., AAUW (sec. Auburn U. br. 1968-72, chmn. edn. founds. Pensacola br. 1974-76), Psi Chi, Phi Delta Kappa, Delta Kappa Gamma. Democrat. Baptist. Editor: Readings for Psychology and Youth, 1973. Home: Route 2 Box 25 D Gulf Breeze FL 32561 Office: 1000 College Blvd Pensacola FL 32504

SPECIAN, ROSEMARIE THERESE, pharm. co. devel. exec.; b. Somerville, N.J., Nov. 4, 1944; d. William Michael and Maryann (Dudek) S.; B.S. in Home Econs. (Ella Mae Shellshy Holmes award), Albright Coll., Reading, Pa., 1966; M.S. in Human Behavior and Devel., Drexel U., Phila., 1971; M.B.A., Loyola-Marymount U., Los Angeles, 1980. Sales rep. Atlas Crown Brokerage, Los Angeles, 1973-75; regional rep. Reynolds Metals Co., Los Angeles, 1975-77; mktg. mgr. nat. accounts Glass Containers Corp., Anaheim, Calif., 1977-79; sr. package developer Lederle Labs., Pearl River, N.Y., 1980—. Recipient various sales awards. Mem. Am. Mktg. Assn., Packaging Inst., N.J. Mktg. Assn., N.J. Packaging Assn. Home: 604 Bergen Blvd Ridgefield NJ 07657 Office: Lederle Labs N Middletown Rd Pearl River NY 10965

SPECTOR, JOHANNA LICHTENBERG, musical educator; b. Libau, Latvia; d. Jacob C. and Anna (Meyer) Lichtenberg; came to U.S., 1947, naturalized, 1954; D.H.S., Hebrew Union Coll., 1950; M.A., Columbia U., 1960; m. Robert Spector, Nov. 20, 1939 (dec. 1941). Research fellow Hebrew U., Jerusalem, 1951-53; faculty Jewish Theol. Sem. Am., N.Y.C., 1954—, dir., founder dept. ethnomusicology, 1962—, asso. prof. musicology, 1966-70, Sem. prof., 1970—. Fellow Am. Anthrop. Assn.; mem. Am. Musicol. Soc., Internat. Folk Music Council, World Union Jewish Studies, Asian (pres. 1973-78), African mus. socs., Soc. Ethnomusicology (sec.-treas. N.Y. chpt. 1960-64), Soc. Preservation Samaritan Culture (founder). Author: Ghetto und Kzlieder, 1947; Samaritan Chant, 1965; Musical Tradition and Innovation in Central Asia, 1966; Bridal Songs from Sana Yemen, 1960; producer documentary films: The Samaritans, 1971; Middle Eastern Music, 1973; About the Jews of India; Cochin (Cine Golden Eagle award 1979), 1976; The Shanwar Telis of India (Cine Golden Eagle award 1979), 1978; contbr. articles to profl. jours.; editorial bd. Asian Music. Home: 400 W 119th St New York NY 10027 Office: 3080 Broadway at 122d St New York NY 10027

SPECTOR, PAULA SYLVIA, occupational therapist; b. Boston, Jan. 30, 1927; d. John and Eva (Lebow) Nathan; student Mass. Sch. Art, 1946-48, Fashion Inst. Tech., 1957-59; B.S. cum laude, N.Y. U., 1964; m. Albert Spector, Oct. 2, 1947; 1 son, Michael. Sr. occupational therapist Mt. Sinai Hosp., Elmhurst Gen. Hosp., 1964-67; chief occupational therapist Orthopedic and Rehab. Inst., Jamaica, N.Y., 1967-69; asst. chief occupational therapist L.I. Jewish Hosp./Queens Hosp Center Affiliation, Jamaica, 1969-76; supr. clin. affiliations Hempstead (N.Y.) Park Hosp., 1976—. Mem. Am., N.Y., L.I. occupational therapy assns. Contbr. articles to profl. jours. Home: 69-31 222 St Bayside NY 11364 Office: 800 Front St Hempstead NY 11550

SPEEDLIN, SHIRLEY ANNE, civic worker; b. Fayetteville, Ark., Feb. 18, 1935; d. William Edward and Viola (Hulsey) Wines; student U. Ark., 1953-55; m. Kenneth Speedlin, Apr. 6, 1958; 1 dau., Vicki. Bookkeeper, Kelley Bros. Lumber (now Hillcrest Lumber), Fayetteville, 1955-79; office mgr. Joe Brennan Gen. Contractor, Fayetteville, 1980—. Chmn. Cystic Fibrosis Dr., Springdale, Ark., 1973; co-chmn. Springdale Centinal Pageant, 1978; co-chmn. Washington County Jr. Miss Pageant, 1978, chmn., 1979, 80; judge Ft. Smith Jr. Miss Pageant, 1979, 80; pres. Central Jr. High PTA, 1975-76; deaconess First Christian Ch., Springdale, also tchr. Sunday sch., youth sponsor. Mem. Nat. Women in Constrn., Epsilon Sigma Alpha (sec. city council 1971-72, pres. 1972-73, dist. coordinator state bd. 1972-73, pres. Region 5, 1979-80, regional parliamentarian 1980-81, state ednl. dir. 1980-81, pres. Gamma Alpha sorority 1971-72, parliamentarian, 1972-73, philanthropic chmn., 1973-74, awards chmn. 1974-75, sec. 1975-76). Home: 705 Sherman St Springdale AR 72764 Office: PO Box 657 2401 N Gregg St Fayetteville AR 72701

SPEER, RITA DIANNE, nurse; b. San Diego, Nov. 22, 1941; d. Clifford D. (stepfather) and June Catherine (Jebsen) Winbolt; student Hastings (Nebr.) Coll., 1959-60, 63; R.N., Mary Lanning Hosp., Hastings, 1962; B.S., Ft. Hays (Kans.) State U., 1970; m. Robert P. Speer, June 9, 1963; children—Rebecca Ruth, Allison Marie, Matthew Thomas. Staff nurse pediatrics Mary Lanning Hosp., 1962-63, Glenwood (Iowa) State Hosp., 1963, U. Chgo. Hosps., 1963-65, West Nebr. Gen. Hosp., Scottsbluff, 1966-67, Valley Hope, 1968-74; dir. nurses Valley Hope Alcoholism Treatment Center, Norton, Kans., 1974—. Advancement chmn., treas. Cub Scout pack, 1981—; mem. com. to organize community day care center, 1978-79; brownie leader, 1976-78. Mem. Am. Nurses Assn., Kans. Nurses Assn. Democrat. Episcopalian. Club: Order Eastern Star (past matron). Author newspaper articles, fiction and poetry. Home: 1008 Hartford St Norton KS 67654

SPEIR, BETTY SMITH, ednl. counselor; b. Bethel, N.C., Mar. 3, 1928; d. William Jasper and Carolyn (Pollock) Smith; A.B., Duke U., 1949; M.A., East Carolina U., 1963; m. David Ordway Speir, June 10, 1950; children—Carolyn G. Speir Brown, Christine St. Clair Speir Price. Tchr. English, Farmville (N.C.) High Sch., 1949-50, Bain High Sch., Charlotte, N.C., 1950-51, Bethel High Sch., 1961-70; cotton buyer Bethel Mfg. Co. (N.C.), 1958-60; guidance counselor North Pitt High Sch., Bethel, 1970—. Sec., N.C. Commn. on Edn. and Employment of Women, 1970-74; mem. N.C. State Bd. Edn., 1982—, N.C. Gov.'s Crime Commn., 1977-82, N.C. Commn. on Length of Sentencing, 1981-82; vice chmn. N.C. Democratic Com., 1978-80, 81-82, chmn., 1980; mem. Dem. Nat. Com., 1978-82; del. Dem. Nat. Conv., 1980. Named one of Winning Dem. Women of Decade, Nat. Fedn. Dem. Women, 1980. Mem. NEA, N.C. Assn. Educators, Delta Kappa Gamma. Methodist. Home: PO Box 340 Bethel NC 27812 Office: Route 1 Box 313 Bethel NC 27812

SPEIRS, CAROL LUCILLE, nurse, naval officer; b. Plainfield, N.J., Apr. 20, 1942; d. Alexander Walker and Catherine Lucille (McGovern) S.; diploma St. Peters Med. Center Sch. Nursing, New Brunswick, N.J., 1963; student Seton Hall U., 1966-72; B.A., San Diego State U., 1976; M.A., Webster Coll., 1980. Staff nurse Muhlenberg Hosp., Plainfield, N.J., 1963-64, Burdette Tomlin Meml. Hosp., Cape May Court House, N.J., 1964, 65, Georgetown U. Hosp., Washington, 1964-65; pvt. duty nurse, North Plainfield, N.J., 1965-66; staff nurse, charge nurse Raritan Valley Hosp., Greenbrook, N.J., 1966-72; commd. lt. (j.g.) U.S. Navy, 1973, advanced through grades to lt. comdr., 1979; charge nurse Naval Regional Med. Center, San Diego, 1973-76, Iwakuni, Japan, 1977-78, Long Beach, Calif., 1978—. Mem. Founders Ball Com., City of Cypress (Calif.), 1981. Recipient Outstanding Cath. Young Adult award Diocese of Trenton, 1970. Mem. Nat. League Nursing, Nat. Assn. Female Execs., Crocker Art Mus. Assn. Republican. Roman Catholic. Bd. dirs. Cypress Boys Club, Cypress Civic Theatre Guild. Home: 4457 Casa Grande Circle #443 Cypress CA 90630 Office: NRMC Long Beach 7500 E Carson St Long Beach CA 90822

SPEIRS, DORIS HUESTIS (MRS. J. MURRAY SPEIRS), artist, author; b. Toronto, Ont., Can.; d. Archibald Morrison and Florence Gooderham (Hamilton) Huestis; student Toronto Model Sch., 1900-02, Havergal Ladies Coll., 1902-15, U. Toronto, 1914-16, U. Ill., 1940-41; m. Wilfrid Gordon Mills, May 2, 1916 (div. June 1939); children—Adele Barbara (Mrs. Norman J. Hearn), Iris Florence (Mrs. John Leslie Weir); m. 2d, John Murray Speirs, Aug. 1, 1941. Exhibited one-man shows studio J.E.H. MacDonald, Toronto, 1925, Prouts Neck, Maine, 1929, Jerrold Morris Gallery, Toronto, 1970, Toronto Heliconian Club, 1970, Robert McLaughlin Gallery, Oshawa, Ont., 1971, Lyceum Club Can. and Women's Art Assn., 1975; exhibited in group shows Art Gallery of Toronto, Bklyn. Mus. Art, Albright Art Gallery, others; represented in permanent collections Nat. Mus. Can., Art Gallery Ont., McMichael Canadian Collection, Kleinburg, Ont. Named hon. diplomate philosophy, 1973; co-recipient Ont. Conservation Trophy, 1974; honoree Can. Mus. Sci., 1975, Fedn. Ont. Naturalists, 1977. Mem. Royal Ont. Mus., Art Gallery Ont., Fedn. Ont. Naturalists, Am., Brit. ornithologists' unions, Wilson Ornithol. Soc., World Federalists Can., Theta Beta Sigma. Clubs: Hamilton Nature, Heliconian of Toronto, Margaret Nice Ornithological. Author: Exercise for Psyche, 1922-72, 1973. Translator: (poems from Swedish of Lars von Haartman) The Forehead's Lyre, 1962, Black Sails, 1976; Life History of the Evening Grosbeak, 1968. Contbr. poems, essays to mags., profl. jours. Home: Cobble Hill 1815 Altona Rd Pickering ON L1V 1M6 Canada

SPELLMAN, CATHY CASH, advt. agy. exec.; b. N.J., June 27, 1942; d. Harry A. and Catherine (Gibbons) Cash; student Vassar Coll., 1959-60, Trophagen, 1960-62, Art Students League, 1960-62; m. Joseph

X. Spellman, Feb. 21, 1975; children—Bronwyn, Catherine. Public relations dir. Revlon, 1970-75; v.p., dir. Bloomingdale's, 1975-76; pres. McGlone, Nightingale, Rheingold and Spellman, 1976-77; pres. Cathy Cash Spellman, Inc., N.Y.C., 1977—. Mem. Fashion Group, Authors Guild, Am. Cosmetic Women. Author: Notes to My Daughters, 1981; So Many Partings, 1983; contbr. articles to mags. Office: 11 E 26th St New York NY 10010

SPELLMAN, KIRA BURDICK, bus. machine co. exec.; b. Montreal, Que., Can., Mar. 6, 1950; came to U.S., 1959, naturalized, 1974; d. Timothy and Margaret (Villa) B.; B.A., Hope Coll., 1971; M.A., Rutgers U., 1973; m. James J. Spellman, June 28, 1980. French tchr. Zeeland (Mich.) High Sch., West Ottawa High Sch., Holland, Mich., 1973; adminstrv. asst. to pres. U.S.-U.S.S.R. Trade & Econ. Council, N.Y.C., 1973-74; with IBM, N.Y.C., 1974-82, nat., internat. account mgr. 1975-82; project mgr. computer ops. Bus. Systems div. Perkin-Elmer Corp., Little Silver, N.J., 1982—. Mem. Nat. Assn. Female Execs., Am. Mgmt. Assn. Episcopalian. Home: 1235 Ash Ln Yardley PA 19067 Office: 2 Tinton Ave Little Silver NJ 07739

SPENCE, JANET BLAKE CONLEY (MRS. ALEXANDER PYOTT SPENCE), civic worker; b. Upper Montclair, N.J., Aug. 17, 1915; d. Walter Abbott and Ethel Maud (Blake) Conley; grad. Masters Sch., 1933; student Vassar Coll., 1933-35; cert. Katharine Gibbs Sch., 1936; m. Alexander Pyott Spence, June 10, 1939; children—Janet Spence Kerr, Robert Moray, Richard Taylor. Active Jr. League, Neighborhood House, ARC, 1950-65, Girl Scouts U.S.A., 1950-60, various community drives; chmn. Darien (Conn.) Assembly, 1955-56; sec., chmn. Wilton Jr. Assembly, 1961-63; subscription chmn. Candlelight Concerts Wilton, Conn., 1963-65; rec. sec. Public Health Nursing Assn. Wilton Bd., 1964-67; corr., rec. sec. Royle Sch. Bd., Darien, 1952-55; mem. Washington Valley Community Assn., 1973—; vol. N.J. Symphony Orch., 1974—, corr. sec., 1982—; treas. Morris County League, 1978-83, now corr. sec. Mem. Vassar (council rep. from Class of '37 1973-77), Dobbs alumnae assns., Washington Valley Home Econs. Club (corr. sec. 1977-82, pres. 1982—), Morris County Art Assn., Morris Mus. Arts and Scis. Congregationalist. Home: Washington Valley Rd Morristown NJ 07960 and 8 Evergreen Ave Kennebunk ME 04043

SPENCE, PEGGY MARIAN, pianist, educator; b. Cushing, Okla., Nov. 28, 1938; d. Merle Otto and Ula Marian (Hancock) Pickering; Mus.B., U. Okla., 1960, Mus.M., 1962, postgrad., 1974-76; postgrad. Southeastern State Coll., Durant, Okla., 1963; children—Stephanie Rochelle, James Theodore. Grad. asst. in piano U. Okla., Norman, 1960-61, staff accompanist, 1961-62, grad. asst. in piano, 1975-76; music coordinator Head Start project, Ardmore, Okla., 1963-64; lectr. applied piano, music lit., music history and music theory Central State U., Edmond, Okla., 1972—; adjudicator for music contests; ch. pianist; asst. music dir. Okla. Theatre Center; pianist Lyric Theatre of Oklahoma City, Okla. Musical Theatre, Inc.; soloist Okla. Art Mus. Recitals; soloist with Central State Symphony Orch., U. Okla. Symphony Orch. Mem. Am. Guild Piano Tchrs., Okla. Music Tchrs. Assn., MacDowell Club Okla., Pi Kappa Lambda, Alpha Lambda Delta, Mu Phi Epsilon. Democrat. Baptist. Club: Oklahoma City Pianists'. Home: 5817 Seminole Ct Oklahoma City OK 73132 Office: Music Dept Central State U 100 N University St Edmond OK 73034

SPENCE, SANDRA, transp. exec.; b. McKeesport, Pa., Mar. 25, 1941; d. Cedric Leroy, Jr. and Suzanne (Haudenshield) S.; B.A. in Polit. Sci., Allegheny Coll., Meadville, Pa., 1963; M.A. (Eagleton fellow 1963-64), Rutgers U., 1964. Various positions with Pa. Govt., 1964-68, Appalachian Regional Commn., 1968-75; legis. rep. Nat. Assn. Counties, 1975-77; fed. rep. Calif. Dept. Transp., 1977-78; dir. congl. affairs Amtrak, 1978-81, corp. sec., 1981—; mem. transp. adv. council D.C. Adv. Neighborhood Commns., 1976-78; bd. dirs. Nat. Council Transp. Disadvantaged, 1976-78; tchr. lobbying Open U., Washington, 1980—. Mem. Am. Soc. Corp. Secs., Women's Transp. Seminar (founder, chmn. legis. com. 1977-79, bd. dirs. 1982—, chmn. Edn. Com. 1982—). Am. Mgmt. Assn., Nat. Women's Polit. Caucus, Phi Beta Kappa, Alpha Chi Omega, Pi Gamma Mu, Pi Delta Epsilon, Pi Sigma Alpha. Author articles in field. Home: 3010 Porter St NW Washington DC 20008 Office: 400 N Capitol St Washington DC 20001

SPENCE, WYNNA JO, clin. social worker; b. Hollis, Okla., Apr. 22, 1926; d. William Roy and Alice Izora (Bolles) S.; A.A., Sacramento City Coll., 1948; B.A., Calif. State U., Long Beach, 1970; M.S.W., U. So. Calif., 1972; children—Kimberley Hunt-Williams, Cynthia Hunt-Donohoe. Intern Dept. Mental Health Los Angeles County, Calif., 1970-71, intern Centinella Valley Union High Sch. Dist., 1971-72; clin. social worker psychiatry Med. Center U. Calif., Irvine, 1972-76, service chief clin. social work, psychiatry, 1976—; clin. instr. dept. psychiatry and human behavior, co-dir. sex edn., Coll. Medicine U. Calif., Irvine, 1973—; vis. lectr. U. So. Calif., Calif. State U., Fullerton, Orange County Community Colls., Orange County Mental Health Services; mem. faculty Chapman Coll., 1974-77. Bd. dirs. Big Sisters of Orange County, 1974-79, pres., 1977-78; mem. Los Amigos de la Humanidad, U. So. Calif., Mental Health Assn. Orange County, Long Beach Grand Opera Assn. NIMH fellow, Inst. for Sex Research, Ind. U., 1973; recipient Clevenger awards, U. So. Calif., 1970, 71; lic. clin. social worker, Calif., marriage family child counselor. Fellow Soc. for Clin. Social Work; mem. Nat. Assn. Social Workers, Acad. Cert. Social Workers. Democrat. Club: U. So. Calif. Alumni. Office: U Calif Irvine Med Clinic 101 City Dr S Orange CA 92668

SPENCER, ANNE HARRIMAN, mgmt. cons.; b. Royal Oak, Mich., Jan. 1, 1936; d. John Dennis and Eva Pauline (Workman) Harriman; B.A., Marygrove Coll., 1957, M.Ed., 1975; div.; children—Joseph V. Alvaro, Timothy Alvaro, Marie Alvaro, Christina Alvaro. Adminstr. edn. program Laurel Montessori Center, Drayton Plains, Mich., 1973-75; edn. cons. Comprehensive Learning Inst., Detroit, 1975-76; outside sales rep. Pacific Mut. Life Ins. Co., Southfield, Mich., 1976-79; dir. mktg. First Call Realty Assn., Inc., Southgate, Mich., 1979-80; pres., dir. Infinity Inst., Royal Oak, Mich., 1980—; stress mgmt. cons. Bio Med. Center; ednl. cons. Marygrove Coll., 1980-81, adj. prof. bus., 1980-81. Detroit del. Mich. Alliance of Small Bus., 1981-82. Recipient Personal Power Unltd. award for seminar excellence, 1981; Agt. of the Yr., Pacific Mut. Life Ins. Co., Detroit Lambert Agy., 1977. Mem. Nat. Fedn. Bus. and Profl. Women Clubs, Nat. Assn. Women Bus. Owners, Nat. Speakers Assn., Am. Soc. Tng. and Devel., Southfield Bus. and Profl. Women's Club (pres. 1981-83), World Congress of Profl. Hypnotists (pres. 1982-84). Unity Ch. of Today. Columnist, Phenome News, 1980-83.

SPENCER, BARBARA Z., data services co. exec.; b. Ponce de Leon, Fla., July 21, 1939; d. J.P. and Alvesta (Simmons) Paul; student Santa Monica City Coll., 1968-70, UCLA, 1961-63; m. Walter F. Spencer, Oct. 5, 1981; children—Matthew Zuiderhof, Noah Zuiderhof, Heather Zuiderhof. Vice pres. Mgmt. Scis. Corp., Santa Monica, Calif., 1967-69; v.p. Profl. Computer Services, Anaheim, Calif., 1970-73; cons. data services, Springfield, Va., 1974; pres. Postal Data Corp., LaPlata, Md., 1976-80; pres. Mailing Data Services East, Inc., Waldorf, Md., 1980—. Pres., Port Tobacco PTA, 1978; chmn. Sch. Adv. Council, 1978-79; chmn. Parent Adv. Council, 1979-80; chmn. membership Charles County LWV, 1980. Mem. Mail Advt. Services Assn. (pres. Chesapeake chpt. 1979-80), Direct Mail Mktg. Assn., Fullfillment Mgmt. Assn., Zonta Internat Office: 901 N Columbus Alexandria VA 22134

SPENCER, BETTY GAISFORD, writer, public relations specialist; b. American Fork, Utah, July 12, 1925; d. Charles Joseph and Nellie La Rue (Spratley) Gaisford; student Brigham Young U., 1970-73, Utah Tech. Coll., 1972-73, U. Utah, 1973-74, Utah State U., 1975; m. Lawrence W. Hansen, June 7, 1943 (div. 1948); 1 son, Larry J.; m. 2d, Ralph H. Spencer, Dec. 9, 1949; children—Brent Guy, Alan Charles, Marsha. With gen. offices Columbia Steel, Hansen Bros., Dr. W.W. Ricks, 1943-51; reporter, photographer, columnist The Daily Herald, American Fork (Utah) Citizen, 1962, 71; info. and tng. officer Utah State Tng. Sch., American Fork, 1972-74, dir. info. services, 1974-77; columnist, editorial writer, freelance mag. writer, 1968-79; public relations dir. Utah Pageant of the Arts, 1972-80, script writer, 1972—; public relations cons., 1968-79; editor six publs. fields of mental retardation and communications; dir. workshops in fields. Utah del. Nat. Arts for Handicapped Com., 1975-78; bd. dirs. Alliance of Arts Edn., Utah, 1975-78; mem. Miss American Fork Scholarship Com., 1966-71, American Fork Library Com., 1967-68, American Fork Republican Party, 1960—. Winner first prize hist. article writing contest, 1976, various prizes for exhibits Utah State Fair; recipient citation State Forester, 1965; service award American Fork City, 1972; writing awards Utah State Inst. Fine Arts, 1970, 73; journalism Beehive award, 1974, 76, 78; profl. service award Mental Retardation Assn. Utah, 1978; other awards. Mem. Nat. Fedn. Press Women (historian 1979-83), Utah Press Women (state pres. 1975-76, Utah Woman of Achievement 1973), League of Utah Writers (pres. 1970-71), Utah State Poetry Soc., Nat. Writers Club, League Am. Pen Women, Utah State Hist. Soc., Am. Assn. Mental Retardation. Mormon. Club: Philadea Study Group. Co-author, producer documentary film: That Faraway Prize (winner four nat. awards including Best TV Documentary, Nat. Fedn. Press Women 1975); poetry included in Utah Sings, 1964, 74; contbr. articles to mags., regional and nat. publs. Home: 180 South 500 East American Fork UT 84003

SPENCER, CAROLINE M., fashion designer; b. Dallas, Nov. 22, 1932; d. Harold Austin and Anna M. Spencer; B.F.A., Mpls. Coll. Art and Design, 1955. Guest fashion editor Mademoiselle mag., 1955; designer Wonderalls, Mpls., 1958-62; sportswear designer Jr. House Milw., 1962-63; sr. fashion designer (clothes and accessories for Barbie Doll) Mattel Toys, Hawthorne, Calif., 1963—, dir. Volitan, Inc., Van Nuys, Calif. Recipient Best Toy award Mattel Toys, 1973, 77. Mem. Fashion Group, Women at Mattel, Mattel Mgmt. Assn., Nat. Assn. Female Execs. Democrat. Roman Catholic. Office: 5150 Rosecrans Ave Hawthorne CA 90250

SPENCER, DEBORAH LYNN, nurse; b. Pikeville, Ky., Oct. 17, 1954; d. Charles Edward and Martha Euline (Swiney) Anderson; A.A. in Nursing, Morehead (Ky.) State U., 1975; m. Joe Spencer, Aug. 11, 1976; children—Charles, Brian. Charge nurse hosps. in Ky. and Tex., 1975-79; mem. nursing staff Buchanan Gen. Hosp., Grundy, Va., 1979—, asst. dir. nursing, 1980—, also inservice edn. dir. Recipient award Woodmen of World, 1972; Basic Edn. Opportunity grantee, 1972. Home: Box 459 Grundy VA 24614 Office: Route 4 Box 335-E Grundy VA 24614

SPENCER, DIANNE WINTER, public relations co. exec.; b. Cin., Aug. 15, 1936; d. George Wolters and Mary Magdalen (Enzweiler) Winter; student U. Cin., 1954-57; 1 dau., Sheba. Account rep. J. Walter Thompson, N.Y.C., 1961-62; v.p. Schless & Co., N.Y.C., 1963-67; dir. Strauchen & McKim, N.Y.C., 1968-71; account supr. Manning, Salvage & Lee, N.Y.C., 1975-79; pres. Spencer-Wood, Inc., N.Y.C., 1979—. Mem. Nat. Home Fashions League, Pres.'s Assn., Am. Mgmt. Assn. Office: 1501 Broadway Suite 1519 New York NY 10022

SPENCER, ELEANOR BESS, waste mgmt. co. exec.; b. Cleve., Oct. 20, 1942; d. William C. and Eleanor A. (Rychlik) Lodwick; B.S., Mt. Union Coll., 1967; postgrad. U. Akron, 1969; m. Donald J. Spencer, Jan. 20, 1979; children—Jennifer, John. Analytical chemist Morgan Adhesives, Stow, Ohio, 1966-69; research and devel. chemist, analytical chemist Inmont Corp., Cin., 1974-79; environ. engr. Carrier Air Conditioning Co., Collierville, Tenn., 1979-80; adminstrv. asst. to dir. research and devel. Chapman Chem. Co., Memphis, 1981; chemist, safety officer, mgr. lab. chems. program Earth Indsl. Waste Mgmt. Co., Millington, Tenn., 1981—; dir. L & S Splty. Products, Inc. Resource family Memphis Boys Town, 1981-82; active children's worship Norwood (Ohio) Bapt. Ch., 1974-78, Bartlett (Tenn.) United Meth. Ch., 1979—; mem. Bartlett Jr. Pro Sports Booster Club, Shelby Youth Sports, Ellendale Athletic Assn. Mem. Am. Chem. Soc., Coblentz Soc., Memphis Chromatography Group, Alpha Delta Pi (pres. Cin. alumnae assn. 1975-78, adv. 1970-82). Republican. Clubs: Cuyahoga Falls Jr. Women's (charter, treas. 1969-70), Memphis Christian Women's After 5 P.M. (treas. 1982—), Order Eastern Star. Home: 8280 Bon Lin Dr Memphis TN 38134 Office: Earth Indsl Waste Mgmt Co 3536 Fite Rd Millington MN 38053

SPENCER, ELIZABETH FRANCES, educator; b. Edina, Mo., Apr. 4, 1922; d. Harry Frances and Elizabeth Ellen S.; student Quincy Coll., 1939-40, N.E. Mo. State Tchrs. Coll., B.S., 1945; M.S., U. Mo., 1951; D.Ed. (Delta Kappa Gamma scholar, U.S. Office Edn. fellow), U. Ill., Urbana, 1962. Tchr., Knox County, Mo., 1941-43, elem. sch., Hannibal, Mo., 1944-46; tchr. educable mentally retarded, Quincy, Ill., 1951-60; mem. faculty Ball State U., Muncie, Ind., 1962—, now prof. spl. edn., chmn. dept. spl. edn., 1967-74. Mem. Am. Assn. Mental Deficiency, Council Exceptional Children (Tchr. of Yr. award chpt. 495, 1981), Delta Kappa Gamma, Phi Delta Kappa. Club: Altrusa. Home: 2208 Yorkshire Dr Muncie IN 47304 Office: 2000 University Ave Muncie IN 47306

SPENCER, KAROLYN ANN, social worker; b. Kansas City, Mo., Mar. 22, 1932; d. George Louis and Annette Christine (Baum) Horst; B.A., Ohio Wesleyan U., 1954; M.A., U. Chgo., 1961; cert. child therapy program Chgo. Inst. Psychoanalysis, 1975; m. Gilbert Lowell Spencer, Aug. 3, 1968; 1 son, David Lowell. Caseworker, LaRabida Children's Hosp., Chgo., 1961-66; caseworker II, United Charities Family Service, Chgo., 1966-68; supr. med. casework Wyler Children's Hosp., U. Chgo. Hosps. and Clinics, 1968-72; psychiat. caseworker Evanston (Ill.) Hosp., 1973-74; cons., pvt. practice social work, 1974-76; supr. foster care dept. Children's Home and Aid of Ill., Chgo., 1976-77; chief social worker joint service program for adolescents Comprehensive Community Services of Chgo., 1977—; adminstrv. dir. Profl. Services to Youth, 1981—; cons. Bd. dirs. Catalyst for Youth. Cert. social worker, Ill. Mem. Nat. Assn. Social Workers, Assn. Child Psychotherapists. Democrat. Unitarian. Home: 1211 Michigan St Evanston IL 60202 Office: Comprehensive Community Services of Chgo 64 E Jackson Blvd Chicago IL 60604

SPENCER, LILLIAN MARIE, mfg. co. public relations exec.; b. Tuscaloosa, Ala., Aug. 7, 1954; d. John Herbert and Lillian Marie (Brown) S.; B.A. in Mass Communications, U. Ala., 1975. Sr. research asso. Colo. Legis. Council, 1975-78; public adminstrn. intern Denver Manpower Adminstrn., 1978; public relations asso. Western Electric Co., Aurora, Colo., 1978—; speaker in field. Sec. bd. Big Sisters Colo., 1982, Artreach, Inc., 1982; active allocations coms. United Way. Recipient Jefferson medal for community service; named One of 9 Who Care for community service. Mem. Internat. Assn. Bus. Communicators, Delta Sigma Theta. Democrat. Baptist. Home: 630 S Dayton St Apt 6-304 Denver CO 80231 Office: Western Electric Co 111 Havana St Aurora CO 80010

SPENCER, MARY EILEEN, biochemist, educator; b. Regina, Sask., Can., Oct. 4, 1923; d. John J. and Etta Christina (Hamren) Stapleton; A.A., Regina Coll., 1942; B.A. with high honors in Chemistry, U. Sask., 1945; M.A. in Chemistry, Bryn Mawr Coll., 1946; Ph.D. in Agrl. Chemistry, U. Calif., Berkeley, 1951; m. Henry Anderson Spencer, July 3, 1946; 1 dau., Susan Mary. Chemist, Ayerst, McKenna and Harrison Ltd., Montreal, Que., Can., summer 1945, full time, 1946-47, Nat. Canners Assn., San Francisco, 1948; teaching fellow U. Calif., Berkeley, 1949, instr. food chemistry, 1951; faculty U. Alta., Edmonton, Can., 1953—, instr., asst. prof., asso. prof., acting head biochem. dept., 1960-61, plant sci. dept., 1962, prof. plant sci., 1964—; sec.-treas. Spencer-Lemaire Industries Ltd.; mem. Nat. Research Council Can., 1970, 70-73, 73-76, Task Force on Post-Secondary Edn., Alta. Govt. Commn. on Ednl. Planning, 1970-72; chmn. Nat. Adv. Com. on Biology, Nat. Research Council; adv. bd. Prairie Regional Lab.; bd. govs. U. Alta., 1976-79; chmn. ad hoc vis. com. in forestry research NRC, 1975-76; mem. Agr. Can. Cons. Com. IBT Pesticides, 1981-82. Recipient Queen's Jubilee Medal. Mem. Can. Soc. Plant Physiologists (pres. 1971-72), Can. Biochem. Soc., Am. Soc. Plant Physiologists, Can. Assn. Univ. Tchrs., Japanese Soc. Plant Physiologists, Internat. Assn. Plant Tissue Culture, AAAS, Growth Regulators Working Group. Office: Univ Alberta Dept Plant Sci Faculty Agr and Forestry Edmonton AB T6G 2E3 Canada

SPENCER, MARY LOUISE WAKEFIELD, civic worker; b. St. Louis, Mar. 31, 1909; d. Ralph and Mary Catherine (Black) Wakefield; B.A., Northwestern U., 1930; M.A., U. Chgo., 1932; m. Harry Chadwick Spencer, May 26, 1935; children—Mary Grace Spencer Lyman, Ralph Wakefield. Circle leader Women's Soc. Christian Service of Calvary Methodist Ch., Nashville, 1954-56, pres., 1956-58; pres. United Ch. Women Nashville and Davidson County, 1959-61, chmn. nominating com., 1965-66; v.p. Nashville Assn. Chs., 1959-61; public relations chmn. United Ch. Women Tenn., 1958-61, pres., 1962-65, constn., by-laws chmn., 1965-67; v.p. Tenn. Council Chs., 1962-65; lead tchr. ch. sch. Calvary United Meth. Ch., 1955-80; chmn. Coop. Bd. Hillsboro Chs.; vol. tchr. remedial reading program Buena Vista Sch., 1964-65, enrichment program for tchrs. Carter Lawrence Sch., 1965-70; mem. Nashville Community Relations Council, Tenn. Council Human Relations, Internat. Christian U. Tokyo Women's Planning Com., Wesley Found. Aid; mem. nominating com. Scarritt Aid, 1964, pres., 1968-70; active YWCA; bd. dirs. Bethlehem Center, 1961-66, sec., 1963-66. Mem. UN assns. U.S. (state bd. dirs. 1964-65), Nashville, Tenn. Bot. Gardens and Fine Arts Center, Northwestern U. Alumni Assn., Goodwill Industries Aux., PEO (pres. chpt. Sisterhood 1965-67), Woman's Club of Nashville (pres. 1971-73), Tenn. Fedn. Women's Clubs (Dist. V pres. 1974-76, chaplain 1980-82, historian 1982—, state 2d v.p. 1975-78, state rec. sec. 1978-80, state historian 1980—), Metaphys. Club (pres. 1978-80, v.p. 1980-82), Ladies Hermitage Assn., Alpha Omicron Pi. Editor Tidings, 1974—; contbr. articles to religious publs. Home: PO Box 150063 Nashville TN 37215 also 610 Westview Ave Nashville TN 37205

SPENCER, MARY MILLER, civic worker, club woman; b. Comanche, Tex., May 25, 1924; d. Aaron Gaynor and Alma (Grissom) Miller; B.S., North Tex. State U., 1943. 1 dau., Mara Lynn. Cafeteria dir. Mercedes (Tex.) public schs.; 1943-46; home economist coordinator All-Orange Dessert Contest, Fla. Citrus Commn., Lakeland, 1959-62, 64. Tchr. purchasing sch. lunch dept. Fla. Dept. Edn., 1960. Clothing judge Polk County (Fla.) Youth Fair, 1951-68, Polk County Federated Women's Clubs, 1964-66; pres. Dixieland Elem. Sch. PTA, 1955-57, Polk County Council PTAs, 1958-60, dist. 7. Fla. Congress Parents and Tchrs., 1961-63; chmn. public edn. com. Polk County unit Am. Cancer Soc., 1959-60, bd. dirs., 1962—; charter mem., bd. dirs. Lakeland YMCA, 1962-72; sec. Greater Lakeland Community Nursing Council, 1965-72; trustee, vice chmn. Polk County Eye Clinic, Inc., 1962-64, pres., 1964-82; public relations chmn. Fla. Congress Parents and Tchrs., 1962-66; bd. dirs. Polk County Scholarship and Loan Fund, 1962-70; mem. exec. com. West Polk County (Fla.) Community Welfare Council, 1960-62, 65-68; mem. budget and audit com. Greater Lakeland United Fund, 1960-62, bd. dirs., 1967-70, residential chmn. fund drive, 1968; mem. adv. bd. Polk County Juvenile and Domestic Relations Ct., 1960-69; worker children's services dist. II, unit 3, Div. Family Services, Dept. Health and Rehab. Services, State of Fla., 1969-70, social worker region 7, unit 62, 1970-72, 74-82, social worker OFR unit, 1977-81. Mem. exec. com. Suncoast Health Council, 1968-71; mem. Polk County Home Econs. Adv. Com., 1965-71; sec. bd. dirs. Fla. West Coast Ednl. Television, 1960-81; bd. dirs. Lake Region United Way, Winter Haven, 1976-81; mem. Polk County Community Services Council, 1978—. Mem. Nat. Welfare Fraud Assn., Fla. Congress Parents and Tchrs. (hon. life), AAUW (pres. Lakeland br. 1960-61), Polk County Mental Health Assn., Fla. Health and Welfare Council, Fla. Health and Social Service Council, North Tex. State U. Alumni Assn. Democrat. Methodist. Mem. Order Eastern Star. Home: 535 W Beacon Rd Lakeland FL 33803 Mailing Address: PO Box 2161 Lakeland FL 33803

SPENLINHAUER, GEORGIA MYRNA, printing co. exec.; b. Cheyenne, Wyo., June 12, 1909; d. Leonard and Rose Mangiaracine; grad. Boston State Coll., 1931; m. John Edward Spenlinhauer, June 30, 1938; children—John 3d, Robert, Stephen. Tchr. elementary sch., 1931-33; asst. buyer photog. equipment R.H. White Philately, Boston, 1934-35, buyer, 1935-37; sales promotion asst. Cedric Chase Photo Finishers, Waltham, Mass., 1937-45; co-founder with husband Spencer Press, Inc., Hingham, Mass., 1942, pres., 1945—, chmn. bd., 1972—. Chmn., St. Sebastian's Country Day Sch., Newton, Mass., 1959-61, pres. 1961-62; bd. dirs. Matre Dei Guild for Blind, Newton, 1962-64, Big Brother Assn. Boston, 1977—; mem. New Eng. regional auditions com. Met. Opera, 1976-77. Mem. Internat. Platform Assn.

SPERANZO, CAROLANN MARIE, optician; b. Brookline, Mass., Mar. 2, 1954; d. Fred P. and Madeleine Elizabeth (Harrington) S.; B.A., Emmanuel Coll., 1975; postgrad Boston Coll., 1976—. Research aide, Med. Library, Harvard U., part-time 1972-75; optician, office mgr. William H. Fehrnstrom Inc., Optician, Milton, Mass., 1972-79; owner, optician Second Sight, Boston, 1979—; mem. adv. bd. med. assts. program Aquinas Jr. Coll., 1979—; vol. emergency med. technician Boston Ambulance Squad. Mem. Mayor's Commn. on Status of Women, 1982-83; bd. dirs. DOVE, Inc. Fellow Contact Lens Soc. Am.; mem. New Eng. Contact Lens Soc., Mass. Assn. Registered Dispensing Opticians, New Eng. Women Bus. Owners, AAUW. Democrat. Roman Catholic. Club: Altrusa. Home: 150 Bromfield St Quincy MA 02170 Office: 299 Newport Ave Quincy MA 02170

SPERLICH, LINDA LEE, elec. engr.; b. Chgo., May 18, 1953; d. Fred Alan and Helen Mae Hazeltine; B.S. in Computer Sci., Calif. State U., Fullerton, 1975; M.S. in Elec. Engring. (Hughes fellow), U. So. Calif., 1980. Staff engr. Hughes Aircraft Co., Fullerton, 1975—. Mem. Assn. Computing Machinery (vice chmn. Orange County chpt. 1981-82, chmn. 1982-83), IEEE, Soc. Women Engrs., Eta Kappa Nu. Office: PO Box 3310 618/M311 Fullerton CA 92634

SPERLING, JOANN, businesswoman, writer/editor; b. Paterson, N.J., May 6, 1938; d. Charles F. L. and Else T. M. (Sothmann) S.; B.A., Fairleigh Dickinson U., 1960. Personnel asst. Pepsi Cola Co., N.Y.C., 1960-61; with Am. Mgmt. Assns., N.Y.C., 1961-74, sr. research assoc., 1971-72, supr. exec. services, 1972-74; editor publs. Exec. Assns., ITT, N.Y.C., 1974-79, adminstr. Exec. Assn. activities, 1977-79; asst. to v.p. mktg. Research Inst. Am., N.Y.C., 1981—; Freelance writer and editor,

1979—. Democrat. Lutheran. Home: 80 Central Park W New York NY 10023

SPERO, RUTH L., symphony orch. adminstr.; b. N.Y.C., Oct. 18, 1932; d. Eva Zarrow; B.A., Tufts U., 1953; postgrad. U. Miami, 1961-63; m. Robert D. Spero, Dec. 21, 1964 (dec.); children—Ilene, Karen, Janice Berger. Music therapist S. Fla. State Hosp., 1958-60; dir. cultural arts and vol. services Jewish Center of Buffalo, N.Y., 1965-68; dir. creative arts therapies Children's Rehab. Center, Buffalo, 1968-70; dir. creative arts therapies research Exceptional Edn. div. Niagara Falls Schs., 1970-71; exec. dir. Day Care Council of Erie County, N.Y., 1971-73; head div. social rehab. and creative arts therapies dept. Buffalo Psychiat. Center, Mental Hygiene, State of N.Y., Buffalo, 1973-76; dir. devel. Buffalo Philharm. Orch., 1976-77, mgr., 1977-80, exec. dir., 1980—; mem. faculty SUNY, Buffalo, 1974-76; mem. U.S. Pres. Com. on Employment of Handicapped, 1975—. Mem. nat. exec. council Am. Jewish Com., 1966—; mem. adv. bd. Erie County Manpower, 1976—, Erie Community Coll., 1974—, Daemon Coll., 1978—. Mem. Major Mgrs. of Am. Symphony Orch. League, Nat. Rehab. Assn., Nat. Assn. Music Therapy, Inc. (registered music therapist), Am. Assn. Music Therapy Inc. (cert. music therapist), Am. Dance Therapy Assn., N.Y. State Assn. for Edn. of Young Children. Democrat. Jewish. Club: Zonta. Office: 26 Richmond Ave Buffalo NY 14222

SPERRY, JEAN ELIZABETH, educator; b. Des Moines, July 30, 1951; d. Herbert J. and Helen (Anderson) S.; B.S., Drake U., 1972; M.A., Coll. St. Thomas, 1980. Tchr. spl. edn. W. St. Paul Ind. Sch. Dist. 197, 1973—; mgr. concessionary St. Paul Civic Center, 1976—; seminar leader Coll. St. Thomas, 1980—; mktg. asso. ARP Enterprises, Learning Programs Am., Performax, 1982—. Mem. Task Force, United Handicapped Fedn. Mem. Am. Bus. Women Assn., Am. Soc. Tng. and Devel., Minn. Fedn. Tchrs., Assn. Retarded Citizens, NOW, Abortion Rights Council. Democrat. Presbyterian. Club: Women's Network. Home: 1355 Dodd Rd West Saint Paul MN 55118

SPERRY, S. BAXTER, pub.; b. Wurzburg, Ger., July 10, 1914; d. John Augustus and Lillian (Mason) S.; B.A., San Francisco Coll. Women, 1956; M.A., San Francisco State Coll., 1958; postgrad. Wash. State U., 1960-62. Women's editor Utah mag., 1937-38; tchr. U.S. Army, Okinawa, 1951, writer, 1952-53; tchr. U.S. Navy, Philippines, 1956; editorial writer, asst. dir. public relations Calif. Redwood Assn., 1963; counselor Calif. Dept. Rehab., 1966-67; owner, pub. Covenant Press, Laurel Hill Press, Galt, Calif., 1968—. Chmn., Galt Property Owners Council, 1969—; mem. Sacramento Regional Arts Council, 1978-80. Mem. Dry Creek Antiquarian Soc. (sec. 1968—), Archives Assos., Psi Chi. Office: PO Box 202 Galt CA 95632

SPETCH, DORIS EDNA JACKSON, educator; b. Hudson, S.D., Mar. 2, 1920; d. Olin DeBuhr and Edna Anna (Hanson) Jackson; B.A., Hamline U., St. Paul, 1942; M.A., Northeastern Ill. U., 1970; m. William B. Spetch, Dec. 23, 1942; children—Barbara Spetch Mader, John. Tchr. schs. in Minn. and Ohio, 1942-45; newswriter Richfield Messenger, Mpls., 1945-46; tchr., choir dir., Appleton, Wis., 1958-66; tchr., Oak Lawn, Ill., 1966-74; with alumni dept. Lawrence U., Appleton, 1956-58; tchr. English and Communications Alan B. Shepard High Sch., Palos Heights, Ill., 1966-81; lectr. speech dept. Moraine Valley Coll., 1976—; cons. workshops, coach forensics teams. Pres. Winona (Minn.) YWCA, 1955. Named Woman of Year, Winona Bus. and Profl. Women, 1955; Ill. Coach of Yr., Northeastern Ill. U., 1976; recipient degree of distinction Nat. Forensic League; 1976. Mem. NEA, Ill. Edn. Assn., Ill. Speech and Theatre Assn., Ill. Tchrs. English, AAUW (pres. Winona 1954, mem. Minn. bd. 1953-55), Speech Communications Assn., Nat. Reading Assn.

SPICER, EMILY TAYLOR, ednl. adminstr.; b. Versailles, Ky., July 25, 1926; d. Larry Duncan and Arega (Owens) Harris; B.S. in Edn., U. Cin., 1948, M.Ed., 1963; m. Roy J. Spicer, Dec. 18, 1976; 1 son, Mac D. With Cin. Pub. Sch. System, 1958—, tchr. health and phys. edn. Heinold Jr. High Sch., 1959-62, tchr. health, phys. edn. and driver edn. Aiken High Sch., 1962-65, counselor Aiken High Sch., 1965-68, guidance coordinator Woodward High Sch., 1968-71, asst. prin., 1971-76, prin. Merry Jr. High Sch., 1976-78, prin. Robert A. Taft High Sch., Queen City Vocat. Center, 1978-81, dir. staff devel. br. Cin. Pub. Sch. System, 1981-82, dir. secondary edn., 1982—. Bd. dirs. YMCA; mem. social devel. com. Emanuel Community Center Exec. Bd.; mem. exec. com. Billy Graham Crusade, vice chmn.; trustee Ohio Lung Assn.; mem. adv. bd. Black Career Women, Inc.; mem. Adv. Youth Services Juvenile Ct. Recipient numerous awards including: Outstanding Educator trophy Ohio Elks Assn., 1979; Ethelrie Harper Human Relations award Cin. Human Relations Commn., 1980. Mem. Ohio Assn. Secondary Sch. Prins., Cin. Assn. Adminstrs. and Suprs., Ohio Edn. Assn., Nat. Assn. Secondary Sch. Prins., Cin. Guidance and Personnel Assn., Delta Sigma Theta, Delta Kappa Gamma, West End Community Council. Presbyterian. (deacon, elder). Home: 11289 Lockport Ct Cincinnati OH 45240 Office: 230 E 9th St Cincinnati OH 45202

SPICER, FLORENCE LEVAN, genealogist; b. Simpson, Minn., Oct. 4, 1907; d. Clinton Ambrose and Clara Augusta (Johnson) LeVan; student U. Oreg., 1925-26; m. Ivan Rea Spicer, May 18, 1929; children—Jean Marie Spicer Smith, James Ivan. Partner, office mgr. Spicer Lumber Co., Eugene, Oreg., 1939-51; genealogist, compiler geneal. works. Named Woman of Achievement, Council Women's Orgns. in Eugene, 1972; cert. geneal. record searcher. Mem. Nat. Assn. Parliamentarians, Hugenot Soc. Oreg. (pres. 1976), Oreg. Geneal. Soc. (charter, parliamentarian, 1968-72), Lane County Hist. Soc., Oreg. Hist. Soc., Colonial Dames XVII Century (state pres. 1972-75), Daus. Am. Colonists, Daus. Colonial Wars, DAR (Oreg. state regent 1964-66, v.p. gen. Oreg. Nat. Soc. 1966-69, Western Div. chmn. Am. History month 1968-74, Western Div. lineage researcher 1977-80 nat. speakers staff 1966— Soc. Mayflower Desc. Oreg. (dep. gov.-gen. 1981-84), Order Ams. of Armorial Ancestry (councillor 1982-84), Oreg. Assn. Parliamentarians (treas. 1981-82), Nat. League Am. Pen Women. Mem. Christian Ch. (Disciples of Christ). Clubs: Soroptimist of Eugene (charter; pres. 1955-56). Compiler: The Spicer Family; Campbell-Rea Families, 1973; LeVan Johnson Families, 1977. Home: 2247 Bedford Way Eugene OR 97401

SPIEGEL, JEANNE S., economist; b. Merion, Pa., Oct. 23, 1926; d. Stanley R. and Julia (Nusbaum) Sundheim; B.A., Wellesley Coll., 1948; postgrad. U. Pa., 1976-78; m. Walter F. Spiegel, Oct. 8, 1950; children—Walter D., Karen J., James R. Economist Dept. Labor, Washington, 1949-50; with Walter F. Spiegel, Inc., Cons. Engrs., Jenkintown, Pa., 1963—, office mgr., 1965-78, contract adminstr., 1965-75, energy analyst, chief economist, 1975—, corp. sec., 1967—. Mem. Nat. Assn. Women in Constrn. (chpt. pres.). Home: 405 Lodges Ln Elkins Park PA 19117 Office: 321 York Rd Jenkintown PA 19446

SPIEGEL, SUSAN LYNN, mfg. co. exec.; b. N.Y.C.; d. Irving and Beatrice (Albert) Jaffe; B.S., Boston U., 1964; postgrad. Hofstra U., C. W. Post U.; m. Maurice Spiegel, Aug. 31, 1975; children by previous marriage—Robert Wayne, Stephen Mark. Elementary sch. tchr., Long Beach, N.Y., 1964-67; pres. Fashions by Appointment, Glen Cove, N.Y., 1967-71; pres. North Shore Sales, Glen Cove, N.Y., 1972-73; adminstrv. asst. Peerless Sales Corp., Elmont, N.Y., 1967-71; sales mgr., then mktg. dir. United Utensils Co. Inc., Port Washington, N.Y., 1973-78, v.p. ops. and control, 1978—; v.p. ops. and control United Molded Products, 1978—; dir. Peerless Sales Corp. Fundraiser, Glen Cove Community Hosp., Glen Cove Library. Mem. Hadassah, NOW, Am. Meat Inst., Bus. Persons Advt. Assn., Nat. Trade Show Exhibitors Assn., Women's Am. ORT, Boston U. Women Grads. Club. Home: 159 Brookville Ln Old Brookville NY 11545 Office: United Utensils Co Inc Yennicock Ave Port Washington NY 11050

SPIEGEL, VIRGINIA ANN, nurse; b. N.Y.C., Oct. 20, 1952; d. Charles Martin and Sophie (Kuzmyn) S.; R.N., Queens Hosp., Jamaica, N.Y., 1974; B.S. in Nursing, Seton Hall U., 1978; M.S.N., Hunter Coll., 1981. Staff nurse Columbia-Presbyterian Hosp., N.Y.C., 1974, Meml. Sloan-Kettering Cancer Center, N.Y.C., 1975; staff nurse Lyons (N.J.) VA Hosp., 1975-79, nursing supr., 1979-80; nurse recruiter Bergen Pines Hosp., Paramus, N.J., 1980—; speaker in field. Mem. Am. Nurses Assn., N.J. State Nurses Assn., N.J. Assn. Hosp. Recruiters, Nat. Assn. Nurse Recruiters, Costeau Soc., ASPCA, Sigma Theta Tau. Roman Catholic. Office: Bergen Pines County Hospital Paramus NJ 07652

SPIERS, NEDRA BROWN, psychologist; b. Kansas City, Mo., Nov. 3, 1929; d. Milton Bird and Blanche Sadie (McHenry) Brown; student Hendrix Coll., 1944-45; B.S., Austin Peay State U., 1975, M.A., 1976; m. James Allyn Spiers, Mar. 17, 1950; children—James Allyn, Lynn, Susan, Richard, Nancy, Jennifer, JoAnn. Substitute tchr. Wayne County (Ga.) Bd. Edn., 1970-71; dir. counseling services Ky. Better Living Center, Hopkinsville, 1976-79; dir. Community Mental Health Center, Jesup, Ga., 1979—. Vol. ARC, Ala. and Ga., 1960-72, Girl Scouts U.S.A., Ala. and Ga., 1965-72. Mem. Am. Psychol. Assn. (asso.). Methodist. Club: Order Eastern Star. Home: 235 S Bamboo St Jesup GA 31545 Office: 244 Peach Tree St Jesup GA 31545

SPILKER, BARBARA JO, Mont. state rep.; b. Alliance, Nebr., Feb. 13, 1938; d. Lamoine James and Loretta (Kunc) Bible; B.A., U. Nebr., Lincoln, 1960; m. William McBride Spilker, 1960. Mem. exec. bd. Model Cities Devel. Corp.; mem. Mont. Ho. Reps., 1979—; tchr. English, Jordan Vocat. High Sch., Ga., 1960-61; instr. journalism Kearney State Coll., Nebr., 1963-64; dir. pub. info. Westside Community Schs., 1966-69; dir. First Nat. Bank, Helena, Mont. Bd. dirs. YMCA. Mem. Lewis and Clark County Republican Women (dir.), Theta Sigma Phi, Gamma Alpha Chi, Alpha Chi Omega. Office: Mont Ho of Reps Capitol Sta Helena MT 59620 *

SPILLER, ELLEN BRUBAKER, educator; b. San Marcos, Tex., July 17, 1932; d. George Nunley and Lou Emma (Greathouse) Brubaker; B.J. (T.R. Larsen scholar 1952-53), U. Tex., 1954; M.A. in English, U. Houston, 1965, M.A. in Coll. Teaching, 1980; m. Sam Christopher Spiller, Nov. 21, 1954; children—Katherine, Georgianne. Mem. public info. office Tex. Hwy. Dept., 1954-55; editor Tex. Future Farmer, Austin, 1955-57; editor house organs St. Luke's, Tex. Children's hosps., Houston, 1959—; tchr. English Aldine Jr. High Sch., 1959-61; tchr. English Waltrip Sr. High Sch., Houston, 1961-65; instr. English, Lee Coll., Baytown, Tex., 1965—. Mem. Am. Assn. Coll. Tchrs., Tex. Jr. Coll. Tchrs. Assn., Council of Coll. Tchrs. of English, AAUP, Women in Communications. Democrat. Episcopalian. Clubs: Faculty Women's (v.p. 1980-81, pres. 1981-82), Altar Guild. Home: 211 Rue Orleans Baytown TX 77520 Office: Box 818 Baytown TX 77520

SPILLER, MIRIAM BRITTON, fine arts appraiser; b. Reading, Pa., Sept. 4, 1926; d. William Wainwright and Katie Irene (Miller) Britton; student ceramics and sculpture Fleisher Art Meml., Phila., 1958, interior design Phila. Coll. Art, 1961; m. Raymond M. Spiller, Nov. 17, 1956. Practice interior design, 1958—; antiques cons., 1958—; officer R.M. Spiller & Assos., appraisal, conservation and restoration fine arts, Haverford, Pa., 1960—; mem. Strawberry Mansion, historic preservation; slide lectr. in field. Certified fine arts appraiser, Pa. Mem. Appraisers of Fine Arts Soc. (dir., sec., treas. 1975—), Phila. Mus. Art. Republican. Address: 741 Millbrook Ln Haverford PA 19041

SPILSETH, TERRI VIRGINIA, air force officer; b. Johnson AB, Tokyo, Apr. 29, 1954; d. Sidney Milo and Auby Virginia (Rudy) S.; B.S. in Bus. Adminstrn., So. Ill. U., Edwardsville, 1976. Commd. 2d Lt. USAF, 1976, advanced through grades to capt., 1980; exec. support officer 6112th Air Base Misawa, Japan, 1981; chief central base adminstrn., 1981-82; with Mil. Airlift Command, Insp. Gen. Team, Scott AFB, Ill., 1982—. Recipient Gerritt D. Foster award, 1980. Mem. Air Force Assn., Nat. Assn. Female Execs. Republican. Lutheran. Office: HQ MAC IGIBA Scott AFB IL 62225

SPINELLI-NANNEN, ANTOINETTE ANN, sch. psychologist; b. Springfield, Mass., Feb. 9, 1951; d. Stephen and Camilla Grace (Latino) Spinelli; B.A., Am. Internat. Coll., 1971; M.Ed., Westfield State Coll., 1974; M.S., Am. Internat. Coll., 1977; postgrad. U. Mass. Bilingual Inst., 1972; m. Gerald William Nannen, Oct. 28, 1978; 1 son, Matthew Spinelli. Spanish tchr. Fed. Bilingual Project, Springfield, 1971-75, Springfield Tech. Community Coll., 1975-76; psychol. and personality assessment cons. Mass. Rehab. Commn., Springfield, 1975—; psychol. examiner, sch. psychologist, Springfield, 1975—; counselor Youth Resource Bur., 1974, Holyoke Boys Club, 1976. Mem. Am. Psychol. Assn., Phi Delta Kappa, Alpha Chi. Club: Amoro-Rosicruz. Home: 384 Converse St Longmeadow MA 01106 Office: 195 State St Springfield MA 01105

SPINNEY, VIVIEN BEATON, hosp. exec.; b. Winchester, Mass., d. Ernest G. and Minnie C. (Cantwell) Beaton; Licensure in opticianry; m. Russell G. Spinney, June 21, 1953 (dec.); children—Debra Jeanne Spinney Morrison, Russell G. Asst. office mgr. Winchester Hosp., 1953-54; med. asst. to gen. surgeon, Arlington, Mass., 1965-68; exec. asst. to owner N.E. Rehab. Hosp., Woburn, Mass., 1968—, dir., 1975—, now sr. v.p.; lic. real estate broker. Mem. Am. Bd. Opticianry, Soc. Notary Publics. Roman Catholic. Home: 14 Chestnut St Woburn MA 01801

SPIRE, NANCY WOODSON (MRS. LYMAN SPIRE), civic worker; b. Wausau, Wis., May 6, 1917; d. Aytchmonde Perrin and Leigh (Yawkey) Woodson; B.S., Radcliffe Coll., 1939; postgrad. Syracuse U., 1957—; m. Lyman J. Spire, June 29, 1940; children—Stephen Crittenden Woodson, Abigail Lyman. Vice pres. Woodson Fiduciary Corp., Wilmington, Del. Trustee Aytchmonde Woodson Found., pres., 1963—; trustee Corinthian Found., 1958-63, 68—, Syracuse Child and Family Service, 1957-62; trustee, sec. Crouse-Irving Meml. Hosp., Syracuse; trustee Onondaga Symphony Orch.; mem. exec. com. Syracuse U. Library Assos., 1958-63, trustee, 1958—. Bd. visitors N.Y. State Tng. Sch. for Girls; v.p. bd. dirs. Leigh Yawkey Woodson Art Mus. Mem. Onondaga Symphony Guild (treas. 1958-59), U.S. Trotting Assn. Republican. Universalist (trustee). Club: Virgin Islands Game Fishing. Home: Highbridge Rd Fayetteville NY 13066 also Lagoon Marina Red Hook St Thomas US Virgin Islands 00801 Office: Yawkey Lumber Co Box 65 Wausau WI 55401

SPIRER, JUNE DALE, exec.; b. N.Y.C., May 14, 1943; d. Leon and Gloria (Wagner) Spirer; B.A., Adelphi U., 1965; M.S., Yeshiva U., 1980, postgrad., 1981—. TV/radio buyer BBD&O, 1965-66, SSC&B, 1966-68; sr. media planner Norman, Craig & Kummel, N.Y.C., 1968-71; asso. media dir. Ted Bates Co., 1971-72; v.p., account supt. C.T. Clyne Co., N.Y.C., 1972-74; dir. advt. Am. Express, 1974-75; corporate dir. advt. Del Labs., Farmingdale, N.Y., 1975-78; pres. J. Spirer & Assos., Inc., N.Y.C., 1978—. Mem. Tng. Inst. of Nat. Psychol. Assn. Psychoanalysis, Am. Psychol. Assn. (asso.), Nassau County Psychol. Assn., Soc. Personality Assessment (asso.). Office: 31 Jane St New York NY 10014

SPITLER, CAROLYN SUE, food cons.; b. Ft. Wayne, Ind., Dec. 31, 1937; d. Gordon Pifer and Lola Ruth (Buckley) S.; B.S. in Home Econs. Edn., Ball State U., 1960. Tchr. home econs., Auburn, Ind., 1960-63; exec. dietitian Stouffer's, Chgo., 1963-69; sr. home economist Armour & Co., Chgo., 1969-71; food editor Sphere mag., Chgo., 1971-77; pres. Incredible Edibles, Ltd., Chgo., 1977—; instr. cooking sch. Cooks Mart, Chgo. Bd. govs. Mus. Contemporary Art. Mem. Am. Home Econs. Assn., Home Economists in Bus., Chgo. Council Fgn. Relations, Internat. Assn. Cooking Schs. Author: Bagels, Bagels and More Bagels, 1979; The New French Cooking, 1980; Hallmark Celebrate the Four Seasons, 1980, 81. Home and office: 6033 N Sheridan St Chicago IL 60660

SPITTLER, BETTY JANE, motel mgr.; b. Terre Haute, Ind., Nov. 12, 1922; d. John Thomas and Nellie (Brough) Jones; grad. high sch.; m. Fenton Eugene Spittler, Feb. 19, 1942 (div. July 1968); children—Robert Eugene, Karen Lynn. Mgr., Terrace Inn and Restaurant, Terre Haute, 1964-65, Hickory Manor Hotel, Crystal Lake, Ill., 1965; mgr., buyer St. Mary's Hotel, Evansville, Ind., 1965-72; mgr. Donna Ct. Motel, Evansville, 1972—; owner Riverboat Motor Inn, Evansville, 1974—; mem. Evansville Conv. and Tourism Bur. Mem. Evansville C. of C. (com. mem. 1969—), Evansville Hotel-Motel Mgrs. Assn. (treas.). Republican. Lutheran (ch. council 1962-65, mem. parish bd. 1951-65, supt. Sunday sch. 1950-65). Address: Riverboat Motor Inn 2804 S Kentucky Ave Evansville IN 47714

SPITZER, SUSAN KATE, social worker; b. St. Louis, Aug. 11, 1953; d. Norman H. Spitzer and Barbara B. Lieberman; B.A., Ohio Wesleyan U., 1975; M.B.A., Washington U., St. Louis, 1977; postgrad. Fla. State U. Med. social worker Jewish Hosp. of St. Louis, 1977-79; coordinator Cleft Palate and Craniofacial Deformities Inst., St. Louis Children's Hosp., 1980-82. Mem. Acad. Cert. Social Workers, Am. Cleft Palate Assn., Kappa Kappa Gamma Alumni Assn. Home: 10439 Willowdale Saint Louis MO 63141

SPITZ-YOUNG, PAMELA JEAN, interior archtl. designer; b. Cleve., May 4, 1953; d. Gerald Isreal and Mary Jo Spitz; student Ohio U., 1971-72; B.S. in Design, U. Cin., 1977; m. Leonard Dorsey Young, Sept. 10, 1977. Architect, space planner Rode Kaplan Curtis Woodard, Architects and Planners, Cleve., 1976-78; pres. Pamela Spitz-Young: Space Planning and Design Cons., Cleve., 1978-80; dir. The Design Group subs. F.W. Roberts Co., Solon, Ohio, 1980—. Baptist. Clubs: Back Wall Racquet, Park East Tennis. Home: 2661 Ashton Rd Cleveland Heights OH 44118 Office: 32333 Aurora Rd Solon OH 44139

SPIVACK, CHARLOTTE, educator; b. Schoharie, N.Y., July 23, 1926; d. William L. and Laura (Snyder) Roscoe; B.A., SUNY, Albany, 1947; M.A., Cornell U., 1948; Ph.D., U. Mo., 1954; m. Bernard Spivack, Oct. 17, 1956; children—Carla Naomi, Loren Adlai. Asst. prof. Coll. William and Mary, 1954-56; assoc. prof. Fisk U., 1956-64; mem. faculty U. Mass., Amherst, 1964—, now prof. English. AAUW fellow, 1959-60. Mem. MLA, Dante Soc. Am. Author: (with William Bracy) Early English Drama, 1966; George Chapman, 1967, The Comedy of Evil on Shakespeare's Stage, 1978; Ursula K. Le Guin, 1983. Office: University of Massachusetts Amherst MA 01003

SPIVEY, STEPHANIE RAY, found. exec.; b. N.Y.C., Feb. 29, 1948; d. Joseph and Ann (Dreeben) Neufeld; B.A., Queens Coll., City U. N.Y., 1972; postgrad. New Sch., Golden Gate U. Grants analyst Wenner-Gren Found. Anthrop. Research, N.Y.C., 1969-72; grants adminstr., publs. mgr. Mus. Am. Indian/Heye Found., N.Y.C., 1972-74; coordinator CETA program Human Services Adminstrn., N.Y.C., 1974-76; adminstr. S.H. Cowell Found., San Francisco, 1976—; chmn., founder Bay Area Women in Philanthropy, 1979-80; charter mem. Women and Founds./Corp. Philanthropy, 1977—; steering com. No. Calif. Grantmakers, 1980; cons. mgmt./fundraising for non-profit orgns. Bd. govs. Navy/Marine Corps Mus.; trustee J.F. Kennedy U. Mem. NOW. Office: SH Cowell Found 350 Sansome St Suite 620 San Francisco CA 94104

SPLANE, BEVERLY J., commodity exchange exec.; b. Santa Monica, Calif., Dec. 5, 1943; d. Donald E. and Eleanor Anne (McInnes) S.; B.A., U. Chgo., 1967, M.B.A., 1969. Mgmt. cons. Boston Cons. Group, 1969-73; staff asst. to the Pres., The White House, Washington, 1974-75; exec. dir. Commodity Futures Trading Commn., Washington, 1975; exec. v.p. Chgo. Merc. Exchange, 1975—; mem. bd. dirs. Chgo. Fin. Exchange, 1979—. Mem. exec. com. U. Chgo. Alumni Cabinet, 1978-80, pres., 1980—. Mem. Chgo. Network. Clubs: Econ. (Chgo.); Met. Office: Chgo Merc Exchange 444 W Jackson Blvd Chicago IL 60606

SPLITT, CODY, lawyer; b. Wausau, Wis., Aug. 13, 1919; d. Anne Monahan Wendt; B.A., U. Wis., 1947, LL.B., 1949; m. Harley B. Splitt, Apr. 17, 1948; 1 dau., Leigh Rogers. Admitted to Wis. bar, 1949; individual practice, Appleton, 1949—; asst. dir. U.S. Agrl. Census, 1955; dist. dir. U.S. Census, 1960; mem. Wis. Equal Rights Commn., 1966-73, Appleton Equal Opportunities Commn., 1973-81; dir., gen. counsel Appleton Packing and Gasket, Inc., 1970-78; lectr. Law for Laymen, 1975, 79, moderator, 1980; instr. wills Fox Valley Tech. Inst., 1979-80. Vice chmn. Outagamie County Republican Club, 1965; pres. Outagamie County Republican Women's Club, 1951; co-pres. Appleton PTA, 1971; v.p. Appleton Big Sisters, 1974. Served with WAVES, 1942-45. Named Woman of Yr. for Outagamie County, NOW, 1974. Mem. State Bar Wis. (sec. sect. individual rights and responsibilities 1974), Outagamie County Bar Assn. (exec. com. 1978-83), Fed. Bus. and Profl. Women (v.p. Wis. 1978). Home: 1611 W Glendale Ave Appleton WI 54911 Office: 1213 N Superior St Appleton WI 54911

SPOEHEL, JERRI HOSKINS, broadcasting exec.; b. Oak Park, Ill., Mar. 13, 1932; d. George Alex and Myrtle Jean (McBean) Hoskins; B.A. in English cum laude, Coll. Wooster; m. Edwin H. Spoehel, Apr. 16, 1955; children—Ronald Ross, Jacqueline Jean. Instr., Success-Plus, 1974; columnist Daily News, San Fernando Valley, Van Nuys, Calif., 1970—; now community relations dir. Sta. KCSN-FM, Nat. Pub. Radio, Northridge, Calif.; panelist/seminar instr. Nat. Devel. Conf., Corp. Pub. Broadcasting. Recipient Nat. Abe Lincoln Merit award So. Baptist Radio and TV Commn.; named Disting. Citizen of Northridge; other awards. Mem. AAUW, Publicity Club Los Angeles, Pub. Relations Roundtable, Bus. and Profl. Women's Club, Dirs. Vols. in Agys. Clubs: Valley Press, Soroptimists, Toastmasters, Northridge Cultural Arts, Devonshire Dames. Methodist. Home: 9615 Shoshone Ave Northridge CA 91325 Office: Sta KCSN Northridge CA 91330

SPOMER, MARYLYN JEAN BRADLEY, ednl. psychologist; b. Fresno, Calif., Mar. 14, 1937; d. Harry Robert and Eleanora Mary (Zerrell) Bradley; B.A., Portland U., 1966; M.Ed., Loyola U., 1973; M.A., Loyola/Marymount, 1975; Ph.D., Laurence U., 1977; m. Delbert Eugene Spomer, June 17, 1978. Tchr., Catholic schs., Boise, Ida., 1957-58, Colusa, Calif., 1958-61, Woodland, Calif., 1961-65, tchr., vice prin., Los Angeles, 1965-67; prin. St. Agnes Sch., Los Angeles, 1967-71; owner, adminstr. M.J. Bradley Tutoring Service, Fresno, Calif., 1971-79, St. Therese Kindergarten Sch., Fresno, 1971-79; curriculum coordinator, sch. psychologist Diocese of Fresno, 1973—; lectr. in field various univs. Exec. sec. Mayor's Com. for Redevel., City of Los Angeles Greater Normandie Project, 1966-71; chmn. Vt. Community Council, 1966-71; mem. lay adv. bd. Los Angeles Police Sta., 1969. Recipient Spl. award for outstanding contbn. to Community of Los Angeles, Exposition Coordination Council, 1969; Exposition Community Coordinating Council award of recognition Diocese of Fresno, 1977. Mem. Am.

Psychol. Assn., Calif. Psychol. Assn., Nat. Cath. Edn. Assn., Calif. Assn. Sch. Psychologists and Psychometrists, Calif. Personnel and Guidance Assn., Council for Exceptional Children, Feingold Assn., Calif. Assn. Neurol. Handicapped, Kappa Delta Pi. Roman Catholic. Office: PO Box 4273 Fresno CA 93744

SPONNOBLE, SUSAN, telephone co. exec.; b. Williamsport, Pa., June 24, 1947; d. John Dodge and Hildegarde Marie (Derwig) S.; A.B., U. Miami, Coral Gables, Fla., 1969. Public relations writer Miami-Metro Publicity and Tourism Dept., 1969-73; v.p., accounts mgr. John Crouse Assos., Miami, Fla., 1973-76; account exec. Cameron-Friedlander Inc., Ft. Lauderdale, Fla., 1976-80; field cons. Hydroplanes, Inc., 1980-81; asst. mgr. public relations So. Bell Tel. & Tel. Co., Ft. Lauderdale, Fla., 1981—. Recipient nat. promotional award Unlimited Racing Commn., 1971; Commendation award City of Miami, 1973; Arthur W. Page award AT&T, 1982; named Ky. col., 1978. Mem. Fla. Public Relations Assn. (spl. govt. promotions award 1975, spl. events award 1978), Delta Zeta. Office: 300 NE 3d Ave Fort Lauderdale FL 33301

SPONTAK, BARBARA ANN, nurse; b. Pottstown, Pa., Nov. 10, 1943; d. Wellington Farel and Mary Eleanor (Hampton) Davidheiser; A.S., Coll. DuPage (Ill.), 1974; B.S. in Nursing, U. Ill., 1978; m. Stephen John Spontak, Aug. 18, 1962; children—Stephen F., Gregory A., Mark T., Michael A. Charge nurse burn unit, then staff nurse emergency dept. Loyola U. Med. Center, 1974-77; nursing supr., asst. dir. nursing Good Samaritan Hosp., Downers Grove, Ill., 1978; asst. dir. nursing medicine U. Ill. Med. Center, 1979-81, asst. dir. nursing, coordinator nursing resources, 1981—; instr. nursing Coll. DuPage, 1981—. Sec., Park View Sch. PTA, 1975. Mem. Ill. Nurses Assn., Lombard Nurses Club. Lutheran. Club: Rams Gymnastics (pres. 1980-82). Home: 332 W Sunset Ave Lombard IL 60148 Office: 1740 Taylor St Chicago IL 60612

SPOONER, SUSAN ELIZABETH, counseling psychologist; b. Indpls., Feb. 14, 1939; d. Hugh Jacob and Dorothy Cooper (Genung) Baker; B.S., Purdue U., 1960, Ph.D., 1975; M.S. in Counseling, U. Wis., Madison, 1961; m. John Alfred Spooner, June 30, 1962; 1 son, Kevin Jon. Counselor, instr., acting dir. Counseling Center, Colo. Coll., Colorado Springs, 1962-63; asst. dir. Office of High Relations, U. Wis., Madison, 1967-70, counselor Counseling Center, 1961-62, 69-70; exec. dir. Sycamore council Girl Scouts U.S.A., Lafayette, Ind., 1970-72; student personnel intern, registrar, asst. to dir. Univ. Placement Service Purdue U., West Lafayette, Ind., 1972-75, vis. prof., 1975-76; asst. and assoc. prof. counselor edn. U. Wis., Oshkosh, 1976—. Exploring chairperson Bay Lakes council Dist. 7 Boy Scouts Am., chmn. com. Explorer Post 2600. Cert. psychologist, Ind.; lic. psychologist, Wis. Mem. Am. Personnel and Guidance Assn., Am. Coll. Personnel Assn., Am. Psychol. Assn., Assn. of Counselor Educators and Suprs., Wis. Personnel and Guidance Assn., Wis. Coll. Personnel Assn., Wis. Psychol. Assn., Wis. Assn. of Counselor Educators and Suprs. Contbr. articles to profl. jours. Home: 2500 Shorewood Dr Oshkosh WI 54901 Office: 002 N/Ed Bldg U Wis Oshkosh WI 54901

SPOOR, LAVINA IRENE, civic worker; b. Leonia, Idaho, Jan. 23, 1915; d. Edward Elijah and Hester Maybelle (Coats) Krom; student Kellogg (Idaho) public schs.; m. Robert Franklin Spoor, Mar. 5, 1932; children—Robert Franklin, Nancy, Sally, Terry, Cheryl. Vol., Sr. Citizens of Shoshone County, Idaho, 1973-74, county coordinator, 1974-77; co-founder Shoshone County Sr. Citizen Council, 1975, county adminstr., 1977-80; pres. Camp Fire Assn., 1966-69, leader, 1963-72, recipient Wo-He-Lo medalion, numerous other awards; sponsor Blue Birds, 1972-80; post office Santa Claus, 1969-81. Named Elks Citizen of Yr., Western Shoshone County, Idaho, 1976; recipient Citizen award Pinehurst C. of C., 1975; First Lady of Yr. award Beta Sigma Phi Internat., 1981. Mem. Nat. Council Camp Fire Girls, Am. Assn. Ret. Persons. Mormon. Clubs: Eagles, Ret. Eagles, Pinehurst Sr. Citizens. Home: Weir Gulch Pinehurst ID 83850 Office: Lions Community Bldg Pinehurst ID 83850

SPORAR, MARY JANE, assn. exec.; b. Joliet, Ill., Feb. 29, 1920; d. Arnold Frederick and Helen Louise (Wolling) Muhlig; student Joliet Jr. Coll., 1938-40; m. Stanley J. Sporar, Aug. 11, 1969; children by previous marriage—Jill Telfer, James, John (Hamrin). Proofreader, Joliet Republican Printing Co., 1940-41; sec. Ruberoid Roofing Co., 1941-42; statis. typist, sec. Am. Steel & Wire Co., 1943-48; proofreader, sec. Peterson Printing Co., 1964-71; pres. Joliet Area Women's Bowling Assn., 1957—; sec.-treas. Greater Joliet Area Bowling Council, 1959-81; bowling columnist Joliet Herald-News, 1956—; editor Will County Bowler, 1971-75; 11-time weekly bowling program WJRC Radio, 1977—; producer, announcer bowling shows cable TV, 1976-77. Bd. dirs. Will County unit Am. Cancer Soc., 1964—. Recipient various awards in field. Mem. Nat. Women's Bowling Writers Assn. (life mem.; pres. 1965-71), Bowling Writers Assn. Am., World Bowling Writers Assn., Women's Internat. Bowling Congress (dir. 1977—), Ill. Women's (dir. 1967-81, sgt.-at-arms 1981—), Ill. State Jr. (dir. 1971-81) bowling assns. Republican. Lutheran. Home: 1010 Richmond St Joliet IL 60435

SPRAFKIN-KAHN, JOYCE, psychologist; b. N.Y.C., Apr. 21, 1949; d. Isaac and Toby Sprafkin; B.A., Queens Coll., 1971; Ph.D. in Clin. Psychology, SUNY, Stony Brook, 1975. Sr. research scientist L.I. Research Inst., also adj. asst. prof. psychiatry and psychology SUNY, Stony Brook, 1975—; chief lab. communications L.I. Research Inst., 1977—. Grantee NIMH, ABC, AMA, United Methodist Communications. Mem. Am. Psychol. Assn., Phi Beta Kappa. Author book; contbr. articles, chpts. to books on effects of TV on children. Office: LI Research Inst SUNY Stony Brook NY 11794

SPRAGUE, AMARIS JEANNE, real estate broker; b. Jackson, Mich., Feb. 18, 1935; d. Leslie Markham and Blanche Lorraine (Basnaw) Reed; student Mich. State U., 1952-53; B.S., Colo. State U., 1965; children—Anthony John, James Stuart. Real estate sales Seibel and Benedict Realty, Ft. Collins, Colo., 1968-69; salesman Realty Brokers Exchange, Ft. Collins, 1969-72; broker, pres. Sprague and Assos., Inc., Realtors, Ft. Collins, 1972-80; broker Van Schaack & Co., Ft. Collins, 1980—; dir. Univ. Nat. Bank. Mem. bus. adv. council Colo. State U., 1976—, chmn. 1979-80, mem. adv. council Coll. of Engring., 1981. Cert. real estate broker. Mem. Nat. Assn. Realtors, Colo. Assn. Realtors, Ft. Collins Bd. Realtors, Ft. Collins C. of C. (dir. 1975-78, pres. 1982). Republican. Episcopalian. Home: 2718 Aberdeen Ct Fort Collins CO 80525 Office: 417 S Howes St Fort Collins CO 80521

SPRAGUE, MARY G., retail exec.; b. N.Y.C., Sept. 10, 1943; d. James Joseph and Mary Catherine (Rabbett) Gribben; A.B., Sarah Lawrence Coll., 1971; M.A., N.Y. U., 1973; m. R. Paul Sprague, Sept., 1970; children—William, Jennifer. Pres., White Oak Profl. Properties, Inc., Bronxville, N.Y., 1972-74; pres. Victory Shirt Co., N.Y.C., 1974—. Arbitrator, Am. Arbitration Assn. Mem. N.Y. Assn. Women Bus. Owners. Office: 345 Madison Ave New York NY 10017

SPRAGUE, MELBA RUZICKA, broadcaster; b. Elk City, Okla., Apr. 6, 1921; d. Henry and Lora (Ellison) Ruzicka; B.S. in Bus. cum laude with spl. mention, Okla. State U., 1942; student Okla. Coll. for Women, 1938-39; m. William P. Sprague, Dec. 21, 1940; children—Douglas Lawrence, James Randolph. Sec. to pres. Farmers Bank, Elk City, 1938-39; free-lance profl. book reviewer, 1949—; book rev. editor, reporter Sta.-WOLS, Florence, S.C., 1969-77; book editor, roving reporter Sta.-WDAR, Darlington, S.C., 1971—, free-lance advt. copywriter, 1969—; supr. stat. analysis for econ. and social conditions Dept. Commerce, 1972—; AAUW grantee UN, 1977. Bd. dirs., regional dir. for unit devel., regional dir. for public info. S.C. div. Am. Cancer Soc.; bd. dirs., chmn. public info.-public edn. com. S.C. Mental Health Assn.; bd. dirs. Greater Florence Family YMCA; v.p. Pee Dee Presbyterial, Florence; vol. tchr. for lang. arts in low socio-econ. areas; initiator Hot Line Crisis Intervention Service, Florence, 1972. Named Woman of Yr., City Fedn. of Women's Clubs, Florence, 1969; recipient commendation Florence Mental Health Assn., 1973; Nat. award for Am. Cancer Soc., 1973, S.C. Div. Vol. of Yr., 1975; named Mem. AAUW (pres. Florence br. 1966-68, pres. S.C. div. 1977-79), Am. Women in Radio and TV (bull. editor Palmetto chpt. 1974-75). Republican.

SPRAGUE-FRINK, RUTH MARIE, electron microscopist, histologist; b. Barre, Vt., Aug. 26, 1927; d. Ernest Alonzo and Marion Evelyn (Perry) Sprague; B.S., U. Vt., 1949, M.S., 1964; children—Dennis, Douglas, Sharon, Terry. Electron microscopist U. Vt., 1963-66; electron microscopist Ladd Research Inc., Burlington, Vt., 1966-67; biol. electron microscopy cons. Los Alamos Sci. Lab., also Ernest F. Fullam, Inc., Schenectady, 1967; electron microscopist, research technologist, instr. med. histology U. Vt., 1967—, mem. staff council, 1978—, pres. staff council, 1979—. Mem. Women's Network. Contbr. numerous articles to profl. jours. Home: 52 Hayden Pkwy South Burlington VT 05401 Office: Dept Anatomy U Vt Coll Medicine Given Bldg Burlington VT 05401

SPRAINGS, VIOLET EVELYN, psychologist; b. Omaha, Aug. 1, 1930; d. Henry Elbert and Stravnella (Hunter) S.; A.B., U. Calif., Berkeley, 1948, M.A., 1951; Ed.D., U. San Francisco, 1982. Tchr., Oakland (Calif.) Public Schs., 1951-58; psychologist Med. Edn. Diagnostic Center, San Francisco, 1959-62; dir. psychol. edn. and lang. services Calif. Dept. Edn., 1963-71; asst. prof. San Francisco State U., 1964-71; asso. prof. ednl. psychology Calif. State U., Hayward, 1971-79; dir. Lang. Assos., Orinda, Lafayette and Redwood City, 1971-79; psychologist in pvt. practice, 1962—; dir. Western Women's Bank; mem. adv. bd. Bay Area Health Systems Agy.; instr. U. Calif., Berkeley extension, 1964—; mem. Oral Bd. Ednl. Psychologists, 1972—; mem. adv. com. Foothill Jr. Coll. Dist. Recipient Phoebe Apperson Heart award San Francisco Examiner, 1968. Mem. Am. Psychol. Assn., Internat. Neuropsychol. Assn. (charter), Calif. Psychol. Assn., Calif. Assn. Sch. Psychologists and Psychometrists, Western Psychol. Assn., Nat. Council Negro Women, AAUP, Delta Sigma Theta, Psi Chi, Pi Lambda Theta. Contbr. articles to profl. jours. Home: 170 Glorietta Blvd Orinda CA 94563 Office: 3408 Deer Hill Rd Lafayette CA 94549

SPRAWKA, EDNA W., lawyer; b. Columbus, Ohio, May 11, 1950; d. William August and Sylvia Fay (Graff) Sprawka; B.A., Ohio State U., 1972, J.D., 1975. Admitted to Ohio bar, 1975, U.S. Dist. Ct. Ohio, 1975, U.S. Supreme Ct. bar, 1979. Assoc. firm Smathers, Green and Foster, Columbus, 1975-79; assoc. firm Jordan, Langley & Potter, Cin., 1979-82, ptnr., 1982—; vol. atty. Cin. Legal Aid Soc., 1979—. Bd. dirs. Jones Settlement House, 1980—. Mem. ABA, Ohio Bar Assn., Cin. Bar Assn., Assn. Trial Lawyers Am., Am. Judicature Soc., Kappa Kappa Gamma. Republican. Lutheran. Club: Cin. Lawyers. Home: Werik Apt 2327 Park Ave Cincinnati OH 45206

SPREI, JUDITH ELLEN, psychologist; b. Jamaica, N.Y., Mar. 19, 1950; d. Emanuel and Zelda (Hartman) Sprei; B.A. with honors, U. Md., 1972, M.A., 1974, Ph.D., 1979. Student intake officer Dept. Juvenile Services, Hyattsville, Md., 1971-72; teaching asst. dept. psychology U. Md., 1972-73; psychology trainee VA Hosp., Martinsburg, W.Va., 1973-74; instr. U. Md., 1980—, Cath. U., 1980; counseling psychology intern Counseling Center, So. Ill. U., Carbondale, 1975-76; sr. counselor and coordinator of services to adults Prince George's County Sexual Assault Center, Cheverly, Md., 1976—; pvt. practice, 1977—; pres. Snowden Oaks Assos., Inc., 1980—; dir. So. Md. Community Services Corp., 1980—. Mem. Am. Psychol. Assn., Md. Psychol. Assn., Assn. for Women in Psychology (treas. 1978-81), Coalition of Sexual Assault Centers. Home: 8321 Snowden Oaks Pl Laurel MD 20708 Office: Sexual Assault Center Dept Psychiatry Prince George's Gen Hosp Cheverly MD 20785

SPREMULLI, LINDA LUCY, chemist; b. Sept. 6, 1947; d. Paul Francis and Gertrude (Haspeslagh) S.; B.A., U. Rochester, 1969; Ph.D., M.I.T., 1973. Postdoctoral research assoc. Clayton Found. Biochem. Inst., U. Tex., Austin, 1973-74; NIH postdoctoral fellow, 1974-76; asst. prof. chemistry U. N.C., Chapel Hill, 1976-81, assoc. prof., 1981—. Mem. AAAS, Am. Chem. Soc., Am. Soc. Biol. Chemists, Am. Soc. Microbiology, Assn. Women in Sci., Research in nucleic acid and protein biosynthesis. Office: Dept Chemistry U NC Chapel Hill NC 27514

SPRENGER, DIANE GAIL, beverage co. exec.; b. Milw., Oct. 14, 1953; d. Roland Alvin and Lillian Ruth (Bowers) S.; B.A., U. Iowa, 1976. Supr. spl. events Miller Brewing Co., Milw., 1976-77, sr. supr. convs., 1977-78, retail sales adminstr., 1978-80, asst. brand mgr. Lowenbrau div., 1980—. Layout editor Milwaukee Jr. League News Mag., 1981—. Mem. Kappa Alpha Theta. Office: 3939 W Highland Blvd Milwaukee WI 53201

SPRING, SHARON DOYLE, lawyer; b. Mpls., July 28, 1939; d. Walter Anthony and Margaret Mary (Murphy) Doyle; student Barnard Coll., 1957-60; J.D. cum laude, N.Y. Law Sch., 1969-72; m. Justin M. Spring, Apr. 23, 1960 (div. 1972); children—Margaret Faith, Justin Doyle, Arthur John. Admitted to N.Y. bar, 1973, U.S. Dist. Ct. bar, 1974; clk., then asso. firm Poletti, Freidin, Prashker Feldman & Gartner, N.Y.C., 1971-76; gen. atty. Sea-Land Service, Inc., Menlo Park, N.J., 1976-78, gen. atty. personnel/labor Sea-Land Industries, Inc., 1978-79, counsel Atlantic div. Sea-Land Service, Inc., 1979—. Democratic dist. leader, Manhattan, 1967-71; Dem. state Committeewoman, 1968-70; mem. N.Y.C. Community Planning Bd. 12, 1967-72, chmn. parks com., 1968-71. Recipient Am. Jurisprudence awards, 1971. Mem. Assn. Bar City N.Y. (admitting com. 1982—), ABA, Maritime Law Assn., Order of Barristers, Barnard Coll. Alumni Assn. Roman Catholic. Office: PO Box 800 Iselin NJ 08830

SPRINGER, ANN MURPHY, mgmt. cons., fire chief; b. Boston, Apr. 13, 1935; d. William James, Jr. and Katherine Mary (Danehy) Murphy; B.S., Simmons Coll., Boston, 1956; M.S. (teaching asst.), Purdue U., 1958; m. David Alan Springer, Nov. 27, 1971. Home economist, 1956-59; program developer U.S. Spl. Services, W.Ger., 1959-62; with Ford Found. project, Oakland, Calif., 1962-65; mem. staff War on Poverty, 1965-67; tng. cons. Western Community Action Tng., Oakland, 1967-69; dir. tng. Internat. Tng. Cons., Berkeley, Calif., 1969-71; ind. mgmt. cons., Bodega, Calif., 1971—; prof. mgmt. studies Sonoma (Calif.) State U., 1979—; adj. faculty Nat. Fire Acad., Md., 1978—; chief Bodega Vol. Fire Dept., 1979—; adv. com. re-entry and women's studies Santa Rosa Jr. Coll., 1977—, mem. fire tech. adv. com., 1982—. First chairperson Sonoma County Commn. Status Women, 1975-76. Grantee Indian Valley Colls., Novato, Calif., 1977, 79. Mem. Internat. Assn. Fire Chiefs, Internat. Assn. Fire Service Instrs., Calif. Fire Chiefs Soc., Calif. Tng. Officers Assn., Sonoma County Fire Chiefs Assn. Co-author: The Organizational Operations Process, 1972; Management for the Fire Officer, 1981; contbr. articles to profl. publs. Address: 1931 Joy Rd PO Box 139 Bodega CA 94922

SPRINGER, JANET VIVIAN CASHMAN, bldg. co. exec. sec.; b. Kingston, N.Y., Mar. 18, 1937; d. James Erne and Vivian Amelia (Beatty) Cashman; student public schs., Phila.; m. Wolfe Ernest Springer, July 18, 1959; children—James E., Christopher D., Andrew K. Sec. to mgr. real estate Esso Standard Oil Co., Bala Cynwyd, Pa., 1954-59; sec. to dean students and admissions office U. Richmond (Va.), 1959-61; asst. sec. to chief exec. officer Gilbane Bldg. Co., Providence, 1976-79, sec. constrn. dept., 1979-80, exec. sec. to v.p. constrn. ops., 1980—. Mem. Simsbury Vol. Ambulance Squad, 1969-72; clk. N. Cumberland Fire Dist., 1978—; mem. Cumberland Republican Town com., 1974—, sec., 1976—. Mem. Women in Constrn., LWV. Clubs: Simsbury Jr. Women's (pres. 1967-68), Gen. Fedn. Women's Clubs (state bd. 1968-69, asst. jr. dir. Conn. 1970-71). Home: 17 Intervale Dr Cumberland RI 02864 Office: 7 Jackson Walkway Providence RI 02940

SPRINKLE, SYLVIA YVONNE, librarian; b. Winston-Salem, N.C., Apr. 25, 1945; d. Arthur William, Jr. and Thelma Norwood (Holtzclaw) S.; B.S. in Edn., Winston-Salem State U., 1967; M.L.S., Atlanta U., 1968; m. Larry Leon Hamlin, Aug. 29, 1981. Elem. sch. tchr., Goldsboro, N.C., 1967; grad. library asst. Atlanta U., 1967-68; children's librarian Free Library, Phila., 1968-70; info. specialist Benjamin Banneker Urban Center, Phila., 1970-73; sch. librarian Phila. public schs., 1973-77; entrepreneur Fashion Two Twenty Cosmetics, 1977-81; asst. librarian Winston-Salem State U., 1978-79; coordinator children's outreach Forsyth County Public Library, Winston-Salem, 1979-80, head extensions div., 1980—. Bd. dirs. N.C. Black Repertory Co., 1980—; mem. adv. council N.C. Library Services and Constrn. Act, 1981-83. Recipient cert. of merit Bennett Coll., Greensboro, N.C., 1963; Expt. in Internat. Living scholar, 1966; Joseph Ruzicka Library scholar, 1967; Library Services and Constrn. Act continuing edn. grantee 1981. Mem. ALA, N.C. Library Assn. (scholar 1967), Forsyth County Library Assn., Delta Sigma Theta (chpt. corr. sec. 1980-82). Episcopalian. Home: 2677 Oak Grove Circle Winston-Salem NC 27106 Office: 660 W 5th St Winston-Salem NC 27101

SPROLES CARR, LELIA ELIZABETH, med. technologist; b. Oakland, Md., Oct. 1, 1921; d. Rolland Grover and Margaret Josephine (Glotfelty) Schoch; student Tex. A&I U., 1938-40, U. Houston, 1950-52; M.T., Allegheny Valley Hosp., 1953; m. Herbert Sproles, July 29, 1939; children—Clara J.; m. 2d, Teddy R. Carr, Feb. 20, 1954; 1 son, Teddy R. With King Ranch, Kingsville, Tex., 1940-43, Tex. Agr. Exptl. Substa. No. 3, Angleton, 1943-46; med. technologist Angleton Clinic, 1947-54, part-time, 1954—; cattle rancher. Mem. DAR, Brazosport Geneal. Soc. (treas. 1978-80), Am. Soc. Clin. Pathologists. Democrat. Methodist. Club: Mineral Moochers of Brazoria County.

SPROUSE, MARY ELIZABETH, electric co. exec.; b. Klondike, Tex., Mar. 24, 1935; d. Wesley Oscar and Robbie Elizabeth Wallace; nursing home adminstrn. cert. Paris Jr. Coll., 1970; student East Tex. State U., 1953-54; m. Ted Sprouse, Apr. 14, 1973; children by previous marriage—Gary Neal Click, Julie Ann Click. Budget sec. U. Utah, Salt Lake City, 1963-66; sec. Bonjour Engring. Firm, Shawnee Mission, Kans., 1966-67, Shawnee Mission High Sch., 1967-69; nursing home adminstr. Klondike (Tex.) Nursing Home, 1969-71, Deerings Nursing Home, Odessa, Tex., 1971-75; sec. corp. Monahans Electric Co., Inc. (Tex.), 1975—. Edn. chmn. Am. Cancer Soc., 1976-80. Recipient cert. of merit Am. Council Nursing Homes, 1969-72. Mem. Women's Div. C. of C. Mem. Ch. of Christ. Clubs: Desert Sands Garden (pres. 1978-80), Sands Art Assn. (treas. 1978-79), Tau Lambda Study Club (sec. 1980-82, pres. 1982-84), Order Eastern Star. Home: 1405 S Dwight St Monahans TX 79756 Office: 3000 S Stockton St Monahans TX 79756

SPRUCE, FRANCES BLYTHE, ins. co. mgr.; b. Washington, May 4, 1927; d. Samuel Stewart and Nell Trabue (Anderson) S.; A.A., Mt. Vernon Jr. Coll., 1947; B.A., George Washington U., 1950; postgrad. Cath. U., 1953. With Group Hospitalization, Inc., Washington, 1950—, field rep., 1958-72, jr. enrollment field rep., 1972, small group coordinator, 1972-74, mgr. mktg. services, 1974—, currently hospitalization account exec. Past v.p. Montgomery Players. Mem. Washington Theater Alliance (past pres.), Pi Beta Phi. Democrat. Club: Arts. Home: PO Box 9882 4518 Drummond Ave Chevy Chase MD 20815

SPRUILL, CONNIE MARIE, wholesale co. exec.; b. Cleveland, Tenn., Oct. 19, 1950; d. Orville Porter and Wilma Nadine (White) Porter; student Columbus Coll. Art and Design, 1968-69; LaSalle Extension, 1966-68, AA in Interior Design, 1970; grad. Patricia Stevens Modeling and Finishing Sch., 1964; m. 2d, James C. Spruill, July 21, 1979; stepchildren—James C. Spruill Jr., Tina M. Spruill, Tiffeney Spruill; children by previous marriage—Heidi Marie Short, Brandy Renee Short. Sales and sales mgmt. positions Squires of Ohio, Columbus, 1970-71, Crown Life Ins. Co., 1971-72, European Health Spa, Columbus, 1974-75; owner, mgr. Viviane Woodward Cosmetic Distbrship, 1971-74; freelance model and comml. artist; adminstrv. asst. to purchasing agt. Columbus Wood Preserving Co., 1976-78; owner, chief exec. officer Central Ohio Forest Products, Inc., Columbus, 1979—. Coordinator, constrn. explorer post Boy Scouts Am., 1980. Named Women Bus. Advocate of Yr., Central Ohio region SBA, 1982. Mem. Assn. Bus. and Profl. Women in Constrn. (pres., founder Central Ohio, dir. Ohio region), Am. Wood Preservers Assn., Central Ohio Builders Exchange. Democrat. Office: 2871 Brice Rd Brice OH 43109

SPRUILL, DIANE BERNADETTE, bank exec.; b. L.I., N.Y., Jan. 27, 1950; d. Lloyd William and Mary (Fitzsimmons) Nulty; A.A., Brevard Jr. Coll., 1970; B.S., U. South Fla., 1975; student U. Colo., 1978; 1 son, Marshall. Teller, bookkeeper, Master Charge clk. First Peoples Bank, Fort Walton Beach, Fla., 1970-72; customer service supr., loan officer Sun Coast Bank, St. Petersburg, Fla., 1973-75, mktg. officer, 1975-78, asst. v.p. mktg., 1978-79, v.p. mktg. dept., 1979—; tchr., cons. St. Petersburg Jr. Coll. Mem. Am. Inst. Banking, Sales and Mktg. Execs., Bank Mktg. Assn. Democrat. Methodist. Club: Northeast Racquet. Home: 10755 Village Club Circle Saint Petersburg FL 33702 Office: PO Drawer G Saint Petersburg FL 33731

SPRUYT, KATHLEEN THERESE, social work adminstr.; b. Bklyn., Apr. 14, 1943; d. Emiel and Margaret (O'Connor) S.; B.A., St. Joseph's Coll. for Women, 1965; M.S.W., Fordham U., 1968. Lay extension vol., Casper, Wyo., 1965-66; social worker Meth. Hosp., Bklyn, 1968-72, supr. social work dept., 1972-77; dir. social work St. John's Queens Hosp., Elmhurst, N.Y., 1977—; field instr. Fordham U. Sch. Social Service, 1969-77; mem. social work adv. com. Bklyn. Tb. and Lung Assn., 1976—; mem. social work adv. com. Queens County Profl. Standards Rev. Orgn., 1977—. NIMH grantee, 1966-68. Mem. Nat. Assn. Social Work, Am. Hosp. Assn., Soc. Hosp. Social Work Dirs., Am. Public Health Assn. Home: 1225 86th St Brooklyn NY 11228 Office: St John's Queen's Hospital 90-02 Queens Blvd Elmhurst NY 11373

SPURLOCK, RACHEL YVONNE, banker; b. Princeton, Ark., Sept. 16, 1937; d. Willie Roscoe and Croma Lee (Gresham) Hughes; cert. Am. Inst. Banking, 1979; grad. Southwestern Grad. of Banking, 1982; m. Burk Hobson Spurlock, Oct. 7, 1956; children—William Marcus, Gregory Morgan. Officer mgr. Salling Wiping Cloth Co., Shreveport, La., 1960-63, So. Towel, Shreveport, 1963-64; clerk Comml. Nat. Bank, Shreveport, 1964-73, mgr. ops. consumer loans, 1973—, asst. cashier, 1978—. Mem. Am. Bus. Women's Assn., Nat. Assn. Bank Women. Democrat. Baptist. Home: Route 9 Box 850 Shreveport LA 71107 Office: 329 Texas St Shreveport LA 71152

SPYCHE, AGNES MAGDELENE (PITTNER), health services assn. exec., nurse; b. Buffalo, Oct. 27, 1936; d. Peter John and Agnes Rose (Kolasz) Pittner; diploma Sisters of Charity Hosp. Sch. Nursing, Buffalo,

1954-57; B.S. in Nursing, SUNY, Buffalo, 1961, M.S. in Health Care Planning and Mgmt., 1981; m. Gerald John Spyche, Feb. 23, 1963; children—Gerald John, Peter J., Mary A. With Sisters Hosp., Buffalo, 1957-64, 65-66, in-service coordinator, 1960-61, supr. spl. dept. emergency room, urology, out-patient dept. and ICU, 1961-64, staff nurse, 1965-66; night supr. St. Joseph's Intercommunity Hosp., Cheektowaga, N.Y., 1961-64; with Emergency Hosp., Buffalo, 1964-65; 67-78, asst. dir. nursing service, 1969-71, dir. nursing service, 1971-78; asst. dir. nursing service DeGraff Meml. Hosp., North Tonawanda, N.Y., 1979, dir. nursing service, 1979-80; dir. blood service nursing ARC, Buffalo, 1981—; bd. dirs. Western N.Y. High Blood Pressure Screening; cons. for developing ICUs. Mem. Erie County (N.Y.) CD Com.; mem. Erie County Disaster Com. Recipient Med. award Sisters Hosp., 1957; Hill Burton Act of 1956 trainee, 1957—. Mem. Alumni Sisters of Charity Hosp. Sch. Nursing, Alumni Sch. Nursing SUNY Buffalo, Am. Assn. Blood Banks. Roman Catholic. Home: 124 Cresthaven Dr West Seneca NY 14224 Office: 786 Delaware Ave Buffalo NY 14209

SQUAIR, JEAN MARIE, ednl. adminstr.; b. Vancouver, B.C., Can., Jan. 19, 1925; came to U.S., 1943; d. Alfred Ernest and Bertha Edith (Bailey) Hall; student Stanford U., 1943-47, Boston U., 1964-65, U. Calif., Berkeley, 1965-68; m. Stuart Davidson Squair, Feb. 14, 1948; children—Roslyn Marie, Elizabeth Ann. Mgr., Oakland (Calif.) Symphony Chorus, 1963-70; dir. vol. services Goodwill Industries, Oakland, 1970-80; professorial lectr., dir. Grad. Sch. Arts Adminstrn., Golden Gate U., San Francisco, 1976—. Bd. govs. San Francisco Symphony, 1976-81; bd. dirs. San Francisco Opera Western Opera Theater, 1970-78; trustee Calif. Hist. Soc., 1970-76; co-chmn. Piedmont Arts Festival, 1970-78; pres. San Francisco Symphony League, 1973-76. Recipient Disting. Service award Oakland Symphony, 1966; award Nat. Aux. to Goodwill Industries, 1978. Mem. Assn. Arts Adminstrn. Educators (dir.), Assn. Calif. Symphony Orchs. (founding pres.), Am. Symphony Orch. League (mem. vol. council bd.). Home: 6001 Acacia Ave Oakland CA 94618 Office: 536 Mission St San Francisco CA 94105

SQUARE, HELEN ELVE, educator, nursing home adminstr.; b. Houston, July 4, 1929; d. Albert William and Alice Clara (King) Johnson; A.A., Houston Comml. Coll., 1975; B.B.A., Prairie View A&M U., 1977; M.B.A., 1979; children—Vertis, Emit, Clara, Robert, Sonia. Worker Sunshine Laundry, Houston, 1944-50; instr. driving Halliston Driving Sch., Houston, 1954-56; nurse aide North Houston Hosp., Houston, 1956-59; nurse in dr.'s office, 1960-63; mgr. I-H Hotel, Houston, 1963-64; sec. Tex. Star Enterprises, Houston, 1963-64; asst. adminstr. Leisure Arms Nursing Home, Inc., Houston, 1966-69; with Ripley Rust Credit Union, Houston, 1970; adminstrv. aide Houston Community Coll., 1972-79, Mem. Nat. Assn. Female Execs., Assn. for Study Negro Life and History, Nat. Council Negro Women, Houston Apt. Assn., Nat. Black Caucus on Aging, E.J.C. Vol. Aux., Delta Mu Delta, Phi Theta Kappa. Club: La Esponal (Houston Community Coll.). Home: 8002 Shotwell St Houston TX 77016 Office: 10012 Cullen Blvd Houston TX 77051

SQUIRE, LAURIE RUBIN, broadcasting co. exec.; b. N.Y.C., Jan. 30, 1953; d. Daniel and Ruth Thelma (Deutsch) Rubin; B.A. cum laude (scholar), Finch Coll., 1974; M.A., N.Y. U., 1976; postgrad. Tchrs. Coll. Columbia U., 1977—; m. Herbert E. Squire, Jr., Aug. 6, 1975; children—Amy Ruth and Julie Wynn (twins). Actress, TV commls., 1960-65; arts editor Finch/Metro N.Y.C. newspaper, 1970-74; co-editor Finch Alumnae Mag., 1971-72; intern producer WBAI-FM, N.Y.C., 1973; music prodn. coordinator WNET TV Ballet Theatre spl., 1973; Coll. Bd. writer Mademoiselle Mag., 1973; intern asst. public affairs dir. N.Y. Cultural Center, 1974; mdse. coordinator WOR-AM, N.Y.C., 1974-76, contbg. writer Bob and Ray's Mary Backstayge serial, contbr. nostalgia features Joe Franklin Show; producer Jean Shepherd Show, WOR-AM and syndicated markets, 1975-77; prodn. coordinator Texaco Met. Opera broadcasts, 1976—; producer Bernard Meltzer What's Your Problem, WOR-AM, 1977—; dance critic Show Bus., theatre newspaper; dir. publicity and advt. L.I. Playhouse, 1982—. Recipient commendations for Leukemia Radiothons, 1975, 77. Mem. Internat. Radio and TV Soc., Friends of Ballet Theatre, Baker St. Irregulars, N.Y. U. Alumni Club, Friends of Animals, Great Neck Hist. Soc. Home: 11 Welwyn Rd Apt 1C Great Neck NY 11021

SQUIRES, PATRICIA EILEEN, freelance journalist; b. Beaver Falls, Pa., Jan. 28, 1927; d. John Wiley and Helen Marie (Barstow) Purtell; B.A. in Journalism, Ind. U., 1949; m. Mark B. Squires, Sr., June 30, 1951; children—Sally Regan, Mark B., Susan Barstow. Staff reporter LaPorte (Ind.) Herald-Argus, 1949-51, daily columnist, 1950-51, sect. editor, 1949-51; women's news and feature writer Muskegon (Mich.) bur. Grand Rapids Herald, 1956-57; editor suburban sect. North Shore Line, Chicagoland Mag., Chgo., 1967-69; staff writer Fairpress, Westport, Conn., 1972-73; regular contbr. New Canaan (Conn.) Advertiser, 1975-78, Bridgeport (Conn.) Sunday Post, 1976-78, Soundings, Essex, Conn., 1977-78, N.Y. Times, N.Y.C., 1976—; tchr. English, journalism, social studies jr. and sr. public high schs., Jackson, Mich., 1966-67, Niles Twp., Skokie, Ill., 1967-68; vol. tutor Social Cultural Ednl. Enrichment Program, Protestant Community Center, 1979—. Public relations, promotion dir. Ella Sharp Mus., Jackson, 1964-66; publicity chmn. New Canaan Soc. for Arts, 1977-78; bd. dirs. Centennial Celebration Com., Winnetka, Ill., 1968-69; Community Council New Canaan, 1972-75; New Canaan Bicentennial Com., 1975-76; publicity chmn. parent-tchr. council Frost Jr. High Sch., Jackson, 1963-64; active Girl Scouts Am. Mem. Women in Communications, AAUW, Ind. U. Alumni Assn. Presbyterian. Clubs: Cedar Point Yacht (Westport, Conn.); Lake Mohawk Golf (Sparta, N.J.). Home and Office: 688 West Shore Trail Sparta NJ 07871

SREDL, DARLENE RITA (MAJKA), aviation nursing cons.; b. Chgo., Feb. 20, 1943; d. Joseph Harry and Bernice Catherine (Pacyna) Majka; B.S. in Nursing, Loyola U., Chgo., 1964; M.A. in Hosp. Adminstrn., Webster Hosp., St. Louis, 1979; Ph.D. candidate St. Louis U.; m. Frederick Henry Sredl, Oct. 17, 1964; children—Steven, Michael, Stacy Jolie, Thomas. Dir. nursing Regency Extended Care, 1974, Clayton-On-The-Green, St. Louis, 1977, St. Joseph Hosp., Alton, Ill., 1978; edn. asso. Washington U. Med. Sch., St. Louis, 1975; dir. nursing Friendship Village, 1979—; founder, pres. AV-Nurse, Ltd., Ballwin, Mo., 1977—; founder Aerohemodynamics Inst., 1980; bd. dirs. Madison County chpt. Am. Cancer Soc., 1978; CPR coordinator Madison County chpt. Am. Heart Assn. Recipient Outstanding Alumna award Loyola U., 1978. Mem. Aerospace Med. Assn., Soc. Nursing Service Adminstrs., Oncology Nurses Soc., Long Term Care Dirs. Nursing Assn. (pres. 1981), Council Nursing Research, Mo. Nurses Assn., Alpha Tau Delta. Roman Catholic. Author: Air Transport of the Critically Ill and Injured; also numerous articles in field. Office: PO Box 1247 Ballwin MO 63011

SRIGLEY, CONNIE LEE, mfg. personnel exec.; b. Lansing, Mich., Feb. 2, 1943; d. Theron Kingsley and Leolyn Lorena (Scheurer) Slade; B.A. in English Edn., Mich. State U., 1964; profl. designation in personnel mgmt. UCLA Extension, 1980; m. William Richard Srigley, Apr. 3, 1965; children—Karen Marie, Teresa Rochelle. Personnel asst. Coldwell, Banker & Co., Los Angeles, 1969-70; personnel interviewer City Nat. Bank, Beverly Hills, Calif., 1972-73; personnel asst. Products Research & Chem. Corp., Glendale, Calif., 1973-75; employment rep. Metro-Goldwyn-Mayer Inc., Culver City, Calif., 1975-80; employment mgr., then employee relations mgr. Seven-Up Bottling Co. of So. Calif., Vernon, 1980—. Mem. Personnel and Indsl. Relations Assn., NOW, AAUW. Office: 3220 E 26th St Vernon CA 90023

STAAS, GRETCHEN LEE, librarian; b. Dallas, Oct. 1, 1938; d. Fred Raike and Martha (Garten) Hyde; B.S., Tex. Christian U., 1961; M.S. in Library Sci., East Texas State U., 1974; postgrad. North Tex. State U.; m. Gene L. Staas, Aug. 29, 1959; 1 dau., Gayla Lynn. Classroom tchr. Garland (Tex.) Ind. Sch. Dist., 1967-74, librarian, 1974-78, cons. library and media services, 1978—. Mem. ALA, Tex. Library Assn., Learning Resource Program Dirs. Tex., Tex. Assn. Ednl. Tech., Phi Delta Kappa, Kappa Delta Pi, Delta Kappa Gamma. Home: 2702 Country Club Pkwy Garland TX 75043 Office: 720 Stadium Dr Garland TX 75040

STABENOW, DEBORAH ANN, state legislator; b. Gladwin, Mich., Apr. 29, 1950; d. Robert Lee and Anna M. (Hallmark) Greer; B.A., Mich. State U., 1972, M.A. in Social Work, 1975; m. Dennis Richard Stabenow, June 12, 1971; children—Todd Dennis, Michelle Deborah. Commr., Ingham County, Mich., 1975-78, chmn. bd. commrs., 1977-78; mem. Mich. Ho. of Reps., 1979—, vice chmn. mental health, public works coms., mem. taxation, judiciary and corrections com., chmn. Judiciary Subcom. on Domestic Relations; chairperson exec. com. State Foster Care Rev. Bd.; sec. Ho. of Reps. Democratic Caucus, 1980—. Co-chmn. Mich. Dem. Citizens Caucus, 1980—; mem. Dem. Women's Polit. Caucus, 1979—; mem. Ingham County Dem. Women; active Lansing Boys' Club. Recipient Diana award, Lansing Area YWCA, 1977, leadership award, Ingham County Soil Conservation Dist., 1979; named Legislator of Yr. Mich. Assn. Children's Agys. Mem. Council Against Domestic Assault (co-founder), Nat. Assn. Social Workers (named outstanding student social worker, 1975), Am. Bus. and Profl. Women Assn. (named Woman of Yr. Cedar Circle chpt. 1981), Dem. Bus. and Profl. Assn., Mich. Consortium for Rights Protection and Advocacy, Mortar Bd., Phi Beta. Methodist. Club: Zonta. Office: State Capitol Lansing MI 48909

STABILE, ROSE TOWNE (MRS. FRED STABILE), bldg. and mgmt., public relations cons.; b. Sunderland, Eng.; d. Stephen and Amelia Bergman; student English schs., Tchrs. Coll., Columbia; m. Wilfred Kermode (dec. Feb. 1934); m. 2d, Arthur Whittlesey Towne, May 29, 1936 (dec. 1954); m. 3d, Norbert Le Veillie, June 10, 1961 (div. Feb. 1969); m. 4th, Fred Stabile, May 30, 1970. Formerly auditor Brit. Govt., Whitehall, London; activities and membership dir. N.Y. League of Girls Clubs, N.Y.C.; real estate exec., now semi-ret. bldg. mgr. State Tower Bldg., Syracuse, N.Y.; cons. public relations, office designer and decorator; lectr. real estate dept. Syracuse U. An initiator Syracuse Peace Council; mem. area sponsoring com. Assn. for Crippled Children and Adults. Mem. Syracuse Real Estate Bd., English Speaking Union (membership com.), Nat. N.Y. assns. real estate bds., Nat. Assn. Bldg. Owners and Mgrs., N.Y. Soc. Real Estate Appraisers, Syracuse C. of C., League Women Voters, Assn. UN, Women of Rotary, Bus. and Profl. Women's Clubs, Everson Mus. Art Friends of Reading, Mus. Modern Art (N.Y.C.), Internat. Center of Syracuse. Unitarian (chmn. service com. 1956-57.). Club: Corinthian. Home: 304 Malverne Dr Syracuse NY 13208 Office: State Tower Bldg Syracuse NY 13202

STABLER, MABEL IRENE KINKADE (KAY), writer; b. Decatur, Ill., Oct. 22, 1910; d. Arthur and Rose Mae (Phillips) Kinkade; student Butler U., 1937-38, Ind. U., Indpls. Center, 1939-40; m. Sammie D. Stabler, July 5, 1927; children—Stanley Dean, Norman Karl, Sandra Sue Stabler Yates. With Western Union, Chgo., 1926, Bell Telephone Co., Decatur, Ill., 1927; instr. first aid ARC, Ind. U. Med. Center, 1940-41; program chmn. Ind. Assn. History of Medicine, 1947; contbr. articles mainly on history of medicine to publs., 1941—, letters to newspapers, mags.; editor Indpls. Pen Women, 1950; responsible for exhibits Student Union Bldg., Ind. U. Med. Center, Indpls.; contbr. column to church publs., 1952-57; bd. dirs. John Shaw Billings Med. History Soc., 1967-73. Mem. Republican Nat. Com., 1977. Recipient silver bar for 500 hours teaching, ARC, World War II, engraved medal Am. Security Council, 1967; Founder's Cert., Center for Internat. Security Studies, 1977; medal of merit as charter mem. Republican Task Force; (with husband) Presdl. Achievement award, 1982. Mem. Nat. League Am. Pen Women (br. pres. Indpls. 1958, pres. Ind. 1960). Mem. Christian Ch. (Disciples of Christ). Founder (with husband) infant care home, Fla., 1973-82. Address: 1109 River Dr 10th St SW Ruskin FL 33570

STABY, JUDITH LINA, computer co. exec.; b. Plainview, Nebr., Mar. 12, 1941; d. Andrew Paulsen and Martha (Rasmussen) S.; B.A., U. Colo., 1964; postgrad. U. Denver, 1966-68; 1 dau., Kirsten Esther Little. Sr. engr./mgr. IBM, Boulder, Colo., Tucson and San Jose, Calif., 1968-79; adv. engr./mgr. Storage Tech. Corp., Louisville, Colo., 1979-81; pres., chief exec. officer Boulder Systems Group, Inc., 1981-82; owner Rasmussen Computer; partner XYZZY. Boettcher Found. scholar, 1959-64. Mem. Soc. Women Engrs., Boulder Woman's Network. Republican. Lutheran. Clubs: 99's Flatirons Ski. Home: 5322 Gallatin Pl Boulder CO 80303 Office: 5375 Western Ave Boulder CO 80301

STACEY, EVA DRUMM, journalist; b. Cedar Vale, Kans., Apr. 29, 1904; d. Frank Tilden and Myrta Lodema (Cross) Drumm; B.A., U. Kans., 1925, postgrad., 1926; m. Maro Hunting Stacey, Apr. 17, 1927; children—Martha (Mrs. William A. King), Donald Norman. English tchr. Lawrence (Kan.) Jr. High, 1925-27; freelance feature writer for various newspaper and mags., 1934—; by-line feature writer for area newspapers, Chautauqua County, Kans., 1973-80; now hist. writer St. Matthew's Episcopal Ch., Cedar Vale. Publicity writer Cedar Vale Hist. Soc.; sec.-treas. Friends of the Library. Mem. Cedar Vale Hist. Soc. (book editor), Tuesday Writers Club, Tulsa, Okla. writers clubs, Tuesday Writers Cedar Vale (co-founder 1977), Women in Communications. Home and office: 402 Maple St Cedar Vale KS 67024

STACEY, NORMA JEANNE, nurse; b. Houlton, Maine, Aug. 20, 1927; d. Lisle Fulton and Rena Alice (Hannigan) Hallett; R.N., Mercy Hosp. Sch. Nursing, Portland, Maine, 1947; student E. Tex. State U., 1977—; m. James Edward Stacey, Oct. 26, 1948; children—James Edward, Royal K. II, Marsha Stacey Carmichael, Catherine Stacey Shrode, John Douglas, Mark Allen, Mary Margaret, Rebecca Jane. Nurse, Maine, 1947, Tex., 1950-51, Mo., 1953-55, Colo., 1958-60, Ga., 1964-66, Okinawa, 1966-67, Hawaii, 1967-68, Ariz., 1968-70, Ky., 1970-71; nursing supr. Children's Med. Center, Oklahoma City, 1971-74, Dallas, 1975-78; adminstrv. asst. Med. Center Hosp., Garland, Tex., 1980-81; dir. nurses Raleigh Hills Hosp., Dallas, 1981—. Active, Girl Scouts U.S.A., 1962-64, 66-67, 71-74, Nat. Council Cath. Women, 1962-64, 68-70, AAU, 1977—. Mem. Smithsonian Assos. Roman Catholic. Home: 6211 W Northwest Hwy G315 Dallas TX 75225 Office: 2345 Reagan St Dallas TX 75219

STACH, CYNTHIA MELANIE, communications co. mgr.; b. Chgo., May 3, 1952; d. Adalbert Aloysius and Florence Helen (Niwinski) S.; student Hamilton Coll., 1972-73; B.A. in Econs. and Internat. Studies, Am. U., 1974; postgrad. U. Chgo. Ops. supr. AT&T Long Lines, Washington, 1974-75, service cons., 1975-77, supr. promotions, Chgo., 1977-78, bus. analyst, 1978-80, industry devel. supr., 1980—. Recruiter alumna Am. U., 1979-82, chairperson Univ. Alumnae Recruiting Com., 1980—. Mem. Assn. M.B.A. Execs. Am. Soc. Profl. and Exec. Women, Nat. Assn. Female Execs. Office: 101 N Wacker Dr 17th Fl Chicago IL 60606

STACHOWSKI-CHMIEL, CLAUDIA C., speech and lang. pathologist; b. Buffalo, Feb. 4, 1950; d. Edward Harry and Sylvia Angela (Brzeski) Chmiel; B.S., SUNY, Buffalo, 1972; M.S. in Edn., Wayne State U., 1978; postgrad. Inst. for Myofunctional Therapy, summer 1974. Speech and lang. pathologist Warren (Mich.) Consol. Schs., 1973-78; myofunctional therapist for Dr. Harold G. Nixon, D.D.S., Warren, 1974-75; dir., therapist Macomb Myofunctional Therapy Clinic, Warren, 1975-78; speech and lang. pathologist lang. devel. program, Tonawanda, N.Y., 1979; speech and lang. pathologist Clarence (N.Y.) Central Schs., 1978-80. Bd. dirs. Family Counseling Center, Sterling Heights, Mich., 1977-78. Permanent cert. for speech and hearing handicapped, N.Y. State; continuing cert. for speech correction, elem. edn., 9th grade social scis., Mich. Mem. Myofunctional Therapy Assn. Am., Am. Speech, Lang. and Hearing Assn. Home: 3 Naramore Dr Batavia NY 14020 Office: 4343 Union Rd Cheektowaga NY 14225

STACKHOUSE, SUSAN HALE, export co. exec.; b. Knoxville, Tenn., Feb. 11, 1954; d. William C. and Linda (Rust) Hale; A.B. in Jour., U. Ga., 1975; student DeKalb Community Coll., 1972-73, Alliance Francais, Paris, 1972; m. Thomas B. Stackhouse, Nov. 22, 1975. Asst. buyer Furchgott's of Fla., Jacksonville, 1975-76, buyer, 1976-78; vice-pres. merchandising Potpourri of Fla., Tampa, 1978-80; gen. mgr. Bonanni Exports, Inc., Tampa, Fla., 1980—. Mem. Network of Exec. Women, NOW. Democrat. Methodist. Home: 3416 Barcelona St Tampa FL 33609 Office: Tampa Internat Airport Tampa FL 33607

STADLER, KATHERINE LOY, advt. exec.; b. N.Y.C., Mar. 26, 1930; d. William L. and Catherine (Schmidhauser) Stadler; student St. John's U., 1948-49, Hunter Coll., 1957-59, N.Y. U. Mgmt. Inst., 1963-69. Br. mgr. Hull Travel Service, Inc., N.Y.C., 1959-63; with Loire Imports, Inc., N.Y.C., 1963-69; dist. mgr. McGraw-Hill Info. Systems Co., Sweet's Div., N.Y.C., 1969-74; nat. sales mgr. Floor Covering Weekly, N.Y.C., 1974-76; account exec. Ziff-Davis Pub. Co., Hotel & Travel Index, Los Angeles, 1976-81; founder Katherine Stadler & Assocs., 1981— . Mem. Med. Mission Sisters, Roman Catholic Ch., 1949-57. Named Sweet's Eastern Region Salesman of Yr., 1972. Mem. Los Angeles Advt. Women, Mag. Reps. Assn. So. Calif., Nat. Assn. Pubs. Reps., Nat. Home Fashions League. Clubs: Los Angeles Ad, Toastmasters. Home: 504 S Ogden Dr Los Angeles CA 90036 Office: PO Box 480013 Los Angeles CA 90048

STAEBELL, SANDRA LYNNE, hosp. pub. relations exec.; b. St. Louis, July 14, 1947; d. Louis Joseph, Jr. and Maureen (Barry) S.; B.L.S., St. Louis U., 1981. From exec. staff asst. to public relations coordinator, pub. relations dept. Seven-Up Co., St. Louis, 1972-80; dir. pub. relations Newcomb House, Inc., St. Louis, 1980, St. Mary on the Mount Hosp./Rehab. Center, St. Louis, 1981—; instr. advt. prins. and practices St. Louis U., 1981. Mem. Advt. Fedn. St. Louis (dir. 1978-80), Nat. Assn. Female Execs., Am. Soc. Profl. and Exec. Women, St. Louis Hosp. Public Relations Soc., Am. Soc. Hosp. Pub. Relations, Mo. Assn. Hosp. Pub. Relations. Democrat. Lutheran. Home: 2829 Raritan Dr Webster Groves MO 63119 Office: 9101 S Broadway Saint Louis MO 63125

STAEHLE, SANDRA, lawyer; b. Bridgeport, Conn., Feb. 11, 1952; d. Otto John and Pearl Julia (Toth) S.; B.A. cum laude, Temple U., 1973, J.D., 1976, LL.M. in Taxation, 1978. Admitted to Pa. bar, 1976, N.J. bar, 1976; sr. trust adminstr. Phila. Nat. Bank, 1976-77; chief house counsel Birchminster Industries, Inc., Telford, Pa., 1977-78; atty. RCA, Camden, N.J., 1978-81, atty. RCA-RCA Internat. Ltd., Sunbury-on-Thames, Eng., 1981-82, counsel for Europe, Africa and Middle East, 1982—. Mem. Am. Bar Assn., Pa. Bar Assn., Phila. Bar Assn., Am. Soc. Internat. Law, Am. C. of C. (U.K.) (liaison to internat. trade com.). Phi Alpha Delta, Sigma Delta Pi. Address: RCA Bldg 2-4 Front & Cooper Sts Camden NJ 08102

STAFFLER, DOMINICIA MARIE, clin. psychologist; b. Silver Springs, N.Y., Feb. 3, 1911; d. Fred J. and Eva (Ribaud) S.; B.A., Syracuse U., 1931, M.A., 1940. Asso., Marcy and Utica (N.Y.) Psychiat. Centers, 1951-69; asso. prof. psychology Utica Coll., Syracuse U., 1942-74; supervising clin. psychologist Wyoming County Mental Health Clinic, Perry, N.Y., 1978-80; ret., 1980; pvt. practice clin. psychology, Arcade, N.Y. Home: 43 Liberty St Arcade NY 14009

STAFFORD, ANITA FAYE, educator; b. Newport News, Va.; d. Sid Friend and Nina Eileen (Johnson) Rutherford; B.S., Central State U., Edmund, Okla., 1970, M.Ed., 1971; Ed.D., Okla. State U., 1975; m. J.L. Stafford; children—David Wayne, Stephen Lee. Lectr. family relations Central State U., 1971-73; asst. prof. home econs. Okla. Christian Coll., 1973-75; instr. early childhood edn. Oscar Rose Jr. Coll., Midwest City, Okla., 1975-76; asso. prof. human devel., chmn. dept. Tex. Woman's U., Denton, 1976—; cons. Five Senses, Inc. Mem. Nat. Assn. Edn. Young Children, Nat. Council Family Relations, AAUP, Nat. Assn. Gifted and Talented Children, Assn. Ednl. Communications and Tech., Assn. Spl. Edn. Tech., So. Assn. Children Under Six, Denton Assn. Edn. Young Children, Tex. Council Family Relations, Tex. Assn. Coll. Tchrs., Okla. Assn. Edn. Young Children (charter), Phi Delta Kappa. Republican. Baptist. Author: Human Technological Systems Series (4 vols.); also articles in field. Home: 1228 Stanley St Denton TX 76201 Office: Texas Woman's Univ PO Box 23975 Denton TX 76204

STAFFORD, DOT MELBA, banker; b. Brownwood, Tex., Feb. 27, 1928; d. A. R. and Julia M. (Sherrod) Elliott; student public schs., Pecos, Tex.; m. Joe M. Stafford, June 11, 1946; children—Ray M., Bobby G., Cindy S. Hubbs, Michelle S. Acker. Sec., CPS Utility Co., Pecos 1954-61, W. W. Teague Real Estate, Pecos, 1962-63; v.p. First Nat. Bank of Pecos, 1963—. Recipient Outstanding Merit award City of Pecos, 1980. Mem. Nat. Assn. Bank Women, Bank Adminstrn. Inst. (Permian Basin group 1981), Pecos C. of C. (pres. women's div. 1980, dir. 1981). Mem. Ch. of Christ. Clubs: Bus. and Profl. Women's, Nat. Fedn. Women. Address: PO Box 2077 Pecos TX 79772

STAFFORD, HELEN ELIZABETH THOMSON, mgmt. cons.; b. Port Chester, N.Y., Mar. 1, 1926; d. James Ramage and Helen Cunningham (McGill) Thomson; B.S. in Psychology, Coll. William and Mary, 1948; m. Paul Tutt Stafford, Dec. 14, 1951; children—Paul Tutt, Timothy Alden, Mark Thornton, Todd Lawton. Exec. asst. commn. on worship Nat. Council Chs., N.Y.C., 1950-51; co-founder, officer Paul Stafford Assos., Ltd., Mgmt. Cons., N.Y.C., 1959—, dir., treas., sr. v.p., 1977—. Mem. Assn. Exec. Recruiting Cons. (dir. 1968-70), Mortar Board, Phi Beta Kappa, Kappa Kappa Gamma. Republican. Presbyterian. Clubs: Apawamis (Rye); Princeton of N.Y., Coral Beach (Bermuda); Hillsboro (Pompano Beach, Fla.). Office: Paul Stafford Associates Ltd 45 Rockefeller Plaza New York NY 10111

STAFFORD, PEGGY KIRBY, reading specialist; b. Dillon, S.C., July 27, 1938; d. Duncan K. and Lillian Leona (Herring) Kirby; B.S., Francis Marion Coll., 1973, M.S., 1976; postgrad. U. S.C., Coastal Carolina U.; m. Richard Francis Stafford, Nov. 6, 1955; children—Richard Francis, Gwendolyn Neil. Pvt. music tchr., 1960-73; elem. sch. sec., 1966-68; 3d grade classroom tchr., 1973-75; reading specialist Dillon Public Schs., 1976-79, bldg. reading coordinator, 1977-79, Right to Read dir., 1977—; boys baseball coach, girls softball coach. Heart Fund rep.; mem. St. Eugene Hosp. Aux. Club, Jr. Charity League; bd. dirs. Dillon County Arts Council. Named Bldg. Tchr. of Yr., 1974; cert. tchr., elem. prin., reading specialist, S.C. Mem. Nat. Social Sci. Honor Soc., Dillon County Ednl. Assn., S.C. Ednl. Assn., NEA, Internat. Reading Assn., Dillon Hist. Soc., Pi Gamma Mu. Baptist. Clubs: Palmetto, UDC, Bus. and Profl. Women's (named Career Woman of Yr.). Author: I Can Read a Book - One, 1978; I Can Read a Book - Two, 1979; Easy as A B See, 1978; editor Easy as A B See Newsletter, 1978—. Home: Route 2 Box 169 Dillon SC 29536 Office: E Harrison St Dillon SC 29536

STAFFORD, REBECCA, ednl. adminstr.; b. Topeka, July 9, 1936; d. Frank Clinton and Anna Elizabeth (Larrick) S.; B.A. magna cum laude, Radcliffe Coll., 1958; M.A., Harvard U., 1961, Ph.D., 1964; m. Willard Van Hazel, Apr. 12, 1973. Research sociologist Harvard U. Health Services, Cambridge, Mass., 1964-69, lectr. sociology Sch. Edn., 1969-70; asso. prof. sociology U. Nev., Reno, 1970-74, prof., chmn. dept., 1974-77, dea Coll. Arts and Scis., 1977-80; pres. Bemidji (Minn.) State U., 1980-81; exec. v.p. Colo. State U., Fort Collins, 1982—. Recipient McCurdy-Rinkle prize Eastern Psychiat. Assn., 1970. Mem. Am. Sociology Assn. (council sect. edn. 1971-74), Pacific Sociol. Assn. (session chmn. 1975, program com. 1975, sect. orgn. 1976, election com. 1979), NEA, N. Central Sociology Assn., Council Colls. Arts and Scis. (dir.), Nat. Council Family Relations, Phi Beta Kappa, Phi Kappa Phi. Contbr. articles on sociology to profl. jours. Office: Colo State U Fort Collins CO 80523

STAFFORD, VIRGINIA FRANCES, sorority adminstr.; b. Burlington, Iowa, Feb. 21, 1927; d. Neils Alfred and Florence Cecelia (Johansen) Rosenberg; B.A., U. Iowa, 1948; postgrad. U. Maine, 1950-51; m. Robert William Stafford, Aug. 29, 1948; children—Marcia Stafford Jorgensen, Craig William, Brian James, Maren Stafford Smith. Sub. tchr., tchr. speech Des Moines Public Schs., 1948-50; chmn. Iowa state membership Alpha Delta Pi, Ames, 1955-58, nat. chmn. membership selection, 1958-67, nat. chmn. pledge edn., 1967-73, grand sec., 1973-77, v.p. collegiate chpts., 1977-79, grand pres., 1977—; del. Nat. Panhellenic Conf., 1977—. Bd. dirs. Ames Internat. Festival Assn., sec., 1972-78; chmn. Ames Bicentennial Commn., 1974-76; bd. dirs. Ames Found., 1976—; bd. dirs. Mamie Eisenhower Birthplace Found., 1979—; bd. dirs. Ames Art Council. Mem. Nat. Assn. Women Deans, Adminstrs. and Counselors (asso.), Assn. of Frat. Advs. (asso.), LWV, U. Iowa Alumni Assn. (com. to provide A. Craig Baird Endowment, speech dept. 1977—), Phi Beta Kappa, Delta Sigma Rho, Zeta Phi Eta. Republican. Presbyterian. Club: P.E.O. Home: 421 Briarwood Pl Ames IA 50010 Office: Alpha Delta Pi 1386 Ponce de Leon Ave NE Atlanta GA 30306

STAFFORD-GARRISON, SANDRA ELAINE, ins. underwriter; b. Detroit, Sept. 23, 1949; d. Leland Delbert and Amy Dorothy (Hudson) Stafford; gen. cert. of edn. Oxford (Eng.) U., 1966; student Olivet Coll., 1966-67, 67-69, Wayne State U., 1980—. Asst. bookkeeper stock, trust, transfer dept. Nat. Bank Detroit, 1970-72; med. transcriber Henry Ford Hosp., Detroit, 1972-75; resident br. multiline underwriter Bay City div. Auto Club of Mich., 1975—. Mem. Huber Com., Mich. colls. and univs., 1969-70; corr. sec. women's caucus Democratic Party Mich., 1971; ex officio nat. bd. for 8 states YWCA, 1969-71, voting del. nat. conv., 1970, chmn. social action ann. meeting, fin. com., 1975—, 2d v.p. Detroit Bd. Mgmt., 1979—; chpt. organizer, media chmn. Detroit NOW, del. nat. minority leadership conf., Washington, 1979, mem. nat. media reform com., 1980—, also mem. state nominating com.; mem.-at-large, bd. dirs., pres. NW chpt. Women's Conf. of Concerns; del. U.S. Dept. Labor regional conf. on working minority women, 1980; del. White House Conf. on Families, 1980; state moderator White House Conf. on Small Bus., 1980. Mem. Nat. Assn. Female Execs., (charter; regional network dir.), Women's Econ. Club (membership com.), Coalition of Black Trade Unionists (participant study tour of Greece 1979), NAACP, Nat. Assn. Black Social Workers, Alpha Lambda Epsilon (historian), Alpha Kappa Alpha, Hodegus (ofcl. hostess); Ivy Leaf Reporter, treas., 1967-69). Club: Zonta Internat. Home: 814 Center Ave Apt H Bay City MI 48706 Office: 1111 S Euclid Ave Bay City MI 48706

STAGGS, LOLA LOUISE, telephone co. exec.; b. Burlington, Colo., June 28, 1946; d. Duane Winfield and Nelle W. (Wright) Fox; student Colo. Women's Coll., 1978; 1 child, Teri. Telephone operator Mountain Bell Telephone Co., Greeley, Colo., 1967-70, sec., 1970-73, network supr., Denver, 1973-74, staff mgr., 1974-79, dist. mgr., Colorado Springs, 1979-81, dist. ops. mgr., 1981—. Mem. Pikes Peak Y/Jr. Achievement Capitol Com., 1981—; pres. Women's Resource Agy., 1980—; co. chmn. United Way, 1980; sec.-treas. Ski Cooper Nat. Ski Patrol, 1978—; bd. dirs. Jr. Achievement, 1979—; mem. Nat. Ski Patrol System, 1978—; CPR instr. ARC, 1979—; pres. Park Plaza Homeowners Assn., 1980—, Wide Acres Homeowners Assn., 1975-79. Named Employer of Yr., Internat. Assn. Personnel Women, 1981. Mem. Colorado Springs C. of C., Colorado Springs Execs. Assn., Women in Mgmt. Republican. Baptist. Club: Lynmar Racquet. Home: 2039 Sussex Ln Colorado Springs CO 80909 Office: 308 E Pikes Peak Colorado Springs CO 80903

STAHL, MARILYN BROWN, interior designer; b. Boston, Dec. 11, 1929; d. Benjamin H. and Nettie D. (Glazer) Brown; B.S. in Art Edn., Mass. Coll. Art, 1951; m. Alvan L. Stahl, July 1, 1951; children—Robert, Barry, Kim. Instr. painting, Newton, Mass.; free-lance fabric designer, 1960-63; owner gallery, Newton, 1963-66, M.B. Stahl Interiors, Chestnut Hill, Mass., 1966; founder, pres. Maab Inc., mfrs. French furniture, 1979; founder showroom Boston Design Center; pres. Decorators' Clearing House, Newton Upper Falls, Mass. Mem. Nat. Home Fashions Council, Am. Soc. Interior Designers Found., Nat. Home Fashions League Found. Home: 15 Manet Circle Chestnut Hill MA 02167 Office: Decorators' Clearing House 1029 Chestnut St Newton Upper Falls MA 02164

STAHL, RUTH MCNEIL, art gallery exec.; b. Clarks Summit, Pa.; d. Martin F. and Beatrice (Walton) McNeil; m. William W. Stahl; 2 sons. Owner, mgr. Deerfield Fine & Decorative Arts, Dalton, Pa., 1958—. Chmn., founder Puppet Theatre, Everhart Mus., Scranton, Pa., 1948-50; active Florence Crittenden Missions 1946-48. Mem. Internat. Platform Assn. Home: 475 E Main St Dalton PA 18414

STAHLER, MARGARET ENGLER, nurse; b. Palmerton, Pa., Dec. 10, 1942; d. Samuel David and Eva Margaret (Walk) Engler; nursing diploma Allentown Hosp. Sch. Nursing, 1963; student Moravian Coll., 1964-65; m. William Quintus Stahler, Mar. 12, 1966; children—Patricia Lynne, Deborah Jeanne, Julianne Kay, Timothy Mark. Instr., Allentown (Pa.) Hosp. Sch. Nursing, 1963-66; procedures com., 1963-64, admissions com. Sch. Nursing, 1964-65; staff nurse cancer surgery and intensive care units NIH, Bethesda, Md., 1966-69; office evening nurse LaPlata (Md.) Med. Center, 1973; relief nurse Home for the Aged, Frederick, Md., 1979-81; dir. nursing, 1981—, mem. pharmacy, admissions and infections coms., bd. mgrs., 1981—; nurse CAP, 1964-65. Chmn., Arts Com., 1976-77, sec., 1977-79, v.p., 1979-80, dean, dept. chmn., 1979-80; mem. Task Force on Battered Spouses, 1977-78; pres. Urbana Sch. PTA, 1976-77, bd. dirs., 1977-78; mem. Supts. Task Force on Housing Frederick High Sch. Students During Renovation, 1976-77; mem. Adv. Com. on Sch. Redistricting, 1979-80; bd. dirs., childhood coordinator Hyattstown United Methodist Ch., 1975-79, mem. long range planning com., 1976-78; troop leader Girl Scouts U.S.A., 1977—, service team and camping cons., 1981—. Mem. Nat. League Nursing, Pa. Nurses Assn. (area sec. 1964-66), Allentown Hosp. Alumnae Assn. Republican. Methodist. Clubs: Jr. Women's (Frederick, Md.); Charles County (Md.) Homemakers; Md. Jr. Women's (chmn. dist. II family living div. 1978-80). Home: 2047 Fire Tower Ln Ijamsville MD 21754 Office: 15 Record St Frederick MD 21701

STAKER, LYNNE KAYE LORENZ, social worker; b. Cedar Falls, Iowa, Apr. 28, 1947; d. Noel I. and Alice Lorenz; B.A., U. Iowa, 1970, M.S.W. (HEW fellow), 1973; m. Daniel Staker, Feb. 5, 1968; children—Danielle Lorenz, Justin Lorenz. Sch. social worker Joint County Schs. Fayette and Chickasaw (Iowa) counties, 1973-75; supr. sch. social worker, program social worker severe emotional disabilities Area Edn. Agy. 7, Cedar Falls, Iowa, 1975—. Pres. bd. dirs. Reinbeck Nursery Sch., 1978-79. Mem. Nat. Assn. Social Workers, Acad. Cert. Social Workers. Home: 701 Blackhawk St Reinbeck IA 50669 Office: 3712 Cedar Heights Dr Cedar Falls IA 50669

STALEY, MARTHA MCHENRY GREEN (MRS. WALTER G. STALEY), civic worker; b. Kirkwood, Mo., Oct. 22, 1905; d. Allen Percival and Josephine (Brown) Green; A.A., Hardin Coll., 1925; postgrad. Art Student's League N.Y.C., 1925-28, 50, Acad. Julian, Paris, 1950; m. Walter Goodwin Staley, Dec. 25, 1928; children—Martha Staley Marks, Walter Goodwin, Allen Percival Green. First v.p. Mo. Assn. Mental Health, 1960-64, bd. dirs., 1958-64; v.p. East Central Mo. Mental Health Assn., 1969—; v.p. Presbyn. Home for Children Mo., 1962-63, bd. dirs., 1968-71; chmn. Audrain Fine Arts Council, 1965-70; pres. Audrain County Hist. Soc., 1965-70; mem. advisory council Mo. Arthritis Center, 1971—. Bd. dirs. Allen P. and Josephine B. Green Found; trustee Mexico-Audrain County Library, 1959-66. Life mem. St. George Village Bot. Garden of St. Croix, Landmarks Soc. of St. Croix, Island Center of St. Croix; mem. Nat. Soc. Colonial Dames Am., Nat. Soc. Magna Charta Dames, Huguenot Soc. S.C. Presbyterian. Home: 15 S Jefferson Rd Mexico MO 65265 also (winter) PO Box 2334 Frederiksted St Croix VI 00840

STALHEIM, DONNA LOU, cosmetics co. exec.; b. Richland Center, Wis., May 14, 1930; d. Joseph V. and Veronica E. (Reuter) Neu; student Madison Area Tech Coll., 1950-51, 76-77; m. Richard Stalheim, Oct. 25, 1952; children—Richard, Randall, Ronald, Roxanne. Distbn. cutlet mgr. Viviane Woodard Corp., Madison, Wis., 1963-77; exec. asst. Tola Inc. div. Elysee Cosmetics, Madison, 1979—, sec.-treas., 1980—. Recipient Achievement award Viviane Woodard Corp., 1968-70, 74. Roman Catholic. Asso. editor Tola Inc. Newsletter, 1979; columnist Beauty News, 1980—. Home: 5220 Maher Ave Madison WI 53716 Office: 6804 Seybold Rd Madison WI 53719

STALLING, PAULETTE ROBINSON, audiologist; b. Washington, July 22, 1948; d. Marion Bryant and Vivian Amy (Weedon) Robinson; B.A., Howard U., 1970; M.S., Gallaudet Coll., 1972; postgrad. U. Md., 1973-74; m. Ronald Eugene Stalling, June 23, 1973; children—Kali Genienne, Dana Marie. Trainee in audiology Rehab. Services Adminstrn., 1970-72, VA, 1972-74; audiologist Children's Hearing and Speech Center, Washington, 1972, VA Hosp., Washington, 1972-73; dir. audiol. services Md. Sch. for Deaf, Columbia, 1973—; audiol. cons. Howard County Health Dept.; mem. Md. State Bd. Examiners in Audiology. Mem. Am. Speech-Lang.-Hearing Assn., Md. Speech-Lang.-Hearing Assn., D.C. Assn. Retarded Citizens. Episcopalian. Home: 905 Elm Ave Takoma Park MD 20912 Office: Md Sch for the Deaf Route 108 and Old Montgomery Rd Columbia MD 21044

STALLINGS, NETA SMITH, banker; b. Aubrey, Tex., Sept. 13, 1925; d. Joe Bailey and Naomi Azlee (Turner) Smith; student N. Tex. State U., 1942-45, B.S., 1945; cert. Am. Inst. Banking, 1969, 74; m. Weldon Bailey Stallings, Dec. 23, 1944; children—Ronald Bailey, Dennis Weldon, Sherry Dawn Stallings Berend. Tchr., Aubrey Sch. Systems, 1945-46; with 1st State Bank, Denton, 1958—, v.p., loan officer, 1976—. Bd. dirs. N. Tex. Higher Edn. Authority, 1979, United Way Denton, 1978. Mem. Am. Inst. Banking, Nat. Assn. Bank Women, Bus. and Profl. Women's Club (pres. 1972-73). Club: Soroptimist (pres. 1973-74). Democrat. Baptist. Home: Rt 1 Box 183A Aubrey TX 76227 Office: Box 100 Denton TX 76201

STALLINGS, VIOLA ANN, systems engr.; b. Norfolk, Va., Nov. 6, 1946; d. Harold Albert and Marie Blanche (Welch) S.; B.S. in Psychology, Va. State U., 1968; postgrad. Calif. State U., 1973, Temple U., 1972-74; M.B.A. with distinction, U. Pa., 1975. Peace Corps vol., Liberia, West Africa, 1968-71; tchr. Day Care Center, Tioga Community Youth Center, Phila., 1972-73; tchr. jr. high sch. math., Phila., 1972-76; account systems engr., info. center specialist, IBM, Phila., 1976—; cons. to small bus.; asst. supr. Shaklee Corps. Mem. fin. and bus. com. of bd. dirs., mem. personnel com. Woodrock Inc., Phila., 1974—; bus. mgr. on bd. dirs. Hospitality Com., Inc., 1975-77, 80; pres. Black Worker Alliance, IBM Employees of Delaware Valley Area, 1980—; acting sec. Black United Fund Movement, Phila., 1982; dir. Christian edn. dept., asst. supt. Sunday sch., adult class tchr. Sunday sch., sec. bus. com. Philippian Baptist Ch., Phila. Mem. Inst. Mgmt. Scis., Assn. M.B.A. Execs., Nat. Assn. Female Execs. (dir. Phila. network), Ops. Research Soc. Am., NAACP, Beta Gamma Sigma. Home: 5450 Wissahickon Ave Philadelphia PA 19144 Office: IBM Corp NAD CSC 1700 Market St Philadelphia PA 19103

STALEY-EVANS, PHYLLIS DIANE, title co. exec.; b. Denver, Feb. 6, 1949; d. Stanley Dean and Phyllis Mable (Green) Mikelson; m. Roger Lee Evans, Aug. 1, 1981; children by previous marriage—Kristi Ann, Rory Paul. Mgr./title officer Western Title Corp., Castle Rock, Colo., 1970-79, N.W. Colo. Title Co., Steamboat Springs, 1979-81, Land Title Guarantee Co., Castle Rock, Colo., 1981—. Named Asso. of Year, Douglas/Elbert Bd. Realtors, 1978. Mem. Bd. Realtors, C. of C. (treas. 1978). Republican. Methodist. Office: 200 Wilcox St Castle Rock CO 80104

STAMATAKIS, DEBORAH WILKINS, publishing co. exec.; b. Phila., Mar. 6, 1946; d. Alfred Charles and Geraldine Lillian (Purdy) Wilkins; B.A. in English Lit., Pa. State U., 1968, M.A., 1969. With Chilton Co., Radnor, Pa., 1969—, mktg. services mgr. transp. publs., 1975-79, adminstrv. mgr. automotive and transp. publs., 1979-82, fin. analyst automotive and transp. publs., 1982—. Mem. Nat. Assn. Female Execs., Am. Soc. Profl. and Exec. Women. Republican. Office: Chilton Publs Chilton Way Radnor PA 19089

STAMBAUGH, HELEN HUNTLEY, journalist; b. Clearwater, Fla., Aug. 18, 1949; d. Julius Everett and Alice P. (Zine) Huntley; A.A., St. Petersburg Jr. Coll., 1968; B.S. in Journalism, U. Fla., 1970; M.A. in Polit. Sci., U. South Fla., 1978; m. Thomas Christopher Stambaugh, July 31, 1971; 1 son, Andrew Huntley. Reporter, copy editor Clearwater (Fla.) Sun, 1965-68; reporter Fla. Alligator, Gainesville, 1969-70, asst. editor, 1969-70; reporter St. Petersburg (Fla.) Times, 1970—, edn. writer, 1974-78, energy writer, 1980—, staff writer, 1970—; speaker to various confs. and programs, 1977-81. Recipient William Randolph Hearst Found. award for editorial writing, 1970; Elmer J. Emig award, U. Fla., 1971; Fla. Sch. Bell award Fla. Edn. Assn./Fla. affiliate Am. Fedn. Tchrs., 1975; Fla. Teaching Profession Newsmaker award Fla. affiliate NEA, 1978; Council for Advancement and Support Edn. award Southeastern div., 1976, 77; 1st prize in nat. edn. reporting Edn. Writers Assn., 1982. Mem. Women in Communications (chpt. pres. 1977-78), Soc. Profl. Journalists (chpt. pres. 1977-78), Fla. Press Club, Alligator Alumni Assn. (pres. 1981—), U. S.Fla. Alumni Assn., Leadership St. Pete Alumni Assn. (program grad. 1981), Mortar Board, Phi Kappa Phi, Phi Theta Kappa, Kappa Tau Alpha. Presbyterian. Home: 1000 Serpentine Dr South St Petersburg FL 33705 Office: PO Box 1121 St Petersburg FL 33731

STAMPLER, RENEE, chiropractor; b. N.Y.C., Mar. 3, 1934; d. Abraham and Minnie (Stein) S.; cert. in art (Union scholar) Cooper Union, 1958-62; D. Chiropractic, Cleve. Chiropractic Coll., 1973. Practice chiropractic, Los Angeles, 1973—; founder and chiropractor Children's Free Chiropractic Clinic, Los Angeles, 1975—; exhibited oils and woodcuts in one-woman shows at Kottler Gallery, N.Y.C., others; also exhibited in group shows; represented in pvt. collections. Research on club feet, learning disabled, hyperkinesis and Down's Syndrome. Office: 8576 Melrose Ave Los Angeles CA 90069

STAMPOLIS, MARJORIE FRIEDL, lawyer; b. Oak Park, Ill., Dec. 19, 1942; d. Stanley and Helen Friedl; B.B.A., U. Iowa, 1965, J.D., 1968; LL.M. Urban Affairs, U. Mo., 1972. Asst. prof. bus. law and real estate East Carolina U., Greenville, N.C., 1968-70; admitted to Iowa bar, 1968, Mo. bar, 1972, Ill. bar, 1977; asst. prof. fin. Central Mo. State U., Warrensburg, 1970-71; atty. HUD, Kansas City, Kans., 1973-74; asso. prof. law Coll. Law, Lewis U. (name now No. Ill. U.), Glen Ellyn, Ill., 1974-78; Mem. Women Bar Assn. Ill. practice law, Chgo. Ill., Iowa, Mo. bar assns., Chgo. Bar Assn. Office: 1 N LaSalle St Suite 1700 Chicago IL 60602

STANDART, DENALEE JOAN, nurse; b. Olney, Ill., Dec. 3, 1935; d. George Almon and Mildred Louise (Crome) Kitchene; R.N., Lilly Jolly Sch. Nursing, 1957; B.S.N., Calif. State U., 1970; M.B.A., Golden Gate U., 1982; m. Melvin Wesley, May 9, 1957; children—Jerrilee, Stephanie. Supr., Permanente Med. Group, Sacramento, 1970-75; asst. dir. Kaiser Found. Hosp., Sacramento, 1975-80; dir. nursing, 1981—; policy and procedure analyst Kaiser Permanente Health Plan, Oakland, Calif., 1980; Mem. adv. bd. Los Rios Community Coll., 1981—. Recipient Calif. Assembly commendation, 1972. Mem. Nurses Assn. of Am. Coll. Obstetricians and Gynecologists, Calif. Soc. Nursing Service Adminstrs., Sigma Theta Tau. Republican. Home: 2634 El Segundo Dr Rancho Cordova CA 95670 Office: 2025 Morse Ave Sacramento CA 95825

STANDLEY, SHERRIANNE MADDOX, univ. ofcl.; b. Biloxi, Miss., Apr. 12, 1945; d. Tom Smith and Mary Anna (Jenkins) Maddox; B.S. in Edn., Ind. U., 1967; M.P.A., Ind. State U., 1980; m. Barry Layne Standley, May 12, 1942; 1 dau., Sloane. Pub. relations asst. Ind. Democratic Central Com., Indpls., 1967-68, youth dir., 1968, pub. relations dir., 1968-71; dir. pub. relations Ind. Motor Truck Assn., Indpls., 1971; claims supr. Deist, Hopson & Assocs., Cin., 1972; dir. pub. relations and devel. No. Ky. U., 1972-76; publs. dir. Ind. State U., Evansville, 1976-77, asst. to pres., 1977—, adj. instr. communications, 1977; workshop instr. Ohio River Writer's Conf., 1981. Adv. bd. Foster Grandparent Program of Evansville, chmn., 1979; bd. dirs. Vol. Action Center; mem. schs. com. Operation City Beautiful; mem. pub. affairs com. Planned Parenthood Southwestern Ind.; Dem. precinct committeeman Vanderburgh County, 1978, precinct vice committeeman Marion County, 1970-71; treas. Connie Davis for State Rep., 1978. Recipient Disting. Service award Ind. State U. Evansville Alumni Assn., 1979, Outstanding Advisor award Ind. Collegiate Young Dems., 1970; named Ky. col. Mem. Council Advancement and Support of Edn., Women in Communications, Ind. U. Alumni Assn. (life), M.P.A. Club (past v.p.), Network of Evansville Women. Democrat. Methodist. Club: Oak Meadow Golf and Country. Home: 7320 Greenbriar Dr Evansville IN 47710 Office: Indiana State University 8600 University Blvd Evansville IN 47712

STANFIELD, ELIZABETH DEAVER, nurse; b. Fayetteville, N.C., July 15, 1953; d. Jennings Edward and Alberta (Lancaster) Deaver; grad. Rex Hosp. Sch. Nursing, 1974; student N.C. State U., 1971-72; B.S.N. with high honors, U. Fla., 1979; M.S.N. with honors, U. Ala., Huntsville, 1982; m. James Malcolm Stanfield, June 8, 1974; children—Joel Michael, Lauren Elizabeth. Staff nurse St. Mary's Hosp., West Palm Beach, Fla., 1974-75; office nurse West Palm Beach, Fla., 1971-72, Cocoa, Fla., 1972; teaching nurse pediatric intensive care unit Shands Teaching Hosp. and Clinics, Gainesville, Fla., 1975-76, teaching nurse, charge nurse, 1976-79, pediatric nurse clinician for cardiology and cardiovasular surgery, 1979—. Mem. Am., Fla. nurses assns., Critical Care Nursing Assn., Sigma Theta Tau, Phi Kappa Phi. Democrat. Home: 1034 Sharpsburg Dr Huntsville AL 35803

STANFIELD, ELIZABETH POPLIN, educator; b. Jacksonville, Fla., Aug. 9, 1930; d. Thomas William and Mattie Olene (Padgett) Poplin; B.A. magna cum laude, U. N.C., Greensboro, 1952; M.A., Emory U., 1966; m. William Thomas Stanfield, June 30, 1956; children—C. Freeman, William Thomas. Tchr., fgn. langs. Atlanta City Schs., 1952-57, Fulton County (Ga.) High Sch., 1963-69; instr. Spanish, Ga. State U., Atlanta, 1968-78, asst. prof., 1978—. AAUW fellow, 1964-65. Mem. Am. Assn. Tchrs. Spanish and Portuguese (pres. Ga. 1979-81), MLA, So. Conf. Lang. Teaching, Fgn. Lang. Assn. Ga., 19th Century Studies Assn., Phi Beta Kappa, Sigma Delta Pi, Phi Sigma Iota, Lambda Iota Tau. Mem. Ch. of Christ. Club: Peach State Depression Glass. Office: Dept Fgn Langs Ga State U Atlanta GA 30303

STANFILL, DOROTHY MCMAHEN, author; b. Stanton, Tenn., Dec. 22; d. William Scott and Irma Josephine (Galloway) McMahen; B.A., Lambuth Coll., 1962; m. Charles Stanfill, June 21, 1941; 1 son, Arthur Hall Stanfill. Tchr. various locations, Tenn., Jackson (Tenn.) public schs., 1961-64; free-lance writer, 1964—; works have appeared in So. Humanities, Miss. Rev., Sam Houston Lit. Rev., Twigs, Eclectic, Delta Scene, New Laurel Reu, others; editor Old Hickory Rev., Jackson; condr. workshops U. Tenn., Christian Bros. Coll., 1973—. Active Jackson Dem. Party. Recipient 2d prize Ozark Writers and Writers Conf., 1969; 1st prize De South Writers Conf., 1971, 73, 2d prize, 1969. Mem. Nat. League Am. Pen Women, Tenn. Press and Authors Club, Jackson Writers Group, Tenn. Arts Commn. Lit. Assn., Joseph E. Martin Shakespeare Soc., Friends of the Jackson Library, Alpha Omicron Pi. Democrat. Methodist. Author: Collection of Short Stories, 1978. Home: 1 Mimosa Dr Jackson TN 38301

STANFORD, PATRICIA ANN, med. technologist; b. Poplarville, Miss., Oct. 24, 1937; d. Herman Thomas and Anna M. (Lee) Holden; A.A., Pearl River Jr. Coll., 1957; B.A., Miss. So. Coll., 1959; cert. med. tech., Miss. Bapt. Hosp. Sch. Med. Tech., 1959; m. Hiram B. Stanford, July 3, 1962; children—Herman Curtis, Lawanna Lee. Med. technologist Pearl River County Hosp., Poplarville, Miss., 1959—, chief lab. and x-ray technologist, 1959—; vol. local sch. sci. dept. Active PTA; mem. Pearl River County Hosp. and Extended Care Facility Aux. Mem. Am. Soc. Clin. Pathologists (assoc. mem., cert. med. technologist), Nat. Certification Agy. for Med. Lab. Personnel (clin. lab. scientist), Miss. State Soc. for Med. Tech., Am. Soc. Med. Tech., U. So. Miss. Alumni Assn. Beta Beta Beta, Alpha Epsilon Delta. Baptist. Home: Rt 3 Box 94 Poplarville MS 39470 Office: PO Box 392 Poplarville MS 39470

STANGO, ALEXANDRA ROSE MARIE, human resources exec.; b. Glen Cove, N.Y., June 18, 1939; d. Henry A. and Frances S.; B.A., Molloy Coll., 1965; M.S.W. (Catholic Charities fellow), Fordham U., 1967. Community worker St. John's Acad., Kitwe, Zambia, 1960-62; dir. Grant Houses, community center, N.Y.C., 1967-69; founder, exec. dir. CONNECT, Inc., N.Y.C., 1969-74; ind. cons., 1975-76; mgr. organizational devel. Corning Glass Works (N.Y.), 1976-78, mgr. personnel devel., 1978-80; dir. human resources Am. Can Co., Greenwich, Conn., 1980-82, dir. exec. devel., 1982—; field instr. Fordham U., N.Y.C., 1968-74; profl. trainer Nat. Tng. Labs., Inst. Applied Behavioral Scis.; organizational cons. Procter & Gamble, 1974-77, Office Edn., HEW, 1975-76. Bd. dirs. Yorkville Civic Council, N.Y.C., 1969-75; bd. dirs. Gregg Smith Singers, 1982—. Mem. Nat. Orgn. Devel. Network, Inst. Human Devel. (dir. 1968-76), N.Y. Human Resource Planners. Home: 11 Field Point Dr Greenwich CT 06830 Office: Am Can Co Greenwich CT 06830

STANIFORTH, SUSAN LYNN HASSLOCHER, restaurateur, bus. exec.; b. San Antonio, June 8, 1948; d. G. and Veva (Ball) Hasslocher;

B.B.A., U. Tex., Austin, 1970, M.B.A., 1971; children—Sarah, Graham. Mgmt. cons. Frontier Enterprises, Austin, 1970-73; mgr. Steak Island Restaurant, Austin, 1973-75; div. mgr. Jim's Coffee Shops of Austin, 1976-79; corp. vp. and Austin Area mgr. Frontier Enterprises, 1979—; dir. Unilife Ins. Co., San Antonio, Tex. Commerce-Bank-Barton Creek, Austin. Alumni vice-chmn. Leadership Austin, 1981-82, mem. curriculum com., 1982-83; Jewel Ball treas. Women's Symphony League Austin, 1977, 78, 79; treas. Women's Art Guild Laguna Gloria, 1979, Fiesta treas., 1980, 82; v.p. bd. corp. Alpha Phi Omega House, 1972—; treas. Jr. Austin Woman's Club, 1982-83. Recipient Ursa Major award Alpha Phi Internat., 1980. Mem. Austin Restaurant Assn. (pres. 1980-81, dir. 1978—; by-laws com. 19-, exec. com. and chmn. industry relations 1982-83, named Outstanding Restaurateur 1982), Tex. Restaurant Assn. (dir. 1979—, v.p. 1982), Nat. Restaurant Assn. (conv. speaker 1979), Austin C. of C. (tourism com. 1977-80), Austin Better Bus. Bur. (dir. 1982—), Ex-Students Assn. U. Tex. Austin (life). Methodist. Home: 2614-B Jefferson St Austin TX 78703 Office: 2700 Bee Cave Rd Suite 200 Austin TX 78746

STANLEY, BARBARA HREVNACK, psychologist; b. Hillside, N.J., Aug. 13, 1949; d. John and Marie C. (Wnukowski) H.; B.A., Montclair (N.J.) State Coll., 1971; M.A. (NIMH trainee), N.Y. U., 1975, Ph.D., 1979; m. Michael Stanley, Mar. 26, 1970; 1 dau., Melissa. Clin. psychologist, then research psychologist L.I. Jewish-Hillside Med. Center, 1978-81; clin. instr. N.Y. U. Med. Sch., 1979-81; asst. prof. psychiatry Wayne State U. Sch. Medicine, Detroit, also dir. psychiatry, ethics and law program Lafayette Clinic, 1981—; cons. Mem. Am. Psychol. Assn., AAAS, N.Y. Acad. Scis. Author papers in field. Office: Lafayette Clinic Wayne State U 951 E Lafayette St Detroit MI 48207

STANLEY, CAROL ANN JEAN, sporting goods co. exec.; b. Syracuse, N.Y., June 12, 1949; d. John Francis and Cassie Marie Stanley; B.A., SUNY, Fredonia, 1971; M.S., SUNY, Cortland, 1974. Asso. dir. S.R.R. Office SUNY, Binghamton, 1974-81, head softball coach, 1976-81; asst. softball coach Ohio State U., 1981-82; pres. Stash Sporting Goods, Inc.; softball cons. Nat. Softball Commn., Peru, 1977-82, Jamaica, 1982. Recipient Diploma of Honor Nat. Softball Commn., Peru. Mem. Nat. Collegiate Athletic Assn., Sporting Goods Dealers Assn. Clubs: Moose, Eagles. Patentee Stan-Mill mitt. Office: PO Box 56 Collingswood NJ 08108

STANLEY, JUDITH ANN, mental health adminstr.; b. Buffalo, Apr. 1, 1944; d. Stanley A. and Phyllis (Surma) S.; B.A. cum laude, D'Youville Coll., 1969; M.S. in Counseling Psychology-Rehab. Counseling, SUNY, Buffalo, 1971. Rehab. counselor E. J. Meyer Meml. Hosp., Buffalo, 1970-73; psychologist Adirondack Correctional Treatment and Evaluation Center, Dannemora, N.Y., 1973-74, Attica (N.Y.) Correctional Facility, 1974-75; program coordinator elderly and handicapped unit Fishkill (N.Y.) Correctional Facility, 1976; psychologist Matteawan State Hosp., Fishkill, 1975-76, acting unit chief, 1976-77; extramural program coordinator Central N.Y. Psychiat. Center, Marcy, 1977-81; mental health satellite unit chief Ossining (N.Y.) Correctional Facility, 1981—; cons. to N.Y. State Dept. Correction, 1980—. Mem. Am. Psychol. Assn., Am. Corrections Assn., N.Y. State Corrections Assn., Secular Franciscan Order. Roman Catholic. Office: Ossining Correctional Facility Ossining NY 10562

STANLEY, KATHLEEN FRANCES GOOLD, state legislator; b. Montour Falls, N.Y., Sept. 24, 1943; d. Howard and Charlotte (Carmen) Goold; B.A. in History, Muskingum Coll., 1965; M.S., Syracuse U., 1967; postgrad. U. Hawaii, 1970; m. Patrick A. Stanley, Feb. 6, 1971; 1 son, Ryan Patrick. Tchr., Liverpool (N.Y.) Intermediate Sch., 1966-67; VISTA vol., Honolulu, 1967-68; coordinator OEO Community Action Program, Honolulu, 1968-69; program specialist Social Welfare Devel. and Research Center, U. Hawaii, Honolulu, 1969-74; mem. Hawaii Ho. of Reps., 1974—, chmn. com. public assistance and human services, 1974-76, chmn. com. public employment and govt. ops., 1977-81, majority floor Leader, 1981-82. Bd. dirs. Health and Community Services Council, Honolulu Med. Group Research and Edn. Found.; adv. council Queen Liliuokalani Children's Center, Liliuokalani Trust; adv. com. Sex Abuse Treatment Center, Kapiolani Hosp.; bd. dirs. Windward Child Care Fedn.; Punchbowl adv. com. Honolulu City Council; Oahu adv. council State Vol. Services; mem. Hawaii Com., Hunger Project, Punchbowl Community Assn., LWV. Named one of ten most effective legislators in Hawaii, Honolulu Star-Bull., 1976; one of ten most outstanding women in Am., 1978. Mem. Nat. Assn. Social Workers, Hawaii Correctional Assn. Contbr. articles to profl. jour., reports to Social Welfare Devel. and Research Center. Office: State Capitol Room 315 Honolulu HI 96813

STANLEY, MARY CAROLYN, vocat. rehab. counselor; b. Carthage, Mo., Nov. 15, 1948; d. Ralph Eugene and Marian Jean (Van Buren) Reynolds; B.A., Marymount Coll., Salina, Kans., 1970; postgrad. Ariz. State U., Tempe, S.W. Mo. State U., Springfield. Supr. work adjustment Goodwill Industries, Phoenix, 1971-75; vocat. counselor Ariz. Found. Handicapped Maryvale, Phoenix, 1975-76, Kans. Vocat. Rehab. Center, Salina, 1977, Yuma WORC Center (Ariz.), 1977-78; project aide U. Mo. Extension Services, Springfield, 1978; case mgr. Lakes County Rehab. Center, Springfield, 1979-81; field counselor Mo. Vocat. Rehab., Springfield, 1981—; mem. council Region VI Adv. Council Devel. Disabilities, Springfield, 1979-81. Vice chmn. Ozarks Area Community Action-Family Planning Program, Springfield, 1980-81. Cert. Nat. Commn. Rehab. Counselors. Mem. Nat. Rehab. Assn. (cert.). Office: 149 Park Central Sq Suite 526 Springfield MO 65801

STANLEY, MARY FRANCES, writer, assn. exec.; b. Dallas, May 31, 1938; d. Robert Lee and Ruby Lee (Glasscock) Stanley; B.A. in English, U. Tex., 1961; postgrad. U. Tex., 1982. Counselor, asst. mgr. Snelling & Snelling, Austin, Tex., 1965-68; dir. spl. projects Assn. of Tex. Electric Cooperatives, Inc., Austin, 1969—. Vice pres., Austin Livestock Show bd., 1969-73. Recipient Disting. Service and Hon. State Lone Star Farmer award Future Farmers of Am., 1971; hon. mention Alma award Assn. Home Appliance Mfrs., 1970. Mem. Elec. Women's Round Table (nat. treas. 1975-77), Future Homemakers (hon. mem.), Tex. Assn. and Young Homemakers of Tex. (hon. mem.), Am. Soc. Tng. and Devel., Women in Communication, Nat. Assn. Female Execs. Democrat. Contbr. articles to profl. jours.; lifestyles and energy mgmt. editor Co-op Power Mag., 1969—; compiler, editor: Typically Texas Cookbook, 1970; editor: My Favorite Recipe, 1976; editor: (with Jane Jordan) Today's Kitchen Cookbook, 1979. Home: 6602 Branching Oak Ct Austin TX 78759 Office: PO Box 9589 8140 Burnet Rd Austin TX 78766

STANLEY, MARY KATHRYN, educator; b. Charleston, W.Va., Jan. 6, 1928; d. Isaac Bruce and Helen (McIntire) Poe; B.A., Glenville State Coll., 1976; m. Forrest Eugene Stanley, Oct. 14, 1950; children—Susan Leigh, Michael Eugene. Sec. local 9, Textile Workers Union Am., 1947-71; exec. sec. Chessie System, 1972-76; asst. prof. ct. and conf. reporting Bus. div. Parkersburg (W.Va.) Community Coll., 1976—. Active Girl Scouts U.S.A.; youth program coordinator Methodist Ch. Cert. profl. sec. Mem. Nat. Bus. Educators Assn., W.Va. Educators Assn., Profl. Secs. Internat., Nat. Shorthand Reporters Assn. Home: 3210 Elm St Parkersburg WV 26101 Office: Route 5 Box 167A Parkersburg WV 26101

STANLEY, REBECCA ANN, banker; b. South Bend, Ind., Apr. 8, 1947; d. Edward Clinton and DaMaris Ellen (Troyer) S.; student Ind. U., South Bend, 1972-78, grad. U. Wis. Bank Adminstrn. Inst. Sch. Banking. Relief mgr. Western Union Telegraph Co., Ohio, 1965-71; trust ops. officer St. Joseph Bank & Trust Co., South Bend, 1971-78, Union Bank & Trust Co., Bethlehem, Pa., 1978—. Mem. Nat. Assn. Bank Women, Nat. Assn. Female Execs., Am. Soc. Profl. and Exec. Women. Home: 1247 Knossos Dr Whitehall PA 18052 Office: 52 W Broad St Bethlehem PA 18018

STANLEY, SANDRA ORNECIA, ednl. researcher; b. Jersey City, July 6, 1950; d. McKinley and Thelma Louise (Newberry) S.; B.A., Ottawa (Kans.) U., 1972; M.S. in Edn., U. Kans., 1975, Ph.D. (fellow), 1980. Dir., head tchr. Salem Bapt. Nursery Sch., Jersey City, 1972-73; spl. ednl. instr. Joan Davis Sch. Spl. Edn., Kansas City, Mo., 1975-76; instructional media/materials trainee, then research asst. U. Kans. Med. Center, 1976-79; research asst. U. Kans., Lawrence, 1979; dir., coordinator tng. and observation Juniper Gardens Children's project Bur. Child Research, U. Kans., Kansas City, 1979—, research assoc., 1980; lectr., speaker, cons. edn. and med. sci. Coll. Women Inc. scholar, 1977; Easter Seal grantee, 1975; recipient various certs. of recognition. Mem. Council Exceptional Children, Council Learning Disabilities, Assn. Supervision and Curriculum Devel., Women's Ednl. Network, Coll. Women Inc., Nat. Assn. Female Execs. Democrat. Baptist. Author papers in field. Home: 5305 Oak Leaf Dr Apt 14 Kansas City MO 64129 Office: 1980 N 2d St Kansas City MO 66101

STANLEY, SHEILA FORSTER, psychologist; b. Boston, July 8, 1942; d. Malcolm North and Anita (McKeen) S.; B.A. in Sociology cum laude, Allegheny Coll., 1964; M.Ed. in Counseling, Boston U., 1965, Ed.D. in Counseling Psychology, 1975; m. David Stuhr, July 30, 1977; children—Mark, Michael. Fed. grantee East West Center, U. Hawaii, 1965-66; dir. U. Pitts. YWCA, 1967-69; guidance counselor Sharon (Mass.) Public Schs., 1969-71; counselor/cons. Parent Counseling Program, Wayland, Mass., 1971-75; asst. prof. psychology Boston U., 1975-78; psychologist/dir. Contoocook Valley Mental Health Center, Henniker, N.H., 1978—; mem. faculty Boston U.; instr. Northeastern U., Boston State Coll. Mem. service and rehab. com. Am. Cancer Soc., Boston, 1978—; mem. N.H. Commn. on Status of Women, 1979-82; mem. adv. bd. Womankind, Concord, N.H., 1979-81. Named to Outstanding Young Women in Am., U.S. Jaycees, 1977; lic. psychologist, Mass.; cert. psychologist, N.H. Mem. Am. Psychol. Assn., N.H. Psychol. Assn., N.H. Women Psychotherapists, Parent Counseling Assn. N.E., N.H. Assn. Mental Health, NOW. Contbr. articles to profl. jours. Home: 43 Rumford Concord NH 03301 Office: PO Box 117 Henniker NH 03242

STANSFIELD, ARLENE LAVONNE, food processing co. exec.; b. Cloquet, Minn., Apr. 20, 1926; d. Adolph Gustav and Dorothy Bertha (Hein) Franzen; student St. Olaf Coll., 1944-46; B.S., U. Minn., 1948; m. Russell Vernon Stansfield, June 10, 1950; children—Lory Lee, Patti Jo. Home economist Swift & Co., 1948-50, Internat. Harvester Co., 1950-52, No. States Power Co., 1952-55; home econs. cons. Minn. Turkey Growers, St. Paul, 1959-71, Minn. Dept. Agr., St. Paul, 1960-68, Litton Industries, Mpls., 1969-70, Am. Dairy Assn., St. Paul, 1958-68, Minn. Mining, St. Paul, 1963-64; dir. consumer affairs Land O'Lakes, Inc., Mpls., 1970—. Vice-chmn. U. Minn. Adv. Council Inst. Agr., Forestry and Home Econs., 1975—; mem. U. Minn. Adv. Com., Crookston, 1974—; mem. Adv. Com. for Vocat. Edn., Sch. Dist. 281, 1979-81; mem. Consumer Adv. Council Ednl. Home Econs., 1979-81. Mem. Soc. Consumer Affairs Professionals in Bus. (nat. sec. 1977, internat. bd. dirs. 1980—, chpt. pres. 1981), Grocery Mfrs. Am. (mem. exec. com. consumer affairs), Am. Home Econs. Assn., Soc. Nutrition Edn., Home Economists in Bus., Community Nutrition Inst., Minn. Nutrition Council, U. Minn. Alumni Assn. (life), Gamma Omicron Beta, Phi Upsilon Omicron. Republican. Lutheran. Home: 2410 Brunswick Ave N Minneapolis MN 55422 Office: 4001 Lexington Ave N Arden Hills MN 55112

STANTON, GRACE PATRICIA, public relations co. exec.; b. Jersey City, Dec. 17, 1951; d. John Joseph and Marjorie Theresa (Nolan) S.; B.A., Fairleigh Dickinson U., 1973; M.A., Seton Hall U., 1974; Ph.D., U. Denver, 1979; m. Mark E. Rieger, July 11, 1976. Editor, IBM, Franklin Lakes, N.J., 1973; univ. relations mgr. Fairleigh Dickinson U., Rutherford, N.J., 1973-75; editor Kraft, Inc., Glenview, Ill., 1976-77; public relations dir. Indian Head, Denver, 1977-78, CML, Denver, 1979-81; v.p. The Johnston Group, Denver, 1981—; faculty U. Denver, 1975-76. Bd. dirs./public relations chmn. Arapahoe Mental Health Center, 1981—; active Leadership Denver, 1981—; active fund raising Denver Center for Performing Arts, 1981. Recipient Publ. award Kraft News, 1976. Mem. Denver C. of C., Colo. Press Women (dir. 1981—), Public Relations Soc. Am., Internat. Assn. Bus. Communicators, Speech Communication Assn. Home: 7985 S Field St Littleton CO 80123 Office: 200 Colorado Press Bldg 1340 Glenarm Pl Denver CO 80204

STANTON, JANE GRAHAM, trade assn. exec., writer, advt. exec.; b. Rice, Tex., Mar. 4, 1922; d. William Edward and Kathryn Ruth (McKay) Tidwell; student Tex. State Coll. Women, 1938-39, Abilne Abilene Christian Coll., 1939-40, N. Tex. State Coll., 1941; m. Joseph Wesley Graham, Jan. 5, 1946 (div. Aug. 1974); 1 dau., Kathryn Ann; m. 2d, Hinds Victor Thomas, Dec. 18, 1975 (div. 1977); m. 3d, Hank Stanton, June 10, 1980. Profl. singer on radio, 1941-49; producer, writer radio-TV drama, N.Y.C., 1948-56; v.p. United Nat. Films, Dallas, 1957-59; with Tracy-Locke Advt., Dallas, 1964-66; owner Jane Graham Advt., 1967—; exec. dir. S.W. Apparel Mfrs. Assn., Dallas. Active United Fund. Recipient numerous awards Dallas Advt. League. Mem. Fashion Group. Editor S.W. Advt. & Mktg., Am. Fashion mag., 1974—; contbr. articles to profl. jours.; columnist Dallas Times Herald. Home: 4727 N Central Expy Dallas TX 75205

STANTON, JEANNE FRANCES, lawyer; b. Vicksburg, Miss., Jan. 22, 1920; d. John Francis and Hazel (Mitchell) Stanton; student George Washington U., 1938-39; B.A., U. Cin., 1940; J.D., Salmon P. Chase Coll. Law, 1954. Admitted to Ohio bar, 1954, U.S. Dist. Ct. (so. dist.) Ohio, 1956; chief clk. Selective Service Bd., Cin., 1940-43; instr. USAAF Tech. Schs., Biloxi, Miss., 1943-44; with Procter & Gamble, Cin., 1945—, legal asst., 1952-54, head advt. services sect. legal div. trade practices dept., 1954-73, mgr. advt. services legal div., 1973—. Team capt. Community Chest Cin., 1953. Mem. AAAS, Am., Ohio (chmn. uniform state laws com. 1968-70), Cin. (sec. law day com. 1965-66, chmn. com. on preservation hist. documents 1968-71) bar assns., Vicksburg and Warren County, Cin. hist. socs., Internat. Oceanographic Found., Otago Early Settlers Assn. (assoc.), Intercontinental Biog. Assn. Clubs: Cin. Lawyers (exec. com. 1978—, sec. 1980, 1st v.p. 1982, pres. 1983), Cin. Women Lawyers (treas. 1958-59), Cincinnati; Terrace Park Country. Home: Easthill Ave Cincinnati OH 45208 Office: 301 E 6th St Cincinnati OH 45202

STANTON, JULIET ELLEN (MRS. JOHN SCHOEDINGER), physician; b. Columbus, Ohio, Nov. 9, 1914; d. Frederic M. and Nellie Darling (Swartzel) Stanton; A.B., Ohio State U., 1935, M.D., 1938; m. John Frederick Schoedinger, June 11, 1938; children—John A., David S., Steven P. Intern, Grant Hosp., Columbus, 1938-42, tchr. family practice sect., 1973—; practice gen. medicine, Columbus, 1939-82, physician Franklton Health Center, part-time 1982—; physician Planned Parent Clinic, Columbus, 1940-60, Univ. Sch., Columbus, 1942-48, Juvenile Ct., Franklin County, 1947-59; clin. instr. dept. family practice Ohio State U. Coll. Medicine, also Riverside Meth. Hosp. Adv. bd. Girl Scouts U.S.A., Columbus, 1939-42, Planned Parenthood, Columbus, 1942-50. Fellow Am. Acad. Gen. Practice, Acad. Family Physicians; mem. Am., Pan Am., Ohio med. assns., Am. Women's Med. Assn. (pres. br. 1952, 62), Columbus Acad. Medicine, Delta Gamma, Alpha Epsilon Iota, Delta Gamma Alumni Assn. (pres. 1942). Presbyn. Club: Pilot (Columbus). Home: 4167 Nottinghill Gate Rd Columbus OH 43220

STANTON, PAMELA ELIZABETH, pub. co. exec.; b. Detroit, Nov. 19, 1947; d. Eugene Joseph and Elinor Grace (Olszewski) Kornmeier; B.A., Aquinas Coll., 1966-69; m. Roger Stanton, Dec. 19, 1970. With Visual Aids, Inc., Detroit, 1965-66; with Nat. Bank of Detroit, 1966-70; journalist Football News, Detroit, 1970—, v.p., 1972—, executor pension and profit sharing plans, 1972—. Mem. public relations com. Decorators Showhouse, 1980; vol. ARC, 1980; mem. Jr. League Detroit, 1975. Mem. Profl. Football Writers Assn., Nat. Assn. Sportswriters and Sports Broadcasters, Nat. Football Writers Assn. Clubs: Lochmoor Golf, Carlton, Racquet, Palm Bay. Editor: Christ Child Yearbook, 1976; Tennis and Crumpets Program, 1979. Home: 7 Stratford Pl Grosse Pointe MI 48230 Office: 17820 E Warren St Detroit MI 48224

STANTON, SALLY A., sales exec.; b. Norfolk, Va., Jan. 17, 1948; d. Robert Edward and Sarah Nelle (Lloyd) S.; student Agnes Scott Coll., 1966-68; B.A., U. N.C., Chapel Hill, 1970; postgrad. St. John's U., 1980, U. Va., 1976, George Washington U., 1975. Art tchr. Clarke County Schs., Athens, Ga., 1970-71, Williamsburg (Va.) Public Schs., 1971-74; med. accounts rep. Log Etronics, Inc., Springfield, Va., 1974-77; sales rep. Savin Bus. Machines, Lake Success, N.Y., 1977-78, Itek Corp., N.Y.C., 1978; mktg. rep. N.Y. Times Info. Bank, N.Y.C., 1978-81; dir. sales Billboard Info. Network, Billboard Publs., Inc., N.Y.C., 1981—. Mem. Nat. Assn. Female Execs., Kappa Kappa Gamma. Republican. Methodist. Club: St. Bartholomews Community, Sand Bar Beach. Office: 1515 Broadway New York NY 10036

STAPLETON, JEAN (JEANNE MURRAY), actress; b. N.Y.C.; d. Joseph E. and Marie (Stapleton) Murray; student Hunter Coll., N.Y.C.; student Am. Apprentice Theatre, Am. Actors Co., Am. Theatre Wing and with Harold Clurman; L.H.D. (hon.), Emerson Coll.; hon. degrees, Hood Coll., Monmouth Coll.; m. William H. Putch, Oct. 26, 1957; 2 children. First N.Y. stage role in The Corn is Green, Equity Library Theatre; starred as the mother in Am. Gothic, Circle-in-the-Sq.; Broadway debut with Judith Anderson in In The Summer House; also appeared on Broadway in Damn Yankees, Bells Are Ringing, Juno, Rhinoceros and Funny Girl; first major break in comic ingenue role as Myrtle Mae with Frank Fay in Harvey; played with nat. tour of Come Back, Little Sheba starring Shirley Booth; starred in tour of Morning's at Seven; appeared in motion pictures including Damn Yankees, Bells Are Ringing, Up the Down Staircase, Cold Turkey; appeared in numerous TV shows including Studio One, Naked City, Armstrong Circle Theater, The Defenders, Jackie Gleason Show, with guest appearances on Laugh-In, Sonny and Cher, Mike Douglas, Dinah, The Carol Burnett Show, Tailgunner Joe; starred in the title role of Aunt Mary on Hallmark Hall of Fame, 1979; her most famous TV role was Edith Bunker on All In The Family, 1971-79; TV films include Isabel's Choice, Angel Dusted, Eleanor, First Lady of the World; appears regularly at the Totem Pole Playhouse, Fayetteville, Pa., starred in Daisy Mayme, 1978, The Late Christopher Bean, 1982 (both at Kennedy Center). Bd. dirs. Women's Edn. and Research Inst., Eleanor Roosevelt's Val-Kill; U.S. commr. to Internat. Woman's Year Commn. and Nat. Conf. Women, Houston, 1977. Mem. Actors Equity, Screen Actors Guild, AFTRA. Office: care Arcara Bauman & Hiller 9220 Sunset Blvd Los Angeles CA 90069

STAPLETON, KATHARINE HALL, TV personality; b. Kansas City, Mo., Oct. 29, 1919; d. William Mabin and Katharine (Foster) Hall; B.A., Vassar Coll., 1941; m. Benjamin Franklin Stapleton, June 20, 1942; children—Benjamin Franklin, III, Craig Roberts, Katharine Hall. Cookbook reviewer Denver Post, 1974—; producer, writer, host On the Front Burner, daily radio program Sta. KOA-CBS, Denver, 1976-79, Sta. WGAN, Portland, Maine, 1979—, Cooking with Katie, live one-hour weekly, Sta. KOA, 1979—; guest broadcaster London Broadcasting Corp., 1981, 82; tour leader culinary group to Cornwall, Eng., 1978. Chmm. women's div. United Fund, 1955-56; founder, chmn. Denver Debutante Ball, 1956, 57; regional v.p. Nat. Travelers Aid Assn., 1952-56; commr. Denver Centennial Authority, 1958-60; trustee Washington Cathedral, regional v.p., 1967-73; mem. world service council YWCA, 1961—; trustee, Colo. Women's Coll., 1975-80. Decorated Chevalier de L'Etoile Noire (France); recipient People-to-People citation, 1960, 66, Beautiful Activist award Altrusa Club, 1972. Mem. Alliance Française (hon., pres. 1968-70). Democrat. Episcopalian. Clubs: Denver Country, Denver. Author: Denver Delicious: 150 Past and Present Recipes from the Queen City, 1980, 2d rev. edit., 1981. Home: 8 Village Rd Englewood CO 80110

STAPLETON, KATHLEEN M., automobile financing co. exec.; b. 1938; student St. Joseph's Coll. With Gen. Motors Acceptance Corp., N.Y.C., 1959—, corp. sec., 1978—. Office: Gen Motors Acceptance Corp 767 Fifth Ave New York NY 10022 *

STAPLETON, MAUREEN, actress; b. Troy, N.Y., June 21, 1925; d. John P. and Irene (Walsh) S.; student Siena Coll, 1943; m. Max Allentuck, July 1949 (div. Feb. 1959); children—Daniel, Katharine. Debut appearance in Playboy of the Western World, 1946; other plays include tour with Barretts of Wimpole Street, 1947, Anthony and Cleopatra, 1947, Detective Story, The Bird Cage, Rose Tatoo, 1950-51, The Sea Gull, Orpheus Descending, The Cold Wind and the Warm, 1959, Toys in the Attic, 1960-61, Plaza Suite, 1969, The Gingerbread Lady, 1970, Country Girl, 1972, Secret Affairs of Mildred Wild, 1972 The Gin Game, 1978; motion pictures include: Lonely Hearts, The Fugitive Kind, A View from the Bridge, Bye Bye Birdie, Plaza Suite, The Fan, 1981, Reds, 1981, On the Right Track, 1981; TV drama Tell Me Where It Hurts, 1974. Recipient Nat. Inst. Arts and Letters award, 1969, Tony award for the Gingerbread Lady, 1970, Acad. Award for Best supporting actress for Reds, 1981. Address: care Internat Creative Mgmt 8899 Beverly Blvd Los Angeles CA 90048 *

STAPLETON, RUTH CARTER, evangelist, therapist; d. James Earl and Lillian (Gordy) Carter; student Ga. State Coll. for Women; m. Robert Stapleton; children—Lynn, Scott, Patti, Michael. Creator, developer Inner Healing, psychotherapy based on Christian principles; workshops and meetings conducted throughout Europe, Australia, Far East and the Americas; pres. Behold, Inc. Founder quar. newsletter Behold and Be Whole. Author: The Gift of Inner Healing, 1976; The Experience of Inner Healing, 1977; Billy Book, 1978 In his Footsteps, 1979. Address: Box H Denton TX 76201

STAPP, WILLIE LEE, accountant; b. Snyder, Okla., Mar. 4, 1913; d. William Benjamin and Kate (Ross) Broome; grad. Draughan's Bus. U., 1936; student Okla. State U., 1936-37, U. Okla., 1936-44, 57-69; m. Carl Herbert Stapp, Nov. 23, 1938; children—Bruce Michael, Patricia Kay (Mrs. Bert Walker Jr.), Roger Leon (dec.). 1 stepdau., Evelyn Ruth Stapp Manning. Sec. to pastor Bible Baptist Ch., Oklahoma City, 1935-36; office sec. Okla. Congress of Parents and Tchrs., Oklahoma City, 1936-44, asst. editor, bus. mgr., 1936-44, asso. exec. sec., 1957-59, exec. sec., 1959-69, mng. editor Okla. Parent-Tchr., 1963-69; real estate salesperson Carl H. Stapp Co., Oklahoma City, 1948-56; chief acct. account sponsor athletic dept. U. Okla., Norman, 1969-83. Recipient Merit award U. Okla. Athletic Council, 1982. Mem. Okla. Edn. Assn. (asso.), Okla. Congress Parents and Tchrs. (life). Democrat. Baptist. Mem. Order Eastern Star. Home: 200 W Symmes St Norman OK 73069

STAR, BARBARA GAIL, social worker, educator; b. Niagara Falls, N.Y., May 21, 1939; d. William Victor and Edith (Monoson) Star; B.S., SUNY Coll. at Buffalo, 1961; M.S.W., UCLA, 1966; Ph.D., Ohio State U., 1973. Tchr. elem. edn. Inglewood (Calif.) Unified Sch. Dist., 1961-62; ednl. therapist Marianne Frostig Clinic, Los Angeles, 1962-65, West Valley Center for Ednl. Therapy, Canoga Park, Calif., 1965-66; psychiat. social worker State of Calif., Los Angeles, 1966-71; program cons. Jr. League, Columbus, Ohio, 1972; teaching asso. Sch. Social Work, Ohio State U., Columbus, 1972-73; adminstrv. cons. United Cerebral Palsy Assn. Franklin County, Columbus, 1973; asst. prof. Sch. Social Work, Mich. State U., East Lansing, 1973-75; asso. prof. Sch. Social Work, U. So. Calif., Los Angeles, 1975—; clin. pvt. practice, 1966—; cons. to various orgns. Co-founder, v.p. So. Calif. Coalition on Battered Women, 1976-79; mem. adv. bd. Rosa Sharon Shelter, 1977—; mem. Los Angeles County Task Force on Domestic Violence, 1978-79; mem. adv. planning com. Mid-Am. Inst. on Violence in Families, 1978—; mem. adv. bd. Los Angeles Commn. on Assaults Against Women, 1981—. Mem. Nat. Assn. Social Workers, Acad. Cert. Social Workers, Am. Orthopsychiat. Assn., Council Social Work Edn. (com. on use of non-print media in social work edn.), Calif. Psychol. Assn. (com. on legal and social issues concerning mental health of children and families 1980). Author: Services for Abusers in Family Violence Situations, 1980; Helping the Abuser: Effective Intervention in Family Violence, 1982; contbr. articles to profl. jours., anthologies. Office: Sch of Social Work Univ So Calif Los Angeles CA 90007

STARBUCK, DOROTHY LAUREEN, govt. adminstr.; b. Denver, Oct. 17, 1917; d. Clyde Cyril and Kathryn Honora (Hanson) S.; B.A., Loretto Heights Coll., 1940; L.H.D. (hon.), Nat. U., 1981. With VA, field dir. VA Central Office, Washington, dir. VA Regional Office, chief benefits dir., 1977—. Served with WAC, U.S. Army, 1942-45. Decorated Bronze Star medal; recipient Pres.'s award, 1978; named VA Employee of Yr., Air Force Assn., 1980. Mem. Am. Legion, AMVETS (Silver Helmet 1978). Clubs: Soroptomists, Bus. and Profl. Women's (Denver). Office: 810 Vermont Ave NW Washington DC 20420

STARBUCK, JO JO (ALICIA JO), figure skater; b. Birmingham, Ala., Feb. 14, 1951; d. Hal F. (dec.) and Alice (Plunkett) Starbuck Sells; student Long Beach State Coll.; m. Terry Bradshaw, June 6, 1976. Skater, Winter Olympics, Grenoble, France, 1968, Sapporo, Japan, 1972, U.S. Nat. Pair Championships, 1970-72, N.Am. Championships, 1971-72, Stars of Ice Capades, 1972-76; co-star (with John Curry) Ice Dancing (on Broadway), 1978-79; TV commentary includes CBS figure skating on Superskates, European Championships, Challenge of Sexes; free lance performing artist on TV shows, religious shows and comms. Bd. dirs. So. Calif. Olympians, 1972—; spl. rep. for Kennedy Found. Spl. Olympics, 1972—. Recipient Gold medals in figure skating and pair skating U.S. Figure Skating Assn.; named Athlete of Yr., Helms Found., 1972. Mem. U.S. Figure Skating Assn., Arctic Blades Figure Skating Club, Los Angeles Figure Skating Club, DAR. Mem. Christian Ch. Author: (with Nina Ball) Jo Jo Starbuck. *

STARER, RUANA MAXINE, clin. psychologist; b. N.Y.C., Dec. 30, 1946; d. Emanuel and Zoe (Cibul) S.; B.A. in Psychology summa cum laude, Hunter Coll., City U. N.Y., 1974; M.A., Calif. Sch. Profl. Psychology, 1977, Ph.D., 1980; m. Jed H. Weitzen, Oct. 27, 1979; 1 son, Jason Seth. Psychol. asst. in pvt. practice, Upland, Calif., 1977-79; parent tng. specialist Via Avanta, Didi Hirsch Community Mental Health Center, Pacoima, Calif., 1979-80; staff clin. psychologist So. Reception Center and Clinic, Calif. Dept. Youth Authority, Norwalk, 1980—. Mem. Am. Psychol. Assn., Psi Chi. Office: 13200 Bloomfield Ave Norwalk CA 90650

STARESINA, DENISE MARIE, mfg. co. exec.; b. Cleve., May 18, 1951; d. Nicholas Edward and Lucille Cecelia (Horley) S.; B.A. in Office Adminstrn., Mich. State U., 1974. With Pitney Bowes, Inc., Stamford, Conn., 1974—, bus. segment mgr. meters and mailing machines, 1981—; program mgr. remote meter resetting system Pitney Bowes Can., Toronto, Ont., 1979-81. Mem. Nat. Assn. Female Execs., Mich. State U. Alumni Assn., Phi Gamma Mu. Home: 1941 Hudson Glen Bethel CT 06801 Office: Pitney Bowes Walter Wheeler Jr Dr Stamford CT 06926

STARK, BETTY WALKER, mktg. exec.; b. Manitowoc, Wis., Sept. 18, 1940; d. Woodrow Nelson and Mary Ann (Sieracki) Walker; B.A., U. Wis., 1962, M.S.W., 1971; m. Richard Paul Stark, Apr. 20, 1974. Social worker, pub. info. officer Dane County (Wis.) Social Services, Madison, 1962-72; sales asso. and mgr., cons. Stark Co., Madison, 1972-75; account exec., media dir., v.p. ops. Stephan & Brady Advt., Madison, 1975-78; pres. B.W. Stark Cons., Madison, 1978—; prin. Sahr Seminars Inc., 1978—; v.p. sales and mktg. Condominium Ventures Ltd., Madison, 1980-82; v.p. Rainbow Resortsharing Internat., Madison, 1982—. Bd. dirs. Wis. Arthritis Found., Jonah House, Madison, 1974—; adv. Madison Civic Repertory Theatre, 1979—. Lic. salesperson, Wis. Real Estate Bd. Mem. Meeting Planners Internat., Nat. Assn. Social Workers, Wis. Pub. Welfare Assn., Madison Advt. Fedn. Home: 12 Blue Spruce Trail Madison WI 53717 Office: 2423 American Ln Madison WI 53704

STARK, CAROL LOUISE HATFIELD, nurse; b. Canton, Ohio, Nov. 16, 1946; d. Paul Riley and Jeannette Louise Riley; grad. Massillon St. Hosp. Sch. Practical Nursing, 1968; B.A., Mt. Union Coll., 1978; m. Roger Stark, Feb. 20, 1976; 1 dau., Jacqueline Christine. Charge nurse Massillon (Ohio) State Hosp., 1968-72; dir. nursing services Jean Carol Nursing Home, Canton, 1972-77; charge nurse Stark Nursing Home, Canton, 1976—; pvt. duty nurse Quality Care Nursing Inc. Cert. parapsychologist Nat. Parapsychol. Research Found., 1978—. Mem. Licensed Practical Nurse Assn. Ohio, Nat. Psychiat. Found. (life), Nat. Assn. for Practical Nurse Edn. and Service, East Central Coll. Consortium. Democrat. Roman Catholic. Home: 809 5th St NW Canton OH 44703

STARK, JOAN SCISM, univ. dean; b. Hudson, N.Y., Jan. 6, 1937; d. Ormonde F. and Myrtle Margaret (Kirkey) S.; B.S., Syracuse U., 1957; M.A. (Hoadly fellow), Columbia U., 1960; Ed.D., SUNY, Albany, 1971; m. William L. Stark, June 28, 1958 (dec.); children—Eugene William, Susan Elizabeth, Linda Anne, Ellen Scism; m. 2d, Malcolm A. Lowther, Jan. 31, 1981. Tchr., Ossining (N.Y.) High Sch., 1957-59; freelance editor Holt, Rinehart & Winston, Harcourt, Brace & World, 1960-70; lectr. Ulster County Community Coll., Stone Ridge, N.Y., 1968-70; asst. dean Goucher Coll., Balt., 1970-73, asso. dean, 1973-74; asso. prof., chmn. dept. higher postsecondary edn. Syracuse (N.Y.) U., 1974-78; dean Sch. Edn. U. Mich., Ann Arbor, 1978—. Leader Girl Scouts U.S.A., Cub Scouts Am.; coach girls Little League; dist. officer PTA, intermittently, 1968-80; bd. dirs. Environ. Sci. Inst.; mem. adv. com. Gerald R. Ford Library, U. Mich., 1980—; trustee Kalamazoo Coll., 1979—; mem. exec. com. Inst. Social Research, U. Mich., 1979-82; bd. dirs. Mich. Assn. Coll. Tchr. Edn., 1979-81. Mem. Assn. Study Higher Edn. (dir. 1977-79), Soc. Coll. Univ. Planning, Assn. Innovation Higher Edn. (nat. chmn. 1974-75), Am. Assn. Higher Edn., Am. Ednl. Research Assn., Assn. Instnl. Research, Am. Conf. Acad. Deans, Am. Assn. Environ. Edn. (trustee 1979-81), Assn. Colls. and Schs. Edn. State Univs. and Land Grant Colls. (dir. 1981—), Phi Beta Kappa, Phi Kappa Phi, Sigma Pi Sigma, Eta Pi Upsilon, Lambda Sigma Sigma, Phi Delta Kappa, Pi Lambda Theta. Contbr. numerous articles in field to profl. jours. Office: 1110 School of Education University of Michigan Ann Arbor MI 48109

STARK, PATRICIA ANN, psychologist; b. Ames, Iowa, Apr. 21, 1937; d. Keith C. and Mary L. (Johnston) Moore; B.S., So. Ill. U., Edwardsville, M.S., 1972; Ph.D., St. Louis U., 1976; m. Edward Milton Stark, June 13, 1959. Counselor to alcoholics Bapt. Rescue Mission, East St. Louis, 1969; researcher alcoholics Gateway Rehab. Center, East St. Louis, 1972; psychologist intern Henry-Stark Counties Spl. Edn. Dist. and Galesburg (Ill.) State Research Hosp., 1972-73; instr. Lewis and Clark Community Coll., Godfrey, Ill., 1973-76, asst. prof., 1976-82, assoc. prof., 1982—, coordinator child care services, 1974—; mem. staff dept. psychiatry Meml. Hosp., St. Elizabeth's Hosp., 1979—; supr. various workshops in field, 1974—; dir. child and family services Collinsville Counseling Center, 1978-82; clin. dir., owner Empas-Complete Family Psychol. and Hypnosis Services, Collinsville, 1982—; cons. community agys., 1974—; mem. adv. bd. Madison County Council on Alcoholism and Drug Dependency, 1977-80. Mem. Am. Psychol. Assn., Ill. Psychol. Assn., Midwestern Psychol. Assn., Nat. Assn. Sch. Psychologists, Am. Soc. Clin. Hypnosis. Home: 202 Bill Lou Dr Collinsville IL 62234 Office: 407 E Main St Collinsville IL 62234

STARKS, ANDRIA BROUSSARD, nurse; b. New Orleans, Sept. 26, 1935; d. Theogene and Philomene (Biagas) Broussard; student Dillard U., New Orleans, 1954-56; R.N., St. Johns L.I. City Hosp., N.Y., 1959; postgrad. Cath. U. Am.; m. Otto Dethaniel Starks, July 25, 1959; children—Otto Dethaniel, II, Pamela Michele. Staff nurse hosps. in N.Y. and D.C., 1959-64; occupational health nurse Dept. Health and Human Services, Washington, 1964—, asst. chief nurse div. fed. employees occupational health, 1972-80, adminstr., 1980—; cons., tchr. in field. Recipient various service awards; registered nurse. Mem. Met. Washington Assn. Occupational Health Nurses (past pres.), Public Health Service Nurse Career Devel. Program. Democrat. Roman Catholic. Office: Parklawn Bldg 5600 Fishers Ln Rm 13A55 Rockville MD

STARLING, DAWN ALLISON, interior designer; b. Miami, Fla., Feb. 15, 1952; d. Thomas and Ruth Arlene (Terhune) Foster; B. Design with high honors, U. Fla., 1976. Interior designer Jeffery Howard & Assocs., Coral Gables, Fla., 1977-80; corp. pres., head designer Starling Fattahi Assocs., Inc., Coral Gables, 1980—. Mem. Inst. Bus. Designers (programs. dir 1980-82), Am. Soc. Interior Designers (profl. mems. com. 1981—). Office: 4203 Ponce de Leon Blvd Suite B Coral Gables FL 33146

STARLING, MARGARET IRENE, title ins. co. exec.; b. Warren, Ark., Oct. 12, 1946; d. Joe Russell and Margaret Maxine (Davidson) Sharp; student Massey Bus. Coll., 1964; 1 dau., Tammy Lynn. Sec., Gulf Coast Investment Co., Houston, 1965; legal sec. Renfrow, Zelesky, Lufkin, Tex., 1966-69; bookkeeper U.S. Life Title, Houston, 1969-71; with Guardian Title Ins., Houston, 1971; legal sec. Ft. Worth (Tex.) Mortgage Co., Houston, 1972-73; county mgr. TransAm. Title Ins. Co., Stafford, Tex., 1973—. Mem. East Ft. Bend C. of C., Ft. Bend Bd. Realtors, Greater Houston Builders Assn (asso.). Republican. Baptist. Office: 10701 Corporate Dr Suite 101 Stafford TX 77477

STARR, JENNIE SPRING, archtl. designer, advt. exec.; b. Columbus, Ohio, Jan. 7, 1935; d Ralph Downing and Mary Alice (Gard) Spring; student Columbus Coll. Art and Design, 1960-62, Wittenberg U., 1962-65, Penland Sch. Crafts, 1963, Inst. Irish Studies, 1979; m.. John C. Starr, June 14, 1958; children—Victoria Prince, Cynthia Mickey, Teresa Gaa, Kristi Hodge, Holly Schuler, Tina, Charles, Penny; foster children—Hans Jurgen Zander, Edwardo V. Rahal. Art tchr. St. Patrick Sch., 1964-65; exec. sec. Madison County Continuing Med. Edn. Dept., 1967-71; owner London Internat. Travel, Inc. (Ohio), 1967-73; art dir. Madison County Schs., 1973-74; archtl. designer, art dir. Starr Studios, 1973—; advt exec., art dir Starr Advt., Public Relations and Mktg., 1979—; one-woman shows sculpture and mixed media: Huntington Nat. Bank, Columbus, 1967, 74, Internat. Platform Assn., Washington, Madison County Sch Bd., 1969, 75, 76, Ohio State U., 1973; lectr. Art dir., bd. dirs. Madison County Arts Guild, 1975-76; news editor Project HOPE, 1973-74; adv. bd. dirs. Quality of Life Found., Inc., 1982. Recipient Spark Plug award City of London, 1967; named Hon. Kiwanian, 1971. Mem. Contractors Assn. Sarasota, Manatee, Hardee and Lee Counties, Sarasota Advt. Club, Internat. Platform Assn. Episcopalian. Club: London County. Contbg. editor: Madison County History, 1976; garden editor Madison Press, 1962-67; author numerous articles on Irish history, arts and crafts of Ireland. Address: 2334 Siesta Dr Sarasota FL 33579

STARR, JOYCE R., fgn. affairs specialist; b. Phila., Mar. 15, 1945; B.A. in History, U. Mich., Ann Arbor, 1963-67; Ph.D., Northwestern U., 1973. Program officer Drug Abuse Council, Washington, 1971-74; asst. to v.p. Nat. Urban Coalition, Washington, 1975; policy analyst U.S. Privacy Protection Commn., Washington, 1975-76; adviser to Office of Chmn., Nat. Endowment for Humanities, Washington, 1976; dep. dir. Carter-Mondale Campaign, Atlanta, 1976; asst. to counsel Carter-Mondale Transition Team, Washington, 1976-77; asso. spl. asst. The White House, 1977-79; overseas rep. middle east Center for Strategic and Internat. Studies, Washington, 1979—; TV and radio appearances. Adviser, Nat. Democratic Com., 1981—; bd. dirs. Jerusalem Women's Seminar, 1980—. NIMH grantee, 1969-72; NSF award, 1971. Mem. Nat. Assn. Female Execs. Editor: (with N. Novick) Challenges in the Middle East, 1981; author Joyce Starr Reports newsletter; Peace through Economic Security, 1983. Office: Suite 400 1800 K St NW Washington DC 20006

STARRATT, PATRICIA ELIZABETH, energy cons., author, actress; b. Boston, Nov. 7, 1943; d. Alfred Byron and Anna (Mazur) S.; A.B., Smith Coll., 1965; grad. prep. dept. Peabody Conservatory Music, 1961. Teaching asst. Harvard U. Grad. Sch. Bus. Aminstrn., 1965-67; mng. dir. INS Assos., Washington, 1967-68; adminstrv. asst. George Washington U. Hosp., 1970-71; legal asst. Morgan, Lewis & Bockius, Washington, 1971-72; profl. staff energy analyst Nat. Fuels and Energy Policy Study, U.S. Senate Interior Com., 1972-74; cons., exec. asst. energy resource devel. Fed. Energy Adminstrn., Washington, 1974-75; sr. cons. energy policy Atlantic Richfield Co., 1975-76; energy cons., Alaska, 1977-78; govt. affairs asso. Sohio Alaska Petroleum Co., Anchorage, 1978—; mem. Econ. Devel. Commn., Municipality of Anchorage, 1981; appeared Off-Broadway in To Be Young, Gifted and Black; performed as Angela in Papa's Wine, Elizabeth Procter in The Crucible, Candida in Candida, Zeuss in J.B., Martha in Who's Afraid of Virginia Woolf, Amy in Dinny and The Witches, as Columbina in Servant of Two Masters, as Singer in Death of Morris Biederman, as Joan in Joan of Lorraine, as Mado in Amadee, as Mrs. Rowlands in Before Breakfast, as the girl in Hello Out There, as Angela in Bedtime Story, as Hannah in Night of the Iguana, as Lavinia in Androcles and the Lion, as Catherine in Great Catherine, as Julie in Lilliom, as First Nurse in Death of Bessie Smith, as Laura in Tea and Sympathy, as Amelia Earheart in Chamber Music; appeared at Detroit Summer Theatre in Oklahoma, Guys and Dolls, Carousel, Brigadoon, Kiss Me Kate, Finnian's Rainbow; asst. to dir. Broadway plays A Cry Of Players, A Way Of Life, Off-Broadway play To Be Young, Gifted, and Black. Bd. dirs. Anchorage Community Theatre; industry rep. Alaska Eskimo Whaling Commn.; mem. Alaska New Music Forum. Mem. Actors Equity. Episcopalian. Author book. Contbr. articles on natural gas and Alaska econ. policy to profl. jours. Home: SRA Box 372-B Anchorage AK 99507

STARRETT, AGNES LYNCH (MRS C. V. STARRETT), ret. educator, editor, author; b. Peru, Ind.; d. Jerome and Nancy X. (ReMine) Lynch; A.B., U. Pitts., 1920, M.A., 1925; Litt.D., Waynesburg Coll., 1960; m. Clare V. Starrett, July 29, 1923; children—Clare (Mrs. Walter L. Thompson III), David D. Tchr. Lemington Sch., 1918-22; prof. dept. English, U. Pitts. 1922-64, prof. emeritus English and humanities, 1964—, dir. Univ. Press, 1952-64, emeritus dir. and editor, 1964—, editor Pitt, 1939-59; mem. Irish Scholarship Awards Com. Free lance editor, writer, book designer, 1964—. Named Disting. Dau. of Pa. by Gov., 1954. Mem. Hist. Soc. Western Pa. (trustee 1960-82), Gaelic Art Soc., Quens, Mortar Bd., Women in Communications, Phi Beta Kappa, Phi Alpha Theta. Roman Catholic. Clubs: Faculty (U. Pitts.). Womens Press, Zonta Internat., Pitts. Bibliophiles. Author: Through One Hundred Fifty Years, 1937; Falk Foundation, A Private Fortune, A Public Trust, 1967; Henry C. Frick Educational Commission Historical Record 1909-1974, 1975. Editor, designer, coordinator, author colophon Appendix, Elena Lucrezia Conaro Piscopia 1646-1684, Prima Donna Laureata nel Mondo, 1976; co-author, editor: Pittsburgh Bibliophiles Pilgrimage to Italy, 1976; books represented in Fifty Books of Year selection, 1954, 64. Contbr. articles to jours. Address: 415 Bigham St Pittsburgh PA 15211

START, BRENDA ALICE, computer cons. co. exec.; b. Hamilton, Ont., Can., Mar. 21, 1949; d. Earl William and Dorothy Ellen (Moser) Start; student Automation Inst., 1969. Mgr. edn. Boeing Computer Services, Inc., Kent, Wash., 1973-74; data base adminstr. Western Bancorp Data Processing, Los Angeles, 1975-77; system performance supr. Blue Cross So. Calif., Woodland Hills, 1978-79; pres. Start Systems, Arleta, Calif., 1979—, Sojourner Data Systems, Inc., Rowland Heights, Calif., 1981—. Bd. dirs. Madwoman Book Center, Seattle, 1974-75, Seattle Woman's Center, 1974-75. Recipient Scholastic Merit award City of La Verne, 1967. Mem. NOW, Alliance for Survival, Cousteau Soc., Nat. Wildlife Assn., Greenpeace, Union Concerned Scientists, Nat. Assn. Female Execs., Data Processing Mgmt. Assn., Boeing Mgmt. Assn., ACLU, Sierra Club, Whale Protection Fund, Nat. Audubon Soc., Wilderness Soc., People for Am. Way. Democrat. Home and office: 18203 Dusk St Rowland Heights CA 91748

STASI, LINDA, author, producer; b. N.Y.C., Apr. 14, 1947; d. Anthony John and Florence (Barbera) Stasi; B.F.A., N.Y. Inst. Tech., 1970; postgrad. Hofstra U., 1971; m. John Rovello, Nov. 22, 1970 (div.); 1 dau., Jessica Stasi. Edn. editor Seventeen Mag., N.Y.C., 1970-74; freelance writer, 1974-79; producer, creator, host Good Looks Line, 1979-81; pres. Linda Stasi & Assocs., Inc., 1978—; author: Simply Beautiful, 1983, Looking Good is the Best Revenge, 1983. Mem. Writer's Guild. Address: 20 Waterside Plaza New York NY 10010

STATEN, MARCEA BLAND, lawyer; b. Chgo.; d. Ralph and Beatrice (Lucas) Bland; B.S., Knox Coll., 1968, B.A., 1968; J.D., Northwestern U., 1971. Admitted to Ill. bar, 1971, Minn. bar, 1974; gen. atty. Pilsbury Co., Mpls., 1972-74; sr. atty., Montgomery Ward & Co., Chgo., 1974-78; internat. counsel Medtronic Inc., Mpls., 1978—; regional counsel Nat. Democratic Party, Chgo., 1972; staff counsel ACLU, 1971-72. Mem. allocations com. United Way, Mpls.; mem. Minn. Dem. Central Com.; trustee Mpls. YWCA; bd. trustees Mpls. Legal Aid, Mpls. Urban Coalition. Mem. Am. Bar Assn., Nat. Bar Assn., Hennepin County Bar Assn., Minn. Assn. Black Lawyers, Iota Phi Lambda. Office: 3055 Old Hwy 8 Saint Anthony MN 55440

STATHIS, GEORGIA ANNA, real estate agt., astrologer; b. Chgo., Mar. 1, 1949; d. Gus and Mary (Diakomis) S.; B.S. in Speech, Northwestern U., 1970; M.B.A., Pepperdine U., Malibu, Calif., 1978 m. John Nunes, Jr.; 1 dau., Alexandra Maria. Public relations asst. Arnold & Palmer & Noble, San Francisco, 1971-72; freelance designer, Martinez, Calif., 1972-74; profl. astrologer, Concord, Calif., 1974—; advt. rep. Lesher Newspapers, Walnut Creek, Calif., 1974-77; advt. asst. Lewis/Benedict Advt., Concord, 1977-78; realtor asso. Saxe Real Estate, Walnut Creek, 1979-81, Gt. Am. Real Estate, Lafayette, 1981—; condr. seminars, lectrs. in astrology and bus. Asso. mem. Am. Fedn. Astrologers. Club: Diablo Champagne Breakfast Toastmasters (pres. Pleasant Hill, Calif. 1980, asst. gov. Area 6, Dist. 57 1980-81, gov. 1981-82 dist. top evaluation winner 1979). Home: 6645 Waverly Rd Martinez CA 94553 Office: Gt Am Real Estate 3435 Mt Diablo Blvd Lafayette CA 94549

STATON, DORA JANE, nurse; b. New Columbia, Ill., July 16, 1933; d. Tom and Arbie Mae (Sharpe) Staton; diploma Bapt. Hosp. Sch. Nursing, 1958; B.S. with honors, Murray State U., 1965; M.S. in Nursing, U. Ky., 1974. Commd. capt. U.S. Army, 1968, advanced through grades to maj., 1978—; asst. chief nurse Hawly Army Hosp., Ft. Benjamin, Indpls., 1973-74; head nurse med. wards, Ireland Army Hosp., Fort Knox, Ky., 1974-76, chief nursing edn. and training, 1976-78; oncology nurse William Beaumont Army Med. Center, El Paso, 1978-81; oncology clin. nurse specialist, chief ambulatory nursing sect. Army Hosp., Ft. Benning, Ga., 1981—. Decorated Army Commendation medal with oak leaf cluster, Meritorious Service medal. Mem. Internat. Assn. Enterostomal Therapists, Oncology Nursing Soc., Nat. League for Nursing, Assn. U.S. Army, U. Ky. Coll. Nursing Honor Soc. Baptist. Home: 7710 Crescent Dr Columbus GA 31904

STATZELL, MARGARET ANN, govt. ofcl.; b. Washington, Jan. 22, 1931; d. Ona Roy and Ilvie Bertha (Henritzy) Hoover; B.A., William and Mary Coll., 1952; postgrad. Pasco Hernando Jr. Coll., 1973, Ind. U., South Bend, 1977; m. Robert William Statzell, Apr. 25, 1979; 1 son, Michael Alan Gordon. Flight instr., charter pilot Logansport Flying Service (Ind.), 1963-67; flight instr. Grissom AFB, 1967-73; chief flight instr., chief pilot Glenndale Aviation, Kokomo, Ind., 1973-76; prin. ops. insp. FAA, South Bend, Ind., 1976—; airline transport pilot (single and multiengine). Named Flight Instr. of Yr., 1973. Mem. Airplane Owners and Pilots Assn., 99's, Delta Delta Delta, Kappa Kappa Kappa. Lutheran. Address: 51666 Trowbridge Ln South Bend IN 46637

STAUBLIN, JUDITH ANN, computer co. mgr.; b. Anderson, Ind., Jan. 17, 1936; d. Leslie Fred and Esta Virginia (Ringo) Wiley; student Ball State U., 1954-55, 69-70, Savs. and Loan Inst., 1962-67, U. Ga., 1974, Wright State U., 1975; children—Juli Jackson, Scott Jackson. Teller, Anderson Fed. Savs. and Loan Assn., Anderson, 1962-64, data processing mgr., 1965-70, loan officer, 1970-72, v.p. systems, 1972-74, fin. systems mktg., 1974-76; fin. dist. mgr. data centers div. NCR Corp., Atlanta, 1977-81, nat. mgr. EFT Services data center div., Dayton, Ohio, 1981-82, fin. dist. mgr. data center div., Atlanta, 1982—. Active United Way. Mem. Am. Savs. and Loan Inst., Fin. Mgrs. Soc., Anderson C. of C. Home: 6115 Woodmont Blvd Norcross GA 30092 Office: NCR Corp 5 Executive Park Atlanta GA 30329

STAUDENMAIER, MARY LOUISE, banker; b. Marinette, Wis., Apr. 13, 1938; d. Louis William and Hildegarde C. (Schmit) S.; B.A., Mt. Mary Coll., Milw., 1960; J.D., Marquette U., 1971. Tchr. math. Milw. Public Sch. System, 1960-66; trust adminstr. First Wis. Trust Co., Milw., 1966-70; v.p. Am. City Bank and Trust, Milw., 1970-75; trust adminstr. Marine Nat. Exchange Bank, Milw., 1975; v.p. Heritage Trust Co., Milw., 1975-77; pres., trust officer Stephenson Nat. Bank and Trust, Marinette, 1977—, also dir. Bd. dirs. United Way of Marinette, Marinette Catholic Central Found. Mem. State Bar Wis., Marinette County Bar Assn. (pres.), Ind. Bankers Assn. Am., Wis. Bankers Assn., Wis. Trustees Assn. Roman Catholic. Office: Stephenson Nat Bank and Trust 1820 Hall Ave Marinette WI 54143

STAUTAMOYER, GAIL LYN, educator; b. Muncie, Ind., Sept. 2, 1953; d. Joe Donald and Nada Jean (Doolittle) Stautamoyer; B.A. in Bus. Edn., Ball State U., 1975, postgrad. 1979; M.S. in vocat. Bus. and Office Edn., Ind. U., 1976; postgrad. Ind. Central U., 1981. Assoc. instr. Ind. U. Sch. Bus., Bloomington, 1975-76, grad. asst., 1976; asst. to controller Hermanson Constrn. Co., Inc., Hartford City, Ind., 1976-77; bookkeeper-office mgr. Weldors Inc., Muncie, 1977-81; bookkeeper Fine Art Assocs., Muncie, part-time, 1979-81; cons. Curtis Pub. Co., Indpls., 1980; econ. research analyst Ind. Nat. Bank, Indpls., 1981; instr. mktg. Ball State U. Coll. Bus., Muncie, 1977—; coordinator seminars for women. Active 1st United Cerebral Palsy Telethon, Delaware County, 1981; mem. Republican Women's Club. Mem. Nat. Assn. Female Execs., Inc., Nat. Bus. Edn. Assn., Ind. U. Alumni Assn., Alpha Lambda Delta, Delta Pi Epsilon (chpt. historian 1978-79), Phi Delta Kappa, Pi Omega Pi. Clubs: Riley-Jones, Inc. (charter), Ball State Transnational Business (charter). Contbr. articles on bus. to profl. jours. Home: 2001 W Memorial Dr Muncie IN 47302 Office: Mktg Dept Coll Bus Ball State U Muncie IN 47306

STAY, BARBARA, zoologist, educator; b. Cleve., Aug. 31, 1926; d. Theron David and Florence (Finley) Stay; A.B., Vassar Coll., 1947; M.A., Radcliffe Coll., 1949, Ph.D., 1953. Entomologist, Army Research Center, Natick, Mass., 1954-60; vis. asst. prof. Pomona Coll., 1960; asst. prof. biology U. Pa., 1961-67; asso. prof. zoology U. Iowa, Iowa City, 1967-77, prof., 1977—; Fulbright fellow to Australia, 1953; Lalor fellow Harvard U., 1960. Mem. Am. Soc. Zoologists, Am. Inst. Biol. Scis., Am. Soc. Cell Biology, Entomol. Soc. Am., Iowa Acad. Scis., Sigma Xi. Office: Dept Zoology Univ Iowa Iowa City IA 52242

STEAHLY, VIVIAN EUGENIA EMRICK, emeritus educator, author, cons.; b. Wapakoneta, Ohio, July 10, 1915; d. Daniel and Katharine (Bush) Emrick; B.S., Ohio State U., 1936, B.A. cum laude, 1936; M.A., U. Cin., 1941; postgrad. U. Va., 1941-42, Mich. State U., 1961; m. Frank Lester Steahly, Oct. 17, 1936 (dec. May 1967); 1 son, Lance Preston. Tchr. Latin, French, English, Grant High Sch., Georgetown, Ohio, 1936-39; instr. English, Seaford (Del.) High Sch., 1942-43; instr. English, U. Tenn., Knoxville, 1948; tchr. Latin, French, English, Winfield (W.Va.) High Sch., 1955-58; asst. prof. English, French, Morris Harvey Coll. (now U. Charleston), Charleston, W.Va., 1958-66, chmn. dept. modern langs., 1962-64, asst. prof. edn., 1964-65; asst. prof. English, Ohio State U., 1967-78, emeritus, 1978—; editing cons. W.Va. U. bd. govs., W.Va. Dept. Edn., 1966-67; free-lance writer, book reviewer, monologuist, tech. writing cons. Mem. AAAS, N.Y. Acad. Sci., Ohio Acad. Sci., Nat. Trust Historic Preservation, Early Am. Soc., Ohio State U. Assn., U. Cin. Alumni Assn., Scholaris, Phi Beta Kappa, Pi Lambda Theta, Eta Sigma Phi. Republican. Presbyn. Author: Fanny Burney; Seven Steps to Sensible Structure and Style; Stories for Little People; I Always Wanted to Live in the Chicken Yard; The Gift and Other Tales; Seek and Find. Home: 206 Stinebaugh Dr Wapakoneta OH 45895

STEARLEY, MILDRED SUTCLIFFE VOLANDT, found. exec.; b. Ft. Myer, Va., Aug. 3, 1905; d. William Frederick and Mabel Emma (Sutcliffe) Volandt; student George Washington U., 1923-24, 25-28; m. Ralph F. Stearley, Sept. 19, 1931. Elementary tchr. Brent Sch., Baguio, Philippines, 1929-30; staff aide vol. services ARC, also acting chmn., Charlotte, N.C., 1943, staff asst., Washington, 1943-47, Gray Lady vol., Okinawa, 1950-53, Brazil, Ind., 1954; trustee Air Force Village Found., San Antonio, 1975-78, sec. bd., 1975-77; sustaining mem. Tex. Gov.'s Com.; mem. 300 com. Bexar County Republican Com. Recipient commendation ARC, 1943. Mem. Army Daus., Am. Legion Aux., Army-Navy Club Aux., P.E.O. (life), Am. Security Council (nat. adv. bd.), Pi Beta Phi. Episcopalian. Clubs: Shakespeare Circle. Ladies Reading (Brazil, Ind.); Lackland Officers Wives, Bright Shawl (San Antonio). Home: 4917 Ravenswood Dr San Antonio TX 78227

STEARNS, ELISABETH GENE, librarian; b. Monte Vista, Colo., Sept. 30, 1920; d. Eugene Lamar and Olive (Hammond) Carter; A.B. (scholar), Mills Coll., U. Colo., 1942; M.Ed., U. Fla., 1970; m. James Coleman Stearns, June 11, 1943; children—Anne Stearns Lindberg, Beth Carter. Elem. tchr. Venetia Sch., Jacksonville, Fla., 1962-63; librarian Duval County (Fla.), 1963—; head librarian Fletcher Sr. High Sch., Neptune Beach, Fla., 1963-82. Mem. So. Assn. Colls. and Schs. (head media evaluation cons. 1979), Duval County Library Assn. (sec. 1963). Episcopalian. Clubs: St. John's Dinner, Kappa Alpha Theta Alumnae (pres. 1967). Researcher, author computerized project Reading Interests of Black Students, 1970. Home: 2637 Apache Ave Jacksonville FL 32210

STEARNS, E(LIZABETH) CAROLYN, med. adminstrv. officer; b. Mooresville, Ind., Aug. 16, 1928; d. Gale Able and Ercie Louise (Smith) Rose; grad. Mooresville public schs.; m. William Joseph Sawyers, Sept. 6, 1946, (div. May 1951); children—William Joseph, Sherry Lou; m. John Pershing Stearns, Oct. 4, 1954 (div. Mar. 1980); 1 son, Dennis Gale. Sec., Lab. Equipment Corp., Mooresville, 1946-49; sec. to chief surg. service VA Hosp., Indpls., 1950-57, sec. radiology service, 1963-64, sec. to chief med. service, 1964-66, adminstrv. asst. to chief med. service, 1966-70, adminstrv. officer med. service, 1970-72; staff asst. med. service VA Hosp., Tampa, Fla., 1972-80, adminstrv. officer, med. service, 1981—; adminstrv. officer dept. internal medicine U. So. Fla. Coll. Medicine, Tampa, 1972—. Mem. bus. edn. adv. com. J. Everett Light Career Center, Indpls., 1969-72. Mem. Adminstrs. of Internal Medicine Assn., Med. Group Mgmt. Assn., Nat. Notary Assn., Nat. Assn. Female Execs. Inc., Am. Soc. Profl. and Exec. Women, Hillsborough County Med. Assts. Assn. Office: Dept Internal Medicine 12901 N 30th St Box 19 Tampa FL 33612

STEBBINS, LOU HIRSCH, ednl. adminstr.; b. Los Angeles, Sept. 20, 1930; d. Harold H. (stepfather) and Pauline (Lazenby) Hirsch; grad. with honors Amarillo (Tex.) Coll., 1961; B.S. in Med. Record Adminstrn., Incarnate Word Coll., 1963; M.B.A., La. Tech. U., 1976; children by previous marriage—Sherra, Holly, Scott, Kirk. Asst. med. record librarian St. Anthony Hosp., Amarillo, 1964-66, U. Miss. Med. Center, Jackson, 1966-67; chief med. record adminstr. Schumpert Meml. Hosp., Shreveport, La., 1967-72; dir. med. record adminstrn. program div. allied health La. Tech. U., Ruston, 1972—; instr. med. terminology Shreveport-Bossier Tech. and Vocat. Tng. Center, 1969, 71, 72; cons. nursing home med. records, 1972; lectr. div. continuing edn. La. Nursing Home Assn., 1970-71. Bd. dirs. Southeastern Conf. of Med. Record Adminstrs., 1973. Mem. Am. Med. Record Assn. (council on certification 1981—), La. Med. Record Assn. (pres. 1975, mem. exec. bd. 1974-76), NW La. Med. Record Assn. (pres. 1970). Lutheran. Home: Route 4 PO Box 102 Ruston LA 71270 Office: PO Box 3171 Tech Station Ruston LA 71272

STEBER, ELEANOR, soprano; b. Wheeling, W.Va., July 17, 1916; d. William Charles and Ida A. (Nolte) Steber; Mus.B., New Eng. Conservatory Music, 1938, hon. Mus.D.; Mus.D. (hon.), Bethany Coll., U. W.Va., Fla. So. Coll., Temple U., Ithaca Coll.; L.H.D. (hon.), Wheaton Coll., 1966; A.F.D., U. Oklahoma City. Singer, 1935—; won Met. Auditions of Air, spring 1940; with Met. Opera Co., 1940-66, San Francisco Opera Co., 1945, Central City Opera Festival, 1946, Cin. Summer Opera, 5 summers; appeared with all maj. Am. opera cos., and all maj. European festivals including Glynbourne, 1948, Bayreuth, 1953, Florence (Italy), 1954, Salzburg, 1959; sang with 7 opera cos. in Yugoslavia, 1955, Vienna Staats Oper, 1956; soloist with N.Y. Philharmonic, NBC, Boston, Mpls., Chgo., Cin., Kansas City, Denver, Montreal, Phila. Symphony orchs., others; makes radio, TV appearances; star of TV's Voice of Firestone, 10 yrs. Concert tours throughout U.S., Can., Europe, Orient; head vocal dept. Cleve. Inst. Music, 1963-73; voice faculty Julliard Sch. Music, 1971—, New Eng. Conservatory Music, 1971—, Phila. Music Acad., 1975. Bd. dirs. Bklyn. Opera Co., Opera Soc. Washington; founder, pres. Eleanor Steber Music Found., 1975—. Mem. Delta Omicron, Pi Kappa Lambda. Lutheran. Home: Box 342 Port Jefferson NY 11777 Office: 2109 Broadway New York NY 10023

STEBINS, JANET H., consumer educator, legal sec.; b. N.Y.C., Jan. 17, 1939; d. Irving and Irma Margaret (Gross) S.; student Los Angeles City Coll., 1956-58, CUNY, 1958-62; paralegal cert. L.I. U./Bklyn. Center, 1978. Stewardess, reservations rep. United Air Lines, N.Y.C., 1966-71; free lance legal sec., N.Y.C., 1971-79; founder, exec. dir. GET Consumer Protection, Inc., N.Y.C., 1971—; expert witness on utility matters N.Y. State Senate and Assembly, Public Service Commn., Fed. Energy Adminstrn., Dept. Energy, FTC. Active N.Y. sect. Nat. Council Jewish Women, chmn. program and public affairs com. bus. and profl. br., 1979-80; coordinator consumer edn. programs Phoenix House, drug and fed. re-entry male prisoners, also Daytop Village; Consumer and Credit Info. Cons. Chase Exchange Program, Chase Manhattan Bank. Recipient vol. award for consumer edn. Mem. Soc. Consumer Affairs Profls. in Bus., Internat. Platform Assn., Am. Soc. Profl. and Exec. Women, Am. Council Consumer Interests, Networks Unltd. Republican. Author: Shedding Light on Electricity (Major Appliance Consumer Action Panel award), 1974; columnist: Government, Business & You, N.Y. Womensweek; contbr. weekly column: Utility Watch, The Township, Bklyn.; appeared radio and TV; arranged spl. electric billing for sr. citizens by Consol. Edison, 1979; revised form letters sent by N.Y. State Public Service Commn. to consumers regarding complaints, 1978; featured in articles in publs. including N.Y. Times, Daily News, Miami Herald, Nat. Observer, Newsday, Barron's. Office: PO Box 37 Ansonia Sta New York NY 10023

STECKEL, BARBARA JEAN, city ofcl.; b. Los Angeles, Mar. 9, 1939; d. John Herschel and Bernice Evelyn (Selstad) Webb; B.A. in Acctg., U. Alaska, Anchorage, 1980; m. Dale R. Steckel, Mar. 16, 1962; children—Leanna Virginia, Debra Lynn, Richard Alan. Adminstrv. officer dept. public works Govt. Am. Samoa, Pago Pago, 1967-69; sec. to sch. bd. supt. Nome (Alaska) public schs., 1970-72; city clk.-treas. City of Kotzebue (Alaska), 1973-74, city mgr.-treas., 1974-76; grants adminstr. Municipality of Anchorage, 1976-79, controller, 1979-82, mcpl. mgr., 1982—; v.p. P.G. Hupperten & Assos., Inc.; dir. Star Investment, Inc. Mem. Am. Soc. Women Accts., Am. Soc. Public Adminstrn., Mcpl. Fin. Officers Assn., Nat. Council Govtl. Acctg., Internat. City Mgmt. Assn. Club: Women of Moose. Office: 632 W 6th Pouch 6-650 Anchorage AK 99502

STECKEL, JANET LOUISE, lawyer; b. Allentown, Pa., Aug. 26, 1951; d. George William and June Louise Steckel; A.B., Smith Coll., 1973; J.D., George Washington U., 1976. Admitted to D.C. bar, 1976; law clk. D.C. Ct. Appeals, 1976-77; atty. Regulatory Litigation Sect., Office Gen. Counsel, Dept. Energy, 1977-80; asst. counselor Office Profl. Responsibility, Dept. Justice, atty. Appellate Sect., Land and Natural Resources Div., 1982—. Mem. Choral Arts Soc. Washington, 1976—, Polyhymnia, (a capella chamber chorus), 1981—. Mem. D.C. Bar Assn. Democrat. Address: Dept Justice 10th St and Constitution Ave NW Washington DC 20530

STECKEL, JULIE RASKIN, psychotherapist; b. Los Angeles, Jan. 3, 1940; d. Edward M. and Selma (Romm) Raskin; B.A., UCLA, 1960; M.A.T., Harvard U., 1961; M.S.W., UCLA, 1975; m. Richard J. Steckel, June 16, 1960; children—Jan Marie, David. Pvt. practice psychotherapy, Los Angeles, 1975—; clin. social worker Centinela Hosp., Inglewood, Calif., 1975-76; clin. social worker Bio-Med. Applications Dalysis Units, Los Angeles, Torrance, 1976—, dir. social work, Torrance, 1980—; field adv. Antioch West U., 1979-80. Co dir. Pacific Palisades Democratic Hdqrs., 1972. Mem. Nat. Assn. Social Workers, Soc. Clin. Social Work, So. Calif. Psychotherapy Assn. Editorial bd. Contemporary Dialysis Mag. Home: 248 24th St Santa Monica CA 90402 Office: 12301 Wilshire Blvd West Los Angeles CA 90025

STEED, DIANE KAY, govt. ofcl.; b. Hutchinson, Kans., Nov. 29, 1945; d. Charles Lee and Heleh Ruth S.; student Hutchinson Jr. Coll., 1964; B.S. in Edn., U. Kans., 1967; postgrad. in Mgmt. Sci., George Washington U. Congressional intern, summer 1966; mgmt. intern Def. Supply Agy., 1967-68; mgmt. analyst Def. Contract Adminstrn. Services, Washington, 1968-72; sr. budget analyst ACTION, 1972-73; mgmt. asso. Office Mgmt. and Budget, 1973-79, chief regulatory policy, 1979-81; dep. adminstr. Nat. Hwy. Traffic Safety Adminstrn., Dept. Transp., Washington, 1981—; lectr. univ. courses. Mem. Women in Transp., Alpha Phi. Republican. Mem. Christian Ch. (Disciples of Christ). Office: 400 7th St SW Room 5220 Washington DC 20590

STEEL, CLAUDIA WILLIAMSON, artist; b. Van Nuys, Calif., Mar. 19, 1918; d. James Gordon and Ella (Livingston) Williamson; B.A. in Art, U. Calif., Berkeley, 1939, secondary credential, 1940; M.F.A., Mills Coll., 1978; m. Lowell F. Steel, Aug. 15, 1941; children—Claudia Steel Rosen, Douglas Lowell, Roger Conant. Tchr. art Greenville Jr./Sr. High Sch., Calif., 1940-42; faculty Calif. State U., Chico, 1967-69; pvt. tchr. art, Chico; one-woman shows include: Laboudt Gallery, San Francisco, 1958, Witherspoon Bldg., Phila., 1959, traveling show with old Bergen Guild to nat. galleries, 1971, Redding (Calif.) Mus., 1973, Central Wyo. Mus. Art, Casper, 1976, U. Portland 1976; U. Wis., LaCrosse, 1978, Purdue U., West Lafayette, Ind., 1979, Pratt Inst., Manhatten Gallery, N.Y.C., 1980; exhibited in group shows at: Santa Barbara Art Mus., 1951, San Francisco Arts Festival (award), 1953, Oakland Art Mus., 1954, San Francisco Women Artists juried shows, 1958, 68, 72, 73, 75, 76, Crocker Mus., Sacramento, 1958, 59, 60, 65, 67, 73, Richmond (Calif.) Mus., 1960, DeYoung Mus. Art, San Francisco, 1960, San Francisco Mus. Art, 1959, 61, Mills Coll. Gallery, 1962, 67, 78, Berkeley (Calif.) Art Center Gallery, 1969, San Francisco Art Commn. Gallery, 1972, Brandeis U., Mass., 1973, Ohio State U., Columbus, 1973, Brandt Gallery, Glendale, Calif., 1978, Chico State U., 1979, Fisher Gallery, Chico, Walnut Creek Art Gallery and Sonoma State U., 1979, Pratt Inst., Manhattan Gallery, N.Y.C., 1980, others. Bd. dirs. Creative Art Center, Chico, 1977-81, Omni Arts, Chico, 1979-82. Recipient San Francisco Mus. of Art Serigraphy award, 1961; trustees' scholar, Mills Coll., 1935, others. Mem. Calif. Soc. Printmakers (v.p., dir. 1973-77), others. Republican.

STEEL, DANIELLE FERNANDE, author; b. N.Y.C., Aug. 14, 1947; d. John and Norma (Stone) Schuelein-Steel; student Parsons Sch. Design, 1963, N.Y. U., 1963-67. Vice pres. public relations and new bus. Supergirls Ltd., N.Y.C., 1968-71; copywriter Grey Advt., San Francisco, 1973-74; novels include: Going Home, 1973, Passion's Promise, 1977, Now and Forever, 1978, The Promise, 1978, Season of Passion, 1979, Summer's End, 1979, To Love Again, 1980, The Ring, 1980, Loving, 1980, Love, 1981, Remembrance, 1981, Palomino, 1981, Once in a Lifetime, 1982, Crossings, 1982, A Perfect Stranger, 1982; contbr. poetry to mags., including: Cosmopolitan, McCall's, Ladies Home Jour., Good Housekeeping.

STEEL, JOYCE MARIE, realtor, ins. agy. exec.; b Anson, Tex., Jan. 2, 1937; d. Herman Thell and Gladys (Propst) S.; student Ranger Jr. Coll., 1954-55, Tex. Tech. U., 1956-59, U. Houston, 1965-67. With Panhandle Abstract Co., Anson, 1955, Wayne Durham & Co., Abilene, Tex., 1955-56, Pan-Am. Petroleum Corp., Lubbock, Tex., 1956-60, Cabot Corp., Pampa, Tex., 1960-61, Hunt Oil Co., Dallas, 1961-62, James E. Kemp, Dallas, 1962-63, Vinson, Elkins, Weems & Searls, Houston, 1963, Wells Stewart Interests, 1963-66; real estate broker Joyce Steel, Realtor Houston, 1966—; dir. Home Savs. Assn. Dallas County, 1969-70; chmn., pres. Ambassador Gen. Ins. Agy., Inc., Houston, 1971-76, dir., 1976-78, cons., 1978-80; chmn., ops. mgr. First Am. Title Co. of Houston, 1972-73; adv. dir. Bankers Capital Corp., 1974; exec. v.p. Republic of Tex. Savs. Assn., 1973-74, dir., 1974-78, vice-chmn. bd., 1975-78; chmn. Bankers Investment Bldg. Corp., 1978-80, Property Dynamics, Inc., 1978-80; owner, designer Joyce Steel Interiors, 1970—; owner Joyce Steel d.b.a. Steel & Assos., Houston, 1965—; v.p., dir., sec. Alamo Ins. Agy. Inc. (and predecessor cos.), 1969—, Tex. Asso. Agy. Inc., 1980-81. Sustaining mem. Republican. Nat. Com.; founder Westheimer Art Festival, Houston, 1973. Mem. Houston Fin. Council for Women (founding chmn. 1974, pres. 1975), Harris County Heritage Soc., Houston C. of C., Houston Bd. Realtors, Tex. Assn. Realtors, Nat. Assn. Real Estate Bds., Am. Inst. Mgmt., Houston Assn. Ins. Agts., Ind. Profl. Agts. Houston, Tex. Assn. Ins. Agts., Nat. Assn. Ins. Agts., Am. Judicature Soc., Beta Sigma Phi. Republican. Clubs: Braeburn Country, Warwick, Elan's. Author: The Son of Mary, Books I, II, III, 1975-77; The Daughter of Atlantis, 1977; The Children of Eden, 1978. Office: 811 Westheimer St Suite 106 Houston TX 77006

STEEL, MIRIAM ANDERSON, conservationist; b. Madera, Pa., Nov. 19, 1895; d. David W. and Nineveh Diana Anderson; student Northwestern U. Sch. Speech and Music, 1912-13, Goucher Coll., 1913-16, Peabody Conservatory of Music, 1913-16; m. Maxwell Wensel Steel, Dec. 2, 1916; children—Maxwell W., Barbara Meza, David, Patricia. Pres., Garden Club Fedn. Pa., 1956-58, hon. life pres., 1976—; v.p., dir. Pa. Roadside Council, 1953—; pres. Nat. Council State Garden Clubs, 1971-73, trustee, chmn. trustees, 1973-79; conservation lectr. Pa. Game Commn. County Insts., 1943-45, 75—; chmn. Huntingdon Borough Tree Commn., 1942—. Named Disting. Dau. Pa. Mem. Pa. Environ. Council (dir.), Pa. Roadside Council. Republican. Methodist-Episcopal. Home: 226 Penn St Huntingdon PA 16652

STEELE, DIANA ALEXANDER, lawyer; b. Phila., Oct. 3, 1946; d. Joseph Middleton Steele and Martha Cynthia Pound; B.A., Wellesley Coll., 1968; J.D., N.Y. U., 1971, LL.M. in Taxation, 1982. Admitted to N.Y. State bar, 1971; atty. appeals bur. Legal Aid Soc., N.Y.C., 1971-74, sr. supervising atty., 1974-78; counsel women's rights project ACLU, N.Y.C., 1978-81; asso. firm Reid & Priest, N.Y.C., 1981—; trustee, counsel Women's Equity Action League, Washington, 1979-80. Mem. Am. Bar Assn., N.Y. State Bar Assn., Assn. Bar City N.Y. Democrat. Office: 40 Wall St New York NY 10005

STEELE, EVELYN JANE, public relations and advt. agy. exec.; b. Berkeley, Calif., Feb. 14, 1911; d. Carlos Louis and Jane Catherine (Jensen) de Clairmont; student Munson Bus. Coll., San Francisco, 1929-30; m. Donald Dickinson Steele, May 8, 1932; 1 son, Donald de Clairmont. Pvt. sec., 1930-32; engaged in public relations, publicity and advt., 1940—; v.p., dir. Steele Group, San Francisco, 1977—; sec.-treas. Internat. Pub. Relations Co., Ltd., San Francisco; sec.-treas. Internat. Bus. Interface, Inc., Don Steele Advt. Pres. Ladies Aid Retarded Children, San Francisco, 1977-78, bd. dirs., 1978-82. Mem. Fashion Group (regional dir. 1965-67). Republican. Unitarian. Clubs: Metropolitan (dir. 1961-68), Order Rainbow Girls. Office: 703 Market St San Francisco CA 94103

STEELE, HÉLÉNE LISA, architect; b. Westchester, N.Y., June 11, 1943; d. Leo J. and Rose Lillian (Birk) Kimmel; A.B., B.S., McGill U., Montreal, Que., Can., 1962; M.F.A., Yale U., 1966; m. Apr. 3, 1966; 1 dau., Gabrielle Gillian. Architect firms in N.Y.C., 1966—; architect Robert L. Steele, 1963—; v.p. Roblis Corp., 1969—; prin. works include Leather stocking Farm, Easton, N.Y., 1968, various residences. Mem. alumnae exec. com. Yale U., 1967—; chmn. class of 1966, Yale U., 1969. Mem. AIA, ASID. Republican. Jewish. Clubs: Yale (N.Y.C.), Women's League of Temple EmanuEl, 1965—.

STEELE, HILDA HODGSON, ret. home economist, educator; b. Wilmington, Ohio, Mar. 24, 1911; d. George and Mary Jane (Rolston) Hodgson; certificate Wilmington Coll., 1931, B.S., 1935; M.A. in Home Econs. Edn., Ohio State U., 1941; postgrad. Ohio U., 1954, Miami U., 1959; m. John C. Steele. Tchr., Brookville (Ohio) Elementary Sch., 1932-37; tchr. home econs., Lincoln Jr. High Sch., Dayton Public Schs., 1937-40, coordinator home econs. dept., travelling exptl. home econs. tchr., 1940-45, supr. home econs., 1945-81. Mem. Ohio Farm Electrification Com., 1964-66. Jr. adv. com. Montgomery County chpt. ARC, 1940-70; mem. town and country br. career com. Miami Valley br. YMCA, 1948-59; adv. bd. Dayton Sch. Practical Nursing, 1951—; adv. com. Dayton Miami Valley Hosp. Sch. Nursing, 1951-67; mem. child care adv. com. Central State U., 1973—; bd. dirs. mem. for youth group FHA-HERO of Ohio, 1979—; mem. legis. network com. Dept. Vocat. Home Econs., State of Ohio, 1979-81; mem. adv. com. community and home service Sinclair Community Coll. Mem. Montgomery County Nutrition Council (Dayton area. 1st vice-chmn. 1967), Am. (del. 1961-76), Ohio (chmn. elementary and secondary edn. com. 1947-51, co-chmn. ann. conv. 1961-77, mem. housing, equip. com. 1965-68), Dayton Met. (pres. 1949-50, 60-61) home econ. assns., Am. (life mem.), Ohio (Disting. Supr. Home Econs. award 1981), Western Ohio (sec. 1977) vocational assns., Am. Vocat. Home Econs. Assn., Nat., Ohio edn. assns., Dayton Sch. Adminstrs. Assn. (past sec., past v.p., pres. 1960-61), Dayton Sch. Mgmt. Assn. (program com. 1971), Elec. Women's Round Table, Ohio Assn. Childhood Edn. Mem. Ch. of Christ. Mem. Order Eastern Star. Club: Zonta (pres. Dayton 1950-52). Research in public sch. food habits, 1957. Home: 1443 State Route 380 Xenia OH 45385

STEELE, MILDRED ROMEDAHL, educator; b. Boone, Iowa, Jan. 13, 1924; d. Joe and Gladys (Cree) Romedahl; B.A., Simpson Coll., 1946; M.A., Drake U., Des Moines, 1968, Ed.S., U. Iowa, 1973, Ph.D. (Higher Edn. fellow), 1982; m. Otto S. Steele, Jr., Sept. 4, 1947; children—Martha Steele Knepper, John, Timothy. Instr. English, Des Moines Area Community Coll., 1972-73; instr. English, Drake U., 1973-77, asst. to v.p. acad. adminstrn. 1976-77; coordinator communications skills Central Coll., Pella, Iowa, 1977—, asst. prof. English, 1978—; cons., speaker in field. Grantee Drake U., 1974, 76, Central Coll., 1980. Mem. MLA, Nat. Council Tchrs. English, Iowa Council Tchrs. English, Conf. Coll. Composition and Communications, Writing Program Adminstrs., AAUW, Nat. Assn. Remedial/Devel. Studies in Postsecondary Edn., Pella Hist. Soc., Christian Benevolent Assn., Sigma Tau Delta, Pi Lambda Theta. Democrat. Methodist. Author articles in field. Home: 402 N Monroe St Monroe IA 50170 Office: Central Coll Pella IA 50219

STEELEYSMITH, DEBORAH LYGIA, ednl. adminstr.; b. N.Y.C., Oct. 6, 1951; d. Ellis Robert and Deressa Doris (Moultrie) Steeley; B.A. in Psychology, Coll. Mt. St. Vincent, 1974; M.S.Ed., Fordham U., 1981; m. Allan David Smith, Oct. 14, 1978. Mental health counselor Harlem Hosp., N.Y.C., 1973-74, Project Create, N.Y.C., 1974-77; tng. specialist N.Y. State Bur. Tng. and Resource Devel., N.Y.C., 1978-82; dir. tng. and staff devel. Manhattan Psychiat. Center, N.Y. State Office Mental Health, 1982—. Cons. Nat. Inst. Drug Abuse, Adelphi U. Nat. Tng. Inst., others, 1977—; Active PBS-Channel 13, N.Y.C., 1971—. Cert. trainer Nat. Drug Abuse Tng. Center. Mem. N.Y. Zool. Soc., Planetary Soc., Am. Soc. Tng. and Devel. Democrat. Office: Ward's Island New York NY 10035

STEEMER, ALMETA DANIELS, health care exec.; b. Montgomery, Ala., Mar. 30, 1924; d. Roosevelt and Marie (Glenn) Daniels; student Ala. Tchrs. Coll., 1940-41, Clark Coll., Atlanta, 1941-42; grad. Homer G. Phillips Hosp. Sch. Med. Record Sci., St. Louis, 1960; B.A., Roosevelt U., 1974, M.P.A., 1980; m. Herbert Smith, Feb. 12, 1944 (div.); children—Michele Adrian Smith Johnson, Michael Julian Smith, Marcia Juanyta Smith Lanier; m. 2d, Elwood Steemer, Dec. 23, 1961 (dec. 1968). Dir. med. record dept. U. Nebr. Hosp., Omaha, 1960-63, Nat. Jewish Hosp., Denver, 1963-66, Fitzsimmons Army Hosp., Denver, 1966-69, Wright Patterson AFB Hosp., Dayton, Ohio, 1969-71; dir. med. records systems Charles R. Drew Neighborhood Health Center, Dayton, 1969-72; med. record cons. HEW Regional Office, Chgo., 1972—; evaluator State Health Dept. Survey Agys. Mem. Am. Med. Record Assn., Nat. Assn. Health Service Execs. Mem. Unity Ch. Contbr. articles to profl. publs. Home: 9252 S Michigan Ave Chicago IL 60619 Office: 175 W Jackson St Chicago IL 60604

STEFFEN, SHARRON VERLAIN, govt. adminstr.; b. Hillsboro, Oreg., Oct. 12, 1940; d. David Betrand and Marguerite Lucille (Carpenter) Heidinger; student Walla Walla Coll., 1958-61; m. Donald Roderick Steffen, July 28, 1961; 1 dau., Teresa Ann. Asst. fire underwriter Internat. Underwriters Am., Walla Walla, 1961-63; clk. Walla Walla dist. C.E., 1963-70, Bonneville Power Adminstrn., Walla Walla, 1970-74, adminstrv. technician, 1974-80, transmission maintenance asst., 1980—, fed. womens program mgr., 1976-80; Owner Tole-N-Things. Mem. Federally Employed Women (treas. 1982-83), Walla Walla Bus. and Profl. Women's Club (pres. 1978-80), Nat. Soc. Tole and Decorative Painters. Home: 960 Brickner Rd College Place WA 99324 Office: PO Box 1518 101 W Poplar St Walla Walla WA 99362

STEFFENS, DOROTHY RUTH, coll. ofcl.; b. N.Y.C., May 5, 1921; d. Saul M. and Pearl Y. (Reiter) Cantor; B.S., City Univ. N.Y., 1941; M.S., Temple U., 1962; Ph.D. in Polit. Economy, Susan B. Anthony U., 1982; m. Jerome Steffens, Nov. 19, 1940; children—Heidi Sue, Nina Ellen. Economist, U.S. Bur. Labor Stats., 1941-42; economist Nat. War Labor Bd., 1942-44; labor rep. United Elec., Radio and Machine Workers Am., 1944-46; instr. Temple U., 1954-57; lectr. U. Md., 1957-60; dir. Quaker Seminar Program, 1959-61; conf. dir. United Planning Orgn., Washington, 1967-68; dir. tng. Nat. Council Negro Women, Washington, 1967-68; exec. dir. Women Internat. League for Peace and Freedom, Phila., 1971-77; exec. dir. Fund for Open Info. and Accountability, Inc., N.Y.C., 1978-80; conf. dir. Haverford (Pa.) Coll., 1980—; cons. in field. Bd. dirs. Fund for Open Info., N.Y.C. N.Y. State Regents scholar, 1937-41; U.S. C. of C. scholar, 1937-41; Disting. Pa. Woman of Yr. citation, 1977; Disting. Service award U.S. sect. Women's Internat. League for Peace and Freedom, 1977. Democrat. Quaker. Contbr. in field. Home: PO Box 97 Douglassville PA 19518 Office: Haverford College Haverford PA 19041

STEHLIN, SAUNDRA ROSE, dental lab. technician; b. Cin., Oct. 7, 1953; d. Wilbur William and Mary Louise (Ollier) S.; grad. in dental tech., Career Acad., 1972; student U. Cin., 1976-79. Dental technician Towne Dental Lab., Racine, Wis., 1972-73, Artizan Dental Lab., Cin., 1973-77; owner, operator S S Dental Lab., Cin., 1977—. Cert. Nat. Bd. Dental Labs. Mem. Greater Dental Lab. Assn. (treas. 1980), Soc. Occlusal Studies, Nat. Assn. Female Execs. Club: Bus. and Profl. Women's. Office: 5233 Glenway Ave Cincinnati OH 45238

STEIDINGER, ANNE, med. social worker; b. Wilsonville, Ala., Sept. 2, 1949; d. Wesley Reid and Anne (Bell) Smith; B.S.W., U. Montevallo (Ala.), 1971; m. Warren Barber Steidinger, Sept. 2, 1967; children—Warren Barber, Wendy Jenae. Med. social worker U. Ala. Hosp., Birmingham, 1971—, also counselor heart transplant patients and family, tchr. patient and family edn. class cardiac patient and family. Mem. Nat. Assn. Social Workers, Med. Social Service Orgn., Ala. Soc. Hosp. Social Workers. Club: Birmingham Pilot (corr. sec. 1980). Home: 2956 Pine Haven Dr Mountain Brook AL 35223 Office: 619 S 19th St Social Service Dept Birmingham AL 35233

STEIGER, DONNA MARIE, travel and tourism adminstr.; b. Fort Scott, Kans., Dec. 12, 1921; d. Donald and Helen V. (Matthewson) Pickard; B.A. in Drama and Bus., U. Kans., 1942; student Theatre Arts Colony, 1945-47; m. Nathan Bernard Steiger, July 5, 1952; 1 son, Bradley Joseph. Vice pres., co-propr. Travel Advisors, Sunnyvale, Calif., 1958-65; mgr. Edmonds Travel, Inc., 1966-69; nat. conv. sales dir. and area mgr. Loyal Travel, Inc. div. Greyhound Corp., Seattle, 1972-77; propr., pres. Northwest Hosts Conv. and Tour Corp., Seattle, 1977-79; pres. Travel Central Tng. Sch. Inc., Seattle, 1977—; dean of travel and tourist Travel U., Colorado Springs, 1979-81; lectr. and trainer in customer service Mexicana Airlines Inc., Los Angeles, 1979-81; tchr. drama and speech San Francisco Center for the Blind, 1949-52; actress San Jose (Calif.) Light Opera, 1963-66; founder Los Gatoes Community Theatre, Los Gatos, 1962, actress, 1962-75; adv. bd. travel curriculum Edmonds Community Coll., 1972-78. Mem. Pacific Area Travel Assn., Am. Soc. Travel Agts., Washington Soc. Assn. Execs., Am. Soc. Tng. and Devel., Hotel Sales Mgrs. Assn., Travellarians (founder Seattle chpt. 1972). Home: PO Box 2624 Lynnwood WA 98036 Office: 530 Joseph Vance Bldg Seattle WA 98101

STEIN, ADLYN ROBINSON (MRS. HERBERT ALFRED STEIN), jewelery co. exec.; b. Pitts., May 8, 1908; d. Robert Stewart and Pearl (Geiger) Robinson; Mus.B., Pitts. Mus. Inst., U. Pitts., 1928; m. J. Francis Hollearn, 1929 (dec.); children—Adlyn (Mrs. Brandon J. Hickey), Frances (Mrs. Ralph A. Gleim); m. 2d, Allen Burnett Williams, Dec. 5, 1955 (dec.); m. 3d, Herbert Alfred Stein, Nov. 28, 1963; 1 adopted dau., Rachel Lynn (Mrs. Stephen M. Kampfer). Treas., R.S. Robinson, Inc., Pitts., 1947—. Mem. Pitts. Symphony Soc., Tuesday Musical Club, Pitts.; mem. women's com. Cleve. Symphony. Mem. D.A.R. Republican. Episcopalian. Clubs: Duquesne, University, Lakewood Country; Clifton; South Hills Country. Home: 22200 Lake Rd Cleveland OH 44116 Office: Clark Bldg Pittsburgh PA 15222

STEIN, ADRIENNE, lawyer; b. N.Y.C., Nov. 15, 1924; d. Isidore and Lena (Florea) Bakst; B.B.A., City U. N.Y., 1944; J.D., Pacific Coast U., 1967; m. Jack M. Stein, June 18, 1946; children—Gilbert, Peggy, Harvey. Admitted to Calif. bar, 1967, since practiced in Long Beach; asso. firm Gyler & Gottlieb, Inc., Long Beach, 1967-73; partner firm Gottlieb, Gottlieb & Stein, 1974—. Past pres. Long Beach Jewish Community Center; bd. dirs. Long Beach Jewish Community Fedn., Long Beach chpt. ACLU. Mem. Calif., Los Angeles County, Long Beach bar assns. Office: 675 E Wardlow Rd Long Beach CA 90807

STEIN, BLANCHE, lawyer; b. Chgo., Apr. 4, 1922; d. Abe and Ida (Mash) Stein; B.A., U. Chgo., 1943; J.D., Columbia U., 1948; m. Philip H. Vision, Sept. 30, 1967. Admitted to Oreg. bar, 1949, D.C. bar, 1950; house counsel Goldblatt Bros. Dept. Stores, Chgo., 1950-51; dir. sta. relations Keystone Broadcasting System, Inc., Chgo., 1952-60; sr. atty. FTC, Chgo., 1961-80; adminstrv. law judge Office of Hearings and Appeals, Social Security Adminstrn., Chgo., 1980—. Mem. Am. Bar Assn., D.C. Bar Assn., Oreg. Bar Assn., Phi Beta Kappa. Office: Office of Hearings and Appeals Social Security Adminstrn 55 E Monroe St Chicago IL 60603

STEIN, ELLEN GAIL, urban planner; b. N.Y.C., May 19, 1951; d. Manuel W. and Bella (Skutel) Stein; B.A., SUNY, Stony Brook, 1972; M.U.P., Hunter Coll., 1976. Sr. research assoc. Nassau Suffolk (N.Y.) Regional Med. Program, 1976-77; sr. planner N.Y.C. Dept. Correction, 1977-79; group leader criminal justice Mayor's Office Ops., N.Y.C., 1979-81, dep. asst. dir. citywide spl. projects, 1981, dir. citywide audit implementaion, 1981—. Mem. Am. Soc. for Pub. Adminstrn., Am. Planning Assn. Home: 67 Park Terr E New York NY 10034 Office: 100 Church St New York NY 10007 *

STEIN, GERTRUDE EMILIE, educator, soprano, pianist; b. Ironton, Ohio; d. S.A. and Emilie M. (Pollach) Stein; Mus.B., Capitol Coll., 1927; B.A., Wittenberg Coll., 1929, M.A., 1931, B.S. in Edn., 1945; Ph.D., U. Mich., 1948; piano and voice student Cin. Coll. Conservatory Music. Music supr. Centralized County Schs. Ohio, Williamsburg, 1932-37; dir. jr. high sch. music, 1937-68; mem. faculty Adult Evening Sch. Springfield (Ohio) Public Schs., 1951-68; head dept. music, asso. prof. piano and music edn. Tex. Luth. Coll., Seguin, 1948-49. Donor, founder Rev. Dr. and Mrs. S.A. Stein Meml. Funds, 1955—. Mem. AAUW, Am. Symphony Orch. League, Nat., Ohio edn. assns., Asso. Council Arts, Met. Opera Guild, Assn. Tchr. Educators, Am. Film Inst., Ohio Music Tchrs. Assn., Nat. Story League, Music Tchrs. Nat. Assn., Music Educators Nat. Conf., N.Y. Writers' Guild (Local pres.), Nat. Assn. Schs. Music, Nat. Fedn. Music Clubs (spl. mem. Ohio, Tex.), Amateur Chamber Music Players, Nat. Fedn. Bus. and Profl. Women, Zonta Internat., Phi Kappa Phi, Pi Lambda Theta. Lutheran. Contbr. articles to profl. jours. Home: 133 N Lowry Ave Springfield OH 45504

STEIN, GLADYS MARIE, pianist, educator; b. nr. Meadville, Pa., Oct. 19, 1900; d. Henry and Albertha (Hood) Stein; grad. Pa. Coll. Music, 1922, New Eng. Conservatroy Music, 1924; grad. Aeolian Hall Sch. Music Research, 1927; pvt. student of pipe-organ and violin. Pvt. tchr. of piano, Meadville, 1921-22, Boston, 1923-24, Erie, Pa., 1925-29; organizer, dir. Stein Sch. Music, Erie, 1930-50; pvt. tchr., Erie, 1950—; lectr. on rhythm band for Ludwig & Ludwig Co., 1936-45, also author rhythm band book Tuned Time Bell, 1936, Rhythm Band Instr., 1936; author articles, stories for Kindergarten-Primary mag., Erie Daily Times, Christian Sci. Monitor, Music Tchrs. Rev., Etude mag., others, 1927—; condr. piano tchr. workshops; trained and directed children in radio programs, 1928-35. Mem. Music Tchrs. Nat. Assn., Pa. (Distinguished Service award 1973), Erie (organizer 1970. pres. 1970-72, certification officer 1972—), music tchrs. assns., Internat. Platform Assn., Nat., Walnut Creek rifle assns. Author: Keyboard Tunes, 1949; composer numerous piano pieces, also for rhythm bands. Address: 427 W 31st St Erie PA 16508

STEIN, SANDRA MERLE, civic worker; b. Tucson, Sept. 23, 1942; d. Norman J. and Rhoda Leona (Hayutin) Fuchs; B.A. in Edn., U. Colo., 1964; m. Marvin N. Stein, Oct. 24, 1964; children—Shari Lynn, Mindy Kay. Pres., Pueblo (Colo.) Newcomers Club, 1965-66, Temple Emmanuel Sisterhood, 1966-68, Pueblo Met. Mus. Aux., 1969-71, Pueblo Jr. League, 1980—, Rotary Ann Club, Pueblo, 1969-70; trustee, pres. aux. St. Mary Corwin Hosp., Pueblo, 1966-70; pres., bd. dirs. Pueblo Symphony Guild, 1973-76; chmn. for dinner Nat. Jewish Hosp., Denver, 1972-75; bd. dirs. Parkview Hosp. Found., 1976-80; chmn. bd. Sangre de Cristo Arts Conf., 1977-79, Pueblo United Fund, 1968; v.p. Pueblo Symphony Assn., 1979-80, Pueblo chpt. Am. Cancer Soc., 1969-74, Pueblo chpt. Am. Heart Assn., 1970-75; sec., bd. dirs. Pueblo Therapy Center, 1969-73, Sacred Heart Home, Pueblo, 1969-73; adv. bd. PBS Sta. KTSC, 1978-80, auction '77 chmn.; sec.-treas. Stein Food Co., Inc., 1979-80. Recipient Community Service medal U. Colo. Alumni Assn., 1975, Community Service award U. So. Colo., 1975; named Colo. Stylemaker of Yr., 1978. Mem. Pueblo Creative Arts Alliance (founder). Clubs: Pueblo Country, Minnequa. Address: 109 Cornell Circle Pueblo CO 81005

STEINBACHER, MARTHA JANE, civic worker; b. Los Angeles, Aug. 29, 1921; d. Fred Drummond and Hazel Naomi (Gentry) Lutes; student Los Angeles public schs.; m. Edgar Lewis Steinbacher, May 9, 1943; children—Kathryn, Robert, Mary, Anne, Joseph, Michael, Thomas. Vol. dir. Pioneer Mus., Sweet Home, Oreg., 1976; pres. Archdiocesan Council Cath. Women, Portland, Oreg., 1974-76; chmn. bd. dirs. Linn County ARC, 1979-81; mem. Portland Archdiocese Marriage and Family Bd., 1980-83; mem. Am. Field Service Com., 1969-79. Named Oreg. Merit Mother, 1977, Woman of Yr., Sweet Home Bus. and Profl. Women, 1979. Republican. Author: Echoes from East Linn County, 1979. Home: 26262 Fern Ridge Rd Sweet Home OR 97386 Office: 746 Long St Sweet Home OR 97386

STEINBERG, MERRY LANDIS, art gallery dir.; b. Phila., Aug. 17, 1940; d. Samuel Joseph and Marion (Kaysen) Landis; B.A. with honors in History, U. Pa., 1962; M.A., U. Md., 1963; postgrad. U. Mex., UCLA, 1964-65; m. Alan Steinberg, Dec. 12, 1968; children—Alan Randall, Victoria. Social studies tchr. Phila., 1964; teaching asst. UCLA, 1965; social studies tchr., Phila., 1966; asst. to adminstr. Children's Bur., HEW, Washington, 1967; investigator U.S. Dept Labor, College Park, Md., 1967-69; co-dir. Open Space/Fine Art Resources, Allentown, Pa., 1980—. Mem. Mayoral Adv. Com. on Consumer Protection, Ft. Lee, N.J., 1972-73; sec. Bergen County Women's Polit. Caucus, 1970, coordinator, 1971, newsletter editor, 1972; founder Women's Polit. Caucus of Lehigh Valley, 1975; convener Ft. Lee Action for Individual Rights, 1971; sec. Allentown NOW, 1974; vice chmn. Allentown Human Relations Commn., 1977—; chmn. bd. dirs. Turning Point of Lehigh Valley, Inc., 1979—; mem. Mayor's Adv. Com. for the Arts, Allentown, 1982. 1982). Mem. Nat. Women's Studies Assn., Allentown-Lehigh County C. of C. (exec. women's task force 1982). Office: 808 Hamilton Mall Allentown PA 18101

STEINBERG, SUE KNIGHT, garment mfg. co. exec.; b. Haleyville, Ala., Dec. 23, 1934; d. Talmadge M. and Gladys (Cummins) Knight; grad. Haleyville Public Schs., 1953; m. Jack J. Steinberg, Dec. 31, 1956; 1 dau., Mindy Lou Steinberg Agler. With Mojud Mills, Decatur, Ala., 1954-55; with Waynesboro Garment Co. (Ga.), 1956-57; payroll clk. Burke Mfg. Co., Waynesboro, 1965-67, prodn. mgr., 1967-76, sec.-treas., 1976—. Mem. vocat. tng. com. Burke County Schs., 1975. Mem. Am. Apparel Mfrs. Assn. Jewish. Office: Burke Mfg Co PO Box 613 Waynesboro GA 30830

STEINBRING, YVONNE JEANNE, orgn. extension agt.; b. Isanti, Minn., Aug. 31, 1944; d. Alton E. and Eva Henrietta (Boettcher) Steinbring; B.S., U. Minn., 1969, M.S., 1980. Instr. fashion merchandising Alexandria (Minn.) Area Vocat. Inst., 1970-73; Rice county extension agt. Minn. Extension Service, Faribault, 1973-81; 4-H home adv., Yreka, Calif., 1981—. Mem. Nat. Assn. Extension Home Economists, Minn. Assn. Extension Home Economists (pres. 1980), Calif. Assn. Extension Home Economists, Minn. Weavers Guild, Epsilon Sigma Phi. Office: 1655 S Main Yreka CA 96097

STEINBRONN, KAREN KRAEMER, pathologist, educator; b. Phoenix, Apr. 4, 1949; d. Harold A. and Lillian J. Kraemer; B.S., No. Ariz. U., 1971; M.D., U. Ariz., 1975; m. Del V. Steinbronn, June 30, 1973; 1 dau., Valerie. Research assoc. dept. surgery U. Ariz. Health Sci. Ctr., Tucson, 1975-77, resident in anatomic and clin. pathology, 1977-81, asst. prof. pathology, 1981—; pathologist VA Hosp., 1981—. Diplomate Am. Bd. Pathology. Mem. Am. Soc. Clin. Pathologists, Coll. Am. Pathologists, Ariz. Soc. Pathologists, AMA, Ariz. Med. Assn., Pima County Med. Soc., Am. Med. Women's Assn. Contbr. articles to med. jours. Office: VA Hosp Tucson AZ 85723

STEINECKE, MAUREEN KANE, assn. exec.; b. Boston, Dec. 18, 1932; d. Martin and Helen (Leonard) Kane; A.B. in Am. Lit., Middlebury Coll., 1954; M.S. in L.S., Pratt Inst., 1956; m. Charles Steinecke, July 7, 1956; children—John, Ann, Patricia. Asst. to coordinator children's services D.C. Pub. Library, Washington, 1956-59; free-lance indexer, 1959-65; exec. dir. Md. Assn. Bds. of Edn., Annapolis, 1978—. Vice pres. LWV of Prince George's County, 1971-73; mem. Prince George's County Bd. Edn., 1973-78; bd. mgmt. Prince George's County YMCA, 1979-82. Named Prince Georgian of yr., Sentinel Newspapers, 1977. Mem. Am. Soc. Assn. Execs., Md. Soc. Assn. Execs., Md. Congress Parents and Tchrs. (hon. life). Democrat. Episcopalian. Office: 130 Holiday Ct Suite 105 Annapolis MD 21401

STEINEM, GLORIA, writer, editor, lectr.; b. Toledo, Mar. 25, 1934; d. Leo and Ruth (Nuneviller) Steinem; B.A., Smith Coll., 1956; postgrad. (Chester Bowles Asian fellow), India, 1957-58; D. Human Justice, Simmons Coll., 1973. Co-dir., dir., ednl. found. Ind. Research Service, Cambridge, Mass. and N.Y.C., 1959-60; editorial asst., editorial cons., contbg. editor, free-lance writer various nat. and N.Y.C. publs., 1960—; co-founder, contbg. editor New York mag., 1968—; feminist lectr., 1969—; co-founder, Ms. mag., 1971, editor, from 1971, columnist, 1980—. Active various civil rights and peace campaigns including United Farmworkers, Vietnam War Tax Protest, Com. for the Legal Def. of Angela Davis (treas., 1971-72); active polit. campaigns of Adlai Stevenson, Robert Kennedy, Eugene McCarthy, Shirley Chisholm, George McGovern. Co-founder, chairperson bd. Women's Action Alliance, from 1970; convenor, mem. nat. advisory com. Nat. Women's Polit. Caucus, 1971—; co-founder, mem. bd. Ms. Found. for Women, 1972—; founding mem. Coalition of Labor Union Women, 1974; mem. Internat. Women's Yr. Commn., 1977. Recipient Penney-Missouri Journalism award, 1970; Ohio Gov.'s award for Journalism, 1972; Bill of Rights award ACLU of So. Calif., 1975; named Woman of Yr. McCall's mag., 1972; fellow Woodrow Wilson Internat Center for Scholars, 1977. Mem. Nat. Orgn. for Women, AFTRA, Nat. Press Club, Soc. Mag. Writers, Authors' Guild, P.E.N., Phi Beta Kappa. Author: The Thousand Indias, 1957; The Beach Book, 1963. Contbr. to various anthologies. Address: Nat Women's Polit Caucus 1411 K St NW Suite 1110 Washington DC 20005 *

STEINER, DIANA, concert violinist; b. Portland, Oreg., July 17, 1932; d. Ferenz and Elizabeth (Levy) Steiner; diploma Curtis Inst. Music, Phila., 1949, Mus.B., 1957; M.M., U. So. Calif., 1970; m. Edward R. Dickstein, Dec. 13, 1956; children—Sallie Marcia. Concert violinist, tchr. Columbia Artists Mgmt., 1953-56; violin soloist at festivals, including Tanglewood, Marlboro, Hollywood Bowl, others, 1950-75, with maj. symphony orchs., including N.Y. Philharmonic, Phila. Orch., others, 1943-80; rec. artist Orion Records, 1974—; mem. Steiner-Berfield Trio, 1966—; faculty Loyola Marymount U., Los Angeles; tchr.; writer ednl. books for performing students; books include: Violin Classics, Books I and II, 1972; String Orchestra Classics, Book I, 1975, Book II, 1979; Lessons with the Master, NFMC Showcase, 1960; condr. master classes and workshops; host, producer radio show Air for Strings. Bd. dirs. Curtis Inst. Music. Recipient W.W. Naumburg Found. award, 1952, Young Artists award Nat. Fedn. Music Clubs, 1959. Mem. Curtis Alumni Assn. S.W., Curtis Alumni Assn. (nat. v.p.), Nat. Assn. Composers U.S.A. (nat. dir.), Nat. Fedn. Music Clubs, Music Tchrs. Nat. Assn., Am. String Tchrs. Assn., Am. Fedn. Musicians, Music Tchrs. Assn. Calif., Calif. Profl. Music Tchrs. Assn., Mu Phi Epsilon. office: 223 S Bundy Dr Los Angeles CA 90049

STEINER, GITTA HANA, composer, pianist, poetress; b. Prague, Czechoslovakia, Apr. 17, 1932; came to U.S., 1939, naturalized, 1945; d. Eric Erhard and Erna (Bondy) S.; diploma in composition (Abraham Ellstein scholar) Julliard Sch. Music, 1963, Mus.B., 1967, M.S., 1969; studied with Vincent Persichetti, Gunther Shuller, Elliot Carer. Compositions include: Suite for Flute, Clarinet and Bassoon, 1958; Suite for Orch., 1958; Three Songs for Medium Voice, 1960; Three Pieces for Piano, 1961; Concerto for Violin and Orch., 1963; String Trio, 1964; Pages From a Summer Jour., 1963; Piano Sonata, 1964; Fantasy for Clarinet and Piano, 1964; Brass Quintet, 1964; Jouissance for Flute and Piano, 1965; Five Choruses, 1965; Movement for Eleven, 1966; Tetrark for String Orch., 1965; Fantasy Piece for Piano, 1966; Two Songs, 1966; Concerto for Piano and Orch., 1967; Refractions for Solo Violin, 1967; String Quartet, 1968; Percussion Quartet, 1968; Three Pieces for Solo Vibraphone, 1968; Concert Piece for Seven, 1968; Interludes for Voice And Vibraphone, 1968; Concert Piece for Seven II, 1968; Trio for Two Percussionists and Piano, 1969; Four Bagatelles for Solo Vibraphone, 1969; Five Poems for Mixed Chorus, 1970; Duo for Horn and Piano, 1970; Four Songs for Medium Voice and Vibes, 1970; Settings for Chorus, 1970; Duo for Cello and Percussion, 1971; Percussion Music for Two, 1971; Trio for Voice Piano and Percussion, 1971; Four Choruses, 1972; Four Settings for A Capella Chorus, 1973; New Poems for Voice and Vibes, 1974; Dream Dialogues for Voice and Percussion, 1974; Duo for Vibe and Marimba, 1974; Cantos, 1975; Dialogue for Two Percussionists, 1975; Music for Four Players, 1976; Eight Miniatures, 1976; Night Music, 1977; 8 Miniatures for Vibraphone, Fantasy for Solo Percussion, Night Music for Marimba Solo, 1977; Fantasy for Percussion, 1978; Contemporary Solos for Vibe and Marimba, 1979; Vibe Sonata, 1980; 2 vols. piano music, 1982, Duo (2), 1982; commd. by N.Y. Percussion Trio, 1969, by mems. of Boston Symphony Orch., 1971, by various soloists; works included in Lincoln Center Repertoire Project, 1967; performed orchestral and chamber music throughout U.S., abroad; pvt. tchr. piano, 1960—; faculty Bklyn. Conservatory Music, 1963-65; dir. Contemporary Ensemble, 1982; co-dir. Composer's Group for Internat. Performance, 1968. Recipient Gretchaninoff Meml. prize for string orch. work, 1966; Marion Freschl award for vocal works with original texts, 1966-67; Standard Ann. award ASCAP, 1972—; awarded Composer's Forum, Donell Library, 1966; Berkshire Music Center, Tanglewood fellow, 1967. Address: 71-81 244th St Douglaston NY 11362

STEINER, GLORIA LITWIN, psychologist; b. Newark, Oct. 12, 1922; d. David and Minna (Krasner) Litwin; B.A., U. Pa., 1944; M.S., CCNY, 1956; Ed.D., Columbia U., 1965; m. Charles Steiner, Aug. 29, 1942; children—Charles, Susan, Jeanne. Prof. psychology Kean Coll., Union, N.J., 1971-78; cons. staff United Hosps., Newark, 1965—; dir. tng. N.J. Center Family Studies, Chatham, 1976—; clin. asso. prof. psychiatry N.J. Med. Sch., Newark, 1978—; sec. N.J. State Bd. Psychol. Examiners, 1979. Mem. Am. Psychol. Assn., N.J. Psychol. Assn., N.J. Acad. Psychology, N.J. Acad. Medicine, Acad. Psychosomatic Medicine, Am. Orthopsychiat. Assn., Am. Assn. Marital and Family Therapy. Home and Office: 35 Sequoia Dr Watchung NJ 07060

STEINER, NANCY MILLER, educator, civic worker; b. Denver, June 6, 1930; d. Philip and Ruchiel C. (Simmons) Miller; B.A., U. Denver, 1951, cert. in edn., 1963, M.A., 1967; Ph.D., U. Colo., 1977; m. Jay A. Steiner, Aug. 24, 1956 (dec.); children—Sally, Susan, Robert. Credit mgr. Miller Stockman, Denver, 1952-53; asst. to asst. comptroller Katz Agy., N.Y.C., 1953-56; asso. prof. reading Met. State Coll., Denver, 1969-79; coordinator tchr. edn. Loretto Heights Coll., Denver, 1980; reading and study skills instr. Arapahoe Community Coll., 1981; with systems reorgn. dept. Miller Internat., 1982—; cons. adult ednl. tutorial Colo. Right to Read. Sec., Police-Community Coop. Endeavor, 1972-75; chairperson regional bd. dirs. Anti-Defamation League of B'nai B'rith, 1975-80. mem. nat. exec. com., 1976—, vice chairperson nat. program com., 1976-78, Western Area chmn. community service div., 1978-80; apptd. by gov. to Colo. Career Info. Service, sec., 1979, sec., 1979—; bd. dirs. Rose Meml. Hosp., Nat. Conf. Soviet Jewry (exec. com.), Allied Jewish Fedn. Mem. Internat., Nat., Colo. (chmn. coll. com. 1974-76),

Denver (dir. 1975-76) reading assns., Nat. Council Tchrs. of English, Western Reading Coll. Assn. (state chmn.), Colo. Lang. Arts Soc., NEA, Colo. Edn. Assn. (dir. 1977), Kappa Delta Pi. Democrat. Jewish. Home: 2901 S Fillmore Way Denver CO 80210

STEINER, ROBERTA PEARL, assn. adminstr.; b. N.Y.C., July 11, 1948; d. Charles and Ethel (Fier) Steiner; B.A., U. Calif., Berkeley, 1969, M.L.S., 1973. Community resource specialist Sch. Resource Vols., Berkeley public schs., 1969-70; chief librarian Am.Insts. for Research, Palo Alto, Calif., 1973-77; asso. in bibliography, instr. Library Sch., U. Calif., Berkeley, 1975-77; Central Pacific regional dir. B'nai B'rith Women, Daly City, Calif., 1977—. Mem. Am. Soc. Assn. Execs., Conf. Jewish Communal Service, Phi Beta Kappa. Jewish. Home: 57 Wilshire Ave Daly City CA 94015

STEINHAUSER, CYNTHIA SUZANNE, psychiat. social worker; b. N.Y.C., Apr. 9, 1950; d. Carl Philip and Marie (Bauer) Steinhauser; B.A. cum laude, Park Coll., 1972; postgrad. Goethe Institut, Schwabisch Hall, W. Ger., 1972; M.S.W., Tulane U., 1974; postgrad. N.Y. Center Psychoanalytic Tng., 1975-78. Psychiat. technician N.Y. Hosp., Cornell Med. Center, White Plains, 1973; lectr. Weight Watchers Internat., Oakland, N.J., 1978—; program dir. Acad. House Partial Hospitalization Program, Jersey City, 1975—; field instr. Kean Coll., Union, N.J., 1979—. Cert. social worker, N.Y. Mem. Nat. Assn. Social Workers, Acad. Cert. Social Workers, Delta Tau Kappa. Democrat. Lutheran. Home: 564 Godwin Ave Midland Park NJ 07432 Office: 308 Academy St Jersey City NJ 07306

STEINKE, PATRICIA JEANNE, orch. adminstr.; b. Omaha, Apr. 8, 1947; d. Frederic Dennison and Betty Elizabeth (Kellogg) Hemphill; B.A., U. Nebr., 1971, postgrad., 1977—; children—Laura, Benjamin and Jonathan (twins). Claims sec. State Farm Ins., 1968-69; sec. dept. English, U. Nebr., Lincoln, 1970-72; exec. dir. mem. Lincoln Symphony Orch., 1979—. Mem. Trenton (Nebr.) Sch. Bd., 1975-77; mem. Trenton Library Bd., 1976-77. Mem. Bus. & Profl. Women, Am. Symphony Orch. League. Office: 1315 Sharp Bldg Lincoln NE 68508 *

STEINMAN, SHERRY FRANCESCA POULOS, state ofcl.; b. Chgo., Nov. 21, 1951; d. Hercules Paul and Shirley (Murphy) Poulos; B.A. in Journalism, Drake U., Des Moines, 1973; m. Feb. 13, 1982. With Sta. KCBC, Des Moines, 1973-74; continuity dir. Sta. WCLT, Newark, Ohio, 1974-77; communications officer Central Ohio Rural Consortium Employment and Tng. Adminstrn., Newark, 1977—; freelance writer, design cons., 1972—. Chmn. publicity Licking County (Ohio) Census Com., 1980. Recipient Outstanding Scholastic Achievement in Advt. award Advt. Women Des Moines, 1973; named Newark Outstanding Young Career Woman, Bus. and Profl. Women Newark, 1982; Outstanding Young Woman of Licking County, Jaycee-ettes, 1982. Mem. Internat. Assn. Bus. Communicators, Ohio Manpower Assn., Newark Bus. and Profl. Women's Club. Newark C. of C., Gamma Alpha Chi. Office: 33 W Main St Newark OH 43055

STEINMANN, ELCENA TAGGART, educator; b. Seattle, May 15, 1915; d. William John and Margaret Louise (Shadle) Taggart; B.E., U. Wash., 1953, M.A., 1960; m. Samuel Algot Steinmann, Sept. 14, 1940; children—Elcena Olga Steinmann Standish, Margaret Louise Steinmann Irvine, Rae Christine Steinmann Allen. Sec., Wash. Athletic Club, Seattle, 1933-35; civil service clk. div. disbursements U.S. Treasury Dept., Washington, 1935-43; telephone operator Pacific N.W. Bell Telephone Co., Seattle, 1944-47; tchr. Seattle Public Schs., 1953—, Sch.-Age Parent Continuation High, 1973—; instr. Seattle Community Coll., 1962-65; prof. Everett Jr. Coll., 1965-66; advisor, instr. office mgmt. Seattle U., 1967-68; instr. Shoreline Community Coll., 1968-70; tchr. Crittenton Home for Unwed Mothers, 1968-73. Trustee, Kalm Brae Christian Sch., Redmond, Wash.; mem. exec. bd. Wash. Alliance Concerned with Sch.-Age Parents, 1975—. Mem. NEA, Nat. Ret. Tchrs. Assn., Nat. Bus. Edn. Assn., AAUP, Am. Assn. Higher Edn., Am. Bus. Communication Assn., Am. Vocat. Assn., Wash. Edn. Assn., Seattle Tchrs. Assn., Western Bus. Edn. Assn., Wash. Bus. Edn. Assn., Western Wash. Bus. Edn. Assn., Wash. Vocat. Assn., Council for Exceptional Children, U. Wash. Alumni Assn., Seattle U. Alumni Assn., Seattle and King County Mcpl. League, DAR, Pioneer Assn. State of Wash., Internat. Platform Assn., Delta Kappa Gamma, Club: Order Eastern Star. Home: 19623 27th Ave NW Seattle WA 98177

STEINMEIER, DOROTHY ELIZABETH, public relations cons.; b. Indpls., Dec. 2, 1916; d. Albert Lee and Fannie Elizabeth (Wilson) S.; student Butler U., 1934-37; B.A., U. Wis., 1938. Asso. editor The Hoosier Farmer, Ind. Farm Bur., Inc., Indpls., 1939-44; feature writer U.S. Army Public Info. Office, U.S. Constabulary, W.Ger., 1946-48; customer relations staff The Bookwalter Co., Indpls., 1948-56; editorial staff Indpls. Times, 1948; with Indpls. Star, 1956-60; coordinator mfr. dept. Bobbs-Merrill Co., Indpls., 1960-64; asso. dir. info. Ind. Dept. Commerce, Indpls., 1965-67; asst. editor, public relations staff Ind. Tchrs. Assn., Indpls., 1967-71; free lance writer, public relations cons., Indpls., 1971—. Democratic precinct committeewoman, 1977—; del. Dem. State Conv., 1978, 82; public relations dir. women's affairs Ind. Dem. Campaign Hdqrs., fall 1964; asst. in public relations legis. Ind. Dem. State Central Com., 1965. Mem. Women in Communications (pres. Indpls. chpt. 1954-55, Kleinhenz award 1979), Woman's Press Club Ind. (pres. 1972-74, Kate Milner Rabb award 1977), Women for Better Govt. (pres. 1977-79), Nat. Fedn. Press Women (regional dir. 1965-67, 75), Ind. Bus. Communicators, U. Wis. Alumni Assn., Indpls. Mus. Art, Women's Polit. Caucus, Sigma Kappa. Methodist. Address: 5821 Bywood Dr Indianapolis IN 46220

STEINMETZ, DEBORAH SUSAN, interior designer; b. New Orleans, Nov. 29, 1951; d. Donald Frederick and Estelle Margaret (Ulmer) Tossell; B.F.A., La. State U., 1973; m. Robert Steinmetz, Dec. 29, 1973. Interior designer David Grinnell Architect, 1973-75; ind. design cons., Columbus, Ga., 1975-77; designer Dameron-Pierson, New Orleans, 1977-79; v.p. interior design Interior Environments, Inc., New Orleans, 1979—; mem. interior design curriculum com. Dominican Coll., New Orleans, 1981-82; mem. interior design adv. com. Delgado Community Coll., New Orleans, 1982—. Mem. visual arts com. Contemporary Art Center, 1980-81. Mem. Am. Soc. Interior Designers (Presdl. citation; chmn. New Orleans assn. 1980-81, dir. La. chpt. 1982—, newsletter editor La. Chpt. 1982), Nat. Trust Hist. Preservation, La. Landmarks Soc. Roman Catholic. Home: 2850 Annunciation St New Orleans LA 70115 Office: 111 Rue Iberville Suite 707 New Orleans LA 70130

STEINMETZ, KAYE HERRMAN, state legislator Mo.; b. Kansas City, Mo., Mar. 5, 1938; d. Frederick R. and Ida Louise (Franklin) Herrman; A.A., Columbia (Mo.) Coll., 1958; postgrad. Mo. U.; m. C. Robert Steinmetz, Aug. 30, 1958; children—Mark, Steven, Richard, Stacey. Sports editor Rolla (Mo.) Daily News, 1950-55; nursey sch. mgr. Lucky Strike Lanes, Hazelwood, Mo., 1963-73; exec. v.p. Florissant Valley C. of C., Florissant, Mo., 1973-76; mem. Mo. Legislature from 57th dist., 1976—, mem. govt. rev., edn., coms., vice chmn. social services, and medicaid coms., mem. joint House and Senate met. airport com., task force on adoptions, coalition on foster care. Mem. Florissant Planning and Zoning bd., 1973-76; bd. dirs. Mo. Jr. Miss. Scholarship Program, United Way Greater St. Louis; mem. Gov.'s Conf. on Edn.; chmn. Florissant Sr. Citizens Council, 1972-76; mem. Florissant Community Betterment Com.; bd. dirs. Mo. PTA, 1973-77. Recipient several achievement awards from orgns.; Outstanding Young Woman, 1972; Woman of Yr., Florissant, 1975. Mem. Advt. Women St. Louis, Florissant Bus. and Profl. Women, St. Louis County League of Chambers. Democrat. Roman Catholic. Club Sorptimist Internat. Pres., founder Missourian Aid for Am. Indians mag. Office: State Capitol Room 103-B Jefferson City MO 65101 *

STEINMILLER, ANITA MARY, nurse; b. Pitts., Feb. 4, 1951; d. Henry James and Ann Frances S.; diploma Ohio Valley Gen. Hosp. Sch. Nursing, 1972; B.S.N. magna cum laude LaRoche Coll., 1981, B.A., 1979; postgrad. U. Pitts. 1981—. Staff nurse Ohio Valley Gen. Hosp., McKees Rocks Pa., 1972-75, patient care coordinator infection control, audit inservice edn., 1975-81, asst. dir. nursing, 1981—; vol. instr. nursing service ARC; vol. lectr. Am. Cancer Soc. Mem. Nat. Orgn. Practitioners in Infection Control, Ohio Valley Nurses Alumni Assn. Roman Catholic. Home: 334 Bascom Ave Pittsburgh PA 15214 Office: Ohio Valley Hosp Heckel Rd McKees Rocks PA 15136

STEMMER, HELEN MARIE, mfg. co. exec.; b. Utica, N.Y., June 22, 1928; d. Gerald Garfield and Christina Katherine (Rock) Coon; grad. public schs., Utica, N.Y., 1945; m. Donald Joseph Stemmer, Jan. 31, 1948; children—Dorothy Gail, Janet Marie, Paul Donald, Judith Ann. Keypunch operator, N.Y.C. R.R., Utica, and Griffith Air Base, Rome, N.Y., 1945-51; head cashier Oneida (N.Y.) Foodland, 1967-70; sr. clk., buyer GAF Corp., Vernon, N.Y., 1970-76; asst. buyer DND Teletronics, Utica, N.Y., 1978-79; purchasing agt. Divine Brothers Co., Utica, 1979—. Mem. Purchasing Mgmt. Assn. Utica, Rome and Mohawk Valley. Home: 36 Woodberry Rd New Hartford NY 13413 Office: 200 Seward Ave Utica NY 13503

STEMPNIAK, AGNES MARIE FOWLES, mcpl. ofcl.; b. Oak Park, Ill., Sept. 23, 1945; d. James A. and Agnes M. (Bruha) Fowles; B.S. in Journalism and Communications, U. Fla., Gainesville, 1967; M.P.A. with honors, Roosevelt U., Chgo., 1975; m. Martin J. Stempniak, May 8, 1982. Asst. account exec. Bozell & Jacobs, Inc., Chgo., 1967-69; mktg. asst. Oak Park Trust & Savs. Bank, 1969-70; public info. officer Village of Oak Park, 1970-75, adminstrv. asst. to village mgr., 1975-78, dir. personnel and communications, 1979—. Div. head Oak-Park-River Forest Community Chest, 1976; bd. dirs. Way Off Broadway Theatre Group, 1975-76; mem. Oak Park/River Forest Civic Theatre. Mem. Ill. League Municipal Employees (past pres. Oak Park), Internat. City Mgmt. Assn., Women in Communications, Women in Mgmt., Internat. Personnel Mgmt. Assn., Publicity Club Chgo. (Disting. Service award 1980, Spl. Person award 1982; dir. 1982—), Ill. Mgmt. Assts. Assn. Roman Catholic. Contbr. to Developing the Municipal Organization, 1974; contbr. articles to profl. jours. Home: 245 S Maple Ave Oak Park IL 60302 Office: 1 Village Hall Plaza Oak Park IL 60302

STENCHEVER, DIANE H., social worker; b. Buffalo, Aug. 10, 1933; d. Hanford Willard and Rose (Backer) Bilsky; B.S., U. Buffalo, 1955; M.S.W., U. Utah, 1975; m. Morton Albert Stenchever, June 19, 1955; children—Michael Alan, Marc Russell, Douglas Andrew. Pvt. practice marriage and family counseling, Seattle and Renton, Wash., 1976—; group leader Divorce Life Line. Mem. Nat. Assn. Social Workers. Club: Mercer Island Country. Author articles in field. Address: Suite 212 3216 NE 45th Seattle WA 98105

STENGLEIN, JANE, astrologer; b. Wilkes-Barre, Pa., Aug. 28, 1940; d. Stephen and Sophie (Garbartovich) Alba; grad. Coll. S.I., 1981; postgrad. L.I. U., 1982—; m. Barth John Stenglein, Oct. 20, 1962; children—Sandra Ann, Sharon Margaret, Bart John. Sec., Thomas & Betts Co., Elizabeth, N.J., 1958-63, 73-75; caseworker to case mgr. Anna Erika Home for Adults, S.I., N.Y., 1979—; now pres. bd. dirs., instr. S.I. Astrologers Guild; asst. to v.p. Great Eastern Assos., N.Y.C., 1981—. Mem. Am. Fedn. Astrologers (accredited advanced astrologer). Home: 60 Galloway Ave Staten Island NY 10302 Office: 110 Henderson Ave Staten Island NY 10301

STENROSE, MARIE DOYLE, nurse; b. Lowell, Mass., Aug. 20, 1917; d. Morill Joseph and Alberta Marie (Marquis) Doyle; R.N., B.S.N., Simmons Coll., 1945; postgrad. Boston U., 1947-48, U. Tex., El Paso, 1962-64; m. Arnold Wilhelm Stenrose, Oct. 16, 1945; children—Paul, Kenneth, Mark, Karen. Nursing arts instr. Simmons Coll., Boston, 1940-45, St. Joseph's Hosp., Lowell, Mass., 1940-45; clin. instr. Baylor U., Dallas, 1946; ednl. media coordinator Hotel Dieu Hosp., El Paso, 1963-72; ednl. media dir. nursing U. Tex., El Paso, 1972—, founder Microcomputer Research Lab., Microcomputer Users Lab. (both Coll. Nursing and Allied Health); leader workshops, insts., faculty inservice tng. on media in nursing; cons. instructional designs of Media Center. HEW grantee, 1974-77; HHS grantee, 1979-82. Mem. Am., Tex., Dist. 1 nurses assns., Assn. Ednl. Communication and Tech., Photog. Soc. Am., Health Edn. Media Assn. Republican. Roman Catholic. Co-inventor 3 obstet. simulators, pulse simulator, ear simulator, others; research on simulation labs. and peer-tutoring. Co-author: Compendium of Simulaids for Nursing Practice, 1982. Home: 5147 Timberwolf Dr El Paso TX 79903 Office: 1101 N Campbell St El Paso TX 79902

STEORTS, NANCY HARVEY, consumer affairs specialist; B.S., Syracuse U., 1959. Public relations coordinator Woodward & Lothrop Dept. Stores, Washington, 1958-61; home economist Washington Gas Light Co., 1961-64; sales asso. Naomi B. Faison, Inc., Realtors, Summit, N.J., 1967-68; staff asso. Com. for Exec. Reorgn. of Govt., Washington, 1971; asst. nat. dir. of vols., nat. dir. women's speakers bur. Nat. Presdl. Campaign, 1971-72; nat. dir. candlelight dinners Inaugural Com., 1972-73, vice-chmn., dir., 1981—; U.S. expositions officer Dept. Commerce, 1973; spl. asst. to sec. agr. for consumer affairs Dept. Agr., 1973-77; chmn. U.S. Consumer Product Safety Commn., 1981—; founder, pres. Nancy Harvey Steorts & Assos., Washington, nat. spokesman Procter and Gamble Ivory Centennial, closure com. Glass Packaging Inst.; co-host consumer segment Panorama TV Show, Sta. WTTG-TV, Washington; testifys on consumer issues to Congress and Exec. Dept. Dean Bernice M. Wright Guest Meml. lectr. Syracuse U., 1976. Mem. Montgomery County Commn. for Women, 72-74, Montgomery County Manpower Commn., 1973-74; pres. Welcome Wagon Clubs, Washington and Summit, 1965-69; chmn. fund raising benefits embassies of Iran, Turkey and Uruguay, 1968-70; del. Summit Community Council, 1964-66; bd. dirs. Women's Inst., Am. U.; active Conf. on Consumer Orgns., Nat. Consumers League; bd. dirs. Sumner Village Condominium Assn., Elem. Schs.; chmn., nat. adv. com. Flammable Fabrics Act, Consumer Product Safety Commn.; exec. com. Food Safety Council; dir. Women's Surrogate Program, Republican Nat. Com. and Reagan-Bush campaign, 1980-81; trustee Am. Nat. Standards Inst., Inc., Internat. Platform Assn. Recipient Selleck prize Syracuse U., 1959, Spl. award for consumer concern Nat. Diet Workshop, 1976, George Arents Pioneer medal Syracuse U., 1976. Mem. Nat. Council Career Women (pres., dir.), Soc. Consumer Affairs Profls. (dir.), Nat. Assn. Career Women (dir.), Nat. Press Club, Am. Home Econs. Assn., AAUW (pres., dir., chmn. nat. conv.), Inter-Am. Choral Soc. (dir.), Syracuse U. Alumni Assn. (past dir.). Contbr. articles on consumer subjects to profl. jours. Address: 1111 18th Street NW Washington DC 20207

STEPHANY, JUDITH BUCKLEY, state legislator; b. Jamaica, N.Y., June 1, 1944; d. John Aloysius and Agnes Estelle (Larmour) Buckley; B.S. in Econs., LeMoyne Coll., 1965; m. William A. Stephany, Sept. 3, 1966; children—David, Kathleen, Brian, Nicholas. Research economist Mfrs. Hanover Trust Co., N.Y.C., 1965-66; tchr. St. Elizabeth's Sch., Wilmington, Del., 1966-67; mem. Vt. Ho. of Reps., 1976—, vice chmn. judiciary com., 1979-80, clk. Democratic caucus, 1979-80, Dem. leader, 1981-82. Vice pres., treas. Howard Mental Health Services, 1979—; del. Dem. Nat. Conv., 1980. Mem. Vt. Fedn. Dem. Women, LWV (past chpt. dir.), Women of U. Vt., Pi Gamma Mu. Roman Catholic. Office: State House Montpelier VT 05602

STEPHEN, MAE, social psychologist; b. Manchester, N.H.; d. Simon Y. and Victoria (Saigh) Estfan; A.B., U. N.C., 1940; postgrad. U. Chgo., 1939-41, U. Buffalo, 1942, Am. U., 1959; children from former marriage—Anita Joan, Franklin David, Lisa Jeanne, Sharon E., Robert Michael. Group worker, Greensboro, N.C., 1936-37, Hiram House Settlement Camp, summer 1937; departmental asst. psychology dept. U. N.C., 1937-39, sociology dept. U. Chgo., 1940; social worker Internat. Inst., Buffalo, 1941-42; vocational adviser VA, Manchester, 1945-46; personnel technician AGO Dept. Army, 1942-44, 47-48; social sci. analyst NIMH, HEW, Bethesda, Md., 1959-61, pub. health analyst, 1966-67, program analyst Nat. Inst. Child Health and Human Devel., 1967-70; sociologist Stanford Research Inst. Edn. Policy Research Center, 1970-73, edn. research dept. Stanford Research Inst., Menlo Park, Calif., 1973-78, Center for Health Studies, 1978—. Leader, Capitol council Girl Scouts U.S.A., 1959-62, organizer, 1962; regional chair Am. Arab Antidiscrimination Com., 1981—. Recipient Superior Service award HEW, 1967. Mem. Am., Pacific sociol. assns., World Affairs Council, Am. Public Health Assn., Fedn. Am. Scientists, AAAS, Union Concerned Scientists, Alpha Kappa Delta. Club: Commonwealth. Author: A Brief Look at the State of Reading Research, 1961, rev. 1962; Career Education: Limitations and Possibilities, 1971; Early Childhood Education: Perspectives on the Federal and Office of Education Roles, 1972. Contbr. articles to profl. publs. Home: 1611 Castilleja Ave Palo Alto CA 94306 Office: Center for Health Studies SRI Internat Menlo Park CA 94025

STEPHENS, ALFREDA MICHELLE, system engr.; b. Balt., Sept. 21, 1959; d. Alfred and Elizabeth (Whitaker) S.; B.A., Mills Coll., 1980. System engr. phase I Electronic Data Systems, San Francisco, 1980; indsl. engr./systems EG&G Idaho Inc., Idaho Falls, 1981, systems engr., 1981—. Sec. bd. Solid Rock Ch., Idaho Falls. Mem. Am. Mgmt. Assn., Soc. Women Engrs. Club: Touch of Class Social. Home: 209 S Adam Ln Idaho Falls ID 83401 Office: PO Box 1625 Idaho Falls ID 83415

STEPHENS, DOROTHY CELESTE, ins. cons.; b. St. Louis; B.A., Marymount Coll., Tarrytown, N.Y.; M.A., St. Louis U. Researcher, U. Mo., 1969-70; asst. prof., 1970-73; chief staff asst. to Hon. Wm. L. Clay of Mo., 1973-76; v.p. govt. relations Hellmuth, Obata & Kassabaum, Architects and Engrs., 1976-78, v.p. corp. devel., 1978-79; founder, pres. D.C. Stephens, Ltd., Ins. Cons., Washington, 1980—; dir. Woman's Nat. Bank, Washington. Bd. govs. USO, exec. com., asst. treas., 1980; bd. dirs. Washington Internat. Horseshow, chmn. nominating com., vice chmn. budget and fin. com. Contbr. articles to profl. jours. Office: 1742 N St NW Washington DC 20036

STEPHENS, JANE STEWART, career planning cons.; b. N.Y.C., Nov. 10, 1941; d. Roy McCutcheon and Alice (Denice) Stephens; grad. Wood Sch., 1960. Adminstrv. asst. CBS, N.Y.C., 1960-64; trainee Revlon Co., N.Y.C., 1964-65; adminstrv. asst. ITT Corp., N.Y.C., 1965-73, research analyst-recruiting, 1973-74, research analyst-staffing, 1974-75, staffing analyst-personnel, 1975-79; dir. research Eastern region Korn/Ferry Internat., N.Y.C., 1979-80; ind. cons. career planning and adminstrv. mgmt., 1980—. Mem. Bronxville League for Service. Club: St. Bartholomew Community (N.Y.C.). Author: Staffing Procedures Handbook, 1972. Address: 25 Parkview Av Bronxville NY 10708

STEPHENS, JUDY RUTH, mgmt. cons. co. exec.; b. Chgo., Aug. 28, 1947; d. Moses and Jimmie (Powers) S.; student U. Ill., 1972-75; M.B.A., U. Chgo., 1977; 1 son, James Clifford Boone. Exec. sec. Maremont Corp., Chgo., 1970-72; exec. asst. to v.p. group ops. CNA Fin. Corp., Chgo., 1977-78, mgr. planning and budgeting, 1978-79; sr. mgmt. cons. Internat. Harvester, Chgo., 1979-80, mgr. tech. and adminstrv. services, Hinsdale, Ill., 1980-81; pres. The Stephens Group, Chgo., 1981—; lectr. in field. Research chairwoman League of Black Women, 1979—; bd. dirs. YWCA Met. Chgo., 1981—. Zenith Radio Corp. fellow 1975-77. Mem. U. Chgo. Alumni Assn., Nat. Black M.B.A. Assn., Inc., Am. Soc. Profl. and Exec. Women, Assn. Internal Cons., Assn. M.B.A. Execs., Alpha Lambda Delta. Office: PO Box 49285 Chicago IL 60649

STEPHENS, JULIE VERRETTE, personnel cons.; b. Iron Mountain, Mich., Mar. 19, 1941; B.A., U. Miami 1962; M.A., Mich. State U., 1963; children—Elisabeth, Timothy, Michael Cade. Counselor, No. Mich. U., 1963-65, Mich.. Tech. U., 1966-72; risk mgr., personnel dir. Champion, Inc., Iron Mountain, 1976-81; owner, pres. Personnel Assos., Iron Mountain, 1980—. Bd. dirs. Iron Mountain United Way; past bd. dirs. Dickinson County YMCA Mem. Nat. Assn. Female Execs. Episcopalian. Club: Zonta (charter pres. Iron Mountain-Kingsford area). Address: PO Box 534 Iron Mountain MI 49801

STEPHENS, MILDRED BASON, ednl. corp. exec.; b. Greensboro, N.C., Oct. 25, 1928; d. Thomas and Claretta Bason; student Pa. State Coll., 1944-45; B.S., Morgan State Coll., 1948; m. Oct. 1, 1949; children—Cheryl, Frank, Thomas. With Ednl. Testing Service, Princeton, N.J., 1948—, dir. fin. div., 1980—. Pres., Ewing Twp. (N.J.) Bd. Edn., 1975-77. Mem. Nat. Assn. Accts. (dir. 1977-79, nat. v.p. 1982-83). Methodist. Club: Ewing Community (dir. 1969—, recipient citizens award 1971). Home: 408 Hazel Ave Trenton NJ 08638 Office: D042 Rosedale Rd Princeton NJ 08541

STEPHENSON, BETTE M., Can. provincial ofcl., physician; b. Aurora, Ont., Can., July 31, 1924; d. Carl Melvin and Clara Mildred (Draper) S.; grad. Earl Haig Coll. Inst.; M.D., U. Toronto, 1946; m. Gordon Allan Pengelly, 1948; children—J. Stephen A., Elizabeth Anne A., C. Christopher A., J. Michael A., P. Timothy A., Mary Katharine A.; Mem. med. staff Women's Coll. Hosp., 1950—, chief dept. gen. practice, dir. outpatient dept., 1954-64; mem. med. staff N.Y. Gen. Hosp., 1967-76; elected Ont. Legislature for York Mills, 1975, 77—, Ministry of Labor, 1975-78; minister edn., minister colls. and univs., 1978—. Bd. dirs. Ont. Med. Found.; active Can. Mental Health Assn. Fellow Coll. Family Physicians Can. (chmn. nat. coordinating com. on edn. 1961-64, chmn. confs. on edn. for gen. practice 1961, 63), Acad. Medicine Toronto; mem. Ont. Med. Assn. (bd. dirs. 1964-72, pres. 1970-71), Can. Med. Assn. (bd. dirs. 1968-75, pres. 1974-75), Art Gallery Ont., Royal Ont. Mus. Office: Parliament Bldgs Toronto ON M7A 1A1 Canada *

STEPHENSON, HELEN ROSE, writer; b. Pitts.; d. Charles E. and Ruth L. (Bowers) Gibson; B.A., U. Pitts.; m. George M. Stephenson, June 10, 1961; children—Rosalind, Karen. Account supr. Ketchum, MacLeod & Grove, Inc., Pitts., 1955-61; editor-supr. printed materials Gen. Foods Corp., White Plains, N.Y., 1964-73; free-lance writer, 1973—, contbr. articles to various publs., including N.Y. Times, Wall St. Jour., Ladies Home Jour., Town & Country. Recipient Golden Quill award Sigma Delta Chi, 1960. Mem. Conn. Press Women, Nat. League Am. PEN. Editor, author various cookbooks Gen. Foods Corp., 1964-73. Home and Office: 190 Chestnut Ridge Rd Bethel CT 06801

STEPHENSON, MARIE CHASE, health care exec.; b. Mars Hill, Maine, June 15, 1927; d. C. Dudley and Laura H. Chase; A.A., Lasell Jr. Coll., Auburndale, Mass., 1947; postgrad. Columbia U., U. Maine; m. William Bartley Stephenson, Dec. 6, 1954; children—Gary Chase, Linda L. Asst. mgr. Hotel Ansonia, N.Y.C., 1955-59; publ. coordinator Maine Dept. Edn., 1975-78; staff asst. to gov. of Maine, 1978-79; mgr., adminstrv. asst. Kennebec Valley Mental Health Center, Augusta, Maine, 1979—. Bd. dirs. Am. Field Service, 1975; past pres. Jefferson Library Assn. Mem. Bus. and Profl. Women's Club Augusta. Club: Jefferson Woman's (past pres.). Home: RFD 1 Box 136B Waldoboro ME 04572 Office: Kennebec Valley Mental Health Center 66 Stone St Augusta ME 04330

STEPHENS-ROBERTS, ELIZABETH ANNE, workshop dir.; b. Bklyn., Oct. 23, 1942; d. Edward Joseph and Mary Agnes (Donlon) Stephens; B.A., Seat of Wisdom Coll., 1967: M.A., Hunter Coll., City U. N.Y., 1972; P.D., C.W. Post Coll., L.I. U., 1976; m. James Patrick Roberts, July 31, 1976; children—Sean Michael, Kerri Elizabeth. Tchr., Christ the King High Sch., N.Y.C., 1964-73, asst. prin., 1973-74; tchr. Elwood Jr. High Sch., Huntington, N.Y., 1974-75, asst. adminstr., 1975-79; team leader for group dynamics workshops Diocese of Rockville Centre, 1970—, group trainer for pre-marriage edn. program, 1974—. Cert. sch. dist. adminstr. Democrat. Roman Catholic. Conv. presenter on role of women in edn1. adminstrn., 1975-76. Home: 24 Platt Pl Huntington NY 11743

STERBENZ, JOANNE RUTH, accountant; b. New Orleans, June 16, 1947; d. Joseph Roch and Merlin (Prieto) S.; B.S., U. Southwestern La., 1969; M.B.A., Tulane U., 1971. With Arthur Young & Co., Los Angeles, 1971—, mgr., 1976-80, coordinator computer auditing, 1976-79, prin., 1980—, office dir. edn., 1979. C.P.A., Calif.; Tulane U. fellow, 1969-71. Mem. Am. Inst. C.P.A.s, Nat. Assn. Female Execs., Am. Women's Soc. C.P.A.s, EDP Auditors Assn., NOW, Tulane Assn. Bus. Alumni, Greater Los Angeles Zoo Assn., Smithsonian Assos. Democrat. Roman Catholic. Club: University. Home: 222 7th St Apt 107 Santa Monica CA 90402 Office: Arthur Young Co 515 S Flower St Los Angeles CA 90071

STERLING, AUDREY MAY, vintner; b. San Francisco, May 5, 1931; d. Joseph and Charlotte (Raff) Shapiro; student Mills Coll., 1948-51, Stanford U., 1951-52; m. Barry H. Sterling, Aug. 30, 1952; children—Joy Anne, Laurence Garrett. Mem. Calif. Fair Employment Practices Commn., 1964-66; co-mgr., partner Iron Horse Vineyards, Sonoma County, Calif., 1976—. Dir. Sonoma Marin State Fair, Sonoma County Harvest Fair; founder, Los Angeles Music Center, Los Angeles County Mus. Art; bd. dirs. San Francisco Art Inst., 1981—. Mem. Wine Inst. Jewish. Club: Hillcrest Country. Address: 9786 Ross Station Rd Sebastopol CA 95472

STERLING, JOANNE WINIFRED, psychologist; b. Titusville, Pa., Nov. 29, 1934; d. George W. and Anne Elizabeth (Dowling) S.; B.A., Chatham Coll., Pitts., 1956; M.A., U. N.Mex., 1964, Ph.D., 1970. Probation officer Allegheny County Juvenile Ct., Pitts., 1956-58; clin. dir. Girls' Welfare Home, Albuquerque, 1959-64; dir. mental health and manpower project U.S. Dept. Labor, Colo. State U., Fort Logan Mental Health Center, Denver, 1964-66; sr. counselor Packard-Bell Corp., Job Corps Center, Albuquerque, 1966-67; instr. dept. psychiatry U. N.Mex. Med. Sch., Albuquerque, 1969-71, asst. prof., 1971—; coordinator rehab. services Bernalillo County Mental Health/Mental Retardation Center, Albuquerque, 1968-72, dir. spl. programs div., 1972-76, asso. dir., 1975-77, dep. dir., 1977-78, dir., 1978—. Mem. Met. Criminal Justice Coordinating Council, 1972-79; mem. rehab. study com. Gov's. Council on Criminal Justice Planning, 1973-76; mem. nat. adv. com. Center Prevention and Control Rape NIMH, HEW, 1976-78, 80-81; mem. Gov's. Mental Health, Drug Abuse Alcoholism/Devel. Disabilities Adv. Council State N.Mex., 1979-81; mem. profl. adv. bd. All Faith's Receiving Home, 1973-75; trustee Suicide Prevention and Crisis Center, 1975-76; mem. sci. staff Bernalillo County Med. Center, 1975—; bd. dirs. Nat. Council Alcoholism, Albuquerque chpt., 1976-78; resource person Albuquerque Urban Obs., 1977—; mem. Health Issues Council, Community Council Albuquerque, 1977-79; mem. legis. com. N.Mex. Council Community Mental Health Services, 1978-79, mem. exec. com., 1979—; judge Central N.Mex. Civitan Citizenship Essay Contest, 1979; bd. dirs. Albuquerque Mus. Found., 1979-82. Recipient Disting. N.Mex. Woman award Internat. Women's Yr. Com., 1977. Mem. Am. Psychol. Assn. (state rep. com. on women in psychology 1975-77), Am. Correctional Assn., Am. Orthopsychiat. Assn., Nat. Council Crime and Delinquency, Am. Assn. Correctional Psychologists, Assn. Mental Health Adminstrs., N.Mex. Psychol. Assn. (state coordinator com. on health planning 1979—). Contbr. articles to profl. jours. Office: U NMex Dept Psychiatry 620 Camino de Salud Albuquerque NM 87131

STERN, CAROL SIMPSON, educator; b. Newcastle-on-Tyne, U.K., June 22, 1942; came to U.S., 1946; d. Alan and Mary (McEdlowney) Simpson; A.B. with honors, U. Chgo., 1963; M.A., Northwestern U., 1964, Ph.D. (Woodrow Wilson fellow), 1968; m. J. Allyson Stern, June 5, 1963. Asst., then asso. prof. and chmn. dept. english Roosevelt U., Chgo., 1967-74; asso. prof. dept. interpretation Northwestern U., Evanston, Ill., 1974—; cons. in field. Trustee, Roosevelt U., 1970-74. Woodrow Wilson fellow, 1963-64. Mem. AAUP (1st v.p. 1978-80), Speech Communication Assn., Midwest Victorian Studies Assn., Ill. Speech & Theatre Assn. Contbr. articles to profl. jours.; reviewer Victorian Studies, 1978-81; book reviewer for The Daily News (now Chgo. Sun Times, 1974. Home: 2521 Wilmette Ave Wilmette IL 60091 Office: 1979 Sheridan Rd Evanston IL 60201

STERN, DALIA VIVAS, community coll. ofcl.; b. Lorain, Ohio, Dec. 29, 1926; d. Julius and Mirta (Campos) Vivas; A.B., Baldwin-Wallace Coll., Berea, Ohio, 1948; m. Lester M. Stern, May 1, 1949; children—Richard Alan, Lorette Ines, Howard Andrew. Various secretarial positions, 1948-51; sales mgr. Fair Housing, Inc., Cleve., 1964-71; exec. sec. president's office Cuyahoga Community Coll., Cleve., 1971-77, coordinator human resources, 1977—; cons. Women's Equity Action Program, U.S. Dept. Edn., 1980-82. Trustee WomenSpace, 1980-82. Mem. Am. Soc. Personnel Adminstrn., Women's Equity Action League, Fedn. Bus. and Profl. Women, Am. Jewish Congress, ACLU, NOW. Home: 14630 Shaker Blvd Shaker Heights OH 44120 Office: 700 Carnegie Ave Cleveland OH 44115

STERN, MADELEINE BETTINA, rare book dealer, writer; b. N.Y.C., July 1, 1912; d. Moses Roland and Lillie (Mack) S.; B.A., Barnard Coll., 1932; M.A., Columbia U., 1934. Tchr. English, N.Y.C. high schs., 1934-43; partner Leona Rostenberg & Madeleine B. Stern, Rare Books, 1945—; author: The Life of Margaret Fuller, 1942; Louisa May Alcott, 1950; Purple Passage: The Life of Mrs. Frank Leslie, 1953; Imprints on History: Book Publishers and American Frontiers, 1956; We The Women: Career Firsts of 19th Century America, 1962; The Pantarch: A Biography of Stephen Pearl Andrews, 1968; So Much in a Lifetime: The Story of Dr. Isabel Barrows, 1965; Queen of Publishers' Row: Mrs. Frank Leslie, 1966; Heads and Headlines: The Phrenological Fowlers, 1971; Books and Book People in 19th Century America, 1978; (with Leona Rostenberg) Old and Rare: Thirty Years in the Book Business, 1974, Between Boards: New Thoughts on Old Books, 1977, Bookman's Quintet: Five Catalogues About Books, 1980; editor: Women on the Move, 4 vols., 1972; The Victoria Woodhull Reader, 1974; Louisa's Wonder Book—An Unknown Alcott Juvenile, 1975; Behind a Mask: The Unknown Thrillers of Louisa May Alcott, 1975; Plots and Counterplots: More Unknown Thrillers of Louisa May Alcott, 1976; Publishers for Mass Entertainment in 19th Century America, 1980; A Phrenological Dictionary of 19th-Century Americans, 1982. Guggenheim fellow, 1943-45; recipient Medalie award, 1982. Mem. Antiquarian Booksellers Assn. Am., Internat. League Antiquarian Booksellers, MLA, Manuscript Soc. (trustee), Am. Printing History Assn., Authors League, Phi Beta Kappa. Address: 40 E 88th St New York NY 10028

STERN, MYRA, health care adminstr.; b. Phila., Sept. 25, 1939; d. Israel Abraham and Freda (Sanders) S.; R.N., Albert Einstein Med. Center, 1964; B.A., Temple U., 1961. Head nurse Michael Reese Hosp., Chgo., 1965-68, clin. coordinator nephrology program, 1968-73; clin. adminstr. North Central Dialysis Centers, Chgo., 1973-79, dir. adminstrv. devel., 1979—; lectr. health systems Northwestern U. Bd. dirs. Nat. Kidney Found. Ill., 1971-79. Mem. Am. Mgmt. Assn., Women in Health Care, Am. Bus. Women's Assn., Am. Nurses Assn., Am. Assn. Nephrology Nurses and Technicians. Home: 5445 N Sheridan Rd Apt 812 Chicago IL 60640 Office: 55 E Washington St Chicago IL 60640

STERN, PAULA, govt. ofcl.; b. Chgo., Mar. 31, 1945; d. Lloyd and Fan (Wener) S.; B.A., Goucher Coll., 1967; M.A. (Nat. Def. Fgn. Lang. fellow), Harvard U., 1969; M.A. (scholar), Tufts U., 1970, Ph.D., 1976; m. Paul A. London, Dec. 28, 1971; children—Gabriel Stern, Genevieve Stern. Staff writer New Republic mag., 1969; legis. asst. to U.S. Senator Gaylord Nelson, 1972-74, 76; guest scholar Brookings Instn., 1975-76; mem. Carter-Mondale transition team, 1976-77; internat. affairs fellow Council Fgn. Relations, 1977-78; sr. commr. U.S. Internat. Trade Commn., Washington, 1978—; adj. asso. prof. urban and policy scis. program Averill Harriman Sch., SUNY, Stony Brook, 1974-75. Bd. dirs. Inter-Am. Found., 1980-81. Recipient Alicia Patterson Found. award, 1970-71; U.S. Dept. State fellow Arabic Lang. Study, Am. U., Cairo, 1968. Mem. Nat. Women's Polit. Caucus, Exec. Women in Govt. Democrat. Jewish. Author: Water's Edge: Domestic Politics and the Making of American Policy, 1979; contbr. articles to Atlantic Monthly, New Republic, Washington Post, Washington Star-News, Middle East Jour., New York Times, others. Office: 701 E St NW Washington DC 20436

STERN, SANDRA SILVERSTONE (MRS. ROBERT LOWELL STERN), television actress; b. London, Eng.; d. Arthur Joseph and Pearl (Finkelstein) Silverstone; A.B., Vassar Coll., 1955; m. Robert Lowell Stern, June 19, 1955; children—Antony Ian, Michael Keith, Wendy Joy, Peter Jonathan, Valery Jennifer. Summer stock actress, Ogunquit, Maine, 1954; apprentice actress, 1955-56; writer, performer children's TV program Jr. Clubhouse, Sta. CHCT-TV, Calgary, Alta., Can., 1957-59, Romper Room hostess, 1959-60, writer, producer, performer Teddy Bear Quiz and 12 and Under, 1960-61; writer, producer, performer children's TV program TV Partytime, CFCN-TV, Calgary, 1962-65, writer, producer, hostess Rocket IV Club, 1965-67; pres. R.L. Stern Mgmt. Co. Ltd., Calgary, 1967—; co-owner Court Stars, active sportswear boutiques, West Vancouver and Vancouver; pres. Exec-Suite, Calgary. Mem. Jr. League Calgary and Vancouver; bd. dirs. Calgary Dance Theatre, 1974, Festival Calgary, 1975; pres. West Vancouver Newcomers Club, 1977, Can't Wait Tennis Assn., 1981; mem. Amnesty Internat. Club Author: (ballet play) The Absent-Minded Sorcerbird. Home: 889 Farmleigh Rd West Vancouver BC V7S 1Z8 Canada

STERN, SUE STEWART, lawyer; b. Casper, Wyo., Oct. 9, 1942; d. Fraizer McVale and Carolyn Eliabeth (Hunt) Stewart; B.A., Wellesley Coll., 1964; postgrad. Harvard U. Law Sch., 1964-65; J.D., Georgetown U., 1967; m. Arthur L. Stern, III, July 31, 1965; children—Anne Stewart, Mark Alan. Admitted to N.Y. bar, 1968; clk. to Judges Juvenile Ct., Washington, 1967-68; mem. firm Nixon, Hargrave, Devans & Doyle, Rochester, N.Y., 1968-74, partner, 1975—; lectr. in field; trustee Found. of Monroe County (N.Y.) Bar, 1976—. Sec., dir. United Community Chest of Greater Rochester, 1977—; trustee, sec. Internat. Museum Photography at George Eastman House, Rochester, 1974—, Genesee Country Mus., Mumford, N.Y., 1976—. Mem. Am. (chmn. task force on charitable giving, exempt orgns. com. tax sect. 1981—), N.Y. State (exec. com. tax sect., 1974-76, chmn. com. exempt orgns. 1975-76), Monroe County (trustee 1974-75) bar assns. Office: Nixon Hargrave Devans & Doyle Lincoln First Tower Rochester NY 14603

STERNBERG, CORA N., physician; b. Phila., Oct. 21, 1951; d. Samuel and Barbara S.; B.A. summa cum laude, U.Pa., 1973, M.D., 1977. Resident, Stanford (Calif.) Hosp., 1979-80, Mt. Sinai Hosp., N.Y.C., 1980-81; research and clin. fellow in hematology and oncology Sloan-Kettering Cancer Center, N.Y.C., 1981—; teaching asst. Cornell-N.Y. Hosp., N.Y.C., 1981—. Mem. AMA, N.Y. Acad. Scis. Jewish. Office: Sloan-Kettering Cancer Center 1275 York Ave New York NY 10021

STERNBERG, SIMONE ELSA, psychoanalyst, educator; b. Newark, Nov. 18, 1933; d. Norman and Anita (Chivian) S.; B.A., Antioch Coll., 1955; postgrad. Inst. de Phonetique Sorbonne, Inst. des Hautes Etudes, 1960-68; M.A., New Sch. Social Research, 1971; Ed.D., Columbia U., 1976; cert. New Hope Guild Therapist Tng. Program, 1976, N.Y. Center for Psychoanalytic Tng., 1978; m. Robert Morris Feinstein, Nov. 12, 1973; 1 son, Noah Carl. Actress/mime, Theatre de la Mandragore, France, 1958-68; research assoc. psychol. cons. Teaching and Learning Research Corp., N.Y.C., 1971-73; coordinator, instr. Inst. Study for Older Adults, N.Y.C., 1973-79; prof. Brookdale Center, Hunter Coll., N.Y.C., 1976-77, New Sch., N.Y.C., 1977-78; pvt. practice psychoanalysis and psychotherapy, N.Y.C. and Elmwood Park, N.J., 1978—; adj. assoc. prof. Fordham U. Sch. Social Service; faculty Ctr. Human Devel., L.I. U., Bklyn.; dean students, bd. dirs. N.Y. Ctr. Psychoanalytic Tng.; clin. instr., supr. New Hope Guild, N.Y. Center Psychoanalytic Tng.; cons. New Hope Guild Assos. Lic. psychologist, N.J., Pa.; cert. sch. psychologist, N.Y. State; HEW grantee, 1975. Mem. Soc. Psychoanalytic Tng. (exec. bd.), Am. Psychol. Assn., Council Psychoanalytic Psychotherapists, N.Y. Soc. Clin. Psychologists, Nat. Psychol. Assn. for Psychoanalysis, Inst. Clin. Social Work (trustee). Author: She Must Have Been a Beautiful Woman Once, 1975; An Exploration of the Cognitive and Personality Functioning of Older Adults, 1976; (with others) Fear of Flying High: Fear of Success in Women, 1978. Home: 225 West End Ave New York NY 10023 Office: 300 West 72d St Suite 2F New York NY 10023 also 131A River Dr Elmwood Park NJ 07407

STERNHAGEN, FRANCES, actress; b. Washington, Jan. 13; d. John Meyer and Gertrude S.; B.A., Vassar Coll., 1951; attended Catholic U. Am., 1952. Profl. stage debut in The Glass Menagerie and Angel Street at Bryn Mawr (Pa.) Summer Theatre, 1948; N.Y.C. stage debut in Thieves' Carnival at Cherry Lane, 1955; other stage appearances include: The Admirable Bashville (Clarence Derwent award, Obie award), The Country Wife, Ulysses in Nighttown, Great Day in the Morning, The Room, A Slight Ache, The Right Honourable Gentleman, The Displaced Person, Blood Red Roses, The Playboy of the Western World, All Over, Mary Stuart, The Sign in Sidney Brustein's Window, Enemies, The Good Doctor, Equus, Angel; film debut in Up the Down Staircase, 1967; other films include: The Tiger Makes Out, 1970, The Hospital, 1971, Two People, 1973, Fedora, 1979; TV debut on Omnibus in The Great Bank Robbery, 1955; appeared on TV serials Love of Life and The Doctors; numerous other TV appearances. Recipient Obie award for performance in The New Pinter Plays, Antoinette Perry (Tony) award for performance in The Good Doctor; Delia Austrian medal for On Golden Pond. *

STERRETT, FRANCES SUSAN, chemist, educator; b. Vienna, Austria, Sept. 25, 1915; came to U.S., 1944; d. Edmund and Klara (Handl) Krauss; Ph.D., U. Vienna, 1938; m. Anthony H. Sterrett, May 29, 1939; children—Jane E., Elizabeth A. Research asst. Columbia U. Med. Center, N.Y.C., 1939-40; research chemist Fritsche Bros., Inc., N.Y.C., 1943-49, Woburn Degreasing Co., Harrison, N.J., 1943, Van Amerigen & Haebler, Inc., 1940-41; lectr. Hofstra U., Hempstead, N.Y., part-time, 1953-57, 57-62, asst. prof., 1962-69, asso. prof., 1969-73, prof. chemistry, 1973—; cons. in field; adv. to Congressman J. Ambro, Am. Chem. Soc., 1976. Recipient Cert. of Appreciation, Fed. EPA, Region II, 1975, 76. Fellow N.Y. Acad. Sci., Am. Inst. Chemists; mem. Am. Chem. Soc. (dir.-at-large N.Y. sect.), AAUP (pres. 1968), History of Sci. Soc., AAAS. Contbr. articles to profl. jours. Home: 64 Hathaway Dr Garden City NY 11530 Office: Fulton Ave Hempstead NY 11550

STEAN-SOLIS, DEBRA-LYNNE ANN, mktg. devel. cons.; b. Toms River, N.J., Mar. 12, 1954; d. Samuel Robert and Sylvia Dorothy (Bushing) Stean; B.A., Gettysburg Coll., 1976; postgrad. in bus. adminstrn. U. So. Calif., 1981—; m. Carlos Solis, Aug. 15, 1981. Real property analyst, La Jolla, Calif., 1976-77; comml. loan officer/analyst Union Bank, Los Angeles, 1977-80; bus. devel. officer First Los Angeles Bank, 1980-81; profl. evaluation cons. Seven-Up Bottlers div. Westinghouse Beverage, Los Angeles, 1981-82; mktg. devel. cons. Sav-On Drugs Inc. div. Jewel Corp., Anaheim, Calif., 1982—. Chmn. mgmt. devel. com. Los Angeles Jr. C. of C., 1980-81, chmn. exec. devel. program, 1980-81, bd. dirs., 1981-83, Century of Pacific del., 1982; mem. U. So. Calif. Student Adv. Council. Named to Career Bd., Mademoiselle Mag., 1976-83. Mem. Am. Mktg. Assn., Entertainment Mgmt. Assn., Am. Fin. Assn., Los Angeles Credit Assn., Univ., Profl., and Businesswomen's Assn., Alpha Xi Delta. Clubs: Los Angeles Athletic, Westside Young Profls. (pres. 1979-81). Home: 590 Bradford Pasadena CA 91105 Office: 1500 S Anaheim Blvd Anaheim CA 92805

STEVENS, ALTHEA WILLIAMS, educator; b. Norfolk, Va., Oct. 23, 1931; d. Richard Dawson and Virginia (Creekmore) Williams; B.S. in Mgmt., Calif. State U., 1969; M.Ed., Rutgers U., 1974, postgrad., 1974—. Statis. coordinator Los Angeles County (Calif.) Probation Dept., 1966-68; instr. Camden (N.J.) High Sch., 1970-75; prof. bus. adminstrn. Bergen County Community Coll., Paramus, N.J., 1977—; prof. bus. edn. and office systems adminstrn. Montclair State Coll., Upper Montclair, N.J., 1975-78; asso. prof. computer sci., curriculum devel., Western Wyo. Coll., Rock Springs, 1978—, chmn. div. bus. and mgmt., 1979-81; computer cons. Sweetwater County Planning Office, 1979. Ednl. Profl. Devel. grantee, 1975. Mem. Wyo. Bd. C.P.A.s (gen. public mem. 1980-83), Am. Vocat. Assn., Nat., Mountain, Wyo. bus. edn. assns., Assn. for Computing Machinery, Data Processing Mgmt. Assn., Vocat. Edn. Assn. Wyo., Omicron Tau Theta. Lutheran. Home: 1414 Raindance Dr Rock Springs WY 82901 Office: Western Wyo Coll Rock Springs WY 82901

STEVENS, ELAINE BURR, mktg. exec., b. Coshocton, Ohio, Jan. 11, 1942; d. Earl Radcliffe and Jeanette Isbelle (Spies) S.; student Northwestern U., 1960-63 Harvard Grad. Sch. Bus., 1968-70, Case Western Res. Sch. Mgmt., 1975; m. James D. Angle, Sept. 13, 1980; children by previous marriage—Steven Burr Erikson, Michael Brandt Erikson; stepchildren—Laura Angle, Mark Angle, Scott Angle. Sales rep. Hilton Hotels, Chgo., 1963-64; div. mgr. Maxwell Sroge, Chgo., 1964-68; cons. Store Front Learning Center, Boston, 1968-70; product mgr. Disston, Inc., Pitts., 1975-78; exec. dir. Health Maintenance Orgn., Akron, Ohio, 1978-80; v.p. strategic mktg. team Bus. Support Group, Hudson Ohio, 1980-82; pres. Home Mgmt. Technologies Inc., 1982—. Mem chief exec. officers roundtable Council Small Enterprise, 1980—; bd. dirs. Chamber Music Soc., 1976-78, vice-chmn. bd. 1978-79; bd. dirs. Jr. League Akron, 1981-82, exec. bd., 1981-82; mem. health maintenance orgn. adv. council Case Western Res. U., 1978-79. Health Maintenance Orgn. Devel. grantee, 1978. Mem. Direct Mail Advt. Assn. (dir. 1966-69), Council Small Enterprise, Woman's Network Speakers Bur., Greater Cleve. Growth Assn. Mem. Christian Ch. Patentee in field. Office: 76 Church St Hudson OH 44236

STEVENS, ELIZABETH DREW, lawyer, univ. union exec.; b. Syracuse, N.Y., Dec. 19, 1946; d. Phil Franklin Blum and Helen Marie (Yarwood) Drew; B.A. (Nat. Merit scholar), U. No. Iowa, 1973; postgrad. Schoitz Hosp. Sch. Med. Tech., 1973-74; J.D. (research scholar), Washburn U., 1981; m. Carl A. Stevens, Jr., Dec. 13, 1975; children by previous marriage—Denise Anne Beving, Cynthia Marie Beving. Quality supr. U.S. Gypsum Co., Ft. Dodge, Iowa, 1974-75, employment supr., 1975-77; realtor assoc. Toothaker Real Estate Co., Manhattan, Kans., 1978, Anderson Realty Agy., Manhattan, 1978-79; research asst. Washburn U. Sch. Law, Topeka, 1979-80; law clk. Kans. Corp. Commn., Topeka, 1980-81; admitted to Kans. bar, 1981; individual practice law, Manhattan, 1981—; mgr. personnel Kans. State Union, Manhattan, 1981—, mem. univ. staff devel. task force, 1981—, mem. univ. appeal and rev. com., 1982—. Active LWV, 1977-80; mem. adv. bd. 4-H Club, 1981—; solicitor United Way, 1981, 82, Cancer Crusade, 1975. Mem. ABA, Kans. Bar Assn., Riley County Bar Assn., Am. Trial Lawyers Assn., Kans. Trial Lawyers Assn., North Central Iowa Personnel Assn. (sec. 1976-77), Manhattan Personnel Assn., Bus. and Profl. Women, Washburn Women's Legal Forum (v.p. and pres. 1979-80), Manhattan C. of C. (various coms.), Am. Legion Aux., Phi Delta Phi. Republican. Methodist. Club: Pilot. Home: 816 Mimosa Ln Manhattan KS 66502

STEVENS, ETHEL PATRICIA, med. soc. exec.; b. Newark, June 20, 1924; d. George Patrick and Gladys Christy (Stanaback) O'Reilly; student St. Michael's Hosp. Sch. Nursing, 1941-42; cert. hosp. mgmt. Rutgers U., Newark, 1971; m. Stephen G. Szczepaniak, Aug. 18, 1944; children—Patricia, Stephen, Laura, Kathleen, Irene, Jodie, Margaret. Dir. admissions, communications and physician-adminstrv. relations Alexian Brothers Hosp., Elizabeth, N.J., 1963-73; exec. dir. Union County Med. Soc., Cranford N.J., 1973—; Union County adv. council, regional health planning council Health Systems Agy., Newark, 1976—; adv. PSRO, Fanwood, N.J., 1976—. Pres., Linden (N.J.) Bd. Edn., 1968; cons. Jr. League of Union County, 1977-78. Mem. Am. Assn. Med. Soc. Execs. Home: 705 Willow St Cranford NJ 07016 Office: 347 E Lincoln Ave Cranford NJ 07016

STEVENS, EVELYN TRUSSELL STILLE, mfg. co. ofcl.; b. LaGrange, Ga., July 4, 1921; d. Daniel Coley and Winnie Mae (Phillips) Trussell; A.A., La Grange Coll.; diploma Druitt Sch. Speech, Atlanta, 1953, Patricia Stevens Modeling Sch., Atlanta, 1954, Viviane Woodard Acad., Panorama City, Calif. 1963; cert. Ga. State U., Atlanta, 1959; m. Edward Jackson Stille, Aug. 21, 1942 (div. 1949); children—Deanna Lynn Stille Strickland, Fredrick Vaughn; m. 2d, Evan Jack Stevens, Dec. 28, 1980. Tchr., Hogansville, Ga., 1943-51; exec. sec., safety coordinator Atlanta Newspapers, Inc., 1951-64; office mgr., personnel dir. Manpower, Inc., Atlanta, 1964-65; adminstrv. div. mgr. James Pair Personnel Service, Atlanta, 1965-66; personnel and indsl. relations dir. Westab div. Mead Corp., Atlanta, 1966-73, Atlantic Envelope Co., Atlanta, 1973—. Mem. Atlanta Area Employment Adv. Council, 1970-73, 75-77, Mayor's Com. Manpower Area Planning, 1973-74; mem. job placement and adv. com. Atlanta Public Schs., 1974-76; mem. adv. com. Nat. Alliance Businessmen, 1970-72, Comprehensive Career Edn. Model Program, 1973; organizer, dir. Grace Players of Grace United Methodist Ch., 1960-70; coordinator alumni class, mem. adv. council LaGrange Coll.; mem. Ga. Employment and Tng. Council, 1979—; steward Am. Horse Shows Assn. Recipient cert. of appreciation Ga. Bus. Industry and Trade Indsl. Relations Com., 1974, 75, Good Guy award, 1976; recipient honorable designation Gov. of Ga., 1979. Mem. Adminstrv. Mgmt. Soc. (pres. 1978-79, internat. dir. Area 8, merit award 1978, plaque for outstanding leadership, 1979, cert. of appreciation Athens chpt. 1976, Diamond Merit award 1980), Indsl. Relations Assn., Ga. Bus. Industry and Trade, Atlanta Women's C. of C. (cert. of appreciation 1974-75), Atlanta Personnel Club. Democrat. Author: The Posed Princess, 1943. Home: 442 Saint Patrick Dr Mableton GA 30059 Office: 1700 Northside Dr NW PO Box 1267 Atlanta GA 30301

STEVENS, GWENDOLYN RUTH, psychologist; b. Los Angeles Feb. 29, 1944; d. Oscar and Alice (Whalen) Stevens; B.A., Calif. State U., Los Angeles, 1973, M.A., 1974; Ph.D., U. Calif., Riverside, 1978; m. Sheldon Gardner, Oct. 27, 1972; children—Lorin Ann, Stephen Forrest. Research asst. Los Amigos Hosp., Downey, Calif., 1973-75; research dir. Client Assistance Program, Downey 1975-77; psychotherapist, psychodiagnostician Luth. Family and Children's Services, Cape Girardeau, Mo., 1978-82; mem. humanities faculty U.S. Coast Guard Acad., New London, Conn., 1982—; mem. faculty East Los Angeles Community Coll., 1975, Cypress (Calif.) Community Coll., 1975, Whittier (Calif.) Coll., 1976; mem. psychology faculty S.E. Mo. State U., 1978-82. Mem. Am. Psychol. Assn., Nat. Women's Studies Assn., Cherion, Mo. Psychology Assn., Eastern Psychol. Assn., Assn. Women Psychologists, Eastern Ednl. Research Assn., Internat. Council Psychologists. Author: Care and Cultivation of Parents, 1979; Women of Psychology: Pioneers and Innovators, 1981; Women of Psychology: Refinement and Elaboration, 1981; A Feminist Bibliography; 1979; Hyperkinesis: A Parent Guide, 1979; contbr. articles to profl. jours. Home: 75 Hilltop Rd Mystic CT 06355 Office: Dept Humanities US Coast Guard Acad New London CT 06320

STEVENS, HELEN ANN, hosp. staff devel. coordinator; b. Midland, Pa., Mar. 11, 1921; d. Harry John and Helen Alexandria (McCune) Wiedenbeck; student No. Ill. U., 1939-40; R.N., Garfield Park Community Hosp., Chgo., 1943; m. Robert E. Akins, 1945 (dec.); children—Robert E. (dec.), Catherine Ann, John W.; m. 2d, Robert Ware Stevens, Sept. 25, 1976. Staff nurse Meml. Hosp. of Michigan City (Ind.), 1966-71, day supr., 1971-74, staff devel. coordinator, 1974-76. Served as lt. Nurse Corps, AUS, 1943-45; New Guinea Decorated Bronze Star. Episcopalian. mem. P.E.O. Chpt. G Atlanta. Home: 3611 Teal Rd Atlanta GA 30341

STEVENS, KAREN LANG, govt. adminstr.; b. St. Petersburg, Fla., Nov. 10, 1949; d. James Talley and Dorothy Louise (Gustafson) Lang; student U. N.C., Chapel Hill, 1967-70; B.A., U. Md., 1971. Aide to Congressman C.W. Young, 1972-73; aide consultation and Guidance Center, 1973-76; legis. rep. Nat. Assn. Small Bus. Investment Cos., 1976-78; asso. dir. regulatory affairs Nat. Assn. Mfrs., 1978-79; congressional liaison U.S. Regulatory Council, 1979-81; spl. asst. to adminstr. for info. and regulatory affairs Office of Mgmt. and Budget, Washington, 1981; dept. dir. Office Congressional Relations, FTC, Washington, 1981—. Dep. dir. Rockville Free Clinic, Planned Parenthood, 1975-76. Mem. Women in Govt. Relations, Alpha Delta Pi. Republican. Methodist. Club: Jr. League (Washington). Office: Office Congressional Relations FTC 6th and Pennsylvania Ave NW Washington DC 20580

STEVENS, KAY FRANCES, TV exec.; b. Hamburg, Iowa, Jan. 31, 1947; d. Roy Harland and Wanita (Killion) Sparks; children—Douglas Kent, Michelle De'Ann. With Warner Cable Co., Atchison County, Mo., 1965-78, system mgr., 1974-78; office mgr., gen. mgr. tng. Am. Heritage Cablevision, Council Bluffs, Iowa, 1979; gen. mgr. United Cable TV Sarpy County, Bellevue, Nebr., 1979-82; gen. mgr. United Cable TV of Scottsdale (Ariz.), 1982—. Bd. dirs., sec. Bellevue Crimestoppers, 1981-82. Mem. Nebr. Cable Communications Assn. (dir. 1980-81, v.p. 1981-82), Mid Am. Cable TV Assn. (dir. 1981-82), Women in Cable, Nat. Assn. Female Execs. Clubs: Lioness, Eagles, Parents Without Partners. Office: 7100 E Lincoln Dr Suite C-130 Scottsdale AZ 85253

STEVENS, MARGARET MARIE, nurse; b. Frederick, Md., May 10, 1947; d. John Clayton and Ruby Marie (Bourne) Phillips; B.S. in Nursing, U. Md., 1969, cert. nurse practitioner, 1980; 1 son, John Phillip. Staff nurse Wichita Gen. Hosp., Wichita Falls, Tex., 1969-71, head nurse intensive care, 1971-72; staff nurse Brackenridge Gen. Hosp., Austin, Tex., 1972-74, also charge nurse intensive care unit; head nurse critical care recovery unit Maryland Inst. Emergency Med. Services, Balt., 1977-78, neurotrauma nurse coordinator, 1978-79, neurosurgery nurse practitioner, 1980—; tchr. trauma nursing various workshops State of Md., 1974—. Mem. Am. Assn. for Critical Care Nurses, Am. Assn. for Neurol. Nurses, Am. Nurses Assn. Democrat. Mem. Ch. of Brethren. Contbr. articles to profl. jours. Home: 25 Lerner Ct Baltimore MD 21236 Office: Maryland Inst Emergency Med Services 22 S Greene St Baltimore MD 21201

STEVENS, MARGOT DUBOSE SEMPLE, mortgage co. exec.; b. Waco, Tex., Nov. 18, 1929; d. John Dick and Maryliza (Figuers) DuBose; student U. Houston, 1948-49, Howard Payne U., 1963-65, Pa. State U., 1965-66, 73-74; m. William Stilwell Semple, Apr. 17, 1948; children—Toni, Jock Stilwell (dec.) Todd Bertrand, Robin Scot; m. 2d, Keith Frederick Stevens, Oct. 19, 1974. Prodn. mgr. Sta. KEAN, Brownwood, Tex., 1963-65; bus. mgr. Sta. WMAJ, State College, Pa., 1965-67; rental agt. Federated Home & Mortgage Co., Inc., State College, 1967-68, rental mgr., 1968-70, asst. v.p., 1970-76, v.p. rental div., 1976—; mem. housing adv. panel McGraw Hill Publs. Bd. dirs. Skills Inc., Vacationland Council. Lic. real estate salesman, Pa.; cert. property mgr. Mem. Inst. Real Estate Mgmt., State College Area C. of C. (dir., mem. exec. bd.). Republican. Presbyterian. Club: Square Dance. Home: 16 High Meadow Ln State College PA 16801 Office: Federated Home & Mortgate Co Inc 810 Cricklewood Dr State College PA 16801

STEVENS, MARILYN RUTH, publishing co. exec.; b. Wooster, Ohio, May 30, 1943; d. Glenn Willard and Gretchen Elizabeth (Ihrig) Amstutz; B.A., Coll. Wooster (Ohio), 1965; M.A.T., Harvard U., 1966; J.D., Suffolk U., 1975; m. Bryan J. Stevens, Oct. 11, 1969; children—Jennifer Marie, Gretchen Anna. Tchr., Lexington (Mass.) Public Schs., 1966-69; in various editorial positions Houghton Mifflin Co., Boston, 1969—, editorial dir. sch. depts., 1978-81, editorial dir. math. and scis. Sch. Div., 1981—; admitted to Mass. bar, 1975. Mem. Mass. Bar Assn., Am. Bar Assn. Office: One Beacon St Boston MA 02106

STEVENS, MAVIS ELAINE, educator; b. Corinth, Miss., Oct. 19, 1947; d. Burley S. and Emma Blanch (Austin) S.; student N.E. Miss. Jr. Coll., 1966-68; B.S., Blue Mountain Coll., 1970. Eligibility worker asst. Prentiss County (Miss.) Welfare Dept.; now spl. edn. tchr. Prentiss County Bd. Edn.—Prentiss County Child Devel., Mem. Miss. Assn. Educators, Am. Bible Soc., Nat. Assn. Female Execs. Methodist. Address: Route 1 Box 142 Booneville MS 28839

STEVENS, NORMA YOUNG, educator; b. Canton, Ga., Oct. 23, 1927; d. Sherman Taylor and Cora Lee (Stephens) Young; B.F.A., U. Ga., 1949; M.R.E., New Orleans Bapt. Theol. Sem., 1956; Ed.D., U. Ga., 1970; m. Howard Lamar Stevens, Sept. 6, 1949; children—Catherine Lynn Stevens Self, Karen Leigh Stevens Cantrell, Kristen Leslie. Landscape architect Jones Ornamental Nursery, Nashville, 1950-54; missionary, Torreon, Coahuila, Mexico, 1962-74; prof. edn. Belmont Coll., Nashville, 1975—; cons. sch. psychologist Colegio Americano, Mexico, 1970-74. Mem. Am. Psychol. Assn., Tenn. Psychol. Assn., Internat. Platform Assn., Nat. Council Measurement in Edn., Tenn. Assn. Tchr. Educators, Kappa Delta Pi. So. Baptist. Author: Go Out With Joy, 1966; co-author: The Christian and Divorce, 1980. Home: 2715 Hemingway Dr Nashville TN 37215 Office: Belmont Coll Nashville TN 37203

STEVENS, RISË, mezzo-soprano; b. N.Y.C.; d. Christian Steenberg; student Juilliard Sch. of Music, N.Y.C., Mozarteum, Salzburg, Austria; studied singing with Mme. Anna Schoen René and Mme. Vera Schwarz; m. Walter G. Surovy, Jan. 6, 1939; 1 son, Nicolas Vincent. Made debut as Mignon, Prague, Czechoslovakia, 1936; 1st appearance with Metropolitan Opera Co. in Mignon, Dec. 1938; has sung at Prague Opera, Vienna State Opera, Teatro Colon, Buenos Aires, Cairo, Egypt, Glyndbourne Mozart Festival England, San Francisco Opera Co., Athens, Greece, Paris Grand Opera; created title-role in world premiere of Virgilio Mortari's opera La Figlia del Diavolo at La Scala, Milan, 1954; prin. roles in Mignon, Der Rosenkavalier, Carmen, Samson et Dalila, La Gioconda, Hansel and Gretel, Le Nozze di Figaro, Die Walküre, Cosi Fan Tutte, Orfeo ed Euridice, Khovanchina (Met. opera premiere), Tales of Hoffmann, Die Fledermaus; created Carmen in new Met. Opera prodn.; in motion pictures The Chocolate Solider, Going My Way, Carnegie Hall; opened Music Theater of Lincoln Center starring in The King and I, 1964. Co-general mgr. Metropolitan Opera Nat. Co., 1963-66; lectr. New Sch., N.Y.C.; pres. Mannes Coll. of Music, N.Y.C. Traveled extensively with the Hollywood Victory Caravan during World War II; headed own radio programs; starred regularly on TV programs; concertized yearly throughout U.S. and Canada; recordings for Columbia Records and RCA Victor. Mem. music panel Nat. Endowment for Arts. Bd. dirs. Met. Opera Guild. Recipient Citation for U.S. Treasury Dept.; Certificate of Honor from ARC; Citation from Greater N.Y. Fund; Distinguished Service Award, N.Y. Cancer Com.; Box Office Blue Ribbon Award for picture, Going My Way; voted best female vocalist in radio by Motion Picture Daily and Musical America, 1947 and 1948. Established Risë Stevens Scholarships, Adelphi Coll., 1947. Hon. mem. Wagnerian Soc. (Buenos Aires), Sigma Alpha Iota. Address: Metropolitan Opera Association New York NY 10023 *

STEVENS, ROSALIE MARIE, court reporter; b. Wheeling, W.Va., Jan. 29, 1939; d. Severine Harry and Kathryn (Redosh) Niekro; student in ct. reporting Columbus Bus. U., 1958; m. Berton Binet Stevens, Sept. 26, 1959; children—Brian Binet, Jon Brenden, Bruce Berton. Legal sec. firm Lane, Huggard & Alton, Columbus, Ohio, 1957-58; ct. reporter Hancock County (Ohio) Common Pleas Ct., 1958-63, Defiance County (Ohio) Common Pleas Ct., 1963-71; adminstrv. ct. reporter Wood County (Ohio) Common Pleas Ct., 1971—. Ch. Women United del. to Ohio Gov.'s Com. on Migrant Problems, 1963-64; liaison vol. worker Hancock County Summer Migrant Sch., 1965-66; active Cub Scouts Am., 1967-70, 4-H, 1973-76. Mem. Nat. Shorthand Reporters Assn. (registered profl. reporter, del. nat. com. state assns.), Ohio Shorthand Reporters Assn. (chmn. com. cert. shorthand reporter, pres.), Nat. Assn. Ct. Adminstrs., Nat. Assn. Female Execs., Lutheran Ch. Women (life). Home: 15076 County Rd 37 Arlington OH 45814 Office: Common Pleas Ct #2 Courthouse Bowling Green OH 43402

STEVENS, ROSEMARY ANNE, health educator; b. Bourne, Eng.; d. William Edward and Mary Agnes (Tricks) Wallace; B.A., Oxford (Eng.) U., 1957; Diploma in Social Adminstrn., Manchester (Eng.) U., 1959; M.P.H., Yale U., 1963, Ph.D., 1968; m. Robert B. Stevens, Jan. 28, 1961; children—Carey Thomasine, Richard Nathaniel. Came to U.S., 1961, naturalized, 1968. Various hosp. and adminstrv. positions, Eng., 1959-61; research asso. Yale Med. Sch., 1962-68, asst. prof., 1968-71, asso. prof., 1971-74, prof. pub. health, 1974-76, prof. health systems mgmt., Sch. Public Health and Topical Medicine, 1976-79, prof. history and sociological services, U. Penn., 1979—, chmn. dept., 1980—, mistress Jonathan Edwards Coll., 1974-75; vis. lectr. Johns Hopkins U., 1967-68; guest scholar Brookings Instn., Washington, 1967-68; acad. visitor London Sch. Econs., 1962-64, 1973-74. Mem. Inst. Medicine, Nat. Acad. Sci., Am. Pub. Health Assn., Sigma Xi. Author: Medical Practice in Modern England: The Impact of Specialization and State Medicine, 1966; American Medicine and the Public Interest, 1971; (with Joan Vermeulen) Foreign Trained Physicians and American Medicine, 1972; (with Robert Stevens) Welfare Medicine in America, 1974. Contbr. articles to profl. jours. Address: Dept History and Sociological Services U Penn D6 Philadelphia PA 19104 *

STEVENS, SUSAN YVONNE REESEMAN, nursing educator; b. Bklyn., Oct. 19, 1944; d. Harry Bernard and Helen Vaughn (Horton) Thomsen; B.S., Adelphi U., 1966, M.S., 1968; postgrad. U. Ala., Birmingham, 1977—. Asst. prof. Nassau Community Coll., Garden City, N.Y., 1968-71; asso. in psychiat. group practice, Buffalo, N.Y., 1971-75; pvt. practice individual and family psychotherapy, Atlanta, 1976—; asst. prof. SUNY, Buffalo, 1973-76; asso. prof. Ga. State U., 1976-77; asso. prof. nursing programs Emory U., Atlanta, 1980—; cons. in field. USPHS, HEW fellow, 1978; cert. for excellence in practice. Mem. Mental Health Assn. Met. Atlanta, Am. Nurses Assn., Council on Specialists in Psychiat.-Mental Health Nursing, N.Y. State Nurses Assn., Mensa, Sigma Theta Tau. Clubs: Southeastern Savoyards, Southern Ballet. Home: 3650 Ashford Dunwoody 10F Atlanta GA 30319 Office: Sch of Nursing Emory U Atlanta GA 30322

STEVENSON, BARBARA JEAN, sales exec.; b. Tucson, Apr. 3, 1955; d. Carl Glenn and Barbara Patricia (Fritz) Stevenson; student U. Ariz., 1972-74; B.S. in Animal Sci., Wash. State U., 1976. Area sales rep. Syntex Agribusiness, Wash., Oreg., Idaho, 1977-78, area sales cons. for Tex. Panhandle and N.Mex., 1980—, nat. accounts coordinator Western region, 1982—; office mgr. Red Rock Feeding Co. (Ariz.), 1978-79. Vice pres. Cattle Capital Cowbelles, 1981, pres., 1982; mem. Pres.'s Council, 1981-82. Named Outstanding Sales rep. Syntex, 1978, 80, 81, 82. Mem. Am Nat. Cowbelles, N.Mex. Cowbelles, Cattle Capital Cowbelles, Tex. Cattle Feeders' Assn., N.Mex. Cattle Growers' Assn., Ariz. Cattle Feeders' Assn., Bus. and Profl. Women. Republican. Methodist. Home: PO Box 1825 Clovis NM 88101 Office: PO Box 653 Des Moines IA 50303

STEVENSON, BETTY LEWIS, mgmt. cons.; b. Wenona, Ill., Oct. 22, 1915; d. George D. and Erma D. (Swartz) Butcher; student Pleasant View Luther Coll., 1933-35; A.A., N.Mex. State U., 1972; 1 son, Scott L. Dep. county clk. LaSalle County, Ottawa, Ill., 1937-46; asst. exec. dir. LaSalle County Fed. Public Housing Authority, 1937-43; steno pool supr. Manhattan Project, Hanford Engr. Works, Richland, Wash., 1944; various secretarial positions, Chgo., 1945-48; sec. White Sands (N.Mex.) Missile Range, 1948-50; asst. adminstr. phys. sci. lab. N.Mex. State U., Las Cruces, 1951-59, adminstr. research center, 1959-69, adminstr., dir. Office of Grants and Contracts, 1969-79; pres. Lewis Ltd., Las Cruces, 1978—, Double L Constrn., 1979—. Mem. exec. bd. Las Cruces Girls and Boys Club, 1976—; pres. Dona Ana County Republican Women, 1982. Mem. Soc. Research Adminstrs., The Assn., Las Cruces C. of C. (pres. women's div. 1980-82), Delta Zeta. Presbyterian. Contbr. articles to profl. jours. Office: Lewis Ltd PO Box 3009 Las Cruces NM 88003

STEVENSON, ELIZABETH, writer, educator; b. Ancon, Panama C.Z., June 13, 1919; d. John Thurman and Bernice (Upshaw) S.; B.A. magna cum laude, Agnes Scott Coll., Decatur, Ga., 1941. Clk., Trust Co. Ga., 1941; stats. clk. So. Bell, 1941-42; auditor War Prodn. Bd. & War Assets Adminstrn., 1942-47; library asst. order dept. Atlanta Public Library, 1948-56; sec., asst. to dean Emory U., 1960-74, research asso., 1974-77, asst. prof. Grad. Inst. Liberal Arts, 1977-78, asso. Prof., 1978-82, prof., 1982—. Guggenheim fellow, 1951-52, 55-56; Am. Council Learned Socs. grantee, 1974-75; Nat. Endowment Humanities Stipendee, 1974; recipient Bancroft prize, 1956. Mem. Am. Studies Assn., Authors Guild, Phi Beta Kappa. Democrat. Author: The Crooked Corridor, A Study of Henry James, 1949; Henry Adams, 1955; A Henry Adams Reader, 1958; Lafcadio Hearn, A Biography, 1961; Babbitts & Bohemians, The American 1920's, 1967; Park Maker, A Life of Frederick Law Olmsted, 1977; Return to Montana, 1983. Home: 532 Daniel Ave Decatur GA 30032 Office: Inst Liberal Arts 308 Physics Bldg Emory U Atlanta GA 30322

STEVENSON, FERDINAN BACKER, lt. gov. S.C.; b. N.Y.C., June 8, 1928; d. William Bryant and Ferdinanda Legare (Backer) Waring; B.A., Smith Coll., 1949; LL.D. (hon.), U. S.C., 1979, Columbia Coll., 1979; children—David, Ferdinan, Norman Williams, Josephine. Staff, N.Y. Herald Tribune Book Rev., 1951-53; mem. S.C. Ho. of Reps., 1975-78; lt. gov. S.C., 1978—; mem. exec. com. Nat. Conf. Lt. Govs.; mem. strategy council Dem. Nat. Com. Mem. Bus. and Profl. Women's Club. Democrat. Episcopalian. Office: Office of Lt Governor Columbia SC 29201

STEVENSON-MICHENER, DEBORAH GRANVILLE, broadcast journalist; b. E. Orange, N.J., July 4, 1951; d. Albert Granville and Stella Margaret (Laube) Stevenson; student Georgian Ct. Coll., 1969-70; B.A. cum laude, U. Conn., 1975; postgrad. Fairfield U., 1979; m. Alan Howard Michener, Dec. 28, 1974. With Woodbury Ice Cream Shop (Conn.), 1969-71; sec., editor Colonial Bank, Waterbury, Conn., 1972; reporter WQQW Radio, Waterbury, 1973, Town Times Newspaper, Watertown, Conn., 1973; news dir. WINE Am-FM Radio, Brookfield, Conn., 1974-75; asst. news dir., mgr. intern program, producer pub. affairs programs WMMM/WDJF Radio, Westport, Conn., 1975-78; capitol reporter, mgr. pub. affairs show Hotseat, WDRC-AM-FM Radio, Bloomfield, Conn., 1978-81; reporter U. Conn. Newspaper, Storrs, 1972-74; page editor Georgian Ct. Coll. Newspaper, 1969-70; editor Colonia News, Bank Newspaper, 1971, Leaves of Laurel, 1971-72, Conn. Artists and Writers Inc. Newspaper, 1977-78. UPI Thomas C. Phillips New Eng. Broadcasting award citation for excellence for pub. affairs show Enterprise, 1976; Conn. Safety Commn. spl. award, 1977; others. Mem. Radio and TV News Dirs. Assn., Am. Fedn. TV and Radio Announcers, Am. Bus. Women's Assn., DAR, Pi Delta Phi, Phi Alpha Theta. Co-creator: WMMM Radio mini-documentary mag. show Enterprise, 1975; author, dir.: Trouble at the North Pole, 1978, others; author short stories for children. Home: Flag Swamp Rd Southbury CT 06488 Office: 869 Blue Hills Ave Bloomfield CT 06002

STEVES, GALE C., editor; b. Mineola, N.Y., Dec. 20, 1942; d. William Harry and Ruth (May) S.; B.S., Cornell U., 1964; M.A., N.Y. U., 1966. Editorial asst. Ladies Home Jour., N.Y.C., 1966-69; seafood consumer specialist U.S. Dept. Commerce, N.Y.C., 1969-73; food editor Homelife Mag., N.Y.C., 1973-74; food and equipment editor Co-ed Mag., N.Y.C., 1974-77, Am. Home Mag., N.Y.C., 1977-78; equipment editor Woman's Day Mag., N.Y.C., 1979—; adv. Mid Atlantic Fisheries Commn., 1977—; mem. marine fisheries adv. com. Sec. Commerce, 1973-77. Mem. Am. Home Econs. Assn., Am. Dietetics Assn., Home Economists in Bus., Food and Nutrition Council Greater N.Y., Elec. Women's Roundtable, Les Dames d'Escoffier, Am. Inst. Kitchen Dealers, Omicron Nu. Author: Game Cookery, 1979; Campbell Soup's International Cookbook, 1980; Campbell's Microwave Cookbook, 1980; editorial adv. bd. Assn. Home Appliance Mfrs. Office: care Woman's Day mag 1515 Broadway New York NY 10036

STEWARD, PATRICIA ANN RUPERT, real estate cons.; b. Panama City, Panama, Apr. 20, 1945 (parents Am. citizens); d. Paul S. and Ernestina M. (Ward) Rupert; grad. Sch. of Mortgage Banking, Grad. Sch. of Mgmt., Northwestern U., 1979; m. Robert M. Levine, Oct. 28, 1978; children by previous marriage—Donald F. Steward, Christine Marie Steward. Vice pres. Asso. Mortgage & Investment Co., Phoenix, 1969-71; v.p., br. mgr. Sun Country Funding Corp., Phoenix, 1971-72, Freese Mortgage Co., Phoenix, 1972-74, Utah Mortgage Loan Corp., Phoenix, 1974-81; owner Elles Co., 1982—. State chmn. Ariz. Leukemia Dr., 1977-78, mem. exec. com., 1979—; troop leader Cactus Pine council Girl Scouts U.S.A., 1979-80. Recipient cert. of appreciation Multiple Listing Service, Phoenix Bd. Realtors, 1975, Multiple Listing Service, Glendale Bd. Realtors, 1977. Mem. Mortgage Bankers Assn. Am., Ariz. Mortgage Bankers Assn. (dir., chmn. edn. com. 1981-82), Young Mortgage Bankers Assn. (chmn. exec. com. 1980-81), Phoenix C. of C., Phoenix Real Estate Bd., Glendale Real Estate Bd., Central Ariz. Homebuilders Assn., Scottsdale Real Estate Bd. Republican. Office: 10823 N 66th St Scottsdale AZ

STEWARD, SANDRA LILLIAN, county govt. ofcl.; b. Chgo., Oct. 25, 1953; d. Edmund Lemont and Elzadia (Cprsey) S.; B.A. (Ill. State Tchr. scholar 1971-75), U. Ill., Chgo., 1975; M.A., Roosevelt U., 1976. Tchr., Chgo. public schs., 1975-78; program coordinator, producer sta. WBBM-TV, Chgo., 1978-80; freelance public relations exec., 1980-81; civil service recruiter Cook County, Chgo., 1981—; TV ednl. cons., freelance publicist, 1978—. Adminstrv. asst. spl. childrens charities Spl. Olympics, 1978—; judge Bd. Election Commrs., Chgo., 1979-82. Recipient Spl. Olympics award, 1980. Mem. Links, Ill. Affirmative Action Officers Assn., Chgo. Urban League, Chgo. Affirmative Action Assn., Govt. Coll. Relations Council (v.p. 1982). Roman Catholic. Office: 119 N Clark St Room 834 Chicago IL 60602

STEWART, ARLENE JEAN GOLDEN, designer; b. Chgo., Nov. 26, 1943; d. Alexander Emerald and Nettie (Rosen) Golden; B.F.A. (Ill. state scholar), Sch. of Art Inst. Chgo., 1966; postgrad. Ox Bow Summer Sch. Painting, Saugatuck, Mich., 1966; m. Randall Edward Stewart, Nov. 6, 1970; 1 dau., Alexis Anne. Designer, stylist Formica Corp., Cin., 1966-68; with Armstrong World Industries, Lancaster, Pa., 1968—, interior furnishings analyst, 1974-76, internat. staff project stylist, 1976-78, sr. stylist Corlon flooring, 1979-80, sr. exptl. project stylist, 1980—. Home: 141 E Marion St Lancaster PA 17602 Office: Armstrong Tech Center 2500 Columbia Ave Lancaster PA 17604

STEWART, BARBARA DEAN, writer, musician, ednl. cons.; b. Rochester, N.Y., Sept. 17, 1941; d. George Adgate and Louise (Griswold) Dean; B.A., Cornell U., 1962; M.S., Simmons Coll., 1964; diploma with honors in flute, Eastman Sch. Music, 1958; m. James C. Stewart, May 30, 1963; children—Allison, Whitney. Asst. law librarian Cornell U., 1963-64; writer/performer Kazoophony, Rochester, N.Y., 1972—; pres. Stewart Assos. Ednl. Systems Group, Rochester, 1979—; flutist La Jolla Civic Orch., 1966-68. Dir. jr. devel. U.S. Squash Racquets Assn.; pres. bd. dirs. Rochester Chamber Orch.; bd. dirs. Rochester chpt. English Speaking Union, 1982—. Recipient Achievement Bowl U.S. Squash Racquets Assn., 1981. Mem. Am. Fedn. Musicians, ASCAP. Home and Office: 3485 Elmwood Ave Rochester NY 14610

STEWART, BARBARA HOME, info. specialist, writer, lectr., photographer; b. St. Augustine, Fla., Mar. 10, 1931; d. Peter Stewart and Lala Home Schouten; B.A., ., U. Fla., 1952, postgrad., 1952-53; m. Orin Good Fogle, May 9, 1954 (div. May 1961); m. 2d, Edmund S. Rogalski, May 18, 1972. Owner, editor, pub. Newberry (Fla.) News, 1948-53; asso. mgr. Fla. Bldg. Jour., 1953-54; asst. dir. public relations Miami Seaquarium, 1954-55; writer television scripts Sea Scope Prodns., Inc., 1955-56; producer survival film in Everglades, 1957-60; asso. editor Fla. mag., 1961-63; dir. publicity D. Van Nostrand Co., Inc., Princeton, N.J., 1963-66; library public relations rep. J.B. Lippincott, Phila., 1966-75; lectr. book pub. Calif. State U., Long Beach, summers 1973-75; condr. public relations seminars Pa. Library Assn./Pa. State Library, 1975; sales exec., info. specialist Inst. for Sci. Info., Phila., 1976—; film producer, lectr. Nat. Audubon Soc. Wildlife Film Tours, 1969-71. Recipient First Place award Fla. Outdoor Writers Assn., 1959. Mem. Outdoor Writers Assn. Am., Sigma Kappa. Home and office: 870 Ronnie Ln Philadelphia PA 19128

STEWART, EDNA MAE, nurse; b. Liberty Twp., Ill., Jan. 16, 1915; d. Samuel Francis and Letah W. (Coats) McBride; diploma Parkview Hosp., Pueblo, Colo., 1944. Head nurse Meml. Hosp., Topeka, 1951—.

Vol. ARC, 1945—; life trustee Cedars Home for Children, Lincoln. Served as 1st lt. Nurse Corps, U.S. Army, 1945-49. Named Hon. Co-founder Coll. of Ams., 1978; recipient cert. of appreciation Holy Land Christian Mission, 1978. registered nurse, Colo., Kans. Mem. Am., Kans. nurses assns., Nat. Audubon Soc., Am. Legion, St. Francis Hosp. Aux. (life), Nat. Wildlife Fedn. (life). Democrat. Home: 1616 Webster St Topeka KS 66604

STEWART, GRACE, educator; b. Rahway, N.J.; d. Marshall and Rachel Harriet (Clark) Stewart; B.A., Wayne State U., 1968, M.A., 1969, Ph.D., 1977; children—Mark David Wurster, Kevin Wurster. Mem. faculty Wayne State U., Detroit, 1968-76; mem. faculty Henry Ford Community Coll., Dearborn, Mich., 1978—, dir. Focus on Women program, 1978—; dir. Computech Services, Inc., 1982—. Bd. dirs. Villa Pointe Condominiums, 1980, YWCA of Western Wayne County, 1980—, Detroit Women's Forum, 1980—. Wayne State U. fellow, 1972, 73, 76. Mem. MLA, Mich. Women's Studies Assn. (dir. 1976—), Nat. Assn. Women Deans, Adminstrs. and Counselors, Phi Beta Kappa. Episcopalian. Author: A New Mythos: The Novel of the Artist as Heroine, 1979; contbr. articles to profl. jours. Office: 5101 Evergreen Rd Dearborn MI 48128

STEWART, GRACIE MAE, ednl. guidance counselor; b. Gainesville, Ala., Mar. 8, 1933; d. Frank and Lizzie Mae (Guy (Hall) Maniece; student Miles Coll., 1951-53; B.Edn., U. Toledo, 1955, M.Ed. in Guidance and Counseling, 1961, postgrad., 1974—; Reading Specialist (ednl. grantee), Bowling Green State U., 1974-75; m. Leonard D. Stewart, Sr., June 22, 1957; 1 dau., Deborah J. Tchr. Newnan (6a.) Elementary Sch., 1954-55, James Madison Jr. High Sch., Pontiac, 1956-57; math. tchr. J.W. Scott High Sch., Toledo, 1957-63, guidance counselor, 1963-69, asst. prin., 1969-75; guidance counselor T.A. DeVilbiss High Sch., Toledo, 1975—. Mem. Gov.'s Adv. Commn. on Drug Abuse, 1975, 78—; mayoral appointee Bd. Community Relations, 1978—; trustee v.p. program, YWCA, del. to leadership conf., 1972, rec. sec. bd. dirs., 1982-83; active Maumee council Girl Scouts U.S.A., 1975-78; bd. dirs. Econ. Opportunity Planning Assn., 1979; fin. sec. Union Grove Bapt. Ch.; mem. Dem. Bus. and Profl. Women's Club. Recipient cert. of appreciation, YWCA, 1975. Mem. NAACP, Toledo Mus. Art, New Union of Blacks to Improve Am., Phi Delta Kappa, Delta Kappa Gamma (1st v.p. Gamma Omega chpt.). Clubs: Nat. Assn. Bus. and Profl. Women's (life, profl. award, 1970, local pres., 1977-79, 71-73, dist. fin. sec., 1973-77, youth advisor, bd. dirs. credit union), Order Eastern Star (asso. conductress, asso. matron), Daus. of Isis (ceremonial dau. Mecca Ct. 73, oriental guide), Order Golden Circle (La Paz Assembly), Prince Hall Affiliate. Home: 530 Colonial Ct Toledo OH 43620 Office: DeVilbiss High School 3301 Upton Ave Toledo OH 43613

STEWART, INA MAY, nutritionist; b. Leicesterfield, Clarendon, Jamaica, W.I., Oct. 20, 1916; came to U.S., 1966, naturalized, 1979; d. Oliver Percival and Mary Ann (Webb) Martin; B.Sc. with distinction, McGill U., 1948; M.S., Howard U., 1949; Ph.D. (fellow), Yale U., 1953; m. Eldon Stewart, Jan. 31, 1970. Food microbiologist Processed Foods div. Ministry of Trade and Industry, Jamaica, 1954-58, controller food standards, dept. head, 1958-63; asst. prof. botany and biology L.I. U., 1963-64; asst. prof. biochemistry and nutrition Pratt Inst., 1964-70, asso. prof. nutrition, 1970-72, prof., chmn. dept. food sci. and mgmt., 1972—; lectr., cons., researcher; organizer nutrition symposia. Registered dietitian; lic. clin. lab. supr. Fellow Royal Soc. Health; mem. Hosp. Food Adminstrs. Assn. (adv. bd. 1975-77), AAUP, Am. Dietetic Assn., N.Y. State Dietetic Assn., L.I. Dietetic Assn., N.Y. Acad. Scis., Inst. Food Technologists, AAAS, Am. Public Health Assn., Profl. Women's Assn., Kappa Lambda Mu. Democrat. Anglican. Research on lipid metabolism. Contbr. articles to Jamaican publs. 11433 Office: 215 Ryerson St Rm 305 DeKalb Brooklyn NY 11205

STEWART, JEANNE GABRIELLE, transp. co. exec.; b. N.Y.C., Nov. 14, 1946; d. Henry John and Erna Hedwig (Nagel) Burger; student Fordham U., U. B.C., No. Va. Community Coll.; m. Robert A. Stewart, Jan. 31, 1979. Mgr., Four Winds, N.Y.C., 1969-72; chief agy. and tour sales Amtrak, Washington, 1972-81; dir. sales Eastern U.S., Via Rail Can., Inc., N.Y.C., 1981—. Republican. Writer, editor trade manuals. Home: 1403 1/2 Turner St Alentown PA 18102 Office: 1 World Trade Center Suite 7969 New York NY 10048

STEWART, MARY AGNES, music critic, journalist; b. Battle Creek, Mich., Feb. 25, 1899; d. William Ray and Mary Ann (Hays) Simpson; ed. Pacific Union Coll., U. Wash., U. Md., Am. U., Southeastern U., Washington, San Diego State U.; m. William Robert Stewart, May 4, 1918; children—William Robert, Ray Simpson, Stanley Hays. Asso. editor Calif. Hawaii Hotel-Life and Ocean Travel, 1925-36; impresario L. E. Behymer, Honolulu, 1926-29, La Jolla, Calif., 1941-44; San Diego rep. Pacific Coast Musician, 1945-54; La Jolla corr. Los Angeles Times, 1952-60; interior decorator Mary Stewart Interiors, La Jolla, 1942-82; researcher books The Spanish West, 1976, San Diego County Pioneer Families, 1976; free-lance writer, La Jolla, 1982—. Historian, San Diego Opera Guild; chmn. San Diego Woman's Philharm. Com., La Jolla, Los Angeles Philharm. Orch., 1975-78. Recipient Letter of Commendation, USN, 1972. Mem. Nat. League Am. Pen Women (br. pres. 1960-62), DAR (chpt. registrar 1966-67), Women in Communications, Nat. Geneal. Soc., Nat. Soc. Colonial Dames Am., First Families Va., San Diego Geneal. Soc., Social Service League La Jolla (life), Library Assn. La Jolla (life), Scottish Record Soc., Friends of Glasgow Cathedral (life), Sigma Alpha Iota. Clubs: Woman's (La Jolla); Clan Hay (life). Home: 7118 Olivetas Ave La Jolla CA 92037

STEWART, MARY AMANDA, social services adminstr.; b. Kansas City, Mo., Oct. 22, 1947; d. George Griffis and Mary Eugenie (Voorhis) Fowler; student Colo. State U., 1966-69; B.S., Okla. State U., 1972; M.S.W., Ind. U., 1977; children—Corin Justine, Benjamin George. Adminstrv. asst. Ind. Family Health Council, Indpls., 1977—; social worker Koala Center Alcohol Treatment Center, Lebanon, Ind., 1977; coordinator staff devel., cons. and edn. Crisis Unit, Midtown Community Mental Health Center, Indpls., 1977-80, case mgr. inpatient services, 1980-81, crisis unit team dir., 1981—; tng. faculty Marion County Mental Health Assn. Crisis & Suicide Intervention Service, 1972-80, mem. crisis and suicide intervention com., 1976-80, chmn., 1980. Recipient 2000 hr. Vol. award, Marion County Mental Health Assn., 1979. Mem. Ind. Crisis Resource Fedn. (treas. 1979-80, dir. 1979-82), Nat. Assn. Social Workers. Democrat. Roman Catholic. Home: 5929 Deerwood Ct Indianapolis IN 46254 Office: 1001 W 10th St Indianapolis IN 46202

STEWART, MARY CATHERINE, psychologist; b. Sault Ste. Marie, Mich.; d. Alexander Pringle and Marguerite Louise (Mc Carron) S.; A.B., U. Miami, 1941, M.S., 1960; m. Charles William Marker, Nov. 14, 1942 (div.); 1 son, Kevin Charles Stewart Marker. Human engring. analyst Boeing Co., Seattle, 1960-69; cons. MITRE Corp., McLean, Va., 1970, tech. staff, 1971-74; research contract mgr. U.S. Dept. Transp., Washington, 1974-76; supervisory auditor psychologist GAO, Washington, 1976-78; established human factors group Idaho Nat. Engring. Lab. EG&G Idaho, Inc., Idaho Falls, 1978, mgr., 1978-82; profl. staff TRW Ballistic Missile Div., Norton AFB, Calif., 1982—. Mem. Human Factors Soc. (founder, 1st pres. chpt.), Assn. Women in Sci., Evaluation Research Soc., Am. Nuclear Soc., Audubon Soc., LWV. Home: 1980 Moran St Idaho Falls ID 83401

STEWART, MEREDITH LEE, hosp. adminstr.; b. Kellogg, Idaho, Aug. 20, 1940; d. Norval Rupert and Dorothy Jean (Cameron) Jones; grad. high sch.; m. Donald Eugene Stewart, June 17, 1972; children—Jamie, Jennifer, Jeffery, Jean, Jason. Bookkeeper, Deaconess Hosp., Spokane, Wash., 1970-71, supr. accounts payable, 1971-73, echocardiographer and cardiovascular coordinator, 1973-79, mgr. central supply, 1979—; part time instr. Spokane Community Coll., 1977-79, pres. echocardiography com., 1979, adv. com. cardiopulmonary and echocardiography program, 1977-79; guest speaker, organizer seminars in field. Registered diagnostic med. sonographer. Mem. Echocardiography Soc., Am. Hosp. Assn. Home: Route 1 Box 282 A Colbert WA 99005 Office: W 800 5th Ave Spokane WA 99210

STEWART, ORO ROZELLA, retail exec.; b. Pendleton, Oreg., July 8, 1917; d. Joseph Allen and Oro Rozella (Overholtzer) Holaday; B.E., Oreg. State Coll., 1940; postgrad. Wash. State Coll., 1940-42; m. Ivan Stewart, Apr. 4, 1943. Owner, mgr. Stewart's Photo Shop, Anchorage, 1943—; co-owner Stewarts Jewel Jade Mine, 1970—; instr. TV Sch. Photography. Mem. Anchorage Centennial Com., 1967, organizer time capsule to be buried in Juneau. Recipient various awards, gem and mineral shows. Mem. Anchorage C. of C., Chugach Gem and Mineral Soc. (pres. 1967, chmn. field trips 1965-78, internat. chmn. 1967-82), Master Photo Dealers Assn., Profl. Photographers Alaska, Alaska Miners Assn., Am. Fedn. Lapidary Socs. (internat. relations com. 1977-80), Pioneers of Alaska, Nat. Businessmens Assn., Alaska Geol. Soc., Riflemans Assn., N.W. Fedn. Mineral Socs., Anchorage Downtown Assn., Fairview Homeowners Assn., Tropical Fish Club. Democrat. Mem. Soc. Friends. Clubs: Zonta (v.p. 1971), Scottish. Writer Alaskan directory on rockhound locations. Home: 1008 A Anchorage AK 99501 Office: 531 4th Ave Anchorage AK 99501

STEWART, PATRICIA ANN, clin. psychologist; b. Tulsa, Feb. 25, 1931; d. Jack Truman and Anna Mae (Smith) Paris; B.A., U. Denver, 1963, M.A., 1965, Ph.D., 1968; m. A. Frank Knotts, Oct. 15, 1976; children—Ralph Steven, Jacqueline Suzanne. USPHS fellow U. Colo. Med. Sch., Denver 1968-69; clin. psychologist Arapahoe Mental Health Center, Englewood, Colo., 1969-71, Profl. Psychiat. and Guidance Clinic, Denver, 1971-73; pvt. practice clin. psychology, Littleton, Colo., 1973—; lectr. U. Colo., 1969, Regis Coll., 1970; cons. Coors Wellness Center, Golden, Colo., 1981-82; coordinator gifted children Colo. Mensa, 1978—. Mem. Am. Psychol. Assn., Colo. Psychol. Assn., Am. Bd. Profl. Psychology, Mensa, Intertel, Phi Beta Kappa. Home: 420 S Marion Pkwy #1802 Denver CO 80209 Office: 2305 E Arapahoe Rd #119 Littleton CO 80122

STEWART, PATRICIA ANN, forest industries co. exec.; b. Phoenix, Nov. 3, 1953; d. Travis Delano and Ann Helen (Lopez) Hill; B.S., Ariz. State U., 1975. Programmer, analyst Victor Comptometer Corp., Phoenix, 1975-77, Lewis & Roca, Attys., Phoenix, 1977-79; data processing mgr. Central Mgmt. Corp., Phoenix, 1979-80; corp. systems cons. S.W. Forest Industries, Phoenix, 1981—; partner Abacus Group, 1980—. Mem. Data Processing Mgmt. Assn. (pres. Phoenix chpt. 1982). Home: 15849 N 20th Pl Phoenix AZ 85022 Office: SW Forest Industries Co 6225 N 24th St Phoenix AZ 85011

STEWART, PATRICIA CARRY, found. ofcl.; b. Bklyn., May 19, 1928; d. William J. and Eleanor (Murphy) Carry; student U. Paris, 1948-49; B.A., Cornell U., 1950; m. Charles Thorp Stewart, May 30, 1976. Fgn. corr. Irving Trust Co., N.Y.C., 1950-51; with Janeway Research Co., N.Y.C., 1951-60, sec., treas., 1955-60; dir. Galt Malleable Iron Ltd., 1958-60; with Buckner & Co., N.Y.C., 1961-71, partner, 1962-71; pres., treas. Knight, Carry, Bliss & Co., Inc., N.Y.C., 1971-73; pres., treas. G. Tsai & Co., Inc., 1973; v.p. Edna McConnell Clark Found. Inc., 1974—; dir. Trans World Airlines, Borden Inc., Continental Corp., Bankers Trust Co.; allied mem. N.Y. Stock Exchange, 1962-73; mem. nominating com., arbitration com. Am. Stock Exchange, N.Y. Stock Exchange; past chmn., dir. Investor Responsibility Research Center. Trustee Cornell U., vice chmn. investment com., mem. exec. com.; vis. com. Grad. Sch. Bus., Harvard U., 1974-80; vice chmn. CUNY, 1976-80; mem. bd. advisers Baruch Coll.; bd. dirs. United Way of Tri-State, 1977-81, Inst. for Edn. and Research on Women and Work; voting mem. Blue Cross and Blue Shield Greater N.Y., 1975-82; trustee N.Y. State 4-H Found., 1970-76, Internat. Inst. Rural Reconstruction, 1974-79; mem. bd. overseers Cornell U. Med. Coll. mem. N.Y.C. panel White House Fellows, 1976-78. Recipient Elizabeth Cutter Morrow award, 1977; Catalyst award, 1978. Mem. Pi Beta Phi. Club: Cosmopolitan. Home: 135 E 71st St New York NY 10021 Office: 250 Park Ave New York NY 10017

STEWART, PHYLLIS ANN, motion picture co. exec., educator; b. Decker, Ind., Feb. 17, 1939; d. Loren and Jennie (Key) Purcell; B.S., Ind. State Tchrs. Coll., 1961; M.S., Ind. State U., 1968; m. Eddie C. Stewart, Aug. 12, 1961. Co-owner Stewart Theatres, 1961-79; tchr. S. Knox Sch. Corp., Knox County, Ind., 1962-63, 64-66; with Gimbel Bond, Vincennes, Ind., 1963-64; tchr. N. Knox Sch. Corp., 1966-67; tchr. Vincennes Community Sch. Corp., 1967—, Vincennes Lincoln Sch., 1967—; pres. Exclusive Internat. Pictures, Vincennes, 1977—. Recipient Rose award Alpha Omicron Pi, 1961; Parker fellow, 1967-68. Mem. NEA, Am. Vocat. Assn., Nat. Assn. Vocat. Home Econs. Tchrs., Am. Home Econs. Assn., AAUW, Nat. Broadcasting Assn., Nat. Assn. Theatre Owners, Nat. Ind. Theatre Owners, Theatre Owner Coop., Ind. Motion Picture Producers Assn., Ind. Tchrs. Assn., Vincennes Edn. Assn., Ind. Vocat. Assn., Ind. Home Econs. Assn. (pres. dist. 7, 1974), Ind. Vocat. Home Econs. Assn. (Merit award), Delta Kappa Gamma. Home: 1410 McKinley Ave Vincennes IN 47591 Office: Suite 509 Am Nat Bank Bldg Vincennes IN 47591

STEWART, RACHEL ANN, educator; b. Burlington, Iowa, Mar. 12, 1943; d. Clarence Robert and Rachel Elizabeth (Miner) S.; B.A., Coe Coll., 1965; postgrad. Western Ill. U. Tchr., Gulf Oil Co., Puerto La Cruz, Venezuela, 1967-70, Ft. Madison (Iowa) Community Schs., 1970—; mem. Ft. Madison City Council, 1980—; mem. Iowa Profl. Practice Commn., 1981—. Bd. dirs. Friends Reach Out, 1981—, Lee County Restitution Bd., 1981—. Mem. NEA, Iowa Edn. Assn., Ft. Madison Edn. Assn. Republican. Presbyterian. Home: 406 17th St Fort Madison IA 52627

STEWART, RITA JOAN, conf. center adminstr.; b. Muncie, Ind., June 6, 1945; d. John Marion and Crystalee (Shirley) Masterson; B.S., Ball State U., 1967, M.A., 1974; children—Jon Lewis, Robert Forest. Tchr., Sunnyside Elem. Sch., New Castle, Ind., 1967, Blue River High Sch., Mt. Summit, Ind., 1969; substitute tchr. Union Twp. High Sch., Modoc, Ind., 1971-72; copywriter/announcer Sta. WTIM, Tyalorville, Ill., 1974-75; mgr. Kitselman Conf. Center, Ball State U., Muncie, 1978—. Democratic precinct committeewoman, 1970; precinct chmn. March of Dimes, 1975; chmn. com. edn. Westview Sch. Council. Mem. Ind. Conf. Dirs., AAUW, Am. Home Econs. Assn., Kappa Delta Pi. Democrat. Methodist. Club: Order Eastern Star. Home: 3401 University Ave Muncie IN 47304 Office: Kitselman Conf Center Ball State Univ Muncie IN 47306

STEWART, SUZANNE, service co. exec., ins. agt.; b. Schenectady, June 3, 1948; d. George Curtis and Janet (Gurney) S.; B.A., U. Pa., 1970, M.S. in Cardiovascular Physiology (teaching fellow), 1978. Plan adminstr. Todd Service Corp., Greenwich, Conn., 1978-80; spl. agt. Northwestern Mut. Life Ins. Co., Milw., 1980—; sec.-treas. John O. Todd Orgn., Stamford, Conn., 1981—, Servestate Corp., Stamford, 1981—, Todd Service Corp., Stamford, 1981—; sr. asso. John O. Todd Orgn., 1981—. Mem. Nat. Assn. Life Underwriters. Office: 524 Glenbrook Rd Stamford CT 06906

STEWART, WILLA ELIZABETH, soprano, music educator; b. Lockwood, Mo., Mar. 8, 1917; d. George and Ethel (Cunningham) S.; B.A., S.W. Mo. State U., 1956; degree in voice, Curtis Inst. Music, 1941; m. Michael Setseak, Jan. 26, 1941. Appeared in leading soprano roles San Carlo Opera, 1945-48, City Center Opera, N.Y.C., 1947, Covent Garden, London, 1948-50, Staatsoper, Vienna, Austria, 1950-52; solo appearances with symphonies, 1946-52, including London Symphony, Detroit Symphony, Phila. Symphony, Dallas Symphony, CBS Symphony, NBC Symphony; asst. prof. voice N. Tex. State U., Denton 1954-57; asso. prof., U. Tex., Austin, 1957-65, prof., 1965-80; prof. U. Ill., Urbana, 1982—; former vocal coach apprentice program Santa Fe Opera Co.; judge Met. Opera Regional Auditions; condr. master classes. Mem. Nat. Assn. Tchrs. Singing, Mu Phi Epsilon. Republican. Roman Catholic. Home: 4613 D Pinehurst Dr S Austin TX 78747 Office: Dept Music U Ill Urbana IL 61801

STICH, PEGGY ANN STIMMEL, automobile co. ofcl.; b. Darbyville, Ohio, Aug. 25, 1931; d. Wilbur Smith and Bernice Edna (Hott) Stimmel; missionary diploma with honor Moody Bible Inst., 1952; B.A. cum laude in Econs. (scholar), Ohio Wesleyan U., 1965; M.B.A. with distinction, Xavier U., 1977; m. George R. Stich, Mar. 7, 1953; 1 son, Mark Stephen. Missionary in S. Am., Evang. Alliance Mission, 1956-61; cost acct. Western Electric Co., 1965-66; acctg. mgr. Ohio Wesleyan U., 1966-73; fin. specialist NCR Corp., 1973-74, systems analyst, 1974-75, supr. inventory planning, 1975, mgr. material planning and purchasing control, 1976-78; materials mgr. U.S. Elec. Motors Co., 1978; with Gen. Motors Corp., 1978—, shift supt. materials, Lakewood, Ga., 1979-80, gen. ops. supr. material data base mgmt. Central Office, Warren, Mich., 1980, dir. material and prodn. control GM Assembly Div., Balt., 1980—. Mem. Am. Prodn. and Inventory Control Soc., Am. Soc. Women Accts., AAUW. Baptist. Home: 1207 Turnbridge Rd Forest Hill MD 21050 Office: Gen Motors Assembly Div 2122 Broening Hwy PO Box 148 Baltimore MD 21203

STICKLE, MARGARET ALICE, controller; b. Russell, Ky., Oct. 3, 1934; d. Russell De Atley and Lorah Ellen (Ferrell) Kegley; B.A., Marshall Coll., 1956; postgrad. UCLA 1973-75; 1 son, David Brent. Asst. controller R & B Devel., Los Angeles, 1973-78; pres. Evergreen Realty Corp., and Evergreen Realty Corp., Tex., Los Angeles, 1978-80; v.p., controller Consol. First Nat. Corp., Los Angeles, 1980—; controller western div. Niagara Cyclo Massage, 1968-70; sec. various corps. Treas., Boy Scouts Am., 1965-68; mem. election bd. Republican Party, 1968-71. Mem. Nat. Acctg. Assn., Nat. Notary Assn. Presbyterian. Club: Northridge Woman's (sec. 1967). Home: 23500 The Old Rd Newhall CA 91321 Office: 10880 Wilshire Blvd Suite 2100 Los Angeles CA 90024

STICKLE, MARILYN GREGER, clin. social worker; b. Johnson City, N.Y., Jan. 20, 1947; d. George William Beers and Mary (Breckner) Thomas; B.A., George Washington U., 1968; M.Ed., Am. U., 1971; M.S.W., Ind. U., 1974; m. Warren E. Stickle, III, Aug. 15, 1970. Tchr.-counselor Todd County High Sch., Mission, S.D., 1969-70; social worker Logansport (Ind.) State Hosp., 1971-73; clin. social worker Guidance Center, Logansport, 1973-75, Arlington (Va.) Guidance Assn., 1976-78; clin. social worker, coordinator services Arlington Counseling Center, 1978—. Active polit. campaigns for Dem. candidates, 1972, 81. Lic. clin. social worker. Mem. Greater Washington Soc. Clin. Social Work (v.p. 1980—), Nat. Assn. Social Workers (chmn. Va. Pace com. 1981). Home: 1911 Rhode Island Ave McLean VA 22101 Office: 5319 Lee Hwy Arlington VA 22207

STICKLES, BONNIE JEAN, nurse; b. Waukesha, Wis., Nov. 24, 1944; d. Donald William and Betty Jane Stickles; B.S. in Nursing, U. Wis., 1967; M.S. in Nursing, Midwifery, Columbia U., 1974. Mem. nursing staff Grace Hosp., Detroit, 1970-73; mem. faculty and staff U. Minn. Sch. Nursing and Nurse-Midwifery Service, Mpls., 1974-76; chief nurse-midwife, clin. instr. St. Paul-Ramsey Med. Center, 1976—; mem. consumer adv. pool FDA; adv. bd. Childbirth Edn. Assn., 1980—. Served with USNR, 1965-70. Decorated Letter of Commendation. Mem. Am. Coll. Nurse-Midwives (chmn. profl. affairs com. 1975-80), Nurses Assn. Am. Coll. Obstetricians and Gynecologists (charter), Aircraft Owners and Pilots Assn., Gt. Plains Perinatal Orgn., Alpha Tau Delta. Author articles in field. Office: 640 Jackson Ave St Paul MN 55701

STIDGER, RUTH WILLMAN, editor; b. Rodney, Iowa, Sept. 20, 1939; d. Kenneth Wilbur and Eileen Lucille (Walton) Willman; student U. Iowa, State Coll. Iowa, Northwestern U.; m. 2d, Howe C. Stidger; children by previous marriage—Ellen Joyce, Susan Grace. Constrn. field mgr. Saul Cohen Realty, Gary, Ind., 1965-67; editor house mag. Dilts Equitable Life Assurance Agy., Gary, 1967-68; staff editor Instns., Chgo., 1968-70; features editor Nation's Schs., Chgo., 1970-71; editorial dir. internat. group Tech. Pub. Co., N.Y.C., 1975—. Recipient Jesse H. Neal Editorial award, 1969 cert. merit, 1978 80; Nat. Merit scholar, 1957. Mem. Am. Bus. Press (past chmn., editorial bd.), N.Y. Bus. Press Editors (past pres.), Mensa. Author: Cost Reduction From A to Z, 1975; Inflation Management, 1976; Mining Equipment Handbook, 1982; The Compentence Game, 1981; Automation and Robotics Handbook 1982. Editor Mining Equipment Internat., 1977-78; asso. editor World Constrn. 1975-77. Office: 875 3d Ave New York NY 10022

STIEFEL, BETTY KRAEUCHE, nurse, clothing co. exec.; b. Hartford, Wis., May 24, 1941; d. George Roland and Delores (Horst) Kraeuche; R.N., Mt. Sinai Hosp. Sch. Nursing, 1962; grad. Patricia Stevens Sch., 1963; student U. Wis., 1962-63, 69—; m. William James Stiefel, May 20, 1964; children—John Benjamin, James Gottfried, Elisabeth Kraeuche, William George. Model various firms, Milw., Chgo. and Green Bay, Wis., 1962-78; staff nurse med. surg. floor to asst. head nurse Mt. Sinai Med. Center, Milw., 1962-64; weekend night nurse Ivanhoe Sanitarium, Milw., 1962-64; vol. research asst. Marquette U., Milw., 1962; occupational nurse Stiefel Clothing Co., Green Bay, 1965-79, office/personnel mgr., 1976-79, dir., 1969—, v.p., 1976—; pres., owner Betty K Stiefel & Assos., Green Bay, 1980—; librarian Green Bay Montessori Soc., 1970-78; librarian Brown County Library, chmn. taping for blind and handicapped, 1973-79, cons., 1981—. Vol., Blood Donor Center, ARC, Green Bay, 1965-75; treas. Cnesses Israel Sisterhood, 1981—; pres. Green Bay Symphony Orch. Women's Guild, 1980—, also bd. dirs.; pres., bd. dirs. City of Hope; mem. adv. bd. Green Bay Symphony Orch. Assn., bd. dirs., 1980—; bd. dirs. YWCA; bd. dirs., sec. Service League Green Bay; pres., bd. dirs. Green Bay Montessori Soc.; bd. dirs. Brown County Civic Music Assn., also mem. adv. bd.; mem. sustaining com. Peninsula Music Festival; trustee Peninsula Arts Assn., 1980—. Served to 2d lt., Nurse Corps, U.S. Army, to 1964. Recipient Jaycettes Community Appreciation award, 1969; others. Mem. Beta Sigma Phi. Office: PO Box 123 Green Bay WI 54301

STIEFEL, MARIGENE HOKE, real estate broker; b. Greenville, Ohio, Oct. 3, 1921; d. John M. and Mary (Shaner) Hoke; grad. Realtors Inst., Bert Rodgers Sch. Real Estate, 1977; m. Arthur Anthony Stiefel, May 24, 1952; 1 dau., Erica Charleen Stiefel Dickerson. Adminstrv. asst. FAO, Washington, 1945-52; owner, mgr. Stiefel Art Shop, Bradenton, Fla., 1962-71; personnel adminstr., public relations officer, asst. v.p. Palmetto Fed. Savs., Holmes Beach, Fla., 1971-78; owner S.I.D. Group Interiors; broker, office mgr., public relations officer, Realtor, Des Champs & Gregory, Inc., Bradenton, 1978—; free lance interior designer; instr. Savs. & Loan Inst. Served with USMC, World War II.

Mem. Women's Council Realtors (pres.). Club: Ret. Officers' Wives. Home: 5200 Gulf Dr Holmes Beach FL 33510 Office: 1812 Manatee Ave W Bradenton FL 33505

STIEGHORST, JUNANN JORDAN, seed co. exec.; b. Hydro, Okla., June 8, 1923; d. John Wallace and Myrtle Mae (Harrison) Jordan; student Southwestern Coll., Weatherford, Okla., 1940-41; B.A. in L.S., U. Okla., 1944, B.A. in English, 1947, postgrad., 1959-60; postgrad. So. Meth. U., 1945; m. Guenther Paul Stieghorst, Aug. 13, 1955; 1 son, Theodore Mark. Stewardess, Braniff Airways, 1944-45; advt. copywriter, model Neiman-Marcus, Dallas, Tex., 1945-46, dir. clientele and charge account promotion, 1947-55; advt. copywriter Wilhelm-Laughlin-Wilson, Dallas, 1946; dir. public relations and clientele Lichensteins, Corpus Christi, Tex., 1955-56; clientele dir. Joskes of Tex., San Antonio, 1957-58; children's librarian Jefferson County Public Library, Golden, Colo., 1967-69; co-owner Stieghorst Seed Co., Golden, 1973—. Recipient award for outstanding book U. Okla., 1966. Mem. AAUW, Colo. Archaeol. Soc., DAR (nat. chairman's award 1975; nat. vice-chmn. public relations, state chmn., chpt. regent), Alpha Chi Omega. Republican. Lutheran. Club: Soroptimist. Author: Bay City and Matagorda County: A History, 1965; Colorado Historical Markers, 1978; contbr. articles on retail bus. to various mags. Home and Office: Golden CO 80401

STIEGLER, CHRISTINE BROWN, educator; b. Lumberton, N.C., Dec. 9, 1940; d. Leo M. and Ann Lane Brown; B.S. in Bus., Appalachian State U., 1962, M.A., 1963; Ed.D., U. No. Colo., 1969; postgrad. N.C. State U., 1971-72, U. Wis., summer 1981; m. James R. Stiegler, Apr. 4, 1974. Instr., Appalachian State U., Boone, N.C., 1963; tchr. Lake-Sumter Jr. Coll., Leesburg, Fla., 1963-68; instr. U. No. Colo., Greeley, 1968-69; researcher and instr. mgmt. tng. programs GT&E Data Services Corp., Tampa, Fla., 1970; asst. prof. U. S. Fla., Tampa, 1970; prof. econs. dept. Sandhills Community Coll., Southern Pines, N.C., 1970-72; lectr. U. Cin., 1972-74; editor South-Western Pub. Co., Cin., 1972-77; lectr. Edgecliff Coll., Cin., 1976-77, U. Cin., 1976-77; asso. prof. bus. edn. No. Ky. U., Highland Heights, 1978—. Named Woman of Yr., City of Leesburg, 1966; Bus. Woman of Yr., State of Fla., 1965; recipient Helen Eisenhower award, 1966. Mem. Am. Mgmt. Assn., Bus. Communication Assn., Am. Vocat. Assn., Nat. Assn. Female Execs., Adminstrv. Mgmt. Soc., Am. Soc. Tng. Devel., Nat. Bus. Edn. Assn., Nat. Assn. Tchr. Educators for Bus. and Office Edn., Office Systems Research Assn., Nat. Assn. Profl. Saleswomen, Delta Pi Epsilon. Democrat. Methodist. Author: Office Systems and Procedures, 1982; editor 12 books on communications; contbr. articles on bus. edn. to profl. publs. Home: 8474 Farm Pond Ln Maineville OH 45039 Office: Bus Edn No Ky U Highland Heights KY 41076

STIEHL, CELESTE M., state legislator; b. Belleville, Ill., Sept. 7, 1925; student Katherine Gibbs Sch., N.Y.; m. William D. Stiehl; children—William David, Susan. Active civic, polit. affairs, including Cub Scouts, PTA, Belleville Meml. Hosp., Belleville Community Concert Assn., others; pres. St. Clair County Republican Women; co-chmn. Ill. Positive Action Task Force; mem. Ill. Ho. Reps., 79th, 80th, 81st Gen. Assemblies, apptd. asst. minority leader. Mem. St. Clair County Lawyers' Wives Assn. (past treas.), Order Women Legislators, LWV, Delta Kappa Gamma. Club: Zonta. Office: Ill Ho Reps State Capitol Springfield IL 62706

STIETZ, LUCILLE ELIZABETH, banker; b. Wis., July 4, 1931; d. Henry C. and Leona M. (Gille) S.; ed. Grad. Sch. Mgmt., Northwestern U., 1978. With Monroe (Wis.) Evening Times, 1952-58; loan clk. Crocker Bank, Stockton, Calif., 1958-61, note dep. supr., 1962-67; teller Nat. Bank Alaska, Anchorage, 1961-62; with Public Service Co. N.Mex., Albuquerque, 1967-70; with Nat. Bank Alaska, 1970—, mgr. mortgage loan dept., 1978—; tchr. workshops, seminars in field. Mem. Mortgage Bankers Assn. Am. (rep.), Soc. Real Estate Appraisers (affiliate), Alaska Mortgage Bankers Assn. (pres. 1979-80). Office: Pouch 7-025 Anchorage AK 99510

STILL, KAY HIGHTOWER, banker; b. Ashepoo, S.C., July 1, 1940; d. Harold Elmore and Julia Kathleen (Delk) Hightower; m. Merrell Christopher Still, Aug. 24, 1958; children—Merrell C., Stephen Cooper. Bookkeeper, Brooker Hardware, Denmark, S.C., 1958-61; cost. clk. Shuron, Barnwell, S.C., 1961-64; planning clk. Barnwell Mills, 1964-69; asst. v.p., br. mgr. Tri County Bankers Trust, Barnwell, 1970—. Chmn. regional edn. funds crusade Am. Cancer Soc., Barnwell, 1974-82, chmn. S.C. div., 1982. Recipient Career Woman of Yr. award Barnwell County Bus. and Profl. Women, 1978, Barnwell C. of C., 1978-79. Mem. Am. Inst. Banking (pres. Edesto chpt. 1980-81), Nat. Assn. Bank Women (chmn. LowCountry group 1980-81), Barnwell County C. of C., Barnwell County Bus. and Profl. Women, S.C. Bankers Assn. Baptist. Office: 1108 Dunbarton Blvd Barnwell SC 29812

STILLMAN, MARY ELIZABETH, librarian, educator; b. Phila., Oct. 31, 1929; d. Ernest E. and Rosalie (Burhans) Stillman; B.A., Wilson Coll., Chambersburg, Pa., 1950; M.S., Drexel U., Phila., 1952; Ph.D. (fellow), U. Ill., 1966. Librarian, USAF, 1953-63, Export-Import Bank U.S., 1965-68; asst. prof. Drexel U., 1968-72; mem. faculty Albright Coll., Reading, Pa., 1972—, prof., librarian, 1975—; editor Drexel Library Quar., 1969-72; cons. research info. system Social and Rehab. Service, 1972-74; del. Pa. Gov.'s Conf. on Libraries, 1977; chmn. Pa. Library Week, 1978, 79. Mem. ALA (reviewer Subscription Books Bull. 1969—), Pa. Library Assn. (dir. pub. relations task force 1974-79, editor bull. 1973-79, treas. colloquium on info. retrieval 1978-79), AAUP. Contbr. articles to profl. jours. Home: 1516 Greenview Ave Reading PA 19601 Office: Albright Coll Reading PA 19604

STILWELL, EDNA MAE, gerontologist, editor, educator; b. Indpls., Mar. 22, 1931; d. James William and Ada A. (Spears) Brown; R.N., Knoxville Gen. Hosp., 1952; B.S., U. Md., 1962, M.S., 1972, Ph.D. in Health Edn. and Gerontology, 1981; m. William E. LeBow, Jan. 5, 1953 (div. 1957); m. 2d, James J. Stilwell, Nov. 22, 1962; children—Elizabeth J., James F., Robert R., William M., Linda L., James R., James J. Instr. Anne Arundel Gen. Hosp., Annapolis, Md., 1953-61, 69-71; field adviser Community Health Facilities, 1967-68; instr. U. Md., College Park, 1971-73; editor Jour. Gerontol. Nursing, 1974—; project leader Center on Aging U. Md., Annapolis, 1975-77; prin. investigator nursing project, instr. Johns Hopkins U., 1978-79; coordinator gerontol. nursing U. Md. Sch. Nursing, Balt., 1979—. Cons. Gov.'s Comm. to Study Nursing Homes, 1971-75; mem. expert panel on long term Care Md. State Office on Aging. Mem. Am. (exec. com. div. gerontol. nursing 1980—), Md. (past pres. dist. 3, chmn. div. gerontol. nursing) nurses assns., Nat. League Nursing, Gerontol. Soc., Am. Geriatrics Soc., Am. Public Health Assn. Democrat. Home: 916 Ridgewood St Annapolis MD 21401 Office: 655 W Lombard St Baltimore MD 21201

STIMACH, JANET LOUISE, real estate, comml.; b. Seattle, Oct. 29, 1939; d. Carl J. and Josephine A. (Baranzini) Carulli; 1 son, Craig B. Property mgr. Clarke-Ruble & Assos., Seattle, 1970-71; property mgr. commercial brokerage News Realty, Seattle, 1971-73; pres., owner, comml. broker, cert. property mgr., cert. bus. counselor Western Investment & Mgmt., Inc., Seattle, 1973—. Mem. Inst. Real Estate Mgmt., Seattle/King County Bd. Realtors, Internat. Platform Assn., Pacific NW Ballet. Republican. Roman Catholic. Club: Wash. Athletic, Variety (life, patron). Office: 2030 9th Ave Suite 202 Seattle WA 98121

STIMPSON, CATHARINE ROSLYN, educator, writer, editor; b. Bellingham, Wash., June 4, 1936; d. Edward Keown and Catharine Charlotte (Watts) S.; A.B., Bryn Mawr Coll., 1958; B.A. (Fulbright fellow), Cambridge (Eng.) U., 1960, M.A., 1965; Ph.D., Columbia U., 1967. Mem. faculty English dept. Barnard Coll., N.Y.C., 1963-80; prof. English, Douglass Coll./Rutgers U., New Brunswick, N.J., 1980—; founding editor Signs: Jour. of Women in Culture and Society, 1974-80; author: Class Notes, 1979; (novel) J.R.R. Tolkien, 1969; cons. Nat. Inst. Edn., 1978—, UNESCO, 1979, various colls. and univs. on women's studies, 1972—. Mem. nat. adv. bd. Southwest Inst. for Research on Women, 1979—; mem. nominating com. Nat. Medal for Lit., 1980; mem. nat. com. Emergency Civil Liberties Com., 1975—; mem. com. on status of women U.S. Commn. on UNESCO, 1979—. Nat. Humanities Inst. fellow, 1975-76. Mem. Nat. Abortion Rights Action League, NOW, MLA. Democrat. Office: Dept English Douglass College/Rutgers U New Brunswick NJ 08903

STIMSON, MIRIAM MICHAEL, ednl. adminstr.; b. Chgo., Dec. 24, 1913; d. Frank Sharpe and Mary Frances (Holland) S.; B.S., Siena Heights Coll., 1936; M.S., Instn. Divi Thomae, Cin., 1939, Ph.D., 1948. Joined Adrian Dominican Sisters, Roman Catholic Ch., 1935; mem. faculty Siena Heights Coll., Adrian, Mich., 1939-68, chmn. chemistry dept., 1948-68, dir. grad. studies, 1978—; research asso. Fla. State U., Tallahassee, 1969; prof. Keuka Coll., Keuka Park, N.Y., 1969-78; lectr. Canisius Coll., 1961; mem. screening panel NSF, 1963. Speaker Ch. Women United, Penn Yan, N.Y., v.p., 1973-74, pres., 1974-76; chmn. pub. events com. Keuka Coll. Campaign 1970, Penn Yan, 1970-72; chmn. Lenawee County Profl. Devel. Policy Bd., 1979-80. Mem. Am. Chem. Soc., Nat. Assn. Women Deans, Mich. Assn. Women Deans, AAUW. Home: 1126 E Siena Heights Dr Adrian MI 49221 Office: 1247 E Siena Heights Dr Adrian MI 49221

STINE, MADELINE IRENE, elem. sch. tchr., prin.; b. Bloomington, Ill., Nov. 1, 1937; d Richard and Lena (Kutz) S.; B.S. in Edn., Ill. State U., Normal, 1959; M.A. in Edn., Concordia Coll., River Forest, Ill., 1978. Tchr. phys. edn. Plaintiff (Ill.) Sch. Dist. 202, 1959-73; prin. St. Peter's Lutheran Sch., Joliet, Ill., 1980—, tchr. 4th and 5th grade, 1980-81, tchr. 3d and 4th grades, 1981—; pres. Assn. Plainfield Tchrs., 1970-71; tchr. adult fitness classes, workshop leader in field. Active local Girl Scouts; pres. altar guild St. Peter's Evang. Luth. Ch., 1980-82, sec. missions soc., 1982—, adv. mem. bd. Christian edn., 1980—; lay del. No. Ill. Dist. Luth. Ch.-Mo. Synod, 1980. Ill. Lambda scholar, 1977. Mem. AAHPER, Luth. Edn. Assn. (life), NEA (life), Aid Assn. Lutherans (chpt. sec.-treas. 1979-82), Delta Kappa Gamma. Republican. Home: Plainfield IL 60544

STINE, MARTHA GRACE, nurse; b. Marion, Ohio, Apr. 30, 1925; d. Orval Halsey and Sylvia (McEldowney) Emberton; L.P.N., Bartholomew County Sch. Practical Nursing, Columbus, Ind., 1968; R.N., Ind. U.-Purdue U., Indpls., 1975; m. Oren Clinton Callon, Apr. 7, 1939; children—James C. Callon, Kenneth Lee Callon, Judith M. Zook, Ralph S. Callon, David L. Callon, Wilma L. Choi. Nursing asst. Methodist Hosp., Indpls., 1955; dir. nursing Welcome Nursing Home, Franklin, Ind., 1976-80; charge nurse Johnson County Meml. Hosp., Franklin, 1980—; cons. in field. Grantee Meth. Hosp., 1974. Home: 121 Jordan Dr Franklin IN 46131 Office: 1125 W Jefferson St Franklin IN 46131

STINES, MARVELLA NORMA, machine shop exec., artist; b. Escondido, Calif., Sept. 8, 1945; d. Henry Amusden and Etha Mae (Bowling) Brown; student Palomar Jr. Coll.; m. Grant Edward Stines, Sept. 5, 1964; 1 son, Edward Grant. Library aide Escondido Public Library, 1960-63; repair part mgr. Sears Roebuck, 1964-69; apt. mgr., 1964-77; acct. S & S Machine Shop, 1969-76; acct. Stines Machine, 1977; pres. Stines Design, Inc., 1979—; porcelain artist. Mem. Am. Soc. Women Accts. (publicity chmn. 1982-83), Calif. China Painters Art Assn., North San Diego County China Painters Art Assn., World Orgn. China Painters, Internat. Porcelain Art Tchrs. Home: 1610 Friendship Ln Escondido CA 92026 Office: 1340 La Mirada Dr San Marcos CA 92069

STINSON, CAROLYN HOLLEY, research inst. bus. exec.; b. Paris, Tex., Nov. 23, 1936; d. Wilbert Willis and Treva May (Young) Holley; student Los Angeles City Coll., 1954-55; m. Charles David Stinson, Nov. 11, 1966; 1 son, Eric Zsasha. Acctg. mgr. Amax Aluminum Co., Riverside, Calif., 1956-67; asst. treas. Archtl. Enging. Products Co., Inc., San Diego, 1967-68; asst. treas., asst. sec. Salk Inst., La Jolla, Calif., 1969—; founder Salk Inst. Fed. Credit Union, 1972; treas.-mgr. Torrey Pines Fed. Credit Union, 1972-75, bd. dirs., 1976-78. Served with USAF, 1955-56. Decorated Am. Spirit of Honor medal. Mem. Soc. Research Adminstrs., Nat. Assn. Coll. and Univ. Bus. Officers, Nat. Council Univ. Research Adminstrs., Nat. Assn. Accts. Democrat. Mem. Ch. Religious Sci. Home: 2118 Belloc Ct San Diego CA 92109 Office: PO Box 85800 San Diego CA 92138

STIPE, JEAN ELIZABETH, nurse; b. Easton, Pa., Sept. 23, 1933; d. Charles and Margaret (Schnell) Boyer; diploma St. Lukes Hosp. Sch. Nursing, 1954; m. Edwin Stipe, Aug. 14, 1954; children—Daniel, Kelly. Staff nurse community hosps., Easton, Pa., 1957-59, Phillipsburg, N.J., 1961-62, Mt. Kisco, N.Y., 1964-66, Needham, Mass., 1969-71; head nurse neurology unit Lyons (N.J.) VA Hosp., 1971—. Mem. Nurses Orgn. VA (chpt. officer). Home: 70 Queen Ann Dr Basking Ridge NJ 07920 Office: Lyons VA Hospital Lyons NJ 07939

STIRN, REBECCA ATKINSON, optical co. exec.; exec.; b. Kansas City, Mo., Feb. 23, 1953; d. Russell Jay and Virginia (Cox) Atkinson; B.A., Smith Coll., 1975; M.B.A., Stanford U., 1978; m. Bradley Albert Stirn, Aug. 30, 1975. Asst. mgr. market devel. So. Pacific Transp. Co., San Francisco, 1978-79, fin. analyst, fin. adminstrn., 1979-80, asst. mgr. fin. adminstrn., 1980-81; mgr. market research Cooper Vision Optics div. Cooper Labs., Palo Alto, Calif., 1981—; market researcher Saga Corp., Menlo Park, Calif., summer 1977; research asst. Fed. Res. Bank of San Francisco, 1975-76. Mem. devel. com. Nairobi Day Sch., 1978; bd. dirs. Wilmer Eye Inst. at Johns Hopkins Hosp., Peninsula Smith Coll. Club, 1977-80. Home: 172 Stockbridge Ave Atherton CA 94025 Office: 2801 Orchard Pkwy San Jose CA 95134

STITT, KATHLEEN ROBERTA, nutritionist; b. Roanoke, Ala., Dec. 27, 1926; d. Mabrey and Bertha (Green) S.; B.S., U. Ala., 1946, M.S., 1955; dietetic intern Case Western Res. U., 1947; Ph.D., Ohio State U., 1965. Adminstrv. dietitian Case Western Res. U. Hosp., Cleve., 1947-49; dir. dietetics Selma (Ala.) Bapt. Hosp., 1949-53; prof., head dept. food, nutrition, and instn. mgmt. U. Ala., University, 1965-79, prof., coordinator research, 1980—. Recipient Hazel Lapp award, 1963-65; Mead Johnson award, 1964. Mem. Am. Dietetic Assn., Am. Home Econs. Assn., Am. Public Health Assn., Am. Sch. Food Service Orgn., AAAS, Ala. Public Health Assn., Nutrition Today Soc., Soc. Nutrition Edn., Sigma Xi, Phi Upsilon Omicron. Contbr. articles to profl. jours. Home: 125 Fox Run Tuscaloosa AL 35406 Office: PO Box 1488 University AL 35486

STITT, SUSAN MARGARET, mus. adminstr.; b. East Liverpool, Ohio, Jan. 24, 1942; d. Wilson Montgomery and Cora Blanche (Link) S.; B.A. in Am. History, Coll. William and Mary, 1964; M.A. in Am. Civilization, U. Pa., 1966. Asst. to dir. Hist. Soc. of Pa., Phila., 1966; dir. Mus. of Albemarle, Elizabeth City, N.C., 1967-68; adminstr. Mus. of Early So. Decorative Arts, Winston-Salem, N.C., 1969-71; asst. to dir. Bklyn. Mus., 1971-72; project dir. survey of placement and tng. Nat. Endowment for Humanities, Old Sturbridge Village, Sturbridge, Mass., 1972-74; dir. Museums at Stony Brook (N.Y.), 1974—; adj. asso. prof. dept. art SUNY, Stony Brook, 1975-78. Mem. Am. Assn. Mus., N.E. Mus. Conf. (v.p.), Am. Assn. State and Local History, L.I. Mus. Assn., N.Y. State Assn. Mus. (council). Office: The Museums at Stony Brook 1208 Route 25A Stony Brook NY 11790

STIVER, INEZETTA OREL ELIASON, accountant; b. Centerville, Ind., Mar. 26, 1916; d. Wood Esta and Pearl Mae (Davis) Eliason; diploma Ind. Bus. Coll., 1948; m. Roy Carl Stiver, Nov. 24, 1940. Pvt. practice acctg., Centerville, 1955—; instr. acctg. Richmond (Ind.) Bus. Coll., 1945-48. Clk., Centerville Christian Ch., 1955—; bd. dirs. Historic Centerville, Inc., 1969—; mem. Centerville Planning Com., 1975-77. Recipient civic award Centerville Jaycees, 1971; This Is Your Life award, 1978; Scouters Wife Heart of Gold award, 1979. Mem. Nat., Ind. socs. public accts., Soc. Ind. Pioneers, Am. Legion Aux. Republican. Author: Wilderness Opportunity, 1964. Address: 116 E Plum St Centerville IN 47330

STIVERS, ANN EVELYN, delivery co. exec.; b. Casper, Wyo., Oct. 26, 1948; d. Winthrop Newcomb and Merva (Culver) S.; B.S., Tex. Woman's U., 1970. Tchr., Dallas, 1971-75; with United Parcel Service, 1975—, mgr., Little Rock, 1978—. Republican. Presbyterian. Home: 9000 Longacre St Little Rock AR 72205 Office: 8121 Distribution Dr Little Rock AR 72209

STIVERS, SUE CRAVENS, home economist; b. Russell County, Ky., June 8, 1936; d. Jason Everett and Zellah (Cunningham) Cravens; A.A., Campbellsville Coll., 1954-55; B.S., U. Ky., 1957; postgrad. George Washington U., U. Ky.; m. Robert P. Stivers, Jr., Feb. 16, 1966. Home economist Coop. Extension Service U. Ky., Cumberland County, 1957-66, Adair County, 1966—. Founder, exec. dir. Miss Lake Cumberland Scholarship Pageant, 1973—, bd. dirs., 1973—. Mem. Columbia C. of C. (cultural arts chmn.), Ky. Assn. Extension Home Economists, Nat. Assn. Extension Home Economists, Ky. Home Econs. Assn., Am. Home Econs. Assn., Bus. and Profl. Women Club, U. Ky. Alumni Assn., Epsilon Sigma Phi. Baptist. Clubs: Womans, Order Eastern Star. Home: PO Box 231 Columbia KY 42728 Office: 202 Public Square Columbia KY 42728

STOCK, ANNE ALDEN, city exec.; b. Wilkes-Barre, Pa., Feb. 9, 1941; d. George Edward and Thelma Ayre (Cooper) S.; student San Diego State Coll., 1959-63, cert. in gen. secondary teaching, 1967; B.A. in Music, UCLA, 1965. Choir dir. First Evangelical United Brethren Ch., San Diego, 1965-68; purchasing clk. City of San Diego, 1968-77, buyer, 1977-80, sr. buyer, sewage and water treatment equipment and chems., 1980—. Fundraiser, Mothers March, March of Dimes, San Diego, 1975; polit. campaigner for candidates for San Diego City Council, U.S. Congress. Mem. Calif. Women in Govt., Nat. Mgmt. Assn., San Diego Opera Assn., San Diego Zool. Soc., LWV, Sigma Alpha Iota (pres. Iota Delta chpt. 1963). Republican. Presbyterian. Office: City Purchasing Dept 1222 1st Ave San Diego CA 92101

STOCK, BARBARA M., psychologist; b. Pitts., May 4, 1943; d. Samuel M. and Hilda (Marmins) Morris; B.A., Chatham Coll., 1964; Ph.D., U. Mich., 1972; div.; children—Aric, Adam, Michael. Cons., Ky. Infant Presch. Project, Dept. Econ. Security, Frankfort, 1972; asst. prof. dept. spl. edn. Eastern Ky. U., Richmond, 1972-74; instr. parent courses, Lexington, Ky., London, Eng., 1972-75; stringer, feature writer Suburban Tribune, Hinsdale, Ill., 1977-81; pvt. practice clin. psychology, Wilmette, Ill., 1980—; instr. Oakton Community Coll.; staff psychologist One to One Learning Center, Wilmette, 1980—. Mem. Ky. Gov.'s Ad Hoc Com. for Programs for Children with Behavioral Disorders, 1972. Mem. Am. Psychol. Assn., Ill. Psychol. Assn., Internat. Transactional Analysis Assn., Phi Beta Kappa. Home: 930 Linden Ave Wilmette IL 60091 Office: One to One Learning Center Highcrest Center 702 Locust St Wilmette IL 60091

STOCK, WENDY L., banker; b. Detroit, Jan. 24, 1950; d. Harry J. and Bette E. Stock; B.B.A., Western Mich. U., 1972; diploma Grad. Sch. Bank Mgmt., U. Mich., 1978; m. Charles R. Howie, Jan. 17, 1981. With Union Bank & Trust Co., N.A., Grand Rapids, Mich., 1972—, mgmt. devel. officer, then regional br. adminstr., 1979—, v.p., 1980—. Chmn. Babe Zaharias Gulf Invitational, Am. Cancer Soc., 1982. Recipient Disting. Contbr. award Grand Rapids C. of YWCA, 1982. Mem. Nat. Assn. Bank Women (chmn. 1983 state conf., membership chmn., mem. council Mich. chpt. 1981—), Am. Bankers Assn. (br. adminstrn. div. 1981—), Grand Rapids C. of C., Econ. Club Grand Rapids. Republican. Episcopalian. Office: 200 Ottawa St NW Grand Rapids MI 39503

STOCKER, BEATRICE HANNAH, speech pathologist; b. N.Y.C., Nov. 20, 1909; d. Tobias and Ida (Weinstein) Klipstein; B.A., Barnard Coll., 1931; M.A., Tchrs. Coll. Columbia U., 1936; m. Jule E. Stocker, Mar. 26, 1932; children—Maida Stocker Abrams, Michael. Adminstrv. asst. Speech and Hearing Center Queens Coll., CUNY, 1949-78, lectr., 1968-78; pvt. practice speech pathology, N.Y.C., 1978—; cons. in field. Axe-Houghton Found. grantee, 1973; City U. N.Y. Research Found. grantee, 1971—. Mem. Am. Speech, Lang. and Hearing Assn. (cert. clin. competence in speech and audiology), N.Y. State Speech and Hearing Assn., N.Y.C. Speech, Lang. and Hearing Assn., AAUP. Author: The Stocker Probe Technique for Diagnosis and Treatment of Stuttering in Young Children, 1976, rev. edit., 1980. Home and Office: 17 W 54th St New York NY 10019

STOCKLER, JULIE RENEE, free-lance writer, producer; b. Detroit, Nov. 12, 1954; d. Morton Israel and Ruth (Racklin) S.; B.A., U. Mich., Ann Arbor, 1975; m. Roger Green, Apr. 1, 1979. Copywriter, William Douglas McAdams, N.Y.C., 1976-77; project mgr. Health Edn. & Tng., N.Y.C., 1977-78; project mgr. KPR Infor/Media Corp., N.Y.C., 1978-79, editorial dir., 1979, v.p., dir. publs., 1980-82; free-lance writer. Mem. Assn. Multi Image, Women in Communications, Healthcare Businesswomen's Assn. Jewish. Home: 150 Essex Ave Glen Ridge NJ 07028

STOCKMAN, JUDITH KOVIS, interior designer; b Bamberg, W.Ger., May 29, 1946; came to U.S., 1948; d. Michael and Elizabeth Kovis; B.F.A., Pratt Inst., 1968. Interior designer George Nelson & Co., N.Y.C., 1971; prin. Judith Stockman & Assos., N.Y.C., 1971—; designed restaurants Mus. Modern Art, N.Y.C.; First Women's Bank, N.Y.C.; lectr. in field. Recipient Interior Design award for Luchow's, Institutions, 1980. Contbr. articles to profl. jours. Office: 111 Wooster St New York NY 10012

STOCKTON, BEVERLY ANN, physiologist, educator; b. Indianola, Iowa, June 6, 1939; d. Frank Ray and Freda Ann (Courtney) Stockton; R.N., Iowa Meth. Hosp. Sch. Nursing, 1960; B.A., Simpson Coll., 1963; M.A., U. Oreg., 1965, Ph.D., 1972. Instr. med.-surg. nursing Iowa Meth. Hosp., Des Moines, 1960-63; emergency rm. nurse Sacred Heart Hosp., Eugene, Oreg., summers 1964, 65, 66; teaching asst. biology U. Oreg., Eugene, 1963-65; instr. med.-surg. nursing Borgess Sch. Nursing, Kalamazoo, 1965-66; curriculum coordinator med.-surg. nursing Iowa Meth. Hosp., summer 1967; asst. prof. biology Simpson Coll., Indianola, Iowa, 1966-69, asst. prof. biology, 1975-76; asso. prof. physiology/pharmacology, U. Osteo. Medicine and Health Scis., Des Moines, 1976—, discipline head, 1979—, dir. continuing nursing edn., 1980—; asst. prof. biology Tabor Coll., Hillsboro, Kans., 1972-75; mem. Am. Osteo. Assn. site accreditation teams for osteo. med. schs. Mem. adv.

com. continuing nursing edn. Drake U., 1979—; mem. Indianola Drug & Alcohol Abuse Commn., 1982—, others. Mem. Student Osteo. Med. Assn. (editorial adv. bd.), Soc. for Study of Reprodn., Am. Inst. Biol. Scis., Inst. of Soc., Ethics and the Life Scis., Hastings Center. Democrat. Baptist. Contbr. articles to profl. jours. Home: 106 S J St Indianola IA 50125 Office: 3200 Grand Ave Des Moines IA 50312

STODDARD, JEAN ELIZABETH, investment broker; b. Portland, Oreg., Mar. 24, 1950; d. Bruce O. and Mary Jo (Gemmer) Stoddard; student Boise State Coll., 1970-72; 1 son, Travis L. Caudle. Registered rep. Foster & Marshall Am. Express Inc., Juneau, Alaska, 1979-82; registered rep. Piper Jaffray and Hopwood, Idaho Falls, Idaho, 1982—; partner No. Restaurants, Inc., Juneau, 1973-76; sales rep. S.E. Alaska Empire, Juneau, 1976-79. Bd. treas. Big Bros./Big Sisters of Juneau, 1981-82; mem. Juneau Visitors Info. Council, 1980-82. Club: Soroptomists (corr. sec. 1981-82). Home: 129 E 23d St Idaho Falls ID 83401

STODDARD, KAREN ANN, auto sales co. ofcl.; b. Twin Falls, Idaho, Jan. 4, 1942; d. Donald and Merle N. (Nelson) Stoddard; B.F.A., U. Utah, Sale Lake City, 1963; tng. certifications, est, 1975, 77; m. Francis Belinne, June 12, 1962 (div., 1971); children—Adrian George, Daryl Jarvis. Dancer U. Utah Ballet Co., 1962-63; owner, operator art and dancing sch., Alamogordo, N.Mex., 1965-68; counselor Sonoma County Juvenile Hall, Santa Rosa, Calif., 1970-74; adminstrv. asst. Acad. and Tng. Div., est, San Francisco, 1974-76; sales agt. Colonial Realty, San Francisco, 1976-78; cons. to Heyneman Assos., San Francisco, 1976; employment and tng. Medicon, Inc., San Francisco, 1977-78; employment, planning, tng. Praedium, Inc., San Francisco, 1978; personnel, sales tng., advt., mgmt. planning Wills Motor Co., Twin Falls, Idaho, 1979—; cons. in field various firms. Vol. at Center and fund drives Easter Seals; mem. Opera Guild; public relations chmn. Twin Falls bd. LWV, 1980; mem. Hunger Project, World Runners for Hunger. Cert. leader seminars. Republican. Club: Toastmistress. Choreographer Jr. Miss Pageant for Optimist Club, 1979; tchr. aerobic exercise YFCA. Home: Box 1762 161 Pierce St Twin Falls ID 83301 Office: Box 1866 or 236 Shoshone St W Twin Falls ID 83301

STODDARD, MARGERY MIESSNER, editor; b. St. Louis, May 26, 1929; d. George Emil and Myrtle Antoinette (Wolf) Miessner; A.A., Santa Monica Coll., 1948; student U. So. Calif., 1948-50; m. Scott Powell Stoddard, Nov. 5, 1955; children—Scott Wilcox, Janet Faye Stoddard Bouweraerts. Photo and fashion model (part-time) Caroline Leonetti Studios, Hollywood, Calif., 1948-51; tech. artist and scene coordinator Metro-Goldwyn-Mayer Motion Picture Studios, Culver City, Calif., 1951-54; story editor Playhouse 90, CBS-Television City, Los Angeles, 1954-56; free-lance non-fiction and features writer various publs., 1956-78; mng. editor Plastics mag. (Western Plastics News, Inc.), Santa Monica, Calif., 1978—, public relations and press rep. Western Plastics Expns., Santa Monica, also creative advt. and graphics artist. Patron Santa Monica Coll. Mem. Soc. Plastics Engrs., Soc. Advancement of Material and Process Engring., Los Angeles Soc. Coatings Tech., Nat. Assn. Female Execs., Inc. Republican. Presbyterian. Home: 502-26th St Santa Monica CA 90402 Office: 1704 Colorado Ave Santa Monica CA 90404

STOECKMANN, ETHEL DOLORES, fin. exec.; b. N.Y.C., July 4, 1922; d. Albert Lewis and Ethel Carol (Wade) Infantas; student public schs., N.Y.C.; m. Sept. 17, 1944; 1 son, Robert W. Sec./treas. Stoeckmann Land Co., Inc., Baudette, Minn., 1972—, Stoeckmann Ranches, Inc., Red Bluff, Calif., 1976—, Stoeckmann Farms, Inc., Pecos Tex., 1977—, dir., 1951—; partner Stoeckmann & Co., 1972—, S & S Enterprises, Baudette, 1976—, Stoeckmann Investment Co., Red Bluff, 1976—. Democrat. Home: PO Box 2017 Pecos TX 79772 Office: Route 2 PO Box 24 Red Bluff CA 96080

STOKES, ELIZABETH HENDON, psychologist, educator; b. Tex., June 5, 1922; d. Walter Lee and Gertrude (McCord) Hendon; B.S., Sam Houston State U., Huntsville, 1942; M.A., 1947; Ed.S., George Peabody Coll., Nashville, 1956; Ed.D., N. Tex. State U., Denton, 1960; m. William Glenn Stokes, May 1, 1942; children—William Glenn, III, Sara Lynne. Social worker, Tex., 1942-44; public sch. tchr., Tex., 1945-46, 51-53; appraiser VA Vocat. Evaluation Center, 1949-50; sch. psychologist, Clarksville (Tenn.) City Schs., 1955-57; asst. prof. psychology Northwestern State Coll., Natchitoches, La., 1957-58; mem. faculty Austin Peay State U., Clarksville, 1960—, prof. psychology, 1963—; bd. dirs. Tenn. Vocat. Tng. Center, 1969-71, 76-78; cons. in field. Chmn., Clarksville Human Relations Council, 1969-71; pres. Montgomery County Assn. Retarded Citizens, 1969-71; bd. dirs. Tree House, day care center, 1981—. Named Disting. Prof., Austin Peay State U., 1976; Educator of Yr., Tenn. Assn. Retarded Citizens, 1976. Mem. Nat. Assn. Sch. Psychologists, Am. Psychol. Assn., Tenn. Personnel and Guidance Assn. (editor newsletter 1964-66, pres. 1966-67), Tenn., Assn. Psychology in Schs. (pres. 1978-79). Democrat. Presbyterian. Home: 316 Irene Dr Clarksville TN 37040 Office: Psychology Dept Austin Peay State U Clarksville TN 37040

STOKES, LILLIAN SCOTT, nurse, educator; b. Greenville, N.C., Feb. 18, 1942; d. John Thomas and Lillian Catherine (Thompson) Gatlin; diploma Kate Bitting Reynolds Sch. Nursing, 1963; B.S. in Nursing, N.C. Central U., 1966; M.S. in Nursing, Ind. U., 1969; m. Robert Everett Stokes, Aug. 7, 1965; children—Everett Scott, Robyn Catherine. Nurse, Norfolk (Va.) Community Hosp., 1963-64, Silver Cross Hosp., Joliet, Ill., 1966-67; asst. prof. nursing Purdue U., Indpls., 1969-72; asso. prof. nursing Ind. U., Indpls., 1974—. Chairperson audit com. Home Care Agency of Marin County, 1973-76. Recipient Disting. Service award Girls Clubs Greater Indpls., 1982. Mem. Am., Ind., Dist. V nurses assns., Nat. League for Nursing (Lucile Petry Leone award 1975), Ind. Citizens League for Nursing, Ind. U. Sch. Nursing Alumni Assn. (pres. 1978—), Womens Aux. Indpls. Dist. Dental Soc., Chi Eta Phi (Spl. Achievement award 1975), Alpha Kappa Alpha, Sigma Theta Tau. Co-author: Adult and Child Care: A Client Approach to Nursing, 2d edit., 1977; Medical-Surgical Nursing: Common Health Problems of Adults and Children Across the Life Span, 1982; editorial bd. Family and Community Health.

STOKOWSKI, ANNE K., state senator; widow; children—Barbara, Steven, Laura, Robert, Jean Anne. Mem. Minn. Senate, St. Paul, 1979—, vice chairperson gen. legis. and adminstrv. rules, com., chairperson post-secondary and higher edn. subcom. of edn. com. mem. energy and housing, govtl. ops. coms. Bd. dirs., v.p., sec. Mpls. council Camp Fire Girls, Recipient Luther Halsey Gullock award Nat. Camp Fire Girls. Clubs: Dome, Senate. Office: 29 State Capitol Saint Paul MN 55155 *

STOLL, CAROLINE JEAN, nurse, naval officer; b. St. Charles, Mo., Oct. 17, 1935; d. Emil Joseph and Alice Anna (Meyling) S.; B.S.N. cum laude, St. Louis U., 1960, M.S.N., 1976. Staff nurse Mt. St. Rose Hosp., St. Louis, 1960-63, Barnes Hosp., St. Louis, 1963-64; charge nurse Med. Ward, St. John's Mercy Hosp., St. Louis, 1964; dir. nurses Chesterfield Manor, St. Louis, 1964-65; supr. St. Louis City Hosp. #2, Tuberculosis Sanitarium and Rehab. Center, 1965-68; commd. lt., U.S. Navy, 1968, advanced through grades to comdr., 1979—, charge nurse U.S. Naval Hosp., San Diego, 1968-71, U.S. Naval Hosp., Great Lakes, Ill., 1971-75, nurse midwife Naval Regional Med. Center, New Orleans, 1977-78, Naples, Italy, 1978-81, Groton, Conn., 1981—. Decorated Naval Commendation medal. Mem. Am. Nurses Assn., Nurses Assn. of Am. Coll. Ob-Gyn, Am. Coll. Nurse Mid-Wives, Naval Inst., Sigma Theta Tau. Home: 78-8 Buddington Rd Groton CT 06340

STOLL, JEAN ETHEL, bldg. materials mfg. co. exec.; b. Passaic, N.J., Nov. 13, 1945; d. Dominic and Ethel (Feher) Stamato; B.A., U. Vt., 1965; postgrad. U. Calif., Berkeley, 1967, Temple U., 1968; m. Jean Stamato Hoover, Dec. 29, 1969; children—Melissa, Deborah. Tchr., Morris Catholic High Sch., Denville, N.J., 1965-67, High Point Regional High Sch., Sussex, N.J., 1967-68, St. Rose of Lima Sch., Denver, 1968-69, Tampa Public Schs., 1975-76; treas. D. Stamato & Co., Inc., Andover, N.J., 1976, pres., 1977-80; pres. Andover Industries Inc. (N.J.), 1982—. Mem. Indsl. Commn. Andover Twp., 1977-78, chmn., 1979-80. Mem. N.J. Redi Mix Assn., Builders Assn. Home: Route 1 Box 224 Newton NJ 07860 Office: Route 206 Box U Andover NJ 07821

STOLLER, BARBARA, exec. recruiter; b. N.Y.C.; d. Robert and Mildred (Juceam) Weinberg; B.A. in English, Hofstra U., Hempstead, N.Y., 1969. Editorial asst. Redbook mag., 1969-70; adminstrv. asst. McGraw-Hill Films, N.Y.C., 1970-72; sr. assoc. E.G. Todd Assocs., N.Y.C., 1977—. Office: 535 Fifth Ave New York NY 10017

STOMP, PATRICIA GAMON, registrar; b. Chgo., Mar. 8, 1936; d. Phillip and Josephine Gamon; B.G.S. in Psychology, Roosevelt U., 1982; m. Lawrence Stomp, Dec. 29, 1974; children—Rudy, Robert, James, Sharon, Rebecca. Registrar, Ill. Coll. Optometry, Chgo., 1969—. Mem. Am. Assn. Collegiate Registrars and Admissions Officers, Ill. Assn. Collegiate Registrars and Admissions Officers. Office: 3241 S Michigan Ave Chicago IL 60616

STONE, BARBARA FROST, speech pathologist; b. Robinson, Ill., Feb. 13, 1929; d. Virgil Elsworth and Nancy Brittimer (Sutfin) Frost; B.S., Eastern Ill. State Coll., 1951; M.A., St. Louis U., 1965; m. Neville Stone, Feb. 2, 1974; children—Nancy, Michael. Instr., St.-Mary of-the-Woods (Ind.) Coll., 1953-55; speech clinician Spl. Sch. Dist. St. Louis County (Mo.), 1958-63; instr. St. Louis U. Sch. Medicine, 1963-65; cons. Mo. Crippled Children's Service, St. Louis, 1967-74; instr., exec. dir. cleft palate div. Washington U. Sch. Medicine, 1974-75; cons. speech pathology, Chesterfield, Mo., 1981—. Asst. to dep. dir. George Bush Nat. Polit. Campaign, Alexandria, Va., 1980. Mem. Am. Speech, Hearing, Lang. Assn., Am. Cleft Palate Assn. Republican. Presbyterian. Clubs: Forest Hills Country, Clayton. Home: 14928 Manor Lake Dr Chesterfield MO 63017

STONE, BETTY RUTH BOYLS, editor; b. West Point, Miss., Mar. 3, 1930; d. Gaston Dean and Mary Frances (Yeates) Boyls; A.B., Miss. U. Women, 1951, M.S., 1972; m. Douglas Clyde Stone, July 8, 1951; children—Nora Frances Stone McRae, Kate Terrell Stone Rogers, Diana Gaston Futrell Stone. Med. lab. technologist, 1951-53; recruiting counselor Miss U. Women, Columbus, 1965-67, instr. physiology lab., 1972-74; editor Showcase publ. Columbus Civic Arts Council, 1981—. Pres., Columbus Jr. Aux, 1963, Demonstration PTA, 1966, Les Amis Club, Four Seasons Club, Lawyers Wives Club. Mem. Beta Beta Beta, Gamma Sigma Epsilon, Pi Kappa Delta. Methodist.

STONE, DIANA BARRY, rehab. counselor; b. Elizabeth, N.J., Jan. 10, 1944; d. John B. and Jane D. (Barry) S.; B.A. in Psychology, San Francisco State U., 1974, M.S., 1976; children by previous marriage—Christopher John, Mark Stephen. Supr., Avis Rent-a-Car, Newark, 1964-67; tour guide Am. Express Co., Geissen, W.Ger., 1968; dept. supr. data processing European Exchange System, Geissen, 1969; bank teller Gt. Western Savs. & Loan Assn., Berkeley, Calif., 1970-72; vocat. counselor Goodwill Industries, Oakland, Calif., 1972-74; vocat. rehab. counselor Dept. Vocat. Rehab., San Pablo, Calif., 1974-75; group facilitator U. Calif., Berkeley Extension, 1974-76; vocat. rehab. counselor Rehab. Cons., Inc., Emeryville, Calif., 1975-76; propr., dir. Diana B. Stone, Inc., Rainbow Assos., San Rafael, Calif., 1976—, supr. vocat. rehab. counselors, 1976—. Coordinator fund raiser Community Vol. Services, Myrtle Beach, S.C., 1966-68. Cert. rehab. counselor, Calif.; cert. community coll. tchr., Calif. Mem. Am. Personnel and Guidance Assn., Nat. Assn. Rehab. Profls. (membership chairperson 1980-81), Calif. Assn. Rehab. Profls., Nat. Assn. Rehab. Counselors (dir region 9, 1981-82, editor-in-chief newspaper 1981-82), NOW, Hebrew Free Loan Assn., Nat. Wildlife Fedn., NOW, Polit. Caucus, Nat. Audubon Soc. Democrat. Home: 98 Berkeley Ave San Anselmo CA 94960 Office: 1518 5th Ave San Rafael CA 94901

STONE, DONNA JESSIE, found. exec.; b. Evanston, Ill., May 23, 1935; d. W. Clement and Jessie V. (Tarson) S.; student Northwestern U., 1954-56; Baldwin-Wallace Coll., 1956-58; children by previous marriage—Christopher Kneifel, Linda Kneifel; m. 3d, LeRoy A. Pesch, Dec. 28, 1975; step-children—Christopher Pesch, Brian Pesch, Daniel Pesch. Pres., W. Clement and Jessie V. Stone Found., Chgo., 1970—; founder Nat. Com. for Prevention of Child Abuse, Chgo., pres., 1972-78. Chmn. Alliance for Arts Edn., 1976-78; John F. Kennedy Center for Performing Arts, Washington, 1972—; sec. Child Welfare League Am.; chmn. Internat. Standing Com. Child Abuse, Geneva, 1981—; life mem. bd. govs. Art Inst. Chgo., 1966. Republican. Presbyterian. Clubs: Capitol Hill, La Concha, Club de Yates, MidAm. Home: 333 N Mayflower Rd Lake Forest IL 60045 Office: 111 E Wacker Dr Suite 510 Chicago IL 60601

STONE, ELAINE MURRAY, author, TV producer, musician; b. N.Y.C., Jan. 22, 1922; d. H. and Catherine (Fairbanks) Murray-Jacoby; student Juilliard Sch. Music, 1939-41; diploma N.Y. Coll. Music, 1942; licentiate in organ Trinity Coll. Music, London, 1947; student U. Miami, 1952, Fla. Inst. Tech., 1963; m. F. Courtney Stone, May 30, 1944; children—Catherine Margaret (Mrs. Robert Louis Rayburn), Pamela Elizabeth (Mrs. Don Webb), Victoria Francis. Organist, choir dir. St. Ignatius Episcopal Ch., 1940-44; accompanist Strawbridge Ballet on Tour, N.Y.C., 1944; organist All Saints Episcopal Ch., Ft. Lauderdale, Fla., 1951-54, St. John's Episcopal Ch., Melbourne, Fla., 1956-59, 1st Christian Ch., Melbourne, 1962-63, United Ch. of Christ, Melbourne, 1963-65; piano studio, Melbourne, 1955-70; editor-in-chief Cass, Inc., 1970-71; dir. continuity Sta. WTAI-AM-FM, Melbourne, 1971-74; mem. sales staff Engle Realty, Inc., Indialantic, Fla., 1975-78; v.p. public relations Consol. Cybertronics, Inc., Cocoa Beach, Fla., 1969-70; writer/producer Countdown News, KXTX-TV, Dallas, 1978-80; asso. producer Focus-News, 1980—. Mem. exec. bd. Women's Assn., Brevard Symphony, 1967—; mem. heritage com. Melbourne Bicentennial Commn. Recipient 1st place in piano Ashley Hall, 1935-39, S.C. State Music Contest, 1939, numerous other awards, Mem. Nat. League Am. Penwomen (1st place awards Tex. 1979, v.p. Dallas br. 1979-80, pres. 1980—), Women in Communications, DAR (Fla. state chmn. music 1962-63, organizing regent Rufus Fairbanks chpt. Satellite Beach, Fla. 1982-83), Children Am. Revolution (past N.Y. state chaplain), Am. Guild Organists (organizing warden Ft. Lauderdale), ASCAP, Space Pioneers, Fla. Press Women's Assn. Episcopalian. Author: The Taming of the Tongue, 1954; Love One Another, 1957; Menéndez de Avilés, 1968; Bedtime Bible Stories, Travel Fun, Sleepytime Tales, Improve Your Spelling for Better Grades, Improve Your Business Spelling, Tranquility Tapes, 1970; The Melbourne Bi-Centennial Book, 1976; Uganda: Fire and Blood, 1977; Tekla and the Lion, 1981; contbr. feature articles in nat. mags., newspapers including N.Y. Herald Tribune, Guidepost Mag., Logos Jour.; space corr. Cape Kennedy, for Religious News Service, 1962-78. Home: 1945 Pineapple Ave Melbourne FL 32935 Office: Three Rivers Realty Inc 500 N Harbor City Blvd Melbourne FL 32935

STONE, ELIZABETH WENGER, librarian; b. Dayton, Ohio, June 21, 1918; d. Ezra and Anna Bess (Markey) S.; A.B., Stanford U., 1937, M.A., 1938; M.L.S., Catholic U. Am., 1961; Ph.D., Am. U., 1968; m. Thomas A. Stone, Sept. 14, 1939; children—John Howard, Anne Elizabeth, James Alexander. Tchr. pub. schs., Fontana, Calif., 1938-39; asst. state statistician State of Conn., 1939-40; librarian New Haven Pub. Libraries, 1940-42; dir. pub. relations, asst. to pres. U. Dubuque (Iowa), 1942-46; substitute librarian Pasadena (Calif. Pub. Library System, 1953-60; instr. Cath. U. Am., 1962-63, asst. prof., asst. to chmn. dept. library sci., 1963-67, asso. prof., asst. to chmn., 1967-71, prof., asst. to chmn., 1971-72, prof., chmn. dept., 1972-80, dean Sch. Library and Info. Scis., 1981—; exec. dir. Continuing Library Edn. Network and Exchange, 1975-79. Program mgr. Nat. Rehab. Center, 1977—; mem. Pres.'s Com. on Employment of Handicapped, 1972—. Recipient Pres.'s medal Cath. U. Am., 1982. Mem. ALA (council 1976-83, v.p. 1980-81, pres. 1981-82, exec. bd. 1980-83), D.C. Library Assn. (pres. 1966-67), Spl. Libraries Assn. (pres. D.C. chpt. 1973-74), Assn. Am. Library Schs. (pres. 1974), Am. Soc. Info. Sci., Cath. Library Assn., Adult Edn. Assn., Am. Soc. Assn. Execs., Phi Sigma Alpha, Beta Phi Mu, Phi Lambda Theta. Presbyterian. Author: Factors Related to the Professional Development of Librarians, 1969; (with James J. Kortendick) Job Dimensions and Educational Needs in Librarianship, 1971; Continuing Library Education as Viewed in Relation to Other Continuing Professional Movements, 1975; Motivation: A Vital Force in the Organization, (with F. Peterson and M. Chobot), 1977; American Library Development 1600-1899, 1977; (with others) Model Continuing Education Recognition System in Library and Information Science, 1979; (with M.J. Young) A Program for Quality in Continuing Education for Information, Library and Media Personnel, 1980; others; editor D.C. Libraries, 1964-66; contbr. articles to profl. jours. Home: 4000 Cathedral Ave NW Washington DC 20016 Office: Cath U Am Washington DC 20064

STONE, ETHEL BELLE, educator; b. Galveston, Tex., Jan. 15, 1929; d. Ralph William and Ethel Belle (Johnson) Trout; B.S. in Edn., Southwestern U., 1950; M.Ed., U. Houston, 1951; postgrad. U. Tex., Austin, 1965, San Jose State U., 1970-71; m. Robert Melvin Stone, Mar. 20, 1952; children—Suzanne, Robert Melvin, John David. Asst. mgr. Circle S Ranch, Zerhyr, Tex., 1954-65; tchr. rural schs., Tex., Calif., 1954-72; tchr. Public Schs. Clear Creek (Tex.), 1972—. Troop organizer Girl Scouts U.S.A., Tex., 1952-65, v.p., 1953-54; pres. ch. women (Ch. of Good Shepherd, Brownwood, Tex., 1956-57. Recipient commendation U.S. Army, 1953. Mem. Tex. State Tchrs. Assn. (life), NEA, Tex. PTA (hon. life), Delta Kappa Gamma, Delta Delta Delta. Club: Order of Eastern Star. Office: P H Greene Elementary Sch Webster TX 77598

STONE, KAREN SUE SEDGWICK, state edn. specialist; b. Riverside, Calif., Aug. 3, 1934; d. Joel Garrett and Lola Mae (Hansen) Sedgwick; B.S., Brigham Young U., 1965, M.S., 1968; m. Douglas Leslie Stone, Aug. 8, 1955; children—Rebecca, Douglas Reed, Adam Leslie. Mem. faculty Latter-day Saints Sem., 1964; tchr. Utah Tech. Sch., Provo, 1965; faculty Brigham Young U., 1965-72; state specialist in consumer home econs. edn. Utah Office Edn., Salt Lake City, 1972—; adv. Utah Future Homemakers Am. Assn.; speaker Am. Mothers, 1982. Mem. Am. Vocat. Assn., Utah Vocat. Assn., Am. Home Econs. Assn. (yearbook com. 1979—), Utah Home Econs. Assn., Nat. Assn. Vocat. Home Econs. Edn. Suprs. Republican. Mormon. Author curriculum guides, 1974-82. Office: 250 E 500 S Salt Lake City UT 84111

STONE, KATHRYN DOLORES, credit union exec.; b. Pontiac, Mich., June 12, 1929; d. Durward South and Betty Marie (LaVelle) Young; student public schs.; m. James Macklin Stone, Oct. 19, 1946; children—James Durward, David Allan. With T&C Fed. Credit Union, Pontiac, 1955—, asst. gen. mgr., teller mgr., acctg. mgr., 1972-77, treas. bd. dirs., exec. gen. mgr., 1977—; exec. com. Credit Union Data Acctg. Council, 1972-74, mem. exec. com. Oakland County (Mich.), chpt. Credit Unions, 1980—; exec. bd. Credit Union Met. Area Advt. Council, Detroit; dir. Joint Advt. Bd., Flint, Mich. Chmn. community div. Pontiac United Way, 1972. Recipient various service awards, certs. appreciation. Mem. Credit Union Execs. Soc., Jayno Heights Women's Assn., Epsilon Sigma Alpha (chpt. pres. 1966, 76-77, pres. Mich. council 1968-69). Episcopalian. Author manuals, policy books in field. Office: 939 S Woodward Ave Pontiac MI 48056

STONE, LAJANACE, univ. adminstr.; b. Buford, Ga., Sept. 19, 1938; d. Buford and Josie (Alexander) Butler; B.S., U. Kan., 1973; student Iowa State U., 1973-74. Asst. to dir. fin. aid U. Kans., Lawrence, 1970-73; asst. coordinator fin. aid Iowa State U., Ames, 1973-74; dir. fin. aid Lincoln U., Jefferson City, Mo., 1974-76, U. Mich., Dearborn 1976—; lic. rep. Investors Diversified Services, Detroit, 1982—; owner, founder LaStone Assos.-Money Mgmt. Inst., Detroit, 1982—; fin. cons.; fin. planning seminar instr. Mem Nat. Assn. Student Fin. Aid Adminstrs., Mich. Assn. Fin. Aid Adminstrs., Midwestern Assn. Fin. Aid Adminstrs., South Oakland County Bd. Realtors, Fin. Aid Adminstrs. (dir. Region V), Women's Econ. Club, Nat. Assn. Female Execs. Office: 4901 Evergreen Rd Dearborn MI 48128

STONE, MARY OVERSTREET, macrame designer, journalist; b. Auburndale, Fla., Mar. 17, 1924; d. Leroy Blan and Aldah (Myrick) Overstreet; student Orange County Vocat. Sch., 1954-55, Loch Haven Art Center, 1960, U. Tenn., 1979; m. Robert Myron Stone, Sept. 8, 1942; children—Lily Sue, Mary Lou. Macrame designer, Madisonville, Tenn., 1970-81; tchr. adult edn. Hiwassee Coll., Madisonville, 1977—, Monroe Vocat. Tech. Sch., Madisonville, 1976—; with Mountain Press, 1982—; Mem. E. Tenn. Crafts Council (rep. 1976-78), Sequoyah Arts and Crafts (v.p. 1975-76), Nat. Writers Club, Internat. Platform Assn., Soc. Craft Designers. Republican. Author instructional booklets including: Basic Macrame, Illustrated; Mary Stone's Macrame Cradle, Swing and Table; At Home With Macrame; These Are Knot Flowers; A Tisket, A Tasket, A Macrame Basket. Home: 6 Sunnydale Dr Sevierville TN 37862

STONE, NANCY GUNDERSEN, apparel mfg. co. exec.; b. S.I., Apr. 13, 1940; d. Walter Taft and Winifred (Wood) Gundersen; B.A., Fairleigh Dickinson U., 1960; postgrad. New Sch. Social Research; m. Martin L. Stone, Sept. 5, 1976; 1 stepson, Robert. Account exec. Rowland Co., N.Y.C., 1972-74; dir. public relations Ship N' Shore, N.Y.C., 1974-77; dir. merchandising Miss O by Oscar de la Renta, 1977-78; v.p. merchandising Jondel, Inc., 1978—. Asst. producer, fund raiser The People's Ticket for Gov. Hugh Carey; mem. women's com. fund raising Southampton Hosp. Mem. Fashion Group. Clubs: Water Mill Beach (dir., treas.), Harmonie. Office: Jondel Ind 525 7th Ave New York NY 10018 *

STONE, RUTH MAY, army non-commd. officer, recruiter; b. Shreveport, La., July 2, 1941; d. Vernon Lee and Thena Margaret (Robinson) Payne; A.A. in Bus., Columbia Coll., 1975-77, B.A. in Bus., 1980; m. Allen Perry Stone, May 15, 1969; 1 son, Scott Thomas White. Entered U.S. Army, 1968, non-commd. officer, 1980; non-commd. officer charge dermatology Med. Clinic, Ft. Gordon, Ga., 1968-71; WAC counselor, Albany, Ga., 1973-75; field recruiter, Miami, Fla., 1975-78; guidance counselor U.S. Army, Miami, 1977-80, Richmond, Va., 1980-82; sta. comdr. Chesterfield Recruiting Sta., 1982—; sec. Army Adv. Council; mem. U.S. Army Recruiting Command Comdr. Adv. Council. Decorated Meritorious Service medal, Army Commendation medal; recipient various awards, including U.S. Army Recruiting Ring, U.S. Army Recruiting Command, 1978. Mem. Women's Army Corps Museum, Non Commd. Officers Assn., Fla. Vocat. Assn. Home: 21 Buford Rd Richmond VA

STONE, SUSAN RUTH, mortgage banking exec.; b. Madison, Wis., Sept. 11, 1946; d. John Mather and Lois Marie (Wiessinger) Murray; student U. Wis., 1964-66, U. Wis., Milw., 1976-78, U. Tex., El Paso, 1981-82; m. Raymond William Stone, Sept. 13, 1964; children—Lora Rae, Julie Lynn. Adminstrv. asst. Madison C. of C., 1967-72; mgr. processing dept. Kensington Mortgage & Fin. Corp., Milw., 1972-73, gen. mgr. adminstrn., 1973-75, asst. v.p., 1975-76, v.p., 1976-79; asst. v.p., auditor Mortgage Investment Co., El Paso, 1979-81, v.p. loan adminstrn., 1981—; cons. new cos. in govt. fin. mobile homes. Mem. Mortgage Bankers Assn., Personnel Adminstrn. Assn., Nat. Assn. Female Execs. Author poems and short stories. Home: 10500 Ashridge St El Paso TX 79925 Office: 5801 Trowbridge El Paso TX 79999

STONE, VIRGINIA EILEEN COOPER, piano tchr.; b. Sedan, Kans., Apr. 28, 1919; d. Emery Franklyn and Myrtle Emily (Ostland) Cooper; B.S. in Edn., Kans. State Coll., Pittsburg, 1941; m. Richard Linn Stone, Nov. 21, 1943; children—Richard Linn II, Stanley Craig. Pvt. tchr. piano, Pittsburg, 1941-43, Battle Creek, Mich., 1948-63, Katonah, N.Y., 1964—; tchr. music and English pub. schs., Agenda, Kans., 1941-43; clk.-typist U.S. Army Air Force, U.S. Army, 1943-46, 51-53; organist, choir dir. Katonah Methodist Ch., 1965-68; vacation organist 1st Baptist Ch., White Plains, N.Y., 1968—; vol. music tchr. for retarded children Bd. Coop. Ednl. Services of Westchester County, 1966-68. Pres., Battle Creek Music Tchrs. Club, 1957-58, Morning Mus. Club, Battle Creek, 1955-56; organizer, counselor Little Notes Club, 1957-59. Certified Mich., N.Y. (sec. 1978-82) State music tchrs. assns. Mem. Music Tchrs. Nat. Assn., Am. Guild Piano Tchrs., Sigma Alpha Iota (life), Sigma Tau Delta. Baptist. Home: 91 Harris Rd Katonah NY 10536

STONEHILL, MARJORIE LEAMNSON, coll. dean; b. Boone County, Ind., Jan. 10, 1925; d. Charles Arthur and Gertrude Leona (Burns) Phillips; B.S., Butler U., Indpls., 1947; M.S., Purdue U., 1973; m. Robert B. Stonehill, Sept. 2, 1978; children by previous marriage—John Phillips Leamnson, George F. Leamnson. Co-pub., editor Zionsville (Ind.) Times, 1955-68, editor, 1968-69; mem. adminstrv. staff Ind. U., Indpls., 1970—, asso. dean, dir. Ind. U. Sch. Continuing Studies, 1981—; rep. Ind. Council Continuing Edn. Recipient 1st pl. award for weekly newspaper column Women's Press Club, 1965-67; 1st pl. award for news story Nat. Women's Press Club, 1966; 1st pl. award for weekly newspaper Hoosier Press Assn., 1965-68; named Woman of Yr., Network Women in Bus., 1981. Mem. Nat. Univ. Continuing Edn. Assn., Women in Communications (past pres.), Nat. Fedn. Press Women (nat. conv. workshop chmn. 1979). Home: 581 S Century Oaks St Zionsville IN 46077 Office: 1300 W Michigan St Indianapolis IN 46202

STONER, DOROTHY ELEANOR, editor; b. Rowan, Iowa, Feb. 25, 1916; d. Leon Loney and Mabel (Henry) Curtis; m. Ross Arnold Stoner, Sept. 26, 1936; 1 dau., Sybil Jeanne Stoner Carter. Owner, operator grocery store, Charles City, Iowa, 1933-39; bookkeeper, office sec. Scott Barnett Plumbing and Heating, Charles City, 1948-61; bookkeeper Dobbs Coal & Oil Co., Charles City, 1950-53; soc. editor Charles City Press, 1961—, feature editor and ch. pages, 1965—. Leader, Charles City council Girl Scouts U.S.A., Charles City; treas. YWCA, Charles City. Mem. Iowa Press Women, Nat. Fedn. Press Women, Nat. League Am. Pen Women. Republican. Clubs: Rainbow Girls, Soroptimist, Pythian Sisters. Home: 403 1/2 S Main St Charles City IA 50616 Office: 100 N Main St Charles City IA 50616

STONER, JOYCE HILL, art conservator, painting restorer, editor; b. Washington, Oct. 9, 1946; d. I. William and Catherine (Dawson) Hill; B.A. summa cum laude, Coll. of William and Mary, 1968; M.A., Inst. Fine Arts, N.Y.U., 1970, diploma in art conservation, Conservation Center, 1973; m. William Patrick Stoner, July 4, 1970; 1 dau., Catherine Rebecca. Paintings conservator U. Va. Mus., 1970-73; asst. dir., actress Albemarle Playhouse, Charlottesville, Va., 1970-73; paintings conservator N.Y.C., 1973-74; dir., composer, lyricist Off-Broadway Show —I'll Die If I Can't Live Forever—, 1973-74; asst., then asso. prof. Va. Commonwealth U., 1975-76; cons. conservator of paintings Freer Gallery, Washington, 1975-76; paintings conservator, sr. conservator Wintherthur (Del.) Mus., 1976—, asso. dir. Art Conservation Program, 1980—; mng. editor Art & Archaeology Tech. Abstracts, 1969—; cons. in field. Founder Better Parents of Wilmington, 1979; mem. Com. for Excellence, Inst. for Achievement of Human Potential, Phila., 1980—. Kress Found. vis. scholar, Met. Mus. Art, 1980; named Outstanding Sr. Woman, Phi Beta Kappa, 1967; Outstanding Young Woman of Del., 1979. Fellow Am. Inst. Conservation, Internat. Inst. Conservation; mem. Washington Conservation Guild, Am. Assn. Mus., Found. of Am. Inst. for Conservation (exec. dir. 1975-79), Phi Beta Kappa. Methodist. Contbr. articles to profl. jours. Office: Winterthur Mus Winterthur DE 19735

STONER, VIRGINIA WADSLEY FULLER, cons.; b. Winston-Salem, N.C., July 4, 1949; d. Donnell Curtis and Louise Virginia (Teague) Wadsley; B.S. in Edn., East Carolina U., 1971; postgrad. Ga. Coll., 1974, Augusta Coll., 1975; m. Michael Alan Stoner, June 1, 1979. Tchr., Greene County (N.C.) Bd. Edn., 1971-72, Charlotte/Mecklenburg County (N.C.) Bd. Edn., 1972-74; math. coordinator Bibb County (Ga.) Bd. Edn., 1974-75; sales rep. East Ednl. Services Co., Columbia, S.C., 1975-78; basic skills cons. EDL/McGraw-Hill, Atlanta, 1978—. Mem. NOW, Nat. Council Tchrs. Math., Internat. Reading Assn., The Exec. Female, Atlanta C. of C., Nat. Assn. Profl. Saleswomen. Episcopalian. Home: 375 Wyth Way Atlanta GA 30342 Office: 2310 Parklake Dr Suite 520 Atlanta GA 30345

STOOKER, ALISON REESE, public relations exec.; b. Oklahoma City, Nov. 6, 1950; d. Robert Simeon and Alice Virginia (Mantz) S.; B.S. magna cum laude, Boston U., 1973. Public relations asst. Morgan Meml. Goodwill, Boston 1972-73; sr. account exec. The Softness Group, Inc., N.Y.C., 1973-76; N.E. regional public relations officer Ford Motor Co., N.Y.C., 1976—. Mem. Public Relations Soc. Am., Women in Communications, Inc. Home: 315 E 70th St New York NY 10021 Office: 1345 Ave of Americas New York NY 10105

STOOP, NORMA MCLAIN, editor, author, photographer; b. Panama, C.Z., July 20, 1910; b. Harry Edward and Gladys (Brandon) McLain; student Penn Hall Jr. Coll., Carnegie Inst. Tech., New Sch., N.Y. U.; m. William J. Stoop, Jr., Sept. 20, 1932. Contbg. editor Dance Mag., N.Y.C., 1969-71, asso. editor, 1971-79, sr. editor, 1979—; sr. editor After Dark, 1978—, also feature writer; also photographer, theater, ballet and film critic; entertainment editor sr. edit. WNYC-AM, 1980—; mem. nat. adv. bd. TV Arts Studio, Inc. Mem. Poetry Soc. Am., Dance Masters Am., Dance Critics Assn., TV Acad. Arts and Scis., Sigma Delta Chi. Clubs: N.Y. Womens Press, Overseas Press. Contbr. poems to Tex. Quar., Chgo. Rev., N.Y. Times, Arts in Society, Quest, Atlantic Monthly, Christian Sci. Monitor, others, 1958—, essays to Book Week in N.Y. Herald Tribune; represented in Best Poems of 1973, Exhibit of Dance Photography, Harvard U., Tufts Coll., 1975. Recipient award Dance Tchrs. Club Boston, 1977. Office: 1180 Ave of Americas New York NY 10036

STOOPS, LOUISE, librarian; b. Honolulu; d. Robert Earl and Ethel (Saunders) Stoops; B.A., U. Ariz.; M.S., Simmons Coll., 1952. Asst. librarian Popular Library, 1952-53; bus. and econs. div. Enoch Pratt Free Library, Balt., 1953-54; librarian, advt. and information services and office of adviser non-theatrical films Eastman Kodak Co., Rochester, N.Y., 1954-57; librarian Wilson, Haight, Welch & Grover, advt. agy., Hartford, Conn., 1957-58; asst. librarian U.S. Steel Corp., N.Y.C., 1958-60, head librarian, 1960-68; chief librarian Bache & Co., Inc., N.Y.C., 1968-70, chief librarian Cities Service Co., N.Y.C., 1970-71; chief librarian Dominick & Dominick, Inc., N.Y.C., 1971-72; librarian Baker, Weeks & Co., N.Y.C., 1972-77; chief librarian Lehman Bros., Kuhn Loeb, Inc., N.Y.C., 1977—. Mem. Spl. Libraries Assn. (editor Conn. Valley Chpt. News 1957-58; hospitality chmn. N.Y. chpt. 1959-60, sec. 1960-61, dinner chmn. 1961-62, chmn. internat. vis. librarians 1960-62, recruitment com. 1960-61, program chmn. N.Y. chpt. 1965-66, sec. advt. and marketing div. 1964-67, chmn. bus. and finance div. 1968-69), Financial Women's Assn., Chi Omega. Indexed English-Speaking Union International Cookbook, 1962, The Dollars and Sense of Business Films (Assn. Nat. Advertisers), 1954. Home: 211-A Rossmoor Dr Jamesburg NJ 08831 Office: 55 Water St New York NY 10041

STORAASLI, MARIE ELIZABETH, med. technologist, educator; b. Milw., June 26, 1945; d. Tollef Bardolf and Ruth Elizabeth (Storvick) S.; B.S. in Med. Tech., Northwestern U., 1967; M.S. in Clin. Sci., San Francisco State U., 1978; m. Jörn Olaf Thomas von Ramm, July 12, 1981. Chemist, Rikshospital Sentrallaboratoriet, Oslo, 1967-68; med. technologist Clinic Internal Medicine, Wauwatosa, Wis., 1968-69; med. technologist U. Minn., Mpls., 1969-71; supervisory med. technologist Hoag Hosp., Newport Beach, Calif., 1971-73; supr. hematology Project HOPE, Maceio, Brazil, 1973; staff research asso. dept. medicine U. Calif., San Diego, 1974-77; instr. hematology San Francisco State U., 1977-78; edn. coordinator Sch. Med. Tech., Scripps Clinic and Research Found., LaJolla, Calif., 1978-80; asst. prof. med. tech. U. N.C., Chapel Hill, 1980—. Mem. Durham (N.C.) Arts Council, Project HOPE Alumni Assn. Mem. AAUP, Am. Soc. Clin. Pathology (asso.), Am. Soc. Med. Tech., N.C. Soc. Med. Tech., Triangle Weavers Guild. Republican. Lutheran. Club: Univ. Women's (U. N.C.), Univ. Women's (Duke U.). Home: 3433 Dover Rd Durham NC 27707 Office: U NC Med Sch Wing B113 207-H Chapel Hill NC 27514

STORANDT, MARTHA, psychologist, educator; b. Little Rock, June 2, 1938; d. Farris and Floy (Montgomery) Mobbs; A.B., Washington U., St. Louis, 1960, Ph.D., 1966; m. Duane Storandt, Dec. 15, 1962; 1 son, Eric. Staff psychologist VA, St. Louis, 1966-68; mem. faculty Washington U., 1968—, assoc. prof. psychology, 1977—. Mem. Am. Psychol. Assn., Gerontol. Soc. Am., Mo. Psychol. Assn., Sigma Xi. Author: Therapy and Counseling with Older Adults, 1983; co-author: Memory, Aging and Related Functions, 1972; co-editor: The Clinical Psychology of Aging, 1978; editor-in-chief Jour. Gerontology, 1981-83. Home: 12 Hanley Downs St Louis MO 63117 Office: Dept Psychology Washington U St Louis MO 63130

STORB, URSULA, immunologist, educator; b. Stuttgart, Ger., July 6, 1936; came to U.S., 1966; d. Walter Maria and Marianne Margarethe (Kaemmerer) Stemmer; M.D., U., Tuebingen (Ger.), 1960. Intern, city hosps., Munich, Stuttgart, 1960-63; postdoctoral resident in immunology Pasteur Inst., Paris, 1963-65; postdoctoral resident dept. microbiology U. Wash., Seattle, 1966-68, mem. faculty dept. microbiology, 1968—, now prof. microbiology and immunology. NATO fellow, 1963-65; W.Ger. Govt. fellow, 1966-68; NIH grantee, 1972-87; NSF grantee, 1978-82. Mem. Am. Assn. Immunologists, Am. Soc. Cell Biology, Assn. for Women in Sci., NOW. Contbr. articles in field to profl. jours. Office: Dept Microbiology and Immunology U Wash Seattle WA 98195

STORM, HARRIET NACHMAN, writer; b. Newport News, Va., Sept. 26, 1942; d. Abe and Isabel (Levy) Nachman; student U. Md., 1960-62; B.A., Coll. William and Mary, 1964; m. Charles Ray Storm, Feb. 16, 1967; children—Lisa Ann, Laura Elizabeth. Reporter, women's editor Daily Press, Newport News, Va., 1964-72; freelance writer, public relations cons., 1972—. Mem. bd. visitors Coll. William and Mary, Williamsburg, Va., 1979—, pres. Soc. Alumni, 1978; pres. Peninsula unit Am. Cancer Soc., 1979-80; chmn. Hampton-Newport News Community Services Bd., 1982—; sec.-treas. Peninsula Legal Aid Center. Recipient Community Service award Woodmen of World Life Ins. Soc., alumni medallion Coll. William and Mary, 1981, Div. Vol. award Va. div. Am. Cancer Soc., 1981. Mem. Va. Press Women, Nat. Fedn. Press Women (dir. 1973-75), Nat. Council Jewish Women (v.p. Hampton Roads 1978-80), Reading is Fundamental (fund raising coordinator), Peninsula Jr. Arts Series (pres. 1980-81), William and Mary Athletic Ednl. Found. (trustee). Address: 36 Albany Dr Hampton VA 23666

STORY, ALICE JOSEPHINE, educator; b. DeArmanville, Ala., July 3, 1926; d. Joseph Benjamin and Lucille Bonner S.; B.S. cum laude, Fla. State U., 1948, M.S., 1953; postgrad. U. Cin., 1949-50, La. State U., 1958, U. Wash., 1964. Sci. and math. tchr. Meml. Jr. High Sch., Orlando, Fla., 1948-49; math. and phys. edn. tchr. Chapman High Sch., Apalachicola, Fla., 1950-52; math. instr. Fla. State U., Tallahassee, 1953-55; math. prof. Chipola Jr. Coll., Marianna, Fla., 1955-78, chmn. div. natural sci. and math., 1978—. Vice pres. Lula Rawls Service Guild, 1977; mem. adminstrv. bd. First United Meth. Ch., 1975-78. Fla. Ho. of Reps. scholar, 1944-46, Lewis State scholar, 1946-48, U. Cin. univ. scholar, 1949-50. Mem. Fla. Assn. Community Colls., Fla. Assn. Jr. Coll. Tchrs. Math., Marianna Bus. and Profl. Women's Club (pres. 1962), Delta Kappa Gamma (Phi pres. 1968-70), Alpha Lambda Delta, Kappa Delta Pi, Phi Kappa Phi. Club: Chipola Dames (pres. 1957). Home: 706 4th St Marianna FL 32446 Office: Chipola Jr Coll Marianna FL 32446

STORY, CYNTHIA STINSON, govt. ofcl.; b. Siler City, N.C., July 28, 1956; d. Benner H. and Evangeline D. Stinson; A.A., Elon Coll., 1976; m. Douglas T. Story, June 27, 1981. With Faison M. Hicks, atty., Raleigh, N.C., 1976-77; regional audit team mem., asst. del. team E.F. Hutton & Co., Inc., Raleigh, 1977-82; spl. asst. to U.S. Sen. John P. East, Greenville, N.C., 1982—. Dist. dir. N.C. Fedn. Young Republicans, 1976-77, exec. sec., 1977-79, nat. committeewoman, 1979—, Woman of Yr., 1980. Named Woman of Yr., Young Reps. Nat. Fedn., 1981. Baptist. Club: Toastmasters. Home: 101 David Dr Apt 4 Greenville NC 27834 Office: PO Box 8087 Greenville NC 27834

STORY, MARILYN DARLENE, educator; b. Dayton, Ohio, Nov. 23, 1941; d. Earl C. and Opal O. (Myers) Welshimer; B.A. with high honors, Ohio Wesleyan U., 1962; postgrad. (fellow), Merrill Palmer Inst., 1962; M.A. with honors, 1963; Ph.D. with honors, Mich. State U., 1967; m. Norman Lee Story, Oct. 14, 1962; children—Dewayne Martel, Dean Russell. Tchr. home econs. Niles (Mich.) Public Schs., 1962-63; lectr. family sociology U. Mich., Ann Arbor, 1962-63; tchr. home econs. S. Lyon (Mich.) Community Sch., 1963-65; instr. family life Mich. State U., East Lansing, 1966-67, dir. Head Start Evaluation Center, 1967-68; asso. prof., head dept. home econs. U. No. Iowa, Cedar Falls, 1968-76, prof. family studies, 1976—; vis. asso. prof. Calif. State U., Long Beach, 1973, Calif. State U., Los Angeles, 1973-74; cons. family life texts William C. Brown Co. and Wadsworth Pub. Co., 1976—; guest speaker on human sexuality various radio and TV programs, 1976—. Bd. dirs. Cedar Valley Hospice, 1978—, v.p., 1979—; v.p. State Hospice Orgn., 1981—. Mem. Am. Home Econs. Assn. (asso. editor newsletter 1973-74, chmn. coll. and univ. sect. 1978-80, offices on state council 1968—, del. to nat. meetings 1969-80), Nat. Council Family Relations (Iowa v.p. 1969), NEA, Am. Vocat. Assn., Assn. Humanistic Psychology, Soc. Sci. Study of Sex, Nat. Council Adminstrs. Home Econs., Home Econs. Edn. Assn., Iowa Home Econs. Edn. Assn. (exec. council 1968-72), Am. Assn. Sex Educators, Counselors and Therapists (cert.), Phi Upsilon Omicron, Omicron Nu, Kappa Delta Pi, Alpha Xi Delta. Mem. Christian Ch. Contbr. articles on home econs., Sex research, family life, hospices to profl. jours. Home: 205 Loma St Waterloo IA 50701 Office: Wright Hall Univ No Iowa Cedar Falls IA 50613

STOSUR, APRIL MARIE, assn. exec.; b. Chgo., Dec. 2, 1955; d. Donald Eugene and Marie Annette (Thilmont) S.; B.A. in Polit. Sci., No. Ill. U., DeKalb, 1977, M.P.A., 1979; m. Perry Martin Bassett, Feb. 14, 1981. Evaluation and planning project asso. N.W. Criminal Justice Commn., Dixon, Ill., 1977-78; circuit ct. dep. Ogle County Circuit Ct., Oregon, Ill., 1977-78; uniform crime report field rep. Wash. Assn. Sheriffs and Police Chiefs, Olympia, Wash., 1979—. Mem. ednl. policies com. Shimer Coll., Mt. Carroll, Ill., 1975. Title IX Public Service Edn. fellow 1978. Mem. Am. Soc. Public Adminstrn., Nat. Assn. Female Execs., Bus. and Profl. Women's Club, Pi Sigma Alpha, Pi Alpha Alpha. Club: Toastmasters. Home: 904 E Bay Dr Olympia WA 98506 Office: WASPC/WUCR PO Box 826 Olympia WA 98507

STOTHART, ROBERTA BATES, bookstore mgr.; b. Long Beach, Calif., Mar. 29, 1934; d. Morley DaCosta and Dorothy Clarice (Graham) Bates; student U. Ariz., 1952-53; children—Lisa Camille, Anna, Elizabeth. Library asst. Am Sch. Switzerland, Lugano, 1967-70; mus. bookstore mgr. J. Paul Getty Mus., Malibu, Calif., 1974—. Mem. Mus. Stores Assn. (dir.). Republican. Episcopalian. Home: 22560 Carbon Mesa Rd Malibu CA 90265 Office: 17985 Pacific Coast Hwy Malibu CA 90265

STOTLER, ALICEMARIE HUBER (MRS. JAMES ALLEN STOTLER), judge; b. Alhambra, Calif., May 29, 1942; d. James Russell and Loretta (Montoya) Huber; A.B., U. So. Calif., 1964, J.D., 1967; m. James Allen Stotler, Sept. 11, 1971. Admitted to Calif. bar, 1967; prosecutor Orange County Dist. Atty.'s Office, Santa Ana, Calif., 1967-73; mem. firm Stotler & Stotler, Tustin, Calif., 1973-76; judge Harbor Jud. Dist., Orange County, Calif., 1976—, Orange County Superior Ct., 1978—; pres. Calif. Judges' Found., 1980-82; assoc. dean Calif. Jud. Edn. and Research, Coll. Trial Judges, 1982-83. Mem. Victim/witness adv. com. Calif. Office Criminal Justice Planning Com., 1980—; bd. dirs. U. So. Calif. Legion Lex, 1981-82. Named Judge of Yr. Orange County Trial Lawyers Assn., 1978. Mem. Nat. Assn. Women Judges, Women in Bus. (bd. dirs. 1982), Mortar Bd., Kappa Alpha Theta. Office: 700 Civic Center Dr W Santa Ana CA 92701

STOTT, FRANCES MAKRIS, psychologist; b. Berwyn, Ill., Aug. 20, 1941; d. Gust and Constantina (Giannakos) Makris; B.A., U. Chgo., 1963, M.A., 1974; Ph.D. (univ. fellow 1977-79), Northwestern U., 1980; divorced; 1 son, Jason Allen. Tchr. 5th grade, Homewood, Ill., 1963-66; tchr. emotionally disturbed children, Pritzker Children's Hosp., Chgo., 1966-76; instr. Nat. Coll. Edn., also Northwestern U., 1978-79; mental health cons. Head Start, 1979-81; research/clin. psychologist Thresholds Mothers' Project, Chgo., 1979-81; mem. faculty Erikson Inst. Advanced Study Child Devel., Chgo., 1979—; adv. bd. early intervention project, div. child psychiatry Children's Hosp., Chgo. Mem. Am. Psychol. Assn., Soc. Research Child Devel., Nat. Assn. Edn. Young Children. Home: 128 S Stone Ave LaGrange IL 60525 Office: 233 N Michigan Ave Suite 2200 Chicago IL 60601

STOTT, MARY LOU, real estate broker; b. Washington, Mar. 2, 1933; d. Martin Anthony and Mary Louise (Berberich) Dempf; B.S. in Edn., D.C. Tchrs. Coll., 1955; M.S.W., U. Hawaii, 1972; m. George W. Stott, Jr., Aug. 4, 1956; children—Michael, Helen, Tracey Anne. Tchr. public schs., 1955-69; family therapist Catholic Social Service, Honolulu, 1972-74; public relations dir. Sheraton Hotel Disco, 1975; dir. counseling Chaminade U., 1975-76, dir. women's programs, 1976-77; v.p. Stott Real Estate, Inc., Kailua, Hawaii, 1978—; guidance dir. St. Anthony Sch.; condr. U. Hawaii Career Seminar; mem. Gov.'s Com. on Children and Youth, 1974-75. Recipient Fed. grant for services to women re-entering career world, 1976. Mem. Am. Bus. Women's Assn., Acad. Cert. Social Workers, Nat. Assn. Social Workers, Am. Assn. Sex Educators and Counselors, Nat. Assn. Realtors, Hawaii Assn. Realtors, Honolulu Bd. Realtors. Republican. Roman Catholic. Club: Cath. Daus. Home: 360 Dune Circle Kailua HI 96734

STOUGHTON, JANET MAURY, travel corp. exec.; b. W.Palm Beach, Fla., Apr. 3, 1936; d. Thomas Peter and Geraldine (Green) Maury; B.A., Marjorie Webster Coll., 1954; m. John Eliot Stoughton, Aug. 31, 1957; children—Thomas Frost, Janet Maury, Anne Boushelle. Office mgr. Bert Roberts Real Estate, Nassau, Bahamas, 1954-56; exec. sec. firm McLean & Stacy, attys. at law, Lumberton, N.C., 1958; travel agt. Quixote Travels, Inc., Greenville, N.C., 1971-75, pres., 1975—; dir. N.C. Nat. Bank. Governing com. Greenville Found.; mem. Stallings Field adv. devel. com.; mem. fin. bd. St. Paul's Episcopal Ch. Mem. Am. Soc. Travel Agts., Travel Agts. of the Carolinas, Greenville Area C. of C. (air service task force). Republican. Clubs: Greenville Country, Baywood Tennis. Office: PO Box 465 319 Cotanche St Greenville NC 27834

STOUT, DONNA KARY, mfg. co. exec.; b. Balt., Aug. 16, 1954; d. Donald Angelo and Anna May (Vollenweider) Kary; B.Biology, Western Md. Coll., 1976; M.S., George Washington U., 1980; m. David M. Stout, Aug. 13, 1977. Microbiologist, McCormick & Co., Balt., 1976-79, specifications coordinator, Hunt Valley, Md., 1979-80, supr. tech. services, indsl. bus., Balt., 1980—. Mem. Inst. Food Technologists. Home: 602 Coventry Rd Towson MD 21204 Office: 414 Light St Baltimore MD 21202

STOUT, GLORIA BETH, real estate exec.; b. Dayton, Ohio, June 30, 1927; d. James Madox and Helen Irene (Fearn) McCormick; student U. Dayton, 1946, Dayton Art Inst., 1947; m. Donald E. Stout, Apr. 12, 1947; children—Holly Sue, Scott Kenneth. Partner, Wright Gate Indsl./Office Research Devel., Dayton, 1965—, Falls Devel. Co., Vandalia, Ohio, 1977—; v.p., dir. Harshman Valley Transp. Center, Dayton, 1954-60, Develop Dayton Corp., 1975—; real estate appraiser; antique appraiser; precious stones, metals appraiser; buyer silver, china and crystal Jaccards Jewelers. Past bd. dirs. Dayton Opera Guild. Mem. Dayton Art Inst., Dayton Philharm., Victory Theater Assn., Granada Hist. Soc. Home: 759 Plantation Ln Dayton OH 45419

STOUT, JOAN, educator; b. Ft. Madison, Iowa, Sept. 9, 1932; d. Guy H. and Thelma N. (Bowker) Ollis; B.S., Western Ill. U., 1954; M.L.S., U. Wash., 1968; postgrad. U. Ill., U. Chgo.; M.S.T., Portland State U., 1977; m. Charles E. Stout, June 5, 1955; children—Greg, Mitch, Amy, Matt. Tchr. English, secondary schs., Ill., 1954-55, 60-62; librarian/adult basic edn. coordinator Clark Coll., 1967-80, asst. dean Learning Resource Center, 1980—; mem. Wash. Equity Funding Task Force, 1978—; mem. various state task forces on budget formula and job specifications. Mem. NEA, Assn. Higher Edn. (chpt. pres. 1977-78, state v.p. 1977-78), AAUP, Wash. Library Assn., Community Coll. Librarians and Media Specialists, Wash. Continuing Edn. Assn., N.W. Adult Edn. Assn., Beta Phi Mu. Democrat. Home: 9714 NW 31st Ave Vancouver WA 98665 Office: 1800 E McLoughlin Vancouver WA 98663

STOUT, MARTHA ANN, clin. psychologist; b. Greensboro, N.C., Aug. 12, 1953; d. Adrian Phillip and Martha Eva (Deaton) S.; B.A., U. Pa., 1975; Ph.D., SUNY, Stony Brook, 1979. Fellow in psychology dept. psychiatry, Harvard U. Med. Sch., Boston, 1978-79, instr. psychology, 1981—; asst. prof. psychology grad. faculty New Sch. for Social Research, N.Y.C., 1979-80; asst. prof. psychology Wellesley (Mass.) Coll., 1980-81; pvt. practice clin. psychology, Boston; attending psychologist McLean Hosp. Lic. psychologist, Mass. Mem. Am. Psychol. Assn. (divs. clin. psychology and psychology of women). Contbr. articles to profl. publs.; contbr. colloquia at schs. Office: 121 Mt Vernon St Boston MA 02108

STOVER, BETSY MAE JONES, pharmacologist; b. Salt Lake City, May 13, 1926; d. Richard Hugh and Bessie Ina (Miers) Jones; B.A., U. Utah, 1947; Ph.D., U. Calif., Berkeley, 1950; m. (div. Mar. 1980); children—Susan, Steven Nathan. Mem. faculty U. Utah, Salt Lake City, 1950—, cons. Radiobiology Lab., 1970—; asso. research prof. dept. chemistry, 1958-70, adj. research prof. anatomy, 1975-79, adj. research prof. dept. pharmacology, 1979—; asso. prof. pharmacology U. N.C., Chapel Hill, 1970-76, prof., 1976—, dir. grad. tng. program pharmacology, 1974-80, faculty mem. curriculum in toxicology, 1979—; mem. panel to evaluate grad. fellowships applications for NSF, NRC, 1974-76; mem. adv. com., health physics div. Oak Ridge Nat. Lab., 1975; mem. NRC panel to evaluate postdoctoral fellowship applications NSF, 1978-80; panel to evaluate associateship applications, 1982—. Mem. AAAS, AAUP, Am. Chem. Soc., Am. Phys. Soc., Am. Soc. Bone and Mineral Research, Am. Soc. Pharmacology and Exptl. Therapeutics (subcom. on women in pharmacology 1979—), Assn. Women in Sci., Radiation Research Soc., Soc. Exptl. Biology and Medicine, Soc. Toxicology, Phi Beta Kappa, Sigma Xi, Alpha Lambda Delta, Phi Kappa Phi. Co-author 3 books; co-editor 3 books; contbr. articles to profl. jours.; mem. editorial bd. Proc. of Soc. Exptl. Biology and Medicine, 1980—. Home: 103 Marion Way Chapel Hill NC 27514 Office: Dept Pharmacology Med Sch U NC Chapel Hill NC 27514

STOVER, BONNIE, bank exec.; b. Corsicana, Tex., Dec. 19 1949; d. Virgle Edell and Ruby Juanita Widener; B.S., Tex. Woman's U., 1971; postgrad. U. Tex., Arlington, 1972-73. With First Nat. Bank of Corsicana, 1974—, asst. v.p., 1977-79, v.p., 1979—; dir. Old Reliable Mortgage Co., Inc., Corsicana. Bd. dirs. Camp Fire Inc., Corsicana, 1981; co-chmn. United Fund Residential Dr., Corsicana, 1981. Nat. Assn. Bank Women regional scholar, 1979. Mem. Nat. Assn. Banking Women Mortgage Bankers Assn. Am., Nat. Homebuilders Assn., Tex. Mortgage Bankers Assn., Nat. Fedn. Bus. and Profl. Women (dist. dir.). Baptist. Office: 100 N Main Corsicana TX 75110

STOWERS, BARBARA, microbiologist; b. Oklahoma City, Sept. 14, 1927; d. Lee Wiley and Mary Marle (Elliott) Woods; student Seminole Jr. Coll., 1944-45, Okla. U., 1947; B.S. in Biology, Okla. A. and M. U., 1950; postgrad. U. N.Mex., 1948, 49, 77, 78, Coll. St. Francis; m. Harry Edward Stowers, Mar. 25, 1950; 1 dau., Faye Marie. Sec., Lee Wood Agy., Albuquerque, 1950; med. technologist for Herbert Abramson, M.D., Washington, 1951-52, George Washington U. Hosp., 1952-53, Warwick Meml. Cancer Clinic, Washington, 1952-53, Walter Reed Army Hosp., Washington, 1953-55, St. Joseph Hosp. Clin. Lab., Albuquerque, 1955-58; microbiologist, med. technologist clin. lab. VA Hosp., Albuquerque, 1971—, supr. Tb mycology, 1973-77. Mem. Rehab. Center, vol. chmn. Aux., Albuquerque, 1964-66, 1st v.p. Aux., 1966-67, pres. Aux., 1967-69, bd. dirs., 1965-75, sec. bd., 1974-75; active Camp Fire Girls, 1967-78, bd. dirs. Albuquerque council, 1969-77, pres. bd., 1973-75; bd. dirs. Albuquerque chpt. Amigos de las Americas, 1975-82, pres., 1978-80, trustee internat. orgn., 1980-82. Recipient U.S. Govt. Performance award, 1974; Vol. participation award Gov. N.Mex., 1981. Mem. Am. Soc. Microbiology (sec.-treas. N.Mex. chpt. 1974-78), Am. Soc. Clin. Pathologists, U. N.Mex. Kappa Kappa Gamma Alumni Assn. (chmn. Meml. Loan Fund 1970-79), Alpha Pi Mu. Democrat. Episcopalian. Home: 2112 Dietz Pl NW Albuquerque NM 87107

STÖWHAS, MARGARITA CLARA, educator; b. Santiago, Chile, Nov. 18, 1937; came to U.S., 1971; d. A. Raul and Graciela S. (Sánchez) S.; B.S., Escuela Normal Santa Teresa, Santiago, 1958; Ph.D., U. Chile, Santiago, 1961; divorced; 1 son, Chris M. Tchr., Escula San Patricio, Santiago, 1959; prof. Spanish, Universidad Católica, 1960-64; charge social dept. CORVI, Santiago, 1964-71; laborer Childres Canvas, Dallas, 1971; order filler Paradise Corp., 1972; mem. office staff Franklin Stores Corp., Dallas, 1972-73; night tchr. Dallas schs., 1973-75; tchr., translator, Dallas, 1973-77; lang. instr. Easfield Coll., Dallas County, 1975-77; exec. dir. Dallas Internat. Lang. Center, 1975—. Mem. Nat. Assn. Female Execs. (dir. 1979—), Am. Translators Assn., L'Alliance Française, N. Dallas C. of C. Mormon. Office: 1450 Preston Forest Sq Dallas TX 75230

STOZEK, MARY ALODIA, psychologist, nun; b. Chgo., Dec. 15, 1922; d. John Joseph and Mary Anne (Kuczaj) Stozek; B.S., Loyola U., Chgo., 1958; M.A., Marquette U., 1962; Ph.D., U. Chgo., 1966. Joined Sisters of St. Felix of Cantalice, Roman Catholic Ch., 1941; tchr. elem. sch. Archdiocese of Chgo., 1943-60; asst. to dir. Reading Clinic Marquette U., Milw., 1961-64; dir. Felician Coll. Psychoednl. Center, Chgo., 1965—; mem. temp. faculty Loyola U., Northeastern Ill. U.; mem. State of Ill. Adv. Com., Right to Read, 1972-73, adv. com. Cert. Standards and Curriculum Devel., 1972-73; del. chpt. Chgo. Province of Felician Sisters, 1975, 81, to gen. chpt., 1982; chmn. communications com. Chgo. Province of Felician Sisters, 1970-75; cons. to Alcohol Safety Edn. Program (Central States Inst. of Addiction and Circuit Ct. of Cook County), 1974. Mem. Am. Psychol. Assn., Ill. Sch. Psychologists Assn., Internat. Reading Assn., Pi Lambda Theta. Contbr. articles in field to profl. jours.; editor: Elan (publ. of Chgo. Province of Felician Sisters), 1970-75. Home and Office: 3800 W Peterson Ave Chicago IL 60659

STRAATMAN, MARCELLE DOROTHEA, home economist; b. Red Wing, Minn., May 15, 1920; d. Frederick Edward and Helen Anna (Buchholtz) Bollum; B.S., U. Wis., 1943; fifth yr. cert. U. Wash., 1965; M.Ed., Central Wash. State U., 1972; postgrad. U. So. Calif., 1973, U. Minn., 1948; m. Zeger William Straatman, Dec. 23, 1948; children—James Brian, Steven Pol. Tchr. vocat. home econs., secondary public schs., Wash. State, 1943-52, 67-71; asst. prof. family studies Central Wash. State U., 1971-74; asso. prof. home econs., family life Oreg. State U., 1974—, extension human devel. specialist, 1974—; adult educator Bellevue Community Coll., 1960-70. Bd. dirs. Benton County (Oreg.) Family Planning, 1979-80; mem. Oreg. Gov.'s Task Force, White House Conf. on Families, 1979-80. Mem. Nat. Council Family Relations, Oreg. Council Family Relations, Am. Home Econs. Assn., Oreg. Home Econs. Assn. Nat. 4-H Assn. Extension Agts., Oreg. Extension Assn. (New Staff award 1978), P.E.O. Methodist. Club: Order Eastern Star. Author: Oregon's Children, 1982; also extension publs.; editor Specially For You Young Homemaker, 1974-79. Home: 2950 13th St Corvallis OR 97330 Office: 153 Milam Hall Oreg State U Corvallis OR 97331

STRAHM, NINA JEAN, Kans. state rep.; b. Pomona, Calif., Sept. 19, 1934; d. William Thomas and Virginia Carolyn (Sharp) Beard; B.A., U. So. Calif.; m. Hal Kingon Strahm, 1957; children—Mark William, Michele, Clarissa. Mem. state steering com. Citizens for Reagan, 1975-76, 79-80; pres., sec. Nemaha County Republican Women's Club Fedn., 1975; candidate 2d Dist. Congressional Primary, 1976; precinct committeewoman Berwick Twp., Kans., 1976; del. Internat. Woman's Yr. Conv., Houston, 1977; mem. Kans. Ho. of Reps., 1979—. Mem. Bus. and Profl. Women. Mem. Ch. of Christ. Office: Kans Ho Reps State Capitol Topeka KS 66612

STRAIGHT, BEATRICE WHITNEY (MRS. PETER COOKSON), actress; b. Old Westbury, L.I., N.Y.; d. Willard Dickerman and Dorothy (Whitney) S.; student pvt. schs.; m. Peter Cookson, June 2, 1949; children—Gary, Tony, stepchildren—Peter, Brookse. Appeared in Broadway prodns. The Crucible, Eastward in Eden, The Innocents, Twelfth Night, The Heiress, Macbeth, Sing Me No Lullaby, Everything in the Garden; appeared in off-Broadway prodn. Phedre, All My Sons, 1974; toured with Streetcar Named Desire, 1969-70; motion picture appearances include Phone Call From A Stranger, Patterns, The Silken Affair, The Nun's Story, The Promise, Bloodline, Endless Love, 1981, Poltergeist, 1982; appeared TV series Beacon Hill, 1975, Kings Crossing, 1982; founder Michael Chekov Studio, Eng., U.S.; co-founder Theatre, Inc., 1946. Recipient Antionette Perry award for role in The Crucible, 1953, Acad. award for supporting actress in Network, 1977. Address: 156 E 62d St New York NY 10021

STRAIGHT, CHARISSE LYNN, ins. agt.; b. Parkersburg, W.Va., July 21, 1949; d. William H. Meredith and Helen (Janetos) Meredith Knaus; student pub. schs. Parkersburg; m. Jerry W. Russell, Apr. 8, 1967 (div.); 1 dau., Christine Renee; m. 2d, Charles H. Straight, Jr., Dec. 30, 1978. Sec., Walker Parkersburg div. Textron, 1971; owner, mgr. El Rancho Restaurant, Parkersburg, 1971-74; agt. Allstate Ins. Co., Vienna, W.Va., 1974—. Mem. Parkersburg Assn. Life Underwriters, Parkersburg Art Center, NOW. Methodist. Home: 803 46th St Vienna WV 26105 Office: 500 Grand Central Mall Vienna WV 26105

STRAIN, PAULA MARY, librarian; b. Brooke County, W.Va.; d. Paul Russell and Margaret (Evans) Strain; A.B., Bethany Coll., 1937; B.S., Carnegie Inst. Tech., 1938; student U. Pitts., 1940-41. Asst. librarian Westminster Coll., 1939-40; asst. librarian Carnegie-Ill. Steel Corp., Pitts., 1940-42, librarian, 1942-44; librarian U.S. Naval Photog. Interpretation Center, Washington, 1946-48, liaison and selection officer Library of Congress, 1948-57; sr. research analyst Library of Congress, 1957-60; tech. librarian Electronics Systems Center, IBM, Owego, N.Y., 1960-68; head librarian Booz Allen Applied Research, Inc., Bethesda, Md., 1968-70; mgr. info. services MITRE Corp., McLean, Va., 1970—. Served with USNR, 1944-46. Mem. bd. mgrs. Finger Lakes Trail Conf., 1962-68, pres., 1966-67. Mem. Appalachian Trail Conf. (bd. mgrs. 1979-80), Spl. Libraries Assn. (various offices). Clubs: Potomac Appalachian Trail (council 1957-60, 69-80, pres. 1970-72), Adirondack Mountain. Author articles various periodicals and jours. Home: 4522 Avondale St Bethesda MD 20814 Office: 1820 Dolley Madison Blvd McLean VA 22102

STRAIN, SIBYL MARJORIA SHIPP (MRS. NUMA ALONZO STRAIN), educator; b. Hiram, Ga.; d. John Seaborn and Nell (Barber) Shipp; A.B. summa cum laude, Berry Coll., 1942; M.A., Columbia U., 1955, profl. diploma secondary sch. and coll., 1956; Ph.D., U. So. Calif., 1976; postgrad. Whittier Coll., UCLA Calif. State Coll., Loyola U., Los Angeles; m. Numa Alonzo Strain, Aug. 19, 1944 (dec. July 1969); 1 dau., Laura Marjoria. Tchr., Hiram (Ga.) High Sch., 1942-43; exec. asst., research dept. J.M. Mathes, Inc., N.Y.C., 1947-49; reading specialist John Muir High Sch., Pasadena, Calif., 1957-60, John Marshall Jr. High Sch., Pasadena, 1960-66; asst. dir. Nat. Charity League, U. So. Calif. Reading Center, Los Angeles, 1966-67; prof. psychology and reading, chmn. dept. Los Angeles S.W. Coll., 1967-72, 77-78, chmn. behavioral sci. dept., 1978—, sec. acad. senate, 67-68, 80-82, v.p., 1979-80, exec. council, 1970—. Active various community drives; asso. mem. Am. Mus. Natural History, Smithsonian Instn.; patron Friends Pasadena Library, Los Angeles County Mus. Art. Served to lt. WAVES, 1943-47. Mem. Nat. Soc. for Study Edn., NEA, Internat., Western reading assns., AAUW (br. newsletter editor 1965-66), Pasadena Assn. Career Tchrs. (co-founder 1964, sec.-treas. 1964-65), U. So. Calif. Hon. Assn. Women in Edn. (charter mem.), Calif., Los Angeles (exec. council 1967—) (pres. SW coll. chpt. 1975—), coll. tchrs. assns., Calif. Higher Edn. Assn. (del. SW Community Coll. 1969—), Nat. Council Adminstrv. Women in Edn., LWV, AAUP, Women's Caucus, NOW, Nat. Hist. Soc., U. So. Calif., Berry Coll. (v.p. 1944-45) alumni assns., Calif. Women in Higher Edn. (charter, state steering com. 1974-76, chmn. panel on women's studies for state conf. 1976), Kappa Delta Pi, Pi Lambda Theta (chpt. pres. 1962-63), Phi Delta Gamma. Democrat. Presbyterian. Home: 2236 Las Lunas St Pasadena CA 91107 Office: 1600 W Imperial Hwy Los Angeles CA 90047

STRAND, ANN SCOTT, coll. ofcl.; b. Mt. Airy, Ga., Dec. 13, 1929; d. Ralph Clifton and Agnes (Cone) Scott; B.A., Piedmont Coll., 1948; m. Berger A. Strand, May 13, 1959; children—Stephen, Scott, Craig, Shaun, Bret, John, Ann. Corr., Casper (Wyo.) Star-Tribune, 1968-73; publicist, then fed. projects writer Western Wyo. Coll., Rock Springs, 1978-82, coordinator devel. and giving, 1980—. Mem. Wyo. Ho. of Reps., 1979-80; mem. Gov. Wyo. Commn. Women, 1977—; insp. of mines State of Wyo.; mem. hazardous wastes com., western region Council State Govts. Mem. Western Wyo. Coll. Faculty Assn., LWV, Sweetwater County Resource Conservation Dist. Democrat. Roman Catholic. Office: Western Wyo Coll Box 428 Rock Springs WY 82901

STRAND, NANCY MARIE, nurse; b. Phila., Dec. 27, 1926; d. Edward Joseph and Ella Frances (Waldron) McNelis; student in Nursing, Coll. St. Rose, 1944-47; B.S., N.Y.U., 1951, M.A. in Counseling, 1954; m. Bart Strand, Jan. 15, 1955; children—Deirdre, Maureen, Sheila. Staff nurse, relief supr. VA Hosp., Bronx, N.Y., 1947-59; staff nurse Children's Hosp., Buffalo, 1959-61, VA Hosp., Buffalo, 1961-62; with U. Ark. Hosp., 1962-77, asso. dir. nursing, 1966-73, dir. nursing, 1973-77; clin. coordinator nursing VA Hosp., Little Rock, 1977—; mem. nursing curriculum project So. Regional Edn. Bd.; mem. faculty research workshop U. N.C. R.N. Mem. Am. Nurses Assn. (cert. nursing adminstr.), Ark. State Nurses Assn., Nat. League Nursing, Ark. League Nursing (Ann. award of Merit 1971), AAUW. Roman Catholic. Home: 464 Midland Ave Little Rock AR 72205

STRANG, SANDRA LEE, airline exec.; b. Greensboro, N.C., Apr. 22, 1936; d. Charles Edward and Lobelia Mae (Squires) S.; B.A. in English, U. N.C., 1960; M.B.A., U. Dallas, 1970. With American Airlines, Inc., 1960—, mgr. career devel. for women, N.Y.C., 1972-73, dir. selection and tng., 1974-75, sr. dir. selection, tng. and affirmative action, 1975-79, sr. dir. compensation and benefits, Grand Prairie, Tex., 1979—. Mem. Am. Mgmt. Assn., Assn. Advancement of Women into Mgmt., Am. Soc. Tng. and Devel., Am. Compensation Assn. Home: 4521 Rawlins St Dallas TX 75219 Office: 4200 American Blvd Euless TX 76039

STRANGE, CLEO B. (MRS. JOHNNIE CHESTER STRANGE), educator, civic worker; b. Alexandria, La., Jan. 1, 1916; d. Thomas J. and Clara (Bessonett) Bryant; A.B., La. State U., 1936; Master in Elem. Edn., Memphis State U., 1970; m. Johnnie Chester Strange, Oct. 9, 1937 (dec.); children—Charles Thomas (dec.), Barbara Diane (Mrs. Billy Ray Fellers), John Edward, Donna Jean (Mrs. James M. Neal), Janet Claire (Mrs. Ed Wilson). Sci. tchr. Vinton (La.) High Sch., 1936-38, Corpus Christi (Tex.) High Sch., 1941-42; asst. chemist Ethyl Corp., Baton Rouge, 1942-43; dir. Navy Nursery and Kindergarten-Naval Air Station, Memphis, 1954-72; day care specialist Tenn. Dept. Public Welfare, Memphis, from 1972; now community services rep. Tenn. Dept. Human Services. Active Girl Scouts U.S.A., Boy Scouts Am. Recipient Outstanding Service award Tenn. Assn. Young Children. Mem. AAUW (br. v.p. 1964-66), Assn. Childhood Edn. (br. v.p. 1968-72), Memphis and Shelby County Tchrs. Day Care Fedn. (pres. 1967-69), Tenn. Assn. Children under Six (v.p. 1968-70, pres. 1970-72), Memphis Assn. Young Children (pres. 1979-80), Memphis Kindergarten Study Group, Kappa Delta Pi. Presbyterian. Home: 4833 Easley St Millington TN 38053 Office: 170 N Main State Office Bldg Memphis TN 38101

STRASINGER, SUSAN KING, med. technologist; b. Boston, July 2, 1939; d. Francis Boland and Dorothy Inez (Okey) King; B.A., U. Maine, 1961; M.S., Va. Poly. Inst., 1974; m. Harry L. Strasinger, Sept. 8, 1972. Research technologist Bowman-Gray Sch. Medicine, Winston-Salem, N.C., 1961-65; supr. chemistry DeWitt Army Hosp., Ft. Belvoir, Va., 1966-72; program dir. med. lab. technician program No. Va. Community Coll., Alexandria, 1972—. Mem. Am. Soc. Clin. Pathologists, Delta Zeta. Republican. Methodist. Home: 307 Yoakum Pkwy Apt 223 Alexandria VA 22304 Office: 3001 N Beauregard St Alexandria VA 22311

STRATFORD, CAROL ANN DEERING (MRS. FRANCIS ARTHUR STRATFORD JR.), occupational therapist; b. Columbus, Ohio, Dec. 17, 1946; d. Earl Brent and Gladys May (Wade) Deering; A.A., Brevard Jr. Coll., 1966; B.S., U. Fla., 1968; m. Francis A. Stratford, Jr., Aug. 4, 1973. Staff occupational therapist Hosp. Albert Einstein Coll. Medicine, Bronx, N.Y., 1968-74; sr. research therapist Inst. Rehab. Medicine N.Y. U. Med. Center, N.Y.C., 1975-81, mem. developmental team voice recognition, wheel chair and environ. control system; supr. dept. occupational therapy Danbury (Conn.) Hosp., 1982—; cons. environ. controls. Registered occupational therapist. Mem. Am., Conn. occupational therapy assns., Rehab. Engring. Soc. N. Am. Co-author, editor: (monograph) Environmental Control Systems and Vocational Aids for Persons with High Level Quadriplegia, 1979; contbr. articles to profl. jours. Methodist. Home: Shady Knolls Danbury CT 06810 Office: Danbury Hosp 24 Hospital Ave Danbury CT 06810

STRATHDEE, ESTHER LINNEA ROSWALL, nurse; b. Twin Falls, Idaho, Apr. 19, 1944; d. Winfrid and Louise Elizabeth Roswall; A.A., Los Angeles Valley Coll., 1964; B.S. in Nursing and Pub. Health Nursing, Stanford U., 1967; m. Frederick R. Strathdee, Feb. 14, 1960; children—Mark C., Brian F. Staff nurse Stanford (Calif.) Med. Center, 1967-71, adminstrv. and clin. nursing supr., 1971—, also editor Nursing at Stanford, 1978-82. Mem. Com for Recognition of Nursing Achievements, chmn., 1969-71. Mem. Salvation Army Nurses Fellowship. Mem. Peninsula Covenant Ch. Club: Stanford Nurses. Home: 186 Alameda Atherton CA 94025

STRATMAN, MAXINE THEOBALD, banker; b. Brigham, Wis., May 22, 1938; d. Max L. and Gladys B. (Olson) Theobald; student Barneveld (Wis.) public schs.; children—Julie Lynn, Jodie Lynn. With Barneveld State Bank, Ridgeway, Wis., 1956—, beginning in bookkeeping dept., successively teller, asst. br. mgr., mgr. and asst. cashier 1956-80, asst. v.p., br. office mgr., 1980—. Chair Meml. Hosp. Campaign Fund 1980, Ridgeway Salvation Army, 1981—; treas. Methodist Ch. Mem. Iowa County Bankers Assn. (sec.-treas.), Nat. Assn. Bank Women. Republican. Home: Rt 1 Box 170 Barneveld WI 53507 Office: Barneveld State Bank Main St Ridgeway WI 53582

STRATTON, LILLIAN, musician, composer, philanthropist; b. Vienna, Austria, Jan. 9, 1905; d. Isadore and Anna (Hannover) Stignitz; ed. Conservatory of Music, Vienna; m. Henry M. Stratton, Sept. 6, 1925. Composer songs including Schoen bist Du, suess bist Du, 1926, Wien, dich gruesse ich wieder, 1949; founder, v.p. Henry M. and Lillian Stratton Found., 1956—; sustaining patron Met. Opera, N.Y.C. Dept. pathology of Mt. Sinai Med. Sch. named in her honor (with Henry M. Stratton), 1981. Home: 118 E 60th St New York NY 10022

STRATTON, LOIS JEAN, Wash. state rep.; b. Springdale, Wash., Jan. 5, 1927; d. Charles B. and Ann (Hill) Brunton; student Kinman Bus. U., 1944-45; m. Allen F. Stratton, 1946; children—Alan Edward, Kathleen Prayer, Mark Charles, Scott D., Karen Jeanne. Precinct committeewoman Spokane County Democratic Com., 1958—, now mem. exec. bd.; alt. del. Dem. Nat. Conv., 1976; co-chmn. Gov. Dixy Lee Ray Com., 1976—; committeewoman Wash. State Dem. Com, 1977—; mem. Wash. Ho. of Reps.; exec. sec. pub. affairs Kaiser Aluminum & Chem. Corp., Spokane, 1963—. Adminstrv. asst., exec. sec. to pres. Expo '74 World's Fair, Spokane. Mem. Spokane County Dem. Club (sec.), Jane Jefferson Dem. Club (1st v.p.). Roman Catholic. Office: Wash State Ho Reps State Capitol Olympia WA 98504

STRAUBER, GRACE FRANCES, hosp. adminstr.; b. N.Y.C., Oct. 24, 1927; d. Jerome James and Grace Frances (Martin) S.; B.B.A., Siena Coll., Loudonville, N.Y., 1963; M.H.A., St. Louis U., 1968. Joined Order Franciscan Sisters of Poor, Roman Catholic Ch., 1947; bus. mgr. St. Francis Hosp., Bronx, N.Y., 1954-56; asst. adminstr. St. Clare Hosp., Schenectady, 1956-59, St. Michael's Med. Center, Newark, 1960-61; asst. adminstr. St. Clare Hosp., Schenectady, 1961-65; provincial treas. Province of St. Anthony, Franciscan Sisters of the Poor, 1966-68; gen. treas. Franciscan Sisters of Poor, 1968-70; exec. dir. St. Mary Hosp., Hoboken, N.J., 1971-80, pres., 1980—, bd. dirs., 1970—; bd. dirs. St. Anthony Community Hosp., Warwick, N.Y., 1966—, pres. bd., 1980—; bd. dirs. St. Francis Community Health Center, 1981—, Hudson Health Systems Agy., 1976-82; dir. Hudson United Bank, 1979—. Named to Hudson County Health Hall of Fame, 1975; named Hudson County Woman of Achievement, 1976. Mem. N.J. Hosp. Assn. (dir. 1977-79), Am. Coll. Hosp. Adminstrs., Am. Hosp. Assn., Cath. Hosp. Assn., Hosp. Fin. Mgmt. Assn., Hosp. Trustees N.Y. State, Nat. Assn. Female Execs., Hudson Hosp. Council, Met. N.Y. Hosp. Fin. Assn. Office: 308 Willow Ave Hoboken NJ 07030

STRAUS, A. SUSAN, journalist; b. Chgo., Aug. 16, 1950; d. Herman and Ruth (Krisky) S.; B.A., Northeastern Ill. U., 1973. Collator, Adams Press, Chgo., 1972; payroll clk. Oxford Clothes, Chgo., 1973-75; sec. Liquid Carbonic, Chgo., 1975-76; file clk. Philip H. Corboy & Assos., Chgo., 1976—; mem. newsletter staff NOW, Chgo., 1974—; mem. prodn. staff Come for To Sing mag., Chgo., 1975—. Mem. Women in Communications, Inc., Women Employed. Home: 5205 N Bernard Chicago IL 60625 Office: 33 N Dearborn St Chicago IL 60602

STRAUSS, DOROTHY BRANDFON, marital, sex and family therapist; b. Bklyn.; d. Marcus and Beatrice (Wilson) Brandfon; B.A., Bklyn. Coll.; M.A., N.Y.U., Ph.D., 1963; m. Hyman Strauss, Oct. 19, 1947; 1 dau., Josette. Instr., Hunter Coll., City U. N.Y., 1960-63; research asst. Center for Human Relations Studies, N.Y.U., 1962, instr., 1963; prof. Kean Coll. N.J., 1963-77; spl. instr. U.S. Army Signal Corps Sch., 1967-71; now instr. dept. psychiatry U. Pa. Sch. Medicine, mem. NIH research team dept. psychiatry; clin. asso. prof. dept. psychiatry SUNY Downstate Med. Center, also asso. dir. Center for Human Sexuality; cons. sch. and community agys.; pvt. practice marital, family, and sex therapy, Bklyn. Mem. Am. Psychol. Assn., N.J. Psychol. Assn., Am. Assn. Marital and Family Therapists, Soc. for Sex Therapy and Research, Am. Assn. Sex Educators and Therapists, Am. Psychosomatic Soc., Soc. Clin. and Exptl. Hypnosis, N.J. Gerontol. Soc., Kappa Delta Pi, Pi Lambda Theta. Home: 2221 Quentin Rd Brooklyn NY 11229 Office: Dept Psychiatry Downstate Med Center SUNY Brooklyn NY 11203

STRAUSS, ESTHER HELEN, psychologist; b. Montreal, Que., Can., Nov. 18, 1948; d. Edgar Josef and Lily (Stein) Strauss; Ph. D., U. Toronto, 1980; m. Josef Cherniawsky, Dec. 7, 1980. Neuropsychologist Aphasia Research Center, Boston, 1973-76; prof. psychology U. Victoria (B.C., Can.), 1979—; hon. asst. prof. dept. pediatrics U.B.C., 1979-81—. Mem. AAAS, N.Y. Acad. Sci., Can. Psychol. Assn., B.C. Psychol. Assn., Internat. Neuropsychol. Soc. Contbr. numerous articles in field to profl. jours. Office: Dept Psychology U Victoria PO Box 1700 Victoria BC V8W 2YZ Canada

STRAUSS, JANE ALYSON, publishing co. exec.; b. Cleve., Feb. 11, 1947; d. George Albert and Dorothy Jane (Davie) S.; B.A., Smith Coll., 1969; M.B.A., Stanford U., 1974. Mgmt. intern HEW, Washington,

1969-72; mgmt. cons. McKinsey & Co., Inc., N.Y.C., 1974-76; strategic planner Pfizer Inc., N.Y.C., 1977; advt. mgr. Newsweek, Inc., N.Y.C., 1978-81, dir. sales planning and analysis, 1981—; cons. Am. Women's Econ. Devel. Corp., 1977-78. Stanford U. grantee. Mem. Women in Communications, NOW, Stanford Alumni Assn., Smith Alumnae Assn., Smith Club N.Y. Office: 444 Madison Ave New York NY 10022

STRAUSS, JEANNE H., tech. translator; b. Hamburg, Germany, Mar. 5, 1928; came to U.S., 1948, naturalized, 1954; d. Frederic and Julie Strauss; B.A., Roosevelt U., 1956; M.A., Loyola U., Chgo., 1960; doctoral candidate U. Wis., Madison. Legal sec. Montgomery Ward, Chgo., 1957-60; instr. Creighton U., Omaha, 1961-63; teaching asst. U. Wis., Madison, 1964-65; asst. prof. U. Wis., Stevens Point, 1965-69, Western Ill. U., Macomb, 1969-71, U. Wis., Superior, 1973-75; tech. translator, interpreter Phillips Petroleum Co., Bartlesville, Okla., 1975—. Mem. Am. Assn. Tchrs. French, Am. Assn. Tchrs. Spanish and Portuguese, MLA, Women in Energy, Philbrook Art Museum. Republican. Home: PO Box 78 Bartlesville OK 74005

STRAUSS, PATRICIA SHELDON, bus. exec.; b. Greenville, Miss., Feb. 7, 1941; d. Anson Hoisington and Beatrice Everett Sheldon; student Miss. State Coll. for Women, 1958-59; B.A., U. Miss., 1962; 1 dau., Anne Michelle. With U. Miss. Med. Center, Jackson, 1965-75, grant coordinator, workshop coordinator, in-house instr., 1975; legal sec., office mgr. Parks & Moss, Houston, 1975-77; adminstrv. asst. 3D/ Internat., Houston, 1977-79, spl. facilities coordinator, 1979-81, asso., 1980—, exec. asst., 1981—. Pres., bd. trustees Jackson Ballet Guild; co-founder, trustee Jackson Ballet Guild Sch., 1973-75; mem. Jackson Civic Arts Council, 1971-73; auction co-chmn. Jackson Symphony League, 1967-75. Republican. Episcopalian. Office: 1900 W Loop S Suite 2100 Houston TX 77027

STRAW, BARBARA CURTIS, mgmt. analyst; b. Phila., Nov. 22, 1950; d. James Robert and Marie Lily (Phillips) Curtis; B.S. with distinction, Pa. State U., 1973; M.S., Drexel U., 1978; m. Ronald Charles Straw, June 29, 1974; 1 son, Jonathan David. Mgmt. analyst mgmt. analysis br. Navy Ships Parts Control Center, Mechanicsburg, Pa., 1973-78, orgn. and manpower devel. sect., 1978-80, supr. orgn. and position mgmt. sect., 1980-82, head orgn. planning br., 1982—; mem. fed. women's program subcom., 1975-79; career counselor, 1979—. Mem. Federally Employed Women (program chairperson Almech chpt. 1978-79, pres. 1979-81, treas. 1982-83, mem. nat. awards com. 1982-83), Nat. Ichthyosis Found., Nat. Assn. Female Execs., Psi Chi. Roman Catholic. Home: 3615 Dwayne Ave Mechanicsburg PA 17055 Office: PO Box 2020 Code 7631 Mechanicsburg PA 17055

STRAWGATE-KANEFSKY, LAURIE ELLEN, social worker; b. N.Y.C., Sept. 8, 1952; d. Justin Herbert and Betty (Heller) S.; B.A. cum laude, Brandeis U., 1974; M.S. in Social Work, Columbia U., 1977; m. E. Paul Kanefsky. Fellow dialysis unit Bronx VA Hosp., 1976-77; intake and group worker 92d Street Y, 1976-77; sex therapist trainee, dept. psychiatry Center for Human Sexuality, Downstate Med. Center, SUNY, Bklyn., 1979-81, sex therapist Center for Human Sexuality, 1981—; nephrology social worker Rogosin Kidney Center, N.Y. Hosp., N.Y.C., 1977—. Cert. social worker N.Y. State. Mem. Nat. Assn. Social Workers, Acad. Cert. Social Workers, Nat. Assn. Patients on Hemodialysis and Transplantation (exec. bd. 1980-81), Am. Soc. for Sex Therapy and Research, Council of Nephrology Social Workers (sec.-treas. N.Y. chpt. 1978-80). Home: 138 Atlantic Ave Brooklyn NY 11201 Office: NY Hosp 525 E 68th St Room M 708 New York NY 10021

STRAWINSKY, ELIZABETH ROWE, psychiatrist; b. Gainesville, Fla., Aug. 31, 1925; d. Albert Reed and Elizabeth Ellen (Rowe) Caro; B.S., Coll. William and Mary, 1948; M.D., Med. Coll. Va., 1948; m. Albert Strawinsky, Dec. 28, 1957. Intern, St. Elizabeths Hosp., Washington, 1948-49, resident in psychiatry, 1949-52, clin. dir., 1962-69, dir. forensic programs, 1969-73; psychiatrist No. Va. Mental Health Inst., Falls Church, 1974—; Recipient Superior Performance award, HEW, 1962. Diplomate Am. Bd. Psychiatry and Neurology. Fellow Am. Psychiat. Assn.; mem. AMA, Med. Soc. Va., Washington Psychiat. Soc., Am. Acad. Psychiatry and Law, Am. Group Psychotherapy Assn., Am. Med. Women's Assn., N.Y. Acad. Scis. Democrat. Home: Route 2 Box 98H Waldorf MD 20601 Office: 3302 Gallows Rd Falls Church VA 22042

STREATER-ACKER, MARY NOËL, educator; b. N.Y.C., Feb. 21, 1945; d. Charles Hayden and Mary Elizabeth (Gehrig) Streater; B.S., SUNY, Cortland, 1967; M.L.A., SUNY, Stony Brook, 1971; m. David Henry Acker, Mar. 28, 1980. Tchr. 5th grade Nassakeag Sch., Setauket, N.Y., 1967—. Bd. mgrs. Sagamore Hill Condominium Assn., 1976-77; bd. dirs. Miller Place Homeowners Assn., 1979-82. Mem. Three Village Tchrs. Union (bldg. rep., chmn. curriculum com.). Home: 6 Miller Ct Miller Place NY 11764 Office: Nassakeag Sch Pond Path Setauket NY 11733

STRECKER, FRANCES IRENE BROWN, civic worker; b. Denver, Aug. 28, 1896; d. Edward Newton and Frances Evelyn (Hittson) Brown; student Colo. Woman's Coll., 1917; m. George O. Strecker, Oct. 21, 1922 (dec. May 1962); children—Muriel Frances, Roger William. Pres. women's aux. Highland Park (Ill.) Hosp., 1956-60, Northwestern U. Settlement, 1960-64; pres. Glencoe (Ill.) Sr. Aux. Infant Welfare Soc. Chgo., 1968-71; corr. sec. Eng. women HEW, 1978-80, chaplain, 1980-82. Mem. Colonial Dames Am. (pres. chpt. 1965-71), Women's Descs. Ancient and Hon. Arty. Co. (pres. Ill. chpt. 1968-71, v.p. Conn. chpt. 1977-80, dep. 1980-83), Greenwich New Eng. Women (librarian 1982—), Ill. Soc. Daus. Colonial Wars (rec. sec. 1968-71, chaplain 1974-77, corr. sec. Conn. 1977-80), Nat. Soc. Daus. Founders and Patriots Am. (pres. Ill. chpt. 1964-67, council Conn. chpt. 1975-78, 81—), Conn. Soc. Genealogists, Colo., Stamford (pres. 1975-77) geneal. socs., Colo. Hist. Soc., Conn. Hist. Soc., Stamford Hist. Soc., Conn. Daus. Am. Colonists (v.p. 1976-78, 82-84, pres. 1978-80), DAR (N. Shore regent 1946-48, 53-54, chaplain Stamford chpt. 1975-77, librarian 1977-79, chmn. manuals 1979—), Pilgrims. Episcopalian. Clubs: Stamford Woman's; Denver Athletic. Republican. Home: 83 Morgan St Stamford CT 06905

STRECKER, SUSAN LINNEA, assn. exec.; b. Aurora, Ill., Aug. 22, 1941; d. John Anthony and Doris (Connery) S.; student Coll. of St. Teresa, 1959-61; B.A. in English, So. Meth. U., 1963. Area supr. Am. Field Service, N.Y.C., 1964-66; adminstrv. sec. B.D./M.T.S. com. Harvard U. Div. Sch., Cambridge, Mass., 1967-68; tchr. Boston Public Schs., 1968-73, Albert Inst. and Am. Sch., Madrid, 1973-75; office mgr. Allende & Brea, N.Y.C., 1975-77; analytic asst. Citibank, N.Y.C., 1977-78; v.p. publs., mng. editor Exec. Female and More Money mags., Nat. Assn. Female Execs., 1978—; start-up cons. mags.; freelance editor, writer; feature stories pub. The Exec. Female, Collector Editions Quar. Mem. Women in Communications (head mag. roundtable N.Y. chpt.). Home: 324 E 77th St New York NY 10021 Office: 123 E 54th St Suite 9C New York NY 10022

STREEP, MERYL (MARY LOUISE STREEP), actress; b. Summit, N.J.; d. Harry Jr. and Mary W. Streep; B.A., Vassar Coll., 1971; M.A. in Fine Arts, Yale U., 1975; Ph.D. (hon.), Dartmouth Coll., 1981; m. Donald J. Gummer, 1978; 1 son, Henry. Appeared with Green Mountain Guild, Woodstock, Vt.; debut at Lincoln Center Beaumont Theater in Trelawny of the Wells, 1975; N.Y.C. theatrical appearances include: 27 Wagons Full of Cotton (Theatre World award), A Memory of Two Mondays, Henry V, Secret Service, The Taming of the Shrew, Measure for Measure, The Cherry Orchard, Happy End, Wonderland, Taken in Marriage, Alice in Concert; movie appearances include: Julia, 1977, The Deer Hunter (Best Supporting Actress award Nat. Soc. Film Critics), 1978, Manhattan, 1979, The Seduction of Joe Tynan, 1979, Kramer vs. Kramer (N.Y. Film Critics' award, Los Angeles Film Critics' award, both for best actress, Acad. Motion Picture Arts and Scis. award for best supporting actress), 1980, The French Lieutenant's Woman, 1981, Still of the Night, 1982, Sophie's Choice, 1982; TV film: The Deadliest Season, 1977; TV mini-series: Holocaust (Emmy award), 1978; TV dramatic spls.: Secret Service, 1977, Uncommon Women and Others, 1978. Recipient Mademoiselle award, 1976; Woman of Yr. award B'nai Brith, 1979, Hasty Pudding Soc., Harvard U., 1980. Office: care Internat Creative Mgmt 40 W 57th St New York NY 10019

STREET, JULIA MONTGOMERY (MRS. CLAUDIUS AUGUSTUS STREET), writer; b. Concord, N.C., Jan. 19, 1898; d. Samuel Lewis and Elizabeth Blanche (Norris) Montgomery; A.B., U. N.C., Greensboro, 1923; m. Claudius Augustus Street, Sept. 13, 1924; children—Carol Street McMillian, Claudius Augustus. Tchr. public schs., N.C., 1918-20, 23-24; field worker N.C. Children's Home Soc., Greensboro, 1924; faculty U. N.C., Greensboro, summers 1922-23; cons. N.C. History-in-Sch. Radio, 1970—; script writer N.C. History (radio) State of N.C., 1970—. Mem. Winston-Salem (N.C.) Radio Council, 1940—. Recipient award AAUW, 1956, 63, 66; Alumni Service award U. N.C., Greensboro, 1967. Mem. N.C. Poetry Soc., N.C. Writers Conf., N.C. Folklore Soc., N.C. Lit. and Hist. Assn. Author: Fiddler's Fancy, 1955; Moccasin Tracks, 1958; Candle Love Feast, 1959; Drovers' Gold, 1961; Dulcie's Whale, 1963; (with Richard Walser) North Carolina Parade, 1966; (poetry) Street Lights, 1949; Salem Christmas Eve, 1955; Judaculla's Handprint, and Other Mysteries from North Carolina, 1975. Contbr. articles to various mags. Home: 545 Oaklawn Ave Winston-Salem NC 27104

STREETER, ANNE PAUL, former mayor, TV co. exec.; b. Phila., July 21, 1926; d. Henry Neill and Marianne Frazer (Harris) Paul; B.A., Smith Coll., 1948; m. Ronald Mather Streeter, June 18, 1949; children—Jean M., Deborah H. Lane, Stephen M., Richard H., Jonathan P. Mem. town council Town of West Hartford (Conn.), 1973-81, mayor, 1975-81; chmn. Capitol Region Council of Govts., 1979-81; pres. West Hartford Community TV, Inc., 1979—. Candidate for Conn. Senate, 1982. Named Man of Yr., West Hartford C. of C., 1979. Mem. LWV (pres. Central San Mateo, Calif. 1966-67, pres. West Hartford 1970-73). Republican. Congregationalist. Office: Town of West Hartford 28 S Main St West Hartford CT 06107

STREGE, MARILYN THERESA, communications co. exec.; b. Medford, NY., Mar. 11, 1937; d. Charles A. and Margaret (Beck) Geide; student U. Md., 1960-63; divorced; children—Sherrie Lynne, Lori Ann. With N.Y. Telephone Co., Riverhead, 1954-59; adminstrv. asst. Edn. Center, Spangdahlem, W. Ger., 1960-63; sales rep. Central Telephone Co., Las Vegas, 1963-68, mktg. mgr., 1973-79; chief operator Caesars Palace, Las Vegas, 1968-73; div. v.p. Telecom, Las Vegas, 1979—; v.p. Am. Security Systems. Mem. Ind. Telephone Pioneers Am., Am. Bus. Women's Assn., Nat. Assn. Female Execs., Las Vegas C. of C. Republican. Lutheran. Home: 5248 Stacey St Las Vegas NV 89108

STREHLAU, BETTY GENE, educator; b. Seattle; d. John A. and Clara (Wabraushek) S.; B.A., U. Wash., 1944, M.A., 1954. Asst. advt. and asst. sales promotion dir. The Bon Marche, Seattle; sales promotion dir. Western Hotels Internat., Seattle; propr., dir. Strehlau Publicity and Advt. Services, Seattle; co-pub. West Woodland-Fremont News, Seattle; prof. journalism and mass media Highline Coll., Midway, Wash., 1962—. Mem. Wash. Press Women (Superior Performance award 1965, Torchbearer award 1979), Community Coll. Journalism Assn. (nat. pres. 1979—), Pacific N.W. Assn. Journalism Educators (regional pres. 1979-80), Am. Women in Radio and TV (Wash. State pres. 1979), Nat. Council Coll. Publ. Advisors (Nat. Disting. Advisor 1977), Nat. Press Women Assn., Women in Communications (Founders' award for leading communicator 1980), Pi Lambda Theta, Alpha Delta Pi. Club: Wash. Athletic.

STREIKER, CONNIE LORRAINE, exec. suites, secretarial services co. exec.; b. Redding, Calif., Apr. 23, 1940; d. Glen Dale and Betty (Aberg) Johnson; student Sacramento State Coll., 1958-59, Sacramento City Coll., 1959-60, 1973-74; m. Lowell Dean Streiker, Aug. 1, 1975; children—Todd Paul Blankenship, Matthew Dale Blankenship. Exec. dir. Mental Health Assn., Yolo County, Calif., 1972-74; crusade coordinator Am. Cancer Soc., Wilmington, Del., 1974-76; exec. sec. Am. Motel Brokers, Burlingame, Calif., 1976-77; owner, mgr. The Home Office, Burlingame, 1977—. Mem. Yolo County Mental Health Advisory Bd., 1973-74; v.p. Mental Health Assn., 1972; mem. allocation and orgns. com. United Way, 1972, town chmn. fund dr., 1973. Mem. Profl. Assn. Secretarial Services (No. Calif.), Women Entrepreneurs, Fedn. of Women's Clubs (sec. Sutter dist. 1973, v.p. 1971, pres. 1972), Fedn. Women's Clubs (sec. dist. 1973). Office: 1633 Old Bayshore Hwy Suite 265 Burlingame CA 94010

STREISAND, BARBRA JOAN, singer, actress; b. Bklyn., Apr. 24, 1942; d. Emanuel and Diana (Rosen) S.; student Yeshiva of Bklyn.; m. Elliott Gould, Mar. 1963 (div.); 1 son, Jason Emanuel. N.Y. theatre debut Another Evening with Harry Stoones, 1961; appeared Broadway musical I Can Get It for You Wholesale, 1962, Funny Girl, 1964-65; rec. artist Columbia Records; motion pictures include: Funny Girl, 1968, Hello Dolly, 1969, On a Clear Day You Can See Forever, 1970, The Owl and the Pussy Cat, 1970, What's Up Doc?, 1972, Up the Sandbox, 1972, The Way We Were, 1973, For Pete's Sake, 1974, Funny Lady, 1975, The Main Event, 1979, All Night Long, 1981; star, producer film A Star is Born, 1976; TV spls. include: My Name is Barbra (5 Emmy awards), 1965, Color Me Barbra, 1966; Gold record albums include: People, 1965, My Name is Barbra, 1965, Color Me Barbra, 1966, Stoney End, 1971, Barbra Joan Streisand, 1972, The Way We Were, 1974, A Star is Born, 1976, Superman, 1977, The Stars Salute Israel at 30, 1978, Wet, 1979, (with Barry Gibb) Guilty, 1980. Recipient Acad. award as best actress of 1968 (Funny Girl); Georgie award AGVA, 1977; Grammy awards for best female vocalist, 1964, 65, 78, for best song writer (with Paul Williams), 1978, for album of yr., 1963. Address: care Press Relations Columbia Records Inc 51 W 52d St New York NY 10019

STRENCIWILK, JANE (STELLA), holding co. fin. exec.; b. Detroit, Feb. 18, 1923; s. George and Julia (Maczko) S.; acctg. cert. Walsh Coll., 1955. Jr. acct. Lawrence Scudder & Co., Detroit, 1955-60, sr. acct., 1960-64, sr. supr., 1964-68; with Trans-Industries, Inc., Waterford, Mich., 1968—, asst. controller, 1968-69, treas., 1969—. C.P.A. Mem. Am. Inst. C.P.A.'s, Mich. Assn. C.P.A.'s, Am. Soc. Women C.P.A.'s. Republican. Roman Catholic. Clubs: Detroit Boat, Altrusa (pres. local club). Office: 3777 Airport Rd Waterford MI 48095

STRETCH, SHIRLEY MARIE, textiles educator; b. Wauneta, Nebr., May 6, 1949; d. Lloyd Ray and Roberta Marie (Schroeder) S.; B.S., U. Nebr., 1971; M.S., Kans. State U., 1972; M.B.A., Ohio State U., 1977, Ph.D., 1982. Instr. clothing and textiles Bowling Green (Ohio) State U., 1972-75; grad. adminstrv. asso. Univ. Coll., Ohio State U., 1976-78, 80; asso. mgr. direct mktg. div. Ashland Petroleum Co. (Ky.), 1979-80; asst. prof. clothing and textiles Tex. Tech. U., Lubbock, 1980—. Pres., mem. bd. adminstrn. Sunport Condominium. Ednl. Profl. Devel. fellow, 1971-73. Mem. Am. Mktg. Assn., Lubbock Assn. M.B.A. Execs., Nat. Assn. Female Execs., Am. Home Econs. Assn., Assn. Coll. Profs. Textiles and Clothing, Omicron Nu, Phi Upsilon Omicron. Republican. Methodist. Home: 4604C 55th Dr Lubbock TX 79414 Office: PO Box 4170 Tex Tech U Lubbock TX 79409

STREY, MICHELE YVETTE, utility co. exec.; b. St. Paul, June 14, 1950; d. Virdon Alfred and Camille Eugenie (Gabrio) Strey; B.S. with high honors in Acctg., San Diego State U., 1975. Acct., Gilbert Vasquez & Co., San Diego, 1974-75; auditor Peat, Marwick, Mitchell & Co., San Diego, 1976-78; acct. San Diego Gas & Electric Co., 1978—, mem. mgmt. forum steering com., 1980-82, credit union mktg., edn. and pub. com., 1980-82, Employees Fed. Credit Union Supervisory com., 1980-81. Publicity chmn. Mexican and Am. Found., 1980-81, hospitality chmn., 1981-82; publicity chmn. 1981 An Evening with the Star. (Named Dama de Distincion, Mexican and Am. Found., 1982. C.P.A., Calif. Mem. Calif. Scholarship Fedn., Calif. Soc. C.P.A.s, Beta Alpha Psi, Beta Gamma Sigma. Republican. Home: 6615-161 Canyon Rim Row San Diego CA 92111 Office: PO Box 1831 San Diego CA 92112

STRICKLAND, ALLEN MCGILL (MRS. GEORGE M. STRICKLAND), artist; b. Washington; d. I.J. Nota and Frances M. (Maloy) McGill; student pvt. schs.; m. George Marlon Strickland. Salon in Paris Artistes Francais; one-woman shows Daytona Beach and Ormond Beach, Ormond Library, 1979; numerous group shows; represented in pvt. collections in U.S. and France. Recipient numerous awards in painting. Mem. Nat. League Am. Pen Women (pres. Daytona Beach br., 1961-64), Fla. Fedn. Art, Daytona Beach Art League, St. Augustine Art Assn., Garden Club Am., Beaux Arts Volusia County. Home: 487 John Anderson Hwy Ormond Beach FL 32074

STRICKLAND, MARY LOU, corp. exec.; b. Ivydale, W.Va., June 20, 1937; d. Robert Lee and Gladys Valerie (Wood) Wilmoth; B.S., Auburn U., 1971; M.S., W.Va. Coll., 1975; Ph.D., Va. Poly. Inst. and State U., 1979; m. Steve R. Strickland, June 11, 1955; children—Pamela, Mark, David. Chmn. lang. arts dept. Putnam County Bd. Edn., Hurricane, W.Va., 1971-75; adj. prof. W.Va. Coll., Charleston, 1976; dir. of gifted children Regional Ednl. Service Agy., Charleston, 1977-79; pres. MJ, Inc., Hurricane, MultiLine Sales and Services, Inc., Hurricane, 1978—; dir. SEARCH Agy., Hurricane, 1978—. Trustee, Thomas Meml. Hosp. South Charleston, W.Va., 1979—. Mem. Putnam County C. of C. (dir. 1979—), Assn. Community Edn. W.Va. (pres. 1979-81), AAUW, Phi Delta Kappa. Presbyterian. Office: 4005 Teays Valley Rd Scott Depot WV 25560

STRICKLAND, PATRICIA LAFORE, data processing exec.; b. Hanau, Ger., Oct. 12, 1952; came to U.S., 1958, naturalized, 1961; d. Jack Harold and Thelma Fern (Allen) L.; student Hillsbourgh Community Coll., 1977-78, Nova Community Coll., 1979-81; m. James E. Strickland, Feb. 27, 1972 (div.); 1 dau., Christina Lynn. Account analyst Gen. Portland, Inc., Tampa, Fla., 1971-77; acctg. mgr. Best Steel Products, Inc., Tampa, 1977-78; data processing mgr. Smacna, Vienna, Va., 1979-81; software specialist KDK Enterprises, Inc., McLean, Va., 1981-82; customer service specialist Insurnet, Inc., Atlanta, 1982—; dir. Micro Internat., Chgo., 1981. Mem. Nat. Capitol Area Microdata Users Group (sec.-treas. 1980—). Home: Lake Village Terr Atlanta GA 30346 Office: 8 Perimeter Center Atlanta GA 30346

STRICKLER, DIANA HOLE, investment banker; b. N.Y.C., July 25, 1951; d. Richard Witherspoon and Tacey (Belden) Hole; student Wellesley Coll., 1969-71; B.A., magna cum laude, Williams Coll., 1973; M.B.A., Columbia U., 1979; m. Richard Stoner Strickler, Jr., June 11, 1977; 1 dau., Margaret Evans Hennen. Comml. officer First Pa. Bank, Phila., 1974-77; cons. Booz Allen & Hamilton, N.Y.C., 1978; assoc. corp. fin. dept. First Boston Corp., N.Y.C., 1979—. Mem. fin. adv. bd. Columbia U. Grad. Sch. Bus.; trustee Williams Coll., 1977-81. Mem. Phi Beta Kappa, Beta Gamma Sigma. Republican. Episcopalian. Clubs: Merion Cricket (Haverford, Pa.); Williams (N.Y.C.). Home: 55 East End Ave 2-H New York NY 10028 Office: Park Avenue Plaza New York NY 10055

STRICKLIN, ALICE ROSEMARY, nurse; b. Ajo, Ariz., Oct. 21, 1942; d. Daniel John and Susan Ellen (Breen) O'Connor; student U. Ariz., 1967-68; B.S.N., Incarnate Word Coll., San Antonio, 1964; m. John David Stricklin, May 31, 1964; children—John Eric, Michael Morrow. Mem. surg. cardio-vascular research team SW Research Inst., San Antonio, 1962-64; nurse Highsmith-Rainey Hosp., Fayetteville, N.C., 1964-65; operating room supr. New Cornelia Hosp., Ajo, 1966-69, asst. dir. nurses, 1968-69; with Hillcrest Gen. Hosp., Silver City, N.Mex., 1969-81, supervisory nurse, 1969-81, asst. chmn. nursing div., 1979-81, dir. in-service edn., 1979-81; ind. nursing research, writer, lectr., 1978—. Chmn. Grant County chpt. Am. Heart Assn.; concert chmn. Grant County Choral Union; coordinator, resource person Medic Alert Program, 1976-79. Mem. Assn. Critical Care Nurses. Republican. Roman Catholic. Contbr. articles to profl. jours. Home: 44100 Blackhwak Silver City NM 88061

STRIDIRON, JUDITH JAMISON, assn. exec.; b. Phila., Feb. 7, 1950; d. James Russell and Betty (McNeal) Jamison; B.S., Cheyney State Coll., 1971; certificate Inst. of Psychotherapy/Psychodrama, 1971-72; M.Ed., Temple U., 1974. Tchr., Sch. Dist. of Phila., 1971-74, elem. sch. counselor, 1975-77; dir. Youth Directions, Phila., 1978-80; dir. teen services Crime Prevention Assn. of Phila., 1980—; adj. prof. Brandywine Coll., 1977-79. Supt. Sunday sch. Holy Cross Bapt. Ch., 1980—. Mem. Nat. Assn. Univ. Women (chmn. scholarship com. 1979—; Woman of Yr. 1980), Nat. Assn. Female Execs., Nat. Assn. Bus. and Profl. Women, Am. Inst. Fgn. Study, Edn. Task Force of Phila. Urban Coalition, League Women Voters. Baptist. Contbr. articles to profl. jours. Home: 16 Concord Rd Darby PA 19023 Office: 3512 Haverford Ave Philadelphia PA 19104

STRINGER, ROXANNE RICHARDS, educator; b. Hartford, Conn., Feb. 3, 1936; d. George Jerre and Ruth Patz Richards; B.A. in Psychology, U. Hartford, 1969, M.Ed., 1972; 6th Yr., Central Conn. Coll., 1976; m. Norman John Stringer Jr., Sept. 7, 1957; children—Norman John III, George Richards, Marc Williams. Tchr., Samuel Huntington Sch., Meriden, Conn., 1969-72; reading cons. Benjamin Franklin Sch., also Thomas Hooker Sch., Meriden, 1972-76, John Barry Sch., Meriden, 1976—; lectr. to parent groups, vol. tutors, high sch. and coll. classes; cons. to pub. cos. Vice pres., treas. Meriden Hosp. Women's Aux., 1966-68. Conn. Right to Read grantee, 1974. Mem. NEA, New Eng. Reading Assn., Internat. Reading Assn., Greater Hartford Area Reading Councils of Conn., Conn. Edn. Assn., Meriden Edn. Assn. Republican. Roman Catholic. Clubs: Home; Windham Heights Country (Windham, Vt.). Home: 69 Butternut Dr Meriden CT 06450 Office: John Barry Sch 124 Columbia St Meriden CT 06450

STRINGHAM, JUDITH MITCHELL, equipment sales exec.; b. Hartford, Conn., May 9, 1939; d. William Joseph and Irene Elizabeth (Campion) Mitchell; A.A.S., Fashion Inst. Tech., 1959; B.S., Cornell U., 1961; M.S., SUNY, New Paltz, 1964; m. Varick Van Wyck Stringham, Jr., June 15, 1963; children—Amanda, Pamela, Varick Van Wyck III, Rebecca. Tchr., Fishill (N.Y.) Elem. Sch., Lamar Elem. Sch. and Presbyn. High Sch., Kingsville, Tex., 1961-65; sec.-treas. North Atlantic Equipment Sales, Inc., Wappingers Falls, N.Y., 1972—. Former bd. dirs. Jr. League Poughkeepsie; former bd. dirs. LWV; past treas., bd. dirs. and pres. Community Children's Theatre; pres., past sec. Community Exptl. Repertory Theatre; sec., former mem. bd. dirs., now sec. adv. com.

Dutchess County Arts Council Adv. Com.; charter bd. dirs. Cunneen-Hackett Cultural Complex; former crew Hudson River Sloop Clearwater; former mem. bd. dirs. PTA; mem. Cornell Secondary Schs. Com.; Paul Harris sustaining mem. Rotary Found. of Rotary Internat. Mem. Nat. Assn. Female Execs., NOW, Cornell U. Alumni Assn., Cornell Coll. Human Ecology Alumni, Cornell Chorus Soc., Dutchess County Hist. Soc., Fishkill Hist. Soc., Bardavon 1869 Opera House, Hudson Valley Philharm., County Players, Dutchess County Landmarks, Mt. Gulian Soc., Mental Health Assn. Dutchess County, Century Circle of Vassar Bros. Hosp. Assn., Dutchess County Soc. for Prevention Cruelty to Animals. Mem. Reformed Ch. in Am. Club: Mid-Hudson Cornell. Home: Dogwood Hill Rd Wappingers Falls NY 12590 Office: PO Box 619 Route 376 Wappingers Falls NY 12590

STRINGER-MOORE, DONNA M., city govt. ofcl.; b. Forest Grove, Oreg., June 30, 1942; d. Lester L. and Viola M. (Bean) Stringer; B.A. with honors in Psychology, Sacramento State U., 1971; M.A., U. Calif., Davis, 1973, Ph.D., 1981; children—Scott Alan, Mark Edward, David Todd. Research coordinator Berkeley (Calif.) Public Schs., 1973-74; dir. Women's Resources and Research Center, U. Calif., Davis, 1974-78; affirmative action and human resources officer Mont. State U., 1978-81; dir. City of Seattle Office Women's Rights, 1981—; tchr., speaker in field. Mem. Am. Assn. Women Psychologists, NOW, AAUW, Nat. Women's Polit. Caucus, Seattle Mcpl. League, Seattle Mgmt. Assn., ACLU. Author papers, articles in field. Editor: Battered Women, 1979. Office: 400 Yesler St 5th Floor Seattle WA 98104

STRIPLING, JOHNNIE RUTH ERVIN, educator; b. Gilmer, Tex., Aug. 14, 1934; d. John Henry and Lela Belle Ervin; B.A., Tex. Coll., 1956; M.Ed., N. Tex. State U., 1970; m. June 29, 1957. Tchr., Goldsberry Elem. Sch., Joinerville, Tex., 1956-59, Lincoln High Sch., La Marque, Tex., 1959-70, Boulter Jr. High Sch., Tyler, Tex., 1970-72; tchr. Whitehouse (Tex.) Ind. Sch. Dist., 1972—; part-time counselor Tyler (Tex.) Jr. Coll., 1978-79. Mem. exec. adv. bd. Nat. Security Bank, 1975—; sec., bd. dirs. North Tyler br. YMCA, 1977-79. Recipient Century Club award YMCA, 1979, Service to Youth award, 1979; Friends of Tex. Coll. award, 1980. Mem. NEA, Tex. Tchrs. Assn., Tex. Classroom Tchrs. Assn., Smith County Tchrs. Assn., E. Tex. Council of Reading, Internat. Reading Assn., Mental Health Mental Retardation Assn. (pres. 1977-79), AAUW N. Tex. State Alumni Assn., Delta Sigma Theta. Baptist. Clubs: Tex. Coll. Explorers, Heroines of Jerico. Home: 3005 N Whitten St Tyler TX 75702

STRITZEL, URSULA ELISABETH, internal auditor; b. Essen, Germany, Nov. 24, 1951; came to U.S., 1955, naturalized, 1965; d. Hubert Paul and Elisabeth Gertrud (Thiel) S.; B.S., Quinnipiac Coll., 1982. Exec. sec. to corp. med. dir. Uniroyal, Inc., Middlebury, Conn., 1971-73; exec. asst. to pres. and vice chmn.-fin. Timex Corp., Waterbury, Conn., 1973-74; internal auditor Yale U., New Haven, 1974—, sec.-treas. Communications Bd., 1976—; sec. Yale U. Alumni Publs., Inc., 1976—. Mem. Nat. Assn. Female Execs. Roman Catholic. Home: 23 Silver St Branford CT 06405 Office: 155 Whitney Ave New Haven CT 06520

STROHM, LILLIAN ANN, home economist; b. South Bend, Ind, Oct. 17, 1914; d. John and Sadie (Kelley) Murphy; B.S., Purdue U., 1938; M.A., George Washington U., 1941; m. John Strohm, Sept. 8, 1941; children—Terry, Karen, Robert, Cheryl, Dave, Colleen. Head home econs. dept. USDA, Bainbridge, Ind., 1938-39, home demonstration agt., Vigo County, Ind., 1938-41; homemaking editor Ford Almanac, Woodstock, Ill., 1954—. Exec. sec., then pres. Woodstock Opera House Community Center, Inc., 1970-80. Purdue U. scholar, 1928-32; USDA fellow, 1939-40. Mem. AAUW, Omicron Nu, Kappa Delta Pi, Alpha Lambda Delta. Roman Catholic. Clubs: Garden (pres.), Book (v.p.), Investment (sec.). Address: 515 W Jackson St Woodstock IL 60098

STROKOFF, SANDRA LEE, lawyer; b. Phila., Jan. 19, 1950; d. Edward and Lillian (Katz) S.; B.A., U. Pa., 1971, J.D., 1975; M.A., King's Coll. U. London, 1973; m. Jay Richard Gordon, Apr. 12, 1981. Admitted to Pa. bar, 1975, D.C. bar, 1976; law intern Phila. Pub. Defenders Assn., 1973; staff firm Kominers, Fort, Schlefer and Boyer, Washington, summer 1974; intern Center for Law & Social Policy, Washington, 1974; legal asst. Office Legis. Counsel U.S. Ho. Reps., 1975-77, asst. legis. counsel, 1977—. Mem. Pa. Bar, D.C. Bar, Women's Legal Def. Fund, Phi Beta Kappa. Office: 136 Cannon House Office Bldg United States House of Representatives Washington DC 20515

STROMFELD, DIANNE LOU, Realtor; b. Bklyn.; d. Irving and Sally (Goldstein) Tillman; student pub. schs.. Bklyn.; m. Lawrence Stromfeld, Feb. 27, 1960; children—Jeffery, Lisa, Stephen. With I.C. Isaacs Co., sportswear sales and design, N.Y.C., 1957-60; pres. Century 21 D.L.S. Realty Corp., Huntington, N.Y., 1968-80; v.p., mem. edn. com. Multiple Listing Service of L.I., pres., 1979-80, chairperson advt. com., 1981-82; Realtor; pres. Century 21 Brokers Council L.I., 1978-79; v.p., regional mktg. dir. Partners of No. N.J.; mgr. Merrill Lynch Realty/Carl Burr, Inc., Commack, N.Y. Mem. L.I. Bd. Realtors (treas., v.p., pres. Huntington chpt., mem. arbitration com.). Mem. Nat., N.Y. State assns. Realtors. Jewish. Home: 15 Markwood Ln East Northport NY 11731 Office: 50 Commack Rd Commack NY 11725

STROMP, PHOEBE A., twp. trustee; b. Wyandotte, Mich., July 23, 1932; d. Frank A. and Elizabeth M. (Rushlow) Beaker; student Wayne County Community Coll., 1974—; m. William J. Stromp, Sept. 22, 1951; children—Elizabeth, Christine, John, Francis, Phoebe M., Renee, William J. Mgmt. info. coordinator Detroit Edison Co.; trustee Brownstown Twp., Trenton, Mich., 1976—. Mem. Engring. Soc. Detroit. Democrat. Roman Catholic.

STRONG, ALDA (MRS. LAVERN STRONG), community service vol., realtor; b. Menan, Idaho, Sept. 22, 1911; d. William D. and Margaret (Hunting) Watson; grad. high school; nat. grad. Realestate Inst., 1977; m. LaVern Strong, June 14, 1930; children—Nalda (Mrs. Richard C. Powell), Harvey, Deanna (Mrs. Douglas Vollmer). Active Internat. Toastmistress Clubs, 1951—, organizer 4 local clubs, pres. council number 9, No. region, 1959-60, parliamentarian No. region, 1960-61; legislative chmn. Idaho Bus. and Profl. Women's Clubs, 1958-59, chmn. pub. relations, 1959-61, pres.; safety chmn. Idaho Gen. Fedn. Women's Clubs, 1960-61, Idaho chmn. crime prevention, 1964, state safety chmn.; sec. dist. South Central Bus. and Profl. Clubs, 1967; pres. 20th Century, Twin Falls, Idaho, 1962-63; bd. dirs. Twin Falls Salvation Army, chmn., 1975-78, life mem. Salvation Army Help; state rep. to President's Safety Conf. Mich. State U. Organizer 5 safety clubs Nat. Safety Council; safety chmn. So. Idaho Citizens Safety Council; regional dir. Idaho Women's Hwy. Safety Leaders, 1971-74; bd. dirs. Twin Falls Civic Auditorium, 1959-61; chmn. Twin Falls County chpt. Nat. Found.; sec. Idaho Hosp. Auxiliaries, 1959-60; pres. Twin Falls YWCA; sponsor Sigma chpt. Beta Sigma Phi; sec.-treas. Twin Falls County Civil Def.; past pres. Gem. State Writers Guild, editor Gem State News Letter, 1970-71; mem. Nat. Assn. Parliamentarians (Idaho pres. 1977—). Democratic candidate Idaho Ho. of Reps., 1960. Recipient Certificate of Merit award Nat. Safety Council, 1959; named Woman of Year, Bus. and Profl. Women's Clubs, 1960, Magic Toastmistress Club, Number 1002, No. region, 1959; Disting. Service award Jr. C. of C., 1960, merit award Idaho Safety Council; registered parliamentarian. Mem. Idaho Bd. Realtors (parliamentarian 1976—). Clubs: Altrusa (internat. chmn.); 20th Century Federated (fine arts chmn. 2d v.p.) Home: 2016 Stadium Blvd Twin Falls ID 83301

STRONG, DIANE PATRICIA, accountant; b. San Diego, Dec. 13, 1945; d. Emma Wanda Brown; B.A., U. Calif., San Diego, 1979; 1 dau., Debra Lynn Hammond. Staff bookkeeper Smathers & Nutter, C.P.A.s, San Diego, 1974-77; staff acct. Levitz, Zacks & Ceceric, Inc., San Diego, 1977-79, Ford, Hickman, Gibbs & Massinger, Accts., Inc., San Diego, 1979-80; supr. small bus. dept. West, Johnston, Turnquist Accountancy Corp., San Diego, 1980—. Vol., United Way campaign, 1979, 80, 81. C.P.A., Calif. Mem. Nat. Assn. Accts., Calif. Soc. C.P.A.s, Nat. Assn. Female Execs., Internat. Assn. Fin. Planners, Giving and Receiving Orgn. for Women, Alumni and Friends U. Calif. San Diego. Office: 2550 5th Ave Suite 1009 San Diego CA 92103

STRONG, JOYCE ELIZABETH, pianist, educator; b. Kansas City, Mo., May 26, 1933; d. Melvin Witzel and Lucy Mae (Adams) S.; student U. Pitts. 1951, Eastman Sch. Mus., Rochester, N.Y. 1951-53; B.S., Juilliard Sch. Music, 1957, M.S., 1959. Piano debut, Pitts., 1952; recitalist primarily in So. and Eastern U.S., also Lincoln Center for Performing Arts, N.Y.C., Hartford, Conn., Columbus, Ohio, Dallas, Austin, Tex., U. Mich. Internat. Conf. on Women in Arts, 1982; tchr. Kent Place Sch., Summit, N.J. 1959-60; asst. prof. Huntingdon Coll., 1961-63; instr. U. Ala., 1963-67; prof. Tex. Woman's U., Denton, 1967—. Recipient Alta. Symphony Assn. award 1948, Pitts. Concert Soc. award 1952, award of merit Nat. Fedn. Music Clubs 1977. Mem. Women in Arts, Coll. Music Soc., Am. Music Scholarship Assn., Tex. Assn. Coll. Tchrs., Music Tchrs. Nat. Assn., Pi Kappa Lambda. Home: 1804 Teasley Ln Denton TX 76201 Office: Music Department Texas Woman's University Denton TX 76204

STRONG, JUDITH ANN, chemist, educator; b. Van Hornesville, N.Y., June 19, 1941; d. Philip Furnald and Hilda Bernice (Hulbert) S.; B.S. cum laude (N.Y. State regents scholar), SUNY, Albany, 1963; M.A., Brandeis U., 1966, Ph.D., 1970. Asst. prof. chemistry Moorhead State U. (Minn.), 1969-73, acting chmn. chemistry dept., 1976, asso. prof., 1973-81, prof., 1981—. Recipient Tietzen Meml. award SUNY, Albany, 1963; NSF fellow, 1965-67. Mem. Am. Chem. Soc., NEA, Minn. Edn. Assn., Minn. Acad. Sci., Sigma Xi. Home: 1209 12th St S Moorhead MN 56560 Office: Chemistry Dept Moorhead State U Moorhead MN 56560

STRONG, LEAH AUDREY, educator; b. Buffalo, N.Y., Mar. 14, 1922; d. Robert LeRoy and Dorothy Sinclair (Kennedy) S.; A.B., Allegheny Coll., 1943; A.M., Cornell U., 1944; Ph.D., Syracuse U., 1953. Instr. dept. English, Syracuse U., 1947-52; asst. prof. Cedar Crest Coll., 1953-61; prof. Am. studies Wesleyan Coll., Macon, Ga., 1961—, chmn. div. humanities, 1981—. Mem. So. Humanities Conf. (exec. sec. 1980—), Southeastern Am. Studies Assn. (pres. 1981—), MLA, South Atlantic MLA, Am. Studies Assn., Popular Culture Assn. South, Am. Motorcyclist Assn. Conglist. Clubs: Altrusa, Order Eastern Star. Author: Joseph Hopkins Twichell: Mark Twain's Friend and Pastor, 1966; contbr. articles to mags. Home: 1173 Forest Hill Rd Macon GA 31210 Office: Dept Am Studies Wesleyan Coll Macon GA 31297

STRONG, MAYDA NEL, psychologist, educator; b. Albuquerque, May 6, 1942; d. Floyd Samuel and Wanda Christmas (Martin) Strong; B.A. cum laude, Tex. Western Coll., 1963; M.Ed., U. Tex., Austin, 1972, Ph.D. in Counseling Psychology (AAUW fellow), 1978; m. Ronald Soechting, Aug. 21, 1977; 2 sons. Asst. instr. in ednl. psychology U. Tex., Austin, 1974-78; instr.psychology Austin Community Coll., 1974-78, Otero Jr. Coll., La Junta, Colo., 1979—; dir. outpatient and emergency services S.E. Colo. Family Guidance and Mental Health Center, Inc., La Junta, 1978-81; pvt. practice psychol. therapy, La Junta, 1981—. Co-star The Good Doctor, Picketwire Theatre, La Junta, 1980, On Golden Pond, 1981. Mem. Bus. and Profl. People (legis. chairperson 1982-83), Colo. Psychol. Assn. Contbr. articles in field to profl. publs. Home and Office: 910 San Juan Ave La Junta CO 81050

STROPUS, JUDITH VICTORIA (JURA), public relations cons., race driver; b. Kaunas, Lithuania, Oct. 7, 1943; came to U.S., 1949, naturalized, 1963; d. Algirdas and Malvina Brucas (Bubelevicius) S.; student public and parochial schs., N.Y.C. Public relations sec. Western Electric Co., N.Y.C., 1960-64; legal sec. Bucknum & Archer, N.Y.C., 1964-67, Dills & Schelker, N.Y.C., 1967-70; public relations rep. Fred Opert Racing, N.J., 1971, Mobility Systems Co., N.Y.C., 1971-75; founder, owner JVS Enterprises, Ridgefield, Conn., 1976—; profl. timer and scorer for U.S. auto racing teams including Lincoln-Mercury's Cougar Team, Am. Motors Javelin Team, Penske Racing Team, Peter Gregg's Brumos Racing Team, BMW Motorsports Team, Toyota Factory Team, Bob Akin Motor Racing, Holbert Racing, 1967—; profl. race driver, 1973—, sponsored by Dunlop Tire Co., 1975-80; asst. to author Karl Ludvigsen, 1968-73. Mem. Internat. Motor Press Assn. (dir.), Auto Racing Writers and Broadcasters Assn., Internat. Motor Sports Assn., Sports Car Club Am., Madison Ave. Sports Car Driving and Chowder Soc., Motor Racing Safety Soc., Vintage Sports Car Club Am. Author: The Stropus Guide to Auto Race Timing & Scoring, 1975; mem. cross country contingent demonstrating Run-Flat tire, Dunlop Tire Co., 1980; star in dealer promotional film for Volvo, 1981. Home and Office: 19 Cook Close Ridgefield CT 06877

STROTHER, PAT WALLACE, author; b. Birmingham, Ala., Mar. 11, 1929; d. Claude Hunter and Gladys Eleanor (English) Wallace; student U. Tenn., Knoxville, 1947-51; m. Lee Levitt, 1951 (div. 1957); m. 2d, David G. Latner, 1958 (div. 1968); m. 3d, Robert A. Strother, 1980. Dir. women's programs WGNS Radio, Murfreesboro, Tenn., 1951-52; continuity dir. WMAK Radio, Nashville, 1952-54; asst. editor Civil Service Leader, N.Y.C., 1955-57; adminstrv. sec. Local 237 Teamsters, N.Y.C., 1957-76; works include: House of Scorpio, 1975, This Willing Passion, 1978, The Wand and the Star, 1978; Traitor in My Arms, 1979; The Voyagers, 1980; Once More the Sun, Silver Fire, 1982; My Loving Enemy, Summer Kingdom, 1983. Mem. Am. Astrological Assn., Authors Guild. Democrat.

STROTHER, VIRGINIA, artist; b. Fort Worth, July 19, 1920; d. Sterling Maddison and Ethel Leona (Freeman) Vaughn; B.F.A., Tex. Christian U., 1950; m. Aubrey Leon Strother, Apr. 17, 1938; 1 dau., Delores Ann. Dir. workshop art classes Tex. Christian U., 1950-54; one woman shows Ridglea Country Club, Fort Worth, 1971, 79 Latch String Gallery, Fort Worth, 1974, Danciger Center, Fort Worth, 1975; exhibited in group shows Heritage Hall Gallery, Fort Worth, 1968, Patio Gallery, Fort Worth, 1971-72, Fort Worth Art Mus., 1968, 70, 73, Okla. Art Center, Ark. Art Center, 1973, El Paso (Tex.) Mus. Art, 1972-76, others; represented in permanent collections Tex. Fine Arts Assn., Fort Worth Women's Club, Tex. Christian U., U. Tex. at Arlington. Mem. Tex. Fine Arts Assn. (awards, state adv. bd. 1968-75), Tex. Watercolor Soc. (awards), Fort Worth Art Mus. (awards), Nat. League Am. Pen Women (awards). Club: Fort Worth Women's. Home: 4109 Shannon Dr Fort Worth TX 76116

STROTHMAN, LINDA JEAN, social worker; b. Wheeling, W.Va., June 13, 1943; d. Ferdinand and Margaret Esther (Lohrey) S.; B.G.S., Roosevelt U., Chgo., 1970; postgrad. U. Ill., 1971; M.A. in Social Work, U. Chgo., 1976; m. John Charles Stokes, IV, June 3, 1977. Mem. leadership staff Ill. Ho. of Reps., Springfield, 1970-71; pvt. practice legis. cons., Chgo., 1971-72; mem. staff Black Legis. Clearinghouse, 1971; instr. women's studies Roosevelt U., 1970-71; dir. legis. intern program Chgo. State U., 1972-74; therapist The Depot, Chgo., 1974-76, 77-79, Oak Lawn (Ill.) Family Service, 1978-81; NIMH fellow Mt. Zion Hosp., San Francisco, 1976-77; clin. dir. Constance Morris Family Crisis Center of Des Plaines Valley Community Center Hull House Assn., Summit, Ill., 1979—; pvt. practice psychotherapy, specializing in domestic violence, child psychotherapy, cons., Chgo., 1979—; psychotherapy cons. Uptown Center Hull House, Chgo., 1980—. Ford Found. fellow, 1970-71. Mem. Nat. Assn. Social Workers, Ill. Soc. Clin. Social Workers, Chgo. Psychoanalytic Study Group, NOW (Ill. legis. coordinator 1971-73). Lutheran. Editor: Illinois Women's Legislative Bulletin, 1971-73; contbr. in field. Home: 5445 S Harper Ave Chicago IL 60615 Office: 6125 S Archer Rd Summit IL 60501 also 55 E Washington St Suite 1521 Chicago IL 60602

STROUT, JANIS LYNN, ednl. adminstr.; b. Altadena, Calif., Dec. 24, 1947; d. George Augustus and Dorothy Dean (Wiseman) S.; B.A. in History, Calif. State U., Long Beach, 1970; M.S. in Edn., So. Ill. U., Edwardsville, 1975. Asst. program dir. Univ. Center, So. Ill. U., Edwardsville, 1973-75; program dir. Hewitt Union SUNY, Oswego, 1975-77; 504 coordinator Equal Opportunity Office, U. Mont., Missoula, 1977-78; dir. programming services Mont. State U., Bozeman, 1978—, dir. Women's Resource Center, 1982—. Founder, bd. dirs. Bozeman Battered Women's Network, 1978—, pres., 1982—; bd. dirs. Mont. Environ. Info. Center, v.p., 1980—; producer Mont. Woman Radio Program, 1978—; coordinator Bozeman Film Festival, 1979—; mem. Mont. Spouse Abuse Task Force, 1980—; founder, mem. Women's Community Center, 1980—; mem. Madison Gallatin Alliance, 1979—; mem. Alliance for a Nuclear Free Future, 1981—. Recipient Woman of Achievement for Gallatin County, Bus. and Profl. Women, 1981. Mem. Affiliated Women of Mont. State U., Nat. Assn. Women Deans, Adminstrs. and Counselors, Assn. Coll. Unions (Internat.), Am. Coll. Personnel Assn., HERS/West, Gallatin County Women's Polit. Caucus. Office: Women's Resource Center Mont State U Bozeman MT 59717

STRUB, LINDA ELAINE, pharm. co. ofcl.; b. Jersey City, Mar. 10, 1948; d. Charles Christian and Esther Louise (Haerle) S.; B.A. in Econs., Rutgers U., 1969; M.B.A. in Fin., Fairleigh Dickinson U., 1976. With mem. firms dept. N.Y. Stock Exchange, 1969-72, ops. coordinator, 1971-72; adminstrv. asst. to v.p. ops. and fin. Laird Inc., N.Y.C., 1972-74; supr. records mgmt. Pfizer Inc., N.Y.C., 1974-75, mgr. graphic communications, 1975—. Mem. Assn. Multi-Image, Nat. Assn. Female Execs., Nat. Micrographics Assn., Assn. M.B.A. Execs. Lutheran. Club: Order Rainbow Girls. Home: 68 South Dr Rochelle Park NJ 07662 Office: 235 E 42d St New York NY 10017

STRUM, PHILIPPA, polit. scientist, educator; b. N.Y.C., Dec. 14, 1938; d. Joseph Bernard and Ida Strum; B.A., Brandeis U., 1959; Ed.M., Harvard U., 1960; Ph.D., New Sch., 1964; m. Herbert F. Weiss, July 28, 1976; children—Laura Segelstein, Eric Segelstein, David Strum. Successively instr., asst. prof., asso. prof. Rutgers U., Newark, 1964-72; asso. prof., then prof. Bklyn. Coll., City U.N.Y., 1972—; vis. prof. Barnard Coll., 1978-79. Mem. Am. Polit. Sci. Assn., AAUW, Women's Caucus for Polit. Sci., ACLU (acad. freedom com. 1973—, dir. 1979—), Am.-Israeli Civil Liberties Coalition (pres. 1981—). Co-author: On Studying Political Science, 1969; author: Presidential Power and American Democracy, 1972, 1979; The Supreme Court and Political Questions, 1974; contbr. articles in field to profl. jours. Office: Dept Polit Sci Bklyn Coll Brooklyn NY 11210

STRUVE, SANDRA FORTENBERG, title co. exec.; b. Three Rivers, Tex., Aug. 26, 1944; d. Glad and Louise Ila (Sparks) Fortenberg; B.S. in Bus., U. So. Miss., 1965; m. Charles W. Struve, Nov. 27, 1965; 1 dau., Julianne Hillary. Closing clk. Stockton-White & Co., Raleigh, N.C., 1968-71; part-owner Mountain Vintners, Ltd., 1971-76; br. mgr. Uslife Title Ins. Co. Dallas, 1976; br. mgr. Mountain Title Co., Western Divide Title Cos., Breckenridge, Colo., 1977-79, chief exec. officer, 1979—; alt. title assn. com. HUD. Precinct chmn. Republican party, 1976-78; leader Girl Scouts U.S.A., 1979-80. Mem. Am. Land Title Assn., Colo. Land Title Assn., Pi Beta Phi, Phi Chi Theta. Republican. Roman Catholic. Office: 111 Ski Hill Rd Breckenridge CO 80424

STRYKER, RHOSAN DOBBEN, educator; b. Jackson, Mich., May 19, 1934; d. George J. and Audrey (McKinlay) D.; B.A., Mich. State U., 1956, M.A., 1967, Ed.S., 1980; postgrad. Calif. State Coll., Bakersfield, Central Mich. U., Fashion Inst. Tech.; m. James G. Stryker, Sept. 7, 1957; children—Audrey, Gordon, Gregory. Nat. traveling sec. Delta Zeta, Columbus, Ohio, 1956-57; promotion sec. Mich. State U. Alumni Mag., 1957-58; co-owner, mgr. Stryker Hardware Co., Grand Rapids, 1958-62; coordinator mktg. programs Grand Rapids (Mich.) Jr. Coll., 1963-69; prof. bus. Delta Coll., University Center, Mich., 1970—; dir. Markey Elliott Co., Trikelion Consignment Shop. Pres., United Ch. of Christ, Midland, 1975. Mem. AAUP (state council 1975-78), Bus. Edn. Assn. Mich., Nat. Bus. Edn. Assn., Am. Assn. Women in Jr. and Community Colls., Nat. Assn. Female Execs., Eastern Mich. Interior Design Soc., Mich. Assn. Distributive Edn. Tchrs., Mortar Board, Phi Kappa Delta, Delta Pi Epsilon, Phi Kappa Phi, Delta Zeta. Home: 1117 Airfield Ln Midland MI 48640 Office: Delta Coll University Center MI 48710

STUART, BETTY CLYMER, cosmetic products co. exec.; b. Mayfield, Ky., Aug. 26, 1932; d. Burl Samuel and Ocie Beard Clymer; B.A., Murray State U., 1954; M.A., Peabody Coll., 1958; m. Ronald Lynn Stuart, Dec. 24, 1954; children—Jennifer Lynn, Jon Gregory. High sch. tchr., Wolfe Lake, Ill., 1954-55, Randle, Wash., 1956-59, White Swan, Wis., 1959-61, San Leandro, Calif., 1962-63; with Avon Products, Inc., 1963—, mgr. recruiting, N.Y.C., 1975-76, br. tng. and devel. mgr., Newark, Del., 1976-80, group mgr. sales tng. design and devel., 1980—. Mem. Community Devel. Com., State Senator Roy Goodman, 1981. Mem. Am. Soc. Tng. and Devel. (chair program planning com. N.Y. Met. chpt.), Nat. Assn. Exec. Females, Alpha Sigma Alpha. Republican. Christian. Office: 9 W 57th St 32d Floor New York City NY 10019

STUART, COLLEN MURRAY, mfg. co. exec.; b. Wheeling, W.Va., Oct. 8, 1945; d. Edward James and Margaret Hanna (Parker) M.; B.A., W. Liberty State Coll., 1964; postgrad. CCNY, 1969-70; m. Walter Tomasulo, Jr., Sept. 4, 1980; 1 son, Thomas Beecher Stuart. Tchr., Coop. Nursery Sch., Ringwood, N.J., 1968-69; mgr. R & R Printing Co., Wayne, N.J., 1976-78; sales mgr. Technicorp, Wayne, 1978-79, v.p., 1979—; freelance graphic artist. Vice pres. Ringwood Manor Arts Assn., 1974-75; sec. Ringwood Jaycettes, 1968-69. Mem. Am. Soc. Quality Control, Am. Soc. Metals, ASTM, Instrument Soc. Am., Nat. Audubon Soc., The Planetary Soc. Democrat. Presbyterian. Club: PEO. Contbr. to trade publs. Home: 16 Knox Terr Wayne NJ 07470 Office: 2140 Hamburg Turnpike Wayne NJ 07470

STUART, GAIL ELAINE WISCARZ, nurse, mental health cons.; b. Jersey City, Dec. 6, 1949; d. August Joseph and Genevieve (Szymanski) Wiscarz; B.S. cum laude, R.N., Georgetown U., 1971; M.S. summa cum laude, U. Md., 1973; postgrad Sch. Public Health, Johns Hopkins U., 1979—; m. Robert K. Stuart, June 12, 1971; children—Robert Morgan, Elaine Catherine. Psychiat. nurse therapist, cons. Southwestern Community Mental Health Center, Catonsville, Md., 1972-78; asst. prof. Sch. Nursing, U. Md., 1973-79; psychotherapist, mental health cons., Balt., 1980—; cons. Inst. Medicine, Nat. Acad. Sci., Washington, 1981. Recipient Lucile Petry Leone award Nat. League Nursing, 1977; cert. recognition U. Md., 1976; grantee NIMH, 1971-73, scholar, 1970-71; scholarship student Georgetown U., 1967-70; Johns Hopkins U. Alumni Assn. award, 1981; Nat. Research Service award NIMH, 1981—. Mem. Am. Nurses Assn. (cert. psychiat. nurse specialist), Md. Nurses Assn., Nat. League for Nursing, AAUP, Council Specialists in Psychiat. and Mental Health Nursing, Gamma Pi Epsilon, Sigma Theta Tau, Phi

Kappa Phi. Author: Nurse-Client Interaction, 1976, 2d edit., 1981. Principles and Practice of Psychiatric Nursing, 1979, 2d edit., 1983. Home: 4215 Wickford Rd Baltimore MD 21210

STUART, HELEN GWINN, vocat. coll. adminstr.; b. Poplar Bluff, Mo., Nov. 13, 1920; d. Frank Abner and Ida Leona (Hickman) Gwinn; A.B., U. Miami (Fla.), 1943; student LaSalle Extension U., 1958-60; grad. N.Y. Inst. Photography, 1957; m. Hardin V. Stuart, Sept. 1, 1945 (dec.); 1 son, Jonathan Vereen. Nat. field rep. Girl Scouts U.S.A., N.Y.C., 1955-60, United Cerebral Palsy, Columbia, S.C., 1960-65; exec. dir. S.C. Retarded Children, 1965-73; program coordinator S.C. Heart Assn., Columbus, 1973-74, dir. hypertension control project, 1974-78; mem. adminstrv. staff Horry-Georgetown Tech. Coll., Conway, S.C.; 1978—. Chmn. S.C. Adv. Council on Vocation and Tech. Edn.; mem. adv. councils The Blind and Deaf Child, the Handicapped Child, Dept. Edn. Stuart Manor for retarded women, halfway house, named in her honor, 1971; recipient S.C. Gov.'s award for disting. service in vocation and tech. edn., 1978; Order of Palmetto award, 1981. Mem. Nat. Council for Resource Devel., Nat. Rifle Assn., Nat. Wildlife Fedn., Nat. Platform Assn., Delta Zeta. Democrat. Episcopalian. Home: PO Box 277 Murrells Inlet SC 29576

STUART, JOAN MARTHA, advt./pub. relations exec.; b. Huntington, N.Y., June 2, 1945; d. Ervin Wencil and Flora Janet (Applebaum) Stuart; student Boston U., 1963-67. Prodn. asst. Random House, N.Y.C., 1968-69; book designer Simon & Schuster, N.Y.C., 1969-71; feature writer Palm Beach Post, West Palm Beach, Fla., 1971-72; co-founder, communications dir. Stuart, Gleimer's Assos., West Palm Beach, 1973—, pres., 1982—. Mem. crusade com. Am. Cancer Soc. Bd., 1981—; bd. dirs. Theatre Arts Co., 1980-81; community services chmn., bd. dirs. B'nai B'rith Women, 1980-82. Recipient Nat. award B'nai B'rith Women, 1978, Regional award, 1979; certificate of merit Big Bros./Big Sisters, 1976. Mem. Palm Beach C. Of C., Palm Beach Gardens C. of C., Palm Beach County Council of the Arts, Theatre Arts Co. Republican. Jewish. Clubs: Poinciana, Lake Worth Racquet and Swim, Eastlakes Country. Contbr. articles to profl. jours. Office: 745 US Hwy One Global Bldg North Palm Beach FL 33408

STUART, JOANNA DALRYMPLE, social worker; b. Bklyn., Nov. 13, 1933; d. Henry Raymond and Dorothy Marion (Campbell) Dalrymple; B.A., Swarthmore Coll., 1955; postgrad. U. Wis.; M.S.W., Portland State Coll., 1964; m. William J. Stuart, June 5, 1969; 1 adopted son, G. Wally. Caseworker, Lane County Dept. Public Assistance, Eugene, Oreg., 19S6-57, caseworker, child welfare worker, 1958-62; psychiat. social worker Multnomah County Mental Health Clinic, Madison, Wis., 1964-72; med. social worker Bess Kaiser Hosp., Portland, Oreg., 1972-73; dir. Home Health Agy. Kaiser-Permanente (Oreg. Region), Portland, 1973-80; social worker Kaiser-Permanente Mont. Clinic, 1980—. Bd. dirs. Guttnam Rehab. Program, 1972-76; alumni interviewer Swarthmore Coll., 1972—. Mem. Nat. Assn. Social Workers (med. dir. 1979-80), Acad. Cert. Social Workers. Home: 6015 SE Salmon St Portland OR 97215 Office: 3414 N Montana Portland OR 97217

STUART, MARY TERESA, nursing edn. dir.; b. Dublin, Ireland, May 26, 1926; d. Cornelius and Sarah (Burke) O'Shea; came to U.S., 1952, naturalized, 1958; M.A. Ed., U. San Francisco, 1977; m. William Stuart, June 4, 1966. Instr. nursing Los Angeles Community Coll., 1965-69; dir. nursing edn. Berkeley Sch. Nursing Art, Santa Monica, 1970-79, dir. nursing continuing edn. Stuart Enterprises, Santa Monica, 1979—; cons. nursing edn. Nat. Assn. Practical Nurse & Service Inc., N.Y.C., 1979—; ednl. cons. Surgeon Gen. USAF, 1980. Disaster nurse, disaster health services Am. Nat. Red Cross, Los Angeles, 1978-82. Served with USAF, 1960-63, USAFR, 1963—. Mem. Am. Nurses Assn., Calif. Nurses Assn., Air Force Assn., Res. Officers Assn. Home: 235 15th St Santa Monica CA 90402 Office: PO Box 1893 Santa Monica CA 90406

STUART, SIGNE, artist; b. New London, Conn., Dec. 3, 1937; d. Carl Einar and Anna Nelson; B.A., U. Conn., 1959; M.A., U. N.Mex., 1960; m. Joseph Stuart, June 18, 1960; 1 dau., Lise Nelson. Artist, painter; tchr. art Eastern N.Mex. U., 1961-64, Maude I. Kerns Art Center, 1963-64, S.D. State U., 1974—. Bd. advs. S.D. Public Radio; bd. dirs. Brookings Area Humane Soc., Brookings Area Arts Council. Recipient Ford Found. purchase award, 1964; Nat. Endowment Arts fellow, 1976, purchase award, 1977; S.D. Biennial purchase award, 1977. Mem. Artists Equity, Coll. Art Assn., Women's Caucus for Art, Phi Beta Kappa. Home: 718 8th St Brookings SD 57006 Office: SD State U Brookings SD 57007

STUART-OTTO, SUSAN, public TV exec.; b. Amsterdam, N.Y., Apr. 5, 1935; d. Ralph Harold and Leao Jean (McNeil) Kurlbaum; B.A. in English, Duke U., 1957; postgrad. U. Minn.; m. David Otto, July 14, 1973; children by previous marriage—Frank Allan, Christopher and Lisbeth Stuart. Coordinator vol. services U. Minn. Hosps. 1970-72; dir. public relations U. Minn. Hosps. and Clinics, 1972-78; cons. mktg. and public relations, 1978-79; v.p. info. services Twin Cities Public TV, St. Paul, 1979—. Mem. White House advance staff for Mrs. Joan Mondale, 1978-80; nat. public issues com. Am. Cancer Soc., 1978—, bd. dirs. Minn. div., public info. chair, 1976-80; bd. dirs. ARC, 1978—, also nominating and public relations coms.; adv. bd. U. Minn. Continuing Edn. for Women; trustee Mpls. Inst. Arts, 1978-79, Washburn Child Guidance Center, 1978-80; pres. Minn. Arts Forum, 1977-79. Mem. Am. Women in Radio and TV, Public Relations Soc. Am., Women in Communications, Minn. Women's Econ. Roundtable. Democrat. Club: Minn. Press. Editor: The Facts About Cancer (Charles McKhann, M.D.), 1981. Home: 1915 Knox Ave S Minneapolis MN 55403 Office: KTCA-TV 1640 Como Ave Saint Paul MN 55108

STUBAUS, KAREN RUTH, ednl. adminstr.; b. Englewood, N.J., June 12, 1950; d. Kenneth L. and Margaret S. (Dunning) S.; B.A. cum laude, Douglass Coll., 1972; M.A., Rutgers U., 1975; m. Stephen M. Goldfarb, May 6, 1978. Adminstrv. asst. to v.p. univ. personnel Rutgers U., 1976-77; program devel. specialist Bur. Research, N.J. Div. Youth and Family Services, 1977-78; asst. to dean, dir. continuing edn. Coll. Allied Health Scis., Thomas Jefferson U., Phila., 1978-81; exec. asst. Office Vice Chancellor, N.J. Dept. Higher Edn., 1981-82; acad. planning asso. Rutgers U., New Brunswick, N.J., 1982—; mem. history faculty Douglass Coll., 1973-76. Mem. Am. Hist. Assn., Orgn. Am. Historians, Nat. Coordinating Com. Promotion History (pres. N.J. chpt. 1982), Phi Beta Kappa. Co-editor: The American Revolution: Whose Revolution?, 1977. Office: Rutgers U New Brunswick NJ 08903

STUBBART, AUDREY FAY, newspaper exec.; b. Newman Grove, Nebr., June 9, 1895; d. Francis Arlando and Etta Belle (Lyon) Morford; Tchrs. Cert., U. Wyo., 1923; m. John Perry Stubbart, Feb. 2, 1911; children—Enid Irene, Veryl Winston, Donald Perry, Carol Ardyce, Kenneth James. Tchr., U. Wyo. and various schs., Wyo., 1918-25; proofreader, copy editor Herald Pub. Ho., Independence, Mo., 1945-62; proofreader, copy editor, book rev. editor, editorial writer, reporter Independence, (Mo.) Examiner, 1962—. Chmn. Found. for Archaeol. Research; editor asst., bd. dirs. Jackson County Hist. Soc. Mem. Profl. Tchrs. Assn. Republican. Reorganized Ch. Jesus Christ of Latter Day Saints. Club: Knife and Fork. Office: 410 S Liberty St Independence MO 64051

STUBBLEFIELD, BEVERLY ANN, psychometrist; b. New Albany, Miss., Nov. 2, 1952; d. Charles LePrade and Marie Alma (Hall) S.; B.A. with honors, Miss. Coll., 1974; M.A., U. Miss., 1979, postgrad., 1979—. Grad. asst. dept. psychology U. Miss., University, 1975-77, instr., student counseling center, 1977-79; psychometrist Region VI Mental Health, Greenwood, Miss., 1979—. Active Greenwood Little Theatre; choir men. First Bapt. Ch., Greenwood. Mem. Am. Psychol. Assn. (asso. div. 29), Miss. Psychol. Assn. (asso.), AAUW (pres. Greenwood br.). Republican. Contbr. writings to publs. in field. Home: 106 E Monroe Greenwood MS 38930 Office: Box 1505 Browning Rd Greenwood MS 38930

STUBBLEFIELD, JENNYE LEE WASHINGTON, home economist; b. Jacksonville, Fla., Mar. 6, 1925; d. Marion and Ira (McCombs) Washington; B.A. in Instn. Mgmt., Tuskegee (Ala.) Inst., 1946; M.S. in Nutrition, Rutgers U., 1966; m. Charles Stubblefield, June 26, 1954. Dietitian, Lincoln Hosp., Durham, N.J., 1946-48; instr. vets. cooking and baking schs., 1948-50; tchr. vocat. foods, cafeteria mgr. William Jason High Sch., Georgetown, Del., 1950-56; asst. dietitian Mercer Hosp., Trenton, N.J., 1957; instr. nutrition St. Francis Hosp. Sch. Nursing, Trenton, 1957-64, Helene Fulde Hosp. Sch. Nursing, Trenton, part-time 1965-71; dir. food service Middlesex County Head Start, New Brunswick, N.J., 1965-66; tchr. foods and nutrition Nottingham Jr. High Sch., Trenton, 1966-71; dir. dept. health, recreation and welfare City of Trenton, 1971-74; dir. Aid to Low Income Alcoholics Mercer County, Trenton, 1974-76; supr. consumer and homemaking edn. Trenton Bd. Edn., 1976—; co-adj. instr. Douglass Coll., 1964-65; adv. council Sch. Vocat. Edn., Rutgers U., 1977—. Chmn. bd. dirs. United Progress, Inc., Trenton, 1974-76; mem. Trenton City Council, 1976—, Black Women for Democratic Action, 1978—; vice chairperson Mercer County Dem. Com., 1981—; bd. dirs. Trenton chpt. ARC, 1972-77, chmn., 1976-77. Mem. Am. Dietetic Assn., Am. Home Econs. Assn., Home Econs. Edn. Assn., Vocat. Edn. Assn., Am. Vocat. Assn., N.J. Assn. Secondary Sch. Prins. and Suprs., NAACP. Home: 21 Alden Ave Trenton NJ 08616 Office: 108 N Clinton Ave Trenton NJ 08609

STUBBS, FRANCES EVELYN, banker; b. N.Y.C., Dec. 7, 1926; d. Cyrilo Juan and Madeline Orenina (Bowman) Lima; student public schs.; diploma Am. Inst. Banking, 1963; m. Andrew Stubbs, Nov. 25, 1946; children—Steven, Andrea. With Home owners Loan Corp., 1944-47, Kay Jewelers, N.Y.C., 1948-58; with NBW div. Lincoln First Bank, N.A., New Rochelle, N.Y., 1959—, asst. v.p., mgr. comml. loan ops., 1981—. Treas. Family Services Westchester, 1980—. Mem. Nat. Assn. Bank Women (chpt. chmn. 1979-80), Westchester County Bankers Assn. (treas. 1979—), Bus. and Profl. Women New Rochelle (1st v.p. 1980—), Negro Bus. and Profl. Women New Rochelle (fin. sec. 1980—). Presbyterian. Office: 270 North Ave New Rochelle NY 10801

STUBBS, KAREN KIRTLEY, county ofcl.; b. Kansas City, Mo., Sept. 23, 1938; d. John Marcus and Hazel Alice (Nickell) Kirtley; student U. Mo., Columbia, 1956-59; B.S., U. Mo., Kansas City, 1961, M.P.A., 1978, J.D., 1977; m. Donald George Stubbs, Apr. 4, 1959; children—David, Laura, Julie. Chmn. Highlawn Montessori Sch., Shawnee Mission, Kans., 1967-68; pres. Planned Parenthood of Western Mo./Kans., 1971-72; dir. records County of Jackson, Mo., Kansas City; mem. Mo. local records bd. for Sec. of State. Chmn., Jackson County Welfare Commn., 1967-71; dir. Mayor's Corps of Progress, Kansas City, Mo.; v.p. Kansas City Energy Commn., 1979—. Mem. Nat. Micrographics Assn., Am. Records Mgmt. Assn., Pi Beta Phi. Democrat. Unitarian. Home: 1000 Brentwood Circle Kansas City MO 64112 Office: 415 E 12th St Kansas City MO 64106

STUBBS, LINDA GAIL, banker; b. Greenville, Ky., Apr. 19, 1947; d. Warren Gayle and A. Marlene (Bivens) Wood; student Moser Bus. Coll., 1965-66, U. Okla., 1977; m. William Frederick Stubbs, Sept. 3, 1976; children—Sherry, Krista, Brent. Supr., Sears, Roebuck and Co., Peoria, Ill., 1966-74; supr. Jefferson Bank, Peoria, 1974-75, lending officer, 1976, ops. officer, asst. v.p., 1977, v.p. ops., 1978—; pres. Peoria Assn. of Banks. Mem. Bank Adminstrn. Inst., Am. Inst. Banking, Nat. Assn. Bank Women, Peoria C. of C. Clubs: Creve Coeur (Peoria); Sunset Country (Pekin, Ill.). Office: Jefferson Bank 124 SW Adams St Peoria IL 61554

STUBER, BETTIE JEAN, chiropractor; b. Harrisonville, Mo., June 26, 1929; d. Arthur Vernon and Mary Betty (Brown) Barker; Dr. Chiropractics summa cum laude, Cleve. Chiropractic Coll., 1967; postgrad. Tex. Chiropractic Coll., 1973-74, Nat. Chiropractic Coll., 1973, 76, Logan Chiropractic Coll., Columbia (Mo.) Coll.; m. George Edgar Stuber, Sept. 4, 1948; children—Dennis, Debra Stuber Rearick, Diana. Clk., typist, stenographer, nurses aid IRS, 1948-52; gen. practice chiropractics, Kansas City, Mo., 1967—. Mem. Am. (council roentgenology, chiropractic council on sports injuries, council on chiropractic technique, council on chiropractic physiotherapy, council on nutrition, council on chiropratic neurology), Mo. (v.p. dist. 2), Kans. (asso.) chiropractic assns., Am. Chiropractic Council Diagnosis and Internal Disorders, Am. Council Women Chiropractors, Wyandotte Johnson Chiropractic Assn., Assn. for Research and Enlightenment (asso.). Home: 8910 Western Hills Dr Kansas City MO 64114

STUCKEY, JOHANNA HEATHER, educator; b. Gananoque, Ont., Can., Sept. 5, 1933; d. William Henry Stuckey and Mary (Smith) Diplock; B.A., U. Toronto, 1956, M.A., 1960; postgrad. Univ. Coll., London, 1956-57, 60-64; Ph.D. (fellow), Yale U., 1965. Lectr., York U., Founders Coll., Downsview, Ont., Can., 1964-65, asst. prof., 1965-72, asso. prof. English and humanities, 1972—, chmn. div. humanities, 1974-79, adv. to pres. on status of women, 1981—. Mem. New Feminists, 1969-71, Feminist Party of Can., Women for Polit. Action, Nat. Action Com. on Status of Women, Ont. Commn. on Status of Women. Mem. MLA, Can. Research Inst. for Advancement of Women. Author: (with G. Schmeling) Bibliography of Petronius, 1977; contbr. articles in field to profl. jours.; asso. editor Can. Woman Studies, 1982—. Office: Founders Coll York U Downsview ON Canada

STUDEBAKER, JOYCE CAROLYN, art auditor; b. Richmond, Ind., Dec. 6, 1938; d. Albert Joseph and Esther Beulah (Bowers) Witte; student Pepperdine U., 1957-59; A.A., Moorpark Community Coll., 1975, A.S. in Alcohol Studies, 1976; postgrad. Calif. State U., 1977—; m. Richard Studebaker, Mar. 16, 1962; children—Steven Jon, Michele Lee. Draftsman, Gilfillan Bros., Los Angeles, 1959-60, 61, Coastal Publs., Fullerton, Calif., 1960, Tridea Electronics Co., Pasadena, Calif., 1960-61, Rocketdyne, Canoga Park, Calif., 1961-66, Naval Base, Port Hueneme, Calif., 1973-76; instr. Alcohol Info. Sch., Ventura County, Calif., 1978-80; tech. writer-editor, art auditor Stanwick Corp., Ventura, Calif., 1979—. Home: 2099 Glenbrook Camarillo CA 93010 Office: 3503 Arundell Ventura CA 93003

STUDIN, LORRAINE R., indsl. chem. co. exec.; b. Hartford, Conn., May 8, 1939; student U. Ala., 1967-68, U. New Orleans, 1981; children—Andrea Anton, Robert Studin, Karen Studin. Indsl. chem. sales rep. Malter Internat. Corp., Gretna, La., 1962-77; pres. Stutton Corp., Metairie, La., 1977—. Pres. Women's group Knesseth Israel Synagogue, Birmingham, Ala., 1961-62. Mem. Women in Constrn., Nat. Assn. Women Bus. Owners. Democrat. Jewish. Office: PO Box 7913 Metairie LA 70010

STUDY, MARY MARGARET (TELLER), print service center exec.; b. Oklahoma City, Dec. 3, 1945; d. Ernest Leonard and Mary Ann Teller; B.A., U. No. Colo., 1967; M.A. in Public Relations, M.A. in Journalism, Ball State U., 1970; m. Larry Lee Study, Jan. 3, 1970; 1 son, Darren Boyd. Report specialist, adminstrv. specialist, Avionics Research, Ohio U., Athens, 1971-73, exec. sec. dean Coll. Engring. and Tech., 1973-74; instr.-lectr. public relations Sch. Mass Communications, Mara Inst. Tech., Shah Alam, Malaysia, 1974-76; owner-mgr. Alpha Graphics Ltd., Print Media Service Center, Muncie, 1976—; free lance public relations writer, cons., Athens, 1970-74; free lance writer, pub. periodicals on small bus., graphics, advt. Chmn., Oktoberfest, 1979—; mem. Downtown Bus. Council Retail Promotions and Spl. Events Com., 1978—, chmn., 1979—; mem. Public Relations Task Force, 1972. Mem. Women in Communications (advisor Ball State U. chpt. 1969), C. of C. Muncie-Delaware County (small bus. council 1979), Alpha Gamma Delta. Editor, pub. Muncie Marketeer, 1978. Office: 111 E Adams Muncie IN 47305

STULL, CAROL GANSZ, chemist; b. Chgo., Feb. 11, 1936; d. Charles William and Ruth Emma (Waddell) Gansz; B.S. in Chemistry, U. Ill., Urbana, 1958; M.S. in Chemistry, Baylor U., 1960; m. Robert L. Stull, June 22, 1958; children—Charles Allen, Steven Dale, Scott David. Chief research chemist dept. ob-gyn Deaconess Hosp., Buffalo, 1967-75, clin. chemistry supr., med. tech. edn. coordinator, 1975-79; clin. chemistry dept. head, med. tech. edn. coordinator Deaconess div. Buffalo Gen. Hosp., 1979-80, supr. immunopathology Buffalo Gen. Hosp., 1980—; clin. instr. Daemen Coll., Amherst, N.Y., 1975—. Chmn., Erie County Abates, 1970; charter mem., bd. dirs. Environ. Clearing House, 1970; mem. plan devel. com. Western N.Y. Health Systems Agy., 1978—, chmn., 1980-81, chmn. systems planning and devel. com., 1981—; mem. High Risk Pregnancy Med. Team, 1967—. Mem. Am. Chem. Soc., Can. Soc. Clin. Chemists, AAUW (pres. Buffalo br. 1972-74, pres. N.Y. State, 1976-78, co-dir. project WIDE, N.Y. State 1980-82, Achievement award Buffalo br. 1978, ednl. found. grantee 1980-81), Nat. Assn. Female Execs. Methodist. Home: 110 Saratoga Rd Snyder NY 14226 Office: Deaconess Div Buffalo Gen Hosp 1001 Humboldt Pkwy Buffalo NY 14208

STULL, PATRICIA MYERS, chem. co. exec.; b. Albany, Calif., May 17; d. Gilbert W. and Catherine L. (Indilicato) Myers; A.A., Stephens Coll.; married. Sec. treas., dir. D.H. Sutton Co., 1958—, Gen. Am. Tank Corp., 1960—; adminstrv. mgr. Pacific Coast Chems. Co., Berkeley, Calif., 1970—. Mem. Golden Gate Paint and Lacquer Assn., Golden Gate Soc. Paints and Coatings, Pacific Traffic Assn., Exec. Women Internat. Office: 2424 4th St Berkeley CA 94710

STUMP, SANDRA SUE, med. technologist; b. Ft. Wayne, Ind., Feb. 11, 1936; d. Hubert A. and D'Maris A. (Smith) S.; B.A., DePauw U., 1958; M.T., Borgess Hosp., Kalamazoo, Mich., 1959. Clin. microbiologist Borgess Hosp., Kalamazoo, Mich., 1960-63; chief med. technologist Luth. Hosp., Ft. Wayne, 1964-65, clin. microbiologist, 1965-74, program dir., 1975—. Mem. Am. Soc. Clin. Pathologists, Am. Soc. Microbiology, South Central Assn. Microbiology, Consortium Ind. Med. Lab. Educators. Methodist. Office: 3024 Fairfield Ave Fort Wayne IN 46807

STUMP, SUSAN LYNNE, food store ofcl.; b. Murfreesboro, Tenn., Aug. 17, 1954; d. Thompson Bragg and Anna Lee (Knight) S.; B.S. in Elem. Edn., Middle Tenn. State U., Murfreesboro, 1977. Mktg. asst. Commerce Union Bank of Rutherford County, Murfreesboro, 1977-80; dir. public relations Spartan Food Systems, Inc., Spartanburg, S.C., 1980—. Named Outstanding Young Career Women, Bus. and Profl. Women, 1980. Home: 151 Fernwood Dr Apt 165 F Spartanburg SC 29302 Office: PO Box 3168 Spartanburg SC 29304

STURDEVANT, ANNETTE KORMANIK, mgmt. cons.; b. Akron, Ohio, Feb. 14, 1951; d. Edward and Bettye Jo Kormanik; B.A. summa cum laude, Ohio U., 1973, M.A., 1974, Ph.D., 1978. Asst. to dir. extended learning program Ohio U., Athens, 1972-73, dir. coll. work-study, 1974-77, dir. coll. work-study and student employment, 1977-79; mgmt. cons. in higher edn. sr. asso. Human Dynamics, Inc. and Organizational Leadership, Inc., Washington, 1979-80; pres. Orgn. Devel., Inc., Human Resources Mgmt. Cons., Athens, 1980—; mem. task force on student employment HEW. Recipient Outstanding Service award Am. Work-Edn. Found., 1979. Mem. Ohio Assn. Student Fin. Aid Adminstrs. (tng. com.; chmn. research com. 1978-80), Am. Assn. Higher Edn., Nat. Assn. Women Deans, Adminstrs. and Counselors, Midwest Assn. Student Employment Adminstrs. (chmn. research com. 1979-80), Nat. Assn. Student Employment Adminstrs., NOW (v.p. Athens chpt. 1976), Women's Equity Action League, Phi Beta Kappa (chpt. v.p. 1978—, chpt. treas. 1977-78, pres. Ohio U. chpt. 1979-80), Phi Delta Kappa (v.p. for programming 1977-79, pres. 1979-80), Phi Kappa Phi, Pi Gamma Mu. Democrat. Office: 2 Valley View Dr Athens OH 45701

STURDIVANT, KARON ANN, univ. adminstr.; b. Abilene, Tex., Mar. 30, 1954; d. James Arvin and Hazel (Griffin) Sturdivant; B.S.E., Ark. State U., 1976, M.S.E., 1977; postgrad. U. Miss., 1981—. Instr., So. Ark. U., El Dorado Br., 1977-78; asst. mgr. El Dorado C. of C., 1978-79; dir. admissions Ark. State U., 1979—; coordinator state-wide high sch. sponsored coll. programs, participant at So. Assn. Collegiate Registrars & Admissions Officers, 1981; lectr. in field. Recipient Highest Achievement award, Dale Carnegie Couse, 1981. Mem. Ark. Personnel and Guidance Assn., Ark. Assn. Coll. Admissions Officers, Nat. Assn. Coll. Admissions Counselors, Am. Assn. Collegiate Registrars and Admissions Officers, Nat. Assn. Women Deans, Adminstrs. and Counselors, Nat. Assn. Student Personnel Adminstrs., Phi Delta Kappa, Delta Pi Epsilon, Alpha Gamma Delta. Home: PO Box 588 State University AR 72467 Office: PO Box 1630 State University AR 72467

STUREK, JORJA KAYE, pharmacist; b. O'Neill, Nebr., June 2, 1948; d. George Edwin and Lillian Vernice (Zimmerman) S.; student Kearney State Coll., 1966-67; B.S. in Pharmacy, U. Nebr., 1971; M.S. in Pharmacy, Ohio State U., 1976. Staff pharmacist Sacred Heart Hosp., Cumberland, Md., 1971-73; asst. mgr. Potomac Valley Pharmacy, Cresaptown, Md., 1973-74; asst. dir. pharmacy services Riverside Methodist Hosp., Columbus, Ohio, 1976—; clin. instr. pharmacy Ohio State U.; active community outreach for medication edn. for sr. citizens. Mem. Am. Pharm. Assn., Am. Soc. Hosp. Pharmacists, Central Ohio Soc. Hosp. Pharmacists, Rho Chi. Democrat. Methodist. Office: 3535 Olentangy River Rd Columbus OH 43214

STURGES, FLORENCE MARGARET (MRS. DWIGHT RICHARD STURGES), librarian; b. Boston, July 2, 1908; d. Edgar Saxon and Charlotte Jane (Case) Stanley; student New Eng. Conservatory, 1928-30; student Boston Public Library Tng. Sch., 1931-33; diploma Curry Coll., 1940; m. Dwight Richard Sturges, Oct. 12, 1935. Children's librarian Boston Public Library, 1932-41; children's librarian Wellesley (Mass.) Free Library, 1943-70, reference librarian, 1943-70; children's librarian, asst. librarian Skidompha Library, Damariscotta, Maine, 1970—; cons. in establishment of library at Children's Hosp., Boston, 1956-60; pres. New Eng. Round Table of Children's Librarians, 1960-62; mem. Sci. Mus. Book Com., Boston, 1962-68; Caroline M. Hewins lectr., Boston, 1959. Mem. Bronte Soc. of Eng., Nat. Book League, Am. Pen Women (book rev. editor 1968-70). Clubs: Saturday Morning of Boston, Women's Club. Author: Elizabeth Coatsworth Beston, A Brontë Tapestry, History of Newcastle-Damariscotta Area, History of the Skidompha Library. Contbr. articles to lit. publs. Home: Old County Rd Damariscotta ME 04543 Office: Skidompha Library Damariscotta ME 04543

STURGES, SANDRA JEANE, commodity exchange adminstr.; b. Basin, Wyo., Nov. 2, 1940; d. Howard D. and Wilma E. Sturges; B.A.,

U. Wyo., 1963. Account exec. 1st Nebr. Securities, Omaha, 1968-70; asst. v.p. 1st Mid Am., Inc., Lincoln, Nebr., 1970-75; asst. dir. div. trading and markets Commodity Futures Trading Commn., N.Y.C., 1975-77; dir. spl. project N.Y. Coffee & Sugar Exchange, N.Y.C., 1977-79; dir. commodity brokerage ops. Mocotta Metals and Brody, White & Co., Inc., N.Y.C., 1979—. Mem. Nat. Assn. Securities Dealers (registered prin.). Contbr. articles to Consensus mag. Home: 10 Waterside Plaza Apt 24A New York NY 10010 Office: New York NY

STURGIS, JANE PHILBECK, fed. govt. library ofcl.; b. St. Louis, May 3, 1936; d. Robert Hoyle and Ruby Lillian (Glawe) Philbeck; student Am. U., 1976-80; children by previous marriage—Gene Mark, Donna Susan, Christopher Drew; m. 2d, Ralph M. Sturgis, Jan. 12, 1980. Sec., Dept. Agr., 1954-58, IRS, Dept. Treasury, Washington, 1971-72; sec. Nat. Library Medicine, NIH, Bethesda, Md., 1972-74, adminstrv. intern, 1974-76, contract specialist, 1976—. Mem. Am. Contract Bridge League. Methodist. Home: 4806 Davron St Laurel MD 20707 Office: Nat Library of Medicine NIH 8600 Rockville Pike Bethesda MD 20209

STURM, GWENDOLYN LEE, nurse; b. Petoskey, Mich., May 11, 1936; d. Elliot Leland and Eva E. (Lewis) Ostrum; R.N., West Suburban Hosp., 1957; B.S., Mich. State U., 1961; M.S., Loyola U., Chgo., 1967; m. Gus Charles Sturm, Oct. 23, 1970; children—Cynthia Marie, Christine Lynn. Nurse, West Suburban Hosp., Oak Park, Ill., 1957-62; operating room supr. Swedish Covenant Hosp., 1962-67; asst. prof. Chgo. City Coll., 1967-71; nurse Luth. Gen. Hosp., 1971-76; asst. prof. nursing North Park Coll., Chgo., 1976—. Evanston area coordinator Camp Fire, Inc.; bd. dirs. Dawes and Chute Schs. PTA, Evanston. Mem. Am. Nurses Assn., Nat. League Nursing, Internat. Order Foresters, Sigma Theta Tau. Office: 5125 N Spaulding Ave Chicago IL 60625

STURTEVANT, BRERETON, govt. ofcl.; b. Washington, Nov. 24, 1921; d. Charles Lyon and Grace (Brereton) Sturtevant; B.A., Wellesley Coll., 1942; J.D., Temple U., 1949. Research chemist E.I. duPont de Nemours & Co., Inc., Wilmington, Del., 1942-50; admitted to D.C. bar, 1949, Del. bar, 1950; law clk. Del. Supreme Ct., 1950; gen. practice law, Wilmington, 1950-57; partner firm Connolly, Bove & Lodge, Wilmington, 1957-71; examiner-in-chief Bd. Appeals, Patent Office, Commerce Dept., Washington, 1971—; adj. prof. law Georgetown U., 1974-79. Trustee, Holton Arms Sch., Washington, 1977—. Mem. Am. Bar Assn., Del. Bar Assn., Govt. Patent Law Assn., Patent Office Soc., AAUW, Exec. Women in Govt. (founding mem. chmn. 1978-79). Episcopalian. Club: Wellesley Coll. Home: 1227 Morningside Ln Alexandria VA 22308 Office: Patent and Trademark Office Washington DC 20231

STURTEVANT, CLARA BARES, med. social worker; b. Cleve., Aug. 12, 1917; d. John J. and Rose L. (Novotny) Bares; A.B., Notre Dame Coll., 1939; M.S. in Social Work, Cath. U. Am., 1941; m. Frederick C. Sturtevant, Jan. 8, 1944; children—Suzann Garson, Rick, Rosanna Sprague, Mary-Jo Schiefer, John, Peter, Patrick, Mariclare McCann, Thomas. Social worker Humane Soc., Cleve., 1941-43, Cath. Family and Children's Services, Cleve., 1963-67, Catherine Horstmann Home, Cleveland Heights, Ohio, 1967-69; med. social worker St. Vincent Charity Hosp., Cleve., 1971-76, asst. dir. social service, 1976—; student field supr. Cleve. State U., 1975—, Case-Western Res. U., Cleve., 1976—. Mem. Acad. Cert. Social Workers, Nat. Assn. Social Workers. Home: 2257 Coventry Rd Cleveland Heights OH 44118 Office: 2351 E 22d St Cleveland OH 44115

STUTT, MARILYN JEAN, publisher; b. St. Croix Falls, Wis., Aug. 25, 1927; d. Myron Lawrence and Margaret Julia (O'Neil) Heebink; student Stout Inst., Menomonie, Wis., 1945-46; divorced; children—Dena Margaret Oliver, David Michael Stutt, Scott Patrick Anderson. Musician, arranger, vocalist with all girl orch. Sweethearts of Swing, 1947-53; music dir., disc jockey sta. KNIT, Abilene, Tex., 1958-59, writer sta. KRBC-TV, Abilene, also sta. KOAT-TV, Albuquerque, 1959-61; writer, editor U.S. Civil Service, Sandia Base, N.Mex., 1962-63; advt. dir. Roger Cox & Assos. Enterprises, Albuquerque, 1974-77; owner Marilyn Stutt Advt. Agy., Albuquerque, also pres. Marilyn Stutt Enterprises, Inc., Albuquerque, 1977—; founder, 1979, since publisher Albuquerque Singles Scene mag.; pres. Singles Scene Mag., Inc., nat. licensing network, 1981-82. Mem. Mag. Pubs. Assn., N.Mex. Advt. Fedn., Albuquerque Women in Bus. Democrat. Club: N.Mex. Press. Office: 5600-T McLeod St NE Albuquerque NM 87109

STUTZ, DIANN PULLIAM, city ofcl.; b. Norfolk, Va., June 12, 1947; d. William Merton and Lena Mae (Eaton) Pulliam; student Old Dominion U., Norfolk, 1965-66; m. Kenneth Wayne Stutz, Aug. 11, 1965. Sec., Investment Corp., Norfolk, 1966-68; with City of Norfolk, 1968-74; dir. public relations, asso. producer Va. Entertainment Corp., 1974-77; dir. tourism Norfolk Conv. and Visitors Bur., 1977—. Mem. Travel Industry Assn. Am., Nat. Tour Brokers Assn., Va. Travel Council, Am. Bus. Assn. Office: 208 E Plume St Monticello Arcade Norfolk VA 23510

STUTZMAN, SANDILEE, choreographer; b. Cleve., June 28, 1942; d. Charles J. and Stella A. S.; student Case Western Res. U., 1961-62, John Carroll U., 1962-63. Profl. performer The Ponitails, 1960, The Rudy Noel Dancers, 1962-64, Dance Connection, Ltd., 1970-73; dir. Suburban Cultural Arts Inst., Cleve., 1962—; dir., producer, choreographer Expositions, Inc., Cleve., 1974-76; dance dir. Glen Oak Sch., Gates Mills, Ohio, 1976-78; dir., choreographer, tchr. Dance Connection Ltd., Los Angeles, 1977—; dir., choreographer, tchr. Startracks Gymnastics Camp, Gates Mills, Ohio, 1977—; pres. Unique Talent Agy., Los Angeles, 1981—, Gymjazz, exercise program, Los Angeles, 1982—; tchr. master classes, Los Angeles, N.Y.C., 1965—. Mem. Nat. Assn. Female Exes. Home: 8016 Via Verona St Burbank CA 91504 Office: 8157 Lankershim Blvd North Hollywood CA 91605

STYLES, DOROTHY GENEVA, musician, educator, mathematician, artist; b. Eldorado, Ark., Dec. 13, 1922; d. Alfred Alexander and Minnie Amy (Shelnut) Styles; diploma Detroit Inst. Mus. Art, 1945; Mus.B., U. Detroit, 1947; B.S. in Math., Columbia, 1954; M.A. in Lit., Eastern Mich. U., 1970, M.A. in Edn., U. Mich., 1970. Pvt. tchr. piano, Hazel Park, Mich., 1934—; pianist, organist Hazel Park Bapt. Tabernacle, 1932-43, 1st United Meth. Ch., Wayne, Mich., 1975—; choir dir. St. Timothy's Evang. Luth. Ch., Oak Park, Mich., 1970-71. Mem. Ruth Giese Com. for Needy Children, Hazel Park, 1971—. Mem. Am. Coll. Musicians (cert.), Am. Guild Organists, Nat. Assn. Organ Tchrs., Nat. Guild Piano Tchrs., Detroit Musicians League (licentiate), Delta Omicron, Mensa. Composer: Lullaby, 1966; I Sing a Song, 1975; The Pledge of Allegiance to the Flag, 1976; Mrs. Santa Claus Loves Mr. Santa Claus, 1976; Mother, Tell Me, 1977. Author: (poetry) Young Verses for the Early Old; An Extension of the Idea of Countability as Applied to Real Numbers, 1966; A Prime Number Theorem, 1971; Projections of the Natural Harmonic Series: Some Implications, 1978; A Simplified Method for Computing All Factors of Any Odd Number (Including Two Ways of Obtaining the Series of Prime Numbers, 1981. Home and office: 443 W Evelyn St Hazel Park MI 48030

STYRES, KATHRYN SMELLEY, nurse; b. Hale County, Ala., Apr. 11, 1938; d. Ervin Clyde and Retha Jewel Smelley; diploma Druid City Hosp. Sch. Nursing, 1959; A.A., Clarke Coll., 1971; B.S.N., Samford U., 1975; M.S., Miss. U. for Women, 1977; m. Lloyd Wayne Styres, May 6, 1959; children—Pamela Kay, Cynthia Leigh. Staff nurse Druid City Hosp., Tuscaloosa, Ala., 1961-62; instr. and nursing supr. Bryce Hosp., Tuscaloosa, 1963-68; staff psychiat. nurse VA Hosp., Tuscaloosa, 1969; unit chief nurse and instr. Bryce Hosp., Tuscaloosa, 1972-76; instr. Capstone Coll. Nursing, U. Ala., Tuscaloosa, 1977-78, instr. and family nurse practitioner Coll. Community Health Scis., 1978-81, asst. prof. nursing Capstone Coll., 1980-81; family nurse practitioner, asso. Gordo (Ala.) Family Practice Center, 1981-82; instr. nursing Shelton State Community Coll., 1982—; adj. asst. prof. nursing Miss. U. for Women. Mem. Health Occupations Edn. Adv. Council. Mem. Am. Nurses Assn. (cert. family nurse practitioner), Ala. Nurses Assn. (cert. family nurse practitioner), Sigma Theta Tau. Baptist. Home: Route 4 Box 106 Northport AL 35476

SU, HELEN CHIEN-FAN, chemist; b. Nanping, Fujian, China, Dec. 26, 1922; came to U.S., 1949, naturalized, 1963; d. Ru-chen and Sieu-Hsien (Wong) S.; B.A., Hwa Nan Coll., Fuzhou, Fujian, China, 1944; M.S., U. Nebr., 1951, Ph.D., 1953. Asst., instr. chemistry Hwa Nan Coll., 1944-49; prof. chemistry Lambuth Coll., Jackson, Tenn., 1953-55; research asst. Auburn Research Found., Auburn U., 1955-57; sr. chemist, project leader Borden Chem. Co., Phila., 1957-63; scientist Lockheed-Ga. Research Lab., Marietta, Ga., 1963-67; research chemist Agrl. Research Service, U.S. Dept. Agr., Savannah, Ga., 1968—. Fellow Am. Inst. Chemists, Ga. Inst. Chemists; mem. Am. Chem. Soc., AAAS, N.Y. Acad. Sci., Entomol. Soc. Am., Ga. Entomol. Soc., Sigma Xi, Sigma Delta Epsilon, Iota Sigma Pi. Author articles in field. Home: 610 Highland Dr Savannah GA 31406 Office: PO Box 22909 Savannah GA 31403

SUAREZ, ALMA LATIMER, social worker; b. Boston, May 7, 1920; d. George and Emma (Parsons) Latimer; B.A., Calvin Cooledge Coll., Boston, 1942; M.A., New Sch. Social Research; M.P.A., N.Y. U., 1978. Social worker N.Y.C. Civil Service, 1948-62; religious dir. Community Ch. of N.Y., 1968-71; social worker, health cons. Community Health Center, Jamaica, N.Y., 1970—. Mem. Nat. Assn. Social Workers, Am. Public Health Assn., Am. Acad. Scis., Coalition of 100 Black Women. Episcopalian. Author monographs: The Black Family, 1974; The Legal Aspects of Insanity, 1978. Office: 97-04 Sutphin Blvd Jamaica NY 11435

SUAREZ, MYRIAM, tire wholesale co. exec.; b. Havana, Cuba, Sept. 15, 1940; d. Gustavo Adolfo and Mignonne (Menendez) S.; came to U.S., 1960, naturalized, 1974; student Merici Acad., Havana; children from previous marriage—Alejandro Jose, Jose Antonio. With Pitts. Plate Glass Co., Havana, 1960-62; asst. to br. mgr. Mercedes Benz P.R., 1962-63; asst. sales mgr. P.R. div., Colgate Palmolive Co., 1963-65; sales staff Koehring Overseas, P.R., 1965-67; asst. to fin. comptroller Rohm & Haas Co., Miami, 1968-73; sales corr., adminstrv. asst. Internat. B.F. Goodrich Co., Miami, 1973-76; adminstrv. asst. TCM Internat., Miami, 1976—. Mem. Nat. Tire Dealers and Retreaders Assn., Orgn. Women Execs. Republican. Roman Catholic. Clubs: Lit. Guild, Rosicrucians. Home: 3090 SW 84th Ct Miami FL 33155 Office: 3466 N Miami Ave Miami FL 33127

SUCHER, DOROTHY GLASSMAN, psychotherapist; b. Bklyn., May 18, 1933; d. Henry and Shirley (Hankin) Glassman; B.A., Bklyn. Coll., 1954; M.M.H., Johns Hopkins U., 1975; m. Joseph Sucher, Aug. 10, 1952; children—Gabriel, Michael, Anatole, Anne. Psychotherapist, Group Health Assn., Washington, 1975-81; pvt. practice psychotherapy, Greenbelt, Md., 1981—. Mem. Am. Assn. Marriage and Family Therapy, Am. Mental Health Counselor Assn., Am. Assn. Sex Educators, Counselors and Therapists, NOW (Md. consciousness raising chmn. 1978-80, Md. ERA chmn. 1979-80).

SUCHINA, LUCILE FENZL, bus. ofcl.; b. Houston, Dec. 18; d. Gustav John and Sarah (Ludtke) Fenzl; student Southwestern Bus. U., 1941-42; m. Andrew Harry Suchina, Aug. 29, 1942; children—Carole Ann Robertson, Pamela Jean Suchina Gillan, John Andrew. Stenographer C.E., U.S. Army, Galveston, Tex., 1942; sec. Aviation Enterprises, train-air ferry, Houston, 1943-44; sec. to supt. maintenance Pioneer Air Lines (now Continental Air Lines), Houston, 1944-47; account payable clk. Tellepsen Constrn. Co., Houston, 1950-51; stenographer City of Houston, 1953-54; sec. Exxon Co. U.S.A., Houston, 1954—. Nat. chmn. So. Conf. Youth Activities and Voice of Democracy Scholarship, 1973-74; mem. Tex. Medal of Honor Grove Com., 1976; nat. chmn. So. Conf. for Jr. Girls, 1977-78; hon. mayor of El Paso (Tex.), 1976. Named hon. citizen Lubbock, Tex., 1974, El Paso, 1976, hon. mayor of San Antonio, 1976. Mem. Am. Mgmt. Assn., Internat. Platform Assn., Am. Inst. Parliamentarians, Profl. Secs. Internat., Am. Soc. Profl. and Exec. Women, Houston Parliamentary Soc., VFW Aux. (asst. condr. So. conf. 1977-78, nat. chmn. pages 1977, Outstanding State Pres. Ladies Aux. award 1977, nat. chaplain 1982). Republican. Roman Catholic. Clubs: Toastmistress (chpt. pres. 1969-70), VFW Aux. (pres. Tex. 1976-77, treas so. conf. 1978-81). Home: 7314 Cayton St Houston TX 77061 Office: PO Box 2180 Houston TX 77001

SUDAKOFF, MARLENE MITCHELL MOOERS, lawyer; b. Mpls., Feb. 22, 1938; d. Henry Joseph and Frances O'Byrne Mitchell; J.D., U. Minn., 1958; postgrad. U. Pitts., U. London, 1977; m. Edwin Stanton Mooers II, July 31, 1965 (dec. 1970); 1 son, Edwin Stanton III; m. 2d, Michael Richard Sudakoff, Jan. 22, 1977. Admitted to Minn. bar, 1959, Fla. bar, 1980; former partner firm Mitchell & Pierce; partner Golden Apple Dinner Theatre, Mpls., from 1971; now partner firm Lancer, Vanclroff, Sudakoff, P.A., Sarasota, Fla.; dir. Three Arts Prodns. Inc., Coastal Prodns. Inc. Asst. treas. Miller for Congress campaign, 1974; active Women Minn. Symphony Orch.; bd. dirs., historian Sarasota Opera Soc.; bd. dirs. Fla. Ballet, Inc., Women's Center, Family Counseling Center; treas. San Remo (Fla.) Assn., 1980-81. Mem. Am., Minn., Fla., Sarasota County bar assns., Am. Judicature Soc., Am. Assn. Trial Lawyers, Criminal Cts. Bar Assn., St. Andrew's Soc., Kappa Beta Pi, Beta Sigma Pi. Club: Century. Home: 3647 San Remo Terr Sarasota FL 33579 Office: 527 S Washington Blvd Sarasota FL 33577

SUDIA, MARY EILEEN, nursing adminstr.; b. Denver, Oct. 18, 1922; d. Joseph and Perenella (McDonald) Tenhaeff; R.N., Mercy Hosp. Sch. Nursing, 1944; B.S. in Nursing Edn., Colo. U., 1950; m. Andrew T. Sudia, Dec. 30, 1949; children—Thomas M., Joseph A., Patricia Sudia Bittner. Nurse, VA Hosp., Ft. Lyons, Colo., 1946-50; instr. San Antonio Jr. Coll., 1951-53, Union Meml. Hosp., Balt., 1961-66; asso. dir., dir. nursing Pickersgill Inc., Balt., 1971—. Served with U.S. Army, 1944-46. Mem. Am. Nurses Assn., Nat. League Nursing. Club: Am. Nurses Found. Century (founding mem. 1981). Home: 1556 Putty Hill Ave Baltimore MD 21204 Office: 615 Chestnut Ave Baltimore MD 21204

SUDLER, BARBARA WELCH, assn. exec.; b. Honolulu, Apr. 20, 1925; d. Leo F. and Barbara (Petrikin) Welch; B.A., U. Colo., 1944; m. James Stewart Sudler, Dec. 30, 1950; children—Eleanor, James. Book critic Denver Post, 1955-75; exec. adminstr. Hist. Denver, 1974-79; pres. Colo. Hist. Soc., Denver, 1979—; founder, dir. Women's Bank. Coordinator Colo. Adv. Com. Nat. Hist. Publs. and Records; bd. dirs. Denver Symphony; mem. Loretta Heights Leadership Council; mem. 2d cir. Jud. Nominating Com.; mem. Gov.'s Council Tourism. Recipient award Soroptimist Internat., 1978; named Woman of Yr. AIA, 1981. Mem. Women's Forum, Denver Women's Press. Editor: Nothing is Long Ago, 1976. Office: 1300 Broadway Denver CO 80203

SUELTENFUSS, SISTER, ELIZABETH ANNE, univ. pres.; b. San Antonio, Apr. 14, 1921; d. Edward L. and Elizabeth (Amrein) S.; B.A. in Botany and Zoology, Our Lady of the Lake Coll., 1944; M.S. in Biology, U. Notre Dame, 1961, Ph.D. in Biology, 1963. Joined Sisters of Divine Providence, 1939; tchr. high schs., Okla. and La., 1942-49, Our Lady of the Lake Coll., San Antonio, 1940-59, chmn. biology dept., 1963-73, pres., 1978—; adminstrv. staff Superior Gen. of Congregation of Divine Providence, 1973-77; sec. Tex. Ind. Coll. Fund. Bd. dirs. Sta. KLRN Public TV, S.W. Research Found., Trim and Swim, Friends of Library. Recipient award of yr. for achievement and leadership U. Notre Dame, 1978-79, Headliner award for profl. achievement Women in Communications, 1980; Atomic Energy grantee. Mem. AAAS, Am. Soc. Microbiology, AAUP, AAUW, Nat. Assn. Women Religious, Tex. Acad. Sci. Club: Zonta (pres. San Antonio). Office: 411 SW 24th St San Antonio TX 78285

SUGARMAN, JUNE BESKIN, speech pathologist; b. Bronx, Sept. 2, 1936; d. Abraham David and Sara (Litzky) Beskin; B.A., Bklyn. Coll., 1957, M.A., 1964; m. Wallace Sugarman, Sept. 4, 1955; children—Rhonda Gail, Marc Adam. Tchr., College Park (Md.) Elem. Sch., 1957-58, Bedford Stuvesant, Bklyn., 1958-60; speech therapist Bklyn. Coll., part-time 1962-67; speech therapist Randolph (N.J.) Twp. Schs., part-time 1967-68; speech pathologist dept. communication disorders, dept. rehab. Morristown (N.J.) Meml. Hosp., 1968—; cons. nursing homes. Mem. Am. Speech Lang. Hearing Assn., N.Y. State Speech Hearing Assn., N.J. Speech and Hearing Assn. Jewish. Club: Livingston Community Players. Home: 51 Rockledge Dr Livingston NJ 07039 Office: 100 Madison Ave Morristown Meml Hosp Morristown NJ 07960

SUGHRUE, JOAN MARGARET, acct.; b. Whitinsville, Mass., Dec. 1, 1932; d. James John and Julia Elizabeth (Healey) Sughrue; B.S. in Acctg., Hill Coll., 1953; postgrad. George Washington U., 1960-61, U. Md., 1962-63, U. So. Calif., 1976. Bookkeeper, Worcester (Mass.) County Trust, 1951-53; with Whitins-Machine Wks., Whitinsville, Mass., 1953-58; acct. Lawyers Title Ins. Co., Washington, 1958-60; payroll supr. NBC TV, Washington, 1960—; pvt. practice acctg., tax cons., Washington, 1965—; faculty Montgomery Community Coll., 1969-71. Vol., Ednl. TV, Channel 53/14, Va., 1979; tutor Inner City Youth, Washington, 1969-74; vol. Dem. Party, 1960—, Anderson for Pres., 1980. Mem. Nat. Assn. Female Execs. Democrat. Roman Catholic. Club: Pinehurst Country. Home: 10103 Mosby Woods Fairfax VA 22030 Office: 4001 Nebraska Ave NW Washington DC 20016

SUGHRUE, KATHRYN EILEEN, state legislator; b. Oketo, Kans., May 2, 1913; d. John and Charlotte Peterman; B.S. in Home Econs., Kans. State U., 1937; M.S. in Adminstrn., Colo. State U., 1962; m. Herbert Sughrue, May 3, 1941; children—Kathleen, Margaret, Patricia, John, Tim. Extension home economist, Ford County, Kans., 1937-41, Dodge City, Kans., 1949-61; dist. supt., asso. state leader Kans. State U., 1962-69; adv. Home Econs. Coll., Andra Pradesh U., Hyderabad, India, 1969; state leader N.D. State U., Fargo, 1969-73; freelance profl. speaker, 1973-76; mem. Kans. Ho. of Reps., 1976—. Vice pres., sec. Ford County Democratic Party. Recipient Top award Kans. 4-H Club Program, Finney County, 1958; Disting. Service award Kans. State U., 1981. Mem. Home Econs. Extension (pres. state chpt. 1957-58), Nat. Home Econs. Assn. (pres. state chpt. 1956-57), Kans. Home Econs. Assn. (pres. 1976-77), Home Econs. Club, Arts Council Speakers Guild, AAUW, Delta Kappa Gamma, Epsilon Sigma Phi (pres. state chpt. 1959-60). Roman Catholic. Clubs: Bus. and Profl. Women's, Women's Democratic. Philomat, PEO. Contbr. articles to mags. Office: 1809 La Mesa Dodge City KS 67801

SUGUITAN, CAROL ANNE, dietitian, food co. exec.; b. Mesa, Ariz., Dec. 4, 1938; d. Earl Perry and Hazel (De Rosier) Snoddy; B.S., U. Ariz., 1960; M.P.H., U. Calif., Berkeley, 1970; m. Manuel G. Suguitan, May 8, 1971. Dietetic intern Mass. Gen. Hosp., Boston, 1960-61; sr. research dietitian N.Y. Hosp., N.Y.C., 1961-64; clin. dietitian Hammersmith Hosp., London, Eng., 1964-65; nutritionist N.S.W. Dept. Health, Sydney, Australia, 1966; nutritionist Maricopa County Health Dept., Phoenix, 1967-69; dietetic internship dir. ARA Services, Omaha, 1971-74, regional dietitian, 1975-77; mgr. nat. health care accounts Armour & Co., Phoenix, 1977—. Mem. Omaha Mayors Task Force on Youth and Aging, 1974. Mem. Nebr. Dietitians Assn. (pres.-elect 1974), Omaha Dietetic Assn. (pres. 1973-74), Heard Mus. Guild, Phoenix Art Mus., Am. Dietetic Assn., Ariz. Dietetic Assn., Dietitians in Bus. and Industry (nominating com. 1982), Am. Public Health Assn., Ariz. Public Health Assn., Soc. for Food Service Research, Am. Home Econs. Assn., Ariz. Home Econs. Assn., Home Economists in Bus. (nominating com. 1981-82), Am. Soc. Hosp. Food Service Adminstrs. (nominating com. 1980), Am. Sch. Food Service Assn., Soc. Nutrition Edn., AAUW, Kappa Alpha Theta, Omicron Nu, Alpha Lambda Delta. Club: Altrusa Internat. Address: 2005 Greyhound Tower Phoenix AZ 85077

SUITS, DIANE STEWART, librarian; b. Norwich, N.Y., Dec. 9, 1939; d. Clarence Eugene and Margaret Alice (Carr) Stewart; B.S. in Child Devel. and Family Relationships, Cornell U., 1962; m. Allen P. Suits, Nov. 29, 1968; children—Brian, Andrew; stepchildren—Catherine, Valerie, Stephen, Jeanne. Kindergarten and elem. sch. tchr., N.Y. and Mass., 1962-70; asst. librarian Brookline (Mass.) schs., 1970-72; tchr. 2d grade, Salem, N.H., 1972-73; sch. librarian, Windham, N.H., 1973-80; librarian Meml. High Sch., Manchester, N.H., 1980—. Mem. N.H. Ednl. Media Assn., Cornell U. Alumni Secondary Schs. Com. Home: 38 Bedard Ave Derry NH 03038 Office: Memorial High Sch S Porter St Manchester NH 03103

SUJECKI, JOY MARY, med. technologist; b. Milw., Nov. 29, 1935; d. John Henry and Helen Eleanor (Bronikowski) Jakubowski; B.S. in Med. Tech., Marquette U., Milw., 1957; M.A. in Health Adminstrn., Central Mich. U., 1979; divorced; children—Ellen, Michael, Laura, Paul, Carol, Nancy, Thomas. Med. technologist for physicians and hosps., Milw., 1957-59; med. technologist Trinity Meml. Hosp., Cudahy, Wis., 1969—, adminstrv. technologist, lab. mgr., 1975—; mem. insp. team Coll. Am. Pathology. Bd. dirs. South div. Am. Cancer Soc., 1975-79; asso. editor news Our Lady of Lourdes Roman Cath. Ch., Milw., 1974-75. Mem. Am. Soc. Clin. Pathology, Clin. Lab. Mgmt. Assn., Nat. Assn. Female Execs., Wis. Assn. Med. Technologists (chmn. edn. com. 1976). Editorial bd. Med. Lab. Observer. Office: 5900 S Lake Dr Cudahy WI 53110

SUKOL, SHERRY MERLE, psychologist, educator; b. Phila., June 29, 1951; d. Austin Lewis and Elvera (Promisloff) S.; B.A., Carnegie-Mellon U., 1973; M.S., Ohio U., 1975, Ph.D. in Clin. Psychology, 1978. Clin. fellow psychology Harvard Med. Sch., 1977-78; clin. intern Children's Hosp. Med. Center, Boston, 1977-78; asst. prof. counseling psychologist West Chester (Pa.) State Coll., 1978-79; fellow Counseling Assos., Paoli, Pa., 1979-81; consulting psychologist Interac Community Mental Health Center, Phila., 1979-81; pvt. practice psychology, Wayne, Pa., 1980—; asst. prof. Grad. program in counseling and human relations Villanova (Pa.) U., 1980—. Advisor Women Against Rape, Athens, Ohio, 1977. Lic. psychologist, Pa.; cert. sch. psychologist, Pa. Mem. Am. Psychol. Assn., Phila. Soc. Clin. Psychologist, Phi Kappa Phi. Editor: Consumer's Guide to Psychotherapy, 1980. Office: Villanova University 304C Falvey Hall Villanova PA 19085

SUKONECK, HARRIET, psychologist, computer scientist; b. Newark, Jan. 30, 1945; d. Edward and Mae S.; B.A., Rutgers U., 1966; M.A., U. So. Calif., 1968, Ph.D. (NIMH fellow), 1971. Lectr., Calif. State U., Los Angeles, 1971-76; mem. research faculty Calif. Sch. Profl. Psychology, 1973-76; NIH postdoctoral fellow Childrens Hosp. of Los Angeles, 1971-73; vis. asst. prof. Loyola Marymount U., Los Angeles, 1976-78; research asso. Neuropsychiat. Inst., UCLA, 1978-80; sr. mem. tech. staff, project leader Computer Scis. Corp., El Segundo, Calif., 1980-81; mgr. systems test 1st Interstate Services Co., El Segundo, 1982—. Lic.

psychologist, Calif. Mem. Assn. Computing Machinery, Am. Psychol. Assn., AAAS. Contbr. articles to profl. jours. Editor et. al, social sci. jour., 1971-76. Office: Systems Test 1st Interstate Services Box 935 El Segundo CA 90245

SUKUP, MARY ELIZABETH, mfg. co. exec.; b. Hampton, Iowa, Oct. 29, 1932; d. Walter F. and Bessie May Bielefeld; A.A., Mason City Jr. Coll., 1952; m. Eugene George Sukup, Feb. 24, 1952; children—Charles Eugene, Steven Eugene. Tchr., 1951-52; corp. sec. Sukup Mfg. Co., Sheffield, Iowa, 1965—, Sukup Enterprises Inc., Sheffield, 1968—, also dir. Vice pres. Mason City conf. Am. Luth. Ch. Women, 1962-63; pres. Zion St. John Am. Luth. Ch. Women, 1959-60. Republican. Club: F & S Study (pres. 1978-80). Home: Dougherty IA 50433 Office: Sukup Pkwy Sheffield IA 50475

SULERZYSKI, MARGARET DOROTHY, acct.; b. N.Y.C., Mar. 14, 1951; d. Thomas Edward and Margaret Dorothy (Quinlan) Sulerzyski; student Skidmore Coll., 1969-71; B.A., Barnard Coll., 1973; M.B.A., U. Pa., 1975; certificate in profl. accountancy with honors Northwestern U. Grad. Sch. Bus., 1976. Jr. acct. Arthur Young & Co., N.Y.C., 1975-76; sr. acct. Arthur Young & Co., 1977-79, audit mgr., 1980—; lectr. in field. C.P.A., N.Y. Mem. Am. Women's Soc. C.P.A.s, N.Y. State Soc. C.P.A.s, Am. Inst. C.P.A.s. Clubs: Wharton Bus. Sch., Barnard Coll. Home: 57 Park Terr E New York NY 10034 Office: 277 Park Ave New York NY 10172

SULIIN, SHEILA GWEN MILLER, psychologist, educator; b. North Adams, Mass., Apr. 12, 1939; d. Joseph B. and Wenonah Violet (Longstreet) Miller; B.S., Henderson State U., 1971, M.S., 1972; Ed.D., U. Okla., 1978; children—Paul Scott, Robert Barry. Spl. edn. tchr. Little Rock (Ark.) public schs., 1972-73, Ark. Girl's Tng. Sch., Alexander, 1973-74, Hot Springs (Ark.) public schs., 1974-75; cons. tchr. and diagnostician Poyen (Ark.) public schs., 1975-76; instr. dept. spl. edn. Henderson State U., Arkadelphia, Ark., 1976; grad. asst., supr. student tchrs. U. Okla., Norman, 1977-78; ednl. diagnostician Hot Spring County Exceptional Center, Malvern, Ark., 1979; adj. prof. spl. edn. U. Ark., Fayetteville, 1979—; psychol. examiner Ark. Childrens Colony, Arkadelphia, 1979—. Den mother Boy Scouts Am., 1967-72; leader Evergreen council Girl Scouts U.S., 1956-63; Sunday sch. tchr. St. John's Episcopal Ch., 1965-70. Will Rogers scholar, 1977. Mem. Nat. Council Tchrs. English, Council for Exceptional Children, Assn. for Children with Learning Disabilities, Nat. Assn. for Retarded Citizens and Adults, Council for Ednl. Diagnostics, Phi Delta Kappa, Alpha Chi Alpha. Home: 1513 Dogwood Trail Malvern AR 72104 Office: Arkansas Childrens Colony Arkadelphia AR 71923

SULLIVAN, ALBERTA CONSTANCE, speech pathologist; b. Providence, Dec. 12, 1935; d. James Gabriel and Alberta Ellen (O'Connor) Landrigan; B.A., Coll. New Rochelle, 1957; M.Ed., Boston U., 1960; m. Joseph Leo Sullivan, Aug. 12, 1961; children—Catherine, Elizabeth, James. Tchr., Cumberland (R.I.) High Sch., 1957-65, Providence Sch. Dept., 1965-67, Warwick (R.I.) Sch. Dept., 1967-69; tchr. drama Young Peoples Sch. for the Performing Arts, Seekonk, Mass., 1971—; pvt. practice speech pathology, East Providence, R.I., 1969—; sr. speech lang. hearing pathologist Barrington (R.I.) Sch. System, 1980—. Mem. R.I. Speech, Lang. and Hearing Assn., Am. Speech, Lang. Hearing Assn., R.I. Ednl. Assn., NEA. Home: 226 Wilson Ave Rumford RI 02916 Office: 310 Maple Ave Barrington RI 02806

SULLIVAN, ANN CATHERINE, hosp. adminstr.; b. N.Y.C., June 8, 1947; d. Joseph Peter and Catherine Janet (Wolt) S. Mem. Hosp. Care Fin. Mgmt. Assn., N.Y. Assn. Ambulatory Care. Home: 20-16 Parsons Blvd Whitestone NY 11357

SULLIVAN, BARBARA ANN, ins. co. exec.; b. Boston, July 6, 1928; d. Richard Wesley and Monica (McCoy) S.; B.A., Mt. Holyoke Coll., 1950. With John Hancock Mut. Life Ins. Cos., Boston, 1950—, actuarial clk., 1950-55, supr., 1955-58, asst. mgr., 1958-60, mgr., 1960-70, adminstrn. dir., 1970-78, 2d v.p., 1978—. Active Fine Arts Chorale, New Eng. Gilbert and Sullivan Soc. Clubs: Appalachian Mountain, South Shore Country. Office: John Hancock Pl PO Box 111 Boston MA 02117

SULLIVAN, BARBARA BOYLE, mgmt. cons.; b. Scranton, Pa., Apr. 12, 1937; d. Edmund F. and Mary R. (O'Connell) Boyle; B.S. in Bus. Adminstrn., Drexel U., 1958; Ph.D. (hon.), Newton Coll., 1975, Gwynedd Mercy Coll., Pa., 1975; m. John L. Sullivan, Jr. With IBM Corp., 1959-72, systems engring. mgr. Eastern and Central Europe, Vienna, 1967-70, mgmt. devel. mgr., 1970, mgr. spl. programs, 1970-71, mktg. mgr., asst. br. mgr., 1971-72; pres. Boyle/Kirkman Assos., Yarmouthport, Mass., 1972—; trustee Equitable Gas Co., Pitts., 1979—; cons. maj. corps. on affirmative action programs, condr. exec. awareness seminars Harvard Bus. Sch., Internat. Mgmt. Conf., several nat. confs. on equal opportunity for women. Vice-chmn. bd. trustees Marymount Manhattan Coll., N.Y., 1980; bd. regents Mt. St. Mary's Coll., Los Angeles, 1982—. Named Bus. Person of Year, St. Johns U., 1973, to Drexel U. Hall of Fame, 1976. Featured in numerous mags., books, radio and TV programs, including Time mag. and CBS 60 Minutes; named one of 50 Leaders for Future, Time Mag., 1979; Mktg. Exec. of Yr., Drexel U., 1982. Office: Boyle Kirkman Assos 244 Willow St Yarmouthport MA 02675

SULLIVAN, CARLEY HAYDEN, polit. party orgn. exec.; b. Elko, Nev.; student U. Oreg., 1945-47; m. Will Sullivan; children—Blaine Sullivan Rose, Valerie Sullivan Mitchell, Dan, Peggy Sullivan Hagen. Mgmt. asst. State of Nev., Elko, 1967—; sec. Elko County (Nev.) Democratic Central Com., 1972-82; treas. Nev. Dem. Com., 1980-82, co-chmn. state conv., 1980, mem. state cons. planning com., 1982; mem. state hosp. adv. bd., 1964-66, adv. council on children and youth, 1970-80; mem. gov.'s State Sch. Survey Com., 1975-77, Gov.'s Drug Abuse Adv. Bd., 1974-76; gov.'s del. to Nev. Library Conf., 1981; alt. del. White House Conf. on Libraries, 1982; Nev. del. to Presdl. White House Conf. on Children and Youth, 1970; life mem. Gov.'s Youth Traffic Safety Assn.; exec. sec., interim mgr. Elko C. of C., 1961-68. Pres. Elko Dem. Women, 1970; bd. dirs. Elko Dem. Club, 1970-82; chmn. Rural Nev. Mental Health Adv. Bd., 1973-78; bd. Nev. PTA, 1962-72, pres., 1972-74; v.p. Am. Lung Assn. of Nev., 1972-82, pres.-elect, bd., 1982—; coordinator Youth Traffic Safety Confs., 1968-78; bd. mgrs. Nat. Com. Health and Welfare, PTA, 1972-74; adv. bd. Nat. Council Juvenile Ct. Judges, 1972-74; mem. 8 state project Designing Edn. for the Future, 1965-68; Nev. rep. to nat. ALA conv., 1981; vol. Elko Hosp. Aux.; co-chmn. 1st Rural Nev. Women's Conf., 1980; mem. Nev. Adv. Council for Vocat. Tech. Edn., 1982—; mem. Nev. State Bd. Edn., 1982—. Recipient honors Am. Lung Assn. Nev., C. of C., Nev. Dept. Edn., Gov.'s Office State of Nev. Mem. Elko Bus. and Profl. Women (state legis. chmn., scholarship award com.), Sigma Kappa.

SULLIVAN, DONNA MARIE, med. adminstr.; b. Medford, Mass., Feb. 9, 1947; d. William Henry and Kathleen Francis (Travers) Sullivan; diploma lab. tech. Northeastern U., 1966; B.A. B.A., Emmanuel Coll., 1982; M.B.A., Anna Maria Coll., 1983. Staff technologist Choate Hosp., Woburn, Mass., 1966-72, asst. chief med. technologist, 1972-81; lab. mgr. Choate Symmes Health Services Inc., Woburn, 1981—. Mem. Soc. Clin. Pathologists, Clin. Lab. Mgrs. Assn. Democrat. Roman Catholic. Office: 21 Warren Ave Woburn MA 01801

SULLIVAN, DOROTHY RONA, state ofcl.; b. Boston, Jan. 7, 1941; d. Lewis Robert and Dorothy (Hopkins) Sullivan; B.A., Boston U., 1963, C.A.G.S., 1972; M.Ed., State Coll. Boston, 1966; postgrad. Northeastern U., Boston Coll. Research asst., lay med. editor Boston Lying-in Hosp., 1963-64; employment counselor Mass. Div. Employment Security, Boston, 1964-66, sr. employment counselor, 1966-67, prin. employment counselor, 1967-70, employment office mgr., 1970-75, supervising employment office mgr., 1975-78, chief supr. labor research, 1978—; supr. community counselor interns and rehab. adminstrn. intern Northeastern U. Grad. Sch. Edn., 1968-72; supr. public adminstrn. interns Suffolk U., 1976; supr. econ. interns Boston U., 1979; mem. regional adv. subcom. on mental retardation Mass. Dept. Mental Health, 1969; mem. White House Conf. on Small Bus., 1978. Mem. Jamaica Plain Community Council Health, Edn. and Welfare Subcom., 1967-69; recorder Gov.'s Conf. on Rehab., 1970; assoc. mem. Gov.'s Commn. on Employment Handicapped, 1972-78; mem. Pres.'s Com. on Employment of Handicapped, 1976-78; mem. adv. com. Boston Commn. Affairs of Elderly, 1977-78; bd. dirs. Greater Boston council Camp Fire Girls, 1972-75; exec. bd. local chpt. Am. Fedn. State, County and Mcpl. Employees, AFL-CIO, 1972-76. Mem. Am. Acad. Polit. and Social Sci., Nat. Vocat. Guidance Assn., Nat. Rehab. Assn. (sec. Mass. chpt. 1971-72, exec. bd. chpt. 1971-74, pres. 1975-76, recorder, awards chmn. Northeast Regional Conf. 1971), Nat. Employment Counselors Assn., Am. Personnel and Guidance Assn. (nat. recorder conf. 1968), Rockport Art Assn., Smaller Bus. Assn. New Eng., Chatham Conservation Found., Am. Soc. Public Adminstrn., Am. Bus. Women's Assn. (pres. Boston chpt. 1982-83), Internat. Platform Assn. Author: Boston Employment Service Guide, 1969, Massachusetts/Cities and Towns (monthly), 1980—; editor: Massachusetts Trends (monthly), 1978—; contbr. articles to profl. jours. Office: Employment Security Bldg Govt Center Boston MA 02114

SULLIVAN, HAZEL ERICKSEN, civic worker; b. Bklyn., Mar. 28, 1916; d. Christian and Tonny (Abrahamsen) Ericksen; student Jamaica (N.Y.) public schs.; m. Daniel Sullivan, Oct. 5, 1935; children—Daniel, Lawrence, Terrence. Bd. dirs. Republican Party, 1980—; pres. Penataquit Aux. to Southside Hosp., 1978-79, recipient aux. recognition award; active ARC, Sagtikos Hist. Soc., Library. Recipient Heritage and Arts awards L.I. Fedn. Women's Clubs. Mem. Am. Bell Assn., Republican Islip Women. Methodist. Clubs: Bayshore Garden, Bayway Tennis. Home: 78 Bayway Ave Brightwaters NY 11718

SULLIVAN, ISABELLA AGNES, assn. exec.; b. Seney, Mich., July 31, 1904; d. Antoni and Jadwiga (Wozniak) Krzyminski; A.B., U. Mich., 1937; B.S., U. Denver, 1942; m. R. Herbert Sullivan, Apr. 5, 1952. Librarian, Grand Rapids (Mich.) Public Library, 1928-36, 38-42, Ottawa Hill High Sch., Grand Rapids, 1942-67; pres., curator Alger County Hist. Soc., 1971—; mem. rev. com. Alger County Courthouse, 1979—; mem. Alger County Housing Commn., 1971-77, Munising Partnership Com., 1979—, Alger County Underwater Preserve Com., 1980—. Recipient Mich. Week Gov.'s Minuteman award, 1973; Alger County Woman of Yr. award, 1979; Charles Follo award Hist. Soc. Mich., 1982. Mem. Hist. Soc. Mich., Mich. Mus. Assn., Mich. Archival Soc., Delta County Hist. Soc., Luce County Hist. Soc., Seney Hist. Soc., Marshall Hist. Soc. Roman Catholic. Hist. columnist Munising News, 1968—. Home: 411 Birch St Munising MI 49862 Office: Alger County Historical Soc PO Box 201 Munising MI 49862

SULLIVAN, JOYCE A(NN), mgmt. cons.; b. Cleve., Mar. 18, 1931; s. Benjamin F. and Leonora E. (LePontois) Reed; B.S., Kent State U., 1952, M.A., 1963; Ph.D., Ohio State U., 1971; m. Lawrence J. Sullivan, Aug. 23, 1952; children—Larry, Deborah, Diane. Head human ecology U. Akron, 1967-76; co-dir. interdivisional program in individual and family counseling Fla. State U., 1976-79; cons. Batten, Batten, Hudson & Swab, Irvine, Calif., 1979-81; cons. Fred Pryor Seminars, 1981—; ednl. adv. J.C. Penney Co., Parents' Mag. Enterprises. Mem. Nat. Council Family Relations, Am. Soc. Tng. and Devel., Phi Delta Kappa. Author coll. texts; contbr. numerous articles to profl. jours.; asso. editor Jour. Edn., Counseling and Services, 1980—. Home: 1903 Bay Crest Santa Ana CA 92704 Office: 2000 Johnson Dr Shawnee Mission KS 66205

SULLIVAN, JUDITH PATRICE ELDRIDGE, social worker; b. Texarkana, Ark., Jan. 28, 1945; d. Joseph and Agnes (Wilson) Eldridge; B.A., U. Tex., Austin, 1966; M.S.W., SUNY, Buffalo, 1972; m. John Patrick Sullivan, Apr. 7, 1967 (div. 1972). Sensory tng. tchr. Devereaux Found., Devon, Pa., 1966-67; counselor Clergy Counseling Service, Buffalo, 1969-70, research cons., London, 1970; adminstrv. asst. to exec. officer Sch. Social Work, SUNY, Buffalo, 1971; supr. counseling services Erie Med. Center, Buffalo, 1972-74; program dir. dept. child psychiatry and behaviorial scis. Buffalo Children's Hosp., 1974-79; pvt. practice psychotherapy and consultancy, Williamsville, N.Y., 1979—; clin. instr., SUNY Sch. Medicine, Buffalo, 1974-79, mem. com. on human values and meth. ethics, 1977—, clin. asst. prof., 1979, clin. instr. pediatrics, 1974-79, clin. instr. family planning, nurse practioner program, 1973-76. Vice pres. Abortion Rights Assn. N.Y., 1971-73, bd. dirs., 1969-70, Western N.Y. polit. coordinator, 1969-70. Cert. social worker, N.Y.; lic. psychotherapist, N.Y. Mem. NOW (v.p. 1969-70), Nat. Assn. Social Workers, Acad. Cert. Social Workers, Am. Hosp. Assn. Soc. for Hosp. Social Work Dirs., Am. Public Health Assn., Zero Population Growth, Planned Parenthood/World Population Growth, Sex Edn. and Info. Council of U.S. Home: 600 Parkside Ave Buffalo NY 14216

SULLIVAN, KAREN HARRIS, retail chain exec.; b. St. Louis, Dec. 12, 1954; d. William Clinton and Elsie (Jackson) Harris; B.F.A., S.W. Mo. State U., 1976; m. John Lorenz Sullivan, Feb. 3, 1978; 1 dau., Lauren Marie. Dept. mgr. Famous-Barr, St. Louis, 1976-77, dept. mgr. budget store, 1977, asst. buyer designer sportswear and accessories, 1977-78, dept. mgr. designer sportswear, dresses, furs, coats, FB Ltd., Frontenac, Mo., 1978-79, dept. mgr., 1979-80, sr. asst. buyer, 1980-81; dist. mgr. Libson's, Inc., St. Louis, 1981, dir. store supervision, 1981-82, asso. gen. mdse. mgr., 1982, gen. mdse. mgr., 1982—. Mem. Alpha Delta Pi. Roman Catholic. Office: 1209 Washington St Saint Louis MO 63103

SULLIVAN, KATHLEEN ANN, clin. audiologist; b. Ludlow, Mass., May 31, 1950; d. Thomas Francis and Agnes S.; B.A. cum laude, U. Mass., 1973, M.A., 1975. Clin. audiologist Robert N. Speth, Montague, Mass., 1973-75; pediatric audiologist Dartmouth Hitchcock Med. Center, Hanover, N.H., 1976; dir. audiol. services Belchertown (Mass.) State Sch., 1976-81; clin. audiologist UCLA Med. Center, 1981—; tchr. speechreading; cons. edn1. collaboratives, Mass. Rehab. Commn.; mem. Mass. Statewide Task Force on Deafness, 1978—, Mayor's Com. on Handicapped, Northampton, 1979—. Mem. Am. Speech, Lang. and Hearing Assn. (cert.), Hampshire Choral Soc. Home: 1224 24th St Santa Monica CA 90404

SULLIVAN, KATHLEEN CLAIRE, state legislator; b. Meeker, Colo., Oct. 8, 1954; d. Joseph Burton and Claire Marie (Obuchowski) S.; B.A., Mesa Coll., 1977; M.A. in Communications, U. No. Colo., 1980. Wheat farmer, Meeker, Colo., 1980—; now mem. Colo. Ho. of Reps. from 57th Dist., mem. Agr., Livestock, and Natural Resources Com., Game, Fish, and Parks Com., Local Govt. Com.; mem. Colo. Employment and Tng. Council, Romcoe, Abandoned Mines Adv. Com. Democrat. Methodist. Office: State Capitol Denver CO 80203

SULLIVAN, MARGARET PATRICIA, pediatric oncologist, educator; b. Lewistown, Mont., Feb. 7, 1922; d. William A. and Mabel Cooper (Conrad) S.; B.A., Rice Inst., Houston, 1944; M.D., Duke U., 1950. Intern, Duke Hosp., Durham, N.C., 1950-51, asst. resident 1951-52; resident St. Louis Children's Hosp., St. Louis, 1952-53; asst. resident Tex. Children's Hosp. Houston, 1955; pediatrician Atomic Bomb Casualty Commn., Hiroshima and Nagasaki, Japan, 1953-55; pediatrician, asst. prof. pediatrics U. Tex. M.D. Anderson Hosp. and Tumor Inst., Houston, 1956-61, asso. pediatrician, asso. prof. pediatrics, 1961-73, pediatrician, prof. pediatrics, 1973—. Diplomate Am. Bd. Pediatrics. Mem. Am. Acad. Pediatrics, Harris County Med. Soc., Tex. Med. Assn., Am. Assn. Cancer Edn., Am. Assn. Cancer Research, AMA, Am. Soc. Clin. Oncology, Houston Pediatric Assn., Phi Beta Kappa, Sigma Xi, Alpha Omega Alpha. Presbyterian. Editor: (with J. van Eys) Status of Curability of Childhood Cancers, 1980; mem. editorial bd. Year Book of Cancer, 1959—. Home: 4606 Waynesboro St Houston TX 77035 Office: MD Anderson Hosp and Tumor Inst 6723 Bertner Ave Houston TX 77030

SULLIVAN, MARY ROSE, educator; b. Boston, May 13, 1931; d. John Joseph and Elinor Mary (Grotty) S.; B.A., Emmanuel Coll., Boston, 1952; M.A., Cath. U. Am., 1957; Ph.D., Boston U., 1964. Instr. English, Emmanuel Coll., 1960-66; mem. faculty U. Colo., Denver, 1966—, prof. English, 1970—. Served as officer USNR, 1952-56. Fellow Am. Council Learned Socs., 1973. Mem. AAUP, AAUW, MLA, Browning Inst., Naval Inst., Nat. Book Critics Circle. Clubs: Altrusa, Denver Woman's Press. Author: Browning's Voices in the Ring and the Book, 1969; editor: People and Policy, 1979-80; mem. editorial bd. English Lang. Notes, 1972—, Browning Inst. Studies, 1974—. Home: 2443 S Colorado Blvd Apt 213 Denver CO 80222 Office: 1100 14th St Denver CO 80202

SULLIVAN, MARY W(ILSON), author; b. Grants Pass, Oreg., Dec. 25, 1907; d. Roy Stanley and Adelia (Harth) Wilson; student U. Oreg., 1926-28; m. Paul Dennis Sullivan, Apr. 15, 1931; children—Mary Anne, Mildred, Denis, Francis, Margaret. Freelance writer, Pasadena, Calif., 1965-78, Laguna Beach, Calif., 1978—; author: Happenings, 4 readers and tchrs. man., 1970, Danish transl., 1978, Indestructible Old Time String Band, 1975, Bluegrass Iggy, 1975, What's This About Pete?, 1976, Brian-Foot-In-The-Mouth, 1978, The VW Connection, 1980, Earthquake 2099, 1982. Mem. PEN (v.p. Los Angeles chpt. 1978, del. Internat. conf. London 1976, Sydney, Australia 1977, Paris, 1981, co-chmn. writers in prison com.), Quill Pen (pres. 1976-77), Soc. Children's Book Writers, Friends of Children and Lit., So. Calif. Council Lit. for Children and Young People, Alpha Phi. Democrat. Home and Office: 8811 Coast Hwy #118 Laguna Beach CA 92651

SULLIVAN, MAUREEN ELIZABETH, sales exec.; b. Hempstead, N.Y., July 10, 1946; d. John Andrew and Helen Margaret (Canivan) Sullivan; B.A. in English, C.W. Post Coll., 1969. Adminstrv. asst. Basford, Inc., N.Y.C., 1969; gen. mgr. Nat. Retail Mchts. Assn., N.Y.C., 1970-74; sales trainer Am. Express Co., N.Y.C., 1974-77, dist. sales mgr., Hackensack, N.J., 1978-80, dir. sales, N.Y.C., 1980—. Named Asso. Mem. of Yr., Pocono Mountains Vacation Bur., 1979. Mem. N.Y. Restaurant Assn., Nat. Retail Mchts. Assn., N.Y.C. C. of C., N.Y. Hotel/Motel Assn., Women in Sales Assn., Restaurant League of N.Y., Westside C. of C. Editor: Credit Mgmt. Yearbook, 1969-70. Home: 425 E 63d St New York NY 10021 Office: 708 3d Ave 9th Floor New York NY 10017

SULLIVAN, PAMELA GRACE, engr., research specialist; b. Rio de Janeiro, Brazil, Apr. 11, 1945 (parents Am. citizens); d. Lloyd Charles and Helen Postill Hawken; A.S., Long Beach (Calif.) City Coll., 1968; B.S.M.E., Calif. State U., Long Beach, 1971, M.S.M.E., 1978; m. Charles J. Sullivan, Feb. 22, 1962 (div.); 1 dau., Catherine Anne. Engr., Nevada Engrng. & Tech. Corp., Long Beach, 1971-79, also sec.; research specialist Lockheed Missles & Space Co., Sunnyvale, Calif., 1979—. Mem. ASTM, ASME, AIME, Am. Ceramic Soc. Contbr. articles to profl. publs. Home: 544 W Latimer Campbell CA 95008 Office: Lockheed Missles & Space Co 62-60 104 1 PO Box 504 Sunnyvale CA 94086

SULLIVAN, PATRICIA ANN, social work cons.; b. Queens, N.Y., Oct. 17, 1948; d. Patrick Henry and Mary Margaret (Lefebure) S.; B.A., Queens Coll., 1972; M.S.W., Columbia U., 1974; m. Edward J. Bealler, Jr., Feb. 7, 1975; 1 dau., Julia Sullivan. Social worker Angel Guardian Home, Bklyn., 1974-77, Vis. Nurse Assn., of Bklyn., 1977-79; social work cons. MIC Family Planning Projects, N.Y.C., 1979-81. Mem. Nat. Assn. Social Workers, Acad. Social Workers, Acad. Cert. Social Workers. Home: 459 12th St Brooklyn NY 11215

SULLIVAN, PATRICIA MAUREEN, psychologist; b. Des Moines, June 24, 1946; d. Paul John and Maureen (Tighe) S.; B.A., Marycrest Coll., 1968; Ed.S., U. Iowa, 1977, Ph.D., 1978. Secondary sch. tchr., Mo., 1969-70; coordinator dormitory counselors Pa. Sch. Deaf, Phila., 1970-74; tchr. autistic and emotionally disturbed children, supr. spl. edn. student tchrs., pediatric psychology grad. asst. U. Iowa Grad. Sch. Employment, 1974-78; coordinator psychoednl. services for hearing-impaired Boys Town Inst. Communication Disorders in Children, Omaha, 1978—; sec. Nebr. Commn. Hearing Impaired, 1979-82, chmn., 1982-84; adv. council edn. and welfare of deaf Nebr. Bd. Edn., 1981. Mem. Am. Psychol. Assn., Nat. Assn. Sch. Psychologists, Internat. Neuropsychol. Assn., Nebr. Psychol. Assn., NOW, Delta Epsilon Sigma. Democrat. Roman Catholic. Author articles, films in field. Office: 555 N 30th St Omaha NE 68131

SULLO, DONNA ROSE, product mgr.; b. College Point, N.Y., Apr. 20, 1952; d. Joseph Anthony and Rose Ann (Pesce) Sullo; B.B.A. in Fin. and Investments, Bernard M. Baruch Coll., 1973, postgrad., 1973-77. Central treas. Bernard M. Baruch Coll., N.Y.C., 1973-74; telecommunications technician Met. Life Ins., N.Y.C., 1974-77; staff mgr. mktg. AT&T, Basking Ridge, N.J., 1977-80, dist. mgr. mktg., 1980-82; dist. mgr. Advanced Network Services Am. Bell, Inc., 1982—; guest lectr. Bell System, 1979. Mem. Assn. Data Communications Users, Am. Mensa Soc. Home: 320 South St Apt 11-N Morristown NJ 07960

SULLO, ROSE ANN, sculptor, artist; b. N.Y.C., Mar. 27, 1919; d. Saverio and Rosina (Palumbo) Pesce; student Leonardi DaVinci Cultural Center, N.Y., 1934-37, Poppenhusen Inst., N.Y., 1936-37, Delphic Studios, N.Y., 1937, Cooper Union Inst., N.Y., 1937-39; m. Joseph A. Sullo, Oct. 12, 1947; children—Susan Ann, Donna Rose, Peter Adam. Free-lance profl. sculptor and artist; one woman shows include: Halifax Hist. Soc., Daytona Beach, Fla., 1978, Ormond Meml. Art Gallery, Ormond Beach, Fla., 1979; group shows: Brockton (Mass.) Art Center, 1972, United Fedn. Doll Clubs, Detroit, 1970, Los Angeles, 1971, Omaha, 1972, Louisville, 1973, Miami, 1974, San Francisco, 1976, San Diego, 1977, Hartford, Conn., 1973, 77, Seattle, 1972, Denver, 1978, N.Y.C., 1979, Akron, Ohio, 1979, Flushing (N.Y.) Council Women's Clubs, 1977, 78, Nat. League Am. Pen Women, 1974, 75, 76, 77, 78; represented in permanent collections: Wee Lassie Doll Mus., Mus. City N.Y., Homestead, Fla., Strong Mus., Pittsfield, N.Y., Morristown (N.J.) Mus. Arts and Scis.; presented work to Pres. Nixon, 1972. Del. Flushing Council Women's Clubs, 1975—. Recipient many awards for art works and sculpture; Internat. Women's Year award, 1975. Mem. Nat. Inst. Am. Doll Artist, Inc. (award of excellence 1970), Nat. League Am. Pen Women, (spl. award 1974), United Fedn. Doll Clubs, Dollology Club Washington, Doll Collector's Guild N.Y., Flushing Art League, Internat. Doll Clubs, Dutchess Art Assn. Home: RD 3 Box 68 Bria Hill Rd Route 52 Hopewell Junction NY 12533

SULTON, ANNE THOMAS, educator; b. Racine, Wis., Oct. 24, 1952; d. William Henry and Esther (Phillips) Thomas; B.S., Wash. State U., 1973; M.A., SUNY, 1975; postgrad. U. Md., 1978—; student U. Wis., 1970-71; dipl. ordinario de lengua y cultura espanos, Universidad de la Salamanca (Spain), 1975; postgrad. Pacific Luth. U., summer 1972, Instituto Tech. y Superious Estudious Monterrey, Mexico, summer 1970; m. James E. Sulton, Jr.; 1 son, James E. III. Instr., ANAFCO CETA Fliers, Atlanta, summer 1977; faculty Atlanta U., summer 1977; instr. Atlanta Fed. Penitentiary, 1978; faculty Spelman Coll., Atlanta, 1976-78; instr. Balt. City Police Tng. Acad., 1979-80; asst. instr. U. Md., College Park, 1979; lectr. Howard U., Washington, 1980—; research asso. Nat. Orgn. Black Law Enforcement Execs. LEAA Tech. Assistance Project, Balt., 1978-80; lead cons. Nat. Crime Prevention Inst., U. Louisville, 1979; cons. ANAIFCO CETA Fliers, Atlanta, 1978. Pres., Willard L. Thomas Scholarship Found., Inc., Racine, 1973—. Recipient Spl. Friend of NAACP award Atlanta Penitentiary br. NAACP, 1978; cert. of appreciation Atlanta's Crime Analysis Team, 1978, Atlanta's First Cert. Black Aviatrix award Atlanta Negro Airmen Internat. Flying Club Orgn., 1978; named Fulton County Outstanding Citizen, 1977; SUNY research fellow, 1973-75. Mem. Police Exec. Research Forum, AAUP, Help Urban Balt., NAACP, Am. Soc. Criminology, Acad. Criminal Justice Scis., Alpha Phi Sigma. Editor: Contemporary Issues in Criminology, Law Enforcement and Corrections; contbr. articles to profl. jours. Address: PO Box 861 N College Park State College Park MD 20740

SULZBERGER, ROBERTA ZECHIEL, writer, producer ednl. films; b. Stoutsville, Ohio, Dec. 5, 1913; d. Edward Emanuel and Ethel Claire (Smith) Zechiel; A.B., Heidelberg Coll., 1935; M.A. in English Lit., U. Chgo., 1936; m. Marion Baldur Sulzberger, 1958. Tchr. English lang. and lit. Louisville (Ohio) High Sch., 1936-37, Alliance (Ohio) High Sch., 1937-38; staff writer, producer ednl. and indsl. motion pictures Audio Prodns., Inc., N.Y.C., 1940-45, 51-61; staff writer Am. Film Center, N.Y.C., 1945, Young America Films, N.Y.C., 1946; staff writer and producer motion pictures for coll. textbook pubs. and various industries, Pathescope Corp., N.Y.C., 1946-50; co-founder, exec. sec. Inst. for Dermatologic Communication and Edn., San Francisco, 1962—, producer and script writer numerous motion pictures for dermatologists, 1960—, also script writer and producer color sound AV teaching aids for med. students, dermatologists, children, 1970—; asst. univ. extension specialist, dept. continuing edn. in health scics. U. Calif., San Francisco, 1964-69; producer AV programs Am. Acad. Dermatology, 1970—. Recipient All-European Sci. film award, 1963. Mem. Info. Film Producers of Am., Am. Med. Writers Assn., Royal Soc. Medicine (asso.) (London), Pi Kappa Delta, Kappa Delta Pi. Democrat. Mem. United Ch. of Christ. Club: Cosmopolitan. Address: 2785 Jackson St San Francisco CA 94115

SULZBY, ELIZABETH FAY, educator; b. Walker County, Ala., Feb. 25, 1942; d. Phillip Glen and Ophelia Sulzby; B.A., Birmingham-So. Coll., 1963; M.Ed., Coll. William and Mary, 1969; Ph.D., U. Va., 1977; m. Mitchell Frank Rouzie, July 8, 1980. Tchr. public schs., 1966-75; instr. Jacksonville (Fla.) U., 1970-71, R.I. Coll., Providence, 1973-74, U. Va., Charlottesville, 1975-77; asst. prof. edn. Northwestern U., Evanston, Ill., 1977—. Mem. adv. bd. One-To-One Learning Center, Wilmette; Ill., 1980-82. Woodrow Wilson fellow, 1963-64; Nat. Council of Tchrs. of English grantee, 1980-81; Nat. Inst. Edn. grantee, 1980-82; Spencer Found. grantee, 1981-82. Mem. Am. Ednl. Research Assn., Am. Psychol. Assn., Internat. Reading Assn., Nat. Council of Tchrs. of English, Nat. Reading Conf., Soc. Research in Child Devel. Contbr. articles in field to profl. pubis. Home: 2537 Prospect Ave Evanston IL 60201 Office: 2003 Sheridan Rd Evanston IL 60201

SUMMER, CAROL ROCHELLE, publisher, exec. editor; b. San Francisco, Apr. 28, 1937; d. Harry and Sophie (Kaufman) Cohen; diploma George Washington High Sch., 1954; m. Arthur Summer, June 19, 1955; children—Mark, Mitchell, Julie. Asst. pub. Tech. Pub. Corp., Los Angeles, 1963-70; pub., exec. editor Creative Age Publs., North Hollywood, Calif., 1970—. Mem. Am. Trauma Assn., Western Publs. Assn. (Editorial Leadership award 1975, 78, 79, Maggie award 1982), Illustrators West, Los Angeles Advt. Club. Home and Office: 12849 Magnolia Blvd North Hollywood CA 91607

SUMMERFIELD, ELLEN, ednl. adminstr.; b. Chgo., Aug. 7, 1944; B.S. in Edn., Chgo. State U., 1965, M.A. in English, 1972; postgrad. U. Chgo., 1974—. Tchr., Chgo. Public Schs., 1966-78; coordinator dept. mgmt. devel. and long range planning Chgo. Bd. Edn., 1978-80, coordinator dept. intergovtl. relations, 1980—. Scott Foresman scholar, 1964-65; Noyes scholar, 1976-77; recipient Outstanding Tchr. of Yr. award, 1975. Mem. Nat. Soc. Study Edn., Am. Ednl. Research Assn., Pi Lambda Theta, Phi Delta Kappa. Office: 160 W Wendell St Chicago IL 60610

SUMMERFIELD, FAYE VERNICE, med. technologist; b. Houston, Sept. 25, 1939; d. Jesse Lee and Bertha Louise McAllister; B.S., Bennett Coll., Greensboro, N.C., 1960; m. John Summerfield, Aug. 26, 1961; children—Bertha, Belinda. With Dexar County Hosp. Dist., San Antonio, 1961—, now supr. hematology coagulation. Home: 1819 Dawson St San Antonio TX 78202 Office: 4502 Medical Dr San Antonio TX 78284

SUMMERS, ELAINE, choreographer; b. Perth, Australia, Feb. 20, 1925; d. James and Lillian (Lane) Smithers; B.S. in Art Edn., Mass. Coll. Art, 1947; postgrad. U. Iowa, 1975, 82; m. Davidson Gigliotti, Oct. 1975; 1 son, Kyle Summers. Artistic dir. Exptl. Intermedia Found., N.Y.C., 1968—; founding mem. Judson Dance Theatre, 1960-64; artistic dir. Fantastic Gardens Concert, 1964; asst. prof. film C.W. Post Coll., 1969-70; founder EIF, 1968, Kinetic Awarness Center, 1970, Elaine Summers Dance and Film Co., 1968; artistic dir. 1st Intermedia Art Festival, N.Y.C., 1980; artist-in-residence Iowa U., 1978, Mills Coll., 1980, U. Calif., San Diego, 1980; works include Energy Changes, 1973, Crow's Nest, 1980, Skyline, 1982. Illuminated Workingman, 1975; tours Europe, Australia. Grantee Nat. Endowment Arts, N.Y. State Council Arts, William Hassett Found., Seymour Knox, Jr. Found., Friends of New Cinema, Martha Baird Rockefeller Fund Music; CAPS Multimedia fellow, 1981. Mem. Actors Equity, Am. Assn. Dance Cos., Assn. Ind. Film and Video, Dance Theatre Workshop.

SUMMERS, MARY ELLEN, city ofcl.; b. Purcell, Okla., Dec. 21, 1932; d. Nick A. and Jessie Lee (Fleming) Arms; student public schs.; m. Raymond Leslie Summers, July 3, 1950 (dec.); children—Susan, Vickie, Leslie, John. Bookkeeper, Purcell Med. Center, 1967-70; accounts receivable mgr. Purcell Mcpl. Hosp., 1970-72; city clk.-treas. City of Purcell, 1972—. Mem. Okla. Assn. Mcpl. Clks., Treasurers and Fin. Ofcls., State Okla. Mcpl. Clks. and Treasurers, Internat. Inst. Mcpl. Clks., Okla. Mcpl. League. Democrat. Baptist. Clubs: Okeyha Mother's, Order Eastern Star. Home: 710 W Adams St Purcell OK 73080 Office: 223 W Main St Purcell OK 73080

SUMMERS, PATTI PRATT, hosp. adminstr.; b. Uniontown, Pa., Jan. 14, 1938; d. M. Wayne and Helen J. (Burke) Pratt; R.N., Presbyn. Hosp.-U. Pitts. Sch. Nursing, 1958; B.A., Marietta (Ohio) Coll., 1976; postgrad. W.Va. U., 1976—; m. James C. Summers, June 14, 1977; children—William W., Marian L., Douglas L. Med.-surg. clin. instr. Presbyn.-U. Pitts. Sch. Nursing, 1960-64; instr. staff devel., human resources dept. Camden-Clark Hosp., Parkersburg, W.Va., 1976-78; account exec. Fahlgren & Ferris Advt., 1978-80; dir. public relations Greensboro (N.C.) Hosp., 1980—; past bd. dirs. Mid-Ohio Valley chpt. ARC. Mem. Pitts. Symphony Women's Aux., 1970-72, Parkersburg Art Center, 1974-77; mem. alumni council Marietta Coll., 1978-81, 1st v.p., 1979-80; mem. Greensboro Civic Ballet Guild, 1980—. Recipient commendation Freedoms Found. Mem. AAUW (dir. Parkersburg 1977-79, 1st v.p. 1979), Republican. Presbyterian. Club: Parkersburg Country. Address: 3617 Gramercy Rd Greensboro NC 27410

SUMMERSELL, FRANCES SHARPLEY, club woman; b. Birmingham, Ala.; d. Arthur Croft and Thomas O. (Stone) Sharpley; student U. Montevallo, Peabody Coll., Nashville; m. Charles Grayson Summersell, Nov. 10, 1934. Partner, artist, writer Asso. Educators, 1959—. Mem. D.A.R., Magna Charta Dames, U. Women's Club (pres. 1957-58), U.D.C. (state historian 1956-58, pres. Robert Emmet Rodes chpt. Tuscaloosa 1953-55), Daus. Am. Colonists (organizing regent Tuscaloosa 1956-63), English Speaking Union, Marquis Biog. Library Soc. (adv. mem.). Vice-chmn. Ft. Morgan Hist. Commn., 1959-63. Mem. Tuscaloosa County Preservation Soc. (trustee 1965-78, service award 1975), W. Ala. Art Assn., Nat. Trust Historic Preservation, Birmingham-Jefferson Hist. Soc. Clubs: Country, University (Tuscaloosa). Co-author: Alabama History Filmstrips, 1961; Viewing Alabama History Filmstrips, 1961; Florida History Filmstrips, 1963; Texas History Filmstrips, 1965-66; Ohio History Filmstrips, 1967 (Merit award Am. Assn. State and Local History 1968); California History Filmstrips, 1968; Illinois History Filmstrips, 1970. Home: 1411 Caplewood Tuscaloosa AL 35401

SUMMY, ANNE TUNIS, artist; b. Balt.; d. Archer Carlton and Ethel Cleveland (Farlow) Tunis; student Pa. Acad. Fine Arts, 1933-36, Edison Community Coll., 1975-78; further studies at Inst. Allende (Mex.), Millersville (Pa.) Coll., Franklin and Marshall Coll; m. C. Frank Summy, Jr., Jan. 21, 1939. One-woman shows include: York Mus., 1968, William Penn Mus., Harrisburg, Pa., 1970, Goethaen Gallery Art, Lancaster, Pa., 1970, Millersville State Coll., 1980, Bradley Gallery, Naples, Fla., 1982; group shows include Edison Community Coll., Ft. Myers, Fla., 1977; represented in permanent collections: William Penn Meml. Mus., Court Art Trust, Washington, Bloomsburg (Pa.) Coll., Franklin and Marshall Coll., Millersville Coll., Armstrong Cork Co., Rehoboth (Del.) Art League, Landscape Painters Pa.; pres. Art Encounter, Inc.; juried shows include: Pa. Acad. Fine Art, 1969-70, Balt. Mus. Art, 1969-74, Butler Inst. Am. Art, 1968, Soc. Four Arts, Palm Beach, Fla., 1975-78, Sarasota Arvida Show, 1979-82, Jacksonville Art Mus., 1976, Met. Mus. and Art Center, Miami, Fla., 1977. Recipient Neuman medal Nat. Soc. Painters in Casein, 1968; Lorne medal, 1969; 1st award Cape Coral Nat., 1974; 1st award Naples Art Assn., 1979; 1st award Fla. Artists Group Area VII, 1977; awards Bloomsburg Coll., 1970, Harmon Gallery Maj. Fla. Artists, 1976, 80; Hamel award Fla. Artists Group Statewide Show, 1980. Mem. Fla. Artist Group, Inc. Club: Naples Yacht. Home: 2885 Gulf Shore Blvd N Apt 501 Naples FL 33940

SUMNER, ELAINE MARY GERHARD, educator; b. Pasadena, Calif.; d. C.F. and I.M. Gerhard; B.A., Calif. State Coll. at Los Angeles, 1962, M.A., 1968; postgrad. Whittier Coll., 1969, U. Calif. at Los Angeles, 1970; children—Valerie Elaine, Richard Joseph. Sec. Calif. Inst. Tech., 1951-52; elementary tchr. Los Angeles City Schs., 1962—. Brownie leader Pasadena council Girl Scouts U.S., 1960. Mem. Assn. for Childhood Edn. (v.p. 1963), AAUW. Home: 8502 Los Olivos Dr San Gabriel CA 91775

SUMNER, MARION KAYE, social worker; b. Ocala, Fla., July 30, 1944; d. Marion Wilbert and Agnes Kaye (Johns) Mann; B.S., Fla. State U., 1966; m. Kenneth Gilbert Sumner, Feb. 16, 1971; children—Robert Matthew, Vanessa Kaye. With Fla. Health and Rehab. Services, 1966—, counselor II for adoptions, Ocala, 1978—. Baptist. Club: Ocala Jr. Woman's (corr. sec. 1979-80). Home: 4519 NE 9th St Ocala FL 32671 Office: 3001 SW Broadway Ocala FL 32670

SUN, COSSETTE TSUNG-HUNG, library dir.; b. Taipei, Taiwan, July 14, 1937; came to U.S., 1960, naturalized, 1972; d. Lin Tuang Hsieh and Chiu Chin Wu; LL.B., Nat. Taiwan U., 1960; M.A., U. Houston, 1963; M.S., Simmons Coll., 1965; m. Stanley Shang-Shian Sun, Nov. 23, 1961; children—Louise Caroline, Marina Sheree, Olivia Cossette. Asst. prof. law, asso. librarian St. Louis U., 1965-73; asso. reference librarian U. Calif., Berkeley, 1974-75; br. librarian Alameda County (Calif.) Law Library, Hayward, 1975-77, law library dir., Oakland, 1977—. W.H. Anderson scholar, 1966; Matthew Bender scholar, 1971. Mem. Am. Assn. Law Libraries (cert. law librarian), ALA, Spl. Library Assn., Asian/Pacific Librarians Assn. Editor State Ct. County Law Libraries Newsletter, 1979; chmn. Law Library Services to Instl. Residents, 1979-80; contbr. article to legal review. Office: 1225 Fallon St Oakland CA 94612

SUN, SHIRLEY HSIAO-LING, Asian culture and art specialist, writer, filmmaker; b. Shanghai, China, June 19; d. Anthony Tsang-nien and Pauline (Pao-ling) Sun; M.A. in Asian Regional Studies, Stanford U., 1969, M.A. in History of Art, 1971, Ph.D., 1974. Exec. dir. Chinese Culture Found., San Francisco, 1974-79; dep. dir. public programs Nat. Endowment Humanities, 1979-82; fellow Aspen Inst. Humanistic Studies, Washington, 1982—. Recipient Bronze Hugo award Chgo. Internat. Film Festival, 1977; Calif. Mus. Found. award, 1976; Chester Dale fellow Nat. Gallery Art, 1971-72. Mem. Center Advanced Studies in Visual Arts, Nat. Gallery Art. Author: Mine Okubo, 1972; Three Generations of Chinese-East and West, 1973; Modern Chinese Woodcuts, 1979; contbg. author: Journey into China, 1982; dir. documentary films including: Cities in China series, 1980, Chinese Americans: The Second Century, 1979, Old Treasures from New China, 1976. Office: 2010 Mass Ave Washington DC 20036

SUNDBERG, NORMA ELIZABETH JOHNSON (MRS. COLLINS Y. SUNDBERG), funeral dir.; b. Rockford, Ill.; d. Conrad Walfred and Olga (Pierson) Johnson; student Brown's Bus. Coll., 1928-30; m. Collins Y. Sundberg, June 20, 1942. Partner Sundberg Funeral Home, Rockford, 1952—. Sec.-treas. Col-Nor Corp., Rockford, 1961—. Mem. Winnebago County Women's Republican Club, 1948—, v.p., 1956, 57. Mem. Nat., Ill. funeral dirs. assns., Rockford Humane Soc. Aux. (v.p.). Lutheran. Clubs: Zonta (dir.), Rockford Woman's, Ostende, Forest Hills Country, Am. Legion Aux., Women of Moose, Daus. of Nile, Order Eastern Star, Order White Shrine of Jerusalem. Home: 5431 Einor Ave Rockford IL 61108 Office: 215 N 6th St Rockford IL 61107

SUNDBY, DIANNE YVONNE, clin. psychologist; b. Mpls., Nov. 2, 1942; d. Olaf E. and Mavis Elizabeth (Prichard) S.; B.S., U. Wis., Superior, 1964; M.S. (univ. fellow 1964-65), Purdue U., 1965, Ph.D. (NDEA fellow 1966-69), 1971; m. Michael J. Driver, May 29, 1976; children—Steven Thor, Maia Perelandra. Girls counselor Lombard (Ill.) and Westlake jr. high schs., 1965-66; asst. prof. counselor edn. Calif. State U., Los Angeles, 1969-71, dir. guidance clinic, 1970-71; psychotherapist Los Angeles Psychosocial Center, 1971-72; lectr. U. So. Calif., 1972-78; psychotherapist Inst. Humanistic Psychology, Beverly Hills, Calif., 1972-74; postdoctoral intern Northridge (Calif.) Hosp. and Mental Health Center, 1973; pvt. practice clin. psychology, Los Angeles, 1974—; dir. Career Counseling and Assessment Assos., Los Angeles, 1976—; asso. dir. career and edn. research project, career research program U. So. Calif., 1975-79, dir. fin. analyst profile study, 1977-79; cons. in field. Mem. Am. Psychol. Assn., Calif. Psychol. Assn., Los Angeles County Psychol. Assn. Author papers in field, editor handbook. Office: 9229 W Sunset Blvd Suite 502 Los Angeles CA 90069

SUNDEL, SANDRA STONE, behavior therapist, cons.; b. Chgo., Oct. 8, 1948; d. Harry Bernard and Lillian (Kantor) Stone; B.A. with distinction, U. Mich., 1970, postgrad., 1970-71; M.S.S.W., U. Louisville, 1973; m. Martin Sundel, Aug. 22, 1971; children—Adam Daniel, Jenny Rebecca. Pvt. practice psychotherapy, Louisville, 1973-77, Chevy Chase, Md., 1977-80, Arlington, Tex., 1980—; asst. dir. research and tng. Ky. Children's Home Day Treatment Center, Louisville, 1974-76; adj. instr., lectr. Kent Sch. Social Work, U. Louisville, 1974-77; instr. continuing edn. U. Tex., Arlington, 1980—. Mem. Nat. Assn. Social Workers, Acad. Cert. Social Workers, Assn. Advancement Behavior Therapy, Social Work Group Study Behavioral Methods (sec. 1977-79), Registry Health Service Providers in Social Work, NOW, Hadassah, Nat. Council Jewish Women. Co-author: Behavior Modification in the Human Services: A Systematic Introduction to Concepts and Applications, 1975, Be Assertive: A Practical Guide for Human Service Workers, 1980; Behavior Modification in the Human Services, 2d edit., 1982; author column Coping with Kids, 1978-80; co-author newspaper series, Supermom, 1980—. Address: 406 Rockgate Ct Arlington TX 76011

SUNDERMAN, MAY MURRAY, nurse; b. Niles, Ohio, Apr. 7, 1924; d. George and Euphemia (Sterling) Murray; R.N., Warren City Hosp. Sch. Nursing, 1945; B.S.P.A., St. Joseph's Coll., 1981; 1 son, Kurt Vaughn. Staff nurse Warren (Ohio) City Hosp., 1945, Fed. Machine & Welding, Warren, 1945-47; office nurse, Warren, 1947-57; pvt. duty nurse, Warren, 1957-62; head nurse Packard Electric div., GMC, Warren, 1962-75, staff nurse, biol. testing OSHA standards, 1975-79, head nurse, 1979—. Cert. occupational health nurse. Mem. NOW, Sierra Club, ACLU, Handgun Control, Inc., Equal Rights Am., Nat. Abortion Rights Action League, Am. Assn. Occupational Health Nurse, Am. Pub. Health Assn., Nat. Assn. Female Execs. Home: 3073D Ivy Hill Circle Cortland OH 44410

SUNDICK, SHERRY SMALL, author, journalist, poet; b. Washington, July 17, 1946; d. Charles Haskell and Ruth (Behrend) Small; B.A., Am. U., 1970; m. Gary Norman Sundick, Aug. 3, 1969; children—Amy Beth, Suzanne Faye. Columnist, Today Newspapers, Rockville, Md., 1973-75; tchr. guitar pvt. students Open U. of Washington, 1975—; journalist The Jour. Newspapers, Chevy Chase, Md., 1975—, The Potomac Almanac, 1976—. Recipient N.Am. Mentor Mag. Ann. Mentor Poetry award, 1973. Mem. Nat. League Am. Pen Women, Writers Center, World Poetry Soc. Jewish. Author: Celebration, 1977; (with Ruth Small) Potpourri, 1978; contbr. articles to various mags. and jours. including Md. Mag., No. Va. Mag. Design, Maine Life, others. Address: 11809 Hunting Ridge Ct Potomac MD 20854

SUNDQUIST, BARBARA LOUISE, personnel exec.; b. Grand Forks, N.D., Feb. 10, 1934; d. Elmer Ferdinand and Carolyn Johanna (Schmidt) Anderson; student Northwestern U., 1952-53; B.A. cum laude, U. Minn., 1956; m. John Lewis Sundquist, Oct. 13, 1956. Civil service technician Minn. Civil Service Dept., St. Paul, 1956-58; personnel officer Minn. Dept. Hwys., St. Paul, 1959; personnel dir. Minn. State Prison, Stillwater, 1959-67; suggestion system adminstr. Minn. Dept. Adminstrn., St. Paul, 1970-71; dir. Minn. merit system Minn. Dept. Pub. Welfare, St. Paul, 1967-77, personnel dir., 1977-79; commr. Minn. Dept. Employee Relations, St. Paul, 1979—; mem. adv. council U. Minn. Indsl. Relations Sch. Recipient cert. of appreciation Internat. Personnel Mgmt. Assn., citation of honor Office of Gov., State of Minn. Mem. Internat. Personnel Mgmt. Assn., Am. Soc. Personnel Adminstrn., Twin City Personnel Assn., Nat. Pub. Employer Labor Relations Assn., St. Paul Personnel Dirs., Indsl. Relations Exec. Council, Alpha Omicron Pi. Republican. Lutheran. Home: 579 Westwood Village II Roseville MN 55113 Office: 444 Lafayette Rd Saint Paul MN 55101

SUNLIGHT, CAROLE, psychologist; b. DuBois, Pa., Aug. 19; d. Andy and Mary Ann Gaborick; Med. Technologist, Carnegie Inst., 1959; B.A., Cleve. State U., 1971; M.A., Pepperdine U., 1973; Ph.D. in Profl. Psychology, U.S. Internat. U., 1980. Med. technologist, Cleve., 1959-67; chief technologist med. dept. U.S. Steel Corp., Lorain, Ohio, 1967-69; office mgr. dept. philosophy and religious studies Cleve. State U., 1969-70; counselor Gardena (Calif.) Valley Counseling Service, 1971-72; testing technician Norco-Corona (Calif.) Sch. Dist., 1973; dir. treatment services Unfinished Symphony Ranch Inc., Agoura, Calif., 1973-77; staff Kaiser Permanente Mental Health Center, Los Angeles, 1977—; pvt. practice clin. psychology, Torrance, Calif., 1980—; speaker in field. Bd. dirs. COMOSI Mental Health, Thousand Oaks, 1977-78. Registered med. technologist; lic. marriage, family and child counselor, Calif.; recipient pub. award Ohio soc. A.M.T., 1972. Mem. Am. Psychol. Assn., Calif. Psychol. Assn., Western Psychol. Assn., Los Angeles County Psychol. Assn. (editor newsletter 1982—), Am. Med. Technologists, Calif. Neuropsychol. Soc., Assn. for Women in Sci., Psi Chi. Home: 4772 Vangold Ave Lakewood CA 90712 Office: 765 W College St Los Angeles CA 90012 also 3250 W Lomita Blvd Suite 305 Torrance CA 90505

SUNNERGREN, MARIAN BROWN UPDEGRAFF, businesswoman, promotions specialist; b. Sewickley, Pa., Feb. 6, 1923; d. Kenneth Phillip and Emilie Elizabeth (Starr) Updegraff; A.B., Pa. Coll. for Women, 1945; m. Carl Edward Sunnergren, Jan. 14, 1947; children—Jeffrey Edward, Kenneth Peter, Amy Brown. Asst. publicity dir., fashion coordinator Jonasson's, Pitts., 1945-47; owner mgr. advt. agy., Pitts., 1947-51; editorial asst. Bethlehem (Pa.) Globe-Times, 1969-70; copy chief Ritter-Berger, Inc., Allentown, Pa., 1970-72; freelance promotions, writing, 1972-74; promotions dir. Palmer Park Hall, Easton, Pa., 1974-76; promotions dir. Lehigh Valley Mall, Allentown, 1976-77; owner, mgr. The Gentleman Framer and Art Gallery, Allentown, 1978—; freelance promotions, writing, 1978—. Chmn. promotions com. Allentown Center City Assn., 1979-80; bd. dirs., 1980—. Mem. Pa. Press Club (pres. 1975-77, v.p. 1973-75), Nat. Fedn. Press Women (budget dir. nat. conv. 1981), Pa. Press Women (treas. 1981—), Profl. Picture Framer's Assn., Allentown C. of C., Writer's Guild, Hist. Print Soc., Lehigh Valley Council for the Arts, LWV. Democrat. Episcopalian. Home: Saucon Ln RD 7 Bethlehem PA 18015 Office: The Gentleman Framer 955 Hamilton Mall Allentown PA 18101

SUNSTEIN, CAROLYN RUTH NETTER, antique dealer; b. Phila., Jan. 5, 1922; d. Morton Angelo and Dorothy G. (Goldsmith) Netter; B.S. in Edn., Temple U., Phila., 1942; m. Charles Gerstley Sunstein, Aug. 22, 1941; children—Florence Gertsley Sunstein Begun, Lynn Carol, Charles Gerstley, Jr. Antique miniature collector, 1942—; dealer, show coordinator Phila. Miniature Show, 1972—; lectr., appraiser, 1977—; adv. bd. Warmans Antique Guild, 1981. Sec., Adoption Center Del. Valley, 1982—; bd. dirs. Samuel Paley Day Care Center, 1942—, Albert Einstein Med. Center, 1975—. Mem. Pa. Antique Assn., Nat. Assn. Miniature Enthusiasts. Republican. Jewish. Office: PO Box 26734 Elkins Park PA 19117

SUPINSKI, CATHERINE JOSEPHINE CURRAN (MRS. EDMUND SUPINSKI), ret. librarian; b. N.Y.C., Aug. 27, 1915; d. Francis Joseph and Mary (Jordan) Curran; B.A., Hunter Coll., 1936; M.A., Columbia, 1937, B.S. in Library Sci., 1943; m. Edmund Supinski, June 2, 1951. Asst. librarian Nat. Indsl. Conf. Bd., N.Y.C., 1943-48; librarian N.Y. C. of C., N.Y.C., 1948-64, Dumont (N.J.) High Sch., 1964-80. Mem. Spl. Libraries Assn. (N.Y. pres. 1950-51, internat. 2d v.p. 1953-54), ALA, NEA, N.J., Bergen County, Dumont edn. assns., N.J.,

Bergen County (rec. sec. 1967-68) sch. librarians assns., N.J. Secondary Tchrs. Assn. Home: 30 Kinderkamack Rd Woodcliff Lake NJ 07675

SUPLEE, KAREN APRIL, sch. adminstr.; b. San Juan, P.R., Apr. 22, 1954; d. James Reed and Carol Janet (Cunningham) S.; B.A. magna cum laude, Lycoming Coll., 1975. Sales mgr., cert. moving cons. McCollister's Moving & Storage, United Van Lines, Burlington, N.J., 1975-77; music engraver, new product design promotion Music Press, Inc., Collingswood, N.J., 1977-78; sales rep. safety products for heavy industry Wilkie Optical Inc., Barrington, N.J., 1978-79; asso. dir. admissions, flute instr., academic advisor, residence hall tchr. George Sch., Newtown, Pa., 1979—. Flutist, Cherry Hill Wind Symphony, 1967—, pres. bd. dirs. 1978—, 1st v.p. publicity, 1976-78. Address: George Sch Newtown PA 18940

SURPITSKI, ELLEN, artist; b. Dracut, Mass., Sept. 26, 1917; d. John and Despo Cutrumbes; R.N., Lowell (Mass.) Gen. Hosp., 1944; m. Kastanty Joseph Surpitski, June 24, 1945; children—Gwen, John. Saleswoman, S.S. Krege Co., 1936-44; nurse hosps. in Mass., 1944-75; charge CCU and ICU, Cable Meml. Hosp., Ipswich, Mass., 1970-75; freelance artist, 1976—; one-woman exhbns. include: Anna Jacques Hosp., Newburyport, Mass., Harvard Community Plan, Boston, Bay Bank & Trust, Hamilton, Mass., Bay State Nat. Bank, Andover, Mass., Union Hosp., Lynn, Mass.; group exhbns. include: Guild of Beverly (Mass.) Artists, Newburyport Art Assn., Lynfield (Mass.) Art Guild, Andover Artist Guild, N. Shore Art Assn., Gloucester, Mass., Ogonquit (Maine) Art Gallery. Recipient 2d pl. award oil painting, Rockport (Mass.) Art Exhbn., 1978. Mem. Guild Beverly Artists, Newbury Art Assn., Lynfield Art Guild, Copley Soc., Andover Artists Guild, N. Shore Art Assn., Polish Legion Am. Vets. Women's Aux. Address: 7 Ortins Rd Hamilton MA 01936

SUSALLA, ANNE AGNES, biologist; b. Mich., Jan. 24, 1934; d. Lucian and Gertrude Susalla-Messing; A.B., Madonna Coll., Livonia, Mich., 1962; M.S., U. Detroit, 1967; Ph.D., Ind. U., 1972. Tchr. parochial schs., Mich., 1956-67; teaching asst. Georgetown U., 1967-68; research asst. NASA, Ind. U., 1969-70, asso. instr. botany, 1970-71; asst. prof. biology St. Mary's Coll., Notre Dame, Ind., 1972-75, asso. prof., 1975—, chmn. dept. biology, 1977-80. Mem. Ind. Acad. Sci., Bot. Soc. Am., AAAS, Ind. U. Alumni Assn., Sigma Xi, Beta Beta Beta. Home: 1515 Marigold Way Apt 506 South Bend IN 46617 Office: 212 Sci Bldg Biology Dept St Mary's Coll Notre Dame IN 46556

SUSE, RUTH E., data processor; b. Jackson, Mich., Jan. 11, 1910; d. Howard A. and Bessie (Oliver) Matthews; student MacMurray Coll., Jacksonville, Ill., 1928-29, U. Mich., 1929-33; A.B., U. So. Calif., 1942; certificate Los Angeles Sch. Lab. Tech., 1946; postgrad. Am. U.; m. Edmund T. Suse, July 20, 1935 (div. Sept. 1940); 1 dau., Barbara J. Tchr., Am. Sch., Colombia, 1933-35, schs. in Guatemala, 1939-40; geodesist U.S. Govt., 1942-44, 54-57, 58-61; clin. pathologist Pasadena (Calif.) Hosps., 1945-54; med. technologist, tchr. Am. Hosp., La Paz, Bolivia, 1957-58; math. linguistics U.S. Govt. and Gen. Elect., 1961-62; educator langs. U.S. Army Okinawa, 1962-64; tech. asst., dept. dir. biomed. div. Documentation, Inc., Bethesda, Md., 1964-66; systems analyst U.S. Army, Washington, 1966; tech. dir. edn. resources br. Nat. Naval Med. Sch., Bethesda, Md., 1967-68; computer systems analyst Naval Air Systems Div. Integrated Logistics Support Center, 1968-70; computer specialist U.S. Army Computer Systems Support and Evaluation Command, Washington, 1970-72, computer systems br. U.S. Forest Service, 1972-73, now cons. data processing mgmt.; exec. dir. Pacific Grove Art Center (Calif.), 1974-75; project coordinator Vols. Intervening for Equity of Jr. Leagues; tchr. data processing; substitute tchr. Va. Schs. Fairfax County. 1966. Bd. govs. U. Mich. Alumni Club, Alumni Devel. Council; active Girl Scouts U.S.A.; mem. adv. bd. Vol. Service Bur., Human Services Planning Council; mem. Linguistic U. Mich. Alumni Club, devel. council U. Mich.; commr. Va. Commonwealth Health Regulatory Bds., 1980—. Recipient citation for meritorious service Dept. Army; Ruth Suse award established in her honor U. Mich., 1973. Mem. Linguistic Soc. Am., Am. Documentation Inst., Am. Fedn. Information Processing, Data Processing Mgmt. Assn. (chpt. award Outstanding Service in Edn. 1978, v.p. edn. Richmond chpt. 1982—), Federally Employed Women, Soc. for Applied Learning Tech., C. of C. of Winter Park, Sigma Kappa, Phi Delta Gamma. Club: Univ. Mich. Alumni of Washington (bd. govs. 1967-73, pres. Richmond chpt. 1982). Home: 1718 Cloister Dr Richmond VA 23233

SUSSMAN, LYNDA, personnel exec.; b. Bklyn., July 7, 1938; d. Oscar and Florence Seif; student Cortland State Tchrs. Coll., 1956-57; B.A., Bklyn. Coll., 1960; m. Alvin Sussman, June 24, 1973. Personnel interviewer Met. Life Ins. Co., N.Y.C., 1961-63; personnel mgr. Macmillan, Inc., 1963-72; mgr. staffing ITT World Hdqrs., N.Y.C., 1972-77; v.p., dir. adminstrn. and personnel ITT Def. Communications Div., Nutley, N.J., 1977-82, mgr. tech. and engring. personnel ITT World Hdqrs., N.Y.C., 1982—; mem. adv. bd. The Effective Mgr. Bd. dirs. Passaic-Clifton-Garfield YMCA. Recipient Twin award YWCA, 1979, Acad. Women Achievers award YWCA of N.Y., 1980. Mem. N.Y. Personnel Mgmt. Assn. Office: ITT World Hdqrs 320 Park Ave New York NY 10022

SUSTENDAL, DIANE MARIE, fashion editor; b. New Orleans, Aug. 30, 1944; d. George and Mary (Anderson) S.; student La. State U., 1963-64; certificate John McCrady Sch. Fine Arts, 1966; Asst. art critic Times-Picayune, New Orleans, 1966-68; asst. mng. editor spl. studies div. Frederick A. Praeger, N.Y.C., 1969; fashion and beauty editor Times-Picayune Pub. Corp., New Orleans, 1970—, women's news editor, 1974-75. Bd. dirs. New Orleans Ballet, 1971-73. Recipient award La. Press Anns., 1972. Mem. Fashion Group (dir. New Orleans chpt. 1973-74), New Orleans Symphony (women's com.), New Orleans Mus. Art, La. Council Music and Performing Arts, Art Assn. New Orleans. Republican.

SUTCLIFFE, MARILYN CASE, research technician; b. New Haven, Apr. 20, 1936; d. Warren Evans and Esther Mary (Snow) Case; B.A. summa cum laude, U. Bridgeport, 1957; postgrad. Sorbonne, Paris, 1957-58, Duke U., 1958-59; m. William Manchester Sutcliffe, Dec. 27, 1958; children—Stacy Ellen, James Sheldon. Substitute tchr. Broward County, Fla., 1966-67; tchr. chemistry Nova Sr. High Sch., Ft. Lauderdale, Fla., 1967-68; research technician Dept. Infectious Diseases, VA Med. Center, Nashville, 1968—. Fulbright scholar, 1957-58; James B. Duke fellow, 1958. Mem. Am. Soc. Microbiology. Republican. Contbr. articles to profl. jours. Home: 6824 Highland Park Dr Nashville TN 37205 Office: 1310 24th Ave S Nashville TN 37203

SUTHERLAND, CAROL ANN, constrn. mgmt. exec.; b. Saskatoon, Sask., Can., June 14, 1946; came to U.S., 1962; d. Harry Hugh and Evelyn Anna S.; student pub. schs., Vancouver, B.C., Can. Sec., Internat. Securities Corp., Seattle, Newport Beach, Calif., 1967-71; design coordinator AMFAC Fin. Corp., Honolulu, 1971-73; pres. Bright Ideas, Inc., Honolulu, 1973-81. Mem. Am. Soc. Interior Designer (affiliate). Home: 2029 Nuuanu Ave Honolulu HI 96817 Office: 1415 Kalakaua Ave Suite 201 Honolulu HI 96826

SUTHERLAND, JOAN, coloratura soprano; b. Sydney, Australia, Nov. 7, 1926; d. McDonald Sutherland; student Royal Coll. Music, London, 1951; m. Richard Bonynge, 1954; 1 son. Appeared concert and oratorio performances, Australia; appeared in opera Judith, Syndey Conservatory of Music; debut Covent Garden in Magic Flute, 1952; other operatic performances include: Lucia di Lammermoor, La Traviata, La Sonnambula, Handel's Acis and Galatea, heroine roles operas by Bellini and Donizetti; Italian debut in Handel's Alcina, Teatro la Fenice, Venice, 1960; appeared in Bellini's Puritani, Glyndebourne Festival, Sussex Eng., 1960, Bellini's Beatrice di Tenda, La Scala, 1961, Rossini's Semiramide, La Scala, 1962, Meyerbeer's Les Huguenots, La Scala, 1962; N.Y. debut, Carnegie Hall, 1961; Opera debut, Lucia, 1961; opened Sutherland-Williamson Opera Co. tour, Australia, 1965, appeared Handel's Julius Caesar, Hamburg Co. tour, Australia, 1965, appeared Handel's Julius Caesar, Hamburg Opera, 1969, Bellini's Norma, Met Opera, 1970; opened Lyric Opera Chgo. with Semiramide, 1971, San Francisco Opera with Norma, 1972, San Francisco Opera with Trovatore, 1975, Met. Opera with I Puritani, 1976, Met. Opera with Esclamode, 1976, Vancouver Opera with Le Roi de Lahore, 1977; premiered new prodn. Met. Opera in Tales of Hoffmann, 1973; premiered 1st prodn. in Am. in 80 years, Esclarmonde, Massenet, San Francisco Opera, 1974. Winner Sun Aria competition; recipient Mobil Quest award, 1951; decorated comdr. and dame comdr. Order Brit. Empire, Order Australia. Address: care Colbert Artists Mgmt 111 W 57th St New York NY 10019

SUTHERLAND, LYNETTE ELIZABETH, physiologist; b. Toronto, Ont., Can., May 11, 1917; d. Charles Thompson and Laura Frances (MacDonald) Roddy; B.A. in Honour Sci., U. Toronto, 1937, M.D., 1959, Ph.D. in Physiology, 1966; m. James Sutherland, Aug. 22, 1938; children—Sara Jane, Charles, Walter, Michael, Irene Sutherland Singleton, Joseph, Robert, Ian. Intern, Toronto Gen. Hosp., 1959-60; asst. scientist Research Inst., Hosp. for Sick Children, 1960-70; practice medicine, specializing in physiology, Kirkfield, Ont., 1972—; dir. Kirkfield and Dist. Med. Centre, 1972—; mem. teaching staff dept. family and community medicine U. Toronto, 1975—. Med. Research Council Can. scholar, 1965-70. Mem. Can., Ont. med. assns., Acad. Medicine (Toronto), Assn. Women in Sci., Alpha Omega Alpha. Roman Catholic. Club: Univ. Women's (Toronto). Contbr. articles to profl. jours. Home and office: Kirkfield ON K0M 2B0 Canada

SUTHERLAND, MARY LOUISE WADDELL, communication cons., counselor; b. St. Clairsville, Ohio, Feb. 6, 1930; d. Paul V. and Grace (Robinson) Waddell; B.S., Ohio State U., 1952; M.A., Mich. State U., 1975; m. Dale E. Sutherland, Dec. 28, 1951 (dec.); children—Timothy, Paul, Patricia, Robert, Matthew, Michael. Health edn. dir. YWCA, Lansing, Mich., 1952-55, adult activities dir. N.W. br., Detroit, 1956; tchr. pre-sch., elem., secondary, adult edn. Ednl. Instns., Mich., 1957-73; free-lance writer, 1968-73; communications cons., Traverse City, Mich., 1976—; co-owner, dir. Retreat for Growth, Glen Arbor, Mich., 1981—; profl. public speaker; instr. Northwestern Mich. Coll., Traverse City. Campaign mgr. Leelanau County Probate Judge, 1974. Mem. Nat. Speakers Assn., Mich. Woman's Studies Assn., NOW (v.p. Traverse City chpt. 1979-80). Club: Glen Arbor Woman's. Home: 5685 Manitou View Blvd Glen Arbor MI 49636 Office: 230 Brooks St Traverse City MI 49684

SUTHERLAND, SUSAN CARRI, research microbiologist; b. Barre, Vt., Oct. 9, 1948; d. Hugo E. and Marie H (Abare) Carri; B.S. in Med. Tech., U. Tenn., 1972, M.S. in Microbiology, 1977; m. William James Sutherland, Aug. 1, 1969; children—Ann-Marie, Teresa Lynn. Med. technologist Sequatchie Gen. Hosp., Dunlap, Tenn., 1972-73, Moccassin Bend Psychiat. Hosp., Chattanooga, 1973-74; microbiologist Erlanger Hosp., Chattanooga, 1977; med. technologist Parkridge Hosp., Chattanooga, 1975, Chattanooga State Tech. Community Coll., 1978-81; research microbiologist U. Tenn. Coll. Medicine, Chattanooga, 1981—. Served with U.S. Army, 1966-68. Mem. Tenn. Soc. Clin. Microbiology, Am. Soc. Clin. Pathologists, Southeastern Assn. Clin. Microbiology. Roman Catholic. Club: Scuba Diving. Home: 1617 Montlake Rd Daisy TN 37317 Office: 921 E 3d St Chattanooga TN 37403

SUTTER, CAROLYN OPTHOFF, city ofcl.; b. Kalamazoo, Oct. 9, 1942; d. John Martin and Lorraine Eleanor (Kloosterman) Opthoff; B.S., Calvin Coll., 1964; M.S., Western Mich. U., 1970; M.P.A., Calif. State U., Long Beach, 1981; children—Chandra, Stephan. Dir., Library System of Southwestern Mich., 1974-76; asso. dir. Long Beach (Calif.) Public Library, 1977-79; dir. library and mus. services, Long Beach, 1979-81, dir. communications, 1981-82; now gen. mgr. Tidelands Agy., Long Beach. Chairwoman Mich. 4th Dist. Tricounty Women's Polit. Caucus, 1972-76. Mem. ALA, Public Library Execs. Assn. So. Calif., Library Info. and Tech. Assn., Am. Soc. Public Adminstrs., Urban Libraries Council, Long Beach C. of C. (dir. women's council). Office: Long Beach City Hall 333 W Ocean Blvd Long Beach CA 90802

SUTTER, ELIZABETH HENBY (MRS. RICHARD A. SUTTER), civic leader, mgmt. co. exec.; b. St. Louis, May 15, 1912; d. William Hastings and Alvina (Steinbreder) Henby; A.B., Washington U., St. Louis, 1931; m. Richard A. Sutter, June 15, 1935; children—John Richard, Jane Elizabeth, Judith Ann (Mrs. William Hinrichs). Sec.-treas. Sutter Mgmt. Co., St. Louis, Sutter Clinic, St. Louis; v.p. Downtown Med. Bldg., Inc., St. Louis. Chmn. com. on mental health AMA Aux., 1960-62, v.p., 1962-63, 64-64, pres. 1965-66, editor Direct Line newsletter, 1967-74; asso. editor MD's Wife, 1973—; mem. adv. bd. Deaconess Hosp. Sch. of Nursing, St. Louis; trustee John Burroughs Sch., 1958-61, v.p. 1959, devel. commn., 1960-61; mem. Historic Bldgs. Commn. St. Louis County, 1957—, chmn., 1973—; chmn. Com. for Preservation Children's Teeth; mem. planning bd. Health, Hosp. Health, Welfare Council Met. St. Louis, 1955-64; pres. Aux. Central States Soc. Indsl. Medicine and Surgery, 1960-61; pres. St. Louis County Med. Soc. Aux., 1948-49, Mo. Med. Soc. Aux., 1952-53; sec. St. Louis County Health and Hosp. Bd., 1956-60, chmn., 1961; bd. dirs. Am. Lung Assn. Eastern Mo., exec. com., 1956—, v.p., 1960-61; pres. Tb and Health Soc. of St. Louis, 1962-65; adv. council vol. services Nat. Assn. Mental Health, 1962-64; bd. dirs. Am. Cancer Soc., St. Louis, exec. com., 1954-64; bd. dirs. Mental Health Assn. St. Louis, 1960-61; mem. Practical Nursing Edn. Council, chmn. exec. com., 1959-60; mem. AMA Council on Mental Health Planning for Nat. Conf. on Mental Health, 1961; mem. adv. com. on women in services Dept. Def., 1969-72, vice chmn., 1971; participant 24th ann. global strategy discussion U.S. Naval War Coll., 1972; bd. govs. Washington U. Alumni, 1970-71, 75—, vice chmn. 1979-80, chmn., 1980-81; trustee Washington U., 1979-81; pres. Washington U. Arts and Scis. Century Club, 1970-71; bd. dirs. St. Louis Conv. and Tourist Bur., 1975—, sec., 1980-82; bd. dirs. Health Services Agy., 1975—; mem. East West Gateway Coordinating Council Task Force on Historic Preservation, 1975-81, University City Historic Preservation Commn., 1977. Named 1 of 10 Women of Achievement in good citizen category St. Louis Globe-Democrat, 1961; Alumna of Yr., Gamma Phi Beta, St. Louis, 1966; recipient St. Louis County Med. Soc. award of merit, 1964; Disting. Alumni citation Washington U., 1968, Disting. Alumni Service citation, 1977; Life Style award Eastern Mo. chpt. Am. Lung Assn., 1982. Mem. Mo. Hist. Soc., St. Louis Symphony Soc., AMA Aux. (hon. life), Mo. Med. Aux. (hon. life), Met. St. Louis Med. Aux. (hon. life). Presbyterian. Home: 7215 Greenway Dr Saint Louis MO 63130

SUTTINGER, MARY CATHERINE, educator, media specialist; b. Chgo., Aug. 5, 1945; d. Edward Lawrence and Juanita (LaValle) White; B.A., St. Joseph's Coll., 1967; M.A., Purdue U., 1973, M.S., 1981, postgrad. 1981—; m. Leonard W. Suttinger, Nov. 5, 1966. Juvenile cataloger Hammond (Ind.) Public Library, 1967-68; substitute tchr. public schs., Highland, Ind., 1968-71, tchr. English, 1973-79; teaching asst. Purdue U.-Calumet, Hammond, 1971-73, 79—, media specialist, 1979—. Mem. ALA, Am. Assn. Sch. Librarians, MLA. Roman Catholic. Home: 9015 Hess Dr Highland IN 46322 Office: 2233 171st St Hammond IN 46323

SUTTLES, VIRGINIA GRANT, advt. exec.; b. Urbana, Ill., June 13, 1931; d. William Henry and Lenora (Fitzsimmons) Grant; student pub. schs., Mahomet, Ill.; m. John Henry Suttles, Sept. 24, 1977; step-children—Linda Suttles, Peg Suttles Hanly, Pamela Suttles Diaz, Randall. Media estimator and Procter & Gamble budget control Tatham-Laird, Inc., Chgo., 1955-60; media planner, supr. Tracy-Locke Co., Inc., Dallas and Denver, 1961-68; media dir., account exec. Lorie-Lotito, Inc., 1968-72; v.p., media dir. Sam Lusky Assos., Inc., Denver, 1972—; lectr. sr. journalism class U. Colo., Boulder, 1975-80; condr. class in media seminars Denver Advt. Fedn., 1974, 77; Colo. State U. panelist Broadcast Day, 1978, High Sch. Inst., 1979, 80, 81, 82. Mem. Denver Advt. Fedn. (dir. 1973-75, 80-82, exec. bd., v.p. ops. 1980-81, chmn. Alfie awards com. 1980-81, advt. profl. of yr. 1981-82), Denver Advt. Golf Assn. (v.p. 1976-77, pres. 1977-78), Colo. Broadcasters Assn. Republican. Congregationalist. Club: Denver Broncos Quarterback. Home: 503 Nile St Aurora CO 80010 Office: Suite 1616 First of Denver Plaza Bldg 633 17th St Denver CO 80202

SUTTON, BEVERLY JEWELL, psychiatrist; b. Rockford, Mich., May 27, 1932; d. Beryl Dewey and Cora Belle (Potes) Jewell; M.D., U. Mich., 1957; m. H. Eldon Sutton, July 7, 1962; 2 daus. Intern, St. Joseph Mercy Hosp., Ann Arbor, Mich., 1957-58; resident Hawthorn Center, U. Mich., Ann Arbor, 1959-61, Northville (Mich.) Hosp., 1958-62; resident Austin (Tex.) State Hosp., 1962-64, chief child psychiatry, 1964—, dir. Children's Psychiat. Unit, 1966—, dir. Child Psychiatry Tng. Program, 1971—; mem. clin. staff U. Tex., Galveston, San Antonio, Houston. Recipient Commendation, State of Tex. Senate, 1971; Austin Child Guidance Center Service award, 1978. Fellow Am. Psychiat. Assn., Am. Acad. Pediatrics, Am. Acad. Child Psychiatry; mem. Am. Soc. Human Genetics, AMA, Tex. Soc. Child Psychiatry (pres. 1980), Travis County Med. Soc. Contbr. articles in field. Office: 4110 Guadalupe St Austin TX 78751

SUTTON, GERALDINE SPEARS, educator; b. Washington, Oct. 24, 1946; d. Preston and Evelyn Beatrice Spears; B.S., D.C. Tchrs. Coll., 1968; M.A., Fed. City Coll., 1976; postgrad. Pepperdine U., 1982; m. Verbe Sutton, Jr., Feb. 26, 1966; children—Vera, Veronica, Vernita, Verna. Instr., Project Win, Washington, 1968-72; instr. Calif. State U., Dominquez Hills, Carson, Calif., Banning Adult Sch., Wilmington, Calif. Dist. insp. Voter Registration, Carson, Calif.; leader Potomac dist. Campfire Girls; youth dir. Greater New Canaan Ch.; vol. Green Valley Sr. Citizens Home. Mem. Nat. Assn. Women Deans, Adminstrs. and Counselors, Calif. Women in Higher Edn., Los Angeles Task Force on Human Relations. Home: 1236 E Denwall Dr Carson CA 90746 Office: 1000 E Victoria St Carson CA 90747

SUTTON, ROSE, real estate co. exec.; b. Astoria, Queens, N.Y., May 15, 1926; d. Angelo and Domenica (Curzio) Fidelo; student pub. schs. N.Y.C.; m. Delbert Gene Sutton, Sept. 1, 1956; children—William J. Sutton, Linda R., Delbert Gene. With Tompkins Realty, Inc., Tucson, 1964-72; owner, mgr. Sutton Realty Co., Inc., Tucson, 1973; owner, pres., mgr. Red Carpet Rose Sutton & Assocs., Tucson, 1973—. Mem. Nat. Assn. Realtors Inst., Ariz. Assn. Realtors, Tucson Bd. Realtors, Tucson C. of C. Republican. Roman Catholic. Home: 3131 N Swan Rd Bldg 2 Tucson AZ 85712 Office: Red Carpet Rose Sutton & Assos 3131 N Swan Rd Bldg A1 Tucson AZ 85712

SUYDAM, EUNICE MORGAN, ins. co. exec.; b. Newark, May 16, 1906; d. Edward and Minnie Belle (Cheek) Morgan; R.N., St. Barnabas Hosp., 1926; m. Abram J. Suydam, Mar. 2, 1929; children—Abram J., Ann Suydam Klapper. Ins. agt. Franklin Mut. Ins. Co., Branchville, N.J., 1944—, dir., 1949—, chmn. bd. dirs., 1979—; co-owner Suydam Farms, Somerset, N.J., 1950—. Judge, Bd. Registry and Elections, 1st Election Dist., Franklin Twp., Somerset County, N.J., 1956—; pres. Missionary Soc., Six Mile Run Dutch Ref. Ch., Franklin Park, N.J. Republican. Home: Suydam Farms RD 3 PO Box 342 Somerset NJ 08873

SVEINSSON, LINDA RODGERS, computer scientist; b. Tuscaloosa, Ala., July 1, 1938; d. Eric and Sarah Ella (Haughton) Rodgers; B.A. in Math., Birmingham-So. Coll., 1960; M.S. in Indsl. Engring. (NSF trainee 1970-72), U. Ala., 1972; m. Hjalmar Sveinsson, May 29, 1971; children—Martha M. Reed, Stephen R.M. Moreno, III. Systems analyst U. Ala. Med. Center, Birmingham, 1967-69; systems mgr. Internat. Data Systems, New Orleans, 1969-70; computer scientist Computer Scis. Corp., Silver Spring, Md., 1973-76; computer systems specialist System Devel. Corp., McLean, Va., 1976-78; mem. tech. staff Bell Labs., Columbus, Ohio, 1978—, tech. supr., 1979—. Mem. Assn. Computing Machinery, Phi Beta Kappa, Alpha Pi Mu. Republican. Methodist. Home: 7196 Lee Rd Westerville OH 43081 Office: 6200 E Broad St Columbus OH 43213

SVETLOVA, MARINA, choreographer, ballerina, educator; b. Paris, France, May 3, 1922; d. Max and Tamara (Andreieff) Hartman; came to U.S., 1940, naturalized, 1946; student Vera Trefilova, Paris, 1930-36, L. Egorova and M. Kschessinska, Paris, 1936-39, A. Vilzak, N.Y.C., 1940-57. Debut Paris Opera, 1932; baby ballerina, original Ballet Russe de Monte Carlo, 1939-41; guest ballerina Ballet Theatre, Met. Opera tour, 1942; prima ballerina Met. Opera Co., N.Y.C.. 1943-50, N.Y.C. Opera, 1950-52; appeared Jacob's Pillow Summer Festival, 1949; own concert group under mgmt. Columbia Artists Mgmt., 1944-58, Nat. Artists Corp., 1958-69; ballet tours in U.S., 1944—, Far East, 1953, Middle East, 1954, Europe, 1955, 59, S. Am., 1962; guest ballerina London's Festival Ballet, 1953, Teatro dell Opera, Rome, 1953. Nat. Opera, Stockholm, 1955, Suomi Opera, Helsinki, Finland, 1956, Het Nederland Ballet, Holland, 1954, Cork Irish Ballet, 1955, Paris Opera Comique, 1958, London Palladium, 1959-60; appeared in Les Sylphides, 1943, Bluebeard, 1943, Balustrade, 1940, Giselle, 1953, Pas de Quatre, 1943, Swan Lake, 1941, Graduation Ball, 1940, also various classical ballets, 1939-69; choreographer Dallas Civic Opera, 1964-67, Seattle Opera, 1961-62, Houston Opera, 1965, Kansas City Performing Arts Found., 1965-67, Ft. Worth Opera, 1967—; ballet dir. So. Vt. Art Center, Manchester, 1959-65; dir. Svetlova Dance Center, Dorset, Vt., 1963—; prof. ballet Ind. U., Bloomington, 1969—. Mem. Am. Guild Mus. Artists (dir. 1943), Nat. Soc. Arts and Letters (nat. dance chmn.). Contbr. articles on theatre, choreography and ballet works to newspapers and various mags. Home: Dorset VT 05251 Office: 2100 Maxwell Ln Bloomington IN 47401 also 25 W 54th St New York NY 10019

SWAFFORD, EDNA ANN O'DELL, journalist; b. Excelsior Springs, Mo., Jan. 8, 1918; d. Willie Everett and Sarah Alice (Siegel) O'Dell; corr. student Central Bus. Coll., Kansas City, Mo., 1932-34; m. Wilfred Floyd Swafford, Nov. 7, 1941 (dec.); 1 dau., Beverly Sue Swafford Barron. Editor society page Daily Standard, Excelsior Springs, 1938-42, city editor, 1942-43, editor people page, 1962—; dep. collector City of Excelsior Springs, 1952-54; office mgr. Excelsior Springs Water Dept., 1954-62. Recipient Appreciation award Excelsior Springs Lions Club, 1977, 81; named Citizen of Yr., Excelsior Springs C. of C., 1981. Mem. Nat. Fedn. Press Women, Mo. Press Women (1st pl. news story, publicity, editorial 1970, 1st pl. women's page 1972, 1st pl. makeup page 1976, 1st pl. sports, publicity 1980), Mo. Press Assn., Nat. Fedn. Bus. and Profl. Women (Woman of Yr. award Excelsior Springs 1977, editor Mo. Bus. Woman, dir. Mo. fedn. 1978-80), Am. Legion Aux., Excelsior Springs Hist. Mus. Soc., Beta Sigma Phi (Woman of Yr. 1978).

Republican. Club: Lioness. Home: 508 Isley Blvd Excelsior Springs MO 64024 Office: 417 Thompson Ave Excelsior Springs MO 64024

SWAILS-MORAH, TANYA MARIA, univ. ofcl.; b. Cleve., Jan. 7, 1954; d. Nathaniel and Jane (Lane) Swails; B.A., Ohio State U., Columbus, 1974, M.A. in Black Lit., 1976, M.A. in Journalism, 1976; m. Emeka Ogbogu Morah, July 9, 1981. Moderator, producer talk show sta, WVKO, Columbus, 1976; communicative skills instr. Ohio State U., 1976; mng. editor Columbus Onyx News, 1975-77; asst. to news dir. sta. WTVN-TV, Columbus, 1977; news reporter sta. WBIE/WCOB, Marietta, Ga., 1977, Atlanta Daily World, 1977; newscaster sta. WCSU, Wilberforce, Ohio, 1979; staff writer Dayton (Ohio) Black Press, 1979-80; news corr. Daily Gazette, Xenia, Ohio, 1980; instr. English, Wilberforce U., 1977-78, dir. mass media communications program, also asst. prof. English, 1978-81; instr. dance Central State U., Wilberforce, 1978-81, adj. prof. English, 1981—, coordinator publs., 1981—. Mem. exec. bd. Universal Liberty in Christ Truth Kingdom, 1981—. Recipient Outstanding faculty award Wilberforce U., 1980, Disting. Service award, 1981. Mem. Nat. Council Tchrs. English, AAUP, Black Women Academicians, Delta Sigma Theta. Democrat. Home: 888 N Bickett Rd Xenia OH 45385 Office: Office Univ Relations Central State U Wilberforce OH 45384

SWAIM, ALICE MACKENZIE, poet; b. Craigdam, Scotland, June 5, 1911; came to U.S., 1928, naturalized, 1939; d. Donald Campbell and Alice Annand (Murray) Mackenzie; B.A., Wilson Coll., Chambersburg, Pa., 1932; m. William Thomas Swaim, Dec. 27, 1932; children—Elizabeth Anne, Kathleen Mackenzie. Newspaper columnist, 1953-70; poetry therapy cons., 1971—; public relations dir. 2d World Congress Poets, 1973; contest and mktg. editor N.H. Poetry Soc., 1975-82; writer Concordia Greeting Card Co., 1981-82; contest judge, 1954—; author: Let The Deep Song Rise, 1952; Up To The Stars, 1954; Sunshine in a Thimble, 1958; Crickets Are Crying Autumn, 1960; The Gentle Dragon, 1962; Pennsylvania Profile, 1966; Here on the Threshold, 1966; Scented Honeysuckle Days, 1966; Beneath a Dancing Star, 1968; Beyond My Catnip Garden, 1970; Unicorn and Thistle, 1981; And Miles to Go, 1981. Recipient Am. Heritage award, 1974, award Leonardo Da Vinci Acad., 1982; named Scottish Am. Poet Laureate, 1953; Alumna of Yr., Tain Royal Acad., 1958; Poet Laureate of the Sonnet, 1963; Poet of Yr., Ill. Poetry Soc., 1982. Mem. Poetry Soc. Am., Acad. Am. Poets, Poetry Soc. Pa., Poetry Soc. Ky., Poetry Soc. Tex., Poetry Soc. N.H., Poetry Soc. Calif., Nat. Fedn. State Poetry Socs., United Poets Laureate Internat., Studie Scambi Internat. Presbyterian. Address: 322 N 2d St Harrisburg PA 17101

SWAIN, ANNA CHAMBLEE, mktg. cons.; b. N.Y.C., Mar. 31, 1954; d. Carrie Chamblee Cutts; B.B.A. in Internat. Mktg., Bernard M. Baruch U., 1983. Sec. to pres. Bleuette, Inc., N.Y.C., 1970-73; asst. to dir. classified advt. Fairchild Publs., N.Y.C., 1974-75, asst. mgr. real estate advt., 1976-77; asst. to publs. dir. and nat. sales mgr. Lebhar-Friedman Pub., N.Y.C., 1975; asst. account exec. Gaynor & Lucas Advt., N.Y.C., 1976; research analyst, asso. client service rep. Time, Inc., N.Y.C., 1977-80; mktg. cons., N.Y.C., 1980—. Public relations liaison Black Liberation Thru Action, Colletiveness and Knowledge, 1979-80. Mem. Am. Soc. Personnel Adminstrn. (pres. Baruch U. chpt. 1980-81; Harry M. Sherman award 1981), Baruch Arts and Letters Soc. (founder), Women for Racial and Econ. Equality, Nat. Council Culture and Art, Nat. Bus. League, Internat. Arts Forum (founder), Smithsonian Instn. Office: PO Box 1142 Ansonia Station New York NY 10023

SWAIN, JOYE RAECHEL BOULTON, writer, researcher; b. Oklahoma City, Jan. 1, 1940; d. Opal Cowan Garland; student U. B.C., 1957-58, U. Nacional Autonoma, Mexico City, summer 1958, Instituto Technologico y de Estudios Superiores, Monterrey, Mex., 1958-59; B.A., Oklahoma City U., 1960; postgrad. Ecole des Interpretes, U. Geneva, 1959-61; M.A., U. Okla., 1965, postgrad., 1965-70; m. Dwight V. Swain, Feb. 12, 1969; children—Rocio, Antonia, Ronald. Asst. camp dir. Lager Asten, refugee camp, Linz-Ens, Austria, 1960; grad. asst. in French, U. Okla., 1961-64, spl. instr. French extension div., 1964-65, instr. French; dir. modern lang. Okla. Coll. Liberal Arts, 1965-68; researcher Okla. solar energy plan, 1977; lang. instr. Peace Corps, Norman, Okla., 1962-64; book reviewer, free-lance contbr. Star-Telegraph, Ft. Worth, 1971-77; free-lance writer Okla. Today, Solar Engring., Atencion, Neohelican, others, 1971—; UN accredited reporter Internat. Women's Yr. Conf., 1975; coordinator Spanish lang. program Instituto Allende, San Miguel de Allende, Mex., 1972-74; translator, editor, adminstrv. asst. Dando, S.A., mgmt. cons., San Miguel Allende, 1972-74; Title IV film coordinator Assn. Am. Indian Physicians, Norman, 1976; writer audio-visual tng. programs for U.S. Postal Service, film for Okla. Dept. Tourism and Recreation; free-lance editor, 1966—, fiction course Palmer Writers Sch., 1966-67; ct. interpreter Caddo and Grady Counties, Okla., 1980—. Mem. MLA, World Sci. Fiction Assn., Internat. Platform Assn., PEN Women Internat., AAUW. Club: Amaranth. Home: 1304 McKinley Ave Norman OK 73069

SWAIN, MADELEINE TRAUBE, exec. outplacement cons.; b. N.Y.C., Jan. 15, 1938; d. Leonard and Marjorie (Bercovici) Traube; A.S., Endicott Coll., 1956; m. Robert Louis Swain, Oct. 25, 1975; children—Lisa D. Swain, Eric Swain. Research asst., project coordinator several graphic design firms, N.Y.C., 1965-75; mng. dir. Perfect Projects, N.Y.C., 1975-78; prin., head cons. services, dir. pub. relations Eaton Swain Assos., N.Y.C., 1978—. Mem. Nat. Assn. Female Execs., Assn. Outplacement Cons. Firms (chair pub. relations com.). Home: 420 E 72d St New York NY 10021 also 1 Autumn Ridge Rd Weston CT 06880 Office: 405 Lexington Ave New York NY 10174

SWAIN, NANCY JANE COX (MRS. JAMES OBED SWAIN), former educator; b. Elwood, Ind., Dec. 19, 1901; d. Alfred Thomas and Emma (Allen) Cox; A.B. with high distinction, Ind. U., 1923, postgrad., 1928; M.A., U. Tenn., 1951, postgrad., 1953; m. James Obed Swain, June 24, 1923; children—J. Maurice, J. Robert. Teaching missionary M.E. Ch., Costa Rica, 1923-28; instr. U. Tenn., Knoxville, 1943, 45, non-resident instr. corr. Extension Div., 1959-71; tchr. Oak Ridge High Sch., 1943-67, Hollins Coll., 1967. Mem. Am. Assn. Tchrs. Spanish and Portuguese, E. Tenn. Edn. Assn., S. Atlantic Modern Lang, Assn., Phi Beta Kappa, Phi Kappa Phi, Sigma Delta Pi, Pi Delta Phi, Pi Lambda Theta. Republican. Methodist. Mem. P.E.O. Home: 414 Forest Park Blvd Knoxville TN 37919

SWANN, BLANCHE ARCENEAUX, newspaper editor; b. Lafayette, La., Feb. 22, 1904; d. Emile Galbert and Rose Lima (Mouton) Arceneaux; student U. Southwestern La., 1922-25, Peabody Tchrs. Coll., 1927; Colo. A & M Coll., 1953, La. State U., 1927-29; m. Fenwick Appleton Swann, Aug. 19, 1930 (dec.); children—June Rose, Fenwick Appleton. Tchr. various public and pvt. schs., 1925-27, 42-51; home demonstration extension agt. Avoyelles Parish, Marksville, La., 1928-30, 54-57, community devel. agt., 1958-59; with Weekly News, Marsville, 1958—, editor, 1959—. Recipient numerous awards in newspaper communication writing. Mem. La. Press Women's Assn., Library Bd. Control, C. of C., Conseil pour le Développement du Français en Louisiane. Democrat. Roman Catholic. Author: Louisiana, the Community, 1959; The House of Bread, 1964. Home: 609 S Washington St Marksville LA 71351 Office: 205 N Washington St Marksville LA 71351

SWANN, RUTH NEELY, ednl. adminstr.; d. Thomas H. and Mary (Howard) Neely; M.A., U. Mich., 1950; postgrad. Boston U., 1959-66; Ed.D., Va. Poly. Inst. and State U., 1976; m. Gadson N. Swann; 1 foster dau., Amanda L. Cason. Tchr., counselor Norfolk (Va.) City Schs., 1950-55, guidance dir., 1955-70; trainer, cons. Southeastern Tidewater Opportunity Project, 1965-70; instr. community devel. project Norfolk State U., 1959-68, asso. dir. project, 1959-68; research asso. Va. Poly. Inst. and State U., 1973-76; dir. faculty devel. Hampton Inst., 1976—; cons., trainer, counselor in field. Bd. dirs. Am. Cancer Soc., Norfolk, Va., 1969-73, Va. Council on Alcoholic and Drug Dependency, 1972-76, YWCA, Norfolk, 1974—, Peninsula Office Manpower Mgmt., Hampton, Va., 1977—, Norfolk Com. for Improvement Edn., 1977—; active Tidewater Mental Health Assn., 1954-72, treas., 1970-72; chmn. edn. com., women's div. Norfolk C. of C.; chmn. employment com. Citizen's Adv. Council of Norfolk. Ford fellow, 1975-76. Mem. Va. Vocat. Guidance Assn. (pres. 1971-73), Am. Assn. Higher Edn. (nat. coordinator women's caucus), Nat. Vocat. Guidance Assn. (sec. 1976-79, trustee 1979—, designer Nat. Career Guidance Week Poster Contest 1972), Nat. Soc. Study Edn., Am. Personnel and Guidance Assn., Va. Assn. Non-White Concerns (parliamentarian 1980-81), Profl. and Organizational Devel. Network, Phi Lambda Theta, Phi Delta Kappa. Democrat. Baptist. Clubs: Federated Women's, Ladies of Distinction, Order Eastern Star. Author tchrs.' guides; contbr. articles to profl. publs.; editor, co-author: Financial Aid for Minorities Series, 1980; editor Data, 1976—. Home: 2713 Mapleton Ave Norfolk VA 23504 Office: Faculty Devel Center Hampton Inst Hampton VA 23668

SWANSON, BARBARA EDNA, ins. co. exec.; b. Modesto, Calif., Sept. 16, 1934; d. Robert Raymond and Edna Christine (Dahlgren) Niel; student pub. schs., Modesto, Calif.; children—Randal N., Donald L., Sandra Gail. With Royal Neighbors of Am., 1975—, state supr. Calif., Denair, 1979—; owner, breeder thoroughbred horses, 1960-82; Dir. Fraternal Ins. Council, 1979-80, pres., 1982—, del. So. Calif. State Conv., 1978; chmn. Com. on Rules and Order of Bus. Nat. Fraternal Congress Am. and alternate del., Milw., 1978; 4-h Leader, 1960-70. Mem. Denair C. of C., Am. Legion. Clubs: Toastmistress, Am. Bus. Women's. Home: P O 67 3724 San Joaquin St Denair CA 95316 Office: 303 Wayside St Turlock CA 95380

SWANSON, BARBARA STEELE, psychologist; b. Pitts.; Feb. 14, 1924; d. John Floyd and Augusta Stanlietta (Jarrett) Steele; A.B., Bryn Mawr Coll., 1945; M.A., U. Pitts., 1962, postgrad., 1962—; m. Ragnar G. Swanson, May 25, 1947; children—Linda Lee, Reed Gary. Research analyst mil. intelligence div. U.S. War Dept., Washington, 1945-46; intelligence officer CIA, Washington, 1947-50; asst. to dir. Am. Inst. for Research., Pitts., 1950-51; test item writer Psychometric Techniques Assocs., Pitts., 1952-59; owner, tchr. Tot Town Nursery Sch., Pitts., 1960-61; grad. asst. U. Pitts., 1961-66; mgr. testing and tng. div. Psychol. Service of Pitts., 1969—. Mem. Mt. Lebanon Twp. Election Bd., Mt. Lebanon, Pa., 1970. Mem. LWV (chmn. membership com. 1956), Am. Soc. Tng. and Devel. (publicity chmn. Pitts. chpt. 1979, sec. 1980, pres.-elect 1981, pres. 1982, Contbr. to Chpt. award 1980, asst. to regional v.p. 1982—), Am. Psychol. Assn., Greater Pitts. Psychol. Assn. (newsletter chmn. 1973-75), Am. Mgmt. Assn., Soc. for Advancement Mgmt. (pres. Pitts. chpt. 1982—), Exec. Women's Council. Republican. Presbyterian. Club: Bryn Mawr Coll. (pres. 1958-59). Home: 89 Seneca Dr Pittsburgh PA 15228 Office: 100 5th Ave Pittsburgh PA 15222

SWANSON, BERNICE MARIAN OLSON, psychologist; b. Taft, Calif., Jan. 30, 1924; d. Albert B. and Bertha G. (Jacobsen) Olson; B.S., U. Oreg., 1951; M.Ed. (Tex. Soc. Crippled Children scholar, Midland Council Retarded Children scholar), Tex. Wesleyan U., 1956; Ph.D. (Will Rogers Service scholar), U. Okla., 1969; m. Louis M. Swanson, Dec. 23, 1943; 1 son, Gregory K. Tchr. exceptional children, Ft. Worth, 1953-55, Midland, Tex., 1955-61; prin., dir. spl. edn., Midland, 1961-66; clin. coordinator Muskogee (Okla.) Guidance Center, 1969-70; prof. psychology Northeastern State U., Tahlequah, Okla., 1970—; cons. psychologist Cherokee County Guidance Center. Mem. adv. bd. Okla. Assn. Citizens with Learning Disabilities, 1972—; bd. dirs. Muskogee Sheltered Workshop Activity Program, 1979—. Recipient Disting. Internat. award for noble achievement Epsilon Sigma Alpha, 1972. Mem. Okla. Psychol. Assn., Am. Psychol. Assn., Council Exceptional Children, Okla. Assn. Citizens with Learning Disabilities, Nat. Health Register, Delta Kappa Gamma, Phi Delta Kappa. Author: The Instructor, 1965; Ginger and The Little Lost Kitten, 1974; Understanding Exceptional Children and Youth—An Introduction to Special Education, 1979. Home: 3001 Chandler Rd Muskogee OK 74401 Office: College Ave Northeastern State University Tahlequah OK 74464

SWANSON, CLAUDIA JEAN, social worker; b. Chgo., July 8, 1944; d. Trois William and Alpine Edna S.; M.S.W., Loyola U., Chgo., 1972. Geriatric med. social worker Chgo. State Hosp., 1967-70; psychiat. social worker Loyola U. Med. Center, Maywood, Ill., 1972-74; sr. sch. social worker Chgo. Bd. Edn., 1974—; instr. socialwork fieldwork U. Ill., 1982—; cons. Ill. Assn. Sch. Social Workers, 1982—. Cons. sch. personnel, adminstrn., parents of children. Mem. Nat. Assn. Social Workers, Ill. Assn. Sch. Social Workers, Acad. Cert. Social Workers, Assn. Black Social Workers (chmn. profl. experiences com. Chgo. chpt. 1973-75). Democrat. Office: Bur Social Work Chgo Bd Edn 228 N LaSalle St Chicago IL 60601

SWANSON, DEBORAH LEE, orgn. exec.; b. Brockton, Mass., Sept. 4, 1953; d. Ralph Philip and Patricia Louise Swanson; B.A. in Bus. Adminstrn. magna cum laude, Bryant Coll., Smithfield, R.I., 1975. Gen. acct. Textron Inc., Providence, 1975-76; auditor Price Waterhouse & Co., Providence, 1976-80; asst. controller Foster Parents Plan Internat., Warwick, R.I., 1980—. Bd. dirs. Trinity Sq. Repertory Theatre, Providence, 1977—, sec., 1977-80. C.P.A. Mem. Am. Soc. Women Accts. (v.p. 1979-80), Nat. Assn. Accts. Office: 155 Plan Way Warwick RI 02886

SWANSON, FERN ROSE (MRS. WALTER E. SWANSON), former educator; b. Kalmar Twp., Minn.; d. Henry E. and Susie (Hastings) Rose; student Winona (Minn.) Normal Coll., 1918-20; B.S., St. Cloud (Minn.) State Coll., 1955, M.S., 1958; m. Walter E. Swanson, June 24, 1928. Tchr. high sch. English, Latin, Eyota, Minn., 1920-21; tchr. jr. high sch. English, Appleton, Minn., 1921-22; tchr. elementary schs., Harmony, Minn., 1922-23; tchr. high sch. English, Latin, Augusta, Wis., 1923-24, South Haven, Minn., 1924-26; tchr. elementary and high sch. dramatics, Waterville, 1926-27; tchr. elementary schs., South Haven, 1927-41, 43-51, Silver Creek, Minn., 1941-43; tchr. elementary schs., Annandale, Minn., 1951-53, prin., 1953-67; tchr. elementary reading, Belgrade, Minn., 1967-71. Organizer, South Haven council Girl Scouts U.S.A., 1927, leader, 1927-30. Mem. Minn. Elementary Sch. Prins. Assn. (charter mem. 25 Year Club), NEA, Nat. Assn. Elem. Sch. Prins., Ret. Educators Assn. Minn., Minn. Edn. Assn., Nat. Council Tchrs. English, Central Minn. Reading Council (past dir.), Internat., Minn. reading assns., DAR, Ladies of Grand Army Republic (registrar Lookout Circle, dept. pres. Minn. 1974-77, nat. pres. Betsy Ross Club 1978, nat. patriotic instr. 1981—), Minn. Hist. Soc., Rebekah, Delta Kappa Gamma (past chpt. pres.). Episcopalian. Home: 541 Fairhaven Av South Haven MN 55382 Office: South Haven MN 55382

SWANSON, HELEN WADSWORTH, mfg. co. exec.; b. Cattaraugus, N.Y., Nov. 12, 1940; d. Marc E. and Jenny F. (Wilder) Wadsworth; student Palm Beach Jr. Coll., 1978-80; B.S., Barry Coll., Miami, 1982; m. Lyle B. Swanson, Nov. 28, 1975; children by previous marriage—Jennifer M. Allsop, Melanie Allsop. Parts book draftsman Clarke Bros., Inc., Olean, N.Y., 1966-73; designer-draftsman Lab. Data Control, Rivera Beach, Fla., 1973-78, engring. records supr., 1978-81, cost analyst, 1981—. Mem. NOW. Democrat. Lutheran. Club: Zonta (corr. sec. 1981). Office: Interstate Indsl Pkwy Riviera Beach FL 33404

SWANSON, JENNIE ELIZABETH, educator; b. Atlanta, Aug. 5, 1932; d. Chester Arthur and Cleo Annie (McEachern) Williams; B.S., Northwestern U., 1954; M.S., No. Ill. U., 1972, Ed.D., 1976; m. Richard Edward Swanson, Apr. 24, 1954; children—Laurel Dee, Jeffrey Richard, Scott Edward. Public sch. tchr., 1954-69; psycho-ednl. diagnostician, 1969-72; mem. faculty Loyola U., Chgo., 1976-82, asst. prof. ob-gyn and pediatrics, 1979-82, dir. pre-start project depts. ob-gyn and pediatrics Stritch Sch. Medicine, 1978-82; dir. spl. services Community Unit Sch. Dist. 220, 1982—; mem. Gov. Ill. Com. Preventive Services, 1979-80; chmn. B-3 subcom. First Chance Consortium, 1978-80; chmn. INTERACT, 1979-80; cons. in field. Grantee HEW, 1973-76, 78-82. Mem. Council Exceptional Children, Assn. Maternal and Child Health, Nat. Perinatal Assn., Nat. Assn. Edn. Young Child, Northwestern U. Alumni Assn., Delta Delta Delta, Delta Kappa Gamma (scholar 1974). Lutheran. Author: (with others) Partners in Child Development, 1978. Office: 310 E James St Barrington IL 60010

SWANSON, MARY ELIZABETH, banker; b. Lake Como, Fla., Feb. 10, 1930; d. John Caldwell and Ethel Elizabeth (Baker) Mayfield; student St. Johns River Community Coll., Palatka, Fla., Daytona Beach (Fla.) Jr. Coll.; m. Stanley Edward Swanson, Sept. 7, 1947; children—Carolyn, Sarah, Anna, Mary K.; 1 foster dau., Chauthi Do. Mgr., Leatherleaf Fernery, Crescent City, Fla., 1969; with Flagship Bank Putnam County, Crescent City, 1970—, cashier, 1978—, v.p., 1980—; mem. Putnam County Bus. Edn. Adv. Com., 1980-82. Pres. Brevard County Democratic Women's Club, 1959-63, Grandview Garden Club, 1956. Mem. Bus. and Profl. Women's Club. Lutheran. Home: 326 S Prospect St PO Box 223 Crescent City FL 32012 Office: 1 N Summit St Crescent City FL 32012

SWANSON, PHYLLIS GERTRUDE STEWART, accountant; b. Dos Palos, Calif., Nov. 28, 1932; d. Donald Steven and Kathleen Mary (Sutcliffe) Stewart; certs. bus. mgmt. and acctg. with honors, Canada (Calif.) Jr. Coll., 1980; student Notre Dame Coll., Belmont, Calif., 1980—; divorced; children—Alicia Marie, Lorene Diane Swanson Black. Acct., Cuesta La Honda Guild, La Honda, Calif., 1970-72, Lloyd B. Mingay, P.A., Redwood City, Calif., 1973-75; propr. Phyllis Swanson Bookkeeping Service, Menlo Park, Calif., 1975—; notary public. Sec.-treas. La Honda Fire Brigade, 1967-73. Mem. Taxpreparers Assn. Am. (charter), Nat. Assn. Tax Cons., Nat. Fedn. Small Bus., Am. Mgmt. Assn., Delta Epsilon Sigma. Democrat. Roman Catholic. Office: 1178 Chestnut St Menlo Park CA 94025

SWANSON, ROCHELLE ANITA, recreation coordinator; b. Kenmare, N.D., Apr. 16, 1949; d. Arthur Reuben and Verna Waneta (Nederbo) S.; student Phoenix Coll., 1968-69; B.S. in Public Adminstrn., U. Ariz., 1971; postgrad. U. So. Calif., 1972. Recreation specialist Los Angeles County Parks and Recreation, 1974-82; program coordinator ARCO Jesse Owens Games, Los Angeles, 1982—; lectr. Calif. State U., Northridge, 1981—; cons. Fountain Valley Parks and Recreation, 1979—; coordinator, computer specialist Calif. Spl. Olympics Gymnastics, 1972—. Calif. bowling state handicapper Assn. for Retarded Citizens, 1979-82, dist. IX bowling chmn., 1978—; youth adv. com. Nat. Youth Sports Program, U. So. Calif., 1977—. Registered recreation therapist. Mem. Calif. Parks and Recreation Soc. (dist. XIII sec., therepeutic sect., awards chmn., dep. dir., ways and means chmn.), Chi Kappa Rho (scholarship chmn. Alpha chpt.). Republican. Lutheran. Clubs: Wildcat (U. Ariz.), Sons of Norway (cultural dir. Edvard Grieg Lodge), Vasa Lodge. Contbr. article in field to publ. Home: 1430 A Rock Glen Ave Glendale CA 91205

SWANSON, ROSEMARIE (MURDOCK FROST), protein crystallographer; b. Taylorville, Ill., Dec. 17, 1942; d. Keith and Dolores (Kennerly) Murdock; S.B., U. Chgo., 1965; Ph.D. (McBain fellow 1965-66), Stanford U., 1969; m. Stanley M. Swanson, Aug. 29, 1968. Research fellow Stanford U., 1969-70, Calif. Inst. Tech., Pasadena, 1970-74; research asso. Tex. A&M U., 1974—. NIH fellow, 1972-74; recipient George Gamow award in theoretical molecular biology, 1981. Mem. Sigma Xi, Phi Lambda Upsilon. Club: Circle Squares (sec.-treas. 1978). Author articles in field. Home: 3604 Cavitt St Bryan TX 77801 Office: Chemistry Dept Tex A&M U College Station TX 77843

SWANSTROM, KATHRYN RAYMOND, conv. mgmt. exec.; b. Milw., Sept. 5, 1907; d. William Hyland and Jessie Viola (Bliss) Raymond; student Bryant and Stratton Bus. Coll., 1927-28; m. Luther D. Swanstrom, Aug. 27, 1937; 1 son, William Hyland Raymond. Caterer, Racine, Wis., 1926; field rep., asst. mgr. Master Reporting Co., 1936-52; dir., sec. Diesel-Ritter Corp., 1942-46; pres. Kay C. Raymond Assos., 1952—; v.p., treas. Kenneth G. Mackenzie Assos., 1954—. Asst. sec. nat. com. U.S.A. 3d World Petroleum Congress, 1950-51. Sec. Ridge Civic Council, 1940-69, Police Traffic Safety Com., Mayor's Com. Keeping Chgo. Clean; state chmn. legislation Ill. Congress Parents and Tchrs. Rep. Ill. Central Republican party committeewoman, 1938-44; asst. ofcl. reporter Rep. Nat. Conv., 1940-48. Mem. Anti-Cruelty Soc., AIM, Soc. Mayflower Descs. (dep. gov.-gen.), DAR, Nat. geog. Soc., ASTM, Ladies Oriental Shrine N.Am. Founders, Patriots and Aux. Ancient Honorable Arty. Co. of Boston (nat. treas. 1971-77, nat. pres. 1977-80), John Alden Kindred, Colonial Dames Am., Magna Charta Dames, Internat. Platform Assn., Hugenot Soc. (1st v.p. gen. 1975-79, pres. gen. 1979—), Sons and Daus. of Pilgrims (organizing sec. gen. 1975—), Ams. of Armorial Ancestry (1st v.p.), Pi Omicron (nat. pres. 1950-54). Episcopalian. Clubs: Beverly Hills, Woman's Crescendo. Address: 9027 S Damen Ave Chicago IL 60620 also 3 Old Hill Farms Rd Westport CT 06880

SWART, HANNAH WERWATH (MRS. GEORGE J. SWART), museum curator; b. Milw., Mar. 21, 1913; d. Oscar and Hannah (Seelhorst) Werwath; student Milw. Downer Coll., part-time 1931-34, U. Wis., 1933-36, Milw. Sch. Engring., 1933-46; m. George Jerry Swart, Oct. 7, 1937; children—Greta Toni, JoHannah Werwath Nickolai, George Jerry Jr., Paul Oscar. Head dept. records, registrar coll. engring. Milw. Sch. Engring., 1931-51, mem. corp., 1952—, also cons. dept. alumni affairs; curator Hoard Hist. Mus., Fort Atkinson, Wis., 1967—. Co-chmn. heritage Wis. Bicentennial Commn.; Bd. dirs. Girl Scouts Am. Recipient Bronze Statue, Girl Scouts U.S.A., Nat. Thanks badge, 1967. Mem. State Hist. Soc. Wis. (past pres. women's aux., life mem.), Watertown (hon. life), Fort Atkinson (program chmn.) hist. socs., Wis. Acad. Scis., Wis. Council Writers, Nat. Trust Hist. Preservation. Clubs: Tuesday, Quarter Century, Woman's Club of Wis. Author: Footsteps of our Founding Fathers, 1963; Biography of General Henry Atkinson, 1964; Margarethe Meyer Schurz, 1967; Koshkonong Country: A History of Jefferson County; Koshkonong Country Revisited, 1981. Home: Rural Route 3 Box 27 Fort Atkinson WI 53538 Office: Hoard Historical Museum Merchants Ave Fort Atkinson WI 53538

SWART, JANICE LIGHTNER, mfg. co. exec.; b. Amwell Twp., Pa., Nov. 22, 1933; d. Fred B. and Edna (Sowers) Lightner; student Penn Comml. Bus. Coll., 1953-54; m. Robert E. Swart, June 15, 1956. Clk. typist Washington and Jefferson Coll., Washington, Pa., 1954-69; receptionist, sec. Bennet Real Estate, Washington, Pa., 1970-74; receptionist, sec. Washington Mould Co. (Pa.), 1974-78, purchasing agt., 1978—. Office: Greene and Madison Aves PO Box 518 Washington PA 15301

SWARTZ, CAROLINE, economist, educator; b. Salamanca, N.Y., May 17, 1952; d. Paul Stanley and Magdalene Frances (Lenda) S.; B.S., SUNY, Fredonia, 1973; M.A. in Econs., Duke U., 1975, Ph.D. in Econs., 1979. Research assoc. Inst. for Devel. Studies, U. Nairobi (Kenya), 1976-78; asst. prof. econs. Notre Dame U., 1979-80, Emory U., 1980—. Mem. So. Econs. Assn., Am. Econs. Assn., Population Assn. Am. Office: Dept Econ Emory U Atlanta GA 30322

SWARTZ, GENEVA MAE, Girl Scout exec.; b. Topeka, Jan. 24, 1927; d. Kerby Lee and Maude Nettie (Harding) Smith; B.S.L., San Jose (Calif.) Bible Coll., 1948; B.A., Valley Coll., Reseda, Calif., 1950; m. Jack C. Swartz, Feb. 14, 1959. Tchr., San Fernando (Calif.) Christian Sch., 1950-57; exec. dir. Wasatch council Girl Scouts U.S.A., Ogden, Utah, 1957-61, field adv., camp adminstr. Utah council, Salt Lake City, 1961-70, exec. dir., 1970—, trainer Girl Scouts U.S.A., 1967; ednl. adv. bd. J.C. Penney Co., 1970-77; participant corp. mgmt. seminar Harvard U., 1980. Mem. devel. com. Sr. Citizens Center, Ogden, 1958-59. tchr., choir dir. First Christian Ch., Ogden, 1960—; women's cons. Christian Chs. Utah-Idaho; mem. adv. com. Weber County (Utah) Library, 1962-65; Recipient Thanks badge Girl Scouts U.S.A., 1967. Mem. Am. Camping Assn. (pres. Utah chpt. 1960-66), Christian Women's Fellowship (pres. 1963-64, 70-71). Club: Zonta. Office: 2386 East 2760 South Salt Lake City UT 84109

SWEEN, JOYCE ANN, sociologist, psychologist; b. N.Y.C.; d. Sigfried Joseph and Julie (Hollins) Ellmer; B.S. in Math., Antioch Coll., 1960; M.S. in Exptl. Psychology, Northwestern U., 1965, Ph.D. in Social Psychology, 1971; children—Terri Lynn, James Michael. Univ. fellow Northwestern U., Evanston, Ill., 1960-63, dir. computer ops. Inst. Met. Studies, Northwestern U., 1965-70; asst. prof. sociology DePaul U., Chgo., 1971-74, asso. prof., 1974-80, prof., 1980—; cons. Nat. Commn. on Violence, 1968; cons. in field. NIH grantee, 1971-75, 78-81; NSF grantee, 1979-82. Mem. Internat. Sociol. Assn., Am. Sociol. Assn., Am. Psychol. Assn., Midwest Sociol. Soc., Sociologists for Women in Soc., AAAS, Sigma Xi. Research, publs. on fertility, African polygyny, childlessness, urbanization, social effects of assassination, evaluation methodology. Office: Dept Sociology DePaul U 2323 N Seminary Ave Chicago IL 60614

SWEENEY, R. CAROL, cons. firm exec.; b. Bklyn., d. Benjamin and Dorothy Helen (Leboe) Leinseider; B.S. cum laude, Pepperdine U., 1976, M.S., 1978; postgrad. Claremont Grad. Sch.; m. Neil Gordon Sweeney, Mar. 25, 1951; children—Steven, Jeffrey, Russell. Sch. sec. Los Angeles Unified Sch. Dist., 1966, adminstrv. asst., 1971, classified tng. officer, 1977—; owner Strategies for Success, Tng. and Cons. Firm, Chatsworth, 1977—; cons. in field; faculty U. Redlands, 1979, Pepperdine U., 1978, U. San Francisco, 1980. Mem. Commn. for Sex Equity Los Angeles City Schs. Named Nat. Ednl. Sec. of Yr., 1974; recipient resolution City Council Los Angeles; Woman of Year, Sylmar Bus. and Profl. Women, 1974. Fellow Inst. Ednl. Leadership; mem. Am. Soc. Tng. and Devel., Assn. Calif. Sch. Adminstrs., Calif. Assn. Ednl. Office Employees (pres. 1978), Nat. Assn. Female Execs., Phi Delta Kappa. Contbr. articles to profl. jours. Author: Transition: Secretary to Manager; (with Emery Stoops) Handbook for Educational Secretaries and Office Personnel. Home: 20248 Labrador St Chatsworth CA 91311 Office: 450 N Grand Ave Los Angeles CA 90012

SWEENEY-RADKE, KATHLEEN ANN, clin. social worker; b. Spring Valley, Wis., May 27, 1947; d. Leo M. and Florence E. (Blegen) Sweeney; student U. Wis., Madison, 1965-69; B.S. in Labor Econs., U. Wis., Parkside, 1974; M.S.W., U. Wis., Milw., 1980; m. Ronald E. Radke, Oct. 15, 1977. Vocat. counselor Gateway Tech. Inst., Racine, Wis., 1975-78; clin. social work cons. Milw. Psychiat. Hosp., Wauwautosa, Wis., 1980-81; psychiat. social worker Washington County Mental Health Center, West Bend, Wis., 1980—, also vol. services coordinator. Mem. planning and workshop coms. ann. Woman to Woman Conf., 1980; chmn. directory com. Woman's Resource Network, 1980. Gen. Mills Nat. scholar, 1965. Mem. Nat. Assn. Social Workers (dir. Wis. chpt.), Am. Assn. Marriage and Family Therapy, Phi Kappa Phi, Alpha Delta Mu. Author monograph. Home: 3153 S 25th St Milwaukee WI 53215 Office: Washington County Mental Health Center West Bend WI 53095

SWEET, DEE (MRS. HERBERT A. SWEET), bus. owner; b. Muskogee, Okla., June 3, 1913; d. Walter Oliver and Lola R. (Morris) McDaniel; student Butler U., 1931, 33; m. Herbert A. Sweet, Aug. 28, 1935; children—Judee Lo, Jill B. Sweet Bowles. Asst. to interior decorator L.S. Ayres & Co., Indpls., 1930-33; co-dir. Acorn Farm Camp, Carmel, Ind., 1933-77; owner Acorn Farm Antiques, Carmel, 1960—, Acorn Farm Workshops, 1972—; dir. TV programs WFBM, Indpls., 1949-54, WISH, Indpls., 1955-60; lectr. adult edn. Ind. U., Purdue U. Mem. Appraisers Assn. Am. (sr.), Antique Dealers Nat. Assn., Am. Camping Assn., Am. Women in Radio and TV, Ind. Hist. Soc., C. of C., Asso. Antique Dealers Am. Author newspaper column Ind. Soc. Auctioneers. Home: 15466 Oak Rd Carmel IN 46032

SWEET, JANET ANN, nurse; b. Terre Haute, Ind., Jan. 3, 1942; d. Wilbur Raymond and Gladys Lucille (Modesitt) Hoffman; R.N., Union Hosp. Sch. Nursing, 1963; B.S.N., Ind. State U., 1967, M.S., 1971; m. Hershel Ray Sweet, Apr. 25, 1964; children—Hershel Ray, Michelle Lynn. Staff nurse Union Hosp., Terre Haute, Ind., 1963-64, 67; clin. instr. practical nursing students Union Hosp., 1967-68; dir. nursing services Daviess County Hosp., Washington, Ind., 1971—. Pres., Northside Elem. PTA, Washington, 1972-73; den mother, instr.-trainer Boy Scouts Am., Washington, 1972-77; leader, asst. leader Girl Scouts U.S.A., 1977—; CPR instr. Daviess County, Ind., 1977—; bd. dirs. Daviess County Heart Assn., 1976—, Twin Rivers Vocat. Sch., 1977—; adv. com. Vincennes (Ind.) U. Nursing Programs, 1971—, Adult Continuing Edn. programs, 1975—. Recipient Jane award Daviess County Homemakers, 1977; 5 Yr. award Am. Heart Assn., 1981. Mem. Am. Nurses Assn., Ind. Soc. Hosp. Nursing Services Adminstrs., Am. Soc. Hosp. Nursing Services Adminstrs., Ind. Fedn. Bus. & Profl. Women (pres. 1977-79, dist. dir. 1980—). Club: Order Eastern Star. Home: 1201 Grand Ave Washington IN 47501 Office: 1314 Grand Ave Washington IN 47501

SWEET, MARTHA HERBERT, bus. equipment co. exec.; b. San Francisco, Oct. 21, 1949; d. Charles Aldrich and Elizabeth (Herbert) Sweet; student U. Calif., Davis, 1967-69; B.S. in Bus. Mgmt., Pepperdine U., 1979. Personnel supr. Calif. Canners & Growers, San Francisco, 1971-74; employee relations and compensation mgr. Xerox Corp., El Segundo, Calif., 1974—. Republican. Episcopalian. Home: 26010 Crenshaw Blvd Apt 217 Palos Verdes Peninsula CA 90274 Office: 701 S Aviation Blvd El Segundo CA 90245

SWEET, VIRGINIA KROENKE, educator; b. New Orleans, Dec. 16, 1948; d. Frederick Herman and Doris Overton (Brooks) Kroenke; student U. So. Miss., 1966; B.A., La. State U., 1969, M.S.W., 1971; m. William Ross Sweet, Aug. 15, 1970; children—Jennifer Marion, Ashley Elizabeth. Dir. family services Irene Wortham Center, Inc., Asheville, N.C., 1973-76; guest lectr. Developmental Disabilities Tng. Inst., Chapel Hill, N.C., 1976-77; social worker Mountain Youth Resources, Inc., Sylva, N.C., 1979-80; asst. prof. social work, coordinator field instrn. Western Carolina U., Cullowhee, N.C., 1980—; presenter Internat. Conf. on Pediatric Social Work; cons. Youth Services Program, Macon County, Franklin, N.C., 1980, Macon Program for Progress, Franklin, 1982—; mem. bd. Chysalis, Macon County, N.C., 1981. Com. chmn. Macon County Family Life Council, Franklin, 1979-80; mem. Macon County Youth Adv. Council, Franklin, 1979-80; com. chmn. edn. Patton United Meth. Ch., Franklin, 1980-81, com. chmn. missions, 1982; bd. dirs. Patton Community Devel. Assn., Franklin, 1981. Mem. NOW, Acad. Cert. Social Workers, Nat. Assn. Social Workers (past program chmn. western dist.), Assn. Retarded Citizens (past mem. program, funding coms. 1973—), Council Social Work Edn., La. State U. Alumni Assn. Democrat. Methodist. Home: Route 10 Box 84D Franklin NC 28734 Office: Social Work 120 McKee Cullowhee NC 28723

SWEETER, CAROLE LEA, home economist; b. Canton, S.D., Oct. 11, 1952; d. Gerhard and Esther Maxine (Johnson) S.; B.S., S.D. State U., 1974. Recreation counselor juvenile treatment center Woodfield Center, Beresford, S.D., 1975-76; extension home economist, Ipswich, S.D., 1976—. Active Ipswich Hosp. Aux., Community Concert Assn. Mem. Am. Home Econs. Assn., Nat. Assn. Extension Home Economists, S.D. Home Econs. Assn., S.D. Assn. Extension Home Economists, Dist. D and Aberdeen Area Home Economists, Chi Omega. Republican. Lutheran. Club: Ipswich Jaycettes. Home: Box 113 Oak St Ipswich SD 57451 Office: Box 345 Courthouse Ipswich SD 57451

SWEETING, LINDA MARIE, educator; b. Toronto, Ont., Can., Dec. 11, 1941; came to U.S., 1965, naturalized, 1979; d. Stanley H. and Mary (Robertson) S.; B.Sc., U. Toronto, 1964, M.A., 1965; Ph.D., UCLA, 1969. Asst. prof. chemistry Occidental Coll., Los Angeles, 1969-70; asst. prof. chemistry Towson (Md.) State U., 1970-75, prof., 1975—; guest worker NIH, 1976-77; program dir. chem. instrumentation NSF, 1981-82. Bd. dirs. Chamber Music Soc. Balt. Mem. Md. Acad. Scis. (mem. sci. council 1975—), Assn. for Women in Sci. (treas. 1977-78), Am. Chem. Soc., AAAS, Sierra Club, Wilderness Soc., Sigma Xi (sec. TSU Club 1979-81). Office: Dept Chemistry Towson State U Baltimore MD 21204

SWEETSER, MARIE-ODILE GAUNY, educator; b. Verdun, France, Dec. 28, 1925; came to U.S., 1949, naturalized, 1960; d. Eugène and Madeleine (Schwab) Gauny; Licence ès lettres, U. Nancy (France), 1944, diplôme d'études supérieures, 1945; M.A., Bryn Mawr Coll., 1950; Ph.D., U. Pa., 1956; m. Franklin Pratt Sweetser, Dec. 17, 1955; 1 dau., Caroline Gauny. Lectr., McGill U., Montreal, Que., Can., 1950-52; asst. instr. U. Pa., Phila., 1952-56; instr. Cedar Crest Coll., Allentown, Pa., 1956-57, Mills Coll., Oakland, Calif., 1957-60; instr. CCNY, City U. N.Y., 1960-63, asst. prof., 1963-68, asso. prof., 1968-69; asso. prof. U. Ill., Chgo., 1969-79, prof. French, 1979—; cons. Nat. Endowment Humanities, La. Bd. Regents Mem. MLA, Am. Assn. Tchrs. of French, Sociétédes Professeurs Français en Amérique, N.Am. Soc. for Seventeenth Century French Lit., Sociétéd'Etude du XVIIe Siècle, Association Internationale des Etudes Françaises. Author: Les Conceptions Dramatiques de Corneille d'après ses Ecrits Théoriques, 1962; La Dramaturgie de Corneille, 1977; co-editor: Papers on French Seventeenth Century Literature, 1977-78. Home: 311 Hirst Ct Lake Bluff IL 60044 Office: Dept French U Ill Chicago IL 60680

SWEGEL, DOROTHY, personnel service corp. exec.; b. Forest City, Pa., Dec. 23, 1932; d. John J. and Anna T. (Loush) Swegel; student Chestnut Hill Coll., Phila., 1950-51. Periodicals librarian Charles M. Schwab Meml. Library, Bethlehem (Pa.) Steel Co., 1952-55; with spl. sales Nat. Airlines, Miami, Fla., 1955-58; sr. supr. TWA Ambassadors Club, Kennedy Airport, Jamaica, N.Y., 1959-66; owner, pres. Cover Girl Temporary Office Personnel, Inc., and Gateway Careers, Inc., White Plains, N.Y., 1969—. Mem. White Plains Regional C. of C. (dir.), New Rochelle C. of C., Westchester County Assn. Mem. Adminstrv. Mgmt. Soc. (pres. Westchester chpt.), Sales and Mktg. Execs. of Westchester/Fairfield (dir.), Soroptimist Internat. (2d v.p. Central Westchester). Republican. Roman Catholic. Office: 235 Main St White Plains NY 10601

SWEITZER, BETTY JO, mfg. co. exec.; b. Cartersville, Ga., Nov. 19, 1932; d. James William and Mattie Modene (King) Puckett; grad. Polk Coll., 1970; m. R.J. Sweitzer, 1973, 1 dau., Cathie Marie. Reservations mgr. Marlin Beach Hotel, Ft. Lauderdale, Fla., 1955-57; bldg. mgr. Sunrise Profl. Bldg., 1957-60; v.p., gen. adminstr. Race & Race, Inc., equipment mfg. co., Winter Haven, Fla., 1966—, dir., 1970—; dir. AFFCO, Winter Haven; sec. U.S. Utilities Co., Ft. Lauderdale, Palmdale, Inc., Ft. Lauderdale, Broward Water Supply Co., Ft. Lauderdale. Served with USMCR, 1952-54. Mem. Nat. Assn. Credit Women, Nat. Secs. Assn. (chpt. sec. 1969), Fla. Irrigation Soc. (officer and dir. 1977-80, pres. 1980—). Address: PO Box 1400 Winter Haven FL 33880

SWENHOLT, BONNIE KINDIG, photog. scientist; b. Otsego, Mich., May 24, 1925; d. Charles and Selma (Basinger) Kindig; B.S., Fla. State U., 1945; M.S. in Physics, Northwestern U., 1958; m. John H. Swenholt, Apr. 9, 1962. Physics instr. Fla. State U., 1945-47; spectographic technician Kodak Research Lab., 1948-50, photog. technician color control dept., 1950-57, photog. engr., 1957-75, sr. engr., 1975-81, tech. assoc., 1981—. Mem. Optical Soc. Am., Soc. Photog. Scientists and Engrs., Internat. Soc. Color Council, Am. Contract Bridge League. Contbr. articles to profl. jours. Office: Bldg 9 Kodak Park Rochester NY 14650

SWENSON, ELIZABETH VON FISCHER, psychologist; b. Cleve., Mar. 4, 1941; d. William and Cordelia (Thacker) von Fischer; B.S., Tufts U., 1963; M.A., Case Western Reserve U., 1974, Ph.D., 1974; m. Paul F. Swenson, Aug. 26, 1961; children—Karen, Connie, Kirsten. NDEA fellow Case Western Reserve U., Cleve., 1971-74; asst. prof. dept. psychology John Carroll U., 1975-80, asso. prof., 1980—, chairperson dept. psychology, 1978—; adj. prof. Ursuline Coll.; pvt. practice forensic child psychology, Cleve. Trustee Ruffing Montessori Sch. Mem. Am. Psychol. Assn., Ohio Psychol. Assn., Cleve. Psychol. Assn., Am. Psychology Law Soc., Phi Beta Kappa. Home: 20431 Almar Dr Shaker Heights OH 44122 Office: Dept Psychology John Carroll U University Heights OH 44118

SWENSON, GAY LEAH, psychologist, educator; b. St. Paul, Jan. 21, 1936; d. Robert and Sarah Winifred (Gridley) Fisher; Diplôme Supérieure avec honneurs, Sorbonne, Paris, 1960; B.A. cum laude, U. Calif., Berkeley, 1958; M.A., San Francisco State U., 1966; Ph.D., Union Grad. Sch., 1977. Tchr., Aragon High Sch., San Mateo, Calif., 1966-73; human relations trainer/facilitator Coll. of San Mateo, 1971-73; founder Women's Center, La Jolla, Calif., 1973-77; founder, dir. Living Now Inst. of Center for Studies of the Person, La Jolla, 1977—; internat. cons. in field; lectr. in field. Mem. Belmont City Fair Housing Commn., 1965-69, San Mateo County Human Rights Commn., 1967-69; mem. Community Congress of San Diego, 1978—, San Diego County Regional Consortium on Aging, 1975—, Common Cause, 1980—. Mem. ACLU, AAUW, NOW, Nat. Assn. Female Execs., Assn. for Humanistic Psychology, Western Gerontol. Soc., Alpha Omicron Pi. Democrat. Club: Charter 100. Contbr. articles to profl. jours. Home: 1235 Olivet St La Jolla CA 92037 Office: 1125 Torrey Pines Rd La Jolla CA 92037

SWENSON, LINDA LINN, home economist; b. Eldora, Iowa, Apr. 17, 1947; d. Howard A. and Bernice Linn; B.S., Mankato State U., 1973; M.S., Iowa State U., 1980; m. Glen V. Heitritter, Aug. 10, 1977; 1 dau., Amy; 1 dau. by previous marriage, Staci Swenson. Bookkeeper, Mankato Free Press Office Supplies (Minn.), 1969-70, 71; sales staff Dayton's, Fargo, N.D., 1973; dist. mgr. Woodmen Accident & Life Ins. Co., Fargo, 1974-75; Woodbury County extension home economist, Sioux City, Iowa, 1975-82. Recipient Outstanding Educator award Iowa State U. Extension, 1981. Mem. Nat. Assn. Extension Home Economists (Iowa public relations chmn., nat. Florence Hall award, 1979, Iowa Communications award, 1981), Sioux City C. of C., Am. Home Econs. Assn., Iowa Home Econs. Assn., Iowa State U. Extension Assn., Greater Siouxland Press Club, Epsilon Sigma Phi. Lutheran. Club: Sioux City Home Ec. Home: 2602 Wilde St Sergeant Bluff IA 51054

SWENSON, RUTH ISABEL, educator; b. Buffalo, May 4, 1924; d. Henry Nicholas and Muriel (Beattie) Christman; B.S., Buffalo State Tchrs. Coll., 1945; m. William Warrenm June 29, 1946; children—Melinda Marie, Claudia Elizabeth. Tchr., 1945-47; adult edn. tchr., 1954-63; tchr. kindergarten Smallwood Dr. Sch., Snyder, N.Y., 1972—. Chmn. UNICEF, 1957. Mem. Alpha Sigma Alpha. Clubs: College, PTO. Home: 102 Foxcroft Ln Buffalo NY 14221 Office: 300 Smallwood Dr Snyder NY 14226

SWENSON, STEPHANIE SUE, agr. mktg. specialist; b. Pomona, Calif., Aug. 1, 1955; d. William Wheeler and F. Sue (Perkins) S.; B.S., Calif. State U., Fresno, 1976; postgrad. Calif. State U., Sacramento, 1980—. Grain mcht. Cargill, Inc., Kern County, Calif., 1976-79, field mgr., Colusa, Glenn and Tehema Counties, Calif., 1979-81; field rep. Valley Grain Mktg., Inc., Colusa, Calif., 1981—; cons. to agrl. industry. Mem. Nat. Assn. Female Execs., Calif. Women for Agr. (pres., co-founder Colusa chpt.), Am. Agri-Women, East Bay Agrl. Roundtable, Dale Carnegie Alumni. Research on children's lit. relating to agr. Home and Office: 1208 Second St Colusa CA 95932

SWENSSON, ELSIE LOUISE, state legislator; b. Braintree, Mass., Aug. 20, 1922; d. Joseph Schofield and Lillian Margaret (Berry) Drinkwater; student public schs., Braintree, Mass.; m. Joseph Leggett Swensson, June 1, 1951; children—Elaine Flynn, Joseph Leggett; 1 stepson, Kurt J. Sec. J. L. Swensson, Inc., Manchester Conn., 1973—; now mem. Conn. Ho. of Reps. Republican. Methodist. Club: Manchester Country.

SWERDA, PATRICIA FINE, artist, author, educator; b. Ft. Worth, Aug. 10; d. William Emerson and Margaret Ellen (Cull) Fine; B.S. cum laude, Tex. Woman's U., 1941; student Ikenobo U., Tokyo, 1965-66, Ikenobo Dojo, Kyoto, Japan, 1976, 77; m. John Swerda, July 7, 1941; children—John Patrick James, Susan Ann Mary Swerda Foss, Margaret Rose Swerda Yovino. Pres., Ikenobo Ikebana Soc., Seattle, 1960—; exhibited ikebana in one-person shows including: Bon Marche, Tacoma, 1966, Seattle, 1967, Gallery Kokoro, Seattle, 1972-78; exhibited in group shows including: Takashimaya Dept. Store, 1965, Matsuzakaya Dept. Store, Tokyo, 1966, Ikenobo Center, Kyoto, 1966, Seattle Art Mus., 1974-82, Sangyo Kaikan, Kyoto, 1976, Ikenobo Center, Kyoto, 1977; demonstrations in field for various groups. Master of Ikebana of Ikenobo Ikebana Soc. Mem. Ikenobo Ikebana Soc. (pres. Seattle-NW Sakura chpt. 1965—), Ikebana Internat., Bonsai Clubs Internat., Puget Sound Bonsai Assn., Japan-Am. Soc., Seattle-Kobe Affiliation, Seattle Rose Soc., Seattle Chrysanthemum Soc., Bellevue-Yao Sister-City Affiliation, AAUW, Good Shepherd Movement. Democrat. Roman Catholic. Author: Japanese Flower Arranging: Practical and Aesthetic Bases of Ikebana, 1969; Creating Japanese Shoka, 1979; contbr. articles to mags. in field. Home and Office: 23025 NE 8th St Redmond WA 98052

SWERGOLD, MARCELLE MIRIAM, sculptor; b. Antwerp, Belgium, Sept. 6, 1927; came to U.S., 1939, naturalized, 1947; d. Gillel and Sarah (Matuzewitz) Elfenbein; student N.Y.U., Art Students League, Sculptors Workshop; m. Maurice Swergold, June 12, 1949; children—Diane Botnick, Henry, Gary, Paul Kogan, George Kogan. Sculptor, 1965—; one-woman exhbns. include Studio 12, N.Y.C., 1980, 82; group exhbns. include Farleigh Dickinson U., Teaneck, N.J., 1972, Audubon Artist Ann., N.Y.C., 1978—, Internat. Treasury Fine Arts, Plainview, N.Y., 1979, New Britain (Conn.) Mus., 1980, also Cork Gallery, Lincoln Center, N.Y.C., Allied Artists Nat. Acad. Galleries, N.Y.C., U.S. Custom House, N.Y.C., others; represented in permanent collection New Britain Mus. Am. Art. Recipient Best in Show award for Tetons, Women's Art Gallery, N.Y.C., 1977. Mem. N.Y. Soc. Women Artists (pres. 1979-81, exec. v.p. 1981—), Artists Equity, Contemporary Artists Guild. Jewish. Home: 450 West End Ave New York NY 10024 Studio: 246 W 80th St New York NY 10024

SWETHARANYAM, LALITHA, educator; b. Trivanduum, India; naturalized U.S. citizen, 1980; d. Ramanathan and Subhadra (Sesha Iyer) Parameswaran; M.A. and M.Sc., U. Madras, India, 1955; Ph.D., Annamalai U., 1966; m. Sundaram Swetharanyam, Aug. 23, 1971. Lectr., head dept. math. L.V.D. Coll., Raichur, India, 1957-61; lectr. dept. math. Annamalai U., India, 1965-69; assoc. prof. dept. math. McNeese State U., Lake Charles, La., 1969-73, prof., 1973—. Govt. of India research scholar, 1961-64; Univ. Grants Commn. research fellow, 1964-66. Mem. Math. Assn. Am., Am. Math. Soc., Indian Math. Soc., Assn. for Women in Math., Pi Mu Epsilon. Club: India Assn. Lake Charles. Contbr. articles to profl. jours. Home: 525 E Jefferson St Lake Charles LA 70605 Office: 137 F McNeese State U Lake Charles LA 70609

SWIBOLD, BARBARA JEANNE, retail exec.; b. Pekin, Ill., Dec. 30, 1935; d. Joseph Francis and Dorothy Rosemond (Oltman) Doubet; student pub. schs. Pekin; m. Jack Star Swibold, Oct. 2, 1955; children—Gregory, Garry. Sec., Caterpillar Tractor Co., East Peoria, Ill., 1953-59; sec., state desk editor Pekin Daily Times, 1962-63; sec. law firm Clevenger, Smith & Bunch, Pekin, 1963; sec. Office Tazewell County States Atty., Pekin, 1963-64; sec., ct. reporter Tazewell County Zoning Bd. Appeals, Pekin, 1964-72; owner, operator Barbara's Uniforms Shop, Pekin, 1972-77, Karmelkorn Shoppe, Pekin, 1977—; exec. dir. Miller Sr. Citizen Center, Pekin. Bd. mem. Tazewell County Assn. for the Handicapped, Tazewell County Disaster Agy.; mem. adv. council Ill. Assn. for Sr. Citizens Dirs. Piano accompanist, tchr. Sunday Sch., fin. sec., chmn. meml. com., chmn. Stewardship and Fin. Com., 1st Christian Ch., Pekin; charter mem., pres., sec. Pekin Safeguard Against Crime Com.; mem. City Planning Com. Mem. Pekin Women's Civic Fedn., Pekin Mall Mchts. Assn. (dir.), Pekin Downtown Businessmen's Assn., ARC (bd. mem. CIC chap.), Pekin Public Library (v.p. Friends of Library com.) Pekin Women's Bowling Assn. (pres.), Nat. Women Bowling Writers, Beta Sigma Phi (treas., pres.). Club: Altrusa (pres. Pekin). Home: 2606 Willow St Pekin IL 61554

SWICK, LUCILLE, performing artist; b. Athens, Ala., Aug. 31, 1930; d. James H. and Agnes E. (Neely) Sims; student Orlando (Fla.) Jr. Coll., 1949-50, Orlando Sch. Modelling, 1951; m. Thomas Swick, Mar. 22, 1958 (dec. Jan. 1976); children—Nanette M., Carol Anne. Singer, guitarist Radio Sta. WORZ, Orlando, 1956-58, WLOF, Orlando, 1955-56, WDBO, Orlando, 1950-54; mem. N.J. Council on the Arts, 1977-81; mem. adv. bd. Public TV Sta. WNET/13, 1979—; pres. Warren County Summer Festival Assn., 1978—; bd. dirs. Pa. Stage Co., 1982—, State Theatre Easton, Pa., 1981—. Mem. Phillipsburg (N.J.) Town Council, 1977—. Recipient numerous awards for country and western music performances. Mem. So. Quartets Assn., Models Guild Phila., AFTRA. Home: 651 Elder Ave Phillipsburg NJ 08865

SWIFT, DOLORES MONICA MARCINKEVICH (MRS. MORDEN LEIB SWIFT), pub. relations exec.; b. Hazleton, Pa., Apr. 3, 1936; d. Adam Martin and Anna Frances (Lizbinski) Marcinkevich; student McCann Coll., 1954-56; m. Morden Leib Swift, Dec. 18, 1966. Pub. relations coordinator Internat. Council Shopping Centers, N.Y.C., 1957-59, Wendell P. Colton Advt. Agy., N.Y.C., 1959-61, Sydney S.

Baron Pub. Relations Corp., N.Y.C., 1961-65, Robert S. Taplinger Pub. Relations, N.Y.C., 1965-66; prin. Dolores M. Swift, Pub. Relations, Chgo., 1966—. Bd. dirs. Welfare Pub. Relations Forum, 1971-79, treas., 1975-77; mem. pub. relations adv. com. Mid-Am. chpt. ARC, 1973—; mem. women's com. Mark Twain Meml., 1968-69; pub. relations dir. N.J. Symphony, Bergen County, 1969-70, mem. pub. relations/promotion com.; mem. Wadsworth Atheneum, 1968-69; bd. dirs. Youth Guidance, 1972-75; mem. NCCJ Labor, Mgmt. and Pub. Interest Conf., 1977-79; mem. pub. relations com. United Way/Crusade of Mercy, 1979—. Mem. Pub. Relations Soc. Am. (accredited, chmn. subcom. Nat. Center for Vol. Action 1971-72, pub. service com. Chgo. chpt. 1971-72, dir. 1975-81, chmn. counselors sect. 1976-78, assembly del. 1976, 79-81, sec. 1977-78, v.p. 1978-79, pres.-elect 1979-80, pres. 1980-81, host chpt. chmn. nat. conf. 1981), Clubs: Women's (publs. chmn. Englewood, N.J., 1970-71); Publicity (chmn. pub. info. com. 1975-76) (Chgo.) Mem. editorial bd. Pub. Relations Jour., 1978. Address: 525 Hawthorne Pl Chicago IL 60657

SWIFT, ELIZABETH ROSS THOMPSON, bus. exec.; b. Washington, Oct. 16, 1916; d. John William and Elizabeth Noyes (Hempstone) Thompson; certificate Kelsey-Jenney Bus. Sch., San Diego, 1937; m. Garfield Christian Swift, Sept. 16, 1939; children—Theodore Noyes, Justin Ransom II, Garfield Christian, William Byrne III. Sec. to drama critic Washington Star, 1938-40; asst. to Eastern advt. mgr. Charm Mag., 1941-43; owner Request Records, 1943-46; picture researcher, photog. br., internat. press and publs. div. State Dept., Washington, 1950-51; communications and records supr. Mut. Security Agy., Hague, Holland, 1952-54, Army-Navy-Air Force Register, Washington, 1955-58; service club dir. Soesterberg Air Base, Huis Ter Heide, Holland, 1958-61; adminstrv. asst. Cath. Coll. Admissions and Information Center, Washington, 1964-66; co-dir., pres. Edu-Data Service Center, Washington, 1966-75; real estate investment and remodeling, 1975-77; owner/mgr. The Greystone, country inn, 1977—. Recipient Letter of Commendation for outstanding service USAF, 1960. Republican. Episcopalian. Home: Highfield House Highfield MD 21753

SWIFT, EVANGELINE WILSON, lawyer; b. San Antonio, May 2, 1939; d. Raymond E. and Josephine (Woods) Wilson; student So. Methodist U., 1956-59, UCLA, 1959; LL.B., St. Mary's U., 1963; 1 son, Justin Lee. Admitted to Tex. bar, 1963, U.S. Ct. Appeals bar, 1972, U.S. Supreme Ct. bar, 1980; atty., advisor ICC, 1964-65; staff atty. headstart program OEO, 1965; exec. legal asst. to chmn. and spl. asst. to vice chmn. EEOC, 1965-71, chief decisions div., 1971-75, asst. gen. csl., 1975-76; cons. to sec. Employment Standards Adminstrn., Dept. Labor, Washington, 1977-79; ptnr. firm Swift & Swift, P.C., Washington, 1976-79; gen. csl. Merit Systems Protection Bd., Washington, 1979—; guest lectr. Drake U., U. Pa., M.I.T.; mem. U.S. del. 23d Session of UN Econ. and Social Council Commn. Status of Women, Geneva, 1970. Recipient Fed. Govt. Meritorious Service award, 1967; Fed. Women's award, 1975; Performance award Merit Systems Protection Bd., 1981. Methodist. Office: 1120 Vermont Ave NW Washington DC 20419

SWIFT, MARY GRACE, historian, educator; b. Bartlesville, Okla., Aug. 3, 1927; d. Frank William and Helen (Moran) S.; B.S., Creighton U., Omaha, 1956; M.A., 1960; Ph.D. (NDEA fellow 1962), U. Notre Dame, 1967. Elem., then secondary sch. tchr., 1950-62; mem. faculty Loyola U., New Orleans, 1966—, prof. history, 1981—. Recipient De la Torre Bueno award Wesleyan U. Press-Dance Perspectives Found., 1973; NDEA fellow, summers 1968, 69; grantee Loyola U., summers 1967, 70, 77, 80; grantee Nat. Endowment Humanities, 1979. Roman Catholic. Author: The Art of the Dance in the USSR, 1968; A Loftier Flight: The Life and Accomplishments of Charles-Louis Didelot, Balletmaster, 1974; With Bright Wings, 1976; Belles and Beaux on Their Toes, 1980; also articles. Address: Box 192 Loyola U New Orleans LA 70118

SWIGERT, ALICE HARROWER (MRS. JAMES MACK SWIGERT), civic worker; b. Montrose, Pa., Dec. 18, 1908; d. Lewis Titcomb and Margaret (Ayars) Harrower; student U. Tenn., 1927-29; m. James Mack Swigert, July 7, 1931; children—Oliver, David Ladd, Sally Harper (Mrs. Swigert Hamilton). Sec. to profs. Harvard Law Sch., Cambridge, Mass., 1932-35; pub. relations U. Chgo. Press, 1935-36. Mus. panoramas chmn. Cin. Symphony Orch. Women's Com., 1963-65; founder, treas. Citizens Crusade, 1967-77; vol. Children's Convalescent Hosp., 1969-75; founder, corr. sec. New Life for Girls, Inc., Cin., 1971-75, trustee, 1971-82, hon. trustee and adv. 1982—. mem. adv. council Ohio Presbyn. Home, 1973-75; trustee emeritus Cin. Speech and Hearing Center; trustee, scholarship chmn. 3 Arts Scholarship Fund, 1972-75; Mem. DAR, Mensa, Chi Omega. Republican. Presbyterian. Clubs: Cincinnati Womans, Cincinnati Country, Queen City, Town. Home: 196 Green Hills Rd Cincinnati OH 45208

SWINK, RHONDA LYNN, data processing cons., software co. exec.; b. Ft. Dodge, Iowa, Mar. 15, 1954; d. Robert Leo and Donna Jean (Nordstrom) S.; student Calif. State U., Fresno, 1972-73, Rio Hondo Community Coll., 1973-77; cert. in programming Basic Four Corp., 1975. With Nev. Meats Inc., Las Vegas, 1973; computer operator, collections Monfort Food Distbg. Co., Long Beach, Calif., 1973-75; computer operator, programmer accounts receivable Rod's Food Products, Inc., Los Angeles, 1975-77; data processing mgr., statistician Wilcour Food Products, Inc., Los Angeles, 1977-80; systems analyst Monogram Aerospace Fasteners, City of Commerce, Calif., 1980; pres. owner Basic 4 Software and Ops. Cons., Hacienda Heights, Calif., 1980—; lectr. to fgn. students. Mem. Data Processing Mgmt. Assn., Nat. Assn. Female Execs., Am. Entrepreneurs Assn., Library Computer and Info. Scis., Am. Mgmt. Assn., Western Basic Four Users Group, Am. Assn. Aviculture, Am. Lovebird Soc., Am. Cockatiel Soc. Republican. Roman Catholic. Club: Orange County Bird Breeders. Office: 17044 E Colima Rd 169 Hacienda Heights CA 91745

SWIT, LORETTA, actress; b. N.J., Nov. 4; student Am. Acad. Dramatic Arts, Gene Frankel Repertoire Theatre, N.Y.C. Stage appearances include: Any Wednesday, The Odd Couple, Mame, The Apple Tree, Same Time Next Year; films include: Stand Up and Be Counted, 1972, Freebie and the Bean, 1974, Race with the Devil, 1975, S.O.B., 1980; star TV series MASH, 1972—; TV movies: Shirts/Skin, Hostage Heart, Coffeeville, Superman, The Loveboat Movie, Mirror, Mirror, Valentine, The Walls Came Tumbling Down, The Love Tapes, TV series: Gunsmoke, Mannix, Hawaii Five-O, Mission Impossible, The Doctors, Cade's County, Love, American Style, Bonanza; star on maj. dramatic shows and musical variety shows, including Cagney and Lacey, The Kid From Nowhere, The Muppet Show, Bob Hope Christmas Spl. Mem. AFTRA, Screen Actors Guild, Actors Equity. Office: care Internat Creative Mgmt 8899 Beverly Blvd Los Angeles CA 90048 *

SWITTEN, MARGARET LOUISE, educator; b. Chgo.; B.Mus., Westminster Choir Coll., 1947; B.A., Barnard Coll., 1948; M.A., Bryn Mawr Coll., 1949, Ph.D., 1952; m. Henry N. Switten (dec.). Asst. prof. music and French, assoc. prof., then prof. French, Hampton (Va.) Inst., 1952-63; mem. faculty Mt. Holyoke Coll., South Hadley, Mass., 1963—, Alumnae Found. prof. French, 1975—, chmn. dept., 1969-76, 82-83. Mary Andersen fellow, 1951-52; Fulbright fellow, 1956-57; Am. Council Learned Socs. fellow, 1969-70. Mem. MLA, Am. Assn. Tchrs. French, Medieval Acad., Modern Humanities Research Assn. Author book on Raimon de Miraval, articles on Diderot, medieval music and poetry. Address: 16 N Sycamore Knolls South Hadley MA 01075

SWITZER, ELAINE ALICE, social worker; b. Chgo.; d. Edgar Julius and Blanche Bertha (Schoenlank) S.; B.S., Northwestern U., 1936; M.S.W., U. Ill., 1954. Asso. dir. Hull House, Chgo., 1943-52; asso. div. dir. Welfare Council Metro. Chgo., 1954-63; asso. prof. field work U. Chgo., 1963-79; supr. profl. program devel. Council for Jewish Elderly, Evanston, Ill., 1979—; cons. in field. Mem. Nat. Assn. Social Workers, Council Social Work Edn. Contbr. articles to profl. jours. Office: 1015 Howard St Evanston IL 60202

SWITZER, GWENDOLYN JOHAN, nurse; b. Ada, Okla., Oct. 24, 1935; d. Claud B. and May Alice (Bratcher) Smith; student Bethany Peniel Coll., 1953-54; B.S., E. Central State Coll., 1957; R.N., St. Anthony's Hosp. Sch. Nursing, 1962; 1 dau., Janet Dianne. Office nurse Dr. C.B. Dawson, Oklahoma City, 1962-63; pvt. duty nurse St. Anthony Hosp., Oklahoma City, 1963-64; staff nurse Valley View Hosp., Ada, 1964-66, house supr., 1966-68; dir. nursing Holdenville (Okla.) Gen. Hosp., 1968-69, coronary care nurse, 1969-76, unit dir. med. floor, 1976-78, dir. pediatrics, 1978-79, house supr., 1979—; cons. nurse Stonegate Nursing Home, Stonewall, Okla., 1974-77. Leader Camp Fire Girls, 1970-76, counselor, 1971-72; ch. choir dir. Ch. of the Nazarene, 1968, children's dir., 1974-77; first aide instr. ARC, 1966-68, disaster-nurse, 1964—. Recipient ARC Nursing Student award, 1962. Mem. Nat. League for Nursing, Am. Assn. Critical Care Nurses, Okla. Nurses Assn. Democrat. Ch. of the Nazarene. Home: 2629 E 14th St Ada OK 74820 Office: 1300 E 6th St Ada OK 74820

SWOPE, SUZANNE, univ. adminstr.; b. Lakewood, Ohio, Nov. 7, 1941; d. Armstead Miller and Diana (Waits) Swope; B.S., Ohio State U., 1963, M.A., 1964; Ed.D., Boston U., 1974; m. Carlyle D. Eckstein, May 21, 1977; 1 dau., Diana Caryl Eckstein. Pub. sch. speech/hearing therapist Groton (Conn.) Public Schs., 1964-65, Burlington (Mass.) Public Schs., 1965-67; instr. Emerson Coll., Boston, 1967-70, asst. prof., 1970-73, asso. prof., 1973-79, prof., 1979-80, asst. to pres., 1980, asso. dean, 1980—, v.p. adminstrn., 1982—; lang. cons. Behavioral Devel. Center, 1978-81; cons. Zenker Assos., 1973-79. VA rehab. trainee/fellow, 1964-65; Am. Council on Edn. fellow, 1981—. Mem. AAUP (v.p. 1972-73, 78-79), Mass. Speech and Hearing Assn., Am. Speech and Hearing Assn., Internat. Assn. Logopedics and Phoniatrics, Pi Lambda Theta, Sigma Alpha Eta. Conglist. Contbr. articles to profl. jours. Home: 55 Fiske Rd Wellesley MA 02181 Office: 100 Beacon St Boston MA 02116

SWYDAN, ANNE, mfg. co. mgr.; b. Worcester, Mass.; d. Shokri K. and Hafeeza Swydan; student New Eng. Sch. Acctg., 1939, Clark U., evenings, 1939-50. With Norton Internat. Inc., Worcester, 1948—, asst. mgr. advt. and sales promotion, 1965-71, mgr. advt. and sales promotion, 1972—. Club: Soroptimists (v.p.). Home: 61 Hillcroft Ave Worcester MA 01606

SYDOR, DARIA DOROTHY, accountant, flower shop exec.; b. Germany, May 22, 1946; came to U.S., 1949, naturalized, 1956; d. Michael and Maria (Stadnyk) S.; student Spencerian Bus. Coll., 1965-68, No. Mich. U., 1970-72, Milw. Area Tech. Coll.; children—Angela Marie, Chad Michael. Acct., Diocensan Office of Edn., Marquette, Mich., 1971-78; service rep. Kramer Machinery, Marquette, 1978-79; acct. Rexnord, Milw., 1979-82; owner, operator Sadie's Flower Shop, Milw., 1982—. Lic. real estate broker, Wis. Mem. Beta Sigma Phi. Ukrainian Catholic. Clubs: Ukrainian Dance Group, Ukrainian Lang. Home: 3811 S 94th St Milwaukee WI 53228 Office: 4800 W Mitchell St Milwaukee WI 53214

SYER, DIANE SUE, clin. psychologist; b. Hamilton, Ont., Can., Apr. 15, 1945; d. Charles Luke and Doris Evelyn Mullenax; B.A., U. B.C., 1966, M.A., 1969; Ph.D., York U., 1973. Mem. staff Crisis Intervention Unit, Dept. Psychiatry, Toronto (Ont., Can.) E. Gen. Hosp., 1972-74, dir., 1974—; supr. clin. internships and lectr. abnormal psychology York U., Toronto, 1974—; dir. Council on Suicide Prevention, chmn., 1976-77, chmn. sub-com. on police tng.; supr. clin. internships Ont. Bd. Examiners in Psychology. Registered psychologist, Ont., Can. Mem. Am. Assn. of Suicidology, Internat. Assn. Suicide Prevention, Am. Psychol. Assn., Ont. Psychol. Assn. Contbr. articles in field to profl. jours. Club: 21 McGill Street (Toronto). Office: Crisis Unit 825 Coxwell Ave Toronto ON M4C 3E8 Canada

SYKES, MAYME JEAN PHARIS, ednl. adminstr.; b. Pineville, La., Feb. 21, 1928; d. Henry Garland and Ethel Fern (Mandeville) Pharis; B.A., La. Coll., 1949; M.Ed., U. Houston, 1954; m. Stephen McKenzie Sykes, Dec. 21, 1950; children—Stephen McKenzie, Sandra Jean. Tchr. all levels and home econs. schs. La. and Tex., 1949-73; prin. Jefferson Elem. Sch., Temple, Tex., 1973—; cons. Edn. Service Center. Pres., Opti-Mrs.; mem. City Commn. on Safety; supt. children's Sunday Sch. Meth. Ch. Mem. NEA, Tex. State Tchrs. Assn., Assn. Supervision and Curriculum Devel., Nat. Assn. Elem. Prins., Prins. Research Assn., Tex. Elem. Prins. Assn. (dist. pres.), Phi Delta Kappa, Delta Kappa Gamma, Alpha Delta Kappa. Clubs: Order Eastern Star, PEO. Home: 3305 Buckeye Temple TX 76502 Office: 400 W Walker Temple TX 76502

SYLVANDER, CAROLYN WEDIN, educator; b. Frederic, Wis., Oct. 2, 1939; d. Reuben Peter and Ruth Elizabeth (Hane) Wedin; B.A., Gustavus Adolphus Coll., 1961; M.A., U. Kans., 1964; Ph.D., U. Wis., Madison, 1976; m. Stefan Sylvander, Aug. 26, 1961; children—Monika, Mario, Brendan. Instr., Shaw U., Raleigh, N.C., 1964-66; instr. humanities Project Upward Bound, Greensboro, N.C., 1966-69; instr. English, U. Wis., Whitewater, 1966-68, asst. prof., 1968-77, asso. prof., 1977-80, prof., 1980—; bd. dirs. Alternative Directions, Inc. Woodrow Wilson fellow, 1961-63, 75-76. Mem. Phi Beta Kappa, Phi Kappa Phi. Democrat. Lutheran. Author: James Baldwin, 1980, Jessie Redmon Fauset, 1981; contbr. articles in field. Home: Rural Route 2 E La Keshore Dr Whitewater WI 53190 Office: Heide 434 U Wis Whitewater WI 53190

SYLVESTER, IRENE LEHMAN, aircraft co. exec.; b. Mexico City, Mexico, Jan. 24, 1946; came to U.S., 1954, naturalized, 1966; d. Paul Ernest and Esta Shirley (Vanderhoef) Lehman; B.S., Northrop U., 1972, M.S., 1975; m. Richard R. Sylvester, Apr. 17, 1976; children—Bonnie Ann, Vicky Ellis, Juliesta Elaine. Test engr. space div. Rockwell Internat., Downey, Calif., 1972-75; project engr. Hughes Helicopters, Summa Corp., Culver City, Calif., 1975-77; sr. engr. propulsion systems Northrop Corp., Century City, Calif., 1977—. Mem. Christian Ch. Home: 10860 Arizona Ave Culver City CA 90230

SYLVESTER, MABEL ELTON, real estate broker; b. Sherborn, Mass., Oct. 17, 1900; d. David Judson and Lena (Elton) Stark; student U. Mass., 1925-26, Bates Coll., 1926-27, U. Pitts., 1975; m. Lionel N. Sylvester, Dec. 8, 1917; children—Laura, Ward (dec.). Editor, Onsted News and Grand Ledge Ind. (Mich.), 1934-44; dist. mgr. House of Stuart, So. Mich., 1945-50; dir. mus. comedies, 1950-53; dir. advt. sales Woman's Cook Book, 1969-70; real estate broker Sylvester Realty Co., Lansing, Mich., 1948—. Dir. Centennial, Cambridge Twp., 1936; head Men's Orgn., Onsted, 1934-43; expert witness Circuit Ct. mem. U.S. Senate from Mich., 1979-82. Mem. Liberty Lobby Bd. Policy. Republican. Clubs: Rep. Senatorial, Odd Fellows. Author: Red Leaves, 1927; Scenic Irish Hills, 1937. Home: 110 W Maple Lansing MI 48906 Office: Sylvester Realty Co 110 W Maple Lansing MI 48906

SYMONDS, GENEVIEVE ELLEN, leather goods bus. exec.; b. Wilson Boro, Pa., Mar. 1, 1931; d. Jacob Rush and Ellen Maria (Brackmann) Twining; student Mercer County Coll., 1974, 76; m. Howard Eugene Symonds, May 21, 1950; children—Jess Howard, Bryce Dale. Acct., Miller's Chrysler Plymouth, Glen Gardner, N.J., 1950-55; officer mgr. Centrum Constrn. Corp., Clinton, N.J., 1969-76; owner, mgr. S & S Bus. Services, Clinton, 1976-81, Gen's Shop for Pappagallo, Clinton, 1982—; corp. sec. Nat. Sporting Frat. Ltd. Pres., Lebanon Twp. (N.J.) Vol. Fire Co. Aux., 1960-64, treas., 1964-68; pres. Lebanon Twp. PTA, 1965-69; committeeperson Hunterdon County Republican Party, 1968—, vice chmn., 1974-77; state committeeperson Rep. Party N.J., 1977-81; mem. com. George Washington council Boy Scouts Am., 1974-78. Recipient Service award PTA, 1969, Spl. Service award Boy Scouts Am., 1974. Methodist. Clubs: Hunterdon County Women's Rep. (pres. 1970-74, treas. 1978-82), African Safari of N.Y. Weekly columnist Star newspaper, Washington, N.J., 1964-68; monthly columnist What's In The Pot, Today In Hunterdon Mag., 1977-80. Home: Mountain Top Rd RD #1 Glen Gardner NJ 08826 Office: #1 Main St Clinton NJ 08809

SYMONS, JOYCE, state legislator; b. Detroit, Sept. 10, 1927; ed. Detroit pub. schs.; m. 1945; children—Jill, Gary, Mark. Mem. Mich. Ho. of Reps., 1964. Mem. 16th Congl. Dist. Democratic Orgn., Mich. Dem. Central Com., Allen Park Dem. Club, Lincoln Park Dem. Club, Mich. Kidney Found. Mem. Nat. Order Women Legislators (historian), Women of Moose. Presbyterian. Office: Michigan House of Representatives State Capitol Bldg Lansing MI 48909 *

SYPERT, NANCY SUSAN, nurse; b. Chgo., July 30, 1948; d. Oscar Jimenez and Mary Jane (Wahl) Rojo; B.S.N., U. Wash., 1970, M.Nursing, 1974; m. George Walter Sypert, Dec. 10, 1971; children—Kirsten Diane, Shannon Ruth. Staff nurse Univ. Hosp., U. Wash., Seattle, 1970-74; instr. Coll. Nursing, U. Fla., Gainesville, 1975-78, asst. prof., 1978-80, adj. asst. prof., 1980—; dir. surg. nursing Shands Hosp., Gainesville, 1980—, mem. search com. for Shands Hosp. Vice-pres. for Nursing, 1979. Mem. Speakers Bur., Mental Health Assn. Alachua County, 1979—; bd. dirs. N. Central Fla. Kidney Found., 1978—. Named Tchr. of Yr., U. Fla. Coll. Nursing, 1978-79. Mem. Am. Nurses Assn., Am. Assn. Nephrology Nurses and Technicians (nat. chmn. learning insts. 1979-80, nat. chmn. ednl. programming 1980-81), Am. Assn. Critical Care Nurses, Nat. League for Nursing, Aux. of Congress of Neurol. Surgeons, Sigma Theta Tau. Contbr. articles to profl. jours., chpts. to books. Home: 3729 SW 65 Ln Gainesville FL 32608 Office: PO Box J335 JHMHC Univ of Fla Gainesville FL 32610

SYTEK, DONNA PAGE, state legislator; b. Haverhill, Mass., Dec. 14, 1944; d. Louis Donald and Mary Frances Page; A.B., Regis Coll., Weston, Mass., 1966; m. John J. Sytek, Jr., Feb. 4, 1967; 1 dau., Mary Caroline. Blood bank technician Hale Hosp., Haverhill, 1966-67; chief technician blood bank Peter Bent Brigham Hosp., Boston, 1967; blood bank technician Portsmouth (N.H.) Hosp., 1967-70; med. technician Pentucket Med. Assos., Haverhill, 1974-82; mem. N.H. Ho. of Reps. from Rock Dist. 5, 1977—. Mem. Citizens Adv. Bd. Community Devel., Salem, N.H., 1976-77; mem. Salem Republican Town Com., 1975—; v.p. Salem Rep. Women's Club, 1976—; chmn. N.H. Rep. State Com., 1982—. Mem. Salem Bus. and Profl. Women's Club (past pres.). Roman Catholic.

SYWAK, ZOFIA, archivist, coll. ofcl.; b. Mosciska, Poland, Mar. 26, 1941; d. Wasyl I. and Aniela (Lyszczek) S.; came to U.S., 1949, naturalized, 1955; B.A., Albertus Magnus Coll., 1964; M.A., St. John's U., 1966, Ph.D., 1975. Research asso. Yale Med. Sch., New Haven, 1962-64; tchr. Bklyn. Diocese, 1964-66; mgr. N.Y. Telephone Co., N.Y.C., 1966-68; lectr. Poznan U. (Poland), 1969; free-lance translator, interpreter, Warsaw, Poland, 1968-70; free lance translator, researcher, New Haven, 1970-74; archivist New Haven Colony Hist. Soc., 1975-78; archivist James A. Kelly Inst. Local Hist. Studies, St. Francis Coll., Bklyn., 1978-79; dir., archivist R.I. Hist. Records Survey, Office of Gov., Providence, 1979-81; registrar records Kean Coll. N.J., 1982—; mem. R.I. Pub. Records Commn. Trustee, mem. exec. com. Ukrainian Mus., N.Y.C. Mem. Am. Assn. Advancement Slavic Studies, Am. Hist. Assn., Jozef Pilsudski Inst. Am., Polish Inst. Arts and Scis. Am., Soc. Am. Archivists, New Eng. Archivists Soc., New Eng. Slavic Assn., Ukrainian Nat. Women's League Am. Co-author: Poles in America: Bicentennial Views, 1978; Am. editor: Paderewski, 1980; contbr. articles to profl. jours. Home: 888 Westfield Ave Apt 5C Elizabeth NJ 07208

SZAPA, DORIS CAROLINE, social worker; b. Stephenson, Mich., Oct. 3, 1920; d. Henry J. and Jennie M. (Doucette) DeMille; ed. Badger-Green Bay Bus. Coll., Bay de Noc Community Coll.; m. Edward J. Szapa, Nov. 26, 1938; children—Gary, Scott, Bruce. Sec., DeMille Trucking, Stephenson, 1937-38; hearing and vision technician Delta-Menominee Dist. Health Dept., Escanaba, Mich., 1961-69; outreach social worker Menominee-Delta-Schoolcraft Community Action, Escanaba, 1969-75, outreach supr., 1975-79, community services dir., 1979—. Bd. dirs., steering com. Mich. Coalition Food and Nutrition; mem. Menominee County Easter Seal Soc. Mem. Upper Peninsula Central Area Rep. Assn. (sec. 1971-73), Upper Peninsula Central Assn. Para-Profls. (pres. 1973-74), Mich. Assn. Social Workers. Democrat. Roman Catholic. Clubs: Lake Twp. Civic, Longrie Home Extension. Home: Box 2 Star Route Stephenson MI 49887 Office: 507 1st Ave N Escanaba MI 49829

SZEKELY, DEBORAH SHAINMAN, health and beauty resort exec.; b. Bklyn., May 3, 1922; d. Harry and Rebecca (Seidman) Shainman; student pub. schs., Calif.; Litt.D. (hon.), Calif. Sch. Profl. Psychology, 1978; children—Livia, Alex. Founder, Rancho La Puerta, Tecate, Baja, California, Mexico, 1940—; founder pres. Golden Door, Escondido, Calif., 1958—; chmn. bd. govs. San Diego Stadium Authority, 1975-78; mem. President's Council Phys. Fitness and Sports, 1975-78. Bd. dirs. Old Globe Theatre, San Diego, Travelers Aid Soc., Boy Scouts Am., San Diego Council; mem. exec. com. Combined Arts and Edn. Council; chmn. bd. overseers U. Calif., San Diego, 1977, 78; mem. adv. bd. U. San Diego Sch. Bus. Adminstrn.; bd. trustees San Diego Center for Children. Mem. Cancer Research Found. Univ. Calif., Menninger Found. (trustee, mem. exec. com.), Calif. Sch. Profl. Psychology (trustee), Calif. Press Women, Com. of 200. Author: Secrets of the Golden Door, 1977. Office: 3085 Reynard Way San Diego CA 92103

SZEKELY-SHELLEY, MARIA MAGDALENA, chem. engr.; b. Timisoara, Romania, Apr. 21, 1931; came to U.S., 1974; d. Sigmund and Maria (Konnerth) Kohn; M.S. in Chem. Engring., Kazan (USSR) Inst. Chem. Tech., 1955; m. John Szekely, Sept. 2, 1954; 1 son, Attila. Project engr., Iprochim Central Project Inst. Chem. Industry, Bucharest, Romania, 1955-62, project mgr., 1962-74; project mgr. E.R. Squibb Co., Princeton, N.J., 1975-81; plant engr. Hoffmann La Roche, Belvidere, N.J., 1981—. Recipient Romanian Govt. decoration for starting of Romanian synthetic fiber plant, 1962. Mem. Am. Inst. Chem. Engrs. Home: 288 Fieldboro Dr Lawrenceville NJ 08648 Office: Belvidere NJ 07823

SZEWCZYK, JACQUELYNN RAE, nurse; b. Libertyville, Ill., Mar. 3, 1952; d. Earl F. and Ann L. (Klee) Levandowski; student Coll. of Lake County, 1970-71; m. Julian J. Szewczyk, July 13, 1974; 1 son, Joseph M. Nurses aide Lake County Nursing Home, 1968-69; nurses aide, student nurse Pavillian Nursing Home, Waukegan, Ill., 1970; lic. practical nurse Parkview Nursing Home, Zion, Ill., 1971-74, Lillian Kerr Nursing Home, Phelps, Wis., 1982—. Cert. of completion Rehab. Workshop for Lic. Practical Nurses Ill., 1973. Roman Catholic. Home: 8984 County

Hwy H Eagle River WI 54521 Office: Lillian Kerr Nursing Home Phelps WI 54554

SZOLD, RUTH, modeling agy., cosmetic co. and sch. exec.; b. Bronx, N.Y., Oct. 14, 1929; d. Albert and Margaret (Karl) Nussbacher; student Hunter Coll., N.Y.C., 1947; m. Martin Szold, Apr. 10, 1949 (div. Sept. 1978); children—Lauren, Terry. Exec. legal sec. to sr. partner firm Paul, Weiss, Rifkind, Wharton & Garrison, N.Y.C., 1958-62; asst. to pres. M.E. Green & Co., brokerage co., N.Y.C., 1962-65; demonstrator and cons. for various cosmetic cos., 1965—; founder, pres. Ruth Szold Promotional Models, N.Y.C., 1968—, Cosmetic Art, Inc., cosmetic and theatrical workshops, N.Y.C., 1979—; founder, pres., designer, promoter cosmetic line Cosmetic Art, 1979—; demonstrator-lectr. for TV, also video tapes; condr. cosmetic workshops for N.Y. Salute to Fashion Industries, 1981; cons. in field. Mem. council Girl Scouts U.S.A., 1964-69; bd. dirs. Bleecker Tower Tenants Corp., N.Y.C., 1979-80, chmn. architecture and design com., 1979—, chmn. maintenance, 1980—, pres., 1981-82; lectr., mem. panel Am. Women's Econ. Devel. Corp., 1981. Recipient Gold medal Deborah Fund Raising Dinner, 1955. Mem. Foragers of Am., Nat. Retail Mchts. Assn. Clubs: Brandeis U., Hadassah. Home and Office: 644 Broadway New York NY 10012

TABACHUK, EMELIA, banker; b. Passaic, N.J., Aug. 3, 1926; d. Michael and Fannie (Stefanyk) T.; student N.Y. Inst. Credit, 1978-80. With Marine Midland Bank, N.Y.C., 1946—, adminstrv. asst., 1975-76, ops. asst., 1976-78, comml. banking officer, 1978-82, asst. v.p., 1982—. Mem. Nat. Assn. Bank Women, Nat. Assn. Female Execs. Home: 78 Stadtmauer Dr Clifton NJ 07013 Office: 140 Broadway New York NY 10015

TABER, CAROL ANDERSON, pub. co. exec.; b. Paterson, N.J., Mar. 29, 1945; d. Walter F. and Eleanor L. Anderson; A.A., Green Mountain Coll., 1965. Sales mgr. Media Networks, Inc., N.Y.C., 1970-75; N.Y. advt. sales mgr. Ladies Home Jour. mag., N.Y.C., 1975-79; asso. pub., advt. dir. Working Woman Mag., N.Y.C., 1979—. Mem. Acad. Women Achievers, Advt. Women N.Y. Office: 1180 Ave of Americas New York NY 10036

TABER, LINDA PERRIN, public relations exec.; b. Marshalltown, Iowa, Dec. 30, 1941; d. Burr H. and Luella M. (Memler) Perrin; B.A., U. Iowa, 1964; M.A., Syracuse U., 1969. Women's editor Cedar Rapids (Iowa) Gazette, 1964-67; writer Inst. Life Ins., N.Y.C., 1969-70; account supr., v.p. Carol Moberg Communications, N.Y.C., 1970-78; dir., sr. v.p. Ketchum Public Relations, N.Y.C., 1978—. Mem. Public Relations Soc. Am., Fashion Group, Nat. Home Fashions League, Women in Communications, Nat. Acad. TV Arts and Scis. Home: 160 West End Ave New York NY 10023 Office: 1133 Ave of Americas New York NY 10036

TABER, NAOMA PEARL, ret. banker; b. Kirksville, Mo., July 17, 1920; d. Thomas Edwin and Ruby Melvina (Holderby) Dodson; student Marycrest Coll.; m. Rudolph Wright Taber, May 4, 1974; children by previous marriage—Ruby Jo Ponce Gustofson, Monica Ponce; stepsons—Rudolph, Ronald, Thomas, Theodore, Eric, Jeffrey Taber. Founder, mgr. United Realty & Investment Co., Davenport, Iowa, 1955-60; co-founder United Home Builders, Inc., Davenport, 1957-65; with 1st Fed. Savs. & Loan Assn. Davenport, 1966—, corp. officer, 1967—, v.p., 1975—. Bd. dirs. Mental Health Assn., 1968-71. Mem. Davenport C. of C. (dir. womens div.), Davenport Bd. Realtors, Iowa Real Estate assn., Nat. Assn. Home Builders, Soc. Residential Appraisers, Iowa Savs. and Loan League, U.S. Savs. and Loan League. Episcopalian. Home: Bettendorf IA

TABLAZON, MARILOU TAN, mech. engr.; b. Iloilo City, P.I., July 23, 1951; came to U.S., 1974, naturalized, 1979; d. Juanito T. and Amparo T. (Tan) T.; B.S. in Arch., U. San Agustin, Iloilo City, 1973; B.S.M.E., Villanova U., 1979. Draftsperson, Westinghouse Elec. Corp., Essington, Pa., 1974-76; designer QYX div. Exxon Enterprises, Lionville, Pa., 1976-80; sr. mech. engr. Boeing Comml. Airplane Co., Seattle, 1980—. Mem. ASME, Nat. Assn. Female Execs. Home: 1111 N Montgomery Ave Bremerton WA 98310

TABNER, MARY FRANCES, educator; b. Rochester, N.Y., Dec. 11, 1918; d. William Herman and Mary Frances (Willenbacher) Arndt; B.A., State U. N.Y., Albany, 1940, M.A., 1959; postgrad. U. Rochester, 1944, 45, Northwestern U. (John Hay fellow), 1963-64, U. Manchester (Eng.), 1971-72; m. James Gordon Tabner, June 27, 1942; 1 dau., Barbara Jean. Tchr. history pub. schs., Mattituck, N.Y., 1940-43, Gorham, N.Y., 1943-46; tchr. pub. schs., Waterford, N.Y., 1949-55; tchr. social studies Shaker High Sch., Latham, N.Y., 1959—, now also dir. Russian studies seminar; tchr. ch. history Our Lady of Assumption Ch., Latham. N.Y. State Regents independent study grantee, 1966. Mem. Nat. Council Social Studies, N.Y. State Tchrs., Assn. Advancement Slavic Studies, State U. N.Y., Albany Alumni Assn., History and Art Council Albany, Am., N.Y., Capital Dist. councils for social studies. Republican. Roman Catholic. Author bibliographies on Russian history, Am. studies. Home: 557 Columbia St Extension Cohoes NY 12047 Office: Shaker High Sch Latham NY 12110

TABOR, DORIS DEE, educator; b. Maryville, Mo., Sept. 17, 1918; d. Mark R. and Golda M. (Roache) Hiles; B.S. in Edn., N.W. Mo. State Coll., 1939; M.S., U. Nebr., Omaha, 1958; Ed.D., U. Nebr., Lincoln, 1967; m. John S. Tabor, June 28, 1942 (dec.); children—Teresa Ann Tabor Griffith, Patricia Annette Tabor Vallat. Tchr., Omaha Public Schs., 1955-57; prof. U. Nebr., Omaha, 1957-67, U. No. Iowa, summer 1967; prof. Calif. State U., Long Beach, 1967—, UCLA Extension, 1968, Pepperdine U. Extension, Los Angeles, 1968; cons. Calif. State Dept. Edn., 1968—, Calif. Commn. for Tchr. Preparation and Licensing, Redondo Beach (Calif.) Public Schs. Life mem. Nebr. Congress Parents and Tchrs. Mem. Internat. Orgn. Tchr. Educators in Reading (pres.), Calif. Assn. Profs. Elem. Edn. (pres.), Calif. Profs. Reading (pres.), Mid Cities Reading Council (pres.), Orange County Reading Assn. (dir.), Kappa Delta Pi (nat. v.p. 1975-78, honor key 1974), Phi Kappa Phi, Phi Delta Kappa, Pi Lambda Theta, Sigma Sigma Sigma (nat. parliamentarian 1952-60, Emily Gates outstanding alumnae achievement award 1970). Presbyterian. Club: Zonta of Long Beach (pres. 1971-73). Author: The Teaching of Reading, transparencies with script, 1971; contbr.: An Annotated Bibliography: Selected Books on American Indians for Children and Young Adults, 1978. Home: 6000 Stearns St Long Beach CA 90815 Office: 1250 Bellflower Blvd Long Beach CA 90840

TACKITT, HARRIET MARTIN, journalist; b. Franklin, Ind., May 1, 1909; d. Harry Jackson and Estelle C. (Clark) Martin; A.B., DePauw U., Greencastle, Ind., 1931; m. W. Barton Cartmel, Aug. 5, 1947 (dec.); m. 2d, Sylvan W. Tackitt, May 13, 1972. News and feature writer Reporter-Times, and predecessor, Martinsville, Ind., 1931-72; corr. Indpls. News, 1946-70; dir., corp. sec. Reporter-Times, 1971—. Pres., Martinsville Public Library Bd., 1968-69; bd. dirs. Morgan County Cancer Soc., 1971-72; trustee, mem. bd. First United Methodist Ch., Martinsville. Mem. Nat. Fedn. Press Women, Nat. League Am. Pen Women (sec.-treas. Ind. chpt. 1976-78, sec. 1982), Women in Communications, Woman's Press Club Ind. (pres. 1944-46), Kappa Kappa Kappa (Ind. treas. 1939-41), Kappa Alpha Theta. Republican. Home: 1307 E 2d St Bloomington IN 47401

TADLOCK, BARBARA ELAINE, nurse; b. Dallas, Feb. 9, 1954; d. Henry Harold and Jimmie Lyndell (Hood) T.; A.A., Richland Jr. Coll., 1975; B.S., Tex. Woman's U., 1977. Student asst. Richard Jr. Coll., 1972-75; student nurse Meml. Hosp., Garland, Tex., 1976; staff nurse neurosurg. ICU, Parkland Hosp., Dallas, 1977—, mem. staff nurse council, 1979-81. Mem. Am. Assn. Nuerosurg. Nursing. Baptist. Home: 734 McLemore Dr Garland TX 75040 Office: 5201 Harry Hines Dallas TX 75225

TADLOCK, GISELA DARDON, educator; b. Guatemala City, Guatemala, June 18, 1936; d. Agusto Dardon Betancourt-Ayau and Alicia Padilla Acuna; came to U.S., 1954, naturalized, 1968; B.A., San Francisco Coll. Women, 1968; Ph.D., U. Ariz., 1976; children—Charles, Hazel, Gisele. Tchr., Marl Twain Jr. High Sch., Modesto, Calif., 1968-69; teaching asso. U. Ariz., 1969-72, U. Calif., Santa Cruz, spring 1973; asst. prof. Spanish, Calif. State Coll., Stanislaus, 1973-77, asso. prof., 1977—. Nat. Endowment Humanities fellow, summer 1979. Mem. AAUW, United Profs. Calif., Calif. Tchrs. Assn., Sigma Delta Pi (1st prize essay 1972, 1st prize short story 1973, v.p. West 1977-80), Pi Delta Phi. Author articles, short stories. Address: Calif State Coll Stanislaus 800 Monta Vista Rd Turlock CA 95380

TAEGE, MARLYS SCHMIDT, nursing home exec.; b. Milbank, S.D., Mar. 21, 1928; d. Daniel Arthur and Lulu Irene (Hoy) Schmidt; Ph.B., Marquette U., 1950; m. Jack F. Taege, Sept. 6, 1952 (dec. 1973); children—Linda Jean, Lauren, James. Journalism tchr. Barron (Wis.) High Sch., 1950-51; women's news editor Badger Luth. newspaper, 1951-53, Milw., editor newspaper, 1971-74; spl. features writer Waukesha (Wis.) Daily Freeman, 1957-59, home sect. editor, 1968-71; mem. editorial staff Luth. Women's Quar., St. Louis, 1963-66, editor-in-chief, 1966-77; public relations dir. Bethesda Luth. Home, Watertown, Wis., 1974-81, devel. dir., 1981—. Mem. Bd. Communication Services, Luth. Ch.-Mo. Synod, 1981—; pres. Kettle Moraine Ednl. Found., 1977-78, bd. dirs., 1972-78; charter mem. Hawks Inn Hist. Soc., 1960—, Honor award, 1969; v.p. Friends of Delafield Public Library, 1980-82. Recipient Gold Quill award Internat. Assn. Bus. Communicators, 1980. Mem. Women in Communications (Clarion award 1980), Public Relations Soc. Am., Assn. Luth. Devel. Execs., Delta Zeta. Republican. Clubs: Milw. Press, Concordia Coll. Century (pres. 1981-82). Author: And God Gave Women Talents, 1978, Why Are They So Happy, 1979. Contbr. articles to religious mags. Home: N5W29116 Venture Hill Rd Waukesha WI 53186 Office: Bethesda Luth Home 700 Hoffmann Dr Watertown WI 53094

TAFF, JULIA EDITH, med. technologist; b. Ft. Bragg, N.C., Apr. 16, 1927; d. John Baskerville and Elmer Lucille (Myers) Joyner; B.S., U. Tulsa, 1971; M.A., Central Mich. U., Mt. Pleasant, 1977; m. Francis Malcolm Taff, Aug. 18, 1946; children—David Malcolm, Sheila Marie, Randall Martin. Med. technologist microbiology St. John Med. Center, Tulsa, 1961-73, program dir. Sch. Med. Tech., 1973—; adv. bd. Tulsa Jr. Coll.; cons., lectr. in field. Named Med. Technologist of Yr. in Okla., 1978. Mem. Am. Soc. Microbiologists, Am. Soc. Med. Technologists, Am. Soc. Clin. Pathologists, Okla. Soc. Med. Tech. Educators (scholarship 1980), Alpha Sigma Alpha. Democrat. Methodist. Office: 1923 S Utica St Tulsa OK 74104

TAFFE, BETTY JO, state legislator; b. West Chester, Pa., Nov. 18, 1942; d. Albert Joseph and Elizabeth Adelaide (Ottey) Miller; B.A. summa cum laude, Juniata Coll., Huntingdon, Pa., 1964; M.A. in Teaching, U. Chgo., 1968; m. William John Taffe, Dec. 27, 1965; children—Daniel David, Michael Andrew. Tchr. German, Barrington (Ill.) High Sch., 1965-66; substitute tchr. Dunbar Vocat. High Sch., Chgo., 1966-67; co-head resident Foss Hall, Colby Coll., Waterville, Maine, 1969-71; mem. Rumney (N.H.) Sch. Bd., 1974-83, chmn., 1976-81, 82-83; mem. Grafton County (N.H.) Exec. Com., 1977—, clk., 1979—; mem. N.H. Ho. of Reps., 1977—, vice chmn. edn. com., 1979—. Bd. dirs. Lakes Region Mental Health Center, Laconia, N.H., 1979-81, Sceva Speare Hosp., Plymouth, N.H., 1980—. Mem. Nat. Order Women Legislators, N.H. Sch. Bd. Assn. (exec. council 1981-83). Republican. Office: Ho of Reps State House Concord NH 03301

TAGALA, ISABEL MARTINEZ, lawyer, ins. co. exec.; b. Philippines, Oct. 12, 1930; naturalized, 1964; d. Gaspar P. and Vicenta (Martinez) T.; LL.B., Far Eastern U., 1956; postgrad. Law Sch., U. Calif., Berkeley, 1958; children—Wenceslao T. Vinzons, Gavino T. Vinzons, Alexander T. Vinzons. Admitted to Philippine bar, 1957; aide Hawaii Legislature, Honolulu, 1966-67; law clk. Hawaii Atty. Gen. Office, Honolulu, 1967-69; mem. exec. sales staff Mfrs. Life Ins. Co., Honolulu, 1969—. Vice pres. Honolulu Commn. on Status of Women, 1975; v.p. Honolulu Mayor's Com. on Community Relations, 1982. C.L.U. Mem. Fil-Am. Assn. (pres.), Waikiki Bus. and Profl. Women (v.p. 1978), Philippine Bar Assn., Hawaii Bar Assn., Filipino Lawyers Assn. (v.p.), Honolulu C. of C., Million Dollar Round Table (life), Filipino C. of C. (v.p. 1982). Democrat. Roman Catholic. Office: 745 Fort St Suite 1600 Honolulu HI 96813

TAGGART, DOROTHY HARRIS, investment counselor; b. Hartford, Conn., June 5, 1927; d. Lester Lee and Hester Barber Harris; B.A., Wellesley Coll., 1949; M.A., Columbia U., 1966; children—Rush III, Alison B., Stewart W. History tchr., Weston, Conn., 1967-69; v.p. investments Scudder Stevens & Clark, N.Y.C., 1969-82, Shearson/Am. Express Asset Mgmt. Inc., N.Y.C., 1982—. Mem. Wellesley in N.Y.; mem. Nat. Com. U.S./China Relations, Inc. Mem. N.Y. Soc. Security Analysts (edn. and seminar com., dir.), Fin. Women's Assn. N.Y. (chmn. China del., co-chmn. edn. com.). Republican. Clubs: Cosmopolitan; Country (New Canaan, Conn.). Office: Shearson/Amer Ex 2 World Trade Center 106th Floor New York NY 10048

TAI, JULIA CHOW, chemist; b. Shanghai, China, Dec. 15, 1935; came to U.S., 1957, naturalized, 1970; d. Fei-Tsen and Jean Tson (Liao) Chow; B.S., Nat. Taiwan U., 1957; M.S., U. Okla., 1959; Ph.D., U. Ill., 1963; m. Hung-Chao Tai, Aug. 14, 1960; children—Eve, Helen, Michael. Research asso. Wayne State U., 1963-66, 67-68; vis. asso. prof. Nat. Taiwan U., 1968-69; asst. prof. chemistry U. Mich., Dearborn, 1969, asso. prof., 1973-79, prof., 1979—. Mem. Am. Chem. Soc., AAUP. Contbr. articles profl. jours. Office: 4901 Evergreen Rd Dearborn MI 48128

TAIT, CORNELIA DAMIAN (MRS. JOY NELSON TAIT), artist, author, lectr.; b. Phila.; d. Mihai Traian and Sofia Maria (Bogdan) Damian; student Stella Elkins Tyler Sch. Fine Arts, 1940-46; B.F.A. (scholar), Temple U., 1944, B.S. in Edn., 1945, M.F.A., 1946; m. Joy Nelson Tait, Feb. 27, 1953. Exhbns. include Phila. Art Alliance, 1950, Woodmere Art Gallery, 1966, 73, also in Bucharest, Cluj and Timisoara, Romania, 1973, Romanian Library, N.Y.C., 1974, in Biarritz and Paris, France, 1975; exhibited art in nat. traveling exhibitio exhbns.; artist Phila. Redevel. Authority; represented in permanent collection Temple U.; art commissions various religious groups; faculty supr., reorganizer Abington (Pa.) Cultural Center, 1962-63; organizer internat. exhbn. Romanian Contemporary Art, Phila., 1973; participant Voice of Am. broadcasts, 1978; condr. slide-lectures to coll., art, and lit. groups; Am.-Romanian rep. 2d Internat. Arts Festival, Princeton, 1980; mem. steering com., chmn. program com. Upper Moreland Council for Arts, 1980. Nominee several art prizes; recipient diploma of merit Universitá della Arti Accademia Italia, 1982. Mem. Artists Equity Assn., Phila. Art Alliance, Woodmere Art Gallery, Violet Oakley Meml. Found., Internat. Platform Assn. Author: Spirals, 1976; Art into Fourth Dimension, 1976; graphic series Folk Fantasy and Romania, 1978. Recorded memoirs of muralists Edith Emerson and Violet Oakley. Home and studio: 10 Armour Rd Hatboro PA 19040

TAIT, MARGARET JENNINGS, cellist; b. Harrisonburg, Va., Nov. 21, 1947; d. Jack V. and Dorothy Coleman (Jennings) T.; B.Mus. U. So. Calif. 1970, M.Mus. San Francisco Conservatory of Music 1974; m. Mitchell I. Ross, May 29, 1977. Cellist, Birmingham Symphony Orch. 1970-73, prin. cellist 1972-73; cellist San Francisco Symphony 1973—; mem. Aurora String Quartet; lectr. in field.

TAITANO, MAGDALENA SANTOS, librarian; d. Jose S. and Josefa (Ignacio) Santos; B.A., Mt. Mary Coll., 1955; M.L.S., Tex. Woman's U., 1959; m. Richard F. Taitano, June 20, 1959; children—Taling Maria, Richard, John Joseph, Carmen Teresita. Reference librarian Office Tech. Services, Dept. Commerce, Washington, 1962-64; chief librarian U. Guam, Mangilao, 1964-66; territorial librarian Guam Public Library, Agana, 1966—. Sec., Guam council Girl Scouts U.S.A. Mem. Guam Library Assn., ALA. Clubs: Guam Women's, Soroptimist. Address: Nieves M Flores Memorial Library Box 652 Agana Guam 96910

TAKACH, MARY HUDCOVIC, mus. dir.; b. N.Y.C., Sept. 22, 1932; d. Gabriel and Mary (Sudjak) Hudcovic; B.A., Harpur Coll., Binghamton, N.Y., 1967; M.A. (Jennie F. Snapp scholar) in Art History, SUNY, Binghamton, 1973; m. Michael T. Takach, Jan. 31, 1953; 1 son, David T. Asst. art dept. SUNY, Binghamton, 1966-67; art tchr. Endicott (N.Y.) Public Schs., 1967-74; asst. prof. art history Syracuse U., 1974-77; curator, asst. dir. Joe and Emily Lowe Art Gallery, Syracuse U., 1974-77; cons. Nat. Endowment Humanities, 1978; ind. exhbn. cons. U.S. Ho. of Reps., 1978-79; cons. N.Y. State Council on Arts, 1980; dir. Pensacola (Fla.) Mus. Art, 1980—; small mus. com. N.E. Regional Conf. Mus., 1974-77; reader Nat. Endowment Humanities, 1981—; guest lectr. colls., hist. socs. Bd. dirs. Pensacola People to People, 1981—; mem. regional library bd. Friends of W. Fla. Regional Library Bd., 1981—; commr. Galvez Celebration, Pensacola, 1980. Ruth Frazer scholar, 1974. Mem. Am. Assn. Mus., Coll. Art Assn., S.E. Mus. Conf., LWV, Delta Kappa Gamma. Democrat. Roman Catholic. Club: Altrusa. Author: The Mural Art of Ben Shahn, 1977; contbr. chpt. in book. Research on letters of Benjamin West. Home: PO Box 641 Pensacola FL 32593 Office: Pensacola Museum of Art 407 S Jefferson St Pensacola FL 32501

TAKEUCHI, VICKI MITSU, social worker; b. Los Angeles, May 13, 1952; d. Mikio Mickey and Joyce Nobuko (Kamiyama) T.; A.B. cum laude, Princeton U., 1974; M.S.W., UCLA, 1977. Social work intern Keiro Minami Nursing Home, City View Hosp., 1975-76; St. Johns Hosp., Kennedy Child Study Center, Santa Monica, Calif., 1976-77; clin. social worker El Nido Services, Los Angeles, 1977-80; asst. city mgr. PSI World, Los Angeles, 1980-82, coordinator, Honolulu, 1982—; resident dir. semester-at-sea Inst. Shipboard Edn., U. Pitts., 1982. Intercultural coordinator Pasadena Urban Coalition; mem. adv. bd. Asian Am. Community Mental Health Tng. Center, 1975-76; co chmn. UCLA Asian Caucus, 1975-77. Lic. clin. social worker. Recipient Miller-Schroeder Meml. prize Princeton U., 1974. Mem. Acad. Cert. Social Workers, Nat. Assn. Social Workers, Asian Am. Social Workers, Japanese Am. Democratic Club, Asian Am. Community Mental Health Tng. Center, Princeton U. Alumni Assn. (schs. com.), PSI World. Home: care Kumoto 4069 Guilford Ave Livermore CA 94550 Office: PSI World of Hawaii 2929 Kapiolani Blvd Honolulu HI 96826

TALBERT, MARNEY DYESS, oil shale co. public relations exec.; b. Memphis, Sept. 30, 1942; d. Coley Doston and Mercedes Maude (Hughs) Dyess; student Ottawa (Kans.) U., 1963; emergency med. technician cert. Mesa Coll., 1978; children—G. Bunk, R. Coley. Para-legal, King and Spalding, attys., Atlanta, 1968-71; exec. asst. legal dept. Zoller and Danneberg, Denver, 1971-73; adminstrv. asst. Occidental Oil Shale, Inc., Grand Junction, Colo., 1974-78, mgr. public relations, 1978—. Recipient award for writing Colo. West Advt. Fedn., 1978. Mem. Public Relations Internat. Assn., Grand Junction C. of C. (dir. 1979-81), Nat. Assn. Female Execs. Republican. Club: Lioness (charter 1st v.p. 1978-79) (Grand Junction). Contbr. stories, articles to newspapers and publs., 1976—. Home: 400 Bookcliff Dr Grand Junction CO 81501 Office: PO Box 2687 Grand Junction CO 81502

TALBOTT, EUNICE TILLMAN, clubwoman; b. Springfield, Mo., Jan. 25, 1911; d. Sidney Ellis and Nancy Elizabeth (Denney) Tillman; B.S. (Ed.), U. Tampa, 1947; postgrad. U. Fla., 1959-61; m. William W. Talbott, June 23, 1933; 1 dau., Sharon Lynn Webb. Tchr., Hillsborough County, Fla., 1947-68; lectr. table settings; poet. Recipient awards flower shows, 1968—. Mem. NEA, Fla. Edn. Assn., English Council (program chmn. Hillsborough County 1963-65), DAR (regent 1970-72), Colonial Dames (pres. 1977-79), Magna Charta Dames, Tampa and Fla. Fedn. Garden Clubs, Plantagnet Soc., Tri Sigma. Democrat. Methodist. Clubs: Sundial Garden (pres. 1970-72), State Jr. Garden (chmn. 1945-47), Tampa Woman's (librarian 1979-80), Jasmine Garden, Order of Crown. Home: 2810 Parkland Blvd Tampa FL 33609

TALBOTT, LINDA HOOD, educator, found. exec., communications exec., lectr.; b. Kansas City, Mo., Dec. 29, 1941; d. Henry H. and Helen E. (Hamrick) Hood; B.A. with highest distinction, U. Mo., 1962, M.A. (grad. fellow), 1964, Ph.D., 1973; postgrad. (postdoctoral fellow) Harvard U. Inst. Ednl. Mgmt., 1974; m. Thomas H. Talbott, Mar. 5, 1965. Prof. English, Met. Jr. Coll., Kansas City, Mo., 1963-67; prof. English, Queensborough Community Coll., Bayside, N.Y., 1967-68; prof. English, editor Nassau Rev., Nassau Community Coll., Garden City, N.Y., 1968-69; prof. English, adminstr. Lesley Coll., Cambridge, Mass., 1969; founding editor Tempo mag. and devel. officer U. Mo., Kansas City, 1969-76, dir. spl. projects Office of Chancellor, 1976—, adj. prof. edn., 1975—; pres. Talbott & Assocs., Kansas City, 1975—; exec. dir. Clearinghouse for Midcontinent Founds., Kansas City, 1975—; lectr., cons. in field. Bd. dirs. Women & Founds./Corp. Philanthropy, Inc., N.Y.C., 1976-79, United Community Services/Heart of Am. United Way, 1974-82, exec. com. The Central Exchange, 1978—, Dimensions Unltd., Kansas City, 1973-77; commr. Kansas City Commn. on Status of Women, 1978—; adminstrv. dir. Mid-Am. Assembly on Future of Performing Arts, 1979; chmn. Internat. Women's Yr. in Mid-Am. Symposium, 1975; del. Nat. Women's Conf., Houston, 1977; bd. advisors Center for Mgmt. Assistance, Kansas City, 1979—, bd. advs. Kansas City Arts council, 1980—, Long Term Care Project for Elderly Nat. Demonstration, Mid-Am. Regional Council, 1981—, Women's Resource Service, U. Mo., Kansas City, 1971—; hon. dir. Rockhurst Coll., 1977—; hon. trustee Truman Med. Center Found., 1980—; bd. dirs. Greater Kansas City Mental Health Found., 1980—, Starlight Theatre Assn., 1980—; bd. advisors Greater Kansas City Community Found., 1980—; cons. R.A. Long Found., 1982—; mem. Community Care Funding Partners Council, 1982—. Named Kansas City Tomorrow Leader, 1978; Chi Omega Pub. Service award, 1962; Outstanding Young Woman of Mo., 1967; Woman of the Yr. award, VFW, 1972; Outstanding Achievement award, U. Mo., Kansas City Sch. Edn., 1973; publ. awards, Nat. and Regional Council for Advancement and Support of Edn., 1971, 72, 73; Regional Citizen of Yr. award Mid Am. Regional Council, 1982; Am. Inst. for Public Service award, 1982; Harvard U. fellow, 1974, others. Mem. Am. Assn. Higher Edn. (coordinator 1973-75), AAUW, Council for Advancement and Support of Edn., Council on Founds., Women and Founds./Corp. Philanthropy, Mortar Bd., Phi Kappa Phi, Phi Theta Kappa, Phi Delta Kappa, Pi Lambda Theta, Delta Kappa Gamma, Chi Omega. Presbyterian. Clubs: Univ. Women's, Woodside Racquet, Kansas City, Central Exchange. Author: The Community College in Community Service, 1973; Grantmaking in Greater Kansas City: The Philanthropic Impact of Foundations, 1976-80; editor: The Foundation Exchange, 1976—; A History of the University of Kansas City: Prologue to a Public University, 1976; A

Brief History of Philanthropy in Kansas City, 1980; The Case for the Community Foundation, 1981; Perspectives on Trusteeship for the 80s, 1981; contbr. articles to profl. jours. Office: PO Box 7215 Kansas City MO 64113

TALESE, NAN AHEARN, pub. co. exec.; b. N.Y.C., Dec. 19, 1933; d. Thomas James and Suzanne Sherman (Russell) Ahearn; B.A., Manhattanville Coll. of Sacred Heart, 1955; m. Gay Talese, June 10, 1959; children—Pamela Frances, Catherine Gay. Fgn. exchange student 1st Nat. City Bank, London, Paris, 1956; editorial asst. Am. Eugenics Soc., N.Y.C., 1957-58; editorial asst. Vogue mag., N.Y.C., 1958-59; copy editor Random House Pubs., N.Y.C., 1959-64, asso. editor, 1964-67, sr. editor, 1967-73; sr. editor Simon & Schuster Pubs., N.Y.C., 1974-81, v.p., 1979-81; exec. editor, v.p. Houghton Mifflin Co., Boston and N.Y.C., 1981—. Home: 109 E 61st St New York NY 10021 Office: 666 Third Ave New York NY 10017

TALLAU, CARLA JANE, broadcasting exec.; b. Orange, N.J., Feb. 6, 1950; d. Howard Gilbert and Lillian Marie (Hollander) T.; B.A. in Social Scis., Muhlenberg Coll., Allentown, Pa., 1972; M.A. in Media Studies, New Sch. Social Research, 1980. Adminstrv. aide U.S. Ct. Appeals, 2d Circuit, N.Y.C., 1974-75; coordinator adminstrn. CBS/Epic Records, N.Y.C., 1975-79; research asso. ON TV, Ltd., N.Y.C., 1979; supr. night programs ABC Radio Network, N.Y.C., 1980—. Mem. AAUW, Nat. Assn. Female Execs., Muhlenberg Coll. Alumni Assn. Lutheran. Office: 1926 Broadway New York NY 10023

TALLCHIEF, MARIA, ballerina; b. Fairfax, Okla., Jan. 24, 1925; d. Alexander Joseph and Ruth Mary (Porter) T.; student public schs., Calif.; A.F.D. (hon.), Lake Forest Coll. (Ill.), Colby Coll., Maine, 1968, Ripon Coll., 1973, Boston Coll., Smith Coll., 1981; hon. degree Northwestern U., 1982; m. Henry Paschen, Jr., June 3, 1957; 1 dau., Elise. Joined Ballet Russe de Monte Carlo, 1942; prima ballerina N.Y.C. Ballet, 1947-60; guest star Paris Opera, 1947; prima ballerina Am. Ballet Theater, 1960; with N.Y.C. Ballet Co. until 1965; now artistic dir. Chgo. City Ballet. Recipient Achievement award Women's Nat. Press Club, 1953; Dance mag. award, 1960; Capezio award, 1965; named Hon. Princess-Osage Indian Tribe, 1953; Disting. Service award U. Okla., 1972; Jane Addams Humanitarian award Rockford Coll., 1973; award Dance Educators Am., 1956. Mem. Nat. Soc. Arts and Letters. Office: care Chgo City Ballet 223 W Erie St Chicago IL 60610

TALLEY, CAROLYN SUE, controller; b. Cin., Sept. 30, 1945; d. LeRoy Millard and Betty Jane (West) Hughes; student Secord's Bus. Coll., 1963-64; m. Jerry Dale Talley, May 17, 1967; stepchildren—Julie Ann, Jonie Gail, Jodie Ellen. With Shilliot's, Cin., 1964-65, R.L. Polk Co., Cin., 1965, Cin. and So. Bell Telephone Co., Cin., 1965-66; buyer Sterling Electric Motors, Los Angeles, 1966-67; credit union clk. Beckman Instruments, Fullerton, Calif., 1967-68; with Federated Dept. Stores, Cin., 1968-69, Macpro, Inc., Loveland, Ohio, 1969-71, Orange Coast Advt., Inc., Santa Ana, Calif., 1971-73; pvt. practice acctg., Orange County, Calif., 1973-75; office mgr./acct. L. Blain Co., Paramount, Calif., 1975-77; owner Jer-Jon Motors, Inc., Garden Grove, Calif., 1976-79; controller Relkoff Constrn., Santa Ana, Calif., 1977; controller Framing div. Warmington Devel., Irvine, Calif., 1977, Brattain Contractors, Inc., Santa Ana, Calif., 1977-78; v.p., controller L. Blain Co., Paramount, 1978-82; owner C.T. Constrn., Inc., Paramount, 1977—, Fine Line Co., Paramount, 1982—; v.p. Hawkeye Equipment Co., 1982—; notary public, Calif. Lic. gen. contractor, Calif. Mem. Nat. Assn. Women in Constrn. (chpt. pres. 1979-81, corr. sec. 1982-83, treas. 1979-80), Internat. Platform Assn., Exec. Women Internat., Nat. Assn. Female Execs., Household Goods Forwarders Assn. Am., Nat. Notary Assn., Silver Lakes Assn., N.Am. Hunters Assn. Home: 2735 E Hill St Signal Hill CA 90804 Office: 16247 Illinois Ave Paramount CA 90723

TALLEY, RONDA CAROL, ednl. adminstr.; b. Glasgow, Ky., Nov. 21, 1951; d. Jack Howard and Ronda Mae (McCoy) T.; B.S., Western Ky. U., 1973; M.Ed., U. Louisville, 1974, Ed.S., 1976; Ph.D., Ind. U., 1979. Spl. edn. tchr. Jefferson County Public Schs., Louisville, 1973-77; research assoc. U. Calif., Riverside, Ind. U., Bloomington, 1977-78; adminstrv. intern Bur. Edn. Handicapped, HEW, Washington, 1978-81; adj. prof. dept. spl. edn. U. Louisville, 1981—; coordinator assessment/placement services exceptional child edn. Jefferson County Public Schs., Louisville, 1981—; founder, pres. Tri-T Assocs., 1982—. Sta. WHAS Crusade for Children grantee, 1974-76; Bur. Edn. for Handicapped student research grantee, 1978; lic. sch. psychologist. Mem. Am. Psychol. Assn. (chmn. student affiliates in sch. psychology), Am. Ednl. Research Assn., Nat. Assn. Sch. Psychologists, Council Exceptional Children, AAUP, Phi Delta Kappa, Kappa Delta. Republican. Methodist. Editor: Special Education in Transition: Administrator's Handbook on Integrating America's Mildly Handicapped Students, 1982. Home: 1114 Whetstone Way Louisville KY 40223 Office: 4409 Preston Hwy Louisville KY 40213

TALLMAN, KATHRYN KAY KLECKLEY, civic worker; b. Greenwood, S.C., Oct. 3, 1939; d. Henry Dailey and Madelyn (Griffith) Kleckley; A.B., Vassar Coll., 1961; m. James Richard Tallman, June 29, 1961; children—Brian and Margaret (twins). Bd. dirs. Planned Parenthood League Dutchess County (N.Y.), 1966-73, fund drive chmn., 1969, 74; bd. dirs. Rehab. Programs, Inc., 1975-79, exec. com., 1978-79, v.p., 1979; v.p. Jr. League of Poughkeepsie, Inc., 1976-77, instr. mgmt., 1975-78; mem. area I council Assn. Jr. Leagues, Inc., 1978; chmn. fund raiser Poughkeepsie Day Sch., 1976; mem. Child Devel. Com. Dutchess County, 1975-79, vice chmn., 1979; mem. Crime Victims Research Com., 1976; mem. task force on families in crisis, adv. body to Dutchess County Legislature, 1979; bd. dirs. Broome County Child Devel. Council, Inc., 1980—, Roberson Center Arts and Scis., Binghamton, 1981—, chmn. ann. giving fund dr., 1981; mem. Broome County Mental Health Adv. Bd., 1981—; mem. community adv. bd. Binghamton Urban Youth Homes, N.Y. State Div. Youth, 1981—. Home: 21 Grand Blvd Binghamton NY 13905

TALLMAN, RUTH MARCHAK (MRS. FRANK G. TALLMAN III), aviation exec.; b. Scranton, Pa., July 18, 1929; d. Michael and Mary (Hosko) Marchak; student Seton Hall Coll., 1948; m. Frank Gifford Tallman, III, Feb. 18, 1968. Fashion model Blue Book Modeling, Hollywood, Calif., 1944-48; sec. to controller, personnel mgr Sta. KTLA-TV, Hollywood, 1955-63; owner Tallmantz Aviation Inc. Frank Tallman's Movieland of the Air Aircraft Mus., John Wayne Airport, Santa Ana, 1968—. Mem. Soc. Exptl. Test Pilots, Newport Harbor Art Mus., Ladies Aux. Whirly Girls. Roman Catholic. Clubs: Balboa Bay, Indian Wells Racquet. Home: 1973 Vista Caudal Newport Beach CA 92660 Office: 19711 Airport Way S John Wayne Airport Santa Ana CA 92707

TALLY, LURA SELF, state legislator; b. Statesville, N.C., Dec. 9, 1921; d. Robert Ottis and Sara (Cowles) Self; A.B., Duke U., 1942; M.A., N.C. State U., Raleigh, 1970; m. J.O. Tally, Jr., Jan. 30, 1943 (div. 1970); children—Robert Taylor, John Cowles. Tchr., guidance counselor Fayetteville (N.C.) city schs.; mem. N.C. Ho. of Reps. from 20th Dist., 1971-83, chmn. com. higher edn., from 1975, also 1980-83, vice chmn. com. appropriations for edn., 1973-83; state senator from 12th Dist. N.C., 1983—. Past pres. Cumberland County Mental Health Assn., N.C. Historic Preservation Soc.; trustee Fayetteville Tech. Inst., 1981-84. Mem. Am. Personnel and Guidance Assn., Fayetteville Bus. and Profl. Women's Club, Kappa Delta, Delta Kappa Gamma. Methodist. Club: Fayetteville Woman's (past pres.). Office: NC Legis Bldg W Jones St Raleigh NC 27611

TALMAGE, GRACE J., editor, publisher; b. Kearny, N.J., Dec. 5, 1923; d. John William and Celesta Jane (Clark) Crown; student Temple U., 1947-49, Rutgers Univ. Coll., 1941-43; m. George S. Talmage, Jan. 19, 1946; children—Jayne S., Richard G., Lisa R. With Conmar Zipper, Newark, 1946; with Ohio Chem. Co., Phila., 1946-47; owner, partner Talmage Tours, Inc., Phila., 1949-77; editor, pub. Ofcl. Domestic Tour Manual, G & G Talmage Assos., 1977—, editor Ofcl. Travel Industry Resource Manual, 1978—. Publicity chmn. Women's Center of Montgomery County, 1979-80. Served with USNR, 1943-46. Mem. Phila. Woman's Network, Phila. Women's Travel Club, Delaware Valley chpt. Am. Soc. Travel Agts. Republican. Roman Catholic. Home: 2600 Martin Rd Willow Grove PA 19090 Office: PO Box 39 Abington PA 19001

TALMAN, MARILEE PAYTON, mktg. dir.; b. Richmond, Va., July 22, 1946; d. L(eland) R(odman) and Mary (Hicks) Payton; A.B. cum laude, Goucher Coll., 1968; M.A. (gov.'s fellow), U. Va., 1970; 1 dau., Anne May. Adj. instr. in English, Cleve. State U. and Cuyahoga Community Coll., Cleve. and Burlington County (N.J.) Coll., 1970-73; mktg. dir., mgr. David Day Advt. Agy., contracts mgr., mem. editorial bd. Stein and Day/Pubs., Inc., Briarcliff Manor, N.Y., 1975-81; former mktg. cons. Feminist Press, Tarrytown, N.Y., now dir., mem. mgmt. com.; co-producer, host: Focus on Women, McLean Cable TV, Tarrytown, 1981. Mem. Women in Communications, Women's Nat. Book Assn., Women in Sales Assn. Editor: Love and Limerence: The Experience of Being in Love (Dorothy Tennov), 1979; The Starr-Weiner Report on Sex and Sexuality in the Mature Years (Bernard D. Starr, Marcella Bakur Weiner, 1981. Office: 298 Fifth Ave New York NY

TAM, TERESA M., med. social worker; b. China, June 20, 1946; d. Chung Yin and Siu Ling (Lee) Yip; B.A., D'Youville Coll., Buffalo, 1968; M.S.W., Hunter Coll., City U. N.Y., 1976; m. Robert Y. Tam, 1968; children—Raymond, Terrence. Social worker Spence-Chapin Adoption Service, N.Y.C., 1968-70, Salvation Army Foster Care, N.Y.C., 1972-73; summer worker N.Y. Hosp., 1975; med. social worker N.Y. Infirmary-Beekman Downtown Hosp., 1976—. Organizer, N.Y.C. Chinatown Health Council; bd. advs. Asian Am. Student Project Hunter Coll. Sch. Social Work; supr. undergrad. psychology and social work students Project Ahead, Chinatown Health Clinic. Vol., Vietnamese Chinese Benevolent Assn., 1976-79. NIMH grantee, 1974-76. Mem. Nat. Assn. Social Workers, Social Work Vocat. Bur., Pacific Asian Am. Social Workers (sec. 1979—). Contbr. articles, translations to China Post. Office: 170 William St New York NY 10038

TAN, JOYCE M., mfg. co. exec.; b. Gloucester, Mass., May 7, 1935; d. Leon Maxim and Mary Catherine (McDonald) LaFlam; diploma nursing Newton-Wellesley Hosp. Sch. Nursing, 1959; m. Bienvenido Tan, Feb. 5, 1955; children—Bienvenido, Jeanette Carol, Karen Segunda, Jacqueline Leona. Lab. technician Mass. Gen. Hosp., Boston, 1956-57; night charge nurse West Valley Community Hosp, Encino, Calif., 1959-60; purchasing agent, asst. dir. Newhall (Calif.) Community Hosp., 1966-68; pres., chief exec. officer MC Industries, Glendale, Calif., 1975—; dir. Benjoy Devel. Corp., Jette, Inc., Magellan World Travel Agy. Bd. dirs. Hamiltair Property Owners Assn., Lake Arrowhead, Calif., 1977-81; del. White House Conf. on Small Bus., 1980. Office: 625 Thompson Ave Glendale CA 91201

TAN, JULIA, cardiologist, internist; b. Kunming, China, Mar. 1, 1943; came to U.S., 1949, naturalized, 1961; d. Pia Chu and Alice (Wong) Tan; A.B., Wilson Coll., 1965; M.D., Med. Coll. Pa., 1969. Intern, resident Med. Coll. Va., Richmond, 1969-71; resident N.Y. Med. Coll. Hosps., 1971-73; resident in cardiology Case-Western Res.-Cleve. Met. Gen. Hosp., 1973-75; practice medicine specializing in internal medicine and cardiology, Visalia, Calif., 1975—, pres. Julia Tan, M.D., Inc.; dir. CCU Visalia Community Hosp., 1975—; mem. staffs Kaweah Delta Dist. Hosp., Visalia County Hosp.; cons. staff Exeter Meml. Hosp., Tulare Dist. Hosp.; mem. Calif. 9th Dist. Med. Quality Rev. Com., 1976—. Diplomate Am. Bd. Internat. Medicine. Fellow Am. Coll. Cardiology (assoc.); mem. Am. Heart Assn. (dir. Central Valley chpt. 1975-80), Calif. Med. Assn., AMA, Tulare County Med. Soc. Office: 1633 S Court St Visalia CA 93277 *

TAN, SHIRLEY, anesthesiologist; b. Djakarta, Indonesia, Oct. 1, 1943; came to U.S., 1965; d. Philip Harry and Shui Yu (Ou) Tan; student La Sierra Coll., 1965-67; M.D., Loma Linda U., 1971. Intern, Glendale (Calif.) Adventist Hosp., 1971-72; resident in anesthesiology U. Louisville, 1972-74, instr. anesthesiology affiliated hosp., 1974-75; mem. clin. faculty anesthesiology Loma Linda (Calif.) U., 1975, asst. prof. anesthesia Sch. Allied Health Professions, 1978—; practice medicine specializing in anesthesiology Loma Linda, Calif., 1975—; asst. prof. anesthesiology U. Colo. Med. Center, Denver, 1976-79; acting chief anesthesia Denver VA Hosp., 1976-77. Mem. Am. Soc. Anesthesiologists, Internat. Anesthesia Research Soc., Am. Soc. Regional Anesthesia, Calif. Med. Soc. Seventh-Day Adventist. Contbr. articles to profl. jours. Home: 11642 Pecan Way Loma Linda CA 92354 Office: 25333 Barton Rd Loma Linda CA 92354

TANA, ALICE MCFADDEN, bus. services firm exec.; b. Freeland, Pa., Oct. 17, 1935; d. Adrian W. and Alice T. (Campbell) Carr; student Georgetown U., 1968-70, Catholic U. Am., 1967-69, U. Mich., 1963-67, Eastern Mich. U., 1963-67, U. Calif., San Diego, 1977-79; also numerous workshops, symposiums; m. Yasuto Tana, Oct. 13, 1973. Supr. order dept. Gallant Inc., Washington, 1954-58; tchr. Mary Anne Baldwin Sch., Pitts., 1958-60; dir. sr. citizen and women City of Ypsilanti (Mich.), 1961-67; regional dir. Nat. Council on Aging, Washington, 1967-70; liaison officer congl./pvt. sector Exec. Office of Pres., Washington, 1971-72; dir. Pres.'s Task Force on Aging, Washington, 1972-73; tng. specialist Japanese Self Def. Force/Sumitomo Corp., Taura, Japan, 1973-76; econ. devel. specialist County San Diego (Calif.), 1977-80, project dir. transp. research and mktg. study, 1980, budget analyst, 1981-82; founder Ask Alice, bus. and personal services for profls., San Diego, 1982—; mem. adv. bd. Women and Mgmt., Georgetown U.; mem. women in politics and govt. Rutgers U., 1980-81. Founder, pres. Diversified Bus. Women, ednl. orgn., San Diego; trustee World Family Living, San Diego, Internat. Student Exchange Program TZ Assos., San Diego. Recipient B-MAC award Mich. Recreation and Parks Assn., 1967, Disting. Service in Disaster Ops. award Pres. U.S., 1972, cert. appreciation Japanese Self-Def. Force, 1975. Mem. Calif. Women in Govt. (pres. 1980-81), San Diego C. of C. (Econ. Research Council), Am. Soc. Public Adminstrs., Nat. Assn. Female Execs., San Diego Women Execs. Network GROW (dir.), Republican Bus. and Profl. Women, Eastern Mich. U. Alumni Assn. (condr. ann. events 1967—), Econ. Research Bur. Clubs: Exchange (Outstanding award 1967), Optimists (Outstanding award 1963). Contbr. articles to profl. jours. Home: 1280-124 River Vista Row San Diego CA 92111 Office: 1600 Pacific Hwy MS-214 San Diego CA 92101

TANCZAK-DYCIO, MARY, physician; b. Rybnyky, Ukraine, July 10, 1922; came to U.S., 1950, naturalized, 1955; d. Basil and Helen (Cisyk) Tanczak; student U. Lviv, 1940-41, Med. Sch., 1942-44, U. Erlangen (Germany), 1945-49; m. George Dycio, Nov. 11, 1949; children—George Myron, Mark Roman. Resident, Contagious Disease Hosp., Belleville, N.J., 1951-52; intern Mercy Hosp., Canton, Ohio, 1952-53, resident anesthesia, 1952-55; practice medicine specializing in anesthesiology, 1955-58; mem. staff Irvington (N.J.) Gen. Hosp., 1955-58; staff St. Mary's Gen. Hosp., Lewiston, Maine, 1958—, chief anesthesia dept., 1960—, also dir. Sch. Nurse Anesthetists. Fellow Am. Coll. Anesthesiologists; mem. AMA, Am.-Ukrainian, Maine. Androscoggin County med. socs. Office: 300 Pine St Lewiston ME 04240 also 3 Bayberry Ln Lewiston ME 04240

TANDBERG, AURORA CLAUDETTE PALMIERI, ins. co. exec.; b. N.Y.C., Apr. 7, 1946; d. Emanuel and Josephine (Gallante) Palmieri; student Bergen Community Coll., 1970-72; m. Douglas Tandberg, Oct. 17, 1965 (div. 1975). With Garden State Nat. Bank, Hackensack, N.J., 1963-73, asst. treas., 1969-73; sales rep. N.Y. Life Ins. Co., N.Y.C., 1973-76, asst. sales mgr., 1976-80, dir. sales personnel devel., 1980-81, gen. mgr., New London, Conn., 1981—. Mem. Nat. Assn. Life Underwriters. Home: 100 Sheffield St Old Saybrook CT 06475

TANDY, JESSICA, actress; b. London, June 7, 1909; d. Harry and Jessie Helen (Horspool) Tandy; student Dame Alice Owens Girls Sch., also Ben Greet Acad. Acting, 1924-27; LL.D. (hon.), U. Western Ont., 1974; m. Jack Hawkins, 1932 (div. 1940); 1 dau., Susan (Mrs. John Tettemer); m. 2d, Hume Cronyn, 1942; children—Christopher Hume, Tandy. First profl. acting role in Manderson Girls, later appeared in Comedy of Good and Evil, Alice Sit-by-the-Fire, Yellow Sands: London debut in The Rumor, 1929, other theatre appearances in Twelfth Night, 1930, Man Who Pays the Piper, Autumn Crocus, Port Said, 1931; various engagements Old Vic, London, including Midsummer Night's Dream, Hamlet, King Lear, 1933-40; first stage appearance U.S., 1930, on Broadway in Time and Conways, 1938, White Steed, 1939, Yesterday's Magic, 1942, Streetcar Named Desire, 1947, Four Poster, 1951-53, Madame Will You Walk, 1953, The Honeys, 1955, A Day by the Sea, 1955, The Man in the Dog Suit, 1958, Five Finger Exercise, 1959, The Physicists, 1964, Noel Coward in Two Keys, 1974; played in Mpls. in Hamlet, Three Sisters, Death of a Salesman, 1963, in Way of the World, The Cherry Orchard, The Caucasian Chalk Circle, 1965; summer theatre prodns., 1950-55; appeared Triple Play, 1958-59, Big Fish, Little Fish, London, 1962; reading tour U.S. (with husband), Face to Face, 1954, A Delicate Balance, 1966-67, The Miser, 1968, Heartbreak House, Shaw Festival, 1968; Tchin-Tchin, Chgo., 1969, Camino Real, Lincoln Center, N.Y.C., 1970, Home, Morosco, N.Y., 1971, All Over, N.Y.C., 1971; appeared (with husband) in Samuel Beckett festival, Lincoln Center, N.Y.C., 1972; tour of Promenade All, 1972-73, Tour Not I, 1973; limited concert recital tour Many Faces of Love, 1974, 75, 76, also Seattle Repertory theatre; tour Noel Coward in Two Keys, 1975; tour The Gin Game, U.S., Toronto, London, USSR, 1978-79; appeared (with husband) in Foxfire, Stratford (Ont.) Festival, 1980, Guthrie Theatre, Mpls., 1981, Long Day's Journey into Night, also in Rose, N.Y.C., 1981; appeared in The Way of the World, A Midsummer Night's Dream, Eve, Stratford (Ont.) Festival, 1976, Long Day's Journey Into Night, London, Ont., 1977, The Gin Game, New Haven, 1977, N.Y.C., 1978; motion pictures include Valley of Decision, Green Years, Desert Fox, A Light in the Forest, 1958, The Birds, 1962, Butley, 1973, Honky Tonk Freeway, 1980, Stab and Garp, 1981; TV prodns., Portrait of a Madonna, 1948, Christmas 'Till Closing, 1955, Marriage, series, 1954, The Fallen Idol, 1959, The Moon and Sixpence, 1959. Dramatic adv. Goddard Neighborhood Center, N.Y.C., 1948. Recipient ann. Antoinette Perry award for performance Streetcar Named Desire, 1948; Twelfth Night Club award for performance Streetcar Named Desire; Della Austria Medal from the Drama League N.Y.; bronze medallion (with husband) for performance The Four Poster, Comedia Matinee Club, 1952; Obie award for Not I, 1973; Drama Desk award for Happy Days and Not I, for best actress in The Gin Game, 1978; Los Angeles Critics award, 1979; Sarah Siddons award, 1979; Theater Arts medal for lifetime of disting. achievement Brandeis U.; elected to Theatre Hall of Fame, 1979.

TANENBAUM, CAROL BINDER, lawyer; b. Zurich, Switzerland, June 15, 1935 (parents Am. citizens); d. Oscar J. and Mary G. (Bodenstein) Binder; B.A. magna cum laude (Elisha Benjamin Andrews scholar), Brown U., 1956; J.D., Case Western Res. U., 1975; m. B. Samuel Tanenbaum, Aug. 26, 1956; children—Laurie Binder, Stephen Jonathan, David Michael. Tchr. public schs., Guilford, Conn., 1956-60, Wayland, Mass., 1960; reading specialist, Cleveland Heights, Ohio, 1965-69; instr. Cuyahoga Community Coll., Cleve., 1972; law clk. Zipkin & Greene, Cleve., 1974-75, William A. Shernoff, P.C., Claremont, Calif., 1975-76; admitted to Calif. bar, 1976; asso. firm Stafford, Buxbaum and Chakmak, Claremont, 1975-77; individual practice law, Claremont, 1977-81; asso. firm Allard, Shelton & O'Connor, 1981—. Mem. Calif. State Bar Assn., Los Angeles County Bar Assn., Eastern Bar Assn. Los Angeles County (trustee 1977—), Calif. Women Lawyers, Inland Counties Women-at-Law, Am. Bar Assn., Campus Women of Claremont Colls., LWV, Galileo Soc. Office: 100 Pomona Mall 6th Floor Pomona CA 91766

TANKE, MARJORIE M., antique dealer; b. Harrington, Wash., Aug. 6, 1917; d. William B. and Maude (Turner) Armstrong; student Wash. State U., 1935-37; m. Robert W. Tanke, Oct. 2, 1937 (dec.); children—Judith, William; m. 2d, F.E. Peters, Apr. 24, 1981. Vice-pres., Tanke Farms, Inc., Harrington, Wash., 1966—; pres. The Horse Collar, Inc., Harrington, 1968—. Mem. exec. bd. Lincoln County Overall Econ. Devel. Program, 1979—; mem. Harrington Planning Commn., 1971-75, Harrington City Council, 1976—; chmn. bd. trustees Eastern Wash. State U. Mem. Wash. Assn. Wheat Growers, Harrington C. of C., Chi Omega. Democrat. Lutheran. Club: PEO Sisterhood. Address: 507 S 2d St Harrington WA 99134

TANKOOS, SANDRA RICH, ct. reporting agy. exec.; b. Bklyn., Nov. 12, 1936; d. Stanley Jacob and Ethel (Seltzer) Rich; A.A.B., The Stenotype Inst., 1957; B.A. cum laude, Queens Coll., 1968; M.A., C.W. Post Coll., 1975; m. Mar. 17 1957; children—Robert, Gary, Jenine. Ct. reporter, N.Y.C., 1957-68; tchr. Spanish, high schs., L.I., 1968-77; ct. reporting tchr. The Stenotype Inst., 1977-79; pres. Tankoos Reporting Co., Inc., Mineola, N.Y., 1978—, Ar-Ti Recording, Inc., Mineola, 1979—. Bd. dirs. Temple Sinai, Roslyn Heights, 1980—, chmn. social action com., 1980—; mem. Planned Parenthood of Nassau County, 1978—; mem. Steering Com. of Task Force on Equality of Women in Judaism, 1978—. Mem. N.Y. Fedn. Ct. Reporters, Prins. Assn. of Reporting Agencies, NOW, Nat. Shorthand Reporters Assn., L.I. Assn. Govt. Contractors. Democrat. Jewish. Club: Roslyn Coin (pres. 1974-78). Contbr. articles to profl. jours. Home: 77 Shepherd Ln Roslyn Heights NY 11577 Office: 223 Jericho Turnpike Mineola NY 11501 also 150 Nassau St New York NY 10038

TANNENBAUM, BERNICE SALPETER, assn. exec.; b. N.Y.C.; d. Isidore and May Franklin; B.A., Bklyn. Coll.; m. Nathan Tannenbaum; 1 son, Richard Salpeter. Mem. exec. bd. Nat. Conf. Soviet Jewry; v.p. Am.-Israel Public Affairs Com.; mem. exec. bd. Am. sect. World Jewish Congress, chmn. internat. affairs com.; mem. presidium Zionist Gen. Council, World Zionist Orgn.; mem. gen. assembly Jewish Agy.; bd. dirs. United Israel Appeal, Jewish Nat. Fund; mem. exec. com. Am. Zionist Fedn.; mem. Conf. of Pres. of Maj. Jewish Orgns.; nat. pres. Hadassah, N.Y.C., 1976-80, immediate past pres., 1980—. Office: 50 W 58th St New York NY 10019

TANNER, HELEN HORNBECK, historian; b. Northfield, Minn., July 5, 1916; d. John Wesley and Frances Cornelia (Wolfe) Hornbeck; A.B. with honors, Swarthmore Coll., 1937; M.A., U. Fla., 1949; Ph.D. (AAUW fellow), U. Mich., 1961; m. Wilson P. Tanner, Jr., Nov. 22, 1940

(dec. 1977); children—Frances, Margaret Tanner Tewson, Wilson P., Robert. Asst. to dir. public relations Public Schs. Kalamazoo, 1937-39; with sales dept. Am. Airlines, Inc., N.Y.C., 1940-43; teaching fellow, then teaching asst. U. Mich., 1949-53, 57-60, lectr. extension service, 1961-72, asst. dir. Center Continuing Edn. Women, 1964-68; project dir. Newbery Library, Chgo., 1976-81, research asso., 1981—; cons., expert witness Indian treaties; mem. Mich. Commn. Indian Affairs, 1966-70. Grantee Nat. Endowment Humanities, 1976. Mem. Am. Soc. Ethnohistory (pres. 1982-83), Western Writers Am., Conf. Latin Am. History, Soc. History Discoveries, Can. Cartographic Assn., Fla. Hist. Soc., Hist. Soc. Mich. Author: Zespedes in East Florida, 1784-1790, 1963; General Green Visits St. Augustine, 1964; The Greeneville Treaty, 1974; The Territory of the Caddo Tribe of Oklahoma, 1974. Home: 1319 Brooklyn Ave Ann Arbor MI 48104 Office: 60 W Walton St Chicago IL 60610

TANNER, LAUREL NAN, educator; b. Detroit, Feb. 16, 1929; d. Howard Nicholas and Celia (Solovich) Jacobson; B.S. in Social Sci., Mich. State U., E. Lansing, 1949, M.A. in Edn., 1953; Ed.D., Columbia U., 1967; m. Daniel Tanner, July 11, 1948. Public sch. tchr., 1950-64; instr. tchr. edn. Hunter Coll., 1964-66, asst. prof., 1967-69; supr. Milw. Public Schs., 1966-67; mem. faculty Temple U., Phila., 1969—, prof. urban edn., 1974—; vis. professorial scholar U. London Inst. Edn., 1974-75; curriculum cons., 1969—. Faculty research fellow Temple U., 1970, 80, 81; John Dewey research fellow, 1981-82. Mem. Soc. Study Curriculum History (founder, 1st pres. 1978-79), Am. Ednl. Research Assn., Profs. Curriculum Assn., Am. Ednl. Studies Assn. Author: Classroom Discipline for Effective Teaching and Learning, 1978; co-author: Classroom Teaching and Learning, 1971, Curriculum Development: Theory into Practice, 1975, 2d edit., 1980. Home: Highwood Rd Somerset NJ 08873 Office: Coll Edn Temple Univ Philadelphia PA 19122

TANNER, MARJORIE JEAN, aircraft corp. communications ofcl.; b. Wichita, Kans., Dec. 12, 1925; d. Vic A. and Evelyn C. Tanner; student U. Wichita, 1943-45; B.A., U. Colo., 1947. Librarian, Wichita (Kans.) City Library, 1947-49; communications operator Pioneer Airlines, Dallas, 1950; communications operator Beech Aircraft Corp., Wichita, 1950—, now supr. communications center. Mem. Wichita Bus. and Profl. Women's Club, DAR, Beechcraft Suprs. Club, Beech Employees Club. Office: PO Box 85 Wichita KS 67201

TANNER, PATRICIA, psychologist; b. Grosse Pointe, Mich., July 3, 1939; d. Edward James and Mary Arlene (Bowers) Tanner; B.A., U. Ariz., 1964, M.Ed., 1964; Ph.D., Oreg. State U., 1977; children—Mary Christina Hahn, Lauretta Alane Hahn, Cathryn Elizabeth Hahn. Sch. psychologist Anchorage Borough Sch. Dist., 1972-73; Sunnyside Sch. Dist., Tucson, 1974-76; lectr. U. Alaska, 1972-73; pvt. practice women's therapy, children's learning and behavior disorders, Tucson, 1977—. Mem. Am. Psychol. Assn., Ariz. Psychol. Assn. Republican. Baptist. Editor: Alaska Psychol. Assn. Newsletter, 1971-73. Office: 6605 E Calle Cavalier Tucson AZ 85715

TANNER, SALLY M., state legislator; b. East Chicago, Ind., Dec. 28; student Art Center Coll. of Design, Pasadena City Coll.; children—Tim, Chris. Former adminstrv. asst. to Assemblyman Harvey Johnson, (Calif.), Congressman Danielson; mem. Calif. Assembly, 1978—. Bd. dirs. San Gabriel Valley Boys Club; mem. Mid Valley Democratic Club, Friendly El Monte Dem. Club. Named Legislator of Yr., Calif. Assn. Physically Handicapped, 1980. Mem. Nat. Assn. Women Legislators, Council State Govts. Roman Catholic. Office: 11100 Valley Blvd Suite 106 El Monte CA 91731

TANNER, SHARON MARIE, assn. adminstr.; b. Fort Wayne, Ind., May 8, 1949; d. Robert Milton and Marie Anna (Mullen) Tanner; B.S. in Advt., U. Fla., 1971; M.S.A., George Washington U., 1980; m. B. J. Sherwin. Mgmt. trainee, teller supr. Security Fed., Miami, 1972-75; personnel mgr. Diners Club, Miami, 1975; personnel rep., mgr. tng. and devel. Am. Auto Assn., Falls Church, Va., 1976-78; dir. personnel Chestnut Lodge, Inc., Rockville, Md., 1978-80; dir. personnel Suburban Hosp. Assn., Bethesda, Md., 1980-82; v.p. research Hosp. Council Nat. Capital Area, 1982—. Mem. Am. Soc. Personnel Adminstrn., Am. Soc. Hosp. Personnel Adminstrn., Hosp. Council Nat. Capital Area, Nat. Assn. Female Execs., NOW. Home: 7401 Westlake Terr 1115 Bethesda MD 20817 Office: 8600 Old Georgetown Rd Bethesda MD 20814

TANOUS, EVELYNE NAJLA, lawyer; b. Zanesville Ohio, Feb. 11, 1947; d. Joseph and Rose (Mokarzel) Tanous; B.A., U. Tex., 1961-65; J.D., South Tex. Coll. Law, 1972; 1 dau., Chantal. Admitted to Tex. bar, 1973; pros. trial atty. Dist. Atty's Office, Houston, 1973-75; asst. dist. atty. U.S. Small Bus. Adminstrn., N.Y.C. and Houston, 1977-81; mem. legal staff Union Oil Co. Calif., Houston, 1981—. Recipient French Lit. award U. Tex., 1962. Mem. Am., Tex., Houston bar assns., Nat. Assn. Dist. Attys., Tex. Dist. Atty. Assn., Sigma Delta Pi, Pi Delta Phi, Iota Tau Tau. Maronite Catholic. Clubs: World Wing Internation; Metropolitan Racquet. Office: 4635 Southwest Freeway 900 Executive Plaza West Houston TX 77027

TANOUS, HELENE MARY, physician; b. Zanesville, Ohio, Oct. 22, 1939; d. Joseph Carrington and Rose Marie (Mokarzel) Tanous; B.A., Marymount Coll., 1961; M.D., U. Tex., 1967. Intern, County Hosp., Los Angeles, 1967-68; resident in radiology U. So. Calif. Hosp., Los Angeles, 1969-71; practice medicine specializing in radiology, Los Angeles, 1972-73; instr. radiology U. So. Calif. Med. Sch., Los Angeles, 1971-72; asst. prof. diagnostic radiology Baylor Med. Sch., Houston, 1973-75; dir. med. student elective in diagnostic radiology Ben Taub Hosp., Houston, 1973-75; pvt. practice diagnostic radiology, Largo, Fla., 1975—; asst. prof. diagnostic radiology U. South Fla. Med. Sch., 1980—. Pres., founder Children's Advocates, Inc.; bd. dirs. Fla. Endowment for Humanities. Diplomate Am. Bd. Radiology. Mem. Am. Med. Women's Assn. Office: Dept Radiology U South Fla Med Sch Tampa Fla 33620

TANSEY, IVA LEE MARIE, state legislator; b. Elyria, Ohio, Jan. 6, 1930; d. Edwin Jacob and Fern L. (McKee) Law; student Lorain Bus. Coll., 1965; m. Charles J. Tansey, Sept. 7, 1948; children—Mark, Dennis, Richard. Sec., Vermilion (Ohio) High Sch., 1959-64; exec. sec. Vermilion C. of C., 1964-67; br. sec., asst. mgr. Cardinal Fed. Savs. & Loan Assn., 1967-76; mem. Ohio Ho. of Reps., 1978—. Republican. Congregationalist. Office: State House Columbus OH 43215

TANT, EMMA JEAN, therapist; b. Miami, Fla., Dec. 21, 1928; d. Roy Hamilton and Clara Agnes (Thomason) Green; B.S., Auburn U., 1950; M.A.T., U. N.Mex., 1970; postgrad. U. N.Mex., 1970-71, Tex. Christian U., 1972-78; m. James P. Tant, Feb. 9, 1968; 1 son, Billy Gene. Tchr. pub. schs., Ala., 1950-54, N.Mex., 1956-65; dist. mgr. Field Enterprises, Albuquerque, 1955-57; planner, coordinator family living program Albuquerque Job Corps for Women, OEO, 1964-65; owner, mgr. Temporary Help Service, 1965; pvt. practice marriage and family counseling, Ft. Worth, 1973—; dir. Get Slim Internat., Inc.; instr. Tex. Christian U., 1976—. Chmn. Democratic Precinct Com., 1960-62; mem. Gov.'s Commn. on Status of Women N.Mex., 1969-71; mem. Ft. Worth Mayor's Com. on Status of Women 1973-77; mem. Mech. Bd. Ft. Worth, 1973-79; bd. dirs. Ft. Worth Ballet. Mem. AAUW, Am., Tex. home econs. assns., Am. Humanistic Psychology Assn., Am. Assn. Marriage and Family Therapists, Internat. Transactional Analysis Assn. Clubs: Petroleum, El Paso, Elks. Home: 2325 Edwin St Fort Worth TX 76110 Office: 1606 Mistletoe Blvd Fort Worth TX 76104

TANZMANN, VIRGINIA WARD, architect; b. Tuxedo Park, N.Y., July 6, 1945; d. John A. and Helen L. (Pfund) Ward; B.A. in Architecture, Syracuse U., 1968, B.Arch., 1969. Apprentice architect Burke, Kober, Nicolais Archuleta, Los Angeles, 1969-72; architect D.L. Dworsky & Assoc., Beverly Hills, Calif., 1972-74, SUA, Inc., Los Angeles, 1974-75, S. Calif. Rapid Transit Dist., Los Angeles, 1975-78; owner The Tanzmann Assos., Los Angeles, 1978—; speaker, cons. in field. Bd. dirs. Los Angeles Voluntary Action Center, 1973—, v.p., chmn. exec. com., 1973—; mem. adv. bd. Architects, Designers and Planners for Social Responsibility; active mem. Los Angeles Area C. of C., 1973—; bd. dirs. YWCA Los Angeles, 1980—. Recipient Achievement award Soroptimist Internat., 1972. Mem. AIA (chmn. nat. task force women in architecture, 1978-80, dir. Los Angeles chpt. 1980—), Assn. Women in Architecture (dir. 1973—, pres. 1976-77), Archtl. Guild (dir. 1982—), L'Union Internat. des Femmes Architectes (chmn. U.S.A. tour, 1979), Soroptomist Internat. Works included archtl. exhibits in Iran, 1976, Los Angeles, 1975, 1978, 1979, and Paris, 1978. Office: 304 S Broadway Suite 320 Los Angeles CA 90013

TAPP, BILLIE JEAN, human resources co. exec.; b. Oklahoma City, Aug. 8, 1946; d. William W. and Jean F. Towe; student Okla. State U., 1974-75. Ins. coordinator Aero Commander, Oklahoma City, 1965-68; advt. sec. university Sound, Oklahoma City, 1968-69; adminstrv. mgr. Hewlett-Packard Co., Oklahoma City, 1969-75; eastern regional mgr. Diversified Human Resources Group, Houston, 1976—. Mem. Nat. Assn. Female Execs. Office: 1980 Post Oak Blvd Suite 2170 Houston TX 77056

TARAZI, LINDA, psychologist, educator; b. Chgo., Nov. 19, 1928; d. Albert and Gerlinde (Friedrich) Mueller; B.S., Northwestern U., 1948, M.S., 1950; Ph.D., Ill. Inst. Tech., 1981; m. Kamal Tarazi, Mar. 23, 1956; children—Laila, Martin. Exptl. biologist Baxter Labs., Morton Grove, Ill., 1952-57; researcher Ency. Brit., Chgo., 1960-61; tchr. biology Roosevelt High Sch., Chgo., 1963—; tchr. parapsychology adult continuing edn. program, Des Plaines, Ill., 1979; pvt. practice psychology and hypnotherapy, Glenview, Ill., 1979—. Mem. Am. Psychol. Assn., Am. Soc. Clin. Hypnosis, Soc. Clin. and Exptl. Hypnosis, Nat. Wildlife Fedn., Am. Mus. Natural History. Home: 2527 Bel-Air Dr Glenview IL 60025 Office: 3436 W Wilson Chicago IL 60625

TARBOX, PATRICIA ANN, psychiat. social worker; b. Queens, N.Y., Mar. 9, 1948; d. Frank Lester and Mary Ellen (Powell) Tarbox; B.S., U. Buffalo, 1969; M.S.W., Syracuse (N.Y.) U., 1976; 1 son, Vaughn Andrew. Caseworker children's div. Jefferson County Dept. Social Services, Watertown, N.Y., 1969-75; psychiat. social worker Community Mental Health Center, Mercy Hosp., Watertown, 1976—; lectr., cons. in field; mem. Legis. Forum Women and Alcohol; adv. steering com. Child Protective Services. Community rep. Jefferson County Head Start Policy Council; bd. dirs., mem. com. Jefferson County Women's Center. Mem. Acad. Cert. Social Workers, Nat. Assn. Social Workers, Childbirth Edn. Assn. Lutheran. Home: 1316 Marra Dr Watertown NY 13601 Office: 218 Stone St Watertown NY 13601

TARGOW, JEANETTE GOLDFIELD, clin. social worker; b. Chgo., May 21, 1910; d. Isadore and Rebecca Covici Goldfield; Ph.B., U. Chgo., 1934; M.S.W., UCLA, 1953; children—Patricia Skinner, Richard Targow. Social worker U. So. Calif. Psychology Clinic, Los Angeles, 1953-55; clin. social worker Psychol. Service Center, Los Angeles, 1955-60; pvt. practice clin. social work, Los Angeles, 1960—; instr. Calif. Sch. Profl. Psychology; mem. faculty dept. psychology Loyola-Marymount Coll., 1981—; supr. Didi Hirsch Mental Health Center, Culver City, Calif., 1977-81. Fellow Am. Group Psychotherapy Assn., Soc. for Clin. Social Work; mem. Los Angeles Group Psychotherapy Soc., Nat. Assn. Social Workers, ACLU. Democrat. Jewish. Home: 1835 N Doheny Dr Los Angeles CA 90069 Office: 648 N Doheny Dr Los Angeles CA 90069

TARLTON, SHIRLEY MARIE, coll. dean; b. Raleigh, N.C., Aug. 8, 1937; d. Lloyd E. and Mary O. (Suycott) Tarlton; diploma Peace Coll., Raleigh, N.C., 1957; B.A. in French, Queens Coll., Charlotte, N.C., 1960; M.S.L.S., U. N.C., Chapel Hill, 1966. Head tech. services div. U. N.C., Charlotte, 1961-68, asst. librarian, 1961-63; asso. dir. tech. services Winthrop Coll. Library, 1968-73, acting dir., 1971, 73-74, dean library services, 1974—; mem. bd. Southeastern Library Network; mem. council Online Computer Library Center. Mem. ALA, Southeastern N.C., S.C., Metrolina, Mecklenburg library assns., Am. Soc. Info. Sci., Rock Hill C. of C., Sigma Pi Alpha, Phi Theta Kappa, Beta Phi Mu, Phi Kappa Phi. Home: 7406 Windyrush Rd Matthews NC 28105 Office: Winthrop College Rock Hill SC 29733

TARNOFF, DIANE SEAMAN, broadcasting co-exec.; b. Watseka, Ill., Mar. 25, 1946; d. William George and Louise Imogene (West) Seaman; B.A., Smith Coll., 1968; M.A., Columbia U., 1969; M.B.A., N.Y.U., 1976; m. Jeffrey Tarnoff, Mar. 15, 1975; 1 dau., Sarah West. Tchr., Madison, N.J., 1969-70; sales promotion coordinator WPIX-TV, N.Y.C., 1970-72; dir. mktg. WMCA, Straus Communications, N.Y.C., 1972-75; mgr. fin. analysis and pricing NBC-TV, N.Y.C., 1975-77, mgr. children's program sales, 1977-81, dir. daytime program sales, 1981—. Bd. dirs. Brownstone Learning and Daycare Center, 1980—, pres., 1981—. Mem. fin. com. Smith Coll. Alumnae Assn., 1976-78. Presbyterian. Club: Smith Coll. of N.Y. Home: 470 West End Ave New York NY 10024 also Averill Park NY 12018 Office: 30 Rockefeller Plaza New York NY 10020

TARPEY, MARIE VERONICA, ednl. adminstr.; b. Boston, Apr. 12, 1924; d. Bernard Michael and Veronica Mary (Hirl) Tarpey; B.A. in English, Manhattan Coll., 1953; M.A. in History, St. John's U., 1959, Ph.D., 1970. Tchr., Resurrection-Ascension Sch., Rego Park, N.Y., 1944-54, Seton Hall High Sch., Patchogue, N.Y., 1954-65; Bishop Reilly High Sch., Fresh Meadows, N.Y., 1965; asst. prof. Wilmington (Del.) Coll., 1969, dean faculty and acad. affairs, 1970-76; v.p. acad. affairs, prof. history Pikeville (Ky.) Coll., 1976-79; acad. dean, prof. history Elmira (N.Y.) Coll., 1979—. Chmn. bd. dirs. Del. Humanities Council, 1975—; mem. Ky. Humanities Council Bd., 1977-79; mem. St. Patrick's Parish Council. Fulbright Scholar, 1965. Mem. Am. Assn. Univ. Adminstrs., Am. Hist. Assn., Am. Com. for Irish Studies, AAUP, Irish-Am. Cultural Inst., Eastern Assn. Deans, Nat. Assn. Women Deans, Am. Assn. Higher Edn., AAUW, Chemung County Humane Soc. (dir., sec. 1980—), Bus. and Profl. Women's Club. Roman Catholic. Clubs: Torch, Zonta. Author: The Role of Joseph McGarrity in the Struggle for Irish Independence, 1976. Home: 320 W 7th St Elmira NY 14901 Office: Elmira Coll Park Pl Elmira NY 14901

TARR, ELVIRA R, educator; b. Bklyn.; d. Max and Minnie (Skolnick) Rosenfeld; B.A. Hunter Coll. 1944, M.S. in Edn., Queens Coll. 1958, diploma in adminstrn. 1958, Ph.D., N.Y.U. 1968; m. Philip Tarr; children—Leslie Laurie, Lawrence D. Tchr., New Hyde Park (N.Y.) Schs. 1953-60; faculty Queens Coll. 1960-61, Hofstra U. 1961-62; faculty Bklyn. Coll. 1963—, now prof. dept. edn., asst. dean students. Mem. exec. bd. Nat. Congress Neighborhood Women 1978-80, Shelter for Battered Women 1978-80. Recipient Founders Day award N.Y.U. 1968. Mem. Am. Assn. Coll. Profs., Soc. Am. Philosophers, Pierce Soc. Contbr. in field. Office: Brooklyn Coll Bedford Ave Brooklyn NY 11210

TARR, MARGO PAQUETTE, public relations and mktg. exec.; b. Hull, Que., Can., Sept. 26, 1934; came to U.S., 1956; d. Alfred W. and Germaine A. Paquette; student Thomas More Coll.; children by previous marriage—Caroline, William Lewis Tarr, Jr., Julie Tarr. Asst. dir. John Robert Powers Sch., Rochester, N.Y., 1969-72; dir. Miss America Pageant, also Jr. Miss Pageants, Rochester, N.Y., 1970; dir. sales Ramada Inn, Sharonville, Ohio, 1973; dir. public relations, editor Cin. Bd. Realtors, 1974-82; dir. mktg. Chelsea Moore Corp., Cin., 1982—; tchr. French folklore dances St. Lawrence High Sch., Ont., Can., 1954. Mem. public relations com. Arthritis Found., 1981; judge various pageants, N.Y. State. Mem. Internat. Assn. of Bus. Communicators (dir. Cin. chpt. 1981—), Women in Communications, Cin. Editors Assn. (dir. 1979—), Exec. Women's Network, Victorian Soc., Alliance Francaise, Lookout Farm Homeowners Assn. (dir. 1981—). Home: 121 Lookout Farm Dr Crestview Hills KY 41017 Office: Chelsea Moore Corp 105 W 4th St Cincinnati OH 45202

TASH, SUSAN SHIELDHOUSE, publishing co. exec.; b. Washington, Mar. 14, 1945; d. Sol Schildhause and Phyllis R. (Sydell) Stambler; B.S. in Journalism, Boston U., 1967; m. Ronald Tash, July 29, 1977; children— Kate Allison, Gabriel James. Mgr. sta. publicity Metromedia Producers Corp., N.Y.C., 1971-73; mgr. bus. info. ABC-TV, N.Y.C., 1973-77, dir. bus. info., 1977; mgr. press info. Sta. WLS-TV, Chgo., 1977-78; mgr. corp. communication Playboy Enterprises, Inc., Chgo., 1978-79, dir. corp. communication, 1979—. Mem. Publicity Club Chgo., Nat. Acad. TV Arts and Scis., Public Relations Soc. Am. Office: Playboy Enterprises Inc. 919 N Michigan Ave Chicago IL 60611

TASHJIAN, HELEN ELIZABETH, nurse, educator; b. Worcester, Mass., May 31, 1926; d. Peter and Nora Margaret (Surabian) T.; A.B. in Geography, Clark U., 1946; M. Nursing, Yale U., 1949; M.S. in Adminstrn. Ednl. Programs in Nursing, Boston U., 1968, Ed.D. in Ednl. Adminstrn. and Supervision (Nurses' Ednl. Funds Nurses' Scholarship and Fellowship Fund grantee), 1971. Instr. in nursing arts Worcester Hahnemann Hosp. Sch. Nursing, 1949-55, asso. dir. edn., 1951-55; instr. nursing, head nursing dept. New Eng. Bapt. Hosp. Sch. Nursing, Boston, 1955-56, asst. dir. in charge health and guidance, 1956-66; asst. prof. nursing Quinsigamond Community Coll., 1966-68; research asso. U.S. Office Edn. and PHS Project, Boston U. Sch. Nursing, 1968-69, cons. W. K. Kellogg Project, 1969; dir. nursing, asso. prof. nursing U. Maine, Augusta, 1970-73; asso. prof., chmn. dept. nursing U. Hartford Coll. Arts and Scis., 1974; prof. nursing, curricula coordinator Ind. State U., 1975-79; dir. nursing program, prof. Anna Maria Coll., 1979-80, Becker Jr. Coll., 1981—; v.p. New Eng. Inst. Comparative Medicine, West Boylston, Mass., 1975—. Mem. Am. Nurses' Assn., Mass. Nurses' Assn., Nat. League for Nursing, Mass./R.I. League for Nursing, AAUW, Adult Edn. Assn. U.S.A., Boston U. Alumni Assn., Boston U. Sch. Nursing Alumni Assn., Clark U. Alumni Assn., Yale U. Sch. Nursing Alumnae Assn., Am. Guild Organists, Am. Assn. Community and Jr. Colls. Club: Boston U. Women's (Worcester County, Mass.). Home: 363 Prospect St West Boylston MA 01583

TASKEY, KAREN JEAN, clin. psychologist; b. Portsmouth, Va., July 28, 1953; d. Stanley Robert and Ruth Naomi Taskey; B.S. summa cum laude in Psychology, Old Dominion U., 1975; M.A. in Clin. Psychology, Indiana U. Pa., 1979; postgrad. Ohio U., 1979—. Research asst. dept. psychology Indiana U. Pa., 1975-76, teaching asst., 1976-77; test adminstr. Applied Sci. Assos., Inc., Valencia, Pa., 1976-77; psychology asso. Coshocton (Ohio) Counseling Center, 1978-81, county dir., 1981—; leader assertion tng. groups YWCA, 1979—. Bd. dirs. Eastern Ohio Regional Alcoholism Council; trustee Coshocton chpt. Big Bros.-Big Sisters. Mem. Am. Psychol. Assn. (asso.), Ohio Psychol. Assn. (affiliate), Pa. Psychol. Assn. (asso.), Psi Chi, Alpha Chi. Methodist. Home: 329 S 9th St Coshocton OH 43812 Office: 226 N 4th St Coshocton OH 43812

TATE, BARBARA LOUISE, nurse, univ. dean; b. Warwick, N.Y., Aug. 6, 1921; d. James Pronk and Caroline May (Still) T.; B.A., Elmira Coll., 1945; M.A., Columbia U., 1951, Ed.D., 1961. Ednl. dir. St. Luke's Hosp. Sch. Nursing, N.Y.C., 1952-56; nursing research editor Am. Jour. Nursing, 1959-62; asst. dir. Nat. League Nursing, N.Y.C., 1959-64, dir. research, 1964-69; dean, prof. Coll. Nursing, U. R.I., 1969—; sec. bd. trustees South County Hosp., Wakefield, R.I.; mem. Nurse Edn. Funds Bd., 1969—, pres., 1976-80. Mem. Nat. League Nursing, Am. Nurses Assn., Am. Psychol. Assn. Contbr. articles to profl. jours. Office: White Hall Kingston RI 02881

TATE, CAROL FAY, social worker; b. Mitchell, Nebr., Apr. 5, 1937; d. Laurence and Vivian Joan (Powell) T.; B.S., Sioux Falls (S.D.) Coll., 1959; postgrad. Kent State U., 1961-64; M.S.W., Fla. State U., 1969. Asst. dir. health, phys. edn. YWCA, Akron, Ohio, 1959-61; home vis. tchr. Summit County Assn. Retarded Children, Akron, 1961-62, Summit County Child Welfare Bd., Akron, 1962-63; instr. Youngstown (Ohio) U., 1964-65; dir. sch. for trainable mentally retarded Scotts Bluff County (Nebr.) Assn. Retarded Children, 1964-65; tchr. Scotts Bluff County Sch. Bd., 1965-66; with Fla. Dept. Health and Rehab. Services, Tampa, 1966-69; pvt. practice social work, Tampa, 1970-75; dir. social work Hope Haven Children's Hosp., Jacksonville, Fla., 1975; dir. Gulf County Activity Center for Retarded Adults, Port St. Joe, Fla., 1976-77; pvt. practice med. social services, St. Petersburg, Fla., 1977-78; staff social worker Bay Area Home Health Services, St. Petersburg, 1978-79; dir. social services Global Home Health Services, Inc., Treasure Island, Fla., 1979—. Mem. Nat. Assn. Social Workers, Acad. Cert. Social Workers, NOW (pres. Pinellas chpt. 1979-80), Fla. Assn. Health and Social Services. Democrat. Home: 589 59th St S Saint Petersburg FL 33707

TATE, EVELYN MARIE, dietitian; b. Houston, Aug. 13, 1954; d. Frederic Carl and Erna Evelyn (Ziebarth) Peters; B.S. in Home Econs., Tex. Tech. U., Lubbock, 1977; m. Gary Wayne Tate, June 6, 1980; 1 son, Eric Scott Winchell. With ARA Food Services, 1977—, asst. dir. food services John Knox Village, Lubbock, 1977-78, chief clin. dietitian Shannon W. Tex. Meml. Hosp., San Angelo, 1978—. Mem. Am. Dietetic Assn., Big Country Dietetic Assn. Lutheran. Club: Altrusa. Home: 723 W Highland St San Angelo TX 76903 Office: PO Box 1879 San Angelo TX 76902

TATE, EVELYN RUTH, real estate broker; b. Ottumwa, Iowa, Sept. 21; d. Frank Edward and Ella Belle (Smith) Ross; student public schs., Huntington Park, Calif.; m. William Tate (dec.); 1 son, William. Owner, mgr. Evelyn R. Tate Realty Co., Sherman Oaks, Calif., 1943-53, Beverly Hills, Calif., 1942—; owner, mgr. Evelyn Tate Fine Arts, San Francisco, 1976—; mgr. Beverly Hills Galleries, Hyatt Regency Hotel, San Francisco, 1979—; mgr. art gallery Fairmont Hotel; owner, mgr. Tate Gallery, Jack Tar Hotel, San Francisco, Hyatt Regency Hotel, San Francisco. Mem. Nat. Assn. Female Execs., The Exec. Female. Home: 999 Green St Apt 1003 San Francisco CA 94133

TATE, MARGOT STEELE, computer services co. exec.; b. Rochester, N.Y., Jan. 16, 1946; d. John David and Jeanne Marie (O'Brien) Hutchinson, student Ithaca Coll., 1963-64, Rochester Inst. Tech., 1965-68, 78-80; m. William C. Tate, Nov. 19, 1966; children—Brien Steele, Antoinette Cooper. With Home Service Dept., Rochester (N.Y.) Gas & Electric, 1964-68; systems cons. I.P. Sharp Assoc., Rochester, 1975-78, facilities mgr., 1979-80, tech. asst., 1979, 80-81, asst. mgr., 1981—. Adviser, Explorer Scouts, 1980-81; bd. dirs. YWCA, Rochester, 1971-76, treas., 1974-76. Mem. Rochester Engring. Soc., Nat. Assn. Female Execs., Assn. for Computing Machinery (sec. 1980-81, chmn. 1981—). Roman Catholic. Home: 11 Dogwood Glen Rochester NY 14625 Office: 1200 First Federal Plaza Rochester NY 14614

TATE, MERZE, educator; b. Blanchard, Mich., Feb. 6, 1905; d. Charles H. and Myrtle Katora (Lett) T.; B.A. Western Mich. U. 1927, D.Litt. 1948, M.A. Columbia U. 1930, B.Litt. Oxford U. 1935, Ph.D. Harvard U. 1941; LL.D. (hon.) Morgan State U., Bowie State Coll. 1977, Lincoln U. 1978. Tchr., Crispus Attucks High Sch., Indpls. 1927-32, Barber Scotia Coll. Concord, N.C. 1935-36, Bennett Coll. 1936-41, Morgan State U. 1941-42; faculty Howard U. 1942—, now prof. emeritus; Fulbright prof. India 1950-51. Fellow and grantee in field; recipient Nat. Urban League Disting. Achievement award 1948; Western Mich. U. Disting. Alumna award 1970; Mayor of Detroit award 1978; Am. Black Artist's Pioneer award 1978; award The Prometheans, Inc., 1980. Mem. Am. Hist. Assn., Assn. Study Afro-Am. History, AAUW, Phi Beta Kappa, Alpha Kappa Alpha. Roman Catholic. Clubs: Radcliffe of Washington, Harvard of Washington, Writers, Howard U. Women's, Howard U. Retirees, Bridge Builders, Bridge Eights. Author: The Disarmament Illusion—The Movement for a Limitation of Armaments to 1907; The United States and Armaments 1948, The United State and the Hawaiian Kingdom 1965, Hawaii: Reciprocity or Annexation 1968; contbr. numerous articles to profl. jours.

TATE, SHEILA BURKE, press sec. to First Lady U.S.; b. Washington, Mar. 3, 1942; d. Eugene L. and Mary J. (Doherty) Burke; B.A. in Journalism, Duquesne U., 1964; postgrad. U. Denver, 1975-76; m. William J. Tate, May 2, 1981; children—Hager Patton, Courtney Patton. Research asst. Westinghouse Air Brake Co., Pitts., 1964-65; copywriter Ketchum, MacLeod & Grove, Pitts., 1965; asst. account exec. Fahlgren & Assos., Parkersburg, W.Va., 1966; account exec. Burson-Marsteller Assocs., Pitts., 1967; public relations mgr. Colo. Nat. Bank, Denver, 1967-70; v.p. Hill and Knowlton, Houston and Washington, 1977-81; press sec. to First Lady Nancy Reagan, Washington, 1981—. Mem. Public Relations Soc. Am., Nat. Press Club. Republican. Presbyterian. Club: Duquesne U. Century. Office: 1600 Pennsylvania Ave NW Washington DC 20500

TATOM, JUDY ELLARD, welfare adminstr.; worker; b. Cornelia, Ga., Aug. 18, 1926; d. William Benton and Margaret Louise (Overton) Ellard; B.A., U. Montevallo, 1948; postgrad. U. Ala., 1950; M.S.W., U. Ala., 1979; m. Marx F. Tatom, June 14, 1953; children—D. Margaret, Marx F. II. Caseworker, Houston County Dept. Public Welfare, Dothan, Ala., 1948-50; child welfare worker Elmore County Dept. Public Welfare, Wetumpka, Ala., 1950-52, county welfare dir., 1952-53; child welfare worker Houston County Dept. Pensions and Security, Dothan, 1963-66, welfare supr. II, 1966-79, welfare supr. III, 1979—. Mem. adv. com. Ala. Ednl. TV; bd. dirs. SE Ala. Youth Services. Mem. Ala. State Employees Assn. (pres. Houston County chpt.), Assn. Service Agys., Am. Bus. Women's Assn., Nat. Assn. Social Workers, Ala. Conf. Social Work, AAUW, Ala. Conf. Child Care, Am. Public Welfare Assn., Beta Sigma Phi. Methodist. Home: Rt 9 Box 295-A Dothan AL 36303 Office: PO Box 2027 Dothan AL 36301

TATUM, MARGARET EUGENIA, retail music co. exec.; b. Waxachachie, Tex., Nov. 26, 1917; d. James Logan and Lola May (Curlin) Wright; B.A., Trinity U., San Antonio, 1938; postgrad. counseling and guidance, Stephen F. Austin U., Nacogdoches, Tex., 1971; m. Thaddeus Alto Tatum, Jr., June 4, 1943; children—Thaddeus Alto III, Judith Wright Tatum Schrader. Tchr. public schs., Tex., 1938-43; v.p., co-owner Tatum Music Co., Inc., Longview and Tyler, Tex., 1948—; genealogist. Mem. AAUW, DRT (chpt. pres. 1977-79), DAR (chpt. registrar 1977-79), Daus. Am. Colonists (chpt. regent 1981-83), Colonial Dames 17th Century (chpt. v.p. 1981-83), Am. Contract Bridge League (life master, life mem.), U.D.C., Huguenot Soc. Founders Manakin (Va.) (Tex. State registrar 1981-83), Nat. Soc. Magna Charta Dames, Colonial Dames Am., Gregg County Hist. Soc., Tex. Geneal. Soc., Bus. and Profl. Men's Club Beaumont. Presbyterian. Club: Pinecrest Country, Summit, Reservation, Longview. Address: 718 Sylvan Dr Longview TX 75602

TATUM, SUE, chem. co. exec.; b. Hickory, Miss., Aug. 1, 1923; d. Marion Clyde and Susie Anna (Biggs) T.; A.A., E. Central Jr. Coll., Decatur, Miss., 1942. Sec., U.S. Govt., Meridian and Jackson, Miss., 1942-46; sec.-treas. Miss. Farm Bur. Fedn., Jackson, 1946-49; with Miss. Chem. Corp., Yazoo City, 1949—, sec.-treas. Coastal Chem. Corp. subs., corp. asst. sec.-treas., 1956-70, corp. sec., 1970—. Mem. Nat. Assn. Corp. Dirs. Baptist. Home: 521 E 18th St Yazoo City MS 39194 Office: Hwy 49 E Miss Chem Corp Yazoo City MS 39194

TAUBER, INGRID DIANE, clin. psychologist; b. Washington, Jan. 30, 1952; d. Laszlo Nandor and Lilly Katherine (Manovill) T.; B.A., Boston U., 1973; M.A., U. Md., 1976; Ph.D., Calif. Sch. Profl. Psychology, 1980. Counselor youth services Area B Community Mental Health Center, Washington, 1974-76; psychology intern Gladman Meml. Hosp., Oakland, Calif., 1976-77, San Francisco Gen. Hosp., 1976-77; pre- and post-doctoral trainee VA Med. Center, San Francisco, 1977-81; pvt. practice clin. psychology Women for Women Psychotherapy Inst., San Francisco, 1977—; tchr. psychol. testing VA Med. Center. Bd. overseers Tauber Inst. Holocaust Studies, Brandeis U. Lic. marriage, family and child counselor, Calif. Mem. Am. Psychol. Assn., Calif. Psychol. Assn., Am. Orthopsychiat. Assn., Am. Group Psychotherapy and Psychodrama Assn., Assn. Mental Health Affiliation with Israel. Home: 2090 Green St 26 San Francisco CA 94123 Office: 421 Locust St San Francisco CA 94118

TAUBERER, GALE MERLIS, speech pathologist; b. Omaha, Jan. 20, 1949; d. Sidney and Annette (Forbes) Merlis; B.A., Case Western Res. U., 1971; M.S., Columbia U., 1976; m. Peter R. Tauberer, May 7, 1978. Speech pathologist transdisciplinary mini-team Willowbrook Devel. Center, United Cerebral Palsy N.Y., Staten Island, 1976-77; asso. dir. inservice edn. U.C.P. Karl Warner Center, Staten Island, 1977-79; speech pathologist U.C.P. Post Instnl. Placement Program, N.Y.C., 1979-80; pvt. practice speech therapy, 1980—. Lic. speech pathologist, N.Y. Mem. Am. Speech, Lang. and Hearing Assn., N.Y. State Speech and Hearing Assn. Office: 2040 Deer Park Ave Deer Park NY 11729

TAUBITZ, FREDRICKA, fin. exec.; b. Los Angeles, Feb. 25, 1944; d. Ferdinand C. and Marie L. (Stewart) T.; A.A., Pasadena City Coll., 1963; B.S. in Bus. Adminstrn., U. Calif., Berkeley, 1965; M.S. in Bus. Adminstrn., UCLA, 1967; grad. Advanced Mgmt. Program, Harvard U., 1980. Acct., Coopers & Lybrand, Los Angeles, 1965-75, partner, 1976—; founding dir. First Women's Bank Calif., Los Angeles, 1974-76. Bd. dirs. Soroptimist Found. Los Angeles, 1978-79, Calif. Mus. Found. Adv. Bd., 1978-81; bd. dirs. Girls' Club, Pasadena, Calif., 1973—, pres., 1981—. Recipient Outstanding Young Bus. Leader award Los Angeles Jr. C. of C., 1978, Internat. Achievement award Soroptimist Internat., 1977. C.P.A., Calif. Mem. Am. Inst. C.P.A.s, Calif. Soc. C.P.A.s, Los Angeles C. of C. (dir. women's council 1978-81), Inst. Internal Auditors (dir. chpt. 1982—), Beta Kappa. Office: 1000 W 6th St Los Angeles CA 90017

TAUBMAN, NAOMI MOLLY, accountant, realtor; b. West Alexandria, Ohio, Jan. 13, 1926; d. David and Edith (Goldstein) Blum; student public schs.; m. Daniel Taubman, Aug. 26, 1945; children—Martin, Harold, Stanley, Brenda. Pvt. practice acctg., Dayton, Ohio, 1942—; realtor DBA Cert. Realty Co., Dayton, 1942—. Mem. Nat. Assn. Public Accts., Public Accts. State Ohio, Enrolled Assn., Dayton Area Bd. Realtors, Nat. Assn. Realtors, Tax Accredation Soc. Democrat. Jewish. Home: 762 Clarendon Rd Troy OH 45373 Office: 206 N Dixie Dr Vandalia OH 45377 also 1312 McKaig Ave Troy OH 45373

TAUNTON, WANDA CARDA, govt. agy. ofcl.; b. Pickstown, S.D., Aug. 24, 1949; d. Lloyd Louis and Viola Vera (Thaler) Carda; B.S. in Bus. Mgmt. magna cum laude, Met. State Coll., 1971; postgrad. in edn. and public adminstrn., U. Colo., 1975—; m. Richard Way Taunton, Jan. 31, 1976; stepchildren—Victoria, Wayne, Jennifer, David. Bus. tchr. Woodland Park (Colo.) High Sch., 1971-72; tchr. bus. and adult edn. Basseterre (St. Kitts, B.W.I.) as Peace Corps vol., 1972-74; clk.-typist Denver Public Schs. and Channel 6 Public TV, 1974-75; sec. EPA, Denver, 1975-76, environ. protection specialist, 1976-80, staff asst. to div. dir. budget, fin. and program analysis, 1980—, co-chair Fed. Women's Program Region VIII, 1982—. Recipient Bronze medal for commendable service EPA, 1979. Mem. Am. Soc. Public Adminstrn., Nat. Assn. Female Execs., Nat. Wildlife Fedn. Methodist. Home: 2368 S Holland Ct Lakewood CO 80227 Office: 1860 Lincoln St Denver CO 80295

TAUSIG, JANE ELLEN, social worker; b. Milford, Conn., May 12, 1954; d. Ted Hans and Dinah Stern Tausig; B.S. in Social Welfare, Adelphi U., 1976, M.S.W., 1977; postgrad. Bryn Mawr Coll.; m. Jeffrey Paul Garelik; Unit psychiat. social worker Hedges Treatment Center, Devereux Found., Devon, Pa., 1977-80, residence dir., 1980—, supervising psychiat. social worker, 1980—; mem. retrospective audit com. Devereux Found., 1978—, chmn. liason com., 1979—. Bd. dirs. World Fellowship, Inc., 1974-77. Mem. Acad. Cert. Social Workers, Nat. Assn. Social Workers. Home: 373D Willowbrook Dr Norristown PA 19403 Office: Hedges Treatment Center Devereux Found Devon PA 19333

TAUSSIG, HELEN BROOKE, former pediatric cardiologist; b. Cambridge, Mass., May 24, 1898; d. Frank William and Edith (Guild) T.; student Radcliffe Coll., 1917-19, D.Sc. (hon.), 1978; A.B., U. Calif., 1921; postgrad. Harvard U., 1921, D.Sc. (hon.), 1959; postgrad. Boston U. Sch. Medicine, 1922-24, D.Sc. (hon.), 1948; M.D., Johns Hopkins U., 1927; hon. degrees include: D.Sc. Goucher Coll., 1949, Women's Coll. of U. N.C., 1950, Northwestern U., 1951, Columbia U., 1951, Women's Med. Coll. Pa., 1951, Middlebury Coll., 1952, Western Coll. for Women, 1959, Gottingen U., 1960, Randolph-Macon Woman's Coll., 1966, Cedar Crest Coll., 1966, U. Mass., Amherst, 1966, Jefferson Med. Coll. and Med. Center, 1967, Duke U., 1968, Med. Coll. Wis., 1972, LL.D., Hood Coll., 1950, D.Sc., M.D., U. Athens (Greece), 1956, M.D., U. Vienna (Austria), 1965, H.H.D., Colby Coll., 1966, Archibald fellow in medicine, 1927-28; intern in pediatrics Johns Hopkins Hosp., Balt., 1928-30, physician-in-charge Harriet Lane Home, Cardiac Clinic, 1930-63, instr. pediatric cardiology, 1930-46; assoc. prof. pediatrics Johns Hopkins U. Sch. Medicine, Balt., 1946-59, prof., 1959-63, prof. emeritus, 1963—; Thomas M. Rivers Meml. research fellow, 1963-68; pediatric cons., staff Balt. City Hosps.; clin. prof. medicine Georgetown U. Sch. Medicine, 1969—; mem. Presdl. Commn. on Heart Disease, Cancer and Stroke, 1964; alt. U.S. del. XXth Internat. Conf. Red Cross, 1965; bd. dirs. Internat. Cardiology Found., from 1967; hon. chmn. Com. of Responsibility on War-Injured Children, Vietnam, 1967; mem. U.S. del. 20th WHO Assembly Conf., 1967; bd. mgrs. Harriet Lane Home, 1972—; Frances Rather Seybold lectr., Tex. Med. Center, Houston, 1973. Honors include: chevalier Legion d'Honneur (France), 1947; Passano award, 1948; Feltrinelli Prize (Italy), 1954; Medal of Freedom, U.S., 1964; Carl Ludwig Medal of Honor, Deutsche Gesellschaft für Kreislaufforshung, 1967; Howland award Am. Pediatric Soc., 1971; William F. Faulkes award Nat. Rehab. Assn., 1971; Drake award Maine Heart Assn., 1974; Award of Excellence Washington Coll., 1977; Sci. Achievement award AMA, 1977, Physicians Award of Excellence, Med. Times, 1978; presdl. citation Am. Coll. Cardiology, 1980, gifted tchr. award, 1981; award Asian Pacific Congress of Cardiology, 1979; hon. centers dedicated: Helen B. Taussig Cardiac Clinic, Gottingen, Ger., 1964, Helen B. Taussig Children's Pediatric Cardiac Center, Johns Hopkins Hosp., Balt., 1970; Helen B. Taussig Internat. Fellowship founded by AAUW, 1973; recipient Milton Stover Eisenhower gold medal, Johns Hopkins U., 1976; honoree symposia Deborah Heart and Lung Center, Albert Einstein Med. Center, N.Y.C., 1975, Johns Hopkins Hosp., 1976, Helen B. Taussig Abteilung Kardiologie, U. Gottingen; co-recipient (with Alfred Blalock) Albert Lasker award, 1954, Gairdner Found. award, 1959. Fellow ACP (John Phillips Meml. bronze medal, 1966), Coll. Physicians Phila. (hon.), Royal Coll. Medicine and Surgery of Glasgow (hon.); mem. Am. Heart Assn. (award of merit, 1957, Gold Heart award, 1963, pres. 1965-66, dir.-at-large 1967-70, Helen B. Taussig lectureship founded 1973, James B. Herrick award 1974), Heart Assn. of Md.; formerly active profl. assns. including Am. Pediatric Soc., Am. Coll. Cardiology, N.Y. Acad. Scis., AAAS, Phi Beta Kappa, Alpha Omega Alpha. Democrat. Unitarian. Conceived blue baby operation; investigator babies in Ger.; active in prevention of distbn. thalidomide in U.S.; author: Congenital Malfunction of the Heart, 2 edits.; contbr. articles in field to profl. publs. U.S. and abroad, also profl. confs. Home: Crosslands Apt 158 Kenneth Sq PA 19348

TAUTFEST, CARLA ANN, writer, editor; b. Twin Falls, Idaho, Aug. 10, 1948; d. Charles and Ellen Kodesh; B.S., Okla. State U., 1971; m. Rexford Tautfest, June 14, 1967; children—Kirsten, John, Charly Ann. Dental asst., Tonkawa, Okla., 1971-72; free-lance writer, 1977—; editor, writer Farming Today, Tonkawa, 1980-82. Dist. committeewoman Noble County Republican Com., 1970-72, chmn. Noble County Rep. Women's Club, 1972; pres. Marland PTO, 1980. Mem. Bliss Ext. Homemakers Group (pres.). Mem. Christian Ch. (Disciples of Christ) (Sunday sch. supt. 1968—). Lodge: Women of the Elks. Articles, photographs to Farm and Ranch Living, High Plains Jour., Okla. Farmer Stockman, Farming Today, Perry Daily Jour., Ponca City News. Address: Route 1 Box 27 Marland OK 74644

TAUTFEST, PATRICIA BOND, ednl. adminstr.; b. Indpls., Jan. 6, 1928; d. William Watson and Margaret (MacCallum) Bond; A.B., Butler U., 1949; M.S., Purdue U., 1953, Ph.D. (Univ. fellow), 1960. Dean girls Harry E. Wood High Sch., Indpls., 1953-56; asst. prof. counseling and guidance Purdue U., 1959-60; asst. dean women U. Wis., Madison, 1960-62, acting dean women, 1963-66, asst. dean students, 1966-70, asst. vice chancellor student affairs, 1970-74, asso. prof. div. social studies, asst. dean Coll. Letters and Sci., 1974—; cons., evaluator North Central Assn. Colls., Secondary Schs. Mem. Nat. Assn. Women Deans, Adminstrs., Counselors (v.p. profl. relations 1975-77), Am. Psychol. Assn., Am. Assn. Higher Edn., Mortar Bd., Kappa Delta Pi, Pi Beta Phi. Contbr. articles to higher edn. jours. Home: 2930 Arbor Dr Madison WI 53711 Office: 2930 Arbor Dr Madison WI 53711

TAYLER, JOAN MCLELLAN, real estate co. exec.; b. San Francisco, Apr. 11, 1928; d. Roderick McLellan and Vivian (Goddard) Irwin; B.A., Sarah Lawrence Coll., 1950; children—James D., Wendy Tayler Clarke, Roderick T., Garratt M. Dir., costume designer various TV stas., 1950-53; real estate sales asso. William Wright & Co., Burlingame, Calif., 1966-69, mgr., 1974-76; sales asso. Grubb & Ellis, Burlingame, 1969-74; adminstr., pres. Joan M. Tayler Inc., Burlingame, 1976—; dir. McLellan Estate Co., Rod McLellan Co. Mem. San Mateo County Growth Council. Mem. Sales and Mktg. Exec. Assn., Burlingame C. of C. Republican. Episcopalian. Clubs: Commonwealth, Town and Country. Home: 241 Telegraph Hill Blvd San Francisco CA 94133 Office: Joan M Tayler & Co 100 El Camino Real Burlingame CA 94010

TAYLOR, ALICE HUBBARD, city mgr.; b. New Orleans, Dec. 30, 1942; d. Hughie Emmanuel and Ira Bell (Hitchens) Hubbard; A.S., Harris Tchrs. Coll., 1962; student U. New Orleans, 1974; B.S., Lindenwood Coll., 1981; divorced; 1 dau., Josette Onnetta Manning. Asst. mgr. Am. Thrift Fin. Plan, Inc., New Orleans, 1965-71; pres., owner H & L Bus. Devel. Inc., New Orleans, 1971-74; venture analyst E. Ark. Planning and Devel. Dist., Jonesboro, 1974-76; dir. A.M.E. Ch. Ext. Dept., St. Louis, 1976-79; city clk. City of Maplewood, Mo., 1980-81, city mgr., 1981—; cons. community devel., bus. devel. Treas., NAACP, 1974-76; adv., den mother Girl Scouts U.S.A., 1967-74. Mem. Am. Bus. and Personnel Assn., St. Louis County and City Mgrs. Assn., Internat. City Mgrs. Assn., Mo. Mcpl. League, St. Louis County Mcpl. League, Internat. Personnel Mgmt. Assn., Mo. City Clks. and Fin. Officers Assn., Internat. Inst. Mcpl. Clks. Democrat. Methodist. Club: Order Eastern Star. Home: 7554 Polk Ave Maplewood MO 63143 Office: 7601 Manchester Rd Maplewood MO 63143

TAYLOR, ANNA DIGGS, fed. judge; b. Washington, Dec. 9, 1932; d. Virginius Douglass and Hazel (Bramlette) Johnston; B.A., Barnard Coll., 1954; LL.B., Yale U., 1957; m. S. Martin Taylor, May 22, 1976; children—Douglass Johnston Diggs, Carla Cecelia Diggs. Admitted to Mich. bar, 1961; atty. Office Solicitor, Dept. Labor, Washington, 1957-60; asst. prosecutor Wayne County (Mich.), 1961-62; asst. U.S. atty. Eastern Dist. Mich., 1966; ptnr. firm Zwerdling, Maurer, Diggs & Papp, Detroit, 1970-75; asst. corp. csl. City of Detroit, 1975-79; U.S. dist. judge Eastern Dist. Mich., Detroit, 1979—; adj. prof. law Wayne State U., Detroit, 1976. Trustee, Det. Receiving Hosp., Met. Hosp., Detroit, Health Alliance Plan, Detroit, Detroit Sci. Center, Planned Parenthood League Detroit, Neighborhood Service Orgn. Mem. Fed. Bar Assn., Nat. Lawyers Guild, State Bar Mich., Wolverine Bar Assn., Women Lawyers Assn. Mich. Democrat. Episcopalian. Office: 235 Federal Courthouse Detroit MI 48226 *

TAYLOR, ANNE, educator, environ. designer; b. Sayre, Pa., May 19, 1933; d. Fred B. and Marion E. Parker; B.A., Wells Coll., 1955; M.A., Ariz. State U., 1966, Ph.D., 1971; m. William C. Taylor, July 30, 1955 (div.); children—Kimberly, Susan, Meredith; m. 2d, Donald E. Kelly, Jan. 1, 1972. Tchr., All Saints Episcopal Day Sch., Phoenix, 1962-66; tchr. Campus Lab. Sch., Ariz. State U., Tempe, 1966-68, grad. asst. Coll. Edn., 1968-70, lectr. Coll. Architecture, instr. art, 1970-71; preschool coordinator Palo Alto Ednl. Systems, (Phoenix) 1971; dir. learning environments Southwestern Coop. Ednl. Lab., Albuquerque, 1971-74; prof. Sch. Architecture and Planning, co-dir. Inst. Environ. Edn. U. N.Mex., 1975-82, prof. architecture, 1974-82, asso. dean Grad. Sch., 1975-77, dir. Inst. Environ. Edn., 1977—; pres. School Zone, Inc., Child's Room Inc., School Zone Inst.; designer sch. environments for severely handicapped, day care, preschs. Mem. Nat., N.Mex. (pres. 1972-74) art edn. assns., Environ. Design Research Assn. (bd. dirs.), N.Mex. Alliance Arts Edn. (pres. 1974-76). Unitarian. Author books; contbr. articles to profl. jours. Home: Box 603 Corrales NM 87048 Office: Sch Architecture U N Mex Albuquerque NM 87131

TAYLOR, BARBARA ALDEN, public relations exec.; b. Dallas, Aug. 21, 1943; d. Harold Earl and Sally Alden (Howard) T.; B.A., Smith Coll., 1965; M.A., Antioch Coll., 1971. Vol., Peace Corps, India, 1966-68; tchr. Upper Merion Sch. Dist., King of Prussia, Pa., 1969-70; tchr. Cheltenham Sch. Dist., Elkins Park, Pa., 1970-74; public relations dir. Princess Hotels Internat., N.Y.C., 1974-75; pres. Alden Taylor and Assos., Ltd., N.Y.C., 1975—. Bd. dirs. Madison Square Boys' Club N.Y., also mem. women's bd. Boys' Club N.Y. Mem. Women in Communications, Public Relations Soc. Am. Clubs: Doubles Internat., Smith Coll. Club N.Y. (dir.), Jr. League City N.Y. Office: 39 E 51st St New York NY 10022

TAYLOR, BARBARA JEAN, oil industry assn. exec.; b. White Plains, N.Y., Feb. 3, 1933; d. Charles George and Gladys Isobel (Winch) Watkins; B.A. in English, SUNY, New Paltz, 1974; m. Richard Taylor, Apr. 10, 1955 (div. 1977); children—Mark Evan, Linda Elizabeth, Janice Barbara, Nancy Jane. Advt. copywriter McCann-Erickson, N.Y.C., 1953-55; newspaper reporter Patent Trader, Mt. Kisco, N.Y., 1962-63, Evening Star, Peekskill, N.Y., 1963-65; founding editor The Yorktowner (N.Y.), 1965-66; gen. news reporter Westchester/Rockland (N.Y.) newspapers, 1966-70, bur. chief, editor No. Westchester Bur., 1970-72; communications specialist fed. Community Devel. Program, Yorktown, 1975-77; asso. dir. N.Y. State Petroleum Council (arm of Am. Petroleum Inst. trade assn.), N.Y.C., 1977—, founder, mgr. speakers bur. in field; freelance writer for New Dawn, Feminist Bull., The Entertainer; tchr. creative writing adult edn. classes; speaker civic and edn. groups. Bd. dirs. Food for the Hungry; adv. Citizens Commn. on Urban Renewal. Mem. Nat. Assn. Female Execs., Publicity Club of N.Y., Bus. and Profl. Women. Presbyterian. Office: 551 Fifth Ave New York NY 10017

TAYLOR, BARBARA JO ANNE HARRIS (MRS. RICHARD POWELL TAYLOR), educator civic and polit. worker; b. Providence, Sept. 9, 1936; d. Ross Cameron and Anita (Coia) Harris; student Tex. Christian U., 1952, Salve Regina Coll., 1952-53, Our Lady of the Lake Coll. and Convent, 1953-54, St. Mary's U., summer 1954, Incarnate Word Coll., 1954-55; student, Georgetown U., 1956-59, 62-63, B.S., 1963; m. Richard Powell Taylor, Dec. 19, 1959; 1 son, Douglas Howard. Adminstrv. asst. profl. devel. and welfare NEA, Washington, 1956-59; asst. to dir. Georgetown U., Washington, 1956-59; exec. asst. All Am. Conf. to Combat Communism, Washington, 1960; spl. legis. asst. for. mil. affairs to chmn. mil. research and devel. subcom. U.S. Senate Armed Services Com., 1971-72; apptd. U.S. nat. commr. to UNESCO, 1982—; mem. exec. bd. Salvation Army Aux., D.C., 1967—, chmn. fund-raising, 1968, co-chmn. fundraising, 1972, 74, chmn. membership com., 1969-70, co-chmn., 1972-74, mem. exec. com. of exec. bd., 1970—, treas., mem. fin. com., 1970-71, v.p., 1971-72, historian, 1972-73, editor Our Watchword Newsletter, 1968-69, chmn. Christmas Toycenter com., 1972—; mem. exec. bd. Welcome to Washington Internat., 1969-72, bd. advs., 1969-72, dir. workshop, 1969—, tchr. English and Spanish lit., 1970—; exec. bd. Am. Opera Sch. Soc., Washington, 1970—, v.p., program chmn., 1973—; exec. bd. Women's Aux., St. David's Episcopal Ch., Washington, 1970-75, v.p., 1970-71, 73-74, chmn. program com., 1970-71, 73-74; exec. bd. Women's Aux. Episcopal Center for Emotionally Disturbed Children, Washington, 1970—, Women's Aux. Episcopal Ch. Home for Aged, 1970—. Mem. exec. bd. League Republican Women D.C., 1964-67, 75-77, treas., 1964-67; mem. nat. council Womens Nat. Rep. Club, N.Y.C., 1969—; mem. Nat. Fedn. Rep. Women, 1964—; mem. Md. Fedn. Rep. Women, 1969—, state regents chmn., 1981; mem. Nat. Reagan for Pres. Fin. Com., 1979-80, chmn. Md. Reagan Bush Effort Com., 1980; coordinator for Md., Reagan-Bush Inaugural Com., 1980-81; Md. Rep. State fin. chmn., 1980. Recipient spl. award for vol. Salvation Army, 1969, 72. Mem. Internat. Platform Assn., Spanish-Portuguese Study Group (dir. 1969-74, treas. 1970-73, fin. chmn. 1972), DAR (nat. vice chmn. mus. docent com. 1974-77, nat. vice chmn. meml. service com. 1977—, chmn. nat. resolutions com., 1980—, mem. state bd. mgmt. 1973-80, state exec. com. 1978-80, state historian 1978-80, other offices, nat. campaign chmn.), Nat. Capital Law League, Nat. Assn. Parliamentarians, Nat. Soc. Children of the Am. Revolution, Sr. Nat. Bd. Mgmt. Clubs: Internat., Nat. Lawyers Wives, Capitol Hill, Capital Speakers, Congressional Country, Washington (internat. com. 1971-75), Am. News women's. Editor, Museum Newsletter, 1978-79; sr. editor, sr. publs. chmn. D.C. Children of the Am. Revolution, 1978-79. Home: 8801 Belmart Rd Potomac MD 20854

TAYLOR, BARBIE J., clin. psychologist; b. Glendale, Calif., Sept. 13, 1943; d. Clarence S. and Eileen M. (Cook) Merrill; student Calif. State Poly. Coll., 1968-70; B.A. magna cum laude, Calif. State U., Long Beach, 1973; Ph.D., U. Wash., 1978; children—Steven P., Tamalynn S. Co-therapist in various pvt. practices, 1971-76; research coordinator Center Marital and Sexual Studies, 1978-79; pvt. practice psychology, Beverly Hills, Long Beach, Calif., Scottsdale, Ariz., 1978-80; pvt.

practice sex therapy and hypnotherapy psychologist, Morgantown, W.Va., 1980—; faculty asso. Ariz. State U., 1980; mem. med. staff Monongalia Riding for the Handicapped Assn., 1981—; mem. continuing edn. faculty W.Va. U., 1982. USPHS fellow, 1973-77. Mem. Am. Psychol. Assn., W.Va. Psychol. Assn., Phi Kappa Phi. Contbr. articles to profl. jours. Home: 500 Jefferson St Morgantown WV 26505 Office: Monongahela Bldg 235 High St Office 506 Morgantown WV 26505

TAYLOR, BERNIECE POLLOCK, lawyer; b. Foosland, Ill., Sept. 6, 1904; d. Ulyssis Sidney Grant and Iva May (Miles) Pollock; B.A., U. Ind., 1927; J.D. (scholar 1929-30), U. Chgo., 1931; m. Herman Lamon Taylor, Sept. 26, 1931; children—Jane Ann Taylor Johns, William. Tchr. schs. in Ind., 1922-28; admitted to Ill. bar, 1931; editorial writer Callaghan Law Pub. Co., 1931-34; law clk. 7th Circuit Ct. Appeals, 1934-36; gen. practice law, Flossmoor, Ill., 1953—. Bd. dirs. Citizens Greater Chgo., 1968-74. Mem. Women's Bar Assn. Chgo., S. Suburban Bar Assn., Alpha Delta Pi (chpt. pres. 1970-71). Clubs: Flossmoor Country, Flossmoor Book (pres. 1962-64), Flossmoor Garden (pres. 1977-79). Editor 20 vols. of Ind. law. Address: 1610 Brassie Ave Flossmoor IN 60422

TAYLOR, BETH HOBBS (MRS. MORRIS HARDING TAYLOR), former convalescent center adminstr.; b. Nephi, Utah, Apr. 21, 1917; d. George Lloyd and Jennie V. (Maimgren) Hobbs; student U. Utah, 1935-36; grad. Latter-day Saints Hosp. Sch. Nursing, Salt Lake City, 1938; student George Washington U. Extension, 1966; B.S., Utah State U., 1971; m. Morris Harding Taylor, June 5, 1940; children—Gordon Morris, Gary Lloyd, Loren Craig Genan, Grant Paul, Mary Gay. Adminstr. Sunshine Terrace Found., Logan, 1959-68, Hillhaven Convalescent Center, Ogden, 1972-74; chmn. Nursing Home Task Force on Study Nursing, Utah. Fellow Am. Coll. Nursing Home Adminstrs.; mem. Utah State Nurses Assn. (hon. life; chmn. geriatric sect.), Utah State U. Faculty Woman's Assn., Asso. Extension Women's Assn. Mormon. Home: 131 E 2d S Hyde Park UT 84318

TAYLOR, CAROL ANN, food service exec.; b. Phila., Nov. 11, 1938; d. Isaac Earl and Theresa Mary (Fitzpatrick) T.; student Drexel Inst. Tech., 1956-58; B.S. in Home Econs., Pa. State U., 1960. Home economist Acme Markets, Inc., Phila., 1961-63; homeservice rep. Phila. Gas Works, 1963-68; home economist SCM Proctor Silex, Inc., Phila., 1968-71; sr. project mgr. ARA Food Services Co., Phila., 1971-81; dir. staff resources The Freshie Co., Phila., 1981—. Mem. Am. (registered), Phila. dietetic assns., Nat. Assn. Female Execs. Home: 4980 State Rd 1 607 Drexel Hill PA 19026 Office: 200 Pattison Ave Philadelphia PA 19148

TAYLOR, CAROL ANN, social services adminstr.; b. Phillipsburg, N.J., June 2, 1944; d. John Clifton and Verna G. (Mock) Hart; B.A., Albright Coll., 1966; M.S.W., Rutgers U., 1970; M.A. in Adminstrn., Rider Coll., 1980; m. G. Douglas Taylor, Mar. 9, 1974. Intake worker Sussex/Warren County Office, N.J. Bur. Children's Services, 1966-68, asst. supr., 1968-69, casework supr. Burlington County Office, 1970-71; dist. office supr. Hunterdon/Somerset County Office, N.J. Div. Youth and Family Services, 1971-74, asst. chief bur. family services, program assistance sect., 1974-77, adminstr. office program adminstrn., Trenton, 1977—. Gov.'s del. N.J. Adv. Council on Title XX; trustee Somerset Home for Temporarily Displaced Children; adv. bd. Hunterdon Community Mental Health Clinic; adv. bd. Women Moving Up Grant. Mem. Nat. Assn. Social Workers (chmn. Mercer County 1976-77), Acad. Cert. Social Workers. Home: 15 Holder Dr Trenton NJ 08628 Office: 1 S Montgomery St Trenton NJ 08625

TAYLOR, CAROLE ANN, temporary help service co. exec.; b. Harrisburg, Pa., Jan. 25, 1940; d. C. Ross and S. Isabella (Mullen) Boyer; student public schs.; divorced. Various clerical and secretarial positions, 1957-65; with Manpower Temp. Services, 1965-69, 71—, v.p., Harrisburg, Pa., 1974—, gen. mgr., 1981—; office mgr. Covenco, Inc., Harrisburg, 1969-71. Treas., Vote Yes Com., Dauphin County, Pa., 1980; bd. dirs. Opportunity Industrialization Center, 1973-74, Wheels, Inc., 1979-81, Ams. for Competitive Enterprise System, 1979—, Tri County United Way, 1981—, ARC, 1977-81. Mem. Harrisburg C. of C. (dir. 1973-76, 82—, treas. 1982—), Adminstrv. Mgmt. Soc. (chpt. pres. 1975-76), Exec. Women Internat. (founder Harrisburg chpt. 1979, 1st pres. 1979-80, dir. corp. membership 1982). Republican. Author articles in field. Home: 7313 Sleepy Hollow Rd Harrisburg PA 17112 Office: 2929 N Front St Box 807 Harrisburg PA 17108

TAYLOR, CAROLE LILLIAN, edn1. adminstr.; b. Pitts.; d. John and Lillie Thompson; B.S., U. Pitts., 1971, M.Ed., 1972, Ph.D., 1973, specialist diploma, 1975; children—Colette, Yvette. Instr. curriculum and supervision U. Pitts., 1972-74; tchr., researcher Pitts. Public Schs., 1975-78; exec. dir. Ednl. Projects and Info. Cons. Center, Pitts., 1975—; founder, pres. Tolate Acad., pre-sch. through 12th grade, 1979—; cons. in field. Recipient Robert L. Vann award for ednl. achievement Pitts. Courier, 1978; Achievement award Young Bus. and Profl. Women's Club, 1978; Woman of Achievement award Career Guild of N.Y., N.J., and Pa., 1981. Mem. Internat. Platform Assn., AAUP, Doctorate Assn. U. Pitts. Author: Lolette Wears a Patch, 1975; A,B,C Count with Me, 1976; Just for Fun, vols. I and II, 1975; Dark Ectasy, Oh! How I Love that Man, 1977. Office: PO Box 4692 Pittsburgh PA 15206

TAYLOR, CAROLE RHUNETTE, librarian; b. Barnesville, Ga., Sept. 19, 1937; d. John B. and Lillie May (Few) T.; A.B., Clark Coll., 1958; M.L.S., Atlanta U., 1963; M.L.S., Fla. State U., 1974, Ph.D., 1980. Acad. librarian, evaluator, cons. So. Assn. Colls. and Schs., tchr.-librarian Palmer Meml. Inst., 1958-61; acquisitions librarian Va. State U., 1962-63; head public service Dillard U., 1963-69, acting head librarian, 1969-73, library dir., 1974—. Pres., bd. dirs. Cooperative Coll. Library Center; cons. New Orleans YWCA, bd. dirs. 1971-73, 76-78; cons. So. Assn. Colls. and Schs.; mem. La. Com. for Humanities. Recipient United Methodist Ch. for Homeland Ministries Fellowship award, 1973-74. Mem. La. Library Assn., ALA, Southwest Library Assn., AAUP, Greater New Orleans Library Assn., Phi Alpha Theta. Baptist. Home: 3622 Virgil Blvd New Orleans LA 70122 Office: 2601 Gentilly Blvd New Orleans LA 70122

TAYLOR, CORA HODGE, social worker; b. Fayetteville, N.C., Nov. 25, 1942; d. John Marlin and Cora Louise (Mitchell) Hodge; B.S., N.C. Coll., Durham, 1963; M.S.W., U. N.C., Chapel Hill, 1965; m. Charles L. Taylor, June 26, 1965; children—Charles L., John M. Clin. social worker VA Hosp., Bedford, Mass., 1965-68, 73-79; chief social worker Regional Health Center, Wilmington, Mass., 1978-79; clin. social worker VA Hosp., Bedford, Mass., 1979—; field instr. Boston U. Sch. Social Work, 1979—; instr., cons. primary care residents Tufts U. Med. Sch., Regional Health Center, Wilmington, Mass., 1978-79. Mem. Town Meeting, Billerica, Mass., 1981—; precinct clk., 1981, 82. Recipient Superior Performance award VA Hosp., Bedford, 1966. Mem. LWV (dir. 1970-73), Acad. Cert. Social Workers, Nat. Assn. Social Workers. Home: 35 Wildwood Rd Pinehurst MA 01866 Office: 200 Springs Rd Bedford MA 01730

TAYLOR, DELLA MAE, nurse; b. Johnson City, Tenn., Apr. 13, 1932; d. Lee Roy and Honolulu Cornelius (Holly) Brewer; R.N., Meml. Hosp., Johnson City, 1953; student E. Tenn. State U.; diploma newspaper writing Newspaper Inst. Am., 1968; B.S., Steed Coll., 1978; m. John R. Taylor, Jr., Feb. 12, 1955; children—Aliesa Benea, Celeste Taylor, Pediatric polio head nurse Meml. Hosp., Johnson City, 1953-54; staff nurse VA, Mountain Home, Tenn., 1954-55, 1961-64, part-time pvt. duty. 1964-78; staff nurse Meml. Hosp., Clarksville, Tenn., 1955-56; pediatric nurse U.S. Army Hosp., Augsburg, Germany, 1957-61; paramed. registered nurse for life ins. exams, Jonesboro, Tenn., 1978—. Pres., Pageants III, Jonesboro, 1980-82; coordinator Pageants III Nationwide Youth Scholarship Pageant Corp., 1980-82. Chmn. precinct, 15th Dist. Democratic Com., 1977-78; mothers' chmn. Washington County March of Dimes; youth coordinator Washington County Heart Assn. Registered nurse, Tenn. Mem. Nurses Christian Fellowship, E. Tenn. State U Alumni Assn., Steed Coll. Alumni Assn., Nat. Assn. Female Execs., Unicoi C. of C., U.S. Pageants Assns., Bus. and Profl. Women's Club. Washington County Farm Bur. Democrat. Baptist. Home: Rt 8 Box 37 Taylor Dr Jonesboro TN 37659

TAYLOR, ELAINE CLAIRE NELSON, exptl. psychologist; b. Meadville, Pa., Dec. 2, 1927; d. John David and Martha Margaret (Zurfluh) Nelson; B.S., Pa. State U., 1949; M.A., Bowling Green (Ohio) State U., 1951; Ph.D., State U. Iowa, 1954; divorced; children—Jenny, Jess. With Human Resources Research Orgn., 1954—, sr. scientist, sr. staff scientist, Monterey, Calif., 1968-80, sr. staff scientist, Louisville, 1980—. Fellow Am. Psychol. Assn. (pres. div. mil. psychology 1978-79), Inter-Univ. Seminar Armed Forces and Society; mem. Human Factors Soc., AAAS, Sigma Xi. Republican. Author reports in field, chpt. in book. Home: 3802 Goldstein Ln Louisville KY 40272 Office: 633 Knox Rd Radcliff KY 40160

TAYLOR, ELINOR ZIMMERMAN, state legislator; b. Norristown, Pa., Apr. 18, 1921; d. Harold I. and Ruth Amanda (Rahn) Zimmerman; B.S., West Chester State Tchrs. Coll., 1943; M.Ed., Temple U., 1958; m. William Morrison Taylor, Aug. 23, 1947; 1 dau., Barbara Ruth. Tchr., Dewey-Mann Elem. Sch., Chester Sch. Dist., 1943, Ridley Park Jr./Sr. High Sch., 1943-46, West Chester (Pa.) Area Sch. Dist., 1946-50; asso. prof. West Chester State Coll., 1955-69, dean student services, 1969-70, dean of adminstrn., 1970-76; mem. Pa. Ho. of Reps., 1976—. Councilwoman, Borough of West Chester, 1974-77, chmn. mcpl. services, 1974-75, chmn. zoning and housing, 1978-79; mem. West Chester Recreation Commn.; trustee Dr. Charles S. Swope Found.; bd. dirs. March of Dimes, United Way Chester County. Recipient Disting. Alumnus award West Chester State Coll., 1977; Order of Owl award Temple Alumni Assn., 1982; hon. award Pa. Health, Phys. Edn., Recreation Assn., 1962, Phila. Bd. Women Ofcls., 1978. Mem. AAUW (pres. 1967-68), Order Women Legislators, Delta Kappa Gamma. Republican. Presbyterian. Club: Soroptimist (hon.; Women Helping Women award 1980). Nat. hon. ofcl. U.S. Field Hockey. Office: Main Capitol Bldg Harrisburg PA 17120

TAYLOR, ELIZABETH, actress; b. London, Feb. 27, 1932; d. Francis and Sara (Sothern) T.; ed. Byron House, Hawthorne Sch., Metro-Goldwyn-Mayer Sch.; m. Conrad Nicholas Hilton, Jr., May 6, 1950 (div.); m. 2d, Michael Wilding (div.); 2 sons; m. 3d, Mike Todd, Feb. 2, 1957 (dec. Mar. 1958); 1 dau., Liza; m. 4th, Eddie Fisher, May 1959 (div.); m. 5th, Richard Burton, Mar. 15, 1964 (div. June 1974), remarried, Oct. 10, 1975 (div. 1976); 1 dau., Maria; m. 6th, John William Warner, Dec. 1976. Motion pictures include: Lassie Come Home, 1942; The White Cliffs of Dover, 1943; Jane Eyre, 1943; National Velvet, 1944; Life With Father, 1946; Courage of Lassie, 1946; Cynthia, 1947; A Date With Judy, 1948; Julia Misbehaves, 1948; Litte Women, 1948; Conspirator, 1949; The Big Hangover, 1949; Father of the Bride, 1950; Father's Little Dividend, 1950; A Place in the Sun, 1950; Love is Better Than Ever, 1951; Ivanhoe, 1951; Elephant Walk, 1954; Rhapsody, 1954; Beau Brummel, 1954; The Last Time I Saw Paris, 1955; Giant, 1956; Raintree County, 1957; Cat on a Hot Tin Roof, 1958; Butterfield 8 (Acad. award best actress), 1960; Cleopatra, 1962; The V.I.P.'s, 1963; Sandpiper, 1965; Who's Afraid of Virginia Wolfe (Acad. award 1966); Taming of the Shrew, 1967; The Comedians, 1967; Reflections in a Golden Eye, 1967; Dr. Faustus, 1968; Boom, 1968; Secret Ceremony, 1968; The Only Game in Town, 1969; X, Y and Zee, 1971; Under Milk Wood, 1971; Hammersmith is Out, 1972; Night Watch, 1973; Ash Wednesday, 1974; The Driver's Seat, 1975; The Blue Bird, 1976; A Little Night Music, 1977; Victory at Entebbe, 1977; Return Engagement, 1978; The Mirror Crack'd, 1980; stage appearances include: The Little Foxes, Ft. Lauderdale, Fla., Washington, N.Y.C., New Orleans, Los Angeles, 1981, London, 1982. Author: Nibbles and Me; (with Richard Burton) World Enough and Time (poetry reading), 1964; Elizabeth Taylor, 1965. Office: care Chen Sam & Assos 315 E 72d St Suite 19 G New York NY 10021

TAYLOR, ELLEN BORDEN BROADHURST, civic worker; b. Goldsboro, N.C., Jan. 18, 1913; d. Jack Johnson and Mabel Moran (Borden) Broadhurst; student Converse Coll., 1930-32; m. Marvin Edward Taylor, June 13, 1936; children—Marvin Edward, Jack Borden, William Lambert. Bd. govs. Elizabethan Garden, Manteo, N.C., 1964-74; mem. Gov. Robert Scott's Adv. Com. on Beautification, N.C., 1971-73; mem. ACE nat. action com. for environ. Nat. Council State Garden Clubs, 1973-75; bd. dirs. Keep N.C. Beautiful, 1973—; mem. steering com., charter mem. bd. dirs. Keep Johnston County (N.C.) Beautiful, 1977; life judge roses Am. Rose Soc.; chmn. local com. that published jointly with N.C. Dept. Cultural Resources: An Inventory of Historic Architecture, Smithford, N.C., 1977; co-chmn. local com. to survey and publish jointly with N.C. Div. Archives and History: Historical Resources of Johnston County, 1980-82. Mem. Nat. Council State Garden Clubs (life; master judge flower shows), Johnston County Hist. Soc. (charter), N.C. Geneal. Soc. (charter), Hist. Preservation Soc. N.C. (life), N.C. Art Soc. (life). Democrat. Episcopalian. Clubs: Smithfield (N.C.) Garden (charter; pres. 1969-71), Smithfield Woman's (v.p. 1976), DAR (organizing vice-regent chpt. 1976), Gen. Soc. Mayflower Descs. (life), Descs. of Richard Warren, Nat. Soc., Colonial Dames Am. (life), Magna Charta Dames. Home: 616 Hancock St Smithfield NC 27577

TAYLOR, ESTELLE WORMLEY, educator; b. Washington, Jan. 12, 1924; d. Luther Charles and Wilhelmina Wormley; B.S. magna cum laude, Miner Tchrs. Coll., 1945; M.A., Howard U., 1947; Ph.D., Catholic U. Am., 1969; m. Ivan Earle Taylor, Dec. 26, 1953. Instr. English, Howard U., 1947-52; tchr. Langley Jr. High Sch., Washington, 1952-55, Eastern Sr. High Sch., Washington, 1955-63; instr. D.C. Tchrs. Coll., 1963-66, asst. prof., 1966-69, asso. prof., 1969-71, prof., 1971—, acad. dean, 1975-76; asso. provost Fed. City Coll., Washington, 1974-75; prof., chmn. dept. English, Howard U., 1976—; mem. Folger fellowships selection com., 1976-79, chmn., 1978-79. Vice pres. Capitol City chpt. Links, Inc., 1979-80; trustee U. D.C., 1979-83. So. fellow, 1968-69; Rockefeller Found. fellow, 1978-79. Mem. Coll. Lang. Assn., Nat. Council Tchrs. Am., Modern Lang. Assn., Assn. Advancement Humanities, Shakespeare Assn. Am. Democrat. Contbr. articles to profl. jours. Home: 3221 20th St NE Washington DC 20018

TAYLOR, FANNIE TURNBULL, educator; b. Kansas City, Mo., Sept. 11, 1913; d. Henry King and Fannie Elizabeth (Sills) Turnbull; B.A., U. Wis., Madison, 1938; L.H.D. (hon.), Buena Vista Coll., Storm Lake, Iowa, 1975; m. Robert Taylor, Dec. 2, 1938 (div. 1974); children—Kathleen Muir Taylor Isaacs, Anne Kingston Taylor Wadsack. Mem. faculty U. Wis., Madison, 1941—, prof. social edn., 1949—, emeritus, 1979—, dir. Wis. Union Theatre, 1946-66, coordinator univ. systems arts council, 1967-70, assoc. dir. Center Arts Adminstrn., 1970-72, coordinator Consortium Arts, 1976—; program dir. music Nat. Endowment Arts, 1966-67, program info. dir., 1972-76; bd. dirs. Wis. Arts Council, 1964-72, Wis. Found. Arts, 1976—, Madison Civic Music Assn., 1976—, Elvejhem Mus. Art, 1976—; mem. grant rev. panel Madison Civic Center, 1981—; cons. in field. Bd. dirs. Wis. chpt. Nature Conservancy, 1963—, chmn., 1976-77; bd. dirs. Shorewood Hills Found., 1976—, pres., 1976-81. Recipient Oak Leaf award Nature Conservancy, 1981. Mem. Assn. Coll., Univ. and Community Arts Adminstrs. (exec. dir. 1970-72; Fannie Taylor award 1972), Am. Assn. Dance Cos. (dir. 1967-72), Nat. Assn. Regional Ballet (dir. 1975-77), Nat. Guild Community Schs. Arts (dir. 1977-80), Women in Communications (Writers' Cup 1980), U. Wis. Alumni Assn. (Disting. Service award 1979), Mortar Bd. Clubs: Madison Civics (pres. 1969-70), Madison, University. Author articles in field, handbook. Home: 1213 Sweet Briar Rd Madison WI 53705 Office: 5525 Humanities U Wis Madison WI 53706

TAYLOR, FLORENCE IRENE WAUL (FROSTY), editor; b. Montrose, S.D., Apr. 9, 1937; d. Emmett Alphonso and Rena Gerdena (Reeves) Waul; student Scottsdale Community Coll., 1972-73, Rio Salado Coll., 1979; m. Duane Mervin Taylor, Aug. 18, 1957; children—Kent Duane, Dana Sue. Telephone operator, Wiota, Iowa, 1953-55, Maryvale, Mo., 1957-59; bookkeeper Walnut Grove Products Co., Atlantic, Iowa, 1955-57; owner, operator portrait studio, Bellevue, Nebr., 1957-67, Phoenix, 1967-75; columnist Paradise Valley News-Progress, Phoenix, 1970-74, asso. editor, 1974-81; editor Paradise Valley Press and N.W. News, Phoenix, 1981—. Sec. Little League East, 1973, Paradise Valley Athletic Assn., 1974, Paradise Valley Community Edn. Adv. Council, 1978; mem. Paradise Valley Vocat. Edn. Adv. Council, 1978—. Recipient Outstanding Service award Little League, 1973; Community Service award Girl Scouts U.S., 1974, 80; Outstanding Community Service award Jaycees, 1977; Little Angel award Sr. Citizens, 1979; named Mrs. Nebr. Mrs. America Pageant, 1964. Mem. Nat. Photographers Assn., Copperstate Photographers Assn., Ariz. Press Women (writing award 1977, 78), Ariz. Press Club (writing award 1975), Paradise Valley C. of C., Sigma Delta Chi. Republican. Methodist. Clubs: Lioness (charter mem.), Paradise Valley Bus. and Profl. Woman's (charter mem.). Home: 3521 E Gold Dust St Phoenix AZ 85028 Office: Paradise Valley Press Box 30286 Phoenix AZ 85046

TAYLOR, GAIL BATTLES, state ofcl.; b. Oklahoma City, Oct. 15, 1943; d. Sam O. and Dorothy (Blackwell) Battles; B.A., Oklahoma City U., 1964; M.Ed., Central State U., 1965; 1 dau., Laura Gail. Records officer Oklahoma County Assessor's Office, Oklahoma City, 1968-69; program mgr. ednl. programs Okla. Hwy. Safety Office, Oklahoma City, 1975-81; info. officer Okla. Tax Commn., Oklahoma City, 1981—. Program chmn. Women's Dem. Club, 1970. Served with USAF, 1970-72. Mem. Women Hwy. Safety Leaders, Women in Communications, Delta Zeta. Democrat. Methodist. Club: Faculty House. Office: 2501 N Lincoln Blvd Oklahoma City OK 73194

TAYLOR, GLADYS GILLMAN, educator; b. Bloomfield, N.J., Dec. 6, 1926; d. Fred Charles and Katherine Mary (Ulrich) Gillman; A.B., Skidmore Coll., 1948; M.A., Radcliffe U., 1952; Ph.D., Ind. U., 1980; m. Harold Edwin Taylor, June 27, 1952 (div. 1971); children—John Gillman, Steven Gillman, Jill Bolte. Tchr., The Winsor Sch., Brookline, Mass., 1949-52, Franklin (Mass.) High Sch., 1952-55; faculty Ind. State U., Terre Haute, 1963—, asso. prof. math., 1980—. Bd. dirs. Wabash Valley ARC, 1966-71; bd. dirs. Terre Haute Symphony. Mem. Philosophy of Sci. Assn., Nat. Council Tchrs. Math., Pi Mu Epsilon, Ind. Assn. Mental Health. Home: 2711 Wilson Dr Terre Haute IN 47803 Office: Dept Math Ind State U Terre Haute IN 47809

TAYLOR, GRACE ELIZABETH WOODALL, law librarian, educator; b. Butler, N.J., June 14, 1926; d. Frank E. and Grace (Carlyon) Woodall; A.B. with honors (Lewis scholar), Fla. State U., 1959, M.A., 1950; J.D., U. Fla., 1962; m. Edwin S. Taylor, Feb. 4, 1951 (dec.); children—Carol Lynn Taylor Crespo, Nancy Ann. Asst. in library U. Fla., Gainesville, 1950-56, asst. law librarian, 1956-62, asso. law librarian, 1962-66, librarian, 1966-73, dir. Legal Info. Center, 1962—, prof. law, 1976—; hearing officer Career Service Grievance Hearings; speaker in field. Bd. dirs. SOLINET, 1981-84; chmn. LAWNET Com. Nat. Endowment Humanities grantee, 1980-81. Mem. Am. Assn. Law Libraries (exec. bd. 1981-84), Am. Assn. Library Sci., Am. Bar Assn., Am. Soc. Info. Sci., Fla. Library Assn., Order of Coif, Beta Phi Mu. Contbr. articles to profl. jours. Home: 2116 NE 7th Terr Gainesville FL 32601 Office: Legal Info Center U Fla Gainesville FL 32611

TAYLOR, HEATHER MACDONALD, life ins. rep.; b. West Warwick, R.I., Feb. 9, 1943; d. Milton Earl and Audrey (Spencer) MacDonald; student Crozer Theol. Sem., part-time 1966-68; B.A., Alderson Broaddus Coll., 1965; A.A., Cushing Jr. Coll., 1964; m. Warren F. Taylor, Jr., June 11, 1966; 1 dau., April Charlene. Dir. religious edn. Fountain Meml. Bapt. Ch., Washington, 1965; program worker Rankin (Pa.) Christian Center, 1965-66; dir. youth service programs YWCA, Chester, Pa., 1966-68; receptionist Washington Center for Met. Studies, 1969; tour desk clk. Grand Canyon Nat. Park, Ariz., 1970; program dir. YWCA, Glendora, Calif., 1974-75, exec. dir., Fontana, Calif., 1976-80; field asso. Fidelity Union Life, Pomona, Calif., 1980-81; regional rep. Ministers Life Ins. Co. of Mpls., Claremont, Calif., 1981—; instr. Chaffey Jr. Coll., Altaloma, Calif., part time, 1978—. Enablement chmn. Greater Fontana Town Hall Com., 1976; cofounder Project I.D.E.A., Goleta, Calif., 1973; mem. Family Service Agy. Bd., Chaffey Coll. Adv. Council. Recipient Howard K. Williams award Phila., 1964; R.I. Bapt. Ednl. Soc. grantee, 1962-66; Grey scholar, Chgo., 1961. Mem. AAUW. Methodist. Home: 462 Carleton Ave Claremont CA 91711 Office: 462 Carleton Ave Claremont CA 91711

TAYLOR, HELEN JEAN, health services adminstr.; b. Dixonville, Pa., May 14, 1927; d. Robert Clyde and Helen (Coalmer) Sickenberger; R.N., Jefferson Med. Coll., 1948; B.A. in Health Edn., Calif. State U., Northridge, 1971, M.S. in Health Sci., 1976; postgrad. UCLA, 1978 U. So. Calif., 1982—; 1 son, Brian Robert. Staff nurse Santa Monica (Calif.) Hosp., 1948-51; sch. nurse St. Martin's in the Fields, Canoga Park, Calif., 1963-65; sch. nurse, health educator, tchr., dist. health supr. William S. Hart Union High Sch. Dist., Newhall, Calif., 1971-79; adminstr. Mgmt. Health Services, Glendale (Calif.) Unified Sch. Dist., 1979—; cons. AIMS Cahill Films, Bur. Indsl. Edn., Calif. Dept. Edn.; vol. clinic nurse Intensive Vaccination Program, Los Angeles County Health Dept., 1961-63. Mem. community edn. task force United Way Planning Council of Los Angeles County; mem. Glendale Community Coordinating Council, v.p., 1982-83; active ARC Disaster Nursing; mem. Am. Lung Assn.'s Children Health Com.; active Valley Symphony Guild, Tree People (Calif Conservation project). Mem. Assn. of Calif. Sch. Adminstrs., Calif. Sch. Nurses Orgn., Los Angeles County Sch. Nurses Assn., Glendale Mgmt. Assn., Calif. State U., Northridge Alumni Assn., Jefferson Med. Coll. Nurses' Alumni Assn., Delta Kappa Gamma. Home: 7249 Quartz Ave Canoga Park CA 91306 Office: 223 N Jackson St Glendale CA 91206

TAYLOR, JEANNETTE CHARLOTTE PALMER, ednl. adminstr.; b. Moultrie, Ga., June 2, 1940; d. James Hasker and Alice (Harrington) Palmer; B.A., Del. State Coll., 1963; M.S.W., Atlanta U., 1965; Ph.D., U. Cin., 1979; m. Solomon Taylor, Dec. 6, 1969; 1 son, Nyamekye Kwesi. Clin. instr. Ohio State U., Columbus, 1968-73; instr. Career Tng. program, City of Cin., 1971-73; field instr. U. Cin., 1972-73, adj. asst. prof., 1972-73, 75—, dir. division continuing edn., 1979—; youth worker Seven Hills Neighborhood Houses, Cin., 1965-67, program supr., 1967-69, program dir., 1969-72, asso. dir., 1972-76; city dir., program developer Univ. Without Walls-Cin./Union for Experimenting Colls. and Univs., 1976-79; cons. in field. Bd. dirs. ARC, Cin., 1977-78, Cin.

Community Adv. Council, 1977-78, Cin. Minority Women's Com., 1981—, Greater Cin. Cancer Control Center, 1981—, Ohio Black Women Leadership Caucus, 1982—. Recipient Woman of Yr. award Del. State Coll., 1963, Greyhound Corp., 1971; Outstanding Humanitarian of Yr. award Hamilton County Black Caucus, 1973, Disting. Citizen award Woman's Alliance, 1974; named Essence Woman, Essence Mag., 1974; Jeannette Charlotte Taylor Day proclamation Mayor of Cin., 1974; recipient Cin. Black Achiever award Cin. Black Achiever Orgn., 1981. Mem. Assn. Women Ohio Council on Higher Continuing Edn., Council for Advancement Exptl. Learning. Author: My Family, 1968; contbr. articles in field to profl. publs. Home: 4550 Paddock Rd Cincinnati OH 45229 Office: Univ Cin Office of Continuing Edn ML # 146 Cincinnati OH 45221

TAYLOR, JOAN KISSNER, home economist; b. Delaware, Ohio, July 4, 1925; d. Russell DeWitt and Grace Mae (Pocock) Kissner; student Fla. So. Coll., 1944-46; B.A., Ohio Wesleyan U., 1948; m. Phillip Otto Taylor, Apr. 9, 1949; children—Bradley Douglas, Russell Gregory, Phillip Steven. Home economist San Diego Gas and Electric Co., 1948-50; home economist So. Calif. Edison Co., Inglewood, 1950-52; microwave home economist Tappan Distbr., Fresno, Calif., 1956-58; home economist Bendix Home Laundry Inst., Fresno, 1959-61; microwave home economist Gen. Electric Co., San Joaquin Valley, Calif., 1966-67; owner, instr. microwave Jo Taylor's Microwave Cooking Sch., Fresno, 1975—; pub., editor Microwave News, 1975—; pub. mem. Calif. Dried Fig Adv. Bd., 1982—; microwave cons. food cos., mfrs. microwave and cooking utensils; presentations TV, radio. Public mem. Melon Research Bd. Calif., 1975—. Mem. Wives of Profl. Engrs. (pres., publicity dir. 1962, 64, v.p. 1963), AAUW, Home Economists in Bus., Am. Home Econs. Assn., Calif. Home Econs. Assn., Internat. Microwave Power Inst., Ohio Wesleyan U. Alumni Assn., Chi Omega. Club: Annapolis Parents No. Calif. Address: 1446 W Stuart St Fresno CA 93711

TAYLOR, JOANN GILBERT, home economist; b. Marion, La., Nov. 5, 1938; d. Arvel and Nellie Orene Gilbert; B.S. in Home Econs. Edn., N.E. La. State U., 1959; M.S. in Home Econs. Edn., La. Tech. U., 1966; m. Richard Earl Taylor, June 6, 1958; 1 dau., Linda Gray. Asst. home economist La. State U. Extension Service, West Carroll Parish, 1961-62; asst./asso. home economist La. State U. Extension Service, Lincoln Parish, 1962-69, area clothing agt. Lincoln and Jackson Parishes, 1969—. Mem. Am. Home Econs. Assn., Nat. Assn. Extension Home Economists, La. Home Econs. Assn., La. Assn. Extension Home Economists, Epsilon Sigma Phi. Baptist. Clubs: Quota (dist. gov. 1978-79) (Ruston, La.). Home: 2703 Hundred Oaks Dr Ruston LA 71270 Office: Courthouse Ruston LA 71270

TAYLOR, JOHNNYE LOU, educator; b. Stamford, Tex., July 24, 1939; d. Johnnie Anderson and Alpha (Stephens) White: B.S., Hardin Simmons U., 1961; M.Ed., Sul Ross State U., 1972; m. Joe Don Taylor, Aug. 28, 1960; 1 dau., Johnna Jo. Tchr. 4th grade, Abilene, Tex., 1961-62; elem. tchr. Public Schs. Odessa (Tex.), from 1964; now elem. spl. edn. counselor Ector County Schs., Odessa. Adv., Tekisha Tri-Hi-Y Girls, Odessa, 1977-80; v.p. Burnet PTA, Odessa. Named Outstanding Adv., Tri-Hi-Y, 1977, 78. Mem. NEA, Tex. State Tchrs. Assn. (dist. 18 treas. 1980-81), Odessa Classroom Tchrs. Assn. (sec. 1973-74, 3d v.p. 1974-75), Ector County Tchrs. Assn. (pres. 1978-79), Beta Gamma Kappa, Kappa Iota (pres.). Democrat. Baptist. Address: 3975 Lakeside Odessa TX 79762

TAYLOR, KATHLEEN OWEN, nurse; b. Milw., Mar. 22, 1935; d. Thomas Jackson and Frieda Anna (Kamin) Wilson; diploma vocat. nursing Houston adult edn. program Meml. Bapt. Hosp., 1959; children—Judith Ann, Donald Eugene, Carolyn Ruth, Wanda Kay; m. Bruce F. Taylor, June 28, 1982. Staff nurse Meml. Bapt. Hosp., Houston, 1959-60; emergency room nurse Height Hosp., Houston, 1960-72; emergency room nurse Twelve Oaks Hosp., Houston, 1972-77, orthopedics staff nurse, 1977-79, outpatient dept. Mem. Tex. Lic. Vocat. Nurses Assns., Emergency Dept. Nurses Assn., Harris County Vocat. coordinator, 1979—. Nurses Assn., Am. Heart Assn. Baptist. Home: 6730 Acorn Houston TX 77092

TAYLOR, LAURIE ANNE, consumer products and services mktg. mgr.; b. Lake Forest, Ill., May 23, 1952; d. Lewis Treat and Virginia Dean (Steele) T.; B.S. cum laude in Econs. (scholar), U. Pa., 1974, M.B.A., 1975. Asst. to internat. v.p. Towers, Perrin, Forster, Crosby, Phila., 1972-75; asst. account exec. Benton & Bowles, N.Y.C., 1974-75; asst. product mgr. women's fashion eyewear and sports eyewear Warner-Lambert, Inc., Boston, 1976-77; mktg. mgr. fashion eyewear Marine Optical, Inc., Boston, 1978; dir. mktg. Pro Air Services, 1982—. Served with USNR, 1981—. Rotary Club Internat. Exchange fellow, 1969-70. Mem. Association International des Etudes Economique et Comercial (Exchange fellow 1972-74; pres. 1974), Am. Mktg. Assn., DAR, Council of Internat. Visitors, AAUW. Republican. Episcopalian. Clubs: Jr. League, St. Bartholomew's, Wharton Grad. Sch. Home: 3 Andorra Ln Hingham MA 02043

TAYLOR, LILLIAN ELIZABETH, adminstrv. asst.; b. Elizabeth City, N.C., Sept. 10, 1946; d. Pringle and Bessie Virginia (Barco) Woodson; student U. Md., Ft. Meade, 1968; m. Frederick Jones Taylor; children—Angela Renee, Ingrid Christine. Sec., analytical asst. Nat. Security Agy., Ft. Meade, Md., 1964-69; sr. legal sec., adminstrv. asst. firm Manger & Dees, Balt., 1969-70; adminstrv. asst. firm Wilkinson, Cragun & Barker, Washington, 1970—. Adv., sec. Columbia Highlands Neighborhood Com., 1976—. Recipient 1st pl. award classical piano recital Elizabeth City State U., 1958; various awards charitable and civic orgns. Democrat. Methodist. Club: Charmoniques (treas. 1972-78). Home: 6108 Osborn Rd Cheverly MD 20785 Office: 1735 New York Ave NW 6th Floor Washington DC 20006

TAYLOR, LOUISE ERDEY, importing co. exec., civic worker; b. Cleve., Nov. 28, 1921; d. Alexander and Anne M. (Nemeth) Erdey; student Cleve. Coll., Western Res. U., 1940-44, UCLA Extension, 1945-47; m. Edward Winthrop Taylor, Jr., Sept. 12, 1953; children—Mary Lou, Mark Alexander, Paul Winthrop. Office service mgr. Sta. WHK, Cleve., 1943-45; sec. to Mrs. Samuel Goldwyn, 1945-46; prodn. asst. to Leopold Stokowski, 1946; women's editor, reporter The Tidings, 1948-52; vol. coordinator Florence Crittenton, 1975-77; exec. sec., advt. mgr. World Imports, Alhambra, Calif., 1977—, also treas., dir. Pres. Democratic Dames, 1962-63; chmn., coordinator Portraits of Am. Women Panel, 1974-75; pres. Civic Center Toastmistress Club, 1952, Christines, 1961-62; bd. dirs. Altos de Monterey Assn., 1973-79; Benedictine oblate St. Andrew's Priory (Valyermo, Calif.); active Venture Club, Archdiocesan Council Cath. Women (award), Arroyo League, Los Angeles County Human Relations Council. Recipient Pius X award for religious edn. instrn., 1980. Office: World Imports Inc 400 S Date St Alhambra CA 91803

TAYLOR, LUCILE KAY WILCOX, mgmt. services officer; b. Ft. Collins, Colo., Dec. 6, 1944; d. William Walter and Eva Viola (Degney) Bradshaw; student U. Wyo., 1963-64, Scottsbluff Jr.Coll., 1965-66; m. D. Dennis Taylor, Jan. 16, 1982; children by previous marriage—Wendy Lizette, Stephanie Kay, Jeffrey Scott. Tchr.'s aide Converse County Sch. Dist. No. 1, Douglas, Wyo., 1972-73; sec. dairy mktg. order State of Wyo., Douglas, 1973-74; mgmt. services officer Wyo. Law Enforcement Acad., 1976—. Leader, 4-H Jr. Leaders, 1980-81. Mem. Wy. Public Employees Assn. (sec.), Wyo. Peace Officers Assn. (mem. cons.). Republican. Club: Women of Moose. Home: Box 588 Douglas WY 82633 Office: Box 1020 Douglas WY 82633

TAYLOR, LYNNETTE DOBBINS (MRS. HOBART TAYLOR, JR.), educator, civic worker; b. Birmingham, Ala.; d. Albert Greene and Louise (Brown) Dobbins; B.S., Ala. State U., 1938; M.Ed., Wayne State U., 1948; m. Hobart Taylor, Jr., Jan. 26, 1950; children—Albert, Hobart III. Tchr. Detroit Pub. Schs., 1945-49; adminstr. elementary schs., 1949-63; exec. dir. Delta Sigma Theta; program analyst, field rep. Midwest region Office Econ. Opportunity, Washington, 1965—; woman's editor N.Y. edit. Chgo. Defender, Detroit Tribune; edn. editor children's page feature and columnist Mich. Chronicle; dir. Jefferson Fed. Savs. and Loan. Adv. com. Truth in Lending, Fed. Res. Bd. Mem. exec. bd. United Found., 1960—; mem. bd. edn. research council YMCA; bd. dirs. Hillcrest Children's Center, A.R.C. Mem. Friends Soc. Detroit Inst. Arts, Nat. Council Vol. Action, Nat. Friends Pub. TV. Mem. Internat. Soc. Women Educators, N.A.A.C.P., Urban League, Washington Ednl. TV Assn. (dir.), Am. Newspaper Women's Club, Women in Community Service (dir.), Delta Kappa Gamma, Phi Delta Kappa, Delta Sigma Theta. Democrat. Unitarian. Club: Nat. Women's Dem. (Washington), Old Acquaintance (Detroit). Home: 203 Yoakum Pkwy Alexandria VA 22304 Office: 1707 New Hampshire St NW Washington DC 20009

TAYLOR, MABEL RUTH, educator; b. McPherson, Kans., Dec. 15, 1924; d. Oscar A. H. and Mildred Marie (Johnson) Larson; B.A., U. Kans., 1948; M.T., Central State Coll. Okla., 1965; Ed.D., U. Okla., 1971; m. John Taylor, Jr., Sept. 7, 1947; children—John Larson, Susan Louise Taylor Painter, Robert Lewis. Tchr. public schs., 1959-61; counselor, psychometrist Oklahoma City Public Schs., 1961-70; mem. faculty Central State U., Edmond, Okla., 1970-74, 1980—, also program dir. tng. sch. psychologist and sch. psychometrists; dir. diagnostic prescriptive learning center Tulsa Jr. Coll., 1976-80. Mem. Okla. Sch. Psychol. Assn. (state sec. 1976-78, exec. bd. 1981, Fay G. Catlett award 1981), Okla. Psychol. Assn. (pres. elect), Nat. Assn. Sch. Psychologists, Okla. Psychol. Assn., Okla. Assn. Gifted Creative Talented Inc., Delta Kappa Gamma. Author: (with N. Ferguson and M. Scott) New Discoveries in Early Education, 1968. Home: 2604 NW 58th Pl Oklahoma City OK 73112 Office: Dept Psychology Central State U Edmond OK 73034

TAYLOR, MAGGIE HENRIETTA PRICE, govt. ofcl.; b. La Grange, Ga., Feb. 18, 1936; d. Nathan and Maggie (Lee) Price; B.S., D.C. Tchrs. Coll., 1969; M.Ed., Fed. City Coll., Washington, 1974; Ed.D., George Washington U., 1978; m. James Taylor, Jr., Jan. 29, 1956 (dec.); 1 dau., Constance Marie. Grants adminstrn. specialist NSF, 1970-71; grants mgmr. officer Dept. Commerce, 1971-73; contract specialist Nat. Inst. Edn., 1973-75; contract and grant specialist U.S. Office Edn., 1975-78; bus. liaison specialist Dept. Energy, 1978-79; dir. community services div. Office Procurement and Contracts, HUD, 1979—; workshop leader, speaker in field. Recipient Outstanding Performance award NSF, 1971, HUD, 1980; named Am. Businessperson of yr. in D.C., Future Bus. Leaders, 1978. Mem. Am. Bus. Women's Assn. (corr. sec. 1978-79; Woman of Year award D.C. chpt. 1979), D.C. Bus. Edn. Assn. (pres. 1977-78, 79-82, dir. 1981—), Nat. Assn. Female Execs., Nat. Contracts Mgmt. Assn., Nat. Council Career Women, Nat. Bus. Edn. Assn., Nat. Assistance Mgmt. Assn., Phi Delta Kappa, Delta Pi Epsilon. Republican. Roman Catholic. Author career booklets. Home: 1031 Michigan Ave NE Washington DC 20017 Office: 451 7th St SW Washington DC 20410

TAYLOR, MARJORIE LEE, investment advisor; b. Springfield, Mo., Apr. 26, 1923; d. James Leonard and Lena Mae (Baker) Johnson; B.A., Wichita State U., 1944; children—James Christopher, David Bryan, Kent Matthew. Exec. sec. Center for Urban Studies, Wichita (Kans.) State U., 1965-69, program exec., 1969-72, asst. dir., 1972-75, acting dir., 1975-76, asso. dir., 1976-78, dir. Office Public Affairs Edn., 1978-82; investment advisor E.F. Hutton & Co., Inc., Wichita, 1982—. Mem. Kans. Adv. Council on Intergovtl. Relations, 1969-75, chmn., 1972; mem. Wichita-Sedgwick County Met. Area Planning Commn., 1969-78, chmn., 1974, 77; mem. Wichita Bd. Zoning Appeals, 1973-79, chmn., 1975-76; mem. Kans. Adv. Com. on Community Service and Continuing Edn., 1968—. Mem. Am. Planning Assn., Am. Soc. for Public Adminstrn. (chpt. pres. 1979-80), Nat. Mcpl. League (mem. governing council 1974—, regional v.p.). Democrat. Congregationalist. Office: EF Hutton & Co Inc 200 W Douglas St Suite 120 Wichita KS 67202

TAYLOR, MARY CULBERTSON, educator; b. Rowan County, N.C., Aug. 13, 1939; d. Marvin and Essie Mae (Oakley) Culbertson; B.S., Barber-Scotia Coll., 1965; M.S. in Edn., Queens Coll., 1974; m. John Taylor, July 1, 1960; children—Beverly Amelia, Evelyn Veronica. Therapeutic dietitian Meml. Hosp., N.Y.C., 1965-66; tchr. home econs., N.Y.C., 1966—. Mem. Assn. Home Econs. Tchrs. N.Y.C. Home: 65 Gormley Ave Roosevelt NY 11575 Office: 111 Columbia St New York NY 10002

TAYLOR, MARY JOAN (MRS. EDWARD MCKINLEY TAYLOR JR.), lawyer; b. Kenton, Ohio, Dec. 24, 1926; d. Maurice A. and Martina (Dolan) McMahon; student St. Mary Springs Coll., 1944-45; Asso. Degree in Bus. Adminstrn. Franklin U., 1946-49; J.D. with high distinction, Ohio No. U., 1951; postgrad., U. Wyo., 1954-56; m. Edward McKinley Taylor, Jr., Apr. 23, 1952; 1 dau., Mary Margaret. Admitted to Ohio bar, 1951; gen. practice law, Kenton, 1951-52, Wichita Falls, Tex., 1953—; mem. law firm Taylor and Taylor, Dayton, Ohio, 1957—; law librarian Franklin U., 1948-49. Trustee, Harrison Twp., 1980—. Mem. Ohio Bar Assn., Montgomery County Law Library Assn., Ohio No. U. Alumni Assn. (sec. Miami Valley 1958-60), Iota Tau Lambda, Kappa Beta Pi. Club: Soroptimist. Address: 7417 N Main St Dayton OH 45415

TAYLOR, MILDRED HENDERSON, recreation specialist; b. Newberry, S.C., May 15, 1925; d. John and Rachel Elizabeth (Reeder) Henderson; ed. Howard U., 1944-46, N.Y. U., 1948-53, Am. U., 1960, Md. U., 1962-64, Catholic U. Am., 1976, 79; m. Dec. 11, 1949; 1 dau., Brenda Christina Taylor Kellogg. Clk., GAO, Washington, 1943-44; with D.C. Dept. Recreation 1945—, recreation supr., 1945-73, recreation adminstr., asst. dir. Before/After Sch. Care Program, 1974—; tutor; counselor; vol. Reading Is Fundamental; bd. dirs. Georgetown Children's House. Vice pres. Georgetown Community Parents Council, Washington, 1957-60, Block Community Orgn., Washington, 1960-62; pres. Ladies Usher Bd., Vermont Ave. Baptist Ch., Washington, 1972—, dir. Children's Worship Hour, 1962—. Recipient Kennedy Found. award, 1964; Disting. Service award Kiwanis Internat., 1970; Beautification award White House, 1973; Outstanding Performance award D.C. Dept. Recreation, Thirty Yr. Service in Govt. award 1975. Mem. Nat. Recreation and Park Assn., D.C. Recreation and Parks Soc. (life), Smithsonian Assos., AAPHER, Friends Nat. Zoo. Better Edn. for Children, Nat. Assn. Edn. Young Children. Clubs: Ladies Needlework, Brooks Meml. (fin. sec.). Home: 6109 7th Pl NW Washington DC 20011 Office: 3149 16th St NW Washington DC 20010

TAYLOR, MILDRED LOIS, nursing home adminstr.; b. Conroe, Tex., July 23, 1927; d. George Carl and Bertha Elizabeth (Swift) Ferguson; student Hunter Coll., 1944, U.S. Navy Hosp. Corps Sch., Bethesda, Md., 1944, corr course Am. Sch., Chgo., 1971, Central Tex. Coll., 1971, U. Tex., Austin, 1975; m. Thomas Nielsen Taylor, Dec. 1, 1945; children—Linda Sue, Thomas Grant, Charles Nielsen. Nurse aide St. David's Hosp., Austin, Tex., 1965-67; adminstr.-in-tng. North Lamar Nursing Home, Austin, 1971-72, adminstr., 1973-75; adminstr. Austin Nursing & Convalescent Center, 1976—, sec., treas., 1976—. Pres. Episcopal Women of the Ch., Austin, 1966; mem. Tex. Nursing Home Adminstrs. Polit. Action Com., 1976—. Served with WAVE, USNR, 1944-45. Lic. nursing home adminstr., Tex. Mem. Tex. Nursing Home Assn., Am. Health Care Assn., Austin C. of C., U.S. C. of C. Clubs: Lost Creek Country, Order Eastern Star, St. David's Hosp. Women's Aux. (Austin). Home: 1909 Glencliff Dr Austin TX 78704 Office: 110 E Live Oak Austin TX 78704

TAYLOR, MURTIS HOWARD, social worker; b. Macon, Ga., Aug. 7, 1911; d. Luther Payne and Pearl (Holloman) Howard; B.S.Ed., Case Western Res. U., 1934, postgrad., 1962-63; postgrad. Ohio State U., 1959, Duke U., 1972-74; m. Richard D. Mills, May 27, 1978; children—Howard F., Bruce C. Edn. dir. Karamu House, Cleve., 1938-44; mgmt. asst. Outhwaite Homes, Cleve., 1944-46; dir. Kinsman br. Hiram House, Cleve., 1946-48; dir. Mt. Pleasant Community Centers, Cleve., 1956-66, Community Services Center Mt. Pleasant, 1966-71; dir. project aging Fed. Community Planning, Cleve., 1971-76, planning asso., 1976—; cons. on aging, Cleve., 1977—; guest German Govt., social work study, 1960. Program chmn. Mt. Pleasant Block Club, 1979—. Recipient Catholic Inter-racial Justice award, 1967; Social Worker of Yr. Merit award Nat. Assn. Social Workers, 1969; Community Services Center Mt. Pleasant re-named Murtis H. Taylor Multi-Service Center, 1976; inducted into Ohio Sr. Citizens' Hall of Fame, 1980. Mem. Nat. Assn. Social Workers, Acad. Cert. Social Workers, Council Human Relations, Hospice Council N.E. Ohio, NAACP, Mt. Pleasant Community Council. Mem. Ch. Religious Science. Home: 3886 E 147th St Cleveland OH 44128

TAYLOR, NANCY JANE, hosp. exec.; b. Gowanda, N.Y., Feb. 17, 1941; d. Bedford D. and Helen Pickup; M. Health Care Adminstrn., U. Buffalo, 1969; m. O.P. Taylor, Jr., May 20, 1978; stepchildren—Gale, Michael, Wayne. Instr. psychiat. nursing Buffalo State Hosp., 1962-70; supr. mental health unit Lake Sumter Community Mental Health Center, Eustis, Fla., 1970-72; exec. dir. Lake Community Hosp., Leesburg, Fla., 1972—. Trustee, Wildwood Manor Nursing Home; chmn. public relations Dixie Youth Baseball League; mem. Nursing Home Authority Bd. Sumter County, 1981-82; mem. adv. bd. Lake-Sumter Community Coll. Am. Acad. Med. Adminstrs. fellow, 1981. Mem. PSRO (dir.), Health Services Area Adminstrs. Council, Fla. League Hosps., Fla. Hosp. Assn., Leesburg Bus. and Profl. Women, Career Guild, E. Central Fla. Hosp. Adminstrs. Council (past pres.), Sumter County Hosp. Cost Containment Bd., E. Central Fla. Hosp. Council (pres. 1980), Am. Acad. Med. Adminstrs. (state dir. 1981-83). Republican. Methodist. Club: Order Eastern Star. Home: PO Box 688 Leesburg FL 32748 Office: PO Box 750 Leesburg FL 32748

TAYLOR, NETTIE BARCROFT, librarian; b. Bronsville, Tenn., Aug. 6, 1914; d. Charles W. and Nettie (Barcroft) Taylor; A.B., Fla. State U., 1936; B.S. in Library Sci., U. N.C., 1942; postgrad. U. Md., 1950-60; M.S., Johns Hopkins, 1967. Librarian, Taylor County High Sch., Perry, Fla., 1936-40, Leon County High Sch., Tallahassee, Fla., 1940-42; library dir. various U.S. Army libraries, U.S. and Germany, 1942-47; dir. Pamunkey Regional Library System, Ashland, Va., 1947-48; supr. pub. libraries Md. Dept. Edn., 1948-60, asst. state supt. for libraries, div. library devel. and services, Balt., 1960—; pres. Continuing Library Edn. Network Exchange, 1976. Mem. ALA, Am. Library Trustees Assn. (2d v.p. 1965), Assn. State Libraries (pres. 1969-70), Md. Library Assn. (pres. 1960), ACLU, Common Cause, League Women Voters. Contbr. to publs. in field. Office: Md State Dept Edn Div Library Devel and Services 200 W Baltimore St Baltimore MD 21201 *

TAYLOR, ROBERTA MIRIAM KENNEY, advt. agency exec.; b. Boston, June 21, 1935; d. Benedict E. and Frances (Siegel) Hirshon; student U. Lowell, 1953-54; m. Donald Kenney, Jan. 12, 1955 (div. 1972); children—Valerie, Mark, Jonathan; m. 2d, David Taylor, May 16, 1982. Founder, pres. Roberta Kenney Advt., Inc., Natick, Mass., 1966—. Mem. South Middlesex Area C. of C. (dir. 1981—), Smaller Bus. Assn. New England, Nat. Fedn. Ind. Bus., New Eng. Women Bus. Owners, Women Entrepreneurs, Old Girls Network. Jewish. Office: 43 Main St Natick MA 01760

TAYLOR, ROSEMARY, potter; b. Joseph, Oreg.; d. Theodore and Sarah A. (Lambright) Resch; student Cleve. Inst. Art, 1937-40, N.Y. U., 1947; m. Robert Hull Taylor; children—Barbara Taylor Ryalls, Robert H. Tchr. pottery Rahway (N.J.) Art Center, 1950-55; one-woman shows: Paterson (N.J.) Coll., 1964, Westchester (Pa.) Coll., 1970, Gallery 100, Princeton, N.J., 1967, George Jensen's, N.Y.C., 1972, Artisan Gallery, Princeton, 1974, Am. Crafts (Ohio), 1979, Taylor Gallery, Balt., 1981; group shows include: Mus. Natural History, N.Y.C., Newark Mus., Trenton (N.J.) Mus., Montclair (N.J.) Mus., Phila. Art Alliance, Nat. Design Center, N.Y.C.; represented in permanent collection Westchester Coll.; pottery cons. McCalls Mag., 1962-72. Pres., LWV, Plainfield, N.J. Mem. Am. Craft Council, N.J. Designer-Craftsmen, Phila. Craft Group, Bucks County (Pa.) C. of C., N.J. Mycological Assn. Democrat. Unitarian. Home and Office: PO Box 46 River Rd Lumberville PA 18933

TAYLOR, SARAH ELLEN, ednl. adminstr.; b. Pitts., July 23, 1928; d. George Francis and Catherine (Dwyer) Carroll; student Community Coll. of Allegheny County, 1965-69; children—Richard D., James W., Mark T., Kathleen L. Mng. acct. Leybold Hereaus, Inc., Monroeville, Pa., 1964-70; treas. Pitts. Metal, Inc., Export, Pa., 1970-72; v.p., controller Art Inst. Pitts., 1972—. Mem. Nat. Assn. Accts. (asso. dir. membership Pitts. chpt.), Nat. Assn. Female Execs. (network dir.). Roman Catholic. Office: Art Inst Pitts 526 Penn Ave Pittsburgh PA 15222

TAYLOR, SHELLEY ELIZABETH, psychologist; b. Mt. Kisco, N.Y., Sept. 10, 1946; d. Charles Fox and Pearl May (Harvey) Taylor; A.B. in Psychology, Conn. Coll., 1968; Ph.D. in Social Psychology, Yale U., 1972; m. Mervyn Francis Feranandes, May 1, 1972; 1 dau., Sara Fernandes Taylor. Asst. prof. dept. psychology and social relations Harvard U., Cambridge, Mass., 1972-77, asso. prof., 1977-79; prof. psychology UCLA, 1979—; NIMH grantee, 1974-86. Mem. Acad. of Behavioral Medicine Research, Am. Psychol. Assn., AAAS, Soc. for Psychol. Study of Social Issues, Soc. for Research in Child Devel., Soc. of Exptl. Social Psychology, Western Psychol. Assn., Jonsson Cancer Center (UCLA). Contbr. articles in field to profl. jours. Office: 4611 Franz Hall Psychology Dept UCLA Los Angeles CA 90024

TAYLOR, SUSAN CAROL HAYMAN, publishing co. exec.; b. Rockville Center, N.Y., Aug. 10, 1948; d. Robert Charles and Carol Hope (Wyman) Hayman; student Cambridge (Eng.) U., summer 1969; B.S., U. Kans., 1970; postgrad. Eastern Mich. U., summer 1971, Pace U., 1977-78; Francis Mortimer Taylor, Jr., Oct. 28, 1979. Tchr., Fauldhouse (Scotland) Jr. Secondary Sch., 1970; corr. Playboy Internat., Chgo., 1971-72; with Reader's Digest, Pleasantville, N.Y., 1972—, mgr. trade sales, 1975-78, dir. market devel., 1978—. Mem. Nat. Assn. Female Execs., Am. Mgmt. Assn., Am. Booksellers Assn., ALA, Assn. Am. Pubs., Pub. Advt. Club, Christian Booksellers Assn., U. Kans. Alumni Assn., Religious Pubs. Club. Republican. Methodist. Home: 96 Louise's Ln New Canaan CT 06840 Office: Reader's Digest Pleasantville NY 10570

TAYLOR, SUSAN GEBHARDT, nurse educator; b. Milw., June 8, 1935; d. Edward Anthony and Janet Meta (Ruhe) G.; B.S.N., Alverno Coll., 1957; M.S.N., Cath. U. Am., 1963, Ph.D., 1972; m. Thomas James Taylor, Oct. 19, 1973; children—Brian Gregory, Daniel Edward. Instr., Sch. Nursing, Georgetown U., Washington, 1963-65, Capital City Sch. Nursing, D.C. Gen. Hosp., 1965-66; asst. prof. No. Va. Community Coll., Annandale, 1966-69; asso. prof. nursing Lucy Webb Hayes Sch. Nursing, Am. U., Washington, 1970-71; univ. prof. health scis. Govs. State U., Park Forest South, Ill., 1971-74; research asso. U. Ill., Chgo., 1975; asso. prof. nursing, acad. asst. to asso. dean grad. study Coll. Nursing, U. Ill. Med. Center, Chgo., part-time, 1975-76; asst. project dir. Ill. Implementation Commn. on Nursing, Chgo., 1976; asso. prof. nursing U. Mo. Columbia, 1976—. Served with USNR, 1958-60. Recipient Excellence in Writing award Mo. Nurses Assn./Am. Jour. Nursing, 1978. Mem. Nat. League Nursing, Am. Nurses Assn., Mo. Nurses Assn., Nat. Soc. Study Edn., Kappa Gamma Pi, Sigma Theta Tau. Roman Catholic. Home: 7 Gipson Ct Columbia MO 65202 Office: Sch Nursing U Mo Columbia MO 65211

TAYLOR, TAMARA SUE, TV news producer; b. Rapid City, S.D., Nov. 11, 1953; d. James E. and Jeanne K. (Kell) Taylor; student U. Kans., 1972-74, Morningside Coll., 1977-78. News reporter Sta. KIMM, Rapid City, 1975-76; anchor, reporter, asst. news dir. Sta. KCAU-TV, Sioux City, Iowa, 1976-78; news writer KNXT-TV, Los Angeles, 1978-80, mgr. news adminstrn., 1980-82, producer, 1982—. Mem. Am. Film Inst., Hollywood Radio, TV and Film Soc., Am. Assn. Female Execs. Office: 6121 Sunset Blvd Los Angeles CA 90028

TAYLOR, YVONNE KEYS, educator; b. St. Louis, July 4, 1938; d. John and Ebie (Summers) Keys; B.A., Harris-Stowe State Coll., 1962; M.A., St. Louis U., 1972; adminstrn. cert. U. Mo., St. Louis, 1979; m. Aug. 17, 1963 (div.); 1 dau., Ingrid. Tchr., St. Louis Public Schs., 1962-63, Kansas City (Mo.) Public Sch., 1963-69, San Diego Unified Schs., 1975-76; tchr. University City (Mo.) Public Sch., 1969-75, 76—, now tchr.-in-charge Nathaniel Hawthorne Sch., chairperson ann. Brotherhood Program. Chairperson, Harris-Stowe State Coll. Alumni Scholarship Dr.; active local polit. campaigns; lectr. on fgn. travel to ch. groups, schs. Mem. NEA, Mo. State Tchrs. Assn., Jack and Jill Am. (journalist), Harris-Stowe State Coll. Alumni Assn. (dir.), Delta Sigma Theta. Club: Les Joviales St. Louis. Curriculum specialist for elem. grades; contbr. to Dictionary Lit. Writers. Home: 4946 Wabada Saint Louis MO 63113 Office: 1351 N Handley Rd University City MO 63130

TAYLOR-DESELL, JOAN-ALICE, phys. therapist; b. Hartford, Conn., Oct. 30, 1946; d. Jack Edward and Edith Alice (Gilbert)Taylor; B.S., Sargent Coll., Boston U., 1968, cert. in phys. therapy, 1969; M.S. in Counseling, U. Hartford, 1979; postgrad. Conn. Soc. Bioenergetic Analysis, 1978-82, Hartford Family Inst., 1980—; m. Dwight Henry Desell, Aug. 1, 1981. Staff phys. therapist Rehab. Services, Inc., Belmont, Mass., 1968-69, St. Joseph's Infirmary, Atlanta, 1970-72; chief phys. therapy Cobb Gen. Hosp., Austell, Ga., 1972-73; cons. phys. therapy Conn. Dept. Health Services, Hartford, 1973-75; dir. rehab. services Brittany Farms Health Center, New Britain, Conn., 1975-80; cons. phys. therapy div. Pa. Health Dept., 1980-81; pvt. practice psychotherapy, Newington, Conn., 1979-82; dir. rehab. Hebrew Home & Hosp., Hartford, 1980-82; partner, therapist Glastonbury (Conn.) Health Assos., 1982—; clin. asst. prof. U. Conn., Storrs, 1975—Quinnipiac Coll., 1975—. Congl. liaison to Rep. Cotter from Am. Phys. Therapy Assn., 1978-81; lobbyist Conn. Chpt. Am. Phys. Therapy Assn. to state legis., 1979—; del. Pres.'s Council on Phys. Fitness and Aging, 1981. Mem. Am. Phys. Therapy Assn. (sec. Conn. polit. action com. 1981-82), Nat. Assn. Female Execs., Internat. Soc. Bioenergetic Analysis, Conn. Soc. Bioenergetic Analysis. Republican. Congregationalist. Clubs: Grange, Newington Choral Home: 372 Willard Ave Newington CT 06111 Office: 131 New London Turnpike Glastonbury CT 06033

TAYMOR, BETTY, educator; b. Balt., Mar. 22, 1921; d. William and Tillie (Blum) Bernstein; A.B., Goucher Coll., Balt., 1942; M.A., Boston U., 1967; m. Melvin L. Taymor, June 7, 1942; children—Michael, Laurie, Julie. Instr. govt. Northeastern U., 1969-71; instr. Met. Coll., Boston U., 1973-74; cons. Office of Pres., U. Mass., 1973-74; dir. Program for Women in Polit. and Govt. Careers, Boston Coll., Newton, Mass., 1973—; mem. Council of Univs., John F. Kennedy Library. Mem. U.S. Nat. Commn., UNESCO, 1960-66, Gov.'s Commn. on Status Women, 1975-77; mem. Democratic Nat. Com., 1976. Elizabeth King Ellicott fellow Goucher Coll., 1959. Mem. Am. Polit. Sci. Assn., Americans for Dem. Action. Home: 14 Eliot Memorial Rd Newton MA 02158 Office: Boston Coll Newton Campus 885 Centre St Newton MA 02159

TAYRIEN, DOROTHY PAULINE, nurse, educator; b. Bartlesville, Okla., June 15, 1921; d. William Cyprian and Ida May (Bennett) Tayrien; student Bartlesville Jr. Coll.; diploma in nursing St. John's Hosp., Tulsa, 1945; B.S., U. Colo., 1948; M.A., U. Chgo., 1959; postgrad. U. S.C., 1980-81. Teaching fellow Vanderbilt U., 1948-49; instr. Sch. Nursing, U. Okla., Oklahoma City, 1948-50; instr. surg. nursing Fla. State U., Tallahassee, 1951-52; asst. prof. nursing fundamentals Northwestern State Coll., Natchitoches, La., 1950-51; asst. prof., dir. clin. edn. Monroe (La.) Div., 1952-54; asst. prof., asst. dean Sch. Nursing, Baylor U., Waco, Tex., 1954-55; asst. dir. nursing service Washington Meml. Hosp., Bartlesville, 1955-57; asst. prof. nursing fundamentals S.W. La. U., Lafayette, 1957-59; asso. prof. med. surg. nursing E. Tenn. State U., Johnson City, 1960-65, So. Ill. U., Edwardsville, 1965-67, Forest Park Jr. Coll., St. Louis, 1967-68; prof., dir. asso. degree nursing program Kankakee (Ill.) Community Coll., 1968-70; asso. prof., dir. continuing edn. Coll. Nursing, Med. U. S.C., Charleston, 1970-81; ret., 1982; dir nursing Tallahassee chpt. ARC, 1951-52; cons. in nursing, Belleville (Ill.) Meml. Hosp., 1966-67; public mem. Palmetto-Low Country Health Systems Agy., 1977—; mem. S.C. Regional Med. program grantee to train nurses in newborn care, 1974-80. Mem. AAUP, Am. Nurses Assn., S.C. Nurses Assn. (council on continuing edn. 1976-80), S.C. Assn. Continuing Higher Edn., Am. Indian Nurses Assn., Nat. Platform Assn., Adult Edn. Assn., AAUW. Democrat. Roman Catholic. Clubs: Cooper Civic, Coin of Charleston, Quota. Contbr. articles to profl. jours.; initiated and established Asso. Degree in Nursing Program, Kankakee (Ill.) Community Coll., 1968-70. Home: 660 Pawley Rd Mount Pleasant SC 29464

TCHERKASSKY, MARIANNA ALEXSAVENA, ballerina; b. Glen Cove, N.Y., Oct. 28, 1952; d. Alexis and Lillian (Oka) Tcherkassky; student Washington Sch. Ballet (scholar), 1965-67, Sch. Am. Ballet and Profl. Children's Sch., 1967-70; pupil of Edward Caton. Appeared with Bolshoi Ballet in Ballet Sch., 1961, 62, N.Y.C. Ballet in A Midsummer Night's Dream, 1963; profl. debut with Andre Eglevsky Ballet Co., 1968; mem. Am. Ballet Theatre, 1970—, soloist, 1972—, prin. dancer, 1976—; guest appearances throughout U.S. and in Europe, also on TV. Winner Nat. Soc. Arts and Letters competition, 1967; Ford Found. scholar, 1967-70. Address: care Am Ballet Theatre 890 Broadway New York NY 10003 *

TEAL, JACQUELYNE SUE, recruiting co. exec.; b. Wadesboro, N.C., Nov. 1, 1946; d. Benjamin Robert and Beatrice Mae (Cole) T.; student public schs. Asst. cryptanalyst/programmer NSA, Ft. Meade, Md., 1964-66; asst. dir. casting Cinderella Finishing and Modeling Sch., Washington, 1966-67; part-owner, asst. dir. Byron Modeling Sch. and Agy., Washington, 1967-69; self-employed in public relations and mktg., 1969-72; bus. mgr., controller, sec.-treas. Valentines, Inc., Mobile, 1972-78; recruiter Employment Specialists, Inc., New Orleans, 1978-80; pres. Corp. Cons., Inc., New Orleans, 1980—. Cert. personnel cons. Mem. Nat. Assn. Female Execs., Am. Soc. Profl. and Exec. Women, Nat. Assn. Personnel Cons. (state cert. chmn.), La. Assn. Personnel Cons. (treas.), Cert. Personnel Cons. Soc. La., Council Ind. Bus. (vice chmn.), C. of C. New Orleans and River Region, Bus. Devel. Bd. (dir.), Mensa. Club: Ambassadors. Office: Corp Cons Inc 419 Carondelet 4th Floor New Orleans LA 70130

TEAL, JANICE REBECCA, educator; b. Carrollton, Ga., Apr. 11, 1939; d. Lunie Everette and Jimmie Lee W. Teal; B.S., U. Ga., 1961, M.S., 1963, Ph.D., 1970. Asst. prof. psychology West Ga. Coll., Carrollton, 1963-68; asso. prof. Samford U., Birmingham, Ala., 1970-73, prof. psychology, 1973—. Mem. Am. Psychol. Assn., Southeastern Psychol. Assn., So. Soc. Philosophy and Psychology. Baptist. Office: Samford University Dept Psychology 800 Lake Shore Dr Birmingham AL 35209

TEARE, MARALYN LOIS, marriage, family, and child counselor; b. Montclair, N.J., Sept. 2, 1937; d. Malcolm and Dolores (Griffin) T.; B.S., Fla. State U., 1959, M.S., 1978; m. William E. Jacobs, Jan. 30, 1959 (div. 1974); children—Cheri Kay, Shanna Lynn. Intern, Parent Tng. Clinic, Neuropsychiat. Inst., UCLA, 1977-79; pvt. practice counseling, specializing in treatment of anxiety and phobias, especially environ. phobias, Beverly Hills, Calif., 1980—; lectr. to state, nat. orgns., on TV. Mem. Mental Research Inst. Palo Alto, Phobia Soc. Am. (charter), Assn. Humanistic Psychology (clin.), Calif. Assn. Marriage and Family Therapists (clin.). Episcopalian. Office: 383 S Robertson Blvd Suite A Beverly Hills CA 90211

TEAT, BETTY MONTGOMERY HOPKINS, convalescent care exec.; b. Baton Rouge, June 10, 1931; d. William Arthur and Sarah Irene (Palmer) Montgomery; B.S. in Commerce, La. State U., 1952; children—Gram Hopkins, Sandra Hopkins Moore, Ellen Hopkins Steen. Pres., gen. mgr. B M H Enterprises, Inc., doing business Better Sitters, Jackson, Miss., 1968—; sales assoc. Bill J. Smith, Realtor, Jackson, 1976-81. Mem. Nat. Assn. Companion Sitter Agys. and Referral Services (charter), Sales and Mktg. Execs. Jackson (chmn. today's career woman seminar V), Jackson C. of C., Miss. Econ. Council, Nat. Assn. Female Execs., Alpha Chi Omega. Republican. Methodist. Club: Magnolia Ladies Civitan (charter mem., dir.). Home: PO Box 184 Ridgeland MS 39157 Office: 350 N Mart Plaza Jackson MS 39206

TEATOR, DAWN NEWNHAM, health services coordinator; b. Gloversville, N.Y., Oct. 28, 1928; d. Albert G. and Ethel May (Rodber) Newnham; R.N., Columbia U. Presbyn. Hosp.; B.S. in Nursing, Columbia U., 1951, postgrad., 1951-52; postgrad. in Edn., SUNY, New Paltz, 1960-61; M.A.T. in Health Edn., U. S.C., 1976; m. Roger F. Teator, Sept. 7, 1950; children—Linda Anne, Sherrie Lee, Penny Marie. Gen. duty nurse Mary Harkness Convalescent Home, Port Chester, N.Y., 1951-52, Newport Gen. Hosp., 1952-53; asst. hosp. supr., head nurse psychiatry Roper Hosp., 1953-55; coordinator vol. sch. nurses Naval Dependents Sch., Nfld., 1958-60; coll. evening relief nurse, Bard Coll., 1960-61; coordinator health services Cooper River Sch. Dist. 4, North Charleston, S.C., 1961-68, Charleston (S.C.) County Schs., 1968—. Bd. dirs. Low Country chpt. Am. Cancer Soc., 1977-81, Lung Assn., 1981—; shelter worker, multi-media first aid instr., bd. dirs. Low-Country chpt. ARC, 1977—; bd. dirs. Tb Assn. Recipient Ann Magnussen Nat. Vol. Nurse award, ARC, 1978; State Soc. of Dentistry for Children awards, 1975. Mem. S.C. Nursing Assn. (chmn. sch. nurses sect. 1974-76, adv. bd.), Am. Sch. Health Assn. (state rep. 1975-76, 79-80), AAHPER, Nat. Assn. Sch. Nurses. Contbr. articles to profl. publs.; speaker confs., workshops; active state orientation for new sch. nurses, 1978-80. Home: 5030 Ashby Ave North Charleston SC 29406 Office: 3 Chisolm St Charleston SC 29401

TEBALDI, RENATA, opera singer; b. Pesaro, Italy, Feb. 1, 1922; d. Teobaldo and Giuseppina (Barbieri) T.; student Arrigo Boito Conservatory, Pesaro Gioacchino Rossini Conservatory, Parma, Italy; pupil of Carmen Melis, Giuseppe Pais. Lyric soprano; profl. debut in Mefistofele, Rovigo, 1944; debut at LaScala, 1946; singer opera houses of Naples, Rome, Venice, Bologna, Florence, Moderna, Cesana, Turin, Venice, Pompeii; Am. debut in Aida, San Francisco Opera Co., 1950; debut in Otello, Met. Opera House, N.Y.C., 1955; singer operatic roles in La Boheme, Madama Butterfly, Tosca. Roman Catholic. Office: care Herbert H Breslin 119 W 57th St New York NY 10019

TEBBETTS, DIANE RUTH, librarian, educator; b. Buffalo, N.Y., May 3, 1943; d. Bernard John and Ruth Amy (Arlin) T.; B.A. cum laude, U. N.H., 1965; M.L.S., Simmons Coll., 1972, postgrad., 1981—; M.L.A., Boston U., 1978. Cataloging library asst. U. N.H., 1965-71, asst. reference librarian, 1971-81, asst. dir., 1981—; asst. prof., 1971-78, assoc. prof., 1978—; reviewer Nat. Endowment for the Humanities, 1982—. N.H. Council Humanities grantee, 1979-81. Mem. New Eng. Library Assn. (dir. 1981—), Assn. Coll. and Research Libraries, NEC (sec. treas. 1979-81), N.H. Library Assn. (v.p. 1977-78, pres., 1978-79), ALA, N.H. Conf. on Library and Info. Services. Contbr. in field. Home: PO Box 593 Dover NH 03820 Office: Adminstrn Office U NH Library Durham NH 03824

TECALA, MILA RUIZ, clin. social worker, psychotherapist; b. Cebu, Philippines, Nov. 26, 1942; came to U.S., 1961; d. Juan Ruiz and Maria Nazaret; A.A., Graceland Coll., 1963; B.A., U. Mich., 1964, M.S.W., 1966; m. Inocentes Tecala, Feb. 11, 1966; children—Raoul, Christopher. Social worker Lapeer (Mich.) State Home & Tng. Center, summer 1965; clin. social worker Children's Convalescent Hosp., Washington, 1966-67, Georgetown U. Hosp., Washington, 1968-77; clin. dir. St. Francis Inst., Washington, 1977-78; pvt. practice clin. social work, Washington, 1979—; cons. to numerous orgns.; clin. asst. prof. community medicine and internat. health Georgetown U., 1977—; instr. Met. Mental Health Skills Center, Washington Sch. Psychiatry, 1973—. Mem. Nat. Assn. Social Workers (dir. 1979—), Acad. Cert. Social Workers, Found. Thanatology, Forum for Dealth Edn. and Counseling. Roman Catholic. Contbr. articles to profl. jours. Home: 3120 Maries Dr Falls Church VA 22041 Office: 1500 Massachussetts Ave Suite 39 Washington DC 20005

TEDESCO, ELEANOR MARTHA HOLLIS, educator; b. N.Y.C.; d. Earl Anthony and Eleanor Martha (Jevons) Hollis; B.S., Cedar Crest Coll., 1949; M.Ed., Boston U., 1950; Ed.D., Mich. State U., 1967; m. Paul H. Tedesco, Jan. 24, 1953; children—Steven Anthony, Sara Adams, James Beattie. Instr., Elizabethtown (Pa.) Coll., 1950-52, Laselle Jr. Coll., Auburndale, Mass., 1953-55, Mich. State U., East Lansing, 1956-60; tchr. Carmel (N.Y.) High Sch., 1952-53; chmn. dept., adult edn. coordinator Quincy (Mass.) Jr. Coll., 1962-68; div. dir. Northeastern U., Boston, 1968-69; prof. Wheaton Coll., Norton, Mass., 1969-74; dean of instrn. Becker-Leicester Jr. Coll., Leicester, Mass., 1974-76; prof. dept. bus. Plymouth State Coll. of U. N.H., Plymouth, 1976-81, head dept. bus. edn. and office adminstrn. N.E. La. U., Monroe, 1981-82; prof. Boston U., 1982—; ednl. cons., mgmt. cons. Mem. N.H. Council Econ. Edn. (dir.), Delta Pi Epsilon. Episcopalian. Author: (with Paul Tedesco) The Creative Social Studies Teacher, 1974; The Secretary Today—An Integrated Block Program, 1978; Administrative Office Management: Systems and Services, 1983. Office: Boston U 605 Commonwealth Ave Boston MA 02215

TEEL, JOYCE, clin. psychologist; b. Fairfield, Ala., May 10, 1939; d. James Ernest and Annie Elizabeth (Fudge) Seay; B.A., Agnes Scott Coll., 1961; M.A., U. Ala., 1975; m. William Dickason Rankin, Aug. 5, 1961; children—Elizabeth Ann, Rebecca Lynn; m. 2d, Sidney Kreider Teel, July 2, 1975. Dir. staffing project West Ala. Mental Health Center, Demopolis, 1972; dir. children's services, dir. partial hospitalization program Sampson County Human Devel. Center, Clinton, N.C., 1975; pvt. practice clin. psychology, Fayetteville, N.C., 1976—; sch. psychologist Fayetteville City Schs., 1977-81, Ft. Bragg (N.C.) Schs., 1981—; cons. sch. systems, vocat. rehab.; part-time faculty Meth. Coll., Fayetteville, 1977—. Recipient award Ga. Psychol. Assn., 1961. Mem. Am. Psychol. Assn., N.C. Psychol. Assn., N.C. Sch. Psychology Assn., Cumberland County Mental Health Assn., Cumberland County Assn. Psychologists, Phi Beta Kappa. Republican. Presbyterian. Home: 2014 Forest Hills Dr Fayetteville NC 28303

TEES, SANDRA KAY MARTIN, program evaluator; b. Omaha, Apr. 18, 1944; d. Leslie B. and Ruth Lillian (May) Martin; B.A. magna cum laude, Tex. Christian U., 1965, M.A., 1972; postgrad. Washington U., St. Louis. Adminstrv. asst./research coordinator Hosp. Improvement Project, Wichita Falls (Tex.) State Hosp., 1968-69; caseworker adoptions Edna Gladney Home, Ft. Worth, Tex., 1970-71; psychologist Mexia (Tex.) State Sch., 1971-72; sch. pshchologist Ft. Worth Ind. Sch. Dist., 1971-78, spl. edn. evaluator, 1978—; project mgr. Growth Center Project, 1975-77, lectr. in field. Founder, leader Alateen Group, Wichita Falls, 1969. Dallas Tex. Christian U. Women's Club creative writing scholar, 1962-64, Virginia Alpha scholar, 1963; NASA research asst., 1965-67; USPHS trainee, 1967-68; cert. Am. Montessori Soc., 1977. Mem. Ft. Worth Public Schs. Adminstrs. Assn., Mortar Bd., Mensa, Alpha Chi, Phi Alpha Theta, Psi Chi, Phi Delta Kappa. Contbr. articles to profl. publs. Home: 5432 Fursman Fort Worth TX 76114 Office: 3210 W Lancaster St Ft Worth TX 76107

TEETERS, LINDA MARIE, educator; b. Cin., Aug. 22, 1945; d. Irvin Louis and Shirley H. (Huenefeld) T.; cert. dental asst. U. N.C., 1973. Pharmacy intern Edward W. Wolff Pharmacy, 1963-67; dental asst. to dentists, 1967-73; coordinator, dental asst. clinics Hamilton County (Ohio) Bd. Health, 1973-76; sr. dental instr. Western Hills Vocat. High Sch., Cin., 1976—, chmn. adv. bd. for dental program, 1976—; mem. Ohio Commn. Dental Assisting Cert., 1981—. Mem. Am. Dental Assts. Assn., Ohio Dental Assts. Assn. (pres. 1982-83, editor newsletter 1979—), Cin. Dental Assts. Assn. (pres. 1971-72, 77-78). Democrat. Roman Catholic. Club: Internationally Yours. Home: 1828 Sunset Ave Apt 32 Cincinnati OH 45238 Office: 2144 Ferguson Rd Cincinnati OH 45238

TEETERS, NANCY HAYS, govt. ofcl.; b. Marion, Ind., July 29, 1930; d. S. Edgar and Mabel (Drake) Hays; A.B. in Econs., Oberlin (Ohio) Coll., 1952, LL.D. (hon.), 1979; M.A., U. Mich., 1954, postgrad., 1956-57; LL.D. (hon.), Bates Coll., 1981; m. Robert Duane Teeters, June 7, 1952; children—Ann, James, John. Staff economist govt. fin. sect., bd. govs. FRS, 1957-66, bd. govs., 1978—; economist on loan Council Econ. Advs., 1962-63; fiscal economist planning and analysis staff Office Mgmt. and Budget, 1966-70; sr. fellow Brookings Instn., 1970-73; sr. specialist Congressional Research Service, Library of Congress, 1973-74; asst. staff dir., chief economist com. budget U.S. Ho. of Reps., 1974-78; instr. U. Md., overseas, 1955-56, U. Mich., 1956-57. Recipient Disting. Alumni award U. Mich., 1980, 82. Mem. Nat. Economists Club (past pres.), Am. Fin. Assn. (dir. 1969-71), Am. Econ. Assn., Exec. Women in Govt., Nat. Assn. Bank Women, Women in Housing and Fin. Democrat. Author articles in field. Office: Bd Govs Fed Res System 20th and Constitution Ave NW Washington DC 20551

TEFFERTELLER, RUTH SINOVOY (MRS. RALPH B. TEFFERTELLER), social worker; b. Albany, N.Y., Aug. 28, 1917; d. Samuel and Jennie (Katz) Sinovoy; B.A., N.Y. State Coll. for Tchrs., 1939; postgrad. Iowa U., 1939-40; M.S.W., Columbia, 1955; m. Ralph B. Tefferteller, Sept. 5, 1941. Social worker A.R.C., St. Louis, Denver, Roswell, N.Mex., Ft. Bragg, N.C., 1942-46; dir. children's div., camp dir., program dir., dir. spl. project for delinquency prevention and control Henry Street Settlement, N.Y.C., 1946-68; asst. chief Unitarian-Universalist Service Com. Project in Vietnam, in cooperation with U.S. AID Mission, 1968-71; asso. area dir. Danvers-Salem area Mass. Dept. Mental Health, 1971-78, area dir., 1978—; cons. Astor Project, 1961-62. Recipient Florence Luscomb award for outstanding achievement, 1980. Mem. Nat. Assn. Social Workers, Nat. Acad. Social Workers. Contbr. articles to profl. jours. Address: 127 Front St Marblehead MA 01945

TEICHMAN, SABINA GOLDMAN, artist; b. N.Y.C.; B.A., Columbia U., 1941, M.A., 1943. One-man shows Salpeter Gallery, 1947, 49, 52, 54, A.C.A. Gallery, 1957, 60, 63, 69, Fairleigh Dickinson U., 1963, ACA Gallery, Rome, Italy, 1965, Orpheus Ascending Gallery, Stockbridge, Mass., 1972, N.Y. Cultural Center, N.Y.C., 1975, St. Mary's Coll. of Md., 1977, Shore Galleries, Boston, 1978, Tower Gallery, Southampton, N.Y., 1978, Phoenix Gallery, N.Y.C. (continuous shows); exhibited in group shows Salpeter Gallery, 1946-55, A.C.A. Gallery, 1955—, Whitney Mus., 1957, John Herron Mus., Butler Inst. Am. Art, Mint Mus., ann. shows Audubon Artists, N.Y.C., 1967-74, Silvermine Guild, New Canaan, Conn., 1970-78, U. Tex. Art Gallery, Austin, Phoenix Gallery, N.Y.C.; paintings in permanent collections Balt. Mus. Art, Bklyn. Mus., Carnegie Inst., Pitts., Butler Inst. Am. Art, Nat. Mus. Israel, San Francisco Mus. Art, Syracuse U. Mus., Whitney Mus. Am. Art, George Vincent Arthur Smith Mus., Springfield, Mass., U. Mass., Brandeis U., Tel-Aviv Mus., U. Puerto Rico Mus., Living Arts Found. Collection, Vatican Mus., Norfolk Mus. Art, James A. Michener Found. Collection, Sheldon Swope Art Mus., Colby Coll. Mus., others, also pvt. collections. Mem. Nat. Assn. Women Artists, Artists Equity Assn., Provincetown Art Assn., Silvermine Guild, Audubon Artists. Studio: 1120 Fifth Ave New York NY 10028

TEICHMANN, DIETRA DUFFALA, psychologist; b. Cleve., Sept. 9, 1946; d. Stephen Harold and Mary (Hrivnak) Duffala; B.A. in Math., Valparaiso U., 1969; B.S. in Psychology, Mills Coll., 1974; M.S. in Counseling and Sch. Psychology, Calif. State U., Hayward, 1976; Ph.D. in Psychology, Calif. Sch. Profl. Psychology, 1978; m. Nelson E. Teichmann, Aug. 30, 1980. Staff psychologist, head injury treatment program Santa Clara Valley Med. Center, San Jose, Calif., 1976-79; psychol. asst. Behaviordyne, Inc., Palo Alto, Calif., 1978-79; staff psychologist Inst. Phys. Medicine and Rehab., Peoria, Ill., 1979—; speaker; tchr. neuropsychology Bradley U., 1979—; resource person rehab. centers. Mem. Am. Psychol. Assn., Ill. Psychol. Assn., Central Ill. Psychol. Assn., Internat. Neuropsychol. Soc., Neuropsychologists in Rehab. (charter). Lutheran. Office: Institute of Physical Medicine and Rehabilitation 619 NE Glen Oak St Peoria IL 61603

TEILHET, HILDEGARDE TOLMAN, author; b. Tucson, Nov. 22, 1906; d. Cyrus Fisher and Hannah Marthe (van Steen) Tolman; B.A., Stanford U., 1926, postgrad., 1926-27; postgrad. U. Heidelberg (Ger.), 1927-28; m. Darwin L. Teilhet, Oct. 28, 1927; children—Marta, Saral, Jehanne. Manuscript editor Center for Advanced Study of Behavioral Scis., Stanford, Calif., 1964-72. Mem. Pen and Brush, Authors Guild, Mystery Writers Am., Internat. Bibl. Centre, IPA, World Affairs Council, Assos. of Stanford U. Libraries (dir. 1976—, chmn. 1979-81, chmn. pub. Imprint 1976-79, 81—), Alpha Phi. Democrat. Episcopalian. Author: (with Darwin L. Teilhet) The Ticking Terror Murders, 1935; The Crimson Hair Murders, 1936; The Feather Cloak Murders, 1938; The Broken Face Murders, 1940; Hero by Proxy, 1941; The Double Agent, 1945; The Assassins, 1946; The Terrified Society, 1947; The Rim of Terror, 1950; A Private Undertaking, 1953; Trouble Shooters, 1958. Address: 14141 Miranda Rd Los Altos Hills CA 94022

TEIXEIRA, LINDA CAROLYN, govt. public affairs officer; b. Harwich, Mass., May 17, 1946; d. Eugenio L. and Frances A. (Raneo) T.; A.B. in Lit., Clark U., Worcester, Mass., 1968. Urban intern HUD, 1968-69, public affairs writer, 1969-70, public info. specialist, 1970-72; legis. research asst. U.S. Senate Labor & Public Welfare Com., 1972-74; freelance writer and legis. cons., 1974-76; legis. asst. internship U.S. Ho. of Reps. Majority Leader, 1976; freelance writer and communications cons., 1976-77; public affairs info. officer Urban Mass Transp. Adminstrn., U.S. Dept. Transp., Washington, 1977—. Bd. dirs. Nat. Women's Health Network, 1976-77. The Ella Lyman Cabot Fund grantee, 1974; recipient Washington Area Fedn. Garden Clubs Public Service award, 1976. Mem. Nat. Press Club, Women in Films, Washington Ind. Writers, Nat. Assn. Govt. Communicators. Home: 3003 Van Ness St Washington DC 20008 Office: 400 7th St SW Washington DC 20590

TE KANAWA, KIRI, opera and concert singer; b. Gisborne, N.Z.; d. Thomas and Elanor Te K.; student St. Mary's Coll., Auckland, N.Z., 1957-60, London Opera Centre, 1966-69; m. Desmond Park, Aug. 30, 1967; children—Antonia Aroha, Thomas Desmond. Joined Royal Opera House, London, 1971, appeared in role of Countess in Le Nozze di Figaro, 1973; U.S. debut in Le Nozze di Figaro, Sante Fe Festival, 1971; Met. Opera debut as Desdemona in Otello, 1974; appears regularly with all major European and Am. opera houses, also Australian opera companies; appeared in film Don Giovanni as Elvira. Decorated comdr. Order Brit. Empire 1973, D.B.E., 1982. Office: care Basil Horsfield Estoril B Ave Princesse Grace 31 Monte Carlo Monaco

TEKIELI, DELORES LORETTA TOCCO, mcpl. ofcl.; b. Youngstown, Ohio; d. Dominic and Annette Pauline (Naples) Tocco; B.S. in Bus. Edn. and Bus. Adminstrn., Youngstown State U., 1963; postgrad. Kent State U., 1964, Northwestern U., 1965, Lakeland Coll., 1980, John Carroll U., 1981; m. Edward Thomas Tekieli, Sr., July 2, 1966; children—Edward Thomas, Michele, Tiffany. Instr. bus. edn. Euclid (Ohio) Sr. High Sch., 1963-67; instr. TRW, Inc., 1967-69; bus. instr. Cuyahoga Community Coll., 1967-70; instr. Lakeland Community Coll., 1975-78; owner, pres. Custom Cover Leasing, 1976-78; coordinator Downtown Euclid Assn., 1979-80; comml. affairs coordinator City of Euclid, also dir. community festival, 1980—; cons. to mchts. assns., festival sponsors, coms. Co-founder Euclid Women's Caucus, dir., 1978-81; mem. Euclid Democratic Caucus Coalition Club; trustee Euclid Devel. Corp.; adv. bd. site com. Euclid Day Care Center; co-founder Euclid Conservation Assn.; founder, prin., mem. staff St. Robert's Catholic Pres-Sch.; mem. Euclid Cultural Council. Named Outstanding Citizen of Yr., Euclid post Am. Legion, 1976; cert. Devel. Council. Mem. Realtors Assn., Sigma Sigma Sigma. Columnist Ecology Corner for Euclid News Jour., 1971-73. Home: 5 E 221st St Euclid OH 44123 Office: Euclid City Hall Annex 21331 Wilmore Ave Euclid OH 44123

TELAK, MARLENE MARY, interior decorator, color cons.; b. Balt., May 18, 1950; d. Casimir S. and Wilhelmina (Balling) T.; B.S., U. Md., 1972; M.Ed., Am. U., 1976; postgrad. George Washington U., 1980—. Interior designer Montgomery Ward & Co., also Hecht Co., Washington, 1972-74; adminstrv. sec. Internat. Student and Faculty Exchange, Am. U. Washington, 1974-76; fin. aid adminstr. No. Va. Community Coll., Alexandria, 1976-81; interior decorator Duron Paints & Wallcoverings, Wheaton, Md., 1981-82, Balt., 1982—. Mem. So. Assn. Student Fin. Aid Adminstrs., Va. Assn. Student Fin. Aid Adminstrs., Del.-D.C.-Md. Assn. Student Fin. Aid Adminstrs. Democrat. Roman Catholic. Home: 1601 Weyburn Rd Baltimore MD 21237 Office: 2407 Cleanleigh Dr Baltimore MD 21234

TELBAN, MARY KATHLEEN, computer software co. exec.; b. Cleve., Dec. 6, 1954; d. Stanley T. and Evelyn L. (Lutes) Telban; B.A. in Bus. Adminstrn., Ohio State U., 1976. Computer programmer Lincoln Nat. Life, Ft. Wayne, Ind., 1977-78; computer analyst Progressive Ins., Cleve., 1978; tech. support rep. Applied Data Research, Princeton, N.J., 1979-80, support specialist, 1980-81, sr. tech. educator, 1982—. Active, Big Bros./Big Sisters, Ft. Wayne, 1977—; vol. Battered Women's Shelter, Cleve., 1979—. Recipient Marion award, Roman Cath. Ch., 1967, also Cath. medal. Office: 8515 Greenville Ave Dallas TX 75243

TEMPLE, FRANCES ELIZABETH, elec. distbr. exec.; b. Marlin, Tex., June 9, 1923; d. A.W. and Louise (Czirr) Meyer; grad. high sch.; m. L.O. Temple, 1944 (dec. 1975); children—Lee O., Terri Temple Bratton. With Gen. Electric Supply, San Antonio, 1942-46; chmn. bd. Temple Inc., San Antonio, 1955—. Mem. Tex. Research League, Am. Soc. Profl. and Exec. Women, San Antonio Council Pres.'s. Methodist. Clubs: Altrusa Internat., Order Eastern Star. Office: 4314 Dividend Dr San Antonio TX 78219

TEMPLIN, ETHELYN MERLE, nurse; b. Giltner, Nebr., Nov. 2, 1928; d. John Pearson and Odessa Merle (Hendrickson) Anderson; student Hastings Coll., 1947-48; R.N., Mary Lanning Meml. Hosp., 1950; B.S. in Psychology, Kearney State Coll., 1976; m. William Samuel Templin, Nov. 3, 1951; children—Samuel Ray, Daniel Caye, Roger Lee. Head nurse, clin. instr. Hastings (Nebr.) Regional Center, 1956-59; staff nurse VA Med. Center, Grand Island, Nebr., 1952-55, head nurse, 1960-74, staff nurse intensive care, 1975-76, staff, supr., 1976—. Cert. Reach to Recovery vol. Am. Cancer Soc., 1974—; Nebr. civil def. nurse, 1963-65. Recipient Cert. of Recognition, Nebr. Nurses Assn. Commn. on Edn., 1976, 78, 80, Disting. Service award, 1977. Mem. ARC, Nat. Assn. Orthopedic Nurses, Assn. Operating Room Nurses, Nebr. Nurse Assn., Mary Lanning Meml. Hosp. Alumnae Assn. Republican. Methodist. Clubs: Ladies Aux. of Eagles, Order Eastern Star, AAUS. Home: 1335 W 5th St Hastings NE 68901 Office: 2201 N Broadwell St Grand Island NE 68801

TEMPLIN, MARTHA SILVIS, nurse, educator; b. Greensburg, Pa., July 7, 1944; d. Gerald Steel and Mae (McColly) Silvis; diploma in nursing Westmoreland Sch. Nursing, 1967; B.A., MacMurray Coll., 1969; B.A. in Nursing, Sangamon State U., 1975; M.S. in Nursing, St. Louis U., 1982; m. Thomas Joseph Templin, June 7, 1968; children—Lydia Ann, Patrick Thomas. Staff nurse Our Savior's Hosp., Jacksonville, Ill., 1967-68; nursing instr. Jacksonville State Hosp., 1968-70; nursing instr. Passavant Meml. Sch. Nursing, 1970-81; instr. med. surg. nursing MacMurray Coll., Jacksonville, 1982—; cert. instr.-trainer CPR, Ill. Heart Assn., 1975-80. Pres., Morgan County Mental Health Assn., 1975. Registered nurse. Mem. Am. Nurses Assn., Ill. Nurses Assn., Sigma Theta Tau, Delta Lambda, Pi Epsilon Delta. Contbr. articles to profl. jours. Office: MacMurray Coll Dept Nursing Jacksonville IL 62650 *

TENCZYNSKI, DOLORES HELENE, psychologist; b. Scranton, Pa., Nov. 5, 1943; d. Leon Francis and Helen Dolores (Tomaszewski) Tenczynski; B.A. cum laude, Seton Hill Coll., 1966; M.A., Fordham U., 1968, postgrad. Vocational counselor Cath. Charities, N.Y.C., 1967-69; psychol. cons. N.Y. U. Med. Center, 1968-69; psychologist Counseling Center Fordham U., Bronx, N.Y., 1969-73, asst. dir., 1974-76; asst. team leader inpatient unit South Beach Psychiat. Center, 1976-77, asst. dir. Day Hosp., 1978-79; dir. Coney Island Acute Day Hosp., 1979—; instr. psychology Coll. New Rochelle, 1968-69, Fordham U., 1969-73. Mem. Am. Psychol. Assn., Am. Group Therapy Assn., Am. Assn. Partial Hospitalization, Eastern Psychol. Assn. Home: 341 E 81st St New York NY 10028 Office: South Beach Psychiatric Center 2508 Coney Island Ave Brooklyn NY 11223

TENER, MONICA ROCHELLE, social worker; b. Brazil, Ind., Mar. 11, 1950; d. Gerald Everett and Dorothy Annadelle (Butts) Deakins; B.S., Ind. State U., 1972, M.A., 1975; m. Thomas Wayne Tener, Sept. 18, 1970; 1 son, Marcus Antonne. Social service dir. Clay County Hosp., Brazil, Ind., 1973-76; dir. Clay County Welfare, Brazil, 1976; social service dir. Dunn Meml. Hosp., Bedford, Ind., 1976-77; dir. Lawrence County Welfare Dept., Bedford, Ind., 1977; supr. child welfare div. Vigo County Welfare Dept., Terre Haute, Ind., 1977—. Bd. mem. Alternatives to Living and Learning. Mem. Nat. Assn. Social Workers, Brazil Bus. and Profl. Women's Club (v.p. 1978-80), Ind. Conf. Social Concerns, Alpha Kappa Delta. Office: PO Box 1584 429 S 6th St Terre Haute IN 47808

TENNILLE, MARGARET ROSE, state legislator; b. Hopewell, Va., Mar. 25, 1917; d. Robert Wilson and Byrd (McClure) Rose; student Salem Coll., 1934-36; m. Norton F. Tennille, Apr. 22, 1939 (dec.); children—Norton F., Wilson R., Ben F. Sec., Noland Co., Inc., Winston-Salem, N.C., 1937-39; adminstrv. asst. to mayor City of Winston-Salem, 1961-71; mem. N.C. Ho. of Reps., 1975—; dir. Forsyth Bank & Trust Co. Mem. Winston-Salem Bd. Edn., 1956-61. Mem. Women's Forum N.C., Phoenix Orgn., Forsyth County Democratic Women. Methodist. Clubs: Capital City, UDC. Home: 2307 Greenwich Rd Winston-Salem NC 27104 Office: PO Box 5988 Winston-Salem NC 27103

TENNILLE, TONI, singer, rec. artist; b. Montgomery, Ala., May 8, 1943; m. Daryl Dragon, Feb. 14, 1974. Mem. duo The Captain and Tennille, 1974—; single recs. include: The Way I Want to Touch You, Love Will Keep Us Together, Lonely Nights, Shop Around, Muskrat Love, Can't Stop Dancing, Come in From the Rain, I'm On My Way; albums include: Come in From the Rain, Love Will Keep Us Together, Greatest Hits, Dream, Make Your Move; host The Toni Tennille Show, NBC-TV, 1980-81. Office: care William Morris Agy Inc 151 El Camino Beverly Hills CA 90212 *

TENOPYR, MARY LOUISE WELSH (MRS. JOSEPH TENOPYR), psychologist; b. Youngstown, Ohio, Oct. 18, 1929; d. Roy Henry and Olive (Donegan) Welsh; A.B., Ohio U., 1951, M.A., 1951; Ph.D., U. So. Calif., 1966; m. Joseph Tenopyr, Oct. 30, 1955. Psychometrist, Ohio U., Athens, 1951-52, also housemother Sigma Kappa; personnel technician to research psychologist USAF, 1953-55, Dayton, Ohio, 1952-53, Hempstead, N.Y.; indsl. research analyst to mgr. employee evaluation N.Am. Rockwell Corp., El Segundo, Calif., 1956-70; asso. prof. Calif. State Coll. at Los Angeles, 1966-70; asso. research educationist U. Calif. at Los Angeles, 1970-71; program dir. U.S. CSC, 1971-72; mgr. human resources research AT&T, N.Y.C., 1972-—; lectr. U. So. Calif., Los Angeles, 1967-70; vice chmn. research com. Tech. Adv. Com. on Testing, Fair Employment Practice Commn. Calif., 1966-70; adviser on testing Office Fed. Contract Compliance, U.S. Dept. Labor, Washington, 1967-73. Fellow Am. Psychol. Assn. (bd. profl. affairs, pres. div. indsl. organizational psychology, mem. employment and human resources com.); mem. Eastern Psychol. Assn., Internat. Council Psychologists, Nat. Council Measurement in Edn., Psychomatic Soc., Met. N.Y. Assn. Applied Psychology, Am. Ednl. Research Assn., Sigma Xi, Sigma Kappa, Psi Chi, Alpha Lambda Delta, Kappa Phi. Editorial bd. Jour. Applied Psychology; contbr. articles to profl. jours. Home: 557 Lyme Rock Rd Bridgewater NJ 08807 Office: 1776 On the Green Morristown NJ 07960

TEPPER, BLOSSOM WEISS, clin. psychologist; b. Bklyn., Oct. 15, 1921; d. Meyer and Anna (Lax) Weiss; B.A., Bklyn. Coll., 1942; M.Ed., Lehigh U., 1962, Ed.D. in Clin. and Counseling Psychology, 1967; m. Louis Tepper, Apr. 17, 1942 (dec. August 1978); children—Irene Tepper Homa, Allan M. Tchr. sci., guidance counselor Blue Mountain Sch. Dist., Schuylkill Haven, Pa., 1958-64; successively grad. asst., instr., asst. prof. Lehigh U., Bethlehem, Pa., 1964-71; dir. home and sch. visitor project Luzerne County Schs., Wilkes-Barre, Pa., 1968-71, also adj. prof. Wilkes Coll., Wilkes-Barre, 1969-71; clin. psychologist base service unit, dir. Schuylkill County Mental Health/Mental Retardation, Pottsville, Pa., 1971-72; clin. psychologist Northampton County Mental Health/Mental Retardation, Easton, Pa., 1972-75; clin. psychologist, mental retardation and devel. disabilities specialist, cons. community living program for mental retardation Northampton County Mental Health/Mental Retardation, Bethlehem and Easton, 1975—. Lic. psychologist, Pa.; cert. sch. psychologist, Pa. Fellow Pa. Psychol. Assn.; mem. Am. Personnel and Guidance Assn., Pa. Personnel and Guidance Assn., Am. Psychol. Assn., Eastern Psychol. Assn., Am. Assn. Mental Deficiency, Am. Assn. Psychiat. Services for Children, Pa. Assn. Sch. Psychologists (charter), Nat. Register Mental Health Providers in Psychology, Am. Assn. Higher Edn. (charter, life), Hadassah (life). Developer exptl. program tng. sch. social workers. Home: Bridle Path Woods Apt C12 Bethlehem PA 18017 Office: 2009 Lehigh St Easton PA 18042

TEREBAYZA, EVELYN DOROTHY, chef; b. Mpls., Nov. 2, 1943; d. Frank Aloysius and Helen (Bendik) Terebayza; student pub. schs., Hill City, Minn. With Silver Grill, Hill City, 1958-63, Quadna Mountain, Hill City, 1963-69; with The Harbor restaurant, Grand Rapids, Minn., 1969—, now head chef. Mem. Democrat Farm Labor Party. Roman Catholic. Clubs: VFW Aux., Am. Legion Aux., Cath. Order Foresters. Home and Office: 5656 Hwy 169 S Grand Rapids MN 55744

TERMINI, CHRISTINE, artist; b. Bklyn., Sept. 30, 1947; d. Thomas and Josephine (Sara) T.; B.F.A., Pratt Inst., 1969; M.A., Hunter Coll., 1973. Dir. Circle Gallery, N.Y.C., 1975-76, Jack Gallery, N.Y.C., 1976-77, Gallerie La Grande Illusion, N.Y.C., 1977-78, Neill Gallery, N.Y.C., 1978-79, Atelier Royce, N.Y.C., 1980-81; one-woman shows: N.Y.C., 1975, U. Pa. Gallery, 1982; group shows include: Nat. Acad. Galleries, N.Y., 1977, Heckscher Mus., Huntington, N.Y., 1978, 80, Long Beach Mus., 1981; lectr. Found. for Community Artists, community schs. Mem. Found. for Community Artists, Artists Equity Assn. N.Y.; assoc. mem. Audubon Artists, Women in the Arts, Nat. Soc. Painters in Casein and Acrylic. Home: 243 E 78th St New York NY 10021

TERPENING, VIRGINIA ANN, artist; b. Lewistown, Mo., July 17, 1917; d. Floyd Raymond and Bertha Edda (Rodifer) Shoup; studied with William Woods, Fulton, Mo., 1936-37; student Washington U. Sch. Fine Arts, St. Louis, 1937-40; m. Charles W. Terpening, July 5, 1951; 1 dau. by previous marriage, V'Ann Baltzelle Dlatrick. Exhibited in one-man shows at Culver-Stockton Coll., Canton, Mo., 1956, Creative Gallery, N.Y.C., 1968, The Breakers, Palm Beach, Fla., 1976; others; exhibited in group shows, including Mo. Annual, City Art Mus., St. Louis, 1956, 65, Madison Gallery, N.Y.C., 1960; Ligoa Duncan Gallery, N.Y.C., 1964, 78, Two Flags Festival of Art, Douglas, Ariz., 1975, 78-79, Internat. Art Exhibit, El Centro, Calif., 1977, 78; lectr. on art; jurist for selection of art for exhibits Labelle (Mo.) Centennial, 1972; chmn. Centennial Art Show, Lewiston, 1971, Bicentennial, 1976; dir. exhibit high sch. students for N.E. Mo. State U., 1974; supt. ann. art show Lewis County (Mo.) Fair; executed Mississippi RiverBoat, oil painting presented to Pres. Carter by Lewis County Dem. Com., Canton, 1979. Mem. Lewistown Bicentennial Hist. Soc. Recipient certificate of merit Latham Found., 1960-63, Mo. Women's Festival Art, 1974, Bertrand Russell Peace Found., 1973; gold medallion award Two Flags Festival Art, 1975; Safeco purchase award El Centro (Calif.) Internat. Art exhibit, 1977; 1st pl. award LaJunta (Colo.) Fine Arts League, 1981; diploma Universita Delle Arti, Parma, Italy, 1981; Purchase award Two Flags Art Festival, 1981; award Assn. Conservation and Mo. Dept. Conservation Art Exhbt., 1982. Mem. Artist Equity Assn., Inc., Internat. Soc. Artists, Internat. Platform Assn., Animal Protection Inst. Mem. Disciples of Christ Ch. Address: Lewistown MO 63452

TERRELL, ETHEL, state legislator; b. Uniontown, Ala., Feb. 28, 1926; d. Julius and Alberta (Wave) Miller; ed. Art Center Music Sch., 1944, Wayne State U., 1964, Bapt. Tng. Union, 1978; widow. Mgr. Sec. of State's Office, Highland Park, Mich., 1962-77; mem. Mich. Ho. of Reps., 1979—. Trustee, deaconess Springhill Missionary Baptist Ch.; dir., founder Terrell's Day Care Nursery Sch.; founder, mem. Highland Park Ciucus Club; mem. pub. relations dept. Nat. Bapt. Conv.; pres., mem. Highland Park City Council, 1968-78. Recipient Humanitarian Service award Gospel Music Workshop Am., 1977, Outstanding Br. Mgr. Service award Mich. Sec. of State, 1977, Outstanding Achievement award in religion, civic and cultural affairs Hartford Bapt. Ch., 1977, Proclamation award Ethel Terrell Day, 1978, Disting. Service award Wings of Truth Gospel Ch., 1978. Mem. Nat. League Cities, Nat. Council Negro Women (life), NAACP. Baptist. Home: 12209 Woodward Ave Highland Park MI 48203 Office: Michigan House of Representatives State Capitol Bldg Lansing MI 48909 *

TERRELL, JEWEL ALTAMAI, educator; b. Nashville, Oct. 25, 1925; d. Ambrose and Evelyn Rosalie (Rucker) Caliver; B.S. in Home Econs., Howard U., 1947, M.S. in Child Devel., 1970; postgrad. in child devel. Merrill-Palmer Inst., 1947-48; m. Richard Austin Terrell, Jr., June 26, 1948; children—Linda Eileen, Richard Austin III, Tracy Ann. Instr. home econs. dept. Nursery Sch., Howard U., Washington, 1949-58, lectr., head tchr., 1958-73, coordinator Nursery Sch., Sch. Human Ecology, 1973-78, instr., head tchr. Nursery Sch., Sch. Human Ecology, 1978—; cons. D.C. Head Start Program, 1969. Supr., Neighborhood Youth Corps Personnel, 1966-71. Recipient cert. of appreciation D.C. Dept. Human Resources Social Services Adminstrn., 1971. Mem. Am. Home Econs. Assn., Nat. Assn. for Edn. Young Children, Assn. for Childhood Edn. Internat., NEA, D.C. Home Econs. Assn., Washington Assn. for Edn. Young Children, Omicron Nu. Co-author pamphlets. Home: 1210 Lamont St NW Washington DC 20010 Office: 2400 6th St NW Washington DC 20059

TERRIS, LILLIAN DICK, psychologist; b. Bloomfield, N.J., May 5, 1914; d. Alexander Blaikie and Herminia (Doscher) Dick; B.A., Barnard Coll., 1935; Ph.D., Columbia U., 1941; m. Louis Long, Apr. 22, 1935 (dec. Sept. 11, 1968), 1 son—Alexander Blaikie Long; m. 2d. Milton Terris, Feb. 6, 1971. Instr. psychology Sarah Lawrence Coll., Bronxville, N.Y., 1937-40; jr. personnel tech. SSA, Washington, 1941; sr. personnel clk. OWI, N.Y.C., 1941-43; dir. profl. examination service Am. Public Health Assn., N.Y.C., 1943-70, pres., 1970-79, pres. emeritus, 1979—; asso. editor Jour. Public Health Policy, 1979—. Recipient Nat. Environ. Health Assn. award, 1976; Cert. of Service award Am. Bd. Preventive Medicine, 1979. diplomate Am. Bd. Examiners in Profl. Psychology. Fellow Am. Psychol. Assn.; mem. Am. Public Health Assn., N.Y. State Psychol. Assn., Am. Coll. Hosp. Adminstrs. (hon. fellow), Phi Beta Kappa, Sigma Xi. Contbr. articles in field to profl. jours. Home: 23 Pheasant Way South Burlington VT 05401 Office: 475 Riverside Dr New York City 10027

TERRIS, SUSAN, physician; b. Morristown, N.J., Sept. 5, 1944; d. Albert and Virginia T.; B.A. in History, U.Chgo., 1967, Ph.D. in Biochemistry, 1975, M.D., 1976. Resident in internal medicine Barnes Hosp., Washington U., St. Louis, 1976-78; fellow in endocrinology U. Chgo., 1978-80, fellow in cardiology, 1980-82, research fellow in cardiology, 1982—. Recipient USPHS award, 1980-81, 82; Juvenile Diabetes Assn. fellow, 1979-80; diplomate Am. Bd. Internal Medicine. Mem. Chgo. Heart Assn., ACP, N.Y. Acad. Scis., Assn. Women in Sci., Am. Med. Women's Assn., Am. Coll. Cardiology (asso.). Research, publs. on metabolism of insulin by whole liver and hepatocytes, on mechanism of modulation of sensitivity to insulin in liver. Office: U Chgo Dept Medicine-Cardiology 950 E 59th St Chicago IL 60637

TERRY, INCI INCIKAYA, psychologist; b. Istanbul, Turkey, Nov. 18, 1932; came to U.S., 1956; d. Sevket and Mucella Incikaya; B.A., Am. Coll. for Girls, Instanbul, 1951; lic. U. Istanbul, 1956; M.A., State U. Iowa, 1958; Ph.D., U. Okla., 1967; m. Richard Allan Terry, June 3, 1959; 1 son, Deniz Terry. Clin. psychologist Lyon (Calif.) Mental Hygiene Clinic, 1959-63; dir. S.W. Center Gerontol. Studies, U. Okla., 1967-69; vis. asst. prof. Hacettepe U., Ankara, Turkey, 1969-70; clin. psychologist Tulsa Comprehensive Health Center, 1970-73; instr. psychology SUNY, Oswego, 1974-75; dir. Orleans County Mental Health Center, N.Y., 1976-78; pvt. practice clin. psychology, Rochester, 1976-78; psychologist Rochester Psychiat. Center, 1978; instr. psychology So. Conn. State Coll., 1979—; clin. dir. Greenshire Sch. Mentally Retarded and Autistic Children. Mem. Am. Psychol. Assn., Gerontol. Soc. Home: 159 Tom Swamp Rd Hamden CT 06518

TERRY, MARY ELLEN, personnel exec.; b. Mpls., Nov. 23, 1951; d. David Edmond and Gail Margaret (Walbom) Terry; B.A., Coll. of St. Catherine, 1973. Personnel dir. Marsh & McLennan, Mpls., 1977—, now asst. v.p.; personnel adminstr. Travelers Express Co., Inc., Mpls., 1973-77; workshop facilitator. Active, United Way of Mpls., 1980—. Accredited personnel mgr. Personnel Accreditation Inst., 1980. Mem. Am. Mgmt. Assn., Am. Soc. Personnel Adminstrn., Internat. Assn. Personnel Women (pres. 1981-82), Twin Cities Personnel Assn. (chmn. 1981-83, v.p. adminstrn. 1983), Speakers Bur. Roman Catholic. Club: Blaisdell Women's. Home: 4443 Cedar Ave S Minneapolis MN 55407 Office: 1500 Northstar Center Minneapolis MN 55402

TERRY, MARY SUE, Va. Democratic state legislator; b. Martinsville, Va., Sept. 28, 1947; B.A., Westhampton Coll., U. Richmond; M.S., J.D., U. Va. Admitted to Va. bar; practice law, Stuart, Va.; chmn. bd. First Nat. Bank of Stuart; mem. Va. Ho. of Reps., 1978—. Mem., West Piedmont Planning Dist. Crime Commn., 1974-77; mem. pres.'s bd. advs. Ferrum Coll.; mem. West Piedmont Health Planning Council, 1975-77; bd. dirs. Patrick Henry Mental Health Center, 1975-77, Va. YMCA. Recipient Disting. Alumna award Westhampton Coll., 1979; Service to Youth award Va. YMCA, 1981. Mem. Patrick County-Stuart C. of C., Am. Bar Assn., Va. Trial Lawyers Assn., Omicron Delta Kappa. Office: Va Ho Dels State Capitol Richmond VA 23219

TERRY, SANDRA DOLORES, health care exec.; b. Bronx, N.Y., Mar. 16, 1942; d. Samuel G. and Annie M. (Edmond) Gay; B.A., Bklyn. Coll., 1963, M.A., 1966; cert. advanced grad. study N.Y. U., 1966; m. Douglas Terry, Aug. 27, 1966; children—Kimberly, Keeva, Kazandra. Adminstrv. asst. to prin. Intermediate Sch. Dist. 55, Bklyn., 1970-74; exec. dir. Brown U./Fox Point Day Care Center, Providence, 1975-76; personnel dir. Opportunities Industrialization Center R.I., Providence, 1976-81; personnel mgr. R.I. Group Health Assn., Providence, 1981—; vice chmn. community relations com. Southeastern New Eng. Long Term Care Gerontology Center, 1981—; cons. in field. Co-chmn. gen. community gifts div. John Hope Settlement House, 1981. Fellow Internat. Understanding Through Edn., New Delhi, 1965; Group Health Assn. Am. fellow, 1982. Mem. Am. Soc. Personnel Adminstrs., Greater Providence C. of C., Alpha Kappa Alpha. Baptist. Editor R.I. Black Heritage Quar., 1980-81. Home: 141 Dexterdale Rd Providence RI 02906 Office: 530 N Main St Providence RI 02904

TERRY-MOTON, SARA, social worker; b. Ala., Dec. 25; d. Jay Cee and Betty Elizabeth Terry; B.S., Tuskegee Inst., 1960; M.S.W., U. Mich., 1970; m. John A. Moton, June 20, 1965. Tchr. elem. schs., Sarasota, Fla., 1960-66, Saginaw, Mich., 1966-68; sch. social worker, Saginaw, 1968-77; coordinator continuation sch. Saginaw City Sch. System, 1977—. Bd. dirs. Saginaw Symphony, YWCA, Mich. Assn. Sch. Aged Parents. Mem. Nat. Assn. Social Work, AAUW, Mich. Assn. Sch. Social Workers, NEA, Mich. Edn. Assn., Saginaw Edn. Assn., Nat. Orgn. Adolescent Pregnancy and Parenting. Democrat. Mem. A.M.E. Ch. Office: 550 Millard St Saginaw MI 48607

TESA, TANYA K(OVACH), law firm exec.; b. N.Y.C., June 24, 1947; d. Stephen P. and Tessie R. Kovach; A.A.S., N.Y.C. Community Coll., 1967; B.A., Bernard M. Baruch Coll., 1974; postgrad. CUNY, 1976-79. Owner, operator Tanya K. Tesa doing bus. as Mint Condition, Inc., antiques, N.Y.C., 1969-72; disbursing agt. U.S. Bankruptcy Ct., So. Dist. N.Y., 1976—; exec. asst. to sr. mng. partner firm Burns Summit Rovins & Feldesman, N.Y.C., 1972—, spl. projects mgr., 1980—: exec. asst. to nat. chmn. Union Coll. 64th and 65th Ann. Funds, 1976-77; exec. asst. to chmn. Union Coll. Terr. Council, Schenectady, 1977-78; exec. asst. to chmn. Cornell U. Law Sch. Met. Campaign for Funds, 1979—; exec. asst. to chmn. Defenders of Freedom, Freedoms Found., Valley Forge, Pa., 1979—; exec. asst. to nat. asso. and fundraiser Boys Clubs Am., 1980—; exec. asst. to mem. bd. dirs. and fundraiser I Love A Clean New York, Inc., N.Y.C., 1981—; exec. asst. to chmn. bd. trustees Union Coll. Schenectady, 1982—. Mem. exec. bd., sec. Ocean Bay Park Assn., Inc., Fire Island, N.Y., 1980—; mem. exec. bd. Fire Island Assn., Inc., 1981—. Club: Murray Hill Com., Inc. Home: 20 Park Ave New York NY 10016 also Ocean Bay Park Fire Island NY 11770 Office: 445 Park Ave New York NY 10022

TESMER, LOUISE M., lawyer, state legislator; b. Milw., Dec. 25, 1942; d. Edward W. and Genevieve (Mitdbow) T.; B.A., U. Wis., 1964, J.D., 1967. Admitted to Wis. bar, 1967; mcpl. justice St. Francis (Wis.), 1966-67; asst. dist. atty., Milw., 1967-72; individual practice law, Milw., 1972—; mem. Wis. Assembly, 1972—. Mem. Wis. Bar Assn., Nat. Order Women Legislators, Mcpl. Justice Assn. (hon.), Kappa Beta Pi. Democrat. Lutheran. Office: 606 W Wisconsin Ave Milwaukee WI 53203

TESMER, NANCY ANN STUTLER, librarian; b. Akron, Ohio, Aug. 25, 1934; d. Ernest Lynn and Sophrona Rebecca (Pepper) Stutler; student U. Akron, 1952-54; B.A., Kent State U., 1956; m. Clifford Frank Haines, Aug. 20, 1960 (div.); m. 2d, John A. Tesmer, Sept. 10, 1980. Jr. asst. librarian E. Br. Library, Akron, 1956-59; hosp. librarian VA Hosp., Northampton, Mass., 1959-61; med. librarian VA Hosp., Brecksville, Ohio, 1961-65, chief librarian, 1965-73; asso. chief librarian Cleve. VA Hosp., 1973-75, chief librarian, 1975—. Mem. Med. Library Assn., N.E. Ohio Med. Library Assn., Zeta Tau Alpha. Home: 6558 Brecksville Rd Independence OH 44131 Office: 10701 East Blvd Cleveland OH 44106

TESON, JEAN M., savs. and loan exec.; b. Erie, Pa., July 29, 1924; d. William John and Rachel (Murray) T.; student Ohio State U., 1951-52; B.B.A., U. Miami, 1957; grad. diploma Inst. Fin. Edn., Chgo., 1969, 74, diploma of distinction, 1977. Secretarial positions Reed, Lear & Co., Meadville, Pa., 1941-42, U.S. Army Engrs., Meadville, 1942-44, U.S. Army Ordnance, Meadville, 1946, State Farm Ins., Meadville, 1946-47, Ry. Express Agy., Ft. Lauderdale, Fla., 1947, M. Jack Kaiser & W.V. Doran, real estate, Ft. Lauderdale, 1947-48, First Fed. Savs. & Loan Assn., Ft. Lauderdale, 1948-51, Ohio State U., Columbus, 1951-52, Tubing Appliance, Los Angeles, 1952, Marquesee Assos., Ft. Lauderdale, 1953; with Atlantic Fed. Savs. & Loan Assn., Ft. Lauderdale, 1953—, v.p., sec., asst. treas., 1974—. Served with USN, 1944-46. Mem. Profl. Secs. Internat. (cert. profl. sec., past dir. Ft. Lauderdale, named Exec. of Yr., Ft. Lauderdale 1976), Fla. Soc. Cert. Profl. Secs., Am. Bus. Women's Assn., Inst. Fin. Edn., Nat. Forum Exec. Women, Am. Legion, VFW Aux., Ft. Lauderdale C. of C. Democrat. Roman Catholic. Office: Atlantic Fed Savs & Loan Assn 1750 E Sunrise Blvd Fort Lauderdale FL 33304

TESSITORE, (ALESSI) KATHRYN, home economist; b. Trinidad, Colo., Feb. 2, 1953; d. Joseph John and Velma Elizabeth (Morlan) Alessi; A.A.S., Trinidad State Jr. Coll., 1973; B.S., Colo. State U., 1975; m. Nick Tessitore, Jr., Aug. 6, 1977; 1 son, Nicholas III. Home economist Chaffee County, Salida, Colo., 1975-76; extension agt. Colo. State U. and Chaffee County Coop. Extension Service, Salida, 1976-80; home econs. tchr. Kesner Jr. High Sch., Salida, 1980-82. Pres., Salida Community Choir; ch. and civic soloist; 4-H teen leader; council adviser Women's Aglow, Heart of the Rockies Right to Life Com. Mem. Am. Home Econs. Assn., Colo. Home Econs. Assn., Nat. Assn. Ext. 4-H and Youth Agts., Colo. Assn. Extension 4-H and Youth Agts., Colo. Assn. Extension Home Economists, Nat. Assn. Extension Home Economists, NEA, Colo. Edn. Assn., Salida Edn. Assn. Club: Salida Christian Women's (pres.). Home: 130 Eaton Salida CO 81201 Office: Kesner Jr High Sch 9th and C Sts Salida CO 81201

TESTA, ELAINE SILVA, educator, civic worker; b. Watsonville, Calif., Oct. 21, 1942; d. Julius Raymond and Mary Dolores (Fuller) Silva; B.A. in Edn. and Psychology (Rotary scholar), San Jose State U., 1965; m. John Vincent Testa, Feb. 6, 1965; children—Laura Marie, Linda Antoinette, John Peter. Elem. tchr. Gilroy (Calif.) Sch. Dist., 1966-68. Chair environ. exec. com. South Lake Tahoe, Calif., 1972-73; mem. state and local environ. coms. AAUW, 1970-80; mem. Lake Tahoe Unified Sch. Dist. Bd. Edn., 1979—; realtor/asso.; vol. tchr. local schs. Recipient Bank of Am. award, 1960, cert. parent adv. com. Lake Tahoe Community Coll., 1972; hon. lt. col. U.S. Army Pershing Rifles, 1964. Mem. AAUW, Calif. Sch. Bds. Assn., South Lake Tahoe Bd. Realtors. Republican. Roman Catholic. Author: Our Environment—No Deposit, No Return, 1973; author environ. and recycling lessons, environ. radio spot announcements. Home: PO Box 13274 South Lake Tahoe CA 95702

TESTA, MARY ANN, former social service agy. exec.; b. Flemington, N.J., Sept. 24, 1955; d. Albert and Christina (D'Ambramo) T.; B.S., Pa. State U., 1977. Dir., Assn. Retarded Citizens, Lycoming County, Pa., 1978-79; dir. Developmental Disabilities Community Living Arrangement, Williamsport, Pa., 1979-81. Recipient Chmn. award Job Fair, 1978, 79. Mem. Nat. Assn. Female Execs., Nat. Assn. Retarded Citizens Advocate Orgn., Gov's. Com. for Employment of Handicapped, Lycoming-Clinton Interagy. Council. Author: The Advocates Training Handbook, 1979. Home: RD 4 Box 41A Jersey Shore PA 17740

TESTERMAN, DANITA GAY, accountant; b. Altus, Okla., June 30, 1954; d. Kenneth Clyde and Sally Laverne (Burge) Hickerson; B.S., Okla. State U., 1975; m. Robert DuWayne Testerman, Aug. 16, 1974. Sr. acct., analyst Sohio Petroleum Corp., Oklahoma City, 1975-78; mgr. fin. reporting and revenue, acctg. NFC Petroleum Corp., Oklahoma City, 1978-79; staff acctg. supr. Tex. Internat. Petroleum Corp., Oklahoma City, 1979—. C.P.A., Okla. Mem. Am. Inst. C.P.A.s, Okla. Soc. C.P.A.s, Petroleum Accts.' Soc. Okla., Am. Soc. Women C.P.A.s. Republican. Baptist. Home: 12017 N Morgan Rd Yukon OK 73099 Office: 3535 NW 58th St Oklahoma City OK 73112

TETRICK, ANNE PAULA, social worker, adminstr.; b. Lawrence, Mass., Jan. 22, 1918; d. Paul Basil and Katherine Paula (Kaplon) Tutko; B.S.W., Simmons Coll., 1939; M.S.W., 1940; m. William Mavern Tetrick, June 9, 1940; children—Deanne E., William Mavern, Nathaniel J., Margaret F., Paul A. In-patient social worker Newton-Wellesley Hosp., Newton, Mass., 1940-42; research social worker dept. community psychiatry Harvard Med. Sch., Boston, 1973; supr. social work Mass. Rehab. Hosp., Boston, 1973-76; dir. human services New Eng. Area Comprehensive Hemophilia Center and hematology clinics Meml. Hosp., Worcester, Mass., 1977—; social work cons. comprehensive hemophilia clinics in New Eng. states, 1977—, nursing com. and mental health com. Nat. Hemophilia Found., 1979—. Lic. ind. practitioner clin. social work. Mem. New Eng. Regional Genetics Group, World Hemophilia Fedn., Nat. Assn. Social Workers, Acad. Cert. Social Workers, Am. Hosp. Assn., Am. Soc. Hosp. Social Work Dirs., Simmons Coll. Alumni Assn. (Harriet Bartlett award 1978). Republican. Episcopalian. Club: Algonquin (Boston). Home: 255 Ridgeway Rd Weston MA 02193 Office: 119 Belmont St Worcester MA 01605

TEUFEL, PATRICIA ANN, actuary; b. Greenwich, Conn., Sept. 30, 1950; d. Robert Joseph and Virginia Adelaide (Hill) T.; B.A. in Math., Trinity Coll., Washington, 1972. With Aetna Ins. Co., Hartford, Conn., 1972—, sr. actuarial asst., 1978-79, asst. actuary, 1979-81, asso. actuary, 1981—. Fellow Casualty Actuarial Soc.; mem. Am. Acad. Actuaries, Casualty Actuaries New Eng., Phi Beta Kappa. Office: 55 Elm St Hartford CT 06115

TEUTSCH, DELORES ELLEN, state legislator; b. Seattle, Sept. 9, 1935; d. Harold Raymond and Laura (Richards) Stone; student U. Wash., 1953-54; m. John Milton Teutsch, Jr., 1954; children—Terri Ellen Teutsch Kalan, John Milton, Jill Margaret. Pres., King County East Conv. and Visitors Bd.; mem. bd. trustees Community Coll. Dist. 8, 1974-78, chairperson, 1976-78; mem. Wash. Ho. Reps., 1978-82, chmn. higher edn. com., 1980-82. Pres., Citizens Adv. Council, 1971-73; chmn. Northshore Community Plan Com., 1976-78; founding pres. Kathryn Glenn Kerry Orthopedic Hosp. Guild. Mem. Wash. State Assn. Community Coll. Trustees (pres. 1977-78), Wash. Council Internat. Trade, Mcpl. League, Wash. Trade Employment Council. Clubs: Wash. Athletic (sec.-treas. Women's adv. bd. 1969-71), Bus. and Profl. Women's. Office: Wash State Ho Reps State Capitol Olympia WA 98504

TEVELOW, ROSEMARIE, bank exec.; b. N.Y.C., Oct. 7, 1936; d. Jacob and Sonia F. Pinsker; B.B.A. magna cum laude, City U. N.Y., 1957, M.B.A., 1965; m. Oscar Tevelow, Dec. 24, 1958; children—Bradley Joseph, Sonia Alexandra. Acct., Alexander Grant & Co., N.Y.C., 1957-61; securities analyst Loeb Rhoades & Co., 1961-71; advisor to acctg. prins. bd. mem. First Manhattan Co., 1971-72; with Bankers Trust Co., 1972—, v.p., 1977—. C.P.A., N.Y. Mem. Am. Inst. C.P.A.s, N.Y. Soc. C.P.A.s, N.Y. Soc. Security Analysts, Fin. Analysts Fedn., Fin. Women's Assn. Office: Bankers Trust Co 280 Park Ave New York NY 10015

TEWKESBURY, JOAN F., screenwriter, dir.; b. Redlands, Calif., Apr. 8, 1936; d. Walter S. and Frances M. (Stevenson) T.; student Am. Sch. Dance, 1947-54, Mt. San Antonio Jr. Coll., 1956-58, (univ. drama scholar) U. So. Calif., 1958-60; m. Robert F. Maguire III, Nov. 30, 1960 (div.); children—Robin Tewkesbury Maguire, Peter Harlan Maguire. Dancer film Unfinished Dance, 1946; dancer, flying understudy play Peter Pan, 1954-55; choreographer, mem. dance and drama faculty U. So. Calif., 1967-69, Immaculate Heart Coll., 1960-63, Am. Sch. Dance, Los Angeles, 1960-68; choreographer, dir., actress U. So. Calif. Repertory Co., 1966-69, London and Edinburgh Festival, 1966-68; script girl film McCabe & Mrs. Miller, 1970; writer screen plays: Thieves Like Us, 1973, Nashville (Los Angeles Critics Best Screenplay 1975), 1974; playwright, dir. Off-Broadway play Cowboy Jack Street, 1977; dir. film Old Boyfriends, 1978; writer, dir. film 10th Month, 1978, Acorn People, 1980; dir. documentary film The Hampstead Center, 1976. Named Outstanding Jr. Coll. Alumnus, Mt. San Antonio Jr. Coll., 1979. Mem. Writers Guild Am., Dirs. Guild Am., ACLU, Nat. Abortion Rights Action League. Author: (book) Nashville, 1976. Home: Santa Monica CA Office: care J Berg 8899 Beverly Blvd Los Angeles CA 90048 *

TEWKSBURY, CAROL ANN, private detective; b. Mexico City, Dec. 13, 1947 (parents U.S. citizens); d. Everett Sawyer and Ruth Kile (Boston) T.; A.B., Duke U., 1968. Copywriter, John Knox Press, Richmond, Va., 1968-69; promotion mgr. Fortress Press, Phila., 1969-72; adminstr. Imaginal Systematics, Inc., Ann Arbor, Mich., 1972-74; freelance journalist, Calif. and Ind., 1974-76; asst. mgr. data research and counter intelligence Wittlinger Agy., Indpls., 1976-79, partner, mgr., 1979—. Recipient award excellence Phila. Club Advt. Women. Mem. Am. Soc. Profl. Investigators, Phi Beta Kappa. Address: 8734 Log Run Dr Indianapolis IN 46234

THALACKER, BARBARA ELIESE, assn. exec.; b. Wisconsin Rapids, Wis., Jan. 16, 1946; d. Harold William and Dorothy Elizabeth (Rickman) Thalacker; B.S., Valparaiso U., 1968; M.S., Ariz. State U., 1970; Ed.D., No. Ariz. U., Tempe, 1979. Tchr. Phoenix Union High Sch., 1968-69; research asst. Ariz. State U., 1969-70; tchr., coach phys. edn. liaison Scottsdale (Ariz.) Public Schs., 1970-78; curriculum specialist Midwest Race and Sex Desegregation Assistance Center, Kans. State Univ., Manhattan, 1978-79; program coordinator, program evaluator Sex Desegregation Assistance Center Project Equity Calif. State U., Fullerton, 1978-82; exec. dir. Sacramento YWCA, 1982—; cons. state depts.Calif., Ariz., Iowa, Maine, Nev., Nebr., also sch. dists. various states, 1970—. Named Outstanding Young Educator, Jr. C. of C., 1976. Mem. Assn. Calif. Sch. Adminstrs., Am. Ednl. Research Assn., NOW, Assn. Supervision and Curriculum Devel., Am. Alliance Health Phys. Edn. Recreation and Dance, Nat. Women's Polit. Caucus, Nat. Coalition for Sex Equity in Edn. Lutheran. Home: 609 40th St Sacramento CA 95819 Office: Sacramento YWCA 1122 17th St Sacramento CA 95814

THARP, NORMA LEE, advt. and public relations cons.; b. Hammond, Ind., Feb. 7, 1952; d. James Francis and Livia Lorraine (Giannini) T.; B.A. in Communication, Purdue U., 1973; m. Robert K. Avery, July 25, 1981. Producer, announcer Sta. WBAA, Nat. Public Radio, West Lafayette, Ind., 1974-75; promotion dir. Sta. WNMU-TV, PBS, Marquette, Mich., 1976-78; advt. mgr. Sta. KUED-TV, PBS, Salt Lake City, 1978-80; account exec. Gardiner Advt., Salt Lake City, 1980-81; public relations dir. Utah distbrs. Adolph Coors Co., Salt Lake City, 1981—; advt. and public relations cons., 1982—. Mem. Women in Communications (pres. Utah chpt. 1981-82), Public Relations Soc. Am.

THARP, TWYLA, dancer, choreographer; b. Portland, Ind., July 1, 1941; student Pomona Coll., Am. Ballet Theatre Sch.; grad. Barnard Coll.; D. Performing Arts (hon.), Calif. Inst. Arts, 1978; hon. degrees Brown U., 1981, Bard Coll., 1981; student Richard Thomas, Merce Cunningham, Igor Schwezoff, Louis Mattox, Paul Taylor, Margaret Craske, Erick Hawkins; m. Robert Huot (div.); 1 son, Jesse. With Paul Taylor Dance Co., 1963-65; freelance choreographer with own modern dance troupe and various other cos. including Joffrey Ballet and Am. Ballet Theatre, 1965—; teaching residencies various colls. and univs. including U. Mass., Oberlin Coll., Walker Art Center, Boston U.; major works choreographed: Tank Dive, 1965; Re-Moves, 1966; Forevermore, 1967; Generation, 1968; Medley, 1969; Fugue, 1970; Eight Jelly Rolls, 1971; The Raggedy Dances, 1972; As Time Goes By, 1974; Sue's Leg, 1975; Push Comes to Shove, 1976; Once More Frank, 1976; Mud, 1977; Baker's Dozen, 1979; When We Were Very Young, 1980; film Hair, 1979; videotape Making Television Dance, 1977, CBS Cable Confessions of a Corner Maker, 1980. Recipient Creative Arts award Brandeis U., 1972; Dance Mag. Annual award, 1981. Office: care Twyla Tharp Dance Found 38 Walker St New York NY 10013

THATCHER, AILEEN ANNE, psychologist; b. Chgo., Oct. 19, 1943; d. Andrew J. and Cecilia Anne (Rooney) Petergal; B.A. (Ill. State scholar), U. Ill., 1969; M.A. with honors in Psychology, Roosevelt U., 1973; Ph.D. in Psychology, Mich. State U., 1976; postgrad. Isaac Ray Ctr., Rush-Presbyn.-St. Luke's Hosp.; m. Roy C. Thatcher, Aug. 10, 1968; 1 dau., Victoria Anne. Grad. teaching asst. Mich. State U., East Lansing, 1973-76; trainee VA Hosp., North Chicago, Ill., 1976-77; pvt. practice clin. psychology, Chgo., 1978—; instr. stats., tests and measurements Roosevelt U., Chgo., summers 1974-75, instr., fall 1975; instr. St. Xavier Coll., Chgo., 1978-79; chmn. child care Beverly Family Center, 1977-78; chmn. human rights com., cons. McKinley Aztlan Community Industries, 1979-80; bd. dirs. Learning Disabilities Center, St. Xavier Coll.; mem. Nat. Register Health Service Providers; cons. Rimland Sch. for Autistic Children, 1980-82, Golfview Devel. Center, 1980—. Registered psychologist, Ill. Mem. Am. Psychol. Assn., Midwestern Psychol. Assn., Ill. Psychol. Assn. (membership chmn.), Chgo. Psychol. Assn. (sec., membership chmn.). Home and office: 9440 S Leavitt St Chicago IL 60620

THATCHER, MARY JO, producer; b. Des Moines, Dec. 24, 1951; d. Ben and Barbara Jean (Ward) Thatcher; student Citrus Coll., 1970-72. Actress, various parts, incl. part in Helter Skelter, 1975; with Denny Harris Inc. of Calif., Los Angeles, 1977—, exec. producer, 1979—. Mem. Screen Actors Guild, Am. Film Inst., Nat. Notary Assn., Women in Film, NOW. Office: 12166 Olympic Blvd Los Angeles CA 90064

THAXTON, ELIZABETH DYER, social worker; b. Roanoke, Va., Feb. 10, 1932; d. David Allison and Ruth Elizabeth (Laughon) Dyer; A.B., Randolph-Macon Woman's Coll., 1953; M.S.W., U. N.C., Chapel Hill, 1973; children—Cynthia Thaxton Norris, David Robert, Mary Elizabeth. Clin. social worker, mental health team of adult div. Durham County (N.C.) Dept. Social Services, 1973-77; dir. dept. social work Pulaski (Va.) Community Hosp., 1977-80; dir. dept. social work Deaconess Hosp., Cleve., 1980—; pvt. practice clin. social work, 1979—; mem. adj. faculty Radford U.; examiner for licensure Va. Bd. Social Workers. Lic. clin. social worker, Va. Mem. Nat. Assn. Social Workers, Soc. Hosp. Social Work Dirs., Acad. Cert. Social Workers, Phi Mu. Home: 15103 Lake Ave Lakewood OH 44107 Office: Deaconess Hosp 4229 Pearl Rd Cleveland OH 44109

THAYER, EDNA ISABELLE, nurse; b. Manchester, N.H., July 25, 1923; d. Charles Everett and Maude Isabelle (Messenger) Trask; R.N., Elliott Community Hosp., 1944; B.S.N., UCLA, 1953; m. Charles Albert Thayer, Feb. 18, 1946; 1 dau., Linda Louise. Supr., Meriden (Conn.) Hosp., 1950-53, Inst. Living, Hartford, Conn., 1954-59; vol. tchr. educationally handicapped Brockton Sch., West Los Angeles, 1972-78; dir. nurses Canoga Terr., Canoga Park, Calif., 1979-80; dir. nurses Corbin Convalescent Hosp., Reseda, Calif., 1981-82; dir. nurses Sun Air Convalescent Hosp., 1982—. Served with Nurse Corp, AUS, 1945-46. Recipient Golden Apple award Los Angeles Unified Sch. Dist., 1976. Mem. Am., Calif. nurses assns., Nat. League Nursing Edn., Calif. Congress Parents and Tchrs., Bus. and Profl. Womens Club, Am. Legion. Republican. Baptist. Club: Emblem. Home: 7819 Ponce Ave Canoga Park CA 91304 Office: 7120 Corbin Ave Reseda CA 91335

THEILING, JANE HODGES, state legislator; b. Morgantown, W.Va., Jan. 10, 1929; d. Charles Edward and Florence Kirtland (Conant) Hodges; B.A., W.Va. U., 1950; m. Louis Foster Theiling Jr., Aug. 6; children—Elizabeth Hayes, Karen Marie, Louis Foster, Jennifer Ann. With, Trans World Airlines, N.Y.C., 1950-54; partner Grosscup-Hodges Travel Bur., Charleston, W.Va., 1954-57; dir. Consumer Protection Dept., City of Charleston, 1973—; mem. W.Va. Ho. of Dels., 1980—. Mem. Nat. Assn. Consumer Agy. Adminstrs., Jr. League Charleston, Delta Gamma. Democrat. Presbyterian. Club: Altrusa. Office: PO Box 2749 Charleston WV 25330

THEIMER, RAMONA KAYE RAGSDALE, psychologist; b. Muskogee, Okla., Oct. 25, 1948; d. Ramon D. and Mary Lou (Steele) Ragsdale; B.S., Okla. U., 1970, M.S., 1972, Ph.D., 1974; m. Jack W. Theimer, Aug. 22, 1970; children—Hillary, Jeffrey. Research asso. Okla. U., Norman, 1973-74; counselor Indian pupil edn., Tulsa, 1975-76; psychologist, asst. prof. Tulsa U., 1976—; coordinator psychol. testing Mary K. Chapman Center, Tulsa, 1976-80; project dir. Bur. Edn. for Handicapped Presch. Demonstration Center, 1979-82, outreach dir., 1982—. Vice pres. bd. dirs. Mental Health Assn.; bd. dirs. Rainbow House Inc. Ednl. Psychology fellow, 1971-72; Sequoyah fellow, 1972-73; postdoctoral fellow U. Calif., Santa Barbara, 1982-83; lic. psychologist, Okla. Mem. Am. Psychol. Assn., Am. Ednl. Research Assn., AAUP, Kappa Kappa Gamma. Democrat. Lutheran. Home: 655 Parra Grande Santa Barbara CA 93108 Office: Dept Spl Edn U Calif Santa Barbara CA 93106

THEMAL, VERA ROSA, social work psychotherapist; b. Berlin, Germany, Dec. 9, 1928; immigrated to U.S. from Argentina, 1971, naturalized, 1975; d. Werner F. and Frieda E. (Levy) Holz; B.S.W., U. Buenos Aires, 1953; diploma in public health and social welfare (Swedish Govt. scholar), U. Gothemburgh (Sweden), 1960; M.S.W. (Fulbright, Ford Motor Co. and OAS scholar), U. Calif., Berkeley, 1964; m. Henry J. Themal, July 27, 1971. Caseworker, Bur. Tb, Montevideo, Uruguay, 1955-57, supr., 1957-66, also field instr., lectr. social work U. Montevideo, 1957-66; social work cons., adv. Sec. Health and Welfare, also mem. Comprehensive Health Planning Bd., Dept. Health and Welfare of Province of Buenos Aires, 1966-70; social worker, coordinator Tb and Chest Clinic, Met. Hosp., N.Y.C. Dept. Health, 1971; social worker City Hosp. Center of Elmhurst, N.Y.C., 1973-75; dir. social work Day Hosp., Burke Rehab. Center, White Plains, N.Y., 1975-79; pvt. practice counseling and psychotherapy (elderly, ill, disabled), dir. Themal Liaison Counseling, Hartsdale, N.Y., 1979—. Adv. bd. VISTA/RSVP, 1978—; mem. Mid-Westchester Mental Health Coordinating Council, also mem. network com. Coordinating Council Disabled in Westchester County, 1979—; founder, cons. Touch and Go, Westchester, 1977—; mem. adv. bd. various community services for the blind Eastchester Project, 1981—; mem. Central and No. Westchester geriatric coms., 1981—. Cert. social worker, N.Y.; cert. Acad. Cert. Social Workers. Mem. Nat. Assn. Social Workers Soc. Clin. Social Work, Workshop Inst. Living Learning. Democrat. Clubs: High Point Social, YWCA, Women's Am. ORT, B'nai B'rith. Author: Social Work Research, 1966. Home: 200A High Point Dr Suite 501 Hartsdale NY 10530

THEODORE, CRYSTAL, educator; b. Greenville, S.C., July 27, 1917; d. James Voutsas and Florence Gertrude (Bell) T.; A.B. magna cum laude, Winthrop Coll., 1938; M.A., Columbia U., 1942, Ed.D., 1953; postgrad. U. Ga., 1947. Instr. art Winthrop Coll., 1938-43; prof. art, head dept. Huntingdon (Ala.) Coll., 1946-52; prof. art, head dept. E. Tenn. State U., 1953-57; prof. art, head dept. Madison Coll., 1957-68; vis. prof. art World Campus Afloat, Chapman Coll., Calif., 1967; prof. art James Madison U., Harrisonburg, Va., 1968—. Bd. dirs. Rockingham Fine Arts Assn., 1980-82, Women's Coop. Council Harrisonburg and Rockingham County, 1976-79; cons. Valley Program for Aging Services, 1976. Served with USMC, 1944-46. Gen. Edn. Bd. of Rockefeller Found. fellow, 1952-53; award Carnegie Found. Advancement of Teaching, 1947, 48, 49, 50; Ednl. Found. Program grantee AAUW, 1981-82. Mem. AAUW (cultural interests rep., dir. 1980-82) Coll. Art Assn., Southeastern Coll. Art Conf., Mensa, Kappa Delta Pi,

Kappa Pi, Delta Kappa Gamma, Sigma Phi, Pi Lambda Theta. Democrat. Lutheran. Contbr. articles to profl. jours. Home: Route 5 Box 202 Harrisonburg VA 22801 Office: Dept Art James Madison U Harrisonburg VA 22807

THERIOT, JOYCE MAE DOUET, bank exec.; b. St. Martinville, La., Nov. 6, 1939; d. Arville and Theresa (Morvant) Douet; student U. So. La., Lafayette, 1982—; m. Nolan P. Theriot, Oct. 10, 1959; children—Nolan P., Lorne, Kevin, Neil, Jody. Bookkeeper, People's Nat. Bank, New Iberia, La., 1957-59; with St. Martin Bank & Trust Co., St. Martinville, La., 1959-60; cashier, v.p. Teche Bank & Trust Co., St. Martinville, 1969—. Home: 2043 Gerard St Saint Martinville LA 70582 Office: 606 S Main St PO Box 78 Saint Martinville LA 70582

THIBODEAU, DIANE VIRGAL, educator; b. Little Falls, Minn., Apr. 6, 1943; d. Wilbur Benjamin and Adeline Marguerite (Karpinski) Stroschein; B.S., Mankato U., 1965; m. James Thibodeau, July 16, 1966; children—Troy, Chad, Nicole. Elem. sch. tchr., Richfield, Minn., Robbinsdale, Minn., 1965-70, res. tchr., 1970-81; elementary tchr., Robbinsdale, 1982—; pres. Wayzata chpt. Gifted and Talented, 1981-82; chmn. chpt. maintenance and devel. Minn. Council Gifted and Talented, also dir., 1982—; chief negotiator Robbinsdale Res. Tchrs., 1978—; omnibus coordinator Wayzata Sch. System, 1981-82. Chmn. ways and means Mpls. Children's Hosp., 1979-80; founder Summer Pre-sch. Bible Sch., St. Joseph's Parish. Mem. NOW, AAUW, Women's Network All the Good Old Girls, Nat. Fedn. Tchrs., Minn. Fedn. Tchrs., Minn. Educators Gifted-Talented, Robbindale Fedn. Tchrs. Democrat. Roman Catholic. Home: 2504 Cherrywood Rd Minnetonka MN 55343 Office: 5657 Duluth St Golden Valley MN 55422

THIEDE, KATHRYN ANN WARE, coll. adminstr.; b. West Chester, Pa., June 6, 1949; d. Harris Oliver and Marion Antoinette (Dennert) Ware; B.S., Ashland Coll., 1971; M.Ed., Bowling Green State U., 1977; postgrad. U. Toledo, 1978—; m. Robert Harold Thiede, Jr., Aug. 4, 1973; 1 dau., Meredith Margaret. Tchr., Margaretta local schs., Castalia, Ohio, 1971-74, Sandusky (Ohio) City Schs., 1974-76; nutrition cons. Erie County (Ohio) Title I, 1975, Adrian (Mich.) Head Start, 1977-79; lectr. home econs. Adrian Coll., 1976—, asst. to v.p. for bus. affairs, 1976—; doctoral grad. asst. U. Toledo, 1981-82. Nat. Inst. Food Service Industry teaching grantee, 1978. Mem. Am. Home Econs. Assn., Mich. Home Econs. Assn., Toledo Home Econs. Assn., AAUP, Am. Vocat. Assn., Adrian Coll. Womens League, Ashland Coll. Alumni Assn., Delta Zeta, Kappa Omicron Phi. Republican. Roman Catholic. Home: 3811 Kimberley Oaks Lambertville MI 48144 Office: 113 North Hall Adrian Coll Adrian MI 49221

THIELEN, DELLA KRAUSE, corp. dir., civic worker; b. Lake Charles, La., July 11, 1930; d. Rudolph Edward and Della (Bel) Krause; B.A., Cornell U., 1951; children—Katherine Bel (Mrs. H.M. Julian), John Chadick. With land dept. Humble Oil & Refining Co., New Orleans, 1951-52; dir. Gulf Nat. Bank, 1975—; pres. Jr. League of Lake Charles, Inc., 1963-64; pres. Lake Charles Ballet Soc., 1969-71; chmn. Southwestern Regional Ballet Festival, 1972, co-chmn., 1980; pres. Womans Aux., La. Med. Soc., 1972-73, conv. co-chmn., 1974; corr. Alumni News, Cornell Assn. Class Officers, 1971-76; mem. Jr. League steering com. Lake Charles Bicentennial Commn., 1975-76; chmn. Symphony Antique Show, 1976; exec. dir. Calcasieu Arts Council; coordinator Olin Affiliate Artist program, 1977-78; chmn. trustee sect. La. Library Assn., 1979-80. Bd. dirs. Lake Charles Symphony, 1974-80, pres., 1977-79; trustee Calcasieu Parish Public Library System. Mem. Kappa Kappa Gamma. Episcopalian. Home: 320 Drew Park Dr Lake Charles LA 70601 Office: PO Box 1334 Lake Charles LA 70602

THIELMAN, DOROTHY LOUISE, coll. dean; b. Paris, Tex., Sept. 12, 1919; d. Albert Birtes and Olga (Rutherford) Webb; B.A., Tex. Women's U., 1949; M.A., George Peabody Coll., Nashville, 1947; m. Charles Eugene Thielman, June 1, 1947; 1 son, Albert Lee. Librarian, Paris Jr. Coll., 1941-69, dir. Learning Resources Center, 1969—, dean instructional support services, 1977—, also mem. adv. com. Center for Women; chmn. adv. com. A.M. and Welma Aikin, Jr. Regional Archives, also R.F. Voyer Mus. Mem. Am. Assn. Women in Community and Jr. Colls., Nat. Council Staff, Program and Organizational Devel., Tex. Jr. Coll. Tchrs. Assn., Tex. Assn. Jr. Coll. Instructional Adminstrs., Jr. Coll. Student Personnel Assn. Tex., Tex. Library Assn., Tex. Assn. Ednl. Tech., Lamar County C. of C. Presbyterian. Office: 2400 Clarksville St Paris TX 75460

THIEMAN, REGINA SUE, constrn. equipment co. exec.; b. Batesville, Ind., Apr. 3, 1945; d. Raymond F. and Irma M. (Greive) T.; student Valparaiso (Ind.) U., 1963-64, Ind. U., 1965-66. Asst. comptroller Kocolene Oil Corp., Seymour, Ind., 1964-70; corp. sec., dir. Swanston Equipment Co., Fargo, N.D., 1970-79; v.p. Prodn. Centre, Honolulu, 1979—; dir. Rental Investment, Inc., Traffic Marking & Striping Co.; co-owner Typesetting Unlimited, Inc. Mem. Cass County Safety Council, 1970-72, F-M Centennial Organizational Com., 1974. Mem. N.D. Fedn. Bus. and Profl. Womens Clubs (pres. 1977-78, nat. com. 1978-80), Nat. Assn. Accountants (v.p. Red River Valley chpt. 1977-79, dic Hawaii chpt. 1979—), Nat. Assn. Women in Constrn. (pres. F-M chpt. 1978), Nat. Assn. Credit Mgmt., Sales and Mktg. Execs. Honolulu, Downtown Bus. Council Honolulu. Lutheran. Home: Route 4 Box 319 Detroit Lakes MN 56501 Office: 1015 Bishop St Honolulu HI 96734

THIESSEN, JO CAULA, med. technologist; b. Covington, Ky., Jan. 19, 1931; d. Joe and Mildred (Payne) Gregg; B.S., Wheaton Coll., 1952; M.B.A., U. So. Calif., 1976; m. Jacob I. Thiessen, Apr. 23, 1954; children—Heather, Jacob. Med. technologist Los Angeles County/U. So. Calif. Med. Center, Los Angeles, 1953-58; supervising med. technologist Thatcher Labs., Pasadena, Calif., 1959-65; chief technologist Meth. Hosp. So. Calif., Arcadia, 1965-74; adminstrv. chief technologist, program dir. Sch. Med. Tech., Huntington Meml. Hosp., Pasadena, 1975—; seminar leader, counselor. Mem. Am. Mgmt. Assn., Am. Soc. Med. Tech., Huntington Meml. Fed. Credit Union (pres. 1978-80), U. So. Calif. M.B.A.'s, U. So. Calif. Alumni Assn., Beta Gamma Sigma. Presbyterian. Home: 444-109 W Huntington Dr Arcadia CA 91006 Office: 100 Congress St Pasadena CA 91105

THIRSK, JOAN EDGERTON, mail order co. exec.; b. Hollis, N.Y. Dec. 22, 1932; d. Benjamin Martin and Florence Alexandra (Bertrand) Edgerton; B.S. in Commerce and Econs., Mt. St. Mary Coll., Hooksett, N.H., 1955; m. David S. Thirsk, June 18, 1955; children—Susan, William, Amy. Founder, treas. China Chasers Inc., Dunwoody, Ga., 1972—; lectr. on use and selection of tableware Dekalb County Schs.; tchr. remedial reading Dunwoody Elem. Sch. Treas. Dunwoody Elem. Sch. PTA, 1976. Democrat. Roman Catholic. Club: Chestnut Ridge Garden (Dunwoody). Home: 4121 Chestnut Ridge Dr Dunwoody GA 30338 Office: PO Box 88214 Dunwoody GA 30338

THISIUS, JOAN LORETTA, elem. sch. prin.; b. Easton, Minn., Aug. 19, 1930; d. Lawrence William and Theresa Margurite (McGoff) Ascheman; B.S., San Francisco State U., 1966, M.S., 1973; m. Orville Lawrence Thisius, Aug. 29, 1950; children—Ann Louise, Timothy Neil, Rebecca Gail, Maxine Therese, Edward John, Jennifer Kay. Sch. sec., 1951-54; public sch. tchr., 1959-63, 66-69; resource tchr., 1969-74; prin. Hidden Valley Elem. Sch., Concord, Calif., 1974—, adminstr. Title IV project; condr. leadership seminars. Pres. ch. aux., 1955-56. Mem. Assn. Calif. Sch. Adminstrs., Elem. Sch. Prins. Assn., Calif. Assn. Gifted, Diablo Assn. Calif. Sch. Adminstrs., VFW Aux. (pres. 1953-55), Sea Scout Aux. (pres. 1968), Delta Kappa Gamma (past pres.). Republican. Roman Catholic. Club: Jr. Women's. Author articles in field, also poetry. Home: 23 Kirkwood Ct Concord CA 94521 Office: 1936 Carlotta Dr Concord CA 94520

THOLEN, SARAH MARIE, insulation mfg. co. exec.; b. Leadville, Colo., Oct. 3, 1950; d. Harold Joseph and Mary Bernadette (Fouhy) Tholen; B.S. in Bus. Adminstrn. (Boettcher Found. scholar), U. Denver, 1974. Northwestern regional dir. Center for Prospective Students, U. Denver, Portland, Oreg., 1974-75; asst. dir. admissions U. Denver, Denver, 1975-77; sales rep. associated and original equipment materials Manville Corp., Oakbrook, Ill., 1977—. Pres. Republican Assos. of Colo., 1977. Mem. Thermal Insulation Mfrs. Assn., Am. Soc. Gas Engrs., Nat. Women's Polit. Caucus, Nat. Assn. Female Execs., Mortar Bd., Sigma Iota Epsilon, Beta Gamma Sigma. Roman Catholic. Home: 17 W 704 Butterfield Rd Oakbrook Terrace IL 60181 Office: 2222 Kensington Ct Oakbrook IL 60521

THOMAN, EVELYN BUTLER, educator; b. Washington, Mar. 18, 1922; d. James Alva and Lila Jean (Walters) Butler; B.A., U. Nebr., 1951, M.A., 1963, Ph.D., 1965; m. Clemens Bernard Thoman (div.); children—Lila Anne, Lynda Jean, Luisa Kim, Marta Ruth, Roger Bernard, Eric James; m. 2d, Victor Denenberg, Nov. 23, 1975. Instr., U. Nebr., 1964-65; Public Health Service postdoctoral fellow dept. psychiatry Stanford U. Sch. Medicine, 1965-67, bioscis. postdoctoral fellow, 1967-69, postdoctoral fellow dept. pediatrics, 1969-70, research asso. dept. psychiatry and pediatrics, 1970-72; asso. prof. dept. biobehavioral scis. U. Conn., Storrs, 1972-79, prof. dept. biobehavioral scis., 1979—. Mem. Soc. for Research in Child Devel., Am. Psychol. Assn., Internat. Soc. Devel. Psychobiology, Soc. Neurosci., Animal Behavior Soc., Assn. for Psychophysiol. Study of Sleep. Contbr. numerous articles to profl. jours.; mem. editorial bd. Am. Jour. Mental Deficiency, 1978, Child Development, 1976—, Infant Behavior and Development, 1977-79. Office: Dept Biobehavioral Scis Box U-154 U Conn Storrs CT 06268

THOMAS, ALICE WATERS, former educator, assn. exec.; b. Memphis; d. Warren and Jennie (Ogilvie) Waters; B.S., Tenn. State U., 1939; M.A. in Edn., Fisk U., 1948; cert. of advanced study in reading U. Chgo., 1964; postgrad. Peabody Coll., 1968; m. Joseph A. Thomas, Sept. 27; children—Jackie M., Alice Thomas Mayhew. Tchr., Nashville public schs., 1943-75; pres. Nashville sect. Nat. Council Negro Women, 1963—, coordinator nat. immunization program, 1979, 80, recipient various service awards at local and nat. level; past mem. del. assembly Tenn. Edn. Congress. Named Tenn. Woman of Yr., Order Eastern Star, 1979, hon. del. U.S. Ho. of Reps., 1982. Mem. adminstrv. bd. YWCA, Nashville, 1961-66, chair vol. leadership com., 1961-66; mem. judging panel Internat. Yr. of Disabled Persons, Met. Nashville Office of Handicapped, 1982; LWV rep. Emergency Sch. Aid Act adv. com. Met. Nashville Pub. Schs., 1981-82. Mem. NEA (conv. del. 1959, 65-71, 74), Met. Nashville Edn. Assn. (honor award 1970, 71, dir.), Nat. Ret. Tchrs. Assn., Nashville Ret. Tchrs., Middle Tenn. Ret. Tchrs., Nashville Fisk Club, AAUW, LWV, UN Assn., Phi Delta Kappa Profl. Frat., Phi Delta Kappa (service award, chair human relations com. Alpha Beta chpt., Soror of Yr. award Southeastern region 1981). Home: 831 Kirkwood Ln Nashville TN 37204

THOMAS, ALMA LUCILLE, fgn. service officer; b. Raleigh, N.C., Aug. 5, 1944; d. Luther and Hazel F. Thomas; B.A., St. Augustine's Coll., Raleigh, 1966; M.P.A., Harvard U., 1980. Researcher, Library of Congress, 1967-69; joined U.S. Fgn. Service, 1970; service in Paris, Tunis, Dakar; dep. exec. dir. Bur. Intelligence and Research, Dept. of State, 1980—. Mem. Am. Fgn. Service Assn., Am. Soc. Public Adminstrn., Bus. and Profl. Women, Women's Action Orgn., Harvard U. Alumni Assn., St. Augustine's Coll. Alumni Assn., NAACP, Urban League, Alpha Kappa Alpha. Office: Bur Intelligence and Research Dept State Washington DC 20520

THOMAS, BARBARA ANN, librarian; b. Gallipolis, Ohio, July 20, 1948; d. Donald Barry and Lillian Ruth (Church) T.; student U. Evansville, 1966-68, U. Oreg., 1969; B.S. cum laude in Speech/Drama, Rio Grande Coll., 1970; postgrad. Sch. Religion, Earlham Coll., 1971-72, Ohio U., 1980—; student Augusta Heritage Arts Workshop, Elkins, W.Va., summer 1976. Coordinator, Ohio Hills Folk Arts and Pioneer Skills project Ohio Arts Council, 1972-74; coordinator Wood Thrush Folk Arts Council, Jackson, Ohio, 1974-75; instr. continuing edn. Rio Grande (Ohio) Coll., 1977-78, acquisitions asst. Davis Library, 1978—; participant African ethnic heritage seminar, Tunisia, Morocco, summer 1980; tchr. pvt. violin lessons; violinist with various orchs., ensembles; cons. Ohio U.; coordinator Cross-Cultural Communication Conf., 1979. Recipient Nat. Sch. Orch. award, 1966. Mem. Council Appalachian Women, Women's Studies Assn., Internat. Soc. for Comparative Study Civilizations, Center for Sci. in Public Interest, Amnesty Internat., Rio Grande Coll. Faculty Assn. (sec. 1979-80), Applachian Studies Council. Club: Rio Grande Coll. Internat. (adv.). Editor, Wood Thrush Notes, 1972-74, River Valley Food Coop. Newsletter, 1979—, Rio Grande Coll. Lit. Rev., 1980—. Home: Route One Box 1515 Cheshire OH 45620 Office: Davis Library Rio Grande Coll Rio Grande OH 45674

THOMAS, BARBARA SINGER, commr. SEC; b. N.Y.C., Dec. 28, 1946; d. Jules and Marcia Singer; B.A. cum laude, U. Pa., 1966; J.D. cum laude, N.Y. U., 1969; m. Allen L. Thomas, Mar. 12, 1978. Admitted to N.Y. bar, 1969, D.C. bar, 1981; asso. firm Paul Weiss Rifkind Wharton & Garrison, N.Y.C., 1969-73; asso. firm Kaye Scholer Fierman Hays & Handler, N.Y.C., 1973-77, partner, 1978-80; commr. SEC, Washington, 1980—. Bd. overseers Wharton Sch. Fin., U. Pa.; trustee Inst. East-West Securities Studies, Youth for Understanding, Washington Opera; mem. secondary sch. com. U. Pa. John Norton Pomeroy scholar; recipient Am. Jurisprudence prizes, 1964-66. Mem. Internat. Bar Assn., Am. Bar Assn. (com. fed. regulation of securities, ad hock task force internat. aspects of U.S. law), N.Y. State Bar Assn. (securities regulation com.), Fin. Women's Assn. N.Y., Assn. Bar City N.Y. (chmn. corp. law com. 1969-80), Council Fgn. Relations, U. Pa. Alumni Assn. N.Y.C. (trustee), N.Y. U. Law Alumni Assn., N.Y. U. Law Rev. Alumni Assn., Order of Coif. Club: Economic (N.Y.C.). Contbr. articles to profl. jours. Home: 2500 Virginia Ave NW Washington DC 20037 Office: 450 5th St NW Washington DC 20549

THOMAS, BETTY MARIE DORTON, state legislator; b. Shelby, N.C., Sept. 10, 1923; d. J.S. and Marie Biggerstaff Dorton; B.S., U. N.C., Greenboro, 1944; m. A.W. Thomas Jr., Apr. 3, 1948 (dec.); children—Bettina Marie Thomas Smith, Terre Thomas Bullock Arthur Webster. Pres., A.W. Thomas & Son; mem. N.C. Ho. of Reps., 1975-76, 77-78, 79-80, 81—, chmn. natural and econ. resources com., vice-chmn. banks and thrift instns. com., vice-chmn. human resources com., mem. com. on Aging, others; mem. Local Govt. Advocacy Council. Named Concord (N.C.) Woman of Yr., 1976; N.C. Legislator of Yr., 1980. Mem. Bus. and Profl. Women, Am. Legion Aux., Nat. Orgn. Women Legislators. Methodist (all offices Sunday Sch. class 1948-60, sec. Women of Ch. 1969, trustee 1975-76, mem. Council on Ministries 1974-76, adminstrv. bd. 1975, 81). Office: NC Ho Reps State Capitol Raleigh NC 27602

THOMAS, BILLIE JANICE, banker; b. Jonesboro, La., Jan. 8, 1950; d. Robert Leonard and Margie (Foster) McCain; student public schs.; m. Dale Eugene Thomas, Jr., June 9, 1968; children—Dale Eugene, III, Robert Sean, Cody Foster. Asst. cashier, personnel adminstr. Bossier Bank & Trust Co., Bossier City, La., 1978—. Pres. Meadowview Elem. PTA, 1976-78; 2d v.p. Bossier Dist. PTA, 1977; mem. pupil progression plan com. Bossier Parish Sch. Bd. Mem. N.W. La. Personnel Assn. (sec. 1981), Am. Soc. Tng. and Devel. Baptist. Home: 407 Post Oak Bossier City LA 71111 Office: PO Box 5667 1325 Barksdale Blvd Bossier City LA 71111

THOMAS, CAROL LOUISE JOSEPH (MRS. CHARLES RAYMOND THOMAS), community planning co. exec.; b. Poughkeepsie, N.Y., Aug. 29, 1923; d. Harold Kritzman and Charlotte Carolyn (Freiberg) Joseph; student Vassar Coll., 1941-43, Boston U., 1943, 49; A.B. cum laude, Syracuse U., 1948; M.A., U. Conn., 1950; postgrad. Mass. Inst. Tech., 1950; m. Charles Raymond Thomas, Mar. 21, 1943; children—Charles Joseph, Katharine Louise. Free-lance community planner, 1950-58; partner Sonthoff & Thomas, community planners, 1958-61; pres., treas. Thomas Assos., community planners, 1961-69; dir. Thomas Assos. div. Universal Engring. Corp., Boston, 1969-78, pres. Thomas Planning Services, Inc., 1978—; mem. faculty U. R.I. Grad. Curriculum in Community Planning and Area Devel.; lectr. Boston State Coll., 1970-78, Grad. Sch. Design, Harvard U., 1975—. Active various community drives; mem. Gov.'s Advisory Com. on Planning, 1963-68, Gov.'s Advisory Com. on Civil Def., 1966-68, Wayland (Mass.) Town Govt. Com., 1958-72; chmn. scholarship awarding com. PTA, Wayland, 1965-72. Active local Republican party. Mem. Am. Planning Assn. (pres. N.E. chpt. 1979-81), Am. Inst. Cert. Planners (pres. New Eng. chpt. 1965-67, chmn. jury of awards 1969-71), Mass. Fedn. Planning Bds. (dir. 1970-75). Republican. Unitarian (mem. parish com. 1958-60, adult edn. com. 1973—). Author articles in field. Home: 151 Tremont St Apt 23P Boston MA 02111 Office: 46 Church St Boston MA 02116

THOMAS, CAROLYN ELISE, educator; b. Mt. Clemens, Mich., Mar. 8, 1943; d. Jack W. and Agnes E. (Anderson) T.; B.A., Western Mich. U.; M.S., U. Wash.; Ph.D., Ohio State U. Instr., U.Idaho, 1966-70; asst. prof. phys. edn. Denison U., Brockport State U., 1972-73; asst. prof. SUNY, Buffalo, 1973-76, asso. prof., 1976—, chmn. dept. phys. edn., 1976—. Mem. Philosophic Soc. for Study Sport (pres.), Nat. Assn. Sport and Phys. Edn., Nat. Assn. Phys. Edn. in Higher Edn. Author: Sport in a Philosophic Context, 1983; editor: Aesthetics and Dance, 1980. Office: 209 Clark Hall SUNY Buffalo NY 14214

THOMAS, CLAUDIA LEE BONDS, ednl. adminstr.; b. Shannon, N.C., Sept. 20, 1930; d. Robert Claud and Mary Lee (McGirt) Bonds; B.S., Bennett Coll., 1952; student U. Tex., 1960-61, Pacific Luth. U., 1963, U. Oreg., 1968-69; M.A. in Adminstrn., Seattle U., 1974; Ph.D. in Organizational Devel. and Mgmt., U. Experimenting Colls., 1979; children—Bryan Lee, Lisa Ann. Tchr. home econs. Allen High Sch., Ashville, N.C., 1952-54; supr. home econs. Agr. Extension Service, Clinton, N.C., 1954-59; tchr. spl. edn. Meridian Jr. High Sch., Kent, Wash., 1962-63; tchr. chemistry Lydia Patterson High Sch., El Paso, Tex., 1959-61; tchr. chemistry, head sci. dept. Kubasaki High Sch., Okinawa, 1964-66; tchr. home econs., reading, spl. edn. Kentridge High Sch., Kent, 1968-73; tchr. spl. edn. and history Kent-Meridian Sr. High Sch., Kent, 1968-71; communications cons. for sch. dists., pvt. and pub. agys., 1973—; asst. prin. Kent Jr. High Sch., 1974-77; adj. prof. Central Wash. U., Ellensburg, 1977—; prin. Sequoia Jr. High Sch., Kent, 1978—. Vol. handicapped program City of Tacoma. Recipient Acorn award PTA, 1972, 82; Human Relations award Wash. Tchrs. Assn., 1972. Mem. Nat. Assn. Secondary Sch. Prins., Assn. Adminstrv. Women, NAACP, Urban League Phi Delta Kappa, Kappa Delta Pi, Alpha Kappa Alpha (pres. Tacoma chpt.). Democrat. Methodist. Home: 11222 96th Ave SW Tacoma WA 98493 Office: 11000 SE 264th St Kent WA 98031

THOMAS, CLAUDIA LYNN, orthopaedic surgeon; b. N.Y.C., Feb. 28, 1950; d. Charles Mitchell and Daisy Mae T.; B.A., Vassar Coll., 1971; M.D., Johns Hopkins U., 1975. Intern, Yale-New Haven Hosp., 1975-76, resident in surgery, 1976-77, resident in orthopaedic surgery, 1977-80; orthopaedic trauma fellow Md. Inst. Emergency Med. Services Systems, Balt., 1980; asst. prof. orthopaedic surgery Johns Hopkins Hosp., 1981—, Balt. City Hosp., 1981—; mem. staff Children's Hosp., Provident Hosp., Wyman Park Health System, Inc. (all Balt.). Mem. Yale Orthopaedic Assn., Newington Alumni Assn., Nat. Med. Assn., Monumental Med. Assn. Democrat. Author: (with A.A. White, M.M. Panjabi) Clinical Biomechanics of the Spine, 1978; (with P. Leppert, E. Siff, C. Thomas) Being a Woman: Your Body and Birth Control, 1979. First black female orthopedic surgeon. Office: 4940 Eastern Ave Baltimore MD 21224

THOMAS, DIAHANN WYKE, mfg. co. exec.; b. Norfolk, Va., Sept. 25, 1951; d. Christopher Jack and Audrey Lee (Suhr) Wyke; A.A., Fla. Jr. Coll., 1973; student U. N. Fla., 1973-74; B.S., Fla. State U., 1976, M.B.A., 1977. Adminstrv. coordinator Xerox Corp., Jacksonville, Fla., 1971-75; employee ins. coordinator Mobile Home Industries, Tallahassee, 1975-76; grad. asst. U. N. Fla., Jacksonville, 1976-77; with Western Electric Co., Inc., New Orleans, 1977-79, electronic switching systems installation supr., 1979, account analyst, Birmingham, Ala., 1979-80, dept. chief service, New Orleans, 1980—; instr. U. New Orleans, 1978-79. Chmn. company campaign United Way, 1980. Mem. Am. Mgmt. Assn., Nat. Assn. Female Execs., Am. Soc. Profl. and Exec. Women, Assn. M.B.A. Execs., Common Cause, Friends of Earth, Ala. Womens Polit. Caucus, NOW, Crises Center, Sigma Iota Epsilon, Beta Gamma Sigma. Address: 1111 S Broad St New Orleans LA 70125

THOMAS, DORIS R., legis. adminstrv. asst.; d. Simon S. and Rosa (Henry) Thomas; 1 dau., Tandi Deirdre. B.S., Hampton Inst.; LL.B., Howard U., 1955. Probation officer Women's Ct., N.Y.C., 1956-58; group worker All Nation Found., 1959-61; community orgn. specialist Bay Area Urban League, San Francisco, 1961-62; adminstrv. asst. to Phillip Burton, state assemblyman, 1962-64; now adminstrv. asst. to Rep. Burton, Washington. Mem. Bus. and Profl. Women's Club, Calif. State Democratic Central Com., Chinese Am. Dem. Club, Women's Dem. Polit. Workshop, Howard U. Alumni Club. Office: Room 1714 Longworth House Office Bldg Washington DC 20515

THOMAS, DOROTHY, indexing cons.; b. N.Y.C., Mar. 3, 1923; d. Hyman and Clara (Lond) Fisch; student Hunter Coll., 1940-43; cert. N.Y. U. Sch. Bus., 1944; m. Sidney Thomashower, Sept. 2, 1944; children—William Jay, James Evan. Personnel troubleshooter W.P.B., 1943; employment mgr. Emerson Radio & Phonograph Corp., 1943-47; editor, author, 1947—; indexer, cons., N.Y.C., 1960—; biographer, lectr., radio producer and moderator; specialist in history of women in legal profession; dir. spl. projects Found. Continuing Legal Edn.; cons. indexing Lond Publs., 1970—; lectr. colls., clubs, orgns. Active legis. reform and women's movement; mem. Nat. Women's Polit. Caucus, NOW. Mem. AFTRA, Am. Soc. Indexers (pres. elect 1982-83), Coalition of Labor Union Women, Friends of Columbia Libraries, Friends of Schlesinger Library of Harvard U., N.Y. Biog. and Geneal. Soc., N.Y. Hist. Soc. Ind. Democrat. Club: Women's City (N.Y.C.). Author: Women Lawyers in the U.S., 1957; Women, The Bench and The Bar, in preparation; contbr. articles and biographies to Notable American Women, 1607-1950, 1971; author indexes and tables. Home and Office: 123 W 74th St New York NY 10023

THOMAS, E. KIKI, educator; b. New Orleans, Feb. 15, 1946; d. Warren F. and Rose Mary (Wilson) Rylander; B.S. in Sociology and Psychology, Dillard U., 1967; M.S.W., Atlanta U., 1970; postgrad. Ga. State U., 1982—; m. Antonio Thomas, Sept. 4, 1971; 1 son, Krantki Thomas. Counselor, program asst. Upward Bound Program, Dillard U.,

1966, library asst., 1967-67; tchr. La. Public Sch. System, Plaquemine, 1967-68; social work field placement Dept. Welfare County of Fulton, Ga., 1968-69; social work trainee VA Hosp., Marion, Ind., 1969-70; psychiat. social worker Grady Meml. Hosp., Atlanta, 1970-71; social worker Central Meth. Ch., Atlanta, 1971-72; psychiat. social worker Econ. Opportunity Atlanta, Inc., 1972-73; assoc. prof. dept. mental health Ga. State U., Atlanta, 1973—. Mem. Ga. Coalition on Consultation Edn. and Parenting, Nat. Assn. Social Workers, Nat. Assn. Black Social Workers, Black Educators Council Human Services, Nat. Assn. Public Adminstrn., Council Social Work Edn., So. Orgn. Human Service Educators, Assn. Social and Behavioral Scientists. Address: 2734 Ben Hill Rd East Point GA 30344

THOMAS, ELINDA PATRICIA GRAFTON (MRS. LEWIS EDWARD THOMAS), educator; b. Michigan City, Ind., Sept. 30, 1921; d. Robert Wadsworth and Elinda (Opperman) Grafton; student (Adolph Dehn fellow water color 1939), Stephens Coll., 1936-39, Purdue U., summer 1938; B.Ed. magna cum laude, U. Toledo, 1966; postgrad. (NDEA fellow) Green U., 1968; m. Lewis Edward Thomas, Dec. 21, 1939; children—Linda L. (Mrs. John R. Collins), Stephanie A., (Mrs. Andrew M. Pawuk), I. Kathryn (Mrs. James N. Ramsey), Deborah. Tchr., Toledo Bd. Edn., 1959-82, tchr. lang. arts and art Harvard Sch., 1966-76, tchr. lang. arts Byrnedale Sch., 1976—; mem. lit. curriculum com. Toledo Pub. Schs., 1969, mem. grammar curriculum com., 1976. Dist. capt. Planned Parenthood, 1952-53, ARC, 1954-55; bd. dirs. Elizabeth Wayne Nursery Sch., 1982—, Toledo Symphony Orch. Women's League, 1982—. Mem. Toledo Soc. Profl. Engrs. Aux., Helen Kreps Guild, AAUW, Toledo Symphony League, Phi Kappa Phi, Phi Delta Kappa, Kappa Delta Pi, Pi Lambda Theta (sec. 1976—, pres. 1978—), Delta Kappa Gamma (chpt. pres. 1976-78, membership chmn. 1978—). Republican. Episcopalian. Home: 4148 Deepwood Ln Toledo OH 43614

THOMAS, ETHEL COLVIN NICHOLS (MRS. LEWIS VICTOR THOMAS), educator; b. Cranston, R.I., Mar. 31, 1913; d. Charles Russell and Mabel Maria (Colvin) Nichols; Ph.B., Pembroke Coll. in Brown U., 1934; M.A., Brown U., 1938; Ed.D., Rutgers U., 1979; m. Lewis Victor Thomas, July 26, 1945 (dec. Oct. 1965); 1 son, Glenn Nichols. Tchr. English, Cranston High Sch., 1934-39; social dir. and adviser to freshmen, Fox Hall, Boston U., 1939-40; instr. to asst. prof. English Am. Coll. for Girls, Istanbul, Turkey, 1940-44; dean freshman, dir. admission Women's Coll. of Middlebury, Vt., 1944-45; tchr. English, Robert Coll., Istanbul, 1945-46; instr. English, Rider Coll., Trenton, N.J., 1950-51; tchr. English, Princeton (N.J.) High Sch., 1951-61, counselor, 1960-62, 72—, coll. counselor, 1962-72. Mem. N.E.A., AAUW, Nat. Assn. Women Deans Adminstrs. and Counselors, Am. Personnel and Guidance Assn., Bus. and Profl. Women's Club (named Woman of Yr., Princeton chpt. 1977), Met. Mus. Art, Kappa Delta Pi. Presbyn. Clubs: Brown University (N.Y.C.); Nassau. Home: 154 Prospect Ave Princeton NJ 08540 Office: Princeton Regional Schs Box 711 Princeton NJ 08540

THOMAS, FRANCES ELAINE, ins. co. exec.; b. Winfield, Kans., June 27, 1932; d. Harold W. and Sarah R. (Linnens) Moon; student Southwestern Coll., 1951-57, Butler County Jr. Coll., 1969; m. William J. Thomas, Mar. 2, 1979; children by previous marriage—Jerome Herman Anglemyer, Constance Lynne Wolf, David Lee Anglemyer. Sec., Simmons Realty, Inc., Augusta, Kans., 1967-69, Eureka Fed. Savs. and Loan, Augusta, 1967-69, mgr. ins. dept., 1967-69; propr., mgr. Anglemyer Ins., Inc., Augusta, 1969-73; mgr., v.p. Simmons Ins., Inc., Augusta, 1973-75; mgr. Dannar Ins. Inc., Wichita, Kans., 1975-76; exec. sec. to v.p. Fin. Guardian, Wichita, 1976-77; mgr. Prairie Ins., Inc., Augusta, 1977—. Mem. Bd. Edn., Augusta, 1971—, pres., 1976-77; sec. Butler County (Kans.) Sch. Bd. Council, 1979—; pres. PTA, 1962-71; sec. Butler County Fair Assn., 1975—. Recipient Project Bus. award Am. Assn. Mng. Agts., 1979, Mr. Chairman award, 1972. Mem. Kans. Assn. Ind. Ins. Agts., Kans. Assn. Mut. Ins. Agts. (dir. 1971-75), Bus. and Profl. Women, Profl. Ins. Agts. Kans. Republican. Mem. Christian Ch. Club: 4-H. Home: Rural Route 1 PO Box 96 Augusta KS 67010 Office: 415 State St Augusta KS 67010

THOMAS, FRANCES JONES, social worker/adminstr., educator; b. St. Louis, Oct. 9, 1942; d. William A. and Sadie Jones; A.A., Harris Jr. Coll., 1962; B.S., St. Louis U., 1964; M.S.W., 1968; m. Robert Banks, June 20, 1965; 1 son, Donovan; m. 2d, Maurice Thomas, Nov. 30, 1969; 1 son, Darrell. Intake specialist Human Devel. Corp., St. Louis, 1965-67; med. social worker, St. Louis City Hosp., 1967-75; dir. social services dept. all divs. DePaul Community Health Center, Bridgeton, Mo., 1975—; adj. asst. prof. St. Louis U.; field work instr. St. Louis U., Washington, U., U. Mo., Southern Ill. U., 1977—. Bd. dirs. Am. Cancer Soc., 1977—; mem. Cardinal Ritter Inst. Home Health Care Adv. Council, 1980—; apptd. cons. spl. concerns St. Louis Office Human Rights, 1981—; bd. dirs. Birthright, 1982-84. Zeta Phi Beta scholar, 1962-64; USPHS stipend, 1965. Mem. St. Louis Soc. Hosp. Social Work Dirs. Am. Hosp. Assn. (pres. 1979-80), Nat. Assn. Social Workers (Register of Clin. Social Workers), Acad. Cert. Social Workers, Council Social Work Edn., Zeta Phi Beta. Democrat. Baptist. Home: 7135 Winchester Dr Northwoods MO 63121 Office: 12303 DePaul Dr Bridgeton MO 63044

THOMAS, GEORGELLE, psychologist, educator; b. Jacksonville, Fla.; d. George Leonard and Mary (McNair) Thomas; A.B. in Psychology, Queens Coll., 1949; M.S. in Exptl. Psychology, U. Ga., 1965, Ph.D., 1967. Psychometrist, Queens, Coll., Charlotte, N.C., 1950-52, admissions counselor, 1955-57; dean of residence Salem Acad., Winston-Salem, N.C., 1953-55, successively asst. prof., asso. prof., prof. psychology Ga. So. Coll., Statesboro, 1967—, acting head dept., 1976-77; cons. psychologist Tng. and Evaluation Group, Dept. Navy. Mem. Am. Psychol. Assn., Soc. for Behavioral Medicine, Sigma Xi. Contbr. articles in field to profl. jours. Home: Rt 7 PO Box 253 Grove Lakes Statesboro GA 30458 Office: Dept Psychology Ga So Coll Statesboro GA 30460

THOMAS, GRACE FERN, physician, psychiatrist; b. Gothenburg, Nebr., Sept. 23, 1897; d. George William and Martha C. (Johnson) Thomas; B.S., U. Nebr., 1924; M.A., Creighton U., 1926; M.D., U. So. Calif., 1935; postgrad. U. Colo., 1942-43, Inst. of Living, 1943, U. So. Calif., 1946, UCLA, Angeles, 1947-50, Columbia U., 1953; M.A. in Religion, U. So. Calif., 1968. Instr. chemistry, biology Duchesne Coll., 1924-27; lab. technician various hosps., 1927-32; intern Los Angeles County Hosp., 1934-35; resident physician Riverside County Hosp., 1935-36; resident psychiatrist Los Angeles County Psychopathic Hosp., 1936-37; staff psychiatrist Calif. State Hosp. System, 1937-42, Glenside Hosp., 1943-44; pvt. practice neuropsychiatry, Long Beach, Calif., 1946-51; chief mental hygiene clinic VA, Albuquerque, 1951-54; dir. psychiat. edn. Miss. State Hosp., Jackson, 1955; dir. Stark County Guidance Center, Canton, Ohio, 1956-58; dir. Huron County Guidance Center, Norwalk, Ohio, 1958-61, Arrowhead Mental Health Center, San Bernardino, Calif., 1962-64; dir. Mendocino County Mental Health Services, Ukiah, Calif., 1964-65; chief psychiat. edn. Porterville (Calif.) State Hosp., 1965-66; dir. Tuolumne County Mental Health Services, Sonora, Calif., 1966-70; psychiatrist-cons. Emanuel Hosp. Mental Health Center, Turlock, Calif., 1970-71; pvt. practice psychiatry, Turlock, 1970-73, Modesto, Calif., 1973—; cons. psychiatrist Stanislaus County Mental Health Dept., Modesto, 1972-73; alienist to Stanislaus County Superior Ct., Modesto, 1972—; psychiatrist-cons. Cath. Social Service Agency, 1974-78. Ordained to ministry United Meth. Ch., 1968. Served as capt. M.C., AUS, 1944-46. Diplomate Am. Bd. Psychiatry and Neurology. Mem. AMA, Stanislaus Med. Soc., Central Calif. Psychiat. Assn., Inst. Religion and Health, Am. Psychiat. Assn., Am. Med. Women's Assn. Am. Legion, AAUW, fellow of Internat. Biographical Asso., Soroptimists, Phi Delta Gamma, Phi Beta Kappa, Sigma Xi, Phi Kappa Phi, Nu Sigma Phi. Methodist. Home: 2001 LaJolla Ct Modesto CA 95350 Office: 1130 Coffee Rd Suite 8B Modesto CA 95355

THOMAS, JACQUELINE ANN SMITH, educator; b. Little Rock, Ark., Jan. 10, 1936; d. William Harrison and Blanche (Elliott) Smith; A.B., Ark. Baptist Coll., 1955; B.S. in Elem. Edn., Ark. A&M Coll., 1957; M.S. in Curriculum and Instrn., U. Wis., 1969; m. Norman M. Thomas, June 5, 1960; children—Michael M., Michelle A. Elem. sch. tchr. in Ark., Ill., Md., N.J. and Wis., 1957—; tchr. 3d grade Blackhawk Elem. Sch., Park Forest, Ill., 1977-78, 80—; sec. bd. dirs. Thomas Distbg. Co., Chgo., 1976—. Vice pres., treas. sr. usher bd., chmn. jr. ushers, chmn. theatre guild, sec. steering com. bldg. fund New Faith Baptist Ch., Chicago Heights, Ill., 1979— ; v.p. Women's Missionary Soc. Mem. Am. Fedn. Tchrs., Alpha Kappa Alpha. Home: 21020 Cambridge St Olympia Fields IL 60461

THOMAS, JANICE LINDA, communications exec.; b. Brockton, Mass., Oct. 25, 1949; d. George Sidney and Jean Louise (Currier) McLean, Jr.; B.A. magna cum laude, Framingham State Coll., 1976; student Boston State Coll., 1967-68; children—Michelle, Kristin. Public info. officer Mass. Dept. Edn., Bur. Fire Tng., Sudbury, Mass., 1976-77, dir. info., 1977-78; public info. officer Internat. Soc. Fire Service Instrs., Hopkinton, Mass., 1976-79; asst. editor Internat. Assn. Fire Chiefs, Washington, 1979-80; mgr. Fire Edn. Resource Network, 1980-82, Fed. Emergency Mgmt. Agy., Office of Planning and Edn., U.S. Fire Adminstrn.; cons. Paradigm, Inc., Potomac, Md., 1981-82; cons. Energy, Mgmt. and Mktg. Div., IMR Corp., Falls Church, Va., 1982—; lectr. in field. Precinct leader for local, congressional campaigns, 1970-74. Recipient Spl. award, 7th Annual Public Fire Educators Conf., 1981. Mem. NOW, Am. Mgmt. Assn., Internat. Assn. Bus. Communicators, Internat. Soc. Fire Service Instrs., Nat. Assn. Female Execs., Nat. Fire Protection Assn., Washington Women in Public Relations, Women in Communications. Unitarian Universalist. Contbr. articles to profl. jours. Home: 10511 Cambridge Ct Gaithersburg MD 20879

THOMAS, LOUANN CAROL, health care co. exec.; b. Willmar, Minn., Aug. 19, 1943; d. Norris E. and Geneva J. (Berg) Johnson; M.T., Pacific Luth. U., 1966; m. Marshall M. Thomas, Apr. 23, 1971. Med. technologist Sacred Heart Hosp., Eugene, Oreg., 1966-68; supr. chemistry Good Samaritan Hosp., Portland, 1968-72, supr. research/devel., 1972-74; dir. customer service Microform Data Systems, Mountain View, Calif., 1974-80; br. mgr. HBO & Co., San Mateo, Calif., 1980—; condr. workshops in field. Mem. Nat. Bd. Am. Soc. Med. Technologists, Am. Soc. Clin. Pathologists, Calif. Soc. Med. Technologists, Soc. for Computer Medicine, Am. Mgmt. Assn. Republican. Lutheran. Club: Belleek Collector's Soc. Office: 2929 Campus Dr Suite 300 San Mateo CA 94403

THOMAS, LUCILLE MATHEWS, assn. and corp. exec.; b. Kingsland, Ga., Nov. 21, 1945; d. Thomas and Joe Ethel (Streeter) Mathews; grad. in Psychology with honors, Miami-Dade Community Coll., 1973; grad. in Psychology, Nova U.; postgrad. U. Ga.; 1 dau., Jamila. Youth coordinator North Dade Manpower, Opa Locka, Fla., 1973; program dir. Culmer Jobs Program, Miami, Fla., 1979-81; exec. dir. Opa Locka C. of C., 1981—; v.p. Classic Stationers, Inc., Opa Locka, 1981—. Mem. Democratic exec. com. Dade County; bd. trustees North Dade Hosp.; mem. advisory com. YWCA; bd. dirs. North Dade Homeowners Assn.; mem. Neighborhood Crime Watch, Dade Partners Assn. Mem. Phi Lambda Phi. Address: 8541 NW 24th Ave Miami FL 33056

THOMAS, LUCINDA ELLEN, psychologist; b. Ft. Collins, Colo., May 21, 1932; d. Glen Vincent Swearingen; B.S. in Psychology, Colo. State U., 1953, M.Ed. in Coll. Student Personnel Adminstrn., 1968; cert. Am. Inst. for Fgn. Trade, 1957; children—Nicholas Paul Thomas, Terence Philip. Tchr., Agana Jr. High Sch., Guam, Marianas Islands, 1953-54; dir. guidance services Am. Community Sch., Buenos Aires, Argentina, 1962-64; dir. testing center and staff psychologist Univ. Counseling Center, Colo. State U., Ft. Collins, 1968—; mem. Larimer County (Colo.) Mental Health Bd., 1979-84, pres., 1981, 82. Mem. City of Ft. Collins Personnel Bd., 1973-79, chmn., 1979. Mem. Am. Psychol. Assn., Rocky Mountain Psychol. Assn., Am. Coll. Personnel Assn., Nat. Vocat. Guidance Assn., Colo. Personnel and Guidance Assn., Colo. Coll. Personnel Assn., Assn. of Women Psychologists, Phi Delta Kappa. Contbr. articles in field to profl. jours. Home: 104 N Roosevelt St Fort Collins CO 80521 Office: Univ Testing Service C-81 Clark Bldg Colo State U Fort Collins CO 80523

THOMAS, MARGARET JEAN, clergywoman, ch. adminstr.; b. Detroit, Dec. 24, 1943; d. Robert Elcana and Purcella Margaret (Hartness) T.; B.S. with honors, Mich. State U., 1964; M.Div., Union Theol. Sem., Va., 1971. Ordained to ministry United Presbyterian Ch. U.S.A., 1971; dir. for research Bd. Christian Edn., Presbyterian Ch., U.S. Richmond, Va., 1965-71, gen. council, Atlanta, 1972-73; mng. dir. research div. United Presbyn. Ch., U.S.A., N.Y.C., 1974-76, dep. exec. dir. ch., 1977—. Mem. Religious Research Assn. (officer), Religious Edn. Assn. (officer), Soc. for Sci. Study Religion, ACLU, Democratic Action Group. Democrat. Contbr. articles to religious mags.; editorial adv. bd. Character Potential, 1973—. Office: 475 Riverside Dr Room 1020 New York NY 10115

THOMAS, MARLO, actress; b. Detroit, Nov. 21, 1943; d. Danny Thomas; ed. U. So. Calif.; m. Phil Donahue, May 22, 1980. Theatrical appearances in Broadway prodn. Thieves, 1974, London prodn. Barefoot in the Park; star TV series That Girl, 1966; conceived book and record, starred in TV spl. Free to Be...You and Me (Emmy for best children's show), 1974; films include Jenny, Thieves, 1977. Recipient George Foster Peabody award; named Most Promising Newcomer, Fame, also Photoplay. Address: care Michael Ovitz Creative Artists, Agy Inc 1888 Century Park East Los Angeles CA 90067 *

THOMAS, MARTHA BROWN, home economist; b. Yalobusha County, Miss., July 31, 1939; d. Hardy and Veola (Hervey) Brown; B.S., Alcorn State U., 1963; M.Ed. (Kellogg fellow), N.C. State U., 1978; m. James Edward Thomas, May 19, 1966; children—Kim Yolando Milton, Kiyoko Kay, Kristina Yvette. Asst. negro home demonstration agt. Miss. Coop. Extension Service, Cohoma County, 1963-64, asso. extension home economist Tate County, Miss., 1964-70; home econs. extension agt. N.C. Agr. Extension Service, Goldsboro, 1970—. Bd. dirs. Operation Bootstrap, Wayne Action Group for Econs. Solvency; mem. liaison council Goldsboro Community Sch., 1978—. Mem. Am. Home Econs. Assn., Nat. Assn. Extension Home Economists, N.C. Home Econs. Assn., N.C. Assn. Extension Home Economists, N.C. Adult Edn. Assn., N.C. Headstart Assn., N.C. Family Life Council, N.C. Fedn. Extension Agts. Assn., Asso. Couples for Marriage Enrichment, Epsilon Sigma Phi. Democrat. Baptist. Office: North Carolina Agricultural Service PO Box 68 Goldsboro NC 27530

THOMAS, MARY ELLEN, stockbroker; b. St. Paul, Mar. 1, 1943; d. William R. and Rose G. Walters; student N.Y. Inst. Fin., 1970, Coll. Fin. Planning, 1982; m. James L. Thomas, June 2, 1962; children—John William, Steven Wayne. Various clerical positions, 1961-69; sec., registered rep., v.p. Schneider Bernet & Hickman, Houston, 1969-81, sr. v.p., 1981—. Cert. fin. planner. Mem. Internat. Soc. Registered Reps., Internat. Assn. Fin. Planners, Houston Security Dealers Assn., Amex Club Houston. Roman Catholic. Office: 3050 S Post Oak Suite 100 Houston TX 77056

THOMAS, MARY LYNN, nurse; b. Monongahela, Pa., Jan. 19, 1948; d. Clarence A. and Sally Ann (Hannan) Sterner; L.P.N., Indian River Jr. Coll., Ft. Pierce, Fla., 1971; A.S. in Nursing Sci., Indian River Community Coll., 1975; m. Ronald Allen Thomas, Dec. 16, 1965; 1 son, Ronald Allen. Mem. staff hosps. in Fla., 1971-73; nurse Indian River Community Mental Health Center, 1977-81; mem. part-time staff Easter Manor Nursing Home, Ft. Pierce, 1976-81; dir. nursing services Hardee Manor Nursing Home, Wauchula, Fla., 1981—. Mem. Fla. Nurses Assn. Democrat. Baptist. Home: 345 Willow Ave Bowling Green FL 33834 Office: 401 Orange Pl Wauchula FL 33873

THOMAS, MAXINE FREDDIE, judge; b. Los Angeles, May 31, 1947; d. Mack and Freddie (Thompson) Thomas; student Los Angeles City Coll., 1965-67; B.A. (Stanley Meml. scholar), Calif. State Coll. at Los Angeles, 1968; postgrad. U. So. Calif., summer 1969; J.D., U. Iowa, 1971. Sec., Joseph Mayfield Realty Co., Inglewood, Calif., summers 1968-69; research asst. Meardon, Sueppel & Downer, Iowa City, 1970-71; admitted to Iowa bar, 1971, Calif. bar, 1972; mem. legal div., corp. fin. dept. Atlantic Richfield Co., Los Angeles, 1972-74; atty. legal div. gen. corp. dept., litigation dept. Pacific Lighting Corp.-So. Calif. Gas Co., Los Angeles, 1974-80; Los Angeles Mcpl. Ct. judge, 1980—; commr. adoptions County of Los Angeles; chmn. subcom. on summons and small claims Adv. Com. on Legal Forms; established night small claims ct., 1981. Chmn. bd. dirs. Community Legal Awareness Corp., 1974-78; bd. dirs. Black Law Center, 1972-74, Crenshaw Family YMCA; mem. legal redress com. NAACP, 1973, br. treas. Los Angeles, 1975, 76, 3d v.p. 1978-80, dir. nominations-image awards, 1979; bd. dirs. Bridgeback, 1975—; mem. pro bono legal council Multiservice Family Center, 1976-78; mem. Citizens Adv. Council on Corps. for Sec. State's Office, 1975-80; mem. So. Calif. Democratic Women's Caucus, 1975—, alt. del. 1976 Dem. Nat. Conv., mem. 1976 Dem. Nat. Credentials Com., mem. Calif. State Central Com., 1977-79. Mem. Am., Calif. (pub. affairs com. 1974-75, legal services exec. com. 1977-80, preliminary disciplinary investigation com. 1975-80), Los Angeles County (trustee 1976, vice chmn. human rights com. 1977), Iowa, John M. Langston (pres. 1974-76, Outstanding Service award 1976), Minority (pres. 1979-80), Nat. (bd. dirs. women's div. 1978—) bar assns., Africare, Calif. Assn. Black Lawyers (pres. 1978-79), Black Women Lawyers of Calif., Calif. Women Lawyers, Los Angeles Urban League, Los Angeles Women Lawyers Assn., Nat. Conf. Black Lawyers, Calif. Judges Assn., Jud. Council Calif., Nat. Assn. Women Judges, Calif. Assn. Women Judges, Phi Alpha Delta. Baptist. Clubs: Women Elks, Black Women's Forum. Office: Los Angeles Mcpl Ct 110 N Grand Ave Los Angeles CA 90012

THOMAS, MILDRED REINWALD (MRS. LLEWYN U. THOMAS), ret. educator; b. Galeton, Pa., Apr. 11, 1912; d. Walter J. and Nora (Woodhouse) Reinwald; B.S., Mansfield State Tchrs. Coll., 1933; M.S., Syracuse U., 1954; postgrad. Alfred U., 1947-48, Buffalo State U., 1947; m. Llewyn U. Thomas, June 3, 1936; 1 son, Llewyn Walter. Tchr., Potter County (Pa.) Schs., 1933-42, N.Y. State Public Schs., 1942-63; asst. prof. and primary edn. supr. State U. N.Y. at Cortland, 1963-74, emeritus, 1974—. Leader Girl Scouts, 1942-63; active YWCA; mem. Animal Welfare League Charlotte County; children's work chmn. Geneva-Lyons Presbyterial Assn., 1956-58; pres. Cortland County Women's Republican Club, 1969, 70; mem. exec. com. N.Y. State Fedn. Rep. Women; del.-at-large Nat. Fedn. Rep. Women Conv., 1971; sec. Charlotte County Rep. Club, 1980-81; pres. Federated Rep. Women's Club, 1982; mem. Spl. Persons Advocacy League Charlotte County; deacon, ordained elder Presbyterian Ch.; mem. exec. com. Susquehanna Valley Presbyterial, 1975-77; ch. sch. supt. First Presbyn. Ch. of Port Charlotte, 1980-81. Mem. DAR (past regent Tioughnioga chpt.), NEA, Assn. Higher Edn., Internat. Reading Assn., Retarded Children's Assn. Cortland County, Cortland County Hist. Soc., AAUW (pres.; chmn. resolutions com. state div. bd.), Yates-Ontawa Tchrs. Assn. (pres. 1961), LWV. Presbyterian. Club: Order Eastern Star. Home: 338 Lasayette Dr Port Charlotte FL 33952

THOMAS, MIRIAM MASON HIGGINS, chemist; b. Chgo., June 22, 1920; d. William Henry and Mame (Mason) Higgins; B.S., Bennett Coll., 1940; M.S., U. Chgo., 1942; m. Lucius Howard Thomas, Sept. 6, 1947; 1 son, Brian Kevin. Research asst. U. Chgo., 1942-45; research chemist Quartermaster Food & Container Inst., Chgo., 1945-62; research chemist U.S. Army Natick Research and Devel. Labs., Natick, Mass., 1962—; vis. lectr. M.I.T., 1974—. Sec. of Army research and study fellow, 1975-76. Mem. Assn. Vitamin Chemists, AAAS, Inst. Food Technology, Animal Nutrition Research Council, Coblentz Soc., Soc. Nutrition Edn., Sigma Xi, Sigma Delta Epsilon, Delta Sigma Theta. Contbg. author: Methods of Vitamin Assay, 1951, 66; Encyclopedia of Food Technology, 1974; Nutritional Evaluation of Food Processing, 1975; Encyclopedia of Food Science, 1978. Home: 57 Eaton Rd Framingham MA 01701 Office: US Army Natick Research and Devel Labs Sci and Advanced Tech Lab Natick MA 01760

THOMAS, NANCY NOBLE, councilwoman; b. Pitts., Aug. 18, 1928; d. Albert Garfield and Neva (Loomis) Noble; student Md. Coll. for Women, 1946-47, Curry Coll., 1947-48; m. Donald Bartlett Thomas, June 11, 1949; children—Douglas, Cynthia, Cathryn, Gregory. Mem. Town Bd. of Webster (N.Y.), 1976-83, dep. town supr.; owner, operator One to One Miniatures; cons. Rochester Women's Career Devel. Center. Bd. dirs. Webster Community Chest; town co-chmn. ARC Blood Drive, 1978-80; chmn. Bicentennial Ball, 1976; parade chmn. Independence Day, 1978-80; memls. chmn. Ch. of the Good Shepherd, 1978-82; Monroe County committeewoman, 1975-82. Recipient hon. mention as Woman of Yr., N.Y. State Fedn. Women's Clubs, 1977; Webster Bus. and Profl. Women, 1976. Mem. State Fedn. Women's Clubs (state protocol chmn. 1981-84), Nat. Assn. Miniature Enthusiasts, Webster C. of C. (chmn. planning 1978-80). Republican. Episcopalian. Clubs: Webster Bus. and Profl. Women, Guardians 1978-80), Women's of Webster (founding mem.). Home: 402 Bittersweet Ln Webster NY 14580 Office: 1000 Ridge Rd Webster NY 14580

THOMAS, NELDA JO HALL, nurse; b. Vernon, Tex., Dec. 21, 1923; d. Joseph Lonzo and Sallie Verona (Bolton) Hall; student Vernon Regional Jr. Coll., 1973-74; Asso. degree in Nursing, Midwestern State U. Sch. Nursing, 1976; m. Charles S. Thomas, Apr. 12, 1942; children—Sylvia, Randy, Greg, Scotty, Gordon. Secretarial position, 1940-41; employee SSS, 1941-42; hostess Canton Cafe, 1972-73; specialist I, Mental Health-Mental Retardation Center, Vernon, 1972-76; nurse supr. Chillicothe Hosp., Chillicothe, Tex., 1976-78; staff nurse Wilbarger Gen. Hosp., 1978-80; dir. nurses Home Health Agy. Tex., 1981—. Pres. Northside Parent Tchr. Orgn., 1969-71; bd. dirs. Campfire Girls, 1956-59; den mother Boy Scouts Am., 1970-72; dir. Fargo United Methodist Vacation Ch. Sch., 1960-63; tchr. Sunday sch. Fargo United Meth. Ch., 1966-72; pres. United Meth. Women, 1969-73. Recipient Service award Boy Scouts Am., 1971; registered nurse, Tex. Club: Northside Booster. Home: Route 2 Box 106 Vernon TX 76384

THOMAS, PATRICIA ANNE, law librarian; b. Cleve., Aug. 21, 1927; d. Richard Joseph and Marietta Bernadette (Teevans) T.; B.A., Case Western Res. U., 1949, J.D., 1951. Admitted to Ohio bar, 1951, U.S. Supreme Ct. bar, 1980; librarian Arter & Hadden, Cleve., 1951-62; asst. librarian, then librarian IRS, Washington, 1962-78; library dir. Adminstrv. Office, U.S. Cts., 1978—. Mem. Am. Assn. Law Libraries, Law Librarians Soc. D.C. (pres. 1967-69). Office: Adminstrv Office US Cts Washington DC 20544

THOMAS, PEGGY RUTH, railroad exec.; b. Granite, Okla., Dec. 19, 1933; d. Sidney Durrell and Ruth Mae (Tuley) Coffman; student U. Okla., 1951-52, Southwestern State Coll., Okla., 1952-53; m. Donald Edward Thomas, Feb. 26, 1969; children—Gene Lowell Gustafson, Richard Lynn Gustafson. Procurement specialist U.S. Air Force, Altus AFB, Okla., 1953-55, contract specialist, 1962-66; procurement specialist U.S. Air Force, Dyess AFB, Tex., 1955-58, Clinton-Sherman AFB, Okla., 1960-61, chief supply procurement br. Altus AFB, Okla. and Mountain Home AFB, Idaho, 1966-71; dep. chief base procurement div. Mountain Home AFB, 1972-76, chief services and constrn. contracts div. Alaskan Air Command, Elmendorf AFB, Alaska, 1976-78; chief contracting and gen. services div. U.S. Fish and Wildlife Service, Anchorage, 1978-79; chief purchasing div. Municipality of Anchorage, 1979; mgr. supply and procurement div. Alaska R.R., Anchorage, 1979—. Recipient Air Force Civilian Service award, 1966, 75; Air Force Incentive award, 1967, 72; Air Force Cert. of Achievement for Resources Conservation, 1968, 75, 76; Military Airlift Command Personal Achievement award, 1971; Tactical Air Command Personal Achievement award, 1973; Gov.'s Disting. Public Service award State of Idaho, 1973; nat. program award for Keeping Am. Beautiful, 1973. Mem. Nat. Assn. Female Execs., Am. Bus. Women's Assn., Nat. Fedn. Bus. and Profl. Women, Fed. Exec. Assn. Home: Star Route A Box 85T Anchorage AK 99507 Office: Supply Management Division Alaska Railroad Pouch 7-2111 Anchorage AK 99510

THOMAS, RHONDA MARIE, state legislator; b. Lawton, Okla., June 17, 1944; d. Harold S. and Augusta M. (Carter) Cox; student Glendale (Ariz.) Community Coll.; m. Ronald E. Thomas, Mar. 31, 1961; children—Mark H., Alicia M., Eric J. Mem. Ariz. Ho. of Reps., 1981—, mem. transp., health, agr. coms., vice chmn. com. on tourism, professions and occupations; del. Nat. Conf. State Legislatures, 1981, Western Conf. Council State Govts., 1981, Am. Council Young Polit. Leaders, 1981. Bd. dirs. YMCA Model Legislature; mem. Ariz. Health Care Cost Containment System, Commn. on Natural Healing Arts; mem. Nat. Council State Govts.; mem. Commn. on Organizational Planning. Pres. Roadrunner Republican Women; v.p. Pop Warner Football Assn.; bd. dirs. Palo Verde Sch. Parent Tchrs. orgn.; mem. Theodore Roosevelt Council Boy Scouts Am.; mem. Coordinating Council of Women; state del. Ariz. Rep. Conv., 1980, precinct committeeman, dep. registrar Dist. 16, 1979-81. Mem. Nat. Rep. Legislators Assn., Am. Legis. Exchange Council, Orgn. Women Legislators. Office: 1700 W. Washington Phoenix AZ 85007

THOMAS, ROCHELLE KATHRYN, govt. ops. cons.; b. Shreveport, La., Oct. 18, 1941; d. Stuart B. and Christine D. (Kozeal) Stafford; B.S., U. Nebr., 1963; children—John, Michael. Project mgr. Nat. Airlines-Pan Am. merger Steel Hector Davis law firm, Miami, Fla., 1978-80, mgr. spl. projects, 1980-81; pres. Rochelle K. Thomas, Inc., Coral Gables, Fla., 1981—. Mem. Lehland Commn., Dem. Nat. Com., 1981-82. Mem. Hist. Soc. S. Fla., Ins. Exchange of the Ams., Greater Miami C. of C. (legis. com. 1979-80), Am. Pub. Transit Assn. Democrat. Club: Bankers. Address: 3618 Palmarito St Coral Gables FL 33134

THOMAS, SANDRA (SANDY) JORDAN, educator; b. Greenville, Miss., Feb. 5, 1947; d. Charles M. and Zell (Williams) Jordan; B.A., U. Miss., 1969; postgrad. U. S.W. Fla., 1970, Ouachita Bapt. U., 1971, Ark. State U., 1972, 78; m. Wallace Thomas, Apr. 11, 1974 (div. 1978); 1 dau., Sonya Kaye; m. James Cook Read, May 9, 1981; 1 son, Jordan Andrew. English tchr., sponsor sch. paper Pryor Jr. High Sch., Ft. Walton Beach, Fla., 1969-70; tchr., drama prodn. coach Choctaw High Sch., near Philadelphia, Miss., summer 1970; tchr., sponsor sch. paper Wynne (Ark.) High Sch., 1970-79; tchr. remedial English, journalism and psychology, Newton (Miss.) High Sch., 1979—, sponsor sch. paper and lit. jour.; columnist, feature writer, photographer Wynne Progress, 1972-79; public relations rep. for Newton City Schs.; condr. workshops in field. Active Ark. affiliate Am. Heart Assn., 1973-79, state publicity bd., 1974, city chmn., 1978, organizer Bikeathon, 1977, Skateathon, 1978, Danceathon, 1979, county co-chmn., 1979; substitute Sunday Sch. tchr., mem. choir Bapt. Ch., active Bapt. Young Women. Named young career woman of yr., Bus. and Profl. Women, 1974. Mem. Ark. Edn. Assn., Nat. Press Women Assn. (awards 1974), Ark. Press Women's Assn. (awards 1974). Clubs: Order Eastern Star, Beta Sigma Phi (Girl of Year, 1978, pres., 1979). Home: 205 E Church Newton MS 39345 Office: Box 150 Newton High School School St Newton MS 39345

THOMAS, SUSAN JANE, mktg. exec.; b. Omaha, Sept. 20, 1953; d. Earl Wayne and Helen Marie (Muller) T.; A.B., Vassar Coll., 1975; M.B.A., Harvard U., 1980; student Macalester Coll., 1971-73. Asst. treas. Morgan Guaranty Trust Co., N.Y.C., 1975-78; cons. The Boston Cons. Group, 1979; asso. Booz, Allen & Hamilton, Inc., N.Y.C., 1980-82; mktg. mgr. Merrill, Lynch Pierce Fenner & Smith, N.Y.C., 1982—; N.Y.C. div. head Macalester Coll. Campaign for the 1980's, 1981-82. Mem. Fin. Women's Assn. N.Y., Women's Econ. Roundtable, Nat. Abortion Rights Action League, NOW. Democrat. Clubs: Harvard of N.Y., Harvard Bus. Sch. N.Y., Vassar of N.Y., Macalester of N.Y., N.J. and Conn. Home: 247 E 28th St New York NY 10016 Office: 165 Broadway New York NY 10080

THOMAS, SUSAN JOYCE, educator; b. Eau Claire, Wis., Feb. 18, 1943; d. William C. and Dorothy C. Moore; B.A., Wis. State U., 1965; M.S., Purdue U., 1967, Ph.D., 1969; m. Hollie Thomas, Mar. 26, 1970; children—Tamara, Tiffany. Instr., Purdue U., 1969; asst. prof. U. Ill., 1969-74, asst. dir. research and testing, 1969-71; asst. dir. ERIC Clearinghouse Early Childhood Edn., 1971-74; asst. prof. Fla. State U., Tallahassee, 1974-76, asso. prof. child devel., 1976—, dir. Resource Center Woman's Programs, 1978—, dir. Center Human Devel., 1982—; cons. Nat. Displaced Homemaker Network. Social chmn., historian Tallahassee Newcomers, 1975-76. Recipient Developing Scholar award Fla. State U., 1978-79. Mem. Am. Psychol. Assn., Am. Ednl. Research Assn. (newsletter editor 1978-80, chmn. research on women and edn. 1981-82; div. program chair 1982-84), Soc. Research in Child Devel., Nat. Council Measurement in Edn. Methodist. Co-author: Evaluation without Fear, 1980; also articles. Home: 3747 Shamrock St W Tallahassee FL 32308 Office: 103 Sandels Fla State Univ Tallahassee FL 32306

THOMAS, SYLVIA JEAN, nurse; b. Texarkana, Ark., Sept. 9, 1947; d. Charles Carroll and Cornelia Alyne (Davis) Sprague; A.D. in Nursing, Texarkana Community Coll., 1972; student Paris Jr. Coll., 1974, 75; B.S. in Health Care Adminstrn., East Tex. State U., 1979; m. James Richard Thomas, Dec. 18, 1971; children—Stephanie Lynn, Stacy Glen. X-ray technician instr. St. Michaels Hosp., Texarkana, 1968, asst. chief technologist, radiology dept., 1968-70, nurse emergency dept., 1972; charge nurse David Granberry Meml. Hosp., Naples, Tex., 1972-77, edn. dir., 1977—, infection control nurse, 1977, coordinator edn., quality assurance, infection control, 1981—. Basic life support instr. Am. Heart Assn., 1979; former instr. swimming ARC; sec. local unit Am. Cancer Soc., 1981; v.p. Young Homemakers Am., 1982; active Girl Scouts U.S. Registered radiologic technologist Am. Registry Radiol. Tech.; cert. in advanced cardiac life support. Mem. Tex. Soc. Radiologic Technologists, Hopsco Shared Services Ednl. Adv. Com., East Tex. Div. Hosp. Educators of Am. Hosp. Assn. (sec.-treas. 1981). Roman Catholic. Home: Route 2 Box 169 Omaha TX 75571 Office: David Granberry Meml Hosp Naples TX 75568

THOMAS, TERESA ANN, biologist, educator; b. Wilkes-Barre, Pa., Oct. 17, 1939; d. Sam Charles and Edna Grace Thomas; B.S. cum laude, Coll. Misericordia, 1961; M.S. in Biology, Am. U. Beirut, 1965; M.S. in Microbiology, U. So. Calif., 1973. Tchr., sci. supr., curriculum coordinator Meyers High Sch., Wilkes-Barre, 1962-64, Wilkes-Barre Area Public Schs., 1961-66; research asso. Proctor Found. for Research in Ophthalmology U. Calif. Med. Center, San Francisco, 1966-68; instr. Robert Coll. of Istanbul (Turkey), 1968-71, Am. Edn. in Luxembourg, 1971-72, Bosco Tech. Inst., Rosemead, Calif., 1973-74, San Diego Community Coll. Dist., 1974-80; instr. math-sci. div. Southwestern Coll., Chula Vista, Calif., 1980—; adj. asst. prof. Chapman Coll., San Diego, 1974-80; asst. prof. San Diego State U., 1977-79; chmn. Am. Colls. Istanbul Sci. Week, 1969-71; mem. adv. bd. Chapman Coll. Community Center, 1979-80. Pres. Internat. Relations Club 1959-61; mem. San Francisco World Affairs Council, 1966-68; mem. exec. bd. U.S. Orgn. Med. and Ednl. Needs No. Calif., 1967-68. NSF fellow, 1965; USPHS fellow, 1972-73; Pa. Heart Assn. research grantee, 1962. Mem. Am. Soc. Microbiology, Nat. Sci. Tchrs. Assn., Nat. Assn. Biology Tchrs. San Diego Natural History Mus., S.D. Zool. Soc., Calif. Tchrs. Assn., NEA, MENSA, Arab Am. Med. Assn., Arab Am. Univ. Grads., San Diego Ecology Center, Am.-Lebanese Assn. San Diego (chmn. scholarship com.), Kappa Gamma Pi, Sigma Phi Sigma. Club: Am. Lebanese Syrian Ladies (pres. 1982-84). Office: Southwestern College 900 Otay Lakes Rd Chula Vista CA 92010

THOMAS, VICKI ANN, communications co. exec.; b. Chgo., Jan. 7, 1946; d. Charles K. and Lillian T. (Chuckwins) Pazar; B.S., U. Wis., Stevens Point, 1968; m. Stephen J. Thomas, Sept. 19, 1970. Feature editor Credit Union Nat. Assn., Madison, Wis., 1971-75, dir. advt., 1975-77, v.p. mktg. and advt., 1971-80; account exec. ABC, Chgo., 1980—; tchr. Madison Area Tech. Sch., 1979-80. Mem. Profl. Communicators Wis. (v.p. 1979-80). Republican. Roman Catholic. Club: Chgo. Ad. Author: How to Make Advertising Work for Your Financial Institution, 1977. Home: 7264 Mile Rd Sun Prairie WI 53590 Office: 233 N. Michigan Ave Suite 1923 Chicago IL 60601

THOMAS, VIRGINIA LEE, microscopist; b. Traer, Iowa, Sept. 22, 1916; d. Paul and Zenaide Vonhesion (Kahler) T.; grad. Gates Coll., 1939, U. Mich., 1943. Spectrographer Rock Island (Ill.) Arsenal, 1943-45; electron microscopist U.S. Rubber Research Labs., Passaic, N.J., 1945-54; group leader Interchem. Research Labs., N.Y.C., 1954-62; research scientist Am. Standard Research Lab., Piscataway, N.J., 1962-68; lectr., supr. microscopy U. Medicine and Dentistry, Rutgers U. Med. Sch., Piscataway, 1968—. Active Westfield Human Rights, Plainfield Joint Def., Rainbow Food Coop, ACLU. Fellow N.Y. Microscopical Soc. (pres. 1960-61, Ashby award 1962); mem. Electron Microscopical Soc. Am., N.Y. Soc. Electron Microscopists. Clubs: Sierra, Porsche Club Am., Nat. Wildlife Assn., Nature Conservancy. Contbr. chpts. to books in field, articles to profl. jours. Home: 2369 Whittier Ave Westfield NJ 07090 Office: Rutgers Med Sch Dept Microbiology Piscataway NJ 08854

THOMAS, WANDA GAYLE, electric co. exec.; b. Shreveport, La., Apr. 12, 1951; d. Dallas Cleveland and Annie Jean (Basinger) Robinette; grad. in acctg. Vocat. Tech. Center, 1970; student La. State U., 1969-71; m. George C. Thomas, June 5, 1970; 1 son, G. Christopher. Bookkeeper, Interstate Electric Co., Inc., Shreveport, 1971-74, asst. controller, 1974—. Jr. Achievement adviser, 1980-81; active ERA, 1980—. Named An Outstanding Young Woman of Am., 1980. Mem. Nat. Assn. Female Execs. Democrat. Baptist. Club: Shreveport Bus. and Profl. Women (treas. 1979-80, pres. 1981-82). Home: 7217 Louise St Shreveport LA 71108 Office: Interstate Electric Co Inc PO Box 31094 Shreveport LA 71130

THOMASON, WILMA FULKS, ins. co. exec.; b. Oklahoma City, Feb. 25, 1932; d. Willard Gordon and Eddie May (Norvell) Fulks; B.B.A., U. Okla., Norman, 1953. With various oil cos., 1953-73; with Modern Woodmen of Am., Oklahoma City, 1974—, life underwriter, estate and fin. planner, 1982—. Recipient Disting. Life Underwriters award Liberty Bank, Oklahoma City, 1982; nat. speaker Nat. Conv. Life Underwriters, Boston, 1977, 78, 79. Mem. Oklahoma City Assn. Life Underwriters, Nat. Assn. Life Underwriters, Million Dollar Round Table (Nat. Sales Achievement award 1982, Nat. Quality award 1982. Women Leader award 1982). Congregationalist. Clubs: Oklahoma City Women's Forum, Desk and Derrick, Modern Woodmen Am. Contbr. articles in field to profl. publs. Home: 5906 N Vermont St Oklahoma City OK 73112 Office: 2403 NW 39th Expressway Oklahoma City OK 73112

THOMAS-PHILLIPS, LINDA, multimedia prodn. co. exec.; b. Chgo., Mar. 29, 1940; d. William David and Christina (Yonan) Thomas; B.S., Northwestern U., 1963; m. Michael Terrance Phillips, Dec. 4, 1976. Research asst. CBS, 1962-63; sr. research analyst, mktg. research specialist Bell & Howell Co., Chgo., 1963-68; project dir., writer Instructional Dynamics Inc., Chgo., 1969-78, dir. multimedia prodn. and mktg., 1978—. Republican. Presbyterian. Author: Educator's Guide to Creative Audio Tape Techniques, 1973; Allied Health Occupations Series, 1975-76; Energy Now and in the Future, 1977; The On-Site Residential Manager Self-Study Program, 1977; Food and Energy, 1978; Adult Writing and Reading Experiences, 1980; producer: (multi-image presentation) Journey Toward 2000, 1981; contbr. articles to various publs. Office: 666 N Lake Shore Dr Chicago IL 60611

THOMASSEN, JANE, educator; b. Tracy, Iowa, July 28, 1932; d. Gerritt Edward and Bertha Ethel (Davis) Thomassen; B.S. cum laude SUNY, New Paltz, 1965, M.S. summa cum laude, 1973; m. Sylvester D. Van Oort, Sept. 3, 1950 (div. 1968); children—Janis K., Kathleen V.O. Davis, Marcus K. Tchr., South Orangetown Public Schs., 1965-66; tchr., union rep. Ramapo Public Schs., Suffern, N.Y., 1966-71; tchr. Clarkstown Public Schs., 1971—; radio announcer, 1975-76; instr., cons. Evelyn Wood Reading Dynamics, 1967-71. Pres. bd. mgrs. Bon Aire Three Condominium, 1978-81; choir dir. Reformed Ch., Beacon and Glenham, N.Y., 1958-62; mem. human relations com. Clarkstown Schs., 1982—; Mem. United Fedn. Tchrs., AFL-CIO, N.Y. State United Tchrs., Clarkstown Tchrs. Assn., Rockland County Tchrs. Assn., Kappa Delta Pi. Democrat. Home: 16 Somerset Dr Suffern NY 10901 Office: 121 Phillips Hill Rd New City NY 10956

THOMAS-STEED, GWENDOLYN ROSEMARIE, gen. contracting exec.; b. N.Y.C., Aug. 30, 1940; d. Ricardo Nicasius and Virginia Maria (Emanuel) Thomas; B.B.A., Baruch Coll., 1975; divorced; 1 son, Joseph Alphanso Steed. Unit head Citibank, N.Y.C., 1959-65; Interviewer Ace Industries, W. Africa, 1967-68; supr. Chase Manhattan Bank, N.Y.C., 1975-80; pres. St. Croix Realty Corp., N.Y.C., 1979—; speaker, cons. in field. Mem. Assn. Bus. and Profl. Women in Constrn., Westchester Minority Contractors Assn. Office: PO Box 839 Boulevard Station Bronx NY 10459

THOMAS-ZIMMERMAN, SHARI ANN, communications co. exec.; b. Bakersfield, Calif., July 27, 1946; d. Vernon David and Jacqueline Sharon (Kramer) Hobbs; A.A., West Valley Jr. Coll., 1968; B.S., San Jose State U., 1972; children by previous marriage—Michelle, Richard, Garld. Asst. dir. core area devel. San Jose C. of C., 1969-71; asst. dir. health occupations Modesto Jr. Coll., 1971-75; mgr. Microwave Assos. Communications Co., Sunnyvale, Calif., 1978-81; field engring. supr. Four Phase Systems, Inc., Cupertino, Calif., 1981—. Mem. Nat. Assn. Female Execs. (network dir.). Home: 410 Auburn Way Apt 33 San Jose CA 95129 Office: 10700 N De Anza Blvd Cupertino CA 95014

THOMPSEN, JOYCE ANN, mfg. co. exec.; b. Owatonna, Minn., Mar. 21, 1946; d. Stanley Albert and Elda Margaret (Buehring) Moeckly; B.S. in Mass Communications/Bus. Adminstrn., Mankato (Minn.) State U.; m. Paul Jerome Thompsen, Jan. 21, 1967; children—James P., Matthew J. Exec. sec. Jostens, Inc., Owatonna, 1964-71; univ. relations supr. U. Minn., Waseca, 1971-72; corp. sec., asst. to chmn. and pres. E.F. Johnson Co., Waseca, 1972—, v.p. adminstrn., corp. sec., 1981—; owner Thompsen Alternator Rebuilders Co., Owatonna and Waseca, 1976—; v.p. and dir. P.J. Thompsen, Inc., 1980—; lectr. U. Minn.; adv. schs. on bus. programs. Pres. Am. Lutheran Ch. Women, Waseca, 1980; bd. dirs. Waseca Concert Assn.; soloist Waseca Chorale; mem. Com. to Settle Dislocated S.E. Asian Families. Mem. Women in Mgmt. Group, Am. Electronics Assn. (human resources com. of Minn. Council), Nat. Assn. Women Bus. Owners. Clubs: Minn. Ind. Republican Century; Waseca Lakeside. Home: 26 Valleyview St Waseca MN 56093 Office: 299 10th Ave SW Waseca MN 56093

THOMPSON, ANNE ELISE, judge; b. Phila., July 8, 1934; d. Leroy H. and Mary E. (Jackson) Jenkins; B.A., Howard U., 1955, LL.B., 1964; M.A., Temple U., 1957; m. William H. Thompson, June 19, 1965; children—William H., Sharon A. Admitted to N.J. bar, 1966; judge Mcpl. Ct., 1972-75, U.S. Dist. Ct., Trenton, N.J., 1979—; Mercer County prosecutor, 1975-79. Recipient Disting. Service award Nat. Dist. Attys. Assn., 1979. Mem. Am. Bar Assn., N.J. Bar Assn., Mercer County Bar Assn. Democrat. Office: PO Box 401 Trenton NJ 08618

THOMPSON, ANNIE LAURA, educator; b. Henderson, Tenn., July 8, 1937; d. Wesley Sylvester and Letha Irene (Jones) T.; student U. Ala., 1956-59; B.A. magna cum laude, M.A., Duke U., 1960; Ph.D., Tulane U., 1973; postgrad. U. Noroeste of Argentina, 1980; m. Edward L. Patterson, June 7, 1980. Instr. Spanish, U. Miss., 1960-64, Auburn (Ala.) U., 1964-66; asso. prof. Delgado Community Coll., New Orleans, 1970—. Recipient Outstanding Tchr. award Delgado Coll., 1974; Woodrow Wilson fellow, 1959-60. Mem. AAUP, MLA (2d v.p. Miss. sect. 1961-62), Phi Beta Kappa, Sigma Delta Pi, Phi Alpha Theta, Spring Fiesta Assn. Mem. Ch. of Christ. Author: Religious Elements in the Quijote, 1960; The Attempt of Spanish Intellectuals to Create a New Spain: 1930-36, 1973; asso. editor The Crusader, 1962-64. Home: 7008 Memphis St New Orleans LA 70124 Office: Dept Spanish Delgado Community Coll New Orleans LA 70119

THOMPSON, BARBARA RICKS, govt. ofcl.; b. Washington, May 3, 1933; d. Vernon Heubutt and Eleanor Velario (Coburn) Ricks; B.S., Howard U., 1954, M.S., 1956; m. Alfred E. Thompson, June 27, 1970. With IRS, Washington, 1957—, dir. program staff resources mgmt., 1978—, coordinator fed. women's program, 1970-73. Bd. dirs. Wider Opportunities for Women, Washington, 1975-80, chairperson, 1979-80; v.p. U.S. conf. World Council Chs., 1978—; pres. commn. on status and role of women United Methodist Ch., 1972-78. Mem. Fed. Exec. Inst. Alumni Assn., Howard U. Alumni Assn. Club: Order Eastern Star. Home: 11215 Oakleaf Dr Apt 1902 Silver Spring MD 20901 Office: 1111 Constitution Ave NW Washington DC 20224

THOMPSON, BARBARA STORCK, state ofcl., educator; b. McFarland, Wis., Oct. 15, 1924; d. John C. and Marie Ann (Kassabaum) T.; B.S., Wis. State U.-Platteville, 1956; M.S., U. Wis.-Madison, 1959, Ph.D., 1969; postgrad. U. Iowa, Mt. Mary Coll., U. Wis.-Milw.; L.H.D., Carroll Coll., Waukesha, Wis.; m. Glenn T. Thompson, July 1, 1944; children—David C., James T. Tchr. elementary schs., Mt. Horeb, Wis., 1944-56; instr. Green County Tchrs. Coll., Monroe, Wis., 1956-57; curriculum coordinator Monroe Public Schs., 1957-60; instr. U. Wis.-Platteville, 1960; supr. schs., psychologist, reading specialist Waukesha (Wis.) Public Schs., 1960-62; adminstr., prin. Fairview Elementary Schs., Brookfield, Wis., 1962-64; adminstrv. cons. Wis. Dept. Public Instrn., Madison, 1964-72, state coordinator individually guided edn., 1971-72, state supt. public instrn., 1973-81; instr. supervision instrn. U. Wis.-Madison, 1972. Participant White House Conf. Children, Washington, 1970; mem. Wis. Gov.'s Com. State Conf. Children and Youth, 1970, Wis. Gov.'s Manpower Council, 1973—; mem. Wis. State Adv. Bd. Early Childhood Edn., from 1971; bd. dirs. Vocat., Tech. and Adult Edn., 1973—, Ednl. Communications, 1973—, Higher Edn. Aids, 1973—, Agy. Instructional TV, 1975—. Recipient State Conservation award Lions, Madison; named Your Madisonian, Wis. State Jour., 1970; named hon. state farmer Future Farmers Am., 1975, recipient Distinguished Service award Bloomer (Wis.) chpt., 1974; award of distinction Nat. Council Adminstrv. Women, 1974; Spl. Service award Vocat. Indsl. Clubs Am., 1974; Distinguised Service award Badger Boys State, Am. Legion, 1975; Outstanding Service award Wis. Assn. Vocat. Agr. Tchrs., 1974; Distinguished Alumnus award U. Wis.-Platteville, 1974; various 4-H awards; named life mem. Wis. Congress Parents and Tchrs. Mem. Nat. Council Adminstrv. Women in Edn. (Woman of Year), Nat. Council State Cons. in Elementary Edn. (pres.), Wis. Assn. Sch. Dist. Adminstrs., Nat., Wis. assns. supervision and curriculum devel., Nat., Wis. elementary sch. prins. assns., Nat., Wis. secondary prins. assns., Nat., Wis. sch. bus. ofcls., PTA, NEA, Wis. (life) Edn. So. Wis. Edn. Assn., Wis. Ednl. Research Assn., Internat. Assn. Childhood Edn., Pi Lambda Theta, Alpha Beta. Address: 3591 Sabaka Trail Verona WI 53593

THOMPSON, CAROLYN ANN, antique dealer; b. Pitts., Nov. 27, 1922; d. Ralph Henry and Velda C. White; nightstudent Cleve. Coll.; m. John Chambers Thompson, Nov. 10, 1945; children—John Chambers, Woodson Mark. With Mantaline Corp., Mantua, Ohio, 1969-71; owner Thompson Antiques, Mantau, 1974—; zoning commnr. Mantua Twp., 1958-66; mayor of Mantua Village, 1976—. Past pres. Mantua Village PTA, Crestwood Band Patrons; past chmn. Mantua Beautification Com.; chmn. Mantua Village Cemetery Assn., 1974—; past co-leader Mantua Center Chi Rho; past den mother and mem. pack com. Mantua Center Cub Scouts. Mem. Mantua Grange (past master). Republican. Presbyterian. Clubs: Mantua Center Garden (charter officer), Mantua Village Garden (past officer). Address: 4514 W Prospect St Mantua OH 44255

THOMPSON, DEBORAH KEMP, neighborhood resource center exec.; b. Mobile, Mar. 3, 1947; d. Hattie Robinson Kemp; B.A. in French and English, U. Minn., 1970; married; children—Michelle Rae, LuVeidya. Data processing clk. Cargill, Inc., Mpls., 1969-71; program dir. NAACP, Mpls., 1971; universal teller Northwestern Nat. Bank, Mpls., 1971-73; procedures writer Lutheran Brotherhood Ins. Co., Mpls., 1973; adminstr. asst. Jacksonville (Fla.) Urban League-Bus. Devel. Center, 1974-75; dir. housing counseling program Jacksonville Urban League, 1975-80; exec. dir. Neighborhood Resource Center, Jacksonville, 1980—; instr. Fla. Jr. Coll.; cons. in field. Recipient various certs. appreciation. Mem. Nat. Assn. Female Execs. (network dir.), Consumer Credit Counseling Service (chairwoman), N.E. Fla. Planning and Zoning Assn. Home: 8220 Kensington Sq Jacksonville FL 32211 Office: 333 Laura St Jacksonville FL 32202

THOMPSON, DIDI (MARY BENNETT) CASTLE, writer, editor; b. Terre Haute, Ind., Feb. 7, 1918; d. Robert Langley Bennett and Marjorie Rose (Tyler) Bennett Castle; student U. Ill., Champaign, 1935-36, U. Ky., 1936-39; m. Jamie Campbell Thompson, Jr., June 24, 1939; children—Jamie, Julia King Thompson Balko, Marjorie Castle. News editor Glen-Echoes, Glencoe, Ill., 1930; columnist Ky. Kernel, U. Ky., Lexington, 1937-39; radio script writer Modern Am. Music, 1940-42; asst. pub. relations dir. Salem Coll., Winston-Salem, N.C., 1945; pub. relations chmn. Barrington (Ill.) Horse Show, 1959-67; staff writer, columnist Barrington Press Newspapers, 1958—; editor ECHO, Defenders of the Fox River, Inc. newsletter, 1970—; travel editor Barrington Press Newspapers, 1973—; freelance writer, 1943—. Past bd. mem. Barrington chpt. Lyric Opera Guild Chgo., Barrington Sr. Center, Infant Welfare Soc. Chgo., Art Inst. Chgo., Barrington Assos.; elected trustee Village of Barrington Hills, 1969-73, health, pub. relations chmn., 1969-73. Mem. Women in Communications (past dir.), Citizens for Conservation, Inc. (past dir.), Barrington Countryside Assn. (past dir.), Barrington Hist. Soc., Spring Creek Basset Hounds Club, Barrington Hills Riding Club (past dir.), Pan Hellenic Council, DAR, Chgo. Press Club, Chi Omega. Episcopalian. Address: 94 Otis Rd Barrington IL 60010

THOMPSON, DOROTHY BROWN, writer, poet; b. Springfield, Ill., May 14, 1896; d. William Joseph and Harriet (Gardner) Brown; A.B., U. Kans., 1919; m. Dale Moore Thompson, July 2, 1921; 1 son, William Brown Began writing professionally, 1931; contbr. verse to nat. mags. and newspapers including Saturday Rev., Sat. Evening Post, Va. Quar. Rev., Poetry (Chgo.), Commonweal, Good Housekeeping; author research articles for hist. jours.; poems pub. in numerous collections and textbooks, mags. and textbooks in Eng., Can., Australia, Sweden, N.Z., 26 in Braille; poems selected for art exhbt. Contemporary Gallery, Jewish Community Center, Kansas City, Mo., 1976, 77, 78, 79, 80; 10 poems pub. as songs; leader poetry sect. Writers' Conf., U. Kans., 1953-55, McKendree Coll., 1961, 63, Creighton U., 1966, Central Mo. State U., 1974, Am. Poets Series, Kansas City, Mo., 1972-73; residency Mo. Council Arts, 1975; workshop leader U. Mo. at Kansas City, 1975. Recipient Mo. Writers Guild award, 1941, awards poetry socs. Ga., 1955, Va., 1956, La., 1958, also Poetry Soc. Am. and various local awards, including Kansas City Star award, 1975, Order First Families of Va., 1607-22. Mem. Diversifiers, Poetry Soc. Am., Nat. Soc. Colonial Dames. Mem. Christian Ch. Clubs: Woman's City, Filson. Author: (poetry) Subject to Change, 1973. Address: 221 W 48th St Apt 1402 Kansas City MO 64112

THOMPSON, ELSIE DUNN WILSON, lawyer; b. Washington, Dec. 8, 1950; d. Orme and Mildred Eddy (Dunn) W.; A.B. cum laude, Radcliffe Coll., 1972; J.D., U. Va., 1975; m. William McIlwaine Thompson, Jr., May 16, 1981. Admitted to Va. bar, 1975, N.Y. bar, 1976, Tex. bar, 1978; assoc. firm Lord, Day & Lord, N.Y.C., 1975-78; corp. sec., asst. gen. counsel Gulf Resources & Chem. Corp., Houston, 1978—. Mem. Am. Bar Assn., Gulf Coast Council Fgn. Affairs (bd. dirs. Houston chpt.), Houston Fgn. Policy Seminar Assn., Am. Soc. Corp. Secs. Episcopalian. Clubs: Signet Soc., Colony (N.Y.C.), Harvard of N.Y. Office: 1100 Milam Bldg 47th Floor Houston TX 77002

THOMPSON, ERNESTINE LAVAN, edn. cons.; b. Milano, Tex., Apr. 30, 1929; d. John and Essie Lee (Scott) Lavan; B.A., Samuel Huston Coll., 1950; M.A., U. Mich., 1976; m. William M. Thompson, Feb. 2, 1953. Program dir. Temple U.S.O. Club, Temple., Tex., 1951-53; case worker Dept. Social Services, Battle Creek, Mich., 1953-55; with Calhoun County, Marshall, Mich., 1969-75; dir. Head Start, Calhoun County Intermediate Sch. Dist., Marshall, 1967-68; tchr. Pennfield Schs., Battle Creek, 1959-70; counselor, work study coordinator, adminstr. Calhoun Area Vocat. Center, Battle Creek, 1970-77; cons. Tex. Edn. Agy., Austin, 1977—. Sec. Assn. Retarded Children, 1972-74; mem. manpower adv. council Calhoun County Bd. Commrs., Marshall, 1974; chmn. adv. bd. Huston-Tillotson Coll. Parent-Family Life Center, Austin, 1979—. Mem. AAUW, Alpha Delta Kappa. Democrat. Baptist. Home: 6603 Ashland Dr Austin TX 78723

THOMPSON, ESTHER MARYE, psychotherapist, cons.; b. Springfield, Mass., Nov. 29, 1927; d. Benjamin Arthur and Esther Elizabeth (Brown) Peters; B.A., U. Mass., 1979; M.Ed. in Psychol. Services, Springfield Coll., 1980; m. Robert J. Thompson, Nov. 30, 1946; children—Celeste, Robert J., Cheri Lynn, Kim Jose. Dir. tenant relations Springfield Housing Authority, 1963-66; exec. dir. Hill-McKnight Community Councils Inc., Springfield, 1966-73; propr. Esther M. Thompson Assos., Springfield, 1976—; founder, dir. Sr. Citizens Social Service Program, Springfield, 1972; social service planner, cons. Teen Pregnant Ednl. Services, Springfield YWCA, bd. dirs. Adolescent Program Devel., 1970-81; coll. lectr., 1962-81; mem. Springfield Human Service Adv. Bd., 1978-79, Title I Ednl. Commn., Springfield, 1965-67. Founder Head Start program, Springfield, 1966; corporator Hill-Top Children's Services, 1965-79, Child Guidance Clinic, 1975-80. Recipient various citations. Mem. Nat. Assn. Female Execs. (network dir.), AAUW, Am. Psychol. Assn., NOW, NAACP. Baptist.

THOMPSON, GLADYS TAYLOR, histo-technologist; b. Perry, Fla., Dec. 25, 1928; d. Joshua and Elise (Cooper) Taylor; student U. Fla., 1967-68; children—Seabie Troy, Jo Ann Litman, Johnny C. Lloyd. Lab. asst. Vet. Sci., U. Fla., Gainesville, 1961-67, with Shands Teaching Hosp., 1967-73; histo-technologist N. Fla. Regional Hosp., Gainesville, 1973—. Cert. histo-technician. Mem. NAACP, Nat. Soc. Histo-Technicians, State Soc. Fla. Histo-Technicians, Regional Histo-Technicians Soc. Baptist. Clubs: Matron Soc., Bethune Cookman Alumni Assn., Elks (dau. ruler 1967-70). Office: PO NFRH Gainesville FL 32601

THOMPSON, GLENDA AUDREY, furniture co. exec.; b. Santa Ana, Calif., June 28, 1950; d. Gilmer Blaine and Edith Jewell (Belcher) T.; student in bus. mgmt. Patrick Henry Community Sch. Sewing machine operator Pannill Knitting Co., Martinsville, Va., 1968-70; from cashier to dept. supr. Gibson Products Co., Collinsville, Va., 1970-72; credit asst., customer repair coordinator J.C. Penney's, Martinsville, 1972-74; asst. personnel dir. Gravely Furniture Co., Inc., Ridgeway, Va., 1974—. Bd. dirs. Martinsville-Henry County Clean Community Commn., 1979. Recipient Disting. Service citation Keep Am. Beautiful. Mem. Blue Ridge Personnel Assn. (v.p.), Am. Soc. for Personnel Adminstrn. Republican. Baptist. Clubs: Collinsville Lioness (treas., dir. 1979-81), Martinsville Toastmasters, Blue Ridge Ski. Home: 1300 Spruce St Apt 7 Martinsville VA 24112 Office: PO Box 407 Ridgeway VA 24148

THOMPSON, HAZEL PAULISON (RUSTY), sch. dist. adminstr.; b. Passaic, N.J., Feb. 4, 1928; B.S. in Edn., Glassboro Coll., 1949; M.A. in Adminstrn. and Supervision, Columbia U., 1960; m. W. Stuart Thompson; 3 children. Tchr., Ridgewood (N.J.) Bd. Edn., 1949-61; tchr. Bloomfield (N.J.) Bd. Edn., 1964-66, reading specialist, 1966-70, adminstrv. asst. in curriculum and instrn., 1970—, also coordinator recruitment, affirmative action officer for hiring policies and procedures; TV coordinator between sch. dist. and N.J. Public TV. Elder, Ref. Ch. in Am. Mem. N.J. Assn. Curriculum Devel., Am. Assn. Curriculum and Supervision, Am. Assn. Sch. Personnel Adminstrs., Mid-Atlantic Assn. Sch. Coll. Univ. Staffing, NEA N.J. Edn. Assn., Internat. Reading Assn., N.J. Reading Tchrs. Assn. Co-author numerous curriculum guides and writings for title funds. Certified as prin., supr., N.J.; specialist in reading, lang. arts, kindergarten through 12th grades, curriculum devel., kindergarten through 12th grades, adminstrv. supervision for classroom instruction, kindergarten through 12th grades, elementary and secondary libraries coordination. Home: Jacquelin Ave Ho-Ho-Kus NJ 07423 Office: 155 Broad St Bloomfield NJ 07003

THOMPSON, JANE SEARS, advt. and sales exec.; b. Tulsa, Mar. 2, 1946; d. Clyde Lee and Lucy (Blackman) Sears; student U. Tulsa, 1965-69; m. David Y. Thompson, Nov. 28, 1975. Asst. dir. promotion dept. Sta KOTV, Tulsa, 1967-68; dir. audiovisual dept. nat. hdqrs. Girl Scouts U.S.A., 1969; asst. pub. Clipper mag. Pan Am. World Airways, 1970-72; sr. v.p. Thompson Communications, Inc., 1972—, dir. Thompson Travel Mktg., Thompson Advt. and Sales Promotion. Office: 90 Park Ave New York NY 10016 *

THOMPSON, JO ANN, utility co. ofcl.; b. Petty, Tex., Dec. 13, 1932; d. Newton Franklin and Myrtle Lorene (Dellinger) Rutherford; A.A., Paris Jr. Coll., 1951; B.S., East Tex. State U., 1964; m. Bill H., July 29, 1951 (dec.); children—Gregory, Mark, Jeffrey Todd. Mgr., Mallory Studio, Paris, Tex., 1951-54; home economist Lone Star Gas Co., Paris, 1966-67; home service advisor Tex. Power and Light Co., Dallas, 1967—, dir. home service, 1972-80, asst. mgr. Sherman dist., 1980-82, mgr. Commerce (Tex.) dist., 1982—. Mem. interior design adv. com. El Centro Coll.; nat. dir. Elec. Womens' Round Table, Inc., 1977-80; 1st v.p. North Tex. Elec. Womens' Round Table, Inc., Recipient ALMA award Am. Home Appliance Mfrs., 1973; Service award State Future Farmers Am., 1976. Mem. Home Economists Bus. (North Tex. chmn. 1976-77, regional adv. 1977-79), Nat. Home Economists Bus. (chmn. 1980-81), Nat. Home Fashions League (chpt. pres. 1977-79), Tex. Home Econs. Assn. (pres. 1980-82), Young Homemakers Tex. (hon.). Home: 2812 Windy Dr Commerce TX 75428 Office: PO Box 468 Commerce TX 75428

THOMPSON, JOANNE, artist, porcelain mfg. co. exec.; b. Chgo., Nov. 2, 1922; d. George A. and Mary Louise Thompson; student U. Colo., Boulder, 1940-42; divorced; children—Barrett, Marc, Stacy. Exhibited group shows Nat. Arts Club Gallery, N.Y.C., 1965-69; Mus. Fine Arts, Springfield, Mass., 1965-70; Am. Artists Profl. League Grand Nat., N.Y.C., 1966-70; Hammond Mus., Westchester, N.Y., 1968; owner, artist, tchr. Joanne Thompson Studio, Scottsdale, Ariz., 1979—. Mem. Am. Artists Profl. League, Artists Guild Chgo., Acad. Artists. Author, illustrator: Fun to Sketch With Pencil and Crayon, 1973; illustrator Love Circles, 1978. Office: PO Box 4042 Scottsdale AZ 85261

THOMPSON, JOYCE ANN, fin. computer co. exec.; b. Haskell, Tex., July 5, 1947; d. Robert Thomas and Ela Aletha (Stanley) Smith; student Midwestern State U., 1968, U. Houston, 1977; m. Jon Collins Thompson, Aug. 19, 1977; children—Robert Tilden Cotton, Darrell Wayne Cotton. Asst. bookkeeper Sheppard Civilian Credit Union, Wichita Falls, Tex., 1966-69; systems mgr. Sheppard Area Fed. Credit Union, Wichita Falls, 1969-78; nat. mgr. system support Summit Info. Systems Corp., Corvallis, 1978—; lectr. in field; cons. in field. Vice pres. Dept. Def. Credit Unions Employees Group, 1971-72. Mem. Nat. Assn. Female Execs., Beta Sigma Phi (chpt. girl of yr. 1969-70, 71-72). Democrat. Christian Ch. Clubs: Spring Hill Country, Timberhill Athletic and Court. Office: 150 A NW Lewisburg Rd Corvallis OR 97330

THOMPSON, JOYCE CAROLYN, elec. contracting co. ofcl.; b. Houston, Aug. 7, 1923; d. Robert Harris and Ruth Morse (Fisk) Davis; B.B.A., Baylor U., 1944; m. Billy Morris Thompson, Dec. 27, 1946. Acctg. clk. comptroller dept. Texaco, Inc., Houston, 1944-45; office mgr., dir., sec.-treas. Fisk Electric Co., Houston, 1945—. Coordinator Reach to Recovery program Am. Cancer Soc., 1981, bd. dirs. Houston div., 1982—. Cert. Nat. Inst. Credit, 1971, cert. in parliamentary law, 1975; recipients awards Reach to Recovery program, Tex. Cancer Control Program, Am. Cancer Soc. Mem. Nat. Assn. Women in Constrn., Exec. Women Internat., Houston Assn. Credit Mgmt. Methodist. Office: 111 T C Jester St Houston TX 77007

THOMPSON, LAURETTA NAYLOR (MRS. GEARS H. THOMPSON), educator; b. Chgo.; d. Arthur W. and Ada (Ferrell) Peterson; grad. Wilson Jr. Coll., 1944; B.E., Chgo. Tchrs. Coll., 1949; M.Ed., Northwestern U., 1953; Ed.D., George Peabody Coll., Vanderbilt U., 1982; m. Gears H. Thompson. Tchr., McCosh Elementary Sch., Chgo., 1949-60, adjustment tchr., 1954-60; asst. prin. McCosh Primary Sch., 1960-70; area A sch. mental health dir. Chgo. Bd. Edn., 1970-73; parent coordinator Dumas and McCosh Spl. Summer Schs., 1965, 67; asst. prin. Wendell Smith Sch., 1973—; drama coordinator Dist. 16 Ednl. Curriculum Council, 1978; v.p. Thompson Limousine Service. Mem. adv. bd. Woodlawn Mental Health Center, 1964, vice chmn. community bd., 1970; faculty adviser McCosh Sch. PTA, 1954-69; mem. Beatrice Caffrey Youth Service; v.p. Berean Credit Union, 1978; edn. chmn., then v.p., then pres. Berean Credit Union, 1968—; 2d v.p. Wendell Smith Sch. and Home Assn.; bd. dirs. Piano Child Devel. Center. Mem. Chgo. Assn. Elementary Asst. Prins., Mental Health Assn. Greater Chgo., Chgo. Ednl. Dirs. Assn., AAUW, NAACP, Nat. Council Negro Women, Chgo. Urban League, Alpha Kappa Alpha (nat. sec. 1966-70 fin. sec. 1970-74), Alpha Gamma Pi, Kappa Delta Pi. Baptist (gen. supt. Sunday sch. 1971—). Home: 7257 S Dr M L King Dr Chicago IL 60619

THOMPSON, LEONA POLINER, social worker, educator; b. Ogden, Utah, June 22, 1911; d. Joseph and Freda (Muldavin) Poliner; B.S., N.Y. U., 1932, M.A., 1933; M.S.W., Columbia, 1959; m. Robert George Thompson, Oct. 13, 1939 (div. Nov. 1961); children—Ellen, James. Psychotherapist, Wiltwyck Sch. for Boys, N.Y.C., 1958-60; dir. social service Knickerbocker Hosp., N.Y.C., 1960-80; psychotherapist Morningside Mental Hygiene Clinic, N.Y.C., 1960-66; asst. prof., then asso. prof. sociology dept. Lehman Coll., N.Y.C., 1968-80, dir. social work program, 1973-80; cons. Sr. Citizen Peer Counseling Tng. Program, East Harlem, N.Y.C., 1976-77. Mental health cons. Caribbean Fedn. Mental Health, from 1965; mem. adv. bd. Manhattanville Community Health Service Center, 1968-69, Manhattanville Head Start, from 1969; mem. dean's steering com. Council Teaching Agys. N.Y.U. Grad. Sch. Social Work. Mem. Am. Soc. Dirs. Social Service, Am. Hosp. Assn., Nat. Assn. Social Workers, Nat. Council Social Work Edn., Nat. Welfare Assn. Home: 225 W 25th St New York NY 10001 Office: Lehman Coll Bedford Park Blvd W Bronx NY 10468

THOMPSON, LINDA RUTH, psychiatrist; b. Bristol, Va., May 17, 1941; d. Eugene Cassidy and Kitty Ruth (Corum) T.; A.B., King Coll., 1962; M.D., U. Va., 1966; 1 adopted son, Ethan Eugene. Intern, State U. of Iowa Hosp., Iowa City, 1966-67; resident in psychiatry U. Va. Hosp., Charlottesville, 1967-71; practice medicine specializing in psychiatry, Chevy Chase, Md. Diplomate Am. Bd. Psychiatry and Neurology. Mem. AMA, Am. Psychiat. Assn., Washington Psychiat. Soc., Med. Soc. of D.C., Am. Psychoanalytic Assn., Washington Psychoanalytic Soc. Home: 7454 Westlake Terr Bethesda MD 20817 Office: 5480 Wisconsin Ave Suite 1129 Chevy Chase MD 20815

THOMPSON, MARGO P., adminstrv. research cons.; b. The Dalles, Oreg., Sept. 25, 1939; d. Uren Jones and Mildred Edna (Tyler) Leonard; student San Bernardino Valley Coll., 1961-62, Eastern Oreg. Coll., 1962-63; 1 son, Kendall Alan. Exec. sec., asst. mgr. Kah-Nee-Ta Vacation Resort, Warm Springs, Oreg., 1963-67, mgr. sales, catering, pub. relations and front desk, 1972-74; exec. sec. Lawrence Livermore (Calif.) Lab., 1968-72; exec. sec. Chemawa Adv. Sch. Bd., Salem, Oreg., 1974-76; tech. assistance dir. for parts B & C Title IV for Oreg., Washington, Idaho, United Indians of All Tribes Found., Seattle, 1976-77; edn. planner, internal evaluator Puyallup Tribal Adminstrn., Tacoma, 1977-78, CETA services coordinator, 1977-79, dir. planning, 1979-81; research cons., adminstrv. Dillon's Enterprises Tucson, 1981—. Mem. Nat. Congress Am. Indians, Affiliated Tribes Northwest Indians, United Indian Planners Assn., Exec. Females, Smithsonian Assn. Nat. Home: 908 N Sheridan St Tacoma WA 98403 Office: 5505 20th St E Tacoma WA 98224

THOMPSON, MARGUERITE MYRTLE GRAMING (MRS. RALPH B. THOMPSON), librarian; b. Orangeburg, S.C., Apr. 23, 1912; d. Thomas Laurie and Rosa Lee (Stroman) Graming; B.A. in English cum laude, U. S.C., 1932, postgrad., 1937; B.L.S., Emory U., 1943; m. Ralph B. Thompson, Sept. 17, 1949 (dec. Oct. 1960). Tchr. English public high schs., S.C., 1932-43; librarian Rockingham (N.C.) High Sch., 1943-45, Randolph County (N.C.) Library, Asheboro, 1945-48, Colleton County (S.C.) Library, Walterboro, 1948-61; dir. Florence (S.C.) County Library, 1961-78. Sec. com. community facilities, services and instns. Florence County Resources Devel. Com., 1964-67; vice chmn. Florence County Council on Aging, 1968-70, exec. bd. 1968-82, bd. treas., 1973-75, bd. sec., 1976-77, bd. v.p., 1979; mem. Florence County Bicentennial Planning Com., 1975-76; mem. relations and allocations com. United Way, 1979-80. Named Boss of Year Nat. Secs. Assn., 1971. Mem. ALA (council 1964-72), Southeastern, S.C. (pres. 1960, chmn. assn. handbook revision com. 1967-69, 80, sect. co-chmn. com. standards for S.C. public libraries 1966-75, fed. relations coordinator 1972-73, planning com. 1976-78) library assns., Greater Florence C. of C. (women's div. chmn. 1969-70, dir. 1975-77), Southeast Regional Conf. Women in Chambers Commerce (dir. 1970-71), Florence, Bus. and Profl. Women's Club (2d v.p. 1975-76, Career Woman of Year 1974, parliamentarian 1980-81, chmn. scholarship com. 1981-82), Delta Kappa Gamma (county chpt. charter pres. 1963-65, treas. 1966-70, chmn. com. on expansion 1977-80, 82—, state chpt. chmn. state scholarship com. 1967-73, state 2d v.p. 1971-73, state 1st v.p. 1973-75, state pres. 1975-77, chmn. policy manual 1977-81, chmn. adv. council 1978—, chmn. fin. com. 1981—, dir. SE Region 1978-80, coordinator SE Regional Golden Anniversary Conf. 1979, internat. scholarship com. 1970-74, internat. exec. bd. 1975-77, 78-80, internat. adminstrv. bd. 1978-80, internat. constn. com. 1980-82) Methodist (chmn. ch. library com. 1965-71, chmn. com. ch. history, 1968-69, sec. adminstrv. bd. 1979-82). Club: Florence Literary (sec. 1964-66, 79-82, pres. 1970-72). Home: Route 2 Box 1000 Apt 8B Orangeburg SC 29115

THOMPSON, MARY ANN ELIZABETH, educator; b. Oklahoma City, Feb. 16, 1948; d. William Best and Ann (Giddings) T.; B.S., Tex. Woman's U., 1969; M.Ed., Central State U., Okla., 1972; Ed.D., Okla. State U., 1978. Tchr. phys. edn. Putnam (Okla.) City Schs., 1969-73; instr. phys. edn. Oklahoma City U., 1973-76; instr. Okla. State U., 1976-78, asst. prof., 1978—. NE area meet dir. Okla. Spl. Olympics, 1972—, state meet dir., 1982—. Mem. Okla. Assn. Health Phys. Edn. Recreation Dance (v.p. gen. div. 1979-81, editor jour. 1973-77, 81—), AAHPERD, Nat. Assn. Sport and Phys. Edn. (asso.), Okla. Assn. Phys. Edn. for Coll. Women. Republican. Roman Catholic. Home: 4817 N Washington St #40 Stillwater OK 74074 Office: 108 Colvin Center Dept Phys Edn Okla State U Stillwater OK 74074

THOMPSON, MARY KRUSE, artist, educator; b. Mankato, Minn., Oct. 22, 1931; d. Cyril Frederic and Ramona (Shepherd) Kruse; B.A., U. Minn., 1954, M.A., 1957; m. Russell A. Thompson, Sept. 12, 1975; children—Julie Ann, Peter Joseph, Mary Susan. Tchr. art Taylors Falls (Minn.) High Sch., Blake Sch. for Boys, Hopkins, Minn., Richfield (Minn.) High Sch.; instr. Gustavus Adolphus Coll., St. Peter, Minn., U. Minn., Mpls., 1970-75; mem. faculty Willmar (Minn.) Community Coll., 1958—; one woman shows include Gustavus Adolphus Coll. Gallery, Gallery 401, Willmar; group shows include: Willmar Community Coll., Women in Art, Marshall (Minn.) State U. Bd. dirs. Women's Assn. Mpls. Symphony Orch., Mpls. Women's Club, Kandiyoki Art Assn. Mem. Southwestern Minn. Art and Humanities Council, Minn. Edn. Assn., Nat. Art Edn. Assn., AAUP, U. Minn. Alumnae Assn., Mpls. Woman's Club, Minn. State Med. Aux., Delta Phi Delta, Club: Minneapolis Woman's. Home: 1000 SW 14th St Willmar MN 56201 Office: Fine Arts Bldg Willmar Community Coll Willmar MN 56201

THOMPSON, MARY LORRAINE, engring. technician; b. Tulsa, Oct. 14, 1938; d. Aubrey Ray and Dixie Lee (Mills) Harris; A.A. in Engring. Tech., N.Mex. State U., 1978; m. Jesse Ward Thompson, Apr. 4, 1958; children—Sylvia Lorraine, Michael Edward. Polit. campaign coordinator, 1978; engring. technician System Devel. Corp., 1979-80, Lockheed/Engring. Mgmt. Systems Corp., 1980—; mem. N.Mex. Ho. of Reps. from 36th Dist., 1980—. County chmn. White House Conf. Children and Youth; bd. dirs. Dona Ana County Cancer Soc. Recipient Amigo de 4-H award, 1982. Mem. Am. Legis. Exchange Council, Assn. Republican Legislators, LWV. Address: 1915 La Jolla St Las Cruces NM 88005

THOMPSON, MAVIS SARAH, physician; b. Newark, June 22, 1927; d. Nathaniel Albert and Mavis Carolyn (Smart) T.; B.A., Hunter Coll., N.Y.C., 1947; M.D., Howard U., 1953; m. James Blaize, Apr. 17, 1955; children—Clayton, Marcia, Sidney, Ronald, Kevin. Intern, then resident in internal medicine Kings County Hosp., Bklyn., 1953-57; practice medicine specializing in internal medicine, Bklyn., 1957-76; med. dir. Lyndon B. Johnson Health Complex, Inc., Bklyn., 1970-71, 74-76; sch. med. insp. N.Y.C. Bd. Edn., Bklyn., 1962—; family physician Kingsboro Med. Group, Bklyn., 1976—; tchr. dept. nursing Medgar Evers Coll., 1975-76; mem. adv. com. Gerontol. Services Adminstrn. program New Sch. Social Research, N.Y.C.; cons. in field. Bd. dirs. Camp Minisink, 1973—; active local Boy Scouts Am.; lic. lay reader St. George's Eplsc. Ch., Bklyn. Recipient Community Service award St. Mark's Meth. Ch., N.Y.C., 1973; Alberta T. Kline service award Camp Minisink, 1980. Mem. Am. Public Health Assn. (pres. Black caucus health workers 1976-77), Nat. Med. Assn., Am. Mgmt. Assn., Am. Geriatrics Soc., Am. Med. Women's Assn., Kings County Med. Soc., Delta Sigma Theta. Episcopalian. Contbr. articles to med. jours. Office: 1000 Church Ave Brooklyn NY 11218

THOMPSON, MAXINE MARIE, horticulturist, educator; b. Bloomington, Ill., Nov. 3, 1926; d. Earnest William and Mare Amelia (Cowen) Moeller; B.S., U. Calif., 1948, M.S., 1951, Ph.D., 1960; m. Harry S. Thompson, Apr. 4, 1953 (div. 1960); children—Michael Allen, Laurie Marie. Viticulturist, U. Calif., Davis, 1962-63; biologist Wis. State U., Oshkosh, 1963-64; faculty Oreg. State U., Corvallis, 1964—, prof. horticulture, 1980—. Mem. Am. Soc. Horticultural Sci., AAAS, Am. Pomological Soc. Democrat. Unitarian. Contbr. articles in field to profl. jours. Home: 2715 NW Frazier Creek Dr Corvallis OR 97330 Office: Dept Horticulture Oreg State U Corvallis OR 97331

THOMPSON, MERNA RUTH, social worker; b. Oconee, Ill., Feb. 25, 1918; d. Edgar and Clara M. (Neathery) Bass; B.A., Wayne State U., 1956; M.A., U. Mich., 1960, Ed.S., 1971; postgrad. Mich. State U., 1978; m. Frank L. Thompson, June 7, 1942 (dec.); children—Carol, Janice (dec.). Elem. classroom tchr., Ill., 1938-42, Walled Lake (Mich.) Schs., 1954-59, sch. social worker, 1959-81; cons. in field; coordinator spl. edn. programs. Mem. Youth Assistance Camping Program Com., 1975-76. Cert. social worker. Mem. Mich. Assn. Emotionally Disturbed Children, Nat. Assn. Social Workers, Mich. Assn. Sch. Social Workers, Mich. Soc. Mental Health, NEA, Mich. Edn. Assn., Walled Lake Edn. Assn. Baptist (Sunday sch. tchr., class sec.-treas.). Home: 13730 Crooked Creek Dr South Lyon MI 48178

THOMPSON, MIREILLE WALDEN, former mfg. co. exec.; b. Paris, Apr. 9, 1920 (parents Am. citizens); d. William Walden and Augustine Isabelle (Girod) Kester; B.S. in Mgmt. and Housing Devel., Va. Poly. Inst. and State U., 1941, M.S. in Mgmt. and Housing Devel., 1951; m. Frederick William Thompson, Jan. 31, 1942; children—Rosalind Dianne Thompson Burt, Roger Geoffrey. With Gen. Electric Co., 1956-82, adminstr. medium gas turbine dept., 1967-73, specialist in program planning dept. gas turbine engring., Schenectady, 1974-75, adminstr.

support tng. and procedures dept. ordnance systems, Pittsfield, Mass., 1975-82. Staging chmn. N.C. Apple Festival, 1963-67; vol. Recs. for Blind, Lenox, Mass., 1977-79. Recipient Go-For-Five Cordiner award Gen. Electric Co., 1964, Best Buy award Gen. Electric Gas Turbine Products div., 1971; lighting award Nat. Illuminating Engring. Soc., 1961, 62, 63, 64. Mem. Navy League U.S. (chmn. public relations Berkshire council 1980-81). Roman Catholic. Contbr. articles to profl. publs.; author co. vendor adminstrv. software specification, adminstrv. procedures. Home: 33 Lake Dr Apt G-4 Hendersonville NC 28739

THOMPSON, OPAL TREADWAY, former nursing services adminstr.; b. Smokemont, N.C., May 27, 1928; d. Henry Coleman and Lena Josephine (Waldrup) Treadway; R.N., S.C. Bapt. Hosp., 1949; A.S., U. S.C., 1975; B.S. in Nursing, Med. Coll. Ga., 1976, M.S. in Nursing, 1977; m. Theron Theodore Thompson, Mar. 26, 1959; children—Stephanie Dawn, Kelly Lyn, Theron Treadway. Pvt. duty nursing, Columbia, S.C., 1949-50; staff nurse Fort Jackson Base Hosp., 1950-53; staff nurse Savannah River Plant, Aiken, S.C., 1953-60; charge nurse Univ. Hosp., Augusta, 1975-76; instr. Coll. Nursing, U. S.C., Columbia, 1978-79, asst. prof. div. nursing, 1979-81; dir. nursing services Blair House, Inc., Augusta, Ga., 1981-82. Pres., Carolina Hospitality Club, 1960-70; mem. Aiken County Health Dept. Vol. Services, 1959—; vol. services ARC, 1959—. Mem. Nat. League of Nurses, S.C. Nurses Assn. United Methodist. Club: North Augusta Women's Club (sec. 1960-65). Home: 1560 Litina Dr Alamo CA 94507

THOMPSON, PAULINE CARMEN, Realtor; b. Lewiston, Maine, Sept. 1, 1941; d. Ralph Ovide and Yvonne Blanche (Gousse) Labbe; student George Washington U., 1962-63, U. Va. Real estate salesman Routh Robbins Real Estate, 1969-70; founder, pres. Tysons Realty, Inc., McLean, Va., 1971—, real estate investment counselor, 1975—. Membership chmn. No. Va. Mental Health Assn. Mem. Nat. Assn. Realtors, No. Va. Bd. Realtors, No. Va. Apt. Assn., Fairfax County C. of C., No. Va. Builders Assn., McLean Bus. and Profl. Assn., Apt. and Office Bldg. Assn. Club: Soroptimist. Office: Tysons Realty Inc 1984 Chain Bridge Rd McLean VA 22101

THOMPSON, PHEBE KIRSTEN, physician; b. Glace Bay, N.S., Can., Sept. 5, 1897; came to U.S., 1923, naturalized, 1937; d. Peter and Catherine (McKeigan) Christianson; M.D., C.M., Dalhousie U., Halifax, N.S., 1923; m. Willard Owen Thompson, M.D., June 21, 1923 (dec. Mar. 1954); children—Willard Owen, Frederic, Nancy, Donald. Intern, Children's Hosp., Halifax, N.S., 1922-23; asst. bio-chemistry, dept. applied physiology Harvard Sch. Public Health, 1924-26; research fellow in medicine, thyroid clinic Mass. Gen. Hosp., Boston, 1926-29; asst. in metabolism dept., endocrinology Rush Med. Coll. U. Chgo. and The Central Free Dispensary, Chgo., 1930-46; asso. with husband in pvt. practice medicine, Chgo., 1947-54; mng. editor Jour. Clin. Endocrinology and Metabolism, 1954-61, cons. editor, 1961-65; cons. editor Endocrinology, 1961-65; editor Jour. Am. Geriatrics Soc., 1954—; freelance editor and writer, 1961—. Recipient Appreciation cert. Am. Thyroid Assn., 1966. Fellow Am. Geriatrics Soc. (Thewlis award 1966), Gerontol. Soc., Am. Med. Writers Assn. (adv. com. 1958-61, v.p. Chgo. 1962-63); mem. Endocrine Soc., AAAS, Am. Genetic Assn., Am. Public Health Assn., Ill. Acad. Scis., Ill. Public Health Assn., Chgo. Hist. Soc. (life), Art Inst. (life). Clubs: Harvard, University (Chgo.); Canadian (Chgo. corr. sec. 1968-73, dir. 1973-76). Address: 2300 Lincoln Park W Chicago IL 60614

THOMPSON, SADA CAROLYN, actress; b. Des Moines, Sept. 27, 1929; d. Hugh Woodruff and Corlyss Elizabeth (Gibson) Thompson; B.F.A., Carnegie Inst. Tech., 1949; m. Donald E. Stewart, 1949; 1 dau., Liza. Stage debut in The Time of Your Life at Carnegie Inst. Tech. Drama Sch., 1945; co-founder Univ. Playhouse, Mashpee, Mass., 1947; appeared at Pitts. Playhouse, The Playhouse, Erie, Pa., summer stock prodns. at Henrietta Hayloft Theatre, Rochester, N.Y., Brattle Theatre Co., Cambridge, Mass.; speech tchr. 92d St. YMHA, N.Y.C.; New York debut at YMHA in Under Milk Wood, 1953; appeared in Off-Broadway revival at Circle in the Sq. Theatre, 1961 and Nat. Edn. Television presentation, 1966; appeared in plays The Clandestine Marriage, Provincetown Playhouse, N.Y.C., 1954, The White Devil and The Carefree Tree at Phoenix Theatre, N.Y.C., 1955, The Misanthrope, Off Broadways Theatre East, 1956, The River Line, Carnegie Hall Playhouse, 1957; joined Am. Shakespeare Festival, Stratford, Conn., 1957, appearing in Othello, Much Ado About Nothing, 1957-58, The Merry Wives of Windsor, Alls Well That Ends Well, 1959, Twelfth Night, The Tempest and Antony and Cleopatra, 1960; appeared in Off Broadway prodn. of Chekhov's Ivanov, 1958, Broadway prodn. of Juno and the Paycock, 1959; appeared in Tartuffe at Lincoln Center Repertory Theatre, 1965, Johnny No-Trump, 1967, The American Dream, 1968, The Effect of Gamma Rays on Man-in-the-Moon Marigolds, 1970, Twigs, 1971, Mourning Becomes Electra, 1971; appeared in motion picture Desperate Characters, 1971; star TV series Sandburg's Lincoln, 1974-76, Family, 1976-79; TV spl. The Entertainer, 1976. Recipient Tony award, 1972, New York Drama Critics award for best actress of year Variety, 1971-72, also 2 Obie awards, Emmy award for outstanding actress on a dramatic series, 1979. Address: care Arcara Bauman and Hiller 9220 Sunset Blvd Los Angeles CA 90069 *

THOMPSON, SALLY DRISCOLL, educator; b. Machias, Maine, Apr. 21, 1943; d. Kenneth S. and Minnie E. (Oliver) Driscoll; B.S., U. Maine, Machias, 1965; postgrad. U. Maine, Orono, 1980—; m. Earland Leroy Thompson, June 13, 1965; children—Kenneth Frank, Katrina Ellen. Tchr., Maine Sch. Adminstrv. Dist. 37, Harrington, 1979-80; learning disabilities tchr. D.W. Merritt and Columbia Falls elem. schs., 1979—. Chmn. bd. of assessors Municipality of Columbia Falls (Maine), 1970-78, mcpl. welfare dir., 1975-78, 1st selectman, 1975-76, selectman, 1976-78. Mem. NEA, Maine Tchrs. Assn., Maine Municipal Assn. Home: Columbia Falls ME 04623

THOMPSON, SALLY ELIZABETH, accountant; b. Spokane, Wash., Feb. 17, 1940; d. Logan Charles and Ava Lea (Phillips) Engstrom; B.S. magna cum laude, U. Colo., 1975; children—Laura, Tammera, Thomas. Asst. to math. coordinator Boulder Valley Sch. Dist., Boulder, Colo., 1971-72; audit mgr. Touche Ross & Co., C.P.A.s, Denver, 1975—; mem. Colo. Bd. Accountancy, 1981-85. Bd. dirs., chmn. resource com. Big Sisters Colo., 1980-83, pres., 1982-83. Recipient Outstanding Student award Beta Alpha Psi and Am. Soc. Women Accts., 1975. C.P.A., Colo. Mem. Am. Inst. C.P.A.s, Women in Mining, Nat. Assn. Women Constrn., Colo. Soc. C.P.A.s, Savs. and Loan League Colo., Mortar Bd. Club: Soroptimist. Home: 4338 S Atchison Circle Aurora CO 80015 Office: 400 United Bank Center Denver CO 80290

THOMPSON, SENFRONIA PAIGE, state legislator; b. Booth, Tex.; d. Lindsey and Thelma (Waterhouse) Paige; B.S. in Biology, Tex. So. U., 1961, J.D., 1977; M.Ed., Prairie View (Tex.) A&M U., 1964; m. W.M. Carrington, 1978; children—Jobie, Jr., Sarah Marie, Jarvis. Public sch. tchr., 1964-72; mem. Tex. Ho. of Reps. from 141st Dist., 1973—, past chmn. joint comm. jud. redistricting, vice chmn. com. jud. affairs; practice law, 1978—. Bd. dirs. United Negro Coll. Fund, Save Johnson Farm Fund; adv. bd. Big Bros./Big Sisters, Houston, Salvation Army, Houston. Mem. Nat. Order Women Legislators, Nat. Council Negro Women, NOW, Black Women Lawyers Assn., Tex. Women's Polit. Caucus, NAACP, Harris County Democrats, Harris County Council Orgns., Vols. Am., Alpha Kappa Alpha, Phi Alpha Delta, Beta Phi Delta. Roman Catholic. Clubs: Triangle Civic, Order Eastern Star. Office: 10518 Homestead St Houston TX 77016

THOMPSON, SUSAN PROBASCO, acctg. co. exec.; b. Bloomington, Ill., Aug. 8, 1946; d. Lewis William and Barbara Claire (Welles) Probasco; student U. Wis., 1965; B.A. in English, Rollins Coll., 1968; m. Thomas Miller Thompson, Aug. 22, 1967; 1 dau., Ruth Helen. Research assoc. Heidrick and Struggles, Chgo., 1969-70, assoc., Houston, 1981-82; v.p. mktg. L. N. Smith, Inc., Houston, 1976-78; pres., owner, cons. Suzy Thompson Personnel Service, Inc., and Susan P. Thompson and Assocs., Houston, 1977-82; mgr. Peat, Marwick, Mitchell and Co., Houston, 1982—. Mem. grievance com. State Bar Tex., 1979-82; bd. dirs. Mental Health Assn. Houston and Harris County, 1979—, v.p., 1980-82; trustee Rollins Coll., 1980—. Mem. Houston Bus. Exchange Club, Profl. Women Execs., Exec. Forum. Episcopalian. Office: 4300 One Shell Plaza Houston TX 77002

THOMPSON, VIVIAN OPAL, nurse; b. Lebanon, Va., Nov. 30, 1925; d. Luther Smith and Cora Belle (Baugh) Thompson; R.N., Knoxville (Tenn.) Gen. Hosp., 1947. Supr. obstetrical dept. Knoxville Gen. Hosp., 1947-48; gen. duty nurse Clinch Valley Clinic Hosp., Richlands, Va., 1948-52, supr., 1957-61, 68-78, 78—; indsl. nurse, Morocco, Africa, 1952-56; charge nurse Bluefield Sanitarium, W.Va., 1961-65, Rockingham Meml. Hosp., Harrisonburg, Va., 1965-68. Democrat. Presbyterian. Home: 205 Pennsylvania Ave Richlands VA 24641

THOMSON, THYRA GODFREY, state ofcl.; b. Florence, Colo., July 30, 1916; d. John and Rosalie (Altman) Godfrey; B.A. cum laude, U. Wyo., 1939; m. Keith Thomson, Aug. 6, 1939 (dec. Dec. 1960); children—William John II, Bruce Godfrey, Keith Coffey. With dept. agronomy and agrl. econs. U. Wyo., 1938-39; writer weekly column Watching Washington pub. in 14 papers, Wyo., 1955-60; planning chmn. Nat. Fedn. Republican Women, Washington, 1961; sec. state State of Wyo., Cheyenne, 1962—; mem. exec. com. Nat. Conf. Lt. Govs., 1976, 81. Mem. Marshall Scholarships Com. for Pacific Region, 1964-68; del. 72d Wilton Park Conf., Eng., 1965, Nat. Women's Conf., 1977; mem. youth commn. UNESCO, 1970-71, Allied Health Professions Council HEW, 1971-72. Recipient Disting. Alumni award U. Wyo., 1969; named internat. woman of distinction Alpha Delta Kappa; recipient citation Omicron Delta Epsilon, 1965, Beta Gamma Sigma, 1968, Delta Kappa Gamma, 1973; Internat. Women's Yr. guest Fed. Republic Germany, 1975. Mem. N.Am. Securities Adminstrs. (pres. 1973-74), Nat. Assn. Secs. of State, Council State Govts. (chmn. natural resources com. Western States 1966-68), AAUW, Wyo. Press Women, Spurs, PEO, Pi Beta Phi, Alpha Kappa Psi, Psi Chi. Office: Capitol Bldg Cheyenne WY 82001

THONIS, GINA DUBRAVKA, writer; b. Washington, Oct. 27, 1952; d. Nenad Dusan and Tanya Popovic; B.A. with honors, Syracuse U., 1972; M.A., Harvard U., 1978; m. Michael Thonis, June 6, 1971. Dir. Hicks House and Roosevelt Meml. Library, Harvard U., Cambridge, Mass., 1974-78; teaching fellow Harvard Coll., 1976-77, editor-in-chief The Harvard Arts Spectrum, 1976; coordinator Eliot Norton Lectures, Harvard U., 1973, 75; exec. dir. Newton (Mass.) Arts Center, 1978-79; coordinator City of Boston's Jubilee 350: 17th Century Market Fair, also Boston's 350th Birthday Celebration, 1980; chmn. Kirkland House Golden Jubilee, 1981; free-lance editor, translator, speech writer, 1974—; dir. Guaranty First Trust Co. Recipient 2d prize prose div. Summer Arts Competition, Harvard U., 1974. Mem. Alpha Lambda Delta, Chi Omega. Author (pamphlets): Crime at Harvard 1974, 75. Home and Office: 16 Kirkland Rd Cambridge MA 02138

THORN, ISABEL MARLENE, psychologist, adminstr.; b. Chgo., Oct. 12, 1947; d. Floyd John and Isabel Ana (Rodriquez) T.; B.A., U. Fla., 1969, M.A., 1970; Ph.D., U. Md., 1980. Rehab. counselor Bur. Rehab. Services, Washington, 1971-73; counselor, cons. Gallaudet Coll., Washington, 1973-78; counseling psychologist GAO, Washington, 1978-80; dir. tng. and devel. service Corp. Public Broadcasting, Washington, 1980—; pvt. practice psychology, Washington, 1982—. Mem. Am. Mgmt. Assn., Am. Psychol. Assn., Am. Women in Radio and TV, Soc. Intercultural Edn., Tng., and Research, Am. Soc. Tng. and Devel. Contbr. articles to profl. jours. Home: 5350 Nebraska Ave NW Washington DC 20015 Office: 1111 16th St NW Washington DC 20036

THORNE, DENISE LYNN, fin. services/mktg. co. exec.; b. Elizabeth, N.J., June 11, 1947; d. Brenton G. and Bessie O. (Thompson) T.; A.B., Beaver Coll., 1967; m. Bruce W. Johnson, Aug. 6, 1977; 1 son, Nicholas Thorne. Research asso. J. Walter Thompson, N.Y.C., 1967-69; research supr. FCB-Honig, San Francisco, 1969-72; product mgr. Internat. Playtex, N.Y.C., 1972-74; acct. supr. Botsford Ketchum Advt., San Francisco, 1974-75; asst. v.p. Citicorp Services Inc., N.Y.C., 1975-77, v.p., mktg. dir. Citicorp/Citibank, 1977—; treas. 670 Apts. Corp. Mem. NOW. Office: 575 Lexington Ave New York NY 10022

THORNE, MARY EARLENE BRANNON, former nurse, civic worker; b. Langdale, Ala., Oct. 25, 1942; d. Earl William and Mary Nae Brannon; A.A. in Nursing, Columbus Coll., 1969; m. James Robert Thorne, Mar. 19, 1969; children—Traci, Stephen Ashley. Dir. nursing service Opelika (Ala.) Nursing Home, 1970-71; staff nurse Scott and White Hosp., Temple, Tex., 1971-74; dir. nursing service Haven Manor Convalescent Center, Waco, Tex., 1974-76; nurse cons. Retama Manor Nursing Home, Pleasanton, Tex., 1978-79. Chmn. organizing com. Longhorn Museum Soc., Pleasanton, Tex., 1978, treas., 1980-82. R.N., Tex., Ga. Mem. Nurses in Geriatric Settings (organizer 1974). Baptist. Club: Woman's (pres. 1978-80) (Pleasanton). Home: 1106 Oak Ridge Pleasanton TX 78064

THORNHILL, LOIS, photographer; b. Boston, Apr. 7, 1945; d. Fred S. and Mary (Evans) Thornhill; B.A., Middlebury Coll., 1966; postgrad. U. St. Thomas, Houston, 1967-69; M.A., N.Y. U., 1971; m. Edward J. McCluskey, Feb. 14, 1981. Research technician dept. virology Baylor Sch. Medicine, Houston, 1966-68; with Kelly Girls, Palo Alto, 1971-72; slide curator dept. art Stanford (Calif.) U., 1972-80; founder, pres. Stanford Design Assos., Palo Alto, 1981—; cons. copy and museum photography. Mem. Smithsonian Assos., Coll. Art Assn. Am. Home: 895 Northampton Dr Palo Alto CA 94303 Office: PO Box 11451 A Palo Alto CA 94306

THORNTON, CORA ANN, educator; b. Washington, June 13, 1941; d. George Francis and Pearl Geneva (Cunningham) Barringer; B.S., D.C. Tchrs. Coll., 1964; postgrad. Howard U., 1966-67, George Washington U., 1970-72; M.A., Trinity Coll., 1982; m. Johnnie Richard Thornton; children—Johnnie Richard, Joseph Teacosia, Jerome Francis, Jenese Elaine. Instr. math. Taft Jr. High Sch., Washington, 1964-73; proprietor J.C. Enterprises, Washington, 1966-75; instr. math. St. Mary's Catholic Sch., Rockville, Md., 1976-79; instr. Eastern High Sch., Washington, 1979—; propr. Barr-Thorn Enterprises, Inc., 1981. Recipient Supt.'s Incentive award, 1982. Mem. NEA, Nation Council Tchrs. Math., Delta Sigma Theta. Author math. games and lessons, 1981. Office: 17th St and E Capitol St NW Washington DC 20003

THORNTON, FLORENCE EMMA (MRS. LAURANCE C. THORNTON), free-lance writer, lectr.; b. Boston, May 9, 1897; d. August L. and Emma (Ericson) Tobin; student Emerson Coll, Boston, 1917-18; m. Laurance C. Thornton, Oct. 19, 1946 (dec. 1952). With U.S. Govt. in Alaska, 1921-53; sec. Bethlehem Shipbuilding Corp., 1917-191 bookkeeper Granite Trust Co., Quincy, Mass., 1920-21; chief civilian personnel USCG, 1940-51; acting mgr. OPS, Fairbanks, Alaska, 1952-53; pvt. tchr. of violin 1921-30; co-founder Orthopedic and Tech. Center, Kottayam, Kerala, India, 1963-64; lectr. on her extensive world travels, also art and religion, U.S., Alaska, 1953—; humorist. Pres., alaska Fedn. Music Clubs, 1928-34. Mem. Dept. of Alaska Am. Legion Aux. (life, pres. 1935-36), W.C.T.U. (sec. Alaska 1950-53), Nat. Assn. Ret. Fed. Employees (past pres.), World War I Vets. Aux. Republican. Methodist. Clubs: Writers, Alaska (Woodburn, also Salem). Home: 1291 Princeton Rd Woodburn OR 97071

THORNTON, JUDY CARRUTH, printing co. exec.; b. Andrews, Tex., Sept. 19, 1950; d. Odis O. and Edith Jessie (Clem) Carruth; student U. Tex., Arlington; m. James W. Thornton, Nov. 22, 1969; children—Michael Paul, Elisa Jennifer, Formerly with City Dallas, Tex., Metroplex Nat. Bank, Arlington; now owner Stockton Printing Co., Fort Stockton, Tex., 19 —. Den leaders coach Cub Scouts Am., 1981—. Mem. Nat. Assn. Printers and Lithographers, Fort Stockton C. of C., Xi Zeta Lambda (v.p. 1981—). Republican. Methodist. Office: 109 N Nelson St Fort Stockton TX 79735

THORNTON, SANDRA WINTERBERGER, lawyer, educator; b. Binghamton, N.Y., Dec. 24, 1935; d. Elmer R. and Gertrude (Crowley) Winterberger; B.A., U. Vt., 1958; Ph.D. (NDEA fellow), Georgetown U., 1964; J.D., Woodrow Wilson Coll. Law, 1981; 1 dau., Lee W. Asso. prof. polit. sci. Ga. Inst. Tech., 1962—; admitted to Ga. bar, 1981; partner firm Thornton & Rose, 1982—; vis. prof. Emory U., 1967, U. Ga., 1967-68. Bd. dirs. Ga. affiliate ACLU, 1974-78, cooperating atty., 1981—. Recipient Disting. Tchr. award Ga. Inst. Tech., 1969; grantee Inst. Internat. Studies, HEW, 1973-75, Nat. Endowment Humanities, summer 1977. Mem. AAUP (nat. council 1974-77, nat. treas. 1977-78, nat. 2d v.p. 1982-84), Am. Polit. Sci. Assn., So. Polit. Sci. Assn., Am. Bar Assn. Home: 1406 Harvard Rd NE Atlanta GA 30306 Office: Sch Social Scis Ga Inst Tech Atlanta GA 30332

THORNTON, YVONNE SHIRLEY, physician, musician; b. N.Y.C., Nov. 21, 1947; d. Donald E. and Itasker F. (Edmonds) T.; B.S. in Biology, Monmouth Coll., 1969; M.D., Columbia U., 1973; m. Shearwood McClelland, June 8, 1974; children—Shearwood III, Kimberly Itaska. Resident in ob-gyn Roosevelt Hosp., N.Y.C., 1973-77; fellow maternal-fetal medicine Columbia-Presbyn. Med. Center, N.Y.C., 1977-79; commd. lt. comdr. M.C., USN, 1979; asst. prof. ob-gyn Uniformed Services U. Health Scis., 1979-82, Cornell U. Med. Coll., N.Y.C., 1982—; dir. clin. services dept. ob-gyn N.Y. Hosp.-Cornell Med. Center, 1982—; asst. attending N.Y. Lying-In Hosp., 1982—; staff Nat. Naval Med. Center, Bethesda, Md.; saxophonist Thornton Sisters ensemble, 1955-76. Diplomate Am. Bd. Ob-Gyn, Nat. Bd. Med. Examiners. Fellow Am. Coll. Obstetricians and Gynecologists; mem. AMA, N.Y. Acad. Scis., Am. Fertility Soc., Soc. Perinatal Obstetricians, Am. Fedn. Musicians. Lambda Sigma Tau. Democrat. Baptist. Office: 525 E 68th St New York NY 10021

THORNTON-CARTER, MARGARET ALICIA JOAN, mgmt. co. exec., retail exec.; b. Gt. Brit., Dec. 23, 1937; d. James and Doris (Bajana) C.; came to U.S., 1961; Royal Soc. Arts degree, 1954. Real estate broker, Providence, 1970—; registered apt. mgr., Providence, 1969-70; foreman constrn. site; owner, operator mgmt. co., Providence, 1973—. Mem. C. of C. U.S., Johnston (R.I.) C. of C. (pres. 1981-82), Nat. Assn. Home Builders, Nat., R.I. builders assns., SBA. Episcopalian. Home: 52 Rotary Dr Johnston RI 02919 Office: 1145 Hartford Ave Johnston RI 02919

THORPE, ALMA LANE KIRKLAND, broadcaster; b. Sylacauga, Ala., Dec. 20, 1941; d. Pierce and Dolly Odessa (Pardue) Kirkland; student Trevecca Nazarene Coll., 1961, Columbia Sch. Broadcasting, 1974; m. Jim Thorpe, Oct. 8, 1961; 1 dau., Margie. With W.T. Grant, Anniston, Ala., 1957-59; with So. Bell Telephone Co., Atlanta, 1963-65; religious broadcaster, Atlanta, 1974—. Office: PO Box 10634 Station A Atlanta GA 30310

THORPE, BETTY LEE, nurse; b. Orange, N.J., Aug. 18, 1942; d. Frederick William and Yolanda Maria (Cella) Rawles; B.A. magna cum laude, Jersey City State Coll., 1980; m. Wayne Thorpe, Mar. 2, 1962; children—Wayne, Glenn, Elizabeth. Pediatric nurse Orange (N.J.) Meml. Hosp., 1965-67; med. surg. nurse Morristown (N.J.) Meml. Hosp., 1967-69; staff nurse Welkind Neurol. Hosp., Chester, N.J., 1971-79; sch. nurse, tchr. health edn., spl. edn. Lakeland Sch., Chester, 1977-79; dir. nursing Welkind Neurol. Hosp., Chester, 1979-81; team leader The Matheny Sch.; Peapack, N.J., 1981—. Den mother, den leader coach Boy Scouts Am., merit badge counselor public health and safety. Mem. Am. Assn. Rehab. Nurses, N.J. League Nursing, Kappa Delta Phi. Presbyterian. Home: 9 Forest View Dr Long Valley NJ 07853 Office: The Matheny Sch Peapack NJ

THORSON, EDNA MARIE, ham radio operator, doll artist and collector; b. Winger, Minn., Aug. 9, 1937; d. Knute and Marie Thorson; student Grand Meadow (Minn.) Public Schs. Charter mem. Handi-Ham System of Minn., 1970—, also trustee; mem. Mil. Affiliate Radio System, 1969-71; instr., tutor, dir. Handi-Ham Amateur Radio Tng. Camps; mgr. Minn. Slow Speed Net, 1968-69, asst. mgr. communications Minn. sect., 1970, mgr. Minn. sect., 1974. Recipient awards in public service and emergency communications. Mem. Courage Handi-Ham System, Am. Radio Relay League, Original Doll Artist Council Am. Home: Box 355 Grand Meadow MN 55936

THORSON, ELOISE, newspaper editor/publisher; b. Knoxville, Iowa, Apr. 21, 1930; d. Adrian Tunis and Naomi Marguerite (Jones) Vander Linden; student Simpson Coll., Indianola, Iowa, 1947-49, Drake U., summer 1954; m. Richard J. Thorson, Dec. 22, 1952 (dec.); children—Todd Alan, Krisann. Elem. tchr., Zearing, Iowa, 1949-51, Story City, Iowa, 1951-53; bookkeeper, appliance store, Ft. Worth, 1953-54; elem. tchr., Colo., Iowa, 1954-55, Story City, 1955-60; co-owner Story City Reminder, 1958-67; bookkeeper Story City Farmers Coop., 1970-71; tchr. aide Roland-Story High Sch., 1971-72; co-owner Story City Herald, 1973-75, owner/pub., 1975—. Sec., Story City Mchts. Aux., 1976-77; bd. dirs., sec. Story City Greater Community Congress, 1981-83; mem. S.C. Adult Edn. Bd., 1981—, Story City Sister City Com., 1979-82, Story City Scandinavian Days Com., 1976-82, Story City-Roland Sch. Reorgn. Bd., 1969-70 Mem. Nat. Newspaper Assn., Iowa Press Assn., PEO. Republican. Lutheran. Clubs: Fine Arts, Story City Federated Woman's Questers. Story City IA 50248 Office: 511 Broad St Story City IA 50248

THRALL, MARY ANNA, veterinarian; b. Montreal, Que., Can., July 4, 1944; d. John Floyd and Mariella (Godfrey) Hull; B.A., U. Evansville, 1966; D.V.M., Purdue U., 1970; M.S., Colo. State U., 1977; m. F.G. Freemyer, Mar. 21, 1975; children—Joseph Paul, Anna Marie, Sarah Elizabeth. Pvt. vet. practitioner Eldred Animal Hosp., Greeley, Colo., 1970-74; resident in clin. pathology Colo. State U., Fort Collins, 1974-77; asst. prof. clin. pathology, 1978—, dir. lab., 1981—. Mem. Am. Coll. Vet. Pathologists, AVMA, Colo. Vet. Med. Assn., Am. Animal Hosp. Assn., Colo. Vet. Med. Assn., Am. Animal Hosp. Assn., Am. Soc. Vet. Clin. Pathology, Womens Vet. Med. Assn., Colo. Soc. Cytology, Colo. Assn. Continuing Med. Lab. Edn., Am. Soc. Cytotechnology, Assn. Am. Vet. Med. Colls., Phi Kappa Phi, Phi Zeta. Office: Dept Pathology Colo State U Fort Collins CO

THREATT, VITA, mgmt. cons.; b. Fort Worth, May 16, 1951; d. David and Mildred C. (Thomas) Threatt; M. City and Regional Planning, Howard U., 1975; 1 dau., Gena. Dir. lab. tng. Howard U., Washington, 1975; dir. hosp programs and evaluation Planned Parenthood of Met. Washington, 1976-78; exec. dir. Nat. Family Planning and Reproductive

Health Assn., Inc., Washington, 1978-80; pres. Bus., Office, Conf. Inc., 1980—. Mem. adv. bd. Improved Pregnancy Outcome Project, 1978-79; bd. dirs. Family Planning Council D.C., 1979-80, Center City Devel. Corp., 1981—, Washington Council Agys., 1982—, Rape Crisis Center D.C., 1981—; mem. com. on women YWCA, 1981—; Mid-Atlantic rep. Nat. Student Planning Network, 1974-75. Named Outstanding Young Woman Am., 1979; Ford Found. fellow, 1973-74; Am. Inst. Planners research fellow, 1974. Mem. Nat. Family Planning and Reproductive Health Assn., Nat. Assn. Female Execs., Am. Mgmt. Assn. Contbr. articles to various publs.

THRESHMAN, (JOAN) ISABELLE KATHERINE, ins. agt. and broker; b. Bronx, N.Y., Mar. 4, 1925; d. Thomas Edwin and Isabelle Stuart (Lyden) Euell; student Ins., Rutgers U., 1967-68; m. Morton George Threshman, Sept. 25, 1943; children—George Thomas, Joann Patrice, Euell Robert. Actress, 1937-51; co-owner M.G. & I.K. Threshman & Co., Inc., Bergenfield, N.J., 1971—, coordinator, 1971—, sec., 1978—. Sec. Bergen County (N.J.) Joint Vets. Legis. Com. Mem. Ins. Women No. N.J. (Internat.) (pres. 1978-79), Profl. Ins. Agts., Bergen County Assn. Ind. Ins. Agts., Brokers Assn. Roman Catholic. Clubs: DAV Aux. (chaplain Dept. N.J. Aux. 1977-78, comdr. 1979-80), Supreme Emblem Club of U.S.A. (pres. Englewood Emblem Club 1968, 78-79, supreme press corr. 1970-71, supreme chaplain 1969-70, dist. dep. dir. N.J. 1979-80). Home: 79 Stillman Ave Bergenfield NJ 07621

THROCKMORTON, JOAN HELEN, advt. and mktg. exec.; b. Evanston, Ill., Apr. 11, 1931; d. Sydney Lilly and Anita Helen T.; B.A., Smith Coll., 1953. Copywriter, Doubleday Book Clubs, N.Y.C., 1954-57; asso. promotion dir. Am. Heritage Pub. Co., 1957-59; circulation promotion mgr. Sports Illus. mag., 1959-60; asst. to chmn. bd. Time, Inc., 1960-65; dir. mktg. planning Lawrence G. Chart & Co., Inc., 1965-68; mgr. mdse. services Cowles Communications, Inc., 1968-70; founder, pres. Throckmorton Assos., Inc., N.Y.C., 1970—; speaker/lectr. Mail Advt. Clubs, Chgo., Boston, Washington, 1971-73, Am. Mgmt. Assn., 1973, Practising Law Inst., 1973. Named One of 100 Top Corp. Women in Am., Bus. Week mag., 1976. Mem. Direct Mail/Mktg. Assn. (speaker Nat. Conv. 1971-79, dir. 1971-77, exec. com. 1974, creative council bd. liaison 1972-77, long range planning com. 1977-78), Women's Direct Response Group, Women's Forum, Phi Beta Kappa. Office: Throckmorton Assos Inc 152 Madison Ave New York NY 10016

THROOP, BEATRICE TERRY, educator; b. Raymond, Ill.; d. John Charles and Therese (Mathis) Terry; B.E., Ill. State U., 1930; M.S. (fellow), U. Chgo., 1938; postgrad. U. Oreg., summer 1939, Oreg. State U., summer 1953, Colo. U., summers 1955-56, U. Caen (France), summers 1965-66, U. Md., summer 1963, 65-66; m. Vincent Medville Throop, May 29, 1940 (dec. Oct. 1968); children—Medville Jay, Alice Milberry, David Edmund, Annette Beatrice, Julian. Tchr., Lima (Peru) High Sch., Women's Fgn. Missionary Soc. of Meth. Ch., 1930-36; instr. Stephens Coll., 1938-40; tchr. public schs., Portland (Oreg.) Air Base, 1941; bibliographer Library of Congress, Washington, 1960-61; tchr. Prince George's County Schs., Brandywine, Md., 1961-77; George Washington U., summers 1967-69. Bd. dirs. Suitland Manor Owners Assn., 1981—. Mem. AAUW, Assn. Am. Geographers, NEA, Md. Edn. Assn., Prince George's County Tchrs. Assn., Am. Assn. Tchrs. Spanish and Portuguese, Alliance Francaise, Sigma Delta Epsilon. Contbr. articles to local publs. Home: 5609 Delaware Dr Forest Heights MD 20745

THURLOW, HEIDA LEHNERT, cookware designer and mfr.; b. Sylt, Ger., July 14, 1943; came to U.S., 1969, naturalized, 1970; d. Hans H. and Gisela E. (Weerpas) Lingen; Dipl. Ing., Mashcinen Bau Schule, Essen, 1965; Dipl. Econs., Oscar von Miller Poly., Munich, 1966; m. Thomas N. Thurlow, Nov. 20, 1976; children—Natasha G., Norman R., Regina E.T. Exec. v.p., then part owner Weerulin GmbH, Muelheim, Ger., 1966-69; founder, 1971, since pres. Lentrade, Inc., Houston. Lutheran. Patentee in field. Office: 10649 Haddington St Suite 1200 Houston TX 77043

THURMAN, JUDITH RAE, restaurant adminstr.; b. Houston, Sept. 28, 1938; d. Claude Fred and Johnnie Bess (Hall) Pitts; B.A., U. Houston, 1961; children—Mark Thurman, Matthew, Stephen. With Paragon Enterprises, Inc., Aspen, Colo., 1975—, mgr., 1980-82. Past pres. Jr. Achievement; past worthy adv. Order Rainbow for Girls. Betty Crocker Homemaker of Yr. scholar. Mem. Nat. Restaurant Assn., NOW, Women Asso. Alcoholic Beverages Colo., Aspen Women's Forum, Beta Sigma Phi. Methodist. Home: PO Box 10725 Aspen CO 81611 Office: PO Box 9064 Aspen CO 81611

THURMAN, MARY EVELYN, librarian; b. Burkesville, Ky., Nov. 23, 1921; d. William Edward and Rosa Simpson T.; student Bowling Green Bus. U., 1945-46; A.B., Asbury Coll., 1951; M.A. in Library Sci., George Peabody Coll., 1962. Tchr., Am. Dependent Schs., U.S. Army, Hokkaido, Camp Crawford, Honshu, Sendai, Kyoto, Tokyo, Simpson County (Ky.) Schs., 1951-57, Bad Kreznach (Germany) Am. Dependent Sch., 1957-59, Franklin (Ky.) Elem. Sch., 1959-62; librarian Fort Knox (Ky.) High Sch., 1962-65, Bermuda Dependent Sch., USAF, 1965-66; librarian Western Ky. U., Bowling Green, 1966—, asso. prof. library sci., 1982—. Ky. Library scholar, 1961. Mem. Laura Ingalls Wilder Meml. Soc. (life), Ky. Library Assn. (life), Ky. Sch. Media Assn. (life). Methodist. Author: The Canary Who Wants to Talk, 1975; Christmas in Kentucky with Little Bernel, 1976; A Pioneer Civil War Story for Molly and Ben, 1979; The Ingalls-Wilder Homesites: A Diary of Visits, 1972-81, 1982; contbr. articles in field to profl. jours. Home: 908 Merideth Dr Bowling Green KY 42101 Office: Helm Library Western Ky U Bowling Green KY 42101

THURMAN, NORMA JEAN, nurse; b. Hannibal, Mo., Feb. 24, 1927; d. David Robert and Sylvia Martha (Sonner) Shuck; R.N., Hillcrest Med. Center, Tulsa, 1955; B.S., St. Mary-of-the-Woods Coll., 1978; postgrad. U. Okla., 1978—; m. Andrew Frank Thurman, July 11, 1959. Head nurse emergency room Hillcrest Med. Center, 1957-63; surg. nurse to Herman Flanigan, M.D., Tulsa, 1956-57, to Robert Spencer, M.D., Tulsa, 1958-59; public health nurse Tulsa City and County Health Dept., 1963; adminstr. med. services Rockwell Internat., Tulsa, 1963—. Named Employee of Month, Rockwell Internat., 1966; R.N., Okla.; cert. occupational health nurse. Mem. Am. Assn. Occupational Health Nurses, Am. Nurses Assn. (chmn. Okla. occupational nurse sect. 1966), Okla. Nurses Assn., Rockwell Internat. Mgmt. Assn. Tulsa, Nat. Mgmt. Assn., Alumnae Assn. St. Mary-of-the-Woods Coll. Club: Tulsa County Democratic.

THURN, VICKIE ANN, electronics corp. ofcl.; b. Long Beach, Calif., Oct. 20, 1953; d. Marlan B. and Carole Ann Rhodes; B.A. in Communication, U. Central Fla., 1975; postgrad. in bus. mgmt. and psychology, U. South Fla.; m. Walt Thurn, Apr. 11, 1981. Communications specialist Fla. Power Corp., St. Petersburg, 1975-80; mgr. tng. and devel. E-Systems, Inc., St. Petersburg, 1980—; public relations adv. council U. Fla. Mem. Internat. Assn. Bus. Communicators (pres., dir.), Am. Soc. Tng. and Devel., AAUW, Suncoast Mgmt. Inst. (dir.), Women in Communication. Republican. Methodist. 1759 Lakewood Dr S Saint Petersburg FL 33712 Office: PO Box 12248 Saint Petersburg FL 33733

TIBBETTS, CHARLENE HANSEN, educator; b. Grand Island, Nebr., Mar. 10, 1921; d. Henry Charles and Nelle Pace (Dellinger) Hansen; B.A., Nebr. State Coll., Kearney, 1942; M.A., Peabody Coll., 1964; m. Arnold M. Tibbetts, Oct. 12, 1951; children—Susan, Alice, John, Caroline. Tchr., Floyd Jr. High Sch., Montgomery, Ala., 1960-61, North High Sch., Nashville, 1961-63; asso. prof. Coll. of Edn., U. Ill., Urbana, 1964—; cons. curriculum devel., teaching of composition. Title IV grantee, 1975-76. Mem. Nat. Council Tchrs. English, AAUP, Ill. Assn. Tchrs. English. Author: (with A.M. Tibbetts) Strategies of Rhetoric, 3d edit., 1983; The Critical Man, 1972; What's Happening to American English, 1978; contbr. articles to profl. jours. Home: 1902 G Huff Dr Urbana IL 61801 Office: 1212 W Springfield Ave Urbana IL 61801

TIBBETTS, JOAN CROSBY, visual arts exec.; b. Washington, Sept. 21, 1932; d. Percy Leo and Agnes Dale (Locke) Crosby; B.A., Vassar Coll., 1954; student Georgetown U., 1955-56, U. Maine, 1970-71, U. St. Andrews, Scotland, 1973; m. Waldo E. Tibbetts, June 22, 1957; children—Jeffrey Locke, Waldo Edward, Melanie Dale, Kimberley Cummings. Multi-lingual interpreter Turkish Embassy and Pan-Am. Union, Washington, 1955-57; field guide, interpreter CARE, Inc., Israel, Greece, Guatemala, 1957-64; adminstratrix Percy Crosby Estate, 1964-68; tchr. dance U. Maine 1971-73; pres. Skippy, Inc., Reston, Va., 1968—, also dir.; dir. Skippy Enterprises, Inc.; cons., patient advocate Nat. Inst. Mental Health, 1979. Co-chmn. N.Y.-Westchester Hwy. Studies, 1965-67; pres. Eddington (Maine) PTA, 1971; mem. adv. council Girl Scouts, 1972; bd. dirs. Eddington Maine Sch., 1970-73. Mem. Nat. Cartoonists Soc., Nat. Women's Polit. Caucus, Nat. Assn. Female Execs., N.S. Dance Fedn., Royal Scottish Country Dance Soc. Unitarian. Club: Vassar of Washington. Editor: Percy Crosby Poetry and Memoirs, Smithsonian Archives of Am. Art, 1978-79; editor, reviser Halt Legal Guide, 1979. Home: 11900 St Johnsbury Ct Reston VA 22091

TIBBETTS, LAURENE, poet, ednl. dir., artist, dancer; b. Mpls.; d. Samuel Elgin and Irene (Lyons) Tibbetts; student U. Minn., 1946-48, Mpls. Sch. Art, 1956, Harvard, 1955. Writer poetry, stories, essays, plays; dancer in Kiddie Revs., Greenwich Village Follies, specialty dances for Twin City programs; appearances in various dramatic roles; dramatic recitals, 1963—; dir. Radio Theatre Playhouse sta. KDHL, 1949-52; mem. Wandering Troubadours, 1940-43; dir. edn. St. Paul Art Center; now dir. Minn. Mus. Art Sch.; poet laureate Minn., 1974—. Counselor, Girl Scouts in Minn., Wis., N.J., N.Y., 1945-55, jr. staff mem. Camp Edith Macy, N.Y., 1949-50, Internat. Camp Andre; chmn. Settlement House Dinners for needy children; capt. of hostesses Mpls. Art Inst. Festival, 1957; drama chmn. Minn. Centennial, chmn. Minn. Outdoor Poetry Festival, 1958; chmn. Salute to Youth, 1970; pres. Inter-Club Council, 1974—; active ARC, Community Chest, Jr. Group of Mpls. Symphony, Womens Soc. Mpls. Symphony, St. Stephens Choir; mem. Mayor's Council Human Relations, Recreation Council St. Paul; edn. com. Econ. Opportunity Project; bd. advisers Montessori La Pepiniere Acad.; trustee KTCA Ednl. TV; bd. dirs. Minn. Terr. Pioneers. Recipient Frank H. Peavy 9100 award, 1947, 1st prize Poetry award, 1950, 51; winner Premio Internazionale di Poesia, Rome, Italy, 1951, various essay contest, including How to Be A Good Am. Citizen, Midwest Druggist essay contest; 1st prize Calif. Poetry Contest, 1949, Frank O. Lowden award, 1947; winner in Am. Weekly Poetry Competition, 1950. Rep. from Minn. to Archbishop John Ireland celebration; named Poet Laureate of Minn. Mem. Internat. Platform Assn. (Carl Sandburg award 1974, Poet Laureateship in Washington 1974), Midwestern Assn. Internat. Chaparral Poets (pres. 1958—), League Minn. Poets (state sec. 1952-58), Am. Poetry League, Mpls. Poetry Soc. (pres. 1953-56), Campers and Counsellors Assn., English Speaking Union, Alliance Francaise, Nat. Forensic League (bd. mgrs. 1946), Nat. Arts Club Am., Western Arts Council, Am., Mo. Valley, Minn. (dir.) edn. assns., Nat. (chmn. liberal arts sect. 1970), Minn. (dir., gen. chmn. ann. spring conf.) adult edn. assns., Adult Educators Am., Western Art Edn. Assn., Minn. Speakers Assn., Panhellenic (chmn. 1946), Delta Zeta. Clubs: Beaux Arts (pres. 1946), Harvard. Author: Be All You Can Be; Blooming in the Shade. Composer song Miss Minn. Lit. editor Minn. Feature. Home: The Fair Oaks 310 E 25th St Minneapolis MN 55404

TIBERIO, FAITH KURT, metal stamping co. exec.; b. St. Augustine, Fla., Jan. 23, 1926; d. Raymond Theodore and Marguerita (Phillips) Kurt; student John B. Stetson U., 1944-45; B.A., Boston U., 1965, M.A., 1967; m. Joseph William Tiberio, May 18, 1945; children—Frederick Morris, Faith Phillips. With Western Union, Phila., 1943-44, So. Bell Telephone Co., St. Augustine, 1944-45; co-founder, mgr. Ty-Car Mfg. Co., Holliston, Mass., 1946-49; partner Century Mfg. Co., Holliston, 1949—, dir., 1970—; v.p. Ty-Wood Corp., Holliston, 1965—. Trustee, Hillside Sch., 1977-80. Mem. Bus. and Profl. Women's Club, DAR (state regent 1977-80, nat. curator gen.). Office: Ty-Wood Corp 383 Fiske St Holliston MA 01746

TIBURCIO, CARMEN TORRES, nurse; b. Bayamon, P.R., July 15, 1921; d. Aniceto To and Hemenegilda (Santiago) Torres; A.Nursing, Bklyn. Coll., 1958; B.S. Nursing, Tchrs. Coll., Columbia U., 1964; M.Nursing and Nurse Midwifery, N.Y. Med. Coll., 1965; postgrad. Columbia U., 1972-78; m. Angel Luis Tiburcio, Oct. 29, 1953; 1 dau., Doris Finnemore Meade. Staff nurse Columbia-Presbyn. Med. Center, N.Y.C., 1958-60, Metro. Hosp., N.Y.C., 1960-64; dir. nurse midwifery sch. New Med. Coll., Grad. Sch. Nursing, Ponce, P.R., 1965-68; dir. dept. nursing P.R. Jr. Coll., Rio Piedras, 1968-69; instr. U. P.R. Sch. Nursing, Hato Rey, 1969; prof., dir. Hostos Community Coll., Dept. Nursing, N.Y.C. U., 1972-74; dir. Inter-Am. U. P.R., Metro. Campus, Sch. Nursing, Hato Rey, 1976-81, asst. dean, 1981—; cons. Pan Am. Health Orgn., WHO. Bd. dirs. Operation for Nursing Success for Minority, Inc., N.Y.C., 1972-73: People to People Goodwill ambassador to Australia and N.Z. as mem. Nat. League Nursing, 1980. Mem. Am. Nurses Assn., Nat. League Nursing, P.R. Coll. Profl. Nurses, Am. Public Health Assn., Spanish Surnamed Nurses Assn. (co-founder), Am. Assn. Advancement Sci. Club: Altrusa. Contbr. articles to profl. jours. Address: Inter Am Univ Metro Campus PO Box 12 93 Hato Rey PR 00919

TICE, JESSICA IRENE SPRUILL, extension home economist; b. Ft. Gordon, Ga., Mar. 21, 1952; d. William Edward and Erma Irene (Phelps) Spruill; A.A., Coll. of the Albemarle, 1973; B.S. in Home Econs. Edn., East Carolina U., 1975; postgrad. N.C. State U., 1979; m. Roger Jeffrey Tice, Aug. 4, 1979; 1 son, Brandon Jeffrey. Asso. home econs. extension agt. N.C. Agrl. Extension Service, N.C. State U., 1977—; liaison agt. extension homemakers clubs, coordinator expanded food and nutrition edn. program. Mem. Albemarle Craftsman Fair Bd., 1979. Mem. Watermark Assn. Artisans (charter), Currituck Friends of Library, Currituck Hist. Soc., Am. Home Econs. Assn., N.C. Home Econs. Assn., Nat. Assn. Extension Home Economists N.C. Assn. Extension Home Economists (sec. N.E. dist. 1978, 2d v.p. 1979, 1st v.p. 1980, pres.-elect 1981, pres. 1982 Young Agts. Service award 1980), Phi Upsilon Omicron. Democrat. Baptist. Clubs: Currituck Ski and Outing (sec.-treas. 1979), Moyock Women's. Office: PO Box 10 Currituck NC 27929

TICHMAN, NADYA ERICA, violinist; b. N.Y.C., June 12, 1958; d. Herbert L. and Ruth (Budnevich) T.; B.Mus., Curtis Inst. Music, 1980. Violinist, Aspen Music Festival 1975, 76, Opera Co. Phila. 1978, 79, Concerto Soloists of Phila. 1979-80, Santa Fe Opera Orch. 1979-81, San Francisco Symphony 1980—, Grand Teton Music Festival 1982; numerous solo and chamber music recitals.

TIDWELL, CHRISTINA BERNICE, public relations counsel, photographer; b. Arkansas City, Kans., May 2, 1946; d. Arlyss Eckard and Martha Josephine (Hughes) Springgate; student Cowley County (Kans.) Community Coll., 1964, U. Kans., 1967-68; m. Terry Lee Tidwell, June 5, 1964 (div. Nov. 1975); children—Matthew Reed, Kristyn Teresa. Reporter, Arkansas City Traveler, 1973-76; community editor Townsend Communications, Kansas City, Mo., 1976-78; features editor/layout editor The Kansan, Kansas City, Kans., 1978-81; advt. mgr. Inland Industries, Lenexa, Kans., 1980-81; free-lance writer/photographer, corp. communications, advt., public relations. Co-dir., Telephone Concern Center, Arkansas City, 1973; exec. adv. Jr. Achievement, Kansas City, Kans., 1979-80; bd. dirs. Wyandotte Players, Kansas City, Kans., 1979. Recipient 2d pl. award Kans. Better Newspaper Contest, 1975; hon. mention Mo. Better Newspaper Contest, 1977. Mem. Kansas City Press Club (dir. 1979-81), Sigma Delta Chi. Mem. Christian Ch. (Disciples of Christ). Club: Soroptimist. Home: 238 N 15 St Kansas City KS 66102 Office: 238 N 15th St Kansas City KS 66102

TIEDEMAN, GRETCHEN THOMAS, artist; b. Washington, June 9, 1919; d. Dorsey Opie and Gretchen (Gorton) Thomas; student Mt. Vernon Jr. Coll., Washington, 1936-38, Corcoran Sch. Art, 1939-40; m. Robert Komfort Tiedeman, Aug. 23, 1941; children—Trudi Tiedeman Puravs, Thomas Van Dohlen. Art tchr. Mt. Vernon Jr. Coll., 1939-40; designer, 1943-45; founder, tchr. Packahack Coop. Nursery Sch., Wayne, N.J., 1953-59; exhibited paintings in shows including Wayne Library; pvt. art tchr.; portraits in collections Navy Mus., Packanack Community Ch., St. Michael's Episcopal Ch., Wayne. Mem. Wayne Hist. Commn., 1969—, chmn., 1972; Wayne chmn. Am. Bicentennial Commn., 1973—, designer Wayne Bicentennial medallion; mem. Citizen's Adv. Com., 1974-75; a founder Wayne chpt. Fedn. Republican Women; mem. county com. Rep. Party, 1960-68; chmn. Nixon Now, 1968; co-chmn. Nixon campaign, 1968; bd. govs. Rep. Club; bd. dirs. United Givers Packanack Lake; co-chmn. Packanack Lake 50th Anniversary Com., 1978. Recipient certificate of merit League Hist. Socs. N.J., 1977. Mem. DAR, Daus. Am. Colonists, Colonial Dames 17th Century. Episcopalian. Clubs: Packanack Lake Golf, Zonta. Home: 23 Spruce Terr Wayne NJ 07470

TIEDEMANN, KATE M., mfg. co. exec.; b. Hackemuhlen, W. Ger., Apr. 21, 1936; came to U.S., 1955, naturalized, 1968; d. Klaus and Maria A. (Doescher) T. Co-founder Eye Ear Nose and Throat Instrument div. Edward Weck & Co., Inc., L.I. City, N.Y., 1966-71; v.p., co founder Sparta Instrument Corp., Fairfield, N.J., 1971-75; pres. Katena Products, Inc., East Hanover, N.J., 1975—, also v.p. Link Am., Inc., 1975—. Mem. Bus. and Profl. Womens Club. Home: RD 1 DeCamp Dr Boonton NJ 07005 Office: 10 Great Meadow Ln East Hanover NJ 07936

TIEGS, CHERYL, model; b. Calif.; d. Theodore and Phyllis Tiegs; student Calif. State U., Los Angeles; m. Peter Beard, 1981. Profl. model, appearing in mags. including Bazaar, Glamour, Time, Life, Seventeen, Sports Illustrated; also appearing in TV commls. for Olympus Camera Corp., Cover Girl; producer Cheryl Tiegs women's apparel for Sears, Roebuck and Co. Author: The Way to Natural Beauty, 1980. Address: care Good Morning America 1 Lincoln Plaza New York NY 10023

TIEMANN, GEORGANNE, med. technologist; b. Jefferson City, Mo., Dec. 20, 1928; d. George Wesley and Marvel (Biglow) Greene; student U. Ill., 1946-47, Ind. State U., 1950-51; B.S. in Health Adminstrn., Lindenwood Coll., 1979; diploma Gradwohl Sch. Lab. Tech.; m. Robert Charles Tiemann, Sept. 11, 1953. Technician Union Hosp., Terra Haute, Ind., 1949-51; technician Barnes Hosp., St. Louis, 1951-52, asst. chief technician, 1952-60, chief technician serology lab., 1961—; civilian supr. serology lab. U.S. Army 5th Area Med. Lab., 1960-61; instr. St. Louis U. Continuing Edn., 1970-71. Bd. dirs. Madison County Easter Seal Soc., 1965-67; bd. dirs. Southwestern Ill. Family Service Agency, 1965-71; bd. dirs., sec. Citizens Com. for Collinsville (Ill.) Hosp., 1965-68. Mem. Am. Med. Technologists, Internat. Soc. Clin. Lab. Technologists (recipient certificate of merit, 1972), Am. Bd. Bioanalysts, Am. Pub. Health Assn., Am. Soc. Microbiologists, UN Assn., Gradwohl Alumni Assn. (pres. 1967-69; achievement award 1967), Nat. Fedn. Bus. and Profl. Women's Clubs. Republican. Lutheran. Contbr. articles to profl. jours., poetry to anthologies. Home: 17 Lake Dr Troy IL 62294 Office: Barnes Hosp Lab Barnes Hosp Plaza St Louis MO 63110

TIEMEYER, HOPE ELIZABETH JOHNSON, advt. co. exec., club woman; b. Ft. Wayne, Ind., May 20, 1908; d. Edward Tibbens and Burton (Meyers) Johnson; B.A., U. Cin., 1932; m. Edwin H. Tiemeyer, Oct. 30, 1929 (dec. Apr. 1955); children—Ann Elizabeth (Mrs. G. L. Lewin, Jr.), Edwin Houghton (dec.). Pres., owner Mail-Way Advt. Co., Cin., pres., 1955—. Regent, Cin. chpt. D.A.R., 1956-58, chmn. nat. sch. survey com., 1961-62, nat. vice chmn. Americanism Manual for Citizenship, 1962-65, Continental Congress program com., 1962-65, Congress Marshall Com., 1966-68, mem. Congress hostess com., 1969-77; rec. sec. Nat. Chmn.'s Assn., 1969-71, pres. Ohio State Officers Club, 1975-77; sr. nat. membership chmn. Children Am. Revolution, 1958-60, sr. nat. rec. sec., 1960-62, nat. chmn. Mountain Sch., 1962-64, hon. sr. nat. v.p., 1963-64, sr. nat. 1st v.p. 1964-66, sr. nat. pres., 1966-68, hon. nat. life pres., 1970—, 1st v.p. Nat. Officers Club, 1965-69, pres., 1970-73, hon. sr. life pres. Ohio soc.; hon. life mem. Ohio Congress PTA, treas., 1957-62, v.p., dir. dept. health, 1962-63; hon. life mem. Nat. Congress PTA; life mem. Kappa Alpha Theta Mothers Club, pres., 1958-59; v.p. women's com. Cin. Symphony Orch., 1964-65; pres. U. Cin. Parents Club, 1959-61, v.p., 1963-64; area chmn. State House Conf. on Edn., 1953; dir. Am. Assn. U. Women, 1963-64; mem. Cin. Social Health Bd., 1950—, exec. com., 1965-70, v.p., 1973-75, treas., 1975-78, life trustee, 1978—; pres. Singleton's of Cin. Club, 1969-71, 73-76, mem. travelers bd., pres., 1973-74, art com., 1971—, mem. membership com., 1973-78; pres. Newtown Garden Club, 1947-49, City Panhellenic Assn., 1951-52, Ohio Hobby Club, 1958-59, Sigma Nu Mothers Club, 1963-65, pres. Alumnae chpt. Alpha Omicron Pi, 1930-32, nat. admissions com., 1933-35; life mem. Craftshops for Handicapped; chmn. Amelia Earhart Fellowship com. Zonta Club, Cin., 1963-64, program chmn., 1964-65, orientation chmn., 1965-67, internat. relations chmn., 1967-68, dir., 1969-74, mem. exec. com., 1969-74, mem. nat. nominating com., 1970-74, v.p., 1971-73; mem. music com., mem. tea room com. Cin. Woman's Club, 1969—; treas. Queen City chpt. Nat. Assn. Parliamentarians, 1965-69; v.p. Greater Cin. area women's chpt. Freedoms Found. at Valley Forge, 1975-77, sec. 1977—, pres., 1978-80. Mem. Nat. Platform Assn., Nat. Gavel Assn., English Speaking Union. Recipient Jonathon Moore citation and award Ind. Soc. S.A.R., 1967; Good Citizenship medal Nat. Soc., 1967; named Ky. col. Home: 2786 Little Dry Run Rd Cincinnati OH 45244 Office: 229 426-30 Plum St Cincinnati OH 45202

TIER, SUSAN BECKER, editor; b. N.Y.C., June 19, 1938; d. Maxwell Arthur and Mildred S. (Strackner) Becker; B.A., Wells Coll., 1959; postgrad. Hofstra U., 1959-60; m. Richard Scott Tier, Jan. 28, 1973; children—Elizabeth Becker Resen, Stafanie Kitt Tier. Asst. editor Indsl. Design mag., 1960-62; free-lance writer, public relations, 1965-72; editor Long Beach Voice, 1975; editor Electronic Buyers/News, 1976-82, also v.p., gen. mgr. TEG Communications subs. Avnet, Inc. Recipient Disting. Service award Electronic Distbrs. Research Inst., 1981. Mem. NOW, Nat. Electronics Distbrs. Assn. Office: 70 Marcus Blvd Hauppage NY 11787 *

TIERNEY, JOAN DOHERTY, communications com. exec.; b. Jersey City, Mar. 6, 1929; d. Hugh Francis and Elsie (Starz) Doherty; B.Sc., Seton Hall U., S. Orange, N.J., 1953, M.A., 1967; Ph.D. (research fellow, HEW scholar 1969-71), Ind. U., 1972; divorced; children—Patrick,

Hugh, Robert, Mary Louise. Various writing positions, 1959-69; cons. Children's TV Workshop, 1971; guest editor Prospectives, Center Research Devel. in Edn., Montreal, Que., Can., 1972; designer, developer tng. films and videotapes City of Montreal Transit Authority, 1972, self-teaching course for R.J. Brady & Co., 1975; cons. Neurol. Inst., Montreal, 1975; spl. adv., v.p. Tele-Metropole Co., Montreal, 1971-75; pres. J.D. Tierney Enterprises, Ltd., Montreal, 1971-76, Joan D. Tierney Enterprises, Inc., Jensen Beach, Fla., 1981—; mgr. div. employee communications Pratt & Whitney Aircraft Co., 1979; asst. prof. edn. tech. U. Montreal, 1971-73; asso. prof. communications, chmn. dept. Concordia U., Montreal, 1973-78; vis. prof. U. Tex., 1978; workshop leader, cons. in field. Grantee Concordia U., Com. Aid Scholarly Activity, Can. Radi-TV and Telecommunications Commn. Mem. Nat. Assn. Female Execs., Am. Bus. Women's Assn., Bus. and Profl. Women's Assn., Internat. Assn. Mass. Communications Research. Author articles, revs. in field. Address: 1077 Hawaii Dr Nettle's Island Jensen Beach FL 33457

TIFFANY, BETTYE JANE, ednl. adminstr.; b. Fayetteville, Ark., Sept. 10, 1925; d. Samuel Rodman and Ruth (Hyatt) Stout; B.A. summa cum laude, Ouachita Bapt. U., 1945; M.A., UCLA, 1971; children—Timothy Neale, Rodman Dana, Bettye Lorraine. Tchr. ungraded spl. edn. Ormsby Village Sch., Anchorage, Ky., 1948-51; cons. primary and intermediate edn. Ark. Bapt. State Conv., 1952-57; tchr., counselor China Lake (Calif.) Elem. Sch. Dist., 1959-65, dir. guidance, 1965-69, vice prin., 1969-71, prin., 1971-74; prin. Murray Jr. High Sch., Sierra Sands Unified Sch., China Lake, 1971—; Sierra Sands Unified Sch. Dist., Ridgecrest, Calif., 1974—. Bd. dirs. Desert Area Counseling Clinic; pres. PEO Sisterhood. Mem. Am. Ednl. Research Assn., Nat. Soc. for Study Edn., NEA (life), Assn. Calif. Sch. Adminstrs., AAUW, Bus. and Profl. Women's Club, Phi Delta Kappa, Pi Lambda Theta. Republican. Episcopalian. Home: 305 E Church St Ridgecrest CA 93555 Office: 921 E Inyokern Rd Ridgecrest CA 93555

TIGERMAN, JO ANN, advt. exec.; b. Chgo., June 16, 1941; d. Harry and Elaine Kinzelberg; B.A., U. Ill., 1965. Interior designer, Chgo., 1970-73; mem. woman's bd. Chgo. Mus. Contemporary Art, 1971-73; sr. sales/mktg. cons. Dun & Bradstreet, Oak Brook, Ill., 1974-79; indsl. real estate salesman Arthur Rubloff & Co., Chgo., 1979-80; Midwest advt. salesperson Crain Communications, Inc., Chgo., 1980—. Recipient Nat. award AIA, 1970. Home: 2053 Broadway San Francisco CA 94115

TIGHE, KATHLEEN ANN, advt. agy. exec.; b. Newark, June 9, 1953; s. Robert Edward and Marie (Schmidt) T.; B.A. in Communications and Polit. Sci., Lycoming Coll., 1975. Reporter, writer Daily Record, Morristown, N.J., 1975-76; community affairs coordinator, advt. rep. Sta. WWPA, Williamsport, Pa., 1976-78; account exec. Hutchins/Young & Rubicam Advt. Agy., Rochester, N.Y., 1978—. Mem. adv. bd. Williamsport Area Community Coll. Career Devel. Center. Mem. Women in Communications, Mktg. Communications Execs. Internat. (sec. Rochester chpt.), Ad Council Greater Rochester. Home: 1132 East Ave Rochester NY 14607 Office: 400 Midtown Tower Rochester NY 14604

TIGNOR, BEATRICE PROCTOR, educator; b. Washington, June 2, 1940; d. Ralph and Sarah Ann (Watson) Proctor; B.S. in Edn., Bowie State Coll.; M.A., George Washington U., Ed.S., Ed.D. Instr. reading Allen U., Columbia, S.C.; asst. prof. reading off-campus div. George Washington U., Washington; lectr. Grad. Sch., U. Md., College Park; instr. adult literacy program Prince George's public sch. system, Upper Marlboro, Md.; dir. acad. reinforcement program Dental Sch., Howard U., Washington; reading specialist D.C. public sch. system, Washington, 1969; reading cons. Prince George's public sch. system, 1969-71, asst. supr., 1971-72; asso. prof. reading Prince George's Community Coll., Largo, Md., dir. developmental studies, 1977—; cons. reading to various ednl. instns. Mem. Internat. Reading Assn., NEA, Coll. Reading Assn., Md. Community Coll. Reading Assn., Nat. Council English Tchrs., Council for Exceptional Children. Roman Catholic. Home: 170 Old Enterprise Rd South Upper Marlboro MD 20772 Office: 301 Largo Rd Upper Marlboro MD 20772

TILLER, OLIVE M., church worker; b. St. Paul, Dec. 13, 1920; d. Otto W. and Myrtle (Brougham) Foerster; B.S., U. Minn., 1940; m. Carl W. Tiller, June 21, 1940; children—Robert W., Jeanne L. Peterson. Chmn. Christian social relations Nat. Council Am. Baptist Women, 1959-63, v.p. Christian service, 1964-68; tchr. handicapped children, Prince Georges County, Md., 1953-54, 58-62; public relations specialist, staff asst. for profl. services Kendall Demonstration Elem. Sch. for Deaf, Washington, 1971-78; staff specialist Ch. Women United, 1979-80; ops. asst. to gen. sec. Nat. Council Chs. of Christ in U.S.A., 1981—. Bd. dirs. Phyllis Wheatley YWCA, Washington, 1961-64; trustee Cheverly-Tuxedo Elementary Sch., Cheverly, Md., 1960-69. Mem. Am. Bapt. Conv. Council on Christian Social Progress, 1959-63; world relief com. Am. Bapt. Conv., 1961-72, Washington rep. div. Christian social concern, 1965-69, mem. gen. council, 1969-72; vice chmn. Bapt. Joint Com. Public Affairs, 1963-64; chmn. Washington Pacifist Fellowship, 1963-65; program bd. div. overseas ministries Nat. Council Chs., 1965-68; bd. mgrs., exec. com. Ch. Women United, 1967-77; mem. Ch. World Service Com., 1971-77; mem. Prince George County Human Relations Com., 1967-73; v.p. Am. Bapt. Chs. U.S.A., 1976-77; pres. Am. Bapt. Peace Fellowship, 1977-81; bd. dirs., sec. Am. Leprosy Missions, Inc., 1981—; chmn. bd. dirs. Internat. Program for Human Resource Devel., 1977-78. Home: 528 Cumberland Ave Teaneck NJ 07666

TILLEY, ELIZABETH ROBERTS CORNWALL (MRS. THOMAS CLARK TILLEY), astronomer, civic worker; b. New Haven, Sept. 23, 1914; d. Charles Edward and Millicent (Johnson) Cornwall; B.A., Vassar Coll., 1935; postgrad. Yale U., 1935-36; M.A., Wellesley Coll., 1939; Ph.D., U. Mich., 1942; m. Thomas Clark Tilley, Oct. 31, 1942; children—Thomas Clark III, Anne Bradford. Computer, Mt. Wilson Obs., Pasadena, Calif., 1936-37; asst. tchr. Wellesley (Mass.) Coll., 1937-40, U. Mich., Ann Arbor, 1940-42; editor, supr. computers OSRD Rocket Project, Calif. Inst. Tech., Pasadena, 1943-44; tchr. St. John's Prep. Sch., San Juan, P.R., 1958-60; supr. lab. tests Analysts, Inc., San Juan, 1961-63; mem. altar guild St. John's Cathedral (Episcopal), 1964-80, pres., 1968-69, mem. vestry, 1974-80, mem. cathedral chpt., 1974-80, parish treas., 1974-80; mem. bishop's council advice Diocese P.R., 1968-69; vice chmn. St. Cecilia Guild All Saints Ch., 1982—. Bd. dirs. Ladies Aux. Presbyn. Hosp., San Juan, 1964-79, pres., 1966-70, treas., 1972-79, trustee hosp., 1970-80. Mem. Am. Astron. Soc., Phi Beta Kappa. Club: Vassar Central Fla. (pres. 1982—). Home: 360 Sylvan Blvd Winter Park FL 32789

TILLINGHAST, META IONE, civic worker; b. Newark, Nov. 14; d. Ralph Vincent and Florence Virginia (MacDonald) Muldoon; student Leland Powers Sch. of Spoken Word, Boston; m. Frederick William Tillinghast, Apr. 20; children—Anne (Mrs. Robert Riley), Patricia (Mrs. Charles McLaughlin). Bd. dirs. Balt. chpt. ARC, 1955-58, chmn. Queen Anne's chpt. 1964-66, nat. bd. govs., 1966-69, Md. state fund chmn., 1969-71, Delmarva div. chmn. mems., funds, 1971-73, vols., 1971-74, coordinator community relations Eastern area, 1975-76; chmn. vols. nat. field office (now Eastern field office) ARC, Alexandria, Va., 1976—. dir. ch. plays; chmn. United Fund Baltimore County (Md.) Women's div., 1950. Named vol. of year Md., ARC, 1965; recipient award Gen. Fedn. Women's Clubs, 1952. Mem. Md. No. Dist. Fedn. Women's Clubs (pres. 1953-55). Clubs: Women's Glyndon (pres. 1949-51), Talbot County Women's (pres. 1962-64), Women's Ten Hills (pres. 1940-42). Home: Queenstown MD 21658 Office: 615 N St Asaph Alexandria VA 22314

TILLMAN, LINDA RUTH, exec. asst.; b. Orlando, Fla., June 3, 1943; d. Thomas John and Stella Frances (Block) Tillman; student Valencia Community Coll., Orlando, 1973-74, Fla. Jr. Coll., Jacksonville, 1976-78. Exec. sec. to mgr. advance systems engrng. Martin Marietta Aerospace Corp., Orlando, 1963-69; exec. sec. to pres., also office mgr., fashion coordinator and writer Act II Jewelry Inc., Orlando, 1969-76; legal asst., sec. Howell, Howell, Liles, Braddock & Milton, Jacksonville, Fla., 1976-78; exec. asst. to owners and developers Regency Sq. Shopping Center, Jacksonville, 1978-79; free-lance legal sec. and asst., Jacksonville, 1979-80; exec. sec. to sr. v.p. personnel labor relations Seaboard System R.R., Jacksonville, 1980—. Hospitality chmn., v.p. Women of Jacksonville Art Mus., 1977-80, publicity chmn., 1981-82; mem. Republican Nat. Com. Nat. Secs. Assn. (asst. treas. 1973-74, sec. 1974-75), Women's Guild of Cummer Gallery, Women's Guild Jacksonville Mus. Arts and Scis., LWV, Women's Info. Exchange, Nat. Assn. Ry. Bus. Women (community affairs, publicity chmn. 1981-82), Jacksonville Wine and Food Soc. (sec.-treas.), Les Amis du Vin. Mem. Ch. Religious Sci. Home: 2361 St John Ave Apt 3 Jacksonville FL 32204 Office: 500 Water St Room 209 Jacksonville FL 32202

TILLMAN, MARY ANNE TUGGLE (MRS. DANIEL TILLMAN), pediatrician; b. Bristow, Okla., Sept. 4, 1935; d. Thomas Gus and Ruthie (English) Tuggle; B.S., Howard U., 1956, M.D., 1960; postgrad. Harvard Grad. Med. Sch., 1965; m. Daniel Tillman, Apr. 20, 1957; children—Dana, Daniel. Intern, Homer G. Phillips Hosp., St. Louis, 1960-61, resident pediatrics, 1961-63; practice medicine, specializing in pediatrics, St. Louis, 1963—; dir. nurseries Homer G. Phillips Hosp., St. Louis, 1964-79, St. Louis City Hosp., 1979—; mem. staffs St. Louis Children's, Deaconess, Barnes, Jewish hosps.; asst. prof. Washington U. Sch. Medicine, St. Louis, 1963—, pediatric cons. Project Head Start, 1969—. Recipient Woman of Year award Zeta Phi Beta, 1970; Woman of Achievement, St. Louis Globe Democrat, 1982. Diplomate Am. Bd. Pediatrics. Fellow Am. Acad. Pediatrics (nat. com. adoptions 1969—); mem. Am., Nat. med. assns., Am. Med. Women's Assn. Presbyterian. Contbr. articles to profl. publs. Home: 26 Washington Terr Saint Louis MO 63112 Office: Room 201 4511 Forest Park Blvd Saint Louis MO 63108

TILLMAN, MARY NORMAN, urban affairs cons.; b. Atlanta, Jan. 31, 1926; d. Mary Nellie Shehee; B.A., Morris Brown Coll., 1947; postgrad. U. Minn., 1964, Old Dominion U., 1975—; m. James A. Tillman, Jr., Apr. 11, 1952; children—James A., Gina G. Asst. bus. mgr. Morris Brown Coll., Atlanta, 1947-53; race relations and urban affairs cons. Tillman Assos. Cons. Social Engrs., Atlanta and Syracuse, N.Y., 1963—, sr. partner, treas., from 1965, now pres.; clin. prof. United Theol. Sem., New Brighton, Minn.; adj. prof. Gordon-Conwell Theol. Sem., South Hamilton, Mass. Mem. adv. council to urban ministries dept. So. Bapt. Conv. Mem. Tidewater Assn. Public Adminstrs. (dir.), Am. Acad. Consultants, Nat. Black Writers Consortium (v.p.). Author: What is Your Racism Quotient?, 1964; (with James A. Tillman, Jr.) Why America Needs Racism and Poverty, 1972; (with J.A. Tillman, Jr.) Black Intellectuals, White Liberals and Race Relations: An Analytic Overview, 1973. Office: 1765 Glenview Dr SW Atlanta GA 30331

TILLMAN, MAYRE LUTHA, polit. cons.; b. Dover, Fla., Aug. 24, 1928; d. Luther E. and Marietta T. Wheeler; student Fla. State U., 1945-46, Alladin Bus. Coll., 1963-64; m. Paul D. Tillman, Apr. 7, 1947 (div.); children—Daniel Paul, Shayla Denise Tillman Nail. Credit investigator Maas Bros., Tampa, 1946-47; sec.-bookkeeper Dover Sch., 1950-53; adminstrv. asst. Dave Gordon Enterprises, Tampa, 1965-68; office mgr. Bumby & Stimpson, Inc., Plant City, Fla., 1968-70; tax clk., clk. of circuit ct. Hillsborough County (Fla.) Courthouse, 1970-73; adminstr. property mgmt. Tampa-Hillsborough County Expressway Authority, 1973-74; exec. asst. Fla. Democratic Party, Tallahassee, 1976-78; adminstrv. asst., office mgr. E. F. Hutton & Co., Tampa, 1979-80; cons. politics, meeting planning, Dover, 1980—; consumer advocate Fla. Dept. Ins., Tampa, 1982—. Mem. Precinct 67 Com., Hillsborough County Dem. Exec. Com., 1964—, sec., 1965-68, state committeewoman, 1974-77, 80—, state liaison for county conv., 1979; active Dem. Women's Clubs Fla., 1968—, pres., 1979-81, bd. dirs., 1969—; Fla. coordinator for ERA, Dem. Nat. Com., 1982; active Dem. Exec. Com. Fla., 1974—, vice chmn. 7th Congl. Dist. on Central Com., 1974-76, 80—, nat. committeewoman for Fla., 1980-84; dir. So. region Nat. Fedn. Dem. Women, 1981-82, mem. nat. credential com., 1980, chmn., 1981; mem. Duke U. Forum on Presdl. Nominations; candidate Fla. Ho. of Reps., 1980; participant Fla. Gov.'s Challenge Conf., Fla. Endowment for Humanities, 1981. Named Hon. Col., State Miss., 1980, State Ky., 1981. Mem. Fla. Fedn. Bus. and Profl. Women's Clubs (pres. Plant City club 1967-69, parliamentarian Plant City club 1980-82, dist. com. chmn. 1969-71, organizer chmn. talent bank 1970, state chmn. legis. 1970-73, chmn. state conv. 1982), East Hillsborough County Hist. Soc. Home: PO Box 97 Dover FL 33527

TILLMAN, NAOMI LATINSKY, govt. affairs and mgmt. adminstr.; b. Bklyn., Apr. 22, 1929; d. Benjamin and Gussie (Toback) Latinsky; B.A., Hunter Coll., 1950; M.S.W., U. Ill., 1961; postgrad. U. Chgo., 1969-70; cert. U. Pa., 1970; m. Raymond Robert Tillman, Jan. 27, 1951. Community orgn. worker Hull House Assn., Chgo., 1961-63; dir. project on family urbanization Assn. Family Living, Chgo., 1963-64; planning asso., adminstrv. asst. Welfare Council Met. Chgo., 1965-67; asst. prof., adminstrv. asst. U. Ill., 1967-69; treas., asst. mgr. Accent Shop, Chgo., 1970-72; dir. public affairs dept. Council for Community Services of Met. Chgo., 1972-77; dir. dept. public affairs, asso. dir. govt. affairs div. United Way Met. Chgo., 1977-79; dir. Office State Guardian Ill. Guardianship and Advocacy Commn., Chgo., 1979-80; mgr. consumer services Chgo. Transit Authority, 1980—. Chmn. Ill. Citizen Adv. Council on Title XX; bd. dirs. 5th Ward Citizens Commn., Chgo., 1979—. Cert. social worker, Ill. Mem. Nat. Assn. Social Workers, Acad. Cert. Social Workers, Am. Public Welfare Assn., Ill. Welfare Assn. Home: 5145 S Cornell Ave Chicago IL 60615 Office: Mdse Mart PO Box 3555 Chicago IL 60654

TILMA, JANICE MAE, ednl. adminstr.; b. Elk City, Kans., July 1, 1942; d. Stanley and Anise Goldena Foster; student Tex. Woman's U., 1960-62, M.S., 1970; B.S., Tex. Tech. U., 1964; ranch mgmt. cert. Tex. Christian U., 1977; m. Geurt Levi Tilma, May 2, 1964. Tchr., Oxnard (Calif.) High Sch., 1964-66, Grapevine (Tex.) Middle Sch., 1968-69, Denton (Tex.) Ind. Sch. Dist., 1969-76; tchr.-coordinator Grand Prairie (Tex.) High Sch., 1978-80; dir. Southwest Okla. Skills Center, Altus, Okla., 1981—. Pres. Students Assos. Aux., Tex. Coll. Osteo. Medicine, 1975-76, adv., 1978-80. Named Tchr. of Month, Sta.-KDNT, 1971. Mem. NEA, Am. Home Econs. Assn., Am. Vocat. Assn., Am. Osteo. Assn. Aux., Classroom Tchrs. Assn., Delta Kappa Gamma, Beta Sigma Phi. Republican. Presbyterian. Club: Officers Wives (2d v.p. Altus AFB). Home: 101 Fir St Altus OK 73521 Office: 1117 N Spurgeon St Altus OK 73521

TILTON, BERNICE ELIZABETH SHEPPARD (MRS. EARLE BARTON TILTON), civic worker; b. Chgo.; d. Samuel Charles and Elizabeth (Keith) Sheppard; Mus.B., Wis. Coll. Music, 1954; m. Earle Barton Tilton, Mar. 12, 1940. Performed as soloist and two-piano team for orgns., Ill., Wis., Fla., 1947—. Pres., Symphony Club, Clearwater, Fla., 1958-60; founder Mus. Arts Soc., Clearwater, 1960, pres., 1960-62, 82—; chpt. pres. Delta Omicron, 1964-66, Fla. chmn. alumnae-at-large, 1965-67, internat. v.p. alumnae, internat. bd. dirs., 1967-71; pres. Fla. West Coast Panhellenic Assn., 1967-68, chpt. adv. bd., 1968—. Bd. dirs. Clearwater Community Concert Assn., 1963-74. Recipient Gold Star Delta Omicron, 1967, Recognition award, 1971. Mem. Nat. Soc. Arts and Letters (local sec., v.p. 1972-73), Henry Solomon Lehr Soc. (life), Delta Omicron (alumnae chpt. pres. 1973-74, 81-83). Home: 6 Belleview Blvd Apt 608 Belleair FL 33516

TIMBERLAKE, NANCY JANE, banker; b. Stevenson, Ala., June 26, 1923; d. Claude Russell and Bessie (Haddon) T.; student public schs. With First Nat. Bank, Stevenson, 1942—, asst. cashier, 1950-70, asst. v.p., 1970-82, v.p., 1982—. Mem. Nat. Bus. and Profl. Women's Assn. (charter; chpt. treas. 1976-78). Methodist. Home: 220 E Main St Stevenson AL 35772 Office: First Nat Bank Hwy 72 Stevenson AL 35772

TIMES, MISBREW LOUISE, educator; b. Sumter, S.C., Sept. 14, 1950; d. Adam and Edna (Lowery) T.; B.S., S.C. State Coll., 1972; M.Ed., U. S.C., 1976. Music dir. Lee County (S.C.) Schs., 1972-75; fine arts dir., tchr. Clarendon Sch. Dist., Summerton, S.C., 1975-82; cons. ch. choral music, time mgmt. Del., N.Y. Nat. Democratic Com., 1980; mem. S.C. State Dem. Exec. Com.; exec. 1st v.p. Sumter County (S.C.) Dem. Com., 1978-82, mem. council, 1982; bd. dirs. P.D. Regional Health Systems Agy., exec. com., chmn. project rev. com., 1981, 82. Mem. S.C. Edn. Assn., NEA, S.C. Assn. Supervision and Curriculum Devel., Nat. Assn. Supervision and Curriculum Devel., Internat. Platform Assn. Democrat. Mem. African Methodist Episcopal Ch. Office: PO Box 2691 Sumter SC 29150

TIMM, JEANNE ANDERSON, musician; b. Sioux City, Iowa, Aug. 15, 1918; d. Milton Earnest and Hazel Fern (Cunningham) Anderson; B.Mus., Morningside Coll., Sioux City, 1940; postgrad. Eastman Sch. Music, La. State U.; m. Everett L. Timm, Aug. 5, 1940; children—Gary Everett, Laurance Milo. Prof. woodwind instruments Morningside Coll., 1943-45, 48—; staff flutist Sta. KSCJ, Sioux City, 1941; prin. flutist Sioux City Symphony, 1943-45; vis. flutist New Orleans Philharm., New Orleans Opera Orch; prof. flute and chamber music La. State U., 1968—; cons., clinician flute co.; editor Armstrong Edu-tainment Co., 1976—; flutist Baton Rouge Little Theater, summers 1965-81. Mem. Nat. Assn. Wind and Percussion Players, Nat. Flute Assn., Music Educators Nat. Conf., Music Tchrs. Nat. Assn., La. Music Educators Assn., Baton Rouge Music Club, Pi Kappa Lambda, Mu Phi Epsilon. Roman Catholic. Home: 465 Magnolia Woods Baton Rouge LA 70708 Office: 269 Music and Dramatic Arts Bldg La State U Baton Rouge LA 70803

TIMMONS, EVELYN DEERING, pharmacist; b. Durango, Colo., Sept. 29, 1926; d. Claude Elliot and Evelyn Allen (Gooch) Deering; B.S. cum laude in Chemistry and Pharmacy, U. Colo., 1948; children—Roderick D., Steven P. Chief pharmacist Meml. Hosp., Phoenix, 1950-54; med. lit. research librarian Hoffman-LaRoche, Nutley, N.J., 1956-57; mgr. Profl. Pharmacies Inc., Phoenix, Airz., 1968-72; owner, mgr. Mt. View Pharmacy, Phoenix, 1972—; pres. Ariz. Apothecaries, Inc., 1976—. Mem. platform com. State of Ariz., Nat. Rep. Conv., 1964; asst. sec. Young Rep. Nat. Fedn., 1963-65; active county and state Rep. coms. Named Outstanding Young Rep. of Yr., Nat. Fedn. Young Reps., 1965; recipient Disting. Public Service award Maricopa County Med. Soc., 1966, 67; Disting. Alumni award Wasatch Acad., 1982. Fellow Am. Coll. of Apothecaries (edn. com. 1979-80, pres. Ariz. chpt. 1979-81, Ariz. state dir. 1981—, nat. 1st v.p. 1982—); mem. Ariz. Soc. of Hosp. Pharmacists, Am., Ariz. (Pharmacist of Yr. 1976, 81), Maricopa County (pres. 1977) pharmacy assns., Am. Soc. of Hosp. Pharmacists, Aux. to County Med. Soc. (pres. 1967-68), Am. Aircraft Owners and Pilots Assn., Nat. Assn. of Registered Parliamentarians. Contbr. articles to profl. jours. Home: 5302 N 69th Pl Paradise Valley AZ 85253 Office: 10565 N Tatum Blvd Paradise Valley AZ 85253

TIMPANARO, PATRICIA LYNN, computer software mgr.; b. East Orange, N.J., July 8, 1951; d. George and Jule Ethel Timpanaro; B.S. in Chemistry, Coll. William and Mary, 1973, M.S. in Applied Sci., 1978. Grad. asst. UCLA, 1973-74; research asst. Northrop Services, Hampton, Va., 1974-76; mem. tech. staff Computer Scis. Corp., Hampton, 1976-78; sr. programmer, analyst LEXICO Enterprises, Inc., Washington, 1978-79, project mgr., 1979-81, group mgr., 1981-82, tech. dir., 1982—; adj. faculty Christopher Newport Coll., 1975-78. Mem. Assn. Computing Machinery, IEEE Computer Soc., Assn. Women in Computing (sec. Nat. Capital chpt., ctbg. editor nat. newsletter), Kappa Delta. Office: 1333 New Hampshire Ave NW Suite 510 Washington DC 20036

TINDAL, CAROLYN LEE, nurse cons.; b. Balt., Dec. 5, 1946; d. Henry Whitfield and Ola Mae (Hilton) Tindal; R.N., Luth. Hosp. Sch. Nursing, 1967; B.S.N., Hampton Inst., 1975; M.S., U. Md., 1976; postgrad. Am. U. Head nurse, U. Md., Balt., 1968-75; staff asst. for edn. Johns Hopkins Hosp., Balt., 1975-77; edn. specialist Howard U. Hosp., Washington, 1977-79; dir. continuing edn. Walter Reed Army Med. Center, Washington, 1979-81, nurse cons. Tri-Service Med. Info. Systems, 1981—; cons. continuing edn. Resource Applications, Inc., 1981—. Served to maj. USAR, 1981—. Recipient Luth. Mission Soc. of Md. honor award, 1967; Purdue-Fredericks Co. scholarship, 1975. Mem. Am. Nurses Assn., Am. Soc. for Training & Devel., Md. League for Nursing, Alpha Kappa Mu, Sigma Theta Tau. Mem. Ch. of God of the Ams. Contbr. articles to profl. jours. Home: 3401 Yataruba Dr Baltimore MD 21207 Office: Trimis Army Bldg T 60A Walter Reed Army Med Center Washington DC 20012

TINGEY-MICHAELIS, CAROL, educator; b. St. James, Mo., Sept. 24, 1933; d. Willis Alma and Lola (Madsen) Tingey; B.S. magna cum laude, U. Utah, 1970, M.Ed., 1971, Ph.D., 1976; children—Richard, Blaine, James, Neil, Trish. Tchr. public schs., Salt Lake City, 1970, spl. edn. tchr., 1971-72; clin. instr. spl. edn. U. Utah, Salt Lake City, 1972-74; dir. staff devel. Utah State Tng. Sch., American Fork, Utah, 1974-75; asst. prof. spl. edn. U. No. Iowa, Cedar Falls, 1975-77; asst. prof. spl. edn. Trinity Coll., Washington, 1977-78; asst. prof. spl. edn. of severely handicapped George Mason U., Fairfax, Va., 1978-79; asso. prof. edn. and tng. physically and multi-handicapped Northwestern State U. of La., Natchitoches, 1979-81; asso. prof. spl. edn. Ill. State U., Normal, also coordinator program for physically handicapped, 1981—; cons. in field. Mem. Assn. for Severely Handicapped, Council for Exceptional Children (pres. Utah chpt. 1974-75), Am. Assn. on Mental Deficiency (sec. Utah chpt. 1975, ednl. chmn. region VIII 1976-77, treas. edn. div. 1979-80), Assn. for Retarded Citizens, Phi Delta Kappa, Phi Kappa Phi. Author: Home and School Partnerships in Exceptional Education; Handicapped Infants and Children: Handbook for Parents and Professionals; contbr. articles to profl. jours.; recorded albums: Self Help Skills, Adaptive Behavior; Socialization Skills; Adaptive Behavior; Daily Living Tasks, Housekeeping Skills, Vocational Awareness, Community Helpers; editorial adv. bd. Exceptional Parent mag. Home: 903 N Linden Apt 19 Normal IL 61761 Office: 313B Fairchild Hall Normal IL 61761

TINKER, LILLIAN MAUDE NIGHTENGALE, nurse; b. Isabella, Okla., Aug. 6, 1921; d. Jacob Benjamin and Catherine Amanda (Isbell) Nightengale; diploma nursing Emanuel Hosp., Portland, Oreg., 1950; B.A., Linfield Coll., 1978; m. Harold Everett Tinker, Apr. 12, 1958. Operating rm. staff nurse Emanuel Hosp., Portland, Oreg., 1950-51; operating rm. staff nurse Physicians and Surgeons Hosp., Portland, 1951-53, McMinn (Oreg.) Hosp., 1953-54; nursing supr. William Baumont Army Hosp., El Paso, Tex., 1965-70; dir. nursing service Silverton (Oreg.) Hosp., 1975-80; mem. adv. council nursing program

Chemeketa Community Coll. Vol. ARC Bloodmobile. Served to capt. AUS, 1954-61. Mem. Oreg. (pres. 1953-54, 78-80, sec. 1982—) Am. nurses assns., Am. Assn. Nurse Anesthetists, World Without War Council, Emanuel Hosp. Alumni Assn., Willamette Council Nursing Adminstrs., Humane Soc. Willamette Valley. Democrat. Mem. Assembly of God. Home: 375 Clackamas Circle W Woodburn OR 97071 Office: 342 Fairview St Silverton OR 97381

TINKHAM, MYRA CELESTE MELTON, nurse; b. Galesburg, Ill., Oct. 9, 1954; d. Roy Ray and Junella (Wilson) Melton; Asso. in Sci., Carl Sandburg Coll., 1977; m. Todd Tinkham, June 19, 1982. With Belscot Dept. Store and Bonanza Sirloin Pit, Galesburg, 1972-73; nurse's aide Americana Health Care Center, Galesburg, 1975-77, R.N., night supr., 1980—; R.N., Cottage Hosp. and pvt. care, 1978-80. Mem. Pres. Council for Phys. Fitness and Health in Am., 1970-73. Baptist. Address: 1451 Lindsey Ln Galesburg IL 61401

TINSLEY, KAREN ROSS, savs. and loan assn. exec.; b. Columbus, Ohio, Feb. 21, 1953; d. Waverly Clarence and Betty Lass Ross; B.S. in Bus. Adminstrn., Ohio State U., 1975; m. Robert W. Tinsley, Jr., June 5, 1976; children— Robert W. III, Rashaun D. With Buckeye Fed. Savs. & Loan Assn., Columbus, 1969—, asst. br. mgr., 1976-77, br. mgr., 1977—. Mem. validation com. Columbus Dept. Devel. Recipient Model Cities Outstanding Youth Achievement award, 1972. Mem. Nat. Assn. Female Execs., Women in Mgmt., Nat. Mgmt. Assn., Mt. Vernon Improvement Dist. Assn. Republican. Home: 3238 Latonia Rd Columbus OH 43227 Office: 1245 E Long St Columbus OH 43203

TIPPETT, CHRISTINE LYNN, psychiat. social worker; b. Tacoma, Nov. 14, 1950; d. James Karl and Joanne Ruth (Abrahamson) Talmage; B.A. in Sociology, U. Calif., Santa Barbara, 1974; M.S.W., Calif. State U., Sacramento, 1977; m. Craig Lawrence Tippett, July 1, 1971. Psychiat. social work intern Napa State Hosp., Imola, Calif., 1975-76; clin. social work intern U. Calif. Sch. Medicine, Davis and Sacramento Med. Center, 1976-77; program social worker Gheel House, County of Sacramento, 1977-79, sr. mental health counselor div. mental health, 1979—; pvt. practice, 1982—; chmn. bd. dirs. About Face Inc., vets. advocates, 1976-77. NIMH grantee, 1977; lic. clin. social worker and marriage, family and child counselor, Calif. also 711 University Ave Sacramento CA 95825

TIPPIT, ANN TOMPKINS PEARCE, stenography service exec., investment co. exec., counselor; b. Lake City, Fla., Oct. 26, 1934; d. Zack Brown and Lelia Iva (Langford) Tompkins; Ph.D., Neotarian Coll. Philosophy, Kansas City, Mo., 1979; 1 stepson, George A. Pearce. Ct. reporter, Fla. and La., 1950-70; owner, operator telephone answering service, Jacksonville, Fla., 1951-53; corp. officer A to Z Driving Schs., Tampa, Fla., 1951-53; com. sec. Fla. Legislature, 1960; engrossing clk. Ala. Legislature, 1963; co-owner Globe Tank Constrns., Houston, 1962-65; owner, operator Ann Tompkins Services, public stenography service, New Orleans, 1970-72, Tampa, 1972—, Lantom Properties, Odessa, Fla., 1979—, Balanced Living, spiritual counseling, Odessa, 1978—; owner MTP Prodns., entertainment bur., 1979—; co-owner Custom Services Unlimited, Specialized Personal Services, Inst. Individuality, Odessa, 1982—. Roads chmn. Keystone Civic Assn., Odessa, 1979-81; bd. dirs. Gunn Hwy. Vol. Fire Dept., Odessa, 1979-81; mem. adv. com. N.W. Hillsborough Expy. Authority; hon. county commr. Hillsborough County, 1981—. Mem. Internat. Entrepreneurs Assn., Nat. Assn. Female Execs. (charter), Am. Soc. Profl. and Exec. Women, Internat. New Thought Alliance, Alcoholism and Drug Addiction Profls'. Assn., Internat. Clergy Assn., Parapsychology Research Assn., Assn. Research and Enlightenment, LWV, Hillsboro County Mental Health Assn., Fla. Sheriffs Assn. Mem. Unity Ch. Clubs: Lutz-Lake Fern Garden, Keystone Homemakers Extension.

TIPTON, ANN BAUGH, phys. chemist; b. Freeport, Tex., Sept. 4, 1938; d. Dewey Lawrence and Ruth Elizabeth (Tipton) Baugh; B.S., Southwestern U., 1960; M.A., U. Tex., Austin, 1963, Ph.D., 1966; M.B.A., Pepperdine U., 1982; m. Van Collier Tipton, Jr., Jan. 30, 1963. Asst. prof. chemistry Southwestern U., Georgetown, Tex., 1964-67; tech. specialist chemistry research dept., Lockheed Propulsion Co., Redlands, Calif., 1969-75; sr. research scientist synthetic fuels, energy, geothermal and phosphates depts., Occidental Research Corp., Irvine, Calif., 1975—. Univ. Honor scholar, Southwestern U., 1956-57; recipient Citation of Merit in Chemistry, Southwestern U. Alumni Assn., 1972; Woman of Achievement, Irvine Bus. and Profl. Women's Club, 1980, Woman of the Yr., San Orco Dist., 1980; Robert A. Welch fellow, U. Tex., Austin, 1963-66, postdoctoral fellow, 1966-69. Mem. Am. Chem. Soc., Am. Inst. Chem. Engrs., Geothermal Resource Council, Am. Inst. Chemists (fellow), Assn. for Women in Sci., NOW, Bus. and Profl. Women's Club, Delta Delta Delta, Iota Sigma Pi. Profl. Women's. Contbr. articles to profl. jours.; patentee in field. Home: 1615 Butternut Way Diamond Bar CA 91765

TIPTON, JENNIFER, lighting designer; b. Columbus, Ohio, Sept. 11, 1937; d. Samuel Ridley and Isabel (Hanson) Tipton; B.A., Cornell U., 1958; m. William F. Beaton, Aug. 29, 1976. Lighting designer Paul Taylor Dance Co., Twyla Tharp and Dancers, 1965, Pa. Ballet Co., 1966, Macbeth, Am. Shakespeare Festival, Stratford, Conn., Harkness Ballet Co., 1967, Dan Wagoner Dancers, Richard II, Love's Labour's Lost, Am. Shakespeare Festival, HB Studios N.Y., 1968, Horseman Pass By, Fortune Theatre, Les Grands Ballet Canadiens, Yvonne Rainer Co., City Center Joffrey Ballet, Our Town Anta Theatre, 1969, Anta Theatre Dance Series, 1971, 72, Eliot Feld Ballet Co., Am. Ballet Theatre, 1971, Kazuko Hirabayashi Dance Co., A Ballet Behind the Bridge, Negro Ensemble Co., Delacorte Dance Festival, Houston Ballet Co., 1972, Nat. Ballet Co., Hartford Ballet Co., Celebration: The Art of Pas de Deux, Jerome Robbins, Jose Limon Dance Co., 1973, Tempest, Macbeth, Midsummer Night's Dream, N.Y. Shakespeare Festival-Newhouse Theatre, The Killdeer, Newman Theatre, Jerome Robbins' The Dybbuk, N.Y.C. Ballet, Dreyfus in Rehearsal, Barrymore Theatre, 1974, San Francisco Ballet Co., Anthony Tudor's The Leaves Are Fading, Am. Ballet Theatre, Habeas Corpus, Martin Beck Theatre, Murder Among Friends, Biltmore Theatre, 1975, Rex, Lunt-Fontanne Theatre, For Colored Girls Who Consider Suicide When the Rainbow is Enuf, Booth Theatre, Cleve. Ballet Co., Mikhail Baryshnikov's The Nutcracker, Am. Ballet Theatre, 1976, The Landscape of the Body, Newman Theatre, The Cherry Orchard, Agamemnon, Beaumont Theatre, Happy End, Martin Beck Theatre, Agamemnon, Delacorte Theatre, 1977, Museum, Public Theatre; Runaways, Public Theatre and Plymouth Theatre, All's Well That Ends Well, Taming of the Shrew, Delacorte Theatre, After the Season, Academy Festival Theatre, A Month in the Country, Williamstown Theatre Festival, Mikhail Baryshnikov's Don Quixote, Am. Ballet Theatre, The Goodbye People, Westport Playhouse, Funny Face, Buffalo Studio Arena, Drinks Before Dinner, Public Theatre, Alice in Wonderland, Public Theatre, 1978. Recipient Drama Desk award for For Colored Girls, The Cherry Orchard, 1977; Tony award for the Cherry Orchard, 1977; Joseph Jefferson award for the Landscape of the Body, 1977. Office: 25 E 10th St New York NY 10003

TIPTON, RHONDA JEANOLA WILLIAMS, statis. analyst; b. Columbus, Ohio, Jan. 16, 1952; d. Freddie Darryl and Iona (Shamlin) Williams; B.A. in Polit. Sci., So. U., 1973; M.B.A. in Mktg., Capital U., 1981; m. John Cornell Tipton, Apr. 9, 1977. Law clk. Public Utilities Commn. Ohio, Columbus, 1974-78; planner Ohio Dept. Energy, Columbus, 1978-79, lobbyist, 1979-82; statis. analyst pricing div. Rockwell Internat., Columbus, 1982—. Fiscal specialist United Way (Catholic Services), Columbus, 1981, program specialist cancer clinic, 1982; mem. adv. com. on women Ohio State U.; mem. com. to re-elect Senator William F. Bowen to Ohio Senate, Central Ohio Young Republican Orgn.; bd. dirs. Options, Inc., adult career counseling service, Columbus. Mem. Nat. Assn. Female Execs., NAACP, Assn. M.B.A. Execs., Alpha Kappa Alpha. Lutheran. Editor, author Capital U. Grad. Sch. Adminstrn. Newsletter, 1980-81. Home: 571 S Hampton Rd Columbus OH 43213

TIRAKIS, JUDITH ANGELINA, chem. co. ofcl.; b. Bristol, Conn., Oct. 11, 1938; d. Dante and Ines (Paravella) Follandri; B.A., St. Joseph Coll., West Hartford, Conn., 1956-60, postgrad., 1960-61; m. George Tirakis, July 15, 1967. With Engelhard Minerals and Chem. Corp., Menlo Park, N.J., 1964-67; supr. Sci. Info. Center, Ciba Geigy Pharm. Co., Summit, N.J., 1967-78; records mgr. research info. Ortho Pharm. Corp. div. Johnson & Johnson, Raritan, N.J., 1978—. Mem. Assn. Records Mgrs. and Adminstrs., Nat. Micrographic Assn., Drug Info. Assn., Am. Mgmt. Assn., Nat Assn. Female Execs. Office: Route 202 Ortho Pharm Corp Raritan NJ 08869

TIRRE, BARBARA CARAMELLA, educator; b. Paterson, N.J., May 5, 1935; d. William Joseph and Mafalda Ermina (Benedetto) Caramella; B.S., Syracuse (N.Y.) U., 1957, M.A., 1966; children—Conrad J., William Christopher. Women's editor, continuity dir. Sta. WWBZ, Vineland, N.J., 1957-58; publicity dir. Conti Advt., Ridgewood, N.J., 1958; copywriter sta. KLNY, San Marcos, Tex., 1959; adminstrv. asst. Univ. Coll., Syracuse U., 1965-66; tchr. speech Henninger High Sch., Syracuse, 1966-67; instr. Belleville (Ill.) Area Jr. Coll, 1967-68; instr., then asst. prof. mass communications So. Ill. U., Edwardsville, 1968-74, asso. prof. mass communications, 1975—; trainer producers and dirs. Nat. Iranian Radio and TV, Tehran, 1974-76; prof. Nat. Film and TV Inst. Grad. Sch., Tehran, 1975; prof. U. Md., program in Tehran, 1975. Mem. Am. Women in Radio and TV (pres. St. Louis chpt. 1980-82), Alpha Chi Omega, Sigma Delta Rho. Republican. Home: 6 Hawthorne Ct Oakland MO 63122 Office: Box 73 So Ill U Edwardsville IL 62026

TIRRELL, JANET ANTHONY, pub. relations generalist; b. Piedmont, Calif., July 13, 1938; B.A. in Polit. Sci., U. Calif., Berkeley, 1961, Teaching credential, 1962, M.A. in Edn., 1968; postgrad. in bus. adminstrn., Fordham U. Tchr. English, Orinda (Calif.) Union Sch. Dist., 1962-68; coordinator ednl. research, edn. counselor Hill & Knowlton, Inc., N.Y.C., 1968-70; pub. relations cons., writer Ednl. Systems & Designs, Inc., Westport, Conn., 1974; writer, producer Producers Row, Inc., N.Y.C., 1975. Recipient Helms award, 1963 (All-American 1956-60). Mem. Calif. Tchrs. Assn., Orinda Educators Assn. (past v.p., pres. elect), Delta Gamma, Pi Lambda Theta. Traveled with championship synchronized swimming team; appearances include Australian Olympics, Brussels World Fair, Ed Sullivan Show.

TISCHLER, NANCY MARIE PATTERSON, educator; b. DeQueen, Ark., Mar. 20, 1931; d. Charles Edward and Allen (Steel) Patterson; B.Sc., Wilson Tchrs. Coll., Washington, 1952; M.A., U. Ark., 1954, Ph.D., 1957; Fulbright scholar, Univ. Coll. S.W., Exeter, Eng., 1952-53; m. C. Merle Tischler, Nov. 26, 1958; children—Carl Eric, Dale Grant. Grad. asst. U. Ark., 1953-56; asst. prof. English, George Washington U., 1956-62; asso. prof. Susquehanna U., Selinsgrove, Pa., 1962-66; prof. English and humanities Pa. State U., Capitol campus, Middletown, 1966—; invitational humanist Pa. Council Humanities. Author: Tennessee Williams: Rebellious Puritan, 1960; Black Masks: Negro Characters in Modern Southern Fiction, 1968; Legacy of Eve: Images of Women in Scripture, 1977; Dorothy L. Sayers: A Pilgrim Soul, 1980. Home: RD 3 643 Elizabethtown PA 17022 Office: Capitol Campus Pa State U Middletown PA 17057

TISHMAN, JUDITH ANN ROTHENBERG, personnel cons.; b. N.Y.C., Mar. 13, 1935; d. Irving and Evelyn (Hirsch) Rothenberg; B.F.A., Cornell U. Coll. Architecture, 1957; m. Peter V. Tishman, Dec. 1, 1974; stepchildren—Steven, Linda, Anita. Mem. staff fashion and art depts. Good Housekeeping mag., N.Y.C., 1957, fashion dept. Capezio, Inc., N.Y.C., 1958-60; art editor Mag. Mgmt. Co., N.Y.C., 1960-65; owner, mgr. Judith Rothenberg Representing, N.Y.C., 1965-80; owner Fabian-Rothenberg, Inc., N.Y.C., 1981—. Mem. friends com. Mus. Am. Folk Art. Mem. Soc. Photographers and Artists Reps., Alpha Epsilon Phi.

TITGEN, BETTY ANN, fin. exec.; b. Artesian, S.D., Oct. 13, 1930; d. Herman R. and Mary (Bruckner) Raether; B.A., Phoenix Coll., 1970; children—Kathleen Ann Isert, Ronni Lou Gathman, Michelle Annette Titgen, Laurie Lynn Titgen. Account exec. Stockton (Calif.) Data Processing, 1964-69; asst. treas. State Savings & Loan Assn., Stockton, 1969-78; controller Tahoe Savings & Loan Assn., S. Lake, Tahoe, Calif., 1978-80; v.p., controller Capital Fed. Savings & Loan Assn., Sacramento, 1980—. Mem. Fin. Mgrs. Soc. for Savs. Instns., Nat. Assn. Accts. Republican. Methodist. Home: 4004 Reggie Way Carmichael CA 95608 Office: PO Box 13326 Sacramento CA 95813

TITLEY, BONNIE SKINNER, coll. adminstr.; b. LaJunta, Colo., Feb. 4, 1939; d. Walter and Katherine (Schweizer) Skinner; B.A., U. Colo., 1959, M.A., 1962; Ed.D., U. No. Colo., 1976; m. Robert Wesley, Sept. 7, 1958; Instr., U. Colo., 1962-65; instr. English, Colo. State U., Ft. Collins, 1965-70, dir. acad. advising, 1970—. Mem. Ft. Collins Planning and Zoning Bd., 1972-74; bd. dirs. Ft. Collins Symphony, 1981—. Boettcher scholar, 1956-59; comml. pilot, cert. basic ground instr. Mem. Nat. Acad. Advising Assn. (charter), Nat. Assn. Student Personnel Adminstrs., Am. Coll. Personnel Assn., Aircraft Owners and Pilots Assn., Phi Beta Kappa, Phi Delta Kappa, Kappa Delta Pi. Methodist. Contbr. articles to profl. jours. Home: 1816 Seminole Dr Fort Collins CO 80525 Office: Colo State U Fort Collins CO 80523

TJADER-HARRIS, MARGUERITE, author, editor; b. N.Y.C., Nov. 24, 1901; d. Richard and Margaret (Thorne) Tjader; B.A., Columbia, 1925; m. Overton Harris, May 23, 1922 (div. 1933); 1 son, Hilary Harris. Lit. sec. Theodore Dreiser, 1933-34, 43-44; editor Direction mag., 1938-45; author: (novel) Borealis, 1929; Theodore Dreiser, A New Dimension, 1975; Mother Elisabeth, 1972; also numerous articles; editor: (Dreiser) Notes on Life, 1974. Mem. Women's Internat. League Peace and Freedom, Fellowship of Reconciliation, Am. European Friendship. Democrat. Roman Catholic. Author: Birgitta of Sweden, 1980. Address: Vikingsborg Tokeneke Trail Darien CT 06820

TOAL, JEAN HOEFER, lawyer, state legislator; b. Columbia, S.C., Aug. 11, 1943; d. Herbert and Lilla (Farrell) Hoefer; B.A., Agnes Scott Coll., S.C., 1965; J.D., U. S.C., 1968; m. William T. Toal, Aug. 24, 1967; children—Jean Hoefer, Lilla Patrick. Admitted to S.C. bar, 1968; assoc. firm Haynesworth Perry Bryant Marion & Johnstone, Columbia, 1968-70, Belser Belser & Baker, 1970-73; partner firm Belser Baker Barwick Ravenel Toal & Bender, Columbia, 1974—; mem. S.C. Ho. of Reps., 1975—, chmn. rules com., mem. judiciary com., chmn. constnl. laws subcom. Named S.C. Legislator of Yr., Greenville News, 1977; recipient Disting. Service award Jaycees, 1976; Legislator of Yr. award S.C. Mcpl. Assn., 1980. Mem. ABA, S.C. Bar, Richland County Bar Assn., S.C. Def. Lawyers Assn. Democrat. Roman Catholic. Home: 2418 Wheat St Columbia SC 29205 Office: 1213 Lady St PO Box 11848 Columbia SC 29211

TOBIAS-BALLESTEROS, FELICITAS D., physician; b. Bani, Pangasinan, Philippines, Oct. 14, 1926; came to U.S., 1954, naturalized, 1963; d. Pascual F. and Pelagia N. (Deogracias) Tobias; A.A., U. Santo Tomas, Manila, 1948, M.D., 1953; m. Joseph C. Ballesteros, May 12, 1962; children—Deanna Lisa, Saul Thomas, Joseph Carl. Rotating intern St. John's Hosp., Yonkers, N.Y., 1954-55, St. Anthony DePadua Hosp., Chgo., 1955-56; resident Women & Children's Hosp., Chgo., 1956-57, Mt. Sinai Hosp., Chgo., 1958-59; practice medicine specializing in bariatrics and preventive medicine, Westchester, Ill., 1968—. Recipient Appreciation award Am. Soc. Bariatrics, 1969. Mem. Internat. Acad. Metabology (treas.), Am. Soc. Bariatric Physician (certified), Internat. Acad. Preventive Medicine, Internat. Coll. Applied Nutrition, Am. Holistic Med. Assn., Acad. Orthomolecular Psychiatry. Roman Catholic. Club: Toastmistress. Office: 947 S Mannheim St Westchester IL 60153

TOBIN, FRANCES KARSCH, psychotherapist; b. N.Y.C., Feb. 4, 1910; d. John Henry and Amelia Frances (Hattemer) Karsch; certificate Sarah Lawrence Coll., 1930; B.A., N.Y.U., 1948; M.S.S., Columbia U., 1950; m. Jerome Ellison, Aug. 4, 1934; 1 dau., Judith; m. 2d, Charles Tobin, Dec. 19, 1959. Mem. staff Yonkers (N.Y.) Family Service, 1950-52, New Rochelle (N.Y.) Child Guidance Center, 1952-56, Waterbury (Conn.) Child Guidance Clinic, 1975—; pvt. practice psychotherapy, Pelham Manor, Rye, N.Y., 1951-73, Southbury, Conn., 1975—; clin. instr. Albert Einstein Coll. Medicine, 1958-68, asst. clin. prof. dept. child psychiatry, 1968-75. Mem. Nat. Assn. Social Workers, Acad. Cert. Social Workers. Democrat. Club: Heritage Village Country (Southbury). Home: 583B East Hill Rd Southbury CT 06488

TOBIN, JOAN FLEISCHMANN, capital venture co. exec.; b. Can., Sept. 17, 1943; B.A., U. Cin., 1967. Engaged in polit. campaigning, 1968, 70, 71-72; owner, operator hotel, Pitlochry, Scotland, 1969-72; chmn. Women's Nat. Talent-Bank, Washington, 1976-77; founder, 1977, since pres. Tobin Enterprises, Inc., Washington. Bd. dirs. ANTA, Fgn. Student Service Council, Children's Hearing and Speech Center, Washington, Vivian Beaumont Theatre, N.Y.C., New Nat. Theatre, Washington; adv. bd. Nat. Women's Polit. Caucus; founding chmn. Com. 200; mem. congressional leadership group Center Strategic and Internat. Studies, Georgetown U. Address: Internat Sq 1850 K St NW Washington DC 20006

TOCCOLI, BETTY JO ANNE, cosmetic co. exec.; b. Caldwell, Idaho, Oct. 28, 1933; s. Robert Emmett and Gladys Lucille (Justus) McGuire; student Coll. Idaho, Idaho State U.; m. Ray Toccoli, Feb. 1, 1963; 1 dau., Gaylene. Bank teller, 1951-54; adminstrv. asst. Dept. Indian Affairs, 1955-57; with Welcome Wagon Internat., 1959-78, v.p. sales, 1970-78; pres., chief exec. officer Laura Lynn Cosmetics, Inc., Los Angeles, 1978—, also dir. Elder, First Presbyn. Ch., Pacific Palisades, Calif., 1982—. Mem. Nat. Assn. Women Bus. Owners, Exec. Female Assn. Office: 5456 McConnell Ave Suite 189 Los Angeles CA 90066

TOCKEY, SALLY ANN, newspaper feature editor; b. Omaha, June 10, 1935; d. Eugene Charles and Gertrude Margaret (Dendinger) Smith; A.A., Chabot Coll., 1974; B.A. with honors, Calif. State U., Hayward, 1976; m. Robert Jay Tockey, May 31, 1954; children—Deborah, Charles, Stephen, Barbara, Karen. Reporter, Tri-Valley News, Danville, Calif., 1976-77; reporter Tri-Valley Herald, Livermore, Calif., 1977-79, feature editor, 1979—. Recipient 1st place award for women's feature Contra Costa Press Club, 1977. Mem. Women in Communications, East Bay Press Club, Sigma Delta Chi. Democrat. Roman Catholic. Office: 7132D Johnson Dr Pleasanton CA 94566

TODD, ANNADEL, bank exec.; b. Jefferson County, Mo., May 9, 1934; d. William Chris and Charlotte Myrtle (Breazeale) Oberhaus; student Rubican Bus. Sch., 1951; m. Harold Dean Todd, June 25, 1955; children—Randall Dean, Janice Elaine. Bookkeeper, teller Bank of Overland (Mo.), 1950-55; teller Vandalia State Bank (Mo.), 1956-57; bookkeeper, teller Middletown Bank (Mo.) (now First Mo. Bank of Montgomery County), 1963-70, asst. cashier, 1970—. Active PTA, 1964-73, v.p., 1969-70, sec., 1968-69, treas. band parents, 1970; den mother Boy Scouts Am., 1966; chpt. mother Future Homemaker of Am., 1976-78; Sunday sch. tchr. Methodist Ch., 1967-68, treas. bldg. fund, 1981-82. Republican. Club: 1st Mo. Bank (dir.). Home: Rural Route 1 Box 20 Wellsville MO 63384 Office: Middletown Bank Box 128 Middletown MO 63359

TODD, BARBARA ANN, Realtor; b. Ft. Wayne, Ind., Mar. 8, 1933; d. Anthony Frances and Margaret Louise (Reid) Schmitt; grad. Ind. U. Realtor Inst., 1972; m. Joseph Keith Todd, Dec. 21, 1962 (div. 1976); children—David Reid Walley, Cathy Elizabeth Walley, Beth Ann Walley, Joseph Keith Todd. Sec., bookkeeper, solicitor Shultz Ins. Agency, Elkhart, Ind., 1948-52; ch. sec., sec. to rector St. Johns Episcopal Ch., 1952-54; partner, gen. mgr., real estate broker Todd Realty, Syracuse, Ind., after 1966; partner, broker Century 21 Domino Real Estate, Bloomington, Ind., 1976-77; field underwriter Mut. N.Y., Anaheim, Calif., 1978—; mgr. Century 21 Allcoast Realty & Investment, Huntington Beach, Calif., 1979-80; gen. partner Real Estate Problem Solvers, Bloomington, Ind., 1980-81; owner/broker Barbara Todd Real Estate Services, Syracuse, Ind., 1981—; real estate investment counselor; dir. Wawasee Village Investment Corp., after 1974; dir. Wawasee Devel. Corp., after 1973. Bd. dirs. Wawasee Arts Found., 1971-72; residential chmn. United Fund, Elkhart, 1959, Kosciusko County, 1972; co-chmn. Elkhart Hosp. Aux., 1960. Cert. real estate broker, mgr. Mem. Warsaw (dir. 1967-74, v.p. 1974), Kosciusko bds. realtors, Syracuse Wawasee C. of C., Calif. Assn. Realtors, Huntington Beach/Fountain Valley Bd. Realtors, Ind. Assn. Realtors, Bloomington Bd. Realtors, Nat. Assn. Realtors, Orange County Assn. Field Underwriters, Realtors Nat. Mktg. Inst., Women's Council Realtors. Republican. Episcopalian. Home: Harborside Condominium Lake Wauasee Syracuse IN 46567 Office: PO Box 37 Syracuse IN 46567

TODD, DEBORAH ANN, project engr.; b. Long Island City, N.Y., June 18, 1955; d. Ralph and Mae Williams (Milligan) T.; B.S.M.E. summa cum laude, Union Coll., 1976; M.S.M.E., Rensselaer Poly. Inst., 1978. Mech. design engr. large steam turbine div. Gen. Electric Co., Schenectady, N.Y., 1976-78, mech. engr. projects engring. ops., 1978-79; mech. engr. Gibbs & Hill, Inc., N.Y.C., 1979-80, project engr. internat. projects dept., 1980—; instr. profl. engring. rev. course, 1980. Recipient Top Managerial award Gen. Electric Internat. Projects Dept.; Top Young Engr. award Gen. Electric Power Systems Sector; registered profl. engr., N.Y. Mem. Nat. Soc. Profl. Engrs., ASME, Tau Beta Pi. Republican. Clubs: Appalachian Mountain, Appalachian Trail Conf., N.Y./N.J. Trail Conf. Home: 39 Netto Ln Plainview NY 11803 Office: 570 Lexington Ave New York NY 10022

TODD, ESTHER STEVENS (MRS. OWEN WILLIAM TODD), former librarian; b. Wenatchee, Wash., Dec. 5, 1914; d. Edward Francis and Loraine Emily (Johnson) Stevens; A.A. (Lanham Found. scholar), Wenatchee Jr. Coll., 1947; B.A., U. Wash., 1949, teaching cert., 1950, M.L.S., 1964; postgrad. U. Minn., 1955; m. Owen William Todd, June 12, 1960. With traffic dept. Interstate Telephone Co., Wenatchee, 1933-54, instr. traffic dept. employees, 1941-45; tchr. typing and lang. arts, librarian Peshastin (Wash.) High Sch., 1950-56, also adviser drama; librarian Eastmont High Sch., East Wenatchee, Wash., 1956-76. Mem. Columbia River Info. Specialists. Active Nat. Polio Week campaign, 1955. Mem. Ind. Telephone Women Employees Assn. (pres. 1935), NEA, Wash., Edn. Assn., Wash. Assn. Sch. Librarians (area-chmn. 1960-62, mem. state constn. com. 1962-64, emeritus 1977—), Adminstrv. Women in Edn. (chmn. N. Central council 1967-69, treas.

Wash. council 1971-72), ALA, Wash. Christian Endeavor Union (devotional chmn. 1935), Heritage Soc. of Mid-Columbia, Pacific NW Assn. Ch. Libraries (chmn. Wenatchee Valley chpt. 1976-78, cert. of appreciation, life mem. 1982). Baptist (chmn. local Pioneer Girls 1956-71, mem. library com. 1970—). Home: 2 S Garfield Ave Wenatchee WA 98801

TODD, LYDA CORNELIUS, nurse; b. Harrodsburg, Ky., Jan. 11, 1924; d. Richard Shouse and Verner (Scrogham) Cornelius; R.N., Nazareth Sch. Nursing, St. Joseph Infirmary, Louisville, 1945; m. Louis Mack Todd, Apr. 21, 1958. Staff, operating room nurse Old A.D. Price Hosp., Harrodsburg, Ky., 1945-50, Ephraim McDowell Hosp., Danville, Ky., 1950-59; operating room nurse St. Lukes Hosp., Ft. Thomas, Ky., 1961-63; staff nurse Garrard County Hosp., Lancaster, Ky., 1964-69; operating room nurse, regular relief 3-11 supr. James B. Haggin Hosp., Harrodsburg, 1969-77; staff nurse surg. floor Methodist Hosp., Indpls., 1977-79, staff nurse diabetic dept., 1979—. Named Ky. Col. Mem. D.A.R. Methodist. Home: 1102 Linden St Indianapolis IN 46203

TODD, MARY ELIZABETH (MRS. ALVA CRESS TODD), engring. coll. ofcl.; b. Lafayette, Ind., Aug. 26, 1920; d. Christian Frederick and Anna Marie (Mahlke) Schelle; diploma Ind. Bus. Coll., 1940; m. Alva Cress Todd, Apr. 17, 1941; children—Richard Schelle, Carol (Mrs. Everett Andrew Biegalski), Joanne (Mrs. Louis Edward Horton), Elizabeth Ann (Mrs. Scott Robert Lowry). Sec., Sears Roebuck & Co., Lafayette, 1940, Riley Poultry Farm, Lafayette, 1940-41; treas. Todd Assos., engrs., Villa Park, Ill., 1961-67; co-founder, bus. mgr., treas. Midwest Coll. Engring., Lombard, Ill., 1967—, trustee, 1973—, sec. bd. trustees, 1974—, acting pres., 1981-82. Mem. Meml. Hosp. Guild, Elmhurst, Ill., 1963—. Mem. Nat. Assn. Coll. and Univ. Bus. Officers, Lombard C. of C., Delta Sigma Kappa. Club: Zonta (charter mem. Oak Brook, Ill.). Home: 827 S Summit Ave Villa Park IL 60181 Office: 440 S Finley Rd Lombard IL 60148

TODD, MARYSNOW STONE (MRS. ZANE G. TODD), educator; b. Owensville, Ind., Apr. 6, 1920; d. Clarence Edgar and Mary Pearl (Knowles) Stone; student Lockyear Bus. Coll., 1945-46, Ind. Central Coll., 1958-62; m. Zane G. Todd, Feb. 8, 1950; 1 dau., Betty (Mrs. William Hudson). Bookkeeper, Mo. Valley Bridge & Iron Co., Evansville, Ind., 1942-45, McCrory's Stores, Indpls., 1947-51; asst. editor Research and Rev. Publs., Inc., Indpls., 1951-55, asso. editor, 1956-58; tchr. Perry Twp. schs., Indpls., 1968—. Counselor in edn., 1965-67. Mem. com. Ind. Symphony Soc., 1960—; area leader Am. Cancer Soc., 1968; mem. Winchester Civic Assn., 1962—, Ind. Hist. Soc., 1959—; volunteer A.R.C., 1970-72; mem. Lions Aux., 1956—. Bd. dirs. Muscular Dystrophy Assn., 1969, Jr. Achievement Aux. Mem. Soc. Comml. Journalists, Internat. Platform Assn., 500 Festival Assos. Republican. Presbyterian. Clubs: Riviera, Indianapolis Athletic, Meridian Hills, Columbia; La Coquille (Palm Beach). Contbr. articles to ins. jours. Home: 7645 Randue Ct Indianapolis IN 46278

TODD, MAY OLA, univ. fundraiser, researcher; b. Okmulgee, Okla., Feb. 3, 1934; d. Farmer and Iola (Sims) T.; cert. Central Bus. Coll., 1957; student Langston (Okla.) U., 1959-61, Howard U., 1962-65, U. So. Calif., Los Angeles, 1969-71; m. Troy James Davis, May 5, 1961 (div.). Stenographer Counuty Supt. Schs., Oklahoma City, 1958-59, Howard U., Washington, 1964-66; computer operator Library of Congress, Washington, 1963-64; asst. dir. research-fund raising U. So. Calif., Los Angeles, 1966—. Mem. Tau Gamma Delta. Office: U So Calif Los Angeles CA 90007

TODMAN, EUNICE CAROL, ednl. service co. exec.; b. Bronx, N.Y., Feb. 8, 1944; d. Carl Edward and Mary (Ellis) Cason; student N.Y.U.; m. Clarence Todman, Aug. 21, 1965; 1 dau., Anissa. Office mgr. Progressive Table Co., Bklyn., 1962-70; adminstrv. asst. ITT Ednl. Services, N.Y.C., 1970-76, fin. aid adminstr., 1977-81, asst. dir., 1977—, fin. mgr., 1981—. Named Fin. Mgr. of Year region I, 1977, 78, 79, Nat. Fin. Mgr. of Yr., 1978, 79. Mem. N.Y. State Fin. Aid Adminstrs., N.Y. State Assn. Two Year Colls. Home: 181 Long Hill Rd Little Falls NJ 07424 Office: One Penn Plaza New York NY 10001

TODORAN-KATZ, PATRICIA LYNN, pharm. co. exec.; b. Warren, Ohio, Apr. 16, 1953; d. George and Madeline E. Todoran; B.S., Pa. State U., 1975; m. Fred F. Katz, Sept. 13, 1981. Traffic analyst chem. div. Borden, Inc., Columbus, Ohio, 1976-77; asst. traffic mgr. Gold Circle Stores div. Federated Stores, Columbus, 1977-79; supr. transp. Ross Labs. div. Abbott Labs., Columbus, 1979-80, mgr. reimbursement, 1980—. Mem. Am. Soc. Traffic and Transp., Kappa Delta. Home: 2865 E Moreland Dr Columbus OH 43209 Office: 6480 Busche Blvd Columbus OH 43215

TOFFLEMIRE, KATHY BYRTILLA, journalist; b. Minot, N.D., Feb. 2, 1950; d. Samuel Theodore and Byrtilla Adeline (Bole) Clark; student public schs., Minot; m. Gary Lee Tofflemire, June 22, 1968; children—Kerry Lynn. Proofreader, Minot Daily News, 1968-74, reporter, 1974-78, AP wire editor, 1978—, bus. page editor, 1979—; freelance writer Velva (N.D.) Jour., 1973-74. Recipient writing awards N.D. Press Women, 1975, 76, 78, 79, 80. Mem. Minot Zool. Soc., N.D. Press Women (pres.), Nat. Fedn. Press Women, Am. Film Inst., Nat. Trust for Hist. Preservation, Minot Press Club (sec.-treas.), Sigma Delta Chi. Methodist. Home: 1111 Soo St Minot ND 58701 Office: 301 4th St SE Minot ND 58701

TOKAR, MAUREEN TANSEY, architect; b. Cin., Mar. 4, 1933; d. Bernard Joseph and Cecile Marie (Sunman) Tansey; B.S. in Architecture, U. Cin., 1955; m. Edward Tokar, June 29, 1974. Job capt. Hixson, Tarter & Merkel, Cin., 1964-68; dir. interior architecture Ferry & Henderson, Springfield, Ill., 1968-72; project coordinator Skidmore, Owings & Merrill, Chgo., 1972-76; rev. architect Ill. Capital Devel. Bd., Chgo., 1977-82; v.p. Planning and Design Cons., 1975—. Mem. AIA, Chgo. Women in Architecture, Art Inst. Chgo., Field Mus., Alpha Omicron Pi. Club: Chgo. Altrusa. Home: 4951 W Melrose St Chicago IL 60641 Office: 180 N LaSalle St Chicago IL 60601

TOKUNAGA, KAZUKO, banker; b. Hoolehua, Molokai, Hawaii, June 24, 1938; d. Torao and Yukie (Taniguchi) Matsuda; student pub. schs., Honolulu; m. Robert Eiji Tokunago, Aug. 19, 1967; children—Eric Yukio, Kent Ken. Bookkeeper, Central Pacific Bank, Honolulu, 1957; bookkeeper Bank of Hawaii, Honolulu, 1958-65, sec. clk., 1965, supr., 1965-73, group mgr., 1973-81, asst. cashier, 1974-81, asst. v.p., 1981—. Office: PO Box 2900 Honolulu HI 96846

TOLAND, FLORENCE WINIFRED, printing co. exec.; b. Paola, Kans., Aug. 6, 1906; d. Frederick W. and Bertha G. (Cartwright) Arzberger; B.A., U. Ariz., 1935, M.S. in Bus. Adminstrn., 1946; m. Jess William Toland, Dec. 23, 1934 (dec. 1954); 1 son, Ronald William. Tchr. grade sch., Dos Cabezos, Willcox and Mascot, Ariz., 1925-32, jr. high and high sch., 1934-36, 38-42; asst. prof. U. Ariz., Tucson, 1942-71, asst. prof. emeritus, 1971—; owner, mgr., pres. Pima Printing Co., Tucson, 1954—. Mem. Ariz. Bus. Educators Assn. (life), Nat. Bus. Educators Assn., Western Bus. Educators Assn., Pi Omega Pi. Democrat. Club: Order Eastern Star. Co-author: Transcription Method Shorthand, 1946. Home: 800 N Houghton Rd Tucson AZ 85710 Office: 110 S Park Ave Tucson AZ 85719

TOLAND, MARY BERNADETTE, social worker; b. Washington, Aug. 7, 1941; d. Edmund Michael and Lenora (Sheehan) T.; B.A., Trinity Coll., 1963; M.S.W., Boston Coll., 1968; postgrad. social work Catholic U. Am., 1976—. Case aide social service dept. Providence Hosp., Washington, 1963-66; home care program social worker Georgetown U. Hosp., Washington, 1967; surg. social worker R.I. Hosp., Providence, 1968-73; chief social worker The Nat. Childrens' Center, Washington, 1974-75; chief social worker, clin. co-ordinator Walden Resource, Wheaton, Md., 1975—. Mem. Md. Com. for Spl. Edn., 1975-77; mem. task force mental health referrals Bd. Edn. Montgomery County, Md., 1979-81, mem. mental health subcom. of med. adv. com., 1982—. Recipient recognition, appreciation award Montgomery County Assn. for Children with Learning Disabilities, 1976; NIMH trainee, 1978-79. Mem. Nat. Assn. Social Workers, Acad. Cert. Social Workers, Register of Clin. Social Workers. Democratic. Roman Catholic. Home: 3412 Garrison St NW Washington DC 20008 Office: 1320 Fenwick Ln Silver Spring MD 20910

TOLAND, MARY EVONNE, museum exec.; b. Waverly, Tenn., Dec. 25, 1935; d. Ernest Aubrey and Annie Pezola (Petty) T.; B.A., Bethel Coll., 1959; M.A., Vanderbilt U., 1961. Tchr. bus. adminstrn. Obion County Bd. Edn., Union City, Tenn., 1956-64; sec. Founders Security Life Ins. Co., Memphis, 1965-67; adminstrv. asst. to pres., exec. v.p. Pace Corp., Memphis, 1967-72; adminstrv. asst. to exec. dir. United Way of Greater Memphis, 1972-82; dir. devel. Brooks Meml. Art Gallery, 1982—. Mem. Am. Soc. Personnel Adminstrn., Exec. Women Internat. (pres. 1977), Memphis Personnel Assn. (sec., treas. 1979), Am. Legion. Republican. Baptist. Home: 5549 Hinton Cove Memphis TN 38117 Office: Brooks Meml Art Gallery Overton Park Memphis TN 38112

TOLBERT, CONSTANCE LYNN, businesswoman; b. Boone, Iowa, Aug. 3, 1945; d. Melvin Emory and Dorothy K. Hitsman; m. James W. Tolbert, Jr., Dec. 30, 1964; children—James, Lisa, Randy Mel. Exec. v.p. Classique Creations, Inc., Dallas, 1976—; bd. mgr. Success, Inc., 1978, v.p. Classique Internat., 1977, Horses, Inc., 1979; exec. v.p. J.W.T., Inc., 1977-80; owner Eagle Ranch, tng. ranch and retreat; Land developer, E.Tex. Republican. Baptist. Home: 5936 Meadowcreek Dallas TX 75248 Office: 14240 Midway Rd Dallas TX 75234

TOLBERT, ROSA JEAN FURR, librarian; b. Fernwood, Miss., Apr. 26, 1925; d. Luther A. and Rosa (Simrall) Furr; B.A., Miss. Coll., 1947; M.L.S., Tex. Woman's U., 1965; m. Charles Madden Tolbert, June 2, 1949; 1 son, Charles Madden II. Tchr. high sch. social studies Copiah-Lincoln Jr. Coll., 1947-49; asst. librarian Miss. Coll., 1950-53; jr. librarian La. State U. Library, Baton Rouge, 1954-57; asst. serials librarian Baylor U. Library, Waco, Tex., 1957-64, tchr. library sci., part-time 1966-67, religion-reference librarian Baylor U. Moody Library, 1969—. Danforth asso., 1964—. Mem. ALA, Southwestern Library Assn. (chmn. 1978-79), Tex. Library Assn. (publicity com. 1978-79), AAUW (officer 1975-76, pres. 1979-80; Outstanding Woman, Waco br. 1981), Beta Phi Mu, Delta Kappa Gamma. Clubs: Baylor Round Table, Baylor Univ. Women (pres. 1969-70). Home: 5206 Lake Arrowhead Dr Waco TX 76710 Office: Baylor U Moody Library Waco TX 76706

TOLBERT, SHARON RENEE, coll. adminstr.; b. Chgo., Feb. 22, 1945; d. Carl and Pearl T.; B.A. in History, Canisius Coll., Buffalo, 1968; M.S. in Edn., SUNY, Buffalo, 1970; M.A. in Sociology, Stanford U., 1975, Ph.D. in Adminstrn., 1975. Mgmt. and edn. specialist HEW, San Francisco, 1970-74; cons. and research asso. San Francisco U., 1974-75; postdoctoral ednl. policy fellow/asst. to chief Nat. Inst. Edn., Washington, 1975-76; sr. research asso. Inst. Services to Edn., Washington, 1976-77; dir. instl. planning and devel. Paine Coll., Augusta, GA, 1977-79; v.p. instl. planning and devel. Edward Waters Coll., Jacksonville, Fla., 1979-81, v.p. instl. advancement Coll. St. Catherine, St. Paul, 1981—; pres. Center Mgmt. Tech. and Policy Analysis, St. Paul, 1981—. Trustee, Sta. KTCA, Public TV, 1981-82. Mem. Econ. Women's Roundtable, Nat. Assn. Women Bus. Owners, Council Advancement and Support of Edn., Phi Delta Kappa. Office: 2004 Randolph Ave Saint Paul MN 55105

TOLIVER, JEAN COVENTRY, nurse; b. Redbird, Okla., May 29, 1932; d. Walter Ramsey and Georgia Ann (Froe) Smith; R.N. diploma Homer G. Phillips Sch. Nursing, 1956; B.S., Kans. State Coll., 1970; M.S.N. in Community Health Nursing (Nurse Traineeship grantee), Catholic U. Am., 1981; m. Adolphus P. Toliver, Aug. 17, 1957. Staff nurse St. Louis Maternity Hosp., 1956-57, Jewish Hosp. of St. Louis, 1957-61, VA Hosp., St. Louis, 1961-62; research asst. in microbiology Purdue U., 1963-67, U. Calif., Davis, 1969-71; public health nursing supr. Scramento Sch. Dist., 1971-75; instr. fundamentals of nursing Howard U. Coll. Nursing, 1975-81, instr. community/mental health nursing, 1981—. Mem. Va. Nurses Assn., Am. Public Health Assn., Am. Nurses D.C. Nurses Assn., Nat. League Nursing. Office: Howard U Coll Nursing Washington DC 20059

TOLL, ROBERTA DARLENE (MRS. SHELDON S. TOLL), social worker; b. Detroit, May 14, 1944; d. David and Blanche (Fischer) Pollack; B.A., U. Mich., 1966; M.S.W., U. Pa., 1971; m. Aug. 11, 1968; children—Candice, John, Kevin. Dir. counselors Phila. Family Planning, Inc., 1971-72; psychologist Lafayette Clinic, Detroit, 1972-73; social worker Project Headline, Detroit, 1973-75; pvt. practice social work, Bloomfield Hills, Mich., 1975—; adj. prof. U. Detroit, Oakland Community Coll. Bd. dirs. Detroit chpt. Nat. Council on Alcoholism. Cert. social worker, Mich. Fellow Masters and Johnson Inst.; mem. Nat. Assn. Social Workers. Democrat. Club: Franklin Hills Country. Home and office: 640 Lone Pine Hill Rd Bloomfield Hills MI 48013

TOLLETT, EILEEN RICE, bus. services owner; b. Little Rock, Mar. 28, 1947; d. Charles J. and Mary Lois (Carroll) Rice; B.S.E., U. Central Ark., 1969; M.L.A., So. Meth. U., 1972; Ph.D., U. Tex., Dallas, 1981; m. Billy E. Tollett, Aug. 16, 1969; 1 dau., Casey Elaine. Pub. relations field cons. Ark. Lung Assn., Little Rock, 1969; instr. McKinney (Tex.) Job Corps Center for Women, 1970-75; clerical staff U. Tex., Dallas, 1976-77, research asst., 1978, 78-79, 79, teaching asst., 1979, research asst., 1980, teaching asst., 1980, 81; owner, operator Tollett Typing & Cons., Allen, Tex., 1977—; copy editor Developmental Learning Materials, Allen, 1981—. Vice pres. Allen Pub. Library Bd., 1980-81; advisor to bd. dirs. Country Day Montessori Sch., Allen, 1980-81, bd. dirs., 1979-80; treas. Montessori Parents Assn., Allen, 1979-80; bd. dirs. Inspired Tchrs. Studio, Inc., Dallas, 1979-80; advisor Allen Pub. Library regarding ref. materials collection on Am. Indians, 1979-80; mem. Allen City Council, 1976-78; mem. Allen Pub. Library Bd., 1975-76. UN and Population Inst. scholar, Europe, 1973. Mem. Am. Bus. Women's Assn., Alpha Chi. Democrat. Address: PO Box 235 Allen TX 75002

TOLMAN, BEVERLY JEAN, educator; b. Silver Creek, N.Y., June 28, 1932; d. Howard Earl and Lucille (Maus) Brevoort; B.A. in Elem. Edn., Fredonia State U., 1966; m. Cecil John Tolman, July 29, 1949; children—Monty, Rex, Kim. Chain store supr. Weber Knapp, Jamestown, N.Y., 1955-56; waitress Hotel Jamestown, 1958-62; playground supr. Sinclairville (N.Y.), summer 1963; tchr. Jamestown Bd. Edn., 1966—. Deaconess, Sinclairville Bapt. Ch., 1959-62, v.p. Missionary Soc., 1980; active YMCA, PTA. Mem. AAUW, NEA, Jamestown Christian Bus. and Profl. Women's Council (chmn. 1978-80), Jamestown Tchrs. Assn., Stonecroft Fellowship. Democrat. Office: Christian Bus and Profl Council 11 Mitchell St Sinclairsville NY 14782

TOLMAN, SUZANNE NELSON, psychologist; b. Omaha, Nov. 8, 1931; d. Raymond LeRoy and Lottie (Kerns) Nelson; B.A. with distinction in Spanish, U. Nebr., Omaha, 1951; M.A., U. Nebr., Lincoln, 1952, Ph.D., 1957; m. Dan Edward Tolman, June 8, 1957; 1 dau., Kimberly Suzanne. Research asst. U. Nebr., Lincoln, 1951-52; tchr. Omaha Pub. Schs., 1952-53, counselor, high sch. instr. history and English, 1953-59; instr. psychology U. Nebr., Omaha, 1957-59; social service worker Mayo Clinic, Rochester, Minn., 1959-60; instr. psychology U. Tampa, 1962-63; sch. psychologist Sch. Dist. 535, Rochester, 1966—. Mem. Rochester Symphony Condr.'s Com., 1976—, pres., 1977; bd. dirs. Jefferson PTA, Rochester, 1966-68; bd. dirs., sec. Family Consultation Center, Rochester, 1970—; bd. dirs. Olmsted County (Minn.) Council Coordinated Child Care, 1971-75, pres., 1973-75; bd. dirs. Olmsted County Assn. Mental Health; pres. Rochester Civic Music Guild, 1981-82. Mem. Minn., Rochester edn. assns., Minn. Sch. Psychologists, Am. Psychol. Assn., AAUW, Zumbro Valley Dental Aux. (pres. 1970-71), Alpha Lambda Delta, Alpha Delta Kappa, Psi Chi, Chi Omega, Phi Delta Kappa. Presbyterian. Mem. Order Eastern Star. Home: 2709 Merrihills Dr Rochester MN 55901 Office: Ind Sch Dist 535 Rochester MN 55901

TOLOCZKO, SANDRA MELANIE, med. technologist; b. Wilkes-Barre, Pa., Dec. 7, 1954; d. Thaddeus Thomas and Cecilia Loretta (Bilski) Toloczko; B.S., King's Coll., 1976; cert. Wilkes Barre Gen. Hosp. Sch. Med. Tech., 1976. Med. technologist Wilkes-Barre (Pa.) Gen. Hosp. Lab., 1976—, supr. clin. microscopy/urinalysis dept., 1980—, clin. lab. instr. clin. microscopy, 1980—. Mem. Am. Soc. Clin. Pathologists (asso.), Nat. Certification Agy. for Med. Lab. Personnel, Women's Internat Bowling Congress, Kings Coll. Alumni Assn., Alpha Mu Gamma. Clubs: The Chrome Card Collectors, Maple City Post Card. Home: 29 E Charles St Plains PA 18705

TOMASZ, MARIA, chemist; b. Szeged, Hungary, Oct. 18, 1932; came to U.S., 1956, naturalized, 1963; d. Ivan and Margit Okalyi; diploma chemistry, Eotvos U., Budapest, 1956; Ph.D., Columbia U., 1962; m. Alexander Tomasz, 1956; children—Martin, Julie. Research assoc. Rockefeller U., N.Y.C., 1962, N.Y.U., 1962-66; vis. research asso. N.Y. Blood Center, 1966; asst. prof., then assoc. prof. Hunter Coll., N.Y.C., 1966-79, prof., 1979—. Grantee, NSF, USPHS. Mem. Am. Chem. Soc., Fedn. Am. Biol. Socs., N.Y. Acad. Scis., Sigma. Author papers in field. Office: 695 Park Ave New York NY 10021

TOMBACK, MARGERY PAT, fin. analyst; b. Bklyn., May 17, 1946; d. Michael William and Sheila T.; B.A. in Psychology, Ithaca Coll., 1968; M.A. in Psychology, Adelphi U., 1975; M.B.A. in Acctg., Baruch Coll., 1976. Auditor, Deloitte Haskins and Sells, N.Y.C., 1976-79; sr. fin. analyst Joseph E. Seagram & Sons, Inc., N.Y.C., 1979-82; asst. dir. fin. Seagram Latin Am., San Francisco, 1982—; adj. instr. Pace U., 1978. Recipient Robert E. Kingsley Meml. award for outstanding service to arts Arts and Bus. Council N.Y.C., 1980; C.P.A., N.Y. Mem. Am. Inst. C.P.A.s. Office: 1255 Columbus Ave San Francisco CA 94133

TOMBAUGH, EULA ROSINA, educator; b. Wray, Colo., July 10, 1921; d. Albert L. and Loma Lucinda T.; B.S., Iowa State U., 1943; M.A., U. Minn., 1961; Intern, Miami Valley Hosp., 1944; dietitian St. Luke's Hosp., Kansas City, Mo., 1944-46, Samaritan Hosp., Nampa, Idaho, 1946-58, Caldwell (Idaho) Meml. Hosp., 1954-58; faculty Northwest Nazarene Coll., Nampa, Idaho, 1958—, head home econs. dept., 1967—. Vol., Mercy Med. Center Hospice. Mem. Am. Home Econs. Assn., Am. Vocat. Assn., Idaho Home Econs. Assn., Idaho Vocat. Assn., Soc. Nutrition Edn. Republican. Clubs: Civitan Internat., Nampa Civitan. Home: 203 S Rowena St Nampa ID 83651 Office: Northwest Nazarene College Dept Home Economics Holly and Dewey Sts Nampa ID 83651

TOMBLIN, ELIZABETH ALENE, ednl. adminstr.; b. Beaumont, Tex., Feb. 25, 1947; d. Hollis David and Mary Risinger; B.A., U. Tex., 1969; M.S., U. Colo., 1972; Ph.D., 1976; m. Douglas Tomblin, Feb. 18, 1970. Tchr., counselor, asst. to dir. eval. Northglenn (Colo.) Schs., 1971-77; asso. dir. eval. research No. Colo. Bd. Coop. Services, 1977-78; program dir., eval. and presenter NW Regional Edn. Lab., 1978-80; prin. investigator, psychologist Navy Personnel Research and Devel. Center, San Diego, 1980; dir. program gifted Escondido (Calif.) Public Schs., 1982; asst. dir. eval. services San Diego City Schs., 1982—; cons. in field. Bd. dirs. Bonita Pet Hosp. Mem. Calif. Assn. Elected Women and Ednl. Research, Assn. Calif. Sch. Adminstrs., Calif. Ednl. Research Assn., San Diego Council Adminstrv. Women in Edn., Am. Soc. Tng. and Devel. Contbr. articles to profl. jours. Office: 4100 Normal St B-8 San Diego CA 92103

TOMCZAK, CHRISTINA MARY, banker; b. Yonkers, N.Y., Sept. 24, 1946; d. Henry Peter and Jane Mary (Brzozowski) T.; B.S., Fla. State U., 1968. Sr. examiner, Fed. Res. Bank Atlanta, 1968-77; v.p. Gt. Am. Banks, Inc., Miami, 1977-79, sr. v.p., 1979—; dir. Gt. Am. Banks of Pinellas, Broward County, Davie, North Miami Beach and Dade County; dir. Am. Bancshares Ins. Agy., Inc. Mem. Bank Adminstrn. Inst., Am. Bankers Assn., Am. Mgmt. Assn., Am. Soc. Profl. and Exec. Women, Gamma Sigma Sigma (nat. pres. 1977-81 nat. dir., 1969—). Home: 10812 Kendall Dr N Q-26 Miami FL 33176 Office: 11755 Biscayne Blvd North Miami FL 33181

TOMECEK, CAROLYN LOUISE, ins. co. exec.; b. Chgo., Dec. 12, 1944; d. Frank Joseph and Louise Mary T.; student U. Chgo., 1965-67; B.S. in Math., Coll. of St. Francis, Joliet, Ill., 1965. Mktg. mgr. IBM, Chgo., 1976-77; exec. asst. to chief exec. officer CNA Ins., Chgo., 1977-78, v.p. personnel, 1978-80, v.p. adminstrn., 1980—. Office: CNA Ins CNA Plaza Chicago IL 60685

TOMICH, LILLIAN, lawyer; b. Los Angeles, Mar. 28, 1935; d. Peter S. and Yovanka P. (Ivanovic) T.; A.A., Pasadena City Coll., 1954; B.A. (LaVerne Noyes scholar 1955, 56), UCLA, 1956, gen. secondary teaching credential (Charles Fletcher Scott fellow), 1957, M.A., 1958; J.D. (Univ. scholar), U. So. Calif., 1961. Admitted to Calif. bar, 1961; practice law, 1961-66, 67-68; mem. firm Hurley, Shaw & Tomich, San Marino, Calif., 1968-76, Driscoll & Tomich, San Marino, 1976—; counsel Mfrs. Bank, Los Angeles, 1966; dir. Continental Culture Specialists, Inc., Glendale, Calif. Recipient Nat. 1st award debating Phi Rho Pi, 1954, Pacific Coast 1st award debating, 1953, 54; Nat. 1st award debating Pi Kappa Delta, 1955. Mem. Calif. State Bar, Am. Bar Assn., Los Angeles County Bar Assn. (arbitration com. 1978—), Women Lawyers Assn., UCLA Alumni Assn., Town Hall Los Angeles, Los Angeles World Affairs Council, Order Mast and Dagger, Iota Tau Tau, Alpha Gamma Sigma (life), Pi Kappa Delta (pres. 1955-56), Phi Rho Pi (pres. 1953-54), Pi Sigma Alpha (v.p. 1957). Mem. Serbian Orthodox Ch. (trustee). Home: 501 N Del Mar Ave San Gabriel CA 91775 Office: 2297 Huntington Dr San Marino CA 91108

TOMIKAWA, SANDRA AKIKO, sch. psychologist; b. Honolulu, July 18, 1953; d. Isao and Grace (Komatsu) T.; B.A. with honors, U. Hawaii, 1974; M.S., U. Utah, 1976, Ph.D., 1979. Ednl. coordinator Children's Center, Honolulu, 1975-76; teaching fellow dept. psychology U. Utah, Salt Lake City, 1977-79; sch. psychologist State Hawaii Dept. Edn., Kaneohe, 1980—; cons. Kaneohe PTA, 1981-82; facilitator Parenting Group, 1982—; cons. Naris Cosmetics, Honolulu, 1979—. NIMH grantee, 1974-75. Mem. Am. Psychol. Assn., Hawaii Psychol. Assn., Hawaii Sch. Counselor Assn., Council Exceptional Children, Hawaii Assn. for Children with Learning Disabilities, Honolulu Japanese C. of C., Phi Beta Kappa, Phi Kappa Phi, Phi Sigma Rho Alumni Assn. Democrat. Club: State Tennis League. Home: 99-650 Aliipoe Dr Aiea HI

96701 Office: State Hawaii Dept Edn 45-955 Kamehameha Hwy Kaneohe HI 96744

TOMINEY, KATHRYN MAURA, quality control engr.; b. N.Y.C., Dec. 21, 1944; d. Patrick Joseph and Virginia (Wooding) Tominey; B.S., U. Ariz., 1968; M.B.A., U. Wash., 1975; m. James S. Dukelow, Jr., Jan. 23, 1981. Sr. engr. reactor analysis, power plant simulation, applied math. WPPSS Co., Richland, Wash., 1968-73; cons. KM Tominey & Assocs., Richland, 1974-78; sr. engr. Radiol. Protection Depot, Rockwell Hanford Co., Richland, Wash., 1978—; prin. Dukelow, Tominey & Assos., Richland, 1981—. Mem. Am. Soc. for Quality Control (exec. com. nuclear div. 1972-77), Am. Nuclear Soc. (exec. com. reactor ops. div. 1981—), Soc. for Risk Analysis. Republican. Episcopalian. Contbr. articles to profl. jours. Home: 1926 Everest St Richland WA 99352 Office: Rockwell Hanford Co PO Box 800 Richland WA 99352 also PO Box 1322 Richland WA 99352

TOMISKA, CORA LORENA, civic worker; b. Fontana, Calif., July 30, 1928; d. Riley Royston and Winifred Lillian (Humphry) Green; A.A., Chaffey Jr. Coll., 1948; B.A., Calif. State Coll., San Bernardino, 1976, postgrad., 1976—; m. Joseph Frank Tomiska, June 19, 1950; children—Jo Ann, William Joseph, Robert Royston, Charity Lillianne, Angelina Kathleen. Owner, mgr. Tomiska Aviaries, Fontana, 1963—. Pres. Redwood PTA, 1976, Sequoia Jr. High PTA, 1969-70, Fontana Council PTA, 1972-74; mem. exec. bd. 5th Dist. PTA, 1972—, historian, 1976-79, v.p., dir. health, 1979-81, v.p., dir. parent edn., 1981—; sec. consol. projects adv. com. Fontana Unified Sch. Dist., 1972-81, sec. family life edn. project, 1982—; mem. Mayoral Candidacy Com., 1978; counselor jr. gardening Fontana Redwood Blue Jays, 1964—; pres. Fontana Garden Club, 1974-77; vol. Fontana Youth Service Center, Am. Heart Fund, Am. Cancer Soc., Christian Youth Edn., Valley Bible Ch., Fontana United Way; scholarship chmn. San Bernardino Valley dist. Calif. Garden Clubs, 1974—; sec.-treas. Fontana Family Service Agy., 1976-79, pres., 1980—. Recipient 1st place award Calif. Jr. Flower Shows, 1969-73. Mem. ARC, San Bernardino County Mus. Assn., Fontana Hist. Soc., AAUW (edn. chmn. 1981—). Address: 8365 Redwood Ave Fontana CA 92335

TOMLIN, LILY, actress; b. Detroit, 1939; student Highland Park Jr. Coll., Wayne State U. Appearances in concerts and colls. throughout U.S.; TV appearances include CBS and NBC spls., from 1973; formerly mem. Laugh in; motion picture debut in Nashville, 1975, The Late Show, Moment by Moment; Nine to Five, Incredible Shrinking Woman; one-person Broadway show Appearing Nightly. Recipient Grammy award, 1971; 5 Emmy awards for CBS and ABC spls., 1973, 75, 81; named Best Supporting Actress, N.Y. Film Critics; spl. Tony, 1977. Records: This Is A Recording; And That's The Truth; Modern Scream; On Stage. Address: PO Box 27700 Los Angeles CA 90027 *

TOMLIN, MARY PHILLIPS, county ofcl.; b. Leesburg, Va., May 16, 1932; d. Lonie John and Bartie Cummings (Clark) Phillips; ed. Leesburg public schs., spl. courses: m. Cyrus Smith Tomlin, Dec. 13, 1952 (dec.); 1 dau., Judy Elizabeth. Clk., U.S. Govt., Washington, 1950-52, Melpar, Falls Church, Va., 1956-58; with County of Fairfax, Va., 1959—, supr., 1960—; tchr. income classes, tng. courses on state and county bus. lics., personal property. Sec. PTA, 1967-69. Recipient Unusual Ability award Fairfax County, 1963, 82. Democrat. Baptist. Club: Rebekah. Author manuals. Home: 161 Edwards Ferry Rd Leesburg VA 22075 Office: 4100 Chain Bridge Rd Fairfax VA 22030

TOMLINSON, CELIA SUVA RUIZ, civil engr.; b. Bulacan, Philippines, Jan. 25, 1942; d. Felix Bernabe and Anacleta (Suva) Ruiz; came to U.S., 1968, naturalized, 1975; B.S. in Civil Engring., Mapua Inst. Tech., 1964; m. Thomas Emery Tomlinson, May 18, 1969; 1 son, Thomas Clay. Surveyor, Bur. Lands, Philippines, 1960-65; engr. H.R. Lopez & Co., 1965; estimator Adrian Wilson & Assos., 1965-66; engr. Atlantica Corp., 1966-68; design engr. City of Albuquerque, 1968—; cons. to land developers. Mem. Adv. Com. Women in City Govt. Registered profl. engr., N.Mex. Mem. ASCE, Nat. Soc. Profl. Engrs., Am. Pub. Works Assn. (chairperson municipal engring. com. N.Mex. chpt.), Filipino Am. Assn. Republican. Author: The Woman's Guide to a Successful Career in Construction, 1979. Home: 10325 Karen Ave Albuquerque NM 87111 Office: Box 645 Albuquerque NM 87103

TOMLINSON-KEASEY, CAROL ANN, psychologist; b. Washington, Oct. 15, 1942; d. Robert Bruce and Geraldine (Howe) Tomlinson; B.A., Pa. State U., 1964; M.S. in Psychology, Iowa State U., 1966; Ph.D., U. Calif., Berkeley, 1970; m. Charles Blake Keasey, June 13, 1964; children—Kai Linson, Amber Lynn. Mem. faculty Rutgers U., 1970-72, U. Nebr., Lincoln, 1972-77; prof. psychology U. Calif., Riverside, 1976—. Named Outstanding Young Individual in Lincoln, 1977. Mem. Am. Psychol. Assn., AAAS, Internat. Neuropsychology Soc., Soc. Research Child Devel., Sigma Xi. Author: Child's Eye View, 1980; also articles, chpts. in books. Home: 6140 Port au Prince Riverside CA 92506 Office: Dept Psychology U Calif Riverside CA 92521

TOMPANE, MARY BETH, Girl Scout exec.; b. Hollywood, Calif., Sept. 27, 1928; d. Richard Earl and Mary Elizabeth (McGregor) Goss; A.A., Phoenix Coll., 1948; postgrad. No. Ariz. U., Ariz. State U., 1946-55; M.Banking Mgmt., U. Calif., Riverside, 1973; m. Eugene F. Tompane, Nov. 4, 1950; children—Michael, Richard, Donald, John. Mgmt. analyst, 1955-69; dept. head Boswell Hosp., Sun City, Ariz., 1969-72; non profit orgn. cons., Phoenix, 1972-80; travel agt., Phoenix and Tempe, Ariz., 1972-81; interim exec. dir. Girl Scouts U.S.A., 1981—; mem. nat. women's bd. Northwood Inst., 1980—. Pres. Maricopa County YWCA, 1962-65, Phoenix Day Nursery, 1965-67, Friends of Thunderbird, 1975-77; pres. Family Service Phoenix, 1980; Horizona chmn. Bicentennial City of Phoenix, 1974-76. Named Woman of Year, Phoenix, 1965. Mem. Internat. Assn. Vol. Edn., Dirs. of Vols., Am. Assn. Assn. Execs. Republican. Episcopalian. Address: Tempe AZ

TOMPKINS, A. KATHLEEN KELLY, civic worker; b. St. Johns, Mich., Jan. 15, 1903; d. William Thomas and Harriet A. (Wright) Kelly; grad. U. Cin. Conservatory of Music, 1926; m. Neil Wright (dec.); children—Neil, Ross; m. 2d, Raymond McLaughlin, June 1961 (dec.); m. 3d, Lawrence E. Tompkins, June 5, 1976. Concert pianist, 1932-37; social dir. Lakeside Hotel, Eaglesmere, Pa., 1938-47; publicity dir. Pocono Manor, 1947-49; resident mgr. apts., St. Petersburg, Fla., 1949-50; social dir. Marshall House, York Harbor, Maine, 1951. Bd. dirs. Sarasota Music Club, 1964—, pres., 1966-68, parliamentarian, 1976-81; bd. dirs. Fla. Fedn. Music Clubs, 1968—; piano chmn., mem. artists selection com. Community Concerts Bd., 1971—; pres. Golden Gate Point Assn., 1962—, cons., 1977-81. Named Realtor of Yr., Sarasota Realtors Assn., 1960. Mem. Delta Omicron (nat. pres. 1931-37). Episcopalian. Club: Intercity Bridge (life historian). Home: 350 Golden Gate Point Sarasota FL 33577

TOMS, KATHLEEN MOORE, nurse; b. San Francisco, Dec. 31, 1943; d. William Moore and Phyllis Josephine (Barry) Stewart; R.N., A.A., City Coll. San Francisco, 1963; B.P.S. in Nursing Edn., Elizabethtown (Pa.) Coll., 1973; M.S. in Edn., Temple U., 1977; children—Kathleen Marie Toms, Kelly Terese Toms. Med.-surg. nurse St. Joseph Hosp., Fairbanks, Alaska, 1963-65; emergency room nurse St. Joseph Hosp., Lancaster, Pa., 1965-69, blood, plasm and components nurse, 1969-71; pres. F.E. Barry Co., Lancaster, 1971—; dir. inservice edn. Lancaster Osteo. Hosp., 1971-75; coordinator practical nursing program Vocat. Tech. Sch., Coatesville, Pa., 1976-77; dir. nursing Pocopson Home, West Chester, Pa., 1978-80, Riverside Hosp., Wilmington, Del., 1980—; mem. Pa. Gov.'s Council on Alcoholism and Drug Abuse, 1974-76; mem. Del. Health Council Med.-Surg. Task Force, 1981—; dir. Lancaster Community Health Center, 1973-76; lectr. in field. Served to capt. Nurse Corps, USAR, 1973—. Decorated Army Commendation medal; recipient Community Service award Citizens United for Better Public Relations, 1974; award Sertoma, Lancaster, 1974; Outstanding Citizen award Sta. WGAL-TV, 1975. Mem. Elizabethtown, Temple U. alumni assns., Pa. Nurses' Assn. (dir.). Inventor auto-infuser for blood or blood components, 1971. Home: 400 Summit House 1450 West Chester Pike West Chester PA 19380 Office: 700 Lea Blvd Wilmington DE 19899

TOMS, SUE ANNE, univ. adminstr.; b. Mansfield, Ohio, Feb. 10, 1947; d. Ray Edward and Ruth Evelyn (Bishop) T.; B.S., Ohio State U., 1969; postgrad. U. of the Am., Mexico, 1968; M.A. (grad. asst.), So. Ill. U., 1975; postgrad. N.Y. U., 1979, Cath. U. P.R., 1979-82; m. T.C. Geat, Dec. 22, 1979. Coordinator exec. English program Honeywell, Madrid, 1970-74; faculty Center of English as a 2d Lang., So. Ill. U., Carbondale, 1975-76; faculty Div. English as a 2d Lang., Ohio State U., Columbus, 1978; dir. Inst. Communicative English, Cath. U. P.R., Ponce, 1978-80, dir. govt. relations, 1980—; USIS linguistics specialist, summer seminar Poznan U. (Poland), 1977; mem. UNESCO Seminar Women, Communications and Community Devel., 1980. Fundraising com. mem. Center Orientation and Services, La Playa, Ponce, 1981; active ARC. Fulbright Hayes lectr., Titograd, Yugoslavia, 1976-77. Mem. P.R. Assn. External Resource Officers (sec. 1981-82), Soc. Intercultural Tng., Edn. and Research, AAUW, Am. Assn. Univ. Adminstrs. (dir. 1982—), Nat. Assn. Fgn. Student Affairs. Methodist. Club: Deportivo de Ponce. Contbr. articles to profl. jours. Home: Alhambra Plaza 703 Ponce PR 00731 Office: Cath Univ PR Govt Relations Ponce PR 00732

TOMSHECK, LYLA ETHEL, educator; b. Conrad, Mont., Oct. 23, 1950; d. Robert Anton and Ethel Johanna (Wallewein) Tomsheck; B.S. in Home Econs., Mont. State U., 1972, postgrad., 1977-79; postgrad. U. Mont., 1977-79; M.S. in Speech Communication, U. Oreg., 1981; Ravalli County extension agt. Mont. Extension Service, Hamilton, 1973-80; instr. dept. speech U. Oreg., Eugene, 1980—. Sunday Sch. and confirmation tchr., fin. sec. Faith Luth. Ch. Recipient Heisey Found. award, 1967; Florence Hall award, 1978; Holmes award for dress design, 1972; Farm Found. fellow, 1980; J.C. Penney fellow, 1980. Mem. Nat. Assn. Extension Home Economists (chmn. public relations com. 1974-77, public affairs com. 1977-80, sec. 1978-80), Mont. Assn. Extension Home Economists, Am. Home Econs. Assn. (nominating com. 1977-78, family and public policy com. 1978-79), Mont. Home Econs. Assn., Mont. Coop. Extension Assn. (dir. 1974-77, sec. 1976-77, chmn. public relations com. 1975-77), Alpha Gamma Delta. Club: Soroptimist (program com. 1976-77, nominating com. 1975-76). Contbr. articles to profl. publs. Home: 1810 Harris Apt 226 Eugene OR 97401 Office: Speech Dept Villard Hall U Oreg Eugene OR 97403

TONCRE, JEANNE BAKER, TV exec.; b. New Orleans, Apr. 9, 1925; d. Claude Leonidas and Gladys Mae (Culver) Baker; student La. State U., 1941-43, Am. Acad. Dramatic Arts, 1943-45; m. Arthur Toncre, 1948; children—Lance, Nanette, Robin. Actress, off-Broadway and summer stock, 1945-48; publicist Sta. KOB, Albuquerque, 1948-50; actress NBC, N.Y.C., 1950-52; asso. producer Sta. KSL-TV, Salt Lake City, 1952-54; free-lance writer, Venezuela, 1955-60; continuity dir. Sta. WWL-TV, New Orleans, 1961-63; publicist Sta. KRON-TV, San Francisco, 1963-68, dir. women's affairs, producer, 1968-78, dir. public affairs programs, producer, host, 1978-82; lectr. in field; communications cons. Bd. dirs. Bay Area Girl Scouts U.S.A., 1975-78; adv. council Marin County Status of Women Commn., 1974. Recipient U.S. Dept. Labor award for Youth Inquires, 1975; Motion Picture/TV Council award for Quality Children's Programs, 1973; Girl Scout Council Community Service award, 1973; Outstanding Contbr. to Broadcasting award Am. Women in Radio-TV, 1982. Mem. Am. Women in Radio and TV (v.p. 1977-79, 82-84), AFTRA, Nat. Acad. TV Arts and Scis. Republican. Clubs: Commonwealth, Soroptimist (pres. 1975). Home: 30 Barbaree Way Tiburon CA 94920

TONDEL, BETTY JANE CAPPS (MRS. LYMAN M. TONDEL, JR.), civic worker, former social services adminstr.; b. Dallas, May 8, 1925; d. James William and Maud Marie (Mode) Brownlee; student U. Colo., 1946-48, B.S. in Home Econs., 1964; postgrad. Colo. State U., 1965-66; children—Timothy James, Joseph Frederick. Adult edn. instr., Boulder, Colo., 1965-66; tchr. home econs. Jr. High Sch., Longmont, Colo., 1965-66; with Colo. State Dept. Social Services, 1966-80, home econs. specialist, Program Planning and Devel. Div., Denver, 1966-73, state dir. nutrition program for the elderly, Div. Services to the Aging, 1973-76, adminstrv. officer tng. program, 1976-77, asst. dir. community care orgn. Div. Med. Assistance, 1977-78, adminstrv. officer long-term care services, 1978-80; mem. Commn. on Med. Profl. Liability, Am. Bar Assn., 1975-78, Commn. on Legal Rights of the Elderly, 1978—; bd. dirs. Citizens Union, also chmn. spl. events, 1981—; v.p. Residence Coop. Bd., 1981—; regent for Colo. Nat. Gerontol. Soc.; membership chmn. for Colo., Am. Council for Consumer Interests, 1969-70; chmn. Colo. sect. Home Economists in Human Services, 1967-69; governing bds. Consumer Credit Counseling Service, 1970-73, Rocky Mountain Assn. Meals for Seniors; mem. adv. bd. to Fed. Region VIII, HEW, 1972-73, fed. exec. bd., consumer com., 1975-77; del. White House Conf. on Nutrition, 1969; arrangements chmn. State House Conf. on Nutrition, 1970; mem. rural devel. com. and tech. action panel State of Colo., law and justice task force, consumer affairs Urban Coalition; vol. standards com. Nat. Bur. Standards; consumer cons. Nat. Can Corp., Chgo., Sears Roebuck & Co., Chgo. and Denver, Carnation Milk Co., Colorado Springs. Vol., Spaulding Rehab. Center; pres. Muscular Dystrophy Assn. Am., Boulder County chpt., 1962-64; Cub Scout den mother Long's Peak council Boy Scouts Am., 1957-60, head den mother, 1959-60; membership chmn. PTA, 1957-58; scorekeeper Boulder Little League Baseball, 1957-64; active fund-raising United Way, Am. Cancer Soc. Named to Gallery of Fame, Denver Post, for devel. Meals on Wheels programs, 1973. Mem. Am. Home Econs. Assn. (governing bd., del. Nat. Health Council 1970-71, coop. relations com. 1970-71, chmn. Home Econs. in Human Services, profl. sect. 1974-76), Am. Home Econs. Assn. Democrat. Episcopalian. Contbr. writings in field to publs. Home: 184 Columbia Hts Brooklyn NY 11201

TONG, MAY LING, assn. exec.; b. Boston, Mar. 30, 1939; d. Soy Soo and Toy (Chou) SooHoo; student Boston U., 1957-60, U. Mass., Boston, 1973-74, Inst. Employment and Tng. Adminstrn., Harvard U., 1979; m. Eugene Y. J. Tong, June 26, 1960; children—Darren Eugene, Gregg. Chmn., vol. dir. Multi-Service Center, Chinese Am. Civic Assn., 1972-74, exec. dir., 1974-77; project cons. Chinese Econ. Devel. Council, Boston, 1977, dir. community devel., 1978—; cons. Medford High Sch., Norwood CETA Consortium, Northeastern U. Mem. Louis B. Russell Award Com., 1976—, chmn., 1978, 79; mem. exec. bd. New Eng. Health Promotion Council; bd. dirs., mem. minority involvement com. Am. Heart Assn., Mass. affiliate, 1974—; mem. corp. Family Services Assn. Greater Boston, 1974—, trustee, profl. services com., 1973—; mem. corp. United Way Mass. Bay, 1975—, bd. dirs., 1980-81; bd. dirs. Boston Community Media Council, 1975—, Nat. Alliance Bus., 1977—; mem. devel. com. Chinese Consol. Benevolent Assn., 1971—. Mem. Nat. Council Urban Econ. Devel. Author: History of Boston's Chinatown, 1976. Office: 20 Hudson St Boston MA 02111

TONIETTE, SALLYE JEAN, physician; b. Sulphur, La.; d. Eugene Augusta and Sallye (Tanner) Toniette; student John McNeese Jr. Coll., 1946-47; B.S., La. State U., 1949; tchrs. certificate La. State U., 1950, M.D., 1955. Intern, Crawford W. Long Meml. Hosp., Emory U., Atlanta, 1955-56, resident in ob-gyn., jr., sr., chief residencies, 1956-59; practice ob-gyn, Sulphur, La., 1959—; bd. dirs. Holly Hill Nursing Home; mem. med. staff West Calcasieu Cameron Hosp., 1959—. Dir. Calcasieu Parish Cancer Soc. 1963-67. Named Woman of Dinstinction, Calcasieu Parish Police Jurors, also Bus. and Profl. Women's Club of West Calcesieu, 1969. Fellow Am. Coll. Ob-Gyn; mem. AMA, So. Med. Assn., La., Calcasieu Parish med. socs., La. Wildlife Fedn., Am. Quarter Horse Assn., Assn. Am. Physicians and Surgeons, Am., La. Paint horse assns., Alpha Chi Omega, Beta Tau Mu, Iota Sigma Pi, Phi Theta Kappa, Beta Sigma Phi. Democrat. Methodist. Clubs: Quota, Bus. and Profl. Women's, Lake Charles Country, Bayou Oaks Country (v.p. bd. dirs. 1974-82). Contbr. articles to profl. jours. Home: 301 W Verdine St Sulphur LA 70663 Office: 521 Cypress St Sulphur LA 70663

TOOKEY, MARCIA HICKMAN, polit. party exec.; b. Van Wert, Ohio, Jan. 3, 1932; d. John A. and Olwen (Jones) Hickman; B.S. in Edn., Wittenberg U., 1954; m. Robert Clarence Tookey, Sept. 15, 1956; children—John Hall, Jennifer Louise, Thomas Anderson. Tchr. speech South Side High Sch., Ft. Wayne, Ind., 1954-56; prodn. mgr. Americana Masterpieces, New Era Prodns., Los Angeles, 1973; lectr. Calif. Circuit, 1974-76; asst. to vice chmn. Calif. Republican Party, Burbank, 1979-80, dir. ops., 1981-82. Pres., La Canada/Pasadena Child Guidance Clinic Guild, 1967, La Canada Elem. Sch. PTA, 1969-70; bd. dirs. La Canada Valley Beautiful, 1972-74, La Canada Scholarship Found., 1972-78. Recipient Hon. Service award, PTA, 1974; named Women of Yr., Town and Country Fine Arts Club, 1975; Outstanding Precinct Worker, Los Angeles County, 1976. Mem. Verdugo Hills Bus. and Profl. Women (bd. dirs.), Theta Alpha Phi, Kappa Delta. Republican. Club: La Canada Thursday. Home: 1249 Descanso Dr La Canada CA 91011

TOOLE, AMY LINDA, ednl. adminstr.; b. Bklyn., Feb. 19, 1948; d. Charles F. and Vera (Malevich) T.; B.A., SUNY, New Paltz, 1969; M.A., Montclair State Coll., 1971. Speech and lang. pathologist Orange County Bd. Coop. Ednl. Services, Goshen, N.Y., 1969-72, diagnostic prescriptive tchr., 1972-74, supr. spl. edn. Putnam/N.W., Yorktown Heights, N.Y., 1974—; adj. lectr. Grad. Sch., Manhattanville Coll., 1975—; project dir. Regional Demonstration Program for Presch. Handicapped Childre, Putnam/No. Westchester, Yorktown Heights; pvt. practice diagnosis of lang. and learning disorders; cons. edn. for handicapped; speaker in field. Lic. speech pathologist, cert. sch. dist. adminstr., N.Y. State. Mem. Am. Speech/Lang. and Hearing Assn. (cert. clin. competence), Council Exceptional Children, Assn. N.Y. State Educators of Emotionally Disturbed, Westchester Speech and Hearing Assn., N.Y. State Speech and Hearing Assn., Delta Kappa Gamma. Home: 77 Coachlight Sq Montrose NY 10548 Office: Bd Coop Ednl Services Yorktown Heights NY 10598

TOOPER, VIRGINIA OLIPHANT, chem. co. exec., ednl. cons.; b. Nashville, June 25, 1928; d. Thomas Alfred and Catherine (Holt) Oliphant; B.S., La. State U., 1949; O.T.R., Tex. Womens U., 1953; M.A., Columbia, 1954; Ed.D., U. Cin., 1973; m. Edward Benjamin Tooper, Aug. 6, 1955; 1 son, Jon Edward. Tchr. pub. schs., Baton Rouge, 1949-52; tchr. VA Hosp., Hines, Ill., 1955-58, Child Guidance Home, Cin., 1963-65; instr. Cleve. State U., 1970-72; asst. prof. spl. edn., also counseling and guidance San Jose (Calif.) State U., 1972-79; v.p. Premier Chem. Corp., 1979—; edn. and communication cons., 1979—. Recipient grants Dept. Mental Hygiene and Correction, 1969, Am. Occupational Therapy Assn., 1970. Nat. Tb. scholar in occupational therapy, 1952-54. Mem. Sales and Mktg. Execs., Nat. Speakers Assn. (bd. dirs., newsletter editor No. Calif. chpt.), Nat. Assn. Profl. Saleswomen (pres. Eastbay chpt.). Author: Motor Skills, 1971; Communication Skills, 1973. Home: 7953 Stonehurst Ct Pleasanton CA 94566

TOPACIO, SALVACION UYGUANCO, physician; b. Manila, Philippines, June 3, 1942; d. Gonzalo Vitug Uyguanco and Lourdes Olalia Puno; A.A., U. Santo Tomas, 1960, M.D., 1965; m. Dionisio Castro Topacio, Apr. 22, 1973; children—Pamela Christine, Annabelle Claire. Intern, Univ. Santo Tomas Hosp., Manila, 1964-65; resident in infectious and tropical medicine San Lazaro Hosp., Philippines, 1965-66; resident in obstetrics and gynecology St. Jude Hosp., Philippines, 1966-67; sr. resident in pediatrics Infant of Jesus Children's Hosp., Philippines, 1967-68; intern Harkness Community Hosp., San Francisco, 1968-69; extern in pediatrics Calif. Hosp., Los Angeles, 1970-71; intern and resident in internal medicine, gen. surgery and orthopedic surgery Santa Fe Hosp., Los Angeles, 1971-73; resident in internal medicine Good Samaritan Hosp., Los Angeles, 1973; family practice medicine, INA-Roos Loos Health Plan, Inc., 1973—. Diplomate Am. Bd. Family Practice. Fellow Am. Acad. Family Physicians; mem. Philippine Med. Assn., Philippine Women's Med. Assn. (Philippines); AMA, Am. Women's, Calif., Long Beach, Los Angeles, Los Angeles Women's med. assns. Philippine Med. Assn. So. Calif. Home: 19006 S Sabrina Ave Cerritos CA 90701 Office: 2220 Clark Ave Long Beach CA 90815

TOPFER, SUE ACE, librarian; b. Media, Pa., Mar. 30, 1925; d. Percy Henry and Dorothy Austin (Redheffer) Ace; B.S., Ursinus Coll., 1946; M.S., Syracuse U., 1951; m. Alvin Richard Topfer, Nov. 27, 1952; children—Edward Henry, Dorothy Sue, Keith Ace, Kurt Alan. Asst. chem. lab. Am. Viscose Corp., Marcus Hook, Pa., 1946-50; librarian electronics and elec. lab. U.S. Naval Air Devel. Center, Johnsville, Pa., 1951-53; asso. librarian Luzerne County Community Coll., Nanticoke, Pa., 1967-78; serials Librarian Wilkes Coll., Wilkes-Barre, Pa., 1979—. Mem. exec. bd. Glen Summit Community Club, Mountaintop, Pa., 1971-72. Mem. ALA, Am. Coll. and Research Libraries. Home: Box 387 Rural Delivery #3 Loop Rd Mountaintop PA 18707 Office: Eugene Shedden Farley Library Franklin at South St Wilkes-Barre PA 18766

TOPINKA, JUDY BAAR, state legislator; b. Riverside, Ill., Jan. 16, 1944; d. William Daniel and Lillian Mary (Shuss) Baar; B.S., Northwestern U., 1966; 1 son, Joseph Baar. Features editor, reporter, columnist Life Newspapers, Berwyn and LaGrange, Ill., 1966-77; with Forest Park (Ill.) Review and Westchester News, 1976-77; exec. v.p. Cicero Radio Corp., 1975-77; coordinator spl. events Dept. Fedn. Communications, AMA, 1978-80; research analyst Senator Leonard Becker, 1978-79; mem. Ill. Ho. of Reps., 1981—. Founder, pres., bd. dirs. West Suburban Exec. Breakfast Club, 1976—. Republican. Office: 6924 W Cermak Rd Berwyn IL 60402

TOPPAN, SANDRA HALL, dancer; b. Atlanta, Oct. 20, 1948; d. Albert Maurice and Barbara Louvree (Coleman) Hall; B.A., Columbia (S.C.) Coll., 1970; m. Peter Christopher Toppan, June 15, 1974; children— Christopher Stephen, Jennifer Lee. With Carolina Ballet Co., 1966-67, Granite State Ballet Co., 1976-77; dir. dance Camp Se-Sa-Ma-Ca, 1969; sec. Senator J. Strom Thurmond, Washington, 1970-72; flight attendant Delta Airlines, 1972-76; owner, dir. Sandra Toppan Studios, Hampton, N.H., 1976-79; founder choreographer Sandra Toppan Dancers, Hampton, 1978—; pres., treas. Sandra Toppan Dance Centre, Hampton, 1979—; dir. dance classes Hampton Recreation Dept., 1976-81; instr. dance YWCA, 1978-81; dir. Miss Dance of New Eng. Pageant, 1980-81. Named Miss Dance of Carolinas, 1970; Miss Congeniality, Miss Dance of Am. Pageant, 1970. Mem. Dance Masters New Eng. (dir. 1978-80, 3d v.p. 1980-81), Dance Masters Am., Nat. Assn. Female Execs., Internat. Graphoanalysis Soc. Republican. Methodist. Clubs: Jr. Women's, Delta Pilot Wives (pres. 1979-80).

TOPPIN, JOYCE, govt. personnel ofcl.; b. N.Y.C., June 29, 1939; d. Josiah and Essie (James) T.; student CCNY, 1957-59; B.B.A., Baruch Coll., 1969; M.A., N.Y.U., 1973. Clk., Met. Life Ins. Co., 1959-61; various clerical and adminstrv. postions NMU Pension & Welfare Plan, N.Y.C., 1961-69; employment interviewer, sr. employment interviewer, employment counselor N.Y. State Dept. Labor, N.Y.C., 1969-72; personnel mgmt. specialist, U.S. Office Personnel Mgmt. (formerly U.S. Civil Service Commn.), asst. area mgr. Newark Area Office, N.Y.C., 1972—; chmn. fed. exec. bd. EEO Subcom. No. N.J. Pres. Riverside Club., Nat. Assn. Negro Bus. and Profl. Women's Club, 1979—; bd. dirs. Ruth Williams Dance Found. Recipient profl. awards Riverside Club, Nat. Assn. Negro Bus. and Profl. Women's Clubs. Mem. Am. Mgmt. Assn., ACLU, Fed. Personnel Assn. N.J., Coalition 100 Black Women. Office: Peter Rodino Jr Federal Bldg 970 Broad St Newark NJ 07102

TORBET, LAURA, graphic designer, author; b. Paterson, N.J., Aug. 23, 1942; d. Earl Buchanan and Ruth Claire (Ehlers) Robbins; B.A., B.F.A., Ohio Wesleyan U., 1964; m. Bruce J. Torbet, Sept. 9, 1967 (div. 1971). Mng. editor Suburban Life mag., East Orange, N.J., 1964-65; asst. public relations dir. United Funds N.J., Newark, 1965-67; art dir. Alitalia Airlines, N.Y.C., 1967-69; propr. Laura Torbet Studio, N.Y.C., 1969—; author: Macrame You Can Wear, 1972, Clothing Liberation, 1973, Leathercraft You Can Wear, 1975, The T-Shirt Book, 1976, The Complete Book of Skateboarding, 1976, How To Do Everything With Markers, 1977; Squash: How to Play, How to Win, 1977; How to Fight Fair With Your Kids...and Win!, 1980; editor: The Encyclopedia of Crafts, 1980; Helena Rubenstein's Book of the Sun, 1979; (with George Bach) The Iinner Enemy, 1982, A Tine for Caring, 1982; (with Hap Hatton) Helpful Hints for Hard Times, 1982; editor, co-author books. Mem. Am. Crafts Council, Am. Women's Econ. Devel. Corp. Club: Nat. Arts (N.Y.C.). Home and Office: 225 E 73d St New York NY 10021

TORDA, CLARA, psychoanalyst; b. Budapest, Hungary, Apr. 1, 1910; came to U.S., 1939, naturalized 1942; d. Joseph and Ilona (Varga) Torda; Ph.D., U. Budapest, 1933; M.D. summa cum laude U. Milan (Italy), 1938; cert. in psychoanalysis N.Y. Med. Coll., 1960; m. Walter Weiss, May 7, 1942; 1 son, Walter. Research asso. Univ. Coll., London, 1938-39, U. Pa., 1939-40, Cornell U. Med. Coll., 1940-52; sr. research asso. Columbia U.-N.Y. State Psychiat. Inst., 1955-57; instr. N.Y. Med. Coll., 1960-65; asso. prof. SUNY Downstate Med. Center, Bklyn., 1964-69, Mt. Sinai Sch. Medicine, 1969-71; prof. N.Y. Sch. Psychiatric Tng., 1965—; vis. prof. U. Argentina, Buenos Aires, 1967, U. Calif., Irvine, 1970, Rockefeller U., 1972, Med. Coll., U. Rochester (N.Y.), 1976, Stanford U., 1975, 80-82, UCLA, 1982—, U. Calif., Berkeley, 1982—; pvt. practice psychoanalysis, N.Y.C., 1955—; civilian with USPHS, AEC, 1951-52; del. World Congress Biol. Psychiatry, 1974. Mem. AMA, Am. Psychiat. Assn., N.Y. County, N.Y. State med. socs., N.Y. County Psychiat. Soc., Am. Acad. Psychoanalysis, Child Psychiat. Soc., Soc. Med. Psychoanalysis, Soc. Am. Group Psychoanalysis, AAUP, Am. Physiol. Soc., Am. Pharm. Soc., Biophys. Soc., Soc. Neurosci., AAAS, Assn. Psychophysiol. Study Sleep, Internat. Brain Research Orgn., Psychophysiol. Soc., N.Y. Acad. Scis., Am. Acad. Child Psychiatry, Soc. Adolescent Psychiatry, Soc. Med. Psychoanalysis, Soc. Med. Group Psychoanalysis, Acad. Psychosomatic Medicine, Assn. for Advancement Psychotherapy, Am. Soc. Pharm. Exptl. Therapy, Soc. Psychoendocrinology, Psychophysiol. Soc., Internat. Soc. Psychoneuroendocrinology, Internat. Soc. Submolecular Biology, Am. Assn. for Artificial Intelligence, AAUP, Macy Found., Markle Found. Author: Depolorization Repolarization Cycle, 1972; Prevention: A Psychophysiological and Psychodynamic Study, 1975; Catecholamines of Developing Brain: Preconditioning for Emotional Disorders, 1977; Memory and Dreams: A Modern Physics Approach, 1980; Information Processing—The Central Nervous System and the Computer, 1982; contbr. over 400 articles to prof. publs.; research on biophys., biochem. and behavioral study of brain, enzymology, neuroses and psychoses, psychoanalytical processes, psychophysiol. studies of mind, brain, memory, sleep and dreaming, artificial intelligence. Address: PO Box 4866 Stanford University Stanford CA 94305

TORGERSON, DOROTHY GERALDINE, radio sta. exec.; b. St. Paul, Feb. 2, 1922; d. Erick Wilhelm and Olga Catherine (Carlson) Anderson; student Minn. Sch. Bus., 1940; m. Stanleigh O. Torgerson, Apr. 19, 1947; children—Larry D., Barbara Ellen. Service rep. N.W. Bell Telephone, Mpls., 1940-47, Mason City, Iowa, 1947-49; sec.-treas., partner WQIC Radio, Meridian, Miss., 1968—; sec.-treas., dir. Torgerson Broadcasting Co., Meridian, 1968—; dir. T & T Promotions, Inc., Meridian, Hot Air Balloonist Corp., Active Lauderdale County Heart Fund Assn., Meridian Mus. Art. Republican. Lutheran. Clubs: Northwood Country, Meridian Little Theatre and Guild (dir.). Home: 2422 26th St Meridian MS 39301 Office: WQIC Radio PO Box 5353 Meridian MS 39301

TORME, MARGARET ANNE, public relations agy. exec.; b. Indpls., Apr. 5, 1943; d. Ira G. and Margaret Joy (Wright) Barker; Coll. San Mateo, 1960-66; children—Karen Anne, Leah Vanessa. With Hoefer, Dieterich & Brown, San Francisco, 1964-73; co-founder, v.p., creative dir. Lowry & Partners, San Francisco, 1975—. Office: Lowry & Partners 921 Front St San Francisco CA 94111

TORRE, ELIZABETH LASSITER, social worker, educator; b. Winston-Salem, N.C., June 17, 1931; d. Vernon Clark and Mary (Pfohl) Lassiter; student Wellesley (Mass.) Coll., 1948-49; B.A., Duke U., 1952; M.R.E., Union Theol. Sem., 1957; M.S.W., Tulane U., 1966, Ph.D., 1972; m. Mottram Peter Torre, Apr. 13, 1957. Field dir. undergrad. admissions Duke U., Durham, N.C., 1952-53; head tchr. primary dept. Riverside Ch., N.Y.C., 1957-60; instr. Sch. Social Work, Tulane U., New Orleans, 1966-72, asso. prof., 1972—; non-govtl. orgn. rep. UNICEF, World Fedn. Mental Health, 1957-61; cons. to v.p. community affairs WETA, Washington, 1979; cons. Office Spl. Symposia and Seminars, Smithsonian Instn., Washington, 1979—. Treas., N.Y. Jr. League, 1961-62, v.p., 1962-63; bd. dirs. Community Vol. Services, New Orleans, 1965-68; mem. profl. adv. com. Project Pre-Kindergarten, Orleans Parish Sch. Bd., New Orleans, 1967-69; mem. adv. bd. DePaul Community Mental Health Center, New Orleans, 1971-72; mem. citizens adv. com. Orleans Parish Juvenile Ct., New Orleans, 1970-73; mem. Council on Social Work Edn. Task Force on Prevention, 1981—. NIMH grantee; Summer Inst. grantee Nat. Endowment Humanities, 1982. Mem. Council Social Work Edn., Nat. Assn. Social Workers, Am. Orthopsychiat. Assn., Nat. Women's Health Network, AAUP, World Future Soc., Phi Beta Kappa. Office: Sch Social Work Tulane U New Orleans LA 70118

TORRES, FELICITA RODRIGUEZ, univ. adminstr.; b. Bronx, N.Y., Sept. 3, 1950; d. Agapito and Ana Silva (Montanez) Rodriguez; B.A. in Urban Studies, SUNY, Old Westbury, 1972; M.S. in Counseling and Student Personnel Services, SUNY, Albany, 1973; m. Julio Torres, Aug. 21, 1976; 1 son, Julio Louie. Mem. adminstrv. staff Hofstra U., Hempstead, N.Y., 1973—, affirmative action officer, 1979-81, dir. Upward Bound program, 1981—; cons. in field. Comptroller, bd. dirs. Hope Community, Inc., N.Y.C., 1974-75. Recipient various service and appreciation awards. Mem. Am. Personnel and Guidance Assn., Assn. Equalty and Excellence in Edn. (chpt. pres. 1982-83), Nat. Assn. Women Deans, Adminstrs. and Counselors, N.Y. State Fin. Aid Adminstrs. Assn. Address: Hofstra U 144 Gallon Wing Hempstead NY 11550

TORRES-MATRULLO, CHRISTINE M., educator, clin. psychologist; b. N.Y.C., Dec. 5, 1948; d. Gilberto and Ondina (Estevez) Torres; B.A., N.Y. U., 1970; Ph.D. (Pub. Health fellow 1970-74), Rutgers U., 1974; m. John Matrullo, Aug. 12, 1972; 1 son, Justin Albert. Cons. psychology Mt. Carmel Guild Comprehensive Community Mental Health Center, Newark, 1970-71; cons. urban univ. program Rutgers U., Newark, 1970-71; cons. psychology Middlesex County Ednl. Opportunities Corp., Newark, 1971-72; mem. faculty Hahnemann Med. Coll. and Hosp., Phila., 1974—, asso. prof. psychology, 1978—, clin. psychologist, 1974—. Bd. dirs. Aspira of Pa.; mem. Coalition of Spanish-Speaking Mental Health Orgns.; cons. to various orgns. Mem. Am. Psychol. Assn., Am. Orthopsychiat. Assn. Contbr. various articles to publs. Home: 1920 Rodman St Philadelphia PA 19146 Office: Hahnemann Med Coll/Coll of Allied Health Professions 201 N 15th St Philadelphia PA 19102

TORRIE, CAROLYN COOPER (MRS. DOUGLAS EDWARDS TORRIE), social worker; b. Laurens, S.C., Aug. 29, 1918; d. Paul Watson and Addie Lucile (Alverson) Cooper; B.A., U. S.C., 1938; postgrad. in child welfare U. Chgo., 1942; M.S.W., Washington U., 1949; m. Douglas Edwards Torrie, Sept. 3, 1949; children—Jane, Susan. Psychiat. social worker Menninger Found., Topeka, 1949-51; family counselor Family Guidance Center, Dallas, 1962-67; social worker Callier Hearing and Speech Center, Dallas, 1968-71; cons. Social Services and Planning S. Central Regional Center, Services to Deaf-Blind Children and their Families, Dallas, 1971-81. Fellow Am. Orthopsychiat. Assn.; mem. Acad. Cert. Social Workers, Nat. Assn. Social Workers, LWV. Unitarian (dir. religious edn. program). Contbr. articles to profl. jours. Home: 2929 Gladiolus Ln Dallas TX 75233 Office: 2930 Turtle Creek Plaza Suite 207 Dallas TX 75219

TORRIELLI, SANDRA ANNE, psychiat. social worker; b. N.Y.C., Apr. 11, 1943; d. Andrew Joseph and Rita Julia (Elacqua) T.; A.B., Barnard Coll., 1965; M.S.W., Boston U., 1967. Caseworker-therapist Ill. Humane Soc., Chgo., 1967-69, Mt. Sinai Hosp., Chgo., 1969-72; psychiat. social worker, team leader Ravenswood Hosp., Chgo., 1972—; field supr. Jane Addams Sch. Social Work, U. Ill., 1973—. Bd. dirs. Alvernia High Sch., Chgo., 1973-74, 77-78, 78-79, sec., 1974-75, v.p., 1975-77. Mem. Acad. Cert. Social Workers, Nat. Assn. Social Workers (mental health council). Clubs: Barnard, Boston U. (program dir.). Home: 655 W Irving Park Chicago IL 60613 Office: 4550 N Winchester Chicago IL 60640

TORRINGTON, MARY CHRISTINE, internat. training cons.; b. Denver, July 20, 1949; d. Warren Rene and Inez Marie (Alexander) T.; B.S. in Zoology, Duke U., Durham, N.C., 1971; M.A., U.S. Internat. U., San Diego, 1973, Ph.D. in Clin. Psychology, 1976; Psychology postdoctoral fellow Devereux Found., Santa Barbara, 1976-77. Vocat. counselor Naval Drug Rehab. Center, Miramar Naval Air Sta., San Diego, 1974; trainee Los Angeles Suicide Prevention Center, 1974; psychologist In Between Social Service Agy., San Diego, 1975; intern Kennedy Child Study Center, Santa Monica, 1975-76; independent travel to 14 Latin Am. countries researching local customs, cultures, and languages, 1978; psychological con. Alysan Center, Santa Clara, Calif., 1979; counselor, cons. employee assistance program Wells Fargo Bank, San Francisco, 1980; participant and intern, The Johnson Inst. Mpls., 1980; Internat. Training Cons., Employee Asst. Program, Standard Oil of Calif., San Francisco, 1980-81; pres., M.C. Torrington & Assos., San Francisco, 1981—. Mem. Am. Psychol. Assn., Calif. Psychol. Assn., San Francisco Bay Area Psychol. Assn., Soc. for Intercultural Edn. Training, and Research World Trade Assn., Internat. Trade Council, Calif. Council for Internat. Trade, Sell Overseas Am., U.S.-Arab C. of C., The Japan Soc. (Internat. Hospitality Center. Club: Commonwealth.) Address: 211 Sutter St Suite 318 San Francisco CA 94108

TOSCHI, PAULINE LOWENTHAL FOSTER, psychologist, educator; b. San Francisco, Apr. 19, 1915; d. Nathan and Lillie (Friedman) Lowenthal; A.B. (Nat. Jewish Found. scholar), U. Calif., Berkeley, 1936, Gen. Secondary Tchrs. credential, 1937; M.A. in Counseling Psychology, 1964, Sch. Psychologist credential, 1965; postgrad. U. Calif., Mills Coll., U. Minn., San Francisco State U., U. of Pacific, 1937-62; m. Louis Toschi, Dec. 23, 1950; foster children—Louise Hopper Fjelstrom, Lynn Forrester. Recreational leader, Albany, Berkeley, Richmond and Oakland, Calif., 1934-65; pioneer dir. recreation program U. Calif. Lair of Golden Bear, 1947-50; dir. ARC Program, London, France and Germany, during World War II; dance specialist in high sch. and coll., 1938-62; athletic and swim dir., 1938-41, 47-48; high sch. and coll. tchr. gen. edn., 1937-62; coach interscholastic football and basketball Corning High Sch., 1942-43; sch. psychometrist and psychologist, Richmond and Oakland, 1963-65; asst. dean student activities, tchr., counselor Coll. of Marin, Kentfield, Calif., 1965—, creator career counseling courses, 1970—, also testing specialist vol. counselor, Womens Center; counselor, lectr. Dominican Coll., 1977-78; mem. Marin County Industry and Edn. Council, 1973-75. Mem. NEA, Calif. Tchrs. Assn., Nat., Calif. assns. sch. psychologists psychometrists, Calif. Personnel Guidance Assn., Calif. Sch. Counselors Assn., U. Calif. Alumni Assn. (life), Nu Sigma Psi, Pi Lambda Theta. Clubs: Mt. Tam Tennis; Richmond Country; Tiburon Peninsula Tennis. Author: Dance Manual for Secondary Teachers in San Francisco, 1955; (with Louis Toschi and Tom Anton) A Practical Approach to Intramural Sports, 1964. Home: 3 Eagle Rock Rd Mill Valley CA 94941 Office: Coll of Marin Kentfield CA 94904

TOSH, JUANITA PRILLAMAN, tire co. exec.; b. Axton, Va., Jan. 13, 1930; d. Stuart Owen and Ann Halvorsen (Jamison) Prillaman; student public schs. Bassett, Va.; m. James Cleavon Tosh, June 5, 1961; children—Rebecca Ann Craze, Cheryl Sue Tuggle, Mark Cleavon. Owner, Russ Auto Service Co., Norfolk, Va., 1954-59; v.p. Russ & Prillaman Auto Service Inc., Collinsville, Va., 1959-68; co-owner John Allen Estates, Collinsville, 1975—; owner Tosh Tire Town, Collinsville, 1969—; sec.-treas. Cash Oil Sales Inc., Collinsville, Va., 1982—. Mem. Retail Mchts. Assn., Va. Tire Dealers and Retreaders Assn., Nat. Tire Dealers and Retreaders Assn. Baptist. Home: 208 Ferndale Dr Collinsville VA 24078

TOTH, DELPHI MELINDA, psychologist, anatomist; b. Cleve., Aug. 22, 1947; d. Bertalan William and Ida (Szachury) T.; B.A. cum laude, Case Western Res. U., 1969; M.A., U. Va., 1972, Ph.D., 1973. Research fellow Harvard Med. Sch., Boston, 1973-75; asst. prof. anatomy U. N.Mex. Sch. Medicine, Albuquerque, 1975-78; asst. prof. anat. scis., psychiatry and behavioral scis. U. Okla. Coll. Medicine, Oklahoma City, 1978—. Mem. Animal Research Council, Oklahoma City Zoo, 1980—. USPHS Research fellow, 1973-75; NIH research grantee, 1973-75, 77-80, 81-82; Nat. Acad. Scis. Travel grantee, 1980. Mem. AAUP, AAAS, Soc. Neurosci., Soc. Cryobiology, Internat. Hibernation Soc., Internat. Union Physiol. Scis., Sigma Xi. Presbyterian. Contbr. articles to profl. jours. Office: Dept Anatom Sci U Okla Health Sci Center Oklahoma City OK 73190

TOTH, GISELLE MARTHA, research scientist; b. Komarom, Hungary, Feb. 6, 1941; came to U.S., June 2, 1970, naturalized, 1979; d. Joseph Istvan and Gizella Rose (Erdey) T.; M.Sc., U. Debrecen, Hungary, 1964, Ph.D. magna cum laude, 1970. Project engr., Hungary, 1964-70; research scientist New Brunswick Sci. Co., Edison, N.J., 1971-75; dir. research and devel. Pharmachem Co., Bethlehem, Pa., 1976-78; mgmt. cons. Hill Inst. Tech., San Francisco, 1978-80, also dir.; research asso. Stauffer Chem. Co., Richmond, Calif., 1980—. Mem. Am. Acad. Polit. and Social Sci., Am. Chem. Soc., Am. Soc. Microbiology, Am. Inst. Chem. Engrs., Tissue Culture Assn., U.S. Yacht Racing Union. Club: Corinthian Yacht. Contbr. articles to profl. jours. Patentee in field. Home: 45 Harbor Oak #32 Tiburon CA 94920 Office: 1200 S 47th St Richmond CA 94804

TOTH, JUDITH COGGESHALL, state legislator; b. Rochelle, Ill., Oct. 21, 1937; d. Robert James and Elita Etzbach Coggeshall; student Mexico City Coll., 1956-57; B.A., Northwestern U., Evanston, Ill., 1959; postgrad. Georgetown U., Washington, 1959-62, Montgomery Coll., 1980-81, U. Md., College Park, 1981—; children—Christina Maria, Adriana Maria. Cons., pres. Commn. on Causes and Prevention Violence, 1969; assoc. Ideas, Inc., Washington, 1970-71; v.p. Politicon Service, Inc., Washington, 1971-74; mem. Md. Gen. Assembly, 1974—, mem. environ. matters com., 1975—, public safety policy com., 1980—; mem. Nat. Conf. State Legislators Task Force Satellite Remote Sensing, 1976—; legis. rep. Gov.'s Commn. to Revise Annotated Code, 1976—; mem. Task Force to Rev. Hosp. Regulation, 1980—. Founding mem. Alliance Democratic Reform, Montgomery County, 1968—; vice-chmn. New Democratic Coalition Md., 1969-70; Democratic precinct chmn. Cabin John-Bannockburn Estates, 1969-74; pres. Montgomery County Civic Fedn., 1973-74; mem. Commn. on Gasohol, 1979-80; mem. Humane Practice Commn., 1979—; mem. Commn. Hispanic Affairs, 1979-82; mem. Council Govts., Met. Washington, 1979-81; bd. dirs. Nat. Consumer Orgn. Hearing Impaired, 1979-80; mem. Washington Deaf Alliance, 1979—; bd. dirs. Md. Assn. Deaf, 1979—. Mem. Hispanic Fedn. Md., Md. State Podiatry Assn., Md. Dental Hygienists Assn., Montgomery County Farm Bur., VFW. Recipient Washington Star Cup, 1974. Democrat. Roman Catholic. Office: Lowe House Office Bldg Annapolis MD 21401

TOTH, MARIAN DAVIES, ednl. adminstr.; b. Gt. Falls, Mont.; d. John and Zetta Allen (Jones) Davies; B.A. magna cum laude, Eastern Coll., 1967; M.A., U. Pa., 1970, Ed.D., 1977; m. Alfred L. Toth, Apr. 21, 1947; children—Jerry Geza, Christopher Keats, Geoffrey Alfred, Richard Kingsley. Tchr., Internat. Sch., Bangkok, Thailand, 1961-64; English tchr. Conestoga High Sch., Berwyn, Pa., 1967-72, vice prin., 1973-77; prin. Juniata Valley High Sch., Alexandria, Pa., 1978; dir. lang. arts East Brunswick (N.J.) Sch. Dist., 1978-82; supr. lang. arts and reading Moorestown (N.J.) Sch. Dist., 1982—; mem. Gov.'s Task Force on Career Edn.; speaker various groups on writing, speaking and composing including U. Pa., 1981, U. Wis., 1981, Assn. Supervision and Curriculum Devel., 1982, Wright State U., 1982; speaker Villanova U., 1976, 78, Rutgers U., 1980, Fordham U., 1980. Bd. alumni trustees Eastern Coll., 1978-80. Recipient Superior Teaching award, Tredyffrin/Easttown Sch. Dist., 1970, 73, Creative Writing award Atlantic Monthly, 1971, Disting. Pub. award, Theta Sigma Phi, 1973; named Outstanding Author, Kutztown State Coll., Pa. Library Assn., 1975. Mem. Nat. Pen Women, Nat. Council Tchrs. English, Nat. Assn. Supervision and Curriculum Devel., Phi Delta Kappa, Phi Lambda Theta. Episcopalian. Author: Tales from Thailand, 1971; Seven Steps to Career Exploration, 1975; contbr. articles to profl. jours. Home: 310 Chamounix Rd Saint Davids PA 19087

TOTMAN, JUDITH JENKINS, inst. exec.; b. Evanston, Ill., Nov. 25, 1932; d. Wilmer Atkinson and Gertrude (Elmore) Jenkins; A.B., Colby Coll., 1954; Ed.M., Harvard U., 1976, Ed.D., 1980; m. Frank Howard Totman, Jr., Nov. 14, 1953; children—Tasha, Frank Howard III, Thomas Atkinson. Tchr., Princess Anne County, Va., 1955-56, tutor handicapped children, 1956-57; adminstr. Follen Community Ch., Lexington, Mass., 1958-72; asst. to asso. dir. Bentley Coll. Center for Continuing Edn., Waltham, Mass., 1972-73, program coordinator, 1973-74, asst. dir., 1974-76, asso. dir., 1976-80, mgr. adult info. and adv. center, summer 1980, dir. curriculum devel. and instrn., asst. prof. continuing edn., 1980-82; cons., Boston, 1981-82; dir. Inst. Banking, Boston, 1982—; mgmt. cons., Boston, 1981-82. Mem., officer Lexington legis. body, 1966—; pres. PTA, 1961-69; active Girl Scouts U.S.A., 1976-80, bd. dirs., 1976-78; mem. Yr. Round Sch. task force, 1974-75. Mem. Assn. for Continuing Higher Edn., Mass. Assn. Tng. & Devel., Am. Assn. of Higher Edn., Adult Edn. Assn. U.S.A., LWV. Contbr. articles to profl. jours. Home: 46 Moreland Ave Lexington MA 02173 Office: 50 Charles River Plaza Boston MA 02114

TOUEY, COLLETTE B., retail clothing store exec.; b. Lancaster, Pa.; d. Joseph B. and Elsie G. (Mueller) T.; B.S. in Bus. Adminstrn., Drexel U., Phila., 1952; postgrad. Wharton Sch., U. Pa.; m. B.H. Kean. Asst. to pres. Fowler, Dick & Walker, Wilkes-Barre, Pa., 1953-56; buyer Lord & Taylor, N.Y.C., 1956-63; sr. div. mdse. mgr. Bergdorf Goodman, 1963-75; v.p., div. mdse. mgr. Wallachs, N.Y.C., 1976-79; v.p., gen. mdse. mgr. women's market Hart, Schaffner & Marx, N.Y.C., 1979—; lectr. Fashion Inst., Lab. Inst. Mdsg., LaGuardia Coll. Trustee Wyoming Sem., Kingston, Pa., 1973-76. Recipient citation for internat. mdsg. Republic of Ireland, 1969, 73. Mem. Internat. Fashion Group (gov. 1968-69), Fashion's Inner Circle, Trends, Inc. Clubs: Deepdale Golf, Eastpointe Country. Home: 435 E 70th St New York NY 10021 Office: 1430 Broadway New York NY 10018

TOUHEY, DOROTHY EVELYN, engring. search cons.; b. Parker's Prairie, Minn., July 1, 1910; d. William and Lillian (Bausman) Black; student Iowa State Coll., 1928-29; B.S., U. Minn., 1938; m. Durant A. Labrie, Nov. 3, 1934 (div. 1943); children—Wilhemine LaBrie Saucier, Mary LaBrie Peterson, Yvonne LaBrie Turner, Valeria LaBrie; m. 2d, Leo F. Touhey, Aug. 9, 1947 (dec. 1972); children—Virginia Touhey, Carol Touhey Burns, Phillip, Maureen Touhey Anderson; m. 3d, Peter S. Gustafson, Aug. 2, 1975 (dec. Nov. 1981). Social worker State of Minn., 1933-40; recruiter Mpls. and St. Paul U.S. Employment Service, 1941-48; personnel dir. St. Barnabas Hosp., Mpls., 1952-53; mgr. Central Personnel and Guardian Personnel, Mpls., 1953-60; engring. cons. Der-Kel Employment Service, Mpls., 1960-75, Dunhill Personnel, San Diego, 1975-77, Westbrooke Search, Inc., San Diego, 1977-82, Profl. Resources, Inc., St. Louis Park, Minn., 1982—; cons. N. Hennepin County Community Coll., State of Minn. Dept. Vocat. Edn., U. Minn. Sch. Bus. and Grad. Sch. Continuing Edn.. Recipient Internat. Merit award and key, Adminstrv. Mgmt. Soc., 1973; WCCO Radio, NW Food Dealers and NW Orient Airlines Good Neighbor award, 1973; first recipient Minn. and Nat. Employment Assn. Counselor of the Yr. award, 1973. Mem. Adminstrv. Mgmt. Soc. Internat. (chpt. dir. 1967-75), Calif. Employment Assn. (state dir. 1975-77), Acad. Cert. Personnel Cons., Am. Soc. Execs. and Profl. Women, Nat. Assn. Female Execs., Nat. Assn. Personnel Cons., U. Minn. Alumni Assn. Republican. Roman Catholic. Clubs: Univ. Minn. Alumni, Pilots Internat. Office: 8085 Wayzata Blvd Suite 206 Saint Louis Park MN 54426

TOULIOS, VASSILIKI ECONOMIDOU, psychiatrist; b. Florina, Greece, Mar. 18, 1937; came to U.S., 1962, naturalized, 1965; d. Dionysios and Eleni (Economidou) Economides; M.D., U. Salonica (Greece), 1961; m. Peter Toulios, Aug. 19, 1962; children—Tom, Katerina, Elena. Intern, West Suburban Hosp., Oak Park, Ill., 1964-65; resident in psychiatry Ill. State Psychiat. Inst., Chgo., 1972-75; practice medicine specializing in psychiatry, Elmhurst, Ill., 1975—; mem. staffs Elmhurst Hosp., Loretto Hosp., St. Anne's Hosp., Chgo., Westlake Community Hosp., Melrose Park, Ill.; chmn., med. dir. psychiat. dept. St. Anne's Hosp., Chgo., 1980—. Mem. Am. Psychiat. Assn., Ill. Psychiat. Assn., Central Neuropsychiat. Soc. Home: 14 Brighton Ln Oak Brook IL 60521 Office: 533 W North Ave Elmhurst IL 60126

TOURETZ, LILLIAN CAROLE CONRAD, psychotherapist; b. N.Y.C., Oct. 17, 1923; d. Philip and Rose Helen Stetsky; B.A., Hunter

Coll., 1944; M.S.W., N.Y.U., 1968; m. Martin Conrad, June 3, 1944; children—David, Donna; m. 2d, Arthur Touretz, May 28, 1977. Asst. mgr. N.Y.C. Housing Authority, 1946-49; pres. Profl. Workers AFL-CIO, 1947-49; lectr., cons. in field, 1952-78; psychotherapist Pelham (N.Y.) Family Service, 1968-77; pvt. practice psychotherapy, Hartsdale, N.Y., 1977—; field instr. Adelphi U., 1972-77. Chmn. United Jewish Appeal; v.p. regional bd. B'nai B'rith; chpt. pres. B'nai B'rith, 1981-82, v.p. Council of Pres. Mem. Nat. Assn. Social Workers, O.R.T., Hunter Coll., N.Y.U. alumni assns. Democrat. Address: 55 Edgewood RD Hartsdale NY 10530

TOURTELOTTE, BARBARA HADEN, sch. adminstr.; b. Atlanta, June 20, 1929; d. William Edward and Alma Clyde (Battle) Haden; student Los Angeles Valley Coll., 1958-61, U. N.C., 1963-64; B.A., U. South Fla., Tampa, 1966, M.A., 1973, postgrad.; children—Terry Thomas, Georgia, Nicole. Writer, TV and stage actress fed. project assisting welfare mothers, 1966-67; tchr. speed reading, TESL, tchr. high sch. English, speech and theater, 1967-73; social dir. Appalachian Hall, Asheville, N.C., 1964-65; supr. community instrnl. services and community schs. Pinellas County Bd. Edn., St. Petersburg, Fla., 1973—; adv. bd. congregate dining centers, St. Petersburg Office Aging; dir. Showcase of Services; bd. dirs. Fla. West Coast Council Adult and Continuing Edn.; host TV show, 1974-78. English Speaking Union Churchill award to study Shakespeare, Stratford-on-Avon, 1972. Mem. Fla. West Coast Adult Adminstrs. (pres. 1975-77), Fla. Press Women (pres. 1977), Fla. Adminstrs. Assn., Fla. Adult Edn. Assn., Fla. Community Edn. Assn., Nat. Press Women, Suprs. Assn. Post-Secondary Adminstrs., Secondary Adminstrs. Assn., Phi Delta Kappa. Clubs: Bath. Treasure Island Tennis and Yacht, YWCA, Isla del Sol Country. Author poetry. Home: 125 94th Ave Treasure Island FL 33706 Office: 709 Mirror Lake Dr St Petersburg FL 33701

TOUSIGNANT, DOROTHY WILTAMUTH (MRS. LEONARD A. TOUSIGNANT), mgmt. exec.; b. East Moline, Ill., Jan. 7, 1920; d. Edward W. and Eleonora (Struss) Wiltamuth; B.S., U. Ill., 1941; M.E., State Tchrs. Coll., Fitchburg, Mass., 1951; postgrad. Am. U., 1959-61; m. Leonard A. Tousignant, June 11, 1949; 1 dau., Carmen Louise. Chief dietitian U.S. Army Hosps., CBI, 1942-45; served to capt.; food service tng. supr. Air Transport Command Hdqrs., Washington, 1946-47; cons. Office Surgeon Gen., Washington, 1948, Inflight Feeding Manual Air Quartermaster, 1948, Office Quartermaster Gen.; ednl. promotion, sales work Basic Vegetable Products, Inc., San Francisco, 1947-49; dietitian resident halls State Tchrs. Coll., Fitchburg, Mass., 1950; ednl. promotion work Dehydrated Food Industries, San Francisco, also Washington, 1950-53; instr. home econs. U. Md., College Park, 1954; nutritional cons., Washington, 1955; asst. prof. nutrition Cath. U. Am., Washington 1954-55; dist. mgr. United Food Mgmt. Services, Inc., Washington, 1955-64, v.p. Hosp. Dietetics, Inc. div. Interstate United Corp., Washington, 1964-67; pres. D.W. Tousignant & Assos., Inc., Washington, 1967—. Served with AUS, 1942-45. Decorated Bronze Star. Mem. Am. Home Econs. Assn. (pres. Washington 1958), Am. Dietetics Assn., Nat. Restaurant Assn., English-speaking Union. Contbr. articles to profl. jours. Research in dehydrated foods. Address: 3919 Watson Pl Washington DC 20016 also Cordova Farm Middleburg VA 22117

TOVSEN, JOAN ESTHER, relocation and welcome service exec.; b. Chgo., Dec. 3, 1950; d. Oliver Kermit and Josephine Esther (Daleo) T.; student Anchorage Community Coll., U. Alaska, 1969-72, night classes, 1973-78; m. Ralph Jones, May 1976 (div. 1977). Procurement and legal clk. Bur. Land Mgmt., Anchorage, 1973-78; pres. Anchorage Welcome Service, 1978—, pres., relocation cons. subs. Anchorage Relocation Center, 1980—, editor Anchorage Blue Book: A Guide to Public Services and Resources and The Anchorage Economic Compass: A Socio Economic Profile, 1980—; relocation cons.; guest speaker community groups. Municipality of Anchorage grantee, 1981-82. Mem. City Hostess Internat. Assn. (pres. 1982-83), Advt. Fedn. Alaska (sec. 1982, dir.), Anchorage C. of C. (co-chmn. hospitality com.), Anchorage Conv. and Visitors Bur. Mem. Worldwide Ch. of God. Home: PO Box 4 1975 Anchorage AK 99509 Office: 524 W 4th Ave Old City Hall Anchorage AK 99501

TOWNE, CLAUDIA CIACCO, data processor; b. N.Y.C., Apr. 6, 1945; d. Francesco and Angelina (Gaultieri) Ciacco; B.A., Hunter Coll., N.Y.C., 1966; m. Gene Leonard Towne, Dec. 23, 1967. Graphics systems analyst Mergenthaler Linotype Co., N.Y.C., 1966-68; systems analyst Service Bur. Corp., Honolulu, 1968-71; systems and programming mgr. Automatic Data Processing, Inc., N.Y.C., 1971-79; data processing mgr. Berol USA, Danbury, 1979—; bd. dirs. Greater Danbury Area Jr. Achievement, 1980—. Mem. Data Processing Mgmt. Assn. Office: Berol USA Eagle Rd Danbury CT 06810

TOWNE, DOROTHEA ALICE, III, chiropractor; b. Easton, Ill., Feb. 1, 1910; d. Elanthan and Fairy Alice (Downey) T.; Ph.C., Cleveland Chiropractic Coll., Los Angeles, 1955, B.S., 1977; student U. Wash., 1928-30; B.A. magna cum laude, U. So. Calif., 1946. Indsl. relations dir. Standard Paper Box Corp., Los Angeles, 1943-54; dean acad. affairs Cleveland Chiropractic Coll., 1956-75, tchr., 1976-82, dir. clin. scis., 1972-78, emeritus, 1981—; lectr. in field. Recipient numerous awards including appreciation award San Francisco Vay Research Assn. Fellow Internat. Chiropractors Assn., Gamma Phi Beta, Psi Chi, Sigma Chi Psi. Contbr. to poetry anthologies. Address: 588 N Larchmont Blvd Los Angeles CA 90004 *

TOWNER, NAOMI WHITING, fiber artist, educator; b. Providence, May 8, 1940; d. Basil J. and Nellie (Woolhouse) Whiting; B.F.A. in Textile Design, R.I. Sch. of Design, 1962; postgrad. (Textron fellow), Foreningen Handarbetets Vanner, Stockholm, 1962-63; M.F.A. in Textile Design, Rochester Inst. Tech., 1965. Teaching grad. asst. Sch. for Am. Craftsmen, Rochester (N.Y.) Inst. Tech., 1963-65, instr. textile design, summer, 1964; instr. Ill. State U., Normal, 1965-68, asst. prof., 1968-72, asso. prof., 1972-76, prof. art, 1976—; lectr. to various art guilds and schs., 1967—; dir. workshops on weaving and textile design, 1964—; exhibited one person shows of art fabrics including Fox Valley Art League, St. Charles, Ill., 1968, Fine Arts Center Clinton (Ill.), 1971, Old Town Gallery, St. Charles, Mo., 1973, Lincoln Coll., Lincoln, Ill., 1974, Craft Alliance Gallery, St. Louis, 1974, Unitarian Ch., Bloomington, Ill., 1975, The Art-In, Riverton, Wyo., 1975; numerous group shows including: Mus. Contemporary Crafts Fabrics Internat. travelling exhibit, 1961-62, Security Trust Co., Rochester, N.Y., 1965, Ill. State U., Normal, 1965-68, 71, 73-81, Old Town Art Center, Chgo., 1967, Brooks Meml. Art Gallery, Memphis, 1967, Lakeview Center for Arts, Peoria, Ill., 1967-68, Ill. State Mus., 1968, Wis. State U., Oshkosh, 1969, Art Inst. Chgo., 1971, No. Ill. U., DeKalb, 1971, U. Mass. Art Gallery, Amherst, 1972, Evansville (Ind.) Mus. Arts and Scis., 1973, Eureka Coll. (Ill.), 1973, Mills Coll., Oakland, Calif., 1974, Columbus (Ga.) Mus. Arts and Crafts, 1974, Wright Art Center, Beloit (Wis.) Coll., 1975, Lowe Art Mus., U. Miami (Fla.) Goldstein Gallery, 1976, U. Minn., St. Paul, 1977, Paul Sargent Gallery, Eastern Ill. U., Charlestown, 1977, Boise (Idaho) State U., 1978, Cin. Art Mus., 1978, Kearney (Nebr.) State Coll. Art Gallery, 1979, others; represented in permanent collections Ill. State Mus., Springfield, Washington U., St. Louis, Eureka (Ill.) Coll., pvt. collections. Recipient numerous awards including Silver Shuttle award U. Rochester, 1964, Owens-Corning Fiberglas competition, 1964, award of excellence Ill. Craftsmen's Council Invitational, 1967, Merit award Springfield Art Assn., 1976; grantee Handweavers Guild Am. and Ill. Arts Council, 1975-78. Mem. Am. Crafts Council, Midwest Weavers Conf., AAUP, Handweavers Guild Am. (rep. 1973-77, bd. dirs. 1978-80), ACLU, Surface Design Assn. Contbr. articles on textile design and weaving to profl. publs.; editor Fiber News, 1975—. Home: 610 E Taylor St Bloomington IL 61701 Office: Art Dept Illinois State Univ Normal IL 61761

TOWNES, MARY MCLEAN, ednl. adminstr.; b. Southern Pines, N.C., July 12, 1928; d. Mitchell and Nora Jane (McPhatter) McLean; B.S., N.C. Central U., 1949; M.S. in Public Health, 1950; M.S., U. Mich., 1953, Ph.D., 1962; m. Ross Emile, Aug. 28, 1954; children—Emilie Maureen, Tricia Lynn. Vis. lectr. to prof. biology N.C. Central U., Durham, 1950—, grad. dean; cons. NIH, NSF, Nat. Research Council. Pres. Durham City PTA Council, 1974-76. Mem. Soc. Gen. Physiologists, Am. Soc. Zoologists, N.Y. Acad. Scis., N.C. Acad. Sci., Sigma Xi, Delta Sigma Theta. Democrat. Methodist. Home: 101 W Alton St Durham NC 27707 Office: NC Central U Durham NC 27707

TOWNLEY, CATHERINE JANET, savs. and loan assn. exec.; b. Atlanta, Apr. 7, 1950; d. William Milton and Audrey (Warnock) T.; student Dekalb Coll., Inst. Fin. Edn.; grad. Sch. Exec. Devel., U. Conn., 1980. Asst. office mgr. First Fed. Savs. & Loan Assn. of Atlanta, 1968-70; sec., teller Decatur (Ga.) Fed. Savs. & Loan Assn., 1970-71, asst. br. mgr., Stone Mountain, 1972-73, asst. v.p., br. mgr., 1973-78, dist. v.p. So. dist. brs., 1978—. Vol., ARC, Aidmore Childrens Hosp., Jr. Achievement, DeKalb County Heart Fund, United Way, Am. Cancer Soc., De Kalb C. of C.; membership chmn. DeKalb County Boy Scouts Am. Mem. Stone Mountain Indsl. Park Assn., DeKalb C. of C., DeKalb Gwinnett Young Realtors, Am. Savs. and Loan Inst. Office: 2942 N Druid Hills Rd NE Atlanta GA 30329

TOWNS, ROSE MARY, librarian; b. Houston, Jan. 7, 1934; d. Arthur and Anna Jewel (Dean) Prince; B.A., San Francisco State Coll., 1955; M.L.S., U. Calif., Berkeley, 1956; m. George Elbert Towns, July 26, 1964; 1 son, Gordon Christopher. With Oakland (Calif.) Pub. Library, 1956-66; asst. city librarian Richmond (Calif.) Public Library, 1966-69, acting city librarian, 1969-70; instr., librarian Contra Costa Community Coll., San Pablo, Calif., 1971-72; public services librarian North Peralta Community Coll., Oakland, Calif., 1972-74; reference coordinator North Bay Cooperative Library, Vallejo, Calif., 1975-79, system programs coordinator, 1979—. Campaign organizer No. Calif. McGovern Campaign, 1972; campaign coordinator Ramsey for Berkeley City Council, 1973; del. Calif. Govs. Conf. on Libraries and Info. Services, 1979. Mem. ALA, ALA Black Caucus, Calif. Library Assn., Calif. Librarians Black Caucus (sec. 1972-73), Calif. Soc. Librarians (sec. 1979), Alpha Kappa Alpha. Democrat. Methodist. Office: 505 Santa Clara St Vallejo CA 94590

TOWNSEND, ALAIR ANE, city ofcl.; b. Rochester, N.Y., Feb. 15, 1942; d. Harold Eugene and Dorothy Sharpe (Daniels) T.; B.S., Elmira Coll., 1962; M.S., U. Wis., 1964; postgrad. Columbia U., 1970-71; m. Robert Harris, Dec. 31, 1970. Asso. dir. budget priorities Com. on Budget, U.S. Ho. of Reps., Washington, 1975-79; dep. asst. sec. for budget HEW, Washington, 1979-80, asst. sec. for mgmt. and budget, 1980-81; dir. N.Y.C. Office Mgmt. and Budget, 1981—. Mem. Am. Public Welfare Assn., Am. Soc. Public Adminstrn., Mcpl. Fin. Officers Assn.

TOWNSEND, DEANNA DEE, elec. engr.; b. Van Nuys, Calif., Oct. 21, 1937; d. Coburn Bud Fisher and Marjorie Vera Lavelle; B.S. in Physics, Calif. Poly U., Pomona, 1968; M.A. History, LaVerne U., 1971; E.E., U. Calif., Davis, 1978; m. Gerald Edward Townsend, Feb. 16, 1957; children—William Casey, Kathleen Ann. Tchr., San Juan (Calif.) Unified Sch. Dist., 1970-78; energy analyst Calif. Energy Commn., Sacramento, 1977-78; asso. system design engr. Gen. Electric Co., Sunnyvale, Calif., 1978-79; mfg. engr., San Jose, Calif., 1979-81, sr. design engr., Sunnyvale, 1981—. Bd. dirs. Tierra Del Oro council Girl Scouts U.S.A.; vol. ARC; mem. sci. adv. com. Mills Coll., women in engring. adv. com. U. Calif., Davis. NSF grantee, 1977-78. Mem. Soc. Women Engrs., IEEE. Republican. Office: 310 DeGuigne Dr M/C S-33 Sunnyvale CA 94086

TOWNSEND, JANE KALTENBACH, zoologist, educator; b. Chgo., Dec. 21, 1922; B.S., Beloit Coll., 1944; M.A., U. Wis., 1946; Ph.D., U. Iowa, 1950; m. 1966. Asst. in zoology U. Wis., 1944-47; asst., instr. U. Iowa, 1948-50; asst., project assoc. in pathology U. Wis., 1950-53; Am. Cancer Soc. research fellow Wenner-Grens Inst., Stockholm, 1953-56; asst. prof. zoology Northwestern U., 1956-58; asst. prof. to assoc. prof. zoology Mt. Holyoke Coll., South Hadley, Mass., 1958-70, prof., 1970—, chmn. biol. scis., 1980—. Fellow AAAS (sec. sect. biol. sci. 1974-78); mem. Am. Assn. Anatomists, Am. Inst. Biol. Scis., Am. Soc. Zoologists, Sigma Xi. Office: Dept of Biology Mount Holyoke College South Hadley MA 01075 *

TOWNSEND, PAMELA GWIN, bus. educator; b. Dallas, Aug. 24, 1945; d. William Thomas and Doris (Gwin) T.; B.A. with distinction in Econs. (Univ. scholar), U. Mo., Kansas City, 1977, M.B.A. (Outstanding Acctg. Grad.), 1980; m. Rae R. Jacobs, July 5, 1975. Real estate sales assoc. KEW Realtors, Austin, Tex., 1967-70; staff mktg. asst. Lincoln Property Co., Dallas, 1970-72; dir. mktg. Commonwealth Devel. Co., Dallas, 1972-73; v.p. market analysis Fin. Corp. N.Am., Kansas City, 1973-75; asst. prof., dir. dept. acctg. Park Coll., Parkville, Mo., 1980—. Coordinator, IRS VITA Program; mem. Friends of Art, Nelson Gallery; mem. Mo. Repertory Theater Guild; Underwriter Folly Theater. C.P.A., Kans.; lic. real estate broker, Tex., Mo., Kans. Mem. Am. Inst. C.P.A.s, Kans. Soc. C.P.A.s, Mo. Soc. C.P.A.s, Am. Acctg. Assn., Nat. Assn. Accts., Alpha Delta Alpha (faculty v.p. chpt.), Beta Alpha Psi Alumnae (pres. 1982), Beta Gamma Sigma, Phi Kappa Phi, Omicron Delta Epsilon, Alpha Chi Omega, Mortar Bd. Episcopalian. Columnist, Tax Tips, Platte County Gazette, 1981. Home: 7262 Mastin Merriam KS 66203 Office: Mackay Hall Box 21 Park College Parkville MO 64152

TOWNSEND, PATRICIA ANN, educator; b. Lufkin, Tex., May 25, 1933; d. Paul Monarch and Clifford Evelyn (Carson) T.; B.S., Stephen F. Austin State U., 1953, M.A., 1956; Ph.D. (Univ. fellow), U. Wis., Madison, 1959. Tchr., Blocker Jr. High Sch., Texas City, Tex., 1954-56; research asst., teaching asst. U. Wis., 1956-59; asst. prof. speech U. No. Iowa, Cedar Falls, 1959-65; asso. prof. U. Wis., Whitewater, 1965-67, prof. speech communication, coordinator speech communication program, coordinator grad. studies in communication, 1967—. Chair bd. dirs. Whitewater ARC, 1970-74. Named Outstanding Educator, U. Wis., 1975; Danforth asso., 1978. Mem. Speech Communication Assn., Central States Speech Assn., Wis. Communication Assn., Rhetoric Soc. Am., AAUP, Wis. Acad. Scis., Arts and Lit., Nat. Assn. Parliamentarians, Wis. Assn. Parliamentarians, Whitewater Assn. Parliamentarians, Nat. Collegiate Honors Council. Club: Whitewater Area Gourmet (chair 1979-80), Emerson. Democrat. Editor Jour. Wis. Communication Assn., 1982—, Women's Caucus Newsletter of Central States Speech Assn., 1981-82, Wis. Communication Assn. Newsletter, 1981-82. Home: 417 S Prince St Whitewater WI 53190 Office: 461 Heide Hall Dept of Communication University of Wisconsin Whitewater WI 53190

TOWNSEND, PATRICIA ANN, nurse, clin. specialist; b. Providence, Dec. 1, 1943; d. William Rolfe and Ann Hutchinson (Ashley) Files; student Furman U., 1975-77; B.S. in Nursing cum laude, Clemson U., 1979; M.S. in Nursing, U. S.C., 1981, Family Nurse Practitioner, 1981; m. James Lester Townsend, Oct. 13, 1963; children—Jill, Christopher Ashley, James Lester. Staff nurse Greenville (S.C.) Gen. Hosp., 1979-81, clin. specialist, 1981—; nurse educator James D. Puckett, M.D., Greenville, 1981; cons., counselor in field. Co-chmn. March of Dimes, 1971; active PTA, Architects Aux., civic groups. Nursing tng. grantee, 1979-81. Mem. Nurses Am. Assn. Council Ob-Gyn, Am. Nurses Assn., S.C. Nurses Assn. and Spl. Interest Group, Grad. Student Nurses Assn. (sec.), Sigma Theta Tau. Republican. Presbyterian. Club: Jr. Women's (pres. 1970-72). Condr. research health behavior R.N.s in S.C. Home: Hathaway Circle Greenville SC 29609 Office: Greenville Gen Hosp Mallard St Greenville SC 29601

TOWNSEND, STORM DIANA, sculptor; b. London, England, Aug. 31, 1937; came to U.S., 1963; d. Douglas A. and Winifred L. Townsend; grad. Goldsmith's Coll. Art, London U., England, 1961, nat. diploma in design. Tchr. art and crafts various London youth clubs, 1960, London Grammar Schs., 1961; tchr. sculpture Marylebone Inst. for Adult Edn., England, 1962, Pojoaque Arts Centre, Santa Fe, 1966, Coll. of Santa Fe, 1974-75; mem. faculty U. Albuquerque, 1976, 80; tchr. pvt. studio classes in Albuquerque, 1976-82; asst. dir. Manchester Gallery, Taos, N.Mex., 1965; mould-maker Shidoni Bronze Foundry, Santa Fe, 1970; mem. faculty (part-time) design U. N.Mex., 1978-82, U. Albuquerque, 1976—; one-man shows of sculpture and drawings include: Maitland-Stokes Gallery, Santa Fe, 1966, West Gallery, Santa Fe, 1970, Artist's Co-op Gallery, Santa Fe, 1973, Discovery Gallery, Santa Fe, 1975, Gallery Marquis, Denver, 1975, Studio Gallery, Albuquerque, 1977, Gallery Eleven, Lubbock, Tex., 1977; numerous group shows, latest being; Mus. of N.Mex., Santa Fe, 1976, 5th Ann. Shidoni Outdoor Exhibition, Santa Fe, 1978, Southwest Arts and Crafts Festival, Albuquerque, 1979, Armijo Gallery of Sculpture, Albuquerque, 1980; executed bronze fountain piece, Denver, 1977; represented in permanent collections: Fine Arts Mus., Santa Fe; also pvt. collections. Jajasan Siswa Lokantara Found. grantee, 1960, Huntington Hartford Found. grantee, 1963; Wurlitzer Found. fellow, 1964. Address: PO Box 1165 Corrales NM 87048

TOWNSEND, TERRY, publisher; b. Camden, N.J., Dec. 14, 1920; d. Anthony and Rose DeMarco; B.A., Duke U., 1942; m. Paul Brorstrom Townsend, Dec. 8, 1961; 1 son, Kim. Public relations dir. North Shore Univ. Hosp., Manhasset, N.Y., 1955-68; pres. Theatre Soc. L.I., 1968-70; pres. Townsend Communications Bur., Plainview, N.Y., 1970—, L.I. Communicating Service, Plainview, 1977—; columnist, writer L.I./Bus., Plainview, 1970-75, pub., 1978—; v.p. Parr Meadows Racetrack, Yaphank, N.Y., 1977—. Asso. trustee North Shore U. Hosp., 1968—; bd. govs. Adelphi U. Friends Fin. Edn., 1978—; chmn. ann. archtl. awards competition N.Y. Inst. Tech., 1970—. Recipient Media award 110 Center Bus. and Profl. Women, 1977; named First Lady of L.I., L.I. Public Relations Assn., 1973; Enterprise award Friends of Fin. Edn., 1981; L.I. Loves Bus. Showcase Salute, 1982. Mem. Public Relations Soc. Am. (pres. L.I. chpt. 1979). Office: 303 Sunnyside Blvd Plainview NY 11803

TOWNSEND, VIRGINIA PAYNE, nurse; b. Shirleysburg, Pa., Apr. 24, 1940; d. Alonzo Roy and Gladys Rebecca (Roth) Payne; R.N., Rockingham Meml. Hosp., Harrisonburg, Va., 1961; m. John D. Driver, Aug. 18, 1961 (div.); children—Crystal Kim, Michelle Robin, Roxanne Dale, Sharlene Kae; m. 2d, George Townsend, Apr. 5, 1980; stepchildren —James, Cynthia, Cheryl, George, Gerald. Asst. head nurse Woodrow Wilson Rehab. Center, Fishersville, Va., 1970-72, head nurse, 1972-75; supr. nursing The Dist. Home, Waynesboro, Va., 1975-78, asst. dir. nursing, 1978-80; dir. nursing Allegheny Lutheran Home, Hollidaysburg, Pa., 1982—. Sunday sch. supt. Dayton (Va.) Ch. of Brethren, 1976-77; officer Port Republic (Va.) Elementary Sch., 1965-66. Mem. Am., Va. (del. 1975-76) nurses assns., Va. Govt. Employees Assn., Rockingham Meml. Hosp. Alumni Assn. Home: RD 2 Box 466 Altoona PA 16601

TOWNSEND, WENDY, orgn. exec.; b. N.Y.C., Nov. 28, 1942; d. Paul Brorstrom Townsend and Ruth Grace (Moerchen) Burgess; B.S., Boston U., 1965; m. Robert Joe Baker, Aug. 2, 1970; children—Lynn, Bob, Michelle. Communications specialist Gen. Electric Co., Lynn, Mass., 1964-67; public relations dir. Unitarian-Universalist Service Com., Boston, 1967-70; communications specialist Gen. Foods Co., Sydney, Australia, 1974-75; public relations and devel. dir. Seattle-King County council Camp Fire, 1976—, mem. nat. tng. staff, 1979-80. Mem. AAUW (chpt. pres. 1972), Women in Communications (chpt. pres. 1981-82), Public Relations Soc. Am. (Totem award 1980), Tau Mu Epsilon. Democrat. Unitarian. Home: 10312 17th St NE Seattle WA 98125 Office: 8511 15th St NE Seattle WA 98115

TOWNSON, MONICA JANE, economist; b. Docking, Eng.; d. Terence Rowland and Dorothy (Batchelor) Wagg; came to Can., 1956, naturalized, 1968; B.S., London Sch. Econs., 1954; children—Diana, David, Rachel, Michael. Econs. editor Fin. Times of Can., Montreal, Que., 1972-75; economist, writer Royal Bank Can., Montreal, 1975-77; v.p. Can. Adv. Council on Status of Women, Ottawa, Ont., 1977-78; sr. econ. adviser Centre Study Inflation and Productivity, Econ. Council Can., 1978-79; sr. adviser communications, 1979-81; pres. Monica Townson Assos. Inc., Ottawa, 1982—. Asst. treas., bd. dirs., exec. com. YWCA, Montreal, 1975-77; bd. dirs. Ottawa Women's Credit Union, 1978-80; mem. research com. Can. Research Inst. Advancement of Women; mem. Can. Human Rights Commn. Task Force on Equal Pay for Work of Equal Value, 1978; coordinator women and pensions workshops Nat. Pensions Conf., 1981. Mem. Ottawa Assn. Applied Econs. (exec. com. 1978-81), Can. Assn. Bus. Econs., London Sch. Econs. Soc. Producer TV programs on women in labour force. Author: The Canadian Woman's Guide To Money, 1982; regular contbr. to Report/Money of Ottawa Citizen, Your Money of Fin. Post. Home: 168 Sunnyside Ave Ottawa ON K1S 0R3 Canada

TOZER, PEGGY MARIE, librarian; b. Shell Lake, Wis.; d. Harold W. and Lucy Anne (Bohn) Tozer; B.S., Wis. State Coll. at Eau Claire, 1943; B.L.S., U. Wis., 1948; M.A. in L.S., U. Mich., 1959. Tchr. high schs., Trempealeau, New Auburn and Sparta, Wis., 1943-48; librarian Meml. High Sch., Beloit, Wis., 1948-52; public services librarian Eastern N.Mex. U., Portales, 1952-73, asst. dir., 1973-75, acting dir., 1975-76, library dir., 1976—. Eastern N.Mex. U. Faculty Senate award, 1976. Mem. Roosevelt County C. of C., Am. Library Assn., S.W. Library Assn., N.M. Library Assn. (pres. 1971-72), AAUP, N.Mex. Media Assn., Delta Kappa Gamma. Club: Altrusa, Order Eastern Star. Home: 1321 W 17th Ln Portales NM 88130 Office: Golden Library Eastern NM Univ Portales NM 88130

TOZZO, LORRAINE MARY, corp. exec.; b. Bklyn., July 11, 1950; d. Palmo Anthony and Helen Sarah (Petraglia) T.; With Arnold Constable Corp. and Noname Stores, Inc., N.Y.C., 1970—, asst. sec. corp., 1972-73, sec., 1973—. Chmn. fund raising N.Y. League for Early Learning, Inc., William O'Connor Sch., Bklyn.; Coordinator fund raising and Tchrs. Coll. Pre-Kindergarten Center, Columbia U. Home: 1013 Shore Pkwy Brooklyn NY 11228 Office: 240 W 40th St New York NY 10018

TRACEY, BEATRICE, law firm adminstr.; b. Boston, Jan. 24, 1922; d. Morris and Eva I. (Rosenberg) Lofchie; dental asst. diploma Forsyth Dental Sch., Boston, 1940; student bus. and mgmt. Harvard U., Boston U.; m. Stanley Trachtenberg, June 22, 1947; children—Mark, Lawrence, Jordan. Dental asst., 1940-44; credit investigator, collector Credit Bur. Greater Boston, 194-47; credit asst. Cable Raincoat Co., Boston, 1947-52; accounts exec. Fin. Collection Agy., Boston, 1967-69; owner, operator Credit Internat., Boston, 1969-74; exec. adminstr. Credit

Control Services, Waltham, Mass., 1975-79; instr. Newbury Jr. Coll., Boston, 1972—; fin. mgr. Peabody & Brown, Boston, 1979—. Pres. Temple Sinai Sisterhood, 1965-67, chmn. fund raising, 1967-69; chmn. fund raising Am. Jewish Congress, 1968-71. Mem. Adminstrv. Mgmt. Soc. (chmn. nat. membership 1973-74), Comml. Law League Am., Am. Collectors Assn. Democrat. Club: B'nai B'rith. Office: Peabody and Brown 1 Boston Pl Boston MA 02108

TRACH, VIRGINIA MARIE, educator; b. Mt. Pleasant, Pa., Aug. 30, 1951; d. John Edward and Bridget Frances (Czaja) T.; B.A. in Psychology, Seton Hill Coll., Greensburg, Pa., 1973; M.Ed. in Counseling (grantee 1981), U. Pitts., 1982. Tchr. 2d grade St. John the Baptist Sch., Scottdale, Pa., 1973-75; tchr. 5th grade Southmoreland Sch. Dist., Scottdale, 1975-82, counselor jr. high sch., 1982—. Mem. Pa. Southmoreland Edn. Assn. (chmn. public relations 1980) Democrat. Home: 103 2d Ave Scottdale PA 15683 Office: Southmoreland Jr High Sch Alverton PA 15612

TRACY, FRANCES LEE, cleaning service exec., steel co. rep.; b. Denison, Tex., May 1, 1926; d. Raymond Evan and Mary Florence (Bock) Tilger; student U. Mexico de San Antonio, San Antonio, 1972, Acad. Real Estate, 1978; m. John L. Tracy, May 6, 1944; children—Thomas Lee, Cynthia A. Tracy Walter, Diane Tracy Richardson, Steven D. Personnel clk., Kelly AFB, San Antonio, 1943-44; sec. Corp. Engrs., Los Angeles, 1955; legal clk. Indsl. Accident Commn., Long Beach, Calif., 1956-58; interviewer Dist. Atty., Santa Ana, Calif., 1959-61; owner, mgr. Tracy Cleaning Service, San Antonio, 1961—; dealer Tri-Steel Structures, Inc., San Antonio, 1981—. Mem. Greater San Antonio Builders Assn., San Antonio Better Bus. Bur., S.W. Tex. Assn. Bldg. Contractors. Democrat. Roman Catholic. Home: 239 Ridge Dr San Antonio TX 78228 Office: 1011 S Main San Antonio TX 78204

TRACY, GRACE CAROL, nurse; b. Clark Field, Minn., Apr. 30, 1931; d. Clifford Harold and Gerda Emelia (Dregseth) Falmoe; student Lutheran Bible Inst., Mpls., 1950-51, Sioux Valley Hosp., 1952; m. Richard Paul Tracy, Mar. 1, 1958 (div. 1965); children—Robert Allan, Bemgecha Marie, Bonnie Kay. Mem. staff Canton Inwood Hosp., Canton, S.D., 1952-54; staff nurse St. Joseph Hosp., Mitchell, S.D., 1955-57, 58-60, Methodist Hosp., Mitchell, 1959-64; nurse, head nurse obstetrics St. Mary's Hosp., Rochester, Minn., 1965-71, nurse coordinator, 1971-82, surg. nurse, 1971-82; obstetrics staff nurse Waterman Meml. Hosp., Eustis, Fla., 1982—; distbr. Amway Corp., Rochester, 1979-82, Eustis, 1982—; Mary Kay beauty cons. Pres., Luther League. Mem. Christian Nurse Assn., Christian Nurses Fellowship (pres.). Lutheran. Office: Waterman Meml Hosp Eustis FL 32726

TRACY, MARY ELIZABETH, librarian; b. Joliet, Ill., Aug. 18, 1922; d. Charles Joseph and Catherine (Fay) Tracy; B.A. cum laude, Coll. St. Francis, 1944; M.A. in L.S., Rosary Coll., River Forest, Ill., 1958. Tchr., Joliet grade schs., 1944-52, 54-61, Am. schs., Bremerhaven, Frankfurt, Ger., 1952-54; librarian Joliet Twp. Central High Sch., 1961—, dist. dir., 1972-73; instr. library tech. Joliet Jr. Coll., 1973—. Pres., Joliet Jr. Catholic Woman's League, 1950-51. Mem. Am., Ill. library assns., Library and Media Assn. Will County (pres. 1976), Ill. Assn. Media in Edn., Ill. Assn. Ednl. Communication and Tech., Chgo. Suburban Audiovisual Roundtable, Alumnae Assn. Coll. St. Francis (sec. 1946-48, v.p. 1957-59, bd. advisers 1965-67, Dist. 204 archives com. 1975—, chmn. 1980—). Home: 1010 Glenwood Ave Joliet IL 60435 Office: 201 E Jefferson St Joliet IL 60432

TRAEGER, BARBARA SHIELDS, public relations exec.; b. Pitts., Oct. 19, 1932; d. Marshall Charles and Margaret Helen (Ward) Shields; B.A., Ripon Coll., 1954; cert. mgmt. U. Chgo., 1965; cert. mktg. Northwestern U., 1978; m. John E. Traeger, Apr. 30, 1971; children—Cynthia Carner, Charles R. Carner, Jr., Henry M. Carner (by previous marriage). Dir. public relations Chgo. unit Am. Cancer Soc., 1964-65; public relations asso., exec. sec. Am. Soc. Hosp. Public Relations of Am. Hosp. Assn., Chgo., 1966-68; dir. public relations U. Chgo. Hosps., 1968-72, Evanston (Ill.) Hosp. Corp., 1972—. Recipient 35 profl. awards. Mem. Acad. Hosp. Public Relations, Am. Soc. Hosp. Public Relations, Internat. Assn. Bus. Communications, Chgo. Hosp. Council Public Relations Assn. Clubs: Publicity, Suburban Press. Office: 2650 Ridge Ave Evanston IL 60201

TRAFTON, BARBARA M., hosp. exec.; b. Rumford, Maine, May 22, 1949; d. George S. and Frances H. (Rolfe) McKnight; B.A. in Psychology, Wellesley Coll., 1971; M.S. in Elem. Edn., U. Maine, Portland-Gorham, 1975; m. Richard Trafton, June 24, 1972; children—Benjamin, Samuel. Research asst. in spl. edn. Cambridge Mental Health Assn., 1971; dir. health, phys. edn. and recreation Lewiston-Auburn (Maine) YWCA, 1971-73, dir. Day Camp, Tri-County Mental Health, 1972-73; tchr. Maine Tchrs. Corps, Buckfield, Auburn, 1973-75; mem. Maine Ho. of Reps., 1976-78, health and instl. services energy coms.; mem. Maine Senate, 1978-82, coms.: judiciary, public utilities, apptd. gov.'s planning com. for Blaine House Conf. on Families, Blue-Ribbon Commn. on Ground Water Protection, Gov.'s Council on Phys. Fitness, chmn. Gov.'s Commn. on Review Dept. of Environ. Protection; dir. community relations and devel. St. Mary's Gen. Hosp., Lewiston, Maine, 1981—. Bd. dirs. YWCA, 1973-75, Androscoggin Valley Red Cross, 1971-76, instr. trainer water safety, 1972-78, chmn. water safety, 1972-78; vice chmn. N.E. Div. Adv. Council ARC, 1975, instr. nat. aquatic sch., 1972-78; CPR instr. Maine Heart Assn., 1974-76, instr. swimming for handicapped, 1971-80, first aid, 1971-78, bd. dirs. Task Force on Human Needs, 1974-76, United Way, 1980; div. chmn. United Way campaign, 1981; trustee Maine Audubon Soc., 1978; chmn. environ. policy, 1978-81, exec. com., 1980; Democratic nat. committeewoman, 1980—; exec. com. Maine Dem. State Com., 1980—; dir. Maine Assn. Women in Fine Performing Arts, 1980. Named Outstanding Public Citizen of Year, Maine chpt. Nat. Assn. Social Workers, 1981. Mem. Nat. Assn. Hosp. Devel., Am. Soc. Hosp. Public Relations. Office: 45 Golder St Lewiston ME 04240

TRAINOR, AGNES MARIE, aviation economist; b. Washington, Nov. 14; d. William Ernest and Agnes Rose (Drew) T.; B.A., Trinity Coll., Washington, 1973. With FAA, U.S. Dept. Transp., Washington, 1973-75, CAB, Washington, 1975-82; sr. air transport ofcl. Internat. Civil Aviation Orgn., Montreal, Que., Can., 1982—; expert witness on air carrier selection; pvt. pilot. asso. transp. research bd. Nat. Acad. Scis. Mem. Internat. Air Transport Assn. (observer Internat. Aviation Club. Roman Catholic. Home: 1250 Ave des Pins Ouest Apt 480 Montreal PQ H3G 2P5 Canada Office: 1000 Sherbrooke St W Montreal PQ H3A 2R2 Canada

TRAMBLE, RENEE, acctg. firm exec.; b. Cleve., June 30, 1954; d. William Pedro and Louise Ellen (McGugan) T.; B.B.A., Kent State U., 1976; M.B.A., Cleve. State U., 1981. Fin. instns. examiner State of Ohio Div. Banks, Columbus, 1976-78; acct. Watson, Rice & Co., Cleve., 1978—, mgr. acctg. staff, 1980—. Treas. bd. dirs. Am. Sickle Cell Anemia Soc., 1980-82; mem. allocations panel United Way Services, 1980-82, mem. audit com., 1980-82; mem. Citizens League of Greater Cleve., 1979-82. C.P.A. Mem. Am. Inst. C.P.A.s, Ohio Soc. Public Accts., Nat. Assn. Black Accts. Baptist. Home: 4186 Eastwood Ln Warrensville Heights OH 44122 Office: Watson Rice & Co Suite 1200 Citizens Federal Tower Cleveland OH 44114

TRANKLE, NANCY KAVAL, computer co. exec.; b. Chgo., Mar. 29, 1938; d. Stanley and Gladys (Kordik) Kaval; student Northwestern U., 1972, Roosevelt U., 1972; B.S., U. San Francisco, 1980; 1 dau., Pamela J. Office positions, Chgo., 1955-62; mem. sales staff Am. Family Assn., Chgo., 1959-65; v.p., 1965-77; editor, exec. dir. Ill. Cemetery Assn., Chgo., 1973-77; mgr. edn. ops. Tandem Computers Co., Cupertino, Calif., 1977-81, mgr. spl. communications, 1981—, sec.-treas., conf. mgr. Internat. Tandem Users' Group, conf. mgr. European div., 1978-83 Chmn. communications Family Services, Wilmette, Ill., 1975-77; bd. dirs. Big Bros. and Big Sisters of Santa Clara County. Mem. Meeting Planners Internat. (v.p. membership No. Calif. chpt. 1981—), No. Calif. Soc. Assn. Execs., Santa Clara County Social Services Vols., Profl. Womens Network (founder, chmn.), Nat. Assn. Female Execs. (network dir.), San Jose C. of C. (dir., exec. com. conv. bur.), Women in Bus., Am. Soc. Tng. and Devel., LWV. Unitarian (steering com. women in religion). Office: 19333 Vallco Pky Cupertino CA 95014

TRAPUCKD, TASNA TAMARREE, microbiologist; b. Bangkok, Thailand, Dec. 18, 1946; d. Thep and Charlouy (Sae Chueng) Tamaarree; Med. Tech. certi. Mahidol Univ., 1968, Robert Packer Hosp., 1971; m. Suriyont Trapuckd, Aug. 7, 1973. Med. technologist chemistry and bacteriology lab. Women's Hosp., Bangkok, 1968; med. technologist bacteriology research lab. South East Asia Treaty Orgn., Thailand, 1968-70; med. technologist Clin. Microbiology Lab., M.S. Hershey Med. Center, Hershey, Pa., 1971-77, sr. tech. specialist, 1977-80, supr., 1981—, tchr. med. technologist, physician asst., 1977, tchr., cons. for med. residents, 1977-82. Mem. Am. Soc. Microbiology, Twin Lakes Park South Civic Assn. Buddhist. Home: 4823 Tamar Dr Harrisburg PA 17111 Office: Clinical Laboratories MS Hershey Med Center Hershey PA 17033

TRASKA, (IRMA) JUNE, artist; b. Bonham, Tex., Apr. 15, 1928; d. Walter J. and Ila Hedgcock; B.F.A., Oklahoma City U., 1941; postgrad. Stanford U., Instituto Allende, San Miguelle d'Allende, Guanajuato, Mexico; m. Henry C. Traska (dec.); children—Henry C., Michel W., Lani Susan. One person shows: Fidelity Bank, Oklahoma City, 1978, Fitzhughe's, Oklahoma City, 1979, Citizens Bank, Oklahoma City, 1980; work shown in Jan Maree Gallery, Oklahoma City, 1980, Mr. J's Gallery, Richardson, Tex., 1980; executed murals Childrens Meml. Hosp., Oklahoma City; represented in permanent collections: Okla. U. Health Sci. Center Med. Library, Okla. Hall of Fame, Oklahoma City U. Vol. tchr. Found. Handicapped Adults; vice chmn. Okla. Statehood Day Com. Recipient Disting. Alumna award Oklahoma City U., 1977. Mem. Okla. Art Guild (recipient Right Hand award 1970), AAUW, Arts Council Okla., Okla. Heritage Assn., Okla. Art League, Oklahoma City U. (exec. bd. alumni relations), Accademia Italia delle Arte e del Lavoro (recipient gold medal), Okla. Watercolor Assn., Internat. Soc. Artists, Southwestern Watercolor Soc., Okla. Mus. Art, Nat. League Am. Pen Women, Okla. Hist. Soc. Clubs: Sooner, Criterion, Town Hall, Ladies Music, Womens Dinner, Civic Music.

TRAUB, LOIS SPECKTER, assn. exec.; b. Cin., Aug. 9, 1931; d. Jack D. and Anna (Blackman) Speckter; student U. Cin., 1949-51; B.A. magna cum laude, Clark U., 1955; student Northeastern U., 1969-72; m. Alan C. Traub, Aug. 5, 1951; children—Lauren Jean, Karen Lynne, Lynda Gail. Legis. aide Sen. Jack Backman, Mass. Senate, 1973-75; dist. office mgr. Congressman Robert F. Drinan, Waltham, Mass., 1975-76, reelection campaign mgr., 1976-77; sr. adminstrv. asst. New Eng. Bd. Higher Edn., Wellesley, Mass., 1977-78, coordinator state del. affairs, 1978-79; coordinator public info. Union Concerned Scientists, Cambridge, Mass., 1980—; adminstrv. dir. Spl. Legis. Commn. Studying Unemployment in Commonwealth of Mass., 1974. Mem. Framingham Town Meeting, 1968-73, 4th Congl. Dist. Midterm Caucus, 1974; mem. Framingham Democratic Town Com., 1976—, chmn., 1980-81; mem. Danforth Art Mus. Council, 1974-76. Recipient Loring E. Dodd Playwriting award Clark U., 1954. Mem. Citizens for Participation in Polit. Action, ACLU, NOW, Women's Nat. Polit. Caucus, Phi Beta Kappa. Home: 56 Donna Rd Framingham MA 01701 Office: 1384 Massachusetts Ave Cambridge MA

TRAUGOTT, ELIZABETH CLOSS, educator; b. Bristol, Eng., Apr. 9, 1939; came to U.S., 1960; d. August and Hannah M. M. (Priebsch) Closs; B.A., Oxford (Eng.) U., 1960; Ph.D., U. Calif., Berkeley, 1964; m. John L. Traugott, Sept., 1967; 1 dau., Isabel M. Asst. prof. English, U. Calif., Berkeley, 1964-70; lectr., then assoc. prof. linguistics and English, Stanford U., 1970-77, prof. linguistics and English, 1977—, chmn. dept. linguistics, 1980-83; lectr. U. Dar-es-Salaam, 1965-66, U. York (Eng.), 1966-67. Am. Council Learned Socs. fellow, 1976-77. Mem. Linguistic Soc. Am. (exec. com. 1982-85), Linguistic Soc. Gt. Brit., Internat. Soc. Hist. Linguistics, AAUW. Author: A History of English Syntax, 1972; (with Mary L. Pratt) Linguistics for Students of Literature, 1980; contbr. numerous articles to profl. jours. Office: Dept Linguistics Stanford U Stanford CA 94305

TRAVAGLINI, BARBARA CARLSON (MRS. ALFONSO FREDERICK TRAVAGLINI), steel co. exec.; b. Easton, Pa., Nov. 4, 1925; d. Gunard Oscar and Margaret Bailey (Berry) Carlson; Bryn Mawr Coll., 1943-44, Moore Coll. Art, 1944-48; m. Alfonso Frederick Travaglini, June 15, 1946; children—Gunard Carlson, Frederick Carlson, Mark Carlson. Vice chmn., sec., dir. G.O. Carlson, Inc., Thorndale, Pa., 1956—. Pres. Coatesville Hosp. Aux., 1967-72, 1st v.p., 1972—; sec. Chester County Airport Authority. Exec. dir., sec., treas. Gunard Berry Carlson Meml. Found.; trustee Saint Francis Coll., Lafayette Coll. Republican. Roman Catholic. Author: The Kelly Green Cow, 1949; Henry Hippo, 1972; columnist A Woman's Pen and As I See It. Home: 4000 Hazelwood Ave Thorndale PA 19372 Office: G O Carlson Inc Thorndale PA 19372

TRAVERS, MARY, singer, recording artist; b. Louisville, Nov. 9, 1936. Vocalist with folk music trio Peter, Paul and Mary, 1961-70; appeared Newport Folk Festival, numerous U.S. coffeehouses during 1960's; albums include: Peter, Paul and Mary, 1962, Peter, Paul and Mary—Moving, 1963, In the Wind, 1963, In Concert, 1965, Song Will Rise, 1965, See What Tomorrow Brings, 1965, Peter, Paul and Mary Album, 1966, Album 1700, 1967, Late Again, 1968, Peter, Paul and Mommy, 1969; single recs. include: If I Had a Hammer, Puff the Magic Dragon; four solo albums since 1970; host radio program The Mary Travers Show, 1975; editor: Knight Flight (Michael R. Conroy), 1977. Address: care K Hunter 9255 Sunset Blvd Los Angeles CA 90069 *

TRAVIS, DOROTHY FRANCES, biologist; b. Atlanta, Dec. 3, 1920; d. James Ernest and Zilpah (Huie) Travis; B.S., George Washington U., 1945; A.M., Harvard U.-Radcliffe Coll., 1950, Ph.D., 1951. Instr., then asst. prof. U. N.H., 1953-58; research fellow Nat. Heart Inst., Harvard U., 1958-60; research fellow dept. orthopedic surgery Harvard U. Med. Sch.-Mass. Gen. Hosp., 1960-62, research asso., 1962-65; asso. dept. orthopedic surgery Harvard U. Med. Sch., also asst. biologist Mass. Gen. Hosp., 1965-69; chief morphology sect. Gerontology Research Center, Nat. Inst. Child Health and Human Devel., NIH, Balt., 1969-74; health scientist adminstr. div. research resources NIH, Bethesda, Md., 1974-80. Thomas Dana fellow 1949-50, E.L. Mark fellow 1949-50; Mees fellow, 1949-50; AEC predoctoral fellow, 1949-51, postdoctoral fellow, 1951-53. Mem. Am. Soc. Cell Biology, Electron Microscopic Soc. Am., Washington-Balt. Soc. Electron Microscopy, N.Y. Acad. Scis., Am. Zool. Soc., AAAS, Am. Inst. Biol. Scis., Woods Whole Marine Biol. Lab. Corp., Bermuda Biol. Sta. for Research, Phi Beta Kappa, Sigma Xi, Alpha Epsilon Delta, Phi Sigma. Contbr. profl. publs. Research in molecular biology of mineralized tissues. Home: 35 Coleridge Dr Falmouth MA 02540

TRAVIS, JANET L., coll. pres.; b. Boston, Mar. 6, 1935; d. Francis Ernest and Dorothy May (Sharkey) Evans; A.B. in Geology, Boston U., 1959, M.A. in Philosophy, 1967, Ph.D., 1969; m. Robert U. Travis, Apr. 26, 1962. Instr., U. Nevada, Las Vegas, 1968-69, asst. prof., 1969-72, asso. prof., 1972-74, chmn. dept., 1969-74, acad. counselor, 1973-74; dean humanities and fine arts, asso. prof. philosophy U. No. Iowa, 1974-75, dean humanities, prof., 1976-77; provost, prof. philosophy No. Ky. U., 1977-79; pres. Mansfield (Pa.) State Coll., 1979—. Mem. Am. Assn. Higher Edn., Am. Philos. Assn., Philosophy Sci. Assn., Soc. Study of Evolution, Personalist Discussion Group, Paleontological Soc., Am. Assn. Univ. Adminstrs., Egypt Exploration Soc., Phi Delta Kappa. Office: Mansfield State Coll Mansfield PA 16933

TRAVIS, JOAN FAYE SCHILLER, lawyer; b. Chgo., Mar. 15, 1939; d. Jack and Betty (From) Schiller; Ph.B. in Psychology, Northwestern U., 1969; J.D., John Marshall Law Sch., Chgo., 1981; m. Maurice Travis, May 31, 1959; children—Jeffrey Bernard, Leonard Edwin, Elizabeth Sue. Elem. sch. tchr., Chgo., 1970-72; admitted to Ill. bar, 1981, U.S. Ct. Appeals, 1981, U.S. Dist. Ct. bar, 1981, U.S. Ct. Mil. Appeals, 1982, since practiced in Chgo.; asso. firm Amirante & Etchingham, Park Ridge, Ill.; speaker, lectr. in field. Mem. Am. Bar Assn., Fed. Defender Panel, Ill. Bar Assn., Chgo. Bar Assn., Def. of Prisoners Com., N.W. Suburban Bar Assn., North Suburban Bar Assn., Nat. Acad. TV Arts and Scis., Delta Theta Phi. Jewish. Author numerous articles in field. Office: 200 S Prospect Profl Center Park Ridge IL 60068

TRAVIS, LEOLA ELIZABETH MADISON, educator; b. Phila., May 22, 1927; d. Alexander and Pauline (Kemp) Madison; B.S., Hampton Inst., 1949; M.A., Marshall U., 1957; Ed.D., Ind. U., 1969; postgrad. W.Va. U., 1955-56, U. Wis., 1960; m. Oneth Morview Travis. Adminstrv. sec. to dean of instrn. W.Va. State Coll., Institute, 1952-58; mem. faculty dept. bus. and econs. Ky. State U., Frankfort, 1958—, prof., 1969—, acting chmn. dept. bus. and econs., 1973—; cons. IBM, N.Y.C., 1969, Kingston, N.Y., 1970; personnel specialist dept. personnel Ky. State Govt., Frankfort, 1972; liaison officer Danforth Fellowship program, 1975—. Mem. Ky. adv. commn. Study of Electric Rates and Regulations, 1975-76, Ky. Minority Bus. Adv. Council, 1974—, Computer Services Policy commn. Ky. Council on Pub. Higher Edn., 1974-77; mem. Gov.'s Sub-com. on Study of Edn. in Ky., 1977—; mem. cable TV adv. commn. Lexington-Fayette Urban County Govt. Urban League fellow NOAA div. Dept. Commerce, 1977. Mem. Nat., So. bus. edn. assns., Am. Vocat. Assn., AAUP, AAUW (corp. rep. Ky. State U.), LWV (treas. bd. dirs. Frankfort-Franklin County Ky. chpt. 1973-77), Nat. Assn. for Tchrs. of Bus. Edn. (sec. bd. dirs. 1975-77), Delta Pi Epsilon, Kappa Delta Pi, Pi Lambda Theta, Alpha Kappa Alpha (chairperson nat. standards com. 1975—). Clubs: Democratic Women's of Ky., Frankfort-Lexington Links. Office: Box 60 Bradford Hall Ky State Univ Frankfort KY 40601 *

TRAVIS, MARY EILEEN (MRS. ARTHUR J. TRAVIS), librarian; b. New Glasgow, N.S., Can., Mar. 16, 1931; d. Louis Michael and Mary Cummane (Hallisey) Connolly; B.A., St. Francis Xavier U., 1952; B.L.S., McGill U., 1953; LL.D. (hon.), St. Thomas U., 1976; m. Arthur J. Travis, Sept. 1, 1958; children—Mary Patricia, John Louis. Librarian bookmobile Pictou County Library, New Glasgow, 1953-55, head children's dept., 1955-58; head children's dept. St. John (N.B.) City Library, 1960-63, city librarian, 1963-67, regional librarian, 1969—. Condr. radio show Book Review, CFBC-FM, St. John, 1966—, TV show Magazine CHSJ-TV, St. John, 1966—. Mem. St. John Mayor's Com., 1972—; mem. St. John Bd. Trade, 1970—, mem. council, 1975—, now 1st v.p. Bd. dirs. Netherwood Sch. for Girls, 1969—, Sch. Dist. 19, Kings County, N.B., 1968—, N.B. Opera Co., 1965-73, St. John Arts Council, 1968—; bd. govs. St. Francis Xavier U., 1978—; v.p. ceremonies Jeux Can. Games Soc. Inc., 1981—. Named Woman of Yr., St. John, 1973; recipient Queen's Silver Jubilee medal, 1977. Mem. Can., Nat. (mem. adv. bd. 1972-74), Ottawa, Atlantic Provinces (pres. 1969-70, co-chmn. bibliog. com. 1975-80) library assns., Can. Assn. Children's Librarians (sec. 1967), Cath. Women's League (pres. Rothesay, N.B. chpt. 1966), N.S. Drama League (pres. 1957), Can. Pony Club, Eclectic Club. Roman Catholic. Home: PO Box 302 Rothesay NB E0G 2W0 Canada Office: Saint John Regional Library 20 Hazen Ave Saint John NB Canada

TRAVIS, VIVIAN KELLY, psychologist; b. Drumright, Okla., Nov. 6, 1926; d. Artie Clarence and Gladys Ham Kelly; B.S., Northeastern Okla. State U., 1948; M.S., Okla. State U., 1966, Ph.D., 1972; m. Vaud Ancil Travis, Jr., Dec. 31, 1947; children—Vaud Ancil III, Daniel Stuart, Patrick Kelly, Mary Margaret. Pvt. practice psychology, Charlotte, N.C., 1972-79; asso. prof. psychology Winthrop Coll., Rock Hill, S.C., 1969—; cons. N.C. Vocat. Rehab., Juvenile Corrections Div., Charlotte, 1967-68, Center for Women in Ednl. Leadership, U. N.C., Chapel Hill, 1980-82. Mem. Assn. Advancement Tension Control, S.C. Psychol. Assn. Democrat. Office: Dept Psychology Winthrop Coll Rock Hill SC 29730

TRAYLOR, CHERYL LEE, psychiat. social worker; b. Oswego, N.Y., June 20, 1944; d. Donald Elton and Harriette (Lee) Gais; B.A., State U. N.Y., Buffalo, 1966, M.S.W., 1972; m. Jean LaRue Traylor, Jr., Nov. 11, 1965 (div. Dec. 1970). With Psychiat. Clinic, Buffalo, 1967-70; psychiat. social worker Hillcrest Childrens Center, Washington, 1972-74; asst. dir. outpatient services Comprehensive Community Mental Health Center #2, Seat Pleasant, Md., 1974-77; psychiat. social worker Arlington (Va.) Mental Health Center, 1977-78, So. Calif. Permanente Med. Group, San Diego, 1978—. NIMH fellow, 1970-72. Mem. Nat. Assn. Social Workers, Nat. Assn. Black Social Workers, Acad. Certified Social Workers. Club: Foxtrappe (Washington).

TRAYLOR, CLAIRE GUTHRIE, state legislator; b. Kansas City, Mo., Jan. 18, 1931; B.S., Northwestern U., 1952; M.A., Washington U., St. Louis, 1955; m. Frank Traylor; children—Nancy, Frank, Susan, David. Primary sch. tchr., St. Louis, 1953-55, Denver, 1955-57; tchr. communications dept. Jefferson County schs., Lakewood, Colo., 1978; mem. Colo. Ho. of Reps., 1978-82; mem. Colo. Senate, 1982—. Mem. Colo. Commn. on Aging; past. mem. Colo. Commn. on Children and Families; mem. steering com. Luth. Hosp. Diamond Jubilee; mem. com. Wheat Ridge Sr. Center. Mem. Wheat Ridge C. of C. Republican. Presbyterian. Clubs: Jr. League (Denver); Clear Creek Valley Med. Aux. Office: Colo Ho of Reps State Capitol Denver CO 80203 *

TREADGOLD, MARTHA LEE, educator; b. Houston, Sept. 1, 1935; d. Emerson Clifford and Margaret A. Irvin; B.S., U. Houston, 1965; M.Ed., Lamar U., Beaumont, Tex., 1977; cert. Elementary Edn., Houston Baptist U., 1970; m. Robert Henry Treadgold, Oct. 28, 1954; children—John Robert, Paul Douglas, Sheila Marie. Tchr., Petersen Elem. Sch., Houston, 1969-72; tchr. Fuqua Sch., Houston, 1972-76, curriculum coordinator, 1974-76; resource tchr. Condit Elem. Sch., Houston, 1976-78, ednl. diagnostician Houston Ind. Sch. Dist., 1978-79, edn. trainer for spl. services, 1980—. Sec., Home Economist in Homemaking, 1966; tchr. Sunday Sch., 1966-80; active Freedom Found. of Valley Forge, 1972-78. Mem. Assn. for Children with Learning Disabilities, Phi Delta Kappa. Office: 5627 Jason Houston TX 77096

TREADWELL, MARY MAUDE (LONE STAR), construction worker; b. L.I., N.Y., Oct. 11, 1945; d. Walter Clinton (Chief Wild Pigeon) and Julia Loise (Viet) Treadwell; A.A.S., Suffolk County Community Coll., 1979; children—Robin Yellow Dawn Lee, James Strong Bow Lee, Robert Spotted Pony Lee. Communications operator Suffolk County Police Dept., Hauppauge, N.Y., 1975; adminstrv. asst., student personnel div. Suffolk County Community Coll., 1977-80; adminstrn. analyst Equitable Life Assurance Soc., Melville, N.Y., 1980; native Am. field rep. Affirmative Action Program, Melville, 1980-81; constrn. worker Dravo Utility Constructors Inc., Wading River, N.Y., 1981—; founder, chmn. bd. Paumanok Algonquin Found. Inc. Suffolk chmn. L.I. Women's Equal Opportunity Council, 1980; treas. Brookhaven Town Minority Bus. Council, 1980. Contbr. articles in field to profl. jours. Office: Dravo Utility Constructors Inc Shoreham Power Sta Box 606 Wading River NY 11792

TREANOR, RUTH PRINGLE D(AUGHERTY), speech-lang. pathologist; b. Girard, Ohio, Sept. 25, 1919; d. Harry Herbert and Ethel Margarite (Bray) Pringle; B.A. (scholarship 1937, asst. 1938-41), Hiram (Ohio) Coll., 1941; M.S. in Speech Pathology (asst. 1946-47), U. Mich., Ann Arbor, 1947; Ed.D. in Edn. (Spl. Edn. scholar Montgomery County, Md. 1970), Am. U., 1970; m. Robert L. Treanor, Oct. 13, 1973; children—Carol, Elizabeth, Christine, Ellen. Tchr. elem. and secondary schs., Ohio and Mich., 1941-46; chief speech Aural Rehab. Center, Walter Reed Army Med. Center, 1947-50; pvt. practice with stroke, aphasia and lang. disordered, 1950-53; tchr. deaf children, 1954-58; speech clinician Montgomery County public schs., 1958-69; supr. speech and hearing programs Prince George's County (Md.) public schs., 1970-79; speech-lang. pathologist, pvt. ednl. cons., Rockville, Md., 1979—; condr. ednl. workshops. Recipient fed. grants. Mem. Am. Speech, Lang. and Hearing Assn., Council Exceptional Children, Alexander Graham Bell Assn. Deaf, Conv. Am. Insts. Deaf, Md. Speech and Hearing Assn. (chmn. com. public sch. speech clinicians 1971-72), D.C. Speech and Hearing Assn., NOW, Foundry Players. Lutheran. Club: Order Eastern Star. Author papers, reports, curriculum guides in field. Home: 3579 Fiske Terr Silver Spring MD 20906 Office: Speech-Lang Center of Olney 17904 Georgia Ave Olney MD 20830

TRECIOKAS, ALODIA DICIUTE, mezzo-soprano, educator; b. Kaunas, Lithuania, Sept. 15, 1905; d. John and Eugenia (Rinkevich) Dicius; came to U.S., 1947, naturalized, 1953; diploma Lithuanian State Sch. of Music, 1930; student of Mme. Gladkaja, Paris, France, 1928-30, Mme. Edwige Ghibaude, Rome, Italy, 1937-38; m. Joseph Treciokes, Oct. 10, 1925; 1 son, Leopold John. Debut in opera as Zibeland Marta in Faust, Lithuanian State Opera, 1930, debut as Carmen, 1935, debut as Delilah in Samson and Delilah, 1938; mem. Lithuanian (Kaunas) State Opera, 1930-44, leading roles in Samson and Delilah, Carmen, Tiefland, Boris Godunov, Prince Igor, Pericola, Faust; appeared as concert soloist numerous concerts Lithuania, Estonia, Germany, U.S.A. including Lithuania Radio Symphony, Lithuania State Opera Orch., Chgo. Symphony Orch.; appeared as soloist in various radio programs in Lithuania, 1923-44, Estonia, 1936—, Germany, 1946-47, U.S., 1949-75; Am. debut as Carmen in Carmen-Bizet, 1949; soloist in recital, Kimball Hall, Chgo., 1951; debut as Catherine in Joan of Arc at the Stake, Orchestra Hall, Chgo., 1952; concert soloist with Nordic Philharmonic Orch., Chgo., 1959; pvt. tchr. voice and opera, Chgo., 1950-65, Tinley Park, Ill., 1963—; dir. opera theatre class Am. Conservatory of Music, Chgo., 1957; recording artist Webb Recording Co., RCA records. Mem. Nat. Assn. Tchrs. of Singing, Nat. Ret. Tchrs. Assn., Musician Club of Women in Chgo. Roman Catholic. Address: 332 26th St Santa Monica CA 90402

TREE, MARIETTA, city planner; b. Lawrence, Mass.; d. Malcolm E. and Mary (Parkman) P.; B.A., U. Pa.; postgrad. Columbia U. Sch. Urban Planning; numerous hon. degrees; m. Ronald Tree, July 28, 1947; children—Penelope Tree, Frances FitzGerald. Commr. human rights City of N.Y., 1958-61; ambassador U.S. Mission to UN, N.Y.C., 1961-65; personal staff of sec.-gen. UN Secretariat, N.Y.C., 1965-67; dir. Llewelyn-Davies, Sahni, Inc., city planners and architects; dir. CBS, Internat. Income Properties, Pan Am. Airways, Lend-Lease Corp. (Australia); cons. Salomon Bros.; trustee U.S. Trust Co. Bd. dirs. Am. Ditchley Found.; mem. vis. com. Sch. Architecture and Planning, M.I.T.; chmn. Citizens Com. for N.Y.C., Inc.; mem. Cooper Hewitt Council, Churchill Found. Mem. Council Fgn. Relations, Pilgrim Soc. Home: 1 Sutton Pl S New York NY 10022

TREECE, MALRA CLIFFT, educator; b. Oxford, Ark., Nov. 19, 1923; d. Joseph A. and Ruth (Thompson) Clifft; B.S., Ark. State U., 1947; M.A., Memphis State U., 1956; Ph.D., U. Miss., 1971; m. Guy Treece, Jan. 18, 1946; children—Diana, Mark David. Prof. bus. communication Memphis State U., 1957—; speaker; cons. Recipient Nat., State, Mid-South Poetry awards. Mem. Am. Bus. Communication Assn., Nat. Bus. Edn. Assn., Nat. League Am. Pen Women, Tenn. Poetry Soc., Phi Kappa Phi, Delta Pi Epsilon. Methodist. Author: Communication for Business and the Professions, 1978; 2d edit., 1982; Successful Business Writing, 1980; Effective Reports, 1982; contbr. articles to profl. jours. Home: 1064 Estate Memphis TN 38117 Office: 317 Bus Adminstrn Bldg Memphis State U Memphis TN 38152

TREFETHEN, FLORENCE NEWMAN (MRS. LLOYD MACGREGOR TREFETHEN), writer, editor; b. Phila., Sept. 18, 1921; d. Otto Carl-Johann and Emma Martha (Paessler) Newman; A.B. magna cum laude, Bryn Mawr Coll., 1943; M. Litt., Cambridge U., 1950; m. Lloyd MacGregor Trefethen, May 17, 1944; children—Gwyned, Lloyd Nicholas. Ops. analyst, ops. research office Johns Hopkins, Chevy Chase, Md., 1950-54; instr. English, Tufts U., Medford, Mass., 1959-66; lectr. Northeastern U. Grad. Sch. Arts and Scis., Boston, 1967-69, Radcliffe Inst., Cambridge, Mass., 1969-70, 72-73; columnist Poet's Workshop, Writer, Boston, 1967—; free lance writer, rewrite editor, Boston, 1966—; editor Council East Asian Studies, Harvard U., 1974—. Served to lt. (j.g.) WAVES, 1943-45. Recipient Arthur Davison Ficke award Poetry Soc. Am., 1969, Consuelo Ford award, 1975; Ann. Lyric prize New. Eng. Poetry Club, 1978, Fox award, 1975, O'Henry Prize Stories, 1982. Mem. NOW, Poetry Soc. Am., New Eng. Poetry Club, Bryn Mawr Alumnae (editorial bd. mem. Bull. 1966—). Author: Writing a Poem, 1970, rev. edit., 1975; (with Joseph F. McCloskey) Operations Research for Management, vol. 1, 1954. Contbr. revs., fiction, poems to lit. jours. Address: 23 Barberry Rd Lexington MA 02173

TREFTS, DOROTHY ELEANORE, computer co. exec.; b. Ithaca, N.Y., Apr. 24, 1953; d. Albert Sharpe and Joan (Landenberger) T.; B.A. cum laude (Coll. scholar), Wellesley Coll., 1974; M.B.A., Harvard U., Boston, 1978. Intern, Wellesley-M.I.T. Urban Legal Studies Project, summer 1973; Washington intern Wellesley Coll., summer 1974; cons. Data Resources, Inc., San Francisco, 1975-76; fin. analyst IBM, Manassas, Va., 1978-79; trainee mgmt. tng. program First Nat. Bank Boston, 1979-80; product mgr. Saddlebrook Corp., Cambridge, Mass., 1980—. Vol., Frontier Nursing Service, Wendover, Ky., spring, 1971, mem. Boston exec. com., recruiting coordinator, 1979—. Mem. Boston Wellesley Career Assos. Republican. Presbyterian. Clubs: DAR, Nat. Soc. Dames XVII Century (charter mem. chpt.) (Cleve.); Harvard Bus. Sch., Wellesley Coll., Harvard (Boston). Office: 76 Rogers St Cambridge MA 02142

TREGELLAS, PATRICIA, musician; b. Kans., Feb. 22, 1936; d. Clarence and Lena T.; B.Mus. in Edn., U. Denver, 1959; scholar, Trossingen, Germany, 1960-61. Concert artist, chamber musician, condr.; music supr. Prowers County (Colo.) High Sch. Band and Chorus, 1962-65; accordionist and orch. leader USO tours abroad, 1966-69; mem. orch., asst. condr. Hal Prince musicals on nat. tours, 1969-71; freelance musician, N.Y.C., 1972—; mus. dir., condr. N.Y. Concerto Orch., 1979—; condr. workshops, Tokyo, London, N.Y.C.; performed in premier performances of new music. Recipient cert. appreciation Gen. Westmoreland and others for work in Vietnam with USO. Mem. Chamber Music Am., Am. Accordion Assn., AAUW, Sigma Epsilon Chi, Kappa Delta, Mu Phi Epsilon. Methodist. Home: 817 West End Ave New York NY 10025

TREGGIARI, SUSAN MARY, educator; b. Moreton-in-Marsh, Eng., 1940; d. Walter Howard and Elizabeth Mary (Washbourn) Franklin; B.A., Lady Margaret Hall, Oxford U., 1962, M.A., 1965, B.Litt., 1967; m. Arnaldo Treggiari, 1964; children—Joanna, Silvia. Vis. prof. Sweet Briar (Va.) Coll., 1969-70; asst. prof. to prof. U. Ottawa, Ont., Can., 1970—, prof., chmn. Dept. Classical Studies, 1981—; prof. Dept. Classics, Stanford (Calif.) U., 1982—. Derby scholar, 1962-63, 63-64; Can. Council and Social Scis. and Humanities Research council grantee, 1971-81. Mem. Soc. for Promotion of Roman Studies, Classical Assn. Can., Assn. Ancient Historians (pres. 1981—), Anglican Ch. Author: Roman Freedmen During the Late Republic, 1969; acting editor Classical News & Views, 1973-74, joint editor, 1974-81. Office: Stanford U Stanford CA 94305

TREI, ALICE ROSALIE, ret. occupational therapist; b. Estonia, Oct. 17, 1909; d. Prüdu and Müna (Kraun) Roost; came to U.S., 1929, naturalized, 1938; certificate occupational therapy, Columbia, 1948; B.S., N.Y. U., 1954; m. Peter Trei, Sept. 20, 1928 (dec. Jan. 1962); children—Astra (Mrs. Felix Bottenhorn), Alan. Occupational therapist N.Y. State Psychiat. Inst., N.Y.C., 1948-53, head occupational therapist, 1953-79; clin. instr. occupational therapy Columbia, 1966—. Recipient Outstanding Employee award N.Y. State Dept. Hygiene, 1975. Mem. Am., N.Y. State (treas. 1959-62, 69-73) occupational therapy assns., Met. N.Y. Dist., World Fedn. Occupational Therapists. Home: 15 Sickles St New York NY 10040

TREICHLER, PAULA ANTONIA, linguistic researcher; b. Dayton, Ohio, Jan. 15, 1943; d. Paul Felix and Jessie Mildred (Cambron) T.; B.A., Antioch Coll., 1965; Ph.D., U. Rochester (NDEA fellow), 1971; postgrad. Madras Christian Coll., 1962-63. Vis. lectr., asso. dir. Unit One program U. Ill., Urbana, 1972-77, asst. dean Med. Coll., 1977-80, assoc. dean, 1980-81, research assoc. Inst. Communications Research and Sch. Humanities, Coll. Medicine, 1981-82; asst. prof. Coll. Medicine, Dept. Speech Communication, Inst. Communications Research, 1982—. Am. Med. Womens Assn. grantee, 1978; U. Ill. Urbana Champaign Research Bd. grantee, 1981; Nat. Council Tchrs. English grantee, 1982-83; U. Ill. research bd. grantee, 1982-83. Mem. MLA (commn. on status of women in profession 1982-85), Internat. Communication Assn., Assn. Am. Med. Colls., Nat. Women's Health Network. Editorial bd. Womens Studies Internat. Quar.; 1978—; co editor Women and Language News, 1981—; For Alma Mater: Theory and Practice in Feminist Scholarship; contbr. articles to profl. jours. Home: 808 S Lynn St Champaign IL 61820 Office: 190 Med Scis Bldg 506 S Mathews St Urbana IL 61801

TREIMAN, JOYCE WAHL (MRS. KENNETH TREIMAN), artist; b. Evanston, Ill., May 29, 1922; d. Rene and Rose (Doppelt) Wahl; A.A., Stephens Coll., 1941; B.F.A. (Grad. fellow 1943), State U. Iowa, 1943; m. Kenneth Treiman, Apr. 25, 1945; 1 son, Donald. One-man shows include Paul Theobald Gallery, Chgo., 1942, John Snowden Gallery, Chgo., 1945, Art Inst. Chgo., 1947, North Shore Country Day Sch., Winnetka, Ill., 1947, Fairweather-Garnett Gallery, Evanston, 1950, Edwin Hewitt Gallery, N.Y.C., 1950, Palmer House Galleries, Chgo., 1952, Glencoe (Ill.) Library, 1953, Elizabeth Nelson Gallery, Chgo., 1953, Charles Feingarten Gallery, Chgo., 1955, 58, Marian Willard Gallery, N.Y.C., 1960, Felix Landau Gallery, Los Angeles, 1961, 64, Adele Bednarz Gallery, Los Angeles, 1969, 74, Forum Gallery, N.Y.C., 1970, La Jolla (Calif.) Mus. 10 year retrospective, 1971; retrospective exhibit Municipal Art Gallery, Los Angeles, 1947-78; exhibited group shows at Met. Mus., 1950, Carnegie Internat., 1955, 57, Whitney Mus., 1951, 52, 53, 58, John Herron Art Inst., 1953, Art Inst. Chgo., 1954-59, Library of Congress, 1954, Corcoran Gallery, 1957, Pa. Acad. Fine Art, 1958, Mus. Modern Art, 1962, Whitney Mus., 1962, Penelope Gallery, Rome, 1964, numerous others; represented in permanent collections Denver Mus. Art, State U. Iowa, Ill. State Mus., Tupperware Art Mus., Orlando, Fla., Art Inst. Chgo., Utah State U., Abbott Labs., Oberlin Allen Art Mus., Internat. Mineral Corp., Pasadena Art Mus., U. Oreg., Whitney Mus. Am. Art, Long Beach Mus. Art; also pvt. collections; artist in residence San Fernando Valley State Coll., 1968; vis. artist Art Center Sch., Los Angeles, summer 1968; vis. prof. San Fernando Valley State Coll., Northridge, Calif., 1969; vis. lectr. U. Calif. at Los Angeles, 1969-70; vis. artist Calif. State U., Long Beach, 1976. Recipient numerous awards including Logan prize and purchase prize Art Inst. Chgo., 1951; Martin B. Cahn prize, 1959, 60; Pauline Palmer prize, 1953; Saratosa Am. Painting Exhbn. award, Ford Found. purchase prize, 1960; Ball State Coll. purchase prize, 1961; La Jolla Art Mus. prize, 1961; Pasadena Art Mus. purchase prize, 1961; named Woman of Year for Arts, Los Angeles Times, 1965. Tiffany fellow, 1947, Tupperware Art Fund fellow, 1955, Tamerino Lithography fellow, 1961. Home: 712 Amalfi Dr Pacific Palisades CA 90272

TRELA, VIRGINIA MAY, publicist; b. Grand Rapids, Mich., Feb. 15, 1925; d. Clair and Sally Jousma; A.A., Green Mountain Coll., 1945; postgrad. U. Calif., Irvine, 1965-66, UCLA, 1978-79; m. Joseph C. Trela, Sept. 11, 1954; children—Christopher Alan, Brian Philip. Profl. actress, 1945-51; exec. adminstrv. asst. McCann Erickson, Inc., 1954-55; sec. Arabian Am. Oil Co., Dhahran, Saudi Arabia, 1951-53; service rep., public relations Champagne Temporary Help, Newport Beach, Calif., 1965-75; publicity coordinator Knott's Berry Farm, Buena Park, Calif., 1975-76; publicity mgr. Five Star Mktg. Services, Santa Ana, Calif., 1976—; coordinator weCan Women's Network. Mem. Calif. Press Women, Nat. Fedn. Press Women, Orange County Press Club, Women in Communications. Home: 8832 Dolphin Dr Huntington Beach CA 92646 Office: 555 Parkcenter Dr Santa Ana CA 92705

TREMULIS, ELIZABETH PICKETT, social worker; b. N.Y.C., June 3, 1928; d. Ralph Edgar and Helen Margaret (Richardson) Pickett; B.A., Stanford U., 1950; M.A., U. Chgo., 1951; m. Demosthenes Tremulis, Dec. 22, 1951; children—Michael Sarantos (dec.), Andrea, Peter Alexander, William Stephen. Caseworker, Family Service Bur., United Charities of Chgo., 1951-54; social worker North Suburban Spl. Edn. Dist., Highland Park, Ill., 1970-72, Sch. Dist. 28, Northbrook, Ill., 1969-70, 72—; cons. St. David's Nursery Sch., 1968, Highland Park Community Nursery Sch., 1969-70, Ravinia Nursery Sch., 1970. Mem. Highland Park Caucus Com., 1977-79; mem. Highland Park Landmark Preservation Com., 1979-80; bd. dirs. Highland Park Community Nursery Sch., 1964-65, Northbrook YMCA, 1961-63. Mem. Acad. Cert. Social Workers, Nat. Assn. Social Workers, Nat., Ill. assns. sch. social workers, Ill. Soc. Clin. Social Work, Council for Exceptional Children. Mem. staff Sch. Social Work Jour., 1979-81. Home: 466 Laurel Ave Highland Park IL 60035 Office: 1600 Walters Ave Northbrook IL 60062

TRENKEL, ARANKA, farmer; b. Diosjeno, Hungary, Mar. 1, 1920; came to U.S., 1937, naturalized, 1943; d. Dezso and Maria (Szaszovszky) Macsicska; student Delehanty Inst., 1940-43; A.A. with honors, Treasure Valley Community Coll., 1970; student N.W. Nazarene Coll., 1971-72; m. Harold F. Trenkel, Dec. 19, 1945; children—Fred D., Barbara M., Harold J., David W. Sec., Trenkel Farming Livestock, Ontario, Oreg., 1945—. Sec., Republican Central Com. of Malheur County, 1960-76, com. woman, 1960-80; chmn. Malheur County Com. for Aged, 1978-80; vice-chmn. Hist. Soc. Malheur County, 1979-80; mem. Malheur County Health Council, Treasure Valley Community Coll. Bd., 1972—; sec. dr. Community Concerts Assn., Ontario; leader Methodist Youth Fellowship, Vale, Oreg., 1960-73. Served with WAC, U.S. Army, 1943-45; Philippine, New Guinea. Mem. Oreg. Sch. Bds. Assn., Assn. Oreg. Community Colls., PTA, Malheur County 4-H Leaders Assn. Club: Malheur Musicale.

TRENT, VIRGINIA RATCLIFF, public relations exec., musician; b. Jasper, Tex., June 3, 1931; d. Bennett S. and Emma L. (Mason) Ratcliff; B. in Music Edn., Lindenwood Coll., 1952; M. in Music Edn., U. Tex., 1953; postgrad. Westminster Choir Coll., 1953, Organ Inst., Mass., 1953, Hardin Simmons U., 1954; m. William Franklin Trent, June 30, 1956; children—Deborah Ratcliff, Faye Brabson. Dir. choral music San Angelo (Tex.) Public Schs., 1953-54; dir. music First Meth. Ch., San Angelo, 1953-54; dir. religious edn. and organist First Meth. Ch., Jasper, Tex., 1954-55; dir. choral music Hillcrest High Sch., Dallas, Tex., 1955-56; organist and dir. music Salem Meth. Ch., St. Louis, 1962-71; dir. public relations Mallinckrodt Inst. Radiology, Washington U. Sch. Medicine, St. Louis, 1971—; pianist-recitalist tours in St. Louis Community, 1956—. Pres., Ladue Chapel Nursery Sch. Bd., 1965-66; mem. aux. bd. St. Louis Conservatory and Sch. for the Arts, 1979—; Ladue Residential chmn. Arts and Edn. Fund Drive, 1965; mem. St. Louis Symphony Rotogravure Com., 1977-80; music chmn. St. Louis Symphony Music Marathon Gala, 1981. Recipient Disting. Alumni award Lindenwood Coll., 1982. Mem. Am. Assn. Hosp. Public Relations Dirs., Internat. Assn. Bus. Communicators, Advt. Fedn. of St. Louis (pres. elect 1982-83), Am. Guild of Organists, Nat. Soc. Arts and Letters, Nat. Fellowship of Meth. Musicians, Hosp. Public Relations Soc. of St. Louis, Women's Assn. of the St. Louis Symphony Soc. (exec. bd. 1960-75, pres. jr. div. 1960-62), Lindenwood Coll. Alumnae Assn. (nat. v.p. 1962-64), Am. Hosp. Assn., Mu Phi Epsilon. Republican. Presbyterian. Contbg. writer and editor Focal Spot, 1971—. Home: 41 N Clermont Ln St Louis MO 63124 Office: 510 S Kingshighway St Louis MO 63110

TREPPLER, IRENE ESTHER, state legislator; b. St. Louis County, Mo., Oct. 13, 1926; d. Martin H. and Julia C. (Bender) Hagemann; student Meramec Community Coll., 1972; m. Walter J. Treppler, Aug. 18, 1950; children—John M., Steven A., Diane V., Walter W. Payroll chief USAF Aero. Chart Plant, 1943-51; enumerator U.S. Census Bur., St. Louis, 1960, crew leader, 1970; mem. Mo. Ho. of Reps., Jefferson City, 1972—; sec. Republican Caucus. Mem. Oak-Le-Mehl Republican Club, Concord Twp. Rep. Club; alt. del. Rep. Nat. Conv., 1976. Mem. Nat. Order Women Legislators (rec. sec. 1981-82), Nat. Fedn. Rep. Women. Republican. Mem. Ch. of Christ. Office: Room 105-E Mo State Capitol Bldg Jefferson City MO 65101

TRESCH, RUBY ELIZABETH, mfg. co. exec.; b. East Concord, N.Y., Sept. 27, 1926; d. Henry Leopold and Irene Belle (Sisson) Schweickert; grad. sec. sci. Chown Comml. Coll., 1944; m. Wesley Milton Tresch, Oct. 30, 1948; 1 dau., Elizabeth Ann. Stenographer, sec. Film Classics Co., Buffalo, 1945-50; bookkeeper Siegfried Constrn. Co., Buffalo, 1951-52; bookkeeper, sec. Roblin Industries, Buffalo, 1959-72, asst. sec., asst. treas., 1972—. Mem. Am. Airlines Fair Ladies (charter), Exec. Female. Republican. Baptist. Home: 18 Jamstead Ct Williamsville NY 14221 Office: 241 Main St Buffalo NY 14203

TRESMONTAN, OLYMPIA DAVIS, psychotherapist; b. Boston, Nov. 27, 1925; d. Peter Konstantin and Mary (Hazimanolis) Davis; B.S., Simmons Coll., 1946; M.A., Wayne State U., 1960; Ph.D. (Schaefer Found. grantee), U. Calif., Berkeley, 1971; m. Dion Marc Tresmontan, Sept. 15, 1957 (dec. Mar. 1961); m. 2d, Robert Baker Stitt, Mar. 21, 1974. Child welfare worker San Francisco Dept. Social Service, 1964-66; sensitivity tng. NSF Sci. Curriculum Improvement Study, U. Calif., Berkeley, 1967-68; individual practice psychol. counseling, San Francisco, 1970—; dir. Studio Ten Services, San Francisco; bd. dirs. Promise for Children; tchr. U. Calif. extension at San Francisco, 1971-72, Chapman Coll. Grad. Program in Counseling, Travis AFB, 1971-74. Active Friends San Francisco Pub. Library, Internat. Hospitality Com. Bay Area; bd. dirs. Childworth Learning Center. Mem. Am. Psychol. Assn., Am. Orthopsychiat. Assn., Am. Assn. Marriage Counselors, Calif. Assn. Marriage, Family and Child Therapists. AAUW. Club: Commonwealth. Author: (with J. Morris) The Evaluation of A Compensatory Education Program, 1967; (Karplus edit.) What is Curriculum Evaluation, Six Answers, 1968. Home: 2611 Lake St San Francisco CA 94121

TRETICK, JOYCE B., psychotherapist, lectr., cons., educator; b. Bklyn., Aug. 29, 1932; d. Jack and Sylvia (Levy) Wien; B.A., Bklyn. Coll., 1953; M.A., U. Chgo., 1956; M.S.W., Columbia U., 1958; postgrad. Center for Psychoanalysis, Ackerman Inst. Family Therapy; m. Gordon Tretick, July 12, 1963. Therapist, Morris County (N.J.) Guidance Center, 1962-64, Beth Israel Hosp., N.Y.C., 1958-62, Hackensack (N.J.) Hosp., 1964-72; prof. family and group therapy Fairleigh Dickinson U., Teaneck, N.J., 1970—; cons., lectr. in field. Poster child March of Dimes, 1933; recipient Theodore Roosevelt award N.Y. State. Mem. Nat. Assn. Social Workers, Am. Family Therapists Assn. (charter), N.J. Assn. Family Therapists, Eastern Group Psychoanalysis Soc., Phi Beta Kappa. Jewish. Home: 313 Con Cors Pl New Milford NJ 07646 Office: 133 Cedar Ln Teaneck NJ 07666

TREVATHAN, SANDRA MAE WOOD, city agy. adminstr.; b. Little Rock, Ark., Sept. 16, 1942; d. Auburn Haskett and Helen Irene (Stuzenbaker) Wood; B.S., Morningside Coll., 1972; student Ark. State U., 1959-60, 64, 65, 66; m. Thomas Rea Trevathan, Mar. 26, 1960; children—Katherine Michelle, Michael Scott. Sec., music therapist Oklahoma City Public Schs., 1966-69; dir. surveys Social Sci. Research Center, Morningside Coll., 1972-73, dep. dir., 1973-75; planner Siouxland Interstate Met. Planning Council, Sioux City, Iowa, 1976-78; adminstrv. asst. to city mgr. EEO, City of Sioux City, 1978—, cons. surveys, 1976, 78; cons. seminars., 1981, 82. Precinct co-chmn. Woodbury County Democratic Central Com., 1980-82; pres. Vol. Bur., 1981, dir., 1976-81; bd. dirs. United Way of Siouxland; mem. adv. com. Woodbury County Employment Tng. Center, 1981—. Mem. LWV, Iowa Women's Polit. Caucus, Siouxland Com. for Handicapped, Am. Interprofl. Inst., Nebr.-Iowa Assn. Human Rights Workers, Psi Chi, Alpha Kappa Delta, Zeta Sigma. Democrat. Presbyterian. Home: 2503 S Newton St Sioux City IA 51106 Office: City of Sioux City PO Box 447 Sioux City IA 51102

TREVINO, CELESTE MARIE, psychotherapist; b. Chgo., Nov. 15, 1952; d. Candido Irnaeo and Charlotte Martha (Vogel) T.; A.A., Coll. DuPage, 1972; B.A. with honors, U. Ill., Chgo., 1974; cert. Inst. Applied Adlerian Tng., 1976; postgrad. Ill. Inst. Tech., 1975-76; M.S., George Williams Coll., 1980, postgrad. degree, 1981. Student counselor Coll. of DuPage, Glen Ellyn, Ill., 1970-72; dir. art therapy Little City, Palatine, Ill., 1973-74; sr. counselor Chgo. Mental Health Clinics, 1974-76; pvt. practice group and individual psychotherapy, 1975—, also assessment psychologist Cook County Jail, Pace Orgn., 1978—; cons. psychol. assessments and programs for inmates Cook County Dept. Corrections; supr. counselors Cook County Jail. Election judge, 1979—. Mem. Am. Psychol. Assn., Ill. Psychol. Assn. Democrat. Research on vol. behavior in correctional systems. Office: Park Professional Bldg 467 W Deming St Chicago IL 60614

TREVINO, MARGARITA CHRISTELA, health care adminstr.; b. Sonora, Tex., Sept. 15, 1943; d. Jose F. and Ysaura (de la Garza) Sanchez; B.S., Tex. Woman's U., 1966, M.S., 1975; Ph.D., U. Tex., 1981;

m. Hugo Cruz, Dec. 23, 1967; children—Margarita Edette, Hugo II. Staff nurse ICU, Methodist Hosp., Houston, Tex., 1966-68; head nurse pediatric div. Arlington (Tex.) Meml. Hosp., 1969; asst. supr. City of Dallas Dept. of Public Health Nursing, Tex., 1969-71; asst. supr. Acute Care Clinic, Children's Med. Center, Dallas, 1971-73; asst. prof. Baylor U. Sch. of Nursing, Dallas, 1973-81; dept. dir. Baylor U. Med. Center, Dallas, 1981—; cons. to various health orgns., 1973—; exchange prof. nursing Autonomous U. Nuevo Leon (Mex.), 1973-80. Vol., ARC, 1966—, Am. Heart Assn., 1973—, Rio Grande River Ministry, Dallas, 1975—; mem. Task Force on the Hispanic Family, 1978—; bd. dirs. Hispanic Bapt. Theol. Seminary, San Antonio, 1982—. Recipient Baylor U. Service Pin, 1977, 79; named Most Outstanding Faculty Mem. of Yr., Baylor U. Sch. Nursing, 1975. Mem. Am. Public Health Assn., Nat. Assn. Hispanic Nurses, U.S.-Mexico Border Public Health Assn. Baptist. Contbr. articles on public health care to profl. publs.

TREWIN, FRANCES ELLEN, accountant; b. Waucoma, Iowa, Jan. 24, 1916; d. Thomas James and Mary Elizabeth (Doyle) Burke; student Waucoma public and parochial schs.; m. Ronald Trewin, Feb. 6, 1937; children—Mary Beth, Richard, Diane, Ronald. Acct., Lynch Enterprises, 1960-70, Jirak Acctg., 1970-75; owner, mgr. Frances Trewin Acctg., Waucoma, 1975—. Mem. Local Election Bd., 1954-72; sec. County Democratic Exec. Com., 1962-66; mem. Waucoma City Council, 1977-82; bd. dirs. Sr. Citizen Housing, 1979—. Recipient Gov.'s award for community betterment program, 1979. Mem. Accts. Assn. Iowa, Nat. Soc. Public Accts., Nat. Assn. Tax Practitioners, Nat. Assn. Enrolled Agts. Roman Catholic. Clubs: Cath. Daus. Am., Waucoma Homemakers. Home and Office: 114 1st Ave NW Waucoma IA 52171

TRIBBLE, DAGMAR HAGGSTROM (MRS. ELSTON J. TRIBBLE), artist; b. N.Y.C.; d. Olaf Albin and Ida (Sabini) Haggstrom; student Parsons Sch. Design, N.Y. and Paris, 1928, Art Students League, 1930-32, Farnsworth Sch. Painting, 1949-50; m. Elston J. Tribble, July 15, 1933; 1 dau., Martha Watkins (Mrs. James Malcolm McKinnon). Tchr. fashion illustration Parsons Sch. Design, 1929-32; designer sportswear and beachwear Travelo Corp., N.Y.C., 1933-45. One-man shows at Beard Sch., Orange, N.J., Monmouth Coll., West Long Branch, The Present Day Club, Princeton, N.J., 1968, 71, 73-75, 77-78, 82, M.S. Kungsholm, 1971-74, M.S. Sagafjord, 1971, United Nat. Bank, Fenwood, N.J., 1972, others; exhibited in group shows at Cape Cod Art Assn., 1963, Knickerbocker Artists Ann. Exhbn., 1963, Westfield Art Assn. State Show, 1963, 64, Hunterdon County Art Center Ann., 1963, 64, Catherine Lorillard Wolfe Art Show, 1964, Nat. Arts Club shows, also Met. Mus. Art, Nat. Acad., N.Y.C., Am. Water Color Soc. Ann., 1978, Nat. Assn. Women Artists Ann., 1967—, Nat. Assn. Women Artists Internat., Paris, 1969, Am. Watercolor Soc. anns., 1967—, Garden State Watercolor Soc. anns., 1970—, Am. Watercolor Soc. Ann. Traveling Exhbn., 1972, N.J. State Cultural Center, Trenton, 1977; represented in pvt. collections. Recipient Agnes B. Noyes award, 1962; Windsor Newton award, 1963; Captain's Barn award for Watercolor Westfield Art Assn. State Show, 1964; Steinback Co. award for watercolor Festival of Fine Art Exhbn., 1964; Am. Artist medal merit, Am. Watercolor Soc., 1965; Jane C. Stanley Meml. prize, Nat. Assn. Women Artists, 1966. Mem. Am. Watercolor Soc., Garden State Watercolor Soc. (pres. 1970—; Squibb award 1973), Nat. Assn. Women Artists, Princeton Art Assn. (pres. 1968-69), Salmagundi Club. Club: Nat. Arts (N.Y.C.). Home: 12 Battle Rd Princeton NJ 08540

TRIEBEL, FRANCES GRANT, assn. exec.; b. Champaign, Ill., Aug. 29, 1916; d. Harry Weston and Laura Alma (Roberts) Grant; student U. Ill., 1934-37; m. Albert Triebel, Jr., Dec. 26, 1937; 1 dau., Marilyn Triebel Burgoyne. Mem. Nat. Soc. DAR, Ill. state officer-registrar, 1977-79, Ill. state chmn. public relations, 1979-81, Ill. state regent, 1981—, mem. nat. bd. mgmt., 1981—; mem. adv. bd., trustee Tamassee (S.C.) DAR Sch., 1981—; mem. endowment com., trustee Kate Duncan Smith DAR Sch., Grant, Ala., 1981—. Mem. Alpha Chi Omega. Presbyterian. Clubs: Rockford Country, Rockford Women's (dir. 1979-81). Home: 3611 Hickory Ln Rockford IL 61107

TRIEMER, CARLA ELAINE, mktg. exec.; b. Palo Alto, Calif., Nov. 12, 1954; d. Francis Willard and Gladys Elaine (Holmes) T.; B.A. with honors, U. Calif., Santa Barbara, 1975; cert. in jud. adminstrn. U. So. Calif., 1978, M.P.A. with honors, 1978. Contract complaince coordinator San Bernardino County, San Bernardino, Calif., 1977-79; criminal justice planner San Bernardino County Criminal Justice and Delinquency Prevention Planning Dist., San Bernardino, 1979-80; ops. analyst Marin County Sheriff's Office, San Rafael, Calif., 1980-81; mktg. rep. IBM, Oakland, Calif., 1981—. Chmn., San Bernardino County Commn. on Status of Women Task Force on Domestic and Social Violence, 1977-80; bd. dirs. San Bernardino County Rape Crisis and Sexual Assault Services, 1979-80; mem. steering com. Western States Shelters Network, 1979-80; chmn. Siegried A. Centerwall Fund Adv. Com., 1977-79. Recipient Cert. of Appreciation, Coalition for Prevention Abuse Women and Children, 1980. Mem. NOW, Nat. Assn. Criminal Justice Planners, Assn. Police Planning and Research Officers, Calif. Women in Govt., Marin County Res. Dep. Sheriffs. Democrat. Lutheran. Home: 26953 Hayward Blvd Suite 305 Hayward CA 94542

TRIGERE, PAULINE, fashion designer; b. Paris, France, Nov. 4, 1912; d. Alexandre and Cecile (Coriene) Trigère; student Victor Hugo Coll., Paris; children—Jean-Pierre, Philippe Radley. Came to U.S., 1937, naturalized, 1942. Began career at Martial et Armand, Place Vendome, Paris; started own bus. with bro. N.Y.C., 1942. Recipient Am. Fashion Critics' award, 1949: Return award, 1951; Neiman-Marcus award, 1950; Cotton award Nat. Cotton Council of Am., 1959; Filene's award, 1959; Hall of Fame award, 1959. Office: 550 Seventh Ave New York NY 10018 *

TRIGLETH, ANTOINETTE, nurse; b. Visalia, Calif., May 7, 1923; d. Nicola and Carmela (Grassi) Giotta; B.S., U. Calif., San Francisco, 1945; cert. public health nursing UCLA, 1951; divorced; children—Brian, Michael. Staff nurse Visalia Community Hosp., 1945-47; with Tulare County (Calif.) Health Dept., 1947-80, supervising public health nurse, 1951-57, dir. public health nursing, 1957-80; dir. pub. health nursing Tulare County Home Health Agy., 1963-80; ret., 1980; mem. Calif. Adv. Council Nursing Edn., Calif. Bd. Nurse Registration; mem. nursing exec. com. AHEC, Fresno, Calif., 1973-80. Mem. Calif. Conf. Local Health Dept. Nursing Dirs.

TRIMBLE, LORA NELLE GARRETSON (MRS. JAMES CURTIS TRIMBLE), writer; b. Wichita Falls, Tex., Aug. 12, 1935; d. Jesse Columbus and Alma Geneva (Higgenbottom) Garretson; student Sul Ross State Tchrs. Coll., 1954, Midwestern U., 1956; B.A., So. Meth. U., 1961; m. James Curtis Trimble, Sept. 4, 1954; children—James Curtis, Mary Christiana. Free lance writer, 1961-67; dir. Royal Lane Lang. Center, Dallas, 1969-77; English lang. tchr. to fgn. adults, 1969-77. Mem. Theta Sigma Phi. Address: Dallas TX 75243

TRIMBY, KATHLEEN, social services adminstr.; b. Moundsville, W.Va., July 3, 1925; d. Carl Wayne and Gertrude Leota (Dowler) Parks; Dipl., Coll. Commerce, Wheeling, W.Va., 1943-45; m. Charles H. Trimby, Sept. 5, 1948; children—Gary Alan, Sharon Kay. Instr., Steubenville Sch. Cosmetology, 1952-57, 67-72; coordinator Jefferson County Sr. Citizens Activities, 1975-79; dir. Jefferson County Office on Aging, Steubenville, Ohio, 1979—. Sec., Regional Area Agy. on Aging Adv. Bd., 1976-79; chmn. for Jefferson County, Ohio Sr. Citizens Day, 1976, regional chmn., 1979, 80, state planning com., 1979, 80; adv. bd. Salvation Army, 1977-80, Mingo Junction Sr. Citizens Assn., 1978-80, Tri-County Nurses Assn., 1980; mem. task force, bd. dirs. Upper Ohio Valley Hospice, Speakers Bur. for C. of C. for Hospice and Advocacy for Older Adults. Mem. Nat. Council on Aging, Am. Assn. Ret. Persons. Methodist. Club: Order Eastern Star. Home: 223 Hollywood Blvd Steubenville OH 43952 Office: Jefferson County Court Ho 301 Market St Steubenville OH 43952

TRIMMER, DOROTHY ANN, nurse; b. Newark, Jan. 28, 1951; d. Robert Stanley and Jane Melissa (Cone) T.; B.S. in Nursing (state scholar), Seton Hall U., 1973; M. Nursing magna cum laude, City U. N.Y., 1976. Staff nurse United Hosp. Med. Center, Newark, 1973-74, St. Barnabas Med. Center, Livingston, N.J., 1974-75; instr. Passaic County Community Coll., Paterson, N.J., 1976-77; dir. staff devel. Riverside Gen. Hosp., Secaucus, N.J., 1977-81; instr. U. Fla., Gainesville, 1981-82, U. Ariz. Coll. Nursing, Tempe, 1982—. Lectr. to civic groups; instr. CPR, Am. Heart Assn.; active Am. Lung Assn. and Am. Cancer Soc. T.J. Kavanagh grantee, 1972; Seton Hall U. grantee, 1973. Mem. Am. Nurses Assn., Am. Assn. Critical Care Nurses, Hudson County Cancer Soc., Am. Soc. Health Edn. and Tng., Hudson County Council Inservice Educators (chmn. 1978-81). Presbyterian (past Sunday sch. tchr.). Home: 4770 N 7th St Apt 2212 Phoenix AZ 85014

TRIPLETT, ARLENE ANN, govt. ofcl.; b. Portland, Oreg., Jan. 21, 1942; d. Vincent Michael and Lorraine Catherine (Starr) Jakovich; B.A. in Bus. Adminstrn., U. Calif., Berkeley, 1963; m. William K. Triplett, Jan. 27, 1962; children—Stephen Michael, Patricia Ann. Budgets and reports analyst Cutter Labs., Berkeley, 1963-66; controller Citizens for Reagan, Washington, 1975-76; dir. adminstrn. Republican Nat. Com., Washington, 1977-80; asst. sec. U.S. Dept. Commerce, Washington, 1981—. Roman Catholic. Home: 6327 Beachway Dr Falls Church VA 22044 Office: US Dept Commerce 14th and Constitution NW Washington DC 20230

TRIPP, MADELYN (MAGGIE) BERESIN, educator; b. Phila., July 7, 1920; d. Jacob and Helen A. (Hexter) Beresin; B.A., U. Pa., 1942, postgrad. in fine arts, 1961-63; postgrad. Barnes Found., 1963-65; m. Alan R. Tripp, Apr. 9, 1941; children—Jeffrey B., Barbara JoAnn. Owner, operator Flowers Every-Friday, Inc. Phila., 1949-54, Four Corners, Inc., Phila., 1955-58, Gallery 252, Phila., 1963-68; mem. Second Career panels U. Pa., 1966-69; originator women's studies programs New Sch. Social Research, 1972, instr. Human Relations Center; founder, tchr. women's center and teaching program Central YWCA, N.Y.C., 1972—; lectr. on status of women for colls., clubs; active Nat. Women's Polit. Caucus, Women's Action Alliance, NOW; coordinator for fine arts Internat. Yr. of Woman, 1975. Mem. Women in Communications. Author: Woman in the Year 2000, 1974; articles on money mgmt.; speeches reprinted in nat. press. Home: 870 United Nations Plaza New York NY 10017

TROCKI, KAREN FRANCES, research psychologist; b. Detroit, July 19, 1944; d. Carl Anthony and Helen Elizabeth (Augustynowicz) T.; B.A., Duquesne U., 1966; M.S., U. Pitts., 1973, Ph.D., 1977; m. Laurence Otis Michalak, June 25, 1977; 1 son, Michael David. Vol., Peace Corps, Tunisia, 1966-68; research asst., asso. research scientist Am. Insts. for Research, Pitts., 1968-76; research specialist, co-prin. investigator Inst. Research in Social Behavior, Oakland, Calif., 1975-80; research analyst U. Calif., Davis, Sch. Medicine, 1981—. Mem. Am. Psychol. Assn., Am. Sociol. Assn. Researcher (NIMH grantee): Sex Role Changes, Peer Influence, Mental Health; contbr. articles to publs. Home: 6425 Irwin Ct Oakland CA 94609

TROISE, AUDREY HELENA, lumber co. exec.; b. Schenectady, Sept. 22, 1934; d. George H. and Emma (Relyea) Flavin; student pub. schs., Mechanicsville, N.Y.; m. Frank Troise, Aug. 1, 1964. Steno-sec. Gen. Electric Co., Waterford, N.Y., 1951-52; sec. Taft Hotel and Republic Pictures, N.Y.C., 1952-54; sec. Walter Schneider Assocs., Inc., N.Y.C., 1954-57; sec. William G. Moore & Son Inc. of Del., N.Y.C., 1957-64, corp. sec., dir., 1965-69, v.p., dir., 1969-76, pres., owner, 1976—. Mem. Am. Wood Preservers Assn., Soc. Am. Mil. Engrs., Assn. Bus. and Profl. Women in Constrn., Assn. of Women Bus. Owners. Office: 4 World Trade Center Suite 6166 New York NY 10048

TROJAN, HILDA ALFREDA, glass co. exec.; b. Fayetteville, Tex., May 21, 1921; d. Hillie Henry and Henrietta (Richter) Kansteiner; student public schs., Columbus, Tex.; m. Joseph Burnard Trojan, Mar. 24, 1940; 1 son, Joseph Burnard, Cecelia. Operator, Southwestern Bell Tel. Co., Robstown, Tex., 1938-40; office staff Agr. Stabilization and Conservation, Columbus, 1960-61, Colo. County Tax Collector, Columbus, 1961; office mgr. Youens Eye Clinic, Columbus, 1965-70; sec.-treas. Columbus Glass Co., 1970—, pres., 1974-75, also dir. Grand regent, dist. dep. Cath. Daus. Am., 1957-61. Mem. Secretarial Ophthalmology Assn., Beta Sigma Phi. Office: 1 Sunset Plaza Columbus TX 78934

TROMBLEY, BARBARA JEAN, nurse; b. Kalamazoo, June 27, 1941; d. Lawrence W. and Florence M. (Shetterly) Cook; R.N., Borgess Sch. Nursing, 1962; postgrad. U. Colo.; m. Brian E. Trombley, Sept. 14, 1963; children—Andrew E., Scott W. Head nurse, pediatric service Borgess Hosp., Kalamazoo, 1964-65; office nurse Frank Harrell, M.D., Kalamazoo, 1965-66; nurse ARC Bloodmobile Program, Lansing, Mich., 1966-67; public health and sch. nurse City/County Health Dept., Colorado Springs, Colo., 1968-72; services adminstr. Rocky Mountain Planned Parenthood, Denver, from 1972; cons. self-sustaining family planning clinics. Cert. ob/gyn nurse practitioner Nurses' Assn. of Am. Coll. Obstetricians and Gynecologists, 1980. Mem. Am. Assn. Sex Educators, Counselors and Therapists. Clubs: Am. Sq. Dance, Am. Round Dance, Rocky Mountain Cloggers. Home: 3626 Indian Pipe Circle Colorado Springs CO 80907

TROOP, VIOLA STASIO, cosmetic co. exec.; b. N.Y.C.; d. Joseph and Rose Stasio; student St. John's U., 1965; m. Roger Joseph Troop, Sept. 12, 1970; stepchildren—Roger, Rawlins, Jessica, Claudia. Sr. market research analyst Colgate-Palmolive Co., N.Y.C., 1965-68; asst. product mgr. Yardley of London, N.Y.C., 1968-69; product counselor Avon Products Inc., N.Y.C., 1969-71; franchise mgr. Revlon Internat. Inc., N.Y.C., 1971-72, mktg. dir., 1975-80, group mktg. dir., 1980-81, v.p., group mktg. dir., 1981—; sr. product mgr. Menley & James, N.Y.C., 1972-75. Mem. The Fashion Group, Cosmetic Career Women's Assn., Soc. Cosmetic Chemists, Am. Mktg. Assn., Advt. Women of N.Y. (past officer). Home: 211 E 77th St New York NY 10021 Office: Revlon Internat Inc 767 Fifth Ave New York NY 10022

TROPP, LOUISE CONSTANCE VELARDI, aircraft spare parts co. exec.; b. Phillipsburg, N.J., Apr. 30, 1942; d. John Francis and Julia Cecilia (Pisaniello) Velardi; B.A., New Sch. Social Research, 1976; m. Howard S. Tropp, June 6, 1964; children—Josephine, Philip. Elem. sch. tchr., Princeton, N.J., 1962-64; owner MPT Enterprises div. Aero. Procurement and Tech. Inc., N.Y.C., 1976—; dir. Jefferson Towers Inc., N.Y.C., 1976—, chmn., 1979-81; dir. Tall Timbers, Sussex, N.Y., 1980—, chmn., 1981—. Mem. bd. Parents Assn. of Columbia Prep. Sch., 1981—. Mem. Am. Women's Econ. Devel. Corp., Women Bus. Owners N.Y., La Leche League (chpt. treas. 1970—). Address: 700 Columbus Ave Apt 7C New York NY 10025

TROPP, YVONNE DAVIES, investment counselor; b. New Rochelle, N.Y., Feb. 25, 1932; d. Bernard and Julia Blanche (Altheimer) Davies; B.A. in Econs. and Psychology, Brown U., 1953; M.B.A. in Fin., N.Y. U., 1975; m. Alan Robbins Tropp, Aug. 25, 1953; children—Karen Julie, Janis Ellen, Dana Robin, Lisa Jill. Market research supr., interviewer W.R. Simmons Assos., N.Y.C., 1970-72; fin. writer, asst. portfolio mgr., mgr. Chartcraft, Inc., Larchmont, N.Y., 1971-77; investment counselor Bank of N.Y., N.Y.C., 1977—. Vice pres. Westchester Shore sect. Nat. Council Jewish Women, 1956-66; founder canteen for retarded young adults, 1956-66; leader Camp Fire Girls, 1962-73; producer N.Y./Westchester Children's Players, 1963-68; v.p. Orienta Point Assn., 1972-74; bd. dirs. Larchmont Temple Youth, 1972-77. Recipient nat. award for excellent and creative leadership Camp Fire Girls, 1965, 68; chartered fin. analyst. Mem. N.Y. Soc. Security Analysts, Fin. Analysts Fedn., Fin. Women's Assn. Club: Brown U. of N.Y. Home: 541 Claflin Ave Mamaroneck NY 10543 Office: Bank of New York 530 Fifth Ave New York NY 10036

TROSIE, VERNITA S., planning officer; b. Wide Ruins, Ariz., July 3, 1958; d. Andrew Edward and Lola Mae (Yazzie) S.; student Central Ariz. Coll., 1976-77. Temporary clk.-typist Navajo Housing Authority, Window Rock, Ariz., 1978, purchasing clk., 1978-79, sec. for dir. adminstrn., 1979, occupancy specialist aide, 1979-80, community housing planner, 1980—.

TROST, KATHRYN CROUCHLEY, home economist; b. East Orange, N.J.; d. Francis David and Kathryn Levina (Quin) Crouchley; B.S., R.I. U., 1955; M.A., Seton Hall U., 1961; married. Tchr. home econs., public schs., Summit, N.J., 1955-58; asso. food editor Good Housekeeping mag., N.Y.C., 1958-60; test kitchen home economist Batten, Barton, Durstine & Osborn, N.Y.C., 1960-62; product publicist Pepperidge Farm, Inc., Norwalk, Conn., 1962-68; consumer sales mgr. Hamilton Beach Co., N.Y.C., 1968-70; mgr. test kitchen Nestle Co., Inc., White Plains, N.Y., 1971-73; sr. research home economist Colgate Palmolive Co., Piscataway, N.J., 1973—. Mem. Am. Home Econs. Assn., Home Economists in Bus., Inst. Food Technologists, Am. Women in Radio and TV. Club: Zonta. Office: 909 River Rd Piscataway NJ 08854

TROTMAN, FRANCES KEITH, psychologist; b. N.Y.C., Sept. 1, 1944; d. Frank R. and Edith C. (Williams) Keith; B.A. (N.Y. Regents scholar) in Sociology, CCNY, 1967, M.S. in Edn., 1972; Ph.D. (Ford Found. fellow) in Counseling Psychology, Columbia U., 1976, M.Phil. in Psychology, 1975; m. Durval Trotman, Aug. 7, 1965; children—Tanya, Tami. Founder, tchr. and dir. Santa Maria de Guido, Morelia, Michoacan, Mexico, 1963-64; tchr. N.Y. Women's House of Detention, 1964-65; asst. program dir. and tchr. Morningside Community Center, N.Y.C., 1966-67, group worker, 1965-66; lectr., counselor Office of Admissions Services City U. of N.Y., 1967-68; guidance counselor Teaneck (N.J.) Jr. High and High Sch., 1971-74; student teaching supr. Fairleigh Dickinson U., Rutherford, N.J., 1974-75; instr. The Tchrs. Inc., N.Y.C., 1974-75; psychotherapist Inst. for Counseling and Psychotherapy, Ft. Lee, N.J., 1976—; chief psychologist Englewood (N.J.) Community Mental Health Orgn., 1978-79; pvt. practice psychotherapy and counseling, Englewood and Teaneck, 1979—; founder, dir. Contemporary Counseling and Psychotherapy Inst., Teaneck. Mem. Am. Psychol. Assn., Assn. of Black Psychologists. Contbr. articles to jours. in psychology. Office: 320 Cedar Ln Teaneck NJ 07666

TROTTER, JANET GAYLE, writer; b. Newark, Oct. 13, 1948; d. Edward and Elizabeth (Henker) Schneider; B.A., Kean Coll., Union, N.J., 1972; m. James Joseph Trotter, Aug. 13, 1977. With Trenton (N.J.) Times Newspaper, 1974-76, feature writer, TV editor N.J. Public TV, Trenton, 1976—, asso. editor, editor The Guide; publicist news and sports programming. Office: NJ Public TV 1573 Parkside Ave Trenton NJ 08638

TROTTER, NANCY LEE, guidance counselor; b. Charleston, W.Va., Nov. 6, 1937; d. Harry Sampson and Blanche Ashley (White) T.; B.S., Morris Harvey Coll., 1959; M.A., W.Va. U., 1961; student Marshall U., 1970, W.Va. Coll. Grad. Studies, 1975, 77. Tchr., Kanawha County Schs., Charleston, 1959-60, counselor, 1961-62, 63-66, psychometrist, 1966-67, guidance counselor, 1968—; counselor Wilmington (Del.) Schs., 1962-63; guidance specialist W.Va Dept. Edn., Charleston, 1967-68; part-time guidance instr. Morris Harvey Coll., 1965. Mem. W.Va. Sch. Counselors Assn. (pres. 1973-74), W.Va. Personnel and Guidance Assn. (v.p. 1976-79), Kanawha County Sch. Counselors Assn. (sec.-treas. 1975-76, v.p. 1976-77, pres. 1977-78), AAUW (v.p. Charleston br. 1974-76, pres. 1979-81, v.p. W.Va. div. 1981—). Democrat. Presbyterian. Home: 1571 Quarrier St Charleston WV 25311 Office: East Bank High Sch 1st Ave and Brannon St East Bank WV 25067

TROUGHTON, SHARON KAY, nurse; b. Rock Springs, Wyo., June 10, 1941; d. Thomas Henry and Tressie May (Bales) Gabbert; grad. magna cum laude Cassia Meml. Hosp., 1974; grad. Newspaper Inst. Am., 1982; m. Barth Louis Troughton, May 8, 1975; children—Alisa, Cathy, Rick, Brian. Dir. med. services Idaho Youth Ranch, Kupert, 1975; charge nurse Minadoka Meml. Hosp., Rupert, Idaho, 1977-79; evening supr. Casabello Estate, 1981-82; staff nurse ob-gyn Cassia Meml. Hosp., Burley, Idaho; also freelance writer. Del., Idaho Easter Seal, 1972-77. Mem. Lic. Practical Nurses Assn. Home: Route 1 Box 222 A-1 Salmon ID 83467

TROUM, REITA ANN MEYEROWITZ, psychotherapist, educator; b. Chgo., Aug. 12, 1933; d. Alfred and Marion (Friedberg) Meyerowitz; B.A. with honors in Philosophy and Psychology, U. N.Mex., 1970; M.S.W. (NIMH fellow), Tulane U., 1971, postgrad. intern counseling and psychiatry, 1972; m. Otho Lee Trick, June 2, 1974; children—William, Deborah, Beth. Chief satellite clinics Chartres Mental Health Center, State of La., 1972-73; pvt. practice, New Orleans, 1972-73; instr. Loyola U., New Orleans, 1972-73; asst. prof., dir. family therapy dept. psychiatry and behavioral medicine Sch. Medicine, W.Va. U., Charleston, 1973-74; joint dir., owner Family Inst. of Southwest, Inc., Houston, 1974—; mem. faculty Grad. Sch. Social Work, U. Houston, 1974-78; cons. staff Sharpstown Gen. Hosp.; pvt. practice psychotherapy. Bell Merit Scholar, 1968-70. Certified La. Bd. Certified Social Work Examiners; lics. Tex. Bd. Examiners in Social Psychotherapy. Mem. Am. (standing research com.), Houston group psychotherapy assns., Nat. Assn. Social Workers, Acad. Certified Social Workers, Am. Pub. Health Assn., Am. Assn. Sex Educators, Counselors and Therapists, AAUP, Tex. Psychotherapy Assn., Phi Beta Kappa. Home: 10002 Green Tree St Houston TX 77042 Office: 6601 Tarnef St Suite 206 Houston TX 77074

TROUT, DIXIE LOUISE, home economist, bus. exec.; b. Grinnell, Iowa, Nov. 21, 1952; d. Morris Elwin and Eleanor Louise (Hill) T.; B.S., Iowa State U., 1975; m. Dennis Gormley, July 17, 1976; 1 step-son, Paul Allen Gormley. With Amana Refrigeration, Inc. (Iowa), 1975—, dir. home econs., 1976-79, dir. consumer affairs, 1979—. Mem. Elec. Women's Roundtable, Home Economists in Bus., Iowa Home Economists in Bus. (chmn.), Am. Home Econs. Assn., Iowa Home Econs. Assn., Soc. Consumer Affairs Profls., Internat. Microwave Power Inst. Methodist. Club: Toastmasters. Home: Box H-37 Amana IA 52203 Office: Amana Refrigeration Inc Amana IA 52204

TROUT, SARA JANE, dietitian; b. Pitts., Sept. 23, 1936; d. Maurice Edwin and Thema Bell (Lowell) T.; B.S. in Home Econs., Carnegie Mellon U., 1958; M.Ed., Duquesne U., 1970. Therapeutic and teaching dietitian Citizens Gen. Hosp., New Kensington, Pa., 1958-65; teaching dietitian, then adminstrv. dietitian Allegheny Valley Hosp. Natrona Heights, Pa., 1961-63, 65-66; clin. and adminstrv. dietitian VA Med.

Center, Pitts., 1967-82, chief nutritional therapy, 1974-82; instr. dietetic tech. program Allegheny Community Coll., 1972-75. Mem. Am. Dietetic Assn., Nutrition Edn. Soc., Am. Assn. Diabetes Educators, Am., Pa. (pres.-elect 1981-82), dietetic assns., Pitts. Dietetic Assn. (past pres., treas.), Sigma Kappa (past chpt. pres.). Author handbook. Died Apr. 7, 1982.

TROUTMAN, CAROL ANN, nurse; b. Lebanon County, Pa., Feb. 3, 1946; d. Paul Andrew and Ruth Suzanne (Kurtz) T.; student Reading (Pa.) Hosp. Sch. Nursing, 1966; A.A.S., Montgomery Community Coll., 1976. Staff nurse operating room Reading Hosp., 1966-72; staff nurse Rolling Hill Hosp., Elkins Park, Pa., 1972-80, clin. coordinator operating room, 1980—, tchr. inservice edn., 1980—. R.N., Pa. Mem. Assn. Operating Room Nurses. Home: 5746 N Front St Philadelphia PA 19120 Office: Operating Room Rolling Hill Hosp 60 E Township Line Rd Elkins Park PA 19117

TROUTWINE, CHARLOTTE TEMPERLEY, psychologist, minister, former ednl. counselor; b. Newton, Mass., Nov. 27, 1906; d. Joseph and Libbie (Kempton) Temperley; B.S., Simmons Coll., 1927; grad. student Boston U., 1947-49; M.A., Northeastern U., 1966; m. Arklay S. Richards, Nov. 28, 1928 (div. 1942); children—Whitman Albin, Lincoln Kempton, Sylvia Caroline; m. 2d, Harry Troutwine, May 3, 1945 (div. 1954); m. 3d, Charles McCrum, 1961 (div. 1966); m. 4th, Lester Lewis Walsh, Feb. 16, 1968 (div. 1972); m. 5th, George Braun, Feb. 6, 1975 (dec. Oct. 1975). Pvt. sec. to pres. Hygrade Sylvania Electric Corp., Salem, Mass., 1927-28; pvt. and dept. exec. sec. Dr. Stanley Cobb, Bullard prof. neuropathology Harvard Med. Sch., 1928-31; part-time work, various positions, 1931-51; exec. dir. Postgrad. Med. Inst., 1951-57; mgr. Postgrad. Info. Service, Lederle Labs. div. Am. Cyanamid Co., Pearl River, N.Y., 1957-61; exec. sec. postgrad. med. edn. Hahnemann Med. Coll. and Hosp., also exec. dir. Mary Bailey Inst. Cardiovascular Research, Phila., 1961; high sch. counselor; instr. psychology Holliston High Sch., 1965-66, Falmouth (Mass.) High Sch., 1966-74; psychotherapist Hallgarth Assocs., 1974-75, Friends of Framingham Reformatory; pastor Internat. Ch. Ageless Wisdom, 1982—; speaker for Am. Epilepsy League. Mem. Simmons Coll. Alumnae Assn., Mass. Psychol. Assn., Am. Assn. Psychical Research, Spiritual Frontiers Fellowship (life), NEA (life), States Med. Postgrad. Assn. (past sec.), Am. Assn. Med. Soc. Execs. (emeritus), Mass. Tchrs. Assn. (life), Nat. Ret. Tchrs. Assn. (life), Nat. Sch. Counselors Assn. (life and charter), Soc. Mayflower Descs. (life), Assn. Research and Enlightenment, World Fedn. Healing, Interface, North Falmouth Village Civic Assn. (life), Am. Spiritual Healing Assn. (advisory bd.). Author articles in field. Home: Carleton Village F-83 100 Old Billerica Rd Bedford MA 01730

TROWBRIDGE, NORMA THOMSEN, educator; b. Audubon, Iowa, Oct. 8, 1921; d. Christian W. and Elena (Jensen) Thomsen; B.S., U. Iowa, 1959; M.S., Drake U., 1961; Ph.D., Iowa State U., 1962; m. Charles Lambert Trowbridge, Mar. 18, 1944; children—Brett Carleton, Lisa Katherine. Instr. Iowa State U., 1961-62; asst. prof. to asso. prof. Drake U., 1962-70; asso. prof. U. Va., 1970-72, Grand View Coll., 1972-79; dir. research Project on retirement and aging, Ann Arbor, Mich., 1979—. Disting. Scholar lectr., 1965, 68; Fulbright-Hays grantee, 1967; Title III grantee, 1966-70. Mem. Am. Psychol. Assn., Am. Statis. Assn., Am. Ednl. Research Assn., NEA, Iowa Edn. Assn., Soc. Research in Child Devel., AAUW, United Ch. Women. Mem. United Ch. of Christ. Contbr. articles to profl. jours. Home and Office: 1126 Warrington Dr Ann Arbor MI 48103

TROY, JANE CAROLYN, govt. ofcl.; b. Washington, Nov. 11, 1935; d. John and Allene (Parry) T.; With Overseas Pvt. Investment Corp., Washington, 1966—, dep. dir., now regional mgr. Europe/Middle East/Africa, Asia, Internat. div. Office: 1129 20th St NW Washington DC 20527

TROYANOS, TATIANA, mezzo soprano; b. N.Y.C., Sept. 12, 1938; d. Nickolas and Hildagod (Langera) Troyanos; diploma Juilliard Sch. Music. Debut N.Y.C. Opera, 1963; singer operas in Hamburg, Berlin, and Munich, Ger., Vienna and Salzburg, Austria, Milan, Rome, Florence and Palermo, Italy, Paris and Strasbourg, France, also London, 1965-75; debut Met. Opera, 1975, San Francisco Opera; prin. roles include Carmen, Marriage of Figaro, Dido in Bluebeard's Castle; rec. artist. Juilliard Alumnae scholar. Office: care Columbia Artists Mgmt Inc 165 W 57th St New York NY 10019 *

TROYER, LOIS JEAN, computer scientist; b. Anderson, Ind., Feb. 7, 1935; d. Leonard Maxwell and Mildred Virginia (Ashby) Newman; B.S., Ball State U., 1956; M.A., U. Colo., 1959; M.B.A., U. Chgo., 1978; m. Bryce Duane Troyer, Feb. 6, 1965. Physicist, Nat. Bur. Standards, Boulder, Colo., 1961-66; sci. programmer Dow Chem. Co., Midland, Mich., 1966-68; asst. computer scientist high energy physics Argonne (Ill.) Nat. Lab., 1969-74, computer scientist, 1974-79, head User Services Central Computing Facility, 1979-81; mgr. Dunhill of Joliet (Ill.), 1981—. Mem. masters swim team YMCA. Mem. Assn. Computing Machinery, Data Processing Mgmt. Assn., Am. Phys. Soc., IEEE, Am. Contract Bridge League. Home: 516 Tana Ln Joliet IL 60435

TROYKA, LYNN QUITMAN, educator; b. Phila., Feb. 21, 1938; d. Sidney L. and Belle (Furman) Q.; B.A., Brandeis U., 1959; M.A., N.Y. U., 1960, Ph.D., 1973; m. David Troyka, Aug. 13, 1965. Tchr., Hastings-on-Hudson (N.Y.) Public Schs., 1960-63; tchr., head jr. high div. Baldwin Sch., N.Y.C., 1963-67; instr. dept. basic ednl. skills Queensborough Community Coll., City U. N.Y., 1967-69, asst. prof., 1969-72, asso. prof., 1972-76, prof., 1976—, supr. writing skills program, dep. dept. chmn., 1967-75; prof. Center for Advanced Study in Edn., City U. N.Y., 1975-78, research asso. Office Acad. Affairs, Bd. Higher Edn., 1980—; cons. The Coll. Bd., 1972-79, N.Y. State Regents, 1978-80, Nat. Endowment Humanities, 1980-81, Nat. Inst. Edn., 1978—, Nat. Assessment of Ednl. Progress, 1980—; chmn. N.E. Regional Conf. on English in 2-Year Coll., 1974-76. Mem. Nat. Council Tchrs. English (dir. 1979-82, exec. com. 1980—), MLA, Conf. Coll. Composition and Communication (chmn. 1979-82), N.Y. State English Council, Internat. Reading Assn. Author: Steps in Composition, 1970, 5th edit., 1982; An A Posteriori Study of the Writing Assessment Test, CUNY, 1982; Taking Action: Writing, Reading, Speaking, and Listening Through Simulation-Games, 1975; A Strategy for Coping with High School and College Remedial English Problems, 1977; Structured Reading, 1978, 2d edit., 1983; editor: Guide to Writing, 1974; two-year coll. editor Freshman English News, 1973-75; editorial bd. Teaching English in the Two-Year College, 1978—; Simulation/Gaming: Jour. of Experiential Learning, 1977-79; columnist English in the Two-Yr. Coll., 1982—. Home: 166-25 Powells Cove Blvd Beechhurst NY 11357 Office: Queensborough Community Coll Bayside NY 11364

TRUAX, MARILYN JULIA SWIFT, educator; b. Cin., Dec. 12, 1940; d. William Henry and Marion Searcy Swift; B.A., U. Ky., 1963; 1 son, William Edward. Tchr. elem. sch., Jefferson County, Ky., 1963—; tchr. Fern Creek Elem. Sch., Louisville, 1969—. Pres., Woodhaven Swim Assn., 1976; bd. dirs. local PTA, 1975-80; mem. chancel choir, asst. dir. pre-sch. choir Walnut Street Baptist Ch. Mem. NEA, Ky. Edn. Assn., Jefferson County Tchrs. Assn. (dir. 1977-79), Ky. Bus. and Profl. Women's Club, Derbytown Bus. and Profl. Women's Club (pres. 1966), Zeta Tau Alpha. Democrat. Club: Woodhaven Country. Home: 9043 Fern Creek Rd Louisville KY 40291 Office: 8073 Fern Dale Rd Louisville KY 40291

TRUAX, SUZY, office complex and secretarial service exec.; b. Reno, Dec. 10, 1939; d. James A. and J. Sue (Hawkins) Smith; A.A. in Bus., Truckee Meadows Community Coll., 1977; m. Ralph Truax, Sept. 27, 1958; children—Coleen Sue, Kevin Todd. Asst. sales mgr. Western div. Banker & Taylor Co., 1968-70; spl. edn. tchrs. asst. Washoe County Sch. Dist., Reno, 1970-75; exec. sec. Heppner & Crofoot, C.P.A.s, 1975-79; sec. to mng. partner Alexander Grant Co., Reno, 1980; owner, operator The Exec. Center, Reno, 1980—. Mem. Reno-Sparks C. of C., Am. Bus. Women's Assn. (past pres. Washoe Zephyrs chpt.), Profl. Assn. Secretarial Services. Democrat. Home: 1070 Foothill Rd Reno NV 89511 Office: 1325 Airmotive Way 1975 Reno NV 89502

TRUCANO, JO ANN, state legislator; b. Early, Iowa, Aug. 30, 1943; d. Joe and Delores Determan; student Iowa State U.; m. Allen Trucano, 1961; children—Suzanne, James, Kathryn, Deanna. With Massey Ferguson-Foam Molding, Des Moines; now mem. Iowa Ho. of Reps. Active Holy Trinity Parish; mem. Bishop's Steering Com. for Women on Justice; active Boy Scouts Am., Girl Scouts U.S.A., camp dir. Mem. Des Moines Panhellenic Assn. (scholarship chmn.). Republican. Office: Iowa State House Des Moines IA 50319

TRUE, MARION (MRS. LAURENCE M. TRUE), civic worker; b. Franklin, N.H., Feb. 16, 1902; d. Ichabod S. and Mary K. (Dunlap) Williams; B.S. in Chemistry, U. N.H., 1923; m. Laurence M. True, Sept. 3, 1927 (dec.); children—Lavinia (Mrs. Paul H. Plough, Jr.), David, Gilbert, Melbern, Katharine (Mrs. Douglas Logan). Tchr. Sanborn Sem., 1923-24, Braintree High Sch., 1924-27. Active Cleve. Girl Scouts, 1942-69, mem. bd. dirs., mem. regional com., 1951-61, mem. group services council, 1943-61, vice chmn., 1943-58, mem. exec. bd., 1955-58; mem. personnel com. Welfare Fedn. of Cleve., 1954-56; mem. Com. on Older Persons; chmn. Com. on Homes for Aged; alumni dir. U. N.H., 1964-70; pres. Aux. Bapt. Home Ohio; trustee, house chmn., sec. of bd., co-chmn. gift shop Judson Park, chmn. work com. Aux., 1973—; trustee First Baptist Ch., 1958-61, 64-70, 74-76, vice chmn. bd., 1975, chmn. bd., 1976, mem. cabinet, 1970-73, 74-77, stewardship com., 1972—. Recipient Alumni Meritorious award 1961; Thanks badge, Lake Erie Girl Scouts. Mem. Nat. Soc. New Eng. Women (pres. Cleve. colony, v.p.) New Eng. Soc. Western Res. Daus. Am. Colonists (v.p.), ASME (woman's aux.), D.A.R., Alpha Xi Delta. Clubs: College (pres., dir.); Canterbury Golf. Home: Jordan-Gardner Tower 2181 Ambleside Rd Cleveland OH 44106

TRUGMAN, RIVA GERTRUDE, educator; b. Bklyn., July 20, 1940; d. Jacob and Netty (Mlotek) Yonks; B.A., Hunter Coll., 1961; M.A., Bklyn. Coll., 1964; postgrad. Montclair State Coll., 1975-77; m. Leonard Trugman, Nov. 22, 1964; children—Jonathon Marc, Robyn Beth. Substitute tchr. N.Y.C. Public Schs., 1961-62, tchr., Bklyn., 1962-66; pvt. practice ednl./learning disability therapy, Ridgewood, N.J., 1971—; cons. No. Valley Regional High Sch., 1980-81; lectr.; cons. editor Clarence Barnhart Pubs. Let's Look at A,B,Cs, 1976, 78. Mem. Orton Soc., Assn. Children with Learning Disabilities, Assn. Learning Cons., Bergen County Speech and Hearing Soc. Jewish. Clubs: Sociology (sec.), B'nai B'rith (pres. 1972-73).

TRUITT, MARY ELLEN, social services adminstr.; b. Madison, Ind., Mar. 19, 1953; d. Herman E. and Rozella (Allen) Hoffman; B.A. in Recreation and Phys. Edn., Purdue U., 1974; m. John Marshall Truitt, Apr. 26, 1975. Counselor, Happening Day Camp, Ind. Extension Service, Marion County, 1975, community devel. program asst., 1975-76, asst. dir. Happening Day Camp, summer, 1976; extension agt.-youth, Hamilton County (Ind.), Noblesville, 1976—, coordinator 4-H Adult Leaders Orgn., Hamilton County, 1976—; supr. Hamilton County 4-H Jr. Leader Orgn.; mem. com. Spl. Services Bur. of Hamilton County, 1979-80; supr. Hamilton County 4-H programs, since 1976—. Recipient Bob Amick award Ind. 4-H Found., 1979; named Outstanding Young Woman, Noblesville Jaycees, 1981. Mem. Nat. Assn. Extension Agts., Ind. Assn. Extension Agts., West Central Camping Assn. (dir. 1978—), Ind. 4-H Found. Roman Catholic. Home: 204 Valley Farm Ct Noblesville IN 46060 Office: 2003 E Pleasant St Noblesville IN 46060

TRUITT-BEAN, GAYLE ARDEN, educator; b. Worthington, Ohio, Nov. 23, 1952; d. John Thomas and Phyllis Ann (Henderson) Truitt; A.B., DePauw U., 1974; M.A. in Athletic Adminstrn., Kent State U., 1979; m. Terrance S. Bean, Dec. 15, 1979. Tchr. math. Bainbridge (Ind.) Elem. Sch., 1974-77; asst. coach women's gymnastics Kent (Ohio) State U., 1977-79; instr., head coach women's gymnastics Clarion (Pa.) State Coll., 1979—; chmn. Eastern Region Div. I Gymnastics Results; chmn. gymnastics com. Pa. State Athletic Conf. Mem. Nat. Assn. Collegiate Gymnastics Coaches/Women, U.S. Gymnastics Fedn., Assn. Pa. State Coll. and Univ. Faculties, Mortar Bd., Phi Beta Kappa, Kappa Delta Pi, Phi Epsilon Kappa, Delta Gamma. Republican. Methodist. Home: Route 1 Strattanville PA 16258 Office: 109 Tippin Gym Clarion State Coll Clarion PA 16214

TRUJILLO, LINDA ANN, computerized adminstrv. services exec.; b. Tulsa, Dec. 28, 1947; d. William C. Lagoni and Mildred A. (Campbell) Wasson; student Coll. Marin, 1965-66, Calif. State U., Long Beach, 1978-82, Calif. State U., Dominiquez Hills, 1978-81; m. Allen H. Trujillo, Jan. 25, 1976; children—Rand B., Allison J., Shawn A., Curtis G. Adminstrv. asst. Kaiser Hosp., Bellflower, Calif., 1976-78; emergency services coordinator City of Long Beach, 1978, supr., 1978-79, mgr./adminstr. Emergency Communications Center, 1979-81; owner, mgr. Exec. Word Systems, Santa Ana, Calif., 1981—; mgmt. cons. Pub. Research Corp., 1982—. Mem. Nat. Assn. Female Execs., WeCan Women's Network, Nat. Notary Assn. Republican. Adventist. Club: Racquetball World Health. Office: 920 W 17th St Suite C Santa Ana CA 92706 also 18700 Beach Blvd Suite 230 Huntington Beach CA 92648

TRULUCK, JANE ANN, civic worker; b. Dallas, Sept. 8, 1925; d. Marshall and Ruth Selwyn (Holliday) McIlhenny; A.A., Edinburg Jr. Coll., 1944; m. John Hinds Truluck, Sept. 25, 1944; children—Janet Ellen, Marsha Joyce, John Marshall, Peggy Ruth. Sec., John H. Truluck Jr., Architect, 1948-56; sec., admitting sec. Colleton Regional Hosp., Walterboro, S.C., 1960-65, sec. vocat. rehab., 1965-66. Hostess, Welcome Wagon, Walterboro, 1974-80; chmn. fund raising Colleton County Cancer Assn.; mem. health adv. com. Low Country Dist. Home; leader Girl Scouts U.S.A.; past bd. dirs. Colleton County Library; v.p. adminstrv. bd. Bethel Meth. Ch., chmn. pastor-parish relations com. 1979, 82; lay del. S.C. Meth. Conf., 1979, 80; v.p. United Meth. Women, pres., 1980—; trustee Greenwood (S.C.) Meth Home, 1980—. Clubs: Woman's (pres.) (Walterboro); Magnolia Garden (pres.). Home: 309 Woodlawn Dr Walterboro SC 29488

TRUMAN, RUTH, writer, lectr., cons.; b. Ashland, Ky., Oct. 5, 1931; d. Rexford Maitland and Allene G. (Barber) Dixon; B.S., Taylor U., 1952; M.S., Calif. State U., 1967; Ph.D. in Higher Edn., UCLA, 1978; m. Wallace Lee Truman, June 5, 1952; children—Mark, Rebecca, Timothy, Nathan. Tchr. Acton (N.J.) Elem. Sch., 1954; tchr. home econs. Chatham (N.J.) High Sch., 1955; counselor, instr. Citrus Coll., Azusa, Calif., 1967-70; dir. counseling Calif. Luth. Coll., Thousand Oaks, Calif., 1971-74; cons. Women's Ednl. Improvement Program, Los Angeles, 1978-80; women's center facilitator Mt. San Antonio Coll., Walnut, Calif., 1981-82; free-lance writer, lectr., cons., 1982—. Trustee Baker Home for Ret. Ministers, Rowland Heights, Calif., 1982—; chmn. Com. Status and Role of Women, Pacific and Southwest Conf., United Meth. Ch., 1980-82; mem. exec. com. Ventura County Council Drug Abuse, 1972-73. Mem. NOW, UCLA Doctoral Assn., Phi Delta Kappa. Democrat. Methodist. Author: How To Be A Liberated Christian, 1981; Mission of the Church College, 1978; Underground Manual for Ministers' Wives and Other Bewildered Women, 1974. Home: 13751 E Philadelphia St Whittier CA 90601

TRUMBO, REDA MAY, motel exec.; b. Braddock Hills, Pa., May 4, 1938; d. Kenneth Keith and Elizabeth Eleanora (Klein) Ellis; R.N., Presbyterian Hosp. Sch. Nursing, 1959; m. Philip Walter Trumbo, Oct. 19, 1962; children—Susan Elizabeth, Walter Ray, Rebecca Ruth. Staff nurse Presbyterian Hosp., Pitts., 1959-60; operating room nurse Children's Hosp., Pitts., 1960-61, Children's Hosp., Denver, 1961-62, Swedish Hosp., Englewood, Colo., 1962-64; co-owner Best Western Red Arrow Motel, Montrose, Colo., 1964—. Active monthly community breakfast program, Montrose. Mem. Montrose Motel Assn. (pres. 1980-81), Colo.-Wyo. Hotel-Motel Assn. Republican. Presbyterian. Clubs: Christian Women's (dir. 1977-78, 80-81, v.p. women's resource center 1980-81), Altrusa of Montrose (dir. 1975-77). Address: PO Box 236 Montrose CO 81401

TRUSCOTT, ADELE ELIZA, banker; b. Salt Lake City, Dec. 4, 1935; d. Earl R. and Eliza (Holley) Groneman; m. Kenneth D. Truscott, Mar. 26, 1954; children—Kathryn, Christina, Marcus. With Continental Bank and Trust Co., Salt Lake City, 1955—, ops. officer, 1974—, asst. v.p., br. mgr., 1976—. Mem. Nat. Assn. Bank Women (chpt. pres. 1980, Utah State Council pres. 1982-83), Ladies of the Guard (pres. 1971). Office: 6940 Highland Dr Salt Lake City UT 84121

TRUSCOTT, DOROTHY HAYDEN, bridge player; b. N.Y.C., Nov. 3, 1925; d. Reginald Lee and Dorothy (Maloney) Johnson; student Smith Coll., 1943-46; B.A., Western Mich. Coll., 1947; m. 3d, Alan F. Truscott, Apr., 1972; children by previous marriage—Catherine Lee Hayden, James Brian Hayden, Margaret Hayden Cooke, Bobette Hayden. Winner Nat. Comml. Teams, 1958, Nat. Women's Pairs, 1959, 61, 66, Nat. Mixed Pairs, 1959, Masters Pairs, 1962, Nat. Blue Ribbon Pairs, 1963, Nat. Life Masters Pairs, 1964, Nat. Women's Teams, 1967, 70, 72, 74, 76; rep. U.S. in Olympiad, 1960, 68, 72-76, in World Women's Pairs, 1962, 74, in World Open Pairs, 1966; rep. N.Am. in Bermuda Bowl Championships, 1965; winner for U.S., Venice Trophy, 1974, 76, 78; grand master. Ranked top woman bridge player in world. Mem. Westchester (bd. dirs. 1965-69), Greater N.Y. (bd. dirs. 1974-77) bridge assns., N.Y. Cavendish Club (dir. 1960-65). Author: Bid Better, Play Better, 1965; Winning Declarer Play, 1968; (with Alan Truscott) Teach Yourself Basic Bidding, 1976.

TRYON, GEORGIANA SHICK, psychologist; b. Glendale, Calif., Mar. 28, 1945; d. Norman Alton and Nancy Emily (Shaffer) Shick; B.A., P. State U., 1966; M.A., Kent State U., 1969, Ph.D., 1971; m. Warren W. Tryon, July 31, 1970; 1 dau., Elizabeth. Psychologist to outpatients, clin. instr. psychology N.Y. Hosp., N.Y.C., 1971-72; dir. Counseling Center Fordham U. Lincoln Center, N.Y.C., 1972-75, Bronx, N.Y., 1975—; pvt. practice psychology, Scarborough, N.Y., 1973—. NDEA fellow, 1966-69. Mem. Am. Psychol. Assn., Eastern Psychol. Assn., N.Y. State Psychol. Assn., Assn. Advancement of Behavior Therapy, Nat. Assn. Women Deans Counselors and Adminstrs., Sigma Xi. Lutheran. Contbr. articles in field to profl. jours. Home: 11 Country Club Ln Scarborough NY 10510 Office: Fordham University Bronx NY 10458

TSAI, ELIZABETH TAN, lawyer; b. Roxas City, Philippines, Nov. 6, 1940; naturalized U.S. citizen, 1973; d. Vicente Robles and Rosario (Gonzaga) Tan; A.A. with honors, U. Philippines, Iloilo City, 1958; B.S. in Jurisprudence, LL.B. (Coll. of Law Golden Jubilee scholar), 1962; LL.M. (Univ. fellow), Yale U., 1965; m. Nien-Tszr Tsai, Dec. 2, 1967; children—Pearl Tan, Andrew Tan. Admitted to Philippine bar, 1963, Calif. bar, 1973, D.C. bar, 1974; assoc. firm SyCip, Salazar, Luna & Assocs., Manila, 1963-64; editor Lawyers Coop. Pub. Co., Rochester, N.Y., 1965-71; individual practice law, San Diego, 1973-74; atty.-adv. Div. Investment Mgmt., SEC, Washington, 1977-81, spl. counsel, 1981—. Democrat. Mem. Chinese Christian Ch. Recent decisions editor Philippine Law Jour., 1961-62; assoc. editor Philippine Internat. Law Jour., 1963-64. Office: 450 5th St Washington DC 20549

TSAKONAS, FRANCES ADELE, psychologist; b. Bronx, N.Y., Jan. 16, 1941; d. Philip and Ethel (Zeltzer) Krupp; B.A. cum laude with honors in Psychology, CCNY, 1970, Ph.D., 1976; postdoctoral study N.Y. U., 1976—. Teaching fellow CUNY, 1970-74; psychol. tester Little Red Schoolhouse, N.Y.C., 1972-74; psychologist inpatient psychiat. unit VA Hosp., N.Y.C., 1974-75, psychologist outpatient psychiat. div., 1975-76; clin. dir. comprehensive drug abuse program Coney Island Hosp., Bklyn., 1976—; pvt. practice, 1978—. Organizer tutorial program No. Student Movement, Balt., 1962-64. Cert. psychologist, N.Y. State. Mem. Am. Psychol. Assn., Phi Beta Kappa, Psi Chi. Home: 113 E 30th St New York NY 10016

TSANGARIS, KALLY J., bank tng. ofcl.; b. Gary, Ind., May 2, 1952; d. John Michael and Mary S. (Kolettis) T.; B.A. in Secondary Edn. and Spanish, Valparaiso U., 1974; M.A. in Secondary Edn. and Spanish, Purdue U., 1979. High sch. Spanish tchr. Crown Point (Ind.) Community Schs., 1974-79; customer service rep. Gary, (Ind.) Nat. Bank, 1979-80, tng. coordinator, Merrillville, Ind., 1980—. Mem. Am. Inst. Banking (instr.). Home: 2360 W 64th Ave Merrillville IN 46410 Office: 8585 Broadway Merrillville IN 46410

TSE, DAPHNE CHIU-FUN, biochemist; b. Hong Kong, Mar. 11, 1939; came to U.S., 1958, naturalized, 1971; d. Kwong Chiu and Yee Wan (Choy) Hui; B.S., UCLA, 1962; m. Tim Tse, Feb. 1, 1964; children—Anthony, Eric. With Hyland Therapeutics div. Travenol Labs., Inc., Glendale, Calif., 1963—, sr. research scientist, 1979-81, research mgr., 1981—. Recipient Inventor's award Baxter Travenol Co., 1979. Mem. Am. Chem. Soc. Methodist. Author articles in field; patentee in field. Office: 444 W Glenoaks Blvd Glendale CA 91202

TSUBOKAWA, AMY, educator; b. Arcadia, Calif., Jan. 10, 1933; d. Seki and Shizue (Miyasaki) Sakamoto; A.A., Cerritos Coll., 1965; B.A., Whittier Coll., 1967; M.A., Coll. St. Thomas, 1980; m. John H. Tsubokawa; children—M. Patricia Reeves, Sandra Whittall, Roger, Lori Williams. Tchr., Norwalk-La Mirada Unified Sch. Dist., 1970—. Mem. Calif. Tchrs. Assn., NEA, Mid-Cities Reading Council. Republican. Presbyterian. Home: 20922 Callaway Ave Lakewood CA 90715 Office: 13510 S Maidstone Ave Norwalk CA 90650

TSUI, PAULINE WOO, ret. govt. ofcl., program dir.; b. Nanking, China, Oct. 2, 1920; d. John Y. and Sarah K. Woo; B.A., St. John's U., 1943; M.A., Columbia U., 1947; m. Tswen Ling Tsui, July 26, 1947; children—Lynnette Tsui Lee, Garrick C.Y. Geographic names specialist Army Map Service, Washington, 1951-62; cartographer Def. Mapping Agy. Hydrographic Topographic Center, Washington, 1963-75, tech. info. specialist, 1975-76, equal employment opportunity specialist, Fed. Women's Program mgr., 1976-80; project dir. Chinese Am. Women Ednl. Equity Program, 1981—. Mem. D.C. adv. com. to U.S. Civil Rights Commn., 1974-78; founding dir. Brookmont Learning Tree Child Care Center, 1979—; bd. dirs. Nat. Com. for Responsive Philanthropy, 1980. Mem. Orgn. Chinese Am. Women (founding nat. pres. 1977—), Fedn. Orgns. for Profl. Women (mem. exec. council 1980). Democrat. Presbyterian.

TUCHMAN, BARBARA WERTHEIM, writer; b. N.Y.C., Jan. 30, 1912; d. Maurice and Alma (Morgenthau) Wertheim; B.A., Radcliffe Coll., 1933; D.Litt., Yale U., Columbia U., others; m. Lester R. Tuchman, 1940; children—Lucy, Jessica, Alma. Research asst. Inst. Pacific Relations, N.Y.C., 1934, Tokyo, 1935; editorial asst. The Nation, N.Y.C., 1936, Spain, 1937; staff writer War in Spain, London, 1937-38; Am. corr. New Statesman and Nation, London, 1939; with Far East news desk OWI, N.Y.C., 1944-45; mem. Smithsonian council, 1971—. Jefferson lectr., 1980. Trustee, Radcliffe Coll., 1960-72. Recipient Order of Leopold 1st class (Belgium). Fellow AAAL (pres. 1979—, Gold medal for history 1978), Am. Acad. Arts and Scis.; mem. Authors Guild (treas.), Authors League (council), Soc. Am. Historians (pres. 1974-76). Club: Cosmopolitan. Author: The Lost British Policy, 1938; Bible and Sword, 1956; The Zimmerman Telegram, 1958; The Guns of August (Pulitzer prize 1963), 1962; The Proud Tower, 1966; Stilwell and the American Experience in China, 1911-45 (Pulitzer prize 1972), 1971; Notes from China, 1972; A Distant Mirror, 1978; Practising History, 1981. Contbr. to Fgn. Affairs, Atlantic Monthly, Am. Heritage, Harper's, N.Y. Times, others. Office: care Russell & Volkening 551 Fifth Ave New York NY 10176

TUCHMAN, PHYLLIS, art critic, art historian; b. Passaic, N.J., Jan. 4, 1947; d. Jack and Evelyn (Sugarman) T.; B.A. with distinction in Fine Arts, Boston U., 1968; M.A., Inst. Fine Arts, N.Y.U., 1973, postgrad., 1973—. Instr., Sch. Visual Arts, N.Y.C., 1972-75; lectr. Hunter Coll., City U. N.Y., 1976-79; art critic, art historian, 1968—; lectr. mus. and univs. including: Detroit Inst. Arts, Los Angeles County Mus. Art, Brown U., 1978—; vis. fellow Princeton U., 1980; Robert Stirling Clarke vis. lectr. Williams Coll., 1981, 82; contbr. articles, revs. and interviews to jours. including Art in Am., Artforum, Art News, Drawing, Marsyas. Nat. Endowment for Arts grantee, 1978-79: Nat. Endowment for Humanities grantee, 1980. Mem. Internat. Assn. Art Critics, Coll. Art Assn. Editor: Sculptors Writings, 1945-70, 1983; author mus. exhbn. catalogues. Home and office: 340 E 80th St New York NY 10021

TUCKER, BARBARA (BEBE LOU MUEHLE) (MRS. RICHARD WALTER TUCKER), arts patron, fashion cons.; b. Des Moines; d. Louis John and Harriett (Shilke) Muehle; student Drake U. Music Sch., Acad. Nvart, Detroit, Center Creative Studies, Detroit, Birmingham-Bloomfield Art Assn.; B.S., Iowa State U.; m. Richard Walter Tucker; 1 dau., Pamela Helen. Fashion writer W.T. Grant, N.Y.C., 1946-47, Kresge Newark, Newark, 1947-50, Best & Co., N.Y.C., 1950-51; millinery designer Chez Nous, Detroit, 1954-57; instr. fashion design Detroit Bd. Edn., 1960-63; fashion lectr. John Robert Powers Sch., Detroit, 1965-68; fashion coordinator Armo Co. of N.Y., 1968-72, Hoechst Fibers, 1972-75; v.p. Richard Tucker & Co., Detroit, 1969—; pres. Barbara Tucker Assos., 1967—. Mem. Met. Opera Com., Detroit, 1962—; charter mem. Am. Symphony Orch. League Vol. Council, nat. pres., 1971-73, instr. mgmt. course, 1975, 76; pres. Detroit Symphony League, 1957, hon. mem. Women's Assn. Detroit Symphony Orch., 1960—, pres., 1963, bd. dirs. Orch., 1969—; bd. dirs. Women's com. Am. Lung Assn., 1967—, Women's Com. for Project Hope, 1966—; trustee Nat. Guild Community Schs. Arts, 1976—; mem. nat. women's bd. Northwood Inst., 1972—; bd. dirs. Am. Symphony Orch. League, 1971-73; bd. dirs. Mich. Orch. Assn., 1976, state pres., 1977—. Mem. Am., Mich. home econs. assns., Founders Soc. Detroit Inst. Arts, Fashion Group Detroit (sec. 1973—), Internat. Platform Assn., Alpha Gamma Delta. Home: 3335 Burning Bush Rd Birmingham MI 48010

TUCKER, BARBARA HARTMAN, pub. relations exec.; b. Hartford, Conn., July 19, 1942; d. Howard Lowell and Mildred Janet (Deady) Hartman; A.A., Briarcliff Coll., 1962; B.S., Rollins Coll., 1964; m. William Quoos Tucker, Dec. 16, 1967; children—Garrett Todd, Lisa Kristan. Tchr., Hartford Pub. Schs., 1965-66; legis. and exec. asst. Conn. Conf. Mayors, 1967; dir., pres., pub. relations spokeperson Shame, Inc., West Hartford, Conn., 1971—; pub. relations lobbyist for Glass Constructors, Inc., 1973-75. Drafter, Endangered Species Bill, State of Conn., 1973; coordinator Worldwide Endangered Species List, 1977; mem. campaign exec. com. Town Council, 1971-73; co-chmn. goods and services com. ann. auction Conn. Pub. TV; treas. campaign com. Ho. of Reps., 1972; gubernatorial campaign chmn., 1974, 77-78; mem. 7th Dist. Republican Com., 1974—; spl. asst. to asst. minority leader Conn. Senate, 1978-79, adminstrv. asst. to dep. minority leader, 1979-80, spl. asst. to senate minority leader, 1980—, also press. sec. Rep. Caucus; mem. Conn. steering com. Reagan for Pres., 1980; sec., mem. exec. bd. West Hartford Rep. Women's Club, 1975-77, 1st v.p., 1977-78, pres., chmn. exec. bd., 1978-79. Episcopalian. Home: 42 Lostbrook Rd West Hartford CT 06117

TUCKER, CAROLYN MAXCINE, clin. psychologist, educator; b. Nottoway, Va., Nov. 17, 1950; d. Thomas Lee and Arethea Elizabeth (Booker) T.; B.S. in Psychology and Guidance summa cum laude (Presdl. scholar), N.C. Agrl. and Tech. State U., 1971; cert. research fellow Howard U., summer 1969, U. S.C., Columbia, summer 1970; Ph.D. in Clin. Psychology, SUNY, Stony Brook, 1976; postgrad. psychology intern U. Fla., 1975-76. Research and parent-tchr. coordinator Univ. Child Devel. Lab., SUNY, Stony Brook, 1972, sex therapist, research program, 1974; part time cons. Bradford-Union Guidance Clinic, Lake Butler, Fla., 1975; part time pvt. practice therapy, Gainesville, Fla., 1976—; asst. prof. dept. behavioral studies U. Fla., Gainesville, 1976-79, counseling center affiliate, 1977—, asso. prof. counseling psychology program, psychology dept., 1979—; co-host, clin. psychologist TV program The Black Family, Jacksonville, Fla., 1977—; part time cons. Westinghouse Health Systems, 1980—; mem. adminstrv. council U. Fla., 1980-81, senate nominating com., 1980-81, pres. Caucus of Black Faculty and Staff, 1978-79, mem. exec. bd., 1980-81, Black Caucus Task Force, 1980-81, minority students subcom. of Student Advisement Self-Study Com. for Univ. Reaccreditation, 1981-82; cons. Duval County Schs., Jacksonville, 1978, Mayor's Regional Conf. on Status of Women, Jacksonville, 1978, Overeaters Anonymous Orgn., Jacksonville, 1978; cons., condr. workshops for profl. assns., colls. and univs., ednl. groups, med. orgns. Fla., Washington, Ill., La., S.C. Advisor U. Fla. Student chpt. NOW, 1979—; active Mt. Olive African Meth. Episcopal Ch., Gainesville; co-founder first Black Women's Self Enrichment Group, U. Fla., 1977. Recipient Delta Sigma Theta scholarship award, 1969; Ford Found. research fellow, summers 1969, 70, NIMH fellow, 1972; summer research fellow Suffolk County Mental Health Dept., 1972; recipient community service awards including Jacksonville Urban League, 1978, bus. community Jacksonville, 1979, Assn. of Patients on Hemodialysis and Transplantation, 1980, So. Union of Churches, Gainesville, 1981; research assistantship award, U. Fla., 1980, faculty research award, 1980; tng.-research grantee Fla. Dept. Health and Rehabilitative Services, 1980-81, 81; cert. lic. clin. psychologist, Fla. Mem. Am. Psychol. Assn., Southeastern Psychol. Assn., Assn. of Women Faculty, Fla. Personnel and Guidance Assn., Am. Personnel and Guidance Assn., Fla. Assn. Non-white Concerns (chmn. constitution com. 1979-80), Soc. Ethnic and Spl. Studies (sec. 1980—), Washington Inst. for Behavior Therapy (dir., 1980—), Alpha Kappa Mu. Club: King David Lodge (Amelia chpt.). Co-author tng. manual Dept. of Health and Rehabilitative Services, Fla., 1980; editorial bd. Jour. Non-white Concerns, 1980—; contbr. chpt. to book, articles to profl. publs. Home: 5210 NW 24th Pl Gainesville FL 32601 Office: Dept of Psychology Univ Fla 253 Psychology Bldg Gainesville FL 32611

TUCKER, DAISY SNELLGROVE, ret. librarian; b. Pinckard, Ala., Dec. 11, 1912; d. LaFayette and Jessie (Bryant) Snellgrove; grad. Columbus (Ga.) City Hosp. Sch. Nursing, 1934; student U. Ga., 1952-67; m. William Clifford Tucker, Jan. 12, 1935 (dec. Apr. 1961); children—William Clifford, Frances. Librarian Ledger-Enquirer Newspapers, Columbus, Ga., 1952-75; book review editor Columbus Enquirer, 1954-75; head research dept. Ledger-Enquirer, 1952-75. Mem. Gov.'s Adv. Com. Mental Instns., 1959-62; bd. dirs. Muscogee Mental Health Assn., 1957-64; bd. dirs. Ga. Assn. Mental Health, sec., 1962. Recipient Cup of Hope award Georgia Assn. Mental Health, 1958. Mem. DAR. Baptist. Home: 1915 Wildwood Ave Columbus GA 31906 Office: Columbus Bank & Trust Co Bldg Columbus GA 31902

TUCKER, DIANE REESE, lawyer; b. Dauphin County, Pa., May 6, 1950; d. Charles Miller and June G. (Anderson) Reese; B.A., Pa. State U., 1971; J.D., U. Tenn., 1974; m. David Creighton Tucker, Dec. 3, 1977. Admitted to Pa. bar, Fla. bar, 1974; asso. firm Brennan, Robins & Daley, Pitts., 1974-76; law clk. Ct. Common Pleas, Allegheny County, Pa., 1976-77; pvt. practice law, Pitts., 1977; asso. arbitration rep. Westinghouse Electric Corp., Pitts., 1978-81. Bd. dirs. Women's Center & Shelter Greater Pitts., 1979-82. Mem. AAUW, Am. Bar Assn., Fla. Bar Assn., Pa. Bar Assn., Allegheny County Bar Assn., Exec. Women's Council Pitts., Phi Alpha Delta. Home: 1877 Stage Ct Allison Park PA 15101 Office: Baskin and Sears PC 10th Fl Frick Bldg Pittsburgh PA 15219

TUCKER, DOROTHY M., educator; b. Spartanburg, S.C., Aug. 22, 1942; d. James Anderson and Cleo Christine (Fant) T.; B.S., Bowling Green State U., 1963; M.Ed., U. Toledo, 1968; Ph.D., Ohio State U., 1972; Ph.D. in Psychology, Calif. Sch. Profl. Psychology, 1976. Coordinator psychiat. services Grad. Psychology Faculty, dir. clin. tng. Wright Inst., Los Angeles, 1978—, dir. clin. tng., clin. and cons. psychologist, 1979—; asso. prof. Charles R. Drew Postgrad. Med. Sch., Los Angeles, 1977-79; instr. dept. human devel. UCLA, 1974—; asso. prof. Fla. Internat. U., Miami, 1971-75. Chmn., bd. dirs. United Negro Coll. Fund; chmn. Black Women's Network, 1979—; spl. asst. to speaker Calif. Assembly, 1981—; mem. nat. continuation com. for Internat. Women's Year, 1977—; del. Calif. State Democratic Com., 1979; commr. Calif. Jud. Evaluation Rev. Commn., 1979-81; mem. Ingelwood Housing Commn., 1980—; bd. dirs. Kwanza Found., 1979—. Ford Found. fellow, 1964-65; NDEA fellow, 1967-68. Mem. Am. Psychol. Assn., Nat. Assn. Black Psychologists, Soc. Pediatric Psychology, Western Psychol. Assn., Assn. Behavioral Scientists, Nat. Women's Studies Assn., Black Women in Psychology (founder/convenor), Calif. State Psychol. Assn., Pi Lambda Theta. Contbr. articles to profl. jours. Home: 3500-29 W Manchester Blvd Inglewood CA 90305 Office: 1100 S Roberston Blvd Los Angeles CA 90305

TUCKER, ELEANOR DOROTHY, educator; b. Orange, N.J., Apr. 27, 1918; d. Andrew Noble and Velma Irene (Gwaltney) Tucker; A.B., Va. Union U., 1942; M.A., Columbia Tchrs. Coll., 1947, profl. diploma, 1950; postgrad. Temple U., 1951, U. Del., 1955-73. Prin., tchr. Prince Edward Elem. Sch., Rice, Va., 1942-43, Hadensville (Va.) Elem. Sch., 1943-46; tchr. Newport News (Va.) elem. schs., 1946-47; mem. faculty Rust Coll., Holly Springs, Miss., 1947-50, Miss. Vocat. Coll., Itta Bena, 1951-53, Morris Coll., Sumter, S.C., 1953-54; asst. prof. edn. William Henry High Sch., Dover, Del., 1954-66, Dover High Sch., 1966-82; asst. supr. migrant edn. State of Del., 1967; asst. supr. migrant edn. program Capital Sch. Dist., Dover, 1969—. Mem. AAUW, NEA, Capital Edn. Assn., Diamond State Reading Assn., LWV, Delta Kappa Gamma, Kappa Delta Pi, Alpha Kappa Alpha, Kappa Alpha. Mem. A.M.E. Ch. Club: Order Eastern Star.

TUCKER, EMMA SCOTT, vol. social worker, nurse, lectr.; b. Chgo., June 19, 1916; s. Reginald Frederic and Alice Ayling (Long) Scott; B.S., George Williams Coll., Chgo., 1941; postgrad. Columbia U., 1942, Highland Community Coll., Freeport, Ill., 1973, No. Ill. U., DeKalb, 1976—, Rockford Coll., 1978; m. Francis C. Tucker, June 14, 1941; children—Elizabeth Tucker Guntermann, Jean Marilyn Tucker Dean, Robert Francis, Joan Eloise Tucker-Sanford, John Frederick. Girls and women's recreation dir. George Williams Coll. Camp, Lake Geneva, Wis., 1938-40; asst. biology George Williams Coll., 1939-41; sec. health edn. Yonkers (N.Y.) YWCA, 1941-42; lab. asst. Pine Mountain (Ky.) Settlement Sch., 1942-43; social work vol. Girl Scouts Am., 1933—, sr. leader, 1958-78, internat. travel guide, lectr., 1955—; missionary, Taitung, Taiwan, Evangel. Alliance Mission, Logefeil Meml. Hosp., 1981—; adv. bd. Salvation Army Welfare, chmn., 1971, mem. bd., 1971-78, pres., 1976; deaconess, del. nat. conv. Park Hills Evangel. Free Ch., Freeport, Ill., 1970—; chmn. for Ill., also art chmn. Am. Mother's Com., 1972-78; Gr. Western Trail chmn. Jane Addamsland Park Fedn., 1974-78, dir., 1976—; sec. bd. Peatonica Prairie Path Soc., 1975—; mem. bd. Am. Field Services; mem. Ill. State-Blackhawk Resource Conservation and Devel. Council. Henry D. Steinhaus research scholar, 1940; recipient Thanks badge Girl Scouts Am., 1969, Disting. Alumnus award George Williams Coll., 1970, A.H. Steinhaus Alumnus of Yr. award, 1980; Disting. Citizenship award Elks Club, Freeport, 1970; named Ill. Mothers of Year, Am. Mothers Com., 1970. Mem. Ill., Stephenson County hist. socs., Am., Stephenson County med. aux., Kings Daus. and Sons Internat., Internat. Platform Assn., Photog. Soc. Am., Audubon Soc., Wilderness Soc., PEO, Chatauqua Lit. and Sci. Soc., Kappa Delta Pi. Republican. Address: 861 W Stephenson St Freeport IL 61032

TUCKER, FLORENCE DENSLOW, govt. ofcl.; b. Greenville, Miss., Nov. 12, 1925; d. Victor Amos and Martha Buchannan (Binkley) Denslow; diploma piano (scholarship 1943), Ward-Belmont Coll., Nashville, 1945; piano pupil of Michael Field, N.Y.C., 1945-46; B.Mus.Edn. (Dean's scholar 1958-60), Delta State U., Cleveland, Miss., 1960; M.S. in Counseling, U. So. Miss., 1971; Hattiesburg; Ed.D., George Washington U., 1982; m. Joseph Nathaniel Tucker, Jr., Nov. 9, 1946; children—Joseph Nathaniel, III, Frederick Steven, James Denslow. Tchr. music Gulfport (Miss.) public schs., 1959-63; recreation therapist VA Hosp., Gulfport, 1964-70; edn. counselor USAF, Miss. and Japan, 1971-74, edn. services officer, Korea, 1974-75, asst. dir. sr. tng. CAP nat. hdqrs., 1975-77; EEO officer D.C. Dept. Labor, 1977-80; bur. chief complaints processing and adjudication Office EEO, U.S. Geol. Survey, Reston, Va., 1980—; dir. Wake Assos., Ltd., mgmt. cons., Washington, 1980—; vis. prof. Kunsan (Korea) Tchrs. Coll., also Kunsan Jr. Coll., 1974-75; workshop leader, cons. in field. Organizer, pres. Gulfport chpt. Parents-Without-Partners, 1962-64; charter mem. Westminster Presbyn. Ch., Gulfport, 1961. Recipient Outstanding Vis. Prof. award Kunsan Tchrs. Coll., 1974, award promoting tchr. exchange program Kunsan Jr. Coll., 1975, also certs. commendation. Mem. AAAS, Am. Soc. Tng. and Devel., Women in Communication, Nat. Assn. Female Execs., Adult Edn. Assn., Am. Soc. Profl. and Exec. Women, Soc. Internat. Devel., Phi Delta Kappa. Clubs: Gulfport Yacht, Bayou View Country (Gulfport). Contbr. articles to profl. jours. Home: 4701 Kenmore Ave Apt 1310 Alexandria VA 22304 Office: Nat Center MS 116 US Geol Survey Sunrise Valley Dr Reston VA 22092

TUCKER, HARRIET EVELYN, lawyer; b. Albany, N.Y., July 21, 1944; d. Charles Marshall and Genevieve Evelyn (Owens) T.; B.A., SUNY, Albany, 1966; postgrad. Howard U., 1966-67; J.D., Albany Law Sch., 1970. Admitted to D.C. bar, 1972; law clk. Hon. Norma H. Johnson, D.C. Superior Ct., 1970-72; contract compliance officer Law Enforcement Assistance Adminstrn., Dept. Justice, 1972-73; regional counsel U.S. Commn. Civil Rights, So. Regional Office, Atlanta, 1973-75; expert cons. Legal Services Corp., Washington, 1975-76; asst. to gen. counsel NSF, Washington, 1976—; spl. asst. to univ. counsel Cornell U., Ithaca, N.Y., 1982-83. Vice-pres. Nat. Teen Conf., 1976-78, bd. dirs., 1979-81. Recipient cash award NSF, 1981. Mem. Nat. Council Negro Women (v.p. membership 1977-78), Am. Bar Assn., D.C. Bus. and Profl. Women's Fedn. (chmn. scholarship com. 1979-81), Bar Assn. D.C. Mem. Ch. of God in Christ. Office: 1800 G St Rm 301 Washington DC 20550

TUCKER, HELEN WELCH, writer; b. Raleigh, N.C., Nov. 1, 1926; d. William Blair and Helen (Welch) T.; B.A., Wake Forest Coll., 1946; postgrad. Columbia U., 1957-58; m. William T. Beckwith, Jan. 9, 1971. Reporter, Burlington (N.C.) Times-News, 1946-47, Twin Falls (Idaho) Times-News, 1948-49, reporter Idaho Statesman, Boise, 1950-51; copy writer Sta. KDYL, Salt Lake City, 1952-53; copy supr. Sta. WPTF, Raleigh, 1953-55; reporter Raleigh Times, 1955-57; editorial asst. Columbia U. Press, 1959-60; dir. publicity and publications N.C. Mus. Art, Raleigh, 1967-70; author books: The Sound of Summer Voices, 1969, The Guilt of August Fielding, 1971, No Need of Glory, 1972, The Virgin of Lontano, 1973, A Strange and Ill-Starred Marriage, 1978, A Reason for Rivalry, 1979, A Mistress to the Regent, 1980, An Infamous Attachment, 1980, The Halverton Scandal, 1980, A Wedding Day Deception, 1981, The Double Dealers, 1982, Season of Dishonor, 1982. Recipient Disting. Alumni award in Journalism, Wake Forest U., 1971. Episcopalian. Home: 2930 Hostetler St Raleigh NC 27609

TUCKER, JEANNE HELEN, hosp. exec.; b. Chgo., Dec. 16, 1922; d. Andrew Jack and Mary Arintha (Gale) Laverty; B.S., U. Central Fla., 1973; widow; children—Terry R. McGee, Barbara Flynn. Asst. adminstr. W. Orange Meml. Hosp., Winter Garden, Fla., 1962-64, med. cons. Fla. Bur. Licensing and Certification, 1973-75; dir. regional data program Fla. Health Data Corp., 1978-79; dir. quality assessment Winter Park (Fla.) Meml. Hosp., 1979—; mem. tech. adv. com. Hosp. Cost Containment Bd., 1981—. Mem. Am. (pres. 1976-77), Southeastern (pres. 1970), Fla. (pres. 1965; Disting. Mem. award 1973) med. record assns., Fla. Hosp. Assn., Assn. Health Care Quality. Presbyterian. Contbr. articles to profl. jours. Home: 1407 Druid Rd Maitland FL 32751 Office: 200 N Lakemont Ave Winter Park FL 32792

TUCKER, JOYCE ELAINE, lawyer, state human rights adminstr.; b. Chgo., Sept. 21, 1948; d. George M. and Vivian Louise T.; B.S., U. Ill., 1970; J.D., John Marshall Law Sch., 1978. Substitute tchr. Chgo. Public Schs., 1970-71; mental health specialist Tinley Park (Ill.) Dept. Mental Health, 1970-74; coordinator Title VII Program, Ill. Dept. Mental Health, Chgo., 1974-76, chief mental health equal employment opportunity officer, 1976-79; acting dir. Ill. Dept. Equal Employment Opportunity, Chgo., 1979-80; dir. Ill. Dept. Human Rights, Chgo., 1980—; admitted to Ill. bar, 1978. Mem. Nat. Bar Assn., Cook County Bar Assn. (Spl. Achievement award 1980), Am. Bar Assn., Chgo. Bar Assn. Mem. African Methodist Episcopal Ch. also 100 N 1st St Springfield IL

TUCKER, KAREN, communications corp. exec.; b. Washington, July 18, 1952; d. Willie and Marie (Roberson) T.; B.A., Trinity Coll., 1974; postgrad. U. Hartford, 1976-78. With Conn. Gen. Life Ins. Co., Hartford, 1974-80, sr. benefits adminstr., 1976-78, staff asst., 1978, mgr. pensions, 1978-80; ops. supr. AT&T, N.J., 1980-81, engring. supr., N.Y.C., 1981—. Class agt. Trinity Coll., 1974—; solicitor, co-capt. United Way, 1976-77. Mem. Nat. Assn. Female Execs., Am. Soc. Profl. and Exec. Women, Internat. Platform Assn., Am. Mgmt. Assn., NAACP. Democrat. Roman Catholic. Club: Trinity (Washington).

TUCKER, LINDA BARNES, educator, mfg. co. exec.; b. Mesa, Ariz., June 1, 1948; d. Alfred Cavis and Leona Cecil (Walters) Barnes; A.A., Stephens Coll., 1969, B.F.A., 1970; M.S., San Diego State U., 1980; m. Arthur Byron Tucker, Nov. 22, 1975; 1 dau., Julie Lin Simon. Exec. trainee Broadway Dept. Stores, 1970; owner, mem. Many Hands Artist's Coop, 1972-75; instr. Palomar Coll., San Diego City Coll., 1974; instr. Southwestern Coll., Chula Vista, Calif., 1974—, curriculum coordinator fashion program, 1976—; v.p. mktg. Sky Tech., Inc., San Diego, 1980—. Mem. Am. Home Econs. Assn., Calif. Home Econs. Assn., Assn. Coll. Profs. in Textiles and Clothing, Am. Assn. Textiles Chemists and Colorists, Costume Soc. Am., Smithsonian Instn. (asso.), Nat. Assn. Female Execs., Am. Vocat. Assn. Office: 900 Otay Lakes Rd Chula Vista CA 92010 also 7270 Engineer Rd #D U San Diego CA 92111

TUCKER, MARCIA, mus. dir., curator; b. N.Y.C., Apr. 11, 1940; d. Emanuel and Dorothy (Wald) Silverman; student Ecole du Louvre, Paris, 1959-60; B.A., Conn. Coll., New London, 1961; M.A., Inst. Fine Arts, N.Y. U., 1969. Curator, William N. Copley Collection, N.Y.C., 1963-66; editorial asso. Art News mag., N.Y.C., 1965-69; collection cataloger Alfred H. Barr, Jr., N.Y.C., 1966-67, Columbus (Ohio) Gallery Fine Arts, 1966-69; catalog raisonée Howald Collection Am. Art, Ford Found., 1966-69; asso. curator Whitney Mus. Am. Art, N.Y.C., 1969-73, curator, 1973-77; dir./founder The New Museum, N.Y.C., 1977—; faculty U. R.I., Kingston, 1966-68, City U. N.Y., 1967-68, Sch. Visual Arts, 1969-73; guest lectr. San Francisco Art Inst., Yale U., New Sch. for Social Research, U. Colo., U. Wis., Princeton U. Mem. Redstockings, 1970, Radical Feminists, 1971. Mem. Coll. Art Assn., Am. Assn. Museums, Phi Beta Kappa. Author: Anti-Illusion: Procedures/Materials, 1969; Catalogue of Ferdinand Howald Collection, 1969; Robert Morris, 1970; The Structure of Color, 1971; James Rosenquist, 1972; Bruce Nauman, 1973; Al Held, 1974; Richard Tuttle, 1975; Early Work by 5 Contemporary Artists, 1977; Bad Painting, 1978; Barry Le Va, 1979; John Baldessari, 1981; Not Just For Laughs: The Art of Subversion, 1981; also articles. Office: New Museum 65 Fifth Ave New York NY 10003

TUCKER, MARION JEAN, human service orgn. exec.; b. Holly Springs, N.C., May 21, 1942; d. Willie Lee and Mamie Richardson (Jones) T.; B.S., Shaw U., 1966. Headstart tchr. Duplin County Sch. System, Teachey, N.C., 1966; home econs. tchr. Halifax County Sch. System, Scotland Neck, N.C., 1966-70; home econs. extension agt. Randolph County Agr. Extension Services, 1970; nosologist Civil Service, Nat. Center Health Stats., Research Triangle Park, N.C., 1971-73; community food and nutrition program coordinator Migrant and Seasonal Farmworkers Assn., Raleigh, N.C., 1973—; chmn. Nat. Farmworker Conduit System. Mem. Nat. Assn. Female Execs. Democrat. Baptist. Club: Light of the Golden West (Lodge 376). Home: Route 1 Box 90 Holly Springs NC 27540

TUCKER, MELODY SUE, social worker, prevention specialist; b. Louisville, Nov. 9, 1947; B.S., Ind. U., 1970; postgrad. Ariz. State U., 1980—. Trainer, U.S. Office Edn. Alcohol and Drug Abuse Prevention Program, Chgo., 1974-77; coordinator prevention activities for alcohol, drug abuse, and mental health prevention activities Ariz. Dept. Health Services, Phoenix, 1978—; staff Gov.'s Task Force on Alcohol and Hwy. Safety, 1982; cons. human services, 1976—. Bd. dirs. Ariz. Right to Choose, 1982-83. Mem. Nat. Assn. Prevention Profls. (coordinator first Ann. Conv. 1978, dir. 1978—), Ariz. Public Employees Assn. (v.p. chpt.). Office: 2500 E Van Buren St Phoenix AZ 85008

TUCKER, NORMA SHEILA, coll. ofcl.; b. Balt., Sept. 14, 1933; d. Sidney Earl and Bessie (Tarses) Tucker; B.S. with honors, Johns Hopkins U., 1974, M.S. with honors in Organizational and Community Systems (Univ. fellow), 1978; postgrad. in counseling and student devel. Am. U.; children—Bart Allan Walker, Robert Edward Walker, Hope Elizabeth Walker. Cons. human resource devel., 1973-74; cons. in curriculum devel. Dundalk (Md.) Community Coll., 1974, asst. in continuing edn., 1974-76, coordinator continuing edn., 1976-78, dir. continuing edn., 1978—, acting dean student services, 1981-82, assoc. dean continuing edn. and community devel., 1982—; mem. adv. bd. Md. Consortium for

Gerontology in Higher Edn.; adv. Md. council Am. Council Edn.; grant dir. Title IA Higher Edn. Act, 1979-80; adv. bd. Singlestep, Edn. for Disabled Adults. Vol. leader VISTA, 1972, mem. staff Nat. VISTA Alliance, 1972; bd. dirs. Mt. Washington Elem. Sch. PTA, Balt., 1966-70. Named Person of Yr. for Region III, Nat. Council Community Services and Continuing Edn., 1981. Mem. Am. Soc. Tng. and Devel., Nat. Council Community Services and Continuing Edn., Nat. Assn. Women Deans, Adminstrs. and Counselors, Am. Personnel and Guidance Assn., Am. Assn. Higher Edn., Md. Group Deans and Coll. Dirs. Continuing Edn. (chmn. 1978), Phi Delta Kappa. Jewish. Contbr. articles to profl. publs. Home: 1 E University Pkwy Baltimore MD 21218 Office: 7200 Sollers Point Rd Dundalk MD 21222

TUCKER, SARAH ANN (SALLY), art appraiser; b. Austin, Tex., Dec. 24, 1934; d. Jim and Lorena (Kinsey) T.; B.A., U. St. Thomas, Houston; m. Peter S. Solito, Aug. 31, 1978; 1 son, Keny Jim. Ind. fine arts appraiser, Houston, 1976—. Mem. Am. Soc. Appraisers, Internat. Soc. Appraisers, Internat. Soc. Fine Arts Appraisers, Harris County Heritage Soc., Mensa, Artists Equity, Tex. Fine Arts Assn., Nat. Assn. Female Execs., Tex. Hist. Commn., Houston Mus. Fine Arts, Phi Alpha Theta. Democrat. Methodist. Club: Riv-O-Lon Garden (pres. 1980-81). Home: 3219 Ella Lee Ln Houston TX 77019 Office: PO Box 13605 Houston TX 77219

TUCKER, SHERRY ELIZABETH, lawyer; b. Guilford County, N.C., July 25, 1947; d. Raymond Jacob and Irma (Davis) T.; B.A. in Sociology, U. N.C., Asheville, 1973; M.A. in Sociology, Appalachian State U., 1974; J.D., N.C. Central U., 1977; m. James D. Coble, Dec. 19, 1979. Admitted to N.C. bar, 1978; individual practice law, Chapel Hill, N.C. 1978—; mem. N.C. Lawyer Referral Service. Mem. Am. Bar Assn., N.C. State Bar, N.C. Bar Assn. Office: PO Box 2504 Chapel Hill NC 27514

TUCKER, TANYA DENISE, singer; b. Seminole, Tex., Oct. 10, 1958; d. Jessie Melvin and Alma Juanita T. Rec. artist, CBS, M.C.A., Artista Records; first album: Delta Dawn; appeared in films The Rebel, Georgia Peaches, Hard Country; TV appearances; also songwriter; owner cattle and horse ranch, Tenn. Recipient 5 Grammy nominations. Office: care William Morris Agy 151 El Camino Beverly Hills CA 90012

TUDINO, ANITA CARBOCCI, bank mgr.; b. N.Y.C., Feb. 28, 1939; d. Lionel Leo and Florence (Spear) Carbocci; student Suffolk County Community Coll.; cert. Am. Inst. Banking; m. Ray Tudino, Feb. 10, 1959; children: Barbara Jeanne, Diane Janet, Raymond Frank. With Oystermen's Bank & Trust Co., Bayport, N.Y., 1969—, beginning as bookkeeper and acct., successively installment loan collector, customer service rep., note teller, asst. credit officer comml. loans, mortgage officer, 1969-81, br. mgr. Bayport office, 1981—. Mem. Blue Point C. of C. (v.p.). Republican. Roman Catholic. Club: Sayville Pilot. Office: Oystermens Bank 925 Montauk Hwy Bayport NY 11705

TUELL, KATHRYN YVONNE (BONNIE), utility co. exec.; b. Hillsboro, Oreg., May 14, 1936; d. Yule Kenneth and Ruth Kathryn (Carr) Austin; B.S. in Home Econs. Edn., Colo. State U., 1958; m. Richard John Tuell, Oct. 23, 1959; children—Terry Kamehameha, Tammy Ruth Poomaikalani, Tiffany Mikiola. Extension home economist U. Hawaii, Kaneohe, Hawaii, 1958-60; home economist Maui Electric Co., Ltd., Kahului, Maui, Hawaii, 1961-68, dir. home service dept., 1968-75, dir. mktg., 1975-78, mgr. adminstrn., 1979—; tchr. adult edn. Baldwin High Sch., 1967-68. Pres., 4-H Leader's Assn., 1977-78; sec. bd. dirs. Jr. Achievement, 1977—; hospitality chmn. St. John's Ch., 1975-78; chmn. Maui County Charter Commn., 1981-82. Mem. Am. Home Econs. Assn., Gen. Fedn. Women's Clubs, Kahului Bus. and Profl. Assn. (pres. 1979), Maui C. of C. (pres. 1980). Republican. Episcopalian. Club: Maui Woman's (pres. 1973-75). Author: Island Cooking, 1966.

TUFTS, JEAN, govt. ofcl.; b. Melrose, Mass., Oct. 7, 1927; B.S., Boston U., 1945, M.A., 1963; married; 4 children. Prin. Rockingham Sch. for Spl. Children, 1961-70; former exec. dir. Greater Manchester Child Care Assn.; sr. project officer New Eng. Program in Tchr. Edn., 1973-79; exec. dir. Rehab. Center, Portsmouth, N.H., 1974-79; former cons. presch. programs for handicapped N.H. Dept. Edn.; asst. sec. for spl. edn. and rehab. services Dept. Edn., Washington, 1982—; mem. N.H. Gov.'s Task Force on Edn. and Spl. Edn., 1970; del Nat. Conf. on Children and Youth, 1972-73. Bd. dirs. Nat. Sch. Bds. Assn., 1970—, pres., 1980—; mem. N.H. Bd. Edn., 1970-75; mem. N.H. Library Commn. Office: Dept Edn 330 C St SW Washington DC 20202 *

TUGGLE, GLORIA MARIA TURK, educator; b. Macon, Ga., Sept. 1, 1936; d. Aurelia Turk; B.S., Fort Valley State Coll., 1957; postgrad. Ga. Coll., 1972-75; children—Tanya Marchanda, Charles Melvin. Media specialist Bibb County Bd. Edn., Macon, 1957—, coordinator instrnl. resource materials Hall Sch.; ann. chmn. Afro-Am. Month. Campaign worker Mayor George Iserial, 1979-80, William Randall for State Rep., 1974, 80. Recipient Storytelling award State Dept. Ga., 1970. Mem. NEA, Ga. Educators Assn., Bibb Educators Assn., Bibb Edn. Media Assn. (v.p. 1978-80), Bibb Assn. Media Specialists (v.p.), Nat. Alumni Assn. Fort Valley State Coll. Democrat. Baptist. Home: 3238 Imperial Dr Macon GA 31211 Office: 2312 Shurling Dr Macon GA 31211

TUITE, KATHY PATRICIA, photographer; b. Mpls., Nov. 2, 1954; d. John Francis and Camille Miriam (Maloof) T.; B.A. in Film Studies, Purdue U., 1976, M.S. in Ednl. Media, 1978. Grad. teaching asst. Purdue U., West Lafayette, Ind., 1977-78, visual aids specialist, audio-visual prodn. dept., 1978-81; staff photographer, writer Lafayette (Ind.) Sport Spirit, 1979-81; cinematographer Central Catholic High Sch., Lafayette, 1978-81; photography editor Natural Bodybuilding mag., 1982—; product photographer Shamrock Labs., Dublin Calif., 1982—; staff photographer: Body Power Mag., Iron Man, Woman and Strength, Lady Athlete, Muscular Development, SPA News; freelance photographer for publs. including NBC SportsWorld, Muscular Development, Powerlifting USA, Muscle Mag., 1979—; participant shows, including Hist. Wabash Valley Photo Contest, Lafayette, 1976, Invitational Diana Show, Berea (Ky.) Coll., 1977, Campus Arts to Community Grant Program, 1977, Open Wall Show, Chgo., 1977, Me-Understanding Myself and Others, Peoria, Ill., 1977, Women See Men, shows N.Y.C. and Boston, 1977, Magic Silver Show, Murray (Ky.) State U., 1978 (award); instr. Olympia Health Club, Oakland, Calif., South Shore Beach and Tennis Club, Alameda, Calif., 1982—. Named Ind. Hoosier Scholar, 1980; recipient Salute to Women sports award, AAUW and Lafayette Bus. and Profl. Women, 1980; named most valuable player Purdue Powerlifting Team, 1980, 81, 82 named Ms. Natural Calif., 1981, Ms. Ironwoman, 1981, Ms. Central U.S.A., 1981, YMCA Nat. Physique Champion, 1980; best lifter Memphis Open, 1980. Mem. Communications and Tech., Univ. Press Photographers Assn., Women in Communications, U.S. Powerlifting Fedn. (nat. powerlifting referee, mem. women's exec. com.), Purdue Powerlifting Team. Democrat. Roman Catholic. Contbr. photographs to books, mags. Home: 484 Capitol St Oakland CA 94610 Office: 6444 Sierra Ct Dublin CA 94566

TULECKE, ROSE OSBORNE, mag. editor; b. Newton, Kans., Dec. 3, 1942; d. Donald A. and Helen M. (Hartman) Osborne; B.S., U. Kans., 1964; m. Jerome B. Tulecke, June 7, 1965; children—Mark, Linda. Free-lance writer Fort Worth Mag., 1973-77, asso. editor, 1980-81, editor, 1981—; asso. editor Tarrant County Med. Soc. Physician, Ft. Worth, 1977-79; editor Focus, Harris Hosp. mag., Ft. Worth, 1979-80. Leader, Girl Scouts U.S.A., 1978-81. Mem. Internat. Assn. Bus. Communicators (dir. 1981-82), Women in Communications, Tarrant County Med. Soc. Aux. Club: Fort Worth Woman's. Home: 5201 South Dr Fort Worth TX 76132 Office: Fort Worth Mag 700 Throckmorton St Fort Worth TX 76101

TULL, PATSY RUTH, graphoanalyst; b. Florey, Tex., Apr. 5, 1935; d. Harris Paul and Irene Matilda (Hinkle) Smith; B.A. in Psychology, Central State U., Edmond, Okla., 1978; graphoanalyst cert., Internat. Graphoanalysis Soc., 1975; m. Troy Tull, July 13, 1960 (div. 1981); children—Susan, Cynthia, Jeanne, Michael. Owner, operator Penlore, graphoanalysis for personnel selection and mgmt. consultation, anonymous letters, forgeries, Oklahoma City, 1979—; lectr., TV series; tchr. in field; jury screening for def. lawyers. Mem. Internat. Graphoanalysis Soc. (pres. Okla. chpt. 1978-79), High Noon Exec. Women (pres. 1981). Democrat. Presbyterian. Graphoanalysis research U. Okla. Office: 2324 NW 115th St Oklahoma City OK 73120

TULLER, WENDY JUDGE, petroleum co. exec.; b. Cranston, R.I., Dec. 17, 1943; d. Alfred Carman and Anna Louise (Waterman) Judge; A.B., Brown U., 1965; M.L.S., U. R.I., 1969. Elem. sch. librarian Providence Public Sch. System, 1965-69; mgr. Xerox Corp., various locations, 1969-75; mgr. Carter Hawley Hale Stores, Inc., Los Angeles, 1976; cons. Sibson & Co. Inc., Princeton, N.J., 1976-78; cons. equal opportunity affairs Atlantic Richfield Co., Los Angeles, 1978—. Named Woman of Yr., YWCA, Stamford, Conn., 1974. Mem. Am. Soc. Personnel Adminstrs., Am. Soc. Tng. and Devel., Internat. Assn. Personnel Women, AAUW (v.p. local chpt.). Club: Los Angeles Athletic. Home: 222 S Figueroa St Los Angeles CA 90012 Office: 515 S Flower St Los Angeles CA 90071

TULLIUS, MARILYN ADELE WINSLOW, mgmt. cons.; b. Grants Pass, Oreg., Sept. 10, 1937; d. Marion Blaine and Hilma Josephine (Hendrickson) Winslow; B.A., Lewis and Clark Coll., 1958; M.S. in Mktg., Grad. Sch. Mgmt., UCLA, 1967; m. James A. Tullius, July 11, 1969; children—Marsten Elissa, Eden Erin. Market analyst, indsl. systems div. Hughes Aircraft Co., 1968-70; market research analyst Arcata Data Mgmt. Co., 1970-71; sr. cons. IMA, Inc., Sherman Oaks, Calif., 1971-72, Marcom Applied Systems, Inc., Sherman Oaks, 1972-73; prin. Tullius and Assos., mgmt. cons., Los Angeles, 1974—; guest lectr. bus. planning topics; instr. mktg. Calif. State U., Long Beach, 1979. Mem. Assn. Corp. Growth, So. Calif. Corp. Planners Assn. (v.p. programs 1982-83), UCLA Sch. Mgmt. Alumni Assn., Mu Phi Epsilon (pres. Beverly Hills chpt. 1969-71). Home: 234 Entrada Dr Santa Monica CA 90402 Office: Tullius and Assos 520 S Sepulveda Blvd Suite 307 Los Angeles CA 90049

TULLOCH-REID, ELMA DEEN, cons.; b. Erie, Pa., June 27, 1938; d. Theodore and Roberta (Hicks) Carlisle; B.S., N.C. Agrl. and Tech. State U., 1960; M.A., Calif. State U., 1977; Ed.D., Nova U., 1981; children—Robynne and Stacey (twins). Staff nurse Michael Reese Hosp., Chgo., 1960-62; instr. Cook County Sch. Nursing, Chgo., 1962-64; tchr. St. Joseph Convent, Trinidad, West Indies, 1964-66; med.-surg. coordinator St. Vincent Coll. Nursing, Los Angeles, 1967-69, me.-surg. coordinator, 1967-69; charge nurse Century City Hosp., Los Angeles, 1971-72; tchr. Los Angeles Unified Schs., 1972-75; instr. inservice dept. St. Vincent Med. Center, Los Angeles, 1972-75; dir. edn. and tng. Imperial Hosp., Inglewood, Calif., 1977-79; pres. Elma Tulloch-Reid Assos., Los Angeles, 1981—; asst. prof. dept. continuing edn. Calif. State U., Long Beach, 1977-81, asso. prof., 1982—; provider Advanced Life Support in Cardiopulmonary Resuscitation, Am. Heart Assn., 1982-84. Community instr. certified basic life support Los Angeles Cardio-Pulmonary Resuscitation Consortium, 1981-82. Mem. Am. Soc. Profl. Cons., Nat. Assn. Mothers Twins and Multiple Births, Nat. Orgn. Mothers of Twins, Am. Nurses Found., Nat. Assn. Female Execs., N.C. Agrl. and Tech. State U. Alumni Assn., Phi Kappa Phi. Club: Westside Mothers Twins (pres. 1971-73) (Los Angeles). Home: 1056 Cochran Ave Los Angeles CA 90019 Office: Wilshire Blvd 36A47 Los Angeles CA 90036

TULLY, CAROL THORPE, social work educator; b. Portsmouth, N.H., Sept. 16, 1946; d. Francis and Laura (Thorpe) T.; B.A., U. Ariz., 1968; M.S.W., Va. Commonwealth U., 1977, now postgrad.; m. J.C. Albro, Nov. 17, 1973. Social worker Richmond (Va.) Dept. Public Welfare, 1971-77; tng. specialist Va. Dept. Public Welfare, Richmond, 1977-79; workshop leader Va. Commonwealth U. Trainer, day camp dir., troop leader Commonwealth council Girl Scouts U.S.A., 1971-74; mem. Richmond Area Community Council, 1972-74; alumni bd. dirs. Va. Commonwealth U., 1979-81. Mem. Nat. Assn. Social Workers (chmn. gay issues com. Va. chpt. 1980—), Council Social Work Edn. (co-chairperson ad hoc gay task force 1976-77, nat. lesbian and gay task force 1980—), Nat. Gay Task Force, Gay Rights Nat. Lobby, NOW, Phi Kappa Phi, Am. Camping Assn. (membership chairperson, public relations chairperson 1969-74). Contbr. articles to profl. jours. Home: 3603 Hawthorne Ave Richmond VA 23222

TULP, GAYE G. K., transp. co. exec.; b. Bismarck, N.D., Aug. 26, 1947; d. Virgil Ralph and Violet Flora (Burg) T.; student Famous Artist Sch., 1975; student in bus. mgmt. Houston Community Coll., 19 , also profl. seminars; m. Richard R. Rogers, Mar. 2, 1979; 1 son, Travor Will Rogers. Sec., Thomas W. Moore, Atty., Houston, 1969-70; underwriter Gt. So. Life Ins. Co., Houston, 1970-71; temporary sec. Top Girls, Houston, 1972-73; sec. to v.p. Rex Supply Co., Houston, 1973; office mgr. John L. Skalla Agy., Houston, 1973-74; traffic adv. Field, Nat. Supply Co. div. Armco Inc., Houston, 19 ; cons. Internat. Transp. Mgmt. Assn. Served with USN, 1965-68; Vietnam. Mem. Internat. Transp. Mgmt. Assn., Nat. Assn. Female Execs. (network dir.). Club: Order Foresters. Home: PO Box 56606 Dept 582 Houston TX 77256 Office: 1455 W Loop S Houston TX 77027

TUMA, JUNE MILDRED, clin. child psychologist; b. Alexandria, La., June 22, 1934; d. Harry and Mary (Pospisil) Tuma; B.A., La. State U., 1958, M.A., 1962, Ph.D. in Clin. Psychology, 1965. Postdoctoral fellow Reiss-Davis Child Study Center, Los Angeles, 1965-67; staff psychologist parent child sect. Mental Health Devel. Center, Los Angeles, 1967-69; dir. tng. and chief psychologist div. child and adolescent psychiatry U. Tex. Med. br. at Galveston, 1969-79; asso. prof., asso. dir. Developmental Psychology Center dept. psychology La. State U. at Baton Rouge, 1979—; examiner La. State Bd. Examiners of Psychologists, 1981-84. Fellow Am. Psychol. Assn., Am. Orthopsychiat. Assn.; mem. Soc. of Personality Assessment, AAAS, AAUP, La. Psychol. Assn. (past pres. sect. clin. child psychology), Soc. Pediatric Psychology (pres.), Sigma Xi, Phi Kappa Phi. Club: Jr. League. Editor: Handbook for Practice of Pediatric Psychology, 1982; editor Jour. Clin. Child Psychology; contbr. articles in field to profl. jours. Home: 318 Stanford Ave Baton Rouge LA 70808 Office: Dept Psychology La State U Baton Rouge LA 70803

TUNG, ROSALIE SUET-YING, educator; b. Shanghai, China, Dec. 2, 1948; came to U.S., 1975; d. Andrew Yan-Fu and Pauline Wai-Kam (Cheung) Lam; B.A. (Univ. scholar), York U., 1972; M.B.A., U. B.C., 1974, Ph.D. in Bus. Adminstrn. (Univ. fellow, Seagram Bus. fellow, H.R. MacMillan Family fellow), 1977; m. Byron Poon-Yan Tung, June 17, 1972; 1 dau., Michele Christine. Lectr., diploma div. U. B.C., 1975, lectr. exec. devel. program, 1975; prof. mgmt. Grad. Sch. Mgmt., U. Oreg., Eugene, 1977-80; vis. scholar U. Manchester (Eng.) Inst. Sci. and Tech., fall 1980; vis. prof. UCLA, spring 1981; prof. mgmt. Wharton Sch. Fin., U. Pa., Phila., 1981—. Mem. Acad. Internat. Bus., Acad. Mgmt., Am. Psychol. Assn., Am. Inst. Decision Scis., Am. Mgmt. Assn., Am. Econ. Assn., Internat. Assn. Applied Psychology. Roman Catholic. Author 3 books; contbr. articles to profl. jours. Home: PO Box 8253 Philadelphia PA 19101 Office: Wharton School U Pa Philadelphia PA 19104

TUNGPALAN, ELOISE YAMASHITA,, state legislator; b. Paia, Maui, Hawaii, July 22, 1945; B.A. with honors in Labor History, U. Hawaii, 1970; m., 2 children. Instr. U. Hawaii, 1969-70; researcher Hawaii Dept. Transp.-U. Hawaii, 1971-72; instr. mgmt. analysis, researcher, Hawaii Dept. Budget and Fin., 1978-80; exec. intern to Gov. Burns, 1970; legis. aide Hawaii House Com. on Hawaiian Homes, 1971, House Com. on Labor/Public Employment, 1974; mem. Hawaii Ho. of Reps., 1980—; del. Hawaii Democratic Conv., 1980; past chmn. Pearl City Neighborhood Bd., Leeward Dist. Sch. Adv. Council; bd. dirs. Pacific Palisades Community Assn.; past dir. Pearl City Community Assn. Mem. Mortar Bd., Phi Beta Kappa, Phi Kappa Phi, Alpha Lambda Delta. Office: Hawaii Ho of Reps State Capital Honolulu HI 96813

TUNICK, PHYLLIS, speech pathologist, educator; b. Bklyn., Mar. 26, 1933; d. Jacob and Rose (Fogelman) T.; B.A., Hunter Coll., 1954; M.A., Columbia U., 1961; postgrad. N.Y. U., 1964-65, 68-69, U. Mich., 1967-68. Tchr., N.Y.C. Bd. Edn., 1955-61, tchr. speech, 1962—; pvt. practice speech pathology, Jamaica, N.Y., 1969—; cons. in field. Mem. Jamaica Civic Community Bd., 1978—. Mem. Am. Speech and Hearing Assn. (cert.), N.Y. State Speech and Hearing Assn., Speech Assn. Eastern States. Jewish. Clubs: Columbia Univ., Adventure. Office: Bur Speech Improvement 110 Livingston St Brooklyn NY 11201

TUNKIEICZ, MARY URSULA, farm co. exec., clown; b. Chgo., Sept. 28, 1937; d. Gunnar and Jennie Adella (Howe) Gram; student public schs., Mich. and Ill.; m. Charles Tunkieicz, Feb. 23, 1957; children—Charlene, John, Jennie, Robert. Vice pres. Charles Tunkieicz Farms, Inc., Kenosha, Wis., 1972—, sec., 1972-80, sec.-treas., 1980—; clown Kenosha Unified Sch. Dist., 1979—; dir. I Am Sorry God, Somers Clowns Circus film, Alpha Film Corp.; clown ambassador Cousin Otto's Alley #22, Franzen Bros. Traveling Circus, Delavan, Wis. Leader for cooking Somers 4-H Club, 1974-75, clown project leader, 1976-80; chairperson Kenosha Farm Bur., 1975-78. Mem. Somers Clowns Clubs (dir.). Democrat. Roman Catholic. Club: Eagles. Contbr. poetry to various publs. Home: 8410 W 60th St Kenosha WI 53142 Office: 8418 38th St Kenosha WI 53142

TUNSKY, PATRICIA A., designer, exec.; b. Manchester, Conn., Sept. 18, 1943; d. William R. and Catherine Tunsky; Cert. Tobe-Colburn Sch., N.Y.C., 1964; 1 dau., Arianna Deyan Tunsky Brashich. Dept. mgr. Saks Fifth Ave., N.Y.C., 1964-67; fashion coordinator Bobbie Brooks, 1967-68; fashion dir. Monsanto Textiles, 1969-71; v.p. Grey Advt., 1972; pres., chief exec. officer Pat Tunsky, Inc., N.Y.C., 1972—, Interior Colors, Inc., 1972—, Color Projections, Inc., 1972—; lectr. in field. Recipient Mehitabel award Tobe Coburn Sch., 1981. Mem. Fashion Group, Fashion Inst. Tech. Author articles in field. Home: 343 E 30th St New York NY 10016 Office: 80 W 40th St New York NY 10018

TUPPER, ELEANOR (MRS. GEORGE O. BIERKOE), former coll. pres.; b. Fitchburg, Mass.; d. Clarence E. and Ella G. (Webster) Tupper; student Bancroft Acad., Worcester, Mass., Wheaton Coll.; A.B. (E. Benjamin Andrews fellow), Brown U.; A.M. and Ph.D., Clark U.; advanced study N.Y. U., Columbia U.; m. George O. Bierkoe, June 21, 1933 (dec.); children—Priscilla Tupper Schneider, Barbara T. Bierkoe-Peer. Prof., dept. head history and govt. Lindenwood Coll., St. Charles, Mo., 1929-30, head history dept., 1933; coll. adminstr. Pine Manor Jr. Coll. and Dana Hall Schs., Wellesley, Mass.; acad. dean Stoneleigh Coll., Rye, N.H.; acad. head Emma Willard Sch., Troy, N.Y.; adminstr. lay council Tchrs. Coll., Columbia U.; dean, v.p. Endicott Coll., 1939-71, pres., 1971-80; lectr. current events, European travels. Mem. Republican Nat. Com.; former mem. div. adminstrn. and communications N.E. Synod Luth. Ch. in Am.; former trustee Upsala Coll.; former mem. archives adv. commn. Commonwealth Mass.; mem. revitalization com. City of Beverly (Mass.). Mem. Am. Acad. Polit. and Social Scis., AAUW, Am. Hist. Assn., Am. Geog. Assn., YWCA, Beverly C. of C., Nat. Council Women U.S., Beverly Hist. Soc., Beverly Improvement Soc., Nat. Soc. DAR, Salem Hosp. Aid Assn., Sandwich Hist. Soc., Rotary Women, Phi Beta Kappa, Phi Beta Kappa Assos., Pi Gamma Mu, Phi Theta Kappa (past dir. nat. bd.). Clubs: North Shore Wheaton (past pres.); Women's (N.Y., Mass.), Zonta (dir.). Author: Syllabus on European History, 1931; Japan in American Public Opinion (with George E. McReynolds), 1937; Tupper Family Genealogy, 1972. Home: 375 Hale St Beverly MA 01915

TUPPER, TERESA LEE, oil co. acctg. mgr.; b. Batavia, N.Y., Feb. 13, 1949; d. Lyle Franklin and Gwen Jane (Day) T.; B.A. in Math., Hastings Coll., 1971; M.B.A., Pa. State U., 1973. With Exxon Co. U.S.A., 1973—, budget analyst, Los Angeles, 1979-80, dist. acctg. supr., Harvey, La., 1980-81, div. mgr. oil and gas acctg., New Orleans, 1981—. Adv., Explorer Post, Houston council Boy Scouts Am., 1974-76. Recipient Good Citizen award DAR, 1967. Mem. Am. Mgmt. Assn., Petroleum Accts. Soc. (council), Nat. Assn. Female Execs. Republican. Presbyterian. Office: PO Box 60626 New Orleans LA 70160

TURANO, JEAN MARIE, banker; b. Trenton, N.J.; d. Marin A. and Jennie (Gantiosa) T.; cert. Sch. Fin. and Public Relations, Northwestern U., 1955. Office mgr. Trenton Area chpt. ARC, 1945-52, chmn. public relations, 1955-66, sec., 1965-75; community relations rep. Trenton Savs. Fund Soc., 1952-53, asst. to pres., 1953-66, v.p., 1966—, bd. mgrs., 1965—. Sec., Dunn Scholarship Fund, 1952-76, Delaware Valley United Fund, 1956, 57, 76; bd. dirs. Community Found. Trenton, Friends of Trenton Library. Recipient Trenton Woman of Yr. award, 1958; award for civic achievement and community service Unico Club of Trenton, 1958; award Savs. Instns. Mktg. Soc. Am., 1970; award Trenton-Mercer County C. of C., 1971; Disting. Citizenship award Sales and Mktg. Execs. Central N.J., 1971; Brotherhood award NCCJ, 1974; Pres.'s award Delaware Valley United Way, 1981. Mem. Nat. Assn. Bank Women, Heart of Trenton Businessmen's Assn. (dir., sec. 1962-67), Greater Trenton C. of C. (chmn. task force on ambulance and emergency service 1971-72), Nat. Secs. Assn. (pres. Trenton chpt. 1951-53), Am. Bankers Assn. (savs. adv. council 1965-69), Savs. Banks Assn. N.J. Club: Soroptimists (pres. 1962-63)(Trenton). Contbr. articles to profl. jours. jours.; mem. com. Mercer Bus. mag. Office: Trenton Savs Fund Soc 123-125 E State St Trenton NJ 08608

TURBEVILLE, DEBORAH, photographer; b. Stoneham, Mass., July 6, 1932; d. Don A. and Martha Turbeville; student Brimmer & May Sch., Boston. Model, Claire McCardell, N.Y.C. 1951; mem. editorial staff Harper's Bazaar from 1963; one-woman shows: U. Wis. 1976, Sonnabend Gallery, N.Y.C. 1977, Galerie Sonnabend, Paris 1978, Exposure Gallery, Wellfleet, Mass. 1978, Paul Cava Gallery, Phila. 1979, La Remise du Parc, Paris 1981, Clock Tower Gallery N.Y.C. 1981, Dalahunty Gallery Dallas 1982, Galleria Il Ponte, Rome 1982, Municipio Di Rimini, Italy 1982; group shows include: Hofstra U. 1975, Jack Glenn Gallery, Newport, Calif. 1975, Women Photographers, Tehran, Iran 1976, Documenta VI, Kassel, W. Ger. 1977, New Gallery, Cleve., 1978, Sonnabend Gallery, N.Y.C. 1978, 79, 81, 82, Cleve. Mus. Art 1980, Grand Palais: Versailles, Montpellier, France 1982; photographs appear in mags. including de Pech Mode, Mademoiselle, Nova, Viva, Vogue; books: The History of Fashion Photography, The World of American Vogue: Fifty Years of Fashion, Allure, Women By Women, Yearbook of Photography. Recipient Grammy award, 1979; Clio award,

1980-81; Am. Book award, 1981. Author: Wallflower 1979; Unseen Versailles 1981.

TURCO, EILEEN, assn. exec.; b. Jersey City, Apr. 29, 1949; d. Arthur and Eileen (Warwick) Kaehler; student public schs.; m. Richard S. Turco, July 18, 1977; children—Robert Turco, Richard Sam II. Legal sec. Deeba, DeStefano, Sauter & Herd, St. Louis, 1976-77; exec. sec., asst. dir. devel. YMCA Greater St. Louis, 1978-80; dir. devel. YWCA, St. Louis, 1980—. Bd. dirs. Indsl. Aid. Mem. Regional Commerce and Growth Assn. (membership leader 1977-81), Nat. Soc. Fund-Raising Execs., Women's Info. Network. Clubs: Direct Mktg. of Am., Elks Ladies Aux., Ad Club of Mo. Office: YWCA Metro St Louis 1015 Locust St Suite 310 Saint Louis MO 63101

TURCOTTE, MARGARET JANE, nurse; b. Stow, Ohio, May 17, 1927; d. Edward Carlton and Florence Margaret (Hanson) McCauley; R.N., St. Thomas Hosp., Arkon, Ohio, 1949; m. Rene Turcotte, Nov. 24, 1961 (div. 1967); 1 son, Michael Lawrence. Gen. duty nurse, central supply staff St. Thomas Hosp., 1949-50; pvt. duty nurse, 1950-57; polio nurse Akron Children's Hosp., 1953-54; operating room, recovery room, emergency room nurse Robinson Meml. Hosp., Ravenna, Ohio, 1961-67, head nurse, 1966-67; staff nurse med. surg. service, head nurse central service Brentwood Hosp., Warrensville Heights, Ohio, 1967—, infections control officer, 1982—; instr. cardiac pulmonary resuscitation; emergency med. technician. Democrat. Roman Catholic. Home: 6037 Highview St Lot 14F Ravenna OH 44266 Office: 4110 Warrensville Center Rd Warrensville Heights OH 44122

TURECK, ROSALYN, pianist, harpsichordist, conductor, author, educator; b. Chgo., Dec. 14, 1914; d. Samuel and Monya (Lipson) T.; student of Sophia Brilliant-Liven, Jan Chiapusso, Olga Samaroff, Theremin; grad. cum laude Juilliard Sch. Music; m. George Wallingford Downs, Sept. 1, 1964. Concert pianist since age of 9, solo recitals with Chgo. Symphony Orch., at Carnegie Hall, Town Hall, Phila. Orch.; European debut, Copenhagen, 1947; conert tours of U.S., Europe, South Africa, S.Am., Israel, Hong King, India, Australia, and with orchs. throughout world; condr./soloist with London Philharmonia, 1958, N.Y. Philharm., 1958, Collegium Musicum, Copenhagen, 1958, Scottish Nat. Symphony, 1963, Israel Philharm., 1963, Internat. Bach Soc. Orch., 1967, 69, 70, Washington Nat. Symphony, 1970, others; with Tureck Bach Players, London, 1958—; TV appearances include Today Show, Camera 3, also in Eng.; mem. faculty Phila. Conservatory of Music, 1935-42, Mannes Coll. Music, 1940-44, Juilliard Sch. Music, 1943-55, Columbia U., 1953-55; vis. prof. Washington U., St. Louis, 1963-64; prof. music U. Calif., San Diego, 1967-72, U. Md., 1982; Regents lectr. U. Calif., San Diego, 1966; Corbett lectr. U. Cin.; lectr. various other colls. and univs.; vis. fellow St. Hilda's Coll., Oxford (Eng.) U., 1974, Wolfson Coll., 1975—; hon. life fellow St. Hilda's Coll.; founder/dir. Composers of Today, 1951-55, Tureck Bach Players, London, 1957—, Internat. Bach Soc., 1966, Inst. Bach Studies, 1968, Tureck Bach Inst., 1981; rec. artist. Recipient 1st prize Greater Chgo. Piano Playing Tournament, 1928; Schubert Meml. Contest, 1935, Nat. Fedn. Music Clubs Competition, 1935; Phi Beta award for Excellence; First Town Hall Endowment award, 1938; MacDowell Colony fellow, 1978; decorated officer Order of Merit (W.Ger.), 1979; nominee Grammy award, 1980; Mus.D. (hon.), Colby Coll., 1964, Roosevelt U., Chgo., 1968, Wilson Coll., 1968, Oxford U., 1977. Mem. Am. Music Scholarship Assn. (pres.), Societe Johann Sebastian Bach de Belgique (hon.), Royal Mus. Assn. (London), Royal Philharm. Soc. (London), Oxford Soc., Inc. Soc. Musicians (London), Am. Musicol. Soc., New Bach Soc. Clubs: Cosmopolitan, Bohemians (hon. life) (N.Y.C.). Author/editor: An Introduction to the Performance of Bach, 3 vols., 1959-60, Japanese edit., 1966, Spanish edit., 1975; Tureck Bach Urtext Series, 1981, 82; also transcriptions, articles. Office: care Columbia Artists Mgmt Inc 165 W 57th St New York NY 10019

TUREN, DONNA ROSE, social worker; b. Washington, Mar. 1, 1950; d. Kurt R. and Gerturde (Latzko; B.A., U. Md., 1972, M.S.W., 1977; 1 dau., Adria Danieele Dobkin. Co-dir./co-founder Time for Livin', Balt., 1972-73, Glaydin Abroad, Florence, Italy, 1973-75; social worker Santa Clara County (Calif.) Schs., 1977-82, Golden Gate Regional Center, San Mateo, Calif., 1982—; parent edn. cons.; pvt. practice psychotherapy. Bd. dirs. CASA S.A.Y., 1980-81; bd. dirs. Vols. for Youth, Stanford U., 1980-81, Time for Livin', 1972-75. Lic. clin. social worker. Mem. Nat. Assn. Social Workers, Calif. Assn. Clin. Social Work. Home: 132 Henry St San Francisco CA 94114

TURLEY, PATRICIA ANN, educator; b. Chesterfield, Mo., Mar. 17, 1938; d. John Carl and Beatrice Delphina (Borchers) Erman; B.S., S.E. Mo. State U., 1960; postgrad. U. Munich (W.Ger.), 1962; M.Ed., U. Mo., 1967, Ph.D., 1978; m. Dave Brian Turley, Apr. 14, 1974. Instr., U. Mo., Columbia, 1963-71, instr. philosophy of edn., 1971-75; supr. student tchrs. of French, student tchrs. of fgn. langs. Columbia Public Schs., 1963-71; prof. philosophy and French, Moberly (Mo.) Coll., 1975-81 cons., co-dir. enrichment program in French; asst. prof. edn. Missouri Valley Coll., Marshall, Mo., 1981—, dir. secondary edn. program, 1981—; instr. sailing. Mem. AAUP, Philosophy of Edn. Soc., Am. Ednl. Studies Assn., Am. Assn. Colls. of Tchr. Edn. (instnl. rep.), Mo. Assn. Colls. of Tchr. Edn. (nominating com. for exec. bd.), AAUP, Valley Philosophy of Edn. Soc. (charter), Assn. Tchr. Educators (com. to select tchr./educator of Yr. Mo. unit), Mo. Tchrs. Assn. (student faculty advisor), Comparative and Internat. Edn. Soc., Nat. Geog. Soc., Kappa Delta Pi, Pi Lambda Theta. Clubs: Thomas Hill Lake Catamaran Fleet (winner 1st pl. summer 1980), Mid-Mo. Yacht. Contbr. articles to profl. publs.; cons. ednl. writings of Montaigne. Home: Thomas Hill Lake Rural Route 1 Callao MO 63534 Office: 205 Baity Hall Missouri Valley College Marshall MO 65340

TURLEY, SHARON STUART, coll. ofcl.; b. Los Angeles, July 5, 1942; d. Raymond C. and Vesta L. (Snethen) Stuart; A.A., Glendale Community Coll., 1977; m. Brian Turley, Nov. 25, 1961; children—Phillip, Cynthia, Damon. Sec., San Bernardino (Calif.) Bus. Men's Assn., 1960-66; asst. dir. fin. aids Eastern Ariz. Coll., Safford, 1977-81, dir. fin. aids and placement, 1982—. Mem. Ariz. Ednl. Assn., Ariz. Community Coll. Placement Assn. (pres. 1981), Safford Bus. and Profl. Women (pres.), Safford Democratic Women's League. Methodist. Club: Emblem (Safford). Home: 1124 10th St Safford AZ 85546 Office: Eastern Ariz Coll Thatcher AZ 85552

TURNBOUGH, PEGGY DIANE, psychologist; b. San Antonio, Oct. 3, 1943; d. Clyde L. and Margaret M. (Moore) Falls; B.A., Eastern Wash. U., 1965, M.S., 1966; Ph.D. (NSF research stipend 1971), Wash. State U., 1972; postgrad. trainee, U. Kans., 1972-73; divorced; 1 dau., Noelle K. Dir. research, staff clin. psychologist Bert Nash Community Mental Health Center, Lawrence, Kans., 1973-74; asst. prof. psychology U. Nev., Las Vegas, 1974—, chmn. dept., 1982—; pvt. clin. practice; mem. Nev. Bd. Psychol. Examiners, 1977—; chmn. program rev. com. Las Vegas Children's Behavioral Services, 1975-77; speaker, cons. in field. Grantee, Nat. Inst. Aging, 1979-82. Cert. psychologist, Nev. Mem. Am. Psychol. Assn., Nev. Psychol. Assn. (pres. 1977-78), Nat. Register Health Service Providers, AAAS, Sigma Xi (pres. U. Nev. 1980-81), Phi Lambda Alpha (award 1979), Psi Chi (past chpt. sec.), Phi Theta Kappa (pres. 1962-63). Democrat. Baptist. Contbr. articles to profl. jours. Office: Dept Psychology Univ Nev 4505 Maryland Pkwy Las Vegas NV 89154

TURNBULL, DOREEN JOYCE, systems analyst; b. Evanston, Ill., Jan. 10, 1938; d. Dale M. and Juliet L. (Van Buskirk) T.; B.S. in Bus. Mgmt., Calif. State Poly., Pomona, 1969; postgrad. Claremont Grad. Sch. Sr. systems analyst Sunkist Growers Inc., Sherman Oaks, Calif., 1968-74; EDP systems analyst Ralphs Grocery Co., Compton, Calif., 1974-77; propr. DJT Cons., 1977-80; project mgr., sr. systems analyst, Xerox Corp., Pasadena, Calif., 1980—. Mem. Data Processing Mgmt. Assn. (chpt. dir.), Am. Mgmt. Assn., Nat. Assn. Female Execs., Women in Mgmt., IS/DP Alumni Assn. (dir.). Club: Altrusa (sec.) (Arcadia, Calif.). Home: 3620 Moreno Ave Space 52 LaVerne CA 91750 Office: 125 N Vinedo St Pasadena CA 91107

TURNER, AVIS BOSAK, librarian; b. Frederic, Wis., June 15, 1949; d. William Leonard and Ruby Myrtle (Johnson) Bosak; B.A., U. Wis., Eau Claire, 1971; m. Richard Wayne Turner, Sept. 3, 1976; 1 dau., Shelby Leigh. Librarian, Fox Valley Tech. Inst., Appleton, Wis., 1971-73; corp. librarian Luth. Brotherhood, Mpls., 1973-80; librarian Rosemount, Inc., Mpls., 1980—. Mem. Spl. Libraries Assn., Minn. Library Assn., Twin Cities Ins. Librarians (co-founder). Clubs: Jaycee Women, Preserve Women's (exec. com. 1978-79), Gourmet. Home: 10895 Fieldcrest Rd Eden Prairie MN 55344 Office: 12001 W 78 St Eden Prairie MN 55344

TURNER, BERNICE COOPER, social services adminstr., social worker; b. Chgo., Jan. 19, 1924; d. Jasper Lorenzo and Jessie Alice (Jones) Cooper; B.S., Wilberforce U., 1947; M.S.W., Loyola U., Chgo., 1952; m. Miles W. Turner, Aug. 4, 1947; 1 son, Miles W., IV. Sr. psychiat. social worker Psychiat. Inst. Circuit Ct. Cook County (Ill.), 1952-67; chief social worker St. Leonards Drug Addiction Center, Chgo., 1967; social worker United Charities, Chgo., 1968-70; family programs coordinator Chgo. Dept. Human Services, 1971—; pvt. practice social work, 1966—; lectr. Central YMCA Coll., Chgo., 1972-81; mem. developmental com. Afro-Am. Community Service, 1972-80; founder, mem. exec. bd. Afro-Am. Family and Community Service, 1972-79; bd. dirs. Woodlawn Maternal and Child Health Center; mem. USPHS Res., 1967—. Mem. Nat. Assn. Social Workers, Internat. Social Workers Conf., Nat. Registry Clin. Social Workers (mem. del. assembly Ill. chpt., past chmn. affirmative action program), Nat. Conf. Social Welfare, Ill. Welfare Assn., Acad. Cert. Social Workers, Delta Sigma Theta. Democrat. Episcopalian. Club: Chums Bridge and Social (pres.). Home: 6232 St Lawrence Ave Chicago IL 60637 Office: 640 N LaSalle St Chicago IL 60610

TURNER, CLEVONNE WATKINS, psychiat. social worker; b. Sumter, S.C., Aug. 14, 1945; d. Lewis Eugene and Isabelle Elizabeth (Davis) Watkins; B.A. in Sociology cum laude with honors, Fisk U., 1966; M.S.W., Ind. U., 1968; m. John B. Turner, June 3, 1967; children—Stephanie, Robin, Bridget. Social worker Indpls. YWCA, 1967-68; psychiat. social worker Ind. U., 1969-74; asst. dean for student affairs M.I.T., 1974-76; psychiat. social worker Wellesley Coll., 1977—; field instr. Boston U. Sch. Social Work, 1978-81; clin. instr. Simmons Coll. Sch. Social Work, 1981—; postgrad. clin. fellow McLean Hosp., Belmont, Mass., 1978-79; pvt. practice psychotherapy; cons. M.I.T. Vol. counselor Planned Parenthood Assn., Bloomington, Ind., 1966-74, bd. dirs., 1972-74; leader Campfire Girls Inc., Lexington, Mass., 1976-78; v.p. Bridge Sch. Assn., Lexington, Mass., 1977; active Black Women for Policy Action, Cambridge, Mass., 1979—. Recipient Outstanding Faculty award Black Student Union, M.I.T., 1976; named to Outstanding Young Women Am., U.S. Jaycees, 1978; lic. clin. social worker, Mass. Mem. Acad. Cert. Social Workers, Nat. Assn. Social Workers, Assn. Black Social Workers, Concerned Black Citizens, Alpha Kappa Alpha. Home: 6 Birch Hill Ln Lexington MA 02173 Office: Wellesley Coll Stone Center Wellesley MA 02173

TURNER, DOROTHA LOUISE, oil co. exec.; b. Clay County, Ark., Feb. 23, 1927; d. Carrel E. and Clara Irene (Cole) Hester; student public schs., Ark.; m. Filbert Turner, Jan. 20, 1945; children—Janice, Phylliss, Gary, Clarissa. Substitute tchr. various schs., 1944-64; purchasing agt. Johanson Shoes, Corning, Ark., 1964-69; sec., bookkeeper Blackman Oil Co., Corning, 1969-70, officer mgr., sec.-treas., 1975—; indsl. engr. computer programming Corning Distbg. Co., 1970-75. Democrat. Baptist. Club: Art. Office: PO Box 105 Corning AR 72422

TURNER, DOROTHY HELEN, profl. sec.; b. Vinita, Okla., Mar. 15, 1922; d. Marion Ellsworth and Elberta Mae (Sparks) Noland; m. Richard K. Turner (dec.). With City of Tulsa Bd. Edn., 1940-41, Boy Scouts Am., Tulsa, 1941-43, First Presbyn. Ch., Tulsa, 1943-45, Fire Cos. Adjustment Bur., Tulsa, 1945-47; with Bank of Okla., Tulsa, 1947—, now exec. sec. to vice-chmn. bd. Mem. Profl. Secs. Internat., Am. Inst. Banking. Republican. Home: 1008 S Troost St Tulsa OK 74120 Office: PO Box 2300 Tulsa OK 74192

TURNER, DORRIS BELLE, architect; b. Santa Anna, Tex., May 12, 1925; d. Arthur Maxwell and Loleita (Hunter) T.; B.Arch., Tex. Technol. U., 1950; M.Arch. in Environ. Design, U. Calif., Berkeley, 1974; D. Environ. Design, Tex. A&M U., 1977. With firm Davis-Foster-Thorpe, architects and engrs., El Paso, Tex., 1950-55, 58-60, Carroll & Daeuble, architects, El Paso, 1955-58; prin. Dorris B. Turner, El Paso, 1960-63; mem. faculty Leyson (Switzerland) Am. Coll., 1963-64; asso. prof. architecture Tex. Technol. U., Lubbock, 1972-74; with dept. architecture and environ. design Tex. A&M U., College Station, 1974—, architect facilities planning dept., 1977—. Bd. dirs. El Paso Research and Treatment Center, 1961-62. Mem. AIA, Tex. Soc. Architects. Home: 1604 Lemontree St College Station TX 77840

TURNER, ELIZA MAE, educator; b. Jackson, Tenn., Jan. 28, 1949; d. David and Lena Taylor; B.A., Lane Coll., Jackson, 1970; m. Walter Turner, Jan. 28, 1980. Tchr., Milw. Public Schs., 1970—. 5877 N 78th St Milwaukee WI 53218

TURNER, ELIZABETH ADAMS NOBLE, realty co. exec.; b. Yonkers, N.Y., May 18, 1931; d. James Kendrick and Orrel (Baldwin) Noble; B.A., Vassar Coll., 1953; M.A., Tex. A&I U., 1964; m. Jack Rice Turner, July 11, 1953; children—Jay Kendrick, Randall Ray. Ednl. cons. Noble & Noble Pub. Co., N.Y.C., 1956-67; psychometrist Corpus Christi Guidance Center, 1967-70; psychologist Corpus Christi State Sch., 1970-72, dir. programs, 1972, dir. vol. service, 1972-76; program cons. Tex. Dept. Mental Health and Mental Retardation and Corpus Christi State U., 1976—; dir. staff devel. Corpus Christi State Sch., 1978-79; coordinator vols. Summer Head Start Program, Corpus Christi, 1967. Mem. allocations com. United Fund, Corpus Christi, 1970; mem. Corpus Christi City Council, 1979-81; mayor pro tem Corpus Christi, 1981—; co-owner Turner, Whittle & Tate, Inc., Realtors. Leadership Corpus Christi, Com. of 100—Goals for Corpus Christi; mem. adv. bd. U. Tex.; bd. dirs. Coastal Bends Council Govts., Conv. and Tourist Bur., Big Bros., YWCA, Corpus Christi Hearing and Speech, C. of C., Coastal Bend Mental Health Assn., Suicide Prevention Inc., Tb Assn. (all Corpus Christi), Corpus Christi Mus., Art Mus. S. Tex., Corpus Christi. Recipient Love award YWCA, 1970. Mem. Tex. Psychol. Assn. (pres., mem. exec. bd.), Psychol. Assos. (pres.), Jr. League Corpus Christi, Tex. Bookman's Assn., C. of C. (dir.), Tex. Assn. Realtors, Kappa Kappa Gamma. Clubs: Corpus Christi Country, Corpus Christi Yacht, Junior Cotillion, Corpus Christi Press. Home: 4466 Ocean Dr Corpus Christi TX 78404

TURNER, ELLEN LATHEAL HOWARD, educator; b. Hollis, Okla., Nov. 18, 1911; d. Cyrus Otto and Cora (Coleman) Howard; B.A., Hardin-Simmons U., 1929; student Abilene Christian Coll., summers 1934, 36; M.A., N. Tex. State U., 1947, postgrad. student, summer, 1968; m. John Edward Turner, Jan. 26, 1944. With Williams Consol. R.R., Quanah, Tex., 1930-31; tchr. Fairview High Sch., Thrift, Tex., 1931-34; Nugent (Tex.) Elem. Sch., 1934-35; Dudley (Tex.) Elem. Sch., 1935-36; prin. Mankins (Tex.) Elem. Sch., 1936-38; tchr. Tuscola (Tex.) High Sch., 1938-41, 42-43; tchr. Woodrow Wilson Jr. High Sch., Port Arthur, Tex., 1943-53; tchr. Abilene (Tex.) High Sch., 1953-67; asst. prof. English, Hardin-Simmons U., 1967-77, part-time asst. prof., 1979—; asst. prof. McMurry Coll., 1978-79; instr. English to Cambodians in Abilene, summer 1979. Mem. Tex. State Tchrs. Assn., Coll. Council Tchrs. English, Nat. Assn. Ret. Tchrs., Tex. Assn. Ret. Tchrs., Delta Kappa Gamma (chpt. pres. 1974-76, chpt. chmn. coordinating council 1976-78, state conv. chmn. 1978, area X coordinator 1979-81, chmn. state personnel com. 1981-82). Baptist. Clubs: Abilene Shakespeare (past pres.), Esther Bible Club (treas. 1980), Univ. Women's (pres. 1981), Abilene Cactus Lioness (pres. 1981-82), River Oaks chpt. Order Eastern Star (past matron, past grand Ruth), Social Order of the Beauceant of Am. (past pres., past supreme dir. music). Home: 1817 Jackson St Abilene TX 79602 Office: C-3 Hardin-Simmons U Abilene TX 79601

TURNER, FRANCES BERNADETTE, clergyman, lectr., author; b. Superior, Wis., June 28, 1903; d. Fyler Bedell and Eleanor Dolores (Donaly) Rainsford; secondary cert. Normal Sch., Superior, 1924; B.S. in Edn., U. Minn., 1926; M.A. in Sociology, Northwestern U., 1938; postgrad. social service adminstrn. U. Chgo., 1941-44; Ph.D. in Sociology and Social Work, Washington U., St. Louis, 1948; m. Delos Ashley Turner, Dec. 8, 1936. Tchr. high sch., Bessemer, Mich., 1924-28; field rep. nat. staff ARC, chpt. exec. sec. Kans., Wash., Nev., 1929-36; psychiat. social worker Chgo. State Hosp., Ill. Inst. Research, Chgo., 1938-41; chief social service Dixon (Ill.) State Hosp., 1945; assoc. prof. sociology and social work Ariz. State Coll., Tempe, 1946-56, also student counselor nursing schs. Good Samaritan, Meml. hosps., Phoenix, 1946-56; student counselor nursing sch. Evang. Hosp., Chgo., 1963; individual practice marriage and family counseling, Phoenix, 1950-62; programmer radio programs radio stas. KTAR, Phoenix, KYND, Tempe, WEAW, WRSV, Chgo., WFIR, Roanoke, Va., 1953-68, KICT, Wichita, Kans., 1974-75, also WTMJ, Milw., 1976-77, KSUL, Calif. State U., 1978, KRUZ, Santa Barbara, Calif., 1979-80, WYMS, Milw., 1981—, WTMJ, 1982—; ordained to ministry, registered pracitioner Divine Sci. Ch., 1965; founder Divine Sci. Center, Evanston, Ill., 1965; pastor Divine Sci. Ch., Roanoke, 1971-72, Evanston, 1971-72; condr. chapel service Carrillo Hotel, Santa Barbara, Calif., 1979-80; resident counselor Retirement Home, Wichita, Kans., 1974-76; instr. div. continuing edn. Marquette U., 1976, 81-82, Calif. State U., 1976; lectr. in field. Bd. dirs. Maricopa council Campfire Girls, Phoenix, 1955-61. Fellow Am. Sociol. Assn.; mem. Nat. Assn. Social Workers, Assn. Cert. Social Workers, Am. Assn. Marriage Counselors, Internat. Assn. Women Ministers, Am. Assn. Pastoral Counselors, Nat. League Am. Pen Women, Kans. Authors Club, World Poetry Soc., Divine Sci. Internat. Fedn., Internat. New Thought Alliance. Club: Daus. of Nile. Author: Happy Is the Man, 1965; God-centered Therapy, 1968; Faith of Little Creatures, 1972; contbr. articles and poetry to newspapers and mags. Address: 1962 N Prospect Ave Milwaukee WI 53202 also 6647 El Colegio Rd Goleta CA 93117

TURNER, GAIL GLORIA, cardiologist; b. Winnepeg, Man., Can., Aug. 15, 1949; came to U.S., 1952, naturalized, 1957; d. Robert E. and Dillie M. (Kraushar) T.; B.S. magna cum laude, Colo. Coll., Colorado Springs, 1971; M.D., U. Minn., 1975; m. Wayne Louis Buesgens, Feb. 14, 1982. Research asso. Mpls. VA Hosp., 1975-76; intern in internal medicine U. Cin., 1976-77, resident in internal medicine, 1977-78; resident in internal medicine U. Minn., 1978-79; cardiology fellow, 1979-81; research asso. in cardiovascular pathology, 1981-82. Mem. ACP, Am. Coll. Cardiology, Phi Beta Kappa.

TURNER, JANET E., artist; b. Kansas City, Mo., 1914; d. James Ernest and Hortense (Taylor) Turner; A.B., Stanford, 1936; diploma, postgrad. Kansas City Art Inst. (under Thomas H. Benton, John de Martelly), 5 years; student art Claremont Grad. Sch. (Millard Sheets, Henry McFee), 2 years, M.F.A., 1947; student serigraphy, Edward Landon; Ed.D., Columbia, 1960. Faculty, Girls Collegiate Sch., Claremont, Calif., 1942-47; asst. prof. art Stephen F. Austin State Coll., Nacogdoches, Tex., 1947-56; asst. prof. Chico State U., 1959-63, asso. prof., 1963-68, prof., 1968-80, emeritus, 1980—. Works have been shown in painting, water colors and prints exhbns. throughout U.S.; exhibited over 140 one-man shows in U.S., Israel, Japan; exhibited in Internat. Biannual of Graphics, Krakow, Poland, Internat. Exchange Exhbn., Seoul, Korea; represented in collections in U.S., fgn. countries. Illustrator The Yazoo, F. Smith. Guggenheim fellow, 1952; Tupperware fellow, 1956—. Recipient prizes including: (painting) 1st prize Tex. Fine Arts Assn., 1948; Dealey purchase prize and Comini popular prize 11th Tex. Gen. Exhbn.; R.D. Straus prize 13th Tex. Gen. Exhbn.; 3 prize oils 50th Anniversary Exhbn. Art Assn. New Orleans; S. Karasick prize 59th Ann. Nat. Assn. Women Artists; (water colors) purchase prize 2d Tex. Water Color Soc.; Sun Carnival prize 3d Ann. Southwestern Sun Carnival Fine Arts Exhbn., El Paso; purchase prize Smith Coll. Mus. Art, 37th Ann. Exhbn. Western Art, Denver; Marcia Tucker prize Nat. Assn. Women Artists; (prints) Nat. Assn. Women Artists 1950; (graphics) 1st prize Painters and Sculptors Soc. N.J., 32d Ann. Springfield (Mass.) Art League, Pen and Brush Black and White Exhbn., N.Y.C.; purchase prize Soc. Am. Graphic Artists 36th Ann. A.N.A., 2d prize, Springfield Art League, Mass., 1955, 1st prize, Pen and Brush, 1956, 8th ann. Boston Printmakers purchase prize; 6th Southwestern Dallas Mus. Fine Arts, 1st prize graphics, Painters Sculptors Soc. of N.J., Tupperware Art Fund Fellowship award for painting, Los Angeles County Nat. purchase prize, purchase prize Calif. State Fair, 1960, Cannon prize N.A.D., 1961; Medal of Honor and Alice S. Buell Meml. prize Nat. Assn. Women Artists, 1963, Katheryn Colton prize, Medal of Honor and Mabel M. Garner award, 1967; A.P. Hankins Meml. prize Print Club Pa., 1972; co-recipient Outstanding Prof. award Calif. State U. and Colls., 1975. Mem. League Am. Pen Women, Los Angeles Printmaking Soc. (Purchase prize 1971), Nat. Assn. Women Artists, Audubon Artists, Am. Color Print Soc., Soc. Am. Graphic Artists, N.A.D. (academician), Nat. Art Edn. Assn., A.A.U.W., Calif. Soc. Printmakers, San Francisco Women Artists, Internat. Arts Guild, Centro Studie Scambi Internazionale, Delta Kappa Gamma, Alpha Omicron Pi, Kappa Delta Pi, Pi Lambda Theta. Home: 567 E Lassen St Sp 701 Chico CA 95926

TURNER, JANIS ELAINE, budget analyst; b. Chattanooga, July 12, 1950; d. Thomas Martin and Elva Marie (Parrot) T.; B.S. in Math., Middle Tenn. State U., 1972; M.B.A. in Mktg., N.Y.U., 1981. Exec. sec. Arlen Shopping Centers Co., Chattanooga, 1973; mgr. loan and discount dept. Commerce Union Bank, Chattanooga, 1974; flight attendant Am. Airlines, N.Y.C., 1975, analyst mktg. dept., 1976-79, budget analyst, 1980—. Mem. Murray Hill. Com. Mem. Assn. M.B.A. Execs. Home: 288 Lexington Ave New York NY 10016 Office: LaGuardia Airport Flushing NY 11371

TURNER, JEAN-LOUISE, press sec.; b. Washington, Sept. 29, 1942; d. Fletcher Wood and Mary Louise (Gant) T.; student Howard U., 1959-62; B.A., Fed. City Coll., 1970; M.A., 1972; children—Nathaniel Anthony Landry, Mark Andrew Landry. Coordinator public relations Sta. WRC-TV, Washington, 1969; adminstr. prodn., 1970-72; mgmt. trainee NBC, Washington, 1972; producer spls. Sta. WRC-TV, 1972-76, asso. producer documentaries, 1972-76; mgr. community affairs and public affairs, host Sta. WRC/WKYS, Washington, 1976-78, producer WRC 1978-79; media rep. PEPCO, Washington, 1979-81; press aide D.C. City Council, 1981—. Judge Gabriel awards; mem. media panel D.C. Arts and Humanities Commn.; bd. dirs. Anchor Mental Health Assn., Epilepsy Found. Am.; career role model St. Anthony's High Sch. Recipient Hallmark award Jr. Achievement, 1976, Public Service award Washington Area Council Alcoholism and Drug Abuse, 1977; Public Interest award Council Better Bus. Burs. Inc., 1977. Mem. Capital Press Club, Washington Assn. Black Journalists, Nat. Acad. TV Arts and Scis., Nat. Assn. Public Continuing Adult Edn., Washington Women's Forum (charter), Alpha Kappa Alpha. Roman Catholic. Editorial bd. NAPCAE Exchange, 1979-81. Home: 2715 31st Pl NE Washington DC 20018 Office: 1350 E St NW Washington DC 20004

TURNER, JOAN GALE, nurse; b. Charleston, S.C., Feb. 12, 1944; diploma in nursing Orange Meml. Hosp., Orlando, Fla., 1964; B.S. with high honors in Nursing, Fla. State U., 1973; M.S. with high honors in Epidemiology and Community Health, U. Md., Balt., 1975; postgrad. U. Ala. Charge nurse emergency room Orange Meml. Hosp., 1968-72; clin. asso. U. Ala., Birmingham, 1974; instr. nursing Tuskegee (Ala.) Inst., 1975; clin. specialist in epidemiology Church Hosp. Corp., Balt., 1976; asst. prof. nursing U. Fla., 1976-80, Sch. Nursing, Grad. Sch., U. Ala., Birmingham, 1980—; nurse cons. in infection control; program designer, writer on infection control Fla. Ednl. Network, 1977, 78. Served with Nurse Corps, USAF, 1966-68; maj. U.S. Army Res. Women of Moose scholar, 1961; Fed. Nurse Traineeship grantee, 1972-75. Mem. Assn. Practitioners in Infection Control, Am. Nurses Assn., Nat. League Nursing, Women Unltd., Sigma Theta Tau. Address: 3636 Belmont Rd Birmingham AL 35210

TURNER, MARGUERITE ROSE COWLES, librarian; b. Port Sulphur, La., June 21, 1941; d. John Clinton and Marguerite Eileen (Slaybaugh) Cowles; B.A., U. New Orleans, 1963; M.L.S., La. State U., 1966; M.A. in History, U. So. Miss., 1970; divorced; 1 son, Jeffrey Jason. Reference librarian edn. div. U. So. Miss., 1966-70; librarian Pascagoula (Miss.) Jr. High Sch., 1970-71, Irwin County High Sch., Ocilla, Ga., 1971-72; dir. Fitzgerald (Ga.) Carnegie Library, 1974-80; adminstrv. librarian Assumption Parish Library, Napoleonville, La., 1980—. Sunday sch. tchr. First Baptist Ch., Fitzgerald, 1978-80, Napoleonville, 1980—. Mem. ALA, La. Library Assn. Democrat. Author poems, contbr. articles profl. jours. Office: Assumption Parish Library Drawer A Napoleonville LA 70309

TURNER, MARIE ROBERTS, bank exec.; b. Hindman, Ky., June 9, 1900; d. John M. and Lauraine (Watts) Roberts; A.B., Morehead U., 1932; m. Ervine Turner, Jan. 23, 1919 (dec.); children—Lois Irene (dec.), John Raymond, Treva Louraine. Dep. law ofcl., supt. Breathitt County Schs., 1931-69; pres. Citizens Bank of Jackson (Ky.), 1968—. pres. Breathitt County Club, 1932-34; Mem. Ky. State Democratic Central Com., 1934—; vice chmn. Ky. Dem. Exec. Com., 1966-81. Office: Citizens Bank of Jackson 1138 Main St Jackson KY 41339

TURNER, MARTHA ANNE, author, educator; b. Warren, Tex.; B.A., Stephen F. Austin U., 1930; M.A. (Grad. fellow), U. Tex., 1945; postgrad. U. So. Calif., summer 1943, U. Tex., 1951-52. Head English dept. Dayton (Tex.) High Sch., 1930-37; dir. English program David Crockett Sr. High Sch., Conroe, Tex., 1940-46; prof. English, Sam Houston State U., Huntsville, Tex., 1946-74, univ. publicist, 1946-64; freelance writer, 1974—. Gen. chmn. Tex. Joint English Com. for Schs. and Colls., 1966. Recipient research grants Sam Houston U., 1967-69; Plaque for 25 years outstanding service to Sam Houston State U.; named Outstanding Woman Huntsville chpt. AAUW, 1971. Author: White Dawn, 1943; The City and Other Poems, 1946; Sam Houston and His Twelve Women, 1966; The Life and Times of Jane Long, 1969; William Barret Travis: His Sword And His Pen, 1972; The Yellow Rose of Texas: The Story of A Song, 1971; Women in Texas, 1972; Texas Epic: An American Story, 1974; Old Nacogdoches in the Jazz Age, 1976; The Yellow Rose of Texas: Her Saga and Her Song with The Santa Anna Legend, 1976; Richard Bennett Hubbard: An American Life, 1979; Clara Driscoll: An American Tradition, 1979; The World of John Thomason, 1983; editor: Tools of the Earthmover, 1951; contbr. articles to profl. jours., also to Marine Corps Gazette, Publs. Tex. Folklore Soc. Home: Huntsville TX 77340

TURNER, MARY LOUISE, librarian, educator; b. Quincy, Ill., Oct. 13, 1925; d. Thelbert R. and Ellen E. (Tucker) T.; A.B., U. Mo., 1967, A.M. (Mo. State Library scholar), 1968, Ph.D. in Ednl. Media, 1978; postgrad. U. Tex., 1973-74, 74-75, U. Nebr., 1976, St. Cloud State U., 1979. Library asst. Little Dixie Regional Library, Moberly, Mo., 1959-62, U. Mo., Columbia, 1962-67; cons. for instl. library services Mo. State Library, Jefferson City, 1968-69; librarian Mo. Tng. Sch. for Boys, Boonville, 1969-71, Parkway N. Sr. High Sch., Creve Coeur, Mo., 1971-73; reference librarian Meramec Community Coll., St. Louis, summer, 1972; head librarian El Paso (Tex.) Community Coll., 1973-74; audiovisual ednl. specialist Grad. Sch. Library Sci., U. Tex., Austin, 1974-75; instr. library sci. Coll. Edn., U. Nebr., Omaha, 1975-76, dir. Ednl. Tech. Center, Coll. Edn., 1976-77; div. leader for instrn. Learning Resource Services, St. Cloud (Minn.) State U., 1978-79; chief edn. and info. Med. Coll. Ga. Library, Augusta, 1979—, asso. prof. library sci., 1979—. Sec. career planning and counseling Huntsville (Mo.) Meth. Ch., 1978. Recipient cert. of recognition Mid-Mo. Mental Health Center, 1967. Mem. ALA, Assn. Ednl. Communication and Tech., Internat. Visual Literacy Assn., Am. Soc. Info. Sci., Assn. for Computing Machinery, NEA, Ga. Health Sci. Library Assn., Mo. Assn. Sch. Librarians, Mo. Library Assn., Ga. Library Assn., Ga. Assn. Instrnl. Tech., Central Savannah Regional Assn., Med. Library Assn., Internat. Platform Assn., AAUW, Bus. and Profl. Women, U. Mo. Alumni Assn., Kappa Delta Pi, Beta Phi Mu. Contbr. articles on ednl. communications and instructional materials to profl. publs. Home: 2534 Yorkshire Dr Augusta GA 30909 Office: Library Medical Coll of Georgia Augusta GA 30912

TURNER, MARY PAULINE CURTIS (MRS. JAMES CASTLE TURNER), artist; b. Lincoln, Nebr., Feb. 14, 1916; d. William Clapp and Nellie (Lee) Curtis; student Wilson Tchrs. Coll., 1940, Corcoran Sch. Art, 1950-54, Am. U., 1955; m. James Castle Turner, Apr. 14, 1934; children—Vivian Lee Turner Polak, Daniel Castle, Brian, Lisa, Lauran. Exhibited at Corcoran Gallery, 1951, Rockville Art Center, 1968, bronze sculpture of Esther Peterson, asst. sec. labor under Kennedy and Johnson at Rehoboth Beach Art League, 1968; retrospective one-man show Labor Tng. Center, Washington, 1978; art tchr. for ret. persons Sargent House Project, 1965-69. Housing chmn. LWV, 1950; U.S del. Trade Union Conf., Blackpool, Eng., 1977; mem. budget com. D.C. Schs., 1969; mem. D.C. Council Arts and Humanities, 1974; membership chmn. Mus. African Art, 1974—; bd. dirs. Washington Ballet, 1976-82. Recipient Ronshein award, 1951, prizes Corcoran Sch., 1951, Washington Area award, 1952. Episcopalian (vestry 1969-71, pres. all women's activities 1969, mem. ch. centennial com.). Home: 6961 32d St NW Washington DC 20015

TURNER, PAMELA JAYNE, Presdl. staff ofcl.; b. Newport, R.I., Oct. 29, 1944; d. Fontaine Stoughton and Irene (Langstaff) T.; B.A., Ind. U., 1966. Legis. asst. to Senator Edward J. Gurney, 1967-75; chief legis. asst. to Senator John G. Tower, 1975-81; dep. asst. to Pres. for legis. affairs, Washington, 1981—. Home: 2126 Connecticut Ave NW Washington DC 20008 Office: The White House Washington DC 20500

TURNER, PAMELA WALKER, educator; b. Montgomery, Ala., July 28, 1943; d. Frederick J. and Yvonne L.B. (Chaplin) Walker; B.A. in Econs., Wellesley Coll., 1965; S.M. in Mgmt., Sloan Sch., M.I.T., 1971; m. F. Cort Turner, III, Oct. 19, 1968; children—Frederica Chaplin, F. Cort, IV. Cons. energy econs. Arthur D. Little, Inc., Cambridge, 1965-67; mem. corp. orgn.-info. staff, dept. mgr. mktg. div. Soc. Nationale de Siderurgie, Algiers, Algeria, 1970-72; dir. recruitment and placement, Sloan Sch. Mgmt., M.I.T., 1975-79, mgr. accelerated master's program, 1978-79, dir. external relations, 1979—, lectr. in mgmt., 1978—; cons. in field. Clubs: Wellesley Coll. (Boston); Longwood Cricket. Address: 1010 Memorial Dr Cambridge MA 02138

TURNER, PATRICIA RAE, ednl. adminstr.; b. Vernon, Tex., May 15, 1935; d. James Ray and Linnie Maria (Corgill) Watson; B.B.A., East Tex. State U., 1971, M.B.A., 1974, postgrad., 1978—; m. Donald H. Turner, Dec. 20, 1969. Program coordinator div. continuing edn. East Tex. State U., Commerce, 1970-72, dir. student devel., 1974-76; asst. dir. community service Mountain View Coll., Dallas, 1972-73; dir. div. adult and continuing edn. Angelo State U., San Angelo, Tex., 1974; mgr. South Central Tex. Regional Tng. Center, Tex. Engring. Extension Service, Tex. A&M U. System, San Antonio, 1978—; mem. region 20 coordinating coop. com. Tex. Edn. Agy., 1982—. Bd. dirs. San Antonio Indsl. Devel. Authority, 1982—; mem. A-95 rev. com. Alamo Area Council Govt., 1981; mem. vocat. and tech. adv. com. United San Antonio; mem. budget allocations panel United Way; mem. S.E. Devel. Found., Gov.'s Com. on Status of Women. Recipient cert. of appreciation U.S. Navy Dept., 1975; appreciation resolution East Tex. State U. Bd. Regents, 1974; named Today Woman, San Antonio Light newspaper, 1982. Mem. Adult Edn. Assn., Tex. Assn. Community Service and Continuing Edn. (dir., research com.), Am. Soc. Tng. and Devel., Tex. Press Women, Nat. Fedn. Press Women, Nat. Community Service Council, Tex. Assn. Continuing Adult Edn. (inter-instl. relations com. 1978-81), Assn. Continuing Higher Edn., C. of C. (com. bus. expansion task force, consular liaison com., legis. com.), San Antonio Mfrs. Assn., San Antonio Bus. and Profl. Women's Fedn., Kappa Delta Phi, Phi Delta Kappa, Alpha Chi, Iota Lambda Sigma. Baptist. Club: Zonta (dir., status of women com., public affairs com.). Editor, contbg. author: Handbook for Employing the Handicap, 1978. Home: 1506 Caper Ln San Antonio TX 78232 Office: PO Box 40 San Antonio TX 78291

TURNER, SHIRLEY KERSEY, coll. adminstr.; b. Dover, N.J., July 3, 1941; d. Robert Nathaniel, Sr., and Catherine Emma (Smith) Kersey; B.S., Trenton (N.J.) State Coll., 1966; M.A., Rider Coll., 1973; postgrad. Rutgers U., 1975-80; m. Donald Ray Turner, June 19, 1965; children—Jacqueline, Donald C. Tchr., Trenton Bd. Edn., 1966-70; asst. dir., counselor equal opportunity program Rider Coll., Lawrenceville, N.J., 1970-74, dir. office career devel. and placement, 1974—; pres. Tri-Kersey, Inc. Mem. N.J. Council on Arts, 1975-79; bd. dirs. Urban League Met. Trenton, 1975—; mem. Lawrence Twp. Zoning Bd. Adjustment, 1979—, Mercer County Improvement Authority, 1979-82; v.p. Lawrence Twp. Democratic Club, 1980—; pres. chpt. N.J. Fedn. Dem. Women, 1982—. Mem. N.J. Bd. Realtors, Am. Personnel and Guidance Assn., Middle Atlantic Placement Assn., Coll. Placement Council. Home: 125 Lawrenceville-Penn Rd Lawrenceville NJ 08648 Office: 2085 Lawrenceville Rd Lawrenceville NJ 08648

TURNER, SHIRLEY SUE, med. technologist, lab. adminstr.; b. Danbury, Iowa, Nov. 17, 1935; d. Wilmer and Aleva Alice (Diment) Earnest; cert. med. tech. St. Joseph Mercy Hosp. Sch. Med. Tech., 1956; student Nebr. State Tchrs. Coll., 1953-55; m. Edmund Bruce Turner, Sept. 30, 1965; 1 dau., Lisa Kay. Gen. lab. technician Magic Valley Meml. Hosp., Twin Falls, Idaho, 1956-57, Buena Vista County Hosp., Storm Lake, Iowa, 1957-59, Rockwood Clinic, Spokane, Wash., 1969-60; lab., x-ray technician Greene County Hosp., Jefferson, Iowa, 1961-65; chief technologist Gt. S.W. Gen. Hosp., Grand Prairie, Tex., 1965-71; technologist spl. chemistry dept., electrophoresis and autoanalyzers, Internat. Clin. Labs., Fort Worth, 1971-73; supr. chemistry dept. Pathology Assos. of Tex., Fort Worth, 1973-75; chief technologist Dallas-Ft. Worth Med. Center, Grand Prairie, Tex., 1975—; mem. med. lab. technician adv. bd. El Centrol Community Coll., Dallas. Mem. Am. Soc. Clin. Pathologists (affiliate mem., cert. med. technologist), Am. Soc. Med. Technologists. Republican. Methodist. Address: 3544 Granada Fort Worth TX 76118

TURNER, SUZANNE, state ofcl.; b. Hollywood, Fla., July 29, 1943; d. John F. and Lucille D. Turner; B.S., Ind. State U., 1964, M.S., 1972; postgrad. Ind. U. Sch. Law, 1964-66; postgrad. John Hopkins U., Mich. State U., Tex. Tech U., Ky. State U. Disability adjudicator Ind. Dept. Public Instrn., 1964-65, vocat. rehab. counselor, 1965-67; counselor women's prison Ind. Dept. Corrections, 1967-68; field cons. Ind. Dept. Health, 1968-69; exec. dir. Johnson County (Ind.) Assn. for Retarded Citizens, 1969-70; asso. dir. Ind. Mental Retardation Planning Project, 1970-72; evaluator Marion County (Ind.) Health and Hosp. Corp., 1972-73; dir. residential services Ohio Devel. Disabilities, Inc., Columbus 1973-76; grants coordinator Epilepsy Found. Am., Washington, 1976-77, dir. tech. assistance, 1977-78; dir. tech. assistance Nat. Assn. Mental Retardation Program Dirs., Arlington, Va., 1978-79; intergovtl. liaison for handicapped HUD, Washington, 1979; spl. asst. to dep. asst. sec. for legislation Dept. Health and Human Services, Washington 1979-81; commr. Dept. Social Services, Commonwealth of Ky., Frankfort, 1981—; mem. Ky. Council on Developmental Disabilities, Ky. Juvenile Justice Commn. Chmn. human resources com. LWV, Arlington County, Va., 1978, chmn. womens rights com., 1979-81; mem. Arlington County Community Block Grant Adv. Bd., 1978-79, 80-81, Arlington County Criminal Justice Com., 1980-81; mem. exec. com. Arlingtonians for a Better County, 1980-81. Named Ind.'s Outstanding Young Woman, 1972; recipient award for outstanding service Ohio Assn. Retarded Citizens, 1974; honored by Ohio Gen. Assembly, 1976; recipient Disting. Alumni award Ind. State U., 1981. Mem. Am. Correctional Assn., Nat. Assn. Juvenile Correctional Agys., Nat. Assn. Retarded Citizens, Ky. Council on Crime and Delinquency, Ky. Assn. Retarded Citizens, Johnson County Assn. Retarded Citizens, Am. Pub. Welfare Assn., Ind. State U. Alumni Assn., AAUW. Democrat. Baptist. Clubs: Badoura Temple, Daus. of Nile. Co-author: Community Living for Ohio Developmentally Disabled Citizens, Vols. I and II; Guide to Epilepsy Services; Housing for Developmentally Disabled Citizens; Our Human Resources; author: Guidelines for the Establishment of a Group Home; Resource Guide for Persons with a Developmental Disability. Office: 275 E Main St Frankfort KY 40621

TURNER, VERA LEE, editor; b. Ottawa County, Okla., Mar. 7, 1930; d. Luther Francis and Grace Rebecca (Kidwell) Smith; student Crowder Coll., Neosho, Mo., 1971; m. Fred Elton Turner, Mar. 4, 1950; children—Katherine Lee Turner Cole, Mary Ellen Turner Fisher. Sec., bookkeeper Milnot Co., Seneca, Mo., 1948-49; with Seneca News-Dispatch, 1969—, society editor, 1980—. Sec., treas. Seneca Sr. Citizens Housing Corp., 1977-80. Mem. Mo. Press Women, Nat. Fedn. Press Women, Mo. Highway Press. Baptist. Clubs: Seneca Study, VFW Aux. Home: 103 Walnut St Seneca MO 64865 Office: Drawer E Seneca MO 64865

TURNIPSEED, DENISE TREMBLY, mktg. exec.; b. San Francisco, June 3, 1950; d. Jean Evan and Mary Frances (O'Connor) Tremley; B.S., Ill. State U., 1973; 1 son, Eric Brading. Customer service/sales rep. StarData, Crystal Lake, Ill., 1976-77; mktg. rep. Datacorp, Chgo., 1977-79, Anacomp Micrographics, Los Angeles, 1978-80, Honeywell, Los Angeles, 1980-81, Automated Concepts, Inc., Century City, Calif., 1981-82; sr. mktg. rep. ICS Group, Inc., Torrance, Calif., 1982—. Pres., Camelot Primary Sch. PTA, Chgo., 1977-78. Mem. Exec. Females, Nat. Assn. Bus. and Indsl. Saleswomen, Data Processing Mgmt. Assn. (dir.). Office: 3848 Carson St Suite 320 Torrance CA 90503

TUROCK, BETTY JANE, info. scientist, educator; b. Scranton, Pa., June 12; d. David and Ruth Carolyn (Sweetser) Argust; B.A. magna cum laude (Charles Weston scholar), Syracuse U., 1955; postgrad. (scholar) U. Pa., 1956; M.L.S., Rutgers U., 1970, Ph.D., 1981; m. Frank M. Turock, June 16, 1956; children—David L., B. Drew. Library and materials coordinator Holmdel (N.J.) Public Schs., 1963-65; story-teller Wheaton (Ill.) Public Library, 1965-67; ednl. media specialist Alhambra Public Sch., Phoenix, 1967-70; br. librarian, area librarian, head extension service Forsyth County Public Library System, Winston-Salem, N.C., 1970-73; asst. dir. Montclair (N.J.) Public Library, 1973-75, dir., 1975-77; asst. dir. Monroe County Library System, Rochester, N.Y., 1978-81; asst. prof. Rutgers U. Grad. Sch. Communications, Info. and Library Studies, 1981—; dir. Grass Roots, Inc., Montclair, 1974—; vis. instr. Rutgers U. Grad. Sch. Library and Info. Studies, 1980—. Trustee, Raritan Twp. (N.J.) Public Library, 1961-62; mem. Bd. Edn. Raritan Twp., 1962-66; mem. Title VII Adv. Bd., Montclair Public Schs., 1975-77; mem. coordinating council Task Force on Women, 1978—; treas. Social Responsibilities Round Table, 1978—. Named Woman of Yr., Raritan-Holmdel Woman's Club, 1975. Mem. ALA, Public Library Assn., NOW, Rutgers U. Grad. Sch. Library and Info. Studies Alumni Assn. (pres. 1977-78), Phi Theta Kappa, Psi Chi, Beta Phi Mu, Pi Beta Phi. Unitarian. Contbr. articles to profl. jours. Home: 11 Undercliff Rd Montclair NJ 07042 Office: Rutgers U 185 College Ave New Brunswick NJ 08903

TUROFF, CAROLE RUTH, lawyer, newspaper columnist; b. Cleve., June 14, 1937; d. Sam and Edna (Siegel) Lecht; B.A., Am. Internat. Coll., 1961; J.D., Cleve. Marshall Law Sch., 1970; m. Jack N. Turoff, Aug. 19, 1961; children—Hyleri Beth, Raechel Dawn, Elana Kay, Avril Jo. Admitted to Ohio bar, 1970; individual practice law, Cleve., 1970—; spl. counsel to atty. gen. Ohio, 1971—; real estate broker Cuyahoga Realty, Cleve., 1976—; columnist Cleve. Press, 1974—; tchr. English, Richmond Heights (Ohio) High Sch., 1961-62; lectr. in field. Chairperson community March of Dimes; active various polit. campaigns; del. Am. Israeli Polit. Affairs com., Israel task force; worker with Ralph Nader in Consumer Fraud; mem. exec. com. Cleve. Congress; founder Women in Divorce; session chairperson Internat. Woman's Yr. UN, Mexico, 1975; TV reporter Nat. Women's Conf., Houston. Recipient trophy as keynote speaker Internat. Woman's Yr. program, NASA. Mem. Internat. Platform Assn., Am. Trial Lawyers, Ohio, Cleve. bar assns., Nat. Women Lawyers. Democrat. Jewish. Club: Nat. Bd. Am. Mizrachi Women. Home: 2569 Snowberry Ln Pepper Pike OH 44124 Office: 24700 Chagrin Blvd #306 Beachwood OH 44122

TURPIN, PATRICIA MARIE GRAY, nurse; b. Flushing, N.Y., Apr. 30, 1946; d. Edward Sumner and Blanche Elizabeth (Wiencke) Gray; B.S.N., U. Tex., 1968, M.S.N., 1978; m. James Leslie Turpin, Nov. 29, 1969. Staff nurse, head nurse, supr. critical care St. David's Community Hosp., Austin, Tex., 1968-77; asst. dir. nursing service-critical care and medicine Seton Med. Center, Austin, 1977-80, dir. nursing critical care, 1980-82; dir. nursing Northwest Mediplex, Austin, 1982—. Mem. Am. Assn. Critical Care Nurses (treas. local chpt. 1975-77), Am. Heart Assn. (v.p., dir. div. level), Am., Tex. (2d v.p., dir. dist. level) nurses assns., Sigma Theta Tau, Phi Kappa Phi. Republican. Episcopalian. Club: Austin Yacht. Home: 11406 Hare Trail Austin TX 78750 Office: 11612 Angus Rd Austin TX 78759

TURZINSKI-DUROVY, PATRICIA ANN, business cons.; b. Milw., Nov. 11, 1950; d. Richard James and Doris Lorene (Smith) Turzinski; student U. Wis., Milw., 1968-69; m. David Michael Durovy, June 25, 1978. Supr. mortgage servicing A.L. Grootemaat & Sons., Milw., 1969-72; legal sec., 1973; exec. sec. Plastronics Inc., Milw., 1974; mgr. mortgage servicing Universal Mortgage Co., Milw., 1975; mgr. Outpost Natural Foods Coop., Milw., 1975-76; owner Genesis, Milw., 1976-79; owner Manifestation Mgmt. Inc., Milw., 1979—; founder, bd. dirs. Women's Resource Network Milw.; bd. dirs. Save-A-Farm, Inc.; co-founder, bd. dirs. Tai Chi Chuan Center, Milw.; instr. Cardinal Stritch Coll., Marquette U., Waukesha County Tech. Coll. Mem. Am. Bus. Women's Assn., Nat. Assn. Female Execs., Am. Soc. Tng. and Devel., Milw. Feminist Therapy Network, Assn. Humanistic Psychology (coordinator Midwest conf. 1981—). Author articles, cassette tapes in field. Address: 2437 N Booth St Milwaukee WI 53212

TUTHILL, BYRDINE HARTMAN, food service adminstr., educator; b. Waldo, Kans., Apr. 27, 1923; d. Roy Martin and Serena Jeanette (Wells) Hartman; B.A., U. No. Iowa, 1945; M.S., U. Wis., 1956; 1 son, John Hartman. Tchr. public schs., Belmond, Iowa, 1946; tchr., dir. pub. sch. food service, Newton, Iowa, 1947; dietitian, head dietitian Weld County Hosp., Greeley, Colo., 1949-52; instr. U. Wis., 1953-56; prof. food systems mgmt., asso. dir. dept. nutrition and dietetics Med. Center, U. Mo., Columbia, 1956-80, adminstr. dept. nutrition and dietetics Univ. Hosp. and Clinics, 1980—; cons./liaison Mo. Dept. Edn., Div. Sch. Food Service, 1956—; cons. Nutrition Program for Elderly, U.S. V.I., 1979. Mem. Am. Dietetic Assn., Mo. Dietetic Assn. (pres. 1966-67), Am. Sch. Food Services, Nutrition Today Soc., Council on Hotel Restaurant and Instl. Edn. Author: Computer Assisted Food Management Systems, 1974; contbr. articles to profl. jours. Home: 1637 Highridge Circle Columbia MO 65201 Office: U Mo Health Scis Center N122 Columbia MO 65212

TUTT, CELESTINE CLARESSA, librarian; b. Winston Salem, N.C., Nov. 9, 1932; d. Arthur Loveliest and Mamie (Guerrant) T.; B.A., Winston Salem State U., 1952; M.L.S., Columbia U., 1971, postgrad., 1981—; m. Henry McNeal Bennett, Dec. 28, 1977; children—Richard Bennett, Kathryn Bennett. Librarian, Urban Center, Columbia U., N.Y.C., 1971-73, asst. librarian Whitney M. Young Jr. Meml. Library Social Work, 1973-77, librarian, 1978—; mem. papers adv. com. Whitney M. Young Jr., 1975-78, chmn., 1979—. Mem. ALA, Council Social Work Edn., Internat. Council Social Welfare, N.Y. Urban League. Home: 456 Riverside Dr New York NY 10027 Office: 420 W 118th St New York NY 10027

TUTTLE, LINDA LOU, real estate broker; b. McBain, Mich., Apr. 24, 1940; d. Lewis Earl and Vonda Virginia (Cavanagh) Corner; ed. spl. courses Central Mich. U., Ferris State Coll., U. Mich., H. & R. Block income tax course; m. Kenneth Charles Tuttle, July 25, 1971; children by previous marriage—Pamela Rae Friess, Bryce Allen Friess. Sales supr. Sandra Co., 1968-73; sales rep. Avon Products, 1968-77; owner small bus. and individual tax service, 1975—, also real estate sales rep. Accent, Cadillac, Mich., 1977—. Sec.-treas. Cadillac Nursery Sch., 1964, bd. dirs. 1967-68; sec. Franklin PTA, 1969, pres., 1970; active Pal Program, 1972. Mem. Paul Bunyan Realtors Bd. Assn., Cadillac Bus. and Profl. Women. Lutheran. Home: 10901 N Diamond Rd Tustin MI 49688 Office: Parkview Palza Harris St Cadillac MI 49601

TUTWILER, MYRA SMITH, personnel cons.; b. Johnson City, Tenn., Oct. 16, 1942; d. Lynn Bachman and Trula Blanche (Irwin) Smith; student East Tenn. State U., 1960-62; Radiologic Technician, Holston Valley Meml. Hosp., 1963; m. Tommy R. Baker, Oct. 13, 1961; children—Kristi Lynn, Laura Marie; m. 2d, Richard G. Tutwiler, June 8, 1979. Radiol. technologist Radiology Cons., Knoxville, 1963-64, Moses H. Cone Meml. Hosp., Greensboro, N.C., 1964; office mgr.

Albany Advt. Assos. (Ga.), 1966-68; adminstrv. asst. Don Richard Assos., Inc., Bethesda, Md., 1976, cons. personnel, 1977—. Vice pres. Sherwood Elem. Sch. PTA, 1970-71; corr. sec. Ayrlawn Elem. Sch. PTA, 1976-78; leader Brownies, 1970-72; mem. Albany Community Council, 1971-72; bd. dirs. Albany Community Drug Abuse Council, 1972-73; pres. Jr. Woman's Club Albany (Ga.), 1971-72, Chevy Chase (Md.), 1976-77; bd. dirs. Montgomery County Fedn. Women's Clubs, 1976—, Ga. Fedn., 1968-73, Md. Fedn. Women's Clubs, 1973—; hdqrs. coordinator, women vols. coordinator Jimmy Carter for Gov. Campaign, Dougherty County, Ga., 1968-70. Recipient Georgia Allie Bates Jolly Poetry Cup, 1972; Community Improvement award Jr. Woman's Club Chevy Chase, 1978; named Md. Jr. Clubwoman of Yr., 1979. Democrat. Episcopalian. Clubs: Bryce Resort (tennis com. chmn.) (Basye, Va.); Montgomery County (Md.) Young Woman's (treas. 1979-80). Home: 5240 Pooks Hill Rd Bethesda MD 20814 Office: 7315 Wisconsin Ave Suite 303E Bethesda MD 20814

TUZIL, TERESA JORDAN, clin. social worker, psychotherapist; b. N.Y.C., May 13, 1948; d. Lester Francis and Kathleen Geraldine (Brady) Jordan; B.A., St. John's U., 1970; M.S.W., Hunter Coll., 1973, certified in gerontology, 1977; m. Joseph Stephen Tuzil, Jan. 15, 1972; children—Joseph IV, Brian Joseph. Social worker Salvation Army Foster Care and Adoption Services, N.Y.C., 1971-72; sr. caseworker Jewish Assn. for Services to the Aged, N.Y.C., 1973-78; program cons. Community Council of Greater N.Y., N.Y.C., 1978-79; pvt. practice individual and family psychotherapy, Seaford, N.Y., 1976—; adj. clin. instr. Hunter Grad. Sch. Social Work, 1975-78; field instr. Grad. Sch. Social Work, Rutgers U., 1975-77; program cons. Assn. for Services to Aged, Bklyn., 1981—. Certified, registered clin. social worker, N.Y. Mem. Nat. Assn. Social Workers, Acad. Certified Social Workers. Editor: Jour. of Gerontological Social Work, 1977—; contbr. articles to profl. publs. in field. Home and Office: 3859 Tiana St Seaford NY 11783

TWA, INEZ LOUISA ARBUTHNOT, writer; b. Boulder County, Colo., Nov. 9, 1905; d. George John and Nancy Louisa (Brammeier) Arbuthnot; student Coll. Commerce, Stockton, Calif., 1929; m. Norman Osbert Twa, Nov. 7, 1929 (dec.); children—Lois, Gordon, Audrey. Office positions, U.S. and Can., 1929-57; with FAA, 1957-75, sec. CAA, Grand Junction, Colo., 1957-63, adminstrv. asst. to dist. chief FAA, Reno, 1963-65, mgmt. tech./specialist area office, Salt Lake City, 1965-68, mgmt. specialist, asst. motor fleet mgr. Dept. Transp., Los Angeles, 1968-72, regional motor fleet mgr. Rocky Mountain Region, Denver, 1972-75, ret., 1975; author short stories pub. 1978, 79, 80, 81, 82; contbr. stories to Colo. Old Times Mag. Active Mental Health Assn., 1958-63, Republican Party. Recipient award C. of C., 1963; service citation CSC, 1975. Mem. Profl. Secs. Internat., Arbuthnot Family International Assn. Aurora Geneal. Soc. Presbyterian. Home: 800 S Ironton St #95 Aurora CO 80012

TWEEDIE, ELEANOR MARGARET, educator; b. Walton, N.Y., Apr. 22, 1931; d. Robert C. and Lenora F. (Forsythe) Tweedie; B.A., SUNY, Albany, 1952, M.A., 1953; Ph.D., Cornell U., 1971. Tchr. secondary schs., N.Y. and Calif., 1953-61; instr. San Jose (Calif.) City Coll., 1961-62; asst. prof. edn. SUNY, Albany, 1962-63; asso. prof. English, Oneonta, 1963-64; lectr. Cornell U., Ithaca, N.Y., 1964-68; asso. prof. English, Calif. State Univ., Los Angeles, 1968-78, prof., 1978—, asst. to v.p. acad. affairs, 1974-81. Mem. Philol. Assn. Pacific Coast, MLA, Calif. Women in Higher Edn., AAUP. Office: California State University 5151 State University Dr Los Angeles CA 90032

TWISS, MAURINE CHRISTMAN, cons. public relations, author's editor; b. Westervelt, Ill., July 4, 1919; d. Paul and Leota Madge (Jenkins) Christman; student Ill. Wesleyan U., 1937-39; m. Armin Russel Twiss, Oct. 16, 1937; 1 dau., Belinda Sue Twiss Allison. Copywriter, Montgomery Ward Corp., Chgo., 1939-41; editorial copy desk Chgo. Tribune, 1948-49; women's editor Jackson (Miss.) Daily News, 1950-54, feature editor, 1954-55; dir. public info. U. Miss. Med. Center, Jackson, 1955-73, dir. spl. services, 1973-78; cons. public relations, author's editor, Jackson, 1978—. Publicist, Miss. Heart Assn., 1953-70, bd. dirs., 1972-78, mem. So. regional evaluation subcom. Am. Heart Assn., 1970-74, chmn., 1973-74; mem. City of Jackson Planning Bd., 1974—; mem. City of Jackson Zoning Bd., 1976-79, 81—, chmn., 1978-79, chmn. comprehensive plan, 1982-83; mem. adv. council Miss. Employment Security Commn., 1978-79, Southeastern Regional Med. Library Program, 1970-72; pres. Miss. Women's Cabinet of Public Affairs, 1963-64; bd. dirs. New Stage, 1965—, pres., 1974-78; bd. dirs. Jackson Arts Alliance, 1979—, pres., 1981-82. Recipient citation Miss. Assn. Mental Health, 1956, Service to Field award Public Relations Assn. Miss., 1981, numerous state, nat. awards for excellence in writing; named Woman of Achievement, Miss. Press. Women, 1973. Mem. Assn. Am. Med. Colls. Group on Public Relations (chmn. 1967-68, Disting. Service award 1978), Nat. Fedn. Press Women (regional chmn. 1961-65), Miss. Press Women (pres. 1958-60). Democrat. Club: Country of Jackson. Home: 1738 Douglass Dr Jackson MS 39211

TWOHIG, DOROTHY ANN, editor; b. Charleston, W.Va., May 10, 1927; d. David Simon and Nell C. Twohig; B.A. summa cum laude, Morris Harvey Coll., 1952; M.A., Columbia U., 1954, postgrad., 1969—. Editorial staff Dictionary Am. Biography, 1957-59; asst. editor Papers of Alexander Hamilton, Columbia U., N.Y.C., 1959-69; asso. editor Papers of George Washington, U. Va., Charlottesville, 1969—, asso. prof., 1980—. Recipient Philip M. Hamer award Soc. Am. Archivists, 1977. Mem. Am. Hist. Assn., Assn. Documentary Editing, Soc. Early Am. Historians. Democrat. Editor: The Journal of the Proceedings of the President, 1793-97, 1981; (with Donald Jackson) The Diaries of George Washington, 6 vols., 1976-79. Home: 609 Malcolm Crescent Charlottesville VA 22901 Office: Alderman Library U Virginia Charlottesville VA 22901

TYLER, ANNE, (MRS. TAGHI M. MODARRESSI), author; b. Mpls., Oct. 25, 1941; d. Lloyd Parry and Phyllis (Mahon) T.; B.A.; Duke U., 1961; postgrad. Columbia U., 1962; m. Taghi M. Modarressi, May 3, 1963; children—Tezh, Mitra. Author: (novels) If Morning Ever Comes, 1964; The Tin Can Tree, 1965; A Slipping-Down Life, 1970; The Clock Winder, 1972; Celestial Navigation, 1974; Searching for Caleb, 1976; Earthly Possessions, 1977; Morgan's Passing, 1980; Dinner at the Homesick Restaurant, 1982. Contbr. short stories to nat. mags. Home: 222 Tunbridge Rd Baltimore MD 21212

TYLER, JACQUELINE, nurse; b. Decatur, Ala., Aug. 3, 1938; d. James H. and Hellon E. (Champion) T.; student Birmingham Sch. Law, 1958-59; diploma Carraway Meth. Hosp. Sch. Nursing, 1964; student Auburn U., 1976, U. Ala., 1977-78, St. Joseph's Coll., 1980—; diploma Acad. of Health Scis., 1981. Sec., Social Security Adminstrn., Birmingham, Ala., 1956-61; staff nurse Vis. Nursing Assn., Birmingham, 1964-65; charge nurse Carraway Meth. Hosp., Birmingham, 1965-72; charge nurse blood program nursing ARC, Birmingham, 1972-74, dir. blood program nursing, Little Rock, 1974-75, dir. blood program nursing, Montgomery, Ala., 1975-77, coordinator center collections, Birmingham, 1977-78, asst. dir. blood services nursing Ala. region, 1978-80, asst. to med. dir. blood services, 1980—; chief nurse Hdqrs. 127th Med. Group, Ala. N.G., 1975—, instr. blood collection procedures N.G. Blood Collection Unit, 1975-80. Recipient Service award Ala. N.G., 1977, 1981; registered nurse. Mem. Am. Nurses Assn., Ala. State Nurses Assn., Am Assn. Blood Banks, Ala. N.G. Assn. (mem. public relations com. 1975-76), Carraway Meth. Nurses Alumni Assn. (sec.-treas. 1965-66). Baptist. Home: 1674 Riderwood Trail Birmingham AL 35214 Office: American Red Cross Blood Services Alabama Region 2225 3d Ave N PO Box 11003 Birmingham AL 35202

TYLER, JOANNA ARMIGER, research and counseling psychologist; b. Balt., Jan. 23, 1943; d. William James Armiger and Marie Eileen (Edmonds) Lowery; A.A., Coll. San Mateo, 1968; B.A. cum laude in Psychology, San Jose State U., 1971, M.A. in Psychology, 1973; Ph.D. in Human Devel. Psychology (grad. fellow), U. Md., 1977; 1 son, Christopher Blair. Research asst., instr. U. Md., 1973-77; adj. asst. prof. Catonsville (Md.) Community Coll., 1973-78; sr. research analyst Teledyne Brown Engring., Rockville, Md., 1976-78; tech. mgr. Applied Mgmt. Scis., Silver Spring, Md., 1978-82; pvt. practice psychology, Columbia, Md., 1978—, also research project mgr. Arbitron Co., Laurel, Md., 1982—; conf. presenter; cons. Mem. Howard County Drug Abuse Adv. Council, 1980—. Cert. community coll. tchr. and counselor, Calif.; lic. psychologist, Md. Mem. Md. Psychol. Assn., Am. Psychol. Assn., Phi Kappa Phi. Democrat. Roman Catholic. Contbg. editor to Md. Psychol. Assn. newsletter, 1980—; contbr. articles to profl. jours. Home: 9647 Green Moon Path Columbia MD 21046 Office: Arbitron Bldg Marshall St Laurel MD 20810

TYLER, JUNE DIANE, software cons.; b. Atlanta, June 25, 1946; d. Rufus Guy and Glenese Naomi (Donald) T.; B.B.A. summa cum laude, Ga. State U., 1974; M.B.A., Ind. U., 1977, D.B.A., 1979; 1 son, John W. DeLamater, Jr. Mgr. decision math lab. Ga. State U., Atlanta, 1973-75; fin. coordinator Am. Inst. Decision Sci., Atlanta, 1975-76; asso. instr. Ind. U. Sch. Bus., Bloomington, 1975-77, lectr. acctg., 1977-79; asst. prof. Emory U. Sch. Bus. Adminstrn., Atlanta, 1979-82; account mgr. mfg. systems div. Mgmt. Sci. Am., Atlanta, 1982—. Mem. Ops. Mgmt. Assn., Nat. Assn. Accts., Am. Prodn. and Inventory Control Soc. (treas. Atlanta chpt. 1980). Presenter research papers, profl. speeches. Home: PO Box 49485 Atlanta GA 90359 Office: MSA 57 Executive Park S Atlanta GA 30329

TYLER, MARGO HILLS (MRS. CONVERSE TYLER), found. exec.; b. Salt Lake City, Sept. 4, 1921; d. Harold Haven and Mary Edith (Roberts) Hills; B.A., U. Utah, 1942; m. Converse Tyler, Sept. 30, 1950. Asst. city editor Salt Lake Telegram, Salt Lake City, 1942-45; adminstrv. asst. safety service ARC, Washington, 1945-55; dir. public relations Am. Cancer Soc., Washington, 1957-65, Am. Assn. Motor Vehicle Adminstrs., Washington, 1966-68; dir. public info. Coll. V.I., St. Thomas, 1968-70; asst. dir. communications div. Nat. 4-H Council. Washington, 1970—. Mem. adv. council nat. orgns. Corp. Public Broadcasting, Washington, 1971-77, exec. com., 1973-75, 77; co-founder Public Info. Assn. St. Thomas, V.I., 1969, sec., 1969. Mem. Public Relations Soc. Am. (chpt. bd. 1962-64, 1967, 72-73, 81, v.p. 1980), Mortar Bd., Phi Beta Kappa, Phi Kappa Phi, Delta Gamma. Clubs: Washington Press; Montgomery County Press (Silver Spring, Md.). Office: 7100 Connecticut Ave Washington DC 20015

TYLER, MARY ANN, social worker; b. Mitchell, S.D., Apr. 21, 1939; d. William Reaves and Matilda Emma (Boeke) Ball; B.A., Macalester Coll., 1960; M.S.W., U. Nebr., 1978; m. Stanley H. Tyler, Aug. 14, 1960 (dec. May 1977); children—William, Michael, Kathy Lynn; m. 2d, Robert Sir Louis, May 23, 1981. Exec. dir. Big Bros./Big Sisters of N.E. Nebr., Norfolk, 1973-75; adminstrv. dir. Alcohol and Drug Treatment unit Clarinda (Iowa) Mental Health Inst., 1977-79; dir. transitions/displaced homemaker program YWCA, Omaha, 1980—; nat. bd. dirs., regional rep. Displaced Homemaker Network, Inc., 1981—. Pres., Nebr. Assn. Mental Health; asst. moderator Nebr. Conf., United Ch. of Christ, 1982—. Grantee, United Ch. of Christ, 1981. Mem. AAUW (nat. dir.; past chmn. nat. com. women; dir. widows network, grantee 1981). Acad. Cert. Social Workers, Nat. Assn Social Workers, Nebr. Assn. Mental Health, Older Women's League, Democrat. Home: 548 S 58th St Omaha NE 68106 Office: 222 S 29th St Omaha NE 68131

TYLER, MARY ELIZABETH, religious orgn. adminstr.; b. New Orleans, Sept. 9, 1930; B.A., La. Coll., Pineville, 1951; M.R.E., Southwestern Baptist Theol. Sem., 1953. Sec. to asst. dist. atty. Rapides Parish, Alexandria, La., 1948-51; sec. to pastor 1st Baptist Ch., Knoxville, Tenn., 1953-75; adminstrv. asst. to exec. dir. Christian Life Commn., So. Baptist Conv., Nashville, 1975—. Mem. Nat. Secs. Assn. (pres. Knoxville chpt. 1974-75, pres. Tenn. div. 1978-79), Nat. Assn. Female Execs. Republican. Baptist. Home: 500 5th Ave N #404 Nashville TN 37219 Office: 460 James Robertson Pkwy Nashville TN 37219

TYLER, PHYLLIS STEPHANIE, monument co. exec.; b. Johnstown, N.Y., Dec. 16, 1943; d. Emerson Stevens and Doris Christina (Busse) T.; Student SUNY, Cortland, 1962-63, Syracuse U., 1963-67, 1981. Foreperson, Letter Memls., Johnstown, N.Y., 1963-67, mgr. alternate days Cherry Valley Memls., 1965-67; salesperson Castle Monument Co., Waltham, Mass., 1967-69, mgr. retail br., 1968; owner, mgr., carver Kellogg Memls., Mexico, N.Y., 1969—. Mem. Vol. Ambulance Corps; trustee Village of Mexico, 1971-77, dep. mayor, 1976-78; deacon 1st Presbyterian Ch., 1971-72, trustee, 1973-74, ruling elder, 1975-79, 82—. Recipient various Skiing medals and trophies. Mem. Monument Builders N. Am., Greater Mexico C. of C., Assn. Profl., Managerial and Exec. Women. Republican. Club: Order Eastern Star. Designer and creator memls. and cast bronze art pieces. Home and office: 5358 Academy St Mexico NY 13114

TYLER, THERESA CAMPBELL, YWCA exec.; b. Knoxville, Tenn., Sept. 22, 1935; d. R. Lynn and Theresa (Hudson) Campbell; B.S. in Med. Tech., U. Tenn., 1956; m. H. Park Tyler, Oct. 12, 1956; children—Victor, Lynn, Amie. Med. technologist, Tenn. and Ohio, 1956-61; program dir. South Bend (Ind.) YWCA, 1971-74; addictions planner Ind. Dept. Mental Health, 1974-75; community services coordinator No. Ind. Drug Abuse Services Mental Health Center, South Bend, 1974-78, public relations coordinator, resource devel. specialist, 1978-79; exec. dir. S. Bend YWCA, 1979—; chmn. Ind. All-State YWCA, 1973; mem. Gov. Ind. Addiction Adv. Council, 1978-80; chmn. adv. bd. St. Joseph County Title XX, 1981-82; cons. in field. Trustee South Bend Community Sch. Corp., 1972-76, pres., 1975; commr. Human Rights Commn., 1978—; v.p. South Bend Art Center, 1973-75; bd. dirs. South Bend Vol. Action Center, 1956-79; pres. area council Assn. Jr. Leagues, 1974; elder Presbyn. Ch.; mem. Ind. Task Force Women's Health Issues. Office: YWCA St Joseph County 802 N Lafayette Blvd South Bend IN 46601

TYNDALL, CONNIE BRITT, soft drink bottling co. exec.; b. Clinton, N.C., Feb. 13, 1949; d. Colonel Ashford and Eunice (Bryant) Britt; student in home econs. Campbell Coll., 1967-70; profl. devel. courses Clemson U., 1977-81; m. Jimmie L. Tyndall, Aug. 29, 1970; 1 son, Stuart Harrison. With Wilmington Coca-Cola Bottling Works (N.C.), 1970—, acctg. auditor, 1973-80, adminstrv. officer, 1981—, asst. to pres. in labor negotiations, 1981—. Mem. human relations task force com. New Hanover County (N.C.); treas. Ch. Circle Group, Wesley Meml. United Methodist Ch., Wilmington, 1979-80; co-chairperson Human Relation Month (Songfest), Wilmington, 1980. Mem. N.C. Coca-Cola Bottlers Council, N.C. Softdrink Assn. Democrat. Home: 2325 Camellia Dr Wilmington NC 28403 Office: 921 Princess St Wilmington NC 28401

TYNER, LORRAINE BYRNE, investment adviser; b. N.Y.C., Sept. 8, 1937; d. Patrick John and Mildred (Caruso) Byrne; student Queens Coll., 1957; bus. degree N.Y.U., 1969; m. Sidney D. Tyner, Sept. 30, 1972; children—Debora A. Cellucci, Michael A. Cellucci, Cherylann, Sidney D., Mark A. Asst. account exec. Warner, Bicking & Fenwick, 1968-70; purchasing agt. Elgin Watch Div., 1970-72; v.p. The Boston Co. Capital Group, Inc., 1978—; v.p. The Boston Co. Fin. Strategies, Inc., 1981—; auditor Taunton Jr. Women's Club, 1975-76. Republican. Episcopalian. Home: 7 Carrlyn Rd Brockton MA 02401 Office: 1 Boston Pl Boston MA 02106

TYNES, KATHERINE MORROW, social worker; b. Dallas, Dec. 6, 1951; d. Walker Aubrey and Susanne (McDonald) T.; A.A., Stephens Coll., 1971, B.A., 1972; postgrad. Drury Coll., 1973-74; M.S.W., Tulane U., 1975. Vol. coordinator Springfield Girls Club, 1969-72; social work intern Fed. Med. Center, 1973; sales rep. Canal Art Galleries, 1974-75; caseworker Kingsley House, New Orleans, 1974-75; dir. social services Milne Boy's Home, 1976-81; case mgr. Regional Diagnostic Center, Springfield, Mo., 1981—; dir. Springfield Grocer Co.; treas., dir. Horizon Inn, S.A. Former Mem. bd. Dogwood Trail council Girl Scouts USA, Springfield, Mo. Mem. Mo. Mental Health Assn., Nat. Assn. Social Workers, Mo. Assn. Social Workers, Acad. Cert. Social Workers, Am. Correctional Assn., NEA, S.W. Mo. Horse Show Assn. Episcopalian. Club: Jr. League.

TYNG, ANNE GRISWOLD, architect; b. Kuling, Kiangsi, China, July 14, 1920; d. Walworth and Ethel Atkinson (Arens) Tyng (parents Am. citizens); A.B., Radcliffe Coll., 1942; M.Arch., Harvard U., 1944; Ph.D., U. Pa., 1975; 1 dau., Alexandra Stevens. Asso., Stonorov & Kahn, Architects, 1945-47, Louis I. Kahn, Architect, 1947-73; pvt. practice architecture, Phila., 1973—; asso. prof. U. Pa. Grad. Sch. Fine Arts, 1968—; vis. disting. prof. Pratt Inst., 1979-81; asso. cons. architect Phila. Planning Commn. and Phila. Redevel. Authority, 1952-54, Mill Creek Redevel. Plan, 1954; vis. critic architecture Pratt Inst., 1969, Rensselaer Poly. Inst., 1969, 78, Carnegie Mellon U., 1970, Drexel U., 1972-73, Cooper Union, 1974-75, U. Tex., Austin, 1976; lectr. Archtl. Assn. London, also numerous univs. through U.S. and Can.; subject of films Anne G. Tyng at Parsons Sch. Design, 1972, Anne G. Tyng at U. Minn., 1974, Connecting, 1976, Forming the Future, 1977; subject of slide/tape talk Perception and Proportion, 1980. Fellow Graham Found. for Advanced Study in Fine Arts, 1965, 79-81; IBM fellow Internat. Design Conf., Aspen, 1980. Fellow AIA (Brunner grantee N.Y. chpt. 1964, dir., mem. exec. bd. Phila. chpt. 1976-78); mem. NAD (asso.), Nat. Assn. Archtl. Historians. Democrat. Episcopalian. Club: C. G. Jung Center of Phila. (mem. planning com.), Form Forum (mem. planning com.). Work included in exhibit Drawing Center, N.Y.C., 1979, under Smithsonian sites, U.S., abroad, 1979-82. Contbr. articles to profl. jours. Patentee Tyng Toy. Prin. works include Walworth Tyng Farmhouse (Hon. mention award Phila. chpt. AIA 1953). Home: 2511 Waverly St Philadelphia PA 19146 Office: Dept Architecture Grad Sch Fine Arts U Pa Philadelphia PA 19107

TYRE, IRMA TYRE, banker; b. Wayne County, Ga., Jan. 27, 1933; d. Felton and Myrtle Ester (Roberson) T.; student public schs., Screven Ga.; m. Carroll Jelone Tyre, June 7, 1950; children—Dennis Clayton, Debra Tyre King. Teller, First Nat. Bank, Jesup, Ga., 1966-73; with Citizens Bank, Hoboken, Ga., 1973—, now asst. cashier, br. mgr. Mem. Brantley County C. of C. Baptist. Club: Blackshear Women's. Office: Citizens Bank PO Box 37 Hoboken GA 31542

TYREE, JUDITH LEE, business services co. exec.; b. Boston, Oct. 1, 1935; d. George Thomas and Christine Ogg Mahar; grad. Hickox Bus. Sch., 1968; children—Michael, Kim. Supr. data processing Lechmere Sales, 1966-68; exec. sec. Gen. Electric Co., 1969-70; v.p. Kino Springs, Tucson, 1970-75; pres. Exec. Suite, Tucson, 1975—. So. Ariz. coordinator Re-Election of U.S. Senator DeConcini, 1982; mem. Ariz. Bd. Pvt., Tech. and Bus. Schs.; mem. adv. com. Pima Community Coll.; mem. bd. 88 Crime; chmn. Pvt. Industry Council, 1980-82. Mem. Tucson Met. C. of C. (dir.), Exec. Women Internat., Exec. Women Council, Bus. Info. Club. Democrat. Roman Catholic. Clubs: Second Tuesday, Soroptimist (Woman Helping Woman award 1981, Excellence award 1982). Home: 2723 N Beverly St Tucson AZ 85712 Office: Exec Suite 5055 E Broadway Room C-214 Tucson AZ 85711

TYRRELL, ELIZABETH ANN, biologist, educator; b. Pittsfield, Mass., Oct. 16, 1931; d. Norman Baker and Mary (Sproule) T.; B.S. in Biology, Simmons Coll., Boston, 1953; M.S. in Bacteriology, U. Mich., 1957, Ph.D., 1962; m. P.C. Rajam, July 7, 1968 (dec.). Research asst. virology Parke, Davis & Co., Detroit, 1953-55; mem. faculty Smith Coll., Northampton, Mass., 1960—, prof. biol. scis., 1979—. Mem. Am. Soc. Microbiology (past br. pres.), AAAS, Assn. Am. Med. Colls., Sigma Xi. Roman Catholic. Club: Connecticut Valley Simmons. Office: Clark Sci Center Smith Coll Northampton MA 01063

TYRRELL, KARINE, tech. writer; b. Saarbrucken, Germany, Nov. 4, 1940; came to U.S., 1968, naturalized, 1978; d. Eduard and Charlotte (Faber) Ambrosius; B.A., McMaster U., Can., 1964; M.A., So. Ill. U., 1972, postgrad., 1977—; m. James Tyrrell, Aug. 27, 1964 (div. 1979); 1 child, Dalton. Tchr., Hamilton (Ont., Can.) Sch. Bd., 1964-65, Ottawa (Ont., Can.) Sch. Bd., 1966-68; research asst. U.S. Grant Assos., So. Ill. U., Carbondale, 1973-74, teaching asst. 1974-77, dissertation fellow, 1977-78; tech. writer Action Data Services, St. Louis, 1979-80, Boeing Computer Services, Wichita, Kans., 1980—. Home: 1235 S Pershing Ave Wichita KS 67218 Office: 3801 S Oliver St M/S K12-06 Wichita KS 67210

TYSER-KRIVO, PATTI E., clin. social worker; b. Houston, Dec. 11, 1952; d. Frederick Stuart and Evelyn Faye (Finkelstein) Tyser; B.A. in Sociology, U. Houston, 1974; M.S.W., Loyola U., Chgo., 1977; m. David Alan Krivo, June 15, 1974; 1 dau., Ariel Sara Part-time group worker Houston Jewish Community Center, 1970-73; child care worker Mary Bartelme Homes, residential treatment, Chgo., 1974-75, social worker dir., 1977-81; social worker, team leader St. Mary of Nazareth Hosp., Chgo., 1977; summer camp counselor, 1968-70. Bd. dirs., vol., casework sec. Jewish Big Sisters, Chgo., 1971—Mem. Acad. Cert. Social Workers, Nat. Assn. Social Workers. Home: 8307 N Kilbourn St Skokie IL 60076

TYSON, CICELY, actress; b. N.Y.C.; d. William and Theodosia Tyson; student N.Y. U., Actors Studio; hon. doctorates Atlanta U., Loyola U., Lincoln U. Former sec., model; stage appearances include The Blacks, 1961-63, Off-Broadway, 1961-63, Moon on a Rainbow Shaw, 1962-63, Tiger, Tiger, Burning Bright, Broadway; star film Sounder, 1972; other film appearances include: Twelve Angry Men, 1957, Odds Against Tomorrow, 1959, The Last Angry Man, 1959, A Man Called Adam, 1966, The Comedians, 1967, The Heart is a Lonely Hunter, 1968, The Blue Bird, 1976, The River Niger, 1976, A Hero Ain't Nothin' but a Sandwich, 1978, The Concorde-Airport '79, 1979; TV appearances include series East Side, West Side, 1963, spl. TV play, The Autobiography of Miss Jane Pittman, 1973, 1974; series Roots, 1977, King, 1978, TV movie Just An Old Sweet Song, 1976. Co-founder Dance Theatre of Harlem; bd. dirs. Urban Gateways; trustee Human Family Inst., Am. Film Inst. Recipient Vernon Price award, 1962; named best actress for Sounder, Atlanta Film Festival, 1972; Nat. Soc. Film Critics, 1972; nominee best actress for Sounder, Acad. awards, 1972; Emmy award for best actress in a spl., 1973; also awards NAACP, Nat. Council Negro Women; Capitol Press award. Address: care Internat Creative Mgmt 8899 Beverly Blvd Los Angeles CA 90048 *

TYSON, HELEN FLYNN, civic leader; b. Wilmington, N.C., Feb. 17, 1913; d. Walter Thomas and Fannie Elizabeth (Smith) Flynn; A.A., Pineland Jr. Coll., 1931; student Guilford Coll., 1932-33, Am. U., Washington, 1961-62; m. James Franklin Tyson, Dec. 25, 1940. Auditor,

Disbursing Office, U.S. Civil Service, AUS, Ft. Bragg, N.C., 1935-46, chief clerical asst. Disbursing Office, Pope AFB, N.C., 1946-49, asst. budget and acctg. officer, 1949-55, supervisory budget officer hdqrs. Mil. Transport Command, USAF, 1955-57, budget analyst Hdqrs. USAF, Washington, 1957-74. Active, Arlington Com. 100, Arlington Vol. Coordinators Roundtable, Alexandria City Hosp. Corp., Ft. Belvoir, U.S. Army Engr. Center, Civilian-Mil. Adv. Council, Salvation Army Women's Aux., Inter-Service Club Council of Arlington; pres. Operation Check-Mate Council of Arlington, 1981—; charter asso. Alexandria City Hosp. Found. Recipient awards U.S. Treasury, 1945, 46, U.S. State Dept., 1970; Good Neighbor award Ft. Belvoir Civilian-Mil. Adv. Council, 1978; awards U.S. First Army, 1973, ARC, 1977; named Inter-Service Club Council Woman of Yr., 1975. Mem. Nat. Fedn. Bus. and Profl. Women's Clubs, Am. Assn. Ret. Fed. Employees, Am. Soc. Mil. Comptrollers, Am. Inst. Parliamentarians, Guilford Coll. Alumni Assn., N.C. Soc. Washington. Club: Altrusa Internat. Va.). Home: 4900 N Old Dominion Dr Arlington VA 22207

TYSON, JOAN SHEPHERD, savs. and loan exec.; b. Ottawa, Kans., Aug. 19, 1926; d. Alvin Carl and Esther Helen (Hendrickson) Shepherd; student Washburn U., 1945, Christ's Hosp. Sch. Nursing, 1945, Ottawa U., 1944-46; m. Evert Earnest Tyson, Aug. 31, 1946; children—Rebecca Helen Tyson Wolfe, Sarah Joan Tyson Meredith. Sec., Willis Nursery Co., Ottawa, Kans., 1946-52; with Franklin Savs. Assn., Ottawa, 1952-53, 62—, v.p., treas., 1980-81, sr. v.p., 1981—. Mem. Fin. Mgrs. Soc. for Savs. Instns., Nat. Assn. Bus. and Profl. Women, Nat. Assn. Female Execs. Democrat. Baptist. Club: Soroptimist. Home: 524 W 15th St Ottawa KS 66067 Office: Franklin Savs Assn 700 S Main St Ottawa KS 66067

TYSON, MARY (MRS. KENNETH W. THOMPSON), artist; b. Sewanee, Tenn., Nov. 2, 1909; d. Stuart L. and Katherine Tyson; student Grand Central Sch. Art, 1928-30, Eastport Sch. Art, 1928, New Sch. Social Research, 1975-76; m. Kenneth W. Thompson, Oct. 1, 1931; children—Kenneth Stuart, Loran Tyson. Exhibited one-man shows: Montross Gallery, N.Y.C., Bruce Mus., Greenwich, Conn., Present Day Club, Princeton, N.J., Pen and Brush Club, N.Y.C., Bodley Gallery, N.Y.C.; exhibited group shows: Balt. Water Color Club, Phila. Watercolor Club, Addison Gallery, Andover, Mass., Bklyn. Mus., Coll. Arts Assn., Morton Gallery, N.Y.C., St. Louis Mus. Contemporary Art, Government House, Nassau, Pen and Brush Club, N.Y.C. (15 awards), New Rochelle (N.Y.) Art Assn., Allied Artists, Knickerbocker Artists, Katherine Lorillard Wolfe, Nat. Arts Club, Lobster Pot Gallery, Nantucket, Am. Watercolor Soc., Easthampton Guild Hall (award), Nantucket Artists Assn.; represented in permanent collections: Guild Hall Mus., Easthampton, Monterey (Calif.) Peninsula Mus., Nantucket Artists Assn., Harrison Meml. Library, Carmel, Calif. Mem. Am. Watercolor Soc., Pen and Brush Club, Nat. Arts Club. Address: 20 W 11th St New York NY 10011

TYSON, PHOEBE WHATLEY, painter; b. Wichita Falls, Tex., May 5, 1926; d. Mertic Boyd and Susie Phoebe (Creath) Whatley; student Abilene Christian U., 1943-45; B.A., North Tex. State U., 1946, M.A., 1951; m. Josiah William Tyson, Jr., Dec. 20, 1946; children—Josiah William III, Phoebe Creath Tyson McDavid. Elem. art tchr. Ft. Worth Ind. Sch. Dist., 1946-47; pvt. tchr. art, Haskell, Tex., 1948-50; painter watercolors, acrylics, Seabrook, Tex., 1971-79; exhibitor Biennial Exhbn., Nat. League Am. Pen Women, Kennedy Center, Washington (award of distinction), 1976, Rocky Mountain Nat. Watermedia Exhbn., Golden, Colo., 1977, 82. Mem. Tex. Fine Arts Assn., McLean (Va.) Art Club (pres. 1970-71), Nat. League Am. Pen Women (nat. art bd. 1972-74, Tex. v.p. 1972-74, Meml. br. pres. 1976-78), Art League Houston, AAUW (v.p. Austin 1955-56), Clear Creek Art League, Watercolor Art Soc. Houston, San Antonio Watercolor Group, Waterloo Watercolor Group, Tex. Watercolor Soc. Mem. Church of Christ. Home: 8600 Appalachian Austin TX 78759

TYTELL, PEARL LILY (MRS. MARTIN KENNETH TYTELL), examiner disputed documents; b. N.Y.C., Aug. 29, 1918; d. Harry and Yetta (Feigenbaum) Kessler; student St. John's U., 1941-43; B.S., N.Y. U., 1962, M.A., 1968; m. Martin Kenneth Tytell, May 23, 1943; children—Peter, Pamela. Examiner disputed documents, N.Y.C., 1950—; lectr. on handwriting, typewriter identification, detection forgery colls., univs., 1955—; lectr. N.Y. U., 1955-57; mem. faculty N.Y. Inst. Criminology, N.Y.C., 1958; cons. govtl. agys., law firms; expert witness in city, state, fed. cts., U.S. and Commonwealth P.R. Sec. Along The Hudson Home Owners Assn., 1960—. Mem. AAAS, Internat. Assn. Chiefs of Police (asso.), Eastern Bus. Tchrs. Assn. Club: N.Y. Univ. Co-author: The Confrontation of Anonymous Letter Writers. Home: 3031 Scenic Pl Riverdale NY 10463 Office: 116 Fulton St New York NY 10038

UCHTMAN, RUTH CAMERON, social work cons.; b. Albany, N.Y., July 20, 1933; d. Truman David and Marion (Scudder) Cameron; B.A., Wellesley Coll., 1955; M.S.W., Smith Coll., 1957; m. Charles C. Uchtman, June 4, 1960; children—Charles C., Barbara Cameron. Social worker Family Service Bur. of United Charities, Chgo., 1957-61; social work cons. N. Ave. Day Nursery, Chgo., 1965-67, Lake Bluff/Chgo. Homes for Children, 1967-70; social service dir. Community Hosp. of Evanston (Ill.), 1973-78, social work cons., 1978—. Chmn. long term care com. Evanston Commn. on Aging, 1979—; bd. dirs. Beacon House of Chgo., 1973-77; mem. women's aux. (pres. 1973) and N. Suburban Tag Day chmn., 1971—; active PTA, 1968—. Mem. Acad. Cert. Social Workers, Nat. Assn. Social Workers, Gray Panthers, Mental Health Assn. Evanston, Ill. Citizens for Better Care, NOW, ACLU, Common Cause. Democrat. Presbyterian. Address: 1131 Ridge Ave Evanston IL 60202

UEHLING, BARBARA STANER, univ. chancellor; b. Wichita, Kans., June 12, 1932; d. Roy W. and Mary Elizabeth (Hilt) Staner; B.A. in Psychology, U. Wichita, 1954; M.A. in Exptl. Psychology, 1956, Ph.D., 1958; L.H.D. (hon.), Drury Coll., Springfield, Mo., 1978; LL.D. (hon.), Ohio State U., 1980; m. Stanley Johnson; children by previous marriage—Jeff, David. Mem. faculty Oglethorpe U., Atlanta, 1959-64, Emory U., Atlanta, 1966-69; adj. prof. psychology U. R.I., 1970-72; mem. faculty, then acad. dean Roger Williams Coll., Providence, 1972-74; dean arts and scis. Ill. State U., 1974-76; provost U. Okla., 1976-78; chancellor U. Mo., Columbia, 1978—; mem. Nat. Council Ednl. Research; dir. Mercantile Bancorp., Inc.; adv. dir. Merc. Trust Co., Columbia, Meredith Corp., Des Moines. Bd. dirs. United Way Columbia; trustee Carnegie Found. Advancement of Teaching. NIHM fellow, 1966-69. Mem. Am. Assn. Higher Edn. (past pres.), Am. Council on Edn. (dir. 1979-82), Columbia C. of C. (dir.), Sigma Xi. Author monograph, chpt. in book. Office: 105 Jesse Hall U Mo Columbia MO 65211

UGGAMS, LESLIE, entertainer; b. N.Y.C., May 25, 1943; d. Harolde and Juanita (Smith) U.; student Juillard Sch. Music, 1961-63; m. Grahame Pratt, Oct. 17, 1965. Appeared on Beulah TV show, 1949; featured on Sing Along With Mitch, 1961-64; starred in Broadway play Hallelujah Baby, 1967, also nightclubs, top television mus. variety shows; appeared in film Skyjacked, 1972; appeared on ABC-TV's Roots, 1977. Recipient Tony award, 1968, Drama Critics award, 1968; Critics Choice award as best supporting actress in Roots, 1977; chosen Best Singer on TV, 1962, 63. Author: The Leslie Uggams Beauty Book, 1966. Address: care William Morris Agy 151 El Camino Beverly Hills CA 90212 *

UGOAGWU, BARBARA JACKSON, chemist; b. Birmingham, Ala., June 24, 1952; d. Louis and Elizabeth J. Davis; lab. cert. Cook County Grad. Sch. Medicine, Chgo., 1969; A.S. with honors (DeWitt Wallace Found. scholar 1972), Central Y Coll., Chgo., 1973; health cert. with honors (Health Edn. Corps. scholar 1976) Harvard U., 1976; B.S. in Biology and Chemistry, Roosevelt U., Chgo., 1977; m. Marcel C. Ugoagwu, Aug. 13, 1976; 1 dau., Vanlynette Bridget. Clin. chemistry technician Ill. Masonic Hosp., Chgo., 1969-70; med. research supr. Ill. Inst. Tech. Research Inst., Chgo., 1970-71; lead poison screening supr. Chgo. Dept. Health, 1972-76; med. coordinator Blue Cross/Blue Shield, Chgo., 1978—; tchr., cons. in field. Mem. Lab. Medicine Assn., Am. Chem. Soc., Harvard U. Alumni Assn., Roosevelt U. Alumni Assn., Park Forest South Women's Assn. (dir. 1981), AAUW, Phi Theta Kappa, Delta Tau. Democrat. Roman Catholic. Home: 759 Burr Oak Ln Apt 2K Park Forest South IL 60466 Office: 10233 S Racine Ave Chicago IL 60643

UHLAND, RUTH ELLEN, educator; b. Escondido, Calif., May 4, 1925; d. William and Ruth (Rooker) U.; A.A., Mira Costa Coll., 1945; B.A., San Diego State Coll., 1947, postgrad., 1948-49, 61, 62, 64, 70-72; postgrad. San Jose State Coll., 1966-67, Fresno State Coll., 1956-57, U. San Diego, 1969, Internat. U., 1971—. Tchr. jr. high sch. Brawley (Calif.) Elem. Sch. Dist., 1947-50, 53-54, 56-64, elem. tchr., 1950-53, 55, 65—, chmn. health-phys. edn. dept., 1960. Active various community drives; adv. bd. Rainbow Girls, 1972—. Mem. Internat. Reading Assn. (sch. rep. 1969-72), Calif., Brawley tchrs. assns., Imperial Valley Girls Phys. Edn. Assn. (pres. 1967-68), Brawley Bus. and Profl. Women's Club (v.p. desert sect. 1968-69, pres.'s ecology citation 1972), Desert Protective Council (life), Nat. Audubon Soc., Cooper Ornithol. Soc. (life), Wilson Ornithol. Soc., Am. Ornithologists Union, Nat. Ret. Tchrs. Assn., Calif. Ret. Tchrs. Assn., Internat. Platform Assn., AAUW, Delta Kappa Gamma. Clubs: Order Eastern Star, Venture (pres. 1954-55) (Brawley); Sierra (San Diego). Home: 158 G St Brawley CA 92227

UHLIG, MARYLOUISE MARGARET, govt. ofcl.; b. Steelton, Pa., July 22, 1946; d. Frank Anthony and Mary (Ivosevich) Cernugel; B.A. in Speech, Pa. State U., 1967; M.P.A., Central Mich. U., 1975; m. Barry Curtis Uhlig, Sept. 2, 1967. Sr. employee devel. specialist Dept. Navy, 1974-76; chief exec. devel. and career systems EPA, Washington, 1976-77, exec. officer, 1977-81, dir. Office of Program Mgmt. and Office of Solid Waste and Emergency Response, 1981—. Mem. nat. alumni council Pa. State U., 1980—; bd. dirs. Friends of Women Prisoners, 1980, EPA Credit Union, 1979-82. Recipient Barbara B. Tennant award, 1979, bronze medal EPA, 1980. Mem. Federally Employed Women, Inc. (pres. 1980-82), Sr. Exec. Assn. (dir. 1981-82), Internat. Personnel Mgmt. Assn., Bus. and Profl. Women Assn., Position Classification and Compensation Soc., Am. Soc. Public Adminstrs., Pa. State Alumni Assn. (pres. D.C. Met. chpt. 1978-81). Office: OSWER WH 562A 401 M St SW Washington DC 20460

UITERMARK, HELEN JOAN, systems cons.; b. Zandvoort, Netherlands, Apr. 5, 1941; came to U.S., 1968, naturalized, 1977; d. Peter Theodore and Maria Francisca (Castien) U.; student schs., London, Ont., Can. File clk. Drug Trading Co., London, 1957-59; with Richard-Wilcox, London, 1959-62, keypunch supr., 1960-62; with Singer Bus. Machines, Toronto, Ont., 1962-68, Los Angeles, 1970-74, systems engr., 1970-74; with Permatex, West Palm Beach, Fla., 1968-70, data processing mgr., 1969-70; with Safariland Leather Co., Monrovia, Calif., 1974-81, v.p. adminstrn., 1975-81, spl. adviser to bd. dirs., 1974-81; ind. cons., systems analyst, 1981—. Mem. Forum Internat. (v.p.), Aircraft Owners and Pilots Assn.

ULICHNY, BARBARA LYNN, state legislator; b. Milw., June 10, 1947; d. Clarence and Karmen Seybold; B.A. in Econs., Northwestern U. Tchr., Nicolet High Sch., Milw., 1969-74; bicentennial adminstr., YWCA program dir.; mem. Wis. Assembly, 1978—, chairperson legis. audit com., crime victims council spl. com. on sexual assault and child sexual abuse, vice chmn. revenue com.; public mem. Wis. State Bar-Govt. Lawyers div. Mem. Milwaukee County Democratic party. Named NOW Woman of Yr., 1980; recipient Environ. Decade award, 1980. Mem. Metro Milw. Fair Housing Council, E. Side Housing Action Com., Women for Soviet Jewry, Wis. Women's Network, Common Cause, Hist. Lower E. Side Neighborhood Assn. Lutheran. Home: 2945 N Prospect St Milwaukee WI 53211 Office: 11 E State Capitol Madison WI 53702

ULLMAN, MARIE, mfg. co. exec.; b. Linlithgo, N.Y., Mar. 19, 1914; d. Max and Sarah (Jaffe) Michaelson; R.N., Bklyn. Hosp., 1935; m. Robert Ullman, Aug. 15, 1935. Pres., sec.-treas. Ullman Devices Corp., Ridgefield, Conn., 1938—; dir. State Nat. Bank Conn., Ridgefield. Mem. C. of C. Ridgefield, Bklyn. Hosp. Nurses Alumnae. Home: 43 Chestnut Hill Rd Wilton CT 06897 Office: PO Box 398 Ridgefield CT 06877

ULLMANN, LIV, actress; b. Tokyo, Japan (parents Norwegian); attended a local pub. sch.; student under a dramatic coach in London, Eng., for 8 months; m. Hans Stang (div.); 1 dau., Linn, by Ingmar Bergman. After dramatic tng. in London, returned to Norway to act; starred in Diary of Anne Frank with a small repertory troupe in Stavanger, Norway; became an established stage actress of classic roles in Norway, also played in Norwegian films; became Bergman's leading lady in film Persona, 1966; appeared in other films directed by Bergman including The Hour of the Wolf, Shame, The Passion of Anna, Cries and Whispers, 1972, Face to Face, Scenes from a Marriage, Serpents, Autumn Sonota; other films include: The Night Visitor, Pope Joan, The Emigrants (directed by Jan Troell), The New Land, and Hollywood films, Lost Horizon, 40 Carats, Zandy's Bride, The Abdication, Richard's Things; starred as Nora in A Doll's House in N.Y. Shakespeare Festival prodn. at Lincoln Center's Vivian Beaumont Theater, N.Y.C.; appeared on Broadway in Anna Christie, 1977, I Remember Mama, 1979. Ofcl. goodwill ambassador UNICEF, 1980—. Recipient Best Actress award for Cries and Whispers, N.Y. Film Critics; was honored for performance in Scenes From a Marriage and Face to Face by N.Y. Film Critics and Nat. Soc. Film Critics; has won either Nat. Soc. Film Critics or N.Y. Film Critics best actress awards for 6 pictures in past 7 years. Author: Changing, 1978 (transl. 20 langs., Book-of-Month club). Office: care Paul Kohner Inc 9169 Sunset Blvd Los Angeles CA 90069 *

ULMER, FRANCES ANN, lawyer; b. Madison, Wis., Feb. 1, 1947; d. George C. and Lois (Radke) U.; B.A., U. Wis., 1969, J.D., 1972; m. William T. Council, Aug. 31, 1977; children—Frances Amelia Council, Louis Charles Ulmer. Admitted to Wis. bar, 1972; with FTC, Washington, 1972-73; legis. counsel Alaska State Legislature, 1973-75, legis. asst. to Gov. Jay Hammond, 1975-77, dir. Div. Policy Devel. and Planning, 1977-81; govt. affairs cons., Juneau, Alaska, 1981—; lectr. mgmt. efficiency and goal setting. Chmn., Juneau Comprehensive Plan Com., 1982—; mem. Council Economic Policy State Alaska, 1982—; chmn. Alaska Coastal Policy Council, 1977-81; mem. Alaska Growth Policy Council and Rural Devel. Council, 1978-81. Mem. LWV, Juneau Lyric Opera Assn., Am. Bar Assn. Presbyterian. Home: 604 E 5th St Juneau AK 99801

ULRICH, GERTRUDE ANNA, nurse; b. Steinauer, Nebr., Oct. 19, 1922; d. Fred, Jr. and Matilda (Rinne) U.; R.N., Lincoln (Nebr.) Gen. Hosp., 1960; postgrad. Wesleyan U., Lincoln, 1960-61, B.S. in Natural Scis., 1972; postgrad. U. Nebr., 1967-68, Omaha U., 1966. Instr. Lincoln (Nebr.) Gen. Hosp. Sch. Nursing, 1960-61, 66-67; staff nurse Lincoln Gen. Hosp., 1961-62, 68-71; missionary nurse to Turkey, United Ch. Bd. World Ministries, N.Y.C., 1963-64; camp nurse Girl Scouts U.S.A., Nebraska City, Nebr., summer 1964; staff nurse Homestead Nursing Home, 1964-66; nursing supr. Tabitha Home, Lincoln, 1972-80, med. record supr., 1975-80; evening nursing supr. Homestead Nursing Home, Lincoln, 1980—. Lincoln Found. ednl. grantee, 1971; named Nurse of Week, Sta. KFOR, 1973, 76. Mem. Am. Nurses Assn. Mem. Reformed Ch. Am. Home: 410 S 41 Lincoln NE 68510

ULRICH, LORRAINE ANNE, editor; b. Chgo., Aug. 24, 1928; d. Ranieri and Anita Carolyn (Benedetti) Bonaguidi; student Northwestern U., 1946; B.S. in Journalism, U. Ill., 1950; postgrad. Moser Bus. Coll., U. Chgo.; m. Gene W. Ulrich, Aug. 30, 1952; 1 son, Christopher. Asst. editor Florists Rev., Chgo., 1950-53, Nat. Underwriter, Chgo., 1955-56; asso. editor Jour. Housing, Chgo., 1956-61; mng. editor Drug and Cosmetic Industry mag., N.Y.C., 1961-62; sr. editor Hearst Mags., N.Y.C., 1962-63; asso. editor Tchr. mag., Darien, Conn., 1963-70; co-founder, mng. editor Early Years, also Early Year's Parent, Darien, 1970-77; mng. editor How To, N.Y.C., 1977—. Recipient awards for stories Edn. Press Assn. Mem. Ednl. Press, Nat. Fedn. Press Women. Clubs: Greenwich Boat and Yacht, Overseas Press. Home: 49 Breezemont Ave Riverside CT 06878 Office: 380 Madison Ave New York NY 10017

UMBER, NOVALINE PIERCE, pharmacist; b. nr. Mangum, Okla., Nov. 13, 1924; d. John Carlton and Anna Lue (Whitmire) Pierce; B.A. in English and Music Edn., Southwestern State U. Okla., 1946, B.S. in Pharmacy (scholar), 1959; m. Herbert Umber, May 29, 1956 (div. 1977). Tchr. Okla. schs., 1943-56; pharmacist Umber Drug, Apache, Okla., 1959-72, Phil's Discount Drug, Carnegie, Okla., 1977, TGY, Wichita, Kans., 1977-78, Tom's Profl. Pharmacy, Andarko, Okla., 1978-79, United Drug, Purcell, Okla., 1980-81; relief pharmacist Marshall Drug, Cyril, 1979-82, Osco Drug, Lawton, 1980-82. Mem. Okla. Pharm. Assn., Mensa, Okla. Poetry Soc., Am. Pharm. Assn., Alpha Phi Sigma. Methodist. Clubs: Apache Study, Rebekahs. Author: Star Dust and Sand Dunes, 1968; Excelsior, 1975. Home: PO Box 379 Apache OK 73006

UMPHRESS, AGNES ELLEN, clin. therapist; b. Ashland, Oreg., June 27, 1925; d. Charles Albert and Mabel (Rice) White; B.A., Willamette U., 1947; M.S.W., U. Wash., 1961; m. Rupert Hampton Umphress, Jan. 20, 1962. Supr., Harry & David, Medford, Oreg., 1947-56; med. social worker Oreg. Welfare Commn., 1956-59; clin. therapist U. Wash., 1961-68; chief therapist Children's Home Soc. Wash., Tacoma, 1968-78; co-owner, therapist Counseling Resource Center, Inc., Chehalis, Wash., 1979—; adv. bd. Child Abuse Program, 1974-78, Sexual Assault Program, 1977-78, Family Planning Assn., 1975-80. Cert. Acad. Cert. Social Workers. Mem. Nat. Assn. Social Workers, Nat. Assn. Clin. Social Workers, Am. Assn. Psychiat. Services for Children, Am. Orthopsychiat. Assn. Republican. Club: Sertoma. Contbr. articles to profl. jours. Research on therapeutic programs in technologically advanced and Third World nations. Home: 625 Tauscher Rd Chehalis WA 98532 Office: 118 N Market Blvd Chehalis WA 98532

UNCAPHER, BARBARA WIDLITZ, educator; b. Cleve., Sept. 9, 1940; d. William F. and Virginia Widlitz; B.A., Denison U., 1962; M.A., W.Va. U., 1965; postgrad. U. Pitts., 1974—; m. Andrew G. Uncapher, Jr., Aug. 26, 1961; children—Leslie, Daniel. Speech therapist Marion County Bd. Edn., Fairmont, W.Va., 1963-65; pvt. practice speech pathology, 1965-67; instr. speech Pa. State U., 1967-71; asst. prof. speech communication Pa. State U., New Kensington campus, 1971—; lectr. in field; sec., treas., dir. Indigo Inc., New Kensington, 1980—. Past bd. dirs. Kiski Valley Vis. Nurse Assn., Kiski Valley Civic League, YMCA; mem. Westmoreland County Republican Com., 1969-72; mem. William Bell's Clown Troop; past leader Girls Scouts U.S.A.. Mem. Eastern Communication Assn., Speech Communication Assn. Pa. (chmn. psychology of speech council). Episcopalian. Club: Order Eastern Star. Contbr. articles to profl. jours. Office: Dept Speech Pa State U New Kensington PA 15068

UNDERHILL, LOUISE FLYNN, poet; b. Du Quoin, Ill., May 17, 1907; d. Edward and Celeste May (Cook) Flynn; A.B., Georgetown (Ky.) Coll., 1930; postgrad. Ohio State U., U. Wis., So. Ill. U., U. Wyo., U. Utah, Columbia U.; m. Charles Glenn Underhill, Oct. 30, 1971. Tchr., DuQuoin (Ill.) High Sch., 1931-44, Julesburg (Colo.) High Sch., 1947, Cheyenne (Wyo.) Schs., 1956-71; corr. ARC, 1944-46; secretarial position, 1948-51; dir. Christmas Seal sale Wyo. Tb and Health, 1951-56; public relations coordinator Laramie County Library, 1973-77; part-time rep. Jelm Mountain Publs., Laramie, 1979—. Recipient Alumni Achievement award Georgetown Coll., 1980. Mem. Nat. Fedn. Press Women, United Presbyn. Women (hon.), Wyo. Press Women (Woman of Achievement award 1980), Wyo. Library Assn., Cheyenne Classroom Tchrs. Assn., Wyo. Edn. Assn., NEA, Nat. Council Tchrs. English, Sch. Broadcast Assn., Alpha Delta Kappa, Alpha Phi Gamma (life). Republican. Presbyterian. Clubs: Thursday Woman's (Du Quoin, Ill.), Order of Does. Author: Red Hollyhocks, 1977; The Moth, 1978; Captain Jason and Other Poems, 1979; (poetry) Wyoming Moods, Reminescences of a Tenderfoot, 1981; editor The Best of Mostly for Men, 1980. Home: 3417 Morrie Ave Cheyenne WY 82001

UNDERWOOD, NANCY MAE, occupational health and safety cons.; b. Vancouver, Wash., Dec. 29, 1944; d. Robert Izea and Jennie Mae (McWhorter) Espie; B.S. in Occupational Health and Safety, Calif. State U., 1974, now post grad.; cert. of proficiency-engring./occupational safety and health, Travelers Ins. Co., 1975, Textron, Inc., 1977; postgrad. U. San Francisco, 1978-81; 1 dau., Apryl. Safety engr. Travelers Ins. Co., Los Angeles, 1975-76; tchr. Los Angeles City Unified Sch. System, 1976; mgr. safety Hydraulic research subs. Textron, Inc., Valencia, Calif., 1977-78; mgr. safety Northrop Aircraft Group, Hawthorne, Calif., 1978—; operator Nancy's Safety Tng. and Cons. firm. Recipient Performance —78— Monthly Cost Reduction/Recognition award, Northrop Aircraft Corp., 1978. Mem. Nat. Safety Council, Am. Soc. Safety Engrs., Am. Indsl. Hygiene Assn., Intersafe Safety Soc., Nat. Assn. Female Execs., Am. Soc. Profl. and Exec. Women, Calif. State Univ. Alumni Assn., Am. Mgmt. Assn. Christian Scientist; Clubs: Wilshire; Tiffanys Social; Eastern Star; Daughters of Isis Court. Home: 1637 Veteran Ave #9 Los Angeles CA 90024 Office: 3516 E Century Blvd Lynwood CA 90262

UNFRIED, DONA LEE, clergywoman, realty saleswoman; b. Los Angeles, Oct. 11, 1928; d. Howard Peter and Helyn Grace (Howson) Wraith; student Santa Monica State Coll., 1948; grad. Unity Sem., 1973, D.D., 1981; diploma in hypnotherapy Ft. Worth Inst., 1970; m. Sept. 1, 1950 (div. 1969); children—Robert F., Teri Lynn. Mgmt. personnel Pacific Telephone, Sacramento, 1947-68; mgr. Match-O-Mates, Ft. Worth, 1968-70; ordained to ministry Unity Ch., 1973; minister Unity Village Chapel, Kansas City, Mo., 1972-75; sr. minister Unity Ch., Overland Park, Kans., 1975-76; sr. minister, chmn. bd. Unity Ch. of Light, Longview, Tex., 1976—; realty mgr. Realty World-Morton and Assos., Longview, 1976—; tchr. in fields; condr. workshops; counselor. Mem. Indsl. relations com., public relations com. Longview C. of C., 1981; bd. dirs. Gateway Found., Sacramento. Mem. Internat. New Thought Alliance, Nat. Assn. Realtors, Tex. Assn. Realtors, Nat. Assn. Female Execs., Assn. Unity Chs., Longview Assn. Realtors, Longview Bd. Realtors (chmn. edn. com. 1982). Club: Toasmistresses (pres. Limerick club 1967; numerous speaking awards 1966-72. Home: 621 Kings Mountain Longview TX 75606

UNG, SANDY ZAMBITO-SCHAEFER, labor relations researcher, orgnl. behavior specialist; b. Cambridge, Mass., May 16, 1942; d. George Harrison and Nina (Augello-Zambito) Schaefer; student Harvard U., 1962-65; B.S. in Indsl. and Labor Relations, Cornell U., 1981; m. 2d John Shew-Kui Ung; children—William Raymond, Sheila Elisabeth. Founder, chief exec. officer, prin. cons. and counselor Selectivity Inc., Natick, Mass., 1968-74, edn. and equal opportunity adminstr. N.E. area office Western Union Telegraph Co., Wesllesley, Mass., 1974-75; prin. cons. Worker Self Renewal Project, Coll. Entrance Exam. Bd., N.Y.C., 1975-76; labor relations research and author 5-yr. history of employee ownership Vt. Asbestos Group, Inc., Lowell, 1975-80; keynote speaker Northeastern U., 1975; lectr. Urban Research Corp., Chgo., 1974; chief planner organizer Career Exploration Conf., S. Middlesex County, Mass. Mem. Am. Friends Service Com. Econ. Alts. Group, Cambridge; bd. dirs. Women's Inner City Ednl. Resource Service, Boston; campaign coordinator mem. staff Barbara Gray, Mass. Rep., 1974—; co-chairperson edn. com. South Middlesex C. of C.; mem. Democratic Socialist Organizing Com., Boston. Recipient Meritorious Service award South Middlesex C. of C., 1970. Mem. Indsl. Coop. Assn. (dir.), Ripon Soc., Catholic Labor Guild, Quality of Working Life Center, Assn. Tng. and Devel., Mass. Personnel and Guidance Assn., NOW, NAACP, Urban League, Assn. Affirmative Action Profls. (co-founder 1975).

UNGAR, FRIEDA STEIN, research scientist, educator; b. Czernowitz, Rumania, Feb. 3, 1910; came to U.S., 1948, naturalized, 1953; d. Salomon and Bertha (Petrover) Stein; M.S., U. of Sci., Czernowitz, 1932; postgrad. N.Y. U., 1955-56, Ill. Inst. Tech., Chgo., 1962-63; m. Jacob Ungar, June 23, 1935; 1 son. Chief chemist Flushing (N.Y.) Hosp., 1954-56; chief clin. chemist St. John's Episcopal Hosp., Bklyn., 1950-54; research asso. Mt. Sinai Research Found., Chgo., 1957-62; research asso. dept. biochemistry Chgo. Med. Sch., 1962-68, instr., 1968-74, asst. prof., 1974-78; instr. nutrition Triton Coll., River Grove, Ill., 1978—. Chgo. Med. Sch. Research grantee, 1975-77. Mem. Am. Soc. Neurochemistry, Sigma Xi. Contbr. 90 research articles to profl. jours., 1958—.

UNGER, BARBARA FRANKEL, educator, poet; b. N.Y.C., Oct. 2, 1932; d. David and Florence (Schuchalter) Frankel; B.A., CCNY, 1955, M.A., 1957; advanced cert. N.Y.U., 1970; children—Deborah, Suzanne. Grad. asst. Yeshiva U., 1962-63; editor County Citizen, Rockland County, N.Y., 1960-63; tchr. English, N.Y.C. Pub. Schs., 1955-58, Nyack (N.Y.) High Sch., 1963-67; guidance counselor Ardsley (N.Y.) High Sch., 1967-69; asso. prof. English Rockland Community Coll., Suffern, N.Y., 1969—, advisor to coll. lit. mag.; poetry fellow Squaw Valley Community of Writers, 1980; contbr. poetry to over 40 lit. mags., including: Kans. Quar., Minn. Rev., Poet and Critic, The Nation, Poetry Now, Invisible City, Thirteenth Moon, So. Poetry Rev.; author books of poems: Basement: Poems 1959-61, 1975; The Man Who Burned Money, 1981; contbr. to Anthology Mag. Verse, Yearbook Am. Poetry, 1981-82. Nat. Endowment for Humanities grantee, 1975; SUNY Creative Writing fellow, 1981-82; finalist W.Va. Writing Competition, 1982. Mem. Poets and Writers, Poetry Soc. Am., Asso. Writing Programs, Women in Media. Office: Rockland Community Coll 145 Coll Rd Suffern NY 10901

UNION, ROBERTA, speech pathologist; b. Worcester, Mass., July 31, 1939; d. Samuel and Frances Rose (Pulda) Mason; B.S. magna cum laude, Worcester State Coll., 1974; M.A. cum laude, U. Mass., Amherst, 1979; m. William Union, Apr. 5, 1959; children—Laurie Beth, David Michael, Terry Ellen. Speech therapist Holden (Mass.) Sch. Collaborative, 1974-76; speech pathologist Fitchburg Leominster (Mass.) Area Rehab. and Work Center, 1976—. Mem. Am. Speech and Hearing Assn., Mass. Speech and Hearing Assn., Mass. Assn. Rehab. Facilities, Assn. Retarded Citizens, Mass. Assn. Speech Pathologists and Audiologists for Developmentally Disabled, Kappa Delta Pi. Jewish. Home: 4 Old English Rd Worcester MA 01609 Office: 564 Main St Fitchburg MA 01420

UNRUH, GERTRUDE H., bank exec.; b. Willard, Ohio, May 20, 1928; d. William and Rose (Reber) Weller; student public schs., Fremont, Ohio; m. Donald C. Unruh, May 25, 1947; children—Jerald A., Barbara J. Unruh Schmitt. Sec. credit dept. Henkel Clauss Co., Fremont, Ohio, 1946-47; bookkeeper Community Hosp., Fremont, 1947-48; with Fremont Savs. Bank, 1961—, v.p. real estate lending, 1976—. Sec., Sandusky County Farm Bur. Council, 1979—. Mem. Nat. Assn. Bank Women. Lutheran. Home: 1419 CR 129 Fremont OH 43420 Office: Fremont Savings Bank 315 Croghan St Fremont OH 43420

UNRUH, PAULA, ofcl.; b. Tulsa, Feb. 13, 1929; d. Paul Mervin and Thelma Opal (Allison) Combest; student U. Ark., 1948-49, U. Tulsa, 1954; m. R. James Unruh, Mar. 21, 1951; children—Jilda Lee, James Kuhns, Allison Page. With Carter Oil Co., 1951-54; campaign mgr. U.S. Rep. Page Belcher, 1960-72; state chmn. Okla. Rep. party, 1975-77; dir. Office Consumer Affairs, Dept. Energy, Washington, 1981—. Co-chmn. Performing Arts Center Bond Issue, Tulsa; pres. Tulsa Philharmonic Women's Assn.; bd. govs. Citizens for Presdl. Primary Reform; bd. govs. Nat. USO; regional v.p., exec. com. USO; mem. Bob Hope USO Center Campaign; bd. dirs., exec. com. ARC, Tulsa. Named Woman of Yr. Women in Communications, 1973. Mem. Women in Energy, Soc. Consumer Affairs Profls., Sigma Alpha Iota, Kappa Kappa Gamma. Republican. Presbyterian. Clubs: Knife and Fork, Town Hall (Tulsa). Office: Dept Energy 1000 Independence Ave SW Washington DC 20585

UNTERBERGER, BETTY MILLER, historian, educator; b. Glasgow, Scotland, Dec. 27, 1923; d. Joseph and Leah Miller; A.B., Syracuse U., 1943; M.A., Harvard U., 1946; Ph.D., Duke U., 1950; m. Robert R. Unterberger, July 27, 1944; children—Glen, Gail Lynn, Gregg Russell. Asst. prof. history E. Carolina U., Greenville, N.C., 1948-50; lectr. Whittier (Calif.) Coll., summers 1950-54; asso. prof., dir. Liberal Arts Center for Adults, 1954-61; asso. prof. Calif. State U., Fulleton, 1961-65, prof., chmn. grad. studies, 1965-68; prof. history Tex. A&M U., College Station, 1968—; vis. prof. U. Hawaii, summer 1967; mem. hist. adv. com. U.S. Dept. Army, 1980-82; mem. adv. com. hist. diplomatic documentation U.S. Dept. State, 1977-81, chairperson, 1981; mem. Nat. Hist. Publs. and Records Commn. Chairperson acad. council Tex. A&M U., 1976. Ford Found. grantee, 1959; Am. Philos. Soc. grantee, 1960-61, 62; Woodrow Wilson Found. fellow, 1979; recipient Disting. Teaching award Calif. State U., 1966, Tex. A&M U., 1975. Mem. Am. Hist. Assn., Orgn. Am. Historians, NOW, Soc. Historians Am. Fgn. Relations, Coordinating Com. on Women in the Hist. Profession, Assn. Pakistan and Indic-Islamic Studies, Conf. on Peace Research in History, Am. Inst. for Pakistan Studies (trustee). Author: America's Siberian Expedition, 1918-1920: A Study of National Policy (Pacific Coast award Am. Hist. Assn.), 1956, 2d edit., 1969; American Intervention in the Russian Civil War, 1969; Woodrow Wilson and the Russian Revolution, 1982; also articles. Editorial bd. Diplomatic History, Red River Valley Hist. Rev., Humboldt Jour. Social Relations, Papers of Woodrow Wilson. Home: Route 3 Box 314 College Station TX 77840 Office: Tex A&M U College Station TX 77843

UNVERFERTH, SUSAN DAVIDSON, retail fabric exec.; b. Ft. Collins, Colo., Apr. 5, 1950; d. Audley Carnahan and Dorothy May (Riley) Davidson; B.S. in Home Econs., U. Calif., Davis, 1971; m. Gerard Patrick Unverferth, Nov. 29, 1974; 1 son, Patrick Ryan. Sensory evaluation asst. Del Monte Corp., Walnut Creek, Calif., 1972-74; sensory evaluation supr., organizer program Riviana Foods, Inc., Houston, 1974-76; owner Eastgate Fashion Fabrics, Grand Junction, Colo., 1977—. Mem. Am. Home Econs. Assn., Home Economists in Bus. Home: 1062 E Pabor St Box 987 Fruita CO 81521 Office: 2830 North Ave Suite 13 Grand Junction CO 81501

UPCHURCH, BARBARA ELLEN, painter; b. St. Louis, Dec. 20, 1948; d. Clelle William and Helen Ione (Wadlow) U.; student (scholar) Carnegie Mus. Art Program, Pitts., 1960-67; B.F.A., Ringling Sch. Art, Sarasota, Fla., 1971; M.F.A. in Painting and Printmaking, U. Miss., 1975; m. Ben Allen Blumberg, Dec. 20, 1980. Photographer, retouch artist Manning Portrait Studio, New Haven, 1971-72; staff artist Johnson-Daniel Graphics, Sarasota, 1970-71, Positively Main St. Graphics, Sarasota, 1972-73, Univ. Publs., U. Miss., Oxford, 1974-75; owner, operator graphics studio, Oxford, 1975-81; freelance artist, Nashville, 1981—; pvt. art tchr., also substitute tchr. U. Miss.; works exhibited in group shows; represented in pvt. collections. Address: Route 3 Box 226 Johns Rd Joelton TN 37080

UPDIKE, HELEN HILL, economist, educator; b. N.Y.C., Mar. 27, 1941; d. Benjamin Harvey and Helen (Gray) Hill; B.S., Hood Coll., 1962; Ph.D., SUNY, Stony Brook, 1978; m. Charles Bruce Updike, Sept. 9, 1963; children—Edith Hill, Nancy Lamar. Asst. prof. Suffolk U., Boston, 1965-67; lectr. SUNY, Stony Brook, 1969-75, vis. asst. prof., 1977-78; asst. prof. U. Mass., 1975-77; asst. prof. econs. Hofstra U., Hempstead, N.Y. 1978—, chmn. dept. econs. and geography, 1981—; dir. Rapid-Am Corp.; cons. in environ. econs., 1973-78. Trustee, v.p. L.I. Forum for Tech., 1979—; trustee Planned Parenthood of Suffolk County, 1980. H.B. Earhart fellow, 1962-63; Georgetown U. fellow, 1963-64. Mem. AAAS, N.Y. Acad. Scis., Am. Econs. Assn. Office: Hofstra University Hempstead NY 11550

UPHOUSE, MIRIAM MCKEEFERY, coll. adminstr.; b. Phila., Sept. 10, 1917; d. William James and Anna (Reichelt) McKeefery; A.B., Grace Coll., 1963; L.P.N., Kirkman Sch., 1952; M.S., St. Francis Coll., 1972; m. Norman H. Uphouse, Nov. 4, 1939; children—Deborah Wingard, Johanna Siebert, Abigail Nahrwold. Asst. to dean women Bryan Coll., Dayton, Tenn., 1945-48; dean women Grace Coll., Winona Lake, Ind., 1964-74, asso. dean students, 1974—, asso. prof. counseling, 1975—. Staff, Blood Bank, ARC, Warsaw, Ind. 1960—. Named Ind. Merit Mother of Yr., 1977; Grace Coll. Alumna of Yr., 1981. Mem. AAUW, Nat. Assn. Women Deans, Adminstrs. and Counselors, Ind. Assn. Women Deans, Adminstrs. and Counselors, Assn. Christians in Student Devel. Republican. Mem. Grace Brethren Ch. Club: Altrusa. Home: Route 8 Box 184 Warsaw IN 46580 Office: Grace Coll Winona Lake IN 46590

UPJOHN, MARY KIRBY, educator; b. Kansas City, Mo., Sept. 30, 1948; d. William Bryant and Mary Analaura (Harrington) U.; B.A., Pomona Coll., 1970; M.S., Boston U., 1977; m. Dean Robert LaCoe, May 23, 1981. Dir. product devel. and promotion Urban Systems, Inc., Cambridge, Mass., 1970-73; pres., co-founder Funktions, Inc., Watertown, Mass., 1973-75; mng. editor Decade Mag., Boston, 1978-79; asst. prof. Boston U. Sch. Public Communication, 1978—; cons. Urban Systems Research and Engring., 1975—, bd. dirs., 1982—. Recipient awards of merit New Eng. Newspaper Execs., 1978, 79, 80, 81, Women Grad. award Boston U., 1981. Mem. Women in Communications, Inc. (Nat. Outstanding Adviser award 1980, Nat. award 1981; v.p. Boston chpt. 1981, pres. 1982), Informational Film Producers Assn., Pomona Coll. Alumni Assn. (bd. mem. New Eng. chpt.). Author: Urban Homsteading: A Guide for Local Officials, 1978; (with Kathleen Heintz) Neighborhood Planning Primer, 1979; (with others) Television Literacy, 1981. Home: 39 Marion Rd Watertown MA 02172 Office: 640 Commonwealth Ave Boston MA 02215

UPSHUR, CAROLE CHRISTOFK, community psychologist, educator; b. Des Moines, Oct. 18, 1948; d. Robert Richard and Margaret (Davis) Christofk; A.B., U. So. Calif., 1969; Ed.M., Harvard U., 1970, Ed.D. (NIMH fellow), 1975; m. Robert Wesley Upshur, July 18, 1970; 1 dau., Emily. Planner, Mass. Com. on Criminal Justice, Boston, 1970-73; licensing specialist, planner, policy specialist Mass. Office for Children, Boston, 1973-76; asst. prof. Coll. Public and Community Service, U. Mass., Boston, 1976-81, asso. prof., 1982—, chmn. Center for Community Planning, 1979-81; cons. to govt. and community agys. on mental health and social service policy and mgmt., 1970—. Lic. psychologist, Mass. Mem. Am. Psychol. Assn., Am. Assn. Mental Deficiency, New Eng. Child Care Assn. Author: How to Set Up and Operate a Non-profit Organization, 1982; cons. editor Mental Retardation. Office: Coll Public and Community Service U Mass Boston 02125

UPTON, LUCILE MORRIS, writer; b. Dadeville, Mo., July 22, 1898; d. Albert G. and Veda (Wilson) Morris; student Drury Coll., 1915-16, S.W. Mo. State Coll., 1917-20; m. Eugene V. Upton, July 22, 1936 (dec. July 1947). Public sch. tchr., Dadeville, Mo., 1917-19, Everton, Mo., 1920-22, Roswell, N.Mex., 1921-23; tchr. creative writing Adult Edn. div. Drury Coll., 1947-52; reporter Denver Express, 1923-24, El Paso (Tex.) Times, 1924-25, Springfield (Mo.) Newspapers, Inc., 1926-64, writer weekly hist. column, 1942-82. Mem. Springfield City Council, 1967-71, Springfield Hist. Sites Bd., 1972-78. Named Woman of Achievement Woman's div. Springfield C. of C., 1967; Ozark Heritage award Mus. of Ozarks, 1978. Mem. Mo. Writers Guild (past pres.), State Hist. Soc. Mo. (life), Greene County (Mo.), White River Valley hist. socs., Nat. Fedn. Press Women, Mo. Press Women, Greater Ozarks Hall of Fame. Congregationalist. Club: Springfield Soroptomist (hon.). Author: Bald Knobbers, 1939; (booklet) Battle of Wilson's Creek, 1950. Contbr. short stories, articles to mags., newspapers. Home: 1305 S Kimbrough Springfield MO 65807

URBAN, JO ANN REBECCA, transp. co. exec.; b. Allentown, Pa., Aug. 24, 1936; d. Joseph Leo and Anna Roslyn (Loftus) McLaughlin; student Drakes Secretarial Sch., 1952-54; m. Victor John Urban, Oct. 3, 1959; 1 son, Victor John. With Armstrong Trucking, Westinghouse Electric, N.Y.C., 1955-58, various trucking cos. including Long Transp., Jersey Truck Center, South Kearny, N.J., 1958-73; terminal mgr. Midwest Seaboard Transp. div. Midwest Emery, Dana Transport, Perth Amboy, N.J., 1973-76; pres. Food Products Refrigerated Express, Inc. South Kearney 1979—; cons. women in transp. field. Active cub scout com. Hazlet chpt. Boy Scouts Am., 1974-75. Mem. Nat. Assn. Female Execs., Delta Nu Alpha. Office: Jersey Truck Center Room 15 South Kearny NJ 07032

URBANOWICZ, CLARENT MARIE, educator, nun; b. Johnstown, Pa., Jan. 2, 1910; d. Stanislaus and Louise (Kalinowski) U.; B.A., DePaul U., 1941; M.A., St. John's Coll., 1946; M.A., Xavier Coll., 1952. Joined Franciscan Sisters of Chgo., 1925; tchr. elem. schs., 1927-52; tchr. Latin and math. Madonna High Sch., Chgo., 1952-57; tchr. math., Am. history Bishop McCort High Sch., Johnstown, Pa., 1957-60; tchr. Polish and math. St. Stanislaus Sch., Youngstown, Ohio, 1960-70; prin. St. Stanislaus Sch., Chgo., 1970-71; tchr. Five Holy Martyr Sch., Chgo., 1971-81, dir. Polish lang. programs, 1960-81, bilingual coordinator, 1971-81; tchr. adult edn. Richard Daley Coll., Chgo., 1975—. Mem. Nat. Cath. Edn. Assn., Ill. Assn. Tchrs. of English as 2d Lang., Polish Am. Hist. Assn. (editorial sec. 1954-56, 1st adv. bd. 1957-59, 81—, treas. 1962-79, auditor, 1979-80), Chgo. Archdiocesan Tchr. Assn., Polish Am. Guardian Soc., Assn. for Advancement of Polish Studies. Office: 4325 Chicago Ave Chicago IL 60632

URBELIS, KATHLEEN, software co. exec.; b. Amsterdam, N.Y., May 20, 1946; d. Henry and Armida M. (Casline) Flesh; B.S. in Mgmt. Sci., U. Rochester (N.Y.), 1968, M.B.A., 1972. Programmer, IAI, Rochester, N.Y., 1971-72; co-founder Integral Systems, Inc., Walnut Creek, Calif., 1972, v.p. product devel., 1977—, corp. sec., 1972—. Home: PO Box 583 Diablo CA 94528 Office: 165 Lennon Ln Walnut Creek CA 94598

URDANG, STEPHANIE MILLER, training center exec.; b. N.Y.C., Mar. 24, 1937; d. Samuel Charles and Mae R. (Rodgers) Miller; student N.Y. U.; children—Scott C. Nevins, Kent S. Nevins. Mgr., dir. Thinking People, Forest Hills, N.Y., 1970-72; adminstrv. dir., v.p. Leisure Learning Center, Greenwich, Conn., 1972-80; dir., pres., creator The Self Paced Learning Center, Stamford, Conn., 1980—. Mem. Am. Soc. Tng. and Devel., Nat. Audio Visual Assn., Southeastern Area Commerce and Industry Assn. Office: 61 4th St Stamford CT 06905

UREEL, PATRICIA LOIS, mfg. exec.; b. Detroit, Nov. 29, 1923; d. Peter Walter and Ethel Estelle (Stewart) Murphy; grad. Detroit Bus. Inst., 1941; student Wayne State U., 1942, U. Detroit, 1943, U. Miami, 1945-46; m. Joseph Ralph Ureel, Jan. 4, 1947; children—Mary Patricia, Ronald Joseph. Exec. sec. to chmn. bd. and pres. Detroit Ball Bearing Co. of Mich., 1965-67; exec. sec. to partner charge Mich. dist. Ernst & Ernst, Detroit, 1967-71, Clubs of Inverrary, Lauderhill, Fla., 1971-72, partner charge of group Coopers & Lybrand, Miami, Fla., 1972-74; corp. sec., personnel mgr. Sanford Industries, Inc. and 4 subsidiaries, Pompano Beach, Fla., 1974-81; corp. sec., asso. Asphalt Assos., Ft. Lauderdale, 1982—. Named Sec. of Yr. for City of Detroit, 1966; cert. profl. sec. Mem. Nat. Secs. Assn., Women's Econ. Club Detroit. Republican. Roman Catholic. Club: Moose. Home: 310 NE 51st St Fort Lauderdale FL 33334 Office: Asphalt Assos Penthouse East Internat Bldg 2455 E Sunrise Blvd Fort Lauderdale FL 33304

URMAN-KLEIN, PHYLLIS, psychotherapist; b. Newark, Nov. 11, 1942; d. George and Jean (Schlein) Urman; B.A., Boston U., 1964; M.S., Columbia U., 1968; postgrad. Union Grad. Sch., Cin., 1979—; m. Peter Klein, June 23, 1978. Casework asst. Mass. Gen. Hosp., Boston, 1964-66; social worker psychiatry Albert Einstein Coll. Medicine, N.Y.C., 1968-70, chief social worker Adult Psychiat. Clinic, 1970-75; asso. dept. psychiatry, 1975—; cons. Assn. Am. Med. Colls. NIH fellow, 1965-66, NIMH fellow, 1967-68; Soc. Psychol. Study of Social Issues for Research grantee, 1976. Mem. Acad. Cert. Social Workers, Soc. Clin. Social Workers, Am. Orthopsychiat. Assn., Nat. Registry of Health Care Providers, Soc. Psychol. Studies of Social Issues. Contbr. articles to profl. jours. Office: 56 E 87th St New York NY 10028

URMSTON, MARILYN MCCARRON, coll. dean; b. Los Angeles, July 1, 1931; d. Cyrus Dennis and Marion Angeles (Sell) McCarron; B.Arch., U. So. Calif., 1954; M.S. in Ednl. Adminstrn., 1974; 1 son, Douglas William. Asso. architect J. George Szeptycki and Assos., Los Angeles, 1956-60; architect, partner Urmston and McCarron, Pasadena, Calif., 1961-65; instr. Los Angeles Trade-Tech. Coll., 1965-68, prof., then asst. dean instrn., 1974-81; dean adminstrv. services Los Angeles Mission Coll., 1981—; del. U.S.-Polish Scholars Exchange Program, 1977. Mem. Mayor Los Angeles Consensus 2000, 1982—. Grantee Nat. Endowment Humanities, 1974. Mem. Assn. Community Coll. Adminstrs., Women of Wall St. West, Los Angeles Community Coll. Dist. Admistrs. Assn., AAUW, Phi Delta Gamma, Pi Lambda Theta, Delta Delta Delta. Office: 1212 San Fernando Rd San Fernando CA 91340

URQUHART, JENNIFER MACK, hotel exec.; b. Annapolis, Md., Sept. 16, 1947; d. William H. and Enid (Williams) Mack; B.A. in Biology, Mary Baldwin Coll., 1969. Circulation mgr. Capitol Publs., Inc., Washington, 1969-70; asst. regional sales mgr. Hilton Internat., Washington, 1970-72; public relations and advt. dir. Holiday Inn, Montego Bay, Jamaica, 1972-74; public relations cons. Holiday Inns of Caribbean, Miami Beach, Fla., 1974-75; group space mgr. Princess Hotels Internat., N.Y.C., 1975-76, dir. mktg. services, 1976-78; dir. mktg. Pinehurst, Inc., N.Y.C. and N.C., 1979-80; pres. JMU Mktg., mktg. cons., 1980—; exec. dir. mktg. services Resorts Internat. (Bahamas) Ltd., Nassau and N.Y.C., 1981-82; v.p. advt. Resorts Internat. Casino Hotel, Atlantic City, 1982—; freelance travel writer. Vol., com. mem. Women's Campaign Fund, 1978-82. Mem. Hotel Sales Mgmt. Assn. (advt. adv. com. 1978), U.S. Tourism Caucus (com. mem.), Travel and Tourism Research Assn., Am. Soc. Travel Agts. (asso.), Jr. League (N.Y.C. chpt.), DAR. Home: 425 E 86th St New York NY 10028 Office: Resorts Internat 555 Madison Ave New York NY 10022

URQUHART, PATRICIA ANN, parks and recreation program coordinator; b. Orange, N.J., Mar. 19, 1935; d. Robert Pervis and Marian Harlow (Chase) Landsperg; B.S. in Elem. Edn., Upsala Coll., 1953; m. Ronald W. Urquhart, Dec. 19, 1959; children—Todd Andrew, Scott Robert. Tchr. Columbian Sch., East Orange, N.J., 1957-59, Fisher Sch., Plimpton Sch., Walpole, Mass., 1959-63; drama cons. Norwood (Mass.) Recreation Dept., 1963-66; program enrichment specialist Syracuse, (N.Y.) Dept. Parks and Recreation, 1966-74; recreation supr. Town of Manlius Parks and Recreation, Fayetteville, N.Y., 1975-81, program coordinator, 1981—; cons. Cultural Resources Council, 1974-75, Central N.Y. Recreation and Park Soc., 1968—; sec. Clairmont Assn., 1968-69; mem. bd. Civic Morning Musicals, 1972-75; mem. adv. bd. Onondaga County Clubs and Centers Council, 1973-80. Recipient Gold U award Upsala Coll., 1957. Mem. Women in Communication, N.Y. State Recreation and Park Soc. (state chmn. sect. on aging 1978-80, mem. state conf. com. 1968-82, adminstrv. council 1978-80), Central N.Y. Recreation and Park Soc., AAUW. Republican. Presbyn. (elder); Club: Long Branch Manor Garden. 7556 Florian Way Liverpool NY 13088 Office: Town of Manlius Recreation Dept 7173 Mott Rd Fayetteville NY 13088

URQUHART-FISHER, CAROL LOANNE, film co. exec.; b. Tex., Dec. 15, 1949; d. John Earl and Marguerite Loanne (Urquhart) Fisher; cert. in Spanish lit. U. Valencia (Spain), 1968; B.A., Rice U., 1970; postgrad. U. Madrid, 1972; M.A., U. Pa., 1973, M.B.A. (Wharton scholar), 1975; m. William Bradley Beam, Feb. 7, 1981. Mgmt. trainee Young & Rubicam (Australia), 1973; founder advt. agy. DeBellegarde NC&P, Phila., 1973-75; dep. mgr. Am. Express Bank A/S, Copenhagen, 1975-77, asst. v.p. Am. Express Internat. Banking Corp.-Global Credit, Treasury), N.Y.C., 1977-79, v.p., 1979-81; founder Carilliam Ltd., 1981—; partner real estate firm, 1978—; guest lectr. City Coll. Phila., 1975; ct. apptd. interpreter (Spanish), U.S. Fed. Dist. Ct. for Eastern Dist. Pa., 1973-75. Mem. Republican Nat. Com., since 1977—, Conservative Party N.Y., 1978—; a founder Center for Internat. Security Studies of Am. Security Council Edn. Found., 1977—. Mem. Am. Mktg. Assn., Fin. Women of N.Y., Assn. M.B.A. Execs. Episcopalian. Home: 200 E 24th St New York NY 10010

USELTON, STELLA MAE, Volunteer b. Washington County, Va., June 9, 1940; d. Clearence P. and Verna Mae (Osborne) Brown; student public schs., Abingdon, Va.; m. Kenneth Elvy Uselton, June 1, 1959; children—Kenneth LeRoy, Theresa Barbar. Auditor, bookkeeper, mgr. Boron Oil Co., Weirton and Chester, W.Va., 1966-73; head cashier K-Mart Corp., Weirton, 1974-75, receiving clk., 1975-81; med. asst., Weirton, 1981—. Pres., PTA, 1973; den mother Boy Scouts Am., 1966-74, trainer Fort Steuben council, 1969—, dist. bd., 1975-80, dist. vice chmn., 1977-78, dist. bd., 1978-80; leader Camp Fire Girls, 1968—, bd. dirs., 1975-80. Served with M.C., U.S. Army, 1958-60. Named Woman of Yr., PTA, 1972, Camp Fire Girls, 1978; recipient awards Boy Scouts Am., 1966-80. Democrat. Methodist. Club: Rebecca (chmn. 1972). Home: 109 Oak St Weirton WV 26062 Office: 2416 Pennsylvania Ave Weirton WV 26062

USHER, ELIZABETH REUTER, librarian; b. Seward, Nebr.; d. Paul and Elizabeth (Meyer) Reuter; diploma Concordia Tchrs. Coll., Seward Litt.D., 1981; B.S. in Edn., U. Nebr., 1942; B.S. in L.S., U. Ill., 1944; m. Harry Thomas Usher, Feb. 25, 1950. Tchr. Zion Luth. Sch., Platte Center, Nebr., St. Paul's Luth. Sch., Paterson, N.J.; library asst. charge res. book reading room U. Nebr., 1942-43; asst. circulation librarian Mich. State U., 1944-45; librarian Cranbrook Acad. Art, Bloomfield Hills, Mich., 1945-48; catalog and reference librarian Met. Mus. Art, N.Y., 1948-53, head cataloger and reference librarian, 1953-54, asst. librarian, 1954-61, chief of art reference library, 1961-68, chief librarian, 1968-80, chief librarian emeritus Thomas J. Watson Library, 1981—. Trustee N.Y. Met. Reference and Research Library Agy., 1968-80, sec. bd. trustees, 1971-77, v.p., 1977-80. Mem. Spl. Libraries Assn. (chmn. mus. div. 1954-55; pres. N.Y. chpt. 1957-58, dir. 1963-65, 75-77; assn. pres. 1967-68, dir. 1960-63, 66-69), Am. Assn. Museums, Coll. Art Assn. (chmn. libraries session 1972-73), N.Y. Library Club, ARLIS/NA, Archons of Colophon (convener 1980-82). Lutheran. Contbr. articles to profl. periodicals. Home: 557A Heritage Village Poverty Rd Southbury CT 06488

UTHE, ELAINE FRANCES, educator; b. Boone, Iowa, Feb. 14, 1930; d. A.R. and Ottilia M. U.; B.A., Marycrest Coll., Davenport, Iowa, 1951; M.A., Cath. U. Am., 1955; Ph.D., U. Minn., 1966. High sch. tchr., Iowa, Ill., France, 1951-64; instr. Mt. Mercy Coll., Cedar Rapids, Iowa, 1959-60; instr., grad. asst. U. Minn., 1964-66; tchr.-educator Mich. State U., East Lansing, 1966-72, U. Ga., 1972-77; head bus. edn. dept. U. Ky., Lexington, 1977—; ednl. cons. Recipient Delta Pi Epsilon research award, 1967; nat. fellow Nat. Center Research in Vocat. Edn., 1980-81. Mem. Nat. Bus. Edn. Assn., Am. Vocat. Assn., Nat. Assn. Tchr. Educators in Bus. Edn., So. Bus. Edn. Assn., Ky. Bus. Edn. Assn., Am. Ednl. Research Assn., Adminstrv. Mgmt. Assn., Am. Soc. Tng. Dirs. Author: (with others) Executive Secretarial Procedures, 5th ed., 1980; Coordinator's Handbook for Cooperative Vocational Programs in Kentucky, 1979; Occupational Opportunities for the Physically Handicapped, 1980; contbr. articles to profl. jours. Office: University of Kentucky 145TEB Lexington KY 40506 0001

UTLEY, LINDA KAY CHALFANT, educator; b. New Kensington, Pa., Oct. 9, 1943; d. Fred and Evelyn V. (Peters) Chalfant; A.B. (scholar), Vassar Coll., 1965; M.S., Georgetown U., 1971; children—Charles V., Yvette Melissa. Tchr. Public Schs. D.C., 1965—; lang. specialist Latin for the Modern Sch., McLean, Va., 1972—. Mem. Fgn. Lang. Action Group (co-founder 1978, chmn. 1978-80), Am. Assn. Tchrs. Spanish and Portuguese, Greater Washington Area Tchrs. Fgn. Lang., Washington Scholastic Press Assn. Roman Catholic. Home: 123 El Camino Way Fort Washington MD 20744 Office: Kramer Jr High Sch 17th and Q Sts SE Washington DC 20020

UTTERBACK, ALICE SKILTON, real estate broker; b. Phila., Mar. 3, 1921; d. Frank Redmond and Mary Ann Verner (Corder) Skilton; student Real Estate Coll., Washington, 1957-58, No. Va. Community Coll., 1971; m. Fred Dailey Utterback, June 15, 1940; 1 dau., Mary Ann Utterback Burritt. With Fairfax County (Va.) Health Dept., 1938, Woodward & Lothrop, Washington, 1939, F. W. Woolworth, Washington, 1940-41, Capital Transit, Washington, 1942-43; with J. H. and O. V. Carper, McLean, Va., 1943-63, office mgr., adminstrv. asst., 1958-63; owner Great Falls (Va.) Realty Assocs., 1958—. Pres., PTA, Great Falls, 1950-52, Fire Dept. Ladies Aux., Great Falls, 1945-47, Meth. Women, 1956-78; bd. dirs. Great Falls Grange; pres. Altar Guild. Mem. Nat. Assn. Realtors, Va. Assn. Realtors, No. Bd. Realtors, Great Falls Hist. Soc. Clubs: Great Falls Lioness (pres.), Forestville Home and Community. Home and Office: 11007 Georgetown Pike Great Falls VA 22066

UTTS, JESSICA MARIE, statistician, educator; b. Niagara Falls, N.Y., Oct. 13, 1951; d. Richard C. and Patricia J. (Highberger) U.; B.A., SUNY, Binghamton, 1973; M.A., Pa. State U., 1975, Ph.D., 1978. Instr. dept. statistics Pa. State U., 1977-78; asst. prof. dept. math U. Calif., Davis, 1978-79, asst. prof. div. statistics, 1979—; cons. in field. NSF trainee, 1973-74. Mem. Biometric Soc., Am. Statis. Assn., Inst. Math Statistics, Phi Beta Kappa. Contbr. articles to profl. jours. Office: Div Statistics Univ Calif Davis CA 95616

UTTS, PATRICIA JANE, social services adminstr.; b. Youngwood, Pa., Apr. 5, 1927; d. Paul Alec and Gertrude Mae (Peoples) Highberger; B.A., Pa. State U., 1948; M.S.W., Rutgers U., 1975; m. Richard C. Utts, July 23, 1949; children—Marsha, Jessica, Paul, Claudia, Melissa. Social worker, tchr., Westmoreland County, Pa., 1948-49, Niagara Falls, N.Y., 1953-55; news corr. Niagara Falls Gazette, 1959-62; dir. public relations United Way, Niagara Falls, 1962-65, asst. exec. dir., 1965-67; social worker N.J. Div. Youth and Family Services, Bridgeton, 1967-68, asst. supr., Atlantic City, 1968-75, protective service specialist So. region, Trenton, 1975-77, coordinator social services Atlantic County, Atlantic City, 1977-80; Atlantic County rep. N.J. Dept. Human Services, Atlantic City, 1980—; mem. Gov.'s Com. on Impact of Casino Gambling, 1979-80, N.J. Task Force on Compulsive Gambling, 1980; mem. So. N.J. Health Systems Agy. Plan Devel. Com., 1978-80, chmn. Atlantic City council, 1980—. Recipient N.J. Mother of Yr. award, 1979. Mem. Nat. Assn. Social Workers (co-chmn. Tri-County chpt. 1979-81), Am. Public Welfare Assn. Club: Bus. and Profl. Women's, Atlantic City (1st v.p.). Home: 925 S Main St Pleasantville NJ 08232

UYENOYAMA, JAYNE HAYDEN, speech/lang. pathologist; b. Hyannis, Mass., Aug. 29, 1940; d. Robert Ferguson and Elizabeth Belvedera (Chartier) Hayden III; B.A., U. Mass., 1962; M.Ed., Boston U., 1964; m. Dennis H. Uyenoyama, May 25, 1968; children—Catharine, Dennis. Speech/lang. pathologist Bedford (Mass.) Public Schs., 1964-67, U.S. Dependent Schs., European Area, Heidelberg, W.Ger., 1967-68, The Children's House, Nursery Sch., 1971-72, Falmouth (Mass.) Nursing Assn. (name now to Community and Home Health Services), 1972—; cons. Centerville (Mass.) Nursing Home, 1979—; pvt. practice speech/lang. pathology, Falmouth, 1969—. Bd. dirs. Cotuit-Santuit Civic Assn., 1974-75; chmn. pastor-parish relations com. Cotuit Federated Ch., 1978—. Vets. Rehab. Assn. grantee, 1963-64. Mem. Am. Speech, Lang. and Hearing Assn., Mass. Speech, Lang. and Hearing Assn. (S.E. Mass. rep. exec. bd. 1977-79, profl. standards rev. bd. 1979-80), Sigma Alpha Eta, Alpha Lambda Delta, Alpha Chi Omega. Home: 19 Ocean View Ave Cotuit MA 02635 Office: 67 Ter Huen Dr Falmouth MA 02540

VACCA, ANNA MARIA, asst. prin.; b. Birmingham, Ala., Jan. 17, 1947; d. Joseph John and Maggie Jo (Petruzella) V.; B.S., Birmingham So. Coll., 1968; M.A., U. Ala., 1972, A.A., 1975, M.A., 1978, now postgrad. Tchr. gen. and advanced biology Minor High Sch., Birmingham. Named Outstanding Tchr. of Yr., Ala. Congress Parents and Tchrs., 1980. Mem. NEA, Nat. Activities Advisers Assn., Nat. Assn. Sci. Tchrs., Ala. Edn. Assn., Jefferson County Edn. Assn., Birmingham Bus. and Profl. Womens Club, Delta Zeta. Roman Catholic. Home: 2301 Winterberry Way Birmingham AL 35216 Office: Minor High School Route 15 Box 342 Birmingham AL 35224

VACCARA, BEATRICE NEWMAN, govt. ofcl.; b. N.Y.C., Sept. 20, 1922; d. Wilfred and Gussie (Tannenbaum) Newman; B.A. cum laude (Adam Smith award 1943), Bklyn. Coll., 1943; M.A. (grad. scholar 1943-44), Columbia U., 1944; postgrad. Columbia U., Am. U.; m. John Vaccara, June 15, 1944; 1 son, Richard John. Research asso. Brookings Instn., 1954-59; with Dept. Commerce, 1959-77, 80—, asso. dir. Bur. Econ. Analysis, 1973-77, dir. Bur. Indsl. Econs., 1980—; dep. asst. sec. econ. policy Treasury Dept., 1977-80. Mem. exec. com. Montgomery County (Md.) LWV, 1959-65. Recipient Silver award Dept. Commerce, 1965, Gold medal, 1974. Fellow Am. Statis. Assn. (v.p. 1979); mem. Am. Econ. Assn., Nat. Economists Club (gov. 1973), Washington Statis. Soc. (pres. 1971-72), Conf. Research Income and Wealth (exec. com. 1972-74), Internat. Assn. Research Income and Wealth, Caucus Women in Stats. (pres.-elect 1980). Author reports, studies, articles in field. Office: Dept Commerce Washington DC 20230

VACCARO, ANNE, cosmetologist; b. Czechoslovakia, Mar. 22, 1930; came to U.S., 1935, naturalized, 1940; d. Peter and Helen (Virostko) Sokol; diploma Robert Fiance Inst. Hair Design, N.Y.C., 1950; m. Joseph Thomas Vaccaro, Oct. 26, 1952. Cosmetologist, 1950—; propr. Joseph Beauty Salon, Newton, N.J., 1969—. Mem. Hampton Twp. Planning Bd., 1973-74, chmn., 1974-75, mem. town governing body, 1975—. Mem. N.J. League Municipalities, Bus. and Profl. Women's Assn., League Profl. Planners, VFW Aux. (past chpt. pres.). Republican. Byzentine Catholic. Home: Rd 4 Box 671 Newton NJ 07860 Office: Big N Plaza Newton NJ 07860

VACCARO, BRENDA, actress; b. Bklyn., Nov. 18, 1939; d. Mario and Christine (Pavia) Vaccaro; student Neighborhood Playhouse, 1958-60. Appeared in Broadway plays Everybody Loves Opal, 1961, The Affair, 1962, Children from Their Games, 1963, Cactus Flower, 1965, The Natural Look, 1967, How Now Dow Jones, 1968, The Goodbye People, 1968, Father's Day, 1971; motion pictures include: Midnite Cowboy, Where it's At, I Love My Wife, Summer Tree, Going Home, Once Is Not Enough, Airport '77, House by the Lake, Capricorn One, House by the Lake, 1977, Capricorn One, 1978, First Deadly Sin, 1980, Zorro, the Gay Blade, 1981; TV appearances in The Greatest Show on Earth, 1963, Fugitive, 1963, Defenders, 1965, Doctors and Nurses, 1965, Coronet Blue, 1967, The FBI, 1969, The Psychiatrist, 1971, Name of the Game, 1971, Marcus Welby, M.D., 1972, Banacek, 1972, McCloud, 1972, McCoy, Streets of San Francisco, Sara, 1976, Dear Detective, 1979; TV movie appearances in Travis Logan, D.A., 1971, What's A Nice Girl Like You, 1971, Honor Thy Father, 1973, Sunshine, 1973, The Big Ripoff, 1975, Julius and Ethel Rosenberg, 1978, Guyana Tragedy—The Story of Jim Jones, 1980. Recipient Theatre World award, 1961-62, 3 Tony nominations, 2 Hollywood Fgn. Press Assn. nominations, Emmy award as supporting actress in The Shape of Things, 1974. Address: care Agy for Performing Arts Inc 9000 Sunset Blvd Suite 315 Los Angeles CA 90069 *

VACCARO, REGINA MARIA, physician; b. Bklyn., May 15, 1953; d. John and Pauline Veronica (Morello) V.; B.S. summa cum laude (scholar), St. Francis Coll., 1975; M.D., N.Y. Med. Coll., 1979. Resident in surgery Meth. Hosp., Bklyn., 1979-80; resident in orthopaedics Cath. Med. Center, Bklyn., 1980-81; resident in radiology Maimonides Hosp., Bklyn., 1982—. Mem. AMA, Am. Coll. Radiology, Radiol. Soc. N.Am. Home: 2183 E 7th St Brooklyn NY 11223

VACHER, CAROLE DOUGHTON, psychologist; b. Rocky Mount, Va., Dec. 31, 1937; d. John Harold and Mamie Katherine (Frith) Doughton; B.A., W.Va. Wesleyan U., 1960; M.A., Ohio U., 1962; Ph.D., N.C. State U., 1973; m. A. Ray Mayberry, Sept. 2, 1978; 1 dau., Elizabeth Michele Vacher. Birth defects coordinator W.Va. U. Med. Sch., Morgantown, 1962-63; research assoc. U. N.C. Med. Sch., Chapel Hill, 1965-70; intermin clin. psychology Vanderbilt U. Med. Sch., 1972-73; psychology research cons. N.C. Dept. Mental Health, Raleigh, 1971-73, research psychologist, 1973-75; asst. prof. psychology family practice residency program East Tenn. U. Med. Sch., Johnson City, 1975-77; cons., edn. and prevention coordinator Overlook Mental Health Center, Knoxville, 1977—; pvt. practice clin. psychology Maryville (Tenn.) Psychiat. Service, 1974—; cons. Knox County Child Abuse Rev. Team, Knoxville, 1977—; asst. prof. psychology U. Tenn., Knoxville, 1976—. Organizer, Community Psychology Task Force, Knoxville, 1977, Mental Health Assns. in Sevier and Monroe Counties, Tenn., 1978, also clinics, workshops; vol. Knoxville Med. Assn. Aux., 1979—, Methodist Ch., 1979; bd. dirs. Orange County Mental Assn., Chapel Hill, N.C., 1967-68. Recipient Wesleyan Key award, 1960; Outstanding Vol. Service award Tenn. Dept. Human Services, 1978; N.C. Dept. Mental Health scholar, 1970-71; lic. clin. psychologist, Tenn. Mem. Am. Psychol. Assn., Tenn. Psychol. Assn., Knoxville Area Psychol. Assn., Phi Kappa Phi, Psi Chi, Alpha Psi Omega. Democrat. Methodist. Author: Consultation-Education: Research and Evaluation, 1976. Researcher, compiler: Self-Help Directory: Knox County and Surrounding Area, 1981. Contbr. articles to profl. jours. Home: Route 23 Topside Rd Knoxville TN 37920 Office: 822 Tuckaleechee Pike Maryville TN 37801

VACHON, CASSANDRASU (SANDI) DHOOGE-QUINN, calligrapher, ednl. adminstr.; b. Moline, Ill., Mar. 4, 1941; d. Albert A. and Phyllis Dian (Witherspoon) Dhooge; student Chgo. Art Inst., 1964-65, Sch. Mus. Fine Arts, 1966-69; m. Marcel O. Vachon, Nov. 26, 1978; 1 dau. by previous marriage, Lewissa Claire. Tchr. calligraphy Cambridge (Mass.) Center Adult Edn., 1971—, Boston Center Adult Edn., 1971—; mem. faculty Decordova Mus., Lincoln, Mass., 1971-74; co-propr., dir. Sch. Calligraphy, Boston, 1974—; mem. faculty Danforth Mus., Framingham, Mass., 1976—; guest lectr. various art socs. and ednl. orgns., 1972—; one-woman shows of calligraphy include: Plymouth Public Library, 1966, Boston Center Adult Edn., 1972, 74, 75, 77, Cambridge Center for Adult Edn., 1972, 73, 76, 80, Atlantic Monthly Bldg., Boston, 1974, Colonnade Hotel Lobby, Boston, 1976—, First and Second Ch. of Boston, 1979; group shows at Boston Marketplace, 1976—; represented in permanent collections: Cambridge Center Adult Edn., Mus. Fine Arts, Boston, Lesley Coll., Sch. Calligraphy, Boston. Mem. Soc. Italic Handwriting, Soc. Scribes and Illuminators. Mem. Christian Ch. Home: PO Box 1546 Brockton MA 02403

VACHON, KATHRYNE FORD, fin. exec.; b. Miami, Fla., Apr. 11, 1915; d. Thomas Floyd and Eva Merle (Harman) Ford; student U. Miami, 1950-52; m. Martin Edgar Vachon, May 30, 1952; children—Betty Jo Jordan, Eugenie Lee Vachon. Owner-operator Service Dry Cleaners, Miami, Fla., 1932-37, Perry (Ga.) Cleaners & Laundry, 1941-46; bookkeeper Tropical Telco Fed. Credit Union, Coral Gables, Fla., 1947-56, gen. mgr., 1956-82, ret., 1982. Mem. budget adv. com. City of Coral Gables, 1977-78. Mem. Nat. Assn. Fed. Credit Unions (dir. 1977, sec. 1978-81), Nat. Credit Union Adminstrs. (nat. dir. 1974-79), Credit Union Execs. Soc., Internat. Telephone Credit Union Assn. (pres. 1968-69), Fla. Central Credit Union (pres. 1972-73, sec. 1974), Credit Union Mgrs. Assn. of Miami (pres. Coral Keys chpt. 1962-63), Nat. Assn. Accts. (dir. 1964-66), Coral Gables C. of C. Republican. Presbyterian. Clubs: Toastmasters, Altrusa. Office: 8000 NW 7th St Miami FL 33152

VAETH, AGATHA MIN-CHUN FANG, nurse; b. Peking, China, Feb. 19, 1935; d. Yung-Cheng and Wen-Pu (Cheng) Fang; came to U.S., 1956, naturalized, 1973; R.N. diploma (Scholar), Maryview Hosp., 1959; postgrad in fine art, Okla. State U., 1969-74, St. Joseph Coll., 1981—; m. Randy H. Vaeth, July 20, 1971; children—David, Elizabeth, Phillip. Staff nurse Mcpl. Hosp., Stillwater, Okla., 1970-73, charge nurse, 1973-74; clin. nurse USINH Hosp., Pawnee, Okla., 1974-75, USPHS Hosp., Carville, La., 1975—. Vol. nurse ARC; mem. Am. Mus. Natural History, La. Art and Artists Guild, Internat. Soc. Artists, Arts and Humanities Council of Greater Baton Rouge. Recipient appreciation award Otoe Missouria Tribal Council, 1974; award for high quality performance USPHS, HEW, 1978, award for service Nat. Hansen's Disease Center, 1981; cert. cardiopulmonary resuscitation instr. Am. Heart Assn. Mem. Am. Nurses Assn., La. State Nurses Assn., Baton Rouge Dist. Assn., Smithsonian Assos. Exhibitor paintings, One Am. Place, Baton Rouge, Art and Artists Guild, Baton Rouge, 1977, 78, 79; biol. illustrator Herpetology Lab. Manual, La. State U., 1978; translator English to Chinese, videocassette tapes on Hansen's Disease. Address: PO Box 45292 Broadview Sta Baton Rouge LA 70895

VAICELIUNAS, CHARLOTTE, nurse; b. Panevezys, Lithuania, Aug. 5, 1922; came to U.S., Sept. 1949, naturalized, 1955; d. Jurgis and Konstancija Dilyte (Daunoriene) Daunoras; diploma in midwifery, Lithuania; B.S. in Nursing, Cleve. State U., 1972; m. Stanley Vaiceliunas-Lunas, Oct. 10, 1943 (div. July 1959); children—Edmund Alexander, Alvin Stanley. Staff nurse St. Catherine's Hosp., East Chicago, Ind., 1952-56, St. Vincent Charity Hosp., Cleve., 1956; staff nurse Highland View Hosp., Cleve., 1959-60, head nurse, 1960, supr., clin. supr., 1962-78, asst. dir. rehab. nursing Cleve. Met. Gen. Highland View Hosp., 1972-82. Health care-provider Lithuanian Lang. Tchrs. Camp Dainava, Manchester, Mich.; active Am. Heart Assn., Inc. Registered nurse, Ohio. Mem. Nat. League Nursing, Lithuanian Cath. Fedn. (Ateitis) (pres. sr. assn. 1974-79), Lithuanian Alliance of Am. (pres. women's 20 chpt.). Roman Catholic. Home: 25250 Benesh Dr Cleveland OH 44122 Office: 3955 Scranton Rd Cleveland OH 44109

VAIL, IRIS JENNINGS, civic worker; b. N.Y.C., July 2, 1928; d. Lawrence K. and Beatrice (Black) Jennings; grad. Miss Porters Sch., Farmington, Conn.; m. Thomas V.H. Vail, Sept. 15, 1951; children—Siri J., Thomas V.H. Jr., Lawrence J.W. Mem. women's council Western Res. Hist. Soc., 1960—; mem. jr. council Cleve. Mus. Art, 1953—; chmn. Childrens Garden Fair, 1966-75, Public Square Dinner, 1975; bd. dirs. Garden Center Greater Cleve., 1963-77, Garden Club Cleve., 1981—; trustee Cleve. Zool. Soc., 1971—; mem. Ohio Arts Council, 1974-76, public sq. com. Cleve. Area Devel. Corp., mem. Chagrin Scenic River Adv. Council, Ohio Dept. Natural Resources. Recipient Amy Angell Collier Montague medal Garden Club Am., 1976, Ohio Gov.'s award, 1977. Episcopalian. Clubs: Chagrin Valley Hunt, Cypress Point, Kirtland Country, Union. Home: Hunting Valley Chagrin Falls OH 44022

VAIL, LOIS MAE, nurse; b. Arcata, Calif., July 5, 1924; d. William A. and Marie Ruby (Peters) Reeves; A.A., Sacramento Coll., 1944; R.N., Sacramento Sch. Nursing, 1945; m. Ronald A. Vail, Mar. 27, 1948; children—Phyllis and Pamela (twins), Cheron, David, Beckey, Bonnie. Dir. nurses Kahuku (Oahu) Hosp., Hawaii, 1945-48; supr. surgery Wahiawa (Oahu) Hosp., Hawaii, 1948-49; dir. nurses Alpine (Calif.) Convalescent Center, 1968-70, Alvarado Convalescent Rehab. Center, San Diego, 1970-71; staff nurse Foothills Hosp., El Cajon, Calif., 1971-72; supr. intensive care unit El Cajon Valley Hosp., 1972—. Bd. dirs. United Cerebral Palsy, 1954. Mem. Assn. Critical Care Nurses. Home: 1301 Bobcat Ln Alpine CA 92001

VAIL, SUSAN MARIE, social work adminstr.; b. Portland, Oreg., Feb. 17, 1943; d. Ralph Orville and Perla Cora Elisabeth (Dobberstein) Clave; B.A., Portland State U., 1965, M.S.W., 1972; children—Catherine Anastasia, Juliana Elisabeth. Caseworker, Multnomah County Welfare, Portland, 1968-69, 69-70; service worker Multnomah County Childrens Services, Portland, 1971; social worker Bess Kaiser Hosp., Portland, 1972; med. social worker Emanuel Hosp., Portland, 1972-73; dir. of social work St. Vincent Hosp. and Med. Center, Portland, 1974—. Bd. dirs. Regional Conf. for Managerial and Profl. Women, 1978, N.E. Portland Mental Health Planning Council, 1973-74; mem. Washington County Home Health Adv. Bd., 1974-77; chmn. Washington County Child Abuse Council, 1975-76; adv. com. St. Vincent Hosp. Home Care, 1978—. Mem. Nat. Assn. Social Workers (Oreg. chpt. pres. 1980-81), Soc. Hosp. Social Work Dirs. (sec.-treas. Oreg. chpt. 1980-81), Acad. Cert. Social Workers, Am. Pub. Health Assn., Oreg. Women's Polit. Caucus, LWV, Alpha Chi Omega. Democrat. Roman Catholic. Club: City of Portland. Home: 3226 NE 19th Ave Portland OR 97212 Office: 9205 SW Barnes Rd Portland OR 97225

VAILE, JEAN ELIZABETH, assn. exec.; b. Cut Bank, Mont., July 18, 1938; d. Leo M. and Evelyn A. (Hensrude) Baker; student Kinman Bus. Sch., 1956-57, Fresno City Coll., 1975-76, U. San Francisco, 1980, State Center Community Coll., Fresno, Calif., 1981-82; m. Alvin L. Vaile (div.); children—Arthur Henry, Sheila Jean, Leo Michael. Mgr., Glacier Drug, Browning, Mont., 1958-60, Club Cafe, Browning, 1960-67; office mgr. J.C. Penny Co., Mont., 1967-69, Bob Ward & Sons, Inc., Missoula, Mont., 1970-73; acct. Sun Fruit, Ltd., Fresno, 1973-76; bus. adminstr. Fresno Assn. for Retarded, 1976—; Amway distbr., 1975—; owner part-time income diversification and 2d income devel. bus. Chmn. supervisory com. Fresno Consumers Credit Union, 1979; voting mem. two social service health orgns., 1979—. Mem. Republican Presdl. Task Force. Lutheran. Club: Toastmasters. Home: 2007 E Austin Fresno CA 93726

VAINA, JENNIE CAROLINE, nurse; b. Arnold, Pa., Aug. 23, 1918; d. Joseph and Anna (Szulinski) Plaszczynski; R.N., Allegheny Valley Sch. Nursing, Tarentum, Pa., 1940; postgrad. U. Pitts.; m. Casimer Charles Vaina, Aug. 23, 1941. Mem. staff Citizens Gen. Hosp., New Kensington, Pa., 1943—, supr., 1945-77, asst. dir. nursing service, 1977—. Roman Catholic. Address: 522 Charles Ave New Kensington PA 15068

VAINE, SHIRLEY ANN, small bus. cons.; b. San Luis Obispo, Calif., Aug. 11, 1944; d. Felix John and Mary Lee (Waddell) Noble; student San Diego State U., 1962; children—Michele, Joann Marie. Br. mgr. Beach N Towne Realty, San Diego, 1973; pres. Womens Broker, San Diego, 1975-76; founder Profl. Women Center, San Diego, 1977, Women's Opportunity Expos, 1979; pres. Shirley Vaine & Assos., San Diego, 1978—. Del. White House Conf. Small Bus., 1978-90; cel., co-chmn. First Calif. Conf. Small Bus., 1981. Named Women in Bus. Advocate of Yr. San Diego C. of C., 1981, certificates Mayor of San Francisco, Pres. Carter. Mem. San Diego Women Council Realtors (charter pres. 1976), League Women Voters (chpt. chmn., pres., 1975), Clairmont C. of C. (v.p. presidents council 1978), Nat. Assn. Women Fed. Contractors (co-founder, mem. bd.), Nat. Assn. Realtors, Nat. Assn. Women Real Estate, Profl. Speakers Assn., NOW. Republican. Contbr. articles to various publs.

VALAD, PAULA TOLTESY, internat. orgn. exec.; b. Bklyn., Sept. 17, 1938; d. Paul Joseph and Hattie Wood Toltesy; B.A., Goucher Coll., 1960; cert. of accomplishment in editorial practices U.S. Dept. Agr. Grad. Sch., 1972; postgrad. George Washington U., Am. U., 1960—; 1 son, Hossain M. Sec., IBRD, Washington, 1960-70, tech. editor, 1970-74, evaluation officer ops. evaluation dept., 1975—, vice-chmn., coordinator career devel. and day care coms., consultation com. Staff Assn., 1973-74. Chmn. subcom. on mobility of status of women working group Personnel Classification Rev. Panel, vice chmn. task force on legal aspects of taxation and pensions, 1981-82. Mem. Soc. Internat. Devel., Assn. Women in Devel., Nat. Assn. Female Execs. Clubs: Toastmasters; Georgetown Women's. Home: 5221 Marlyn Dr Bethesda MD 20816 Office: 1818 H St NW Washington DC 20433

VALADKA, VIRGINIA TELKA, physician; b. Evanston, Ill., Sept. 23, 1954; d. Bruno and Vita Vincenta (Paliokas) V.; B.S., U. Ill., 1976; M.D. cum laude, Loyola U., 1979. Resident physician in gen. surgery Loyola U. Med. Center. Recipient citation Am. Med. Women's Assn. Diplomate

Nat. Bd. Med. Examiners. Mem. ACS, Alpha Omega Alpha. Office: 2160 S 1st Ave Maywood IL 60153 *

VALDES, PAMELA SUE, answering service exec.; b. St. Louis, May 20, 1952; d. Curdeen Lascuscus and Corinne Bernice LaNier; grad. Mary Inst., 1969; m. Julio C. Valdes, June 20, 1974; children—Mariposa, Juan. Co-owner The Bridge Restaurant, Anchorage, 1970-71; dir. The Corn Project, Internat. Friends of Rural India, 1972-73; owner, operator Tel-Us Answering and Communications Service, Oakland, Calif., 1975—; chief exec. officer 800 Line Communications System, 1980—; founder Rent-A-Number, San Jose, Calif., 1981—. Office: 3945 Opal St Oakland CA 94609

VALDES-DAPENA, MARIE AGNES, pathologist; b. Pottsville, Pa., July 14, 1921; d. Edgar Daniel and Marie Agnes (Rettig) Brown; B.S., Immaculata Coll., 1941; M.D., Temple U., 1944; m. Antonio M. Valdes-Dapena, Apr. 6, 1945 (div. Oct. 1980); children—Victoria Maria Valdes-Dapena Grefe, Deborah Anne Valdes-Dapena, Maria Cristina Valdes-Dapena, Andres Antonio, Antonio Edgardo, Carlos Roberto, Marcos Antonio, Ricardo Daniel, Carmen Patricia, Catalina Inez, Pedro Pablo. Intern, Phila. Gen. Hosp., 1944-45, resident in pathology, 1945-49; asst. pathologist Fitzgerald Mercy Hosp., Darby, Pa., 1949-51; dir. labs. Woman's Med. Coll. Pa., Phila., 1951-55, instr. pathology, 1947-51, asst. prof., 1951-55, asso. prof., 1955-59; asso. pathologist St. Christopher's Hosp. for Children, Phila., 1959-76; dir. div. pediatric pathology Jackson Meml. Hosp., Miami, 1976—; cons., lectr. U.S. Naval Hosp., Phila., 1972-76; instr. pathology Sch. Medicine U. Pa., 1945-49, instr. Sch. Dentistry, 1947, instr. Grad. Sch. Medicine, 1948-55, vis. lectr., 1960-62; asst. prof. Temple U. Med. Sch., 1959-63, asso. prof., 1963-67, prof., 1967-76, prof. pediatrics, 1967-76, prof. pathology and pediatrics, 1981—; prof. pathology and pediatrics U. Miami, 1976-81; cons. pediatric pathology div. med. examiner Dept. Pub. Health Phila., 1967-70; mem. perinatal biology and infant mortality research and tng. com. Nat. Inst. Child Health and Human Devel., NIH, 1971-73; mem. sci. adv. bd. Armed Forces Inst. Pathology, 1976—; asso. med. examiner, Dade County, Fla., 1976-81, chmn. med. bd., 1970—; chmn. med. bd. Nat. Sudden Infant Death Syndrome Found., 1961-81. NIH grantee. Diplomate Am. Bd. Pathology. Mem. Internat. Acad. Pathology, Pathol. Soc. Phila., Pediatric Pathology Club (pres. 1980-81), Pediatric Pathology Soc. Gt. Britain and Ireland, Coll. Physicians Phila., Internat. Assn. Pediatric Pathology, Alpha Omega Alpha. Roman Catholic. Contbr. articles to profl. jours. Office: Dept Pathology St Christopher Hosp for Children Philadelphia PA 19133

VALE, MAGDELYN CANDELARI, brokerage firm exec.; b. Houston, Feb. 13, 1941; d. Albert Joseph and Beatrice Magdelyn (Boldreghini) Candelari; student U. St. Thomas, 1961, U. Houston, 62, Zorn Bus. Coll., 1963; m. David Lee Vale, Mar. 15, 1975; 1 dau., D'Anna. Sec., J. Westerfield, C.P.A., Houston, 1961; sec. Hycel, Inc., Houston, 1962, Georgia-Pacific, Houston, 1963; clk. Royal Typewriter, Houston, 1965; mut. fund sales, sec. Fin. Programs Inc., Houston, 1967; with Underwood Neuhaus and Co., Houston, 1968—, v.p., 1982—. Mem. N.Y. Stock Exchange, Am. Stock Exchange, Nat. Assn. Securities Dealers. Roman Catholic. Clubs: Houston Security Dealers, Woman's Syndicate Assn., Zonta Internat. Office: 724 Travis St Houston TX 77002

VALENTINE, CAROL ANN, educator; b. Mt. Clemens, Dec. 5, 1942; d. J.E. and Erna (Brandt) V.; B.A., U. Mich., 1964, M.A., 1965; Ph.D., Pa. State U., 1971; children—Christopher Valentine Hall. Tchr., Oak Park (Iowa) River Forest High Sch., 1965-67; asst. prof. communication Oreg. State U., Corvallis, 1970-74; asst. prof. U. Oreg., Eugene, 1974-75; asst. prof. Ariz. State U., Tempe, 1975—; cons. in communications. Am. Council Edn. fellow, 1973-74; East West Center fellow, 1981-82. Mem. Western Speech Communiction Assn., World Future Soc. Author: (with L. Malandro) Peoplereading, 1977; research on childrens Lang. and nonverbal behavior. Home: 2607 S Forest St Tempe AZ 85282 Office: 412 Stauffer Ariz State U Tempe AZ 85287

VALENTINE, LINDA JEANNE KROES, apparel mfg. co. exec.; b. Kalamazoo, Mar. 9, 1950; d. Keith Edward and Delores June (Burpee) Kroes; student Mich. State U., 1969-70; B.B.A., Western Mich U., 1974; M.B.A., Loyola U. Chgo., 1980; m. Clark McCray Valentine, Jr., Apr. 17, 1971. Sr. tng. specialist Montgomery Ward & Co., Chgo., 1976-79, salary adminstrn. specialist, 1979-80; compensation analyst Hart Schaffner & Marx, Chgo., 1980-81, corp. compensation mgr., 1981—. Mem. Am. Compensation Assn., Chgo. Compensation Assn., Nat. Assn. Female Execs., M.B.A. Network, Loyola Grad Sch. Bus. Alumni Assn., NOW. Office: 101 N Wacker Dr Chicago IL 60606

VALERIO, HELEN JOSEPHINE, restaurant co. exec.; b. Chelsea, Mass., Nov. 23, 1938; d. William P. and Helen (Hoffman) Kazukonis; m. Michael A. Valerio, Oct. 6, 1957; children—Michael A., Laura L., Linda M. Acct., Piece O Pizza, of Am. Inc., Arlington, Mass., 1958-63; treas. Papa Gino's of Am., Inc., Needham Heights, Mass., 1963—, sr. v.p., 1980-81, exec. v.p., 1981—. Bd. dirs. Cath. Charitable Bur. Boston; mem. Nat. Adv. Council Women's Ednl. Programs. Mem. Nat., Mass. restaurant assns., Fin. Execs. Inst. Roman Catholic. Clubs: Weston Community League, St. Julia's Women's (pres. 1977-78). Home: 1064 Grove St Framingham MA 01701 Office: 111 Cabot St Needham Heights MA 02192

VALERIO, NINA DELEON, educator, nutritionist; b. Rizal, Philippines, Aug. 26, 1944; came to U.S., 1968, naturalized, 1978; d. Arcadio O. and Laureta C. (deLeon) Valerio; B.S. in Foods and Nutrition, Philippine Women's U., 1966; M.S., State U. Iowa, 1971; postgrad. U. Wash. Dietetic faculty asst. Philippine Inst. Nutrition and Food Tech., Philippine Women's U., Manila, Philippines, 1966-67; dietetic trainee Mary Johnston Hosp., Manila, 1968; clin. dietitian Univ. Iowa Hosp., Iowa City, 1969-72, relief research dietitian, 1971; nutrition service, continuing edn. coordinator U. Colo. Med. Center, Denver, 1972-74; lectr., clin. instr. clin. dietetics div. human nutrition, dietetics and foods, U. Wash., Seattle, 1974—, nutritionist Nutrition Clinic, 1980—; nutrition cons. U. Iowa Ostomy Group, 1969-72, Seattle Personal Devel. Center, 1979, Shelter for Battered Women, 1980; speaker nutrition topics to various groups. Dietetic Assn. of Philippines fellow for study in U.S., 1967. Mem. TEL-MED, King County Med. Soc., Am. Dietetic Assn., Wash. State Dietetic Assn., Seattle Dietetic Assn., Am. Home Econs. Assn., Nutrition Edn. Soc., NEA, Nutrition Today Soc., Am. Cancer Soc., Am. Heart Assn., Philippine Womens' Univ. Alumni, Floating Home Assn., East Lake Community Council, Omicron Nu, Pi Lamba Theta. Clubs: Beacon Hill Neighborhood, Filipino-American Community, International Circle. Home: 2339 Fairview E Seattle WA 98102 Office: DL-10 Univ of Wash Seattle WA 98195

VALESKA, NEYSA MAXINE, mfg. support analyst; b. Freeport, Ill., Nov. 2, 1927; d. William Joseph and Gladys Marie (Bray) Kirchberg; student U. Ill., 1945-47; m. Melvyn D. Valeska, Sept. 6, 1947; children—David, Daniel, William. Clk., Xerox Electronic Div. (and predecessor firm), El Segundo, Calif., 1969-72, material planner, 1972-80, sr. mfg. support analyst, 1976-80, sr. procurement analyst, 1980—. Vice-pres. Sanitary Laundry & Dry Cleaning, Freeport, Ill., 1978—. Mem. Am. Orchid Soc. Office: 701 S Aviation Blvd M4-06 El Segundo CA 90245

VALETTE, REBECCA MARIANNE, educator; b. N.Y.C., Dec. 21, 1938; d. Gerhard and Ruth Adelgunde (Bischoff) Loose; B.A., Mt. Holyoke Coll., 1959, L.H.D. (hon.), 1974; Ph.D., U. Colo., 1963; m. Jean-Paul Valette, Aug. 6, 1959; children—Jean-Michel, Nathalie, Pierre. Instr., examiner in French and German, U. So. Fla., 1961-63; instr. NATO Def. Coll., Paris, 1963-64, Wellesley Coll., 1964-65; asst. prof. Romance langs. Boston Coll., 1965-68, asso. prof., 1968-73, prof., 1973—; lectr., cons. fgn. lang. pedagogy; Fulbright sr. lectr., Germany, 1974. Am. Council on Edn. fellow in acad. adminstrn., 1976-77. Mem. MLA (task force on commonly taught langs.), Am. Council on Teaching Fgn. Langs., Am. Assn. Tchrs. French (v.p. 1980—), Am. Assn. Tchrs. German, Phi Beta Kappa, Alpha Sigma Nu. Author books, including: Modern Language Testing, 1967, rev. edit., 1977; French for Mastery, 1975, rev. edit., 1982; Contacts, 1976; C'est comme ça, 1978; Spanish for Mastery, 1980; Con Mucho Gusto, 1980; Nouvelles Lectures Libres, 1982; contbr. numerous articles to fgn. lang. pedagogy and lit. publs. Home: 16 Mount Alvernia Rd Chestnut Hill MA 02167 Office: Lyons 313 Boston Coll Chestnut Hill MA 02167

VALLELY, ANNE, fashion merchandiser; b. Natick, Mass., Aug. 2, 1943; d. John Paul and Dorothy (Gray) Vallely; B.A. cum laude, Regis Coll., 1965; M.A., Suffolk U., 1969; certificate Fashion Inst. Tech., 1972; m. Michael Petrucello, Feb. 14, 1974. Chmn., founder fashion merchandising dept. Newbury Jr. Coll., Boston, 1968—; mem. Am. Shoppers Panel; past mem. Mademoiselle Mag. Coll. Bd. Active Democratic congl. campaign, Mass., 1976. Mem. Eastern, New Eng. bus. tchrs. assns., Fashion Group (advisory bd.), Fashion Assos. (adv. bd.), Mass. Tchrs. Assn., Club: Cheerio. Office: 21 Commonwealth Ave Boston MA 02115

VALLERY, JANET ALANE, indsl. hygienist; b. Lincoln, Nebr., Apr. 4, 1948; d. Gerald William and Lois Florence (Robertson) V.; B.S., U. Nebr., Lincoln, 1970; diploma Bryan Meml. Sch. Med. Tech., Lincoln, 1971. Med. technologist Lincoln Gen. Hosp., 1971-72; congressional sec., 1973; lab. scientist Nebr. Dept. Health, 1973-79; safety indsl. hygienist Nebr. Dept. Labor, 1979—; cons. in field. Mem. Am. Conf. Govt. Indsl. Hygienists, Am. Soc. Clin. Pathologists (assoc.), Arabian Horse Assn., Nebr., Nebr. Dressage Assn., Lincoln C. of C., Am. Legion Aux. Republican. Methodist. Home: 4900 S 30th St Lincoln NE 68516 Office: 550 S 16th St Lincoln NE 68508

VALLIN, MARTA E., coll. counselor; b. Panama, Jan. 19, 1936; came to U.S., 1965, naturalized, 1973; d. David Eligio and Isabel Aguilar Dumbar; B.A., U. Panama, 1964; M.S., U. Bridgeport, 1974; Ed.D., Nova U., 1977; m. Karl-Gunnar Vallin, Dec. 16, 1967; 1 son, Lars Eric. Coordinator of services for handicapped, personal, acad. career counseling Panama Bd. Edn., 1956-58; with Panamerican Inst., 1959-65; with New Haven Bd. Edn., 1965-69; with Neighborhood Youth Corps, New Haven, Conn., 1969-73; counselor South Central Community Coll., New Haven, 1973—; adj. faculty N.H. Coll.; cons. U.S. Forest Service. Mem. Am. Personnel and Guidance Assn., Conn. Assn. Latin-Americans in Higher Edn. (pres.), Am. Ednl. Research Assn., Am. Assn. Higher Edn. Christian. Office: 60 Sargent Dr New Haven CT 06511

VALLON, KATHRYN RUDA, clin. social worker; b. Worcester, Mass., June 17, 1948; d. John Joseph and Elizabeth Helen (Carlage) Ruda, Jr.; B.A., Coll. Our Lady of the Elms, Chicopee, Mass., 1970; M.S.W., Boston Coll., 1972; cert. Alliance Francaise, Paris, 1968; m. Ronald Martin Vallon, June 3, 1972; children— Erica Lisbeth, Jordan Ruda. Social worker Mass. Dept. Public Welfare, Southbridge, 1970; caseworker Cath. Charities, Worcester, 1970-71, Mass. Gen. Hosp., Boston, 1971-72; clin. social worker Worcester State Hosp., Mass. Dept. Mental Health, 1972-76; dir. social service Milford-Whitinsville Regional Hosp., Milford, Mass., 1976-78; pvt. practice clin. social work, Medfield, Mass., 1979—; cons. Hubbard Regional Hosp., Webster, Mass., 1973-75, adminstrv. dir. mental health clinic, 1973-76; now cons. Hopedale Garden Nursing Home, Franklin House Healthcare, Milford Public Med. Home, Norfolk-Bristol Home Health Services, Inc., Bancroft House Healthcare. Lic. clin. social worker. Mem. Nat. Assn. Social Workers, Nat. Registry of Health Care Providers in Clin. Social Work. Home: 11 Rolling Ln Medfield MA 02052 Office: 1420 Providence Hwy Norwood MA 02062

VALMY, CHRISTINE, cosmetic co. exec.; b. Bucharest, Romania, Oct. 25, 1926; came to U.S., 1961, naturalized, 1966; d. Cristofor J. and Florika (Zamfiratos) Xantopol; cosmetology degree U. Medicine, Bucharest, 1949; student Law Sch., Bucharest, 1946-50; m. Henry D. Sterian, June 23, 1972; 1 dau. by previous marriage, Marina Valmy. Founder, pres. Christine Valmy, Inc., N.Y.C., 1965—; dir. Christine Valmy Internat. Sch. for Skin Care, 1966—. Named Small Bus. Person of Yr. for State of N.J., SBA, 1976. Mem. Am. Assn. Esthetics (pres.), Cosmetic Career Women. Republican. Author: Esthetics, The Keystone Guide to Skin Care, 1978; Christine Valmy's Skin Care and Makeup Book, 1982. Home: Soundview Castle Route 22 Mount Kisco NY 10549 Office: Christine Valmy Inc 767 Fifth Ave New York NY 10153

VAMMEN, JEAN BROOKS, health agency exec.; b. Phila., Feb. 16, 1929; d. George Albert and Constance Marie (Gossette) Brooks; student Lebanon Valley Coll., 1969-71, Elizabethtown Coll., 1972-74; m. James O. Vammen, May 5, 1975; children—Gail Suzanne Elliott, Richard Brooks Pursell, John Brooks Pursell. Service rep. Bell Telephone of Pa., 1947-49; dir. Pa. Assn. of Residences for Retarded, Harrisburg, 1973-75; dir. Nat. Multiple Sclerosis Soc. SE Colo., Colorado Springs, 1976—; gen. partner J & J Assos., 1978—; pres. Interdependent Service Systems, Inc. (I.S.S.), 1979—; exec. v.p. Individual Child Services, Inc., 1980—; lic. field underwriter Acacia Mut. Life Ins., Colorado Springs, 1980—. Adv. bd. Vol. Action Center, 1977-80. Recipient 7 awards Nat. Multiple Sclerosis Soc.; Citizen Advocacy award, 1978; Sertoma Club award, 1979, Community Service award, 1979. Mem. Colorado Springs C. of C. (chmn. public services com., 1978-80). Republican. Mem. Unity Ch. Club: Soroptimist Internat. (2d v.p. 1979-80). Home and office: 1955 Arapahoe St #101 Denver CO 80202

VAMOS, MAXINE EVELYN, banker; b. Johnstown, Pa., Nov. 19, 1929; d. Walter and Jennie (Wissenbach) Schwer; student pub. schs., Johnstown; m. Stephen E. Vamos, Apr. 17, 1950 (div. 1969); children—Jennifer Lynn Vamos Brown, Eric Vaughn. Saleswoman, Gt. Am. Tea Co., Johnstown, 1950-51; public relations rep. Johnstown Savs. Bank, 1968-71, public relations dir., 1971—, dir. personnel, 1973-77. Mem. Am. Inst. Banking, Greater Johnstown C. of C. Republican. Lutheran. Clubs: Rosicrucian Order. Home: 408 State St Johnstown PA 15905 Office: Market at Main St Johnstown PA 15901

VAN ALSTYNE, MARTHA JAYNE, indsl. designer; b. Delaware, Ohio, Apr. 11, 1923; d. Benjamin Francis and Madelon Suthlerand (Bliss) Van A.; cert. indsl. design, Pratt Inst., 1945; B.F.A., N.Y. State Coll. Ceramics, 1950, M.F.A., 1950. Studio head Gilbert Roade Assos., N.Y.C., 1948; instr. Mont. State U., Bozeman, 1959-54, prof. indsl. design, coordinator profl. design program Sch. Art and Architecture, 1972—; mem. design staff Gen. Motors Corp., 1955-69, asst. dir. safety and human performance lab., 1965-69; asst. prof., mem. faculty Grad. Faculty, Cornell U., 1969-73; cons. to industry, 1972—; exhibited ceramics, 1950—; designer Danforth window Mont. State U., 1954. Recipient Harvey Welch Ceramic award, 1951, diplome ceramique Ville de Cannes, 1955. Mem. Soc. Indsl. Design (charter). Home: 4434 Jackson Creek Rd Bozeman MT 59715 Office: Sch Art and Architecture Mont State U Bozeman MT 59715

VAN APPLEDORN, E(LIZABETH) RUTH, musician; b. Holland, Mich., Dec. 19, 1918; d. John and Elizabeth (Rinck) van Appledorn; Mus.B. (conservatory scholar 1936-40), Oberlin Coll., 1940; Mus.M., Mich. State U., 1942. Music supr. public schs., Newtow Falls, Ohio, 1940-41; mem. faculty N.Mex. State Coll., 1942-43, Washburn Municipal U., Topeka, 1944-46; head dept. music Alma Coll., 1943-44; instr. U. Minn., Duluth, 1946-50, asst. prof. music, 1950-68, asso. prof., 1968-71, prof., 1971—, mem. teaching faculty grad. sch., 1951—, adminstrv. asst., 1967-71; cons. and lectr. in field; participant series Sta. KDAL-TV, 1955-57; recitalist. Recipient Outstanding Tchr. award div. humanities U. Minn., Duluth, 1967, 68. Mem. Coll. Music Soc., Am. Soc. Psychical Research, Psychical Research Found., Mu Phi Epsilon. Mem. Spiritualist Ch. Dir., researcher Duluth's Bicentennial prod.: A Celebration in Sight and Sound, 1976. Home: 5120 Norwood St Duluth MN 55804 Office: Sch Fine Arts U Minn Duluth MN 55812

VANATTA, NANCY NORICEA, cardiology technologist; b. Williamson County, Tenn., Jan. 9, 1942; d. Joe Thomas and Alma W. (Deal) Spicer; student Draughons Bus. Coll., 1970; student cardiopulmonary courses Sch. Medicine, U. Calif., San Diego, 1980-82; m. James Vanatta, Feb. 2, 1957; children—Tony, Janice, Margie, Jeff. Asst. to physicians, Nashville, Tenn., 1970-82; cardiographics supr., Holter monitor technician Goodlark Hosp., Dickson, Tenn., 1982—. Vol. inservice trainer for EKG by telephone, Lewisburg Community Hosp. and Warren County Hosp., McMinnville, Tenn.; den mother Girl Scouts U.S., Boy Scouts Am., 1969-76; softball coach Fairview Recreation Center, 1969-76; hon. sheriff's dep. Sumner County, Tenn. Cert. med. sec., treadmill technician, Ga. Mem. Nat. Assn. Female Execs., Am. Assn. Cardiology Technologists, Nat. Assn. Physicians Nurses, Jaycettes, Moose, Am. Legion, VFW. Democrat. Roman Catholic. Home: Box 321 50th Ave North Nashville TN 37209 Office: 111 Highway 70 E Dickson TN 37055

VAN BEMMEL, DARLENE, educator; b. Hackensack, N.J., May 20, 1950; d. Theodore John and Gwendolyn Adele (Altman) Van Bemmel; A.A., Keystone Jr. Coll., 1970; registered dental hygienist Temple U., 1974, M.Ed., 1981; B.S., West Chester State Coll., 1975. Dental asst., Phila., 1974-75; educator Community Coll. Phila., 1975-77; program dir., asst. prof. dental edn. Harcum Jr. Coll., Bryn Mawr, Pa., 1977—; vis. prof. Community Coll. Phila., 1978-79; writer Dental Assisting Nat. Bd. Exam., 1980, 81. Recipient Legion of Honor award, 1980. Mem. Am. Assn. Dental Schs. Democrat. Roman Catholic. Home: 1000 Conestoga Rd Rosemont PA 19010 Office: Harcum Jr Coll Montgomery Ave Bryn Mawr PA 19010

VANBRAKLE, JOYCE ETHLYN, nursing home adminstr., nurse; b. Washington, Dec. 24, 1944; d. Waldemar Rivelo and Lillian Bernice (Moten) VanB.; B.S., Howard U., 1965; postgrad. in health adminstn. Babson Coll., 1970. Staff nurse Boston VA Hosp., 1965-66; dir. nursing Marlin Nursing Home, Roxbury, Mass., 1966-70; adminstr., inservice edn. coordinator, owner Spruce Haven Nursing Home, Boston, 1970-73; supr. Resthaven Nursing Home, Roxbury, Mass., 1973, asst. adminstr., 1974-75; adminstr. Townsend Nursing Home, Dorchester, Mass., 1973-74; cons. to nursing homes, 1974-75; house supr., inservice coordinator Motion Picture & TV Hosp./Country House, Woodland Hills, Calif., 1975-76; asst. dir. So. Calif. Home Health Assn., Los Angeles, 1976-77; nursing edn. coordinator Western Med. Enterprises, Inc., Los Angeles, 1977-81; dir. nursing Beverly Manor div. Beverly Entrprises, Van Nuys, Calif., 1981—; cons. to staff devel. dirs. of skilled nursing facilities. Mem. exec. bd. Beverly Hills-Hollywood (Calif.) br. NAACP. Lic. nursing home adminstr., Mass.; R.N., Mass., D.C., Calif. Mem. Howard U. Alumni Assn. So. Calif., Council Long-Term Care Nurses San Fernando Valley, Council Black Nurses So. Calif., Roman Catholic. Club: Democratic So. Calif. Home: 636 Hill St Inglewood CA 90302 Office: 6700 Sepulveda Bvld Van Nuys CA 97411

VAN BRONKHORST, ERIN MARIE, journalist; b. Seattle, June 24, 1949; d. John and Edna Marie (de la Torre) Van B.; B.A. in History, U. Wash., 1971, M.Bus. and Econs. Journalism (Bus. and Econs. Reporting fellow), 1982. News writer Sta. KIRO-TV, Seattle, 1970-71; newswoman AP, Seattle and Olympia, Wash., 1971-73; editor, co-pub. Pandora Women's News Jour., Seattle, 1973-76; polit. writer Fairbanks (Alaska) Daily News-Miner, 1976-77; reporter Seattle Post-Intelligencer, 1977-79, copy editor, 1979—; writer Seattle Bus. Jour.; tchr. news writing YWCA, 1974. Recipient Hearst monthly award for spot news, 1977. Mem. Wash. Press Assn., Phi Beta Kappa. Roman Catholic. Author: (with Cara Peters) How to Stop Sexual Harassment: Strategies for Women on the Job, 1980. Office: 521 Wall St Seattle WA 98121

VAN BRUNT, MARCIA ADELE, social worker; b. Chgo., Oct. 21, 1937; d. Dean Frederick and Faye Lila (Greim) Slauson; student Moline (Ill.) Pub. Hosp. Sch. Nursing, 1955-57; B.A. with distinguished scholastic record, U. Wis., Madison, 1972, M.S.W. (Fed. tng. grantee), 1973; children—Suzanne, Christine, David. Social worker div. community services Wis. Dept. Health Social Services, Rhinelander, 1973, regional adoption coordinator, 1973-79, chief adoption and permanent planning No. Region, 1979—; counselor, public speaker, cons. in field. Home: Rural Route 1 Box 2262 Rhinelander WI 54501 Office: Box 697 Rhinelander WI 54501

VAN BUREN, ABIGAIL (PAULINE FRIEDMAN PHILLIPS), columnist, writer, lectr.; b. Sioux City, Iowa, July 4, 1918; d. Abraham and Rebecca (Rushall) Friedman; student Morningside Coll., Sioux City, 1936-39, Litt.D., 1965; m. Morton Phillips, July 2, 1939; children—Edward Jay, Jeanne. Vol. worker for causes of better mental health, Nat. Found. Infantile Paralysis, tng. Gray Ladies ARC, 1939-56; pres. Minn.-Wis. council B'nai B'rith Aux., 1945-49; columnist Dear Abby, San Francisco Chronicle, 1956, syndicated Universal Press Syndicate, now appears in newspapers U.S., Brazil, Australia, Japan, Germany, Holland, Denmark, Can., Korea, Thailand, Italy, Hong Kong, Taiwan, Saudi Arabia; radio program CBS, 1963-75. Nat. chmn. Crippled Children Soc., 1962; hon. chmn. Nat. Soc. Crippled Children and Adults Easter Seal campaign, 1963; del. Democratic Nat. Conv., 1964; bd. dirs. Dr. Franz Alexander Research Found., Los Angeles, Nat. Goodwill Industries, 1968-75, Guthrie Theatre, Mpls., 1970-74; hon. chmn. Cancer Crusade, 1982; participant White House Conf. on Children and Youth, 1970, White House Conf. on Physically Handicapped, 1976; mem. Nat. Adv. Council on Aging, 1978-81; mem. public adv. council Center Study Multiple Gestation, 1981; trustee, adv. bd. Westside Community Ind. Living, 1981; council sponsors Assn. Vol. Sterilization, 1981; women's trusteeship Humanitarian award Braille Inst., 1981. Recipient Mother of Year award, Los Angeles, 1958; Golden Kidney award, Los Angeles, 1960; NCCJ award, 1968; Disting. Service award Suicide Prevention Center, San Mateo, Calif., 1970; Good Samaritan award Salvation Army, San Francisco, 1970; Margaret Sanger award Nat. Planned Parenthood, 1974; Robert T. Morse Writer's award Am. Psychiat. Assn., 1977; Life award Suicide Prevention Center, 1977, spl. citation Am. Cancer Soc., Inc. Paul Harris fellow Rotary Internat. Mem. Women in Communications (hon.), Sigma Delta Chi. Author: Dear Abby, 1957 (also translated Japanese, Dutch, German, Spanish); Dear Teen Ager, 1959; Dear Abby on Marriage, 1962; Best of Dear Abby, 1982; Contbr. to McCall's mag. Home: Beverly Hills CA 90210 Office: 132 Lasky Dr Beverly Hills CA 92012

VAN BUREN, CAROLINE POWERS THOMAS, musician; b. Decatur, Ill., Jan. 18, 1893; d. George Wescott and Hadassah (Bowers) Powers; student Mannes Coll. Music, 1929, Juilliard Coll. Music, 1950; m. James Akin Thomas, Feb. 10, 1917; children—James Akin, Chauncey Powers; m. 2d, Maurice Pelham Van Buren, Nov. 20, 1971. Violin soloist Sousa's Band, 1924; soloist St. Louis Symphony, 1927, Budapest

Philharmonic Orch., 1932, Kansas City Symphony, 1948; concert tour, Europe, 1932, S.Am., 1933; music therapist with war vets; head violin dept. Tulsa Coll. Music, 1925; pvt. tchr. violin, Scarsdale, N.Y., 1928-57. Mem. Musicians Club Am., Musicians Club N.Y., Mu Phi Epsilon, D.A.R., New Eng. Women, Daus. of Holland Dames, Colonial Dames Am. Clubs: Eastern Star, Wychmere Harbor, Hyannis Yacht, Eastward Ho Country, Colony. Address: 1220 Park Ave New York City NY 10028 also 5 Woodland Rd South Chatham MA 02659

VAN BUSKIRK, ANNE MARIE, comml. printing co. exec.; b. Paris, May 29, 1927; came to U.S., 1933; d. Theodore and Georgette (Raphael) Burns; B.A., Los Angeles State Coll., 1949; m. Edward R. Van Buskirk, Nov. 23, 1949 (div.); children—James Edward, John Riley. Owner, mgr. Rainbow Printing, Inc., Seattle, 1977—. Recipient various certs. appreciation. Mem. Wash. Printing Industries, Women's Bus. Exchange, Seattle Women Bus. Owners, Sales and Mktg. Execs., Seattle Mut. Bus. Club, Winners Circle. Mem. Ch. of Religious Sci. Club: Swedish. Home: Northgate Plaza Apt 414 9416 1st Ave NE Seattle WA 98115 Office: Rainbow Printing Inc 2917 1st Ave Seattle WA 98121

VAN CAMP, MABEL MARGARET, justice Ont. Supreme Ct.; b. Blackstock, Ont., Can., May 11, 1920; d. William John Wier and Mary Jane (Smith) Van C.; B.A. with honors, U. Toronto, 1941; postgrad. Osgoode Hall, 1944-47. Called to Ont. bar; assoc. Beaudoin, Pepper & Van Camp, 1947-71; justice Supreme Ct. Ont., Toronto. Pres., YWCA Met. Toronto; del. World Conf. Australia, 1967; com. mem. United Community Fund. Recipient Can. Centennial medal. Mem. Can. Bar Assn. (council), Ont. Women's Law Assn. (past pres.), York County Law Assn., Kappa Beta Pi. Anglican. Clubs: Univ. Women's, Royal Can. Mil. Inst. Office: Osgoode Hall 130 Queen St W Toronto ON Canada

VANCE, ANN BROOKS, lawyer, legis. asst. U.S. Senate; b. Montrose, Colo., Oct. 4, 1949; d. Theodore Lincoln and Marian Ruth (Inhelder) Brooks; B.A., U. Miss., 1972, J.D., 1975. Admitted to Miss. bar, 1975, D.C. bar, 1975, U.S. Supreme Ct., 1981; staff atty. Interior Bd. Land Appeals, U.S. Dept. Interior, Washington, 1975-76, atty. office of solicitor public lands br., 1976-78, minerals br., 1978-81; legis. asst. for energy to U.S. Sen. Malcolm Wallop, Washington, 1981—. Marine Resource Council grantee, 1975. Mem. Am. Bar Assn., Fed. Bar Assn. Republican. Episcopalian. Office: 204 Russell Senate Office Bldg Washington DC 20510

VANDENBERG, HELEN MARIE, psychiat. social worker; b. Paterson, N.J., Aug. 6, 1942; d. James and Helen (Colyer) Rose; B.A., Hope Coll., Mich., 1964; M.S. in Social Work, Columbia U., 1966; m. Peter Vandenberg, Oct. 10, 1969; children—Craig Peter, Stephen James. Social worker Salvation Army Family Service, Bklyn., 1966-68; psychiat. social worker Passaic (N.J.) Mental Health Clinic, 1968-71; cons. Passaic County Probation Dept., 1975-78; nursing homes cons., Clifton and Wayne, N.J., 1977-78; sr. psychiat. social worker-emergency services Community Mental Health Center, Passaic, 1978—; workshop leader. Bd. dirs. CLEAR (Center for Life Enrichment and Renewal), Wyckoff, N.J., 1977—. Cert. sch. social worker-vis. tchr., N.J. Dept. Edn. Mem. Acad. Cert. Social Workers, Nat. Assn. Social Workers. Mem. Ref. Ch. Home: 526 Albert St Wyckoff NJ 07481 Office: 211 Pennington Ave Passaic NJ 07055

VANDERBILT, GLORIA MORGAN, artist, actress, fashion designer; b. N.Y.C., Feb. 20, 1924; d. Reginald Claypoole and Gloria (Morgan) Vanderbilt; attended Mary C. Wheeler, Miss Porter's schs.; studied acting with dir. Sanford Meisner, beginning 1955; m. Pasquale di Cicco (div.); m. 2d, Leopold Stokowski, 1945 (div. 1955); children—Stanislaus, Christopher; m. 3d, Sidney Lumet, 1956 (div.); m. 4th, Wyatt Emory Cooper, 1963; children—Carter V., Anderson H. Exhibited in one-man shows at Rabun Studio, N.Y.C., 1948, Bertha Shaeffer Gallery, N.Y.C., 1954, Juster Gallery, N.Y.C., 1956, Hammer Gallery, N.Y.C., 1966, 68, Cord Gallery, N.Y.C., 1966, Washington Gallery Art, 1968, Neiman-Marcus, Dallas, 1968, Vestart Gallery, N.Y.C., 1969, Parish Museum, Southampton, N.Y., also in Nantucket, Mass., Houston, Reading, Pa., Monterey, Calif., Nashville; exhibited in group shows Washington Gallery Art, 1967, Hoover Gallery, San Francisco, 1971; stage career; acted in summer stock prodn. The Swan; made Broadway debut in The Time of Your Life, 1955; other stage appearances include Picnic, 1955, The Spa, 1956, Peter Pan, 1958, The Green Hat; made TV debut in Tonight At 8:30; other TV appearances include Colgate Comedy Hour, 1955, Flint and Fire on U.S. Steel Hour, 1958, Family Happiness on U.S. Steel Hour, 1959, Very Important People; appeared in film Johnny Concho, 1955; dir. design Riegel Textile Corp., N.Y.C., 1970—; designer stationary and greeting cards Hallmark Co.; designer fabrics Bloomcraft Co. designer bed linens Martex Co., table linens Leacock Co., Gloria Vanderbilt jeans, also china, glassware, scarves. Recipient Sylvania award, 1959, Fashion award Neiman-Marcus, 1969. Mem. Actors Equity, Screen Actors Guild, AFTRA, Authors League Am., Am. Fedn. Arts Author: Love Poems, 1955: (with Alfred Allen Lewis) Gloria Vanderbilt Book of Collage, 1970; Woman to Woman; author play: Three by Two, early 1960's, author poems and short stories. Office: care Murjani USA 498 7th Ave New York NY 10018 *

VAN DER MEER, GRETA, indsl. cons.; b. Chgo., Jan. 15, 1949; d. Walter Henry and Virginia Mae (Olson) Van der M.; Ph.B. in Psychology, Northwestern U., 1974. With Leo Burnett Co., Chgo., 1969-72; personnel asst. Inst. Psychiatry, Northwestern Meml. Hosp., Chgo., 1972-77, coordinator perinatal addiction program, 1975-77; mgr. prodn. and adminstrn., nat. orgnl. surveys Sears, Roebuck & Co., Chgo., 1977-81; nat. sec.-treas. Mayflower Group, 1980-81, nat. vice chmn., 1981-82, nat. chmn., 1982-83; indsl. cons. Harbridge House, Inc., 1981—; v.p. CDS. Grantee, Ill. Dangerous Drugs Commn., 1975. Mem. Am. Assn. Public Opinion Research, Ill. Group Psychotherapy Soc. Home: 222 E Pearson Apt 802 Chicago IL 60611 Office: 150 N Wacker Chicago IL

VANDERPOOL, NATHALIE AKIN, educator; b. Bluegrove, Tex., Apr. 17, 1938; d. George W. and Doris Lurline (Reaves) Akin; B.A., Abilene Christian U., 1960; M.Ed. with high honors, Northeastern U., Boston, 1974; m. Harold Y. Vanderpool, June 10, 1960; children—Jonathan, Katherine, Jay. Elem. sch. tchr., Mass., 1961-63; counselor's asst. Dana Hall Sch., Wellesley, Mass., 1964-67; dir. health and phys. edn. Tenacre Country Day Sch., Wellesley, 1968-74; counselor, support service coordinator Weston (Mass.) public schs., 1974-76; coordinator community tng. programs, asst. prof. pediatrics, div. sch. health and community pediatrics U. Tex. Med. Br., Galveston, 1976—. Mem. exec. com. Galveston Hist. Found. Mem. Ambulatory Pediatric Assn., Am. Sch. Health Assn., Am. Personnel and Guidance Assn., Tex. Sch. Health Assn., LWV, AAUW, East End Hist. Assn. Author papers in field. Home: 2514 Gerol Dr Galveston TX 77551 Office: Dept Pediatrics Univ Tex Med Br Galveston TX 77550

VANDERPOORTE, IDA CORNELIA, restaurant chain fin. exec.; b. Edam, Netherlands, Jan. 27, 1948; came to U.S., 1950, naturalized, 1967; d. Wicher and Ida Cornelia (Hooyberg) VanderP.; student Calvin Coll., 1965-67; B.A. in Math. magna cum laude, Mich. State U., 1973. Sr. audit dept. Price Waterhouse, Los Angeles, 1973-78, mgr. tax dept., 1978-79; chief fin. officer, treas., sec. Hungry Tiger Inc., Van Nuys, Calif., 1979—, also dir.; cons. Project Bus. div. Jr. Achievement. Mem. Fin. Execs. Inst., Am. Inst. C.P.A.s, Calif. Soc. C.P.A.s. Office: 14265 Oxnard St Van Nuys CA 90401

VANDERSLICE, SUELLYN, psychologist, air force officer b. Baytown, Tex., Oct. 10, 1948; d. Thomas J. Vanderslice Jr. and Teodosia E. (Bevers) Loerwald; student Brevard Community Coll., 1966-67; B.A. in Sociology, La. State U., 1970; M.S. in Recreation Therapy, Calif. State U., 1975; Ph.D. in Psychology, U. Hawaii, 1983; m. John Walter Patrick Jr., May 30, 1970 (div. 1975). Community social worker City of Pensacola (Fla.), 1970-71; therapeutic recreation supr. Salvation Army, Honolulu, 1973-74; community social worker Girl Scout Council of the Pacific, Honolulu, 1974-75; psychiat. social worker Mental Health Div., State of Hawaii, summer 1977; lectr. dept. psychology U. Hawaii, Honolulu, 1978-82; state mental health program dir. for women Dept. Health, State of Hawaii, 1979; pvt. practice marriage and family counseling, Honolulu, 1977-82; resident in clin. psychology USAF, Wilford Hall, Lackland AFB, Tex., 1982-83. Mem. Lt. Gov.'s Com. on Women and Family, State of Hawaii, 1979-82. Mem. Am. Psychol. Assn., Western Regional Psychol. Assn., Hawaii Psychol. Assn., Hawaii Assn. for Humanistic Psychology (v.p. 1976-77, sec.-treas. 1977-78), Nat. Assn. Parks and Recreation, Am. Personnel and Guidance Assn., AAUW, Network of Mktg. Women, Gamma Phi Beta. Democrat. Baptist. Contbr. articles to jours. in psychology. Home: 208 Double File Trace Liberty Hall TX 78642 Office: Psychiatry and Psychology Residency Tng CMR 8 Wilford Hall USAF Med Center Lackland AFB TX 78236

VANDERSLUYS, CORA, med. technologist; b. Chester, Pa., Aug. 27, 1923; d. Edward and Florence C. (Murtaugh) Vandersluys; B.S., Fairleigh Dickinson U., 1960. Med. technologist St. Joseph Hosp., Paterson, N.J., 1955-60, asst. chief technologist, head hematology dept., 1960-66; research asst. N.J. Coll. Medicine, Jersey City, 1966-67; mgr. tech. resources Ortho Diagnostic Systems Inc., Raritan, N.J., 1967—; adj. asst. prof. Rutgers Med. Sch., Piscataway, N.J. Mem. Am. Soc. Clin. Pathologists, Am. Soc. for Med. Tech., N.J. Soc. for Med. Tech. (sec. 1958-60) pres. 1960-61). Mem. Christian Reformed Ch. Office: Rt 202 Raritan NJ 08869

VANDERVELDE, MARYANNE, mgmt. cons.; b. Washington, May 31, 1940; d. Arthur and Bertha (Wiersma) Vandervelde; A.B., Calvin Coll., 1960; M.S.W., U. Calif., Berkeley, 1962; Ph.D. (NIMH doctoral tng. fellow), U. Wash., 1978; m. H. Ray Looney, July 7, 1962; 1 son, Spencer Velde. Med. social worker Santa Clara (Calif.) County Hosp., 1962-64; psychiat. social worker Bellevue Psychiat. Hosp., N.Y.C., 1964-66; psychiat. social work supr. Mt. Sinai Hosp., N.Y.C., 1966-69; exec. dir. Stamford (Conn.) Mental Health Center, 1969-70; dir. dept. human resources Hall-Brooke Hosp., Westport, Conn., 1970-75; pres. Pioneer Mgmt. Inc., Seattle and N.Y.C., 1978—; lectr. U. Wash., Seattle, 1976-78. Author: The Changing Life of the Corporate Wife, 1978; Management Preparation for Women, 1979; also articles in profl. jours. Home: 320 E 72d St New York NY 10021

VAN DER VEN, ANNA LUCYLE, banker; b. Des Arc, Ark., Mar. 20, 1924; d. Charles Everet and Irene Evgenia (Thorne) Lawler; student Memphis State U., also various specializing schs.; m. Robert van der Ven, Mar. 23, 1955; 1 son, Eric Allen. Data processing mgr. Hyster N.V., Nijmegen, Netherlands, 1955-62, Chapman Chem. Corp., Memphis, 1962-72; asst. comptroller G.P. Schoenfelder, Rainbows End Ranches, Scottsdale, Ariz., 1972-74; v.p., cashier Bank of Scottsdale (Ariz.), 1974-82, also sec. to bd. dirs.; v.p. cashier Am. Bank, Phoenix, 1982—. Mem. Nat. Assn. Bank Women (past div. dir.), Scottsdale Bus. and Profl. Women's Club, Ariz. Bankers Assn., Paradise Valley C. of C. Home: 5375 E Wallace Ave Scottsdale AZ 85254 Office: 2933 N Central Ave Phoenix AZ 85012

VAN DER WALT, RUTH SELBY, music educator; b. Morgantown, W.Va., Aug. 20, 1923; d. Arthur L. and Amy (Wotring) Selby; B.Mus., W.Va. U., 1944; cert. in elem. music U. Fla., 1950; 1 dau., Judith Amy. Music tchr. public schs., Ft. Lauderdale, Fla., 1950—. Mem. Music Educators Nat. Conf., Broward Music Edn. Assn. (exec. bd.), Broward County Elem. Music Educators Assn. (pres., 1960-61), NEA, Fla. Tchrs. Assn., Classroom Tchrs. Assn., Beta Sigma Phi (pres. 1962-63), Alpha Delta Kappa (chaplain 1980-82). Democrat. Methodist. Clubs: Zonta Internat. (sec. Pompano Beach chpt. 1975-76, v.p. 1980 81, pres. 1981-82), Order Eastern Star (worthy matron 1959-60). Home: 3771 NE 17th Ave Pompano Beach FL 33064 Office: 936 NE 33rd St Fort Lauderdale FL 33330

VANDERWARF, MARILYN, educator; b. Chicago Heights, Ill., May 25, 1920; d. Cornelius and Anna (Hook) Vanderwarf; A.A., Blackburn Coll., 1939; B.S. with honors, U. Ill., 1941; M.S., Cornell U., 1948. Tchr. home econs. secondary schs., Ill., 1941-45; supr., faculty Blackburn Coll., 1945-49; faculty Purdue U., W. Lafayette, Ind., 1949-52; tchr., chmn. dept. home econs. Maine Twp. High Sch., Park Ridge/Des Plaines, Ill., 1952-57; faculty dept. home econs. Calif. State U., Long Beach, 1957—, asso. prof., 19 —; faculty night sch. Northwestern U., Evanston, Ill., 1956. Recipient awards, Calif. State U., Long Beach, Student Dietetic Assn., 1980. Mem. Am. Home Econs. Assn. (membership promotion com. 1973-75), Calif. Home Econs. Assn. (asst. treas. 1967-70), Am. Dietetic Assn., Calif. Dietetic Assn., AAUP, Council on Hotel, Restaurant and Instl. Edn., Calif. Employees Assn., Greater Los Angeles Nutrition Council, Orange County Nutrition Council, Coll. Tchrs. Food and Nutrition (chmn. Pacific region 1968-69), Pi Lambda Theta, Delta Kappa Gamma, Omicron Nu, Sigma Delta Epsilon. Republican. Club: PEO Sisterhood. Home: 9781 Bixby Ave Garden Grove CA 92641 Office: 1250 Bellflower Blvd Long Beach CA 90840

VAN DERWEELE, MARY AMANDA, reporter, editor; b. Lansing, Mich., Jan. 11, 1930; d. Elon Samuel and Helen (Andreas) Bolton; student Western Mich. U., 1956-57; m. Denton Dexter Van DerWeele, May 1, 1970; children by previous marriage—Robert Clarke, Craig Clarke; stepchildren—Sandra Groot, K.S. Van DerWeele. Writer, Sta. WKZO-AM-TV, Kalamazoo, 1958-64, publications coordinator radio and TV, 1968-71; freelance writer Ford Times, Trailer Life, Health, Ladies Home Companion, Golden Mag. for Boys and Girls, 1964-68, also Battle Creek Enquirer and News, The Kalamazoo Gazette; partner, mgr. Van the Printer, Vicksburg Broadcast, Trading Post, Vicksburg, Mich., 1971-77; editor, writer Richland (Mich.) Jour. weekly, 1979—. Area rep. Youth for Understanding, 1978—; St. Joseph County del. State and County Republican Convs., 1974-76; vice chmn. Womens Rep. Com., St. Joseph County, 1975-77; bd. dirs. Constatine Library, 1976. Mem. Mich. Press Assn. Home and Office: 7821 N 37th St Richland MI 49083

VANDERWIER, CONSTANCE JEAN, food co. exec.; b. Muskegon, Mich., Feb. 27, 1921; d. John O. and Anna Marie (Olsen) Loberg; grad. high sch.; m. Henry M. Vanderwier, Mar. 13, 1946. Secretarial positions in law office, Muskegon, 1939-40, Brunswick Corp., Muskegon, 1940-42, Canadian Nat. Ry., Chgo., 1942-46; ct. reporter Marine Corps, 1946; secretarial positions Norge Corp., Muskegon, 1947-50; exec. sec. Gerber Products Co., Fremont, Mich., 1951-68, asst. sec., 1968-73, sec., 1973—. Mem. Am. Soc. Corporate Secs., Bus. and Profl. Women. Club: Ramshorn Country. Home: 1018 Leo St Fremont MI 49412 Office: 445 State St Fremont MI 49412

VANDERWORK, CAROL DEANNE JENKINSON, educator; b. Harper, Kans., Dec. 31, 1945; d. William Manford and Margaret (Davis) Jenkinson; B.S., Okla. State U., 1968; M.Ed., Southwestern Okla. State U., 1972; m. Mickey M. Vanderwork, Aug. 22, 1965; children—Lee Allen, Dell Marvin, Leslie Ann. Adminstrv. asst. Coll. Bus., Okla. State U., Stillwater, 1965-68; bus. tchr. Ripley (Okla.) High Sch., 1968-69; sec. to pres. Am. Fidelity Life Ins. Co., Pensacola, Fla., 1969-70; tchr. bus., English, Reydon (Okla.) High Sch., 1972-74; tchr. English, Taloga (Okla.) High Sch., 1975—. Mem. Nat. Council Tchrs. English, Okla. Tchrs. English Assn. Republican. Mem. Christian Ch. Club: Women's Federated. Home: Route 2 Taloga OK 73667 Office: Taloga High School PO Box 128 Taloga OK 73667

VAN DERZEE, LESLIE MORGAN, fin. mgmt. exec.; b. Albany, N.Y., Jan. 17, 1943; d. George J. and Frances (Fitz) Morgan; B.A., Wellesley Coll., 1965; M.A., Syracuse U., 1968; M.B.A., Columbia U., 1978; m. Pieter S. VanDerzee, Aug. 28, 1965; children—Anne Sanford, Jefferson Morgan. Cons. on higher edn. Bur. Coll. Evaluation, N.Y. State Dept. Edn., 1969-70; asst. to exec. asst. Gov. Nelson A. Rockefeller, N.Y.C., 1970-73; spl. projects asso. Rockefeller Family, N.Y.C., 1973-77; asso. David Rockefeller, N.Y.C., 1977—. Clubs: Met., Lawrence Beach. Office: 30 Rockefeller Plaza Room 5600 New York NY 10020

VAN DEVANTER, ROSE ELLEN TRIMBLE, educator; b. Henry County, Ind., July 1, 1925; d. James Harley and Melva Opal (Moreman) Trimble; B.S., Ball State U., 1965; M.S., Ind. State U., 1970; m. Harold Clyde Dillingham, Aug. 1, 1977; children—Alan Ray, Pamela Ellen Van Devanter Bingham. Dir., Psi Iota Xi Day Care Center, Muncie, Ind., 1948-65; tchr. Madison (Ind.) Consol. Schs., 1965-68, Hawaii State Dept. Edn., Kauai, 1968-69; tchr./coordinator pre-sch. Ind. State U., Terre Haute, 1969-82, asst. prof. early childhood edn., 1975—; con. day care project State of Fla. Mem. Nat. Assn. for Deaf, Nat. Assn. for Edn. of Young Children, Ind. Assn. for Edn. of Young Children (workshop leader). Methodist. Clubs: 4 C of Terre Haute, Order Eastern Star. Home: 2315 Morton St Terre Haute IN 47802 Office: Univ Sch Rm 34 Ind State U Terre Haute IN 47809

VANDEVENTER, JANICE LEIGH, cartographer, orgn. adminstr.; b. Long Beach, Calif., Aug. 10, 1944; d. Owen Jerome and Laurence Elizabeth (Monninger) V.; B.A. in Geography, UCLA, 1966. Cartographer, Automobile Club So. Calif., Los Angeles, 1966-70, sr. cartographer, 1970-72, research coordinator, 1972-74, chief cartographer, 1974—; flight instr. Falcon Air, Long Beach, 1975—. Recipient FAA Safety Pin, 1974. Mem. Am. Congress Surveying and Mapping, Los Angeles Area C. of C., Pilots Internat. Assn., Aircraft Owners and Pilots Assn., UCLA Alumni Assn., Alpha Xi Delta. Home: 3626 Country Club Drive Long Beach CA 90807 Office: 2601 S Figueroa St Los Angeles CA 90007

VANDEVER, LOIS ARLENE LAYCOCK, nurse; b. Milw., Apr. 17, 1931; d. Russell Dana and Thelma Elizabeth (Strodthoff) Laycock; B.S., U. Denver, 1959; pediatric nurse practitioner U. Colo., 1970; m. Mar. 1957 (div. 1981); 1 son, Vincent James. Staff nurse Denver Public Schs., 1959-64; coordinator health services Cherry Creek Schs., Englewood, Colo., 1970-73; cons. U. Colo. Sch. Nursing, Colo. Bd. Nursing, Denver, 1975-79; seminar developer, presenter Invest in Yourself, Arapahoe Community Coll., 1980, pres. bd., 1981—; instr. various colls.; cons. in field; monitor, mem. rewrite com. nurse practice act com. Colo. Bd. Nursing; chmn. fund raiser event Colo. Woman's Coll.; lay minister Stephen Series. Mem. Nat. Assn. Female Execs., U. Denver Alumni Club, Non-Practicing and Part-Time Nurses Assn. (lobbyist), Nat. Assn. Pediatric Nurse Practitioners and Assos., Am. Nurses Assn., Colo. Nurses Assn., Friends U. Denver Sch. Nursing (dir.), Centennial C. of C., Instr. Noetic Scis. Republican. Episcopalian. Clubs: Colo. Columbine Dollogy, Rocky Mountain Standard Schnauzer, Denver Minikins, Zonta (dir. Englewood-Littleton). Editorial bd. Nursing, 1970-75; pioneer in nurse practitioner program in public schs.; co-author: Invest in Yourself, 1982. Home: 835 W Geddes Circle Littleton CO 80120 Office: PO Box 3493 Littleton CO 80161

VAN DINE, HOLLY, steel co. corp. communications mgr.; b. Pitts., Jan. 1, 1943; d. Paul and Elaine (Kinder) Long; B.A., Bennington Coll., 1964; m. Alan Van Dine, Apr. 24, 1977; children—Laura, Alexander. Asst. dir. pub. relations ARC, Allegheny County, 1973-75; asst. mgr. advt. L.B. Foster Co., Pitts., 1975-76, mgr. pub. relations, 1976-77, mgr. advt. and pub. relations, 1977-81, mgr. corp. communications, 1981—. Mem. steering com. Pitts. Children's Mus., 1969-71. Mem. Bus. and Profl. Advt. Assn., Bus. Publ. Audit Assn. Office: 415 Holiday Dr Pittsburgh PA 15220

VAN DOREN, RUTH HENDRICKS, educator; b. Detroit, June 21, 1917; d. Charles S. and Jeannette (Baldwin) Hendricks; B.A. summa cum laude, Smith Coll., 1938; M.A., New Sch. Social Research, 1972; m. W. Dumont Van Doren, Jan. 18, 1939; children—Robin Beebe, Ricky Langford, Guy Van Doren, Amy Van Doren. Mem. faculty N.Y.U., 1940-41, Coll. St. Elizabeth, Morristown, N.J., 1963-65; mem. adminstrv. staff Morris County (N.J.) Mental Health Assn., 1958-60; dir. Human Relations Center, New Sch. Social Research, 1966—. Clk., Quaker's Meeting, Nat. Citizens Com. Edn., 1958-60. Mem. Council Nat. Orgns., NOW, Nat. Council Women (past v.p.), Nat. Assn. Women Deans, Adminstrs. and Counselors, Am. Sociol. Assn., Adult Edn. Assn., Phi Beta Kappa. Home: Ridge Rd Frenchtown NJ 08825 Office: 66 W 12th St New York NY 10011 also 45 W 10th St New York City NY

VANDYK, MARION ALICE, ins. agy. exec.; b. Rocky Ford, Colo., July 11, 1927; d. Murrell Hartley and Mina Elizabeth (Weybright) Anderson; student El Don Bus. Coll., 1944-46; m. Leonard Paul VanDyk, Mar. 15, 1946; children—Neil M., Laurie M. Legal sec., 1947-51; dep. county supt. of schs. Otero County, Colo., 1951-53; real estate and ins. office mgr., 1971-79; owner, mgr. VanDyk-Hancock Ins. Agy., Rocky Ford, 1979—. Mem. Rocky Ford City Council, 1973-77; mem. Otero County Planning Commn., 1974-77, Rocky Ford Planning Commn., 1974-77; pres. Rocky Ford Republican Women's Club. Mem. Rocky Ford C. of C. (dir.). Club: Rocky Ford Elena (past pres.). Mem. Ch. of the Brethren. Address: 705 S 6th St Rocky Ford CO 81067

VAN DYKE, ANNY MARION, telephone co. ofcl.; b. Howard, Ont., Can., Sept. 30, 1928; d. Anthony and Anna (Koolen) Van D.; C.F.A., U. Va., 1969; B.A., Sir George Williams U., 1959. Tchr., Lanoraie Sch. Bd., 1946-47; sec. Can. Nat. Rys., Montreal, Que., Can., 1947-51; sec. Sorel Industries Ltd., Sorel, Que., Can., 1952-53; with Bell Investment Mgmt. Corp. subs. Bell Canada, Montreal, 1953—, now portfolio mgr. U.S. Equities. Mem. Inst. Chartered Fin. Analysts (trustee 1979-80), Montreal Soc. Fin. Analysts (program chmn., pres. 1974-75), Can. Council Fin. Analysts (vice-chmn. 1976-77), Fin. Analysts Fedn. (treas. 1977-78, vice chmn. 1978-79, chmn. 1979-80), Cercle Finance-Placement. Home: 5635 Marie Victorin Blvd Brossard PQ J4W 1A2 Canada Office: Bell Investment Mgmt Corp 1050 Beaver Hall Hill Montreal PQ H2Z 1S4 Canada

VANEK, EVA HEDVIKA, fin. exec.; b. Prague, Czechoslovakia, Oct. 17, 1930; d. Otto and Marie (Topinkova) Fischl; B.S., Charles U., Prague, 1950; postgrad. U. Geneva, 1952-54; M.L.S., C.W. Post Coll., 1972; came to U.S., 1957, naturalized, 1961; m. George J. Vanek, Dec. 1, 1956; children—Helena, Thomas, Philip. Announcer, Radio Free Europe, Munich, 1951-52; research asst. Internat. Labor Office, Geneva, 1953-56; research asst. dept. paleobotany Harvard U., 1958-60; asst. v.p., mgr. info. services Merrill Lynch White Weld, Capital Markets Group, N.Y.C., 1971—. Mem. Spl. Libraries Assn. Republican. Home:

4 Carol Ct Dix Hills NY 11746 Office: 1 Liberty Plaza New York NY 10080

VAN ERP, YMKJE MARLENA, physician; b. Amsterdam, Netherlands, Mar. 27, 1911; d. Anton Pieter Johannes and Jeanette Reina (Keuning) Trap; came to U.S., 1952, naturalized, 1957; M.D., Leiden U., 1937, Ph.D., 1951; m. Johan Willem Theodoor Van Erp, Feb. 5, 1952; 1 son, Pieter George. Resident in pediatrics Sophia Kinderziekenhuis, Rotterdam, 1938-41; practice medicine specializing in pediatrics, Haarlem, Netherlands, 1941-51, Kirtland, Ohio, 1953—; research grantee Columbia U. Med. Center, N.Y.C., 1949-50, Case Western Res. U., Cleve., 1952-53, clin. instr., 1976—; mem. staff Lake County Meml. Hosp.; vis. staff Children's Hosp. (Case Western Res. U.); physician Well Child Clinics, Cleve., 1953-73; sch. physician Cuyahoga County, 1964—; clinic physician East Cleve., 1977—. Chmn., NE Ohio div. Am. Field Service; pres. bd. Mental Health Center, 1966; mem. task force on child abuse Lake County Health and Welfare Council, 1970; med. adv. Teen Listening Post, 1971; med. adv. Lake Geauga County Head Start; Ohio del. White House Conf. on Children, 1970. Mem. AAUW (dir. Ohio 1969-73), Women's Med. Soc. Cleve. (pres. 1954-55, 73-74), AMA, Am. Med. Women's Assn. (dir. 1961-71), Lake County Med. Soc., Ohio Med. Assn., Med. Women's Soc. Cleve., No. Ohio Pediatric Soc. Unitarian. Home and office: 7117 Berkshire Hills Dr RD 4 Kirtland OH 44094

VANESS, MARGARET HELEN, artist, illustrator; b. Seattle; d. Paul Edward and Alma Magdalena Lauch; B.F.A., U. Wash., Seattle, 1970, 71, M.F.A., 1973; cert. bus. Drexel U., Phila., 1975; m. Gerard Vaness; children—Bette, Bruce, Barbara, Helen-Cathleen. Teaching asst. Sch. Art, U. Wash., 1971-73; illustrator DuPont Co., Wilmington, Del., 1973-74, Boeing Vertol Co., Phila., 1974-75; illustrator, program mgr. Boeing Co., Seattle, 1978—; judge art shows, 1969—; executed mural for Dr. L. Mellon-Boeing Vertol Med. Center, 1974; commd. by USIA, 1973. Mem. Coll. Art Assn., Soc. for Tech. Communication, U. Wash. Alumni Assn., U. Wash. Arboretum Found., Lambda Rho (past pres.). Address: 17128 2d St SW Seattle WA 98166

VANEVERY, IVALYN JUNE, educator; b. Dorsey, Nebr., June 24, 1932; d. William Lloyd and Iva Gertrude (Butterfield) Brady; B.S., U. Omaha, 1968; M.S., U. Nebr., 1970, Ph.D., 1976; m. Dean Alan VanEvery, Aug. 2, 1950; children—Elizabeth Ann VanEvery Pittack, Mark Alan, Robert William. Tchr., Omaha Pub. Schs., 1968-69; grad. asst. U. Nebr., Omaha, 1969-70, instr., 1970-76, asst. prof., 1976—. Exec. bd. YWCA, 1958-62; mem. Omaha Women's Polit. Caucus, 1975—; mem. Mayor's Commn. on Status of Women, Omaha, 1977-78; del. Douglas County Republican Conv., 1980. U. Nebr., Omaha gt. tchr. finalist, 1977; Fulbright awardee, summer seminar, India, 1980; Improvement of Instrn. travel grantee, 1980-81. Mem. Nat. Assn. Commns. for Women, Nat. Council Social Studies (nat. chmn. sexism and social justice com. 1980-81), Nebr. Assn. for the Gifted, Nebr. Assn. Tchr. Educators, Mensa, Kappa Delta Pi (nat. exec. bd. 1980-82), Phi Delta Gamma (nat. exec. bd. 1978-80), Delta Kappa Gamma, Pi Lambda Theta, Phi Delta Kappa. Republican. Presbyterian. Contbr. articles to profl jours. Home: 5115 Lake St Omaha NE 68104 Office: U Nebr Kayser Hall 522 Omaha NE 68182

VANGILDER, AMY KATHRYN, designer; b. Somerspoint, N.J., Nov. 27, 1935; d. Ralph Hayes and France (Renshaw) Vangilder; student Dension U., 1963-65; B.F.A., R.I. Sch. Design, 1968, postgrad., 1974; postgrad. Boston Mus. Sch. Fine Arts, 1970; m. Colin Ian Cooke, Dec. 6, 1982. Showroom model Monte & Prusan, N.Y.C., 1968; apparel designer, N.Y.C., 1969; cartoonist ednl. filmstrips Ealing Films, Cambridge, Mass., 1975-82; puppet designer, London, N.Y.C., Toronto; 1975-82; sr. puppet builder Henson Assos., N.Y.C.; designer Muppets. Recipient Emmys (2). Author: Felt Toy Making, Advanced Techniques, 1974. Home: 1300 Bay Ave Ocean City NJ 08226 Office: care Henson Assos 117 E 69th St New York NY 10021

VAN GILDER, BARBARA JANE DIXON, interior designer, cons.; b. South Bend, Ind., Dec. 6, 1933; d. Vincent Alan and Wanda Anita (Rapell) Dixon; student Mich. State U., 1951-55; postgrad. St. Mary's Coll., 1956-57, N.Y. Sch. Design, 1956-58; m. Erwin Dalton VanGilder, May 25, 1959; children—Eric Dalton, Marc David. Factory color cons. Smith-Alsop Paint Co., Terre Haute, Ind., 1955-56; archtl. design cons., Mishawaka, Ind., 1956-58; residential-comml. designer, South Bend, Chgo., 1958-63; designer industrialized housing industry, Ga., Fla., Ind., Mich., 1962—; design cons. Skyline Corp., Ind., Calif., Pa., 1962-66; v.p. design Treasure Chest Corp., Sturgis, Mich., 1969, also dir.; pres., dir. Sandpiper Art, Inc.; v.p. T.C.I. Ltd.; design cons. C.O. Smith Ind. Peachtree Housing, Moultrie, Ga., Nobility Homes, Ocala, Fla.; head merchandising and design Sandpiper Originals, clothing boutique, 1978—; currently pub. relations ofcl. Am. Mktg. Assn., adj. tchr. Lakeshore Sch. System. also coordinator trade show displays; nat. advt. rep. Studebaker-Packard Corp., Mercedes Benz, Clark Equipment, 1959-63; writer series on decorating for 2 Mich. newspapers, 1961-63; participant TV show Know Your Decorator, Calif. and Maine, 1962, 77. Officer, Shoreham Village (Mich.) Bd. Zoning, 1960-63. Named Woman of Year, Profl. Model's Club, 1952; recipient 1st pl. furniture design hardwoods Nat. Hardwoods Assn., 1956; 1st pl. Best in Show award, Louisville, Atlanta, 1964-65, 66, 69, 70-74, 76; others. Mem. Design Council Industrialized Housing (award 1974), Nat. Soc. Interior Designers, Mich. State U. Alumni Assn., Internat. Platform Assn., Internat. Biog. Assn. Contbg. editor Skyliner mag., 1962-66; permanent guest editor, contbr. Today's Home mag., 1974—. Home: 3630 S Lakeshore Dr St Joseph MI 49085 Office: PO Box 244 Stevensville MI 49127 also PO Box 1100 Dunedin FL 33528

VAN GOSSEN, DOROTHY ELAINE, social worker; b. Alexandria, La., June 7, 1928; d. Ernest F. and Irma D. (Greene) Van G.; B.A., Our Lake of the Lake Coll., 1952, M.S.W., 1974; M.A., Catholic U. Am., 1959. Tchr., Sisters of Divine Providence schs., San Antonio, 1948-69, prin., 1966-69; caseworker Goodwill Industries Rehab. Program, Houston, 1969-71; counselor MDTA Tng. Center, San Antonio, 1971-73; clin. social worker with Dr. Robert Rast, San Antonio, 1975-77; clin. social worker Family Counseling Agency, Alexandria, La., 1977-79; pvt. practice social work, 1979—. Cert. social worker, La. Mem. Nat. Assn. Social Workers, Am. Assn. Marriage and Family Therapists, Internat. Transactional Analysis Assn., La. Conf. Social Welfare, La. Mental Health Assn. Roman Catholic. Club: Amicus. Home: 726 Osiris St Alexandria LA 71301 Office: 1545B Jackson St Alexandria LA 71301

VAN HAMEL, MARTINE, dancer; b. Brussels, Nov. 16, 1945; student Nat. Ballet Sch. Can. Debut with Nat. Ballet Can., 1963; guest dancer Royal Swedish Ballet, Royal Winnipeg Ballet, Joffrey Ballet; with Am. Ballet Theatre, soloist, 1971-73, prin. dancer, 1973—. Office: care Am Ballet Theatre 890 Broadway New York NY 10003 *

VANHOOZER, JEAN ELIZABETH, auditor, credit union exec.; b. Marlow, Okla., May 4, 1932; d. Thomas Osa and Gladys Mamie (Sample) McCarley; student Okla. Baptist U., Shawanee, 1951-52; B.S. in Bus Adminstrn., Cameron U., Lawton, Okla., 1978; m. Teddy Gene VanHoozer, Sept 2, 1952; children—Dewayne, David, Nancy. With Lawton (Okla.) Public Schs., 1952-68, bus. office mgr., 1960-68, auditor, 1968—; mgr. Lawton Tchrs. Fed. Credit Union, Lawton, 1968—. Mem. Nat. Edn. Credit Union Council, Data Processing Mgmt. Assn., Okla. Public Acct. Democrat. Baptist. Club: Altrusa. Home: 4227 Camden Way Lawton OK 73501 Office: 1806 Liberty St Lawton OK 73501

VAN HORN, ELAINE CLAUDER, ins. agt.; b. Houston, Nov. 11, 1936; d. Samuel H. and Margaret F. (Hall) Clauder; student Southwestern Jr. Coll., Waxahachie, Tex., 1955-56, U. Houston, 1956-57; completed bus. course, Massey Bus. Coll., 1955; m. Richard W. Van Horn, June 21, 1957 (div., 1968); children—Wesley W., Alex C., Richard A.; m. 2d. George E. Veo, Nov. 13, 1969 (div. 1980). Exec. sec. to officers Sakowitz, Inc., Houston, various years 1957-68; exec. sec. to owner boat co., Houston, 1968-69; agt. Union Central Life Ins. Co., Houston, 1970-75; agt. Sun Life Ins. Co., 1975-77; gen. agt. Gen. Am. Life Ins. Co., Houston, 1977-80; brokerage supr. Union Mut. Life Ins. Co., Houston, 1980—. Dir. secretarial duties Hofheinz for Mayor campaign, 1971. Mem. President's Club, Union Central, 1973-75, Centurian Club, 1972, qualified nat. quality award, 1973-77, Health Ins. quality award, 1974-77; named to Tex. Leaders Roundtable, 1972; recipient nat. sales achievement, 1973-74; named to Women Leaders Roundtable, 1972-74; qualified conf. of champions, Gen. Am. Life, 1977, conv. speaker, 1977. Mem. Nat. Assn. Life Underwriters (program Women's Leaders Roundtable, conv., 1974), Tex. Assn. Life Underwriters, Houston Assn. Life Underwriters (public service award for work with Houston Epilepsy Assn., 1974), Gulf Coast Conservation Assn., Bus. and Profl. Womens Assn. Houston. Pianist, organist, vibraharpist, play various other instruments. Home: 4445 NASA Rd One 204 Seabrook TX 77586

VAN HORNE, HARRIET, journalist; b. Syracuse, N.Y., May 17; d. Victor Cornelius and Gertrude (Theall) Van H.; B.A., U. Rochester (N.Y.); m. David Lowe, Apr. 20, 1956 (dec.). Columnist, N.Y. World-Telegram, then N.Y. Post, now syndicated by N.Y. Times Syndicate; lectr., TV panelist, radio news analyst. Trustee Strange Preventive Medicine Inst., Corr. Fund. Author: Never Go Anywhere Without a Pencil, 1972; also mag. articles. Address: Los Angeles Times Syndicate Times Mirror Sq Los Angeles CA 90053 *

VANIDES, ALEXIA, indsl. mktg. communications exec.; b. Los Angeles, Mar. 11, 1951; d. Thanos Demitrious and Constance (Trigonis) V.; B.A. in English cum laude, Calif. State U., Long Beach, 1973; M.B.A., Pepperdine U., 1980. Vice pres., creative dir. Thanos Vanides & Co., West Los Angeles, 1973-75, Chgo., 1975-77; mktg. communications mgr. Tubular group Hydril Co., Los Angeles, 1977; mktg. communications specialist Hughes Helicopters, Los Angeles, 1977-79; advt. mgr. Electron Device group Varian Assos., Palo Alto, Calif., 1979—. Recipient 1st Pl. award Nat. Agrl. Advertisers Assn., 1978. Mem. Bus./Profl. Advt. Assn. (sec. bd. dirs. 1978-79, 2d v.p. bd. dirs. Los Angeles chpt. 1979-80; sec. bd. dirs. No. Calif. chpt. 1980-81, v.p. programs 1981-82), Am. Mktg. Assn., Am. Helicopter Assn. Writer award-winning ads for indsl. cos., 1977-79, 80-81. Office: 301 Industrial Way San Carlos CA 94070

VAN KLEECK, GAIL HEUSTIS, interior designer; b. Ann Arbor, Mich., Sept. 30, 1938; d. Albert Edward and Catherine Elaine (Greig) Heustis; B.A., Mich. State U., 1960; student LaSalle U., 1972; m. Peter Van Kleeck, Sept. 19, 1959; children—Kimberli, Peter Kenneth. Dir. art and spl. programs Mercer Sch., Newton, Mass., 1960-61; program dir. Nazerine Sch., Des Plaines, Ill., 1962-63; weaver, 1964-66; weaver, display designer Talisman Shop, Boston, 1966-68; display designer Wellesley Shops (Mass.), 1971; apprentice designer Ruth Peakes Assos., Weston, Mass., 1972-73; asso. designer Dover Interiors (Mass.), 1973-75, pres., 1975—; tchr. adult edn. classes in interior design; tchr. weaving and candle making in pub. schs. Episcopalian. Office: Dover Interiors 3 Hartford St Dover MA 02030

VANLEEUWEN, LIZ SUSAN (ELIZABETH), farmer, state legislator; b. Lakeview, Oreg., Nov. 5, 1925; d. Charles Arthur and Mary Delphia (Hartzog) Nelson; B.S., Oreg. State U., 1947; m. George VanLeeuwen, June 15, 1947; children—Charles, Mary, James, Timothy. Secondary sch. and adult tchr., 1947-70; news reporter, feature writer The Times, Brownsville, Oreg., 1949—; co-mgr. VanLeeuwen Farm, Halsey, Oreg.; mem. Oreg. Ho. of Reps., 1981—; weekly radio commentator, 1973-81. Active E.R. Jackman Bd., PTA, sch. adv. com.; precinct committeewoman. Recipient Outstanding service award Oreg. Farm Bur., 1975, Chevron Agrl. Spokesman of Yr. award, 1975. Mem. Oreg. Women for Agr. (pres.), Oreg. Women for Timber, Linn-Benton Women for Agr. (pres.), Linn County Farm Bur., Linn County Econ. Devel. Com., Grange, Am. Agri-Women. Republican. Office: Capitol Bldg H382 Salem OR 97310

VANLIEU, SHIRLEY DEVOL, social worker; b. Los Angeles, Feb. 5, 1933; d. Evander Spalding and Mary Edith (Wilkins) Dixon; A.A., Stephens Coll., 1951; B.A., Calif. State U., Los Angeles, 1956; M.S.W., U. So. Calif., 1969, D.S.W., 1981; m. Kenneth Stowe Devol, Dec. 30, 1951; children—Sharon Marie, Randall Putnam. Tchr., Los Angeles City Schs., 1956-67; foster mother Los Angeles County Bur. Adoptions, 1962-67; clin. social worker (infant specialist) Los Angeles County Dept. Mental Health, San Fernando, Calif., 1969—; asst. clin. prof. nursing UCLA, 1975—; pvt. practice counseling and psychotherapy. Founder mastectomy assistance program Am. Cancer Soc., Los Angeles; bd. dirs. Los Angeles Planned Parenthood, 1978—; mem. adv. bd. Alternatives for Women, Calif., 1980; co-chmn. County Regional Task Force on Mental Health Services for Women. Recipient Planned Parenthood award, 1975; Am. Cancer Soc. award, 1976. Lic. tchr., social worker, Calif. Mem. Nat. Assn. Social Workers, Soc. Clin. Social Work. Office: 601 S Brand San Fernando CA 91340

VAN METER, VANDELIA LAVINA, media specialist; b. Seibert, Colo., July 17, 1934; d. G.W. and Amy Pearl (Mahoney) Klockenteger; A.B., Kans. Wesleyan U., Salina, 1957; M.L.S., Emporia (Kans.) State U., 1970; m. Victor Mearl VanMeter, Jan. 21, 1954; children—Allison Christine, Kristin Charles. Tchr. rural sch., Ottawa County, Kans., 1954-55; tchr. McClave (Colo.) High Sch., 1957-58; tchr. Ellsworth (Kans.) Jr. High Sch., 1960-63, 66-68, media specialist Ellsworth High Sch., 1968—; cons. N. Central Assn. Secondary Schs.; dir. Kans. Demonstration Media Center; cons. libraries; pres. Sch. Dist. 327 Edn. Assn., 1974-75; partner The Workshop: Arts and Crafts, 1978—; instr. Barton County Community Coll. Outreach, 1981—. Mem. Ellsworth City Council, 1975-79, Ellsworth Park Bd., 1975-79, Ellsworth Library Bd., 1977-79; chmn. Ellsworth City Bicentennial Celebration, 1975-76; dir. chancel choir Ellsworth United Methodist Ch., 1960-79. Named Woman of Year, Ellsworth Bus. and Profl. Women, 1976. Mem. NEA, Kans. Edn. Assn., Kans. Assn. Sch. Librarians. Home: 306 N Douglas St Ellsworth KS 67439 Office: Box C Ellsworth KS 67439

VANMINGROOT, NORMA ANN, export co. exec.; b. Bklyn., Oct. 15, 1932; d. Henry Ashley and Iris R. (Hampton) Bryant; B.B.A. magna cum laude (Robert Horowitz fin. award 1975, Wall St. Jour. Student Achievement award 1975), Pace U., 1975, M.B.A. with distinction, 1978; widow. Sec., Davidson Electric Co., Bklyn., 1954-57; adminstv. asst., then corp. sec. Fed. Eastern Corp., N.Y.C., 1957-75, v.p., 1975—; dir. Lien Tung Ltd. Mem. Women's Econ. Roundtable, Women's Polit. Caucus, ACLU, Pace U. Alumni Assn., Phi Chi Theta (alumnae chpt. pres. 1978-80, nat. dir.-at-large 1977—), Sigma Lambda Iota. Clubs: Shanghai Tiffin, Atrium, World Trade Center. Home: 91-08 68 Ave Forest Hills NY 11375 Office: 1 World Trade Center Suite 2447 New York NY 10048

VANN, ROBERTA JEANNE, educator; b. Indpls., Dec. 17, 1947; d. John Robert and Viola Mae (Bannon) V.; B.A., Ind. U., 1970, M.S., 1973, Ph.D., 1978. Vol., Peace Corps, Haile Salaissie U., Gondar, Ethiopia, 1970-71; Fulbright lectr. U. Gdansk (Poland), 1974-76; asst. prof. English, Iowa State U., Ames, 1978—, dir. intensive English and orientation program, 1980—; lang. cons. USICA, Yugoslavia, Poland, Syria, 1975-80. Mem. Nat. Council Tchrs. English, TESOL, Phi Delta Kappa. Democrat. Unitarian. Editor: (with B. Kroll) Exploring Speaking-Writing Relationships: Connections and Contrasts, 1981. Office: Dept English Iowa State U Ames IA 50011

VANNAME, JUDITH ANN, consumer economist, educator; b. Cin., July 14, 1945; d. Glen Albert and Lena Anna (Woerner) Beyring; B.S., Miami U., Oxford, Ohio, 1967; M.S., Ohio State U., 1968. Instr. home econs. U. Del., Newark, 1968-71, asst. prof., 1971-77, assoc. prof. Coll. Human Resources, 1977, chmn. textiles, design and consumer econs., 1978—; dir. Computer Input Services, Inc. Pres., White Haven Poconos Homeowners Assn., 1975-76, dir., 1976-79. HEW grantee, 1974-76. Mem. Am. Home Econs. Assn., Am. Council Consumer Interests, Phi Upsilon Omicron. Author: (with James D. Culley and Barbara H. Settles) Understanding and Measuring the Cost of Foster Family Care, 1975; contbr. articles and revs. to profl. jours. Home: 125 Dallam Rd Newark DE 19711 Office: Textiles Design and Consumer Econs U Del Newark DE 19711

VAN NATTA, ELEANOR SUE POUNDSTONE, nurse; b. Decatur, Ill., Nov. 22, 1932; d. Herbert Lloyd and Blanche Cleo (Zink) Poundstone; diploma nursing, Washington U., St. Louis, 1953, B.S. in Nursing, 1961; B.S. in Nursing, U. Mo., 1956; M.S.Ed., Purdue U., 1970; m. Charles R. Van Natta, Jr., June 12, 1971 (div. 1977); children—Laura, Sue. Staff nurse Barnes Hosp., St. Louis, 1953-54; staff nurse, then head nurse U. Mo. Med. Center, Columbia, 1954-58; instr. Decatur (Ill.) and Macon County Hosp. Sch. Nursing, 1958-60; instr. U. Colo., Denver, 1961-63; asst. prof. U. Mo., Columbia, 1964-66; asst. prof. Forest Park Community Coll., St. Louis, 1967-69; high sch. couselor, Decatur, 1970-71; coordinator diagnostic and evaluation project Comprehensive Devel. Centers, Monticello, Ind., 1975-77; asst. prof. Purdue U. Sch. Nursing, 1980—; pres. White County Registered Nurses Orgn., 1975-76. Vol., Twin Lakes Contact, crisis hotline, Monticello, 1975-76; ednl. coordinator Matrix Lifeline, 1981-82. Mem. AAUW, Am. Nurses Assn., Nat. Assn. Women Deans, Adminstrs. and Counselors, Ind. Nurses Assn., Sigma Theta Tau, Kappa Kappa Kappa. Club: Order Eastern Star. Home: 1137 Hillcrest Rd West Lafayette IN 47906 Office: Sch Nursing 248 Purdue U West Lafayette IN 47907

VAN NEWKIRK, CAROLYN JANE, sch. adminstr.; b. Ephrata, Pa., Sept. 22, 1937; d. Albert Smith and Thelma Rebecca (Watkins) Harris; B.S. in Edn., West Chester State Coll., 1959; M.A. in Edn., Coll. William and Mary, 1978, cert. advanced studies, 1981; m. Jack C. Van Newkirk, June 27, 1959; children—Lauri Lyn, David Collins. Tchr., W. York (Pa.) Area Sch. Dist., 1959-60, 64-65; tchr., team leader Williamsburg (Va.)-James City County Sch. Dist., 1971-78, reading specialist, 1978-82; vice prin. Beth Ifiloh Day Sch., Balt., 1982—; adj. instr. Coll. William and Mary, Williamsburg, 1980, 81. Exec. bd., sec. Ulster County Extension Service, Kingston, N.Y., 1969-71. Mem. NEA, Internat. Reading Assn. (council Md. chpt.), Williamsburg Area Reading Council, Md. Council of Tchrs. of English Lang. Arts, AAUW. Kappa Delta Pi. Home: 860 S Beaver St York PA 17403 Office: Beth Ifiloh Day Sch 3300 Old Court Rd Baltimore MD 21208

VANNIER, ARLENE LINN, investment banker, wholesale tea dealer; b. N.Y.C., Apr. 22, 1933; d. Milton M. and Frances (Stern) Linn; A.B., U. Miami, 1952; postgrad. U. Pa., 1952-53, N.Y. Inst. Fin., 1964; m. Joseph Dale Vannier, Dec. 21, 1969; 1 son by previous marriage, Bruce Mason Malamut. Mannequin, Coronet Agy., Fla., Dior Collections, Cuba, France, 1956-58; owner cattle bus., Colombia, S.Am., 1959-60; account exec. Ted Worner Assos., N.Y.C., 1960-61; v.p. investments Internat. Devel. Corp., N.Y.C., 1962-63; protfolio mgr., registered rep. Oppenheimer & Co., N.Y.C., 1964-71; owner, operator Vannier Ranch, Cool, Calif., 1968—; founder, pres., dir. Vannier Group Inc., N.Y.C., 1969, Folks Mgmt. Inc., N.Y.C., 1971—; founder, sec., treas., dir. Vannier Tea Inc., N.Y.C., 1970—. Mem. N.Y. Acad. Scis. Republican. Clubs: Westchester Country (Rye, N.Y.); Muthaiga Country (Nairobi, Kenya); Atrium (N.Y.C.). Home: Westchester Country Club Rye NY 10580 also 25 E 83d St New York NY 10028 Office: 445 Park Ave New York NY 10022

VAN NORD, JOAN ELAINE, librarian; b. Charlotte, Mich., Aug. 17, 1935; d. Frank William and Alice Caroline (Lewis) Hamilton; B.A., Western Mich. U., 1957; M.S., U. Ill., Urbana, 1963; m. James Irwin, Mar. 29, 1958 (dec.); 1 dau., Diana Christa; m. 2d, Wayne Van Nord, Aug. 19, 1968. Asst. librarian Kalamazoo Central High Sch., 1957-58; librarian USAF Dependents' Schs., Japan, 1959-62; asso. prof. library adminstrn. Univ. High Sch., Urbana, Ill., 1963—; cons. Ill. State Bd. Edn. Mem. AAUP, Ill. Library Assn., Ill. Assn. Media in Edn., Ill. Assn. Ednl. Communications and Tech., Slava, Kappa Delta Pi. Author: The Reading Interests of Gifted Students and Curriculum Adaptations in the Secondary School: A Comparison Over Time, 1980; Reading Interests of Gifted Students in a Special School, 1979; contbr. articles and book revs. to profl. jours.

VAN NORTWICK, BARBARA LOUISE, librarian; b. Johnson City, N.Y., Jan. 3, 1940; d. Joseph John and Mary Louise (Hamzik) Goodwin; B.A., Harpur Coll., 1961; M.L.S., State U. N.Y. at Albany, 1976; postgrad. (U.S. Govt. Title II B fellow in library adminstrn.), Simmons Coll., Boston, 1981—; m. David Harry Van Nortwick, Nov. 17, 1962; children—Kimberly Lynn, Craig Michael. Coordinator ednl. facilities Maine-Endwell High Sch., Endwell, N.Y., 1961-64; tchr. English, Guilderland High Sch. (N.Y.), 1965-66; audiovisual librarian So. Colonie (N.Y.) High Sch., 1974-76; head librarian Westfield (Mass.) High Sch., 1976-78, Columbia High Sch., East Greenbush, N.Y., 1978-79; library dir. N.Y. State Nurses Assn., 1979—; del. Mass. Gov.'s Conf. Libraries and Info. Services, 1978-79; adminstr. HEW grant on self-directed continuing edn. for nurses; mem. New Eng. Interagy. Council on Library Resources for Nursing. Mem. ALA, N.Y. Library Assn., Med. Library Assn., Spl. Library Assn., Regional Med. Library Assn. (N.Y./Ont. Group), N.Y./N.J. Regional Med. Library Assn., Upper Hudson Library Fedn. (rec. sec.), North Atlantic Health Scis. Library Assn., Assn. Specialized and Coop. Library Agys. (com. mem.), Albany Area Health Library Affiliates, Mid-Atlantic Regional Archivists Assn., Bus. and Profl. Women. Methodist. Home: 17 Crescent Dr Castleton-on-Hudson NY 12033 Office: 2113 Western Ave Guilderland NY 12084

VAN NOSTRAND, CASSANDRA PAULA, physician; b. Lethbridge, Alta., Can., Aug. 21, 1947; d. Charles Andrew and June Mable van N.; B.S. magna cum laude, U. Lethbridge, 1968; M.D., U. Alta., 1972; m., 1970. Intern, Misericordia Hosp., Edmonton, Alta., 1972-73; resident in pediatrics U. Alta., 1973-74; resident in radiology U. Minn. Hosp., Mpls., 1975-76; fellow in pediatric cardiology U. Va., Charlottesville, 1975; pediatric cardiovascular pathology trainee Johns Hopkins Hosp., 1976, Armed Forces Inst. Pathology, 1976; trainee radiology U. Minn., 1976-77; cons. Health and Human Scis. Venture Found., Mpls., 1977—. Mayo scholar, 1971; Searle Co. scholar, 1973; diplomate Am. Bd. Pediatrics. Mem. Radiol. Soc. Am., Soc. Nuclear Medicine, Canadian Med. Assn., Friends of Hippocrates, Am. Med. Writers Assn., AAUW, AMA, Am. Heart Assn., Am. Sch. Health Assn. (research council), ACP, So. Med. Assn., Am. Med. Polit. Action Com. Author: Kharma Marga, 1966. Contbr. articles to profl. jours. Address: 2013 4th St S Minneapolis MN 55454

VAN ORDEN, LINDA LOUISE, city ofcl.; b. Garden City, Kans.; Apr. 25, 1936; d. Harold Kenneth and Edna Bernice (Rishell) Umpleby; student Univ. Bus. Coll., 1955; m. Robert R. Van Orden, Jr., Mar. 29, 1958; children—Ronald Dean, Roger David. With Orthopaedic & Fracture Clinic, Eugene, Oreg., 1955, U.S. Nat. Bank of Oreg., Junction City and Corvallis, 1955-58; med. sec./office mgr. H. Lee Harris, M.D., Junction City, 1965-68; med. sec. Westmoreland Med. Clinic, Eugene, 1969-70; adminstrv. asst./office mgr. Drs. Harland, Stansbury & Wright, Dental Clinic, Eugene, 1971-75; office mgr., exec. sec., service coordinator McCormick Swenson Co., elec. contractors, Junction City and Eugene, 1975-79, acct./controller, 1979-81; clk., judge pro tem Mcpl. Ct., City of Junction City, 1981—; cons. career edn. and bus. Mem. Sch. Dist. #69 budget com., Junction City, 1972-76, bd. dirs., 1976-79, vice chmn., 1977, chmn. bldg. and facilities study com., 1979-80. Notary public, Oreg. Mem. Junction City C. of C. (exec. dir. 1980—), Junction City Hist. Soc., Lane County Hist. Soc., Oreg. Hist. Soc., Bus. and Profl. Women. Republican. Mem. Christian Ch. Club: Toastmistresses (charter pres. Scandia Club). Home: 1090 Oak St Junction City OR 97448 Office: PO Box 245 Junction City OR 97448

VAN ORDEN, MARIA CRISTINA, pianist; b. Laredo, Dec. 6, 1945; d. Ralph R. and Minerva Garcia; performer's diploma Palace Fine Arts, Mexico City, 1963; B.Music, N. Tex. State U., 1968; M.Mus., So. Meth. U., 1969; 1 son, Benjamin. Debut Corpus Christi Symphony, 1964; performed in piano recitals throughout the S.W. and Mex.; piano accompanist faculty recitals Tyler Jr. Coll., U. Tex., Tyler, 1978-81; pvt. piano tchr., recitalist, Tyler. Recipient award Am. Legion, 1964, Young Artist award Central W. Tex. Tchrs. Assn., 1967. Mem. Am. Coll. Musicians (bd. judges), Music Tchrs. Nat. Assn., Tex. Music Tchrs. Assn., Tyler Music Tchrs. Assn. (past pres.). Republican. Roman Catholic. Home and office: 2526 Henson St Tyler TX 75701

VANOVERMEIREN, CARYL JANICE, nursing home adminstr.; b. Waterloo, Iowa, Feb. 4, 1938; d. Alwin J. and Frances (Hardwick) Tonn; diploma in nursing Macalester Coll. Northwestern Hosp. Sch. Nursing, 1959; A.S., Elgin Community Coll., 1975; B.S., No. Ill. U., 1979; postgrad. in adminstrn. George Washington U., 1980-81; m. John VanOvermeiren, Nov. 28, 1959; children—Deborah, Thomas. Staff nurse Delnor Hosp., St. Charles, Ill., 1959-60; office nurse, St. Charles, part-time 1960-69; staff nurse, team leader Delnor Hosp., St. Charles, 1972-73; sch. nurse Sch. Dist. 303, St Charles, 1973-74; asst. adminstr., dir. health services Holmstad, Batavia, Ill., 1977—; mem. adv. com. nurse aide tng. Waubonsee Community Coll., Sugar Grove, Ill.; mem. adv. com. health careers Mid-Valley Vocat. Center, Maple Park, Ill., 1978—; guest lectr., instr. gerontology. Bd. dirs. Community Contacts, Geneva, Ill., 1980—; bd. dirs. Bethlehem Luth. Ch., St. Charles, also chmn. Christian edn., chmn. couples fellowship, tchr. Sunday Sch.; v.p., Fox Valley council Girl Scouts U.S.A., also chmn. fin. com., troop leader. Mem. Nat. League Nursing, Ill. League Nursing, Am. Nurses Assn., Ill. Nurses Assn. (sec. gerontol. practice div., publicity newspaper dist. 2), Sigma Theta Tau. Republican. Home: 1442 S 7th Ct Saint Charles IL 60174

VAN PATTEN, MURIEL MAY, educator; b. Quincy, Mich., Apr. 27, 1932; d. Lloyd Delmar and Edwina (Parsons) Van Patten; B.S., Eastern Mich. U., 1954, M.A., 1962; student Wayne State U., 1967—. Art tchr. Fenton (Mich.) Pub. Schs., 1954-56; arts, crafts instr. Chgo. Park Dist., 1955-56; tchr. Wayne (Mich.) Community Sch. Dist., 1956-60, dir. art, 1960-65, elem. sch. prin., 1965-74, learning cons., 1974-75; accountability liaison specialist Mich. State Dept. Edn., Lansing, 1975-77, supr. instructional specialist program, 1977-79, dir. sch. program services, 1979—; dir. secondary edn., coordinator student tchrs. Eastern Mich. U., 1962, vis. guest lectr. edn., art depts. Mem. NEA, Nat., Mich., art edn. assns., Mich. Dirs. Pub. Sch. Art Edn. (chmn. 1966-67), Mich. Assn. Supervision and Curriculum Devel., Mich. Assn. Elem. Prins., Sigma Nu Phi (v.p. 1954). Club: Soroptimist Fedn. Ams., Soroptimist of Wayne (rec. sec. 1967). Home: 5147 E Brookfield Dr East Lansing MI 48823 also 533 Skylark Ln Port Charlotte FL 33952

VAN PELT, CAROLYN SUE, vet. pathologist; b. Orange, Tex., June 25, 1947; d. Eugene and Grace (Ingrahm) Van P.; B.S., Lamar U., Beaumont, Tex., 1969; B.S., Tex. A&M U., 1975, D.V.M., 1976, postgrad., 1979—. Intern, Vet. Teaching Hosp., U. Mo., Columbia, 1976-77; asso. Voss Rd. Animal Clinic, Houston, 1977-79; vet. clin. asso. Tex. A&M U., College Station, 1979-80; postdoctoral fellow dept. tumor biology M.D. Anderson Hosp. Cancer and Research, Houston, 1982—. Served with USNR, 1971-73. Mem. AVMA. Home: 15103 Willowbranch Houston TX 77070 Office: MD Anderson Hosp Houston TX 77030

VAN RAAY, JANICE ELIZABETH, artist, photographer; b. Bklyn., May 27, 1942; d. Gradus Jacobus H. and Mildred Amanda (Buckneberg) van R.; student Sch. Art and Design, 1956-60, Abracheff Sch. Art, 1960-67, N.Y. U., 1960-63, New Sch. for Social Research, 1963-69; m. David Paul Curtis, Mar. 24, 1968; 1 son, Cassidy Jonathan. Numerous one-woman shows, latest being: Bklyn. Public Library, 1977, Hansen Galleries, N.Y.C., 1977, 78, U. Tenn., Chattanooga, 1978, Art Something Gallery, Amsterdam, Holland, 1980, Zimmer Atelier, Mannheim, Germany, 1980, Galerie A, Amsterdam, 1980, Sonja Henie-Neils Onstad Mus., Oslo, 1982, Mus. Modern Art, Stockholm, 1982; numerous group shows, latest being: Librije Beeldende Kunst, Zwolle, Holland, 1977, Smith Coll., 1977, Hansen Galleries, N.Y.C., 1978, 380 Gallery, N.Y.C., 1978, Arte Fiera 78, Bologna, Italy, 1978, Galerie Arkade, Berlin, Germany, 1978, Stedelijk Mus., Alkmaar, Holland, 1978, Galeria Remont, Warsaw, Poland, 1979, Liverpool (Eng.) Acad. Fine Arts, Liverpool, 1979, Foto Gallery, N.Y.C., 1979, Casa Aboy, Miramar, P.R., 1980, Focus Gallery, San Francisco, 1980, Franklin Furnace, N.Y.C., 1982; represented in numerous permanent collections including: U. Tenn., Chattanooga, Parachute Center for Cultural Affairs, Calgary, Can., Art Info. Center, Amsterdam, Holland, Smith Coll., Archiv Sohm, W. Germany. Mem. Beroepsvereniging van Beldende Kunstenaars. Author: Coping and Hoping/Verhaltens Forscher, 1978; Second Coming, 1977; GAAG: The Guerilla Art Action Group, 1978; contbr. feature articles to various mags. and lit. jours.; contbr. photographs to various mags. and art publs. Address: 135 Eastern Pkwy Brooklyn NY 11238

VAN SANT, JOANNE F., ednl. adminstr.; b. Morehead, Ky., Dec. 29, 1924; d. Lewis L. and Dorothy (Greene) Van Sant; B.A., Denison U., 1946; M.A., Ohio State U., 1953; LL.D. (hon.), Albright Coll., 1975. Tchr. health and phys. edn. Mayfield (Ky.) High Sch., 1946-47; instr. Denison U., 1948; instr. Otterbein Coll., Westerville, Ohio, 1948-50, asst. prof. health and phys. edn., 1950-55, asso. prof., 1955—, dean women, 1952-60, 62-64, dean students, 1964—, v.p. for student affairs, 1968—; camp counselor, and dir., Mayfield. Elder Central Coll. Persbyterian Ch., Westerville, 1967-69, trustee, 1975-77; v.p. Friends in Action, Columbus, Ohio, 1981-82; bd. dirs. Westerville Counseling Service, 1978-79; trustee Planned Parenthood Central Ohio, 1976-81; mem. North Area Mental Health and Retardation Bd., 1979—, chmn. planning and research com., 1980-81, chmn. bd., 1981-82. Recipient Citation for service to edn. Pi Lambda Theta, 1979; named Woman of Yr., Otterbein Woman's Club, 1980. Mem. Ohio Assn. Women Deans, Adminstrs. and Counselors (treas. 1972-73), Nat., Ohio assns. student personnel adminstrs., AAUW, Cap and Dagger, Torch and Key, Theta Alpha Phi, Alpha Lambda Delta. Republican. Clubs: Zonta (pres. 1978-80, Dist. V sec. 1981—) (Columbus); Westerville Music, Walnut Valley Boat (sec. 1971-73). Choreographer 24 musical prodns. Otterbein Coll., 1948—. Home: 9100 Oakwood Point Westerville OH 43081 Office: Student Personnel Office Otterbein Coll Westerville OH 43081

VANSICKLER, LINDA ANN, postal service ofcl.; b. Bklyn., Oct. 3, 1951; d. Anthony Alfonse and Lillian Bruno; A.A. in Elem. Edn., Nassau Community Coll., 1971; B.S. in Elem. Edn., SUNY Coll., Oneonta, 1973; postgrad. in liberal studies SUNY, Stony Brook, 1973-75; postgrad. in bus. adminstrn. Suffolk U., 1980. With U.S. Postal Service, 1973—, supr. of mails Postal Inspection Service, 1979-80, postal insp., 1980-81, postal insp.-audit specialist level 23, Boston, 1981—, postal insp.-project coordinator level 24, Washington, 1982—; mgr., co-editor newsletter Boston div. Fed. Women's Program. Recipient cert. appreciation Combined Fed. Campaign, 1975, Women's Day Activities-L.I. Dist., 1977. Mem. Fed. Law Enforcement Officers Assn., Mass. Assn. Women Police Officers, Mensa. Democrat. Roman Catholic. Home: 8138 Carrleigh Pkwy Springfield VA 22152 Office: 475 L'Enfant Plaza Washington DC 20260

VAN SITTERT, CAROL ANN, communications co. exec.; b. Kansas City, Mo., Dec. 18, 1936; d. Clarence Alfred and Adelaide Harriet (Hurst) Hallberg; student Baker U., 1955-56; A.A., Johnson County Community Coll., 1975; m. Joseph Van Sittert Jr., Mar. 18, 1956; children—Sarah Lynn, Jeanne Marie. Lead programmer Pyramid Life Ins. Co., Mission, Kans., 1965-68; programmer Interstate Securities Corp., Kansas City, Mo., 1968-69; sr. programmer Hercules, Inc., De Soto, Kans., 1969-71; lead programmer Wolf & Co., Kansas City, Mo., 1971-74; datapoint ops. supr., programmer Bayvet div. Cutter Labs., Shawnee, Kans., 1974-79; project leader programmer analyst III, North Supply Co. subs. United Telecommunications, Inc., Lenexa, Kans., 1979—. Mem. Nat. Assn. Female Execs., Data Processing Mgmt. Assn. Home: 12714 W 55th Terrace Shawnee KS 66216 Office: North Supply Co Johnson County Indsl Airport Gardner KS

VANSKIVER, MARCIA MARIE, bank ofcl.; b. Augusta, Ga., Nov. 26, 1950; d. Harry Ellsworth and Exa (Clark) Tabor; B.S. in Mgmt. and Acctg., Western State Coll. Colo., 1972; M.S. in Bus. Adminstrn., U. Denver, 1975; m. Mark Wayne VanSkiver, Sept. 9, 1973; children—Kathryn Marie, Marla Kay. Fin. analyst Standard & Poor's Denver, 1972-76; compensation analyst Idaho First Nat. Bank, Boise, 1976-77, mgr. compensation, 1978-79, mgr. placement, 1980-81, sr. human resource planner, 1981—. Chmn. youth UNICEF, 1975, 76. Mem. Am. Soc. Personnel Adminstrs. (treas., regional rep. Boise). Democrat. Office: PO Box 8247 Boise ID 83733

VAN STEENBERGE, VOCKIE, mfg. co. exec.; b. Lodi, Calif., Oct. 29, 1928; d. Everardo and Pia (Guastapaglia) Massoni; ed. pub. schs., Lodi; m. Paul Van Steenberge, Nov. 8, 1947; children—Michael, Kevin. With Lodi Iron Wks., Inc. (Calif.), 1947—, pres., 1963—; chmn. bd. Tokay Savings & Loan, Lodi, 1979—. Mem. Am. Foundrymen's Assn. Home: 1029 S School St Lodi CA 95240 Office: PO Box 71 Lodi CA 95241

VAN STRYKER, CANDACE ANN, advt. agy. exec.; b. Abington, Pa., Aug. 7, 1952; d. George Arthur and Myra Francis (Van Stryker) Gimber; B.F.A. in Graphic Design, Carngie Mellon U., 1973; student Instituto de Cultura Hispanica, N.Y. U., Madrid, 1972. Art dir. Mullen Advt., Boston, 1973-77; sr. art dir. Ogilvy & Mather, Inc., N.Y.C., 1977—. Recipient Effie award, 1981, Andy award, 1980, Clio award, 1980. Home: One Horatio St New York NY 10014 Office: 2 E 48th St New York NY 10017

VANTA, MARLEEN GAYLE, home economist; b. Lakewood, Ohio, July 22, 1951; d. John E. and Esther Margaret (Urban) V.; B.S., Ohio State U., 1973. Tchr. home econs. Cleve. Public Schs., 1973-75; food prodn. supr. Hotel div. Stouffer's, Solon, Ohio, 1975—. Mem. Am. Home Econs. Assn., Ohio Home Econs. Assn., Home Economists in Bus., Greater Cleve. Home Econs. Assn., Northeastern Ohio Group of Home Economists in Bus., Ohio State U. Alumni Assn., Ohio State U. Home Econs. Alumni Assn., Tau Beta Sigma. Home: 15603 Norway Ave Cleveland OH 44111

VAN TYLE, AILEEN LEACH, jewelry co. exec.; b. Arlington Heights, Mass., Apr. 21, 1919; d. Edson Raymond and Louise (Amber) Leach; B.A., Upsala Coll., 1941; M.A., Simmons Coll., 1942; m. Russell Demmon, June 12, 1948; children—William, Peter, Patricia. Buyer Hahne Co., Newark, 1943-45; buyer Gimbels, Pitts., 1945-47; sales promotion mgr., fashion coordinator Sarah Coventry, Newark, N.Y., 1955-69, v.p., 1970—, v.p. advt. and public relations, 1975—, bd. dirs., 1976—; public speaker for various bus. groups; com. head Fashion Group, N.Y.C.; mgmt. classes Sterling Inst.; Mem. Direct Selling Assn. (advancement for women in mgmt. positions com.). Republican. Clubs: Advertising; Newark Country. Office: Route 88 S Sarah Coventry Inc Newark NY 14513

VAN UDEN, JUDY KAY, clin. pharmacist; b. Casper, Wyo., July 19, 1950; d. John Henry and Virginia Mae (Bauer) Van U.; B.S. in Gen. Sci., Oreg. State U., 1972, B.S. in Pharmacy, 1976; M.P.A., Lewis and Clark Coll., 1982. Pharmacy extern, Kaiser-Permanente Research Center, Portland, Oreg., 1974; staff pharmacist Eastern Oreg. Hosp. and Tng. Center, Pendleton, 1976-77; clin. pharmacist Oreg. State Hosp., Salem, 1977—; cons. community nursing homes and small hosps.; instr. hosp. and community programs. NIMH grantee, 1979-80. Mem. Am. Mgmt. Assn., Nat. Assn. Public Asminstrs., Am. Soc. Hosp. Pharmacists, Inst. Managerial and Profl. Women, Oreg. Soc. Hosp. Pharmacists, Assn. Consulting Pharmacists. Democrat. Author patient info. pamphlets on neuroleptic medications, 1981. Office: 2600 Center St NE Salem OR 97310

VAN VALER, BETTY CAROLYN, Realtor; b. Delhi, Calif., May 22, 1936; d. Harold Arthur and Joie Madeline (Harp) Sibell; student West Contra Costa Jr. Coll., 1954-55; m. Richard C. Van Valer, Dec. 1, 1962; children—Jeffrey David, Julia Catherine, John Buchanan. Escrow officer N.Am. Title Guaranty Corp., Richmond, Calif., 1954-58; loan officer/escrow officer Joe B. Powell, realtor, Richmond, 1958, Jones Mortgage Co., Oakland, Calif., 1959; office mgr./escrow officer Surety Title & Guaranty Co., San Jose, Calif., 1959-63; pres., dir. Redwood Escrow Co., San Jose, 1969—; sr. v.p., dir. Van Vleck Real Estate, San Jose, 1966-79, pres., dir., 1979—; owner, operator VV Thrusts, real estate mktg. service; designer and home builder; adv. bd. Pacific Valley Bank. Mem. Calif. Real Estate Polit. Action Com., 1973—; regent Bellarmine Coll. Prep., San Jose; trustee Found. for Med. Care Santa Clara County, 1980—. Mem. San Jose, Los Gatos-Saratoga, Sunnyvale, San Benito bds. realtors, Nat., Calif. assns. realtors, Internat. Real Estate Fedn., San Jose Symphony Assn. Home: 19753 Farwell Ave Saratoga CA 95070 Office: 4950 Hamilton Ave San Jose CA 95130

VAN VALER, CONSTANCE RICHARDSON, physician; b. Utica, N.Y., June 15, 1937; d. Harold Wellington and Mildred (Tourtillott) Richardson; B.A., Franklin Coll., 1959; M.S., Ind. U., 1972, M.D., 1974; m. Joe Ned Van Valer, June 25, 1960; children—Kimberly Joy, Kelli June, Lynn Louise, Joseph Jeffrey. Asso. biochemist Eli Lilly & Co., Indpls., 1959-62; intern Methodist Hosp., Indpls., 1974-75; resident in internal medicine St. Vincent Hosp., Indpls., 1975-76; emergency physician Johnson County Meml. Hosp., Franklin, Ind., 1976—; pres. Johnson County Mental Health Assn. Clinic Bd., 1977—; med. dir. Johnson County Emergency Med. Technician Tng. Program, 1980-81; bd. dirs. Central Ind. Emergency Med. Services, 1979—. Cert. instr. advanced cardiac life support. Mem. Johnson County Med. Soc., Ind. Med. Soc., Am. Coll. Emergency Physicians, AMA. Methodist.

VAN VELDHUIZEN, RUTH MARY JOLLY, educator, home economist, genealogist; b. Marion County, Iowa, Aug. 24, 1932; d. J. Kirtz Smith and Mary Ellen (Hunt) Jolly; A.A., Central Coll., Pella, Iowa, 1951, B.A., 1959; student Colo. U., Boulder, 1953; M.A., U. Alaska, Fairbanks, 1975; m. Philip Androles Van Veldhuizen, June 5, 1952; children—Robert Mark, Jay Andre, Varina Joli. Tchr., Wheatland, Iowa, 1951-52; home econs. tchr. Pella (Iowa) Christian High Sch., 1956-59; nursery sch. co-dir. U. Alaska, Fairbanks, 1964-65, 67-68; co-dir./tchr. Young Learners Presch., Fairbanks, 1968-79; dir./tchr. Young Learners II Presch., Fairbanks, 1979—; tchr. U. Alaska, Fairbanks, 1976—; data collector U.S. Census Bur., Bur. Labor Statistics, 1974-81; fabric cons. Fabulus Fabrics, 1979-81; cons. Fairbanks North Star Bur. Cost of Living Survey, 1977; instr. genealogy Tanana Valley Community Coll., 1979—. Vol., Fairbanks Hosp. Aux., 1969—; vol. leader 4-H, 1964—; chaperone People to People, 1978, 81. Named Tanana Dist. Homemaker of Yr., 1974-75, Alaska State Homemaker, 1975, Dist. 4-H Leader of Yr., 1974, 77, Mrs. Fairbanks, 1980. Mem. Nat. Assn. Edn. Young Children, Am. Home Econs. Assn., Alaska Home Econs. Assn., Iowa Geneal. Soc., Alaska State Hist. Soc., Tanana-Yukon Hist. Soc., Fairbanks Assn. Edn. Young Children, Fairbanks Home Econs. Assn., Fairbanks Geneal. Soc. (pres.), Alaska Extension Homemakers Council, Tanana Valley Homemakers Council, Hilldwellers Homemakers (past pres.), DAR (state regent, chpt. regent). Presbyterian (ruling elder). Clubs: Sweet Adelines, Fairbanks Folkdance, PEO (past pres.). Author: How to Trace Family History by Correspondence, 1978; Record of Daniel Hunt Family including Vanderford, Beitzell, Mills, Brewer, 1965; History of Gilmore Trail; 1972; Jolly Family in America, 1981; contbr. articles in field to profl. jours. and newspapers. Home: Star Route Box 40581 Fairbanks AK 99701 Office: 1 Mile Gilmore Trail Fairbanks AK 99701

VAN VLEET, SUSAN ELLEN, mgmt. cons.; b. Trenton, N.J., Dec. 10, 1946; d. Albert and Marion (Burdman) Bash; B.A. in Sociology, Fairleigh Dickinson U., 1968; M.S.W., Rutgers U., 1974; m. John Van Vleet, Feb. 10, 1979; 1 son, Charles Tyler. Social worker N.J. Bur. Children's Services, Woodbury, 1968-70; social work supr. N.J. Youth & Family Services, Trenton, 1970-73, dir. parent edn., 1973-76; dir. govt. relations Effectiveness Training, Inc., Solano Beach, Calif., 1979—; pres. Susan Van Vleet Cons., Castle Rock, Colo., 1976-79; cons. to corps. and orgns. Mem. edn. com. Nat. Assn. Foster Parents, 1970-76, bd. dirs., 1973-74; chmn. community enrollment program Denver Arca Center. Recipient Cert. of Recognition, Child Welfare League and N.J. State Foster Parents Assn., 1976. Mem. Nat. Assn. Social Workers, Nat. Council Jewish Women (v.p. 1979-80), Nat. Assn. Female Execs. (network dir. 1979-80), Women's Bus. Conf. (exec. bd. 1981—), Exec. and Profl. Women's Council (founding), Am. Soc. Training and Devel., AAUW, NOW. Democrat. Jewish. Club: Temple Sinai Sisterhood. Contbr. articles to profl. jours. Home: Douglas Fir Castle Rock CO 80104 Office: PO Box 213 Castle Rock CO 80104

VAN VLIET, JACQUELINE, broadcasting co. exec.; b. Sioux City, Iowa, Dec. 10, 1943; d. John Huff and Miriam (Samelson) Van Vliet; B.A., Hastings Coll., 1965; postgrad. U. Iowa, 1968-69; m. H.E. Gross, June 16, 1965. Tchr. pub. schs., Omaha, 1965-66, Houston, 1966-67, Iowa City, 1967-71; with communications dept., chmn. bd. Sta. WMFE-TV, Orlando, Fla., 1979—. Vice pres. Human Services Planning Council, 1973-80; mem. Orange County Pollution Control Bd., 1979-80. Mem. LWV, Pub. Broadcasting Service, Sierra Club, Nat. Audubon Soc. Republican. Episcopalian. Home: PO Box 18 Windermere FL 32786 Office: WMFE-TV 11510 E Colonial Dr Orlando FL 32807

VAN VOORHIS, LINDA LYON, poet; b. Rochester, N.Y., May 7, 1902; d. Edmund and Carolyn H. (Talcott) Lyon; student Masters Sch., Dobbs Ferry; m. John Van Voorhis, June 2, 1928; children—Emily (Mrs. Edward Ridgway Harris), June Allis (Mrs. Louis D'Amanda), Eugene. Mem. Women's com. Rochester (N.Y.) Art Gallery, Bausch Meml. Mus. (now Rochester Mus. and Sci. Center), Japan Internat. Christian U. Found., Inc., N.Y.C., Rochester (N.Y.) Civic Music Assn. Bd. dirs. Rochester Sch. for Deaf. Recipient citation for book of poetry St. Lawrence U., 1979. Fellow Rochester Acad. Medicine (hon. life); mem. Poetry Soc. Am., Rochester Poetry Soc., Rochester Jr. League, English Speaking Union, Sigma Alpha Iota. Republican. Episcopalian. Clubs: Century, Chatterbox. Author: June's Verses, 1924, More June's Verses, 1935; June in September, 1973, also numerous poems pub. in popular anthologies, including The Golden Book of Catholic Poetry (by Alfred Noyes), 1946. Home: 714 Rock Beach Rd Rochester NY 14617

VAN VRANKEN, ROSE (MRS. ROBERT C. HICKEY), artist; b. Passaic, N.J.; d. Gilbert and Rose (Camwell) Van Vranken; B.A. cum laude, Pomona Coll., 1939; postgrad. N.Y.U., 1941-42; M.A., State U. Iowa, 1943; study William Zorach, Robert Laurent, Art Students League N.Y., 1939-42; m. Robert C. Hickey, June 11, 1942; children—Kathryn, Robert, Stephen, Dennis, Sarah. One man shows Pasadena (Calif.) Mus. Art, 1945, Dreyer Galleries, Houston, 1963, Little Studio Gallery, Madison, Wis., 1963, U. Wis. Meml. Union, 1964, Nat. Design Center, N.Y.C., 1967, Madison Art Center, 1968, Inst. Texan Cultures, San Antonio, 1970, Barnwell Art Center, Shreveport, La., 1973, Rosenberg Library, Galveston, Tex., 1975, U. Houston Law Sch., 1978, Rosenberg Library, Galveston, 1978, Pomona Coll., Claremont, Calif., 1979; group shows at Nat. Assn. Women Artists, N.A.D., N.Y.C., 1947-76, Beloit Coll., Wis., 1964-66, Audubon Artists Nat. Ann., N.Y.C., 1965, San Diego Mus., 1945, Walker Art Center, Mpls., 1951, 54, Pasadena Art Mus., 1944-46, 62-63, Nat. Assn. Women Artists Travelling Graphic Shows, U.S., 1954, Europe, 1956, Madison Art Center, 1965-67, Denver Mus., Joslyn Mus., Oakland Mus., Mus. Fine Arts, Springfield, 1967-76; represented in permanent collections Coventry (Eng.) Cathedral, Monona Pub. Library, Madison (Wis.) U. Hosps., Madison, U. Iowa, Smith Coll., Tex. Fine Arts Assn., Laguna Gloua Mus., Austin, Texas, Des Moines Art Center, Brand Library Art Gallery, Glendale, Calif., U. Houston Law Sch., Houston Pub. Library, Tex. Commerce Bank, other pub., pvt. collections. Recipient 1st prize Los Angeles Mus. Fine Arts, 1944; Pasadena Art Mus., 1951; Des Moines Art Center, 1953; Iowa State Med. Assn., 1960; Madison Art Guild, 1964; purchase award Baytown (Tex.) Community Center, 1968; 1st prize etching Springfield (Mass.) Mus. Fing Arts, 1968; award for portrait sculpture C.L. Wolfe nat. ann. N.A.D., N.Y.C., 1969; 1st prize sculpture Houston Art League Ann., 1969; Acad. Artists Council award 1979; award for sculpture Nat. Assn. Women Artists, 1980, Internat. Platform Assn., 1981, numerous others. Mem. Nat. Assn. Women Artists (medal honor 1952), So. Assn. Sculptors, Pasadena Soc. Artists, Artists Equity, Acad. Artists Assn. (award for sculpture 1980), Tex. Soc. Sculpture. Club: Salmagundi. Address: 435 Tallowood Houston TX 77024

VAN WINGERDEN, JOAN MARILYN, assn. exec.; b. Detroit, Aug. 5, 1933; d. Frank R. and Geraldine E. (Yake) Schell; student Bob Jones U., 1953-56; m. John Arie Van Wingerden, July 19, 1953; children—Deborah, Irvin, Denise, George, Laura, Dennis, John, Jill. Sec. to supr. purchasing dept. Ford Motor Co., Birmingham, Mich., 1962-63; adminstr. Winning Women, Inc., Farmington, Mich., 1965-74; founder, pres. Family Life Today, Inc., Farmington Hills, Mich., 1974—. Ch. organist, 1961-76. Mem. Nat. Assn. Female Execs. Club: Mothers Club of Detroit (1958-60). Researcher family life, 1958—; author curriculum Family Living in Your Home, 1979, Individual Foundational Instruction, The Uniqueness of You!, 1979; lectr. in field, 1967—; vocalist in Gospelaires, Voice of Christian Youth, Detroit, 1950-51; creator, lectr. TV ednl. series Family Life Today, 1980—; free lance writer. Home: 25645 Kilreigh Dr Farmington Hills MI 48018

VAN ZELST, LOUANN HURTER, ednl. cons.; b. Chgo., May 2, 1928; d. Louis Peter and Anna E. (Lederle) Hurter; B.S., Northwestern U., 1949, M.A., 1951; m. Theodore William Van Zelst, Dec. 29, 1951; children—Anne, Jean, T. David. Ednl. cons., lectr. Am. Indian and Eskimo art and culture to schs. and colls., 1971—; v.p., dir. Testing Scis., Inc., Glenview, Ill., 1969—; v.p., treas., dir. Minann, Inc., ednl. found., 1959—; v.p., dir. Land Services, Inc., 1982—; bd. dirs. Kendall Coll. Indian Museum, Evanston, Ill., 1977—. Trustee Northwestern U., 1980—; pres. Glenview Library Assn., 1979; mem. woman's bd. Field Mus. Natural History, 1982—. Recipient Service award U. Wis., 1971, Northwestern U., 1978. Mem. Northwestern U. Alumni Assn. (dir. 1979-80), Northwestern U. Sch. Speech Alumni Assn. (dir. 1970-79), Phi Beta. Roman Catholic. Club: North Shore Country (Glenview). Founding editor Dialogue, jour. Northwestern U. Sch. Speech Alumni Assn., 1974-79. Office: PO Box 126 Glenview IL 60025

VARADAN, VASUNDARA VENKATRAMAN, physicist; b. Guntur, India, June 10, 1948; d. Mangudi and Haimavathi (Cowsik) Venkatraman; B.Sc., Kerala U., 1967; M.S., U. Ill., Chgo., 1970, Ph.D., 1974; m. Vijay K. Varadan, Oct. 20, 1973; children—Haimavathi, Venkatesh, Sailesh. Postdoctoral asso. Cornell U., 1974-77; asst. prof. engring. mechanics Ohio State U., Columbus, 1977-81, asso. prof., 1981—; cons. Naval Research Lab. Recipient grants Navy, Army, USAF, NSF. Mem. Acoustical Soc. Am., Soc. Engring. Sci. Author: Acoustic, Electromagnetic and Elastic Wave Scattering—Focus on the T-matrix Approach, 1980; Elastic Wave Propagation, 1982. Home: 1916 W Lane Ave Columbus OH 43221 Office: Dept Engring Mechanics Ohio State U Columbus OH 43210

VARMA, RAJENDRA, biochemist, educator; b. Amritsar, India, Dec. 26, 1942; came to U.S., 1967, naturalized, 1972; B.S. with honors, Delhi U., 1958, M.S., 1960; Ph.D., U. New South Wales, Sydney, Australia, 1966; m. Ranbir S. Varma, July 14, 1969; children—Rajeev, Sunil. Lectr., research fellow Delhi U., 1960-62; lectr. Sydney Tech. Coll. Australia, 1963-66; postdoctoral fellow, biochemistry dept. Iowa State U., Ames, 1967, Purdue U., Lafayette, Ind., 1968; asst. prof. Alliance Coll., Cambridge Springs, Pa., 1968-69; asso. prof. Edinboro (Pa.) State Coll., 1969-71; dir. biochemistry dept. Warren (Pa.) State Hosp., 1971—. Fellow Am. Inst. Chemists; mem. Am. Chem. Soc., N.Y. Acad. Scis., Sigma Xi. Author 2 books; contbr. articles to sci. jours. Home: 305 Monroe St Warren PA 16365 Office: Warren State Hosp PO Box 249 Warren PA 16365

VARNER, CHARLEEN LAVERNE MCCLANAHAN (MRS. ROBERT B. VARNER), educator, adminstr., nutritionist; b. Alba, Mo., Aug. 28, 1931; d. Roy Calvin and Lela Ruhama (Smith) McClanahan; student Joplin (Mo.) Jr. Coll., 1949-51; B.S. in Edn., Kans. State Coll. Pittsburg, 1953; M.S., U. Ark., 1958; Ph.D., Tex. Woman's U. 1966; postgrad. Mich. State U., summer, 1955, U. Mo., summers 1952, 62; m. Robert Bernard Varner, July 4, 1953. Apprentice county home agt. U. Mo., summer 1952; tchr. Ferry Pass. Sch., Escambia County, Fla., 1953-54; tchr. biology, home econs. Joplin Sr. High Sch., 1954-59; instr. home econs. Kans. State Coll., Pittsburg, 1959-63; lectr. foods, nutrition Coll. Household Arts and Scis., Tex. Woman's U., 1963-64, research asst. NASA grant, 1964-66; asso. prof. home econs. Central Mo. State U., Warrensburg, 1966-70, adviser to Colhecon, 1966-70, adviser to Alpha Sigma Alpha, 1967-70, 72, mem. bd. advisers Honors Group, 1967-70; prof., head dept. home econs. Kans. State Tchrs. Coll., Emporia, 1970-73; prof., chmn. dept. home econs. Benedictine Coll., Atchison, Kans., 1973-74; prof., chmn. dept. home econs. Baker U., Baldwin City, Kans., 1974-75; owner, operator Diet-Con Dietary Cons. Enterprises, cons. dietitian, 1973—. Mem. Joplin Little Theater, 1956-60. Mem. NEA, Mo., Kans. state tchrs. assns., AAUW, Am., Mo., Kans. dietetics assns., Am., Mo., Kans. home econs. assns., Mo. Acad. Scis., AAUP, U. Ark. Alumni Assn., Alumni Assn. Kans. State Coll. of Pittsburg, Am. Vocat. Assn., Assn. Edn. Young Children, Sigma Xi, Beta Sigma Phi, Beta Beta Beta, Alpha Sigma Alpha, Delta Kappa Gamma, Kappa Kappa Iota, Phi Upsilon Omicron. Methodist (organist). Home: Main PO Box 1009 Topeka KS 66601

VARNER, NELLIE MAE, investment broker, former univ. ofcl.; b. Lake Cormorant, Miss., Aug. 27, 1935; d. Tommie and Essie (Davis) V.; B.S., Wayne State U., 1958, M.A., 1959; Ph.D., U. Mich., 1968. Tchr., Detroit public schs., 1959-64; congressional intern U.S. Congress, 1966; research asso. Russian Research Center, Harvard U., Boston, 1970-71, research fellow Center for Internat. Affairs, 1970-71; faculty asso. Center for Russian and Eastern European Studies, U. Mich., 1968-79, asst. prof. polit. sci., 1968-79, asso. dean Grad. Sch., 1976-79; sales asso. Real Estate One, Detroit, 1971-75; v.p., sec., treas. Precision Group, Inc., 1976—; v.p. and asso. broker Strather & Assos., Detroit, 1976—; v.p. Strather-Varner Properties, Inc., Detroit, Mich., 1978—; chairperson real estate adv. bd. Mich. Dept. Licensing and Regulation, 1978-79; mem. econ. employment com. New Detroit, Inc., 1980—; del. White House Conf. on Small Bus., Washington, 1980. Mem. Mich. Democratic Women's Caucus, 1979—, Mich. Dem. Black Caucus, 1979—; bd. regents U. Mich., 1981—. Wilton Park fellow, 1969, Social Sci. Research Council tng. fellow, 1970-71; U. Mich. research grantee, 1970-71. Mem. Nat. Assn. Realtors, Mich. Assn. Realtors, Detroit Bd. Realtors, NAACP, Phi Kappa Phi, Pi Sigma Alpha. Baptist. Home: c/o Strather & Assoc 16801 Wyoming Ave Detroit MI 48221 Office: 16801 Wyoming Ave Detroit MI 48221

VARNUM, SHARON LORAINE BROWN, psychotherapist; b. Brownwood, Tex., Jan. 7, 1947; d. Loy Darrel and Loraine Louella (Ellis) Brown; B.M.Ed., Okla. Bapt. U., 1969; M.Ed., U. Md., 1973; M.S.W., Nat. Cath. U., 1976; m. Robert V. Varnum, June 13, 1970; 1 son, Robert Bradley. Secondary vocal music tchr. Dallas Sch. Dist., 1969-70; elementary vocal music tchr. Prince Georges County (Md.) Bd. Edn., 1970-73; asst. to legis. aide staff U.S. Congressman Donald D. Clancy, Washington, 1973-74; clin. social worker, psychotherapist Glass Mental Health Center, Balt., 1976-80, dir. social work, 1978-79; pvt. practice psychotherapy, Silver Spring, Md., 1980—. Mem. Nat. Assn. Social Workers, Acad. Cert. Social Workers, Greater Washington Soc. Clin. Social Workers, Mental Health Assn. Montgomery County, Md. Coalition Social Work Licensing (sec.), AAUW (v.p.), LWV. Home and Office: 425 Pershing Dr Silver Spring MD 20910

VARTANIAN, ELSIE VIRGINIA, real estate broker; b. Haverhill, Mass., July 19, 1930; d. Minott LaForest and Nellie Phyllis (Berry) Brown; diploma MacIntish Bus. Sch., Lawrence, Mass., 1949; m. David Vartanian, Nov. 9, 1952; children—David M. (dec.), Corey J. Legal sec., 1951-75; broker asso. Rosemary Green, Realtor, Windham, N.H., 1975-77; account exec. F.L. Putnam & Co., Inc., Boston, 1977-79; owner-operator Elsie Vartanian Realtor, Salem, N.H., 1979—. Mem. curriculum coordination com. Salem High Sch., 1975-76; pres., bd. dirs. Dollars for Scholars, Salem, 1975; mem. N.H. Gen. Ct., 1978-82. Mem. Nat. Assn. Securities Dealers, Nat. Order Women Legislators, Nat. Assn. Realtors, N.H. Assn. Realtors, Salem Area Bd. Realtors. Address: 44 Brady Ave Salem NH 03079

VASARKOVY, DIANE ROSE, computer systems mgr.; b. Newark, June 5, 1943; d. William Louis and Laura Veronica (Fischer) V.; student San Antonio Coll., 1970-73; B.B.A., U. Tex., San Antonio, 1981; children—Robert Frank Montoya, Richard Michael Montoya. Data control clk. AEC, Albuquerque, 1966-67; programmer/analyst Hillcrest State Bank, San Antonio, 1967-69, Alamo Nat. Bank, San Antonio, 1969-71; sr. programmer/analyst Southwest Info. Mgmt. Systems, San Antonio, 1971-74; systems analyst United Services Automobile Assn., San Antonio, from 1974, now project mgr.; v.p., bd. dirs. United Services Automobile Assn. Fed. Credit Union, 1979—. Cert. in gen. ins. Ins. Inst. Am.; cert. in data processing Inst. for Cert. Computer Profls. Mem. San Antonio Women in Processing Data Processing Mgmt. Assn. (dir. San Antonio chpt. 1975-77, 82, sec. 1982-83). Office: United Services Automobile Assn USAA Bldg A-SVC-E San Antonio TX 78288

VASEL, CAROLYNN, health care exec.; b. St. Louis, Oct. 16, 1952; d. Carl Henry and Eleanore Gertrude (Forst) V.; B.S., S.E. Mo. State U., 1974; M.T., St. Luke's Hosp. Sch. Med. Tech., Kansas City, Mo., 1975; M.S.P.H., U. Mo., 1980, M.B.A., 1980. Med. technologist Univ. Hosp. and Clinics, U. Mo., Columbia, 1975-80, planning asst., 1980; asst. adminstr. Boone Hosp. Center, Columbia, 1980—. Mem. Am. Coll. Hosp. Adminstrs., Am. Hosp. Assn., Am. Soc. Clin. Pathologists.

VASQUEZ, SUSAN DELORES, lab. materials mgr.; b. Berkeley, Calif., Nov. 20, 1946; d. Robert Vincent and Gloria M. (Luty) Hughes; student San Francisco State U., U. Calif., Berkeley, Calif. State U., Hayward; m. Gary Vasquez, Jan. 19, 1974. With Bio-Rad Lab., Richmond, Calif., 1966—, purchasing mgr., 1974-78, materials mgr., 1978—. Mem. Nat. Assn. Purchasing Mgmt. (exec. mem. chem. group 1977—, chmn. pub. relations 1980—, William Beckham Pub. Relations award 1982), Purchasing Mgmt. Assn. No. Calif. (dir., officer 1981), Am. Prodn. and Inventory Control Soc. Republican. Roman Catholic. Author articles in field. Home: 205 Iris Rd Hercules CA 94547 Office: 2200 Wright St Richmond CA 94804

VASSAR, BARBARA ANN HENDERSON, educator; b. Clover, Va., May 15, 1925; d. Holt Green and Lena Ann (Sparrow) Henderson; B.S. in Edn., U. South Ala., 1972; M.A. in Edn., Pembroke (N.C.) State U., 1979; m. Clarence Oliver Vassar, Nov. 5, 1949; children—Richard Holt, Hugh Edward, Robert Yancey (dec.). Sec., asst. buyer Thalhimers, Richmond, Va., 1945-49; various secretarial positions, 1950-52; asso. buyer Sanger-Harris Co., Dallas, 1952-55; kingergarten tchrs. Baptist chs. in N.C. and Ala., 1966, 68-69; public sch. tchr., Ala., 1972-74, N.C., 1974-80; tchr. 4th-6th grades Winston-Salem/Forsyth Schs., 1980—; leader various ednl. confs. Mem. NEA, N.C. Assn. Educators, Assn. Classroom Tchrs., Alpha Delta Kappa, Phi Delta Kappa. Democrat. Baptist. Home: 306 Virginia Ave Yadkinville NC 27055 Office: Petree Sch Winston-Salem NC

VASSAR, LINDA SUE, pool co. exec.; b. Luxora, Ark., Sept. 25, 1942; d. Cecil and Doris Mae (Williams) Lawson; student San Jose City Coll., part-time; m. Gary Vassar, Aug. 10, 1960; children—Gary, Rebekah. Exec. sec. to pres. RAM Realtors, San Jose, Calif., 1972-73; mgr. Paul Hammon Real Estate, San Jose, 1974-75; with Blue Fountain Pools, San Diego, 1975—, pres., sec., 1975—. Mem. Swimming Pool Assn. Home: 1961 Willowbrook Ct El Cajon CA 92021 Office: 6403 Mission Gorge Rd San Diego CA 92120

VASSEL, KAREN LOUISE, contractors' assn. exec.; b. Denver, July 27, 1954; d. Henry Ray and Ruth Victoria (Crout) Thompson; student Northeastern Jr. Coll., Sterling, Colo., 1973, U. Colo., 1977—; cert. in mgmt. U. Denver; 1 child, Samie Deon. Registration coordinator Colo. Soc. C.P.A.s, 1975-77; asst. dir. constrn. advancement programs Asso. Gen. Contractors Colo., Denver, 1977—. Cert. Asso. Gen. Contractors. Club: Zonta. Office: 1660 S Albion St Suite 300 Denver CO 80222

VASTOLA, VALERIE, fin. examiner; b. N.Y.C., May 11, 1953; d. Hugo Paul and Gloria Jean (D'Aiuto) Vastola; student (N.Y. State Regents scholar) Harpur Coll., SUNY, 1971-73; B.A. (N.Y. State Regents scholar), Barnard Coll., 1975; M.B.A., Cornell U., 1977; cert. of security analysis and portfolio mgmt. N.Y. Inst. Fin., 1978. Mgmt. intern Bur. of Budget of City N.Y., summer 1974; adminstr. Columbia Law Sch. Alumni Assn., N.Y.C., 1974-75, summer 1975; researcher Donald Sheldon & Co., Inc., N.Y.C., summer 1976; portfolio mgr., security analyst Ferris & Co., Inc., Washington, 1977-79; cons. OAO Corp., Washington, 1979-80; devel. officer Nat. Consumer Coop. Bank, 1981; sr. examiner Nat. Assn. Securities Dealers, N.Y.C., 1981—; radio interviews on investments for women, 1978. Mem. Nat. Council Career Women, Women's Network, Am. Mgmt. Assn. Home: 103 Grandview Ln Smithtown NY 11787 Office: Two World Trade Center 98th Floor New York NY 10048

VATANDOOST, NOSSI MALEK, art sch. adminstr.; b. Teheran, Iran, May 22, 1935; d. Abdullah Goodar and Mahtaban (Goodar) Malek; B.A., Western Ky. U., 1970; m. Ira Vatandoost, May 31, 1964; children—Debbie, Cyrus. Art tchr. Met.-Davidson County Sch. System, Nashville, 1970-71; dir., owner Nossi Sch. Art, Madison, Tenn., 1973—; treas. Malek & Assos. Inc., 1976; dir. EXCEL Edn. Corp., 1980—; vis. lectr., cons. EXCEL Bus. Inst., 1980—. Mem. Hendersonville Art Council, Hendersonville Art Guild (com. chmn.). Club: Soroptimists (Upper Cumberland Valley, Tenn.). Home: 105 Country Club Dr Hendersonville TN 37075 Office: 210 Plaza Professional Bldg Madison TN 37115

VATSURES, LENA SPERO, former advt. art exec.; b. Columbus, Ohio, Nov. 20, 1927; d. Spiro John and Helen (Jerakos) V.; grad. Dallas Art Inst., 1948; postgrad. Dallas Mus. Fine Arts Sch., 1949-55, So. Meth. U., 1975. Art dir. Zale Corp., Dallas, 1950-55, W.A. Green Co., Dallas, 1955-57, Sanger Bros., Dallas, 1957-60; sr. art dir. Bloom Agy., Dallas, 1960-81. Vol. worker Republican party; active Goals for Dallas. Mem. Dallas Soc. Visual Communications, St. Barbara Philoptochos Soc. Greek Orthodox. Home: 1159 Bally Mote Dr Dallas TX 75218 Office: 3000 Diamond Park Dr Dallas TX 75247

VAUGHAN, MARILOU TAYLOR, magazine editor; b. Detroit; d. Robert Adams and Dorothea (Trauffer) Taylor; B.A., Eastern Mich. U., 1958; postgrad. Stanford U., 1959; m. David Rodman Vaughan, Jan. 2, 1960. Asst. editor Smithsonian mag., Washington, 1974-76; asso. editor New West mag., Beverly Hills, Calif., 1976-77, Archtl. Digest, Los Angeles, 1977-79; mng. editor Bon Appetit mag., Los Angeles, 1979—. Mem. Am. Assn. Mag. Editors. Office: 5900 Wilshire Blvd Los Angeles CA 90036

VAUGHAN, NANCY MCBEE, retail exec.; b. Knoxville, Feb. 3, 1951; d. William Lon and Mabel E. (Adkins) McBee; B.S. cum laude, Carson-Newman Coll., 1973; M.S., Va. Tech., 1978; m. Edward L. Vaughan, Dec. 29, 1979; 1 dau., Rebekah Lynn. Extension agt. Va. Coop. Extension Service, Scott County, 1973-75, 4-H coordinator, Virginia Beach, 1975-80; owner Pungo Fabric Barn, Virginia Beach, 1980—. Mem. Va. Assn. Extension Agts., Va. Assn. Extension 4-H Agts. (v.p. 1979-80), Kappa Omicron Phi, Epsilon Sigma Phi. Republican. Methodist. Home: 1628 Mill Landing Rd Virginia Beach VA 23457 Office: Pungo Fabric Barn Virginia Beach VA 23456

VAUGHAN, SARAH LOU, vocalist; b. Mar. 27, 1924; d. Asbury and Ada (Baylor) Vaughan; student pub. schs.; m. George Treadwell; m. 2d, Clyde B. Atkins; m. 3d, Marshall Fisher; 1 dau., Debbie. Joined Earl Hines Orch., 1942, Billy Eckstein Band, 1943; vocalist Mercury Records, Nat. Music Craft, Columbia, Em Arcy Records, Roulette Records, Mainstream Records; recs. include Lover Man, Sometimes I'm Happy, It Shouldn't Happen to a Dream, Alfie, Broken-Hearted Melody, 1959, A Lover's Concerto, 1966, Foggy Day in Londontown. Winner Apollo amateur contest, 1942; recipient ann. vocalist award Downbeat, 1946-52. Office: care Regency Artists Ltd 9200 Sunset Blvd Suite 823 Los Angeles CA 90069 *

VAUGHAN, SHARON KAY, nurse; b. Fairfield, Ill., June 28, 1948; d. Emerial Lee and Dedie Elizabeth (Lanham) Owen; A.A. in Nursing, Frontier Community Coll., Fairfield, 1977; m. Gary Len Vaughan, Dec. 18, 1976; children—Emerial Kent, Kari Sue, Jeremy Len. Obstetrical nurse Good Samaritan Hosp., Mt. Vernon, Ill., 1977-78; staff nurse Fairfield Meml. Hosp., 1978; women, infants and children food supplement dir. Wabash Area Devel., Inc., Mill Shoals, Ill., 1978—. Health Care scholar, 1977. Mem. Maternal and Child Health Assn. Home: PO Box 63 Locust St Mill Shoals IL 62862 Office: PO Box 89 Mill Shoals IL 62862

VAUGHN, DONNA BILTON, physician; b. Albany, Ga., Sept. 6, 1952; d. Frank A. and Caroline (Brandenburf) Bilton; B.S., Tulane U., 1973; M.D., Med. Coll. Ga., 1978; m. Andrew I.S. Vaughn, Apr. 10, 1979. Resident in anesthesia U. Calif. at Davis, 1980-83; practice medicine specializing in anesthesiology, Woodland, Calif.; clin. asso. U. Calif. at Davis. Mem. AMA, Am. Soc. Anesthesiologists. Roman Catholic. Address: 2803 Grinnel Dr Davis CA 95616

VAUGHN, EMMA JUAN BELL (MRS. ERASMUS ROSCOE VAUGHN), librarian; b. Cartwright, Ky., Aug. 23, 1908; d. Henry Clay and Nannie (Cooper) Bell; student Transylvania U., 1925-28, Western State U., 1928; B.S., Tenn. Poly. U., 1940; postgrad. Memphis State U., 1950-52, Catheryn Spalding U., 1957-60; Ph.D. (hon.), Hamilton State Coll., 1973; m. Erasmus Roscoe Vaughn, Sept. 25, 1928; children—George Clay, Ann (Mrs. Jere Calvin Robertson), James Erasmus. Prin., Three Forks Sch., Warren County, Ky., 1942-44, Lamont Sch., Robertson County, Tenn., 1944-46; tchr. Alamo (Tenn.) High Sch., 1946-49, pub. schs., Dyer County, Tenn., 1950-54; tchr. English and French, Heath High Sch., Paducah, Ky., 1948-49; librarian Ballard County High Sch., LaCenter, Ky., 1949-50, Hickman High Sch., Clinton, Ky., 1956-57, Fulton County High Sch., Hickman, Ky., 1957-58; tchr. French, biology Byars Hall High Sch., Covington, Tenn., 1954-56; librarian Lowes (Ky.) High Sch., 1958-69. Trustee Stinnett (Ky.) Settlement Sch. Recipient honor award Lowes High Sch. chpt. Future Farmers Am., 1969. Mem. NEA, Ky. Edn. Assn., Ky. Hist. Soc., D.A.R. Democrat. Mem. Christian Ch. (pianist 1959-69). Clubs: Woodville (Ky.) Home Makers (charter mem.). Home: 827 W Broadway Mayfield KY 42066

VAUGHN, GROVA LEE, nurse; b. Manchester, Ky., Sept. 27, 1922; d. Vernon and Lottie Mae (Halcomb) Reese; R.N., Speers Meml. Hosp., 1944; student Miami U., 1973, U. Cin., 1976-78; m. John Vaughn, Dec. 1, 1945; children—Patricia Gail, Vicki Jo. Staff nurse Bethesda Hosp., Cin., 1946; asst. dir. nursing Bethesda Scarlet Oaks, Cin., 1975-79; dir. nursing Judson Village Retirement Center, Cin., 1980—. Leader, Girl Scouts U.S.A.; bd. dirs. Children's Internat. Summer Villages; treas. North Coll. Hill PTA. Mem. Hamilton County Pharm. Assn. Aux. (v.p.), Ohio Drug Travelers. Baptist. Club: Order Eastern Star. Home: 9622 Millbrook Dr Cincinnati OH 45231 Office: 2373 Harrison Ave Cincinnati OH 45211

VAUGHN, JANETT, lab. technologist; b. Jackson, N.C., Oct. 21, 1949; d. Jarvis and Gertharee (Barnes) Vaughan; A.S., Atlantic Community Coll., 1974; postgrad. E. Carolina U., 1981—. Phlebotomist, Atlantic City Med. Center, 1972-74; lab. technician Halifax Meml. Hosp., Roanoke Rapids, N.C., 1974-75, Ronoke-Chowan Hosp., Ahoskie, N.C., 1975—. Work experience counselor Concern Athletes in Action, Inc., Norfolk, Va., summer 1982; bd. dirs. Employees Credit Union, 1979-8; sch. drug awareness program vol. Roanoke-Chowan Mental Health Services. Mem. Am. Soc. Clin. Pathologists. Democrat. Baptist. Club: Elks (past state pres.). Home: Route 1 PO Box 21 Pendleton NC 27862 Office: Academy St Ahoskie NC 27901

VAUGHN, MARY, health care facilities exec.; b. Trafford, Ala., Apr. 20, 1930; d. Grover Webster and Vivian Lenora (Dorman) V.; student Birmingham Bus. Coll., 1952, Howard Coll., 1959, U. Ala., 1960, 62, Balboa Intermediate Care Facility, San Diego, 1969-76; certificate in therapeutic activities tng. Grossmont Adult Sch., 1975; m. James T. Lovvorn, Mar. 1952 (div. 1959). Owner, pres., treas. Balboa Manor Inc. and Balboa lManor Health Facility, San Diego, 1969-79. Charter pres. Quota Club of Birmingham (Ala.), 1967-68; lt. gov. 8th dist. Quota Internat., 1968-69; supr. adv. com. to Jim Bates, 4th Dist. Supr. San Diego County, 1973—; mem. San Diego County Com. on the Handicapped, 1979—; mem. support com. Community Video Center, pub. access TV, 1979—. Recipient Safety award Indsl. Indemnity, 1973, 75, certificate of appreciation Jim Bates, 1975; notary pub., cert. nursing home adminstr., Calif. Mem. Am. Health Care Assn., Am. Coll. Nursing Home Adminstrs., Am., Calif. nursing home assns., Com. of 100 of San Diego Klee Wyk Soc., San Diego Opera, Bus. and Profl. Women's Club (pres. Birmingham chpt. 1967-69), San Diego Mus. Natural History, San Diego Mus. of Man, Nat. Notary Assn. Republican. Methodist. Author: Exploring Mental Therapy. Home: 2804 C St San Diego CA 92102

VAUGHN, (OLIVE) RUTH, author, playwright; b. Wellington, Tex., Aug. 31, 1935; d. S.L. and Nora Norris (Knowles) Wood; B.A., M.A., U. Kans.; Ph.D., Am. U.; m. Bill Vaughn, Feb. 14, 1955; children—Billy, Ron. Author 35 books, including: Fun for Christian Youth, 1960, Dreams Can Come True, 1964, Portrait in a Nursery, 1965, What I Will Tell My Children About God, 1966, Skits that Win, 1967, No Matter the Weather, 1968, Hey! Have You Heard?, 1969, Playlets and Skits, 1970, Baby's Album, 1973, Even When I Cry, 1975, Proclaiming Christ in the Caribbean, 1976, More Skits that Win, 1977, Celebrate with Words, 1979, What's a Mother to Say?, 1980, Write to Discover Yourself, 1980, To Be a Girl—To Be a Woman, 1982, My God! My God!, 1982; author 46 plays, including: The Living Last Supper, The Man on the Center Cross, Behold a New World!, Lions Can't Eat Truth, Morning Comes at Sunrise, Catherine Marshall's Christy, Eugenia Price's The Beloved Invader; musical stageplays include: God's Dream, To Touch a Rainbow, Once Upon a Hill: The Coward and the Cut-Throat, Please Be King!, Shadow of the Almighty; prof. drama/creative writing Bethany Nazarene Coll., 1968-76; pvt. practice counseling; author numerous short stories and articles. Mem. Women in Communication Internat., Internat. Platform Assn., Pi Lambda Theta, Theta Sigma Phi. Republican. Nazarene. Home: 6151 W Fremont Dr Littleton CO 80123

VAUGHN, RUBY WENTWORTH, artist, real estate exec.; b. Ringwood, Okla., Dec. 18, 1909; d. John Logan and Roberta L. (Courtney) Wentworth; student Ind. U., U. Buffalo, Allegheny Sch. Natural History; m. Thomas H. Vaughn, Sept. 13, 1930; children—Jolan Adele, Vicki Lee, Trudy Gail. Artist, art cons., 1960—; pres. Spltу. Designs Studio, Waretown, N.J., 1970—, Vaughn Realty Corp., Chgo., 1971—; flower arranger, creator artistic and craft designs, 1958—. Mem. women's adv. council U. Notre Dame, 1968—. Recipient numerous awards in art, craft and flower shows. Mem. Soc. Craft Designers, Hackensack (N.J.) Art Club, Bergen Artists Guild, Ridgefield (N.J.) Art Club, DAR. Mem. Christian Ch. (Disciples of Christ). Address: 13 Jolly Roger Way Waretown NJ 08758

VAUGHN, SALLE ALICE WERNER, artist; b. Ennis, Tex.; d. John Patrick and Frances Derden (Horton) Werner; B.S. cum laude, Tex. Woman's U., 1961; postgrad. Rice U., 1978-79, Atelier 17, Paris, 1979; m. James Miller Vaughn Jr. Founder, dir. Art Involvement & Motivation, Dallas, 1970-76; pub. Crystal Press, 1980—; one-woman shows: Courtney Sale Gallery, Dallas, 1972, Tyler (Tex.) Mus. Art, 1973, Pelham Von Stoffer Gallery, Houston, 1977, Helen Serger-LeBoetie Gallery, N.Y.C., 1980, LYC Gallery and Mus., Cumbria, Eng., 1982; group shows include: Oklahoma City Art Center Mus., 1968, Mus. Fine Arts, Dallas, 1968, Pollack Gallery, Dallas, 1970, Whitney Mus., N.Y.C., 1973, Helen Serger-La Boetie Gallery, N.Y.C., 1977, Mus. Contemporary Art, Houston; represented in permanent collections: AT&T, N.Y.C., Wilson Industries, Houston, Akron Art Inst., Lomas Nettleton Mortgage & Banking, Dallas, San Francisco Mus. Modern Art, Bridwell Library, Dallas, Humanities Research Center, U. Tex., Austin. Trustee, Houston Grand Opera, 1974—, mem. repretoire com., 1981—; mem. visitors com. Mus. Fine Art, Boston, 1976—; v.p., trustee Vaughn Found. Fund; mem. collectors com. Nat. Gallery, Washington. Fellow Morgan Library (N.Y.C.). Episcopalian (Altar Guild). Author: Seeds of Snow, 1981; The Illusion of 2, 1982. Address: Helen Serger La Boetie Inc 9 E 82nd St New York NY 10028

VAUGHT, SHERRYL DIANNE, clin. social worker; b. Shiloh County, Ill., Nov. 22, 1953; d. George Madison Vaught and Grace Marion Campfield; A.A., Jefferson Jr. Coll., 1972; B.S. in Psychology, S.W. Mo. State Coll., 1974; M.S.W., St. Louis U., 1976. Clin. social worker S.E. Mo. Mental Health, Kennett, 1976-77; dir. partial hospitalization, Delta Guidance and Counseling, Monticello, Ark., 1977-78; adminstr. Leisure Lodges, Inc., Arkadelphia, Ark., 1978-79; clin. social worker, dir. aging services Central Ark. Mental Health Services, Cabot, 1979—; nursing home cons. Mem. Nat. Assn. Social Workers (chmn. com. on aging Ark.), Ark. Nursing Home Assn. (asso.), Western Gerontol. Soc., Nursing Home Cons. (asso.), Acad. Cert. Social Workers. Republican. Methodist. Clubs: Order Eastern Star, Bus. and Profl. Women. Home: PO Box 423 Cabot AR 72023 Office: PO Box 681 405 N 2d St Cabot AR 72023

VAUGHT, WILMA L., air force officer; b. Pontiac, Mich., Mar. 15, 1930; d. Willard L. and Margaret (Pierce) V.; B.S., U. Ill., 1952; M.B.A., U. Ala., 1968. Commd. 2d lt., U.S. Air Force, 1957, advanced through grades to brig. gen., 1980—; chief Data Services div. 306th Combat Support Group, McCoy AFB, Fla., 1963-67, mgmt. analyst Office of Dep. Chief of Staff, Comptroller, Mil. Assistance Command, Vietnam, Saigon, 1968-69, chief advanced Logistics Systems Plans and Mgmt. Group, Hdqrs. Air Force Logistics Command, Wright-Patterson AFB, Ohio, 1969-72; chief Cost Factors br. Directorate of Mgmt. Analysis, Office of Comptroller, Hdqrs. U.S. Air Force, Washington, 1973-77; dir. programs and budget Office of Dep. Chief of Staff, Comptroller, Air Force Systems Command Hdqrs., 1977-80; dep. chief of staff, comptroller Hdqrs. Air Force Systems Command, Andrews AFB, Md., 1980-82; comdr. Mil. Enlistment Processing Command, Ft. Sheridan, Ill., 1982—; pres. bd. dirs. Pentagon Fed. Credit Union, 1975-82. Decorated Bronze Star. Mem. Am. Inst. Cost Analysis, Am. Soc. Mil. Comptrollers. Home: 6658 Van Winkle Dr Falls Church VA 22044 Office: Comdr Mil Enlistment Processing Command 2500 Green Bay Rd North Chicago IL 60064

VAYDA, VIRGINIA CONYERS, social worker; b. Hamilton, Ohio, Feb. 5, 1953; d. James W. and Doris (Wuest) Conyers; A.Mental Health, Morehead State U., 1973, B.U.S., 1975; M.S.W., W.Va. U., 1977; m. Jeffrey G. Vayda, Aug. 5, 1978. Coordinator family and children services Luth. Social Service, Cin., 1977-78; dir. social service Carlisle (Pa.) Hosp., 1978-79; dir. patient and community services Butler County Meml. Hosp., Butler, Pa., 1979—; part-time faculty U. Pitts. Sch. Social Work, 1979—; faculty Slippery Rock State Coll., 1982—, also adv. bd. social work program. field instr. for area colls., 1977—; social work cons. for nursing home, 1979—. Program chmn. Butler County Health and Welfare Council, pres., 1980—; mem. steering com. Am. Heart Assn.; mem. adv. bd. Hospice of Western Pa.; rep. on bd. United Fund; adv. bd. Butler Meals on Wheels, 1980—, Area Health Edn. Corp., 1981—Mem. Acad. Cert. Social Workers, Nat. Assn. Social Workers, Am. Hosp. Assn. Soc. for Hosp. Social Work Dirs., Southwestern Pa. Soc. for Hosp. Social Work Dirs., Social work Oncology Group, Phi Kappa Phi. Lutheran. Office: Dept Patient and Community Services Butler County Meml Hosp E Brady St Extension Butler PA 16001

VAZIRANI, LOIS MARCIA, real estate salesperson; b. Jersey City, Nov. 14, 1937; d. Henry and Mollie (Radin) Landy; B.A., Cornell U., 1959; M.A., U. Chgo., 1961; m. Hargovind N. Vazirani, June 10, 1961; children—Sondra, Monica. Social worker Mental Health Center, Chgo., 1961-62; tchr. Bombay (India) Internat. Sch., 1962-63; social worker Toronto (Ont., Can.) Bd. Edn., 1964-66, Children's Home, Mt. Holly, N.J., 1966-67, Union County Psychiat. Clinic, Plainfield, N.J., 1967-68, Chatham Twp. (N.J.) Bd. Edn., 1977-80, Mendham Twp. Bd. Edn., Brookside, N.J., 1980; sales rep. Strong Realty, Rolling Hills Estates, Calif., 1981—. Chmn., Passaic Twp. Sr. Citizen Housing Com., 1974-80; treas. Democratic Club Passaic Twp., 1977-80; mem. Bd. Edn. Passaic Twp., 1979-80; pres. Morris County Fair Housing Council, 1975-77. Woods scholar, 1959-60; USPHS fellow, 1961. Lic. asso. realtor, Calif. Mem. Nat. Assn. Social Workers (sec.-treas. 1979-80), Acad. Cert. Social Workers, N.J. Assn. Sch. Social Workers, Mem. Calif. Bd. Realtors, Torrance-Lomita-Carson Bd. Realtors, Rolling Hills Bd. Realtors, N.J. Sch. Bd. Assn. Home: 30755 Via La Cresta Rancho Palos Verdes CA 90274 Office: Strong Realty 777 Silver Spur Rd Suite 101 Rolling Hills Estates CA 90274

VAZQUEZ, AGGIE SUSANA ALFONSO, bookkeeper; b. Havana, Cuba, Feb. 5, 1952; came to U.S., 1962, naturalized, 1972; d. Alvaro Augustine and Eva Nilda (Collado) Alfonso; A.Mgmt., LaSalle U., 1977; 1 son, Joshua Albert. Office mgr. King Meml. Hosp., Opalocka, Fla., 1971-72, Nydia Martin, M.D., Miami, Fla., 1973-76; with U. Tampa (Fla.) Med. Assn., 1976-78; office mgr. Billing Dept.; asst. bookkeeper Stephen Dante Cosmetics, Inc., Flushing, N.Y., 1979—. Mem. Nat. Assn. Female Execs., Smithsonian Assocs. Home: 143 55 41st St Apt 6E Flushing NY 11365 Office: 40 15 Junction Blvd Corona NY 11368

VEACH, BETTY FAYE, educator; b. Mangum, Okla., June 12, 1945; d. Leslie A.J. and Betty Jo Veach; student Altus Jr. Coll., 1963-65; B.S., Southwestern Okla. State U., 1968, M.Ed., 1970; postgrad. Tex. Tech U., 1976. Tchr. Hollis (Okla.) High Sch., 1968-70; tchr., head bus. edn. dept. Clarendon (Tex.) High Sch., 1970—. Soloist, accompanist choirs First Bapt. Ch.; advisor Explorer troop Adobe Walls council Boy Scouts Am., 1973-79. Mem. NEA, Tex. Tchrs. Assn. (rec. sec. Donley County unit, del. dist. conv.), Tex. Bus. Edn. Assn., Mountain Plains Bus. Edn. Assn., Tex. Profl. Educators, Beta Sigma Phi (rec. sec. Xi Lambda Xi chpt. 1978, historian 1979, corr. sec. 1980, pres. 1981). Democrat. Clubs: Rebekahs, 1926 Book (rec. sec. 1978-80, pres. 1981-83). Home: Box 182 Clarendon TX 79226 Office: Box 610 Clarendon TX 79226

VEATCH, RITA RIES, nurse; b. O'Niel, Nebr., Sept. 17, 1926; d. John F. and Loretta G. (Brennan) Ries; R.N., Queen of Angels Coll. Nursing, 1948; B.S., Mt. St. Mary's Coll., 1951; M.A., Tchrs. Coll., Columbia U., 1956; m. Gordon L. Veatch, Feb. 4, 1961; 1 son, John. Staff nurse Queen of Angels Hosp., Los Angeles, 1948-49; mem. faculty Queen of Angels Coll. Nursing, Los Angeles, 1951-64, 68-73; mem. staff Los Angeles Unified Sch. Dist., 1974-76; asst. chairperson, dir. Asso. Degree Program in Nursing, Mt. St. Mary's Coll., Los Angeles, 1976—. Mem. Am. Nurses Assn., Nat. League for Nursing, Orgn. Dirs. Asso. Degree Programs for Nursing in Calif., Phi Lambda Theta. Republican. Roman Catholic. Office: 10 Chester Pl Los Angeles CA 90007

VECCHIO, LISA ANN, ednl. adminstr.; b. Marshall, Mich., June 4, 1944; d. John Bernard and Mary Louise Wasleski; B.A., Western Mich. U., 1966, M.A. (grad. fellow, 1967-69), 1969; m. Thomas J. Vecchio, July 16, 1977; 1 dau., Sarah Elizabeth. Tchr. spl. edn./speech and lang. therapist, Kalamazoo, summers 1967-74; tchr., Headstart for Adults/Basic Skills Adults, Hilo, Hawaii, 1968-69; tchr. spl. edn., Newport, Ky., 1969-70, Mayer, Ariz., 1971-73; dir. Allegan County Devel. Center, Allegan, Mich., 1974—; Child Find coordinator for Allegan County. Active, Kalamazoo Acad. Medicine Aux. Mem. Mich. Assn. for Emotionally Disturbed Children, Spl. Edn. Suprs. of Mich., Assn. for Edn. Severely/Profoundly Handicapped. Contbr. articles to publs. in field. Office: 212 Grove St Allegan MI 49010

VECCHIOLLA, FRANCINE JUNE, social worker; b. Hartford, Conn., June 16, 1950; d. Frank Joseph and Germaine Viola (Blouin) V.; B.S. magna cum laude, Springfield Coll., 1972; M.S.W., U. Conn., 1974; postgrad. in child devel. Yale U. Child Study Center, 1976-78; m. Duncan Coolidge Reid, May 25, 1974. Social work cons. Onondaga County Health Dept., Syracuse, N.Y., 1974-75; med. social work cons. Conn. State Dept. Health, Hartford, 1976-79; project dir. Conn. State Dept. Children and Youth Services, Hartford, 1979—; mem. Conn. Child Abuse Com. Mem. adv. bd. Parents Anonymous of Conn.; mem. Vernon (Conn.) Econ. Devel. Commn., 1978-80. Registered social worker, N.Y. Mem. Acad. Cert. Social Workers, Nat. Assn. Social Workers, Clin. Assn. Social Workers, Psi Chi. Democrat. Roman Catholic. Office: 375 Main St Hartford CT 06115

VEDDER, MARION GRIFFIN, elementary sch. prin.; b. Oswego, N.Y., June 11, 1914; d. James John and Helen Frances (LaGoe) Griffin; B.S. in Edn., Oswego State Tchrs. Coll., 1938; M.A., N.Y. U., 1945; m. Ross John Vedder, Dec. 9, 1949. Spl. edn. tchr. schs. in N.Y. State, 1936-54; prin. schs. in North Babylon, N.Y., 1954—, prin. Deer Park Ave. Elementary Sch., 1959—; cons. in field. Chmn. N. Babylon Sch. Dist. Bicentennial, 1975-76. Recipient Am. Edn. award, Babylon, 1964; Disting. Alumnus award SUNY, Oswego; 1982. Mem. Suffolk County, N. Babylon adminstrs. assns., PTA (hon. life), Catholic Daus. Am. Democrat. Club: Arethusa. Author tchrs. guides, articles. Home: 108 Ketewamoke Ave Babylon NY 11702 Office: 794 Deer Park Ave North Babylon NY 11703

VEENSTRA, KATHLEEN ANNE, artist, ednl. adminstr.; b. Grand Rapids, Mich., Oct. 18, 1948; d. Melvin H. and Mildred I. (Stelma) V.; B.F.A., Mich. State U., 1970; M.F.A., Miami U., 1974; postgrad. U. Calif., Berkeley, 1971, U. N.Mex., 1979—; m. William B. Ott, Mar. 20, 1976; children—Julia Beth, William Jason. Grad. research asst. sci. library dept. Miami U., Oxford, Ohio, 1972-74; mem. faculty Nat. Music Camp, Interlochen, Mich., summers 1974, 75; instr. painting, drawing, design, sculpture and history of art Trinity Christian Coll., Palos Heights, Ill., 1974-76; instr. continuing edn. Coll. Santa Fe (N.Mex.), 1977-78; instr. art No. N.Mex. Community Coll., Espanola campus, 1977—, coordinator continuing edn. and community services, 1978—; one-woman shows of paintings and/or drawings include: Trinity Christian Coll., 1974, Calvin Coll. Fine Arts Center, Grand Rapids, Mich., 1975; group shows include: Miami U., Ohio, 1974, Wayne State U., Detroit, 1974, Nat. Music Camp, Interlochen, 1974, Appalachian State U., N.C., 1975, Moraine Valley Community Coll., Palos Park, Ill., 1976, Town and Country Art League, Matteson, Ill., 1976, Los Llanos Gallery, Santa Fe, 1976, 77, Out-of-Hand Crafts Gallery, Santa Fe, 1977; represented in permanent collection, Calvin Coll., also pvt. collections. Mem. Coll. Art Assn. Am., AAUW. Democrat. Office: 1570 Pacheco St Suite E1 Santa Fe NM 87501

VEHRENCAMP, SANDRA LEE, educator; b. Glendale, Calif., Feb. 11, 1948; d. John Edward and Dorothy Louise (Lee) Vehrencamp; B.A., U. Calif., Berkeley, 1970; Ph.D., Cornell U., 1976; m. Jack W. Bradbury, Dec. 27, 1973; children—Kristin Lee, Katrina Lee. Lectr. dept. biology U. Calif., San Diego, 1976-79, asst. prof., 1979—; cons. NIMH panel on basic behavioral processes, 1980-84. Regents summer faculty fellow, 1976-77; Nat. Geographic Soc. grantee, 1978-79; Affirmative Action Program grantee U. Calif., 1978-82; NSF grantee, 1979—. Mem. British Ornithol. Union, Am. Ornithol. Union, Ecol. Soc. Am., Animal Behavior Soc., Soc. for Study of Evolution. Contbr. articles to profl. jours. Home: 228 Winterhawk Ln Olivenhain CA 92024 Office: Dept Biology C016 U Calif San Diego LaJolla CA 92093

VEILLETTE, ELIZABETH, electronic instrumentation co. exec.; b. Meriden, Conn., July 16, 1953; d. William Henry and Norma Margaret (Dahler) Meyers; cert. Export Mktg., Quinnipiac Coll., 1977; m. Patrick Veillette, Nov. 26, 1971. Export coordinator Internat. Silver Co., Meriden, Conn., 1974-77; sales coordinator Global Specialties Corp., New Haven, 1977-79, export sales mgr., 1978-80, sales mgr., 1980—. Mem. Nat. Assn. Female Execs., Electronic Industry Assn., Nat. Electronic Distbrs. Assn. Roman Catholic. Home: Northwood Dr Guilford CT 06437 Office: 70 Fulton Terr New Haven CT 06509

VEIZER, CAROL LEE, public relations and advt. co. exec.; b. Bayville, N.J., Dec. 28, 1949; d. Joseph Michael and Ethel Beatrice (Clyde) V.; cert. photography learning systems Minn. Art Inst., 1969; B.A., Temple U., 1974, postgrad., 1976-78; postgrad. Glassboro State Coll., 1978-79. Asst. to editor Jour. Modern Lit., Temple U., 1969-75; editor mag. State Farm Ins. Co., Springfield, Pa., 1975-76; editor, publisher What's New News, Delaware County, Pa., 1976; editor Tracks Literary mag., Temple U., 1976; instr. Temple U., 1976-78; instr. communications skills Glassboro State Coll., 1978-79; mng. dir., pres. Veizer Assos., Inc., Public Relations & Advt., Winslow Twp. and Cherry Hill, N.J., 1979—; dir. Rainbow Graphics and VAI Seminars, 1981; pub. New Horizons Newsletter, 1982; freelance artist, photographer and public relations cons. Mem. N.J. Assn. Women Bus. Owners, Am. Mgmt. Assn., Internat. Entrepreneurs Assn., Nat. Sch. Public Relations Assn., Nat. Assn. Female Execs. Presbyterian. Home: 4 Buttonwood Rd Voorhees NJ 08043 Office: Sicklerville NJ also Cherry Hill NJ

VELA, REBECCA ESCAMILLA, state ofcl.; b. Mission, Tex., Dec. 5, 1934; d. Patricio and Aurora (Solis) Escamilla; student Tex. A&I U., 1969; B.S., Pan Am. U., 1974; m. Humberto Vela, July 20, 1953; children—Elizabeth Vela Huerta, Humberto, Cynthia Vela Lerma. Receptionist, dental asst. Hugo Dominguez, Mission, Tex., 1952-54; saleslady Aaronson Bros., McAllen, Tex., 1964-65; tchr. aide Mission Ind. Sch. Dist., 1965-68; tchr. Office of Econ. Opportunity Day Care Center, 1968; clk. Tex. Employment Commn., summer 1978; tchr. aide Mission Ind. Sch. Dist., 1968-69; community service aide Tex. Employment Commn., McAllen, 1969-76, employment interviewer I, 1976-79, employment interviewer II, 1979-80, III, 1980—. Leader, Girl Scouts U.S., 1966-67; v.p. PTA, 1967; pres. Mission Band Boosters, 1977-79; mem. ch. choir El Mesias Methodist Ch., 1949-53. Mem. Internat. Assn. Personnel in Employment Security, Tex. Public Employees Assn. Democrat. Home: 1000 Matamoros St Mission TX 78572 Office: Texas Employment Commission 15 S 15th St McAllen TX 78501

VELA, ROSEANNE, actress, model; b. Galveston, Tex., Dec. 18, 1952; d. Hector and Nancy (Barginear) V.; student U. Ark., Little Rock, 1971-74. Model; appeared on 15 Vogue mag. covers, 1975-81, also numerous TV commls.; actress in Heaven's Gate, 1981; nutritional counselor Internat. Health Inst. Roman Catholic. Office: 344 E 59th St New York NY 10022

VELDE, GAIL PATRICK, TV producer; b. Birmingham, Ala., June 20; d. Lawrence C. and LaValle (Smith) Fitzpatrick; A.B. with honors, Samford U.; m. John E. Velde, Jr., Sept. 28, 1974; children by previous marriage—Jennifer, Thomas. Actress, Paramount Studios, 1932-39; motion pictures include Mississippi, My Man Godfrey, Death Takes a Holiday, Stage Door; free lance actress, 1939-47, pictures include My Favorite Wife, Kathleen, Claudia and David; propr. Gail Patrick's Enchanted Cottage, children's shop, Beverly Hills, Calif., 1945-54, Gail Patrick's Enchanted Weavers, Beverly Hills, 1950-51; exec. producer Perry Mason Show, Paisano Prodns., Hollywood, Calif., 1957-66, mng. partner, 1957—; pres. Paisano Prodns., Inc., 1966—; exec. cons. The New Perry Mason, 1973-74. Sec., Los Angeles Sister City Exec. Com., 1964-65; co-chmn. Mayor's Celebrity Com.; treas. women's div. Los Angeles County chpt. Freedoms Found. at Valley Forge, 1967-68; nat. hon. Christmas Seal chmn. Nat. Tb and Respiratory Disease Assn., 1970-71; bd. dirs., mem. fin. com. YMCA of Met. Los Angeles, 1974—; co-chmn. bd. trustees, bd. dirs. Center for Ulcer Research and Edn. Found., 1977—; nat. bd. dirs. Am. Diabetes Assn., 1972-76, chmn. bd., 1973-74, chmn. pub. affairs com., 1972-76, nat. adv. council, 1979—, bd. dirs. So. Calif. affiliate, 1977—, goals com., 1979-80; mem. nat. arthritis, metabolism and digestive diseases adv. council NIH, 1972-76; mem. Nat. Commn. Digestive Diseases, 1977-79, v.p. bd. dirs. Digestive Diseases Info. Center, 1978—; bd. councilors Brain Research Inst., U. Calif. at Los Angeles, 1977—; 1st vice chmn. bd. dirs. Calif. Mus. Sci. and Industry, 1979-80; mem. adv. council U. Mid Am., 1974—. Mem. Nat. Adv. Com. for Reelection Pres., 1972; trustee Columbia Coll.; bd. regents Immaculate Heart Coll., Los Angeles, 1968-73. Recipient Woman of Year award Woodbury Bus. Coll., Los Angeles, 1950, Howard Coll. Outstanding Achievement award, 1955, Nat. Assn. Women Lawyers Justicia award, 1960, Humanitarian award City of Hope, 1961, Radio and TV Woman of So. Calif. award, 1961, Eve award as one So. Calif. best-dressed women Mannequins of The Assistance League, 1961, Woman of Year award Los Angeles Times, 1961, Businesswoman of Year award Nat. Assn. Accountants, 1962, Raven award for Perry Mason series, 1962, Mother of Year award Helping Hand of Los Angeles, 1962. Mem. Acad. TV Arts and Scis. (nat. trustee bd. govs. 1959-60, 60-61, 61-62, 62-63, nat. v.p. 1960-61, 61-62, pres. Hollywood chpt. 1960-61, 61-62), Am. Women for Internat. Understanding, Les Dames de Champagne (Los Angeles), Delta Zeta (v.p. Found. 1961-62, dir. Found. 1961-65, 68—, Woman of Year 1962), Zeta Phi Eta. Deceased July 6, 1980.

VELLENGA, KATHLEEN ANNE, state rep.; b. Alliance, Nebr., Aug. 5, 1938; d. Howard Benson and Marjorie Charlotte (Menke) Osborne; B.S., Macalester Coll., 1959; m. James Vellenga, Aug. 9, 1959; children—Thomas, Charlotte, Carolyn. Tchr., St. Paul Public Schs., 1959-60, Children's House Montessori, St. Paul, 1974-79; mem. Minn. Ho. of Reps., 1981—. Mem. LWV, Common Cause, Kappa Delta Pi. Democrat. Office: House of Reps Minnesota State Capitol Saint Paul MN 55155

VELLER, MARGARET PAXTON, physician; b. Beaver Dam, Ky., Dec. 14, 1925; d. Darrell K. and Gladys (Myers) V.; B.A., Vanderbilt U., 1947, M.D., 1950. Intern, resident Vanderbilt U. Hosp., Nashville, 1950-54; practice medicine, 1954—. Mem. Am., Miss. (com. maternal and child care 1956-72), Homochitto Valley med. assns., Miss. Obstet. and Gynecol. Soc., Natchez Assn. Commerce, Phi Beta Kappa, Alpha Omega Alpha. Baptist. Club: Pilgrimage Garden. Home: 28 S Circle Dr Natchez MS 39120 Office: Natchez Med Clinic 49 Sgt S Prentiss Dr Natchez MS 39120

VELUSWAMY, ANGAMMAL NANJAPPASARI, psychiatrist; b. Coimbatore, India, Feb. 22, 1940; came to U.S., 1964, naturalized, 1976; s. P. and Parvathi (Krishnaswamy) Nanjappasari; M.D., U. Madras (India), 1963; m. V. P. Veluswamy, Apr. 23, 1965; children—Murali, Asha. Intern, resident, Troy, N.Y., 1964-65; resident in psychiatry Clinton Valley Center, Pontiac, Mich., 1966-69; staff psychiatrist Clinton Valley Center, Pontiac, 1969-76; chief substance abuse program VA Hosp., Allen Park, Mich., 1976-78; pvt. practice psychiatry, Southfield, Mich., Mount Clemens, Mich., 1978—; mem. staff Kingswood Hosp., Ferndale, Mich., St. Joseph Hosp., Mount Clemens. Mem. Am. Psychiat. Assn., Mich. Psychiat. Assn., Mich. Neuropsychiat. Hosp. and Clin. Physicians (pres. 1978-79). Home: 2150 Shore Hill West Bloomfield MI 48033 Office: 30161 Southfield Rd Southfield MI 48076

VENAAS, GLADYS ADELINE, nurse; b. Badger, Minn., Jan. 28, 1919; d. Alfred and Louise (Jacobson) Anderson; A.S., Anoka Ramsey Community Coll., 1976; L.P.N., Alexandria Area Tech. Sch., 1972; m. Oliver J. Venaas, Dec. 31, 1937 (1969); children—Shirley Sunsten, Meridel Sherwood, Thomas Venaas, Roderick. Nursing asst. Roseau Area Hosp., 1955-62; receptionist Harris Dental Clinic Roseau, 1962-71; nurse Roseau Area Hosp., 1972-74, staff supr., 1976-78, nursing care supr. Long Term Care Unit, 1978—. Del., Farmers Union Action Com., 1955; chmn. Rose Ladies Aid; tchr. Rose Lutheran Ch.; pres. Dorcas Circle, Lutheran Ch., also chmn. and tchr.; leader 4-H Club. Home: Box 75 Rt 1 Roseau MN 56751 Office: Roseau Area Hosp Long Term Care Unit Roseau MN 56751

VENABLE, NELL SMITH (MRS. AUSTIN L. VENABLE), ret. educator, clubwoman; b. Butler County, Ala., Nov. 24, 1904; d. William Ward and Elizabeth (Presley) Smith; B.A., U. Ala., 1930; M.A., Vanderbilt U., 1953; m. Austin L. Venable, Dec. 21, 1930. Instr. Coll. of Ozarks, 1943; tchr. Sidney Lanier High Sch., Montgomery, Ala., 1955-72. Mem. Nat., Ala. (v.p. social studies dept. 1958-60), Montgomery (curriculum steering com. 1959-61, chmn. high sch. div. 1959-60) edn. assns., AAUW (exec. bd. 1955-59), Montgomery County Joint Legislative Council (pres. 1955-57), D.A.R. (corr. sec. 1960-64, chaplain 1973-76, Ala. officers' club 1974-80, historian), Nat., Ala., Montgomery ret. classroom tchrs. assns., Old South Hist. Soc. (corr. sec. 1961-62, 64-66), English-Speaking Union, Mortar Bd., Phi Beta Kappa. Episcopalian. Home: Hickory Hill 753 Old Jasmine Rd Wetumpka AL 36092

VENDLER, HELEN HENNESSY, educator; b. Boston, Apr. 30, 1933; d. George and Helen (Conway) Hennessy; A.B., Emmanuel Coll., 1954; Ph.D., Harvard, 1960; Ph.D. (hon.), U. Oslo; D.Litt. (hon.), Smith Coll., Kenyon Coll.; 1 son, David. Instr., Cornell U., Ithaca, N.Y., 1960-63; lectr. Swarthmore (Pa.) Coll. and Haverford (Pa.) Coll., 1963-64; asst. prof. Smith Coll., Northampton, Mass., 1964-66; asso. prof. Boston U., 1966-68, prof., 1968—; Fulbright lectr. U. Bordeaux (France), 1968-69; vis. prof. Harvard U., 1981—; reviewer N.Y. Times Book Review, 1968—; poetry critic New Yorker, 1978—. Fulbright fellow, 1954; Guggenheim fellow, 1971-72; Am. Council Learned Socs. fellow, 1971-72; AAUW fellow, 1959; Nat. Endowment Humanities fellow, 1980; Overseas fellow Churchill Coll., Cambridge, 1980; recipient Lowell prize, 1969, Explicator prize, 1969, award Nat. Inst. Arts and Letters, 1975; Nat. Book Critics Circle award, 1980, 81. Mem. MLA (exec. council 1972-75, pres. 1980), English Inst. (trustee 1977—), Am. Acad. Arts and Scis., Phi Beta Kappa. Author: Yeats's Vision and the Later Plays, 1963; On Extended Wings: Wallace Stevens' Longer Poems, 1969; The Poetry of George Herbert, 1975; Part of Nature, Part of Us, 1980; The Odes of John Keats, 1983. Home: 16 A Still St Brookline MA 02146

Office: 236 Bay State Rd Boston MA 02215 also Warren House Harvard U Cambridge MA 02138

VENNARD, PENNY BAKER, psychotherapist; b. Atlantic City, N.J., June 14, 1945; d. Seth Noel and Geraldine (Sullivan) Baker; B.A., Jackson Coll. Tufts U., 1967; M.S.W., Rutgers U., 1979; 1 son, Christopher. With anti poverty programs, Charleston, S.C. and Newark, 1967-70; developer Community Day Care Program, Newark, 1971-74; inter psychotherapist Pequannock Valley Mental Health Center, Pompton Plains, N.J., 1978-79; pvt. practice psychotherapy specializing in family and individual therapy, Morristown, N.J., 1979—; clin. social worker Child Study Team, Randolph, N.J., 1979—; mental health profl. emergency psychiat. services Morristown Meml. Hosp., 1979—; co-dir. Family and Mgmt. Relocation Assos., Morristown, 1980—; cons. N.J. Div. Youth and Family Services, 1976-78. Pres., Morris Area NOW, 1974-75. Mem. Nat. Assn. Social Workers, N.J. Assn. Sch. Social Workers, Nat. Humanist Assn. Home: 33 Hill St Morristown NJ 07960 Office: Office Instruction Randolph Child Study Team Schoolhouse Rd Randolph NJ

VENNING, ELEANOR HILL, ret. biochemist; b. Montreal, Que., Can., Mar. 16, 1900; d. George William and Elsie Annette (Kent) Hill; B.A., McGill U., Montreal, 1920, M.S.C., 1921, Ph.D. in Exptl. Medicine, 1933; m. E. A. Venning, June 29, 1929. Assoc. prof. exptl. medicine McGill U., 1950-60, prof., 1960-65; dir. endocrine labs. Royal Victoria Hosp., Montreal, 1950-65. Fellow Royal Soc. Can.; emeritus mem. Can. Soc. Biochemistry, Can. Soc. Physiology, Endocrine Soc. U.S. (Fred Comad Koch award 1962), N.Y. Acad. Scis., Can. Soc. Endocrinology and Metabolism. Contbr. chpts., numerous articles to profl. publs.

VENRICK, ELIZABETH LOUISE, oceanographer; b. Chgo., May 21, 1941; d. Charles Franklin and Louise (Morin) V.; B.A., Pomona Coll., 1962; Ph.D. in Marine Ecology, Scripps Inst. Oceanography, 1969. Research oceanographer, lectr. Scripps Inst. Oceanography, La Jolla, Calif., 1969—; mem. Calif. Fish & Game Commn., 1976—, pres., 1980; mem. Nat. Marine Sanctuary Regional Resource Evaluation Team, 1982. Mem. Pacific Fishery Mgmt. Council, Am. Soc. Limnology and Oceanography. Contbr. numerous articles in field. Home: 2159 Glasgow St Cardiff CA 92007 Office: A-001 Scripps Institution of Oceanography La Jolla CA 92093

VENTRESCA, DIANE ROSE, permuthane chem. co. exec.; b. Lynn, Mass., May 29, 1948; d. John H. and Barbara (DeVoe) VenTresca; student Sch. Design, Bryant Coll. Bus., N.Y. Sch. Interior Design, Harvard U. Extension. Owner, Van Tresca Career Schs. for Women, Marblehead, Mass., 1966-71; devel. stylist United Finish Co., Peabody, Mass., 1968-74; dir. new product devel. and design Center Permuthane Worldwide div. Beatrice Foods Co., Peabody, 1974—; cons. maj. cos. for plastics application devel. and mktg. Instr. CPR ARC. Mem. Color Mktg. Assn. U.S. (chmn. com.), Internat. Color Authority, Am. Color Assn., Detroit Color Council, Footwear Industries Am., Internat. Platform Assn., Smithsonian Instn., House and Garden Mag. (profl. mem.). Contbr. articles to trade jours. and mags. Office: 13 Corwin St Peabody MA 01960

VENTURA, ANGELITA DIMAGUILA, social worker; b. Manila, Oct. 12, 1936; came to U.S., 1958, naturalized, 1974; d. Leonardo Abella and Luz Carmona (Polistico) Dimaguila; B.Social Work, Centro Escolar U., Manila, 1957; M.S.W. (scholar 1958-60), Adelphi Coll., N.Y., 1960; m. Abraham M. Ventura, Sept. 3, 1963; children—Sharon, Faith, Roderick, Stephen. Social worker Salvation Army Family Service, S.I., N.Y., 1960-74; dir. Family Counselling Service, Manila, 1962-63; asso. prof. Centro Escolar U., Manila, 1962-63; dir. Child and Family Welfare Service, Richmond Home Needs, S.I., 1974-76, developer Homemaker Service in the Prevention of Juvenile Justice System, 1975-76; social worker Mount Loretto, S.I., 1976-78, N.Y.C. Bd. Edn., Student Support Services, S.I., 1979—. Trustee, Love Mission, N.Y.C., 1976—; mem. com. on aging S.I. Community Chest and Council, 1960-62, mem. com. on child abuse and neglect, 1965-68. Cert. social worker, N.Y. Mem. Acad. Cert. Social Workers, Nat. Assn. Social Workers. Home: 17 Middle Loop Rd Staten Island NY 10308 Office: 211 Daniel Low Terr Staten Island NY 10301

VENUTOLO, ELISABETH CHARLOTTE (MRS. FELIX J. VENUTOLO), physician; b. Barmen, Germany, Aug. 16, 1923; came to U.S., 1953, naturalized, 1962; d. Paul H. and Felicitas (Möller) Willemsen; Abitur, U. Hamburg Med. Sch., Germany, 1946-50; M.D., U. Munich, 1950; m. Felix J. Venutolo, Jan. 31, 1959 (div. 1979); children—Elisabeth, Felicia, Maria, Catherine. Intern, U. Hosp., Hamburg, 1950-52, resident, 1952-56; practice medicine specializing in ophthalmology, Paramus, N.J., 1961—; mem. staff Newark Eye, Ear, Nose and Throat Infirmary, Bergen Pines Hosp., Paramus. Mem. AMA, Bergen County Med. Soc., Am. Med. Women's Assn. Address: 410 Farview Ave Paramus NJ 07652

VEON, DOROTHY HELENE, educator; b. Oxford, Nebr., May 31, 1914; d. John B. and Ella V. (Robertson) V.; B.Sc., U. Nebr., 1935; M.A., George Washington U., 1939; Ed.D., Columbia U., 1947; M. Med. Sci. (fellow), Tulane U., 1969. Asst. prof. edn. dept. George Washington U., Washington, 1941-50; prof. edn. Pa. State U., Phila., 1950-66; asst. dir. Sch. of Nursing, Thomas Jefferson U., Phila., 1966-68; vis. prof. Ariz. State U., 1959-60, Drexel U., Phila., 1973-74, Temple U., Phila., 1974-75; ednl. and bus. cons., Phila., 1972—; prof., dir. div. econs. and bus. adminstrn. Community Coll. Phila., 1976—; vis. prof. U. Vt., summer 1966, Bradley U., summers 1956-58, U. Oreg., summer 1964. Bd. dirs. Va. Guildersleeve Internat. Found. for Univ. Women, 1982—. Recipient Nat. Research award Delta Pi Epsilon, 1949. Mem. AAUW (v.p. Pa. div. 1964-66), Am. Acad. Natural Scis., Am. Mgmt. Assn., Am. Mktg. Assn., Am. Bus. Communications Assn. (v.p. 1962-65, nat. fellow 1970), Internat. Soc. Bus. Edn. (pres. 1958-60), Am. Econ. Assn., World Affairs Council Phila., Phila. Mus. Art, Kappa Delta (province pres. 1948-50, 62-64, 70-72), Phi Delta Gamma, Pi Omega Pi, Am. Acctg. Assn. Republican. Episcopalian. Editor Am. Bus. Edn. Home: 2200 Benjamin Franklin Pkwy Philadelphia PA 19130 Office: 34 S 11th St Philadelphia PA 19107

VERDON, GWEN (GWYNETH EVELYN), actress, dancer, choreographer; b. Los Angeles, Jan. 13, 1925; d. Joseph William and Gertrude (Standring) V.; ed. pub. schs.; m. James Henaghan, 1942 (div. June 1947); children—James O'Farrell, Nicole; m. 2d, Robert Louis Fosse, Apr. 3, 1960 (div.). Broadway debut in Alive and Kicking, 1950; appeared in musical plays including Can Can, 1953-54, Damn Yankees 1955-56, New Girl in Town, 1957; appeared motion picture Damn Yankees, 1958, On The Riviera, 1951; David and Bathsheba, 1952; appeared in play Sweet Charity, 1966; star play Chicago, N.Y.C., 1975; staged musical Dancin, also acted as dance mistress. Bd. dirs. Postgrad. Center for Mental Health. Recipient Donaldson award for acting and dancing, Lambs Gambol award for acting; Grammy award, 1959; Silver Bowl award Dance Mag., 1961; Antoinette Perry award for Can Can, 1954, Damn Yankees, 1956, New Girl in Town, 1958, Red Head, musical, 1959. Office: care Shapiro Taxon and Kopell 1180 Ave of Americas New York NY 10036

VERDY, VIOLETTE, ballerina; b. Pont-L'Abbe, France, Dec. 1, 1933; d. Renan and Jeanne (Chateaureynaud) Guillerm; ed. in Paris; L.H.D. (hon.), Skidmore Coll., 1971. With Ballet des Champs Elysees, 1945-51, Ballet de Paris de Roland Petit; headed London Festival Ballet on tour U.S.; appeared La Scala, Milan, 1955-56, also Ballet Rambert Co., Eng., Am. Ballet Theatre on tour U.S., Europe and Iron Curtain countries, 1957-58; prin. ballerina N.Y. City Ballet, 1958-77; dir. Paris Opera Ballet, 1977-80; artistic dir. Boston Ballet, 1980—; guest ballerina Royal Ballet, 1958; guest appearances include Munich, Stuttgart opera ballets, Jacob's Pillow Festival, others; roles include Miss Julie, Cinderalla, Sleeping Beauty, Nutcracker, Romeo and Juliette, Carmen, Giselle; movie roles in Ballerina, 1948, The Glass Slipper, 1954; TV appearances in U.S., Eng., France, Belgium, Germany. Recipient Silver Medallion award Annual Dance Mag., 1968; decorated chevalier de l'Ordre et Lettres (France), 1971. Office: care Boston Ballet 553 Tremont St Boston MA 02116

VERE, MARY A., mfg. co. exec.; b. N.Y.C., Sept. 21, 1945; d. Victor J. and Dorothy (Pigowski) Iorizzo; B.A., Queens Coll., 1967; J.D., Rutgers U., Newark, 1980; m. James H. Vere, Jan. 8, 1965; children—Kimberley, James P. Chemist, package coordinator E.R. Squibb & Sons, New Brunswick, N.J., 1967-69; package engr. Bristol Myers Products Co., Hillside, N.J., 1969-72; sr. package engr., mgr. Lehn & Fink Products Co., Montvale, N.J., 1972-78; mgr. packaging, Johnson & Johnson Baby Products Co., Skillman, N.J., 1979—; admitted to N.J. bar, 1980; tech. adv. com. poison prevention packaging Consumer Product Safety Commn., Washington, 1974-77; speaker profl. assns. Cert. secondary sci. tchr., N.J. Mem. N.J. Packaging Execs. Club, N.J. Bar Assn. Republican. Presbyterian. Clubs: Flemington Health and Racquet, Hillsborough Racquet. Patentee child resistant closure. Office: Johnson & Johnson Baby Products Co Grandview Rd Skillman NJ 08558

VERESH, CAROLYN KAY, psychologist; b. Detroit, Dec. 29, 1945; d. Willard Louis and Dorothy Francis (Powell) Hart; B.A., Mich. State U., 1968; M.A., Tex. Women's U., 1971; post master's cert. (Inst. scholar) Merrill-Palmer Inst., 1977; Ph.D., Humanistic Psychology Inst., 1981; 1 son, Jacob Andrew. Tchr., Macomb County (Mich.) Intermediate Sch. Dist., 1972-76, also coordinator continuing edn. for youth; instr. Wayne State U., 1972-78; sr. instr., cons. foster parent edn. program, lectr. social work program Eastern Mich. U., 1976—; individual practice Counseling and Evaluation Assos., Davisburg, Mich., 1978—; cons. in field. Adj. adv. youth group Univ. Presbyn. Ch., Rochester, Mich. Mem. Am. Psychol. Assn., Soc. for Sci. Study Sex, Am. Assn. Sex Educators, Counselors and Therapists. Clubs: Rochester Jr. Women's; Deer Lake Racquet and Country. Author: Guiding the Sexual Development of the Foster Child, 1978; Communicating As Part of the Professional Team, 1979; staff writer The Reminder, 1979. Home: 312 Griggs Rochester MI 48063 Office: 12733 Andersonville Rd Davisburg MI 48019

VERHELST, CHRISTINE MICHELE, telephone co. mgr.; b. Oak Park, Ill., Mar. 28, 1950; d. Jerome T. and Patricia (Piesciuk) Gober; B.S., U. Ill., 1972, M.S.T., 1973; postgrad. Advanced Mgmt. Program, Mich. State U., 1979-81; m. Eduardo A. Verhelst, Oct. 3, 1981. Tchr. math. Niles East High Sch., Skokie, Ill., 1973-74; asst. prof. math U. Ill., Chgo., 1975-76; with AT&T Long Lines, Chgo., 1976-79, nat. account mgr., Troy Mich., 1979-81, staff supr. mgmt. employment, Chgo., 1981—; treas. bd. dirs. Imperial Inc., Chgo. Mem. Assn. M.B.A.s, Advanced Mgmt. Alumni Club, Econ. Club Detroit. Office: 10 S Canal St Chicago IL 60606

VER LEE, FRANCES ESTER, nursing home adminstr.; b. Ottawa County, Mich., Sept. 26, 1921; d. Elmer and Carrie Ardelian (Timmerman) Christler; grad. Blodgett Med. Ctr. Sch. Nursing, Grand Rapids, Mich., 1943; R.N. in Adminstr., Mich. State U.; m. Franklin G. VerLee, Jan. 6, 1944 (dec.); children—Ronald, Paul. Surg. nurse, then asst. dir. nurses Pontiac (Mich.) Gen. Hosp., 1944-65; co-adminstr. Curtis Nursing Home, Pontiac, 1966-67; adminstr. Grovecrest Nursing Home, Pontiac, 1969—; pres. bd. govs. Grovecrest Convalescent Ctr. Inc.; pres. Grovecrest Med. Nursing Research Found., Grovecrest Continuing Care, Grovecrest Leasing Co., Knarf Inc.; seminar presenter. Sunday sch. instr., organist, vice chmn. bd., treas.-sec. Community Wesleyan Ch., Pontiac. Lic. nursing home adminstr. Fellow Am. Coll. Nursing Home Adminstrs. (cert.); mem. Am. Health Care Assn., Nat. League Nursing Edn., Health Care Assn. Mich. (Adminstr. of Yr. award 1977), Oakland County Nursing Home Assn., Oakland County Nursing Assn., Wesleyan Women's Missionary Soc. Author manuals. Home: 1295 Fieldway Ct Bloomfield Hills MI 48013 Office: 121 Prall St Pontiac MI 48053

VERMETTE, CARLOTTA ROSE (MRS. JOSEPH SERGE VERMETTE), exec. sec.; b. Detroit, Nov. 30, 1944; d. Dario D. and Rosa Gertrude (Shortt) Bautista; student St. Petersburg Jr. Coll., 1972-82; m. Joseph Serge Vermette, June 20, 1964; children—Joseph Paul, Matthew Allen. Vol., Rehab. Inst. Detroit, 1959-60; with Grace Hosp., 1963-64, with St. Joseph Mercy Hosp., 1964-66; med.-surg. asst. Dr. Jaime Florez, 1972-73; med.-surg. asst. Dr. David Hill, St. Petersburg, Fla., 1973-77; med. asst. Dr. David Hubbell, St. Petersburg, 1977-78; med.-surg. asst. Drs. Bell & Bell, P.A., St. Petersburg, 1978-81; exec. sec. Park Bank of Fla., St. Petersburg, 1982—. Bd. dirs. St. Petersburg chpt. Am. Cancer Soc., 1970—, sec., chmn. public edn., 1970-74. Mem. Assn. Surg. Technologists. Home: 729 18th Ave N Saint Petersburg FL 33704 Office: One Plaza Pl NE Saint Petersburg FL 33701

VERMEULE, EMILY DICKINSON TOWNSEND, classicist, educator; b. N.Y.C., Aug. 11, 1928; d. Clinton Blake and Eleanor Mary (Meneely) Townsend; A.B., Bryn Mawr Coll., 1950, Ph.D., 1956; M.A., Radcliffe Coll., 1954; D.Litt., Douglass Coll., 1968; D.F.A., U. Mass., 1970; LL.D., Regis Coll., 1970, Tufts U., 1980; D.Litt., Smith Coll., 1971, Wheaton Coll., 1973; L.H.D., Trinity Coll., 1974, Emmanuel Coll., 1980; m. Cornelius Clarkson Vermeule III, Feb. 2, 1957; children—Emily Dickinson Blake, Cornelius Adrian Comstock. Instr. Greek, Bryn Mawr Coll., 1956-57, Wellesley Coll., 1957-58; asst. prof. classics Boston U., 1958-61, asso. prof., 1961-64; prof. Greek and fine arts Wellesley Coll., 1965-70; fellow for research mus. Fine Arts, Boston, 1965—; James C. Loeb vis. prof. classics Harvard U., Cambridge, Mass., 1969, Samuel E. Zemurray and Doris Zemurray Stone-Radcliffe prof., 1970—; Sather prof. classical lit. U. Calif., Berkeley, 1975; Geddes-Harrower prof. Greek art and archaeology U. Aberdeen (Scotland), 1980; Jefferson lectr. Nat. Endowment for Humanities, 1982. Alumnae dir. Bryn Mawr Coll., 1965-70; trustee Radcliffe Coll., 1974-82. Recipient Gold medal Radcliffe Grad. Soc., 1968; Fulbright scholar, 1950-51, Catherwood fellow, 1953-54, Guggenheim fellow, 1964-65; Am. Council Learned Socs. grantee, 1963. Fellow Brit. Acad., Soc. Antiquaries; mem. Am. Philos. Soc. (grantee 1959, 71, v.p. humanities div. 1978), Am. Acad. Arts and Scis., Archaeol. Inst. Am., Am. Philol. Assn., Soc. Promotion Hellenic Studies, Deutsches Archaeologisches Instituts. Republican. Episcopalian. Club: Cosmopolitan (N.Y.C.). Author: Euripides V, Electra, Complete Greek Tragedies, 1959; Greece in the Bronze Age, 1964; The Trojan War in Greek Art, 1964; The Mound of Darkness, 1974; Götterkult, 1974; Death in Early Greek Art and Poetry, 1979; (with V. Kara-georghis) Mycenaean Pictorial Vase-Painting, 1982; contbr. articles to profl. jours. Home: 47 Coolidge Hill Rd Cambridge MA 02138 Office: Dept Classics 319 Boylston Hall Harvard U Cambridge MA 02138

VERMIGLIO, JANICE ANNA, nurse; b. Boston, Aug. 6, 1948; d. Rocco Jerome and Hannie (Joseph) V.; A.S., Massasoit Community Coll., 1972; B.S. with honors, Southeastern Mass. U., 1974; M.S. with honors, Ariz. State U., 1977. Counselor, trainer drug and alcohol abuse Tri City Mental Health, Mesa, Ariz., 1975-78; clin. specialist behavioral health St. Lukes Hosp., Phoenix, 1978-79; asst. dir. nursing Ariz. State Hosp., Phoenix, 1980-82; instr. Mesa (Ariz.) Community Coll., 1978-79; dir. nursing Scottsdale Camelback Hosp., 1981—. Mem. Soc. Nursing Service Adminstrs., Ariz. Nurses Assn., Am. Nurses Assn., Nat. Assn. Female Execs., Alpha Nu Omega. Office: 7575 E Earl Dr Scottsdale AZ 85251

VERNADAKIS, ANTONIA OCKERMAN, pharmacologist, educator; b. Canea, Crete, May 11, 1930; B.A., U. Utah, 1955, M.S., 1957; Ph.D. in Anat. Pharmacology, 1961. Research assoc., research instr. anatomy and pharmacology U. Utah, 1961-64; interdisciplinary tng. program fellow in pharmacology U. Calif. San Francisco Med. Center, 1964-65; asst. research physiologist U. Calif., Berkeley, 1965-67; asst. prof. psychiatry and pharmacology U. Colo., Denver, 1967-70, assoc. prof., 1970-78, prof., 1978—. Recipient Research Scientist Devel. award NIMH, 1969-79. Mem. Am. Soc. Pharmacology and Exptl. Therapeutics, Am. Physiol. Soc., Am. Neurochem. Soc., Internat. Soc. Neurochemistry, Internat. Soc. Psychoneuroendocrinology. Office: University of Colorado School of Medicine 4200 E 9th St Denver CO 80220 *

VERNICK, ANDREA MERRILL, cosmetic co. ofcl.; b. Newark, Nov. 18, 1949; d. Harold David and Ada Beatrice (Lipnik) V.; B.A., Sch. Communications, Am. U., 1971. Clerical Asst. promotion dept. Estee Lauder, Inc., N.Y.C., 1971-72, dir. promotions, 1975-82, dir. promotions and coop. print advt., 1982—. Mem. Nat. Assn. Female Execs. Home: 311 E 71st St New York NY 10021 Office: 767 Fifth Ave New York NY 10153

VERNICK, SHEILA K., clin. psychologist; b. Boston, Nov. 23, 1939; d. David and Bertha (Ruby) Kunian; B.A. cum laude, Wheaton Coll., 1961; M.A., Harvard U., 1963; M.Ed., Salem State Coll., 1975; Ph.D., U. Fla., 1979; children—Robyn, David. Psychotherapist Behavioral Devel. Assos., Boston, 1978-79; mem. staff psychol. testing New Center for Psychotherapies, Boston, 1979-80; psychotherapist Bay Area Psychiat. Assos., Lowell, Mass., 1980-81; pvt. practice clin. psychology, Lexington, Mass., 1979—; instr. Framingham (Mass.) State Coll., 1979—; psychotherapist, psychol. tester F. Khajavi, M.D., Mass., 1980—. Mem. Am. Psychol. Assn., Mass. Psychol. Assn., Am. Orthopsychiat. Assn., Mensa, Pi Lambda Theta. Home and Office: 9 Turning Mill Rd Lexington MA 02173

VEROFF, AMY ESTHER, neuropsychologist; b. Hartford, Conn., Jan. 19, 1950; d. Harold and Bernice Charlotte (Lippman) V.; B.A., U. Pa., 1970; Ph.D. U. Rochester, 1976. Research asso. dept. neurology Boston U. Med. Sch., 1976-79, clin. neuropsychologist Neurol. Referral Center, 1979; asst. prof. Johns Hopkins U. Med. Sch., Balt., 1979-81; clin. neuropsychologist Casa Colina Hosp., Pomona, Calif., 1981—. Mem. Am. Psychol. Assn., Internat. Neuropsychol. Soc. Home: 3686 Barham Blvd Apt H212 Los Angeles CA 90068 Office: Casa Colina Hosp 255 E Bonita Ave Pomona CA 91767

VERRETT, SHIRLEY, mezzo-soprano; b. New Orleans, May 31, 1931; attended Juilliard Sch. Music; studied with Anna Fitziu (Hollywood), Marion Freschl (N.Y.C.); m. Louis Lomonaco; 1 dau. Frequent appearances opera houses, U.S. and Europe, also festival appearances; has made concert and recital tours, including performances in orotorio; roles include: Carmen: Amneris, Aida; Eboli, Don Carlos; Lady Macbeth, Macbeth; Dido, Les Troyens. Address: care Columbia Artists Mgmt Inc 165 W 57th St New York NY 10019 *

VER STEEG, DONNA FRANK, nurse, educator; b. Minot, N.D., Sept. 23, 1929; d. John Jonas and Pearl H. (Denlinger) Frank; B.S. in Nursing, Stanford, 1951; M.S. in Nursing, U. Calif. at San Francisco, 1967; M.A. in Sociology, U. Calif. at Los Angeles, 1969, Ph.D. in Sociology, 1973; m. Richard W. Ver Steeg, Nov. 22, 1950; children—Juliana, Anne, Richard B. Clin. instr. U. N.D. Sch. Nursing, 1962-63; USPHS nurse research fellow U. Cal. Los Angeles, 1969-72; spl. cons., adv. com. on physicians' assts. and nurse practitioner programs Calif. State Bd. Med. Examiners, 1972-73; asst. prof. U. Calif. at Los Angeles Sch. Nursing, 1973-79, assoc. prof., 1979—; co-prin. investigator PRIMEX Project, Family Nurse Practitioners, UCLA Extension, 1974-76; asso. cons. Calif. Postsecondary Edn. Commn., 1975-76; spl. cons. Calif. Dept. Consumer Affairs, 1978. Mem. Am., Calif. (pres. elect 1977, pres. 1979-81) nurses assns., Am. Sociol. Assn., Stanford Nurses Club, Sigma Theta Tau. Contbr. articles to profl. jours. Home: 708 Swarthmore Ave Pacific Palisades CA 90272 Office: Sch Nursing U Calif Los Angeles CA 90024

VERSTRATEN, CHAROLETTE, accountant, fin. planner; b. Memphis, Sept. 20, 1942; d. Aaron Loyd and Elsie Elizabeth (Asher) Richardson; student Boise State Coll., 1965-68, Grossmont Community Coll., 1973; children—Rusty Driscoll, Robin Driscoll, Quint Driscoll. Jr. acct., Don W. McDougal, C.P.A., Emmett, Idaho, 1964-67; service rep. Pacific Telephone Co., Boise, 1967-68; acctg. clk. Security Industries, Boise, 1968-69; jr. acct. Charles O. Brady, C.P.A., Boise, 1969-70; sr. acct. M. Kornfeld & Co., San Diego, 1971-73; mgr. small bus. dept. Moody & Bucher, C.P.A.'s, San Diego, 1973-79; owner, mgr. Charolette Verstraten, Enrolled Agt., bookkeeping and tax service, San Diego, 1979—. Enrolled to practice before IRS. Mem. Am. Soc. Women Accts., Nat. Assn. Enrolled Agts., Internat. Assn. Fin. Planners, Nat. Assn. Accts., Calif. Soc. Enrolled Agts. Office: 3505 Camino del Rio S Suite 220 San Diego CA 92108

VER VYNCK-POTTER, VIRGINIA MARY, gen. contractor, builder, designer; b. Chgo., Sept. 30, 1940; d. Anthony James and Virginia Ann (O'Day) DePadro; student Rosary Coll., 1958-60, Loyola U., Chgo., 1960-62, Coll. of DuPage, 1969-72; m. Ronald Lloyd Potter, May 7, 1977; children—Elizabeth Marie, Michael Anthony, John Patrick. Constrn. apprentice, draftsman Utility Engring Co., Oak Park, Ill., 1956-61; draftsman, 1960-66; color coordinator Hoffman Rossner, Lombard, Ill., 1966-67; constrn. supr., draftsman, designer De Padro Engring. Co., Woodridge, Ill., 1967-70; interior designer Brady Wyte Furniture, Lombard, Ill., 1967-68, Carson Pirie Scott & Co., Downers Grove, 1967-70; head interior designer, head dept. rehab. and remodeling House of Woods and Wovens, Lisle, Ill., 1970-74; pres., owner Archtl. Designers & Assocs., Lisle, 1974—; leader seminars. Recipient Silver Key Award, 1982, Cert. of Merit Home Builders Assn. Greater Chgo., 1981, key awards, 1982, only women builder-owner to recieve key awards for Excellence in Housing Design from Home Builders Assn. of Greater Chgo. for the categories of Remodeling/Rehab./conversions; recipient grand prize for best builder exhibit Home Show, 1982. Mem. Nat. Assn. Women in Constrn. (pres. Oakbrook chpt.), No. Ill. Home Builders Assn., Home Builders Assn. Ill., Profl. Remodelers Assn. Ill.

VESPOLI, PATRICIA ANNE, business exec.; b. New Haven, Sept. 14, 1939; d. Salvatore Charles and Angeline Marie (Ippolito) V.; student So. Conn. U., 1957-59; children—James, Anne Marie, Karin, Charles, Pamela. Dental technician, New Haven, 1968-69, 70-74; with Karp Distbg., New Haven, 1974-76; mgr. Service Scientific, Hamden, Conn., 1976-77; pres. Conn. Diagnostics, West Haven, 1977—. Mem. Nat. Assn. Female Execs., New Haven C. of C., Conn. Assn. Purchasing Mgmt., West Haven C. of C. (dir. 1979-80, 2d v.p. 1980-81). Home: 152 Lane St Hamden CT 06514 Office: Connecticut Diagnostics Frontage Rd West Haven CT 06516

VEST, MARY ELIZABETH, newspaper editor; b. Roanoke, Va., Nov. 19, 1954; d. Robert Ellsworth and Margaret (Taylor) V.; student St. Andrew's Coll., Laurinburg, N.C., 1972-74, Coll. of Journalism, U. S.C., 1976. Mng. editor Richlands (Va.) News-Press, 1976-78, Delmarva News, Millsboro, Del., 1979—; part-time journalism tchr. Del. Tech. and Community Coll., 1981—; profl. cons. sch. publs.; dir. Millsboro Hut, Inc. Recipient awards for spot news, series, and photo story, Va. Press Assn., 1977; award for layout, design, and photo series Md.-Del.-D.C. Press Assn., 1980, 81. Mem. Millsboro C. of C. (treas. 1981), Sigma Delta Chi. Roman Catholic. Home: 41 C Blue Teal Rd Selbyville DE 19975 Office: Box 665 Millsboro DE 19966

VETCHER, ALICIA, benefits cons.; b. Bklyn., Oct. 2, 1948; d. John and Irene Veronica (Gerus) V.; B.A. in English and Speech, Montclair (N.J.) State Coll., 1970. Sales rep. L'Eggs Products Co., 1973, 3M Co., 1973-76; group sales rep. Hartford Ins. Co., 1977-79; internat. benefits cons. Am. Internat. Group, N.Y.C., 1979-81, Alexander & Alexander, Inc., N.Y.C., 1981—. Mem. Nat. Assn. Female Execs., Group Ins. Assn. Greater N.Y., Screen Actors Guild, Actors Equity Assn. Methodist. Club: Toastmistress. Office: 1185 Ave of Americas New York NY 10036

VEY, MILDRED JOANE, educator; b. Pitts., Pa., Mar. 16, 1929; d. Eugene Charles and May Julia (Thunell) V.; B.A. in Math., Benedictine Coll., 1959; M.A. in Math., Montclair State U., 1970; A.A. in Nursing, Forest Park Coll., 1976; postgrad. Peru State Coll., 1963-64, U. Colo., 1965-66, U. Kans., 1967-68, U. Mo., 1969-70, Creighton U., 1971-72; postgrad. in spl. edn. St. Louis U., 1978—. Joined Benedictine Order, Roman Catholic Ch., 1948; tchr. math., art, parochial and pub. schs., Kans., Colo., Nebr., Mo., 1949-71; nurse aide St. Catherine's Hosp., Omaha, 1970-72; nurse aide Alexian Bros. Hosp., St. Louis, 1974-79; tchr. spl. edn., alt. sch. for pregnant girls St. Louis Pub. Schs., 1978—, head dept., 1978—; oil painter. Chairperson United Way, St. Louis, United Negro Coll. Fund, St. Louis. Carnegie Mus. scholar, 1943-46; NSF scholar, 1965-68; Parsons-Blewett scholar, 1979-81; cert. tchr., Mo. Mem. Nat. Council Tchrs. Math., Am. Assn. Ret. Persons, Am. Fedn. Tchrs., Benedictine Alumni, Montclair Alumni, Forest Park Alumni. Democrat. Club: Social. Home: 54A Repertory Walk Saint Louis MO 63103 Office: Continued Edn Project 1615 Hampton Saint Louis MO 63139

VEZEAU, SISTER, JEANNETTE EVA, coll. pres.; b. Rochester, N.H., May 11, 1913; d. Edward U. and Laura Ann (Richey) Vezeau; B.S., Boston U., 1948, M.Ed., 1955, Ed.D., 1960. Joined Sisters of Holy Cross, 1933; tchr. high sch., Manchester, N.H., 1937-45, North Grosvenordale, Conn., 1945-49, New Bedford, Mass., 1949-57; prin. St. George High Sch., Manchester, N.H., 1960-64; supr. schs. for Sisters of Holy Cross in New Eng., Pittsfield, N.H., 1964-67; pres. Notre Dame Coll., Manchester, 1967—; bd. corporators Amoskeag Savs. Bank, 1981—. Mem. Christian Unity Commn., 1965-71, Diocesan Sch. Bd., Manchester, 1965-71, adv. bd. Elliott Sch. Nursing, Manchester, 1968-71; exec. bd. N.H. Coll. and Univ. Council, 1967—, Council for Better Schs. in N.H., 1975—; mem. Gov.'s Commn. on Post Secondary Edn., 1973—; bd. incorporators Cath. Med. Center, 1979—; bd. dirs. NE Regional Exchange, 1981—. Recipient Woman of Achievement award N.Y. Fedn. Bus. and Profl. Women's Clubs, Inc., 1974. Mem. Am. Council Edn. Author: (with others) 10,000 Legal Words, 1971. Address: 2321 Elm St Manchester NH 03104

VE ZOLLES, JANET MARIE, home economist; b. Glens Falls, N.Y., June 6, 1940; d. Elwood Monroe and Winona Elizabeth (Caummisar) VeZ.; B.A., Usuline Bellarmine Coll., Louisville, 1963; M.A. in Home Econs. and Child Devel., U. Miss., 1973, Ed.S. cum laude, 1977. Tchr. schs. in Ky. and Miss., 63-71, 74-76; dir., tchr. Eastview Enrichment Center, Oxford, Miss., 1972-74; extension home economist Miss. State U. Coop., Benton County, 1976—. Bd. dirs. Benton County Early Childhood Edn. Center; pres. United Ch. Women, Oxford, 1976; vol. Benton County Ambulance-Registered Emergency Med. Technicians. Mem. Nat. Extension Home Economists, Am. Home Econs. Assn., NEA, Miss. Extension Home Economists, LWV (past chpt. v.p.), DAR. Address: 110 Meloy North Vernon IN 47265

VIAL, PAULA ANTONINA, constrn. co. exec.; b. Warsaw, Poland; came to U.S., 1941, naturalized, 1946; d. Mieczyslaw and Helena Vial; student U. Warsaw; m. Joseph Bernham, Jan. 17, 1973. With Kosciuszko Found., 1944; with Jonathan Woodner Co., N.Y.C., 1947—, v.p., 1952-60, exec. v.p., 1960—. Pres. Vial-Bernham Found., 1952. Named Master Builder, 1979. Mem. Associated Builders and Owners (dir.), 8th Ave Assn. Office: 660 Madison Ave New York NY 10021

VICARS, MARGARET ELAINE, research inst. exec.; b. Poplar Bluff, Mo., Dec. 3, 1947; d. Jeffrey Clifford and Velma Jean Louise (Davis) Dearing; B.A. in Econs., U. Mich., 1970; M.P.A., Golden Gate U., 1973; postgrad. paralegal cert. program San Francisco State U., 1976-77; m. Dec. 19, 1970 (div.). Bookkeeper, Royal Castle, Inc., Cleve., 1970; bookkeeper/mgr. Feiner's Inc., Ann Arbor, Mich., 1971-72; acctg. asst. Lee Wilson, C.P.A., Oakland, Calif., 1974; grant programs coordinator Calif. Coll. Podiatric Medicine, San Francisco, 1974-78; controller Inst. for Research in Social Behavior, Oakland, 1978—. Mem. speakers bur. Planned Parenthood, Oakland, 1973-74; founder, coordinator Bed and Breakfast Program, San Francisco League Women Voters, 1977-80; bd. dirs. Vernon Villa Homeowners Assn., Oakland, 1979-81, pres., 1980-81; fin. dr. coordinator Oakland League Women Voters, 1981—; mem. Hearst Castle com. Calif. State Parks Found., 1982—. Mem. Am. Soc. Public Adminstrn. Democrat. Office: 456-22d St Suite 405 Oakland CA 94612

VICK, MARIE, ret. educator; b. Saltillo, Tex., Jan. 22, 1922; d. Alphy Edgar and Mollie (Cowser) Pitts; B.S., Tex. Woman's U., Denton, 1942, M.A., 1949; m. Joe Edward Vick, Apr. 5, 1942; children—Mona Marie, Rex Edward. Instr., Tex. Woman's U., Denton, 1948-50; tchr. Harlingen (Tex.) High Sch., 1959-62, Harlingen Bonham Elem. Sch., 1958-59, San Angelo (Tex.) Sr. High Sch., 1957-58, San Angelo (Tex.) Jr. High Sch., 1950-52, Monroe Jr. High Sch., Omaha, 1947-48, Crozier Tech. High Sch., Dallas, 1946-47, Santa Rita Elem. Sch., San Angelo, 1943-45, Coahoma (Tex.) High Sch., 1942-43; prof. health sci. Coll. Edn., U. Houston, 1962-80, prof. emeritus, 1980—. artist in oil, watercolor and acrylic. Chmn., Council V, Sch. and Coll. Task Force, Am. Heart Assn.; Reach to Recovery vol. Am. Cancer Soc.; active Houston Planned Parenthood. Mem. AAHPER (dance editor 1971-74), Am. Sch. Health Assn., Nat. Assn. Health, Phys. Edn. and Recreation, NEA, So. Assn. Health, Phys. Edn. Coll. Women (sec. dance sect. 1970-73), Tex. State Tchrs. Assn. (sect. chmn. 1964-65), Tex. Assn. Health, Phys. Edn. and Recreation (chmn. dance sect. 1968-69), Tex. Assn. Coll. Tchrs., Delta Kappa Gamma. Democrat. Baptist. Author: A Collection of Dances for Children, 1970; Health Science in the Elementary School, 1979; contbr. articles to profl. jours. Home: 238 Ravenhead St Houston TX 77034

VICKERY, BYRDEAN EYVONNE HUGHES (MRS. CHARLES EVERETT VICKERY, JR.), library services adminstr.; b. Belleview, Mo., Apr. 18, 1928; d. Roy Franklin and Margaret Cordelia (Wood) Hughes; student Flat River (Mo.) Jr. Coll., 1946-48; B.S. in Edn., S.E. Mo. State Coll., 1954; M.L.S., U. Wash., 1964; postgrad. Wash. State U., 1969-70; m. Charles Everett Vickery, Jr., Nov. 5, 1948; 1 dau., Camille (Mrs. Wayne Loren Flaten). Tchr., Ironton (Mo.) Pub. Schs., 1948-56; elem. tchr. Pasco (Wash.) Sch. Dist. 1, 1956-61, jr. high sch. librarian, 1961-68, coordinator libraries, 1968-69; asst. librarian Columbia Basin Community Coll., Pasco, 1969-70, head librarian, dir. Instructional Resources Center, 1970-78, dir. library services, 1979—; chmn. S.E. Wash. Library Service Area, 1977-78. Bd. dirs. Pasco-Kennewick Community Concerts, 1977—, pres., 1980-81; trustee Wash. Commn. Humanities, 1982—. Recipient Woman of Achievement award Pasco Bus. and Profl. Women's Club, 1976. Mem. AAUW (2d v.p. 1966-68, corr. sec. 1969), Wash. Dept. Audio-Visual Instrn., ALA, Wash. Library Assn., Am., Wash. assns. higher edn., Wash. State Assn. Sch. Librarians (state conf. chmn. 1971-72), Tri-Cities Librarians Assn., Am. Assn. Research Libraries, Soroptimist Internat. Assn. (rec. sec. Pasco-Kennewick chpt. 1971-72, treas. 1973-74, pres. 1978-80), Columbia Basin Coll. Adminstrs. Assn. (sec.-treas. 1973-74), Pacific N.W. Assn. Ch. Libraries, Women in Communications, Pasco Bus. and Profl. Women's Club, P.E.O. Beta Sigma Phi, Delta Kappa Gamma, Phi Delta Kappa (sec. 1981-82). Author, editor: Library and Research Skills Curriculum Guides for the Pasco School District, 1967; author (with Jean Thompson), also editor Learning Resources Handbook for Teachers, 1969. Home: 4016 W Park St Pasco WA 99301 Office: 2600 N 20th Ave Pasco WA 99301

VICTOR, CHARLENE HARRIS, arts exec.; b. Chgo., Mar. 16, 1919; d. Joseph H. and Anna (Kahn) Harris; student Chgo. public schs.; m. Eugene Victor, Apr. 30, 1948; children—Adam H., Damon Brian. Actress, comedienne on Broadway, TV, vaudeville and night clubs, 1933-53; co-mgr. Kutay's Summer Resort, 1953-62; producer, dir. Charlene Victor Prodns., 1962-65; asso. prof. Bklyn. Coll., 1971-73; founder, exec. dir. Bklyn. Arts and Culture Assn., Inc., 1965—; cons. Syracuse U., Bklyn. Coll., Chem. Bank. Co-founder Reform Ind. Democratic Club of Flatbush, 1960, exec. com., 1960-77; founding mem. Flatbush Community Council, 1965, Alliance N.Y. State Arts Councils, Inc., 1976; bd. trustees Bklyn. Inst. Arts and Scis.; bd. dirs. Magnolia Tree Earth Center. Club: Soroptomists. Home: 65 Rugby Rd Brooklyn NY 11226 Office: 200 Eastern Pkwy Brooklyn NY 11238

VICTOR, MARY O'NEILL, museum exec.; b. Boston, Dec. 27, 1924; d. James Daniel and Mary Ellen Beatty (McLaughlin) O'Neill; student Boston U., 1943-47; m. John Victor, Nov. 25, 1971. Adminstrv. asst. to dean Sch. Pub. Health Harvard, 1949-62; bus. mgr. Girl Scouts Am., Washington, 1963; registrar Mus. Fine Arts, Boston, 1964-69; dir., art adminstr. Mobile (Ala.) Art Gallery (name changed to Fine Arts Mus. of South at Mobile 1975), 1969—. Cons. Allied Arts Council, Mobile, 1969—. Bd. dirs. Friends of Mobile Pub. Library, Mobile Opera Assn. Mem. Mobile Area C. of C. Office: Langan Park Mobile AL 36608

VICTORSON, JANET HARRIS, mfg. co. exec.; b. Pitts., Aug. 18, 1954; d. Stuart and Ina Lenore (Trosky) H.; A.A., U. Fla., 1974, B.A., 1976, M.B.A., 1979. Residence hall dir. student and staff devel. U. Fla., Gainesville, 1976-79; employee relations cons. mgmt. and tng. cons. Union Carbide Corp., South Charleston, W.Va., 1979—; exec. advisor Jr. Achievement, 1979-81. Mem. Am. Soc. Tng. and Devel., Nat. Assn. Female Execs., Am. Soc. for Personnel Adminstrs. Office: PO Box 8004 South Charleston WV 25303

VICTORY, LUANN JEANETTE, health care ofcl.; b. Mpls., May 3, 1955; d. John F., Jr., Theresa A. Victory; A.A., North Hennepin Community Coll., 1975; B.A. (scholar), St. Cloud State U., 1976; M.A. with high honors, S.W. Mo. State U., 1978; m. Donald F. Williams, 1982. Grad asst. S.W. Mo. State U., Springfield, 1976-77; dir. public relations Park Central Hosp., Springfield, 1977-79; dir. community relations and devel. Mt. Carmel Med. Center, Pittsburg, Kans., 1980-82; dir. med. staff devel. Coordinated Services, Wichita, Kans., 1982—; public relations cons. Am. Diabetes Assn.; instr. creative dramatics; TV and radio host weekly program. Bd. dirs. ARC, Pittsburg Community Theatre, 1980, 81; coordinator CPR community cert. program. Recipient cert. for contbn. to field of oral interpretation; cert. of excellence for informative speaking. Mem. Am. Soc. Hosp. Public Relations, Mo. Assn. Hosp. Public Relations, Internat. Assn. Bus. Communicators, Pittsburg C. of C. (Dir.). Editor Inner View, 1977-78, Spectrum, 1980-82, Hints for Health, 1980-82, Community, 1981-82. Home: 505 N Rock Rd Wichita KS 67206 Office: Coordinated Services 3720 E Bayley Wichita KS 67218

VIEIRA, SHARON ANN, fin. analyst; b. New Bedford, Mass., Aug. 23, 1954; d. Daniel Thomas and Norma Dorothy (McCabe) V.; B.S. cum laude in Acctg., Providence Coll., 1976; M.B.A., Northeastern U., 1977. M.B.A. intern Lauenthal & Norwath, C.P.A., Providence, 1977; jr. fin. analyst Polaroid Corp., Waltham, Mass., 1977-78, fin. analyst, Freetown, Mass., 1978-79, Cambridge, Mass., 1979-81; sr. fin. analyst Digital Equipment Corp., Stow Mass., 1981—; v.p. fin., treas. Edizioni, Ltd., Boston, 1981-82; lectr. fin. acctg. Southeastern Mass. U., 1979-81; lectr. managerial fin., mgmt. and cost acctg. Northeastern U., 1979—; lectr. communications Shirley C. Martin Modeling Studio, New Bedford, 1979—. Chmn. public support and fund raising com. New Bedford chpt. ARC. Mem. Nat. Assn. Female Execs. (dir.), Providence Coll. Alumni Assn. (treas. 1981-82), Phi Sigma Tau. Roman Catholic. Home: 226 Rockland St South Dartmouth MA 02748 Office: 40 Old Bolton Rd Stow MA 01775

VIERA, GRELA HERNANDEZ SANTA CRUZ, govt. ofcl.; b. Havana, Sept. 5, 1950; came to U.S., 1960, naturalized, 1971; d. Ary Hernandez and Odalina (Costa) Hernandez Santa Cruz; A.A., Miami (Fla.) Dade Community Coll., 1973; postgrad. U. Fla., Fla. Internat. U.; div.; children—Jose C., Francisco J. Nursery sch. tchr. Catholic Spanish Center, Miami, 1970-72; with Social Security Adminstrn., Miami, 1972—, ops. officer, Tampa, 1979-81, mgr., quality assurance officer for State of Fla., St. Petersburg, 1981—. Mem. Nat. Assn. Female Execs., Tampa Bay Fed. Exec. Assn., Fed. Safety and Health Council. Republican. Roman Catholic. Office: PO Box 21000 St Petersburg FL 33742

VIERECK, HELEN RAAZ, univ. adminstr.; b. Houston, Oct. 19, 1937; d. O.F. and Vera (Williams) Raaz; student Rice Inst., 1955, Canal Zone Jr. Coll., 1956-57, U. Tex., 1957-58, U. Mich., 1958-59, B.A. magna cum laude in English, U. Houston, 1973, M.A. in Am. Lit., 1975, postgrad., 1975-76; children—Johanna, William Frederick. Exec. sec. to Detroit dist. mgr. Nat. Cylinder Gas div. Chemetron Corp., 1960-61; real estate mgr., Fairfax County, Va., 1967-72; mgr. Raaz Property, Kerrville, Tex., 1970—; tchr. U. Houston, 1974-76; dept. adminstr. T.W. Bonner Nuclear Labs., Rice U., Houston, 1976—. Recipient commendation Internat. Red. Cross, 1956. Mem. Am. Mensa Soc., English-Speaking Union, Elizabeth Baldwin Literary Soc., Mus. Fine Arts of Houston, Rice U. Alumni Assn., Rice U. Women, Phi Kappa Phi. Methodist. Home: 5518 Ariel Houston TX 77096 Office: T W Bonner Nuclear Laboratories Rice University 6100 S Main St Houston TX 77005

VIEREGG, VIRGINIA ANDERSON (MRS. JAMES WILBUR VIEREGG), civic worker; b. Aurora, Nebr., Sept. 14, 1916; d. Charles Olaf and Minnie Marie (Isaacson) Anderson; student U. Omaha, 1934-35; B.A., U. Nebr., 1938; m. James Wilbur Vieregg, Sept. 21, 1940; children—Anne Vieregg Urick, James, William, Gretchen Vieregg Olenberger, John. Chmn., State Adv. Council Vocat. Edn., 1970—; mem. Nebr. Council for Tchr. Preparation, U. Nebr., 1969-70; mem. State Manpower Council, 1971-72; mem. Gov.'s Block Grant Adv. Council, 1981. Pres. Grand Island Bd. of Edn., 1963—; trustee Mid-continent Regional Ednl. Lab., 1971—; trustee Nebr. State Drug Abuse Found., dir. 1971— mem. external adv. bd. Tchrs. Coll., U. Nebr. Mem. State Sch. Bd. Assn. (pres. 1969-70), AAUW, PEO, Theta Sigma Phi, Kappa Alpha Theta, Delta Kappa Gamma (hon.). Presbyterian. Home: 1016 W Division St Grand Island NE 68801

VIG, ELAINE JOHNSON, state legislator; b. St. John, N.D., Sept. 12, 1920; d. Alfred H. and Irene Mabel (Shaver) Johnson; B.S. in Foods and Nutrition, U. N.D., 1940; m. Kenneth S. Vig, Sept. 4, 1942; children—Jill, Gary, Joel, Guy, Tracy, Leah. Mem. N.D. Ho. of Reps., 1978—. Mem. exec. com. Agassiz Health Systems Agy., 1979-83. Mem. PEO. Republican. Presbyterian.

VIG, KATHERINE WINTER LETA, dentist, educator; b. Hampshire, Eng., June 22, 1938; d. Leslie Watson James and Annie Murray Jean (Cowie) Dryland; B. in Dental Surgery with honors, U. St. Andrews, Eng., 1961; diploma orthodontics Royal Coll. Surgeons of Eng., 1964; m. Peter Vig, June 1970; children—Caroline, Amanda. Practice dentistry specializing in orthodontics, 1965—; cons. Eastman Dental Hosp., London, 1973-76; lectr. in orthodontics U. London Postgrad. Med. Fedn., 1973-76; clin. asst. prof. orthodontic dept. U. N.C., Chapel Hill, 1977-79, asst. prof., 1979—, co-dir. dentofacial program, 1979—, mem. oral facial and communicative disorders team, 1979—; curator Brit. Soc. Study Orthodontics Mus., 1974-76. Recipient Faculty Devel. award U. N.C., 1982. Mem. Am. Dental Assn., Am. Assn. of Orthodontists, Am. Cleft Palate Assn., Royal Coll. Surgeons of Eng., Brit. Soc. for the Study of Orthodontics, Royal Soc. Medicine. Episcopalian. Club: Overseas (London). Contbr. articles on orthodontics to profl. jours. Office: Dept Orthodontics Univ North Carolina Sch of Dentistry 209-H Chapel Hill NC 27514

VIGIL, TERRY ANNE, urban planner; b. Detroit, July 25, 1946; d. Charles Howard and Margo (Carroll) Peake; A.B., Brown U., 1968; M.R.P., Syracuse U., 1970; m. Roy Max Vigil, June 27, 1970; children—Kiara Maria, Ryan Howard. Planner, Mass. Dept. Community Affairs, Boston, 1970-72; regional planner Bur. Transp. Planning and Devel., Mass. Dept. Public Works, Boston, 1972-79; supr. State Transp. Plan Staff for Bur. Transp. Planning and Devel. in cooperation with Exec. Office Transp. and Constrn., Boston, 1979-81; pres., chmn. bd. Kidpool, Inc., 1982—; planning cons., freelance writer, 1982—; Sec.-treas. Brookline Council for Planning and Renewal, 1980-82, vice chmn., 1979-80; founder, treas. Friends of Lost Pond, Chestnut Hill, Mass., 1981; pres. Chestnut Hill Village Assos., 1974-76. Mem. Am. Planning Assn., Women's Transp. Seminar Greater Boston. Christian Scientist. Author: Citizen's Transportation Handbook, 1975; Regional Transportation Plan Guidelines, 1978; I-93 Joint Transportation Study, 1980. Home: 10 Craftsland Rd Chestnut Hill MA 02167

VILIMAS, JACQUELINE SMITH, counselor, educator; b. Chgo., Jan. 22, 1931; d. James Leo and Catherine Ann (Schaack) Smith; B.A., DePaul U., 1954; M.Ed., Boston Coll., 1972, postgrad., 1972—; m. Joseph Vilimas, Sept. 6, 1952; 1 dau., Joanna Marie. Asst. dir. Office Student Devel., Bentley Coll., Waltham, Mass., 1972-74; treatment/process cons. Community Alcoholism Services, Portland, Maine, 1972-74; program devel. specialist Alcoholism Research and Tng. Center, Framingham, Mass., 1974-77; psychol. asst. Asso. Psychologists Inc., 1976—, Therapeutic Tutors and Counseling, Westford, Mass., 1982—; curriculum devel. specialist Boston State Coll., 1977—, adj. asso. prof. psychology, 1977—; cons. J.F. Kennedy Multi-Service Center, Hope House, Inc., Steppingstone, Inc.; speaker Emmanuel Coll., U. Maine, 1975, Boston Coll., 1976—. Program leader Great Books Program, 1967-70; mem. Watertown (Mass.) Town Meeting, 1965-67. Recipient Disting. Columnist award DePaul U., 1952, 53, 54. Mem. Am. Psychol. Assn., Am. Personnel and Guidance Assn., Assn. for Advancement Behavior Therapy. Home: 67 Marlboro St Newton MA 02158 Office: 625 Huntington Ave Boston MA 02111

VILLADSEN, ALICE WILDES, educator; b. Bessemer, Ala., June 6, 1943; d. Paul J. and Susie Dell (Ray) Wildes; B.S., U. Ala., 1964, M.A., 1965; postgrad. Fla. State U., 1970-71, U. West Fla., 1971-72; Ph.D., U. Ala., 1980; m. W. Wayne Villadsen, Jr., Aug. 30, 1963; children—Mary Jacquelin, Michael Wayne. Teaching grad. asst. U. Ala., 1964-65; tchr. Mowat Jr. High Sch., Panama City, Fla., 1965-66; asst. prof. Gulf Coast Community Coll., Panama City, 1966-73; instr. English, U. West Fla., Panama City, 1975, U. Ala., 1976-77, grad. asst., 1977-78, pre-doctoral scholar, 1978-79, post-doctoral scholar, research asso. Inst. Higher Edn. Research and Services, 1979-80; div. chmn. humanities John C. Calhoun State Community Coll., Decatur, Ala., 1980—. Vol., United Cerebral Palsy, 1970-80, sec. bd., Tuscaloosa/W. Ala., 1979-80; pres.-elect PTA, Panama City, 1975-76; mem. Fla. Task Force for Cerebral Palsy Five Yr. Plan, 1975; bd. dirs. W. Ala. Rehab. Center, 1980—, others. Recipient Outstanding Young Woman of the Yr. award, Panama City, Fla., 1975; Most Outstanding Student award Program in Higher Edn., U. Ala., 1979; Ruth Strang Research award for young profls. Am. Assn. Women Deans, Adminstrs. & Counselors, 1980; H. Ray Loree award U. Ala., 1980. Mem. Calhoun Edn. Soc., Capstone Coll. Edn. Soc., Ala. Assn. Women Deans, Adminstrs. and Counselors (v.p. 1980-81), Ala. Assn. Community and Jr. Colls., AAUW, Ala. Assn. Univ. Women, Community Coll. Humanities Assn. (state dir. 1981-82), Phi Delta Kappa, Chi Delta Phi, Pi Tau Chi, Phi Mu Alumni Assn. Democrat. Baptist. Clubs: P.E.O., Decatur Civic Chorous. Contbr. articles to profl. jours. Home: 1706 Carriage Way SE Decatur AL 35601 Office: PO Box 2216 Decatur AL 35602

VILLA-KOMAROFF, LYDIA, microbiologist, educator; b. Las Vegas, N.Mex., Aug. 7, 1947; d. John Dias and Drucilla (Jaramillo) Villa; A.B., Goucher Coll., 1970; Ph.D., M.I.T., 1975; m. Anthony Leader Komaroff, 1970. Research fellow in biology Harvard U., 1975-78; asst. prof. microbiology Med. Sch., U. Mass., 1978-81, asso. prof. microbiology, 1982—; vis. fellow Cold Spring Harbor Lab., 1976-77; fellow Helen Hay Whitney Found., 1975-78. Mem. Am. Soc. Microbiology, Am. Soc. Cell Biology, AAAS, Fedn. Am. Sci., Sigma Xi. Research structure of DNA encoding brain-specific peptides; structure of DNA encoding developmentally regulated genes. Office: Dept Molecular Genetics and Microbiology 55 Lake Ave N Worcester MA 01605

VILLANI, SUSAN, sch. adminstr.; b. Bklyn., July 4, 1950; d. Jerry C. and Helen (Hartzman) V.; B.A., Harpur Coll., SUNY, Binghamton, 1970; M.Ed., Tufts U., 1971; C.A.G.S., Northeastern U., 1979, now Ed.D. candidate; m. Harvey T. Buford, Aug. 3, 1980. With Havils Jewelers, Riverhead, N.Y., 1958-71, Meenan Oil Co., Hicksville, N.Y., 1967; substitute tchr. Somerville (Mass.) Public Schs., 1971; tchr., cons. to adminstrs. Batchelder Sch., North Reading, Mass., 1971-78; prin. Hazard Elementary Sch., Wakefield, R.I., 1978—; cert. instr. Parent Effectiveness Tng., 1977. Mem. Bus. and Profl. Women and Young Career Women of R.I., North East Coalition of Ednl. Leaders (pres. 1981-83), R.I. Assn. Sch. Prins., Nat. Assn. Elem. Sch. Prins., Assn. Supervision and Curriculum Devel., Am. Assn. Sch. Adminstrs., Small Farmers Assn. So. R.I., Kappa Delta Pi, Phi Delta Kappa. Home: Route 1 Box 681 Ashaway RI 02804 Office: 67 Columbia St Wakefield RI 02879

VILLARREAL, MARIA BERTA, brewing co. ofcl.; b. Galveston, Tex., Jan. 15, 1952; d. Domingo and Carolina V.; B.A.T., Sam Houston State U., 1974, M.S., 1976; postgrad. Tex. A&M U., 1977-78. Mem. faculty S.W. Tex. State U., San Marcos, 1976-77; bus. devel. mgr. Credit Bur. Greater Houston, 1978-80; mktg. research and info. mgr. Lone Star Brewing Co., San Antonio, 1980—. Grantee for study of assimilation and acculturation rates of Mex. Ams. in East Tex. Mem. S.W. Sociol. Assn., Am. Mktg. Assn., Mktg. Research Assn., Beta Sigma Phi, Alpha

Kappa Delta, Phi Gamma Mu, Sigma Delta Phi. Home: 9579 Bowen St San Antonio TX 78250 Office: PO Box 2060 San Antonio TX 78297

VILLAZON, LINDA PROW, health care adminstr.; b. Sea Isle City, N.J., July 31, 1950; d. Robert Francis and Madelyn Elizabeth (Ciufo) Prow; B.S. in Med. Tech. cum laude, Gwynedd-Mercy Coll., 1973; M.S. in Clin. Microbiology, Thomas Jefferson U., 1978; m. J.R. Villazon, Apr. 29, 1977. Research technologist dept. med. genetics Thomas Jefferson U., Phila., 1974-75, med. technologist clin. microbiology, 1975-78; supr. clin. microbiology Roxbourgh Meml. Hosp., Phila., 1978-79; program dir., edn. coordinator Med. Lab. Tech. Program, Gwynedd-Mercy Coll., Gwynedd Valley, Pa., 1979—. Mem. Am. Soc. Clin. Pathologists, Am. Soc. Med. Technologists, Am. Assn. Allied Health Professions. Club: Sandy Run Country. Office: Gwynedd Mercy Coll Sumneytown Pike Gwynedd Valley PA 19436

VILLIS, CYNTHIA ANN, counseling psychologist; b. Chgo., July 30, 1952; d. Frank Alexander and Eleanore Marie (Paprицка) V.; B.A. cum laude in Psychology, U. Mo., Columbia, 1974; M.A. in Counseling Psychology, So. Ill. U., Carbondale, 1977, Ph.D. in Counseling Psychology, 1981. Adminstrv. asst. to dean So. Ill. U. Office Dean of Student Services, 1976-78; counseling intern Counseling and Consultation Service, Ohio State U., 1978-79, staff programming assoc., staff psychologist Office Women's Services, 1979; coordinator groups and workshops, staff psychologist Tex. Tech. U. Counseling Center, 1979-82, dir. tng., 1982—; staff counselor Carbondale Women's Center, 1977-78; intern Randolph County Community Counseling Services, 1975-76; cons. Lic. psychologist, Tex.; grantee Ohio State U. Office of Women's Studies, 1979. Mem. Am. Psychol. Assn., Am. Coll. Personnel Assn., Am. Personnel and Guidance Assn., Assn. Women in Psychology (corr. 1976-81), Assn. Women in Sci., Tex. Psychol. Assn., Am. Bus. Women's Assn., Lubbock Assn. Psychologists (sec.-treas. 1982-83). Roman Catholic. Club: Tex. Tech. U. Recreational Center. Author videotapes. Office: PO Box 4160 Lubbock TX 79409

VILLWOCK, MARY KATHERINE, psychologist; b. Barnesville, Ohio, July 11, 1913; d. John Jeffrey and Nancy Mary (Miller) Smith; B.A., Muskingum Coll., 1935; M.A., Ohio State U., 1937; Ph.D., Northwestern U., 1940; m. Arthur Eugene Villwock, June 29, 1957; children—John, Kenneth, Cynthia. Asst. Prof. Central State Tchr.'s Coll., Mt. Pleasant, Mich., 1938-39, 40-44; staff psychologist State Bur. Juvenile Research, Columbus, Ohio, 1941-42, Athens, Ohio, 1942-47; asst. prof. psychology U. Ill., Champaign, 1947-49; psychologist Whitefish Bay Public Schs., Milw., 1949-52; asso. prof. psychology Muskingum Coll., 1952-59; chief psychologist Guidance Center, New Philadelphia, Ohio. 1954-69; dir. Personal and Family Counseling Service, New Philadelphia, 1970-80, clin. supr., 1979—; pvt. practice psychol. counseling, New Philadelphia, 1969—. Mem. AAUW (pres. Dover br. 1967-69), Am. Psychol. Assn., Am. Assn. Mentally Retarded, Sigma Xi. Democrat. Methodist. Home: 243 Beaver Ave NE New Philadelphia OH 44663 Office: 219 W Third St Dover OH 44622

VILOTT, CATHERINE LAVON ELDER (MRS. L. DALE VILOTT), real estate broker; b. Oregon, Mo., Feb. 25, 1911; d. David Harlen and Edith Mae (Culp) Elder; student Coll. of Desert, 1963-64; m. L. Dale Vilott, June 25, 1932; adopted children—Lawrence G., Theodore E. Buyer, J.C. Penney Co., Anaheim, Calif., 1933-43; owner Vilotts Variety Stores, Long Beach and Whittier, Calif., 1945-60; salesman Art Katje Realty, Yucca Valley, 1961-65; owner Circle K. Realty, Yucca Valley, 1965—; chmn. San Bernardino County Solar Research Symposium, 1976—. Chmn., House Beautiful Tour, 1963-72; area chmn. San Bernardino Heart Assn., 1965, 66; trustee Copper Mountain Coll.; Hi Desert rep. to Nat. Prayer Breakfast and Symposium, 1982. Named Yucca Valley Outstanding Citizen, 1975; Most Valuable Citizen, Coll. of Desert, 1981. Mem. Bus. and Profl. Women's Club (charter pres. 1962-66, Woman of Achievement award 1979), C. of C. Club: Soroptimist (charter pres. Yucca Valley 1963-64). Home: 7465 La Vina Country Club Yucca Valley CA 92284 Office: 55379 29 Palms Hwy Yucca Valley CA 92284

VINCENT, CAROLINE CHARLENE, lawyer; b. Los Angeles, Feb. 12, 1950; d. George Calvin and Charlene (Taylor) V.; B.A., Tulane U., 1971; J.D., U. So. Calif., 1978. Corporate paralegal Lillian McHose & Charles, Los Angeles, 1974-75; admitted to Calif. bar, 1978; asso. firm Morrison & Foerster, Los Angeles, 1978-79, Rogers & Wells, Los Angeles, 1979-80; individual practice law, Santa Monica, Calif., 1980—. Mem. Am. Bar Assn., Los Angeles County Bar Assn., Santa Monica Bar Assn., Beverly Hills Bar Assn., Los Angeles World Affairs Counsel, Women in Bus., Women Lawyers Assn. Los Angeles, Main St. Assn., Santa Monica C. of C. Office: 169 Pier Ave Santa Monica CA 90405

VINCENT, CLARE, museum curator; b. Jersey City, Aug. 30, 1935; d. Harold and Lorena (Cole) V.; A.B., Coll. William and Mary, 1958; M.A. Inst. Fine Arts, N.Y. U., 1963; cert. mus. tng. Met. Mus. Art and Inst. Fine Arts, 1963. Cataloguer slides Cooper Union Sch. Architecture, 1959-60; asst. curator decorative arts Cooper Union Mus. Arts of Decoration, 1960-61; curatorial asst. western European arts Met. Mus. Art, N.Y.C., 1962-67, asst. curator, 1967-72, asso. curator European sculpture and decorative arts, 1972—. Mem. Antiquarian Horological Soc. (v.p. Am. sect. 1977—), N.Y. Acad. Sci., Furniture History Soc., Société Internationale de l'Astrolabe, Internat. Union History and Philosophy of Sci. (sci. instrument commn.), History Sci. Soc., Renaissance Soc. Am., Coll. Art Assn. Author: European Clocks in New York Collections, 1972; Rodin at the Metropolitan Museum Art, 1981; contbr. in field. Home: 326 E 85th St New York NY 10028 Office: Metropolitan Museum of Art 5th Ave and 82d St New York NY 10028

VINCENT, HELEN, editor; b. Elizabeth, N.J.; d. James Burlin and Eva Harriet (Winter) V.; B.A. with honors, Elmira Coll., 1942; student Columbia, 1940, N.Y. U., 1949. Asst. editor Your Life and Your Health mags., 1943-50; spl. editorial assignments Wilfred Funk, Inc., publisher, 1943-50; asso. editor Intimate Romances, Ideal Pub. Corp., N.Y.C., 1950-53; True Life Stories, Pines Publs., N.Y.C., 1953-54; free-lance editor, writer Pocket Books, Inc., N.Y.C., 1953-57; mng. editor True Confessions, Macfadden-Bartell Corp., N.Y.C., 1954-73, editor, 1973-75; editor True Story, 1975—. Home: 10 Mohawk Trail Westfield NJ 07090 Office: 215 Lexington Ave New York NY 10016

VINCENT, ROSE HELEN (MRS. LYLE CLEMENT VINCENT), realtor; b. San Luis Potosi, Mexico, Aug. 8, 1923; d. Carl Richard and Hortensia Minerva (Esquivel) Samuelson; came to U.S., 1928, naturalized, 1944; student (Calif. Fedn. scholar), San Francisco State Coll., 1941-42; m. Lyle Clement Vincent, Mar. 17, 1956. Bus. mgr., profl. entertainer, 1945-56; with Lyle C. Vincent, Inc., Wahiawa, Hawaii, 1956—, corporate exec., 1961—. Mem. Nat. Assn. Real Estate Bds., Honolulu Bd. Realtors, Bus. and Profl. Women's Club (pres. 1964). Home: 98-1386 Kaonohi St Aiea HI 96701 Office: 55 Westervelt St Wahiawa HI 96786

VINE, JANET DIANA, educator, author; b. Albany, N.Y., Apr. 6, 1937; d. Harold Arthur and Dora Mary (Meyer) Vine; B.A., Syracuse U., 1959; M.A., SUNY, 1964. Tchr. English, Herbert Hoover Jr. High Sch., Kenmore, N.Y., 1959-66; tchr. Kenmore E. Sr. High Sch., 1966—, chmn. dept. English, 1970—; cheerleading coach, 1959-77; sr. asso. Write Assos., 1982—. Mem. Am. Fedn. Tchrs., N.Y. State United Tchrs., Kenmore Tchrs. Assn., NEA, Nat. League of Am. Pen Women, Assn. Profl. Women Writers, The Write People, World Poetry Soc., Ky. State Poetry Soc., Pi Lambda Theta, Eta Pi Upsilon, Sigma Kappa. Methodist. Club: Kenmore Women Tchrs. Bowling Assn. Author: English: A Comprehensive Review, 1982; Discovering Literature, Reading Guide and Review Tests, 1968; Exploring Literature, Reading Guide and Review Tests, 1968; contbr. articles to newspapers and mags. Office: 350 Fries Rd Tonawanda NY 14150

VINES, DIANE WELCH, psychotherapist, educator; b. Rochester, Minn., Apr. 3, 1945; d. Howard Henshel and Edna (Steck) Welch; B.A., St. Petersburg Jr. Coll., 1964; B.S. magna cum laude, Vanderbilt U., 1967; M.A. with honors, N.Y.U., 1973; postgrad. Boston U.; 1 son, Juan Antonio. Coordinator emotionally disturbed children unit state hosp., Phila., 1967-68; instr. nursing Mt. Sinai Hosp. Sch. Nursing, N.Y.C., 1968-69; asst. dir. nursing Vista Hill Psychiat. Hosp., Chula Vista, Calif., 1969-70; chmn. dept. New Rochelle (N.Y.) Hosp. Sch. Nursing, 1970-71; part-time staff nurse Manhattan Bowery Project, N.Y.C., 1971-72; evening supr. state hosp. for emotionally disturbed children and adolescents, 1972-73; psychotherapist Albert Einstein Med. Center, Bronx, 1973-74; instr. Faulkner Hosp. Sch. Nursing, Boston, 1974-75; instr. students preparing for licensure exam. Mass., Boston, 1974-75; pvt. practice psychotherapy, co-founder Beacon Assos., Brookline, Mass., 1976—; dir. ambulatory nursing Boston Children's Hosp. Med. Center, 1975-78; asst. prof. grad. program psychiat. community mental health nursing, Boston, 1978—; White House fellow, spl. asst. to undersec. edn., Washington, 1982-83; adv. com. Mass. Bd. Registration in Nursing; co-founder sexual abuse program Children's Hosp. Med. Center, Boston, 1977, cons., 1978; psychiat. nurse cons. Criminal Victimology Cons., Inc., Boston, 1978. Active, YMCA, Germantown, Pa.; vol. activities dir. Boys' Club, National City, Calif. Recipient Nat. Research Service award, 1981; cert. psychiat. nurse, psychotherapist, Mass.; cert. secondary sch. tchr., Pa. Mem. Am. Nurses Assn., Am. Orthopsychiat. Assn., Nurses United for Reimbursement of Services, Advanced Council on Psychiat. Mental Health Nursing (Am. Nurses Assn.), Mass. Nurses Assn. (ambulatory spl. interest group 1976-78, program planner 1977-78, program planning sub-com. spl. interest group 1978), Advocates for Child Psychiat. Nursing, Am. Sociol. Assn., Mass. Sociol. Assn., Sigma Theta Tau (treas. 1966-67). Contbr. articles to profl. jours. Home: 3521 S Wakefield St Arlington VA 22206 Office: US Dept Edn Office of Undersec 400 Maryland Ave SW Suite 6402 Washington DC 20202

VINES, LOIS CELESTINE, law firm exec.; b. N.Y.C., Oct. 3, 1943; d. Loftin and Laura Emily (Felton) McIntyre; A.A.S., N.Y. U., 1978; m. Louis E. Vines, Oct. 6, 1962; children—Etiene Loftin, Deneen Merri. Sec., U.S. Dept. Agr., Fruit and Vegetable Market News, 1961-63; asst. supr. Protestant Council N.Y., N.Y.C., 1964-67, sec./editor dept. public relations, 1965-66, exec. sec. to asst. dir., 1966-67; exec. sec. to dir. devel. Presbytery N.Y.C., 1967-69; secretarial and word processing mgr. Fried, Frank, Harris, Shriver & Jacobson, N.Y.C., 1969—. Mem. Suprs. and Adminstrs. Assn. of Profl. Bus. Women's Assn., Female Execs. Inc., Legal Mgrs. Assn. Democrat. Baptist. Home: 19 Greenwood Dr Goshen NY 10924 Office: 1 New York Plaza New York NY 10004

VINEYARD, GERRY LYNN LESTER, educator; b. Monroe, La., Aug. 28, 1938; d. A.J. and Mattie Lou (Oliver) Lester; B.A., NE La. U., 1959, M.A., 1963; student Saltillo Tchrs. Coll., Mex., Southwestern Theol. Sem., Ft. Worth; m. Percy Ray Vineyard, July 7, 1962; children—William Webster, Margaret Loraine, Elizabeth. Tchr. West Monroe (La.) Jr. High Sch., 1959-61, Crosley Elementary Sch., West Monroe, 1961-62, Ouachita (La.) Parish Jr. High Sch., 1963-65, Ponchatoula (La.) High Sch., 1968-69, Natalbany (La.) Bapt. Sch., 1970-74, Madisonville (La.) Jr. High Sch., 1975-80, Covington (La.) High Sch., 1980—. Nat. Def. Act grantee, 1960. Mem. Council Exceptional Children, Assn. Children with Learning Disabilities, La. Edn. Assn., NEA, DAR (state chmn. 1972-75, librarian 1976-78). Democrat. Baptist. Clubs: Les Medames, Womans Missionary Union. Home: Route 2 Box 90 Hammond LA 70401 Office: PO Box 838 Covington LA 70440

VINEYARD, MARGARET JUNE, automobile service co. exec.; d. Hewel Jefferson and Opel Vera (Long) Stewart; student Bakersfield (Calif.) Jr. Coll., 1952-53, Long Beach (Calif.) Jr. Coll., 1967-70; m. Richard O. Vineyard, Aug. 11, 1964; 1 dau. Dist. agt. Constitution Life Ins. Co., 1952; fashion model Lakewood Agy., 1952-55; pvt. practice modeling, part-time, 1952-77; with Rogers & Assos. Detective Agy., Lakewood Detective Agy., 1955-60; owner, operator Maggies Mufflers, Hawaiian Gardens, 1964—. Mem. Hawaiian Gardens City Council, 1980—. Mem. Hawaiian Gardens C. of C., Calif. Med. Assistance Assn. Republican. Clubs: Old Ranch Tennis and Country, Downey Tennis, Sunset Aquatic Yacht. Office: 21734 Norwalk Blvd Hawaiian Gardens CA 90716

VINEYARD, PHYLLIS SMITH, maternal and child health cons.; b. Ridgefield, Conn., Nov. 22, 1923; d. John William and Alice (Thomas) Smith; student Simmons Coll., Boston U., 1941-44, U. Mo., 1945, SUNY, Empire State Coll., 1982; m. George Vineyard, Feb. 3, 1946; children—John, Barbara. Chmn., Suffolk (N.Y.) Community Council, 1977-79, Nassau-Suffolk Health Systems Agy., 1979-80; mem. council Coll. of Old Westbury, SUNY; chmn. N.Y. Statewide Health Coordinating Council; dir. L.I. Lighting Co.; lectr. and analyst on health policy UN Conf. for Women, Copenhagen, 1980, White House Conf. on Families, 1980; leader in China for family planning workers, 1977, 78, 81. Recipient Humanitarian award ARC. Mem. Am. Pub. Health Assn., Nat. Assn. Corp. Dirs., NOW, L.I. Network. Democrat. *

VINING, JEAN WINGATE, educator; b. Atlanta, Aug. 1, 1938; d. Wiley Oscar and Mildred Daisey (Rowland) W.; B.S. in Bus. Edn. cum laude, U. Ga., 1960; M.Ed., Ga. So. Coll., Statesboro, 1966; Ed.D., U. New Orleans, 1976; m. William Sitz Vining, Jr., Dec. 15, 1962; 1 dau., Ashley Jeannine. Instr., then asst. prof. bus. adminstrn. Armstrong State Coll., Savannah, Ga., 1960-69; mem. faculty U. New Orleans, 1969-81, asst. prof., then asso. prof. office adminstrn. Coll. Bus. Adminstrn., 1976-82; lead instr., program coordinator tech. communications Houston Community Coll., 1981—; curriculum devel. cons. in field. Supt. study program, mem. adminstrv. bd. Munholland Methodist Ch., Metairie, La., 1977-79; active local March of Dimes, Am. Cancer Soc. Grad. Faculty grantee Armstrong State Coll., 1964-66; grad. asst. U. New Orleans, 1975-76. Mem. AAUW, Nat. Bus. Edn. Assn., So. Bus. Edn. Assn., Mountain Plains Bus. Edn. Assn., La. Tchrs. Assn., Am. Bus. Communication Assn., La. Assn. Higher Edn., Am. Soc. Tng. Dirs., Soc. Tech. Communication. Phi Kappa Phi, Kappa Delta Pi (past sec.). Author papers, reports, tng. manuals. Home: 2827 Fontana Dr Houston TX 77043 Office: Room 126 Tech Edn Center Houston Community Coll 4310 Dunlavy Houston TX 77006

VININGS, MARY MALINDA, home economist; b. Chillicothe, Ohio, Feb. 17, 1947; d. Eugene Gail and Bonagene Elizabeth (Dunlap) V.; B.S. in Fine and Profl. Arts, Kent (Ohio) State U., 1969; postgrad. Ind. U., 1974-77. Home service rep. Ohio Power Co., Tiffin, 1969-72; elec. living cons. Public Service of Ind., Franklin, 1972-75, sr. elec. living cons., 1975-81, sr. consumer relations cons., 1981—. Publicity chmn. Johnson County Bicentennial Com., 1976. Recipient 4-H leadership award, 1975; named Citizen of the Day, Sta. WIFN, 1979. Mem. Am. Home Econs. Assn., Home Economists in Bus., Am. Bus. Women's Assn., Elec. Women's Roundtable, Am. Inst. Kitchen Designers. Republican. Methodist. Author learning package, recipes and crafts brochures. Office: 2515 N Morton St Franklin IN 46131

VINSON, WANDA MAY, youth dir.; b. Kansas City, Mo., Nov 25, 1916; d. Clarence C. and Maybelle Sarah (Prindle) Vinson; A.B., Baker U., 1938, L.H.D. (hon.), 1979; postgrad. U. Wis., 1938-39; M.A., U. Kans., 1949. Prin. Antioch Grade Sch., 1938-39; instr. social sci. Wellsville High Sch., 1939-42; tchr. social sci. and speech Wellington High Sch., 1942-45; instr. social sci. Wichita East High Sch., 1946-47; adminstrv. asst. Kans. High Sch. Activities Assn.; youth dir. Kans. Assn. for Youth, 1946—; dir. speech activities state, 1957-67, dir. student council program, 1950-56. State dir. 2 Kayette Leadership Camps; state citizenship chmn. White House Conf. on Youth; state pres. Kans. Assn. Sch. Health; trustee, Baker U. Recipient Alumni citation Baker U., 1958; nat. citations Cerebral Palsy, CARE, Meals for Millions; Wanda May Vinson Scholarship Fund established by Kays and Kayettes; Wanda May Vinson Seminar Room given to 4-H Citizenship Bldg. by Kays and Kayettes; named Kans. Woman of Yr., Cardinal Key Women of Kans. State Tchrs. Coll., 1971; recipient citation for youth leadership Nat. Fedn. of Activities Assn., 1980; Disting. Service citation Ky. Assn. Sch. Health, 1980; named to Kans. Tchrs. Hall of Fame, 1981. Mem. Kans. Assn. Sch. Health (pres. 1976-77), State Tchrs. Assn., AAUW, Pi Lambda Theta, Pi Kappa Delta, Delta Kappa Gamma (1st state v.p. 1971-73 state leadership chmn. 1979—). Methodist. Clubs: Topeka Woman's; Kansas Dinner. Home: 1200 College St Topeka KS 66604 Office: 520 W 27th St Topeka KS 66601

VIOLETT, ELLEN MCCARTER, author; b. N.Y.C., Apr. 7, 1925; d. Atwood and Ellen George (McCarter) Violett; B.A., Barnard Coll., 1946. First short story published in Harper's Bazaar, 1944; founding editor Hudson Rev., 1948; assoc. editor, critic Theatre Arts, 1949-51; author novel: Double Take, 1977; freelance dramatist for stage and TV, 1950-82, including TV shows The Lottery (recipient Single Program award NCCJ 1951), The Experiment (Emmy nominee for writing), 1969, Go Ask Alice (Emmy nominee for writing), 1973, Big Blonde (PBS), 1980; author Broadway musical Copper and Brass, 1956; author numerous off-Broadway plays including Brewsie and Willie Theatre de Lys, N.Y.C., 1955 plays for stage and TV published in 5 anthologies. Life mem. Writers Guild E. (council); mem. Nat. Acad. TV Arts and Scis. (past bd. govs.), Dramatists Guild, Authors League. Democrat. Address: 230 E 50th St New York NY 10022

VIRGO, JULIE ANNE CARROLL, librarian, assn. exec.; b. Adelaide, South Australia, Australia, June 14, 1944; came to U.S., 1966; d. Archibald Henry and Norma Mae (Gillett) Noolan; registration cert. Library Assn. Australia, 1965; A.M. in Librarianship (Univ. fellow, Nat. Library of Medicine fellow), U. Chgo., 1968, Ph.D. in Librarianship, 1974; m. Daniel T. Carroll, Aug. 20, 1977. Librarian, State Library of South Australia, 1962-63; librarian dept. repatriation, South Australia, 1963-66; librarian gen. reading collection U. Chgo., 1966-67, asst. dir. tng. program in med. librarianship Grad. Library Sch., 1969-72, lectr. Grad. Library Sch., 1968—; dir. edn. Med. Library Assn., Chgo., 1972-77; exec. dir. Assn. of Coll. and Research Libraries div. ALA, Chgo., 1977—; bd. dirs. Continuing Library Edn. Network and Exchange. Higher Edn. Act fellow, 1969-72. Nat. Library of Medicine Research grantee, 1973-75. Mem. Adult Edn. Assn. U.S.A., AAAS, ALA, Am. Soc. Assn. Execs., Am. Soc. Info. Sci. (mem. bd. 1979-82), Assn. Ednl. Communications and Tech., Assn. Am. Library Schs., Am. Assn. Advancement Humanities, Med. Library Assn., Spl. Libraries Assn., Beta Phi Mu. Contbr. in field. Office: 50 E Huron St Chicago IL 60611

VIRNICH, S. JOYCE, mktg. exec.; b. Ft. Lauderdale, Fla., Apr. 15, 1941; d. James Barney Wetherington and Bonnie Maxine (Hull) Wetherington Murphy; B.S., U. Tulsa, 1963; postgrad. Northwestern U., 1964, DePaul U., 1966; 1 son, Patrick Eugene. Leasing mgr. Apeco Corp., Des Plaines, Ill., 1963-70; regional credit mgr. Bell & Howell Corp., Chgo., 1971; adminstrv. sales mgr. Oce-Industries, Inc., Chgo., 1971-73, product mgr. design and engrng. div., 1977—; pres. Genesis Group, Inc., Waukegan, Ill., 1973-77. Treas., Lake Forest Condominium Assn. Mem. Am. Mgmt. Assn., Internat. Entrepreneur's Assn., Nat. Assn. Female Execs. Republican. Home: 1301 North Western Ave Apt 333 Lake Forest IL 60045 Office: 6500 N Lincoln Ave Chicago IL 60645

VISCO, SUSAN JOSEPHINE, ednl. adminstr.; b. East Boston, Mass.; d. Hugh and Rose M. (Sacco) V.; A.A., Mass. Bay Community Coll., 1965; B.S., Suffolk U., 1967; Ed.M., Boston Coll., 1969, Ph.D., 1973. Instr. music theory and appreciation Faelten Pianoforte Sch., Boston, 1960-65; tchr. elem. public schs., Saugus, Mass., 1967-68; learning disabilities tchr., Wakefield, Mass., 1968-70; cons. and adv. in spl. needs programming of individual psychoednl. evaluations various public sch. systems, 1968-78; tchr. of brain-damaged children Brookline (Mass.) public schs., 1969-71; vis. prof. Southeastern Mass. U., 1969, Salem State Coll., 1971-72, Lowell (Mass.) U., 1973-77; organizer and mgr. pvt. psychoednl. evaluation Psychoednl. Evaluation and Learning Center, Boston, 1970—; asst. prof. Stonehill Coll., 1971-76, dir. child devel. dept., 1971-76; asso. prof. edn. Suffolk U., Boston, 1976-78; psychologist-coordinator presch. evaluation program Medford (Mass.) Sch. System, 1978-79; dir. coll. learning program Bradford (Mass.) Coll., 1980—; guest lectr. various communities in Mass., Conn., N.H., N.Y., R.I., 1968—. Cert. psychologist, Mass. Mem. Assn. Children with Learning Disabilities, Mass. Assn. Children with Learning Disabilities, Council on Exceptional Children. Contbr. articles on spl. edn. to profl. jours. Home: 438 Essex St Saugus MA 01906 Office: Psychoeducational Evaluation Center Saugus MA

VISOS, CLARA LOIS KANDARIS (MRS. CHARLES D. VISOS), former advt. exec.; b. Wheeling, W.Va., Oct. 24, 1928; d. Louis E. and Elizabeth (Haniotis) Kandaris; student Straubenmueller Textile High Sch., N.Y.C.; m. Charles Dennis Visos, June 3, 1945; children—John, Larry, Dennis. Various secretarial positions until 1972; br. mgr. Trading Times, Inc., St. Louis, 1972-75; cons., office mgr. White Glove Systems, comml. cleaning, Kansas City, Mo., 1975-79; office mgr. R.L. Polk & Co., St. Louis, 1977-80. Mem. Nat. Assn. Female Execs., Mo. Notary Assn. Mem. Hope Chapel Interfaith Fellowship. Home: 817 Big Bend Woods Dr Ballwin MO 63011

VISSCHER, SARALEE NEUMANN, devel. physiologist; b. Lewistown, Mont., Jan. 9, 1929; d. Otto August and Sarah Rebecca (Mershon) Neumann; A.B. in Biology, Mont. State U., 1949; M.S. in Entomology, Mont. State Coll., 1958, Ph.D., 1963; postgrad. (NIH fellow) U. Va., 1965-66; m. Paul H. Visscher, Nov. 11, 1969; children—Kirby A. Van Horn, Constance Van Horn, Amy Roena Visscher, Ernst Warren Visscher. Asst. prof. entomology Mont. State U., Bozeman, 1962-67, asso. prof., 1967-72, prof., 1972—; convener-moderator symposium 15th Internat. Congress Entomology, Washington, 1976. NSF grantee, 1960-61, 64, 66, 77-79, 80—; grantee NIH, AID, Dow Chem. Corp., Rockefeller Found. Fellow AAAS, Mont. Acad. Scis. (pres. 1979-80), Sigma Xi (pres. chpt. 1975-76); mem. Am. Soc. Zoologists, Soc. Devel. Biology, Entomol. Soc. Am., Pan Am. Acridological Soc., Plant Growth Regulator Soc. Am. Episcopalian. Editor, author Aspects of the Embryonic Physiology of Insects. Contbr. articles to profl. jours. Home: 516 S 6th Ave Bozeman MT 59715 Office: Dept Biology Mont State U Bozeman MT 59715

VISSER, AUDRAE EUGENIE, educator, poet; b. Hurley, S.D., June 3, 1919; d. Harry John and Adeline Mae (Perryman) V.; B.S., S.D. State U., 1948; M.A., U. Denver, 1954; 1 son, Harry Gerritt. Tchr. 27 yrs. in S.D., 10 yrs. in Minn. and Japan; tchr. Verdi (Minn.) High Sch., 1974-81; apptd. poet laureate of S.D. by Gov. Richard F. Kneip, 1974. Mem.

United Poets Laureate Internat., Nat. League Am. Pen Women, S.D. State Poetry Soc., Nat. Fedn. Press Women, NEA, S.D. Edn. Assn., Minn. Edn. Assn., Bus. and Profl. Women's Clubs, Gen. Fedn. Women's Clubs, AAUW, Delta Kappa Gamma. Democrat. Presbyterian. Author: Rustic Roads, 1961; Poems for Brother Donald, 1974; Meter for Momma, 1974; Poems for Pop, 1976; South Dakota, 1980; Honyocker Stories, 1981. Home: Elkton SD 57026

VITAL, TINA JEAN, chem. engr.; b. Atlantic City, Dec. 22, 1953; d. Andrew and Dorothy (Clark) Vital; B.S., U. Pitts., 1976; M.S. in Chem. Engring., Lehigh U., 1979. Research asst. dept. chem. engring. U. Pitts., summer, 1975, dept. biochemistry, 1977, research asst. Lehigh U., Bethlehem, Pa., 1977-79, teaching asst., 1980; engring. intern Hoffman LaRoche, Inc., Nutley, N.J., summer, 1980; control engr. Exxon Chem. Ams., Baytown, Tex., 1980—. Mem. Soc. Women Engrs., Am. Inst. Chem. Engrs., Am. Chem. Soc., Nat. Soc. Profl. Engrs. Contbr. articles to profl. jours.

VITALE, MARY ELIZABETH, food co. exec.; b. Detroit, Jan. 13, 1954; d. Joseph and Margaret Ann (Hayes) V.; B.A. teaching cert., Hillsdale (Mich.) Coll., 1975; M.S., U. Colo., 1976. Teaching asst. U. Colo., 1975-76; with Carnation Co., 1978—, sr. group mgr., Phoenix, 1979-80, dist. mgr., Denver, 1980—. Recipient cert. of merit Wyo. Sch. Food Service Conf., 1981, Sales Mgr.'s award Carnation Co., 1978, 80. Mem. Nat. Orgn. Female Execs., Chi Omega (chmn. blood drive 1971). Republican. Roman Catholic. Club: Racquet World. Office: 2280 S Xanadu Way Suite 280 Aurora CO 80014

VITENAS, BIRUTE KAZLAUSKAS, systems engr.; b. Los Angeles, Feb. 12, 1949; d. Vincent and Valeria (Dambrauskaite) Kazlauskas; B.S. in Stats., Stanford U., 1970; M.S. in Ops. Research, Columbia U., 1972; postgrad. Rutgers U., 1976; m. Almis T. Vitenas, July 4, 1970; 1 son, Aleksas Joseph. Mem. of tech. staff-switching maintenance Bell Labs., Holmdel, N.J., 1970-71, mem. tech. staff PAR Radar Evaluation, Whippany, N.J., 1971-74, mem. tech. staff, operator services planning, Holmdel, 1974-77; supr. operator services planning, 1977-81, dept. head network project planning, 1981—. Mem. Ops. Research Soc. Am., Am. Statis. Assn. Republican. Roman Catholic. Office: Bell Labs Rm 2E606 Holmdel NJ 07733

VITTUM, MAGGIE INEZ, mfg. co. exec.; b. Lowndes County, Ga., Jan. 14, 1934; d. Leon Wesley and Chloe (Wilkinson) Coppage; student public schs., Adel, Ga.; m. Chester Alpheus Vittum, Jr., Mar. 19, 1954; 1 dau., Judy Lynne. With U. Ga. Extension Service, Adel, 1951-55, Cook County C. of C., Adel, 1955-57, Gen. Gas Corp., Camilla, Ga., 1957-59; Mitchell County clk. of Superior Ct., Camilla, 1959-61; with Credit Cons., Inc., Moultrie, Ga., 1961-70; acct. Kaiser Aluminum & Chem. Corp., Moultrie, 1970—. Fund raiser, vol. Aidmore Children's Hosp., Atlanta, 1965—, Aidmore Children's Home, Conyers, Ga., 1977—; clothing chmn. Aidmore Hosp., 1974-75. Democrat. Methodist. Clubs: Ga. Aidmore Aux. (state v.p. 1976-77, chaplain 1977-78), Moultrie Aidmore Aux. (pres. 1973-74, 78-79, trustee 1975—), United Meth. Women, Ga. PTA. Home: Route 3 Moultrie GA 31768

VIVIANO, ANN TERESA, psychologist; b. Bklyn., Aug. 26, 1952; d. Salvatore Peter and Yolanda Katherine (Lombardi) V.; B.A., Pace U., 1974; M.A., Adelphi U., 1976, Ph.D., 1979. Research asst. dept. epidemiology Columbia U., 1975-76; instr. psychology dept. Pace U., Pleasantville, N.Y., 1977—; asso. indsl. cons. Mitchell & Assos., Caldwell, N.J., 1979—; partner Behavior Resources, N.Y.C., 1980—. Pace U. research grantee, 1980-81. Mem. Am. Psychol. Assn., Eastern Psychol. Assn., N.Y. State Psychol. Assn., Assn. Women in Psychology, N.Y. Acad. Scis., Internat. Communication Assn., Am. Bus. Communication Assn. Contbr. articles to profl. jours. Co-author: Introduction to Statistics.

VIZINA, KAREN DELORES, med. technologist; b. Rock Springs, Wyo., Dec. 30, 1942; d. Kenneth Harlan and Evangeline Conception (Gold) Collier; B.A., St. Mary Coll., 1965; M.T., St. Joseph Hosp., 1966; m. Donald F. Vizina, Oct. 1, 1966; children—Brian, Michele and Monica (twins). Med. technologist St. Joseph Hosp., Denver, 1966, St. Anthony Hosp., Denver, 1966; tchr. sci. Sacred Heart Elem. and Jr. High Sch., L'Anse, Mich., 1967-69; med. technologist Baraga County Meml. Hosp., L'Anse, 1968—, sr. med. technologist, edn. coordinator; clin. teaching supr., med. lab. technician program No. Mich. U., 1979—. Mem. parent adv. com. spl. edn., Copper County Intermediate Sch. Dist., 1979-82; mem. St. Ann's Parish Council, 1980-82, 2d vice chmn., 1982-83; mem. Sacred Heart Sch. Bd., 1970-73; 4-H Leader, 1979-82. St. Mary Coll. scholar, 1961-65; Bausch and Lomb Medallion, 1961. Mem. Am. Soc. Clin. Pathologists. Roman Catholic. Home: PO Box 288 Baraga MI 49908 Office: 770 N Main St L'Anse MI 49946

VLACHOS, ESTELLA MARIA, constrn. co. exec.; b. Santa Monica, Calif., Oct. 24, 1939; d. Rudolph John and Estelle Smith (Scott) Carlson; A.A., Long Beach City Coll., 1959; student Long Beach State Coll., 1959-60; m. Emanuel James Vlachos, Feb. 19, 1966. Accountant, Smith & Smith, public accountants, Long Beach, 1959-65; auditor, tax accountant Lyons, Bandell & Bryant C.P.A.s, Santa Ana, Calif., 1965-67, Diehl, Evans & Co., Santa Ana, 1967-69; controller, C.R.S. Inc., Mikkelson Enterprises Inc., and San Bernardino Bus. Men's Assn., computerized credit reporting and collection, 1969-73; controller Griffith Bros., constrn., farming and fruit packing houses, Placentia, Calif., 1973—; controller Trans Western Airlines of Utah, Logan, 1978—. Mem. parish council, treas. St. John's Greek Orthodox Ch. Mary E. Baker Meml. scholar, 1957; Am. Soc. Women Accts. scholar, 1959. Licensed collector, tax preparer. Mem. Am. Soc. Women Accts. (pres. chpt.), Nat. Notary Assn., Taxpreparers Assn. Calif. (charter), Soc. Calif. Accts. Nat. Soc. Public Accts., Internat. Platform Assn., Smithsonian Assos. Designer computerized accounting program for collection agencies. Home: PO Box 6094 Anaheim CA 92806 Office: 181 W Orangethorpe Ave B Placentia CA 92660

VOEKS, VIRGINIA WILNA, educator; b. Champaign, Ill., May 9, 1921; d. B. Forrest and Dorothy (Wade) V.; B.S. summa cum laude, U. Wash., 1943, M.S., 1944; Ph.D., Yale U., 1947; m. William McBlair IV. Research asso. Yale U., New Haven, 1944-45; asst. prof. U. Wash., 1947-49; asst. prof. San Diego State U., 1949-55, asso. prof., 1955-58, prof., 1958-71, prof. emeritus, 1971—. Recipient Pres. medal U. Wash., 1943; Sterling award Yale, 1945. Fellow N.Y. Acad. Scis., Am. Psychol. Assn. (sec.-treas. div. I 1965-77, editor Newsletter); mem. Western Psychol. Assn., AAUP, AAAS, Nat. Geog. Soc., Psychonomic Soc. (charter), UN Assn. San Diego, U.S. Olympic Soc., San Diego Ballet Assn. (charter), Asso. Council Arts, Phi Beta Kappa, Sigma Xi, Psi Chi (pres. U. Wash. chpt. 1942-44), Phi Kappa Phi, Sigma Epsilon Sigma, Alpha Lambda Delta. Episcopalian. Club: Heritage. Author: On Becoming an Educated Person, 1957, 64, 70, 79; contbr. article to Internat. Ency. Social Scis., 1971; contbr. articles to profl. jours. Editorial bd. Teaching Psychology. Home: PO Box 877 4319 Explorer Rd La Mesa CA 92041 Office: Dept Psychology San Diego State U San Diego CA 92182

VOELKER, LOUISE FROMM, civil engr.; b. Milw.; d. Edward William and Edna (Eadus) Fromm; B.S., U. Wis., 1939, M.S. in Math., 1951; M.S. in Engring. Mgmt., U. Alaska, 1966; m. Harry E. Voelker, Jan. 2, 1942 (div. Apr. 1959); 1 son, John Alan. Tchr. pub. schs., Two Rivers, Wis., 1939-43, Ashland, Wis., 1944-45; instr. U. Wis., 1946-48; asst. prof. Elmhurst Coll., 1954-55; civil engr. U.S. C.E., Camp Atterbury, Ind., 1943; cartographic engr. U.S. Lake Survey, Detroit, 1951; geodetic engr. Tokyo, Japan, 1952-53; computer Western Electric, Anchorage, 1955-56; supr., civil engr. U.S. Army C.E., 1957-66, chief control and photogrammerty sect., Anchorage, 1958-66; project officer DMAAC Geodetic Survey Squadron, Warren AFB, Wyo., 1966-74; geodesist Def. Mapping Sch., 1974-81. Mem. Am. Soc. Photogrammetry, Soc. Am. Mil. Engrs. (treas. Anchorage Post 1965), Am. Congress Survey and Mapping, Am. Soc. Engring. Mgmt., Mensa, Phi Beta Kappa, Pi Lambda Theta. Club: Zonta Internat. (sec., v.p. Anchorage 1962-63, pres. Cheyenne 1972-73, dist. treas. 1974, pres. Fairfax County 1977-79).

VOGEL, DONNA MARIE, mgmt. cons.; b. Monroe, Wis., Aug. 14, 1954; d. Robert John and Delores Kathleen V.; B.A. in Econs., U. Wis., Madison, 1975. With unit buying control div. Sears Roebuck, Madison, 1974-75; research analyst Pres.'s Commn. on Marihuana and Drug Abuse, HEW, U. Wis., Madison, 1975; area mgr., asst. buyer H.C. Prange Co., Green Bay, Wis., 1975-78; sr. mgmt. cons. SYCOM, Madison, 1978—; mem. practice mgmt. faculty Loyola U. Sch. Dentistry, Chgo. Named Mktg. Support Rep. of Year, SYCOM, 1981. Mem. Am. Mgmt. Assn., Am. Soc. Profl. Cons.

VOGEL, IRENE SUSAN KUZMINSKY, psychologist; b. N.Y.C., Jan. 12, 1936; d. Alex and Nettie (Klein) Kuzminsky; B.A., Am. U., 1956, M.A., 1971, Ph.D., 1972; m. Leonard Vogel, Apr. 7, 1957; children—Kenneth, Jay, Dianna. Asst., Am. U., Washington, 1969, 70, 71; fellow Johns Hopkins Med. Sch., Balt., 1970-71; dir. Prince George County Drug Rehab., 1973; dir. Alcohol and Drug Abuse Program, Walter Reed Army Med. Center, Washington, 1973; asso. prof. Montgomery Coll., 1973; dir. Stress Mgmt. Inst., Bethesda, Md., 1978-80, Hypnosis and Psychotherapy Center, Bethesda, 1979—; pvt. practice clin. psychology, Bethesda, Md., 1975—; mem. adj. faculty U. Md., 1972-74, Am. U., 1978-79. Mem. Montgomery County Citizens Bd. Mem. Am. Psychol. Assn., Md. Psychol. Assn., Assn. Practicing Psychologists, Prince George and Montgomery County Soc. Psychologists in Pvt. Practice, Assn. for Advancement of Psychology, Assn. Advancement Behavior Therapy, Soc. Clin. and Exptl. Hypnosis, Am. Soc. Clin. Hypnosis, Internat. Soc. Clin. Hypnosis, Am. Assn. Sex Educators, Counselors and Therapists, LWV, NAACP, Bethesda Chevy Chase C. of C., Montgomery County C. of C. Clubs: B'nai B'rith, Hadassh. Home: 9624 Annlee Terr Bethesda MD 20034 Office: 7708 Greentree Rd Bethesda MD 20034

VOGT, JUDITH CLARA, microbologist; b. Hutchinson, Kans., Oct. 2, 1939; d. Albert and Leona Helena (Reimer) V.; registered med. technologist, Methodist Hosp., Houston, 1960; B.S., Kans. State U., 1961; M.S., Wash. State U., 1966; Ph.D., Oreg. State U., 1975. Vol., Peace Corps, Togo, 1962-64; sales rep. Pfizer Diagnoitics Co., Los Angeles, 1966-67; food chemist Petersville Pty. Ltd., Melbourne, Australia, 1967-68; tchr. chemistry and sci. Convent of Sacre Coer, Melbourne, 1968; lectr. chemistry Taylor's Coll., Kuala Lumpur, Malaysia, 1969-71; asst. prof. biology St. Francis Coll., Biddeford, Maine, 1974-75, Ft. Hays (Kans.) State U., 1975—; chmn. Kans. Med. Tech. Edn. Conf., 1978-80. USPHS fellow, 1965; research trainee N.W. Coll. and Univ. Assn., 1973-74. Mem. Am. Soc. Clin. Pathologists, Am. Soc. Mircobiology, Am. Soc. Med. Tech., Kans. Acad. Sci., LWV, Earthwatch, Sigma Xi, Phi Delta Kappa, Phi Kappa Phi. Methodist. Office: Biology Dept Fort Hays State U 600 Park St Hays KS 67601

VOIGHT, NANCY LEE (MRS. JAY VAN HOVEN), psychologist; b. Kansas City, Mo., Nov. 24, 1945; d. Paul and Leona Alvina (Schultz) V.; B.A., Wittenberg U., 1967; M.A., Ball State U., 1971; Ph.D., Mich. State U., 1975; m. Jay Van Hoven, June 27, 1975; children—Joshua, Janna. Tchr. lang. arts Ashland (Ohio) City Schs., 1967-68; tchr. English, Speedway (Ind.) City Schs., 1969; basic literacy instr. Army Edn. Center, Gelnhausen, Germany, 1969-70; individual assistance Bethel Home for Boys, Gaston, Ind., 1970-71; counselor Wittenberg U. Ohio, 1971-72; staff psychologist Ingham County Probate Ct., Lansing, Mich., 1972-74; asst. prof. U. N.C., Chapel Hill, 1975-79, counseling psychologist, 1976-79; psychologist for employee devel. Gen. Telephone Electronics, No. Region Hdqrs., Indpls., 1979-80; behavioral sci. coordinator Family Practice Center Community Hosp., Indpls., 1980—; media talk show psychologist Sta. WIFE, Indpls., 1982—; v.p. Westlake Profl. Services, 1981—; treas. Med. Splty. Disability Ins. Corp., 1982—; commentator WISH-TV, Indpls., 1982—. Chmn. housing bd. U. N.C., 1976-79; bd. dirs. Behavior Therapy Center, Indpls., 1982—. Diplomate Acad. Behavioral Medicine; cert. sex educator; cert. sex therapist. Office Edn. grantee, 1977-78, 78-80; Spencer Found. young scholars grantee. Mem. Am. Psychol. Assn., Ind. Psychol. Assn., Assn. Advancement Behavior Therapy, Am. Assn. Marriage and Family Therapists. Lutheran. Author: Becoming, 1978; Becoming: Leader's Guide, 1978; Becoming Aware, 1979; Becoming Informed, 1979; Becoming Strong, 1979; also articles. Home: 600 N High School Rd Indianapolis IN 46224 Office: 6357 W Rockville Rd Indianapolis IN 46224

VOLKERT, DORIS CAMPBELL, microbiologist; b. Youngstown, Ohio, Apr. 1, 1923; d. Frank Dickson and Frances Fitgerald (Baker) Campbell; B.S., Pa. State U., 1944; M.S. in Bacteriology, U. Pitts., 1950; m. Charles Fredric Volkert, Oct. 11, 1947; children—Fredric Campbell, Christy Campbell. Research asst. N.Y. State Dept. Health, Albany, 1944-48; research fellow West Penn Hosp., Pitts., 1948-50; office mgr. West Penn Dailies, Gibsonia, 1960-64; asso. prof. biology Monmouth Coll., West Long Branch, N.J., 1965—; microbiologist Paul Kimball Hosp., Lakewood, N.J., 1970—. Pres., North Suburban Fine Arts League, Richland, Pa., 1958-59. NASA grantee, 1960-61. Mem. Am. Soc. Med. Tech., AAUP, N.Y. Acad. Sci., Am. Soc. Microbiology, Am. Women in Sci., Theobald Smith Soc., Phi Sigma, Beta Beta Beta. Club: Monmouth College Faculty. Home: 2031 New Bedford Rd Spring Lake Heights NJ 07762 Office: Biology Dept Cedar Ave Monmouth College West Long Branch NJ 07764

VOLKERT, RUTH E., auto mfg. co. exec.; b. Dayton, Ohio, Oct. 11, 1943; d. Joseph E. and Marguerite M. (Jackson) V.; B.B.A. cum laude, U. Cin., 1979. Sec., Delco Products div. Gen. Motors Corp., 1962-75; program coordinator profl. devel. program U. Cin., 1976-78; mktg. asst. Writer's Digest Books, Cin., 1978; mktg. cons. Sanborn & Volkert Cons., Cin., 1979; dist. mgr. Chevrolet Motor div. Gen. Motors Corp., Parma, Ohio, 1979—. Clairol Loving Care scholar, 1978; Profl. Bus. Women's Assn. scholar, 1976-78. Mem. Am. Mktg. Assn., Am. Mgmt. Assn. Lutheran. Home: PO Box 396 Bolivar OH 44612

VOLKMANN, FRANCES COOPER, psychologist, educator; b. Harlingen, Tex., May 4, 1935; d. Edward O. and Elizabeth (Bass) Cooper; A.B. magna cum laude, Mount Holyoke Coll., 1957; M.A., Brown U., 1959, Ph.D., 1961; m. John Volkmann, Nov. 1, 1958; children—Stephen Edward, Thomas Frederick. Research asso. Mt. Holyoke Coll., South Hadley, Mass., 1964-65; lectr. (part-time) U. Mass., Amherst, 1964-65; lectr. (part-time) Smith Coll., Northampton, Mass., 1966-67, asst. prof. psychology dept., 1967-72, assoc. prof., 1972-78, prof., 1978—, acting dean faculty, fall 1981; vis. asso. prof. Brown U., 1974, vis. prof., summer, 1978, 79-82; vis. scholar U. Wash., Seattle, summer 1977. USPHS fellow, 1961-62; NSF grantee, 1974-78; Nat. Eye Inst. grantee, 1979-82. Fellow Am. Psychol. Assn.; mem. Eastern Psychol. Assn., Assn. for Research in Vision and Ophthalmology, Soc. for Neurosci., Optical Soc. Am., Psychonomic Soc., Assn. for Women in Sci., AAAS, Sigma Xi. Contbr. numerous articles on research in vision and physiol. psychology to profl. jours. Home: 40 Arlington St Northampton MA 01060 Office: Clark Science Center Smith College Northampton MA 01063

VOLL, SARAH POTTS, economist; b. Wilmington, Del., Nov. 13, 1942; d. Robert Curtis and Dorothy Ruth (Counahan) Potts; B.A., Goucher Coll., 1964; A.M. (fellow), Harvard Center for Middle Eastern Studies, 1966; Ph.D. (dissertation fellow), U. N.H., 1977; m. John Obert Voll, June 12, 1965; children—Sarah Layla, Michael Obert. Exec. sec. N.H. Council on World Affairs, 1966-68; mem. N.H. Ho. of Reps., 1977-78; ind. econ. cons., Cairo, 1978-79; dist. mgr. U.S. 1980 Census, 1st Congressional Dist. N.H., Portsmouth, 1979-80; asst. budget dir. N.H. Gov.'s Office, Concord, 1980-81; economist Public Utilities Commn., Concord, 1981—. Mem. budget com. Town of Durham, 1975-78; co-chmn. Jimmy Carter Primary Campaign for Durham, Lee and Madbury, N.H., 1975-76; sec. Strafford County Democratic Party, 1977-78. Nat. Def. Fgn. Lang. fellow, 1965-66. Mem. DAR (chpt. regent 1976-80, state corr. sec. 1980—), Phi Beta Kappa. Home: 4 Croghan Ln Durham NH 03824 Office: 8 Old Suncook Rd Concord NH 03301

VOLNER, JILL WINE, lawyer; b. Chgo., May 5, 1943; d. Bert Stanford and Sylvia Dawn (Simon) Wine; B.S., U. Ill., 1964; J.D., Columbia U., 1968; LL.D., Hood Coll., 1975; m. Ian David Volner, Aug. 21, 1965. Asst. dir. press and relations Assembly of Captive European Nations, N.Y.C., 1965-66; research asst. columbia Law Shc., N.Y.C., 1967-68; admitted to N.Y. State bar, 1969, also D.C. bar, U.S. Supreme Ct. bar; spl. atty. criminal div. organized crime and racketeering sect. U.S. Dept. Justice, Washington, 1969-70; trial atty. criminal div. mgmt. and labor sect., 1970-73, trial atty. strike force 18 organized crime and racketeering sect., 1973, asst. spl. prosecutor Watergate spl. prosecution force, 1974-75; asso. firm Fried, Frank, Harris, Shriver & Kampelman, 1975-77; gen. counsel Dept. Army, Washington, 1977-79; practice law, Chgo., 1979—. Recipient Spl. Achievement award for sustained superior performance Dept. Justice, 1972, Meritorious award, 1973. Mem. D.C., Fed. bar assns. *

VOLTMER, RITA KAY, educator; b. Maryville, Mo., Mar. 11, 1954; d. Evan Henry and Lucille A. Voltmer; B.A. in Chemistry, Tarkio (Mo.) Coll., 1974; M.S. in Edn., N.W. Mo. State U., 1976; Ph.D. in Curriculum and Instrn., Kans. State U., 1980. Grad. teaching asst. N.W. Mo. State U., 1974; tchr. high sch. sci., Mo. and Iowa, 1976-78; grad. teaching and research asst. Kans. State U., 1978-80; asst. prof. sci. edn./physics U. No. Iowa, Cedar Falls, 1980—, asst. prof. teaching sci. Malcolm Price Lab. Sch., 1981—. Mem. Sch. Sci. and Math. Assn., Assn. Ednl. Data Systems, Nat. Sci. Tchrs. Assn., Iowa Acad. Scis., Phi Delta Kappa, Phi Alpha Theta. Democrat. Lutheran. Author articles in field. Office: U No Iowa Dept Teaching 19th and Campus Cedar Falls IA 50613

VOM EIGEN, ANN HADLEY, govt. ofcl.; b. Worcester, Mass., July 9, 1952; d. John Albert and Anna (Clifford) Hadley; B.S., Tufts U., 1973; M.C.P., Harvard U., 1976; m. Robert P. vom Eigen, Jan. 3, 1981. Budget analyst D.C. Office Budget and Mgmt. Systems, 1976-78; analyst commerce, housing and credit Senate Com. on Budget, Washington, 1978—. Mem. Am. Assn. Public Adminstrn., Washington Women in Housing and Fin. (treas.). Democrat. Office: Senate Com on Budget Washington DC 20510

VON BEROLDINGEN, DOROTHY, judge; b. Chgo.; d. Alex R. and Anna E. (Stastny) Gundelfingen; student Northwestern U., U. Calif.; LL.B., J.D., U. San Francisco; 1 son, Paul. Admitted to Calif. bar, 1955, IRS and Tax Ct., 1955; cert. tax specialist, Calif., 1973-77; judge Mcpl. Ct., San Francisco, 1977—, presiding judge, 1982-83; prof. taxation Lincoln U. Sch. Law, San Francisco, 1959-69, prof. legal acctg., 1965-69, 1973-74. Mem. San Francisco CSC, 1964-66; v.p. Econ. Opportunity Council, 1964-66; mem. San Francisco Bd. Suprs., 1966-77, chmn. fin. com., 1967-75; bd. dirs. Golden Gate Bridge, 1975-77; mem. Gov.'s Commn. on Law of Pre-emption, 1966-67. Mem. Am. Bar Assn., Calif. Judges Assn., Calif. Council Jud. Edn. and Research (chmn. planning com.), Bus. and Profl. Women, Women's Forum West, St. Thomas More Soc., Dem. Women's Forum, Queen's Bench. Office: Hall of Justice 850 Bryant St San Francisco CA 94103

VON DAMM, HELENE A., govt. ofcl.; b. Linz, Austria, May 4, 1938; d. Josef and Helene (Pehamberger) Winter; grad. Waidhofen Commerce Sch.; m. Byron Leeds, May 6, 1981. Former Personal sec., exec. asst. to Gov. Ronald Reagan; N.E. regional fin. dir. Reagan for Pres. Campaign; assoc. dir. for Presdl. personnel, Reagan Transition Office; spl. asst. to the Pres., now dep. asst. to the Pres., dir. Presdl. personnel, Washington. Bd. of govs. USO; mem. Pres.'s Commn. on Exec. Exchange. Coro Found. public leadership trainee. Mem. Coro Assocs. Roman Catholic. Clubs: Harmonie, Sierra, Pvt. Pilots Assn. Author: Sincerely, Ronald Reagan, 1975, 2d edit., 1979. Office: White House Washington DC 20500

VONDERHEID, ARDA ELIZABETH, nursing adminstr.; b. Pitts., June 19, 1925; d. Louis Adolf and Hilda Barbara (Gerstacker) V.; diploma Allegheny Gen. Hosp. Sch. Nursing, 1946; B.S. in Nursing Edn., Coll. Holy Names, Oakland, Calif., 1956; M.S. in Nursing Adminstrn., U. Calif., Los Angeles, 1960. Head nurse Allegheny Gen. Hosp., Pitts., 1946-48; staff nurse Highland-Alameda County Hosp., Oakland, Calif., 1948-51, staff nurse poliomyelitis units, 1953-55; pvt. duty nurse Directory Registered Nurses Alameda County, Oakland, 1951-53; adminstrv. supervising nurse Poliomyelitis Respiratory and Rehab. Center, Fairmont, Alameda County Hosp., Oakland, 1955-58; night supr., relief asst. dir. nursing Peninsula Hosp., Burlingame, Calif., 1960, adminstrv. supr., 1961-62, inservice educator, 1963-69; staff nurse San Francisco Gen. Hosp., 1969, asst. dir. nurses, 1969-72; mem. faculty continuing edn. U. Calif., San Francisco, 1969-71; dir. nursing services Kaiser Permanente Med. Center, S. San Francisco, 1973-1982, asst. adminstr. Med. Center Nursing Services, 1982—. Chmn. edn. com. San Mateo County (Calif.) Cancer Soc., 1962-69; bd. dirs. San Mateo County Heart Assn., 1968-71. Cert. advanced nursing adminstrn. Mem. San Mateo County (dir. 1964-69, pres. elect 1967-68, pres. 1968-70), Golden Gate (1st v.p. 1974-78, dir. 1974-78), Calif., Am. nurses assns., Nat. League Nursing, Soc. for Nursing Service Adminstrs., State Practice and Edn. Council, AAUW, Sigma Theta Tau. Republican. Lutheran. Club: Kai-Perm. Contbr. articles in field to profl. jours. Home: 1047 Aragon Ct Pacifica CA 94044 Office: 1200 El Camino Real South San Francisco CA 94080

VONDREHLE, MARY ELIZABETH, lawyer; b. Davenport, Iowa, Apr. 27, 1950; d. William D. and Edna Elizabeth (Chapman) VonD.; B.A., Millsaps Coll., 1972; J.D., U. Tulsa, 1976. Admitted to Okla. bar, 1976; atty. Public Service Co. of Okla., Tulsa, 1976-78; gen. csl. Transok Pipeline Co., Tulsa, 1978-80; gen. csl. Dalco Petroleum Inc., Tulsa, 1980—. Guest speaker Women Unlimited Conf., 1981; Women's Law Caucus, 1981; Law Placement Symposium, 1981. Mem. Okla. Bar. Assn., Women Lawyers Assn., Tulsa County Bar Assn. Republican. Methodist. Home: 3131 E 26th Pl Tulsa OK 74114 Office: 2431 E 51st St Tulsa OK 74105

VON ERDBERG, JOAN PRENTICE, mus. curator; b. Princeton, N.J., Mar. 3, 1908; d. William Kelly and Aline Burwell (Glenny) Prentice; student Bryn Mawr Coll., 1926-27, Radcliffe Coll., 1937-39; grad. Fogg Mus. Tng. Course, 1939; m. Xaver von Erdberg, Aug. 16, 1949. Asst. Phila. Mus. Art, 1939-42, asst. curator decorative arts, 1942-43, asso. curator, 1943-46, curator ceramics and metalwork, 1946-47; chargée de mission dept. des objets d'art Musée du Louvre,

1947-49; mem. arts com. N.J. State Mus., 1955-68; trustee Historic Fallsington, Inc., Pa., 1971-75, curator, 1975-80, cons., 1980—. Republican. Presbyterian. Clubs: Colony (N.Y.C.), Present Day, Nassau (Princeton). Home: Medford Leas Medford NJ 08055

VON FURSTENBERG, DIANE SIMONE MICHELLE, fashion designer; b. Brussels, Dec. 31, 1946; came to U.S., 1969; d. Leon L. and Liliane L. (Nahmias) Halfin; student U. Madird, 1965-66, U. Geneva, 1966-68; m. Eduard Egon von Furstenberg, July 16, 1969; children—Alexandre, Tatiana. Founder, pres. Diane Von Furstenberg, Ltd., mfr. ladies clothing, N.Y.C., 1970—, Diane Von Furstenberg Cosmetics div. Diane Von Furstenberg, Inc., N.Y.C., 1974—, also chmn. Diane Von Furstenberg Studio div. Office: 745 Fifth Ave New York NY 10022 *

VON HESS, LOUISE MC CLURE, educator; b. Nashville, Dec. 11, 1900; d. Thomas Garland and Louise (McClure) Tinsley; student pvt. schs., Dobbs Ferry, N.Y.; m. Richard C. von Hess, July 20, 1972; m. J.H. Steinman; children—Louise, Caroline, Beverly. Dir., co owner Lancaster (Pa.) Newspaper, 1962—, WGAL TV, 1962—, Intell Printing Co., Lancaster, 1972—. Founder, chmn. Louise Steinman von Hess Found., Louise von Hess Found. for Med. Edn.; chmn. James Hale Steinman Found. Recipient Red Rose award City of Lancaster. Mem. Lancaster County Hist. Soc., Rockford Found., Valley Forge Hist. Assn., Nat. Trust Historical Preservation, Hist. Soc. Pa., Am. Mus. in Bath (Eng.), Winterthur Guild, Colonial Dames, Daus. of Cin., Order of Magna Charta. Republican. Episcopalian. Clubs: Sulgrave, Bath Tennis, Everglades, Lyford Cay, Mt Vernon. Instrumental in restoration: Wrights Ferry Mansion, Columbia, Pa., Am. Queen Anne collection, Sehner Ellicott von Hess House, Lancaster, Pa. Home: Conestoga House 1608 Marietta Ave Lancaster PA 17603

VON HOLT, LAEL POWERS, psychotherapist, psychiat. social worker; b. Boston, Apr. 9, 1927; d. Merritt Adams and Rea Francisca (Hunt) Powers; B.A., U. Mass., 1950; M.S., U. Mo., 1972, postgrad., 1978; postgrad. Menninger Found., Topeka, 1977-81; m. Henry William Von Holt, Jr., Sept. 18, 1954; children—Gardner, Dudley, Edward. Psychiat. social worker N.Y. Dept. Mental Hygiene, Wingdale, 1950-51, Mass. Dept. Mental Health, Worcester, 1951-54; instr., social worker U. Oreg., Eugene, 1954-59; psychiat. social worker Mo. Dept. Mental Health, Fulton State Hosp., 1973-81, Columbia (Mo.) Regional Hosp., 1977-82; with Family Mental Health Assn., Jefferson City, Mo., 1982—. Bd. dirs. PTA, 1970-74, 77-78; mem. health com. Boone County Community Services Council, 1975-76; vol. Meals on Wheels, 1972-73, 76-79; den mother Boy Scouts Am., 1968-69, 71-72; mem. by-laws com. Springdale Neighborhood Assn., 1977. Mem. Nat. Assn. Social Workers, Am. Acad. Psychotherapists, Acad. Cert. Social Workers, Registry Clin. Social Workers, Boone County Assn. Mental Health, LWV (city council observor 1976-82, chmn. local action com. 1979-80, sec. 1974-77, chmn. Observer Corps 1981-82), Kappa Kappa Gamma. Republican. Methodist. Club: Stephens Coll. Faculty Wives (pres. 1979-80). Home: 378 Crown Point Columbia MO 65201 Office: Family Mental Health Center 1905 Stadium Jefferson City MO 65101

VON OHLEN, BEATRIZ RODRIGUEZ, nurse; b. Brownsville, Tex., June 6, 1935; d. Antonio C. and Petra S. Rodriguez; A.A., Waubonsee Community Coll., 1974; childbirth educator cert. U. Tex., San Antonio, 1979; m. Alwin C. von Ohlen, June 1, 1957; children—Herman C., Mary H., Michael A., Patricia L., David L. Staff nurse med-surg. floor St. Joseph's Med. Center, Aurora, Ill., 1974; charge nurse, alcoholic counselor Psychiat. Alcoholic unit, Aurora, Ill., 1975; house supr., head nurse Brownsville (Tex.) Med. Center, 1975-76; health educator Lay Midwifery program Health Dept., Brownville, 1976-81; home health supr. Tex. Vis. Nurse Service, Brownville, 1981-82; ob supr. Dolly Vinsant Hosp., San Benito, Tex., 1982—. Mem. Am. Nurses Assn., Am. Public Health Assn., Assn. Psychoprophylactics in Obstetrics, Tex. Nurses Assn., Tex. Public Health Assn. Democrat. Roman Catholic. Home: 7426 Villa Pancho Dr Brownsville TX 78521 Office: Bus 77 San Benito TX

VON SELDENECK, JUDITH METCALFE, search firm exec.; b. High Point, N.C., June 6, 1940; d. Frederick and Harriet C. (Metcalfe) Metcalfe; B.A., U. N.C., 1962, A.A., St. Mary's Coll., 1960; postgrad. Am. U. Coll. Law, 1963-64; m. G. Clay von Seldeneck, Apr. 8, 1972; children—Rodman C., Kevin Clay. Exec. asst. to Senator Walter F. Mondale, Washington, 1963-73; with Diversified Search, Inc., Phila., 1973—, pres., 1980—; dir. Central Pa. Nat. Bank. Bd. dirs. Greater Phila. Partnership, 1980—, Pvt. Industry Council, WHYY-TV; mem. Mayors Small Bus Adv. Council, 1978—, Phila. Tri-Centennial Com., 1978—; trustee St. Mary's Coll., Raleigh, N.C., 1980—. Mem. Nat. Assn. Personnel Adminstrn., Forum of Exec. Women, Com. of 200. Democrat. Episcopalian. Clubs: Phila. Cricket, Country, Phila. Racquet, Sea Pines Country, Cosmopolitan. Home: 8124 Saint Martins Ln Philadelphia PA 19118 Office: 2 Girard Plaza Suite 1804 Philadelphia PA 19102

VON STADE, FREDERICA, mezzo-soprano; b. Somerville, N.J., June 1, 1945; student Mannes Coll. Music, N.Y.C.; m. Peter Elkus. Former nanny, salesgirl; sec. Am. Shakespeare Festival; debut in Zauberfloete with Met. Opera, 1970, now resident mem.; appeared with opera cos., including Paris Opera, San Francisco Opera, Salzburg Festival, London Royal Opera, Spoleto Festival, Boston Opera Co., Santa Fe Opera, La Scala; recital artist, soloist with symphony orchs.; appeared in: The Marriage of Figaro, Faust, The Magic Flute, Don Giovanni, Tales of Hoffmann, Rigoletto. Mem. Am. Guild Mus. Artists. Roman Catholic. Albums: French Opera Arias; Frederica Von Stade Sings Mozart-Rossini Opera Arias. Office: care Columbia Artists Mgmt 165 W 57 St New York NY 10019 *

VON TUNGELN, HAZEL (POLLY) RENDER, human services adminstr.; b. Lake City, Ark., Jan. 13, 1929; d. Sammie T. and Myrtle May (Elder) Render; student Cuzzins Bus. Sch., 1953; m. James Earl von Tungeln, Sept. 1, 1956; children—Sujane, Kenneth; stepchildren—Jim, Mike. Various office positions, Tenn., Ark., Mich. and Tex., 1946-73; broker Joshua Real Estate Co. (Tex.), 1973-75, Tex. Realty, Cleburne, 1975-77; project dir. Johnson County (Tex.) Com. on Aging, Inc., 1977—. Vice pres. Cleburne (Tex.) Ind. Sch. Dist. Community Edn. Adv. Council, 1980-82; treas. LWV, Cleburne, 1981. Mem. Tex. Assn. Nutrition and Aging Programs (sec.), Nat. Assn. Nutrition and Aging Programs, S.W. Soc. on Aging, Fedn. Bus. and Profl. Women. Presbyterian. Club: Zonta. Home: 1212 Hilltop Cleburne TX 76031 Office: PO Box 671 Cleburne TX 76031

VOORDE, FRANCES M., staff White House Office; b. South Bend, Ind., Oct. 28, 1939; d. Edward F. and Theresa (Muszik) V.; B.A., St. Mary's Coll., Notre Dame, Ind., 1961; M.A., George Washington U., 1978. Personal and appoinment sec. Rep. J. Edward Roush of Ind., 1961-64; exec. sec. to Sen. Birch Bayh of Ind., 1965-71; asst. chief Office of Records and Registration, Ho. of Reps., Washington, 1972-75; spl. asst. Office of Disclosure and Compliance, Fed. Election Commn., Washington, 1975-76; dep. dir. Office of Voter Registration, Democratic Nat. Com., 1976; dir. scheduling and advance Carter Campaign, 1976; dir. of scheduling White House Office, Washington, 1977-78, dep. appointments sec. to pres., 1978—. Democrat. Roman Catholic. Address: The White House Washington DC 20500

VOORHIS, BRENDA HEATH JACOBSEN, psychiatrist; b. Buffalo, Feb. 22, 1930; d. Alfred Wilmot and Evelyn (Heath) Jacobsen; B.A., Wellesley Coll., 1951; M.D., Johns Hopkins U., 1955; children—Catherine, Mary Jo, Brenda, Ann, Edward, Karin. Intern in pediatrics Johns Hopkins Hosp., Balt., 1955-56, fellow in pediatric cardiology, 1957; resident in psychiatry Gowanda Psychiat. Center, Helmuth, N.Y., 1967-69, mem. staff, 1969—, unit chief, 1979, dep. program dir., 1980; practice medicine specializing in psychiatry, Gowanda, N.Y.; mem. staffs Tri County Hosp., Gowanda, Lakeshore Hosp., Irving, N.Y. Bd. dirs. Cattaraugus County Council on Alcoholism and Substance Abuse, 1979—. Mem. Cataraugus County Mental Health Assn. Democrat. Roman Catholic. Home: 45 Memorial Dr Gowanda NY 14070 Office: Gowanda Psychiat Center Helmut NY 14079

VORBACH, RENEE LENA RELYEA, newspaper editor; b. Bklyn., Sept 28, 1946; d. Ford S. and Jeanne (Magill) Relyea. A.A. in English, Orange County Community Coll., Middletown, N.Y., 1967; B.A. in English, SUNY, New Paltz, 1969; m. Joseph R. Vorbach; 1 dau. by previous marriage, Vanna Jeanne Cuddeback. Gen. assignment reporter Help columnist Newburgh (N.Y.) Evening News, 1969-74, food columnist, editor, 1974—, asst. editor family and food, 1974—. Publicist, United Fund, 1979-81. Recipient 2d place award N.Y. State Dental Soc. contest, 1977; Cert. of Appreciation, U.S. Navy, 1981. Mem. Newspaper Food Editors and Writers Assn. (charter). Republican. Office: 85 Dickson St Newburgh NY 12550

VOREIS, MARILYN LOUISE, retail div. merchandise exec.; b. Plymouth, Ind., Aug. 10, 1941; d. Orville Jacob and Nita Louise (Leland) V.; B.S. in Home Econs., Purdue U., 1963. Home economist, 4-H Club agt., USDA, U. Ariz., 1963-65; trainee, dept mgr., asst. buyer, buyer L.S. Ayres, Indpls., 1965-76; with Liberty House Calif., 1976, buyer, 1978-79, br. divisional merchandise mgr., 1977-79, buyer cosmetics, Oakland, 1981, divisional merchandise mgr. fashion accessories and cosmetics, 1981—; buyer R.H. Macy, San Francisco, 1979-81; bd. dirs. Luggage and Leathergoods Mag., 1973-76. Home: 933 Shoreline Dr Apt 104 Alameda CA 94501 Office: 1501 Broadway Oakland CA 94612

VORWERK, E. CHARLSIE, artist; b. Tennga, Ga., Jan. 28, 1934; d. James A. and Hester L. (Davis) Pritchett; A.B., Ga. State Coll. for Women, 1955; m. Norman T. Vorwerk, Feb. 9, 1956; children—Karl, Lauren, Michael. Billboard design artist Vanesco Poster, Chattanooga, 1955; cartographic draftsman TVA, Chattanooga, 1955; fashion illustrator Loveman's, Chattanooga, 1956; free lance comml. artist, 1957—; pvt. art instr. children and adults, all media, 1966—; art instr. continuing edn. Bapt. Coll. Charleston, S.C., 1979—. Mem. Bd. Archtl. Rev., Summerville, 1976—; YMCA Flowertown Festival Art Exhibit chmn., 1972-82; mem. women's bd. St. Paul's Episcopal Ch. 1968—; active Boy Scouts Am., Girl Scouts U.S.A.; vol. Mental Health Clinic, 1972-74, others. Mem. Charleston Artists Guild, League of Charleston Artists, Minature Art Soc. Fla., Blue Ridge Art Assn., Beaufort Art Assn., Am. Art Soc., Italian Art Acad. Illustrator: Tales and Taradidales; St. Paul's Epitahs; Captain Tom, others. Address: 315 W Carolina Ave Summerville SC 29483

VOSBURGH, SANDRA JOAN, mfg. co. exec.; b. Cleve., July 31, 1939; d. Courtland Jackson and Margaret Esther (Regal) V.; student Hiram Coll., 1957-60, Baldwin Wallace/Western Res. U., 1977-79; cert. employee benefit specialist Wharton Sch., U. Pa., 1981. Asst. to comptroller Clark Reliance Corp., 1963-65; adminstrv. mgr. firm Goldfarb & Reznick, Cleve., 1970-74; adminstrv. mgr. firm Persky, Marken, Konigsberg & Shapiro, Cleve., 1974-79; dir. hunam resources Work Wear Corp., Inc., Cleve., 1980—. Mem. adv. council Gt. Lakes Assn. Industry and Rehab.; mem. exec. bd. Hiram Coll. Recipient Vol. Service award United Services, 1980-81. Mem. Citizens League, Council World Affairs, Jobs Council Greater Cleve., Beck Center Cultural Arts, Am. Mgmt. Assn., Am. Soc. Personnel Adminstrn., Am. Bus. Women's Assn., Resource. Republican. Club: Women's City of Cleve. Recipient Journalism award Ohio State U., 1957; contbr. articles to profl. jours. Home: 17920 Detroit Ave Lakewood OH 44107 Office: Work Wear Corp 1768 E 25th St Cleveland OH 44113

VOSS, JUDITH ANN, mgmt. co. ofcl.; b. Milford, Ill., Aug. 10, 1939; d. Lawrence Martin and Dorothy Estella (Fleming) Henke; student schs. Milford; m. Robert Clifford Voss, May 26, 1957; children—Dawn Ann, Sharon Sue. Clk. typist, hwy. div. State of Ill., Springfield, 1961-63; credit and personnel reporter, asst. mgr. Fond du Lac (Wis.) Credit Bur., 1966-68; sec., asst. to pres., purchasing agt. Delft Blue-Provimi, Inc., Watertown, Wis., 1969-77, gen. mgr., Concord, Calif., 1977-79; adminstrv. mgr. Bay Area div. EkoTek, Inc., Oakland, Calif., 1979-80; exec. v.p. Diablo Mgmt., Inc., Walnut Creek, Calif., 1980-81; office adminstr. Camp Dresser & Mc Kee Inc., Walnut Creek, 1981—. Home: 1790 Getoun Ct Concord CA 94518 Office: 710 S Broadway #201 Walnut Creek CA 94596

VOSS, RUTH MARILYN, public relations mgr.; b. Cin., July 22, 1928; d. Michael Joseph and Catherine (Reichadt) Hemmert; B.A. U. Cin., 1950; m. Robert Joseph Voss, Sept. 10, 1949; children—Michael, Richard, Peter, Mary, Daniel, Catherine, Andrew, Joseph. Sch. columnist, editor Cin. Times-Star, 1946-58; public relations writer U. Cin., 1958-65; teenager editor Cin. Enquirer, 1965-75; mgr. public relations Kings Island (Ohio) Family Entertainment Center, 1975—; editor New Life Services, Inc., newsletter. Mem. Women in Communications. Roman Catholic. Home: 2480 Socialville-Foster Rd Maineville OH 45039 Office: Kings Island Kings Island OH 45034

VOUGHT, KATHRYN DEBAUN, editor; b. Ridgewood, N.J., Feb. 19, 1952; d. Norman and Harriet (Davison) Vought; B.A. with honors, Skidmore Coll., 1974. Proofreader, Data Communications, Parsippany, N.J., 1975; editorial asst. Avon Books, N.Y.C., 1976-77, asso. editor, 1977-80, mng. editor, 1981—. Mem. NOW. Clubs: Mt. Lakes Badminton (sec. 1980-81), Glenburnie Cottager's Assn. (sec. 1981—). Editor: Nan, Sarah & Clare: Letters Between Friends, 1980. Office: care Avon Books 959 8th Ave New York NY 10019

VOURNAS, ANASTASIA PETROW, mktg. cons.; b. Washington, Aug. 28, 1946; d. George Christian and Helen Jean (Petrow) V.; B.A., U. Denver, 1969, M.B.A., 1970. From account coordinator to account exec. Young & Rubicam, Inc., N.Y.C., 1971-77; account mgr. Compton Advt., Inc., N.Y.C., 1977-78; account supr. SSC&B, Inc., N.Y.C., 1978-80; v.p., account supr. Benton & Bowles, Inc., N.Y.C., 1980-82; mktg. cons. Phoenix House Found., Inc., N.Y.C., 1982—; cons. in field. Democrat. Home: 230 E 50th St New York NY 10022 Office: 164 W 74th St New York NY 10023

VOWELL, DOVIE JEAN, nurse; b. Loyall, Ky., Aug. 11, 1942; d. Shelby C. and Della (Fletcher) Collette; student Berea Coll., 1960-61; A.A.S. in Nursing with honors, Belleville Area Coll., 1977; m. Edward Franklin Vowell, Aug. 28, 1961; children—Edward Franklin, Tamara Francine, Eric Kristian. Sec., George C. Marshall Space Flight Center, NASA, Huntsville, Ala., 1962-63; acctg. asst. CONARC, Ft. Monroe, Va., 1966-68, 21st AF, McGuire AFB, N.J., 1968-70, asst. historian, 1970-72; auditor's asst. Mil. Airlift Command, Scott AFB, Ill., 1972-74; nurse Intensive Care Unit, Centreville Twp. Hosp., East St. Louis, Ill., 1977—, ICU liaison with bd. dirs., 1980-81. ARC vol., 1969-72; den mother Boy Scouts Am., 1969-74; active Girl Scouts U.S.A., 1972-74. Fed. Nursing scholar, 1976-77; St. Clair County Med. Soc. scholar, 1976-77. Mem. Ill. Nurses Assn., Am. Nurses Assn., Am. Assn. Critical Care Nurses. Democrat. Roman Catholic. Club: Nurses for Life. Asst. editor: History of 21AF (MAC), 1970-72. Home: 1104 N 39th St Belleville IL 62223 Office: 5900 Bond Ave East Saint Louis IL 62207

VOWELS, ELEANOR ELAINE, speech pathologist; b. Pitts., Mar. 10, 1937; d. Arnett Lloyd and Amanda (Anthony) Wooding; B.S. in Psychology, Howard U., 1962; M.A. in Speech Pathology and Audiology (Vocat. Rehab. fellow 1965-67), Catholic U. Am., 1967; postgrad. U. Md.; m. Aug. 27, 1960; 1 son, David Scott. Speech pathologist Prince George County (Md.) Diagnostic Teaching Center, 1967-70; speech pathologist Dept. Human Resources D.C., 1970-72, dir. speech pathology and audiology, 1972—; dir. speech pathology and audiology children and youth project D.C. Gen. Hosp., 1972—, dir. handicapped infant intervention project, 1977—, dir. tng. grant, 1980—; v.p. D.C. Consortium Handicapped Children's Programs, 1979, pres., 1980. Pres., D.C. Area chpt. Children Internat. Summer Villages, Inc., 1981, 82-83, mem. expansion com., trustee-at-large Nat. Children's Internat. Summer Villages, Inc. 1982—, also mem. long range planning com.; chmn. com. on handicapped Commn. Pub. Health, 1982. HEW Bur. Edn. grantee, 1977—. Mem. Am. Speech and Hearing Assn. (cert. clin. competence), D.C. Assn. Retarded Citizens (dir. 1972—), D.C. Speech and Hearing Assn., Md. Speech and Hearing Assn., Nat. Assn. Retarded Citizens, Zeta Phi Beta. Democrat. Baptist. Producer audio visual slide presentations on handicapped children, 1962, 70. Home: 7718 Jaffrey Rd Fort Washington MD 20744 Office: 1900 Massachusetts Ave SE Washington DC 20003

VREELAND, DIANA DALZIEL, mag. editor, fashion cons.; b. Paris, France; d. Frederick Y. and Emily Key (Hoffman) Dalziel; m. Thomas Reed Vreeland, Mar. 1, 1924; children—Thomas Reed, Frederick D. Brit. subject, until 1925. Fashion editor Harper's Bazaar, 1937-62; with Vogue mag., 1962—, editor-in-chief, 1962-71, cons. editor, 1971—. Cons. Costume Inst., Met. Mus. Art, 1972. Decorated Legion of Honor (France). Office: Metropolitan Museum Art 1000 Fifth Ave New York NY 10028 *

VRTAR, ROSE MARIE, constrn. co. exec.; b. Jamesburg, N.J., Nov. 30, 1946; d. John C. and Florence (Kesead) Gruca; B.A. in Edn., Trenton State Coll., 1968; postgrad. Calif. State U., Los Angeles, 1976—; m. Jacob Vrtar, Apr. 24, 1972. Cashier/bookkeeper Howard Johnson Restaurant, Cranbury, N.J., 1963-68; clk. McGraw Hill Inc., Hightstown, N.J., 1968-71, car plan adminstr., 1971-72; accounts payable clk. Fla. Realty Bldg. Co., West Palm Beach, Fla., 1972-73, full charge bookkeeper/supr. acct., 1973-75; accounts payable clk. Majestic Realty Co./Commerce Constrn. Co., Inc., Los Angeles, 1975-76, acctg. supr., 1976-78, controller, 1978—. Sec., Pastoral Council, Archdiocese of Los Angeles, 1982-83. Mem. Soc. Am. Exec. and Profl. Women, Am. Rose Soc., Pacific Rose Soc. (corr. sec.), Greater Los Angeles Rose Council, Inland Valley Rose Soc. (sec.), San Gabriel Valley Rose and Hort. Soc. Roman Catholic. Club: El Monte Rose/Garden (editor newsletter 1977-78). Office: 6252 E Telegraph Rd Los Angeles CA 90040

VUCKOVICH, CAROL YETSO (MRS. MICHAEL VUCKOVICH), librarian; b. East Liverpool, Ohio, Sept. 23, 1940; d. Stephen A. and Louise (Sever) Yetso; B.S., Geneva Coll., 1966; M.L.S., U. Pitts., 1968; m. Michael Vuckovich, Sept. 24, 1970. Computation analyst Crucible Steel div. Colt Industries, Midland, Pa., 1958-62; library dir. Community Coll. Beaver County, Monaca, Pa., 1968—, instr. human anatomy and physiology, 1970—. Mem. Am., Pa. library assns., Spl. Libraries Assn., Am. Inst. Biol. Scis., Am. Anti-Vivisection Soc., Nat. Wildlife Fedn., Coll. and Research Libraries. Home: 21 Elm St Midland PA 15059 Office: Center Grange Rd Monaca PA 15061

VYNER, MARY BAINBRIDGE, pianist, composer; b. Uniontown, Pa., Sept. 4, 1933; d. John Andrew and Mary (Anderson) Bainbridge; student Carnegie Tech. U., 1946-50; Mus.B., Phila. Musical Acad., 1952, Mus.M., 1953, Mus.D., 1954; m. Louis Vyner, Feb. 20, 1960. Concert pianist, numerous locations, 1950—; composer 19 concertos for piano and orch., 6 symphonic tone poems for orch., 8 sonatas for piano, 4 preludes for piano, Bicentennial symphony with narrator; mem. faculty Phila. Musical Acad., 1961—, Franklin and Marshall Coll., Lancaster, Pa., 1968-71; founder, dir. Lancaster Conservatory of Music, 1953—. Mem. AAUP, Lancaster Musical Art Soc. (pres. 1962-64), Nat. Fedn. Music Clubs, Musicians Union Local 294. Presbyterian. Author: Creative Harmony, 1953; Creative Counterpoint, 1954. Office: PO Box 1152 Lancaster PA 17603 *

WACHTENDORF, CHRISTINE ANN, pediatrician; b. Bklyn., Mar. 30, 1951; d. Basil Steven and Mary P. Goerner; B.S. cum laude, U. Houston, 1972; M.D., U. Tex., 1976; m. Henry Jacob Wachtendorf, June 7, 1973; 1 son, Henry James. Resident in pediatrics U. Tex. Health Sci. Center st San Antonio, 1976-79; dir. Ottis Media Study Center, NIH, San Antonio, 1980—; clin. faculty. Recipient Physician Recognition award, 1979. Mem. Am. Acad. Pediatrics, Tex. Pediatric Soc., An Antonio Pediatric Soc. Republican. Roman Catholic. Contbr. articles to profl. jours. Home: 15514 Long Creek San Antonio TX 78247 Office: 519 W Houston San Antonio TX 78285

WACHTER, ORALEE ROBERTS, media co. exec.; b. Los Angeles, Apr. 16, 1935; d. Bob and Florence G. (Lederer) Roberts; B.A., U. Calif., 1958; M.A., San Francisco State U., 1978; m. Mark R. Wachter, Aug. 12, 1955; children—Stephen, Paul, Beth. Dir. gen. edn. Brandeis Day Sch., San Francisco, 1965-67; instr. U. Calif., Berkeley extension, 1969-72; communications specialist Berkeley Unified Schs., 1969-75; instr. Calif. Instn. Women, Frontera, 1975; pres., dir. O.D.N. Prodns., Inc., 1974—, creative dir. film and publs. Cert. tchr., Calif.; cert. Am. Mental Health Assn.; finalist Am. Film Festival. Author: Acquaintance Rape Prevention, 1978; Spouse Abuse Handbook, 1981; The Abusive Partner, 1982; Talking Helps, 1983. Office: 74 Varick St New York NY 10013

WACHTER, WANDA VALERIE, acct.; b. Enda, Okla., Dec. 5, 1952; d. Robert J. and Jean M. (Debold) W.; B.B.A. with honors, George Washington U., 1978. With Telesec Temporaries, Falls Church, Va., 1972; mgmt. accountant Am. Assn. Coll. Registrars and Adminstrs., Washington, 1973; accountant technician Am. Council on Edn., Washington, 1973-74, Naval Regional Med. Center, Washington, 1974-77, Immigration and Naturalization Service, Washington, 1978; staff accountant Assn. Advancement of Med. Instrumentation, Roslyn, Va., 1978-79, Honeywell Info. Systems, Inc., McLean, Va., 1979-80; asst. controller Fairmac Realty Corp., Arlington, Va., 1980—.

WADDINGTON, BETTE HOPE (STAGE NAME ELIZABETH CROWDER), violinist; b. San Francisco, July 27, 1921; d. John and Marguerite (Crowder) Waddington; A.B., U. Calif. at Berkeley, 1945, postgrad.; postgrad. Juilliard Sch. Music, 1950, San Jose State Coll., 1955; M.A., San Francisco State Coll., 1953; life cert. music and art Calif. Jr. Coll. Violinist, St. Louis Symphony, 1958—. Cert. tchr., Calif. Mem. U. Calif., San Francisco State Coll., San Jose State U. alumnae assns., Sierra Club, Alpha Beta Alpha. Home: 2800 Olive St Saint Louis MO 63103 Office: Powell Hall Grand Ave and Delmar Blvd Saint Louis MO 63103

WADDLE, AUDREY STERLING, nurse; b. Gloucester County, Va., June 20, 1932; d. James Edward and Ethel Hayden (Williams) Sterling; R.N., Riverside Sch. Profl. Nursing, 1952; student Hampton Inst., 1971-72, Thomas Nelson Community Coll., 1973; B.S. in Health Adminstrn., St. Joseph's Coll., 1980; m. Travis Gene Waddle, May 4, 1952; children—Pamela Gayle Waddle Furr, Anita Darlene Smith. Head nurse Riverside Hosp., Newport News, 1953, Onslow County Hosp., Jacksonville, N.C., 1954; pvt. duty, relief dir. Gray's Clinic & Hosp., Springhill, La., 1955-57; gen. duty nurse Eastern State Hosp., Williamsburg, Va., 1957-58, head nurse, 1958-59, nurse supr., 1959-65, mental health nurse instr. and tng. coordinator, 1982—, chmn. ward manual com., 1967-81, others. Adv. bd. and selection com. Lafayette Practical Nurse Program, Williamsburg, 1972-82; mem. State of Va. Dept. Mental Health/Mental Retardation Individualized Treatment Planning Com., 1979-80; chmn. Eastern State Hosp. United Fund drive, 1978-79. Registered profl. nurse, Va.; U. Md. grantee, 1964. Mem. Va. Govt. Employees Assn., Nat. Soc. Registered Nurses. Presbyterian. Developer psychiat. practical nurse program Eastern State Hosp., 1967; co-author manuals. Home: 108 Underwood Rd Williamsburg VA 23185 Office: Drawer A Williamsburg VA 23187

WADDLE, SANDY DEAN, psychologist; b. Asheboro, N.C., May 28, 1945; d. John Arthur and Rebecca (Lewis) Dean; B.A., U. N.C., Greensboro, 1968, M.A., 1973; Ph.D., N.C. State U., Raleigh, 1982; m. Jerome Alan Waddle, Sept. 18, 1976; children—Lisa Dawn, Susan Lindsay. With Western Electric Co., Inc., Greensboro, 1968—, dept. chief human resources research and devel., 1976-79, nat. adminstr. corp. personnel devel. program Sales div., 1979—; cons. Gov.'s Conf. on Leadership Devel. for Women, Meredith Leadership Inst. First v.p. N.C. Women's polit. Caucus, 1979-80; program chmn., steering com. Guilford County Women's Polit. Caucus, 1979-80; vice chmn. employment task force Greensboro Council on Status of Women, 1979-80. Recipient awards Gov. James B. Hunt, 1979, 82. Mem. Am. Psychol. Assn., Am. Soc. Tng. and Devel. (dir., Human Resource Devel. Profl. of Yr. award), Guilford County Psychol. Soc. (pres.), Phi Kappa Phi. Methodist. Home: 4501 Wiley Davis Rd Greensboro NC 27407 Office: Western Electric Co PO Box 25000 Dept 20GG10001 Greensboro NC 27420

WADE, BARBARA LOUISE, county ofcl.; b. Choctaw, Ala., Aug. 14, 1938; d. Joe Siah and Fannie Mae Rodgers; B.S., Roosevelt U., 1971; M.A. Governor's State U., 1977; m. Thomas Robert Wade, Dec. 24, 1974; children—Diann, Tyree, Kim, Carolyn. Co-chmn. housing, chmn., youth community organizer TWO, Chgo., 1960-72; planning intern City of Chgo.; probation officer Juvenile Ct., Cook County, Ill., 1971-75; clin. supr., Jacksonville, Fla., 1976-77, juvenile ct. unit supr. post arrest unit, domestive intervention Dade State's Atty. Office (Fla.), 1977-78, 78-80, dir. pretrial diversion, Miami, Fla., 1980—, cons. Miami chpt. SCLC of Dade County, Urban League of Jacksonville. Pres. AO Sexton Sch. Council; bd. dirs. Harris YWCA. Cert. social worker, Ill. Mem. Urban League, Women in Criminal Justice, Probation and Parole, Am. Probation and Parole Assn., Nat. Assn. Female Execs., Roosevelt U. Alumni Assn., Governor's State U. Alumni Assn. Address: 11125 SW 156th Terr Miami FL 33157

WADE, CAROLE, interior designer; b. Fairmont, W.Va., Apr. 5, 1947; d. Lewis H. and Hazel M. (West) Manko; B.A., Fairmont State Coll., 1970; postgrad. N.Y. Sch. Interior Design, 1974-75; m. Michael R.A. Wade, Aug. 25, 1974. Public affairs asst. Export-Import Bank of U.S., Washington, 1970-72; owner, interior designer Carole Wade Concepts, N.Y.C., 1975-78, Carole Wade Interior Design, Chgo., 1978—. Bd. dirs. Mus. Contemporary Art, 1980—. Office: 25 E Washington St Chicago IL 60602

WADE, JULIA HOWARD, interior designer; b. Alexandria, La., Dec. 2, 1928; d. Samuel Eugene and Louis D'Or (Moore) Howard; B.A., Baylor U., 1948; student La. Coll., 1946; m. Nelsyn Ernest Brooks Wade, June 29, 1948; children—Sylvia Laureen, Lisa Frances, William Alan, David Eugene. Organizer, dir. Children's Theatre, San Augustine, Tex., 1948-52; tchr. English San Augustine High Sch., 1948; partner, decorator, advt. mgr., buyer Nelsyns Furniture Store, San Augustine, 1958—; lectr. in field. Hist. chmn. 8-County Deep E. Tex. Devel. Assn., 1975; bd. dirs. San Augustine Public Library, 1980-82; bd. devel. E. Tex. Bapt. Coll., 1978-82. Named Outstanding Small Retailer, S.W. Home Furnishings Assn., 1979; Pres.'s award, C. of C., 1973; Rotary award, 1980. Mem. C. of C. (v.p. 1972-77), S.W. Home Furnishings Assn., Nat. Assn. Retail Dealers of Am., Nat. Assn. Female Execs., Tex. Old Missions and Forts Restoration Assn., Nat. Trust Hist. Preservation, Baylor U. Alumni Assn., Tex. Forestry Assn., DAR, San Augustine County Hist. Soc. Republican. Baptist. Clubs: Heritage (pres. 1963), Bible (pres. 1953, 57). Home: 412 Baxter Ln San Augustine TX 75972 Office: 128 E Columbia St San Augustine TX 75972

WADE, MARIE CHAMPION, beauty salon exec.; b. Henderson, N.C., June 12, 1930; d. Walter Edward and Nora May (Roberts) Champion; m. Johnnie Daniel Wade, June 7, 1947, (dec. 1977); children—Steven Daniel, Donna Marie, Lisa LeMay. Owner, mgr. Marie's Hair Fashions. Notary Public, N.C. Mem. N.C. Hairdressers and Cosmetologists Assn., Nat. Hairdressers and Cosmetologists Assn., Nat. Fedn. Ind. Bus., Nat. Fedn. Bus. Women. Mem. Ch. of Christ. Home: 1240 Jefferson St Roanoke Rapids NC 27870

WADE, MARTHA GEORGIE, ednl. adminstr.; b. Memphis, May 27, 1939; d. William Edward and Martha (Moulder) Wade; A.B., U. Tenn., 1961; M.Ed., Ind. U., 1965. Field sec. Phi Mu Frat., Memphis, 1961-63; asst. dean students for freshmen Stephens Coll., Columbia, Mo., 1965-68, asst. dean students, dir. student activities, 1968-71, dean student life, 1971-77, exec. v.p., 1977-79, v.p., dean admissions, 1979—. Mem. Mayor's Adv. Com. on Labor Relations, 1979-80. Mem. Nat. Assn. Coll. Admissions Counselors, Am. Assn. Collegiate Registrars and Admission Officers, Mortar Bd., Alpha Lambda Delta (nat. council 1976—), Delta Kappa Gamma. Episcopalian. Office: PO Box 2121 Stephens Coll Columbia MO 65215

WADE, MARY CARROLL, educator; b. Rome, Ga., Sept. 1, 1909; d. Seaborn Rosa and Dollie Savannah (Hill) Carroll; student Maryville Coll., 1926-28, B.A., 1931; postgrad. U. of the South, summer, 1938; M.A., George Washington U., 1948; Ed.D., Am. U., 1970; m. Richard Rudolph Wade, Apr. 1, 1967. Tchr., Hawkins County, Tenn., 1934-36, Pittman Center, Tenn., 1937-38, Chattanooga, 1938-42, Meigs County, Tenn., 1936-37; with War Dept., Washington, 1942-43; library asst. Library of Congress, Washington, 1943-44; planner, U.S. Govt. Printing Office, Washington, 1944-67, planner-in-charge, 1967-72, chief marginally forms continuous forms sect., Specifications Div., 1972-80, chmn. Fed. Women's Program, 1972-73; cons. psychologist Vocational Rehab. Dept., 1954-57; lectr. Montgomery Coll., Rockville, Md., 1981—; lectr. Fed. Office Systems Expo, 1982. Active Girls Scouts U.S.A.; bd. dirs. United Cerebral Palsy, D.C., 1970—; active ARC; hon. staff mem. Tenn. State Senator Annabelle Clement O'Brien, 1982. Recipient United Service Orgn. award, 1946; Superior Service award, U.S. Govt. Printing Office, 1963, 66, 67, 68, Spl. Achievement award, 1971-72, others. Mem. Am. Psychol. Assn., Va. Psychol. Assn., D.C. Psychol. Assn., Soc. for Personnel Adminstrn., Nat. Vocat. Guidance Assn., Am. Personnel & Guidance Assn., Public Personnel Assn., Franklin Tech. Soc., Bus. Forms Mgmt. Assn. (recording sec. 1980-81), Am. U. Alumni Assn., George Washington U. Alumni Assn., Maryville Coll. Alumni Assn., Nat. Trust Historic Preservation, Poetry Soc. Va., Kappa Delta Epsilon, Psi Chi, Phi Delta Gamma (nat. council rep.). Presbyterian. Clubs: Wash. Club of Printing House Craftsmen, Wash. Litho, George Washington Univ., Americana, Toastmistress, Altrusa, Columbian Women, Interservice Club Council of Alexandria (recording sec. 1981), Fairfax County Bus. & Profl. Womens (pres. 1975-76). Contbr. articles to profl. jours.

WADE, MARY LOUISE POWELL, counselor; b. Springfield, Ohio, Sept. 25, 1932; d. Gamaliel Wyatte Holmes and Lucy Maxwell (Sloan) Powell; A.A., Meridian Jr. Coll., 1951; B.A., U. So. Miss., 1953, M.A., 1954; counselor cert. U. So. Ala., 1979; m. Walter B. Wade, Aug. 25, 1956 (div. July 1980); children—Susan Sloan Wade Massey, Holly Bibb Wade Crane, Walter Wyatte. Speech therapist Moultrie Ga. Speech Clinic, 1954-55, U. Tenn. Speech and Hearing Center, 1955-56, Jackson County Exceptional Sch., 1957-58; vending machine sales Morrisons Co., Pascagoula, 1974; newspaper dealer, Clarion Ledger, Jackson, Miss., 1974-75; audiologist, hearing aid salesman Beltone Co., Hattiesburg, Miss., 1975-77; receptionist Singing River Mental Health Services, Pascagoula, 1977; youth services counselor Jackson County Youth Ct., Miss. Dept. Youth Services, Pascagoula, 1977—, also chief counselor, probation officer. Neighborhood chmn. Girl Scouts, 1958-68; trombonist Gulf Coast Symphony, 1981—; asst. coach Aquatic Club swim team, 1960-70; dir. youth choir 1st Presbyn. Ch., Pascagoula; elder 1st Presbyn. Ch., Ocean Springs, Miss., 1982—; instr. water safety ARC; rape crisis counselor Gulfcoast Women's Center, Biloxi, Miss.; mem. Pas-Point Singers. Mem. Miss. Assn. Clin. Counselors, State Employees Assn. Miss. Democrat. Presbyterian. Home: Rt 3 Box 210C Ocean Springs MS 39564 Office: 4903 Telephone Rd Pascagoula MS 39567

WADE, MELISSA ANN MARQUART, architect; b. Crestline, Ohio, Aug. 26, 1952; d. Paul Frederick and Anna Marie (Perito) Marquart; B.Design-Interior Design with high honors, U. Fla., 1974, B. Design-Architecture with honors, 1975, M.A. in Architecture, 1976; m. Raymond John Wade, Jr., May 2, 1981. Design draftsman Schweizer Assos., Inc., Orlando, Fla., 1977-78; job capt. Catalyst, Inc., Orlando, 1978-79; project coordinator Lynn M. Teneyck Architect, Inc., Orlando, 1979-80; architect, project coordinator Duer & Assos. Architects, Inc., Winter Park, Fla., 1980—. Cert. class A gen. contractor, Fla.; registered architect, Fla. Mem. AIA. Lutheran. Home: 940-E Lake Destiny Rd Altamonte Springs FL 32701 Office: 301-B Park Ave N Winter Park FL 32789

WADLAND, BEATRICE FLAGG, ins. agy. exec.; b. Melrose, Mass., Feb. 12, 1922; d. Arthur Samuel and Glenna Beatrice (Towner) Flagg; student Secretarial Sch. of Cambridge, Boston U.; m. Robert Lewis Wadland; children—Lawrence Arthur, Carolyn Beatrice, Kenneth Robert, Judith Dianne. With John Hancock Life Ins. Co., Boston, A.S. Flagg Ins. Agy., Inc., Melrose, W.C. Huntress Ins. Agy., Inc., Melrose. Christian educator First United Meth. Ch., Melrose; active Kappa Swap Shop, Upham Family Soc., Mem. Internat. Transactional Analysis Assn., Kappa Delta Psi (past pres.). Clubs: Melrose Mother's (past pres.).

WAELTI-WALTERS, JENNIFER ROSE, educator; b. Wolverhampton, Eng., Mar. 13, 1942; came to Can., 1968; naturalized; d. Thomas Gilbert and Joan Ellen (Mills) Walters; B.A. with honors, U. London, 1964, Ph.D., 1968; L'es'L Inst. Francais Du RoyauMe U., 1966; m. Frank Carl Waelti, Dec. 30, 1972. Lectr., U. Paris, 1967-68; asst. prof. French, U. Victoria, B.C., after 1968, prof., 1980—, chairperson dept. French, 1979—. Mem. Canadian Fedn. Humanities (dir. 1980-83), Association des Professeurs de Française des Universités et Collèges Canadiens, Can. Compartive Lit. Assn., Humanities Assn. Can., NE Modern Lang. Assn. Author: Alchimie et Litterature, 1975; Michel Butor, 1977; J.M.G. Le Clezio, 1977, Icare ou L'Evasion Impossible: Etude Psychomythique De L'Oeuvre De J.M.G. Le Clezio, 1981; The Mirror Cracked: Fairytales and the Female Imagination, 1982.

WAGENER, MAGGIE MARY, editor, monthly bus., Publ.; b. North Kingston, R.I., Feb. 12, 1954; d. Richard V. and Lucille M. Wagener; B.A. in English and Communication Arts, St. Mary's Coll., Winona, Minn., 1975. Reporter, photographer, anchorperson Sta.-WKBT-TV, La Crosse, Wis., 1975-78; salesperson Anything Groes Corp., La Crosse, 1978-79; audio-visual scriptwriter Trane Co., La Crosse, 1979-81, mgr. dept. service lit., 1981—. Mem. alumni bd. dirs. St. Mary's Coll. Office: 3600 Pammel Creek Rd La Crosse WI 54601

WAGGONER, NANCY MANN (MRS. EDWARD L. WAGGONER), curator; b. Boston, Nov. 16, 1924; d. Alden T. and Olive A. (Huegely) Mann; B.A. magna cum laude, Smith Coll., 1946; M.A., Columbia, 1963, Ph.D. with distinction, 1968; m. Edward L. Waggoner, Mar. 27, 1948; children—Martha M., Amelia M. Asst. curator Greek coins Am. Numis. Soc. Mus., N.Y.C., 1968-70, assoc. curator, 1970-76, curator, 1976—. Am. Numis. Soc. grad. fellow, 1966-67; Am. Philos. Soc. grantee, 1970. Fellow Am. Numis. Soc. (life); mem. Am. Schs. Oriental Research, Archaeol. Inst. Am., Royal Numis. Soc., Royal Belgian Numis. Soc. Episcopalian. Author: (with Martin Price) Archaic Greek Silver Coinage, 1975; editor: (with Otto Morkholm) Greek Numismatics and Archaeology, Essays in Honor of Margaret Thompson, 1979; Early Greek Coins in the Collection of Jonathan P. Rosen, 1983. Home: 184 Purchase St Rye NY 10580 Office: Broadway at 156th St New York NY 10032

WAGNER, ANNE MARGARET, electronics co. exec.; b. Jordan, Minn., Dec. 11, 1952; d. Herbert Robert, Jr. and Delores Gertrude (Eischens) Wagner; B.A. in Journalism and Advt., U. Minn., 1975. Advt. and sales promotion coordinator, photog. products div. 3M Co., 1976; mktg. adminstr. Syntex Med. Systems Co., 1976-77; tactical mktg. coordinator Nat. Semicondr. Co., 1977-78; microprocessor mktg. mgr., Santa Clara Calif., 1978-82, market area mgr. devel. systems, 1982—. Mem. Bay Area Women's Exec. Forum. Democrat. Roman Catholic. Office: 2900 Semiconductor Dr Santa Clara CA 95051

WAGNER, AYLENE PARKER, speech pathologist; b. Murfressboro, Tenn., Apr. 5, 1939; d. James Russell and Serena Edella (Blackburn) Parker; student Georgetown Coll., 1957-59; B.A., Carson-Newman Coll., 1961; M.A., Northwestern U., 1964; m. Martin Gerald Wagner, Apr. 15, 1965; children—Gaylia Lynn, Samantha Katherine (dec.), Deborah Michelle (adpoted), Aaron Parker. Speech pathologist Sch. Dist. 28, Northbrook, Ill., 1964-66; chief speech pathologist Del. Curative Workshop, Wilmington, 1967-69; asst. prof. speech pathology West Chester State Coll., 1975, 76, 81; pvt. practice speech pathology, Wilmington, 1977—; cons. in field. Mem. Am. Speech-Lang. Assn., Del. Speech and Hearing Assn., Internat. Assn. Logpedics and Phoniatrics, Alexander Graham Bell Assn. Home and Office: 1013 Overbrook Dr Wilmington DE 19807

WAGNER, BARBARA ALLEN, designer, illustrator; b. Mill Valley, Calif., Jan. 20, 1927; d. Verner and Shirley Robeson (Sanders) Allen; B.A., Stanford U., 1948, postgrad., 1949; postgrad. Calif. Sch. Fine Arts, 1951, San Francisco Acad. Art, 1977, San Francisco Tapestry Workshop, 1978; m. Henry Weinhard Wagner, Jr., Dec. 2, 1955; 1 son, Henry Weinhard III. Partner, Van Benthem/Allen Assos., San Francisco, 1953-55; ofcl. designer of canvaswork Grace Cathedral, San Francisco, 1970—; ofcl. designer of canvaswork for sale from the Collections of the DeYoung Mus., Calif. Palace of the Legion of Honor and Asian Art Mus., San Francisco, 1975—; needlepoint designer Haas-Lilienthal House (San Francisco Heritage Found.), 1976; designer Calif Design Group, San Francisco, 1977—; exhibited Form and Freedom, Legion of Honor, San Francisco, 1978; dir. Nat. Standards Council of Am. Embroiderers, 1978—; dir. San Francisco Tapestry Workshop; freelance canvaswork and Aubusson tapestry designer; tchr., judge in field. Pres. DeYoung Mus. Soc. Aux., 1963, 64; bd. dirs. DeYoung Mus. Soc., 1964-70; founding dir. docent council Avery Brundage Collection of Asian Art, 1965-70; trustee Cathedral Sch. for Boys, 1969. Recipient Blue Ribbon, St. Matthew's Needlework Exhibit, San Mateo, Calif., 1970, San Francisco Festival of Needlework, 1972, 74. Mem. Embroiderer's Guild Am., Am. Needlepoint Guild (Bicentennial Ecclesiastical award 1975), San Francisco Women Artists. Contbr. articles in field to profl. jours.; work selected for Fiberarts Design Book.

WAGNER, DOROTHY MARIE, ct. reporter, service exec.; b. Milw., June 8, 1924; d. Theodore Anthony and Leona Helen (Ullrich) Wagner; grad. Milw. Bus. U., 1944; student Marquette U., U. Wis., Milw. Stenographer, legal sec., Milw., 1942-44; hearing reporter Wis. Workmen's Compensation Dept., 1944-48; ofcl. reporter to judge Circuit Ct., Milw., 1952-53; owner, operator ct. reporting service Dorothy M. Wagner & Assos., Milw., 1948—; asst. ofcl. reporter State of Wis. Recipient Gregg Diamond medal Gregg Pub. Co., 1950. Mem. Nat. (registered profl. reporter, certificate of proficiency), Wis. shorthand reporters assns., Am. Legion Aux. Roman Catholic. Home: 214 Williamsburg Dr Thiensville WI 53092 Office: 135 Wells St Suite 400 Milwaukee WI 53203

WAGNER, ELLEN CAROL, bus. exec.; b. New Britain, Conn., Oct. 11; d. Paul and Charlotte Helen (Gloersen) Wagner; B.F.A., Boston U., 1960; M.B.A., Fordham U., 1975. Adminstrv. and prodn. asst. Hurok Concerts Inc., 1960-70; fund adminstr. pension and welfare funds Am. Guild Mus. Artists, N.Y.C., 1971—. Mem. nat. alumni council Boston U., 1981, chmn. Theatre Network, 1980-81. Mem. Am. Mgmt. Assn., Fordham U. Alumni Assn. (Fedn. dir. 1976-80), Assn. M.B.A. Execs., Am. Soc. Profl. and Exec. Women. Office: care AGMA Pension & Welfare Funds 1841 Broadway Room 507 New York NY 10023

WAGNER, ELLEN PAYNE, telephone co. exec.; b. Rome, Ga., June 15, 1945; d. Richard William and Helen (Hatch) Payne; B.A., Shorter Coll., Rome, 1966; M.S. (Belle Baruch fellow 1966-68), Clemson U., 1968; postgrad. Auburn U.; m. Conrad John Wagner, Oct. 21, 1978; 1 adopted son, Conrad John, II; 3 stepchildren. Exec. sec. Milner Corp., Opelika, Ala., 1969; legal researcher Ga. Law Dept., 1973; scientist Ga. State Crime Lab., 1973-74; mgr. network design So. Bell Telephone Co., Atlanta, 1974-78, staff asso. minicomputer support, 1978-82, minicomputer project mgr., 1982—; cons., speaker in field. Organizer, vol. rape crisis center Grady Hosp., Atlanta, 1974; alt. del. Ga. Democratic Conv., 1975; mem. Internat. Women's Yr. task force Ga. Commn. Status Women, 1977. Recipient Outstanding Leadership award Atlanta chpt. AAUW, 1976. Mem. Bus. and Profl. Women (pres. Atlanta chpt. 1978-79), Atlanta Women's C. of C. (editor newsletter 1982—), Nat. Assn. Bus. Owners, Atlanta Bd. Realtors. Unitarian. Clubs: Quota (2d v.p. Northside 1981-82), Women's Commerce (Atlanta). Home: 3478 Honeysuckle Ln Smyrna GA 30080 Office: 22V50 675 W Peachtree St Atlanta GA 30375

WAGNER, FAYE LOUISA, gen. contractor; b. New Orleans, July 10, 1949; d. Louis Frank and Leila Mae (Cornay) W.; student New Orleans public schs.; m. Barry J. Nunez, July 2, 1975 (div.); 1 son, Chad Joseph. Owner, pres. Touch of Class Homes, Inc., Metairie, La., 1977—; founder Flair Constrn. Co., Inc., Metairie, 1982—. Roman Catholic. Club: New Orleans Ski. Office: Touch of Class Homes 3201 Tolmas Dr Metairie LA 70002 also 801 Nursery Ave Metairie LA 70005

WAGNER, ISABELLE AUSTIN, retail exec.; b. Boston, Mar. 26, 1918; d. Alva Carlos and Ada Florence (Stevens) Austin; student Fla. So. Coll., 1936-39; m. Francis William Wagner, Sept. 16, 1938; children—Evelynn Dora Wagner Hotz, Karen Ada. With J.C. Penney Co., 1950-55, Maas Bros., 1955-57; dept. mgr. C.E. Chappel & Sons, Syracuse, 1957-58; mgr. Lerner Shops, Lakeland, Fla., 1958-67, Burlington-High Point, N.C., 1967-70; dept. mgr. Woolco Stores, Lakeland, 1970-74; traveling supr. tng. store openers, suprs. Apparel Buying Assos., 1974—. Leader, Girl Scouts U.S.A., 1947-50; chmn. fund raising coms. PTA. Mem. Nat. Assn. Female Execs., Nat. Wildlife Fedn., The Exec. Program. Republican.

WAGNER, JUDITH L., govt. ofcl.; b. Washington, Feb. 26, 1947; d. Henry C. and Pauline O. (Woodruff) W.; B.S., Madison Coll., 1968; M.S.A., George Washington U., 1970. Mgmt. analyst Office Sec. Army, Washington, 1968-73, U.S. Secret Service, Washington, 1973-74, chief mgmt. programs and studies br., mgmt. and orgn. div., 1974-77, chief paperwork mgmt. br., 1977-78; chief mgmt. and orgn. div. Bur. Mint, Washington, 1978-79, asst. dir. mgmt. services, 1979—. Collegiate profl. teaching cert., Va. Mem. Am. Soc. Public Adminstrn., Am. Mgmt. Assn. Office: 501 13th St NW Washington DC 20220

WAGNER, LINDA CAROLYN WELSHIMER, educator; b. St. Marys, Ohio, Aug. 18, 1936; d. Samuel Anderson and Esther Caroline (Scheffler) Welshimer; B.A., B.S. in Edn. magna cum laude with honors in English, Bowling Green (Ohio) State U., 1957, M.A., 1959, Licentiate, 1961, Ph.D., 1963; m. Paul Wagner, Jan. 22, 1957 (div.); children—Douglas, Thomas, Andrea. Public sch. tchr., 1957-60; mem. faculty Bowling Green State U., 1962-65, Wayne State U., Detroit, 1966-67; mem. faculty Mich. State U., 1968—, prof. English, 1972—. Recipient Disting. Faculty award Mich. State U., 1980; Guggenheim fellow, 1975-76, Bunting Inst. fellow, 1975-76. Mem. MLA, Nat. Council Tchrs. English, Detroit Women Writers. Author books, 1964—, latest being Ernest Hemingway: A Reference Guide, 1977; William Carlos Williams: A Reference Guide, 1978; Dos Passos: Artist as American, 1979; American Modern, Selected Essays in Poetry and Fiction, 1980; Songs for Isadora: Poems, 1981; also essays, monograph, chpts. in books. Editor books, 1973—, latest being Robert Frost: The Critical Heritage, 1977; Denise Levertov: In Her Own Province, 1979; Joyce Carol Oates: Critical Essays, 1979. Office: 211 Morrill Hall Mich State U East Lansing MI 48823

WAGNER, LOUISE HEMINGWAY BENTON, ednl. co. exec.; b. Chgo., July 29, 1937; d. William and Helen (Hemingway) B.; student Skidmore Coll., Saratoga Springs, N.Y., 1955-57; B.A. in English, Finch Coll., N.Y.C., 1960; m. Ralph C. Wagner, May 23, 1979. Pub. relations asst. Look mag., N.Y.C., 1960-62, Compton Ency., Chgo., 1962-63; mktg. services Ency. Brit. Press, Chgo., 1963-66; dir. exhibits Ency. Brit. Ednl. Corp., Chgo., 1966-70, v.p. mktg. services, 1970—, also dir. Bd. dirs. Mus. Contemporary Art, Chgo. Lying-In Hosp., Columbia Coll., Chgo., Cradle Soc., Evanston, Ill., Reading is FUNdamental, Chgo.; mem. women's bd. U. Chgo.; trustee Orchestral Assn. Chgo.; governing mem. Art Inst. Chgo. Mem. Publicity Club Chgo., ALA, Assn. for Edn. Communication Tech., Assn. Supervision and Curriculum Devel. Episcopalian. Clubs: Racquet, Mid-Am., Arts (Chgo.); Country of Fairfield (Conn.); Thorngate Country (Deerfield, Ill.). Home: Southport CT and Chicago IL Office: Ency Brit Edn Corp 425 N Michigan Ave Chicago IL 60611

WAGNER, MARIA MARGARETE, educator; b. Kosice, Czechoslovakia, Nov. 20, 1920; came to U.S., 1960, naturalized, 1966; d. Geza Josef and Albine (Szentgyorgyi) Franze; Ph.D., Leopold Franzens U., Innsbruck, Austria, 1944; m. Eric R. Wagner, Aug. 24, 1944; children—Burkhard, Wilfried, Reinhold. Research asst. U. Innsbruck, 1942-46; tchr. Mt. St. Mary's Acad. and Coll., North Plainfield, N.J., 1960-64; tchr. Highland Park (N.J.) High Sch., 1964-67; mem. German faculty Rutgers U., 1967—, prof., 1980—, chairperson fgn. lang. dept., 1978-81, coordinator open univ. program, 1972-80. Mem. AAUP, MLA, Am. Assn. Tchrs. German, Women in German, German Am. Studies Assn., Droste Hülshoff Gesellschaft, Theodor Storm Gesellschaft, Lessing Soc., Soc. Multi-Ethnic Lit. Studies in Am., NOW. Author: Mathilde

Franziska Anneke, 1980; contbr. articles to nat., internat. profl. jours.; editor: (with others) Basic Concepts in the Humanities, 1977; Problems and Personalities in Modern German Literature, 1978. Home: 35 Gordon Way Princeton NJ 08540 Office: German Dept Rutgers U 64 College Ave New Brunswick NJ 08903

WAGNER, MARJORIE COOGAN DOWNING, educator; b. N.Y.C., Mar. 16, 1917; d. Charles A. and Marguerite C. (Ohland) Coogan; B.A., Coll. Mt. St. Vincent, 1938; M.A., Cath. U. Am., 1939; Ph.D., Yale U., 1942; LL.D., Chapman Coll., 1975; m. M. John Wagner, June 6, 1974; children—Francis, Margaret, Nicholas. Dean, Sarah Lawrence Coll., Bronxville, N.Y., 1961-65; dean of faculty Scripps Coll., Claremont, Calif., 1965-71, Frederick Hard prof. English Lit., 1971-74; pres. Calif. State Coll. Sonoma, Rohnert Park, 1974-76; vice chancellor faculty-staff affairs Calif. State U., Long Beach, 1976-80; dir. Insts. for Chief Acad. Officers, Am. Council Edn., 1980—; cons. Ednl. Inst. Bd. dirs. United Way, 1975; trustee Mt. St. Mary's Coll., Los Angeles, 1979—. Mem. Western Coll. Assn. (dir. 1969-71), Western Assn. Schs. and Colls. (sr. commn. 1968-71, 76—), Am. Council Edn. (dir. 1977-79, commn. on leadership).

WAGNER, MARY KATHRYN, state legislator; b. Madison, S.D., June 19, 1932; B.A., U. S.D., 1954; M.Ed., S.D. State U., 1974, Ph.D., 1978; m. Robert T. Wagner, June 23, 1954; children—Christopher John, Andrea Browning. Tchr., Watertown (S.D.) Public Sch., 1968-71, Brookings (S.D.) High Sch., 1971-75; mem. faculty Huron Coll., 1976; humanist-in-residence S.D. State U., 1977-78; mem. faculty Dakota State Coll., 1978-79, Augustana Coll. 1979; adminstrv. asst. S.D. Com. on Humanities, 1981—; mem. S.D. Ho. of Reps., 1981—. Mem. Brookings Sch. Bd., 1975-80; bd. dirs. Brookings/St. Paul Chamber Orch. Soc.; city chmn. Am. Cancer Soc. Drive. Mem. Population Assn. Am., Rural Social Soc., Midwest Sociol. Soc., PEO, Tau Kappa Alpha, Zeta Phi Eta, Alpha Kappa Delta, Gamma Sigma Delta, Phi Kappa Phi, Pi Gamma Mu. Republican. Episcopalian. Office: SD House of Representatives Pierre SD 57501

WAGNER, MARY KAY, state legislator; b. Burlington, Wis., Jan. 14, 1949; d. Leo John and Eleanor Mary (Cox) W.; B.S. in Elem. Edn., U. Wis., Madison, 1971, J.D., 1982. Tchr. elem. edn., Bristol, Wis., 1971-76; Kenosha County (Wis.) clk., 1976-78; mem. Wis. Assembly, 1978—, sec. Democratic Majority Caucus, 1978—. Mem. Paddock Lake Bus. and Profl. Women, AAUW. Roman Catholic. Office: 108 N Capitol St Madison WI 53703

WAGNER, SUE ELLEN, civic worker, former state legislator; b. Portland, Maine, Jan. 6, 1940; B.A. in Polit. Sci., U. Ariz.; M.A. in History, Northwestern U.; m. Peter Byrne; children—Kirk, Kristine. Successively tchr. Am. govt. and world history, public schs., Tucson, reporter Tucson Daily Citizen, asst. to dean of women Ohio State U., mem. Nev. Assembly, 1975-79; mem. Legis. Commn., 1975-79; Nev. state senator, 1980—; with Western Nev. Community Coll., 1976; mem. Reno (Nev.) Mayor's Citizen Adv. Com.; bd. dirs. Sierra Arts Found.; mem. adv. bd. U. Nev. Coll. Engring.; mem. service adv. bd. Western Nev. Community Coll.; v.p. bd. dirs. Am. Field Service, 1972-73; mem. Washoe County Republican Central Com., Nev. Rep. Central Com.; Nev.'s rep. Western Conf., Council of State Govts.' Com. on Social Services; Recipient Woman of Yr. award Reno Bus. and Profl. Women, 1975; Outstanding Legislator award Nev. Young Republicans, 1976; named Outstanding Young Woman in Am. from Nev., 1976; Outstanding Legislator, Nev. Sch. Counselors' Assn. Mem. Delta Kappa Gamma (hon.), Kappa Alpha Theta (adv. bd. 1966-71). Club: Soroptimists (hon.). Office: Nev Senate State Capitol Carson City NV 89710 *

WAGNER, VIRGINIA MEADE, physician; b. Lebanon, Ind., Feb. 6, 1940; d. Richard Carl and Virginia Evelyn (Adney) W.; B.S., Purdue U., 1962; M.D., Ind. U., 1965. Intern, Marion County (Ind.) Gen. Hosp., 1965-66; resident in pediatrics Ind. U. Med. Center, Indpls., 1966-68, chief resident pediatrics, 1968-69, fellow in pediatrics and hematology-oncology, 1969-71; pvt. practice medicine specializing pediatrics, gen. and hematology oncology, Speedway, Ind., 1971—; clin. investigator Nat. Children's Cancer Study Group, 1972—; instr. Ind. U. Sch. Medicine, Indpls., 1970-72, clin. asst. prof. pediatrics, 1972-78, clin. asso. prof., 1978—. Mem. Indpls. Symphonic Choir, 1966—, bd. dirs., 1976—, pres., 1980—; bd. dirs. Marion County Cancer Soc., 1971—, sec., 1976-80, pres., 1980-82; chmn. adv. com. Vis. Nurses Assn., 1974-78, bd. dirs., 1978—; ruling elder 1st Meridian Heights (Ind.) Presbyn. Ch., 1975-78. Recipient Service to Mankind award Golden Circle Sertoma Club (Indpls.) and N.E. Dist. Sertoma, 1982. Fellow Riley Meml. Assn.; mem. Am. Acad. Pediatrics, Am. Med. Women's Assn., Marion County Med. Soc., Ind. State, Am. med. assns., Ind., Purdue alumni assns. Club: Soroptimist (pres. Indpls. 1976-77; gov.-elect Midwest 1980-82, gov. 1982— ; Outstanding Profl. Woman of Year 1982). Home: 510 Country Club Rd Indianapolis IN 46234 Office: 2840 N High School Rd Speedway IN 46224

WAGNER, WILMA WARDEN, investment counselor; b. Coronado, Calif., June 17, 1942; d. William and Nola Warden; student San Diego Mesa Coll., 1969-72, Am. Inst. Banking, 1971-72, Houston Community Coll., 1974; children—Nola Ann, Scott E. Sec., settlement dept. Guild Mortgage Co., Arlington, Va., 1972-73; asst. loan officer Berens Assn. Washington, 1973; v.p., part-owner Houston Income Properties, 1973—. Named an Outstanding Woman of Am., Tex. Jaycees, 1979. Mem. Harris County Heritage Soc., Theatre Under the Stars, Young Women of the Arts, Cancer Assistance League, Tex. Circle R, Houston West Bus. Club, Profl. Women Execs., Am. Businesswomen's Assn. (named 1 of 10 top businesswomen in U.S. 1980), Sales and Mktg. Execs. Houston, Meml. Execs. Club. Republican. Methodist. Clubs: 100 of Houston, Toastmasters (outstanding communicator award 1979). Office: 10500 Westoffice Dr Suite 101 Houston TX 77042

WAGONER, BETTIE RODERMUND, govt. adminstr.; b. Detroit, May 29, 1923; d. Carl William and Vina (Powell) Rodermund; student Anderson Coll., 1940-41; certificate U. S.C., 1956; m. Donald W. Wagoner, Apr. 26, 1947. Sec. Sumter (S.C.) City Schs., 1941-42; traffic mgr. Pan Am. Airways, Miami, Fla., 1942-44; cost accountant Coble Dairies, Lexington, N.C., 1944-47; adminstrv. officer Dept. Army, Ft. Jackson, S.C., 1955—. Mem. Riverbanks Zool. Soc., Smithsonian Assos., Am. Rose Soc. Presbyterian. Home: 142 Miot St Columbia SC 29204 Office: Fort Jackson Columbia SC 29207

WAGONER, GERALDINE CAROL, music educator; b. Kankakee, Ill., Sept. 16, 1931; d. Ralph and Josie (Mieras) Vanderpol; B.A., Central U. of Iowa, 1954; M.A., Montclair State Coll., 1968; postgrad. Juilliard Sch. Music, 1955, 66, N.Y.U., Royal Conservatory, Toronto, 1971, Mozart EEM, Salzburg, Austria, 1972; children—Joel Timothy, Stephanie Anne. Music coach, piano pedagog, cons. Bd. Edn., Edison, N.Y., Englewood and Ridgewood, N.J., 1954-74; music specialist Ridgewood, 1975—; cons. N.Y.U. spl. project; cons. Project Impact. Trustee, Hudson Symphony Orch., 1965-71; mem. Met. Mus. of Art. Mem. Profl. Music Tchrs. Guild (cert. for highest goals and achievements 1966), Music Educators Assn., Nat. Music Tchrs. Assn., N.J. Music Tchrs. Assn., Am. Orff Schulwekk Assn., N.J. Edn. Assn., NEA, Music Educators Assn. of Am., Bergen County Music Educators Assn., Choristers Guild, Theater Devel. Found., Met. Opera Guild. Club: Les Amis du Vin. Composer sequential tonal and rhythm curriculum for children.

WAHL, JOAN CONSTANCE, tech. writer, editor; b. Phila., Dec. 23, 1921; d. Frank L. and Sara E. (Timoney) O'Brien; B.A., Rosemont Coll., 1943; postgrad UCLA, 1960-61; m. John Carl Wahl, Jr., Dec. 31, 1943 (div. 1959); children—John, Mark, David, Lawrence, Thomas, Jeanne Wahl Pearling, Madeleine Sophie, Eugene. Substitute tchr. Los Angeles City Bd. Edn., 1961; editor, proofreader Renner/Cal-Data Corp., Los Angeles, 1962-63; editor, tech. writer Volt Tech. Corp., 1964-66; sr. tech. writer, sr. project editor Aerospace Corp., El Segundo, Calif., 1966—. Sect. chmn. United Way, Los Angeles, 1963-64; mem. communications com. St. Paul the Apostle Roman Cath. Ch., Westwood, Calif., 1976-78. Recipient Outstanding Service award United Way, 1964. Mem. Soc. Tech. Communications, Aerospace Women's Com., Mental Health Assn. Los Angeles County, Kistler Honor Soc. Contbr. articles to profl. jours. Office: Aerospace Corp 2350 El Segundo Blvd El Segundo CA 90245

WAHL, ROSALIE, asso. justice Supreme Ct. Minn.; b. Gordon, Kans., Aug. 27, 1924; d. Claude William and Gertrude (Patterson) Erwin; B.A., U. Kans., 1946; J.D., William Mitchell Coll. Law, 1967; children—Christopher Rosell, Sara Emilie, Timothy Eldon, Mark Patterson, Jenny Caroline. Admitted to Minn. bar, 1967; practice law, Mpls., from 1967; adj. prof. criminal law U. Minn., 1972-73; clin. prof. law William Mitchell Coll. Law, 1973-77; asso. justice Minn. Supreme Ct., 1977—; del. Nat. Inst. Trial Advocacy, 1973; instr. Minn. Inst. Criminal Justice, 1976; instr. ann. criminal justice course Continuing Legal Edn. div. U. Minn. and Minn. State Bar Assn., 1973-76; lectr. seminar on misdemeanors Continuing Legal Edn., 1974-75. Mem. Am. Bar Assn., Minn. Bar Assn. (former mem. criminal law sect., sub-coms. on penal reform and specialization and com. on delivery of legal services), Am. Judicature Soc., Nat. Assn. Women Lawyers, Minn. Assn. Women Lawyers, Minn. Trial Lawyers Assn. Author: Misdemeanors and Moving Traffic Violations Manual, 1973; Minnesota Criminal Appeal Handbook, 1975. Office: State Supreme Ct 230 State Capitol Saint Paul MN 55155

WAHSHAVSKY, SUZANNE MAY, lawyer; b. N.Y.C., July 22, 1944; d. Charles Finke and Charlotte (Ceaser) Goldman; A.B., Vassar Coll., 1965; J.D. cum laude, N.Y.U., 1968; m. Mordechai S. Warshavsky, June 7, 1964; children—Oren, Adam, Claire. Admitted to N.Y. bar, 1968, since practiced in N.Y.C., founder, 1976, since prin. firm Washavsky, Hoffman & Cohen, P.C.; small claims arbitrator Civil Ct. N.Y.C., 1975—; mem. comml. arbitration panel Am. Arbitration Assn., 1976-79. Mem. Am. Bar Assn., N.Y. State Bar Assn., Assn. Bar City N.Y. Home: 158 Gates Ave Montclair NJ 07042 Office: 500 Fifth Ave New York NY

WAID, MARIANNE NATHAN, advt. exec.; b. Berlin, Nov. 10, 1935; came to U.S., 1937, naturalized, 1947; d. Walter L. and Annemarie (Lotge) Nathan; student Emerson Coll., Boston, 1957; m. Richard F. Waid, Feb. 3, 1967; 1 son, Mark William. Account exec. Sakel-Jackson Co., Boston, 1960-62; creative dir. Kennedy's of New Eng., Boston, 1962-63, Raymond's, Boston, 1963-65; southeastern publs. dir. Dealerscope mag., 1973-79; propr. Stanley Assos. Advt., Atlanta, 1965—; propr. M.W. Mktg. Mem. Atlanta Advt. Club. Republican. Presbyterian. Address: 150 Bocage Walk NW Atlanta GA 30305

WAIDE, SUSAN INK, owner retail store; b. Duluth, Minn., Aug. 20, 1945; d. Lewis Frank and Frances K. (Ring) Ink; B.A., Hamline U., 1967; postgrad. Inst. for Am. Univ. Aix-En Provence, 1966; m. R.E. Waide, Dec. 31, 1968. Program cons. U. Minn., Mpls., 1967-68; unit mgr. Mercy Hosp., Iowa City, Iowa, 1968-69; asst. buyer Famous-Barr Co., St. Louis, 1969-70; buyer Montaldo's, St. Louis, 1970-71; community club awards dir. Sta.-KGNC-TV & Radio, Amarillo, Tex., 1971-74; program dir. YWCA, Duluth, 1974-76; owner The Mad Islander, Bayfield, Wis., 1976—; partner Elijah Pikes, Bayfield, 1976—; cons. in field; profl. model. Amarillo Little Theater vol., 1972-73; mem. Voluntary Action Center com., 1974-75, Discover Duluth, 1974; mem. Duluth Bicentennial Festival com., 1975; adv. bd. Mademoiselle Mag., 1968. Recipient Gold award, Mad Islander logo, Lake Superior Ad Club, 1976; Soneson scholar, 1963-67; Bush Found. grantee, 1963-67; Nat. Endowment for Humanities grantee, 1974-75. Mem. Bayfield C. of C. (pres. 1978), Agy. Exec. Assn., Nat. C. of C., Women's Network, Assn. Coll. Unions Internat., Alpha Phi Theta (v.p., social chmn.). Methodist. Club: Job's Daus. Contbr. articles to profl. jours. Home: La Pointe WI 54850 Office: 2 N 2d St Bayfield WI 54814

WAIDLEY, ERICKA KRISTINE, nurse; b. Los Angeles, May 18, 1949; d. William Rudolf and Grace Clara (Fiskin) Leibold; B.S. in Nursing, San Diego State U., 1972; M.S., U. Calif., San Francisco, 1976; m. Richard Eugene Waidley, June 13, 1970; children—Cole William, Tyler Christopher. Staff nurse Kuakini Hosp., Honolulu, 1972-73; staff nurse/adult surgery Scripps Hosp., San Diego, 1973; rehab. nurse therapist Children's Hosp. and Health Center, San Diego, 1973-74; sr. staff nurse adult surgery Moffitt Hosp., San Francisco, 1975-76; asst. clin. prof. dept. biol. dysfunction U. Calif., San Francisco, 1977-80, instr. dept. staff devel., 1976-79, asst. dir. nursing for univ., 1979-80; lectr. in field. Mem. U. Calif., San Francisco Child Care/Child Study adv. bd., 1978-80; pres. No. Calif. affiliate Assn. Care of Children in Hosps., 1978-80. HEW trainee, 1975-76. Mem. Hawaii Nurses Assn., Calif. Nurses Assn., Assn. Care of Children in Hosps. (pres. 1978-80), Sigma Theta Tau (officer exec. bd. 1980-81). Contbr. articles to profl. jours. Home: 9 Fallbrook Irvine CA 92714 Office: Long Beach Meml Millers Children's Hosp Long Beach CA

WAINDLE, MAUREEN F., telephone co. exec.; b. Chgo., Apr. 4, 1945; d. Frank J. and Eileen (Hartnett) W.; B.A., U. Ga., 1968; grad. advanced mgmt. program, Rutgers U., 1978. Staff programming cons. Arthur Andersen & Co., Atlanta, 1969-70; with AT&T Co., 1970—, dist. ops. mgr. for Ala., Birmingham, 1977-79, dist. data systems mgr., head system design and programming effort in support corp. mktg. and plant ops. depts., Washington, 1979—. Pres. Courts Homeowners Assn. Mem. Nat. Assn. Female Execs. Office: 3033 Chain Bridge Rd Oakton VA 22185

WAINER, DOROTHY RUTH, communications co. exec.; b. Huntington, N.Y., May 3, 1938; d. Stanley A. and Helen V. (Greason) W.; B.F.A. cum laude, Syracuse U., 1960; M.B.A., N.Y.U., 1974. Art. dir. Dale & Finkels, N.Y.C., 1961-65; account exec. Byrde Richard & Pound, Inc., N.Y.C., 1965-70, gen. mgr., 1970-75, v.p., 1975-82; v.p., mgmt. supr. Sawdon & Bess div. Ted Bates, N.Y.C., 1982—; pres. Author! Author! Pub. Co., Inc., N.Y.C., 1973—Dorothy's Party Kids, 1982—; v.p. Program Scouts, 1982—; dir. Solar Fund, Inc.; lectr. in field. Public info. dir. Breast Health Program of N.Y.; advisor Jr. Achievement, N.Y.C.; officer WRATH-Working Rights of the Handicapped. Mem. Advt. Women of N.Y., Women Bus. Owners of N.Y., Nat. Advt. Female Execs. Assn., Sales Execs. Club N.Y. Home: 210 E 58th St New York NY 10022 Office: 444 Madison Ave New York NY 10022

WAINER, MARGARET ANNE, coll. adminstr.; b. Galesburg, Ill., Dec. 5, 1944; d. Martha C.; B.S., Western Ill. U., 1966; M.L.S., North Tex. State U., 1968; m. Burrel Wainer; children—Tamara C., Hilary A. Librarian, Glenbrook North High Sch., Northbrook, Ill., 1966-67; dir. Learning Resources Center, Carl Sandburg Coll., Galesburg, 1968—, asst. dean, 1977—; tchr. Western Ill. U. HEA fellow, 1967-68; Ill. Legis. scholar, 1981-82. Mem. ALA, Ill. Library Assn., Beta Phi Mu, Delta Kappa Gamma. Episcopalian. Office: 2232 S Lake Storey Rd Galesburg IL 61401

WAINES, MARGARET MARY, acct.; b. Loreburn, Sask., Can., Apr. 14, 1928; d. Willard John and Mary Elizabeth (Roddick) Keys; A.T.C.M. (piano), Toronto Conservatory Music, 1944; B.A. with honors (Edward Blake scholar, Thomas Wesley McCallum scholar), U. Toronto, 1950; m. Wesley John Waines, Aug. 4, 1956; children—Kenneth, Harriet, Carolyn, Bruce. With extension dept. U. B.C., Vancouver, 1950-52; home econs. tchr., New Westminster, B.C., 1952-54, Jr.-Sr. High Sch., Jasper, Alta., 1954-55, 57-58; with F and W Holdings Ltd. and Jasper Sports Centre Ltd. (both Jasper), 1962-74; public acct. in pvt. practice, Jasper, 1974—; instr. Yellowhead Region Ednl. Consortium. Mem. Jasper Sch. Bd., 1964-77. Recipient Service award Alta. Sch. Trustees Assn., 1974. Mem. Soc. Indsl. Accts. Alta. Prog. Conservative. Mem. United Ch. Clubs: Order Eastern Star, Jasper Lioness (past pres.). Home and Office: Box 622 Jasper AB T0E 1E0 Canada

WAITE, ELOISE BROWN, charitable orgn. exec.; b. Kalispell, Mont., June 10, 1918; d. Waverly Lee and Martha Ellen (Costich) Brown; B.A., U. Mont., 1939; M.S.S.W., Columbia U., 1954. Served with ARC, Japan and P.R., 1945-59, with disaster service Midwestern area, St. Louis, 1960-63, dir. service to mil. families, Washington, 1963-68, nat. dir., Washington, 1968-76, nat. v.p., Washington, 1976—. Bd. dirs. Travelers Aid Soc., Washington, 1980—; exec. group Nat. Collaboration for Youth, 1976—. Mem. Nat. Conf. Social Welfare, Council Social Work Edn. (ho. dels. 1973-77), Internat. Conf. Social Welfare. Club: Internat. (Washington). Home: 1801 16th St NW Washington DC 20009 Office: American Red Cross 18th and E Sts NW Washington DC 20006

WAITE, GLORIA E., optometrist; b. Rochester, N.Y., May 12, 1943; d. Warren Henry and Frieda (Plapp) Horn; B.S., U. Calif., Berkeley, 1965, O.D., 1966; m. Ray L. Waite, Aug. 20, 1966. Pvt. practice optometry, Pinole, Calif., 1977—. Recipient Cert. of Appreciation Richmond Unified Sch. Dist., 1978-81. Mem. Alameda-Contra Costa Counties Optometric Soc. (dir. 1975-83, pres. 1981-82), Calif. Optometric Assn. (mem. exec. com. 1978-83, Speaker award 1979-82), Pinole-Hercules C. of C. (dir. 1977-83), AAUW (mem. Richmond-El Cerrito chpt. hosting com. 1978, treas. 1979), Am. Optometric Assn., Calif. Optometric Assn. Republican. Lutheran. Club: Soroptomists (chmn. El Pinablo nominating com. 1980, Woman of Achievement award 1977). Contbr. articles in field to profl. publs. Office: 635 Tennent Ave Pinole CA 94564

WAITE, SCOTIA BALLARD KNOUFF, criminal justice specialist; b. Willis Wharf, Va., Apr. 8, 1909; d. Warren Alan and Lotta Mondera (Chard) Ballard; B.L.I., Emerson Coll., 1931; M.Ed., Boston U., 1933; diploma Sch. Social Work, Columbia U., 1939; m. William Francis Knouff, Oct. 9, 1943 (dec. Jan. 1968); children—Mary Francis Knouff Linn, Warren Irving Knouff; m. 2d Frederick Waite, Jan. 3, 1976. Dir., Mathews County (Va.) Relief Office, 1932-35, Rappahanock County Relief Office, 1935-36, dir. relief offices Norfolk County and City of S. Norfolk (Va.), 1936-37, case worker Henry Watson Children's Aid Soc., Balt., 1937, with New Orleans Council Social Agys., 1940, dir. Social Service exchange and family and child welfare div., 1940-44, asst. dir. Detroit Council Social Agys., 1944-45, tech. cons. juvenile delinquency Dept. Justice, Washington, 1948-50, instr., dir. Sociology Research Lab. CCNY, 1950-55, faculty dept. Sociology Adelphi U., 1955-63; dir. research and staff devel. Nassau County (N.Y.) Probation Dept., 1963-78; co-dir. Improving Victim Services Through Probation project Am. Probation and Parole Assn. of Aberdeen (N.C.) and Blackstone Inst. of Washington, 1978-80; cons. criminal justice, Pinehurst, N.C., 1980—; examiner Nat. Commn. on Accreditation for Corrections, 1979—; adj. asso. prof. Sch. Criminal Justice, C.W. Post Coll., L.I.U., 1967—; mem. Child Placement Rev. Com. Moore County, N.C.; chmn. Youth Services Commn., Moore County. Mem. Nat. Republican Com. Recipient Outstanding Achievement award C.W. Post Coll. Sch. Criminal Justice, 1977, Spl. award Nassau County Probation Dept., 1978. Mem. Am. Probation and Parole Assn. (Walter Dunbar award 1977), Am. Correctional Assn., Northeastern Assn. Correctional Educators, Tex. Correctional Assn., AAUW. Episcopalian. Clubs: Pinehurst Country. Author numerous reports in corrections, victim services. Home: PO Box 456 McDonald Rd Pinehurst NC 28374

WAITE, SHIRLEY ELEANOR, nurse, nursing adminstr.; b. Gloucester, Mass., Jan. 4, 1925; d. Walter Dunlap and Ida Estelle (Robinson) Collins; R.N., Truesdale Hosp. Sch. Nursing, Fall River, Mass., 1946; student Miami Dade Community Coll., 1963-68, Fla. Internat. U., Miami, 1974-77; cert. in nursing adminstr., 1980; m. Horatio Simmons Waite, Feb. 15, 1946; children—Bruce F., Cheryl J. Waite Kapit, Charles W., David W., Gayle I. Staff nurse, St. Luke's Hosp., New Bedford, Mass., 1946; nurse premature and new born nursery Union Hosp., Fall River, Mass., 1947-48; supr. Newport (R.I.) Hosp., 1951-52; staff nurse, supr. Jackson Meml. Hosp., 1953-63; supr. Meml. Hosp., Hollywood, Fla., 1964-65; supr., asst. dir. nursing, dir. nurse recruitment Cedars of Lebanon Health Care Center, Miami, Fla., 1966-77; supr. North Miami Gen. Hosp., 1978; asst. adminstr., dir. nursing service DeSoto Meml. Hosp., Arcadia, Fla., 1978—; mem. adv. com. South Fla. Jr. Coll.; Charlotte Vo-Tech. Sch.; 2d v.p. Cedars of Lebanon Credit Union. Mem. Nat. League Nursing, Fla. League Nursing, Fla. Soc. Hosp. Nursing Service Adminstrs., Charsoto Council Continuing Edn. for Nurses (pres. 1981-82), Dade County Practitioners in Infection Control (past v.p.). Home: Route 1 Box 411 Herbert Rd Arcadia FL 33821 Office: PO Box 2180 Arcadia FL 33821

WAITS, CLAUDIA BESS, adminstrv. nurse; b. Tyler, Tex., Sept. 22, 1943; d. Tommie Houston and Alma (Olive) McKay; student Tyler Jr. Coll., 1962-64; R.N., Tex. Eastern Sch. Nursing, 1965; student Park Coll., 1981—; m. Buford Benjamin Waits, Mar. 17, 1978; children—Jason Fortenberry, Joel Fortenberry, Amy Fortenberry. Dir. nursing service Med. Surg. Clinic, Tyler, 1965-66; dir. nursing service So. Heritage Retirement Home, Palestine, Tex., 1967-68; relief supr. ICU, Med. Center Hosp., Tyler, 1969-70; in-service edn. Augusta, Ga., 1971; dir. nursing service Rikard Nursing Home, Lexington, S.C., 1976-81; dir. inservice edn., relief adminstr. Forest Hills Nursing Center, Columbia, S.C., 1981—. Cub Scout den mother council Boy Scouts Am., 1971-74. Mem. Am. Nurses Assn., Central Council Nurses in Long-Term Care (pres. 1979-80, state v.p. 1980-81, mem. exec. bd. 1979—), S.C. Nurses Assn., S.C. Forum of Nursing Orgns., Am. Health Edn. Council. Democrat. Baptist. Home: 114 Laurel Bluff Dr Lexington SC 29072

WAKELEE, ADAH MAE, microbiologist; b. Conneaut, Ohio, Apr. 6, 1935; d. Walter Ivan and Arleen Louise (Beach) Terrill; B.S. in Med. Tech., Wittenberg U., 1960; m. Robert L. Wakelee, Jr., May 23, 1963; children—Kieth Robert, Kent Walter. Staff technologist, Mercy Hosp. Lab., Springfield, Ohio, 1959-63, Grant Hosp. Lab., Columbus, Ohio, 1963-64, J. Mark Handley, M.D., Santa Maria, Calif., 1965-69; microbiologist Rome (N.Y.) City Hosp. Lab., 1972-79; chief technologist MDS Health Systems Inc. (formerly Lorkim Labs.), Rome, 1980—; cons. in microbiology Rose Hosp., Rome, Slocum-Dickson Med. Group, Utica, N.Y. Mem. Oneida County Profl. Adv. Council, 1977, 78; trustee Rome Acad. Scis., 1978—, pres., 1979-81. Cert., registered Am. Soc. Clin. Pathologists; lic. clin. med. technologist, Calif. Mem. Am. Soc. Clin. Pathology, Am. Soc. Microbiology, N.Y. State Assn. Public Health Labs., Mohawk Valley Engrs. Exec. Council (chmn. 1981-82), AAUW (pres. Rome br. 1980-82). Republican. Congregationalist. Clubs: Order Eastern Star, Daus. of the Nile. Determined causes of illnesses, Rome, 1975, Holland Patent (N.Y.) area, 1976; co-author article in field for profl. jour. Home: 123 Glen Road S Rome NY 13440

WAKELIN, DIANE ALEEN, social worker, psychotherapist; b. Los Angeles, Nov. 9, 1937; d. Sidney and Helen Moosnick; B.A., UCLA, 1969, M.S.W., 1971; m. Michael H. Wakelin, June 11, 1971; children—Randal, Cheryl, Jill. Dir. tng. Hamburger Home for Girls, Los Angeles, 1971-78; asst. prof. Calif. State U., Los Angeles, 1973-76; field work supr. Calif. Sch. Profl. Psychology, Los Angeles, 1973-77; cons. to exec. dir. Optimist Boys Home and Ranch, Los Angeles, 1977—; psychotherapist Canyon Center Psychotherapy and Counseling, Studio City, Calif., 1974—; contract family therapist, mem. adv. bd. The Family Connection, San Rafael, Calif.; cons. Calif. Assn. Children's Residential Centers, 1976, Guadalupe Boys Home, Yucaipa, Calif., 1979; del. Los Angeles Mayor's Conf. on Children, Adolescents and Sr. Citizens, 1974; mem. Marin County Child and Youth Mental Health Com. Mem. Nat. Assn. Social Workers. Democrat. Jewish. Home: 26 Cloud View Rd Sausalito CA 94965 Office: 3959 Laurel Canyon Blvd Suite I Studio City CA 91604

WAKELY, BARBARA MARIE, ins. co. exec.; b. Palermo, Maine, Aug. 27, 1934; d. Walter Claude and Laura Mae (Given) Clark; grad. Ins. Inst. Am., 1973; m. Timothy Kenneth Wakely; children—Nancy Anne, Sally Jane, Mary Margaret, Christopher Kenneth. Legal sec. Ralph Ferris Jr., Augusta, Maine, 1951-52, Baker, Hostetler & Patterson, Cleve., 1952-53; office mgr. New Hampshire Ins. Co., Augusta, 1953-59, Macomber, Farr & Whitten Ins., Augusta, 1959-66; office mgr. Jones-Hoxie Corp., Augusta, 1966-73, v.p. adminstrn., 1973-79, pres., 1979—. Bd. dirs., chmn. legis. com. Asso. Gen. Contractors of Maine, Inc., 1977—. Mem. Nat. Assn. Ins. Women, Ind. Ins. Agts. Assn., Ind. Ins. Agts. Maine, Kennebec Valley Ind. Ins. Agts. Assn., Asso. Gen. Contractors Am., Life Underwriters Am., Ins. Women Central Maine, Maine Publicity Bur., Kennebec Valley C. of C. (pres. 1981—, dir. 1975—). Republican. Home: PO Box 2264 Augusta ME 04330 Office: Jones-Hoxie Corp PO Box 2519 Augusta ME 04330

WALBER, CATHERINE ANN, communications co. exec.; b. Cleve., Aug. 18, 1924; d. Charles Joseph and Ann Elizabeth (Wilkinson) Mayers; B.A., Duke U., 1946; M.A., CCNY, 1963; postgrad. St. John's U., 1975; m. John W. Walber, May 19, 1949; children—Elizabeth Ann, Catherine Patricia, Bryan Herbert. Journalist, reporter, feature writer, columnist newspapers, Ohio and N.Y., 1940—; advt. copywriter B. Altman & Co., N.Y.C., 1946-50; freelance advt. copywriter, N.Y., N.J., 1950-58; English tchr. Nanuet (N.Y.) Sr. High Sch., 1962-82; tchr. composition and lit. Rockland Community Coll., 1969-76; fellow Bay Area Writing Project, 1976—; writing cons. Nat. Council Tchrs. English, 1978-79; partner Communications Cons., Mt. Kisco, N.Y., 1979—; co-author Just Writing series Oceana Press, 1982; dir. public relations, writer newsletters and brochures various orgns., instns.; writing cons.; curriculum and publs. adv. Bd. dirs., edn. dir. Rockland County Cancer Soc., 1950-61; troop leader, public relations dir. Rockland County council Girl Scouts U.S.A., 1958-62; pres., public relations dir. Chestnut Grove-Rockland County PTA, 1957-61. Mem. Am. Soc. Profl. Cons. Nat. Assn. Female Execs. Inc., Am. Mgmt. Assn., Am. Soc. Tng. and Devel., Am. Soc. Profl. and Exec. Women, N.Y. State Tchrs. Assn., Kappa Alpha Theta. Republican. Roman Catholic. Home: 3 Stratford Pl New City NY 10956 Office: Box 456 Mount Kisco NY 10549

WALBRAN, BONNIE (JANE) BREAUX, psychologist; b. Little Rock, Feb. 23, 1938; d. Bertin Joseph and Jeanne Rita (LaNasa) Breaux; A.B. cum laude, Vassar Coll., 1960; Ph.D., Washington U., 1975; postgrad. St. Louis U.; children—Stephanie Jane, Alexa Suzanne. Research asst. Milbank Meml. Fund, Hudson River St. Hosp., Poughkeepsie, N.Y., 1960-61, Tufts U. Med. Sch., Boston, 1961-62, Harvard U. Sch. Public Health dept. epidemiology, Boston, 1962-64; research asst. Washington U. Sch. Medicine dept. psychiatry, St. Louis, 1965-69, 75-77, research asso., 1978-79; dir. New Hope Learning Center, St. Louis U., 1979-81; unit psychologist, acting coordinator psychol. services St. Louis Developmental Disabilities Treatment Center; instr. Lindenwood Coll., Webster Coll. Mem. Am. Psychol. Assn., Am. Assn. Mental Deficiency, Valley Sailing Assn., Sigma Xi. Democrat. Contbr. articles in field to profl. jours. Home: 215 Jefferson Rd Webster Groves MO 63119 Office: MS 429 5400 Arsenal St St Louis MO 63139

WALBRIDGE, RUTH P., state legislator; b. Rutland, Vt., Oct. 6, 1924; student Lasalle Jr. Coll., Auburndale, Mass.; m. Richard P. Walbridge; 2 sons, 1 dau. Mem. Vt. Ho. of Reps., 1981—. Pres., Northwest Sch. PTA, Parents Group Vt. Achievement Center. Mem. Am. Legion Aux., VFW Aux. Congregational (former Sunday sch. tchr., supt. Sunday sch., mem. mem. Ch. Diaconate.) Republican. Office: Vt Ho Reps State House Montpelier VT 05602 *

WALBURG, JUDITH ANN, fund raiser; b. N.Y.C., Feb. 19, 1948; d. Charles Albert and Florence Blanche (Perry) Walburg; B.A., Fisk U., 1969. Customer relations rep. Olivetti Corp., N.Y.C., 1970-72; dir. alumni groups and nat. orgns. United Negro Coll. Fund, N.Y.C., 1972—. Mem. sponsoring com. Opera Ebony. Mem. N.Y. Fisk Alumni Assn., Nat. Assn. Media Women. Episcopalian. Home: 284 Convent Ave New York NY 10031 Office: 500 E 62nd St New York NY 10031

WALBY, SANDRA LEE, civic worker; b. Amesbury, Mass., Nov. 23, 1943; d. Clarence Colby and Agnes Elizabeth (Bruce) Wheeler; student Lee Inst. Real Estate Tng., Boston, 1965; m. Ralph William Walby, Sept. 12, 1970; children—Julie, Scott, Jennifer, Kristina. Legal sec. Louis Cyr, Atty., Amesbury, 1961-63; sec., clk. Dist. Ct., Haverhill, Mass., 1967-69; legal researcher, exec. sec., office mgr. Infosearch, Inc., Albany, N.Y., 1969-71; sec. Capital Formation Counselors, Belleair, Fla., 1978-80; mem. customer adv. bd. Maas Bros. Dept. Store, 1978-79. Telethon worker Am. Cancer Soc.; vol. Upper Pinellas Assn. Retarded Citizens, Sci. Center, Child Abuse Center, Hunter Blood Bank; first v.p. Oakhurst Elem. PTA, 1980-82; vol. Upper Pinellas Spouse Abuse Center. Mem. Gen. Fedn. Women's Clubs, Fla. Fedn. Women's Clubs (chmn. jr. state meetings 1982-84, chmn. registration and credentials 1980-82), Republican. Methodist. Club: Largo Jr. Woman's (parliamentarian 1979-80). Home: 14423 Neptune Rd Seminole FL 33542

WALCOTT, CYNTHIA ANN, nurse, surg. products ofcl.; b. Troy, N.Y., Sept. 16, 1948; d. Walter William and Anna (Tanchak) Wilsnack; R.N., New England Bapt. Hosp., 1969. Operating room specialist Columbus (Ga.) Med. Center, 1970-71, Meml. Hosp., Albany, N.Y., 1971-73, Holyoke (Mass.) Hosp., 1974-77; asst. head nurse operating room Noble Hosp., Westfield, Mass., 1973-74; nurse operating room, product evaluation specialist Newton (Mass.) Wellesley Hosp., 1977-78; nurse specialist Davol, Inc., Cranston, R.I., 1978-79, area sales mgr., 1979-80, profl. edn. dir., 1980-82; mgr. profl. services surg. products USCI Internat. div. C.R. Bard, Inc., Burlington, Mass., 1982—; cons. in field. Mem. Assn. Operating Room Nurses, Nat. Assn. Female Execs., Assn. Advancement of Med. Instrumentation. Home: 72 Prescott Dr North Chelmsford MA 01863 Office: PO Box 436 2 Burlington Woods Dr Burlington MA 01803

WALCZAK, ELIZABETH JANICE, commodity broker; b. Passaic, N.J., Feb. 16, 1952; d. Robert Michael and Grace Randall (Schumann) W.; B.A., Elmira (N.Y.) Coll., 1974; postgrad. various specialized courses. Sales asst. Merrill Lynch, Pierce, Fenner & Smith, N.Y.C., 1975-76; adminstrv. asst. Nelson Fund, N.Y.C., 1976; account exec. E.F. Hutton Co., N.Y.C., 1976-78; broker asst. Agcom, N.Y.C., 1978-80; mem. N.Y. Cotton Exchange, 1980-82.

WALD, FRANCINE JOY WEINTRAUB (MRS. BERNARD J. WALD), physicist; b. Bklyn., Jan. 13, 1938; d. Irving and Minnie (Reisig) Weintraub; student Bklyn. Coll., 1955-57; B.E.E., CCNY, 1960; M.S., Poly. Inst. Bklyn., 1962, Ph.D., 1969; m. Bernard J. Wald, Feb. 2, 1964; children—David Evan, Kevin Mitchell. Engr., Remington Rand Univac div. Sperry Rand Corp., Phila., 1960; instr. Poly. Inst. Bklyn., 1962-64, adj. research asso., 1969-70; lectr. N.Y. Community Coll., Bklyn., 1969, 70; instr. sci. Friends Sem., N.Y.C., 1975-76, chmn. dept. sci., 1976—. NDEA fellow, 1962-64. Mem. Am. Phys. Soc., Am. Assn. Physics Tchrs., Assn. Tchrs. in Ind. Schs., N.Y. Acad. Scis., Nat. Sci. Tchrs. Assn., AAAS, Sigma Xi, Tau Beta Pi, Eta Kappa Nu. Home: 520 LaGuardia Pl New York NY 10012

WALD, PATRICIA M., judge; b. Torrington, Conn., Sept. 16, 1928; d. Joseph F. and Margaret (O'Keefe) McGowan; B.A., Conn. Coll., 1948; LL.B., Yale, 1951; m. Robert L. Wald, June 22, 1952; children—Sarah, Douglas, Johanna, Frederica, Thomas. Admitted to D.C. bar, 1952; clk. U.S. Ct. Appeals judge, 1951-52; asso. firm Arnold, Fortas & Porter, Washington, 1952-53; mem. D.C. Crime Commn., 1964-65, Dept. Justice, 1967, Neighborhood Legal Service, D.C., 1968-70; co-dir. Ford Found. Project Drug Abuse, 1970, Center for Law and Social Policy, 1971-72, Mental Health Law Project, from 1972; asst. atty. gen. legis. affairs Dept. Justice, 1977-79; judge U.S. Ct. Appeals for D.C., 1979—. Trustee Ford Found., Conn. Coll., Exeter Acad.; mem. Carnegie Council Children. Mem. Am., D.C. (dir.) bar assns., Inst. Medicine, Am. Law Inst. (council). Author: Law and Poverty, 1965; co-author: Bail in the United States, 1964; Dealing with Drug Abuse, 1973. Mem. bd. editors Am. Bar Assn. Jour. Office: US Courthouse John Marshall Pl Washington DC 20001 *

WALD, SYLVIA, artist; b. Phila., Oct. 30, 1915; ed. Moore Inst. Art, Sci. and Industry. Exhibited one-man shows: U. Louisville, 1945, 49, Kent State Coll., 1945, Nat. Serigraph Soc., 1946, Grand Central Moderns, 1957, Devorah Sherman Gallery, 1960, New Sch., 1967, Book Gallery, White Plains, N.Y., 1968, Benson Gallery, Bridgehampton, N.Y., 1977, Knoll Internat., Munich, W.Ger., 1979, Amerika Haus, Munich, 1979, Aaron Berman Gallery Constrns. & Sculpture, N.Y.C., 1981; group shows include: Nat. Sculpture Soc., 1940, Sculpture Internat., Phila., 1940, Chgo. Art Inst., 1941, Bklyn. Mus., 1975, Library of Congress, 1943, 52, 58, Internat. Print Exhbn., Salzburg and Vienna, 1952, 2d São Paulo Biennial, 1953, Smithsonian Instn., 1954, N.Y. Cultural Center, 1973, Mus. Modern Art, N.Y.C., 1975, Artists Choice traveling exhbn., 1976-77, Wall Dimensions, Sid Deutch Gallery, N.Y.C., 1977, Penthouse Gallery, Mus. Modern Art, N.Y.C., 1977-78, Collage and Assemblage, Summit (N.J.) Art Center, 1980, Suzuki Gallery, N.Y.C., 1981, Linden Gallery, N.Y.C., 1981, Aaron Berman Gallery, N.Y.C., 1981, 82, Genson Gallery, Bridgehampton, 1982; represented in permanent collections Aetna Oil Co., AAUW, Ball State Tchrs. Coll., Bibliotheque Nationale, Bklyn. Mus., Howard U., State U. Iowa, Library of Congress, U. Louisville, Nat. Gallery, Mus. Modern Art, Phila. Mus., N.C. Mus., Rose Mus. Art at Brandeis U., Whitney Mus., N.Y.C., Finch Coll. Mus., N.Y.C., U. Nebr., Ohio U., U. Okla., Princeton U., Victoria and Albert Mus., Guggenheim Mus., Walker Gallery, Worcester (Mass.) Art Mus. Contbr. to profl. publs. Address: 417 Lafayette St New York NY 10003

WALDAU, HELEN FRANCES, educator; b. Torrington, Conn., Mar. 21, 1925; d. Teofil and Michaelena (Plaga) Budney; B.A., U. Conn., 1953, 6th yr. cert., 1968; M.A., U. Hartford; divorced; children—Geoffrey, Christopher, Peter, Sandra. Tchr., Hopewell Sch., Glastonbury, Conn., 1966-82, tchr. academically talented, 1982—, supr. U. Conn. open edn. interns, 1971-75, Task Force Gifted Edn., 1976-81. Fellow U. Conn., 1967-68. Mem. NEA, Conn., Glastonbury edn. assns., Greater Conn. Council for Open Edn. (charter), Conn. Tchr. Center for Humanistic Edn., Psi Upsilon Omicron. Home: 1808 Main St Glastonbury CT 06033

WALDAUER, KAREN, publisher; b. N.Y.C., Jan. 13, 1938; d. Max and Sylvia Gordon; student CCNY, 1955-58; m. Charles Waldauer, May 8, 1958; children—Jan, Kim. Head art dept. Bohanon Printing, Syracuse, N.Y., 1960-64, A.S. Barnes Co., 1964-65; prodn. dir., regional editor, mng. editor Rutgers U. Press, 1965-68; pres. Middle Atlantic Press, Wallingford, Pa., 1968—; pub. cons. Wilmington (Del.) News Jour., Corp. Service Co.; v.p., dir., cons. ValleyDel Publs. Bd. dirs. Sch. in Rose Valley. Mem. Pubs. Alliance, Phila. Pubs. Group, Brandywine Valley Press Assn. Clubs: Phila. Skating, Skating of Radnor (past pres.). Office: Box 263 Wallingford PA 19086

WALDBAUM, JANE COHN, educator; b. N.Y.C., Jan. 28, 1940; d. Max Arthur and Sarah (Waldstein) Cohn; A.B. summa cum laude, Brandeis U., 1962; M.A., Harvard U., 1964, Ph.D., 1968. Research fellow Fogg Art Mus. Harvard U., 1968-70, 72-73; asst. prof. dept. art history U. Wis., Milw., 1973-78, assoc. prof., 1978—, chmn., 1982—; vis. assoc. prof. dept. fine arts Ind. U., 1978-79. Bd. dirs. Milw. Soc. Archeol. Inst. Am. Woodrow Wilson fellow, 1962-63, 65-66; Am. Philos. Soc. grantee, 1972; NEH stipend, 1975. Mem. Archeol. Inst. Am. (mem. exec. com. 1975-77, chmn. com. membership programs 1977-81), Am. Schs. Oriental Research, Assn. Field Archaeology, Soc. Archaeol. Sci., Phi Beta Kappa. Author: (with others) Sardis Final Reports I: A Survey of Sardis and Major Monuments Outside the City Walls, 1975; From Bronze to Iron: The Transition From The Bronze Age to the Iron Age in the Eastern Mediterranean, 1978; Sardis Monograph 8: Metalwork from Sardis, The Finds Through 1974, 1982; contbr. articles to profl. jours. Office: Department of Art History University of Wisconsin Milwaukee MI 53201

WALDEN, AMELIA ELIZABETH, author; b. N.Y.C.; d. William A. and Elizabeth (Wanner) Walden; B.S., Columbia, 1934; certificate Am. Acad. Dramatic Arts; m. John William Harmon, Feb. 9, 1946 (dec. 1950). Author: Gateway, 1946; Waverly, 1947; Sunnycove, 1948; Skymountain, 1950; A Girl Called Hank, 1951; Marsha, On-Stage, 1952; Victory for Jill, 1953; All My Love, 1954; Daystar, 1955; Three Loves Has Sandy, 1955; The Bradford Story, 1956; I Found My Love, 1956; My Sister Mike, 1956; Palomino Girl, 1957; Flight Into Morning, 1957; Today is Mine, 1958; Queen of the Courts, 1959; (duo of novels) An American Teacher: Where is My Heart?, 1960, How Bright the Dawn, 1962; A Boy to Remember, 1960; Shadow on Devils Peak, 1961; (trilogy) The American Shakespeare Festival: When Love Speaks, 1961, So Near the Heart, 1962, My World's the Stage, 1964; My Dreams Ride High, 1963; To Catch A Spy, 1964; The Spy on Danger Island, 1965; Race the Wild Wind, 1965; The Spy with Five Faces, 1966; In Search of Ophelia, 1966; A Spy Called Michel-E, 1967; A Name for Himself, 1967; The Spy Who Talked Too Much, 1968; Walk In A Tall Shadow, 1968; A Spycase Built For Two, 1969; Same Scene, Different Place, 1969; The Case of the Diamond Eye, 1969; Basketball Girl of the Year, 1970; What Happened to Candy Carmichael?, 1970; Valerie Valentine is Missing, 1971; Stay to Win, 1971; Play Ball, McGill, 1972; Where was Everyone when Sabrina Screamed?, 1973; Go, Phillips, Go, 1974; Escape on Skis, 1975; Heartbreak Tennis, 1977. Amelia Walden collection personal, profl. papers, original manuscripts, research data established at U. Oreg., Eugene, 1982; pioneer young adult novel. Home: 89 N Compo Rd Westport CT 06880

WALDEN, LINDA LEE, lawyer state ofcl.; b. Dallas, Aug. 16, 1951; d. Leslie L. and Neva Irene (McBee) W.; B.A., Tex. Woman's U., Denton, 1972; J.D., St. Mary's U., San Antonio, 1975. Admitted to Tex. bar, 1975, U.S. Supreme Ct. bar, 1978, U.S. Dist. Cts., 1976; asst. city atty. City of Amarillo (Tex.), 1976-78; 1st asst. dist. atty. 84th Jud. Dist., 1978-79; asst. atty. gen. City of Austin (Tex.), 1979—; chief prosecutors assistance div. Office Atty. Gen. of Tex., 1981—; instr. Tex. Jud. Council. Cert. criminal law specialist Tex. Bd. Legal Specialization. Mem. Am. Bar Assn., Nat. Dist. Atty. Assn., Tex. Dist. and County Attys. Assn., Assn. Bd. Cert. Attys. Club: Altrusa. Home: 7117 Wood Hollow Apt 1716 Austin TX 78731 Office: PO Box 12548 Austin TX 78711

WALDER, LORETTA, psychologist, lawyer; d. Jack and Fay (Wernik) Berkowitz; B.A., Hunter Coll., 1953; Ph.D., Columbia U., 1959; cert. specialization in psychoanalysis N.Y.U., 1975; J.D., N.Y. Law Sch., 1980. Psychotherapist, Bleuer Center, Jamaica, N.Y., 1961-64; pvt. practice clin. psychology, N.Y.C., 1962—; supervising psychologist Roosevelt Hosp., N.Y.C., 1964-68; chief sch. psychologist Bethpage (N.Y.) Public Schs., 1960-63; cons. psychologist Easton-Redding (Conn.) Schs., 1971-72; psychotherapist Community Guidance Service, 1975-79; admitted to N.Y. State bar, 1981; affiliate BAR/BRI, psychol. cons., N.Y.C., 1980—. Mem. Am. Psychol. Assn., N.Y. State Psychol. Assn., Sigma Xi. Author: Pass This Bar, 1981; contbr. articles to mags.

WALDMAN, ANNE LESLEY, poet, editor, pub., ednl. adminstr.; b. Millville, N.J., Apr. 2, 1945; d. John Marvin and Frances (Le Fevre) W.; B.A., Bennington Coll., 1966; m. Reed Eyre Bye; 1 son, Edwin Ambrose. Dir. The Poetry Project, St. Marks Ch. In-the-Bowery, N.Y.C., 1968-78; co-dir. Jack Kerouac Sch. of Poetics at Naropa Inst., Boulder, Colo., 1974—; author books of poetry: Baby Breakdown, 1970, Giant Night, 1970, No Hassles, 1971, Life Notes, 1973, Fast Speaking Woman, 1975, Journals and Dreams, 1976; editor anthologies: The World Anthology, 1969, Another World, 1972; Talking Poetics From Naropa Institute vol. 1, 1978, vol. 2, 1979; publisher Angel Hair Books, N.Y.C., Full Ct. Press, N.Y.C. Recipient Dylan Thomas Meml. award New Sch., N.Y.C., 1967; Cultural Artists Program grantee, 1976-77; Nat. Endowment for Arts grantee, 1979-80. Mem. PEN Club. Office: care Naropa Inst 1111 Pearl St Boulder CO 80302

WALDMAN, GLORIA FRANCES FEIMAN, educator, journalist; b. N.Y.C., Mar. 10, 1947; d. Harry and Helen (Pfeffer) Feiman; B.A. (Regents scholar), CCNY, 1966; M.A. (NDEA grantee), Cornell U., 1968; Fulbright scholar U. San Carlos, Guatemala, 1966; student U. Madrid, 1964-65; Ph.D., City U. N.Y., 1978. Radio commentator Sta. WOSO, P.R., 1979-80; video filmmaker, P.R., 1979-82; co-founder Producciones Guariquen, P.R., 1979; drama critic El Nuevo Día, P.R., 1979-82; asst. prof. fgn. lang. York Coll., City U. N.Y., 1982—. Grantee Jewish Found. Edn. of Girls, 1963-66, Nat. Endowment for Humanities, 1979. Mem. P.E.N. Club, Overseas Press Club, Latin Am. Studies Assn., Assn. Caribbean Studies, MLA (regional del.), Am. Assn. Tchrs. Spanish and Portuguese, AAUP, Feminstas Unidas, MLA Womens Caucus. Author: (with others) Feminismo ante el franquismo, 1979; author film: Habla Lolita Lebrón, 1979; editor Teatro Contemporaneo, 1983. Office: York Coll 150-14 Jamaica Ave Jamaica NY 11451

WALDO, SALLY (MRS. CLAUDE A. WALDO), ins., real estate broker; b. Seattle, Jan. 8, 1903; d. Hyman and Lena (Kaplan) Rosenstein; student Modesto Jr. Coll., 1930; m. Claude A. Waldo, Nov. 6, 1925 (dec. 1969). Exec. sec., co-owner firm Claude A. Waldo, land surveyor, Martinez, Calif., 1945-69, bus. opportunity broker, real estate broker, 1949—, ins. broker, 1950—. Mem. Calif. 50-50 Bill Com., 1937; mem. constn. revision com. nat. conv. Young Democratic Clubs Am., 1937, nat. committeewoman, 1937-39, 1st v.p., 1936-37, chmn. woman's activities, 1936; Calif. chmn. circulation Nat. Young Dem. Paper, 1937; adv. bd. women's div. Calif. Dem. Central Com., 1936-38; organizer three young Dem. clubs in Stanislaus County, 1935; mem. Calif. Dem. Campaign Com., 1936; v.p. San Joaquin dist. Fed. Dem. Women's Study Clubs, 1940; mem. Civic Arts League, Walnut Creek, Calif. Mem. AIM (asso.), San Joaquin Dist. Conv. Fedn. Women's Clubs (pub. chmn. 1935, legislation chmn. Stanislaus County 1934), Women's Improvement Club, Modesto, Calif. (sec. 1933), Women's Progressive Club (charter), Modesto (sec. 1933), Tres Artes (organizer 1935), Modesto Art League (charter), Martinez Grange, Town Hall Forum Los Angeles, Irish-Israeli-Italian Soc. San Francisco, Civic Arts League Walnut Creek, Internat. Platform Assn., Nat. Women's Polit. Caucus. Clubs: Toastmistress (charter mem. Modesto); Order Eastern Star; San Francisco Press (hon.) (San Francisco); Berkeley, City Commons, Polit. Sci. (Berkeley, Calif.). Address: Box 1023 Lafayette CA 94549

WALDO, TOMMY RUTH BLACKMON (MRS. SELDEN FENNELL WALDO), educator; b. Dallas, Jan. 14, 1916; d. Gulie Hargrove and Mary Lee (Craig) Blackmon; B.A., Agnes Scott Coll., 1938; M.A., U. Fla., 1955, Ph.D., 1961; m. Selden Fennell Waldo, Oct. 28, 1941 (dec. Nov. 1950); children—George Selden (dec.), Andrew Blackmon. Grad. asst. U. Fla., Gainesville, 1952-55, instr., 1955-61, asst. prof. English, 1961-68, asso. prof. English, 1968-76, prof., 1976—; pvt. tchr. piano and organ, 1938-55. Mem. So. Atlantic Modern Lang. Assn., Modern Lang., Assn., Fla., Gainesville music tchrs. assns., Southeastern Renaissance Conf., Phi Beta Kappa, Sigma Alpha Iota (patroness), Delta Kappa Gamma. Author book on Shakespeare. Contbr. articles to profl. jours. Address: 719 NE 1st St Gainesville FL 32601

WALDON, VIVALORIA YNESTRA, pharm. sales rep., mortgage broker, real estate asso.; b. Bartow, Fla., Sept. 22, 1949; d. Leo W. and Eldora S. W.; B.A., Wayne State U., 1972; 1 son, Russell Lamar. Sales rep. Xerox Corp., Atlanta, 1972-78; partner Waldon's Bus. Cons. Service, Charlotte, N.C., 1978-79; real estate asso. J. Bolinger Inc., Orlando, Fla., 1979—; owner Ideal Mortgage Co., Orlando, Fla., 1981—. Mem. Leadership Ga. Program, 1975. Mem. Nat. Assn. Female Execs. (dir.), Emerald Ring Club of McNeil Consumer Products Co., Fla. Assn. Mortgage Brokers, Boynton Beach Bd. Realtors, Nat. Geog. Soc., Delray Beach C. of C. Baptist. Home: 3017 Tradewinds Trail Orlando FL 32805

WALEN, ELIZABETH ROWE (BENSON), civic worker; b. West Somerville, Mass., Jan. 25, 1915; d. Frederick Smallwood and Susan (Rowe) Benson; R.N., Mass. Gen. Hosp., Boston, 1937; B.S. in Public Health Nursing, Simmons Coll., 1937; m. Harry Leonard Walen, June 26, 1939; children—Harry Benson, Kimball Frederick, Robert Leonard. Staff nurse Boston Community Health Nursing Assn., 1937-39; tchr. nurses' aide course ARC, Ayer, Mass., 1945-52, Community Meml. Hosp.; charge nurse Briarwood Nursing Home, Needham, Mass., 1974-75; mem. edn. com. N.E. region NCCJ, 1972—, mem. husband-wife team on study mission to examine intergroup relations within Israel, 1974; bd. dirs. Family Service Bur., Newton, Mass., 1940's; sec. Friends of Jackson Homestead hist. soc., Newton, 1968-73; past chmn. bd. deaconesses Newton Highlands Congregational Ch.; chmn. Harry Walen for Sch. Com., Newton, 1959. Mem. Los Alamos (N.Mex.) Hist. Soc. (life), Sandy Bay Hist. Soc., Pilgrim John Howland Soc. (asso.), DAR (regent chpt. 1960-62, 68-70, rec. sec. state 1965-68, chmn. state coms. pres. Mass. State Officers Club 1970-72, mem. Mass. Ex-Regents Club 1962-78, vice chmn. nat. flag com. 1980—), Daus. Colonial Wars (lady of council 1972-75), Daus. Am. Colonists (hon. state regent 1973—, state regent 1970-73), Nat. Soc. Women Descs. Ancient and Hon. Arty. Co. (pres. Mass. Ct. Assistance 1974-77). Clubs: Harvard Woman's (rec. sec.), Sandy Bay Yacht, Newell (past pres.); Rockport Woman's (v.p.). Home: Penzance Rd Rockport MA 01966

WALES, M(ARY) ELIZABETH, acad. dean; b. Wichita, Kans., Dec. 5, 1932; d. Jesse Lee and Olive F. (Bryant) Moore; B.A., U. Kans., 1949;

M.A., U. Cin., 1963, Ph.D., 1967; children—Dirk Oliver, Jessica Wordin, Stacey Elizabeth. With U. Cin. Sch. Medicine, 1967-71, dept. psychology, 1971-76, Wright State U. Sch. Medicine, 1976-82; acad. dean Calif. Sch. Profl. Psychology, Los Angeles, 1982—; cons. to orgns. Named Tchr. of Yr., Wright State U. Sch. Medicine, 1980; NIMH tng. grantee, 1979-82; diplomate Am. Bd. Profl. Psychology. Mem. Am. Psychol. Assn., Acad. Profl. and Research Psychology, Ohio Psychol. Assn., Nat. Tng. Labs. Home: 341 W California Blvd Pasadena CA 91105

WALKENHORST, DORIS MILLIGAN, mental health adminstr., therapist; b. Daytona Beach, Fla., Jan. 18, 1922; d. John Sterry and Eirene (Esch) Milligan; B.M.E. cum laude, Stetson U., 1943; M.S.W., Ohio State U., 1970; m. Walter Walkenhorst, Jr., Oct. 27, 1945; children—Walter, John Scott, Richard Mark, Robert Wright. Inpatient treatment team, aftercare coordinator Rollman Psychiat. Inst., Cin., 1970-74; sr. planner, program planning dept. Bethesda Hosps., Cin., 1974-77; planner-evaluator, asso. dir. Mental Health Bd. of Health and Rehab. Services, Dist. IV, Daytona Beach, Fla., 1977-79; dir., co-founder Family Inst. of Daytona Beach, 1979—; adv. bd. Mental Health Assn. Bds. dirs. Halifax Urban Ministries, Human Resources Community Mental Health Center, Civic Music Assn., The House Next Door-Family Resource Center; mem. Council of Ministries, adminstrv. bd. Meth. Ch. Mem. Acad. Cert. Social Workers, Register of Clin. Social Workers, Nat. Assn. Social Workers, Fla. Council Community Mental Health, Family Mediation Assn., Phi Beta, Sigma Delta Pi, Alpha Xi Delta. Home: 300 Auburn Dr Daytona Beach FL 32018 Office: Suite 435 444 Seabreeze Blvd Daytona Beach FL 32018

WALKER, ANITA MARIE RANSDELL, educator; b. Dallas, Feb. 13, 1957; d. Palmer Norman and Shirley Ann (Harding) Ransdell; student Marquette U., Ger., 1976; B.A. summa cum laude, So. Meth. U., 1978, B.S. summa cum laude, 1978; postgrad. Goethe-Inst., Freiburg in Breisgau, W. Ger., 1978, Johannes Gutenberg-Universität, Mainz, W. Ger., 1978-79; M.A. in Math., U. Okla., Norman, 1980, postgrad., 1981—; m. Billy Kenneth Walker, Mar. 8, 1980. Pvt. practice tutoring, 1976-78; grader dept. math. So. Meth. U., 1976-78, tutor, 1977, summer orientation leader, 1977-78, registration clk., 1977-78; grader dept. math. U. Okla., 1979-80, tutor, 1980-82, instr. math. Am. Indian Bus. and Engring. Edn. Center, 1981, Karcher grad. teaching fellow, 1979—. Nat. Indian seminar instr. Boy Scouts Am. Order of the Arrow; mem. Okla. Masters Swim Team, 1981—. Mem. Am. Math. Soc., Am. Indian Sci. and Engring. Soc., Math. Assn. Am., Phi Beta Kappa. Republican. Presbyterian. Clubs: German Tex. Heritage Soc., Dallas Goethe Center (dir. 1977-81), Order Eastern Star, Internat. Order Rainbow Girls (adv.). Home: PO Box 2806 Norman OK 73070 Office: Department of Mathematics University of Oklahoma Norman OK 73019

WALKER, ANNE SHIRLEY, women's devel. support resource adminstr.; b. Melbourne, Australia, June 4, 1937; d. Charles Fitzroy and Ethel Ada (Ingamells) Walker; citizen of Fiji, 1972; diploma Inst. for Early Childhood Edn., Melbourne, 1956; M.S. in Edn., Ind. U., 1974, Ph.D., 1976. Dir. Lady Northcote Kindergarten, Melbourne, 1956-59; nat. program dir. YWCA of Fiji, Suva, 1962-72; dir. Internat. Women's Tribune Centre, N.Y.C., 1976—. Sec., Treas. Fiji Nat. Youth Council, 1968-72; World YWCA rep. UN, 1977—. Recipient Fiji Independence medal, 1970. Mem. Soc. Internat. Devel., Assn. Educators in Communications Technology. Democrat. Methodist. Author: Youth Club Ideas for the Pacific, 1972; A Study of Relationships Between Mass Media, Community Involvement and Political Participation in Fiji, 1976. Home: 310 E 46th St Apr 11V New York City NY 10017 Office: 305 E 46th St 6th Floor New York NY 10017

WALKER, CAROL MARSHALL, mfg. co. ofcl.; b. Great Barrington, Mass., Dec. 14, 1937; d. Enoch Raymond and Margaret Josephine (Courtney) Marshall; student Am. Inst. Banking, 1960-62, U. Bridgeport, 1978; children by previous marriage—Marshall Ernest Walker. Sect. head, Union Trust Co., Stamford, Conn., 1959-67; exec. dir. Leukemia Soc. Am., Stamford, 1967-69; neighborhood div. asst. United Way Stamford, 1969; statis. typist Xerox Corp., Stamford, 1970-73, exec. sec. 1973-75, communications coordinator, Greenwich, Conn., 1975—. Pres., Stamford Young Republican Club, 1964; co-chmn. 4th Congressional Dist. Young Rep. Orgn., 1964-65; del. Conn. Young Rep. Bd., 1964, 65, 66; del. Conn. Rep. Women's Orgn., 1964, 65; founder Stamford Teen Age Rep. Club, 1968; mem. Stamford Fair Rent Commn., 1981-82, vice chmn., 1982. Mem. Am. Mgmt. Assn., Internat. Platform Assn., Am. Soc. Profl. and Exec. Women, Springdale Fire Dept. Ladies Aux., Greenwich Hist. Soc., Nat. Trust Hist. Preservation, Early Am. Soc. Roman Catholic. Home: 160 Highview Ave Springdale CT 06907 Office: Xerox Latinamerican Group 3 Pickwick Plaza Greenwich CT 06830

WALKER, CAROLINE ANN, utility co. exec.; b. Seattle, Nov. 16, 1944; d. Charles Leonard and Ann Phyllis (Dziedzic) W.; B.A. in Econs., U. Wash., 1966; M.A. in Econs., UCLA, 1968; m. James C. Sudduth, Mar., 1971 (div. Mar. 1978). Regional economist U.S. Army C.E., Los Angeles, 1969-70, Seattle, 1971-73, 78-79; econ. analyst Library of Congress, Congl. Research Service, Washington, 1970-71; project coordinator Pierce County (Wash.) Wash., Alaska Regional Med. Program, 1974-75; market adminstr. Pacific N.W. Bell Telephone Co., Seattle, 1979, staff specialist, 1979—; lectr. 13th Ann. Pacific N.W. Regional Econ. Conf., 1979. Campaigner mem. Republican Nat. Com. Mem. Seattle Economists Club, Alumni Assn. U. Wash. Clubs: Wash. Athletic, Women's University. Won appeal against Sec. of Wash. State on anti-fluoridation measure, 1976. Home: 24645 8th Ave S Kent WA 98032 Office: 2914 Bell Plaza Seattle WA 98199

WALKER, CAROLYN ANN, telephone co. ofcl.; b. Lynchburg, Va., July 24, 1945; d. Charlie Stencil and Virginia May (Scruggs) W.; student No. Va. Community Coll., 1972—. Long distance operator C & P Telephone, Arlington, Va., 1966-69, employment interviewer, 1969-75, supr. service order typists, 1975-76, govt. liaison, Washington, 1976-78, staff supr., Silver Spring, Md., 1978-82, Washington, 1982—. Adv., exec. adv. Jr. Achievement. Mem. Nat. Assn. Female Execs. Office: 1710 H St NW Washington DC 20006

WALKER, CAROLYN PEYTON, univ. ofcl.; b. Charlottesville, Va., Sept. 15, 1942; d. Clay M. and Ruth (Newman) Peyton; B.A. in Am. History and Lit., Sweet Briar Coll., 1965; cert. in French, Alliance Francaise, Paris, 1966; Ed.M., Tufts U., 1970; M.A. in English and Am. Lit., Stanford U., 1974, Ph.D. in English Edn., 1977. Tchr. Elem. and jr. high schs. in Switzerland, 1967-69; tchr. elem. grades Boston Sch. System, 1969-70, Newark (Calif.) Unified Sch. System, 1970-72; instr. div. humanities Canada Coll., Redwood City, Calif., 1973, 76-78; instr. Sch. Bus., U. San Francisco, 1973-74; evaluation cons. Inst. Profl. Devel., San Jose, Calif., 1975-76; asst. dir. Learning Assistance Ctr., Stanford (Calif.) U., 1972-77, dir., 1977—, lectr. Sch. Edn., 1975—, dept. English, 1977—, supr. counselors, tutors and tchrs., 1972—; condr. reading and writing workshops, 1972—; reviewer Random House Books, 1978—; cons. Basic Skills Task Force, U.S. Office Edn., 1977-79, Right to Read, Calif. State Dept. Edn., 1977—, Program for Gifted and Talented, Freemont (Calif.) Unified Sch. Dist., 1981-82. Mem. MLA, Calif. Profs. of Reading, Western Coll. Reading Assn. (treas. 1982), Nat. Council Tchrs. English, No. Calif. Coll. Reading Assn. (sec.-treas. 1976-78). Author: (with Patricia Killen) Handbook for Teaching Assistants at Stanford University, 1977; How to Succeed As a New Teacher: A Handbook for Teaching Assistants, 1977; (with others) Academic Tutoring at the Learning Assistance Center, 1980; also articles. Home: 2350 Waverley St Palo Alto CA 94301 Office: Learning Assistance Center 123 Meyer Library Stanford U Stanford CA 94305

WALKER, CONSTANCE MAE, librarian; b. Providence, July 22, 1928; d. Bayden Powell and MaeEliza (Hobson) Taylor; B.A., U. Tex. at Austin, 1954, M.L.S., 1956; m. Billy Jack Walker, Nov. 17, 1956. Reference librarian, Houston Pub. Library, 1956-60; asst. librarian South Tex. Jr. Coll., Houston, 1960-67, librarian, 1967-74; librarian U. Houston, Downtown Coll., 1974-80, U. St. Thomas, Houston, 1980—. Mem. ALA, Tex. Library Assn. (chmn. scholarship awards com., 1965-66), Cath. Library Assn., Phi Beta Kappa, Beta Phi Mu. Contbg. author: Magazines for Libraries, 3d edit. Home: 8117 Albacore Dr Houston TX 77074 Office: 9845 Memorial Dr Houston TX 77024

WALKER, CYNTHIA, clin. psychologist; b. Barre, Vt., Aug. 16, 1936; d. Joseph Francis and Catherine Clark (Cousins) W.; B.A., Pomona Coll., 1962; M.A., Pepperdine U., 1974; Ph.D., Calif. Sch. Profl. Psychology, 1977; 1 son, Adrian. Exec. dir. San Diego (Calif.) Hospice, 1977; pvt. practice clin. psychology, San Diego, 1977-79, Costa Mesa, Calif., 1980—; staff oncology psychologist St. Jude Hosp., Fullerton, Calif., 1980. Mem. Am. Psychol. Assn., Orange County Psychol. Assn. (dir.). Democrat. Irvine CA 92715 Office: 1533 W Baker St Costa Mesa CA 92626

WALKER, ELJANA M. DU VALL, civic worker; b. France, Jan. 18, 1924; came to U.S., 1948, naturalized, 1954; student Med. Inst., U. Paris, 1942-47; m. John S. Walker, Jr., Dec. 31, 1947; children—John, Peter, Barbara. Pres., Loyola Sch. PTA, 1958-59; bd. dirs. Santa Claus shop, 1959-73; treas. Archdiocese Denver Cath. Women, 1962-64; rep. Cath. Parent-Tchr League, 1962-65; pres. Aux. Denver Gen. Hosp., 1966-69; precinct committeewoman Arapahoe County Republican Women's Com., 1973-74; mem. re-election com. Arapahoe County Rep. Com., 1973-78; pres. Denver U. Art Conservation Center, 1980-82. Recipient Disting. Service award Am.-by-choice, 1966; named to Honor Roll, ARC, 1971. Mem. Cherry Hills Symphony, Lyric Opera Guild, Alliance Franciase (life mem.), ARC, Civic Ballet Guild (life mem.), Needlework Guild Am. (v.p. 1980-82), Kidney Found. (life), Denver Art Mus., U. Denver Art and Conservation Assns., U. Denver Women's Library Assn., Childrens Diabetes Found. Denver, Internat. Club Welcome to Colo., Nat. Jewish Hosp. Aux., Beth Israel Hosp. Aux., Central City Assn. Guild, Cancer Aux. Colo. Roman Catholic. Clubs: Union (Chgo.); 26, Denver Athletic (Denver). Address: 6185 S Columbine Way Littleton CO 80121

WALKER, ELVA MAE DAWSON, cons. health, hosps., aging; b. Everett, Mass., June 29, 1914; d. Charles Edward and Mary Elizabeth (Livingston) Dawson; R.N., Peter Bent Brigham Hosp., Boston, 1937; student Simmons Coll., 1935, U. Minn., 1945-48; m. Walter Willard Walker, Dec. 16, 1939 (div. 1969). Supr. nursery Wesson Maternity Hosp., Springfield, Mass., 1937-38; asst. supr. out-patient dept. Peter Bent Brigham Hosp., Boston, 1938-40; supr. surgery and out-patient dept. Univ. Hosps., Mpls., 1945. Chmn. Gov.'s Citizens Council on Aging, Minn., 1960-68, acting dir., 1962-66, Econ. Opportunity Com. Hennepin County, 1964-69; v.p., treas. Nat. Purity Soap & Chem. Co., 1968-69, pres., 1969-76, chmn. bd., 1976—; cons. on aging to Minn. Dept. Pub. Welfare, 1962-67; mem. nat. adv. Council for Nurse Tng. Act, 1965-69, Com. Status on Women in Armed Services, 1967-70; dir. Nat. Council on the Aging, 1963-67, sec., 1965-67; dir. Planning Agy. for Hosps. of Met. Mpls., 1963—, United Hosp. Fund of Hennepin County, 1955—, Nat. Council Social Work Edn., 1966-68; vice chmn. Hennepin County Gen. Hosp. Adv. Bd., 1965-68; sec. Hennepin County Health Coalition, 1973; chmn. bd. dirs. Am. Rehab. Found, 1962-68, vice chmn., 1968-70; pres. bd. trustees Northwestern Hosp., 1956-59, Children's Hosp. Mpls., 1961-65; dir. Twin Cities Internat. Program for Youth Leaders and Social Workers, Inc., 1965-67; mem. community adv. council United Community Funds and Council Am., Inc., 1968, Nat. Assembly Social Policy and Devel., Inc., 1968—; mem. priorities determination com. United Fund Mpls., 1971; vice chmn. govt. specifications com. Soap and Detergent Assn., 1972-76, vice-chmn. indsl. and instn. com., 1974-76, chmn., 1976-78, bd. dirs., 1974—; candidate for Congress, 3d Minn. Dist., 1966; trustee Macalester Coll., Archie D. and Bertha H. Walker Found.; chmn. St. Mary's Jr. Coll. Bd., 1970-74, 78-81; pres. U. Minn. Sch. Nursing Found., 1958-70. Mem. Am. Pub. Welfare Assn., Mpls. Med. Research Found., Internat. Council Social Work (asst. treas. N.Am.), Minn. League Nursing (pres. 1971-73), Jr. League Mpls. Democrat. Presbyterian. Home: 3655 Northome Rd Wayzata MN 55391 Office: Nat Purity Soap & Chem Co 110 SE 5th Ave Minneapolis MN 55414

WALKER, EUNICE MIRIAM ARNAUD, writer; b. Monett, Mo.; d. Emile and Pauline (Barriquand) Arnaud; student S.W. Mo. State U.; B.A., U. Ark.; postgrad. George Washington U., 1956; m. Joseph Edward Walker (div.); children—Diane Leigh Walker Smith, Carole Cecile Walker Baker; m. 2d, William Roy Little. Reporter, feature writer Monett Times, Kansas City (Mo.) Star; publs. writer Woodrow Wilson Centennial Celebration Commn., Washington, 1957; pub. relations writer Senator Joseph S. Clark, Washington, 1958-59; asst. pub. relations Ho. of Reps. Com. on Sci. and Astronautics, 1959-61; info. specialist U.S. ACDA, Washington, 1961-65, policy reports officer, Washington, 1965-70; pub. info. officer U.S. Dept. Agr., Washington, 1970-76; free lance writer, 1956—. Mem. LWV, Nat. League Am. Penwomen, Nat. Fedn. Press Women, Nat. Press Club, Assn. Agr. Coll. Editors, Nat. Hist. Soc., Am. Hist. Soc., Nat. Archives, Smithsonian Assos., Nat. Trust Historic Preservation, Nat. Cathedral Assn., Huguenot Soc., Kappa Delta Pi, Lambda Tau. Episcopalian. Club: City Tavern (Washington). Author: Woodrow Wilson, 1958; contbr. articles to various publs. Home: 205 James Thurber Ct Falls Church VA 22046

WALKER, EVELYN, ret. ednl. radio-TV broadcasting exec.; b. Birmingham, Ala.; d. Preston Lucas and Mattie (Williams) Walker; A.B., Huntingdon Coll., 1927, L.H.D. (hon.), 1974; postgrad. Cornell U., 1927-29; M.A., U. Ala., 1963, postgrad., 1965-75; spl. TV course U. Ill., summer 1953. Tchr. speech Phillips High Sch., Birmingham, 1930-34; head speech dept. Ramsay High Sch., Birmingham, 1934-52; chmn. schs. radio, TV, 1944-75, producer, coordinator TV-radio Birmingham Pub. Schs., 1952-69; head instrnl. TV programming services, 1969-75; broadcaster daily children's program, Birmingham, 1946-57; staff producer Birmingham Ednl. TV Studio for Ala. Pub. TV Network, 1954-75. Mem. Def. Adv. Com. on Women in Services, 1958-60; chmn. TV and radio competition Festival of Arts, 1962-65; bd. dirs. Women's Com. of 100 for Birmingham, 1968—, Ala. Humane Soc.; TV radio co-chmn. Gov's Adv. Bd. to State Safety Com., 1965-68; nat. del. Asian-Am. Women Broadcaster's Conf. 1966; mem. Salvation Army Aux.; audio visual chmn. Birmingham Council PTA, 1966-75; mem. acad. jurors Obelisk Awards, 1978—; media Chmn. Gov.'s Commn. on Ala. Yr. of Child; bd. dirs. Women's Army Corps Found. Recipient Educator's Medal award Freedoms Found., 1963; Spl. award for Arts Birmingham Festival of Arts, 1962; Red Cross TV award, 1964; Nat. Headliner award Women in Communications, 1965; Key to City of Birmingham, 1966; Ala. service award Nat. Exchange Club, 1969; named Tops in Our Town, Birmingham News, 1957, Ala. Woman of Achievement, 1964, Birmingham Woman of Yr., 1965; Ala. Woman of Yr., Progressive Farmer mag., 1966; named hon. col. Ala. militia, hon. lt. a.d.c.; 20-Year Service award Ala. Ednl. TV Commn.; Obelisk award Children's Theatre, 1976. Mem. Nat. League Am. Pen Women, Nat. Eagle Forum, Am. Women in Radio and TV (local pres. 1959-60; past trustee area ednl. found.; dir.), Marquis Biog. Library Soc., Ala. Hist. Assn., Colonial Dames XVII Century, DAR (state program chmn.), Daus. Am. Colonists (state TV chmn. 1966-76), Noble Order of Crown, Colonial Order of Crown, Am. United Daus. 1812, Huntingdon Coll. Alumnae Bd. (achievement award, 1958, 1st nat. v.p. 1959-60, internat. pres. 1961-63, 2d v.p. 1973-76), Ams. Royal Descent, Royal Order Garter, Magna Charta Dames (sec.-treas. 1963-64), UDC, Ret. Tchrs. Assn. (past state chmn. internat. travel), Plantagenet Soc., Freedom Ednl. Found. (dir.), Ala. Congress PTA (audio visual chmn. 1966-75), Arlington Hist. Assn. (pres. 1981-83), (dir. 1969—), Greater Birmingham Arts Alliance, English Speaking Union, Nat. Trust for Historic Preservation (Arlington adv. bd.), Ala. Dist. Exchange Clubs (hon. life, bronze plaque award 1969), Internat. Platform Assn., Birmingham-Jefferson Hist. Assn. (trustee), Art Assn., Art Mus., Bot. Soc., Symphony Women, Golden Circle, Delta Delta Delta Alumna. Methodist. Clubs: Press, The Club, Downtown, Birmingham Country (mem. Ladies Golf Assn.). Home: 744 Euclid Ave Mountain Brook Birmingham AL 35213

WALKER, GAIL JUANICE, electrologist; b. Bosque County, Tex., Sept. 3, 1937; d. Hiram Otis and Hazel Ruth (Carmichael) Gunter; cert. Shults Inst. Electrolysis, 1971; children—Lillian Ruth, Deborah Lynn. In quality control Johnson & Johnson, San Angelo, Tex., 1962-70; with Electrolysis of Scottsdale (Ariz.), 1970-80; owner, pres., electrologist Ariz. Inst. Electrolysis, Scottsdale, 1979—. Mem. Ariz. Assn. Electrologists (pres. 1980—), Am. Electrolysis Assn., Internat. Guild Profl. Electrologists, Nat. Fedn. Ind. Businessmen, Ariz. Assn. Electrologists (organizer 1980), Nat. Electrology Educators (sec.). Republican. Baptist. Club: Order of Eastern Star. Area corr. Hair Route mag. Office: 7033 E Indian Sch Rd 2 Scottsdale AZ 85251

WALKER, IRENE ELIZABETH BAKER (MRS. EARNEST ARTMAN WALKER), ret. govt. ofcl.; b. Niagara Falls, N.Y., Dec. 17, 1905; d. Chalice Whitmore and Mattie Louise (Weybright) Baker; student Johns Hopkins U., summer 1925; A.B., Goucher Coll., 1927; M.A. (Harriet Remington Laird fellow), U. Wis., 1928; postgrad. Am. U., 1949-52; m. Earnest Artman Walker, Aug. 28, 1929; 1 dau., Elizabeth Ann. Teaching asst. dept. history U. Wis., Madison, 1927-29; statistician REA, Washington, 1936-42; economist WPB, Washington, 1942-45, policy analyst Civilan Prodn. Adminstrn., Washington, 1945-47; historian Office Chief of Engrs. Def. Dept., Balt., 1947-49; economist AID (and predecessors agy.), Washington, 1949-73, internat. trade and devel. economist, 1951-55, internat. relations officer, 1955-62, sr. mgmt. analyst, 1962-65, supervisory mgmt. analyst, 1965-67, acting chief Program Devel. div. Population Service, Office War on Hunger, 1967-68, chief Program Implementation div., 1968-69, chief Program Grants div., Office Population, 1969-71, asst. dir. spl. projects, 1971-73, chmn. women's adv. com. AID, 1971-72; cons. on women, population and devel. programs, 1973—; congl. rep. Greenbelt Coop. Inc.; sec. D.C. Area Council, 1974-75, chmn., 1975-81; dir. Consumer Services Coop., Inc., legal services, 1977-81; dir. various investment cos.; lectr. AID Career Devel. Sch., 1959-68, Mil. Assistance Inst., Washington, 1960-62; U.S. del. XIII Pan Am. Child Congress, Quito, Ecuador, June 1968. Bd. dirs. Internat. Center for Dynamics of Devel., 1973—, Washington Coop. Forum. Mem. Soc. Internat. Devel. (pres. Washington chpt. 1969-70, council 1967-73), Polit. Sci. Acad., Am. Econs. Assn., Am. Statis. Assn., Am. Hist. Assn., AAUW (various chairmanships 1933—), Phi Delta Gamma (pres. Alpha chpt. 1955-57, 74-76, Nat. achievement award 1972), Goucher Coll. Alumnae Assn. (pres. 1970-71, exec. com. 1968-73), U. Wis. Alumni Assn., Delta Gamma (pres. Beta Sigma House Corp. 1977-81). Methodist. Contbr. monographs and digests to profl. publs. Home: 6903 Carleton Terr College Park MD 20740

WALKER, ISABELLA BROCKWAY, artist, printmaker; b. Dunkirk, N.Y.; d. Thomas C. and Isabella (Parmelee) Brockway; student U. Vt., 1920-21, Boston Mus. Sch. Fine Arts, 1921-25, Boston Designers Art Sch., 1925; m. Wallace Haynes Walker, June 16, 1928; children—Peter Brockway, Clinton Brockway. Cartographic-photo compiler Army Map Service, Washington, 1951-63; free lance illustrator and designer; one man shows Newport Art Assn., Silver Spring (Md.) Art Gallery, Longwood Sch., Arts Club; exhibited group shows D.C. Arts Club, Balt. Art Mus., Newport Art Assn., U. Va., Albany Print Club, Corcoran Gallery, Smithsonian Instn.; represented in permanent collections Nat. Collection of Fine Arts, Smithsonian Instn. Mem. Artists Equity, Washington Art League, Washington Water Color Assn., Arts Club D.C., Washington Print Club, Soc. Washington Printmakers (v.p. acting corr. sec. 1958-73). Home: 5315 Massachusetts Ave NW Washington DC 20016 *

WALKER, JACQUELINE CLARKE, govt. ofcl.; b. Summit, N.J., May 7, 1926; d. Allen Hillyer and Evelyn (Cook) Clarke; R.N., Buffalo Children's Hosp., 1951; B.A., U. Conn., 1972, M.S.W., 1975; m. James Walker, Dec. 29, 1951 (div.); children—Michael Clarke, John Howland, Naomi Silliman. Pediatric nurse Buffalo Children's Hosp., 1951-52; charge nurse local nursing home, 1973-75; state ombudsman Conn. Dept. Aging, Hartford, 1975—; cons. Greater Hartford Process Community Life Assn., 1975. Founder, pres. Glastonbury Human Rights Council, 1968; mem. Glastonbury Citizens Adv. Council, 1964, Glastonbury Charter Revision Comn., 1965. Mem. LWV (chpt. pres. 1961-63), Nat. Caucus of Black Aged (dir. 1976-80), Am. Gerontol. Assn., Northeastern Gerontol. Soc., Nat. Assn. Ombudsman/Advocates (dir. 1978—). Democrat. Contbr. chpt.: Victimization of the Elderly: Causes and Intervention, 1982. Home: 1083 Main St South Glastonbury CT 06073 Office: 80 Washington St Hartford CT 06106

WALKER, JACQUELYN TOUCHSTONE, religious ofcl., public speaker; b. Gainesville, Ga., Jan. 29, 1939; d. Ben Harold and Mildred Charlene (McDonald) Touchstone; student Lee Coll., Cleveland, Tenn., 1956-57; m. Donald M. Walker, June 7, 1958; children—Donalyn, Denise. Sec., Dept. of Interior, Atlanta, 1958; exec. sec. Soo Line R.R., Minot, N.D., 1958-60; state exec. sec. Ch. of God, Indpls., 1960-64, Pontiac, Mich., 1970-72, Akron, Ohio, 1974-76; exec. sec. to pres. Ch. of God Sch. Theology, Cleveland, Tenn., 1978-82; state dir. Ch. of God Young Ladies Aux., Akron, 1974-78, Tenn., 1978-82; sec. to dir. devel. Northwest Bible Coll., Minot, N.D.; internat. bd. dirs. Dept. Ladies Ministries, Ch. of God, Cleveland, Tenn.; public speaker; tchr. Christian edn.; family and marriage counselor. Former PTA officer, S.C., Mich. and Ohio; vol. ARC; notary public, Mich., Ohio, Tenn. Democrat.

WALKER, JESSIE, writer, photographer; b. Milw.; d. Stuart Richard and Loraine (Freuler) Walker; B.S., Medill Sch. Journalism, Northwestern U., also M.S. First major feature article appeared in The Am. Home mag.; contbr. numerous articles to nat. mags. including Am. Heritage's Americana, Better Homes and Gardens, McCall's, House and Garden, Good Housekeeping, others; midwest editor Am. Home mag.; contbg. editor Better Homes & Gardens. Mem. Ill. Opera Guild; mem. N. Shore jr. bd. Northwestern U. Settlement, 1949-59. Recipient Dorothy Dawes award for distinguished journalistic coverage in home furnishing, 1976, 77. Mem. Am. Soc. Interior Designers (press mem.), Women in Communications. Author: How to Plan a Trend Setting Kitchen, 1962; How to Make Window Decorating Easy, 1969; Shaker Design-150-year-old Modern, 1972; Good Design—What Makes It Last?, 1973; Junking Made Easy, 1974; Poster Power, 1976; For Collectors Only, 1977; Bishop Hill-Utopian Community 1978; also articles. Photographer cover photo Better Homes & Gardens, Sept. 1982, Oct. 1980, House Beautiful, Dec. 1981, Country Living, Feb., Jan. 1983. Address: 241 Fairview Rd Glencoe IL 60022

WHO'S WHO OF AMERICAN WOMEN 834

WALKER, JO ANN HOOVER, nurse anesthetist; b. St. George, Kans., Dec. 20, 1931; d. Joel Louis and Juanita Fern (Shelton) Hoover; R.N., Stormont-Vail Sch. Nursing, 1952; cert. registered nurse anesthetist Charity Hosp. Sch. Anesthesia for Nurses, 1969; m. Rankin T. Walker, Jr., Nov. 27, 1955; 1 dau., Victoria Ann. Office nurse, med. sec., asst. office mgr. Manuel De J. Castillo, M.D., Los Angeles, 1952-60; office nurse, med. sec., David Brobeck, M.D., Inglewood, Calif., 1959-60; emergency rm. nurse Centinela Hosp., Los Angeles, 1963-64; staff nurse Bd. Nat. Missions, United Presbyn. Ch., Ganado Mission, Ganado, Ariz., 1964-67; surg. intensive care nurse VA Hosp., Albuquerque, 1969; staff cert. registered nurse anesthetist U., N.Mex. Hosp., Albuquerque, 1969—. Mem. N.Mex. Assn. Nurse Anesthetists (pres.), Am. Assn. Nurse Anesthetists, Bus. and Profl. Women's Club. Republican. Presbyterian. Club: Quester Single Adults. Home: 225 Sycamore St NE Albuquerque NM 87106 Office: 2211 Lomas Blvd NE Albuquerque NM 87106

WALKER, JOYCE LEHMAN, mag. exec.; b. Georgetown, Tex., May 9, 1947; d. Wilfred Paul and Pauline Anne (Cell) Lehman; student Alvin Community Coll., 1965-66, Fordham U., 1978, N.Y. U., 1980—; m. Russell L. Walker, Nov. 29, 1969 (div.). Asst. to dir. recruiting DuPont Glore Forgan, Dallas, 1973-74; sales rep., Southwest mgr. Cathy Corp., Dallas, 1974-77, Eastern regional mgr., N.Y.C., 1977; advt. sales rep. Instl. Investor mag., N.Y.C., 1978-79; nat. sales mgr. Registered Representative mag., N.Y.C., 1979-80; advt. sales N.Y. Times, 1980-81; corp. advt. mgr. Omni mag., N.Y.C., 1981—; lectr. in field. Mem. Fin. Communications Soc. N.Y., Advt. Sales Club N.Y., Advt. Women N.Y. Democrat. Lutheran. Home: 282 W 4th St New York NY 10014 Office: 909 Third Ave New York NY 10022

WALKER, LENORE E., psychologist; b. N.Y.C., Oct. 3, 1942; d. David and Pearl (Moncher) Auerbach; A.B., Hunter Coll., 1962; M.S., City U. N.Y., 1967; Ed.D., Rutgers U., 1972; children—Michael, Karen. Psychologist, Coney Island Hosp., N.Y.C., 1967-69; psychologist Middlesex County Mental Health Clinic, 1969-72; asst. prof. psychiatry Rutgers Med. Sch., dir. ednl. outreach services Rutgers Mental Health Center, 1972-75; asso. prof. psychology Colo. Women's Coll., Denver, 1975—; prin. investigator, dir. Battered Women Research Center, 1978—. Mem. Am. Psychol. Assn., Assn. for Women in Psychology, Feminist Writers Guild. Author: The Battered Woman, 1979; contbr. articles to profl. jours. Home: 440 Fillmore St Denver CO 80206

WALKER, LORNA ANN, nutrition/allergy cons.; b. Newport, R.I., June 19, 1950; d. Orville Henry and Clara (D'Alessio) Hussey; B.S., U. R.I., 1971; M.T., Newport Hosp. Sch. Med. Tech., 1972; postgrad. Antioch Internat. U.; m. Philip Mac Walker, July 16, 1972; 1 son, Brent Alan. Med. technologist Chula Vista (Calif.) Community Hosp., 1972-74, Tri-Counties Blood Bank, Santa Barbara, Calif., 1974; instr. lab. scis. Charron-Williams Coll., Ft. Lauderdale, 1981-82; nutrition/allergy cons., Sunrise, Fla., 1979—, Chiropractic Care Center, Lauderhill, Fla., 1982—; lectr./cons. Hypoglycemia Research Found., Inc., 1982—. Recipient Newport Engring. Soc. award for promotion of the arts/scis., 1968; Lambda Tau Hon. Med. Tech. Soc. award, 1972. Mem. Am. Soc. Clin. Pathologists, Am. Soc. Med. Tech., Internat. Acad. Nutritional Cons., Human Ecology Action League. Contbr. articles to profl. jours. Home: 11091 NW 21st Ct Sunrise FL 33322

WALKER, LYNN JONES, lawyer, found. adminstr.; b. Ft. Lee, Va., Jan. 24, 1946; d. Lawrence Neal and Mary Ellen Jones; student Fisk U., 1963-65; A.B. in Sociology, Barnard Coll., 1967; J.D. cum laude, Columbia U., 1970. Admitted to N.Y. bar, 1971; law clk. to Chief Judge U.S. Dist. Ct. of So. Dist. N.Y., 1970; atty. NAACP Legal Def. and Ednl. Fund, Inc., N.Y.C., 1971-73, 75-78; gen. counsel N.Y.C. Commn. on Human Rights, 1973-75; sect. chief, dep. asst. atty. gen. Civil Rights div. U.S. Dept. Justice, Washington, 1978-82; program officer Ford Found., N.Y.C., 1982—. Recipient Outstanding Performance award Dept. Justice, 1980, 81, 82. Mem. Nat. Bar Assn., Assn. Black Found. Execs. Office: Ford Found 320 E 43d St New York NY 10017

WALKER, LYNN LOUISE, health center adminstr., health activist; b. Orange, Calif., July 20, 1951; d. James Ross and Velma Louise (Koontz) W.; B.A., Calif. State U., Fullerton, 1973; secondary edn. cert. Chapman Coll., 1975; postgrad. Sch. Law, Western State U., 1982; 1 son, Tru. Health staff Feminist Women's Health Center of Orange County (Calif.), 1974-76, dir., 1976—. Community organizer Women Against Violence Against Women, Orange County, 1975-76; bd. dirs. Nat. Abortion Fedn., 1978-79. Recipient Margret Sanger award Fedn. of Feminist Women's Health Centers, 1976. Mem. NOW, Internat. Childbirth Edn. Assn., Am. Public Health Assn., Nat. Assn. Parents and Profls. for Safe Alternatives in Childbirth, Assn. for Childbirth at Home Internat., Abortion Rights Movement. Home: 601 N Clementine Anaheim CA 92805 Office: 406 S Main St Santa Ana CA 92701

WALKER, MARGARET LINZEL, govt. ofcl.; b. Washington, Feb. 22, 1921; d. Frank A. and Verna (Diecks) Linzel; B.A., Stetson U., DeLand, Fla., 1942; divorced; 1 son, Paul L. With Treasury Dept., 1961-81, chief stats. and research staff Bur. Mint, 1970-79, chief program evaluation div., 1979-81, also mgr. fed women's program. Recipient Meritorious Service award Treasury Dept., 1975, Sec's award, 1975; Disting. Alumni award Stetson U., 1977. Mem. Federally Employed Women, Treasury Dept. Hist. Assn., Pi Beta Phi. Presbyterian. Club: Stetson U. Alumni.

WALKER, MARGIE MARIE, sch. counselor; b. Elizabethton, Tenn., May 7, 1931; d. Noah Ezikeel and Essie Rose (Lovelace) Webb; B.S., E. Tenn. State U., 1955; M.R.E., New Orleans Bapt. Theol. Sem., 1960; M.A., E. Tenn. State U., 1964. Tchr., Ft. Payne (Ala.) Schs., 1952-55; tchr. sr. high sch., Hampton, Tenn., 1955-57; tchr., coach Ocala (Fla.) High Sch., 1957-58; tchr., coach, Melbourne (Fla.) Schs., 1960-63; dir. guidance McDowell County, N.C. Schs., 1963-64; counselor Asheville (N.C.) Schs., 1964-65; acting dean of women Montreat-Anderson Coll., 1965; counselor, adminstr. Duval County, Fla., 1965—; adv. Fla. Jr. Coll., Jacksonville. Mem. Am. Personnel and Guidance Assn., Fla. Personnel and Guidance Assn., NEA, Delta Kappa Gamma, Beta Sigma Phi (rep. city council 1977—). Baptist. Home: 7440 Leroy Dr Jacksonville FL 32210 Office: 1700 Old Middleburg Rd Jacksonville FL 32244

WALKER, MARIAN COOPER, phys. therapist; b. L.I., Apr. 13, 1928; d. Frank Loyal and Marguerite Mary (McClain) Cooper; B.S. in Zoology, U. Pitts., 1949, grad. D. T. Watson Sch. Phys. Therapy, U. Pitts. Sch. Medicine, 1950; div.; children—Christine, Patricia. Chief phys. therapist Knoxville (Tenn.) Cerebral Palsy Center, 1959-63; regional phys. therapy cons. Tenn. Dept. Public Health, Knoxville, 1967-80; phys. therapist VA Hosp., Murfreesboro, Tenn., 1980—. Mem. Am. Phys. Therapy Assn. Home: 1203 Taylor Pl Murfreesboro TN 37130

WALKER, MARJORIE BRENNAND, journalist; b. Sweetwater, Tex., Aug. 6, 1934; d. Jess and Dorothy Louise (Askins) Brennand; student Durham Bus. Coll., Albuquerque, 1952-53; m. James Blakely Walker, Apr. 14, 1974; 1 dau. by previous marriage, Debra Lee Seeley. Receptionist, payroll clk. R.E. McKee, gen. contractor, 1952-53; acct. Phelps-Dodge, El Paso, Tex., 1957-58; sec. to editor Herald-Post, El Paso, 1950-52, reporter, 1969-75, women's page editor, 1974-80; dispatcher IBM, El Paso, 1965-66. Mem. Pan Am. Round Table El Paso (hon.), SW Quarter Horse Assn. Democrat. Club: Fort Bliss Officers' Wives (hon.). Home: 10733A Horn Circle El Paso TX 79927 Office: PO Drawer 20 El Paso TX 79999

WALKER, MARY ALICE, educator; b. Warrenton, Ga., Feb. 5, 1941; d. Pierce and Bessie (Pitts) Hill; B.S., Brockport State U., 1963; M.Ed., Nazareth Coll., Rochester, N.Y., 1975; m. James Walker, June 29, 1963. Tchr., Jonathan Child Sch., Rochester, N.Y., 1963-66; dir. Work Edn. Teaching Center, Rochester, 1966-68; tchr. Project Follow Through, John Williams Sch., Rochester, 1968-77, tchr. reading, 1977—. Treas., United Ch. Ministry, Rochester; chmn. bd. Rochester Opportunities Industrialization Center; chairperson fin. com. N.Y.-Wash. Missionary Soc. Mem. N.Y. State Tchrs. Assn., Rochester Tchrs. Assn., Reading Tchrs. Assn. Methodist-Episcopal. Address: 797 Arnett Blvd Rochester NY 14619

WALKER, MARY CUNNINGHAM, lawyer; b. Cleve., Sept. 4, 1944; d. Geoffrey Everett and Katherine E. (Danforth) Cunningham; J.D., U. Tenn., 1975; B.A., Smith Coll., 1966; M.A.T. in French, Wesleyan U., 1967; m. John Albert Walker, Jr., Nov. 26, 1977; children—Christopher Danforth Swann, John Albert III. Admitted to Tenn. bar, 1975; atty. fin. div. Office Procs., ICC, Washington, 1975-76, Office Gen. Counsel, 1976-77; atty. U.S. Dept. Energy, Oak Ridge, 1977-78; mem. firm Fowler & Rowntree, Knoxville, Tenn., 1979—. Bd. dirs. Children's Center, Inc., Knoxville, 1980—; regional dir. Am. Field Service, N.Y.C., 1974—. Mem. Am. Bar Assn., Tenn. Bar Assn., Knoxville Bar Assn., Phi Delta Phi. Clubs: LeConte, Knoxville Symphony League. Home: 800 Blows Ferry Rd Knoxville TN 37919 Office: 700 First Tennessee Bank Bldg Knoxville TN 37902

WALKER, MARY ELLA, nurse; b. St. Louis, Aug. 23, 1945; d. Earl Earnest and Mrytle Emma (Agnew) W.; B.S. in Nursing, Tex. Christian U., 1967; M.S. in Nursing, U. Tex., 1972, Ph.D., 1976. Staff nurse, asst. head nurse, head nurse Barnes Hosp., St. Louis, 1967-71; staff nurse Brackenridge Hosp., Austin, Tex., 1972; research asso. U. Tex. System, 1973-74; research asso. Center Study of Human Resources, Austin, 1975-76, So. Regional Council, Inc., Atlanta, 1975-76; nurse cons. Tex. Med. Found., Austin, 1976-77; vis. lectr. U. Wis., Oshkosh, 1977-78; program dir. Southwest Rural Health Field Services Program Nat. Rural Center, Austin, 1977-78; program dir. Tex. Rural Health Field Services Program, 1979—; lectr. U. Tex., 1979—. Mary Gibbs Jones scholar, 1976. Fellow Am. Acad. Nursing; mem. Am. Nurses Assn., Am. Rural Health Assn., Sigma Theta Tau, Phi Kappa Phi. Contbr. in field. Office: U Texas Sch Nursing Texas Rural Health Field Services Program 1700 Red River St Austin TX 78701

WALKER, MAY ELLA, city ofcl.; b. New Orleans, Dec. 18, 1943; d. Thomas James and Beatrice Jackson; B.S. in Bus. Edn., Tex. So. U., 1969; 1 son, Jamel Raphael. Librarian, Lockwood Andrews & Newman, Inc., Houston, 1965-71; tchr. Houston Ind. Sch. Dist., 1971-72; adminstrv. asst. Light House for Blind, Houston, 1972-74; with Police Dept., Houston, 1967—, officer, 1974—. Recipient cert. Nat. Council Negro Women for Community Service, 1967, 68, 69, 70. Mem. Afro Am. Police Officers League (v.p. 1980-81, dir. 1981—), Women in Community Service, Nat. Bus. League, Inc., Nat. Child Care Assn. Clubs: Hiram Clarke Civic, Catholic Newman, St. Benedict Womens. Home: 3810 Belgrade St Houston TX 77045 Office: 61 Riesner St Houston TX 77002

WALKER, NANCI TRIVERS, travel agt.; b. N.Y.C., Jan. 28, 1935; d. Samuel E. and Claire (Miller) Trivers; student SUNY, Albany, 1953-54; children—Carin Ann, Christopher George. Travel agt. Luck Travel, Poughkeepsie, N.Y., 1954-55; ticket agt. Am. Airlines, N.Y.C., 1955-56; mgr. Travelcade Tours, N.Y.C., 1961-64; owner Pougkpeepsie Travel Center, 1964—, Travel Tips Advt. Agy., Poughkeepsie. Mem. Am. Soc. Travel Agts., Assn. Westchester Travel Agts., Assn. Retail Travel Agts., Mid-Hudson Communicators. Club: Zonta. Contbg. editor, columnist Travel Trade Mag. Home: 70 Nimham Ave Wappingers Falls NY 12590 Office: 3 Spackenkill Rd Poughkeepsie NY 12602

WALKER, NORMA ELIZABETH PEDEN, educator; b. Grove City, Pa., Sept. 26, 1921; d. David Stanton and Mary Louella (Giebner) Peden; B.S., Indiana U. of Pa., 1958; M.S., Pa. State U., 1961, Ph.D., 1968; m. Charles Linn Walker, May 14, 1940 (dec.); children—Edward Erdman, Charles Linn, Rebecca Walker Mihelcic, Ellen Walker Torrey, Esther Walker Habla, Charlotte Walker Whatley. Homemaking tchr. Marion Center (Pa.) Area High Sch., 1958-60, tchr., head homemaking dept., 1961-63; grad. research asst. Pa. State U., 1960-61, instr., 1963-68; asso. prof. clothing and textiles Tex. Tech. U., 1968-69, asso. prof., chmn. clothing and textiles, 1969-70, prof., chmn., 1970-75, Margaret W. Weeks prof., 1975-77; prof. consumer services Indiana U. of Pa., 1977—. Mem. AAUW, Am. Cancer Soc., Am. Assn. Textile Chemists and Colorists (council for profl. devel. 1973-75), Am. Home Econs. Assn. (ofcl. bd. 1973-75, state adv. student membership sect. 1979—), ASTM, Assn. Coll. Profs. Textiles and Clothing (sec. 1977, rep. central region 1976-78), Indiana County Hist. Soc. (curator of costume), Kappa Delta Pi, Kappa Omicron Phi, Delta Kappa Gamma, Phi Delta Kappa. Republican. Methodist (bd. edn. Western Pa, lay del. ann. conf. Western Pa., mem. Council of Ministries, various bds. and coms.). Club: Current Events (pres.). Home: 10 LaVista Dr Indiana PA 15701

WALKER, PATRICIA LILLIAN, editor; b. Chgo., Jan. 2, 1943: d. Robert Warren and Virginia Margaret Walker; B.A., U. Ill., 1965; M.S. in Communications, Mich. State U., 1967; m. Peter Klaus Jeziorski, Aug. 28, 1971; 1 son, Peter. Reporter, Chgo. Tribune, 1967-69, Metalworking News, Chgo., 1969-71; mng. editor Am. Metal Market and Metalworking News, N.Y.C., 1971-74, editor-in-chief, 1974—. Office: 7 E 12th St New York NY 10003

WALKER, PATRICIA SEARS CHALLENDER, govt. ofcl.; b. Sunfield, Mich., Apr. 7, 1934; d. Verle Eugene and Rhoda Leora (Sweet) Sears; B.A., Golden Gate U., 1976, M.B.A., 1978; m. Wilford J. Challender, Apr. 13, 1952 (dec. Oct. 1960); children—Wilford, Patricia; m. 2d, Russell E. Walker, Sept. 28, 1963 (dec. May 1971); 1 son, Russell. Contract specialist U.S. Army, Presidio of San Francisco, 1956-63; contracting officer Naval Supply Center, U.S. Navy, Oakland, Calif., 1964—, now dir. contracts. Mem. Nat. Contract Mgmt. Assn. (pres. Golden Gate chpt., 1978, dir. 1979, 80, v.p. N.W. region 1981-83), Federally Employed Women, NOW, ACLU, Nat. Women's Polit. Caucus. Democrat. Unitarian. Club: Am. Contract Bridge League. Home: 14 Cheyenne Way Corte Madera CA 94925 Office: Code 201 A Naval Supply Center Oakland CA 94625

WALKER, PAULINE BUXTON, gift shop exec.; b. Norman, Okla., Jan. 21, 1922; d. Oscar Henry and Ida Mae (Dorrell) Buxton; student public schs. Norman; m. Paul H. Walker, Jan. 26, 1955; 1 stepdau., Penelope. Co owner, Fish Peddlars Restaurant, Pier, Redondo Beach, Calif., 1958-61; founder, mgr. Framarts, Redondo Beach, 1962—. Pres. Redondo Village Assn.; v.p. City of Hope, recipient Humanities Spirit of Life award, 1975. Outstanding Achievement award VFW, 1950, award 4H. Mem. Better Bus. Bur., Redondo Beach C. of C. Mormon. Clubs: Altrusa (dir.), Deers, Woman's of Redondo Beach. Home: 450 N Paulina Ave Redondo Beach CA 90277 Office: 1262 Beryl St Redondo Beach CA 90277

WALKER, PEGGY ANN, mktg. exec.; b. Sullivan, Ill., Dec. 13, 1934; d. W. Charles and Early Elizabeth Walker; B.A., Wayne State U., Detroit. Various secretarial positions, 1953-64; mortgage closer Curnow Mortgage Co., Detroit, 1964-66; 2d v.p., mktg. officer Mfrs. Nat. Corp., Detroit, 1966—; mem. faculty Am. Inst. Banking, 1969-76. Bd. dirs. Birmingham (Mich.) Day Care Center, 1975-78. Mem. Women's Econ. Club, Women's Advt. Club. Methodist. Office: 100 Renaissance Center Detroit MI 48243

WALKER, PEGGY JEAN, social work agy. adminstr.; b. Carbondale, Ill., Aug. 9, 1940; d. George William and Lola Almeda (Black) Robinson; B.A., So. Ill. U., 1962; M.S.W., Washington U., St. Louis, 1967; children—Edith Nell and Keith Alan. Caseworker, casework supr. Ill. Dept. Public Aid, 1964-71; child welfare adminstr. Ill. Dept. Children and Family Service, 1971-75; mem. faculty social work program So. Ill. U., 1975-79; adminstrv. dir. Western div. Children's Home Soc. of Fla., Pensacola, 1979—; appointed to Ill. Juvenile Justice and Delinquency Prevention Adv. Council, 1978-79. Bd. dirs. Hoyleton (Ill.) Children's Home, 1975-79. Mem. Nat. Assn. Social Workers, Acad. Cert. Social Workers, Council Social Work Edn., Fla. Assn. Health and Social Services. Mem. United Ch. of Christ. Club: Pensacola Yacht. Home: 107 Florida Ave Gulf Breeze FL 32561 Office: 5375 N 9th Ave Pensacola FL 32504

WALKER, SALLY BARBARA, glass co. exec.; b. Bellerose, N.Y., Nov. 21, 1921; d. Lambert Roger and Edith Demerest (Parkhouse) W.; diploma Cathedral Sch. St. Mary, 1939; A., Finch Jr. Coll., 1941. Tchr. interior design Finch Coll., 1941-42; draftsman AT &T, 1942-43; with Steuben Glass Co., N.Y.C., 1943—, exec. v.p., 1959-62, exec. v.p. ops., 1962-78, exec. v.p. operations and sales, 1978—. Mem. Fifth Ave. Assn. Republican. Episcopalian. Clubs: Rockaway Hunting, Lawrence Beach, U.S. Lawn Tennis, Colony, English-Speaking Union, Women's Nat. Republican. Home: 26 Ontario Rd Bellerose Floral Park NY 11001 Office: 715 Fifth Ave New York NY 10022

WALKER, SUZANNE STEWART, nurse; b. Alexander City, Ala., Feb. 2, 1950; d. Charles William and Frances Henry (Nail) Stewart; diploma Sylacauga Hosp. Sch. Nursing, 1975; B.S.N. cum laude, Samford U., 1978; M.S.N., U. Ala., Birmingham, 1980; children—Devanie Alexa, Michael Frederick. Staff nurse Russell Hosp., Alexander City, 1975-76; instr. nursing Sylacauga Hosp. Sch. Nursing (Ala.), 1976-77; staff nurse Brookwood Med. Center, Birmingham, 1979-80; instr. nursing Purdue U., West Lafayette, Ind., 1981-82; coordinator clin. care instrs. Carraway Meth. Med. Center, U. Ala., Birmingham, 1982—. Brownie leader Sycamore council Girl Scouts U.S.A., 1976-77; social chmn. Sunday Sch. class, 1979-80; instr. CPR, Am. Heart Assn., 1979—, ARC, 1977-82. Recipient Acad. Achievement award Sylacauga Hosp. Sch. Nursing, 1975. Mem. Am. Nurses Assn., Am. Assn. Critical Care Nurses, Pi Gamma Mu, Sigma Theta Tau. Presbyterian. Home: 3623 H Snapwood Rd Birmingham AL 35216 Office: Carraway Meth Med Center U Ala 1600 N 26th St Birmingham AL 35294

WALKER, SYLVIA CHRISTINE, research engr.; b. Orange, Calif., July 4, 1954; d. Clarence Loring and Dorothy Mary (Greenwood) Hall; B.S. in Animal Sci., Calif. State Poly. U., 1974, M.S., 1979, postgrad., 1982—; postgrad. San Diego State U., 1979-81, San Jose State U., 1981-82; m. Ronald Raymond Walker, Sept. 9, 1978. Chem. technician Occidental Research Corp., La Verne, Calif., 1974-76; lectr. dept. chemistry. Calif. State Poly. U., Pomona, 1978; chemist Lockheed Aircraft Service Co., Carlsbad, Calif., 1979-81; research engr. Lockheed Missiles and Space Co., Sunnyvale, Calif., 1981-82. Mem. Am. Chem. Soc., Nat. Assn. Corrosion Engrs., Gamma Sigma Delta, Phi Kappa Phi. Home: 10034 Olive St Bloomington CA 92316

WALKER, SYLVIA HUTTER (MRS. JOSEPH R. WALKER), educator; b. St. Gallen, Switzerland, June 2, 1932; came to U.S., 1950, naturalized, 1954; d. Paul and Laura (Schwegler) Hutter; student Conservatory Music, Zurich, Switzerland, 1945-47, Polyclinic Zurich, 1947-48; B.A., UCLA, 1958, M.A., 1965, Ph.D., 1972; m. Joseph R. Walker, Feb. 16, 1950. Adminstrv. sec. Bircher Klinic, Zurich, 1948-50, Univ. Elementary Sch., UCLA, 1952-53; teaching asst. UCLA, 1961-63, 64-65, lectr. French, adminstr. Ecole Française, French dept., 1966—; curriculum coordinator Marymount Internat. Schs., Bel Air, Cal., 1974-81; lectr. French, Mount St. Mary's Coll., Los Angeles, 1980—. Mem. Am. Assn. Tchrs. French (vice pres. chpt.), U. Calif. Women's Faculty Assn., AAUP, Pi Delta Phi. Home: 15306 Del Gado Dr Sherman Oaks CA 91403 Office: Fgn Lang Dept Mount St Mary's Coll 12001 Chalon Rd Los Angeles CA 90049

WALKIR, KAREN KAIGLER, ednl. cons.; b. Lubbock, Tex., Oct. 22, 1946; d. Thomas A. and Mary Lynn (Homesley) Kaigler; B.S. in Home Econs., Tex. Tech. U., 1969, M.S. in Home Econs., 1972; Ph.D. in Home Econs., Ohio State U., 1975; m. M.E. Walker, Aug. 1, 1979. Adminstrv. and teaching asso. Ohio State U., Columbus, 1973-74; asst. prof. dept. home econs. U. Tex., Austin, 1974-81; owner, cons. Network Resources, 1981—. Mem. Assn. Coll. Profs. of Textiles and Clothing (mem. planning council 1978—, pres.-elect 1980), Am. Gerontol. Soc., Western Gerontol. Soc., Am. Home Econs. Assn., San Marcos Heritage Soc. Republican.

WALL, CAROLYN RAIMONDI, publishing co. exec.; b. Springfield, Mass., July 2, 1942; d. Amedio Giacomino and Celestina Francesca (Penna) Raimondi; B.A., Trinity Coll., 1964; children—Christina Ann, Suzanne Caroline. Advt. dir. Beldoch Industries, N.Y.C., 1972-74; promotion dir. W Fairchild Publs., N.Y.C., 1974-76; v.p., pub. AD-WEEK, N.Y.C., 1976—. Bd. advisors Lubin Schs. Bus., Pace U., N.Y.C., 1981—. Mem. Advt. Women N.Y. (pres.), N.Y. Women in Communications. Home: 66 Linwood Rd New Rochelle NY 10804 Office: 820 2d Ave New York NY 10017

WALL, ISABELLE LOUISE WOOD, clergywoman, author; b. Wilkes County, N.C., Oct. 26, 1909; d. Charlie William and Nelia Elizabeth (Wood) Wood; student Appalachian State Tchrs. Coll., 1928-33, Draughn's Bus. Coll., 1944-45, Lee Coll., 1950-51, Franklin Inst., 1952, High Point Coll., 1959-60; m. Albert S. Wall, Feb. 16, 1929; children—Fred Wade, Bernice Adelene Wall Gengo, Tommye. Tchr. public schs. in Surry, Randolph and Davie counties, N.C., 1929-61, also prin. in elem. public schs., 1929-31; head Jr. High Sch. Dept. Miracle Valley, Ariz., 1958-59; instr. visual arts Miracle Valley Bible Coll., 1958-59; propr., dir. Wall's Service and Grocery, Winston-Salem, N.C., 1945-52; ordained to ministry Ch. of God, 1950; missionary trips to Germany, 1952; pastor Ch. of God, Bklyn., 1953, Internat. Miracle Fellowship, Greensboro, N.C., 1962, Winston-Salem, 1961—; del. to Internat. Full Gospel Fellowship, London, Eng., 1952; founder, pres. Internat. Miracle Fellowship, 1959—. Mem. Internat. Platform Assn. Republican. Author: Spiritual Steps, 1948; Sandstones of Time, 1980; contbr. numerous poems and articles to jours. and anthologies; editor World Deliverance Jour., 1960-65, Sandstones Jour., 1977—; also songwriter. Address: 3231 High Point Rd Winston-Salem NC 27107

WALL, JUDITH MARSHBURN, communications cons.; b. Bronx, N.Y., June 26, 1945; d. William Francis and Rita Theresa (Clifford) Marshburn; B.A. in Communications, U. Ga., 1969; M.B.A., City Coll. Seattle, 1982; m. Peter John Wall, May 2, 1970; 1 dau., Heather Dawn. Public info. dir. Bee County Coll., Beeville, Tex., 1970-72; women's editor Whidbey News Times, Oak Harbor, Wash., 1974-75; bd. dirs. Intruder Apparel, Inc., also owner Wrangler Wranch, Federal Way, Wash., 1975-78; asst. editor Federal Way News, 1976-78; communications coordinator Ednl. Service Dist. 121, Seattle, 1978—; communications cons. Bethel Sch. Dist., 1981—. Info. dir. Island County chpt. March of Dimes, 1974-75. Mem. Nat. Sch. Public Relations Assn., Wash. Press Women (various awards for photography and writing), Federal Way C. of C., Wash. Sch. Public Relations Assn. Republican.

Roman Catholic. Club: Federal Way Soroptimists (nat. del. 1980, v.p. 1982). Home: 30002 2d Pl SW Federal Way WA 98003 Office: 1410 S 200th St Seattle WA 98148

WALL, LINDA STANCIL, nurse; b. Raleigh, N.C., Nov. 30, 1948; d. Reuben Russell and Nettie Bell (Walters) Stancil; diploma in nursing Cabarrus Meml. Hosp., 1972; m. Rondal J. Wall, Aug. 1, 1971; children—Jay, Parker Caroline. Staff nurse Hartsville (S.C.) Hosp., 1972-73, also office nurse; family planning team leader dept. health and environ. control Darlington County Health Dept., Darlington, S.C., 1973—. Vice pres. Thomas Hart Acad. PTO, 1980-81. Mem. Hartsville Jaycee-ettes (v.p. 1978-79 Jaycee-ette of dist. 4, 1979), Pee Dee Health Systems Agy., S.C. Employment Assn. Baptist. Home: Route 5 Box 316 Hartsville SC 29550 Office: PO Box 147 Darlington SC 29532

WALL, NANCY LEE, pharm. co. ofcl.; b. Chesnee, S.C., June 28, 1944; d. Albert Lee and Sara Eleanor (Bush) Wall; student Furman U., 1962-63; B.S. in Med. Tech. and Chemistry, Lander Coll., 1966. Med. technologist Self Meml. Hosp., Greenwood, S.C., 1966-67; missionary med. technologist So. Bapt. Conv., Ghana, West Africa, 1967-69; chemistry technologist Alexandria (Va.) Hosp., 1969-70; spl. chem. tech., chemistry supr. Bapt. Hosp. System, Houston, 1970-71, med. tech. teaching coordinator, 1971-72; tech. sales rep. Abbott Labs., Houston, 1972-73, tech. liaison, 1974-76, internat. mktg. mgr. diagnostics div., South Pasadena, Calif., 1976-78; regulatory mgr. Alpha Therapeutic Corp., Pasadena, Calif., 1978-80, dir. quality mfg. and productivity dept., Los Angeles, 1980—; pres. LeLynn Internat., 1982—. Bd. dirs. Via Verde Homeowners Assn., 1980, Erwin Lake Homeowners Assn., 1982; active Fight Against Multiple Sclerosis, 1978—. Recipient Abbott Labs. Presdl. award, 1975; Alpha Therapeutic Pres.'s award, 1981. Mem. Am. Assn. Clin. Chemists, Am. Assn. Clin. Pathologists, Am. Blood Resources Assn., Indsl. Soc. Pharm. Engrs., Nat. Assn. Female Execs., NOW. Home: 1640 Calle Miradero San Dimas CA 91773 Office: 5555 Valley Blvd Los Angeles CA 90032

WALLACE, AURELIA DUNSTAN, author, poet; b. Madison, Wis., Aug. 1, 1925; d. Robert Tayloe and Katherine Lucille (Brenke) Dunstan; A.B., U. Ga., 1945, M.A., 1946; S.S.Ed., U. Fla., 1956; m. Alvin T. Wallace, June 9, 1945; (dec. 1971); children—Robert Dunstan, Katherine A. Tchr. English, St. Mary's Coll., Raleigh, N.C., 1946-47; instr. journalism N.C. State U., Raleigh, 1947-50; tchr. English, journalism and French, Gainesville (Fla.) High Sch., 1955-56; prof. English and tech. writing Santa Fe Community Coll., Gainesville, 1971—; cons. Atkins, Wallace & Assocs., 1981—; books of poetry include: Widow's Weeds and How They Grew, 1974, Reflexions on Everything and the Kitchen Cynic, 1974, Husbands, Lovers and Other Perishables, 1978; author: (textbook) Write, You Are!, 1976; (with P. Beattie) Art and Aesthetics, 1980; editor: (essays) Man's God and God's Man, 1970; contbr. numerous sci.-tech. articles, 1944—; editorial cons., 1945—. Mem. Women in Communications, Am. Assn. Tech. Writers, Am. Assn. Humanistic Edn., Fla. Coll. English Assn., Southeastern Conf. on English in Two-Year Coll., Fla. Assn. Community Colls., MLA, AAUP, So. Conf. Human Welfare, Phi Beta Kappa, Phi Kappa Phi, Alpha Lambda Delta, Theta Sigma Phi. Methodist. Home: 2381 NW 18th Pl Gainesville FL 32605

WALLACE, BOBBIE FRANK, med. technologist; b. Golden, Tex., Feb. 20, 1932; d. Frank Messick and Charlotte Evelym (Cathey) Wallace; B.A., Tex. Women's U., 1953. Chief med. technologist Callison Meml. Hosp., San Francisco, 1958-67; adminstrv. technologist Solano Labs., Berkeley, Calif., 1967-72; chief med. technologist M.D. Anderson Hosp., Houston, 1972-79; mgr. quality control ops. Technicon Corp., Middletown, Va., 1979-82; mgr. quality control Coulter Immunology, Hialeah, 1982—; clin. instr. U. Tex. Sch. Allied Health Scis., Houston, 1977-79. Vol. energy conservation workshop trainer Va. State U., Va. Tech. Extension Service, 1981. Lic. clin. lab. technologist, Calif. Mem. Am. Soc. for Med. Tech., Nat. Assn. for Female Execs. Home: 611 SW 71st Way Pembroke Pines FL 33024 Office: 440 W 20th St Hialeah FL 33010

WALLACE, DEBORAH SUE, educator; b. Columbus, Ohio, Apr. 16, 1947; d. Richard S. and Mary E. (Clarke) W.; B.S. in Edn., Ohio U., 1969; M.A., Ohio State U., 1974, Ph.D., 1976. Tchr., Lancaster (Ohio) Public Schs., 1969-73, tchr. summer sch. program, 1971, 72; tutor neurologically handicapped, Lancaster, 1970-73; grad. research asst. Ohio State U., Columbus, 1973-74, grad. research asso. sch. projects, 1974, student tchr. supr., 1975-76, team leader parent tng. program, 1976; instr. Kent (Ohio) State U., summer, 1976; asso. prof. dept. spl. edn. Ga. State U., Atlanta, 1976—; ccns. to various colls., schs. and rehab. instns., 1976—; panelist Sta. WOSU, 1975; reviewer The Directive Teacher, 1979—. Rep., Gov.'s Conf. Edn., State of Ga., 1980, 81, 82; v.p. Fulton County (Ga.) Young Democrats, 1977-78, pres., 1978-79; bd. dirs. Tommy Nobis Center for the Mentally Retarded, 1980—. Recipient Alumni Teaching award Ga. State U., 1982; Martha Holden Jennings scholar, 1972. Mem. Council for Exceptional Children, Council for Children with Behavior Disorders, NAACP, Pi Lambda Theta, Kappa Delta Epsilon. Methodist. Author teaching manuals; contbr. articles on edn. to profl. publs. Office: Georgia State U University Plaza Atlanta GA 30303

WALLACE, FRAN ANDRON, coll. adminstr.; b. Oceanside, N.Y., July 3, 1955; d. Arnold I. and Shirley Andron Wallace; B.S. with distinction, Cornell U., 1977; M.Ed., Harvard U., 1978; postgrad. Stanford U. Asst. dir. career planning Ithaca (N.Y.) Coll., 1978-79, dir. career planning, 1979-81; staff mem. Nat. Career Devel. Project, Walnut Creek, Calif., 1981—; asst. dean students Mills Coll., Oakland, Calif., 1981-82. Mem. Am. Coll. Personnel Assn. (mem. directorate, standing com. on women), Nat. Vocat. Guidance Assn. (mem. com. on occupational status of women), Assn. Sch., Coll. and Univ. Staffing, Coll. Placement Council, Nat. Orientation Dirs. Assn. Contbr. articles to profl. jours. Editor: Career Counseling and Placement, 1980-81. Home: 1431 Beach Park Blvd #216 Foster City CA 94404

WALLACE, JANE HOUSE, geologist; b. Ft. Worth, Aug. 12, 1926; d. Fred Leroy and Helen Gould (Kixmiller) Wallace; A.B., Smith Coll., 1947, M.A., 1949; postgrad. Bryn Mawr Coll., 1949-52. Geologist, U.S. Geol. Survey, 1952—, chief Pub. Inquiries Offices, Washington, 1964-72, spl. asst. to dir., 1974—, Washington liaison Office of Dir., 1978—. Recipient Meritorious Service award Dept. Interior, 1971, Distinguished Service award, 1976. Mem. geol. socs. Am., Washington (treas. 1963-67), Sigma Xi (asso.). Home: 2450 Huidekoper Pl NW Washington DC 20007 Office: Interior Bldg 19th and C Sts NW Washington DC Mail Address: US Geol Survey 103 Nat Center Reston VA 22092

WALLACE, JOYCE IRENE MALAKOFF, physician; b. Phila., Nov. 25, 1940; d. Samuel Leonard and Henrietta (Hameroff) Malakoff; A.B., Queens Coll., City U. N.Y., 1961; postgrad. Columbia U., 1962-64; M.D, SUNY, 1968; m. Lance Arthur Wallace, Aug. 30, 1964 (div. 1974); 1 dau., Julia Ruth; m. Arthur H. Kahn, Oct. 7, 1979; 1 son, Aryeh N. Kahn. Intern, St. Vincent's Hosp. Med. Center, N.Y.C., 1968-70; resident Manhattan VA Hosp., N.Y.C. and Nassau County Med. Center, East Meadow, N.Y., 1972-73; practice medicine, N.Y.C., 1970-71, North Conway, N.H., 1974-75; practice medicine specializing in internal medicine, N.Y.C., 1976—; mem. attending staff Nassau County Med. Center, 1974, St. Vincent's Hosp. and Med. Center, N.Y.C., 1976—. Diplomate Am. Bd. Internal Medicine. Fellow ACP; mem. Am. Med. Women's Assn., N.Y. County, N.Y. State med. socs. Office: 225 W 12th St New York NY 10011

WALLACE, KRISTIE LEE, hotel mgr.; b. Santa Monica, Calif., Sept. 19, 1955; d. Gary Emory and Katherine Phylis (Monos) W.; A.A., San Diego State U., 1976; B.A., San Francisco State U., 1977. Pre-sch. tchr., San Francisco, 1976; substitute tchr., Palm Springs, Calif., 1979; adminstrv. asst. Marina City Club/Hughes Aircraft, Marina Del Rey, Calif., 1978; sales sec. Hyatt Hotels, Los Angeles, 1978-80; asst. mgr. Melting Pot Restaurant, Encino, Calif., 1980; conv. coordinating, sales Detroit Products Co., Inc., 1978-80; account exec., sales mgr. Hacterda Hotel, El Segundo, Calif., 1980-82; dir. sales Holiday Inn Downtown, Los Angeles, 1982—. Treas., Los Angeles Airport Area Awareness Assn. Mem. Hotel Sales Mgmt. Assn., Travel and Transp. Council. Episcopalian. Club: Manhatten Athletic. Office: 750 Garland Blvd Los Angeles CA 90017

WALLACE, LYSBETH MAI, educator, artist; b. Hopkinsville, Ky., Dec. 7.; d. William A. and Lucile (Van Cleve) Wallace; B.A., U. Ky., 1943; M.F.A., Kansas City Art Inst., 1946; M.F.A., Cranbrook Acad. Art, Bloomfield Hills, Mich., 1951. Grad. asst. Kansas City Art Inst., 1945-46; instr. Washburn U., Topeka, Kan., 1946-48; handweaving expert UN Tech. Assistance Program, Philippine Islands, 1951-53; asst. prof. dept. art., So. Ill. U., Carbondale, 1955-60; asst. prof. dept. art Ill. State U., Normal, 1961-65; prof. weaving Western Ky. U., Bowling Green, 1965—. Kansas City Art Inst. scholar, 1945-46; recipient Purchase Award, Mid-State Craft, Evansville, Ind., 1967, many others. Mem. Coll. Art Assn., Am. Craft Council, AAUP, Textile Mus., Smithsonian Inst. Democrat. Author: Handweaving in the Philippines, 1953; contbr. articles to profl. jours.; commd. works include wall hangings, tapestries.

WALLACE, MARTHA REDFIELD, found. exec.; b. Omaha, Dec. 27, 1927; d. Ralph J. and Lois (Thompson) Redfield; B.A. (Durant scholar), Wellesley Coll., 1949; M.A., Fletcher Sch. Law and Diplomacy, Tufts U., 1950; Litt. D. (hon.), Converse Coll., 1975; LL.D. (hon.), Occidental Coll., 1975, Pace U., 1975, Manhattan Coll., 1977. Instr. econs., asst. to dean Fletcher Sch. Econs., 1950-51; economist Dept. State, 1951-53; with RCA Internat., 1954-55; mem. editorial staff Fortune mag., 1955-57; with IBM, 1960-61; asst. dir. corp. devel. Time Inc., 1963-67; exec. dir., bd. dirs. Henry Luce Found., Inc., N.Y.C., 1967—; dir. Am. Can Co., Am. Express Co., Bristol-Myers Co., Chem. N.Y. Corp., N.Y. Stock Exchange, N.Y. Telephone Co.; trustee Bowery Savs. Bank 1972-81; mem. Conf. Bd., 1974—, Nat. Com. U.S.-China Relations, 1975—, Temp. Commn. N.Y.C. Fins., 1975-77, Brit.-Am. Com., 1976—, Trilateral Commn., 1978—. Trustee Cultural Resources City of N.Y., 1977-81, chmn., 1978-81; trustee Williams Coll., 1974—, N.Y.C. Citizens Budget Commn., 1976—; bd. dirs. Greater N.Y. Fund/United Way, 1975—, Am. Council/W. Ger., 1980—, N.Y.C. Partnership, 1980—. Mem. Am. Judicature Soc. (v.p., exec. com., dir. 1978, chmn. 1981—), Council Fgn. Relations (dir. 1972—), Council Founds. (dir. 1971-77), Found. Center (dir. 1971-77), Japan Soc. (dir. 1975-81), N.Y. Racing Assn. (dir. 1976—), Am. Acad. Polit. Scis., Phi Beta Kappa. Clubs: River, Mashohack Fish and Game Preserve, Board Room, Hemisphere. Home: 435 E 52d St New York NY 10022 Office: 111 W 50th St New York NY 10020

WALLACE, MICHELE FAITH, writer, lectr.; b. N.Y.C., Jan. 4, 1952; d. Robert Earl Wallace and Faith Elizabeth (Jones) Ringgold; B.A., CCNY, 1974. Book rev. researcher Newsweek Mag., N.Y.C., 1974-75; instr. journalism N.Y.U., 1976-78; author Black Macho and the Myth of the Superwoman, 1979; contbr. articles, essays, short stories and poetry to newspapers and popular mags. including Ms., Esquire, The Village Voice, various anthologies; editor Women in Art, 1971. Pres., Art Without Walls, 1974; founding mem. Nat. Black Feminist Orgn., 1974; pres. WSABAL, 1970-76.

WALLACE, MIMI, advt. co. exec.; b. Englewood, N.J., Apr. 7, 1932; d. Jerome and Helen (Hirsch) Kolberg; B.A., N.Y. U., 1954; 1 son, David. Asst. radio-TV comml. bus. mgr. Batten, Barton Durstine & Osborne, Inc., N.Y.C., 1955-62; talent agt. Lester Lewis Assos., N.Y.C., 1964-68; with Ted Bates & Co., Inc., N.Y.C., 1968—, v.p. in charge radio-TV comml. bus. affairs, 1973, pres., pres., 1975-81; pres. Channelex, Inc., Calla Music, Inc., N.Y.C., 1973—. Office: Ted Bates & Co Inc 1515 Broadway New York NY 10036

WALLACE, VONNA SYVETT, aerospace co. ofcl.; b. Columbus, Ohio, June 11, 1947; d. Paris Allen and Dorothy Wallace; B.B.A., Ohio State U., 1969; M.S., Ga. Coll., 1976. Urban intern HUD, Chgo., 1969; asst. dept. mgr. ladies blouses and accessories Lazarus-Federated Dept. Stores, Columbus, 1970-73; buyer, cons. agreements and research and devel. agreements in semicondr. tech. Ford Motor Co., Dearborn, Mich., 1977-80; mgr. subcontract adminstrn. Space div. Gen. Electric Co., King of Prussia, Pa., 1980—. Served to capt. USAF, 1973-77. Mem. Nat. Contract Mgmt. Assn., NOW, Nat. Assn. Female Execs. Home: 30 Woodstream Dr Apt 5 Jeffersonville PA 19403 Office: Gen Electric Co Space Div Goddard Blvd King of Prussia PA 19406

WALLACH, BARBARA PRICE, philologist, educator; b. Roanoke, Va., Aug. 31, 1946; d. Benjamin Thomas and Geneva Mae (Bittinger) Price; B.A., Mary Washington Coll., 1968; A.M., U. Ill., 1970, Ph.D. in Classical Philology, 1974; m. Luitpold Wallach, Aug. 22, 1970. Vis. lectr. in Classics, U. Ill., Urbana-Champaign, summer 1977; vis. asst. prof. Classics, U. Pitts., 1979-80; asst. prof. Classical studies U. Mo., Columbia, 1980—. Mem. Am. Philol. Assn., Women's Caucus of Am. Philol. Assn., Soc. Ancient Greek Philosophy, Classical Assn. Middle West and South. Author: Lucretius and the Diatribe Against the Fear of Death, 1976; contbr. articles to profl. jours. Office: Classical Studies Dept 420b Gen Classroom Bldg U Mo Columbia MO 65201

WALLACH, DAVIDA ANN, ins. broker; b. Copiague, N.Y., Mar. 8, 1954; d. Frank Henry and Carol Jo (Matteson) Fonda; student Duchess Community Coll., 1972-73, Nassau Community Coll., 1981; m. Robert Wallach, Apr. 16, 1977 (div.). Clk., Emery & Webb, Rhinebeck, N.Y., 1975-76; underwriter Newman Greenfield & List, Lynbrook, N.Y., 1976-77, Robert Plan Corp., Lynbrook, 1977; underwriter, gen. mgr. Ambassador Brokerage Corp., Lynbrook, 1977-81; ins. broker John Hancock Life Ins. Cos., Holbrook, N.Y., 1982—. Mem. Nat. Assn. Female Execs., L.I. Sports Car Assn. Democrat. Jewish. Office: PO Box 381 Holbrook NY 11741

WALLAR, BETTY JANE, nurse; b. Detroit, Apr. 3, 1924; d. Earl Edgar and Clara May (Henkel) W.; R.N., St. Luke's Hosp.; B.A., San Francisco State U., 1950, M.A., 1970. Nurse, St. Luke's Hosp., San Francisco, 1947-50, clin. instr., 1950-60, dir. nursing services, 1960-76; psychiat. supr. Cambridge (Ohio) Mental Health Hosp., 1981—. Served with M.C., U.S. Army, 1945-47. Mem. Am. Nurses Assn. Republican. Episcopalian. Home: 136 S 12th St Cambridge OH 43725 Office: Cambridge Mental Health Center County Rd 35 N Cambridge OH 43725

WALLBAUM, JOAN MARGARET, computer co. exec.; b. Decatur, Ill., Dec. 18, 1938; d. Ralph Melvin and Margaret Bernice (Goveia) Funk; student parochial schs.; divorced. Tech. cons. State of Ill., Springfield, 1970-73; info. systems exec., data base adminstr. Ill. Dept. Public Aid, 1973-77; mgr. data base info. systems Philip Morris, Inc., Richmond, Va., 1977-81; mgr. info. mgmt. Prime Computer Co., Natick, Mass., 1981—; mem. faculty Electronic Computer Programming Inst., 1972. Mem. Data Processing Mgmt. Assn. (v.p. 1982), Am. Mgmt. Assn., Inst. Cert. Computer Profls., Council Cert. Data Processing, Am. Contract Bridge League. Club: Framingham (Mass.) Bridge. Home: 48 Tanglewood Dr Milford MA 01757 Office: Prime Computer Co Prime Park Natick MA 01760

WALLENT, JOAN FRANCES, bus. cons.; b. Taunton, Mass., Nov. 3, 1945; d. John and Frances (Tumonis) Wallent; B.A., U. Chgo., 1966; postgrad. Harvard U., 1967-68 Psychol. Inst. N.Y.C., 1970. Research asst. Arthur D. Little, Inc., Cambridge, Mass., 1967-71; asso. dir. admissions Emerson Coll., Boston, 1971-76; dir. admissions Bennett Coll., Millbrook, N.Y., 1976-77, Lake Erie Coll., Painesville, Ohio, 1977-79, Ottawa (Kans.) U., 1979-81; profl. cons. career mktg., 1982—; part-time faculty Newbury Jr. Coll., Boston, 1969-72. Mem. Nat. Assn. Coll. Admissions Counselors, New Eng. Assn. Coll. Admissions Counselors, N.Y. Assn. Coll. Admissions Counselors, Gt. Plains Assn. Coll. Admissions Counselors (pres.), Am. Assn. Coll. Registrars and Admissions Officers, Am. Personnel and Guidance Assn., Nat. Assn. Women Deans, Adminstrs. and Counselors, Am. Soc. Psychical Research, Am. Parapsychol. Assn., Am. Astrological Assn. Roman Catholic. Home: 1517 S Oak St Ottawa KS 66067

WALLER, WILHELMINE KIRBY, civic worker, orgn. ofcl.; b. N.Y.C., Jan. 19, 1914; d. Gustavus Town and Wilhelmine (Claflin) Kirby; ed. Chapin Sch., N.Y.C.; m. Thomas Mercer Waller, Apr. 7, 1942. Conservation chmn. Garden Club Am., 1959-61, pres., 1965-68, dir., 1968-71, chmn. nat. affairs com., 1968-74; mem. adv. com. N.Y. State Conservation Commn., 1959-70, dist. dir. Soil and Water Conservation, Westchester County, 1967-74, recipient Francis K. Hutchinson medal, 1971; mem. Nat. Adv. Com. Hwy. Beautification, 1965-68; mem. Lyndhurst council Nat. Trust Hist. Preservation, 1965-74; mem. Conservation Adv. Council, Bedford, N.Y., 1968-70; mem. Westchester County Planning Bd., 1970—; dir. Westchester Council Social Agys., 1970-72; mem. Rachel Carson council Nat. Audubon Soc., 1964—; v.p. Bedford Farmers Club, 1954-74; mem. Planning Bd. Bedford, 1953-57; mem. adv. com. to sec. of state UN Conf. on Human Environment, 1971-72; mem. N.Y. State Parks Adv. Com., 1971-72; adviser Gov. Rockefeller's Study Commn. Future of Adirondacks, 1968-70; mem. Citizens Adv. Com. on Environ. Quality, 1973-77; bd. govs. Nature Conservancy, 1970-77, vice chmn. Lower Hudson chpt., 1982—; trustee Mianus River Gorge. Recipient award for More Beautiful America, Holiday mag., 1972; Conservation award Am. Motors, 1975. Mem. Nat. Soc. Colonial Dames, Huguenot Soc. Am., Daus. Cincinnati. Episcopalian. Club: Colony (N.Y.C.). Address: Tanrackin Farm Bedford Hills NY 10507

WALLFISCH, LORY, pianist, harpsichordist, educator; b. Ploesti, Romania, Apr. 21, 1922; came to U.S., 1947, naturalized, 1953; d. Samson and Carola Florin; ed. Royal Conservatory of Music, Bucharest, pvt. piano studies with Florica Muzicescu; m. Ernst Wallfisch, Nov. 12, 1944 (dec. May 1979); 1 son, Paul. Pianist, Wallfisch Duo, appearing in Europe, U.S., Israel and North Africa, 1947-79; pvt. tchr., Romania, Switzerland and U.S., 1938-60; prof. music Smith Coll., Northampton, Mass., 1964—; performer, condr. master classes, S.Am., 1982, Australia, 1983; participant Casals, Edinburgh, York, Venice, Besancon and Menuhin festivals; TV appearances; rec. artist Vox/Turnabout, DaCamera, Musical Heritage, Advance and Concert Hall Soc. labels. Mem. European Piano Tchrs. Assn., Mass. Music Tchrs. Assn., Friends of Kennedy Center, Northampton Fedn. Musicians, George Enescu Soc. U.S. (founder). Contbr. articles mags. Office: Sage Hall Smith College Northampton MA 01063

WALLIN, ANN LEWIS, educator; b. Haverstraw, N.Y., Dec. 9, 1937; d. Ernest Dalzell and Margaret Frances (Konecni) Lewis; B.S., U. Vt., 1958; M.S. in Counseling, U. Bridgeport, 1962, M.S. in Reading, 1976; 1 son, Jeffrey Orrick. Tchr., Fairfield (Conn.) Public Schs., 1959-61; free lance tchr. service workshops, Fairfield, 1974-77; pvt. practice diagnostic assessment and prescriptive teaching services, Fairfield, Westport, Conn.; lectr. in field; coordinator Mid-Fairfield County Com. on Learning, 1974-77; sec. Council Exptl. Research in Reading, 1975-76; ednl. therapist Learning Help, Inc. and Ednl. Consulting Center, Westport, Conn., now pres. Learning Help Inc. Cert. tchr., Conn. Mem. AAUW, Orton Soc., Conn. Assn. Children with Learning Disabilities. Clubs: Ausable, Adirondack Mountain Res. Home: 1 Merwins Ln Fairfield CT 06430 Office: 237 Post Rd W Westport CT 06880

WALLIN, JUDITH KERSTIN, pediatrician, educator; b. Paris, Apr. 23, 1938; d. Theodore Bror and Ella Charlotte (Butler) Wallin; came to U.S., 1938; B.S. in Chemistry, Elizabethtown (Pa.) Coll., 1960; M.D., Temple U., 1964. Intern, Bellevue Hosp., N.Y.C., 1964-65, resident in pediatrics, 1965-67, attending pediatrician, 1967—; instr. pediatrics N.Y. U., 1967-71, asst. prof. clin. pediatrics, 1971-74, asso. prof., 1974—. Recipient Educate for Service through Profl. Achievement award, O.F. Stambaugh Alumni award Elizabethtown Coll., 1978. Diplomate Am. Bd. Pediatrics. Home: 300 E 33d St New York NY 10016 Office: Dept of Pediatrics Bellevue Hosp 27th St and 1st Ave New York NY 10016

WALLING, GEORGIA, psychotherapist b. Cedarhurst, N.Y.; d. William English and Anna (Strunsky) W.; student U. Paris, 1931-32, Vassar Coll., 1932-34; B.A., Rollins Coll., 1935; M.A., Columbia U., 1937, M.S. in Social Work, 1947. Caseworker, Family Service Soc., Atlanta, 1948-49, Bklyn. Bur. Social Service, 1951-53, Inwood House, N.Y.C., 1954-58; sr. psychiat. casework therapist Childrens Village, Dobb's Ferry, N.Y., 1959-60; asso. staff mem. Postgrad Center for Mental Health, N.Y.C., 1960-65; pvt. practice psychoanalysis, N.Y.C. Mem. Nat. Assn. Social Workers, Acad. Cert. Social Workers, N.Y. State Soc. Clin. Social Work Psychotherapists, Postgrad. Psychoanalytic Soc., Nat. Accreditation Assn. for Psychoanalysis.

WALLING, LOTTIE B., acctg. firm exec.; b. Hickman County, Ky., Oct. 8, 1930; d. Charles Rivers and Irene Bellew; student Miss Wylie's Office Tng. Sch., Memphis, 1949, U. Tenn., Martin, part time 1974—; m. John Russell Walling, Aug. 19, 1951; children—Vickie, Donna, Bill. Receptionist, bookkeeper Albert B. Maloney & Co., C.P.A.'s, Memphis, 1950-51; sec., bookkeeper R.J. Cheeseman, Union City, Tenn., 1953-60, Cheeseman, Thompson & Co., C.P.A.'s, 1960-76; adminstrv. asst., bookkeeper R.D. Cheeseman & Co., Martin, Tenn., 1977—. Chmn., March of Dimes Drive, 1959, Heart Drive, 1960, Martin Heart Meml., 1978-82, Sr. Parents Activities, 1977; pres. PTA, 1962-64; sr. leader Girl Scouts, 1968-70; den mother Boy Scouts, 1964-65. Cert. profl. sec. Mem. West Tenn. Heart Assn. Methodist. Clubs: Order Eastern Star, Poplar Meadows Country (sec. treas. 1963-77). Home: PO Box 529 Union City TN 38261 Office: PO Box 436 Martin TN 38237

WALLING, SUSAN EILEEN FEMRITE, interior designer; b. Glenwood, Minn., Oct. 4, 1944; d. Sigvold Elmer and Sally Evangeline (Amundson) Femrite; B.S., U. Minn., 1966, cert. interior design, 1980; m. Greg Thomas Walling, Aug. 13, 1966; children—Christopher, Kari. Tchr., Roseville (Minn.) Public Schs., 1966-68, St. Louis Park (Minn.) Public Schs., 1968-73; interior designer Sue Walling Interiors, Edina, Minn., 1978-81; pres., interior designer SW Design, Inc., Mpls., 1981—. Active, Children's Health Center Aux., Friends of Inst.; vol. Blake Schs. Lutheran. Club: Edina Country. Office: 925 Southgate Office Plaza 5001 W 80th St Minneapolis MN 55437

WALLIS, SHARON K., legislative asst.; b. Phila., July 26, 1943; d. Louis and Kathryn (Madden) Kaplan; B.A., St. John's Coll., 1964; LL.B., U. Pa., 1967; married. Admitted to bar; atty. Community Legal Services, Inc., Phila., 1967-69, Lawyers' Com. for Civil Rights, Phila., 1970-71; pvt. practice law, Phila., 1971-77; atty. Phila. Dist. Atty.'s Office, 1978-79; asst. to dean Med. Coll. Pa., 1978-80; legis. asst. to Rep. Foglietta of Pa., Washington, 1980—. Mem. Pa. Human Relations Commn., Phila. Bar Assn., United Communities of S.E. Phila. (dir. 1972—), Fellowship Commn. Bd., U. Pa. Law Alumni Assn. (dir. 1974-80), Phila. Women's Polit. Caucus (pres. 1970-75). Jewish. Office: Longworth Ho Office Bldg Room 1217 Washington DC 20515 *

WALLS, BETTY L., psychologist; b. Kansas City, Mo., Oct. 26, 1932; d. Austin Truman Webb and Gladys Opal (Gillespie) Webb Morrison; diploma in Nursing, Kansas City Gen. Hosp., Mo., 1957; B.A., U. Mo., 1967, M.A., 1971, Ph.D. in Psychology, 1974; m. William Cliebern Walls, Apr. 6, 1954 (div. 1961); 1 son, Paul Kevin. Clin. instr. maternity nursing St. Margaret's Hosp., 1957-60; dir. inservice edn. Research Hosp., Kansas City, 1962-65; instr. anatomy and physiology Sch. of Record Librarians, Kansas City, Mo., 1965; research asst. dept. psychology U. Mo., Kansas City, 1968-70, instr., 1971-73, 76-80, vis. prof., 1980—; asst. prof. dept. psychology Park Coll., Parkville, Mo., 1973-80, chmn. dept. psychology, 1973-75, 78-80; clin. psychologist, cons. Catholic Charities, Kansas City, 1980—; instr. U. Mo.-Kansas City, 1976-80, Benedictine Coll., Atchison, Kans., 1980—; cons. to Kansas City Found. for Retardation, 1978—. Bd. dirs. Operation Discovery Sch., Kansas City, Mo., 1974—, Inst. for Alcoholic Recovery, Kansas City, 1976—; bd. dirs. Sherwood Center for Exceptional Children, Kansas City, 1978—, v.p., 1979—. Recipient Service award City of Kansas City, 1962. Cert. behavior analyst I. Mem. Am. Psychol. Assn., Assn. of Behavior Analyst, AAAS, Am. Assn. for Tension Control, Mo. Psychol. Assn., N.Y. Acad. Sci., U. Mo. Alumni Assn., Psi Chi. Democrat. Methodist. Contbr. articles to jours. in psychology. Home: 8019 Kenwood Kansas City MO 64151

WALLS, VERNA WILLIETTE, educator; b. Port Gibson, Miss., Feb. 6, 1917; d. Scott and Georgia (Trevillion) Carpenter; A.B., Dillard U., 1941; M.A. in English, DePaul U., 1966; m. William Franklin Walls, June 16, 1951. English tchr., Cherry St. Sch., Vicksburg, Miss., 1942-45; ward sec. Cook County Hosp., Chgo., 1948-54; tchr. Froebel Elem. Sch., Chgo., 1954-55; tchr. English, DuSable High Sch., Chgo., 1955-65; tchr. English, chmn. Forrestville-Martin Luther King High Sch., Chgo., 1965—. Mem. Nat. Assn. Women Deans, Adminstrs. and Counselors, Nat. Council Tchrs. English, Chgo. Area Reading Assn., Aux. Sammy Dyer Sch. Theatre, Phi Delta Kappa. Methodist. Office: 4445 S Drexel Blvd Chicago IL 60653

WALNE, PATRICIA LEE, botanist; b. Newark, Nov. 27, 1932; d. George T. and Katherine G. Walne; B.S. magna cum laude, Hanover (Ind.) Coll., 1954; M.S., Ind. U., 1959; Ph.D., U. Tex., Austin, 1965. Mem. faculty U. Tenn., Knoxville, 1966—, prof. botany, 1973—, Chancellor's research scholar, 1980; Univ. Macebearer, 1982; cons. Oak Ridge Nat. Lab., 1966-75; adv. panel NSF, 1976-78; adv. com. Council Internat. Exchange Scholars, 1978-81. Recipient Darbaker award Bot. Soc. Am., 1978; Fulbright research scholar, Denmark, 1974-75; AAUW postdoctoral fellow, 1975; NSF grantee, 1969—. Mem. Phycological Soc. Am. (pres. 1974), Internat. Phycological Soc., Brit. Phycological Soc., Soc. Evolutionary Protistology, Am. Soc. Cell Biology, Electron Microscopy Soc. Am., Am. Soc. Photobiology, Sigma Xi. Author papers in field. Office: Dept Botany U Tenn Knoxville TN 37996

WALPOLE, SHERLU RARDIN, broadcasting exec., writer; b. Kirksville, Mo., Mar. 7, 1924; d. Nelson Gailord and Shirley Lou (Humphrey) Rardin; A.A., U. Chgo., 1943, B.A., 1945; M.A., S.W. Mo. State U., 1979; m. Hugh R. Walpole, Sept. 28, 1946 (div. 1954); 1 son, Hugh Nelson. Continuity writer Sta. KWTO, Springfield, Mo., 1951; continuity writer, women's program dir. Sta. KGBX, Springfield, 1952-54; continuity dir. Sta. KTTS-AM-FM-TV, Springfield, 1954-61; promotion mgr., merchandising dir. Sta. KOLR-TV/KTTS-AM-FM-TV, Springfield, 1962-75; account exec., spl. asst. to pres. MAP Advt. Agy., Springfield, 1975-77; promotion dir. Sta. KSMU, Springfield, 1978-80; mem. adj. faculty S.W. Mo. State U., Drury Coll.; feature writer Springfield! mag. Mem. Mo. Press Women, DAR, Mensa, Alpha Epsilon Rho. Democrat. Home: 3237 E Berkeley St Springfield MO 65804

WALSCH, NELLIE LEE, steel warehousing exec.; b. Garrison, Ky., Mar. 18, 1920; d. Thomas Edgar and Essie Beatrice (Akers) Martin; student public and pvt. schs., also various coll. courses; m. Herman W. Walsch, Nov. 19, 1949; 1 son, Daniel Lee. With United Iron & Metal Co., Inc., Balt., from 1946, office mgr., bookkeeper div. Curtis Steel products Co.; corp. sec., bookkeeper Marlen Trading Co., Inc., Balt., Chesapeake Internat. Corp., Balt.; bookkeeper Curtis Export Corp., Balt., LSL Assos., Balt. Democrat. Methodist. Office: 4101 Curtis Ave Baltimore MD 21226

WALSH, ANNMARIE HAUCK, research orgn. exec.; b. N.Y.C., May 5, 1938; d. James Smith and Annmarie (Kennedy) Hauck; B.A., Barnard Coll., 1961; M.A., Columbia U., 1969, Ph.D., 1971; m. John F. Walsh, Jr., Aug. 20, 1960; children—Peter Hauck, John David. Dir. Govs. N.Y., N.J. and Conn. Task Force Regional Planning, 1979-81; asso. prof. polit. sci., dir. Center Urban and Policy Studies, City U. N.Y. Grad. Sch., 1972-79; mem. sr. staff Inst. Public Adminstrn., N.Y.C., 1971-72, pres., 1982—. Rep. N.Y. Fin. Control Bd., 1979—; resource leader Presl. Mgmt. Intern Program, 1978-80. Mem. Nat. Acad. Public Adminstrn., Phi Beta Kappa. Roman Catholic. Club: Princeton (N.Y.C.). Author: Urban Government for the Paris Region, 1968; The Urban Challenge to Government: An International Comparison of Thirteen Cities, 1969; The Public's Business: The Politics and Practices of Government Corporations, 1978; also articles, monographs. Office: IPA 55 W 44th St New York NY 10023

WALSH, BARBARA MARIE, accountant; b. Pueblo, Colo., Nov. 30, 1931; d. Edward Patrick and Emma Dorothy (Trejfa) W.; A.A., U. So. Colo., 1951. With CF & I Steel Corp., Pueblo, 1951—, beginning as key punch operator, successively tab machine operator, sec. indsl. relations dept., payroll tax acct., jr. staff acct., staff acct., 1951-79, staff acct., 1979—; operator tax and acctg. service. Roman Catholic. Home: 502 E Abriendo St Pueblo CO 81004

WALSH, BEATRICE METCALFE PASSAGE (MRS. THOMAS JOSEPH WALSH), civic worker; b. Schenectady, Mar. 6, 1917; d. William Riley and Jessamine (Littlefield) Passage; student Western Res. U., 1941-42, Cleve. Community Coll., 1980—; m. Thomas Joseph Walsh, July 12, 1941; 1 dau., Joan Beatrice (Mrs. Peter Michael Waltz). Vol. worker ARC, 1941-46, 47-53; leader council Cleve. Beachwood (Ohio) Girl Scouts, 1952-57; vol. worker Community Chest, 1947-50; mem. women's com. Cleve. Orch., 1962—; ladies program chmn. Am. Chem. Soc., 1960, Am. Inst. Chem. Engrs., 1961, ladies program conv. com., 1969; mem. Orange Community Arts Council, 1969—, Pepper Pike Civic League, 1966—; ladies program co-chmn. Nat. Heat Transfer Conf., 1964; mem. women's com. Chagrin Valley Little Theater. Mem. Nat. Huguenot Soc., Nat. Soc. Founders and Patriots, Nat. Soc. New Eng. Women (sec. Cleve. Colony 1980—), Shaker Heights LWV, Case Faculty Wives (pres. 1958-59), Western Res. Rep. Women's Club, DAR, (Shaker chpt., corr. sec. 1962-64, registrar 1964-69, publicity chmn. 1968-70, chaplain 1969-71, librarian 1972-73, vice regent 1973-74, regent 1974-76, del. state conv. 1963, 64, 66, 69, 73, 74, 75, chmn. reception, del. nat. conv. 1964, 73, 74, 75), Friends of Orange Community Library, Daus. Am. Colonists (regent Charter Oak chpt. 1977-79), Order Crown of Charlemagne, Soc. Magna Charta Dames, Nat. Soc. New Eng. Women, Colonial Dames 17th Century, Western Res. Hist. Soc., Garden Center Greater Cleve. Presbyn. Clubs: Blackbrook Country, Landerhaven Golf, Moreland Hills Golf, Landerwood Swim, Suburban Garden, Green Valley Garden (club rep. 1972-73, corr. sec. 1976-77); Case-Western Res. U. (exec. bd. 1981—). Home: 32555 Creekside Dr Pepper Pike Cleveland OH 44124

WALSH, DIANE, pianist; b. Washington, Aug. 16, 1950; d. William Donald and Estelle Louise (Stokes) W.; Mus.B., Juilliard Sch. Music, 1971; M.M., Mannes Coll. Music, 1982; m. Richard Pollak, 1982. N.Y.C. debut Young Concert Artists Series, 1974; other appearances include: Kennedy Center for Performing Arts, Washington, 1976, Met. Museum, N.Y.C., 1976, Wigmore Hall, London, 1979; appeared with maj. orchs. worldwide, including St. Louis Symphony, Indpls. Symphony, San Francisco Symphony, Buffalo Philharmonic, Bavarian Radio Symphony of Munich, Berlin Radio Symphony, Radio Symphony Frankfurt, Radio Symphony Stuttgart; has toured Europe, N. Am., S. Am., Central Am.; mem. piano faculty Mannes Coll. Music. Recipient 3d prize Busoni Internat. Piano Competition, Italy, 1974; 2d prize Mozart Internat. Piano Competition, Salzburg, Austria, 1975; 1st prize Munich Internat. Piano Competition, 1975; Nat. Endowment Arts. grantee, 1981.

WALSH, ELIZABETH ANN, planning analyst; b. N.Y.C., July 4, 1950; d. John Joseph and Mary Margaret (Creehan) W.; B.A. in Edn., Montclair (N.J.) State Coll., 1972; M.B.A. in Econs., Seton Hall U., South Orange, N.J., 1979. With Prudential Ins. Co., Holmdel, N.J., 1976-80, sr. staff auditor comptroller's dept., 1978-80; ops. planning analyst Johnson & Johnson, New Brunswick, N.J., 1980—. Mem. Inst. Internal Auditors, Nat. Assn. Female Execs., AAUW, Nat. Bus. and Profl. Women's Orgn., Mensa. Democrat. Roman Catholic. Home: 4 Gander Ln Englishtown NJ 07726 Office: 501 George St New Brunswick NJ

WALSH, EVELYN CORNELIA, bus. exec., former banker; b. Paterson, N.J., Jan. 14, 1931; d. Cornelius and Dorothy May (Howes) Struyk; grad. Packard Jr. Coll., 1950, N.Y. U., 1957-60; m. Francis Walsh, Sept. 14, 1971; 1 dau., Debra Lynne Bush. Adminstrv. asst. N.J. Bank, Paterson, 1950-54; adminstrv. officer Ford Found., N.Y.C., 1956-69; dir. mktg. and personnel Westinghouse Learning Corp., N.Y.C., 1969-71; mktg. cons., N.Y.C., 1971-73; asst. v.p. Central Savs. Bank, N.Y.C., 1973, v.p., 1975-76, sr. v.p., 1976-79, exec. v.p., 1979-81; chmn. Savs. Banks Assn. N.Y. State Mktg. Forum, 1979-80; co-founder, dir. Celtique Spring Water Bottling Co., Ltd., Ballygown-Piltown, County Kilkenny, Ireland; speaker arts and bus. council, N.Y. U. Sch. Edn. spl. seminars. Mem. Women Execs. in Public Relations, Nat. Assn. Female Execs.

WALSH, GRETCHEN EMIDY, educator; b. Providence, Mar. 21, 1929; d. Herman Lorenzo and Theresa Gertrude (Kerr) Emidy; student U. Rochester, 1947; B.Ed., R.I. Coll., 1950; postgrad. Providence Coll., 1953; M.S., Central Conn. State Coll., 1976; m. Raymond F. Walsh, Mar. 2, 1953; children—Bethany Walsh Ingriselli, Christopher, Timothy, Margaret, Katherine. Elem. tchr., Woonsocket, R.I., 1950-53, Staffordville, Conn., 1954-55, Southington, Conn., 1965—; tchr. learning disabilities Southington (Conn.) High Sch., 1976-77, Milldale Elem. Sch., Southington, 1976-78, William Strong Sch., Southington, 1976—. Mem. NEA, Conn. Edn. Assn., Southington Edn. Assn., Council for Exceptional Children, Conn. Assn. Children with Perceptual Learning Disabilities, Southington Learning Disabilities Assn., Assn. Children with Learning Disabilities. Home: 88 Edgewood Circle Southington CT 06489 Office: William Strong Elem Sch Marion Ave Plantsville CT 06479

WALSH, JANE ELLEN, health care ofcl.; b. Uniontown, Pa., Jan. 16, 1941; d. Albert Benton and Dorothy Rose (Ruble) McCann; B.A., Hood Coll., 1963; postgrad. Northwestern U., 1964-65; M.A., Antioch Coll., 1978; m. John Daniel Walsh, June 8, 1973; stepchildren—Christopher, Mark, Jonathan, Jennifer. Research asst. Cert. Nat. Interviewers, Chgo., 1963-64; project dir. Assn. Am. Med. Colls., Evanston, Ill., 1965-68; systems analyst Research Found. Mental Hygiene, Inc., Orangeburg, N.Y., 1968-72; systems analyst Nat. Center Health Services Research, Rockville, Md., 1972-73; research cordinator U. Calif., Berkeley, 1973-75; coordinator Pvt. Initiative in PSRO, San Francisco, 1975-76; cons., 1977-78; asso. dir. tech. services Western Consortium for Health Professions, Inc., San Francisco, 1978—; cons. health info. systems, health care evaluation, data sources. Recipient Martha Schaeffer Shaw award, 1960. Mem. Am. Public Health Assn., AAAS, Assn. Computing Machinery, Advs. Public Health, Assn. Health Services Research, Common Cause, Mus. Soc. San Francisco, Smithsonian Instn. Democrat. Presbyterian. Club: Highlands Country. Author: Introduction to Standard Mumps, 1978; developer automated system for storage and retrieval of clin. psychiat. data, 1969; research on multi-splty. group practices delivering primary care, procedures for conducting concurrent quality assurance. Home: 50 Schooner Hill Oakland CA 94618 Office: 703 Market St Suite 535 San Francisco CA 94103

WALSH, JULIA MARGARET CURRY (MRS. THOMAS M. WALSH), investment co. exec.; b. Akron, Ohio, Mar. 29, 1923; d. Edward A. and Catharine V. (Skurkay) Curry; B.B.A. magna cum laude, Kent (Ohio) State U., 1945; postgrad. N.Y. Inst. Fin., 1956; grad. Advanced Mgmt. Program, Harvard U., 1962; LL.D., Hood Coll., 1969, Regis Coll., 1973; m. John G. Montgomery, Apr. 7, 1948 (dec. Dec. 1957); children—John, Stephen, Michael, Mark; m. 2d, Thomas M. Walsh, May 18, 1963; 1 dau., Margaret; stepchildren—Mary Francis Walsh Ferencle, Patrick Joseph, Kathleen Walsh Carr, Thomas D., Joan Walsh Cassedy, Daniel, Ann Walsh Walton. Personnel officer Am. counsulate gen., Munich, Germany, 1945-48; probation officer Wash. State Sch. Girls, Centralia, 1948-50; exec. officer U.S. Ednl. Commn., Ankara, Turkey, 1952-54; registered rep. Ferris & Co., Inc., Washington, 1955-59, gen. partner, 1959-70, sr. v.p., 1971-73, vice chmn., 1973-77; chmn. Julia M. Walsh & Sons, Inc., 1977—; mem. Am. Stock Exchange, 1965-75, bd. govs., 1972, exchange ofcl., 1973-76; adv. bd. Union 1st Bank Washington; dir. Pitney Bowes; mem. Sec. State's Spl. Adv. Com. on Public Opinion; mem. adv. com. loan guarantee programs in health HEW; mem. D.C. Judiciary Selection Com. Bd. dirs. Kent State U. Found., Nat. Shrine Immaculate Conception, St. Mary of the Woods Coll., Georgetown U.; dir.-at-large Met. Washington Bd. Trade; mem. Washington bd. Nat. Multiple Sclerosis Soc.; bd. govs. East-West Center, Honolulu; mem. Tax Revision Commn. D.C. Recipient Disting. Alumna award Kent State U., 1967; Bus. and Profl. Leader in Finance award Religious Heritage Am., 1973. Mem. U.S. C. of C. (nat. dir.), AAUW. Clubs: Bus. and Profl. Women's Potomac, Harvard Bus. Sch. Assn. (exec. council), Women's Nat. Democratic, Am. News Women's, Harvard Bus. Sch. (past pres.), Zonta Internat. (Washington). Home: 5001 Millwood Ln NW Washington DC 20016 Office: Julia M Walsh & Sons Inc 910 17th St NW Washington DC 20006

WALSH, SISTER, MARGARET JOSEPHINE, coll. adminstr.; b. Peekskill, N.Y., Nov. 30, 1923; d. Patrick J. and Mary J. (Butler) Walsh; student Columbia U., 1947-49, 62; B.A., Ohio Dominican Coll., 1970; M.B.A., Xavier U., 1980. Mem. staff, acctg. dept. Standard Brands, Inc., 1941-47; with William J. Donovan, Inc., Peekskill, 1947-58, pres., gen. mgr., 1958-63; joined Dominican Sisters of St. Mary of the Springs, Roman Catholic Ch., 1963; devel. dir. Congregation of St. Mary of the Springs, 1966-69; fin. cons. Cath. Diocese of Columbus (Ohio), and ednl. instns. of Dominican Sisters, 1970-74; treas., bus. mgr. Albertus Magnus Coll., New Haven, 1975-82; adv. bd. Colonial Bank, New Haven. Mem. bd. edn. Archdiocese of Hartford (Conn.); trustee Ohio Dominican Coll. Lic. master plumber. Mem. Nat. Assn. Coll. and Univ. Bus. Officers, Eastern Assn. Coll. and Univ. Bus. Officers. Roman Catholic. Home: Saint Mary of the Springs Columbus OH 43219

WALSH, MARGARET M., answering service exec.; b. Appleton, Wis., Nov. 26, 1920; d. Eugene J. and Anna M. (Finnegan) W.; student U. Wis. Extension, 1939, Spencerian Coll., 1940-41. Pres., owner Tel/Sec Inc., Appleton, 1949—; dir. Asso. Bank of Appleton. Mem. ATAE Inc. (pres. 1972-73), Sales and Mktg. Assn. NE Wis. (pres. 1979-80). Republican. Roman Catholic. Club: Riverview Country (pres. 1982-83). Home: 1001 S Oneida St Appleton WI 54915 Office: Tel/Sec Inc 516 W 6th St Appleton WI 54911

WALSH, MARGARET MARY, telephone co. ofcl.; b. Bronx, N.Y., July 13, 1951; d. John Joseph and Mary Margaret (Creehan) W.; B.A. in Math., Montclair State Coll., 1973. Buyer, Rike's, Federated Dept. Stores, Dayton, Ohio, 1973-77; regional distbr. The Limited Stores, Columbus, Ohio, 1977-80; project leader, mem. programming staff AT&T, Piscataway, N.J., 1980-82, staff tech. devel. Standards, Orlando, Fla., 1982—. Active Franklin Community Players, fundraising for Yr. of the Handicapped; adviser Jr. Achievement. Mem. Nat. Assn. Female Execs., AAUW. Home: 6039 S Rio Grande Ave Orlando FL 32809

WALSH, MARIE THERESE, editor spl. publs.; b. Cambridge, Mass., Oct. 13, 1935; d. Joseph Francis and Alice (Dullahan) W.; B.S. magna cum laude in Home Econs., Marywood Coll., Scranton, Pa., 1957. Home economist Best Foods div. Corn Products Co., 1957-59; asso. food editor Family Circle mag., N.Y.C., 1959-68, dir. test kitchen, 1971-75, editor, head dept. spl. mags. and books, including Great Ideas mag., 1975—; freelance home economist, 1968-71; guest lectr. N.Y.U., 1977, U. Mass., 1978; appearances on TV programs, 1971—; author: Casserole Cookery, 1975, Carefree Crockery Cookbook, 1976, Family Circle Cookie and Cake Book, 1977, Family Circle Creative Crafts, 1978, Quick and Easy Christmas Crafts, 1978, Decorative Crafts for the Home, 1979, The Natural Way to Beauty, 1979, Classic One-Dish Meals, 1978, Crafts for All Seasons, 1979, Simply Delicious Meals, 1978. Named Disting. Grad., Marywood Coll., 1976. Mem. Am. Home Econs. Assn., Home Economists in Bus., Elec. Women's Round Table (chmn. N.Y. chpt. 1977-78), Marywood Coll. Alumnae Assn. (pres. N.Y. chpt. 1963-64). Republican. Roman Catholic. Office: Family Circle Mag 488 Madison Ave New York NY 10022

WALSH, MARILYN, lawyer, broadcasting co. exec.; B.A., Grinnell Coll., 1950; J.D., N.Y. U., 1957, LL.M., 1958, M.B.A., 1963. With U.S. Trust Co., 1951-53, Irving Trust Co., 1953-57; tax atty. Davies, Hardy, Ives and Lawther, 1958-64; with CBS, Inc., N.Y.C., 1964—, sr. tax atty., 1965-66, tax counsel, 1966-67, asst. treas., dir. tax sect., 1967-72, corporate v.p., dir. taxes, 1972—. Office: CBS Inc 51 W 52d St New York NY 10019

WALSH, MARY D. FLEMING (MRS. F. HOWARD WALSH), civic worker; b. Whitewright, Tex., Oct. 29, 1913; d. William Fleming and Anna Maud (Lewis) Fleming; B.A., So. Meth. U., 1934; LL.D., Tex. Christian U., 1979; m. F. Howard Walsh, Mar. 13, 1937; children—Richard, Howard, D'Ann Walsh Bonnell, Maudi Walsh Willson, William Lloyd. Pres. Fleming Found.; v.p. Walsh Found.; partner Walsh Co.; mem. Lloyd Shaw Found., Colorado Springs, Colo. Guarantor, Ft. Worth Arts Council, Ft. Worth Opera, Ft. Worth Symphony Orch. Ft. Worth Ballet, Tex. Boys Choir Community Theater; mem. Opera Bd., 1960-81, hon. v.p.; co-founder Am. Field Service in Ft. Worth; mem. Tex. Commn. for Arts and Humanities, 1968-72, mem. adv. council, 1972-82; bd. dirs. Van Cliburn Internat. Piano Competition, Colorado Springs Day Nursery, Colorado Springs Symphony, Ft. Worth Arts Council, Ft. Worth Symphony, William Edrington Scott Theater; hon. chmn. Opera Guild Internat. Conf., 1976; 1st hon. chmn. Opera Ball, 1975; guarantor through the Walsh Found. the presentation of The Littlest Wiseman annually to City of Ft. Worth. Recipient numerous awards, including Altrusa Civic award as 1st Lady of Ft. Worth, 1968, Streams & Valleys award, 1976-77, 78-79, 80, Opera award Girl Scouts, 1977; (with husband) Disting. Service award So. Bapt. Radio and TV Commn., 1972, NCCJ Brotherhood Citation, 1978, Royal Purple award Tex. Christian U., 1979; (with husband) appreciation award Southwestern Baptist Theol. Sem., 1981; Med. Bldg. at Southwestern Bapt. Theol. Sem. and Library at Tarrant County Jr. Coll. N.W. named in honor (with husband); named (with husband) Patron of Arts in Ft. Worth, 1970, Edna Gladney Internat. Grandparents of 1972. Friends of Tex. Boys Choir, 1981. Mem. Ft. Worth Boys Club, Ft. Worth Children's Hosp., Jewel Charity Ball, Ft. Worth Pan Hellenic (pres. 1940), Opera Guild, Fine Arts Found. Guild Tex. Christian U., AAUW, Child Study Center, Tarrant County Aux. of Edna Gladney Home, YWCA (life), Ft. Worth Art Assn., Ft. Worth Ballet Assn., Tex. Boys Choir Aux., Round Table, Colorado Springs Fine Art Center, Am. Automobile Assn., Nat. Assn. Cowbelles, Rae Reimers Bible Study Class (pres. 1968), Tex. League Composers (hon. life), Chi Omega (pres. 1935-36), others. Baptist. Clubs: Kappa Sigma Wives and Mothers, The Woman's (Club Fidelite). Home: 2425 Stadium Dr Fort Worth TX 76109 also 1801 Culebra Ave Colorado Springs CO 80907

WALSH, ROSALIE KAY, coll. adminstr.; b. Butte, Mont., Sept. 7, 1951; d. Walter C. and Dorothy I. (Baravetto) W.; student Seattle U., 1969-71, Gonzaga U. in Florence, 1971-73; B.A., Carroll Coll., 1977. Sec., receptionist SW Mont. Mental Health Center, 1973-77; mgr., applied behavior analyst Progress, Inc., Helena, Mont., 1977-79; dean of women Carroll Coll., Helena, 1979-81, dir. career counseling, 1981—; mem. Mont. Regional Council for Developmental Disabilities, 1980—. Mem. Nat. Assn. Female Execs., Civitan Club of Helena, NOW (Jeanette Rankin Chpt.), Mont. Assn. Behavior Analysis, Helena Woman's Center. Home: Carroll Coll Box 93 Helena MT 59625 Office: O'Connell Hall Carroll Coll Helena MT 59625

WALSH, RUTH MURPHY, educator; b. Utica, N.Y.; d. Edward Simon and Elizabeth (Stack) Murphy; A.B., Barnard Coll., Columbia U., 1947; M.A., State U. N.Y., Buffalo, 1964; Ph.D., U. South Fla., Tampa, 1976; m. John Kevin Walsh, Sept. 20, 1952; children—Joyce G., Gregory S., Kyle Ann, Constance M. Tchr. English, Holy Angels Acad., 1958-59; instr. bus. adminstrn., asst. to dean Coll. Bus. Adminstrn., State U. N.Y., Buffalo, 1960-69; asst. prof. mgmt. U. South Fla., 1969-77, asso. prof., 1977—; cons. to industry. Former mem. Hillsborough County Bd. Cath. Edn.; vol. fund raiser Heart Fund, Multiple Sclerosis, Am. Cancer Soc., others. Mem. So. Mgmt. Assn., Am. Bus. Communications Assn., Phi Chi Theta, Phi Kappa Phi, Beta Gamma Sigma. Author: Communications...Public and Private Sectors, 1974; co-editor, compiler Job Satisfaction and Motivation, 1979; Business Communications, 1980 editor South Fla. Bus. News, 1971-74. Contbr. numerous articles to profl. jours. Home: 14814 Daisy Ln Tampa FL 33612 Office: 3527 Coll Bus Adminstrn U South Florida Tampa FL 33620

WALSH, SUSAN FRANCES, psychiat. social worker; b. Fostoria, Ohio, Apr. 5, 1943; d. Edward Doty and Frances Elizabeth (Storey) W.; B.S., Ind. U., 1965; A.M., U. Chgo., 1968, postgrad., 1977—. Instr. social work Northwestern U. Med. Sch., also staff social worker Northwestern Meml. Hosp., Chgo., 1968-75; pvt. practice psychotherapy, Chgo., 1974—; asso. dept. psychiatry Northwestern U., also coordinator outpatient services Inst. Psychiatry, Northwestern Meml. Hosp., 1975—; field instr. U. Chgo., U. Ill., Chgo. Circle; pres. Susan Walsh, ACSW, Ltd. Mem. Nat. Assn. Social Workers. Research on alternative to psychiat. hospitalization. Home: 3180 N Lake Shore Dr Chicago IL 60657 Office: 333 E Ontario St Chicago IL 60611

WALSH, WINIFRED CAMPBELL, nursing adminstr.; b. Pawtucket, R.I., Nov. 10, 1919; d. Frank Owen and Charlotte Rose (Clark) Campbell; R.N., Roger Williams Sch. Nursing, 1940; postgrad. Yale U., 1941; m. Joseph A. Walsh, Oct. 30, 1943; children—Joseph A., Patrick F., Thomas J., E. Michael, Richard C., William A., Lawrence P. Staff nurse Homeopathic Hosp. R.I., 1940-41; head nurse Nat. Tumor Clinic, USPHS, Balt., 1941-44; supr./coordinator dept. phys. medicine and rehab. Mercy Hosp., Scranton, Pa., 1968—. Vice pres., Goodwill Industries of Scranton, Inc., 1951-52; bd. dirs. Lackawanna County Welfare Council, Scranton Philharmonic Orch., Pa. Ballet Festival; active Friends of Scranton Public Library, Scranton chpt. ARC. Mem. Nat. Assn. Orthopedic Nurses (del./dir.), Orthopedic Nurses Assn., Assn. Rehab. Nurses, Nat. Assn. Female Execs., AMA Aux., Pa. Med. Soc. Aux. (treas., v.p.), Lackawanna Med. Soc. Aux. (pres.), Am. Mus. Natural History, Am. Assn. Ret. Persons, Am. Security Council Found., Irish Am. Cultural Inst., U.S. Congressional Adv. Bd. (charter), Early Am. Soc., Everhart Mus. Natural History, Sci. and Art, Smithsonian Assn., Internat. Platform Assn., Broadway Theater League. Roman Catholic. Clubs: Scranton, Parliamentary Law, Country (Scranton); Skytop (Pa.). Home: 337 1st St Blakely PA 18447 Office: Mercy Hosp Jefferson Ave Scranton PA 18503

WALTER, ELISSE BARBARA, lawyer; b. N.Y.C., Apr. 14, 1950; d. Arthur Milton and Shirley Charlotte (Melnitsky) W.; student Brown U., 1967-69; B.A., Yale U., 1971; J.D., Harvard U., 1974; m. Ronald Alan Stern, June 1, 1974; 1 son, Jonathan Leo Walter Stern. Admitted to D.C. bar, 1975, U.S. Supreme Ct. bar, 1980; asso. firm Arent, Fox, Kintner, Plotkin & Kahn, Washington, 1974-77; atty. office gen. counsel SEC, Washington, 1977-78, spl. counsel, 1978-79, asst. gen. counsel, 1979—. Recipient Manuel F. Cohen Outstanding Younger Lawyer award SEC, 1981. Mem. Am. Bar Assn., D.C. Bar. Jewish. Office: 450 D St NW Washington DC 20549

WALTER, EVA LOU, mathematician; b. Corliss, W.Va., Jan. 13, 1939; d. Roy Franklin and Nancy Virginia Pearl (Kincaid) McClelland; B.A. in Math., Berea (Ky.) Coll., 1961; M.S., Purdue U., 1963; m. Kenneth Gaines Walter, June 10, 1965; children—Regina Eileen, Kevin Michael. Grad. teaching asst. Purdue U., 1961-63; instr. math. Ohio U., Athens, also instr. off-campus acad. programs, 1963-67; instr. math. Ga. So. Coll., Statesboro, 1979—. Mem. Math. Assn. Am. Baptist. Club: Ga. So. Coll. Faculty Dames (pres. 1978-80). Home: 113 Benson Dr Statesboro GA 30458 Office: Math Dept Landrum Box 8074 Ga So Coll Statesboro GA 30460

WALTER, JESSICA, actress; b. Bklyn., Jan. 31; student Bucks County Playhouse, Neighborhood Playhouse. Broadway debut in Advise and Consent, 1961; films include: Lilith, 1964. The Group, 1966, Grand Prix, 1966, Bye Bye, Braverman, 1968, Number One, 1969, Play Misty for Me, 1971; regular TV series Love of Life; ltd. series Amy Prentiss (Emmy award for Outstanding Lead Actress in Ltd. Series), 1974-75; other TV appearances include: The FBI, Mission Impossible, Cannon, Medical Center, Mannix, Visions, Barnaby Jones, Hawaii Five-O, Wheels; TV movies Hurricane, 1974, Having Babies, 1976. Office: care William Morris Agy Inc 151 El Camino Beverly Hills CA 90212 *

WALTER, LISETTE, educator; b. Boston, Sept. 16, 1938; d. Karl H. and Mary D. (Davidson) W.; B.S., U. Mass., 1961; M.Ed., Boston U., 1972, Ed.D. candidate. Asso. prof. U. Mass., 1960-61; tchr. Walpole (Mass.) Public Schs., 1962—, ESEA Title III project dir., 1974-75; field hockey coach U.S. Olympic Devel.; nat. umpire for U.S. Lacrosse, U.S. Field Hockey. Mem. U.S. Women's Lacrosse Assn. (pres. 1980—, editor-founder Cover Point newsletter 1979-81), N.E. Field Hockey Assn. (pres. 1975-82; hon.), Boston Field Hockey Assn. (hon.). Home: 339 Plain St Millis MA 02054

WALTER, MARCIA KAY, state legislator; b. Omaha, Apr. 3, 1950; d. Robert Earl and Helen (Stuart) Gambrel; student Iowa Western U., 1976-77; m. Craig Douglas Walter, Sept. 6, 1969; children—Craig Justin, Melisa Kay. Adminstrv. asst. Iowa Ho. of Reps., 1974-80; mem. Iowa Ho. of Reps., 1980—. Pres., Pottawattamie County Democratic Women, 1972-75. Mem. Bus. and Profl. Women, Nat. Order Women Legislators, LaLeche League, Legis. Ladies League, S.W. Iowans for Talented and Gifted, Hist. Soc. Pottawattamie County. Democrat. Congregationalist.

WALTER, MARJORIE GIBSON, govt. ofcl.; b. Opelika, Ala., Jan. 11, 1923; d. Frederick Meyer and Lottie Belle (Hearn) Gibson; student U. Ala., 1965, 66, Macon Jr. Coll., 1968-71; children—William Guy, Ralph Gibson. Contract negotiator trainee Robins AFB, Ga., 1966-68, contract negotiator, 1968-71; fin. analyst HUD, Birmingham and Washington, 1971-75; contract price analyst U.S. Army, Washington, 1976-77; contract price analyst U.S. Marine Corps, Albany, Ga., 1977-80, head contracts support br., contracts div. Marine Corps Logistics Base, Albany, Ga., 1980—. Vice pres. Woman's Caucus, HUD, 1975. Recipient Sustained Superior Performance award U.S. Marine Corps, 1978. Mem. Nat. Contract Mgmt. Assn., Fed. Mgrs. Assn. Home: 337 E Church St Dawson GA 31742 Office: PO Box 3125 Marine Corps Logistics Base Albany GA 31704

WALTER, MARY MINAHAN, newspaper editor; b. Battle Creek, Mich., Apr. 19, 1919; d. Victor Ivan and Bertha (Bush) Minahan; student Vassar Coll., 1937-39, St Norbert Coll., part-time 1950s; B.A., U. Wis., Green Bay, 1975; m. John M. Walter, Aug. 19, 1939; children—Wendy, Michael, Dinah, Anthony, Heidi, Tara, Rory. Reporter, editorial writer Green Bay Press-Gazette, 1950-79; editorial writer, then asso. editor Appleton (Wis.) Post Crescent, 1950—; sec., dir. Green Bay Newspaper Co., 1960-64; dir., v.p., Post Corp., 1964—, exec. com., 1981—. Girl Scout troop leader Green Bay, DePere, Wis., Mineral Wells, Tex., 1940-62; Girl Scout commr., 1955; mem. DePere (Wis.) Dist. 1 Bd. Edn., 1956-63; mem. Wis. Coordinating Com. Higher Edn., 1958; Brown County rep. CESA Bd., 1963-68; bd. regents Wis. State Coll., 1956-64, U. Wis. System, 1974-81; mem. jud. selection com. Wis. Eastern Dist., 1979—; bd. dirs. Sunshine House, Sturgeon Bay, Wis., 1978-81. Mem. PEO. Episcopalian. Home: Box 155 Bailey's Harbor WI 54202 Office: Post Crescent Appleton WI 54911

WALTER, MAY ELIZABETH, retail co. exec.; b. N.Y.C.; d. Peter J. and Elizabeth (Shaub) W.; student N.Y. U., Columbia U., 1920-30. Co-founder, treas., exec. v.p., vice chmn. Mut. Buying Syndicate, Inc., 1931-65; pres. Retail Marketers Advt., Inc., N.Y.C., 1966-67, cons., adviser, 1968-71. Sec., trustee, mem. exec. com. Am. Crafts Council, N.Y.C., 1962-77, hon. trustee, 1977—; adv. council Art Gallery U. Notre Dame. Recipient Salute to Women award Republican Women in Bus. and Professions, 1962. Home: 923 Fifth Ave New York NY 10021 also Siscowit Rd Pound Ridge NY 10576

WALTERS, ANNA LEE, writer, ednl. adminstr.; b. Pawnee, Okla., Sept. 9, 1946; d. Luther and Juanita Mae (Taylor) McGlaslin; student U. N.Mex., 1977—; m. Harry Walters, June 1965; children—Anthony, Daniel. Dir. public relations Navajo Community Coll. Press and Print Shop, Tsaile (Navajo Nation), Ariz., from 1977; now tech. writer; freelance writer, 1973—; contbg. author: The Man to Send Rainclouds, 1974, Warriors of the Rainbow, 1975, Shantih, 1976, The Third Woman, 1979, The Remembered Earth, 1979, American Indians Today, Thought, Literature, Art, 1981; co-author textbook: The Sacred Ways of Knowledge, Sources of Life, 1977; author: The Otoe-Missiouria Tribe, Centennial Memoirs, 1881-1981, 1981; contbr. articles to jours. in field; guest editor Frauen Offensive, 1978; also poet, feature writer. Grantee, Nat. Anthrop. Archives, Smithsonian Instn.; Delta Kappa Gamma scholar. Office: Navajo Community Coll Public Info Office Tsaile AZ 86556

WALTERS, BARBARA, TV personality; b. Sept. 25, 1931; d. Lou and Dena (Selett) Walters; grad. Sarah Lawrence Coll., 1953; L.H.D., Ohio State U., 1971, Marymount Coll., 1975; m. Lee Guber, Dec. 8, 1963 (div. 1976); 1 adopted dau. Jacqueline Dena. Formerly writer producer Sta. WNBC-TV then with Sta. WPIX and CBS-TV; joined Today Show, 1961, regular panel mem., 1963-74, co-host, 1974-76; newscaster ABC Evening News (now ABC World News Tonight), from 1976; moderator Not for Women Only, nationally syndicated TV program; TV spls. include: Battle for the White House, 1976, Fidel Castro Speaks, 1977, A Farewell Visit with President and Mrs. Ford, 1977, Barbara Walters Specials. Hon. chmn. Nat. Assn. of Help for Retarded Children, 1970. Named to 100 Women of Accomplishment, Harper's Bazaar, 1967, 71, 200 Leaders of the Future, Time, 1974; America's 75 Most Important Women, Ladies' Home Jour., 1970, Woman of Yr. in Communications, 1974, Broadcaster of Yr. Internat. Radio & TV Soc., 1975, Woman of Yr. Theta Sigma Phi; recipient award of yr. Nat. Assn. TV Program Execs., 1975; Mass Media award Am. Jewish Com. Inst. Human Relations, 1975; Emmy, Nat. Acad. TV Arts and Scis., 1975, Matrix award N.Y. Women in Communications, 1977; Hubert H. Humphrey Freedom prize Anti-Defamation League-B'nai B'rith, 1978, others. Author: How To Talk With Practically Anybody About Practically Anything, 1970; contbr. articles to Good Housekeeping, Family Weekly, Ladies Home Jour., Reader's Digest. Barbara Walters coll. scholarship in broadcast journalism established by Ill. Broadcasters Assn., 1975. Address: care ABC 1330 Ave of Americas New York NY 10019 *

WALTERS, DIANNE, architect; b. Whitehall, Pa., Dec. 5, 1944; d. Merlin Paul and Margaret Roberta (Jacoby) W.; B.Arch., Va. Poly. Inst. and State U., 1967, M.B.A., 1979. Draftsman, Saunders & Pearson, Alexandria, Va., 1967-68, Bailey & Pye, Fairfax, Va., 1968-69, Cohen, Haft & Assos., Silver Spring, Md., 1969-70; instl. planner, constrn. engr. Va. Poly. Inst. and State U., Blacksburg, 1970-71; project architect H.D. Nottingham & Assos., McLean, Va., 1971-74; architect GSA, Washington, 1974-80, chief design programs br., 1980—; mem. Nat. Evaluation Bd. on Architect-Engr. Selection. Recipient 2d Biennial Design award Gen. Services Adminstrn., 1975, Outstanding Performance award, 1978, 79; registered architect, Va. Mem. Nat. Acad. Sci., Alpha Rho Chi, Tau Sigma Delta. Author: (with others) Energy Conservation Guidelines for Existing Office Buildings, 1974. Editor: Day on Wheels, 1975. Home: 7915 Treeside Ct Springfield VA 22152 Office: General Services Administration 18th and F Sts NW Washington DC 20405

WALTERS, DORIS FAY, retail exec.; b. Dekalb County, Ind., Apr. 11, 1923; d. Arthur Hugh and Trella Fern (Priser) Clabaugh; student public schs. Garrett, Ind.; m. George William Walters, Mar. 25, 1950; 1 son, Leslie Arthur. With Nature's Rival Co., 1941-42, 45-46; with Gen. Electric Co., 1942-45; clk., cost acct. Midwestern Foundries, Garrett, Ind., 1946-63; co-owner, mgr. George's Sport Spot, Garrett, 1954—. Mem. adv. bd. CD, 1978—; bd. dirs. Garrett Hist. Soc., 1974—; mem. Park Bd., 1978. Mem. Garrett Bus. and Profl. Women's Club, Garrett C. of C. (dir.). Methodist. Club: Rebekah. Sports columnist Garrett Clipper, 1965—. Home: 1325 S Randolph St Garrett IN 46738 Office: 1321 S Randolph St Garrett IN 46738

WALTERS, HELEN HAMER, broadcasting exec.; b. Alton, Ill.; d. Isaac Cloyd and Lydia (Rain) Hamer; Ph.B., Shurtleff Coll., Alton, 1939; m. Charles R. Walters, June 14, 1944; children—Michael Hamer, Isabel Walters Ruedin. High sch. tchr., 1939-44; mgr. Tom Boy Grocery Store, Alton, 1944-45; agt. Fin. Security Life Ins. Co., Moline, Ill., 1962-67; v.p. Sta. WOKZ AM, Alton, 1972-78, v.p., 1978—, also condr. interview and audience participation show. Mem. Ill. Pub. Aid Commn., also Alton Citizens Better Govt., 1953-55; campaign chmn. women's div. Madison County Cancer Crusade, 1953. Recipient Liberty Bell award Madison County Bar Assn., 1976; Voice of Democracy award VFW, 1977, 78, 79; Woman of Achievement award Alton Bus. and Profl. Women, 1965; Nat. Assn. Life Underwriters Quality award, 1964, 65, 66. Mem. Internat. Platform Assn. Author: Bobo, The Elephant. Home: 3106 Leverett Ave Alton IL 62002 Office: WOKZ Box 615 Alton IL 62002

WALTERS, KATHRYN SUSANNE, librarian; b. Fort Bragg, Calif., May 29, 1938; d. Henry and Lydia Maria (Liimatainen) Kujala; student public schs.; m. Robert V. Walters, July 28, 1956; children—Suzanne, Carol, Robert, Amy. Librarian, Tenakee (Alaska) Public Library, 1972—. Mem. City Council, 1972-79, sec. planning commn., 1972-75; sec. Vol. Fire Dept., 1971-79; state voting registrar, 1974-79; vice chmn. Democratic League, 1971-80; bd. dirs. Seacap, 1974-80; mem. adv. sch. bd., 1977-78. Home: 6 Tenakee Ave Tenakee Springs AK 99841 Office: Shamrock Bldg Tenakee Ave Tenakee Springs AK 99841

WALTERS, KAY LYNN, software devel. co. exec.; b. Big Spring, Tex., Nov. 27, 1942; d. Lesley Albert and La Verne (Holden) Clawson; B.A. in English, U. Tex., Arlington, 1974; M.B.A., So. Meth. U., 1978; children—David Ryan, Stephen Paul. Programmer, Bank of A. Levy, Oxnard, Calif., 1966-68; project leader 1st Data Processing, Big Spring, 1968-70, Results, Inc., Dallas, 1970-72; dir. application systems ENSERCH Corp., Dallas, 1973-80; mgr. devel. Performance Assos., Inc., Plano, Tex., 1980-81; v.p. Directions, Inc., Dallas, 1981—. Mem. So. Meth. U. M.B.A. Assn. Baptist. Office: 1740 N Collins St Richardson TX 75081

WALTERS, SANDRA LEE NORKUS, nursing adminstr.; b. Gary, Ind., Feb. 25, 1942; d. John Joseph and Vivian Loretta (Lindzy) Norkus; grad. Chgo. Wesley Meml. Hosp., 1962; student Moraine Valley Coll., Triton Coll., Governors State U.; children—Jeff, Scott, Randy. Obstetrics nurse Carle Hosp., Urbana, Ill., 1962-63; staff nurse Christ Community Hosp., Oak Lawn, Ill., 1964; asst. dir. nurses Resthaven, Palos Heights, Ill., 1967-72; supr. intensive care unit, clin. mgr., dir. nursing S. Suburban Hosp., Hazelcrest, Ill., 1972-74; dir. nursing Med. Center Hosp., Largo, Fla., 1978—; mem. Adv. Com. for Continuing Health Edn., Pinellas County. Mem. Am. Assn. Critical Care Nurses, Am. Soc. Nursing Service Adminstrs., Fla. Soc. Hosp. Nursing Service Adminstrn., Nat. League for Nursing, Nat. Forum for Adminstrs. of Nursing Services, Am. Mgmt. Assn. Office: Med Center Hosp 201 14th St SW Largo FL 33540

WALTHER, NANCY ELLEN, mgr. med. office; b. Iowa City, Iowa, Jan. 15, 1942; d. Carl Edward and Dorothy (Sparks) Hagemann; A.A., Colo. Womans Coll., 1962; B.A., Tulane U., 1966; postgrad. U. So. Calif., 1967-70; m. Neal J. Walther, May 26, 1962; children—Robert, Richard. Office mgr. Dr. Neal J. Walther, Dr. Julia Tann, Internal Medicine, Cardiology, Visalia, Calif., 1975—. Mem. Am. Assn. Med. Assts. Republican. Lutheran. Club: PEO. Home: 3311 W Cambridge St Visalia CA 93277 Office: 1633 S Court St Visalia CA 93277

WALTNER, BEVERLY RULAND, artist; b. Kansas City, Mo.; d. Harry George and Ruth Anna (Laitner) Waltner, Jr.; student Columbia U., 1950-51, Yale U., 1951-53; B.A., U. Miami, Fla., 1955; M.F.A., No. Ill. U., 1968; postgrad. Kent State U., summer 1968. Tchr. art pub. schs. of N.Y., 1960-61, Fla., 1961-62, Mo., 1962-63, Ill., 1963-65; instr. art Barry Coll., Miami Shores, Fla., 1970-71; artist-designer, Coral Gables, Fla., 1972—; one person shows: Art Gallery, No. Ill. U., DeKalb, 1968, Lyons Meml. Library, Point Lookout, Mo., 1968, Jewish Community Center Gallery, Kansas City, Mo., 1969; juried exhbns. include: New Horizons in Painting, N. Shore Art League, 1966, 68, Chautauqua Exhbn. Am. Art, 1968-73, 10th Mid-Western Bienniel, Joslyn Mus., 1968, Mid-Am. I, Nelson Gallery and St. Louis Mus., 1968, Nat. Soc. Painters in Casein and Acrylic, 1969, 70, 72, 73, Ark. Nat., Ark. State U., 1970, 35th Ann. Mid-Yr. Show, Butler Inst. Am. Art, 1970, Ann. Exhbn. Am. Painting, Soc. Four Arts, 1971, 74, IV and V Ann. Pan Am. Exhbns., 1972, 73; represented in permanent collections: No. Ill. U., Arlen Realty Mgmt., Inc., Alexander Muss and Sons, Equitable Life Assurance Soc. of the U.S., Gen. Devel. Corp., Zuckerman-Vernon Corp., also numerous private collections. Recipient First Place award Ann. Chautauqua Exhibition of Am. Art, 1968, Louis E. Seiden award, 1972; Top award New Horizons in Painting Show, 1966, honorable mention, 1968. Mem. Artists Equity Assn., Visual Arts Coalition, Cultural Execs. Council (ex-officio mem. 1978—), Profl. Artists Guild (treas. 1977-78, v.p. 1978—), Chautauqua Art Assn. Mem. editorial staff PAG Newsletter, 1977—. Address: 7500 Almansa St Coral Gables FL 33143 *

WALTON, CARMELITA NOREEN, nurse; b. Chgo., Nov. 15, 1926; d. Elmo Augusta and Evelyn Mae (Terry) Desobrey; student St. Marys Coll., U. Notre Dame, 1943-45; grad. Cook County Sch. Nursing, 1949; student DePaul U., 1978-79; children from previous marriage—Michael Jerome. Head nurse, supr., nurse clinician Cook County Hosp., Chgo., 1951-71; supr. U. Chgo. Hosps./Clinics, 1963-68; dir. nursing Woodlawn Child Health Center, Chgo., 1968-69; dir. nursing prison health care Cermak Hosp., Chgo., 1973—. Mem. Am. (cert. in nursing adminstrn., mem. Council Nursing Adminstrn.), Ill. nurses assn., Nat. League Nursing, Am. Pub. Health Assn. Democrat. Roman Catholic. Home: 5050 LakeShore Dr S Apt 1608 Chicago IL 60615 Office: 2900 California Ave S Chicago IL 60608

WALTON, CAROLE LORRAINE, social worker; b. Harrison, Ark., Oct. 20, 1949; d. Leo Woodrow and Arlette (Armstrong) W.; B.A., Lambuth Coll., 1971; M.A., U. Chgo., 1974. Social worker Community Mental Health, Flint, Mich., 1971-72; dir. self-travel program Chgo. Assn. Retarded Citizens, 1973; clin. social worker Community Mental Health, Westchester, Ill., 1974-76; coordinator family services Anneewakee Treatment Center, Douglasville, Ga., 1976—. Mem. Nat. Assn. Social Workers, Acad. Cert. Social workers, Ga. Assn. Clin. Social Workers (bd. dirs., pres. 1982). Democrat. Episcopalian. Club: Sierra. Home: 5555 Roswell Rd Apt K-2 Atlanta GA 30342 Office: 4771 Anneewakee Rd Douglasville GA 30135

WALTON, ELSIE RAE, social worker, educator; b. Copenhagen, Feb. 15, 1921; naturalized U.S. citizen, 1928; d. Carl Fromberg and Emmy (Ericksen) Rasmussen; B.S., Columbia U., 1944; M.S.W., Cath. U. Am.-Tulane U., 1948; m. Thomas S. Walton, June 1, 1948; children—David, Rebecca, Bruce. Mem. staff Girl Scouts U.S.A., 1944-46, 48-53; tchr., sch. social worker Montgomery County (Md.) public schs., 1955-58, 66—; field instr. Catholic U., 1968-82. Life mem. Md. PTA; bd. dirs. Family Service Assn. Montgomery County, 1979-82. Mem. Nat. Assn. Social Workers, NEA, Md. Tchrs. Assn., Montgomery County Edn. Assn., Council Exceptional Children, Acad. Cert. Social Workers. Unitarian. Office: McKenney Hills Learning Center Montgomery County Public Schools 2600 Hayden Dr Silver Spring MD 20902

WALTON, FANNIE DELORES, researcher; b. Memphis, July 13, 1941; d. Bruce Norris and Irma Mary (Scott) Boyd; student Tenn. State U., 1959-60, Merritt Coll., 1969-75, U. Calif., Berkeley, 1970-73, Stanford U., 1977; B.S., U. San Francisco, 1980; m. Herman C. Walton, Jan. 29, 1962; children—Vanessa E. Boyd, Cheryl E., Gary J. Research clk. Calif. Transp. div., Berkeley, 1965-69; researcher, data mgr. Far West Edn. Lab., San Francisco, 1969-79; researcher Social Issues Research Assos., Berkeley, 1979—; data mgmt. cons. Mem. Nat. Assn. Female Execs., Am. Contract Bridge League. Democrat. Methodist. Author: Evaluation of the Four-Day Week, 1972; (with others) Early Childhood and Drug Education Information Units. Home: 6609 Thornhill Dr Oakland CA 94611 Office: 2490 Channing Way Berkeley CA 94704

WALTON, JOAN LIZABETH, publishing co. ofcl.; b. Chgo., Sept. 7, 1952; d. Herbert Dana and Carolyn Jane (Agnew) Walton; B.S., Miami U., Oxford, Ohio, 1974. Staff home economist Maytag Co., Newton, Iowa, 1974-76; advt. sales exec. Scholastic Mags., Inc., Chgo., 1976-78; advt. sales exec. McCall's Mag., Chgo., 1978-82, Southern Living mag., 1982—. Mem. Home Economists in Bus. (legis. chmn. 1976-77), Agate Club Chgo., Women in Print, English Speaking Union, Phi Upsilon Omicron, Kappa Alpha Theta. Presbyterian. Home: One E Scott St Apt 1109 Chicago IL 60610 Office: 401 N Michigan Ave #830 Chicago IL 60611

WALTON, KARYL LAMONT, clin. social worker; b. Salt Lake City, Dec. 16, 1929; d. Robert Maxwell and Lucille Jane (Petersen) Lamont; B.A., U. Utah, 1951, cert. in social work, 1952, M.S.W., 1957; m. Kent L. Walton, Apr. 17, 1958; children—Kirk Lamont, Kristopher Leon, Katie Lynne. Caseworker adoption and foster care Ch. Jesus Christ of Latter-day Saints Relief Soc., 1951-56; probation officer Utah Juvenile Ct., 2d Dist., 1956-62; psychiat. social worker Family Service Soc., 1962-69, Head Start, 1965; psychiat. social worker Youth Services, 1969-70; pvt. practice clin. social work, Salt Lake City, 1970—; pre-trial cons.; guest lectr. health class Hyland High Sch. Active PTA, 1967—; mem. Utah Heritage Found., 1976-78; pres. young women South 2d ward Ch. Jesus Christ of Latter-day Saints, 1959-61. Mem. Nat. Assn. Social Workers (state com. licensure), Phi Mu (pres. 1950-51), Lambda Delta Sigma. Home: 3068 Cascade Way Salt Lake City UT 84109 Office: 585 3d Ave Salt Lake City UT 84103

WALTON, LOUISE MARIE, psychiat. social worker; b. Chatham, Va., Oct. 26, 1940; d. Alfred Luke and Alberta Ruth (Tarpley) W.; B.A., Va. State Coll., 1963; M.S.W., Va. Commonwealth U., 1968. Child welfare worker Va. Dept. Welfare, Richmond, 1963-66, child welfare cons., 1968-71; clin. instr. U. Va., Charlottesville, 1971-73, clin. asst. prof. social work, 1974-76, project dir., 1972-75, chief social worker, 1975-76; psychiat. social worker Cornell U. Health Services, 1976—; field work supr.; mem. Va. Gov.'s Commn. on Handicapped Children, 1971; founding mem. and asst. dir. bd. dirs. Westminster Child Care Center, 1972-75. Founding mem., adv. Foster Parent Assn., Richmond, Va., 1969; mem., adv. Adoptive Parent Group, Ithaca, N.Y., 1980. Univ. Yr. for Action grantee, 1973-74. Mem. Acad. Cert. Social Workers, Am. Personnel and Guidance Assn. Democrat. Baptist. Research on nonintellectual correlates of black student adjustment. Home: PO Box 3713 Univ Sta Charlottesville VA 22903 Office: Gannett Med Clinic Cornell U Ithaca NY 14853

WALTON, MARGURITE ALBERTSON, navy officer; b. Mobile, Ala., Aug. 26, 1938; d. Frederick Alexander Albertson and Norma Woodroe (Williams) Lane; B.A., U. Montevallo, 1959; student U. Ala., 1963-64, U. Md. Ext. Center, London, 1968-69; U.S. Naval Schs.,

1964-65, 72-73, 74-75, 77-78. Tchr., Mobile County Public Sch. System, 1959-63; commd. ensign U.S. Navy, 1964, advanced through grades to comdr., 1978; Latin Am. desk officer Directorate for Attaches and Tng., DIA, Washington, 1982—. Decorated Nat. Def. Service medal, Navy Achievement medal, Armed Forces Expeditionary medal, Joint Service commendation. Mem. U.S. Naval Inst., U. Montevallo Alumni Assn., Nat. War Coll. Alumni Assn. Democrat. Episcopalian. Clubs: Federal Toastmistress, Internat. Toastmistress. Home: PO Box 1559 Washington DC 20013

WALTON, MAUREEN CECELIA, corp. exec.; b. Phila., Jan. 18, 1954; d. James Richard and Cecelia Ann (Neary) W.; B.S. in Adminstrv. Mgmt., St. Joseph's U., 1978. With Scott Paper Co., 1971-79; research asst. Sun Co., Radnor, Pa., 1979-80, asso. communications rep., 1980-81, communications rep., 1981—, mgr. Speakers Bur.; tchr. energy conservation course, local continuing edn. programs. Office: 100 Matsonford Rd Radnor PA 19087

WANCEL, LINDA, mktg. exec.; b. N.Y.C., Mar. 30, 1951; d. Ralph Rodriguez and Constance Isabel Bennett; B.A., Fordham U., 1974; A.A.S., Parsons Sch. Design, 1977; M.A., Columbia U., 1978; m. Alfred Wancel, Mar. 22, 1976; children—Alexander Bennett, Victoria Alexandra (twins). Error control coordinator Bonwit Teller, N.Y.C., 1977-78, exec. trainee, 1978, asst. buyer, 1978-79; group mgr. Gimbels East, N.Y.C., 1979-80, sr. asst. buyer, 1980-81; asso. market rep. May Merchandising Co., N.Y.C., 1981-82. N.Y. State Regents scholar, 1969-74; Columbia U. Tchrs. Coll. minority scholar, 1977-78. Mem. Am. Mgmt. Assn., Mensa. Club: Williams.

WANG, AMY LAN-CHING, librarian; b. Chunking, China, Aug. 20, 1943; came to U.S., 1962, naturalized, 1972; d. Kui-En and Hwa-Tin (Chen) Chiang; A.B., Baylor U., 1965; M.S. in Library Service, Atlanta U., 1966; m. Abraham K.M. Wang, Sept. 3, 1966; children—Andrea, Allen. Asst. reference librarian Bapst Library, Boston Coll., 1966-67; asst. librarian, bus. library New Eng. Mut. Life Ins. Co., Boston, 1967-68; asst. librarian John Hancock Mut. Life Ins. Co., Boston, 1968-70, co. librarian, 1971—. Mem. citizens rev. com. United Way of Mass. Bay, 1979-81. Mem. Spl. Libraries Assn. (officer Boston chpt. 1973-81 chmn. ins. and employee benefits div. 1980-81). Mng. editor Ins. Lit., 1975-78, editor, 1978-79, contbr., 1978-82. Office: John Hancock Mut Life Ins Co PO Box 111 Boston MA 02117

WANG, CHARLENE, computer scientist; b. Kaoshiung, Taiwan, Mar. 20, 1952; d. Chih Wong and Amy Ch-Wen (Liang) W.; B.S., Tufts U., 1975. Mktg. rep. Burroughs Corp., Boston, 1976-77; regional mgr. field applications NCR Corp., Newton, Mass., 1977-79; comml. software product mktg. specialist Data Gen. Co., Westboro, Mass., 1979—. Mem. Data Processing Mgmt. Assn. Office: 4400 Computer Dr MS-B211 Westboro MA 01580

WANNEMACHER, JILL THERESE, psychologist; b. N.Y.C., Mar. 31, 1947; d. Louis John and Jacqueline Mary (Burke) W., Jr.; B.A. magna cum laude, Mt. Holyoke Coll., 1968; M.A., Brown U., 1971, Ph.D., 1973. Asst. prof. psychology Bryn Mawr (Pa.) Coll., 1973-78; orgn. and manpower rep. Gen. Electric Co., Lynn, Mass., 1978—. NIMH grantee, 1974-78. Mem. Am. Psychol. Assn., Eastern Psychol. Assn., Sigma Xi, Phi Beta Kappa. Roman Catholic. Home: 29 Chestnut St Salem MA 01970 Office: 1000 Western Ave Suite 240G3 Lynn MA 01910

WARBASSE, ELIZABETH BOWLES, social scientist; b. Summit, N.J., Nov. 25, 1927; d. Harry Hallowell and Elizabeth Caroline (Phraner) Bowles; B.A., Wellesley Coll., 1949; M.A., Radcliffe Coll., 1951, Ph.D., 1960; m. James Richard Warbasse, June 23, 1951; children—Kristin, Karin, Bradford, James. Instr. history Howard U., Washington, 1960-62; lectr. Wagner Coll., S.I., N.Y., 1962-66; asso. prof. Community Coll. Balt., 1975—. Md. Dept. Edn. grantee, 1979. Mem. Am Hist. Assn., So. Assn. Women Historians. Coordinating Com. Women in Hist. Profession, Chesapeake Area Group Women Historians. Democrat. Office: Dept Social Scis Community Coll Baltimore Baltimore MD 21215

WARBURG, STEPHANIE WENNER, painter, educator; b. Kalamazoo, Dec. 29, 1941; d. William Franklin and Charlotte Sophia (Rossi) Wenner; B.F.A., U. Mich., 1963; M.A. in Fine Arts, Columbia U., 1965; m. Jonathan Frederick Warburg, Oct. 8, 1978; 1 son, Benjamin Max. Mem. art dept. Latin Sch. of Chgo., 1965-66, chmn. art dept., 1969-72; mem. Lord & Taylor Gallery, N.Y.C., 1968-78, Thee Gallery, Chesterfield, Mo., 1968-78; instr. design Chamberlayne Jr. Coll., Boston, 1975—; one-woman shows include: Lord & Taylor Gallery, 1970, 73, 75, Thee Gallery, Chesterfield, 1970-78, Goodman Gallery, Chgo., 1972; group shows include: Gilman Gallery, Chgo., 1971, Funchal, Madeira, Portugal, 1974; art cons. New Eng. Conservatory of Music, 1976. Mem. service league bd. Mus. Sci., Boston, 1974-80, chmn. focus programs, 1976-80; bd. dirs. Boston Jr. League, 1975-77; mem. Beacon Hill Circle for Charity, 1974—. Recipient award Am. Cancer Soc., New London, Conn., 1968, East Lyme Art Assn., 1969, Hadlyme Art Assn., 1969. Mem. Women Exhibiting in Boston. Club: Vincent (Boston). Home: 179 Commonwealth Ave Boston MA 02116 Office: 128 Commonwealth Ave Boston MA 02116

WARD, CAROL ESTHER, ceramic supply co. exec.; b. Phoenix, Oct. 14, 1930; d. Stephen Raymond and Marjorie Edith (Taylor) Brooks; student public schs.; divorced; children—Eileen Shepherd, Elaine Asmus, Stephen Hieb, Leslie Speissegger, Dawn Ward. With Marjon Ceramic, Inc., Phoenix, 1957—, pres., owner; an organizer, dir. Phoenix Nat. Bank; condr. seminars, cons. in field; del. White Conf. Small Bus., 1980; moderator weekly bus. roundtable, 1978-79. Mem. Mayor Phoenix Com. Future Budget and Fin., 1980, Gov. Ariz. Blue Ribbon Com. Edn., 1979. Mem. Ariz. C. of C. (Small Bus. Person of Yr. award 1982), Ariz. Small Bus. Council (pres. 1979), Ariz. Ceramic Assn. (pres. 1964), Ariz. Bus. Alliance (pres. 1982), Ceramic Distbrs. Am. (pres. 1969), Nat. Ceramic Tchrs. Assn., Nat. Speakers Assn., Nat. Assn. Female Execs., Sales and Mktg. Execs. Assn., Bus. and Profl. Women. Republican. Club: Toastmasters. Author: Original Designs by Carol, 1968, Ceramic Business Survival Kit, 1976; contbr. articles to profl. jours. Office: 3434 W Earll Dr Phoenix AZ 85017

WARD, CELIA AARON, clin. psychologist; b. Bklyn., Aug. 8, 1938; d. Philip and Frieda Aaron; B.B.A., City U. N.Y., 1960, M.S. in Edn., 1963; Ph.D., Yeshiva U., 1975; m. Henry Post Ward, Nov. 2, 1968; children—Lawrence David, Michael Jeffrey. Research asst. Yeshiva U., 1964; intern clin. psychology St. Elizabeth's Hosp., Washington, 1965-67, staff psychologist, 1967-69; mem. faculty Met. Mental Health Skills Center, The Washington Sch. Psychiatry, 1972-75; pvt. practice clin. psychology, Washington, 1967—; founder, dir. Psychol. Center for Loss, Washington; asst. prof. George Washington U., 1982—. USPHS fellow, 1964-65. Recipient Cert. of Leadership and Accomplishment D.C., State Fedn. Bus. and Profl. Women's Club. Mem. Nat. Assn. Women Bus. Owners, Washington Profl. Women's Coop., Am. Psychol. Assn., D.C. Psychol. Assn., Am. Group Psychotherapy Assn., Psychologists Interested in Study of Psychoanalysis. Home and Office: 3030 Q St NW Washington DC 20007

WARD, DORIS ELIZABETH, biologist, fed. agy. adminstr.; b. Charlotte N.C., Jan. 11, 1935; d. James Hopkins and Florie Kathryn Cofield; B.S., Howard U., 1966, postgrad. 1967-70; m. Eddie Eugene Ward, Sept. 18, 1954; children—Eddie Eugene, Tanya Devonne, Tracia Lynnore, Tamara Elizabeth. Med. technician U.S. Dept. Agr., Washington, 1958-64, biol. lab. technician, Bethesda, Md., 1964-65; histologic tech. lab. instr. Howard U., Washington, 1966-67; biologist (histopathology technician) NIH, Bethesda, 1969-71; tchr. Our Lady Queen of Peace Sch., Washington, 1972-74; program analyst/mgmt. analysis Dept. Health and Human Services, Washington, 1974—. Hospice vol.; active United Communities Against Poverty, Inc., 1982. Recipient Tchr. Appreciation award Our Lady Queen of Peace Sch., 1974. Mem. Nat. Soc. Histotech., Am. Soc. Clin. Pathologists, Am. Soc. Med. Tech. Democrat. Roman Catholic. Home: 13003 Keverton Dr Upper Marlboro MD 20772

WARD, DOROTHY BALL, psychologist; b. Cuyahoga Falls, Ohio, Aug. 24, 1928; d. William Arthur and Effa Gay (Lee) Ball; B.A. in English Lit., U. Akron, 1949; M.A. in Psychology (State of Fla. Council on Tng. in Mental Health fellow 1963-67), U. Fla., 1966, Ph.D. in Clin. Psychology, 1968; m. John E. Ward, Aug. 18, 1950. Part time psychologist Sunland Tng. Center, Gainesville, Fla., 1967; intern Volusia County (Fla.) Mental Health Center, 1967-68; staff psychologist Henderson Clinic, Ft. Lauderdale, Fla., 1968-74, chief psychologist, 1974-77, chief adult unit, cons. psychologist, 1977—; pvt. practice clin. psychology, Ft. Lauderdale, 1970—. Grad. sch. fellow U. Fla., 1967-68. Mem. Am. Acad. Psychotherapists, Am. Psychol. Assn., Broward County Soc. Profl. Psychologists, Fla. Psychol. Assn., Southeastern Psychol. Assn. Club: Mensa. Home: 2509 Middle River Dr Fort Lauderdale FL 33305 Office: 1100 E Oakland Park Oakland Park FL 33334

WARD, DOROTHY SCHERER, ret. savs. and loan assn. exec.; b. Port Allegany, Pa., Sept. 12, 1911; d. Robert Abraham and Ellen Cornelia (Johnson) Scherer; B.A., Beaver Coll., Jenkintown, Pa., 1933; bus. cert. Cox Comml. Coll., Tucson, 1940; m. James A. Ward, Mar. 15, 1935. Office mgr. United Mortgage Co., Norfolk, Va., 1961-67; adminstrv. asst. to mgr. Weaver Bros., Inc., Norfolk, 1967-71; with Mut. Fed. Savs. & Loan Assn., Norfolk, Va., 1971-81, v.p., exec. loan officer, 1974-81. Mem. Nat. Assn. Mortgage Bankers (instr. loan processing courses 1979—), Va. Mortgage Bankers Assn., Tidewater Mortgage Bankers Assn. (dir. 1979-80, treas. 1979-80), Norfolk Bd. Realtors, Virginia Beach Bd. Realtors, Inst. Fin. Edn., U.S. Savs. and Loan League, AAUW, Am. Assn. Ret. Persons. Presbyterian. Club: Order Eastern Star. Office: 225 W Olney Rd Norfolk VA 23510

WARD, JANE PAMELA, social worker; b. Sioux City, Iowa, Feb. 10, 1948; d. Robert James and Alice Noreen (Gullickson) W.; B.A., Wartburg Coll., 1970; M.S.W., U. Iowa, 1975. Psychiat. therapist Community Mental Health Center of Scott County, Davenport, Iowa, 1975-76, coordinator of consultation and edn., 1976-77; dir. social work program Viterbo Coll., LaCrosse, Wis., 1977-79; asst. exec. dir., dir. social services Bremwood Luth. Children's Home, Waverly, Iowa, 1979-82; dir. Three Crosses Ranch, Strawberry Point, Iowa, 1982—; adj. prof. U. No. Iowa, Cedar Halls, 1983—. Mem. Gov.'s Commn. Planning Com. for Conf. on Children, Iowa, 1976; cons. South Central Community Justice Planning Commn., La Crosse, 1977, Viterbo Coll., 1979. Mem. Nat. Assn. Social Workers (dir. 1978-79), Bi-County Mental Health Assn. (dir. 1976), Acad. Cert. Social Workers, Nat. Registry Clin. Social Workers. Lutheran. Home: 1420 Byron Ave Waterloo IA 50702

WARD, JANIS ANN, social worker; b. Waco, Tex., Apr. 25, 1950; d. Wayne Leslie and Rebecca Louise (Harris) McDonald; B.A., Baylor U., 1972; M.S.W., La. State U., 1975; m. Robert Mitchell Ward, Aug. 16, 1974; 1 son, Robert Matthew. Fin. services worker Dept. Public Welfare Waco, 1972-73, family services worker, 1974; instl. liaison worker Dept. Human Resources Waco, 1975-76, regional adoption worker, 1976—; field instr. dept. social work Baylor U., 1980—. Family life chmn. First Meth. Ch., Waco, 1978, tchr., 1979. Recipient Dept. Human Resource stipend, 1974-75. Mem. Acad. Cert. Social Workers, Nat. Assn. Social Workers. Democrat. Baptist. Home: 701 N 60th St Waco TX 76710 Office: PO Box 977 Waco TX 76703

WARD, J(ERELEINE) DELARYCE, fast food corp. exec.; b. Cleve., Oct. 21, 1955; d. Eugene Washington and Jereline W.; B.A., Stephens Coll., 1977. Asst. buyer Stix, Baer & Fuller, St. Louis, 1977-78; asst. dir. tng. Holly Enterprises, Inc., Alexandria, Va., 1978—. Bd. dirs. ARC, 1981-82. Mem. Nat. Assn. Female Execs., Am. Soc. for Tng. and Devel. Home: 1323 N Van Dorn St Alexandria VA 22304 Office: Holly Enterprises Inc 4141 Duke St Alexandria VA 22304

WARD, JOAN GAYE, psychologist; b. Englewood, N.J., May 22, 1934; d. James A. and Eda W.; B.A., Miami U., 1956; M.A., New Sch. Social Research, 1965; Ph.D., N.Y.U., 1973, cert. in psychotherapy and psychoanalysis, 1981. Research asso. Mktg. Survey & Research Corp., N.Y.C., 1962-67; counselor N.Y.U., 1967-68, instr., 1970-71; psychologist Bur. Child Guidance, Bronx, N.Y., 1968—; pvt. practice psychotherapy, N.Y.C., 1969—. N.Y.U. fellow, 1967-68. Mem. Am. Psychol. Assn., N.Y. State Psychol. Assn., Assn. Humanistic Psychology, Eastern Psychol. Assn., N.Y.C. Assn. Sch. Psychologists. Home: 395 Riverside Dr New York NY 10025 Office: 239 Central Park West New York NY 10024

WARD, JUDITH LINDA BURTON, clin. psychologist; b. Des Moines, Apr. 20, 1953; d. David Marvin Ward and Carolyn Strimple (Burton) Gillespie; B.A. in Psychology, Alma Coll., 1975; M.A. in Clin. Psychology, Marshall U., 1978. Psychology intern children's unit Community Mental Health Center, Huntington, W.Va., 1977; sr. therapist, adult out-patient unit Jefferson County Comprehensive Mental Health Center, Steubenville, Ohio, 1978-81, acting unit chief, 1981-82; prin. psychologist Martha's Vineyard Mental Health Center, Edgartown, Md., 1982—; cons., condr. workshops in field. Mem. Am. Psychol. Assn. (asso.). Democrat. Episcopalian. Home: Newton Rd Oak Bluffs MA 02557 Office: 86 Main St PO Box 1089 Edgartown MA 02539

WARD, LARRIETTA DALE, clin. social worker; b. Balt., July 24, 1943; d. Lawrence and Lilly (Townsend) W.; B.A., Ohio No. U., 1967; M.S.W., U. Md., 1971, postgrad., 1975—. Research asst. Fels Inst., Yellow Springs, Ohio, 1967; social worker Montgomery County (Ohio) Welfare Bd., Dayton, 1967-68; sr. social worker Meth. Bd. Child Care, Balt., 1968—; sr. cons., partner InterStaff-Human Services Cons., Stevenson, Md., 1979—; field instr. Western Md. Coll., Westminster, 1975—; cons. Title XX; cons. Chapel Hill Convalescent Center, Randallstown, Md., 1980—, Westminster (Md.) Convalescent and Nursing Center, 1981—. Sponsor, Save the Children, 1978—; mem. planning com. Hunger Project, 1978-79; sponsor Md. Mental Health Assn., 1979-80. Mem. Acad. Cert. Social Workers, Nat. Assn. Social Workers (legis. task force Md. chpt.), Md. Conf. Social Concerns (state legis. coordinator 12th dist.), Balt. Camera Club, Alpha Omicron Pi. Democrat. Methodist. Club: Symposium. Office: 3300 Gaither Rd Baltimore MD 21207

WARD, MARGARET LOUISE, social worker; b. Fayetteville, Tenn., Nov. 26, 1946; d. John and Lorine (Owens) Parks; B.S., Tenn. State U., 1971; M.S.W., U. Tenn., 1974; m. William Robert Ward; 1 dau., Shana Verna. Computyper operator Pace Warehouse, Inc., Chgo., 1966-69, Enesco, Chgo., 1969; asst. tchr. Donner Belmouth Child Care Center, Nashville, 1971; social worker Public Health Team, Nashville, 1971-72; coordinator Robertson/Cheatham County Satellite Mental Health Center, Springfield, Tenn., 1974—; mem. Springfield Health Care Community Adv. Bd., 1980—, Robertson/Cheatham County Child Abuse and Neglect Adv. Com., 1978—. Mem. Acad. Cert. Social Workers, Nat. Assn. Social Workers, Mental Health Assn. Methodist. Home: 308 Skyline Dr White House TN 37188 Office: 101 7th Ave Springfield TN 37172

WARD, MARGARET MOTTER, violist, violinist; b. Grand Rapids, Mich., Sept. 21, 1928; d. Gerrit and Dorris Alberta (Gilbert) VanRingelesteyn; student Mich. State U., 1946-49; Mus.B., Eastman Sch. Music, U. Rochester, 1952; m. Robert Paul Ward, June 17, 1978; children—Eva Lynne Motter, Phoebe Motter Baldini, Antonia Lee Motter, Charles Frederick Motter. Violinist, violist Grand Rapids (Mich.) Symphony, 1942-51; violist faculty quartet Mich. State U., 1947-49, Rochester (N.Y.) Philharm., 1951-53; instr. violin and viola U. N.C., Chapel Hill, 1953-56; violist Miami (Fla.) Symphony, 1962-64, LaQuartette, Miami, 1963-64; prof. violin and viola Conservatoire Nationale du Liban, Beirut and violist chamber orch. and quartet of Lebanese Conservatory, Beirut, 1964-66; pvt. tchr. violin and viola, Washington, 1967-78; instr. viola Montgomery Coll., 1970-74; violist Kennedy Center Opera House Orch., Washington, 1970—, Wolf Trap Filene Center Orch., Vienna, Va., 1970—, Balt. Symphony, 1973-74, Am. Camerata for New Music, Wheaton, Md., 1974—; founder, violist New String Art Quartet, 1982—; mem. Amateur Chamber Music Players, Inc. Mem. Alumni Assn. U. Rochester, Chamber Music Am. Home: 1101 Playford Ln Silver Spring MD 20901 Office: Opera House JF Kennedy Center Washington DC 20566

WARD, MARY ALICE, govt. EEO exec.; b. Austin, Tex., Apr. 30, 1934; d. Chester Ahart and Williene (Ates-Holmes) Smith; student U. Tex., Austin, 1968-70, Austin Community Coll., 1974, St. Edwards U., 1978—; m. Henry Ward, Nov. 16, 1953; children—Henry Jerome, Eric Nathan, Sandra Elise. Sec., Atlanta Life Ins. Co., Austin, 1956-60, health claims adjuster, 1960-62, bookkeeper, 1962-64; with IRS-Austin Service Center, 1964—, coordinator Fed. Women's Program, 1974-78, coordinator Handicap Program, 1974-78, coordinator Upward Mobility Program, 1972-78, EEO officer, 1973—; organizer Black Employment Program Council, Hispanic Employment Program Council; adv. Fed. Women's Program Council, Black Program Council, Hispanic Program Council. Mem. budget subcom. United Way, Austin, 3 yrs. Recipient Outstanding Performance award IRS, 1968, Spl. Achievement award, 1972, 1975; Outstanding Iota award, 1978; Spl. award Hispanic Council, 1979. Mem. Am. Bus. Women's Assn., Federally Employed Women (organizing pres. Austin chpt. 1972-74), Austin Personnel Assn., Urban League, NAACP, Iota Phi Lambda. Democrat. Episcopalian. Club: Toastmistress (organizing v.p. club 1975-76). Home: 10106 Faylin Dr Austin TX 78753 Office: PO Box 934 Austin TX 78767

WARD, NATALIE JOY, secondary sch. adminstr.; b. Los Angeles, July 6, 1922; d. Leon and Bess Stromberg; B.A. magna cum laude, Pomona Coll., Claremont, Calif., 1943; M.A. with honors, Calif. State U., Los Angeles, 1956; Ed.D. with honors, UCLA, 1960; m. Oran W. Ward, June 3, 1943; children—Richard, Brian, Robert Wesley. Tchr., Pasteur Jr. High Sch., Los Angeles, 1945-56; mem. staff Los Angeles Unified Sch. Dist., 1956—, prin. Sepulveda Jr. High Sch., 1974-82, dir. instrn. region E, 1982—; coll. instr., cons. in field. Mem. Los Angeles City Bicentennial Commn., 1974-76, Futures Com. San Fernando Valley, 1981-82. Mem. Nat. Assn. Social Studies, Nat. Assn. Adminstrs. in Edn., Phi Beta Kappa, Delta Kappa Gamma, Pi Lambda Theta. Author: American History, Crisis and Conflict, 1971. Home: 1620 Pandora Ave Los Angeles CA 90024 Office: 6621 Balboa Blvd Van Nuys CA 91406

WARD, SHARON THOMPSON, home furnishings distbr.; b. Brigham, Utah, Aug. 27, 1925; d. Roy L. and Lavon (Stayner) Thompson; student (Box Elder scholar 1943), Utah State U., Logan, 1946; m. Grant Charles Ward, Aug. 4, 1944; children—Charles Thompson, Lauri Harriette, Michael Lamar. With Utah Optical Assn., Brigham City, 1942, Intermountain Theaters Co., Salt Lake City, 1942, Brigham City Corp., 1943, RCA Rubber, Akron, Ohio, 1948; pres. Owen Distbrs., Inc., Idaho Falls, Idaho, 1970—; cons. decorator. Mem. Nat. Assn. Home Builders, Nat. Distbrs. Floor Coverings, Eastern Idaho Home Builders Assn., Idaho Falls C. of C., Alpha Chi Omega. Republican. Mormon. Club: Idaho Falls Country. Office: 295 S Eastern Ave Idaho Falls ID 83401

WARD, SHIRLEY ANN, counselor; b. Dallas, Jan. 27, 1933; d. George Walter and Mildred Maggie (Rawdon) Martin; B.A., Austin Coll., 1955; M.A., So. Meth. U., 1963, counseling cert., 1974; Ph.D., N. Tex. State U., 1979; m. Paul Morris Ward, May 1, 1964 (div.); 1 dau., Lisa Lynn. Tchr. phys. edn. Dallas Public Schs., 1955-56; program dir. U.S. Dept. Army in Europe, 1956-57; tchr. Hockaday Sch., 1958-61, Richardson, Tex., 1961-64, Webster Groves, Mo., 1966-68, New Orleans, 1968-73; lang. trainer Center for Behavioral Studies, Denton, Tex., 1975-77; psychologist Pupil Appraisal Center, Denton, 1976-77; tchr. psychology Richland Coll., 1976-79; cons. psychologist The Dallas Agy., Dallas, 1976-78, Fin. Services Network, Dallas, 1976—; research dir. Total Life Care, Dallas, 1980—; pvt. practice counseling, Dallas, 1980—. Cert. tchr., Calif., Mo., Tex., La.; adminstr., counselor, cons., Tex., La. Republican. Research in biochem. treatment of children and adults with hyperkinesis, learning disabilities, behavior disorders, depression, and drug addiction. Home: 3206 Drexel Dr Dallas TX 75205 Office: Total Life Care PO Box 41708 Dallas TX 75080

WARDEN, ELIZABETH (BETTY) PAULA, direct mail mktg. co. exec.; b. Chgo., July 14, 1941; d. Albert A. and Gertrude (Zakin) Toben; B.A., Roosevelt U., 1963; 1 son, Adam. Copywriter, catalog advt. Montgomery Ward, Chgo., 1963-68, catalog advt. specialist, 1969-72, asst. buyer, 1972-75, asso. buyer, 1975-77; asst. mktg. mgr., mdse. Signature Direct Response Mktg. subs. Montgomery Ward, Evanston, Ill., 1977-79, gen. mgr. Wards Credit Card Security Service, 1979-81, v.p., gen. mgr., 1981—. Mem. Wardpac polit. action com., Chgo., 1979-81; founder, chairperson Signature Employee Community Relations Com., 1978-80. Mem. Chgo. Assn. Direct Mail (dir.), Direct Mail Mktg. Assn. Jewish. Office: 2020 W Dempster Evanston IL 60202

WARDEN, WALDIA ANN, dietitian, educator; b. New Orleans, Jan. 15, 1933; d. Walter Emmer and Lydia Eugenie (LeBlanc) W.; B.S., St. Mary's Dominican Coll., 1961; M.S. in Dietetics, St. Louis U., 1964. Joined Dominican Sisters, Congregation of St. Mary, Roman Cath. Ch., 1953; tchr. elem. schs., 1954-62; instr. foods and nutrition Dominican Coll., New Orleans, 1964-66, chmn. home econs. dept., 1966-69, asst. dean students, 1969-75, chmn. dept. home econs., 1975-78, chmn. Coll. Planning Council, 1972-76; dir. Rosaryville Center, Ponchatoula, La., 1979-81; cons. Pike Meml. Hosp. Trustee, St. Mary's Dominican Coll., 1973-79. Mem. La. Dietetic Assn. (editor jour. 1966-68), La. Leadership Conf. Women Religious, Am. Dietetic Assn., Am. Home Econs. Assn. Address: 580 Broadway New Orleans LA 70118

WARD-MCLEMORE, ETHEL, research geophysicist, mathematician; b. Sylvarena, Miss., Jan. 22, 1908; d. William Robert and Frances Virginia (Douglas) Ward; B.A., Miss. Woman's Coll., 1928; M.A., U. N.C., 1929; postgrad. U. Chgo., 1931, Colo. Sch. Mines, 1941-42, So. Meth. U., 1962-64; m. Robert Henry McLemore, June 30, 1935; 1 dau., Mary Frances. Head math. dept. Miss. Jr. Coll., 1929-30; instr. chemistry, math. Miss. State Coll. for Women, 1930-32; research mathematician Humble Oil & Refining Co., Houston, 1933-36; ind. geophys. research, Tex. and Colo., 1936-42, Ft. Worth, 1946—;

geophysicist United Geophys. Co., Pasadena, Cal., 1942-46; tchr. chemistry, physics, Hockaday Sch., Dallas, 1958-59, tchr. math., 1959-60; tchr. chemistry Ursuline Acad., Dallas, 1964-67, Hockaday Sch., 1968-69; geophys. cons., Dallas, 1957-77. Mem. Am. Math. Soc., Math. Assn. Am., Am. Geophys. Union, Seismol. Soc. Am., Soc. Exploration Geophysicists, A.A.A.S., Soc. Indsl. and Applied Math., Am. Chem. Soc., Inst. Math. Statistics, Tex Acad. Sci., Sigma Xi. Contbr. various articles to profl. jours. Home: 11625 Wander Ln Dallas TX 75230

WARDROPE, KAY-FRANCES MINGOLLA, social worker; b. Keene, N.H., June 6, 1939; d. Joseph Michael and Mary-Frances (Bolles) Mingolla; B.A. in Psychology, U. Vt., 1961; M.S.W., U. S.C., 1980; m. Donald A. Wardrope, Jan. 9, 1965; children—Susan A., Michael J. Social worker Eastern area hdqrs. ARC, Alexandria, Va., 1962-69, Md. Dept. Social Services, Rockville, 1969-71, Pennhurst State Sch., Spring City, Pa., 1972-73, Cumberland County Sch., Fayatteville, N.C., 1973-76, U. Hosp., Augusta, Ga., 1976-78, Health Help Services, Augusta, 1978-80; exec. dir. Central Savannah River Area Counseling and Family Service, Augusta, 1980—; cons. ARC, Richmond County Recreation Com., Augusta, 1979—. Mem. Nat. Assn. Social Workers, Sr. Enrichment Council, N.C. Assn. Retarded Children, Nat. Assn. Vol. Coordinators, Ga. Hosp. Assn. Social Workers, Med. Officers Wives Club, Nat. Soc. Sons and Daus. of Pilgrims, Nat. Soc. New Eng. Women. Creator, tchr. first sex edn. course for mentally retarded, Pennhurst State Sch., Pa. Home: 3059 Westwood Rd Augusta GA 30909 Office: 1467 Harper St Suite 406 Augusta GA 30902

WARING, ANN MCINTOSH, psychologist; b. Portsmouth, Va., Feb. 9, 1948; d. David Milton and Mary Rose (Coll) McIntosh; student Miss. Coll. for Women, 1966-68; B.A., U. Miss., 1970; M.A., East Carolina U., 1974; Ph.D., N.C. State U., Raleigh, 1980; m. Robert Edmund Waring, Jr., Sept. 4, 1970; 1 dau., Mary Elizabeth. Psychologist intern Wayne County Mental Health Center, Goldsboro, N.C., 1973; staff psychologist Children Services, Wayne County, 1974-75; psychologist intern Dorothea Dix Hosp., Raleigh, N.C., 1977-79; psychologist Cary Psychol. Services, Raleigh, 1978—; coordinator demonstration nursery sch. Project Enlightenment, Raleigh, 1978—. Nat. Merit scholar, 1966. Mem. Am. Psychol. Assn., N.C. Psychol. Assn., Southeastern Psychol. Assn., Psi Chi. Democrat. Roman Catholic. Home: 1613 Sherburg Ct Raleigh NC 27606 Office: 4900 Waters Edge Dr Suite 240 Raleigh NC 27606

WARMAN, THELMA LAVEDA, farm mgr.; b. Iowa Falls, Iowa, Mar. 10, 1904; d. John C. and Nettie Lucille (Winans) Hamilton; student Iowa Falls Public Schs., also Ellsworth Coll.; m. Leonard Orville Warman, Nov. 7, 1928; children—Craig Hamilton, Karren Lee Warman Hayes, Gary Douglas, Constance Lucille Warman Hoelscher. Tchr. public schs., 1925-29; farm mgr., operator, Alden, Iowa, 1950—. Republican del. Hardin County and Iowa convs.; trustee Iowa Conf., United Methodist Ch., 1967-74, mem. task force to study camp sites, 1977-78; trustee Alden United Meth. Ch., 1970-73, 80—; mem. Mason City Dist. Parsonage Com., United Meth. Ch., 1967-70, Ft. Dodge Dist. Com., 1970—. Mem. Farm Bur., Nat. Corn Growers Assn., Am. Soybean Assn., United Meth. Women. Republican. Home and Office: RFD Alden IA 50006

WARMINGTON, CATHY A., lawyer, bus. exec.; b. Madison, Wis., Oct. 19, 1948; d. Edward M. and Opal C. Huettner; B.S., U. Wis., Madison, 1970, student Milw., 1969, 71; J.D., Marquette U., 1979; m. Thomas E. Warmington, Aug. 1, 1970. Tchr. biology and sci. New Berlin (Wis.) Public Schs., 1970-74; v.p. 20th Century Homes, Inc., Waukesha, Wis., 1974—; office mgr. Fair Oaks Realty Inc., Waukesha, 1974—; v.p. Tomcat Constrn. Corp., Waukesha, 1978—, Homebuilders, Inc., Waukesha, 1978—; admitted to Wis. bar, 1980; pres. Warmington & Warmington, S.C., Waukesha, 1980—. Counselor, Meml. Ch., 1972-73, adminstrv. bd., 1972-75; active YWCA Big Sister Program, 1974-75. Wis. Honor scholar, 1966 Recipient Am. Jurisprudence award, 1980. Mem. Smithsonian Inst., Internat., Nat. wildlife fedns., Phi Delta Phi, Delta Zeta. Office: 152 W Main St Waukesha WI 53186

WARMS, BETH LEE, psychologist; b. N.Y.C., Oct. 10, 1941; d. Abraham and Molly (Rothenberg) Jacobs; A.B., Barnard Coll., 1963; M.A. (NIMH grantee 1963-65, 66-67), Columbia U., 1964, M.Phil., 1976; m. Tom M. Warms, June 13, 1965; 1 dau., Rebecca. Sch. psychologist Haverford (Pa.) Twp. Sch. Dist., 1968-74, Radnor Twp. Sch. Dist., Wayne, Pa., 1974—; mem. long range planning com. Springfield-Montgomery County Sch. Dist., 1979-80. Mem. Internat. Transactional Analysis Assn., Am. Psychol. Assn., Pa. Psychol. Assn. Democrat. Jewish. Home: 113 Shippen Rd Erdenheim PA 19118 Office: 135 S Wayne Ave Wayne PA 19087

WARNCKE, EDNA WAGSTAFF, educator; b. McKenney, Va., Apr. 28, 1935; d. Chester Royal and Anna Virginia (Jones) W.; B.S., Westhampton Coll., 1956; M.A., U. Richmond, 1965; Ed.D., U. Ga., 1972. Tchr., Richmond, Va., 1956-63; asst. prin. Henrico County (Va.) Public Schs., 1963-67; mem. faculty Ball State U., Muncie, Ind., 1967—, asso. prof. edn., 1977-80, prof., 1981—; cons. in field. Mem. Internat. Reading Assn., Nat. Council Tchrs. English, Assn. Supervision and Curriculum Devel. Presbyterian. Author: The What and How of Reading Instruction, (with Cooper, Shipman and Ramstad), 1979; co-editor: Ind. Reading Quar., 1981-84. Home: 3310 N Tillotson Ave Muncie IN 47304 Office: Sch Edn Ball State U Muncie IN 47306

WARNELL, MARY VIRGINIA, home economist; b. Groveland, Ga., Dec. 23, 1949; d. Charles Frederick and Martha Virginia (Moody) Warnell; B.S., Ga. Coll., 1971. With Dairy & Food Nutrition Council, Atlanta, 1971—, program coordinator, 1974—. Mem. Ga. Gov.'s Youth Council, 1966-68; Girls State rep., 1966. Named Outstanding Home Economist in Bus., Atlanta chpt. Phi Upsilon Omicron, 1970; Outstanding Home Econs. Alumni Ga. Coll., 1982. Mem. Am. Home Econs. Assn., Home Economists in Bus., Ga. Home Econs. Assn. (pres. 1981), Ga. Nutrition Council, Beta Sigma Phi. Democrat. Baptist. Clubs: Master 4-H, Beta. Home: 200 Franklin Rd NE Apt R2 Atlanta GA 30342 Office: 5825 Glenridge Dr NE Bldg 1 Suite 108 Atlanta GA 30328

WARNER, CAROLYN, state govt. ofcl.; b. Aug. 5, 1930. Supt. public instrn. State of Ariz., 1974—. Mem. Council of Chief State Sch. Officers, Ariz. Bdn. Edn., Ariz. Bd. Regents, Council on Econ. Edn., Western Correctional Assn., Govtl. Commn. on Environment, Gov.'s Adv. Com. on Mgmt., LWV. Clubs: Phoenix Execs., Democratic Women's. Office: 1535 W Jefferson Phoenix AZ 85007 *

WARNER, GLORIA MARMAR (MRS. RICHARD R. PICHEL WARNER), psychiatrist; b. N.Y.C., July 24, 1933; d. William W. and Celia (Dantzig) Marmar; B.A., Barnard Coll., 1952; M.D., N.Y. U., 1959; postgrad. Columbia Psychoanalytic Clinic for Tng. and Research, 1972-76; m. Richard R. Pichel Warner, July 4, 1953; children—Jon J.P., Keith R.P., Douglas C.P., Lynn S.P. Intern Montefiore Hosp., N.Y.C., 1959-60; research fellow medicine and gastroenterology Mt. Sinai Hosp., N.Y.C., 1961-63, resident psychiatry, 1963-66, staff psychiatrist, 1966-69, asst. attending psychiatrist, 1969-76; asst. attending psychiatrist N.Y. Hosp. Med. Center, 1976—; instr. Mt. Sinai Sch. Medicine, City U. N.Y., 1965-69, clin. asso. psychiatrist, 1967-73, asst. clin. prof. psychiatry, 1973-76; asst. clin. prof. psychiatry Cornell U. Med. Sch., 1976-78, adj. asst. prof. 1978—; asst. clin. prof. psychiatry Columbia Coll. of Physicians and Surgeons; sch. psychiatrist Mt. Sinai Hosp. Sch. Nursing, 1966-69. Diplomate Am. Bd. Psychiatry and Neurology. Mem. AMA, N.Y. State, N.Y. County med. socs., Am. Psychoanalytic Assn. (asso.), Am. Psychiat. Assn., Am. Fedn. Clin. Research, Am. Assn. Group Psychotherapy, Am. Med. Womens Assn., Assn. for Psychoanalytic Medicine, N.Y. Acad. Scis., Alpha Omega Alpha. Contbr. articles to profl. jours. Office: 18 E 87 St New York City NY 10028

WARNER, SALLY SLADE, carillonneur, ch. musician; b. Worcester, Mass., Sept. 6, 1932; d. Harold Stephen and Anna Mae (Snow) Slade; student New Eng. Conservatory Music, 1950-52; Carillonneur's diploma with gt. distinction, Royal Carillon Sch., Mechelen, Belgium, 1979; cert. Dutch lang. Stedelijk Inst. voor Tech. Onderwijs, 1979. Organist, Ch. of St. John the Evangelist, Beacon Hill, Boston, 1955—, dir. music, 1964—; record librarian Phillips Acad., Andover, Mass., 1973—, carillonneur, 1975—; carillon recitalist, U.S.A., Can., Belgium, Netherlands. William R. Kenan Jr. Fund grantee, 1978-79; recipient Adele Colson prize Carillon Sch., Belgium, 1979. Mem. Am. Guild Organists, Guild Carillonneurs in N.Am. (chmn. public relations com. 1977—), Organ Hist. Soc., Assn. Anglican Musicians, Belgische Beiaardiersgilde, Nederlandse Klokkenspel-vereniging, Danish Guild Carillonneurs. Episcopalian. Club: Boston Organ. Composer for carillon: Variations on old Flemish song Die alder soetste Jesus, 1978, Passacaglia on E.A.C., 1979. Address: Phillips Acad Andover MA 01810

WARNES, DEANNA SUZANNE, ins. co. exec.; b. London, Jan. 29, 1945; came to U.S., 1967, naturalized, 1970; d. Ralph and Violet Wood; LL.B., U. London, 1966, J.D., 1967. With Allstate Ins. Co., Menlo Park, Calif., 1967—, dist. sales mgr., San Jose, Calif., 1970—. Mem. San Jose Housing Commn. Mem. Nat. Assn. Ins. women (officer), Am. Bus. Women's Assn. (v.p. 1979-80), Am. Arbitration Assn., Ins. Co. Edn. Dirs. Soc., Nat. Assn. Life Underwriters, Am. Soc. Tng. Dirs. Republican. Office: Allstate Ins 2882 Sand Hill Rd Menlo Park CA 94025

WARNKEN, CHARLENE SCOTT, editor, columnist; b. Tulsa, Sept. 30, 1938; d. Homer Talton and Kathleen Jane (Taylor) Scott; B.A. in English, Benedictine Heights Coll., 1960; m. Gary Michael Warnken, Feb. 16, 1963; children—Christopher Michael, Anne Kathleen. Reporter, Livingston (Mont.) Enterprise, 1959; reporter, bur. chief Miami (Fla.) Herald, 1960-63; religion editor Tulsa Tribune, 1963-64; reporter Tex. Cath. Herald, Houston, 1969-72; religion editor Houston Post, 1972-77; asso. editor The Eastern Okla. Cath. Tulsa, 1978—; public info. specialist City of Tulsa Dept. Human Rights, 1979-80; writer feminist column, Women, 1979—. Sec., Religious Public Relations Council, Gulf Coast chpt. 1974-76. Recipient award Guideposts mag., 1975, Cath. Press Assn., 1970, Religion Newswriters Assn., 1973; Disting. Merit award Tulsa chpt NCCJ, 1980. Democrat. Roman Catholic. Office: EOC 122 W 8th St Tulsa OK 74101

WARNKEN, VIRGINIA MURIEL THOMPSON, social worker; b. Anadarko, Okla., Aug. 13, 1927; d. Sam Monroe and Ruth L. (McAllister) Thompson; A.B., Okla. U., 1946; M.S.W., Washington U., 1949; m. Douglas Richard Warnken, Sept. 16, 1957; 1 son, William Monroe. Med. social cons. Crippled Children's Services, Little Rock, 1950-54; supr. VA Hosp., Little Rock, 1954-55; asst. prof. U. Tenn. Sch. Social Work, Nashville, 1955-57; dir. social services N.Y. State Rehab. Hosp., Rockland County, 1957-58; asst. prof. U. Chgo. Sch. Social Service Adminstrn., 1958-59; free lance editor, 1960—; instr. evening div. Coll. of Notre Dame, Belmont, Calif., 1967-68; asso. Mills Hosp., San Mateo, Calif., 1978—; med. aux. Community Hosp., Pacific Grove, Calif., 1980—. Com. mem. C. of C. Miss Belmont Pageant, 1971—, co-chmn., 1975-78. U.S. Children's Bur. scholar, 1947-49. Mem. Assn. Crippled Children and Adults (dir. 1952-55), Assn. Mentally Retarded (dir. 1953-55), Am. Assn. Med. Social Workers (practice chmn. 1954-55), Nat. Assn. Social Workers (dir. 1962-66), Acad. Cert. Social Workers, Am. Assn. Med. Social Workers, Nat. Rehab. Assn., Am. Psychol. Assn., Am. Orthopsychiat. Assn., Council Social Work Edn. Democrat. Presbyterian. Clubs: Carmel Valley Golf and Country, Peninsula Golf and Country. Author: Annotated Bibliography of Medical Information and Terminology, 1956. Address: 1399 Bel Aire Rd San Mateo CA 94402

WARNS, MARIAN KINCAID, labor relations arbitrator; b. Louisville, Oct. 3, 1923; d. Horace L. and Laura (Law) Kincaid; B.A., U. Louisville, 1944, M.Ed., 1972, Ph.D., 1976; m. Carl Arthur Warns, Jr., Sept. 14, 1946. Asst. tng. dir. Richard Store Co., Miami, Fla., 1947-48; personnel and tng. dir. Kaufman Straus Co., Louisville, 1948-52; tchr., asst. coordinator Ahrens Trade High Sch., 1952-56; personnel, tng. dir. H.P. Selman Co., 1956-57; research asso. in arbitration Carl A. Warns Jr., 1957-64; indsl. psychology cons. Raymond Kemper & Assos., 1970-72; instr. psychology U. Louisville, 1972-76; pvt. practice labor relations arbitrator, 1971—. Mem. Nat. Acad. Arbitrators (gov.), Am. Psychol. Assn., Am. Soc. Tng. Dirs., Indsl. Relations Research Assn., Mortar Bd., Phi Kappa Phi, Psi Chi. Episcopalian. Contbr. articles in field to profl. jours. Home and Office: 312 Brunswick Rd Louisville KY 40207

WARREN, JANICE ELAINE, nurse; b. Newton, Miss., Feb. 23, 1947; d. William Courtney and Aletha Jane (Richmond) Reid; R.N., So. Baptist Hosp., New Orleans, 1968; m. E. Selwyn Warren, III, June 27, 1981; 1 stepson, Chad. Staff nurse hosps. in La., Ala. and Tex., 1968-69, 70-74; service dir. Homemakers Upjohn Health Agy., New Orleans, 1974-75; supr., adminstrv. dir. student health service Loyola U., New Orleans, 1975—, coordinator univ. blood donor program, 1977—, chairperson safety com. Mem. Southwestern Coll. Health Assn. (v.p. 1980, pres. 1981-82), Am. Nurses Assn., Am. Coll. Health Assn., Profl. Traveling Nurse Assn. Democrat. Baptist. Home: 4313 Courtland Dr Metairie LA 70002 Office: 6363 Saint Charles Ave New Orleans LA 70118

WARREN, JEWEL DEAN, learning center exec.; b. Monticello, Fla., July 9, 1944; d. Grover and Bessie M. (Alexander) Norman; B.S., Tuskegee Inst., 1966; postgrad. Fla. A&M U., 1971; m. Carl Marion Warren, June 7, 1969; children—Carl Gregory, Conrad Pierre. Home mgmt. technician Neighborhood Service Center, Tampa, Fla., 1966-68, parent-tchr. coordinator, 1968-72; child care instr. Tampa Bay Vo-Tech. Sch., 1972-76; pres., founder, dir. N & W Early Childhood Learning Center, Inc., Tampa, 1976—; child care cons.; religious lectr. and speaker. Chmn. child care directory LWV, 1978. Named Outstanding Community Leader, 1979, Outstanding Bus. Woman, 1980, Outstanding Tchr., 1979, Outstanding Mistress of Ceremonies, 1976; recipient pres. pin Desota PTA, 1979. Mem. So. Assn. Children Under Six, Pvt. Day Care Owners Assn., Nat. Assn. Female Execs., Ladies Guild, Alpha Kappa Alpha. Roman Catholic. Clubs: Kappa Silhouettes, Aurora Social-Civic (pres. 1977-79). Home: 738 N Pearl Circle Brandon FL 33511 Office: 2709 34th St Tampa FL 33605

WARREN, JUNE ROCHELLE, state ofcl.; b. Detroit, Mar. 23, 1935; d. Frank J. and Lula B. Warren; B.S. in Occupational Therapy, Wayne State U., Detroit, 1959. Rehab. counselor, So. Calif., 1966-71; rehab. supr. Calif. Dept. Rehab., 1971-75, asst. dist. adminstr., 1975-76, dist. adminstr., Riverside, 1976-79, Los Angeles, 1979-81, asst. to dep. dir. adminstrv. services, Sacramento, 1981—; mem. Los Angeles County Commn. Disabilities, 1979-81. Mem. Nat. Rehab. Assn., Nat. Rehab. Counselor Assn., Alpha Kappa Alpha. Methodist. Office: 830 K St Mall Sacramento CA 95814

WARREN, MADELINE, motion picture exec.; b. Greenport, N.Y., Sept. 10, 1949; d. Monte M. and Jean Warren; student Skidmore Coll., 1976-69; B.A. magna cum laude, N.Y.U., 1971, M.A., 1973. Freelance writer, N.Y.C., 1973-75; story analyst Am. Internat. Pictures and Filmways, Inc., Los Angeles, 1975-77; dir. devel. for producer Freddie Fields, 1977-78; v.p. prodn. and devel. Begelman/Fields Co., Burbank, Calif., 1978-80; prodn. exec. MGM Film Co., Culver City, Calif., 1980, v.p. prodn., 1980—. Mem. Women in Film. Office: 342 Thalberg Bldg 10202 W Washington Blvd Culver City CA 90230

WARREN, MARY BERNADETTE, bus. cons.; b. N.Y.C., Apr. 7, 1934; d. Albert Oscar and Lily Frances (Graham) Johnson; student Queens Coll., 1957-60; m. Albert E. Warren, Jr., June 4, 1955; children—Albert E., Walter O., William J. J., Mary Theresa. Adminstrv. asst. Barnard Coll., N.Y.C., 1952-53; sec. plumbing and heating bus., N.Y.C., 1953-55; legal sec. firm Everett Johnson & Breckinridge, N.Y.C., 1959-60; sec. Market Facts Inc., Houston, 1971-72; sec. Pennzoil Co., Houston, 1973, advanced clk., 1974, sr. clk., 1976, analyst human resources info. system, 1978-80, supr., 1980-81, co-pioneer human resources info. system, 1976; cons. Warren Assos., Friendswood, Tex., 1981—.

WARREN, MARY BONDURANT, writer, publisher; b. Athens, Ga., Feb. 5, 1930; d. John Parnell, II and Mary Claire (Brannon) Bondurant; B.S. in Physics, U. Ga., 1951; postgrad. Inst. Nuclear Studies, Oak Ridge, 1952; m. James Randolph Warren, Nov. 27, 1953; children—Eve B., Mark S., Amy M., Stuart H., Lisa B. Spectrochem. analyst Union Carbide Corp. Y-12 Plant, Oak Ridge, 1950-51; mem. staff Med. Div., Oak Ridge Inst. Nuclear Studies, 1951-53; mem. staff dept. physiology Emory U. Med. Sch., Atlanta, 1953; tech. editor Engrng. Expt. Sta., Ga. Inst. Tech., 1954; cons. VA Hosp., Atlanta, 1955-56; editor weekly Family Puzzlers, 1964—, also quar. periodicals: The Carolina Genealogist, 1969—, The Ga. Genealogist, 1969—; lectr. geneal. workshops. Chmn., Clarke County (Ga.) Civil War Centennial Commn. Mem. Athens Hist. Soc. (past pres.), Ga. Geneal. Soc., Athens Jr. League. Author: Marriages and Deaths from Extant Georgia Newspapers, 1763-1820, 1820-1830; South Carolina Jury Lists, 1718-1783; South Carolina Wills, 1982. editor, compiler various geneal. works on Ga. counties. Office: Heritage Papers Route 2 Box 65 Danielsville GA 30633

WARREN, PATRICIA ARMSTRONG, fin. cons.; b. Los Angeles, Jan. 29, 1932; d. Paul Lincoln and Marie (Collison) Armstrong; student Mills Coll., 1949-51, U. Calif., Berkeley, 1951-52; B.A., Calif. State U., Los Angeles, 1965, M.A., 1967; M.B.A., Pepperdine U., 1978; Ph.D., Pacific Western U., 1981; children—William, Tiffany, John, Wendy Warren Mullender. Hist. curator County Los Angeles, Dept. Arboreta and Botanic Gardens, Arcadia, Calif., 1967-75; account exec. Merrill Lynch, Pierce, Fenner and Smith, Sherman Oaks, Calif., 1975-77; instr. Pasadena City Coll., 1968-75, U. Calif. at Los Angeles, 1969-75; pres. Armstrong Warren Assos., Marina del Rey, Calif., 1977—; v.p. Armstrong Investments Co., 1977—, Armstrong Farms, 1981—; instr. UCLA Extension, 1982. Mem. Los Angeles City Hist. and Cultural Properties Survey. Nat. Mus. Act grantee, 1973. Mem. Am. Assn. Mus., Nat. Assn. Female Execs., Assn. M.B.A.s, Inst. Cert. Fin. Planners, Am. Mgmt. Assn., Internat. Assn. Fin. Planners, Women of Wall St. West (dir.), Soc. Archtl. Historians, Women in Bus. (treas. chpt. 1978-80), Calif. Hist. Soc. (merit award 1974), Asso. Hist. Socs. Los Angeles County (pres. 1971-73), Hist. Soc. So. Calif. (v.p. 1971), Conf. Calif. Hist. Socs. (awards chmn./museums chmn. 1971-73), Phi Alpha Theta. Club: University (Los Angeles). Author: California Architecture, 1971; Santa Anita Depot, 1970; Elias Jackson Baldwin, 1973; A Time of Change: Hugo Reid, 1973; Motivation and the Museum Volunteer, 1978. Office: PO Box 9638 Marina del Rey CA 90291

WARREN, SANDRA KAY, ednl. cons.; b. Grand Rapids, Mich., Oct. 17, 1944; d. Marinus and Adrianne Jeanne (Mol) Dieleman; B.S., Mich. State U., 1966; m. Roger Dennis Warren, Sept. 10, 1966; children—Kerri Sue, Leslie Ann, Michelle Lynn. Vol., tchr. Livonia (Mich.) Family Y, 1970-74; tchr. preschool gymnastics Southland YWCA, Middleburg Heights, Ohio, 1976-77; U.S. gymnastics ofcl., 1976—; parent advocate, cons. gifted children Ohio Assn. Gifted Children, 1977—, N.E. Ohio Assn. Gifted Children, 1977—; mem. Com. to Save Cleve. Major Work Program, 1978-79; founder, pres. Strongsville Assn. for Gifted and Talented, 1977-79, cons., 1979—. Mem. N.E. Ohio Assn. for Gifted Children (1st v.p.). Presbyterian. Address: 17035 Raccoon Trail Strongsville OH 44136

WARREN, THELMA CRANDLE, fin. exec.; b. Rayne La., Dec. 29, 1925; d. Arthur and Lucille L. Crandle; cert. bus. adminstrn. So. U., 1944; cert. La. Trade Tech., 1959; m. John E. Warren, May 13, 1950; 1 dau., Tracy. Sch. tchr., La., 1944-45; full charge mgr. fin. Julie Miller of Calif., Inc., Los Angeles, 1950-74; comptroller Richland Industries, Los Angeles, 1974—. First v.p. Pyramid 1000, 1980-81. Recipient cert. of Appreciation, City of Los Angeles, 1981. Mem. Black Women's Forum. Democrat. Methodist. Home: 3617 W 60th St Los Angeles CA 90043 Office: 9000 Sunset Blvd Suite 915 Los Angeles CA 90069

WARRES, MARGIE BLACK, social service exec.; b. Phila., Feb. 17, 1918; d. Harry M. and Eva (Stulbaum) Black; student Goucher Coll., 1936-38; B.A. magna cum laude, Bklyn. Coll., 1941; M.S.W. (Del. fellow 1942-44), U. Pa., 1944; m. H. Leonard Warres, June 11, 1939; children—Stephen Elliot, Neil Eric. Foster home caseworker Del. Dept. Welfare, Dover, 1942-44; exec. sec. public welfare com. Md. Conf. Social Welfare, 1948-50; exec. dir. Central Scholarship Bur., Balt., 1952—; cons. in field. Mem. Nat. Assn. Social Workers, AMA Aux. (chmn. internat. health com. 1973-75), So. Med. Assn. Aux. (state councilor 1977-81, regional coordinator 1981—), Child Study Assn. Md. (pres. 1957-58, chpt. pres. 1950-52, state adv. bd. 1963—), Balt. Med. Soc. Aux. (pres. 1965-66), Aux. to Med. and Chirurg. Faculty Md. (pres. 1968-69). Club: Green Valley Swimming. Author papers, bulls. in field. Home: 3314 Fallstaff Rd Baltimore MD 21215 Office: 4001 Clarks Ln Apt 108 Baltimore MD 21215

WARRINGTON, DEBORAH ANNE, univ. adminstr.; b. Hohenwald, Tenn., Oct. 17, 1949; d. Edward Young and Mattie Nelle (Staggs) W.; B.A., Memphis State U., 1971, postgrad., 1977-78. Asst. editor Holiday Inn Mag. for Travelers, 1971-73, mng. editor, 1973-74; editorial asst. Memphis State U. News Bur., 1975-76; asst. dir. Memphis State U. Office Media Relations, 1976-78; dir. communications and public relations Mid-South Fair, Libertyland, Inc., Memphis, 1978-79; dir. media relations Memphis State U., 1979—. Mem. publicity com. Am. Cancer Soc.; active Heart Fund. Mem. Public Relations Soc. Am., Tenn. Coll. Public Relations Assn. (sec. 1982). Democrat. Club: Memphis State U Tiger. Home: 3479 Fairoaks St Memphis TN 38122 Office: Adminstrn Bldg Rm 322 Memphis State U Memphis TN 38152

WARTA, MARJORIE HAMON, home economist; b. Fredonia, Kans., Sept. 2, 1935; d. John M. and Bertha L. (Cook) Hamon; B.S. in Home Econs. Edn. and Extension, Kans. State U., 1957, M.S. in Home Econs. and Family Econs., 1961; m. Byron Warta, June 2, 1957; children—Steven, Keith. 4-H extension agt. Rutgers U., Mt. Holly, N.J., 1957-58; tchr. schs. in Ill. and Kans., 1966-74; instr. home econs. Hesston (Kans.) Coll., 1971-79; asso. prof. home econs., chmn. dept. Bethel Coll., N. Newton, Kans., 1974—; past mem. extension exec. bd. Harvey County; chmn. West Conf. Hunger Task Force; chmn.-elect Kans. Extension Adv. Council. Mem. Am. Vocat. Assn., Am. Home Econs. Assn., Nat. Council Adminstrs. Home Econs., Home Econs. Edn. Assn., Kans. Vocat. Assn., Kans. Home Econs. Assn. (past pres.), PEO, Mortar Bd.,

Delta Kappa Gamma, Kappa Omicron Phi. Methodist. Office: Bethel Coll North Newton KS 67117

WARWICK, DIONNE, singer; b. East Orange, N.J., Dec. 12, 1941; ed. Hartt Coll. Music, Hartford, Conn.; m. Bill Elliott (div. 1975); 2 sons. As a teen-ager formed Gospelaires, then sang background for rec. studio; debut Philharmonic Hall, N.Y. Lincoln Center, 1966; appearances include London (Eng.) Palladium, Olympia, Paris, France, Lincoln Center Performing Arts, N.Y.C.; hostess weekly variety show Solid Gold; records include: Alfie, Do You Know the Way to San Jose, Valley of the Dolls, What the World Needs Now, I'll Never Love This Way Again (Grammy award 1980), Deja Vu (Grammy award 1980); albums include: Valley of the Dolls and Others, 1968, Promises, Promises, 1968, Then Came You, Dionne; screen debut The Slaves, 1969. Recipient Grand Prize, 9th Ann. Tokyo Music Festival. Address: care Press Relations Arista Records 6 W 57th St New York NY 10019 *

WASHBURN, JANET ARDELL, advt. exec.; b. Corunna, Mich., Jan. 22, 1935; d. Chester Dwight and Armina Pauline (Bouck) Walker; student public schs. Corunna; children—Don, Cynthia, Joan. Designer, advt. mgr. Robbins Furniture Co., Owosso, Mich., 1962-80; owner, exec. dir. J. Washburn Agy., Corunna, 1981—. Mem. vocat. edn. bd. Corunna High Sch., 1970-76. Recipient Advt. Excellence award Retail Advt. Conf. Chgo., 1979. Mem. Owosso-Corunna Area C. of C., Interior Design Soc. (nat. dir.), Eastern Mich. Interior Design Soc. (treas.), Flint Area Advt. Fedn., Am. Bus. Women's Assn. Club: Zonta. Office: PO Box 142 Corunna MI 48817

WASHBURN, URSEL IRENE (MRS. HOWARD C. WASHBURN), church worker; b. Ind., Apr. 22, 1900; d. Charles Evington and Blache (Griffith) McCoy; student Earham Coll., 1918-20, 21-22, Purdue U., 1922, U. Mich., 1925; B.A., Earlham Coll., 1926; m. Howard Caldwell Washburn, July 28, 1927; children—Angus David, Samuel Howard. Tchr., Washington Twp. High Sch., Logansport, Ind., 1920-22, Walton (Ind.) High Sch., 1922-26, Mt. Ayr (Ind.) High Sch., 1926-27, Kentland (Ind.) High Sch., 1950-51. Mem. nat. exec. com. United Presbyterian Women, 1954-58; pres. Ind. chpt. Ch. Women United, 1967-70, mem. nat. bd. mgrs., 1967-70; v.p. Ind. Council Chs., 1967-70; vice moderator Ind. Synod United Presbyn. Ch. U.S.A., 1972—, mem. Synod Lincoln Trails Council, 1973—. Dist. cookie chmn. Girl Scouts U.S., 1961-66; Ind. clothing chmn. Christian Rural Overseas Program, 1972—; chmn. nominating com. Wabash Valley Presbyterial Assn., 1975-76. Trustee Kentlan Pub. Library, pres., 1973, 74. Mem. Ind. Library Trustee Assn. (pres. 1967, Library Trustee of Year 1972), ALA, Ind. Library Assn., Ind. Hist. Soc., Newton Country Hist. Soc., Ind. Fedn. Women's Clubs (pres. dist. 10, 1980—). Republican. Presbyn. (pres. Ind. Synodical 1957-60, mem. nat. bd. pensions, 1965-71). Club: Federated Womens (pres. 1945-46, 70-71, county chmn. 1974-75, dist. chmn. 1976, dist. pres. 1982) (Kentland). Home and Office: 307 6th St Kentland IN 47951

WASHINGTON, CONSUELA M., mem. congressional staff; b. Chgo., Sept. 30, 1948; d. Hilliard L. and Conzoella Emanuelita (Brulee) W.; B.A. cum laude, Upper Iowa U., 1970; J.D., Harvard U., 1973. Admitted to bar; law clk. Mass. Law Reform Inst., 1970-71; asso. firm Kirkland & Ellis, summer 1972, 73-74; counsel corp. law dept. Allis-Chalmers Corp., 1975; atty. adviser div. corp. finance SEC, 1976, spl. counsel, atty. adviser office of chief counsel, 1976-79; mem. staff Ho. Com. on Interstate and Fgn. Commerce, 1979-80; profl. staff mem. Ho. Com. on Energy and Commerce, Washington, 1980—. Mem. Am. Bar Assn., Ill. Bar Assn., D.C. Bar Assn., Harvard Law Sch. Assn. Mem. United Ch. Christ. Office: Rayburn Ho Office Bldg Room 2145 Washington DC 20515 *

WASHINGTON, DOLORES ELIZABETH, home economist; b. Fresno, Calif., Nov. 3, 1936; d. John Earl and Claudine Elizabeth (Brandon) Abernathy; A.A., Reedly (Calif.) Coll., 1956; B.A., Fresno State Coll., 1958; M.A., Calif. State U., Sacramento, 1979; m. Herman Douglas Washington, Jr., June 13, 1970; 1 dau. by previous marriage, Marlene Crystal Boone. Counselor, YWCA Camp, 1957-58; tchr., Public Schs., Corcoran, Calif., 1958-60, Riverside, Calif., 1960-61, Stockton, Calif., 1962-69; food inspector USDA, Stockton, 1962-68; instr. consumer edn. and foods San Joaquin Delta Coll., Stockton, 1969—; microwave food demonstrator, Stockton, 1979—. Judge food, crafts, County Fair; mem. adv. bd. Foster Grandparents, Stockton State Hosp., 1971—; bd. dirs. Better Bus. Bur., 1976-80. Home: 2546 W Hammer Ln Stockton CA 95207 Office: 5151 Pacific Ave Stockton CA 95207

WASHINGTON, VIVIAN EDWARDS, social worker, former govt. ofcl.; b. Claremont, N.H., Oct. 26, 1914; d. Valdemar and Irene (Quashie) Edwards; A.B., Howard U., 1938, M.A., 1946, M.S.W., 1956; m. George Luther Washington, Dec. 22, 1950; 1 son, Valdemar Luther. Tchr., guidance counselor, sch. social worker, asst. prin., prin. Edgar Allan Poe Sch. Program for Pregnant Girls, Balt., 1939-73; cons. Office Adolescent Pregnancy Programs, HEW, Washington, 1978-80, program devel. specialist, 1980-81; cons. to adolescent parents. Bd. dirs. Nat. Alliance Concerned with Sch.-Age Parents, 1970-76, pres., 1970-72; bd. dirs. YWCA, Balt., 1966-69, United Way Central Md., 1971-80; bd. visitors U. Balt., 1978-80; adv. commn. on social services City of Balt., 1978—; chmn. Md. Gov.'s Commn. on Children and Youth, 1972-77. Recipient Alumni award Howard U. Sch. Social Work, 1966; Clementine Peters award United Way, 1980; Sojourner Truth award Nat. Bus. and Profl. Women, 1979; Vashti Turley Murphy award Balt. chpt. Delta Sigma Theta, 1981. Mem. Nat. Assn. Social Work, LWV, Nat. Council Negro Women (life), Balt. Urban League, Balt. Mus. Art, Delta Sigma Theta (nat. treas. 1958-63, Las Amigas service award Balt. chpt. 1973). Democrat. Episcopalian. Club: Pierians. Contbr. articles to profl. jours. Home: 3507 Ellamont Rd Baltimore MD 21215

WASIK, BARBARA HANNA, psychologist; b. Douglas, Ga., May 29, 1942; d. Frank Joseph and Josephine (Nahoom) Hanna; B.A. in Psychology, U. Ga., 1963; M.S. (USPHS fellow 1963-66), Fla. State U., 1965, Ph.D., 1967; m. John Louis Wasik, June 26, 1966; children—John Gregory, Mark Timothy, Jeffrey Joseph. Nat. Inst. Child Health and Human Devel. postdoctoral fellow Duke U., 1967-68, dir. research edn. improvement program, 1968-69, univ. instr., 1968-69; vis. instr. N.C. State U., 1968-69; mem. faculty U. N.C., Chapel Hill, 1969—, prof. Sch. Edn., also asso. dean, 1977—, sr. investigator Frank Porter Graham Child Devel. Center, 1972—, also mem. univ. adminstrv. bds. Mem. Am. Psychol. Assn., Soc. Research Child Devel., Assn. Advancement Behavior Therapy, Southeastern Psychol. Assn., N.C. Psychol. Assn. (dir. 1981—), Phi Delta Kappa, Alpha Omicron Pi. Democrat. Roman Catholic. Author articles in field; asso. editor Jour. Applied Behavior Analysis, 1972-73. Home: 609 Brookview Dr Chapel Hill NC 27514 Office: 103 Peabody U NC Chapel Hill NC 27514

WASILEWSKI, BOZENA, TV dir.; b. Eng., June 22, 1953; came to U.S., 1958, naturalized, 1973; d. Witold and Helena (Zyczynski) W.; A.A., Coll. Boca Raton, 1973; B.A. in Theatre Arts, L.I. U., 1976. Research analyst ABC-Radio Network, N.Y.C., 1973-74, asso. dir., 1977-78; asso. dir. NBC-Radio Network, 1977; stage mgr. ABC-TV Network, Los Angeles, 1979-80; asso. dir. CBS-TV Network, Los Angeles, 1980—; free-lance asso. dir. CBS-TV, ABC-TV, 1979-80. Mem. Dirs. Guild Am., Acad. TV Arts and Scis., Am. Film Inst., Nat. Assn. Female Execs., Phi Theta Kappa (treas.).

WASINGER, VIRGINIA LEE, quality engr.; b. Paris, Tex., Sept. 21, 1932; d. Theo Lee and Elizabeth Virginia (Cartter) White; B.B.A., Tarleton State U., 1978; children—Janet Wasinger Dickson, James, Richard, Lee Anne, Cynthia. Counselor, Nat. Bus. Con., Dallas, 1969; indsl. relations mgr. Voltaic Internat. Corp., 1969-71; property mgr. Sky-Harbour Lake Property, Granbury, Tex., 1974-75; owner Granbury Picture Framing, 1973-76; quality engr., documentation specialist Brown & Root Constrn., Glen Rose, Tex., 1979—. Mem. AAUW, Nat. Carvers Mus. Home: PO Box 129 Church and Warnock Bluffdale TX 76433 Office: PO Box 1001 Glen Rose TX 76043

WASKIEWICZ, JOYCE ANN, psychologist; b. Lawrence, Mass., Feb. 25, 1943; d. Alvin and Doris Martha (Wormwood) Magoon; B.A., U. Mass., 1964, M.S., 1966; Ph.D., U. N.H., 1978; m. Dennis Waskiewicz, Dec. 26, 1966; children—Jon, James. Sch. psychologist Bd. Coop. and Ednl. Services, Ithaca, N.Y., 1967-68; instr. psychology Tompkins, Cortland Community Coll., Groton, N.Y., 1968-72; sch. psychologist, Somersworth, N.H., 1978-81; pvt. practice psychology, Dover, N.H., 1981—; cons. Strafford Learning Center; instr. U. N.H.; bd. dirs. Kelly Brook Day Care Center. Acting sec. Joint Legis. Com., 1982; mem. Seacoast Women's Network. NDEA fellow, 1964-66; cert. psychologist, N.H. Mem. Am. Psychol. Assn., N.H. Soc. Psychologists. Author research studies in field. Home: 49 Oyster River Rd Durham NH 03824 Office: 10 Second St Dover NH 03820

WASKO, KAREN BARBARA, dental mgmt. co. exec.; b. Phila., Oct. 20, 1948; d. Stanley J. and Claire (Woodson) W.; student Monmouth Coll., 1966-68; B.B.A., U. Miami, Coral Gables, Fla., 1971. Exec. sec., v.p. sales Delaware Mgmt. Corp., Phila., 1966; mem. staff, margin dept. Butcher & Sherrard, Brokers, Phila., 1968-69; dept. asst. mgr. Burdines Dept. Store, Miami, 1970-71; mem. budget mktg. staff So. Bell Tel. & Tel. Co., Miami, 1971-77; exec. dir., sec.-treas. Wasko Enterprises Ltd., Phila., 1978—, also dir. Lic. gen. contractor, Fla. Mem. N.E. Phila. C. of C., Am. Mgmt. Assn., Am. Assn. Dental Group Practice, Chi Omega. Clubs: Sailing, Scuba, Huntingdon Valley Country. Home: 1338 Rydal Rd Rydal PA 19136 Office: 3428 Rhawn St Philadelphia PA 19046

WASOWICZ, LIDIA CHERIE, editor, reporter; b. Krakow, Poland, Apr. 3, 1951; came to U.S., 1960, naturalized, 1967; d. Kazimierz and Janina (Wronska) Wasowicz; B.A. with honors, U. Utah, 1973. Reporter, Deseret News, 1970-72; intern Salt Lake City Tribune, 1972, copy editor, 1972-73; UPI reporter, Salt Lake City, 1973-75; news reporter, broadcast editor Pacific div. UPI, San Francisco, 1975-78, news reporter, editor, 1978—. Rotary Club scholar, 1969; Russel S. Marriott scholar, 1969-73; Westminster Coll. Honors at Entrance scholar, 1969-70; Minute Women scholar, 1970-71; Maude May Babcock scholar, 1971-72; Sherwood Music Sch. scholar, 1969-73; Outstanding Calif. Journalist award, 1979; award for outstanding coverage Mt. St. Helens Volcano, 1980; award for outstanding coverage of drug abuse in Marin County, 1980; 1st place competition in news reporting Peninsula Press Club, 1981, feature writing competition Calif. State Fair, 1981; award for outstanding investigative reporting on Calif. prisons, 1981; Stanford U. profl. journalism fellow, 1981-82. Mem. Women in Communications, Mortar Board, Internat. Platform Assn., Smithsonian Assos., Phi Beta Kappa, Kappa Tau Alpha, Sigma Delta Chi. Democrat. Roman Catholic. Author (with others): Violence in the 60's, 1972. Home: 949 Via Casitas Greenbrae CA 94904 Office: 1390 Market St San Francisco CA 94102

WASS, HANNELORE LINA, educator; b. Heidelberg, Ger., Sept. 12, 1926; came to U.S., 1957, naturalized, 1963; d. Herman and Mina (Lasch) Kraft; B.A., Tchrs. Coll., Heidelberg, 1951; M.A., U. Mich., 1960, Ph.D., 1968; m. Irvin R. Wass, Nov. 24, 1959 (dec.); 1 son, Brian C.; m. 2d, Harry H. Sisler, Apr. 13, 1978. Tchr., W.Ger. Univ. Lab. Schs., 1958-60; faculty U. Mich., Ann Arbor, 1958-60, U. Chgo. Lab. Sch., 1960-61, U. Mich., 1963-64, Eastern Mich. U., 1965-69; prof. ednl. psychology U. Fla., Gainesville, 1969—; cons., lectr. in field. Mem. Am. Psychol. Assn., Gerontol. Soc., Internat. Work Group Dying, Death and Bereavement, Forum Death Edn. and Counseling, Nat. Council on Aging, Fla. Council on Aging. Methodist. Author: The Professional Education of Teachers, 1974; Dying-Facing the Facts, 1979; Death Education: An Annotated Resource Guide, 1980; Helping Children Cope With Death, 1982; Death Education: An Annotated Resource Guide, vol. 2, 1982; Childhood and Death, 1983; founder, editor Death Education, 1977—; cons. editor Ednl. Gerontology, 1977—, Hemisphere Pub. Corp. and McGraw Hill Internat.; contbr. articles to profl. jours. Home: 6014 NW 54 Way Gainesville FL 32606 Office: 293 Norman Hall Univ Fla Gainesville FL 32611

WASSEF, GLADYS EASTWOOD, career and personnel cons.; b. Hardy, Ark.; d. William Arthur and Ethel Ettie (Figgins) Eastwood; B.S., Washington U., 1960, M.A. in Edn., 1963; postgrad. St. Louis U., 1963-65, U. Man. (Can.), 1966-68; m. Wassef Y. Wassef, July 31, 1965 (dec.); 1 dau., Mary Alice. Acct., Rosen Brokerage Co., St. Louis, 1954-61; tchr. Ladue Sch. Dist., 1961-65; instr. English, U. Man., 1966; teaching fellow, 1966-67; instr. Wayne State U., Detroit, 1969-70, 70-71; instr. U. Windsor, summers 1971, 72; asst. prof. English, Millersville State Coll., 1974-75; pvt. practice bus. and personal tax cons., Lancaster, Pa., 1975-79; asso. Visions Assos., Lancaster, 1979-80; owner Personnel Cons. Services, 1981—. Can. Council fellow, 1967-68. Mem. Sales and Mktg. Execs. Club, Alpha Sigma Lambda, Kappa Delta Pi. Republican. Club: Pilot (treas. 1977-78, v.p. 1979, pres. 1980). Home: 61 Oak Ridge Dr Lancaster PA 17603 Office: 8 N Queen St Lancaster PA 17603

WASSERMAN, ELVIRA, psychiatrist; b. N.Y.C.; d. Charles W. and Zena (Berlin) W.; A.B., Hunter Coll., 1933; M.D., Women's Med. Coll. Pa., 1938; cert. N.Y. Sch. Psychiatry, 1962, Postgrad. Center for Mental Health, 1965; children—James G. Wallach, Lewis R. Wallach. Intern, Wilkes Barre (Pa.) Gen. Hosp., 1938-39; resident Creedmoor State Hosp., N.Y.C., 1959-62, supervising psychiatrist, 1962-65; practice medicine specializing in psychiatry, psychoanalysis and hypnoanalysis, N.Y.C., 1959-76, West Palm Beach, Fla., 1976—; asst. prof. guidance and counseling L.I.U., 1972-76. Mem. Am. Psychiat. Assn., Internat. Soc. Clin. and Exptl. Hyponosis, Soc. Med. Analysts, Nat. League Am. Pen Women.

WASSERMAN, LINDA MORGAN, clin. psychologist; b. Los Angeles, Apr. 3, 1943; d. Albert William and Mildred Emma (Lloyd) Morgan; A.B. in Psychology, Stanford U., 1964, Ph.D. in Psychology, UCLA, 1968; m. Stephen Wasserman, Aug. 22, 1964; children—Matthew, Zachary. Staff psychologist dept. psychiatry Mass. Gen. Hosp., Boston, 1968-70, dir. research project on patient as customer, 1972-73; staff psychologist Solano County Mental Health Services, Fairfield, Calif., 1970-72; coordinator tng. Bunker Hill Health Center, Charlestown, Mass., 1973-79; chief psychologist Children's In-Patient Unit, San Diego County Mental Health Services, San Diego, 1979-81; core faculty Calif. Sch. Profl. Psychology, San Diego, 1981—; instr. in psychology dept. psychiatry Harvard Med. Sch., 1972—; asst. clin. prof. dept. community medicine U. Calif., San Diego, 1982—. Diplomate Am. Bd. Profl. Psychology; lic. psychologist, Mass., Calif. Mem. Am. Psychol. Assn., Mass. Psychol. Assn. Home: 8420 Cliffridge Ln La Jolla CA 92037 Office: Calif Sch Profl Psychology San Diego CA

WASSERSTROM, EVELYN YAFFE (MRS. DEXTER JEROME WASSERSTROM), civic worker; b. Boston, Sept. 11, 1927; d. Joseph Harry and Tena (Drew) Yaffe; student Kansas City Art Inst., 1946-47, Kansas City Jr. Coll., 1946-47; m. Dexter Jerome Wasserstrom, Dec. 25, 1948; children—Tena Lynn (dec.), Bruce Alan. Project dir. Housing Survey for Retarded, Kansas City Assn. for Retarded, 1969; pres. YWCA, Kansas City, Mo., 1964-65; co-chmn. Met. Action, 1969-80; mem. Kansas City Commn. Human Relations, 1979—; bd. dirs. Kansas City region NCCJ, 1963—, dir., 1980—, Jewish chmn., 1973-76; bd. dirs. Jewish Community Relations Bur., 1969—. United Community Services, Inc., 1981—; bd. dirs. Jewish Ednl. Council, 1970—, chmn., 1973-77; mem. adv. group Met. Jr. Coll., 1967-69; co-chmn. High Sch. Jewish Studies of Greater Kansas City, 1971-73; mem. Panel of Am. Women, 1966—; v.p. woman's div. Jewish Fedn. and Council of Greater Kansas City, bd. govs., 1974—; bd. dirs. Vol. Action Center, 1974—, Jewish Community Center, 1977—; chmn. Kansas City Mayor's Commn. Human Relations, 1982—. Recipient Citation and Brotherhood award Kansas City sect. NCCJ, 1971, Disting. Missourian award Kansas City, 1980; Disting. Alumnus award BBG, 1977; Matrix award Kansas City chpt. Women in Communication, 1979. Jewish (mem. bd. edn. 1970—). Mem. B'nai B'rith Women (internat. pres. 1978-80, counselor 1980-82). Home: 449 W Dartmouth Rd Kansas City MO 64113

WASUTA, STEFANIA ANN, telephone co. exec.; b. Chicopee, Mass., Aug. 4, 1928; d. Zachary and Helen Monica (Skibel) Wasuta; student pub. schs., Chicopee, Mass. With New Eng. Telephone Co., Springfield, Mass., 1947—, instr., 1957-60, supr., 1960-68, tng. supr., 1968-70, mgr. bus., 1973—; rep. for communications exhbns. USSR, 1964-65; corporator Chicopee Savings Bank, 1979—. Bd. dirs. United Way, Chicopee, 1979-81. Mem. C. of C. (dir. 1976-79), Telephone Pioneers of Am. Republican. Roman Catholic. Clubs: Kosciusko, Old Sturbridge Village. Home: 138 Delaney Ave Chicopee MA 01013 Office: 1000 Wilbraham Rd Springfield MA 01109

WATANABE, RUTH, librarian, educator; b. Los Angeles, May 12, 1916; d. Kohei and Iwa (Watanabe) W.; B.Mus., U. So. Calif., 1937, A.B., 1939, A.M., 1941, M.Mus., 1942; student Eastman Sch. Music, 1942-46, Columbia U., 1947; Ph.D., U. Rochester, 1952. Instr. piano, music theory, Los Angeles, 1934-41; counsellor, personnel work Eastman Sch. Music, U. Rochester, 1943-46, instr. music history, 1946-61, asso. prof. musicology, 1961-78, prof. music bibliography, 1978—, instr. English, 1946-47, dir. music library workshop, 1956—, also lectr. music U. Sch.; staff mem. in charge circulation Sibley Music Library, Rochester, N.Y., 1943-47, acting librarian, 1947-48, librarian, 1948—; lectr. on music appreciation and music history, 1956—; lectr. Sch. Library Sci., Kent State U., summer 1968; cons. music libraries, 1968—; program annotator Rochester Philharmonic Orch., 1959—; in charge adult edn. Rochester Civic Music Assn.; adj. prof. Sch. Library Sci., SUNY, Geneseo, 1975—. Pa.-Del. fellow AAUW, 1949-50. Mem. AAUW (v.p. Rochester br. 1964-65, mem. state bd. N.Y. State div. 1965-66, pres. Rochester br. 1969-71, fellowship com. 1968-74), Internat., Am. musicological socs., Music Library Assn. (v.p. 1968-69, program chmn. 1970, pres. 1979-81), Internat. Assn. Music Libraries (2d v.p. commn. on conservatory libraries 1971-79), Assn. Coll. and Reference Librarians, U. Rochester Alumni Fedn. (bd. govs. 1958-61), Rochester Oratorio Soc. (dir. 1961-63, 70-74), Delta Kappa Gamma (v.p. chpt. 1973-76), Phi Beta Kappa (dir. Iota of N.Y. 1962-65, pres. 1977-78), Phi Kappa Phi, Mu Phi Epsilon (gen. chmn. nat. conv. 1956, nat. librarian, 1958-61), Pi Kappa Lambda (sec.-treas. chpt. 1975—), Delta Phi Alpha, Epsilon Phi. Club: Soroptimist (sec. 1956-57, pres. 1963-64). Author: Five Books of Italian Madrigals, 1956; Introduction to Research in Music, 1967; Antonio Il Verso: Madrigali a 5 voci, 1590, 1978; contbg. author: Music Library Handbook, 1966; Essays in Honor of Pauline Alderman, 1977; editor: Music Received. Home: 111 East Ave Rochester NY 14604 Office: 26 Gibbs St Rochester NY 14604

WATERS, DOROTHY LOOSE (MRS. PAUL R. WATERS), educator; b. Pitts., June 18, 1919; d. Otto Walter and Wilhelmina (Doepke) Loose; B.S. in Edn., U. Pitts., 1937, M.Ed., 1961; m. Paul R. Waters, June 29, 1946 (dec.); children—Doreen, Paul David, Devin. Sec., Westinghouse, East Pittsburgh, Pa., 1942-47; tchr. Turtle Creek (Pa.) Pub. Schs., 1957-58, Gateway Union Sch., Monroeville, Pa., 1958—. Tchr., Westinghouse Tech. Night Sch., Turtle Creek, Pa., 1959-60; instr. Community Coll., Monroeville, 1967-68. Pres., Monroeville Women's Club, 1959-60. Mem. Eastern Bus. Tchrs. Assn., Western Pa. Bus. Educators Assn., Nat. Assn. Exec. Females, Internat. Platform Assn., Tri-State Educators, Delta Delta Lambda. Lutheran. Home: 1321 Corkwood Dr Monroeville PA 15146 Office: Gateway Union Sch Moss Side Blvd Monroeville PA 15146

WATERS, EDNA W., psychologist, educator; b. Ft. Worth, Nov. 13, 1947; d. James L. and Mary Jane (Simmons) W.; B.A., U. Tex., Austin, 1969, M.A. in Psychology, 1972, Ph.D. in Ednl. Psychology, 1975. Instr. psychology U. Houston, 1975-79, asst. prof., 1979-81, assoc. prof., 1981—, mem. faculty senate, 1982—; prin. Werik Assocs., Houston, 1975—. Bd. dirs. Crisis Intervention Center, Houston, 1980—, Women's Ednl. Workshop, 1981—. Mem. Am. Psychol. Assn., Tex. Psychol. Assn., Houston Psychol. Assn. Democrat. Baptist. Club: Quota (Houston). Address: Werik Assocs 2727 Kirby Dr Suite 201 Houston TX 77098

WATERS, ELEANOR LOIS YOUMANS, librarian; b. Waycross, Ga., Aug. 25, 1928; d. Jacob Edward and Hazel Lois (Hendrix) Youmans; student Perry Bus. Sch., 1944-45, U. Wis., 1966, Loyola U., 1968; m. Thomas Edward Waters, Mar. 28, 1948; children—Belinda Waters Wheeler, Thomas Bruce, Sharon Waters Faircloth, Steven Edward. Sec. to supt. shipbuilding Brunswick Marine Constrn. Corp., Brunswick, Ga., 1945; library technician Nat. Marine Fisheries Service, Brunswick Lab., 1959-73, Ga. Dept. Nat. Resources Coastal Research Div., 1974—. Recipient Superior Performance award U.S. Dept. Interior, 1965, 68. Mem. Ga. Library Assn., Soc. for Bibliography Natural History. Presbyterian. Home: 2606 Starling St Brunswick GA 31520 Office: Ga Dept Natural Resources Coastal Resources Div 1200 Glynn Ave Brunswick GA 31520

WATERS, HENRIETTA EMMALINE, educator; b. Augusta, Ark., July 4, 1927; d. William and Hazel Eason; B.S., Central State U. (Ohio), 1949; postgrad. Loyola U., Chgo., 1950; M.S.W., U. Kans., 1961; m. Robert H. Waters, Sr., June 8, 1951; 1 son, Robert H. Child welfare worker Ill. Child Welfare Div., Chgo., 1950-52; child welfare supr. Chgo. Div. Welfare, 1953-58; dist. office supr./child welfare cons. Kans. Dept. Social Welfare, Kansas City, 1958-66; asst. prof. U. Kans., Lawrence, 1966-72; asso. prof. Barry U. Sch. Social Work, Miami, Fla., 1972—; cons. Dade County Community Action Agy. Pres. bd. dirs. Greater Miami Urban League, 1974-78, Greater Miami YWCA, 1974-76; exec. com. Children's Psychiat. Center, Miami, 1978—; trustee Bd. PUblic Health Trust, 1978—. Recipient Profl. Achievement award Barry Coll., 1979. Mem. Council Social Work Edn. (ho. of dels.), Nat. Assn. Black Social Workers (chpt. Service award 1976, 79), Nat. Assn. Social Workers, Acad. Cert. Social Workers, Behavioral Sci. Inst., Alpha Kappa Alpha. Methodist. Club: Links (Miami). Home: 6515 SW 116 St Miami FL 33156 Office: 11300 NE 2d Ave Miami FL 33161

WATERS, LOIS KENISTON, educator; b. Rumney, N.H., Sept. 30, 1921; d. Charles Edward and Ginevra Ethel (Bailey) Keniston; B.S. in nursing, U. Colo., 1963; M.S. in nursing, U. Pa., 1967, M.Ed., 1972; Ed.D., Tchrs. Coll. Columbia U., 1975; m. Clifton N. Waters, Oct. 9, 1943; children—Clifton N., Mary Elizabeth. Dir. nursing Allentown (Pa.) State Hosp., 1967-69; asst. prof. nursing Pa. State U., asso. prof. James Madison U., Harrisonburg, Va., 1980—. NIMH grantee. Mem. Am. Nurses Assn., Sigma Theta Tau, pi Lambda Theta. Home: 11

Gatewood Ct Massanutten Village McGaheysville VA 22840 Office: James Madison University School of Nursing Harrisonburg VA 22801

WATERS, MARIE WELCH, cosmetics co. exec.; b. Madison, Fla., Sept. 5, 1944; d. William Leon and Eula Sevor Welch; student Tallahassee Community Coll., 1967, Fla. State U., 1973; m. Kenneth W. Waters, Sept. 8, 1962; children—Gina, Kimberly. Sec. IV, Fla. Devel. Commn., Tallahassee, 1967-70; personnel mgr. State U. System Fla., Tallahassee, 1971-76; sales rep. Mgmt. Growth Tech., Tallahassee, 1976;

sr. dir. Mary Kay Cosmetics, Inc., Tallahassee, 1977—; ann. coordinator profl. devel. Seminar, Tallahassee, 1979—. Mem., adv. youth com. Immanuel Bapt. Ch. Mem. Am. Assn. Female Execs. Democrat. Baptist. Club: Shrine Aux. Home: 2357 Arendell Way Tallahassee FL 32308

WATERS, MARY —MICKIE— MAURINE, educator; b. Ft. Worth, June 20, 1944; d. Kennedy King and Mary Maurine (Davenport) McElroy; B.A., U. Tex., 1966, M.A., 1970; m. Michael John Edwards Waters, Dec. 13, 1975. Office mgr. First Federated Securities, Austin, Tex., 1968-69; tchr. Clear Creek Ind. Sch. Dist., Houston, 1970-76; legal sec. Key, Carr, Evans & Fouts, Lubbock, Tex., 1977; tchr. Greenwood Ind. Sch. Dist., Midland, Tex., 1977-79; instructional cons. Region 18 Edn. Service Center, Midland, 1979—; tchr. Bellevue (Wash.) Schs., 1980-81, Annie Wright Sch., Tacoma, 1981—. Chmn. activities Servetus, Houston, 1974-75. Mem. Tex. Tchrs. Assn. (pres.-elect dist. 18, public and profl. relations com.), Tex. Assn. Suprs. Math., Am. Assn. Supervision and Curriculum Devel., AAUW, LWV (program v.p. Midland chpt. 1978-80), Nat. Council Tchrs. Math., Puget Sound Council Tchrs. Math. (program chmn. 1981-82). Democrat. Unitarian. Address: 7321 137th Ave Redmond WA 98052

WATERS, NUALA MARY KILBRIDE (MRS. FRANCIS P. WATERS), psychiatrist; b. Longford, Ireland; d. Bernard J. and Anna (Ledwith) Kilbride; M.B., U. Coll., Dublin, Ireland, 1969, B.Ch., 1969, B.A.O., 1969; m. Francis P. Waters, Oct. 2, 1965. Mem. Irish Med. Assn., Royal Coll. Psychiatrists (London). Address: 1 Hainault Park Foxrock Dublin 18 Ireland

WATERS, RUTH CRAMER, librarian, mayor; b. Mifflin, Pa., Dec. 15, 1916; d. William McCahan and Clara Esther (Hench) Cramer; A.B., Juniata Coll., Huntingdon, Pa., 1939; M.S., Pa. State U., 1957; m. James Kirk Waters, June 11, 1943 (div. 1950); children—James Kirk, Curtis William. Tchr. schs. in Pa., 1940-42, 44-53; chemist Carnegie Ill. Steel Co., Duquesne, Pa., 1942-43; librarian, 1953—; librarian Juniata High Sch., Mifflintown, Pa., 1970-80; ret., 1980; participant Kent U. seminar in socialist edn., Szeged, Hungary, and Moscow, USSR, 1970; mem. Juniata County Library Bd., 1972-78, pres., 1973-78; mem. Mifflin Borough Council, 1974-78, mayor, 1978—. Mem. Pa. Resolutions and Policy Com., 1976—; del. Pa. Borough Assn., 1976-78; past pres. Mifflin-Juniata Heart Assn.; chmn. public relations com. Juniata County Bicentennial Com., 1972-76; chmn. Juniata County cancer campaign Mifflin-Juniata Cancer Soc., 1982; mem. Mifflin-Juniata-Huntingdon County Mental Health/Mental Retardation, 1981—, Mifflin-Juniata-Huntingdon County Family Planning Bd. (now Women's Health Services), 1980—. Mem. Pa. Edn. Assn., NEA, Juniata County Edn. Assn. (past editor newsletter), ALA, Pa. Library Assn., Juniata County Hist. Soc. (pres. 1979—), Lewistown Bus. and Profl. Women's Club, Delta Kappa Gamma (past chpt. pres.). Democrat. Lutheran. Clubs: Mifflintown Women's Civic (past pres.); East Juniata Women's (past pres.). Author local newspaper column Purely Personal, 1971—; also radio programs. Home: 2 Main St Mifflin PA 17058 Office: Juniata High Sch Mifflintown PA 17059

WATERS, VIRGINIA, clin. psychologist; b. N.Y.C.; d. Richard Duer and Sally (Vass) W.; B.A., Finch Coll., 1969; M.A., Columbia U., 1972, Ph.D., 1973. Psychologist, Spence Sch., N.Y.C., 1974-75; dir. children's services Inst. for Rational Emotive Therapy, N.Y.C., 1977—; pvt. practice clin. psychology, N.Y. and N.J., 1978—. NIMH fellow, 1970-73; Inst. for Rational Emotive Therapy fellow, 1974-76. Mem. Am. Psychol. Assn., Am. Assn. Marriage and Family Counselors, Am. Personnel and Guidance Assn., Assn. Humanistic Psychology, Assn. Advancement Psychology, Am. Assn. Sex Educators, Counselors and Therapists (cert. sex therapist), Sigma Xi. Author: Color Us Rational, 1979; also pamphlets. Home: 18 Springfield Ave 2D Cranford NJ 07016 Office: 19 E 73rd St New York NY 10021 also The Mill 347 Lincoln Ave E Cranford NJ 07016

WATERS-ZAMORA, KATHLEEN ANN, educator; b. San Gabriel, Calif., June 20, 1947; d. David Merlin and Leta Wendellyn (Corbett) Waters; A.A., Mt. San Antonio Coll., 1967; student U. Calif., Santa Barbara, 1967-69; B.A., Calif. Poly. U., 1971; M.Ed., U. Las Vegas, 1973, M.Ed. in Spl. Edn., 1976; m. Steven F. Zamora, Sept. 15, 1973; 1 dau., Maureen; 1 stepson, Alan. Tchr. intern Tchr. Corps, Las Vegas, Nev., 1971-73; with Marvin Strusser, Las Vegas, 1973-74, Central Telephone Co., Las Vegas, 1974-76; behaviorist retarded adults So. Nev. Assn. Handicapped Tng. Learning Center, Las Vegas, 1976-79; tchr. mentally handicapped-phys. handicapped Clark County Sch. Dist., Las Vegas, 1979—. City of N. Las Vegas alt. rep. to So. Nev. Com. on Employment of Handicapped, 1978-81; bd. dirs. So. Nev. Assn. for Handicapped, 1981—; bd. dirs. Spanish Trails council Girl Scouts U.S.A., Pomona, Calif., 1970-71, mem. com. on minority involvement Frontier council, Las Vegas, 1975; bd. dirs. Service Employment Redevel., 1977—, vice chmn., 1980; treas. bd. dirs. So. Nev. Health Systems, 1978—; del. Clark County Dem. Conv., 1982. Mem. Nev. Assn. Latin Ams., United Latin Ams., NEA, Nev. State Edn. Assn., Clark County Classroom Tchrs. Assn. Democrat. Methodist. Clubs: Order of the Amaranth (asso. conductress 1979, conductress 1980, royal matron 1981). Home: 2900 Magnet St North Las Vegas NV 89030 Office: 2601 Sunrise St Las Vegas NV 89101

WATFORD, JEANETTE PATTERSON, educator; b. Graceville, Fla., Aug. 18, 1928; d. Ezra Dalton and Ida Corinne (Finley) Patterson; B.A., U. Fla., 1949; M.S. (Experienced Tchr. English fellow), Fla. State U., 1968; postgrad. Columbia U., 1948, Chipola Jr. Coll., 1957-58; m. Charles Lamar Watford, Sept. 5, 1948; children—Patsy Corinne Watford Mixon, Martha Kathryn Watford Whittemore, Margaret Nannette, Melissa Anne Watford Faucheux. Tchr. Graceville (Fla.) High Sch., 1959-69, head English dept., 1967-68; instr. Chipola Jr. Coll., Marianna, Fla., 1969—; v.p. Patterson Hardware and Furniture Co., Graceville, Fla., 1974-76. Mem. Jackson County (Fla.) Democratic Exec. Com., 1979—; committee woman Jackson County, 1980—; vice chmn. Dist. 2, Fla. State Dem. Central Com., 1980—, mem. state rules com., 1979—; del. Nat. Dem. Conv., N.Y.C., 1980. Recipient Fla. Speech Teaching award Fla. Speech and Communication Assn., 1980. Mem. Fla. Assn. Community Colls. (pres. Chipola chpt. 1976-77), NEA, Fla. Teaching Profession (dir. 1980-82), Chipola Educators Council (dir. 1977-79). Methodist. Club: United Meth. Women (pres. 1950-51, vice chmn. adminstrv. bd. 1977—, chmn. Pastor-Parish relations com. 1980-82, life mem.). Author: (with Dorothy T. Clemmons) Here's How: A Guide to Improving Language Habits, 1981. Home: 902 Brown St Graceville FL 32440 Office: College St Marianna FL 32446

WATFORD, VIRGINIA LEIGH, clin. psychologist; b. N.Y.C., Mar. 10, 1944; d. Donald Joseph and Virginia Edith (Poole) Walters; B.S., Cornell U., 1966; Ph.D., U. Calif., Irvine, 1976; m. Walter T. Watford, Jr., July 8, 1968; children—Paul Jeffrey, Lisa Regina. Social worker Orange County Dept. Social Services, Santa Ana, Calif., 1967-71; clin. supr. Straight Talk Clinic, Cypress, Calif., 1976-78; staff psychologist Long Beach (Calif.) Neuropsychiat. Inst. and Hosp., 1977, People's Clinic, Santa Ana, 1976-78; chief psychologist People's Clinic, Santa Ana, 1978—; psychologist Intergrated Personality Resources, 1978—; pvt. practice psychology So. Orange County Pediatrics, El Toro, Calif., 1979-81, Saddleback Pediatrics, Mission Viejo, Calif., 1979—; instr. Santa Ana Coll., 1979—. Mem. Am. Psychol. Assn., Calif. State Psychol. Assn. Home: 3096 Nestall Rd Laguna Beach CA 92651 Office: 27862 Puerta Rd Suite 109 Mission Viejo CA 92691

WATKINS, CAROLE REGINA, ednl. adminstr.; b. Balt., Feb. 17, 1947; d. Winfield Augustus and Regina Helen (Garner) W.; B.S., Morgan State U., 1971; M.Ed., U. Mass., 1975, Ed.D., 1980. Adminstrv. asst. Chem. Bank, N.Y.C., 1972-73; tng. instr. Lighted House Manpower Training Program, Community Coll. of Balt., 1974; exec. sec. Parks Sausage Co., Balt., 1974; area supr. Com. for Collegiate Edn. of Black Students, U. Mass., Amherst, 1974-75, fin. aid counselor, 1975, counselor/acad. advisor, 1975-78, asst. dir. acad. services, 1978-81; asso. dean of coll. Simmons Coll., Boston, 1981—. Mem. New Eng. Minority Women Adminstrs., Nat. Assn. Women Deans, Adminstrs. and Counselors. Office: 300 The Fenway Boston MA 02115

WATKINS, ELEANOR JANE, stockbroker; b. Toronto, Ont., Can., Mar. 12, 1932; came to U.S., 1960, naturalized, 1965; d. Anthony and Anne (Cucman) Chudzik; student U. Toronto, 1951-53; 1 son, Christopher Anthony Tallon. Account exec. E.F. Hutton & Co., Glens Falls, N.Y., 1974—. Pres., Queensbury Young Republican Club, Glens Falls, 1961. Home: 4 Queens Way Glens Falls NY 12801

WATKINS, HALCYON OLIVETTE, veterinarian; b. Bryan, Tex., June 14, 1939; d. Oliver W. and Sylvia V. (Sealey) Sadberry; B.Sc., Tex. So. U., 1961; D.V.M., Tuskegee Inst., 1968; m. Aubrey B. Watkins, June 1, 1968; children—Russell S., Shane O. Vet. officer Republic of Guyana; asst. prof. biology Prairie View A&M U. (Tex.); veterinarian Stirling (N.J.) Animal Hosp.; now asst. prof. biology Tex. So. U., Houston; cardiovascular research, dept. pharmcology U. Houston; fellow virology dept. Baylor U., Houston, summer 1965. Pres.'s asso. Tuskegee Inst., 1982; recipient Tchr.'s Appreciation award Prairie View A&M U., 1969-70. Mem. Coll. Tchrs. Adv. Assn., Nat. Inst. Sci., Beta Kappa Chi. Democrat. Roman Catholic. Club: NWJJ's. Office: 3200 Cleburn Ave Houston TX 77004 *

WATKINS, HELEN HUTH, psychologist; b. Augsburg, Germany; B.A., Pa. State U., 1946; M.A., U. Denver, 1949; m. John G. Watkins, Dec. 28, 1971; children from previous marriage—Marvin Huth, Karen Huth Eiblmayr. Psychologist, Center for Student Devel., U. Mont., 1959—; adj. prof. psychology Fla. Inst. Tech., 1979—; instr. workshops. Lic. psychologist, Mont. Mem. Am. Psychol. Assn., Soc. Clin. and Exptl. Hypnosis, Internat. Soc. Hypnosis, Am. Personnel and Guidance Assn., Phi Beta Kappa, Phi Kappa Phi, Psi Chi. Democrat. Contbr. articles to profl. jours. Home: 413 Evans Missoula MT 59801 Office: Univ of Mont Missoula MT 59801

WATKINS, JANICE MARIE REGENOS, educator; b. Twelve Miles, Ind., Oct. 18, 1931; d. G. Virgil and Edith Mae (Holland) Regenos; A.B., Westmar Coll., 1953; postgrad. U. Tex., 1969; M.S. in Edn., U. Kans., 1971; children—Kathleen Ann Watkins Burns, Karil Marie. Tchr. music, high sch. English, pub. schs., Nebr., 1953-56; spl. edn. diagnostic/evaluation tchr. Kans. Children's Receiving Home, Atchison, 1965-72; instr. spl. edn. Benedictine Coll., Atchison, Kans., 1972-76; asst. prof. edn. Hastings (Nebr.) Coll., 1976—; mem. Nebr. Consortium Coll. in Spl. Edn.; state adv. Nebr. Student Edn. Assn.; cons. in field. Bd. dirs. Coop. Urban Tchr. Edn., Kansas City, Mo., 1978—, Gingerbread Pre-sch., Hastings, 1981—. Named Outstanding Coll. Tchr., Alpha Chi, 1982. Mem. AAUP, Nebr. Edn. Assn., Am. Assn. Coll. Tchr. Edn., Council Exceptional Children, Embroidery Guild Am., Delta Kappa Gamma. Presbyterian. Editor: The Poetry and Prose of the Handicapped, a collection, 1979. Office: Hastings Coll 7th and Turner Sts Hastings NE 68901

WATKINS, NORMA JEAN, med. record cons.; b. Waldron, Kans., May 10, 1931; d. Harold Edward and Hazel Eva (Welch) Peitz; grad. corr. course Am. Med. Records Assn., 1969; m. Max L. Watkins, Dec. 1, 1967; children—Lori Susan Witters Stallard, Sandy Lee Witters, Matt Shane. Med. records supr. Anthony Hosp. and Clinic, Anthony, Kans., 1962-73; cons. nursing homes and hosp., Anthony, 1977—; inservice tchr. homes and hosp. Mem. Am. Med. Record Assn. (accredited), Okla. Med. Record Assn. Home and Office: Rural Route 3 Box 179 Harrah OK 73045

WATKINS, SARA VAN HORN, oboist; b. Chgo., Oct. 12, 1945; d. John Edward and Virginia Pentland (Marthens) W.; B.Mus., Oberlin Conservatory Music, 1967; m. John Shirley-Quirk, Dec. 29, 1981; 1 son, Benjamin Watkins Shirley-Quirk. Prin. oboist Honolulu Symphony Orch., 1969-73, Nat. Symphony Orch., Washington, 1973-81; solo oboist, Europe, U.S., 1981—; condr. Mem. Chgo. Fedn. Musicians.

WATLINGTON, JANET BERECIA, govt. ofcl.; b. St. Thomas, Virgin Islands; d. Roy A. and Camilita E. (Gabriel) Harrigan; student Pace Coll., George Washington U.; m. Michael F. MacLeod; children—Gregory Scott, Kafi Damali. Adminstrv. sec. to asst. regional counsel HUD, N.Y.C., 1960-63; exec. sec. to legis. counsel V.I. Legislature, 1968-72; adminstrv. asst. to V.I. Washington rep., 1973-78; asst. dir. Office Legis. and Govtl. Affairs, ACTION, Washington, 1979—; mem. S.E. regional adv. com. Nat. Park Service. Candidate, Ho. of Reps. from V.I., 1977; mem. Democratic Nat. Com., 1972—. Mem. ACLU, Am. Judicature Soc., Nat. Council Negro Women, League Women Voters, Bus. and Profl. Women's League, Virgin Islands Conservation Soc. Home: 4324 Westover Pl NW Washington DC 20016

WATMAN, CAROLYN PRESCOTT, educator; b. Altus, Okla., July 5, 1944; d. John Carl and Helen Lorraine (Eikner) Prescott; B.B.A., U. Okla., 1966; postgrad. North Tex. State U., U. N.Mex.; m. Gerald S. Watman, July 31, 1975; 1 dau., Carrie Michele. Personel mgr. Neiman-Marcus, Dallas, 1966-72; dir. records and research Hockaday Sch., Dallas, 1972; dir. personnel and payroll Herman Marcus, Inc., Dallas, 1972-75; pvt. personnel cons., 1973-75; v.p. dir. Santa Fe Merc. Co., Inc., 1975-81; instr. mktg. mgmt. No. N.Mex. Community Coll., Espanola, 1981—. Mem. N.Mex. Bus. Edn. Assn., Profl. Distributive Edn. Clubs Am.

WATRING, BERENICE ANN LACKEY, cardiovascular specialist; b. Chgo., June 2, 1941; d. Robert Charles Niendorf and Evelyn Dolores (Pecho) Vitarelli; grad. Elgin Community Coll. Sch. Nursing, 1973; student No. Ill. U., 1974, 75, U. Ill., 1959, 60; m. Richard L. Watring, June 7, 1980; children—Sandra Lynn, Patricia Ann. Clin. instr. CCU, Sherman Hosp., Elgin, Ill., 1976-78; staff nurse CCU-ICU, 1973-78; cardiovascular specialist Roche Med. Electronics, Cranbury, N.J., Avco Med. Products, Everett, Mass., Kontron Cardiovascular Inc., Everett, 1978—; speaker cardiovascular symposiums. Mem. Am. Assn. Critical Care Nurses (cert.), Chgo. Heart Assn., Sigma Kappa, Phi Kappa Theta. Office: 9 Plymouth St Everett MA 02149

WATROUS, ELEANOR BURNS, wholesale co. exec.; b. New Orleans, Nov. 9, 1914; d. John Thomas and Ellen Lacey (Burns); student Mercy Hosp. Sch. Nursing, 1930-32, Soule Bus. Coll., 1932-33; m. Herbert Leland Watrous, Dec. 5, 1960. Clk., Aleck Mattes, New Orleans, 1932-34; asst. purchasing agt. Hart Enterprises, New Orleans, 1934-39; price and quotation clk. Elec. Supply Co., New Orleans, 1939-49; sec., treas. Long Elec. Supply Co., New Orleans, 1949—, chmn. bd.; pres. Eleanor B. Long Realty Co., New Orleans, 1960—, chmn. bd. Named Citizen of Yr., Patrolmen Assn. New Orleans, 1970; recipient Humanitarian award Nat. Assn. Elec. Distbrs. Mem. Nat. Assn. Elec. Distbrs., So. Ind. Elec. Distbrs., La. Angus Assn., Nat. Angus Assn. Democrat. Roman Catholic. Clubs: Covington Square C, Bogalusa Jeans and Queens, Eastern Star. Home: Rt 1 Box 212 Folsom LA 70437 Office: PO Box 30320 New Orleans LA 70190

WATROUS, LYLE CROOK, librarian; b. East Haddam, Conn., July 19, 1919; d. Joseph Bruce and Henrietta (More) Crook; A.B., Women's Coll., U. N.C., 1940; B.S. in L.S., Carnegie Inst. Tech., 1941; sch. librarian certificate So. Conn. Coll., 1959; M.A. in Edn., Ariz. State U., 1968; m. Claude Philip Watrous, Jr., Oct. 6, 1942; children—Kathryn (Mrs. Raul Ybarra), Cynthia (Mrs. James Long), Jay B., Marion (Mrs. Kurt Henstorf), Claude Philip III. Asst. children's librarian Osterhaut Library, Wilkes-Barre, Pa., 1941-42; acting head librarian East Haddam Pub. Library, 1943; librarian Charles McKew Parr Library, 1955-57, librarian pub. secondary schs., Old Saybrook, Conn., 1957-62; reference specialist and librarian Ariz. State U., Tempe, 1962—, reference specialist in Edn., 1971—, head curriculum and microform services, 1974-81, head curriculum service, 1982—, chmn. Coll. Edn. library devel., 1973-78, mem. faculty senate, 1969-75. Mem. personnel com. Hayden Library, 1973-76. Pres., PTA, Chester, Conn., 1958-59; clk. vestry Episcopal St. Stephens and Ch. of Resurrection, 1981-82, vestry, 1982—; bd. dirs. Continental Villas East II, 1980—. Mem. NEA, Ariz. Edn. Assn., Ariz. State U. Library Assn. (pres. 1972-73), Ariz. Library Assn. (pres. div. colls. and univs. 1969-70), Ariz. State U. Faculty Assn., Ariz. State U. Faculty Women's Club (sec. 1972-73), Kappa Delta Pi. Republican. Club: Soroptimist (1st v.p. 1977-78, pres. 1978-79). Author: Guide for Education Students, Know Your Library, 1969, rev. and expanded edit., 1977, 82. Home: 7810 E Wilshire Dr Scottsdale AZ 85257 Office: Hayden Library Ariz State Univ Tempe AZ 85281

WATSKY, DONNA LOUISE, microbiologist; b. Lackawanna, N.Y., Aug. 4, 1944; d. Fred and Ida Caroline (Columbus) Kubiak; B.S., SUNY, Buffalo, 1966; M.S., Med. Coll. Va., Va. Commonwealth U., 1971; m. Michael Jay Watsky, Nov. 29, 1972; children—Joel Frederick, Tema Marie. Blood bank technician St. Joseph Mercy Hosp., Ann Arbor, Mich., 1966-67, asst. supr. chemistry, 1967-69; nightshift technologist St. Marys Hosp., Richmond, Va., 1969-71; supr. microbiology Anne Arundel Gen. Hosp., Annapolis, Md., 1971—, tchr. microbiology to nursing students, 1971-72; clin. instr. med. lab. tech. Prince Georges Community Coll., 1975-79. Mem. Am. Soc. Clin. Pathologists, Am. Soc. for Med. Tech., Md. Soc. Med. for Tech. (dir. 1981-82), Omicron Sigma. Home: 290-C Hilltop Ln Annapolis MD 21403 Office: Anne Arundel Gen Hosp Franklin and Cathedral Sts Annapolis MD 21401

WATSON, ANDREA LOUISE, economist; b. Plymouth, Mass., Ape. 22, 1947; d. John Charles and Julia Louise (Avery) W.; B.A., U. Mass., 1969; M.A., Johns Hopkins U., 1972. Officer internat. staff Citibank, N.A., 1972-74; research assoc. Internat. Research & Tech., 1974-78; sr. analyst Bechtel, San Francisco, 1978-80, economist-fin., 1980—. Mem. Nat. Assn. Bus. Economists, World Affairs Council No. Calif., Soc. Internat. Devel., Corp. Planners Assn. Democrat. Unitarian. Club: Commonwealth of Calif. Home: 1380 Sacramento St San Francisco CA 94109 Office: PO Box 3965 San Francisco CA 94119

WATSON, BARBARA M., former ambassador; b. N.Y.C., Nov. 5, 1918; d. James S. and Violet (Lopez) W.; B.A., Barnard Coll., 1943; LL.B., N.Y. Law Sch., 1962; LL.D., U. Md.; L.H.D., Mt. St. Mary Coll. Propr., Barbara Watson Models-Barbara Watson Charm and Model Sch., N.Y.C., 1946-56; charity work and travel, 1956-58; fgn. student adviser Hampton (Va.) Inst., 1958-59; admitted to N.Y. State bar, 1962; atty. Bd. Statutory Consolidation, City of N.Y., 1962-63; asst. atty. law dept. Office Corp. Counsel N.Y.C., 1963-64; exec. dir. N.Y.C. Commn. to UN, 1964-66; spl. asst. to dep. under sec. for adminstrn. Dept. State, Washington, 1966, dep. adminstr. Bur. Security and Consular Affairs, 1966-67, acting adminstr., 1967-68, adminstr., 1968-74, asst. sec. of state for consular affairs, 1977-80; ambassador to Malaysia, 1980-81; pvt. practice law, 1975-76. Bd. dirs. Wolf Trap Found. for Performing Arts, Mus. African Art. Decorated Nat. Order Ivory Coast Republic; recipient Luther I. Replogle award Dept. of State, 1974, award United Seamen's Service, 1970, Women's Div. United Hias Service award, 1970, Spl. Merit award Am. Caribbean Scholarship Fund, Inc., 1969, Myrtle Wreath Achievement award Hadassah, N.Y.C., 1968; Distinguished Service award Nat. Council Negro Women, 1971; Woman of Yr. award Utility Club Inc. N.Y., 1979; awards Internat. Aviation Club of Washington, 1971, Deliverance Evang. Center N.Y., 1971, Am. Immigration and Citizenship Conf., 1972, Jr. Citizens Corps Inc., 1972, Caribbean-Am. Intercultural Orgns. Inc., 1972, State Beauty Culturist Assn. Inc., 1973; Rev. Hirsch Masliansky award, 1972. Fellow Internat. Consular Acad., 1971. Mem. N.Y. County Lawyers's Assn., Internat. Women's Lawyers Assn., Am. Bar Assn., Fed. Women's Assn., Am. Fgn. Service Assn., Harlem Lawyer's Assn., Urban League Guild, Delta Sigma Theta (hon.). Clubs: Profl. Women's, Women's City (N.Y.); Internat. (Washington); Cosmopolitan (N.Y.). Office: Dept State 2201 C St NW Washington DC 20520 *

WATSON, BETTY SIMMONS, chem. co. exec.; b. Christiansburg, Va., May 30, 1939; d. James E. and V. Claudine (Cole) Simmons; B.S., Concord Coll., Athens, W.Va., 1960; postgrad Delta Coll., 1968-72, Saginaw Valley State Coll., 1977; children—James Robert, Cambrian Lou. With Dow Chem. Co., Midland, Mich., 1960—, biochemist, 1960-73, product rep. functional products and systems, 1974-76, sr. product rep., 1976-79, sales rep. agrl. products dept., Atlanta, 1979—. Mem. So. Agrl. Chem. Assn., Career Women in Industry, Ga. Plant Food Edn. Soc., Ga. Weed Control Soc., Ga. Entomol. Soc. Home: Walnut Dr Americus GA 31709 Office: Suite 2005 20 Perimeter Center E Atlanta GA 30346

WATSON, CAROL DIANE, educator; b. Akron, Ohio, Oct. 30, 1946; d. Donald Devere and Edwina Marie Watson; B.A., U. Akron, 1968; M.A., Stanford U., 1975; Ph.D., Columbia U., 1980; 1 son, Thomas Tarikh Korula. Staff psychologist N.Y. U. Dental Sch., 1979-80; asst. prof. grad. sch. mgmt. Rutgers U., Newark, 1980—; vis. asst. prof. Amos Tuck Sch. Bus. Adminstrn., Dartmouth Coll., Hanover, N.H., 1981-82. Mem. Am. Psychol. Assn., Acad. of Mgmt. Contbr. articles to profl. jours. Office: Rutgers Univ Grad Sch Mgmt Newark NJ 07102

WATSON, CAROLYN GARRETT, univ. adminstr.; b. Tuscaloosa, Ala., Sept. 22, 1941; d. Marcus O. and Willie J. (Burns) Garrett; B.S., U. Ala., 1977, M.S., 1981; divorced; children—Lynn, Brian. Various secretarial positions, 1961-72; successively exec. sec., staff asst., asst. to dean U. Ala. Med. Sch., 1972-81; bus. mgr. dept. pediatrics Emory U. Med. Sch., 1981—. Mem. Assn. Am. Med. Colls., Beta Alpha Psi. Office: 2040 Ridgewood Dr NE Atlanta GA 30322

WATSON, CATHERINE ELAINE, journalist; b. Mpls., Feb. 9, 1944; d. Richard Edward and LaVonne (Slater) W.; B.A. in Journalism, U. Minn., 1967, also postgrad.; M.A. in Teaching, Coll. of St. Thomas, 1971. Reporter, Mpls. Tribune, 1966-72, editor Picture mag., 1972-78, Travel-Adventure sect., 1978—; part-time instr. U. Minn. Sch. Journalism, 1974-78. Recipient Minn. School Bell award for edn. writing NEA, 1968-69. Mem. Am. Newspaper Guild, Phi Beta Kappa, Kappa Tau

Alpha, Alpha Omicron Pi. Contbr. articles to nat. mags. Office: 425 Portland Ave Minneapolis MN 55418

WATSON, CONNIE CLEO, real estate broker; b. Lubbock, Tex., Nov. 7, 1952; d. Cleo Thomas and Jo Rita (Ray) Lowe; L.V.N., Lubbock Nursing Sch., 1973; student S. Plains Coll., Levelland, Tex., 1974-76; grad. Real Estate Sch., 1976; m. Danny Watson, Aug. 3, 1973; 1 son, Aaron Jeffrey. Nurse, Tex. Tech. U. Med. Sch., 1973-74; office nurse, 1974-76; real estate broker Century 21 Big State, Lubbock, 1977—. Recipient various sales awards. Mem. Nat. Assn. Realtors, Nat. Women's Council Realtors, Tex. Vocat. Nurses Assn., Tex. Assn. Realtors, Tex. Women's Council Realtors (v.p. 1978-79), Lubbock Bd. Realtors, Antique Car Club. Office: 4704 67th St Lubbock TX 79414

WATSON, DIANA DYER, internat. banking exec.; b. Bronxville, N.Y., Aug. 21, 1947; d. Daniel Lamborn and Yvonne (Leggett) Dyer; B.A., Skidmore Coll., 1969; m. Andrew Orr Watson, Mar. 3, 1979; 1 dau., Allison Dyer. Asst. on trading desk in mcpl. bonds Matthews & Wright, Inc., N.Y.C., 1972-73; loan officer covering Malaysia, Singapore, Thailand, Asia Group, Bankers Trust Co., N.Y.C., 1974-78, v.p., sect. head covering Latin Am., Middle East, Can., Internat. Risk Mgmt. div., 1978-82, v.p., internat. loan officer, 1982—. Featured in book Women in Finance (Dian G. Smith), 1981. Office: Bankers Trust Co 280 Park Ave New York NY 10017

WATSON, DIANE EDITH, state senator; b. Los Angeles, Nov. 12, 1933; d. William Allen and Dorothy Elizabeth (O'Neal) W.; B.A. in Edn., UCLA, 1956; M.S. in Sch. Psychology, Calif. State U., Los Angeles, 1967. Mem. staff Los Angeles Public Schs., 1956-76, sch. psychologist 1975-76; dep. dir. secondary schs. allied health professions project UCLA, 1969-71; health occupation specialist Calif. Dept. Edn., 1971-72; assoc. prof. edn. Calif. State U., Los Angeles, 1976; mem. Los Angeles City Bd. Edn., 1975-78; mem. Calif. Senate from 30th Dist., 1978—; trustee Blue Shield. Chmn., Calif. Forestry Adv. Council; mem. Ednl. Innovation and Planning Commn.; bd. dirs. Urban League, Steven's House. Recipient various service awards; hon. life mem. Calif. PTA. Author instructional and curriculum materials in health care occupations. Office: Room 4090 State Capitol Sacramento CA 95814

WATSON, GEORGIA BROWN, author; b. Atlanta; d. George C. and Willie (Willingham) Watson; B.S., Ga. So. Coll., 1946; M.A., George Peabody Coll., 1947, Ph.D., 1949. Tchr., Ga. pub. schs., 1931-42; prof. psychology Ga. So. Coll., Statesboro, from, 1949, now emeritus prof., emeritus chmn. psychology dept.; postdoctoral research fellow Yale U., 1961-62. Served to maj. with WAC, 1942-46. Methodist. Author: How to Enjoy Retirement: Climb a Tree and Holler, 1979; Life in the Retirement Bed of Roses, 1982. Home: 4 Preston Dr Statesboro GA 30458

WATSON, GLADYS HAZEL, educator, polit. worker; b. Shiloh, Okla., Mar. 3, 1908; d. Thomas and Laura (Knowles) Dabner; grad. Kans. State Tchrs. Coll., 1933; m. Harold Edmond Watson, Dec. 27, 1937 (dec. Dec. 1967). Tchr. pub. schs., Kansas City, Mo., 1933-39, also after 1968, now res. tchr.; supply tchr. all grades, Kansas City, 1947-49; tchr. U.S. census takers, 1960. Speaker pub. meetings, ch. related schs. State committeewoman Mo. Republican Party, 1960-64; vol. worker ednl., civic, charity orgns., 1953—; sec. bd. dirs. Big Sister Home, 1955-58; life mem. Wheatley Provident Hosp. Assn., 1960—; mem. Univ. Assos., U. Mo., Kansas City; mem. Bapt. Woman's Missionary Council Mo. Recipient Franklin Delano Roosevelt citation, 1946, numerous other awards and citations. Mem. Am. Assn. Ret. Persons (local bd.). Baptist. Home: 2631 Tracy Ave Kansas City MO 64108

WATSON, JEAN KATHRYN, telephone co. exec.; b. Southbend, Ind., Nov. 29, 1928; d. Thomas and Rachel Evelyn (Murphy) Noonan; student Tyler Jr. Coll.; m. Jim Pat Watson, Jan. 4, 1974; children—Robert Anderson, Thomas Lee, Joseph Alan. With United Telephone Co., Palestine, Tex., 1954—, traffic tng. supr., 1972-76, dist. comml. mgr., 1976-79, service center adminstr., 1979-80, tng. dir., 1980—. Bd. dirs. United Way, Athens, Tex., 1980—, Am. Heart Assn., State of Tex., 1980; area dir. Parents Without Partners, 1973. Mem. Am. Soc. Tng. and Devel., Am. Bus. Women's Assn. (treas., program chmn.), Bus. and Profl. Women's Orgn., Nat. Assn. Female Execs. Republican. Baptist. Home: Box 6955 Tyler TX 75711 Office: PO Box 860 Palestine TX 75801

WATSON, LITA LEA, employment co. exec.; b. Lovettsville, Va., May 28, 1931; grad. pub. schs., Lovettsville; m. Robert J. Watson, Jan. 20, 1951; children—Jeannine Roberta, Robert Neal, James Kevin, Mary Elizabeth, Frederick Michael. Sec., Household Finance Co., Silver Springs, Md., 1948-52, El Paso Natural Gas Co. (Tex.), 1956-59: mem. sales staff, sales mgr. Sarah Coventry Jewelry, Newark, 1959-67; Calif. regional mgr. Snelling and Snelling Employment Agency, 1967-71; owner, mgr. Dennis & Dennis Personnel Service, Anaheim, Santa Ana, Irvine, Huntington Beach, Long Beach and Cerritos, Calif., 1971—; pres. Dennis and Dennis Inc. Franchising; pres. B&W Enterprises; sec.-treas. Robert J. Watson Enterprises. Mem. Am. Soc. Personnel Adminstrn., Am. Mgmt. Assn., Personnel Women of Orange County, Internat. Platform Assn., Calif. Employment Assn. (dir.), Calif. Assn. Personnel Cons. (2d v.p., J.R. Pierce award 1982), Am. Employment Assn., Orange County C. of C., Better Bus. Bur., Nat. Employment Assn. Republican. Roman Catholic. Home: 594 Turnabout Rd Orange CA 92669 Office: 1600 N Broadway Suite 110 Santa Ana CA 92706

WATSON, MAE F., educator; b. Myrtle Beach, S.C., July 31, 1942; d. James Thomas and Ollie Mae (Bellamy) Randall; B.S., Barber-Scotia Coll., 1970; M.Ed., CCNY, 1977, M.S. in Spl. Edn., 1982; student St. John's U., 1981-82; m. Bradley Watson, Nov. 10, 1963; 1 son, Michael. Tchr., Baisley Day Care Center, Jamaica, N.Y., 1969-76; tchr. N.Y.C. Public Schs., 1976-79, tchr. spl. edn., 1979—. Coordinator Tree Top Nursery Sch.-Rochdale, Queens, N.Y.; sec. Flushing br. NAACP, 1978—. Mem. Black Profl. Women Assn. N.Y., Phi Delta Kappa. Home: 156-15 134th Ave Jamaica NY 11434

WATSON, MARY STONE, educator; b. Marcellus, N.Y., May 24, 1909; d. James Horace and Ethel (Cowles) Stone; B.Oral English, Syracuse U., 1931; M.A., U. Md., 1965; m. Harry P. Watson, June 27, 1936; children—Ruth Watson Lancaster, Robert S., Rollin J., Harry P., Douglas J., Donald M., Sara L. High sch. tchr. English, speech, drama, N.Y., Pa., Md., 1931-37, 62-64; prof. speech Essex Community Coll., Baltimore County, Md., 1965-79, now emeritus, part-time instr., former head speech and drama dept.; lectr., condr. workshops in communications and therapeutic communication, 1965—; producer, anchor person Cable TV show The Best Is Yet To Be. Home: 108 W 39th St Apt 8 Baltimore MD 21210

WATSON, NANCY BELCHER, judge; b. Pomona, Cal., July 14, 1926; d. Frank Baker and Ruth Barbara (Reynolds) Belcher; B.A., Stanford U., 1947; J.D., UCLA, 1958; m. Philip Eugene Watson, June 4, 1970; children—Marcia, Brian, Harvey, Jr., Diane. Admitted to bar; law clk. Belcher, Kearney & Fargo, 1955-58; assoc. mem. Belcher, Henzie & Fargo, 1959-68; judge Mcpl. Ct., Los Angeles Jud. Dist., 1968-73; judge Superior Ct. Los Angeles County, 1973—, supervising judge family law dept., 1975-76. Mem. Calif. State Judges Coll., 1973; bd. visitors Stanford U. Law Sch., 1978-80. Mem. Am. Bar Assn., Am. Judicature Soc., Los Angeles County Bar Assn., Calif. Judges Assn., Stanford Profl. Women, Kappa Alpha Theta. Republican. Episcopalian. Contbr. articles in field. Office: County Courthouse 111 N Hill St Los Angeles CA 90012

WATSON, PAMELA GAHERIN, rehab. nurse; b. N.Y.C., Oct. 5, 1941; d. John Joseph and Rita (O'Brien) Gaherin; diploma Mass. Gen. Hosp. Sch. Nursing, 1964; B.S. in Nursing, Boston U., 1971, M.S., 1972, Sc.D. in Rehab. Counseling, 1982; m. Barron C. Watson, May 4, 1970; 1 child, Willis Fanning. Head nurse Yale-New Haven Hosp., 1964-66, Tufts-New Eng. Med. Center, Boston, 1966-67; instr. Boston U. Sch. Nursing, 1973-77, asst. prof., 1977—, chmn. dept. rehab. nursing, 1978—. Bd. dirs. PTA, Peirce Sch., Newton, Mass., 1981-82; bd. dirs., cons. Extended Day Program, Newton, 1982-84. Mem. Am. Nurses Assn., Am. Congress Phys. Medicine and Rehab., Assn. Rehab. Nurses, Boston U. Sch. Nursing Alumni Assn. (dir. 1982-84), Internat. Assn. Enterostomal Therapy. Club: Cambridge Boat. Editor N.E. region Internat. Assn. Enterostomal Therapy Newsletter, 1981—; book rev. editor Rehab. Nursing, 1979—; mem. editorial bd. Cancer Nursing, 1979—, Rehab. Nursing, 1979—; contbr. articles in field to profl. publs. Office: Boston U Sch Nursing 635 Commonwealth Ave Boston MA 02215

WATSON, SHARON GITIN, psychologist; b. N.Y.C., Oct. 21, 1943; d. Louis Leonard and Miriam (Myers) G.; B.A., Cornell U., 1965; M.A., U. Ill., 1968, Ph.D., 1971; m. Eric Watson, Oct. 31, 1969; 1 dau., Carrie. Psychologist, City N.Y. Prison Mental Health, Riker's Island, 1973-74, Youth Services Center, County of Los Angeles Dept. Public Social Services, Los Angeles, 1975-77, dir. clin. services, 1978, dir. youth services center, 1978-80; exec. dir. Los Angeles Florence Crittenton Services, 1980—. USPHS fellow, 1965-68. Mem. Am. Psychol. Assn., Assn. Advancement Behavior Therapy, Calif. Women in Govt. Home: 4056 Camino Real Los Angeles CA 90065 Office: 234 East Ave 33 Los Angeles CA 90031

WATSON, SHARON MYERS, journalist; b. Shreveport, La., Feb. 19, 1947; d. James S. and Myra (Posey) Myers; B.S. in Math., McNeese State U., Lake Charles, La., 1969, postgrad. in English, 1970-71; m. Larry Conrad Watson 1 son, Byron Lee. Edn. writer, Lake Charles (La.) American Press, 1969-70; copy editor, Dallas Morning News, 1971-72, club editor, 1972-76; pub. info. writer Blue Cross and Blue Shield of Tex., 1976—. Adv. com., Early and Periodic Screening - Diagnosis and Treatment Program, Tex. Dept. Human Resources, 1975—; exec. com. Bootstrap Ranch for Boys, 1970—; bd. sponsors Big Sisters of Dallas. Recipient AP award for team reporting, 1974, Austin Headliners award, 1973, AP award for spot news reporting, 1971, La. Press Women's awards, 1971. Mem. Women in Communications (Matrix award, 1976). Democrat. Baptist. Home: 9314 Raeford Dallas TX 75243 Office: 9550 Forest Suite 407 Dallas TX 75243

WATSON, SHEILAH SUE, educator; b. Oklahoma City, Jan. 20, 1958; d. Kenneth M. and Maria Dorothy (Ploransky) Watson; A.A., Oscar Rose Jr. Coll., 1977; B.B.A., Central State U., 1979, M.B.A., 1980; M.P.A., U. Okla., now postgrad. Grad. teaching asst. U. Okla., Oklahoma City, 1981—; adj. polit. sci. instr. South Oklahoma City Jr. Coll., summer 1982; with Genie Personnel Services, Midwest City, Okla., 1979-81, Midwest City Police Dept., summer 1975, Kelly Personnel Services, Oklahoma City, 1981—. Recipient Mgmt. Faculty Scholastic award, Central State U., 1979, Grad. Mgmt. Scholarship award, 1979. Mem. Alpha Chi. Home: 1400 SW 44th St Oklahoma City OK 73119 Office: 455 W Lindsey St Norman OK 73019

WATSON, SKIRMANTE SEMETA, editor, freelance writer; b. Lithuania, Apr. 24, 1934; came to U.S., 1949, naturalized, 1955; d. Aleksas and Anele (Kruglinskaite) Semeta; corr. student Famous Writers Sch.; m. William Callear Robert Watson, Sept. 9, 1971. Dir. Gallery Gemini, Inc., Palm Beach, Fla., 1972-76; freelance art cons., Houston and N.Y.C., 1976-79; account exec. Spencer-Wood, Inc., public relations, N.Y.C., 1980—; N.Y.C. editor Palm Beach Mirror, weekly, 1980—; author articles on art, 1979—. Club: Ponciana (Palm Beach). Office: 1501 Broadway New York NY 10036

WATT, ANN, travel agy. exec.; b. N.Y.C., Aug. 15, 1952; d. Anita Watt; B.F.A. (tutition scholarship 1970-74), Sch. Visual Arts, N.Y.C., 1974; teaching cert., Hunter Coll., N.Y.C., 1975; M.F.A., Alfred U., Inverness, Scotland, 1975. Tchr. art Washington Irving High Sch., N.Y.C., 1974; mgr. Internat. Escorts and Promotional Agy., N.Y.C., 1974-76; dir. Barbizon Internat. Model Agy., N.Y.C., 1976-78; owner, dir. Quality Planning, pvt. tour service, Hollywood, Fla., 1979—.

WATT, BARBARA RAE, advt. exec.; b. Allegheny County, Pa., Dec. 3, 1947; d. George T. and Lucille V. Watt; student Robert Morris Coll., 1965. Mgr., Wall St. Jour., Pitts., 1967-69; exec. sec. Pitts. Playhouse, 1969-78; pres. Main Line Advt. Spltys. and Entertainment, Pitts., 1978—. Mem. Nat. Assn. Female Execs. (dir.). Office: Main Line Rd 1074 Greentree Rd Pittsburgh PA 15220

WATTERS, MARY THERESE, ednl. adminstr.; b. Plymouth, Mich., Jan. 22, 1930; d. Arthur E. and Florence (Miller) W.; A.B., Mich. State U., 1954; cert. elem. edn. Wayne State U., 1966. Asst. to audio visual dir. Burroughs Corp., Detroit, 1954-56; prodn. mgr. Video Films, Detroit, 1957; tchr. elem. schs., Dearborn Twp., Mich., 1958-62; producer, writer Jam Handy Orgn., Detroit, 1964-65; dir. edn. measurement dept. ESEA Title I, Grand Haven (Mich.) Public Schs., 1965-78, also coordinator Indian edn.; dir. state and fed. compensatory programs, 1978—. Hinman scholar, 1953-54. Bd. dirs. Kiddie Carousel Day Care Center, 1979-80. Mem. Am. Assn. Sch. Adminstrs., Am. Mgmt. Assn., Mich. Assn. State and Fed. Program Specialists, Nat. Assn. Adminstrs. State and Fed. Edn. Programs, Nat. Indian Edn. Assn., Nat. Sch. Public Relations Assn., Irish Setter Club Am. (rec. sec. 1979, 80, 1st v.p. 1982), Greater Muskegon Kennel (v.p. 1976), Irish Setter of Mich. Office: 1415 Beech Tree St Grand Haven MI 49417

WATTLETON, ALYCE FAYE, assn. exec.; b. St. Louis, July 8, 1943; d. George Edward and Ozie (Garrett) Wattleton; B.S. in Nursing, Ohio State U., 1964; M.S. in Nursing, Columbia U., 1967; 1 dau., Felicia Megan. Instr. nursing Miami Valley Hosp. Sch. Nursing, Dayton, Ohio, 1964-66; asst. dir. nursing Dayton Public Health Nursing Assn., 1967-70; exec. dir. Planned Parenthood Assn. Miami Valley, Dayton, 1970-78; pres. Planned Parenthood Fedn. Am., Inc., N.Y.C., 1978—; adv. council Peace Corps, 1980—. Bd. dirs. Ind. Sector, 1979—; adv. com. Women's Leadership Conf. on Nat. Security. Recipient citation for outstanding achievement Ohio State U., 1979; N.J. chpt. ACLU Ann. award, 1980. Mem. bd. Nat. Urban League. Mem. Am. Coll. Nurse-Midwives, Am. Public Health Assn., Ohio State U. Alumni Assn. (bd. dirs.), Nat. Acad. Scis. (study com. Inst. Medicine), Nat. Urban Coalition. Democrat. Mem. Ch. of God. Office: 810 7th Ave New York NY 10019

WATTS, EMILY STIPES, educator; b. Urbana, Ill., Mar. 16, 1936; d. Royal Arthur and Virginia Louise (Schenck) Stipes; student Smith Coll., 1954-56; A.B., U. Ill., 1958, M.A. (Woodrow Wilson Nat. fellow), 1959, Ph.D., 1963; m. Robert Allan Watts, Aug. 30, 1958; children—Benjamin, Edward, Thomas. Instr. English, U. Ill., Urbana, 1963-67, asst. prof. English, 1967-73, assoc. prof., 1973-77, prof., 1977—, dir. grad. studies dept. English, 1977-79; bd. dirs. U. Ill. Athletic Assn., chmn., 1981—. John Simon Guggenheim Meml. Found. fellow, 1973-74. Mem. Author's Guild, Ill. Writers' Assn., Phi Beta Kappa, Phi Kappa Phi, Republican. Presbyterian. Author: Ernest Hemingway and The Arts, 1971; The Poetry of American Women From 1632 to 1945, 1977; The Businessman in American Literature, 1982; contbr. articles on Jonathan Edwards and Anne Bradstreet to lit. jours. Home: 1009 W University Ave Champaign IL 61820 Office: 208 English Bldg U Ill 608 S Wright St Urbana IL 61801

WATTS, MARIE ELIZABETH (MITZI WATTS), mining and heavy constrn. co. exec., artist; b. Dallas, Feb. 17, 1936; d. Milan and Marie Elizabeth Martha (Eichinger) Furtula; student St. Mary's Coll., Notre Dame, Ind., 1954-55; student art Dallas Mus. Fine Art, Ark. Art Center, Honolulu Art Center; m. Cleal Thomas Watts, Jr., July 28, 1956; children—Cleal Thomas, III, John Milan, Elizabeth, Lawrence Budd. A founder, 1962, since v.p. H.F. Constrn. Co., Inc., Dallas; a founder, 1970, since v.p. HFCO, Inc., Dallas; a founding partner Cleal T. Watts, research, design, rental and purchasing internat. sales and services, Dallas, 1962—; profl. artist, 1979—; group exhbns. include Lynn Kattler Gallery, N.Y.C., 1981, Florence Gallery, Dallas; one-woman exhbn. Georgetown Gallery, Atlanta, 1980; pres. Ark. Art Center, 1965; co-founder San Marcos Art League, 1962; represented in permanent collections including metal mobile of three kings and annunciation statues St. Mary's Coll., Notre Dame Ursuline Acad., Dallas; public speaker; also personal appearances radio and TV. Dist. dir. Tex. Republican Party, 1963; mem. bd. Ursuline Acad. Sch., 1978-80, mem. alumnae bd., 1976-80. Recipient Tops in Town award N.Y.C., 1981. Linz scholar, 1950-54. Mem. Assn. Gen. Contractors Am., Am. Mining Congress Tex. Fine Arts Assn., Internat. Platform Assn. Office: PO Box 1227 Dallas TX 75225

WATTS, MARY ANN, educator; b. Harrisburg, Pa., Sept. 13, 1927; d. Major Allan and Ellana Susan (Robinson) Brown; B.S., Cheyney State Coll., 1949; student Temple U., 1965-67, Pa. State U., 1969-72; m. Spencer R. Watts, June 23, 1951; children—Shelley Lynn, Allison Dee, Howard Allan. Tchr., Harrisburg Sch. Dist., 1949-51, 59-69, Balt. Sch. Dist., 1951-57, tchr. Reading (Pa.) Sch. Dist., 1969—, mem. sch. dist. dress and discipline code com., 1977-79. Mem., Bernville Borough Council, 1976—; treas. Berks County Boroughs Assn., 1977—. Mem. Reading Edn. Assn., Pa. Edn. Assn., NEA, AAUW, Berks County Boroughs Assn., NAACP, LWV, Delta Sigma Theta. Democrat. United Ch. Christ. Clubs: Bernville Woman's (pres. 1978-80), GNO of Harrisburg. Office: Reading Sch Dist 8th and Washington Sts Reading PA 19602

WATTS, NELL JACKSON, assn. exec.; b. Detroit; d. Norman Smith and Lillie (Adams) Jackson; B.S., Ind. U., 1953, M.S., 1956; m. Leslie J. Watts, Sept. 5, 1953; children—Cynthia, Anita. Mem. faculty Good Samaritan Hosp. Nursing Sch., Lexington, Ky., 1950-52; nurse Louisville VA Hosp., 1953-55; asst. prof. Ind. U. Sch. Nursing, Indpls., 1955-62; exec. dir. Ind. League Nursing, Indpls., 1967-74, editor newsletter Interaction, 1968-73, bd. dirs., 1962-65; exec. officer Sigma Theta Tau, nat. honor nursing soc., Indpls., 1974—, mem. bd. Alpha chpt., 1957-59; mng. editor jour. Image, 1975-78, editor newsletter Reflections, 1975-78; bd. dirs. Ind. chpt. Am. Lung Assn., 1978—. Named Ind. Nurse of Year, Allstate Found. and Ind. Citizens League Nursing, 1975; recipient Disting. Alumni award Ind. U. Sch. Nursing, 1976. Mem. Am. Nurses Assn., Nat. League Nursing, Ind. U. Alumni Assn., Pi Lambda Theta, Sigma Theta Tau. Club: Ind. U. Women's. Home: 6926 Dover Rd Indianapolis IN 46220 Office: 1100 W Michigan St Indianapolis IN 46223

WAUGH, ELIZABETH ANN, social worker; b. Houston, Feb. 6, 1940; d. B. Eugene and Ruth Duffield Parker; B.A. in Biol. Scis., Tex. Woman's U., 1961; M.Ed. in Guidance and Counseling, U. Houston, 1970. Biochemistry technician Southwest Med. Sch., Dallas, 1961-62; bacteriologist Alcon Labs., Ft. Worth, 1962-63; bacteriologist Terrell Lab., Ft. Worth, 1964; employment counselor Employment Commn. State of Tex., San Angelo, Houston and Big Spring, 1964-76; project adminstr. Harris County Psychol. Hosp., 1974-75; supr. emergency social services Ben Taub Gen. Hosp., Houston, 1973-79; pvt. practice social work, Houston, 1975—; field instr. U. Houston, 1977-79. Mem. Nat. Acad. Cert. Clin. Mental Health Counselors, Nat. Assn. Social Workers, Am. Personnel and Guidance Assn., Nat. Vocat. Guidance Assn., Assn. Measurement and Evaluation, Assn. Specialists in Group Work, Am. Mental Health Counselors Assn., Mensa. Office: 2708 Weslayan St 12 Houston TX 77027

WAUGH, JUDITH RITCHIE, broadcaster; b. Indpls., June 5, 1939; d. Wallace Norris and Louise Hern (Green) W.; B.A., Ind. U., 1961, M.A., 1969; John Hay fellow, Northwestern U., 1964-65. Tchr. English and humanities John Marshall High Sch., Indpls., 1969-73, Crispus Attucks High Sch., 1961-69; dir. public affairs McGraw-Hill Broadcasting Co., Inc., WRTV6, Indpls., 1973—; vis. prof. Nat. Urban League Black Exec. Exchange Program. Life mem. NAACP; bd. dirs. YWCA, 1974-80, Urban League, 1973—, Ind. Repertory Theatre, 1979—, Met. Arts Council, Indpls. Ballet Theater; mem. women's com. Ind. Symphony, 1976—. NDEA grantee, 1966; Lilly grantee, 1967. Mem. Nat. Broadcast Assn. Community Affairs, Nat. Council Negro Women, Coalition of 100 Black Women (chmn. arts/culture com.), Indpls. Links (pres.). Democrat. Unitarian. Home: 3965 N Meridian St 3F Indianapolis IN 46208 Office: 1330 N Meridian St Indianapolis IN 46206

WAX, ROSALIE HANKEY, anthropologist, educator; b. Des Plaines, Ill., Nov. 4, 1911; d. Richard B. and Anna (Orb) Hankey; B.A. in Anthropology, U. Calif., Berkeley, 1942; Ph.D., U. Chgo., 1950; m. Murray L. Wax, Mar. 5, 1949. Chmn., Social Scis. II Coll., U. Chgo., 1956, examiner, 1947-55; acad. teaching asst. anthropology, 1946-47, instr. social scis., 1947-49, asst. prof., 1950-57; dir. Workshop on Am. Indian Affairs U. Colo., 1959-69; research assoc. Ogala Sioux Ednl. Research Project Emory U., 1962-64; assoc. prof. U. Kans., 1964-69, prof., 1970-73, assoc. dir. Indian Edn. Research Project, 1966-69; prof. dept. anthropology and sociology Washington U., St. Louis, 1973—; vis. lectr. U. Miami, 1959-62. Rockefeller Found. Humanities fellow, 1981-82; grantee in field. Fellow Am. Anthrop. Assn., AAAS (councilor 1973-74), Soc. Study Social Problems; mem. Am. Ethnol. Soc., Central States Anthrop. Soc., Soc. Applied Anthropology. Author: Magic, Fate and History: The Changing Ethos of the Vikings, 1969. Office: Dept Anthropology Washington U Saint Louis MO 63130

WAXMAN, MARGERY HOPE, lawyer; b. N.Y.C., Oct. 21, 1942; d. Lee and Florence (Jackel) W.; A.B., Smith Coll., 1964; J.D. with honors, George Washington U., 1967; m. Willard H. Mitchell, Apr. 4, 1982. Admitted to D.C. bar, 1968, U.S. Supreme Ct. bar, 1971; law clk. Honorable Spottswood W. Robinson III, U.S. Ct. Appeals for D.C. Circuit, 1967-68; asso. firm Covington & Burling, 1968-72; asst. gen. counsel Office Consumer Affairs, 1972-73; asso., dept. gen. counsel Cost of Living Council, 1973-74; exec. asst. to chmn. FTC, 1975, asst. dir., dep. dir., acting dir. Bur. of Consumer Protection, FTC, 1976-77, exec. dir. FTC, 1977-79; gen. counsel Office of Personnel Mgmt., Washington, 1979-81; dep. gen. counsel Dept. Treasury, 1981—. Recipient Sr. Exec. Service Meritorious Rank award, 1980. Mem. D.C. Bar, Adminstrv. Conf. U.S. (chmn. com. on. pub. access and info.), Am. Bar Assn. (chmn. spl. com. on lawyers in govt. 1982-83). Office: United States Treasury Department Washington DC 20220

WAYMIRE, ROBERTA ARLENE, constrn. co. exec.; b. Wimbledon, N.D., June 20, 1936; d. Gaylord and Huldah Evelyn (Ekstrand) Thorne; student Brigham Young U., 1953-54; m. Kenneth L. Waymire, Feb. 26, 1955; children—Thorne L., Kent L. Reporter, Democrat Herald, Albany, Oreg., 1955-56; with Waverly Constrn. Co., Inc., Hubbard, Oreg., 1964—, v.p., 1982—. Mem. Portland Metro Homebuilders Assn.

Republican. Home and office: 11903 Broadacres Rd NE Hubbard OR 97032

WAYNE, JANE ELLEN, mfg. co. exec.; b. Phila., Apr. 6, 1936; d. Jesse Allen and Eleanor Mae (Brundle) Stump; student Grove City Coll., 1956, N.Y. U., 1956, Am. Acad. Dramatic Arts, 1957; m. Ronald R. Wayne, May 26, 1958 (div. 1967); 1 dau., Elizabeth Jo. Mem. promotion staff NBC, N.Y.C., 1957-65; mgr. V.I.P. div. N.Y. World's Fair, 1966; v.p. Abbot & Abbot Corp., wood mfrs., N.Y.C., 1974—; creator Beauty and Poise pvt. classes for bus. women, 1963-66. Mem. Sigma Delta Phi. Republican. Author: The Life of Robert Taylor, 1977; Kings of Tragedy, 1977; Tiffany, 1979; Lividia, 1979; The Love Gap, 1979; Kings of Tragedy II, 1982. Contbr. to Nat. Enquirer, Harvey Mag. Home: 223-09 56th Rd Bayside NY 11364

WAYNE, MARGARET ANN, social worker; b. St. Louis, Oct. 4, 1943; d. Archie Lee and Margaret (Montgomery) Wayne; A.B., Washington U., St. Louis, 1965, M.S.W., 1967. Social worker Dept. Social Work, Dept. Health and Hosps., St. Louis, 1965-74; social worker Health div., St. Louis, 1977; instr. Sch. Social Service, St. Louis U., 1978-80; dir. dept. social service Meml. Hosp., Belleville, Ill., 1980—. VA Doctoral Tng. grantee, 1974-77. Mem. Nat. Assn. Social Workers (dir. 1978—, George Warren Brown Sch. Social Work Alumni Assn. (pres., dir. 1977), Acad. Cert. Social Workers, Am. Public Health Assn., Am. Hosp. Assn., Soc. Hosp. Social Work Dirs. Home: 4119 Magnolia Ave Apt 3 Saint Louis MO 63110 Office: 450 N Park Dr Belleville IL 62223

WAYNE, SUSAN, criminal justice agy. adminstr.; b. Wilkes-Barre, Pa., Mar. 16, 1942; d. Samuel S. and Esther (Bohorad) W.; A.B., Bryn Mawr Coll.; M.S.W. (Pa. Lung Assn. fellow), Temple U. Dep. commr. Mass. Dept. Community Affairs, 1972-73; asso. area dir. Dept. Mental Health, Boston, 1973-74; dir. spl. programs Middlesex County Hosp., Waltham, Mass., 1974-76; dep. commr. Mass. Dept. Youth Services, 1976-79; exec. dir. Justice Resource Inst., Boston, 1979—; mgmt. cons. social service agys. Bd. dirs., officer Council Human Services; active Beacon Hill Civic Assn. Mem. Nat. Assn. Social Workers, Nat. Assn. Social Welfare. Office: 530 Atlantic St Boston MA 02210

WEADOCK, LOUISE WEEKS, health manpower supply co. exec.; b. Greenwich, Conn., May 5, 1952; d. John Cullen and Sewall Boardman (Weeks) Weadock; B.S. in Nursing, Cath. U. Am., 1974; M.P.H., Johns Hopkins U., 1979. Clin. coordinator and head nurse Forbush Children's Center, Sheppard Pratt Hosp., Balt., 1976-78; dir. nursing Kimberly Nurses div., 1979-81; regional mgr. Nat. Med. Cons., N.Y.C., 1981, v.p. sales and ops., Overland Park, Kans., 1981—. Named top nat. saleswoman, 1980, 81. Mem. Am. Nurses Assn., Assn. for Exec. Females, Jr. League N.Y. Democrat. Roman Catholic. Clubs: L'Hirondelle Country, First Avenue Squash. Home: 400 E 71st St Apt 11-K New York NY 10021 Office: 8500 W 110th St Suite 600 Overland Park KS 66201

WEAR, THERESA SUTTER, ins. co. exec.; b. Birmingham, Ala., July 15, 1938; d. Paul Allen and Charlotte (Burns) Sutter; B.S. in Edn., U. Ala., Birmingham, 1980; children—Richard Lee, Terri Lynn. Office mgr. Edmiston & McGhin, C.P.A.s, St. Augustine, Fla., 1967-71; public stenographer, 1971-74; cons. in word processing mgmt., 1974—; adminstrv. officer word processing Liberty Nat. Life Ins. Co., Birmingham, 1974—; owner Mgmt. Services, Cons., Birmingham, 1979—. Mem. bus. edn. adv. com. Jefferson County Bd. Edn., 1979—, City of Birmingham Bd. Edn., 1979-82. Cert. Profl. Sec., Adminstrv. Mgr. Mem. Internat. Info., Word Processing Assn., Nat. Assn. Female Execs., Adminstrv. Mgmt. Soc., Profl. Secs. Internat. Methodist. Author: TypeWriter to TypeSetter, 1981; mus. compositions include My Special Friend, 1977, Aloha, Hawaii, Mahalo, 1979, There's No Friend Like An Old Friend, 1980. Home: 811 Golden Crest Circle Birmingham AL 35209 Office: 2001 3d Ave S PO Box 2612 Birmingham AL 35202

WEATHERFORD, SYLVIA, elec. engr.; b. Los Angeles, Dec. 2, 1951; d. James Emmett and Berniece W.; B.S.E.E., M.I.T., 1974; M.S.E.E., U. So. Calif., 1975; postgrad. Loyola-Marymount. Engring. instr. Howard U., Washington, 1975-76; digital design engr. Hughes Aircraft, Culver City, Calif., 1973-75; mgr. engring. projects office Xerox, El Segundo, Calif., 1976—. Bd. dirs. Ebonics, v.p., 1982-83. Hughes fellow, 1973-75; Delta Sigma Theta scholar, 1967-73. Mem. Los Angeles Council Black Profl. Engrs. (pres. 1980-82), IEEE, Black Women's Forum, Los Angeles Leadership Coalition. Office: 701 S Aviation Blvd M/S Ni-ol El Segundo CA 90245 *

WEATHERHOLTZ, JOAN HUTTER, educator; b. Moorefield, W.Va., Nov. 10, 1933; d. Adolphus Gottlieb and Velma K. (Woerner) Hutter; A.A., Potomac State Coll., 1954; B.S., W.Va. U., 1954-56; M.Ed., U. Md., 1966; m. Clyde M. Weatherholtz, June 9, 1956. Tchr., Howard County High Sch., Ellicott City, Md., 1956-62; supr. Howard County Bd. Edn., 1962-74; specialist food and nutrition programs Md. State Dept. Edn., Balt., 1974-78, chief food and nutrition programs, 1978—. Sec. Atholton Community Assn., 1964-67. Mem. Am. Sch. Food Service Assn., Am. Home Econs. Assn. (mem. nominating com.), Am. Vocat. Assn., Md. Sch. Food Service Assn. (advisor 1978—), Md. Home Econs. Assn. (pres. 1975-76), Md. Vocat. Assn. (pres. 1969-70), Home Econs. Edn. Assn., Delta Kappa Gamma. Democrat. Presbyterian. Home: 10184 Owen Brown Rd Columbia MD 21044 Office: 200 W Baltimore St Baltimore MD 21201

WEATHERS, MARGARET ALICE, restaurateur; b. Forest City, Ark., Feb. 9, 1922; d. Oscar Russell and Lillie Addlaid (Bass) Allamn; student Lincoln U. Mo., 1937-39, Miss. Indsl. Coll., 1939-40, Western Res. U., 1964-65; B.A., Capital U., 1980; m. Ernest A. Weathers, Jan. 29, 1951; 1 dau., Margaret Kathryn. Tchr., counselor, social service agy. exec., bus. services and mgmt., leadership edn. devel.; now co-owner, mgr. Weathers House of Food, Cleve. Mem. Republican City Com.; trustee Hough Multi Service Center; Christian Meth. Episcopal Ch. rep. Cleve. Inner Ch. Council, 1973—; field coordinator Lake Erie council Girl Scouts U.S.A., mem. commn. health concerns; mem. childrens work dept. Ohio Conf. Christian Meth. Episcopalian Ch., Cleve. Pitts. Dist. Recipient Achievement award U.S. Congress, Congratulatory award City of Cleve. Mem. NAACP. Home: 1610 Ansel Rd Cleveland OH 44106 Office: 1001 Huron Rd Cleveland OH 44115

WEAVER, BARBARA FRANCES, librarian; b. Boston, Aug. 29, 1927; d. Leo Francis and Nina Margaret (Durham) Weisse; B.A., Radcliffe Coll., 1949; M.L.S., U. R.I., 1968; M.Ed., Boston U., 1978; m. George Briggs Weaver, June 6, 1951 (dec. 1970); 1 dau., Valerie Susan. Tech. writer EG&G, Inc., Boston, 1951-59; head librarian Thompson (Conn.) Public Library, 1961-69; dir. Conn. State Library Service Center, Willimantic, 1969-72, regional adminstr. Central Mass. Regional Library System, Worcester, 1972-78; state librarian N.J. State Library, Trenton, 1978—; library cons., 1975—; pres. Val-A, Inc., Thompson, Conn., 1980—. Mem. ALA, N.J. Library Assn., Aircraft Owners and Pilots Assn. Office: New Jersey State Library 185 W State St Trenton NJ 08625

WEAVER, GLADYS PEARL, vocat. rehab. counselor; b. Sangerville, Maine, Dec. 26, 1922; d. Adelbert Valdessa and Alice Marjery (Kneeland) Bradeen; Asso. Sci., Blinn Coll., 1961; B.A., U. Tex., 1965; M.S., Okla. State U., 1967; m. James Andrew Weaver, Jr., Apr. 15, 1972; 1 dau., Sandra Faye. Sec., Army Exchange Camp Drum, N.Y., 1955; sr. vol. U.S.O. Service Club, Ayer, Mass., 1955-56; psychiat. nurse technician Austin (Tex.) State Hosp., 1959-62; eye med. social worker Blind Commn., Austin, 1965; vocat. rehab. counselor Tex. Rehab. Commn., Victoria, 1966—. Bd. dirs. Head Start, 1975-76. HEW grantee, 1965. Mem. Am. Bus. Women's Assn. (mem. adv. com. sr. citizens 1973-75), Nat. Rehab. Assn., Tex. Public Employees Assn., Tex. Rehab. Assn., Tex. Rehab. Counseling Assn., Ex-Students Assn. U. Tex., Okla. State U. Alumni Assn., Am. Profl. and Bus. Women's Assn. Club: Soroptomist (pres. 1976-77) (Victoria, Tex.). Home: 2702 College Dr Victoria TX 77901 Office: 2002-C Commerce St Victoria TX 77901

WEAVER, GLENDA ROSE, nurse; b. Liberty, Tex., Jan. 2, 1944; d. Glenn Wood and Esther Augusta (Becker) W.; student Lamar U., 1961-62; diploma Hotel Dieu Sch. Nursing, 1963. Supr., Kersting Meml. Hosp., Liberty, Tex., 1963-65; sch. nurse Liberty Ind. Sch. Dist., 1965-71; dir. nursing service Chambers Meml. Hosp., Anahuac, Tex., 1971-76; asst. dir. nursing service North Shore Med. Plaza, Houston, 1976-78; dir. nursing service Kelsey-Seybold Clinic, Houston, 1978-82; nurse specialist-adminstrn. Baylor U. Coll. Medicine, Houston, 1982—. Mem. Tex. Hosp. Assn.-Nursing Service Adminstrs., ARC (past county first aid chmn. and disaster nurse chmn.). Methodist. Home: Box 467 Liberty TX 77575 Office: 1200 Moursund Suite 185A Houston TX 77030

WEAVER, JENNIE FAUN, educator, editor; b. Gaston, Ind., Oct. 11, 1901; d. William Hillis and Fannie (Johnson) Cox; B.A., Ind. U., 1923, M.S., 1955; m. Oran L. Weaver, Dec. 23, 1934 (div. 1957); children—Linda Lee Weaver Hays, Susan Jane Weaver Pleasant. Tchr., Eaton (Ind.) High Sch., 1929-35, Marion (Ind.) High Sch., 1949-53, Pendleton High Sch., S. Madison Community Schs., Pendleton, Ind., 1953-69; asst. reference librarian Anderson (Ind.) Pub. Library, 1969-73; newsletter editor Ind. Artists-Craftsmen, 1975—. Mem. Women in Communications, Ind. Artists-Craftsmen, Nat., Ind. ret. tchrs. assns., St. Vincent's Hosp. Guild, Theta Sigma Phi, Pi Beta Phi. Methodist. Club: Ind. U. Women's. Home: 1952 D Canary Ct Indianapolis IN 46260

WEAVER, L. RUTH RUNDLE (MRS. C.H. WEAVER), lawyer; b. St. Joseph, Mo.; d. Charles Vail and Anna (Wist) Rundle; B.A., Nebr. State Tchrs. Coll., 1923; J.D., Akron Law Sch., 1955; m. Clyde Hulbert Weaver, Feb. 28, 1931 (dec. June 1951). Tchr. Chase County High Sch., Imperial, Nebr., 1923-24, Biwabik (Minn.) High Sch., 1924-25, Child High Sch., Edgerton, Wis., 1925-28, Central High Sch., Akron, Ohio, 1928-30; supr. personnel record sect. Goodyear Tire and Rubber Co., Akron, 1942-47; teller Evans Savs. Assn., Akron, 1951-56; admitted to Ohio bar, 1956, practiced in Akron. Mem. adv. com. Coll. Law, Akron U.; mem. Stan Hywet Hall Found., Akron Mus. Art. Named Woman of Year, Summit chpt. Am. Bus. Women's Assn., 1961. Mem. Am. Judicature Soc. Fedn. Women's Clubs, Am. Trial Lawyers Assn., ABA (com. estate and gift tax 1962—, family com. of gen. practice sect. 1974-75), Ohio, Akron (chmn. speakers bur. com. 1958-61, 65-67, probate court com. 1967-68, mem. ethics com., inquiry com. 1967-76, chmn. necrology com. 1973-76) bar assns., Cuyahoga Falls LWV, Am. Bus. Women's Assn., Nat. Trust for Hist. Preservation, Western Res. Hist. Soc., Akron Dist. Golf Assn., (tournament chmn. 1939-41, pres. 1941-49), Phi Delta Delta (pres. Beta Xi chpt. 1969-70). Clubs: Quota (chmn. community service 1964-65), Akron Woman's City (1st vice chmn. six-thirty sect. 1967-68), Business Women's Current Events (1st v.p. 1959, pres. 1964-66).

WEAVER, RITA MARGARET, assn. exec.; b. N.Y.C., Oct. 28, 1925; d. Newcomb and Lucy Elizabeth (Roche) Gaylord; B.A., N.Y. U., 1945; postgrad Lady Margaret Hall, Oxford (Eng.) U., 1945-46; m. Robert A. Weaver (dec.); children—Richard L.N., Michael Cameron. Concert pianist, 1940; reporter Nuremberg trials, 1946-48; syndicated columnist Fashions from New York, Escort Publs., London, 1949-51; actress, Off Broadway productions and summer stock, 1952-56; pres. Empire State chpt. Nat. Soc. Arts and Letters, N.Y.C., 1978-80, chmn. ballet career awards conv., 1980, v.p. and chmn. lit. career awards dinner and music career awards dinner, 1980-82; chmn. ways and means Eleanor Gay Lee Gallery Found., N.Y.C., 1977, membership chmn., 1978-80, chmn. benefit com., 1981-82. Methodist.

WEAVER, ROSE SHARON, tech. researcher; b. Oak Ridge, Tenn.; B.S. in Sociology and Psychology, Berea Coll., 1975; postgrad. U. Tenn., 1976-78. Tech. asst. tech. info. ctr. Dept. Energy, Oak Ridge, 1971-75; part time instr. Multi Service Assn., Scarboro Study Hall, 1973-74, dir., adv., 1973-74; tech. researcher Union Carbide Corp., Oak Ridge Nat. Lab., 1975—. Historian Anderson County Democratic Women; del. Mid-Yr. Dem. Nat. Conv., Phila., organizer, leader troop Tanasi Council Girl Scouts U.S.A.; chairperson community devel. com. NAACP, treas., trustee, youth adv., pianist Spurgeon Chapel A.M.E. Zion Ch., del. to confs., 1975-78; phys. fitness aerobics and dancercise instr., 1981—; bd. dirs., exec. mem. YWCA, Oak Ridge, 1980—. Named Outstanding Woman in Oak Ridge Community, 1981. Mem. Assn. Am. Geographers (dir. energy specialty group), AAAS, Am. Sociol. Assn., Am. Soc. Info. Sci., Am. Poet Soc. Author articles, reports in field. Home: 115 Bethune Circle Oak Ridge TN 37830 Office: Union Carbide Corp Oak Ridge Nat Lab Oak Ridge TN 37830

WEBB, BERNICE LARSON, educator; b. Ludell, Kans.; d. Carl Godfred and Ida Genevieve (Tongish) Larson; A.B., U. Kans., Lawrence, 1956, M.A., 1957, Ph.D., 1961; postgrad. (scholar), U. Aberdeen, Scotland, 1950-60; m. Robert MacHardy Webb, July 14, 1961; children—William Carl Schear, Rebecca Rae Schear Gentry. Asst. instr. English U. Kans., 1958-59, 60-61; asst. prof. U. Southwestern La., Lafayette, 1961-67, asso. prof., 1967-80, prof., 1980—, dir. grad. seminars NDEA Inst. Intellectual & Cultural History of U.S., summer 1966, coordinator Poetry in the Schs., 1974, acting dir. English Reading-Writing Lab., summers 1977, 78, 79; vis. asso. prof. World Campus Afloat, 1972; actor Playwrights Theater of La., 1978—. Outdoor leader troop Bayou council Girls Scouts Am., 1962-64, editor newsletter, 1964-66. Recipient numerous awards for writing. Mem. MLA, Coll. English Assn., Am. Folklore Soc., Nat. Fedn. State Poetry Socs., Inc., South Central Modern Lang. Assn., South Central Coll. English Assn., La. Folklore Soc., La. Assn. Post Secondary Lang. Arts, La. State Poetry Soc. (pres. 1978-79, 81—), Southwest La. Poetry Soc. (treas. 1975—), AAUW (state div. editor 1967-71), Deep South Writers Conf., Inc. (dir. 1979—), Popular Culture Assn. (book reviewer 1980—), Am. Culture Assn. (book reviewer 1980—), Phi Beta Kappa (pres. Southwestern La. assn. 1976-77, v.p. 1975-76, 82—). Roman Catholic. Author: The Basketball Man: James Naismith, 1973; Beware of Ostriches, 1978; Poetry on the Stage: William Poel, Producer of Verse Drama, 1979, Thursday Verse, 1982; editor: La. Poets, 1970—; contbr. poems, short stories, articles. Home: 159 Whittington Dr Lafayette LA 70503 Office: University of Southwestern Louisiana Lafayette LA 70504

WEBB, FAYE MUELLER, nurse; b. Grand Junction, Colo., Dec. 29, 1918; d. Edward Louis and Florence Amanda (Phillips) Mueller; R.N., Washington U., St. Louis, 1941; postgrad. U. Calif., Riverside, 1971, Chapman Coll., 1974, Riverside City Coll., 1976, Calif. State Coll., San Bernadino, 1982; m. Charles Robert Webb, Apr. 19, 1941 (dec.); children—Charles Robert, Tony Kirk. Dir. nursing Beverly Manor Enterprises, Redlands, Calif., 1963-75, Hill Haven Health Care, Highland, Calif., 1975-76, Heritage Gardens, Inc. (Olivewood Convelescent Home), Colton, Calif., 1979—. Mem. Council Long Term Care Nurses Calif., Calif. Assn. Regional Occupational Centers and Programs, Nat. League Nurses. Republican. Mormon. Office: 23185 Washington St Colton CA 92324

WEBB, JANIS LEE, banker; b. Dumas, Tex., July 27, 1941; d. William Lee and Frances Inez (Tidwell) W.; student Draughons Bus. Coll., Amarillo, Tex., 1960-61; divorced. Various clerical and bookkeeping positions, 1961-62, with First Nat. Bank, Dumas, 1962—, asst. v.p. installment loan dept., 1962—; seminar leader, 1980—. Co-chmn. bd. dirs. Moore County Art Assn.; mem. Dumas Sr. High Sch. Bd. Spl. Adult Edn. Mem. Nat. Assn. Bank Women, Bus. and Profl. Women's Club, Dumas C. of C. Republican. Lutheran. Office: PO Box 1117 500 Main St Dumas TX 79029

WEBB, KAREN BOYER, speech pathologist; b. Arco, Idaho, May 25, 1942; d. Ira Wayne and Elsie Bertha (Pieper) Boyer; B.S., Utah State U., 1960, M.S., 1965; 1 son, Kevin Michael. Speech therapist Cache County (Utah) Sch. Dist., 1964-65; speech pathologist N.Y. Eye and Ear Infirmary, N.Y.C., 1965-67; speech pathologist Eastchester (N.Y.) Sch. Dist. 2, 1967-68; tchr. Centro Venezolano Americano, Caracas, Venezuela, 1968-71; sr. speech clinician N.Y. League for Hard of Hearing, N.Y.C., 1972-76; pvt. practice speech pathology, N.Y.C., 1976—; dir. deaf infant program St. Francis de Sales Sch. for Deaf, 1977—. Robert Shaw fellow, 1963. Mem. Am. Speech-Lang. and Hearing Assn.

WEBB, LINDA IRENE, home economist; b. Caldwell, Idaho, Sept. 9, 1948; d. Earl Leroy and Stella Mae (Ireland) Ward; B.S. U. Idaho, 1971; m. Garry Robert Webb, Dec. 28, 1966; children—David, Debra, Brenda. Tchr. home econs. Bonners Ferry (Idaho) High Sch., 1971-75; day care mgr. Gingerbread House Day Care Center, Cascade, Idaho, 1977; substitute tchr. Cascade High Sch., 1977-78; extension home economist U. Idaho Coop. Extension Service, 1978—. Pres. Cascade PTA, 1981-82; Sunday sch. supr. Community Christian Ch., Cascade, 1978, deaconess, 1980; former 4-H leader. Mem. Am. Home Econs. Assn., Nat. Assn. Extension 4-H Agts., AAUW, Idaho Home Econs. Assn., Idaho Extension Home Econs. Assn., Idaho 4-H Agts. Assn., Phi Upsilon Omicron. Club: Order Eastern Star (past matron). Home: Box 734 Cascade ID 83611 Office: Box 337 Donnelly ID 83615

WEBB, NANCY ELIZABETH RUNDQUIST, ophthalmologist; b. Chgo., Oct. 24, 1948; d. Ragnar Arthur and Dorothy Elizabeth (Anderson) Rundquist; B.A., U. Tex., 1970; M.D. with high honors, Baylor Coll. Medicine, 1974; m. David F. Webb, Dec. 17, 1971; children—Elizabeth Lauren, Alexander David. Asst. prof. ophthalmology Baylor Coll., 1979-82; asst. chief ophthalmology VA Hosp., Houston, 1979-82; chief ophthalmology Kelsey-Seybold Clinic P.A., 1981-82; cons. in field. Mem. Southgate Civic Club, ACLU, Am. Acad. Ophthalmology, AMA, Houston Ophthalmol. Soc., Internat. Assn. Ocular Surgeons, Phi Beta Kappa, Alpha Omega Alpha, Phi Chi, Delta Gamma. Home: 2168 Swift St Houston TX 77030 Office: 6624 Fannin Houston TX 77030

WEBB, VIRGINIA RUTH, tech. writer/editor; b. Maryville, Tenn., Sept. 28, 1955; d. Eugene Leslie and Ruth Lillian (Freeman) Webb; B.A. in English magna cum laude, U. Tenn., 1977, M.A. in English, 1979. Asst. dir. engring. central services Washington U., St. Louis, 1979-81; tech. writer/editor Action Data Services Control Data Corp., St. Louis, 1981—. Mem. South Atlantic Modern Lang. Assn., SE Conf. Linguistics, Phi Beta Kappa, Phi Kappa Phi, Alpha Lambda Delta. Home: 7334 Forsyth #102 St Louis MO 63105 Office: 7822 Bonhomme St Clayton MO 63105

WEBB, WILMA, state legislator; b. Denver, May 17, 1943; d. Frank W. and Faye Elizabeth (Wyatt) Gerdine; student Central Bus. Coll., 1962, U. Colo., 1970-78; m. Wellington E. Webb, Sept. 18; children—Keith, Stephanie, Anthony, Allen. Former exec. sec., adminstrv. asst. Mobil Oil Corp., Denver; adminstrv. asst. Colo. Minority Bus. Devel. Agy., 1979; adminstrv. assoc. United Bank of Denver, 1980; mem. Colo. Ho. of Reps., 1980—; dir. Matrix Multi-Media Corp. Chmn. Colo. Caucus of Black Elected Ofcls., Colo. Black Caucus; bd. dirs. St. Joseph Hosp., N.E. Denver Youth Services; vice chmn. Black United Legal Def. Fund; mem. NAACP, Urban League Met. Denver, People United To Save Humanity. Recipient community service award Urban League Met. Denver. Mem. Colo. Black Women for Polit. Action. Democrat. Baptist.

WEBBER, PAMELA CLARK, constrn. scheduling co. exec.; b. Ft. Hood, Tex., Apr. 20, 1947; d. John Lanham and Alice Paula (Collier) Clark; student Radford Coll., 1965-68; m. David L. Webber, Sept. 24, 1976; 1 dau., Stacey Michele. Civil engring. technician with various cons. engrs., 1969-75; critical path method tech. adviser Winn & Assos., Richardson, Tex., 1974-75; v.p., sec.-treas. DLW Infosystems, Inc., Richardson, 1975—. Mem. Beta Sigma Phi (sec. 1973). Republican. Episcopalian. Office: 1216 Executive Dr W Richardson TX 75081

WEBBINK, PATRICIA GLIXON, psychologist; b. N.Y.C., Feb. 13, 1943; d. S. Arthur and Jane (Amberg) Glixon; B.A., Conn. Coll., 1965; M.A., Duke U., 1970, Ph.D., 1974. Asst. dir. Dept. Recreation Day Camp, Washington, 1963; research asst., infant evaluator Edn. Improvement Project, Durham, N.C., 1965-66, 68; organizer Prince Georges County (Md.) Free Clinic, 1970-71; psychologist Prince Georges County Health Dept., Cheverly, 1970-71; pvt. practice psychotherapy, Bethesda, Md., 1971—; mem. faculty U. Md., 1973, 78, Am. U., 1976, George Washington U., 1977. Bd. dirs. Growing Women, Inc., 1979-80. USPHS fellow, 1967-69, stipend, 1969-70; lic. psychologist, Md., D.C. N.C.; Mem. Am. Psychol. Assn. (participant confs. 1977-79), Md. Psychol. Assn., D.C. Psychol. Assn., Assn. Women in Psychology, Assn. Feminist Therapists, Am. Soc. Psychologists in Pvt. Practice, Internat. Platform Assn. Office: 6109 Broad St Bethesda MD 20816

WEBER, CATHERINE LYNN, nurse; b. Chgo., Apr. 29, 1955; d. Richard and Lois (Seeling) W.; B.S.N. with honors, U. Ill., 1977. Staff nurse orthopedic and rehab. unit Grant Hosp., Chgo., 1977-79, cardipulmonary rehab. unit, 1979-81, asst. head nurse rehab. unit, 1981-82, head nurse, 1982—. Registered nurse. Mem. Am. Nurses Assn., Am. Red Cross Vols., Sigma Theta Tau. Lutheran. Home: 3121 N Elston Ave Chicago IL 60618 Office: 550 Webster St Chicago IL 60614

WEBER, DARLENE, restaurant exec.; b. Milw., Jan. 5, 1930; d. Bert B. and Blanche (Corne) Harvey; student public schs., also specialized courses; m. Kurt Weber, Aug. 16, 1964; children—Kim, Jay, Kurt. Engaged in restaurant bus., 1948—; owner-mgr. White Tablecloth Restaurant, Cedarburg, Wis., 1966-69; pres., mgr. The Nantucket, Mequon, Wis., 1969-79; owner, mgr., corp. v.p. Nantucket Shores Restaurant, Milw., 1973—. Regional dir. Milw. Crusade, 1979; mem. council Christ Luth. Ch., Mequon, 1979. Mem. Wis. Restaurant Assn. (dir., v.p. Milw. chpt. 1982), Tempo. Club: Mequon Racquet.

WEBER, HARRIETTE B. SKLADD, bus. exec., real estate broker, appraiser; b. Detroit; d. Alexander and Victoria (Lesnik) Skladd; student Wayne U., 1937-39, U. Mich., 1950-52; m. E. George Weber (dec.). Real estate broker H. B. Weber, Realtor, Detroit, 1953—; fee appraiser, per diem appraiser FHA, Detroit, 1958—; builder. Mem. Detroit Real Estate Bd., Nat. Assn. Real Estate Bds., Internat. Platform Assn., Founders Soc. Detroit, Inst. Arts. Club: Detroit Yacht. Inventor beaute specs, turkey jackets. Home: 18230 Ten Mile Rd East Detroit MI 48021 Office: 14427 E Seven Mile Rd Detroit MI 48205

WEBER, JILL SUSAN, architect; b. Newark, Apr. 5, 1939; d. Alfred M. and Beatrice (Hartman) Weber; B.S., Cornell U., 1960; M.Arch., SUNY, Buffalo, 1980; children—Jennifer, James. Arts editor Info. Services, SUNY, Buffalo, 1971-76; designer Stievater & Czaja, Architects, Buffalo, 1980-81; public relations coordinator, archtl. designer Robert Traynham Coles, Architects, Buffalo, 1981—; archtl. critic/contbg. writer Buffalo News, 1978—, Progressive Architecture, 1979—. Mem. Soc. Archtl. Historians. Democrat. Contbr. articles to profl. jours. Home: 140 Brantwood Rd Snyder NY 14226 Office: 730 Ellicott Sq Buffalo NY 14203

WEBER, JUDITH ANN, nutrition and food mktg. specialist; b. Milw., June 19, 1944; d. William L. and Ruth Barbara (Leon) W.; B.S. with honors, U. Wis., Madison, 1966; postgrad. Mpls. Sch. Design, 1966-67. Home economist Pillsbury Co., Mpls., 1966-68; head Martha Logan Food Info. Service, mgr. publicity Martha Logan Kitchens, Swift & Co., Chgo., 1968-69; dir. food info. service, asst. to dir. food service systems Pronto Food Corp., Chgo., 1969-72; group products mgr. Infra-Red Foods, Chgo., 1972-74; cons. dietitian Wico Corp., Niles, Ill., 1973-74; group products mgr. nutrition products, Midwest rep. Seabrook Farms, Finer Foods, Inc., Chgo., 1974-76; editor Woman mag. Perkins & Co., Inc., Chgo., 1975-76; prin. Judith A. Weber Creative Services, Chgo., 1976-79, owner, Oak Park, Ill., 1981—; owner J.W. Designs, jewelry design and mfg., 1974—; nutrition info. specialist Nat. Dairy Council, Rosemont, Ill., 1979-81. Mem. Home Economists in Bus., Am. Home Econs. Assn., Restaurant Women's Club of Chgo., Women's Advt. Club of Chgo., Phi Kappa Phi, Omicron Nu, Phi Upsilon Omicron, Sigma Epsilon Sigma.

WEBER, LORETTA ANNE, fin. exec.; b. San Francisco, Mar. 25, 1945; d. Bernard Thomas and Esther Margretta (Hedman) Graham; student U. Fla., 1963-67; m. Ronald William Weber, Sept. 2, 1967. Office mgr. Rivkin/Carson, Washington, 1968-69; officer mgr. PADCO, Inc., Washington, 1969-72, adminstrv. officer, 1976-78; adminstrv. officer Nat. Assn. Coll. and Univ. Bus. Officers, Washington, 1972-74, Mid-Atlantic Research Inst., Bethesda, Md., 1974-76; dir., sec.-treas. Center for Internat. Tng. and Research in Urban Devel., Washington, 1978-80; dir. fin. Kendrick & Co., Washington, 1980-82; fin. officer Epis. Ctr. for Children, 1982—. Mem. Nat. Assn. Accts. Democrat. Presbyterian. Home: 2230 Rollins Dr Alexandria VA 22307 Office: 5901 Utah Ave NW Washington DC 20015

WEBER, MARTHA GESLING, educator; b. Lancaster, Ohio, Apr. 10, 1912; d. William and Sue (Crump) Gesling; A.B., Ohio No. U., 1935, Pd.D. (hon.), 1971; A.M., Ohio State U., 1941; fellow edn. Duke, 1944-46, Ph.D., 1951; m. Dr. Joseph Elliott Weber, Dec. 1956. Tchr. history and music, grad. schs., 1933-40, history, English, debate, high schs., 1940-44; asst. prof. edn., ednl. psychology Bowling Green State U., 1946-49, asso. prof. edn., 1949-53, prof. edn., 1953-75, prof. emerita, 1975—, dir. reading center, 1946-65. Reading cons. basic reading series for slow learners. Recipient Distinguished Alumnus citation Ohio No. U., 1954; Distinguished Faculty award Bowling Gree U., 1963, Coll. of Edn. Outstanding Teaching award, 1968. Mem. Am. Assn. U. Women, Internat. Reading Assn. (pres. Ohio council 1957-58), Am. Ednl. Research Assn., Nat. Soc. Study Edn., Nat. Council Tchrs. English, Coll. Reading Assn. (nat. dir. 1965-68), Mortar Board, Phi Kappa Phi (chpt. pres. 1965-67), Chi Omega, Kappa Delta Pi, Delta Kappa Gamma. *

WEBER, MARY ELLEN HEALY, economist; b. San Francisco, May 28, 1943; d. Ignatius Bernard and Grace Marie (Hogan) Healy; B.A., Dominican Coll., 1965; postgrad. Nat. U. Mex., 1967, (vis. scholar) Stanford U., 1969-70, Cath. U. Chile, 1970-71, U. Chile, 1971-72; Ph.D., U. Utah, 1974; m. Stephen Francis Weber, Dec. 21, 1971. U. Utah teaching fellow, 1965-68; asst. prof. Smith Coll., 1972-75; country economist World Bank, IBRD, 1975-76; sr. economist Internat. Research & Tech. Corp., McLean, Va., 1976-78; dir. regulatory analysis, chief economist Occupational Safety and Health Adminstrn., U.S. Dept. Labor, Washington, 1979—. Social Sci. Research Council fgn. area fellow 1969-71. Mem. Am. Econ. Assn., Nat. Economists Club, Nat. Assn. Bus. Economists, Soc. Govt. Economists, Washington Women's Network. Roman Catholic. Office: US Dept Labor 200 Constitution Ave NW Washington DC 20210

WEBER, RUTHANNA MAXWELL, (MRS. CHARLES SWAN WEBER), civic worker; b. May 31, 1915; d. John Bell and Grace (Wisely) Maxwell; B.S. in Edn., Findlay Coll., 1936; postgrad. U. Colo., U. Wis.; m. Charles Swan Weber, Oct. 3, 1968; 1 son, Thomas Marshall Brushart; stepchildren—William Weber, Charles Weber, Diana Palms. Tchr. music and English, pub. schs., Ohio, 1936-42; pres. Hospitality and Info. Service, Washington, 1975-77; pres. Woman's Heart Bd., past chmn. Heart Luncheon; mem. adv. com. HOPE, past ball chmn.; mem. nat. service council YWCA, mem. dist. bd., past chmn. Internat. Fair, Washington; past bd. govs. St. Alban's Sch., Washington; mem. Meridian House Internat. Bd., Washington; past chmn. bd. Wolf Trap Assos., co-chmn. Wolf Trap Ball, chmn. February with the Arts luncheons; chmn. Goodwill Industries Tour, 1969-70; past pres. Seymour Study Club, Washington; founder, past pres. Kenwood Garden Club, Chevy Chase, Md. Served to lt. WAVES, World War II. Recipient Human Service award Nat. Grad. U., 1976. Home: 6412 Highland Dr Chevy Chase MD 20015

WEBER, SHEILA K., educator; b. N.Y.C., d. Morris and Rose (Maclert) Kaufman; A.A.S., N.Y.C. Community Coll., 1954; B.S., N.Y. U., 1959; M.L.S., Pratt Inst., 1961; postgrad. in spl. edn. Yeshiva U., 1959-60, in lit. and adminstrn. U. Calif., Berkeley, 1962-64, in folklore and mythology U. Calif., Los Angeles, 1967-70, U. So. Calif., 1968, in ednl. adminstrn., advanced media concepts Long Beach State U., 1974-75; Ph.D., U.S. Internat. U., 1977; m. Irwin J. Weber, 1956, children—Michele Janette, Robert Leslie. Asst. to chief librarian Bklyn. Pub. Library System, 1949-54; librarian Queens Coll. Edn. Library, 1960-62; coordinator children's services Menlo Park (Calif.) Pub. Library, 1962-64; dir. sch. libraries Los Altos (Calif.) Sch. Dist., 1964-66; sci. tchr. Bethpage (N.Y.) Sch. Dist., 1954-58, East Meadow (N.Y.) Sch. Dist., 1958-61; lectr. U. Santa Clara, 1964-66; lectr. children's lit. Coffee Cup Coll., Torrance, Calif., 1967; lectr. storycraft Glendale (Calif.) City Coll., 1967; lectr. children's lit. and storytelling Pepperdine U., 1966-69; cons. children's services Redondo Beach (Calif.) Pub. Library, 1967-70, Marianne Frostig Center Exceptional Children, Los Angeles, 1970-72; library cons. Long Beach Unified Sch. Dist., 1972—; lectr. children's lit. and dramatic play North Orange Coll., 1974-79; asst. to dir. Calif. State Coll., Bakersfield, 1979-80; lectr. children's lit. and dramatic play Santa Ana Coll., 1975-78; mem. Staff N.Y. World's Fair Library Center of Future, 1964. Mem. Am., Calif. library assns., Calif. Assn. Sch. Librarians, Calif. Tchrs. Assn., NEA. Home: 3402 Gage Pl San Diego CA 92106

WEBER, WINIFRED P., state legislator; b. Ellington, Mo., July 4, 1936; B.S. in Edn., S.W. Mo. State U.; M.A. in Guidance Counseling, U. Mo., Columbia. Mem. Mo. Ho. of Reps., 1970-74, 76—, majority whip; counselor Arnold C-6 Sch. Dist., 1974-76. Del., Democratic Nat. Conv., 1968; pres. 8th Dist. Women's Dem. Club; vice chmn. Jefferson County Dem. Com.; pres. Meramec Twp. Dem. Club; candidate Mo. Senate, 1974. Mem. NEA, Mo. State Tchrs. Assn. Methodist. Club: Order of Eastern Star. Office: Mo State Ho of Reps Jefferson City MO 65101 *

WEBER, YVONNE ROEBUCK, research ofcl., educator; b. McKeesport, Pa., Oct. 22; d. Raymond Henry and Clara Maria (Roberts) Roebuck; B.A., U. Pitts., 1947, M.Litt., 1952, Ph.D., 1973; postgrad. Kent State U., 1950; Ecole Normale, Paris, 1953, Goethe Institut, 1960; m. William Frederick Weber, June 16, 1961; children—Laurel, Wendy. Tchr. French, German, English, history Carrollton (Ohio) High Sch., 1947-51, Canton, Ohio, 1951-52, Munhall (Pa.) High Sch., 1952-58, Wilkinsburg (Pa.) High Sch., 1958-61, Upper St. Clair (Pa.) High Sch., 1963-65; asst. prof. French and German, California (Pa.) State Coll., 1965-66, Point Park (Pa.) Coll., 1968-72; asst. prof., Supr. edn. Washington and Jefferson Coll., 1976-79; head research project Delta Kappa Gamma Soc., Internat., Pitts., 1979-82. Recipient Good Citizenship award DAR, 1943; U. Pitts. scholar, 1943-47, Panhellenic Assn. scholar, 1946-47, Fulbright grantee to Germany, 1960; named Disting. Alumna, U. Pitts., 1971-82. Mem. Modern Lang. Assn., Doctoral Assn. Educators, Pa. State Modern Lang. Assn., Pa. Assn. Tchr. Educators, Delta Kappa Gamma Soc. Internat. (Scholarship 1972-73, Eunah Temple Holden Golden Anniversary award 1979), Mensa Internat., Pi Lambda Theta, Phi Delta Gamma, Zeta Tau Alpha. Club: McKeesport Coll. Contbr. articles in field to profl. jours. Home: 43 Dutch Ln Pittsburgh PA 15236

WEBSTER, JEAN BROOKS, middle sch. adminstr.; b. Rock Hill, S.C., Jan. 21, 1926; d. Roger Malcolm, Sr. and Myrtle Thornton (Naylor) Brooks; A.B., Winthrop Coll., 1950; M.A., George Peabody Coll., 1957. Tchr., Mocksville (N.C.) High Sch., 1947-48, Lexington (N.C.) High Sch., 1948-54, Bartow (Fla.) Jr. High Sch., 1954-56, Rogers Jr. High Sch., Ft. Lauderdale, Fla., 1956-58; dean Rogers Jr. High Sch., 1958-68, asst. prin., 1968-73; prin. McNicol Middle Sch., Hollywood, Fla., 1973-76, Crystal Lake Middle Sch., Pompano Beach, Fla., 1976-80; adminstrv. asst. Ramblewood Middle Sch., Coral Springs, Fla., 1980—; dir. Ft. Lauderdale Oral Sch., 1964-70. Chmn., Am. Heart Assn. fund drive, Lexington, 1952-53. Mem. Broward County Asst. Adminstrs. Assn. (chmn. 1965-66, dir. 1970-73), NEA (life), Nat., Fla. assns. secondary sch. prins., AAUW, Broward Prins. and Assts. Assn., Fla. League Middle Schs., Assn. Supervision and Curriculum Devel., Broward County Middle Sch. Prins. Assn., Kappa Delta Pi, Sigma Epsilon Alpha. Democrat. Baptist. Home: 192 SW 62d Ave Plantation FL 33317 Office: 8505 W Atlantic Blvd Coral Springs FL 33065

WEBSTER, SHARON B., polit. economist; b. Wildwood, Fla., Aug. 23, 1937; d. James McWilliams and Marion (Haulbrook) Boen; B.A., U. Fla., 1959; Ph.D., U. Va., 1965. Asst. prof. No. Mich. U., Marquette, 1962-64, U. Md., Marquette, 1964-66, Hollins (Va.) Coll., 1966-71; prof. Fed. Exec. Inst., Charlottesville, Va., 1971-72; program mgr. IRS, Washington, 1972-74; economist Econs., Statistics and Coop. Service, Washington, 1974-79; mem. Presdl. Commn. for Exec. Exchange, 1979-80; dir. internat. econs. Occidental Petroleum Corp., Los Angeles, 1980—. Mem. adv. bd. Pres.'s Carribbean Basin Initiative, 1982. Mem. Internat. Policy Inst. (v.p. 1977—), Internat. Assn. Energy Economists, Am. Assn. Agrl. Economists, Am. Polit. Sci. Assn., Nat. Assn. Bus. Economists, Internat. Studies Assn., Soc. Internat. Devel., Nat. Council Career Women. Contbr. articles to profl. jours. Address: Occidental Intl Corp 1747 Penn Av #375 Washington DC 20006 Also: 10889 Wilshire Blvd Los Angeles CA 91504

WEBSTER-DAVIS, MABEL LOUISE, psychiat. social worker; b. Kiblah, Ark., May 22, 1933; d. Lawyer W. and Lena (Abraham) Webster; B.S., Prairie View A&M Coll., 1958; M.S.W., U. Kans., 1961; m. Roy Harold Davis, Jr., Jan. 16, 1966; children—Mona L.; stepchildren—Karene, Rochelle. Public welfare worker Child Welfare Services Jackson County, Kansas City, Mo., 1958-63; screening clinic coordinator admissions services Western Mo. Community Health Center, Kansas City, 1963-67; supr. dept. children and adolescent services Kansas City Mental Health Found., 1967-69; psychiat. social work cons., 1967—. health and welfare specialist Automated Services Inc., Washington, 1975—; dir. social work dept. Trenton Psychiat. Hosp. (N.J.), 1978—; adj. prof. Rutgers U., 1977-79, Trenton State Coll., 1977—; mem. profl. adv. bd. Vis. Nurses, Assn., Trenton. Mem. Nat. Assn. Social Workers, Acad. Cert. Social Workers, Clin. Social Workers, Am. Hosp. Assn. Soc. for Hosp. Social Work Dirs., Female Exec. Assn. Home: 9 Darby Circle E Mount Holly NJ 08060 Office: Trenton Psychiat Hosp Box 7500 Trenton NJ 08625

WEDDINGTON, SARAH RAGLE, lawyer, assn. exec.; b. Abilene, Tex., Feb. 5, 1945; d. Herbert Doyle and Lena Catherine (Morrison) Ragle; B.S. magna cum laude, McMurry Coll., 1965; J.D., U. Tex., Austin, 1967; H.H.D. (hon.), Hamilton Coll., 1979. Admitted to Tex. bar, 1967; individual practice law, Austin, 1967-77; gen. counsel Dept. Agr., Washington, 1977-79; asst. to Pres. U.S., 1979-80; mem. exec. com. Population Council of N.Y.C., 1977—; mem. bus. adv. council Legis. 50. Mem. Tex. Ho. of Reps., 1972-77; bd. dirs. Zero Population Growth, 1972-74. Recipient Woman of Year award Tex. Women's Polit. Caucus, 1973. Mem. Am., Tex. bar assns., NOW, AAUW, Women's Equity Action League. Address: Office of Asst to Pres 1600 Pennsylvania Ave NW Washington DC 20500 *

WEDDON, WILLAH MARY, journalist; b. Oakland County, Mich., Sept. 1, 1925; d. Clifford Admiral and Helen Freda (Jones) Skinner; B.A., Western Mich. U., 1944; postgrad. U. Mich., 1944-47; m. Edward Weddon, Sept. 19, 1942; children—Todd, Bradley, Patrice, Alex, Amy. Pub., Comstock (Mich.) Coronet, 1946; Willow Run editor Ypsilanti (Mich.) Press, 1947-50; corr. Jackson Citizen Patriot, Lansing State Jour., Detroit Free Press, 1960-70; founder, owner, mgr. Women's News Bur., Lansing, Stockbridge, Mich., 1970—; rural health columnist Mich. Farmer mag., 1976—; founder E&W Speakers Bur., 1980. Mem. bd. advs. Eberly's Mich. Jour., East Lansing. Mem. Mich. Women's Press Club (pres. 1976-78), Mich. State Med. Soc. Aux. (pres. 1978-79), Nat. Fedn. Press Women (dir. region 6, 1980-82), Tau Kappa Alpha, Sigma Delta Chi. Methodist. Author: First Ladies of Michigan, 1977; How to Heat and Eat with Woodburning Stoves, 1980. Address: 4891 Dexter Trail Stockbridge MI 49285

WEDEL, MILLIE REDMOND, educator; b. Harrisburg, Pa., Aug. 18, 1939; d. Clair L. and Florence (Heiges) Aungst; B.A., Alaska Meth. U., 1966; M.Ed., U. Alaska, Anchorage, 1972; postgrad. in communications Stanford U., 1975-76; m. Frederick L. Wedel, Jr., Nov. 2, 1974; 1 son, Tom Redmond. Profl. model Charming Models & Models Guild of Phila., 1954-61; public relations staff Haverford (Pa.) Sch., 1959-61; asst. dir. devel. in charge public relations Alaska Meth. U., Anchorage, 1966, part-time lectr., 1966-73; communications tchr. Anchorage Sch. Dist., 1967—; owner Wedel Prodns., Anchorage, 1976—; public relations staff Alaska Purchase Centennial Exhibit, U.S. Dept. Commerce, 1967; writer gubernatorial campaign, 1971; part-time instr. U. Alaska, Anchorage, 1976-79; cons. Cook Inlet Native Assn., 1978, No. Inst., 1979; legal asst., research writer Vinson & Elkins, Houston, 1981. Bd. dirs. Sta. KAKM, Alaska Public TV, membership chmn., 1978-80, elected 2d lay rep. to Public Broadcasting Service, 1979; bd. dirs. Ednl. Telecommunications Consortium for Alaska, 1979, Mid-Hillside Community Council, Municipality of Anchorage, 1979-80. Recipient awards for newspapers, lit. mags., Nat. Scholastic Press Assn., 1968, 74, 77; lic. 3d class broadcasting, FCC. Mem. Assn. Public Broadcasting (charter mem., nat. lay del. 1980), Indsl. TV Assn. (San Francisco), Alaska Press Club (chmn. high sch. journalism workshops, 1968, 69, 73, awards for sch. newspapers, 1972, 74, 77), Alaska Fedn. Press Women (dir. 1978—, youth projects dir., award for brochures, 1978), NEA, Am. Educators in Communications Tech., World Affairs Council, Alaska Council Tchrs. of English, Delta Kappa Gamma. Presbyterian. Club: Capt. Cook Athletic. Office: Box 8169 Anchorage AK 99508

WEDGEWORTH, ANN, actress; b. Abilene, Tex., Jan. 21; attended U. Tex.; B.A. in Drama, So. Methodist U.; m. Rip Torn (div.); 1 child, Danae; m. 2d, Ernest Martin; 1 dau., Dianna. Broadway debut in Make A Million, 1958; other Broadway appearances: Thieves, Blues for Mr. Charlie, The Last Analysis, Chapter Two (Tony award); off-Broadway appearances: Chapparal, The Crucible, Days and Nights of Beebee Fenstermaker, Ludlow Fair, Line; toured with nat. cos. of The Sign in Sidney Brustein's Window and Kennedy's Children; appeared in TV series: The Edge of Night, Another World, Somerset, Three's Company; other TV appearances: The Defenders, Bronk, All That Glitters; TV film The War Between the Tates; movies: Thieves, Bang the Drum Slowly, Scarecrow, Catamount Killing, Law and Disorder, Dragon-Fly, Birch Intervals, Handle With Care (Nat. Soc. Film Critics award). Office: care Blake Agency Ltd 409 N Camden Dr 202 Beverly Hills CA 90210 *

WEDGWORTH, RUTH SPRINGER, fertilizer co. exec.; b. Eaton Rapids, Mich., May 10, 1903; d. Clarence P. and Minnie L. (Washburn) Springer; student Mich. State U., 1921-23; LL.D. (hon.), U. Fla., 1965; H.H.D. (hon.), Fla. So. Coll., 1976; m. Herman H. Wedgworth, June 23, 1923; children—Helen Jean, George H., Barbara Ann. Pres., Wedgworth Farms, Inc., Belle Glade, Fla., 1938-80, Wedgworth's Inc., Belle Glade, 1954—, pres. Wedgworth Produce, Inc., Belle Glade, 1955-65; sec. Seminole Life Ins. Co., West Palm Beach, Fla., 1955-65; dir. Fla. Nat. Bank, Belle Glade, 1979—. Mem. Palm Beach County (Fla.) Bd. Edn., 1947-53; bd. dirs. Western Palm Beach County Hosp. Dist., 1940-47; chmn. Highlands Glades Drainage Dist., 1942-68; mem. Gov.'s Com. on Migrant Work, 1942-46; trustee Fla. So. Coll., 1970—; mem. migrant work com. Nat. Council Chs., 1948-56; leadership mem. Boy Scouts Am., 1979. Recipient Award of Merit, Gamma Sigma Delta, 1978; Council of Farmers Cooperatives award, 1979; named Woman of Yr. (Progressive Farmer, 1947), Belle Glade, Fla., 1975; award for excellence in industry and bus. Palm Beach County Com. on Status of Women, 1978; Disting. Service award, Fla. Farm Bur., 1979, Fla. Fruit and Vegetable Assn., 1958; Outstanding Service award for employment and community leadership Everglades Progressive Citizens, 1970; Achievement award, Lions, 1961. Mem. Fla. Fruit and Vegetable Assn., Fla. Hort. Soc., Fla. Soils Sci. Soc., Beta Sigma Phi. Methodist. Clubs: Belle Glade Women's, PEO, Lions. Office: 651 NW 9th St Belle Glade FL 33430

WEDMAN, ELIZABETH LUCY ST. LOUIS, nutritionist; b. Annapolis, Md., May 28, 1946; d. Joseph I. and Elizabeth C. (Chowanetz) St. Louis; student Berry Coll., 1964-65; B.S., U. Minn., 1968; M.S., No. Ill. U., 1973. Home economist Swift & Co., Chgo., 1968; asst. extension advisor U. Ill. Coop. Extension Service, Tinley Park, 1969; home economist Am. Dry Milk Inst., Chgo., 1970; food service supr. Saga Foods, Inc., Aurora, Ill., 1972-73; coordinator nutrition info. Am. Dietetic Assn., Chgo., 1974-76; nutritionist Hinsdale (Ill.) Med. Center, 1976—; cons. in field. Mem. Am. Dietetic Assn., Am. Diabetes Assn., Am. Assn. Diabetes Educators, Am. Soc. Parenteral and Enteral Nutrition, Soc. for Nutrition Edn. Club: Four Winds Ski. Contbr. articles to profl. jours. Office: Hinsdale Medical Center 40 S Clay St Hinsdale IL 60521

WEDMORE, JOYCE ANN HOLCOMB, journalist; b. Cromona, Ky., Feb. 12, 1941; d. Virgil and Nola Nora (Isabell) Holcomb; student public schs., Muncie, Ind.; m. Jack Edward Wedmore, Sept. 1, 1961; children—Tracy Allen, Bryan Logan. Producer spl. sects. Muncie (Ind.) Newspapers, Inc., 1969—. Adv. Jr. Achievement; bd. dirs., publicity chmn. Delaware County Hist. Festival; co-chmn. copywriting com. PBS-TV, 1979-81; active Renaissance Fair Com., Try Muncie First Com. Mem. Nat. Fedn. Press Women, Women in Communications, Woman's Press Club of Ind. (3d v.p., 3d place award 1976, 81, 1st place award 1977, 78, 80, 81, 82, 2d place 1980, 81, 82). Home: 3812 S Ebright St Muncie IN 47302 Office: Muncie Newspapers Inc 125 S High St Muncie IN 47302

WEDRAL, ELAINE REGINA, food chemist; b. Detroit, Feb. 29, 1944; d. Albert and Anna Amelia (Stalc) Maesso; B.S. with honors in Biochemistry, Purdue U., 1966; M.S. in Microbiology, Cornell U., 1968, Ph.D. in Food Chemistry, 1970; m. William Wedral, May 23, 1970. Quality control foreman, supr. Holloway House (Green Giant Food), Lafayette, Ind., 1964-65; chemist Campbell Soup Co., Chgo., 1966; mgr. microbiology Western Farmers Assn., Seattle, 1970-71; project coordinator nutrition and prodn. safety Libby McNeill & Libby Inc., Chgo., 1972-74, asso. dir. product devel., 1974-76, dir. research and devel., 1976, v.p. research and devel., 1979-80; v.p., dir. Westreco (Western Hemisphere Research Co. div. Nestle Inc.), New Milford, Conn., 1981—. Mem. Nat. Food Processors (sci. affairs council), Am. Meat Inst. (sci. research com. 1976-81), Grocery Mfrs. Am. (tech. rep. 1974-77). Contbr. articles to various publs. Office: Westreco Inc Boardman Rd New Milford CT 06776

WEED, BESSIE WHITE, social worker; b. Winslow, Ariz., Oct. 17, 1929; d. Wallace Watson and Mary Virginia (Marley) White; student Tex. Women's U., 1946-47; B.A. in Psychology, U. Tex., Austin, 1950; postgrad. North Tex. State U., 1974; M.S.S.W., U. Tex., Arlington, 1976; m. Earl Dudley Weed, Jr., Nov. 17, 1951; children—Earl Dudley, Wallace Bruce, Daniel Clay. Psychol. examiner Dallas Ind. Sch. Dist., 1950-51; gravity computer Atlantic Oil Co., Dallas, 1951-52; display advt. State Times & Morning Advocate, Baton Rouge, 1952-53; psychol. examiner Preston Hollow Presbyn. Ch. Weekday Sch., Dallas, part-time 1958-74, Dallas Soc. Crippled Children, part-time 1973-75; social work cons. Region X, Edn. Service Center, Tex. Edn. Agy., Richardson, 1976-78; instr., field supr. dept. sociology and social work Tex. Woman's U., Denton, 1978-80; dir. social service dept. Dallas Soc. Crippled Children, 1980-81; social worker Hope Cottage Children's Bur., Dallas, 1981—. Rep., City Council PTA, 1970-72; pres. Arapaho Elem. PTA, 1966-69; vol. hypertension screening program Am. Heart Assn., 1975-78, disaster counselling tng. program ARC, 1979—. Mem. Acad. Cert. Social Workers, Nat. Assn. Social Workers (state conf. planning com. 1978, nominating com. for Dallas steering com. 1980), NOW Alpha Chi, Alpha Delta Mu. Democrat. Methodist. Office: Hope Cottage Children's Bureau 4209 McKinney St Dallas TX 75205

WEED, MRS., CLYDE PITTMAN, ins. exec., club woman; b. Ballinger, Tex., Mar. 7, 1906; d. Benjamin Stanford and Minnie Belle (West) Long; B.A., Tex. Christian U., 1927; m. Clyde Pittman Weed, July 13, 1929; children—Marilyn (Mrs. William P. Aycock), Kathryn (Mrs. James E. Vittetoe). Vice pres. Bandera Hat Co., Fort Worth, 1945-63, Hatters, Inc., Fort Worth, 1945-61; owner, mgr. Clyde P. Weed & Co., Ins. Agy., Fort Worth, 1965—; bd. dirs. Fort Worth Assn. Ins. Agents, 1967-69. Liaison officer Opera Guild of Fort Worth, 1957-58, v.p., 1958-59, treas., 1959-61; bd. dirs. Fort Worth Opera Assn., 1958-61, 1961-64; active Tarrant County Assn. Mental Health, Camp Fire Girls, United Fund, PTA. Democrat. Methodist. Mem. Order Eastern Star. Clubs: Colonial Country, Woman's of Fort Worth (chmn. speech dept., 1956-58, dir. 1976-78, corr. sec. 1976-77), Fidelite (pres. 1956-58, treas, 1963-64, reporter 1972-73), Friday Lecture (pres. 1959-60, sec. 1974-77), Fort Worth Lecture Found., Fort Worth Garden, Met. Dinner, Knife and Fork, Kappa Kappa Gamma. Club: Mothers of Fort Worth (pres. 1957-58). Home: 5032 Arborlawn Dr Fort Worth TX 76109 Office: 3400 Hulen St Fort Worth TX 76107

WEEDMAN, JOYCE JANE, pub. co. exec.; b. Jackson, Mich., July 8, 1942; d. Ralph Benton and Juanita Dorothea (Hoagland) Weedman; B.J., U. Tex., Austin, 1960-65. Reporter, Houston Chronicle, Austin and

Houston, 1964-68; writer Rice U., Houston, 1968-69; editor Tex. Exec. mag. and Tex. Bus. and Industry mag., Houston, 1970-72; copywriter Ketchum MacLeod & Grove Advt., Houston, 1972-74; pres. Ampersand Inc., Houston, 1975—, chmn. bd., 1981—; partner Colophon Ltd., 1981—; editor, pub. S.W. Racquetball mag., 1980-81, Creative Directory of Sun Belt, 1978-81, Houston Home Improvement Guide, 1980-81, Texas Media Guide, 1981—. Home: 2247 Colquitt St Houston TX 77098 Office: 1103 S Shepherd Dr Houston TX 77019

WEEKES, SHIRLEY M., artist; b. Buffalo, May 9, 1917; d. Ray Roscoe and Loretta Marie (Ent) Thompson; grad. Detroit Art Acad., 1939; m. Thomas Weekes, Mar. 27, 1942; children—Judith, Thomas. One woman shows: Frye Mus., Seattle, 1967, 72, Haines Gallery, Seattle, 1973, 75, Challis Gallery, Laguna Beach, Calif., 1970, 72, 74; group shows include: Frye Mus., 1965-69, 71-75, Seattle Art Mus., 1972; represented in permanent collections Frye Mus., Laguna Beach Mus. Art. Mem. N.W. Watercolor Soc., San Diego Watercolor Soc. Home: 40451 Calle Fiesta Rancho California CA 92390

WEEKS, ANNIE RUTH, civic worker; b. Anadarko, Okla., Apr. 30, 1928; d. James Edwin and Blondine (Jordan) Moore; student Massey Bus. Coll., Marietta, Ga., 1962-63; m. Moses McKinly Weeks, Jan. 2, 1943; children—Jimmy McKinly, Lory Ann, Beverly Sue. Substitute tchr. Canton Elem. Sch., 1952-60, Cherokee High Sch., 1970-74. Pres. Cherokee High Sch. P.T.A., 1965-67, dist. dir. 14th dist., 1967-69; bd. mgrs. Ga. P.T.A., 1967-79; pres., 1975-77; nat. bd. mgrs. P.T.A., 1975-79, mem. nat. leadership and membership com., 1979-80, nat. v.p., 1978-80; edn. chmn. Keep Ga. Clean and Beautiful; chmn. Cherokee Cancer Soc., 1972-74; bd. trustees Nat. Youth Courtesy Soc., 1972-79; founder Cherokee County Humane Soc., 1971, Cherokee County Little Theatre, 1972; candidate Ga. Ho. of Reps., 1974; dir. info. Ga. State Senate, 1977; hon. founder Ga. P.T.A.; hon. life mem. Nat. P.T.A.; Ann Weeks music scholarship named in her honor, 1977; recipient Liberty Bell award Cherokee County, 1976, award Cherokee Humane Soc., 1972. Mem. Ga. United for Edn., Ga. Council for the Arts, Cancer Soc. Democrat. Methodist. Club: Lake Arrowhead. Author: The Real Annie, in progress. Home: Station 136 Lake Arrowhead Waleska GA 30183

WEEKS, JANET HEALY, judge; b. Quincy, Mass., Oct. 19, 1932; d. John Francis and Sheila Josephine (Jackson) Healy; A.B. in Chemistry, Emmanuel Coll., Boston, 1954; J.D., Boston Coll., 1958; m. George Weeks, Aug. 29, 1959; children—Susan, George. Admitted to Mass. bar, 1958, Guam bar, 1972; trial atty. Dept. Justice, Washington, 1958-60; trial atty. firm Trapp & Gayle, Agana, Guam, 1971-73; partner firm Trapp, Gayle, Teker, Weeks & Freidman, Agana, 1973-75; judge Superior Ct. Guam, Agana, 1975—; chmn. task force cts., prosecution and defense Terr. Crime Commn., 1973-76; mem. Terr. Crime Commn. Bd., 1975-76, Guam Law Revision Commn., 1981—; rep. Nat. Conf. State Trial Judges, 1982. Mem. Catholic Sch. Bd. Guam, 1973. Mem. Nat. Assn. Women Judges (charter), Am. Judges Assn., Am. Bar Assn., Fed. Bar Assn. (chpt. sec. 1974), Guam Bar Assn. Club: Internat. (Guam). Office: Superior Ct Guam 110 W O'Brien Dr Agana Guam GU 96910

WEEKS, LIN CARNEY, nurse; b. Boston, Oct. 7, 1943; d. Thomas H. and Ann (Day) Carney; R.N., Burbank Hosp. Sch. Nursing, 1964; B.A., Dominican Coll., 1968; M.S., Boston U., 1974; m. Buddy L. Weeks, May 21, 1971. Clin. instr. cardiac nursing Tex. Heart Inst., Houston, 1966-71; clin. supr. critical care Henry Ford Hosp., Detroit, 1971-73; cardiovascular clinician Mass. Gen. Hosp., Boston, 1974-75; surgical clinician Hartford (Conn.) Hosp., 1975-76; clin. dir. surg. spl. care areas, dir. edn. St. John Med. Center, Tulsa, 1976-78; asst. prof. grad. sch. nursing U. Okla., 1977-78; dir. med. nursing Hermann Hosp., Tex. Med. Center, Houston, 1978—; instr. U. Tex. Med. Sch.; adj. asst. prof. Tex. Women's U., 1978—; guest lectr. nat. confs. Am. Heart Assn., Am. Nurses Assn., others. Mem. Am. Assn. Critical Care Nurses, Am. Nurses Assn., Am. Heart Assn., Sigma Theta Tau. Democrat. Contbr. chpt. to nursing book. Home: 12022 Indian Wells St Houston TX 77066 Office: Hermann Hosp 1203 Ross Sterling Ave Houston TX 77030

WEEKS, MARCIA GAIL, state senator; b. Greenbush, Minn., Jan. 19, 1938; d. Casper Lewis and Laura (Wallin) Spangrud; B.A., U. Ariz., 1967; m. James W. Weeks, 1958; 1 son, Chad. Substitute tchr. Phoenix City Sch. System; mem. Ariz. Senate, 1975-78, 80—; owner, mgr. printing firm. Mem. LWV, Nat. Conf. State Legislators. Democrat. Methodist. Office: 1700 W Washington St Senate Wing Phoenix AZ 85007

WEEKS, PHYLLIS ERLENE, educator; b. Gray, Okla., Mar. 21, 1934; d. Alexander and Elsie Ida Pugh; B.S. in Home Econs., Okla. Panhandle State U., 1958, B.S. in Elem. Edn., 1967; m. Alvin Weeks, Dec. 24, 1958 (div.); children—Charles Alan, Earl Lynn. Tchr. public schs., Adams, Okla., 1960-61; tchr. kindergarten public schs., Balko, Okla., 1967-72, tchr. 2d grade, 1973—. Asst. sec. Balko Apotolica Faith Ch., 1978-81, Sunday sch. tchr., 1976-78. Mem. NEA, Okla. Edn. Assn., Okla. Reading Assn. Hi Plains Reading Council (corr. sec. 1980-81), Beaver County Edn. Assn. (rep. 1981-82). Home: Route 1 Box 54 Balko OK 73931 Office: Route 1 Box 37 Balko OK 73931

WEEMS, KATHARINE LANE, sculptor; b. Boston, Feb. 22, 1899; d. Gardiner Martin and Emma Louise (Gildersleeve) Lane; prep. edn. May Sch., Boston; art edn. Sch. of Museum of Fine Arts, Boston; pupil of Charles Grafly, Anna Hyatt Huntington, George Demetrios and Brenda Putman; m. F. Carrington Weems, Nov. 15, 1947. Prin. works include Dog Narcisse Noir, Museum Fine Arts, Boston, and Reading (Pa.) Mus., Kanagroo, Pa. Acad. Fine Arts, 12 foot bronze group Dolphins of the Sea Water Plaza, New Eng. Aquarium, Boston; rep. permanent collection: Greek Horse, Balt. Mus. Art; Bear, Spee Club, Harvard; Whippet, Glenbow Found. Mus.; Whippet and Fox, Colby Coll. Art Mus., Waterville, Maine; brick carvings and entrance doors, and 2 bronze rhinoceroses, Inst. of Biology, Harvard; sculpture on Lotta Fountain, Boston; small bronzes in pvt. collections; permanent exhbn. Weems Gallery Animal Sculpture, Mus. Sci., Boston; sculptor Goodwin medal Mass. Inst. Tech.; sculptor for U.S. Legion of Merit medal and medal for Merit, also Fincke Meml. medal Groton Sch. Mem. Mass. Art Commission, 1941-47. Decorated chevalier L'Ordre Nat. Merit (France); recipient bronze medal Sesqui-Centennial Exposition, Phila., 1926; Widener Meml. gold medal Pa. Acad. Fine Arts, 1927; honorable mention Paris (France) Salon, 1928; Joan of Arc gold medal Nat. Assn. Women Painters and Sculptors, 1928; hon. mention Grand Central Galleries, N.Y.C., 1929; bronze medal Boston Tercentenary Fine Arts Exhbn., 1930; Anna Hyatt Huntington prize Nat. Assn. Women Painters and Sculptors, 1931; Speyer prize NAD, 1931, 63, 72, Barnet prize, 1932; hon. mention Archtl. League of N.Y., 1942; Anonymous prize Nat. Assn. Women Artists, 1946; Saltus gold medal for merit Nat. Acad. Design, 1960; Lindsey Morris Meml. prize Nat. Sculpture Soc., 1960, Kalos Kagathos Found. sculpture prize, 1981; gold medal Nat. Arts Club, N.Y.C., 1961. N.A. Fellow Nat. Sculpture Soc. (council 1949); mem. Guild Boston Artists, Nat. Assn. Women Artists, Nat. Inst. Arts and Letters, Grand Central Art Galleries, Archtl. League, Am. Artists Profl. League, N. Shore Arts Assn., Huguenot Soc., Lords of Colonial Manors. Mass. Soc. Colonial Dames Am. Allied Artists Am. Clubs: Chilton (Boston); Cosmopolitan, Pen and Brush (N.Y.C.); Catherine Lorillard Wolfe. Home: PO Box 126 Manchester MA 01944

WEGNER, PATRICIA ANN MALO, genealogist; b. Fairmont, Minn., Feb. 20, 1947; d. Marvin Henry and Betty Jean (Wedoo) Malo; student public schs., Fairmont, 1951-65; m. Dallas J. Wegner, Apr. 8, 1967; children—Wendy Ann, Becky Lynn, Kathy Jean. Nurse's aide Lakeview Home for Elderly, Fairmont, 1972-73; geneal. researcher, 1976—. Leader Girl Scouts U.S.A., 1974-75; tchr. Sunday sch., 1976-77. Mem. Minn. Geneal. Soc., New Eng. Geneal. Soc., Nat. Trust for Hist. Preservation, Sons of Norway. Democrat. Lutheran. Home and Office: 1528 Albion St Fairmont MN 56031

WEGNER, PATSY RUTH, constrn. co. ofcl.; b. Ratcliff, Tex., July 18, 1940; d. Ralph Walter, Jr., and Thelma Lee (Myers) Jackson; adopted dau. of Elliott Denman and Annie Bella (Myers) Coffer; comml. art degree Regal Sch. Art, Houston, 1959; m. Raymond Wegner, Mar. 27, 1960; children—Sheila Ann, Damon Ray, Larry Wayne, Christopher Mark. Acctg. dept. staff T.J. Bettes Co., Houston, 1959-60; bookkeeper, office mgr. Old Brazos Forge, Brenham, Tex., 1962-68; acct. Otto Lehrmann, Brenham, 1972-73; claims officer Tex. Dept. Mental Health, Brenham State Sch., 1973-77; co-owner, office mgr. Raymond Wegner Constrn., Brenham, 1977—. Sec. edn., bd. parish edn., stewardship com., Sunday Sch. tchr. St. John's Luth. Ch. of Prairie Hill, Brenham; pres. Am. Luth. Ch. Women, Brenham Conf., 1980—. Mem. Nat. Fedn. Ind. Bus. (San Mateo, Calif., and Washington), Washington County C. of C. Club: Brenham Fortnightly (sec.-treas. civic dept. 1964). Home and Office: 1303 Washington Rd Brenham TX 77833

WEHRER, CATHERINE MARY, coll. adminstr.; b. Paterson, N.J., Sept. 15, 1944; d. William J. and Catherine (Jager) W.; B.A., William Paterson Coll., Wayne, N.J., 1966; M.A., Syracuse (N.Y.) U., 1968; postgrad. Rutgers U., 1976. Asst. dir. residences SUNY; Binghamton, 1968-69; mem. adminstrv. staff Kean Coll. N.J., Union, 1969—, coordinator law enforcement edn. program, 1970-74, asst. to dean div. acad. services, 1973—. Recipient Leadership award Kean Coll. Adminstrs. Assn., 1977. Mem. NEA, N.J. Edn. Assn., Kean Coll. Faculty Assn. (corr. sec. 1973-74), Assn. State Coll. Adminstrs. (pres. 1975-77), N.J. Council Ednl. Instns. Law Enforcement (v.p. 1973-74), Nat. Assn. Women Deans, Adminstrs. and Counselors, Nat. Indsl. Relations Research Assn., New Brunswick Indsl. Relations Assn., Am. Soc. Tng. and Devel., Nat. Assn. Student Personnel Adminstrs., Phi Delta Kappa. Office: Kean Coll Morris Ave Union NJ 07083

WEHRLE, MARTHA GAINES, state legislator; b. Charleston, W.Va., Nov. 30, 1925; d. Ludwell Ebersole and Betty (Chilton) Gaines; A.B., Vassar Coll., 1948; M.A., Harvard U., 1954; m. Russell Schilling Wehrle, Oct. 16, 1954; children—Michael H., Ebersole Gaines, Katherine S., Philip N., Martha Chilton. Tchr., W.Va. schs., 1949-50, Belmont (Mass.) Day Sch., 1951-53; mem. W.Va. Ho. of Dels., 1974—, vice chmn. edn. com., 1976, chmn. constl. revision com., 1977-80. Bd. W.Va. Vocat. Edn. Found.; mem. adv. council W.Va. Woman's Commn. Mem. LWV. Democrat. Episcopalian. Clubs: Kanawha Garden, Charleston Jr. League. Office: State Capitol Charleston WV 25305

WEIBLEN, JANET KATHERINE, mfg. co. exec.; b. Englewood, N.J., Feb. 16, 1941; d. Alfred Herman and Augusta Alma (Schellack) Weiblen; student Rapid Advancement program N.Y. U., 1957-58, Wittenberg U., 1958-59, Barnard Coll., 1959-61; B.A. summa cum laude, Fairleigh Dickinson U., 1976; m. Nov. 4, 1962 (div. 1974); children—Scott William Rusterholz, Lisa Michele Rusterholz. Asst. to dir. Fairleigh Dickinson U. Mental Health Center, Teaneck, N.J., 1973-76; asst. to v.p. Hanover Sq. Realty Investors, N.Y.C., 1976-78; traffic mgr. Kingsley & Keith Chem. Corp., Englewood Cliffs, N.J., 1978-79; corp. traffic mgr. Maidenform, Inc., Bayonne, N.J., 1979—; adj. prof. New Sch. Social Research. N.J. chmn. Nat. Humanities series Nat. Endowment for the Arts, 1971-72; pres. PTA, Waldwick, N.J., 1972-73; bd. dirs. YWCA, Bayoone, 1981. Mem. Nat. Council Phys. Distbn. Mgmt. (v.p.), Newark Traffic Club, Raritan Traffic Club, Hudson County Traffic Club, Nat. Assn. Female Execs., Delta Nu Alpha (local dir.). Lutheran. Contbr. article to profl. jour. Office: 154 Ave E Bayonne NJ 07002

WEIDA, DONNA LEE, computer co. exec.; b. Logansport, Ind., Oct. 29, 1939; d. Donald L. and Leila J. (Sweet) Kleckner; A.A., Orange Coast Coll. and Saddleback Coll., Mission Viejo, Calif., 1980; children—Mark, Traci, Teri, Sec., K.L.K. Mfg. Co., Logansport, 1957-60, 63-65; sec. Sch. Edn., Mich. State U., 1962-63; sec. Sch. Fine Arts, U. Calif., Irvine, 1966-69; co-organizer Plaza Vet. Clinic, Upland, Calif., 1969-70; mgr. Bob Bondurant Sch. High Performance Driving, Ontario (Calif.) Motor Speedway, 1970-73; mgr./pub. relations exec. Chuck Jones Racing, Costa Mesa, Calif., 1973; exec. sec. Dana Steel, Newport Beach, Calif., 1974; estimator/office mgr. Hardy & Harper, Tustin, Calif., 1975-76; controller/mgr. Gillen/Kloss Advt., Newport Beach, 1977-78; purchasing adminstr. Butler Housing, Irvine, 1979; controller/mgr. XMark Corp., Costa Mesa, 1980-81, adminstrv. mgr. concept devel., 1981; corp. sec., adminstrv. mgr. Personal Systems Tech., Inc., Laguna Hills, Calif., 1982, founder/owner Numbers & Words, Irvine, 1982—. Mem. Nat. Assn. Female Execs., Am. Soc. Profl. and Exec. Women, Beta Sigma Phi. Republican. Episcopalian. Home: 14241 Utrillo Dr Irvine CA 92714 Office: Personal Systems Technology Inc 22957 La Cadena Laguna Hills CA 92653

WEIDENFELLER, GERALDINE CARNEY, speech therapist; b. Kearny, N.J., Oct. 12, 1933; d. Joseph Gerald and Catherine Grace (Doyle) Carney; B.S., Newark State U., 1954; postgrad. Northwestern U., summer 1956, U. Wis., summer 1960; M.A., N.Y. U., 1962; m. James Weidenfeller, Apr. 4, 1964; children—Anne, David. Speech pathologist Kearny (N.J.) Public Schs., 1954-61, North Brunswick (N.J.) Public Schs., 1961-65, Bridgewater (N.J.) Public Schs., 1969-72; pvt. practice speech therapy, Somerville, N.J., 1980—. Mem. Am. Speech and Hearing Assn., AAUW (dir. 1968). Republican. Roman Catholic. Home: 3 Banor Dr Somerville NJ 08876

WEIGAND, FLORENCE ALINE, civic worker; b. St. Joseph County, Ind., Jan. 29, 1915; d. Jacob Arthur and Carrie Olive (McBride) Herbster; student public schs.; m. Rudy Albert Weigand, July 16, 1938; children—Ray Albert, Jill Aline Weigand Purkey. Mgr., Robertsons Tea Room, South Bend, Ind., 1940-45; co-owner, mgr. Mishawaka (Ind.) Grain & Feed Co., 1957-69; owner, mgr. farms in St. Joseph County (Ind.), 1940—; bd. dirs. St. Joseph County Farm Bur., 1975—; social and ednl. leader Centre Twp. Farm Bur., 1975—. Mem. Centre Twp. Election Bd., 1970—; spl. vol. South Bend Mental Health Assn., 1974-78; mem. Ind. Cultural Arts Com., 1974-76: chmn. service cart Meml. Hosp. Aux. Bd., South Bend, 1977—; pres. St. Joseph County Extension Homemakers, 1978-79; mem. St. Joseph County 4-H Fair Bd., 1978—; sec. St. Joseph County Extension Bd., 1979—. Republican. Mem. Ch. of Brethren. Address: 63049 Turkey Trail South Bend IN 46614

WEIKEL, ANN, historian; b. N.Y.C., Dec. 26, 1935; d. William Stewart and Reba Gertrude (Tibbetts) Weikel; B.A., Mt. Holyoke Coll., 1957; M.A., Yale U., 1959, Ph.D., 1966. Instr., Mt. Holyoke Coll., 1963-64, Knox Coll., 1964-67; asst. prof. history Portland (Oreg.) State U., 1967-70, asso. prof., 1970-80, prof., 1980—. Vice chmn. 1st Congressional Dist. Democratic Com.; mem. exec. com. Oreg. Dem. Party, 1980-82. Mem. Medieval Acad., Conf. Brit. Studies, AAUP (exec. com. Collective Bargaining Congress, com. chmn. U. Oreg. chpt.). Office: Dept History Portland State U Portland OR 97207 *

WEIL, DEBRA SUE, food service co. exec.; b. Denver, June 28, 1933; d. Nelson and Carolyn Maxine (Meyer) New; student U. Colo., 1951-52; m. Robert Leonard Weil, Dec. 6, 1952; children—Ronald Leon, Richard Floyd, Linda Marie. Sec.-treas., dir. Westman Commn. Co., Denver, 1952—; contest judge HERO, DECA. Mem. bd. Temple Micah Sisterhood, Denver, treas., 1960-62; leader Girl Scouts, Denver, 1964-68; sec. Young Am. League, 1963-69; vol. Head Start, Public TV, Muscular Dystrophy, March of Dimes, Am. Cancer Soc., United Way. Mem. Colo.-Wyo. Restaurant Assn. (dir., treas. aux. bd., recipient disting. service award 1975-76), Nat. Restaurant Assn., Denver C. of C., Denver and Colo. Conv. and Visitors Bur., Foodservice Orgn. Distbrs., Colo. Chefs de Cuisine Assn., Colo.-Wyo. Hotel and Motel Assn. Republican. Clubs: Tennis World Racquet World, Mile High Stadium, Town (dir.). Home: 3766 S Jersey St Denver CO 80237 Office: 4450 Lipan St Denver CO 80211

WEIL, MILDRED WISHNATT, sociologist, educator; b. Newark; d. Benjamin and Esther (Wilson) Wishnatt; B.A., Rutgers U.; M.A. in Sociology, N.Y. U., Ph.D. in Sociology; m. Philip E. Weil, (dec.); children—Ann Dedre, Barbara Jane. Teaching fellow N.Y. U.; mem. faculty Upsala U., East Orange, N.J.; mem. faculty Fairleigh Dickinson U.; asst. prof. sociology Paterson State Coll., Wayne, N.J., after 1959, then asso. prof., now prof., dean Sch. Social Sci.; cons. teaching sociology, 1982—. Chmn. elections com. Excellence in Edn. Orgn., 1970-71; mem. Human Rights Com., Livingston, N.J. Recipient Outstanding Educator's award, 1972. Mem. Am. Sociol. Assn., Eastern Sociol. Assn., Nat. Council on Family Relations, Tri-State Council on Family Relations, AAUW (pres.). Author: Shalom, 1958; Marriage, the Family and Society, 1971; Sociological Perspectives of Marriage and the Family: Concepts and Readings, 1972; editor, contbr.: The Sociology of the Arts; contbr. articles on sociology of the family to profl. jours.; contbr. revs. on books about sociology to profl. jours. Home: 15 Stonewall Dr Livingston NJ 07039 Office: William Paterson College 300 Pompton Rd Wayne NJ 07470

WEIL, NANCY HECHT, psychologist, educator; b. Chgo., Apr. 15, 1936; d. Theodore R. and Jenice (Abrams) Hecht; student Cornell U., 1954-57; M.Ed., Nat. Coll. Edn., Ill., 1974; Ph.D., Northwestern U., 1976; postgrad. Chgo. Inst. Psychoanalysis, 1972-74; m. Edward S. Weil, Mar. 24, 1957; children—Lynda J., Edward S. Asso., Med. Sch., Northwestern U., 1977-80, asst. prof., 1976-77; asst. prof. continuing end. program Chgo. Inst. Psychoanalysis, 1976-77; lectr. Sch. Medicine, U. Chgo., 1978—; attending staff dept. psychiatry Michael Rees Hosp., 1978—; mental health cons.; vice-chair Ill. Mental Health Planning Bd., 1973-75; chair adv. council Ill. Dept. Mental Health 5-Yr. Plan, 1975-80. Bd. dirs. Chgo. Inst. Psychoanalysis, Chgo. Focus. Fellow Am. Orthospsychiat. Assn.; mem. Am. Psychol. Assn., Ill. Psychol. Assn., Chgo. Assn. Psychoanalytic Psychology, AAUP. Contbr. articles to profl. jours. Home: 190 Hawthorn Glencoe IL 60022 Office: 646 Michigan Ave Chicago IL 60611

WEILNAU, NORMA LUELLA, ret. educator; b. Ida, Mich., July 9, 1901; d. William and Nellie Belle (Strack) Drodt; student Mich. Normal Coll., 1920-21; B.S., Eastern Mich. U., 1952; m. Walter David Weilnau, June 15, 1922; children—Walter David, Herbert William. Tchr. rural sch. Ida Public Schs., 1946-70, grades 4-6, 1946-48, grade 5, 1948-70, ret., 1970. Leader 4-H Mich. State U., 1929-79, extension classes at Mich. State U., 1925-42; leader coop. extension service Dept. Agr.-Mich. State U., 1929-79; program coordinator Ida Area Sr. Citizens, 1974-80; mem. Monroe County (Mich.) 4-H Council, 1935-65; Sunday Sch. tchr., 1921-64. Recipient Meritorious Service plaque 4-H, 1955, Monroe County Fair, 1967; honoree for 50 yrs. 4-H leadership at Mich. State U., 1980; other awards, plaques. Mem. Mich. Assn. Ret. Sch. Personnel, Monroe County Extension Council, Ida Edn. Assn. (v.p. 1953-54, sec. 1956-60), Mich. State 4-H Key Club (hon.), Nat. Honor Soc. (hon. mem. Ida chpt.), Monroe County Council of Internat. Reading Council (life), United Meth. Women. Clubs: Christian Bus. and Profl. Women's Group, Eastern Mich. U. Alumni Emeritus. Home: 3234 Lewis Ave Ida MI 48140

WEIMMER, JACQUELINE JUNE, financial market cons.; b. N.Y.C., May 22, 1950; d. Frederick James and Aida (Soto) W.; B.A. in Sociology, Herbert H. Lehman Coll., City U. N.Y., 1975. Mktg. asso. Paine Webber Jackson & Curtis, N.Y.C., 1975-77; jr. securities analyst Paine Webber Mitchell Hutchins, N.Y.C., 1975-78; asst. sales mgr. E.F. Hutton & Co., N.Y.C., 1978-79; mgr. over the counter mktg. Thomson McKinnon Securities, N.Y.C., 1979-82; pvt. practice fin. market cons. Jacqueline Weimmer Assos., Inc., N.Y.C., 1982—. Active Women's Republican Club N.Y. Registered N.Y. Stock Exchange. Mem. N.Y. Soc. Security Analysts, Security Traders Assn. N.Y., Investment Assn. N.Y., Nat. Assn. Security Dealers. Home and Office: 211 E 18th St New York NY 10003

WEINBAUM, ELEANOR PERLSTEIN, estate mgr., writer; b. Beaumont, Tex., Sept. 3; d. Hyman Asher and Mamie (Gordon) Perlstein; student Ward-Belmont Coll., 1920, Benjamins' Coll., N.Y.C., 1922, Boulder U., Noted Writers Conf., 1931; L.H.D., U. Libre, 1972; m. Charles Weinbaum, Aug. 25, 1923 (dec.); 1 son, Charles H. Partner estates mgmt. 23d St. Shopping Center, Beaumont, 1956—; founder Eleanor Poetry Room at Lamar U., 1960, Pulse, lit. mag., 1962. Founder, Music Room, So. Meth. U., Dallas, 1965, sponsor ann. lecture by internat. poet, 1960—. Named D. Modern Humanities, Internat. Acad., 1969, one of internat. women of yr. with laureate honors Poet Laureate Internat., 1975; recipient Disting. Service citation World Poetry Soc., 1970. Mem. Beaumont C. of C., LWV, Big Thicket Assn., Heritage Soc., Tex., Nat. Press Women, Internat. Acad. Poets, Acad. Am. Poets, Tex. Council Promotion Poetry, World and Nat. Poetry Day Com. (hon. life), Sigma Tau Delta. Jewish. Club: Beaumont. Author: From Croup to Nuts, 1941; The World Laughs With You, 1950; Jest for You, 1954; Shalom, America, 1970; Conrad's Scrabble Babble, 1977; God's Eternal Word, 1978. Home: Hotel Beaumont Apt 415 Beaumont TX 77701 Office: 1215 Beaumont Savs Bldg Beaumont TX 77701

WEINBERG, BARBARA BICKERSTAFFE, city ofcl.; b. Boston; d. Herbert Powers and Florence (Jameson) Bickerstaffe; B.S., Boston U., 1958; postgrad. U. Conn., 1969-70; grad. Conn. Realtors Inst., 1973; m. Stanley Weinberg, Nov. 21, 1959; children—Leslie Jeanne, Susan Elizabeth. Sales assoc. T.J. Crockett Agy., Manchester, Conn., 1970-72; founder, pres. B/W Realty Inc., Manchester, 1972—; dep. mayor, Manchester, 1981—. Asst. state coordinator Carter Presdl. Primary, 1976; chmn. com. for 51.3% Conn. presdl. campaign, 1976; bd. dirs. Friendship Force, Atlanta, also state dir., 1977; mem. Winograd Commn., Democratic Nat. Com., 1977-78, Mid-Term Conf., 1978; alt. del. Conn. State Dem. Conv., 1980; del. Dem. Nat. Conv., 1980; bd. dirs. Town Council, Manchester, 1979—, chmn. Housing Com., 1981—; bd. dirs. Manchester United Way. Charles Kettering fellow, 1981. Mem. Nat. Assn. Realtors, Women's Council Realtors (past pres. chpt.; service award), Conn. Assn. Realtors, Greater Hartford Bd. Realtors, Greater Hartford Multiple Listing Corp., Manchester Bd. Realtors (dir.; Realtor of Yr. 1981), Manchester Multiple Listing Corp. (dir.). Democrat. Methodist. Home: 157 Pitking St Manchester CT 06040 Office: 164 E Center St Manchester CT 06040

WEINBERG, HAZEL JOAN, psychiatrist; b. N.Y.C., Apr. 28, 1934; d. Samuel Aaron and Harriet (Mahren) Weinberg; A.B., Vassar Coll., 1953; M.D., Hahnemann Med. Coll., 1968. Intern Roosevelt Hosp., N.Y.C., 1968-69; resident in psychiatry Albert Einstein Coll. Medicine, Bronx Mcpl. Hosp. Center, N.Y.C., 1969-71, chief resident, 1971-72, asst. dir. psychiat. emergency services, clin. instr., 1972-72; candidate

William Alanson White Inst., 1970-75, mem. faculty, 1976—; practice medicine specializing in psychiatry and psychoanalysis, N.Y.C., 1972—; asst. attending dept. psychiatry Roosevelt Hosp., also asso. attending outpatient dept., 1975-76; clin. instr., outpatient psychiatrist Cornell U. Med. Coll., N.Y. Hosp., Payne Whitney Clinic, 1977-80; asst. clin. prof. psychiatry Cornell U. Med. Coll., 1980—; asst. attending in psychiatry N.Y. Hosp., 1980—. Mem. Am. Psychiat. Assn., Am. Acad. Psychoanalysis, N.Y. County Med. Soc., William Alanson White Psychoanalytic Soc. Home and office: 500 E 77th St New York NY 10021

WEINBERG, HELEN ARNSTEIN, educator; b. Orange, N.J., June 17, 1927; d. Morris Jerome and Jeannette (Tepperman) A.; B.A., Wellesley Coll., 1949; Ph.D., Western Res. U., 1966; m. Kenneth G. Weinberg, Sept. 11, 1949; children—Janet S., Hugh Benjamin, John Arnstein. Teaching fellow Ohio State U., Columbus, 1949-50, Western Res. U., Cleve., 1953-55; prof. Cleve. Inst. Art, 1958—; coordinator East Hampton Poetry Series, 1975. Nat. Endowment Humanities fellow, 1977-78. Mem. MLA, Coll. Art Assn. Democrat. Jewish. Author: The New Novel in America, 1970; cons. editor Nova Newsletter, 1977—. Home: 3015 Huntington Rd Shaker Heights OH 44120 Office: 11141 East Blvd Cleveland OH 44106

WEINBERG, STEPHANIE GRANT, psychologist; b. N.Y.C., May 9, 1942; d. William D. and Gertrud Phyllis (Greenberg) Grant; student (Ill. State scholar) Northwestern U., 1959-61; A.B. with distinction in Psychology, Boston U., 1963, A.M. in Psychology (USPHS fellow), 1964, Ph.D. in Psychology, 1970. Teaching fellow Boston U., 1965-68, lectr., 1969-70; lectr. Boston State Coll., 1969; supr. behavior therapy Temple U. Med. Sch., Phila., 1971; asst. prof. psychology Trenton (N.J.) State Coll., 1970-72; research asso. Inst. Behavioral Research, Silver Spring, Md., 1972-73; research scientist, asst. prof. edn. Am. U., Washington, 1973-74; asst. prof. psychology U. Nev., Las Vegas, 1974-76; pvt. practice psychology and hypnosis, Las Vegas, 1974-81; postdoctoral intern in clin., family, and sch. psychology Johnson Assos., Auburn, Maine, 1981-82; asst. prof. psychology U. Maine at Presque Isle, 1982—. Lic. psychologist, D.C., Maine; psychologist cert., Nev. Mem. AAUW, Am. Soc. Clin. Hypnosis, Am. Psychol. Assn., Assn. Advancement of Behavior Therapy, New Eng. Soc. Clin Hypnosis, Internat. Soc. Hypnosis, Maine Psychol. Assn., Sigma Xi, Psi Chi. Address: Box 131 UMPI Presque Isle ME 04769

WEINBERG, SYDNEY STAHL, historian; b. N.Y.C., Oct. 2, 1938; d. David Leslie and Bernice (Jarvis) Stahl; B.A., Barnard Coll., 1960; M.A., Columbia U., 1964; Ph.D., 1969; m. Michael Weinberg, Sept. 1, 1957; children—Deborah Sara, Elisa Rachel. Instr. history N.J. Inst. Tech., 1967-69, asst. prof., 1969-72; asso. prof. history Ramapo Coll. N.J., Mahwah, 1972-74, prof., 1974—. Nat. Endowment for Humanities fellow, 1977-78. Mem. Inst. for Research in History, Middle Atlantic Radical Historians Orgn., Am. Hist. Assn., Orgn. Am. Historians. Contbr. articles to profl. jours. Home: 80 LaSalle St New York NY 10027 Office: Ramapo Coll NJ Mahwah NJ 07430

WEINBLATT, TOBY ANGSTER, psychologist; d. Louis and Bessie Angster; A.A., Community Coll. Balt., 1968; B.S., Towson State U., 1970, M.A., 1972; m. Samuel Weinblatt, Aug. 12, 1941; children—Robert, Janice Altman, Stuart, Paul Neil. Instr. psychology Harford Community Coll., 1972—, Essex Community Coll., 1973—, Anne Arundel Community Coll., 1975—; psychologist Carroll County, Windsor Md., 1973-75, Md. Dept. Juvenile Services, Balt., 1977—. Mem. Am. Psychol. Assn., Md. Psychol. Assn., Md. Sch. Psychol. Assn. Clubs: Hadassah, Order Eastern Star. Office: 50 Cathedral St Annapolis MD 21404

WEINER, CLAIRE ZUNDELL, theatrical dir.; b. Worcester, Mass., June 19, 1933; d. Edward A. and Mary (Abramson) Shapiro; student Clark U., SUNY, Miami-Dade Coll.; m. Michael H. Weiner, Aug. 5, 1972; children by previous marriage—Aaryn Anne, Elliot Michael. Instr. fundamentals of theatre Dade County (Fla.) Community Sch. System, 1965-68; tchr. theatre arts Roberson Centre of the Arts, Binghamton, N.Y., 1969-70; artist-in-theatre Colgate U., Hamilton, N.Y., 1968-70; free lance feature writer Norwich (N.Y.) Eve. Sun, 1969-72; dir. Norwich Sr. High Theatre, 1968-72; dir. cultural activities for youth Norwich Youth Commn., 1969-72; resident dir., actress Gold Crown Dinner Theatre & Touring Co., Downey, Calif., 1972-76; dir. Theatre for Youth, City of Santa Clara (Calif.), 1979-80, The Center Players, Long Beach, Calif., 1977-78; mem. Miami Actors Co., Miami, Fla., 1965-68; mem. Gainesville (Fla.) Little Theatre, 1956-58, Jacksonville (Fla.) Little Theatre, 1958-62, Gallery Theatre, Coral Gables, Fla., 1961-62, Miami Beach Players, 1962-64, Arlington Players, Jacksonville, 1958-61; dir. Norwich Adult Weekly Summer Repertory Theatre, 1969-72, Norwich Weekly Children's Theatre in Mime, 1969-72, Tino WorkShop Theatre, Fremont High Sch. Dist., 1980—; guest dir. West Valley Civic Light Opera, 1982; advisor N.Y. State Council on Arts, 1968-70; tchr. theatre arts Norwich Bd. Edn., summer 1970. Youth leader B'nai B'rith. Mem. Am. Ednl. Theatre Assn. Home: 5791 Rudy Ct San Jose CA 95124

WEINER, FERNE HESSBERG, psychologist; b. N.Y.C., June 14, 1928; d. Irving Kapp and Peggy (Finkelstein) Hessberg; B.A., Skidmore Coll., 1965; M.A., Sarah Lawrence Coll., 1971; Ph.D., U. Hawaii, 1975; m. Howard Robert Weiner, July 20, 1948; children—Irving Kenneth, Laurie Robin. Asst. prof. psychology West Oahu Coll., Aiea, Hawaii, 1975-76, U. Hawaii at Manoa, Honolulu, 1976-77; clin. psychology intern Connecticut Valley Hosp., Middletown, 1977-78; clin. psychologist Community Child Guidance Clinic, Manchester, Conn., 1978—; pres., mem. exec. bd. Westchester chpt. Children's Asthma Research Inst. and Hosp., Denver; mem. speaker's Bur., Skidmore Coll., Chairperson Alumnae Fund, Skidmore Coll., 1968, chairperson Reunion, 1969; alumnae admissions rep. Sarah Lawrence Coll., 1974-77. Lic. psychologist, Conn. Mem. Am. Psychol. Assn., Eastern Psychol. Assn., Conn. Psychol. Assn., Assn. for Advancement Psychology, Assn. to End Violence Against the Next Generation, Hawaii Psychol. Assn., Western Psychol. Assn., Sigma Xi. Democrat. Jewish. Research, publs. in field. Home: Bushnell Towers 1 Gold St Hartford CT 06103 Office: 317 N Main St Manchester CT 06040

WEINER, MARCI, food and instl. products co. exec.; b. Phila., Nov. 1, 1942; d. Jacob and Martha (Blotstein) Cohen; B.S. (scholar), Temple U., 1964; postgrad. UCLA, 1966-68; m. Frederick P. Weiner, Jan. 13, 1975. Maj. stockholder Global Products Corp., Beverly Hills, Calif., 1977—; circulation mgr. Phila. Inquirer, 1970-72; banquet mgr. El Morocco, N.Y.C., 1972-74; semi-profl. singer. Mem. Variety Club, Opera Assos. Mem. Rolls Royce Owners Club, Los Angeles County Art Mus. Clubs: Pres.'s, Thalians. Office: PO Box 3687 Beverly Hills CA 90212

WEINER, MARCIA MYRA, lawyer; b. Chgo., Apr. 12, 1934; d. Adolph Carl and Esther (Kahan) Spitzer; student U. Ariz., 1952, 54, Ind. U. extension, Indpls., 1953; B.A., St. Mary's U., San Antonio, 1965, J.D., 1970; m. Bernard K. Weiner, Sept. 15, 1952; children—Audrey Weiner Scheinberg, Jodi Weiner Groff, Karen Weiner Miller. Tchr. history Congregation Agudas Achim, San Antonio, 1965-69; admitted to Tex. bar, 1971; atty.-adviser HUD, San Antonio area office, 1971—, spl. achievement awards HUD, 1972, 75, 77. Mem. Am., Tex., Fed. bar assns., Pi Gamma Mu, Delta Epsilon Sigma, Phi Alpha Theta, Kappa Beta Pi. Jewish. Club: Hadassah. Home: 6603 Moss Oak Dr San Antonio TX 78229 Office: 800 Dolorosa St PO Box 9163 San Antonio TX 78285

WEINGARTEN, PALOMBA, investment broker; b. N.Y.C., Oct. 25, 1942; d. Sidney and Allegra (Atlas) Charach; B.A., M.A., Queens Coll.; m. Robert Weingarten, Jan. 27, 1962; children—Marc Gordon, Ilene Suzanne. Adj. lectr. Queens Coll., 1971-73; stockbroker Harris, Upham & Co., Inc., N.Y.C., 1974-75; with Dean, Witter, Reynolds & Co., Inc., N.Y.C., 1975-82, v.p. investments, 1977-82; v.p. Chase Investors Mgmt. Corp., N.Y.C., 1982—. Office: 5 World Trade Center New York NY 10048

WEINKAUF, MARY LOUISE STANLEY, educator; b. Eau Claire, Wis., Sept. 22, 1938; d. Joseph Michael and Marie Barbara (Holzinger) Stanley; B.A., Wis. State U., 1961; M.A., U. Tenn., 1962, Ph.D., 1966; m. Alan D. Weinkauf, Oct. 12, 1962; children—Stephen, Xanti. Grad. asst., instr. U. Tenn., 1961-66; asst. prof. English, Adrian Coll., 1966-69; prof., head dept. English, Dakota Wesleyan U., Mitchell, S.D., 1969—. Mem. Mitchell Arts Council. Mem. Nat. Council Tchrs. English, S.D. Council Tchrs. English, Sci. Fiction Research Assn., Popular Culture Assn., Milton Soc., AAUW (div. pres. 1978-80), Delta Kappa Gamma (pres. local chpt., mem. state bd. 1972—, state v.p. 1979—), Sigma Tau Delta, Pi Kappa Delta, Phi Kappa Phi. Republican. Lutheran. Home: 914 University Blvd Mitchell SD 57301 Office: 507 Smith Hall Dakota Wesleyan U Mitchell SD 57301

WEINLANDER, ALBERTINA ABRAMS (MRS. MAX M. WEINLANDER), educator; b. Mecosta, Mich., July 21, 1919; d. Edward and Albertina (Mantai) Abrams; B.S., Central Mich. U., 1942; M.A., U. Mich., 1947; Ph.D., 1955; m. Max M. Weinlander, June 4, 1945; children—Bruce, Annette. Tchr., prin. Mecosta (Mich.) High Sch., 1942-46; tchr. Sherman Twp. Rural Agrl. Sch., Weidman, Mich., 1946-48; instr., asst. prof. edn. and integrated studies Miami U., 1948-55, lectr. extension service, 1955-56; asst. prof. Wittenberg U., 1956-59, asso. prof. edn., 1960-69, prof., 1969—. Mem. NEA, Author's Guild (pres. Sprinfield chpt. 1968-70), Ohio Edn. Assn., Nat. Aerospace Edn. Council, Assn. Learning Disabilities, AAUW (pres. Springfield br. 1962-64), AAAS, Assn. Supervision and Curriculum Devel., Pi Lambda Theta, Kappa Delta Epsilon, Kappa Delta Pi. Clubs: Springfield Women's, Zonta (pres. 1968-70). Author: Your Child in a Scientific World, 1959; How to Prepare for the National Teacher, Examination, 1968, rev. edit., 1980; Education in the Elementary School, 1970; also articles in profl. jours. Composer gospel songs. Home: 290 Ridge Mall Springfield OH 45504

WEINSHIENK, ZITA LEESON, fed. judge; b. St. Paul, Apr. 3, 1933; d. Louis and Ada (Dubov) Leeson; student U. Colo., 1952-54; B.A. magna cum laude, U. Ariz., 1955; J.D. cum laude, Harvard U., 1958; m. Hubert T. Weinshienk, July 8, 1956; children—Edie, Kay, Darcy. Admitted to Colo. bar; probation counselor, legal adv., referee Denver Juvenile Ct., 1959-64; mcpl. judge, Denver, 1964-65; judge Denver County Ct., 1965-71, Denver Dist. Ct., 1972-79; judge, U.S. Dist. Ct. Colo., 1979—. Mem. vis. coms. Harvard Law Sch.; mem. Denver Anti-Crime Council. Named Woman of Yr., Denver Bus. and Profl. Women, 1969, one of 100 Women in Touch with Our Time, Harper's Bazaar mag., 1971. Fellow Colo. Bar Found., Am. Bar Found; mem. ABA, Colo. Bar Assn., Denver Bar Assn. (trustee), Nat. Conf. Fed. Trial Judges, Colo. Women's Bar Assn., Harvard Law Sch. Assn., Denver LWV, Women's Forum Colo., Phi Beta Kappa, Phi Kappa Phi, Phi Alpha Delta. Club: Soroptimist (Denver). Home: 3100 S Monroe St Denver CO 80210 Office: US Courthouse 1929 Stout St Denver CO 80294

WEINSTEIN, GRACE WOHLNER, author; b. N.Y.C., Nov. 19, 1935; d. David and Esther (Lobel) W.; B.A., Cornell U., 1957; m. Stephen D. Weinstein, Feb. 24, 1957; children—Lawrence B., Janet L. Author: Children and Money: A Guide for Parents, 2d edit., 1976; Retire Tomorrow-Plan Today, 1976; A Teacher's World: Psychology in the Classroom, 1977; Money of Your Own, 1977; People Study People: The Story of Psychology, 1979; Life Plans: Looking Forward to Retirement, 1979; columnist for Good Housekeeping, Elks mags.; tchr. nonfiction writing for mags.; lectr., cons. Mem. alumni adv. bd. Cornell U. Recipient nat. media award Am. Psychol. Found., 1975; sci. writer award ADA, 1979. Mem. Am. Soc. Journalists and Authors (pres. 1979-81), Council of Writers Orgns. (pres. 1979-82), Authors Guild/Authors League, Nat. Fedn. Press Women, LWV (v.p. Teaneck, N.J.).

WEINSTEIN, JOYCE, artist; b. N.Y.C., June 7, 1931; d. Sidney and Rose (Bier) W.; student CCNY, 1948-50, Art Students League, 1948-52; m. Stanley Boxer, Nov. 28, 1952. Exhibited in one-women shows: Perdalma Gallery, N.Y.C., 1953-56, L.I. U., Bklyn., 1969, U. Calif., Santa Cruz, 1969, T. Bortolazzo Gallery, Santa Barbara, Calif., 1972, Dorsky Gallery, N.Y.C., 1972, 74, Galerie Ariadne, N.Y.C., 1975, Gloria Cortella Gallery, N.Y.C., 1777, Meredith Long Contemporary Gallery, N.Y.C. 1978, 79, Martin Gerard Gallery, Edmonton, Alta., Can., 1981; group shows: Marlborough Gallery, N.Y.C., 1968, Bula Mus. Art, Calcutta, India, 1970, Rose Fried Gallery, N.Y.C., 1970, Hudson River Mus., 1971, Dorsky Gallery, 1972, Suffolk Mus., Stony Brook, N.Y., 1972, New York Cultural Center, 1973, Stamford (Conn.) Mus., 1973, Landmark Gallery, N.Y.C., 1974, Women's Interart Center, N.Y.C., 1974, 75, 78, New Sch. Social Research, N.Y.C., 1975, Bklyn. Mus., 1975, Galerie Areadne, N.Y.C., 1975, Fairleigh Dickinson U., Hackensack, N.J., 1976, Gloria Cortella, Inc., 1976, Edmonton Art Gallery Mus., 1977, Northeastern U., Boston, 1977, Lehigh (Pa.) U., 1977, Long Contemporary Gallery, 1977, 78, 79, 80, Mus. Modern Art, N.Y.C., 1981, Galerie Wentzel, Cologne, W.Ger., 1981 Martin Gerard Gallery, Edmonton, 1981, Gallery One, Toronto, 1981, also numerous univs. and colls.; represented in permanent collections: Pa. Acad. Fine Arts, N.J. State Mus., Ciba-Geigy Corp., New Sch. Social Research, Bula Mus. Art, U. Calif., Mus. Modern Art, N.Y.C., others; represented by Haber/Theodore Gallery, N.Y.C., Martin Gerard Gallery, Edmonton, Gallery One, Toronto, and Galerie Wentzel, Cologne, W. Ger.; exec. coordinator Women in Arts Found., Inc., 1975-79, 81-82. Recipient Lambert Fund award Pa. Acad. Fine Arts, 1955. Home and Studio: 37 E 18th St New York NY 10003

WEINSTEIN, JUDITH, art cons.; b. Chgo., Feb. 11, 1927; d. Julius and Charlotte (Brandau) Braun; B.S. in Psychology, U. Wis., 1950; m. Irwin Weinstein, Jan. 20, 1951; children—James, David. Tchr., N.Y. State Child Care Center, N.Y.C., 1950-52, U. Chgo., 1952-53; interior designer, color cons. Paul Bennett & Assos., 1953-58; mem. polit campaign coms. for U.S. Senate, mayor of Los Angeles, 1958-63; dir. Ethnic Arts Shop, Bookshop and George Page Mus. Shop, Los Angeles County Mus. Natural History, also producer ethnic art shows and research asst. dept. anthropology, 1971-77; dir., continuing edn. specialist Artsreach program UCLA Extension, also bd. dirs. Los Angeles Mcpl. Art Gallery Assos. and Los Angeles Art Showcase, 1978—; bd. dirs., dir. arts and crafts Los Angeles Street Scene Festival, 1978—; dir. fine arts prodns. T.S.B. Television, 1981—; project developer Zev Braun Pictures; spl. adv. for art U.S. Sen. Alan Cranston, 1978—. Planning com. Dem. Nat. Telethon, 1960; founder, v.p. Brentair Democratic Women, 1958-63; bd. dirs. Calif. Chamber Symphony, 1960-71; v.p. Pacific chpt. UN Assn., 1963-69, adv. bd., 1969-71; co-founder UN Center, Westwood, Calif., 1963, dir., 1965-71; del. 1st women's conf. Dem. Nat. Com., 1971—; bd. dirs. Mus. Alliance, 1971-77, Corp. on Disabilities and Telecommunications, 1981—; adv. com. Los Angeles Children's Mus., 1978; mem. (Calif.) Gov.'s Com. on Art and Media, Internat. Yr. of Disabled Persons, 1981.

WEINSTEIN, LAURA, health scientist adminstr.; b. N.Y.C., Aug. 21, 1927; d. Sol and Mollie Kagan; B.A., Cornell U., 1949; M.A. (NIMH grantee), Vanderbilt U., 1961, Ph.D. (NSF fellow; NIMH fellow), 1963; children—Richard Gordon Heimberg, Steven Andrew Heimberg. Asst. prof. George Peabody Coll. for Tchrs. (Vanderbilt U.), Nashville, 1963-66, asso. prof., 1966-72, prof., 1972-73; dir. research and eval. Edwin Gould Services for Children, N.Y.C., 1973-75; grants asso. NIH, Bethesda, Md., 1976-77; psychology tng. specialist NIMH, Rockville, Md., 1977-81; exec. sec. Behavioral and Neuroscis. Study Sect., NIH, Bethesda, 1981—. Mem. Am. Psychol. Assn., Phi Beta Kappa, Sigma Xi, Phi Kappa Phi. Contbr. articles in field to profl. jours. Home: 7420 Westlake Terr #1211 Bethesda MD 20817 Office: NIH Div Research Grants Westwood/A-25 5333 Westbard Ave Bethesda MD 20205

WEINSTEIN, NANCY ANNE, box mfg. co. exec.; b. Richmond, Va., Oct. 21, 1925; d. Morris Hyman and Bertha (Batkins) W.; cert. commerce, U. Richmond, 1971. With C&O Ry., 1942-57; with Va. folding box div. WESTVACO, Richmond, 1957—, supr. acctg. dept., 1971—. Pres. Highland Springs Civic Assn., 1953-55, Highland Springs Jr. Women's Club, 1951-53; treas. Belmont Meth. Ch., Richmond, 1965-79; mem. budget and allocations com. United Way Greater Richmond, 1981—; trustee Ednl. Found. of Am. Women's Soc. C.P.A.s-Am. Soc. Women Accts., 1982-84. Mem. Am. Soc. Women Accts. (pres. Richmond chpt. 1978-80, chmn. nat. subcom. 1981). Republican. Club: Richmond Coin (past treas.). Home: 3556 Marquette Rd Richmond VA 23234 Office: 320 Hull St Richmond VA 23224

WEINSTEIN, SHARON HARRIET, public relations exec.; b. Newark, Apr. 15, 1942; d. Louis Charles and Ruth Margaret (Franzblau) Schlein; B.A., U. Pa., 1964; m. Elliott Weinstein, May 7, 1978. Sr. editor Merrill Lynch, N.Y.C., 1972-74; public relations officer Chase Manhattan Bank, N.Y.C., 1974-79; v.p. public relations and advt. Blyth Eastman Dillon, N.Y.C., 1979-80; mgr. corp. communications Sanford C. Bernstein & Co., N.Y.C., 1980—. Mem. Women Execs. in Public Relations, Women in Communications, Womens Econ. Roundtable. Home: 161 W 15th St New York NY 10011 Office: 767 Fifth Ave New York NY 10153

WEINTRAUB, RUTH G., educator; b. N.Y.C., Feb. 15, 1909; d. Morris and Pessa (Noah) Goldstein; A.B., Hunter Coll., 1929, D.H.L. (hon.), 1981; J.D., N.Y. U., 1931; A.M., Columbia U., 1932, Ph.D., 1939; LL.D., Skidmore Coll., 1969; fellow Poly. Inst. N.Y., 1980; m. Solomon Weintraub, Aug. 26, 1930; 1 son, Jonathan W. Instr., Hunter Coll., 1929-40, asst. prof., 1940-45, asso. prof. polit. sci., 1946-51, prof., 1951—, coordinator social scis. (T.E.P.), 1951-56, dean grad. studies arts and sci., 1956-68, dean of social scis., 1968-72, dean emeritus, 1972—, chmn. dept. polit. sci., 1956-60; cons. Acad. for Ednl. Devel., 1972—, v.p., 1974, sr. v.p., 1977; asso. dean grad. div. City U. N.Y., 1963-68; vis. prof. N.Y. U. Grad. Sch., 1948-49; admitted to N.Y. bar, 1932. Chmn. N.Y. State Legis. Internship Program, 1961-72; mem. nat. labor panel Am. Arbitration Assn. Bd. dirs. Asso. YM-YWHA's Greater N.Y., 1968—, v.p., 1974. Mem. Am. Polit. Sci. Assn. (nat. com. on advancement teaching 1947-51, nat. council 1956-58, program com. 1960, com. status of women 1972-74, chmn. Charles E. Merriam award com. 1976), Am. Soc. Pub. Adminstrn. (v.p. Met. region 1949-50, sec. 1948-49), Citizens Union (legis. com. 1940-60), ACLU (acad. freedom com. 1947-54), Phi Beta Kappa (com. on qualifications 1973-79), Pi Sigma Alpha (pres. 1964-66; exec. council). Club: Princeton. Author: Government Corporations and State Law, 1939; How Secure These Rights?, 1949; (with others) Goals for Political Science, 1951, Administrative Questions and Political Answers, 1966; also chpts. in books. Contbr. to polit. sci., legal and ednl. publs. Home: 55 Central Park W New York NY 10023

WEIR, BIRDIE OLDOM, librarian, educator; b. West Blocton, Ala.; d. Ollius and Bettie (Duncan) Oldom; B.A., Ala. State U., 1960; M.S., Atlanta U., 1965; cert. in computer sci. Ala. A&M U., 1971; Ed.S., George Peabody Coll. for Tchrs., Vanderbilt U., 1977, Ph.D., 1979; m. Theo Weir, Dec. 3, 1962; 1 dau., Angela. Acting head librarian Mississippi Valley State U., Itta Bena, Miss., 1960-64, asst. librarian, supr. reference sevices and tech. services, 1965-69; intern Austin Peay State U., 1968; cataloger, head tech. services Ala. A&M U., Normal, 1969-72, acting univ. librarian, 1972-73, dir., prof. J.F. Drake Meml. Learning Resources Center, 1973—; lectr., cons. to libraries; cons. workshops; conf. presenter; lectr. Southwestern U., Memphis, 1979; mem. Ala. Center Higher Edn. Council Librarians, N.E. Ala. Library Network System Adv. Com. Active Reading is Fundamental Project, hosp. vol. program of Alpha Kappa Alpha PTA, NAACP, Huntsville Council Human Relations. Recipient Carrie Coleman Robinson ann. achievement award Beta Phi Mu, 1981; Ala. Center Higher Edn. faculty mini-grantee, 1978. Mem. ALA, Ala. Library Assn., Southeastern Library Assn., 1890 Library Dirs. Assn., Ala. Assn. Women Deans, Adminstrs. and Counselors, So. Conf. Afro-Am. Studies, NEA, Ala. Edn. Assn., AAUW, Alpha Kappa Alpha. Democrat. Baptist. Club: Eastern Star. Editor: 1890 Libline Newsletter, 1979—; contbr. articles to profl. jours. Home: 2814 Hilltop Terr Huntsville AL 35810 Office: PO Box 489 Normal AL 35762

WEIR, GLORIA JANE (MRS. N. LYLE EVANS), physician; b. Baton Rouge, Jan. 18, 1921; d. Claude Arnold and Peggy (Downing) W.; student Sullins Coll., 1936-37; B.S., La. State U., 1940, M.D., 1943; m. N. Lyle Evans, July 26, 1952; children—Peggy Jane, David Lyle. Intern, Charity Hosp. La., New Orleans, 1944, resident in pediatrics, 1949-51; pvt. practice medicine specializing in pediatrics, Baton Rouge, 1952-80; staff mem. Baton Rouge Gen. Hosp., vice-chief staff, 1965, vice-chief pediatrics, 1969, chief pediatrics, 1970-71; mem. staff Our Lady of Lake Hosp., Baton Rouge, vice chief pediatrics, 1959-60; mem. staff Women's Hosp., chief pediatrics, 1969-70; mem. staff Drs. Meml. Hosp.; mem. cons. staff Mary Bird Perkins Treatment Center, Cancer, Radiation and Research Found.; vis. staff Earl K. Long Meml. Hosp.; clin. instr. pediatrics La. State U. Med. Sch.; pediatric cons. Baton Rouge Gen. Hosp. Child Day Care Center; chief med. cons. Disability Determination Services, Baton Rouge Area, State of La. Diplomate Am. Bd. Pediatrics. Fellow Am. Acad. Pediatrics (alt. state chmn. La. chpt. 1975-78); mem. AMA, La. 6th Dist., East Baton Rouge Parish med. socs., La. Heart Assn., La., Baton Rouge (v.p. 1968-69, pres. 1969-70) pediatric socs., Cancer Soc. Baton Rouge (dir. 1963-67, 76—), Sullins Alumnae Assn., La. State U. Med. Sch. Alumni Asns., La. Concert Ballet Aux., Baton Rouge Civic Symphony Aux., Delta Zeta (mem. house corp.), La. State U. Alumni Fedn. Episcopalian. Club: Harlequins. Home: 5885 Eastwood Dr Baton Rouge LA 70806 Office: 2730 Wooddale Blvd PO Box 66498 Baton Rouge LA 70896

WEIR, NANCY MILLER, fabric and wallpaper wholesale exec.; b. Milw., Sept. 21, 1938; d. Lee and Agnes (Olson) Miller; student Carleton Coll., 1956-59; grad. Katharine Gibbs Sch., 1960-61; B.A., Miami U., 1960; m. George F. Weir, July 31, 1965. Corp. sec. PMA Ins. Fund, Inc., PMA Assurance Co., Inc., PMA Investment Sales Corp., PMA Ins. Agy. Inc., Milw., 1963-65; corp. sec. Fund Mgmt. Inc., Milw., 1964-65; office mgr. Ross Wilson C.P.A., Atlanta, 1965-66; office mgr. Sterling Offices Ltd., Atlanta, 1966-68; adminstrv. asst. to pres. Value Line Securities, N.Y.C., 1968-69; exec. asst. to chmn. bd. Brunschwig & Fils, N.Y.C., 1969-81, mgr. purchasing, 1981—. Vice-pres. Am. Field Service, 1975-77, bd. dirs., 1975—, student adv. liaison, 1978-79; vol. United Fund, 1976-77. Mem. Nat. Assn. Female Execs., Psi Chi, Kappa Delta. Club: Altrusa. Home: 32 Gramatan Court Bronxville NY 10708 Office: 410 E 62d St New York NY 10021

WEISBERG, JANET SUSAN, psychotherapist; b. N.Y.C., Mar. 21, 1940; d. Morris and Vivian (Wank) Weisberg; B.B.A., CCNY, 1960; M.S., City U. N.Y., 1966; postgrad. Yeshiva U., 1977—. Psychologist, Bklyn. Jewish Hosp., 1969-75; cons. N.Y. State Dept. Mental Hygiene, N.Y.C., 1978, N.Y.C. Bd. Edn., 1977—, Parent-Child Consultation Center, 1980—; psychotherapist Beth Israel Hosp., N.Y.C., 1975—, acting chief psychologist dept. child psychiatry, 1982—, dir. Enuresis Clinic, 1981—; mem. faculty Mt. Sinai Med. Sch., N.Y.C., 1979—. Pres. Singles div. Park Ave. Synagogue, N.Y.C., 1980—. Mem. Am. Psychol. Assn. Jewish.

WEISBERG, LORI ANNE, journalist; b. Los Angeles, Jan. 5, 1954; d. Irving Martin and Sally Joyce (Korsen) W.; B.A. in Communications summa cum laude (Newspaper Fund scholar, Sigma Delta Tau Found. Dora Davis Chapman scholar), UCLA, 1976. Intern, Congressman Mario Biaggi, Washington, summer 1974; reporter Herald Am., Bellflower, Calif., summer 1975; reporting intern Los Angeles Times, 1976; reporter Vista (Calif.) Press, 1976-78, Register, Orange County, Calif., 1978-80, San Diego Union, 1980—; UCLA del. Mademoiselle mag. Coll. Bd.; mem. chancellor' com. on media policy UCLA. Sec. Panhellenic Assn., U. Calif., Los Angeles. Recipient Nathanial R. Dumont Undergard. award; Orange County Press award, 1979; Calif. State Fair award for feature Writing, 1982. Mem. Women in Communications (award for best newswriting San Diego chpt. 1982), UCLA Govt. Internship Assn., Mortar Bd., Phi Beta Kappa, Sigma Delta Chi (Harry E. Morris award 1976, Mark of Excellence contest 1st Pl. award 1975), Alpha Mu Gamma, Sigma Delta Tau. Democrat. Jewish. Home: 1628 Thomas Ave San Diego CA 92109 Office: 350 Camino de la Reina San Diego CA

WEISBERGER, BARBARA, tchr., choreographer, artistic dir.; b. Bklyn., Feb. 28, 1926; d. Herman and Sally (Goldstein) Linshes; B.S., Pa. State U., 1945; L.H.D., Swarthmore Coll., 1970; D.F.A., Temple U., 1973; D.F.A. (hon.), Kings Coll., 1978, Villanova U., 1978; m. Sol Spiller, 1945 (div. 1948); m. Ernest Weisberger, Nov. 15, 1949; children—Wendy, Steven. Performed with Met. Opera Ballet, N.Y.C., 1937, 38, Mary Binney Montgomery Co., Phila., 1940-42; tchr., dir. Wilkes-Barre (Pa.) Ballet Theatre, 1953; artistic dir., founder Wilkes-Barre Ballet Guild, 1957; ballet mistress, choreographer Ballet Co. of Phila. Lyric Opera, 1961-62; artistic dir., founder Pa. Ballet Co., 1962—; choreographic works include: Judgment of Paris (Debussy, Griffes); Gingko Tree (Mendtner, Schubert); The Sorceress (Chopin); Quintet in Gay Minor (Gould); The Endless Curve (Debussy); Symphonic Variations (Franck); Italian Concerto, Bach; also operas for Phila. Lyric Opera Co., choreography for contemporary musical theatre. Ford Found. grantee, 1963, 65, 68, 71. Named Distinguished Dau. Pa., 1972; Distinguished Alumna, Pa. State U., 1972; recipient 46th ann. Gimbel Phila. award, 1978. Mem. Psi Chi. Home: 571 Charles Ave Kingston PA 18704 Office: Pennsylvania Ballet 2333 Fairmount Ave Philadelphia PA 19130

WEISER, MARGARET GOEWEY, educator; b. Binghamton, N.Y., July 7, 1922; d. Harold Webster and Margaret (Eager) Goewey; B.S., Rutgers U., 1943; M.S., Fla. State U., 1959; Ed.D., U. Ill., 1966; children—Robert E., Margaret E. Supr. kindergarten, primary edn. Ill. State U., Normal, 1959-66; prof. early childhood and elem. edn. U. Iowa, Iowa City, 1966—; cons. early childhood and spl. edn. Delta Kappa Gamma scholar, 1965-66, recipient teaching excellence award, 1973. Mem. World Orgn. Early Childhood Edn. (v.p. U.S. nat. com., N.Am. rep. program commn.), Nat. Assn. Edn. Young Children, Day Council Am., Pi Lambda Theta, Delta Kappa Gamma, Phi Delta Kappa. Author: Group Care and Education of Infants and Toddlers, 1982; contbr. articles to profl. jours. Home: 915 Oakcrest St #4 Iowa City IA 52240 Office: Coll Edn U Iowa Iowa City IA 52242

WEISLER, SHERRY JACOBS, psychologist; b. Bklyn., May 18, 1951; d. Barnet and Eve (Rosen) Jacobs; B.S. cum laude in Psychology, Bklyn. Coll., 1972, M.S. in Sch. Psychology, cert., 1974; m. Jeffrey Mark Weisler, Dec. 14, 1974; children— Stacey Melissa, Robert Allen. adj. lectr. psychology Bklyn. Coll., 1972, adj. lectr. counseling Sch. Edn., 1973-74, coll. asst. in testing and research, 1973-75; sch. psychologist-intng. Bur. Child Guidance, N.Y.C. Bd. Edn., 1974-75; sch. psychologist Kennedy Learning Clinic, Bklyn., 1975-76; asst. research scientist child psychiat. evaluation and research unit N.Y. Dept. Mental Hygiene, Bklyn., 1976; instr. social sci. St. Petersburg (Fla.) Jr. Coll., 1977-80; psychologist Comprehensive Mental Health Services, Inc., Clearwater, Fla., 1978-80, Pinellas County Head Start, 1980—. Mem. Am. Psychol. Assn. (asso.), Assn. Sch. Psychologists Bklyn. Coll. Jewish. Home: 2868 Meadow Oak Dr E Clearwater FL 33519

WEISMAN, CAROL DRESCHER, lawyer; b. N.Y.C., July 12, 1946; d. Raymond A. and Ruth W. Drescher; A.B. magna cum laude with high honors in English Lit., Brown U., 1967; M.A.T., Harvard U., 1969; J.D., Cath. U. Am., 1974; children—Stephanie, Deborah. Admitted to Md. bar, 1974, D.C. bar, 1975; law clk. U.S. Ct. of Appeals, D.C. Circuit, Washington, 1974-75; assoc. firm Wilmer & Pickering, Washington, 1975-79; assoc. counsel Washington Post, 1979—. Mem. D.C. Bar, Md. Bar, Phi Beta Kappa. Office: 1150 15th St NW Washington DC 20071

WEISMAN, LESLIE KANES, architect; b. Detroit, Nov. 8, 1945; d. Marvin L. and Mollie M. Kanes; B.F.A., Wayne State U., 1967; M.A. in Urban Studies, U. Detroit, 1973. Asst. prof. architecture and adminstrv. programming coordinator U. Detroit Sch. Architecture, 1968-75; co-founder, coordinator, mem. faculty Women's Sch. Planning and Architecture, 1974—; mem. faculty Woman's Sch., N.Y.C., 1975-76; asso. prof. architecture and environ. design N.J. Inst. Tech. Sch. Architecture, Newark, 1975—; asso. prof. women's studies Bklyn. Coll., 1979—; cons., mem. rev. bd. N.J. Regional Health Planning Council. Mem. Women in Architecture (a founder), NOW (exec. bd. 1970-74), Nat. Women's Polit. Caucus. Author: Flight From Suburbia, 1973; contbr. articles to profl. jours. Home: 99 Bank St New York NY 10014 Office: 323 High St Newark NJ 07102

WEISS, AGATHA LIN, social worker; b. Taipei, Taiwan, Apr. 11, 1944; came to U.S., 1969, naturalized, 1980; d. Tien-Tsai and Siou (Chen) Lin; B.S. with honors, Nat. Taiwan U., 1966; M.S.W. (scholarship), SUNY, Albany, 1971; m. Ernest S. Weiss, June 18, 1972; children—Donna Lin, Tina Claire. Asst. editor Chung Hua Pub. Co., Taipei, Taiwan, 1964-66; psychiat. social worker Nat. Taiwan U. Hosp., Taipei, 1966-69, field instr., 1967-69; social worker Talbot Perkins Children's Services, N.Y.C., 1971-73, dir. intake diagnostic dept., 1975—; psychiat. social worker supr. Corona Clin. Catholic Charities, Queens, N.Y., 1973-75. Cert. social worker, N.Y.; NIH grantee, 1967-69. Mem. Nat. Assn. Social Workers, Nat. Assn. Clin. Social Workers. Buddhist, Jewish. Contbr. articles to profl. jours. Home: 198-39 Pompeii Ave Holliswood NY 11423 Office: 342 Madison Ave New York NY 10017

WEISS, DAVIDA SOLOMON, educator; b. Bklyn., Nov. 11, 1939; d. Jacob and Estelle (Wager) Solomon; student Douglass Coll., 1957-60; B.A., George Peabody Coll. Tchrs., 1960-61; postgrad. Va. Commonwealth U., 1968-70; M.A., U. Tex., Dallas, 1977; m. George B. Weiss, June 5, 1960; children—William, Debra. Tchr. 7th grade, Nashville, 1961-62; adminstrv. asst. U. Pa., 1962-64; participant Ford Found. Exptl. Teaching Program, Richmond, Va., 1965-66; team leader social studies Haggard Middle Sch., Plano, Tex., 1975—, gifted children's program Plano Ind. Sch. Dist.; cons. on time mgmt. Pres. PTA, Richmond Jewish Community Center Nursery Sch., 1968, Prestonwood Elem. Sch., Dallas, 1971-72. Va. Commonwealth U. fellow, 1968-70. Mem. Tex. Council Social Studies, Tex. Tchrs. Assn., NEA, Plano Edn. Assn., Delta Kappa Gamma Soc. Internat. Home: 7605 Pennyburn Dr Dallas TX 75248 Office: 2401 Westside Dr Plano TX 75074

WEISS, DAWN ADRIENNE, flutist; b. Monticello, N.Y., July 11, 1951; d. Jerome and Marcia (Neukrug) W.; student Music Acad. of West, Santa Barbara, Calif., summers 1968, 69, 72, UCLA, 1969-72. Second flutist Miami (Fla.) Philharm., 1974-75; prin. flutist Mex. State Symphony Orch., Toluca, 1975-76; second flutist Oreg. Symphony Orch., Portland, 1977-80, prin. flutist, 1980—; concert soloist with Oreg. Symphony Pops, Pasadena Symphony, Debut Orch. of the YMF; flute instr. Lewis and Clark Coll., Reed Coll., Portland State U., U. Portland. Recipient Frank Sinatra 1st place award, 1970; Atwater Kent grand prize, 1970. Mem. Am. Fedn. Musicians, Greater Portland Flute Soc. Democrat. Jewish. Office: Oreg Symphony Orch 1119 SW Park St Portland OR 97205

WEISS, ELAINE LANDSBERG, community devel. ofcl.; b. N.Y.C., May 4, 1938; d. Louis and Sadie Blossum (Schoenfeld) Landsberg; B.A. in Philosophy and Polit. Sci., Bklyn. Coll., 1960; postgrad. N.Y.U. Law Sch., 1960-62; M.A. in Sociology, Hunter Coll., N.Y.C., 1969; divorced. Social investigator N.Y.C. Dept. Social Services, 1963-64; intern, fellow Eleanor Roosevelt Meml. Found., Nat. Assn. Intergroup Relations Ofcls., 1964-65; asst. dir. housing and asst. project dir. Operation Equality, Nat. Urban League, 1965-67; program asso. housing div. ch. missions Am. Bapt. Home Mission Socs., 1967-70; pres. E.L. Weiss Assos., 1970-76; exec. dir. Suffolk Community Devel. Corp., Coram, N.Y., 1976—; mem. citizens adv. com. N.Y.C. Dept. Housing Preservation and Devel.; exec. com. L.I. Community Devel. Orgn.; past 2d v.p. Suffolk Housing Task Force. Chmn., Suffolk County Citizens Adv. Com., 1981-82. Recipient cert. of commendation L.I. Council Chs., 1981. Mem. Nat. Assn. Housing Ofcls., N.Y. State Assn. Housing and Redevel. Ofcls., Am. Contract Bridge League (life master). Home: 211 E 18th St New York NY 10003 Office: 625 Middle Country Rd Coram NY 11727

WEISS, MADGE WEISBERGER (MRS. ANDREW B. WEISS), occupational therapist; b. Jersey City, Apr. 6, 1943; d. Phillip S. and Faye (Rapoport) Weisberger; B.A. in Psychology, Douglass Coll., 1963; cert. in Occupational Therapy, Columbia U., 1965; m. Andrew B. Weiss, June 14, 1964; children—Adam Matthew, Jennifer Mara, Leah Rebecca. Staff therapist Kenny Rehab. Inst., Mpls., 1965-66, U. Iowa Hosp. Sch. for Handicapped Children, Iowa City, 1966-68, sr. research asso. div. hand surgery U. Iowa Hosps., 1968-70, cons. to research project, 1970-73; asst. prof. occupational therapy U. Ala., Birmingham, 1973-77; cons. hand therapy, 1977—; asso. Hand Rehab. Services, P.A., 1978-82; dir. Hand Rehab. Assos., 1982—; cons.; lectr. Kean Coll. Former bd. dirs. Ala. Zool. Soc. Mem. Am., N.J. (pres.) occupational therapy assns., Am. Soc. Hand Therapists (chmn. research com.). Contbr. articles to profl. publs. Home: 66 Slope Dr Short Hills NJ 07078

WEISS, MARILYN MAGALIFF (MRS. HOWARD JERRY WEISS), artist; b. Bklyn., Sept. 4, 1932; d. Max and Anna (Haber) Ackerman; B.S. magna cum laude, N.Y. U., 1953; m. Howard Jerry Weiss, Nov. 24, 1972; children—Jodi Kim Magaliff and Barry Todd Magaliff (twins). Exhibited one-woman shows: Alper-Goldberg Gallery, Cedarhurst, N.Y., 1977, Fred Leighton Madison Ltd., 1975, Port Washington (N.Y.) Library, 1974, Adelphi U., 1974, Hewlett Woodmere Library, 1972, Bodley Gallery, N.Y.C., 1983; exhibited in group shows Firehouse Gallery Nassau Community Coll., Garden City, 1971, Pallazzio Vechio, Florence, Italy, 1972, Palazzio Nat., Naples, Italy, 1972, Brockton (Mass.) Library, 1972, Roanoke (Va.) Fine Arts Center, 1972, Milliken U., 1972, U. Okla., 1973, Southeastern Ark. Art. and Sci. Center, 1973, Tuskegee Inst., 1974, Albrecht Gallery, 1974, Bergen Community Mus., 1974, Jesse Besser Mus., 1976, Central Wyo. Mus. Art, 1977, U. Wis., 1978, City Gallery, N.Y.C., 1981, Community Mus., 1974, Equitable Gallery, N.Y.C., 1979, Fed. Bldg., N.Y.C., 1979, 81, Traveling Painting Exhbn. U.S.A., 1972-74, Traveling Watermedia Exhbn. U.S.A., 1976-78, 78—, Oil and Watermedia Exhbn., 1978-80, numerous others. Recipient maj. prize Suburban Art League Ann. Show, 1968, 71; award Suburban Art League Show, 1968, 71. Mem. Nat. Assn. Women Artists, Beta Gamma Sigma. Address: 1100 Park Ave New York NY 10028

WEISS, PAULINE EDITH, psychiatrist; b. N.Y.C., Nov. 23, 1931; d. Ellis H. and Freda (Teitlebaum) Liberman; B.A., Bklyn. Coll., 1952, M.S., 1958; M.D., Autonomous U., Guadalajara, Mex., 1973; m. Aaron Weiss, Nov. 26, 1964. Tchr. N.Y.C. Pub. Schs.; resident in psychiatry Roosevelt Hosp., now staff psychiatrist; practice medicine specializing in psychiatry, N.Y.C.; candidate Karen Horney Inst. Recipient cert. of excellence N.Y.C. Bd. Edn. Mem. Am. Psychiat. Assn., Am. Med. Women's Assn., Am. Inst. Psychoanalysis. Democrat. Jewish. Office: 435 W 57th St New York NY 10019

WEISS, RITA SHAPIRO, speech pathologist, educator; b. Newark, Jan. 5, 1922; d. Joseph and Dorothy (Hochberg) Shapiro; B.S., Simmons Coll., 1945; M.A., U. Colo., Boulder, 1957, Ph.D., 1967; m. Lawrence G. Weiss, June 15, 1942; children—Carolyn Judith, Jonathan Lawrence. Speech therapist Laradon Hall Sch. Exceptional Children, Denver, 1956-58; speech correctionist Boulder (Colo.) Valley Schs., 1958-62; mem. faculty dept. communications disorders and speech sci. U. Colo., Boulder, 1962—, prof., 1969—, asst. dean Coll. Arts and Scis., 1982—. Bd. dirs. Boulder Day Nursery, 1974-82; mem. Boulder Child Find Adv. Bd.; mem. Boulder Headstart Health Adv. Bd. Recipient Teaching Recognition award U. Colo., 1969; Outstanding Educator Am. award Nat. Council Edn., 1970, research grant awards U.S. Dept. Edn., 1974-81. Mem. Am. Assn. Mental Deficiency, Am. Speech and Hearing Assn., AAAS, Nat. Assn. Edn. Young Children, Colo. Speech and Hearing Assn., Colo. Assn. Edn. Young Children, Council for Exceptional Children. Democrat. Jewish. Club: Boulder Valley Racquet. Contbr. articles in field to profl. jours. Office: Dept Communications Disorders and Speech Sci U Colo Box 409 Boulder CO 80309

WEISSLER, BEATRICE, nutritionist; b. Bklyn., Jan. 6, 1926; d. Abraham and Sarah (Dreiblatt) Schriftman; B.S. in Home Econs., Bklyn. Coll., 1947; M.S. in Nutrition and Public Health (President's scholar 1951-53), Columbia U., 1954; m. Paul Weissler, Oct. 2, 1948; children—Rona, Edye. Dietitian, Met. Hosp., N.Y.C., 1947-49; sch. lunch mgr. Jr. High Sch. 35, Bklyn., 1949-50; instr. nutrition and diet therapy Prospects Heights Hosp. Sch. Nursing, Bklyn., 1955-59; instr. nutrition Bklyn. Coll., 1959-60, 70-81; instr. to Tb patients Kings County Hosp., Bklyn., 1961-66; instr. nutrition and diet therapy Skidmore Coll. Sch. Nursing, 1965-66; nutritionist, lectr. Bklyn. Tb and Lung Assn., 1955-75; nutritionist N.Y.C. Dept. Health, 1973-75; cons. nutritionist, 1982—; chmn. Bklyn. nutriton com. Food and Nutrition Council Greater N.Y., 1974—. Mem. Am. Dietetic Assn., Am. Public Health Assn., Am. Home Econs. Assn., Greater N.Y. Dietetic Assn., Public Health Assn. N.Y.C., N.Y. State Home Econs. Assn., Food and Nutrition Council Greater N.Y. Address: 2732 Whitman Dr Brooklyn NY 11234

WEISSMAN, NANCY DIANE, data processing co. exec.; b. Phila., Jan. 31, 1956; d. Max and Fredrica G. Weissman; B.S., Pa. State U., 1977; M.B.A., Temple U., 1979. Instr. remote customer edn. Burroughs Corp., Radnor, Pa., 1979-81, customer support rep., Fairfax, Va., 1981, Systems rep., Columbia, Md., 1981—. Mem. Assn. M.B.A. Execs. Clubs: Pa. State Alumni, Temple U. Alumni (Washington). Home: 4904 Herkimer St Annandale VA 22003 Office: 9160 Red Branch Rd Columbia MD 21045

WEISSMAN, RONEE FREEMAN, speech pathologist, owner tour agy.; b. N.Y.C., Apr. 16, 1951; d. Jonas Herbert and Marion (Rosen) Freeman; B.A. magna cum laude, Queens Coll., 1973, M.A. in Speech Pathology, 1978; m. Eugene Weissman, Jan. 28, 1973; children—Ilana Nicole, Adam Scott. Tchr. high sch. speech, theatre and English, N.Y.C., 1973-75; speech pathologist Byram Hills Sch. Dist., Westchester, N.Y., part-time, 1979-80, E. Ramapo Sch. Dist., Rockland, N.Y., 1981—; owner, v.p., dir. Weissman Teen Tours, Inc., Ardsley, N.Y., 1974—. Youth dir., Sunday sch. tchr. Temple Israel, New Rochelle. Speech and hearing handicapped cert., speech arts cert., N.Y.; lic. speech pathologist, N.Y. Mem. Am. Speech, Lang. and Hearing Assn. (cert. clin. competency), N.Y. State Speech, Lang. and Hearing Assn., Internat. Platform Assn., Phi Beta Kappa, Kappa Delta Pi. Jewish. Home and Office: 517 Almena Ave Ardsley NY 10502

WEITZEL, JACQUELINE NECHO, bus. research analyst; b. Phila., Oct. 16, 1927; d. Louis and Marie (Miglio) Necho; B.S. in Chemistry and Microbiology, U. Pa., 1949; M.S. in Info. Mgmt., Drexel U., 1968; m. Raymond A. Weitzel, June 3, 1952 (dec.); children—Pamela, Eric, Grant, James. Research chemist Dept. Agr., 1950-52; engring. librarian Widener U., 1964-66; info. analyst E.I. duPont de Nemours, Inc., 1966-71; sr. bus. research analyst Phila. Quartz Corp. (name now PQ Corp), Valley Forge, Pa., 1971—. Mem. Am. Chem. Soc., Nat. Assn. Bus. Economists, Chem. Mktg. Research Assn., Spl. Libraries Assn. (pres. Phila. chpt.). Home: 508 Lawrence Dr Springfield PA 19064 Office: PQ Corp Box 840 Valley Forge PA 19482

WELCH, ANN-MARIE STEPHENSON, physician; b. Knoxville, Tenn., Aug. 20, 1937; d. Charles Millard and Laura Norwood (Roberson) Stephenson; B.S., Duke U., 1959, M.A. (Gen. Foods fellow in Marine Algology, Fulbright scholar, Internat. Inst. Edn. Research scholar), 1960; M.D. (NIH predoctoral fellow), Johns Hopkins U., 1974; m. Bruce L. Welch, Aug. 23, 1959. Research asst. in pharmacology Duke U., Durham, N.C., 1960-62, Med. Coll. Va., 1962-64; research asso. dept. biology Coll. William and Mary, Williamsburg, Va., 1964-66, U. Tenn. Meml. Research Center and Hosp., Knoxville, 1966-69, Md. Psychiat. Research Center, Balt., 1969-70; intern Yale-New Haven Hosp., 1974-75; resident, 1975-76; resident U. Conn. Health Center, Farmington, 1977-78; practice medicine specializing in internal medicine, New Britain, Conn., 1980—; staff physician Gaylord Hosp., Wallingford, Conn., 1977-78; emergency room physician New Britain Gen. Hosp., 1978-79, jr. attending physician dept. medicine, 1980—; sr. partner Welch Assos., Kensington, Conn. Diplomate Am. Bd. Internal Medicine. Mem. Am. Soc. Pharmacology and Exptl. Therapeutics, A.C.P., AAAS, AMA, N.Y. Acad. Scis., Conn. State Med. Soc., Hartford County Med. Assn., Phi Beta Kappa, Sigma Xi. Co-editor Physiological Effects of Noise, 1970; co-author research reports in biochem. and pharmacol. fields. Home: 1113 High Rd Kensington CT 06037 Office: 40 Hart St New Britain CT 06052

WELCH, BERNICE MARIE, state legislator; b. Middletown, Conn., Aug. 7, 1914; d. Frederick and Ellen (Hayes) Harrison; cert. Bur. Ednl. Research and Testing Service, U. N.H., 1968; student Notre Dame Coll., Manchester, N.H., 1971-73; m. John L. Welch, June 20, 1937; children—John L., George E. Social worker Community Action Program, Manchester, N.H., 1967-69; community health worker Dept. Public Health, Manchester, 1971; social worker Model Cities Program, Manchester, 1971-73; mem. N.H. Ho. of Reps., 1978—. Vice chmn. Ward 4, City of Manchester, 1976—; com. mem. Overall Econ. Devel. Program Hillsborough County (N.H.), 1977-78, So. N.H. Human Services, CETA Planning Council, Hillsborough County, 1978. Mem. Order Women Legislators. Democrat. Office: #4-85 State of NH House of Reps Concord NH 03301

WELCH, JENNIFER GROCE, social service adminstr., writer; b. Columbus, Ohio, Jan. 24, 1945; d. Robert O. and Maryanna (Sharkey) Miller; ed. Ohio State U.; m. Richard Alan Welch, Apr. 25, 1981; children by previous marriages—David Jeffrey DeRhodes, Christopher Daniel Groce. Publs. adminstr. Extension Entomology, Ohio State U., Columbus, 1973-77, project process coordinator Nat. Center for Research in Vocat. Edn., 1978, office supr. Writing Workshop, English dept., 1978-81, adminstrv. dir. Disaster Research Center, Dept. Sociology, 1981—; dir. Ohio Valley Region Certification Training Center and Library, 1978—; mem. Women's Poetry Workshop, Ohio State U., 1978—; reader and tchr. poetry therapy workshops, 1979—; bd. dirs., judge Community of Poets Awards. Mem. Montage, 1979—; chairperson Justice for Jack Com., 1976-79; active First Ch. of Christ, Scientist, Columbus, Ohio, 1965—. Recipient Ohio Legislature Recognition, 1978. Mem. Nat. Assn. for Poetry Therapy (bd. dirs. 1978—, editor NAPT News), Nat. Fedn. of Poetry Socs. (state pres. 1977-79), Alliance of Expressive Art Therapies, Nat. Assn. for Neighborhood Schs., Nat. Ednl. Council Creative Therapies. Author: Earthdays, 1977; 2:36 a.m., 1978; Magic House (with Darryl Price), 1980; All My Designs Turn Out Crooked in the End, 1980; The Pulling, 1981; Topics for Getting in Touch: A Poetry Therapy Sourcebook, 1982; contbr. numerous poetry to various mags. and lit. publs.; editor Pudding Mag., 1979—; columnist Collage, 1977-79, editor 1977-79; editor DRC Publs. Home: 2384 Hardesty Dr So Columbus OH 43204 Office: Disaster Research Center Ohio State U 128 Derby Hall 154N Oval Mall Columbus OH 43210

WELCH, LORA JANELLE, govt. ofcl.; b. Banner, Miss., Aug. 15, 1933; d. Willie Clark and Lora Allie (Moore) Wilson; A.A., Cochise Jr. Coll., 1976; B.S., SUNY, Albany, 1979; postgrad. U. Ariz., 1980; grad. Armed Forces Staff Coll., 1982; m. Bill A. Welch, Aug. 6, 1960 (dec. 1981); children—Karen Sue, Bill A., Richard. Exec. sec. various depts. within the govt. at numerous mil. installations, 1956-74; plans and programs specialist U.S. Army Air Traffic Control Activity, Fort Huachuca, Ariz., 1974-79, mgmt. analyst, comptroller office, 1979—. Mem. Nat. Assn. Female Execs., Am. Soc. Mil. Comptrollers (pres. elect Cochise chpt.), Aircraft Owners and Pilots Assn. Democrat. Home: Route 1 Box 121 Hereford AZ 85615 Office: US Army Communications Command Comptroller Office Fort Huachuca AZ 85613

WELCH, MARY ANN, ednl. adminstr.; b. Rutland, Vt., Feb. 1, 1947; d. John Joseph and Yolanda Frances (Bove) Welch; A.B. in History, Smith Coll., 1969; M.A. in Student Personnel Adminstrn., Columbia U., 1977. Personnel counselor Manpower, Inc., N.Y.C., 1969-71; tchr. social studies Edmunds Jr. High Sch., Burlington, Vt., 1971-72; asst. dean students Smith Coll., Northampton, Mass., 1972-76; asso. dean students Douglass Coll./Rutgers State U., New Brunswick, N.J., 1977-78; dir. Weekend Coll., Trinity Coll., Burlington, 1979—; mem. Burlington Continuing Edn. Consortium. Bd. dirs. Greater Burlington Women's Network, 1981-82; mem. Save The Flynn Theater Project, 1981-82; vol. Vt. ETV Auction, 1981-82. Mem. Nat. Assn. Women Deans, Adminstrs. and Counselors. Home: 11 E Allen St #12 Winooski VT 05404 Office: Trinity Coll Colchester Ave Burlington VT 05401

WELCH, MARY-SCOTT, writer; b. Chgo.; d. William Scott and Myrtle (Ferrin) Stewart; A.B. in English, U. Ill.; m. Barrett F. Welch (dec.); children—Farley, Laura Stewart, Margaret, Mary Barrett. Books include: Your First Hundred Meals, What Every Young Man Should Know, The Family Wilderness Handbook, Networking: The Great New Way for Women to Get Ahead; mem. staff Esquire-Coronet mag., Pageant mag., Look mag.; contbg. editor Glamour mag.; columnist

Seventeen mag., McCall's mag., Vogue mag.; contbr. to mags. including Ladies Home Jour., Redbook, Ms., Modern Maturity, Working Woman, Woman's Day. Bd. advisors Working Women Edn. Fund, Inst. Women and Work of Cornell U. Served with USNR. Mem. Authors Guild, Authors League, Am. Soc. Journalists and Authors, Women in Communications, Women's Inst. Freedom of Press, Nat. Press Club, NOW (adv. bd.; past coordinator rape prevention com. N.Y.C.), Phi Beta Kappa. Home and Office: 30 Waterside Plaza New York NY 10010

WELCH, RAQUEL, actress; b. Chgo., Sept. 5, 1942; d. Armand and Josepha (Hall) Tejada; m. James Westley Welch, May 8, 1959 (div.); children—Damon, Tahnee; m. 2d, Patrick Curtis (div.); m. 3d, Andre Weinfeld, July 1980. Former model for Neiman-Marcus stores; films include Fantastic Voyage, 1966, One Million B.C., 1967, The Biggest Bundle of Them All, 1968, Roustabout, 1964, A House is Not a Home, 1964, Swinging Summer, 1965, Shoot Louder. . . I Don't Understand, 1967, Fathom, 1967, Magic Christian, 1970, Fuzz, 1972, Bluebeard, 1972, Hannie Caulder, 1972, Kansas City Bomber, 1972, Myra Breckinridge, 1970, The Last of Sheila, 1973, The Three Musketeers, 1974, The Wild Party, 1975, The Four Musketeers, 1975, Mother, Jugs and Speed, 1976, Crossed Swords, 1978, L'Animal, 1979; appeared in Broadway musical Woman of the Year, 1982. *

WELCH, SANDRA LYNN, machine shop exec.; b. Gilmer, Tex., Feb. 15, 1946; d. Leo Albert and Mattie Lou (Middlebrook) Lambert; student Massey Bus. Coll., 1963, Conroe Area Vocat. Sch., 1977, Conroe Vocat. Sch., 1978; cert. for completion machine shop programming Mfg. Data Systems, 1981; m. Travis J. Welch, July 8, 1963; children—Donna Marie, Debra Lynne, Deidra Sue, Travis Wayne. Gen. office worker Kelly Girls, Houston, 1963-68; co-owner, gen. mgr. T & S Machine Co., Inc., Cut and Shoot, Tex., 1974—; bd. chmn. Conroe Vocat. Dist. Adv. Council, 1980-82; dir. Conroe Bus. Computing, Inc., Bd. dirs. Conroe Area Girls Softball. Named Woman of Yr., YWCA, 1981. Mem. Am. Bus. Women's Assn. (chmn. bd. Conroe chpt., Boss of Yr. award 1982), Nat. Women in Constrn., Nat. Assn. Female Execs., Desk and Derricks. Office: PO Box 188 Cut and Shoot TX 77303

WELCH, SARAH RAYNOR, clergyman; b. Phila., Nov. 17, 1900; d. Hartley and Daisy (Kercher) Raynor; student Unity Sch. Christianity, Lee's Summit, Mo., 1954-56, Inst. of Religious Sci., Los Angeles; m. Fred W. Welch, Feb. 16, 1954. Ordained to ministry Unity Ch., minister and tchr., Jacksonville, Fla. Mem. New Thought Alliance (life), DAR. Address: 2625 Emily Ln Jacksonville FL 32216

WELCH, SUSAN LUCY, mental health counselor; b. Phila., Nov. 6, 1949; d. Joseph P. and Sue (Pugliese) Pacileo; B.S., Gannon U., 1979; children—Laura Renae Fulford, Alyssa Dawn Welch, Heather Krystie Welch. With Gertrude Barber Center, Erie, Pa., 1978, Stairways, Inc., Erie 1978; founder H.E.L.P. Crisis Center, Erie, 1977-80; mental health counselor Community Country Day Sch., Erie, 1980-81. Mem. Dem. Women's Council, Erie, 1980-81; mem. Downtown Center City Commn., Erie, 1979; Democratic committeewoman, 6th Ward, 6th Dist., Erie County, 1978-82; public relations chmn., mem. adv. bd., v.p. People for Life, 1976-81. Roman Catholic. Club. Calabrese Club Bowling League. Address: 4820 Fillmore Terr L-12 Philadelphia PA 19124

WELCHONS, VIRGINIA RUTH, psychiat. social worker; b. Indpls., July 17, 1930; d. Alvie McGregor and Harriet (Blue) W.; B.S., Ball State U., 1953; M.A. in Social Work, Ind. U., 1963. Social worker Marion County (Ind.) Welfare Dept., Indpls., 1960-61; probation officer Marion County Juvenile Ct., 1963-64, supr. probation officers, 1964-66; supr. counselors Ind. Girls Sch., Indpls., 1966-67, asst. supt., 1967-69; psychiat. social worker Midtown Community Mental Health Center, Indpls., 1969-70, supr. psychiat. counselors, 1970-71, dir. county out-patient team, 1971-73, dir. crisis intervention unit, 1973-75, dir. hosp.-based services, 1975-77, dir. clin. services, 1977—; services devel. coordinator Ind. Council Community Mental Health Centers, 1979-80. Elder, chmn. recruitment and coordination vols. com. Wallace St. Presbyn. Ch., Indpls. Mem. Acad. Cert. Social Workers (cert.), Nat. Assn. Social Workers. Home: 1021 N Downey Indianapolis IN 46219 Office: 1001 W 10th St Indianapolis IN 46202

WELCOME, VERDA F., state senator; b. Lake Lure, N.C.; B.S., Morgan State Coll., 1939; M.S., N.Y. U., 1943; postgrad. Columbia U. Tchr.; mem. Md. Ho. of Dels., 1959-63; mem. Md. Senate, 1963-83, vice chmn. exec. nominations com., mem. fin. com. Public mem. State Dept. Fgn. Service Selection Bds.; mem. Americans for Democratic Action, Valiant Women's Dem. Club, Balt. Urban League, Nat. Order Women Legislators; bd. govs. 4th Dist. Dem. Orgn. Balt. City, Inc.; bd. dirs. Citizens Planning and Housing Assn., LWV; founder, mem. Mondawmin Improvement Assn.; life mem. NAACP; adv. bd. Provident Hosp. Recipient awards and citations. Mem. AAUW, Delta Sigma Theta (life). Office: 101 Presidential Wing James Bldg Annapolis MD 21401

WELD, ELLEN LEE, real estate broker; b. St. Louis, May 8, 1935; d. William Peter and Marjorie (Kingsbury) Carleton; student Manhattanville Coll., 1954; m. William George Weld, June 22, 1954; children—Ellen, William, Thomas, Edward K. Real estate broker Cleveland, Deeble, Arnold, Greenwich, Conn., 1972-75, Newhall and Ogilvy, Greenwich, 1975-81; pres., Lee Weld Inc., Greenwich, 1981—. Docent, Toledo Mus., 1960-63; head docent Mpls. Inst. Arts, 1963, 64. Mem. Nat. Assn. Realtors, Conn. Assn. Realtors, Greenwich Bd. Realtors. Repbulican. Clubs: Round Hill, Garden of Am., St. Andrews, Jr. League, Hortulus (dir., treas.). Home: 120 Zaccheus Mead Ln Greenwich CT 06830 Office: 2 Sound View Dr Greenwich CT 06830

WELDON, ANN BLAIN, journalist; b. Roanoke, Va., June 12, 1911; d. Samuel Stuart and Jean Maurice (Vaughan) Blain; student Nat. Bus. Coll., 1931, U. Va. Extension, 1932-36; m. Jack Weldon, Sept. 11, 1937; children—Ann Stuart, John Blain. mem. secretarial, writing staffs Roanoke (Va.) Times and World News newspapers, 1933-41, also Sta. WDBJ-AM; corr. Times Publ. Co., St. Petersburg, Fla., 1965-70; religion writer St. Petersburg Evening Ind., 1970—; freelance writer on religious events, other subjects, 1969—. Tchr. Sunday Sch. Presbyn. Ch., 1928-64. Mem. DAR, Religion Newswriters Assn., Fla. Press Women, (sec. 1981-83), PEO, Sigma Delta Chi. Democrat. Clubs: garden, womens. Home: 5025 39th St S Saint Petersburg FL 33711 Office: 430 1st Ave S Saint Petersburg FL 33731

WELDON, BERNICE OLIVE MORTON, educator; b. Basin, Wyo., Feb. 25, 1915; d. Ray Royal and Olive Ethel (Robertson) Morton; B.A. in Social Studies and Classical Langs. (tuition scholar), Lewis and Clark Coll., Portland, Oreg., 1936; M.R.E. (William Gray scholar), Boston U., 1937; elem. tchr. cert., Oreg. Coll. Edn., 1955; m. Fay B. Weldon, May 16, 1939; children—Joseph, David, Philip, James, John, Michael. Instr. religion and Greek, Lewis and Clark Coll., 1937-38; dir. religious edn. Sheldon Jackson Sch., Sitka, Alaska, 1938-39; tchr. Liberty Elem. Sch., Sweet Home, Oreg., 1953-58; elem. sch. tchr., Austin, Minn., 1958—, specialist learning disabilities, 1968—. Precinct and county chmn. Minn. Ind. Republicans, 1976—, mem. state central com., 1980—, fin. chmn., 1980. Mem. NEA, Assn. Children Learning Disabilities, Orton Soc., Council Exceptional Children, World Future Soc., AAUW, Minn. Edn. Assn., Austin Edn. Assn., Bus. and Profl. Women, LWV, Audubon Soc. Presbyterian (elder). Home: 1806 5th Ave NW Austin MN 55912

WELKER, JOAN ELIZABETH, social worker; b. Gary, Ind., Oct. 15, 1940; d. Thomas Franklin and Dorothy Jane (Hogenfeld) Taylor; B.S., Ohio State U., 1972, M.S.W., 1973; m. John G. Welker, Dec. 18, 1971 (dec.). Psychiat. social worker Columbus (Ohio) State Hosp., 1973-74; psychiat. social worker Columbus Area Mental Health Center, 1974-75, coordinator intermediate care program, 1975-78, chief day treatment programs, 1976-78; clin. social worker, consultation and edn. specialist KernView Mental Health Center and Hosp., Bakersfield, Calif., 1978—; owner, pvt. practice Canaan Cons.; founder, chairperson Bakersfield Community Rape Treatment Program. adj. instr. Coll. Social Work, Ohio State U., 1975—, Capital U., 1976-77; lectr. in field. Lic. clin. Social Worker. Mem. Acad. Cert. Social Workers, Nat. Assn. Social Workers, Nat. Registry Clin. Social Workers, AAUW. Democrat. Episcopalian. Author articles. Home: 2112 Courtleigh Dr Apt C Bakersfield CA 93309 Office: Suite 205 4949 Buckley Way Bakersfield CA 93309

WELKOWITZ, JOAN, psychologist, educator; b. N.Y.C.; d. Abraham and Ray (Young) Horowitz; B.A., Queens Coll., 1949; M.A., U. Ill., 1952; Ph.D., Columbia U., 1960; m. Walter Welkowitz, June 17, 1951; children—David, Lawrence, Julie Ann. Chief research psychologist Mt. Sinai Hosp., N.Y.C., 1959-62; asst. prof. psychology N.Y. U., N.Y.C., 1964-69, asso. prof., 1969-76, prof. psychology, 1976—, Art & Sci. Research grantee, 1981-82; vis. prof. Princeton U., 1975-77. Mem. Am. Psychol. Assn. Author: Introductory Statistics for the Behavioral Sciences, 3d edit., 1982; cons. editor: Jour. Cons. and Clin. Psychology, 1977-82. Home: 138 Highland Ave Metuchen NJ 08840 Office: NY Univ 6 Washington Pl 4th Floor Dept Psychology New York NY 10003

WELLER, ADA STRAHAN, cosmetics co. exec.; b. Alton, Ill., Aug. 7, 1927; d. Crit and Minnie (Rathgeber) Shaw; grad. Midwestern Broadcasting Sch., 1947, Patirica Stevens Modeling Sch., 1948, Ill. Central Beauty Sch., 1948; m. Gerald E. Weller, July 3, 1974; 1 son by previous marriage, Darrell Lon. Sales rep. Nat. Tape, Inc., Milw., 1966-68; nat. sales supr. Barton's Candy Co., Bklyn., 1968-70; ter. supr. Helena Rubenstein, Inc., Honolulu and Alaska, 1970-77; ter. supr. Del Labs., Ballwin, Mo., 1978—. Recipient various sales awards. Republican. Club: Lambert Field Officers. Address: 307 Quail Village Ct Ballwin MO 63011

WELLER, MARGARET JANET, accountant; b. Jersey City, Mar. 30, 1945; d. Steven and Margaret (Wilson) Kozak; B.A. in Econs., Rutgers U., 1980; m. Huyler D. Weller, June 23, 1968; children—David, Michael, Jennifer. Controller, office mgr. Southland Container, Inc., Avenel, N.J., 1975-80; mgr. acctg. dept. Garden State Bus. Machines, Inc., Mountainside, N.J., 1980-81; plant acct. plastic beverage ops. Owens-Ill., East Brunswick, N.J., 1981—. Mem. Nat. Assn. Female Execs., NOW, Common Cause. Democrat. Roman Catholic. Office: 1090 Bristol Rd Mountainside NJ 07092

WELLES, KELLY, advt. exec.; b. Bellingham, Wash., June 10, 1948; d. Solon Richard and Elva Maria (Dibble) Boynton; student Sorbonne, Paris, 1966-67; B.A., U. Wash., Seattle, 1968; M.A. in Polit. Sci., New Sch. for Social Research, N.Y.C., 1974. Advt. copywriter Norton Simon Communication, N.Y.C., 1974-75; v.p., creative dir. Gordon & Shortt Advt., N.Y.C., 1976-79; exec. dir. advt. Paramount Pictures, N.Y.C., 1979-80; sr. copywriter, asso. creative dir. William Esty Co., 1981-82; v.p., asso. creative dir. Bozell & Jacobs Advt., N.Y.C., 1982—; mass media cons. to Ford Found., 1976. Bd. dirs. Daily-Plan-It Newsletter, 1980; cons. YWCA Contact Career Conf., 1979, 80. Intern, UN, Geneva, SHAPE and NATO, Paris, The Common Market, Internat. Ct. at the Hague, 1966; recipient Casebook Print awards, 1975; The One Show award, 1976; Effie award, 1979. Mem. Advt. Women of N.Y. (dir., 1979-80), N.Y. Women in Communications (dir., 1981), One Club for Art Dirs. and Copywriters, TV Acad. Arts and Scis. (Emmy award judge 1980), Fgn. Policy Assn., Women's Econ. Roundtable, Nat. Women's Polit. Caucus. Author: Analysis of Folk Art in Third World Communications, 1976; Creation and Analysis of African Training and Research Center for Women, 1976. Home: 425 E 63rd St New York NY 10021

WELLMAN, GAIL EUNICE, advt. and sales exec.; b. N.Y.C., July 20, 1937; d. Morris and Barbara (Schwartz) Schechter; B.A., Queens Coll., 1959; children—Matt, Jami. In constrn., advt., sales promotion, Jamaica Estates, N.Y., 1959; v.p. Fla. Atlantic Devel. Corp., Forest Hills, N.Y., 1973-75; v.p. Fla. Atlantic Advt., Inc., Forest Hills, 1973-75, Webb Realty, Inc., Forest Hills, 1973-75; pres. advt. firm, Jericho, N.Y., 1975; sales v.p. Minieri Communities, Inc., Met-Com Mktg., Inc., Hicksville, N.Y., 1975—; pres. Marstar Advt., 1978—; pres., owner, operator GJM Realty, Inc., Flushing, N.Y., 1978—; GM Mktg. Inc., Flushing, 1978-80; div. sales mgr. Gen. Devel. Corp., Valley Stream, N.Y., 1980-81; sales mgr. Fla.'s Mackle Bros. (Deltona Corp.), Rego Park, N.Y., 1981—; seminar speaker on Fla. housing for various cos., 1975-80. Chmn., Israel Bonds, 1969; pres. PTA, 1967-69; v.p. sisterhood edn., 1969; pres. sisterhood Hillcrest Jewish Center, 1968; v.p. Hillcrest Hadassah, Orgn. Retarded Children, 1965-73. Mem. Nat. Bd. Realtors, N.Y. Bd. Realtors, L.I. Bd. Realtors (public relations, yearbook, community service coms.), Com. 100, Advt. Women N.Y., Nat. Home Builders Assn., NOW. Republican. Home: 410 NW 65th Terrace Margate FL 33063 Office: 95-25 Queens Blvd Rego Park NY

WELLS, ALICE BERTHA JOHNSON, former businesswoman; b. Tiffin, Ohio, Dec. 28, 1926; d. Arthur Bernard and Julia Grace (Ellson) Johnson; B.S. in Mktg., U. Ill., 1948; M.A. in Geography, Western Ill. U., Macomb, 1973; m. Norman Dwight Wells, June 20, 1948; children—Ronald Christopher, Jan Diana Wells Hooker. Asst. dir. Tamagawa English Lang. Inst. for Japanese Students in U.S.A., Monmouth (Ill.) Coll., 1966-69, co-dir., 1969-70; v.p. Walt Montgomery Assos., Louisville, 1974-75, also head Aquaculture div., Chgo.; part-owner Wells Mgmt. Group, Inc., Chapel Hill, N.C. Mem. Assn. Am. Geographers, Gamma Phi Beta. Home: 175 E Delaware Pl Apt 8510 Chicago IL 60611 also 888 E Franklin St Chapel Hill NC 27514

WELLS, CAROL LYLE, confectionery co. exec.; b. DuBois, Pa., Aug. 17, 1935; d. Carl L. and Sarah L. (Stanton) Johnson; ed. public schs.; m. Robert A. Wells, June 19, 1954; children—Robin, David, Robert A. Cake decorator Riverside Markets, DuBois, 1964-74; adult edn. instr. Jeff Tech., Reynoldsville, Pa., 1974-79; founder, exec. officer Carol's Cake Decorating & Candy Making Supplies, Reynoldsville, 1975—; co-founder 1st ann. Pa. Cake Decorating Show, 1980, host 3d ann., DuBois, 1982. Mem. Internat. Cake Exploration Soc. Methodist. Address: 360 W Main St Reynoldsville PA 15851

WELLS, CHRISTINE LOUISE, educator; b. Buffalo, Mar. 22, 1938; d. Harold E. and Edythe A. (Burton) W.; B.S. in Edn., U. Mich., 1959; M.S., Smith Coll., 1964; Ph.D., Pa. State U., 1969. Tchr. phys. edn., Grosse Pointe, Mich., 1959-62; instr. phys. edn. Smith Coll., Northampton, Mass., 1964-66; NDEA fellow Pa. State U., 1966-69; asst. prof. Dalhousie U., Halifax, N.S., Can., 1969-71; fellow U. Calif., Santa Barbara, 1971-73; assoc. prof., Temple U., Phila., 1973-76; asso. prof. dept. health and phys. edn. Ariz. State U., Tempe, 1976-80, prof., 1980—. Recipient award Wonder Woman Found., 1982. Fellow Am. Coll. Sports Medicine (trustee 1979—, v.p. edn. 1982-84, position statement com. 1978-80), Am. Acad. Phys. Edn.; mem. AAHPER (pres. research consortium 1978-79), Ariz. State Assn. for Health, Phys. Edn. and Recreation. Mormon. Club: Sierra. Contbr. numerous articles on physiology and phys. edn. Home: 11611 S Maze Ct Phoenix AZ 85044 Office: Dept Health and Phys Edn Arizona State Univ Tempe AZ 85287

WELLS, JEAN HESS, civic vol.; b. Beaumont, Tex., Oct. 12, 1928; d. Aubrey Franklin and Jean (Van Horn) Hess; student Agnes Scott Coll., 1945-46; B.S., U. Ga., 1950; m. Robert E. Wells, June 16, 1949; children—Jere Aubrey, Cathlean Elaine. Chpt. adviser Kappa Kappa Gamma Fraternity, U. Ga., 1950-52, 55-58, U. Miss., 1952-55, Emory U., 1958-62, province dir. chpts., 1962-67, asst. to nat. pres., 1967-70, nat. v.p., 1970-72, nat. dir. chpts., 1972-76, nat. pres., 1976-80. Bd. sponsors Atlanta Symphony Orch., 1970-76; bd. dirs. High Mus. Art, Atlanta, 1973—, v.p., 1978-80, mem. exec. com., chmn. constrn. com. Mem. Nat. Panhellenic Conf., Nat. Assn. Women Deans and Counselors, Psi Chi, Rho Lambda. Republican. Unitarian. Home and Office: 4830 Jett Rd NW Atlanta GA 30327

WELLS, JERELENE DEERING, educator; b. Knoxville, Tenn., July 8, 1931; d. Norman and Anna (Marchman) Deering; B.A., Knoxville Coll., 1954; M.A., Calif. State U., 1969; Ph.D., Claremont Grad. Sch., 1977; m. David Mason Wells, Sept. 25, 1951; children—David Norman, Ronald Charles. Tchr., Los Angeles Unifed Sch. Dist., 1957-67, reading coordinator, 1964-66, Title I coordinator, 1967-68, registrar/adminstrv. dean, 1968-73, asst. prin., Venice High Sch., 1973-82, prin. Dorsey High Sch., 1982—; mem. Western Assn. Schs. and Colls. accreditation team, 1979—; Precinct officer County of Los Angeles, 1967-72; elder Westminster Presbyterian Ch., 1982—; mem. Venice Community Coordinating Council, 1977-79. Recipient Parent, Tchr., Student Assn. Service award, 1976, others. Mem. Knoxville Coll. Alumni Assn. (pres. 1965, 67, 73, 80-81), Los Angeles Assn. Secondary Sch. Adminstrs., Sr. High Asst. Prins. Orgn. (v.p. 1980-81), Assn. Calif. Sch. Adminstrs. (pres. Region 16), Nat. Assn. Secondary Sch. Prins., Council of Black Adminstrs., Women in Leadership (pres. 1978-80), Alpha Kappa Alpha. Democrat. Office: 3537 Farmdale Ave Los Angeles CA 90016

WELLS, MARY ELIZABETH THOMPSON, psychotherapist; b. Dallas, Oct. 9, 1936; d. Owen Perry and Ruth Marie (Baker) Thompson; B.A. in Sociology, Syracuse U., 1958; M.A. in Child Devel., Tufts U., 1964, M.Ed. in Counseling Psychology, Tufts U., 1974; children—Tadd Whitney, Britony Ruth. Asst. public relations dir. Inst. for Crippled and Disabled, N.Y.C., 1958-59; head tchr. Eliot-Pearson Children's Sch., Tufts U., Medford, Mass., 1964-66; psychotherapist Mental Health Center of Greater Cape Ann, Gloucester, Mass., 1974—. Mem. Am. Psychol. Assn., Mass. Psychol. Assn., Am. Orthopsychiat. Assn. Clubs: Essex County (Manchester, Mass.); Manchester Yacht. Home: 52 Central St Manchester MA 01944 Office: Mental Health Center of Greater Cape Ann Addison-Gilbert Hosp 298 Washington St Gloucester MA 01930

WELLS, MARY GEORGENE BERG, (MRS. HARDING L. LAWRENCE), advt. agy. exec.; b. Youngstown, Ohio, May 25, 1928; d. Waldemar and Violet (Berg) Wells; ed. Carnegie Inst. Tech.; LL.D., Babson Coll., 1970, Carnegie-Mellon U., 1974; m. Harding L. Lawrence, Nov. 28, 1967; children by previous marriage—Kathryn, Pamela. With advt. dept. Macy's N.Y.C., fashion advt. mgr., until 1951; copy group head McCann-Erickson, Inc., N.Y.C., 1952-57; with Doyle Dane Berbach, N.Y.C., 1957-64; copy chief, v.p., 1963-64; sr. partner Jack Tinker & Partners, N.Y.C., 1964-66; pres., chief adminstr. Wells, Rich, Greene, Inc., N.Y.C., from 1966, now chmn. bd., chief exec. officer. Mem. Commn. on Critical Choices for Ams., from 1974; speaker Econ. Summitt, Washington, 1974. Address: 575 Fifth Ave New York NY 10022 *

WELLS, PATRICIA ANN, educator; b. Park River, N.D., Mar. 25, 1935; d. Benjamin Beekman Bennett and Alice Catherine (Peerboom) Bennett Breckinridge; A.A., Allan Hancock Coll., Santa Maria, Calif., 1964; B.S. magna cum laude, Coll. Great Falls, 1966; M.S., U. N.D., 1967, Ph.D., 1971; children—Bruce Bennett, Barbara Lea. Fiscal acct. USIA, Washington, 1954-56; public acct., Bremerton, Wash., 1956; statistician U.S. Navy, Bremerton, 1957-59; med. services accounts officer U.S. Air Force, Vandenberg AFB, Calif., 1962-64; instr. bus. adminstrn. Western New Eng. Coll., 1967-69; vis. prof. econs. Chapman Coll., 1971; vis. prof. systems Griffith AFB, 1973-74; asso. prof. bus. Va. State U., 1973-74; assoc. prof. bus. adminstrn. Oreg. State U., Corvallis, 1974-82, prof., 1982—, dir. adminstrv. mgmt. program, 1974-81, pres. Faculty Senate, 1981; cons. process tech. devel. Digital Equipment Corp., 1982. Pres., chmn. bd. dirs. Adminstrv. Office Services, Inc., Corvallis, 1976—. Cert. adminstrv. mgr. Mem. Am. Bus. Communication Assn. (mem. internat. bd. 1980-83, v.p. Northwest 1981, 2d v.p. 1982), Am. Bus. Women's Assn. (named Top Businesswoman in Nation 1980), Internat. Word Processing Assn., Adminstrv. Mgmt. Soc., AAUP (chpt. sec. 1973), Am. Vocat. Assn. (nominating com. 1976), Associated Oreg. Faculties, Nat. Bus. Edn. Assn., Nat. Assn. Tchr. Edn. for Bus. Office Edn. (pres. 1976-77, chmn. public relations com. 1978-81), Sigma Kappa. Roman Catholic. Club: Toastmasters Internat. Contbr. numerous articles to profl. jours. Office: 108 Bexell Sch Bus Oreg State U Corvallis OR 97331

WELLS, SARAH PAULINE, nursing adminstr.; b. Hackensack, N.J., Sept. 18, 1927; d. Nathaniel Dewey and Isabelle Grace (Storms) W.; R.N., Hackensack Hosp. Sch. Nursing, 1948; B.S. in Nursing Edn., Columbia U., 1961; M.S. in Public Health Nursing, U. Colo., 1965. Commd. 1st lt., U.S. Air Force, 1951, advanced through grades to brig. gen., 1979; asst. nursing services Hdqrs. Mil. Airlift Comd., Scott AFB, Ill., 1970-72; Office of Surgeon Gen., Hdqrs. U.S. Air Force, 1972-75; asst. for nursing services Office of Comdg. Surgeon, U.S. Air Forces in Europe, 1975-78; command nurse Air Force Systems Command, Andrews AFB, Md., 1978-79; chief Air Force Nurse Corps, Washington, 1979-82. Chmn. bd. dirs. Air Force Nurse Corps Found., Inc., 1973-75. Mem. Assn. Mil. Surgeons of U.S., Am. Nurses Assn., Nat. League for Nursing, Aerospace Med. Assn., Hackensack Hosp. Alumni Assn., Air Force Inst. Tech. Assn. Grads., Sigma Theta Tau. Club: Volksmarching. Office: HQ USAF SGN Bolling AFB Washington DC 20332

WELLS, TERRY, cosmetics co. exec.; b. Ark., Mar. 13, 1942; d. Leroy and Odessa Mae (Davis) Woods; B.S., U. Wis., Madison, 1964; children—Karen L, Brandy O. Fashion coordinator Burlington Industries, N.Y.C., 1969-71, sales mgr., 1973-79; sales rep. Beach-Nut Inc., Boston, 1971-73; div. sales mgr. Avon Products, Inc., Cin., 1979-82, mgr. rep. motivation, N.Y.C., 1982—. Mem. NAACP, Black Retail Action Group, Black Exec. Exchange Program, Am. Mgmt. Assn., Alpha Kappa Alpha. Mem. Ch. of Christ.

WELLS, THEODORA WESTMONT, communications cons.; b. Niagara Falls, N.Y., Apr. 18, 1926; d. Oscar B. and Marjorie Wells (Fraser) Westmont; B.S., U. Calif., Berkeley, 1947; M.B.A., U. So. Calif., 1965; divorced; children—David Kuettel, Steven Kuettel; 1 stepdau., Deanna Molina. Fin. dir. Los Angeles Council Girl Scouts U.S., 1954-58; asst. v.p., project coordinator, customer relations dir. Lytton Savs. & Loan Assn., Hollywood, Calif., 1961-68; tng. and customer relations mgr. First Charter Fin. Corp., Beverly Hills, Calif., 1968-69; partner Wells-Christie Assocs., 1970-72; propr. Wells Assos., Beverly Hills, 1970—; extension tchr. mgmt. devel. for women UCLA, 1968—. Adv. bd. Los Angeles Commn. on Assaults Against Women. Mem. Acad. Mgmt., Am. Soc. Tng. and Devel., World Future Soc., Assn. Humanistic Psychology, Delta Gamma, Beta Gamma Sigma. Author: Woman—Which Includes Man, of Course, 1970; (with Rosalind K. Loring) Breakthrough: Women into Management (Edn. award Delta Kappa Gamma 1973, Profl. Achievement award Phi Chi Theta 1974), 1972; Keeping Your Cool Under Fire: Communicating Non-Defensively, 1980; also chpts. in books on non-defensive communication, psychology of women. Home: 341 S Swall Beverly Hills CA 90211 Office: Box 3392 Beverly Hills CA 90212

WELLS, VALDA EVELYN, mgmt. cons.; b. N.Y.C., June 23, 1935; d. William Frederick and Valda Elva (Baldwin) W.; B.A. in Econs., N.Y. Sch. Social Research, N.Y.C., 1967. With Gen. Electric Co., N.Y.C., 1964-80, cons. internat. trade policy devel., 1973-75, mgr. internat. research programs, 1975-80; pres. Wellspring, N.Y.C., 1980—; tchr. profl. communication. Mem. Nat. Assn. Female Execs., Am. Soc. Profl. and Exec. Women, Internat. Platform Assn. Democrat. Presbyterian. Home: 36-19 Bowne St Flushing NY 11354 Office: PO Box 310 Flushing NY 11352

WELS, MARGUERITE SAMET (MRS. RICHARD H. WELS), interior decorator; b. N.Y.C.; d. Max and Bertha (Levine) Samet; student N.Y. U., 1937, N.Y. Sch. Interior Design, 1938-41; m. Richard H. Wels, Dec. 12, 1954; children—Susan Rebecca, Amy Elizabeth. Interior decorator—Marguerite Samet, N.Y.C., 1946-60; interior decorator, head Marguerite Samet Assos., 1960—; co-ordinator U.S. Army Spl. Services, 1942-46; cons. United Bowling Centers, Inc., Interboro Gen. Hosp. Active in William Alanson White Inst. Psychiatry, Psychoanalysis and Psychology, Am. Jewish Com., Islands Research Found. Mem. Am. Inst. Interior Designers (exec. bd., v.p. N.Y. Met. chpt.), Democratic Women's Workshop. Jewish. Clubs: Women's City, Woman Pays. Home: 911 Park Ave New York NY 10021

WELSH, JUDITH SCHENCK, educator; b. Bayshore, N.Y., Feb. 5, 1939; d. Frank W. and Muriel (Whitman) Schenck; B.Ed., U. Miami (Fla.), 1961, M.A. in English, 1968; m. Robert C. Welsh, Sept. 16, 1961; children—Derek Francis, Christopher Lord. Co-organizer Cataract Surg. Congress med. meetings, 1963-76; grad. asst. instr. Dale Carnegie Courses Internat., 1967; adminstr. Office Admissions, Bauder Fashion Coll., Miami, 1976-77, instr. communications, 1977—, also pub. coll. monthly paper; guest speaker Optifair Internat., N.Y.C., 1980; guest speaker, mem. seminar faculty Optifair West, Anaheim, Calif., 1980, Optifair Midwest, St. Louis, 1980, Face to Face, Kansas City, Mo., 1981. Mem. Nat. Assn. Female Execs., Delta Gamma. Congregationalist. Clubs: Nat. Writers, Coral Reef Yacht, Riviera Country, Royal Palm Tennis. Co-editor: The New Report on Cataract Surgery, 1969, Second Report on Cataract Surgery, 1974. Home: 1600 Onaway Dr Miami FL 33133 Office: 100 SE 4th St Miami FL 33131

WELSH, SUE ANGELA, devel. and fund-raising specialist; b. N.Y.C., Nov. 10, 1938; d. Edward Thomas and Susan Bridget (Swanton) W.; B.A., Immaculate Heart Coll., 1960, Calif. secondary teaching credential, 1961; children—John Francis, Kieron Michael. Secondary sch. tchr. Los Angeles City Schs., 1960-77; field rep. Inter-Study, Los Angeles, 1977-78; dir. devel./community relations Poseidon Center for Troubled Adolescents with Learning Disabilities, Los Angeles, 1979—; adminstrv. coordinator Danzantes Unidos, 1978-82. Co-chmn. Irish Info. Com.; mem. Calif. Democratic Circle. Recipient Pub. Service to Youth in Watts award, 1964, Los Angeles County Human Relations award, 1965, Mexican Folklorico Arts Adv. award, 1979, Vol. Action Center award, 1982. Mem. Assn. for Children Who Learn Differently, Santa Monica-Westside Community Services Council (pres.). Home: 354 S Harvard Blvd Los Angeles CA 90020

WELT, JOHANNA SINGLETARY, oil and gas co. exec.; b. Tulsa, May 18, 1944; d. Heston Leroy (dec.) and Margaret Singletary (James) Singletary; B.A. in Sociology, The Principia, 1967; m. Leo G. B. Welt, Nov. 28, 1970 (dir. 1981); children—Sabina Margaret, Leo G. Instr. Evelyn Wood Reading Dynamics, St. Louis, 1967-69; method analyst Acro Chem. Co. div. Atlantic Richfield, Chgo., 1969-71; v.p. Welt Internat. Corp., Chgo., 1971-77; v.p. Heston Oil Co., Tulsa, 1980—. Mem. bd. Colonial Dames Am., 1981—; pres. woman's bd. Planned Parenthood, Chgo., 1976. Mem. Jr. League. Office: 2409 E Skelly Dr Suite 102 Tulsa OK 74135

WELTE, VERNA L., health care adminstr.; b. Hopinton, Iowa, Oct. 23, 1933; d. Edmund P. and Marie C. (Nefziger) Rausch; B.S. in Nursing, Briar Cliff Coll., 1955; M.A. in Adult Edn., U. S.D., 1979; m. Dennis G. Welte, Feb. 4, 1956; 8 children. Staff nurse Sioux City (Iowa) Dept. Health, 1955-57; staff nurse St. Vincent Hosp., Sioux City, 1957-58, instr. operating room and med.-surg. nursing, 1958-62, staff nurse ICU, 1965-67, instr. critical care nursing, 1967-70, dir. nursing, 1970-77; staff nurse med.-surg. nursing unit, nursing dir. Luth. Hosp., Sioux City, 1962-65; v.p. inpatient services Marian Health Center, Sioux City, 1977—. Bd. dirs. Servi-Share of Iowa, 1980—. Recipient Disting. Community Service award Briar Cliff Coll., 1972, Mother of Yr. award, 1980. Mem. Am. Hosp. Assn., Iowa Hosp. Assn., Am. Nurses Assn., Iowa Nurses Assn. (dir. dist.), Iowa Heart Assn., Iowa Women's Polit. Caucus, Sioux City C. of C. (govtl. affairs com. 1981—), Am. Soc. Nursing Adminstrs. Roman Catholic. Home: 4022 Teton Trace Sioux City IA 51104 Office: 801 5th St Sioux City IA 51101

WELTING, RUTH LYNN, singer; b. Memphis, Nov. 5, 1948; d. William Edwin and Mary Frances (Pugh) Welting; student Memphis State U., 1966-68, Juilliard Sch. Music, 1968-69; div. Mem. N.Y.C. Opera, 1971-73; appeared with Dallas Opera, Houston Symphony, San Francisco Symphony, Chgo. Lyric Opera, Met. Opera, N.Y. Philharm., Covent Garden, London, Netherlands Opera, San Francisco Opera, Teatro Colón, Buenos Aires, Chatalet Theatre, Paris, others; soloist with Chgo. Symphony, Phila. Orch., San Francisco Symphony. Rockefeller grantee. Mem. Am. Guild Musical Artists. Office: care Columbia Artists Mgmt Inc 165 W 57th St New York NY 10019

WELTY, EUDORA, author; b. Jackson, Miss.; d. Christian Webb and Chestina (Andrews) Welty; student Miss. State Coll. for Women; B.A., U. Wis., 1929; postgrad. Columbia Sch. Advt., 1930-31. Author: A Curtain of Green, 1941; The Robber Bridegroom, 1942; The Wide Net, 1943; Delta Wedding, 1946; The Golden Apples, 1949; The Ponder Heart, 1954; The Bride of the Innisfallen, 1955; The Shoe Bird, 1964; Losing Battles, 1970; One Time, One Place, 1971; The Optimist's Daughter, 1972 (Pulitzer prize 1973); The Eye of the Story, 1978; Collected Stories, 1980; contbr. So. Rev., Atlantic Monthly, Harpers Bazaar, New Yorker. Recipient creative arts medal for fiction Brandeis U., 1966, Presdl. Medal of Freedom, 1979, Nat. medal for lit., 1980. Mem. Nat. Inst. Arts and Letters (Gold medal 1972), Am. Acad. Arts and Letters.

WEN, SHEREE HSIAO-RU, electronics co. mgr.; b. Keelung, Taiwan, May 27, 1951; naturalized, 1982; d. Joong-Yu and Yu-Huang (Wang) Wen; Ph.D. in Materials Sci., U. Calif., Berkeley, 1979. Mgr. materials characterization and analysis Thomas J. Watson Research Center, IBM, Yorktown Heights, N.Y. Recipient Robert Lansing Hardy gold medal, 1979; John E. Dorn Achievement award Am. Soc. Metals, 1978. Mem. AIME. Contbr. articles to profl. jours. Office: PO Box 218 Yorktown Heights NY 10598 *

WENBERG, MARY FRANCES, dietitian, educator; b. Spencer, W.Va., July 7, 1937; d. Robert P. and Thelma E. (Grose) Fockler; B.S. in Home Econs., Ohio U., 1959; M.S., Ohio State U., 1961; m. Richard Dean Wenberg, Nov. 10, 1965; children—R. Brian, Susan Burness. Asst. dir. clin. dietetics and metabolic research W.Va. U. Hosp., Morgantown, 1961-67; mem. faculty, Vocat. Tech. Sch. 916, St. Paul, 1970-73, Tarrant County Jr. Coll., Ft. Worth, 1974-76; asst. prof. dept. home econs., coordinator dietetics program Tex. Christian U., Ft. Worth, 1976—; cons. dietitian White Bear Lake Nursing Home. Mem. Am. Dietetic Assn. (registered dietitian), Am. Home Econs. Assn., Am. Coll. Nutrition, Tex. Nutrition Council, Ft. Worth Dietetic Assn. (pres. 1979-80), Phi Upsilon Omicron. Methodist. Home: 1605 Rockmoor Dr Fort Worth TX 76134 Office: Dept Home Econs Tex Christian U Fort Worth TX 76129

WENDEL, FAYE F., coin equipment mfg. co. exec.; b. Newark, Sept. 16, 1928; d. John Thomas and Sara Rose (Agliozzo) Fiorenza; m. Daniel C. Wendel, Nov. 26, 1949; children—Catherine C., Daniel C. III, Wayne J. Sec., P. Ballantine & Sons, Newark, 1946-49; head hostess, asst. to mgr. Bambergers-Carriage House Restaurant, 1971-74; sec. Peter Wendel & Sons, Inc., Irvington, N.J., 1961-78; sec. Wendel Industries, Inc., Millburn, N.J., 1978-80, pres., 1980—; pres. D.C. Wendel Corp., 1982—. Tchrs. aide St. Ann Sch.; asst. treas. Ladies Aux. St. Rose of Lima Ch., 1963. Mem. Short Hills Assn., Twig Group of Overlook Hosp., Rotary Assn., Am. Soc. Profl. and Exec. Women. Clubs: Republican, Short Hills Racquet. Home: 33 Quaker Rd Short Hills NJ 07078 Office: PO Box 703 Millburn NJ 07041

WENDER, PHYLLIS BELLOWS, lit. agt.; b. N.Y.C., Jan. 6, 1934; d. Lee and Lilian (Frank) Bellows; B.A., Wells Coll., 1956; m. Ira Tensard Wender, June 24, 1966; children—Justin Bellows, Sarah Tensard. Dir. publicity Grove Press, 1958-61; theatrical agt. Artists Agy. Corp., N.Y.C., 1963-66, dir. N.Y. office, 1966-68; agt., pres. Wender & Assocs., 1968-81; lit. agt., partner Rosenstone/Wender, N.Y.C., 1981—. Trustee, Wells Coll., 1981—; bd. dirs. Fortune Soc., 1977-80; adv. council Just Women, Inc., 1982—. Mem. Women's Media Group. Club: Cosmopolitan (N.Y.C.). Home: 555 Park Ave New York NY 10021 Office: 3 E 48th St New York NY 10017

WENDT, ANN CARLSON, univ. adminstr., hearing officer, educator; b. Holmquist, S.D., Sept. 11, 1937; d. Albin C. Carlson and Agnes Johnson Carlson Hillgren; student Gustavus Adolphus Coll., 1955-56, U. Minn., Mpls., 1963-66; B.S. in Polit. Sci. magna cum laude, B.S. in Psychology magna cum laude, U. Utah, 1977, M.S. in Human Resource Mgmt. (Allied Printing Trades scholar), 1980, postgrad. 1980—; m. Roderick N. Wendt, Apr. 20, 1957; children—LeAnn Corinne and LuAnn Victoria Wendt Brigham (twins). Labor relations and compensation analyst N.W. Orient Airlines, Inc., Mpls., 1956-61; exec. sec. to pres. G. M. Stewart Lumber Co., Mpls., 1961-62; adminstrv. asst. to dir. instl. market research Pillsbury Co., Mpls., 1962-63; asst. personnel mgr. Data Products Corp., St. Paul, 1963-64; adminstrv. asst. to v.p. personnel Brown & Bigelow, St. Paul, 1964-66; corp. officer, sec. Applied Mgmt. Sci., Inc., Mpls., 1964-66; adminstrv. asst. to v.p. pub. relations First Bank System, Mpls., 1966-70; human resource mgmt. program coordinator Inst. for Human Resource Mgmt., U. Utah, 1982—, teaching asst. dept. polit. sci., 1976-77, Coll. Bus., 1977-80, teaching fellow Coll. Bus., 1980—; Hearing examiner Utah Personnel Rev. Bd., Salt Lake City, 1982—; personnel cons., 1978—. Vol., Murry-Allen Center for Blind, Salt Lake City; active local, dist. and synod levels Lutheran Ch. in Am. Mem. Am. Soc. Personnel Adminstrn., Soc. Profls. in Dispute Resolution, AAUW, Acad. Mgmt., Indsl. Relations Research Assn. Research on arbitration. Home: 4823 Naniloa Dr Salt Lake City UT 84117 Office: U Utah 412 Coll Bus Salt Lake City UT 84112

WENGER, LOIS HAWBAKER, mfg. co. exec.; b. Mercersburg, Pa., May 10, 1927; d. Daniel M. and Ada B. (Hege) Hawbaker; student Valencia Community Coll., 1975; m. Eugene L. Wenger, May 10, 1945; children—Diana J. Wenger Wilson, LaVonna R. Gamble. With Aerospace div. Martin-Marietta Corp., Orlando, Fla., 1957—, sr. analyst, 1960-70, mfg. engr., then group mfg. engr., 1970-76, mfg. mgr., staff to dir. mfg. div., 1977—. Exec. com. So. Baptist Conv., 1978—. Recipient Top 100 Meritorious award, Martin Marietta, 1980. Mem. Nat. Assn. Female Execs. Club: Order Eastern Star. Home: 4600 Tinsley Dr Orlando FL 32809 Office: PO Box 5837 MP434 Orlando FL 32855

WENGER, MICHELE JAY, ednl. adminstr.; b. Cin., Mar. 29, 1947; d. John Paul and Mildred Elizabeth (Zaus) W.; B.S., U. Cin., 1969, M.Ed., 1970; postgrad Xavier U., 1972-82, Coll. Mt. St. Joseph, 1980-81. With Cin. Public Schs., 1970—, dir. Right to Read, 1972—, project dir. minimum competencies in writing, 1978-81, sex desegregation, 1981-82. U. Cin. scholar, 1969-70; Betty Jane Hull scholar, 1968. Mem. Internat. Reading Assn., Nat. Coalition Sex Equity for Edn., Phi Delta Kappa (pres. U. Cin. chpt. 1982-83). Home: 2435 Mustang Dr #12 Cincinnati OH 45211 Office: 230 E 9th St Cincinnati OH 45202

WENK, JENNY, advt. exec.; b. Pitts., Dec. 29, 1942; d. Samuel Augustine and Jean Lois (Barnes) W.; B.A., U. Calif., Berkeley, 1964; M.B.A., Golden Gate U., 1980; m. Paul R. Allman, Dec. 31, 1981. Advt. promotion and research asst. Richmond (Calif.) Independent, 1965-67; sales promotion writer Dow Jones & Co., Inc., N.Y.C., 1968-70; mem. advt. sales staff Nat. Observer, San Francisco, 1970-74, advt. mgr. Pacific coast, 1974-77; advt. sales rep. Wall Street Jour., San Francisco, 1977—. Mem. San Francisco Women in Advt. (hon. mem., past pres.), San Francisco Advt. Club (dir. 1979-80), Seattle Women in Advt. (hon.). Presbyterian. Office: 220 Battery St San Francisco CA 94111

WENTE, VERGIE DEE, court ofcl.; b. Allison, Kans., Apr. 24, 1936; d. Virgil D. and Hazel (Storer) Wennihan; student Colby Community Coll., 1969-70; m. Lloyd Wente, July 23, 1953 (div. May 1966); children—Allen Charles, Rhonda Marie, Daniel Lloyd, Lynne LaRea. Bookmobile librarian N.W. Kans. Library System, Hoxie, 1968-70; clk. Dist. Ct. of Sheridan County, Hoxie, 1970-76; chief clk. 15th Jud. Dist. Kans., Hoxie, 1976—; mem. clks. adv. council Kans. Supreme Ct., 1979—. Honored by chief justice Supreme ct. for outstanding contbns. to Kans. Dist. Ct. Clks. and Adminstrs. Assn., 1981. Mem. Kans. Dist. Ct. Clks. Assn. (sec.-treas. 1978, v.p. 1979, pres. 1980, legis. chmn. 1981, chmn. 1982—, Mem. public edn. and info. com. 1982—, exec. com. 1982—), Nat. Assn. Ct. Adminstrs. Mem. Ch. of Christ. Home: 1417 Sheridan Ave Hoxie KS 67740 Office: Box 753 Hoxie KS 67740

WENTZ, CHARLOTTE MARIE, librarian; b. Dayton, Ohio, July 25, 1920; d. Walter Grover and Bessie Sunbeam (Stoner) Wentz; B.S. in Edn., U. Dayton, 1942; M.S. in Library Sci., Western Res. U., 1956; postgrad. U. Denver, Western Mich. U., 1966. Sec., Frigidaire div. Gen. Motors Corp., Dayton, 1942-50; tchr. Madison Elem. Sch., Trotwood, Ohio, 1950-52, Garfield Elem. Sch. Mason City, Iowa, 1952-55; librarian Madison High Sch., Trotwood, 1956-58, Madison High Sch., Madison, Ohio, 1958-59, Trotwood-Madison High Sch., Trotwood, 1959-67; library dir. Southwestern Mich. Coll., Dowagiac, Mich., 1967—; bd. dirs. Dowagiac Public Library, 1975—, chmn., 1977, 78. Mem. ALA, Southwestern Mich. Library Coop., Bus. and Profl. Women's Club (treas. 1969). Republican. Mem. Christian Ch. (Disciples of Christ). Home: 606 Fairlawn Dr Dowagiac MI 49047 Office: Cherry Grove Rd Dowagiac MI 49047

WENTZ, JANET MARIE, N.D. state legislator; b. McClusky, N.D., July 21, 1937; d. Charles G. and Martha (Schindler) Neff; student Westmar Coll., 1955-57, U. Minn., 1960-62, Minot State Coll., 1967-70; m. Thomas Arthur Wentz, 1957; children—Elizabeth, Karin, Thomas. Vice-pres. Republican Women of Minot, N.D., 1966-67; mem. N.D. Ho. Reps., 1974—. Mem. Nat. Assn. Securities Dealers. Methodist. Clubs: PEO, Minot C. of C. (public affairs com.), Office: N D Ho Reps State Capitol Bismarck ND 58501

WENTZ-CURTIS, ELENA JEAN MITCHELL, nurse, educator; b. Lacona, Iowa, Sept. 6, 1927; d. Harley Edwin and Elena (Jeffrey) Mitchell; student (Coll. scholar) Simpson Coll., 1944-46, B.A., 1954; cert. in nursing State U. Iowa, 1949, postgrad., summer 1971; M.S.N. (HEW trainee), Wayne State U., 1977; postgrad. Ferris State Coll., summer 1979; children by previous marriage—Marcia Wentz Jackson, Sharon Wentz Capriccioso, Diane Wentz; m. Robert W. Curtis, June 21, 1980; stepchildren—Gary Curtis, Nancy Curtis, Thomas Curtis, Laura Curtis, Ann Curtis McKay. Gen. duty nurse State U. Iowa Hosp., 1949-51, head nurse med. neurology, 1958-61, supr. inservice edn., 1961-63; instr. sci. St. Vincent's Hosp. Sch. Nursing, Indpls., 1951-53; gen. duty nurse Kingston (Pa.) Meml. Hosp., 1953; instr. nursing Lake Superior State Coll., 1971-77, asst. prof. nursing, 1977—; nurse Camp Michigamme, summers 1972-74; cons. procedure com. Plummer Meml. Hosp., Sault Ste. Marie, Ont., Can., 1978. Dir. jr. high Chippewa County council Campfire Girls Am., 1966-68; pres. Sault Ste. Marie (Mich.) Musicale, 1967; chairperson circle United Methodist Women, Central United Meth. Ch., Sault Ste. Marie, 1966-69, pres., 1970-71, chairperson spiritual growth, 1972; mem. exec. bd. Parent's Without Partners, Sault Ste. Marie, 1973-78; chairperson United Meth. Mission Saturation Event, Sault Ste. Marie, 1978; chairperson Questers study group, Sault Ste. Marie, 1979—. Mem. Am. Nurses Assn., Mich. Nurses Assn., Sault Ste. Marie Dist. Nurses Assn., Am. Diabetic Assn., NEA, Mich. Edn. Assn., Internat. Nursing Edn. Council, Pi Beta Phi. Republican. Club: War Meml. Hosp. Aux. (chairperson style show 1970). Home: 1025 Parnell Sault Sainte Marie MI 49783 Office: Dept Nursing Lake Superior State Coll Sault Sainte Marie MI 49783

WERBLOOD, SHERRILL LEE, psychologist; b. N.Y.C., May 17, 1948; d. Samuel S. and Gertrude (Lambert) W.; B.A. cum laude, Queens Coll., 1969; M.A., (fellow), N.Y.U., 1972, Ph.D., 1977. Tchr., Public Schs. N.Y.C., 1969-71; psychometrist, B'nai B'rith Vocat. Guidance, N.Y.C., 1971-72; instr. Washington Sch. Psychiatry, 1973; diagnostic prescriptive tchr. trainer, sch. psychologist Child Study Center, Howard County, Md., 1972-74; psychol. diagnostician New Haven Juvenile Ct., 1975-77; clin. psychology intern Child StudyCenter Yale U., 1975-76; staff psychologist Highland Heights, New Haven, 1976-77; coordinator spl. edn. Redding (Conn.) Schs., 1977-80; coordinator spl. services Redding-Easton Schs., 1980—; clin. psychologist in pvt. practice, New Haven and Westport, Conn., 1976—. Lic. clin. psychologist, N.Y. State, Conn. Mem. Am. Psychol. Assn., Conn. Assn. Pupil Adminstrs., Conn. Assn. Sch. Psychologists, Orton Soc., Phi Beta Kappa, Psi Chi, Kappa Delta Pi. Contbr. articles to profl. publs. Editor: CAPPA Newsletter, 1980—. Home: 180 Imperial Ave Westport CT 06880 Office: Redding Schs Rt 107 Redding CT 06875

WERLIN, ROSELLA HARWOOD, journalist; b. N.Y.C., Sept. 17, 1912; d. Henry J. and Cecilia (Feinberg) Horowitz; B.A., U. Houston, 1946, M.A., 1950; postgrad. Columbia U., U. Mo., U. Tex.; m. Joseph S. Werlin, Dec. 23, 1928 (dec.); children—Herbert Holland, Joella Barbara, Ernest Pyle. Reporter, San Antonio Light, 1924-25, St. Louis Globe Democrat, 1925-27, Galveston News-Tribune, 1927-28, United Press and Houston Press, 1928; corr. Chgo. Jour., 1928-29; publicity writer Mcpl. Advt. Com., Galveston, 1929-30; writer Interocean Syndicate, Chgo., 1931-32; free-lance publicity writer, Chgo., 1934; free-lance writer for newspapers and mags., including N.Y. Times, Chgo. Sun Times, Chgo. Tribune, St. Louis Post Dispatch, Dallas News, Houston Post, Reader's Digest, 1944—; instr. journalism Sam Houston Sch., 1935-38; public relations dir. Galveston C. of C., 1944-50; tchr. retarded children Houston Public Schs., 1961-67. Mem. publicity bd. Houston YWCA, 1936-37; mem. Galveston Com. for Def., 1941; county publicity chmn. Am. Women Vol. Service, 1942; mem. Bundles for Brit.; established Werlin Internat. Culture Tours, 1944-64; del. White House Conf. Aging, 1981; established Joseph S. Werlin Meml. Scholarship Found., U. Houston, 1967. Recipient numerous nat. and state awards in journalism. Mem. Tex. Press Assn., Tex. Woman's Press Assn., Nat. Fedn. Press Women (award 1979), Houston Press Club, Tex. Ex's, Assn. Am. Pen Women, LWV, Bus. and Profl. Women's Club, World Congress of Internat. Journalists, Sigma Delta Chi. Clubs: B'nai B'rith Women, Hadassah. Co-editor: History of Galveston, 1931. Contbr. over 500 articles to numerous mags., newspapers, periodicals. Home: 2340 Underwood Blvd Houston TX 77030

WERNER, BELLA GLORIA, broadcasting co. exec.; b. Bratislava, Czechoslovakia, Nov. 28, 1943; naturalized U.S. citizen, 1957; d. Julius Mathew and Bella Lenke (Toth) W.; B.A., Syracuse U., 1965. Asst. radio research mgr. Peters, Griffin, Woodward, N.Y.C., 1966-67; sr. radio analyst Metromedia, N.Y.C., 1967-68; dir. research John C. Butler Co., N.Y.C., 1968-69, H-R Radio, N.Y.C., 1969-70, Eastman Radio, N.Y.C., 1970-73; sr. v.p. research Christal Co., N.Y.C., 1973—; cons.; mem. Arbitron Radio Adv. Council. Mem. Nat. Radio Broadcasters Assn. (research com.), Radio Advt. Bur./GOALS (research com., tech. sub-com., procedures sub-com.), N.Y. Market Radio, Radio/TV Research Council. Home: 595 Main St Apt 302 Roosevelt Island NY 10044 Office: 919 3d Ave New York NY 10022

WERNER, GLORIA S., librarian; b. Seattle, Dec. 12, 1940; d. Irving L. and Eva H. Stolzoff; B.A., Oberlin Coll., 1961; M.L., U. Wash., 1962; postgrad. UCLA, 1962-63; m. Newton Davis Werner, June 30, 1963; 1 son, Adam Davis. Reference librarian UCLA Biomed Library, 1963-64, asst. head pub. services dept., 1964-66, head pub. services dept., head reference div., 1966-72, asst. biomed. librarian public services, 1972-77, asso. biomed. librarian, 1977-78, biomed. librarian, asso. univ. librarian, 1979—, dir. Pacific S.W. regional Med. Library Service; asst. dean library services UCLA Sch. Medicine, 1980—; adj. lectr. UCLA Grad. Sch. Library and Info. Sci., 1977—. Mem. Med. Library Assn., Assn. Acad. Health Sci. Library Dirs. (dir. 1981—). Editor, Bull. Med. Library Assn., 1979-82, asso. editor, 1974-79; mem. editorial bd. Ann. Stats. Med. Sch. Libraries U.S. and Can., 1980. Office: UCLA Biomed Library Center Health Scis Los Angeles CA 90024

WERNER, HELEN HINCHEY, ednl. adminstr.; b. Salmon, Idaho, May 23, 1919; d. Charles Benjamin and Mildred Hannah (Matthews) Hinchey; student Albion Normal Coll., 1938-39, San Jose State Tchrs. Coll., 1941, Lewis Clark State Coll., 1948-49; B.S., U. Idaho, 1960, M.A., 1966, Ed.D., 1973; m. Daniel Glenn Werner, Nov. 27, 1941; children—Linda Rae Werner Cook, Margaret Ann Werner Epke. Elem. tchr., Glenns Ferry, Idaho, 1939-41; secondary tchr., Weippe, Idaho, 1941-42, Kamiah, Idaho, 1950-55, Stites, Idaho, 1948-50; supt. schs., Kamiah, Idaho, 1955-56, secondary prin., 1956-65; cons., program mgr., bur. chief, asso. state supt. State Dept. Edn., Boise, Idaho, 1965-78, dep. state supt. public instrn., 1979—; mem. sch. accreditation teams, evaluation teams, task force U.S. Office Edn. Mem. bd. Lewis County (Idaho) Library; mem. State Employment and Tng. Adv. Council; mem. State Vocat. Edn. Planning Com.; active PTA. Recipient cert. of outstanding leadership in edn. Women's Commn. in Idaho, 1974, cert. of appreciation Masons, 1956. Mem. Idaho Edn. Assn. (past dist. pres.), Delta Kappa Gamma (cert. achievement leadership in edn. 1979), Phi Delta Kappa. Clubs: Soroptimist (past pres.) (Boise); Order Eastern Star (past worthy matron). Office: Statehouse Boise ID 83720

WERNER, JEANNE ELDER, mgmt. cons.; b. Clarion County, Pa.; d. John O. and Grace Divins Elder; B.S., Clarion State Coll., 1958; M.Ed., SUNY, Buffalo, 1965, Ed.D., 1969; m. Wayne E. Werner, 1965; 1 son, Elon Wayne. Tchr., public schs., Pa., N.Y., 1958-64; counselor West Seneca Schs., Buffalo, N.Y., 1965-68; asst. prof. founds. of edn. Auburn (Ala.) U., 1970-71, coordinator community service and women's programs, 1973-74; asst. prof. Tuskegee Inst., 1972; asst. prof. E. Tex. State U., Texarkana, 1974-79; dir. student devel. service, 1975-79; pres. Werner Assos., Texarkana, Tex., 1979—. Mem. allocations com. United Way, 1976-77, bd. dirs. Greater Texarkana, 1979; bd. dirs. Conifer Girl Scout Council, 1981—, Texarkana Community Concerts Assn., 1978—. NDEA fellow, 1964-67. Mem. Am. Personnel and Guidance Assn., Nat. Vocat. Guidance Assn. (sec. 1979-80), Tex. Personnel and Guidance Assn. (chmn. human relations com.), Am. Soc. Tng. and Devel., Pi Gamma Mu, Am. Personnel and Guidance Assn. (commn. for women 1973-74, 76-77). Address: 1507 Olive St Box 3380 Texarkana TX 75504

WERNER, PHYLLIS TENGDIN, editor, writer; b. Chgo., Dec. 20, 1923; d. Elmer Theodore and Agnes Minne Tengdin; A.A., Kansas City Jr. Coll., 1943; B.A., U. Okla., 1945; postgrad. U. Mo.; m. Dean Franklin Werner, Oct. 14, 1945; children—Nancy Werner Bybel, Sallie Werner Wilson, Lynn Werner Driggers, Barbara Werner Douglas. Asst. prodn. dir. Carter Advt., Kansas City, Mo., 1945; reporter Daily Oklahoman, Oklahoma City, 1946-48; librarian Denver Post, 1948-49; reporter Dispatch Newspapers, North Kansas City, Mo., 1968-69; editor Central States Lutheran, Kansas City, Mo., 1979—; freelance writer, 1948—; del. to Luth. Ch. in Am. Biennial Convs., 1976, 78. Vice pres. bd. govs. Kansas City Philharm., social chmn., 1982—; past vice chmn Cockefair Chair (humanities) U. Mo., Kansas City; past pres. Philharm. Guild N.; past mem. Kansas City Mayor's Commn. for Human Relations, mem. commn. Sister Cities, Corps of Progress; mem. Lyric Opera Guild, Friends of Art, North Kansas City Hosp. Aux., Clay County (Mo.) Med. Aux. (past v.p.). Mem. World Assn. for Christian Communicators, Women in Communications, Inc., AAUW, Hist. Kansas City Found., NCCJ (dir.), Ecumedia, Gamma Phi Beta. Club: Central Exchange. Home and Office: 4609 N Main St Kansas City MO 64116

WERNER, RUTH ANGELA JOSEPHINE, clin. microbiologist, technologist; b. Mexico City, May 13; d. Max Milton and Eva (Goldwater) W.; student Bklyn. Coll., 1968—. Microbiologist, Roosevelt Hosp. Lab., N.Y.C., 1962-65; microbiology lab. technologist L.I. Coll. Hosp., Bklyn., 1965-75, Park West Hosp., N.Y.C., 1975-76, Sydenham Mcpl. Hosp., N.Y.C., 1977-80, Kings County Mcpl. Hosp., N.Y.C., 1980—. Mem. Am. Soc. Microbiology, Am. Clin. Lab. Mgrs. Assn., Am. Pub. Health Assn., N.Y. State Registry Med. Technologists, N.Y. Acad. Sci. Democrat. Roman Catholic. Home: 180 W End Ave Apt 9E New York NY 10023

WERNER, SANDRA LEE, county ofcl.; b. Lake City, Fla., Oct. 10, 1938; d. George Washington and Frances Fair (Clark) Blankenship; student Pasco-Hernando Community Coll.; m. Eugene Vernon Werner, Jan. 31, 1970; children—Clark, Addine, Reed Nessler, Paul Nessler, Jeffrey Nessler, Frances. Legal asst. Delzer, Edwards & Martin, Port Richey, Fla., 1964-71, Roy M. Speer, Holiday, Fla., 1971-72; congressional aide, 1975; county commr. Pasco County, Fla., New Port Richey, 1980—. Sec., chmn. Pasco County Republican Exec. Com., 1974-80; precinct committeewoman; del. Rep. Nat. Conv., 1976; chmn. Pasco County Ford Campaign, 1976. Mem. Pasco County Legal Secs. (charter pres. 1968), Fla. Assn. Legal Secs., Nat. Assn. Legal Secs. (charter), Nat. Assn. Legal Assts. Presbyterian. Home: 19 Marlin Dr New Port Richey FL 33552 Office: 4025 Moon Lake Rd New Port Richey FL 33552

WERNICK, SANDIE ROTHSTEIN, hotel exec.; b. Tampa, Fla., Sept. 13, 1944; d. Nathan and Sylvia (Bienstock) Rothstein; B.A., U. Fla., 1966. Tchr., English and history, Miami Beach Sr. High Sch., 1966-67; asst. dir. public relations Waldorf Astoria, N.Y.C., 1968-70; account exec. Internat. Public Relations Inc., San Francisco, 1972-73; dir. advt. and public relations Hyatt on Union Square, San Francisco, 1974—. Mem. San Francisco Women in Advt., Bay Area Publicity Club, San Francisco Advt. Club, Public Relations Soc. Am., Am. Women in Radio and TV.

WERNIKOFF, NANCY KASDON, speech/lang. pathologist; b. Cleve., Apr. 6, 1938; d. Eli David and Doree (Sands) Kasdon; B.A., N.Y. U., 1962; M.S. in Edn., Queens Coll., 1969; m. Sergio Wernikoff, Oct. 26, 1958; children—Laura Sue, Daniel Mark. Speech pathologist Speech Rehab. Inst., N.Y.C., 1962-63, acting speech supr. speech therapy dept., 1963-65; speech-lang. cons. pre-sch. program Pascack Valley (N.J.) Council Spl. Edn., 1976-77; cons. speech-lang. pathologist Ramsey (N.J.) Public Schs., 1978—; pvt. practice, 1967—; cons. in field. Mem. exec. bd. Archer Nursery Sch., Allendale, N.J., 1973-74; active local Boy Scouts Am., Girl Scouts U.S.A., 1972-78; mem. exec. bd. sisterhood Temple Beth Or, Washington Twp., N.J., 1976-81, mem. exec. bd. Temple Beth Or, 1981—. Recipient Griffith Hughes Meml. prize Washington Sq. Coll. of Arts and Scis., N.Y. U., 1962. Mem. Am. Speech, Lang. and Hearing Assn., N.J. Speech and Hearing Assn., Bergen County Speech and Hearing Assn. (co-founder), Speech and Hearing Study Group (co-founder). Home: 42 Somerset Dr Woodcliff Lake NJ 07675

WERT, LUCILLE MATHENA, librarian, educator; b. Sioux City, Iowa, May 24, 1919; d. Arthur Edmund and Anna Sarah (Harrington) Mathena; B.A., Morningside Coll., 1942; B.S. in L.S., Simmons Coll., 1945; M.A., U. Ill., 1963, Ph.D. 1969; m. Charles Allen Wert, Sept. 7, 1942; children—John Arthur, Sara Ann. Asst. librarian, elec. engring. library M.I.T., Cambridge, Mass., 1944-45; math., physics and astronomy librarian U. Iowa, Iowa City, 1946-48, U. Chgo., 1948-51; research asst. Grad. Sch. Library Sci., U. Ill., Urbana, 1964-65, research asso., 1966-67, vis. lectr., 1968-69, research asst. prof., 1969-71, research asso. prof., dir. library research center, 1971-75, asso. prof., 1975-77, prof. library adminstrn., chemistry librarian, 1977-81, asst. dir. phys. sci. and engring. libraries, 1981—; library cons. Council Ind. Colls. U.S. Office Edn. small research project grantee, 1968-69. Mem. ALA, Assn. Coll. and Research Libraries, Library Adminstrn. and Mgmt. Assn., Assn. Am. Library Schs. (dir.), Am. Chem. Soc., Am. Soc. Engring. Edn., Am. Soc. Info. Scis., Spl. Libraries Assn., Beta Phi Mu. Presbyterian. Editor Jour. Edn. for Librarianship, 1976-80. Office: 257 Noyes Lab U Ill Urbana IL 61801

WERTHEIMER, MINDY RENEE, social worker, educator; b. Bronx, Apr. 1, 1954; d. Benjamin and Claire (Milefsky) W.; B.A., Pa. State U., 1975; M.S., Columbia U., 1976; m. Ira Katz, Nov. 25, 1978. Psychiat. social worker South Shore Child Guidance Center, Freeport, N.Y., 1976-78; med. social worker Nassau County Med. Center, East Meadow, N.Y., 1976-78; cons. Nassau County Coalition Family Planning, 1978; sr. social worker Central Dekalb Mental Health Center, Decatur, Ga., 1979-80; pvt. practice social work, 1980-81; asst. acad. dir. Ga. State U., Atlanta, 1980-81, asst. prof. social work, 1980—. Bd. dirs. Atlanta Council Internat. Programs, 1981—; adv. bd. Eclipse Crisis Center, 1981—. Recipient outstanding service award Ga. State U., 1981. Mem. Acad. Cert. Social Workers, Nat. Assn. Social Workers (bd. dirs. 1981—, chmn. North Ga. unit, coordinator continuing edn. com.), Ga. Women's Polit. Caucus, Phi Beta Kappa, Phi Kappa Phi. Author: (with Sheila Sussman and others) Adolescents are Special—A Handbook for Staff of Health Agencies Serving Youth, 1978. Office: Coll Public and Urban Affairs Ga State U Atlanta GA 30303

WERTZ, OLIVE MARION, psychiat. social worker; b. Buffalo, Dec. 2, 1913; d. John Arthur and Edna Lillian (Garihan) Tonking; B.A. magna cum laude, U. Buffalo, 1934, cert. in social work, 1935; M.S.S.A., Case Western Res. U., 1953; m. John Carl Wertz, Mar. 17, 1938; children—Christopher Allen, Derek Arthur. Social worker Crippled Children's Guild, Buffalo, 1935-37, Ch. Mission of Help, Buffalo, 1937-38, Cleve. State Hosp., 1953-63, dir. social service, 1958-63; instr. to asso. prof. Sch. Applied Social Scis., Case Western Res. U., Cleve., 1963-72; dir., sr. social worker Nord Centers, Elyria, Ohio, 1972-78; part time counselor Westshore Unitarian Ch., Rocky River, Ohio, 1978—, Lakeland Guidance Centre, Lorain, Ohio, 1978—; cons. in field; instr. workshops, seminars, coll. courses. Bd. dirs. LWV, 1981—; active ACLU, Common Cause, Nat. Com. for an Effective Congress. Mem. Nat. Assn. Social Workers (Social Worker of Yr. award Lorain-Elyria program unit 1982, Co-Social Worker of Yr. award Electoral dist. 2, 1982), Acad. Cert. Social Workers. Democrat. Unitarian. Contbr. article to profl. jour. Home: 23637 Concord Dr Westlake OH 44145 Office: 20401 Hilliard Rd Rocky River OH 44116 also 3600 Kolbe Rd Lorain OH 44053

WESEMAN, ROXANNA RUTH WARRINGTON, civic worker; b. Austin, Minn., Dec. 13, 1910; d. Samuel Henry and Nettie (Trowbridge) Warrington; cert. elem. edn. Winona State Tchrs. Coll., 1931; m. Donald H. Weseman, June 30, 1933; children—Amy, Kay, Lana, Douglas. Elem. tchr., Minn., 1931-42; leader, 4-H Club, 1942-59; mem. Mower County Hist. Bd., 1951-80, v.p., 1951-80; chmn. Nat. Barrow Show, 1956-57; Mower County chmn. women's div. Minn. Statehood Centennial Observance, 1958; mem. Bicentennial Commn., City of Austin, Bicentennial Commn. Mower County; organizer Mower County Library, 1967, pres. 1968-80. Recipient North Star award State of Minn., 1958. Mem. DAR (regent Red Cedar chpt. 1968-69, 76-77, Am. heritage chmn. Minn. 1972-78), SE Dist. Hist. Soc. (past pres.), Pythian Order (grand chief Minn. 1969-70). Methodist. Home: 115 Route 3 River Rd Austin MN 55912

WESLEY, ESTHER BESSIE, assn. exec.; b. Westfield, N.J., Sept. 16, 1920; d. Samuel and JoAnna (Stephane) Pasquarella; grad. high sch.; m. Paul Wesley, June 1, 1941; 3 daus., 1 son. Supr., instr. N.J. Bell Telephone Co., 1940-46; vol. tchr. arts and crafts Queens (N.Y.) Elem. Sch., 1952-55; exec. sec. Brevard (N.C.) C. of C., 1977—. Mem. N.C. Assn. C. of C. Execs., Brevard Bus. and Profl. Women. Presbyterian. Office: PO Box 589 Brevard NC 28712

WESS, GRACE IRENE BROWN (MRS. OTTO FRANCIS WESS), estimator, nurse, stables owner; b. Youngstown, Ohio, May 13, 1925; d. Floyd Raymond and Ruth (Walter) Brown; student Bliss Bus. Coll., 1942-43; LL.B., LaSalle U., 1952; grad. nurse's tng. Youngstown Hosp. Assn., 1974; m. Otto Francis Wess, June 11, 1949 (dec. Mar. 1969); children—Raymond Francis, Shannon Grace Wess Gorman, Colleen Melody Wess Bloomingdale, Honey Lucile Wess Biondillo, Alyson Rae Wess Gilpin Carol Lynn Wess Sivley. Nurse's aid St. Elizabeth Hosp., Youngstown, 1938-42; traffic clk. B.F. Goodrich Co., Akron, Ohio, 1942-43; rate clk., traffic dept. Gen. Fireproofing Co., Youngstown, 1947-49; pres., co-owner Jewels by Lady Grace, Detroit, 1949-63, Grayce's Treasure Chests, Youngstown, 1949-63, Grayce's Medicine Chests, Youngstown, 1949-63; indsl. and comml. bldg. estimator Ben Rudick & Son, Inc., Youngstown, 1963-71; freelance estimator, North Lima, Ohio, 1971—; newspaper columnist, various newspapers, 1963-68; nurse, 1974—; now staff nurse Drs. Hosp., Lake Worth, Fla.; owner Grace Wess Stables, Inc., Canfield, Ohio, 1949—. Democratic candidate for Mahoning County commr., 1973. Served with WAVES, 1943-47. Mem. Am. Bus. Women's Assn. (pres. 1969-70, Woman of Yr. award 1970), Youngstown Bus. and Profl. Women's Club, U.S. Trotting Assn., Canfield Harness Horsemen's Assn., Ohio Harness Horsemen's Assn., Am. Legion, VFW, Def. Supply Assn., McGuffey Meml. Assn., Women in Constrn., Constrn. Specifications Inst., Home and Sch. Assn., St. Charles Altar and Rosary Soc., Mahoning County Agrl. Soc., Am. German Club of Palm Beaches (Fla.), Youngstown Playhouse. Democrat. Roman Catholic. Home and office: 1008 Penn Grove Lake Worth FL 33461

WESSEL, NAN MEIER, hosp. adminstr.; b. N.Y.C., Sept. 13, 1929; d. Joshua and Edith Meier; B.S., SUNY, Empire State Coll., 1980; postgrad. N.Y. Inst.; m. Harry Nathan Wessel, Jr. Nov. 25, 1971; children—Peter, David, Thomas, Jo, Elizabeth. Dir. vols. L.I. Jewish-Hillside Med. Center, New Hyde Park, N.Y., 1970-74, adminstrv. asst. dept. surgery, 1974-77, adminstr./coordinator Satellite Dialysis Facility, 1977-80, asst. adminstr. Manhasset (N.Y.) div., 1980—. Mem. Am. Public Health Assn., Am. Hosp. Assn. Home: 57 Kensington Oval New Rochelle NY 10805 Office: 1554 Northern Blvd Manhasset NY 11030

WESSELS, GLADYS CHANEY, educator, film producer; b. Hillsboro, Ohio, Sept. 28, 1922; d. Newton Edwin and Elsie Elizabeth (Hall) Chaney; B.S., U. Cin., 1955; M.S., Fla. State U., 1963; m. Philippus Q. Wessels, Oct. 2, 1952; 1 son, Kim. Dir. health edn. YWCA's in Ohio, N.Y. and Ariz., 1944-50; dir. spl. services U.S. War Dept., W. Ger., 1947-49, Japan, 1950-53; instructional materials coordinator Pinellas (Fla.) schs., 1958-63, Wilmington (Ohio) schs., 1963-68; prof. communications Wright State U., Dayton, Ohio, 1968-74; film producer, media cons. Wes-Len Prodns., Yellow Springs, Ohio, 1978—; producer films for Greene County Recreation Bd.; films include Choices, Jobs in 80s, Mr. Bumble Goes Boating, Women's Issues, Inner Mongolia. Mem. Ohio Equal Rights Bd., 1974-76. Recipient Susan B. Anthony award, 1979; CETA grantee, 1978; Ohio Humanities Council grantee, 1979. Mem. ALA, Women Library Workers, AAUW, AAUP, NOW, Nat. Women's Polit. Caucus, Ohio Media Council, Women Inc. (charter). Address: 509 SW College St Yellow Springs OH 45387

WEST, ANNA LOUCHHEIM, public relations cons.; b. Phila., Dec. 5, 1953; d. Frank Pfeiffer and Betty (Meinel) Louchheim; B.A., Mt. Holyoke Coll., 1975; M.S., Boston U., 1980; m. Edward Faulke West, July 6, 1974; 1 son, David Lauchheim. Public participation coordinator Delaware Valley Regional Planning Commn., 1975-77; public info. rep. New Eng. Power Co., 1977-79; sr. communications cons. Energy Research Group, Inc., 1979—. Mem. Public Relations Soc. Am. (dir. New Eng. chpt.). Home: 210 Litchfield Dr Carlisle MA 01741 Office: 400-1 Toten Pond Rd Waltham MA 02154

WEST, BETTY AARON, banker; b. Chatham, Va.; d. Lester George and Ellen (Crocker) Aaron; grad. Teller Tng. Seminar, Am. Inst. Banking; m. Henry Marvin West, Apr. 21, 1946; children—Mary Elizabeth West Branch, Robert Marvin, Stephen Dale. Successively bookkeeper, teller, head teller, First Nat. Bank of Martinsville (Va.), 1955-77, bank officer, asst. cashier, 1977—. Active Nat. Arthritis Soc., United Fund Campaign. Recipient Boss of Yr. award local chpt. Am. Bus. Women's Assn., 1980. Baptist. Home: Route 6 PO Box 148 Martinsville VA 24112 Office: PO Box 4911 Martinsville VA 24112

WEST, CARIN CHAPMAN, communications and tech. co. exec.; b. N.Y.C., Sept. 16, 1945; d. Edgar Harry Arthur and Eloise (LeTarte) Chapman; B.A., Lindenwood Coll., 1967; M.S., U. So. Calif., Los Angeles, 1970; m. L. Clinton West, Jan. 1, 1972; stepchildren—P. Lee, Richard G. Research asso. Nat. Spl. Media Inst., U. So. Calif., Los Angeles, 1969-70; project officer Bd. Coop. Edn. Services, Nassau County, N.Y., 1970-72; media cons. U. Wis., Calif. State Dept. Edn., U.S. Dept. Edn., 1972-75; edn. specialist Naval Instructional Devel. Center, San Diego, 1975-76; spl. projects coordinator Sensors, Data, Decisions, San Diego, 1976-77; program mgr. ManTech Internat. Corp., Arlington, Va., 1977—; chmn. bd. Transtec Corp. Recipient Gettysburg award for multi-media communications, 1969. Mem. Soc. for Applied Learning Tech., Assn. for Ednl. Communications and Tech., Nat. Assn. Female Execs., Film and Media Educators (sec. 1974), U.S. Internat. Univ. Women (pres. 1975-76). Mem. Christian Ch. (Disciples of Christ). Club: Penasquitos Lioness (charter mem.). Home: 203 Yoakum Pkwy Alexandria VA 22304 Office: ManTech Internat Corp 2341 Jefferson Davis Hwy Suite 1111 Arlington VA 22202 also Transtec PO Box 2769 Arlington VA 22202

WEST, CAROLYN VERONICA, writer, former elec. products mfg. co. exec.; b. Syracuse, N.Y., June 7, 1928; d. Peter J. and Mabel (Feigel) W.; B.S., Syracuse U., 1950. With Crouse-Hinds Co., Syracuse, 1953-78, communications mgr., 1968-73, v.p. press relations, 1973-78; free lance writer, 1978—. Bd. dirs. Opera Theatre of Syracuse, Inc., 1974-79, v.p., 1976-78; bd. dirs. UN Assn. Central N.Y., 1973-78, v.p., 1975; bd. dirs. Republican Citizens Com., 1972-78; vol. public broadcasting WCNY-FM-TV, Syracuse, 1970—; mem. community relations com. Crouse-Irving Meml. Hosp. Found. 1975-81; bd. dirs. Regional Learning Service, 1979-82; mem. Onondaga County Fair Campaign Practices Com., 1978—. Mem. Mfrs. Assn. Central N.Y. (public relations com. 1973-78), Women in Communications, Business-Industry Communicators Council, Soc. Tech. Communication, Greater Syracuse C. of C. (small bus. council steering com. 1982—). Republican. Lutheran. Club: Syracuse Press (dir. 1975-77, sec. 1978-79). Home and Office: Regency Tower 770 James St Syracuse NY 13203

WEST, CATHY MAYNARD, psychologist; b. Los Angeles, July 18, 1945; d. Kenneth Lloyd and Margaret E. (Bell) Maynard; A.B. with honors in psychology, Occidental Coll., 1966; M.A., U. Calif., Berkeley, 1967, Ph.D., 1972; m. Robert Elliott West, Sept. 6, 1969; children—James Arthur, Brian Kendall, Kyle Richard. Clin. intern Bklyn. State Hosp., 1970-71; staff psychologist Fordham Hosp., Bronx, 1972; counseling psychologist Drew U., Madison, N.J., 1973-75; cons. Irvington Mental Health Center, Irvington, N.J., 1973-77; chief psychologist Youth and Family Counseling Service, Westfield, N.J., 1974—; pvt. practice psychology, Summit, N.J., 1977—; psychol. tester Overlook Hosp., Summit, 1979-80; guest lectr. Drew U., various times 1974-79. Lic. psychologist, N.J. Mem. Calif. Scholarship Fedn., Am. Psychol. Assn., N.J. Psychol. Assn., N.J. Assn. Women Therapists (exec. bd.), Am. Soc. Psychologists in Pvt. Practice, Psi Chi. Republican. Presbyterian. Contbr. to profl. publs. Home: 21 Upper Dr Summit NJ 07901 Office: 233 Prospect St Westfield NJ 07090

WEST, DOTTIE (DOROTHY MARIE MARSH), singer; b. McMinnville, Tenn., Oct. 11; d. William and Pelina (Jones) Marsh; B.A. in Music, Tenn. Tech. Coll., 1956; m. William West, 1952 (div. 1972); children—Morris, Kerry, Shelly, Dale; m. 2d, Byron A. Metcalf, Aug. 27, 1973 (div. 1981). Singing debut WEWS-TV, Cleve., 1956-60; singer 5-piece band Cross-Country, 1966—; performances include: Grand Ole Opry, 1962—, Memphis Symphony Orch., 1973, Kansas City Symphony, 1961-74, also Atlanta Symphony, Denver Symphony, New Orleans Symphony, TV appearances include: Eddy Arnold Special, Country Hit Parade, Music Country U.S.A., Hee-Haw, Glen Campbell Show, Jimmy Dean, Mike Douglas, Good Ole Nashville, Tonight Show, Kenny Rogers Spl., Hollywood Squares, Dukes of Hazzard, Barbara Mandrell; rec. artist Staeday Records, 1959-61, Atlantic Records, 1962, RCA, 1962—, United Artists Records. Recipient Grammy award female artist for Here Comes My Baby, 1965; named Number One Female Writer in U.S., Billboard Mag., 1974, Number One Female Performer in Eng., 1973, 74; Country Music Artist of Year, British Country Music Assn.; Coca Cola Country Girl, 1972—; Duet Artist of Yr. (with Kenny Rogers). Address: care Michael Brokaw 1112 N Sherbourne Dr Los Angeles CA 90069

WEST, JESSAMYN, novelist; b. Ind., 1902; student Whittier Coll., U. Calif., also studied in Eng.; hon. doctorates Whittier Coll., Mills Coll., Ind. U., Swarthmore Coll., Western Coll. for Women; m. H.M. McPherson. Tchr. at writers confs. Bread Loaf, U. Notre Dame, U. Wash., Ind. U., U. Utah, Stanford, U. Colo., U. Ky.; former writer in residence Wellesley Coll., Mill Coll. Trustee Whittier Coll. Mem. bd. Foster Parents Plan. Mem. ACLU, NAACP. Mem. Soc. of Friends. Writer movie scripts The Big Country, Stolen Hours. Author: To See the Dream; Cress Delahanty (also pub. as series in New Yorker mag.); Mirror for the Sky, 1948; The Witch Diggers; The Friendly Persuasion (wrote screenplay for motion picture), 1956; Love, Death and the Ladies Drill Team, 1955; Love Is Not What You Think, 1958; South of the Angels, 1960; The Quaker Reader, 1961; A Matter of Time, 1966; Leafy River, 1967; Except for Me and Thee, 1969; Crimson Ramblers of the World, Farewell, 1970; Hide and Seek, 1973; The Secret Look, 1974; Massacre at Fall Creek, 1975; The Woman Said Yes, 1976; The Life I Really Lived, 1979. Contbr. to mags., including McCalls, Good Housekeeping, Red Book, New Yorker. Home: 2480 3d Ave Napa CA 94558 Office: care Harcourt Brace & Co 757 3d Ave New York NY 10017

WEST, JOSEBELL LUCILLE, educator; b. Hialeah, Fla., Dec. 2, 1925; d. Willie and Willie Alfred (Thompson) Akers; student Oakwood Coll. Acad., 1946; early childhood certificate Broward Community Coll., 1963; m. Eddie West, Mar. 28, 1946; children—Frank A., Bernard E., Marva L., Dwayne E. Tchr., Mt. Olivet Seventh-Day Adventist Ch. Sch., Dania, Fla., 1951-52, West's Kindergarten, Dania, 1952-69; social educator Broward County (Fla.) Sch. Bd., Ft. Lauderdale, 1969—. Committeewoman, Dania Democratic Com., 1958-69; pres. Collins Elementary Sch. PTA, Dania, 1960-69, Bethune Elementary Sch. PTA, Hollywood, Fla., 1969-70; bd. dirs. Pathfinder, 1974-81. Mem. NEA, Am. Legion Aux., Concerned Citizens of Dania, Inc. Adventist. Clubs: Cheerful Workers, Westside Civic of Dania (sec. 1959-65, pres. 1974—), Pathfinder (dir.), Dania Dem. Home: 621 NW 3d Terr Dania FL 33004 Office: 701 NW 31st Ave Fort Lauderdale FL 33311

WEST, KATHRYN MARIE, pianist; b. Lansing, Mich., Apr. 15, 1935; d. Harry Allen and Mabel Agnes (Dyer) Strait; student Central Mich. U., 1952-55, Eastern Mich. U., 1979—; m. David Roche West, June 11, 1955; children—Julie, Martha, Nancy, Jean, Mark. Profl. accompanist, Ann Arbor Civic Theatre, U. Mich. Gilbert and Sullivan Soc., U. Mich. Summer Theater, 1965-72; duo pianist with Naomi Donaldson, 1970-76, with Margaret Bond, 1972—; sec. Office of Pres. U. Mich., Ann Arbor, 1976-77, exec. sec., 1978—; concerts in Kansas City, Mo., Ohio, Mich. Mem. Friends of Four Hand Music, Amateur Chamber Music Players, Sigma Alpha Iota. Home: 551 Hunt Pl Ypsilanti MI 48197 Office: Office of Pres U Mich Ann Arbor MI 48109

WEST, MARCIA ANN, broadcasting exec.; b. Seattle, Nov. 27, 1944; d. Byron Hale and Norma Ruth Harvey; B.A., W. Tex. State U., 1966, M.A., 1969; postgrad. U. Colo., 1971-76. Instr. Spanish, W. Tex. State U., 1966-68, U. Evansville (Ind.), 1969-71, U. Colo., Denver, 1971-76; host, co-producer Esta Semana, Sta. KRMA-TV, Denver, 1971-75; asso. editor La Luz mag., 1972—; producer, broadcaster KOA News, Denver, 1972-76; mgr. public affairs KOA Stas., Denver, 1976-78, program and public affairs dir., 1978—; publicity dir. Barney Ford Meml. Assn., 1976—; cons. in field. Bd. dirs. Cystic Fibrosis Found., Denver Opportunities Industrialization Center; mem. selection com. Minoru Yasui Vol. Awards for Denver; adv. bd. Denver Internat. Film Festival; mem. selection com. 10th Nat. Abe Lincoln awards; cons. Gov.'s Conf. Library Services. Recipient Abe Lincoln Merit award, 1977; Tummy award Denver Area Journalists Assn., 1972; Silver Bell award Nat. Advt. Council, 1981; named Outstanding Educator U. Colo., Denver, 1976; Outstanding Tchr. Fgn. Lang., W.Tex. State U., 1966; Best Public Affairs Producer, Denver Catholic Register, 1977; chosen media contributions winner Colo. Salute to Women, 1981. Mem. Am. Women Radio

TV, Nat. Assn. Broadcasters, Colo. Broadcasters Assn., Nat. Alliance Businessmen, Nat. Assn. Program Execs. (selection com. awards 1978), Nat. Broadcasters Assn. for Community Affairs (regional v.p., nat. conf. chairperson 1980-81, pres. 1981-82), Leadership Denver, Denver C. of C. Author articles. Office: 1044 Lincoln St Denver CO 80203

WEST, MARGARET LILA WALKER (MRS. VICTOR ROYCE WEST), ednl. adminstr.; b. Gibbon, Nebr., Aug. 28, 1905; d. James George and Niema Sybil (Converse) Walker; B.A., U. Nebr., 1934; student U. Heidelberg (Germany), 1930-32, 35-36; postgrad. U. Minn., 1948-49, U. Ill., 1952; M.Ed., Nat. Coll. Edn., 1965; m. Victor Royce West, June 3, 1930; children—Sybel West Kimmel, Vicki West Matovic. Tchr. Gibbon (Nebr.) Elementary Sch., 1926-30; tchr. German and Latin Omaha Central High Sch., 1938-40; prin., tchr. Sheltering Arms Hosp. Sch. for Polio Patients, Mpls., 1948-51; supervisory tchr. educable mentally handicapped Evanston (Ill.) Twp. High Sch., 1951-70; supr. student tchrs. in spl. edn. Ill. State U., Normal, 1972—. Bd. dirs. YWCA, Omaha, 1938-40, Evanston, 1965-67, North Shore Assn. for Retarded Children and Shore Tng. Center, Evanston, 1965-67. Am. Assn. Mental Deficiency fellow, 1967. Mem. Internat., Ill. (sec. 1956-58, bd. dirs. 1956-61, chpt. pres. 1960) councils for exceptional children, Am. Assn. Mental Deficiency, AAUW, Gamma Phi Beta (province dir. 1939-41), Delta Kappa Gamma. Methodist. Home: 9310 Lincolnwood Dr Evanston IL 60203

WEST, MARIANNE V., social worker; b. South Bend, Ind., Mar. 29, 1951; d. Leo William and Janet Irene (Grove) West; B.A., Ind. U., 1973; M.S.W., U. Ill., Chgo., 1975. Staff social worker St. Francis Hosp., Evanston, Ill., 1975-77; clin. social worker Health Care Assos. for Women, Grants Pass, Oreg., 1977-78; pvt. practice clin. social work, Grants Pass, 1978-79; clin. social worker, dir. residence Mary Bartelme Home for Girls, Chgo., 1979—; unit dir., 1981—; instr. Rogue Community Coll., Grants Pass, 1978; cons. Josephine County Juvenile Dept., Grants Pass, 1978; fieldwork instr. Loyola U. Sch. Social Work, Chgo., 1979; cons. Chgo. YWCA, Chgo. Women Against Rape, 1976-77, 79—; coordinator Parents Anonymous, Grants Pass, 1979; mem. Cook County Taskforce on Child Sexual Abuse, Chgo., 1980—. Cert. social worker, Ill.; registered clin. social worker, Oreg., 1978. Mem. AAUW, Nat. Assn. Social Workers, Acad. Cert. Social Workers, Assn. Humanistic Psychology, Alpha Xi Delta. Club: Order Eastern Star. Office: Mary Bartelme Home for Girls 2737 W Peterson St Chicago IL 60659

WEST, MAY ELLEN, social worker, bus. exec., profl. fund raiser, grants writer; b. Curtin, Oreg., May 1, 1927; d. Walter Dee and Ethel May (Gilkenson) Skidmore; student Eastern Oreg. Coll. Edn., 1945, Nat. Tng. Inst., UCLA, 1968-69; m. Ernest Glenn West, Jan. 1, 1947 (div. 1969); 1 son, Michael Donovan. Credit mgr. Beamer Motor Co., Sacramento, 1956-58; owner, mgr. Tot Cottage, Carmichael, Calif., 1960-65; exec. dir. Sacramento Assn. for Retarded, 1965-67, bd. dirs., 1960-65, hon. life mem., 1967-68; area dir., campaign A asso. Sacramento United Crusade, 1968-70; exec. dir. Yuba Sutter United Way, Yuba City, Calif., 1970-73; budget dir., agy. relations exec. Sacramento United Way, 1973-75; adv. council Yuba Sutter Council for Retarded; mem. Inter-Agy. Co-ordinating Council, 1970-73; chmn. Calif. project Try Another Way, 1977-78; bd. dirs. Yuba City Vol. Bur., 1970-73, Yuba Sutter USO, 1971-73, Yuba Sutter Commn. on Aging, 1971-73, Placer County Interagy. Council, 1975-79, Legal Aid Services No. Calif., 1980—; bd. dirs., sec. Project Go, 1978-80, pres., 1981-82; exec. dir. Placer Assn. Retarded, Roseville, Calif., 1975-79; Amway dealer, 1979—; owner West Enterprises (Rentals), 1976—; co-owner, bus. mgr. Universal Sch. Master Locksmithing, 1976-80; sec. Sacramento Area United Way Agy. Execs., 1975-76, also mem. area campaign cabinet; mem. Placer County Archtl. Barriers Com., 1976-79; mem. fiscal planning task force Calif. Assn. Retarded, 1976-78, public relations com., 1979-80. Active Yuba Sutter Campfire Girls, 1970-73, hon. mem., 1973—; bd. dirs., editor newsletter, Casilas Mangnanita Homeowners Assn., 1973-74; bd. dirs. Sutter Buttes Regional Theatre, 1971-73, Parents without Partners, 1970-73; chmn. Placer County Coordinating Council for Handicapped, 1978; chmn. Eskaton Needs Assessment Survey for Handicapped, 1977; v.p. conf. execs. Calif. Assn. for Retarded, 1977-78; mem. Placer County Arts Council, 1982—. Mem. Crocker Art Gallery, Roseville C. of C. Clubs: Toastmistress, Soroptomist (dir. Yuba City-Marysville 1970-73, Roseville 1976—). Home: 7632 Hardy Ln Roseville CA 95678

WEST, MILDRED BARRETT, profl. tennis player, athletics adminstr.; b. Cedartown, Ga., Oct. 26, 1934; d. Russell R. and Mildred (Maxwell) Barrett; B.S., Ga. State Coll. for Women, 1957; M.A., U. Md., 1959; m. Marvin F. West, Dec. 17, 1966. Instr. phys. edn. Coll. of William and Mary, Williamsburg, Va., 1959-63, asst. prof. phys. edn., 1963-68, asso. prof., 1968-78, prof., 1978—, chmn. women's phys. edn. dept., 1969-79, dir. women's athletics, 1969—, coach women's tennis varsity, 1965-72, 75-80; aquatic chmn. Va. div. of Girls and Women's Sports, 1967-71; dir. Malta Jr. Wightman Cup Tennis matches, 1970-80; profl. tennis player, Va., 1960—; guest instr. swimming Sargent Coll., Boston U., 1963, 64. Mem. 20th Century Art Gallery, Williamsburg Library, Williamsburg Community Hosp. Aux. Named Outstanding Young Woman in Am., Ga. Coll., Milledgeville, 1968. Mem. U.S. Lawn Tennis Assn., U.S. Profl. Tennis Assn., AAHPER, Va., So. assns. of health, phys. edn. and recreation, Nat., So. assns. phys. edn. for coll. women, Assn. Intercollegiate Athletics for Women (regional tennis chmn. 1979-81, nat. tennis chmn. 1980-81, nat. tennis com. 1982, div. commr. nat. championships 1981-82). Democrat. Baptist. Clubs: Centre Court Racquet, Williamsburg Garden. Home: 310 Nottingham Rd Williamsburg VA 23185

WESTALL, PEGGY BURKE, state legislator; b. Caliente, Nev., Feb. 3, 1929; student U. Nev., Reno; m. Alfred H. Westall; children—Lyn, Ann, Terry, Christine. Pres., Westall Inc.; mem. Nev. Assembly, 1977-81, 81—. Active Sparks (Nev.) Charter Revision Com., Washoe Council Govts., Com. on Sewage and Water Quality. Mem. Reno Bd. Realtors (polit. affairs com.). Democrat. Mormon. Office: Legislative Bldg 401 S Carson St Carson City NV 89710 *

WESTBIE, CONSTANCE VIRGINIA, writer; b. Ft. Pierra, S.D., Oct. 5, 1908; d. Albert George and Adelaide Lucia (Sebree) Loveall; music student of Gyula Ornay, San Francisco, 1927-34; student U. Calif., Berkeley, 1930-33, Marian Madsen's Bus. Coll., 1933-34; student in creative writing Maren Elwood, San Francisco, 1935-37, Lloyd Eric Reeve, Berkeley, 1955-62; m. John Myrrell Westbie, Apr. 5, 1941; children—John Arthur, Donald Kaelber. Legal sec. firm Silver & Hall, 1933-36, firm DeAvila, Roderick, Michaels & Silver, 1936-40; pvt. sec. to Judge Edward J. Silver, Oakland, Calif., 1940-43; music tchr. and organist Ch. of Religious Sci., Paradise, Calif., 1961-76; sec. Paradise Unified Sch. Dist., 1966-76; author: The Birdcage Murders, 1964; Night Stalks the Mansion, 1978; (poetry) Moon Madness, 1980; Once Over Lightly, 1980; editor, re-writer: The Carver Effect, 1979; contbr. articles, short stories to various publs. Pres. guild Ch. Religious Sci., Paradise, 1963-65; sec. Paradise Guild Arts and Crafts, 1973-75; pres. Mary Doyle unit Mt. Diablo Therapy Center, Concord, Calif., 1955-57. Winner Nat. Writers Club Book Contest, 1977, Grand prize Ina Coolbrith Circle State Contest for poetry, 1977. Mem. Nat. Writers Club, Calif. Writers Club, Ina Coolbrith Circle, Calif. Fedn. Chapparal Poets. Clubs: Paradise Writer's, Republican Women, Rosicrucian Order (San Jose, Calif.). Home: 5033 Russell Dr Paradise CA 95969

WESTBROOK, ETTA MAE, educator, extension agt.; b. New Matamoras, Ohio, Dec. 18, 1939; d. Alfred O. and Glenda L. W.; B.S. in Home Econs., Harding Coll., 1961; M.S., Pa. State U., 1967. Tchr. vocat. home econs. Leetonia, Ohio, 1961-65; teaching asst. Pa. State U., 1965-67; asst. prof. home econs. Abilene (Tex.) Christian U., 1967-71; asst. extension agt. Grundy County, Tenn., 1971-73; assoc. prof. agrl. extension service U. Tenn., Knoxville, 1973—. Bible class tchr. Norwood Ch. of Christ, 1973—, coordinator primary classes, 1977—. Mem. Am. Home Econs. Assn., Tenn. Home Econs. Assn. (v.p., 1978-79, state membership chmn., 1979-80, v.p. program, 1980-81, pres. internal affairs 1982—), Knoxville Area Home Econs. Assn. (pres.-elect 1982-83), U.S. Dept. Agr. Club (program chmn. 1981, pres. 1982), Delta Kappa Gamma (pres., 1978-80). Contbr. bulls. for ltd. income/ltd. edn. homemakers. Home: 7745 Cranley Rd Powell TN 37849 Office: Box 1071 University Tenn Knoxville TN 37901

WESTBURY, JUNE ALWYN, mem. Can. legis. assembly; b. Hamilton, N.Z.; came to Can., 1948, naturalized, 1971; d. Philip William and Doris Myrtle (Halcrow) Cantwell; student Brain's Coll., Auckland; voice student of Mina Caldow; m. Peter W.A. Westbury, Oct. 22, 1949; children—Sheila Westbury Raffey, Pamela June Westbury Danwich, Jennifer Doris. Elected alderman, Ward I, Winnipeg (Man., Can.) City Council, 1969, vice chmn. Centennial Celebrations Com., 1970, mem. various Council coms., including Parks and Recreation, Health and Welfare, Housing and Urban Renewal, Utilities and Personnel, chmn. Health and Welfare Com., 1971, councillor, Roslyn Ward, City of Winnipeg, 1971-77, mem. various times Environ. and Works and Ops. Coms., Winnipeg Police Commn., Winnipeg Heritage Corp., chmn. subcom. on Group Homes, elected Corydon Ward, 1977, chmn. Adv. Com. on Hist. Bldgs., 1979; elected Liberal mem. Legis. Assembly, Man., Ft. Rouge Constituency, 1979-81; dir. Via Rail Corp. Founder, chmn. Laurier Club of Man., 1982—; bd. dirs. Winnipeg Mcpl. Hosps., 1970-79, chmn., 1971-75, vice chmn., 1977-78. Elected sec. (first woman) Liberal Party of Man., 1968-69, v.p. Liberal Party of Can., 1970-73; Liberal candidate Osborne Constituency, 1973; bd. dirs. Man. Health Orgns., Inc., 1970-76; bd. dirs. Can. Council Christians and Jews, Central Region, 1972—, chmn. program com., 1979—, mem. Central Exec. Com., 1976—, Nat. Exec., 1979—; bd. dirs. Age and Opportunity Centres, 1972-76; adv. bd. YWCA, 1972-82; exec. Riverview Community Centre, 1973-74; commr. Nat. Capital Commn., Ottawa, 1976-82, mem. adv. com. on design, 1976—; ofcl. Man. Track and Field Assn., 1978; mem. Task Force on Maternal and Child Health and Edn. subcom., 1979-82; dir. Epiphany pageant St. Alban's Anglican Ch., 1954-72; pres. Riverview-Ashland Home and Sch. Assn., 1967-69; edn. chmn. Royal Winnipeg Ballet Women's Com., 1967-69. Named Woman of Yr. in Politics and Govtl. Affairs, YWCA, 1979; recipient Melitta achievement award, 1982. Mem. So. Cross Internat. Assn., Man. Action Com. on Status of Women, Man. Hist. Soc., Heritage Can. Found. (bd. govs. 1982—).

WESTCOTT, JACQUELYN MAUREEN, legis. advisor; b. Vineland, N.J., Aug. 23, 1929; s. John Leslie and Lillian Mary Magdalen (Pearsall) W.; B.A. with honors, Washington Internat. Coll., 1980. Clerk, supr. FBI, Washington, 1950-57; sec., caseworker U.S. Ho. of Reps., Washington, 1957-60; office mgr. Seegmiller, Wilner & Custer, Washington, 1960-63; mgmt. asst. Pres.'s Com. on Equal Employment Opportunity, 1963-64; adminstrv. asst. to asso. counsel to Pres., 1964-65; adminstrv. aide, asst. dir. info. Plans for Progress, 1965-68; adminstrv. asst. Office of Vice-Pres. U.S., 1968-69; research asst. Congressional Quar., Washington, 1969-72; legis. adv. U.S. Ho. of Reps. Com. on Merchant Marine and Fisheries, 1973—; Mem. NOW, Capitol Hill Polit. Caucus, Nat. Women's Polit. Caucus. Democrat. Roman Catholic. Contbr. articles to profl. jours. Home: 560 N St SW Washington DC 20024 Office: Com on Merchant Marine and Fisheries US Ho of Reps H2-543 HOB Annex No 2 Washington DC 20515

WESTER, CAROL MARIE, nurse; Taunton, Mass., Sept. 10, 1954; d. Herbert Lee and Eva Martha (Klausky) W.; B.S.N., Northeastern U., 1977; postgrad. in psychiat. nursing Boston Coll. Team nurse Human Resource Inst., Boston, 1977-78; charge nurse Hall-Mercer Childrens Center, McLean Hosp., Belmont, Mass., 1978-80; hosp. mgr. Paul A. Dever State Sch., Taunton, 1980—. Mem. Am. Nurses Assn., Mass. Nurses Assn., Sigma Theta Tau, Phi Kappa Phi. Home: 214 Bay St Taunton MA 02780 Office: 1380 Bay St Taunton MA 02780

WESTERBECK, PENELOPE BUTTS, advt. agy. exec.; b. Buckinghamshire, Eng., Oct. 24, 1942; came to U.S., 1945; d. Robert and Phyllis Winifred (Crew) Butts; B.A. with honors, Mt. Holyoke Coll., 1964; m. Colin Leslie Westerbeck, May 22, 1965; 1 dau., Katherine Cody. Copywriter, J. Walter Thompson Co., N.Y.C., 1964-67, D'Arcy-MacManus, Adams, N.Y.C., 1967-72; sr. writer DFS Advt., N.Y.C., 1972-73; v.p., creative supr. Grey Advt., N.Y.C., 1973-82; v.p., creative dir. Wm. Esty Advt., N.Y.C., 1982—. Home: 601 West End Ave New York NY 10024 Office: 100 E 42d St New York NY 10017

WESTERMAN, PEGGY DAY, lighting designer; b. Gulfport, Miss., Aug. 11, 1945; d. Warren Francis and Helen Elizabeth (Cubley) Day; B.F.A., La. State U., 1974; student La. Tech. U., 1963-65; m. Robert Dean Westerman, Mar. 2, 1977; 1 dau., Jennie Elizabeth; children by previous marriage—Douglas Howard, Gregory Alan; stepchildren—Rhett Jeffrey, Lecia Kay, Todd Douglas, Sheri Deane. Exec. sec. Sch. of Banking of South, Baton Rouge, 1969-70; lighting designer, project mgr. Levy Kramer & Assos., Baton Rouge, 1974-78; lighting design cons. Peggy D Westerman, Baton Rouge, 1976—; pres., developer Westerman Properties, Inc.; student adv. La. State U. Chmn. architects United Givers Campaign, 1977. Mem. AIA, Illuminating Engring. Soc. (chmn. lighting design awards), Soc. Preservation Historic La., Phi Kappa Pi. Club: Bal Societe.

WESTFALL, CAROL DOOLEY, artist; b. Everett, Pa., Sept. 7, 1938; d. Carroll F. and Doris L. (Hawkins) Dooley; B.F.A., R.I. Sch. Design, 1960; M.F.A., Md. Inst. Coll. Art, 1972; children—Camille, Maigann. Instr., Md. Inst. Coll. Art, Balt., 1968-72; asst. prof. fine arts Montclair (N.J.) State Coll., from 1972, now asso. prof.; instr. Tchrs. Coll., Columbia U., 1976—; crafts cons. Reader's Digest. Crafts grant adv. N.J. State Council on Arts, 1977-80; chmn. resident evaluation com. Peters Valley, 1979—; bd. dirs. Peters Valley Craftsmen, Layton, N.J., 1977—. Council for Internat. Exchange Scholars grantee, 1980-81. Mem. Textile Mus. (asso.), N.Y. Rug Soc., Asia Soc. Author: (with Glashausser) Plaiting - Step By Step, 1976; critical reviewer Craft Horizons, 1973—. Home: 162 Whitford Ave Nutley NJ 07110 Office: Fine Arts Dept Montclair State Coll Upper Montclair NJ 07043

WESTFALL, HELEN NAOMI, microbiologist; b. Grafton, W.Va., June 23, 1933; d. Banks and Thelma Gertrude (Conwell) Roach; student St. Mary's Hosp. Sch. Nursing, Clarksburg, W.Va., 1951-52, Hosp. for Women of Md. Sch. Nursing, Balt., 1952-53; U. Hawaii, 1964-66; Grossmont Coll., El Cajon, Calif., 1967-68; B.S., Old Dominion U., 1971, M.S., 1974; student Cath. U. Am., 1976; Ph.D., W.Va. U., 1980; m. Andrew Robert Westfall, May 13, 1952; children—Steven Neal, Aleta June, Bryce Ruell. Lab. tchrs.'s asst. Old Dominion U., 1969-71, grad. research asst., 1971-72, grad. teaching asst., 1973-74; sci. tchr. Portsmouth (Va.) Cath. High Sch., 1974-75; instr. biology Alderson-Broaddus Coll., Philippi, W.Va., 1975-77; NRC Postdoctoral research assoc. Naval Med. Research Inst., Bethesda, Md., 1980—. Claude Worthington Benedum Found. predoctoral fellowship awardee, 1977-80. Mem. Am. Soc. Microbiology, Am. Leptospirosis Research Conf., Am. Soc. Rickettsiology and Rickettsial Diseases, Assn. Women in Sci., Old Dominion U. Alumni Assn., W.Va. U. Alumni Assn., Sigma Xi, Phi Kappa Phi. Home: 939 Maple Dr Lot 2 Morgantown WV 26505 Office: Lab Chair of Sci Naval Med Research Inst Nat Naval Med Center Bethesda MD 20814

WESTHOFF, JUDITH ANN, banker; b. Waterloo, Iowa, Aug. 3, 1939; d. John F. and Margaret (Boyle) Baker; student Clarke Coll., Dubuque, Iowa, 1957-59; B.A., U. Wis., Madison, 1979; m. J. Cotton Westhoff, Dec. 26, 1964; children—Michael John, Michelle Rene, Megan Cathleen. With First Nat. Bank, Burlington, Iowa, 1959-64; with City Nat. Bank, Pittsburg, Kans., 1965—, vice-pres., cashier, 1979—. Pres. bd. dirs. Help Now Inc.; bd. dirs. Pittsburg United Way. Mem. S.E. Kans. div. Nat. Assn. Bank Women (past pres.), Pittsburg Area C. of C. (treas., dir.), Am. Inst. Bankers, Bank Adminstrn. Inst. Club: Altrusa of Pittsburg (past treas.). Home: 2009 Colonial Dr Pittsburg KS 66762 Office: 522 S Broadway Pittsburg KS 66762

WESTIN, LORI ELISABETH, musician; b. New Haven, May 18, 1954; d. Ralph Gustav and Holly Richards (Burgess) W.; Mus.B., performance cert. Eastman Sch. Music, 1976. Horn player Spoleto Festival, Italy, 1976, Phoenix Symphony Orch., 1976-79; 2d horn San Francisco Symphony Orch., 1979—. Office: Davies Symphony Hall San Francisco CA 94102

WESTLEY, ARLENE, marriage-family-child counselor; b. N.Y.C., June 12, 1938; d. Frank P. and Adele M. (Kawaja) Wolf; student (N.Y. Regents scholar) Queens Coll.; student San Jose State U., UCLA, Azusa Pacific Coll.; m. David Westley, Oct. 20, 1974; 1 son, Eric Sharples. Social case worker Los Angeles County, 1961-62; tchr. Santa Monica Unified Sch. Dist., Los Angeles City Schs., 1963-74; pvt. practice marriage family child counselor, Beverly Hills, Calif., 1975—. Exam. commr. Calif. State Bd. of Behavioral Sci. Examiners. Mem. Am. Assn. Marriage and Family Counselors (clin.). Home and Office: 1908 N Beverly Dr Beverly Hills CA 90210

WESTON, CORINNE COMSTOCK, historian, educator; b. Castle Hill, Maine, Dec. 8, 1919; d. Gerald Gerry and Kit B. (Flanigan) Comstock; B.A. with highest distinction, U. Maine, 1941; M.A., Columbia U., 1944, Ph.D., 1951. Instr., U. Maine, 1946-47, 48-49; lectr. Sch. of Gen. Studies, Columbia U., N.Y.C., 1949-51; instr. Brooklyn Coll., N.Y., 1951-52; asst. prof. history U. Houston, after 1952, then asso. prof., prof.; vis. asso. prof. Hunter Coll., N.Y.C., 1964-65, lectr., 1964, asso. prof., 1965-66; prof. history Herbert H. Lehman Coll., CUNY, 1969—. Am. Council of Learned Socs. grantee, summer, 1962. Am. fellow Royal Hist. Soc.; mem. Am. Hist. Assn. Author: (with Robert Livingston Schuyler) British Constitutional History since 1832; English Constitutional History and the House of Lords, 1965; contbr. articles on English history to scholarly jours. Home: Apt 14G 200 Central Park S New York NY 10019 Office: 298 Corman Herbert H Lehman Coll CUNY Bronx NY 10468

WESTON, DAWN THOMPSON, artist, researcher; b. Joliet, Ill., Apr. 15, 1919; d. Cyril C. and Vivian Grace Thompson; student (scholar) Penn Hall Jr. Coll., Chambersburg, Pa., 1937-38; B.S., Northwestern U., 1942, postgrad. in reading and speech pathology, 1960-61, M.A. in Ednl. Adminstrn., 1970; postgrad. U. Ill., 1964; student Art Inst. Chgo., 1954, Pestalozzi-Froebel, Chgo., 1955, Phila. Inst. for Achievement Human Potential, 1963; m. Arthur Walter Weston, Sept. 10, 1940; children—Roger Lance, Randall Kent, Cynthia Brooke. Therapist, USN Hosp., Gt. Lakes, Ill., 1940-45; tchr. Holy Child and Waukegan (Ill.) High Schs., 1946-54; elem. and jr. high art dir. Lake Bluff (Ill.) Schs., 1954-58; pioneer ednl. dir. Grove Sch. for Brain-Injured, Lake Forest, Ill., 1958-66; art gallery mgr., Wilmette, Ill., 1969-82; one-woman shows: Evanston Woman's Club, Northwestern U., Deer Path Gallery, Lake Forest; The Hein Co., Waukegan; numerous group shows, 1939-76. Represented in permanent collections: ARC, Victory Meml. Hosp., Waukegan, Sierra Assos., Chgo., numerous pvt. collections U.S., Can., Africa; works include: Poisonous Plants of Midwest set of etchings for Country Gentleman mag., 1956, Clouds mural, 1981; ind. researcher on shifting visual imagery due to trauma, 1982—; life mem. corp. Grove Sch., co-chmn. bd., 1958-66. Mem. Presdl. Gold Chain, Trinity Coll., 1979. Named Citizen of Yr., Grove Sch., 1978, room at sch. named in her honor, 1982; cert. tchr., Ill. Mem. Art Inst. Chgo., Deerpath Art League, Pi Lambda Theta. Methodist (del. Ann. Conf. 1982). Research on uneven growth, 1969-70. Home and Office: 349 E Hilldale Pl Lake Forest IL 60045

WESTON, FRANCES, state ofcl.; b. Phila., Sept. 1, 1954; d. Alfred and Patricia Peteraf; B.A., Temple U., 1977; m. Edward Weston, May 20, 1977. Acctg. supr. J C Penney Regional Credit Office, Voorhees, N.J., 1976-80; mem. Pa. Ho. of Reps., 1980—. Committeewoman 41st Ward, Phila., 1973—. Mem. Phila. Council Republican Women, Polish Am. Citizens League. Roman Catholic. Club: Am. Legion Aux. Office: 7115 Torresdale St Philadelphia PA 19135

WESTON, JERRY LEAH, nurse; b. Ardmore, Okla., July 18, 1925; d. Finis Franchett and Susan Mae (Wilson) Newman; B.S.N., Johns Hopkins U., 1955, Sc.D., 1972; M.P.H., Tulane U., 1963. Nurse, M.D. Anderson Hosp., Houston, 1954-56; charge nurse Radiotherapy Dept., Baylor U. Coll. Medicine, Houston, 1956-62; commd. USPHS, 1963, advanced through grades to nurse dir., 1973—; sr. research mgr. Nat. Center for Health Services Research, 1971—; condr. grad. seminars SUNY, Stony Brook, 1975-79, U. Ill., 1978, U. Wash., 1980, others. Recipient Commendation medal USPHS Commd. Corps, 1978. Mem. Nat. League for Nursing, Am. Public Health Assn., AAAS, Am. Nurses Assn., Johns Hopkins U. Alumni Assn., Tulane U. Alumni Assn., Delta Omega. Contbr. articles to profl. jours. Home: 118 Monroe St Rockville MD 20850 Office: 3700 East West Hwy Hyattsville MD 20782

WESTON, MARJORIE MOORE, med. record adminstr.; b. San Antonio, Dec. 19, 1934; d. Jesse and Jewell (Mitchell) Moore; B.S. in Med. Record Adminstrn., Incarnate Word Coll., 1965. Dir. med. record dept. Hays Meml. Hosp., San Marcos, Tex., 1965-69; dir. health records mgmt. Bexar County Hosps., San Antonio, 1969-72; chief clin. records library Wilford Hall USAF Med. Center, Lackland AFB, Tex., 1972-75; asst. to pres. for med. records, med. staff, PSRO, quality evaluation and utilization rev. services St. Joseph Hosp., Denver, 1975—; mem. oral exam. bd. med. record adminstrn. U. Colo. Med. Center; mem. subcom. on quality assurance Colo. Found. Med. Care. Mem. San Antonio Mayor's Commn. on Status Women, 1970-72; bd. dirs. YWCA, San Antonio, 1970-72; liaison Channel 9-TV Health Fair, Denver, 1980-81. Recipient Outstanding Service to Community award City of San Antonio, 1972; USAF citation of noteworthy performance in support of Operation Homecoming, USAF Surgeon Gen., 1976. Mem. Am. Med. Records Assn. (chmn. credentials com. 1980, dir. 1981-84), Colo. Med. Records Assn. (v.p. 1980-82, pres.-elect 1982—). Democrat. Episcopalian. Office: St Joseph Hosp 1835 Franklin St Denver CO 80218

WESTROPE, MARTHA RANDOLPH, clin. psychologist; b. Gaffney, S.C., May 19, 1922; d. Gordon Robert and Hannah (Brown) Westrope; B.S., Winthrop Coll., 1942; M.A., U. N.C., 1944; Ph.D., U. Iowa, 1952; 1 son, Ashley Randolph. Psychologist, Univ. Hosps., Iowa City, 1947; clin. psychologist Spartanburg (S.C.) Mental Hygiene Clinic, 1949-50; chief psychologist Mental Health div. S.C. Mental Health Commn., Columbia, 1952-53; chief clin. psychologist Richland County Mental Health Clinic, Columbia, 1953-55; head psychology sect. dept. psychiatry Med. Sch. U. Miami, Fla., 1956-57; chief clin. psychologist Greenville (S.C.) Mental Health Clinic, 1957-60, part-time clin. psychologist, 1974—, Spartanburg Mental Health Center, 1971-73; lectr. Furman U. evening div., 1957-67; pvt. practice clin. psychology, Greenville, 1960—. Mem. Am. Psychol. Assn., Southeastern Psychol. Assn., S.C. Psychol. Assn., AAAS, Greenville County Mental Health Assn., Am. Group Psychotherapy Assn., Council for Nat. Register of Health Service Providers in Psychology, S.C. Acad. Profl. Psychologists. Democrat. Presbyterian. Home: 11 Darien Way Greenville SC 29615 Office: 618 E Washington St Greenville SC 20602

WESTWATER, MARTHA, educator; b. Boston, Jan. 3, 1929; d. Joseph James and Martha Elizabeth (Early) W.; B.S. in Secondary Edn., St. John's Coll., 1955, M.A., 1957; Ph.D., Dalhousie U., 1973. Joined Sister of Charity, Roman Cath. Ch., 1946; tchr., various locations, 1949-70; with Mt. St. Vincent U., Halifax, N.S., Can., 1973—, prof. English lit., 1978—. Mem. MLA, Assn. Canadian Univ. Tchrs. English, Research Studies in Victorian Periodicals. Author: Nothing on Earth, 1967; Six Victorian Women, 1982; contbr. articles in field. Home: 51 Marlwood Ave Halifax NS B3M 3H4 Canada Office: 150 Bedford Hwy Halifax NS B3M 2J6 Canada

WETHERBY, IVOR LOIS, librarian; b. Louisville, May 22, 1924; d. Luther Silas and Clara Marders (Hite) W.; A.B., Ky. Wesleyan Coll., 1944; M.S. in L.S. (AAUW fellow 1964-65), 1965; m. Herbert Charles Howard, July 4, 1947; children—Ivor Jane, Elizabeth Wetherby, John Allen, Luther Hite, Ann Dell. Various clerical and secretarial positions, 1944-50; tchr. Our Lady of Mercy Acad., Louisville, 1963-64; librarian Palm Beach Jr. Coll., Lake Worth, Fla., 1966-78; head librarian Sebring (Fla.) Public Library, 1978; health scis. reference librarian Miami-Dade Community Coll., Med. Center Campus, Miami, Fla., 1978—. Mem. Southeastern, Fla. library assns., Spl. Libraries Assn., DAR. Episcopalian. Home: 14560 NE 6th Ave North Miami FL 33161 Office: 950 NW 20 St Miami FL 33127

WETMORE, ROSAMOND BAYNE, librarian; b. Middlesboro, Ky., Nov. 1, 1914; d. Herbert E. and Almeda (Mason) Bayne; A.B., Earlham Coll., Richmond, Ind., 1936; B.S. in L.S., Columbia U., 1940; M.A., Ball State U., Muncie, Ind., 1957; m. Thomas H. Wetmore, July 5, 1941; children—Stephen Bayne, Allyn Christophers. Reference asst. Earlham Coll. Library, 1936-37; librarian Lloyd High Sch., Erlanger, Ky., 1937-40, Beechwood Sch., Ft. Mitchell, Ky., 1940-41; cataloging asst. Ball State U. Library, 1946-69, mem. univ. faculty, 1959—, prof. library sci., 1978—. Author: A Guide to the Organization of Library Materials, 3d rev. edit., 1976. Address: 1601 Riverside St Muncie IN 47303

WETTERS, DORIS EVELYN, home economist; b. Huntington, Ind., Jan. 12, 1929; d. John E. and Clara (Witter) Wetters; B.S., Ball State U., 1951; postgrad. Fla. State U., 1952-54, Mich. State U., 1960-64; M.S., Ohio State U., 1958; Ed.D., Pa. State U., 1967. Tchr. home econs. secondary public schs., Gary, Ind., 1951-52; home econs. extension agt. coop. extension service U. Fla., 1952-56; consumer mktg. dist. specialist coop. extension service Mich. State U., 1959-61, asst. state leader adult family living program, 1961-65, asst. dir. coop. extension service for family living edn., prof. family ecology, 1975—; consumer edn. specialist Cornell U., 1967-69; asst. dir. coop. extension service for human resource devel. U. Hawaii, 1969-75; dietetics intern Am. Dietetic Assn., 1958; sec. Commn. on Home Econs., 1979-80, chmn., 1980-82; lectr. fellow dept. univ. extension U. Aukland (N.Z.). 1971, Sch. Home Sci. U. Otago, Dunedin, N.Z., 1971. Recipient Diana award for leadership, 1980; Disting. Service award Mich. Council Family Relations, 1982. Mem. Am. Council Consumer Interest (state del. 1965-69), Mich. (extension chmn. 1977-79), Hawaii (chmn. family econs. 1969-71), Am. (Hawaii del.) home econs. assns., Adult Edn. Assn. (chmn. nat. consumer interest 1971-73), Theta Sigma Phi, Omicron Nu, Phi Upsilon Omicron. Home: 326 Kedzie Dr East Lansing MI 48823 Office: 108 Agrl Hall Mich State U East Lansing MI 48824

WETZEL, ELLEN LIVELY, mgmt. cons.; b. Long Branch, W.Va., Jan. 22, 1936; d. Alfred F. and Sarah Ellen (Pritchard) Lively; student N.Mex. State U.; m. Henry Gilmer Steele, July 20, 1982; children—Gregory Benjamin Pake, Seana Ellen Pake. With Dept. Army, White Sands Missile Range, N.Mex., 1962-68; pres. Lively Enterprises, Inc., Las Cruces, N.Mex., 1967-75; licensee Kelly Services, Inc., Las Cruces, 1967—; pres. Asset and Resource Mgmt. Corp., Washington and N.Mex., 1978—; owner Ellen Lively Wetzel & Assos., lit. agts., 1979—; adv. Dona Ana County Occupational Extension Program, N.Mex. State U., 1975-78; dir. Santa Rosa Resources Corp.; exec. Gasco Internat., Inc., 1981—; v.p. San Augustine Pass Corp., 1981-82; mng. partner AVVA III, 1981—. Mem. Task Force on Public Relations, N.Mex. Republican Party, 1977, ward chmn. Dona Ana County, mem. central com., 1981—; bd. dirs. Am. Cancer Soc., Dona Ana County chpt., 1970-71, fund drive chmn., 1970, v.p., 1970-71; bd. dirs. Planned Parenthood Assn. Dona Ana County, public affairs chmn., 1971-77. Served with USAF, 1954-57. Recipient Community Service Gold medal Kelly Services Inc., 1969-77. Mem. Internat. Assn. Fin. Planners, Am. Mgmt. Assn., DAR, Las Cruces C. of C. (mem. public relations com. 1968-73). Republican. Episcopalian. Clubs: Picacho Hills Country (bd. govs. 1981—), Order Eastern Star. Address: Box 188 Organ NM 88052

WETZEL, MARY CHRISTINE, psychologist, educator; b. Nelson, B.C., Can., Jan. 23, 1935 (parents Am. citizens); d. Robert Harland and Janet (Thomson) Yorke; B.S., U. Wash., 1957, M.S., 1959, Ph.D., 1962; children—Timothy Yorke, Robert Elliot. Sr. psychologist So. Ariz. Mental Health Center, Tucson, 1964-69; research asso. in psychology VA Med. Center, Tucson, 1969-71; asst. prof. dept. psychology U. Ariz., Tucson, 1971-76, asso. prof., 1976-81, prof., 1982—. Mem. Am. Psychol. Assn., Soc. for Neurosci., AAAS, Inst. for Cultural Research. Home: 2841 N Silver Spur Dr Tucson AZ 85745 Office: Dept Psychology U Ariz 250 New Psychology Bldg Tucson AZ 85721

WEWER, DEE J., mfg. co. exec.; b. Mobile, Ala., Apr. 27, 1948; d. Gene B. and Juanita (Schmeckenbecher) Wewer; B.S., U. So. Miss., 1969; M.A., Am. U., 1974; postgrad. Georgetown U., 1981-82. With Dixie Press, Biloxi, Miss., 1968-70; tchr. St. Martin Public Sch., Biloxi, 1970; editor newspaper of Nat. War Coll., Ft. McNair, Washington, 1971-73; press and scheduling asso. and coordinator Nat. Fedn. State Chairmen, Office of Chmn., Republican Nat. Com., Washington, 1972-73; cons. Nat. Women's Edn. Fund, Nat. Women's Polit. Caucus, 1973-74; gen. mgr., treas. Printing Services Unltd., Washington, 1975; instr. Inst. Politics, Harvard U., Boston, 1976; media dir./prodn. mgr./creative group head Bailey, Deardourff & Assos., Washington, 1975-76; dir. mktg./account supr. Weitzman & Assocs., Washington, 1976-78; dir. mktg. Britches of Georgetown, Washington, 1978-79; instr. Coll. Bus. and Mgmt., U. Md., College Park, 1980—; v.p. public affairs AMF Head Sports Wear, Columbia, Md., 1979-81; exec. v.p. Sport-Obermeyer, Aspen, Colo., 1982—; cons. in field. Recipient Creative Design Distinction, Andy, Printing Industries Am., 1981; Distinctive Merit award Advt. Club of N.Y., 1980, Art Dirs. Club of Met. Washington, 1980; Clio awards, 1979; named Outstanding Working Woman, Glamour mag., 1978; Nat. Newspaper Nat. Creativity award, 1974. Mem. Ski Industries of Am., Women in Advt. and Mktg., Am. Women in Radio and TV, Am. Mgmt. Assn., Advt. Club, Art Dirs. Club, NOW. Home: 0226 Kings Row Carbondale CO 81623 Office: 92 Atlantic Ave Aspen CO 81611

WEXLER, ANNE, cons. co. exec.; b. N.Y.C., Feb. 10, 1930; d. Leon R. and Edith R. (Rau) Levy; B.A., Skidmore Coll., 1951, LL.D. (hon.), 1978; D.Sc. in Bus. (hon.), Bryant Coll., 1978; m. Joseph Duffey, Sept. 17, 1974; children by previous marriage—David Wexler, Daniel Wexler. asso. pub. Rolling Stone mag., 1974-76; personnel adv., 1976-77; dep. undersec. Dept. Commerce, 1977-78; asst. to Pres. U.S., 1978-81; pres. Wexler and Assos., Inc., Washington, 1981—; dir. New Eng. Electric System; adj. lectr. Kennedy Sch. Govt., Harvard U. Mem. nat. steering com. Carter/Mondale, 1976; mem. edn. and tng. council Democratic Nat. Com., 1976; bd. dirs. Pennsylvania Ave. Devel. Corp., Center Nat. Policy, Nat. Center Initiative Rev., Wolf Trap Found. Fellow Inst. Politics, John F. Kennedy Sch. Govt., 1973; named Outstanding Alumna, Skidmore Coll., 1972. Mem. Council Fgn. Relations. Jewish. Office: 1616 H St NW Washington DC 20006

WEXLER, HILDA, biologist; b. Bklyn., Apr., 6, 1915; d. Rubin and Adele (Karp) W.; B.A., N.Y. U., 1936; M.A., George Washington U., 1953. Analyst, War Prodn., Washington, 1941-46; analyst U.S. Bur. Census, Washington, 1946-47, research analyst, 1947-48; biologist Army Med. Center, Washington, 1948-55, Nat. Cancer Inst., USPHS, Bethesda, Md., 1955—. Active Am. Cancer Soc. Recipient award for sustained outstanding performance Nat. Cancer Inst., 1965, 69, 77; disting. service award Am. Cancer Soc., 1967, 72, Edward F. Bartelt award, 1967, cert. of merit, 1976, 25 Yr. Service award, 1977, John F. Feeney award, 1979, St. George medal, nat. div. award, 1981, 30 Yr. Service award, 1982. Mem. AAAS, Am. Assn. Cell Biologists. Jewish. Contbr. articles to profl. jours. Home: 1220 Blair Mill Rd Apt 1001 Silver Spring MD 20910 Office: Nat Cancer Inst Surgery Branch Bethesda MD 20014

WEXLER, JACQUELINE GRENNAN, assn. exec., former coll. pres.; b. nr. Sterling, Ill., Aug. 2, 1926; B.A. cum laude, Webster Coll.; M.A., U. Notre Dame; postgrad. St. Louis U.; hon. degree Skidmore Coll., 1967; LL.D., Franklin and Marshall Coll., 1968, Temple U., 1970; Sc.D., Central Mich. U., 1970; D.H.L., Carnegie Inst. Tech., Brandeis U., Colo. Coll., 1967, Syracuse U., 1971; Hum. D., U. Mich.; m. 1969; 2 stepchildren. Joined Sister of Loretto upon completion of undergrad. edn., laicized, 1967; formerly high sch. tchr., El Paso, Tex.; became asst. to pres. Webster Coll., Webster Groves, Mo., 1959, later exec. v.p., then pres., 1965-69; pres. Hunter Coll., N.Y.C., 1970-79; cons., commentator, writer, 1979—; pres. Academic Cons. Assocs., N.Y.C., also NCCJ; dir. United Technologies Corp., Optimum Holding Co., Interpub. Group of Cos.; mem. Pres. Kennedy's Adv. Panel on Research and Devel. in Edn., N.Y.C. Mayor's Commn. City-State Relations; nat. steering com. Project Head Start; v.p., dir., internat. univ. studies Acad. Ednl. Devel., N.Y.C., 1969-70; mem. Pres.'s Task Force on Urban Ednl. Opportunities, 1967; adv. panel to dir. NIH, 1978—; exec. panel Chief Naval Ops.; life trustee U. Pa., 1971. Author: Where I Am Going, 1968. Office: 43 W 57th St New York NY 10019

WEXLER, KAY F., librarian; b. Wildsville, La.; d. Charles W. and Addie (LeBlanc) W.; B.A., Xavier U., 1955; M.A., Ind. U., 1958; Children's librarian Mpls. Public Library, 1956-59, Detroit Public Library, 1959-61; asst. to librarian Gen. Motors Corp., Detroit, 1961-64, librarian, Washington, 1964-66; reference librarian U.S. Commn. on Civil Rights, Washington, 1966-70, chief Documentation Center, 1970-71; asst. chief Catalog Publs. div. Library of Congress, Washington, 1971—. Mem. ALA, D.C. Library Assn., Black Caucus of Am. Library Assn. Office: Catalog Publ Div Library of Congress Washington DC 20540

WEYAND, RUTH, lawyer; b. Grinnell, Iowa, Jan. 14, 1912; d. Lorenzo Dow and May (Grafton) W.; Ph.B., U. Chgo., 1930; J.D. cum laude, 1932; m. Leslie Sterling Perry, Sept. 29, 1947; children—Perry Weyand, Sterling Weyand. Admitted to Ill. bar, 1933, U.S. Supreme Ct. bar, 1936; asso. firm Gardner & Carton, Chgo., 1933, White and Hawxhurst, Chgo., 1933-35, Moses, Kennedy, Stein & Bachrach, Chgo., 1935-38; asst. gen. counsel NLRB, Washington, 1938-50; mem. firm Clifford D. O'Brien, Chgo., 1950-56, Leibik & Weyand, Chgo. and Washington, 1956-65; asst. gen. counsel Internat. Union Elec. Radio and Machine Workers, Washington, 1965-77; supervisory trial atty. Phila. Regional Litigation Center, EEOC, 1977-79, equal pay act counsel Office Gen. Counsel, EEOC, Washington, 1979—. Mem. Am. Bar Assn., Chgo. Bar Assn., Am. Assn. Trial Lawyers, NAACP (mem. nat. legal com. 1945-64). Democrat. Home: 308 N St SW Washington DC 20024 Office: Room 2246 2401 E St NW Washington DC 20506

WEYMOUTH, ETHEL MARION, ret. educator, librarian; b. North Berwick, Maine, May 18, 1894; d. Woodbury Ellsworth and Winnette Evelyn (Hussey) W.; A.B., Bates Coll., 1920; M.S., Cornell U., 1930. Tchr. rural pub. schs., North Berwick, Maine, 1912-13, 15-17, Acton, Maine, 1914; tchr. math., phys. sci., librarian Wells (Maine) High Sch., 1920-64. Mem. NEA, AAAS, Cousteau Soc., Nat. Audubon Soc., Smithsonian Assos., Am. Forestry Assn., Wells Pub. Library, Nat., World wildlife fedns. Congregationalist. Home: Wells ME 04090

WHALEN, CAROL KUPERS, educator; b. Los Angeles, July 20, 1942; d. Edward Carlton and Frances Shirley (Praissman) Kupers; B.A., Stanford U., 1963; M.A., UCLA, 1965, Ph.D., 1967. Research asst. Stanford U., 1961-63; student profl. asst. Neuropsychiat. Inst., UCLA, 1963, USPHS predoctoral fellow, 1964-67; intern Psychology Clinic, U. Calif., Los Angeles, 1964-65, Fernald Sch., 1965-66. Long Beach VA Hosp., 1966, Fairview State Hosp., 1966-67, South Coast Child Guidance Clinic, 1966-67; lectr. social scis. U. Calif., Irvine, 1968-70; research specialist, co-prin. investigator therapeutic pyramids project Fairview State Hosp., Costa Mesa, Calif., 1967-70; research cons. Ednl. Assessment Center for Handicapped Children, Orange County, 1970-71; asst. prof. social ecology U. Calif., Irvine, 1970-73, asso. prof. social ecology, 1973-79, asso. prof. psychiatry and human behavior, Irvine, 1974-79, prof. psychiatry and human behavior, 1979—, prof. social ecology, 1979—; mem. deinstitutionalization panel Nat. Acad. Scis., 1978-81, com. on child devel. research and pub. policy, 1982—; mem. treatment devel. and assessment research rev. panel NIMH, 1980—. NIMH research grantee, 1977-80; Nat. Inst. Drug Abuse research grantee, 1974—; Spencer Found. research grantee, 1980—. Mem. Am. Psychol. Assn., Assn. Advancement Behavior Therapy, Am. Orthopsychiat. Assn., Soc. Pediatric Psychology, Western Psychol. Assn. Author: (with B. Henker) Hyperactive Children: The Social Ecology of Identification and Treatment, 1980; contbr. articles to profl. jours. Office: Social Ecology U Calif Irvine CA 92717

WHALEN, LUCILLE, educator; b. Los Angeles, July 26, 1925; d. Edward Cleveland and Mary Lucille (Perrault) W.; B.A. in English, Immaculate Heart Coll., Los Angeles, 1949; M.S.L.S., Catholic U. Am., 1955; D.L.S., Columbia U., 1965. Tchr. elementary and secondary schs., Los Angeles, Long Beach, Calif., 1945-52; high sch. librarian Conaty Meml. High Sch., Los Angeles, 1950-52; reference/serials librarian, instr. library sci. Immaculate Heart Coll., 1955-58, dean Sch. Library Sci., 1958-60, 65-70; asso. dean Sch. Library and Info. Sci., SUNY Albany, 1971-78, prof., 1978—; dir. U.S. Office Edn. Insts. Mem. ALA (chmn. com. on accreditation 1976-78), Spl. Libraries Assn. (chmn. com. research 1974-80), N.Y. Library Assn. (pres. sect. library educators 1976), Soc. Am. Archivitst, Am. Assn. State and Local History, ACLU, Common Cause, Amnesty Internat. Democrat. Roman Catholic. Office: Sch Library and Info Sci State U NY 135 Western Ave Albany NY 12222

WHALEN, MARION ELIZABETH, ednl. adminstr.; b. Jamaica, N.Y., Jan. 29, 1937; d. Elmer John and Bertha Irene (Beers) W.; B.S., SUNY, Plattsburgh, 1958, M.S., 1967; profl. diploma St. John's U., Jamaica, 1976. Elem. sch. tchr. Freeport (N.Y.) Schs., 1958-66, elem. sch. counselor, 1967-75; asst. dean women SUNY, Plattsburgh, 1966-67; asst. prin. Freeport High Sch., 1975—. Mem. Nat. Assn. Female Execs., Council Adminstrs. and Suprs., Freeport Adminstrs. Assn. (pres. 1982—), SUNY Plattsburgh Alumni Assn., St. John's U. Alumni Assn. Delta Kappa Gamma (chpt. pres. 1976-78; Elsa Brookfield scholar 1975), Phi Delta Kappa. Contbr. articles to profl. jours. Home: 1 Toms Point Ln Bldg 5 Apt 9J Port Washington NY 11050 Office: Freeport High Sch Brookside Ave Freeport NY 11520

WHALEN, PAULINE KATHERINE, librarian; b. Boulder, Colo., May 11, 1921; d. William C. and Naoma S. (Ward) Malzahn; B.A., U. Colo., 1942, M.A., 1946; M.A., U. Denver, 1950. Asst. documents librarian U. Colo. Libraries, Boulder, 1950-51, order librarian, 1955-64; base librarian Ent AFB, Colorado Springs, Colo., 1951-53; documents librarian Colo. Sch. of Mines Library, Golden, 1953-55; sr. reference librarian Santa Rosa (Cal.) Library, 1965-66; humanities bibliographer U. Calif. San Diego Library, La Jolla, 1966-67; sr. librarian Salk Inst. for Biol. Studies, La Jolla, 1968—. Mem. Am., Spl., Med. Library assns. Democrat. Home: 12988 Via Esperia Del Mar CA 92014 Office: Salk Institute PO Box 85800 San Diego CA 92138

WHALEN, SUSAN FRANCES, market devel. exec.; b. Chgo., May 16, 1947; d. Charles Edward and Doris (Atteridge) Whalen; A.A., Va. Intermont Coll., 1967; B.F.A., U. Ga., 1969; B.S., 1974; m. Sidney D. Foldman, Aug. 25, 1982. Credit mgr. Warren's Alexis Co. Inc., 1969-71; customer service rep. Continental Can Co., 1975-76; account exec. Ga. Pacific Corp., 1976-79, sales promotion mgr. printing paper div., 1979-81, market devel. mgr., 1981—. Mem. Univ. and Coll. Designers Assn., Am. Inst. Graphic Arts, Internat. Assn. Bus. Communicators, Art Dirs. Club N.Y., Color Mktg. Group, Zeta Tau Alpha. Republican. Presbyterian. Club: Golden Bridge Hounds. Office: 375 Park Ave New York NY 10022

WHALEY, BARBARA BAYNARD, med. tech. educator; b. Mobile, Ala., Apr. 2, 1945; d. H. Hugh Baynard and Frances Ethel (Deane) Whaley; B.S. in Biology, Spring Hill Coll., 1966; cert. med. tech. Providence Hosp. Sch. Med. Tech., 1967; M.S. in Clin. Pathology, U. Ala., Birmingham, 1970; postgrad. U. S. Ala., 1982—, U. So. Miss., 1982—. Hematology supr. Mobile Infirmary Lab., 1970, ednl. coordinator sch. med. tech., 1970-78, ednl. dir., 1978—; site surveyor Nat. Accrediting Agy. for Clin. Lab. Scis.; vice chmn. hematology exam. sub-com. Nat. Cert. Agy. for Clin. Lab. Personnel; clin. instr. Auburn U., Judson Coll., Livingston U., Millsaps Coll., Miss. Coll., Mobile Coll., Morehead State U., Spring Hill Coll., U. W. Fla. Trustee Wilmer Hall Episcopal Children's Home, Mobile, 1977-80; dir. S.W. Ala. Health Systems Agy., 1977—, mem. exec. com., 1981—; lab. dir. Seale Harris Diabetic Camp, 1972. Cert. clin. lab. scientist Nat. Certification Agy. for Clin. Lab. Personnel. Mem. Am. Soc. Clin. Pathologists (cert. med. technologist), Am. Soc. for Allied Health Professions, Am. Soc. for Med. Tech. (del. annual meeting 1972-78, pres.'s council 1974-76, region III council, 1974-76, competency delineations com. 1975-77), Ala. State Soc. for Med. Tech. (numerous coms. including edn., scholarship, awards, bylaws, Sara Crowson Trust Fund, coordinator hematology sci. assembly 1971-74, pres. 1975, treas. 1978-80, registration chmn. 1979, dir. 1974-80), Mobile Bus. and Profl. Women's Club (v.p. 1980), Alpha Mu Tau. Asso. editor Am. Jour. Med. Tech., 1976—. Home: 706 Westmoreland Dr W Mobile AL 36609 Office: PO Box 2144 Mobile AL 36652

WHALEY, ELLEN HIBBARD, newspaper editor; b. Providence, Aug. 12, 1924; d. Robert E. and Jenny Whaley; ed. public schs., profl. schs., Radio-TV Arts Acad. Editor, gen. mgr. Ft. Myers (Fla.) Suburban Reporter, 1978—. Served with WAC, 1941-45. Mem. Fla. Press Club, Nat. Notary Assn., Nat. Assn. Female Execs., Sigma Delta Chi. Club: St. Petersburg (Fla.) Dog Tng. Home: PO Box 05864 Tice FL 33905

WHALEY, JOAN FRANCES, mag. editor; b. Evanston, Ill., Aug. 8, 1935; d. James Templeton and Elizabeth Markley (Dodson) Pettingell; student (scholar) Art Inst. Chgo. Sch. Art, 1949-53; B.A., Fla. Internat. U., 1976; M.A., Fla. Atlantic U., 1981. Promotion writer Edward Petry & Co., Inc., N.Y.C., 1954-56, Sta. WTVD-TV, Durham, N.C., 1956-57; reporter, feature writer Chicago Heights (Ill.) Star, 1958-59; editor, asso. editorial dir. Industry Pubs., Miami, Fla., 1973—; vis. instr. U. Miami, 1981. Janet Rice fellow, 1977. Mem. Women in Communications, Nat. Assn. Exec. Women, Sigma Delta Chi (pub. awareness chmn.), Phi Theta Kappa. Editor, contbg. author: The Idea Book, Planning, Building, Financing Tennis Clubs, Racket and Shoe Factory, 1972—, PGA Product Knowledge Book, 1979. Home: 13801 NE 3d Ct Apt 105B North Miami FL 33161

WHALING, ANNE, educator; b. Houston, Mar. 30, 1914; d. Horace Morland and Annie Byrd (Ward) Whaling; B.A., So. Meth. U., 1933, M.A., 1934; Ph.D., Yale, 1946. Cataloger, specialist in music, fgn. langs., So. Meth. U., 1947-55; tchr., English dept. Arlington State Coll., 1955, instr., 1955-57, assistant professor, 1957-60, associate professor English, 1960-67, asso. prof. English, U. Tex., Arlington, 1967-71, prof. English, 1971-80, ret., 1980. Program annotator for chamber music series Dallas Mus. Fine Arts, 1956-61. Mem. bd. dirs. Dallas Chamber Music Soc., 1954—. Recipient Decima Lantern award So. Meth. U., 1933; Woman of Achievement award So. Meth. U. Alumni Assn., 1968. Mem. Am. Studies Assn. of Tex. (mem. steering com. 1956—, councilor 1961-62), Modern Lang. Assn., AAUW (chmn. fellowship com. Dallas br. 1959-64), South Central Modern Language Assn., The Malone Soc., Phi Beta Kappa. Methodist. Home: 3320 Daniels Ave Dallas TX 75205

WHARTENBY, CATHERINE ENGLISH (MRS. CHARLES ALFRED WHARTENBY), business exec.; b. Wellsboro, Pa., June 30, 1920; d. Robert Dean and Elizabeth Perpetua (Dwyer) English; B.S., Mansfield State Coll., 1941; J.D., Golden Gate U., 1968; m. Charles Alfred Whartenby, Feb. 9, 1946. Office employee Refractory Mica Products, Inc., Newark, 1941; clk. legal dept. 9th Service Command, Presidio of San Francisco, 1942-44; office sec., office mgr. Research Inst. Am., San Francisco, 1945-54; office sec. Conn. Gen. Life Ins. Co., San Francisco, 1954-62, asst. mgr., 1962-72, regional design cons. estate and bus. planning, No. Calif., 1973-74; regional design mgr. Western Regional Design Center, 1975-78, dir., 1981; dir. Southwestern Regional Design Center, Huntington Beach, Calif., 1978-80; dir. Qualified Plans, Design Services, 1982—; admitted to Calif. bar, 1969; lectr. pension courses Am. Coll. Life Underwriters, 1969-71, instr. advanced estate planning course, 1973-74. Mem. Am., San Francisco bar assns., State Bar Calif. (vice chmn. ins. subcom. estate planning com. 1978-81), Am. Soc. C.L.U.s, Peninsula Estate Planning Council. Home: 40 Corte Alegre Millbrae CA 94030 Office: 3000 Sand Hill Rd Bldg 4 Suite 160 Menlo Park CA 94025

WHARTON, DOLORES DUNCAN, fund exec.; b. N.Y.C., July 3, 1927; d. V. Kenneth and Josephine Wells (Bradford) Duncan; B.A., Chgo. State U.; D.H.L. (hon.), Central Mich. U.; m. Clifton R. Wharton, Jr., Apr. 15, 1950; children—Clifton R. 3d, Bruce D. Pres., The Fund for Corp. Interns, Albany, N.Y., 1980—; dir. Phillips Petroleum Co., Kellogg Co., Battle Creek, Mich., N.Y. Telephone Co., Gannett Co., Inc., Key Bank N.A. Mem. Mich. Council for Arts, 1971-75, Nat. Council Arts, 1974-80; trustee Detroit Inst. Arts, 1975-78, China Med. Bd., 1977-81; vice chmn. Mich. Bicentennial Commn., 1972-76; bd.

visitors Tulane U., 1975-77; mem. Mich. Gov.'s Spl. Commn. for Architecture, Nat. Com. Bicentennial Era; trustee Mus. Modern Art, Albany Law Sch., Asia Soc.; bd. dirs. Albany Inst. History and Art; policy studies com. U.S. UN Assn. Mem. Asia Soc., Mich. Soc. Architects (hon.), Phi Beta Kappa. Episcopalian. Club: Cosmopolitan (N.Y.C.). Author: Contemporary Artists of Malaysia: A Biographic Survey, 1972. Home and office: South Tower State University Plaza Albany NY 12246

WHATLEY, JACQUELINE BELTRAM (MRS. JOHN W. WHATLEY), lawyer; b. West Orange, N.J., Sept. 26, 1944; d. Quirino R. and Eliane (Gruet) Beltram; B.A., U. Tampa, 1966; J.D., Stetson U., 1969; m. John W. Whatley, June 25, 1966. Admitted to Fla. bar, 1969, Alaska bar, 1971; practiced in Anchorage, 1971-73; partner firms Gibbons, Tucker, McEwen, Smith, Miller, Whatley & Stein, Tampa, Fla., 1969-71, 73—; dir. Fla. Investment and Devel. Corp.; arbitrator Am. Can Co., Continental Can Co., United Steelworkers Am., Tampa, 1974—. Bd. dirs. Travelers' Aid Soc. Mem. Am., Alaska, Fla., Tampa-Hillsborough County, Anchorage bar assns., Fla. Walking Horse Assn. (pres. 1980), Tenn. Walking Horse Breeders and Exhibitors Assn. (dir. for Fla.), Nu Beta Epsilon, Delta Phi Epsilon, Phi Alpha Theta. Home: PO Box 17595 Tampa FL 33682 Office: 606 Madison St Tampa FL 33601

WHAUN, JUNE M., hematologist; b. North Vancouver, B.C., Can., June 26, 1935; d. Thomas M. and Diamond (Kwan) Whaun; student Faculty Arts, U. B.C., Vancouver, 1953-56, M.D., 1960. Rotating intern U. Md. Hosp., Balt., 1960-61; resident in pediatrics U. Mich. Hosp., Ann Arbor, 1961-62, U. Toronto Hosp. for Sick Children, 1962-64; resident internal medicine Shaughnessy Hosp., Vancouver, U. B.C., 1964-65; clin. research hematology fellow U. Toronto Hosp. for Sick Children, 1965-66; Blood Bank fellow King County Central Blood Bank, U. Wash., Seattle 1966-67; research hematology fellow Hosp. U. Pa., Phila., 1967-69; instr., head coagulation lab. Children's Hosp. Phila., 1969-71; asst. prof. pediatric oncology/hematology U. Calgary (Alta., Can.), 1971-76, asso. prof., 1976-78, dir. dept. pediatric oncology/hematology, 1975-78; lt. col. M.C., research hematologist Walter Reed Army Inst. Research, Washington, 1978—; cons. Alta. Hosp. Services Commn., 1973-78, dir. So. Alta. Pediatric Oncology Program, 1975-77; cons. hematologist, prof. dept. pediatrics Tex. Tech U. Med. Sch., Amarillo, 1981—; asso. prof. Uniformed Services U. Health Scis., Bethesda, Md., 1981—. Diplomate Am. Bd. Pediatrics, subsplty. hematology-oncology. Fellow Royal Coll. Physicians, Surgeons Can.; mem. Am. Soc. Hematology, AAAS, Soc. Pediatric Research, Am. Fedn. Clin. Research, Internat. Soc. Thrombosis and Hemostasis, Am. Soc. for Clin. Oncology, Biophys. Soc., Am. Soc. for Microbiology. Research in pediatric hematology, hemostasis. Home: 336 New Mark Esplanade Rockville MD 20850 Office: Walter Reed Army Inst Research Walter Reed Army Med Center Washington DC 20012

WHEATON, ELIZABETH LEE, educator; b. Sherman, Tex.; d. Percival King and Minerva Fay (Ratzel) Fulton; student Rice Inst., 1920-21, San Angelo Coll., 1949-51; certificate S.W. Tex. State Coll., 1922, Kansas City-Horner Conservatory, 1929; B.S., McMurray Coll, 1952; postgrad. A. and I. Coll., 1953-54; m. Grant Wiltsie Wheaton, Dec. 23, 1923. Tchr. pub. schs., Texas City, Tex., 1922-24; pvt. tchr. speech, 1922-29, voice and speech, 1929-47; reporter, soc. editor Texas City Sun, 1930-36; corr. Galveston (Tex.) News, 1934; dir. The Texas City Hour, radio KGBC, 1947; elementary tchr. La Feria (Tex.) Pub. Schs., 1952—; pvt. tchr. voice, speech, 1956-57; originator, writer, dir., master of Story Book Time TV series, KRGV-TV, 1957; mem. staff S.W. Writers Conf., Corpus Christi, Tex., 1954—. Mem. Composers, Authors and Artists Am. (pres. Rio Grande chpt., mem. nat. pub. com. 1960), Tex. Woman's Press Assn., Tex. State Tchrs. Assn., Tex. Poetry Soc. (charter mem., sec. chpt. 1970—), Tex. Inst. Letters, Am. Legion Aux. (past pres. units Texas City, San Angelo, La Feria; Tex. state dept. music chmn. 1960, past pres.'s parley), Nat. Soc. D.A.R. (chpt. pub. relations), Lower Rio Grande Valley Hist. Soc., Community Concert Assn. (bd. dirs. Harlingen chpt., chmn. La Feria chpt. 1961-62), Rio Grande Valley Internat. Music Festival (sponsor 1961-62), Am. Budgerigar Soc., Tex. Bird Breeders and Fanciers Assn., Tex. Southmost Bird Assn. (sec. 1962-64), Tip-O-Tex. Exhbn. Budgerigar Soc., Delta Kappa Gamma (chpt. publicity com.). Mem. Order Eastern Star (past matron Texas City chpt.). Clubs: P.M., LaFeria Garden, Bailey Dunlap Meml. Library Friends. Author: Mr. George's Joint, 1941; Texas City Remembers, 1948; also poems, articles, reviews in various mags., newspapers. Home: Valley Vista N Beddoes Rd and Expwy Hwy 83 PO Box 1026 La Feria TX 78559

WHEELER, BEVERLY GAIL, physician; b. Fort Knox, Ky., July 15, 1952; d. Jesse Leonard and Magaret (Teabeaut) W.; B.S., Emory U., 1974; M.D., Med. Coll. Va., 1978. Intern, Cin. Gen. Hosp., 1978-79; resident U. Cin. Med. Center, 1979-82, fellow in geropsychiatry, 1982—; psychiatrist Rollman's Psychiat. Inst., 1979—; adj. clin. prof. U. Cin., 1982—. Mem. AMA, Am. Med. Womens Assn., Am. Psychiat. Assn., Ohio Psychiat. Assn., Assn. Advancement Psychiatry, Ohio Med. Assn., Phi Sigma. Presbyterian. Office: Central Psychiatric Clinic 3259 Elland Ave Cincinnati OH 45267

WHEELER, EMMA BELLE, state legislator; b. Hillsboro, N.H., Jan. 24, 1916; d. Alvin A. and Nettie B. (Scruton) Yeaton; B.Ed., Plymouth (N.H.) Tchrs. Coll., 1963; M.Ed., Rivier Coll., 1969; m. Kenneth T. Wheeler, June 30, 1939; children—Kenneth T., Jacquelyn Wheeler Johnston. Tchr. music, N.H., 1936-40, elem. sch. tchr., 1954-64, 67-76, jr. high sch. tchr., 1965-67; mem. N.H. Ho. of Reps., 1977—. Alt. del. Nat. Republican Conv., 1980; vice chmn. Milford Rep. Com., 1957; sec. Milford Bicentennial Com., 1975-77. Recipient Woman of Achivement award Bus. and Profl. Women, 1977, 1st prize piano N.H. Grange, 1978. Mem. Nat. Assn. Women Legislators, Union 40 Tchrs. Assn. (pres. 1960), NEA, N.H. Edn. Assn., Ret. Tchrs. Assn. N.H., Sons Union Vets. Civil War Aux. (past nat. pres.), Grange. Methodist. Address: 64 Amherst St Milford NH 03055

WHEELER, ROBINETTA THERESA, nurse, found. ofcl.; b. N.Y.C., Apr. 19, 1947; d. John Sinclair and Verdelle Josephine (Williams) Wheeler; B.S., N.Y.U., 1969; M.S., San Jose State U., 1972; postgrad. U. Calif., San Francisco, 1974—; m. Lee Van Chilton, Apr. 15, 1978. Nurse, Santa Clara County Drug Abuse Clinic, 1970-71; nurse educator Inst. Study Social and Health Issues, 1971-72; lectr. San Jose State U., 1972-74; nurse, head nurse, clinical coordinator Palo Alto (Calif.) VA Hosp., 1974-78; asst. dir. programs Nat. Center Health Edn., Oakland, Calif., 1978-82; project dir. Regional Cancer Found., Mill Valley, Calif., 1982—. Bd. dirs. Bay Area Big Sisters, 1974-76. Nat. Inst. Aging fellow, 1979-80. Mem. Nat. Assn. Female Execs., Am. Sociol. Assn., Soc. Study Symbolic Interaction, Am. Nurses Assn. (Ethnic Minority fellow, 1976-79), N.Y.U. Alumni Assn., Sigma Theta Tau. Contbg. author: Nursing Assessment, 1977. Home: 2680 Tilton Ct San Jose CA 95121 Office: 80 Lomita Dr Suite 9 Mill Valley CA 94941

WHEELOCK, SHARON MARIE, newspaper pub.; b. Hyannis, Nebr., June 23, 1938; d. Milton Dwight and Lois Mae (Jones) Thomas; student public schs. Denver and Hyannis; children—Robyn Renee, James Sidney, Londa Sue, Christi Marie, Lance Michael. With Grant County News, Hyannis, 1957—, owner, pub., editor, 1976—. Mem. Nebr. Writers Guild, Nat. Fedn. Press Women, Nebr. Press Assn., Internat. Clover Poetry Assn., Soc. Am. Poets, Sigma Delta Chi. Baptist. Poetry pub. in Best Am. Poems, 1967, Clover Collections and Verse, 1972, 74, 20th Century Poets and Their Poems, 1982. Home: PO Box 134 Hyannis NE 69350 Office: PO Box 308 Hyannis NE 69350

WHERLEY, CLARE ELIZABETH, mfg. co. exec.; b. Balt., Dec. 28, 1944; d. David Franklin and Clare Elizabeth (Willeke) W.; student Catholic U. Am., 1962-64; B.S. in Math., Duquesne U., 1966; M.B.A., U. San Francisco, 1973. Computer programmer Bell of Pa., Phila., 1966-67; computer applications/software systems Pacific Telephone & Telegraph Co., San Francisco, 1967-69; systems designer, supr. data processing Bell Telephone Labs., San Francisco, 1969-72; supr. data processing Pacific Telephone & Telegraph Co., San Francisco, 1972-73; supr. corporate planning studies AT&T, N.Y.C., 1973-76; planning and devel. mgr. Western Electric Co., San Francisco, 1976-77, supply distbn. mgr., San Leandro, Calif., 1977-79, mgr. planning and devel., Sunnyvale, Calif., 1979—. Mem. sci. adv. bd. Mills Coll., Oakland, Calif. Mem. Union Square Bus. and Profl. Womens Club of San Francisco. Home: 2501 Shadow Mountain Ct San Ramon CA 94583 Office: 1090 E Duane Ave Sunnyvale CA 94086

WHIGHAM, TERRI LEE, marketing exec.; b. Riverside, Calif., May 8, 1953; d. Gordon Terrance and Virginia Lee (Warren) W.; student Merced Jr. Coll., 1979. Asst. to pres. BAC-Pritchard, Inc., Merced, Calif.; asst. to pres. Valley Sheet Metal, South San Francisco, Calif.; asst. to supt. Herman Christensen & Sons, San Carlos, Calif.; now corp. treas. TransGlobal Mktg. Corp., San Francisco. Mem. Nat. Assn. Female Execs., Nat. Sporting Goods Assn., Far West Ski Assn. Democrat. Methodist. Office: World Trade Center Suite 270 San Francisco CA 94111

WHILEY, JOAN MARGARET, utility cons.; b. Vancouver, B.C., Can. Jan. 4, 1930; d. Alfred Ernest and Mary Margaret Mathews Scoby; B.A., U. B.C., 1951; m. John D. Whiley, Dec. 21, 1957 (div. Jan. 1965); children—Philip Vincent, Louise Margaret, Anthony John. Writer, Chiswell & Assos. Public Relations, London, 1954-57; freelance writer, 1958-65; writer Nordstrom's, Inc., Seattle, 1965-68; creative supr. Cole & Weber, Inc., Seattle, 1968-71; dir. public affairs Seattle City Light, 1973-78; mgr. mem. relations Wash. Public Power Supply System, Seattle, 1978-82; utility cons., 1982—. Mem. bd. Univ. Dist. Community Council, 1979—. Mem. Am. Public Power Assn. (communications com.), Public Relations Soc. Am., Am. Nuclear Soc., Friends of the Earth, Mountaineers. Club: Wash. Athletic. Home: 5823 17th St NE Seattle WA 98105

WHINERY, DOROTHY COOKE (MRS. JAMES C. WHINERY), assn. exec.; b. Louisville; d. Thomas and Abigail (Latimer) Cooke; B.S. in Music, Drake U., 1935; m. James Curtis Whinery, Oct. 9, 1938 (dec. Oct. 1955); 1 dau., Janet (Mrs. Jock Evan Thompson). Tchr. music pub. schs. Somers, Iowa, 1935-38; asst. buyer Younkers, Inc., Des Moines, 1941-45; nat. exec. sec. Sigma Alpha Iota, Des Moines, 1957—, nat. exec. bd., 1957—. Bd. dirs. Des Moines Civic Music Assn., 1950-53, exec. sec., 1953-65. Recipient Sword Honor, 1950, Rose Honor, 1962, Ring Excellence, 1968, all Sigma Alpha Iota. Mem. Nat. Trust Hist. Preservation, Smithsonian Assos., Met. Mus. Art, Am. Bus. Women's Assn. Included in book Iowa Women at Work, 1979. Home: 1447 57th St Des Moines IA 50311 Office: 4119 Rollins Ave Des Moines IA 50312

WHIPPLE, BABETTE SAMELSON, clin. psychologist; b. Memphis, July 22, 1918; d. Monroe M. Goldstein and Dorothy Janet (Samelson) Villmont; B.S., Wellesley Coll., 1939; Ph.D., Harvard U., 1945; m. Fred Lawrence Whipple, Aug. 20, 1946; children—Sandra, Laura. Instr. psychology dept. Wellesley (Mass.) Coll., 1941-47; opinion analyst Russian Research Center, Harvard U., Cambridge, Mass., 1952-55; research fellow child psychiatry dept. Mass. Gen. Hosp., Boston, 1955-62; pvt. practice clin. psychology, ednl. cons., Belmont, Mass., 1965—; research cons. tchr. Newton (Mass.) Public Schs., 1965-71. Co-founder, v.p. Belmont Community Center, Inc., 1965-73. Cert. elem. tchr., Mass.; cert. psychologist, Mass. Mem. Am. Psychol. Assn., Mass. Psychol. Assn., Am. Group Psychotherapy Assn., Northeastern Soc. for Group Psychotherapy, Soc. Clin. and Exptl. Hypnosis, Phi Beta Kappa. Jewish. Home and Office: 35 Elizabeth Rd Belmont MA 02178

WHIPPLE, BARBARA, graphic artist, writer; b. San Francisco, June 16, 1921; d. George Hoyt and Katharine Ball (Waring) W.; B.A., Swarthmore Coll., 1943; B.S., Rochester Inst. Tech., 1956; M.F.A., Temple U., 1961; m. John Schilling, Feb. 13, 1943 (div. 1956); children—Christine, Katharine; m. 2d, Grant Heilman, Aug. 14, 1961; 1 son, Hans. Tchr., Elizabethtown Coll., 1973-76, Franklin and Marshall Coll., 1974-76; grad. asst. Tyler Sch. Art, 1961; graphic artist; one person shows include: Lebanon Valley Coll., 1973, Colo. Mountain Coll., 1979, Foothills Art Center, 1980, Adams State Coll., 1982; numerous invitational and group shows; co-author: Watermedia, 1983; contbr. articles to La Revue Moderne, Colorado Outdoors; contbr. Am. Artist, 1971—, contbg. editor, 1979—; condr. workshops Adams State Coll., 1982, Colo. Graphic Arts Center, 1980, 82. Bd. dirs. Swarthmore Coll., 1970-76; pres. Chaffee County LWV, 1980-81. Recipient 1st prize for prints Lancaster Open Juried Show, 1964, Best of Show award Liberal Religious Art, Denver, 1967, 1st prize for drawing Phila. Watercolor Club, 1979, others. Mem. Phila. Watercolor Club, Artists Equity, Foothills Art Center, Colo. Artists Assn. Home: PO Box 609 Buena Vista CO 81211 Office: 429 E Main St Buena Vista CO 81211

WHIPPLE, CAROL OWEN, rancher, business cons.; b. Amarillo, Tex., Apr. 11, 1940; d. Wiley Ducoe and Marian (Hall) Owen; student U. Ariz., 1957-59, Utah State U., 1960; m. Gordon S. Whipple, Mar. 26, 1980; children—Laura, Katherine, Randall. Owner, operator Creekwood Ranch, farming, horse and cattle breeders, Amarillo, 1960—; dir. Okla. Stud, Inc., Purcell, 1976-78, sec., 1978-80; sec. Rowel, Inc., comml. bldg. and property mgmt., Amarillo, 1975-79, pres., 1979—; owner, operator A New Idea, furniture leasing, 1979-80; pres. Sun Tans Unlimited, Inc., 1979-80; partner Whipple Assos., mgmt. cons., direct sales distbrs., 1981—; tng. cons. Neo-Life Tng. Center, Amarillo. Pres. Amarillo Girl Scout Council, 1974-78. Mem. Am. Soc. Profl. and Exec. Women, Nat. Assn. Female Execs., Am. Quarter Horse Assn., Appaloosa Horse Club, Internat. Entrepreneurs Assn., Nat. Fedn. Ind. Bus., Kappa Alpha Theta. Presbyterian. Home: Route 2 Box 370 Canyon TX 79015 Office: 4551 S Western St Suite 1 Amarillo TX 79109

WHIPPLE, ELEANOR BLANCHE, ednl. adminstr., social worker; b. Bellingham, Wash., June 7, 1916; d. Charles William and Susan Blanche (Campbell) W.; B.A. in Sociology, U. Wash., 1938, M.S.W., 1949; Ph.D., Laurence U., 1982; m. Robert Auld Fowler, Oct. 1, 1938 (div. 1947); children—Lawrence William, Jeanice Marie Fowler Roosevelt. Founder, dir. Camp Cloud's End, Deception Pass, Wash., 1939-42; therapist Family Counseling Service, Seattle, 1949-58; field instr. U. Wash., Seattle, 1954-57; pvt. practice counselling, Burbank, Calif., 1958-60; social service dir. Hollygrove Children's Residential Treatment Center, Hollywood, Calif., 1960-66, exec. dir., 1966-81; adj. faculty Biola U., La Mirada, Calif., 1972-80; dean acad. affairs Calif. Christian Inst., Anaheim, 1981—, chmn. grad. dept. social work, 1981—. Fellow Soc. Clin. Social Work, Royal Soc. Health; mem. Nat. Assn. Social Workers, Acad. Cert. Social Workers, Nat. Assn. Christians in Social Work (immediate past pres. bd. dirs.). Contbr. articles in field to profl. publs. Home: 1105 Mound Ave Apt 9 South Pasadena CA 91030 Office: 1740 S Zeyn St Anaheim CA 91030

WHIPPLE, ELIZABETH LOU, nurse; b. Detroit, Nov. 3, 1942; d. Ralph and Lillian (Pipesh) Degesie; R.N., St. Joseph Sch. Nursing, 1963; student Western Mich. U., 1979—; m. Gerald DeWayne Whipple, June 28, 1967; children—James, Joseph, Jeffrey, Jennifer. Orthopedics staff nurse Edward W. Sparrow Hosp., Lansing, Mich, 1963-64, operating room staff nurse, 1964-65, hemodialysis staff nurse, 1966-78, dialysis asst. dept. head, 1978—; nurse rep. Mich. Dept. Pub. Health Panel, 1979-80; lectr. in field. Mem. planning com. Mich. End Stage Renal Disease Network Coordinating Council, 1977—, exec. com., 1981—; asst. Brownie leader Girl Scouts U.S. A., 1978; vol. Polio Vaccine Program, Ingham County, 1964. Mem. Mich. Nurses Assn., Am. Assn. Nephrology Nurses and Technicians, Am. Kidney Found., Nat. Renal Adminstrs. Assn., VFW 4090 Women's Aux. Contbr. articles to profl. jours. Home: 610 Academy St Portland MI 48873 Office: 1215 E Michigan Ave Lansing MI 48909

WHIPPLE, JACQUELINE CONANT, writer, media specialist; b. Columbus, Ohio, Mar. 31, 1921; d. William Horace and Gertrude Virginia (Bryant) Conant; A.B. magna cum laude, Mt. Holyoke Coll., 1943; postgrad. Art. Inst. Boston, 1974-79; m. David Collins Whipple, Sept. 6, 1944; children—Nancy, Roger, Leah, Benjamin. Reporter, Scarsdale (N.Y.) Inquirer, summers, 1939-43; scriptwriter radio dept. J. Walter Thompson Co., N.Y., 1943-45; reporter Washington Daily News, 1945-47; broadcast journalist, chief editorial writer Sta. WCRB-AM-FM, Waltham, Mass. and Boston, 1960-67; with Sch. div. Houghton Mifflin Co., Boston, 1967—, now audio visual coordinator; jury chmn. excellence in pub. writing/support of edn. Council for Advancement and Support of Edn., Washington, 1981. Chmn. know your town Waltham LWV 1951, v.p., 1953; pres. Cohasset (Mass.) PTA, 1963. Recipient Tom Phillips award, UPI Broadcasters of Mass., 1963; cert. of merit Art Inst. Boston, 1976. Mem. Women in Communications. Democrat. Unitarian. Club: Cohasset Yacht. Contbr. articles to popular mags. Home: 119 N Main St Cohasset MA 02025 Office: 1 Beacon St Boston MA 02108

WHISNANT, LELA RUTH, electronics co. ofcl.; b. Asheville, N.C., Feb. 4, 1950; s. d. Clyde McCiver and Ruth (DePriest) W.; B.A., Eckerd Coll., St. Petersburg, Fla., 1971; M.B.A., Wake Forest U., Winston-Salem, N.C., 1977. Grad. asst. in stats. Wake Forest U., 1976-77; mfg. engr. Tex. Instruments Inc., Dallas, 1977-80, planning mgr. imager br., 1980—. Vice pres. N.C. Teenage Democrats, 1966-67. Mem. Nat. Assn. Female Execs., AAAS, Planetary Soc. Presbyterian. Home: 405 Nottingham Dr Richardson TX 75080 Office: 13500 N Central Expressway Dallas TX 75265

WHISSELL-BUECHY, DOROTHY YVONNE EUGENIE, geneticist; b. St. Louis, Apr. 12, 1926; d. George Brandon and Erna May (Busch) Whissell; B.A., Wellesley Coll., 1948; M.D., U. Tex., 1956; Ph.D., U. Calif., Berkeley, 1968; m. Werner H. Buechy, July 18, 1956; children—Catherine, Barbara, Heidi. Fellow in hematology Children's Hosp., San Francisco, 1959-61; lectr. in pub. health U. Calif., Berkeley, 1964-78, instr. ind. study, extension, 1969—, lectr. genetics, 1969—, research geneticist Inst. Human Devel., 1969—. Mem. Tamalpais Design Review Bd., 1977-79; commr. Tamalpais Parks and Recreation Commn., 1972-74; dir. Tamalpais Community Services Dist., 1979—, pres. bd., 1981—. Home: 408 Spruce St Mill Valley CA 94941 Office: Inst Human Devel 1203 Tolman Hall U Calif Berkeley CA 94720

WHITACRE, CAROLINE CLEMENT, immunologist, educator; b. Cin., Nov. 4, 1949; d. Richard S. and Rosalyn (Wilson) W.; B.A. in Microbiology, Ohio State U., 1971, Ph.D., 1975; m. Michael F. Para, June 28, 1975. Multiple Sclerosis Soc. fellow Northwestern U., Chgo., 1975-78, instr. microbiology and immunology, 1978-81; asst. prof. medicine Ohio State U., Columbus, 1981—; mem. council Mid-west Autumn Immunology Conf., 1981—. Trustee Ohio chpt. Multiple Sclerosis Soc., 1981—. Mem. Am. Assn. of Immunologists, Am. Soc. Microbiology, AAAS, N.Y. Acad. Scis. Republican. Presbyterian. Contbr. numerous articles on comparative immunology to profl. jours. Home: 347 W 7th St Columbus OH 43201 Office: 400 W 12th Columbus OH 43210

WHITAKER, ADELYNNE HILLER, univ. adminstr.; b. Orange Grove, Tex., Aug. 15, 1924; d. Alfred Carl and Caroline Barbara (Arnecke) Hiller; B.A., Central State U., 1964; M.A., Trinity U., 1968; Ph.D., Emory U., 1974; m. Harold William Whitaker, Apr. 8, 1969; 1 dau., Sandra Lynne Castro. Self-employed, 1960-68; dir. Trinity U. Press, San Antonio, Tex., 1964-69; prof. U.S. and women's history U. Md., in W.Ger., 1973-75, area dir. European div., Heidelberg, 1975-77, asst. dir. planning and devel., 1977—, coordinator women's studies, 1975—, dir. internat. programs Center for Instructional Devel. and Evaluation, 1981—. Active, Girl Scouts Am. Nat. Library Medicine grantee, Bethesda, Md., 1972. Mem. NOW, Am. Hist. Assn., Orgn. Am. Historians. Home: 427 W Summit St San Antonio TX 77218 Office: U Md APO New York NY 09102

WHITAKER, CORINNE COOPER, brokerage co. exec.; b. Stamford, Conn., Aug. 31, 1934; d. Samuel and Natalie Gordon; B.A. (Durant scholar), Wellesley Coll., 1956; postgrad. N.Y. Inst. Fin., 1972-73, U. Houston, 1974; m. Don. C. Whitaker, Aug. 31, 1979; children—Nanette Cooper McGuinness, Robin Cooper. Sr. account exec. Eppler, Guerin & Turner, Inc., Houston, 1972-76; fixed income liaison Loeb, Rhodes & Co., Los Angeles, 1976-77; cons. Edward T. Watkins & Co., Houston, 1977; account exec., asso. v.p. Bateman Eichler Hill Richards, Los Angeles, 1977-79; chmn. bd., chief adminstrv. officer Don C. Whitaker, Inc., Los Angeles, 1980—; mem. Pacific Stock Exchange; organized seminars, courses in field; seminar coordinator Investment Dynamics series, Houston, 1975. Bd. dirs. women's div., nat. publicity chmn. Aerospace Med. Assn., 1964; lectr. African art, docent leader Rice U. Media Center Art to Schs. Program, 1974-75; mem. bus. and industry com. women's council Los Angeles Area C. of C., 1978. Recipient John Masefield award Wellesley Coll., 1956, Katherine Lee Bates award, 1956; Vol. Service award N.Y. Med. Coll., Flower and Fifth Ave. Hosps., 1958; Rookie of Yr. award Eppler Guerin & Turner, 1973, award of excellence, 1976, named to Millionaires Club 1973-75; commendation Houston Jr. C. of C., 1975; named to Century Club, Bateman Eichler Hill Richards Inc., 1978. Mem. Pasadena Heritage Soc., Norton Simon Mus., Sierra Club, Friends of Photography, Nat. Assn. Female Execs., Los Angeles Floor Brokers Assn. (founder), Phi Beta Kappa. Clubs: Wellesley Coll. Alumnae (chmn. spl. gifts div. Washington area 1964). Office: 618 S Spring St Los Angeles CA 91106

WHITAKER, EILEEN MONAGHAN, artist; b. Holyoke, Mass., Nov. 22, 1911; d. Thomas F. and Mary (Doona) Monaghan; ed. Mass. Coll. Art, Boston; m. Frederic Whitaker. Ann. exhibits in nat. and regional watercolor shows; represented in permanent collections Charles and Emma Frye Mus., Seattle, Hispanic Soc., N.Y.C., Atlanta Art Mus., U. Mass., Norfolk (Va.) Mus., Springfield (Mass.) Mus. Art, Reading (Pa.) Art Mus., Okla. Mus. Art, St. Lawrence U., Wichita State U., pvt. collections. Recipient numerous major awards, including several awards Allied Artists Am., Providence Water Color Club, several awards Am. Watercolor Soc., Wong award Calif. Watercolor Soc., De Young Mus. award, Springville (Utah) Mus. Art award, Ranger Fund purchase prize, Orbrig prize NAD, silver medal Am. Watercolor Soc., Watercolor West. Fellow Huntington Hartford Found., 1964. Academician NAD; mem. Am. Watercolor Soc. (Western v.p.), Providence Watercolor Club, Soc. Western Artists, Watercolor West (hon.), San Diego Watercolor Soc. (hon.). Home: 1579 Alta La Jolla Dr La Jolla CA 92037

WHITAKER, MARLENE ADKISON, broadcasting exec., announcer; b. Warrington, Eng., Oct. 6, 1954; d. Emory Hoover and Evelyn (Little) Adkison; came to U.S., 1954, naturalized, 1962; B.A. in Journalism in Radio-TV (Ellis-Stewart scholar), Kans. State U., 1976; m. Thomas A. Whitaker, Nov. 1979. Announcer, ops. mgr.-continuity Sta.-KTPK-FM, Topeka, 1976—. Home: 4152 SW 6th St Topeka KS 66606 Office: 910 First Nat Bank Tower Topeka KS 66603

WHITAKER, MARY RUTH, educator; b. Kansas City, Kans., Dec. 5, 1940; d. Floyd Edgar and Ruth Mary Fassnacht; B.S. in Edn., U. Kans., 1962, postgrad. in spl. edn., 1972-76; M.A., U. Mo., 1971; m. John C. Whitaker, Feb. 26, 1972. Tchr., Conn. and Kans., 1962-66; mem. staff Crittendon Center, Kansas City, Mo., 1972—, ednl. evaluation and resource coordinator, dir. edn., 1980, elem. program developer and tchr., 1980—; speaker, cons. in field. Mem. Kansas City Young Matrons, chmn. ways and means com., 1973. Mem. Conf. Exceptional Children, AAUW, Alpha Chi Omega, Alpha Delta Kappa. Republican. Presbyterian. Club: Sertoma (pres. Johnson County 1981-83). Home: 3906 W 103d St Overland Park KS 66207 Office: 10918 Elm St Kansas City MO 64134

WHITAKER, NANCY JOLENE, quality control specialist; b. Minneapolis, Kans., Mar. 11, 1937; d. Loren Allen and Maxine Virginia (Elliott) Morris; B.A., U. Nebr., 1959, postgrad.; m. James D. Whitaker, June 14, 1959; children—Kimberly Anne Nichols, David James. Caseworker, Denver Dept. Welfare, 1959-61; community organizer Nebr. Tech. Assistance Agy., North Platte, 1975-76; coordinator weatherization program Mid-Nebr. Community Action, North Platte, 1979—. Elder, Presbyn. Ch., 1979-81; mem. North Platte Community Playhouse Guild; past mem. adv. bd. Gt. Plains Mental Health Center; former leader Cub Scouts, 4-H, Campfire Girls. Mem. Nat. Assn. Social Workers, PEO. Republican. Club: Christian Women's. Home: 2311 Birchwood Rd North Platte NE 69101 Office: PO Box 945 North Platte NE 69101

WHITCOMB, RAE JEAN, hosp. and lab. supplies co. exec.; b. Sturgis, Mich., Mar. 21, 1940; d. Ralph Wilford and Velma Jeanette (Guernsey) Whitcomb; student Purdue U., 1958-60; M.T., Pontiac Gen. Hosp., 1961; student Robert Morris Coll., 1974-78, Marywood Coll., 1978. Teaching supr. Parkview Meml. Hosp., Ft. Wayne, Ind., 1961-68; sales rep. Gen. Diagnostics, Morris Plains, N.J., 1968-70; chief med. technologist Citizens Gen. Hosp., New Kensington, Pa., 1970-74, Sewickley (Pa.) Valley Hosp., 1974-79; sales rep. Fisher Sci. Co., Pitts., 1979-81, eastern regional sales mgr., 1981—. Mem. Am. Soc. Clin. Pathologists, Am. Soc. Med. Tech., Pa. Soc. Med. Tech. Office: 585 Alpha Dr Pittsburgh PA 15237

WHITE, BARBARA WILLIAMS, educator; b. Macon, Ga., Feb. 26, 1943; d. Ernestine (Cliett); B.S., Fla. Agrl. and Mech. U., 1964; B.S., Fla. State U., 1974, M.S.W., 1975, postgrad., 1979—; m. Julian Earl White, June 26, 1965; children—Tonja Victoria, Phaedra Aurelia. Tchr., Lake County, Fla., 1964-65, Duval County, Fla., 1965-73; sch. social worker/project coordinator Leon Dist. Schs., Tallahassee, 1975-76; dir. Leon County Community Coordinated Child Care Council, Inc., Tallahassee, 1976-77; asst. prof. Fla. A. and M. U., Tallahasse, 1977-1979; asst. prof. Fla. State U., Tallahassee, 1979—. Vice pres. bd. dirs. Center Creative Employment, 1976—; pres. bd. dirs. Leon County 4-C Council, Inc., 1979-80. Univ. competitive fellow, 1974-75. Mem. Acad. Cert. Social Workers, Nat. Assn. Social Workers (pres. Fla. chpt., sec. nat. com. on minority affairs, mem. council on social work edn.), Alpha Kappa Alpha. Club: Links. Home: 1213 Devils Dip Tallahassee FL 32308 Office: Sch Social Work Fla State U Tallahassee FL 32306

WHITE, BERNICE ELIZABETH SMITH, govt. ofcl.; b. Balt., Feb. 27, 1924; d. Oscar and Georgia E. (Bell) Smith; B.S. in Edn., Coppin State Coll., 1945; postgrad. Johns Hopkins U., U. Md., George Washington U., Morgan State U.; m. George Alfred White, July 8, 1945; children—Myra Lorraine, Marlene Lenora White Baskerville. Tchr., Balt. City pub. schs., 1952-64; dir. community edn. div. Balt. City Community Relations Commn., 1964-67; ins. compliance specialist Social Security Adminstrn., Balt., 1967-69, dir. fed. women's program, 1969-72, community relations officer, 1972-78, chief hdqrs. coordination and liaison staff, office of govtl. affairs, 1978—. Bd. dirs. Health and Welfare Council Central Md., 1972-79, Med. Eye Bank of Md., 1973-79, Lexington Market Assn., 1980—, Balt. chpt. Young Audiences Inc., 1981—; past pres. United Presbyn. Women, Trinity Presbyn. Ch.; chmn. pres.'s com. Morgan State U. Choir. Recipient Public Service award Philomathians, 1973; Profl. award of Yr., Nat. Assn. Negro Bus. and Profl. Women, 1973; Disting. Woman award Delta Sigma Theta, 1974; Pres.'s award for disting. service Pres. Balt. City Council, 1981, others. Mem. Federally Employed Women (founder, 1st pres. Greater Balt. chpt.), Nat. Council Negro Women, NAACP, Balt. Urban League, Woman Power Inc. (Cert. of Merit 1973, 74), Les Grandes Dames (founder, pres. 1976—), Herbert M. Frisby Hist. Soc. (pres. 1974-78), Zeta Phi Beta (chmn. polit. action com. Atlantic region 1979-80, Woman of Yr. 1971, Meritorious Service award 1981). Democrat. Office: Social Security Adminstrn Room 4-H-5 West Highrise 6401 Security Blvd Baltimore MD 21235

WHITE, BEVERLY JEAN, state legislator; b. Salt Lake City, Sept. 28, 1928; d. Gustave R. and Helene (Sterzer) Larson; m. M. Floyd White, Apr. 8, 1947; children—Susan White Morris, Douglas Floyd, Robyn White Bauder, David Scott, Wendy Jo White McCleery. Mem. Utah Ho. of Reps., 1971—. State bd. dirs. United Way; sec. Tooele County Merit Commn.; mem. Utah Health Systems Agy.; mem. Prison Halfway Houses Adv. Council, Dist. 12 Law Enforcement Planning Agy.; sec. Utah Dem. Party; Sunday Sch. tchr. Ch. of Jesus Christ of Latter Day Saints. Mem. Nat. Order Women Legislators (past treas.), Utah Orgn. Women Legislators (treas.). Club: Tooele Womans (past pres.).

WHITE, CAROL CUTTER, counselor, univ. ofcl.; b. Milw., Sept. 7, 1943; d. C. Theodore and Sara B. (Bullwinkel) Cutter; B.S., U. Wis., Milw., 1966; M.A., U. Denver, 1969; postgrad. MacMurray Coll., 1971, Sangamon State U., 1972, Western Ky. U., 1979-82; m. Barton C. White, July 24, 1971. Personnel asst. First Wis. Nat. Bank, Milw., 1966-67, market researcher, summer 1968; head resident U. Denver, 1967-69; student activities coordinator U. Wis., Milw., 1969-71; exec. dir. Morgan County Big Bros./Big Sisters Assn., Jacksonville, Ill., 1972-76; social services coordinator/dir. Vista project, Morgan County Housing Authority, 1976-79; asst. dir. Office Coop. Edn., Western Ky. U., Bowling Green, 1979—. Chmn., Human Relations Commn., Jacksonville, 1978-79; vice chmn. Bowling Green. Human Rights Commn., 1981—; pres. First Presbyn. Daycare Bd., 1977-78; deacon, 1977-79; vice chmn., Jacksonville-MacMurray Music Assn., 1977-78; publicity chmn. Jacksonville Conf. Chs., 1976-77. Recipient Outstanding Service award Big Bros./Big Sisters Assn., 1976; Presdl. award Jacksonville Jr. C. of C., 1976; Service award Presbyn. Daycare Center, 1979. Mem. Coop. Edn. Assn. Ky. (dir., editor 1981—), Midwest Coop. Edn. Assn., Social and Community Services Congress of Ill., Women's Alliance Western Ky. U., Alpha Sigma Alpha, Kappa Delta Pi. Presbyterian. Club: Little Sigma Soc. of Sigma Chi. Contbr. articles to profl. jours. Home: 2700 Thompson Dr Bowling Green KY 42101 Office: Office Coop Edn Western Ky Univ Bowling Green KY 42101

WHITE, CAROLYN WEST, historian, educator; b. Marble, N.C., Apr. 19, 1939; d. Venson Frank and Evelyn Lenora (Ford) West; A.B., Woman's Coll. U. N.C., 1961; M.A., Duke U., 1967, Ph.D., 1975; m. John Charles White, July 6, 1963. Instr. history, govt. Clemson U. 1963-64; instr. Oglethorpe U., 1964; instr. to asso. prof. polit. sci. U. Ala., Huntsville, 1967—, chmn. dept. polit. sci., 1972-80, dir. Acad. Advisement Center 1980—. Mem. Community Action Adv. Bd., Huntsville 1976-78. Opdyke scholar 1958-61. Mem. Am. Hist. Assn., So. Assn. Women Historians, N.Am. Conf. British Studies, Soc. Conf. Brit. Studies, Carolinas Symposium on British Studies, Nat. Assn. Academic Advising, Ala. Hist. Assn., Phi Beta Kappa, Phi Alpha Theta, Omicron Delta Kappa. Contbr. articles to profl. jours. Office: Dept History U Ala Hunstville AL 35899

WHITE, CHERYL JEAN, disc jockey, radio announcer; b. St. Louis, Jan. 1, 1956; d. Billy Lorene and Helene Elizabeth (Borman) White; student Ind. State U., Evansville, 1973-74. Producer daily program Woman's World, Sta. WROZ, Evansville, 1974-80, writer, producer weekly show Seeds and Stems, 1977-80, public service dir., 1974-80, disc jockey, 1973—. Vol., Easter Seal Telathon, 1978-81, Career Day Conf., Evansville Human Relations Commn., 1976-77; mem. PBS Spl. Talent Corps, 1981—; troop leader Girl Scouts U.S.A., 1979-80. Recipient cert. of merit Evansville Deaf Social Services Agy., 1980. Home: 1201 SE 1st St Evansville IN 47713 Office: PO Box 139 Evansville IN 47701

WHITE, CYNTHIA ADAMO, clin. psychologist; b. Boston, Jan. 17, 1944; d. Sebastian Anthony and Olga (Rizzo) Adamo; B.A., Fla. Atlantic U., 1966; M.S., U. Miami (Fla.), 1970, Ph.D. in Clin. Psychology, 1973; m. Michael Dale White, Aug. 26, 1972. Asst. prof. psychology Xavier U., Cin., 1975-76; dir. behavior modification adolescent unit Longview State Hosp., Cin., 1975-76; psychologist eating disorders clinic U. Cin. Med. Sch., 1978—; dir. clin. tng., health psychologist VA Med. Center, Cin., 1976—; adj. asst. prof. U. Cin.; cons. in field. Mem. Am. Psychol. Assn., Soc. Behavior Medicine, Ohio Psychol. Assn., Sigma Xi. Author papers in field. Office: 3200 Vine St Cincinnati OH 45220

WHITE, DESPINA STRATOUDAKI, educator; b. Rethymon, Crete, Greece; d. Theodore Emmanuel and Paraskevi (Martinengo) Stratoudakis; came to U.S., 1950, naturalized, 1956; B.A., Our Lady of Lake U., San Antonio, 1956; M.S., Trinity U., San Antonio, 1960; Ph.D., U. Ga., 1972; m. Darrell S. White, July 1, 1949; children—Nora Linda White Gignilliat, Darrell Theodore. Instr. fgn. langs. Wesleyan Coll., Macon, Ga., 1966-69; asso. prof. history and modern langs. Middle Ga. Coll., Cochran, 1973—. Grantee, Am. Philos. Soc., 1976, Andrew Mellon Found., 1977, 78, Nat. Endowment Humanities, summer 1980. Mem. AAUW (dir.), Modern Greek Assn., Ga. Historians, AAUP, Byzantine Studies Conf., LWV (pres. Macon chpt. 1962-64), Phi Sigma Iota, Pi Gamma Mu. Republican. Greek Orthodox. Club: Morning Music (dir). Author: Patriarch Photios—His Times and His Letters, 1980; The Patriarch and the Prince, 1981. Office: Middle Ga Coll Cochran GA 31014

WHITE, DOROTHY SHIPLEY, historian; b. Phila., Jan. 29, 1896; d. Samuel Richards and Agnes Gillespie (Evans) Shipley; B.A., Bryn Mawr Coll., 1917; M.A., Columbia U., 1921; B.F.A., Temple U., 1943; Ph.D., U. Pa., 1954; m. Thomas Raeburn White, Jan. 12, 1924; children—David, Dorothy Gaus, Stephen. Mem. staff Bryn Mawr (Pa.) Coll., 1921-22; author: Seeds of Discord: DeGaulle, Free France, and the Allies, 1964, French transl., 1967; author Black Africa and DeGaulle, 1979. Mem. adv. commn. dean U. Pa., Alliance Française of Phila. Bd. dirs. Atwater Kent Mus., 1966—. Decorated officer French Nat. Order Merit; recipient Silver medal City of Paris; award Phila. Athenaeum, 1964. Mem. Académie des Sciences d'Outre-Mer, (Paris), Comité Universitaire d'Etudes et de Recherches Gaulliennes (Paris), Art Alliance. Republican. Clubs: Acorn, Cosmopolitan, Phila. Cricket. Contbr. articles to jours. Home: 600 Cathedral Rd Apt D214 Cathedral Village Philadelphia PA 19128

WHITE, DOROTHY T., nursing educator; b. N.Y.C., Dec. 11, 1923; d. Joseph V. and Pearle E. (Salter) Raymond; diploma in nursing L.I. Coll. Hosp. Sch. Nursing, Bklyn.; B.S., M.A., Ed.D., Columbia U.; m. Jan. 5, 1952. Prof. nursing Med. Coll. Ga., Augusta, 1971-77, dean Sch. Nursing, 1971-76; prof. Nova U., Ft. Lauderdale, Fla., 1977-78, dir. The Louise Mellen Inst. Nursing, 1977-78; prof. Calif. State U., Sacramento, 1978-79, chmn. div. nursing, 1978-79; prof. Hunter Coll.-City U. N.Y., Hunter-Bellevue Sch. Nursing, N.Y.C., 1979—, dean, 1979-82; cons. Office of Chancellor, City U. N.Y.; dir. Augusta Radiation Center, 1973-76; govtl. appointee Master Planning Com. for Nursing in Ga., 1971-75. Bd. dirs. Nurses House, Nurse Ednl. Fund; trustee Mt. St. Mary Coll., 1960-61, asso. trustee, 1961-65. Recipient citation Office of Sec. State of Ga., 1977; Cert. of Appreciation, U.S. Army Health Services Command, 1977. Mem. Group for Advancement in Nursing (founder), Am. Acad. Polit. and Social Scis., AAUW, Am. Assn. Women in Higher Edn., Am. Assn. Female Execs., Am. Assn. Higher Edn., AAUP, Am. Assn. Univ. Adminstrs., Nat. Assn. Women Deans, Adminstrs. and Counselors, N.Y. Acad. Scis. Author papers in field. Office: 440 E 26th St New York NY 10010

WHITE, EILEEN KNIGHT, dietitian; b. N.Y.C., Dec. 21, 1949; d. Harold Y. and Mildred (Varlack) Knight; B.S., Andrews U., Berrian Springs, Mich., 1971; M.P.H. (USPHS grantee 1972), Loma Linda (Calif.) U., 1974; m. O.C. White, Jr., Sept. 8, 1974; children—O.C. III, Anissa Camille. Intern, then student supr. Loma Linda U. Med. Center, 1972-73; dir. food services San Joaquin Community Hosp., Bakersfield, Calif., 1973-74, San Joaquin Gardens-Retirement Center, Fresno, Calif., 1974-75, State Center Community Coll. Dist., Fresno, 1975—; partner Nutritional Mgmt. Cons.; bd. commnrs. Fresno County EOC Commnr., Fresno City and County Commn. Status Women, 1977-79. Mem. Am. Dietetic Assn., Nat. Assn. Coll. and Univ. Food Service, Seventh-day Adventist Dietetic Assn., Food Service Assn., Calif. Dietetic Assn. Office: 1525 E Weldon St Fresno CA 93704

WHITE, EVA ANDERSON, newspaper pub.; b. Aurora, Ill., Jan. 24, 1913; d. Claus Emil and Anna (Nelson) Anderson; student Stephens Coll., 1931-32, Chgo. Acad. Fine Arts, 1932-33, N. Central Coll., 1934-35; m. Harold Edgar White, July 23, 1937. Tchr., Freeman Sch., Aurora, Ill., 1935-36; with Naperville (Ill.) Sun, 1937—, co-pub., 1937—, sec. bd. dirs., 1937—. Trustee, North Central Coll., Naperville, 1974—, mem. exec. com., 1977—. Methodist. Clubs: 99's Internat. Assn. Women Pilots (chmn. 1961-62), Lioness (charter mem. Naperville chpt., 2d v.p. 1978-79). Home: 9 S 281 Aero Dr Naperville IL 60566 Office: Sun Bldg Naperville IL 60566

WHITE, FONTAINETTE, health care agy. exec.; b. Cameron, Tex., June 10, 1931; d. Henry and Harriet (Fontaine) Parker; student Tex. Coll., 1948; R.N., St. Joseph Hosp., Ft. Worth, 1970; student in health care adminstrn. E. Tex. State U., 1972; m. Douglas White; 1 son, Ronald Thomas. Dir. nursing Four Seasons Convalescent Center, 1970-71; health coordinator Head Start/Day Care Assn. of Tarrant County, Tex., 1971-74; program coordinator Sickle Cell Anemia Assn., Ft. Worth, 1974-75, exec. dir., 1976—; mem. disaster team ARC, Health Fair Council. Precinct chmn., 1966-72; mem. Democratic Precinct Workers Council. Mem. Am. Nurses Assn., Tex. Nurses Assn., Dist. Nurses Assn., Tex. Family Planning Assn., Am. Assn. Female Execs., United Way Exec. Dirs., Minority Leaders and Citizen Council, Network of Exec. Women. Episcopalian. Clubs: Altrusa, F. Brooks/Grays Literary and Art, Eastern Star. Home: 2400 Hillview Dr Fort Worth TX 76119 Office: 2914 E Rosedale St Fort Worth TX 76105

WHITE, GERALDINE POTTS, nurse; b. Bradenton, Fla., Jan. 20, 1941; d. Will and Burnell (Potts) Williams; A.A. in Nursing, Manatee Jr. Coll., Bradenton, 1970; B.S. in Psychology, Barry Coll., Miami, Fla., 1975; B.S. in Nursing, Fla. Internat. U., 1978, M.S., 1980; postgrad. Nova U., 1981—; m. Gladstone Joseph White, July 15, 1973. Dental asst., 1959-63; practical nurse Sarasota (Fla.) Meml. Hosp., 1964-69, registered nurse, 1970-72; asst. head nurse surg. ICU, North Shore Hosp., Miami, 1973-75; psychiat. supr. Highland Park Gen. Hosp., Miami, 1975-77; dept. head health occupations, dir. Miami Lakes practical nursing program Dade County Public Schs., Miami, 1977—. Hartman scholar, 1975. Mem. Am. Nurses Assn., Nat. League Nursing, Am. Heart Assn., Nat. Assn. Female Execs., Fla. Notary Public Soc., Fla. Vocat. Assn., Health Occupations Educators Assn. Fla., South Fla. Consortium Nursing Edn., NAACP, Fla. Bus. and Profl. Women's Assn., United Tchrs. Dade County, Barry U. Alumni Assn., Fla. Internat. U. Alumni Assn., Kappa Delta Pi, Epsilon Pi Tau. Methodist. Club: Ebony (Sarasota). Home: 15120 SW 105th Ave Miami FL 33176 Office: 5780 NW 158th St Miami FL 33014

WHITE, GLORIA WATERS, univ. adminstr.; b. St. Louis County, Mo., May 16, 1934; d. James Thomas and Thelma Celestine (Brown) W.; B.A., Harris-Stowe Tchrs. Coll., 1956; M.A., Washington U., St. Louis, 1963, M. Juridical Studies, 1980; m. W. Glenn White, Jan. 1, 1955; 1 dau., Terry Anita. Tchr., St. Louis Bd. Edn., 1956-63, psychol. counselor, 1963-67; dir. office spl. projects Washington U., 1967-76, asst. to asso. vice chancellor personnel and affirmative action, 1975—. Bd. dirs. Am. Assn. Affirmative Action, 1974-77; instl. chair Arts and Edn. Fund, 1975-82; mem. Eastern Dist. Mo. Desegregation and Adv. Com., 1981-82. Accredited exec. in personnel; cert. life counselor, life tchr; recipient citations Urban League, Pres.'s Council Youth Opportunities. Mem. Coll. and Univ. Personnel Assn. (v.p.; Creativity award 1981), Am. Soc. Personnel Adminstrn., St. Louis Symphony Soc., Delta Sigma Theta. Roman Catholic. Home: 545 Del Price Ct Saint Louis MO 63124 Office: Box 1184 Saint Louis MO 63130

WHITE, IRMA REED, writer, librarian; b. Nebraska City, Nebr., Mar. 4, 1897; d. Eustace Glen and Martha (Soper) Reed; B.A., U. Colo., 1919; M.A., Radcliffe Coll., 1926; m. Wilford L. White, June 12, 1922. Instr. English, U. Colo., 1922-24; instr. report writing Grad. Sch. Bus. Adminstrn. Harvard U., 1925-28; asst. head field sect. Office Price Adminstrn., editor, Washington, 1943-47; public info. specialist Bur. Census, 1958-69; writer Office Sec. Commerce, 1969-71, editor series Do You Know Your Economic ABCs, 1962-70; dir. press room Cost of Living Council, Washington, 1971-74; librarian firm Mayer, Brown & Platt, Washington, 1975—. Recipient Outstanding Achievement award Office Price Adminstrn., 1945; Silver medal Dept. Commerce, 1964, Creative Communication award, 1965; Excellence in Communications award Fed. Editors Assn., 1965, 66, 70; Oustanding Service award Cost of Living Council, 1972, 73; Public Service award SBA, 1978, Internat. Council Small Bus., 1978. Mem. Nat. Press Club, Nat. League Am. Pen Women (Nat. Achievement award 1966), Am. Newspaper Womens Club, PEO, Chi Omega. Contbr. articles to Ency. Brit., London Times, Christian Sci. Monitor, others. Home: 4000 Massachusetts Ave NW Washington DC 20016 Office: 888 17th St NW Washington DC 20006

WHITE, JOHNNIE MAE, educator; b. Sulphur Springs, Tex., Aug. 3, 1923; d. Escol and Ruth Belle (Davis) Williams; B.S., Wiley Coll., Marshall, Tex., 1939; M.S., Prairie View (Tex.) A&M Coll., 1950; M.A., E.Tex. State U., 1976; m. Octurus J. White, Aug. 7, 1948; 1 son, Octurus J. Public sch. tchr., 1942-46; mem. faculty Wiley Coll., Marshall, Tex., 1950—, asso. prof. edn., 1950-67, dir. student tchrs., 1967—. Mem. AAUP, AAUW, Am. Assn. Colls. Tchr. Edn., NEA, Tex. Tchrs. Assn., Tex. Edn. Assn., NAACP, Phi Delta Kappa, Alpha Kappa Alpha. Baptist. Home: 411 University Ave Marshall TX 75670 Office: 7007 Wiley Coll Marshall TX 75670

WHITE, JOYCE L., med. technologist; b. Darlington, Wis., Sept. 2, 1938; d. William E. and Martha E. (Smith) Calverley; B.S., U. Wis., La Crosse, 1967; M.A., Central Mich. U., Mt. Pleasant, 1979; m. Raymond C. White, Jan. 30, 1960; children—Lorelei, Pamela, Lyall. Staff med. technologist Methodist Hosp., Peoria, Ill., 1960, St. Francis Med. Center, La Crosse, 1960-61; staff technologist, then head technologist LaCrosse Clinic, 1964-79; dir. lab. services Skemp-Grandview La Crosse Clinic, 1979—. Chmn. Pops Nite, Gt. River Festival Arts, 1974-82; coordinator Medieval World Banquet, 1979-81; chmn. German dinner Ocktoberfest USA, 1977-81. Recipient various service and appreciation awards. Mem. Am. Soc. Med. Tech., Am. Assn. Clin. Chemists, AAUW, Wis. Assn. Med. Tech. (dir. 1978-82, chmn. govt. liason com. 1980-82). Jehovah's Witness. Club: Jackson Hole (Wyo.) Racquet. Home: 1017 S 7th St La Crosse WI 54601 Office: 212 S 11th St LaCrosse WI 54601

WHITE, JUANITA MITCHELL, state legislator, devel. cons.; b. Savannah, Ga., Oct. 12; d. Willie and Hattie G. Mitchell; student Savannah State Coll.; grad. Eastman Bus. Sch., 1951; m. Ernest White, Apr. 16, 1948; children—Lorraine Veronica, Yvonne Brenee. Chmn. bd. dirs. LLBH Water Co., 1973-77; asst. to spl. projects dir. Beaufort-Jasper Comprehensive Health Service, 1974-76; devel. cons.; mem. S.C. Ho. of Reps., 1980—. Mem. adv. council Beaufort-Jasper Career Devel. Center; mem. S.C. Pvt. Industry Council, S.E. Regional Community Assistance Program; v.p. Coastal Mental Retardation Assn.; mem. Democratic Com., Phila., 1956-64. Mem. NAACP, S.C. Water Assn. Baptist. Office: 530B Blatt Bldg Columbia SC 29211 *

WHITE, JUDITH ANN O'RADNIK, social services adminstr.; b. St. Paul, Oct. 27, 1943; d. Clarence Edwin and Marcella Ann (Cappelle) O'R.; B.A., Quincy Coll., 1965; M.S.W., Ohio State U., 1970; m. Dean H. White, May, 1981. Dep. juvenile officer St. Louis Circuit Ct. Juvenile Div., 1965-68; caseworker Ohio Div. Youth Services, Powell, Ohio, 1968-69; supr. intake delinquency juvenile div. St. Louis Circuit Ct., 1970-76, supr. child abuse and neglect unit, 1976—. Bd. dirs. Council on Child Abuse and Neglect of Met. St. Louis, 1979—. Mem. Nat. Council Crime and Delinquency, Ohio State U. Sch. Social Work Alumni Assn. Home: 138 Manlyn Dr Kirkwood MO 63122 Office: 920 N Vandeventer Ave Saint Louis MO 63108

WHITE, JUDY WINN, computer specialist, govt. ofcl.; b. Lubbock, Tex., May 10, 1943; d. Vaughn Pierce and Gladys Mae (Sledge) Winn; B.A. with high honors, U. Md., 1967; m. Stephen White, June 9, 1972; children—Jeffrey Alan, Craig Parton. Computer specialist GSA, Washington, 1968-71; supr. sci. systems unit Drug Enforcement Adminstrn., 1971-79; dep. dir. div. ADP mgmt. Bur. Public Debt, 1979—. Methodist.

WHITE, KATHLEEN ANN, educator; b. Indpls., Aug. 13, 1944; d. Paul Edwards and Anna Marie (Dziewas) W.; B.S., Ball State U., 1966; M.S., Ind. U., 1968. Tchr. bus. edn. North Central High Sch., Indpls., 1968—. Chmn. Sunday Vols. Rental Gallery, Indpls. Mus. Art. Mem. Ind. Bus. Edn. Assn. (dir. 1980, newsletter editor 1981), Internat. Word Processing (editor newsletter, v.p. 1979), Indpls. Bus. Edn. Council (sec. 1972, v.p. 1980, pres. 1981), Ind. Vocat. Assn., Am. Vocat. Assn., North-Central Bus. Edn. Assn. (dir. 1982—), Nat. Secs. Assn. (edn. com.), Adminstrv. Mgmt. Soc. (edn. com., program dir. 1981), Word Processing Soc., Ind. Bus. Educators Club, Delta Pi Epsilon, Phi Delta Kappa. Mem. United Ch. of Christ. Home: 3025 N Meridian # 804 Indianapolis IN 46208 Office: 1901 E 86th St Indianapolis IN 46240

WHITE, KATHLEEN MAE, social worker; b. Lamar, Colo., Feb. 12, 1941; d. Cornelius William and Lillian Mae (Oswald) Hogan; A.A., U.

Md., 1969; M.S.W., Our Lady of Lake U., 1976; B.S. cum laude, Tex. A. and I. U., 1972; m. Larry F. White, Mar. 30, 1959; children—Thomas William, Richard Edward, Judy Lynn, Ramona Marie. With Vol. Services, ARC, Wright Patterson AFB, Ohio, 1964-65, Randolph AFB, Tex., 1965-66, Sembach AFB, Ger., 1966-69; tchr. St. Augustines Cath. Sch., Laredo, Tex., 1970-71; social worker Tex. Dept. Public Welfare, San Antonio, 1972-74; tchr. Edgewood Ind. Sch. Dist., San Antonio, 1976-78; coordinator teenage mother's sch. Harlandale Ind. Sch. Dist., San Antonio, 1978—; pvt. practice mental health social work, 1976—. VA stipend, 1975-76. Mem. Acad. Cert. Social Workers, Am. Assn. Social Workers, Am. Bus. Women's Assn., Our Lady of Lake U. Alumni Assn. Republican. Roman Catholic. Home: 261 Westway University City TX 78148 Office: 102 Genevieve St San Antonio TX 78285

WHITE, LELIA CAYNE, librarian; b. Berkeley, Calif., Feb. 22, 1921; d. James Lloyd and Eulalia Fulton (Douglass) Cayne; B.A., U. Calif., Berkeley, 1943, M.L.S., 1969; children by previous marriage—Douglass Fulton, Cameron Jane. Bibliographer, lectr., asso. U. Calif. at Berkeley Sch. Library and Info. Studies, 1969-72; reference librarian Berkeley-Oakland (Calif.) Service Systems, 1970-76, supervising librarian, 1973-76; dir. Oakland Public Library, 1976—. Mem. ALA, Calif. Library Assn., Public Library Assn., Calif. Inst. Libraries (pres.), Public Library Execs. Central Calif., LWV, Oakland Dalian (China) Friendship City Soc. (pres.). Contbr. to Public Library User Education, 1981. Office: 125 14th St Oakland CA 94612

WHITE, LINDA DAMER, educator; b. Springfield, Ill., Dec. 5, 1938; d. J. Fred and Mary Jane (Thurmond) Welsh; B.A., William Jewell Coll., 1959; M.A., Boston U., 1967; Ed.D., U. N.C., Greensboro, 1979; m. Dane M. White, May 31, 1980; children—Diana, Cynthia and John Damer. Tchr., Kearney (Mo.) Public Schs., 1959-60, Consolidated Sch. Dist. 1, Kansas City, Mo., 1960-63, Wellesley (Mass.) Pub. Schs., 1963-64, Newton (Mass.) Pub. Schs., 1966-67, Smyth County (Va.) Pub. Schs., 1969-72, Washington County (Va.) Pub. Schs., 1973-76, Burlington (N.C.) Pub. Schs., 1978-79; grad. teaching asst. U. N.C., Greensboro, 1977-78; asst. prof. music Ind. State U., Terre Haute, Ind., 1979—. Bd. dirs. Arts Illiana, Terre Haute, Ind. U. N.C., Greensboro fellow, 1976-77. Mem. Music Educators Nat. Conf., Am. Orff Schulwerk Assn., Pi Kappa Lambda, Phi Delta Kappa. Home: 2707 Oak St Terre Haute IN 47803 Office: Dept Music Ind State U Terre Haute IN 47809

WHITE, LINDA NELL FARLEY, chem. co. exec.; b. Charleston, W.Va., Nov. 24, 1941; d. Frederick Paul and Frances Eloise (Hale) Farley; student Eastern Mont. Coll. of Edn., 1959-60, W.Va. State Coll.; m. Bernard Jerome White, May 27, 1964. Instr. gymnastics Lawrence Frankel Inst., Charleston, 1960-61; sec. Union Carbide Corp., Institute, W.Va., 1961-73, office services supr., 1973-81, mgmt. devel. asso., 1981—, sr. office supr., public relations adminstr., non-exempt tng. adminstrn. Mem. Nat. Assn. Female Execs. Club: Altrusa (corr. sec. 1976-77) (Charleston). Home: 141 Shawnee Estates Winfield WV 25213 Office: PO Box 2831 Charleston WV 25330

WHITE, LORAINE PATRICIA, social worker, educator; b. St. Louis, July 18, 1930; d. John J. and Lucy L. (Brock) Williams; B.S., Calif. Poly. U., Pomona, Calif., 1971; M.S.W., U. So. Calif., 1973; m. Waldo R. White; children—William L., Darryl C., Russlyn D., Bambia E. Psychiat. social worker Tri-City Mental Health Center, Pomona, 1973-74; med. social worker Univ. Hosp., Ariz. Dept. Social Services, Tucson, 1974-76, psychiat. social worker dept. psychiatry, 1976-77; lectr., psychiat. social worker U. Ariz., 1977—; asso. faculty mem. Pima (Ariz.) Community Coll., 1975—, Ariz. State U., 1977—. Bd. dirs., v.p. Ododo Theatre, Tucson, 1977-79. Mem. Ariz. Soc. Clin. Social Work and Psychotherapy, Inc., Nat. Assn. Black Social Workers, Acad. Cert. Social Workers, Nat. Assn. Social Workers, Am. Orthopsychiat. Assn., LWV, AAUW, Alpha Kappa Alpha. Democrat. African Methodist Episcopal. Office: 1501 N Campbell St Tucson AZ 85724

WHITE, LYNETTE MICHELE, histology technologist; b. Lebanon, Oreg., Feb. 16, 1950; d. Chester Lysle and Mable Olive (Wyatt) Smith; student Good Samaritan Hosp. Sch. Nursing, 1969-70; m. Ward Russell White, May 12, 1972; 1 son, Lee Edward. Lab. asst. hematology U. Oreg. Med. Sch. Hosp., Portland, 1969-71; lab. asst. Good Samaritan Hosp., Corvallis, Oreg., 1971, histology technologist, sect. head, 1974—. Sec.-treas. Pacific N.W. Histoloty Soc., Am. Soc. Clin. Pathologists. Democrat. Methodist. Club: Am. Legion Aux. Home: 380 7th St Lebanon OR 97355 Office: 3600 NW Samaritan Dr Corvallis OR 97330

WHITE, MARGARET ELIZABETH, ins. agt.; b. Ranger, Tex., Dec. 23, 1920; d. Russell Worley and Margaret Katerhine (McGaha) White; diploma Met. Bus. Coll., 1940; cert. Dallas Coll/So. Meth. U., 1955, 56; cert. El Centro Community Coll., 1973; Sec., ins. solicitor Hereford Cairns & Co., Dallas, 1955-59; sec., ins. solicitor Cairns-Blakeley & Co., Dallas, 1959-62; ins. agt., adminstrv. asst. Gen. Aviation Underwriting Corp., Dallas, 1963-64; owner, agt. Margaret E. White, Dallas, 1964—. Chmn. Hallmark Art contest Dallas Fedn. Women's Club, 1970, 71; spl. adviser Dallas Public Library Learning Program, 1980; mem. Dallas Commn. Status of Women, 1979; mem. Lone Star council Camp Fire Girls, 1981. Recipient SW Bus. and Profl. Women's Club award, 1978. Mem. Oak Cliff C. of C., Dallas Council Women's Affairs. Republican. Methodist. Home: 4305 Pensacola Ct Dallas TX 75211 Office: 1850 W Commerce St Dallas TX 75208

WHITE, MARGARETTE PAULYNE MORGAN, coll. adminstr.; b. Tattnall County, Ga., Sept. 11, 1934; d. Margrio Riley and Lilliam Ophelia (Bradley) Morgan; diploma Reids Bus. Coll., 1953; B.A., Morris Brown Coll., 1957; cert. U. Tenn., 1966; m. Frank White, July 8, 1961; 1 dau., Lairalaine. Tchr., English and journalism Trinity High Sch., Decatur, Ga., 1957-66; mass media specialist/publs. adv. Charles L. Harper High Sch., Atlanta, 1967-74; dir. public relations Morris Brown Coll., Atlanta, 1974—. Bd. dirs. YWCA of Greater Atlanta. Mem. Women in Communications, Ga. Assn. Broadcasters, Media Women (named Media Woman of Yr. 1978, nat. 2d v.p. 1980—), Nat. Assn. Market Devel., Bus. & Profl. Women, (nat. public relations dir. 1975-80), LWV, NAACP, Democratic Women. Methodist. Address: 257 W Lake Ave NW Atlanta GA 30314

WHITE, MARILYN JANE, fed. agy. adminstr.; b. Morristown, N.J., Dec. 27, 1944; d. Oliver D. and L. Josephine (Winter) Schmidt; B.A., Kans. State U., 1966; M.S., Ind. U., 1972; grad. Armed Forces Staff Coll., 1979, Nat. Def. U., 1981. Field services dir. U.S. Army Recreation Centers, Hdqrs. Dept. Army, Washington, 1972-76; mgmt. analyst Office of Adj. Gen., 1976-77, program analyst, 1977-79, organizational effectiveness specialist, Sec. of Army fellow, 1979-80; productivity improvement officer Office of Sec., Dept. Commerce, 1980-81; chief Organizational Effectiveness br. Office of Comptroller, Def. Communications Agy., Washington, 1981—; pres., chmn. bd. Performance Skills, Inc., Arlington, Va., 1981—; cons. career counseling. Mem. Organizational Devel. Network, Federally Employed Women, Inc. (Pentagon I chpt.), Internat. Personnel Mgmt. Assn., Fed. Organizational Devel. Network. Author: The Upward Mobility Kit, 1979; Moving Up: A Practical Guide for Women and Men Who Want to Move Up in the Federal Govt., 1981; contbr. articles in field to profl. jours. Home: 1204 S Cleveland St Arlington VA 22204

WHITE, MARILYN MILDRED, educator; b. Newark, June 1, 1947; d. Edward Russell and Bertha Susan (Finney) W.; B.A. in English (Inst. scholar), Hampton Inst., 1969; M.A. in Folklore (Univ. fellow), Ind. U., 1971; Ph.D. in Anthropology (grantee), U. Tex., 1982. Instr. English, Central Wash. State Coll., Ellensburg, 1971-73; instr. folk studies, dir. Afro-Am. studies Western Ky. U., Bowling Green, 1977—; cons., evaluator Ky. Humanities Council. So. Fellowships Fund fellow, 1974-75, 76-77. Mem. Am. Anthrop. Assn., Am. Folklore Soc., Assn. African and African-Am. Folklorists, Assn. Black Anthropologists, Ky. Folklore Soc., NAACP, Assn. Aspirations for Real Equality (v.p. 1979-80, 82—), Phi Kappa Phi, Delta Sigma Theta. Democrat. Baptist. Home: 1588 Normal Dr Apt 10 Bowling Green KY 42101 Office: IWFAC 235 Western Ky U Bowling Green KY 42101

WHITE, MARION, nurse; b. Ft. Worth, Apr. 2, 1922; d. Alphonso and Lenollie Elizabeth (Ainsworth) McAfee; R.N., Kansas City Gen. Sch. Nursing, 1943-46; diploma Sacred Heart Dominican Coll., 1957-59; B.S.N., Harris County Sch. Nurse Anesthetists, 1972; m. John White, Aug. 8, 1946; children—John Allen, Charles D. Head nurse operating room St. Elizabeth Hosp., Houston, 1947-65; indsl. nurse A.O. Smith Steel Co., Houston, 1965-66; dir. nursing service Lockwood Gen. Hosp., Inc., Houston, 1966-79; dir. profl. services Riverside Gen. Hosp., Houston, 1980—. Mem. Gulf Coast Assn. Nurse Anesthetists, Am. Assn. Nurse Anesthetists, Am. Acad. Med. Adminstrs., Houston Area Dirs. Assn. Democrat. Roman Catholic. Club: Kansas City Gen. Alumni (pres. 1979). Home: 2515 12th St Galena Park TX 77547 Office: 3204 Ennis St Houston TX 77547

WHITE, MARTHA STURM, psychologist, educator; b. Clarksburg, W.Va., June 4, 1925; d. Harry Gail and Frances Folsom (McGuire) Sturm; B.A., Denison U., 1947; M.A., Columbia U., 1948; Ph.D., U. Mich., 1954; m. Benjamin Ward White, Apr. 8, 1953; children—Christopher Ward, Stacey Elizabeth. Research asso. Stanford (Calif.) U., 1952-55; Community Mental Health fellow Harvard U. Med. Sch., Cambridge, Mass., 1955-56; ednl. guidance asso. Radcliff Inst. (name changed to Bunting Inst.), Cambridge, 1961-66; research asso. Harvard U., 1966-67; postdoctoral fellow in adult devel. U. Calif., San Francisco, 1969-70; asso. research psychologist U. Calif., San Francisco, 1973-78, lectr., 1970—; prof. psychology Calif. Sch. Profl. Psychology, Berkeley, 1972—; cons. in field. Mem. Am. Psychol. Assn., Western Psychol. Assn., Nat. Council for Family Relations, AAAS. Contbr. articles in field to profl. publs. Home: 20 Malvino Ct Tiburon CA 94920 Office: 1900 Addison St Berkeley CA 94704

WHITE, MARY ESTERLYN, chemist; b. Selma, Ala.; d. Frank Herman and Sadalure Elizabeth (Moore) W.; B.A., Dillard U., 1960; M.S., Fairleigh Dickinson U., 1971. Analyt. chemist Bristol Myers, Hillside, N.J., 1960-67; research scientist Lever Bros., Edgewater, N.J., 1968-75; asst. mgr. tapes and backings devel. Johnson & Johnson, New Brunswick, N.J., 1975—. Recipient Samuel B. Ullman award, 1956; mem. Dillard U. Dean's List, 1956-60; Philip B. Hofmann Research Scientist award, 1979. Mem. Am. Chem. Soc., N.Y. Acad. Scis., Soc. Cosmetic Chemists, Sigma Xi, Alpha Kappa Alpha. Democrat. Baptist. Home: 100 Manhattan Ave Union City NJ 07087 Office: 501 George St New Brunswick NJ 08903

WHITE, NANCY (MRS. GEORGE K. THOMPSON), fashion cons.; b. Bklyn., July 25, 1916; d. Thomas J. and Virginia (Gillette) W.; student pvt. schs.; m. Ralph Delahaye Paine, Jr., July 25, 1947 (div. Dec. 1977); children—Gillette Dauphinot Piper, Katharine Delahaye Chapin. Fashion editor Pictorial Rev. mag., 1936-40; asst. fashion editor Good Housekeeping mag., 1940-47, fashion editor, 1947-57; asst. editor Harper's Bazaar, N.Y.C., 1957-58, editor-in-chief, 1958-71; fashion dir. Bergdorf Goodman, N.Y.C., 1972-74; dir. Gen. Mills; fashion cons., N.Y.C., 1974—; cons. Channel 13 Public TV; cons. spl. events Nat. Found. March of Dimes. Former mem. Nat. Council of Arts; mem. women's bd. Lighthouse for the Blind. Decorated knight Order Merit (Italy), Silver medal Merit (Spain); recipient N.Y. Designers award. Mem. Fashion Group (past pres.). Address: 3 E 77 St Apt 5C New York NY 10021

WHITE, ROSALIE VIVIAN, former real estate broker, nurse, antique dealer; b. McClouth, Kans., Mar. 6, 1921; d. Roy H. and Margaret E. DeHoff; R.N., Asbury Hosp., Salina, Kans., 1943; student William Jewell Coll., 1947, Drury Coll., Springfield, Mo.; m. John F. White, June 23, 1948; children—John F., James Ford, Judson Flynn. Supt. drug and alcoholism sanitarium, Kansas City, Mo., 1945; pvt. duty nurse, 1946-47; owner, operator White's Antique Shop, Springfield, 1960-80; sales mgr. White Realty, 1976-82; treas. Hidden Valley Land & Cattle Co., Springfield, 1976-80. Bd. dirs. S.W. Mo. Mus. Assn., 1972-78, pres., 1977-78; active 1st Bapt. Ch., Springfield. R.N., Mo. Mem. Springfield Realtors Assn., Kans. Bd. Nurses, Beta Sigma Phi, Beta Sigma Omicron. Republican. Club: Springfield Collectors (past pres.). Home: 3851 E Sunshine St Springfield MO 65804 Office: 3911 E Sunshine St Springfield MO 65804

WHITE, RUTH BENNETT, nutritionist, educator; writer; b. Howe, Okla., Aug. 18, 1906; d. Ambrose L. and Sarah A. (Blevins) Bennett; B.A. with honors, Okla. Baptist U., 1928; M.S. (fellow), U. Iowa, 1930; postgrad. Cornell U., 1930-34, Columbia, 1955-56; m. Carl Milton White, Aug. 5, 1928; children—Sherril White Spencer, Caroline White Buchanan. Prin. Jr. High Sch., Heavener, Okla., 1926-27; surveyor of diets, research fellow N.Y. State 4-H Club camps, summer 1931-34; instr. nutrition Coll. Home Econs., Cornell U., Ithaca, N.Y., 1931-34; tchr. pub. schs., N.Y.C., 1956-58 Fort Lee (N.J.) High Sch., 1959-60; pub. lectr. foods and nutrition, 1931—; nutrition specialist for community programs N.Y. State Extension, 1931-34, Ankara, Turkey, 1960-61, Lagos, Nigeria, 1962-64; mem. Nat. Commn. on Revision of Home Econs. Curriculum, Fed. Republic of Nigeria, 1962-64. Mem. Leonia (N.J.) Bd. Edn., 1950-54. Recipient Alumni Achievement award Okla. Baptist U., 1975; named Woman of the Year, San Diego dist. Calif. Home Econs. Assn., 1973, 74; Woman of Achievement award Pres.'s Council Womens Service, Bus. and Profl. Clubs San Diego, 1973, 74. Mem. Am., Calif., Channel Islands home econs. assns., Internat. Fedn. Home Econs. (mem. council 1970-76), AAUW, Soc. Nutrition Edn., Nat. League Am. Pen Women, Pi Lambda Theta, Pi Kappa Delta. Democrat. Author: If Food Could Talk, 1932; You and Your Food (text), 4th edit., 1976; Food and Your Future (text), 1972, 2d edit., 1979; contbr. articles on nutrition to profl. jours. and newspapers. Address: 2663 Tallant Rd EV-10 Santa Barbara CA 93105

WHITE, RUTH MIRIAM WEIHS, trade and fin. co. exec.; b. Vienna, Austria; came to U.S., 1947, naturalized, 1952; d. Hugo and Ilka (Herzog) Weihs; B.A. in Bus. Adminstrn., St. John's U., Shanghai, China, 1947; postgrad. N.Y.U., CCNY; m. Paul White, Sept. 18, 1949. Exec. sec. to chmn. bd. Pan Am. Trade Devel. Corp., N.Y.C., 1947-49, mgr., 1949-53, asst. v.p., 1953-58, v.p., 1958-74, sr. v.p., 1974—; pres. Indsl. Crystal Corp. Office: 2 Park Ave New York NY 10016

WHITE, RUTH S., record co. exec.; b. Pitts., Sept. 1, 1925; d. Leon H. and Rose (Stevenson) W.; B.A. in Music Composition, B.A. in Piano, Carnegie Inst. Tech., 1948, M.F.A., 1949. Supr., UCLA Lab. Sch., 1951-59; composer-producer, pres. Rhythms Prodns. Records, Los Angeles, 1955—; v.p. Cheviot Corp., Los Angeles, 1961—; past nat. v.p. Nat. Assn. Rec. Arts and Scis. Inst., also past bd. dirs.; co-founder Electronic Music Assn., 1968. Past bd. govs. Los Angeles v.p. Rec. Acad. Huntington Hartford Found. fellow, 1965. Mem. Nat. Assn. Am. Composers and Condrs. (past dir.), Am. Fedn. Musicians, ASCAP, Audio Engring. Soc., Music Educators Nat. Conf., Sigma Alpha Iota. Composer, producer: Mr. Windbag Stories; composer: Pinions, Seven Trumps from the Tarot Cards, Flowers of Evil, Short Circuits; producer-writer: Garden of Delights; author 10 books and 45 record albums for ednl. use. Office: Whitney Bldg Box 34485 Los Angeles CA 90034

WHITE, SHERYL BARBARA, advt. co. exec.; b. Cleve., Apr. 1, 1948; d. Robert Allen and Mitzi (Pinkus) W.; B.S.C., Ohio U., 1970. Copywriter, BBDO, Cleve., 1970-72, N.Y.C., 1972-73, William Douglas Mc Adams, N.Y.C., 1973-76, Cunningham & Walsh, N.Y.C., 1976-77; v.p. James Neal Harvey, N.Y.C., 1977-80; asso. creative dir., v.p. J. Walter Thompson/Brouillard Communications, N.Y.C., 1980—. Democrat. Jewish. Home: 230 E 30th St N-6A New York NY 10016 Office: 420 Lexington Ave New York NY 10022

WHITE, SHERYL ZENZ, acct.; b. San Diego, Dec. 5, 1945; d. William Donald and Monica Jean (Herney) Zenz; B.S. in Bus. Adminstrn., Calif. State U., San Diego, 1969; m. Don R. White, Apr. 26, 1970 (dec.). Departmental acct. water utilities City of San Diego, 1969-74, asst. coordinator, pub. employment program, 1974-75, fiscal analyst gen. services dept., 1976-77, investment officer treasury dept., 1977-78; owner, operator Fireside Manor Apts., Ontario, Calif., 1977—; prin acct. Sowell & Forsythe, La Jolla, Calif., 1979—; adj. instr. San Diego Community Coll., 1976-77. Bd. dirs. Law Center for Equal Rights, 1979-81. Mem. Young Ams. for Freedom (treas. San Diego chpt. 1965-66, v.p., 1966-67), Young Republicans, Mcpl. Fin. Officers' Assn. (pres. San Diego chpt. 1974), Calif. Women in Govt. (chmn. San Diego chpt. 1979-80), NOW, Ninety-Nines. Home: 8886 Caminito Primavera La Jolla CA 92037 Office: 1141-D W D St Ontario CA 91762 also 8950 Villa La Jolla Dr Suite 2241 La Jolla CA 92037

WHITE, WINIFRED DEMAREST (MRS. HERBERT A. WHITE), ret. assn. exec., editor; b. N.Y.C.; d. Peter Edward and Margaret (McLaughlin) Demarest; A.B., Coll. New Rochelle, 1914; postgrad. in journalism Columbia U. Extension, 1916-18; m. Joseph S. Gifford, Aug. 29, 1925 (dec. Feb. 1948); m. 2d, Herbert A. White, Nov. 14, 1964 (dec. Oct. 1972). Tchr. English, speech Bryant High Sch., N.Y.C., 1914-17; asst. to bursar Rockefeller Inst. Med. Research, 1917-26; asst. editor, asst. to exec. sec. AIME, N.Y.C., 1947-59, editor, 1960—; exec. sec. Soc. Women Engrs., N.Y.C., 1961-73, asso. life mem., 1973—; cons. copy editor IEEE, 1981—; freelance editor miscellaneous papers, 1959—; editorial proofreader, 1978—. Recipient Ursula Laurus citation Coll. New Rochelle, 1974; cert. of recognition and White Glove award Soc. Women Engrs. Editor: Ironmaking Proc., Open Hearth Proc., Honors Book, 1950-63, Proc. Conf. on Women, 1971; copy editor Trans. of ASHRAE, 1976-81. Home: 12 E 97th St New York NY 10029

WHITEBOOK, DENA KOENIGSBERG, psychotherapist; b. N.Y.C.; d. Louis and Yetta (Shapiro) Koenigsberg; B.A., Hunter Coll., N.Y.C., 1940; M.A., Pepperdine U., Los Angeles, 1976; m. Harold Plant, Oct. 30, 1943; children—Janet G., Richard P.; m. 2d, Edward F. Whitebook, Dec. 14, 1963. Sch. tchr., N.Y.C., 1945-47; crisis therapist Los Angeles Suicide Prevention Center, 1964-76; instr. UCLA Extension, 1975-77; pvt. practice psychotherapy, Beverly Hills, Calif., 1977—; dir. counseling Am. Inst. Family Relations, Los Angeles, 1978—; tchr. human sexuality, clin. supr. LaVerne (Calif.) U. Extension, 1980—; radio and TV panelist, 1967—; cons. in field. Mem. Am. Assn. Marriage and Family Therapists, Am. Assn. Sex Therapists, Educators and Counselors, Assn. Humanistic Psychology, Am. Assn. Suicidology, Internat. Assn. Suicide Prevention, Calif. Assn. Marriage and Family Therapists. Home: 320 N Maple Dr Beverly Hills CA 90210 Office: 5287 Sunset Blvd Los Angeles CA 90027 also 9025 Wilshire Blvd Beverly Hills CA 90211

WHITEHEAD, LENORE RUTH, genealogist; b. Friendsville, Tenn., June 14, 1917; d. James Alexander and Elizabeth Susan (Burns) Ridings; student Maryville Coll., 1936-38, Am. U., 1969; cert. genealogist Bd. Cert. Genealogists, 1975; m. Daniel Lee Whitehead, Feb. 14, 1938; children—Barbara Jean, Daniel Lee, Patricia Gail. Pvt. geneal. cons., Export, Pa., 1970—; tchr. adult edn. classes, Sr. Citizens Center, 1978-79. Mem. Republican Town Com., 1962-64, chmn. Franklin Twp. Com., 1964-66. Mem. DAR (state chmn. geneal. records com., 1974-79, state registrar), Nat. Geneal. Soc., Geneal. Soc. Pa., Western Pa. Geneal. Soc., Daughters Am. Colonists, Huguenot Soc., Colonial Dames XV11 Century (life promoter) Children Am. Revolution. Republican. Mem. United Ch. of Christ. Author: Pennsylvania Revolutionary War Pensioners, 1976. Address: Roundtop Rd RD 3 Export PA 15632

WHITEHEAD, ROSA LEA NEWMAN, mayor, journalist; b. Kimberly, Idaho, Oct. 28, 1925; d. Christian Jorgensen and Hattie Olive (Brown) Newman; student Coll. of Idaho, 1943-44; m. Donald R. Whitehead, Dec. 22, 1944; children—James D., H. Bruce. Co-owner Kimberly Drug Co., 1946—, with Weight Watchers of So. Idaho, 1971-75; co-owner, operator East County Chronicle, Kimberly, 1982—; mayor City of Kimberly, 1980—. Mem. Kimberly C. of C. (named Good Neighbor of Yr. 1979, past pres.), Assn. Idaho Cities. Methodist. Clubs: Twin Falls Soroptimists (past pres.), Eastern Star, Social Order of Beauceant, Daus. of Nile (pres. Zenobia Club 2). Office: City of Kimberly Kimberly ID 83341

WHITEHOUSE, MARTHA JO, physician; b. Lexington, Ky., Sept. 23, 1946; d. Scott and Elizabeth (Foley) W.; B.S., U. So. Calif., 1966; M.D., U. Calif., San Francisco, 1970; m. E. Michael Heffernan. Intern, U. Vt., 1970-71; fellow in rheumatology U. Calif., San Francisco, 1971-73, resident, 1973-75, asst. clin. prof. dept. medicine, ambulatory and community medicine, 1975—; internist San Mateo Med. Clinic. Mem. Calif. Med. Assn., No. Calif. Assn. Rheumatologists. Home: 151 Upper Terr San Francisco CA 94117

WHITEHURST, MARION ARD, genealogist; b. West Palm Beach, Fla., Apr. 9, 1935; d. Euzema Garrison and Katherine (Stewart) Ard; B.S. in Social Welfare, Fla. State U., 1957; postgrad. in indsl. mgmt. Clemson U., 1979; m. Clinton Howard Whitehurst, Jr., Mar. 2, 1957; children—Elizabeth Leech, Clinton Howard III. Tchr. English, Greene County (Va.) Sch. System, 1958-60; genealogist, Clemson, S.C., 1962—; instr. continuing edn. program in geneal. research Clemson U., 1980—. Vol. genealogist DAR Hdqrs., Washington, 1974-75; charter mem. Clemson Republican Woman's Club, 1964, sec., 1964, co-chmn. reelect Thurmond com., 1966, fin. chmn., 1979—; bd. dirs. Old Ninety Six council Girl Scouts U.S.A., 1963-67, Tamassee DAR Sch., 1971-74; chmn. S.C. DAR Mus. Com., 1976-79; chpt. regent DAR, 1976-79; pres. local chpt. UDC, 1967-69, 75-77, S.C. registrar, 1976-78; mem. S.C. Gov.'s Fine Arts Com.; mem. Ft. Hill Com. Recipient Thanks Badge, Girl Scouts U.S.A., 1972. Mem. Nat. Geneal. Soc., S.C. Geneal. Soc., Pendleton Hist. Soc., Found. for Historic Restoration, Huguenot Soc. Washington, Delta Gamma. Episcopalian. Co-author: Confederate Soldiers Buried at Old Stone Church, 1981. Home: Box 47 Clemson SC 29631

WHITEMAN, MARIJANE KELLY, computer co. exec.; b. N.Y.C., Mar. 23, 1935; d. James C. and Margaret M. (McGoldrick) Kelly; B.S., A.B., St. John's U., Jamaica, N.Y., 1956; m. John Whiteman; children by previous marriage—Michael John McDonough, Kelly Ann McDonough, Patricia McDonough; stepchildren—David Whiteman, Andrew Whiteman. Systems engr. IBM Corp., N.Y.C., 1956-61; ind. cons., 1962-69; with Mini Computer Systems Inc., Elmsford, N.Y., 1970—, sr. v.p. software research and devel., 1975—, also dir.; dir. Mini Computer Systems U.K., Mini Computer Systems France; lectr. St. John's U. Mem. Am. Mgmt. Assn., Data Processing Mgmt. Assn. Roman Catholic.

Home: 12 South Ln Chappaqua NY 10514 Office: 399 Fairview Park Dr Elmsford NY 10530

WHITESIDES, ELIZABETH IGLER (MRS. LAWSON EWING WHITESIDES), lawyer, club woman; b. Glendale, Ohio, Oct. 12, 1910; d. Herman Einhaus and Matilda (Voegtle) Igler; LL.B., U. Cin., 1932, J.D., 1967; m. Lawson Ewing Whitesides, June 29, 1935; children—Elizabeth Lawson (Mrs. David Garth Holdsworth), Lawson Ewing. Admitted to Ohio bar, 1932, U.S. Supreme Ct., 1968; pvt. practice law, Cincinnati, 1932—. Mem. Cin. Woman's Club; Town Club, Cin., mem. Glendale Lyceum; pres. Monday Class, Glendale, 1948-49, Glendale Village Gardeners, 1966-67. Mem. Cin. Council on World Affairs. Mem. Cin., Ky. hist. socs., Cin. Bar Assn., Order of Coif, Phi Delta Delta, Kappa Alpha Theta (pres. Cin. alumnae 1954-55). Episcopalian. Address: 840 Woodbine Ave Glendale Cincinnati OH 45246

WHITE-WARE, GRACE ELIZABETH, educator; b. St. Louis, Oct. 5, 1921; d. James Eathel, Sr. and Madree (Penn) White; B.A. in Edn., H.B. Stowe Tchrs. Coll., 1943; divorced; 1 son, James Otis Ware II (Oloye Kunle Adeyemon). Mgr. advt. Superior Press, St. Louis, 1935-39; tri-owner, v.p. Carolina Oil Co., St. Louis, 1938-42; with pub. relations Triangle Press, St. Louis, 1939-47, sales promotion, 1939-47; account supr. overtime payroll Bell Tel. Labs., Inc., N.Y.C., 1943-46; tchr. Dunbar Elem. Sch., St. Louis, 1946-47, Garfield Elem. Sch., Chgo., 1948-49, Betsy Ross Elem. Sch., Chgo., 1950-51, Lincoln Sch., Richmond, Mo., 1951, Dunbar Sch., Kinlock, Mo., 1952, Gladstone Elem. Sch., Cleve., 1954-61, Quincy Elem. Sch., Cleve., 1961-78, W.H. Brett Elem. Sch., Euclid Park, Ohio, 1979—; head tchr. Head Start program, 1965; adult edn. tchr. Cleve. Bd. Edn., 1965—; tchr. TV Tonight Sch., lessons for adults, Cleve., 1972; tri-owner, v.p., social editor Style mag., St. Louis, 1947-49; owner/mgr. Wentworth Record Distbrs., Chgo., 1947-51; supr. accounts receivable div. Spiegel, Inc., Chgo., 1947-52; radio panelist Calling All Americans, Cleve., 1957-58; sec. bd. dirs. Hough Pub. Co., also Hough Area Devel. Corp., Cleve., 1968-69. Mem. child devel. parent bd. Greater Cleve. Neighborhood Centers Assn.; mem. fund raising com. Food First Program, co-chmn. woman's aux. Black Econ. Union, Cleve.; vice chmn. Cleve. com. Youth for Understanding Teenage Program; mem. Cleve. Council Human Relations; mem. Cleve. chpt. CORE; charter mem., fin. sec. Tots and Teens, Inc.; treas. Jr. Women's Civic League; mem. Cleve. bd. Afro-Am. Cultural and Hist. Soc.; women's aux. bd. Talbert Clinic and Day Care Center, Cleve.; adv. bd. Langston Hughes Library; mem. Forest City Hosp. Aux. Bd., also Women's Aux. Com. Forest City Hosp.; scholarship com. Women's Allied Arts Assn. Greater Cleve., 1972-74 Mem. spl. com. Lake Erie council Girl Scouts U.S.A., 1982—. Named Most Outstanding Vol. of Year, N.Y. Fedn. Settlements, 1944, Leading Tchr. of Community, Cleve. Call and Post, weekly newspaper, 1958; recipient Martha Holden Jennings scholar award Martha Holden Jennings Found., Cleve., 1966-67, Spl. Outstanding Tchrs. award, 1973; Outstanding Service award Black Econ. Union, 1970; Cert. of Appreciation, City of Cleve., 1973. Mem. Ohio, Cleve. edn. assns., Nat. Assn. Public Sch. Adult Edn., NAACP, Phillis Wheatley Assn., Moreland Community Assn., Nat. Council Negro Women, Phi Delta Kappa (1st v.p. Cleve. 1971-73, Outstanding Achievement award 1975), Delta Sigma Theta (pres. Cleve. 1969-73), Delta Kappa Gamma, Eta Phi Beta (regional treas. 1979-83). Democrat. Clubs: Novelette Bridge (pres. Cleve. 1973-77), Arewa Du-Du Bridge (treas. 1980—). Home: 14701 Milverton Rd Cleveland OH 44120

WHITING, SUSAN FRANCES, hosp. public relations adminstr.; b. St. Cloud, Minn., July 6, 1945; d. Daniel Malachy and Mary Frances (Helget) Higgins; B.A. in Speech and Theatre Arts/Journalism, Mankato (Minn.) State U., 1967; m. Ward Harrison Whiting, May 25, 1968; children—Edward James, Ian Daniel. Copywriter, Better Homes and Gardens, Des Moines, 1967-68; asst. editor IBM, Rochester, Minn., 1968-70; publs. editor, dir. pubic relations Hubbard Milling Co., Mankato, 1970-73; instr. speech, dir. pubic relations Ohio No. U., Ada, 1973-79; dir. public relations St. Luke's Hosp., Maumee, Ohio, 1979—. Mem. AAUW, Women in Communications, Public Relations Soc. Am., Am. Soc. Hosp. Public Relations, Ohio Soc. Hosp. Public Relations, Am. Mktg. Assn. Roman Catholic. Office: 5901 Monclova Rd Maumee OH 43537

WHITLEY, EDYTHE JOHNS RUCKER, genealogist-historian; b. Rural Rutherford County, Tenn., Nov. 3, 1900; d. Archibald Edmondson and Clara Gibson (Johns) Rucker; student Middle Tenn. Coll., 1916-18, Draughon's Bus. Coll., 1918, Blackstone Law Sch., 1930-31, Internat. U., 1929; m. Albert Boyd Whitley, June 25, 1919; children—Sarah Frances Whitley Dillon, Mary Anderson Whitley Hopton, Lillian Boyd Whitley Matamoroz. Genealogist-historian. Mem. DAR (parliamentarian Gen. Francis Nash chpt., state chmn. hist. markers), Magna Charta Dames (state v.p., parliamentarian Middle Tenn. chpt.), U.S. Daus. War 1812 (parliamentarian Nickajack chpt.), Soc. Preservation Va. Antiquity, Hermitage Assn. (life), Sam Davis Assos. (life). Republican. Mem. Christian Ch. Clubs: Order Eastern Star, White Shrine. Author: Sam Davis, Confederate Hero, Coleman's Scouts, 1971; Tennessee Genealogical Records, 1980; The Muster Roll of the Tennessee Soldiers in War of 1812, 1980; Red River Settlers, Montgomery, Robertson and Sumner Counties, Tenn., 1980; also books on county records, including: Tennessee County Records, Archives and Counties, 1980; Marriages of Sumner County, Tennessee, 1787-1838, 1980; Early Marriages of Robertson County, Tennessee, 1980; Marriages of Maury County, Tenn., 1982; Marriages of Williamson County, Tenn., 1982; Marriages of Grainger County, Tenn., 1982. Home and Office: 1604 S Observatory Dr Nashville TN 37215

WHITLEY, ELIZABETH DURRELL, mem. staff U.S. Congress; b. Kiowa County, Okla., May 2, 1953; d. Jesse W. and Ann (Marshall) W.; B.A. in Polit. Sci. and Am. History, Sweet Briar (Va.) Coll., 1975. Staff asst. scheduling office Office of the Vice Pres., Washington, 1973-74; legis. liaison Cook Industries, 1975-77; dir. scheduling John Warner for Senate campaign, Va., 1978; asst. dir., congressional liaison AIA, 1979; legis. dir. Office of U.S. Congressman Barry M. Goldwater, Jr., Washington, 1980—; researcher polit. campaigns; fund raiser. Bd. dirs. Am. Council Young Polit. Leaders, 1981-82; chmn. Sweet Briar Washington Job Resources Council, 1975-77. Mem. Women in Govt. Relations, Sweet Briar Alumnae Assn. Republican. Presbyterian. Club: Capitol Hill. Office: 2240 Rayburn House Office Bldg Washington DC 20515

WHITLOCK, MARY ELLEN JENKINS (MRS. DOUGLAS WHITLOCK), social worker, travel cons.; b. Brownville, Nebr., Sept. 3, 1906; d. John Crisler and Mabel (Sapp) Jenkins; student Sullins Coll., 1923-24, Ferris Inst., 1924; A.B., Ind. U., 1927; m. Douglas Whitlock, June 18, 1929; children—Douglas Whitlock II, Marilyn Whitlock Long, Sandra (Mrs. Theodore G. Driscoll, Jr.). Case worker Children's Aid Soc., Detroit, 1927-28, head adoption dept., 1928-29; case supr. Asso. Charities Washington, 1929-32; co-owner, sec.-treas. Global Travel, Inc.; travel cons., 1973—. Mem. Women's Inaugural Com., Washington, 1953, 57. Chmn. women's com. Devereux Found., Devon, Pa., 1959-61. Mem. League Rep. Women, Nat. Fedn. Rep. Women, Family Service Assn. of Am., Goodwill Industries Assn., Mental Health Assn., Vis. Nurse Assn.; trustee Family and Child Services, Washington, 1951-65, 1st v.p., 1962-65; v.p. Episcopal Ch. Women of Washington, 1963-69, pres., 1969-72. Recipient award Alpha Omicron Pi, 1963; award Episcopal Diocese Washington, 1972. Mem. Ind. Soc. of Washington (mem. exec. bd. 1932—, award 1962), Ind. U. Alumni Assn., Alpha Omicron Pi. Republican. Episcopalian (vestrywoman 1968-71, 74-79). Clubs: Little Garden (pres. 1938-40), Wednesday (pres. 1940-42) (Sandy Spring, Md.); Internat. Neighbors (1st pres. 1956-58)) (Washington); Women of St. Thomas (pres. 1960-62). Home: The Westchester Apt 504-B 4000 Cathedral Ave NW Washington DC 20016

WHITLOCK, RUTH HENDRICKS SUMMERS, music educator; b. McAllen, Tex., May 10, 1934; d. Harold Glen and Lucile (McKee) Hendricks; B.A. (Theodore Presser scholar), Newcomb Coll., New Orleans, 1955; M.A., Occidental Coll., Los Angeles, 1970; Ph.D. (Mu Phi Epsilon grantee), N. Tex. State U., 1981; m. Robert Edward Whitlock, Jr., June 2, 1972; 1 son, Hal; stepchildren—Karen, Robert Edward, III. Music tchr., choral dir., supr. Tex. public schs., 1955-73; teaching fellow music edn. and choral music. N. Tex. State U., 1973-75; asst. prof. music edn. Tex. Christian U., Ft. Worth, 1975—; tchr. clinics and workshops. Mem. Music Educators Nat. Conf., Am. Choral Dirs. Assn., Tex. Music Educators Conf., Tex. Music Educators Assn., Tex. Choral Dirs. Assn., Pi Kappa Lambda, Mu Phi Epsilon (Outstanding Faculty award 1979). Republican. Episcopalian. Author: Choral Insights-General Edition, 1982; Choral Insights-Renaissance Edition, 1982. Editor: Handbook for the Development of the Choral Music Program, 1982. Home: 2712 6th Ave Fort Worth TX 76110 Office: Dept Music Tex Christian U Fort Worth TX 76129

WHITLOCK, SYLVIA VERONICA, ednl. adminstr.; b. N.Y.C., Apr. 28, 1935; d. James Egerton and Clarice Virginia (Foster) Alexander; B.A. in Psychology, Hunter Coll., 1967; M.A. with honors in Edn., Calif. Poly. Inst., 1974; Ph.D. with honors in Edn. (Univ. fellow 1977-78, United Meth. Ch. Bd. Higher Edn. fellow 1977-78), Claremont Grad. Sch. Edn., 1978; children—Arlan Heron, Meredith Lynne, B.G. Edward. Payroll clk. City of N.Y., 1959; statistician UN, N.Y.C., 1959-67; social worker Los Angeles County (Calif.), 1968-69; tchr. Ontario-Montclair Sch. Dist., 1967-78; tchr., adminstr., coordinator instrn. San Bernardino (Calif.) Unified Sch. Dist., 1978—; lectr. U. Calif., Riverside, Calif. Poly. U.; program reviewer Calif. Dept. Edn.; tng. cons. Bd. dirs. Sickle Cell Found. Inland Counties, 1980-81. Mem. Delta Kappa Gamma, Pi Lambda Theta. Methodist. Clubs: Zonta, Campfire. Author reading program for disadvantaged students, 1974; research on multicultural edn. for tchrs., 1978. Office: 777 N F St San Bernardino CA 92410

WHITLOW, MARION VIRGINIA, educator; b. Johnstown, Pa., May 17, 1929; d. William Sercy and Mary Thelma (Hill) Holton; diploma in nursing St. Francis Hosp., Pitts. 1950; B.S. in Nursing, U. Pitts. 1966; M.S., U. Ind.-Purdue U., Indpls., 1977; m. Emery Whitlow, June 28, 1969; children—Cecily Patterson, Gary Patterson, Carol Patterson Upshur. Staff nurse St. Francis Hosp., 1950-52; staff nurse Mercy Hosp., Johnstown, 1956-58, 60-65, instr. pediatrics, 1966-69; assoc. prof. nursing Purdue U., Westville, Ind., 1980—. Mem. AAUW, Am. Nurses Assn., Am. Black Nurses Assn., Harriet Tubman Nurse Assn. Michigan City (organizer), NAACP (sec. Michigan City 1971-73), Sigma Theta Tau. Democrat. Mem. African Methodist Episcopal Ch. Office: Purdue University North Central Westville IN 46390

WHITMAN, GAIL FELICIA, obstetrician/gynecologist; b. Gary, Ind., Sept. 15, 1949; d. David Myers and Annie Margaret (Mott) W.; B.A., U. Chgo., 171, M.D., 1976. Resident in ob-gyn U. Chgo. Hosps. and Clinics/Chgo. Lying-In Hosp., 1976-80; staff obstetrician-gynecologist Hyde Park-Kenwood Community Health Center, Chgo., 1980—; clin. instr. dept. ob-gyn Pritzker Sch. Medicine, U. Chgo., 1980—; dir. young mothers' obstet. program Chgo. Lying-In-Hosp., 1980—; pvt. practice ob-gyn, Chgo., 1980—. Mem. exec. com. bd. mgrs. Chgo. Boys' Clubs; vice-chmn. First Congressional Dist. Health Task Force. Diplomate Nat. Bd. Med. Examiners. La Verne Noyes scholar, 1972-76; Nat. Med. fellow, 1972-73; recipient Searle Chemistry award, 1968. Jr. fellow Am. Coll. Ob-Gyn; mem. Chgo. Med. Soc., Ill. Med. Soc., AMA, Cook County Physicians Assn., Prairie State Med. Soc., Nat. Med. Assn., Internat. Soc. Psychosomatic Ob-Gyn, U. Chgo. Alumni Assn., Chgo. Urban League, St. Jude League, Alpha Kappa Alpha, Alpha Gamma Pi. Mem. United Ch. of Christ. Office: 1515 E 52d Pl Chicago IL 60615

WHITMAN, KATHRYN ELIZABETH, nursing home adminstr.; b. Drewsville, N.H., Aug. 23, 1935; d. Ralph Erwin and Emma Mariam (Galloway) Whitman; R.N., Children's Hosp., 1957; diploma New Eng. Peabody Home for Crippled Children, 1954; cert. Northeastern U., 1961, Quinsigamond Community Coll., 1965; Boston U., 1966. Head nurse Children's Hosp., Boston, 1957-58, clin. instr., 1958-59; asst. adminstr. Grangers Nursing Home, Northboro, Mass., 1959-61; owner, adminstr. Grangers Nursing Home, 1961—; mem. adv. bd. Assabet Regional Vocat. Lic. Practical Nursing Sch., 1969—, chmn., 1969-75. Pres., Northboro Bus. Assn., 1964-65, 68-69; mem. adv. bd. Northboro Citizens Adv. Bd., 1969-81, chmn., 1969-70, 75-76, 78-79. Mem. Am. Coll. Nursing Home Adminstrs., Mass. Coll. Nursing Home Adminstrs., Mass. Mental Health Nursing Assn. Congregationalist. Club: N.H. Pilgrim Fellowship (pres. 1952-53). Home: 116 W Main St Northboro MA 01532 Office: 112 W Main St Northboro MA 01532

WHITMAN, MARINA VON NEUMANN, economist; b. N.Y.C., Mar. 6, 1935; d. John and Mariette (Kovesi) von Neumann; B.A. summa cum laude, Radcliffe Coll., 1956; M.A., Columbia U., 1959, Ph.D., 1962; L.H.D., Russell Sage Coll., 1972, U. Mass., 1975, N.Y. Poly Inst., 1975, Baruch Coll., 1980; LL.D., Cedar Crest Coll., 1973, Hobart and William Smith Coll., 1973, Coe Coll., 1975, Marietta Coll., 1976, Rollins Coll., 1976, Wilson Coll., 1977, Allegheny Coll., 1977, Amherst Coll., 1978, Ripon Coll., 1980, Mt. Holyoke Coll., 1980; Litt.D., William Coll., 1980; m. Robert Freeman Whitman, June 23, 1956; children—Malcolm Russell, Laura Mariette. Mem. faculty U. Pitts., 1962-79, prof. econs., 1971-73, distinguished pub. service prof. econs., 1973-79; v.p. chief economist Gen. Motors Corp., N.Y.C., 1979—; sr. staff economist Council Econ. Advisers, 1970-71; mem. Price Commn., 1971-72; mem. Council Econ. Advisers, Exec. Office of Pres., 1972-73; dir. Mfrs. Hanover Trust Co., Procter & Gamble Co.; mem. President's Commn. for Nat. Agenda for Eighties; mem. Trilateral Commn.; mem. adv. com. on reform internat. monetary system Dept. Treasury, 1977—; econ. adv. com. U.S. Dept. Commerce, 1979—. Bd. overseers Harvard Coll., 1972-78; trustee Princeton U., 1979—. Recipient Columbia medal for excellence, 1973; George Washington award Am. Hungarian Found., 1975; fellow Earhart Found., 1959-60, AAUW, 1960-61, NSF, 1968-70, also Social Sci. Research Council. Mem. Am. Econ. Assn. (exec. com. 1977-80), Commn. on Critical Choices for Ams., Atlantic Council (dir.), Council Fgn. Relations (dir. 1977—), Am. Fin. Assn. (dir. 1979—), Phi Beta Kappa. Author: Government Risk-Sharing in Foreign Investment, 1965; International and Interregional Payments Adjustment, 1967; Economic Goals and Policy Instruments, 1970; Reflections of Interdependence: Issues for Economic Theory and U.S. Policy; also articles; bd. editors Am. Econ. Rev., 1974-77; mem. editorial bd. Fgn. Policy. Office: Gen Motors Corp 767 Fifth Ave New York NY 10022

WHITMIRE, KATHRYN JEAN, mayor; b. Houston, Aug. 15, 1946; B.B.A. with honors, U. Houston, 1968, M.S. in Accountancy, 1970; m. James Whitmire (dec.). Audit mgr. Coopers & Lybrand, C.P.A.s, Houston, 1971-76; controller City of Houston, 1977-81, mayor, 1982—; mem. faculty bus. mgmt. U. Houston, 1976-77, mem. adv. com. Coll. Bus. Adminstrn., 1978-80. Mem. adminstrv. bd. St. Paul's United Methodist Ch., Houston, 1972-75; bd. dirs., treas. Juvenile Diabetes Found., Houston, 1977; adv. bd. Houston YWCA, 1979-81, Houston Area Women's Center, 1978-79. Recipient Disting. Alumna award U. Houston, 1982. C.P.A., Tex. Mem. Am. Soc. Women Accountants (dir. 1972-73), Tex. Soc. C.P.A.s (dir. Houston chpt. 1973-75). Office: PO Box 1562 901 Bagby St Houston TX 77251

WHITMORE, ALICE WADSWORTH, author; b. Dixon, Ill., Dec. 8, 1918; d. Howard Elmer and Ruth Ella (McClanahan) Emmert; student Northwestern U., Rockford Coll.; hon. degree Centro Studie Scambi, Rome, 1977; 1 son, Michael R. Wadsworth. Works include: A Garland of Leis (poetry), 1971; Our Singing States, 1973; also plays and short stories. Recipient Cert. of Merit award Am. Poets Soc., 1973; named Poet of Yr., N.Y. State, 1975; Laurel Crown, Am. Theatre Assn., 1976. Mem. Centro Studi e Scambi Internat. (hon. v.p. 1976-77, poet laureate award 1976), Am. Adventurers Assn. (charter), Nat. League Am. Pen Women, World Poetry Soc., World Congress of Poets, Acad. Am. Poets, Internat. Platform Assn., Rockford Art Assn. Clubs: Dixon Woman's (dir. drama); Mendelssohn Music (Rockford).

WHITMORE, DORIS LOCKHART, mus. dir.; b. Haines City, Fla., Jan. 20, 1914; d. William Clarence and Alta Ann (Cain) Lockhart; B.S. in Design, H. Sophie Newcomb Coll., 1934; postgrad. U. Fla., 1951-56, Fla. State U., 1958-59, Jacksonville U., 1966, Summer Inst. Winterthur Mus., Wilmington, Del., 1980; m. Frederick Leslie Whitmore, Dec. 15, 1951. Tchr., Fla. pub. schs., 1935-44; assoc. dir. Jacksonville (Fla.) Mus. Arts and Scis. and predecessor Jacksonville Children's Mus., 1949-60, exec. dir., 1960—. Mem. Am. Bicentennial Com. of Jacksonville; exec. com. Am. Patriotic Com. Jacksonville, Arts Assembly; charter mem. Round Table of History. Recipient Elsie B. Naumberg award, 1969, 2d place for Eve award for edn., 1970; named one of 20 women who make life better here Jacksonville Monthly Mag., 1982. Mem. Am. Assn. Mus. (council, chmn. children's mus. sect.), Southeastern Mus. Conf. (council), Am. Assn. Youth Mus. (pres. 1976-78), Audubon Soc., African Violet Soc., Fla. Fedn. Garden Clubs, Kappa Alpha Theta. Christian Scientist. Clubs: Garden. Contbr. articles to profl. jours. Home: 4797 Raggedy Point Rd Orange Park FL 32073 Office: 1025 Gulf Life Dr Jacksonville FL 32207

WHITMORE, MARY, nursery sch. exec.; b. Decatur, Ala., June 11, 1936; d. Johnnie Mack and Esker Lee Blanchard; student Kent State U., Cleve. Community Coll.; div.; children—Thomas, Derek, Glenn, Carmalena, Chandra. Real estate broker, Cleve., 1964-67; owner, operator Hayden Day Care Center, Cleve., 1967—. Mem. Nat. Assn. for Edn. Young Children, Ohio Assn. for Edn. Young Children, Cleve. Bus. League, NAACP, East Cleveland Devel. Assn., Black Caucus, Women's Voting League, Bel-Air Civic Club (Woman of Yr. award 1978). Mem. Ch. of Christ. Office: Hayden Day Care Center 14901 Woodworth Ave Cleveland OH 44110

WHITNEY, BARBARA ELVIN, personnel admin. b. N.J., May 30, 1936; d. Kenneth W. and Isabel J. (Creighton) Elvin; B.A. in Econs., Smith Coll., 1957; grad. N.Y. Sch. TV Techniques, 1958; m. Richard P. Whitney, June 24, 1961; children—Patricia, Wendy, Meredith. Asst. producer TV commls. J. Walter Thompson, N.Y.C., 1958-59; market research analyst Richardson Merrell, Inc., N.Y.C., 1959-61; market research supr. Carter-Wallace, Inc., N.Y.C., 1961-63; employment counselor Opportunities for Women, Providence, 1974-75; candidate research cons. Ability Search, Inc., Washington, 1976-78; supr. spl. survey field ops. Arbitrton div. Control Data Corp., Beltsville, Md., 1976-78; cons. for exec. recruiting research, Washington, 1979—; dir. job placement service Public Affairs Council, Washington, 1980—. Mem. Nat. Council Career Women (past adminstr.), Jr. League, LWV (past chpt. dir.). Roman Catholic. Club: Smith Coll. Home: 4527 Jamestown Rd Bethesda MD 20816 Office: 1220 16th St NW Washington DC 20036

WHITNEY, JANE ERDMANN (MRS. MORGAN WHITNEY), civic worker; b. N.Y.C., July 13, 1910; d. John Frederick and Georgia (Wright) Erdmann; student The Spence Sch., N.Y.C.; grad. Nightengale Bamford, N.Y.C.; m. William Lafayette Burton II, 1934 (dec. 1957); children—Beverly Ann, William Lafayette III; m. 2d, Francisco Aurelio Gonzalez, Aug. 13, 1959 (div. Oct. 1965); m. 3d, Morgan Whitney, July 12, 1966. Com. work for numerous charities, mem. Nat. Watershed Congress, 1963-65. Pub. relations work women's br. Navy League, N.Y.C., mem. women's aux. com. World War II; adv. mem. Home for N.Y. Aged and Indigent Females; com. mem. St. Barnabas House, 1962-65; women's aux. bd. William Waldo Burton Meml. Home, New Orleans; bd. dirs. Christian Women's Exchange Herman-Grima House, Friends of the Cabildo, New Orleans, Gallier House, Royal St., New Orleans, Gallier House, New Orleans; trustee Caroline Dormon Nature Preserves, Natchitoches, La., 1968-74, Live Oak Gardens, Jefferson Island, La.; patron, bd. dirs. numerous galleries, mus. and bot. gardens. Fellow Royal Hort. Soc. Eng., Va. Mus. (Richmond), Friends of Am. Wing of Met. Mus. Art (N.Y.C.); mem. Hort. Soc. N.Y., English-Speaking Union, N.Y. Bot. Garden Assos. (native plant garden vol.), La. Soc. Hort. Research (dir.), DAR, Colonial Dames Am., La Causerie de Lundi (New Orleans), La Petite Salon (New Orleans). Republican. Episcopalian. Clubs: Colony, Garden of Am. (vice chmn. conservation 1962-65); Women Flyfishers (charter mem.); Maidstone of East Hampton; Devon Yacht (Amagansett, L.I.). Address: 31 East 79th New York NY 10021 also 502 St Peter St New Orleans LA 70116 also PO Box 1226 Slidell LA 70459 also PO Box 939 East Hampton NY 11937

WHITNEY, LEA CITRIN, personnel adminstr.; b. Germany, Aug. 5, 1946; d. Howard and Shirley (Len) Citrin; B.A., Northeastern U., 1969; m. Kenneth L. Whitney, Dec. 23, 1979. Vice-pres. Anthony Kane Assos., N.Y.C., 1971-75; v.p. mgr. employee resources Blyth Eastman Dillon & Co., N.Y.C., 1975-80; personnel mgr. corp. hdqrs. Revlon, N.Y.C., 1980—. Mem. Am. Soc. for Tng. and Devel., Am. Soc. Personnel Adminstrs., Wall Street Employment Mgr. Assn. Home: 47 Jacobus Ave Little Falls NJ 07424

WHITNEY, RUTH REINKE, mag. editor; b. Oshkosh, Wis., July 23, 1928; d. Leonard G. and Helen (Diestler) Reinke; B.A., Northwestern U., 1949; m. Daniel A. Whitney, Nov. 19, 1949; 1 son, Philip. Copywriter edn. dept. circulation div. Time, Inc., 1949-53; editor-in-chief Better Living mag., 1953-56; asso. editor Seventeen magazine, 1956-62, exec. editor, 1962-67; editor-in-chief Glamour mag., 1967—. Mem. Fashion Group, Am. Soc. Mag. Editors (pres. 1975-77), Women in Communication, Matrix award 1980), Alpha Chi Omega. Home: Riverview Rd Irvington-on-Hudson NY 10533 Office: 350 Madison Ave New York NY 10016

WHITNEY, VIRGINIA KOOGLER, librarian; b. Hillsboro, N.Mex., Feb. 6, 1927; d. Clare V. and Josephine (Clements) Koogler; B.A., Admas State Coll., 1959, M.Ed., 1965; postgrad. Denver U., 1980-81; m. Clifford Whitney, Apr. 6, 1946 (div. 1973); children—Barbara Jo Whitney Petersen, James. Tchr. Aztec (N.Mex.) Public schs., 1959—, media dir. C.V. Koogler Jr. High Sch., 1960—. Mem. N.Mex. Republican State Central Com., 1977-82, precinct chmn., 1974-82; trustee Altrurian Public Library, 1954-82. Birdie Adams scholar, 1980-81; Delta Kappa Gamma State scholar. Fellow N.Mex. Acad. Sci.; mem. N.Mex. Media Assn. (pres. 1982-83), Aztec Edn. Assn. (pres. 1971, N.W. dist. treas. 1979-82), DAR, Kappa Kappa Iota (state pres. 1959-62). Methodist. Author: Women in Education, 1977. Contbr. articles to profl. publs. Home: 502 Orchard St Aztec NM 87410

WHITSON, LINDA JO, univ. adminstr.; b. Brownfield, Tex., Feb. 27, 1944; d. Ray Earl and Pauline Castleberry; B.A. in English, Tex. Tech. U., 1966; M.S. in Ednl. Psychology, Tex. A&M U., 1975, Ph.D. in Ednl.

Adminstr., 1979; m. Robert E. Whitson, Aug. 30, 1963; children—Cristie Lynn, Susan Kimberly. Mem. adminstrv. staff Tex. A&M U. System, 1975-82, asst. to vice chancellor programs, 1978-82; cons. Spring Branch (Tex.) Sch. Dist., 1977; asst. to pres., asst. prof. edn. U. Tex., San Antonio, 1982—. Mem. Am. Assn. Higher Edn., Assn. Study Higher Edn., Am. Ednl. Research Assn., Assn. Women Deans, Adminstrs. and Counselors, Alpha Lambda Delta, Phi Kappa Phi, Kappa Delta Pi. Baptist. Office: Office of Pres U Tex San Antonio TX 78285

WHITTAKER, JUDITH CAMERON, lawyer; b. N.Y.C., June 12, 1938; d. Thomas M. and Mindel (Wallman) Cameron; B.A., Brown U., 1959; postgrad. U. Mich., 1959-60; J.D., U. Mo., 1963; m. Kent E. Whittaker, Jan. 30, 1960; children—Charles E. II, Catherine Cameron. Admitted to Mo. bar; partner firm Sheffrey, Ryder, Skeer, Kansas City, Mo., 1963-72; counsel Hallmark Cards, Kansas City, from 1972, now assoc. gen. counsel; dir. Kansas City Bar Found., 1978—. Dir., Indsl. Devel. Authority Kansas City, 1981-87; trustee Brown U., 1977-82, U. Mo. Law Found., 1971—; bd. dirs., pres. Legal Aid Soc., 1971-77. Mem. ABA, Internat. Soc. Barristers, Mo. Bar, Kansas City Bar Assn., Lawyers Assn. Kansas City (dir. 1974-77), Phi Beta Kappa. Home: 838 W 52d Terr Kansas City MO 64112 Office: PO Box 126 Kansas City MO 64108

WHITTED, JEAN LORRAINE, agri-bus. exec.; b. Sundance, Wyo., July 1, 1924; d. Earl Jennings and Valgene Bertha (Talbot) Hughes; student public schs.; m. Arthur Charles Whitted, Oct. 14, 1947; children—Kathleen Valgene, Mary Kay, Vicki Lynne, Louanne Jane. Bookkeeper, Morey Merc. Co., Denver, 1944-46, Merchant Biscuit Co., Denver, 1947, W.W. Doane & Assos., Decatur, Ill., 1947-49; with Van Horn Hybrids, Inc., Cerro Gordo, Ill., 1964—, sec.-treas., 1976—, also dir.; treas., dir. La Place Water Works, Inc. (Ill.), 1973-79. Republican. Methodist. Home: Box 166 La Place IL 61936 Office: Box 38 Cerro Gordo IL 61818

WHITTEMORE, DOROTHY JANE, librarian; b. San Jose, Calif., Nov. 9, 1920; d. Glen James and Jane Dorothy (Katz) Gordon; A.B., San Jose State Coll., 1941, cert. of librarianship, 1942, postgrad., 1952-53; m. Robert Clifton Whittemore, June 15, 1959; children by previous marriage—Stanley Allen Lawton, Shirley Anne (Mrs. Anthony Kopcych). Sch. library supr. Piedmont (Calif.) Sch. Dist., 1942-43; asst. post librarian Presidio of San Francisco, 1943-49; jr. librarian San Jose (Calif.) State Coll., 1951-53; reference librarian Tulane U. Library, New Orleans, 1953-76, acting dir., 1976-78, asst. dir. public service, 1978-80, dir. Norman Mayer Bus. Library, 1980—. Dir., New Orleans chpt. LWV, 1964-66, dir. La. chpt., 1967-69, 73—; mem. citizens adv. com. City Planning Commn. of New Orleans, 1965-67; sec. New Orleans chpt. La. Consumers League, 1972-74; active Public Affairs Research Council; mem. adv. council La. State Bd. Nursing, 1977—. Council on Library Resources research grantee, 1972. Mem. Spl. Libraries Assn. (pres. La. chpt. 1975-77, sec.-treas. social welfare sect. 1977-79), La. Library Assn. (chmn. coll. and reference sect. 1968-69, exec. bd. 1973-74), New Orleans Library Club (past pres.), Am. Soc. Info. Sci., Nat. Microfilm Assn. Author: (with others) Citizen's Guide to Louisiana Government, 1969. Home: 7521 Dominican St New Orleans LA 70118 Office: Tulane U Library New Orleans LA 70118

WHITTEN, VERA P, banker; b. Hernando, Miss., Feb. 26, 1930; d. Emerson and Freddie Pounders; student Northwest Jr. Coll., 1950; m. Bailey Whitten, May 28, 1950; children—Amy Dale, Robert B. With The Hernando (Miss.) Bank, 1951—, asst. cashier, 1968-72, asst. v.p., 1972-75, v.p., 1975-77, asst. to pres., 1977-81, trust officer, 1981—. Bd. dirs., DeSoto Econ. Council, 1978-80. Mem. Nat. Assn. Bank Women, DeSoto County Econ. Council, N. Miss. Group Nat. Assn. Bank Women (past chmn.), Miss. Bankers Assn. (mem. state trust com.). Democrat. Baptist (treas.). Home: 2135 Hwy 301 Hernando MS 38632 Office: PO Box 328 Hernando MS 38632

WHITTIER, BETH ANN, lawyer; b. Kansas City, Kans., Apr. 26, 1953; d. John Greenleaf and Dorothy Lillian Whittier; B.S. in Bus. Adminstrn. (univ. scholar 1974), Kans. State U., Manhattan, 1974; J.D. with honors (Law Alumni fellow, George A. and Mabel Kline scholar, 1975-76, asst. editor law jour. 1978), Washburn U., Topeka, 1978. Legal intern Office Atty. Gen. Kans., 1976-77; assoc. to George Rosenberg, Vail, 1978-79; admitted to Colo. bar, 1979; county atty. Eagle County (Colo.), 1979—; mem. jud. nominating com. 5th Jud. Dist. Colo., 1982—. Precinct committeewoman Eagle County Democratic Party, 1980. Mem. Am. Bar Assn., Colo. Bar Assn., Continental Bar Assn., Gamma Phi Beta, Phi Alpha Delta (pres.). Democrat. Episcopalian. Author articles in field. Home: PO Box 552 Avon CO 81620 Office: PO Box 850 Eagle CO 81631

WHITTINGTON, ALICE DUKE, utility co. exec.; b. Memphis, May 26, 1951; d. Earle Ligon and Alice Duke (Martin) W.; B.A. in Journalism, Memphis State U., 1973. With Memphis Light, Gas & Water Div., 1973—, supr. communications services dept., 1978—; instr. in field. Chmn. public info. com. Am. Cancer Soc., 1981—. Mem. C. of C., Internat. Assn. Bus. Communicators, Public Relations Soc. Am., Women in Communications, Inc., Memphis State U. Journalism Alumni Assn., Am. Mgmt. Assn. Presbyterian. Club: Gamma Phi Beta. Home: 4536 Sequoia Memphis TN 38117 Office: PO Box 430 220 S Main St Memphis TN 38101

WHITTINGTON, MARY JAYNE GARRARD, journalist; b. Monteagle, Tenn., Aug. 13, 1915; d. William Mountjoy and Mabelle Moseley (Smith) Garrard; grad. Nat. Cathedral Sch., 1934; student King-Smith Studio Sch., 1934-35; m. William Madison Whittington, Jr., Dec. 27, 1945; children—Jamie Garrard Whittington Gasner, William Madison, Anna Aven. Contbg. editor Delta Rev., Memphis, 1964-69, Mississippi mag., 1977-82; freelance writer, columnist, Greenwood, Miss., 1956—. Mem. exec. bd. Greenwood Found. Arts, 1962—; bd. govs. Greenwood Little Theatre, 1956-66, 75-82; trustee Jackson (Miss.) Ballet; bd. dirs. Mimi Garrard Dance Co., N.Y.C., New Stage Theatre, Jackson, Miss., Mississippians for Ednl. TV, Friends of Art in Miss. Served to capt. WAC, 1942-45. Mem. Nat. League Am. Pen Women, So. Debutante Assembly, Delta Debutante, DAR, First Families Va., Delta Cotton Wives, Nat. Soc. Colonial Dames, Order Crown Am. Jr. Aux. (life), Kappa Pi (hon.). Clubs: Greenwood Garden, Greenwood Country. Address: 1000 Grand Blvd Greenwood MS 38930

WHITTLESEY, SUZANNE WOOD, psychiat. social worker; b. Oklahoma City, Sept. 16, 1942; d. William and Beryl Wood; B.S. in Nursing, San Francisco State Coll., 1965; M.S.W., U. Okla., 1975; m. W. A. Whittlesey, Apr. 13, 1963; children—Mark, Timothy. Nursing supr. Doctor's Gen. Hosp., Oklahoma City, 1970-73; psychiat. social worker, clin. instr. U. Okla., Oklahoma City, 1975-78, clin. asst. prof. psychiatry, 1980—. Mem. Nat. Assn. Social Workers, Okla. Health and Welfare Assn., Okla. Mental Health Assn., Assn. Clin. Social Workers. Home: 2313 Old Farm Rd Edmond OK 73034

WHITTON, JOANN LUCILLE, metals co. exec.; b. Detroit, May 7, 1934; d. John S. and Genevieve (Shaw) Smar; student parochial schs.; children from previous marriage—Raymond, Cheryl, Stephen, Diane. Sec., FoMoCo, 1952-54; legal sec. firm Foster, Lutz & Meadows, Detroit, 1954; pvt. sec. Weed & Co., Detroit, 1955; sec. Planning Com. City of Dearborn, 1956-58; repro typist Aero Detroit, Oak Park, 1960-62; pvt. sales sec. Paramount Engring. Co., Madison Heights, 1962-64; collator repro typist Pioneer Engring. Co., Warren, Mich., 1964-73; pvt. sec. Comtel Standards Co., Southfield, Mich., 1973-77; sec.-treas. Sterling Steel Treating Inc., Detroit, 1977—, also sec.-treas. bd. Mem. Detroit Tooling Assn., Am. Soc. Metals, Metal Treating Inst. Home: 17320 Redwood St Southfield MI 48076 Office: 12200 Greenfield St Detroit MI 48227

WHITWORTH, JOHNRUTH, educator; b. Houston, Jan. 31, 1934; d. John Lewis and Nevelyn Kyle (Stanley) Ashen; B.S., Lamar U., 1970, M.Ed., 1974; m. B.F. Whitworth Jr., Aug. 21, 1953; children—B.F. III, Laura Evelyn, Ruth Ellen. Classroom tchr., Jasper, Tex., 1970-71; resource tchr. spl. edn. Rowe Elementary Sch., Jasper, 1971-73; diagnostic tchr. Sam Houston, Baytown, Tex., 1973-74; ednl. diagnostician, cons. Newton-Jasper Coop., Newton, Tex., 1974-78; ednl. diagnostician Williamson County Coop., Georgetown, Tex., 1978-79; cons., ednl. diagnostician, supr. Balcones Spl. Services Coop., Austin, Tex., 1979—. Mem. Am. Psychol. Assn., Tex. Psychol. Assn., Tex. Tchrs. Assn., NEA, Council for Exceptional Children, Austin Area Diagnosticians Assn., Tex. Assn. Children with Learning Disabilities, Kappa Delta Pi. Methodist. Author: WISC-R Compilation What to Do Now That You Know The Score, 1977; co-author: Stanford Binet Compilation. Home: 6303 Highland Hills Dr Austin TX 78731 Office: 204 Eanes School Rd Austin TX 78746

WHITWORTH, KATHRYNNE ANN, profl. golfer; b. Monahans, Tex., Sept. 27, 1939; d. Morris Clark and Dama Ann (Robinson) Whitworth; student Odessa Jr. Coll., 1957. Mem. Ladies Profl. Golf Tour, 1959—; winner more than 80 ofcl. tournaments, 1965-71; winner Vare Scoring Trophy, 1965-67, 69, 71, 72; mem. adv. staff Walter Hagen Golf Co. Named Woman Athlete of Year, A.P., 1965, 66; Player of Year Ladies Profl. Golf Assn., 1966-69, 71-73; elected to Ladies Profl. Golf Assn. Hall of Fame, 1975; first LPGA mem. to win over one million d Mem. Ladies Profl. Golf Assn. (pres. 1967, 68, 70). Address: Ladies Profl Golf Assn 1250 Shoreline Dr Sugar Land TX 77478 *

WHORRALL, KAREN SUE, chem. engr.; b. Middletown, Ohio, Dec. 12, 1943; s. Neal Vincent and Margaret Olive (Long) Farnlacher; B.S.Chem. Engring., U. Cin., 1966; postgrad. Wright State U., 1967-70, Dayton Art Inst., 1966-70, exec. program Ind. U., 1970-71; m. William J. Whorrall, June 10, 1971; 1 son, David William. Process engr. Kimberly Clark Corp., West Carrollton, Ohio, 1966-70; chem. engr. mfg. tech. div., applied scis. dept. Naval Weapons Support Center, Crane, Ind., 1973-75,; pyrotechnic prodn. engr./environ. coordinator Crane Army Ammunition Activity, 1975-81; chem. engr. Naval Ammunition Prodn. Engring. Center, Crane, 1981—; sci. instr. Northwood Inst., West Baden, Ind., 1972-73. Charter mem. Hoosier Hills chpt. Federally Employed Women, 1974—, pres., 1976, v.p., 1977-78, parliamentarian, 1975, rec. sec., 1980. Lic. profl. engr., Ind. Mem. Am. Inst. Chem. Engrs. Patentee ecol. reclamation of pyrotechnic wastes (2). Home: Route 3 Shoals IN 47581 Office: Naval Ammunition Prodn Engring Center Crane IN 47522

WHYTE, PAMELA JEAN, tax cons.; b. Kettering, Ohio, Sept. 26, 1955; d. William Kepler and Mary Lois (Parks) W.; student U. South Fla., 1973-75; B.B.A., U. Oreg., 1977, postgrad., 1980—. Ind. bus./tax cons., Eugene, Oreg., 1977-78; profl. asst. Gen. Bus. Systems Lane County, 1978-80; v.p., treas. Bergmann, Whyte & Assos., Inc., Eugene, 1980—. Bd. dirs. Consumer Credit Counseling Service Lane County, 1980—; mem. Neighborhood Econ. Devel. Corp. and Whiteaker Community Council, 1980-81. Notary public, Oreg., 1978—; lic. tax preparer, Oreg.; lic. tax cons., Oreg. Mem. Assn. Tax Cons., Nat. Soc. Public Accts., Profl. Women's Assn. Democrat. Home: 10 Monroe St Eugene OR 97402 Office: 2190 W 11th St Suite 206 Eugene OR 97402

WIBLE, JUDITH LAINE, psychiatrist; b. Portland, Ind., Oct. 7, 1940; d. John F. and June V. (Young) W.; student U. Houston, 1959-61; M.D., U. Tex., 1965; children—Pamela, Frederick. Intern, Jewish Hosp. and Med. Center, Bklyn., 1965-66; resident in psychiatry Phila. Psychiat. Center, Ancora Psychiat. Hosp., Hammonton, N.J., 1971-72, Phila. State Hosp., 1972-74; research psychiatrist Phila. Gen. Hosp., 1973-75; clin. dir., staff psychiatrist Phila. State Hosp., 1974-76; clin. asst. psychiatrist Pa. Hosp., Phila., 1976-77; inpatient unit dir. Dallas County Mental Health Center, Dallas, 1977-78; practice medicine specializing in psychiatry, Dallas, 1978—. Diplomate Am. Bd. Psychiatry and Neurology, Inc. Mem. Am. Med. Women's Assn., Am. Psychiat. Assn., Pres.'s Assocs. of Woman's Med. Coll. Pa., NOW, Nat. Women Polit. Caucus, Dallas C. of C., Alpha Epsilon Delta. Office: 13601 Preston Rd Dallas TX 75240

WICHMANN, KAREN DAWN, pharm. co. ofcl.; b. Eau Claire, Wis., Mar. 9, 1950; d. Aage Yngvar and Evelyn Arlene (Berg) Wichmann; B.A., U. Wis., 1972. Music therapist Golden Valley Health Center, Mpls., 1973-78; asst. editor Nat. Jour. Music Therapy, Mpls., 1974-76; supr. music and psychotherapy Golden Valley Health Center, Mpls., 1975-78; profl. sales rep. Boehringer Ingelheim, 1978-79, field trainer, 1979-80, mgr. continuing edn. tng. and devel. dept., Ridgefield, Conn., 1980—. Active Community Stress Mgmt. Seminar, 1981. Mem. Nat. Assn. Female Execs., Am. Soc. Tng. and Devel., Women's Working Inst. Author: (with David E. Wolfe) Analysis of Music Therapy Techniques, 1975. Home: 87 Main St Woodbury Ct 06798 Office: 90 E Ridge St PO Box 368 Ridgefield CT 06877

WICK, ALICE JOAN MEAD, educator; b. Marshalltown, Iowa, Jan. 7, 1917; d. Edward Joseph and Alice Catherine (Turner) Mead; B.S.C., State U. Iowa, 1938; M.S., St. Cloud State U., 1964; m. Robert Hobbie Wick, Apr. 25, 1942; children—Ann Louise Roettger, Thomas Mead, William Robert. High sch. bus. tchr., Keota, Newton, Iowa, 1938-42; sec., Macon, Ga., 1942-44; instr. bus. edn. St. Cloud (Minn.) State U., 1960—; tchr. night sch., Newton, Iowa, Area Vocat. Sch., St. Cloud. Mem. St. Cloud City Council, 1972-78, St. Cloud Park and Recreation Bd., 1972-78; mem. legis. com. Minn. State League of Cities, 1975-77, mem. exec. search com., 1977, Ludwig award selection com., 1979; trustee Coll. St. Benedict, St. Joseph, Minn., 1977—; bd. dirs. St. Cloud State U. Found., 1979—. Mem. LWV, AAUW, Delta Kappa Gamma. Roman Catholic. Club: St. Cloud Area Genealogists, St. Cloud Reading Rm. Soc. Home: 1720 N 6th Ave St Cloud MN 56301

WICK, ERIKA ELISABETH, psychologist; b. Basel, Switzerland, July 31, 1937; d. Josef and Martha (Gabriel) W.; came to U.S., 1964, naturalized, 1970; Ph.D., U. Basel, 1964. Prof. psychology St. John's U., Jamaica, N.Y., 1976—. Mem. Am. Psychol. Assn., N.Y. Acad. Sci.; fellow Acad. Psychosomatic Medicine. Office: St John's U Jamaica NY 11439

WICKER, VERONICA DICARLO, judge; b. Monessen, Pa., Nov. 26, 1930; d. Vincent James and Rose Margaret DiCarlo; B.F.A., Syracuse U., 1952; J.D., Loyola U. of the South, 1966; m. Thomas Carey Wicker Jr. U.S. magistrate, La., 1977-79; judge U.S. Dist. Ct. La., New Orleans, 1979—. Office: US Courthouse Room C-508 500 Camp St New Orleans LA 70130

WICKETT, JEAN LAUNER, lay church exec.; b. Fullerton, Calif., Jan. 25, 1921; d. Albert Oscar and Lulu Imogene (Convis) Launer; B.Ed. cum laude, UCLA, 1942; m. William H. Wickett, Jr., June 6, 1942; children—Anne Cross, Albert Rhodes-Wickett, Kay Ostensen, William H. III, Susan. Tchr., Bellflower Schs., Calif., 1942-43; Christian missionary with family, Rhodesia, 1960-61,73; lectr. New Generations in Africa, World Christian Mission Conf., Asilomar, 1971; dir. Bd. Global Ministries, United Methodist Ch., 1972—, pres. Pacific and S.W. Conf., 1972-77, chairperson Africa-Europe region, mem. Africa Task Force, 1976-80, mem. gen. council on ministries; vis. instr., speaker, various churches and univ. groups; trustee Sch. Theology, Claremont U., Calif., 1977—; formerly pres. So. Calif.-Ariz. Conf., Conf. Bd. Missions. Mem. med. adv. council Calif. State U., Fullerton; bd. dirs. Found. Bowers Mus. Mem. Calif. Med. Assn. Aux. (sec., dir., chmn. health careers), Orange County Med. Assn. Aux. (pres., chmn. charitable donations com.), UN Orgn., Women's Internat. League Freedom and Peace, NOW, Ballet Pacific, Am. Ballet Theater, Laguna Beach Art Mus. Assn. Democrat. Home: 631 Cliff Dr Laguna Beach CA 92651

WICKLUND, SHIRLEY MAE, librarian; b. Coleharbor, N.D., Oct. 23, 1935; d. Elton L. and Emma L. (Kraft) Peightal; A.S., Bismarck Jr. Coll., 1955; B.A., Moorhead State Coll., 1960; M.S. (H.W. Wilson scholar), Fla. State U., 1967; m. L. Richard Wicklund, Aug. 17, 1957 (div. 1960); children—Marc, Cheryl. English tchr. Jamestown (N.D.) Jr. High Sch., 1960-62, Hughes Jr. High Sch., Bismarck, N.D., 1962-64, Gt. Falls (Mont.) Dist. 1, 1964-66; grad. asst. Fla. State U., 1966-67; catalog librarian Central Piedmont Community Coll., Charlotte, N.C., 1967-70; library tech. services coordinator Pima Community Coll. Dist., Tucson, 1970—; instr. library tech. program Pima Coll. Mem. NEA, Ariz. Edn. Assn., Ariz. Library Assn. (pres.-elect coll. 2nd univ. div.), Pima Coll. Edn. Assn., Beta Phi Mu. Methodist. Office: 2202 W Anklam Rd Tucson AZ 85709

WICKS, BARBARA CLARK, town ofcl.; b. Buffalo, Feb. 11, 1930; d. Reginald Dillingham and Mary Elizabeth (King) Clark; B.S. with honors, SUNY, Buffalo, 1964, M.S., 1968; m. Harry O. Wicks, III, June 11, 1955; 1 son, Kenneth Burrows. Tchr. Am. studies Kenmore High Sch., Tonawanda, N.Y., 1964-67, Maryvale High Sch., Cheektowaga, N.Y., 1967-70; town historian Town of Hamburg, N.Y., 1974, mem. town bd., 1974—, now town supr.; bd. mgrs. Erie County Sewer Dist. 3, Southtowns Sewer Agy. Former mem. council Hilbert Coll.; bd. dirs. Hamburg Counseling Center, United Methodist Metro., Erie County Democratic Com. Mem. Nat. Fedn. Bus. Women, Hamburg Hist. Soc., LWV, Upstate Mcpl. Risk Assn. (v.p.), Botsford Family Hist. Assn., Kappa Delta Pi. Club: Order Eastern Star. Home: 39 Union St Hamburg NY 14075 Office: S6100 S Park Ave Hamburg NY 14075

WICKWIRE, PATRICIA JOANNE NELLOR, psychologist, educator; b. Sioux City, Iowa; d. William McKinley and Clara Rose (Pautsch) Nellor; B.A. cum laude, U. No. Iowa, 1951; M.A., U. Iowa, 1959; Ph.D., U. Tex., Austin, 1971; postgrad. U. So. Calif., UCLA, Calif. State U., Long Beach, 1951-66; m. Robert James Wickwire, Sept. 7, 1957; 1 son, William James. Tchr., Ricketts Ind. Schs., Iowa, 1946-48; tchr., counselor Waverly-Shell Rock Ind. Schs., Iowa, 1951-55; reading cons., head dormitory counselor U. Iowa, Iowa City, 1955-57; tchr., sch. psychologist, adminstr. S. Bay Union High Sch. Dist., Redondo Beach, Calif., 1962—, dir. student services and spl. edn.; cons. mgmt. and edn.; mem. Calif. Interagency Mental Health Council, exec. bd., 1968-72; chmn. Friends of Dominguez Hills (Calif.), 1981—; mem. exec. bd. Beach Cities Symphony Assn., 1970-82. Lic. ednl. psychologist, marriage, family and child counselor, Calif. Mem. AAUW (exec. bd., chpt. pres. 1962-72), Los Angeles County Dirs. Pupil Services (chmn. 1974-79), Los Angeles County Personnel and Guidance Assn. (pres. 1977-78), Calif. Personnel and Guidance Assn. (exec. bd. 1977-78), Assn. Calif. Sch. Adminstrs. (dir. 1977-81), Los Angeles County SW Bd. Dist. Adminstrs. for Spl. Edn. (chmn. 1976-81), Calif. Assn. Sch. Psychologist (dir. 1981—), Am. Psychol. Assn., Am. Assn. Sch. Adminstrs., Calif. Assn. for Measurement and Evaluation in Guidance (dir. 1981—), Am. Personnel and Guidance Assn., Nat. Assn. Sch. Psychologists, Assn. for Supervision and Curriculum Devel., Pi Lambda Theta, Alpha Phi Gamma, Psi Chi, Kappa Delta Pi, Sigma Alpha Iota. Contbr. articles in field to profl. jours. Home and Office: 2900 Amby Pl Hermosa Beach CA 90254

WIDDER, BETTE WIENBERG, nurse adminstr.; b. Lafayette County, Mo., June 20, 1929; d. Elmer Arthur and Lorene Mathilda (Bodenstab) Wienberg; B.S. cum laude, Linfield Coll., 1976; m. John Arthur Widder, July 7, 1953; children—John A., Anne Whiteley, Susan Jane, Scott Kevin. Acting supr. U. Mo. Hosps., 1951-52; mem. staff Arlington (Va.) Community Hosp., 1960-61, W. Jefferson Gen. Hosp., Marrero, La., 1965, dispensary 8th Naval Dist., 1965; mem. rehab. staff A. Holly Patterson Home, Uniondale, N.Y., 1969-70; mem. staff St. Vincent Hosp. and Med. Center, Portland, Oreg., 1972-78, asst. dir. nursing services, 1978—. R.N., Oreg., N.Y., R.I., Va., La., Mo. Mem. Portland Women's Union, Oreg. Women's Polit. Caucus, AAUW, NOW, SEE Internat., Am. Hosp. Assn., Oreg. Hosp. Assn., Am. Soc. Nurse Adminstrs., Oreg. Soc. Adminstrs. Home: 15095 NW Oakmont Loop Beaverton OR 97006 Office: 9205 SW Barnes Rd Portland OR 97225

WIDDER, RUTH SARAH, economist; b. N.Y.C., Sept. 22, 1932; d. Morris and Frances (Wintner) Blasenheim W.; B.S., Hunter Coll., 1955; student Mannes Coll. Music, N.Y.C., 1959-63; m. Herman A. Widder, Nov. 24, 1955; children—Lynnette, Laurette. Ins. brokerage exec. J. S. Frelinghuysen Corp., N.Y.C., 1955-63; cons. J.S.F. Corp., N.Y.C., 1963-65; prodn. planner and exec. Widder Bros., Inc., N.Y.C., 1966—, also dir. Trustee, Mannes Coll. Music, 1972—; bd. dirs. Widder Found. Inc., 1966—; pres. Hunter Coll. Campus Schs. PTA, 1969-73. Mem. Met. Opera Guild, Lincoln Center (asso.), N.Y. Bot. Garden, Hunter Coll. Alumni Assn., N.Y. State Brokerage Assn., Mus. Natural History. Clubs: City of N.Y., Musicians of N.Y. Home: 210 E 68th St New York NY 10021 Office: 1457 Broadway New York NY 10036

WIDELOCK, MARGARET, mktg. research co. exec.; b. Hollister, Calif., Sept. 9, 1944; d. Charles James and Alice Leah (Southworth) Hawkins; B.A., York U., Toronto, Ont., Can., 1967, M.A., 1969; postgrad. N.Y.U.; m. John Foster Widelock, May 10, 1969. Research asst. Inst. Behavioral Research, Toronto, 1967-68; sr. analyst Asso. Merchandising Corp., N.Y.C., 1968-70; sr. asso. Yankelovich, Skelly & White, N.Y.C., 1971-75; v.p., mng. dir. NOVA Research Group, San Francisco, 1975—; vis. lectr. York U., 1969. Mem. standards com. ARC, 1971, tchr. water safety, 1970-74. Can. Council fellow, 1969-72; Govt. Ont. Grad. fellow, 1967-68. Mem. Am. Sociol. Assn., Am. Mktg. Assn. Address: 575 Sutter St San Francisco CA 95102

WIDGOFF, MILDRED, physicist; b. Buffalo, Aug. 24, 1924; d. Leo and Rebecca (Shulminson) W.; B.S., U. Buffalo, 1944; Ph.D., Cornell U., 1951; divorced; children—Eve, Jonathan B. Research asso. Brookhaven Nat. Lab., Upton, N.Y., 1952-55; research fellow cyclotron lab. Harvard U., 1955-59; mem. faculty Brown U., 1959—, prof. physics, 1974—. Mem. Am. Phys. Soc., Phi Beta Kappa, Sigma Xi, Phi Kappa Phi. Office: Physics Dept Brown U Providence RI 02912

WIDICKER, GLENNA NELL, interior design firm exec.; b. Jamestown, N.D.; d. Herman and Janiece W.; B.S., Andrews U., 1972. Owner, G.N. Designs, Vail, Colo., 1972-76; salesperson Contract Internat., Denver, 1976-79; Colo. real estate salesperson, 1972-79; pres., owner Contract Design Ltd., Denver, 1979—. Office: Contract Design Ltd 1948 S Quebec St Denver CO 80231

WIDMAN, LINDA ELLEN, diversified energy co. ofcl.; b. Phila., Aug. 6, 1953; d. Louis and Laura W.; B.S. with highest honors, Phila. Coll. Textiles and Sci., 1975; M.B.A. with highest honors, Drexel U., 1982. Pvt. practice public acctg., Pa., 1975-78; acctg. specialist Sun Petroleum Product Co., Phila., 1978-79; mgr. internal control and adminstrn. Sun

Co., Inc., Radnor, Pa., 1979—; speaker in field. C.P.A., Pa. Member Am. Inst. C.P.A.s, Pa. Inst. C.P.A.s (chmn. industry com.; Scholastic award 1975), Am. Woman's Soc. C.P.A.s, Am. Mgmt. Assn., Phila. Fin. Assn., Am. Acctg. Assn. Office: 100 Matsonford Rd Radnor PA 19087

WIEBENSON, DORA LOUISE, archtl. historian, educator, pub.; b. Cleve., July 29, 1926; d. Edward R. and Jeannette (Rodier) W.; B.A., Vassar Coll., 1946; M.Arch., Harvard U., 1951; M.A., N.Y. U., 1958, (fellow), Ph.D., 1964. Architect various N.Y.C. offices, 1951-60; pvt. practice architecture, N.Y.C., 1960-66; lectr. (part-time) dept. art and archaeology Columbia U., N.Y.C., 1966-68; asso. prof. Sch. Architecture U. Md., College Park, 1968-72, prof., 1972-77; vis. prof. Cornell U., N.Y., 1974; prof. archtl. history U. Va., Charlottesville, 1977—, chmn. div. archtl. history, 1977-79; dir. Archtl. Publs., Inc.; editorial cons. to various univ. publs. Samuel H. Kress Found. grantee, 1966, 72-73, Am. Council of Learned Socs. grantee, 1976, 81; Am. Philos. Soc. grantee, 1964, 70; Graham Found. grantee, 1982; Yale Center Brit. Art fellow, 1983. Mem. Am. Soc. Archtl. Historians (sec. N.Y. chpt. 1976-77, dir. 1980-83, chmn. edn. com. 1976—), Am. Soc. for Eighteenth Century Studies (chmn. awards com. 1976-78), Victorian Soc. of Am., Coll. Art Assn., Soc. of Archtl. Historians of Great Britain. Editor: Marsyas XI: 1962-64, 1965; Essays in Honor of Walter Friedlaender, 1965. Contbr. numerous articles on European and Am. architecture to scholarly jours. Office: School Architecture U Va Charlottesville VA 22947

WIEDEMANN, FLORENCE LEACHMAN, clin. psychologist; b. Dallas, Mar. 25, 1927; d. Neth Lowe and Mary (Camp) Leachman; B.A., Randolph Macon Womans Coll., 1947; M.A., So. Meth. U., 1970; Ph.D., U. Tex., Dallas, 1975; analyst diploma Inter-Regional Soc. Jungian Analysts, 1979; m. Frederic Franklin Wiedemann, Nov. 1, 1947; children—Frank, Harden, Jonathan. Psychologist, Dallas County Juvenile Dept., 1972, psychiat. emergency rm. and outpatient clinic Parkland Hosp., Dallas, 1972-74, Children's Med. Center Dallas, 1974, biofeedback clinic Parkland Hosp., 1974; clin. psychologist, jungian analyst in pvt. practice, Dallas, 1975—; adj. prof. psychology So. Meth. U., Dallas, 1975—. Pres., Jr. League Dallas, 1967; bd. dirs. Mental Health Assn. Dallas, Dallas Child Guidance Clinic, Creative Learning Center, Women for Change, H.A.R.A., Southwest Family Inst. Mem. Am. Assn. Marriage and Family Therapists, Am. Psychol. Assn., Tex. Psychol. Assn., Dallas Psychol. Assn., Inter Regional and Internat. Socs. Jungian Analysts. Home: 4939 Crooked Ln Dallas TX 75229 Office: 8350 Meadow Rd Suite 162 Dallas TX 75231

WIEDEN, MARION ANNA, microbiologist; b. Cleve., Oct. 16, 1937; d. Joseph Frank and Anna Barbara (Bohac) Rusnak; B.S., U. Ariz., 1959; m. Walter Carl Wieden, Aug. 8, 1959; children—Mark David, Jill Ann, Matthew Joe. Microbiologist, St. Mary's Hosp., Tucson, 1961-63, chief microbiologist, 1963-68; chief microbiology sect. VA Hosp., Tucson, 1968—; chmn. Tucson Inter-hosp. Infections Control Com., 1974-77. Registered microbiologist and clin. lab. specialist Nat. Registry, Am. Acad. Microbiology. Mem. Am. Soc. Med. Tech. (liaison officer for VA in Ariz.), Ariz. State Soc. Med. Tech. (Cert. of Merit 1975, 78, 79, 80, Cert. of Achievement 1980; Outstanding Contbns. to Microbiology award 1981, Mem. of Yr. award 1981, state dir. 1976-79, 80-81, program chmn. 1981 conv., gen. chmn. 1983 conv., pres. Tucson chpt. 1980-81), Am. Soc. Microbiology (cert. specialist), Ariz. Soc. Microbiology (program chmn. Tucson br. 1979-81), Am. Public Health Assn., Ariz. Med. Lab. Assn., Assn. Practitioners in Infection Control, Am. Soc. Clin. Pathologists (various coms.), Smithsonian Instn., U. Ariz. Alumni Assn., Coccidiomycosis Study Group, Beta Beta Beta, Alpha Delta Pi. Roman Catholic. Contbr. articles to profl. jours. Address: 7180 N Cathedral Rock Pl Tucson AZ 85718

WIEDL, SHEILA COLLEEN, biologist; b. Buffalo, Feb. 19, 1950; d. Frank George and Corinne Ruth (Nuskay) Wiedl; B.S., Daemen Coll., 1972; M.S., U. Notre Dame, 1974; postgrad. SUNY, Buffalo, 1975—. Instr., Holy Cross Jr. Coll., South Bend, Ind., 1973-74; research technician SUNY, Buffalo, 1975-78; entomol. asst. N.Y. State Health Dept., 1979-80; entomol. intern Ohio Dept. Health, 1981; prof. natural scis. Trocaire Coll., Buffalo, 1974—. Mem. N.Y. State Assn. Two-Year Colls., Assn. Gnotobiotics, N.Y. State Archeol. Assn. Roman Catholic. Club: Notre Dame Alumni. Contbr. articles to profl. jours. Home: 141 Carefree Ln Cheektowaga NY 14227 Office: 110 Red Jacket Pkwy Buffalo NY 14220

WIEDLEA, JANE LEACH SMITH, civic worker; b. Battle Creek, Mich., Oct. 14, 1910; d. William Reynolds and Edith Pearl (Leach) Smith; A.B., Battle Creek Coll., 1933; postgrad. U. Mich., 1933; m. Clare Edgar Wiedlea, June 30, 1934; children—William Clare, Jane Reynolds, John Towle. Sch. librarian Willard Library, Battle Creek, 1927-29; desk librarian Battle Creek Coll., 1931-33, instr. history, 1933-35. Mem. Sturgis (Mich.) Public Library Bd., 1950—, pres., 1955-60, 75—; mem. Sturgis Hosp. Bd., 1969—, v.p., 1974—; pres. Sturgis Hosp. Aux., 1969-70, life mem., 1970—; sec. S.W. Dist. Hosp. Aux. Bd., 1970-74; active St. John's Guild, St. John's Altar Guild; chmn. planning com. centennial yr. Episcopal Diocese of Western Mich., 1874-1974. Named Citizen of Yr., 1970. Mem. DAR (Ames-Sturgis chpt. regent 1953-55, 73-75, nat. vice chmn. Am. History month 1955-58, state regent Mich. 1961-64, hon. state regent for life), U.S. Daus. of 1812, Daus. Colonial Wars, Daus. Am. Colonists. Republican. Episcopalian. Club: Polit. Study. Home: 400 Cottage Ave Sturgis MI 49091

WIEGAND, VIRGINIA ANN KEISTER, computer co. exec.; b. Buffalo, N.Y., July 21, 1928; d. Forest Glen and Bess Katherine (Baughman) Keister; B.A., U. Calif., Berkeley, 1962, M.A., 1966, Ph.D., 1969; m. William Charles Wiegand, Jr., Feb. 20, 1947; children—William, Cort, Ronn, James, Carley, Scott, Wenden. Asso. dir. Jack and Jill Nursery Sch., Walnut Creek, Calif., 1960-62; tchr. Lafayette (Calif.) Sch. Dist., 1963-64; teaching asst. U. Calif., 1965-69, research asst., 1964-69; asst. prof. ednl. psychology Calif. State U., Hayward, 1969-71; research psychologist Stanford Research Inst., Menlo Park, Calif., 1971-75; pvt. practice cons. psychology, Walnut Creek, 1975-77; pres. Wiegand System Design, Walnut Creek, 1977—; instr. computer sci. Diablo Valley Coll., Pleasant Hill, Calif., 1980. Mem. Am. Psychol. Assn., Western Psychol. Assn., Am. Ednl. Research Assn., AAAS, Assn. Computing Machinery. Democrat. Club: Commonwealth. Author: Social Inquiry: An Overview, 1979; contbr. articles to profl. jours.

WIEMER-SUMNER, ANNE-MARIE, psychotherapist, ednl. adminstr.; b. Ger., Mar. 3, 1938; came to U.S., 1949, naturalized, 1956; d. Franz and Margaret (Neubacher) Wiemer; B.A., Hunter Coll., 1963; M.A., N.Y. U., 1965; cert. Psychoanalytic Individual and Group Therapy, Washington Square Inst. Psychotherapy, 1975, 76; m. Eric Eden Sumner, May 24, 1974; children—Erika, Trevor. Adminstrv. asst., counselor, asst. chmn. admissions N.Y. U., N.Y.C., 1956-69; asst. dean student Hunter Coll., N.Y.C., 1969-71; asso. dean students Cooper Union Advancement Art and Sci., N.Y.C., 1971—; supr. Washington Sq. Inst. for Psychotherapy, N.Y.C., 1977-81; pvt. practice psychotherapy, N.Y.C. Bd. dirs. Washington Sq. Assn. Mem. Council Psychoanalytic Psychotherapists, Am. Psychol. Assn., Am. Group Psychotherapy Assn., Am. Orthopsychiat. Assn., Internat. Assn. Group Psychotherapy, Nat. Accreditation Assn. and Am. Exam. Bd. Psychoanalysis, N.Y. State Assn. Practicing Psychotherapists, Nat. Assn. Women Deans and Counselors, Coll. Placement Council, Eastern Coll. Personnel Officers. Home: 12 Washington Sq N New York NY 10003 Office: Cooper Union Cooper Sq New York NY 10003

WIENER, ANNABELLE, UN ofcl.; b. N.Y.C., Aug. 22, 1922; d. Philip and Bertha (Wrubel) Kalbfield; ed. Hunter Coll.; married, Jan. 1, 1941; children—Marilyn Grunwald, Marjorie Petit, Mark. Chmn. UN Dept. Pub. Info., Nongovtl. Orgns. Exec. Com., spl. adviser to sec. gen. Internat. Women's Year Conf.; mem. exec. bd. Nongovtl. Orgns. Com. on Disarmament UN; bd. dirs. World Fedn. UN Assns., also founder, dir. art and philatelic program. Mem. Am. Fedn. Arts, Mus. Modern Art, Musee Nat. Message Biblique Marc Chagall, Am. Philatelic Soc., UN Philatelic Soc., UN Assn. U.S. Address: UN Hdqrs New York NY 10017

WIENER, JEAN LESSINGER, psychologist; b. N.Y.C., Jan. 2, 1918; d. Samuel and Pauline (Sirkis) Lessinger; student Hunter Coll., 1934-37; B.A. with honors in Psychology, UCLA, 1939, M.A., 1941, Ed.D., 1960; m. Paul Wiener, Feb. 26, 1950; children—Diane, Jeanine, Gerry. Tchr., psychologist, supr. Clin. Sch., UCLA, 1939-41, 46-50, asst. prof. edn., summers, 1962-64; tchr., remedial supr. El Segundo (Calif.) Schs., 1941-44, dir. pupil personnel services, 1960-66; tchr. Los Angeles City Adult Evening Schs., 1954-60; prof., co-dir. fed. project Calif. State U., Dominquez Hills, 1966-68; cons. program evaluation, research and pupil services Los Angeles County Supt. Schs., Downey, Calif., 1968-81; cons. Nat. Tng. Inst. for Gifted, 1978-81. HEW grantee, 1966-68; lic. psychologist. Mem. Am. Psychol. Assn., Am. Ednl. Research Assn., Internat. Psychologists Assn., Calif. Assn. for Gifted (pres. 1966-67), Calif. Soc. for Ednl. Program Auditors and Evaluators (pres. 1976-77), Sigma Xi, Psi Chi, Pi Gamma Mu, Pi Lambda Theta, Delta Kappa Gamma. Co-author: Reading Is Your Business, 1959; co-editor: Manual for Gifted for State of Texas, 1978; contbg. editor Ednl. Research Quar., 1978—; contbr. articles to profl. jours. Home: 87 Carmel St San Francisco CA 94117 Office: 9300 E Imperial Hwy Downey CA 90242

WIENS-TORMEY, DIANA CAROL, office mgr.; b. Dallas, Oreg., June 8, 1945; d. Frank Preston and Esthwr Frieda (Fern) Wiens; student Oreg. State U., 1963-64. Office mgr. Boldt, Carlisle & Smith, C.P.A.'s, Salem, Oreg., 1968—; mem. career edn. adv. com. Salem Sch. Dist. 24J. Cert. profl. sec. Mem. Nat. Secs. Assn. (pres. Marion/Polk County chpt. 1977-78; Sec. of Yr. award 1973), Am. Bus. Women's Assn. (chpt. sec. 1977-78), Adminstrv. Mgmt. Soc. (dir. 1976-77), Internat. Word Processing Assn. (dir. 1975-77). Office: 2001 Front St NE Suite D Salem OR 97303

WIENSTROER, ANN TICHENOR, packaging co. exec.; b. Fairfield, Ky., Sept. 22, 1935; d. John W. and Mary B. (Luckett) Tichenor; student Cath. U., 1951; grad. Florissant Valley Community Coll., 1978, grad. Lindenwood Coll.; postgrad. Webster Coll.; m. Donald Gerhardt Wienstroer, Apr. 25, 1959; children—Michael, Stephen, Christopher, Suzanne, Michelle. Bookkeeper, Heaven Hill Distillery, Bardstown, Ky., 1953-57; with personnel dept. Hussmann Refrigerator, St. Louis, 1957-59; purchasing agt. Beltx Corp., St. Louis, 1960-72; personnel mgr., acct., office mgr. Packaging Corp. Am., St. Louis, 1972—. Am. Bus. Women's Assn. scholar; scholar Journalism Inst., Cath. U.; recipient cert. in journalism U. Ky. Mem. Am. Bus. Women's Assn., NOW. Home: 4265 Manteca St Bridgeton MO 63044 Office: 10750 Baur Blvd Saint Louis MO 63132

WIER, ELEANOR JANE, educator; b. Denver, Oct. 17, 1923; d. Ross J. and Lillian May (Winans) W.; B.A., U. Denver, 1946, M.A., 1968; children—William Eugene, Susan Kay. Tchr., Stanislaus County Schs., Modesto, Calif., 1954-64; reading specialist Colorado Springs (Colo.) Public Schs., 1964-71; asst. prof. Tex. A&I U., Kingsville, 1973; reading cons. Ednl. Service Unit No. 2, Fremont, Nebr., 1972-73; reading specialist Ferguson-Florissant (Mo.) Sch. Dist., 1972—; instr. Webster Coll., St. Louis, 1977—. Mem. Internat. Reading Assn., Mo. Internat. Reading Assn., St. Louis Suburban Council, AAUW, Nat. Council Tchrs. English, Assn. Childhood Edn., Assn. Supervision and Curriculum Devel. Author works in field. Home: 10634 St Edmund Ct Saint Ann MO 63074 Office: 200 Church St Ferguson MO 63135

WIEST, ELIZABETH HERMAN, nursing educator; b. Lancaster, Pa., July 3, 1936; d. Paul Lester and Elizabeth MacDonald (Woodburn) Herman; diploma Lancaster Gen. Hosp. Sch. Nursing, 1957; B.S.N., U. Md., 1966, M.S., 1968; Ed.D., U. Wyo., 1980; m. Donald K. Wiest, Mar. 8, 1980. Staff nurse Lancaster Gen. Hosp., 1957-63, Univ. Hosp., Balt., 1965-66; asst. prof. U. Md., Balt., 1967-74; asst. prof. U. Wyo., Laramie, 1974-80, asso. prof., 1980—, coordinator continuing nursing edn., 1981—. Bd. dirs. Wyo. affiliate Am. Heart Assn., rep. N.W. Regional Heart Com., 1981; exec. bd. Western Council Higher Edn. in Nursing, 1982—. USPHS trainee, 1966-67; Kemper scholar, summer 1969. Mem. LWV, Am. Nurses Assn., Wyo. Nurses Assn. (council on continuing edn.), Nat. League Nursing, Adult Edn. Assn. U.S., Wyo. Commn. Nursing and Nursing Edn., AAUW, Lancaster Gen. Hosp. Nurses Alumni Assn., Summer Sch. Alumni Assn. Rutgers Summer Sch. Alcohol Studies, Sigma Theta Tau. Republican. Lutheran. Editorial adv. bd. PRN Learning Systems. Home: 1930 Sheridan Laramie WY 82070 Office: U Wyo Sch Nursing Box 3065 Univ Sta Laramie WY 82071

WIGGINS, BELLE BUCHMAN, psychologist; b. N.Y.C., Apr. 30, 1927; d. Usher and Dora (Halpern) Buchman; B.B.A., CCNY, 1948; M.A., Tchrs. Coll., Columbia U., 1966; Ph.D., Fordham U., 1978; m. Lee M. Wiggins, May 23, 1955. Research asst. Tchrs. Coll., Columbia U., N.Y.C., 1948-50, research assoc. Bur. Applied Social Research, 1950-62, preceptor Sch. of Social Work, 1962-66; research assoc. Simulmatics Corp., N.Y.C., 1966-67; research assoc. Behaviormetrics, Inc., N.Y.C. and Hartsville, S.C., 1967-71, research dir., 1973—; lectr. Hunter Coll. Sch. Social Work, 1971; research assoc. Nat. Accreditation Council for Agys. Serving the Blind, N.Y.C., 1971-72; research dir. Greenleigh Assos., N.Y.C., 1972-73; assoc. in psychology Coker Coll., Hartsville, 1978; cons., research assoc. Community Services Inst., CCNY and Birmingham (Eng.) Tech., 1981—; research assoc. Brit./Am. Community Services Inst. Mem. Am. Sociol. Assn., Am. Psychol. Assn., Am. Statis. Assn. Author: Dynamics of Public Support of Voluntary Health and Welfare Associations. Home: 225 W 106th St New York NY 10025 Office: Behaviormetrics 225 W 106th St New York NY 10025

WIGGINS, FRANCES KNOTTS, psychotherapist; b. Palmetto, Fla., Mar. 15, 1926; d. Leon Owen and Nettie Ruth (Whittemore) Knotts; R.N., Mercy Hosp. Street Meml. Sch. Nursing, Vicksburg, Miss., 1961; B.A., U. N. Fla., 1975, M.A., 1977; m. Joe Willie Wiggins, Aug. 16, 1950; children—Leslie, Steven, Judith, Sarah, Anne, Joseph. Nurse, Vicksburg Hosp., 1962-64, Alachua Gen. Hosp., Gainesville, Fla., 1965-69, East Jacksonville (Fla.) Neighborhood Health Center, 1970-72; pvt. practice psychotherapy, Jacksonville, 1979—; instr. Center for Continuing Edn. for Women, Fla. Jr. Coll., 1979—; instr. DAWN program Jacksonville U.; cons. USPHS Outpatient Clinic, Jacksonville, 1979—. cert. master practitioner in neuro-linguistic programming. Mem. Am. Personnel and Guidance Assn., Am. Psychol. Assn., Internat. Transactional Analysis Assn., Assn. for Creative Change, Assn. Ind. Psychotherapists, Fla. Nurses Assn. Council of Clin. Specialists in Psychiat.-Mental Health Nursing. Home: 5470 Clifton Rd Jacksonville FL 32211 Office: 5644 Colcord Ave Jacksonville FL 32211

WIGGINS-JONES, KATHLYN YVETTE, telephone system rep.; b. Memphis, Dec. 16, 1950; d. Mack C. and Texana R. (Ricks) Wiggins; B.S. in Fashion Merchandising, Memphis State U., 1972, M.Ed. in Distributive Edn., 1974; postgrad. in Instructional Communications, SUNY, Buffalo; m. Young B. Jones, Feb. 11, 1978; 1 dau., Anaxet Yvette. Communications cons. N.Y. Telephone Co., Buffalo, 1974-76, mktg. adminstr. 1976-81, communications systems rep., 1981—. Active Urban League, NAACP; bd. dirs. Buffalo br. ARC, 1982—. Recipient cert. of appreciation United Negro Coll. Fund, 1979, cert. of salesmanship N.Y. Telephone Co., 1974. Mem. Nat. Assn. Female Execs, Am. Mktg. Assn., Curriculum Devel. and Instructional Media Club, Alpha Kappa Alpha. Democrat. Baptist. Author: Telecommunications Information for the Blind and Visually Impaired, 1981; developer video presentation Bell Mktg. Dept., 1981. Home: 22 University Ave Buffalo NY 14214 Office: 600 Main Pl Tower Main St Buffalo NY 14202

WIGGLESWORTH, HOPE WILLIAMS, hosp. adminstr.; b. N.Y.C., Oct. 14, 1926; d. Andrew Murray and Helen (Ogden) Williams; A.B., Radcliffe Coll., 1948; m. William C. Wigglesworth, Dec. 16, 1950; children—Henrietta Lodge, John, Andrew, David. Asst. editor M.I.T., 1949-51; tchr. children with lang. disabilities, 1969-71; dir. Radcliffe Coll. Fund, 1972-77; dir. devel. and alumnae affairs Radcliffe Coll., 1977-79, chmn. ann. giving, 1969-72; asso. dir. for devel. Brigham and Women's Hosp., 1979-81, dir., 1981—. Trustee Shore Country Day Sch., 1964-70; vestry Ascension Episcopal Ch., 1968-74; standing com., v.p. Trustees of Reservations of Mass., 1972-81, adv. com., 1981—; corp. mem. Beverly (Mass.) Hosp. Cert. fundraising exec. Mem. New Eng. Assn. Hosp. Devel., Nat., Mass. (dir.) socs. fundraisers. Democrat. Club: Harvard (Boston) (dir. 1980—). Asst. editor: Letters of Theodore Roosevelt, 1950. Home: 215 Argilla Rd Ipswich MA 01938 Office: 10 Vining St Boston MA 02115

WIGHTMAN, BETTY JEAN LYON, mobile home community ofcl.; b. Des Moines, Apr. 21, 1922; d. James Everett and Pearl Ione (Eastman) Lyon; grad. high sch.; m. Carl Franklin Wightman, Feb. 21, 1942; children—Carl Franklin III, Denise (Mrs. Monte C. Sims). Membership dir. YMCA, Terre Haute, Ind., 1954-79; service coordinator Island in the Sun Mobile Home Community, Largo, Fla., 1979—. Mem. Beta Sigma Phi. Home: 9 Saint Croix 12100 Seminole Blvd Largo FL 33540 Office: 12100 Seminole Blvd Largo FL 33540

WIIG, ELISABETH HEMMERSAM, educator; b. Esbjerg, Denmark, May 22, 1935; came to U.S., 1957, naturalized, 1967; d. Svend Frederick and Ingeborg (Hemmersam) Nielsen; B.A., Statsseminariet Emdrupborg, 1956; M.A., Western Res. U., 1960; Ph.D., Case Western Res. U., 1967; postgrad. U. Mich., 1967-68; m. Karl Martin Wiig, June 10, 1958; children—Charlotte Elisabeth, Erik Daniel. Clin. audiologist Cleve. Hearing and Speech Center, 1959-60; instr. dept. phonetics Bergen (Norway) U., 1960-64; asst. prof. U. Mich., 1968-70; asst. prof. Boston, 1970-73, asso. prof., 1973-77, prof. dept. speech pathology and audiology, 1977—. Recipient Metcalf Cup and Prize for excellence in teaching Boston U., 1967. Fellow Am. Speech and Hearing Assn. (cert. of clin. competence in speech pathology and audiology); mem. Council on Exceptional Children. Democrat. Lutheran. Author: Language Disabilities in Children and Adolescents, 1976; Language Assessment and Intervention for the Learning Disabled, 1980; CELF Screening Tests: Elementary and Secondary Levels, 1980; Clinical Evaluation of Language Functions, 1980. Office: Boston U 48 Cummington St Boston MA 02215

WIKE, D. ELAINE, business exec.; b. Ridgecrest, Calif., Sept. 26, 1954; d. Robert G. and Jimmie Mae (Sallee) Field; student U. Houston, 1975-77; m. Mike Wike, Oct. 14, 1978; 1 son, Mike II. Legal sec. Morgan, Lewis & Bockius, Washington, 1977-78; legal asst. Alfred C. Schlosser & Co., Houston, 1972-77, 78-81, Jerry Sadler, atty., Houston, 1982—; founder, owner DEW Profl. & Bus. Services, Houston, 1979—. Treas., Wilhelm Schole Parents Orgn., 1981—; vol. campaign worker, (Ron Paul for Congress and Reagan for Pres.), 1975, 76. Mem. Young Ams. for Freedom, Nat. Notary Assn., Nat. Assn. Female Execs. Republican. Mem. Christian Ch. Home: 4122 Dover Houston TX 77087

WILBER, CLARE MARIE O'KEEFE, musician, educator; b. Denver, Mar. 21, 1928; d. Thomas A. and Kathleen M. (Brennan) O'Keefe; A.B., Loretto Heights Coll., 1948; M.S., Fordham U., 1950; M.M., Colo. State U., 1972; m. Charles Grady Wilber, June 14, 1952; children—Maureen, Charles, Michael, Thomas (dec.), Kathleen, Aileen, John Joseph. Instr. biology Webster (Mo.) Coll., 1951-52, Loyola Coll., Balt., 1957-61; instr. in music Colo. State U., Ft. Collins, 1972—; mgr. Ft. Collins Symphony Orch., 1969—, dir., 1969—; adjudicator Stars of tomorrow, 1970; v.p. Elite Music Co., Ft. Collins, 1975—, dir., 1975—; piano adjudicator Rocky Mountain region, 1976—. Mem. adv. council Ft. Collins High Sch., 1972-74; mem. com. Designing Tomorrow Today, 1972-74; adminstr. grants Colo. State Council on the Arts and Humanities, 1974-75. Mem. adv. bd. Children's Sch. of Sci., Woods Hole, Mass., 1965—. Recipient Spl. Service award Delta Omicron, 1974. Mem. Music Tchrs. Nat. Assn., Colo. State Music Tchrs. Assn. (co-chmn. cert. bd. 1980-81), Am. Symphony Orch. League, Delta Omicron, Kappa Gamma Pi. Roman Catholic. Clubs: Colo. State U. Ram, Colo. State U. Women's Assn., Women's Guild of the Ft. Collins Symphony. Composer: musical composition for two pianos; Fantasie Romantique, 1972; Mass in D, 1981. Home: 900 Edwards St Fort Collins CO 80524 Office: Dept Music Colo State U Fort Collins CO 80523

WILBER, MARGIE ROBINSON, editor; b. Florence, S.C.; d. Mack Donald and Bessie (Wright) Robinson; A.B., S.C. State Coll., 1942; student Am. U., 1954-55, George Washington U., 1955-58, Dept. Agr. Grad. Sch., 1961, 62, 65, 66; divorced; children—Norman L., Reginald G. Elementary sch. tchr., Marion, S.C., 1942-44; with State Dept., Washington, 1945—, editor, 1962—, asst. chief documentary editing, 1979—. Founder, exec. dir., pres. Crime Stoppers Club, Inc., 1967—. Mem. Woman's Nat. Democratic Club, Neighborhood Adv. Commn. Bd. dirs. D.C. Women's Commn. Crime Prevention. Recipient Community Service award Boys Club Greater Washington, 1968; commendation from President Nixon, 1970, Sigma Gamma Rho, 1971; Action Fed. Employee Distinguished Vol. Service award, 1973; award Iota Chi Lambda, 1973. Mem. Washington Urban League, Capitol Hill Restoration Soc., D.C. Fedn. Bus. and Profl. Women's Clubs, Delta Sigma Theta. Composer: D.C.—Tribute to Nation's Capital, 1971; We Are Future America, 1972; Safe for the Children, 1972. Home: 1366 South Carolina SE Washington DC 20003 Office: Dept State 21st and Virginia Ave NW Washington DC 20520

WILBOURN-LINGLE, GALE ANN, pvt. portfolio mgr.; b. Long Beach, Calif., Nov. 7, 1946; d. Thomas Robin Young and Nada Jean (Jones) Young Richards; B.A. in Polit. Sci., Mills Coll., 1968; postgrad. Ohio State U., 1968-70; m. Ted R. Lingle, Sept. 21, 1980; 1 son by previous marriage, Christopher Bradley Wilbourn. Tchr. Johnstown (Ohio) Elem. Sch., 1968-70; substitute tchr. San Diego Bd. Edn., 1970-71; pvt. portfolio mgr., Long Beach, Calif., 1976—. Republican. Clubs: Rick Rackers, So. Calif. Catalina 38 (sec.-treas.). Home and office: 131 Bay Shore Ave Long Beach CA 90803

WILBURN, MARY NELSON, lawyer; b. Balt., Feb. 18, 1932; d. David Alfred and Phoebe Blanche (Novotny) Nelson; A.B. cum laude, Howard U., 1952; M.A., U. Wis., 1955, J.D., 1975; m. Adolph Yarbrough Wilburn, Mar. 5, 1957; children—Adolph II, Jason David. Mem. faculty Tex. So. U., 1955, Fla. A&M U., 1955-56, 57-58, Wiley Coll., 1959-60, So. U., 1957, Fed. Sci. Sch., Lagos, Nigeria, 1960-61, Howard U., 1962-64, Cardinal Cushing Coll., Mass., 1964-66; admitted to Wis. bar, 1975, U.S. Supreme Ct bar, 1981; lectr. U. Wis. Law Sch., 1975-77; atty. adv. Bur. Prisons, Dept. Justice, 1977-82; mem. steering com. Network Women Offenders, Women's Bur., Dept. Labor, 1981-82. Mem. Madison Met. Sch. Dist. Bd. Edn., 1975-77; bd. dirs. REP, Inc., Washington,

1978-82. Mem. Fed. Bar. Assn. (nat. council 1981-82), Women's Bar Assn., Nat. Bar Assn., Am. Bar Assn., Am. Correctional Assn., Am. Assn. Access Profls., Nat. Assn. Blacks in Criminal Justice, Howard U. Alumni Assn., Alpha Kappa Alpha. Club: Nat. Lawyers. Home: 11 Road 11 Maadi Egypt Mailing Address: Box FPO New York NY 09527

WILCOX, GLENDA MARY, interior designer; b. Westerly, R.I., Sept. 13, 1943; d. Glenn William and Josephine Corrine (Santos) Wilcox; B.F.A. in Interior Architecture, R.I. Sch. Design, 1965; m. Richard Joseph Milewski, Sept. 2, 1967. Jr. designer, Bus. Interiors div. Bus. Equipment Corp., Boston, 1965, designer, 1966-74, sr. designer, 1974-77, asst. design dir., 1977-80, dir. div., dir. design for corp., 1980—; guest lectr. R.I. Sch. Design, Garland Jr. Coll., Western Carolina U., Newbury Jr. Coll., U. Mass.; guest juror New Eng. Sch. Art, Garland Jr. Coll., Chamberlayne Jr. Coll.; mem. accreditation com. Nat. Assn. Trade and Tech. Schs., 1973; mem. alumni council R.I. Sch. Design, 1976-78. Fellow Inst. Bus. Designers (v.p. 1975-77, sec. 1972-75, trustee 1972-77; mem. numerous coms., rep. to Nat. Council Interior Design Qualifications), Am. Soc. Interior Designers (bd. govs. 1971-74, 1978-79, mem. coms.), Nat. Council of Interior Design Qualifications (sec. 1980-81, dir., 1977-81, chmn. jury task force 1979-81). Contbr. articles in field to profl. jours. Roman Catholic. Home: 13 Pleasant St Lexington MA 02173 Office: 100 Shawmut Ave Boston MA 02118

WILCOX, JEANNE BURDEN, publishing co. exec.; b. Lancaster, Calif., Jan. 23, 1948; d. Lewis Arthur and Roma (Mintun) B.; B.A. in Social Work, Calif. State U., Long Beach, 1971; m. Peter Gavin Wilcox, Oct. 4, 1979. Freelance writer, Holland, Germany, 1971-73; public relations asst. N.Y. Heart Assn., N.Y.C., 1973-75; book editor prodn/preprodn. Marcel Dekker Inc., N.Y.C., 1975-77; publs. specialist N.Y. Assn. for Blind, N.Y.C., 1977-79; mgr. editorial services, editor Connections Mag., Boys Clubs Am., N.Y.C., 1979-81; pres. Jeanne Wilcox Assos., 1981—; public relations dir./editor DMFA Forum, Direct Mail Fund Raisers Assn., 1979-80; editor Intermed Jour., 1980; publicist, writer, editor Motorcycle Woman, 1975-78; freelance writer, editor, photographer. Vol., Citizens for Cleaner N.Y. Recycling Project, N.Y.C., 1973-76; mem. women's prison center project ad hoc com. N.Y.C., NOW, 1974-75; mem. Women Office Workers, N.Y.C., 1974-75, Women in Transition, 1974-75, Health Right Women's Health Forum, 1977-78; bd. dirs. 15th St. Sch., Chelsea Day Sch., 1981—. Mem. Women in Communications, Women's Inst. for Freedom of Press, Bus. and Profl. Women, Editorial Freelancers Assn., Internat. Assn. Bus. Communicators. Home and Office: 130 W 26th St New York NY 10001

WILCOX, MARY ELIZABETH, nurse, educator; b. Fall River, Mass., Nov. 15, 1938; d. James Forest and Sarah Marie (Hession) W.; B.S., Boston Coll. Sch. Nursing, 1960, M.S., Grad. Sch. Arts and Scis., 1966. Staff nurse Union Hosp., Fall River, 1960, faculty Sch. of Nursing, 1960-64; staff nurse intensive care St. Elizabeth's Hosp., Boston, 1966; faculty Coll. of Nursing, Northeastern U., Boston, 1966—, asso. prof. nursing, 1973—; field faculty Goddard Coll., Plainfield, Vt. Active Boston Mus. Fine Arts. Mem. Am. Nurses Assn., Mass. Nurses Assn., Nat. League for Nursing (accreditation visitor, curriculum cons. asso. degree programs 1974—), AAUP, Boston Coll. Alumni Assn., Sigma Theta Tau, Phi Kappa Phi. Condr. research in field. Home: 30 Gardner Rd Brookline MA 02146 Office: 360 Huntington Ave Boston MA 02115

WILCOX, VALDI SUZANN, psychol. treatment center adminstr.; b. Dallas, June 20, 1948; d. Glenn Gordon and Ruth (Wright) Wilcox; B.A. in Psychology, Trinity U., 1970, M.A. in Clin. Psychology, 1976, postgrad. in clin. psychology U. Tex. Health Sci. Center, Dallas, 1974-77; program dir. Cartwheel Devel. Center, Wharton, Tex., 1978-79; unit psychologist Mexia (Tex.) State Sch., 1979-81; team leader San Marcos (Tex.) Treatment Center, 1981-82; cons. San Antonio Free Clinic and Rape Crisis Center. Mem. Am. Psychol. Assn., Tex. Psychol. Assn., Am. Assn. on Mental Deficiency, Tex. Assn. Mental Deficiency, Psi Chi. Democrat. Methodist. Home: 1505 Arizona Ave Dallas TX 75216

WILD, JANICE EILEEN, credit exec.; b. Fremont, Nebr., Dec. 30, 1950; d. Kenneth Eugene and Marguerite Dorothy (Riddle) W.; B.A.E., Wayne State Coll., 1974; postgrad. U. Nebr., Omaha, 1974-76. Phys. edn. tchr., coach Creighton (Nebr.) Community Schs., 1974-76; field rep. Gen. Motors Acceptance Corp., Omaha, 1976-79, credit rep., 1979-80, dist. rep., 1980-81; adminstrv. credit rep., v.p. 3-B Distributing, 1982—. Charter mem. Republican Presdl. Task Force. Mem. Nat. Assn. Female Execs., Am. Entrepreneurs Assn., Smithsonian Assos., Wayne State Alumni Assn. Republican. Baptist. Home: 6766 Wirt St Omaha NE 68104 Office: 2421 S 73d St Omaha NE 68124

WILDER, BERNICE APPLETON, librarian; b. Kansas City, Mo., Aug. 30, 1923; d. Victor Barnes and Ruth (Crowder) Appleton; A.B., Lincoln U., 1945; B.S.L.S., U. So. Calif., 1950; m. Jasper C. Wilder, Nov. 22, 1956; 1 son, Jasper Charles III. Librarian, Western Baptist Coll., Kansas City, Mo., 1947-53; mem. staff Gary (Ind.) Pub. Library, 1954-65, 72-75, library dir., 1978—. Mem. Ind. Library Assn., ALA, Nat. Council Tchrs. English, Eta Chi Kappa Book Club, Alpha Kappa Alpha. Baptist. Office: Gary Pub Library 220 W 5th Ave Gary IN 46402

WILDER, JOYCE ANN, lawyer; b. Mar. 10, 1950; d. Russell Roland and Theresa Marie (Beauregard) Wilder; B.A. magna cum laude, Yale U., 1971; J.D., Cornell U., 1974; LL.M. in Taxation, Boston U., 1977. Admitted to N.H. bar, 1974; asso. firm Bell & Kennedy, Bell & Falk, Keene, N.H., 1974-76; mem. firm Smith, Currier, Connor, Wilder & Lieberman, and predecessors, Nashua, N.H., 1976, partner, 1978—. Mem. Am. Bar Assn., Nashua Bar Assn., N.H. Bar Assn., Am. Trial Lawyers Assn., N.H. Trial Lawyers Assn. Office: 47 Factory St Nashua NH 03061

WILDER, MARION BURT (MRS. RICHARD BETHELL WILDER), civic worker; b. N.Y.C.; d. George Frederick and Grace (Knight) Burt; student pvt. schs.; m. John Williams Morgan; 1 son, George Frederick; m. Richard Bethell Wilder, Oct. 27, 1972. Vice pres. Internat. Garden Club, Pelham, N.Y., 1961—; hon. pres. women's com. Judson Health Center, 1949—, bd. govs., 1946-60, hon. life mem. bd. govs.; bd. dirs. Samaritan Home for Aged, 1950-58; bd. govs. N.Y. Women's Bible Soc., 1947-57. Mem. Nat. Inst. Social Scis., Nat. Soc. Colonial Dames, Nat. Trust for Historic Preservation, Am. Fedn. Arts, Huguenot Soc. Am., Soc. Daus. Holland Dames (bd. govs.). Soc. of Four Arts. Clubs: Colony (N.Y.C.); Bath and Tennis, Everglades (Palm Beach, Fla.). Episcopalian. Home: 20 E 66th St New York NY 10021 also 389 S Lake Dr Palm Beach FL 33480 And Twin Brooks Kent CT 06757

WILDER, SONIA MARLENA, statis. cons.; b. Munich, W. Ger., Jan. 18, 1948; came to U.S., 1950, naturalized, 1957; d. Joseph and Rose Wilder; B.S., Towson (Md.) State U., 1969; M.S.W. (acad. scholar), U. Md., 1976; M.B.A. (Bufton Meml. scholar), Loyola Coll., Balt., 1980. Social work asst. Johns Hopkins Hosp., Balt., 1969-74, clin. social worker, 1976-79, statis. cons., 1979—; asst. to dir. human devel. Office of Mayor Balt., 1980-81; mgmt. analyst Blue Cross & Blue Shield, Towson, Md., 1981—. Active in Sisterhood, Chizuk Amuno Synagogue; mem. young leadership council Associated Jewish Charities and Welfare Fund. Mem. Nat. Assn. Social Workers, Social Work Vocat. Council, Council Nephrology Social Workers, Grad. Bus. Sch. Council Loyola Coll., Psi Chi. Home: 4 Longstream Ct Baltimore MD 21209

WILDMAN, LORETTA JEAN, public relations dir.; b. Pitts., May 11, 1947; d. Anthony and Jane (Romankiewicz) Bonazzo; B.A., Chatham Coll., 1969; m. Gary Wildman, June 7, 1969; children—Angela, Heather. Community relations asst. North Hills Passavant Hosp., Pitts., 1977-79; public relations dir. Vocat. Rehab. Center, Pitts., 1979—; tchr. Sweetwater Art Center, Sewickley, Pa., 1979-80; asst. troop leader Girl Scouts U.S.A., 1981—. Mem. Public Relations Soc. Health Care Orgns., Internat. Assn. Bus. Communicators, Women in Communications (pres.-elect 1982, pres. 1983), Public Relations Soc. Office: 1323 Forbes Ave Pittsburgh PA 15219

WILDMAN, SUZANNE BLANCHARD, composer, educator; b. Boston, Jan. 4, 1940; d. Wells and Helen Lane Blanchard; grad. San Francisco Conservatory Music, Vocal major, 1957; A.B., Classics, Stanford U., 1958; m. Ben. H. Williams, July 28, 1952 (div. 1958); children—Helen LeRoy, Benjamin Henry. Concert pianist performing at Palace of Legion of Honor, San Francisco, 1961, Temple Emmanuel, San Francisco, 1961, Meml. Ch., Stanford U., 1962; tchr. elem. piano San Francisco Conservatory, 1963-64. Foster parent Operation Happy Child, Taiwan; active Met. Opera Raffle, UNICEF; mem. Town Com., Republican Party, Manchester, Mass. Mem. Am. Security Council, Manchester Hist. Soc., Stanford U. Alumni Assn. Republican. Christian Scientist. Clubs: Pebble Beach (Carmel, Calif.); Bath and Tennis (Manchester); Revolutionary Ridge Book (Concord, Mass.). Composer: The Governor Proposes, 1962; Five Christmas Duets for Teacher and Beginner, Preludes 1-3, Fugue, 1962. Home: 27 Pine St Manchester-by-the Sea MA 01944 Office: University Ln Manchester MA 01944

WILEN, DIANE KRIGER, psychologist; b. Memphis, Oct. 20, 1949; d. Abe Herman and Aimee (Herzberg) Kriger; B.A. with distinction, Northwestern U., 1971; M.A., U. Ill., 1973, Ph.D., 1975; m. Barry Alan Wilen, Aug. 12, 1973; 1 son, Jeffrey David. Research cons. Urbana (Ill.) Schs., 1972-73; instr. Fla. Inst. Tech., Ft. Lauderdale, 1976; sch. psychologist Broward County (Fla.) Sch. Bd., 1974—, coordinator in-service edn., 1979-80; cons. psychologist Learning Workshop, Miami, Fla., 1978; mem. state steering com. for specific learning disabilities Fla. Dept. Edn., Tallahassee, 1978-81; part-time pvt. practice psychology; adj. prof. Nova U. Mem. Northwestern U. Alumni Admissions Council, 1976—; asso. mem. Health Planning and Devel. Council of Broward County, 1975-77. NIMH fellow, 1971-74. Mem. Am. Psychol. Assn., Nat. Assn. Sch. Psychologists, Fla. Psychol. Assn., Fla. Assn. Sch. Psychologists, Broward County Assn. Sch. Psychologists (v.p. 1980-81, pres. 1981-82), Nat. Assn. Professions, U. Ill. Alumni Assn., Phi Kappa Phi, Kappa Delta Pi. Jewish. Home: 5107 McKinley St Hollywood FL 33021

WILER, LINDA LOU, librarian; b. Chgo., July 31, 1940; d. Edward and Joyce (Wengert) W.; A.A., Pasadena City Coll., 1960; B.A., U. Calif., Los Angeles, 1962, M.L.S., 1963; postgrad. in history U. Chgo., 1963-65. Sci. librarian John Crerar Library, Chgo., 1963-65; cataloger U. Chgo. Library, 1965-66; librarian I, Chgo. Pub. Library, 1966-70, librarian II dept. history and travel, 1970, librarian III in charge Blackstone br. library, 1970-73; liaison librarian Fla. Atlantic U. Library, Boca Raton, 1973-74, head reference/liaison dept., 1974—, editor Municipal Research News, 1974-79, asst. editor Library News, 1975-79; mem. adv. bd. Boca Raton Public Library. Mem. ALA, Orgn. Am. Historians, Palm Beach County Library Assn., S.E. Library Assn., Calif. Scholarship Assn. (life award 1960). Home: 290 W Palmetto Park Rd Boca Raton FL 33432 Office: Univ Library Florida Atlantic Univ Boca Raton FL 33431

WILES, ANN LOUISA, mgmt. engr.; b. Williamsport, Pa., Apr. 26, 1951; d. E. Robert and Edna (Leinbach) Buzzell; B.S. summa cum laude in Nursing, U. Mich., 1974; M.B.A., Oakland U., 1980; m. Robert Wiles, May 18, 1974. Public health nurse Huron County Health Dept., Bad Axe, Mich., 1974-76; public health nurse Oakland County Health Dept., Southfield, Mich., 1976-78; mgmt. engr. Mt. Carmel Mercy Hosp., Detroit, 1979-80; mgmt. engr. William Beaumont Hosp. Corp., Royal Oak, Mich., 1980—. Mem. Mich. Hosp. Mgmt. Systems Soc., Hosp. Mgmt. Systems Soc., Healthcare Fin. Mgrs. Assn., Mich. Profl. Women's Network. Office: 3601 W 13-Mile Rd Royal Oak MI 48072

WILES, BEATRICE MARIE, escrow co. exec.; b. Eufaula, Okla., Sept. 21, 1923; d. Loyd and Anna Viola (McNatt) Dunegan; student public schs., Eufaula; m. Newton Oneal Wiles, Sept. 6, 1942 (dec. Jan. 1976); children—Roger Neal, Myrna Lynn Wiles Davis. Various secretarial positions, 1942-46; escrow officer Stanislaus County Title Co., Modesto, Calif., 1946, Allen Mortgage Co., La Jolla, Calif., 1948-49; with Allison-McCloskey Escrow Co., San Diego, 1949—, v.p., mgr., 1966—; dir., cons. Art Leitch Escrow Co., Asso. Holding Corp., Real Property Trust Deed Corp.; tchr. escrow classes San Diego City Coll. Mem. ofcl. bd. First Assembly of God Ch., La Mesa, 1979—. Mem. Calif. Escrow Assn. (dir.), San Diego County Escrow Assn. (pres. 1978), San Diego County Inst. Trustees Sales Officers (pres. 1979), San Diego Better Bus. Bur. (dir. 1978—), San Diego Apt. Assn., San Diego Bd. Realtors (affiliate). Republican. Office: 4820 El Cajon Blvd San Diego CA 92115

WILES, MARGARET ISOBEL, violinist; b. Hamilton, Ohio, Dec. 25, 1911; d. Bertram Thompson and Dovie Mae (Osborne) Jones; Mus.B., DePauw U., Greencastle, Ind., 1935; student Royal Acad. Music, London, 1933-34; pupil of Arthur Catterall, Ralphael Bronstein, Cecil Aronowitz; m. Gordon Pitts Wiles, Jan. 6, 1937; children—John Christopher, Peter Thompson. Violinist, Durban (S.Africa) Broadcast Orch., 1940, Durban Symphony Orch., 1941-45; concertmaster Pietermaritzburg (S.Africa) Symphony Orch., 1945-51, Radio String Quartet, Durban, 1942-45; soloist throughout S. Africa, 1937-54; violinist Trenton, Princeton, N.J. and Little Colonial symphony orchs., 1951-57; asst. concertmaster Eastern Conn. Symphony Orch., 1957-71; instr. violin and viola Conn. Coll., 1957-75; condr. Conn. Coll. Symphony Orch., 1957-75, condr. emeritus, 1975—. Recipient Gold diploma in viola Natal (S. Africa) Eisteddfod, 1937. Mem. AAUP, Mu Phi Epsilon, Alpha Phi. Presbyn. Composer string quartets; editor viola instrn. book. Address: 30 Colony Rd East Lyme CT 06333

WILEY, CAROL RICHARDSON, library adminstr.; b. Flushing, L.I., N.Y., Jan. 5, 1946; d. Harry Alvin and Claire Amelia (Sepe) Richardson; A.A., Thomas A. Edison State Coll., 1979, B.S.B.A., 1982; m. Bennett John Wiley, Nov. 28, 1965; children—Jennifer, Julianne, Megan Jean. Sec. to dir. clin. investigation CIBA Pharm. Co., Summit, N.J., 1965-67; sec.-treas. Tuxford Corp., Westfield, N.J., 1971-79; dir. Watchung (N.J.) Public Library, 1980-82. Chmn. adult edn. program Wilson Meml. Ch., Watchung, N.J., 1977-81; sec. Watchung Borough Community Chest, 1977-82; mem. Christian Edn. com. Wilson Meml. Ch., 1977-81, mem. exec. bd., 1979, 80. Mem. ALA, Nat. Assn. Female Execs., N.J. Library Assn., Mensa. Republican. Home: 19 Becker Dr Lititz PA 17543

WILEY, LOY BROWN, magazine editor; b. Hutchinson, Kans., Feb. 18, 1939; d. Wesley E. and Mary A. Brown; B.A. in Psychology, U. Kans., 1962; M.B.A., U. Dayton (Ohio), 1978; m. John K. Wiley, Aug. 1, 1959; children—Jennifer Wesley, Elizabeth Kimmel. Staff editor Consultant, Smith Kline Pharm. Co., Phila., 1962-67; freelance med. editor, San Antonio, 1967-71; asst. editor, then sr. editor Nursing mag., 1971-81; editor Nursing Life mag., Kettering, Ohio, 1981—; pres., chmn. bd. Wiley Assos., Inc., 1980—. Mem. appropriations bd. Dayton United Way, 1977. Mem. Am. Soc. Bus. Press Editors, Assn. M.B.A.s, Dayton M.B.A. Assn., Dayton C. of C. Author articles in field. Office: 28 E Rahn Rd Suite 100 Kettering OH 45429

WILEY, MILLICENT YODER, educator; b. Mercedes, Tex., June 7, 1923; d. Frank and Grace Mae (Setter) Yoder; B.S., Tex. State Coll. Women, 1949; postgrad. U. Houston, 1950-53; m. William Gregory Wiley, Mar. 25, 1946; children—Sandra Kay, Patti Gayle Wiley Diamond. Choral dir., music tchr. schs. in Tex. and La., 1945-60; tchr. Kingsville (Tex.) Ind. Sch. Dist., 1960—, now also trustee; choral dir. H.M. King High Sch., 1964-80, ret., 1980; area admissions adv., adminstr. Pacific Am. Inst., 1976-80; state dir. South Tex. for Am. Internat. Edn. and Tng., 1980—; pianist Kingsville Rotary Club, 1966—. Recipient various certs. appreciation. Mem. Am. Choral Dirs. Assn., Music Educators Nat. Conf., NEA, Tex. Music Educators Assn. (dir. 1973-74), Tex. Choral Dirs. Assn. (state clinic condr. 1977), Tex. Tchrs. Assn., Kingsville Bd. Realtors, Tex. Assn. Realtors, Multiple Listing Service Kingsville, Nat. Bd. Realtors, Fgn. Study League (adv., adminstr. 1971-76). Republican. Methodist. Clubs: Kingsville Music, Exxon Bridge, Monday Night Bridge. Home: 229 Helen Marie Ln Kingsville TX 78363

WILHELM, ALISON BRADLEY, physician; b. Phila., Dec. 4, 1931; d. Edward Sculley and Margaret (Cashner) Bradley; B.A., Coll. for Women U. Pa., 1953; M.D., U. Pa., 1957; m. Frederick Henry Wilhelm, May 9, 1960; children—Barbara Ann, Frederick Henry, Pamela May, Scott David. Intern, Hartford Hosp., 1957, resident in ob-gyn, 1959-60, resident in surgery, 1958-59; resident in anesthesiology Columbia Presbyn. Med. Center, N.Y.C., 1960-62; instr. anesthesiology Georgetown U., Washington, 1962-65, clin. instr., 1965-70; practice medicine specializing in anesthesiology, Washington, 1962—; chmn. dept. anesthesiology Providence Hosp., Washington, 1978-80, vice chmn., 1980—. Diplomate Am. Bd. Anesthesiology. Fellow Am. Coll. Anesthesiologists; mem. AMA, Am. Soc. Anesthesiologists, Md.-D.C. Soc. Anesthesiologists, So. Med. Soc., Am. Med. Women's Assn., Phi Beta Kappa, Phi Gamma Mu. Democrat. Mem. Soc. Friends. Contbr. articles to profl. jours. Home: 9703 Hill St Kensington MD 20795 Office: Dept Anesthesiology 1150 Varnum St NE Washington DC 20017

WILHELM, JULIANNE, broadcasting co. exec.; b. Sondma, Calif., Feb. 15, 1944; d. Robert Gerald and Doris Anita W.; B.A., Coll. Holy Names, 1966; postgrad. Wharton Sch. Mgmt., U. Pa., 1980, Human Resources Mgmt. Program, Harvard U., 1982. Dept. mgr. Bloomingdale's, N.Y.C., 1968-71; office mgr. Corinthian Broadcasting, N.Y.C., 1977-79, dir. adminstrn., 1979-82, v.p. adminstrn. and human resources, 1982—. Mem. Internat. Radio and TV Soc. Office: 280 Park Ave New York NY 10017

WILHELM, WILLA METTA, edn. media specialist; b. Jasper, Oreg., Sept. 10, 1912; d. Charles Elzie and Margaret Sephronia (Jacoby) Logsdon; B.S., U. Oreg., 1933, M.S., 1941; m. George August Wilhelm, June 21, 1941; 1 son, Daren Lyle. Tchr., Sprague River, Oreg., 1934-35, Canyonville (Oreg.) High Sch., 1935-37, Junction City (Oreg.) High Sch., 1937-41; mem. staff bus. office Convair Corp., San Diego, 1942-45; tchr. Riddle (Oreg.) Sch. System, 1945-47, supt., 1946-47; tchr. Lowell (Oreg.) High Sch., 1947-61, media specialist, 1961—, dir. high sch. paper (internat. 1st pl. award), 1947-60. Mem. Delta Zeta, Pi Lambda Theta. Republican. Clubs: Order Eastern Star, Rebekah. Home: 85501 Jasper Park Rd Pleasant Hill OR 97401

WILKEN, DOROTHY HARRIS, graphic designer; b. Annville, Pa., Jan. 2, 1936; d. William Henry and Mary Magdalen (Kreider) Harris; A.B., George Washington U., 1957; M.P.A., Fla. Atlantic U., Boca Raton, 1979; divorced; children—Melany Ruth, Stephany Mary, Marjory Frances, Lorilee Elizabeth. Art dir. Jour. AIA, 1957-59; art editor Qualified Contractor, Nat. Elec. Contractors Assn., 1959-60; studio mgr. graphics dept. Fla. Atlantic U., Boca Raton, 1965—; cons., lectr. in field. Mem. Boca Raton City Council, 1974-78, mayor, 1976-77; mem. Palm Beach County Commn., 1982—; chmn. Boca Raton Com. on Annexation, 1974-75, Complete Count Com. for Census, 1980, Ethical Conduct Bd. Boca Raton, 1980-82; charter bd. dirs. Citizens Crime Watch Boca Raton, 1980—, pres., 1982. Recipient various civic awards; grantee Fla. Bd. Regents, 1978. Mem. Acad. Polit. Sci., Am. Planning Assn., Am. Soc. Pub. Adminstrs., AAUW, LWV, Women's Polit. Caucus, Fla. Atlantic U. Alumnae Assn., Audubon Soc., Sierra Club, Nature Conservancy, Common Cause. Democrat. Clubs: Wells Coll. Alumnae, George Washington U. Alumnae. Home: 490 NW 20th St Apt 311 Boca Raton FL 33431

WILKES, BEVERLY LAKE, lawyer; b. Boston, Apr. 25, 1949; d. Thomas E. and Ann W. Lake; B.A. in Math., Wheaton Coll., Norton, Mass., 1970; J.D., Fordham U., 1976; m. Lawrence R. Wilkes, Oct. 9, 1976. Photog. model Wilhelmina Models, Inc., N.Y.C., 1970-72; stockbroker E.F. Hutton & Co., Inc., N.Y.C., 1972-74; estate planner U.S. Trust Co., N.Y.C., 1974-76; admitted to N.Y. bar, 1977; corp. atty. Davis Polk & Wardwell, N.Y.C., 1976—. Mem. Am. Bar Assn., Nat. Assn. Women Lawyers, N.Y. State Bar Assn., N.Y. Council Law Assos., Assn. Bar City N.Y. Home: 30 Chappaqua Mountain Rd Chappaqua NY 10514 Office: 1 Chase Manhattan Plaza New York NY 10005

WILKES, CHERYL WHELCHEL (MRS. JAMES BURPEE WILKES), coll. adminstr.; b. Alma, Ga., July 20, 1944; d. John Davis and Charnell (Ramsey) Whelchel; A.B. cum laude, U. Ga., 1966, M.A., 1968; m. James Burpee Wilkes, Sept. 10, 1967; 1 son, John William. Research asst. Inst. Govt., Athens, Ga., 1966-67; asso. editor Naval Weapons Evaluation Facility, Albuquerque, 1968-69; dir. student fin. aid and career planning and placement Augusta (Ga.) Coll., 1969-74, instr. journalism, 1971-74; dir. fin. aid Med. Coll. Ga., 1975—; cons. So. regional office Coll. Scholarship Service, 1975-80, also mem. nat. council, 1978-81; mem. application rev. panel Region IV Office Edn., 1975; chmn. Assn. Am. Med. Colls. commn. on student fin. assistance. Vice pres. Augusta Panhellenic Council, 1972-73; bd. dirs., past pres. Augusta Met. YWCA; bd. dirs. United Way. Mem. Nat. Assn. Student Fin. Aid Adminstrs. (nat. council), So. Assn. Student Fin. Aid. Adminstrs. (pres.-elect 1981-82), Ga. Assn. Student Fin. Aid Adminstrs. (pres. 1978-79), Ga. Assn. Women Deans, Adminstrs. and Counselors, Jr. League Augusta, Mortar Bd., Phi Beta Kappa, Phi Kappa Phi, Phi Mu. Office: Office Fin Aid Med Coll Ga Augusta GA 30912

WILKES, HELEN TOWNSEND, artist; b. El Paso, Tex., 1904; d. Wilber and La Belle Frances (Read) Townsend; B.A., U. Calif., Berkeley, 1926; pupil of Sam. H. Harris, Katherine Shackelford, Robert Frame, Gay Maccoy, Lenard Kester; m. Peter F. Wilkes, 1927 (dec. 1969); children—Peter T. (dec.), Patricia Wilkes Wright; m. 2d, Kenneth Thomas Norwood, Aug. 14, 1978. One-woman shows: St. Mark's Gallery, Altadena, Calif., 1960, 62, 64, Main YWCA Gallery, Glendale, Calif., 1963, Tuesday Afternoon Club Gallery, Glendale, 1964, Glendale Fine Arts Gallery, 1968, Glendale Main Library Gallery, 1966; group exhbns. include: Greek Theatre, Los Angeles, 1961, Santa Paula (Calif.) C. of C., 1961, 63, Gallery Cezanne, Laguna Beach, Calif., 1972-74, Glendale Fine Arts Gallery, 1967-71; chmn., exhibit dir. Glendale All-City Art Show, 1960; gallery dir. St. Mark's Episcopal Ch., Altadena, 1957-63; coordinator Vincent Price shows, Glendale and Los Angeles, 1964; co-founder, v.p. Glendale Fine Arts Gallery, 1967; bd. dirs. Glendale Art Assn., 1955-56; mem. Gallery Cezanne, 1972—; art juror, speaker, tchr. in field. Bd. govs. Glendale Symphony Orch. Assn.; mem. women's com. Glendale Philharm. Affiliates. Mem. PEO, Group Four Painters (co-founder 1976), Los Angeles Art Assn., Descanso Garden Guild, Zeta Tau Alpha. Episcopalian. Address: 1831 Crestmont Ct Glendale CA 91208

WILKIN, RUTH MARGARET, state legislator; b. Atchison, Kans., Sept. 9, 1918; d. William T. and Ella (Calvert) Warren; A.B. in Polit. Sci., U. Kans., Lawrence, 1940; m. Donald K. Wilkin, Sept. 28, 1940; children—Janet, Donna, Susan. Mem. Kans. Ho. of Reps., 1973—; sec. to purchasing agt. Montgomery Ward, Chgo., 1941-45; sec. to owner Stokes Constrn. Co., Corpus Christi, Tex., 1945-47; sec. to mgr. Creamery Package Mfg., Kansas City, Mo., 1948-51; sec. to dist. engr. C.E., Topeka, 1951-55. Elder, Potwin Presbyterian Ch., Topeka, 1975-79, pres. women's assn., 1958-60, trustee, 1961-62, chmn. refugee family relocation project, 1979; Kans. chmn. Rhodes Scholarship Selection Com., 1976-79. Mem. AAUW, Women's Polit. Caucus, Common Cause, Topeka League Women Voters (pres. 1968-69), Kans. Council on Crime and Delinquency. Democrat. Club: Exec. Women's Forum (Topeka). Columnist, Topeka Capital-Jour. Newspaper, 1971-72. Home: 1610 Willow St Topeka KS 66606 Office: Statehouse Topeka KS 66612

WILKIN, SHARON LOU, retail exec.; b. Xenia, Ohio, Feb. 20, 1942; d. Eugene Lewis and Mary Katherine (Junk) Smith; student Columbus Bus. U., 1960-61; m. Duane Wilkin, May 20, 1976; children by previous marriage—Jeffrey Todd DeBord, Jennifer Terese DeBord. With display advt. dept. Columbus (Ohio) Dispatch, 1960-62; exec. asst. to pres. Donaldson Baking Co., Columbus, 1962-63; exec. asst. to sales mgr. Columbus Plastic Products, 1963-64; public service dir., mktg. mgr., v.p. WCOL Radio, Columbus, 1967-78; v.p. mktg. services Hameroff/Milenthal, Inc., 1978-81, sr. v.p. consumer retail div., 1981—; freelance public relations and advt. cons. for various orgns. and govtl. agys.; lectr. Franklin U., Rio Grande Coll. Gen. co-chmn. Columbus USA Assn., 1979-80; mem. arbitration panel Better Bus. Bur., 1977—; regional adv. council SBA, 1977—; mem. devel. task force, founder Met. Center for Women, 1979—, charter pres. bd. trustees, 1980—. Recipient Talaria award Am. Women in Radio and TV, 1974; named Career Woman of Yr., Columbus Citizen Jour., 1974; Outstanding Young Citizen, Columbus Jaycees, 1976; Bus and Profl. Woman of Yr. award, 1980. Mem. Women in Bus. (pres. 1978—), Columbus Advt. Fedn. (pres. 1976, Silver medal award 1976), Columbus C. of C. Presbyterian. Contbg. editor Buckeye Bus. Jour., 1980-81. Home: 226 St Pierre St Worthington OH 43085 Office: Hameroff/Milenthal Inc 411 E Town St Columbus OH 43215

WILKINS, CHILTON MINUS, accountant; b. Columbus, Ohio, Nov. 17, 1927; d. Norman and Dorothy Quincy (Loring) Minus; B.A., Mary Baldwin Coll., 1949; postgrad. U. N.C., Greensboro, 1974-76; m. William Y. Wilkins, Mar. 19, 1972; children—Beverly W. Rogers, Chilton Rogers. Bookkeeper, So. Mill Supply Co., Summerville, S.C., 1950-53; free-lance art instr. Dorchester County, S.C., 1954-64; owner, mgr. Picket Fence, Summerville, 1965-70; acct. William Y. Wilkins, atty./C.P.A., Winston-Salem, N.C., 1972—; owner, mgr. Dial A Tax Form, Winston-Salem, 1972—. Sec., S.C. Young Republicans, 1962-64, 1st Dist. Republican Com., 1963-65; mem. S.C. Rep. Com., 1963-65; del. at large Rep. Nat. Conv., 1964; chmn. Dorchester County Mental Health Assn., 1967-70; mem. Tri-Centennial Commn. for S.C., 1968-70. Republican. Episcopalian. Office: 706 1st Center Bldg Winston-Salem NC 27104

WILKINS, LUCY LEE, investment broker; b. Lynchburg, Va., Nov. 11, 1934; d. William Palmer and Lucy Todd (Hundley) W.; A.B., Converse Coll., Spartanburg, S.C., 1957. Tchr. fgn. langs., dir. lang. lab. Hermitage High Sch., Henrico County, Va., 1957-64; stock broker Legg-Mason Co., Richmond, Va., 1965-72; investment broker, account exec. Wheat First Securities, Inc., Lynchburg, 1973—; instr. U. Va., Richmond extension. Mem. Lynchburg City Republican Com., 1973—, Va. Rep. Com., 1980—; bd. dirs. Lynchburg YWCA, 1975-81, United Way Central Va., 1978-80, Jr. Achievement, Lynchburg, 1981—. Presbyterian. Club: Richmond Zonta. Home: 220 Belvedere St Apt A Lynchburg VA 24503 Office: Suite 1900 Fidelity Bank Bldg Lynchburg VA 24505

WILKINS, RILLASTINE ROBERTA, city ofcl., telephone co. ofcl.; b. Taft, Okla., July 24, 1932; d. Willie and Canzaty Smith; student Muskegon Bus. Coll., U. Wis., Eau Claire, 1972; m. Clarence E. Wilkins, Oct. 8, 1955; children—Nathlyn Roberta Wilkins Barksdale, Clarence Henry. With Gen. Telephone Co. Mich., Muskegon, 1957—, service rep., 1962-67, div. comml. instr., 1967-71, tng. office adminstr., 1971-73, contact records supr. bus. accounts, 1973-79, phone mart mgr., 1979-81, customer service mgr., 1981—. Mem. Muskegon Heights (Mich.) City Council, 1974-77, mayor pro-tem, 1977—; regional dir. Nat. Black Caucus Local Elected Ofcls.; vice-chairperson Muskegon County Regional Planning Commn.; co-chairperson Muskegon County Human Resources Commn.; mem. Vice-Pres. Mondale's Task Force on Youth Employment, 1980; chairperson Muskegon Heights Community Devel. Commn.; bd. dirs. Econ. Devel. Commn. Muskegon Heights, Muskegon Area Transp. System; chairperson Muskegon Heights Zoning Bd. Appeals, Community Services Commn. Muskegon County; past pres. Every Woman's Place, Urban League Guild Greater Muskegon; co-chairperson allocations and rev. com. United Way, 1980-81; bd. dirs. Heritage Hosp., Black Women's Polit. Caucus Greater Muskegon; bd. dirs., sec. Greater Muskegon Seaway Festival, 1980-82. Recipient Citizen's award City of Muskegon Heights, 1974; cert. of commendation Muskegon Community Coll., 1979; named Boss of Day, Sta. WZZR, 1980; cert. of merit St. Joseph's Christian Community Center, 1980; Pace award Muskegon Community Coll., 1980; plaque Black Women's Polit. Caucus, 1980. Mem. Urban League (pres. bd. dirs.), NAACP (life), Greater Muskegon C. of C. (dir. women's div.). Club: Tri-City Woman's (past pres.). Democrat. Baptist. Home: 2305 5th St Muskegon Heights MI 49444 Office: 860 Terrace St Muskegon MI 49440

WILKINSON, BARBARA ELLIOTT, Girl Scout ofcl.; b. Peru, Ill., July 28, 1931; d. Clarence Burton and Mary Barbara (Fullenwieder) Elliott; B.A., Rockford (Ill.) Coll., June 4, 1955; m. C.G. Wilkinson, June 4, 1955; children—Nancy A., Robert E. Mem. Inland Empire Girl Scout Council, 1969—, mem.-at-large bd. dirs., 1974, 1st v.p., 1975-78, pres., 1978-81. Pres. Olaf Bustad Spl. Edn. PTA, Coeur d'Alene, Idaho, 1971-73; sec., bd. dirs. Kootenai County (Idaho) PTA Council, 1973-75; bd. dirs. Kootenai County United Way, 1977—, div. chmn. fund drive, 1976—; v.p. Coeur d'Alene Federated Women's Club, 1982—. Club: Order Eastern Star. Home: 830 N 17th St Coeur d'Alene ID 83814

WILKINSON, DORIS YVONNE, sociologist, educator; b. Lexington, Ky.; d. Howard Thomas and Regina Lavonne Wilkinson; Ph.D., Case Western Res. U., 1968. Assoc. prof. med. sociology Macalester Coll. 1970-75, prof. 1975-77; exec. assoc. Am. Sociol. Assn. 1977-80; prof. Howard U. 1980—; cons. in field. Social Sci. Research Council grantee, 1975, Nat. Inst. Edn. grantee, 1978-79. Mem. D.C. Sociol. Assn. (pres. 1982—), Eastern Sociol. Soc. (v.p. 1983—), Soc. Study Social Problems (dir. 1982—), Am. Pub. Health Assn., Assn. Orthopsychiatry, Phi Beta Kappa. Club: D.C. Links. Author: Workbook for Introductory Sociology, 1968; editor: Black Revolt: Strategies of Protest, 1969, Black Male/White Female, 1975; co-editor The Black Male in America, 1977; contbr. articles to profl. jours. Office: PO Box 987 Howard University Washington DC 20059

WILKINSON, HEI SOOK PARK, psychologist; b. Seoul, Korea, Oct. 11, 1947; came to U.S., 1970, naturalized, 1977; d. Woo Young and Seung Ui (Song) Park; B.A., Ewha Womans U., 1969; M.A., George Peabody Coll. Tchrs., 1973; Ph.D., Merill-Palmer Inst., 1981; m. Todd Scripps Wilkinson, Mar. 21, 1973; children—Todd Scripps, Gina Park. Korean lang. instr. Peace Corps, Fairleigh Dickinson U., 1970, cons. Peace Corps, Washington, 1971; tour guide UN, N.Y.C., 1971-72; liaison specialist Met. Davidson County Sch. System, Nashville, 1973-75; ednl. therapist Children's Day Treatment Program, Detroit, 1975-76; psychotherapist Lee M. Shulman Assos., Royal Oak, Mich., 1978—; psychol. cons. Mich. Dept. Social Services, 1978-82; adj. faculty Union Grad. Sch., Cin., 1982—. Mem. Korean Del. to UN World Youth Assembly, 1970. Mem. Am. Psychol. Assn., Assn. Humanistic Psychology. Home: 708 Parkman Dr Bloomfield Hills MI 48013 Office: 751 Hendrie Blvd Royal Oak MI 48067

WILKINSON, JOAN KRISTINE, nurse; b. Rochester, Minn., June 15, 1953; d. A. Ray and Ruth Audrey (Wegwart) Kubly; B.S. in Nursing, U. Wis., Madison, 1975; m. Robert M. Wilkinson, June 14, 1975; 1 son, Michael Robert. Team coordinator Boulder (Colo.) Psychiat. Inst., 1977-78; public health nurse Rocky Mountain Poison Center, Denver, 1978-79, asst. head nurse, toxicology specialist, 1979-80, head nurse, toxicology specialist, 1980—; lectr. in field. Agy. campaign coordinator Mile High United Way, 1980-81. Recipient gold award United Way, Denver, 1981; cert. recognition for outstanding vol. service ARC, 1973. Mem. Am. Assn. Poison Control Centers, Colo. Nurses Assn., Am. Nurses Assn., World Health Assn. Office: 645 Bannock St Denver CO 80204

WILKINSON, KATHERINE KAY, real estate broker, publisher; b. Walker County, Ga., Oct. 6, 1930; d. Fred Steven and Vecil Bryson; diploma LaFayette (Ga.) High Sch., Bus. Coll., Tulsa, 1952; grad. Realtors Inst., 1971; m. Franklin E. Wilkinson, May 13, 1954; 1 son, James Howard. Broker-owner Home Finders Inc., Del City, Okla., 1963—; pres. Del City Publishing Co., 1977—. Chmn. Del City Planning Commn., 1972; sec. Del City Indsl. Trust, 1972-73; mem. Del City Council, 1975-79; del. Democratic Nat. Conv., 1976; spl. events chmn. Okla. chpt. Am. Cancer Soc., 1978. Named Woman of Yr., Del City chpt. Am. Bus. Women, 1972. Mem. Nat. Realtors Assn., Nat. Press Assn., Okla. Press Assn., Midwest City-Del City Bd. Realtors (Realtor of Yr. 1972; pres. 1973-74), Del City C. of C. (1st v.p. 1974; Super Saleswoman award 1974), Del City Hist. Soc. (v.p. 1976), Del City Bus. and Profl. Women (pres. 1970). Baptist. Home: 4800 SE 19th St Del City OK 73115 Office: 4513 SE 29th St PO Box 15221 Del City OK 73115

WILKINSON, NANA MIRIAM SLATEN (MRS. WESLEY O. WILKINSON), realtor; b. Dahlgren, Ill., June 8, 1912; d. John R. and Fleta E. (Berry) Slaten; student Carthage Coll., 1930-32; grad. Real Estate Inst.; m. Wesley Owen Wilkinson, Feb. 14, 1945. Sec. pres.'s office DePauw U., Greencastle, Ind., 1935-37; exec. sec. to v.p. Beach & Arthur Paper Co., Indiana, Pa. and N.Y.C., 1937-45; realtor Henry B. Trachy Real Estate Agy., Franklin, N.H., 1970—; mem. 3d Dist. Belknap County, N.H. Ho. of Reps., 1970-73. Mem. N.H. Fedn. Garden Clubs, 1957—, 1st v.p., 1966-67, state pres., 1967-69, legis. chmn., 1971-74, editor Lilac Letter, 1969-71; mem. Nat. Council State Garden Clubs, 1957—, treas. New Eng. region Symposium, 1969-71, chmn. New Eng. Regional Youth activities, 1969-71, mem. nominating com. New Eng. region 1971—, life mem., 1969—; pres. Tilton-Northfield Woman's Club, 1953-55; pres. Tilton Garden Club, 1959-61, now life mem.; mem. organizational study com., mem. nat. conv. com. Nat. Council State Garden Clubs, 1975—, nat. corr. sec., 1979—, recipient presdl. citation, 1981, parliamentarian New Eng. region, 1979—; mem. Tilton Park Commn., 1963—; mem. Tilton Planning Bd., 1969-70, Tilton Budget Com., 1976-79; mem. Flood Plains Commn. N.H., 1972-74; treas. Tilton Republican Com., 1958—; trustee Arthur S. Brown Found., 1973-79. Recipient Presdl. citation N.H. Fedn. Garden Clubs, 1970, 73, 81, Order Purple Finch for outstanding woman, 1970, cert. of recognition Nat. Rep. Congl. Com., 1981. Mem. Nat. Assn. Realtors, Lakes Region Bd. Realtors (women's council), Nat. Wildlife Fedn., Audubon Soc. N.H., Nat. Resources Council N.H., Tilton Woman's Club, Nat. Assn. Parliamentarians, Mass. Horticulture Soc., Soc. Protection N.H. Forests, Nat. Assn. Women Legislators. Congregationalist (pres. Ladies' Circle 1961-62, 70-71; chmn. music com. 1971—; trustee (1st woman 1965-70). Home: Mountain View Dr Tilton NH 03276 Office: 395 Central St Franklin NH 03235

WILKINSON, NANCY BURCH, art historian; b. Chgo., Sept. 25, 1942; d. Edwin Whitney and Roberta Swartwout (Johnson) Burch; A.B., Randolph-Macon Woman's Coll., 1964; M.A., U. Calif., Berkeley, 1966; Ph.D., UCLA, 1983; 1 son, John Anthony. Peace Corps vol., Bangkok, Thailand, 1967-69; asst. prof. art and humanities Okla. State U., Stillwater, 1969—. Mem. Okla. Symphony Soc., 1972-80; Oklahoma City chair fund drive Randolph-Macon Woman's Coll. Alumnae, 1975. Nat. Endowment Humanities nat. fellow, 1977-78; UCLA Dickson fellow, London, 1982-83. Mem. Am. Oriental Soc., Coll. Art Assn., S.W. Conf. Asian Studies. Home: 1702 Westridge St Stillwater OK 74074 Office: Art Dept 212 Gardiner Hall Oklahoma State University Stillwater OK 74078

WILKINSON, ROSEMARY REGINA CHALLONER, poet; b. New Orleans, Feb. 21, 1924; d. William Lindsay and Julia Regina (Sellen) Challoner; student San Mateo Coll., 1964-66; D.H.L. (hon.), l'Université Libre Asie, Pakistan, 1975; m. Henry Bertram Wilkinson, Oct. 15, 1949; children—Denis James, Marian Regina, Paul Francis, Richard Challoner. Mem. staff hosp. adminstrn. numerous hosps., 1939-47, 58, 59; supr. West Disinfectant Co., San Francisco, 1948-51; pres. 5th World Congress of Poets, San Francisco, 1981; works include: (epic biographies) An Historical Epic, 1975, California Poet, 1976, Epic of Ship's Captain/Artist, 1978, Poet: Uplift Mankind, 1982; (books) A Girl's Will, 1973 (translated into Chinese), Earths Compromise, 1977, It Happened to Me, 1978, I Am Earth Woman, 1979, The Poet and the Painter, 1980, Poetry and Arte, 1982. Pres. Friends of Burlingame Library, 1976-77; bd. dirs. Burlingame Civic Arts Council, 1975-76. Decorated knight grand dame of grace Sovereign Mil. Order St. John of Jerusalem, Knights of Malta; recipient cert. of merit Am. Poets Fellowship Soc. of Ill., 1973; named Internat. Woman of Yr., Philippines, 1975. Fellow Internat. Acad. Poets (founder); mem. Calif. Fedn. of Chaparral Poets (pres. Toyon chpt., press chmn. 1977-79), Poetry Soc. of London-N.Y., Nat. League Am. Pen Women, Ina Coolbrith Circle, World Acad. Arts and Culture, Author's Guild, Author's League Am., Internat. Guild Contemporary Bards, World Poetry Soc. Intercontinental, Accademia Internationale Leonardo da Vinci, Nat. Fedn. State Poetry Socs., Tagore Inst. Creative Writing. Democrat. Roman Catholic. Contbr. poetry to anthologies and quars. Home: 1239 Bernal Ave Burlingame CA 94010

WILKS, JACQUELIN HOLSOMBACK, educator; b. Oakdale, La., Jan. 18, 1950; d. Jack and Ida Mae (Bass) Holsomback; B.S., La. Coll., 1972; M.A.T., Okla. City U., 1982; postgrad. So. Bapt. Theol. Sem., Louisville, 1974, S.E. Mo. State U., 1977; m. Thomas M. Wilks, Jan. 28, 1972; children—Thomas David, Bryan Emerson. Sec. to adminstr. Allen Parish Hosp., Kinder, La., 1968-69; tchr. horseback riding, swimming Triple D Guest Ranche, Warren, Tex., 1969; singer, speaker Found. Singers, including TV and radio appearances, record albums, 1970-71; tchr. English, reading Pine Bluff (Ark.) High Sch., 1972-74; tchr. kindergarten Doyle Elem. Sch., East Prairie (Mo.) R-2 Sch. Dist., 1974-75; tchr. 1st grad Bertrand (Mo.) Elem. Sch., 1975-76; tchr. 6th grade sci. A.D. Simpson Sch., Charleston, Mo., 1976-78; dir. admissions and fin. aid Mo. Bapt. Coll., St. Louis, 1978-80; fin. adminstr. Control Data Inst., Control Data Corp., St. Louis, 1980-81; dir. tutorial services, instr. tutorial methods Okla. Bapt. U., 1981—; instr. horsemanship St. Gregory's Jr. Coll., 1981; counselor Gordon Cooper Area Vocat. Tech. Sch., 1982—; tutor for children under jurisdiction Juvenile Ct., Jefferson County, Ark., 1972-73, leader group counseling/therapy sessions, 1972. Choreographer, First Bapt. Ch. Youth Choir, Pine Bluff; v.p. St. Gregory's Coll. Therapeutic Horsemanship Program; Republican election judge. Recipient Kathryn Carpenter award La. Bapt. Conv., 1971; Real Scope award Realty World, St. Louis, 1980; lic. Realtor, Mo. Mem. Nat. Hist. Soc., Univ. Alliance Okla. Bapt. U., Nat. Assn. Fin. Aid Adminstrs., Nat. Assn. Admissions Counselors, Athenian Lit. Soc., Nat. Geog. Soc., Gamma Beta Phi, Kappa Delta, Phi Kappa Phi. Republican. Baptist. Clubs: Kathryn Boone Music, Civinette Booster. Home: Route 3 Box 143 Shawnee OK 74801 Office: Gordon Cooper Area Vocat Tech Sch Shawnee OK 74801

WILKS, MARY ELIZABETH, ednl. adminstr.; b. Nashville, Tenn., Aug. 14, 1933; d. Thatchers and Ola B. (Owens) Terry; grad. Detroit Bible Coll., 1955; B.A., Wayne State U., 1962; M.A. in Spl. Edn., U. Mich., 1967, Ph.D., 1976. With Detroit Bd. of Edn., 1962—, tchr. elem. schs., 1962-67, summer sch. adminstr., 1970-73, asst. supt. Region 4, 1980—; radio producer/TV program WGPR-TV, 1962; dir. Teen Profile, 1968—; instr. psychology Wayne County Community Coll., 1975-79; cons. mass communication, 1968-82; producer, dir. television program Teen Profile, 1968-82; mem. various coms. Mich. Bd. Edn., 1968-82; lectr. and cons. to Mich. Sunday Sch. Assn., 1965-72, Detroit Urban League, 1970-82, Gospel Workshop Am., 1972-82, Faith Bethany United Meth. Ch., 1973-82, NAACP, 1982; dir. Sylvia Moy Prodns., Muziki Pub., BMI. Bd. dirs. Brightmoor Community Center, 1974—, Boy's-Girl's Club of Met. Detroit, 1975—, Center for Creative Communications, 1974—, Afro-Am. Mus. Bldg. Fund Program, 1978—; bd. dirs., trustee Nat. Conv. Gospel Choirs and Choruses, 1960-82, adminstrv. asst., 1955-79; 3d v.p., bd. dirs. Mich. Metro council Girl Scouts U.S.A. Recipient Community Service award Met. Detroit Boys' Club, 1974, Nat. Conv. Gospel Choirs and Choruses, 1975, Mfrs. Nat. Bank, 1979; Disting. Service award Waterford Sch. Dist., 1979; Spirit of Detroit award Detroit City Council, 1980; Community Edn. award Eastern Mich. U., 1981; resolution Detroit City Council, 1981; spl. tribute State of Mich., 1981; Tide award Wayne State U., 1981; Nat. Endowment Arts fellow U. Calif., San Diego, 1981; Mott Found. grantee, 1981. Mem. Orgn. Sch. Adminstrs. and Suprs., Fine Arts Fellowship Assn., Detroit Black Educators Assn., NAACP, Women in Communication, Nat. Acad. TV Arts and Sci., Detroit C. of C. Democrat. Methodist. Contbr. paper to profl. jour.; author: Black English and the Education of Black Children and Youth; composer: (songs) Thanks for the Gift, 1971, Give a Little Love, 1979, Brick by Brick, 1981. Home: 14049 Whitcomb Detroit MI 48227 Office: 14111 Puritan Detroit MI 48229

WILKS-PENROD, ANN WIKOWSKY, univ. adminstr.; b. Dallas, Feb. 24, 1941; d. Theodore Rodney and Irene Virginia (Bevelhymer) Wikowsky; student Abilene Christian Coll., 1959-60; B.S. in Edn., U. Tex., Austin, 1965; M.S.Ed., Pepperdine U., 1975, M.B.A., 1979; m. James I. Penrod; children— Elizabeth Wilks, James Michael Penrod, Rita Kareen Penrod. Dir. audiovisual dept. Pepperdine U., Los Angeles, 1973-75; asst. to exec. dir., unif. info. services, 1975-77; systems coordinator Security First Group, Los Angeles, 1977-78; sr. adminstrv. analyst dept. physiology Med. Sch. UCLA, 1978-81, mgmt. fellow, office vice-chancellor student affairs, 1981—, also mem. univ. policies commn., chmn., 1980-81. Mem. Soc. Research Adminstrs., Nat. Council Univ. Research Adminstrs., UCLA Staff Assn., Adminstrs. and Suprs. Assn. UCLA. Congregationalist. Office: 2221 Murphy Hall UCLA 405 Hilgard St Los Angeles CA 90024

WILL, JERRIE ANN, psychologist; b. Hazleton, Pa., Apr. 6, 1950; d. Gordon John and Doris Griffiths (Brown) W.; B.A., Bucknell U., 1971; Ph.D., W.Va. U., 1977. Instr., W.Va. U., 1974-75, teaching fellow, 1975-76; intern child clin. psychology U. Md. Hosp., College Park, 1976-77; sr. child clin. psychologist Michael Reese Hosp., Chgo., 1977-82; cons., 1977—; pvt. practice psychology, Chgo., 1982—. Nat. Inst. Child Human Devel. grantee, 1972-75. Mem. Am. Psychol. Assn., Soc. Research in Child Devel., Am. Contract Bridge League. Home: 1360 E 48 St Chicago IL 60615 Office: 1360 E 48 St Chicago IL 60615

WILL, JESSIE GERMAN, handwriting expert, document examiner; b. Muskogee, Okla., Oct. 8, 1912; d. William Paxton Zacheus and Mabel Gussie (Ward) German; student Ward Belmont Coll., 1929-30, Drake U., 1930-32; B.S., Okla. U., 1933; cert. Internat. Graphoanalysis Soc., 1968, master cert., 1973; m. Edward Ray Will, Sept. 29, 1934; children—Henry German, Margaret Ann Will Cornell. Handwriting expert, document examiner, Tulsa, 1970—; lectr. Oklahoma City U., 1972-78, Tri-County Tech. Sch., Bartlesville, Okla., 1977-81. Pres. local PTA, 1948-49, 55-58; bd. dirs. Tulsa WYWCA, 1963, Tulsa Philharmonic, 1964. Mem. PEO, (chpt. pres. 1962-63), Internat. Graphoanalysis Soc., Ind. Assn. Questioned Document Examiners (corr. sec. 1976-77), Tulsa Boys Home Women's Assn. (v.p. 1978-79), Internat. Assn. Forensic Scis., Kappa Alpha Theta (pres. alumni assn. 1961, coll. dist. pres. 1961-63), Mu Phi Epsilon. Republican. Mem. Disciples of Christ Ch. Expert witness in fed. and dist. cts. Okla. and Mo. Home and Office: 1727 E 31st St Tulsa OK 74105

WILL, MARTHA BONNIE, telecommunications corp. ofcl.; b. Phila., Apr. 13, 1947; d. Warren Howard and Martha Kathryn Sayre; student in Bus., Brevard Community Coll., 1979—; m. Manfred Carl Will, June 5, 1976. Sec., Gen. Electric Co., Kennedy Space Center, Fla., 1965-70; mktg. asst. Symetrics Industries, Inc., Satellite Beach, Fla., 1970-71; asst. corp. sec., sec. to pres. Opto-Mechanik, Inc., Melbourne, Fla., 1971-73; sec. quality assurance dept. Pan Am. World Airways, Kennedy Space Center, 1973-77; with ITT North-Internat. Ops., Cape Canaveral, Fla., 1977-82, mgr. compensation and benefits, 1981—. Named clubwoman of yr., Today newspaper, 1978. Mem. Nat. Mgmt. Assn. (chpt. pres. ITT North 1981-82, v.p. Fla. Space Coast Council 1981-82, del. nat. conv. 1981), Nat. Assn. Female Execs., Am. Soc. Personnel Women, Beta Sigma Phi (pres. Delta Omega chpt. 1973-74, Xi Eta Xi Exemplar chpt. 1977-79, council del. 1974-79). Republican. Methodist. Home: 1545 Sykes Creek Dr Merritt Island FL 32952 Office: 7321 N Atlantic Ave Cape Canaveral FL 32920

WILLACY, HAZEL MARTIN, lawyer; b. Utica, Miss., Apr. 20, 1946; d. Julious and Willie Thelma (Barnes) Martin; student Tougaloo Coll., 1963-64; B.A. in Econs., Smith Coll., 1967; J.D., Case Western Res. U., 1976; m. Aubrey Barrington Willacy, Mar. 18, 1967; children—Austin Keith, Louis Samuel. Admitted to Ohio bar, 1976; labor economist Bur. Labor Stats., U.S. Dept. Labor, 1967-70; asso. firm Baker, Hostetler, Cleve., 1976-80; labor relations atty. Sherwin Williams Co., Cleve., 1980—. Bd. dirs. YWCA, 1972, mem. fin. devel. com., 1976-80; mem. Citizens Com. of Cleve. Mem. Am. Bar Assn. (labor law com.), Ohio Bar Assn. (labor law com.), Cleve. Bar Assn., Nat. Assn. Female Execs., Order of Coif. Clubs: Women's City, Law Wives (treas., 1979-80). Contbr. articles to legal publs. Office: 101 Prospect Ave Cleveland OH 44115

WILLARD-GALLO, KAREN ELIZABETH, molecular biologist; b. Oak Ridge, July 8, 1953; d. Harvey Bradford and Isabella Victoria (Tallis) Willard; student in microbiology U. Reading (Eng.), 1973-74; A.B. in Biology, Randolph-Macon Woman's Coll., 1975; M.S. in Immunology, Va. Poly. Inst., 1978, Ph.D. in Molecular Biology, 1981; m. James Paul Gallo, July 31, 1982. Grad. teaching asst. Va. Poly. Inst., 1976-78; fellow Research Inst. in Cell Biology, Argonne (Ill.) Nat. Lab., 1977, lab. resident student asso., 1978-81, postdoctoral fellow, 1981-82; research scientist Ludwig Inst. for Cancer Research, Brussels, 1982—;

cons. in field. Recipient award for teaching excellence Va. Poly. Inst., 1977, 78. Mem. Am. Soc. Cell Biology, Electrophoresis Soc. Contbr. chpts., articles to profl. publs.; patentee method for early detection infectious mononucleosis. Home: Rue de Pinchart 16 1340 Ottignie Belgium Office: Ludwig Inst for Cancer Research Ave Hippocrate 74 UCL 74.59 B-1200 Brussels Belgium

WILLBRAND, MARY LOUISE, speech pathologist, educator; b. Tulsa, Aug. 16, 1936; d. Raymond Richard and Wilma (Collins) Scott; A.A. in Drama, Christian Coll., 1956; student Mary Washington Coll., 1955, Tulsa U., 1957; B.S., U. Mo., 1958, M.A., 1969, Ph.D., 1972; postgrad. Stanford U., 1969; m. Richard D. Rieke, June 24, 1979; 1 dau., Amy Dawn. Speech clinician pub. schs., Moberly, Mo., 1958-61, Columbia, Mo., 1961-65, Cerebral Palsy Center, Fayette, Mo., 1967; tchr. speech and drama summer enrichment program, Columbia Mo., 1963-65; lang. clinician Inst. Childhood Aphasia, Palo Alto, Calif., 1969; instr. speech pathology U. Mo., Columbia, 1969-71; dir. speech-lang. pathology and audiology U. Utah, Salt Lake City, 1976-81, prof. speech pathology, 1973—; cons. to sch. dists. Mo., Wyo., Utah. Vice pres., bd. dirs. Montessori Sch., Columbia, 1969-71; mem. exec. council Nat. Charity League, Salt Lake City, 1974-77; mem. home-sch. bd. Rowland Hall-St. Marks Sch., Salt Lake City, 1975-77; v.p., bd. dirs. Boy's Club Early Childhood Edn. Center, Salt Lake City, 1980—. Coll. Humanities grantee U. Utah, 1975, research com. grantee, 1981-83. Mem. Utah Speech and Hearing Assn. (pres.), Am. Speech-Lang-Hearing Assn. (visitor edn. tng. bd. site). Author: (with M.J. Mecham) Language Disorders in Children, 1979; contbr. numerous articles to profl. jours. Home: 1485 Sigsbee Ave Salt Lake City UT 84103 Office: 1201 Behavioral Sci Bldg Univ of Utah Salt Lake City UT 84112

WILLCOX, CAROLYN, home economist; b. Flushing, N.Y., June 28, 1952; d. Alfred Norman and Ruth Ann (Fuller) W.; B.S., Brigham Young U., 1974. Home economist, designer Craftsman Kitchens, Orem, Utah, 1974-77; real estate agt. Century-21 All Western, Orem, 1977-79; dept. mgr. Zion's Coop. Merc. Instn., Orem, 1978-79, home economist major appliances, 1979, bridal cons., dept. mgr. bridal salon, 1979-80; home economist, designer Heber Cabinets (Utah), 1980-81, Kitchen Concepts, Salt Lake City, 1981-82; sales rep. Office Support Systems, North Salt Lake, Utah, 1982—; cons. home economist, 1977—. Mem. Home Economists in Bus. (chmn. chpt. 1978-79), Elec. Women's Round Table (chmn. Utah chpt. 1976-77). Republican. Mormon. Home: PO Box 151234 Salt Lake City UT 84115 Office: 80 S Redwood Rd Suite 210 North Salt Lake UT 84054

WILLEFORD, CATHERINE PROCTOR, civic worker; b. Greenwood, S.C., Sept. 9, 1935; d. Benjamen Moye and Catherine Proctor; B.S., Winthrop Coll., 1957; M.S., La. State U., 1959; m. Brice J. Willeford, Jr., July 22, 1961; children—Brice J. III, Catherine Elizabeth. Instr., La. State U., 1957-58, Duke U., 1958-61; tchr. Cannon Jr. High Sch., Kannapolis, N.C., 1961-62; bd. dirs. Cabarrus County United Way, 1974-79, ARC, 1976-79, N.C. United Way, 1977-79; chmn. Womens Democratic County Com., 1973; chmn. Gov.'s Involvement Council, 1978-79; vice chmn. Democratic Precinct Com., Kannapolis, N.C., 1970-77; mem. planning bd. So. Piedmont Health Assn., 1978-79; chmn. Tchr. Parent Council, 1978-79; leader Girl Scouts U.S.A., 1970-78, Cub Scouts, 1969; sec. bd. Library Arts Council, 1977-79; bd. dirs. Old Courthouse Theatre, 1977—; chmn. Episcopal Churchwomen, 1982; Art Acquisition (Holt Collection), 1981—, Kannapolis Book Club II, 1982; bd. dirs. Cabarrus County chpt. Am. Cancer Soc., 1981—. La. State U. fellow, 1957-58; recipient Gov.'s Spl. Vol. award, 1979. Mem. N.C. Hist. Assn., DAR. Clubs: Friends of Library, Garden, Parnassus Book (chmn.). Home: 1646 Eastwood St Kannapolis NC 28081

WILLETT, ROSLYN LEONORE, public relations and food service cons.; b. N.Y.C., Oct. 18, 1924; d. Edward and Celia (Stickler) Sternberg; B.A., Hunter Coll., 1944; student Tchrs. Coll., Columbia U., 1944-45, N.Y.U., 1947-48, 51-52, CCNY, 1947-48; m. Edward Willett, June 8, 1949 (separated); 1 son, Jonathan Stanley. Head tech. service and devel., food products Stein, Hall & Co., N.Y.C., 1944-48; editor McGraw-Hill Pub. Co., Laurel Publns., others, 1949-54; head instl. and bus. press dept. Farley Manning Assos., N.Y.C., 1954-58; pres. Roslyn Willett Assos., Inc., N.Y.C., 1959—; lectr. Columbia Sch. Public Health, 1971—, N.Y.U. Sch. Bus., 1969-71; tchr. Hunter Coll., 1955-56; adj. prof. Poly. Inst. N.Y., 1981. Seminar del. White House Conf. Food, Nutrition and Health, 1969, Organizer Nat. Women's Polit. Caucus, 1971—; chairwoman Women's Polit. Caucus, Inc., 1971-73; chairwoman 1st women candidates workshops for polit. candidates, N.Y., N.J., Conn., 1971, 72. Bd. dirs. Women Studies Abstracts, Foodservice Cons. Soc. Internat., IX Investors Corp., Will Inst.; v.p., trustee Mid-Hudson Arts and Sci. Center, 1981—; mem. regional adv. council Fed. SBA, 1977-79. Recipient award Nat. Restaurant Assn., 1968-69, 70-71. Mem. Inst. Food Technologists, Am. Mktg. Assn., NOW (dir. Image of Women program), Am. Home Econs. Assn. Am. Acad. Polit. and Social Scis., Public Relations Soc. Am. (accredited), Assn. Small Bus. Execs. (dir. 1981—). Contbr. articles to profl. publs., essay in book. Home: PO Box 106 Stanfordville NY 12581 Office: 2248 Broadway New York NY 10024

WILLETT, RUTH ELAINE, ednl. library media adminstr.; b. Peoria, Ill., Dec. 1, 1936; d. Edward F. and Mry Elizabeth (Shepherdson) Voss; B.S., U. Ill., 1958; M.A., Ariz. State U., 1966; postgrad. U.S. Internat. U., 1970; m. Lloyd F. Willett, Dec. 29, 1964; children—Jan V., Stephen F., Jolaine H. Tchr. public schs., Peoria, Ill., Anaheim, Calif., Williams AFB, Ariz., 1960-67; Title 1 media specialist Alhambra Sch. Dist., Phoenix, 1967-68; curriculum coordinator Shalimar (Fla.) Elem. Sch., 1969-70; team leader Jefferson Elem. Sch., Carlsbad, Calif., 1970-72; dir. Learning Resource Center, U.S. Internat. U., 1972-74; coordinator library media services Escondido Union Sch. Dist., Escondido, Calif., 1974—; cons. on library skills to sch. dists.; conf. and workshop presentor; team mem. Nat. Council Accreditation Tchr. Edn. Recipient Charles E. Marrion award U. Ill., 1957; San Diego County pilot project grantee, 1977-80. Mem. Calif. Media Librarians and Educators Assn. (v.p. organizational 1978-79), Assn. Ednl. Communications and Tech. (coordinator Region X 1974-78), Assn. Calif. Sch. Adminstrs., North County Adminstrs. (sec.), Phi Kappa Phi, Delta Kappa Gamma. Editor: So You Want to Make a Film, 1972; asst. editor Audiovisual Jour. Ariz., 1967-69; asso. editor AVEAC Jour., 1971-73; editor Jour. Media and Tech., 1973-76. Home: 633 Ranchite Dr Escondido CA 92025 Office: 980 N Ash St Escondido CA 92027

WILLEY, HERMINE (MRS. WALTER C. WILLEY), microbiologist; b. Bklyn., Aug. 25, 1936; d. David and Sylvia Sarah (Heineman) Bernitz; B.S. in Agr., Ohio State U., 1959; m. Walter Calvin Willey, Oct. 4, 1959; children—David Newman, Diane Marie. Microbiologist, lab. supr. in food microbiology Ohio Dept. Agr., Reynoldsburg, 1959—; cons. in field. Ednl. Found. for Jewish Girls grantee, 1956-59. Mem. Am. Soc. Microbiology, Internat. Assn. Milk, Food and Environ. Sanitarians, Inst. Food Technologists, Ohio Civil Service Assn. (2d v.p. 1975-78), Olde Orchard Civic Assn., Assn. Food and Drug Ofcls. Home: 689 Olde Orchard Ct Columbus OH 43213 Office: Ohio Dept Agr Consumer Analytical Labs Reynoldsburg OH 43068

WILLEY, MYRTLE DENNEY, steel co. exec.; b. Jacksonville, Ill., July 7, 1918; d. Benjamin Harrison and Lora Edna (Burke) Denney; student Brown's Bus. Coll., 1935-36; m. George A. Corbett, Sept. 25, 1945 (div. 1964); 1 son, Michael Denney Corbett; m. 2d, Leland B. Willey, Sept. 14, 1972. Fashions buyer Emporium, Jacksonville, 1936-40; photographer Olin Mills Studio, Chattanooga, 1941-45; floor mgr. W.T. Grant Co., Jacksonville, 1945-50; with Peoples Water & Gas Co., Miami Beach, Fla., 1950-56; with T.W. Dick Co., Gardiner, Maine, 1956—, exec. v.p., 1968-76, pres., treas., gen. mgr., 1976—; corporator Gardiner Savs. Inst., 1974—. Chmn. fin. com., treas., exec. bd. Gardiner Gen. Hosp., 1975—; treas. Gardiner Gen. Hosp. Women's Bd. Aux., 1973—; budget com., dir. United Way, Augusta, Maine, 1975—; pres. Kennebec Valley United Way, 1979-80; patron Forum A, U. Maine, Augusta, 1974—, Portland (Maine) Symphony Orch., 1976—. Mem. Augusta Music Jazz Soc. (v.p. 1976—), Maine Good Roads Assn., Asso. Gen. Contractors, Small Bus. Assns. New Eng., Nat. Assn. Women in Constrn. (pres. chpt., mem. liaison com. 1982—), Maine State C. of C. (dir. 1979—). Republican. Episcopalian. Club: Zonta (pres. 1981—), Dist. I treas. 1982—). Home: 2 Ash St Hallowell ME 04347 Office: 1 Summer St PO Box 140 Gardiner ME 04345

WILLEY, SHIRLEY FAYE (MRS. RICHARD WARREN WILLEY), antique dealer; b. Dawson, N.D., Aug. 5, 1933; d. Fern Clifford and Bessie Christine (Nord) Werner; student Pierce Coll., 1952, U. Calif. at Los Angeles, 1961; m. Richard Warren Willey, Feb. 25, 1967. Dir. mktg. and pub. relations Family of Artists, Rockton, Ill.; asst. corp. tng. dir. Bergner-Weise, Rockford, 1979—; program dir. Valley View, Rockford, 1981—; communications cons. Fairmont Hotel, San Francisco and Dallas, 1968-70, Beverly Hilton Hotel, Beverly Hills, Calif., 1964-67; chief communications Better 'n Nothing TV show, Grass Valley, Calif., 1968-69. Mgr. antique show for theatre restoration benefit, 1969; chmn. Nevada County chpt. Heart Assn., 1971—; entertainment chmn. Winnebago (Ill.) Sr. Citizens Days, 1982. Bd. dirs. Nevada County Liberal Arts Commn., cons., 1969-71. Recipient Meritorious service award Am. Heart Assn., 1971. Mem. Ch. of Religious Sci. (dir. 1967). Address: 150 W Russell Apt 9 Rockton IL 61072

WILLHOIT, MARILYN JEAN, med. equipment mfg. ofcl.; b. Paterson, N.J., Aug. 9, 1947; d. Robert and Eleanor Jean (Lewis) Houston; B.A. in Speech Correction, Trenton State Coll., 1968; M.A. in Audiology, U. Conn., 1970; m. Robert Norval Willhoit, Mar. 29, 1969 (div. 1978); m. 2d, Louis Lazar Reidt, Jan. 1, 1982. Teaching fellow U. Conn., Storrs, 1968-69; audiologist Grove Hill Clinic, New Britain, Conn., 1968-77, Hartford Hearing League, W.Hartford, Conn., 1969-71, Gaylord Hosp., Wallingford, Conn., 1971-73, chmn. dept. speech and hearing, 1973-77; ednl. cons. Am. Electromedics Corp., Acton, Mass., 1978-79, nat. sales mgr., 1980—; part time prof. So. Conn. State Coll., 1976-77; cons. Blue Cross of Conn., 1973-77, Pfeizer Industries, North Haven, Conn., Conn. State Dept. Health, Pehlps-Stokes Fund, Washington; profl. adv. Employees Ins. of Wasau, Conn.; public speaker in field; adv. bd. Profl. Standards Rev. Orgn., Conn. Mem. Am. Speech and Hearing Assn. (cert.), Conn. Speech and Hearing Assn. (award for spl. contbn. 1978), Nat. Assn. Bus. Planners, Nat. Assn. Small Bus. Mgrs., Nat. Assn. Female Execs. Author: Guidelines for the Provision of Speech, Hearing and Language Services State of Conn., 1977; contbr. article in field to profl. jour. Home: 9 Pine Hill Ave Nashua NH 03060 Office: American Electromedics Corp 13 Sagamore Park Rd Hudson NH 03051

WILLIAMS, ANDREA CARUSO, clin. social worker; b. Chester, Pa., Apr. 21, 1951; d. Anthony and Evelyn (Boyle) Caruso; B.A. cum laude in Psychology, West Chester State Coll., 1973; M.S.W. summa cum laude, Barry Coll., 1976; m. Eric J. Williams, June 19, 1976. Internat. social service (affiliate UN), Caracas, Venezuela, 1976-77; clin. social worker Children's Psychiat. Center, Hialeah, Fla., 1977-79; pvt. practice specializing in child and family psychotherapy, Miami, Fla., 1980-82; dir. social work services Highland Park Gen. Hosp., Miami, 1982—; adj. instr. dept. psychology and edn. Miami Dade Community Coll., 1980—; vol. Systems and Techs. Effective Parenting instr. Parent Resource Center, Miami, 1980—. Lic. social worker. Mem. Nat. Assn. Social Workers, Am. Orthopsychiat. Assn., Child Welfare League Am., AAUW. Club: Coconut Grove Sailing, Miami. Contbr. articles to profl. jours. Home: 1724 SW 131 Pl Circle S Miami FL 33175

WILLIAMS, ANN MORGAN, actress; b. Washington, May 18, 1935; d. John Oscar and Alys Elizabeth (Gott) W.; A.A. (Univ. scholar), George Washington U., 1957; m. Robert D.P. Welch, Sept. 19, 1964 (dec.); children—Amanda G., Elizabeth M., Daniel M., Diana Rebecca. Appearances include tour with nat. cos. Damn Yankees and Pajama Game, 1957; understudy to Gwen Verdon in New Girl in Town, Broadway, 1958-59; lead ingenue Alley Theatre, Houston including Six Characters in Search of an Author, Ondine, 1960-61; guest star many N.Y.-based TV shows including Kraft Theatre, Kraft Mystery Theatre, CBS Workshop, Naked City, Hawk, 1960-61; stage roles include: Karen in Applause with Lauren Bacall, Broadway, 1970; starred in The Headhunters with Anthony Quayle, Kennedy Center, 1974; Florence Tuckerman in Autumn Garden, Alley Theatre, 1976; TV roles include: Dr. Erica Brandt, Young Dr. Malone, NBC, 1960-62; Frances Black in The Milk Train Doesn't Stop Here Anymore, 1963; Maggie Fielding in The Doctors, NBC, 1963-65; Eunice Wyatt in Search for Tomorrow, CBS, 1975-76; Margot Dorn in The Edge of Night, ABC, 1977-79; Nurse Chastain in As the World Turns. Mem. Actors Equity Assn., Screen Actors Guild, AFTRA, Actors Studio. Episcopalian. Club: Bedford Golf and Tennis. Three times women's golf champion Bedford Golf and Tennis Club.

WILLIAMS, ANN MORGAN, psychologist; b. Wilkes-Barre, Pa., Nov. 5, 1952; d. Thomas Percy and Elizabeth May (Jenkins) W.; B.A. in Psychology, Wilkes Coll., 1974; M.A. in Psychology, Marywood Coll., doctoral candidate Temple U., 1978—. Social service researcher Pa. State U., University Park, 1974-75; instr. Luzerne County Community Coll., Nanticoke, Pa., 1976-81, assoc. prof., 1981-82, dir. ednl. confs., 1982—; research specialist Luzerne-Wyoming County Mental Health Center, Wilkes-Barre, 1978-79, community service specialist, 1979-81; pvt. stress reduction counselor and cons. Bd. dirs. Wyoming Valley Alcohol and Drug Services, Inc. Recipient hon. mention merit award in photography Kodak Co., 1981; cert. counselor, Pa. Mem. Am. Personnel and Guidance Assn., Pa. Personnel and Guidance Assn., Am. Mental Health Counselors Assn., NEA, Nat. Council on Continuing Edn., Am. Soc. Tng. and Devel. Baptist. Home: 10 Lawrence St Nanticoke PA 18634 Office: Prospect and Middle Rds Nanticoke PA 18634

WILLIAMS, ANNE SHIPLEY, sociologist; b. Butte, Mont., Oct. 13, 1940; d. James J. and Margaret E. (Ralph) Shipley; B.A., U. Mont., 1961, M.A., 1963; Ph.D. (Liberty-Hyde Bailey Research award 1977), Cornell U., 1977; m. James R. Williams, Nov. 28, 1964; children—J. Scott, Amanda Lee. Research asst. U. Mont., 1961-63; research asso. Am. Inst. Research, Palo Alto, Calif., 1963-64, Mont. Dept. Public Welfare, Butte, 1964-65; research asso., then dir. Center Interdisciplinary Studies, Mont. State U., Bozeman, 1968-75; research asso. Cornell U., 1975-77; asso. prof. sociology Mont. State U., 1977—; adv. com. Western Rural Devel. Center, 1977—. Grantee NSF, Kellogg Found., U.S. Office Edn., Bur. Reclamation, Dept. Agr. Mem. Rural Sociol. Soc. (council 1975-77), Am. Sociol. Assn. Author papers in field. Asso. editor Jour. Rural Sociology, 1977—. Home: 1915 S Tracy St Bozeman MT 59715 Office: Dept Sociology Mont State U Bozeman MT 59717

WILLIAMS, ANNETTE POLLY, state legislator; b. Miss., Jan. 10, 1937; s. James Wade and Louise Swan Wade; B.S., U. Wis., Milw.; children—Winston II, Mildred Louise, Kimberly Ann, Krystal Renee. Key punch operator J.C. Penney & Co., 1955-68; clk., cashier Kroger Foods, 1968-79; counselor Social Devel. Commn., 1969-71, mem. commn., 1973-76; mental health asst. Med. Coll. Wis., 1971-80; mem. Wis. Ho. of Reps., 1981—. Mem. State Equal Rights Council, Dept. Indsl. Labor and Human Relations, 1975-80; vice chmn. Northside Democratic Party, 1978-79; trustee Commando Acad., chmn., 1976—; chmn. Fabulous 50's Civic Orgn., 1977—; chmn. program com. Inner City Council of Alcoholism, 1978-80. Recipient Community Service award Parkman Jr. High Sch. Students, 1979; Partner of Youth award Met. Milw. YMCA, 1978; Leadership award Inner City Council on Alcoholism, 1979; Mother of Yr. award Women Educating Women, 1980; cert. of recognition Black Women on the Move, 1980. Mem. Black Women's Network. Office: Room 48 N State Capitol Madison WI 53702

WILLIAMS, ANNIE JOHN, educator; b. Reidsville, N.C., Aug. 26, 1913; d. John Wesley and Martha Anne (Walker) W.; A.B., Greensboro Coll., 1933; M.A., U. N.C., Chapel Hill, 1939; postgrad. Appalachian State U., summer 1944, Duke U., summer 1936, (Shell Merit fellow) Cornell U., summer 1961. Tchr. math. Blackstone (Va.) Coll., 1934-35; tchr. public schs., Hoke High Sch., Raeford, N.C., 1935-37, Massey Hill High Sch., Fayetteville, N.C., 1937-42, Alexander Graham Jr. High Sch., Fayetteville, 1942-43, Carr Jr. High Sch., Durham, N.C., 1943-53; supr. math. N.C. Dept. Public Instrn., Raleigh, 1959-62; tchr. math. Durham High Sch., 1953-59, 62-78, ret., 1978; vol. in math. N.C. Sch. Sci. and Math., Durham, 1980—; adj. asst. prof. math. and sci. edn. N.C. State U., Raleigh, 1966-73. Mem. Nat. Council Tchrs. Math. (life), (dir., 1957-60), Math. Assn. Am. (life), N.C. Council Tchrs. Math. (W. W. Rankin Meml. award 1975), Internat. Platform Assn., Delta Kappa Gamma, Mu Alpha Theta (hon.). Methodist. Clubs: Pierian Lit. (sec. 1979-80, pres. 1980-81), Durham Woman's, DAR (chmn. chpt. Am. History Month 1980-82, corr. sec. chpt. 1982—). Author: (with Brown and Montgomery) Algebra, First Course, 1963, Algebra, Second Course, 1963. Home: 2021 Sprunt Ave Durham NC 27705

WILLIAMS, ANNIE KATE, educator; b. Pelham, N.C., Sept. 1, 1938; d. Walter James and Katie Irene Myers; student Youngstown State U., 1970-79; m. Eugene Titus Williams, Jan. 24, 1959; children—Eugenia Earlene, Theadoris Anne, Darryl Titus. Out reach worker Planned Parenthood, Youngstown, Ohio, 1969-74, ednl. asst., 1974-77, health educator, 1977—. Precinct judge Democratic party, 1978—. Mem. Am. Assn. Sex Educators, Counselors and Therapists, Ohio Public Health Assn., Soc. for Sci. Study of Sex, Am. Public Health Assn., Eastern Ohio Counselors Assn. Baptist. Club: Order of Eastern Star. Home: 1106 Stiles Ave Youngstown OH 44505

WILLIAMS, ANNIE RUTH, rehab. corp. exec.; b. Gadsden, Ala., Dec. 24, 1934; d. Erwin and Rosie L. (Sturns) Stevens; B.S. in Nursing Edn., Fresno State U., 1971, M.S. in Mental Health, 1972; M.S. in Counseling, Calif. State U., Los Angeles, 1976. Psychiat. nurse VA Hosp., Denver, 1965-69; supervising counselor Valley Med. Center, Fresno, Calif., 1969-70; asst. prof. Fresno State U., 1971-72; instr. for in-service edn. VA Hosp., Long Beach, Calif., 1972-75; asst. prof. Calif. State U., Los Angeles, 1975-78, also dir. tutorial program for minority students; rehab. counselor Profl. Counselors Inc., Santa Monica, Calif., 1978; pres., owner Rehab. Mgmt. Specialist, Inc., Long Beach, 1978—; cons. Los Angeles Regional Family Planning Council, Inc.; ednl. com. for ednl. seminar Calif. Assn. Rehab. Program, 1980-81. Registered nurse; cert. credentials rehab. counselor, pupil personnel counselor, community coll. instr., coll. counselor, student personnel worker. Mem. Am. Personnel and Guidance Assn., Calif. Personnel and Guidance Assn., Assn. Black Faculty and Staff of So. Calif., Nat. Rehab. Assn., Calif. Assn. Rehab. Profls., Council of Nurses Assn., NAACP, Alpha Nu (pres.), Theta Alpha Omega (rec. sec., com. chmn.). Democrat. Home: 13068 Sutton Cerritos CA 90701 Office: 3605 Long Beach Blvd Suite 201 Long Beach CA 90807

WILLIAMS, ARDELIA RUTH, psychol. asst.; b. Melrose Park, Ill., May 31, 1936; d. Alfred Otto and Pearl Marietta (Coleman) Max; student Am. Conservatory of Music, Chgo., 1954-55, Passavant Meml. Hosp., Northwestern U., 1955-58; B.A., St. Mary's Coll. of Calif., 1975, M.A., 1979; m. Noel A. Williams, June 15, 1957; children—Sean Noel, Stewart James, Anne Arlene. Intern, Lafayette (Calif.) Counseling Center, 1978-80; psychol. asst. Noel A. Williams, M.D., P.C., Walnut Creek, Calif., 1977—. Mem. Am. Psychol. Assn., Calif. Psychol. Assn., Calif. Assn. Marriage and Family Counselors. Office: 130 La Casa Via Bldg 3 Suite 212 Walnut Creek CA 94598

WILLIAMS, ARTHALIA WILL BORDEAUX, ednl. adminstr.; b. Currie, N.C., Nov. 18, 1937; d. John Wesley Alderman and Sadie Bordeaux Robinson; B.S. in Edn., Winston-Salem (N.C.) State Tchrs. Coll., 1960; M.Ed., U. Md., 1967, advanced grad. specialist, 1968; divorced; children—Marcia, Aaron, Jr. Tchr., Charlotte, N.C., 1960-62, D.C. Pub. Schs., 1962-71; grad. tchr. U. Md., 1967-69; tchr., asst. prin. Wilmington (N.C.) Pub. schs., 1971-74; prin. Williston Jr. High Sch., Wilmington, 1974—. Mem. Assn. Supervision and Curriculum Devel., New Hanover County Prins. Assn., Alpha Kappa Alpha. Baptist. Club: Order Eastern Star. Home: Route 6 Box 139-C Wilmington NC 28405 Office: 401 S 10th St Wilmington NC 28401

WILLIAMS, AUDREY JOAN, univ. adminstr.; b. Montreal, Que., Can., Mar. 6, 1929; d. William E. and Florence G. (Cunningham) W.; B.A., Marianopolis Coll., Montreal, 1950; B.Sc., McGill U., 1953, M.Sc., 1955. Tech. and analytical services Merck, Sharp & Dohme, Montreal, 1955-58, adminstrv. asst.-sci. services, 1958-61, market analyst, 1961-62, research group leader, 1962-69, sr. devel. scientist, 1969-71; univ. research officer Concordia U., Montreal, 1971—. NRC Can. Indsl. Research grantee, 1964-70. Mem. Chem. Inst. Can., Can. Assn. Univ. Research Adminstrs., Nat. Council Univ. Research Adminstrs., Soc. Univ. Patent Adminstrs. Roman Catholic. Contbr. articles to sci. jours. Office: 1455 de Maisonneuve Blvd W Montreal PQ H3G 1M8 Canada

WILLIAMS, BARBARA ANN, religious orgn. communications specialist; b. Hinsdale, Ill., Sept. 30, 1952; d. Ralph William, Jr., and Doree Lydia (Duda) Pouk; B.S. cum laude in Edn. (fellow), No. Ill. U., 1974; M.A., Purdue U., 1978; m. Lawrence A. Williams, Aug. 17, 1974. Tchr., Dundee (Ill.) High Sch., 1974-75; office mgr. United Way, Burlington, Iowa, 1975-76; announcer Sta. WXUS-FM, Lafayette, Ind., 1976-77; adminstr., grad. asst., Purdue U., West Lafayette, Ind., 1977-78; instr. Danville (Ill.) Area Community Coll., 1979-81; mgmt. cons. Progressive Mgmt. Techniques, Chgo., 1979-81; dir. field services and communication United Ministries in Edn., Am. Bapt. Ch., Valley Forge, Pa., 1981—. Mem. regional task force on communication Am. Bapt. Ch./GRR; mem. Religious Public Relations Council. Named Outstanding Speech Communication Student, No. Ill. U. Mem. Internat. Communication Assn., Speech Communication Assn., Pi Kappa Delta. Baptist. Contbr. papers to profl. jours. Home: 143 Arden Gulph Mills PA 19428 Office: care Am Bapt Chs USA Valley Forge PA 19481

WILLIAMS, BARBARA ELIZABETH WOMACK, guidance counselor; b. Hollytree, Ala., Feb. 4, 1938; d. William Arthur and Margaret Kathleen (Enochs) Womack; B.A., Am. U., 1966, M.Ed., 1968; postgrad. U. Va.; m. Leon Franklin Williams, Aug. 17, 1957; children—Mark Franklin, Alice Kathleen, Stephanie Todd. With mil. intelligence and security Redstone Arsenal Hdqrs., Huntsville, Ala., 1956-57; charge maintenance of fgn. students in U.S. colls. Dept. Agr., Washington, 1957-59; tchr. English, humanities and psychology Glenvar High Sch., Roanoke County, Va., 1968-72; guidance counselor Hidden Valley Jr. High Sch., Roanoke, Va., 1972—. Founder Farmingdale Civic League;

campaign worker Democratic Party, 1978-79; mem. ofcl. bd. Farley Methodist Ch. Recipient Madison County (Ala.) Leadership award Elks Club, 1966, Americanism award Nat. Sojourners, 1966; lic. family counselor. Mem. NEA (life), Nat. Council Tchrs. English, Va. Assn. Tchrs. English (corr. sec.), Roanoke Valley Mental Health Assn., Roanoke County Edn. Assn., Va. Edn. Assn. Home: 5556 McVitty Rd SW Roanoke VA 24018 Office: 4901 Mount Holland Dr SW Roanoke VA 24018

WILLIAMS, BARBARA JEAN MAY, librarian; b. Alphoretta, Ky., June 5, 1927; d. Andrew Jackson and Bess (Salisbury) May; A.B. in Spanish, Centre Coll., 1949; postgrad. Columbia U., 1957; M.S. in Library Sci., U. Ky., 1963. Tchr. public schs., Ky., 1958-60; librarian Midway Jr. Coll., 1961-63; librarian Ky. Dept. Library and Archives, Frankfort, 1965-68, state librarian, 1977-80; planning librarian Ky. Program Devel. Office, Frankfort, 1968-72; head planning and budgeting collection, exec. dept. fin. and adminstrn. Ky. Office Policy and Mgmt., Frankfort, 1972-75; mem. dean's adv. council U. Ky. Coll. Library Sci.; mem. Depository Library Council to U.S. Public Printer. Mem. ALA, Southeastern Library Assn., Ky. Library Assn. (sec. 1974-75), Chief Officers of State Library Agys., Assn. State Library Agys. (ad hoc adv. com.), Council Planning Librarians (treas. 1970-76), Ky. Hist. Soc., Friends of Ky. Libraries, Friends of Ky. Ednl. TV, Ky. Council on Archives, Assn. Records Mgrs. and Adminstrs., Internat. Personnel Mgrs. Assn., Nat. Micrographics Assn. Presbyterian. Clubs: Filson, Democratic Woman's. Office: Capitol Annex Frankfort KY 40601

WILLIAMS, BARBARA LYNN, Realtor; b. Montrose, Colo., Nov. 25, 1944; d. Joe H. and Elsie Arlene Baldwin; grad. Am. Acad. Real Estate, 1973, Wyo. Real Estate Inst., 1977, Realtors Inst., 1979; children—Christine, Anisa Jo. Saleswoman, Western Realty Co., Durango, Colo., 1970-72; mng. broker Wedgwood Ltd., Realtors, Durango, 1973-74, pres., 1974-75; sales mgr. Coulter Agency, Gillette, Wyo., 1976-77, gen. sales mgr., 1977-78; broker, owner Barbara Williams Brokerage, 1978—. Vice chmn. LaPlata County Republican Central Com., 1973-75, Campbell County Rep. Central Com., 1976-78, 80-82; alt. del. Rep. Nat. Conv., 1980; mem. Region 9 Housing Com., 1974-75; mem. steering com. Sch. Dist. 9R, 1973-74. Lic. real estate broker, Colo., Wyo.; cert. residential specialist. Mem. LaPlata County Bd. Realtors (pres. 1974, dir. 1975—), Colo. Real Estate Bds. Assn. (dir. 1974-75), Nat. Assn. Realtors, Wyo. (dir. 1982), Campbell County bds. Realtors, Wyo. Assn. Realtors (pres. 1982, chmn. profl. standards com. 1980), Nat. Inst. Real Estate Brokers, Durango, Gillette (housing com. 1977-79) chambers commerce. Clubs: Rep. Women's; Emblem (past sec., trustee); Newcomers (past dir.); Empire Investment (pres. 1977). Address: 3 Grandview Circle Gillette WY 82716

WILLIAMS, BETTY JEANE, city ofcl.; b. Los Angeles, Aug. 11, 1948; d. Charles and Jessie Mae (Howard) W.; A.A., Los Angeles Harbor Jr. Coll., 1970; B.A., Calif. State U., Dominguez Hills, 1973. Counselor, Compton (Calif.) Urban Corps, 1973-74, chief counselor, 1974-75, asst. dir., 1975-76, dir., 1976-78; manpower program dir. City of Compton, 1978—; manpower cons. Chmn. Project Hope, Compton Community Coll., 1979—; bd. dirs. Paul Robeson Players, 1979—, Mid-County Action Coalition, Employment Tng. Adv. Com. active Century Club YMCA. Mem. Nat. Assn. Female Execs. Democrat. Baptist. Home: 318 W 121st St Los Angeles CA 90061 Office: 205 S Willowbrook Ave Compton CA 90220

WILLIAMS, BETTY JUNE, accountant; b. Prentis, Miss., Apr. 27, 1941; d. Hoyte Millard and Ellawae (Bryan) Rose; student public schs.; 1 dau., Jana. Asst. to pres. Akin Distbrs. Tulsa, 1969-71; acct. leasing div. Crane Carrier Co., Tulsa, 1971-73; sec. to pres., asst. to treas. Harley Industries, Tulsa, 1974-77; acct. corporate officer Design Properties, Tulsa, 1977—; pres. BJW Enterprises, Inc., Owasso, Okla., 1979—. Mem. Owasso C. of C. Republican. Baptist. Office: 7318 S Yale Ave Tulsa OK 74136

WILLIAMS, BETTY LOU, social worker; b. Marietta, Okla., June 14, 1937; d. Daniel and Hattie Mae (Carter) Jones; B.A., U. Oreg., 1959; M.A., U. Chgo., 1961; m. Kenneth L. Williams, June 13, 1964; children—Cynthia, Michael. Social worker United Charities, Chgo., 1962-64; supr., casework dir. Family Service of Evanston (Ill.), 1964-75; social work cons., fieldwork supr. Dist. 65 Evanston Schs., 1977-79; dir. social policy United Charities Chgo., 1979—; cons.; chairperson Gov.'s Adv. Council to Dept. Children and Family Services, 1977-80. Mem. NAACP (officer), Nat. Assn. Social Workers (chpt. officer), Nat. Assn. Social Workers, Ill. Assn. Sch. Social Workers, Delta Sigma Theta. Democrat. Home: 549 Florence Evanston IL 60202 Office: 14 E Jackson Blvd Chicago IL 60202

WILLIAMS, BETTY SUE, journalist; b. Waverly, Tenn., Aug. 20, 1941; d. Thomas Bruce and Ruby Lee W.; student George Peabody Tchrs. Coll., 1969-70, Fla. Keys Community Coll., 1979; Charles A. Tosch, III, m. Apr. 8, 1979; 1 dau., Lauren Elizabeth. Clearance service rep. Social Security Adminstrn., Nashville, 1961-67; real estate salesperson, public relations rep. Kenneth Boyd and Assos., also Computerized Apt. Locators Inc., Nashville, 1970-72; Sun Life editor Key West (Fla.) Citizen daily newspaper, 1973-80, feature writer, 1980—. Mem. com. United Way Fund, 1979; bd. dirs. Big Bros./Big Sisters Monroe County, 1982—. Recipient public service cert. award Key West Lions Club, 1979. Mem. Key West Art and Hist. Soc., Old Island Restoration Found. Democrat. Club: Key West Woman's. Home: 21 Beachwood Dr Key Haven Key West FL 33040 Office: Key West Citizen 515 Greene St Key West FL 33040

WILLIAMS, BRENDA PAULETTE, TV reporter, anchor; b. St. Louis, July 7, 1946; d. Herman and Hattie Williams; B.J., Ohio U., Athens, 1969; postgrad. U. Mo., Columbia. Newscaster, Sta. KATZ, St. Louis, 1969-70; reporter, talk show producer/host Sta. KPLR-TV, St. Louis, 1973-74, Stas. KSD-TV and Radio, St. Louis, 1974-77; weekend anchor-reporter Sta. KMBC-TV, Kansas City, Mo., 1977-81, weekday co-anchor KMBC-TV 6 p.m. and 10 p.m. news, 1981—. Recipient Cert. of Appreciation, St. Louis Urban League-St. Louis Sentinel, 1975; Human Relaions award Nat. Assn. Colored Women's Clubs, 1975; Documentary Reporting award Mo. Radio and TV Assn., 1979; Consumer Reporting award Mo. Dept. Consumer Affairs, 1979; Achievement award Mo. Black Leadership Assn., 1981, SCLC, 1981. Mem. Alpha Kappa Alpha (Women of Involvement award 1974).

WILLIAMS, CARMELITA KIMBER, educator; b. Kansas City, Mo., Dec. 12, 1932; d. Myron Elico and Hazel Ruth (Meekins) Kimber; B.A., Talladega Coll., 1953; M.A., U. Mo., Kansas City, 1963; Ed.D., SUNY, Buffalo, 1973; m. Paul Garnett Williams, June 9, 1957; children—Paul Garnett, John A., Michael. Tchr. elem. sch., Kansas City, Mo., 1953-67; instr. reading, dir. Reading Center, Norfolk (Va.) State Coll., 1967-78; sr. program asso. in reading Inst. for Services to Edn., Washington, 1979; prof. Sch. Edn., head reading dept. Norfolk (Va.) State U., 1979—; cons. Recipient award Tidewater Black Educators, 1977, 78; Tng. of Tchr. Trainers fellow, 1971-73. Mem. Internat. Reading Assn., Va. Reading Assn., Coll. Reading Educators of Va., Nat. Reading Conf., Coll. Reading Assn., Jack and Jill of Am. Inc. (Disting. Jack and Jill award 1977, 78), Pi Lambda Theta, Alpha Kappa Alpha. Episcopalian. Co-author: Fundamental Reading Skills, 1978; Advanced Reading Skills, 1980. Home: 1300 DePaul Way Virginia Beach VA 23464 Office: Dept Reading Norfolk State U Norfolk VA 23504

WILLIAMS, CAROL LOU, nurse, educator; b. New Britain, Conn., Feb. 20, 1950; d. Robert Llewellyn and Charlotte Louise (Manon) Williams; B.S. in Nursing, Catholic U. Am., 1972, M.S. in Nursing (NIH, NIMH grantee), 1975, D.N.Sc., 1979; m. Theodore P. Barnard, Jr., Aug. 9, 1974; 1 dau., Lauren Llwellyn Williams. Various summer nurse positions, 1966-76, 77-78; teaching asst. psychiat. mental health nursing Catholic U. Am., 1976; asst. prof. nursing Sch. Health Studies, U. N.H., Durham, 1978—; mem. bd. fellows Norwich U., Northfield, Vt. Mem. Am. Nurses Assn., Nat. League Nursing, Am. Heart Assn., N.H. Nurses Assn., N.H. League Nursing, N.H. Heart Assn., Phi Theta Kappa, Sigma Theta Tau, Lutheran. Club: Norwich U. (Boston). Office: Dept Nursing Univ NH Garrison Ave Durham NH 08324

WILLIAMS, CAROLE ANN, cytotechnologist; b. Duquesne, Pa., Apr. 14, 1934; d. Theodore Wylie and Dorothy Belle (Mehrmann) Williams; B.S., Chatham Coll., 1956; postgrad. Case-Western Res. U., 1956-57. Cytotechnologist, Clin. Path. Lab. of Paul Gross, Pitts., 1957-59; chief cytotechnologist, teaching supr. Presbyn. U. Hosp., Pitts., 1959-63; staff Pathology Lab. of Drs. Armanini & Wegner, Stockton, Calif., 1964; chief cytotechnologist, teaching supr. Hosp. of Good Samaritan, Los Angeles, 1964—; conductor workshops in field. Mem. Am. Soc. Clin. Pathologists (cytotech. exam. com. bd. registry 1978), Calif. Assn. Cytotechnologists (pres. 1967-68, 72-73), Internat. Acad. Cytology, Am. Soc. Cytology (Technologist of Yr. award 1981). Republican. Presbyterian. Home: 1200 Tellem Dr Pacific Palisades CA 90272 Office: 616 S Witmer St Los Angeles CA 90017

WILLIAMS, CAROLYN ANTONIDES, nurse, epidemiologist; b. Louisville, Oct. 27, 1939; d. John Dwight and Dorothy Ida Marie (Hoffman) Antonides; B.S. with honors in Nursing, Tex. Woman's U., 1961; M.S. in Public Health Nursing Edn., U. N.C., 1965, Ph.D. in Epidemiology (USPHS fellow), 1969; m. Frank Canon Williams, Dec. 26, 1961. Asst. prof. Nell Hodgson Woodruff Sch. Nursing, Emory U., Atlanta, 1968, asso. prof., 1969, prof., dir. grad. programs and research, 1979-71; asso. prof. nursing, asst. prof. epidemiology U. N.C., Chapel Hill, 1971-81, asso. prof. epidemiology, 1981—, asso. prof. nursing and research asso. Health Services Research Center, 1971—; mem. Pres.'s Commn. Study of Ethical Problems in Medicine and Biomed. and Behavioral Research, 1980-82; chair research adv. com. Am. Nurses Found., 1979-81; mem. planning com. study of nursing and nursing edn. Inst. Medicine of Nat. Acad. Scis., 1980; cons. WHO in S.Am. Fellow Am. Acad. Nursing (pres. elect, governing council), Am. Pub. Health Assn. (publs. bd., Young Practitioner award 1973); mem. Council Nurse Researchers, Am. Nurses Assn. (chair Commn. Nursing Research 1980-82), Soc. Epidemiol. Research, Delta Omega, Sigma Theta Tau. Democrat. Baptist. Editorial bd. Family and Community Health, 1977—, Advances in Nursing Sci., 1979—, Internat. Jour. Nursing Studies, 1981—; contbr. articles to profl. jours., chpts. in books. Home: 4100 Five Oaks Dr Apt 42 Durham NC 27707 Office: Dept of Epidemiology School of Public Health University of North Carolina Chapel Hill NC 27514

WILLIAMS, CASSAUNDRA ANN, social researcher; b. N.Y.C., Sept. 2, 1948; d. Samuel and Mary Sue (Fountaine) W.; student Queensborough Community Coll., 1966-70, Cheyney Coll., 1970-72, Columbia U., 1976-78. Human resources cons. Amalgamated Clothing & Textile Workers Union, N.Y.C., 1977-78; recruiter Graham-Windham, N.Y.C., 1978-80; social researcher Clark, Phipps, Clark & Harris, N.Y.C., 1980—; dir., founder CW Workshops, N.Y.C., 1980—. Recipient award Girl Scouts U.S.A., 1965. Mem. Nat. Assn. Female Execs., Columbia U. Alumni Assn. Club: Tom Skinner Fellowship. Home: 31-07 49th St Woodside NY 11377 Office: 60 E 86th St New York NY 10028

WILLIAMS, CHARLOTTE BROOKS, furniture and interior design firm exec.; b. Milw., Nov. 16, 1920; d. Lewis C. and Marguerite Peil Brooks; student U. Wis., 1941; m. Robert Lee Williams, Jr., Oct. 25, 1944 (dec.); children—Patricia, Melissa Williams O'Rourke, R. Brooks; m. 2d, Fred Korth, Aug. 23, 1980. Vice-pres., co-owner Charlotte's Inc., El Paso, Tex., 1951-76; pres. Paso del Norte Design, Inc., El Paso, 1978—; chmn. bd., chief exec. officer Charlotte's, Inc., El Paso, 1979—; mem. adv. bd. Mountain Bell Telephone Co., 1976-79; First City Nat. Bank, El Paso, 1981—. Mem. women's com. El Paso Symphony Orch.; charter mem. Com. of 200, 1982—. Recipient Silver plaque Gifts and Decorative Accessories mag., 1978; named Woman of Year, Women's Polit. Caucus, 1979, Outstanding Woman Entrepreneur El Paso, Am. Bus. Women's Assn., 1979. Mem. Am. Soc. Interior Designers (dir. Tex. 1977—), El Paso C. of C. (dir. 1976—), El Paso Women's C. of C., Delta Gamma. Roman Catholic. Clubs: Coronado Country, El Paso, Internat. (El Paso). Home: 1054 Torrey Pines El Paso TX 79912 Office: Charlotte's Fine Furniture Pepper Tree Square 5411 N Mesa St El Paso TX 79912

WILLIAMS, CHARLOTTE EVELYN FORRESTER (MRS. WALKER ALONZO WILLIAMS), civic worker; b. Kansas City, Mo., Aug. 7, 1905; d. John Dougal and Georgia (Lowerre) Forrester; student U. Kans., 1924-25; m. Walker Alonzo Williams, Sept. 25, 1926; children—Walker Forrester, John Haviland. Trustee, Detroit Grand Opera Assn., 1960—, dir., 1955-60; chmn. Grinnell Opera Scholarship, 1959-65; founder, dir., chmn. adv. bd. Cranbrook Music Guild, Inc., 1952-59, life mem., 1952—; bd. dirs. St. Peter's Home for Boys, Detroit, 1951-53, Detroit Opera Theater, 1959-61, Severo Ballet, 1959-61; Detroit dist. chmn. Met. Opera Regional Auditions, 1958-66; patron-mem. Met. Opera Nat. Council; mem. Central Opera Service, Met. Opera Guild; mem. Opera Guild Ft. Lauderdale (Fla.); trustee Detroit Grand Opera Assn.; mem. Fla. Atlantic U. Found.; past pres. Friends of Caldwell Playhouse, Boca Raton. Mem. Debbie-Rand Meml. Service League (life), Fla. Atlantic Music Guild (past pres.), DAR, English-Speaking Union, Vol. League Fla. Atlantic U., PEO, Order Eastern Star. Home: 1355 Fan Palm Rd Boca Raton FL 33432

WILLIAMS, CINDY JANE, actress; d. Beachard J. and Frances (Bellini) W.; student Los Angeles City Coll., 1965-68. Co-star, Laverne & Shirley, ABC-TV, Hollywood, Calif., 1975—; motion picture appearances include The Conversation, 1975; TV appearances include Room 222, Nanny and the Professor, Policy Story, The Migrants, Happy Days; star TV movie Suddenly Love, 1977; co-star American Graffiti, also More American Graffiti, 1978. Nat. chairwoman for the Fund for Animals. Address: care ABC Public Relations 1330 Avenue of the Americas New York NY 10019 *

WILLIAMS, DORIS ERNESTINE, accountant; b. Selmer, Tenn., Mar. 12, 1931; d. Neely Carder and Eva Cornelia (Stewart) W.; student U. Tenn., 1958-62. Civilian payroll clk. Naval Air Sta., Millington, Tenn., 1956-72, payroll supr., 1972-77, dir. civilian payroll Chief of Naval Res., New Orleans, 1977-80. Named Outstanding Employee, 1978, 79, 80. Mem. Am. Soc. Mil. Comptrollers, Nat. Assn. Female Execs., Am. Soc. Profl. and Exec. Women. Democrat. Mem. Assembly of God. Author: Financial Information Processing Center Payroll Services Guide, 1978. Home: PO Box 26622 New Orleans LA 70186 Office: 4400 Dauphine St New Orleans LA 70146

WILLIAMS, DORIS MOSS, educator; b. Washington, July 13, 1931; d. William and Lila Lee (Elliott) Moss; R.N., Howard U., 1953; B.A., Am. U., 1960; M.A., U. Chgo., 1962; Ph.D., U. Ala., 1977; m. Lionel Therron Williams, Aug. 10, 1963; children—Lionel Therron and Leah Telesyandra (twins). Program dir. Chgo. Youth Centers, 1963-65; family counselor Family Counseling Assos., Birmingham, Ala., 1965-68; dir. student tng. U. Ala. Med. Sch., Birmingham, 1968-74, asso. dean and dir. M.S.W. degree program, 1977—, interim dean, 1980—; cons. VA Mgmt. Tng. Inst., University, Ala., U. Ala. Mem. Women's Polit. Caucus; dir. personnel women's com. Birmingham Symphony Assn. Mem. Nat. Assn. Social Workers (exec. bd.), Council Social Work Edn., Iota Phi Lambda, Phi Delta Kappa, Kappa Delta Pi. Democrat. Baptist. Clubs: Imperial, Federated. Home: 3817 Jefferson Ave SW Birmingham AL 35221 Office: PO Box 1935 University AL 35486

WILLIAMS, DOROTHY ELLEN, educator; b. San Benito, Tex., July 27, 1940; d. Harry James, Jr. and Josephine Louise (Witherwax) W.; B.S., Tex. Woman's U., 1962; M.Ed., Our Lady of Lake Coll., San Antonio; 1968; mid-mgmt. cert. U. Tex., San Antonio, 1982. Tchr., coach Harlandale Sch. Dist., San Antonio, 1962-68; instr. Sam Houston State U., Huntsville, Tex., 1968-69; tchr. Harlandale Sch. Dist., 1969-75; asst. athletic dir. San Antonio Sch. Dist., 1975-82; vice prin. M.L. King Middle Sch., San Antonio, 1982—. Mem. AAHPER, Nat. Interscholastic Athletic Adminstrs. Assn., Tex. Assn. Health, Phys. Edn. and Recreation (asst. mgr. conv. 1976, 80), Tex. Tchrs. Assn. (pres., sec. dist. 20, 1976-78), Tex. High Sch. Girls Coaches, S.E. Bus. and Profl. Women, Delta Kappa Gamma. Methodist. Author articles in field. Home: PO Box 21292 San Antonio TX 78221 Office: 3501 Martin Luther King Dr San Antonio TX 78220

WILLIAMS, DOROTHY FRANCES, educator; b. Brookline, Mass., Aug. 23, 1918; d. John Joseph and Gertrude (Riley) Williams; student Lasell Jr. Coll., 1938-39; B.S., Simmons Coll., 1941, D.Journalism (hon.), 1978; postgrad. Providence Coll., 1953-56; M.S., Boston U., 1967. Mem. personnel dept. Am. Optical Co., Boston, 1942-43; news editor Raytheon News, Raytheon Mfg. Co., Newton, Mass., 1943-45; editor Hammett Herald, J.L. Hammett Co., Cambridge, Mass., 1945-46; editor Your Home mag., Boston, 1946-50; chmn. dept. communications ret., prof. pub. emeritus, editor Simmons Rev., Simmons Coll., Boston, 1947-78. Communications cons. labor, mgmt., alumni publs., writer-editor; dir. editorial graphic arts workshops; tchr. editorial workshop Council Advancement and Support of Edn., 1982; adviser Leadership Tng. Inst., U.S. Office of Edn. Mem. (ret.) corp. Editorial Projects for Edn., Washington. Formation dir. St. Francis of the Cape Frat., Secular Franciscan Order, 1980-82. Recipient Am. Alumni Council awards for editorial achievement, 1948-74; Internat. Council Indsl. Editors, New Eng. Bus. Communicators, Am. Coll. Public Relations Assn. awards for editorial excellence; Am. Graphic Arts Inst. award for excellence in graphic arts in Simmons Rev.; awards Council Advancement and Support Edn., 1975-77; Sibley award for top alumni mag. Council Advancement and Support Edn., 1977; Eleanor Collier Meml. award for profl. achievement, 1978. Mem. Mass. Indsl. Editors Assn. (treas. 1945-47), Nat. Conf. internat. Council Indsl. Editors (edn. coordinator 1967), Am. Alumni Council (mag. chmn. dist. I conf. 1964, dir. communicators insts. 1964-74), Council for Advancement and Support of Edn., Communication Inst., Advt. Club Greater Boston (ret.), Am. Advt. Fedn., Assn. Edn. in Journalism. Author: The Labor Press in Profile, 1964; A Primer for the Graphically Illiterate, 1966; The Day A Lincoln Was Saved, 1963; Communicating with Alumni, 1979. Home: PO Box 1173 5 Wixon Rd Dennis Port MA 02639 Office: Simmons Coll 300 The Fenway Boston MA 02115

WILLIAMS, DOROTHY MARIE, banker; b. Evansville, Ind., Mar. 11, 1924; d. Roy L. and Marie K. (Bender) Williams; student Ind. State U., 1970—. With Permanent Fed. Savs. & Loan Assn. of Evansville (Ind.), 1943—, asst. sec., 1965, corporate sec., 1977, asst. v.p., sec., 1979—, sec. to pres., 1977—. Vol., Evansville Assn. for Retarded Citizens, 1960—, pres. Aux., 1965-66; active Christ the King Ch., 1974—. Recipient Friend of Retarded award Evansville Assn. Retarded Citizens, 1967. Roman Catholic. Home: 216 S Ruston Ave Evansville IN 47714 Office: 101 SE 3d St PO Box 3407 Evansville IN 47733

WILLIAMS, E. FAYE, assn. exec.; b. Melrose, La., Dec. 20, 1941; d. Vernon Williams and Frances (LaCour) Williams; B.S., Grambling State U., 1962; postgrad. UCLA, 1963-65, Pepperdine U., 1965; M.P.A., U. So. Calif., 1971; postgrad. Atlanta Law Sch., 1971-72, Mich., 1976. Tchr., Los Angeles public schs., 1963-71; dir. Atlanta Assn. Educators, 1971-73; dir. Pacific Div., Overseas Edn. Assn., Far East, 1973-75; dir. United Tchrs. of Flint (Mich.), 1975-77; asst. dir. Mich. Edn. Assn., Southfield, 1977-80; dir. Mich. Edn. Assn.-NEA Met. Detroit Organizing project, Southfield, 1980-81, dir. profl. devel. and human rights, 1981—; franchisee with Success Motivation Inst., 1979—. Bd. dirs. Grambling State U., 1969-71, 82-84; mem. Com. of Labor Union Women, 1977—; Mich. Edn. Assn.'s staff rep. to United Found., 1977—; edn. cons. TV show, Room 222, 1969-71. Recipient Key Woman award, Calif. Dem. Central Com., 1970; Calif. Senate Resolution and Cert. of Merit, Calif. Assembly, 1969; Coe Found. fellow, 1965; Delta Sigma Theta and La. Dept. Edn. scholar, 1959. Mem. Mich. Edn. Assn. Women's Caucus, Nat. Assn. Female Execs., Nat. Assn. Coll. Women, Am. Acad. Human Services, NEA Uniserv Mgrs. Assn., Grambling State U. Alumni Assn. (pres. Detroit chpt., also nat. pres. 1982-84), Delta Sigma Theta. Democrat. Baptist. Club: Order Eastern Star. Home: 6242 Edenhall Way East Lansing MI 48823 Office: 1216 Kendale Blvd East Lansing MI 48823

WILLIAMS, E. VIRGINIA, artistic dir., educator, choreographer, educator; b. Melrose, Mass.; d. Charles F. and Mary Virginia (Evitts) W.; trained in Boston, N.Y.C.; also student piano, drama and art; hon. degrees in the arts. married; 1 child. Tchr. ballet; choreographer; dir. New Eng. Civic Ballet Co., 1958—; founder, artistic dir. Boston Ballet, 1963—. Mem. Dance Tchrs. Club Boston (past pres.; hon. citation). Office: Boston Ballet 19 Clarendon St Boston MA 02116

WILLIAMS, EDNA ALETA THEADORA JOHNSTON, journalist; b. Halifax, N.S., Can., Sept. 19, 1923; d. Clarence Harvey and Edna May (Lewis) Johnston; student Maritime Bus. Coll., 1943; m. Albert Murray Williams, Apr. 16, 1949 (dec.); children—Murleta, Norma, Martin, Charla, Kerrick, Renwick, Julia. Typist, Dept. Treasury (Navy), Halifax, 1944-49; with Bedford (N.S.) Mag., Halifax br., 1954-55, Presbyn. Office, New Glasgow, N.S., part-time, 1965-67, Thompson and Sutherland, New Glasgow, part-time, 1967-69; family editor, columnist and reporter New Glasgow Evening News, 1969—. Baptist rep. Pictou County Council of Churches, 1978—, sec., 1980—; pres. ch. aux. 2d United Bapt. Ch., 1979—asst. organist, 1970—, chorus dir. Men's Choir, 1980—; provincial rep. Women's Inst. of African United Bapt. Assn., 1980—; mem. council Halifax YWCA; founding mem. Pictou County YM-YWCA, 1966—, bd. dirs., 1967-77, corr. sec., v.p., 1975-77, 1974-75; past pres., past provincial dir. Home and Sch.; past officer local interracial com. Mem. Can. Press Assn. Home: 230 Reservoir St New Glasgow NS B2H 4K4 Canada Office: Evening News 352 East River Rd New Glasgow NS B2H 5E2 Canada

WILLIAMS, ELMA, public relations exec.; b. Carroll County, Va.; d. Preston and Macy (Goad) W.; A.B. with spl. honors, George Washington U., 1953; M.A. in Public Adminstrn., Am. U., 1961. Asst. program dir., asst. dir. ops. WTOP, CBS-Radio and TV, 1947-51; mem. pub. relations staff George Washington U., 1951-52; registrar Washington Sch. for Secs., 1953; exec. sec. Joint Econ. Com. of U.S. Congress, 1956-59; legis. info. specialist NEA, Washington, 1960—. Bd. dirs. Edn. Assos. Fed. Credit Union, 1973—, pres., 1975-77; bd. dirs. Met. Area Credit Union Mgmt. Assn., 1977—, sec., 1977—; sec. Kenwood Beach (Md.) Citizens Assn., 1981—. Recipient Alumni Service award George Washington U., 1970. Mem. AAUW (br. publicity chmn. 1956-59), Am.

News Women's Club, NEA (life), Columbian Women George Washington U. (pres. 1965-67), George Washington U. Alumni Assn. (dir. 1965-67, 69-70), Edn. Writers Assn., Ednl. Press Assn., Women's Joint Congressional Com. (chmn. 1974-76), Phi Delta Gamma (chpt. pres. 1973-74, nat. conv. chmn. 1980, nat. treas., trustee 1980—), Pi Sigma Alpha. Mem. Nat. Woman's Party, Woman's Nat. Dem. Club, Twentieth Century Club. Home: 4000 Cathedral Ave NW Washington DC 20016 Office: Div Govt Relations NEA 1201 16th St NW Washington DC 20036

WILLIAMS, FRANCES MAY, printing plant exec.; b. Bklyn., May 20, 1936; d. Max and Nettie Kane; student public schs., Bklyn.; m. Carroll F. Williams, Feb. 22, 1956; children—Cindy Lynn, Roger. Paste-up trainee, typesetter Massapequa (N.Y.) Post., 1962-64; with Accurate Web, Inc., Deer Park, N.Y., 1965—, typesetter, paste-up and estimator, 1965-72, asst. prodn. mgr., 1972-75, prodn. mgr., 1975—, v.p., 1979—. Mem. Printing Industries Met. N.Y., L.I. Graphic Arts (dir.). Home: 48 McKinley Pl Massapequa NY 11758 Office: 335 Marcus Blvd Deer Park NY 11729

WILLIAMS, GEORGIA CHRISTENE BLANTON, psychologist; b. Adams County, Ohio, Dec. 6, 1927; d. John Scott and Frona Ruth (Morrison) Blanton; R.N., Bethesda Sch. Nursing, 1948; B.A., Calif. State U., Sacramento, 1965, M.A., 1969; Ph.D., U. Man., 1971. Head nurse Ohio State U. Hosp., Columbus, 1948-56, Calif. Instn. for Women, Corona, 1956-61; dir. day patient unit Health Scis. Center, Winnipeg, Man., Can., 1971-74, co-dir. sexuality clinic, 1972-79; asso. prof. Faculty of Medicine, U. Man., 1973-79; pvt. practice psychology, Carmichael, Calif., 1980—. Mem. Am. Psychol. Assn., Am. Assn. Sex Educators, Counselors and Therapists, Marriage Family and Child Counselors, Assn. Advancement Psychology. Home: 7041 Lincoln Oaks Dr Fair Oaks CA 95628 Office: 5738 Marconi Ave Suite 5 Carmichael CA 95608

WILLIAMS, HARRIETTE FLOWERS, ednl. adminstr.; b. Los Angeles, July 18; d. Orlando and Virginia (Carter) Flowers; B.S., UCLA, 1952, Ed.D., (HEW fellow), 1973; M.A., Calif. State U., Los Angeles, 1956; m. Irvin F. Williams, Apr. 9, 1960; children—Lorin Finley, Lori Virginia. Tchr., Los Angeles Unified Sch. Dist., 1952-59, counselor, 1954-59; psychometrist, 1958-62, faculty chmn., 1956-57, student activities coordinator, 1955-59, leader insts. and workshops, 1952-76, dir. counseling, 1960-65, supr. Title I programs Elem. Secondary Edn. Act, 1965-68, asst. prin., 1968-76; prin. Foshay Jr. High Sch., 1976-80; prin. Manual Arts High Sch., 1980-82; Dir. of instrn., sr. high schs. div., 1982—. asst. dir. HEW project for high sch. adminstrn. UCLA, 1971-72; adj. prof. Masters in Sch. Adminstrn. program Pepperdine U., Los Angeles, 1974-76. Recipient Sojourner Truth award Nat. Assn. Negro Bus. and Profl. Women's Clubs, Los Angeles, 1968, Life Membership Service award Los Angeles PTA, 1975, 79. Mem. Los Angeles Assn. Secondary Sch. Adminstrs., Assn. Calif. Sch. Adminstrs., Nat. Assn. Secondary Sch. Prins., Sr. High Sch. Prins. Orgn. Los Angeles Nat. Council of Negro Women (life mem.), Lullaby Guild of Children's Home Soc. Los Angeles, Los Angeles PTA, NAACP, Urban League, Delta Sigma Theta (pres. Los Angeles chpt. 1964-66, regional dir. 1968-72, nat. committeewoman 1966-82, recipient Minerva award 1982), Pi Lambda Theta, Phi Delta Kappa, Kappa Delta Pi. Baptist. Office: 644 W 17th St Los Angeles CA 90015

WILLIAMS, HAZEL MAY, real estate exec.; b. San Diego, Oct. 21, 1926; d. William and Alice May (Yarno) Roth; B.A., San Diego State U., 1946; student West Valley Jr. Coll., 1970-73; grad. Realtors Inst.; m. Shelley S. Willians, Jr., Aug. 24, 1947; 1 dau., Christabel May. Vice pres. Shelley Williams Assos., Inc., Saratoga, Calif., 1968—. Active Los Gatos chpt. ARC, Community Hosp. Aux., West Valley Republican Women. Named Woman of Yr., Santa Clara chpt. Women's Council Realtors; cert. residential specialist, Realtor and broker; cert. real estate brokerage mgr. Mem. Nat. Assn. Realtors, Calif. Assn. Realtors (dir. 1974-79, regional v.p. 1981, dir.-at-large 1982), Los Gatos-Saratoga Bd. Realtors (pres. 1978, certs. of merit, Realtor of Yr. 1980), San Jose Real Estate Bd., Women's Council Realtors, Calif. Assn. Real Estate Tchrs., DAR (Los Gatos chpt.). Clubs: Saratoga Foothill, San Jose Women's. Office: 12960 Saratoga Sunnyvale Rd Saratoga CA 95070

WILLIAMS, HELEN ELIZABETH, clin. psychologist; b. Stantonsburg, N.C., Sept. 14, 1914; d. George Short and Helen (Heinzer) W.; B.A., Randolph-Macon Woman's Coll., 1936; diploma Beacom Bus. Coll., 1938; M.A., Columbia U., 1945, Ed.D., 1945. Tchr. English, Bridgeville (Del.) High Sch., 1936-37; congl. sec. U.S. Ho. of Reps., Washington, 1938-40; sec., asst. to dir. retail merchandising, asst. personnel mgr. charge female personnel Am. Viscose Corp., N.Y.C., 1941-43; psychologist, psychotherapist Child Guidance Center, Westchester County Children's Assn., 1945-48; psychologist, psychotherapist Child Guidance Clinic of Pinellas County, Fla., 1948-50, acting dir., 1949-50; sr. clin. psychologist U.S. Naval Hosp., St. Albans, N.Y., 1952-55; guidance dir., sch. psychologist New Lincoln Sch., N.Y.C., 1955-56; chief psychologist out-patient dept. Westchester div. N.Y. Hosp., 1956-57; asst. dean, dir. counseling New Sch. for Social Research, N.Y.C., 1958-60; psychologist Health and Guidance Center, Wilmington (Del.) Pub. Schs., 1960-61; part-time supervising clin. psychologist St. Vincents Hosp., N.Y.C., 1961-77; pvt. practice in psychology, 1961-81. Fellow Am. Psychol. Assn.; mem. N.Y. State Psychol. Assn., Pi Lambda Theta, Kappa Delta Pi. Club: Congressional. Address: 23 W 73d St New York NY 10023

WILLIAMS, HENRIETTA VER MEER, clin. psychologist; b. Pella, Iowa, Apr. 2, 1924; d. Otto Henry and Dena Catherine (Stadt) Ver Meer; B.A. in Philosophy, U. Iowa, 1944; M.A. in Psychology, U. Ill., 1946, Ph.D. in Exptl. Psychology, 1949; postgrad. in clin. psychology U. Md., 1966-67; m. Richard Hays Williams, Feb. 19, 1971; children—Marylie Catherine Williams Karlovac, Robert Harold, Frank Rendler. Counselor, U. Wis., Madison, 1945-51, lectr. dept. psychology, 1951-52; research psychologist NIMH, Bethesda, Md., 1965-67, postdoctoral intern in clin. psychology, 1967-68; staff psychologist, psychologist-in-charge of div. St. Elizabeth's Hosp., Washington, 1969-72, clin. adminstr., 1972-74; dir. psychol. services Pitt County Mental Health Center, Greenville, N.C., 1974-78; pvt. practice clin. psychology, asso. Nelson Clinic, Greenville, 1978—; cons. Alcoholic Rehab. Center, 1977-79, Regional Rehab. Center, Pitt Meml. Hosp., 1977-81, Devel. Evaluation Clinic, Med. Sch., 1980—; clin. asst. prof. psychology Eastern Carolina U. Sch. Medicine, 1977—. Mem. vestry St. Luke's Episcopal Ch., Rockville, Md., 1968-71; mem. incorporating body, chmn. personnel com. St. Luke's Half-Way Houses, Rockville. Mem. Am. Psychol. Assn., Nat. Register Health Service Providers in Psychology, Phi Beta Kappa, Univ. Condominium Assn. (pres. 1980-82). Democrat. Clubs: Pilot, PEO. Contbr. articles in field to profl. jours. Home: 111 Cardinal Dr Greenville NC 27834 Office: Nelson Clinic Suite 9 Med Pavilion Greenville NC 27834

WILLIAMS, JANE WELCH, lawyer; b. Memphis, Feb. 14, 1945; d. Frank P. and Clemmie (Corley) Welch; B.A. cum laude, U. Wis., 1967; J.D., Albany Law Sch., 1974; m. Jim Williams, Dec. 20, 1965 (div. June 1976); m. 2d, Jerome Brownstein, July 25, 1980. Admitted to N.Y. bar, 1975; legis. asst. N.Y. State Legislature, 1968-74; atty. N.Y. State Power Authority, N.Y.C., 1974-76; gen. counsel N.Y. State Higher Edn. Services Corp., Albany, 1976-77; v.p. Gavit & Co., Inc., Albany, 1978—; partner firm Brownstein & Williams, Albany, 1977—; adj. prof. Russell Sage Coll., 1978-79. Mem. Gov.'s Task Force on Energy, 1974. Mem. Women's Bar Assn. N.Y. State (pres. Capital Dist. chpt. 1977-79), N.Y. State Bar Assn., Am. Bar Assn., Albany County Bar Assn. Office: 284 State St Albany NY 12210

WILLIAMS, JEAN TAYLOR, artist; b. Town Creek, Ala., Mar. 27, 1912; d. Woodie Richard and Ella Ross (Harrison) Taylor; B.S., U. Montevallo, 1933; student Chgo. Art Inst., 1936; student of Robert Brackman, Noank, Conn., 1958-60; m. James Hayes Williams, June 18, 1935; children—James Richard, Hayes Taylor, Jean Williams Johnson. Art tchr. high sch., Ala., 1933-35; tchr. pvt. classes own studio, Birmingham, Ala., 1976—; art chmn. Mountain Brook Jr. High Sch., Birmingham, 1966; one-woman shows: Samford U., Nat. Soc. Arts and Letters; exhibited invitational Jerome Hines Exhbn., 1977; represented in numerous pvt. collections. Recipient grand award in oil painting State of Ala., 1961. Recipient Crusade citation for service Am. Cancer Soc., 1979. Mem. Am. Artists Profl. League (life), Nat. League Am. Pen Women (1st v.p. Birmingham br. 1982—), Nat. Soc. Arts and Letters (pres. Birmingham chpt. 1982—; organizer Ala. state art competition 1981, Ala. state piano competition 1982), Ala. Art League, Birmingham Art Assn. Presbyterian. Clubs: Vestavia Country, Turtle Point Yacht and Country, The Club. Address: 2801 Mountain Brook Pkwy Birmingham AL 35223

WILLIAMS, JESSIE RUTH, purchasing exec.; b. Warrensburg, Mo., Dec. 22, 1928; d. Rolla and Daisy Vine (Thomas) Close; B.S. in Bus. Edn., Central Mo. State Coll., 1967; m. Vernon Lyle Williams, May 8, 1950; 1 son, Lyle Eugene. With Montgomery Ward & Co., Kansas City, Mo., 1946-48, clk., Warrensburg, 1968-69; telephone operator United Telephone Co., Warrensburg, Mo., 1952-56, acctg. clk., 1958-62; purchasing dir. Johnson County Meml. Hosp., Warrensburg, Mo., 1969—. Mem. Kansas City Area Hosp. Purchasing Dirs. (sec.-treas. 1976, pres. 1981), Am. Hosp. Assn., Nat. Assn. Hosp. Purchasing Mgmt., Ozark Purchasing Group (sec. 1977). Baptist. Clubs: Club 46 Extention, Bus. and Profl. Women's (2d v.p. 1978—). Home: PO Box 170 Warrensburg MO 64093 Office: Burkarth Rd Warrensburg MO 64093

WILLIAMS, JOAN KAY, purchasing mgr.; b. Richmond, Va., Oct. 12, 1946; d. Walter Bosher and Ruth Lilly Williams; A.A., Shennandoah Coll. Sec., Value Engring., Alexandria, Va., 1967-68; personnel interviewer Montgomery Ward, 1968-69; adminstrv. asst. Data Processing Fin. and Gen. Corp., Alexandria, 1969-70; purchasing mgr. ENSCO, Inc., Springfield, Va., 1970—. Mem. IEEE, Am. Mgmt. Assn., Regional Purchasing Council Va., Nat. Assn. Female Execs., Bus. and Profl. Women's Club, Beta Sigma Phi, Phi Beta Lambda. Home: 6019 Kerrwood St Burke VA 22015 Office: 5400 Port Royal Rd Springfield VA 22151

WILLIAMS, JOAN LEE, educator; b. Clifford, Ill., Sept. 24, 1930; d. Lawrence Singleton and Mabel Marie (Nance) W.; B.S., So. Ill. U. (Normal Sch. scholar), 1954; M.S., 1960, Ph.D. (NDEA fellow), 1963; postgrad. Ind. U., 1961-62. Tchr., North Bend Sch., Carterville, Ill., 1948-50, Colp (Ill.) Standard Sch., 1950-53, Sunnyside Sch., Herrin, Ill., 1954-56, Herrin City Schs., 1956-60; instr. So. Ill. U., Carbondale, 1960-63; asst. prof. edn. U. Conn., Storrs, 1963; mem. faculty Ball State U., Muncie, Ind., 1964—, asso. prof. elem. edn. 1968-72, prof., 1972—. Recipient grant Ball State U., 1970-71. Mem. Internat. Reading Assn., Nat. Council Tchrs. English, AAUP, Ind. Reading Profs., Orton Soc., Pi Lambda Theta, Phi Delta Kappa, Kappa Delta Pi. Home: 2020 N Ball Ave Muncie IN 47304 Office: Sch Edn Ball State U Muncie IN 47306

WILLIAMS, JULIA MARIE, cons., devel. co. ofcl.; b. Vallejo, Calif., June 17; d. L.B. and Almarie (Anthony) W., Jr.; B.A., Calif. State U., San Jose, 1972; M.B.A., UCLA, 1974. Tchr., Compton (Calif.) Unified Sch. Dist., 1974; loan officer Bank of Am., 1975-78; sr. fin. analyst Pacific Coast Devel. Corp., Los Angeles, 1978-80; fin. mgr. Hub City Urban Developers, Inc., Compton, 1980—; owner, pres. Julia Williams and Assos., cons. and devel.; instr. S.W. Coll. Sponsor, Black Women's Forum; bd. dirs. Los Angeles Small Bus. Investment Corp. Mem. Nat. Assn. M.B.A. Execs., UCLA Alumni Assn. Office: 408 E Alondra Blvd Compton CA 90220

WILLIAMS, JULIE BELLE, psychiat. social worker; b. Algona, Iowa, July 29, 1950; d. George Howard and Leta Maribelle (Durschmidt) W.; B.A., U. Iowa, 1972, M.S.W., 1973. Social worker Psychopathic Hosp., Iowa City, 1971-72; OEO counselor YOUR, Webster City, Iowa, 1972; social worker Child Devel. Clinic, Iowa City, 1973; group therapist Cedar Manor Nursing Home, Tipton, Iowa, 1973; therapist Mid-Eastern Iowa Community Mental Health Center, Iowa City, 1973; psychiat. social worker Mental Health Center N. Iowa, Mason City, 1974-79, chief social worker, 1979-80; asst. dir. White Bear Lake (Minn.) Community Counseling Center, 1980—; lectr., cons. in field. NIMH grantee, 1972-73. Mem. Nat. Assn. Social Workers, NOW, Acad. Cert. Social Workers, Am. Orthopsychiat. Assn., Am. Assn. Sex Educators, Counselors and Therapists, Phi Beta Kappa. Democrat. Home: 761 Cannon Ave Shoreview MN 55112 Office: 2129 2d St White Bear MN 55112

WILLIAMS, KAREN NORRIS, social service agy. adminstr.; b. Cleve., July 18, 1943; d. Frederic Douglass and Viola Sears Norris; B.A., U. Pa., 1964; M.Ed., Temple U., 1967; Ed.D., Wayne State U., 1980; children—Kathryn, David, Douglas. Asst. buyer Lit Bros. Co., Phila., 1965-66; tchr. secondary schs., Phila., Cleve., Detroit, 1966-71; mem. faculty Wayne State U., 1971-75, Wayne County Community Coll., 1971-75; planner researcher Wayne County Juvenile Facility Network, 1975; with YWCA of Met. Detroit, 1975—, exec. dir., 1980—. Bd. dirs. WIC Magnet Sch. for Gifted Children, Inkster, Mich.; active Met. Detroit council Boy Scouts Am. Mem. Am. Soc. Tng. and Devel., Women's Econ. Club, Nat. Assn. Black Social Workers, New Detroit Conf. of Black Agy. Exec. Dirs. for Human Services, Delta Sigma Theta. Club: Jack and Jill of Am., Inc. Office: 2230 Witherell St Detroit MI 48201

WILLIAMS, LORRAINE ANN, nurse; b. Mt. Vernon, N.Y., Dec. 11, 1937; d. Thomas Lawrence and Hyacinth Mathilda (Heitzman) W.; R.N., Stamford (Conn.) Hosp., 1958; B.S., Boston Coll., 1962. Mem. faculty Stamford Hosp. Sch. Nursing, 1962-65; from supr. to dir. patient care Peninsula Hosp., Burlingame, Calif., 1965-77; dir. patient care San Jose (Calif.) Hosp., 1977—; cons. in field. Recipient Leadership award Stamford Hosp. Sch. Nursing, 1958. Mem. Am. Soc. Nursing Service Adminstrs., Calif. Soc. Nursing Service Adminstrs. (dir.). Democrat. Roman Catholic. Home: 415 Wave Ave Half Moon Bay CA 94019 Office: 675 E Santa Clara St San Jose CA 95112

WILLIAMS, LOUISE ANITIA, graphic design co. exec.; b. Portland, Oreg., Mar. 31, 1942; d. Homer Bruce and Ora Ellen (Diehl) W.; student public schs., Beaverton, Oreg.; 1 dau., Tiffany Joy Wlecial. Med. asst., physicians' practice, 1963-64; adminstrv. asst. St. Vincent's Hosp., 1964-70; salesman, sales mgr., nat. sales mgr. Indsl. Systems, 1970; regional sales mgr. Peel O'Matique, 1971; bus. devel. rep. Imperial Bank, 1971-72; pvt. practice fin. cons., Los Angeles, 1972-73; sales rep. Printing Services, Granada Hills, Calif., 1976; partner Art, Love, Time & Money, Marina City, Calif., 1978-79; pres., sole stock holder Corporate Creative Services, Sherman Oaks, Calif., 1979—. Served with Hosp. Corps, USN, 1960-63. Mem. Nat. Assn. Female Execs., Los Angeles Ad Club, Sherman Oaks C. of C., Republican Presdl. Task Force. Clubs: Buckley Mother's, Marina City; Mid Town Exec. (Los Angeles). Home: 5316 Sylmar Ave Van Nuys CA 91401 Office: 15301 Ventura Blvd Suite 300 Sherman Oaks CA 91403

WILLIAMS, LYNNE HUIE, psychiatrist; b. Evanston, Ill., Aug. 23, 1943; d. Virgil Clifford and Vivian (Brown) W.; B.A., U. Mich., 1965; M.D., Wayne State U., 1969; children—Tavis Randall, Shepherd Subhan. Intern, Bronx Mcpl. Hosp., 1969-70, resident in pediatrics, 1970-72; resident in psychiatry U. Miami (Fla.), 1973-74, fellow developmental pediatrics, 1972-73; practice medicine, specializing in developmental pediatrics, gestalt therapy, Asheville, N.C., 1974-79; med. dir. Devel. Evaluation Center, Asheville, 1976-79; fellow in child and adolescent psychiatry U. Miami, 1979-81; practice medicine specializing in infant, child, adolescent and adult psychiatry, Spokane, Wash., 1981—. Diplomate Am. Bd. Pediatrics. Mem. Human Potential Inst. Gt. Smokies (dir. 1975—), Am. Soc. Adolescent Psychiatry, Gestalt Therapy Inst. Fla. (asso.), Am. Psychiat. Assn., Am. Orthopsychiat. Assn., N.C. Group Behavior Soc. Research on developmental effects of early parent-infant interactions. Home: E4518 Silver Pine Rd Colbert WA 99005 Office: E 235 Rowan Suite 202 Spokane WA 99207

WILLIAMS, MARCILLE GRAY, mfg. co. exec.; b. Tacoma, Apr. 15, 1947; d. Harold Franklin and Lucille Bessie (Price) Gray; student public schs., Tacoma. Pres., Spectra Advt. Inc., Newport Beach, Calif., 1973-76; exec. v.p. Reiser/Williams/deYong, Costa Mesa, Calif., 1977-79; mgr. mktg. communications Xerox Co., Dallas, 1979—. Bd. dirs. Dallas Opera. Author: The New Executive Woman, 1977. Office: 1341 W Mockingbird Ln Dallas TX 75247

WILLIAMS, MARILYN MURPHY, lawyer; b. Elizabeth, N.J., May 13, 1942; d. Thomas Patrick and Florence Ann (Weickhardt) Murphy; B.S., U. Kans., 1964; M.L.S., Emporia State Coll., 1974; J.D., U. Mo. at Kansas City, 1979; m. John James Williams, July 25, 1964; children—Patrick, Kathryn. Tchr., Shawnee Mission (Kans.) Sch. Dist., 1964-66, Virginia Beach, Va., 1967-68, Newport, R.I., 1969-70; librarian Center Sch. Dist., Kansas City, Mo., 1973-75; admitted to Kans. bar, 1979; partner Williams & Oberhelman, Mission, Kans., 1979—. Bd. dirs. Kans. Legal Services of Olathe, 1981—. NDEA fellow, 1965. Mem. Am. Bar Assn., Kans. Bar Assn., Kans. Trial Lawyers Assn., Kansas City Bar Assn., Johnson County Bar Assn. (bench-bar com. domestic relations 1981—). Republican. Home: 2312 W 96th St Leawood KS 66206 Office: Williams & Oberhelman 6420 W 95th Overland Park KS 66212

WILLIAMS, MARSHA E., data processor; b. Providence, Mar. 18, 1945; d. Charles and Estelle Rose Abrams; B.S. magna cum laude, Northeastern U., 1973; postgrad. Babson Coll.; 1 dau., Jocelyn Diane. Programmer, analyst Citizens Bank, Providence, 1965-66, RAI Cons., Providence, 1966-67, Keane Assos., Boston, 1967-69; systems programmer Rustcraft Greeting Cards, Dedham, Mass., 1969-73, systems and programming mgr., 1973-76; mgr. info. systems Schmid, Inc., Randolph, Mass., 1976-81; sr. systems cons. Digital Equipment Corp., Southboro, Mass., 1981—; data processing cons. Bd. dirs. Easton Girls Soccer League. Lic. real estate broker, Mass. Mem. Data Processing Mgmt. Assn., Women South, Nat. Assn. Female Execs., Am. Mgmt. Assn., Am. Prodn. and Inventory Control Soc., Sigma Epsilon Rho. Home: 108 Black Brook Rd South Easton MA 02375

WILLIAMS, MARTHA DOUGLAS, ednl. coordinator; b. St. Louis, Nov. 22, 1948; d. James Major and Odcal Douglas; B.S. in Sociology (Margaret Elam Bus. scholar), N.E. Mo. State U., Kirksville, 1971; M.Ed., U. Mo., St. Louis, 1982; 1 dau., Candice Brenda. Sec. to advt. mgr. St. Louis Argus Pubg. Co., 1966; telephone clk. customer relations Union Elec. Co., St. Louis, 1966-68; with Hollister's Hosp. Products, Inc., Kirksville, Mo., 1970; sec. Manpower Temporary Help Agy., St. Louis, 1968-71; supervising tchr. St. Louis Agy. on Tng. and Employment, 1980; tchr. St. Louis Pub. Schs., 1972-81; ednl. coordinator Citizenship Edn. Clearing House, St. Louis, 1981—; dept. head. Visual and Performing Arts High Sch. Magnet Program, 1977-80. Sec., Mt. Calvary Lutheran Ch., 1982; bd. dirs. St. Martin's Day Care, 1978-80, Downtown Day Care, 1980-81. Econ. Edn. scholar, 1976; Allen J. Ellender fellow, 1979-80; participant St. Louis Pub. Schs. Partnership Program, 1980-81. Mem. Conf. on Edn., Mo. Council on Social Studies. Home: 5226 Wells Saint Louis MO 63113 Office: Citizenship Edn Clearing House 5331 Enright St Louis MO 63112

WILLIAMS, MARTHA JANE SHIPE, univ. dean; b. Houston, June 28, 1935; d. Charles Edward and Florence Mae (Coons) Shipe; B.A., U. Tex., Austin, 1957, M.A., 1962, Ph.D., 1963; m. John Gregor Williams, June 4, 1958; children—John, David, Susan, Thomas. Sec., U. Tex., Austin, 1954-57; sec. personnel and sales div. Tenneco, 1957-58; teaching asst. U. Tex., Austin, 1958-61, research asso., 1960-65, asst. prof., 1966-69, asso. prof., 1969-75, prof., 1975—; asst. dir. Inst. Higher Edn. Mgmt., U. Tex. System Adminstrn., Austin, 1979—, dean Sch. Social Work, 1981—. Univ. fellow, 1959; NSF fellow, 1960-61. Mem. Am. Psychol. Assn., Tex. Assn. Coll. Tchrs., Tex. Intergovtl. Tng. Council, Sigma Xi. Contbr. articles to profl. jours. Home: 3200 Silverleaf Dr Austin TX 78757 Office: SWB 2-112 U Texas Austin TX 78712

WILLIAMS, MARTHA OLIVER, accountant; b. Aberdeen, Miss., May 15, 1925; d. Christopher Lorenzo and Lydia Ercelle (Brown) Oliver; student So. Ark. U., 1974; m. Carl S. Williams, Dec. 15, 1946; children—Larry Carl, Mark Oliver. Office mgr.-acct. Ark. Chems., Inc., El Dorado, 1971—; broadcaster local TV and radio, 1955-65; tchr. So. Ark. U., El Dorado, 1978—; also lectr. Vice pres., membership chmn. Community Concert Assn., 1972-74; active PTA. Mem. Nat. League Am. Pen Women, Poets Roundtable Ark. Mem. Ch. of Christ. Author: Lines From Living, 1973; Windows, 1976. Home: 1015 Harrison St El Dorado AR 71730 Office: Route 6 Box 98 El Dorado AR 71730

WILLIAMS, MARY EDWINA, mktg. service cons.; b. Worcester, Mass., Jan. 18, 1950; d. Edward Joseph and Mary Theresa (Sullivan) W.; B.A., Clark U., Worcester, 1972; M.B.A., Anna Maria Coll., Paxton, Mass., 1979; grad. Tanglewood listening and analysis seminar Berkshire Music Center, Lenox, Mass., 1975, mgmt. seminar Am. Symphony Orch., 1975; m. Frederick Leroy Monahan, Jr., June 9, 1979. Mental hygiene therapist Hutchings Psychiat. Center, Syracuse, N.Y., 1972-75; bus. mgr., registrar Worcester Community Sch. Performing Arts, 1975-78; long-term substitute tchr. bus. dept. Sheehan High Sch., Wallingford, Conn., 1979-80; mktg. service cons. bus. dept. So. New Eng. Telephone Co., 1980—. Mem. Clark U. Alumni Council, also co-chmn. career counseling com.; trustee, mem. exec. com., chmn. public relations com. Edward St. Day Care Center, Worcester, 1976-78; bd. dirs. Wallingford Symphony Orch., 1980—. Club: Wallingford Jr. Women's (co-chmn. arts com. 1980—). Address: 61 New Place St Wallingford CT 06492

WILLIAMS, MARY ELLEN, nurse; b. Breckenridge, Tex., Feb. 25, 1932; d. Minor Hayden and Lura C. (LeeMasters) Harper; R.N., Parkland Hosp., Sch. Nursing, Dallas, 1953; postgrad. Cisco Jr. Coll., 1955; m. Robert L. Williams, Mar. 4, 1972; children by previous marriage—Jaye Harlene Bollinger, Melody Kim Bollinger, Mary Beth Bollinger. Floor supr. Eastland (Tex.) Meml. Hosp., 1953-54, supr., 1970-72; supr. operating room Ranger (Tex.) Gen. Hosp., 1954-62; dir. nurses Western Manor Nursing Home, Ranger, 1967-70, Eastland Manor Nursing Home, 1973-74, Leisure Lodges, Inc., Eastland; instr. in nursing Ranger Jr. Coll., 1975-76; dir. nurses Cisco (Tex.), Nursing Center, 1977—; supr. Eastland Meml. Hosp., 1978—; speaker in field. Recipient award for continuing edn. West Tex. Rehab. Center, 1975. Mem. Am., Tex. nurses assns. Baptist. Home: PO Box 323 Eastland TX 76448

WILLIAMS, MARY LOU NEWMAN, mus. and archives coordinator; b. Harleton, Tex., Dec. 21, 1918; d. Ray Maxie and Corine (Baker) Newman; A.A., Coll. of Marshall, 1935; B.A., Mary Hardin-Baylor U., 1937; postgrad. U. Tex., Austin, 1937-38; M.A., E. Tex. State U., 1961; m. Louis Booth Williams, Oct. 15, 1938; children—Joanne Williams Click, Louis Booth. English instr. Paris (Tex.) Jr. Coll., 1953-68, chmn. communications div., 1965-68, coordinator for devel. A.M. and Welma Aikin Regional Archives, 1977—; English instr. E. Tex. State U., Commerce, 1970-74; coordinator for devel. R.F. Voyer Regional Mus., Honey Grove, Tex., 1977—. Pres., McCuistion Regional Med. Center Aux., 1975-77; dist. bd. Nat. Multiple Sclerosis Soc.; mem. YWCA, Lamar County Hist. Commn. Winedale Mus. seminar scholar, 1977. Mem. AAUW, Am. Assn. State and Local History, Soc. Am. Archivists, Am. Assn. Museums, Tex. Assn. Museums, Tex. State Hist. Assn., N.E. Tex. Geneal. Soc., LWV, Phi Theta Kappa (hon.). Methodist. Clubs: Cosmos (pres. 1977), Paris Garden (pres. 1944), Garden Study (pres. 1955), Mary Emma Bible (pres. 1975, 80). Home: 3170 Laurel Ln Paris TX 75460

WILLIAMS, MARY LOUISE AUSTIN, accountant; b. Hot Springs, N.Mex., Aug. 2, 1946; d. Jesse Lee and Jeanne Marie (Weger) Austin; B.S., No. Ariz. U., 1968; postgrad. bus. Golden Gate U., 1977—; m. Paul Williams, July 27, 1968; children—Aaron, Michael, Eric. With Nevada Club, Reno, 1968-73; acct. Smith Constrn. Co., Concord, Calif., 1973-74, Shady Grove Inc., Oakland, Calif., 1974—; data processing So. Pacific Co., San Francisco, 1978-81. Bd. dirs. Diablo Parents for Enrichment Edn. Inc. Mem. Am. Soc. Women Accts. Democrat. Methodist. Club: East Contra Costa County Mothers of Twins. Home: 1763 Poplarwood Ct Concord CA 94521 Office: One Market Plaza San Francisco CA 94105

WILLIAMS, MARY NEWBERN, research asso., mental health services center ofcl.; b. Cleve., Nov. 27, 1951; d. Philip and Mary W. Newbern; student Alliance Francaise, Paris, 1972; B.A., Baldwin-Wallace Coll., 1973; postgrad. Princeton U., 1973-74, Austin-Peay State U., 1978; m. Robert S. Williams, Feb. 4, 1974; children—Joy Chandra, Robert Stultz III, Philip Newbern. Adminstrv. asst. Drug Abuse Centers, Inc., Cleve., 1972-73; tchr. Newburgh (N.Y.) City Schs., 1974-75; employee relations coordinator Kaiser Found., Cleve., 1976-77; exec. asst. to pastor Phillips Temple Ch., Toledo, 1977-79; sales asst. U.S. Steel Corp., Cleve., 1979-81; research asso. Murtis H. Taylor Multi-Services Center, Cleve., 1981—; reporter Christian Index, 1970-73; free-lance reporter, 1972. Recipient sales award U.S. Steel Corp., 1979. Mem. Am. Psychol. Assn., Twenty-First Congl. Dist. Caucus, Smithsonian Assos. Mem. Christian Meth. Episcopal Ch. Home: 304 Greenvale Rd South Euclid OH 44121 Office: 13422 Kinsman Rd Cleveland OH 44120

WILLIAMS, MELVA JEAN, oil and gas co. exec.; b. Burke, S.D., June 11, 1935; d. Wayne and Mildred Eva (Graham) Mulholland; grad. Roberta's Finishing Sch., Miami, Fla., 1950, Charron-Williams Comml. Coll., 1954; m. J.B. Williams, Apr. 29, 1977; children—Mark, Doris, Robin, Jeannie. With Southeastern Resources Corp., Ft. Worth and Rising Star, Tex., 1968—, pres., 1979—, also dir.; with Delta Gas Co., Inc., Tchula, Miss., 1973-81, sec., treas., 1974-81, also dir.; with SERPCO, Inc., Fort Worth, 1977—, v.p., 1980—, also dir.; sec., treas. J J & L Drilling Co., Inc., Ft. Worth and Cisco, Tex., 1979-82, also dir.; with Rising Star Processing Corporation, Fort Worth, sec. treas. 1981—, also dir.; with Brownwood Pipeline Corporation, Fort Worth, sec. treas. 1981—, also dir.; gen. partner B & W Real Estate Investments, Nashville, 1980—, F & W Real Estate Investments, Fort Worth, 1981—. Republican. Home: 6150 Indigo Ct Fort Worth TX 76112 Office: 5205 W Freeway Fort Worth TX 76107

WILLIAMS, NANCY KAROLYN KERR, pastor, mental health cons.; b. Ottumwa, Iowa, July 10, 1934; d. Owen W. and Iris Irene (Israel) Kerr; student Boston U., 1953; A.A., U. Bridgeport, 1966; B.A., Hofstra U., 1967; postgrad. in clin. psychology Adelphi U. Inst. Advanced Psychol. Studies, 1968-73; m. Richard Clayton Williams, June 28, 1953 (div.); children—Richard Charles, Donna Louise. Pastoral counselor Nat. Council Chs., Jackson, Miss., 1964; dir. teen program Waterbury (Conn.) YWCA, 1966-67; intern in psychology N.Y. Med. Coll., 1971-72; research cons., 1972-73; coordinator home services, psychologist City and County of Denver, 1972-75; cons. Mennonite Mental Health Services, Denver, 1975-78; asst. prof. psychology Messiah Coll., 1978-79; mental health cons., 1979-81; called to ministry Mennonite Ch., 1981, pastor Cin. Mennonite Fellowship, 1981—, coordinator campus evangelism, adv. ch. curriculum, 1981; mem. Tri-County Counseling Clinic, Memphis, Mo., 1980-81. Mem. Waterbury Planned Parenthood, 1964-67; mem. MW Children's Home Bd., 1974-75; mem. Boulder (Colo.) ARC, 1977-78. Mem. Am. Psychol. Assn., Am. Assn. Mental Deficiency, Soc. Psychologists for Study of Social Issues, Am. Acad. Polit. and Social Scientists, Am. Youth Hostel. Home and office: 407 Warner St Cincinnati OH 45219

WILLIAMS, PATRICIA ANN YETTER, nurse; b. Centerville, Iowa, June 15, 1946; d. Ray A. and Mary Louise (George) Yetter; R.N., Meth. Hosp., Peoria, Ill., 1968; m. Donald James Williams, June 29, 1968. Mem. nursing staff Copley Meml. Hosp., Aurora, Ill., 1968—, asst. dir. nursing ICU-CCU, intermediate care, and emergency rm., 1975-79, asso. dir. med.-surg. nursing, 1979—. Mem. Nat. Assn. Orthopedic Nurses, Am. Soc. Nursing Service Adminstrs., Meth. Hosp. Alumni Soc., McHenry, Kane, Kendall and Lake Counties Health Systems Agy., Alpha Chi. Methodist. Home: 1239 Howell Pl Aurora IL 60505 Office: Copley Meml Hosp Lincoln and Weston Sts Aurora IL 60507

WILLIAMS, PATRICIA RAE, counselor, writer; b. Ft. Pierce, Fla., Mar. 17, 1936; d. Jack and Lucy M. (VanWickler) McGauran; student Stetson U., 1956-58, Columbus Coll., 1960-62, Presbyn. Sch. Christian Edn., 1973; Litt.D. (hon.), Internat. Bible Inst. and Sem., 1981; m. H. Page Williams, Jan. 2, 1955; children—Perry Scott, Jacklyn Plythe. Instr., counselor Indian River Community Coll., Ft. Pierce, 1979-81, coordinator Women's Program, 1981—; author: Husbands, 1976; Hurting and Healing, 1980. Mem. Nat. Council Family Relations, Nat. Fedn. Press Women, Internat. Platform Assn. Democrat. Presbyterian. Home: 1605 Hispana Ave Fort Pierce FL 33450

WILLIAMS, PEGGY FOWLER, mgmt. cons.; b. nr. Seymour, Tex., May 8, 1933; d. Leon Dockrey Fowler and Annie Bell (Williams) Dodd; B.S., North Tex. U., 1954; M.B.A., Rollins Coll., 1963; cert. of advanced study Am. Grad. Sch. Internat. Mgmt., Phoenix, 1980; m. George S. Moranz, June 5, 1953 (div. Aug., 1979); children—Leigh Ann, Walter Lochran. With Tex. Instruments, Dallas, 1957-58; with Temco Aircraft, Dallas, 1951-53, 55-57; owner Williams Cons. (formerly Moranz Cons.), Dallas, 1963—. Mem. UDC, Dallas Hist. Soc., Nat. Assn. Female Execs., Am. Mgmt. Assn. Episcopalian. Club: Listener's. Address: PO Box 7173 Dallas TX 75209

WILLIAMS, PEGGY LENORE, circus clown; b. Madison, Wis., Nov. 5, 1948; d. Richard Eli and Harriet Jane (Edwards) Williams; student U. Wis., 1967-70; grad. Ringling Bros. Barnum & Bailey Clown Coll., 1970. Clown, Ringling Bros. Barnum and Bailey Circus, Washington, 1970-79, asst. performance dir., 1981—, staff instr. Clown Coll., 1974—; cons. in field. Mem. Circus Fans of Am., Nat. Assn. Female Execs. Republican. Mem. Ch. of Jesus Christ of Latter-day Saints. First female to hold positions. Office: Ringling Bros Barnum and Bailey Circus 3201 New Mexico Ave NW Washington DC 20016

WILLIAMS, PENNY BALDWIN, state legislator; b. N.Y.C., May 6, 1937; d. Peter and Polly (Potter) Baldwin; student Sarah Lawrence Coll., U. Tehran (Iran), U. Tulsa; m. Joseph Hill Williams, Nov. 24, 1956; children—Joseph Hill, Peter Baldwin, James Chestnut. Editorial asst. James Joyce Quar., 1977-78; cons. Okla. ERA, 1978-79, state chmn., 1979-80; mem. Okla. Ho. of Reps., 1980—. Mem. community adv. com. Tulsa U. Coll. Edn., 1976—; bd. dirs. Living Arts Council, Tulsa, 1975—; vice chmn. Tulsa Humanities Com., 1976-78. Grantee Nat. Endowment Humanities. Mem. LWV, Common Cause, ACLU, NOW, Nat. Assn. Female Execs., Tulsa Com. Fgn. Relations. Office: 400 NW 23d St Tulsa OK 73103 *

WILLIAMS, PETRA SCHATZ, antiquarian; b. Poughkeepsie, N.Y., Sept. 2, 1913; d. Grover Henry and Mayme Nickerson (Bullock) Schatz; A.B., Skidmore Coll., 1936; J.D., Fordham U., 1940; m. J. Calvert Williams, Nov. 26, 1946; children—Miranda, Frederica, Valerie. Founder, Fountain House, Phoenix, 1953, Fountain House East, Jeffersontown, Ky., 1966. Past pres. Meml. Hosp. Aux., Phoenix, Heard Mus. Guild, Phoenix. Bd. dirs. Ky. Humane Soc. Mem. Nat. Soc. Interior Designers (nat. dir. for Ariz. 1957-58, Ky. 1968, pres. Ky. 1967-68), DAR, Ky. Hist. Soc. Quaker. Club: Filson. Author: Flow Blue China, An Aid to Identification, 1971; Flow Blue China II, 1973; Flow Blue China and Mulberry Ware, 1975; Staffordshire Romantic Transfer Patterns, 1979. Address: 4906 Chenoweth Run Rd Jeffersontown KY 40299

WILLIAMS, PHYLLIS HELEN, artist; b. N.Y.C., June 10, 1913; d. Ernest August and Helena (Ulrich) Zinke; B.A., Atlantic Union Coll., 1934; M.A. in Art History, U. Pa., 1950; postgrad. Temple U., 1963; m. Albert J. Williams, Jr., Dec. 20, 1937; children—Albert J., III, Robert Ernest. Tchr. art Phila. jr. high schs., 1950-72; head art dept. Leeds Jr. High Sch., 1968-72; freelance artist, lectr., 1972—; one-woman exhbns. Phila. jr. and sr. high schs.; murals in chs., schs. and hosps. in Phila. area. Named Pa. Mother of Year, Am. Mothers' Com., 1980. Mem. Art Am. Mothers Assn. (chmn. art Pa. 1978-82), Am. Mothers Inc. (state pres. 1980-82), Phila. Public Schs. Ret. Employees Assn., NEA, Phila. Art Tchrs. Assn., Woodmere Art Gallery, Stagecrafters. Seventh-day Adventist. Author: South of the Border, 1966; illustrator, translator: German Folksongs, 1968. Address: 901 Llanfair Rd Ambler PA 19002

WILLIAMS, RITA CHARLENE, data communications analyst; b. Huntingburg, Ind., Nov. 17, 1946; d. Charles Philip and Mary Marjedene (Miller) Whitsitt; A.B., Ind. U., 1968; M.S., San Jose State U., 1976; children—Geoffrey Starr, Jonathan Carey. Contracts analyst San Jose (Calif.) State U. Found., 1975-76; product mktg. engr. systems div. Hewlett-Packard Co., Cupertino, Calif., 1976-79, software support rep. Neely sales region, 1979-80; sr. systems programmer data communications MacMillan Bloedel Ltd., Vancouver, B.C., Can., 1980-82; section head-communications messages (aviation systems) Macdonald Dettwiler Assos., Ltd., 1982—. Unitarian. Office: 3751 Shell Rd Richmond BC V6X 2Z9 Canada

WILLIAMS, ROSA (ROSALIE) CLAIRE, genealogist; b. Kansas City, Mo., Oct. 13, 1918; d. Travis Z. and Linnie Q. (Wickline) Hurt; Bus. degree Anne Sarachon-Hooley Sch. for Girls, 1938; student George Washington U., 1942; cert. genealogist, Am. U., 1968; m. Marion E. Williams, Mar. 14, 1944; children—David Murray, Philip Neale. Sec., FBI Lab., 1942-44; genealogist DAR, 1970-72, nat. vice chmn. Patriot Index, 1974-77, nat. vice chmn. lineage research, 1977-80, chmn., 1980—; Va. state chmn. lineage research com., 1974-80, state membership chmn., 1980—; nat. registrar Daus. Am. Colonists, 1980—; chpt. pres. Colonial Dames XVII Century; tchr. genealogy YWCA, 1972; lectr. for genealogy and DAR library research. Republican judge for elections, 1962-74; state and nat. sponsor Children Am. Revolution, also sr. nat. asst. registrar; mem. Retarded Adults Parents Group, YWCA; co-organizer Fairfax Br. Unity Sch. of Christianity, Lee Summit, Mo., 1959. Cert. genealogist Bd. Certification for Genealogists. Mem. Nat. Geneal. Soc., Brit. Geneal. Soc., Scottish Geneal. Soc., Va. Genealogists, Germanna Colonists and Va. Huguenot Soc. Clubs: Rep. Women's, Bus. and Profl. Women, Soroptimist, Fedn. of Women's Clubs, Order Eastern Star. Pub. booklets on family lines. Home and Office: 1048 Rector Ln McLean VA 22102

WILLIAMS, ROSE, public relations cons.; b. Chgo., Sept. 24, 1949; d. Bealie and Louise (Billingslea) W.; B.S. in Edn., U. Ill., 1971. Dir. mktg. Chgo. Daily Defender, 1979-80; coordinator, mgr. mdsg. Playboy Enterprises, 1970-74; exec. asst. Bank Mktg. Assn., Chgo., 1974-79; dir. mktg. Chgo. Daily Defender, 1979-80; pres. Rose & Assos., public relations, Chgo., 1980—; mem. speakers bur. Chgo. Bd. Edn., 1981—; mem. host com., public relations co-chmn., Women's Bur., Dept. Labor 1979—; exec. council, chmn. publicity Provident Hosp. Aux., Chgo., 1981—; exec. council, co-chmn, public relations Chgo. PBS Sta. WTTW, 1981—. Recipient Public Service award Nat. Council Negro Women, 1978, Dept. Labor, 1981. Mem. Nat. Assn. Female Execs. (network dir.), Nat. Assn. Media Women, Inc., Chgo. Assn. Commerce and Industry, Publicity Club Chgo., Chgo. Fashion Exchange, Delta Sigma Theta. Address: 3129 W Flournoy St Chicago IL 60612

WILLIAMS, ROSE ANN, educator; b. Paris, Ill., June 2, 1932; d. Roy Lee and Charlotte W.; student Stephens Coll., 1950-51; B.S., Ind. U., 1954; M.S., Butler U., 1958; Ph.D., Ind. State U., 1970; 1 son, Gregg L. Asst. prof. elem. edn. Ind. State U., 1962-68; asst. prof. Ohio State U., Columbus, 1970-73; asso. prof. Ball State U., Muncie, Ind., 1973—, dir. living learning lab. young children, 1973—. Kappa Kappa Kappa scholar, 1954; Danforth asso., 1971-78. Mem. Nat. Assn. Edn. Young Children, Internat. Assn. Childhood Edn., Delta Kappa Gamma, Phi Delta Kappa. Home: 2800 Wellington St Muncie IN 47304 Office: Tchrs Coll Ball State U Muncie IN 47306

WILLIAMS, ROWENA JEAN ROMER, radiologist; b. Kansas City, Mo., Oct. 5, 1919; d. Andrew Ralph and Lorna (Linton) Romer; A.A., San Mateo Jr. Coll., 1938; B.A., Stanford U., 1940, M.D., 1948; m. James A. Williams, Dec. 18, 1948; children—Katherine Louise Williams Murphy, Susan Jean. Intern, Charity Hosp., New Orleans, 1947-48; resident in radiology Stanford Hosps., San Francisco, 1948-50, Baton Rouge (La.) Gen. Hosp., 1950-51; instr. radiology Stanford Hosps., 1952; individual practice medicine, specializing in radiology, Sacramento Valley, Calif., 1953—, Sacramento, 1972—; radiologist McClelland AFB Med. Clinic, 1977—; cons. Chmn. advt. programs Symphony League Sacramento, 1955; pres. Honeybear chpt. Children's Home Soc., 1956; chmn. com. to organize well-baby clinic Sacramento Children's Home Soc., 1957; bd. dirs. Children's Home Soc. No. Calif., 1960-61; deaconess Carmichael Presbyn. Ch., Sacramento, 1964. Named alumnus of yr. Burlingame High Sch., 1977. Diplomate Am. Bd. Radiology. Mem. Am. Coll. Radiology, No. Calif., Calif. radiol. socs., Sacramento, Calif. med. socs., AMA, PEO, Phi Beta Kappa, Alpha Omega Alpha. Republican. Club: Order Eastern Star. Home: 1229 El Toro Way Sacramento CA 95825

WILLIAMS, RUTH H., TV broadcasting exec.; b. Bklyn., Mar. 15, 1938; d. Oscar and Lillian (Steinberg) Forster; student schs., Los Angeles; children—Steven, Richard, Michael. Asst. studio mgr. Columbia Records, Los Angeles, 1966-71; West Coast adminstr. Custom div. RCA Records, Los Angeles, 1972-75; studio mgr. Motown Records, Los Angeles, 1975-80; central scheduling supr. Golden West TV/KTLA, 1980—. Active Los Angeles chpt. Coalition for Econ. Survival. Mem. Nat. Acad. Rec. Arts and Scis. Home: 7548 Lexington Ave Los Angeles CA 90046

WILLIAMS, RUTH YEARSLEY, choral dir.; b. Phila., Jan. 12, 1927; d. James Raymond and Evelyn Pomeroy (Jarden) Yearsley; Mus.B. Beaver Coll., 1948, M.Mus. Westminster Choir Coll., 1950; m. Lewis Bolton Williams, June 27, 1953; children—David Randolph, John Raymond, Elaine Pomeroy. Organist, dir. Roslyn Presbyterian Ch., Pa., 1946-48; organist Bethlehem Presbyn. Ch., Phila., 1948-50; instr. music S.W. Tex. State U., 1950-54, choral dir., 1955-56; choral dir. Victoria (Tex.) Coll., 1954-55, choral dir., voice instr., 1956—; organist, dir. First United Methodist Ch., Victoria, 1956-81; choral dir. First Presbyn. Ch., Victoria, 1982—. Pres. Juan Linn PTA, Victoria, 1968; pres. Victoria Fine Arts Assn., 1969; dir. Victoria Civic Chorus, 1978—. Mem. Tex. Choral Dirs. Assn., Nat. Assn. Tchrs. Singing, Am. Choral Dirs. Assn., Delta Kappa Gamma. Methodist. Clubs: Victoria Music, Aggies Mothers. Office: Victoria College Victoria TX 77901

WILLIAMS, SHIRLEY ANN, edn. mgmt. cons.; b. Houston, May 10, 1954; d. Robert Moses and Blossom (Hutchinson) W.; B.S., Prairie View A. and M. U., 1975, M.S., 1978; Ph.D., Pacific Western U., 1981; m. Isaac Williams, June 27, 1981. Art instr., Central Houston YMCA, 1973-74; asst dean Sch. Agrl. Edn., Prairie view A. and M. U., 1978; tchr. Houston Ind. Sch. Dist., 1976-79, edn. cons., 1979—. Vol., ARC, Houston, 1976-81. Recipient Harris County Bicentennial Youth Fair award, 1976, Perceiver Acad. Award, Selection Research, Inc., 1981; cert. profl. mid-mgmt. adminstr., profl. supr., provisional elem. tchr. Mem. Houston Tchrs. Assn., Internat. Human Relations Assn., Houston Assn for Supervision and Curriculum Devel., Houston Council Edn., Am. Inst. Parliamentarians, Phi Delta Kappa. Democrat. Mem. A.M.E. Ch. Home: 4006 Tiffin St Houston TX 77026 Office: 2011 Solo St Houston TX 77020

WILLIAMS, SUSAN BRITTON, psychologist, educator; b. Pitts., May 20, 1937; d. Donald George and Catherine Ruth (Campbell) Britton; B.S., Grove City Coll., 1959; M.Ed., U. Pitts., 1962, Ph.D., 1971; m. Alan Williams, July 9, 1981. Tchr. high schs., Pa., 1959-63; counselor Oil City (Pa.) High Sch., 1963-66; mem. faculty Clarion (Pa.) State Coll., 1966—, prof. psychology, 1978—, chmn. dept. psychology, 1980—. NDEA grantee, 1964. Fellow Pa. Psychol. Assn.; mem. Am. Psychol. Assn., Eastern Psychol. Assn., Pi Lambda Theta. Home: Box 283 Clarion PA 16214 Office: Clarion State Coll Clarion PA 16214

WILLIAMS, SUSAN LENORE EVENSON, educator; b. Waseca, Minn., Nov. 20, 1944; d. Oswald Sunde and Marjorie Jean (Foels) Evenson; B.A. summa cum laude, U. Minn., 1969, M.A., 1975; divorced; 1 son, Garret Christopher. Teaching asst., then teaching asso. English, U. Minn., 1975-80, instr. communication program, 1980—, rep. scholastic com. Coll. Edn., 1980—, lectr. continuing edn. women extension, 1978-79. Mem. AAUP (chpt. exec. sec. 1977), MLA, Women Historians of Minn., Am. Field Service, Phi Beta Kappa. Mem. Democratic-Farm-Labor Party. Lutheran. Author articles, revs., poems in field; editor: Great River Rev., 1981—. Home: 3424 Garfield Ave S Minneapolis MN 55408 Office: 106 Klaeber Ct 320 16th Ave SE Minneapolis MN 55414 also 1425 University Ave SE Minneapolis MN 55414

WILLIAMS, TERRIE MICHELLE, assn. exec.; b. Mt. Vernon, N.Y., May 12, 1954; d. Charles and Marie Zone (Kearney) W.; B.A., Brandeis U., 1975; M.S., Columbia U., 1977. Med. social worker N.Y. Hosp., 1977-80; program adminstr. Black Filmmaker Found., N.Y.C., 1980-81; exec. dir. Black Owned Communications Alliance, N.Y.C., 1981-82; exec. dir. World Inst. Black Communications, N.Y.C., 1982—. Recipient D. Parke Gibson award for public relations-public affairs Public Relations Soc. Am., 1981; award Afro-Am. Civic Assn., 1982. Mem. Nat. Assn. Media Women, Nat. Acad. TV Arts and Scis. Democrat. Baptist. Office: 10 Columbus Circle New York NY 10019

WILLIAMS, VERONICA MYRES, psychiat. social worker; b. Shreveport, La., May 11, 1947; d. McEura and Margie Virginia (Reagan) Myres; B.A., La. Tech. U., Ruston, 1969; M.S.W., U. Mich., Ann Arbor, 1977; m. John L. Williams, Jr., Nov. 30, 1969; children—Nicole Leann, Jennifer Lyn, Erica Maria. Probation counselor Citizens Probation Authority, Flint, Mich., 1970-72; unit dir., therapist Services to Overcome Drug Abuse Among Teenagers, Flint, 1972-74; psychiat. therapist Psycho-Therapeutic Treatment Clin., P.C., Flint, 1974-77: psychiat. social worker Hurley Med. Center, Flint, 1977-79; field instr. U. Mich., Flint, 1978-79; psychiat. social worker Inst. Mental Health, Flint, 1979-81, Psychotherapeutic Treatment Clinic, 1981—; clin. social worker Flint Bd. Edn., 1979—. Cert. social worker, Mich.; lic. realtor, Mich. Mem. Nat. Assn. Social Workers, Nat. Assn. Advancement of Colored People, Flint Area Med. Social Workers Assn., Young Women's Christian Assn., Mich. Edn. Assn., NEA. Democrat. Baptist. Club: Internat. 700. Office: 1420 W 12th St Flint MI 48507 also Suite 300 N Bank Center 400 N Saginaw St Flint MI 48502

WILLIAMS-MADDOX, JANICE HELEN, nurse; b. Boston, Nov. 27, 1936; d. Arthur Hamilton Wade and Edith Josephine (Weekes) Williams; B.S. in Nursing, Boston U., 1957; M.A., Atlanta U. Sch. Edn., 1971; M.Community Health, Emory U., 1976; m. Larry Maddox, May 21, 1977. Staff nurse Beth Israel Hosp., Boston, 1957-58, N.Y. Hosp.-Cornell U. Med. Center, N.Y.C., 1958-59; ward supr. Jewish Meml. Hosp., Boston, 1959-61; staff and pvt. duty nurse Mass. Gen. Hosp., Boston, 1961-63; public health nurse Boston Health Dept., 1963-64; intravenous nurse Hughes Spalding Hosp., Atlanta, 1964-66; public health nurse Fulton County (Ga.) Health Dept., 1966-69; sr. tchr. Atlanta Southside Comprehensive Health Center, 1970-73, acting dir. edn., 1973-74, asso. dir. clin. nursing, 1974-76; asso. dir. mental health planning project So. Region Edn. Bd., Atlanta, 1976-78; nursing cons. Dept. Health and Human Services, Atlanta, 1978-81; head nurse VA Med. Center, Atlanta, 1982—; evening coordinator, instr. for innovative practical nursing program for health para-profl. Atlanta Area Tech Sch., 1971-81; mem. admissions com. M.Community Health program Emory U. Sch. Medicine, 1979—. Mem. coms., including Women's Day com. Central United Meth. Ch., Atlanta. Recipient spl. recognition Am. Cancer Soc., 1975. Mem. Am. Assn. Health Planners, Nat. Assn. Female Execs. Office: VA Med Center 1670 Clairmont Rd Decatur GA 30030

WILLIAMSON, BETTY JAYNE HUGHES (MRS. JOSEPH ROBERT WILLIAMSON), dietitian, systems design cons.; New Brunswick, N.J., May 29, 1941; d. Ronald Clyde and Esther (Wenzel) Hughes; B.S., Mich. State U., 1963; A.D.A., Duke U. Med. Center, 1964; m. Joseph Robert Williamson, June 3, 1972. Therapeutic dietitian Lankenau Hosp., Phila., 1964-65, asst. chief dietitian, 1965-66, chief dietitian, 1966-68; administrv. dietitian Hahnemann Med. Coll. and Hosp., Phila., 1968-72; asso.-facilities planning E.F. Johnson Co., Inc., Phila., 1972-74; v.p. Dynamic Systems, Inc., Phila., 1974—; cons. Pa. State U. Dept. Food Service and Housing Adminstrn., Community Meml. Hosp., West Grove, Pa., The Larchwood Sch., Phila. Victory Refrigeration Plymouth Meeting, Pa. Mem. Am. Diatetic Assn., Pa. Dietetic Assn. (ann. meeting chmn. 1976, ann. meeting adv. bd. 1977), Phila. Dietetic Assn., (nominating chmn. 1973-74, sec. 1969-71, pres. 1972-73), Dietitians in Bus., Nutrition Today Soc., Pi Beta Phi. Republican. Mem. United Ch. Christ. Contbr. to Cyclopedia of Medicine, also jours. in field. Home: Foxgayte 26 Maryhill Rd Phoenixville PA 19460 Office: PO Box 854 Valley Forge PA 19482

WILLIAMSON, BETTY SPARKMAN, govt. ofcl.; b. Waco, Tex., June 19, 1944; d. Clarence Marvin and Joyce (Wornick) Sparkman; 1 son by previous marriage, Kirk Ernest II. B.S., U. Tex., Austin, 1966; postgrad. So. Meth. U., 1974, Govt. Inst., 1978, Inst. for Participatory Planning, 1978. Spl. asst. Sen. John Tower, Austin, Tex., 1969-73; public affairs dir. EPA, Dallas, 1973-78, chief info. devel. br., 1978-79, coordinator Info. Center, 1979-81, state liaison, 1981—. Mem. Nat. Energy Environ. Task Force, 1974-75, Nat. Prevention of Significant Deterioration Task Force, 1975-76. Mem. Young Women in Arts, Dallas Summer Mus. Guild, Federally Employed Women, Nat. Environ. Communicators Assn., Press Club Dallas. Republican. Episcopalian. Office: 1201 Elm St Dallas TX 75270

WILLIAMSON, EUNICE THERESA, nutritionist; b. Fulton, Ark., July 6, 1945; d. Londell and Christine Evelyn (Woods) W.; B.S., U. Ark., Pine Bluff, 1967; M.P.H., UCLA, 1970. Sci. tchr. Atheimer (Ark.) Sch. Dist., 1967; clk.-dietitian Holy Cross Hosp., Mission Hills, Calif., 1967-68; 4-H youth adv./4-H youth coordinator U. Calif. Coop. Extension, Riverside, 1970-75, family and consumer scis. adv., 1975—; nutrition cons. Supt. Schs. Head Start Program, 1971-78. Vice chmn. City of Riverside Citizens Affirmative Action Adv. Com., 1977-78, regional adv. council Inland Manpower Assn., 1976-78; mem. So. Calif. Area Constrn. Opportunity Program, 1977—, vice chmn., 1979-80; bd. dirs. United Way of Riverside. Recipient award for meritorious service Riverside County Heart Assn., 1972, 75, Klug award Calif. Heart Assn., 1971. Mem. NAACP (membership chmn. 1974-77, pres. Riverside br., outstanding service award 1976), Am. Dietetic Assn., Am. Home Econs. Assn., Am. Soc. Public Adminstrn. Christian Methodist-Episcopal. Clubs: U. Calif. Univ., Campus. Home: 1435 Everton Pl Riverside CA 92507 Office: 21150 Box Springs Rd Riverside CA 92507

WILLIAMSON, JANET ANN K., educator; b. Scranton, Pa., Sept. 5, 1934; d. William and Rachel (Davis) Kay; diploma Geisinger Med. Center, 1955; B.S. in Nursing, Wilkes Coll., 1962; M.A., N.Y.U., 1966; Ph.D., Pa. State U., 1972. Staff nurse Geisinger Med. Center, Danville, Pa., 1955-58, clin. instr., 1960-64; staff nurse VA Hosp., Salt Lake City, 1958-60; asst. prof. Fla. State U., Tallahassee, 1968-70; part-time instr. nursing Pa. State U., University Park, Pa., 1970-72, asst. prof. nursing, 1972-75, prof. in charge undergrad. program, 1974-76, head dept. nursing, 1976-80, assoc. prof., 1980—; manuscript reviewer various pub. companies, 1976—; cons. to various colls. and univs., 1975—. Bd. dirs. Central Pa. Health Systems Agy., 1976-77. Recipient Book of Yr. award Am. Jour. Nursing, 1978. Mem. Nat. League Nursing, Am. Nurses Assn., Council Nurse Researchers, Sigma Theta Tau, Pi Lambda Theta. Author: (with B.A. Therrien and B.L. Metzger) Intensive Care Nursing, 1976; editor: Current Perspectives in Nursing Education, 2 vols., 1976, 1978; contbr. articles on nursing edn. to profl. jours. Home: 1134 Karen St Boalsburg PA 16827 Office: 201 Human Development E University Park PA 16802

WILLIAMSON, LIZ (ELIZABETH ANNE RAY) (MRS. WILLIAM ELLIOTT WILLIAMSON), dancer, choreographer, educator; b. Winston-Salem, N.C.; d. Alexander Hamilton and Maude E. (Young) Ray; A.B., Radcliffe Coll.; M.A., N.Y. U.; m. William Elliott Williamson; 1 dau., Wonza Elizabeth Williamson Sinclair. Tchr., Howard U., Tuskegee Inst., Bennett Coll., Greensboro, N.C., Ethical Culture Sch., high schs. in N.Y.C.; chmn. performing arts dept. Dalton Sch.; artist-in-residence Talladega (Ala.) Coll.; master tchr. in jazz 1st Statewide Dance Conf., Nashville; prof. dance Hostos Community Coll., City U. N.Y.; master tchr. modern and jazz Dance Masters Am., Fla. chpt., Miami Beach, 1971, Halifax, N.S., Can., N.B., Can., 1977, 1st N.Y. State Coll. and Univ. Dance Festival, 1971; master tchr. in jazz U. Alta., Edmonton, Can., 1972, Dresden and Bonn, Germany, 1978, ann. series, N.Y.C.; numerous master classes and workshops; choregrapher Jazz Ballet for Skeel Dancers, Oak Ridge, 1970, Mass. Jazz Ballet, 1970; jazz artist-in-residence Jacob's Pillow, Lee, Mass, 1973; vis. tchr. jazz ballet Moderno Enid Sauer Studio, Rio De Janeiro, Brazil, 1977, N.C. Sch. Arts, Winston-Salem, 1973, 74, Paris, Brussels, 1974; dancer with Donald McKayle and Alvin Ailey cos., 1952-55; appeared in Finian's Rainbow, 1955, Carmen Jones, 1956, The Boy Friend, 1960, Show Boat, 1960, Follies of 1910, Carnegie Hall; appeared on Jackie Gleason TV show; films Edge of the City, A Man Called Adam; rec. artist Hoctor Records. Recipient Elsa Heilich Kempe award Dance Masters Am., 1976; Oak Ridge Commemorative medal, 1970. Mem. Nat. Assn. Regional Ballet (dir. 1977-78), New Dance Group (dir. 1977-78). Author: Fundamentals of Teaching Modern Dance and Modern Jazz, 1956; The History of Jazz Dance, 1978; editor adaptor, writer introduction: Jazz Dance and Jazz Gymnastics, including Disco Dancing, 1978. Address: 1270 5th Ave Apt 5-T New York NY 10029

WILLIAMSON, NANCY DIANE, nurse, educator; b. Little Rock, Sept. 26, 1944; d. Elmer Charles and Agnes Marie (Orten) Burk; R.N., St. Joseph Sch. Nursing, 1965; B.S.N., Med. Coll. Ga., 1977, M.S.N., 1979; m. John Rollen Williamson, Oct. 19, 1968; children—John Russell, Jennifer Leigh, Jessica Marie. Head nurse CCU, St. Joseph Hosp., Wichita, Kans., 1965-69, Commanchee County Hosp., Lawton, Okla., 1969; staff nurse St. Joseph Hosp., Augusta, Ga., 1969, ICU/CCU staff nurse, 1975; emergency room staff nurse Monmouth County Med. Center, Eatontown, N.J., 1970, St. John's Hosp., Salina, Kans., 1970-71; instr. med./surg. and obstetrics Augusta Area Tech. Sch., 1975-76; instr. adult nursing Johnson County Community Coll., Overland Park, Kans., 1979-80; instr. nursing U. Va. Sch. Nursing, Charlottesville, prof., 1981—; relief evening supr. U. Va. Med. Center, Charlottesville, 1981—; cons. in nurse mgmt.; instr. ARC home nursing to Operation Head Start, Wichita, 1966; instr. CPR, Am. Heart Assn., 1981—. Named Bus. and Profl. Women's Assn. Career Girl, 1967. Mem. Am. Nurses Assn., Va. Nurses Assn., Sigma Theta Tau. Republican. Roman Catholic. Contbr. article to profl. jour. Office: Univ Va Sch Nursing McLeod Hall Charlottesville VA 22903

WILLIMANN, PEGGY A(NN) BELLM, retail exec., cons., civic worker; b. Highland, Ill., June 27, 1950; d. Erwin Anthony and Margaret Jane (Knebel) Bellm; B.A. in Theatre, So. Ill. U., Edwardsville, 1976; m. Randy S. Willimann, Sept. 12, 1969. Sec., So. Ill. U., Carbondale and Edwardsville, 1968-71, sec. to dir. Delinquency Study and Youth Devel. Center, Edwardsville, 1971-75; owner Pegalie's, Highland, Ill., 1977—; partner Pig Patch, U.S.A., Highland, 1981—; pres. IMPACT, Highland, 1981—; cons.; public speaker; emcee, coordinator Bridal Showcase, 1980, 81, 82. Mem. Highland Zoning Bd. Appeals, 1980; treas. Highland Hist. Soc., 1979-81; coordinator Volksmarsch Festival, 1982; sec. Friends of Theatre and Dance, So. Ill. U., Edwardsville, 1979-81, dir., 1981-82; pageant author, dir., also festival coordinator Highland Bicentennial Commn., 1975-76; dir., choreographer numerous local and area theatrical prodns.; adv. bd. Highland Area Community Counseling Service div. So. Madison County Mental Health Services 1979—; adv. bd., exec. bd., directorial advisor Highland Summer Theatre, 1981—; vocat. adv. council Highland Community Schs., 1981—. Mem. Highland Bus. and Profl. Women's Club (Young Career Woman 1979, dist. winner 1980), Nat. Assn. Female Execs., Nat. Fedn. Ind. Bus., Highland C. of C. (pres. 1981-82), Highland Mchts. Assn., So. Ill. U. Alumni Assn. Office: 912 9th St Box 294 Highland IL 62249

WILLINGHAM, GLORIA JEAN, nurse; b. Little Rock, Mar. 5, 1945; d. Ellis and Mary Lee Nelson; student So. Ill. U., 1963-66; R.N., St. Vincent Infirmary Sch. Nursing, Little Rock, 1970; B.S.N., SUNY, Albany, 1981; M. Nursing Sci. candidate U. Ark. Coll. Nursing, 1981—; children—Gina Michele, Michael Damon, Christopher. Clin. nurse Brooke Army Med. Center, Ft. Sam Houston, Tex., 1970, 72-75; night charge nurse Albany (N.Y.) VA Hosp., 1971-72; staff nurse VA Med. Center, Little Rock, 1970, 75-78, clin. instr., 1978—, program coordinator, med., 1980—; chief instr. Med. Corpsmen Sch., Ark. Army N.G., now commd. capt. Dir. Christian edn. Miles Chapel, Little Rock, 1975-77; bd. dirs. Franklin Sch. PTA, chmn. City Beautiful, 1979-80; bd. dirs. Terry Sch. PTA, Little Rock, parliamentarian, adv. com., 1978-80, dist. rep., 1979-80; co-chmn. Christmas Bur., United Way Pulaski County, 1981—, mem. research and planning com., 1981-82; v.p. alumni trustee bd.-regents external degrees SUNY, Albany, 1982—. Recipient Public Service award Miles Chapel Meth. Ch., 1976; suggestion awards VA, Little Rock, 1977; R.N., Ark. Mem. Assn. Female Execs., Am. Soc. Profl. and Exec. Women, Am. Assn. Critical Care Nurses, Nat. Guard Officers Assn., Ark. Young Adminstr.'s Forum, Internat. Platform Assn. Methodist. Home: 10923 Beverly Hills Dr Little Rock AR 72211 Office: 300 E Roosevelt Little Rock AR 72203

WILLIS, DIANE JANICE, clin. and pediatric psychologist; b. Tahlequah, Okla., May 9, 1937; d. William Pascal and Zelma Marie (Bynum) W.; B.S. in Biology, Northeastern State Coll., Tahlequah, 1960; M.A. in Psychology, George Peabody Coll., 1965; Ph.D. in Exptl. Psychology, U. Okla., 1970. Intern in clin. psychology U. Okla. Med. Center, 1969-71; med. technologist Am. Soc. Clin. Pathologists, 1960-64; research asst. neuropsychology lab. U. Okla. Med. Center, 1965-66, asst. dir. Child Study Center and asso. prof. dept. pediatrics, 1980—; staff psychologist dept. communication disorders and dept. pediatrics U. Okla. Health Scis. Center, 1966-67 asst. prof., chief clin. psychologist, 1971-74, asst. dir. pediatric psychology, coordinator in-patient psychol. services, also chief pediatric psychol. services Children's Hosp., 1974-75, chief pediatric psychol. services, asso. prof. Child Study Center, 1975—; sec. Okla. Gov.'s Commn. on Children, Youth and Families, 1980-82. cons. in field; public interest dir. Fed. Home Loan Bank of Topeka, 1977—. Democratic precinct co-chmn., 1972, chmn., 1973; co-chmn. Dem. Com. Cleveland County, Okla., 1973-75; voting mem. Kiowa Indian Tribe. Mem. Am. (pres. elect clin. child psychology div. 12, numerous exec. offices), S.W. Okla. psychol. assns., Soc. Pediatric Psychology (council rep. 1972-75, pres.-elect, Disting. Contbn. award 1982), Okla. Assn. Children With Learning Disabilities (adv. bd. 1972-76, Outstanding Profl. award 1976), Soc. Research Child Devel., Assn. for Advancement Psychology (trustee 1978—), Council Exceptional Children, Alpha Sigma Alpha. Baptist. Editor: Jour. Clin. Child Psychology, 1976-81; contbr. articles to profl. jours; co-author textbook. Home: 1132 W Brooks St Norman OK 73069 Office: 1100 NE 13 Oklahoma City OK 73117

WILLIS, JANE MARLOW, newspaper editor, publisher; b. Brandenburg, Ky., Mar. 8, 1942; d. James Mercer and Thelma (Marlow) W.; B.A., So. Meth. U., 1964; postgrad. (Mark Ethridge fellow), U. N.C., 1966, fire prevention and control Eastern Ky. U., 1976-78; mem. staff Meade County Messenger, Brandenburg, 1964—, editor, 1966—, pub., 1978—. Former den mother local Cub Scouts; mem. drive com. Patton Museum Fund, 1965; mem. local com. Ky. Bicentennial, 1973; patron Pioneer Playhouse, Danville, Ky., 1972; mem. Brandenburg Vol. Fire Dept., 1975—, chmn. firemen's ball, 1977, chmn. Brandenburg Fire Sch., 1977, cert. fire fighter; group coordinator Brandenburg Unity Festival, 1975-76; participant 1977 inaugural parade, 1977 part-time instr. fire sci. Ky. Dept. Vocat. Edn. Mem. Ky., Western Ky. (pres. 1971) press assns., Nat. Newspaper Assn., Internat. oc. Fire Service Instrs. (charter mem. Ky. chpt., Dixie Firemen's Assn. (sch. com.), DAR, Women of Moose, Mensa, Sigma Delta Chi. Democrat. Methodist. Clubs: Falls City Corvette, Hillcrest Country. Editor: Since April Third, 1975; Meade County Messenger Happy Holidays Cookbook, 1975; Summertime and The Cookin' Is Easy, 1977. Co-author slide presentation, Does A Water Curtain Really Work?. Home: 321 Main St Brandenburg KY 40108 Office: Box 612 Brandenburg KY 40108

WILLIS, JOAN RIDLEY, social worker; b. Newport News, Va., Nov. 12, 1942; d. Hannibal William and Ruth (Spruill) Ridley; B.A., U. Toledo, 1964; M.S.W., Smith Coll., 1966; C.A.S., SUNY, 1982; m. Charles L. Willis (div.); 1 son, Christophe Hannibal. Clin. instr. dept. psychiatry U. Rochester (N.Y.), 1965-69; cons.-therapist Genesee Mental Health Center, Rochester, 1972-74; sch. social worker Rochester City Sch. Dist., 1974-80, asst. dir. sch. psychol. and social work services, 1980-81; sch./community specialist Fed. Out of Cycle Grant, 1981—; primary mental health project U. Rochester, 1978-80. Bd. dirs. Legal Aid Soc., Community Chest/United Way Rochester; bd. overseers U. Rochester; mem. 21st ward com. Republican party. Mem. Acad. Cert. Social Workers, Nat. Assn. Social Workers, Black Social Workers Rochester, N.Y. State Sch. Social Workers, Jr. League Rochester, Community Players, Inc., Alpha Kappa Alpha, Pi Gamma Mu. Club: Jack and Jill Am. Home: 129 Beckwith Terr Rochester NY 14610 Office: 131 Broad St Rochester NY 14608

WILLIS, MARGARET SCOTT, hosp. food service adminstr.; b. Welland, Ont., Can., Oct. 12, 1928; came to U.S., 1929, naturalized, 1949; d. Ira and Minnie (Marklove) Hickey; student U. R.I. Extension, 1962-74; A.A. in Home Econs., Dean Jr. Coll., 1948; m. James A. Willis, May 13, 1950; children—James A., III, Christopher Scott, Malcolm Kenneth. Asst. dietitian Pawtucket Meml. Hosp., 1948-50, Charles V. Chapin Hosp., Providence, 1950-51, Miriam Hosp., Providence, 1960-62; adminstrv. dietitian Cranston (R.I.) Gen. Osteo. Hosp., 1962-74, food service adminstr., 1974-82, food service cons., 1982—. Adv., Med. Explorer Post #3 Narragansett council Boy Scouts Am., 1979-80. Mem. Internat. Food Service Exec. Assn. (scholarship chmn., mem. exec. bd. R.I. br., pres. R.I. br. 1982, Eastern regional chmn. 1982, cert. food exec.), Nat. Assn. Female Execs., Am. Soc. Hosp. Food Service Adminstrs., R.I. Nutrition Council, Nutrition Today Soc., Hosp. Assn. R.I. (dietary purchasing chmn. 1976). Episcopalian. Club: Order Eastern Star (pres. R.I. assn. grand reps. 1980, past worthy matron). Editor: R.I. Clambake, 1974-79, Food Service Newsletter, 1974-79. Office: Box 9555 Warwick RI 02889

WILLIS, MARLENE ANNE, polit. scientist, govt. ofcl.; b. St. Louis, Feb. 3, 1944; d. Claude Frank and Norma (Sieving) W.; B.A. magna cum laude and B.S. in Edn., N.E. Mo. State U., 1966, M.A., 1967; Ph.D., N. Tex. State U., 1979. Tchr. pub. schs., Harlingen, El Paso, Tex., 1967-69; instr. polit. sci. E. Tex. Bapt. Coll., 1969-71; grad. teaching fellow N. Tex. State U., 1971-74; asst. prof. polit. sci. Cameron U., Lawton, Okla., 1974-80; legal adminstr. Social Security Adminstrn., Dallas, 1980-81; researcher, cons. Dept. State, Dallas, 1981—. Mem. AAUW, LWV (v.p.) El Paso chpt. 1968-69, Denton chpt. 1979-80), Am., Okla., Southwestern polit. sci. assns., Council for Studies of Comparative Legal Systems, Internat. Commn. Justice, Pi Sigma Alpha, Phi Alpha Theta (co-sponsor Pi Mu chpt. 1970-71), Alpha Phi Sigma (v.p. Alpha chpt. 1965-66). Author: Obscenity before the U.S. Supreme Ct., 1968, 72; Statistical Analysis of the Voting Behavior of the Hughes Court, 1979; contbr. articles to profl. jours. Home: 14500 Dallas Pkwy #2035 Dallas TX 75240

WILLIS, NORMA B., state legislator; b. Naples, N.C., Dec. 24, 1931; student Brown U., 1953. Mem. R.I. Ho. of Reps., 1980—. Mem. North Kingstown Sch. Com., 1958-73, mem., vice chmn. bd. regents, 1972-79. Republican. Office: Rhode Island State House Providence RI 02903 *

WILLIS, VERA LOUISE, educator, civic worker; b. Cumberland, Md., Aug. 20, 1930; d. John and Louisa Lottie (Boots) Bestwick; student Md. Coll. for Women, 1949-52; B.A., Mary Washington Coll., 1954; postgrad. U. Va.; m. Rance Rothwell Willis, Apr. 22, 1961. Tchr., Anne Arundel County (Md.) Schs., 1954-55, U.S. Army Dependent Schs., Ft. Belvoir, Va., 1955-67; substitute tchr. U.S. Army Overseas Dependent Schs., Heidelberg, Germany, 1968-72, Alexandria (Va.) Public Schs. and St. Agnes Episc. Sch., Alexandria, 1973—. Chmn. No. Va. Interbr. Council, AAUW, 1979—, pres. Alexandria br., 1977-79, co-chmn. Va. div. conv., 1980, honored with named grant Alexandria br. AAUW Ednl. Found., 1980, chmn. Alexandria br., 1981—; pres. Chpt. IV, Women of the Ch. of Epiphany, Washington, 1975-77, treas. Chancel Guild, 1977—, mem. vestry, 1981—; v.p. for box office Little Theatre of Alexandria, 1980—. Cert. tchr., Va. Episcopalian. Home: 407 Thomas St Alexandria VA 22302

WILLISCROFT, BEVERLY RUTH, lawyer; b. Conrad, Mont., Feb. 24, 1945; d. Paul A. and Gladys L. (Buck) Williscroft; B.A. in Music, So. Calif. Coll., 1967; J.D., John F. Kennedy U., 1977; m. Joe Luma, Sept. 8, 1972. Elem. tchr., Sunnyvale, Calif., 1968-72; legal sec., legal asst. various law firms, Bay Area, 1972-77; admitted to Calif. bar, 1977; asso. firm Neil D. Reid, Inc., San Francisco, 1977-79; individual practice law, Concord, Calif., 1979—; exam. grader Calif. Bar, 1979—; real estate broker, 1980—; partner Office Services Unltd., Concord, 1981—; tchr. real estate King Coll., Concord, 1979-80; lectr. in field; judge pro-tem Small Claims Ct., evenings, 1981-82. Bd dirs. Contra Costa Musical Theatre, Inc., 1978—, v.p. adminstrn., 1980-81, v.p. prodn., 1981—; mem. community devel. adv. com. City of Concord, 1981—, vice chmn., 1982-83, mem. status of women com., 1980-81; co-chmn. Longshore Morning Forum, Concord, 1980—; mem. exec. bd. Mt. Diablo council Boy Scouts Am., 1981—; trustee Mt. Diablo Health Care Found., 1982-84. Named Woman of Achievement, Todos Santos Bus. and Profl. Women, Clayton, Calif., 1980, 81; award of merit, Bus. and Profl. Women, Bay Valley Dist., 1981. Mem. Concord C. of C. (dir., chmn. govt. affairs com. 1981—), Calif. Women Lawyers, Calif. State Bar, Contra Costa County Bar Assn., Contra Costa Barristers, Am. Bar Assn. Clubs: Todos Santos, Bus. and Profl. Women (co-founder, 1st v.p. 1980-81, 3d v.p. 1981-82, public relations chmn. 1982-83), Soroptimists (fin. sec. 1980-81). Office: 2108 Grant St Concord CA 94520

WILLMANN, CAMILLA CLAUDIA, tax preparation co. exec.; b. Greenville, Ill., Jan. 27, 1916; d. Charles Harrison and Dorcas Camilla (Foulon) McLean; m. Frederick E. Willmann, Jan. 27, 1945; children—Charles L., Mary S., William E., Max Louie. Owner, mgr. H & R Block, Greenville. Treas. Bond County Health Improvement; sec. Utlaut Hosp. Aux.; charter mem. Bond County Extension, U. Ill.; mem., Sponsor Illini Midstate Tumblers; sponsor women's slowpitch softball team. Recipient various awards H & R Block. Enrolled agt. IRS, U.S. Treasury Dept. Mem. Greenville C. of C., Bond County Bus. and Profl. Club (charter; treas., chmn. fin. com.), Greenville Retailers Assn. Republican. Roman Catholic. Home: Rt 2 Pocahontas IL 62275 Office: 217 S 3d St Greenville IL 62246

WILLNER, STELLA O'ROURKE, microbiologist, med. biochemist; b. Bronx, N.Y., Oct. 1, 1932; d. J. Joseph and Stella Elizabeth (Ward) O'R.; B.A., Caldwell Coll., 1954; M.S., Wichita State U., 1957; postgrad. Wayne State U., 1954-56; m. Allen E. Willner, Sept. 1, 1956; children—Sharon, Keith, Kenneth. Teaching fellow Wayne State U. Coll. Medicine, Detroit, 1954-56; teaching fellow Wichita State U., 1956-57; med. technologist Thomas M. Gellert, M.D., Huntington, N.Y., 1975—. Pres., Community Nursery Sch. Parent Orgn., Topeka, 1961-63; publicity chmn. Flower Hill Sch. PTA, 1969-71, pres., 1971-73; pres. Finley 6th Grade Sch. Parents Orgn., Huntington, 1973-74; pres. East Neck Assn., 1979-80; mem. Huntington Community First Aid Squad, 1979—. Mem. Nat. Assn. Female Execs., N.Y. Acad. Scis., AAAS, Nat. PTA (life). Roman Catholic. Club: Yacht (Northport, N.Y.). Home: E Neck Rd Huntington NY 11743 Office: 150 Main St Huntington NY 11743

WILLOUGHBY, AVALEE, educator; b. McComb, Miss.; d. John Cletus and Vertner (Tynes) Willoughby; B.S., La. State U., 1942; M.A., U. Fla., 1956; Ed.D., U. Ala., 1972. Tchr. phys. edn. Southwest Miss. Jr. Coll., Summit, 1944-51; phys. dir. YMCA, Birmingham, Ala., 1952-55; instr. phys. edn. U. Md., College Park, 1956-58; prof., chmn. div. health, phys. edn. and recreation Samford U., Birmingham, 1958—; also rehab. work with handicapped. Extensive work Aquatics, Ala. Spl. Olympics, ARC; mem. Gov.'s Commn. on Phys. Fitness. Named to Sports Hall Fame, S.W. Miss. Jr. Coll., 1972. Fellow AAHPER; mem. NEA, Ala. Assn. Health, Phys. Edn. and Recreation (pres. 1973-74, Honor award 1970), Phi Kappa Phi, Delta Kappa Gamma; Kappa Delta Pi. Methodist. Club: Soroptomists. Home: 1841 Burning Tree Circle Birmingham AL 35226

WILLOUGHBY, SARAH MARGARET CLAYPOOL, educator, engring. cons.; b. Bowling Green, Ky.; d. Austin Burrell and Minerva (Renfrow) Claypool; B.S., Western Ky. U., 1938; Ph.D., Purdue U., 1950; m. John Richard Evans II, Aug. 30, 1938 (dec. Dec. 1942); 1 son, Richard Claypool; m. 2d, O. Glenn Willoughby, June 18, 1948 (div. Aug. 1956); children—Sarah Peyton, Stephen Burrell (dec.). Chemist, Devoe-Raynolds, Inc., Louisville, 1941-43; jr. engr. Curtiss-Wright Corp., Louisville, 1943-44; research fellow Purdue U. Sch. Chem. Engring., West Lafayette, Ind., 1946-50; research chemist Monsanto Chem. Co., Boston, 1950-51; asst. prof. chemistry U. Tex., Arlington, 1954-55; asso. prof., 1955—. Profl. engr., Ind., Tex. Fellow Am. Inst. Chemists; mem. Am. Chem. Soc. (sect. sec.-dir. 1967-68), Soc. Women Engrs., Tex. Acad. Sci., Daus. Founders and Patriots Am., Colonial Order of Crown, Colonial Dames Am., Magna Charta Dames (colony regent 1974-76), Soc. Friends of St. George, Peyton Soc. Va. (life), Descs. of Knights of Garter, Ams. of Royal Descent, Plantagenet Soc., D.A.R. (chpt. regent 1967-69, state bicentennial chmn. 1969-70), Children Am. Revolution (sr. state pres. 1969-71), Sigma Xi (pres. U. Tex. club, 1966-68), Alpha Chi Omega. Presbyn. Clubs: Arlington Women's, Arlington City. Home: 1630 Pecan Park Dr Arlington TX 76012

WILLSIE, BERTHA SPOONER, educator; b. Ashville, N.Y., May 15, 1921; d. Frank W. and Jeannette C. (Bergstresser) Spooner; B.A., Coll. Wooster, 1942; A.M., Cornell U., 1947; postgrad. Western Res. U., 1943, U. Buffalo, 1944-45, U. Havana, 1948, St. Bonaventure U., 1964-67; m. Robert L. Willsie, June 30, 1951; 1 dau., Anita Ruth. High sch. English and lang. tchr. Bemus Point High Sch., 1942-47; instr. French and Spanish, Alfred U. Extension, 1948-52; tchr. French, Spanish, Latin Falconer High Sch., 1952-56; tchr. Panama Central Sch., 1958-64; head fgn. lang. dept. Jamestown (N.Y.) Public Schs., 1964-76; instr. Spanish Chautauqua (N.Y.) Instn., 1976—. Mem. Bd. Edn., Chautauqua Central Sch., 1970-77; active Marvin Community House. Recipient Scholarships, Coll. Wooster, 1938-42, Cornell U., 1946-47. Mem. Internat. Order King's Daus. and Sons, Chautauqua County Hist. Soc., Fenton Hist. Soc., DAR (chmn. com. on schs.), Delta Kappa Gamma, Phi Beta Kappa, Phi Sigma Iota, Delta Kappa Gamma. Methodist. Club: Eastern Star (sec.). Home: Box 155 Stow NY 14785

WILMORE, MARIE MCCLURG, govt. ofcl.; b. Tremont, Ohio, Jan. 27, 1940; d. Charles McClurg and Elsie Louisa (Ridder) McClurg Pearis; student No. Va. Community Coll., 1971-75; m. Jon Frederick Mattfeld, Nov. 30, 1957 (div. 1965); 1 son, Jon Frederick; m. 2d, Dhalmas Otto Wilmore, May 29, 1969; 1 dau., Laura Kathleen. Clk. stenographer USAF, Wright Patterson AFB, Ohio, 1957-62, sec.-stenographer, 1967-69, sec.-stenographer, Washington, configuration mgmt. specialist, 1970-72; with Dept. Navy, Washington, mgmt. analyst, 1974-82, dep. OEO officer, 1976-77, reports control analyst Naval Air Systems Command, 1977-82, staff asst. to dep. asst. Sec. Navy for res. affairs,

1982—; petty officer USNR, 1979—; pres. Dhalmar Arabian Farm, Spotsylvania, Va., 1976—. Recipient Zero Defects awards, 1960, 63, 67; Sustained Superior Performance award Dept. Navy, 1966; Air Force Excellence award, 1969. Mem. Federally Employed Women, Va. Arabian Horse Assn., Eastern Amateur Arabian Horse Assn. Baptist. Home: PO Box 135 Thornburg VA 22565 Office: Dept Navy Office Asst Sec Navy Manpower and Res Affairs Washington DC 20350

WILMOTH, CAROLE LINA, pianist, educator; b. Wilkinsburg, Pa., Oct. 25, 1934; d. Paul Arno and Edris Laura (Wilson) Guenther; B.S. in Edn., (scholarship 1952), S.W. Mo. State U., 1955; diploma piano, M.Mus., La. State U., 1957; pupil Ruth Burr, William Van Overeem, William Armstrong, Alfred Mouledous; m. Stephen R. Wilmoth, July 22, 1979; children—Mark Tobin Everett, James Wilson Everett. Head piano dept. Labette County Community High Sch., Altamont, Kans., 1955-56; pvt. piano tchr., Houston and Dallas, then Los Altos, Calif., 1957-62, Sherman, Tex., from 1962, now Richardson, Tex.; mus. dir., pianist musicals Sherman Community Players, 1960-75; composer Children's mus. prodns.; tchr. piano pedagogy, continuing edn. Austin Coll., Sherman, 1974-79; instr. piano Grayson County Coll., Sherman, 1975-79; tchr. Music Master Sch. of Music, Plano, Tex., 1979-80; pres. Bomar Cramer Music Club, 1966-68; bd. dirs. Sherman Mus. Arts, 1966-69, 73-79, charter mem., pres. Women's Guild, 1968-69, 73-74; violist Sherman Symphony Orch., 1973-79. Charter mem., v.p. Sherman Community Players Theater Guild, 1969-70, bd. dirs., 1967-70; mem. bd. Sherman LWV, 1974-75; v.p. Grayson County Humane Soc., 1978-79. Cert. music tchr. Mem. Music Tchrs. Nat. Assn., Tex. Music Tchrs. Assn. (sec. student affiliate 1974-81), Nat. Guild Piano Tchrs. (adjudicator 1972—), Grayson County Music Tchrs. Assn. (charter mem., pres. 1971-73), Dallas Music Tchrs. Assn. (pres. 1980-82), Richardson Music Tchrs. Assn., Plano Music Tchrs. Assn., Metroplex Pres. Council Music Tchrs. Assns. (chmn. 1981-82), Cliburn Council, Dallas Symphony Orch. League, Sigma Alpha Iota, Sigma Sigma Sigma. Address: 919 Vinecrest Richardson TX 75080

WILMOTH, MARY JANELLE, health care exec.; b. Ardmore, Okla., Feb. 21, 1934; d. Charles Dewitt and Susan Ruthelle (Martin) Heartsill; student Hill's Bus. U., 1951; m. William Robert Wilmoth, Oct. 29, 1975; children by previous marriage—Robert Walker, Richard Walker, Charles Walker. Sec., Bill Story Fire & Safety, Oklahoma City, 1963, Greb X-Ray Co., Oklahoma City, 1963-66; sec., bookkeeper Don Hunt Enterprises, Oklahoma City, 1966-75; supr. radiology transcription Bapt. Med. Center, Oklahoma City, 1975—. Mem. Am. Assn. Med. Transcriptionists, Career Guild. Republican. Mem. Christian Ch. Clubs: Bowling League of Ind. Order Foresters. Office: 3300 NW Expressway Oklahoma City OK 73112

WILNER, MARIE SPRING, painter; b. Paris, July 24, 1910; d. Joseph and Helene Spring; came to U.S., 1915, naturalized, 1920; B.A., Hunter Coll., 1927; m. Joseph Walter Wilner, Sept. 4, 1926; children—Helene Victoria, Harvey I., George Dubar. Exhibited one-woman shows Gallery 21, 1959, Bodley Gallery, N.Y.C., 1960, Galeries Raymond Duncan, Paris, 1961, 63, 65, 67-69, Jason Gallery, N.Y.C., 1963, Bridgeport (Conn.) Mus. Art, 1962, Evansville (Ind.) Mus., 1964, Irving Gallery, Milw., 1964, Sheldon Swope Gallery, 1965, Pietrantonio Gallery, West Hampton, 1966, 68, 69, Oliva Gallery, South Hampton, N.Y., 1966, N.Y. U., 1966, La Salle Coll., Phila., 1966-68, U. Del., 1966, Dickson Gallery, Washington, 1968-69, Bohmann's Gallery, Stockholm, Sweden, 1968. Rioboo Nueva Gallery, Buenos Aires, Argentina, 1969, Tweed Gallery, U. Minn., 1969, Karelon Gallery, Provincetown, N.Y., 1970, Galerie fur Zeitgenossische Kunst, Hamburg (Germany) U., 1971, Musee d'Art Moderne, Paris, 1972, Charleroi, Belgium, 1972, Nat. Mus. Arts and Sports, N.Y.C., 1971, Lehigh U., 1972, Galerie Rene Borel, Deauville, France, 1972, La Traboule, Lyon, 1972, Musee de Lyon, Musee d'Art Moderne, Paris, Salon d'Ete, France, Salon d'Automne, France, Salon de l'Ecole de Paris, Salon de Thomas, Salon des Artistes, Paris, Palais de Beaux Arts, Rome, Societe de la Palmes d'Or, Monaco, 1972, 73, Met. Mus. Art, 1979, Salon des Surindépendants, Musée de Luxembourg, 1978, Festivale Internat., Brussels, Paris, Madrid, 1980, others; works included traveling shows; works represented permanent collections Tweed Gallery, Community Coll. N.Y., LaSalle Coll., Evansville Mus., Art Inst. Richmond (Ind.), Norfolk (Va.) Mus. Art, Seton Hall U. Mus., N.Y. U., Fla. So. Coll., Ga. Mus. Art, St. Vincent Coll., Latrobe, Pa., Mus. Ala., Emily Lowe Mus., Bat Yam Mus., Israel, Safad Mus., Israel, Muss d'Angouleme, France, Musee de Cognac, France, S.I. Mus., Musee des Beaux Arts de Montbard. Sec., treas. Rosemarie Holding Inc., N.Y.C. Recipient Gold medal Am. Artist Profl. League, 1965, Grumbacher Purchase prize, 1966; Bronze medal Gran Prix Internationale de Peintures et Scalptures du Pays Noir, Charleroi, Belgium, 1972; named chevalier Societe d'Encouragement au Prog, 1969, chevalier 4th grade Merite Belgo-Hispanique, 1973. Fellow Royal Soc. Art, Nat. Assn. Women Artists (chmn. jury award 1966—, chmn. traveling oil show), Artists Equity Assn. (dir.); mem. Nat. Soc. Arts and Letters, Internat. Arts Guild, Intercontinental Biog. Assn. Address: 77 7th Ave New York NY 10011 *

WILSNACK, SHARON CARLSON, psychologist, educator; b. Manhattan, Kans., July 31, 1943; d. Lloyd Willard and Venita Maxine (Allen) Carlson; B.A., Kans. State U., 1965; postgrad. U. Freiburg, (W.Ger.), 1965-66; M.A., Harvard U., 1968, Ph.D., 1972; m. Richard William Wilsnack, Dec. 29, 1967; children—Joel, Brian, Peter, Kirsten, Jonathan. Research fellow, teaching fellow Harvard U., 1966-71; clin. psychology intern Mass. Mental Health Center, Boston, 1968-69, supervising psychologist, 1971-74; asso. psychology dept. psychiatry Harvard U., 1972-74; dir. Regional Alcoholism Rehab. Program, Bloomington, Ind., 1974-78; adj. asst. prof. psychology Ind. U., 1975-78, co-dir. clin. research tng. program in alcoholism, 1975-78; asso. prof. psychology U. N.D. Sch. Medicine, 1978—, dir. preclinical curriculum div. psychiatry and behavioral sci., 1978—; asso. dir. Internat. Sch. Alcohol Studies, 1978—; cons. in field; mem. Alcohol Tng. and Alcohol Prevention Peer Rev. Coms., Nat. Inst. on Alcohol Abuse and Alcoholism, 1972-76, 76—. Commr. City of Bloomington Alternative Programs Commn., 1975-78, chmn., 1976-78; mem. Monroe County (Ind.) Criminal Justice Task Force, 1975-78. Fulbright fellow, 1965-66; Wilson fellow, 1966-67, NIMH fellow, 1967-71; grantee in field. Mem. Am. Psychol. Assn., N.D. Psychol. Assn., Research Soc. Alcoholism, Soc. Psychologists in Substance Abuse, Assn. Acad. Psychiatry, N.D. Mental Health Assn., Kappa Kappa Gamma. Lutheran. Contbr. articles to profl. jours. Office: University of North Dakota School of Medicine North Unit Room 221 Grand Forks ND 58202

WILSON, ALICE HENRIETTA, civic worker; b. Fort Logan, Colo., Dec. 10, 1913; d. Charles Frederick and Jeannette Pearla (Townsend) W.; B.S., Tex. Woman's U., 1935; postgrad. Columbia U., 1939-40, Juilliard Inst. Mus. Art, 1939-40. Tchr. music, Electra, Tex., 1935-39, Fairbanks, Tex., 1940-42, Freeport, Tex., 1942 (all public schs.); clerical supr., reviewer analyst, FBI, Washington, 1942-73; state regent D.C., DAR, 1978-80. Organist, Presbyn. Ch., 1955—. Mem. Nat. Assn. Parliamentarians, PEO, Nat. Huguenot Soc., Colonial Dames 17th Century, Daus. Am. Colonists, Daus. U.S. Army. Republican. Clubs: 20th Century, Order Eastern Star. Home: 2118 Gaither St Temple Hills MD 20748

WILSON, ALVERDA OLSON, wholesale co. exec.; b. Beloit, Wis., June 1, 1923; d. Bernie and Elsie (Erickson) Olson; student public schs., Hillsboro and La Cross, Wis.; m. John D. Wilson, Sept. 30, 1950; children—Gail Ann, Wendy Jayne, John D. III, Mary Ruth. Dental asst., 1941-50; v.p., gen. mgr. John D. Wilson Co., Pontiac, Ill., 1972—. Founder, 1st pres. Pontiac FISH program, 1970-73; pres. Church Women United, 1969-71, state bd. dirs., 1972-75; bd. dirs. Episcopal Ch. Women Diocese of Chgo., 1974-77, chmn. Kankakee Deanry, 1968-71, 79-80. Mem. Specialty Advt. Assn. Internat., Specialty Advt. Assn. Chgo. Clubs: Elks, Moose. Home: 420 W Lincoln St Pontiac IL 61764 Office: 1000 N Mill St Pontiac IL 61764

WILSON, BARBARA GAYLE, real estate broker/owner; b. Chgo., Jan. 8, 1934; d. Edward Sachem and Juanita Ann (Cantrell) Wilson; student Stephens Coll., 1951-52. Stewardess, Am. Airlines, 1955-67; dir. tng./employee relations Bullocks Dept. Stores, Los Angeles, 1967-69; personnel mgr. Broadway Dept. Stores, Los Angeles, 1969-71; with Bob Crane & Assoc., Los Angeles, 1971-75; real estate owner/broker Gayle Wilson & Assocs., Inc., Los Angeles, 1975—, Gayle Wilson & Assocs., Internat., London, Los Angeles, 1980—. Mem. Fed. Narcotics Prevention Bd. of Los Angeles, 1967-68; co-chmn. Community Guild Los Angeles, 1977-78; bd. dirs. Concerned Voters of Calif., 1977-78; fin. chmn. No on Six Com., 1978; mem. Calif. State adv. bd. on Alcoholism and Drug abuse, 1979-80; adv. bd. Women's Bldg. Los Angeles, 1979-80; bd. dirs. Mun. Elections Com. Los Angeles, 1979-81, adv. bd., 1981—; bd. dirs. Bank of Los Angeles, 1980—; mem. Calif. Commn. on Personal Privacy, 1980—, Los Angeles Conv. Center Commn., 1981—; bd. dirs. El Centro del Pueblo, 1981—; mem. credentials com. Dem. Conv., 1980; fin. com. Calif. Dem. Party, 1981- others. Named Woman of the Yr., Christopher St. W. Orgn., 1979; Citation of Commendation, Los Angeles City Council, 1980. Mem. NOW, Nat. Women's Polit. Caucus. Office: 540 N San Vicente Blvd Los Angeles CA 90048

WILSON, BETTY WOLFENBARGER, real estate broker, gen. contractor, nursing adminstr.; b. Knoxville, Tenn., Mar. 14, 1938; d. Robert Lee and Lillian (Winkler) Wolfenbarger; B.S. in Nursing, U. Tenn., 1961, M.S., 1968; m. Tommy Philip Wilson, Apr. 14, 1966; children—Tommy Philip, Heather Elaine, Bryan Patrick. Dir. nursing Chamberlain Meml. Hosp., Rockwood, Tenn., 1981—; owner, broker Exec. Realty, Inc., 1976—; owner, pres. Crafterhouse, Inc., 1974—. Mem. adv. bd. Carson-Newman Coll., Jefferson City, Tenn.; mem. adv. Don Gally Camp, 1977-78; active local Cub Scouts, Brownie Scouts; music dir. Summertown Youth Camp, 1973-74. Mem Nat. League Nursing, Am. Nurses Assn., Am. Home Bldg. Assn., Tenn. Real Estate Assn., Knoxville Home Bldg. Assn. Republican. Presbyterian. Clubs: Ft. Loudon Yacht, Fox Den Country, U. Tenn. Faculty. Home: PO Box 22698 Concord TN 37922 Office: 241 S Chamberlain Blvd Rockwood TN also Crafterhouse Kingston Pike PO Box 22698 Knoxville TN 37922

WILSON, CAROLE DENISE, security co. exec.; b. New Shrewsbury, N.J., May 12, 1954; d. Jean Thomas and Julia May (Kennedy) W.; B.S., Marquette U., 1977. Asst. to account exec. Moore & Schley, Cameron & Co., N.Y.C., 1978-80; account exec. Racz Internat., N.Y.C., 1980-81; partner Gaines/Rothbard & Assos., N.Y.C., 1981—. Advisor, Cath. Youth Orgn., Notre Dame Parish, North Caldwell, N.J., 1977-78. Republican. Roman Catholic. Club: Montclair Coll. Women's (chmn. women's com. 1980-81). Home: 295 Park Ave S Apt 7R New York NY 10010 Office: 63 Wall St 12th Floor New York NY 10005

WILSON, CAROLE MILDRED, broadcasting co. exec.; b. Bklyn.; d. Morris and Frances Beckerman; student Columbia U., 1970-72; m. B. Andrew Ungar, Aug. 15, 1972; children—Kimberley Jo. Weatherperson, WHNC-TV, New Haven, 1962-64; actress, commls., As The World Turns, Prize Movie, indsl. films, others, N.Y.C., 1964-72; anchorperson Midday, Today in Cin., 1975-78, co-anchorperson 6 P.M. News, WLWT-TV, Cin., 1975-78; freelance TV news journalist, 1978-82; dir. public affairs and spl. programming, news anchorperson WTVX-TV, Ft. Pierce, Fla., 1982—; producer, writer Women USA!. Mem. Am. Women in Radio and TV (dir.), Women in Communications (named outstanding woman in communications Cin. chpt.), AFTRA, Screen Actors Guild. Democrat. Jewish. Office: PO Box 3434 Fort Pierce FL 33450

WILSON, CHERYL SUE JONES, accountant; b. Globe, Ariz., June 20, 1948; d. Elton Roland and Shirley Vivian (Scott) Jones; B.S., No. Ariz. U., 1969; M.B.A., U. Chgo., 1982; m. Gregory S. Wilson, Feb. 14, 1970. Staff acct. Coopers & Lybrand, Chgo., 1970-71, sr. supr., 1972-74, mgr., 1975-77, partner, 1977—, asso. nat. dir. health care services, 1976—. Bd. dirs. Planned Parenthood Assn., Chgo., 1979—. C.P.A., Ill., Iowa, La., N.C. Mem. Am. Soc. Women C.P.A.s, Am. Inst. C.P.A.s, Ill. C.P.A. Soc. (chmn. com. health care instns. 1979-81), Am., Ill. hosp. assns., Hosp. Fin. Mgmt. Assn. (dir. Ill. chpt. 1980—), Chgo. Soc. Assn. Execs., U. Chgo. Women's Bus. Group, U. Chgo. Exec. Club. Presbyterian. Home: 36 Fox Trail Lincolnshire IL 60015 Office: Coopers & Lybrand 222 S Riverside Plaza Chicago IL 60606

WILSON, CLAIRE VIRGINIA, psychologist; b. Phila., Dec. 11, 1946; d. Edwin Howard and Claire Virginia (Schaller) Wilson, Jr.; B.S., Pa. State U., 1969; M.A., Temple U., 1972, postgrad. 1972—. Probation officer I, City of Phila. Ct. of Common Pleas, Family Ct. Div., 1972-73, psychologist I, 1973-75, psychologist II, 1975—; psychologist St. Joseph's Hall for Girls, Phila., part-time, 1974; correctional counselor Commonwealth of Pa. Dept. Justice, Bur. Corrections, Community Treatment Center No. 1, Phila., 1972; teaching asst. Temple U., Phila., 1971, trainee in behavior therapy Behavior Therapy Unit, 1972-73; fellow June Inst. Behavior Therapy, 1973; grad. research asst. dept. gen. ednl. psychology Temple U., 1974—, Eastern Pa. Psychiat. Inst., Phila., 1971, Friend's Hosp., Phila., 1971-72, Temple U. Hosp., 1971-72; pvt. practice psychology, Phila., 1979—. Lic. psychologist, Pa. Mem. Am. Psychol. Assn., Eastern Psychol. Assn., Pa. Psychol. Assn., Soc. for Research in Child Devel., Assn. for Advancement of Behavior Therapy, Assn. for Women in Psychology, NOW (co-convenor N.E. Phila. chpt., mem. nat. edn. discrimination com.), Four Chaplains Legion of Honor, Psi Chi. Contbr. articles to profl. jours. Office: 1305 E Tyson Ave Philadelphia PA 19111

WILSON, CONNIE MARIE, librarian, educator; b. Merced, Calif., Jan. 26, 1950; d. James Lowden and Virginia R. Dennis; B.A., U. Okla., 1972, M.L.S., 1973; m. Steven C. Wilson, Dec. 29, 1973. Librarian, Regional Library Services, U. Okla. Health Scis. Center Library, 1973-76; librarian Area Health Edn. Center-N.W. Library, U. Ark. for Med. Scis., Fayetteville, 1977—, asst. prof. library sci., 1979—; participant TALON core workshops to develop teaching seminars for hosp. library mgrs. Recipient Library Research Round Table research award ALA, 1976. Mem. Med. Library Assn. (cert. Librarian I), Ark. Library Assn., Phi Beta Kappa. Democrat. Presbyterian. Office: 1125 N College St Fayetteville AR 72701

WILSON, CORA LUCILLE MORGAN, educator; b. Cherokee, Ala., Apr. 18, 1918; d. John Henry and Erie Lee (Hargett) Morgan; B.A., George Peabody Coll. for Tchrs., Nashville, 1952, M.A., 1955, postgrad., 1970-72; m. Olen E. Wilson, Aug. 3, 1940; 1 dau., Patricia Ann Wilson Hall. Tchrs., Cherokee (Ala.) Elem. Sch., 1937-45, Joy Sch., Julia Green Sch., Richland Sch., Nashville, 1949-59, Glendale Sch., Nashville, 1959—. Chmn., Bicentennial Com., Nashville, 1976. Recipient Jeffersonian award City of Nashville, 1981. Mem. NEA (life), Tenn. Edn. Assn. (rep. assembly 1975-82, Disting. Classroom Tchr. award 1978, 81), Assn. Childhood Edn. Internat., Met. Nashville Edn. Assn., Middle Tenn. Edn. Assn., Alpha Delta Kappa (chpt. pres. 1976-78, state sgt.-at-arms 1978-80, dist. sec. 1981-83), Kappa Kappa Iota. Democrat. Baptist. Clubs: Woman's (life) (Nashville); Belmont Coll. Aid (life), Mary Shelton Circle (pres.). Home: 895 Thompson Ave Nashville TN 37204 Office: 800 Thompson Ave Nashville TN 37204

WILSON, DIANE MONTGOMERY, human resource devel. exec.; b. Houston, Apr. 25, 1942; d. Ralph Wesley and Anna Ruth (Montgomery) Peterson; A.A. with honors, Johnson County Community Coll., 1973; B.S. in Journalism with highest distinction, U. Kans., 1976; m. James Timothy Wilson, July 25, 1964 (div. June 1981); children—Rebecca Lynn, Anthony Greg, Wendelle Marie. Asso. writer Golf Course Supts. Assn., Lawrence, Kans., 1976-77, asso. editor, 1977-78; copywriter Hallmark Cards, Inc., Kansas City, Mo., 1978-79; v.p. advt. and pub. relations The Wood Works, Inc., Overland Park, Kans., 1979-81; mgr. program devel. Western Auto, Kansas City, Mo., 1981—; pres. Images, Overland Park, 1979-81, Phoenix Unltd., Overland Park, 1981—. Bd. dirs. Mid-Continent council Girl Scouts U.S.A., 1976-80; chmn. Vol. Services Com., 1976-77; dir./producer Cable TV Programming for Leaders, 1974-77. Mem. Nat. Assn. Female Execs., Women in Communications, Phi Beta Kappa. Am. Soc. for Tng. and Devel., Dimensions Unltd., Kappa Tau Alpha, Phi Kappa Phi. Democrat. Mem. Unity Ch. Home: 8478 Carter Overland Park KS 66212 Office: 2107 Grand Ave Kansas City MO 64108

WILSON, DORI, public relations exec.; b. Winona, Miss.; d. William and Fannie (Brown) W.; student Roosevelt U., 1961-62. With Compton Advt., Inc., 1963-68, Foote, Cone & Belding Advt., 1968-79; pres. Dori Wilson Assos., Inc., Chgo., 1979—; hostess TV show Memorandum, 1975-77. Trustee, Columbia Coll., Central YMCA Coll.; v.p., bd. dirs. Chgo. Internat. Film Festival; mem. women's bd. Chgo. Urban League; bd. dirs. The Academy of Art, Dance, Music, Theatre; bd. advs. Chgo. Fashion Exchange, Ray-Vogue Sch. of Fashion Design, Internat. Acad. Fashion Merchandising. Recipient numerous public service awards. Mem. Screen Actors Guild, AFTRA, Fashion Group, Nat. Acad. TV Arts and Scis. Office: 845 N Michigan Ave Suite 903E Chicago IL 60611

WILSON, FRANCES HELEN, occupational therapist; b. Pitts., Oct. 17, 1929; d. J. Vernon and Margaret Hassler (Prugh) W.; B.A., Conn. Coll., 1951; advanced standing cert. Columbia Sch. Occupational Therapy, 1953. Therapist, Washington County Soc. Crippled Children and Adults, Washington, Pa., 1953-54; staff therapist Oakland VA Hosp., U. Pitts., 1955-66; supr. occupational therapy Aspinwall VA Hosp., Pitts., 1966-74, Oakland VA Hosp., Pitts., 1974-80; supr. occupational therapy clinic Aspinwal VA Hosp., Pitts., 1980—. Active Jr. League Pitts., Inc. Mem. Am., Western Pa. (treas. 1967-69) occupational therapy assns. Republican. Presbyn. Clubs: Connecticut College (treas. 1971—), Twentieth Century (Pitts.). Home: 14 Devon Ln Ben Avon Heights Pittsburgh PA 15202 Office: VA Hosp Delafield Rd Aspinwall Pittsburgh PA 15215

WILSON, GENE VARNEY, exploration and tech. systems analyst; b. Sherman, Tex., May 7, 1938; d. Chester Aaron and Opal (Whitehead) Varney; student U. Houston, 1962; children—Kathleen Pearce, Richard Kary. Exploration and tech. programmer analyst Gulf Sci. and Tech. Co., Houston, 1961—; mem. Petroleum Info. Well History Control System Adv. Com., 1979—. Active Achievement Rewards for Coll. Scientists, 1972-73; Harris County Mental Health Assn., 1973-74, Houston Zool. Soc., 1974-75; mem. Gramm for Senate Com., 1976. Mem. Nat. Assn. Female Execs., Met. Employees Recreation Council, Desk and Derrick Club of Houston (pres. 1977, 1st place award best news story 1974, parliamentarian 1981); Gulf Cos. Employees Club (sec. 1982-83), Colonial Dames of 17th Century. Editor: The Catline, 1973; (with others) The Oil and Gas Jour., 1982-83. Contbr. articles to profl. jours. Home: 7118 Bintliff Dr Houston TX 77074 Office: 5959 Corporate Dr Houston TX 77036

WILSON, ILLA ROSALEE, govt. ofcl.; b. McCook, Nebr., Apr. 19, 1930; d. James Hamilton and Sarah (Grinell) W.; B.A., U. Denver, 1950; postgrad. Western State Coll., Colo. Coll., U. Colo., Whittier Coll., Calif. State U., Long Beach. Tchr. public schs., Alaska, Calif., Colo., Oreg., 1954-76; speech pathologist United Cerebral Palsy Center, Denver, 1960-64; research chemist div. indsl. medicine U. Colo. Med. Center, Denver, 1962-64; ednl. cons. Colo. Dept. Instns., Denver, 1971-73; pvt. practice speech pathology, Denver, 1976-78; letter sorting machine clk. U.S. Postal Service, Denver, 1978—. Mem. Colo. Master Planning Task Force on Edn., 1973; trustee Town of Dacano, Colo., 1974-78, police commr., 1974-78. Cert. in spl. edn., speech pathology, and learning disabilities, Calif., Colo., Nebr., Oreg. Mem. Am. Speech and Hearing Assn. (cert. in clin. competence, coordinator handicapped and mental health), Am. Mensa Ltd. Democrat. Home: 716 Glen Moor Dacono CO 80514 Office: 7190 Colorado Blvd Commerce City CO 80022

WILSON, INGEBORG MARGARETE, author; b. Berlin, Jan. 19, 1925; came to U.S., 1950, naturalized, 1954; d. Rudolf Emil and Margarete Alma (Wichura) Beify; grad. Bus. Sch., Berlin; student U. Alaska, Fairbanks; m. Edward S. Wilson, Dec. 20, 1949; children—Bruce D., Beverly M. Wilson Warner, Bryan E. Interpreter, adminstrv. asst. Dept. State, Berlin, 1949-50; freelance writer and novelist, 1960—; employment security specialist, adjudicator Alaska Dept. Labor, 1974—; trustee, corp. sec. Mt. McKinley Mut. Savs. Bank, Fairbanks, 1965—; author: (novels) Nurse in Alaska, 1972, The Long Road to Freedom, 1973, The Secretary, 1974, A Second Chance, 1975, The Divorcee, 1977, Stepmother, 1979, Bank President, 1980, The Promise, 1980, Journey into the Past, 1981, They Fly Around the World, 1982; (non fiction) Alaskans I Have Met, 1967, 20 Jahre in Alaska, 1975, Ingeborg's Metric Bakebook, 1978. Mem. Nat. Fedn. Press Women (life), Alaska Press Women (charter; regional v.p. 1974), Alaska Alumni Assn. Office: Box 468 Fairbanks AK 99707

WILSON, JACKIE LYNN, educator; b. Houston, Sept. 22, 1933; d. John and Elton Jean (Spivey) Harris; B.A., Adelphi U., 1971; M.S., L.I. U., 1974; doctoral candidate U. Colo., 1977—; children—Robert, Patrick, Gregory. Detective, policewoman Nassau County (N.Y.) Police Dept., 1968-76; asst. prof. criminal justice L.I. U., 1973-76; asso. prof., chair dept. criminal justice Met. State Coll., Denver, 1976—. Served with USAF, 1952-57. Mem. Internat. Assn. Black Women for Criminal Justice (pres.), Am. Criminal Justice Assn., Am. Assn. Criminology, Colo. Prison Assn. (exec. bd.), Colo. Assn. Probation Ofcls. (exec. bd.), Colo. Law Enforcement Officers Assn. (exec. bd.), Delta Sigma Theta, Delta Theta Kappa. Home: 255 Holly St Denver CO 80220 Office: 1000 11th St Denver CO 80204

WILSON, JACQUELINE LAURA, air traffic controller; b. Superior, Ariz., June 28, 1940; d. Harold Marcus and Margaret (Minson) Smith; student FAA Sch. Air Traffic Control, 1968, FAA Mgmt. Sch., 1977, Antelope Valley Jr. Coll., 1975-77; m. J. C. Wilson, Jr., May 21, 1978; children by previous marriage—Jeffrey, Russell, William, Laura. Air traffic controller FAA, Los Angeles Center, Palmdale, Calif., 1968-77, supervisory air traffic control specialist, 1977-79, airspace and procedures specialist regional hdqrs., Hawthorne, Calif., 1979-80, air traffic evaluator regional hdqrs., Des Plaines, Ill., 1980-81; dep. chief Cleve. Air Route Traffic Control Center, 1981—; equal employment counselor, 1975-77; mem. women's subcom. FAA, 1979—. Mem. Civil Rights Com., Western region, 1976-79. Served with USN, 1958-61. Recipient Spl. Achievement award FAA, 1975, Cert. of Merit, 1979. Mem. Nat. Profl. Women Controllers (v.p. 1979-80). Republican. Home: 4626 Ashland Ave Lorain OH 44053 Office: 326 E Lorain Rd Oberlin OH 44074

WILSON, JANE FARISS, girls orgn. exec.; b. Adamsville, Tenn., Mar. 6, 1928; d. Hugh David and Myrtle (Griffin) Fariss; A.A., Sullins Coll., 1947; B.A., U. Tenn., Chattanooga, 1949; postgrad. Scarritt Coll., 1973, Vanderbilt U. Grad. Sch. Mgmt., 1975, U. Chgo, 1977, N.Y.U., 1978, Harvard U. Bus. Sch., 1980; div.; children—David Lamar, Deborah Jane. Field dir., supr. Moccasin Bend council Girl Scouts U.S.A., Chattanooga, 1965-72, field exec. Cumberland Valley council, Nashville, 1972-76, exec. dir. Dogwood Trails council, Springfield, Mo., 1976-80, counselor Project Overview, Chattanooga, 1981, interim exec. dir. Flint River council, Albany, Ga., 1981—, Green Hills council, Freeport, Ill., Maumee Valley council, Toledo, Ohio, 1981-82; cons.; ch. sch. and religious edn. trainer. Mem. Springfield Community Planning Council, 1977-80. Mem. Adminstrv. Mgmt. Soc., Assn. Girl Scout Exec. Staff, Am. Guild Organists, Fellowship United Meths. in Music Worship and Other Arts, Bus.and Profl. Women, C. of C., AAUW, Sigma Alpha Iota. Clubs: Zonta, Quota.

WILSON, JANET MARIE, home economist; b. Pawnee City, Nebr., Jan. 11, 1926; d. John H. and Ruby (Nelson) W.; B.S., N.W. Mo. State U., 1946; M.Ed., U. Mo., Columbia, 1950; postgrad. Oreg. State U., U. Ariz. Tchr. high schs., Mo., Iowa, Ill.; mem. faculty Kans. State U., U. Vt., Burlington; adminstrv. dir. home econs. edn. Nebr. Dept. Edn., Lincoln, 1963-71; prof., state extension specialist U. Nebr., Lincoln, 1971—; mem. adv. council Lincoln Public Schs.; cons. bus. and industry. Mem. Nebr. Home Econs. Assn. (exec. bd. 1963-77), Nat. Assn. Suprs. Home Econs. Edn. (pres. 1969-70), Am. Home Econs. Assn., Am. Council Consumer Interests, Nebr. Coop. Extension Assn., LWV, Kappa Omicron Phi, Pi Lambda Theta, Phi Delta Gamma. Club: Altrusa. Office: Coll Home Econs Univ Nebr Lincoln NE 68583

WILSON, JEAN ELIZABETH, mfg. engr.; b. North Tonawanda, N.Y., Dec. 31, 1948; d. Ralph Ashley and Ruth Jean (Spohr) W.; A.A.S. (N.Y. State Regents scholar 1969-71), Erie Community Coll., 1971; B.S., SUNY Coll. at Buffalo, 1977; M.S. Fla. Inst. Tech., 1982. Design draftsman Moog Inc., East Aurora, N.Y., 1973-77; indsl. engr. Chevrolet Tonawanda Motor Plant, 1977-78, sr. indsl. engr. STC Documetion Inc., Palm Bay, Fla., 1978-80, sr. mfg. systems analyst, 1980-82, staff mfg. engr., 1982—. Mem. Melbourne Mcpl. Band. Mem. Am. Inst. Indsl. Engrs., Am. Prodn. and Inventory Control Soc. Republican. Home: 1681 Cownie Ave Palm Bay FL 32905 Office: STC Kirby Ln Palm Bay FL 32905

WILSON, JEAN MARIE HALEY, civic worker; b. Dallas, Oct. 16, 1921; d. William Eldred and Helen Marie (Littlepage) Haley; B.A., So. Meth. U., 1943; m. Edward Lewis Wilson, Jr., Mar. 19, 1943; children—Edward Lewis III, William Haley, Sarah. Bd. dirs. Dallas Symphony Orch. League, 1963—, sec., 1964-68, 1st v.p., 1968-72, vice-chmn. spl. projects, 1977—; trustee Dallas Symphony Orch., 1976—; precinct chmn. Democratic Party, 1952-62; mem. Dallas County Dem. Exec. Com., 1952-62; bd. dirs. TACA (Com. for Fund Raising of the Arts), 1975—; mem. women's bd. Dallas Civic Opera, Dallas Civic Ballet Soc.; mem. Southwestern hospitality bd. Met. Opera; charter mem., bd. dirs., N. Tex. Herb Club, 1974—. Mem. Women in Communications, Kappa Alpha Theta. Methodist. Home: 3501 Lexington Ave Dallas TX 75205 Office: 2909 Maple Ave Dallas TX 75201

WILSON, JEANNE DOLORES, elec. contractor; b. Mpls., June 20, 1920; d. Enoch S. and Dolores E. Engstrom; student U. Minn., m. Vincent E. Wilson, July 26, 1944 (dec.); children—Candyce Ann, Brian Vincent. Sec. treas. Wilson Electric Co., Mpls., 1962-74, pres., 1974—. Apptd. City of Mpls. Women/Minority Bus. Adv. Com. Mem. Nat. Elec. Assn. (Mpls. chpt.), Nat. Assn. Women in Constrn. (chmn. youth info. com., 1981-82), Nat. Elec. Contractors Assn. (v.p. Mpls Chpt., 1980, chmn. EEO com., 1978). Roman Catholic. Club: Decathlon. Home: 11600 W Park Ridge Dr Minnetonka MN 55343 Office: 2902 Lyndale Ave S Minneapolis MN 55408

WILSON, KAREN MIRTH MCKEE, naval officer; b. Hamdem, Conn., Apr. 13, 1945; d. Benjamin Franklin and Dorothy Martha (Schumacher) Moore; A.S. in Acctg., Southwestern Coll., Chula Vista, Calif., 1973; m. Wayne C. Wilson, Nov. 28, 1981; 1 dau. by previous marriage, Billie Jo. Enlisted in U.S. Navy, 1963, commd. chief warrant officer, 1979; personnel officer personnel support activity Naval Submarine Base, Groton, Conn., 1979-82; personnel officer USS Fulton, 1982—. Mem. Nat. Assn. Female Execs., Fleet Res. Assn. Republican. Presbyterian. Home: 49 Osprey Dr Groton CT 06340 Office: X-Div USS Fulton (AS-11) FPO New York NY 09536

WILSON, KAREN SUE, mgmt. cons.; b. Vandalia, Ill., Oct. 2, 1946; d. Eugene H. and Grace (England) Culbertson; B.S., U. Ill., Champaign-Urbana, 1968; M.B.A., Pepperdine U., 1978. High sch. tchr., Norfolk, Va., 1969; pub. relations rep., trainer Va. Nat. Bank, Norfolk, 1969; weather girl Sta. WILL-TV, Urbana, 1967-68; mgmt. cons., trainer CSC, 1969-80, mktg. researcher and merchandiser Sta. KFI, Los Angeles, 1969-71; pres. Another Wilson Enterprise, pubs. and diversified interests, Laguna Beach, Calif., 1974-82; sr. cons. Wilson & Assos., tng. cons., 1969—; mem. faculty U. Calif. Bus. Extension, Irvine, U. So. Calif. Bus. Extension, 1976—. Mem. Am. Soc. Tng. and Devel. (officer), Internat. Assn. Bus. Communicators, Calif. Women in Higher Edn., NOW, Internat. Fedn. Tng. and Devel. Officers, Laguna Greenbelt Assn. Author manuals, articles, books on bus. and public speaking. Office: PO Box 217 Laguna Beach CA 92652

WILSON, KATHERINE ANN, educator; b. Detroit, July 26, 1946; d. Steve and Hedwig (Jablonski) Oros; B.A., U. Detroit, 1968; m. Mark Wilson, Aug. 17, 1968. Tchr., Precious Blood Sch., Detroit, 1968-69; spl. edn. tchr. Fremont (N.C.) Sch., 1969-70; elem. tchr. St. Mary's Sch., Goldsboro, N.C., 1970-74, Broadmeadow Sch., Rantoul, Ill., 1977-81, Merrimack Sch., Hampton, Va., 1982—. Mem. Beta Sigma Phi. Home: 4 G Maria Dr Poquoson VA 23662 Office: Merrimack Sch Hampton VA 23663

WILSON, KATHERINE BURRELL, mgmt. cons.; b. Delaware, Ohio, Mar. 14, 1945; d. Harold Courtland and Mildred (Baker) Burrell; B.A., Ohio Wesleyan U., 1966; M.B.A., Northeastern U., 1981; 1 son, Peter George. Copy editor Jour. Bone and Joint Surgery, 1969-70; exec. dir. Youth Dynamics, Boston, 1971; coop. edn. counselor Northeastern U., Boston, 1971-81; pvt. practice mgmt. cons., 1981—; editorial cons., 1968—. Bd. dirs. Lawrence Extended Day Program, Brookline, Mass., 1978-79, v.p., 1979-80, instr., cons. Managerial and Ednl. Inst. Ltd., Washington, 1980—. Home: 20-B Alton Pl Brookline MA 02146

WILSON, KATHERINE SCHMITKONS, biologist; b. Lorain, Ohio, Jan. 22, 1913; d. H. William and Katherine (Bauman) Schmitkons; A.B., Oberlin Coll., 1933; M.S., Northwestern U., 1935; Ph.D., Yale U., 1944; m. George E. Woodin, Nov. 23, 1961. Instr. biology Muskingum Coll., New Concord, Ohio, 1935-40; bot. researcher Yale U., 1941-44, Sessel fellow in biology, 1948-49, instr. biology, 1953-56; biologist div. research grants NIH, Bethesda, Md., 1956-58, scientist adminstr. genetics, 1958-77; ret., 1977; cons., lectr. genetics, 1978—. Recipient High Quality Service award HEW, NIH, 1966. Fellow AAAS, N.Y. Acad. Sci.; mem. Am. Soc. Human Genetics (spl. citation 1973), Genetics Soc. Am. (Service citation 1979), Environ. Mutagen Soc., Am. Inst. Biol. Scis., Am. Genetic Assn., Sigma Xi. Congregationalist. Club: PEO. Author: Botany—Principles and Problems, 5th ed., 1955; contbr. articles to profl. jours. Home: 77 235 Indiana Ave Palm Desert CA 92260

WILSON, MARCELLE NADEAU, dinner theatre mgr., theatrical producer; b. St. Leonard, N.B., Can., Oct. 24, 1936; came to U.S., 1955, naturalized, 1965; d. Emile and Louise (Bouchard) Nadeau; student Fredericton (N.B.) Bus. Coll., 1954, Vallejo Jr. Coll., 1967, also modeling schs.; m. Charles H. Wilson, Nov. 25, 1970. Various clerical and secretarial positions, 1955-68; mgr. Timbers Cabaret Theatre, Goleta, Calif., 1970-73; owner, mgr. Le P'tit Cabaret, Inc., dinner theatre, Santa Barbara, Calif., 1973—, also corp. sec. Recipient arts commendation plaque Santa Barbara News-Press, 1972, 73, Ventura County Actors award, 1973. Mem. Dramatists Guild (asso.). Roman Catholic. Playwright. Home: 249 Cooper Rd Santa Barbara CA 93109 Office: 1826 Cliff Dr Santa Barbara CA 93109

WILSON, MARGARET SULLIVAN, coll. ofcl.; b. Norwich, Conn., Mar. 21, 1924; d. John Joseph and Margaret Ellen (Connelly) Sullivan; B.S., Eastern Conn. State Coll., 1944; M.A., U. Conn., 1949; m. William Robert Wilson, July 20, 1950 (dec.); children—Margaret Ellen, William Robert. Reading cons. Greenwich (Conn.) Pub. Schs., 1948-50; asst. prof. early childhood, chmn. dept. early childhood Eastern Conn. State Coll., Willimantic, 1967-77, exec. asst. to pres., 1977-78, v.p. adminstrv. affairs, 1978-80, exec. asst. to pres., 1980—; del. White House Conf. on Children, 1970, 80; cons. Windham-Willimantic Child Care, 1971—; corporator Groton Chelsea Savs. Bank, Norwich, Conn. Mem. Conn. Dept. Mental Health Adv. Bd.; mem. Norwich (Conn.) Hosp. Adv. Bd.; mem. Eastern Regional Mental Health Bd., Mohegan Mental Health Council; chairperson rev. com. Conn. Health Coordinating Council; mem. Norwich Bd. Edn.; mem. vestry Ch. of Resurrection, Episcopal ch., Norwich; mem. policy adv. com. Conn. Dept. Human Services. Mem. Norwich Area C. of C. (dir.). Democrat. Home: 27 Canterbury Turnpike Norwich CT 06360 Office: 83 Windham St Willimantic CT 06226

WILSON, MARY EVE, librarian; b. Nashville, May 23, 1943; d. Alwin Curtis and Mary Usula (Glover) Hutcherson; B.S., Miss. State Coll. for Women, 1965; M.L.S., Vanderbilt U., 1968. Librarian, George Washington Carver High Sch., Newport News, Va., 1968-69; children's, young adult librarian Finkelstein Meml. Library, Spring Valley, N.Y., 1970-77; young adult services specialist Tampa-Hills County Pub. Library System, Tampa, Fla., 1977—; adj. prof. Grad. Sch. Library Sci., Fla. State U., 1981. Mem. Hills County Women's Polit. Caucus, 1980; del. Fla. Conf. on Children and Youth, 1981; bd. dirs. Northside Community Mental Health Complex, Tampa, 1981—; mem. Fla. Alliance for Responsible Adolescent Parenting, 1978—. Recipient vol. service award Hills County Children's Services, 1981. Mem. ALA (pres. young adult services div. 1981-82). Democrat. Episcopalian. Contbr. articles to profl. jours. Office: 900 N Ashley St Tampa FL 33602

WILSON, MAXINE FAY, educator; b. Leonardville, Kans., Mar. 25, 1924; d. Roy Elmer and Agnes Marie (Nyberg) Wilson; B.S., Kans. State U., 1946; M.S., Purdue U., 1955. Staff dietitian Colo. State Hosp., Pueblo, 1947-50; mem. faculty Purdue U., Lafayette, Ind., 1950—, dir. food service, 1950-69, asst. dir. residence halls, 1969-75, asst. prof. Restaurant, Hotel Inst. Mgmt. Sch. Consumer and Family Sci., 1975-78, asso. prof., 1978—; cons. food service devel., 1965—. Bd. dirs. YWCA, 1975, 79—, exec. bd., 1979—, recipient Community Service award.; bd. dirs. Westminster Village, 1980—. Mem. Am. Dietetic Assn. (state pres.; ho. of dels.; joint com. nat. sanitation found.), Nat. Assn. Coll. and Housing Officers, Sigma Xi, Sigma Delta Epsilon. Lutheran. Club: Altrusa. Author: Food for Fifty, 6th edit., 1979. Home: 2729 Henderson Ave West Lafayette IN 47906 Office: Stone Hall Purdue U West Lafayette IN 47906

WILSON, MILDRED MCGILL, labor exec.; b. Tifton, Ga., Jan. 1, 1921; d. John D. and Josie Davis McGill; student Abraham Baldwin Coll., 1938-40; m. W. D. Wilson, Aug. 22, 1940; children—Jim L., W. David. Head teller, tng. officer Farmers Bank, Tifton, 1948-68; employment programs coordinator Ga. Dept. Labor, Tifton, 1969—. Chmn., Aidmore Children's Home, 1976-77, March of Dimes, 1955-70. Mem. Internat. Assn. Personnel in Employment Security. Club: Elks Aux. (pres. 1978-79) (Tifton). Home: Old Union Rd Route 2 Box 644 Tifton GA 31794

WILSON, MOLLIE CROSS HALEY, bank exec.; b. Charlotte, N.C., May 5, 1942; d. Shaffer and Mollie Flournoy (Cross) Haley; B.S. with honors in Bus. Adminstrn., U. Ark., Fayetteville, 1963, M.B.A., 1972, Ph.D. in Fin., 1979; m. Jack E. Grober. Grad. asst. U. Ark., Fayetteville, 1971-73, instr., 1974-79; asso. Robert E. Kennedy, Inc., Fayetteville, 1971—; v.p. investment div. Mchts. Nat. Bank, Ft. Smith, Ark., 1979—; fin. cons. for public cos., Ark. Bd. dirs. Ark. Community Found., 1979—, Ft. Smith Heritage Found., 1979—. Chartered fin. planner, 1982. Mem. Inst. Chartered Fin. Planners, Ark. Soc. Fin. Mgrs. (bd. dirs., 1972—), Dallas Soc. Investment Analysts, Fin. Analysts Fedn., Beta Gamma Sigma. Contbr. articles in field to publs. Home: 8401 Mile Tree Dr Fort Smith AR 72903 Office: PO Box 8 Fort Smith AR 72902

WILSON, NANCY, singer; b. Chillicothe, Ohio, Feb. 20, 1937; d. Olden and Lillian (Ryan) W.; ed. Columbus (Ohio) schs.; m. Kenneth C. Dennis (div. 1969); 1 son, Kenneth C.; m. 2d, Wiley Burton, 1974. Began career as singer with local groups, then joined Rusty Bryant band, 1956, and toured Midwest and Can. until 1958; singing independently, 1959—; rec. artist Capitol Records; recs. include But Beautiful; Can't Take My Eyes Off You; Close-Up; For Once in My Life/Who Can I Turn To; How Glad I Am; Hurt So Bad; Now I'm a Woman; Right to Love; Son of a Preacher Man; Come Get To; TV appearances include Bob Hope Show, Danny Kaye Show, Hollywood Palace Show, Carol Burnett Show, Glen Campbell Goodtime Hour, Hawaii Five-O, Flip Wilson Show, Dean Martin Show, The FBI, Police Story, others; hostess TV series KNBC, Los Angeles, 1974-75. Address: care Albatross Mgmt Inc PO Box 66558 Seattle WA 98166

WILSON, OLIVE FULLER (LANDER), librarian; b. Nacogdoches County, Tex., Feb. 18, 1922; d. Fulton and Lillian (Brewer) Fuller; B.Mus., Mary Hardin-Baylor Coll., 1943; M.Librarianship, U. S.C., 1979; postgrad. Clemson U., 1955, 60, Stephen F. Austin State U., 1948, 53; m. William Lander, Jr., 1943 (dec.); children—Susan Lander Dye, Margaret Lander Shaw, Mary Laura; m. 2d, Jack C. Wilson, Feb. 25, 1973. Tchr., Williamston (S.C.) High Sch., 1948-50, Fremont Elementary Sch., Spartanburg, S.C., 1953-54, Pelzer (S.C.) Elementary Sch., 1954-57; tchr. S.C. Opportunity Sch., 1962-68, ofcl. hostess, 1962-68, dean women, 1968; tchr. Palmetto High Sch., Williamston, 1968-70, librarian, 1970—; bd. trustees S.C. Opportunity Sch., 1976—; mem. Young Adult Book Award Com., 1979—. Legis. appointee com. for animal shelter, Anderson, S.C.; bd. dirs. Animal Shelter, 1977—; del. Dem. Conv., 1972, 76, 78, 80, sec. local precinct, 1972. Mem. NEA, S.C. Ednl. Assn., S.C. Library Assn., S.C. Assn. Sch. Librarians, AAUW, Anderson County Edn. Assn. Methodist. Clubs: Williamston Garden (pres., 1962, 69, 74, 80—), Alpha Delta Kappa (pres. Lambda chpt. 1978-80). Author: History of Williamston, South Carolina, 1972. Home: 106 Hardy St Williamston SC 29697 Office: Box 428 Hamilton St Williamston SC 29697

WILSON, PATRICIA BOYD (MRS. ROBERT WILSON), journalist, ednl. adminstr., mus. ofcl.; b. Everett, Wash., Oct. 22, 1911; d. John and Addie Alberta (Foss) Boyd; B.S., N.Y. U., 1943; M.S., Columbia, 1944; m. Robert Wilson, Jan. 18, 1952. By-line on art Christian Sci. Monitor, Boston, 1962—; dean edn. Fine Arts Mus. of South, Mobile, Ala., 1979—; art appraiser. Cons. pilot project M.W. Smith Found., Mobile, Ala. Mem. Intertel. Home: 2769 Chadwick Dr N Mobile AL 36606 Office: PO Box 8404 Mobile AL 36608

WILSON, PATRICIA POPLAR, elec. mfg. exec.; b. Chgo., Sept. 20, 1931; d. George and Leona (O'Brien) Poplar; B.S., U. Wash., 1966, M.A., 1967, Ph.D., 1980; m. Chester Goodwin Wilson, Jan. 30, 1960; children—Susan Spadafora, Chester Wilson. Instr., U. Wash., Seattle, 1967-74; women's editor Nor'westing Mag., Seattle, 1969—; pres. Wilson & Assos. N.W. Inc., Seattle, 1974—; v.p. N.W. Mfg. & Supply, Inc., 1977—; dir. Trydor Sales, Ltd., Can. Mem. Electric League. Episcopalian. Club: Seattle Yacht. Author: Household Equipment, Guide to Surplus Equipment. Contbr. articles to profl. jours. Office: 4045 7th Ave S Seattle WA 98108

WILSON, SANDRA ELAINE, engr.; b. Kansas City, Kans., Feb. 11, 1943; d. Harry and Aline (Sloan) Jackson; B.A. in Bus., Kansas City Jr. Coll., 1962; B.G.S. in Psychology, U. Kans., 1979, B.S. in Bus. Law, 1964; children—Vincent Charles, Michael DeWayne. Fgn. affairs supr. Nat. Bellas Hess Inc., Kansas City, Mo., 1962-63; file clk. AT&T, Kansas City, 1963-64, mktg. asso., 1964-66, sr. engring. clk., 1966-69, sr. engring. asso., 1970-79; circuit designer Pacific Tel. & Tel., Los Angeles, 1979—. Mem. Pasadena (Calif.) Sch. Bd., 1979-82; mem. women's aux. Pasadena Boys' Club, 1979-82; chairperson Pasadena/Altadena Consol. Funding Bd., 1978-81; music coordinator Lincoln Ave. Baptist Ch., Pasadena, 1980—, youth counselor, 1980—. Recipient cert. United Way Calif., Pasadena Sch. Bd. Mem. Profl. Women Calif., Exec. Females Am., Nat. Assn. Female Execs. Democrat. Club: Daus. of Elks. Home: 2370 El Sereno Altadena CA 91001 Office: 3525 W 8th St Los Angeles CA 90005

WILSON, SHARON CECELIA, airlines exec.; b. Long Branch, N.J., Feb. 24, 1946; d. John R. and Ruth Joan (Sweeney) Hendrie; student (N.J. scholar) Rutgers U., 1965, 69-75; B.A. in Econs. with honors, Fla. Internat. U., 1979; m. John V. Wilson, June 24, 1972. Reservations agt. Eastern Air Lines, N.Y.C., 1966-69, fare and rate agt., 1969-71, analyst, planning, N.Y.C., 1971-75, Miami, 1975-80, sr. analyst, planning, 1980—. Ruth Kaplan Meml. scholar, 1965-66. Mem. Miami Mgmt. Council, Nat. Audubon Soc., Egyptology Soc., Mus. Sci., Nat. Assn. Female Execs., Miami Assn. Bus. Economists, Nat. Assn. Bus. Economists, Am. Econ. Assn., Mus. Sci. Miami. Home: 43 Salamanca Ave Coral Gables FL 33134 Office: Eastern Air Lines Miami Internat Airport Miami FL 33148

WILSON, SHIRLEY CAIN, univ. ofcl.; b. Madison, Ala., Apr. 17, 1932; d. John Slaughter and Margaret Lucille (Wade) Cain; B.S. in Edn., U. Ala., Tuscaloosa, 1953; M.A. in Edn., U. Ala., Birmingham, 1979; m. Henry Martin Wilson, Sept. 15, 1956; children—Margaret Susannah, Henry Martin, Elizabeth Corley. Sec. for Thiokol Chem. Corp., Huntsville, Ala., 1953-54, U.S. Senator Lister Hill, Washington, 1954-55; exec. sec. to pres. Brown Engring. Co., Huntsville, 1955-57; adminstrv. sec. dept. anesthesiology U. Ala., Birmingham, 1969-74, adminstrv. sec. div. phys. therapy, 1974-79, adminstrv. asst. div. nephrology, 1979—. Vestry, St. Mary's Episcopal Ch., Childersburg, Ala., 1980—. Episcopalian. Home: Route 2 Box 115 Vincent AL 35178 Office: Div Nephrology Univ Ala Birmingham AL 35294

WILSON, WANDA MARIE, social worker; b. Sharon, Pa., Nov. 13, 1947; d. Clem Cleophus and Rosetta Lucille (Satterwhite) Ragster; B.A. in Sociology and Psychology, Slippery Rock State Coll., 1969; M.S.W., U. Pitts., 1973; m. Maurice Thomas Wilson, Nov. 24, 1974; children—Maurice Thomas, Maureen Marie. Diagnostic and evaluative supr. foster homes Trumbull County Children's Service Bd., Warren, Ohio, 1973-74; social service supr. Asso. Cath. Charities, Balt., 1976-79; dir. outreach and health screening Health Screening Research Found., Pitts., 1974-76; supr. emergency services Cath. Charities, Balt., 1980-81, supr. deaf family service, 1981—, coordinator central counseling services, 1981—. Mem. Emergency Adv. Council, Energy Assistance Program; supt. intermediate dept. Bethel A.M.E. Sunday Sch. Lic. social worker, Md. Mem. Nat. Assn. Social Workers, Balt. Ministers Wives Alliance, Baltimore Interdenominational Ministers Wives Alliance, Altruist Guild (fin. com.). Clubs: Elks, Order Eastern Star. Home: 408 Acadia Dr Joppa MD 21085 Office: 320 Cathedral St Baltimore MD 21201

WILSON DUBLIN, ELVIE, psychologist; b. Athens, Greece, May 18, 1937; d. Anthony I. and Rosa (Protecdicos) Nicolopoulos; B.A., Ind. U., 1966, Ph.D., 1972; m. John Wilson, Oct. 29, 1958 (div. 1967); children—David, Toni; m. 2d James Dublin, Dec. 21, 1973 (div. 1978). Cons., Hospitality House Nursing Home, Bedford, Ind., 1972-73; psychotherapist Choice, Inc., 1973-79, sec.-treas., 1973-79; pres. Studentworld, Inc., 1978-81; pvt. practice psychology, Bloomington, Ind., 1979—; bd. dirs. Midwestern Psychotherapy Inst., 1977. NSF trainee, 1965-67; USPHS trainee, 1967-70. Mem. Am. Psychol. Assn., Ind. Psychol. Assn., Assn. Advancement Psychology, Phi Beta Kappa. Club: Monroe County Saddle. Home: 9401 E St Rd 46 Bloomington IN 47401 Office: 4151 E 3d St Bloomington IN 47401

WILSON-MONIGAN, DAISY MAXINE, public sch. tchr.; b. Flatwood, Ala., Mar. 18, 1949; d. William J. and Mildred L. (Monigan) Creagh; B.S., Ala. A&M U., 1971; M.S., U. Hartford (Conn.), 1975; also pvt. student voice; divorced; children—Maia N., Floyd V. Tutor music Ala. A&M U., 1969; with Conn. Dept. Community Affairs, 1971; tchr. English and music Weaver High Sch., Hartford, Conn., 1971—. Vol. counselor Women in Crisis, 1978—. Mem. Am. Fedn. Tchrs., Hartford Fedn. Tchrs., NAACP, Zeta Phi Beta. Democrat. Baptist. Address: 23 Hill Farm Rd Bloomfield CT 06002

WILTSE, GLADYS MAY, social worker; b. Denmark Twp., Mich., July 2, 1908; d. Norman John and Alice May (Levis) Garner; B.A., Eastern Mich. U., 1948; postgrad. U. Mich., 1955-69; m. Dorr Norman Wiltse, Nov. 11, 1932; children—Dorr Norman, Saire Christina Wiltse Keckler. Tchr. public high sch., Mayville, Mich., 1927-30, Vassar (Mich.) High Sch., 1930-33; social worker Tuscola County (Mich.) Bur. Social Aid, 1937-40, supr., 1940-44; area rep. Mich. Dept. Social Welfare Thumb Area, Caro, 1944-48; tchr. Caro High Sch., 1955-73; mem. Tuscola County Social Services Bd., 1952—, chmn., 1954-68, vice chmn., 1968-79; founder, sponsor Caro High Sch. History Club, 1958-73. Co-founder Watrousville-Caro Area Hist. Soc. and Museum, 1972. Recipient award of commendation Mich. Civil War Centnnial Graves Registration Com., 1965; Merit award Rotary Club, 1975; cert. appreciation Saginaw Inter-Tribal Assn., Inc., 1977; Outstanding Soc. Service award Watrousville-Caro Area Hist. Soc., 1982. Mem. Mich. Counties Social Services Assn. (Meritorious award 1959, cert. commendation 1981), Caro Tchrs. Assn. (pres. 1956-57), Ret. Tchrs.' Assn., Indianfields Questers (pres. 1974-76), Tuscola County Med. Care Facility Forget Me Not Club, Cass River Gem and Mineral Soc., Saginaw Geneal. Soc. Clubs: Caro Garden (pres. 1977-78), DAR, Nat. Soc. Colonial Dames XVII Century, Nat. Soc. Daus. of Barons Runnemede, Huguenot Soc. Mich., Order of Crown of Charlemagne in U.S.A., Nat. Soc. Old Plymouth Colony Descs., Nat. Soc. Daus. Colonial Wars, Order Three Crusades, 1096-1192, Nat. Soc. Sons and Daus. of Pilgrims. Dames of the Court of Honor, Ancient and Honorable Artillery Co., Nat. Soc. of Magna Charta Dames, Colonial Daus., of the XVII Century. Home: 708 W Sherman St PO Box 143 Caro MI 48723

WIMBERLEY, MARY LINDA, coll. adminstr.; b. Choctaw, County, Ala., Apr. 12, 1949; d. Little Tom and Verma Leota (McDaniel) W.; B.A., U. Ala., 1971. Women's editor Cullman (Ala.) Times, 1972,

Athens (Ala.) News Courier, 1972-73; feature writer Decatur (Ala.) Daily, 1973-74; info. specialist Office Info. Services, Samford U., Birmingham, 1974—. Mem. AAUW (membership chmn., program chmn., group leader), Women in Communications (past pres. Birmingham profl. chpt.), Internat. Assn. Bus. Communicators (dir.), Ala. Women's Press Assn. (1st pl. newswriting award 1976), Council Advancement and Support Edn. Baptist. Office: Samford Univ 800 Lakeshore Dr Birmingham AL 35209

WIMBERLEY, RACHAEL LERABETH, social worker; b. Attapulgus, Ga., Mar. 4, 1938; d. Eugene and Ada Elizabeth (Robinson) W.; B.S., Fla. State U., 1960; M.S.W., U. Ala., 1973. Child welfare worker Fla. Dept. Public Welfare, Panama City, 1960-63, public assistance, child welfare worker, Pensacola, 1966-69; recreation specialist, U.S. Dept. Army, Germany, 1963-65; dean women Troy (Ala.) State U., 1969-71; coordinator day care Ala. Sch. Social Work, Tuscaloosa, 1973-77; regional coordinator community services Ala. Dept. Mental Health, Tuscaloosa, 1977-79; caseworker Childrens Home Soc. Fla., Ocala, 1979—. Named Alumnus of Yr., Sch. Social Work U. Ala., 1977. Mem. Acad. Cert. Social Workers, Nat. Assn. Social Workers (editor), Alumni Assn. Sch. Social Work U. Ala., Am. Bus. Women's Assn. (treas.). Democrat. Baptist. Home: 3201 SW 88th St Ocala FL 32671 Office: 401 SE 19th Ave Ocala FL 32674

WIMBERLY, ANNE ELIZABETH STREATY, educator; b. Anderson, Ind., June 10, 1936; d. Robert Harold and Valeska Bea (Cunningham) Streaty; B.Sc., Ohio State U., 1957; M.Mus., Boston U., 1965, postgrad., 1965-72; grad. cert. gerontology Ga. State U., 1979, Ph.D., 1981; m. Edward Powell Wimberly, June 4, 1966; 1 foster son, Michael A. Haynie. Dir. music Harwood Girls' Sch., Albuquerque, 1957-58; music specialist Detroit Public Schs., 1958-64; teaching fellow Boston U., 1964-66; music cons. Newton Public Schs., jr. high vocal music tchr., Newton, Mass., 1966-68; music cons. Worcester (Mass.) Public Schs., 1968-73; asst. prof. music Worcester State Coll., 1973-75; asso. prof. music, instr. gerontology Atlanta Jr. Coll., 1975—, faculty coordinator faculty campus ministry outreach, 1981—, faculty coordinator performing arts series, 1977—. Vol., Pineview Convalescent Center, 1975-78; mem. adv. com. Bethlehem Sr. Center, 1977—; mem. bd. discipleship family life com. United Meth. Ch., 1980-84; mem. World Meth. Family Life Com., 1981-86; bd. dirs. Dekalb Community Council on Aging, Dekalb County, Ga., 1981-84; mem. planning com. N.Am. Family Life Convocation, United Meth. Ch., 1982. Sch. of Theology at Claremont scholar in residence, 1982, Adminstrn. on Aging grantee, Ga. State U., 1979; Nat. Endowment Humanities grantee Atlanta Jr. Coll., 1977-81. Mem. Music Educators Nat. Conf., Internat. Soc. Music Edn., AAUW, Ga. Music Educators Assn. (chmn. state coll. div. 1979-81), Ga. Gerontol. Soc., Kappa Delta Pi, Pi Kappa Lambda. Democrat. Methodist. Club: Knollview Civic (Dekalb County, Ga.). Home: 2738 Aquamist Dr Decatur GA 30034 Office: 1630 Stewart Ave SW Atlanta GA 30310

WIMBY, LENORA YVONNE, med. technologist; b. Orlando, Fla., Jan. 12, 1949; d. Benjamin Harrison and Josephine Lenora (Alexander) W.; A.A., Santa Fe Community Coll., 1968; B.S. in Med. Tech. U. Fla., 1971. Staff med. technologist in spl. hematology Shands Hosp. and Clinics, Gainesville, Fla., 1971—; lectr., instr. in field. Mem. Am. Soc. Clin. Pathologists, Am. Soc. for Med. Tech. Office: PO Box J275 Shands Hosp Archer Rd Gainesville FL 32610

WIMER, CYNTHIA CROSBY, biologist; b. Boston, Oct. 23, 1933; d. Robert Addison and Hazel (Ruggles) Crosby; B.A., Wellesley Coll., 1955; M.A., McGill U., 1958; Ph.D., Rutgers U., 1961; m. Richard Earl Wimer, Dec. 21, 1957; children—John Savage, James Lucas, Mark Crosby. Research asso., ednl. program supr. Jackson Lab., Bar Harbor, Maine, 1962-69; asso. research scientist City of Hope Research Inst., Duarte, Calif., 1969—. Mem. AAAS, Am. Psychol. Assn., Behavior Genetics Assn., Sigma Xi. Club: Channel Island Yacht. Contbr. articles in field to profl. publs. Home: 386 N Lima St Sierra Madre CA 92024 Office: City of Hope Research Inst 1450 E Duarte Rd Duarte CA 91010

WINANT, ETHEL WALD, broadcasting exec.; b. Worcester, Mass., Aug. 5; d. William and Janice (Woolson) Wald; B.A., U. Calif., Berkeley; M.T.A., Whittier Coll.; children—William, Scott, Bruce. Dir. casting Talen Assos., N.Y.C., 1953-56; asso. producer Playhouse '90, CBS, Hollywood, Calif., 1956-60; asso. producer All Fall Down, MGM, Calif., 1960-61; producer Gt. Adventure, DBS, Hollywood, 1961-62; v.p. talent, dir. program devel. CBS, Hollywood, 1962-75; exec. producer Best of Families, PBS, N.Y.C., 1975-77; v.p. talent NBC, Burbank, Calif., 1978—, v.p. mini-series and novels for TV, 1979; sr. v.p. Metromedia Producers Co., 1981—; mem. adv. bd. Center for Advanced Film Studies, Am. Film Inst., 1981—; bd. govs. Nat. Acad. TV Arts and Scis.; bd. dirs. Circle Reperatory Theatre; mem. Pres.'s Commn. for Women; mem. Calif. Arts Council; cons. in field. Recipient Emmy award Nat. Acad. TV Arts and Scis., 1960; Disting. Alumni award Calif. Community Colls., 1981; named TV Woman of Yr., Conf. Personal Mgrs., 1974. Mem. Acad. TV Arts and Scis. (exec. com. 1981—), John Tracy Clinic, Women in Film (Crystal award 1979), Hollywood Radio and TV Soc. (dir. 1981—, sec. 1981—). Office: 5746 Sunset Blvd Los Angeles CA

WINCENC, CAROL, flautist; b. Buffalo, June 29, 1949; d. Joseph Frank and Margaret (Miller) W.; Diploma, Santa Cecilia Acad. Music, Rome, 1967; Diploma d'Honore, Chigiana Acad. Music, Siena, Italy, 1968; student Oberlin Conservatory Music, 1967-69; Mus.B., Manhattan Sch. Music, 1971; Mus. M., Juilliard Sch. Music, 1972; m. Ronald J. Dennis, May 23, 1976. Prin. and solo flutist St. Paul Chamber Orch., 1972-77; solo flute recitalist, soloist with orch. and chamber music groups, 1978—; prin. flutist Aspen (Colo.) Chamber Symphony, Aspen Festival summers 1970-72, Claremont (Calif.) Music Festival, 1973, Grand Teton (Wyo.) Music Festival, 1974-77; prin. and solo flutist-in-residence Marlboro (Vt.) Music Festival, 1978, 79; solo flutist Spoleto (Italy) Festival, in U.S. and Italy, 1977, Mostly Mozart Festival, First Internat. Bach Festival, Madeira, Portugal, 1980, 81, Santa Fe Chamber Music Festival, 1981; founding mem. Musica Camerot ensemble, in residence Merkin Concert Hall, N.Y.C., 1982—; flute tchr. Manhattan Sch. Music, N.Y.C.; recs. for Mus. Heritage Soc. (1st solo album cited as Rec. of Spl. Merit, Sterio Rev. 1980); recorded with St. Paul Chamber Orch., Tashi Chamber Ensemble; appeared on Today Show, NBC, 1981. Recipient Solo Debut Recital award Concert Artists Guild N.Y., 1972, Solo. Recital award Met. Museum N.Y. Introduction Series, 1977, 1st prize Walter W. Naumburg Solo Flute Competition, 1978, citation for bringing world outstanding recognition to Buffalo, Buffalo Area C. of C., 1978; Fulbright-Hayes French Govt. grantee. Mem. Associated Musicians Greater N.Y., Nat. Flute Assn. Home and Office: 875 West End Ave New York NY 10025

WINCH, DEBRA LYNN CHAMPION, indsl. engr.; b. Ishpeming, Mich., Aug. 25, 1956; d. Ruben Richard and Donna Mae (Benson) C.; B.S.B.A., Mich. Tech. U., 1979; m. Raymond F. Winch, Jr. Indsl. engr. Am. Can Co., Menasha, Wis., 1979-80, porcelain div. Franklin Mint Corp., Franklin Center, Pa., 1981—. Mem. Houghton (Mich.) Bus. and Profl. Woman's Club (mem. legislative com. 1978-79), Phi Gamma Nu (v.p. 1977-79, Phila. chpt. alumni 1981—). Home: 138 Ridge Blvd Brookhaven PA 19015 Office: Franklin Mint Corp Porcelain Div Aston PA

WINCHELL, MARGARET ST. CLAIR, realtor; b. Clinton, Tenn., Jan. 26, 1923; d. Robert Love and Mayme Jane (Warwick) Webster; student Denison U., 1940, Miami U., Oxford (Ohio), 1947, 48; m. Charles M. Winchell, June 7, 1941; children—David Alan, Margaret Winchell Boyle; m. 2d, Robert George Sterrett, July 15, 1977 (div. 1979). Salesman, Fred K.A. Schmidt & Shirmer real estate, Cin., 1960-66, Cline Realtors, Cin., 1966-70; owner, broker Winchell's Showplace Realtors, Cin., 1972—; ins. agt. United Liberty Life Ins. Co., 1966—, dist. mgr., 1967-70, 77-82, regional mgr., 1982—; stockbroker Waddell & Reed, Columbus, Ohio, 1972—. Treas., v.p. Parents without Partners, 1969, sec., 1968; pres. PTA; dir. Children's Bible Fellowship Ohio, 1953-76; dir. Child Evangelism Cin.; nat. speaker Child Evangelism Fellowship and Nat. Sunday Sch. Convs., 1955-57; pres. Christian Solos, 1974; chaplain Bethesda N. Hosp. Mem. Nat. Assn. Real Estate Bds. West Shell Realtors (v.p.), Womens Council Real Estate Bd. (treas.). Clubs: Alfonta, Travel go go, Guys and Gals Singles (founder, 1st pres.), Hamilton Singles (sec.). Home and office: 8221 Margaret Ln Cincinnati OH 45242

WINCHESTER, ALMA ELIZABETH TATSCH (MRS. CLARENCE FLOYD WINCHESTER), civic worker, radio writer and broadcaster; b. Fredericksburg, Tex.; d. Otto August and Meta (Hohenberger) Tatsch; spl. student Am. Conservatory Music (Chgo.), 1937-38; m. Clarence Floyd Winchester, Sept. 25, 1943. Singer Chgo. Civic Opera Jr. Chorus, 1937-38; writer radio script Evans Fur Co., Chgo., 1941-42; writer Sta. KTSA, San Antonio, 1942-43; women's dir., writer, broadcaster Sta. KNOE, Monroe, La., 1944-45; writer, music lead ins Boyce Smith Show, Sta. WGN, Chgo., 1944; women's dir., writer, broadcaster Sta. WGGG, Gainesville, Fla., 1948-49; public relations Stokeley-Van Camp, Inc., Washington, 1954-55. Mem. Salvation Army Aux., Washington; mem. women's bd. Providence Hosp., Washington, Pan-Am. liaison com. Women's Orgns., Washington, to 1981; mem. Women's Internat. Religious Fellowship in cooperation with UNESCO, UNICEF, schs., embassies; past pres. City of Hope Med. Research chpt. 56, Washington. Mem. Los Picaros (hon.). Mem. Christian Ch. Home: 2124 Sudbury Pl NW Washington DC 20012

WINCHESTER, LORRAINE PECK, speech pathologist; b. Alcester, S.D., Sept. 25, 1921; d. Andros Otis and Ferne (St. John) Peck; B.A., Coe Coll., 1944; M.A., U. Denver, 1947; m. Richard Albert Winchester, Aug. 24, 1947; children—Anne Lorraine, James Albert, Anthony Richard. Tchr. speech and English, Arlington (Iowa) High Sch., 1943-45, instr. U. Denver, 1946-48; speech pathologist Calif. Sch. Cerebral Palsy Children, Altadena, 1949-50; pvt. practice speech pathology with Margaret Jones, M.D., Glendale, Calif., 1949-50; pvt. practice, Phila., 1951-65; head speech and lang. therapy Vanguard Lower Sch., Paoli, Pa., 1965—. Pres., Rowen Elem. Home and Sch. Assn., 1963-64; v.p. Wagner Jr. High Sch. Home and Sch. Assn., 1964-66. Coe Coll. scholar, 1940-44; U. Denver fellow, 1945. Mem. Am. Speech, Lang. and Hearing Assn., Congress Exceptional Children. Mem. Unity Sch. Christianity. Home: 726 Clyde Circle Bryn Mawr PA 19010 Office: PO Box 730 Paoli PA 19301

WINDELL, MARYMARGARET CREWS, property mgr.; b. San Jose, Calif., Mar. 22, 1938; d. Denzel Calvin and Mary Elizabeth (Blondin) Crews; A.A. in Bus., San Jose City Coll., 1959; m. Harold Cecil Windell, Mar. 22, 1956; children—Helen Mary (dec.), Roger Lee (dec.), Grace Ann Windell Chavez, Suzanne Rose, Tamie Rene Windell Weldon. Dist. mgr. Beauty Counselor Cosmetics, Los Altos, Calif., 1960-63; exec. sec.-adminstrv. asst. T.G. & Y. Stores Co. Dist. Office, Milpitas, Calif., 1969-74; sec. to pres., Roaring Camp, Felton, Calif., 1975; sec.-mgr. Hy Wiesel Properties, Star Lodge Hosp., Scotts Valley, Calif., 1976-79; cons. Con-Stand Industries, Inc., Scotts Valley, 1979-80; asst. property mgr.-coordinator Gandauff Ind., condominium mgmt., Capitola (Calif.) br. office, 1980—. MADD (Mothers Against Drunk Drivers) rep., Santa Clara, Santa Cruz and Monterey counties, Calif., 1980—; sustaining mem. Republican Nat. Com., 1981: Mem. Nat. Assn Female Execs., Scottish Rite Woman's Assn., Relief Soc., Beta Sigma Phi. Mormon. Clubs: Eastern Star, Rosicrucian Order, Rebecca's (Odd Fellows), Job's Daus. Home: 228 San Augustine Way Scotts Valley CA 95066

WINDER, WILMA LOY, nursing home adminstr.; b. Graham County, Kans., Oct. 2, 1937; d. Hubert I. and Gladys Gertrude (Zumwalt) Scranton; R.N. diploma Kansas City (Mo.) Gen. Sch. Nursing, 1958; A.A., Barton County Community Coll., 1979; m. C. Duane Winder, June 3, 1962; 1 son, Douglas Duane. Staff nurse obstetrics Norton County Hosp., Norton, Kans., 1958-70; adminstr. Andbe Home, Inc., Norton, 1970—; mem. adv. bd. for nursing home adminstrs. Barton County Community Coll.; mem. practical nursing adv. bd. Colby Community Coll. Mem. Kans. Profl. Nursing Home Adminstrs. Assn. Methodist. Club: Monday Federated Study. Home: 810 N Wabash Norton KS 67654 Office: 201 W Crane Norton KS 67654

WINDSOR, PATRICIA, author, educator; b. N.Y.C., Sept. 21, 1938; d. Bernhard Edward and Antionette (Gaus) Seelinger; student Bennington Coll., 1956-57; Westchester Community Coll., 1970-71; children—Patience Wells, Laurence Edward. Asst. coll. bds. editor Mademoiselle Mag., N.Y.C., 1956; asst. editor Living For Young Homemakers Mag., 1959-60; mgr. info. Family Planning Assos., London, 1974-75; correspondent Nat. Council Social Services, London, 1975-76; editor in chief Easterner, AT&T, Washington, 1978-80; author: The Summer Before, 1973, Something's Waiting, 1974, Home Is Where Your Feet Are Standing, 1975, Diving for Roses, 1976, Mad Martin, 1976, Killing Time, 1980; contbr. short stories to mags.; mem. faculty Inst. Children's Literature, 1976—; instr. Writers Inst. U. Md., 1981-82; instr. Open U., Washington, 1982. Youth dir. YWCA, Evanston, Ill. Recipient Best Book Am. Library Assn., 1973; Austrian State Award on Books for Children and Youth, 1981. Office: care Writers House 21 W 26th St New York NY 10010

WINDSOR, REBECCA HAHN, trucking co. exec.; b. Md., Sept 19, 1926; d. James Russell and Ruby Virginia (Clark) Hahn; student public schs., m. Robert S. Windsor, Jr., Dec. 19, 1946; children—Barbara Jean Windsor Ketchum, Rosemary Patricia. With Hahn Transp., Inc., New Market, Md., 1943—, treas., chief fin. officer, 1954—. Mem. Am. Trucking Assn., Mid-Atlantic Petroleum Dealers Assn., Md. Motor Truck Assn. Democrat. Episcopalian. Home: 10501 Brenda Ave Ijamsville MD 21774 Office: PO Box 8 New Market MD 21774

WINEGARNER, DOROTHY FRANCES, bus. services co. exec.; b. Marion, Ill., Mar. 29, 1940; d. Windell Kenneth and Helen Clara (Kirshman) W.; student U. Tenn., 1959-64. With Dun & Bradstreet, Inc., various locations, 1959—, mgr. ops. div., Van Nuys, Calif., 1980—. Mem. Nat. Assn. Female Execs. Republican. Methodist. Home: 8030 Langdon St #3 Van Nuys CA 91406 Office: 16600 Sherman Way Van Nuys CA 91406

WINER, JANE LOUISE, educator; b. Albany, N.Y., Nov. 1, 1947; d. Harold and Elizabeth Gertrude (Jensen) Winer; B.A., SUNY, Albany, 1969, M.L.S., 1970; M.A., Ohio State U., 1971, Ph.D., 1975; m. Monty Joseph Strauss, Nov. 4, 1978. Asst. prof. dept. psychology Tex. Tech. U., Lubbock, 1975-81, asso. prof., 1981—. NSF trainee, 1970-73; lic. psychologist, Tex. Mem. Nat. Register Health Service Providers in Psychology, Am. Psychol. Assn., Southwestern Psychol. Assn., Tex. Psychol. Assn., AAUP, Tex. Assn. Coll. Tchrs., Lubbock Assn. Psychologists. Contbr. articles to profl. jours. Home: 7010 Nashville Dr Lubbock TX 79413 Office: Dept Psychology Tex Tech Univ PO Box 4100 Lubbock TX 79409

WING, ANNE MARIE HINSHAW (MRS. LEONARD WILLIAM WING), writer, artist, naturalist; b. Chgo., Oct. 28, 1901; d. William Wade and Anna T. (Williams) Hinshaw; A.B., U. Mich., 1923, M.A., in English and Journalism, 1931, M. in Landscape design, 1937, life certification edn., 1931; m. Leonard W. Wing, Mar. 18, 1936; children—William Hinshaw, Thomas Leonard Hinshaw, Anne (Mrs. Robert Bruce Petters), George Clyde. Author, illustrator nature conservation articles, Ypsilanti (Mich.) Press, 1957, Ann Arbor (Mich.). News, series 1958-64, various other newspapers, mags., others. Chmn., Ann Arbor Garden Club conservation com., Washtenaw Roadside Council, Ann Arbor, 1931-35; landscape architect asst. PWA, Detroit, 1935-36; mem. Superior Twp. (Mich.) Citizens' Adv. Com., 1967; pres. Superior Twp. Civic Assn., 1959. Mem. D.A.R. (chmn. chpt. conservation com. 1960-61), P.E.O., Nat. League Am. Penwomen, Ann Arbor Art Assn., Nat. Audubon Soc., Mich. Audubon Soc., Aiken Audubon Soc. Colorado Springs, Am. Ornithologists Union, Cooper Ornithol. Soc., Wilson Ornithol. Soc., U. Mich. Alumni Assn., Am. Forestry Assn., Wilderness Soc., Colo. Open Space Council Enact Ecology Center, Assn. Interpretive Naturalists, Sierra Club, Washtenaw Hist. Soc., Nat. Soc. New Eng. Women, Nature Conservancy, Pi Lambda Theta, Alpha Phi. Episcopalian. Clubs: Ann Arbor Women's City, Ann Arbor Garden. Research and publs. on musical aspects of bird song. Home: 1333 La Paloma Way Colorado Springs CO 80906

WING, KYLENE SCARBOROUGH (MRS. ROBERT L. WING), columnist; b. Charlotte, N.C.; d. Kyle and Tomi (Riggs) Scarborough; student grad. Stevens Schs. for Models, 1946-47, Ben Bard Acad. Theatre, Hollywood, Calif., 1952, Nat. Acad. Broadcasting Washington, 1957, U. Calif. at Los Angeles Extension, 1965; m. Robert L. Wing, Jan. 16, 1943; children—Susan, Jayme. Columnist, Kylene's Kalifornia Kapers, Inverness, Fla., 1965-66, Kylene's Kontinental Kapers, Berlin, Germany, 1966-68. Founder patron Huntington Hartford Theatre. Mem. Soc. Motion Picture and Television Engrs., Greater Los Angles Press Club, Arcs, Antons, Japan Am. Soc. Presbyn. Clubs: German American Women's, American Women's, American Yacht (all Berlin). Address: 3405 Blair Dr Hollywood CA 90028 also Box 362 Inverness FL 32650

WING, NANCY JANE, physician; b. Bangor, Maine, Nov. 5, 1930; d. Gerald Everett and Katherine Emily (Atkins) Wing; student U. Maine, 1948-50; B.A. in Zoology, U. N.C., 1952; M.D., Med. Coll. Va., 1956; children—Jason, Alan. Intern, Atlanta, 1956; asso. med. dir. Greater Atlanta Blood Bank, Atlanta, 1957-58; staff physician Langley AFB, Va., 1960-62, Forbes AFB, Topeka, 1963-65, Topeka VA Hosp., 1965-76; med. dir. Kans. Medicaide Program, Topeka, 1976, Security Benefit Life Ins. Co., 1977—. Bd. dirs. Girls Club of Topeka, 1979—. Mem. Am. Council Life Ins., Topeka C. of C., Kans. Med. Soc., Shawnee County Med. Soc., AMA, Assn. Life Ins. Med. Dirs. Am., Risk Selectors, Phi Beta Kappa. Republican. Christian Ch. Club: Exec. Women's Forum. Home: 3688 SE Arrowhead Dr Topeka KS 66605 Office: 700 Harrison St Topeka KS 66636

WINGERT, EMILY ANN, pvt. detective; b. N.Y.C., Nov. 24, 1934; d. Edgar S. Peierls and Betsy (Vogel) Peierls Evans; B.S., Columbia U., 1961; widow; children—Laura, Edward, William. Pvt. cons. to art collectors and dealers, 1962-74; sec.-treas. Mark Ten Assos., Inc., Montclair, N.J., 1974-75, pres., 1975—; pres. Centurion Tng. Inst., Inc., 1981— W.C. Pubs., Inc., 1982—. Bd. dirs. Whole Theatre Co., Montclair, 1973, 82—; mem. bd. N. Essex Drug Abuse Council, 1970-73; residential fund chmn. Montclair chpt. ARC, 1972; mem. chmn.'s com. U.S. Senatorial Bus. Adv. Bd., 1981-82; co-founder Republican Presdl. Task Force, 1982—. Mem. Am. Soc. Indsl. Security (cert. protection profl., vice chmn. No. N.J. chpt. 1981, chmn. contract security com. 1980-81, chmn. security seminar com. 1982), Nat. Council Investigative and Security Services, N.J. Pvt. Detectives Assn., Am. Law Enforcement Officers Assn., Acad. Security Educators and Trainers, Nat. Assn. Female Execs., Am. Mgmt. Assn., Nat. Assn. Chiefs Police, Internat. Assn. Chiefs Police. Unitarian. Author basic security officer tng. manual, seminar materials, also audiovisual programs for security personnel. Office: 500 Bloomfield Ave Montclair NJ 07042

WINGFIELD, CANDACE SUZANNE, architect; b. Alexandria, Va., Feb. 28, 1954; d. Joseph Daniel and Betty Jo (Elmore) W.; B.Arch., U. Cin., 1977. Archtl. apprentice J. Joseph Wagner, Assos., Troy, Ohio, 1973-77, architect, 1977—, in charge design, drafting dept., 1977—. Mem. adv. com. Upper Valley Joint Vocat. Sch., 1981—. Mem. Am. Bus. Women's Assn. (v.p. 1980-81, pres. 1981-82; named Woman of Year 1982), AIA, and the Architects Soc. of Ohio. Club: Women of Moose. Home: 542 1/2 S Plum St Troy OH 45373 Office: J Joseph Wagner Assos 25 S Norwich Rd Troy OH 45373

WINGO-DAVIS, MARIAN LEE, feminist therapist; b. Asheville, N.C., Sept. 16, 1944; d. Hugh Albert and Lee Ardis (English) Wingo; B.S. in Edn., Fla. State U., Tallahassee, 1966; M.S. in Human Devel. Counseling with honors George Peabody Coll., 1978; m. H.C. Davis, Aug. 28, 1966; children—Remi, Wade. Feminist therapist, human devel. counselor, San Antonio, 1980-82; dir. women's tng. programs Internat. Trainers, Educators and Cons., Inc., San Antonio, 1980-82, now cons; exec. bd. San Antonio Women's Credit Union, 1981—, San Antonio Women's Law Center, 1981—, Battered Women's Shelter of Bexar County, 1981—. Program chmn. Bexar County Women's Polit. Caucus, 1980-81. Recipient Today's Woman award San Antonio Light. Mem. Nat. Feminist Therapist Assn., Assn. Women in Psychology, Town and Country Bus. and Profl. Women (Outstanding Citizen award), Women in Bus., NOW, Tex. Women's Polit. Caucus, Am. Personnel and Guidance Assn., Older Women's League, Am. Soc. Tng. and Devel. Methodist. Home: 111 Mark Daniel Circle Ocean Springs MS 39564 Office: ITEC Suite 360 5835 Callahgan St San Antonio TX 78228

WINIKOW, LINDA, state legislator; b. N.Y.C., May 9, 1940; d. Barnett and Minna (Rosenberg) Bord; B.A., Hofstra U., Hempstead, N.Y., 1962; M.A. in Social Studies, Queens Coll., 1966; D.Laws, St. Thomas Aquinas Coll., 1979; Dr. Hum. L., Mercy Coll., 1979; m. Arnold Winikow, Dec. 24, 1961; children—Jeffrey Keith, Scott Kenneth. Mem. Ramapo (N.Y.) Zoning Bd. Appeals, 1968-71; councilwoman, Ramapo, 1971-73; chmn. Ramapo Consumer Protection Bd., 1971-75; mem. Rockland County Legislature from Ramapo, 1974-75, N.Y. State Senate from 38th Dist., 1975—; mem. N.Y. State Temp. Commn. Living Costs and Economy, 1973-75. Bd. dirs. United Way Rockland County, 1973; pres. Spring Valley Hadassah, 1970, Eldorado Sch. PTA, 1971, Ramapo Democratic Women's Club, 1970-71. Recipient Humanitarian award Rockland County Bldgs. and Central Trade Council, 1976; named Outstanding Citizen of Year, Rockland region Woman's Am. ORT, 1974; Golda Meir Woman of Valor, United Jewish Appeal, 1979; Woman of Year, Rockland Bus. and Profl. Women's Club, 1981; Martin Luther King, Jr. award Fairview-Greenburgh Community Center, 1982. Mem. Rockland County Hist. Soc., Rockland Bus. and Profl. Women's Club, Phi Alpha Theta. Jewish. Club: B'nai B'rith. Home: 62 Sutin Pl Spring Valley NY 10977 Office: 130 N Main St New City NY 10956

WINKEL, NINA, sculptor; b. Germany, May 21, 1905; d. Ernst and Augustine (Bauer) Koch; came to U.S., 1942, naturalized, 1945; student Staedel Mus. Art Sch., 1929-31; m. George J. Winkel, Dec. 15, 1934.

Trustee, Sculpture Center, Inc., N.Y.C., 1946-69, pres., 1970-73, pres. emeritus, trustee, 1974—; one-man shows: Notre Dame U., 1954, Sculpture Center, N.Y.C., 1944, 47, 58, 72, Adirondack Mus., Elizabethtown, N.Y., 1976, Center Music Drama Art, Lake Placid, N.Y., 1977, Nat. Savs. Bank, Plattsburgh, N.Y., 1979, Carpenter and Painter Gallery, Elizabethtown, 1982, Allentown (Pa.) Art Mus., 1982; group shows: Met. Mus., Whitney Mus., Pa. Acad., San Francisco Mus., Va. Mus. Juror for sculpture competition Winter Olympics 1980 in Lake Placid, 1978—; trustee Keene Valley Library Assn., 1967—, chmn. bi-centennial com., 1973-77; trustee Adirondack Mus., Elizabethtown, N.Y., 1978—. Recipient Samuel F.B. Morse Gold medal NAD, 1964, Artists Fund prize, 1979, Gold medal, 1982; Founders prize, Mrs. Louis Bennett prize Nat. Sculpture Soc.; Pen's Brush award Pen's Brush club, 1982. Fellow Nat. Sculpture Soc. (sec. 1965-68, Bronze medal 1967, 71, Purchase prize 1981); mem. Nat. Acad. Design (E. Watrous Gold medal 1945, 78), Sculptors Guild, Artists Equity, Center Music, Drama and Arts-Lake Placid. Home: Dunham Rd Keene Valley NY 12943 Office: Sculpture Center Inc 167 E 69th St New York NY 10021

WINKLEMAN, ANNE JOYCE, aerospace co. ofcl.; b. Detroit, Oct. 31, 1945; d. Peter Joseph and Inez Marcella (Longville) Feliccia; student in bus. and adminstrn. Mt. San Antonio Coll., 1974-78; Assembler, Hoffman Electronics, El Monte, Calif., 1963-65; meat cutter, clk. P&J Meat Market, La Puente, Calif., 1965-70; with HTL Industries Inc. ATD (formerly Am. Standard), Monrovia, Calif., and Duarte, Calif., 1970—, supr. inventory control, 1978-79, supr. materials handling, 1980-81, program supr. contracts dept., 1981—. Mem. Nat. Assn. Female Execs. Roman Catholic. Office: 1800 Highland Duarte CA 91010

WINNER, ANNE MOORE WINDLE, sch. psychologist; b. West Chester, Pa., Sept. 4, 1921; d. Ernest Garfield and Sylvia Louise (Moore) Windle; B.A. in Philosophy, Swarthmore (Pa.) Coll., 1942; postgrad. scholar, Pa. Sch. Social Work, 1945-46; M.A. in Psychology (scholar), Bucknell U., Lewisburg, Pa., 1961; cert. of advanced study in communication disorders Johns Hopkins U., 1974; doctoral candidate Pa. State U., 1981—; m. Drexel Winner, Apr. 15, 1944 (dec. 1967); children—Catherine Winner Salem, David R., Hanna Winner Dunleavy, Rebecca Winner Diehl. Sch. psychologist II, Balt. City Schs., 1963—; cons. psychologist problems of children, pets; Md. rep. Internat. Sch. Psychology Com., 1981, 82. Mem. Md. Psychol. Assn. (officer 1975, 76), Balt. City Assn. Sch. Psychologists (pres. 1980-82), Pa. Assn. Sch. Psychologists, Md. Assn. Sch. Psychologists, Am. Psychol. Assn. (asso.), Golden Retreiver Club Am. Quaker. Author articles in field. Address: 102 E Chestnut Hill Ln Reisterstown MD 21136

WINNICK, WILMA ARTUS, psychologist; b. N.Y.C., Dec. 8, 1923; d. William Fred and Ruth (Manee) Artus; B.A., Queens Coll., 1944; Sc.M., Brown U., 1945; Ph.D., Columbia U., 1949; m. Louis Winnick, Dec. 26, 1948; children—Pamela Winnick Morril, Holly Cushing. Research asst. Brown U., 1944-45; teaching asst. Columbia U., 1945-49; research cons. Community Services Soc., N.Y.C., 1950-52, Daniel Starch and Staff, Mamaroneck, N.Y., 1960-62; mem. faculty Queens Coll., 1950—, prof. psychology, 1970—; adj. prof. N.Y. Med. Coll., 1980—. Fellow N.Y. Acad. Scis.; mem. Am. Psychol. Assn., Eastern Psychol. Assn., N.Y. State Psychol. Assn., Sigma Xi. Author research papers in field. Home: 23 Nassau Dr Great Neck NY 11021 Office: Dept Psychology Queens Coll Flushing NY 11367

WINOKUR, DENA, communications exec.; b. N.Y.C., July 10, 1949; d. Louis and Silvya (Block) W.; B.F.A., U. Conn., 1970; M.A., Am. U., 1971; Ph.D., Ohio U., 1975. Communications specialist, info. officer Met. Washington Regional Med. Program, 1971-72; instr. journalism Ohio U., Athens, 1972-74; media center coordinator Eastern region AT&T Long Lines, Washington, 1976-79, employee communications specialist, N.Y.C., 1979-81, mgr. transition info., 1981-82, dist. mgr. planning, 1982—; adj. asst. prof. mktg. Pace U., N.Y.C., 1981— ; lectr. Internat. TV Assn., Speakers' Bur. Mem. Internat. Television Assn. (award of merit 1979), Phi Kappa Phi, Kappa Tau Alpha. Contbg. author: The Pollution of Politics, 1971. Home: 201 E 87th St New York NY 10028 Office: 195 Broadway Room 01-1535 New York NY 10007

WINOKUR, MARSHA CHERASKIN, psychologist, pianist; b. N.Y.C., Sept. 27, 1942; d. Max and Rose (Rubin) Cheraskin; B.A., Sarah Lawrence Coll., 1963; B.M., Manhattan Sch. Music, 1963; M.A., Yeshiva U., 1965, Ph.D., 1972; m. Peter Winokur, June 21, 1964; children—Mara, Rachel. Cons. family devel. study Boston Children's Hosp., 1972-73; asst. chief psychologist Jewish Bd. Family and Children Services, N.Y.C., 1972—; cons. psychologist SAR Acad., Riverdale, N.Y., 1973—; chief psychologist Center for Learning and Devel., New City, N.Y., 1977—; mem. Serafin Duo, 1976—, Saxon Wood Chamber Players, 1978—; adj. prof. Tchrs. Coll., Columbia U., 1979—; piano concerts through U.S. and Europe; recs. for Mus. Heritage Soc. Records. Mem. Am. Psychol. Assn., Nat. Register for Health Service Providers in Psychology. Mem. editorial bd. Psychosocial Process. Home: 16 Winthrop Ln Scarsdale NY 10583 Office: 990 Pelham Pkwy S Bronx NY 10461

WINSKI, LOUISE FLORENCE, biologist; b. Phila., June 20, 1950; d. Ladislaus J. and Florence H. (Hejnar) W.; B.Sc. in Med. Tech., Phila. Coll. Pharmacy and Sci., 1972. Med. technologist spl. chemistry dept. Lower Bucks Hosp., Bristol, Pa., 1971-75; staff biologist clin. chemistry safety assessment Merck, Sharp & Dohme, West Point, Pa., 1975—. Mem. Am. Soc. Clin. Pathologists (affiliate; registered med. technologist). Roman Catholic. Club: Polish Intercollegiate (Phila.). Home: 1090 Bayless Pl Eagleville PA 19403 Office: Merck Sharp & Dohme Sumneytown Pike West Point PA 19486

WINSLEY, SHIRLEY JOANN, state legislator; b. Fosston, Minn., June 9, 1934; d. Nordin and Helga (Sorby) Miller; student Tacoma Community Coll., 1970, Pacific Lutheran U., 1970-71; m. Gordon P. Winsley, 1952; children—Alan, Nancy. Precinct committeewoman, 28th dist. Pierce County, Minn., 1960-74, dist. chairperson, 1972-74; mem. Wash. Ho. Reps., 1977—. Mem. C. of C. (Lakewood area mgr. 1975-77, chairperson 1975-77), Cert. Property Appraisers Soc., Jr. Women's League. Columnist, Chamber Action, Suburban Times, 1975-77, Legis. Report, 1977. Office: Wash State Ho Reps State Capitol Olympia WA 98504

WINSLOW, HELEN CAUDLE, artist; b. New Salem, N.C., Mar. 24, 1916; d. Rufus Spurgeon and Nellie Sophia (Richardson) Caudle; B.A., Fla. So. Coll., 1936; student Art Students League, 1936-41, Otis Art Inst., Los Angeles, 1954-57; m. Randolph Winslow, Nov. 30, 1940; 1 dau., Joyce. Artist; juried exhbns. include; Frye Art Mus., Seattle, 1960, 62, 65, De Young Mus., San Francisco, 1968, 69, San Bernardino Mus., 1978; one woman shows include: Roberts Gallery, Los Angeles, 1966, Brentwood Gallery, Los Angeles, 1967-68, Vallis & Jensen, San Francisco, 1967, Gallery Fair, Mendocino, Calif., 1968-80, Austin Gallery, Scottsdale, Ariz., 1974-77; pvt. art tchr., 1956—; tchr. summer painting workshop, Rye, Colo., 1972-80. Recipient purchase award Los Angeles Ann. Art Festival, 1956, 2d prize Calif. State Fair, 1965, Wells Fargo award De Young Mus., 1969, 1st prize Beverly Hills Art League, 1974, spl. award San Bernardino Mus., 1978. Mem. Art Students League (life), Soc. Western Artists, Los Angeles Art Assn. Featured in article in S.W. Art Mag., 1977. Home: 9934 Westwanda Dr Beverly Hills CA 90210

WINSOR, HELEN BRUCE, home economist; b. Carlisle, Ark., Oct. 9, 1923; d. Bernard Carlisle and Ebb Alexander (Miller) Bruce; B.S., U. Central Ark., 1948; M.S., Okla. State U., 1969, Ed.D. (La Verne Noyes scholar), 1974; m. Henry M. Winsor, Jr., May 31, 1950; children—Susan Jeanette, Henry B. Tchr. home econs. high schs. in Ark., 1948-49, 52-53; home economist Coop. Extension Service, Jasper, Ark., 1949-51; adult tchr. Lompoc (Calif.) Unified Sch. Dist., 1966; asst. prof. U. Tenn., Martin, 1969-75; asso. prof. home econs. edn. No. Ill. U., DeKalb, 1975—; mem. Ill. Adv. Council Occupation Homemaking Programs; speaker in field. Recipient Outstanding Tchr. award U. Tenn., Martin, 1971. Mem. Am. Home Econs. Assn., Am. Vocat. Assn., Nat. Assn. Home Econs. Tchr. Educators, Nat. Assn. Vocat. Home Econs., Ill. Home Econs. Assn., Ill. Vocat. Assn., Ill. Vocat. Home Econs. Tchrs. Assn., Phi Upsilon Umicron. Republican. Methodist. Author curriculum materials. Home: 1618 E Stonehenge Dr Sycamore IL 60178 Office: Dept Home Econs No Ill Univ DeKalb IL 60115

WINSRYG, MIRIAM THOMAS, ednl. adminstr.; b. Erick, Ga., July 20, 1912; d. Allen W. and Eva Belle (Faircloth) Thomas; B.S., Ga. State Coll. for Women, 1939; M.S., Fla. State U., 1952, postgrad., 1955; postgrad., Northwestern U., 1967-69; m. Marcus Andreas Winsryg, Dec. 17, 1950; 1 son, Mark Thomas (dec. 1961). Tchr. elem. sch., Hoboken, Ga., 1936-38; tchr. home econs. Emanuel County Inst., Twin City, Ga., 1939; supr. home econs. FHA, U.S. Dept. Agr., Alma and Waycross, Ga., 1940-44, Mt. Vernon, Ga., 1944-46, Waynesboro, Ga., 1946-47; dietitian Ga. State Coll. for Women, 1947-48; tchr. elem. schs. Jacksonville, Fla., 1948-66; coordinator specific learning disabilities exceptional student sect. Duval County Sch. Bd., Jacksonville, 1966-78, area specialist, Jacksonville, Fla., 1978—; adj. prof. Jacksonville U., 1974-76. Mem. DAR (chmn. lineage com. John Floyd chpt. 1978-82, regent 1982—), Huxford Geneal. Soc. (dir. 1976—), UDC, Delta Kappa Gamma, Phi Delta Kappa, Kappa Delta Pi. Democrat. Christian Scientist. Contbg. editor Huxford Geneal. Mag., 1975—. Home: 914 Old Hickory Rd Jacksonville FL 32207 Office: 1701 Prudential Dr Jacksonville FL 32207

WINSTON, CLARA, translator, writer; b. N.Y.C., Dec. 6, 1921; d. Isadore and Lotte (Ginzburg) Brussel; L.H.D. (hon.), Suffolk U., 1980; m. Richard Winston, Sept. 16, 1941; children—Krishna, Justina. Free-lance translator of more than 150 works, chiefly from German, including: Memories, Dreams, Reflections (C.S. Jung), 1961; Glass Bead Game (Herman Hesse), 1969; Inside the Third Reich (Albert Speer), 1970; Letter (Franz Kafka), 1977; author novels: The Closest Kin There Is, 1952; The Hours Together, 1962; Painting for the Show, 1969; author history books: (with Richard Winston) Notre Dame de Paris, 1971, Daily Life in the Middle Ages, 1975. Guggenheim grantee, 1960-61; recipient Nat. Book award, 1978. Mem. Am. Translators Assn. (medal 1960), PEN (award 1972).

WINSTON, JUDITH ANN, lawyer; b. Atlantic City, Nov. 23, 1943; d. Edward Carl and Margaret Ann (Goodman) Marianno; B.A. (Nat. Competitive scholar), Howard U., Washington, 1966; J.D., Georgetown U., 1977; m. Michael Russell Winston, Aug. 10, 1963; children—Lisa Marie, Cynthia Eileen. Dir. EEO Project, Council Great City Schs., Washington, 1971-74; legal asst. Lawyers Com. for Civil Rights Under Law, Washington, 1975-77; admitted to D.C. bar, 1977; spl. asst. to dir. Office for Civil Rights, HEW, Washington, 1977-79; exec. asst., legal counsel to chair U.S. EEO Commn., Washington, 1979-80; asst. gen. counsel U.S. Dept. Edn., 1980—; ednl. cons., 1974-77; guest lectr. Washington Coll. Law of Am. U. Active NAACP Legal Def. and Ednl. Fund, 1968-79, Women's Legal Def. Fund, 1979. Mem. D.C. Bar Assn., Washington Council Lawyers, Washington Bar Assn., Nat. Bar Assn., Phi Beta Kappa, Delta Theta Phi. Democrat. Episcopalian. Author: Desegregating Schools in the Great Cities: Philadelphia, 1970; Chronicle of a Decade 1961-1970, 1970; Desegregating Urban Schools: Educational Equality/Quality, 1970. Home: 1371 Kalmia Rd NW Washington DC 20012 Office: US Dept Edn 400 Maryland Ave SW Washington DC 20202

WINSTON, NANCY LEE, contracting co. exec.; b. Cin., Apr. 1, 1945; d. Alvin B. and Adrienne Carol (Goldstone) Galpren; student U. Ariz., 1963-64; cert. Art Center Coll. Design, Los Angeles, 1968. Freelance graphic artist, 1968—; tchr. pilot program Los Angeles City Sch. System, 1968-70; graphic artist Marie France Mag., Paris, 1973; graphic designer Design and Typog. Co., London, 1974; v.p. Nat. Conservation Co., Inc., Fresno, Calif., 1977—; pres. Valley West Barns and Bldgs., Fresno, 1979—. Recipient Home Fashions League award, 1968; Brit. Art Dirs. award, 1975.

WINSTON, SANDRA, mgmt. cons.; b. Chgo., Jan. 14, 1938; d. David L. and Mae (Lieberman) Yavitt; B.S., Ohio State U., Columbus, 1959; M.Ed., U. Cin., 1973; m. George M. Winston, Oct. 17, 1959; children—Marci, Gregg, Robin. Speech and hearing therapist in Ill. and Ky., 1959-67; pvt. practice marriage, family and children's counseling, Palos Verdes Estates, Calif., 1973—; pres. Step, Inc., adult edn., 1974—, Sandra Winston Assos., Inc., mgmt. cons., 1975—; instr., program cons. UCLA extension, 1974—; instr. women's small bus. programs Los Angeles Community Coll. Dist. Recipient Woman of Achievement award Cleveland Women's City Club, 1979, Woman of Year award Women's World Expo, Pasadena, Calif., 1979. Mem. Internat. Assn. Personnel Women, Nat. Women's Polit. Caucus, Women in Bus. (founder, v.p. 1976, dir. 1977). Author: The Entrepreneurial Woman, 1979. Home: 920 Via Mirada Palos Verdes Estates CA 90274 Office: 401 Via Corta Palos Verdes Estates CA 90274

WINTER, BERNICE HASTON, fin. exec.; b. Albany, Ga., May 4, 1948; d. Paul Henry and Ruth Moore (Haston) W.; B.A., Wellesley Coll., 1970; M.B.A., Harvard U., 1978; m. Michael Anthony Doyle, Nov. 12, 1977. Mgmt. asso. Citizens and So. Nat. Bank, Atlanta, 1971-74, asst. mktg. officer, 1974-76; sr. internat. commodities buyer Coca-Cola U.S.A., Atlanta, 1978-80; treasury specialist Coca-Cola Co., 1980-81, asst. controller, mgr. corp. budget dept., 1981—, mgr. corp. and U.S. Treasury services, 1982. Mem. profl. council Jr. League Atlanta, 1982, mem. leadership council, 1981-82, mem. fin. com., 1981-82. Mem. Nat. Cash Mgmt. Assn. Clubs: Harvard Bus Sch (sec. 1980-81, dir. 1981-82) (Atlanta); Wellesley, Commerce (Atlanta). Home: 63 28th St NW Atlanta GA 30309 Office: 310 North Ave NW Atlanta GA 30313

WINTERS, ALICE GRAHAM BUTLER (MRS. CARL S. WINTERS), civic worker; b. Linton, Ind., July 5, 1907; d. William Austin and Mary (Inman) Butler; A.B., Franklin Coll., 1932; spl. student U. Rochester, 1929-30, Colgate-Rochester Div. Sch., 1929-30; m. Carl S. Winters, May 23, 1925; children—Barbara (Mrs. Robert Kane), Janet (Mrs. Ralph Kuzmic), Linda (Mrs. Allen F. Jones). Minister junior ch., Jackson, Mich., 1931-39, 1st Bapt. Ch. Oak Park, Ill., 1939-59; lectr. Adult Edn. Council Chgo.; also free-lance writer. Organizer, pres. Jackson (Mich.) Peace Council, 1933-35; pres. Jackson County LWV, 1935, Chgo. Drama League, 1948-50, Chgo. Mission Union, 1956-60; treas. Art Assocs. Oak Park, 1961-64; pres. Infant Welfare Soc., 1960-62; mem. Com. of 100, Nat. Council of Chs., 1963—; bd. dirs. Woman's Bd. Salvation Army, Chgo., 1960—, pres. bd., 1969—; bd. dirs. Women's Bd. Mental Health Assn., Chgo.; bd. dirs. Maywood (Ill.) Home and Hosp., 1940-62, v.p. bd., 1958-62; mem. woman's bd. Christian U. of Tokyo, 1963—. Recipient Outstanding Woman award Chgo. Assn. Commerce and Industry, 1976; citation for outstanding contbns. to humanity Franklin Coll., 1978; Disting. Service award Salvation Army Internat., 1980; Cert. of Recognition for outstanding service Comprehensive Community Services of Chgo., 1980; citation for achievement and influence Chautauqua Instn., 1982. Mem. Delta Zeta, Beta Sigma Phi, Kappa Delta. Clubs: Conference Club Presidents (bd. dirs. 1962—, chmn. pub. relations, sec.); 19th Century Women's; Garden; Chautauqua (N.Y.) Women's; Oak Park Country; Zonta. Home: 404 N East Ave Oak Park IL 60602 also Packard Manor Chautauqua NY 14722

WINTERS, BARBARA JO, musician; b. Salt Lake City; d. Louis McClain and Gwendolyn (Bradley) Winters; A.B. cum laude, UCLA, 1960, postgrad., 1961; postgrad. Yale U., 1960. Mem. oboe sect. Pasadena (Calif.) Symphony, 1958-60; mem. oboe sect. Los Angeles Philharm., 1961—, now prin. oboist. Recs. movie, TV sound tracks. Home: 3529 Coldwater Canyon Studio City CA 91604 Office: 135 N Grand Ave Los Angeles CA 90012

WINTERS, BETH ANN, ARC exec.; b. Monroe, Mich., June 12, 1918; d. John Joseph and Edith (Golden) Harrington; student U. Toledo; m. 3d, Edward R. Dobie, May 25, 1979; children—James W. Payne, III, Michael H. Winters, Penelope Ann Winters, Terrence J. Winters. Various clerical, bookkeeping and secretarial positions, 1934-58; clk. Monroe County (Mich.), 1959-63; owner Winters Office Aides, Monroe, Mich., 1963-65; acting exec. dir. Monroe County chpt. ARC, 1964, exec. dir., 1964—, chmn. 1959-62; co-organizer Coordinating Council Agencies, Monroe, 1964. Bd. dirs. Friends Monroe County Zoo Assn., 1958-60, Monroe County Big Bros., 1968, Monroe County OEO, 1969, Mich. Welfare League, 1968, S.E. Mich. Tourist Assn., 1961; chmn. Monroe County Traffic and Safety Com., 1979; mem. Greater Monroe Council Alcoholism; treas. Alcohol and Substance Abuse Center, 1979-80. Recipient award ARC, 1960, 62, Camp Fire Girls, 1960. Mem. Monroe County His. Soc. (sec. 1964-66), Art and Crafts League Monroe (vice chmn. 1958), Monroe County Bus. and Profl. Women, St. Patrick's Soc. Am. Irish (founder 1958, 1st pres. 1958-59), VFW Aux. Democrat. Roman Catholic. Club: Navy Mother's (charter, past dir.). Home: 443 N Macomb St Monroe MI 48161 Office: 202 S Macomb St Monroe MI 48161

WINTERS, DEBORAH ANN, radiologist; b. Garden City, Kans., Aug. 23, 1951; d. Wesley Chester and Ruby Irene (Vaughn) Winter; B.A. cum laude, So. Missionary Coll., 1973; postgrad. Vol. State Community Coll., 1973-74, Middle Tenn. State U., 1974; M.D., Loma Linda U., 1978; m. Clyde Elam Marlin, Dec. 21, 1975. Records librarian Sta. WSMC, Collegedale, Tenn., 1969-71, 1972-73; computer operator Eaton, Yale & Towne, Gallatin, Tenn., 1973-74; resident in radiology Loma Linda U. (Calif.) Med. Center, 1979-82; practice medicine specializing in radiology Kern Radioloy and Nuclear Med. Group, Bakersfield, Calif., 1983—. Cert. secondary tchr., Tenn.; diplomate nat. bd. med. examiners. Mem. Am. Coll. Radiology, Radiol. Soc. of N.Am., Kern County Med. Soc., Calif. Med. Assn., Nat. Soc. of Tole and Decorative Painters, San Diego Zool. Soc. Adventist. Office: 1420 Crestmont Dr Bakersfield CA 92354 *

WINTERS, SUSAN PATRICIA, audiologist; b. Columbus, Miss., June 28, 1952; d. Everett Louis and Louise (Ivy) W.; B.A.E., U. Miss., 1974; M.A., U. Tenn., 1975. Student tchr. Memphis Public Schs., 1974; clin. audiologist U. Tenn., Knoxville, 1976, Dr. R. E. Flatley's Office, Moline, Ill., 1976—. Mem. Am. Speech and Hearing Assn. (cert. clin. competence in audiology), Quad-Cities Speech and Hearing Assn. Republican. Baptist. Home: 13 Blackhawk Hills Dr Rock Island IL 61201 Office: 829 15th St Moline IL 61265

WINTERS, WENDY GLASGOW, coll. dean; b. Norwalk, Conn., June 26, 1930; d. William and Gladys E. (Carter) Russell; B.S. with honors, Central Conn. State Coll., 1952; M.S., Columbia U. Sch. social work, 1954; Ph.D., Yale U., 1975; m. Irving J. Winters, Jr., June 14, 1975; children—Allison Lenore Glasgow, Roger DeCourey Glasgow, Jr. Chief social worker Baldwin-King schs. program Child Study Center, Yale U., 1968-75, instr., then asst. prof. social work, 1968-71, research asso., 1975-78, fellow Pierson Coll., 1969—; asso. prof., asst. dean acad. affairs Sch. Social Work, U. Conn., 1975-78; asso. prof. sociology and anthropology, adj. asso. prof. social work, dean coll. Smith Coll., 1979—; mem. regional adv. council Conn. Dept. Children and Youth Services, 1975-78, chmn. evaluation subcom., 1977-78; adv. com. Conn. Commn. Higher Edn., 1976-77; bd. dirs. Leila Day Nurseries, Inc., New Haven, 1975-78; mem. juvenile justice adv. com. Conn. Justice Commn., 1977; bd. corporators Northampton Instn. Savs., 1979—. Bd. dirs. Greater New Haven Urban League, 1969-71. Recipient various appreciation awards; NIMH research award, 1974; fellow Black Analysis, Inc., 1972-75, Yale U. Inst. Social and Policy Studies, 1974-75. Mem. Am. Orthopsychiat. Assn., Am. Sociol. Assn., Black Analysis, Inc., Nat. Assn. Social Workers, New Eng. Deans Assn., New Eng. Minority Women Adminstrs. Congregationalist. Author articles, co-author book, reports in field. Home: 36 Paradise Rd Northampton MA 01060 Office: College Hall 21 Smith Coll Northampton MA 01063

WINTERS-MALOLEPSY, TERRI, costume designer; b. Omaha, May 8, 1946; d. Henry C. and Mercedes (Royle) Winters; B.A. in Theatre, Edgewood Coll., Madison, Wis., 1968; M.A., U. Wis., Madison, 1972; M.F.A. in Theatre Design, Mich. State U., 1977; m. John F. Malolepsy, June 17, 1967; children—Jennifer Anne, Paul Michael. Instr. costume design Edgewood Coll., 1968-69, U. Mich., Flint, 1972-78; asst. prof. creative drama, costume design Memphis State U., 1979—, costume designer, makeup designer, 1968—; freelance costume designer, creative drama leader; costume designer Memphis Mud Island River Museum, 1981. Bd. dirs. Flint Hist. Theatre Assn., 1974-77, Coop. Threads Inc., 1969-72. Mem. Am. Theatre Assn., Univ. and Coll. Theatre Assn., U.S. Inst. Theatre Tech., AAUP (past univ. rep.). Home: 3545 Stuart St Memphis TN 38111 Office: Dept Theatre and Communication Arts Memphis State U Memphis TN 38152

WINTERSON, HELEN JANE, nurse, adminstr., nun; b. Omaha, July 10, 1937; d. George McPherson and Helen Julia (Patach) W.; B.A., Duchesne Coll., 1958; postgrad. Washington U., St. Louis, 1965-66; M.S., U. Mo., St. Louis, 1969; postgrad. Colo. State U., 1971; R.N., Maryville Coll., 1974; M.S.A., U. Notre Dame, 1981; cert. in coronary intensive care Mercy Regional Med. Center, Vicksburg, Miss. Instr., Republic (Mo.) High Sch., 1959-60; instr. sci. Villa Duchesne Acad. Sacred Heart, 1960-65; instr., asst. to dean Maryville Coll., St. Louis, 1965-68, counselor, 1969-72, asst. prof. biology, 1969-75, dir. student fin. aid, 1972-75; title III grant coordinator Maryville Coll.-Fontbonne Coll. Consortium, 1968-69; mem. staff Jewish Hosp. St. Louis, 1973-74, DePaul Hosp., 1973-74; mem. staff St. John's Mercy Med. Center, 1973-74, med. staff nurse, 1974-75; joined Sisters of Mercy of the Union, 1975; coronary care nurse Mercy Regional Med. Center, Vicksburg, Miss., 1975—; nurse Frisco Day Care Center for Migrant Workers' Children, Plainview, Tex., summer 1975; dir. planning mgmt. and cons. office Sisters of Mercy, St. Louis, 1980—. Sci. fair judge Post Dispatch, 1970-75; sec. bd. Greene County Nursing Home; bd. dirs. St. John's Regional Health Center; trustee Mercy Hosp., Laredo, Tex., 1982—; vol. counselor Good Shepherd Camp, 1964-65; vol. tutor Children's Hosp., 1958-73. Mem. Am. Assn. Critical Care Nurses, Soc. For Hosp. Planning of Am. Hosp. Assn., U. Mo. at St. Louis (mem. scholarship com. 1971-76), Maryville Coll. alumni assns. Home: 1316 Purdue Ave University City MO 63130 Office: 2039 N Geyer Ave Saint Louis MO 63131

WIRE, GAIL JOANNE ELLIOTT, equal employment opportunity officer; b. Bremerton, Wash., Sept. 5, 1940; d. Ellsbury Burt and Alice Josephine (Olsen) Elliott; B.A. in Sociology, Calif. State U., 1962; M.A. in Human Resource Mgmt., Pepperdine U., 1976; 1 dau., Allison Theresa. Intake worker, office mgr. Gailor Mental Health Clinic, U. Tenn., Memphis, 1963-64; spl. services caseworker N.C. Welfare Dept., Carteret County, 1964-67; various clerical and secretarial posts U.S. Civil Service, Calif. and Pa., 1969-75; coordinator fed. women's program Naval Air Engrng. Center, Lakehurst, N.J., 1975-78; mgmt. cons. Shore Equal Opportunity Program, San Diego Region, Naval Material Command, 1978; dep. EEO officer Naval Supply Center, San Diego, 1978-80; personnel staff cons. TVA, Knoxville, 1980-81; command asst. dep. EEO officer Naval Supply Systems Command, Washington, 1981—; mem. women's program adv. com. Ocean County Coll., 1976-78; mem., counselor bus. indsl. council Central Regional High Sch., Toms River, N.J., 1977-78; pres. Fed. EEO Council San Diego County, 1979-80. Served to lt. USMC, 1962-63. Recipient Outstanding Performance award U.S. Civil Service, 1976, 77, Sustained Superior Performance award, 1976. Mem. Calif. State U.-Long Beach, Pepperdine U. alumni assns., Federally-Employed Women Inc. (founder Ocean County chpt. 1976, v.p. 1976-77, chmn. by-laws com. 1977-78, chmn. legis. com. San Diego chpt. 1978-79, chpt. mem.-at-large 1979-80), Image de Calif. (pres. San Diego chpt. 1978-80), Am. Soc. Tng. and Devel., Internat. Platform Assn. Home: 7704 Donnybrook Ct Apt 3 Annandale VA 22003 Office: NAV SUPSYSCOM SUPOOE CM3 Washington DC 20376

WIRKLER, MARY LOUISE, psychologist; b. Garnavillo, Iowa; d. Herbert August Jacob and Irene Emily (Kregel) W.; B.S. in Nursing, U. Iowa, 1948; M.S., San Francisco State Coll., 1962, cert. in sch. psychology, 1966. Staff nurse, Downey (Calif.) VA Hosp., 1948-49; asst. supr. contagious ward Evanston (Ill.) Hosp., 1949-50; psychiat. nurse Langley Porter Clinic, San Francisco, 1950-52; staff nurse VA Hosp., 1957-59; clin. psychologist San Francisco Juvenile Ct., 1962-64; sch. psychologist, Oakland and Fremont, Calif., 1964-69; sch. psychologist Dept. Def. Dependent Schs., Okinawa, 1969-72, Turkey, 1972-73, Italy, 1973-78, Wiesbaden, W. Ger., 1978—. Served with USN, 1952-56. Mem. Am. Psychologists Assn., Internat. Council Psychologists, European br. Guidance Assn., Wiesbaden Humanistic Assn., Beta Sigma Phi. Home: 18 Taunus Ring WI-Delkenheim 6200 Federal Republic Germany Office: PO Box 4806 APO NY 09633

WIRSIG, JANE DEALY, writer; b. Boston, Aug. 22, 1919; d. James Bond and Anna B. (McQuillen) Dealy; B.A., Vassar Coll., 1941; M.S. (Vassar Coll. fellow 1941-42), Columbia U., 1942; m. Woodrow Wirsig, Dec. 11, 1942; children—Alan Robert, Guy Rodney, Paul Harold. Network radio newswriter CBS, 1942-43; free lance writer articles, short stories various mags., 1942—; editor Vassar Alumnae mag., 1952-53; editor, rewriter Companion in Paris, Woman's Home Companion, 1953-56; editor Wirsig, Gordon & O'Connor, Inc., Princeton, N.J., 1956-58; editorial cons. Ednl. Testing Service, Princeton, 1957-60, dir. publs., 1960-70, exec. dir. info. services and publs., 1971-74, sec. corp., 1974-81. Mem. exec. bd. George Washington council Boy Scouts Am., 1976-80. Mem. Am. Assn. Higher Edn., Greater Princeton C. of C. (dir. 1974—, v.p. 1976-80, pres. 1980), Phi Beta Kappa. Club: Vassar (Central N.J. v.p. 1955-57). Home: 25 Gordon Way Princeton NJ 08540

WIRTSCHAFTER, IRENE NEROVE, tax cons., real estate salesman; b. Elgin, Ill., Aug. 5; d. David A. and Ethel G. Nerove; B.C.S., Columbus U., 1942; m. Burton Wirtschafter, June 2, 1945 (dec. 1966). Commd. ensign Supply Corps, U.S. Navy, 1944, advanced through ranks to capt., 1975; sea duty, 1956; comdg. officer Res. Supply Unit, 1974-75; ret., 1976; agt. office internat. ops. IRS, 1967-76, internat. banking specialist, 1972-75; now enrolled agt. IRS, pvt. practice tax cons., Washington. Past adv. Wing Scouts; past troop leader Girl Scouts U.S.A.; lt. col. and mission pilot CAP; comml. instrument pilot; chmn. Coll. Park Airport Johnny Horizon Day, 1975; co-chmn. Internat. Women's Yr. Take Off Dinner, Washington, 1976; mem. Nat. Com. Internat. Forest of Friendship; sr. Senate intern, 1981; founder Sr. Action com., 1981. Named hon. citizen of Winnipeg (Can.), 1966, of Atchison (Kans.), 1979; Ky. col.; winner 17 air races; Internat. Air Race; Sr. intern U.S. Senate, 1981. lic. single-engine pilot, land and sea ratings, lic. accident prevention counselor FAA. Mem. Naval Res. Assn. (nat. treas. 1975-77), Ninety Nines (past chpt. and sect. officer), Ret. Officers Assn. (chpt. officer), Assn. of Enrolled Agts., Assn. of Naval Aviators, Naval Order of U.S. First female Supply Corps officer to be assigned sea duty. Home: 1825 Minuteman Causeway Cocoa Beach FL 32931 and 2500 Q St NW Apt 641 Washington DC 20007

WIRTZ, CAROLYN, speech pathologist; b. Jersey City, Feb. 23, 1949; d. Joseph Francis and Sylvia Mary (Keary) W.; B.A., Livingston Coll., 1974; M.Ed., U. Va., 1975. Speech pathologist Med. Center at Princeton (N.J.), 1975-76; spl. services coordinator Ethan Allen Child Care, Winooski, Vt., 1976-77; tchr., cons. Children's Energy Center, N.Y.C., 1977-78; asst. in literacy Baruch Coll., N.Y.C., 1979; communications cons., N.Y.C. House mgr., prodn. staff, performer Drama Ensemble Repertory Co., Inc., N.Y.C.; communications cons. bus., theater, children; condr. video workshops; writer and speaker in field. Vol. counselor Vets. Counseling Service of Livingston/Rutgers U., 1969-72; active SoHo Citizen's Community Assn., Nat. Abortion Rights Action League, N.Y. Feminist Art Inst., NOW; pres. 108-114 Wooster St. Corp. Lic. speech pathologist, N.Y. Mem. Am. Speech-Lang.-Hearing Assn. (cert. clin. competency), N.Y.C. Speech, Hearing and Lang. Assn., Aphasia Study Group. Address: 108 Wooster St New York NY 10012

WIRTZ, RUTH CATHERINE, newspaper editor; b. Canton, Ohio, Mar. 22, 1924; d. Roman George and Clara Ann (Donant) Zwick; student Canton Actual Bus. Coll., 1942; m. Justin H. Wirtz, Nov. 25, 1948; children—Justin H., Dorothy Marie. Sec., gen. mgr. Evening Ind., Massillon, Ohio, 1942; gen. assignment reporter, feature writer, 1943-55; freelance writer, stringer Cleve. Press and Cath. Exponent, 1955-59; reporter Chagrin Valley Herald, Chagrin Falls, Ohio, 1959-71; news editor Chagrin Valley Herald Sun, Solon (Ohio) Herald Sun, 1971, editor, 1971-78, editor, 1978—; editor Sun Press, Sun Messenger, Beachwood, Ohio, 1978-81; founding editor Bedford Sun Banner, 1981. Co-chmn. Solon's Sesquicentennial, 1970. Recipient state and nat. newspaper writing and editing awards. Mem. Nat. Fedn. Press Women (dir.), Nat. Newspaper Assn., Suburban Newspapers Am., Ohio Newspaper Assn., Ohio Press Women (pres. 1978—), Solon C. of C. (dir. 1979-81). Home: 6800 Solon Blvd Solon OH 44139 Office: 32914 Solon Rd Solon OH 44139

WIRTZ, VIRGINIA WADSWORTH (MRS. ARTHUR M. WIRTZ), civic worker; b. Cleve., Jan. 30, 1903; d. Charles and Anna (Doyle) Wadsworth; student U. Colo., 1920-21; B.S., Northwestern U., 1924; m. Arthur Michael Wirtz, March 1, 1926; children—Cynthia Wirtz MacArthur, William Wadsworth, Arthur Michael, Elizabeth Virginia. Mem. Rush Presbyn. St. Luke's Hosp. Med. Center Women's Bd., 1926—; trustee Ill. Children's Home and Aid Soc., Am. Opera Soc., Bd.; mem. women's council Chgo. Heart Assn., women's bd. USO, Chgo.; mem. Chgo. br. English Speaking Union; bd. govs. Chgo. Symphony. Mem. Mortar Bd., Pi Beta Phi. Clubs: Casino, Women's Athletic, Saddle and Cycle, Racquet, Arts. Deceased.

WISBAR, TANIA, communicative disorders specialist, educator; b. Berlin, Germany; d. Frank and Eva (Kroy) Wisbar; B.A., Mills Coll., 1958; M.A., Calif. State U., Northridge, 1970; Ph.D., Walden U., 1978. Actress and dir. plays and films, W. Ger., U.S., 1958-70; asst. to pres. Worldwide Books, 1964-65; specialist lang. and behavioral disorders, Los Angeles, 1971-75; now owner-dir. Behavior, Edn., and Learning Inst. Inc., Before and Aftersch., Elarca Center, Los Angeles; v.p., treas. Visual Resources, Inc., N.Y.C.; dir. LADDI Farm and Acad., Ramona, Calif.; Mem. Nat. Assn. for Retarded Citizens, Nat. Soc. for Autistic Children, Council for Exceptional Children. Author: LADDI - Language Approach for Developmentally Disabled Individuals, 1978. Researcher in lang. therapy, clin. tech. with Down's Syndrome children; producer: (film) In a World Alone, 1975. Office: Behavior Edn and Learning Inst Inc 3839 Selig Pl Los Angeles CA 90031

WISCH, PATRICIA BOGIN, educator, psychologist; b. Phila., Apr. 17, 1932; d. Barney M. and Dora (Schultzberg) Bogin; B.S. in Edn., Temple U., 1970, M.Ed., 1972, Ed.D. (Univ. fellow), 1976; children—Judith, Benjamin, Elizabeth, David. Tchr., Cedarbrook Jr. High Sch., Wyncote, Pa., 1970-71; pvt. practice psychology Phila., 1977—; dir. Inst. of Awareness, YM-YWHA, Phila., 1975—; asso. Psychology Asso., Inc.; dir Access Centers, Inc. Bd. dirs. Big Bros./Big Sisters, Montgomery County, Pa., 1975-78, Youth Emergency Services, Phila., 1977-79. Named Woman of Yr., Jewish War Vets., 1977, Nat. Brith Sholon Women, 1978. Mem. Am. Psychol. Assn., Assn. for Humanistic Psychology, Am. Assn. Sex Educators, Counselors and Therapists, Phila. Women's Network, Pa. Psychol. Assn., NOW. Home: 2635 Bainbridge St Philadelphia PA 19146 Office: Broad and Pine St Philadelphia PA 19147

WISDOM, GUYRENA KNIGHT, psychologist; b. St. Louis, July 27, 1923; d. Gladys Margaret (Hankins) McCullin; A.B., Stowe Tchrs. Coll., 1945; A.M., U. Ill., 1951; postgrad. St. Louis U., Washington U., St. Louis, Fontbonne Coll., U. Mo., Harris Tchrs. Coll., U. Chgo., Drury Coll. Tchr. elementary sch. St. Louis Public Sch. System, 1945-63, psychol. examiner, 1963-68, sch. psychologist, 1968-74, cons. spl. edn., 1974-77, supr. spl. edn. dept., 1977-79, coordinator div. staff devel., 1979-81 (on sabbatical leave); pvt. tutor, 1971-72; instr. Harris Tchrs. Coll., St. Louis, 1973-74, 79. Mem. Nat. Assn. Sch. Psychologists, Mo. Assn. Children with Learning Disabilities, Council for Exceptional Children, St. Louis Assn. Sch. Adminstrs., United Teaching Profession Orgn., NEA, Mo., St. Louis tchrs. assn., Spl. Edn. Instructional Materials Center, Assn. Supervision and Curriculum Devel., Kappa Delta Pi. Roman Catholic. Home: 5046 Wabada St Saint Louis MO 63113

WISE, HELEN DICKERSON, edn. assn. exec.; b. Sussex, N.J., Sept. 11, 1928; d. Russell Burton and Josephine Cornelia (Miles) Dickerson; B.A., Pa. State U., 1949, M.Ed., 1952, D.Ed., 1969; m. Howard E. Wise, Sept. 17, 1949; children—Dan Howard, David Russell, Dirk Frederick. Tchr. jr. high sch., public schs., Unionville, Pa., 1949-52, State College, Pa., 1958-77; instr. Pa. State U., 1965, trustee, 1969—; mem. Pa. Ho. of Reps., 1976-78; exec. dir. Del. State Edn. Assn., Dover, 1979—. Bd. dirs. Nat. Found. Improvement Edn., 1971-81. Recipient award for excellence in classroom teaching Freedom's Found., 1961; named Speaker of Yr., Pa. Speech Assn., 1970. Mem. Pa. State Edn. Assn. (pres. 1969), NEA (pres. 1973-74), AAUW, LWV, Phi Delta Kappa, Pi Lambda Theta, Delta Kappa Gamma, Pi Gamma Mu, Delta Sigma Rho, Omicron Delta Kappa. Democrat. Lutheran. Author: What Do We Tell The Children? Watergate and the Future of Our Country, 1974. Office: 335 Martin St Dover DE 19901

WISE, JANIE DENISE, communications cons. co. exec.; b. Frankfort, Ky., Dec. 15, 1945; d. Joseph William and Kathryn (Smither) W.; B.A. in Edn. and Psychology, U. Ky., 1971; postgrad. U. Louisville, 1971-72. Tchr., Taylorsville (Ky.) High Sch., 1970-72; mental health specialist mental health-retardation bd. Gardiner Lane Center, Louisville, 1972-73; alcohol counselor W.T. Edwards Hosp., Tampa, Fla., 1973-74; community edn. coordinator, counselor First Step, Inc., Sarasota, Fla., 1974-75; communications cons., coordinator Tri-County Alcoholism Services, Inc., Winter Haven, Fla., 1975-78; communications specialist, select account, area sales rep. Visual Products div. 3/M, St. Paul, 1978-80; owner, pres. Effective Communications, Lakeland and Tampa, Fla., 1980—. Bd. dirs. YMCA, Lakeland. Mem. Fla. Public Relations Assn., Fla. Fedn. Safety Orgns., Nat. Assn. Female Execs., Nat. Task Force on Women and Alcohol (bd. dirs.) Nat. Assn. Bus. and Indsl. Saleswomen (rep. Fla. office on women and alcohol Washington), U. Ky. Alumni Assn., AAUW, Aircraft Owners and Pilots Assn. Club: Porsche Club of Am. Home: 1505 Kipling St Lakeland FL 33803 Office: 4201 W Cypress St Suite B Tampa FL 33607

WISE, SARAH BARBARA, educator; b. S.C., Mar. 25, 1940; d. Lacy Cecil and Edith Louise (Yonce) W.; B.S., U. S.C., 1962, M.A., 1967, Ph.D., 1971. Instr., Columbia (S.C.) Coll., 1968-70; mem. faculty dept. mktg. and retailing U. S.C., Columbia, 1971—, now asso. prof. Mem. Am., So., Mid Atlantic mktg. assns., Am. Collegiate Retailing Assn., Am. Acad. Advt., Phi Beta Kappa, Beta Gamma Sigma, Delta Kappa Gamma, Sigma Alpha Sigma. Presbyterian. Home: Rt 1 Pelion SC 29123

WISHARD, BETTY JANE, mgmt. cons.; b. Detroit, Oct. 12, 1948; d. George Leo and Helen Pijut; B.S., Mich. State U., East Lansing, 1971. Asst. buyer accessories, then corp. dir. tng. and devel. Charles A. Stevens, Chgo., 1971-75; mgr. sales and human relations tng. No. Trust Co., Chgo., 1975-78; asst. v.p., dir. tng. and devel. Hibernia Nat. Bank, New Orleans, 1978; now pres. Betty Wishard & Assos., Inc.; speaker, cons. in field. Bd. dirs. Martha Washington Home Dependent Crippled Children, Chgo., 1977-78. Mem. Am. Soc. Tng. and Devel. (dir. La. chpt. 1978—), Nat. Assn. Bank Women, Am. Inst. Banking, Nat. Assn. Female Execs., Am. Soc. Profl. and Exec. Women, Assn. Multi-Image, Internat. Platform Assn. Home: 2025 Burdette New Orleans LA 70118

WISHNIE, WENDY LYNN, copywriter; b. Forest Hills, N.Y., June 22, 1951; d. Jack and Mildred (Silensky) W.; B.S. magna cum laude, SUNY, Buffalo, 1972; postgrad. Simmons Sch. Social Work, 1972-73; M.S.W., Hunter Coll., 1974. Psychiat. social worker Children's Aid Soc., N.Y.C., 1974-77; psychiat. social worker Sisters of the Good Shepherd, N.Y.C., 1977-78; copywriter SKG Advt., N.Y.C., 1978-79; copywriter TLK Direct Mktg., N.Y.C., 1979-80, Ogilvy & Mather Direct, 1980-81, B & B Direct Inc., 1981—; cons. in field. Nat. Council on Drug Abuse fellow, 1972-73; Children's Aid Soc. fellow, 1973-74. Mem. Nat. Assn. Social Workers, Acad. Cert. Social Workers, Direct Mktg. Writers Guild, Advt. Women of N.Y. Jewish. Home: 333 E 43d St New York NY 10017

WISNIESKI, BERNADINE JOANN, microbiologist; b. Balt., Feb. 26, 1945; d. Anthony Paul and Loretta Joanne (Andrzejewska) W.; B.S., U. Md., College Park, 1967; Ph.D. in Genetics, U. Calif., Berkeley, 1971; postdoctoral fellow UCLA, 1971-74; m. John Shepherd Bramhall, May 28, 1980. Acting asst. prof. microbiology UCLA, 1974-75, asst. prof., 1975-80, asso. prof., 1980—, full mem. Jonsson Comprehensive Cancer Center, UCLA., asso. mem. Molecular Biology Inst., UCLA, 1975—; researcher biochemistry and biophysics. USPHS research career devel. awardee, 1976-81; Damon Runyon Meml. Fund fellow, 1971-73; Celeste Durand Rogers Meml. Found. fellow, 1973-74. Mem. Assn. Acad. Women, AAAS, Phi Beta Kappa, Sigma Xi, Phi Sigma. Club: Manhattan for Women. Contbr. articles sci. jours. Office: Dept Microbiology UCLA Los Angeles CA 90024

WITCHER, BARBARA JEAN MILLER, sales exec., interior designer; b. Chgo., July 1, 1940; d. Roy Clifford and Margaret Genevieve (Dewing) Johnson; student Mt. San Antonio Coll., 1968-70; m. Harvey North Witcher, Aug. 6, 1976; children—Linda Lee Miller, Laurie Ann Miller, Paul Robert Miller. So. Calif. dist. sales mgr. The Hervin Co., Tualatin, Oreg., 1970-74, 76-78; retail sales trainer Crown/BBK Food Brokers, Bell Gardens, Calif., 1974-75; retail sales mgr. Kelley-Clarke Food Brokers, South Pasadena, Calif., 1975-76; West coast regional sales mgr. Sales Maids of Am., Inc., Westport, Conn., 1979—; owner Masterpiece Interiors, San Dimas, Calif., 1980—; motivational speaker to women's orgns. Leader Spanish Trails council Girl Scouts U.S.A., 1969-75; active PTA, 1969-76. Mem. Profl. Women in Food Industry (founding pres.). Republican. Home and Office: 1315 Paseo Corrido San Dimas CA 91773

WITEK RICHARDS, CHRISTINE HELEN, interior designer, TV producer; b. Chgo., May 19, 1940; d. Philip E. and Genevieve (Kruzel) Rogalski; student Loyola U., Chgo., 1958-60; B.S. cum laude, Monmouth Coll., 1963; grad. Harrington Inst. Interior Design, 1971; m. Richard J. Witek, Sept. 4, 1960; children—Andrea, Amy, Ricky. Pres., Designery, Chris Richards Enterprises, Inc., Golf, Ill., 1971—; organizer, producer, host series of programs on interior design Cable TV, 1968-69; staff cons. ABC-TV, Chgo., 1975-80, producer, host segments on consumer advice ABC News, 1978; staff cons. as consumer adv. home furnishings Chgo. Mayor's Model Cities Program, 1978; cons. Decorating Den, Inc., Indpls., 1979-80. Mem. Women in Communications, Nat. Home Fashions League (v.p. consumer affairs 1978-79, exec. v.p. 1982—). Address: Designery Chris Richards Enterprises PO Box 139 Golf IL 60029

WITHERSPOON, FREDDA LILLY, educator; b. Houston; d. Fred D. and Vanita E. (Meredith) Lilly; A.B., Bishop Coll.; M.S.W., Washington U., 1949, M.A. in Guidance and Counseling, 1954; Ph.D., St. Louis U., 1965; m. Robert L. Witherspoon; children—Robert L., Vanita. Social worker, supr. St. Louis City Welfare Office, Homer G. Phillips Hosp., 1943-50; tchr. English, guidance counselor St. Louis Public Schs., 1950-65; prof. student personnel services Forest Park Community Coll., St. Louis, 1965—; cons. Ednl. Testing Service, Princeton, N.J., Head Start program, 1965-68; counseling cons. St. Louis Job Corps Center for Women, 1966-68. Organizer teenage service guild Annie Malone Children's Home, 1964; v.p. St. Louis chpt. NAACP, 1969—, pres. Mo. Conf., 1973—; mem. Challenge of 70's Crime Commn., 1970-75; mem. adv. council Central Inst. for Deaf, 1970-78; mem. Mayor's Council Youth, 1970-75; dir. teens fund drive March of Dimes, 1960-72, Lily Day drive for Crippled Children, 1966-72; chpt. chmn., mem. speakers bur. United Way, 1969—. Bd. dirs. children's services City of St. Louis, Mo. Heart Assn., NAACP, Social Health Assn., Community Assn. Schs. for Arts, St. Louis Heart Assn., Girl Scouts; pres. St. Louis Met. YWCA, 1978-79, bd. dirs.; bd. dirs., vice-chmn. St. Louis Urban League, 1977—. Named woman of Year, Greyhound Bus Corp., 1967, St. Louis Argus, 1968, Nat. Outstanding Woman, Iota Phi Lambda, 1970; named Outstanding Woman of Achievement, Globe Dem., 1970, Outstanding Educator of Am., 1971, Nat. Top Lady Distinction, 1974; recipient Negro History award, 1971; George Washington Carver award, 1976; Health and Welfare Council award, 1975. Mem. NAACP (life, Nat. Outstanding Youth Adv. 1977), Am. Personnel and Guidance Assn., AAUP (pres. 1975—), AAUW, Nat. Assn. Women Deans and Counselors, Am. Sch. Counselors Assn., Am. Vocat. Guidance Assn., Assn. Measurement and Evaluation in Guidance, Nat. Assn. Jr. Colls., Nat. Faculty Assn. Jr. Colls., League Women Voters, Nat. Council Negro Women (life), Mo. Assn. Social Welfare, Jack and Jill, Mound City (pres. 1946-49), Nat. (pres. 1950, 82) bar auxs., Kappa Delta Pi, Iota Phi Lambda (nat. pres. 1977-81), Top Ladies of Distinction (organizer, pres. 1973-77), Continental Socs. (organizer 1981), Sigma Gamma Rho. Research on high sch. drop outs with police records, uses of group guidance techniques in jr. colls. Home: 20 Lewis Pl Saint Louis MO 63113

WITHROW, ANNE LOUISE, med. technologist, univ. adminstr.; b. Akron, Ohio, Sept. 13, 1932; d. Gilbert J. and Gertrude L. (Rogers) Marsh; student Asburg Coll., 1949-52; postgrad. Columbia U., 1953; m. Marvin L. Withrow, Aug. 29, 1954; children—David, Mark. Med. technologist McKennan Hosp., Sioux Falls, S.D., 1954-56, Brookings (S.D.) Clinic, P.A., 1956—; asst. supt. med. tech. S.D. State U., 1974—; cons. in field. Mem. Beta Sigma Phi (adv.). Republican. Methodist. Club: Altrusa (pres. local club). Office: 2005 1st Street Brookings SD 57006

WITKIN, EVELYN MAISEL, geneticist; b. N.Y.C., Mar. 9, 1921; d. Joseph and Mary (Levin) Maisel; A.B., N.Y.U. 1941; M.A., Columbia U., 1943, Ph.D., 1947; D.Sc. (hon.), N.Y. Med. Coll., 1978; m. Herman A. Witkin, July 9, 1943 (dec. July 1979); children—Joseph, Andrew. Mem. staff genetics dept. Carnegie Inst., Washington, 1945-55; mem. faculty SUNY Downstate Med. Center, Bklyn., 1955-71, prof. medicine, 1968-71; prof. biol. scis. Rutgers U., Douglass Campus, 1971-79, Barbara McClintock prof. genetics, 1979—. Postdoctoral fellow Am. Cancer Soc., 1947-49; fellow Carnegie Instn., 1957; Selman A. Waksman lectr., 1960; grantee NIH, 1956—; recipient Prix Charles Leopold Mayer, French Acad. Scis., 1977; Lindback award, 1979. Fellow AAAS; mem. Nat. Acad. Scis., Am. Acad. Arts and Scis., Am. Genetics Soc., Am. Soc. Microbiology, Radiation Research Soc. Author articles, mem. profl. jour. editorial bds. Home: 88 Balcort Dr Princeton NJ 08540 Office: Rutgers U Douglass Campus New Brunswick NJ 08903

WITKIN, LYNNE JOY, social worker; b. Long Beach, N.Y., May 4, 1945; d. Joseph and Eleanor (Kollisch) Lipset; B.A., U. Conn., 1966; student Columbia U. Grad. Sch. Social Work, 1966-67; M.S.W., UCLA, 1969; m. Steven Sol Witkin, Dec. 22, 1966; children—Jolene Beth, Keren Lisa. Child welfare worker, acting supr. County of Los Angeles Dept. Adoptions, Los Angeles, 1968, 69-70; psychiat. social worker Community Mental Health Services for Belleville, Bloomfield and Nutley, Belleville, N.J., 1970-73, chief psychiat. social worker, 1973-76; pvt. practice counseling and psychotherapy, Upper Montclair, N.J., 1979—. Cons., West Essex Community Health Services Hospice; Family and Children's Testing and Counseling Center; Love The Children Adoption Agy. Pres., North Jersey chpt. Concerned Persons for Adoption, 1978-79; mem. steering com. Region II Adoption Resource Center, 1980—. Mem. Nat. Assn. Social Workers, Acad. Cert. Social Workers, Registry of Clin. Social Workers, Mortar Bd., Phi Beta Kappa, Phi Kappa Phi, Alpha Lambda Delta. Home: 17 Oberlin St Maplewood NJ 07040 Office: The Livery Suite 5C Valley Rd at Cooper Ave Upper Montclair NJ 07043

WITSIL, ELIZABETH SMITH ALISON (MRS. WALTER EARLE WITSIL), social worker; b. Wilmington, Del., Sept. 13, 1909; d. Alexander and Katharine Anna (Smith) Alison; A.B., Wilson Coll., 1931; postgrad. Columbia U., 1934-36; m. Walter Earle Witsil, Aug. 27, 1938 (dec. Feb. 1964); 1 dau., Adah Elizabeth Witsil Unger; stepchildren—Walter Earle, Sarah Virginia Witsil Lloyd. Accounting clk. Remington Rand, Inc., Bridgeport, Conn., 1932-33; social case-worker Bridgeport Br.-New Eng. Home for Little Wanderers, 1933-36; social case worker Conn. Children's Aid Soc., Danbury, 1936-38; dir. membership, pub. relations and publicity YWCA, Bridgeport, 1964-75; dir. cultural tours and vols. Bridgeport Mus. Arts, Sci. and Industry, 1975—. Mem. Bd. Fin. Fairfield (Conn.), 1955-79; mem. Fairfield Rep. Town Meeting, 1947-55; pres. bd. mgrs. Woodfield Maternity Home and Adoption Service, Bridgeport, 1954-57, mem. corp.; bd. dirs. Vis. Nurse Assn. Bridgeport, United Fund Council Eastern Fairfield County, Bridgeport Council Ch. Women, Child Guidance Center of Bridgeport, Conn. Conf. Social Work, Mountain Grove Cemetery Assn., Bridgeport, Fairfield Community Services; trustee Greater Bridgeport Symphony Soc., 1978—; mem. Sr. Citizens Tax Relief Com., Fairfield, 1980—, Sr.

Citizens Life Center Study and Bldg. Com., 1981—; bd. assos. U. Bridgeport; mem. Republican Women's Assn. Fairfield. Mem. AAUW, LWV, DAR, Bridgeport Hosp. Aux. (pres. 1961-63), Delta Kappa Gamma (hon.). Presbyterian (trustee, elder). Clubs: Contemporary (sec. 1957-64, pres. 1976), Wilson Coll. Home: 318 Buena Vista Rd Fairfield CT 06432 Office: 4450 Park Ave Bridgeport CT 06604

WITT, JOAN CAROL, nurse, biofeedback therapist; b. Staunton, Va., Feb. 7, 1938; d. Charles Anderson and Nellie Madeline W.; R.N. diploma Rockingham Meml. Hosp. Sch. Nursing, Harrisonburg, Va., 1958; student in nursing Northwestern State U., Shreveport, La., 1972, 73, 79; postgrad. Emory U. Sch. Medicine, 1979. Operating room nurse Rockingham Meml. Hosp., 1958-59, Physicians & Surgeon's Hosp., Shreveport, 1963-64; rehab. nurse, shift supr. Woodrow Wilson Rehab. Center, Fishersville, Va., 1959-60, 64-65; public health nurse Augusta-Staunton (Va.) Health Dept., 1965-70; pulmonary disease nurse VA Hosp., Miami, Fla., 1970, Shreveport, 1970-72; psychiat. nurse, night supr. and adminstrv. supr. adolescent unit Brentwood Neuropsychiat. Center, Shreveport, 1972-78; biofeedback therapist, thermography technician, rehab. nurse Shreveport Pain & Rehab. Center, Shreveport, 1978—; biofeedback nurse cons. Doctors Psychol. Services, Inc.; nurse cons. bd. dirs. Staunton (Va.) March of Dimes, 1969. Vice pres. bd. govs. Gaslight Players Theatre, Shreveport, 1978; active in community theatre, 1971—; counselor Rape Crisis Center, Shreveport. Served to capt. Nurses Corps, USAF, 1960-63. Mem. La. State Nurse's Assn., Am. Soc. Profl. and Exec. Women, Smithsonian Assos., Shreveport Regional Arts Assn., Animal Welfare of Shreveport, Am. Nurse's Assn., Biofeedback Soc. La. (cert., newsletter editor 1981—), Nat. Biofeedback Assn. Am., Theatre Arts Guild, YWCA. Republican. Presbyterian. Home: 840 Martha Ln Shreveport LA 71104 Office: 1128 Louisiana Ave Shreveport LA 71101

WITT, SANDRA JOHNSON, psychologist; b. Sanford, Fla., July 17, 1946; d. Elmer Hunter and Betty Malvina (Beeler) Johnson; B.A. with high honors in German, U. Fla., 1968, M.A. in German, 1969, Ph.D. in Psychology, 1978; M.A. in Psychology, Emory U., 1973; m. William Witt, Oct. 16, 1971; children—Amanda, Katherine. Internat. hostess and in-flight instr. Trans World Airlines, 1969-71; grad. teaching asst. Emory U., 1971-73; staff psychologist, dir. adult edn. Key Tng. Center, Lecanto, Fla., 1973-74; fellow Center for Gerontol. Studies and Programs, U. Fla., Gainesville, 1976, research asst. psychology dept., 1977, adj. asst. prof., 1978-79, asst. dir. testing and evaluation, coordinator basic skills program, 1981—; psychologist, dir. behavior mgmt. therapy Intermediate Care Facility, Sunland Tng. Center, Gainesville, 1979-81; dist. psychologist, devel. services program office Dept. Health and Rehabilitative Services, Gainesville, 1981; cons. psychologist for various orgns., univs., community mental health centers. Active in local elections; active in lobbying efforts for ERA passage in Fla.; sch. adv. council rep. Alachua County Sch. System. Mem. Am. Psychol. Assn., Southeastern Psychol. Assn., Am. Assn. Mental Deficiency, Gerontol. Soc., Nat. Assn. Retarded Citizens, Phi Beta Kappa. Democrat. Lutheran. Contbr. articles to profl. jours. Office: 1012 GPA U Fla Gainesville FL 32611

WITTE, ANN DRYDEN, economist; b. Oceanside, N.Y., Aug. 28, 1942; d. Harry Clifford and Frances Elizabeth (Ferguson) Dryden; B.A., U. Fla., 1963; M.A., Columbia U., 1965; Ph.D., N.C. State U., 1971; m. Charles Leo Witte, June 1, 1969; 1 son, Jeffrey Dryden. Vis. asst. prof. public law and govt. Inst. Govt. U. N.C., Chapel Hill, 1973-74, asst. prof. econs., 1974-79, asso. prof., 1979—; adv. N.C. Gov.'s Office Criminal Justice Planning, 1977; cons., Dept. Justice, HUD, U.S. Congress, N.C. Legislature. Fulbright lectr. Fed. U. Pernambuco, Recife, Brazil, summer 1981; grantee Dept. Justice, N.C. Dept. Correction, NIMH, Fed. Bur. Prisons. Mem. Am. Econs. Assn. (chmn. census adv. com. 1981—), Am. Statis. Assn., Nat. Acad. Scis., Regional Sci. Assn., So. Econ. Assn., Law and Society Assn. (trustee 1982-84), Phi Beta Kappa. Author: The Economics of Crime: Applications, Theory and Methods (with Peter Schmidt), 1982; with Carl Simon) The Underground Economy: A Microeconomic Approach, 1982; contbr. articles to profl. jours. Office: Dept Econs U NC Chapel Hill NC 27514

WITTELES, ELEONORA MEIRA, physicist; b. Jerusalem, July 14, 1938; d. Salomon and Rivka (Komornik) W.; B.S., Fordham U., 1962, M.S., 1963; M.S., N.Y.U., 1965; Ph.D. (research fellow), Yeshiva U., 1969. Postdoctoral fellow Bar-Ilan U., Israel, 1969-70, asst. prof., 1970-72; ind. cons., 1972-80; sr. research scientist Atlantic Richfield Co., Los Angeles, 1980—. Mem. Am. Phys. Soc., AAAS, IEEE, IEEE Engrng. in Medicine and Biology Soc., IEEE Magnetics Soc., Com. on Status of Women in Physics. Research on solid state physics, superconductivity, applied material scis.; inventor med. instrumentation and cryogenic instrumentation. Home: 4714 Browndeer Ln Palos Verdes CA 90274 Office: 515 S Flower St Los Angeles CA 90071

WITTENBERG, NANCY KELLEY, state ofcl.; b. Urbana, Ill., Dec. 30, 1949; d. Byron Maxwell and Marilyn Jeannette (Kerr) Kelley; B.S. in Bus., Fla. State U., 1971, M.S. in Ednl. Adminstrn., 1974; m. Dennis P. Wittenberg, Nov. 9, 1974; children—Owen Patrick, Byron Porteman. Field rep. Kappa Kappa Gamma, 1971-73; govt. asst. Office of Tallahassee, Gov. Fla., 1974-78, exec. staff dir., 1981—; sec. Fla. Dept. Profl. Regulation, 1978-81. Mem. Am. Mgmt. Assn., Tallahassee Women's Network, Women's Polit. Caucus Fla. (treas. 1979-80), Tallahassee Women's Polit. Caucus (treas. 1978-79). Democrat. Mem. Ch. of Christ. Office: Office of Gov The Capitol Tallahassee FL 32303

WITTLER, SHIRLEY JOYCE, state ofcl.; b. Ravenna, Nebr., Oct. 10, 1927; d. Earl William and Minnie Ethel (Frink) Wade; student U. Nebr., 1944-47; m. LeRoy F. Wittler, Dec. 31, 1946; children—Julie Diane, Barbara Liane. Real estate saleswoman Harrington Assos., Lincoln, Nebr., 1965-69; real estate broker Tom Searl Realty, Inc., Cheyenne, Wyo., 1970-76; dep. state treas. State of Wyo., 1976-78, state treas., 1978-83. Pres., LWV, Lincoln, 1965-69, state bd. dirs., 1970-72; fin. chmn. Republican Central Com. Laramie County, 1974-76; chmn. Laramie County Pres. Ford Com., 1976; Rep. precinct committeewoman, 1972-77; mem. Laramie County Library Bd., 1976, Community Devel. Adv. Bd., 1974-77. Mem. Cheyenne Bd. Realtors (pres. 1976, Cheyenne Realtor of Yr. 1974), Women's Civic League (treas. 1974, legis. chmn. 1975-76). Lutheran. Office: State Capitol Cheyenne WY 82001

WITTSTOCK, LAURA WATERMAN, ednl. adminstr., journalist/writer, edn. cons.; b. Cattaraugus, Indian Reservation, N.Y., Sept. 11, 1937; d. Isaac and Clarinda (Jackson) Waterman; student San Francisco State Coll., 1961, Fla. Jr. Coll., 1964; m. Lloyd Wittstock, Aug. 30, 1970; children—Joe, Tedi, Arthur, James, Rosy. Copywriter, The Hecht Co., Washington, 1968-71; editor Legis. Review, Indian Legal Info. Devel. Service, Washington, 1971-73; project MEDIA designer/dir. Nat. Indian Edn. Assn., Mpls., 1973-77; ind. cons., edn. specialist, Mpls., 1976—; adminstr. Heart of the Earth Sch., Mpls., 1982—; mgr. Center V Satellite Office, Native Am. Research Inst., Inc., Mpls., 1981; lectr. in field. Bd. dirs. United Way, Mpls., Christian Sharing Fund, Mpls. Community-Bus. Employment Alliance, Met. U. Minority Services Program, St. Paul. Recipient award Best Merchandising Impression, May Cohens, Jacksonville, Fla., 1969. Mem. Am. Indian Bus. Devel. Corp. (dir. 1979-83), Nat. Commn. on Alcoholism and Alcohol Related Problems, Am. Indian Opportunities Industrialization Center (dir.). Editor, Indian Edn., 1973-74; contbr. articles to profl. jours. Address: 917 21st V SE Minneapolis MN 55414

WITZMAN, AUDREY LORAINE, educator; b. Galva, Ill., July 22, 1937; d. Clarence Gilbert and Gladys Bernice (Westlin) Peterson; B.A., Eureka Coll., 1958; M.Ed., Nat. Coll. Edn., 1962; Ph.D., Northwestern U., 1976; m. Thomas A. Witzman, Aug. 10, 1958; children—Johanna Marie, Jocelyn Anne. Public sch. tchr., Ill., 1958-67; asst. prof. early childhood edn. Northeastern Ill. U., Chgo., 1968-71; developer, owner/dir. Country Woods Nursery Sch. and Day Camp, Valparaiso, Ind., 1971—; asst. prof. early childhood edn. Governors State U., Park Forest South, Ill., 1979—. Chmn., Porter County (Ind.) Child Protection Team, 1980; bd. dirs. Family House, Valparaiso, 1981—. Mem. Am. Assn. for Edn. Young Children, Midwest Assn. Edn. Young Children (co-coordinator conf. Indpls. 1982, Ind. rep. to bd. 1981—), Ind. Assn. for Edn. Young Children. Republican. Methodist. Home: 450 East 725 North Valparaiso IN 46383 Office: Div Edn Governors State U Park Forest South IL 60644

WIX, VICTORIA LEIGH, health care exec.; b. Syracuse, N.Y., Nov. 30, 1947; d. Fred J. Lenway and Betty Francis (DeGarmo) Lenway DePuy; children—Robyn JoAnne Loucks, Christine Elizabeth Loucks, Melissa Anne Loucks. Adminstr., Betta Toy Co., Inc., Chatsworth, Calif., 1976-79; bus. affairs and mgmt. cons. Dr. Didrik Sopler, Los Angeles, 1979-82; pres. Internat. Source of Supply, Ltd., Los Angeles, 1981—, Health Scis. Inst., Inc., Los Angeles, 1982—. Recipient Achievement cert. for outstanding trade advancement Hong Kong Trade Devel. Soc., 1978. Mem. Nat. Assn. Female Execs, Songwriters Resources and Services. Composer songs: China Doll, The Childhood of Miss Lonnie and Me, Time to Move On, Images, One Day Someday's Gonna Up and Pass You By. Office: 10850 Wilshire Blvd Suite 370 Los Angeles CA 90024

WOCKLEY, KATHY KIRRY, coll. adminstr.; b. Cin., Aug. 18, 1931; d. Leon Eugene and Catherine Josephine (Bach) Kirry; A.B., Fla. Atlantic U., 1973, M.A., 1974, Ed.D., 1977; m. Joseph Frank Wockley, Feb. 18, 1956. Exec. asst. to pres. Indian River Community Coll., Ft. Pierce, Fla., 1968-73, dir. devel., 1973—, instr. art layout and design for publs. Pres., Ft. Pierce Meml. Hosp. Women's Aux., 1971-74; mem. Democratic Com., Precinct 11A, 1972-76; mem. Dem. Exec. Com., Ft. Pierce. Mem. AAUW, Nat. Assn. Women Deans, Adminstrs. and Counselors, Nat. Secs. Assn. (pres. Ft. Pierce chpt. 1967-69, Sec. of Yr. award 1965), Nat. Identification Program for Advancement of Women in Higher Edn. Adminstrn., Am. Assn. Women in Community and Jr. Colls., Fla. Assn. Community Colls. (instl. advancement com.), Fla. Assn. Colls. and Univs., Council for Advancement in Support of Edn., St. Lucie County Hist. Soc., Okeechobee County Hist. Soc., St. Lucie County Humane Soc. (dir. 1981—), Martin County Hist. Soc., Fla. Hist. Soc., Phi Alpha Theta. Roman Catholic. Office: Indian River Community Coll 3209 Virginia Ave Fort Pierce FL 33450

WOELLHOF, ELDENE COOK, psychologist, hosp. adminstr.; b. Rock Creek, Ohio, June 15, 1924; d. Edward E. and Annie Myrtle (Oliver) Cook; B.S., SUNY, Buffalo, 1945; M.Ed., Miami U., 1954; Ph.D., Fla. State U., 1961; m. Lawrence Ray Woellhof, Sept. 21, 1962; 1 son, Jeffrey Ray. Tchr. home econs. public schs., N.Y. State, Ill., Ga., Fla., 1945-59; asst. buyer Macy Dept. Stores, Davison-Paxon Co. (subs.), Atlanta, 1957; asst. prof. Grad. Sch. Counselor Edn. Kans. State Tchrs. Coll., Emporia, part-time psychotherapist in counseling bur., 1961-63; dir. dept. psychology Topeka State Hosp., 1972—; mem. adv. council Shawnee County Mental Health Corp., 1965-70; adj. asso. prof. dept. psychology U. Kans., 1970—, ad hoc mem. Grad. Council, 1970; chmn. state research com. instrns., 1968-69, psychology counterpart com., Topeka, 1970-74. Mem. Community Resources Council; active Friends of the Library, Friends of the Zoo. Cert. psychologist, Kans., 1967. Fellow Kans. Psychol. Assn.; mem. Am. Men and Women of Sci., Am. Psychol. Assn. (site visitor com. on accreditation 1974—), Midwestern Psychol. Assn., AAAS, Am. Orthopsychiat. Assn., Kans. Council of Adminstrv. Psychologists (chmn. 1975), Delta Zeta (Topeka alumni). Contbr. articles in field to profl. jours. Home: 4432 Twilight Dr Topeka KS 66614 Office: 2700 W Sixth St Topeka KS 66606

WOFFORD, BUENA GUILFORD, utility co. exec.; b. DeWitt County, Tex., Feb. 2, 1934; d. Richard W. and Audrey L. (Johnson) Wofford; student Tex., Lutheran Coll., 1953-56; m. Charles W. Wofford; children—Donna Michelle, Jacquelyn Ann, Cynthia Kay, Russell W., Charles W. IV. Office mgr., head acct. Valley Telephone Coop., Raymondville, Tex., 1968—. Mem. South Tex. Telephone Accts. Assn. (pres. 1971-72, 80-82), Beta Sigma Phi (corr. sect. Xi Gamma Iota chpt. 1972-73, pres. chpt. 1973-74). Episcopalian. Home: 370 E Sunset Ave Raymondville TX 78580 Office: 480 S 6th St Raymondville TX 78580

WOHLER, MARJORIE LYNN, nurse, educator; b. Gilmer, Tex., Mar. 6, 1948; d. Cleo and Ima Neola (Dean) Coulter; R.N., Bapt. Hosp. Sch. Profl. Nursing, 1970; B.S.N., McNeese State U., 1975; M.S. in Nursing, Tex. Woman's U., 1978; m. Robert Frederick Wohler, Mar. 9, 1979; 1 son, Robert Frederick III. Charge nurse surg. unit Bapt. Hosp. of S.E. Tex., Beaumont, 1970-73, staff nurse surg. unit, 1975; dir. nurses Beaumont Remedial Clinic, 1973-74; relief staff nurse Orange (Tex.) Meml. Hosp., 1974-75; relief staff nurse med.-surg. units Beaumont Med./Surg. Hosp., 1976-78; instr. nursing Lamar U., Beaumont, 1975—, advisor Lamar U. Student Nurses Assn., 1978—, Asso. Degree Student Nurses Assn., 1978—, coordinator Health Career's Day, 1979-81. Bd. dirs. Am. Heart Assn., 1981; chmn. edn. Am. Cancer Soc., North Jefferson County, 1980—, bd. dirs., 1981—; chmn. Youth Against Cancer, 1981—. Mem. Nat. Student Nurses Assn., Tex. Student Nurses Assn., Am. Nurses Assn., Tex. Nurses Assn., Nat. League for Nursing, Tex. League for Nursing, Tex. Assn. Coll. Tchrs. Republican. Roman Catholic. Club: Lamar U. Women's Home: 9498 Doty St Beaumont TX 77707 Office: PO Box 10081 Beaumont TX 77710

WOHLERS, NORMA JEAN, pubs. clearing agy. exec.; b. Charleston, W.Va., Dec. 1, 1935; d. Sterling Patrick and Rosalie Pebble (Anderson) Brown; grad. airline sch. TWA, 1954; m. Gerhard Andrew Wohlers, Mar. 5, 1960 (dec. 1977); children—Gerhard Andrew III, Shannon Diane. Sec., Ohio Nat. Bank, Columbus, 1955-57; mgr. Slenderama, Columbus and Cin., 1957-59; mgr. Civic Reading Club, Look mag., Grand Rapids, Mich., 1959-70, gen. mgr., 1972-77, v.p., 1972; pres., owner Am. Guild Circulation Corp., Detroit, 1972—, chmn. bd., 1977—; pres. Am. Guild Corp., Detroit, 1980—; founder, pres. G.N.S. Publs. Sch. Plan, 1982—. Recipient Presdl. Sports award for tennis, 1973. Mem. Audit Bur. Circulations. Republican. Office: 24453 Grand River Detroit MI 48219

WOHLMAN, LESLIE ELLEN, real estate co. exec.; b. N.Y.C., Mar. 6, 1954; d. Robert F. and Vivian W.; B.A. summa cum laude, U. Pa., 1975; M.B.A. with honors, Harvard U., 1978. Regional v.p. real estate acquisitions and debt placement Integrated Resources, Inc., N.Y.C., 1980—. Mem. Urban Land Inst., Mortgage Bankers Assn., Young Mortgage Bankers Assn., Phi Beta Kappa. Club: Harvard Bus. Sch. (chmn. real estate com. 1980—). Contbr. articles in field. Office: 666 3d Ave New York NY 10017

WOJNICH, ELEANOR MAE BENSON (MRS. WILLIAM WOJNICH), gerontologist, photojournalist; b. Louisville, July 7, 1917; d. Andy T. and Jennie Mae (Venable) Benson; A.B., Allegheny Coll., 1939; postgrad. Boston U., 1947; M.Ed., U. Ark., 1967; m. William Wojnich, June 20, 1946. Social worker Pitts. Assn. for Improvement of Poor, 1940-43; counselor Fla. Employment Service, Miami, 1950-54; asst. dir. Mpls. council Camp Fire Girls, 1954-57; case worker Minn. Div. Child Welfare, St. Paul, 1957-60, University Mound Sch., San Francisco, 1961-63; social worker Ark. Rehab. Services, Little Rock, 1966-67; counselor Minn. Div. Vocat. Rehab., St. Paul, 1967-69; counselor, tchr. Berryville (Ark.) High Sch., 1970-73; photojournalist, Elliam, Seattle, 1973—; co-ordinator social services Source Found., Seattle, 1974-76; Community Outreach developer Sr. Services of Snohomish County, Everett, Wash., 1976—. Served as 1st lt. WAC, 1943-46. Mem. Western Gerontol. Assn., Internat. Platform Assn., AAUW, Am. Personnel and Guidance Assn., Photog. Soc. Am. Home: PO Box 166 Index WA 98256

WOLANIN, SOPHIE MAE, civic worker; b. Alton, Ill., June 11, 1915; d. Stephen and Mary (Fijalka) Wolanin; student Pa. State Coll., 1943-44; cert. secretarial sci. U. S.C., 1946, B.S. in Bus. Adminstrn. cum laude, 1948; Ph.D. (hon.), Colo. State Christian Coll., 1972. Clk., stenographer, sec. Mercer County (Pa.) Tax Collector's Office, Sharon, 1932-34; receptionist, social sec., nurse-technician to Dr., N.Y.C., 1934-37; coil winder, assembler Westinghouse Electric Corp., Sharon, 1937-39; duplicator operator, typist, stenographer, 1939-44, confidential sec., Pitts., 1949-54; exec. sec., charter mem. Westinghouse Credit Corp., 1954-72, sr. sec., 1972-80; reporter WCC News, 1967-68, asst. editor, 1968-71, asso. editor, 1971-74; student office sec. to dean U. S.C. Sch. Commerce, 1944-46, instr. math., bus. adminstrn., secretarial sci., 1946-48. Publicity and pub. relations chmn., corr. sec. South Oakland Rehab. Council, 1967-69; mem. nat. adv. bd. Am. Security Council; founder Center Internat. Security Studies Am. Security Council Edn. Found. Recipient various 1st prize awards Allegheny County Fair, gold plaque Westinghouse Credit Corp., 1968, citation Congl. Record, 1969, TWA, 1969, Medal of Merit, Pres. Regan, numerous other plaques and certificates. Fellow Intercontinental Biog. Assn. (life, patron), Internat. Inst. Community Service (founder, life), U. S.C. Ednl. Found.; mem. Allegheny County Scholarship Assn. (life), Polish-Am. Numis. Assn., Polonus Philatelic Soc., Allegheny County League Women Voters, Am. Judicature Soc., AAUW (life), Internat. Fedn. U. Women, Am. Mus. Natural History, (asso.), N.E. Historic Geneal. Soc. (life), Internat. Platform Assn., Nat. Hist. Soc. of Gettysburg (founding), Nat. Trust Historic Preservation, U. S.C. Alumni Assn. Ednl. Found. (gen. chmn. Tri-State area 1959, Pa. state fund chmn. 1967-68, pres.'s council 1972—), Smithsonian Assos. (charter), UN Assn. U.S., Am. Bible Soc., Hypatian Lit. Soc., Acad. Polit. Sci. (life), Societe Commemorative de Femmes Celebres, Bus. and Profl. Women's Club Pitts. (dir. 1963-80, editor Bull. 1963-65, treas. 1965-66, historian 1969-70, pub. relations 1971-80, Woman of Yr. Award 1972), Liturgical Conf. N. Am. (life), Am. Counselors Soc. (life), Am. Hort. Soc., Westinghouse Vet. Employees Assn., Am. Acad. Social and Polit. Sci., Mercer County Hist. Soc. (life), Nat., Pa. (key club) fedns. bus. and profl. women's clubs, St. Paul's Cathedral Altar Soc., Assn. Nat. Archives, Early Am. Soc., Nat. Soc. Lit. and the Arts, Friends of Churchill Meml. Library in U.S., Met. Opera Guild (asso.). Republican. Roman Catholic. Clubs: Jonathan Maxcy of U. S.C. (charter), University Catholic of Pitts., College of Sharon (hon.). Contbr. articles to newspapers. Home: 5223 Smith-Stewart Rd SE Girard OH 44420

WOLCOTT, NOREEN FERRIS, univ. publs. ofcl.; b. El Paso, Tex., June 29, 1952; d. Joseph Edward and Jean Marie (Kleps) Ferris; B.A. with distinction, U. Mich., 1977; m. Mark Alan Wolcott, May 19, 1979. Communications mgr. Balance Tech., Inc., Ann Arbor, Mich., 1977-78; asso. editor U. Mich. Alumni Assn., Ann Arbor, 1978-81, mng. editor, dir. publs., 1981—. Mem. planning com. U. Mich. Women's Career Fair, 1977; mem. public awareness task force Internat. Year of Disabled Persons, U. Mich., 1981-82, chmn. task force publs. subcom. Mem. Women in Communications, Soc. Profl. Journalists, Council for Advancement and Support Edn. Baptist. Home: 5051 Mast Rd Dexter MI 48130 Office: U Mich Alumni Assn 200 Fletcher St Ann Arbor MI 48109

WOLD, JO ANNE, journalist; b. Fairbanks, Alaska, Apr. 20, 1938; d. Arnold and Eleanor Helen (Gatzek) W.; ed. U. Alaska, L.H.D. (hon.), 1979; m. Lee R. Schroer, Aug. 18, 1979. Producer children's radio program Sta. KFAR, Fairbanks, 1955-60; editor women's page Fairbanks Daily News Miner, 1960-67, columnist, 1976—; editor women's page Jessen's Daily, Fairbanks, 1968-69; reporter All Alaska Weekly, 1969-70; asst. to U.S. Senator Ted Stevens, 1970—; author: Gold City Girl, 1972; Well, Why Didn't You Say So?, 1975; This Old House (1st pl. award Alaska Press Women 1977), 1976; Tell Them My Name is Amanda, 1977. Mem. Nat. Fedn. Press Women (award of excellence 1967, 1st pl. best women's sect. 1969), Alaska Press Women (1st pl. best women's sect. 1965, 67, 68, best mag. story 1967, 1st prize mag. 1973, award of excellence 1976, 1st pl. column 1977, 1st pl. personal column 1978), Alaska Assn. Arts, Tanana Yukon Hist. Soc. (hon.). Republican. Christian Scientist. Club: Fairbanks Soroptimists (hon.).

WOLF, BARBARA ANNE, biol. research adminstr., biologist; b. N.Y.C., July 24, 1947; d. Boris and Molly (Gruberg) W.; B.A. magna cum laude (N.Y. State Regents scholar, Stanley Koncal award 1968), Queens Coll., City U. N.Y., 1968; Ph.D. in Biology, M.I.T., 1973; m. Robert Stanley Spiel, Aug. 25, 1973. Research asst. chem. synthesis Sloan-Kettering Inst. for Cancer Research, Rye, N.Y., 1967; teaching asst. cell biology M.I.T., Cambridge, 1969-70, supr. grad seminars, 1972-73; research asst. virology Rockefeller U., N.Y.C., 1973-75, fellow Nat. Cancer Inst., 1975-77, research asso., oncological studies, summer, 1977; mgr. biol. services Revlon Research Center, Bronx, N.Y., 1977-80, dir. biol. services, 1981—; asso. prof. Coll. Pharmacy St. John's U., Queens, N.Y., 1981—. Mem. Am. Soc. Microbiologists, Soc. Toxicology, Am. Coll. Toxicology, N.Y. Soc. Electron Microscopists, Soc. of Cosmetic Chemists, Genetic Toxicology Assn., Environ. Mutagen Soc., AAAS, N.Y. Acad. Scis., Sigma Xi, Phi Beta Kappa, Beta Delta Chi. Contbr. articles on cell biology and oncology to sci. jours. Office: 945 Zerega Ave Bronx NY 10473

WOLF, CAROLE BRUCE, educator; b. Houston, Mar. 20, 1944; d. Victor Van Buren and Susie Ellen (Fuller) Bruce; B.A., Stephen F. Austin State U., 1965, M.A. in English, 1968; Ph.D. in English (Truman Camp fellow), Tex. Tech U., 1982; m. John Charles Wolf, Oct. 21, 1967; children—Allan Bruce, Anne Elizabeth. Tchr. English, Marshall (Tex.) High Sch., 1965-66; teaching asst. in English, Stephen F. Austin State U., 1966-68; tchr. English, Castleberry Ind. Sch. Dist., Ft. Worth, 1968-72; instr. English, South Plains Coll., 1974, 79; instr. English, Tex. Tech U., Lubbock, 1975-79, lectr., 1980—; instr. Tarrant County Jr. Coll., 1969. Vol., Am. Cancer Soc.; leader South Plains council Cub Scouts Am.; pres. S.C. Episcopal Churchwomen, Lubbock, 1982-83. Mem. South Central Modern Lang. Assn. Episcopalian. Contbr. articles to profl. publs. Home: 3312 40th St Lubbock TX 79413 Office: PO Box 4530 Dept English Tex Tech U Lubbock TX 79409

WOLF, CHARLOTTE ELIZABETH, sociologist; b. Boulder, Colo., Sept. 14, 1926; d. Marion Guy and Ethel Eugenia (Thomas) Rosetta; B.A., U. Colo., 1949, M.A., 1959; Ph.D., U. Minn., 1968; m. Rene Arthur Wolf, Sept. 3, 1952; children—Christopher Robin, Michele Renee. Lectr. sociology U. Md., Tokyo, 1959-62; instr. St. Mary Coll., Leavenworth, Kans., 1962-63; teaching asst. U. Minn., 1963-65; lectr. U. Md., Ankara, Turkey, 1965-67; asst. prof. Colo. State U., 1968-69, Colo. Woman's Coll., 1969-74; asso. prof. sociology Ohio Wesleyan U., Delaware, 1974-80, prof., 1980, chmn. dept. sociology and anthropology, 1974—. Grantee, Shell Oil Co., 1978; recipient Ohio Wesleyan research award, 1982-83. Mem. Am. Sociol. Assn. (chmn. com. status women 1974-76), Soc. Study Social Problems (chmn. budget, audit and fin. com. 1975-79, treas. 1979—), Western Social Sci. Assn. (exec. council

1974-77), Pacific Sociol. Assn., Sociologists Women in Soc. (chmn. nominations com. 1971-73), Soc. Study Symbolic Interaction, N.Central Sociol. Assn. (v.p.-elect 1982), AAUP, ACLU, NOW (pres. Denver 1970-71, nat. dir. 1971-73; Woman of Yr., Denver chpt. 1972). Democrat. Author: Garrison Community: A Study of an Overseas American Military Colony, 1969; also articles. Home: 45 Park Ave Delaware OH 43015 Office: Dept Sociology Ohio Wesleyan Delaware OH 43015

WOLF, DONNA MONGERO, dietitian; b. Yorktown Heights, N.Y., May 11, 1952; d. Anthony and Eleanor F. Mongero; B.S. in Nutrition and Food Sci., Syracuse (N.Y.) U., 1974; m. Clifford J. Wolf, Sept. 12, 1981. Surg. nutritionist U. Colo. Med. Center, Denver, 1974-75; with Profl. Dietetic Counselors, San Bernardino, Calif., 1976-77; cons. nutritionist, Irvine, Calif., 1977-78; clin. nutrition cons. Comprehensive Care Corp., Newport Beach, Calif., 1978—; lectr. in field. Named Young Dietitian of Yr. Calif., 1980. Mem. Am. Dietetic Assn., Nat. Group Cons. Nutritionists (a founder, chmn. Calif. group 1982), Soc. Nutrition Edn., Nat. Orgn. Cons. Dietitians in Health Care Facilities, Calif. Dietetic Assn., Orange Dist. Dietetic Assn., Nat. Assn. Female Execs., Alpha Phi. Lutheran. Clubs: Orange County, Westwood Ski. Home: 906 La Jolla Ave Los Angeles CA 90046 Office: Care Unit Hosp Orange 401 S Tustin Ave Orange CA 92666

WOLF, EDNA JACOBS, religious orgn. exec.; b. Norfolk, Va., Apr. 10, 1932; d. Isaac Westheimer and Marion (Russell) Jacobs; student Wheaton Coll., 1949-52; B.A., George Washington U., 1972; postgrad. Cath. U. Am., 1974; children—Susan Marcia, William B. III, Victoria Katharine. Dir. communications Nat. Children's Island, Washington, 1976; dir. devel. Washington Hebrew Congregation, 1977; exec. dir. B'nai B'rith Women, Washington, 1978—. Mayoral appointee D.C. Commn. for Women, 1980-83; Kennedy del. Dem. Nat. Conv., 1980. Mem. Am. Soc. Assn. Execs., NOW. Democrat. Office: B'nai B'rith Women 1640 Rhode Island Ave NW Washington DC 20036

WOLF, EVELYNE ROBERTS, psychotherapist; b. N.Y.C., Apr. 2, 1921; d. Morris H. and Belle (Mendelsohn) Eddelman; A.B., Hunter Coll., 1941; M.S.W., U. Mich., 1948; Ph.D., Fla. Inst. Tech., 1982; m. Ted George Wolf, Jan. 1, 1970; children—Jane Roberts, Kevin Seth Roberts, Richard Eric Roberts; stepchildren—Amy Wolf Lautin, Steven Alan Wolf. Sr. psychiat. social worker St. Michael Hosp., Newark, 1958-64; clin. dir. N.J. Assn. Retarded Children, 1965-67; exec. dir. Irvington (N.J.) Community Mental Health Center, 1968-70; pvt. practice psychotherapy, Southfield, Mich., 1975—. Bd. dirs. PTA, 1955-60, Children's Inst., West Orange, N.J., 1967-69, Northwestern Guidance Clinic, Garden City, Mich., 1971-73; chmn. ARC, South Orange, 1956. Served as psychiat. social worker ARC, WW II. Wayne County fellow, 1942; U. Mich. fellow, 1942-43; recipient awards Girl Scouts U.S.A., Boy Scouts Am., Am. Cancer Soc., ARC, Community Chests of the Oranges, Mem. Acad. Cert. Social Workers, Nat. Assn. Social Workers, Nat. Clin. Registry of Social Workers, Assn. Children and Adults with Learning Disabilities. Club: California Country (Miami). Office: MRC 21700 Northwestern Hwy Suite 1057 Southfield MI 48075 also 640 NW 183d St North Miami FL 33169

WOLF, GERTRUDE OLSHAKER, librarian, journalist, poet; b. Bklyn., Sept. 27, 1923; d. Morris and Sarah Olshaker; B.A., Bklyn. Coll., 1944; children—Carol Jane, Laura Jean, Nancy Ellen, David Charles. Dir. prodn. Intersci. Pubs., N.Y.C., 1944; reporter, asst. to editor Somerset Messenger-Gazette, Somerville, N.J., 1944-46; asso. editor Cosmetic & Drug Preview, 1946; editor-in-chief Citations, Comml. Investment Trust, N.Y.C., 1946-47; reporter, feature writer, asst. theater editor, drama critic Columbus (Ohio) Citizen, 1947-51; advt. copywriter Eaton Paper Corp., Pittsfield, Mass., 1951-52; suburban newspaper corr. Evening and Sunday Bull., Phila., 1966-69; reporter West Chester Daily Local News, 1966-67, Ardmore Main Line Times, 1968; reception desk clk. LaGuardia Med. Group, Jamaica, N.Y., 1971-80; clk. Queensborough Public Library, 1981—. Recipient writing awards. Author poetry: Golden Tinsel and the Stars, 1980; Seashells at Mantoloking, 1981; The First Snow of Winter, 1982; Lonely Landscape, 1982; Castle of Dreams, 1982. Home: 67-33 Kissena Blvd Apt 2D Flushing NY 11367

WOLF, HELEN(E) COLLINS, govt. ofcl.; b. Uniontown, Ala., Mar. 4, 1934; d. Willie and Katie Collins; A.A., Peters Coll., 1956; student San Diego Coll., 1976-78, Western State U., 1979—; m. Joseph Wolf, July 2, 1958; 1 son, Joseph III. Sec. IRS, Chgo., 1955-56, U.S. Army Fin. Center, Chgo., 1956-58. U.S. Marine Corps., 1958-64, U.S. Navy Bur. Yards and Docks, San Diego, 1964; with U.S. Customs Service, 1964—, fed. women's program mgr., 1974-78, import specialist, 1970—. Pres. adv. council Colonia del Sol Recreation Center, 1980—; mem. Children's Home Soc., 1980; adv. bd. Salvation Army, 1981; mem. Rep. Duncan Hunter's Adv. Conil, 1982. Recipient recognition award Coll., U. Calif., San Diego, 1980, 82. Mem. Pres.'s Council Women's Services, Am. Mgmt. Assn., Nat. Council Negro Women (pres. chpt. 1979-80, Woman of Yr. award, 1979), Career Devel. Assn., Govt. Coll. Assn. Republican. Roman Catholic. Office: U S Customhouse U S Customs Service San Ysidro CA 91073

WOLF, ISABEL DRANE, food scientist, govt. ofcl.; b. Boston, Nov. 21, 1933; d. Louis Andrew and Anna (Whalen) Drane; B.S., Simmons Coll., 1955; M.S., U. Minn., 1971; children—Isabel, August L., Erika M. Instr. dept. food sci. and nutrition U. Minn. 1972-79, asst. prof., 1979-81, asso. prof., 1981—, extension food and nutrition specialist, 1972—; dir. Office of Consumer Advisor U.S. Dept. Agr., 1982—. Mem. Inst. Food Technologists, Soc. Nutrition Edn., Nat. Nutrition Consortium, Minn. State Nutrition Council, Am. Home Econs. Assn. Author: (with N.W. Jerome, J.G. McCleery) Help Yourself - Choices in Food and Nutrition, 1981; contbr. articles to profl. jours. Office: US Department of Agriculture Office of Consumer Advisor 14th St and Independence Ave SW Washington DC 20250

WOLF, JOAN LEVIN, ballet tchr.; b. Richmond, Va., July 28, 1933; d. Simon Jacob and Jean (Sturman) Levin; student Coll. William and Mary, 1951-54; m. Harold Lawrence Wolf, May 6, 1956; children—Eric Andrew, Elizabeth Ann. Soloist, Richmond (Va.) Civic Ballet Co., 1949-57, pres., 1955-56; comml. artist Cargill & Wilson Advt. Agy., Richmond, 1954-56; owner Joan Wolf Sch. Ballet, Riveredge, N.J., 1957-79, Hillsdale, N.J., 1963—; owner, dir. Joan Wolf Ballet Ensemble, 1964-82; artistic dir., choreographer Joan Wolf Ballet Co., Hillsdale, River Edge, N.J., 1972—. Trustee Hackensack YMHA, 1969-70; bd. dirs. Pascack Valley Mental Health Center, 1975-77; chmn. Bikeway Commn. Woodcliff Lake, 1975—; mem. Bergen County Cultural Arts Commn., 1977-80. Recipient cert. of merit as profl. tchr. Nat. Acad. of Ballet, 1960; citation for outstanding cultural contbn. State of N.J., 1981; commendation Bergen County Freeholders, 1981. Mem. Hillsdale C. of C. (pres. 1968-71), Greater Pascack Valley C. of C. (trustee, chmn. Bikeway Commn. 1974—). Subject of book There's Always a Right Job for Every Woman (Roberta Roesch). Home: 12 Anderson Ct Woodcliff Lake NJ 07675 Office: 455 Hillsdale Ave Hillsdale NJ 07642

WOLF, MARY, tng. specialist; b. Camden, N.J., July 7, 1938; d. Harry S. and Reba (Braun) Elkins; B.S. in Edn., Temple U., 1960; M.A. in Human Devel., Fairleigh Dickinson U., 1979; children—Alan Eric, Lisa Caryl, Marla Beth. Tchr., Camden High Sch., 1960-61, W. Phila. High Sch., 1961-64; instr. World-Wide Ednl. Services, Newark, 1979; pres. Dynamic Lifestyles, Inc., Belmar, N.J., 1979—; tng. specialist Ocean County Coll., Toms River, N.J., 1979-81; tng. specialist Ocean County Employment and Tng. Adminstrn., Toms River, N.J., 1981—; cons. in field. Mem. Am. Personnel and Guidance Assn., Am. Soc. Tng. and Devel., Nat. Soc. Performance and Instrn., Nat. Assn. Female Execs., Assn. Humanistic Psychology. Office: Ocean County Employment and Tng Adminstrn Toms River NJ

WOLF, MARY ZIETLOW, mfg. co. exec.; b. New London, Wis., Feb. 26, 1950; d. Gordon Leo and Melane Mary (Simonis) Z.; student U. Wis., Stevens Point, 1968-70, part time, 1977-80; m. Rodney A. Wolf, 1980; 1 son, Dirk. Adminstrv. asst. K.F. Kellogg, Northfield, Ill., 1970-74; prodn. mgr. M.R. Ceramics, Inc., Iola, Wis., 1974-77; plant mgr. Weber Tackle Co., Stevens Point, Wis., 1979-81; v.p. Rodmar Co., Amherst Junction, Wis., 1981—; instr. adult evening tech. sch. Leader local area 4-H Club, 1973-78, key leader county level, 1976-78. Mem. Nat. Assn. Female Execs., Am. Crafts Council. Roman Catholic. Club: Hobbies Unlimited Art League (pres., 1977). Home: Route 1 Box 63A Amherst Junction WI 54407 Office: 8946 Loberg Rd Amherst Junction WI 54407

WOLF, MONICA THERESIA, procedures analyst; b. W.Ger., Apr. 26, 1943; came to U.S., 1953, naturalized, 1959; d. Otto and Hildegard Maria (Heim) Bellemann; student U. Albuquerque, 1981; m. Henry Wolf (div.); children—Clinton, Danielle. Developer Word Processing Center, Public Service of N.Mex., Albuquerque, 1971-74, word processing supr., 1974-78, budget coordinator, 1978-80, lead procedures analyst, 1980—. Adv. bd., student trainer APS Career Enrichment Center. Mem. Internat. Word Processing Assn., Nat. Assn. Female Execs., Nat. Rifle Assn., N.Mex. Shooting Sports Assn. Republican. Club: Sandia Gun (adv. bd., coach). Instr. firearm safety and pistol marksmanship. Home: 912 Washington Ave NE Albuquerque NM 87110 Office: 414 Silver Ave SW Albuquerque NM 87103

WOLF, SUSAN HARTENSTINE, educator; b. West Rockhill Twp., Pa., Jan. 20, 1946; d. Byron Robert and Mildred Irene (Stadon) Hartenstine; B.A. cum laude, Ursinus Coll., 1967; M.A., Gallaudet Grad. Sch., 1970; m. Craig Joseph Wolf, May 24, 1969; children—Melissa Dawn, Evan Curtis Owen. Writer, editor Census Bur., Washington, 1967-68; interpreter, film designer Captioned Films, Washington, 1970; tchr. Arlington (Va.) Pub. Schs., 1970; tchr. N.Y. Soc. for the Deaf, N.Y.C., 1971; tchr. N.Y.C. Bd. Edn., 1971-72; mem. faculty L.I. U., Bklyn., 1974; tchr. of deaf Curtis High Sch., S.I., N.Y., 1978—. Mem. Registry of Interpreters for the Deaf, Internat. Assn. Parents of the Deaf, Council Am. Instrs. of the Deaf, Nat. Cath. Deaf Orgn., Mensa, S.I. Zool. Soc. Quaker. Office: Curtis High Sch 105 Hamilton Ave Staten Island NY 10301

WOLF, VIRGINIA DANFORTH, civic worker; b. N.Y.C., Nov. 20, 1918; d. Francis Jenkins and Leonie (Alexandre) Danforth; m. Stewart George Wolf, Aug. 1, 1942; children—Stewart George, Angeline Griffing, Thomas Danforth. Mem. Snarks Theatre Group, N.Y.C., 1934-52; vol. health worker Sir Wilfred Grenfell Mission, St. Anthony, Nfld., Can., 1940-41; heart sta. technician Cornell-N.Y. Hosp., 1942, 1944-45, Johns Hopkins Hosp., 1943-44; adminstrv. sec. Central Soc. Clin. Research 1958-62; sec. Totts Gap Med. Research Labs., Bangor, Pa., 1977—, acct., treas., 1982—. Sec.-treas. William Temple Found., Galveston, Tex., 1972-77. Mem. Galveston Hist. Soc., Galveston Cultural Arts Council. Episcopalian. Republican. Address: RFD 1 Box 1262 Bangor PA 18013

WOLFE, ANN, sculptor; b. Poland, Nov. 14, 1905; d. Jacob and Sarah (Szulmirski) Wolfe; B.A., Hunter Coll., 1926; studied sculpture Paris, 1932-33; m. Mark Graubard, Mar. 5, 1927; children—Jane Strovas, Maya Jones. One-man shows: Worcester (Mass.) Art Mus., 1939, Grace Horne Gallery, Boston, 1941, Whyte Gallery, Washington, 1946, Hamline U., St. Paul, 1951, Minn. State Fair, 1951, World Gallery, St. Paul, 1954, Walker Art Center, Mpls., 1955, Mpls. Inst. Arts, 1964, Adele Bednarz Galleries, Los Angeles, 1966, Stewart-Verde Galleries, San Francisco, 1966, West Lake Gallery, Mpls., 1970, Jewish Community Center, Mpls., 1970; group shows include Kraushaar Gallery, N.Y.C., Sculpture Center, N.Y.C., Fairweather Hardin Gallery, Chgo., Sears-Vincent Price Gallery, Chgo., 3d Sculpture Internat., Phila. Mus. Art, Pa. Acad. Fine Arts; represented in permanent collections CCNY, Hamline U., Colgate U., Nat. Mus. Korea, Seoul, Mus. Western Art, Moscow, Jerusalem Mus., Israel, Hartt Coll., U. Hartford (Conn.), Children's Hosp., St. Paul, Mt. Zion Temple, St. Paul, U. Minn., U. Calif., Berkeley, and numerous pvt. collections; tchr. sculpture; reviewer art publs. Worcester Telegram-Gazette, 1940-60. Recipient awards Allied Artists Am., 1936, Soc. Washington Artists, 1944, 45, Minn. State Fair, 1949, Mpls. Inst. Arts, 1951, Soc. Minn. Sculptors, 1955, Spring Salon, Mpls., 1957. Mem. Soc. Minn. Sculptors (past pres.). Home: 2928 Dean Pkwy Minneapolis MN 55416

WOLFE, CORINNE HOWELL, ret. social worker; b. El Paso, Tex., Dec. 15, 1912; d. David Emerson and Clara (Schultz) Howell; B.A., U. Tex., El Paso, 1933; M.S.W., Tulane U., 1944; m. Howard Clark Wolfe, Jr., Feb. 29, 1936. Social worker Tex. Dept. Public Welfare, 1933-45, Family Service Assn., Ft. Worth, 1945-46, VA, Dallas, 1946-48; dir. staff devel. and tng. Social and Rehab. Service, HEW, Washington, 1948-72; prof. social work N.Mex. Highlands U., Las Vegas, 1972-82, ret., 1982; cons. social services, social work edn. Mem. Santa Fe Community Devel. Commn. Recipient Disting. Service award HEW, 1973; Outstanding Alumni award Tulane U., 1975. Mem. Nat. Assn. Social Workers, Council Social Work Edn. (Disting. Service award 1972), Santa Fe Mental Health Assn., Am. Public Welfare Assn., Nat. and Internat. Conf. on Social Welfare. Democrat. Methodist. Contbr. articles to profl. jours. Home: 2509 Avenida de Isidro Santa Fe NM 87501

WOLFE, GOLDIE BRANDELSTEIN, realtor; b. Linz, Austria, Dec. 20, 1945; d. Albert and Regina (Sandman) Brandelstein; student U. Ill., Urbana, 1963-64; B.S. in Bus. Adminstrn. cum laude, Roosevelt U., 1967; postgrad. Grad. Sch. Bus. U. Chgo., 1968-69; 1 dau., Alicia Danielle Schuyler. Account research mgr. J. Walter Thompson, advt., Chgo., 1967-71, asso. account exec., 1971-72; account exec. Needham, Harper & Steers Advt. Inc., Chgo., 1972; real estate broker, office leasing dept. Arthur Rubloff & Co., Chgo., 1972—, asst. v.p., 1975-77, v.p. office leasing, 1977-80, sr. v.p., 1980—, also dir. Chmn. services group Chgo. Public TV, 1974-75; bd. dirs. realty div. Jewish United Fund, 1976-77; bd. dirs. Michael Reese Hosp. Med. Research Inst. Council, 1979—. Recipient Salesman of Yr. award Chgo. Real Estate Bd., 1981. Mem. Chgo. Council Fgn. Relations, Young Execs. Club Chgo. (program chmn. 1980-81), Chgo. Real Estate Bd., Nat., Ill. assns. Realtors, Am. Mktg. Assn., Roosevelt U. Alumni Assn. (bd. govs.), Jr. Women's Advt. Club Chgo. Home: 1332 Sutton Pl Chicago IL 60610 Office: care Arthur Rubloff & Co 69 W Washington St Chicago IL 60602

WOLFE, JEAN ELIZABETH, med. artist; b. Newark, Oct. 3, 1925; d. Arthur Howard and Ethel (Harper) W.; B.S., Russell Sage Coll., 1947; student Pratt Inst., 1949-50; diploma U. Rochester Sch. Medicine and Dentistry, 1955; M.F.A. (W. B. Saunders fellow 1955-56), U. Pa., 1973, postgrad., 1980. Exhbns.: Pratt Inst. Galleries, Bklyn., 1958, N.Y. Med. Coll., 1958, Assn. Med. Illustrators, 1961-70, AMA, N.Y.C., 1965, Phila., 1965, ACS, Atlantic City, 1965, Research Study Club Los Angeles, 1966, Phila. Art Alliance, 1967, U. Pa. Opthalmol. Soc., 1967-68, Cayuga Mus. History and Art, 1968, Pensacola Art Center, 1969, FAA Aero. Center, Okla., 1970, Scheie Eye Inst., 1972-75, Assn. Med. Illustrators Traveling Salon, 1977-79; illustrations in med. books, jours., pharm. house publs.; represented in permanent collection Phila. Coll. Physicians, Francis A. Countway Med. Library, Harvard U.; instr. Pembroke Coll. Brown U., 1947-49; mem. faculty Kimberley Sch., Upper Montclair, N.J., 1950-52; free lance med. illustration Studio N.Y. Med. Coll., 1956-60; instr. Pratt Inst., 1958-59; asso. in med. illustration in ophthalmology U. Pa. Sch. Medicine, 1960-72, research asst. prof. med. art, 1972—; guest lectr. Johns Hopkins Med. Sch., 1973, NIH; guest artist U.S. Air Force Acad., 1971. Recipient Merit cert. AMA; Appreciation cert. ACS; 1st prize Pensacola Art Center and Am. Heart Assn., 1969. Mem. Phila. Art Alliance, Assn. Med. Illustrators (bd. govs. 1970—, chmn. bd. govs. 1974-75, vice chmn. bd. 1973-74, chmn. nominating com. 1972-73, Ralph Sweet, Tom Jones awards), Soc. Illustrators N.Y., AAUP, Marquis Biog. Library Soc. Contbg. illustrator: Adler's Textbook of Ophthalmology (Scheie and Albert), 8th edit. Studio: Colonial Towers B-9 27 E Central Ave Paoli PA 19301

WOLFE, JOAN LUEDDERS, environ. activist, writer, consultant; b. Detroit, May 2, 1929; d. William R. and Mary Lucinda (Deane) Luedders; B.A., in Econs., U. Mich., 1951; D.Public Service (hon.), Western Mich. U., 1973; m. Willard Wolfe, June 26, 1953; children—John Roberts, Peter Harper. Vol., PTA, Audubon Soc., LWV, others; founder, 1st chmn. West Mich. Environ. Action Council, exec. dir., 1971-73; mem. Mich. Natural Resources Commn., 1973-82; author: Making Things Happen: The Guide for Members of Volunteer Organizations, 1981. Pres., Belmont Sch.-Community Club, Newcomers Club Grand Rapids, Grand Rapids Audubon Club, Mich. Pesticide Council. Recipient Environ. Quality award Mich. Soc. Internal Medicine, 1970; Conservation award Am. Motors Corp., 1973; others. Mem. AAAS, Mich. Assn. Vol. Adminstrs., Nat. Audubon Soc. (nat. bd. dirs. 1982—), NOW Women in Natural Resources.

WOLFE, KATHLEEN S., banker; b. Erie, Pa., Sept. 29, 1950; d. L. Wilburn and Shirley Ann Wolfe; student U. Central Fla., 1975, Rollins Coll., 1976—. supr.. pension and profit sharing 1st Nat. Bank of Pa., Erie, 1969-73; asst. v.p. Sun Bank, Orlando Fla., 1973—. Active Hotline, crisis counseling, The Bridge, drug counseling. Warrant officer USAR, 1974—. Mem. Res. Officer Assn., Women in Mgmt. Network, Royal Manors Homeowners Assn. (dir.), Central Fla. Mcpl. Bond Club. Roman Catholic. Club: Toastmasters. Author: Fin. Market and Interest Rate Comment weekly, 1980—. Home: 3011 Maybry Ln Orlando FL 32807

WOLFE, MARGARET RIPLEY, historian, educator; b. Kingsport, Tenn., Feb. 3, 1947; d. Clarence Estill and Gertrude Blessing Ripley; B.S. magna cum laude, East Tenn. State U., 1967, M.A., 1969; Ph.D. (Haggin fellow), U. Ky., 1974; m. David Early Wolfe, Dec. 17, 1966; 1 dau., Stephanie Ripley. Instr. history East Tenn. State U., 1969-73, asst. prof., 1973-77, assoc. prof., 1977-80, prof., 1980—. Recipient Disting. Faculty award East Tenn. State U., 1977; East Tenn. State U. Found. research award, 1979. Mem. Orgn. Am. Historians, Cath. Studies Hist. Assn., So. Assn. Women Historians (pres.-elect 1982-83), So. Hist. Assn., Tenn. Hist. Soc. Author: Lucius Polk Brown and Progressive Food and Drug Control; Tennessee and New York City, 1908-1920; 1978; contbr. articles to profl. jours. Office: E Tenn State U Kingsport Center Kingsport TN 37660

WOLFE, NAN THERESIA, social worker; b. Bluffton, Ohio, Aug. 10, 1939; d. Herman G. and Mary (Boerger) Schmidt; B.S., Bluffton Coll., 1961; M.S.W., U. Mich., 1968; m. David F. Wolfe, June 28, 1980; children—Mary Theresa Knee, LeAnne Patricia Knee. Supr., Lucas County Welfare, Toledo, 1961-69; clin. supr. Monroe (Mich.) Mental Health Center, 1969—; owner Union Fire Equipment Co., Monroe, 1972-78. Mem. Nat. Assn. Social Workers, Acad. Cert. Social Workers, Mich. Lic. Cert. Social Workers. Office: 740 N Macomb St Monroe MI 48161

WOLFE, NORMA LEE, constrn. co. exec.; b. Seneca, Mo., Mar. 12, 1932; d. Lawrence L. and Stella Mae Arehart; student Seneca schs.; m. R.E. Wolfe, Mar. 7, 1957; children—Alan E., Deborah L. Corp. sec. Ming of Am. Inc., Prairie Village, Kans., 1969-79, gen. mgr., 1969-75, dir., 1969—; sec.-treas. Alan E. Wolfe Equipment & Constrn. Co., Kansas City, Mo., 1978—; corp. sec., dir., adminstrv. asst. to pres. Tri-City Constrn. Co., Kansas City, Mo., 1973—; commn. officer Joplin (Mo.) Police Dept., supr., 1953-57. Mem. ch. council, treas. Prince of Peace Lutheran Ch., Grandview, Mo., 1970-75; mem. Luth. Ch. Women. Democrat. Office: 3001 E 83d St Kansas City MO 64132

WOLFE, TRACEY DIANNE, distbg. co. exec.; b. Dallas, June 13, 1951; d. George F. Wolfe and Helen Ruth Cline Lemons; B.S. in Edn. and Social Sci., East Tex. State U., Commerce, 1973, M.S. in Elem. Edn., 1976; 1 son, Bronson Alan. Asst. to dir. student devel. East Tex. State U., 1973-74; corp. sec., v.p. Wolfe Distbg. Co., beer distbrs., Terrell, Tex., 1974—. Mem. Kappa Delta (alumnae v.p. 1978-79, alumnae treas. 1979-81, province pres. 1980-82). Republican. Methodist. Home: 3316 Lakeside Dr Rockwall TX 75087 Office: 100 Metro Dr Terrell TX 75160

WOLFORD, MARY S., telephone co. exec.; b. Glasgow, Ky., Feb. 26, 1940; d. Willie and Mary A. (Wilson) O'Neal; B.A., Butler U., 1976; m. Robert O. Wolford, Apr. 17, 1971; 1 dau., Krystal Smith. With Ind. Bell Telephone Co., Indpls., 1963—, operator, 1963-64, service asst., 1964-65, group chief operator, 1965-67, spl. asst., 1967-69, dept. asst., 1969-71, customer service advisor, 1971-77, staff asso., 1977-81, engring. supr., 1981—. Fund raising capt. Am. Cancer Soc., 1980; bd. dirs. Big Sisters of Greater Indpls., 1980-83, March of Dimes, 1981-83. Mem. Am. Bus. Woman's Assn. (dir.; Am. Bus. Woman of Year, New Hope chpt. 1975-76), Network of Women in Bus. (bd. dirs. 1980-83), Ind. Bus. Communicators, Bus. Club (chmn. membership and publs. coms. 1978-79), Coalition of 100 Black Women (bd. dirs. 1981-83), Sigma Gamma Rho. Home: 1752 Kessler Wood Ct Indianapolis IN 46208 Office: 5858 N College Ave Indianapolis IN 46220

WOLICKI, NANCY FRIEDA, staff mem. U.S. Senate, lawyer; b. Chgo., Sept. 8, 1953; d. Samuel and Ingrid (Rappel) W.; B.A. in Journalism and Sociology, U. Ariz., 1974, J.D., 1977. Admitted to Ariz. bar, 1977; law clk. firm Verity, Smith & Kearns, Tucson, 1976-77, Ariz. Ct. Appeals, 1977-78; legis. asst. fgn. policy and armed services health, staff atty. Billy Carter investigation to U.S. Sen. Dennis DeConcini, 1979-81; staff dir. Senate Subcom. on Alcoholism and Drug Abuse, Washington, 1981—. Recipient William Spaid Meml. award U. Ariz. Coll. Law, 1977, Senate commendation for Billy Carter investigation, 1980. Mem. Am. Bar Assn., Ariz. Bar Assn., Phi Kappa Phi. Jewish. Office: 4230 Dirksen Senate Office Bldg Washington DC 20510

WOLIN, GAIL BETH, conf. coordinator; b. Flint, Mich., Mar. 13, 1952; d. Sidney and Ellen (Guz) W.; B.A. in Elem. Edn., U. Mich., 1974; M.S.W., U. Md., 1976; postgrad. George Washington U., 1978. Regional dir. dept. youth activities Seaboard Region, United Synagogue Am., Silver Spring, Md., 1976-77; conf. coordinator Advanced Mgmt. Edn. Center, George Washington U., 1977-78, Nat. Inst. Community Devel., Inc., Arlington, Va., 1978—. Mem. leadership devel. program United Jewish Appeal of Greater Washington, 1979—, fundraising chmn., 1979-80; mem. exec. council and steering com., chmn. young adults program Young Leadership div. USA Fedn., 1980-81. Recipient award of merit United Jewish Appeal of Greater Washington, 1979, 80; cert. social worker, Md. Mem. Meeting Planners Internat., U. Mich. Alumni Assn., Nat. Council Career Women, Nat. Council Jewish Women. Democrat. Office: 1815 N Lynn St Suite 1000 Arlington VA 22209

WOLKONSKY, MARY WARD, civic worker; b. Grand Rapids, Mich., Nov. 24, 1907; d. Clarence Jay and Bernice (Godwin) Van Etten; B.A., Vassar Coll., 1929; D.Humane Arts (hon.), Lake Forest (Ill.) Coll., 1971; m. Peter Wolkonsky, May 2, 1980; children by previous marriage—David Harris, John Anthony. Past founding chmn. women's bd. Lyric Opera Chgo., U. Chgo., Know Your Chgo. lecture and field trip ann. series; founding chmn. Bright New City forum on urban design; past pres. women's bd., trustee Art Inst. Chgo.; bd. dirs. Lyric Opera; trustee U. Chgo.; pres. council Museum Sci. and Industry, Chgo.; past pres. Planned Parenthood Assn. Chgo.; mem. women's bd. Field Mus. Natural Sci., Northwestern U., Harvard Bus. Sch. Assn., Salk Inst., San Diego; mem. internat. com. N.Y.C. Ballet. Republican. Clubs: Casino, Onwentsia, Friday.

WOLLERMAN, PEGGY JANE, food co. exec.; b. Columbus, Ohio, July 12, 1950; d. Edward H. and Dorothy E. Wollerman; student Miami U., 1968-69; B.S., Ohio State U., 1972. Research technician Kellogg Co., Battle Creek, Mich., 1974-76, Washington rep., 1976-77, mgr. govt. relations, 1977-78, dir. public affairs, 1978-79, v.p. public affairs, 1979—. Mem. Mich. Efficiency Task Force, 1976, Battle Creek Internat. Relations Com., 1977. Mem. Women in Govt. Relations. Home: 3801 Willow Lake Dr Apt 316 Kalamazoo MI 49008 Office: 235 Porter St Battle Creek MI 49016

WOLLIN, DOROTHY D., cons. psychologist, educator; b. Louisville, July 17, 1946; d. Lloyd T. and Evelyn R. (Renn) Drane; B.A., U. Louisville, 1968; M.A., SUNY, Buffalo, 1971, Ph.D., 1976. Asst. prof. St. Cloud (Minn.) State U., 1973—; human relations educator, feminist. Mem. Am. Psychol. Assn., Minn. Women Psychologists. Office: Psychology Dept St Cloud State University Saint Cloud MN 56301

WOLMAN, CAROL STONE, psychiatrist; b. Phila., June 22, 1941; d. Irving J. and Roslyn Carol (Stone) Wolman; A.B., Radcliffe Coll., 1962; M.D., Harvard U., 1967. Intern, Stanford U. Hosp., 1967-68; resident in psychiatry U. Pa. Hosp., 1970-73; practice medicine specializing in psychiatry, San Francisco, 1973—; asst. clin. prof. dept. psychiatry Sch. Medicine, U. Calif.-San Francisco, 1977—. Pres., No. Calif. Physicians for Social Responsibility, 1979; bd. dirs. Agape Found., 1978—. Served with div. Indian health USPHS, 1968-70. Diplomate Am. Bd. Psychiatry and Neurology. Fellow Am. Psyciat. Assn. (founder, mem. task force on women 1972-74, mem. com. on constn. and by-laws 1975-77); mem. No. Calif. Psychiat. Soc. (coms. on women, ethics, membership). Home: Box 21 Elk CA 95432

WOLTER, MARY LOU(ISE), distbg. co. exec.; b. Prairie du Chien, Wis., Nov. 24, 1926; d. Ralph Waldo and Dessa May (Brownlee) Lathrop; m. Charles Thomas Wolter, Jan. 20, 1946; children—Thomas Quinn, David Ralph, Cynthia Louise, Martin Bryce. Free lance journalist; producer radio and cable TV shows; co-owner distributorship Amway Corp., Tucson and LaQuinta, Calif., 1969—; pres. Caml'lot Corp., Tucson and LaQuinta, 1976—. Mem. Amway Distbrs. Assn. U.S. Clubs: Diamond, Order Eastern Star, Daus. of Nile. Author newspaper and mag. articles, bus.-related materials. Home: Box 985 54-950 Ramirez LaQuinta CA 92253 also 5160 E Pima Tucson AZ 85712

WOLVEN, ANNE MARTYN, toxicologist; b. N.Y.C., Feb. 2, 1925; d. Michael and Mary (Pzsyk) Martyn; B.A., Hunter Coll., N.Y.C., 1945; m. William A. Garrett, Jan. 14, 1978. Pharmacologist, Schering Corp., Bloomfield, N.J., 1945-47; asst. dir. Contract Lab., Roselle Park, N.J., 1947-72; mgr. toxicology Alza Pharmaceuticals, Palo Alto, Calif., 1972-74; sr. toxicologist Shell Chem. Co., San Ramon, Calif., 1975-77; environ. toxicologist Syntex Corp., Palo Alto, Calif., 1977-78; pres. A.M. Wolven, Inc., toxicology and regulatory affairs cons., Atlanta, 1979—; chairperson Gordon Research Conf. on Toxicology and Safety Evaluation, 1976. Mem. Soc. Toxicology, Soc. Microbiology, Soc. Cosmetic Chemists, AAAS. Author articles in field. Office: 175 W Wieuca Rd Suite 118 Atlanta GA 30342

WOMACK, SHARON GENNELLE, library adminstr.; b. Flora, Ill., June 13, 1940; d. Teddy Roosevelt and Mary Martha (Sale) Martin; B.S. in Bus. Adminstrn., U. Ariz., 1972, M.L.S., 1973; m. Robert Darrol Womack, Jan. 29, 1960 (dec. Dec. 1979). Library asst. Phoenix Union High Sch. Dist., 1958-61; bookmobile librarian Yuma City-County Library, 1962-63; reference librarian Ariz. State Library Extension Service, Phoenix, 1963-67; documents asst. U. Ariz., Tucson, 1967-69; dir. Miami Meml-Gila County, Ariz., 1972-76; dir. Maricopa County Library, Phoenix, 1976-77; dep. dir. Ariz. Dept. Library Archives and Pub. Records, Phoenix, 1977-79, dir., 1979—; vice chairperson State Adv. Council on Libraries, 1974-77; mem. technician adv. com. Mesa Community Coll. Library, 1977—. Chairperson steering com. Gila County Community Coll., 1975. Mem. ALA, Southwestern, Ariz. (pres. 1977—) library assns. Home: 6810 N 29th Ln Phoenix AZ 85017 Office: 3d Floor State Capitol 1700 W Washington St Phoenix AZ 85007

WOMBLE, MELODIE LYNN, utility co. exec.; b. Rockville Centre, L.I., N.Y., Mar. 19, 1945; d. Harold and Sylvia (Ross) Lisses; B.A. in English and Journalism, Fla. State U., 1967; M.Ed., U. Miami, 1970; postgrad. Nova U., 1978; m. Gary W. Womble, June 10, 1967 (dec. 1978). Tchr. Dade County Public Schs., Miami, Fla., 1967-69; asst. communications research Dallas Ind. Sch. Dist., 1970-73; editor Sports Digest, Miami, 1974; evaluation specialist Evaluator Dade County Public Schs., Miami, 1975-77; sr. coordinator Fla. Power and Light Corporate Communications Dept., 1977—; instr. U. Miami, 1979. Charter mem. Fla. AWARE Com., Chmn., 1980, program chmn. state meetings, 1979, 80, 83. NDEA fellow, 1970. Mem. Internat. Assn. Bus. Communication (co-chmn. regional meeting 1979), Women in Communication (moderator seminar 1980, 81), LWV (bd. dirs. legislative liaison 1980-83), Greater Miami C. of C., Leadership Miami Alumni Assn. Jewish. Author profl. papers. Office: PO Box 529100 Miami FL 33152

WONCH, DIANE ELIZABETH, nurse, educator; b. Buffalo, May 24, 1947; d. Charles William and Ruth Catherine (Besser) W.; student Medaille Coll., 1965-69; A.S., Trocaire Coll., 1971; B.S. in Nursing, D'Youville Coll., Buffalo, 1976; M.S. in Nursing, SUNY, Buffalo, 1978, postgrad., 1980—. Elem. sch. tchr., East Aurora, N.Y., 1968-69; nursing asst., practical nurse Orchard Park (N.Y.) Nursing Home, 1969-71; with Roswell Park Meml. Cancer Inst., Buffalo, 1971—, staff nurse, 1971-74, head nurse, 1974-75, clin. nurse specialist, 1975-78, dir. staff devel., 1978—; asst. prof. SUNY, Buffalo, 1981—; cons. law firm for nursing related cases; vol. lectr. Am. Cancer Soc.; vol. instr. ARC; cons. Buffalo and Erie County, Girl Scouts U.S.A. Recipient Anne Walker Sengbusch Leadership award, 1977; Public Health grantee, 1975-76. Mem. Am. Nurses Assn., N.Y. State Nurses Assn. (dir. dist. 1), D'Youville Alumni Assn., Am. Heart Assn., Buffalo Zool. Soc., Nat. Audubon Soc., Buffalo Soc. Natural Scis., SUNY Buffalo Alumni Assn., Sigma Theta Tau. Office: 666 Elm St Buffalo NY 14263

WONG, ELAINE DANG, fin. ofcl.; b. Canton, China, June 3, 1936 (parents Am. citizens); d. Robert G. and Fung Heong (Woo) Dang; A.A. (Rotary scholar), Coalinga Coll., 1956; B.S. (AAUW scholar, Grad. Resident scholar), U. Calif., Berkeley, 1958, teaching credential, 1959; m. Philip Wong, Nov. 8, 1959; children—Elizabeth, Russell, Roger, Edith, Valerie. Tchr. acctg. San Mateo (Calif.) High Sch., 1959-60; acct., 1960-75; substitute tchr. Richmond County Schs., Augusta, Ga., 1975-77; comptroller Central Savannah River Area, United Way, Augusta, 1977—; cons. small bus.; pvt. tutor acctg. Panel judge Jr. Achievement Treas. award, 1980, 81; treas. Chinese Lang. Sch., 1973-75, Merry Neighborhood Sch., 1974-75. Recipient Achievement award Bank of Am., 1954. Mem. Nat. Assn. Accts. (dir. 1978—, treas. 1982—), Chinese Assn. Republican. Presbyterian.

WONG, MARY ANN, info. systems specialist; b. Hartford, Conn., Oct. 14, 1953; d. Toy S. and Bo Yuk (Kwan) W.; B.S. magna cum laude, Bklyn. Coll., 1975; postgrad. Pace U., 1979—. Programmer, Texaco, Inc., N.Y.C., 1975-77; programmer-analyst Inco Inc., N.Y.C., 1977-80, systems analyst, 1980-81, info. systems mgr. Inco U.S. Inc., N.Y.C., 1981—. Mem. Nat. Assn. Female Execs. Inc. Office: One New York Plaza New York NY 10004

WONG, STELLA MEE QUE, educator; b. Honolulu, May 29, 1950; d. Yuen Kong and Margaret M. H. (Lum) W.; B.S., U. Hawaii, 1972, M.S.W., 1976; Lectr. dept. human devel. U. Hawaii, 1974—, dept. acad. adv., 1977—; cons. in field. Treas., Hawaii Council Family Relations, 1977—; sec. Hawaii council Camp Fire, Inc., 1978, 2d v.p., 1979, pres., 1980. Recipient Shawnequas award Hawaii Council Camp Fire, Inc., 1974. Mem. Nat. Assn. Social Workers, Nat. Council Family Relations. Office: U Hawaii Dept Human Devel George Hall 120 2560 Campus Rd Honolulu HI 96822

WOOD, BARBARA ANN, editor; b. Alameda, Calif., May 18, 1943; d. Cecil Charles and Anna Louise (Freeman) Floyd; student Central State Coll., Edmond, Okla., 1961; A.A. in Journalism with honors, Hillsborough Community Coll., Tampa, Fla., 1978; student U. South Fla.; m. G. Don Wood, Oct. 23, 1976. With GTE Data Services Inc., Tampa, 1969—, editor, communications adminstr., 1978—. Bd. dirs. Hillsborough-Manatee County Mental Health Bd., 1981—. Recipient various awards for house mags. and newspapers; lic. real estate salesman. Mem. Internat. Assn. Bus. Communicators (sec.-treas. Fla. Suncoast chpt. 1980, dir.-at-large 1981, dir. 1980-81), Women in Communications. Office: PO Box 1548 Tampa FL 33601

WOOD, BARBARA CHAMPION, state legislator; b. Swampscott, Mass., Jan. 10, 1924; d. John Duncan and Eva (Moore) Champion; R.N., Mary Hitchcock Meml. Hosp., Hanover, N.H., 1945; student Simmons Coll., 1947-48; m. Newall Arthur Wood, 1948; children—Gary D., Craig A., Brian S., Dennis M., Joan Wood Unger. Nursing supr. Mary Hitchcock Meml. Hosp., 1946-47; gen. nurse Gifford Meml. Hosp., Randolph, Vt., 1952-55; sch. dir., Bethel, Vt., 1963-81; mem. Vt. Ho. of Reps., 1981—. Served to 2d lt., Nurse Corps, AUS, 1945-46. Mem. Am. Legion. Clubs: Bethel Women's (pres. 1976-78), Vt. Fedn. Women's (dist. pres. 1978-80). Home: Woodland Rd Bethel VT 05032 Office: Vermont House of Representatives State Capitol Montpelier VT 05602 *

WOOD, BARBARA LOUISE, psychologist; b. Staunton, Va., Nov. 28, 1949; d. William Earle and Caroline Estelle (Marks) W.; B.A. in Psychology, Carnegie-Mellon U., 1971; M.A. in Counseling (EDPA fellow), U. Minn., 1974; Ph.D. in Counseling, U. Md., 1979; m. Philip Bond Ray, Aug. 2, 1981. Counselor Kenyon Coll., Gambier, Ohio, 1976-77; psychol. counselor Am. U., Washington, 1977; cons. Temple Hills (Md.) Counseling Center, 1977-79; profl. asso. Univ. Counseling Center, U. Md., College Park, 1977-79, teaching asst., 1977, 79, instr., 1978—; dir. Greenbelt-College Park (Md.) Counseling Center, 1979—; pvt. practice psychol. counseling, Silver Spring, Md., 1982—. Mem. Am. Personnel and Guidance Assn., Am. Coll. Personnel Assn., Am. Psychol. Assn., Phi Kappa Phi. Democrat. Roman Catholic. Contbr. articles to profl. publs. Home: 117 Hilltop Rd Silver Spring MD 20901 Office: 1738 Elton Rd Suite 127 Silver Spring MD 20903

WOOD, CONSTANCE RICE, psychiat. social worker; b. Marlboro, Mass., Feb. 1, 1922; d. John Edward and Helen Bullard (Ellis) Rice; A.B., Syracuse U., 1943; M.S.W., Boston U., 1973; m. Robert K. Wood, Mar. 18, 1944; children—Robert K. Jr., Jeffrey Bullard, Durinda Rice. Clinician, psychiat. social worker Monadnock Family and Mental Health Service, Keene, N.H., 1972—; pvt. practice psychiat. social work, Keene, 1975—; owner Tavern Antiques, Keen, 1981—. Mem. adv. bd. Monadnock Area Women's Crisis Service, 1980-82; founding mem. Keene Center for Human Concerns, 1969, Women's Crisis Center, Keene, 1977-79; N.H. del. Nat. Democratic Conv., 1968, mem. exec. bd. N.H., Dem. Party, 1969-72, chmn. Cheshire County Dem. Party, 1972; pres. bd. trustees Keene Unitarian-Universalist Ch., 1969; recorder N.H. Women's Polit. Caucus, 1974. Mem. Nat. Assn. Social Workers, NOW, Nat. Women's Polit. Caucus, ACLU, LWV, Women's Internat. League for Peace and Freedom. Home: 63 Arch St Keene NH 03431 Office: 331 Main St Keene NH 03431

WOOD, EDNA LUELLA (SELBE), nurse, educator; b. Phillipsburg, Kans., Apr. 24, 1925; d. John Carlyle and Cora Jane (Reese) Selbe; R.N. diploma St. Francis Hosp. Sch. Nursing, Topeka, 1946; B.S. in Nursing Edn. (Coll. fellow), St. Mary Coll., Leavenworth, Kans., 1948; M.S. in Health Edn., So. Ill. U., Carbondale, 1972; m. Elmer Leroy Wood, June 6, 1948; children—Carolyn Ann, Wanda Lee, John Leslie. Sch. nurse St. Mary Coll., 1946-48; supr. Meml. Hosp. Cheyenne, Wyo., 1947, 48, staff nurse obstetrics, 1951-55; staff nurse Invenson Meml. Hosp., Laramie, Wyo., 1949-51; with VA Nursing Service, 1955—, asst. chief nursing service VA Med. Center, Cheyenne 1962-66, chief nursing service, Grand Junction, Colo., 1967-70, Marion, Ill., 1970-76, asso. chief nursing service for edn. Colmery-O'Neil VA Med. Center, Topeka, 1976—; mem. numerous health-related coms.; mem. Task Force Continuing Edn. for Nurses in Kans., 1980; mem. Kans. Planning Com. for Nurses, 1982; mem. adj. faculty U. Kans. Sch. Nursing. Mem. Gov.'s Com. for Nurses in Wyo., 1960-66; pres. Wyo. League for Nursing, 1962-66; mem. consumer planning com. U. So. Ill. Sch. Medicine, 1970-72. Recipient Dir.'s commendation for superior performance VA Med. Center, Cheyenne, 1964; hon. recognition plaque So. Ill. Nurses, 1976, Washburn U. Honor Soc. for Nursing, 1980; hon. plaque Task Force Continuing Edn. for Nurses, 1982. Mem. Am. Nurses Assn., Kans. State Nurses Assn., Nat. League Nursing, Am. Hosp. Assn. for Health Manpower, Nursing Orgn. VA. Mem. Christian Ch. (Disciples of Christ). Clubs: Toastmistress (Cheyenne); Wider Horizons Toastmistress (Grand Junction). Contbr. articles to profl. jours. Home: 730 NW 35th Topeka KS 66617

WOOD, EMMA LOU, real estate mgmt. corp. exec.; b. Jasonville, Ind., Sept. 29, 1935; d. Leo William and Elizabeth (White) Warrick; student Ind. U., 1957-72; m. C.J. Wood, Jan. 31, 1966 (dec.); children—Elizabeth Marie, Charles John. Bookkeeper, Place & Co., South Bend, Ind., 1959-65; pres. C.J. Wood, Inc., South Bend, 1976—. Mem. South Bend C. of C. Club: Orchard Hills Country (Niles, Mich.). Office: C J Wood Inc 1119 S Franklin St South Bend IN 46624

WOOD, EVELYN NIELSEN, educator; b. Logan, Utah, Jan. 8, 1909; d. Elias and Rose (Stirland) Nielsen; B.A., U. Utah, 1929, M.A., 1947; postgrad. Columbia, 1956-57; m. Myron Douglas Wood, June 12, 1929; 1 dau., Carolyn Wood Evans. Tchr., Weber Coll., Ogden, Utah, 1931-32; girls counselor Jordan High Sch., Sandy, Utah, 1948-57; tchr. jr. and sr. high schs., 1948-59, U. Utah, 1957-59; founder, originator Evelyn Wood Reading Dynamics, 1959—; tchr. rapid reading U. Del., 1961; author, conductor radio programs, 1947; guest lectr. NEA, 1961, Internat. Reading Assn., Tex. Christian U., 1962; faculty Brigham Young U., research specialist for reading, 1973-74. Author: (with Marjory Barrows) Reading Skills, 1958; A Breakthrough in Reading, 1961; A New Approach to Speed Reading, 1962; Speed Reading for Comprehension, 1962; also articles.

WOOD, FAY S(ONIA), television sales and service co. exec.; b. Phila., Aug. 22, 1945; d. Paul and Dorothy (Berkowitz) Wiener; B.A. in English, Pa. State U., 1967; grad. exec. mgmt. course RCA Corp., 1977; children—Deborah, Esther. Real estate sales rep., 1968-70; cons. Hearing Centers, Inc., 1970-72; dist. sales mgr. Beltone Hearing Aid Centers, Inc., 1972-76; v.p. PhD Hearing Centers, Inc.; with RCA Service Co., 1976-79, sales mgr., 1977-79, regional sales mgr., N.Y. dist., 1979—; v.p. sales and mktg. Full Line Repair Centers, Inc., Ridgewood, N.Y. and Linden, N.J., 1979-81, pres., 1981—. Mem. N.Y.C. Commn. on Status of Women, 1981-82. Recipient audiology cert. Dahlberg Electronics, 1974; Master Cons. award Beltone Electronics, 1975; 1st degree Black Belt in Tae Kwon Do Karate, 1975; named Regional Mgr. of Yr., RCA Service Co., 1977-79. Mem. AAUW, LWV, Nat. Assn. Female Execs., Nat. Fedn. Bus. and Profl. Women, NOW, Nat. Fedn. Bus. and Profl. Women. Club: B'nai B'rith. Office: 62-59 Fresh Pond Rd Ridgewood NY 11385 also 238 S Wood Ave Linden NJ 07036

WOOD, JOLEAN MORTON, family counselor; b. Gaffney, S.C., June 23, 1929; d. Joe Roland and Pecolia (Smith) Morton; ed. Torrington (Conn.) Bus. Coll., continuing edn. courses U. S.C., Spartanburg, Greenville (S.C.) Tech. Coll.; m. Walter Ernest Wood, Jr., Feb. 29, 1952; children—Thomas Ryan and Phillip Lester (twins), Karen Michele. Office mgr. Council for Spartanburg County, 1956-58; adminstrv. asst. Milliken Yarn Sales, Inc., Spartanburg, 1958-65; equal opportunity officer Piedmont Community Actions, Inc., Spartanburg, 1967-81; family counselor Green Lawn Meml. Gardens, Inc., Spartanburg, 1981—. Bd. dirs. Council on Aging, 1978—; leader Girl Scouts U.S.A., 1965-75; treas. Food Bank of Piedmont, 1982. Mem. S.E. Assn. Equal Opportunity Officers (dir., plaque for outstanding leadership in human rights), Spartanburg County Nutrition Council, Am. Bus. Women's Assn. (charter v.p., Woman of Yr. 1981), S.C. Equal Opportunity Officers Assn. (past pres.), S.C. Assn. Human Rights Workers (sec.), S.C. Assn. Human Service Agys. (sec. 1980-82), S.C. Ch. Women United (pres.). Democrat. Presbyterian. Club: Huntington Hills Country (Spartanburg). Home: 128 Old Georgia Rd Spartanburg SC 29302 Office: Fernwood Glendale Rd PO Box 2255 Spartanburg SC 29304

WOOD, JOYCE ANN MLAKER, hosp. histologist; b. Warren, Ohio, Mar. 11, 1946; d. John and Anna (Poncer) Mlaker; student Ohio U., 1964-66; cert. Northside Hosp., 1967; m. Robert Vaughn Wood, May 6, 1978. Lab. asst. Northside Hosp., Youngstown, Ohio, 1966-67, histologist, 1967-71; supr. histology Bethesda Meml. Hosp., Boynton Beach, Fla., 1971—. Mem. Am. Soc. Clin. Pathologist (affiliate), Nat. Soc. Histotech. Home: 3919 Edgar Ave Boynton Beach FL 33436 Office: Bethesda Meml Hosp 2815 S Seacrest Blvd Boynton Beach FL 33435

WOOD, JUNE POPHAM (MRS. GLEN NORRIS WOOD), educator; b. Houston, Nov. 27, 1920; d. Jesse Lee and Esther Bailey (Brown) Popham; student Sophie Newcomb Coll., 1936, Tex. Christian U., summer 1936; B.A., Baylor U., 1941; M.A., U. Houston, 1958; m. Glen Norris Wood, Aug. 15, 1942; children—Esther Wood (Mrs. Robert Carter Wilson), Glen Norris. Prof. math. U. Houston, 1947-60, chmn. dept. math. Downtown Coll., 1974—; prof., chmn. dept. math. South Tex. Jr. Coll., Houston, 1960-74. Mem. Com. on Undergrad. Program in Math., 1971—, mem. panel on two-year colls., 1970-73. Sect. chmn. Houston Symphony Soc., 1958; leader Girl Scouts U.S.A., 1950-51; chmn. March of Dimes, City of Bunker Hill, 1960. Named Outstanding Tchr., Tex. Assn. Jr. Colls., 1970, Piper Prof., Minnie Stevens Piper Found., 1975. Mem. Math. Assn. Am. (mem. com. on two yr. colls. 1972-75, mem. Tex. exec. council 1972—, 2d v.p. 1973—), Tex. Assn. Jr. Coll., South Tex. Jr. Coll. Faculty Assn. (pres. 1967), Alpha Chi. Episcopalian. Author: Introductory Algebra, 1969; A First Course in Algebra, 1971; (with David Outcalt) A Second Course in Algebra, 1974; Introductory and Intermediate Algebra, 1982. Editorial bd. Two-Year Coll. Math. Jour., 1972—, book rev. editor, 1974—. Home: 10 Carolane Trail Houston TX 77024

WOOD, KATHERINE ELIZABETH, social worker; b. Saginaw, Mich., July 4, 1950; d. Maurice Myron and June Ella (Hoffman) Finger; B.A., Valparaiso U., 1971; M.S.W., Wayne State U., 1976; m. Michael R. Wood, Apr. 6, 1973 (dec. 1973); 1 son, Jared Michael. Tchr.'s aide Nursery for Emotionally Impaired Children, South Bend (Ind.) Mental Health Center, 1971; sch. social worker Grand Blanc and Goodrich sch. dists. (Mich.), 1972; substitute tchr. Frankenmuth, Birch Run and Clio sch. dists. (Mich.), 1973-74; clin. social worker, pre-intake worker Bay Area Guidance Center, Bay City, Mich., 1976-81; pvt. practice, 1981—. Co-chmn. community-coll. relations com. Valparaiso (Ind.) U., 1970. Cert. social worker, Mich. Mem. Nat. Assn. Social Workers, Internat. Assn. Infant Mental Health. Democrat. Lutheran. Office: 201 N Mulholland 3d Floor Bay City MI 48706

WOOD, KATHLEEN ANN, hair stylist, orgn. exec.; b. Springfield, Ill., Mar. 17, 1951; d. Charles William and Mary Jane (Lovas) W.; student Ill. Coll., 1969-71; B.A., Sangamon State U., 1973. Data analyst, office of gov. State of Ill., Springfield, 1973-75; bus. asst. Ill. Issues mag., Springfield, 1976-77; barber/stylist As You Like It Personal Hairstyling, Springfield, 1978—; grad. asst. Sangamon State U., Springfield. Alt. del. Democratic Nat. Conv., 1972; convener Springfield Women's Polit. Caucus, 1971; chairwoman People's Alliance for Reproductive Choice, 1979, sec., 1980; cashier coordinator King Harvest Food Coop., 1974-76. Mem. Barbers, Beauticians and Allied Industries Internat. Assn., NOW (pres. 1975, treas. 1978-79). Mem. Brainchild women's poetry collective, pub. Brainchild IV, 1977. Home: Rural Route 1 Springfield IL 62707 Office: Women's Studies Sangamon State U Springfield IL 62708

WOOD, KATHLEEN OLIVER, writer and editor; b. Mt. Kisco, N.Y., Sept. 17, 1921; d. Eli Leslie and Melba Antoinette (Gislason) Oliver; student Swarthmore Coll., 1938-39, Antioch Coll., 1940-41, U. N.Mex., 1949, Cleve. Coll., 1960-61; m. John Thornton Wood, June, 1941 (div. 1947); children—Mark Thornton, Jonna Grim, Karen Wood Weston; m. 2d, Clifford Emanuel Huff, June, 1948 (div. 1955). Tech. sec. Gray Iron Founders Soc., Cleve., 1955-57; tchr. Whiting Bus. Coll., Cleve., 1957-62; editorial asst. Chem. Rubber Co., Cleve., 1966; editor, writer Jefferson Ency., World Pub. Co., Cleve., 1967-68; disc jockey, announcer Sta. WCLV-FM, Cleve., 1968-69; communications coordinator, writer, editor Highlights newsletter University Circle, Inc., Cleve., 1971-81; talk-show hostess, announcer Sta. WERE-AM, Cleve., 1972-73; freelance writer, editor, cons., 1981—; tchr. Project LEARN; tutor VIP program. Hostess weekly radio show, CRRS, Cleve. Soc. for Blind; taper books for Library of Congress Service for Visually Handicapped; treas. Cleve. Beautiful Com., 1980, sec., 1982; exec. sec. Cleve. Cultural Garden Fedn.; trustee E. Cleve. Community Theatre. Mem. Pub. Relations Soc. Am., Internat. Assn. Bus. Communicators, Women's Advt. Club Cleve. (past pres., editor Weathervane 1982-83), Women in Communication, World Assn. Women Journalists and Writers (congress coordinator), MENSA, Early Settlers. Quaker. Clubs: Zonta Internat. (past pres. Cleve.), Women's City. Author: Greenwood, 1967; editor, pub. Frog in the Milk Pan (Marie Wallace), 1963; editor Graffiti Mag., 1967, Office Gal Mag., 1962-63, Smorgasbrain Mag., 1968. Home: 3118 E Overlook Rd Cleveland Heights OH 44118 Office: PO Box 5612 Cleveland OH 44101

WOOD, LARRY (MARYLAIRD WOOD), journalist, educator; b. Sandpoint, Idaho; d. Edward Hayes and Alice (McNeel) Small; B.A.

magna cum laude, U. Wash., Seattle, 1938, M.A. with highest honors, 1940; postgrad. Stanford U., 1941-42, U. Calif., Santa Cruz, 1975; postgrad. U. Calif. at Berkeley, 1943-44, cert. of photography, 1971; postgrad. in journalism U. Wis., Madison, 1971-72, U. Ga., 1972-73; children—Mary, Marcia, Barry. By-line columnist Oakland (Calif.) Tribune, San Francisco Chronicle, 1946—; feature writer Western region Christian Sci. Monitor and CSM Syndicate, 1973—, also Donnelly Bus. Publs., Oak Brook, Ill.; stringer Travelday mag., regional corr. Spokane Mag., 1976—; Calif. corr. Seattle Times Sunday mag.; stringer Off Duty, mag. for mil.; free lance writer for various nat. mags. including Parents', Sports Illus., Popular Mechanics, Mechanix Illus., Oceans, Sea Frontiers, TV Guide, Woman's Day, Am. Home, nat. travel, bus., fashion, home/garden and environ. mags., 1946—; writings syndicated Internat. Communications Agy., 1981—; author, reviewer series Focus on Sci., Charles Merrill Pub. Co., 1982—; feature writer Calif. Today; feature and travel writer San Jose (Calif.) Mercury News, 1979—, Odyssey Travel mag., AAA, Motorland, 1982—, Chevron, USA, Accent, People, Your Home, Fodor Guide 1982—. contbg. editor Fashion Showcase, Dallas; dir. public relations No. Calif. Assn. Phi Beta Kappa, 1969—; judge Am. Book Awards, Nat. Assn. Real Estate Editors, others prof. journalism San Diego State U., 1974—; asst. prof. journalism Calif. State U., Hayward, fall 1977; vis. prof. journalism San Jose State U., spring 1976; asst. prof. sci./environ. journalism U. Calif. extension, 1978—; public relations dir./cons. in field of sci., environ. affairs and recreation numerous firms, instns. and assns.; syndicated news stories and features on AM radio, 350 stas. in U.S. and Can.; participant, speaker nat. profl. confs. Public relations dir. YWCA, YM-YW USO, Seattle, 1942-46, YWCA, Oakland, Calif., 1946-56, Children's Home Soc. Calif., 1946-56, Children's Med. Center No. Calif., 1946-70, Eastbay Regional Park Dist., 1946-58, Calif. Spring Garden Show, 1946-58, Girl Scouts U.S.A., Oakland, 1948-56; speaker for ednl. insts., profl. groups, 1946—; sec. Jr. Center of Arts, Oakland, 1952—; vol. public relations Am. Cancer Soc., YMCA, Oakland, 1946-52; public relations writer ARC, 1946-56, cons. Oakland Park Dept.; public relations account exec. March of Dimes, 1946-58; bd. dirs. Camp Fire Girls, Oakland, Joaquin Miller PTA, Oakland; del. 1st Conf. on Sci. in Nat. Parks, San Francisco, 1979, Nat. Park Service-Nat. Trust Historic Preservation joint conf., 1982, 1st Internat., C., Hydrofoil Conf., N.S., Can., 1982. Recipient citations U.S. Forest Service, 1975, Nat. Park Service, 1976; award for feature on Adapt-A-Horse program U.S. Forest Service, 1977-78; citation for Sea Grant, article in Oceans Mag., 1980; Citation Am. Youth Hostels, 1982. Mem. Public Relations Soc. Am., Nat. Sch. Public Relations Assn., Environ. Cons. N.Am., Internat. Environ. Cons., Internat. Oceanographic Soc., Am. Assn. Edn. in Journalism (nat. mag. and newspapers com. 1969—), U. Wash. Ocean Scis. Alumni Assn. (charter), Investigative Reporters and Editors, Soc. Am. Travel Writers, Nat. Press Photographers Assns, Eastbay Women's Press Club, Nat. Assn. Sci. Writers, Calif. Writers Assn., San Francisco Press Club, Mortar Bd., Women in Communication (Woman of Year, Eastbay 1952, regional pres. 1970-71, mem. nat. bd., speaker nat. conv. 1980), Calif. Assn. Environ. Profls., Found. Am. Communications (del.), Phi Beta Kappa (pub. relations dir. No. Calif. 1969—), Phi Beta Kappa Alumni, Chi Omega, Pi Lambda Theta, Sigma Delta Chi. Author: Pacific Coast Waterfronts, 1974; Railroads of the West, 1975; Restoration in the West, 1976; America's Endangered Animals, 1976; Great Zoos of the World, 1976; Showcase Cities of the West, 1977; America at the 1980 Olympics; America's Estuaries; Sylvia Earle—Woman Aquanaut; others Contbg. editor: Science '82, Fodor's Travel Guides, 1982. Address: 6161 Castle Dr Oakland CA 94611

WOOD, MARGARET ANN, advt. exec.; b. Princes Risborough, Eng., May 20, 1934; came to U.S., 1957, naturalized, 1979: d. Montague and Mary Anna (Hennessey) Jones; student Brit. schs.; divorced; children—Mark, Michael, Peter. Vice pres., copy chief, then asso. creative dir. Lennen & Newell, Inc., advt., Honolulu, 1960-70; pres. Environ. Devel. Council, Inc., Honolulu, 1971-73; chmn. bd., pres. Margo Wood Advt., Inc., Honolulu, 1974—; chmn. bd. subs. Pacific Public Relations, 1979—. Trustee, Hawaii Bound, Honolulu Jr. Acad.; bd. dirs. Hawaii Public Radio, Honolulu council Navy League U.S., Hawaii Visitors Bur., C. of C., ARC. Named Advt. Woman of Yr., 1965. Mem. Sales and Mktg. Execs. Honolulu (past pres.), Am. Mktg. Assn. (pres. Honolulu 1979-80, Western regional v.p.), Advt. Agy. Assn. Hawaii, Hawaii Hotel Assn., Pacific Area Travel Assn. (vice chmn.), Internat. Mktg. Authority, Mensa. Roman Catholic. Clubs: Oahu Country, Plaza. Author articles in field. Home: 649 Ulili St Honolulu HI 96816 Office: 841 Bishop St Suite 1501 Honolulu HI 96813

WOOD, MARGARET E., fin. corp. exec.; b. Freeland, Pa., Mar. 21, 1921; d. Thomas J. and Stella R. (Daubert) Williams; Bus. degree, McCann Sch. Bus., 1939; m. Raymond W. Wood, May 20, 1944; children—Thomas H., Richard W. Asst. v.p. Dominick & Dominick, Inc., Boston, 1970-73; v.p., div. mgr. F.L. Putnam & Co., Inc. of Boston, Salem, N.H., 1973-81, Buttonwood Securities Corp. of Mass., Boston, Salem, N.H. div., 1981—; dir. BankEast Guaranty Savs. Bank. Trustee Haverhill YWCA. Office: 1 Manor Pkwy Salem NH 03079

WOOD, MARGARET MEEKS, archtl.-engring. firm exec.; b. Tipton, Okla., July 31, 1932; d. Fred Lionel Meeks and Josie Gladys (Alexander) Meeks Kennedy; A.A., Columbia Basin Coll., 1972, computer sci. cert., 1975; B.P.A., U. San Francisco; m. Leonard Herbert Wood, June 30, 1975 (div.); children—Regina Mary, Robin Theresa. With Burns & Roe, Inc., Richland, Wash., 1975—, computer programmer, 1979—. Treas., Franklin County Democratic Central Com., 1978-80. Presbyterian. Home: 2909 S Elm St Fresno CA 93706

WOOD, MARION PETERS, lectr.; b. Edinburgh, Pa., Mar. 30, 1900; d. Clayton Ames and Mary (McCreery) Peters; B.A., Barnard Coll., 1921; M.A., Cornell U., 1922; m. John M. Wood, June 30, 1923; children—John M., Clayton P., Wendy Wood Chapple. Asst. editor Woman's Home Companion mag., N.Y.C., 1922-24; free lance writer, 1925-30; writer feature articles N.Y. Sun, N.Y. Telegram, 1926-35; writer radio scripts, N.Y.C., 1923-40; asso. Lloyd Hyde Antiques, N.Y.C., 1953-60; head classical dept. Oakwood Sch., Poughkeepsie, N.Y., 1956-58; head dept. English Laycock Sch., Green Farms, Conn.; resident tchr. English and Latin, Miss Hall's Sch., Pittsfield, Mass., 1962-64; lectr. on Eng. and Am. antiques, 1964—. Mem. women's bd. St. Barnabas Hosp., N.Y.C., 1930—, v.p., 1950-55. Mem. D.A.R., Barnard Alumni Assn., Pi Beta Phi. Episcopalian. Club: Fairfield Country Hunt. Address: 206 Godfrey Rd Weston CT 06880

WOOD, MARY LOVEY, speech pathologist; b. McAllen, Tex., Oct. 9, 1942; d. David Gregg and Florella (Salter) W.; B.A. in Speech, U. Tex., 1964, M.A. in Communication Disorders (Vocat. Rehab. Adminstrn. grantee), 1966, Ph.D., 1976. Chief dept. speech pathology Cerebral Palsy Center, Austin, Tex., 1965-67; supr. U. Tex. Speech and Hearing Clinic, Austin, 1967-71; faculty U. Tex., Austin; co-dir., owner, speech pathologist Austin Speech, Lang., and Hearing Center, 1971—; cons. in field; mem. adv. com. Child and Family Service; mem. task force on autism interagy. div. Tex. Gov.'s Adv. Com. on Developmental Disabilities; mem. Profl. Advisory Bd. Autism. Mem. Tex. (pres., exec. council), Am. (cert. clin. competence, fellow standards bds., mem. legis. council) speech, hearing assns., Tex. Com. of Orgns. for Handicapped (pres.), Phi Kappa Phi, Alpha Delta Pi. Methodist. Contbr. articles to profl. publs., chpts. to books. Office: 1209 W 34th St Austin TX 78705

WOOD, NANCY E(LIZABETH), educator; b. Martins Ferry, Ohio; d. Donald Sterret and Orne (Erwin) W.; B.S., Ohio U., 1943, M.S., 1947; Ph.D., Northwestern U., 1952. Tchr., St. Clairsville High Sch., 1943-45, Ohio U., 1946-47, Bethany Coll., 1947-48, Northwestern U., 1948-52; coordinator clin. services, also Lang Found., Cleve. Hearing and Speech Center, 1952, dir. lang. disorders sect., 1959-60; asso. prof. Western Res. U., 1952-60; specialist speech and hearing disorders U.S. Office Edn., Washington, 1960-62; asst. chief research Neurol. and Sensory Disease Service Program div. Chronic Diseases USPHS, Washington, 1963-64; dir. research John Tracy Clinic, Los Angeles 1964-65; prof. lang. pathology and otolaryngology U. So. Calif., 1966-72, chmn. grad. program communicative disorders, 1972-75, prof. journalism, 1975—. Fellow Internat. Council Women Psychologists, Am. Psychol. Assn., Soc. Research in Child Devel., Am. Speech and Hearing Assn. (mem. exec. com.); mem. Council Exceptional Children and Youth, Delta Kappa Gamma. Author: Language Disorders in Children; Delayed Speech and Language Development; Verbal Learning; contbr. articles to profl. jours. Office: 305 Grace Ford Sackatori Hall U So Calif Los Angeles CA 90089

WOOD, ROBERTA SUSAN, fgn. service officer; b. Clarksdale, Miss., Oct. 4, 1948; d. Robert Larkin and Dorothy Eloise (Shelton) Wood; B.A. with distinction, Southwestern U., Memphis, 1970; postgrad. Nat. U. Cuyo, Mendoza, Argentina, 1970-71; M.P.A., Harvard U., 1980. Joined U.S. Fgn. Service, 1972; service in Manila, Naples and Turin, Italy and Port-au-Prince, Haiti; mgmt. analyst Dept. State, Washington, 1980—. Fulbright scholar, 1970-71. Mem. Am. Fgn. Service Assn., Consular Officers Assn., Nat. Assn. Female Execs., DAR, Friends of Kennedy Center, Planned Parenthood Washington, Phi Beta Kappa. Home: 1448 SE 15th St Fort Lauderdale FL 33316 Office: CA/EX Dept State Washington DC 20520

WOOD, SANDRA ELAINE, systems analyst; b. Lynchburg, Va., June 27, 1944; d. William Lewis and Mattie Lou Wood; diploma exec. sec. course Phillips Bus. Coll., Lynchburg, 1970; B.A. in Bus. Adminstrn./Mgmt., Lynchburg Coll., 1982. Various clerical and secretarial positions, 1962-66; with Owens-Ill., Inc., 1966—, data processing supr./programmer, Big Island, Va., 1974-76, data processing systems-analyst/programmer, 1976—. Sec. Bedford County Transp. Safety Commn., 1974—. Mem. Profl. Secs. Internat. (Sec. of Yr. award Lynchburg chpt. 1971, chpt. pres. 1974, coordinator S.E. Dist. Conf. 1981-82), Data Processing Mgmt. Assn. (chpt. pres. 1980), CPS Assos. Democrat. Methodist. Address: Owens-Ill Inc Big Island VA 24526

WOOD, WENDY DEBORAH, filmmaker; b. N.Y.C., Oct. 4, 1940; d. John Meyer and Marion Emily (Peters) W.; B.A. cum laude, Vassar Coll., 1962; M.A., Stanford U., 1964; m. William Dismore Chapple, Dec. 7, 1963; 1 son, Samuel Eliot. Teaching asst. Stanford U., 1962-64; photographer, film editor Bristol (Eng.) U., 1964-66, asst. dir. Internat. Conf. Film Schs., 1966; research asst. biology dept. U. Conn., Storrs, 1970-72; sr. program devel. specialist, writer, producer, dir. video and film audio visual services Aetna Life & Casualty Co., Hartford, Conn., 1972—; pres. Chapple Films, Inc., 1972—; films include: Yankee Craftsman, 1972; Alcoholism, Industry's Costly Hangover, 1974; Dragerman's Haul, 1975; Flight Without Wings, 1977; Auto Insurance Affordability (2 awards), 1981; Where Rivers Run to the Sea (award), 1981; Our Town is Burning Down (6 awards), 1982. Recipient CINE Golden Eagle award Council on Internat. Non-theatrical Events, 1972, 76, 1st Place award Indsl. Photography, 1974, cert. Outstanding Creativity U.S. TV Commls. Festival, 1974, EFLA award Am. Film Festival, 1974, 76, Dir's. Choice award Sinking Creek Film Festival, 1975, award Columbus Film Festival, 1975, award Excellence Life Ins. Advtrs. Assn., 1975, Silver Screen award U.S. Indsl. Film Festival, 1976, 81, 1st place award Conn. Film Festival, 1977, 1st prize Nat. Outdoor Travel Film Festival, 1978, 1st pl. Houston Film Festival, 1982, CINE Golden Eagle, 1982, award Am. Film Festival, 1982, N.Y. Film Festival, 1982; others. Mem. Info. Film Producers Am. (nat. dir.; pres. chpt. 1981-82; Cindy award 1971, 72, 81, 82), Assn. Ind. Video and Film Producers, Internat. Quorum Motion Picture Producers, Women in Communications. Republican. Quaker. Home: Star Route Chaplin CT 06235 Office: Aetna Life & Casualty Co Creative Services-Corp Communications 151 Farmington Ave Hartford CT 06115

WOODARD, BARBARA HELEN THOMAS, govt. ofcl.; b. Havana, Ill., May 31, 1944; d. Robert Lee and Alta Mae (Johnson) Thomas; student U. Nev., part-time, 1974—, Clark County Community Coll., part-time, 1973—. With AEC, Las Vegas, Nev., 1968—, (name changed to Energy Research and Devel. Adminstrn., 1975, Dept. of Energy, 1977—), adminstrv. asst. to dep. mgr., part-time mgr., 1977—. Mem. Nuclear Emergency Search Team, 1978—; vol. So. Nev. Meml. Hosp., Las Vegas. Mem. Fed. Women's Program Adv. Council, 1974-75. Recipient High Quality Achievement award U.S. Dept. Energy, 1979, also Superior Job Performance award, 1981. Democrat. Roman Catholic. Office: PO Box 14100 Las Vegas NV 89114

WOODARD, CAROL JANE, educator; b. Buffalo, Jan. 19, 1929; d. Harold August and Violet Maybelle (Landsittel) Young; B.A., Hartwick Coll., 1950; M.A., Syracuse U., 1952; Ph.D., State U. N.Y. at Buffalo, 1972, postgrad. Bank St. Coll., 1976, Harvard U., 1977; m. Ralph Arthur Woodard, Aug. 19, 1950; children—Camaron Jane, Carsen Jane, Cooper Ralph. Tchr., Orchard Park, N.Y., 1950-51, Danville, Ind., 1951-52, Akron, N.Y., 1952-54, Amherst (N.Y.) Coop. Nursery Sch., 1967-69; dir. Garden Nursery Sch., Williamsville, N.Y., 1955-65; asst. prof. early childhood edn. State U. Coll. at Buffalo, 1969-72, lab. demonstration tchr. and student teaching supr., 1969-76, asso. prof., 1972-79, prof., 1979—; cons. Lutheran Ch. Am., Villa Maria Coll., Headstart Tng. Programs, Niagara Falls (N.Y.) Pre-Sch. Program, numerous workshops. Mem. alumni bd. dirs. Hartwick Coll., Oneonta, 1976, 1977, trustee, 1978—; cons. civic orgns. in child care. Recipient faculty grant State U. N.Y., 1974-75, Shield grant, 1977; certified tchr., N.Y. Mem. Nat. Assn. Edn. Young Children, Early Childhood Edn. Council Western N.Y., Assn. Childhood Edn. Internat., Pi Lambda Theta, Phi Delta Kappa. Author 7 books for young children, 2 textbooks, in field; co-author nat. curriculum for ch. sch. for 3 yr-olds; author booklet for parents: You Can Help Your Baby Learn; contbr. numerous articles in field to profl. jours. Home: 1776 Sweet Rd E Aurora NY 14052 Office: State U Coll 1300 Elmwood Ave Bacon Hall #301 Buffalo NY 14222

WOODARD, DOROTHY MARIE, ins. broker; b. Houston, Feb. 7, 1932; d. Gerald Edgar and Bessie Katherine (Crain) Floeck; student N.Mex. State U., 1950; m. June 19, 1950 (dec.). Partner, Western Oil Co., Tucumcari, N.Mex., 1950—; owner, mgr. Woodard & Co., Las Cruces, N.Mex., 1959-67; agt., dist. mgr. United Nations Ins. Co., Denver, 1968-74; agt. Western Nat. Life Ins. Co., Amarillo, Tex., 1976—. Exec. dir. Tucumcari Indsl. Commn., 1979—; dir. Bravo Dome Study Com., 1979—; regional bd. dirs. N.Mex., Eastern Plains Council Govts., 1979—, Resource Conservation and Devel., El llana Estacado, 1980—; panel mem. N.Mex. R.R. Planning Conf., 1981. Mem. N.Mex. Indsl. Devel. Execs. Assn., Tucumcari C. of C. Club: Mesa Country. Home: PO Box 823 Tucumcari NM 88401 Office: PO Box 1003 Tucumcari NM 88401

WOODARD, ELAINE MARIE, antique store exec.; b. Denver, Oct. 10, 1924; d. Victor Eugene and Alsina May (Smith) Leroy; student U. Minn., 1944; B.S., U. Colo., 1947; M.A., Adams State Coll., 1969; m. John Marold Woodard, June 6, 1948; children—Victoria, Tom, Jim. Tchr., Alamosa (Colo.) High Sch., 1947-48; ct. reporter 12th Jud. Dist., Colo., 1953-54; tchr.'s aide public schs., Saguache, Colo., 1966-67, elem. tchr. Mountain Valley Sch., 1967-72; sec., bookkeeper Family Health Services, Center, Colo., 1972-73, adminstrv. asst., 1973-74, adminstr., 1974-75; bookkeeper Saguache Health Clinic, 1975-77; owner, operator Hay-Sled Heritage, Villa Grove, Colo., 1977—. Sec., bd. dirs. Saguache County Mus., 1959—; mem. Saguache County Housing Authority, 1977-79; sec. bd. dirs. No. Saguache County Fire Protection Dist., 1978—. Recipient Spl. Recognition award Center Soil Conservation Dist., 1972. Mem. San Luis Valley Hist. Soc., Chaffee County Bd. Realtors. Clubs: Fortnightly of Saguache, Order Eastern Star, Alpha Phi. Home and Office: PO Box 285 Villa Grove CO 81155

WOODARD, SUSAN JEANNE, pianist, ednl. adminstr., educator; b. Mineola, N.Y., Aug. 31, 1945; d. Robert Allen and Jeanne Lucy (Wilhelm) W.; student Eastman Sch. Music, 1963-65; B.A., Adelphi U., 1967; M.M., Ohio State U., 1973, D.M.A., 1982. Teaching asso. Ohio State U., 1968-69, teaching asst., 1972-77; music dir. Brookville (N.Y.) Sch., 1969-72; vis. asst. prof. piano Lawrence U., 1977-78, 79-81, asst. dir. admission, conservatory counselor, 1981—; numerous piano recitals, radio and TV performances; adjudicator; condr. master classes; fellow Tanglewood, 1967; mem. Columbus Symphony Orch. Women's Unit, 1976-78; performer Wis. Women in Arts, 1978; Bechstein Restoration performer Outagamie Hist. Soc., 1980, 81. Ohio rep. Fund For Animals, 1972-77; active Am. Diabetes Assn., 1981—. Recipient Samuel Moritz prize in piano Adelphi U., 1966, 67; Lawrence U. research grantee, summer 1980; cert. tchr. secondary music, N.Y. State, Ohio, Wis. Mem. Wis. Music Tchrs. Assn., Coll. Music Soc., AAUP, Delta Omicron, Pi Kappa Lambda, Phi Kappa Phi, Sigma Kappa. Episcopalian. Research on applications of Stanislawski principles. Office: PO Box 599 Appleton WI 54911

WOODARD, WILMA CUMMINGS, state legislator; b. Angier, N.C., Nov. 18, 1934; d. C. Claud and Lutheria (Searcy) Cummings; student U. N.C., Chapel Hill; B.A., N.C. State U., 1969; m. Warden Lewis Woodard, Jr., Mar. 17, 1952; children—Mary Ellen Nixon, Warden Lewis, Albert Searcy, Richard Allen. Mem. N.C. Ho. Reps., 1978, 79-80, 81—; treas. Wake County Democratic Com., 1977. Mem., Democratic Women of Wake County, Wake Women's Polit. Caucus; vice-pres. Wake County PTA Council, 1977; vice-chmn. Garner Planning and Zoning Bd.; mem. Raleigh-Wake Land Use Code Com., 1977; mem. adv. bd. Wake County CETA, 1977; mem. adv. bd. N.C. Student Legislature, 1980; mem. adv. commn. N.C. State Mus. Natural History, 1979; mem. Task Force on Employment, N.C. White Ho. Conf. on Aging, 1980; mem. State-wide Child Abuse and Neglect Prevention Advocacy Com., 1980; bd. dirs. Raleigh-Wake Urban League, Wake County Kidney Council. Mem. N.C. State U. Alumni Assn. (dir. 1974-81), Garner C. of C., Nat. Order Women Legislators, Womens Forum (dir. 1980), Phi Kappa Phi. United Methodist. Office: NC Ho Reps State Capital Raleigh NC 27602

WOODBRIDGE, ANNIE SMITH, library researcher; b. Wingo, Ky., July 7, 1915; d. Ernest Herbert and Flora Susan (Parrish) Smith; B.A., Murray State Coll., 1935; M.A., Peabody Coll., 1936; postgrad. U. Wis., Tex. State Coll. for Women, U. Ky., Sorbonne, Universidad Interamericana; m. Hensley C. Woodbridge, Aug. 28, 1953; 1 dau., Ruby Susan Woodbridge Jung. Tchr. Cadiz High Sch., 1936-37, David Lipscomb Coll., 1937-43, Bethel Coll., 1943-46, Murray State Coll., 1946-54, 59-65; instr. So. Ill. U., Carbondale, 1966-74, researcher Morris Library, 1974—. Mem. NOW, Midwest Latin Am. Studies Assn., Ellen Glasgow Soc., Soc. Study of Midwestern Lit. Democrat. Mem. Ch. of Christ. Editor: (with others) Collected Short Stories of Mary Johnston; contbr. articles jours and newsletters. Home: 1804 W Freeman St Carbondale IL 62901 Office: Morris Library Southern Illinois University Carbondale IL 62901

WOODBURN, MARION RUTH, coll. counselor; b. Tustin, Mich., Apr. 13, 1919; d. Franklin H. and Louisa B. (McDonald) Thompson; B.A., Mich. State U., 1942; certificate Primary and Secondary Tchr., Wayne State U., 1958, M.Ed., 1966; m. Richard B. Woodburn, Dec. 25, 1941; children—Richard F., R. Jeffrey. Reporter The Daily Tribune, Royal Oak, Mich., 1937-41; asst. personnel dir. N.A. Woodworth Co., Ferndale, Mich., 1942-44; sales and office mgr. World Ins. Co., Detroit, 1945-47; tchr. Berkley (Mich.) Elementary Schs., 1958-65; tchr. Warren (Mich.) High Sch., 1966-67; prof./counselor Macomb Community Coll., Warren, 1967—, mem. adv. bd. Community Resource Center. Sec., tchr. v.p. PTA, Berkley, 1955-66. Mem. Am. Assn. Higher Edn., Nat. (treas. 1978 ann. conf.), Mich. (editor Newsletter 1978-80, exec. bd. 1976-80) assns. women deans, adminstrs. and counselors, Am., Mich. coll. personnel assns., Am. Assn. Community and Jr. Colls., Am., Mich. (counselor licensing com.), Macomb County personnel and guidance assns., Mich. Assn. Specialists in Group Work, Mich. Vocat. Guidance Assn., Am. Ednl. Research Assn., NEA (life), Mich. State Alumni Assn., Wayne State Alumni Assn. Contbr. articles to profl. jours. Office: 14500 Twelve Mile Rd Warren MI 48093

WOODBURY, ELEANOR ATKINSON, physician; b. Tilton, N.H., June 25, 1920; s. Bert Palmer and Mary Frances (Smith) Atkinson; B.S., U. N.H., 1942; M.D., U. Rochester, 1946; m. William Walter Woodbury, Dec. 30, 1944; 1 son, Jonathan Hale. Intern, resident in internal medicine Rochester Gen. Hosp., 1946-49, now practice medicine, sr. attending staff; practice medicine specializing in internal medicine, 1950—; teaching staff U. Rochester Med. Sch., 1949-50. Mem. N.Y. State Med. Soc., Am. Soc. Internal Medicine, Rochester Acad. Medicine, U.S. Ski Assn., Meml. Art Gallery, Am. Soc. Archeology. Club: Nordic Ski. Office: 425 Titus Ave Rochester NY 14617

WOODFOLK, PATRICIA VIOLA BLAND, govt. ofcl.; b. Richmond, Va., May 7, 1947; d. Fenton Lee and Virginia (Bouldin) Bland; B.A. in Econs., Va. State U., 1969; M.A., Central Mich. U., 1982; m. Roland Thomas Woodfolk, Nov. 28, 1968; 1 dau., Tomicia Musette. Personnel mgmt. specialist U.S. Mil. Acad., 1972-76; position classification specialist U.S. Army, Mil. Dist. Wash., 1976-78; personnel specialist Exec. Office of President, 1968—; seminar leader, 1968—. Mem. Nat. Assn. Female Execs., Classification and Compensation Soc., Internat. Personnel Mgmt. Assn., Blacks in Govt., NAACP, Nat. Council Negro Women, Nat. Urban League, Va. State U. Alumni Assn. Home: 4981 Landover Ct Woodbridge VA 22193 Office: Room 4013 New Exec Office Bldg 17th and Pennsylvania Ave Washington DC 20503

WOODHOUSE, ROSSALIND YVONNE, state ofcl.; b. Detroit, June 7, 1940; d. Allen P. and Pereditha E. (Wright) Venable; B.A. in Sociology, U. Wash., 1963, M.S.W., 1970; m. Donald Woodhouse, July 19, 1958; children—Joycelyn, Justin. Program coordinator New Careers Project, Seattle, 1968; community orgn. specialist Seattle Housing Authority, 1969-70; exec. dir. Central Area Motivation Program, Seattle, 1971-73; instr./coordinator Edmonds Community Coll., Lynnwood, Wash., 1973-77; dir. Wash. State Dept. Licensing, Olympia, 1977—; adv. Nat. Accident Sampling System Com.; mem. Wash. State Minority and Women Bus. Enterprise Council; mem. states' task force U.S. Consumer Product Safety Commn. Pres. Seattle Women's Commn., 1971-72, 75-76. Recipient service award Iota Phi Lambda, 1979; named one of Ten Outstanding Young Women of Am., 1978; Nat. Fellowship Fund. fellow, 1976-77. Mem. Am. Assn. Motor Vehicle Adminstrs. (pres. western region), N.W. Conf. Black Public Ofcls. (pres. 1979—), Wash. State Black Women Caucus, NAACP, Urban League, Alpha Kappa Alpha. Democrat. Office: Dept Licensing Olympia WA 98504

WOODHULL, NANCY JANE, newspaper editor; b. Perth Amboy, N.J., Mar. 1, 1945; d. Harold and Mertie May Cromwell; student Trenton (N.J.) State Coll., 1963-64; m. William D. Watson, Sept. 24, 1976; 1 dau., Jane Cromwell Watson. Reporter, editor News, Tribune, Woodbridge, N.J., 1964-72; reporter Detroit Free Press, 1973-75; mng. editor Times-Union, Rochester, N.Y., 1979-80, Democrat and Chronicle, Rochester, 1980-82; mng. editor News, U.S.A. Today, Washington, 1982—. Recipient numerous awards N.J. Newspaperwoman's Assn. Mem. Am. Soc. Newspaper Editors, AP Mng. Editors Assn. Office: USA Today Box 500 Washington DC 20044

WOOD-PRINCE, ELEANOR, civic worker; b. Cin., Jan. 25; d. Edward William and Eleanor May (Zimmerman) Edwards; student L'Hermitage, Versailles, France, 1930, Sorbonne, 1930-31; m. William Henry Wood-Prince, Nov. 2, 1940; children—Alain de Ricou, William Norman, Edward Alexander. Vice pres. women's bd., head emergency ward Wesley Meml. Hosp., Chgo., 1953-54; pres. Alliance Francaise, Chgo., 1970; mem. women's bd. U. Chgo., 1976; trustee Chgo. Symphony Assn., 1977; mem. com. of old masters Art Inst. Chgo., 1973; mem. women's bd. Rehab. Inst. Chgo., 1974. Recipient Legion of Merit award French Govt., 1970; Harvard award Chgo. Harvard Club, 1975; Merit award Cliff Hangers, Chgo., 1976; Pucci award Chgo. Wedgewood Soc., 1977. Republican. Christian Scientist. Clubs: Arts, Casino (Chgo.); River (N.Y.C.). Home: 2430 Lakeview Ave Chicago IL 60614

WOODRING, CAROLE LYN, psychologist; b. State College, Pa., Nov. 7, 1945; d. Charles Elmer and Helen Pauline W.; B.A., Pa. State U., 1967; M.A., Columbia U., 1969; m. Eric Marvin Berg, May 30, 1970; children—Nicole Leslie Woodring, Adam Trevor Woodring, Jessica Lynne Woodring. Foster caseworker Dauphin County Child Care Agy., Harrisburg, Pa., 1967-68; personnel asst. dir. Conf. Bd., Inc., N.Y.C., 1969-70; mgr. tng. design and validation Chem. Bank N.Y. Trust Inc., N.Y.C., 1970-73; tng. cons. 1st Union Corp., Charlotte, N.C., 1978-79; adj. prof. Sacred Heart Coll., Belmont, N.C., 1978-80; dir., officer Fortune Cons., 1977—; pvt. cons., Matthews, N.C., 1979—; pres. J.N. Adams & Assos., 1982—. Trustee, Charlotte Montessori Sch., 1980—, pres., 1981—. Mem. Assn. for Psychol. Type, AAUW (past dir.), Am. Psychol. Assn. (asso), Sigma Sigma Sigma (past chpt. pres.). Presbyterian. Home: 2416 Beaucatcher Ln Matthews NC 28105 Office: 5527 Monroe Rd Charlotte NC 28212

WOODRING, PATRICIA ANN, fgn. service officer, diplomat; b. Oakland, Calif., Dec. 1, 1939; d. Loel Steven and Bertha Emilia (Giese) W.; B.A., U. Paris, Sorbonne, 1959, postgrad., 1975, 76-77; m. Robert Silber McGowan, Sept. 5, 1976. Internat. trust investment officer Irving Trust Co., N.Y.C., 1959-61; market research analyst Corning Glass Works, N.Y.C., 1961-63; with U.S. Dept. State, Fgn. Service, 1963—, fgn. service officer for internat. affairs Bur. Internat. Orgns., Washington, from 1972; now with NATO, Brussels, Belgium; guest lectr. internat. affairs colls. and univs. Mem. Am. Fgn. Service Assn. (1st woman pres. 1976-77), Nat. Assn. Female Execs., Women's Action Orgn., Aircraft Owners and Pilots Assn. Lutheran. Address: US NATO APO New York NY 09667 *

WOODRUFF, GEORGIA DELORES (WILBUR), nursing edn. adminstr.; b. Port Arthur, Tex., Mar. 31, 1926; d. Clarence Nelson and Gertrude Alice (Sewell) Wilbur; diploma St. Mary's Hosp. Sch. Nursing, 1948; A.A., Lamar Coll., 1947; m. James Calvin Woodruff, Sept. 27, 1957. Staff nurse various hosps. in Tex. and Ariz., 1948-61; nurse, Park Place Hosp., Port Arthur, Tex., 1961-65; dir. of nurses Newton County (Tex.) Hosp., 1966-67; dir. Home Health Assistance, Inc., Kirbyville, Tex., 1967-71; dir. Home Health-Home Care, Newton, Tex., 1972-76; inservice edn. dir. Mary Dickerson Hosp., Jasper, Tex., 1976—. Mem. Am., Tex. nurses assns., Nat. League Nurses. Democrat. Mem. Pentecostal Ch. Home: 511 Mays St Jasper TX 75951 Office: Mary Dickerson Hospital 1001 Dickerson Dr Jasper TX 75951

WOODRUM, PATRICIA ANN, librarian; b. Hutchinson, Kans., Oct. 11, 1941; d. Donald Jewell and Ruby Pauline (Shuman) Hoffman; B.A. in Lit., Kans. State Coll., Pittsburgh, 1963; M.L.S., U. Okla., 1966; m. Clayton Eugene Woodrum, Mar. 31, 1962; 1 son, Clayton Eugene, II. Mem. staff Tulsa City-County Library, 1964—, asst. dir., 1973-76, dir., 1976—. Bd. dirs. Downtown Tulsa Unlimited, 1976—; mem. Tulsa Area Council Aging, 1974—. Mem. ALA, Public Library Assn. (dir.), Southwestern Library Assn. (exec. bd.), Okla. Library Assn. (past pres.), Tulsa Area Library Coop. (steering com.). Home: 214 E 24th Pl Tulsa OK 74114 Office: 400 Civic Center Tulsa OK 74103

WOODS, DELMA MARIA, psychol. cons.; b. N.Y.C., June 11; d. Edmund and Maria Williams (Tucker) Prioleau; B.S., Howard U., 1962, M.S., 1971; postgrad. George Washington U., 1969, 72, Washington Sch. Psychiatry, 1970, Children's Hosp. Nat. Center for Learning Studies, 1972; m. Roy Woods, Mar. 17, 1974; children—Roy Woods, Edmund Prioleau, Delma Maria Delia. Tchr. children with Downs Syndrome, Washington, 1965; tchr. emotionally disturbed children D.C. Public Schs., 1964-66, clin. psychologist Head Start program, 1969, psychol. cons., 1973, psychologist, 1976-78, 67-74; psychologist Dade County (Fla.) Schs., 1974-76; psychol. cons. to physician, Charleston, S.C., 1979—; staff devel. chairperson, dept. pupil personnel services D.C. Schs., 1971-74; guardian-ad-litem for neglected and abused children, Charleston, 1979, 80; coordinator The Health Line, Radio Sta. WPAI, Charleston; membership chairperson Charleston County Multidisciplinary Com. on Child Abuse and Neglect, 1978-79; organizer, Statehood Party, Washington, 1972-73 bd. dirs. Pam Robinson Contemporary Sch. Performing Arts. Recipient Achievement award Washington Sch. Psychiatry, 1972, Children's Hosp. Nat. Center, 1973. Mem. Am. Psychol. Assn., D.C. Psychol. Assn., Nat. Assn. Sch. Psychologists (award for research on intelligence and creativity 1973), D.C. Assn. Sch. Psychologists, Nat. Assn. Black Psychologists, AAAS, Charleston County Med. Soc. Aux., Palmetto Med. Soc. Aux., Jack & Jill Am., Inc., Psi Chi, Alpha Kappa Alpha (youth leadership com. 1979-80, co-chairperson health edn. com. 1979-80). Democrat. African Methodist Episcopal. Home: 1106 Woodhaven Dr Charleston SC 29407 Office: 19 Hagood Ave Suite 901 Charleston SC 29403

WOODS, DEMETRIOUS LOVELL, univ. purchasing agt.; b. Chgo., Sept. 8, 1946; d. Percy and Christine (Hannibal) Harmon; student U. Ill., Navy Pier, 1964-65, U. Ill., Chgo., 1965-66, 73-75, Chgo. State U., 1978—; m. Melvin Woods, July 24, 1965; children—Lance, Velicia Dawn. Acctg. clk. U. Ill. Chgo. Circle Campus, 1966-76; asst. purchasing agt. Chgo. State U., 1977-79, purchasing agt., 1979—; minority vendors rep. Ill. Dept. Commerce and Community Affairs, Chgo. Bus. Opportunity Fair. Corr. sec., fund raiser West Chatham Little League, 1970-75; active tape ministry and women's fellowship Trinity United Ch. Christ, 1981—. Cert. Nat. Inst. Govtl. Purchasing. Mem. Nat. Assn. Ednl. Buyers, Ill. Ednl. Consortium (purchasing adv. council). Democrat. Club: Chgo. State U. Women's (treas. 1979-80, rec. sec. 1980-81, cert. of appreciation 1980). Mem. subcom. to revise govt. procurement in state univ. systems in Ill. Home: 9126-28 S Wallace Chicago IL 60620 Office: 95th St at King Dr Chicago IL 60628

WOODS, GEORGIA B., banker; b. Millville, Ky., Aug. 12, 1918; d. William Preston and Lillie Mae (Lewis) Shelton; student Am. Inst. Banking, 1970, 71, 75, Ky. Sch. Banking, 1966-67; m. Carl Jackson Woods, Oct. 22, 1956; children—Danny Thomas, Steve Carroll, Patricia Neal. Bookkeeper, Farmers Deposit Bank, Eminence, Ky., 1960-62; teller, asst. cashier Citizens Bank, New Castle, Ky., 1962-71, cashier, 1971-74, v.p., cashier, 1974-75; v.p., cashier United Citizens Bank & Trust Co., New Castle, 1975—. Chmn. Henry County Arthritis Found., 1970—; bd. dirs. Ky. Arthritis Found., 1974—. Mem. Nat. Assn. Bank Women (pres. Louisville group 1974-75), Ky. Bankers Assn. (pres. group V 1978-79), Ky. Col. Assn. Democrat. Baptist. Home: Route 1 Smithfield KY 40068 Office: United Citizens Bank Trust Main St New Castle KY 40050

WOODS, GLORIA JEAN SUGGS, ednl. personnel adminstr.; b. Durham, N.C., Dec. 19, 1948; d. George Lee and Clarice (Cassidy) Suggs; B.A., N.C. Central U., 1971; M.A., Howard U., 1972; adminstrv. and supr. cert. Prairie View A&M U., 1982; postgrad. in edn. Tex. So. U., 1982—; m. Arthur Allen Woods, July 3, 1976. Tchr., Bd. Edn. Norwalk (Conn.), 1973-76; tchr. North Forest Ind. Sch. Dist., Houston, 1976-80, adminstrn. asst. for asst. supt. personnel, 1980—. Mem. Assn. Supervision and Curriculum Devel., Tex. Assn. Sch. Personnel Adminstrs., Nat. Assn. Female Execs., Tex. Assn. Sch. Personnel Adminstrs., Tex. State Tchr. Assn. (faculty rep. 1978-80, conv. del. 1978-80, Outstanding Faculty Rep. 1980). Democrat. Baptist. Office: 10721 Mesa Dr PO Box 23278 Houston TX 77078

WOODS, HARRIETT, state senator; b. Cleve., June 2, 1927; student U. Chgo. Coll.; B.A., U. Mich., 1949; m. James B. Woods, Jan. 2, 1953; 3 children. Newspaper reporter, St. Louis; producer TV sta., St. Louis; mem. Mo. Senate, 1976—; mem. Mo. State Hwy. Commn., Mo. State Transp. Commn., Active University City (Mo.) Council, Nat. League of Cities, Mo. Mcpl. League, St. Louis County Mcpl. League, LWV, civic orgns. St. Louis and University City, St. Louis TV Acad. Democrat. Office: Missouri State House Jefferson City MO 65101

WOODS, KATHY MCCLANAHAN, investment exec.; b. Indpls., Mar. 17, 1952; d. R.M. and Ruth (Strand) McClanahan; B.S., Ball State U., Muncie, Ind., 1974. Asst. dir. admissions Tri-State U., Angola, Ind., 1974-77; sales account exec. sta. WISH-TV, Indpls., 1977-79; prin. distbr. Woman's Learning Center, Indpls., 1978—; account exec. Slade-Best Advt. Agy., Indpls., 1979-80; investment exec. Shearson, Loeb, Rhoades, Indpls., 1980-82; account exec. Dean Witter Reynolds, Inc., Indpls., 1982—. Mem. Nat. Soc. Fin. Analysts, Security Traders Assn., Bond Club Indpls., Women in Communications, Am. Assn. Coll. Admissions Counselors, Mid-West Fin. Aid Assn., Ad Club Indpls. (instr.), Ball State U. Alumnae Assn. (v.p., chmn. publicity 1977-80), Kappa Alpha Theta (v.p. 1980-81, chmn. Santa's House 1977—). Republican. Presbyterian. Club: Job's Daus. Home: 600 N Alabama St Penthouse 2900 Indianapolis IN 46204 Office: One Indiana Sq Indianapolis IN 46204

WOODS, MARGARET BRAUER, former chem. co. exec.; b. Bolivar, Pa., Dec. 24, 1931; d. Francis J. and Elizabeth (Long) Brauer; student public schs. Bolivar, Pa.; m. George L. Woods, July 26, 1952. With SRS, Inc., Linden, N.J., 1949-82, controller, 1971-82, sec.-treas., 1973-82, sec. treas. RaySolv, Inc. subs., Piscataway, N.J., 1975-82. Mem. Linden Adv. Group, 1970-75. Mem. Am. Mgmt. Assn. Republican. Methodist: Home: 376 Midway Ave Fanwood NJ 07023 Office: 1200 Sylvan St Linden NJ 07036

WOODS, MARGARET FARMAN, civic worker; b. Holyoke, Mass., May 24, 1944; d. Robert Burton and Helen Margaret (Magill) Farman; R.N., Holyoke Hosp. Sch. Nursing, 1965; B.A. in Art History, Mt. Holyoke Coll., 1969; m. Gill Woods; children—E.G., Aaron. Mem. Holyoke Model Cities Policy Bd., 1971-74; fund raising chmn. Am. Heart Assn., 1978, bd. dirs., 1976-78; active, public TV auction WGBY, 1975-82, community chmn., 1975-76, county chmn., 1977-78; bd. dirs. Jr. League Holyoke, 1970-72, pres., 1978-79, mem. Mass. public affairs com., 1979-80; bd. dirs. Holyoke Hosp. Aid Assn., 1978—, follies chmn., 1980-81; bd. dirs. United Way of Holyoke, South Hadley and Granby, 1976-82, v.p., 1982; pres. Greater Holyoke chpt. Mt. Holyoke Coll. Alumnae Assn., 1974-77, Nat. Alumnae Scholarship chmn., 1979-82, v.p., 1982-85; bd. dirs. Mt. Tom Ski Area, 1982—; mem. area 1 nominating com. Assn. Jr. Leagues, 1981-83.

WOODS, NANCY ROSE, film producer, realty exec.; Boston, Nov. 24, 1932; s. John James and Belle (Singer) Worswick; student public schs.; m. Alvin M. Roselin, Nov. 3, 1957; children—Phillip, Jonathan, Joel, Stephan. Fashion cons. Catalina, Inc., Boston, 1955-57; prodn. mgr. sunnybrook Sportswear, N.Y.C., 1957-59; asst. editor Printing News, N.Y.C., 1966-76; v.p. Planned Communication Services, N.Y.C., 1976—; pres. Nanal Realty, Spring Valley, N.Y., 1977—; seminar leader in field. Recipient Bronze award Internat. Film Festival, 1981. Home: 4 Lomond Ave Spring Valley NY 10977 Office: 12 E 46th St New York NY 10017

WOODS, PATRICIA ANN, microbiologist; b. Akron, Ohio, Aug. 25, 1953; d. Theodore Nathaniel and Marion Henrietta (Albert) Woods; A.A., Glendale Community Coll., 1974; B.S. in Microbiology, U. Ariz., 1975. Microbiologist, U.S. Dept. Health and Human Services, Centers for Disease Control, Hepatitis Labs., Phoenix, 1976—, mgr. fed. women's program hepatitis lab., 1980. Leader Girl Scouts U.S.A., 1979-81; sec. Fed. Women's Program Interagy. Council, 1981-82. Mem. Am. Soc. Microbiology, Am. Soc. Med. Tech., Ariz. Med. Lab. Assn. (Lawrence Jessop Meml. award for microbiology 1974; pres. 1980). Republican. Clubs: United Fedn. of Doll Clubs. Home: 7734 N 34th Ave Phoenix AZ 85021 Office: 4402 N 7th St Phoenix AZ 85014

WOODS, PHYLLIS KAREN, drycleaning co. exec.; b. Chgo., June 15, 1938; d. Phillip Emery and Mildred Emily (Anderson) Sharrar; student Lindenwood Coll., 1956-57, Silliman U., Philippines, 1957-58; B.S., Carroll Coll., 1960; div.; children—Phillip Howard, Kathryn Sue. Personnel mgr. Glens Falls Ins., Chgo., 1960-64; personnel and office mgr. Artistic Cleaners, Lake Station, Ind., 1965-69, vice-pres., 1969-77, pres., 1977—; mem. adv. bd. Apparelmaster, Cin. Met. div. campaign chmn. Lake Area United Way, 1980, bd. dirs., 1980—, vice-chmn., 1981, chmn. planning and allocation com., 1982. Mem. Internat. Fabricare Inst., Ind. State Drycleaners and Laundry Assn. (dir., v.p. 1977, pres. 1978), Women in Laundry and Drycleaning (treas.). Presbyterian (elder). Club: Altrusa. Home: 725 W 67th Ln Merrillville IN 46410 Office: 2316 Ripley St Lake Station IN 46405

WOODS, SUSAN LERCH, educator; b. Battle Creek, Mich., Oct. 11, 1951; d. Robert Connor and Joretta (Colombo) Lerch; B.S., U. Ill., 1974, M.S., 1976; m. Raymond L. Woods, Sept. 1, 1973; 1 dau., Jennifer, Micjele. Instr. health edn. Eastern Ill. U., Charleston, 1976—; speaker workshop leader in field. Coordinator Coles County Women Against Rape, 1978—. Recipient Outstanding Faculty Service award Eastern Ill. U., 1979, Outstanding Faculty Teaching award, 1981. Mem. Sex Edn. and Info. Council, Ill. Public Health Assn., Ill. Council Family Relations. Home: 1614 Jackson St Charleston IL 61920 Office: 174 Lantz Bldg Charleston IL 61920

WOODS, SUSANNE, educator; b. Honolulu, May 12, 1943; d. Samuel Ernest and Gertrude (Cullom) W.; B.A. in Polit. Sci., UCLA, 1964, M.A. in English, 1965; Ph.D. in English and Comparative Lit. (Woodrow Wilson fellow 1968-70), Columbia U., 1970; M.A. (hon.), Brown U., 1978. Asst. editor Rand Corp., Calif., 1963-65; instr. Ventura (Calif.) Coll., 1965-66; lectr. CUNY, 1967-69; asst. prof. U. Hawaii, 1969-72; asst. prof. Brown U., Providence, 1972-77, asso. prof. English, 1977—; vis. asso. prof. U. Calif., 1981-82. Active various polit. campaigns, 1960-64, 68-76; mem. staff Senator Daniel K. Inouye, 1963. Bronson fellow, 1976; Huntington Library fellow, 1979-80, 81; Clark Library fellow, 1981. Mem. MLA (chmn. div. Seventeenth Century English lit., 1982), N.E. MLA (chmn. English Renaissance sect. 1978), Renaissance Soc. Am., Milton Soc., Spenser Soc., Alpha Gamma Delta. Democrat. Episcopalian. Club: Athenaeum (Pasadena, Calif.). Author: English Versification, 1983; contbr. numerous articles to profl. jours.; reviewer for various profl. jours. including Renaissance Quar., Jour. of English and Germanic Philology; reader for PMLA jour. Office: Box 1852 Brown Univ Providence RI 02912

WOODSIDE, LISA NICOLE, univ. adminstr.; b. Portland, Oreg., Sept. 7, 1944; d. Lee and Emma (Wenstrom) W.; student Reed Coll., 1962-65; M.A., U. Chgo., 1968; Ph.D. (Am. Assn. Papyrology grantee, S. Maude Kaemmerling fellow), Bryn Mawr Coll., 1972; cert. Harvard U. Inst. for Ednl. Mgmt., 1979; m. John S. Bilinski, Jr., June 8, 1973. Mem. dean's staff Bryn Mawr Coll., 1970-72; asst. prof. Widener U., Chester, Pa., 1972-77, asso. prof. humanities, 1978—, asst. dean student services, 1972-76, asso. dean, 1976-79, dean, 1979, asst. v.p., 1980—; accreditor Commn. on Higher Edn., Middle States Assn., 1979—. Active ARC, 1973—; city commr. for community relations Chester, 1980—. Mem. Am. Assn. Higher Edn., Am. Assn. Collegiate Registrars and Admissions Officers, Nat. Assn. Student Personnel Adminstrs., Nat. Assn. Women Deans, Adminstrs. and Counselors, Pa. Assn. Women Deans, Adminstrs. and Counselors, Nat. Assn. Fgn. Student Advisors, AAUW (univ. rep. 1975—), Phi Eta Sigma. Episcopalian. Club: Am. Fox Terrier. Home: 217 Avondale Rd Wallingford PA 19086 Office: Widener Univ Chester PA 19013

WOODS-JONES, DEZIE DELL, coll. adminstr.; b. Ruston, La., Nov. 11, 1941; d. Roy Mayfield and Tena (Lowery) Woods; student Fresno City Coll., 1959-61, Fresno State Coll., 1962-64, U. Calif. at Berkeley, 1971; 1 son, Robert Elroy. Supr. for community relations and spl. community task force Park Job Corps Center, Pleasanton, Calif., 1964-66; dir. Merrit Coll. North Oakland (Calif.) Devel. Center, 1968-70; coordinator community services North Perlata Community Coll., Oakland, 1970—; dir. student activities Coll. of Alameda, 1975—; dir. govtl. affairs Perlata Coll. Dist., 1980—. Community organizer Congress Racial Equality, San Francisco, 1964-67; nat. fund raising chmn., community organizer Student Nonviolent Coordinating Com., Atlanta, 1966-69; chmn. coll. campus United Crusade campaign, Oakland, 1972-73; chmn. Black Women Organized for Polit. Action, 1975—; founder, chair Bay Area Black Women United; mem. legis. com. Council on Black Am. Affairs, 1975-76; mem. Calif. Commn. on Crime Control and Violence Prevention; bd. dirs. Bay Area Black United Fund; active numerous polit. campaigns. Mem. NAACP (pres. 1957-59), Calif. Tchrs. Assn., Perlata Community Coll. Assn., Calif. Community Coll. Community Services Assn., Black Bus. and Profl. Women Assn., Calif. Assn. for Higher Edn., Assn. Calif. Community Coll. Adminstrs. Democrat. Home: 10966 Cliffland Ave Oakland CA 94605

WOODSON, PHYLLIS ANN MCMANAWAY, extension home economist; b. Roanoke, Va., Dec. 14, 1948; d. Charles M. and Zaman (Khan) McManaway; student Radford Coll., 1968-70; B.S. in Human Nutrition, Va. Poly. Inst. and State U., 1972, M.S. in Human Nutrition, 1978; postgrad. Johns Hopkins U., 1975; m. Dillard Davis Woodson, Dec. 15, 1973; 1 dau., Ellen Elizabeth. Cancer researcher, lab. technician Microbiol. Assos., Bethesda, Md., 1972; dietetic extern, dietitian Md. Dept. Health, Balt., 1972-74: substitute tchr. Lawton (Okla.) Public Schs., 1974-75; dietitian Md. Dept. Health, 1975; public health nutritionist Onslow County (N.C.), 1976; extension home economist Okla. State U. Coop. Extension Center, Lawton, 1978-81; home economist Va. Poly. Inst. and State U., 1981-82. instr. nutrition Cameron U., 1979. Bd. dirs. New Directions, Lawton, 1979-81; mem. Quality of Life Outreach Task Force, Ft. Sill, Okla., 1979-81. Mem. Okla. Assn. Extension Home Economists, Am. Dietetic Assn. (registered), Okla. Dietetic Assn., Lawton C. of C., DAR Democrat. Baptist. Clubs: Altrusa Internat. (dir. Lawton 1979-81), Officer Wives (Quantico, Va.); Garden (Camp Le Jeune, N.C.). Contbr. articles on nutrition to profl. jours., to Lawton Constn., Potomac News, 1979-82.

WOODSON, VIRGINIA BURBAGE, shipbuilding and dry dock co. exec.; b. Ft. Eustis, Va., June 16; d. Douglas Johnson and Virginia Parks (Davidson) Burbage; m. Granville Owens Adams, Apr. 6, 1946 (dec. 1974); m. 2d, William Hart Woodson, Nov. 10, 1979 (dec. 1981). Legal sec., sec. to gen. counsel Newport News Shipbuilding and Dry Dock Co. (Va.), 1938-71, asst. sec., corp. sec., 1977—; corp. sec. Newport News Indsl. Corp., Newport News Indsl. Corp. Ohio, Newport News Reactor Services, Inc., Greeneville Metal Mfg., Inc., Newport News Offshore Systems Corp., Asheville Industries, Inc., Newport News Tech. Services, Inc., James River Oyster Corp.; corp. sec., treas. Mariners Mus., Newport News; dir., sec. Newport News Shipbuilding Employees Credit Union. Bd. dirs. Hampton Roads chpt. ARC, 1980—, sec., 1949-55. Mem. PEO, Beta Sigma Phi. Baptist. Club: Soroptimist Internat. Home: 1207 Riverside Dr Newport News VA Office: Newport News Shipbuilding and Dry Dock Co 4101 Washington Ave Newport News VA 23607

WOODSON, WILBERTA, documentation specialist; b. Tecumseh, Nebr., Sept. 7, 1939; d. Charles Wilber and Edith Mildred Woodson; student Coll. of Emporia, 1957-61; B.A., Wichita State U., 1963; M.A., U. Hawaii, 1966; postgrad. U. Conn., 1968, U. Ill., 1969-70; M.S., U. San Francisco, 1981; children— Rebecca Louise. Research asst., computer programmer U. Hawaii, Honolulu, 1964-66; computer programmer Newport News (Va.) Shipbldg., 1967; computer programmer econ. research U. Ill., Urbana, 1969-70; cons. Ventura County Mental Health, Ventura, Calif., 1973-78; tech. writer Mohawk Data Scis., Los Gatos, Calif., 1978-79; sr. tech. writer Tandem Computers, Cupertino, Calif., 1979—. Mem. Nat. Assn. Female Execs., Soc. Tech. Communication. Democrat. Unitarian. Home: 1056 Queensbrook Dr San Jose CA 95129 Office: Tandem Computers 16333 Vallco Pkwy Cupertino CA 95014

WOODWARD, CLAIR DONEY, ednl. adminstr.; b. Franklin, Idaho, Sept. 24, 1928; d. Ivan and Ordel (Doney) W.; B.S. in Music Edn., Utah State U., 1952; M.S. in Secondary Edn. and Music, 1954; Ed.D., U. Colo., 1963; m. Jeri McBride, Aug. 28, 1952; children—Daina, Eric, Nan, April, Annalese, Joel. Dir. instrumental music high schs. in Utah and Nev., 1953-67; asso. prof. music, dir. ind. study and music extension Ind. State U., Terre Haute, 1967—; bd. dirs. Terre Haute Symphony, 1969-71; music adjudicator, 1974—. Served with USAF, 1954-56. Mem. Music Educators Nat. Conf. (div. chmn. 1971-75), Nev. Music Educators Assn. (pres. 1965-67), Nat. U. Continuing Edn. Assn. Mormon. Home: 4430 Alan Dr Terre Haute IN 47802 Office: AC 209 Ind State U Terre Haute IN 47809

WOODWARD, ISABEL AVILA, writer; b. Key West, Fla., Mar. 14, 1906; d. Alfredo and Isabel (Lopez) Avila; student Fla. State Coll. for Women, 1925, A.B. in Edn., 1938; cert. in teaching Spanish, U. Miami, 1961; summer study U. Fla., Eckerd Coll.; postgrad. St. Lawrence U., U. Miami; m. Clyde B. Woodward, June 6, 1944 (dec.); children—Joy Avis Ball, Greer Isabel Woodward Sucke. Tchr., Key West, 1927-42, remedial reading cons., 1941-42; reading tchr., asst. reading lab. and clinic St. Lawrence U., summer 1941; Spanish translator U.S. Office of Censorship, Miami, 1943; tchr. Central Beach Elem. Sch., Miami Beach, Fla., 1943-44, Silver Bluff Elem. Sch., 1943-50, Henry West Lab. Sch., Coral Gables, Fla., 1955-57, Dade Demonstration Sch., Miami, 1957-61; author 125 sch. radio lessons for teaching Spanish, Dade County Elem. Schs., 1961; tchr. Spanish Workshop for Fla.; speaker poetry and short story writing, 1977; guest lectr. on writing the short story Fla. Inst. Tech., Jensen Beach, 1981; freelance writer; contbr. to Listen Mag.,

Sunshine Mag., Lookout Mag., Christian Sci. Monitor, Miami Herald, Three/Four, Child Life, Wee Wisdom, Fla. Wildlife, Young World. Recipient awards for writing Nat. League Am. Pen Women, 1973, 74, 77, Honoris Causa award Alpha Delta Kappa, 1972-74; named one of 5 Outstanding Fla. Tchrs., 1972-74. Mem. Nat. League Am. Pen Women (1st v.p. Greater Miami br. 1974-76, historian 1978—, librarian 1978—), AAUW, Alpha Delta Kappa, Psi Psi Psi. Address: 1950 Palm City Rd Apt 6-301 Stuart FL 33494

WOODWARD, JOANNE GIGNILLIAT, actress; b. Thomasville, Ga., Feb. 27, 1930; d. Wade and Elinor (Trimmier) W.; student La. State U., 1947-49; grad. Neighborhood Playhouse Dramatic Sch., N.Y.C.; m. Paul Newman, Jan. 29, 1958; children—Elinor Terese, Melissa Stewart, Clea Olivia. First TV appearance in Penny, Robert Montgomery Presents, 1952; understudy broadway play Picnic, 1953; appeared in play Baby Want a Kiss, 1964; motion pictures include Three Faces of Eve (Acad. award Best Actress, Nat. Bd. Rev. award, Fgn. Press award), 1957, Count Three and Pray, 1955, Long Hot Summer, 1958, No Down Payment, 1957, Sound and the Fury, 1959, A Kiss Before Dying, 1956, Rally Round the Flag Boys, 1958, The Fugitive Kind, 1960, Paris Blues, 1961, The Stripper, 1963, A New Kind of Love, 1963, A Big Hand for the Little Lady, 1965, A Fine Madness, 1965, Rachel, Rachel, 1968, Winning, 1969, WUSA, 1970, They Might Be Giants, 1971, The Effect of Gamma Rays on Man-in-the-Moon Marigolds (Cannes Film Festival award), 1972, Summer Wishes, Winter Dreams (N.Y. Film Critics award), 1973, The Drowning Pool, 1975, The End, 1978; TV appearances include All the Way Home; TV-film appearances in Sybil, 1976, Come Back, Little Sheba, 1977, See How She Runs (Emmy award), 1978, Streets of L.A., 1979; The Shadow Box, 1980; narrator film documentary Angel Dust. Democrat. Episcopalian. *

WOODWARD, SISTER, M. IRENE, coll. chancellor; b. Laramie, Wyo., Apr. 18, 1933; d. Richard Joseph and Mary Irene (Campbell) W.; B.A., U. So. Calif., 1961; M.A. with distinction, Cath. U. Am., 1963, Ph.D. with distinction, 1967. Joined Sisters of Holy Names; music tchr. St. Elizabeth Sch., Altadena, Calif., 1954-58, Ramona Convent High Sch., Alhambra, Calif., 1958-61; asso. prof. philosophy Holy Names Coll., Oakland, Calif., 1963-72, pres., from 1972, now chancellor. Bd. dirs. Oakland Symphony Assn., 1975—, Jesuit Sch. Theology at Berkeley, 1975-79; mem. nat. adv. council Danforth Found. Assos. Program, 1973-76. Danforth asso., 1968—; Inst. Ednl. Mgmt., Harvard Bus. Sch. grantee, 1973. Mem. Am. Cath. Philos. Soc., Metaphys. Soc. Am., Assn. Ind. Calif. Colls. and Univs. (trustee; exec. com. 1978-82), Ind. Colls. No. Calif. (sec.-treas. 1974-82), Assn. Cath. Colls. and Univs. (dir. 1977-79), Oakland Mus. Assn., Nat. Cath. Edn. Assn. (exec. com. coll. and univ. dept. 1976-79), Regional Assn. East Bay Colls. and Univs. (exec. com., bd. dirs. 1976-82), Western Assn. Schs. and Colls. (exec. com. 1980-82). Editor: The Catholic Church: The United States Experience, 1978. Address: Holy Names Coll Oakland CA 94619

WOODY, ANN LOUISE, social worker; b. St. Louis, Dec. 3, 1946; d. Albert B. and Agnes B. (Wittmann) Ruhl; B.A., U. Mo., Columbia, 1969, M.S.W., 1971; m. Donald Eugene Woody, June 5, 1971; 1 son, Marshall Wittmann. Correctional caseworker Mo. State Tng. Sch. for Boys, Boonville, 1971-72; psychiat. social worker Fulton (Mo.) State Hosp., 1972-73; psychiat. social work supr. Springfield (Mo.) Regional Center, 1973—. Vice chmn., bd. dirs. Springfield Children's Home, SW Mo. Regional Adv. Council for Psychiat. Services; chmn. multi-disciplinary com. Child Adv. Council. NIMH fellow, 1969-71; recipient U. Mo. Curators award, 1965. Mem. Acad. Cert. Social Workers, Nat. Assn. Social Workers, Greene County Assn. Retarded Citizens, Council Exceptional Children, Jr. League. Democrat. Roman Catholic. Home: 3124 E Seminole St Springfield MO 65804 Office: 1515 E Pythian St Springfield MO 65801

WOODY, CAROL CLAYMAN, mfg. co. ofcl; b. Bristol, Va., May 20, 1949; d. George Neal and Ida Mae (Nelms) Clayman; B.S. in Math., Coll. William and Mary, Williamsburg, Va., 1971; M.B.A. with distinction (IBM Corp. fellow 1978, Stephen Bufton Meml. Ednl. Found. grantee 1978-79), Wake Forest U., 1979; m. Robert William Woody, Aug. 19, 1972. Programmer trainee GSA, 1971-72; systems engr. Citizens Fidelity Bank & Trust Co., Louisville, 1972-75; programmer/analyst-tng. coordinator Blue Bell, Inc., Greensboro, N.C., 1975-79; mgr. adminstrv. info. systems and tech. services J.E. Baker Co., York, Pa., 1979-81, mgr. adminstrv. info. systems and tech. services, 1981-82; fin. design supr. Lycoming div. AVCO, Stratford, Conn., 1982—; mem. Data Processing Standards Bd., 1977, CICS/VS Adv. Council, 1975, Health Resources Planning and Devel., 1980—. Bd. dirs. Ruth Gasnell Ednl. Found., 1981—. Mem. Am. Bus. Woman's Assn. (chpt. v.p. 1978-79; Merit award 1978), Nat. Assn. Female Execs., Delta Omicron (alumni pres. 1973-75, regional chmn. 1979—). Republican. Presbyterian. Author various manuals. Home: PO Box 713 Orange CT 06477 Office: 550 S Main St Stratford CT 06497

WOODY, KATHLEEN JOANNA, lawyer; b. Honolulu, May 3, 1949; d. Edward Franklin and Norma Lee (Harris) W.; A.B. magna cum laude, U. Miami, 1973, J.D., 1976; LL.M., Columbia U., 1981. Vice pres., tax cons. Franklin Tax Service, Inc., Silver Spring, Md., 1967-76; real estate agt., sales mgr. Pershing Real Estate Co., Silver Spring, 1972-76; admitted to Fla. bar, 1976, D.C. bar, 1977, U.S. Tax Ct. bar, 1977, U.S. Supreme Ct. bar, 1980; atty. Office Comptroller of Currency, Washington, 1976-78, N.Y.C., 1979-80; mem. faculty New Sch. for Social Research, N.Y.C., 1980; teaching fellow, dir. tng. internat. tax program Harvard Law Sch., 1981-82; mem. faculty Inst. Comparative Law, U. San Diego, 1982; ptnr. firm Woody & Woody, Washington, 1982—. Mem. Internat. Bar Assn., Am. Bar Assn., D.C. Bar Assn., Fed. Bar Assn., Am. Arbitration Assn. (arbitrator), Assn. Bar City N.Y. Baptist. Club: St. Bartholomew's Community (N.Y.C.). Contbr. articles to profl. jours. Home: 9131 Sligo Creek Pkwy Silver Spring MD 20901

WOODY, MARY FLORENCE, nursing educator, univ. adminstr.; b. Chambers County, Ala., Mar. 31, 1926; d. Hugh Ernest and May Lillie (Gilliland) W.; diploma Charity Hosp. Sch. Nursing, 1947; B.S., Columbia U., 1953, M.A., 1955. Staff nurse Wheeler Hosp., Lafayette, Ala., 1947-48; polio nurse Willard Parker Hosp., N.Y.C., 1949; staff nurse, supr. VA Hosp., Montgomery, Ala., 1950-53; faculty mem., field supr., nursing dept. Tchrs. Coll., Columbia U., N.Y.C., 1955-56; asst. dir. nursing Emory U. Hosp., clin. asst. prof. Emory U. Sch. Nursing, Atlanta, 1956-68; asst. dir., then dir. nursing Grady Meml. Hosp., Atlanta, 1968-79; dean, prof. Sch. Nursing, Auburn (Ala.) U., 1979—; chmn. Ga. Statewide Master Planning Com. for Nursing and Nursing Edn., 1971-75; faculty preceptor patient care adminstrn. Sch. Public Health, U. Minn., 1977-79. Recipient Spl. Recognition, 5th Dist. and Ga. Nurses Assn., 1978. Fellow Am. Acad. Nursing (charter); mem. Am. Nurses Assn., Nat. League Nursing, Am. Heart Assn., Sigma Theta Tau. Democrat. Chmn. bd. dirs. Am. Jour. Nursing, 1978-82. Office: Sch Nursing Auburn U Auburn AL 36849

WOODYARD, VIVIAN WELCH, educator; b. Metamora, Ohio, May 31, 1934; d. Elmer E. and Agnes Vivian (Boroff) Welch; student Ohio U., 1958-59, Antelope Valley Coll., 1959-60; B.A., U. Calif., Riverside, 1962, M.A., 1964, postgrad., 1969; m. Richard L. Woodyard, May 31, 1955 (div. 1972); 1 son, Shawn Mark. Med. asst. to gen. practitioner, Manchester, Ohio, 1955-59; teaching asst. in English, U. Calif., Riverside, 1965-68, library asst., 1969; asst. prof. English, Lake Superior State Coll., Sault Ste. Marie, Mich., 1969-73; library asst. State Hist. Soc. Wis., Madison, 1973-75; vol. TEFL instr. U.S. Peace Corps, Bangkok, Thailand, 1975-76; grad. asst. U. Calif., Santa Barbara, 1976-77; asso. dir. GTE TEFL Tng. Sch., Tehran, 1977-79; adminstrv. asst. Intergrated Circuit Engring. Corp., Santa Clara, Calif., 1979-80; asst. to chief div. plastic and reconstructive surgery, Stanford (Calif.) U. Med. Center, 1980—. Recipient Kathleen B. Loly Honor award, 1960; Regents of U. Calif. summer fellow, 1963. Mem. Tech. Writers Assn., MLA, Teaching English as A Second or Fgn. Lang. Democrat. Methodist. Clubs: Sierra, Apres-Ski, The Grads., Schola Cantorum. Author: Thomas Traherne, 1962; (play) Shouting on the Rooftops: An American in Iran, 1980. Home: 2113 Town and Country Ln Apt 3 Santa Clara CA 95050 Office: R213 Div of Plastic Surgery Stanford Univ Med Center Stanford CA 94305

WOOLEY, COLLEEN LEE, health services public relations exec.; b. Wichita, Kans., Dec. 13, 1930; d. Charles Lee and Faye Marie (Hall) Schreffler; B.A., Wichita State U., 1952; m. John B. Wooley, Aug. 30, 1958. Public info. dir. ARC, Wichita, 1952-62, dir. office of public relations, 1974—; acad. sec. Wichita State U., 1966-68; sec. Prestige Engraving and Printing, Wichita, 1968-70; clk. typist U. Kans., 1971-73; public relations dir. ARC, Wichita, 1974—, mem. nat. blood services communications com., mem. nat. public affairs adv. com. Ruling elder Grace Presbyterian Ch., Wichita. Mem. Nat. Fedn. Press Women, Kans. Press Women, Wichita Press Women (past pres., dir.), Am. Women in Radio and TV (charter mem. chpt., dir. 1978-79), Women in Communications (Woman of Achievement award 1982), Public Relations Soc. Am. (dir., sec. chpt.), Wichita Advt. Club Nat. Audio Visual Assn., Wichita State U. Alumni Assn. (dir.). Democrat. Home: 243 S Belmont Wichita KS 67218 Office: Am Red Cross 707 N Main St Wichita KS 67203

WOOLF, ESTHER BARASCH, real estate exec.; b. Russia, Dec. 24, 1913; came to U.S., 1921; d. Hyman and Celia (Mandelbaum) Barasch; grad. high sch.; 1 dau., Louise Gersen Sharir, Dec. 15, 1962. Office asst., then office mgr. F & P Mgmt. Co. 1932-37; asst. to pres. L.V. Hoffman & Co., Inc., 1937-42; with Marx Realty & Improvement, N.Y.C., 1942-43; with Williams & Co., Inc. and Williams Real estate Co., Inc., N.Y.C., 1943—, successively adminstrv. v.p., fin. v.p., also dir.; dir. L.F. Rush, Inc., Fairfax, N.J. Mem. Local Bd. 5, 1982—; mem. Assn. for a Better N.Y.; mem. U.S. Congl. Adv. Bd. Mem. Real Estate Bd. N.Y., Bldg. Owners and Mgrs. Assn. N.Y. (budget com.). Jewish. Home: 240 Central Park S New York NY 10019 Office: 1700 Broadway New York NY 10019

WOOLF, JEANNE AUSTIN, psychologist; b. Memphis, Mo., Nov. 19, 1909; d. Charles Fred and Mary Evelyn (Richardson) A.; B.S., State Coll., Kirksville, Mo., 1931; Ph.D. with honors, U. Chgo., 1960; m. Maurice D. Woolf, July, 1929; children—Donald Austin, Maurice Cameron. Clin. psychologist U. Pitts., 1957-59, Counseling Clinic Honolulu, 1959-77; pvt. practice psychotherapy, psychodiagnosis, Honolulu, 1977—; Mem. Am. Psychol. Assn., Hawaii Psychol. Assn. Author: (with M.D. Woolf) The Student Personnel Program, 1953; Remedial Reading, 1957. Contbr. articles to profl. jours. Home: 2895 Kalakaua Ave Apt 1608 Honolulu HI 96815 Office: 1110 University Ave Suite 310 Honolulu HI 96826

WOOLFE, ELIZABETH ARMSTRONG, community coll. adminstr.; b. Orlando, Fla., Jan. 18, 1929; d. William and Alice Lucy (Metcalf) Armstrong; B.S., Fla. State U., 1950, M.S., 1967; Ed.D. (Charles S. Mott fellow 1974), Fla. Atlantic U., 1979; m. Robert Cecil Woolfe, July 30, 1950; children—Robert Craig, Richard Stephen (dec.), Randall Clark, Russell Cameron. Home service rep. Fla. Power & Light Co., 1960-62; extension home econs. agt. Palm Beach County (Fla.), also U. Fla., 1964-66; from program specialist to tchr. Palm Beach County Sch. Bd., 1966-70, county staff resource tchr. dept. adult and community edn., 1972-74; asst. prof. Indian River Community Coll., 1970-72; part-time instr., then coordinator continuing edn. Palm Beach Jr. Coll., 1976-81, dir. continuing edn. II, North Campus, 1981—. Deacon, Immanuel Presbyn. Ch., Palm Beach Gardens, Fla., 1959-82. Mem. Am. Assn. Community and Jr. Colls., Nat. Assn. Women Deans, Adminstrs. and Counselors, Am. Assn. Women Community and Jr. Colls., Assn. Continuing Higher Edn., Am. Soc. Tng. and Devel., AAUW, Fla. Assn. Community Colls., Fla. Assn. Community Edn., Fla. Fedn. Women's Clubs (jr. dist. dir. 1962-64), Palm Beach County Panhellenic (pres. 1959-60), Greater W. Palm Beach C. of C., Palm Beach Gardens C. of C., Alpha Lambda Delta, Kappa Delta Pi, Omicron Nu, Phi Delta Kappa, Alpha Chi Omega. Democrat. Club: Palm Beach Gardens Soroptomist (chmn. youth citizenship com. 1980-82, dir. 1982—). Home: 6253 Celadon Ct Palm Beach Gardens FL 33410 Office: 3160 PGA Blvd Palm Beach Gardens FL 33410

WOOLLACOTT, MARJORIE HINES, neuroscientist; b. Long Beach, Calif., Aug. 25, 1946; d. Laurence Robert and Helen Virginia (Carson) Hines; student U. Redlands, 1963-65; A.B. magna cum laude with honors extraordinary in organic chemistry, U. So. Calif., 1969, Ph.D. (NIH fellow), 1973. NIH summer trainee in neurophysiology U. So. Calif., 1968; NIH postdoctoral fellow U. Oreg., 1973-76, Alfred P. Sloan postdoctoral research asso. in neurophysiology, 1975-76, asso. prof. phys. edn. and neurosci., 1980—; asst. prof. Va. Poly. Inst. and State U., 1976-77; sr. research asso. Neurol. Scis. Inst., Portland, Oreg., 1977-80; cons. neurophysiologist Biodynamics Corp., Eugene, Oreg.; Arthur Vining Davis fellow in marine invertebrate neurophysiology Santa Catalina Marine Lab., 1971. Mem. exec. com. Siddha Meditation Center, Eugene. M.I.T. Neurosci. Research Program fellow, 1977; NIH grantee, 1978-80; Med. Research Found. Oreg. grantee, 1979-80, 81-82; Fyssen Found. France grantee, 1982; Calif. State Personnel Bd. grantee, 1982. Mem. Soc. Neurosci., AAAS, Am. Coll. Sports Medicine, Phi Beta Kappa. Contbr. chpts., articles to profl. publs. Home: 1628 Lawrence St Eugene OR 97401 Office: Esslinger Hall U Oreg Eugene OR 97403

WOOLLEY, CATHERINE (JANE THAYER), author; b. Chgo., Aug. 11, 1904; d. Edward Mott and Anna L. (Thayer) W.; A.B., U. Calif. at Los Angeles, 1927. Advt. copywriter Am. Radiator Co., N.Y.C., 1927-31; free-lance writer, 1931-33; copywriter, editor house organ Am. Radiator & Standard San. Corp., N.Y.C., 1933-40; desk editor Archtl. Record, 1940-42; prodn. editor SAE Jour., N.Y.C., 1942-43; pub. relations writer NAM, N.Y.C., 1943-47; instr. juvenile writing Cape Cod Writers Conf., 1965, 66; instr. workshop in juvenile writing Truro Center for the Arts, summers 1977, 78. Trustee Truro Pub. Libraries, 1974—; mem. Passaic Bd. Edn., 1953-56, Passaic Redevel. Agy., 1952-53. Mem. Authors League Am., Friends of Truro Libraries, Truro Hist. Soc., Vols. for AIM, Kenilworth Soc. Democrat. Author juvenile books (under name Catherine Woolley): I Like Trains, 1944, rev., 1965; Two Hundred Pennies, 1947; Ginnie and Geneva, 1948; David's Railroad, 1949; Schoolroom Zoo, 1950; Railroad Cowboy, 1951; Ginnie Joins In, 1951; David's Hundred Dollars, 1952; Lunch for Lennie, 1952 (pub. as L'Incontentabile Gigi in Italy); The Little Car that Wanted a Garage, 1952; The Animal Train and Other Stories, 1953; Holiday on Wheels, 1953; Ginnie and the New Girl, 1954; Ellie's Problem Dog, 1955; A Room for Cathy, 1956; Ginnie and the Mystery House, 1957; Miss Cathy Leonard, 1958; David's Campaign Buttons, 1959; Ginnie and the Mystery Doll, 1960; Cathy Leonard Calling, 1961; Look Alive, Libby!, 1962; Ginnie and Her Juniors, 1963; Cathy's Little Sister, 1964; Libby Looks for a Spy, 1965; The Shiny Red Rubber Boots, 1965; Ginnie and the Cooking Contest, 1966; Ginnie and the Wedding Bells, 1967; Chris in Trouble, 1968; Ginnie and the Mystery Cat, 1969; Libby's Uninvited Guest, 1970; Cathy and the Beautiful People, 1971; Cathy Uncovers a Secret, 1972; Ginnie and the Mystery Light, 1973; Libby Shadows a Lady, 1974; Ginnie and Geneva Cookbook, 1975; (under name Jane Thayer) The Horse with the Easter Bonnet, 1953; The Popcorn Dragon, 1953; Where's Andy?, 1954; Mrs. Perrywinkle's Pets, 1955; Sandy and the Seventeen Balloons, 1955; The Chicken in the Tunnel, 1956; The Outside Cat, 1957 (English edit. 1958); Charley and the New Car, 1957; Funny Stories To Read Aloud, 1958; Andy Wouldn't Talk, 1958; The Puppy Who Wanted a Boy, 1958; The Second-Story Giraffe, 1959; Little Monkey, 1959; Andy and His Fine Friends, 1960; The Pussy Who Went To the Moon, 1960 (English edit. 1961); A Little Dog Called Kitty, 1961 (English edit. 1965); The Blueberry Pie Elf, 1961 (English edit. 1962); Andy's Square Blue Animal, 1962; Gus Was a Friendly Ghost, 1962 (English edit. 1971, Japanese edit. 1982); A Drink for Little Red Diker, 1963; Andy and the Runaway Horse, 1963; A House for Mrs. Hopper; the Cat that Wanted to Go Home, 1963; Quiet on Account of Dinosaur, 1964 (English edit. 1965, 74); Emerald Enjoyed the Moonlight, 1964 (English edit. 1965); The Bunny in the Honeysuckle Patch, 1965 (English edit. 1966); Part-Time Dog, 1965 (English edit. 1966); The Light Hearted Wolf, 1966; What's a Ghost Going to Do?, 1966 (English edit. 1972, Japanese edit. 1982); The Cat that Joined the Club, 1967 (English edit. 1968); Rockets Don't Go to Chicago, Andy, 1967; A Contrary Little Quail, 1968; Little Mr. Greenthumb, 1968 (English edit. 1969); Andy and Mr. Cunningham, 1969; Curious, Furious Chipmunk, 1969; I'm Not a Cat, Said Emerald, 1970 (English edit. 1971); Gus Was a Christmas Ghost, 1970 (English edit. 1973); Mr. Turtle's Magic Glasses, 1971; Timothy and Madam Mouse, 1971 (English edit. 1972); Gus and the Baby Ghost, 1972 (English edit. 1973); The Little House, 1972; Andy and the Wild Worm, 1973; Gus Was a Mexican Ghost, 1974 (English edit. 1975); I Don't Believe in Elves, 1975; The Mouse on the Fourteenth Floor, 1977; Gus Was a Gorgeous Ghost, 1978; Where is Squirrel?, 1979; Try Your Hand, 1980; Applebaums Have a Robot, 1980; Clever Raccoon, 1981; Gus Was a Real Dumb Ghost, 1982; contbr. stories to juvenile anthologies, sch. readers, juvenile mags. Home: Higgins Hollow Rd Truro MA 02666

WOOLLEY, DONNA RYDELL, lumber co. exec.; b. Drain, Oreg., Jan. 3, 1926; d. Chester Arthur and Mona B. (Cheever) Rydell; m. Harold Woolley, Dec. 27, 1952; children—Daniel, Debra, Donald. Sec., No. Life Ins. Co., Eugene, Oreg., 1943; bookkeeper Smith River Lumber Co., Drain, 1944; bookkeeper Woolley Logging Co., Drain, 1944, exec. Woolley Enterprises, 1971-77; dir. Douglas Nat. Bank, Roseburg, Oreg., SAIF Corp., Salem, Oreg. Mem. Douglas County Budget Commn., Roseburg, Oreg., 1971-—; mem. Drain Sch. Bd., 1967-80; trustee U. Oreg. Found.; bd. assocs. Linfield Coll. Mem. Sunnydale Grange, Pacific Internat., Amateur trapshooting assns. Mem. Rebekah Lodge. Home: POB 43 Drain OR 97435 Office: Eagle's View Mgmt Co Inc 1577 Pearl St Suite 200 Eugene OR 97401

WOOLSEY, JACQUELYN SUE, former editor; b. Ft. Scott, Kans., Sept. 1, 1931; d. Chester Earl and Mildred Louise (Bainum) Eves; A.A., Ft. Scott Jr. Coll., 1951; B.S. in Journalism, U. Ark., 1953; m. Harvey Norman Woolsey, Nov. 19, 1960. Reporter, Ill. State Jour., Springfield, 1953-56, Topeka State Jour., 1956; writer Salina (Kans.) Jour., 1957—, women's editor, 1957—, Women Today and Living Today editor, 1978-80. Mem. Beta Sigma Phi. Address: E Country Club Rd Rural Route 5 Box 48 Salina KS 67401

WOOLSEY, MARY BETH, food co. fin. analyst; b. Pasadena, Calif., Mar. 20, 1948; d. Charles Cramer and Mary Elizabeth (Sawyer) W.; A.B. in Psychology, UCLA, 1971; M.B.A. in Fin., U. San Francisco, 1980; m. Gary Franklin Calame, Mar. 13, 1982. Sr. buyer Geyser Peak Winery, Geyserville, Calif., 1974-75; buyer Calif. & Hawaiian Sugar Co., San Francisco, 1976-78, fin. analyst, 1978-80; sr. cost acct. Shaklee Corp., San Francisco, 1980-81; regional fin. analyst Foremost McKesson, San Francisco, 1981—; mem. faculty Golden Gate U., 1980-81; condr. small bus. mktg. workshop Alameda C. of C., 1981; cons. to small bus. Mem. allocation panel United Way, San Francisco. Democrat. Christian Scientist. Office: 625 Third St San Francisco CA 94107

WOOSLEY, ELLEN JEAN BOGAN, educator; b. Blumont, Va., July 6, 1941; d. Merle Warwick and L. Irene (Lightner) Bogan; B.A., Longwood Coll., 1963; postgrad. U. Va., 1967-77, James Madison U., 1977—; m. Robert Lawrence Woosley, Jr., June 22, 1963; children—Ellen Cameron, Kristen Paige, Robert Lawrence III. Tchr., Wilson Elem. Sch., Fishersville, Va., 1963-65, Waynesboro (Va.) Schs., 1965-68, 69-71; kindergarten tchr. Berkeley Glenn Elem. Sch., Waynesboro, 1974—. Mem. Waynesboro Bd. Assessors, 1973-76. Mem. Waynesboro Edn. Assn., Va. Edn. Assn., NEA, Mental Health Assn. (lectr. on parenting), AAUW. Republican. Presbyterian. Office: 1020 Jefferson Ave Waynesboro VA 22980

WOOSTER, PAMELA MCCARTHY, banker; b. W. Palm Beach, Fla., Nov. 8, 1953; d. Edward Aloysius and Constance (Bishop) McCarthy; B.S. in Bus. Adminstrn., N.Y.U., 1975, M.B.A., 1975; m. Robert Butler Wooster, Jr., Nov. 27, 1976. Govt. bond rep. Chem. Bank, N.Y.C., 1975-76; govt. bond rep. Citibank N.A., N.Y.C., 1976—, v.p. taxable instruments div., 1981—. Mem. Money Marketeers, Jr. League N.Y.C. Republican. Episcopalian. Home: 131 Garden St Garden City NY 11530 Office: Citibank NA Sort 850 New York NY 10043

WOOTEN, PEGGY PARKER, social worker; b. Bradyville, Tenn., Oct. 17, 1946; d. Leo Beacher and Mae Ola (Perkins) Parker; A.A., Martin Coll., 1966; B.S., E. Tenn. State U., 1968; M.S.W., La. State U., 1970; m. Morris R. Wooten, Jr., Oct. 7, 1972; children—Bryan Parker, Chad Edward. With Meth. Home, Waco, Tex., 1970—, dir. foster care, 1974-76, coordinator social work services, 1976—. Lic. child care adminstr. Mem. Nat. Assn. Social Workers, Acad. Cert. Social Workers, Regional Network for Children. Democrat. Methodist. Office: 1111 Herring Ave Waco TX 76708

WOPPERER-HURLEY, GERTRAUD JOHANNA, psychiat. social worker; b. Munich, Germany, Oct. 26, 1926; d. Anton and Johanna (Ege) Wopperer; Ph.D., Albert Ludwigs U., Freiburg (W.Ger.), 1957; M.S. in Social Service, Boston U., 1973; m. Gerald J. Hurley, Nov. 17, 1973; fostersons—Michael, Jon. Research asst. Inst. for Social Research, Cologne, W.Ger., 1958-62; lectr. social scis. U. Louvanium, Kinshasa, Africa, 1964-65; instr. Sch. Social Work, Freiburg, 1965-70; psychiat. and geriatric social worker Solomon Mental Health Center, Lowell, Mass., 1978-80; geriatric therapy specialist South Shore Mental Health Center, Quincy, Mass., 1980-82. AAUW fellow, 1972. Mem. AAUW, Nat. Assn. Social Workers, Internat. Council Social Welfare, Mass. Gerontol. Assn. Home: 1524 Main St Concord MA 01742

WORDEN, KATHARINE COLE, sculptor; b. N.Y.C., May 4, 1925; d. Philip Gillette and Katharine (Pyle) Cole; student Potters Sch., Tucson, 1940-42, Sarah Lawrence Coll., 1942-44; m. Frederic G. Worden, Jan. 8, 1944; children—Rick, Dwight, Philip, Barbara, Katharine. Sculptures exhibited Royce Galleries, Galerie Françoise Besnard (Paris), Cooling Gallery (London), Galerie Schumacher (Munich), Selected Artists Gallery, N.Y.C., Art Inst. Boston, Reid Gallery, Nashville, Weiner Gallery, N.Y.C., 1976, 77, Desraches Gallery, Montreal, Que., Can., 1977, 78, Boston Athanaeum, 1979, Gilcrease Mus. (Tulsa), Galerie des Capucines (Paris), pvt. collections Grand Palais (Paris), Dakar and Bathurst, Africa. Occupational thrapist psychopathic ward Los Angeles County Gen. Hosp., 1953-57; headstart vol., Watts, Calif., 1965-67; tchr. sculpture Watts Towers Art Center, 1967-69; participant White House Women Doers Luncheon meeting, 1968; dir. Cambridgeport Problem Center, Cambridge, Mass., 1969-71; chmn. bd. Quality Shellfish, Inc.,

1982—; dir. Stride Rite Corp. Trustee, Communication Research Inst., Miami, Fla., 1960-69, chmn. bd., 1966-69; bd. dirs. Boston Center for the Arts; bd. overseers Boston Mus. Fine Arts, 1978—. Mem. Common Cause (Mass. adv. bd. 1971-72, dir. 1974-75), Mass. Civil Liberties Union (exec. bd. 1973-74, 76-78, dir. 1976-77, trustee found. 1977-78). Home: Rural Route 2 Box 127AA Jamestown RI 02835

WORDEN, PATRICIA ANN, fashion exec.; b. Mason City, Iowa, Dec. 30, 1932; d. Albert Emmet and Mary Ellen (Root) Hale; student Clarke Coll., Dubuque, Iowa, 1950-51, 71-72, U. Mich., 1951-52; m. Joseph Edgar Worden, Aug. 23, 1952; children—Joseph P., Jon C., James M., Richard M., David C., Eric A., Erin M. Advt. salesman Decorah (Iowa) Newspapers, 1963-64; advt. mgr. Manchester (Iowa) Pub. Co., 1964-71; advt. mgr., feature writer, editorial writer Dyersville (Iowa) Comml., 1972-75; advt. mgr. Manchester Press & Democrat-Radio & Banner, 1975-80; owner Pat Worden's Wardrobe, Dyersville, 1980—. Condr. advt. workshop West Delaware Jr. High Sch.; bd. dirs. Dyersville Bus. Com.; mem. Iowa Women's Polit. Caucus. Recipient five advt. awards Cedar Rapids Advt. Council, awards Iowa Press Assn. Mem. Iowa Press Women (retail com. advt. seminar), Manchester Area C. of C. (bd. dirs.). Democrat. Roman Catholic. Club: Manchester Golf. Writer series on area churches, hosps., When You're in Trouble Where Do You Turn?, Dyersville Comml., 1972-75. Home: 205 E Union St Manchester IA 52057 Office: 225 1st Ave E Dyersville IA 52040

WORK, JANE ALLEN (MRS. WILLIAM MCCLEAN WORK), psychologist; b. Phila., May 17, 1920; d. Robert Louis and Lois (McKinney) Allen; student Grove City Coll., 1938; B.B.A., Westminster Coll., 1965; M.A., Case Western Res. U., 1967, Ph.D., 1973; m. Homer Richard Allen, Apr. 19, 1941 (dec. Apr. 1963); children—Robert McKinney, Homer Gerald, Emily Jane (Mrs. Joseph Berg); m. 2d, William McClean Work, Jan. 1, 1979. Psychologist, Bd. Edn. Cleve., 1968-70, Spl. Edn. Dist. Lake County, Ill., 1970-73; instr., Roosevelt U., Chgo., Loyola U., Chgo., 1973-74; treas. Chgo. Area Spl. Edn. Services, Ltd., 1973-74; project dir. NSCC Consortium, ESEA, 1974, Psychol. Coop. Edn. Service Agy. 18, Burlington, Wis., 1974-76; psychologist Marion (Ohio) Area Counseling Center, 1976-78; pvt. practice psychology, Pitts., 1979—. Founder, New Group for Adult Singles, Evanston, Ill., 1970; bd. dirs. Pitts. Planned Parenthood Assn. Mem. Am. Psychol. Assn., Pa. Psychol. Assn., Gestalt Inst. (Cleve.). Home: 599 Robinwood Dr Pittsburgh PA 15216 Office: 615 Washington Rd Pittsburgh PA 15228

WORLINE, MARJORIE BESS, social worker; b. Wellston, Ohio, Jan. 9, 1920; d. Victor Lincoln and Carrie Bess (Harper) McCall; B.A., Ohio State U., 1941, B.S. in Edn., 1942; M.S.W., Our Lady of the Lake U., San Antonio, 1974; m. James R. Worline, Apr. 13, 1946; 1 son, Barry Jay. Nurse, Wright-Patterson AFB, Dayton, Ohio, 1942-46; with Cath. Social Services, Albuquerque, 1964-69; social worker Brooke Army Med. Center, Ft. Sam Houston, Tex., 1974—; cons. Crisis Care Center, Albuquerque, 1965-69. Lic. social psychotherapist, Tex. Mem. Nat. Assn. Social Workers, Am. Orthopsychiat. Assn., San Antonio Group Psychotherapy Soc., Am. Assn. Marital and Family Counselors, Sierra Club, S. Tex. Archaeol. Assn. Republican. Club: Toastmistress. Home: 116 Bryker San Antonio TX 78209 Office: Social Work Service Brooke Army Med Center Fort Sam Houston TX 78234

WORMLEY, DOROTHY LEE EATON, ednl. adminstr.; b. Washington, Sept. 14, 1922; d. Saulisberry and Ophelia (Gatewood) Eaton; B.A., Miner Tchrs. Coll., 1953; M.A., N.Y. U., 1957; postgrad. Am. U., Howard U., George Washington U., D.C. Tchrs. Coll.; m. George Dyson Wormley, Sept. 12, 1943; children—George Dyson, Raymond Brett, Marilyn Yvonne. Tchr., D.C. Public Schs., 1953-66, reading specialist, 1966-71, reading cons., 1971-73, asst. prin., 1973-78, prin. Shaed Elem. Sch., 1978-81, Noyes Elem. Sch., 1981—. Mem. Nat. Assn. Elem. Sch. Prins., D.C. Assn. Elem. Sch. Prins., Internat. Reading Assn., Nat. Council Negro Women (chpt. v.p. 1977-79), Phi Delta Kappa. Democrat. Lutheran. Author: Attack, 1975. Home: 7242 15th Pl NW Washington DC 20012 Office: Noyes Elem Sch 10th and Franklin St NE Washington DC 20017

WORNE, PHYLLIS DOLORES, biochem. co. exec.; b. Phila., May 27, 1931; d. Fred S. and Rose J. Garofalo; student Phila. Music Acad., 1949-51; m. Howard E. Worne, Sept. 14, 1962; 1 dau., Elinor D. Sec. preventive clinic Am. Cancer Soc., Phila., 1949-52; with zone office Oldsmobile, Phila., 1952-62; adminstrv. exec. v.p. Worne Biochemicals, Inc., Berlin, N.J., 1970-81; exec. v.p. Bioferm Internat., Medford, N.J., 1981—; owner Food Resources, Inc. Mem. N.J. Assn. Women Bus. Owners (v.p. So. region, state pres., chmn. fin. com. state group), N.J. Coalition Small Bus., Zonta Internat. Food editor Jersey Woman mag., Tangent mag. Home: 205 Sunny Jim Dr Medford NJ 08055 Office: Medford Med Bldg Stokes Rd PO Box 458 Medford NJ 08055

WORRELL, GAIL GARRETT, med. illustrator and graphic designer; b. Queens, N.Y., Apr. 11, 1946; d. Wayne Oliver and Gloria Elizabeth (Titscher) Garrett; B.S. in Design, U. Cin., 1969. Graphic designer Alpha Designs, Inc., Cin., 1969-73; med. illustrator and supr. Good Samaritan Hosp., Cin., 1973—; free-lance cons. designer. Recipient various awards Tulsa Art Dirs. Show, 1977, 1st prize Am. Occupational Med. Assn. exhibit, 1976, 2d prize Ohio Med. Assn. exhibit, 1977, bronze plaque Ohio Med. Assn., 1978, Hull award AMA, 1980. Illustrator: Vascular Surgery, Vol. 2 (John J. Cranley, M.D.); contbr. illustrations to med. texts. Home: 3850 Clifton Ave Cincinnati OH 45220 Office: Good Samaritan Hosp 3217 Clifton Ave Cincinnati OH 45220

WORTH, IRENE, actress; b. Nebr., June 23, 1916; B.Edn., UCLA, 1937; pupil Elsie Fogarty, London, 1944-45. Formerly tchr.; debut as Fenella in Escape Me Never, N.Y.C., 1942; Broadway debut as Cecily Harden in The Two Mrs. Carrolls, 1943; London debut in The Time of Your Life, 1946; following roles include Anabelle Jones in Love Goes to Press, 1946, Ilona Szabo in The Play's The Thing, 1947, as Eileen Perry in Edward my Son, 1948, as Lady Fortrose in Home is Tomorrow, 1948, as Mary Dalton in Native Son, 1948, title role in Lucrece, 1948, as Olivia Raines in Champagne for Delilah, 1949, as Celia Coplestone in The Cocktail Party, 1949, 50; various roles with Old Vic Repertory Co. including Desdemona in Othello, Helena in Midsummer Night's Dream and Lady Macbeth in Macbeth, also Catherine de Vausselles in The Other Heart (on tours S. Africa 1952), as Portia in The Merchant of Venice, 1953; joined Shakespeare Festival Theatre, Stratford, Ont., Can., 1953, as Helena in All's Well That Ends Well, Queen Margaret in Richard III; appeared as Frances Farrar in A Day by the Sea, 1953-54; leading roles in The Queen and the Rebels, 1955, Hotel Paradiso, 1956, as Mary Stuart, 1957, The Potting Shed, 1958, appeared as Albertine Prine in Toys in the Attic (Page One award), 1960; mem. Royal Shakespeare Co., 1962-64, including world tour King Lear, 1964; star Tiny Alice, N.Y.C., 1964, Aldwych, 1970; also appeared as Hilde in A Song at Twilight, Anna-Mary in Come into the Garden Maud (Evening Standard award), Hesione Hushabye in Heartbreak House (Variety Club Gt. Britain award 1967), Jocasta in Oedipus, 1968, Hedda in Hedda Gabler, 1970; with internat. Co. Theatre Research, Paris and Iran, 1971; leading role in Notes on a Love Affair, 1972, Mme. Arkadina in The Seagull, 1973, Gertrude in Hamlet, Mrs. Alving in Ghosts, 1974, Princess Kosmonopolis in Sweet Bird of Youth, 1975-76 (Jefferson award, Tony award), Lina in Misalliance, 1976, Mme. Ranevskaya in The Cherry Orchard, 1977 (Drama Desk award), Kate in Old Times, 1977, Winnie in Happy Days, 1979, Anne in After the Season, 1979, Elizabeth in The Lady from Dubuque, 1980, Ella in John Gabriel Borkman, 1980, Dr. von Zahnd in The Physicists, 1981; films include role of Leonie in Orders to Kill (Brit. Film Acad. award), 1958, The Scapegoat, 1958, King Lear, 1970, Nicholas and Alexandra, 1971, Deathtrap, 1981; also numerous radio, TV appearances Eng., Can., U.S., including Stella in The Lake, Ellida Wangel in The Lady from the Sea (Daily Mail Nat. TV award); also Candida, Duchess of Malfi, Antigone, Prince Urestes, Variations on a Theme, The Way of the World, The Displaced Person; poetry recitals, recs. Decorated comdr. Brit. Empire (hon.); recipient Whitbread Anglo-Am. award outstanding actress, 1967. Address: care Milton Goldman ICM 6th Floor 40 W 57th St New York NY 10019

WORTH, SUSAN EILEEN, psychologist; b. Milw., Mar. 25, 1947; d. J. Allen and Helen Madonna (Marnon) Butler; B.A. in Psychology, Wheeling Coll., 1969; M.Ed. in Counseling Psychology, Boston Coll., 1971, postgrad., 1972—; m. Mark L. Worth, Nov. 24, 1973; children—Jessica Ellyn. Ednl. liaison Boston-Brookline Collaborative Center, Brookline, Mass., 1972-73; coordinator outpatient psychol. services Joseph P. Kennedy Meml. Hosp. for Children, Brighton, Mass., 1974-76; psychologist Newark Devel. Center, 1976-77; coordinator Project II-D, Phila. Elwyn Inst., 1978-81; dir. CEEPS program, 1981—. NDEA fellow, 1969-72. Lic. psychologist, Pa. Mem. Am. Psychol. Assn., Am. Assn. Mental Deficiency, Mass. Psychol. Assn., Pa. Psychol. Assn. Democrat. Roman Catholic. Home: 22 Fitzwatertown Rd E-5 Willow Grove PA 19090 Office: 4017 Ludlow St Philadelphia PA 19104

WORTHINGTON, BARBARA CAVEDO, clin. psychologist; b. Richmond, Va., June 25, 1942; d. William Fitzgerald Cavedo and Edith Earline (Mann) Cavedo Gould; B.A. with high honors, Christopher Newport Coll., 1973; M.A. (Roper Grad. fellow, Williams fellow), U. Richmond, 1974; Ph.D., Va. Commonwealth U., 1978; m. Clarke Worthington III, Dec. 20, 1963; 1 son, Tyler Clarke. Psychol. intern VA Treatment Center, Med. Coll. of Va., Richmond, 1977-78; clin. child psychologist Child Guidance Clinic, Winston-Salem, N.C., 1978-80; pvt. practice clin. psychology, Winston-Salem, 1980—. Mem. bd. dirs. Winston-Salem/Forsyth County Battered Women's Services, 1980-82. Mem. NOW (treas. Winston-Salem chpt. 1979), Forsyth Area Psychol. Assn., N.C. Psychol. Assn., Va. Psychol. Assn., Am. Psychol. Assn. Democrat. Episcopalian. Club: Winston-Salem Jr. League. Contbr. articles in field to profl. publs. Office: 840 W 4th St Winston-Salem NC 27101

WORTHINGTON, MARY EMMONS, clin. psychologist; b. San Jose, Calif., Apr. 17, 1922; d. Grover Carlton and Helen Keith (Boulware) Emmons; B.A., Vanderbilt U., 1942; M.L.A., U. So. Calif., 1972; M.A., Pepperdine U., 1975; Ph.D., Fla. Inst. Tech., 1981; m. John Worthington, July 4, 1942; children—Jon, Gina. Librarian, Internat. Grad. U., Lugano, Switzerland, 1976-77; dir. and clin. psychologist High Plains Comprehensive Community Mental Health Center, Osborne, Kans., 1978—; lectr. Pepperdine U., UCLA, Ft. Hays U., Internat. Grad. U. Founder and pres. Friends of Long Beach Library; neighborhood chmn. Girl Scouts U.S.A., 1978-82; mem. Area Agy. on Aging, Osborne, 1981-82; chair bd. trustees CIFAS Med. Sch., Dominican Republic; mem. Gov.'s Com. on Drunk Driving. Lic. marriage, family and child therapist, Calif. Mem. Am. Psychol. Assn., Osborne C. of C., Hospice, Osborne County Hosp. Aux., Gamma Phi Beta, Sigma Beta Pi, Psi Chi. Democrat. Methodist. Clubs: PEO (chpt. CR), Fidelia (pres. 1981-82). Home: 318 S 2d St Osborne KS 67473 Office: High Plains Comprehensive Community Mental Health Center 121 W Main St Osborne KS 67473

WOULFF, NINA, clin. psychologist; b. Bronx, N.Y., Oct. 5, 1949; d. Sholem and Sylvia (Siegal) W.; B.A. cum laude in Psychology and English, CCNY, 1970; Ph.D. in Psychology, U. Maine, 1975. Staff psychologist Atlantic Child Guidance Centre, Dartmouth, N.S., Can., 1975-80, dir., 1980—; instr. div. family medicine Dalhousie U., Halifax, N.S., Can., 1977—; leader assertiveness tng. Mt. St. Vincent U., Halifax, 1977—; asso. fellow, supr. Inst. Rational-Emotive Therapy, N.Y.C., 1980—. Mem. Am. Psychol. Assn., Phi Beta Kappa. Author papers in field. Office: 277 Pleasant St Suite 204 Dartmouth NS B2Y 4B7 Canada

WRAY, CLAIRE FRANCES LEEDS (MRS. WILSON J. WRAY), public info. rep.; b. San Francisco, Mar. 13, 1923; d. Roy Maxwell and Marie (Coops) Leeds; A.B. in Polit. Sci., U. Calif., Berkeley, 1945; m. Wilson J. Wray, July 21, 1961. Feature writer, reporter San Francisco Examiner, 1944-66, spl. feature writer, 1966-67; nat. dir. publicity, pub. relations, ann. conf. ALA, San Francisco, 1967; public info. dir. Irwin Meml. Blood Bank of San Francisco Med. Soc., 1967-71; freelance com. pub. relations, 1971-73; coordinator publicity Concours d'Elegance, Silverado Country Club, Napa, 1972-73; editor Hosps. and Clinics newsletter U. Calif. San Francisco Med. Center, 1972-73, sr. writer USCF News, 1973-75, pub. info. rep., editor newsletter San Francisco Gen. Hosp., 1972—, sr. writer dept. news services univ., 1975-81; vice chmn. com. pub. relations and info. Am. Assn. Blood Banks, San Francisco, 1969-75, chmn. ad hoc com. pub. sch. edn. programs, 1971-73, editor Reciprocity newsletter nat. clearinghouse program, 1973-76; instr. publicity, pub. relations YWCA, San Francisco, 1963-66. Coordinator women's activities Alioto for Mayor Com., San Francisco, 1967; publicity chmn. San Francisco Women's Com. to Re-elect Gov. Brown, 1966. Bd. dirs. Vol. Bur. San Francisco, 1967-70; 2d v.p., bd. dirs. Aux. to San Francisco Gen. Hosp., 1975-80. Mem. No. Calif. Sci. Writers Assn., Friends San Francisco Library, San Francisco-Oakland Newspaper Guild. Democrat. Home: 4124 21st St San Francisco CA 94114 Office: 1475 4th Ave San Francisco CA 94140

WRENN, ANN SANFORD, newspaper co. exec.; b. Atlanta, Apr. 26, 1936; s. Harold J. and Sarah (Mahone) S.; B.B.A., Ga. State U., 1958, postgrad. U. Miami; m. Charles A. Wrenn (dec.). With Bowles, Andrews & Towne, Atlanta 1957-58, 60-64, The Terriberry Co. 1958-60, Towers, Perrin, Forster & Crosby, Atlanta 1964-65; actuary The Coca-Cola Co., Atlanta 1966-67, mgr. retirement plan 1967-72, staff cons. employee benefits 1972; dir. compensation and employee benefits Knight-Ridder Newspapers, Inc., Miami 1973-74, asst. treas. 1975-78, treas. 1978—. Bd. dirs. South Fla., Inc.; treas. Salvation Army, 1978-81; bd. dirs. United Way Dade County, 1980—; pres. Goodwill Industries South Fla., 1981-82; mem. exec. bd. South Fla. council Boy Scouts Am. 1980, 82. Mem. Fin. Execs. Inst., Nat. Assn. Corp. Treas., Am. Newspaper Assn., Assn. Pvt. Pension and Welfare Plans. Republican. Methodist. Club: Lagorce Country, Surf, Bankers, New World Center. Office: 1 Herald Plaza Miami FL 33101

WRENN, BESSIE MAE NOBLE, social worker; b. Birmingham, Ala.; d. Sam and Eula Mae Noble; B.S. in Sociology, Ala. A&M U.; B.S.W., U. Ala., 1975, M.S.W., 1976, cert. Mgmt. Inst., 1979. Caseworker, Jefferson County Dept. Pensions and Security, Birmingham, 1967-70, casework reviewer, 1970-76, casework supr., 1976-77; dist. supr. Bur. Field Service, Ala. Dept. Pensions and Security, Montgomery, 1977-79, welfare field insp. Office Insp. Gen., 1979—. Cert. social worker. Mem. Nat. Assn. Social Workers, Ala. Conf. Social Work, Jefferson County Human Service Club. Methodist. Office: Room 301 85 Bagby Dr Birmingham AL 35209

WRIGHT, ALMA MCINTYRE, mag. editor; b. Knoxville, Tenn., July 31, 1909; d. William Mobry and Theresa (Biagiotti) McIntyre; B.S. in Edn., U. Tenn., 1932; m. Robert Oliver Wright, Feb. 17, 1931; 1 son, Robert Oliver. Writer stories, articles on African violets, house plants, 1947—; editor African Violet Mag., 1947-63, The Master List of African Violets, 1962, GSN (Gesneriad-Saintpaulia News), 1963—, publs. of Saintpaulia Internat., 1963 (rec. sec. 1963), Am. Gerneria Soc., Inc., 1963; exec. dir. African Violet Soc. Am., Inc., 1960-63; pres. Indoor Gardener Pub. Co., Inc., 1963—. Mem. Am. Hort. Soc., Inc. (hon. v.p. 1954), African Violet Soc. Am., Inc. (hon. life mem., rec. sec. 1946-48, nat. pres. 1948-49, membership sec. 1953-63). Home: The Meadows 7914 Gleason Rd Condominium 1075 Knoxville TN 37919 Office: 1800-1802 Grand Ave Knoxville TN 37901

WRIGHT, BARBARA, nurse, educator; b. Cranbury, N.J., Aug. 3, 1933; d. William Aloysius and Mary (Matlosz) Wincklhofer; B.S., Boston Coll., 1955; M.Ed., Rutgers U., 1969; M.A., N.Y. U., 1976, postgrad., 1979—; m. Walter Olden Wright, Oct. 8, 1960; children—Elizabeth (dec.), Walter, Mary Alice. Instr., head dept. Muhlenberg Hosp. Sch. Nursing, Plainfield, N.J., 1967-71; cons. N.J. State Dept. Higher Edn., Trenton, 1973-75; asst. prof. Rutgers U. Coll. Nursing, Newark, 1976-79; exec. dir. N.J. State Nurses Assn., Trenton, 1980—. Dep. mayor Plainsboro (N.J.), 1977—; trustee United Way of Princeton Area Commn., 1978—. Mem. Am. Nurses Assn., AAUP, Soc. Advancement in Nursing, Am. Soc. Psychoprophylaxis in Obstetrics. Democrat. Home: 20 Davison Rd Box 266 Plainsboro NJ 08536 Office: 320 W State St Trenton NJ 08618

WRIGHT, BESSIE MARGARET, nursery exec.; b. Centralia, Kans., May 23, 1905; d. Onbey Roscoe and Sarah Elizabeth (Shrontz) Roberts; student public schs., Rupert, Idaho; m. Loyd K. Wright, Feb. 6, 1924; 1 son, John Robert. Partner, treas. Kimberly Nurseries, Inc., Twin Falls, Idaho, 1924—. Sunday sch. tchr., 1946-56. Mem. Nat. Fedn. Ind. Bus., Twin Falls C. of C., Am. Nurserymen, Idaho Nursery Assn., Archaeol. Inst. Am., Twin Falls Hist. Soc. (dir.), Nat. Assn. Watch and Clock Collectors, Franklin Mint Collectors Soc., Smithsonian Soc. Republican. Methodist. Club: Daus. of Nile. Author: Me and My Other Self (autobiography). Home: PO Box L Kimberly ID 83341 Office: Kimberly Nurseries Inc Route 3 Addison Ave E Twin Falls ID 83301

WRIGHT, CATHARINE MORRIS (MRS. SYDNEY LONGSTRETH WRIGHT), artist, nat. academician; b. Phila., Jan. 26, 1899; d. Harrison Smith and Anna (Wharton) Morris; ed. pvt. schs., Phila. Sch. of Design for Women, 1916-18; A.F.D. (hon.), Moore Inst., Phila., 1959; m. Sydney Longstreth Wright, Feb. 28, 1925; children—Anna Templeton-Cotill, William Redwood, Harrison Morris, Ellicott. Began career as artist, 1918; represented in Pa. Acad. Fine Arts, Allentown Mus., Moore Inst., U. Pa., Pa. State Coll., Woodmere Gallery, Phila. Mus., Asso. Nat. Acad., 1933; founder Fox Hill Sch. Art, Jamestown, R.I., 1950. Hon. mention Phila. Art Club. 1924, Gimbel prize, 1932, Mary Smith prize Pa. Acad. Fine Arts, 1933, 2d Hallgarten prize Nat. Acad. Design, 1933, Greenough Meml. prize Newport Art Assn., 1933, Germantown Art League prize, 1936, hon. mention Phila. Sketch Club, 1940, Woodmere Gallery, 1941, Allied Artists of Am. prize, 1941, Silvermine Marine prize Guild of Artists, 1955. Mem. Am. Water Color Soc., Audubon Artists, Newport Art Assn., Keats-Shelley Assn. Am. (v.p. 1952-78), Phila. Water Color Club (v.p. 1949-57), Allied Artists Am., Authors League Am., Poetry Soc. Am., Va. Poetry Soc. Author: The Simple Nun (verse), 1929, Princess Anne Prize (verse), 1945, Seaweed Their Pasture, 1946, The Color of Life, 1957, Lady of the Silver Skates, 1979. Home: Fox Hill Farm Jamestown RI 02835

WRIGHT, CLEO ALVA BUCKNER, civic worker, publisher; b. Bertram, Tex.; d. Ira Arthur and Vonnie (Ross) Buckner; B.A. (scholar 1947-51), U. Houston, 1951; m. Merrill Clair Wright. Vice pres. Wright Light, Inc., Houston, 1950-67. Vol. worker hosp. and recreation corps ARC, Atlanta, 1942-43, Houston, 1946-48; charter founder sec. Elva A. Wright Aux. to City Tb Hosp., Houston, 1950-52, pres., 1952-53, bd. dirs., 1950-60, sec., 1975-76, pres. elect, 1976-77; vol. Traveller's Aid, Houston, 1960-66; mem. Past Pres.'s Bd. Hosp. Auxs., 1950-80; sec. Glenbrook Valley Civic Club, 1972-75; owner, pub. Houston Bowling News. Recipient Brunswick NWBW awards. Mem. Bowling Writers Assn. Am. (1st pl. awards for feature, column), Nat. Women Bowling Writers Assn., Women in Communications, So. Bowling Writers Assn. (charter), Am. Bowling Congress (award 1978), Nat. Hist. Soc. (charter founding mem.), Houston Turn Verein Ladies Aux. (historian 1965-66, 68-70), Women of Rotary (vol. and publicity chmn. 1964-65), Turn Verein Ladies Bowling Assn. (pres. 1962-64), Theta Sigma Phi (v.p. 1966-67), Phi Kappa Phi, Gamma Delta Chi. Club: Caprice Dance (sec. 1970-71). Home: 8102 Colgate St Houston TX 77061

WRIGHT, ELEANORE REIDELL, physician; b. Mattoon, Ill., June 17, 1915; d. Joseph Emanual and Mabel Edna (Eckerly) Reidell; B.S., U. Ill., 1938, B.M., 1940, M.D., 1941, cert. hosp. adminstr., 1959; m. Curtis Wright, Mar. 21, 1941; m. 2d, Arthur O. Hecker, Feb. 11, 1955 (dec.); children—Carolyn Pearson, Eleanore H., Sarah Lawrence, Deborah O'Connell, Curtis. Intern, Augustana Hosp., Chgo., 1940-41; resident Ypsilanti (Mich.) State Hosp., 1950-52, Trenton (N.J.) State Hosp., 1952-54; mem. staff Friends Hosp., Phila., 1954-55; asst. supt. Embaeevilor (Pa.) Hosp., 1955-70, supt., 1970-71; dir. Eastern Pa. Mental Health programs, 1962-65; lectr. U. Ill., 1941-43, Women's Med. Coll., Phila., 1954-68. Chmn. Cecil Republicans, Inc., 1973; pres. Cecil County Soc. Prevention Cruelty to Animals, 1973-75, 76-78, 79-81; bd. dirs. Foster Care, Cecil County, Grantee in field. Cert. hosp. adminstr. Md. Mem. AMA, Am. Psychiat. Assn., Pa. Psychiat. Assn., Chester County Med. Soc., Am. Coll. Neurol. Psychiatry. Presbyterian. Contbr. numerous articles in field to profl. jours. Home: 1657 Elk Forest Elkton MD 21921

WRIGHT, ESTELLA VIOLA HARRISON (MRS. WILLIAM M. WRIGHT), sculptor; b. Riceville, Ga.; d. Elijah and Elicia (Butler) Harrison; student Art Student's League, 1937, 48-50, (scholar) Newark Mus., 1961, summer 1962, Nat. Acad. Sch. Fine Arts, 1962, NAD, fall 1962; m. William M. Wright, Apr. 24, 1928 (dec.). One-man shows at various banks, also Scott's Auditorium; exhibited in group shows: Artists of Am. at Master Inst., 1941, Audubon Artists Ann., 1942, NAD, 1962, Art Exhbn. Springfield (Mass.), 1962, Countee Cullen Public Library, 1963, Lynn Kottler Gallery, N.Y.C., 1973 others; commd. work includes bas relief in plaster, 1976, trophy for Boy Scouts Am., Bklyn., 1977; life-size works various persons, including George Washington Carver, Thomas Bethune, also portrait busts including Eubie Blake, Mary McLoed Bethune; represented in permanent collections: Schromberg Collection, N.Y.C. Public Library, Public Sch. 92, N.Y.C. Mus., also pvt. collections. Bd. dirs. Gray lady Harlem Hosp., N.Y.C., 1951—. Recipient certificate of public service State of N.Y., 1958, citation for meritorious service Bklyn. Women's Council, 1963. Mem. Art Students League (life), John Brown Meml. Assn., Rosicrucian Anthrosophic League Sch. Philosophy. Home: 226 W 138th St New York NY 10030 Office: Art Student League 215 W 57th St New York NY 10019

WRIGHT, GRACE ELIZABETH, textiles and clothing specialist; b. Grinnell, Kans., Aug. 15, 1918; d. James Harvey and Sarah Elizabeth (Holaday) Mather; B.S., Kans. State U., 1941; M.S. in Clothing Textiles, U. Mo., 1969; postgrad. U. Ariz., 1966, Columbia Coll., 1979; m. Oscar Thomas Wright, Oct. 11, 1956. Home mgmt. supr. FHA, Emporia, Ottawa, Kans., 1941-47; county home agt. U. Mo. Extension, Sullivan County, 1947-56, clothing and textiles specialist Kansas City Met. area, Liberty, 1958—. Recipient Meretorious award U. Mo., 1971, Vice Pres. award, 1975. Mem. Nat. Assn. Extension Home Economists (Nat. Disting. Service award 1965, regional dir. 1967-69), Am. Home Econs. Assn., AAUW (treas. 1976-80, v.p. 1972-73), Mo. Assn. Extension

Home Economists (pres. 1965), U. Mo. Extension Assn., Greater Kansas City Home Econs. Assn., Mo. Home Econs. Assn. (state honor 1977, dist. pres. 1977-78), dist. pres. 1977-78), Epsilon Sigma Phi (state award 1967, nat. award 1977), Omicron Nu. Methodist. Clubs: Blue Springs Country, Order Eastern Star, Soroptomist (pres. 1971-72) (Liberty). Bd. dirs. Jour. of Extension, 1965-68. Home: 1701 N 3d St Blue Springs MO 64015 Office: 103 E Kansas St Liberty MO 64068

WRIGHT, IRENE HODGE, reporter; b. Kokomo, Ind., Dec. 11, 1929; d. Kert and Esther (McCullum) Hodge; student U. Cin., 1950-53, U. Tulsa, Ind. U.; m. Francis W. Wright, June 16, 1962; children—Pamela, Scott; children by previous marriage—Michael Barr, Deborah Barr. Reporter, Middletown (Ohio) Jour., 1957-62; reporter Suburban Group Newspapers, Cherry Hill, N.J., 1966-68; bur. chief Cin. Enquirer, 1968—, med. reporter, 1975—. Founder, Middletown Actors Theater, 1958. Mem. Ohio Press Women, Ohio Newspaper Womens Assn. (pres. 1982-83). Republican. Presbyterian. Club: Soroptimist. Home: 500 Aberdeen Dr Middletown OH 45042 Office: Enquirer Bureau 1919 Central Ave Middletown OH 45042

WRIGHT, ISABELLE H., civic worker; b. Manito, Ill., Mar. 31, 1903; d. Peter John and Kate A. (Krie) Helst; student schs. Mason County, Ill.; m. Norval Wright, May 15, 1921 (dec. 1966); 1 son, Norval (dec., 1953). Owner apt. house, Peoria, Ill., 1923-79. Treas. Peoria (Ill.) Leatherneck Club, 1941—, unit pres., 1945-46, state pres., 1950-51, nat. pres., 1956; sec. Am. War Dads Aux., 1944-80; rifle instr. G.A.R. Aux., 1970—; jr. pres. South Side Republican Club, 1923-24, sec., 1926-80; judge, election bd.; precinct committeeman, 1936-38; vol. Old State Hosp., 1970-76; mem. Am. Legion Aux. Recipient awards for vol. work with vets. Lutheran. Home: 301 W Second St Peoria IL 61605

WRIGHT, JEAN VERLICH, writer, public relations exec.; b. McKeesport, Pa., July 5, 1950; d. Matthew Louis and Irene (Tomko) Verlich; student Bucknell U., 1968-69; B.A., U. Pitts., 1971; m. S(tanley) Wayne Wright, Sept. 29, 1979. Press sec. Com. to Re-elect President, S.W. Pa., 1972; adminstrv. asst. Pa. Rep. James B. Kelly III, 1972-73; reporter Beaver (Pa.) County Times, 1973-74; proofreader Ketchum, MacLeod & Grove, Pitts., 1975-76; community relations specialist, PPG Industries, Pitts., 1976-77, editor PPG News, 1977-79, sr. staff writer, 1979—. Mem. Internat. Assn. Bus. Communications (dir. Pitts. chpt. 1981, v.p. public relations Pitts. chpt. 1982), Phi Beta Kappa, Delta Zeta. Office: One Gateway Center 10 North Pittsburgh PA 15222

WRIGHT, JOANNE LUTZ, nuclear industries exec.; b. Richland, Wash., July 5, 1955; d. George Edward and Clara Veda (Maxwell) Lutz; student Columbia Basin Coll., 1976—; m. Samuel Andrew Wright, May 9, 1981. Sec. trainee Exxon Nuclear Co., Inc., Richland, Wash., 1972-75; with UNC Nuclear Industries, Richland Wash., 1975—, communications rep., 1979—, also editor The Nucleus. Public relations vol. Energy Fair, 1983. Cert. profl. sec., 1979. Mem. Internat. Assn. Bus. Communicators (judge Pacesetters awards com.), Women in Communications. Home: 1423 Arbor St Richland WA 99352 Office: UNC Nuclear Industries PO Box 490 Richland WA 99352

WRIGHT, JOSEPHINE ROSA BEATRICE, musicologist; b. Detroit, Sept. 5, 1942; d. Joseph Le Vander and Eva Lee Garrison W.; Mus.B., U. Mo., Columbia U., 1963, M.A., 1967; Mus.M., Pius XII Acad., Florence, Italy, 1964; Ph.D., N.Y.U., 1975. Instr. music York Coll., CUNY, 1972-75, asst. prof., 1975; asst. prof. Afro-Am. studies in musicology Harvard U., Cambridge, Mass., 1976-81; asso. dir. integration of Afro-Am. folk arts with music project, Nat. Endowment Humanities, 1979-82; asso. prof. music Coll. of Wooster, 1981—; panelist, cons. on music Mass. Council of Arts and Humanities, 1978-80; cons. Nat. Endowment Humanities, 1982. Mem. AAUW, Am. Musicol. Soc., Internat. Musicol. Assn., Coll. Music Soc., Assn. for Study of Afro-Am. Life and History, Nat. Assn. Female Execs., Sonneck Soc. Democrat. Episcopalian. Author: Ignatius Sancho (1729-1780), An Early African Composer in England: The Collected Edition of His Music in Facsimile, 1981; editor of new music; The Black Perspective in Music, 1979—; co-editor: The Bicentennial Issue of The Black Perspective in Music, 1976. Contbr. articles to profl. jours. Office: Dept Music Coll of Wooster Wooster OH 44691

WRIGHT, JUDITH MITCHELL, mgmt./mktg. cons.; b. Balt.; d. John Armitage and Mary (Bowen) Mitchell; R.N., Church Home and Hosp. Sch. Nursing, 1970; m. Harold Russell Wright, Jr., Aug. 15, 1970; 1 son, Alexander Bowen. Team leader Good Samaritan Hosp., Balt., 1970-73; patient care coordinator Keswick Home for Incurables, Balt., 1974-76; owner, pres. The Wright Group. Co chmn. Druid Hill tennis project Jr. League Balt., 1977, 78, bd. dirs., 1980—, asst. treas., 1982-83, also mem. exec. bd.; chmn. security Balt. Internat. Indoor Tennis Championships, 1978; co-chmn. ops. 1st Nat. Grand Prix Tennis Classic, 1979, chmn. ops., 1980, asst. chmn., 1981. Republican. Episcopalian. Club: Woman's of Roland Park (pres. jr. dept. 1982-83, bd. govs. 1982—). Home and office: 146 Murdock Rd Baltimore MD 21212

WRIGHT, KAREN MIRIAM, metal fabricating co. exec.; b. Chgo., Sept. 12, 1938; d. Rhody Rodney and Caroline Henrietta (Kloppman) Gates; student Walton Acctg. Sch., 1978; Wright Jr. Coll., 1979; m. Porter F. Wright, Jan. 31, 1959; children—Kimberly Gail, Michael Patrick. Order editor Doremeyer Electric Co., Chgo., 1956-59; insp. Modine Co., Ringwood, Ill., 1965-68; office mgr. Lee Optical, Chgo., 1968-69; with Mellish & Murray, Chgo., 1969—, trustee profit sharing, 1977—, treas., 1978—, office mgr., 1979. Mem. Ill. Mfrs. Assn., Chgo. Assn. Commerce and Industry. Clubs: Metro, Postle Health. Office: 1720 W Fulton St Chicago IL 60612

WRIGHT, KATHLEEN KAY, banker; b. Evanston, Ill., Mar. 2, 1949; d. William P. and Joan (Mohring) W.; B.S., Fla. State U., 1971; M.B.A., N.Y.U., 1977; J.D., Fordham U., 1981; postgrad. N.Y. U. Mem. audit staff Peat, Marwick, Mitchell & Co., Miami, 1971-73; with Citibank, N.Y.C., 1973—, now v.p. legal and external affairs/gen. counsel's office; adj. prof. Pace U., N.Y.C., 1981—; admitted to N.Y. bar, 1981. C.P.A., N.Y. Mem. Am. Inst. C.P.A.s, Am. Bar Assn., N.Y. State Soc. C.P.A.s. Club: St. Bartholomew's Community (sports com.). Office: Citibank 399 Park Ave New York NY 10043

WRIGHT, KATIE HARPER, ednl. adminstr., journalist; b. Crawfordsville, Ark., Oct. 5, 1923; d. James Hale and Connie Mary (Locke) Harper; B.A., U. Ill., 1944; M.Ed., 1959; Ed.D., St. Louis U., 1979; m. Marvin Wright, Mar. 21, 1952; 1 dau., Virginia (Mrs. Ed Jordan). Elem. and spl. edn. tchr. East St. Louis (Ill.) Pub. Schs., 1944-65, dir. Dist. 189 Instructional Materials Program, 1965-71, dir. spl. edn. Dists. 188, 189, 1971-77, asst. supt. programs, 1977-79; adj. faculty Harris/Stowe State Coll., 1980; cons. to numerous workshops, seminars in field. Mem. Ill. Commn. on Children, 1973—, East St. Louis Bd. Election Commrs.; pres. bd. dirs. St. Clair County Mental Health Center, 1970-72; bd. dirs. River Bluff council Girl Scouts, 1979—, nat. bd. dirs., 1981—; bd. dirs. United Way, 1979—, Urban League, 1979—; pres. bd. trustees East St. Louis Public Library, 1972-77. Recipient Lamp of Learning award East St. Louis Jr. Wednesday Club, 1965; Outstanding Working Woman award Downtown St. Louis, Inc., 1967; Ill. State citation for ednl. document Love is Not Enough, 1974; Delta Sigma Theta citation for document Good Works, 1979; named Woman of Achievement, St. Louis Globe Democrat, 1974, Outstanding Adminstr. So. region Ill. Office Edn., 1975. Mem. Am. Libraries Trustees Assn. (regional v.p. 1978-79, nat. sec. 1979-80), Ill. Commn. on Children, Mensa, Council for Exceptional Children, Top Ladies of Distinction, Delta Sigma Theta (chpt. pres. 1960-62), Kappa Delta Pi (pres. So. Ill. U. chpt. 1973-74), Phi Delta Kappa, Pi Lambda Theta. Republican. Presbyterian. Club: East St. Louis Women's (pres. 1973-75). Contbr. articles to profl. jours.; feature writer St. Louis Argus Newspaper, 1979—. Home: 733 N 40th St East Saint Louis IL 62205

WRIGHT, LILYAN BOYD, educator; b. Upland, Pa., May 11, 1920; d. Albert Verlenden and Mabel (Warburton) Boyd; B.S., Temple U., 1942, M.Ed., 1946; Ed.D., Rutgers U., 1972; m. Richard P. Wright, Oct. 23, 1942; 1 dau., Nicki Warburton (Mrs. Arthur Scott Vanek). Tchr. health and phys. edn. Woodbury (N.J.) High Sch., 1942-43, Glen-Nor High Sch., Glenolden, Pa., 1944-46, Chester (Pa.) High Sch., 1946-54; chmn. women's dept. health and phys. edn. Union (N.J.) High Sch., 1954-61; with Trenton State Coll., 1961—, head women's program health and phys. edn., 1967-77, chmn. dept. health, phys. edn. and recreation, 1977—; mem. N.J. State Com. Div. Girls and Women's Sports, 1958-80; chmn. New Atlantic Field Hockey Sectional Umpiring, 1981—. Active Chester United Fund; water safety, first aid instr. ARC Scholarship in her honor N.J. Athletic Assn. Girls, 1971; named to Hall of Fame, Temple U., 1976. Mem. AAHPER (chmn. Eastern dist. assn. div. girls and women's sports, sec. to council for services Eastern dist. 1979-80, chmn. 1980-81), N.J. AHPER (pres. 1974-75, past pres. 1975-76, v.p. phys. edn. div., Disting. Service and Leadership award 1969, Honor Fellow award 1977), N.J. Women's Lacrosse Assn. (umpiring chmn. 1972-76), Nat. Assn. Phys. Edn. in Higher Edn., Eastern Assn. Phys. Edn. Coll. Women, AAUP, North Jersey, Central Jersey bds. women's ofcls., Am., Pa. (v.p. 1953-54), Chester (pres. 1949-54) fedns. tchrs., U.S. (exec. com.), North Jersey (past pres.) field hockey assns., Kappa Delta Epsilon, Delta Psi Kappa (past pres. Phila. alumni chpt.), Kappa Delta Pi. Episcopalian. Home: 260 Green Valley Rd Langhorne PA 19047 Office: Trenton State College Trenton NJ 08625

WRIGHT, LINDA JEAN KEMPH, banker; b. Chgo., Dec. 14, 1949; d. Eugene F. and Rosemary M. (Kiely) Kemph; student Loretto Heights Coll., 1967-69, U. Ill., 1970-71; m. Kelly W. Wright, Jr., Feb., 1979. Asst. to v.p. Busey First Nat. Bank, Urbana, Ill., 1969-72; spa mgr., sales tng. supr. Venus & Apollo Health Club, San Antonio, 1973-76; owner retail plant store, San Antonio, 1976-77; with Town & Country Bank, Falls Church, Va., 1977—, now sr. v.p. comml. lending, also sec. bd. dirs.; dir., treas. No. Va. Local Devel. Corp. Vice chmn. exec. com. Fairfax/Falls Church United Way. Mem. Nat. Assn. Bank Women (chmn. No. Va. group 1981), Nat. Assn. Bank Women (chmn. No. Va. group 1981), Fairfax County C. of C. (dir., v.p.). Office: Town & Country Bank 7787 Leesburg Pike Falls Church VA 22043

WRIGHT, MARY JANE, nurse; b. Indianola, Miss., July 15, 1936; d. Johnnie Clarence and Mary Lee (Herrin) Tupman; diploma gen. bus., Memphis Sch. Commerce, 1955; A.D.N., Parkland Coll., Champaign, Ill., 1973; student Eastern Ill. U.; m. Robert Gene Wright, Mar. 13, 1955; children—Cynthia Lea Wright Bodmer, Randal David, Scott Alan, Stephanie Jane. Staff nurse hosps. in Monticello, Ill., 1973-78; dir. nursing Champaign Convalescent Center, Savoy, Ill., 1978-80; nurse cons., regional dir. Am. Healthcare Corp., Monticello, 1980-81; quality assurance coordinator Manor Healthcare, Silver Springs, Md., 1981—; mem. adv. nursing com. bd. Parkland Coll., 1978-80; mem. Champaign-Urbana Continuing Edn. Program, 1978-80. Home: Route 2 Box 6 Mansfield IL 61854 Office: 105 S State St Monticello IL 61856

WRIGHT, MARY RUTH (MRS. WILLIAM KEMP WRIGHT), psychologist; b. St. Louis, Apr. 2, 1922; d. Leon Carl and Gwendolyn (Travis) Brown; R.N., Washington U., St. Louis, 1944; B.S., U. Houston, 1966, M.A., 1967; Ph.D., Union Grad. Sch., 1978; m. William Kemp Wright, Feb. 10, 1945; children—Gwendolyn, Veronica, Victoria, Jennifer. Instr. surgery Washington U. Sch. Nursing, 1944-45, U.S. Cadet Nurse Corps, USPHS, 1944; instr. pediatrics Children's Meml. Hosp., Chgo., 1945-46; teaching fellow U. Houston, 1965-66; instr. S. Tex. Jr. Coll., Houston, 1967-70; mental health cons. St. Joseph Mental Hosp., Houston, 1966-67; staff psychol. services Almeda Clinic, Houston, 1966-70; pvt. practice marriage and family counselor, Houston, 1970—; med.-psychol. researcher and writer, 1970—; psychologist Vasectomy Clinic, Houston Dept. Health, 1971—; clin. asst. prof. psychology, dept. otorhinolaryngology and communicative scis. Baylor Coll. Medicine, Houston, 1979. Recipient spl. award Security Agy., 1945. Mem. Am. Psychol. Assn., Am. Assn. Marriage and Family Counselors, Am. Assn. Sex Educators and Counselors, Internat. Council Psychologists, Nat. Council Family Relations, Nat. Assn. Social Workers, Mental Health Assn. Houston and Harris County (dir.). Contbr. articles to profl. jours. Home: 3671 Del Monte St Houston TX 77019 Office: 633 Hermann Profl Bldg Houston TX 77030

WRIGHT, OLGIVANNA LLOYD, archtl. sch. exec.; b. Cetinje, Montenegro, Yugoslavia; came to U.S., 1924, naturalized, 1933; d. Iovan and Militza (Milianova) Lazovich; student pvt. schs., Russia, Turkey, France; m. Frank Lloyd Wright, Aug. 25, 1926 (dec. 1959); children—Svetlana Wright Peters (dec.), Iovanna Lloyd Wright Schiffner. Co-founder with Frank Lloyd Wright, Taliesin Fellowship, 1932; v.p. Frank Lloyd Wright Found., 1941-59, pres., 1959—; pres. Frank Lloyd Wright Sch. of Architecture, 1959—; pres., cons., adv. Taliesin Associated Architects, 1959—. Mem. Nat. Fedn. Press Women, Am. Soc. Interior Designers (hon.), Nat. League Am. Penwomen (hon.), Women in Communication (hon.). Author: The Struggle Within, 1955; Our House, 1959; The Shining Brow, 1960; Roots of Life, 1963; Frank Lloyd Wright, His Life, His Work, His Words, 1966. Composer of numerous works for chamber orch.

WRIGHT, PATRICIA, state legislator; b. South Bend, Ind., Feb. 28, 1931; d. Chester David and Merle Amelia (Malone) Bryant; student Phoenix Community Coll., Glendale Community Coll.; m. Paul J. Wright, 1951; children—Timothy Paul, Patrick Michael. Mem. Ariz. Ho. of Reps., 1976—. Active Am. Legis. Exchange Council; precinct committeeman, dep. registrar, Republican coordinating council, edn. com., state Americanism com., alt. del. Rep. nat. conv., 1980; mem. Glendale Arts Council, Freedoms Found.; bd. dirs. Girls Ranch. Mem. Nat. Order Women Legislators, Nat. Rep. Legislators Assn. Mem. Christian Ch. Clubs: Glendale Women's, Central Dist. Dental Aux., State Dental Aux. Office: Capitol Bldg House Wing 1700 W Jefferson Phoenix AZ 85007

WRIGHT, ROSE MARIE, controller; b. Boston, July 14, 1947; d. James Melbourne and Viola Margaret Stevenson; B.S.B.A. magna cum laude, Wright State U., 1973; postgrad. Ohio State U., 1979-80; m. Thew Wright, III, July 14, 1971. Sr. acct. Peat, Marwick, Mitchell & Co., Cin., 1973-76; supervising sr. auditor Borden, Inc., Columbus, Ohio, 1976-79; mgr. internal auditing Ohio Med. Indemnity Mut., Columbus, 1979; controller, chief fin. officer Agfoods, Inc., Columbus, 1980—. Trustee, Epilepsy Assn. Franklin County, 1981-82, treas., 1982-83. C.P.A., Ohio. Mem. Am. Inst. C.P.A.s, Ohio Soc. C.P.A.s, Acctg. Research Assn., Nat. Soc. Accts. for Coops., Nat. Council Phys. Distbn. Mgmt., Nat. Council Farmer Coops (legal, tax and acctg. com.). Club: Continental Athletic. Home: 733 Worthington Forest Columbus OH 43229 Office: 3775 Zane Trace Dr Columbus OH 43228

WRIGHT, RUTH M., state legislator; b. Ottumwa, Iowa, Sept. 6, 1928; d. Robert E. and Margaret (Wenzel) Sponner; Ph.B., Marquette U., 1950; postgrad. U. Wis., 1956; J.D., U. Colo., 1972. Mem. Colo. State Health Bd., 1975-79; mem. Colo. State Water Quality Control Commn., 1975-81; mem. Colo. Ho. of Reps., 1981—. Admitted to Colo. bar, 1972; practice law, Boulder, Colo., 1972-81. Mem. ABA, Colo. Bar Assn., Boulder County Bar Assn. (chmn. environ. law com. 1976-79), Internat. Congress on Irrigation and Drainage. Office: Colo Ho of Reps State Capitol Denver CO 80203

WRIGHT, SHARON SUE POTTER, banker; b. Dallas, Mar. 4, 1940; d. Millard M. and Gladys P. (Potter); student N. Tex. State U., 1958-59, U. Tex., Arlington, 1960-62, Am. Inst. Banking, 1963; m. Robert E. Wright, Apr. 28, 1965; children—Deborah Sue, David Michael. Exec. sec. First Nat. Bank, Duncanville, Tex., 1962-63, Trinity Nat. Bank, Dallas, 1963-65; ops. officer Exchange Bank and Trust, Dallas, 1965-76; v.p. Nat. Bank of Commerce of Dallas, 1976-80; sr. v.p., cashier Tex. Am. Bank, Dallas, 1980—. Bd. dirs. Cedar Hill (Tex.) Youth Assn., 1966-78. Mem. Nat. Assn. Bank Women, Am. Inst. Banking, Bankers Adminstrn. Inst., Am. Bankers Assn., Cedar Hill C. of C. Mem. Churches of Christ. Office: Tex Am Bank 6300 Harry Hines Blvd Dallas TX 75235

WRIGHT, SHELLEY FAYE, comml. arts and advt. cons.; b. Berkeley, Calif., Feb. 5, 1956; d. Allen Cheever and Addye Faye (Duke) W.; A.A. in English, Fullerton Coll., 1977; B.A. in Communications/Advt., Calif. State U., Fullerton, 1981; m. Martin G. Rezmer, Oct. 17, 1980. Free-lance photographer, Placentia, Calif., 1976-77; asst. prodn. mgr. Interface Age mag., Cerritos, Calif., 1977-79; contractor service rep. card div. Am. Express Co., Santa Ana, Calif., 1980-81; cons. SHE Prodns., Fullerton, 1979—; lectr. in field; tchr. arts and crafts to children. Vol., Braille Inst. Am., Anaheim, Calif., 1969-70; sec. Volunteers for Retarded, Fullerton, 1970-71. Recipient Service award Braille Inst. Am., 1970, Community Service award City of Placentia, 1973; Bus. Excellence award, 1973. Mem. Am. Advt. Fedn., Women in Communications, Inc. (Photog. award 1980), Nat. Assn. Profl. Saleswomen, Nat. Assn. Female Execs., Woman's World Internat., Inc., Fullerton Alumni Assn.

WRIGHTMAN, CAROLINE MCGHEE, nurse, adminstr.; b. Portland, Oreg., Mar. 14, 1942; d. William Hanen and Lola Jeanette (Oberg) McGhee; B.S. in Nursing, Loma Linda U., 1965; M.Nursing in psychiat. nursing, UCLA, 1975; m. Larry Keith Wrightman, Mar. 24, 1974. Head nurse mental health unit Glendale (Calif.) Adventist Med. Center, 1966-68, Loma Linda (Calif.) U. Med. Center, 1968-69; asst. supr. Glendale Adventist Med. Center, 1969-70; instr. nursing Pacific Union Coll., Glendale, 1970-72, Los Angeles County Hosp. Sch. Nursing, 1972-74; mental health counselor Los Angeles County-San Gabriel Valley Mental Health Center, 1976-79; dir. psychiatry Fla. Hosp., Orlando, 1979—. Mem. Loma Linda U. Sch. Nursing Alumni Assn., UCLA Sch. Nursing Alumni Assn. Am. Assn. Suicidology. Mem. Ch. of Adventist Fellowship. Home: 7748 Waunatta Ct Orlando FL 32807 Office: 601 E Rollins St Orlando FL 32803

WRIGLEY, ELIZABETH SPRINGER (MRS. OLIVER K. WRIGLEY), found. exec.; b. Pitts., Oct. 4, 1915; d. Charles Woodward and Sarah Maria (Roberts) Springer; B.A., U. Pitts., 1935; B.S., Carnegie Inst. Tech., 1936; m. Oliver Kenneth Wrigley, June 16, 1936 (dec. July 26, 1978). Procedure analyst U.S. Steel Corp., Pitts., 1941-43; Research asst. The Francis Bacon Found., Inc., Los Angeles, 1944, exec., 1945-50, trustee, 1950—, dir. research, 1951-53, pres., 1954—. Mem. Renaissance Soc. Am., Modern Humanities Research Assn., Am. Cryptogram Assn., Alpha Delta Pi. Presbyn. Mem. Order Eastern Star, Damascus Shrine. Editor: The Skeleton Text of the Shakespeare Folio L.A. (W. C. Arensberg), 1952; (with David W. Davies) A Concordance to the Essays of Francis Bacon, 1973. Compiler: Short Title Catalogue Numbers in the Library of the Francis Bacon Foundation, 1958, supplement, 1967; Lee-Bernard Collection in American Political Theory, 1972; compiler, pub. Wing Numbers in the Francis Bacon Library, 1959. Home: 4805 N Pal Mal Ave Temple City CA 91780 Office: 655 N Dartmouth Ave Claremont CA 91711

WRINGER, PAULA HARMON, educator; b. Princeton, Ind., Aug. 23, 1945; d. Roderick Allen and Emily Lou (Williams) Harmon; B.Nursing, U. Evansville, 1967, M.S., 1975; m. Ralph Dean Wringer, Dec. 9, 1967; children—Brian Allen, Edra Lynn. Unit supr. Norman Beatty Psychiat. Hosp., Westville, Ind., 1967-70; instr. nursing Purdue-North Central Campus, Westville, 1970-73; instr. nursing U. Evansville (Ind.), 1973-75, Olney (Ill.) Community Coll., 1975-76; asst. prof. nursing Purdue U., West Lafayette, Ind., 1976—, acting head baccalaureate program, 1982-83; cons. Lafayette Home Hosp., 1978. Sec. Am. Heart Assn., Tippecanoe unit, 1979-82, v.p., 1982—; mem. adv. bd. Tippecanoe County Elderly Ombudsman, 1979—. Mem. Nat. League Nursing, Central Ind. Health Systems Agy., Sigma Theta Tau, Alpha Tau Delta. Methodist. Club: Order Eastern Star. Home: 4830 N SR 25 Lafayette IN 47905 Office: Purdue U Sch Nursing West Lafayette IN 47907

WROBEL, ELIZABETH MARY, elec. mfg. co. systems exec.; b. Indpls., Mar. 4, 1944; d. William August and Martha Emma (Struewing) Hoelker; student U. Ottawa (Ont., Can.), 1962-65; B.S. in Math., Purdue U., 1967, M.S. in Indsl. Engring., Purdue U., 1979; m. Robert C. Harold, Aug. 26, 1966; 1 son, Lee C. Harold; m. 2d, Ronald B. Wrobel, Sept. 22, 1979. Computer programmer Western Electric Co., Indpls., 1969-75, engr., 1975-77, computer systems mgr., Reading, Pa., 1977—. Active Western Electric Co. United Way campaigns, including chmn. Reading 1981 campaign; active fund raising Jr. Achievement, Reading, 1978; mem. data processing adv. bd. Reading Area Community Coll. Mem. Assn. Computing Machinery (sec. Central Ind. chpt. 1973-74, 74-75), Data Processing Mgmt. Assn., Purdue Alumni Assn. Republican. Roman Catholic. Office: 2525 N 11th St Reading PA 19603

WU, LINDA YEE CHAU, sculptor; b. Canton, China, July 4; student Calif. Sch. Fine Arts, 1939-42, Nat. Acad. Design, 1942-44, Sch. Painting and Sculpture, Columbia U., 1944-50. Exhibited group shows Allied Artists Am. Ann. Exhibits, 1947—, Audubon Artists Ann. Exhibits, Nat. Acad. Design Ann. Exhibits, Nat. Sculpture Soc. Ann. Exhibits, Internat. Sculpture Third, Phila. Art Mus., 1949; dean students N.Y. Chinese Sch., 1960-74, prin., 1974—; represented collections Bas-relief Chinese Community, N.Y., 1952, portrait Sam Y. Ong, Republican Club, Chinatown, N.Y., 1975. Recipient Dessier Greer prize for sculpture Nat. Acad. Design, 1965; Anna Hyatt Huntington Gold medal Catharine Lorillard Wolfe Art Club, 1968, Gold medal of Honor for sculpture Allied Artists Am., 1973. Mem. Nat. Acad. Design, Nat. Sculpture Soc., Allied Artists Am., Knickerbocker Artists (chmn. jury sculpture awards 1974). Address: 209-10 185 Canal St New York NY 10013

WU, MARGARET ANNE, computer scientist, educator; b. Chgo., Apr. 11, 1935; d. Aloys Joseph and Beatrice Rose (Kubal) Schlosser; B.S. in Math., Ill. Inst. Tech., 1956; M.S. in Math., Northwestern U., 1958; Ph.D. in Computer Sci., U. Iowa, 1980; m. Shih-Yen Wu, June 24, 1967; children—Jennifer, Gregory. Research computer scientist IIT Research Inst., Chgo., 1958-67; research assoc. U. Iowa, 1967-71, vis. asst. prof. mgmt. sci., 1979—. Mem. Assn. Computing Machinery, IEEE Computer Soc. Author: Computers and Programming: An Introduction, 1973; Introduction to Computer Data Processing, 1975, 2d edit., 1979; Introduction to Computer Data Processing with Basic, 1980. Office: Phillips Hall University of Iowa Iowa City IA 52242

WU, NORMA SUH-MEI, real estate broker; b. Tainan, Taiwan, Mar. 26, 1947; came to U.S., 1969, naturalized, 1978; d. Ching Piao and

Hsiang (Kuo) Hwang; B.A. in Public Administrn., Nat. Cheng Chi U., 1969; m. Ping Chih Wu, Oct. 22, 1969; children—Benjamin Yuan-Hsien, Irene Joy, Elaine Sandra. Real estate asso. Sun Realty, Torrance Calif., 1975-76, Hettig & Co., Torrance, 1976-78, Lincoln Realty, Orange, Calif., 1978-80; real estate broker/asso. Park W. Properties, Tustin, Calif., 1980-81; real estate broker/owner Wise Investments, Buena Park, Calif., 1981—. Mem. Nat. Assn. Realtors, Calif. Assn. Realtors, E. Orange County Bd. Realtors, Realty Investment Assn. Orange County. Office: 6965 Aragon Circle Buena Park CA 90620

WUKASCH, DORIS LUCILLE STORK, educator, counselor; b. Somerville, Tex., Dec. 30, 1924; d. Edwin William and Clara Rofine (Fuchs) Stork; B.A. with high honors, U. Tex., 1944, M.Ed., 1969; m. Joe Eugene Wukasch, July 7, 1945 (div. 1971); children—Linda (Mrs. Barry Thiering), Susan, Jean (Mrs. Richard P. Mihalik), Jonathan. Chemist Tex. Dept. Health, Austin, 1944-45; microbiologist Terrell Labs., Ft. Worth, 1946-47; exec. sec. Wukasch Architects and Engrs., Austin, 1954-66; editorial asst. Steck-Vaughn Pubs., Austin, 1966; rehab caseworker, job counselor Mary Lee Sch., Austin, 1969-70; spl. tchr. career edn. Austin Ind. Sch. Dist., 1970—. Instr. A.R.C., 1972—; vol. tchr. Austin State Sch., 1958-68. Area chmn. Am. Cancer Soc., 1970; mem. Women's Archtl. Guild, 1954-71, pres., 1964; mem. Tex. Fine Arts Assn., 1960—, Smithsonian Assos., 1972—, Wycliffe Assos., 1973—. HEW grantee, 1968-69. Certified rehab. counselor. Mem. Austin Mental Health Assn., Nat. Rehab. Counselors Assn., Assn. Supervision and Curriculum Devel., Nat., Tex. State tchrs. assn., Internat. Platform Assn., Am. Judicature Soc., Nat. Trust Hist. Preservation, Christian Bus. and Profl. Women's Council, Nat. Orgn. Women, Phi Beta Kappa. Lutheran. Contbr. poems and articles to mags. and newspapers. Home: 2500 Inwood Pl Austin TX 78703 Office: 6100 Guadalupe Austin TX 78752

WULFF, LOIS YVONNE, med. librarian; b. Seattle, Nov. 23, 1940; d. Arthur Ray and Audrey June (Carpenter) Roark; B.S., Washington State U., 1962; M.L.S., U. Wash., 1963; postgrad. Syracuse U., 1969-70; m. Barry Kahn, Dec. 18, 1971. Intern, then head documents div. Ohio State U., 1963-67; spl. project investigator U. Wash., 1968-69; staff asst., head search unit Johns Hopkins Med. Instns., 1971-72; project coordinator, asst. to dir., coordinator health sci. libraries U. Minn., 1973-77; head librarian Alfred Taubman Med. Library, U. Mich., 1978—, coordinator Med. and Sci./Tech. Libraries, 1981—. Gaylord fellow, 1969-70. Mem. Med. Library Assn., ALA, Assn. Acad. Health Sci. Library Dirs., Assn. Coll. and Research Libraries. Office: 1135 E Catherine St Ann Arbor MI 48109

WURSTER, THELMA PAULINE, nurse; b. Celina, Ohio, June 9, 1932; d. Francis Q. and Mary Lee (Kindel) Wade; R.N., Miami Valley Hosp., Dayton, Ohio, 1953; B.S. in Nursing, Marquette U., Milw., 1961; M.Ed. in Profl. Devel., U. Wis., Whitewater, 1982; postgrad. Coll. of St. Joseph, Joliet, Ill.; m. Charles Wayne Wurster, Aug. 18, 1952. Staff and head nurse hosps. in Ohio and Wis., 1953-80; dir. operating rm. Milw. Children's Hosp., 1966-78, asst. dir. nursing, 1979-80; supr. operating room Eye Inst., Milw. County Med. Complex, Wauwatosa, Wis., 1980—. R.N., Ohio, Wis. Mem. Assn. Operating Room Nurses, Phi Delta Kappa. Republican. Club: Kettle Moraine Curling (Hartland, Wis.). Contbr. articles to profl. jours. Home: 1932 Moraine End Delafield WI 53018 Office: 8700 W Wisconsin Ave Wauwatosa WI 53226

WUSNACK, PRIMA THOMAS, librarian; b. Picayune, Miss., Mar. 14, 1949; d. Charles A. and Jessie Don (Welsh) Thomas; B.A. with honors in Edn., U. Miss., 1974; M.S. in Library Sci., U. So. Miss., 1981; 1 son, Charles Joseph. Librarian, Coast Episcopal High Sch., Pass Christian, Miss., 1974-75, Christ Episcopal Day Sch., Bay St. Louis, Miss., 1974-75; dir. Hancock County Library System, Bay St. Louis, 1975—; mem. adv. com. S. Mi-s. Conf. on Libraries and Info. Sci.; group leader Miss. Gov.'s Conf. on Libraries and Info. Sci. Mem. ALA, Miss. Library Assn., Kappa Delta Pi. Clubs: Altrusa (treas. 1978-79) (Bay St. Louis/Waveland). Office: Hancock County Library System 312 Hwy 90 Bay Saint Louis MS 39520

WYATT, ADDIE L., labor leader; b. Bookhaven, Miss., Mar. 8, 1924; d. Ambrose and Maggie (Nolan) Cameron; student pub. and pvt. schs., Chgo.; LL.D. (hon.), Anderson (Ind.) Coll., 1976; m. Claude S. Wyatt, Jr., 1940; children—Renaldo, Claude S., Emmett Cameron, Willie Cameron, Bluet Cameron (dec.), Audrey Dandridge, Maude Davis. Employee in meat packing and food industry, Chgo., 1941-54; internat. rep. United Packinghouse Workers Union (merged with Amalgamated Meat Cutters 1968), Chgo., 1954-74, pres. local 56, 1953-55; dir. women's affairs dept. Amalgamated Meat Cutters and Butcher Workmen N.Am. (merged with Retail Clks. Internat. Union, name now United Food & Comml. Workers Internat. Union), AFL-CIO-CLC, Chgo., 1974—, internat. v.p., 1976—, also dir. civil rights and women's affairs dept.; exec. v.p. Coalition Labor Union Women; advisor, labor instr. Roosevelt U., Chgo.; labor com. advisor Chgo. Urban League; served as a labor advisor to Dr. Martin Luther King, Jr., Dr. Ralph Abernathy, Rev. Jesse L. Jackson. Mem. Ill. Commn. on Status of Women, Ill. Pub. Health Survey Commn.; youth leader for Altgeld Gardens, Chgo. Housing Authority, 1945-55; apptd. to Internat. Women's Year Commn., 1977; mem.-at-large Democratic Nat. Com.; mem. bd. advisors Alliance to Save Energy, Citizens for Day Care, People United to Serve Humanity; mem., advisor women's orgn. Nat. Assn. Ch. of God; minister of music Vernon Park Ch. of God, Chgo. Recipient Image award League Black Women, 1973; Disting. Labor Leader award Woodlawn Orgn., Chgo.; Service award Women's Bd. NAACP; named one of 12 Women of Yr., Time Mag., 1975; Black Book award, 1977; Ebony Mag. citation, 1977; one of 9 Women of Year, Ladies' Home Jour., 1977; recipient numerous other awards and citations. Mem. Coalition of Black Trade Unionists, Nat. Commn. on Working Women, Ams. for Dem. Action (del.-at-large), NAACP (v.p.), Nat. Council Negro Women, Interdenoml. Ministers Wives. Office: United Food and Comml Workers Internat Union AFL-CIO & CLC 1775 K St NW Washington DC 20006

WYATT, EILEEN LITTON, med. technologist, city ofcl.; b. Zanesville, Ohio, Feb. 19, 1927; d. Hazelwood and Lenore (Arnold) Litton; student Muskingum Coll., 1944-46; B.Sc., Ohio State U., 1947; M.T., Trinity Lutheran Hosp., Kansas City, Mo., 1952; m. William Edward Wyatt, 1947; children—Jeff, Gary, David, Martha, Kim, Erin, William D., Amy, Andy, Howard, Dewey, Beth. Med. technologist Trinity Luth. Hosp., 1950-54, Regional Blood Banks, Inc., Portland, Maine, 1972-74, Maine Med. Center, Portland, 1973-81; donor recruiter N.E. Regional Blood Services, Portland, 1974-76; health officer Town of Cumberland (Maine), 1978—. Sec. Portland chpt. ARC, 1980-81, chmn., 1982, vol. coordinator for blood services, 1981, sec. N.E. Regional Blood Services Dist. IX, 1981-82; bd. dirs. Sch. Adminstrv. Dist. 51, 1968-73. Recipient Disting. Service cert. ARC Blood Services-N.E. Region, 1982. Mem. Maine Assn. Med. Technologist (pres. 1982), Am. Soc. Med. Technologist, Maine Health Officers Assn., Am. Soc. Clin. Pathologists (asso.). Methodist. Home: 363 Tuttle Rd Cumberland ME 04021

WYATT, FARICITA HALL, ednl. cons.; b. Bakersfield, Calif., Oct. 29, 1912; d. William M. and Susie Salindia (Pinkney) Hall; A.B., San Jose State Coll., 1935; teaching credential U. Calif., 1962; m. Thomas Edward Wyatt, Oct. 20, 1953 (dec. 1954). Employment security officer Calif. Dept. Employment, Berkeley, 1946-58; exec. sec. Congressman Jeffery Cohelan, Washington, 1959-61; tchr. Skyline High Sch., Oakland, Calif., 1962-75; employment officer U. Calif., Berkeley, 1968-69; dir., pres. Impact Assos., ednl. cons.'s, San Francisco, 1976—; employment rep. U. Calif., San Francisco, 1979—, coordinator retirees employment program, 1980; cons. affirmative action U. Calif. Davis Med. Center, Sacramento, 1979-80; participant profl. confs. and seminars. Bd. dirs. Vol. Bur. San Francisco, 1976—, v.p., 1978, vice chmn. edn. com., 1976-77; bd. dirs. U. Calif. Hosp. Aux., San Francisco, 1979—, 2d v.p., 1980—; bd. dirs. Communications Inst., San Francisco, 1978—. Served to capt. WAC, 1943-46. Mem. Nat., Central Calif. councils tchrs. English, Calif. Tchrs. Assn., NAACP, Am. Assn. Ret. Persons. Author: The River Must Flow (poems) 1965, By the Banks of the River, 1975; (one-act play) You Gotta Pay Your Dues, 1974. Home and Office: 40 Parkridge Dr #11 San Francisco CA 94131

WYATT, KATHRYN BENTON, psychologist; b. Danville, Va., May 11, 1928; d. Joseph Nelson and Margaret (Davis) Benton; B.A., Randolph Macon Womans Coll., 1949; M.Ed., U. Va., 1952; M.A., U. N.C., 1973, Ph.D., 1977; m. Landon Russell Wyatt, Aug. 30, 1952; children—Margaret Wyatt Scott, Landon Russell III, Elizabeth Benton. Instr. psychology Stratford Coll., Danville, 1949-54, asst. prof., chmn. dept., 1963-73; asso. prof. psychology and sociology Danville Community Coll. Mem. Danville Sch. Bd., Danville Sch. System Planning Council. Mem. Am. Psychol. Assn., Soc. Research Child Devel., Southeastern Psychol. Assn., Va. Acad. Sci., Va. Psychol. Assn., Va. Assn. Social Scis., Phi Delta Kappa. Baptist. Clubs: Jr. Wednesday (pres.), Shakespeare, Alyce Kyle Dist. Jr. Women's, Wayside, Gabriella Garden. Contbr. articles to profl. jours. Home: 301 Magnolia Dr Danville VA 24541 Office: Danville Community College Bonner Ave Danville VA 24541

WYATT-KENNER, ROSE MARIE, psychiat. and med. social worker; b. San Angelo, Tex., Feb. 16, 1937; d. James Odis and Annie LaVernia (Lott) Wyatt; B.A. (Ford Found. scholar, 1953-57), Fisk U., 1957; M.S., U. So. Calif., 1963; M.A., M.S.W. (univ. scholar 1970-72, United Charities scholar 1970-72), U. Chgo., 1972; postgrad. in indsl. psychology Ill. Inst. Tech., 1976—. Elem. tchr. Chgo. Bd. Edn., 1959-63, clin. social worker, 1979—; adult program dir. Chgo. YWCA, 1963-64; youth counselor Chgo. Commn. on Youth Welfare, 1964-66; supervising social worker for Head Start, Chgo. Com. on Urban Opportunity, 1966; social worker Chgo. Commn. on Youth Welfare, 1966-68, Jewish Vocat. Service, 1968; social worker Sch. Community Relations, Detroit Public Schs., 1968-70; social worker United Charities, 1972-74; clin. social worker Kenner-Rosman and Assos., Chgo., 1980—, pres., 1981—; instr. dept. of corrections Chgo. State U., 1972—. Adv. bd. United Charities, Calumet Area, program com. chmn., 1974-80; vol. Assn. of Community Agts. 1968-70, Southside Sr. Citizens Coalition, Chgo., 1963-66, Roseland Health Planning Com., 1974-76, Teen Pregnancy Caucus, 1978-82; mem. social work adv. council Chgo. Bd. Edn., 1976. Recipient Outstanding Employee award for med.-social work services Maternal and Child Health Services div. HEW; 1971. Mem. Nat. Assn. Social Workers, Acad. Cert. Social Workers, Ill. Cert. Social Workers, Chgo. Psychol. Club, Ill Acad. Criminology, NEA, Ill. Assn. Sch. Social Workers, Am. Assn. for Mental Deficiency, Qualified Mental Retardation Profls., Fisk U. Alumni Assn., Alpha Kappa Alpha. Roman Catholic. Clubs: Am. Bridge Assn., Civenos Bridge.

WYCHE, MARY GREEN (MRS. EDMOND WYCHE, JR.), educator; b. Norfolk, Va., Oct. 29, 1938; d. George Herbert and Lillian Louise (Vaughn) Green; student Norfolk State Coll., 1955-57; B.S., Howard U., 1959; postgrad. N.Y. U., 1960; M.Ed., So. U., 1962; postgrad. Ind. U., 1963, U. Ill., 1964, Temple U., 1968, U. Del., 1973; doctoral candidate U. Md., 1978—; m. Edmond Wyche, Jr., June 3, 1978. Health and phys. edn. tchr. Newport News (Va.) City Schs., 1959-61, East Baton Rouge Parrish, 1962-63; instr. health and phys. edn. Dillard U., New Orleans, 1963-65, Va. State Coll., Petersburg, 1965-67; asst. prof. health and phys. edn. Del. State Coll., Dover, 1967-70, asst. prof., chmn. health and phys. edn., 1970—, mem. Grad. Sch. council, 1981-82. Mem. State Health Adv. Com. Recipient award Dover YMCA, 1968, Plaque Phys. Edn. Major's Club, 1970-73, grant, DuPont Co., 1973. Mem. Am. (mem. nat. com. 1969-71), Del. (mem. scholarship com. 1970) assns. health, phys. edn. and recreation, Nat., Eastern assns. health, phys. edn. and recreation, Delta Sigma Theta. Democrat. Roman Catholic. Clubs: Delicadoes (Norfolk); Racquet, Indoor Tennis, Colonial (Dover). Home: 600 Carriage Ln Dover DE 19901

WYCKOFF, CLAIRE MOHNKERN, assn. exec.; b. New Rochelle, N.Y., Oct. 17, 1940; d. McAllister Reynold and Adele Marie (Gennert) Mohnkern; B.A. in History and French, Mt. Holyoke Coll., 1962; M.A. in Edn., N.Y. U., 1969; m. Edward Lisk Wyckoff, May 8, 1965; 1 dau., Jenny Adele. Promotion mgr. Harcourt, Brace, Jovanovich, East, 1966-68; sales dir. Trade and Library div. Scholastic Mag., 1970-75; pres. Claire M. Wyckoff Assos., 1975-78; mktg. and sales dir. Publs. div. Am. Mgmt. Assns., N.Y.C., 1978-82, pub. book div., 1982—. Bd. dirs. N.Y. Jr. League, 1973-74, Vol. of Year award; mem. N.Y. County Republican Com., 1973—; bd. dirs. Lower Eastside Center Drug Abuse, 1974—. Mem. Am. Booksellers Assn., Sales Execs. Club, Children's Book Council (past dir.), Pubs. Library Promotion Group (past dir.). Roman Catholic. Office: 135 W 50th St New York NY 10020

WYCKOFF, JUANITA CHARLENE, educator; b. Luray, Kans., Sept. 24, 1915; d. William S. and Bertha (McKanna) W.; B.S., Kans. State U., 1940; M.S., Colo. State U., 1959. Tchr., Gove (Kans.) Rural High Sch., 1940, Luray (Kans.) Community High Sch., 1941-42, Decatur Community High Sch., Oberlin, Kans., 1944-46, Oswego (Kans.) High Sch., 1946-48, Cherryvale (Kans.) High Sch., 1948-57; asst. prof. textiles and clothing Mankato (Minn.) State U., 1959—; mem. adv. bd. Secondary Home Econs. Dist. No. 77, Mankato. Mem. NEA, Minn. Edn. Assn., Mankato State U. Interfaculty Assn., Am. Home Econs. Assn., Minn. Home Econs. Assn., Assn. Coll. Prof. Textiles and Clothing, Delta Kappa Gamma. Methodist. Home: 105 E Welcome St Mankato MN 56001 Office: Trafton Sci Center Mankato State U Box 44 Mankato MN 56001

WYCKOFF, SUSAN, astronomer; b. Santa Cruz, Calif., Mar. 18, 1941; d. Stephen and Jean (Taft) W.; B.A., Mt. Holyoke Coll., 1962; Ph.D., Case Inst. Tech., 1967; m. Peter A. Wehinger, July 29, 1967. Postdoctoral fellow astronomy U. Mich., 1967-68; asst. prof. physics Albion (Mich.) Coll., 1968-70; research asso. physics-astronomy U. Kans., 1970-72; sr. lectr. Tel-Aviv U., 1972-75, Smithsonian research fellow, 1972-74; U.K. Sci. Research Council prin. research fellow Royal Greenwich (Eng.) Obs., 1975-77; adj. prof. astronomy Sussex (Eng.) U., 1975-77; asst. prof. Ohio State U., 1977-79; asso. prof. physics Ariz. State U., Tempe, 1979-82, prof. physics, 1982—; vis. prof. Inst. Theoretical Astrophysics, U. Heidelberg (W.Ger.), 1980; mem. A.J. Cannon Prize Commn., 1982—; mem. various coms. NASA, 1979—. Mem. Am. Astron. Soc., Astron. Soc. Pacific, Internat. Astron. Union, Royal Astron. Soc., Sigma Xi. Home: 1606 E West Wind Way Tempe AZ 85283 Office: Physics Dept Ariz State U Tempe AZ 85287

WYLAND, CHERYL ANN, escrow co. exec.; b. Los Angeles, Apr. 4, 1941; d. Ellwood Blaine and Mary Estelle (Robinson) Davis; student UCLA, 1958-60; m. Frank Wyland, June 5, 1971; children—Shon, Patrick, Brian. Legal sec. Gordon T. Shepard, Brookhurst, Garden Grove, Calif., 1967-68; escrow sec. Escrow Co., Santa Ana, Calif., 1969-71, escrow officer 1971—, pres., 1971—; lectr. profl. seminars.; tchr. in field. Bd. dirs. Ind. Escrow Licensees State of Calif. Accredited by Dept. Real Estate, Calif. Mem. Escrow Inst. (dir.), East Orange County Bd. Realtors, Am. Contract Bridge League (life master). Office: 2070 N Tustin Santa Ana CA 92711

WYLE, EDITH ROBINSON, artist, mus. dir.; b. San Francisco, Apr. 21, 1918; d. Louis L. and Rose R. Robinson; B.A., U. Calif., Berkeley, 1940; student Chouinard, Otis and Art Center Schs.; m. Frank Wyle, Jan. 25, 1942; children—Stephen, Nancy Wyle Romero, Diana Wyle Munk. Painter, 1936-65; one-person show Preston Gallery, N.Y.C., 1963; founder The Egg and the Eye Gallery/Restaurant, 1965; founder Craft and Folk Art Mus., Los Angeles, 1974, program dir., 1974—, curator, designer Japanese Traditional Toys exhbn., 1978; trustee Calif. Inst. Arts; bd. dirs. Ethnic Arts Council of Los Angeles; adv. panelist Performing Tree, art com. Los Angeles Music Center Performing Arts Council; hon. sponsor Modern and Contemporary Art Council; council mem. Council for the Arts, M.I.T. Mem. Am. Assn. Mus., Am. Women Internat. Understanding. Editorial bd. Craft Internat. Mag., 1979—; reviewer Dorland Mountain Colony. Office: 5814 Wilshire Blvd Los Angeles CA 90036

WYLIE, FLOREAN HOLLENBERGER, nurse; b. Waynesboro, Pa., Oct. 4, 1912; d. John Marshall and Alice Edna (Duffey) Hollenberger; R.N., Med. Coll. Hosp. Sch. Nursing, 1933; grad. x-ray technology U. Pa., 1934; m. Orval Dale Wylie, July 21, 1950; 1 dau., Florean Phyllis. Office mgr., surg. asst. John J. Curry, M.D., Phila., 1935-53; staff nurse Vis. Nurses, Haddonfield, N.J., 1960-62; also pvt. duty nurse, N.J., 1962-63; supr. obstet. dept. Med. Coll. Hosp. Pa., Phila., 1964-70; dir. nurses Meth. Homes N.J.-Pitman (N.J.) Manor, 1971—. Mem. Alumni Med. Coll. Pa. (pres., treas.), South Jersey Gerontol. Nurses Assn. (treas.), Med. Coll. Nurses Assn., Eagles Aux., Am. Legion Aux.

WYLIE, MARY JEAN, textile chemist, educator; b. Bowling Green, Ohio, Mar. 9, 1926; d. W. Elmer and Gladys B. (Stockley) W.; B.S. in Edn., Bowling Green State U., 1948; M.S., U. Wis., 1957; postgrad. U. Ariz., 1962-63. Home demonstration agt. Ohio State U., Auglaize county, 1948-55; grad. research asst. U. Wis., Madison, 1955-57; instr. Syracuse (N.Y.) U., 1957-59; asst. prof. home econs. dept. U. Iowa, Iowa City, 1959-62; grad. teaching asst. U. Ariz., Tucson, 1962-63; mem. faculty home econs. extension Ohio State U., Paulding County, 1965-66; asst. prof. U. Mo., Columbia, 1966-67; asst. prof. Sch. Home Econs., U. Ariz., Tucson, 1967-72, asso. prof., 1972—; adv. Irvin Industries, 1972-73; asst. to Tucson Police Dept., 1975-76, Ariz. State Mus., 1978. U.S. Dept. Agr. research grantee, 1967—. Mem. Am. Assn. Textile Chemists and Colorists, ASTM (textiles com.), Costume Soc. Am., Am. Home Econs. Assn., Ariz. Home Econs. Assn. (mem. exec. bd. 1974-77), AAUP, Assn. Coll. Profs. in Textiles and Clothing (mem. nat. exec. bd. 1974-77, pres. 1972-73, mem. com. to revise handbook 1975-77), Info. Council on Fabric Flammability, Ariz. Consumer's Council, Kappa Delta Pi, Omicron Nu, Sigma Delta Epsilon, Alpha Gamma Delta, AAUW, Phi Upsilon Omicron. Clubs: Order Eastern Star, Altrusa (mem. exec. bd. 1977-79). Contbr. numerous articles to jours. in home econs. Home: 2507 E Forgeus Pl Tucson AZ 85716 Office: School Home Econs U Ariz Tucson AZ 85721

WYLIE, NETA EVANGELINE, psychologist; b. Grapeland, Tex., Sept. 5, 1921; d. John Robert and Edith (Bean) Taylor; B.Mus., Baylor U., 1942; M.A., U. Houston, 1975; Ph.D., Tex. A&M U., 1976; m. Roger Wylie, Dec. 16, 1944 (div. Feb. 6, 1976); children—Pat (dec.), Beth. Instr. violin, piano, music theory East Tex. Bapt. Coll., Marshall, 1944-45; asst. prof. off-campus counselor edn. Prairie View (Tex.) A&M U., 1975-78; pvt. practice psychology, Baytown, Tex., Galveston, Tex., 1975—; speaker, violinist, pianist, vocalist, organist for clubs and chs. in Houston area, 1945—; organist 1st Presbyn. Ch., Galveston. Mem. Am. Psychol. Assn., Tex. Psychol. Assn., Am. Guild of Organists, Mu Phi Epsilon. Presbyn. Composer musical composition Prayer, 1959; rec. album Sounds of Joy and Reverence, 1977. Home: 16 Colony Park Circle Galveston TX 77551 Office: 1903 Church St Galveston TX 77550

WYMAN, LOTTE ANN NOVAK (MRS. RALPH M. WYMAN), civic worker; b. Vienna, Austria, Aug. 15, 1925; d. Josef and Hertha (Wallnstorfer) Novak; B.A., Barnard Coll., 1947; 1 dau., Leslie Andrea. Grey Lady, ARC, 1947-55; treas. Women's Assn. First Presbyn. Ch., Greenwich, Conn., 1963-65, chmn. mission interpretation program, 1975-77; bd. dirs. Friends of Sunny Hill Sch. for Phys. and Emotionally Handicapped Children, Greenwich, 1960—; bd. dirs. YWCA, Greenwich, 1963-78, 81—, chmn. world fellowship, 1965, mem. bldg. com., 1965-70, pres., 1967-70; bd. dirs. Drug Liberation Program of Greater Stamford, 1970-74, Community Chest, Greenwich, 1967-70, Community Forum, Greenwich, 1970—; bd. dirs. Turtle Bay Music Sch., N.Y.C., 1970-80; bd. dirs. Greenwich Arts Council, 1974-79, pres., 1976-79; bd. dirs. Neuberger Mus., SUNY, 1979—, M.I.T. Council for the Arts, 1980—, Met. Opera Assn., 1980—. Mem. N.Y. Zool. Soc., Ch. Women United (v.p. 1971-72). Republican. Presbyterian. Clubs: Greenwich Country; Stratton Mountain (Vt.) Country. Home: Baldwin Farms North Greenwich CT 06830

WYNAR, CHRISTINA LORAINE GEHRT, pub. co. exec.; b. Rockford, Ill., Mar. 14, 1933; d. Francis William and Lydia Ann (Teuscher) Gehrt; B.A. in History, Quincy (Ill.) Coll., 1955; M.S. in Library Sci., U. Denver, 1963; m. Bohdan S. Wynar, Aug. 23, 1965 (div. 1980). Tchr., librarian public schs., Rockford, Ill., 1955-63; dist. librarian Alamitos Sch. Dist., Garden Grove, Calif., 1963-65; mng. editor, sec.-treas. Libraries Unlimited, Inc., Littleton, Colo., 1970-80; pres. Corona Press, Littleton, 1980—. Soviet sect. leader Amnesty Internat./U.S.A., Group 60, Denver, 1978; dir. Ukrainian Research Found., Inc., Englewood, Colo., 1974. Mem. ALA, Swiss Am. Hist. Soc. Contbg. editor Sch. Media Quar., 1973-78; author: Guide to Reference Books for School Media Centers, 1973, Supplement, 1974-75, 1978, 2d edit., 1981; The Ukrainian American Index: The Ukrainian Weekly (ann.), 1978, 79, The Ukrainian American Index: Ukrainian Art Digest 1963-69, 1980; contbr. articles to profl. jours. Home: 7788 S Ogden Way Littleton CO 80122

WYNDEWICKE, KIONNE ANNETTE, educator; b. Preston, Miss.; d. Clifton Thomas and Missouria (Jackson) Johnson; student Columbia Coll., Chgo., 1972; B.S., Ill. State Normal U., 1961; postgrad. Williams Coll., Williamstown, Mass., 1972; M.Ed., Nat. Coll. Edn., 1982; m. Eugene C. Moorer, Sept. 23, 1961 (div.). Social worker Cook County Dept. Pub. Aid, 1961; tchr. reading Chgo. Bd. Edn., 1961—; asst. to news dir. WCIU-TV, 1972-74; asst. women's editor Chgo. Defender, 1970-72; social sec. Dr. William R. Clarke, 1972—; part-time photog. model, fashion commentator, pub. relations cons., pub. speaker. Cochmn. installation Profl. Women's Aux., Provident Hosp., 1961, corr. sec., 1969, publicity chmn., 1969-72, 74-77. Selected one of 13 persons in U.S. to attend Innovative Tchr. Tng. Seminar, funded by Henry Luce Found. at Williams Coll., 1972; one of 25 Black women of Chgo. to receive Kizzy award, 1977; recipient Outstanding Community Service award Beatrice Caffrey Youth Service, Inc., 1978. Mem. Ill. Speech and Theatre Assn., WTTW Channel 11 Ednl. TV, Mus. Contemporary Art, Speech Communication Assn. Am., YWCA. Lutheran. Contbr. articles to local newspapers. Home: 533 E 33d Pl Apt 1100 Chicago IL 60616 Office: 707 E 37th St Chicago IL 60653

WYNETTE, TAMMY, singer; b. Red Bay, Ala., May 5, 1942; d. William Hollis Pugh; m. George Jones, Sept. 1968. Former beauty operator; rec. artist Epic Records, 1967—; regular appearance Grand Ole Opry radio sta. WSM, Nashville, 1969—, tours U.S. and Can.; recs. include Your Good Girl's Gonna Go Bad, My Elusive Dreams, Stand by Your Man, Divorce, Take Me to Your World, Bedtime Story, We're Gonna Hold On; albums include Till I Can Make It on My Own, Let's Get Together, Womanhood. Named Female Vocalist of Year Country Music Assn., 1968, 69, 70. Address: care Jim Halsey Co Inc Corporate Pl Penthouse 5800 E Skelly Dr Tulsa OK 74135 *

WYNIA, ANN JOBE, state legislator, polit. scientist; b. Ft. Worth, July 29, 1943; d. Lewis Harvey and Josephine Jewel (Dibrell) Jobe; B.A., U. Tex., Arlington, 1965; M.A., U. Wis., 1968; m. June 14, 1966. Instr. polit. sci. North Hennepin Community Coll., 1970—; mem. Minn. Ho. of Reps., 1976—. Bd. dirs. Working Opportunities for Women, St. Paul, 1977-80; mem. Minn. Gov.'s Task Force on Families, 1978-79. Recipient Open-Up-The System award Minn. Common Cause, 1979. Mem. Minn. Polit. Sci. Assn., Women's Polit. Caucus. Mem. Democratic Farm Labor Party. Office: Capitol Saint Paul MN 55155 *

WYRICK, PRISCILLA BLAKENEY, microbiologist; b. Greensboro, N.C., Apr. 28, 1940; d. Carnie Lee and Prestine (Blakeney) W.; B.S., U. N.C., Chapel Hill, 1962, M.S., 1966, Ph.D., 1971. Supr. clin. microbiology N.C. Meml. Hosp., Chapel Hill, 1962-66; Med. Research Council fellow Nat. Inst. Med. Research, London, 1971-73; asst. prof. microbiology U. N.C., Chapel Hill, 1973-79, asso. prof., 1979—. Recipient Faculty Teaching award, 1979; Burroughs Wellcome Research travel fellow, 1980-81; NIH grantee. Mem. Am. Soc. Microbiology, Am. Acad. Microbiology. Contbr. articles to profl. jours. Office: Dept Bacteriology U NC Med Sch Chapel Hill NC 27514

WYSE, SHEILA RUTH, ins. co. exec.; b. N.Y.C., Feb. 4, 1950; d. Benjamin Wyse; B.A., Bklyn. Coll., 1972. Underwriting trainee Beneficial Nat. Life Ins. Co. (name changed to Nat. Benefit Life 1980, N.Y.C., 1973-75, mgr., 1975-79, asst. v.p., 1979-80, 2d v.p., 1980-82, v.p., 1982—; chmn. industry adv. com. disability benefits law, 1980-81. Publ. coordinator Statutory Star, 1979—. Office: 2 Park Ave New York NY 10016

XETHALIS, EILEEN SCANLON, acct.; b. New Castle, Pa., May 8, 1943; d. Thomas Edward and Martha Irene (Posivach) Scanlon; B.A., N.Y.U., 1982; m. Demetrios L. Xethalis, July 11, 1966; children—Sofia Demetria, Lambros Demetrios. Sec.-treas. Flowers by Demetrios, Inc., Hightstown, N.J., 1967—. Key leader Capital Funds campaign Princeton Day Sch., 1976-77; v.p. Arts and Exhibits Parents Assn., 1977-79, class parent, 1981. Mem. Am. Mgmt. Assn., Nat. Fedn. Ind. Bus., Mfg. Jewelers Assn. Am. Republican. Greek Orthodox. Club: Skyview Country. Home: 182 Stockton St Hightstown NJ 08520 Office: 182 Stockton St Hightstown NJ 08520

YACABUCCI, ELENA, bus. exec.; b. Jersey City; d. Ralph George and Eleanor Mary (Corvino) Y.; student N.Y. U., 1978, Western Conn. State Coll., 1974-79. With All-Rite Pen Co., Hackensack and Fair Lawn, N.J., 1967-72, adminstrv. asst., 1972-75; sales promotion coordinator Berol USA, Danbury, Conn., 1975—. Democrat. Contbr. articles to profl. jours. and newspapers. Home: 15-7 Pilgrim Trail Woodbury CT 06798 Office: Berol USA Eagle Rd Danbury CT 06810

YACAVONE, MURIEL TAUL, state legislator; b. Hartford, Conn., May 26, 1920; d. William M. and Elizabeth (Griffing) Taul; student schs. W. Hartford, Conn.; children—John Peter, Mark Philip, Teresa Jane, Elizabeth Rose. Commr. health bd. Town of East Hartford, Conn., 1962-63, com. mem. Econ. Opportunity Commn., 1964-65, chmn. Community Council Youth, 1965-68; justice of the peace, 1968-70; mem. Conn. Ho. of Reps., 1971—, asst. majority leader, 1974-78; citizen mem. Drug Adv. Com. State of Conn., 1969—; dir. Greater Hartford Council on Alcoholism. Bd. dirs. George J. Penney High Sch. Parent-Tchr. Orgn.; legis. chmn. Conn. Fedn. Democratic Women's Clubs; mem. East Hartford LWV, Dem. Women's Club E. Hartford. Served with USMC, 1943-45. Roman Catholic. Office: Connecticut House of Reps Hartford CT 06115 *

YACHER, NANCY TERRELL STEERE, educator; b. McMinnville, Oreg., Mar. 22, 1935; d. Horace Clifford and Mary Margaret (Newsom) Terrell; student Linfield Coll., 1953-55; B.A. summa cum laude in English, Lewis and Clark Coll., 1957; M.A. in Am. Studies (Danforth fellow, scholar), U. Pa., 1960; postgrad. (Danforth Grad. Woman fellow), U. Kans., 1972-78; m. Sherman L. Yacher, Oct. 5, 1979; children by previous marriage—John Tierney Steere, Robert Terrell Steere. Program asst. Am. Friends Service Com., Phila., 1957-58, 60-61; asst. instr. English dept. U. Kans., Lawrence, 1975-78; instr. English, Washburn U., Topeka, 1980—. Mem. regional selection com. Danforth Assocs. Program, 1972-74; bd. dirs. Gainesville (Fla.) Women for Equal Rights, 1962-67; chmn. Lawrence Community Nursery, 1968-69; v.p. Schwegler Sch. PTA, Lawrence, 1970-71. Danforth Assoc., 1963-75. Mem. Nat. Council Tchrs. of English, Soc. for Values in Higher Edn., Nat. Inst. for Campus Ministries, Inst. for Theol. Encounter with Sci. and Tech. Home: 1749 W 20th St Lawrence KS 66044 Office: 300 Morgan Hall Washburn U Topeka KS 66621

YACOBACCI, HELEN PATRICIA, educator; b. Moultrie, Ga., Apr. 23, 1947; d. Fred Leslie and Mina Marqurite (Shaver) McDaniel; B.S.Ed., U. Ga., 1969; M.Ed., Smith Coll., 1970; Ph.D., Syracuse U., 1978. Tchr., Callier Speech and Hearing Center, Dallas, 1970-71, instructional mgr., 1971-73; ednl. supr. Houston Sch. for Deaf Children, 1973-75; asst. prof. N.Y. U., N.Y.C., 1978—, coordinator tchr. tng. program in edn. of deaf, 1978—; instr. Syracuse U., fall 1977; research asst. Nat. Tech. Inst. for Deaf, Rochester, N.Y., summer 1976; coordinator spl. summer program for parents of deaf Houston Sch. for Deaf Children, 1974; invited lectr., Athens, Greece, 1982; also cons. HEW fellow, 1975-78; Spencer Found. grantee, 1979-83; N.Y. U. curriculum grantee, 1981-82. Mem. Am. Ednl. Research Assn., Conv. Am. Instrs. of the Deaf, Assn. Edn. and Communication Technologists, Northeastern Ednl. Research Assn., A.G. Bell Assn. Edn. of Deaf, Internat. Fedn. of Hard of Hearing, Council Edn. of Deaf. Unitarian. Contbr. articles to profl. jours. Home: 100 Bleecker St L4 New York NY 10012 Office: 829 Shimkin Hall New York NY 10012

YACURA, MARY ELLEN, oil co. exec.; b. Tarentum, Pa., Nov. 11, 1952; d. Michael and Mary Dolores (Virostek) Y., B.A. magna cum laude, U. Pitts., 1974, M.P.I.A., 1978, M.B.A., 1979. With Office of Senator H. John Heinz, III, 1977; sr. advisor Gulf Oil Corp., 1979-80, spl. asst. to pres. Gulf Trading & Transp. Co., Pitts., 1979-80, dir. strategy devel., Houston, 1980-81, dir. strategy devel. Gulf Trading Co., Houston, 1981—. Fulbright scholar, Nat. Def. Fgn. Lang. fellow, 1977-79; Kosciuszko Found. summer scholar in Poland, 1973; U. Pitts. Russian and E. European fellow, 1976-77. Mem. Am. Assn. M.B.A. Execs., Internat. Assn. Energy Economists, Nat. Assn. Female Execs. Democrat. Roman Catholic. Home: 2100 Tanglewilde St Apt 592 Houston TX 77063 Office: PO Box 3726 Houston TX 77253

YAJNIK, SUSAN TRUITT, petroleum geologist; b. Phoenixville, Pa., Aug. 30, 1952; d. Eugene Alfred and Dolores (Barnes) Truitt; B.S. in Geology, Dickinson Coll., 1974; m. Rashmi N. Yajnik, Aug. 4, 1979. Geologist, Ralph H. Hamblin, Marion, Ohio, 1974-77, United Petroleum Corp., Columbus, Ohio, 1977-78; cons. geologist and oil and gas leasing R. & S. Enterprises, Columbus, 1978—; v.p. Rashmi Research, Inc., Columbus, 1978—. Mem. Am. Assn. Petroleum Geologists, Ohio Geol. Soc., Ind. Petroleum Assn. Am., Ohio Oil and Gas Assn., Desk and Derrick Assn. Presbyterian. Address: PO Box 896 Mount Vernon OH 43050

YALOW, ROSALYN SUSSMAN, med. physicist; b. N.Y.C., July 19, 1921; d. Simon and Clara (Zipper) Sussman; A.B., Hunter Coll., 1941; M.S., U. Ill., 1942, Ph.D., 1945, D.Sc. (hon.), 1974; hon. degrees: D.Sc., Phila. Coll. Pharmacy and Sci., 1976, N.Y. Med. Coll., 1976, Med. Coll. Wis., Milw., 1977, Yeshiva U., 1977, Southampton Coll., 1978, Bucknell U., 1978, Princeton U., 1978, Jersey City State Coll., 1979, Med. Coll. Pa., 1979, Manhattan Coll., 1979; D.Hum.Lett., Hunter Coll., 1978, Sacred Heart U., Conn., 1978, St. Michael's Coll., Vt., 1979, Johns Hopkins U., 1979, U. Vt., U. Hartford, Rutgers U., 1980, Rensselaer Poly. Inst., St. Lawrence U., Colgate U., U. So. Calif., 1981, Clarkson Coll., 1982, U. Md. at Balt., 1982; D.Honoris Causa, U. Claude Bernard, Lyon, France, 1979; D.Med., Med. U. S.C., 1981; D.LL., Beaver Coll., 1982; m. A. Aaron Yalow, June 6, 1943; children—Benjamin, Elanna. Asst. in physics U. Ill., Urbana, 1941-43, instr., 1944-45; lectr., temp. asst. prof. physics Hunter Coll., N.Y.C., 1946-50; physicist, asst. chief radioisotope service VA Hosp., Bronx, N.Y., 1950-70, chief nuclear medicine service, 1970-80, dir. Solomon A. Berson Research Lab., 1973; sr. med. investigator VA, 1972; research prof. dept. medicine Mt. Sinai Sch. Medicine, City U. N.Y., 1968-74, Disting. Service prof., 1974-79; Disting. Prof.-at-large, Albert Einstein Coll. Medicine, Yeshiva U., N.Y.C., 1979; chmn. dept. clin. scis. Montefiore Hosp. and Med. Center, Bronx, 1980—; cons. radioisotope unit VA Hosp., Bronx, 1947-50, Lenox Hill Hosp., N.Y.C., 1952-62; mem. subcom. 13, Nat. Com. Radiation Protection, 1957—; sec. U.S. Nat. Com. Med. Physics, 1963-67; med. adv. bd. Nat. Pituitary Agy., 1968-71; endocrinology study sect. NIH, 1969-72; IAEA expert Instituto Energia Atomica, Sao Paulo, Brazil, 1970; cons. subcom. human applications of radioactive materials N.Y.C. Dept. Health, 1972—; bd. sci. counselors NIAMD, NIH, 1972-75; mem. task force immunology and disease NIAID, NIH, 1972-73; mem. com. for evaluation of NPA, NRC, 1973-74; WHO cons. Radiation Medicine Center, Bombay, India, 1978. Bd. dirs. N.Y. Diabetes Assn., 1974. Recipient Nobel prize, 1977; Dickson prize U. Pitts., 1971; Gairdner Found. Internat. award, 1971; Koch award Endocrine Soc., 1972; Commemorative medallion Am. Diabetes Assn., 1972, Rosalyn S. Yalow Research and Devel. award, 1978; Anachem award Detroit Assn. Analytical Chemists, 1973; Dr. Albion O. Bernstein award Med. Soc. N.Y. State, 1974; Sci. Achievement award AMA, 1975; VA Exceptional Service award, 1975, 78; A. Cressy Morrison award N.Y. Acad. Scis., 1975; Disting. Achievement award Modern Medicine, 1976; Albert Lasker Basic Med. Research award, 1976; La Madonnina Internat. prize, Milan, 1976; Torch of Learning award Am. Friends of Hebrew U., 1978; Gratum Genus Humanum Gold medal World Fedn. Nuclear Medicine and Biology, 1978; Virchow Gold medal Virchow-Pirquet Med. Soc., 1978; G. von Hevesy medal, 1978; citation of esteem St. John's U., 1979; Achievement in Life award Ency. Britannica, 1980; ann. gold medal award Phi Lambda Kappa, 1980. Fellow Clin. Soc. of N.Y. Diabetes Assn. (hon.), N.Y. Acad. Sci. (chmn. biophysics div. 1964-65), Am. Coll. Radiology (asso.); mem. Radiation Research Soc., Am. Assn. Physicists in Medicine, Biophys. Soc., Am. Diabetes Assn., Am. Physiol. Soc., Endocrine Soc. (council; pres.-elect 1977, pres. 1978), Soc. Nuclear Medicine, Nat. Acad. Scis., Am. Acad. Arts and Scis., Harvey Soc. (hon.), French Acad. Medicine (fgn. asso.), Sigma Xi (hon.), Phi Beta Kappa (hon.), Sigma Pi Sigma, Pi Mu Epsilon, Sigma Delta Epsilon. Editorial bd. Endocrinology, 1967-72; co-editor Hormone and Metabolic Research, 1973—; editorial adv. council Acta Diabetologica Latina, 1975-77; editorial bd. Mt. Sinai Jour. Medicine, 1976-79, Diabetes, 1976-79; editorial adv. bd. Ency. Universalis, 1978; contbr. numerous articles to profl. jours. Home: 3242 Tibbett Ave Bronx NY 10463 Office: 130 W Kingsbridge Rd Bronx NH NY 10468

YAMADA, ANNIE HANAKO KANESHIRO, educator; b. Honolulu, July 7, 1930; d. Seimatsu and Naye (Nakahara) Kaneshiro; B.A., Carleton Coll., 1952; postgrad. So. Oreg. Coll., 1953-54; M.Ed., U. Hawaii, 1968; Ed.D., Nova U.; 1 dau., Annette Shinsato; m. 2d, William Yuuji Yamada, May 3, 1974; adopted children—Grant, Marc, Guy, Dan. Elem. tchr. dept. edn., Honolulu, 1954-58, Wiseburn Sch. Dist., Hawthorne, Calif., 1958-60, dept. edn., Honolulu, 1960-67 supr. student tchrs., dept. edn., 1961-64; counselor U. Hawaii, Honolulu Community Coll., 1968—. Mem. Coll. and U. Profl. Assn., NEA, Hawaii Personnel and Guidance Assn., Hawaii Edn. Assn. Congregationalist. Home: 46-278 Kalaua Pl Honolulu HI 96744 Office: 874 Dillingham Blvd Honolulu HI 96817

YANCY, E(VA) REGINA, mfg. co. personnel ofcl.; b. Athens, Ala., Oct. 12, 1946; d. James Howard and Vera Eva (Boshell) Y.; B.A. in English, Athens Coll., 1968; M.Adminstrv. Sci., U. Ala., Huntsville, 1980. Exec. sec. PPG Industries, Huntsville, 1968-74; adminstrv. asst. Cahoon & Assos., Huntsville, 1974-75; adminstrv. asst. Owens-Corning Fiberglas, Huntsville, 1975-79, personnel asst., 1979-81, personnel dir. Huntsville plant, 1981—. Mem. Pvt. Industry Council, 1981—, Job Service Employers Commn., 1981—. Mem. Am. Soc. Personnel Adminstrs. Mem. Ch. of Christ. Club: Met. Huntsville Bus. and Profl. Women's (v.p. 1979-80). Home: Route 3 Fox Run Athens AL 35611 Office: PO Box 6086 Huntsville AL 35806

YANEZ, LINDA SUE BEMBRY, corp. exec.; b. San Francisco, Aug. 22, 1953; d. Charles M. and Lorraine Deaderick; B.S. in Bus., San Diego State U., 1975; postgrad. UCLA, 1977-80; m. Robert A. Yanez, Dec. 12, 1980. Purchasing agt. Calif. Milling Corp., Los Angeles, 1976-77; sales mgr. Universal Storage Systems, San Gabriel, Calif., 1977-80; ter. mgr. Alcon Labs., Dallas, 1981; sales mgmt. dir. Ladd-Fab Inc, El Monte, Calif., 1981—. Recipient cert. of Achievement award Action In Mgmt. Forum, 1980. Mem. Internat. Material Mgmt. Soc. Conf. (cert. of achievement award 1980), Nat. Assn. Female Execs. Republican. Home: 416 E Duarte Rd Arcadia CA 91006 Office: 4323 N Rowland Ave El Monte CA 91731

YANG, MEI-UIH, med. researcher, educator; b. Taiwan, Republic of China, Nov. 11, 1935; came to U.S., 1963, naturalized, 1975; d. Sun-Lih and Ching-Tz (Huang) Shieh; Ph.D., Columbia U., 1976; m. Chi-Yuan Yang, Nov. 19, 1963. Postdoctoral fellow Inst. Human Nutrition, Columbia U., 1976-77; research asso. dept. medicine Obesity Research Center, Coll. Physicians and Surgeons, Columbia U., N.Y.C., 1977-79, asso. staff nutrition and metabolism dept., St. Luke's Hosp. Center, N.Y.C., 1979—; adj. asst. prof. Bklyn. Coll., 1977—. NIH research trainee, 1976-77, obesity research grantee, 1977—. Mem. Am. Dietetic Assn. Office: WH 1027 St Luke's Hosp Center 114th St Amsterdam Ave New York NY 10025

YANGA, ELIDA DURAN, obstetrician, gynecologist; b. Philippines, Oct. 24, 1942; d. Ismael E. and Sofia R. (Duran) Yanga; came to U.S., 1966; A.A., U. St. Tomas, Manila, 1960, M.D., 1965. Rotating intern Queens Hosp. Center, Jamaica, N.Y., 1966-67; resident in obstetrics and gynecology Jewish Hosp. and Med. Center, Bklyn., 1967-71; clin. fellow in obstetrics and gynecology Albert Einstein Coll. Medicine, Bronx, N.Y., 1971-73; clin. instr. Downstate Med. Center, Bklyn., 1973-77; practice medicine specializing in obstetrics and gynecology, Bklyn., 1973-77, Howell, Mich., 1978—. Diplomate Am. Bd. Obstetrics and Gynecology. Mem. Mich., Livingston County med. socs., Philippines Med. Assn., AMA. Roman Catholic. Home: 1050 Fox Hill Dr Howell MI 48843 Office: 715 Byron Rd Howell MI 48843

YANISH, ELIZABETH YAFFE, sculptor; b. St. Louis; d. Sam and Fannie May (Weil) Yaffe; student Washington U., 1941, Denver U., 1960; pvt. studies; m. Nathan Yanish, July 5, 1944; children—Ronald, Marilyn Ginsburg, Mindy. One-woman shows: Woodstock Gallery, London, 1973, Internat. House, Denver, 1963, Colo. Women's Coll., Denver, 1975, Contemporaries Gallery, Santa Fe, 1963, So. Colo. State Coll. Pueblo, 1967, others; exhibited in group shows: Salt Lake City Mus., 1964, 71, Denver Art Mus., 1961-75, Oklahoma City Mus., 1969, Joslyn Mus., Omaha, 1964-68, Lucca (Italy) Invitational, 1971, others; represented in permanent collections: Colo. State Bank, Bmh Synagogue, Denver, Denver Womens Coll., Har Ha Shem Congregation, Boulder, Colo., Faith Bible Chapel, Denver, others. Chmn. visual arts Colo. Centennial-Bicentennial, 1974-75; pres. Denver Council Arts and Humanities, 1973-75; mem. Mayor's Com. on Child Abuse, 1974-75; co-chmn. visual arts spree Denver Pub. Schs., 1975; trustee Denver Center for the Performing Arts, 1973-75; chmn. Concerned Citizens for Arts, 1976. Recipient McCormick award Ball State U., Muncie, Ind., 1964, Purchase award Colo. Women's Coll., Denver, 1963, Tyler (Tex.) Mus., 1963, 1st prize in sculpture 1st Nat. Space Art Show, 1971; Humanities scholar Auraria Libraries, U. Colo., Denver. Mem. Artists Equity Assn., Rocky Mountain Liturgical Arts, Allied Sculptors Colo., Allied Arts Inc. Hist. Denver, Symphony Guild, Parks People, Beth Israel Aux. Jewish. Home: 131 Fairfax St Denver CO 80220

YANKEY-MARTICH, CAROL KATE, social worker; b. East Chicago, Ind., Oct. 16, 1947; d. Louis Joseph and Helen Ann (Walas) Yankey; B.S., Ball State U., 1969; postgrad. Ind. U. N.W., 1970, 72; M.S.W., U. Chgo., 1976; m. Richard Allen Martich, July 27, 1974; 1 dau., Lauren Yankey Martich. Tchr. public elem. schs., Portage, Ind., 1969-71; sec. to pres. Ency. Brit. Ednl. Corp., Chgo., 1971-72; social worker, crippled children's service Lake County Dept. Public Welfare, Gary, Ind., 1972-74; psychiat. social worker, in-patient psychiat. unit St. Catherine Hosp., East Chicago, 1976-78, psychiat. team leader, 1978-81; psychotherapist Associated Counseling Service, Calumet City, Ill., 1977-78. Mem. Nat. Assn. Social Workers, Acad. Cert. Social Workers, Ball State U. Alumni Assn., U. Chgo. Alumni Assn., Miller Citizens Corp. Roman Catholic.

YANKOWITZ, SUSAN, author; b. Newark, Feb. 20, 1941; d. Irving and Ruby (Katz) Y.; B.A., Sarah Lawrence Coll., 1963; M.F.A., Yale U., 1968; m. Herbert Leibowitz, May 3, 1978; 1 son, Gabriel Sky. Author: (plays) The Ha-Ha Play and the Lamb, 1970, Terminal, 1970, Slaughterhouse Play, 1971, Boxes, 1972, Terminal, 1973, Wooden Nickels, 1973, Still Life, 1977, True Romances, 1978, Qui Est Anna Mark?, 1979; (novels) Silent Witness, 1976, Taking Liberties, 1982; (screenplay) Portrait of a Scientist as a Dumb Broad, 1969, The Amnesiac, 1980; (TV play) Milk and Funny, 1976, The Prison Game, 1977, Charlotte Perkins Gilman: Forerunner, 1979. Recipient Drama Desk award, 1969; Nat. Endowment Arts fellow, 1972, 79; Guggenheim Found. grantee, 1975; Rockefeller Found. grantee, 1973, CAPS grantee, 1974; Eugene O'Neill fellow for A Knife in the Heart, 1982; Mem. PEN, Dramatists Guild, Authors Guild, Writers Guild Am. Address: 205 W 89th St New York NY 10024

YANNELLO, JUDITH ANN, fed. judge; b. Buffalo, Mar. 27, 1943; d. Guy Raymond and Grace Alberta (Barone) Y.; B.A., Barnard Coll., 1964; J.D., Cornell U., 1967. Admitted to N.Y. bar, 1967, D.C. bar, 1970, U.S. Supreme Ct. bar, 1971, also various fed. cts.; law clk. U.S. Ct. Claims, Washington, 1967-68, trial judge, 1977-82, judge, 1982—; trial atty. civil div. Dept. Justice, Washington, 1968-73; asso. firm Hudson, Creyke, Koehler & Tacke, Washington, 1973-76; adminstrv. judge Armed Services Bd. Contract Appeals, Washington, 1976-77; adj. prof. law Potomac Sch. Law, 1980; speaker, lectr. in field. Recipient Meritorious Service award Dept. Justice, 1972. Mem. Am. Bar Assn., Fed. Bar Assn. (chmn. Ct. Claims com. 1974-76, Disting. Service award 1975), D.C. Bar Assn. (Cert. of Appreciation 1976), N.Y. State Bar Assn., D.C. Bar, Exec. Women in Govt. Club: Zonta. Contbr. articles to profl. jours.; co-editor, contbg. author: Manual for Practice in U.S. Court of Claims, 1976.

YANNITELLI, ANITA KATHRYN, civic worker; b. Peekskill, N.Y., Aug. 4, 1918; d. Charles Frederick and Anna (Abele) Huebner; B.A., Barnard Coll., 1939; M.A., Columbia U., 1945; m. S.A. Yannitelli, Dec. 18, 1940; children—Christine, Thomas, Peter. Grad. asst. Barnard Coll., 1939-41; asst. prof. biology Manhattanville Coll. of Sacred Heart, 1941-46. Chmn. bd. Battle Creek (Mich.) Civic Art Center, 1979-81, acting dir., 1981, also bd. dirs., exec. com., long-range planning com. Recipient cert. of recognition and appreciation Mich. Med. Soc., 1976; cert. Community Concerts for Cultural Progress, 1976. Mem. Mich. Press Women's Assn., Art Center League (pres. 1982-83), AMA Aux. (regional chmn. communications 1976-77), Mich. State Med. Soc. Aux. (state pres. 1974-75, adv. com. to pres., cert. of spl. recognition). Republican. Roman Catholic. Club: Battle Creek Country. Editor, Mich. State Med. Soc. Aux. News, 1978—.

YANOFSKY, BRENDA LEE, psychologist; b. Boston, May 10, 1950; d. Abraham and Martha (Yakus) Y.; B.A. cum laude, U. Mass., 1971; M.Ed. cum laude, Tufts U., 1973; A.G.S., Boston U., 1974, Ed.D., 1982. Counselor, Newton North High Sch., Newtonville, Mass., 1972-76; psychologist State of Mass., 1974-76, Oak Park (Mich.) Schs., 1976—; instr. Eastern Mich. U., 1977-81, Mercy Coll., 1982—; psychologist Jensen Counseling, Farmington Hills, Mich., 1980—; bd. dirs. Multi-Service Center, Newton, Mass., 1974-76. Mem. Am. Psychol. Assn., Am. Personnel and Guidance Assn., Mental Health Profs. Assn., Mich. Alcohol and Addiction Assn.

YANTIS, KATHLEEN MARY, naval officer; b. Gouverneur, N.Y., Dec. 15, 1951; d. Clifford Alexander and Isabelle Marjorie (Howard) Hance; B.S. in Psychology, St. Lawrence U., 1974; m. Micheal Dee Yantis, Dec. 28, 1976; Commd. ensign U.S. Navy, 1974, advanced through grades to lt., 1978; communications watch officer, Naval Communications Area Master Sta. Eastern Pacific, 1974-76; message center officer, comdr. Oceanographic Systems Atlantic, 1977-78; asst. officer in charge Nav. Aids Support Unit, 1979-80; asst. officer in charge Naval Telecommunications Center, Hampton Roads, Norfolk, Va., 1980-82; assigned to Naval Postgrad. Sch., Monterey, Calif., 1982—. Mem. Armed Forces Communications and Electronics Assn., Nat. Assn. Female Execs. Home: 1745 Military Ave Seaside CA 93955 Office: SMC 1935 Naval Postgrad Sch Monterey CA 93940

YANTIS, SHAR SOUTHALL, writer; b. Holidays Cove, W.Va., Jan. 28, 1930; d. Edgar C. and Freda Bodell (Kay) Southall; B.A. in Journalism, Bethany Coll., 1952; m. Leech Key Cracraft, Dec. 10, 1956 (dec. Aug. 1961); 1 son, Stuart McLure; m. 2d, John Marshall Yantis, May 7, 1976. Reporter, columnist Wheeling (W.Va.) News Register, 1951-56; soc. editor Palm Springs (Calif.) Life mag., 1959-61, 75-76; social columnist Riverside (Calif.) Daily Enterprise, 1958-63; women's editor The Desert Sun, Palm Springs, 1967-70. Past pres., dir. Palm Springs Pathfinders, 1974-76; bd. dirs. Palm Springs Boys Club, 1972-76. Mem. World Affairs Council (dir.), Phi Mu. Republican. Clubs: Thunderbird Country (Palm Springs); Hardscrabble Country, Fianna Hills Country, Town (Fort Smith, Ark.); Garden of the Gods (Colorado Springs, Colo.); Balboa (Mazatlan, Mex.). Home: 3 Berry Hill Fort Smith AR 72903 also Thunderbird CC PO Box Y Rancho Mirage CA 92270

YAO, HILDA HSIANG, banker; b. Honolulu, Sept. 11, 1956; d. Tze Yee and Dorothy Wen (Wu) Yao; B.A., U. Pacific, 1975; M.S., U. Wis., 1976; postgrad. Stanford U., 1976-77. Project dir. Nat. Endowment Humanities, Washington, 1977; sr. ops., product analyst Visa Internat., San Francisco, 1977-80; asst. v.p. Bank of Am., 1980—; lectr. in field. Vol., San Francisco Bay Area United Way. Nat. Endowment Humanities grantee. Mem. Am. Mgmt. Assn., Calif. Bankers Assn., Am. Bankers Assn., Nat. Assn. Bank Women, Calif. Acad. Scis., Calif. Hist. Soc., U. Pacific Alumni Assn. (dir.). Club: Commonwealth. Contbr. articles to profl. jours. Address: PO Box 261 San Francisco CA 94101

YARBROUGH, JOYCE LENORE, mgmt. cons.; b. Bowling Green, Ky., Oct. 7, 1948; d. William S. Yarbrough and Hortense Lenore (Bullock) Jackson; B.A., Fisk U., 1970; M.B.A., Golden Gate U., 1977. Spl. projects coordinator Econ. Opportunity Council, San Francisco, 1971-77; sales/statistician Macy's of Calif., San Francisco, 1971—; mgmt. cons. C.J. & Assos. Enterprises Inc., San Francisco, 1977-78; pres. Le Nore Co., Inc., 1978—; adminstrv. ops. supr. Bur. Census, U.S. Dept. Commerce, 1980; market researcher Western Pacific Industries, 1981—. Co-founder Scott-Wada Youth Found.; bd. dirs. Urban League San Francisco, 1973-79, Mental Assn. San Francisco, 1972-79; panelist United Way of Bay Area, 1971-76; treas. Westside Community Mental Health Center, 1976-79; sec. Cath. Youth Orgn., 1977—. Mem. Mortar Bd. Home: 100 Font Blvd Apt 1K San Francisco CA 94132 Office: PO Box 15117 San Francisco CA 94115

YARBROUGH, MARTHA CORNELIA, music educator; b. Waycross, Ga., Feb. 8, 1940; d. Henry Elliott and Jessie (Sirmans) Y.; B.M.E., Stetson U., 1962; M.M.E., Fla. State U., 1968, Ph.D., 1973. Choral dir. Ware County High Sch., Waycross, Ga., 1962-64, Glynn Acad., Brunswick, Ga., 1964-70; asst. choral dir. Fla. State U., 1970-72; cons. in music Muscogee County Sch. Dist., Columbus, Ga., 1972-73; cons. in tchr. edn. Psycho-Edno. Cons., Inc., Tallahassee, 1972-73; asst. prof. music edn., dir. univs. choruses and oratorio soc. Syracuse U., 1973-76, asso. prof. music edn., 1976—, acting asst. dean Coll. Visual and Performing Arts, 1980-82, acting dir. Sch. Music, 1980-82, chmn. music edn., 1982—. Mem. Music Educators Nat. Conf., N.Y. State Sch. Music Assn., AAUP, Pi Kappa Lambda, Phi Beta, Kappa Delta Pi. Co-author: Competency-Based Music Education, 1980; mem. editorial com. Jour. Research in Music Edn.; contbr. articles to profl. jours., chpts. in books. Office: Sch Music Syracuse U Syracuse NY 13210

YARBROUGH, SHARON LYNN, ednl. adviser, cons.; b. Dyer, Tenn., Aug. 3, 1948; d. Guy Freeman and Gwendolynn Aileen (Sawyer) Roden; B.S. in Bus. Adminstrn., Carson Newman Coll., 1972; M.S. in Bus. Edn., U. Tenn., 1974; children—Tammye Lynn, James Royce. Adminstrv. asst. Hamblen County Quar. Ct., Morristown, Tenn., 1974-76; field adviser U. Tenn.-County Tech. Assistance Service, Chattanooga, 1976—; instr. Walters State Community Coll., part-time, 1974-76, Columbia Coll., part-time, 1974-76, Chattanooga State Tech. Community Coll., part-time, 1977-81. Rec. sec. adminstrv. bd. St. Johns' United Methodist Ch., 1980-81. Club: Harrison Booster's (rec. sec. 1978). Home: 5836 Pine Lake Dr Harrison TN 37341 Office: Suite 500 226 Capitol Blvd Bldg Nashville TN 37219

YARMOFF, RENEE H., educator; b. N.Y.C., Dec. 4, 1934; d. Morris and Gussie (Nadler) Himmel; B.A., CCNY, 1956; student N.Y. Inst. Fin., 1959; M.S. in Edn., Queen Coll., 1974; Ph.D., St. Johns U., 1982; m. Bernard D. Aroesty, June 9, 1957 (dec. 1966); m. Conrad H. Yarmoff, Sept. 4, 1970; children—Susan Reina, David Bernard. With Hirshon, Roth & Co., N.Y.C., 1959; tchr. N.Y. Public Schs., 1970—, resource room tchr., 1980—, educational evaluator, 1982. Active Am. Red. Magen David for Israel, Hadassah. Mem. Council Exceptional Children, Orton Dyslexia Soc., N.Y. State Reading Assn., Queensboro Reading Council, Center Preventive Psychiatry, Am. Ednl. Research Assn. Democrat. Jewish. Contbg. editor: Learning Styles Newsletter. Home: 96 Phipps Ln Plainview NY 11803 Office: P107Q 167-02 45th Ave Flushing NY 11358

YARN, BARBARA LYNNE IVEY, physician; b. Knoxville; d. Boyd S. and Geraldine Ivey; B.S. U. Tenn., 1962, Knoxville Coll., 1963; M.P.H., U. Minn., 1967; M.D., Meharry Med. Coll., 1973; m. Tyrone Von Yarn, May 17, 1963; children—Tiffany Nicole, Tyrone Lee Livingston. Tchr., Knoxville City Schs., 1963-64; biology asst. Oak Ridge Nat. Lab., 1964-67; intern Howard U., Hosp., Washington, 1974; resident in anesthesiology Emory U. Med. Sch., Atlanta, 1975-78; commd. med. officer USPHS, HHS, 1978, advanced through grades to comdr., 1980; USPHS regional med. clin. coordinator Nat. Health Service Corps Physicians, Atlanta, 1978-82; practice medicine specializing in anesthesiology, Atlanta, 1982—; chief med. officer Cuban Haitian Refugee Camp, Miami, 1981; physician Munich Mil. Hosp., 1974-75. Alpha Kappa Alpha scholar, 1959-63. USPHS scholar, 1967-69; Jesse Smith Noyes fellow, 1969-72; Sloan Found. scholar, 1969-73; recipient Sustained Superior Performance award USPHS, 1979. Mem. AMA, Nat. Med. Assn., Ga. Med. Soc., Alpha Kappa Mu, Beta Kappa Chi. Roman Catholic.

YARNELL, CYNTHIA LOUISE, comml. artist, illustrator, designer; b. St. Paul, June 8, 1955; d. John Warren and Dolores Jeannine (Nelsen) Alexander; student U. Pittsburg (Kans.), 1974-75, Kans. State U., 1976, Wichita State U., 1978, 82, Graphic Arts Seminar on Design, Atlanta, 1979; m. Eric David Yarnell, May 31, 1975; children—Angela Kay, Jonathan Eugene. Artist, typesetter Sunflower Graphics subs. Kreonite, Inc., Wichita, Kans., 1973-74; layout artist Arrow Jet Print, Wichita, 1973-74, newspaper U. Pittsburg, 1974-75; comml. artist Fincom, Inc., Topeka, 1975-76; artist, typesetter, designer St. Joseph Med. Center, Wichita, 1976—; owner, prin. Comml. Graphics & Design, Wichita, 1979—. Bd. dirs. March of Dimes Birth Defects Found., Wichita, 1977—. Recipient Service award March of Dimes, 1973, 79, St. Joseph Med. Center, 1982. Mem. Women in Communications, Inc., Wichita Arts Dirs. Club, Beta Sigma Phi (v.p. Beta Epsilon chpt. 1980—, chpt. Achievement award 1980, Sweetheart for City Wichita 1980-81). Republican. Roman Catholic. Designer corp. logo Coordinated Services, Wichita, 1981. Home and Office: 610 N Crestway Wichita KS 67208

YAROUSH, RITA A., psychologist; b. Bridgeport, Conn., Sept. 7, 1948; d. Wasil and Anna Yaroush; B.A., U. Colo., 1970; M.A., U. Denver, 1973, Ph.D., 1980. Research technician U. Colo. Med. Sch., 1970-73; DAAD fellow, dir. research project Maxmillian U., Munich, W.Ger., 1973-74; research asst. Nat. Jewish Hosp., Denver, 1974-80; asst. prof. psychology U. Tulsa, 1980-81; research asso. U. Colo., Boulder, 1981—; ind. clin. practice psychology, 1981—. Social Sci. Research Council fellow, 1978; NIMH fellow, 1979. Mem. Am. Psychol. Assn., AAAS, Soc. Psychophysiol. Research, Mental Health Assn. Colo., Sigma Xi (grantee 1978). Author research papers in field. Office: Inst Cognitive Sci Box 345 Dept Psychology U Colo Boulder CO 80309

YARYAN, RUBY BELL, psychologist; b. Toledo, Apr. 28, 1938; d. John Sturges and Susan Barrett (Bell) Y.; B.A. in Psychology (NSF fellow), Stanford U., 1960; Ph.D. in Psychology, U. London, 1968; m. John Frederick Buenz, Jr., Dec. 15, 1962 (div. Aug. 1967). Dir. communications research div. U. Calif. at San Francisco, 1963-67; reporter-analyst news KING-TV, Seattle, 1968-69, KIRO-TV, 1968-69; research dir. Univ. Radio and TV programs U. Calif., San Francisco, 1969-70; dir. interdept. council to coordinate all fed. juvenile delinquency programs, Washington, 1970-73; dir. evaluation Calif. Regional Med. Program, Oakland, 1974-76; dir. program evaluation County of San Diego, 1977—; cons. White House Conf. Children and Youth and Follow-Up, 1970-71, HEW Task Force on Classification of Exceptional Children, 1972-73, Calif. Council Criminal Justice, 1973-74; gov. Sci. Analysis Corp., San Francisco, 1969-70. Rotary Found. fellow, 1960-61; recipient Hon. Gold Key to State Capitol, Olympia, Wash., 1970. Mem. Nat. Adv. Commn. Criminal Justice Standards and Goals, 1972-73; del. Nat. Conf. Criminal Justice, 1973. Mem. Am., Western, Calif. psychol. assns., Am. Ednl. Research Assn., Am. Assn. Pub. Opinion Research, Internat. Orgn. Study Group Tensions, AFTRA, Phi Beta Kappa. Contbr. articles to profl. jours. and chpts. to books. Office: Office Program Evaluation 1600 Pacific Hwy San Diego CA 92101

YATES, BARBARA, accountant; b. Red Star, Ark., Apr. 3, 1950; B.S. in Acctg., U. Ark., 1970; married; 2 children. Tax specialist Peat, Marwick, Mitchell & Co., C.P.A.s, Tulsa, 1970-72; sr. acct. Touche Ross & Co., C.P.A.s, Los Angeles, 1972; mgr. tax practice Gaddy & Co., Fayetteville, Ark., 1972-74; sr. acct. E.L. Gaunt & Co., Little Rock, 1974-75; propr. Barbara Yates, C.P.A., Little Rock, 1975-77; mng. partner Yates, Schwartz, Kelly & Co., Little Rock, 1977-78; propr. Yates & Co., Little Rock, 1978-80; pres. Yates & Co., Ltd., C.P.A.s, Little Rock, 1980—; mem. Ark. Bd. Public Accountancy, 1979—; del. Nat. Assn. State Bds. Accountancy, 1980—. Bd. dirs. Suzuki Inst. Mus. Tng., 1978—. C.P.A., Ark., Okla. Mem. Am. Inst. C.P.A.s, Ark. Soc. C.P.A.s (chmn. public relations com. 1981-82, past chpt. pres.), Central Ark. Estate Council (dir.), Am. Soc. Women Accts. (charter pres.), Sales and Mktg. Execs. Assn. (v.p.). Address: 1215 Rebsamen Park Rd Little Rock AR 72202

YATES, BARBARA KOTEL, social worker; b. Youngstown, Ohio, Oct. 21, 1947; d. Louis George and Elizabeth Ann (Savka) Kotel; B.A. (Wm. Courtney scholar), Youngstown State U., 1970; M.S.W. (United Appeal scholar), Fla. State U., 1976; m. William Lewis Yates, Mar. 13, 1976; 1 son, Thomas. Social worker Mahoning County Welfare Dept., Youngstown, 1971, Woodside Receiving Hosp., Youngstown, 1971-74; State of Ohio Grant for Tng., 1974-76; social worker III, Woodside Receiving Hosp., Youngstown, 1976-78, supr., 1978, dir. social service dept., 1978—. Mem. Mahoning County Alcoholism Services Adv. Planning Task Force, 1979-82; mem. Crestview Parent Tchrs. Orgn., 1979-82; v.p. Crestview Baseball Assn., 1980—. Mem. Acad. Cert. Social Workers, Ohio Social Workers Assn. (chmn. social service dirs. com., No. regional coordinator), Nat. Assn. Social Workers, Ohio Assn. Mental Health Adminstrs., Soc. Hosp. Social Work Dirs. Roman Catholic. Co-developer comprehensive treatment psychiat. patients. Office: 800 E Indianola Ave Youngstown OH 44502

YATES, ELLA (MAE) GAINES, librarian; b. Atlanta, June 14, 1927; d. Fred Douglas and Laura (Moore) Gaines; A.B., Spelman Coll., Atlanta, 1949; M.S. in L.S., Atlanta U., 1951; J.D., Atlanta Law Sch., 1979; m. Joseph L. Syndor (dec.); 1 child, Jerri Gaines Sydnor Lee; m. 2d, Clayton R. Yates (dec.). Asst. br. librarian Bklyn. Pub. Library, 1951-54; head children's dept. Orange (N.J.) Pub. Library, 1956-59; br. librarian East Orange (N.J.) Pub. Library, 1960-69; med. librarian Orange Meml. Hosp., 1967-69; asst. dir. Montclair (N.J.) Pub. Library, 1970-72; asst. dir. Atlanta Pub. Library, 1972-76, dir., from 1976; now pres. Yates-Edwards Library Cons., Seattle; co-chmn. Quarles Library Soc., Spelman Coll., 1977—; adv. bd. Library of Congress Center for the Book; cons. in field. Vice chmn. N.J. Women's Council Human Relations, 1957-59; chmn. Friends of Fulton County Jail, 1973—; bd. dirs. United Cerebral Palsy Greater Atlanta, Inc. Named Profl. Woman of Year, N.J. chpt. Nat. Assn. Negro Bus. and Profl. Women's Club, 1964; Outstanding Chum of Year, 1976; Outstanding Alumni, Spelman Coll., 1977; recipient Meritorious award Atlanta U., 1977. Mem. ALA (exec. bd.), Ga., Southeastern library assns., NAACP, Atlanta Women's C. of C., Delta Theta Phi, Delta Sigma Theta. Baptist. Contbr. to profl. jours. Address: Yates-Edwards Library Cons Seattle WA *

YATES, GAYLE GRAHAM, educator; b. Wayne County, Miss., May 6, 1940; d. Robert C. and Gleta (Jones) Graham; B.A., Millsaps Coll., 1961; M.A.T., Vanderbilt U., 1962; Ph.D., U. Minn., 1973; m. Herschel Wilson Yates, Jr., July 21, 1961; children—Natasha, Stiles. Mem. Faculty English dept. Boston U., 1964-67; vis. scholar Cambridge U., 1973-74, 78; chmn. women's studies U. Minn., Mpls., 1976-81, assoc. prof. women's studies and Am. studies, 1981—, founding mem. Big Ten panel on women's studies. Mem. Minn. Gov.'s Adv. Com. on Families, 1980-82. Named Alumna of Yr., Millsaps Coll., 1976. Mem. Am. Studies Assn. (chmn. women's com. 1981-83), Women Historians of Midwest, Nat. Women's Studies Assn. Democrat. Methodist. Author: What Women Want: The Ideas of the Movement, 1975. Office: 474 Ford Hall Women's Studies U Minn Minneapolis MN 55455

YAZZIE, ETHELOU, ednl. adminstr.; b. Chinle, Ariz., Feb. 1, 1943; d. Frank and Bessie (Burbank) Y.; A.A., Hesston Coll., 1966; B.A., Goshen Coll., 1968; 1 dau., Lyndell. Tchr., Rough Rock Demonstration Sch., Chinle, 1968-70, exec. dir. 1973-78; dir. Navajo Curriculum Center, Chinle, 1970-71; prin. Rough Rock Elem. Sch. Chinle, 1971-73; exec. dir. Little Singer Sch., Winslow, Ariz., 1978—; mem. Nat. Task Force on Indian Edn., 1978—. Bd. overseers Hesston Coll.; pres. Navajo Womens Conf., Winslow, Ariz. Mem. Dine Bi Ota Assn., State Planning Adv. Council of Ariz. Author textbooks. Home: PO Box 647 Chinle AZ 86503 Office: St Route Box 239 Winslow AZ 86047

YAZZIE, RENA MERCEDES, human services exec.; b. Little Water, N.Mex., Feb. 8, 1946; d. Reed and Mary (Benally) Henderson; A.A., N.Mex. State U.-San Juan Coll., 1976; B.S. in Elem. Edn., U. N.Mex., 1982; m. Thomas Joe Yazzie, June 2, 1965; children—Tomasita Esparanza, Rufus Reno. Adminstrv. asst. U. Utah Coll. Nursing, Shiprock, N.Mex., 1971-76; adminstrv. sec. office of asst. supt. instrn., Central Consol. Schs. #22, Kirtland, N.Mex., 1977-79; legal sec. Office of Navajo Econ. Opportunity, Navajo Children's Legal Services, Shiprock, 1979; regional coordinator Ednl. Opportunity Center, Navajo Community Coll., Shiprock, 1979-80; health career counselor Navajo Health Authority, Shiprock, 1980-81; bd. dirs. Navajo Nation Family Planning Corp., Ft. Defiance, Ariz., 1980-81, sec. bd., 1981-82. tutor/counselor. Mem. Dine Bi Olta Assn., Navajo Nat., 1973, Nat. Family Planning Forum for Am. Indians, 1975-76; sec. Central Consol. Schs. Dist. 22 Bd. Edn., 1979—; bd. dirs. N.Mex. State U.-San Juan Coll., 1979—. Mem. Nat. Fedn. Bus. and Profl. Women's Clubs, N.Am. Indian Women's Assn. Nat. Indian Edn. Assn., N.Mex. Sch. Bd. Assn. (resolutions com. 1980-81). Republican. Mem. Assemblies of God Ch. Club: Bus. and Profl. Women's. Home: PO Box 1067 Shiprock NM 87420 Office: PO Box 1734 Shiprock NM 87420

YBARRA, EVA, tchr. bilingual edn.; b. Alma, Mich., Aug. 17, 1949; d. Panteleon Belmares and Cesarea Rosario (Cortez) Ybarra; student Marymount-Loyola U., 1970-73, Calif. State U., Fullerton, 1972-73; B.A., Calif. State U., Los Angeles, 1978, M.A., 1981. Exec. sec. Boy Scouts Am., Yakima, Wash., 1965-67; exec. sec. Hops Extract Corp., Yakima, 1967-69; tch. St. Jeanne de Lestonnac Sch., Tustin, Calif., 1971-72, St. Antonio de Padua Sch., Los Angeles, 1973-76; tchr. Los Angeles Children's Mus., 1981; bilingual tchr. Franklin Sch., Pasadena, Calif., 1981, Magnolia Ave. Sch., Los Angeles, 1982—; lectr. in field. BASIC Ednl. Opportunity grantee. Mem. United Tchrs. Los Angeles, Mexican Am. Scholarship Com., Nat. Council Family Relations, Community TV So. Calif. Roman Catholic. Office: 1626 N Orchard Los Angeles CA 90006

YEAGER, PATRICIA MARGARET, univ. adminstr.; b. Detroit, July 24, 1941; d. William Hugh and Kathleen Grace (McKee) Sullivan; B.A. with high distinction, U. Mich., Dearborn, 1973; m. Frederick Carl Yeager, Aug. 17, 1963; children—Gwendolyn Grace, Elizabeth Brooke, Emily Anne. Mem. adminstrv. staff U. Mich., Dearborn, 1973—, adminstrv. asst. II, 1977-79, dir. Engring. Projects Office, 1979—, acting dir. profl. devel. program, 1980—, interim dir. sponsored research, 1981—; trustee Met. Detroit Sci. and Engring. Coalition, 1980—; grant reviewer Nat. Action Council Minorities in Engring., 1982. Recipient Outstanding Engring. Edn. Achievement award Mich. Soc. Profl. Engrs., 1980. Mem. Nat. Assn. Female Execs., Am. Soc. Engring. Edn., Soc. Women Engrs. (asso.), Nat. Assn. Minority Engring. Project Adminstrs., Alumni Assn. U. Mich., Alumni Assn. U. Calif., LWV (chpt. 1st v.p. 1970-72), Gamma Phi Beta. Club: Detroit Yacht. Home: 15818 Longmeadow Rd Dearborn MI 48120 Office: 4901 Evergreen St Dearborn MI 48128

YEAGER, SUZANNE WHITE, writer, communications cons.; b. Scranton, Pa., Dec. 14, 1945; d. Roger Nelson and Dorothy (Jones) White; B.J., U. Mo., Columbia, 1967, M.A. in Communications Research, 1971; m. Jesse Alan Yeager, Aug. 26, 1967; children—D'Arcy Suzanne, Troy Alan. Staff writer The Blade, Toledo, 1968-69, Virginia Gazette, Williamsburg, 1969-70, Toledo Times, 1973-75; journalism faculty U. Toledo, 1976-78; pub., editor Connections, Toledo newspaper for women, 1978-81; writer, communications cons., Toledo, 1981—. Trustee Epworth United Methodist Ch.; active Women Involved in Toledo; mem. women's research project Toledo-Lucas County Community Planning Council. Mem. Women's Inst. for Freedom of Press, Women in Communications (dir.; Woman of Achievement 1980), LWV (dir.), Ohio Newspaper Women's Assn., Sigma Delta Chi. Office: 3311 W Bancroft Toledo OH 43606

YEAKEL, MARGARET CAROLINE, social work educator; b. Fair Oaks, Pa., Jan. 10, 1916; d. Leon and Olga Catherine (Egger) Y.; B.A., Oberlin Coll., 1935, M.A., 1941; M.S.S.W., Case Western Res. U., 1954, D.S.W., 1963. Sch. tchr., Pa., Ohio and Ky., 1935-41; exec. dir., camping dir. and adult edn. dir. Girl Scouts U.S.A., Inc., La Crosse, Wis. and Cleve., 1942-52; dir. group services Detroit Orthopedic Clinic, 1954-56; asst. prof. Wayne State U., Detroit, 1956-57; social worker Cleve. Child Guidance Center, 1957-63, co-dir. NIH clin. research project on intermediate group treatment of inaccessible children, 1961-63; asso. prof. social work SUNY, Buffalo, 1964-66, Smith Coll., Northampton, Mass., 1966-70; dir. social work Magee Meml. Hosp., Phila., 1972-73; prof. West Chester (Pa.) State Coll., 1973-81; prof. Temple U. Extension Degree Program, 1981—. Fellow Am. Orthopsychiat. Assn.; mem. Acad. Cert. Social Workers, Nat. Assn. Social Workers, NAACP (chpt. faculty award). Author: (with Ganter and Polansky) Retrieval from Limbo, 1967; (with Grace Ganter) Human Behavior and the Social Environment: A Perspective for Social Work Practice, 1980; contbr. chpt.: Principles and Methods of Social Work Research, 1975.

YEARGAIN, BETTY JAN, banker; b. Harperville, Miss., July 20, 1942; d. Edgar Jacob and Audrey Belle (Hooks) Fisher; m. Virgil L. Yeargain, Mar. 14, 1971; 1 son, Marvie Allen. Exec. sec. Security Bank of Midwest City, Okla., 1968-69; asst. v.p., employment mgr. Fidelity Bank of Oklahoma City, 1969-77; ops. officer Choctaw (Okla.) State Bank, 1977-78; sr. v.p., cashier Southwestern Bank & Trust Co., Oklahoma City, 1978—, adv. dir., 1980—; guest lectr. Oklahoma City Public Schs., Draughans Sch. Bus. Named Banker of Yr., Central Okla. chpt. Am. Inst. Banking, 1975. Mem. Nat. Assn. Bank Women (vice-chmn. 1980-81, chmn. Western Okla. group 1981-82), Central Okla. Clearinghouse Assn. (sec., chmn. ops. com. and mem. exec. com.), Am. Inst. Banking (chpt. dir. 1979-81). Democrat. Baptist. Office: 6000 S Western St Oklahoma City OK 73144

YEARLING, LOWETA LEE, community agy. exec.; b. Lawrence, Kans., Jan. 1, 1939; d. Leslie Clarence and Minnie Lee (Clayborne) Kimball; B.A., Colo. Women's Coll., Denver, 1982; children—Debra Veola, Denise Kay. With U. No. Colo., Greeley, 1959-62, Compensation Ins. Fund, Denver, 1962-67, Colo. Dept. Health, 1967-77, Colo. Med. Center, Denver, 1977-81; dir. office services Mile Hi council Girl Scouts U.S.A., Denver, 1981—. Bd. dirs. Community Colls. Denver. Active NAACP, YWCA, Democratic Party; reader for visually impaired; ch. sch. supt., ch. clk. A.M.E. Ch. Recipient recognition awards for civic vol. work. Mem. Colo. Public Health Assn. (pres.), Colo. Assn. Public Employees. Office: Girl Scouts Mile Hi Council Denver CO

YEARWOOD, ALMA C., nurse, educator; b. N.Y.C., July 23, 1945; d. Aubrey Francis and Alma Leotta (McIntosh) Y.; B.A. summa cum laude in Psychology, Fordham U., 1976; M.S. in Community Health Edn., Hunter Coll., 1978; M.A. in Adult Edn., Tchrs. Coll., Columbia U., 1982, Ed.D., 1982. Staff nurse N.Y. State Psychiat. Inst., N.Y.C., 1966-68, St. Luke's Hosp., N.Y.C., 1968-69; head nurse outpatient psychiatry dept. Roosevelt Hosp., N.Y.C., 1970-73, nursing care coordinator Smithers Alcoholism Center, 1973-77, nursing care coordinator, ambulatory care services, 1977-78; ednl. programs asso. Nat. Multiple Sclerosis Soc., N.Y.C., 1978-81; adminstr. health info. and guidance services Brownlee, Dolen and Stein, N.Y.C., 1981—; instr. continuing edn. dept. Tchrs. Coll., Columbia U., N.Y.C., 1978-81; cons. to instns. establishing alcoholism units, career counseling for health profls. R.N., N.Y. Mem. Am. Nurses Assn., N.Y. State Nurses Assn., Adult Edn. Assn., Am. Pub. Health Assn. Author articles on alcoholism, career counseling. multiple sclerosis. Office: 70 Pine St New York NY 10005

YEARY, ELIZABETH EINSIEDLER, editor; b. Newark, June 26, 1938; d. Zacharias and Pauline Einsiedler; B.A., Montclair (N.J.) State Coll., 1960, M.A., 1966; m. John C. Yeary, June 9, 1973. Jr. high sch. tchr., Ridgefield Park, N.J., 1960-61, Franklin Sch., Nutley, N.J., 1961-66; asso. editor Junior Rev., Civic Edn. Service, Washington, 1966-68; editorial asso. Todays Edn., NEA Jour., Washington, 1968-72, staff writer, 1972-76, asst. editor, 1976-80, editor, 1980—. Mem. Ednl. Press Assn. Am. (pres. 1975-77). Home: 5317 Truman Ave Alexandria VA 22304 Office: 1201 16th St NW Washington DC 20036

YEAZELL, RUTH BERNARD, educator; b. N.Y.C., Apr. 4, 1947; d. Walter and Annabelle (Reich) Bernard; B.A. with high honors, Swarthmore Coll., 1967; M.Phil. (Woodrow Wilson fellow), Yale U., 1970, Ph.D., 1971; m. Stephen C. Yeazell, Aug. 14, 1969 (div. 1980). Asst. prof. English, Boston U., 1971-74; asst. prof. UCLA, 1975-77, asso. prof., 1977-80, prof., 1980—. Guggenheim fellow, 1979-80. Mem. MLA, AAUP. Author: Language and Knowledge in the Late Novels of Henry James, 1976; Death and Letters of Alice James, 1981; asso. editor Nineteenth-Century Fiction, 1977-80. Home: 555 Midvale Ave Los Angeles CA 90024 Office: Dept English UCLA Los Angeles CA 90024

YECIES, SUSAN MARILYN, real estate co. pub. relations exec.; b. Newark, Dec. 21, 1948; d. Sidney and Thelma (Greenbaum) Y.; B.A., Yale U., 1971; M.A., U. Tex., Austin, 1979. Dir. internat. dept. Am. Assn. Museums, 1973-76; curator Latin Am. collection U. Tex. Art Mus., Austin, 1977-79; cons. communications dept. Internat. Paper Co., N.Y.C., 1980; dir. pub. relations Julien J. Studley, Inc., N.Y.C., 1980—. John Courtney Murray research fellow, Europe and W. Africa, 1971-73; Bicentennial fellow Australian-N.Z. govts., 1976. Mem. Public Relations Soc. Am., Am. Assn. Mus., Internat. Council Mus., Yale U. Alumni Assn., Women Bus. Owners of N.Y., Guggenheim Mus. Friends, Phi Beta Kappa, Phi Kappa Phi. Club: Yale of N.Y.C. Author features, brochures, booklets and mus. catalogues in field. Address: Julien J Studley Inc 333 E 46th St New York NY 10017

YEKO, DORIS CHU, recording and TV co. exec., producer; b. Honolulu, Nov. 17, 1941; d. Paul Enshun and Rose (Shon) Chu; B.A., Fairleigh Dickinson U., Teaneck, N.J., 1964, M.A., 1966; M.A., William Paterson Coll., Wayne, N.J., 1980; m. Bruce David Yeko, Mar. 23, 1968

(div.); 1 dau., Jennifer. Personnel analyst Flower and Fifth Ave. Hosps.-N.Y. Med. Coll., 1966-67; compensation analyst Ciba Corp., 1967-68, Clairol Inc., 1968-70; personnel and fulfillment mgr. Hobby Card House, 1972-82; publisher Broadway/Hollywood Internat. Music Pubs., 1979—, Broadway/Hollywood Prodns., 1979—; founder, dir. C.Y. Mus. Found.; producer Original Cast Records, Film Score Records, Broadway Baby Records; dir. Take Home Tunes! Record Co. Mem. Nat. Acad. Rec. Arts and Scis., Nat. Assn. TV Arts and Scis., Women in Music. Author: How to Produce a Phonograph Record, 1979, (tape) How to Cope with Stress, 1980. Office: Box 1314 Englewood Cliffs NJ 07632 also Box 10051 Beverly Hills CA 90213

YELLIN, JEAN FAGAN, educator; b. Mich., Sept. 19, 1930; d. Peter and Sarah (Robinson) Fagan; B.A., Roosevelt U., 1951; M.A., U. Ill., 1963, Ph.D., 1969; m. Edward Yellin, Dec. 17, 1948; children—Peter Fagan, Lisa Mitchell, Michael Fagan. Teaching asst. U. Ill., 1960-64, N.Y. U., 1966-67; asst. prof. English Pace U., N.Y.C., 1968-74, asso. prof., 1974-80, dir. N.Y.C. Humanities program, 1979—, prof., 1980—. AAUW fellow, 1967-68; Nat. Endowment for Humanities fellow, 1974-75; Nat. Humanities Inst. fellow, 1976-77; Smithsonian Instn. postdoctoral fellow, 1978-79; Nat. Endowment for Humanities grantee, 1979-81; AAUW postdoctoral fellow, 1981-82. Mem. Am. Studies Assn., Assn. Study of Afro-Am. Life and History, Coll. Lang. Assn., Melville Soc., N.E. MLA (exec. bd.), Soc. Study of Multi-Ethnic Lit. of U.S. Author: The Intricate Knot: Black Figures in American Literature, 1776-1863, 1972; contbr. articles to profl. jours. Home: 38 Lakeside Dr New Rochelle NY 10801 Office: Dept English Pace U Pace Plaza New York NY 10038

YENGER, SUE, state ofcl.; b. Ottumwa, Iowa, Aug. 5, 1938; d. James Franklin and Bernice Goldine (Chapin) Peck; B.A. in Elementary Edn., Parsons Coll., 1961; m. Jim Yenger, Mar. 28, 1959; children—Russell, Laura. Tchr., 1961-71; tchr., dir. head start program Wapello County (Iowa) schs., 1971; mgr. Work Incentive Program, 1973-78; mem. Iowa Senate, 1978—; gov. del. White House Conf. Aging, 1981. Bd. dirs. United Way Wapello County; chmn. Ottumwa Day Care Center; chmn. Wapello County Alcoholism Program; commr. Aging Iowa 1979—. Mem. Nat. Conf. State Legislators, Am. Legis. Exchange Council, Nat. Order Women Legislators. Republican. Mem. Diciples of Christ. Club: Eagle Aux. Office: Iowa State Capitol Des Moines IA 52509

YEOMAN, GERALDINE, therapist, educator; b. Scobey, Mont., Nov. 7, 1928; d. William Allen and Lenore Mae (Mahon) MacDougall; B.S., Okla. State U., 1950; M.S.W., U. Ala., 1977, postgrad. 1979-80; m. M.H. Yeoman, May 21, 1950; children—Marc H., Kimberly, Lynne, Leigh, Kelly. Adminstrv. asst. Family Guidance Center, Montgomery, Ala., 1962-64, caseworker, 1963-65, supr., 1968-76; asst. prof. social work Ala. State U., Montgomery, 1977—; cons. Home Health Service and Nursing Home, 1977-80. Bd. dirs. Public TV, WAIQ, Montgomery, 1979-80, Montgomery Urban League, 1978-80; initiator, dir. Great Books Group, Mental Health Assn. Bd., 1968-69; mem. Ala. Comprehensive Mental Health Planning Commn., 1965. Recipient commendation Comprehensive Mental Health Planning Ala., 1965; lic. cert. social worker, Ala. Mem. Acad. Cert. Social Workers, LWV (pres. 1958-60, dir. 1956-62), Nat. Assn. Social Workers (unit co-chmn., mem. exec. bd., chmn. program com. 1981-82, mem. legis. com. 1980-81), Adlerian Soc., Internat. Transactional Analysis Assn., Safe Energy Alliance, Mental Health Roundtable, Ala. Conf. Social Work (nominating com. 1981-82), Congress for Human Services, Council on Social Work Edn., Phi Kappa Phi. Presbyterian. Home: 1442 E Audubon Rd Montgomery AL 36111 Office: PO Box 47 Ala State Univ Montgomery AL 36195

YGLESIAS, ANITA NIETO, mfg. co. mgr.; b. Bklyn., Mar. 5, 1925; d. Jose Antonio and Rosario (Gayo) Nieto; fgn. trade cert. CCNY, 1944; m. James Yglesias, July 14, 1946; children—James, Denise R. With Export & Import Devel. Corp., N.Y.C., 1943-48; with Union Carbide Corp., N.Y.C., 1963—, personnel coordinator, 1965, royalty adminstr., 1970, sr. sales service specialist, 1980, asst. to export mgr., 1981—. Mem. vestry Grace Ch., Brooklyn Heights, 1971-77; pres. Escuela Cervantes Bklyn., 1961-79; com. mem. Bishop of L.I. (Partners in Mission), 1979. Democrat. Episcopalian. Clubs: Lioness of Bklyn., Grace Ch. Woman's Service (pres. 1982-83). Home: 75 Henry St Brooklyn Heights NY 11201

YIH, MAE DUNN, state legislator; b. Shanghai, China, May 24, 1928; d. Chung Woo and Fung Wen (Feng) Dunn; B.A., Barnard Coll., 1951; postgrad. Columbia U., 1951-52; m. Stephen W. H. Yih, 1953; children—Donald, Daniel. Precinct person, Oreg. State Democratic Party; mem. Clover Ridge Elem. Sch. Bd. Albany, Oreg., 1969—; mem. Albany Union High Sch. Bd., 1975—; mem. Adv. Com., Environ. Health Dept., Linn County, Oreg., 1977; mem. Oreg. Ho. of Reps., Dist. 36, 1977—. Mem. AAUW, League Women Voters, Linn County Citizens for Retarded, Linn County Mental Health Assn., Oreg. Sch. Bd. Assn. Episcopalian. Office: Oreg Ho Reps State Capitol Salem OR 97310

YIM, MARY ANCILLA, library dir., educator; b. Honolulu, Feb. 17, 1927; d. Ernest K. and Wai Shan (Ching) Y.; student St. Francis Normal Sch., Maria Regina Coll., 1948-52; B.S. in Edn., U. Dayton, 1957; M.S. in L.S., Cath. U. Am., 1962; postgrad. U. Hawaii, Honolulu, 1961-69; cert. advanced studies in instructional adminstrn. SUNY, Oswego, 1975. Joined Third Order of St. Francis, 1948; sec., receptionist, real estate, ins. and law office, Honolulu, 1944-48; tchr. St. Paul's Ch., Whitesboro, N.Y., 1950-52; tchr.-librarian St. Joseph's High Sch., Hilo, Hawaii, 1952-65, prin., 1965-71; asst. prin. Oswego (N.Y.) Cath. High Sch., 1971-75; dir. library Maria Regina Coll., Syracuse, N.Y., 1975—, instr., 1976-79, asst. prof., 1979-82, asso. prof., 1982—. NDEA grantee in English, U. Hawaii, 1964. Mem. ALA, Cath. (chpt. pres. 1980-82; facilitator continuing edn. program 1982—), N.Y. library assns., Assn. Coll. and Research Libraries. Office: 1024 Court St Syracuse NY 13208

YOAKUM, CYNTHIA JANE COLBY, librarian; b. Hudson, N.Y., Mar. 9, 1952; d. LeRoy Leonard and Jane Marie (Boright) Colby; B.A., U. No. Iowa, 1974; M.A., U. Denver, 1975; m. John H. Yoakum, June 12, 1976. Grad. asst. U. Denver, 1974-75; librarian Scott City (Kans.) Jr. High Sch., 1975-76, Ft. Worth Pub. Library, 1976—. Mem. ALA, Tex. Library Assn., Bus. and Profl. Women. Home: 2821 Autumn Dr Hurst TX 76053 Office: 300 Taylor St Fort Worth TX 76102

YOCHAM, DORIS ROGERS, petroleum co. ofcl.; b. Sapulpa, Okla., Dec. 3, 1926; d. William and Esther M. (Fielding) Rogers; student Okla. State U., 1967-70, Tulsa Jr. Coll., 1979-80; m. George R. Yocham, June 11, 1943; 1 son, Roger A. Secretarial position Gulf Oil Corp., Tulsa, 1950-58, Schermerhorn Oil Corp., Tulsa, 1958-62; adminstrv. asst., asst. corp. sec. Kewanee Oil Co., Tulsa, 1962-78; analyst Warren Petroleum Co., Tulsa, 1978-79, personnel rep., 1979—. Chairperson, Okla. Tribal Assistance Program, Pvt. Industry Council. 1982—. Mem. Tulsa Personnel Assn. (treas. 1979-80, dir. 1980-81), Tulsa EEO Coordinators Assn. Home: 1130 Burroughs Rd Sapulpa OK 74066 Office: PO Box 1589 Tulsa OK 74102

YOCHAM, WANDA JUNE BURLESON, theol. sem. adminstr.; b. Rankin, Tex., Oct. 29, 1934; d. Wesley Hardin and Vivian May Lee (Hickerson) Burleson; student San Angelo Coll., 1953-54, Austin Community Coll., 1974-75, U. Ky. Coll. Bus. Mgmt. Inst., 1977-78, 79; div.; children—James, Kathy. Claims clk. Legal div. Tex. Bd. Hosps. and Schs., Austin Tex., 1959-61; office mgr. George T. Barr Comml. Food Equipment, Orlando, Fla., 1962-64; bus. officer Episcopal Theol. Sem., Austin, Tex., 1964—. Mem. So. Assn. Coll. and Univ. Bus. Officers. Republican. Episcopalian. Address: Episcopal Theol Sem Southwest Box 2247 Austin TX 78767

YOCOM, HELENMAE SOTTER, religious and civic leader; b. Pottstown, Pa., Oct. 11, 1916; d. Walter Philip and Florence May (Hartenstine) Sotter; B.S., West Chester State Coll., 1942; m. James Harold Yocom, July 20, 1940; children—James Harold, Elizabeth May Sotter, Helenmay Sotter, Philip William Sotter. Pres., Jessie Cronk Circle, 1949-51, Emmanuel Luth. Ladies Bible Class, 1955-57, Sister Gladys Circle, 1968-70, Emmanuel Luth. Ch. Women, 1976-78; life mem. Luth. Ch. Women Am.; treas. Pottstown Garden Club, 1962-64, pres., 1978-80; treas. Pottstown Century Club, 1974-76, pres., 1980-82; mem. Freedom Valley council Girl Scouts U.S.A., public relations com. Chester County council; nominating com. bd. dirs. YWCA; asst. treas. Pottstown Hosp. Aux.; bd. dirs. Meml. Hosp. Aux.; edn. chmn. Pottstown chpt. Am. Cancer Soc.; treas. Vis. Nurse Assn.; treas. Jr. High Sch. PTA; sec. Wyndcroft PTA; bd. dirs. Rupert PTA, High Sch. PTA; life mem. Nat. Council PTA, Nat. Council Garden Clubs, Garden Club Fedn. Pa., Woman's Aux. Albright Coll.; vol. Meals on Wheels; key woman Woman's Aux. Muhlenberg Coll.; charter mem., life mem. Pottsgrove Hist. Soc.; charter mem. Pottstown Symphony Orchestra Assn.; mem. Women's Aux. Luth. Theol. Sem., Phila., Valley Forge Hist. Soc., Needlework Guild, Germantown Luth. Home. Recipient Legion of Honor, Chapel of Four Chaplains, Phila. 1980. Club: Brookside Country. Lutheran. Home: 215 Rosedale Dr Pottstown PA 19464

YOCUM, LOUISE JOAN, dance therapist, clergywoman; b. Buffalo, Sept. 22, 1917; d. Frank and Mildred (Rizzo) Guarino; student Trudi Schoop Tng. Center Dance Therapy, N. Hollywood, Calif., 1959-66, Glendale (Calif.) Coll., Mary Whitehouse Dance Studio, Santa Monica, Calif., 1964-67, White Research Center, 1964-68, Nat. Tai Chi Ch'uan Inst., Los Angeles, 1964-72, Los Angeles Coll. Massage, Phys. Therapy, 1973-74, Unity in Diversity Center, Northridge, Calif., 1975—; m. George Vernon Yocum, May 31, 1941; children—Vernise Elaine Yocum Pelzel, Raymond Francis. Profl. dancer, choreographer various theaters, restaurants, hotels in U.S., tchr. Arthur Murray Dance Studio, Statler Hotel, Buffalo, 1943-45; dir. Louise Yocum Dance Studio, Burbank, Calif., 1947-57; dance therapist White Research Center, Hollywood, Calif., 1958-68; dance therapist, Sunair Asthmatic Home Children, Tujunga, Calif., 1964-70; dir. movement for actors Young Players Prodn. Workshop, Hollywood, 1965; dance therapist Los Angeles Day Treatment Center, 1966-69; dir. movement for transpersonal experience Unity in Diversity Center, Beverly Hills, Calif., 1966—; pvt. practice, Burbank, 1966—; ordained to ministry, 1976; mem. faculty, Everywoman's Village, Van Nuys, Calif., 1972—, Women's Workshop, Northridge, 1973-74, Brand Art Center Studios, Glendale, Calif., 1974—; cons., lectr. clin. and ednl. instns., TV. Recipient award Los Angeles Day Treatment Center, 1968; awards Vol. Guild Sunair, 1967, 68, 69. Mem. Am. (registered, dir. 1969-71), So. Calif. dance therapy assns., Am. Assn. Study of Mental Imagery. Mem. Unity in Diversity. Club: Vol. Guild Sunair Asthmatic Home for Children. Contbr. articles to profl. jours. Home: 1131 Sunset Canyon Dr Burbank CA 91504

YODER, SHARYN LEE, food service adminstr.; b. West Liberty, Ohio, July 15, 1939; d. Floyd Emerson and Naomi Helen (Hartzler) King; m. Darrel Robert Yoder, June 24, 1956; children—Vicki Kaye, Rodney Lyn, Brian Keith, Jill Diane. With Jefferson (Ohio) Local Sch., 1969—, dir. food service adminstrn., 1973—. Pres., Band Boosters, 1977-78, 79-80; sec. PTO, 1979-80; bd. dirs. Madison County Cancer Soc., W. Jefferson Bible Ch. Recipient Humanitarian award W. Jefferson High Sch., 1977; named Friend of Edn., 1981. Mem. Am. Sch. Food Service Assn. (cert.), Ohio Sch. Food Service Assn. (dir. Suburbia chpt.), Ohio Assn. Sch. Bus. Ofcls., Mennonite. Clubs: West Jefferson C B'ers Group, West Jefferson Athletic Assn. Home: 600 Middle Pike West Jefferson OH 43162 Office: 561 W Jeff-Kiousville Rd West Jefferson OH 43162

YOKELEY, MARGARET HILL, hosiery mill exec.; b. Thomasville, N.C., Nov. 21, 1925; d. Cleveland C. and Elizabeth B. Hill; student Kings Bus. Coll., 1944; m. Joe H. Yokeley, Mar. 16, 1946 (dec.); children—Joe Stephen, Chris C. Vice pres. Celand Yarn Dyers, Thomasville, N.D., 1976; sec.-treas. Hill Hosiery Mill, Inc., Thomasville, 1978—; dir. Wachovia Bank, Thomasville, 1980—. Methodist. Club: Thomasville Women's. Office: Hill Hosiery Mills Inc 602 Davidson St Thomasville NC 27360

YOLEN, JANE, author, educator; b. N.Y.C., Feb. 11, 1939; d. Will Hyatt and Isabelle (Berlin) Y.; B.A., Smith Coll., 1960; M.Ed., U. Mass., 1976; LL.D. (hon.), Coll. Our Lady of Elms, Chicopee, Mass., 1980; m. David W. Stemple, Sept. 2, 1962; children—Heidi Elisabet, Adam Douglas, Jason Frederic. Mem. staff prodn. dept. Sat. Rev., 1960-61; editorial asst. This Week, 1960; editor Rutledge Press, 1962-63, A.A. Knopf, 1963-65; freelance writer, 1966—; lectr. edn. Smith Coll., 1979—; author 65 books, since 1963, including: The Emperor and the Kite, 1968, The Girl Who Cried Flowers, 1974, Writing Books for Children, 1976, An Invitation to the Butterfly Ball, 1976, The Seeing Stick, 1978, The Gift of Sarah Barker, 1981, Touch Magic: Fantasy, Faerie and Folklore in the Literature of Childhood, 1981, Dragon's Blood, 1982, Neptune Rising, 1982; also poems, articles, short stories, songs. Chmn. bd. trustees Hatfield (Mass.) Public Library, 1977—. Mem. Soc. Children's Book Writers (dir. 1972—; Golden Kite award 1974), Sci. Fiction Writers Am., Authors Guild, Nat. Council Tchrs. English, Children's Lit. Assn., Bay State Writers Guild. Democrat. Address: Box 27 Hatfield MA 01038

YOMANTAS, PATRICIA LYNN, univ. public relations adminstr.; b. Burbank, Calif., Nov. 26, 1950; d. Floyd Clifford and Rose Marie (Baitman) Balding; student Calif. State U., Northridge, 1970-74; B.A. in Journalism, Calif. State U., Long Beach, 1975, postgrad. 1977—; m. Gary Charles Yomantas, Sept. 15, 1973. Community info. specialist Coll. of Canyons, Valencia, Calif., 1973-74; asst. dir. public info. Saddleback Community Coll. Dist., Orange County, Calif., 1974-79; dir. public info. Pepperdine U., Malibu, Calif., 1979—, coordinator, editor Pepperdine U. Press, 1980—; lectr. in field. Mem. public relations com. Am. Heart Assn., 1980—; campaign chmn. United Way, 1980; mem. Orange County Arts Alliance, 1977-78; public relations task force chmn. Western div. Am. Heart Assn., 1981—. Recipient Pro award Calif. Community Colls., 1978. Mem. Women in Communications, Calif. Women in Higher Edn., Am. Heart Assn., Public Interest Radio and TV Edn. Soc., Council for Advancement and Support of Edn. Republican. Presbyterian. Club: Job's Daus. Contbr. articles to profl. jours. Office: 24255 Pacific Coast Hwy Malibu CA 90265 also Pub Info Office Pepperdine U Malibu CA 90265

YONKERS, CATHERINE GITSAS, nurse; b. Bklyn., June 26, 1937; d. Dennis and Lena (Zambooni) Gitsas; A.S., SUNY, Farmingdale, 1976; children—Mary Ann Stellakis, Gregory Stephepn Stellakis, Dennis Yonkers. Staff nurse surg. unit North Shore U. Hosp., Manhasset, N.Y., 1977-78; nurse coordinator Suffold Developmental Center, Melville, N.Y., 1978-80; staff nurse psychiat. unit VA Med. Center, Northport, N.Y., 1980—. Mem. fundraising com. Suffolk County Heart Assn., 1982. Cert. psychiat. and mental health nurse. Home: 16 Catherine St East Northport NY 11731 Office: VAMC Northport NY 11768

YOPCONKA, NATALIE ANN CATHERINE, computer specialist; b. Taylor, Pa., July 21, 1942; d. Michael Joseph and Natalie Ann Lucille (Panek) Yopconka; B.S., U. Md., 1965; M.B.A., George Washington U., 1976. Mgmt. analyst, adminstrv. trainee U.S. Dept. Commerce, Maritime Adminstrn., Washington, 1965-67; computer programmer, computer specialist Dept. Labor, Washington, 1967-78; instr. Assn. for Computing Machinery, Washington, 1978; instr. computer sci. Montgomery Coll., Takoma Park and Rockville, Md., 1979; sr. programmer analyst Dynamic Data Processing, Inc., Silver Spring, Md., 1979; instr. Nat. Bus. Sch., Inc., Alexandria, Va., 1980; cons. McLeod Corp., Washington, 1980; lectr. computer sci., coop. coordinator U. Md., College Park, 1980-81; sr. adminstrv. applications analyst programmer, Data Transformation Corp., Washington, 1981; sr. systems analyst Singer Link Simulation Systems div., Silver Spring, 1981-82; self-employed distbr. and accessory designer, 1979—. Mem. Takoma Park Disability Com.; Mayor's Com. on Energy, Housing and Planning, 1980-81; mem. choir Our Lady of Sorrows Ch. Mem. EDP Auditors Assn., Assn. for Computing Machinery (edn. com., instr. 1978-79, 1980-81), Data Processing Mgmt. Assn., Fed. Automatic Data Processing Users Group, Am. Automobile Assn., Internat. Biog. Assn., Am. Biog. Inst. Research Assn., Phi Delta Gamma (scholarship com., social com., hospitality com. 1977-78, 1980-81, 82—). Clubs: Cath. Alumni, Fed. Poets. Home and office: 7401 New Hampshire Ave Apt 1115 Hyattsville MD 20783

YOPP, RUBYE SIMPSON, author; b. Hornsby, Tenn., July 9, 1924; d. Hiram Franklin and Mattie Lucille (Jernigan) Tennyson; m. Henry Grady Simpson, Jr., Mar. 10, 1946; children—Jacquelyn Anne, James Barry; m. 2d, Charles Edward Yopp, July 3, 1975. Various positions in banking and industry, 1943-74; freelance writer; columnist, 1977—; author: Diamonds on a Chain, 1965, In Hardeman, 1973, Star of Love (illustrated by son), 1978; author poems pub. in anthologies, mags. and newspapers. Mem. Nat. Fedn. Press Women, Poetry Soc. Tenn., Tenn. Women's Press and Authors Club, Nat. League Am. Pen Women, Poets Roundtable Ark., Jackson Writers Group, Tenn. Lit. Arts Assn., W. Tenn. Hist. Soc., Hardeman County Hist. Commn., Hardeman County Arts Council, Am. Poets Fellowship Soc., DAR. Methodist. Address: 624 Clifft St Bolivar TN 38008

YORBURG, BETTY (MRS. LEON YORBURG), educator; b. Chgo., Aug. 27, 1926; d. Max and Hannah (Bernstein) Gitelman; Ph.B., U. Chgo., 1945, M.A., 1948; Ph.D., New Sch. Social Research, 1968; m. Leon Yorburg, June 23, 1946; children—Harriet, Robert. Instr., Coll. New Rochelle, 1966-67; lectr. City Coll. and Grad. Center, City U. N.Y., 1967-69, asst. prof., 1969-73, asso. prof. sociology dept., 1973-77, prof., 1978—; research asst. Prof. Clifford Shaw, Chgo. Area Project, 1946-47. Mem. Am., Eastern sociol. assns., Am. Council Family Relations. Author: Utopia and Reality, 1969; The Changing Family, 1973; Sexual Identity: Sex Roles and Social Change, 1974; The New Women, 1976; Introduction to Sociology, 1982. Home: 20 Earley St City Island NY 10464 Office: Sociology Dept City U NY 133d and Convent Ave New York NY 10031

YORDON, JUDY ELLEN, educator; b. Chgo., Nov. 6, 1946; d. Myron William and Miriam Rochelle (Saltzman) Y.; B.S., Northeastern Ill. U., 1968; M.A., Northwestern U., 1970; Ph.D., So. Ill. U., 1976. Tchr., Hayt Elem. Sch., Chgo., 1968-69; asst. prof. N.E. Mo. State U., Kirksville, 1970-74; asso. prof. theater, dir. oral interpretation Ball State U., Muncie, Ind., 1976—; dir. Children's Theatre Repertory Co., Chgo., 1969-70. Recipient Outstanding Tchr. award Alpha Psi Omega, 1977. Mem. Ind. Speech Assn., Ind. Oral Interpretation Guild, Central States Speech Assn., Speech Communication Assn., Phi Kappa Phi. Author: Roles in Interpretation, 1982. Office: Dept Theater Ball State U Muncie IN 47306

YORK, DENA LYNN WINSLOW, former educator, author; b. Caribou, Maine, Sept. 16, 1953; d. Carl Reginald and Wilma Carolyn (Tompkins) Winslow; B.S. in English, Speech and Drama, U. Maine, Presque Isle, 1975; m. Vaughn P. York, July 16, 1974; children—Christopher Vaughn, Thomas Winslow. Spl. edn. tutor Zipple Elem. Sch., Presque Isle, 1971-72; reading tutor, Presque Isle High Sch., 1972-73, adult edn. tchr., 1973-74; tchr. high sch. English, Penquis Valley High Sch., Milo, Maine, 1975-77; author: Mapleton Maine 1880-1980, 1980. Active local 4-H Club, 1963—; pres. Budget Buyers Food Coop., Presque Isle, 1975, Take Off Pounds Sensibly Club, 1979-82; justice of peace, 1975—. Mem. Haystack Hist. Soc. (librarian, curator 1981-82), N.E. Micro-Mini Tractor Pullers Assn. Address: RFD 1 Box 369 Presque Isle ME 04769

YORK, JANET BREWSTER, nurse, family and sex therapist; b. N.Y.C., Mar. 5, 1941; d. Edward Cox and Janet (Stone) Brewster; A.A. with honors, Briarcliff Coll., 1961; R.N. with highest honors, U. Iowa, 1965; B.A. summa cum laude, Marymount Manhattan Coll., 1975; M.A. with honors, N.Y.U., 1978; m. Albert Thompson York, Mar. 31, 1962 (dec.); children—Clifton Gaston, Torrance Brewster. Nurse, Manhattan Eye, Ear and Throat Hosp., N.Y.C., 1966-74; nurse, counselor Washington Free Clinic, 1969-71; family therapist Ackerman Family Inst., N.Y.C., 1976-80; sex therapist N.Y. Med. Coll., Flower Fifth Ave. Hosp., N.Y.C., 1976-78; individual practice family, marriage and sex therapy, N.Y.C., 1978—. Fellow in sex edn., counseling and therapy, marital and family therapy Internat. Council Sex Edn. and Parenthood, Am. U., 1981. Mem. Am. Soc. Sex Therapy and Research, Am. Assn. Marriage and Family Therapists (asso.), Am. Assn. Sex Edn., Counseling and Therapy, Soc. for Sci. Study Sex, Sex Info. and Edn. Council U.S. Clubs: Lawrence Beach, Rockaway Hunting, Mashomack Fish and Game Preserve. Contbr. articles to profl. jours. Home: 155 E 72d St New York NY 10021

YORK, MARCENE MABRY, oil co. exec.; b. Plainview, Tex., Nov. 17, 1939; d. Glenn Raymond and Berniece Parlee (Thompson) Mabry; student Okla. U., 1958-60; B.A., W. Tex. State U., 1972; children—Gregory, Randal. With Air Speed Oil Co., Amarillo, Tex., 1970—, corp. treas., 1973, v.p., 1978—, dir., 1975—. Mem. Amarillo Symphony Guild, 1981-82; patron Amarillo Symphony; mem. Amarillo Art Center, Amarillo Art Alliance. Mem. Women's Network of Amarillo, Amarillo C. of C. (Women's Div.), Gamma Kappa, Alpha Chi, Kappa Delta Pi. Republican. Baptist. Clubs: Amarillo, Amarillo Country. Home: 4413 Olsen St Amarillo TX 79106 Office: PO Box 2047 1201 NE 3rd St Amarillo TX 79105

YORK, MARGARET RUTH ASHTON (MRS. GORDON C. YORK), ret. occupational therapist; b. Reynoldsburg, Ohio, June 9, 1911; d. George Edward and Mary Ruth (Abbott) Ashton; A.A., Los Angeles City Coll., 1933; postgrad. UCLA, 1940; B.S., U. So. Calif., 1958, certificate occupational therapy, 1959; m. Edward T. Randall, Nov. 2, 1938 (dec. Mar. 1968); m. Gordon C. York, Mar. 26, 1973; 1 stepdau., Paulette Marie. Audio-visual specialist U. Calif. Extension, Los Angeles, 1940-56; registered occupational therapist Bur. Crippled Children Services, Schs. for Physically Handicapped, Calif. Dept. Public Health, El Monte, Burbank and Ontario, 1959-63; supervising occupational therapist Crippled Children Services, Orange County Health Dept., Santa Ana, Calif., 1963-74, ret., 1974. Hon. clin. faculty Sargent Coll. Allied Health Professions, Boston U., Sch. Allied Health Professions, Loma Linda U. Mem. South Orange County Regional Citizens Mental Health Adv. Bd., 1975. Mem. Audio-Visual Assn. So. Calif. (v.p. 1955-56), So. Calif. (sec. 1960-61), Orange County (sec. 1969-70) occupational therapy assns. Episcopalian. Club: Pilot (v.p. 1955)

(Westwood Village, Calif.). Home: 320-F Avenida Carmel Laguna Hills CA 92653

YORSTON, LUCILLE ELIZABETH ROANE NOYES, program analyst; b. Campbellton, Tex., June 6, 1928; d. Tom Harvey and Ollie Elizabeth (Stockhorst) Roane; student S.W. Tex. State U., 1945-47; B.A. in Econs., Trinity U., San Antonio, 1975; m. Dale L. Noyes, Mar. 28, 1958 (dec.); 1 son, Craig Lowell; m. Alfred Yorston, Jr., May 12, 1979. Clk., Dept. of Army, San Antonio, 1944-45; sec., bookkeeper W.R. Quin Oil Co., San Antonio, 1947-49; clerk-typist Dept. Air Force, Kelly AFB, Tex., 1950-53; clk.-steno Humble Oil and Refining Co., Houston, 1953; clk.-typist, statis. clk. Dept. of Army, Ft. Sam Houston, Tex., 1953-63, budget analyst, 1963-67, program analyst, 1967-73, program analysis officer, 1973—. Active Boy Scouts Am., Tex. Folklife Festival. Recipient various Dept. Army achievement certs. and performance awards. Mem. Assn. Govt. Accts. (pres. San Antonio chpt.), Am. Soc. Mil. Comptrollers, Toastmistress Club, Fed. Woman's Program. Methodist. Clubs: Order Eastern Star, Daus. of Nile; Zonta (San Antonio). Home: 5842 Winding Ridge San Antonio TX 78239 Office: Directorate of Plans Training and Security Headquarters Fort Sam Houston TX 78234

YOSHA, LINDA OLIVIERI, banker; b. Chgo., Feb. 25, 1953; d. Joseph John and Adelaide Teresa (Leonard) Olivieri; B.A., Elmhurst Coll., 1976; m. Larry Yosha, Aug. 22, 1981. With East Side Bank & Trust Co., Chgo., 1968—, full-time 1977—, v.p. mktg. and personnel, 1982—. Mem. Nat. Assn. Bank Women, Bank Mktg. Assn., Ill. Bankers Assn., Chgo. Bank Women Assn. Office: 10635 Ewing St Chicago IL 60617

YOST, JUDITH ANN, hosp. lab. manager; b. Hazleton, Pa., Feb. 15, 1947; d. Michael William and Frances M. (Zoltak) Shenesky; B.S., Wilkes Coll., 1969; postgrad. Central Mich. U., 1982—; m. Mar. 7, 1970. Med. technologist Allentown (Pa.) Hosp. Lab., 1969-79, lab. mgr., 1979—; microbiologist Med. Diagnostic Labs., Allentown, 1977-79. Recipient 10 Yr. Service award Allentown Hosp., 1980. Mem. Lehigh Valley Soc. Med. Technologists, Am. Soc. Clin. Pathologists, Pa. Soc. Med. Technologists, Am. Soc. Med. Technologists, Nat. Assn. Clin. Lab. Mgrs. Democrat. Home: Rural Route 2 Box 407 Breinigsville PA 18031 Office: 17th and Chew Sts Allentown PA 18102

YOST, NANCY LYNN, architect; b. Santa Monica, Calif., Mar. 25, 1954; d. Stewart William and Marilyn Austin (Judson) Y.; student Ohio State U., 1972-73, U. Oreg., 1973-76; B.Arch., Boston Archtl. Center, 1981. Designer, William B. Morris, Cleve., 1972, Claude Miquelle Assos., Melrose, Mass., 1976-77; job capt. Kubitz & Pepi, Wellesley, Mass., 1977-78; project mgr. Gelardin/Bruner/Cott, Cambridge, Mass., 1978-80; asso. architect Boston Archtl. Team, Inc., 1980—. Mem. Am. Inst. Architects, Boston Soc. Architects, Nat. Trust Hist. Preservation. Office: 184 High St Boston MA 02110

YOST, NELLIE IRENE, author; b. Lincoln County, Nebr., June 20, 1905; d. Albert Benton and Grace Bell (McCance) Snyder; student public schs.; m. David Harrison Yost, July 6, 1929; 1 son, Thomas Snyder. Bookkeeper, Merrick and Co., Maxwell, Nebr., 1923-25; elem. sch. tchr. Diamond Bar Sch., Flats, Nebr., 1925-26; cashier Miller Dept. Store, Salem, Oreg., 1928-29; freelance writer, 1945—; author: Pinnacle Jake, 1951; The West That Was, 1958; Boss Cowman, 1969; Call of The Range, 1966; Medicine Lodge, 1970; Buffalo Bill: His Family, Friends, Fame, Fortunes and Failures, 1979; No Time On My Hands, 1963; Before Today, 1977; A Man As Big As The West, 1979; Backtrailing An Old Cowboy, 1982; pres. bd. dirs. Nebr. Hist. Soc., 1974-76; bd. dirs., 1966—; mem. Nebr. Hall of Fame Commn., 1973-80. Recipient Eyes of Nebr. award, 1970, Wrangler award Cowboy Hall of Fame, 1975, Best Non-Fiction Book award Soc. Midland Authors, 1979; named Col. in Cody Scouts N. Platte (Nebr.), 1965, Hon. Col., Nebr. N.G., 1980. Mem. Western Writers Am. (sec.-treas. 1972-80; Golden Saddleman award 1975, Golden Spur award 1969), PEO, Buffalo Bill Corral Westerners, Friends Buffalo Bill, Westerners Corrals (dir.), Little Big Horn Assn., Beta Sigma Phi (hon.). Republican. Baptist. Address: 1505 West D St North Platte NE 69101

YOUELL, LILLIAN BELK, educator, civic worker; b. Piedmont, S.C., Mar. 9, 1923; d. John Blanton and Jennie Bruce (Wannamaker) Belk; student Hollins Coll., 1941-42; B.A., Westhampton Coll., 1945; postgrad. U. Va., Santo Tomas; m. Rice McNutt Youell, June 22, 1946; children—John Rice, William Nelson. Tchr. public schs., Hanover County, Va., 1945-47, Henrico County, Va., 1954-56, 63, Alexandria, Va., 1957-61, Fairfax County, Va., 1964-66; coordinator Constn. Week celebration, 1977; vol. Virginia Beach (Va.) City Public Schs.; coordinator bicentennial celebration Battle Off Virginia Capes, Virginia Beach City Commn., 1980-81; including project A Revolutionary Experience. Chmn., Vol. Group Teaching Conversational English in Public Schs., Cavite City, P.R., 1967-68, San Juan, P.R., 1969-70; mem., chmn. public relations com. Bicentennial Commn., Virginia Beach, 1980-81; nat. coordinator Yorktown Bicentennial Events, DAR, 1980-81, nat. vice chmn. George Washington 250th Birth Anniversary; cons. to pres. Up with People, 1982. Recipient Gold medal award Freedom's Found., 1978; Ship's Logo Hist. medal from comdg. officer USS Comte de Grasse, 1982; Hist. Medal of Appreciation DAR, 1981. Mem. AAUW (pres. Richmond br. 1949-50), Westhampton Coll. Alumnae Assn. (nat. pres. 1965-66), Assn. Wives of Civilian and Mil. Lawyers Guam (founder), Ret. Officers Wives Soc. (dir. 1973-74, 82-83), Colonial Dames XVII Century (state officer 1978-83), Carolinas Geneal. Soc., Friends of Virginia Beach Library. Editor Youel Log, 1975—. Address: 4105 Hermitage Point Virginia Beach VA 23455

YOUNATHAN, MARGARET TIMS, home economist, educator; b. Clinton, Miss., Apr. 25, 1926; d. Peter Asbury and Eula Lee (Tatum) Tims; B.A., Miss. So. U., 1946, B.S., 1950; M.S., U. Tenn., 1951; Ph.D., Fla. State U., 1958; m. Ezzat S. Younathan, Aug. 11, 1958; children—Janet Nadya, Carol Miriam. Instr., food and nutrition Oreg. State U., 1951-55; postdoctoral research asso. Fla. State U., 1958-59; sr. nutritional cons. Ark. Dept. Health, Little Rock, 1962-68; instr. pediatrics U. Ark. Sch. Medicine, Little Rock, 1962-65, asst. prof. pediatrics, 1965-68; asso. prof. food and nutrition Sch. Home Econs., La. State U., 1971-79, prof., 1979—. Am. Inst. Nutrition grantee, 1965; La. State U. Council on Research summer faculty grantee, 1980. Mem. Inst. Food Technologists, Am. Dietetic Assn., Am. Home Econs. Assn., La. Home Econs. Assn. (pres. dist. D. 1981-82), Sigma Xi, Phi Kappa Phi, Gamma Sigma Delta, Omicron Nu. Mem. Christian Ch. (Disciples of Christ). Home: 1048 Castle Kirk Dr Baton Rouge LA 70808 Office: Sch Home Econs La State U Baton Rouge LA 70803

YOUNG, ANN ELIZABETH O'QUINN, historian; b. Waycross, Ga.; d. James Foster and Pearl Elizabeth (Sasser) O'Quinn; student Shorter Coll.; B.A., M.A., U. Ga., Ph.D., 1965; m. Robert William Young, Aug. 18, 1968; children—Abigail Ann, Leslie Lynn. Asst. prof. history Kearney (Nebr.) State Coll., 1965-69, assoc. prof., 1969-72, prof., 1972—. Mem. Am. Hist. Assn., Phi Alpha Theta, Delta Kappa Gamma (chpt. pres. 1978—). Republican. Presbyterian. Contbg. author Dictionary of Georgia Biography. Office: Dept History Kearney State Coll Kearney NE 68847

YOUNG, ANNE MARY, nurse, educator; b. New London, Conn., Nov. 19, 1926; d. Bruce A. and Helen Skaling; B.S. in Edn., California (Pa.) State Coll., 1970; M. Health Edn., W.Va. U., 1976, M.S. in Nursing, 1981, postgrad., 1982; m. Alan G. Young, June 26, 1948; children—Bruce (dec.), Gary, Brad, Diane, Pam and Rebecca (twins). Public health nurse OEO, Bellaire, Ohio, 1969; instr. Sch. of Nursing, Ohio Valley Gen. Hosp., Wheeling, W.Va., 1970-78; mem. faculty Sch. of Nursing, West Liberty (W.Va.) State Coll., 1980—, asst. prof. community health nursing, 1982—. Bd. dirs. Am. Cancer Soc., Wheeling; Mem. Am. Nurses Assn., Nat. League for Nursing, W.Va. U. Alumnae Assn., Calif. State Coll. Alumnae Assn., Sigma Theta Tau. Republican. Roman Catholic. Clubs: Wheeling Country, Ye Olde Country. Home: 45 Walnut Ave Wheeling WV 26003 Office: 317 Main Hall West Liberty WV 26003

YOUNG, AUDREY GAYLE, social worker; b. Portland, Maine, Apr. 9, 1947; d. William G. and Elcye M. (Ross) Y.; B.A., U. N.H., Durham, 1969; M.S.W., Boston Coll., Chestnut Hill, 1974. Social worker Children's Protective Services, Worcester, Mass., 1969-73, Salem, Mass., 1974-77; social work intern McLean Hosp., Belmont, Mass., 1973-74; prin. clin. social worker Danvers State Hosp., Hathorne, Mass., 1977-78, clin. social work supr., 1978-79; crisis team worker Project RAP, Beverly, Mass., 1977-81; vis. lectr. Salem State Coll., 1976—; mental health coordinator Dept. Mental Health, Lynn, Mass., 1979-81; asso. area dir. Dept. Mental Health, Lynn, Mass., 1981—; mem. Greater Lynn Sr. Services Adv. Bd., 1982—; also cons. Mem. alumni bd. dirs. Boston Coll. Sch. Social Work, 1976-68, 80-82; bd. dirs. Social Advocates for Youth, 1975-79, pres. 1977-79; bd. dirs. Melrose Hickory Hawks Ski Club, 1976-78, sec., 1977-78. Recipient Outstanding Service award Social Advocates for Youth, 1979; lic. ind. clin. social worker, Mass. Mem. Nat. Assn. Social Workers (dir. N.E. region steering com. 1977-81, vice chmn. 1978-80), Acad. Cert. Social Workers (lic. ind. clin. social worker). Protestant. Home: 7 Laurent Rd Salem MA 01970 Office: 156 Broad St Lynn MA 01901

YOUNG, BARBARA NAIMAN, psychiatrist; b. S.I., N.Y., June 23, 1939; d. John Zygmund and Rose Marie (Burchie) Naiman; A.B., Immaculata Coll., 1961; M.D., Med. Coll. Pa., 1966; postgrad. Phila. Psychoanalytic Inst.; children—Andrew, Christopher, Timothy. Intern, Women's Med. Coll. Pa., 1966-67; resident in adult psychiatry Med. Coll. Pa., Phila., 1969-71, chief resident, 1970-71, instr. child psychiatry, 1973-83, dir. Child and Adolescent Psychiat. Clinic, 1976-79, fellow in child psychiatry Psychiat. Inst., 1971-73; candidate in adult and child psychoanalysis Phila. Psychoanalytic Inst., 1971—; pvt. practice psychiatry, Bala Cynwyd, Pa. and Moorestown, N.J., 1974—; psychiat. cons. Center Early Childhood Services, Phila., 1979-81; sch. cons. Germantown Friends Sch., Phila., 1974-76; adolescent group and individual psychotherapist Cath. Home for Girls, Phila., 1973-77; sch. cons. Eastern Pa. Psychiat. Inst., 1971-73. Mem. Am. Psychiat. Assn., Am. Psychoanalytic Assn., Pa. Psychiat. Soc., New Jersey Psychiat. Assn., Phila. Psychiat. Soc., Phila. Psychoanalytic Inst. Candidates' Orgn. (pres. 1976-77). Roman Catholic. Office: 214 W Main St Moorestown NJ 08057

YOUNG, BETTY STANSBURY, home econs. cons.; b. Columbus, Ohio, Nov. 11, 1940; d. Earl and Helen Marie (Chalfant) Stansbury; B.S., Ohio State U., 1962; m. Robert Anthony Young, Oct. 7, 1967; children—Elizabeth Marie, Jeanne Louise. Acting dir., home economist Home Service dept. Mich. Consol. Gas Co., Detroit, 1962-69; commodity exhibits coordinator Mich. State Fair, 1970; cons. Waste King-Universal, Amana Refrigeration, Crowley's, Franciscan, 1971-79; educator Macomb County Community Coll., Wayne County Community Coll., Henry Ford Community Coll., Marygrove Coll., Hudson's, Grosse Pointe Continuing Edn., 1972—; promotion cons., exec. dir. Mich. Wine Inst., 1975-77; pres. Culinary Consultants, Inc., Detroit, 1980—; advt. dir. Detroit Pub. Cons., 1981—. Mem. Am. Home Econs. Assn., Mich. Home Econs. Assn., Detroit Home Economists in Bus. (chmn. 1979-80), Detroit Home Economists in Action (founder, pres. 1974-76), Internat. Microwave Power Inst., Am. Wine Soc., Les Amis du Vin, Soc. Wine Educators, Women Econ. Club, Detroit Adcraft Club. Editor: The American Wine Soc. Jour., 1978-81; No Second Fiddle Cookbook, 1970. Producer Microwave Show, 1979. Address: 5557 Kensington St Detroit MI 48224

YOUNG, CLORA DUMAS, social worker, adminstr.; b. DeKalb, Ill., Feb. 14, 1924; d. Herchel Andrew Alexander and Gladys (Allen) Dumas; grad. Guidance and Counseling, No. Ill. U., DeKalb, 1962; M.S.W., Jane Addams Sch. Social Work, U. Ill., Chgo., 1964; postgrad. in Social Work, U. Calif., Berkeley, 1971-72; m. Wilbur Young, Feb. 12, 1950 (dec., 1980); children—Judith Ann, Deborah Lamon, Wilbur Herbert, Hadassah Alyne. Social work supr. Ill. Mental Health Dept., Elgin and Chgo. State Hosps., 1953-65; asst. prof. Oakwood Coll., A&M U., U. Ala., Huntsville, 1966-71; study list adv.-in-charge black studies div. U. Calif., Berkeley, 1971-72; child welfare adminstr., day care div. State Dept. Pensions and Security, Huntsville, Ala., 1973—, satelite day care licensing outpost worker; cons. Harris Home for Children, Huntsville; concert artist Negro spirituals; rec. I Talked to God, 1971. Dir. Operation Reformation Research Project; U.S. public relations rep. Mirriwinnie Gardens Aboriginal Acad., Sydney, Australia; speaker Library Forum; vol. Dem. polit. campaigns; dir. ch. collections for United Negro Coll. Funds, Huntsville; asso. supt. Sabbath Sch., First Seventh-day Adventist Ch., Huntsville. Recipient Pi Lambda Sigma award of merit, Danial Payne Coll., 1971; service cert. Boguechitto Community Center, 1977; Internat. Rotary grantee to attend Internat. Conf. on Social Welfare, Finland, 1968. Registered Nat. Assn. Social Workers; cert. social worker, Ala. Mem. Nat. Assn. Social Workers (bd. dirs. Ala. state div.), Acad. Cert. Social Workers, D.B. Reid Oakwood Coll. Alumni Assn. (parliamentarian). Home: 6311 Maywick Dr Huntsville AL 35810 Office: 4603 Governor's Dr Suite O Huntsville AL 35805

YOUNG, DIANA ROSE, electronics co. exec.; b. Kokomo, Ind., July 12, 1942; d. Marian Thomas and Verna Inajean (Davison) Herren; student Ind. U.; B.S. in Bus. Adminstrn., St. Mary of the Woods, Terre Haute, Ind., 1981; children—Raymond, Steven, Jared. Prodn. worker Delco Electronics Co. div. Gen. Motors Corp., Kokomo, 1967-72, prodn. supr., 1972-79, gen. supr. mfg., Milw., 1979—. Coordinating supr. Kokomo chpt. Ind. Research Assn. for Dyslexia, 1976-77, supr. tutorial program, Indpls., 1974-75, bd. dirs., 1977—. Recipient Mem. Nat. Mgmt. Assn. (charter mem.; bd. dirs.; cert. achievement 1977, cert. outstanding service 1978), Kokomo Art Assn. Mem. United Brethren Ch. Home: Route 2 84S 24695 W Pheasant Hill Mukwonago WI 53149 Office: 7929 S Howell Oak Creek WI 53154

YOUNG, DOLORES SALLY, advt. photography co. exec.; b. Camden, N.J., Mar. 4, 1932; d. Herman Carl and Rayetta (Glading) Brandt; B.A. in Journalism and Advt. with honors, Douglass Coll., Rutgers U., 1954; m. Robert Arthur Young, July 17, 1959. Chief copywriter Koos Bros. Furniture Showplace, Rahway, N.J., 1954-62; co-owner, sec.-treas. Bob Young Photography, Inc., Linden, N.J., 1962—; N.J. account exec. Graphics 3 Inc., Jupiter, Fla., 1974-78; trustee Jal-Con, Inc., conv. chmn., 1981. Trustee, First Unitarian Soc., Plainfield, N.J. Recipient Advt. award Asbury Park (N.J.) Press, 1954, Best Lamp Ad award Nat. Lamp Council, 1959, Socrates award for furniture advt., 1956; N.J. State scholar, 1951-54; Desi award, 1978. Mem. AAUW, NOW, Art Dirs. Club N.J. (co-chmn. communications art seminar 1978), N.J. Schola Cantorum, ACLU. Home: 116 Cleveland Ave Colonia NJ 07067 Office: 326 E Elizabeth Ave Linden NJ 07036

YOUNG, DOROTHY WAGNER, ednl. adminstr.; b. Carnegie, Pa., Oct. 22, 1934; d. Fred Charles and Leona (Garlett) Wagner; B.S. in Edn., Slippery Rock Coll., 1956; M.Ed. in Counselor Edn., U. Pitts., 1970, Ph.D., 1973, postgrad., 1975; m. Ronald K. Young, June 15, 1957; children—Susan Elaine, Jon Christopher, Pattilee. Tchr./author Pa. Schs., Frankfurt, W. Ger., 1956-68; instr. U. Pitts., supr. Churchill Schs., McKeesport Schs., learning disability coordinator/specialist Greensburg Salem Schs., 1971-73, central office adminstr., pupil personnel/fed. programs, planning and research, 1973-77; case/info. mgr. Westmoreland Intermediate Unit 7, Greensburg, Pa., 1977-79, dir. supplemental programs, 1979—; lectr. U. Pitts. Co-chmn. Interagency Local Children's Team; mem. multidisciplinary county team for child abuse neglect; bds. Parent/Infant Center, Epilepsy Found., Headstart. Experienced Tchr. fellow, 1968. Mem. Pa. Assn. Fed. Program Coordinators (editor state newsletter), Assn. Supervision/Curriculum, Assn. for Retarded Citizens, Assn. Children with Learning Disabilities (bd.). Developer ind. activity center materials for children. Office: Westmoreland Intermediate Unit Greensburg PA 15601

YOUNG, ELIZABETH BELL, speech pathologist, audiologist; b. Franklinton, N.C., July 2, 1929; d. Joseph Henry and Eulalia Miller Bell; B.A., N.C. Central U., 1948, M.A., 1950; Ph.D., Ohio State U., 1959; m. Charles Alexander Young, Jr., Nov. 27, 1964; Chmn. dept. English Barber Scotia Coll., Concord, N.C., 1949-52; prof. Talladega (Ala.) Coll., 1954-56; prof., dir. speech clinic Va. State U., Petersburg, 1956-57, Fla. A&M U., Tallahassee, 1959; chmn. dept. speech and English Fayetteville (N.C.) State U., 1959-63; prof., speech pathologist Howard U. Coll. Dentistry, Washington, 1963-64; chmn. dept. English and speech U. Md., College Park, 1965-66; prof., supr. speech clinic Cath. U. Am., Washington, 1966-79; staff aide U.S. Ho. of Reps., 1980; cons., workshop leader, lectr., Washington, 1981—. Mem. adv. bd. United Negro Coll. Fund.; mem. Congressional Adv. Council on Edn.; mem. D.C. Voting Rights Service Corp. Fellow Am. Speech-Lang. and Hearing Assn. mem. Internat. Assn. Logopedics and Phoniatrics, Public Mems. Assn. of Fgn. Service, NAACP, Urban League, Nat. Council Negro Women, Alpha Kappa Alpha. Democrat. Baptist. Contbr. articles in field to profl. jours. Home and office: 8104 W Beach Dr NW Washington DC 20012

YOUNG, ELIZABETH LOUISE, radio station mgr.; b. Lafayette, La., Dec. 1, 1950; d. Ralph Raney and Annie Lee (Boutin) Y.; student Ariz. State U.; m. Tommy Russell Vascocu, May 2, 1980. Asst. public relations dir. Lomma Internat., Scranton, Pa., 1970-71, public relations dir., 1972-73; asst. direct mail and broadcast dir. Diamonds Dept. Stores, Phoenix, 1973-74, broadcast dir., 1974-75; account exec. KDKB Radio, Mesa, Ariz., 1975-78, sales mgr., 1979-80, gen. sales mgr., 1980—. Mem. Met. Phoenix Ratings Bd. Cert. radio mktg. cons. Mem. Ariz. Broadcasters Assn., NOW. Republican. Roman Catholic. Office: 1167 W Javelina Mesa AZ 85201

YOUNG, ESTHER CHRISTENSEN (MRS. CHARLES JACOB YOUNG), artist; b. Milw., May 10, 1895; d. Niels Anton and Mathilde (Thomesen) Christensen; student Layton Sch. Art, 1914, Art Student's League, N.Y.C., 1915, Milw. Downer Coll. and Sem., 1915-19; pvt. study; m. Charles Jacob Young, June 15, 1929; stepchildren—John Peter, David Whitman (dec. 1975); children—Niels Owen, Esther Van Horne (Mrs. Giles Constable). Exhibited Layton Art Gallery (Milw.), Chgo. Art Inst., Pa. Acad. Fine Arts, Corcoran Art Gallery, Washington, Phila. Water Color Club, Women's Arts and Industries, N.Y.C., Nat. Assn. Women Artists, N.Y.C., Balt., Cleve. Museums Art, Balt. Water Color Club, Painters and Sculptors Soc. N.J., 1960; designer, craftsman, poet, free-lance fabric designer; composer crossword puzzles N.Y. Herald Tribune, 1953. Recipient numerous prizes in Jr. League Art and Poetry contests; medal for design of U.S. stamp for N.J. Tercentenary, 1964. Mem. Princeton Art Assn., Phila. Water Color Club Acad. Natural Sci. (life). Republican. Episcopalian. Clubs: Present Day; Garden, Nassau (Princeton); Acorn (Phila.); Contbr. poems, drawings to mags. Home: 78 Stockton St Princeton NJ 08540 also Holiday House Van Hornesville NY 13475

YOUNG, EULALIE BARNES, social services cons.; b. New Orleans, Oct. 24, 1942; d. Roy and Lucille (Woods) Barnes; B.A., So. U., 1966; M.S., SUNY, Buffalo, 1976; m. Harris Samuel McGee, July 11, 1963; children—Shawn Arlene McGee, Darren Lance McGee; m. 2d, James Leonard Young, Mar. 24, 1970; 1 dau., Jayanna Lucille, Supervisory recreation specialist Dept. Army, Ft. Polk, La., 1967-72; program coordinator YMCA/Model Cities Teen Center, Buffalo, 1972-74; student intern VA Hosp., Buffalo, 1974-76; program coordinator BUILD Work Assessment Center, Buffalo, 1976-77; sr. rehab. counselor Calif. Dept. Rehab., Los Angeles, 1978-80; social services cons. Calif. Dept. Social Services, 1980—. Calif. coordinator Nat. Hook-up of Black Women, 1979—. Recipient Outstanding Achievement award Calif. State Dept. Rehab., 1980. Mem. Assn. Black Psychologists, Am. Personnel and Guidance Assn., Nat. Rehab. Assn., Aware of Women Orgn. Club: Rosicrucians. Address: 2165 E 19th St A San Bernardino CA 92404

YOUNG, FLOY WOODUL, educator; b. Hope, Ark.; d. John Henry and Lou (Wylie) Woodul; student with Silvio Scionti, Chgo. Musical Coll., 1935, 36, 37, North Tex. Tchrs. Coll., Denton, 1942-49; m. Benjamin Richard Young, Sept. 13, 1924 (dec.); 1 son, John Richard. Field rep., guest tchr. in progressive series of piano Art Pub. Soc., St. Louis, 1926-28; pvt. tchr. piano, Shreveport, La., 1929—; organist Broadmoor Baptist Ch., Shreveport, 1938-78. Certified piano tchr., Music Tchrs. Nat. Assn. Mem. Am. Coll. Musicians, Nat., La. State, Greater Shreveport music tchrs. assns. Democrat. Address: 902 Anniston St Shreveport LA 71105

YOUNG, GERALDINE CAMPBELL, electric utility exec.; b. Emporium, Pa., Sept. 4, 1919; d. Walter Scott and Edna Alice Campbell; student public schs., Morris, Pa.; 1 son, Robert; stepchildren—Philip, Lillian Jean, Mary Catherine. Mgr., Western Auto, Wellsboro, Pa., 1939-49; agt. Wingate Ins. Agy., Wellsboro, 1949-56; owner, operator Young Ins. Agy., Wellsboro, 1956-60; pres., chief exec. officer, chmn. bd. Wellsboro Electric Co., 1960—. Fellow Am. Inst. Mgmt.; mem. Grow Resources, Bus. and Profl. Women (dir., v.p.), Republican Women. Home: 59 Waln St Wellsboro PA 16901 Office: 19 Waln St Wellsboro PA 16901

YOUNG, GERALDINE ELIZABETH HEDGE, govt. ofcl.; b. Norfolk, Va., July 24, 1946; d. Gerald Elmer and Elizabeth Mae (Epperley) Hedge; student Lexington (Ohio) public schs. Miscellaneous positions comml. firms, Ohio and Va., 1964-66; with U.S. Naval Supply Center, Norfolk, 1966—, beginning as clk.-typist, successively mgmt. technician, sec., stenographer, writer, editor, public info. specialist, 1966-80, public info. officer, spl. staff asst. to comdg. officer, 1980—. Sec. bd. dirs. Naval Supply Center Fed. Credit Union. Named Zero Defects Employee of Quarter, Naval Supply Center, 1971, Woman of Yr., 1978, Career Woman of Day, 1981. Contbr. articles to newspapers, mil. publs. Home: 8112 Mona Ave Norfolk VA 23518 Office: Public Affairs Office Code 01 Naval Supply Center Norfolk VA 23512

YOUNG, GERTRUDE GOLDEN, corp. sec.; b. Stockdale, Tex., Aug. 10, 1926; d. John and Agnes (Christa) Golden; student Rhodes Bus. Sch., 1945; m. Beryl Young, Apr. 26, 1945; 1 dau., Sally Ann Young Hoopes. With S.W. Bell Telephone, Houston, 1943-44; receptionist Linde Air Products, Houston, 1945-46; with Selby-Leigh Accts., Houston, 1947; with Courtney & Co., Inc., Houston, 1947—, sec.-treas., 1964—; sec. Courtney Enterprises, Inc., 1982—; dir. Gulf Coast Rentals, Inc., 1962—. Mem. So. Baptist Woman's Missionary Union (past tchr. girls' aux.). Home: 1018 Kern St Houston TX 77009 Office: 5322 Ashbrook St Houston TX 77081

YOUNG, JANIE KATHLEEN CHESTER, museum dir.; b. Port Huron, Mich., Apr. 19, 1949; d. Leonard Arthur Chester and Ruth Chester Krumlauf; B.A. (Regents scholar), U. Mich., 1971, M.Mus.-Practice, 1975. Nettie Poe Ketcham fellow Toledo Mus. Art, 1972-73, fellowship coordinator, 1973-75; curator edn. Rutgers U. Art Gallery, 1975-77; art critic Midland (Mich.) Daily News, 1978-80; dir. Saginaw (Mich.) Art Mus., 1977-80; dir. New Bedford (Mass.) Glass Mus., 1980—; instr. Rutgers U. Grad. Sch. Edn., 1976; chmn. Saginaw Arts Alliance, 1979-80; cons. in field, 1979—; mem. mus. adv. panel Mich. Council Arts, 1979—; art adv. panel Alma (Mich.) Coll., 1978-80. Club: Saginaw Zonta (exec. bd. 1979-80, chmn. Mentor project 1980). Author: What's It To You?, 1977. Office: PO Box F-655 New Bedford MA 02742

YOUNG, JEUNE JOHNSON, hosp. adminstr.; b. Memphis, June 26, 1949; d. James and Inez (Whitworth) Johnson; B.A., Memphis State U., 1971, M.Ed., 1973. Spl. edn. tchr. Shady Oaks Sch., Memphis, 1973-75; tchr.-counselor Memphis Mental Health Inst., 1975-78, program coordinator, 1978-79; dir. community services in adolescent psychiatry Mid-South Hosp., Memphis, 1979-80; asst. dir. children's unit and dir. community services St. Joseph Hosp. Children and Youth Center, Memphis, 1980—; program cons. Memphis State U., W. Tenn. Edn. Assn. Bd. dirs. Rivendell, Inc., Memphis; mem. Memphis Mayor's Youth Guidance Commn., 1981—. Mem. Tenn. Assn. Child-Caring Agys., Council Exceptional Children, Council Ednl. Diagnosticians, Council with Children Behavioral Disorders, Assn. Children with Learning Disabilities. Club: Civitan. Office: 210 Jackson Ave Suite 619 Memphis TN 38105

YOUNG, JOAN CRAWFORD, advt. agency exec.; b. Hobbs, N.Mex., July 30, 1931; d. William B. and Ora Maydelle (Boone) Crawford; student Tex. Tech. U., 1949; B.A. in Journalism, Hardin Simmons U., 1952. Reporter, Lubbock (Tex.) Avalanche-Jour., 1952-54; promotion dir. Sta. KCBD-TV, Lubbock, 1954-61; space buyer, account exec. Ward Hicks Advt., Albuquerque, 1961-71; v.p. Mellekas & Assos Advt., Albuquerque, 1971-78; pres. Young & Gallegly Advt., Albuquerque, 1978—. Bd. dirs. N.Mex. Symphony Orch., 1970-72. Recipient Am. Advt. Fedn. Silver medal award, 1977. Mem. N.Mex. Advt. Fedn. (dir. 1976-78), Am. Women in Radio and TV (dir. Zia chpt. 1978). Republican. Author: (with Louise Allen and Andre Lipscomb) Radio and Television Continuity Writing, 1962. Home: 3425 Avenida Charada NW Albuquerque NM 87107 Office: 303 Roma NW Albuquerque NM 87102

YOUNG, LILLIE DEMPSTER, univ. adminstr.; b. Pitts., May 29, 1947; d. James Garfield and Stephanie (Lockwood) Dempster; B.B.A., Ohio Wesleyan U., 1969; M.B.A., So Meth. U., 1976; postgrad. U. Tex., Arlington, 1976-77; m. Charles Edward Young, Sept. 19, 1970; children—Christopher Ryan, Erin Leigh. Dir. univ. devel. Transworld Airlines, N.Y.C., 1967; flight attendant Am. Airlines, N.Y.C., 1968, Pan Am. World Airways, N.Y.C., 1969-71; tchr. English, Jacksonville (Fla.) Public Schs., 1971; mgr. acctg. Southwestern Bell Telephone Co., Dallas, 1974-76; asst. dir. univ. devel. So. Meth. U., 1976-77, asso. dir., 1977-78, dir., 1978—. Mem. So. Meth. U. MBA Assn., Exec. Women of Dallas, Council for Advancement and Support of Edn., Delta Delta Delta. Republican. Methodist. Home: 4231 Nashwood St Dallas TX 75234 Office: Southern Meth U PO Box 402 Dallas TX 75275

YOUNG, LORITA ELLEN, coll. adminstr.; b. Broadwater, Nebr., Oct. 4, 1933; d. Oren Rosco and Dessie Elizabeth (Longan) McNurlin; student U. Nebr., 1951, Western Nebr. Tech. Coll., 1979; m. Robert James Young, Oct. 26, 1952; children—Sharon, Lewis, Leslie, Regina, Teresa. Acting store mgr. Montgomery Ward and Co., Sidney, Nebr., 1966-71; receptionist Holechek Funeral Home, Sidney, 1971-73; sec. Sidney Jr. High Sch., 1973-75; adminstrv. asst. Hwy. Aircraft Corp., Sidney, 1975-77; dir. fin. aid Western Nebr. Tech. Coll., Sidney, 1977—. Den mother Cub Scouts; treas. Sidney PTA, 1964-65. Cert. fundamentals of fin. aid mgmt. Midwest Assn. Student Fin. Aid Adminstrs. Mem. Nebr. Assn. Fin. Aid Adminstrs., Rocky Mountain Assn. Fin. Aid Adminstrs. Democrat. Clubs: Order of Eastern Star (worthy matron 1978), Does. Home: 1626 Manor Rd Sidney NE 69162 Office: Western Nebr Tech Coll Sidney NE 69162

YOUNG, MACHERÉ ANONA, hosp. ofcl.; b. Stoneville, N.C., Oct. 23, 1951; d. James Mark and Susie Elenor (Carter) Spencer; Western Mich. U., 1970-72, student Grand Rapids (Mich.) Jr. Coll., 1973-74; m. Westley Al Young, Mar. 29, 1971; 1 son, Allen Ruffin. Interviewer, Nat. Opinion Research Center, 1973-74; pres. Madison/Hall Neighborhood Assn., 1974-76; agt. Pearson-Cook Real Estate, 1975-76; mem. citizens participation task force Grand Rapids City Commn., 1977; adminstrv. asst. Grand Rapids Public Schs., 1976-81; environ. services supr. St. Mary's Hosp., Grand Rapids, 1981—. Democrat. Baptist. Home: 500 Umatilla St SE Grand Rapids MI 49507 Office: 200 Jefferson Ave Grand Rapids MI 49503

YOUNG, MARGARET ALETHA MCMULLEN (MRS. HERBERT WILSON YOUNG), social worker; b. Vossburg, Miss., June 13, 1916; d. Grady Garland and Virgie Aletha (Moore) McMullen; B.A. cum laude, Columbia Bible Coll., 1949; grad. Massey Bus. Coll., 1958; M.S.W., Fla. State U., 1965; postgrad. Jacksonville U., 1961-62, Tulane U., 1967; m. Herbert Wilson Young, Aug. 19, 1959. Dir. Christian edn. Eau Claire Presbyn. Ch., Columbia, S.C., 1946-51; tchr. Massey Bus. Coll., Jacksonville, Fla., 1954-57, office mgr., 1957-59; social worker, unit supr. Fla. div. Family Services, St. Petersburg, 1960-66, dist. casework supr., 1966-71; social worker, project supr., program supr. Project Playpen, Inc., 1971-81, pres. bd., 1982—. Mem. Acad. Cert. Social Workers, Nat. Assn. Social Workers (pres. Tampa Bay chpt. 1973-74), Fla. Assn. for Health and Social Services (pres. chpt. 1971), Fla. Assn. on Children Under Six, Clearwater Audubon Soc. Democrat. Presbyn. Rotary Ann (pres. 1970-71). Home: 330 Roebling Rd N Belleair Clearwater FL 33516 Office: 4140 49th St N Saint Petersburg FL 33709

YOUNG, MARGARET BUCKNER, civic worker, author; b. Campbellsville, Ky.; d. Frank W. and Eva (Carter) Buckner; B.A., Ky. State Coll., 1942; M.A., U. Minn., 1946; m. Whitney M. Young, Jr., Jan. 22, 1944 (dec. Mar. 1971); children—Marcia Elaine, Lauren Lee. Instr., Ky. State Coll., 1942-45; instr. edn. and psychology Spelman Coll., Atlanta, 1958-60; dir. Phillip Morris Inc. Alt. del. UN Gen. Assembly, 1973; mem. public policy com. Advt. Council; bd. dirs. Lincoln Center for Performing Arts, Lincoln Center Inst., UN Assn.; chmn. Whitney M. Young Jr. Meml. Found.; trustee Met. Mus. Art; mem. Rockefeller U. Council; bd. gos. UN Assn.; bd. visitors U.S. Mil. Acad. Author: The First Book of American Negroes, 1966; The Picture Life of Martin Luther King, Jr., 1968; The Picture Life of Ralph J. Bunche, 1968; Black American Leaders-Watts, 1969; The Picture Life of Thurgood Marshall, 1970; public affairs pamphlets. Office: care Whitney M Young Meml Found 100 Park Ave New York NY 10017

YOUNG, MARGARET LAURENE, journalist; b. Galesburg, Ill., Aug. 30, 1948; d. Robert Louis and Margaret Emily (Conley) Y.; student U. London, 1970; B.A., Wash. State U., 1971; M.A. in Theatre, U. Idaho, 1972; m. Rory David Rice, Mar. 27, 1976. Reporter, No. Ireland, 1971; freelance polit. reporter, U.S. and Can., 1972-73; reporter Robinson Syndicate, 1973-76; public relations for City of Seattle, 1976-78; instr. journalism, adv. Seattle Community Coll., 1978-80; owner Source Northwest, public relations-advt. Del., Democratic Nat. Conv., 1972; campaign organizer race for gov. Wash., 1976. Named Woman of Yr., C. of C., 1976. Mem. Wash. Press Women. Author: Mousecapade, 1975; Death Masque, 1980; co-author: White Center Remembers, 1976; Knoxville Through Five Generations. Home: Knoxville IL 61448 Office: Midland Trading Co Box 2 Knoxville IL 61448

YOUNG, MARION RUTH, media cons.; b. Abington, Pa., May 7, 1936; d. Frank Pierce and Agnes Margaret (Roberts) Y.; student Temple U., 1954-60, Beaver Coll., 1959-61, Tyler Sch. Fine Arts, 1961-62; m. William M. Young; children—Richard, Scott, Gregory. Mem. psychol. testing staff Edward N. Hay & Assos., Phila., 1954-55; travel rep. Am. Express Co., Phila., 1955-56; mem. phys. edn. staff Abington (Pa.) YMCA, 1956-58; office mgr. W.G. Knorr, real estate, Glenside, Pa., 1958-59; tchr. retarded and adults Phila. Council of Chs., 1958; tchr. Abington Friends Sch., 1959; asst. dir. admissions Beaver Coll., 1959-61; adult edn. tchr. Dept. Interior, Micronesia, 1965-67; salesperson Vincent Montalto, real estate, Wayne, N.J., 1969-71; exec. v.p. Urban Dynamics, Inc., Oak Park, Ill., 1975—; pres. Studio 909, Inc., Oak Park, 1980—; co-dir. Union Media Project, 1980—. Trustee Wilmington Coll., 1978—; Democratic committeewoman, Oak Park, 1976-78: co-dir. Nat. PTA TV Project, 1977-81. Mem. AAUP. Quaker. Clubs: Met., Ill. Athletic. Editor Televiews, 1976—, PTA TV Rev. Guide, 1977-81, Phi Delta Kappa Critical Viewing Skills Curriculum, Phi Delta Kappa TV Trainers Manual, 1981. Office: Studio 909 Inc 909 S Oak Park Ave Oak Park IL 60304

YOUNG, MARY ELIZABETH, historian, educator; b. Utica, N.Y., Dec. 16, 1929; d. Clarence Whitford and Mary (Tippit) Young; B.A., Oberlin Coll., 1950; Ph.D. (Robert Shalkenbach Found. grantee, Exra Cornell fellow), Cornell U., 1955. Instr., Ithaca (N.Y.) Coll., part-time, 1954-55; instr. Ohio State U., Columbus, 1955-58, asst. prof., 1958-63, assoc. prof., 1963-69, prof., 1969-73; prof. history U. Rochester (N.Y.), 1973—. Recipient Louis Pelzer prize, 1955; Social Sci. Research Council grantee, 1968-69. Mem. Am. Hist. Assn., Orgn. Am. Historians (exec. bd.), Soc. of Historians of Early Republic, Am. Studies Assn. Author: Redskins, Ruffle-shirts and Rednecks, 1961; co-editor and contbr: The Frontier in Am. Devel.: Essays in Honor of Paul W. Gates, 1969. Office: Dept History U Rochester Rochester NY 14627

YOUNG, PATSY K., state senator; b. Maui, Hawaii, Oct. 29, 1929; student U. Hawaii Mem. Hawaii Ho. of Reps., after 1972, now mem. Hawaii Senate. Mem. adv. council Leeward Sch., 1966-70; del. State Constl. Conv., 1968; bd. regents U. Hawaii, 1971; mem. staff Hawaii Senate, 1966-71; active Waipahu Jackrabbits Youth Orgn., Hui Makaala. Club: Zonta (Leilehua). Office: Hawaii Senate State Capitol Honolulu HI 96813 *

YOUNG, PATTI KAY, real estate exec.; b. Quanah, Hardeman, Tex., Dec. 9, 1944; d. Edmund and Mary Beatrice (King) Nuss; student U. Okla., 1963-65, West Tex. State U., 1965, Amarillo Coll., 1965-67. Traffic dir., continuity writer Sta. KIXZ, Amarillo, Tex., 1964-67; continuity writer Sta. WFAI, Fayetteville, N.C., 1968; prodn. scheduler Bell Helicopter, Amarillo, 1968-70, Swearingen Aircraft, San Antonio, 1970; exec. v.p. Kirkland Mortgage Corp., Dallas, 1971-74; v.p. Hibbard, O'Connor & Weeks, Inc., Houston, 1974; half-owner Real Condominiums, Inc., Real Investments, Inc., Real Designs, Inc., INCO, Inc., Dallas, 1974-81; also dir.; owner, pres., dir. Real Realty Corp., 1974—, Internat. Condominium Enterprises, Inc., 1981; half-owner S.W. Hot Tubs & Spas, Inc., Dallas, 1974—, also dir. Mem. Nat. Assn. Realtors, Tex. Savs. and Loan League, Tex. Real Estate Polit. Action Com. (life), Greater Dallas Bd. Realtors (com. on revision Tex. Uniform Condominium Act), Alpha Phi. Republican. Baptist. Home: 8614 Townhouse Row Dallas TX 75225 Office: 3619 Travis St Suite 104 Cedar Springs Dallas TX 75204

YOUNG, PHYLLIS ANNE, sales mgr.; b. Cammeron, Mo., Nov. 3, 1951; d. Thomas Jefferson and Beverly DeMoss (Banks) Grooms; student pub. schs. With Chess King, 1977—, store mgr. Oak Park Mall, Kansas City, Mo., 1977, store mgr., Joplin, Mo., 1978-79, field tng. coordinator, St. Louis, 1979-80, dist. sales mgr. Iowa Dist., Davenport, 1980—, dist. sales mgr. div. Melville Corp., Harrison, N.Y., 1980—. Republican. Episcopalian. Home: 1803 Chateau Knoll Bettendorf IA 52722 Office: Chess King North Park Mall Davenport IA 52806

YOUNG, SALLY PATRICIA, social worker; b. Marquette, Mich., Apr. 12, 1934; d. Albert Henry and Hilda Emily (Waisanen) Keaton; A.A. with high honors, Thornton Community Coll., 1971; B.S. magna cum laude, George Williams Coll., 1973; M.A. (Noyes scholar, acad. fellow), U. Chgo., 1975; m. Clifford J. Young, Sept. 6, 1952; children—Clifford, Kirby, Brian. Clin. social worker DuPage County Convalescent Home, Wheaton, Ill., 1972-73, Des Plaines Valley Community Center, Argo, Ill., 1975-78, Sunnybrook Sch. Dist. 171, Lansing, Ill., 1978—; cons. Active Ill. Coalition on Domestic Violence. Mem. Nat. Assn. Social Workers, Ill. Assn. Sch. Social Workers, Am. Orthopsychiat. Assn., Kappa Beta Phi (Beta chpt.). Home: 15472 Ridgeway St Markham IL 60426 Office: 19250 S Burnham St Lansing IL 60458

YOUNG, SARAH COLGLAZIER, community services exec.; b. Salem, Ind., July 20, 1937; d. Donald Lee and Phyllis Irma (Hansen) Colglazier; B.S.N., Duke U., 1959; postgrad. Holy Names Coll., Oakland, Calif., 1980—. Staff nurse Duke U. Med. Center, Durham, N.C., 1959-60, Riverside Meth. Hosp., Columbus, Ohio, 1961-62; pvt. duty nurse, Columbus, 1962-66, Oakland, 1966-68; asst. dir. nurses Booth Meml. Home, Oakland, 1968-71; program coordinator Creative Health Resources, Walnut Creek, Calif., 1977; adminstrv. asst. Pleasant Hill (Calif.) C. of C., 1978-79; community liaison to Contra Costa County Bd. Suprs., Concord, Calif., 1979-81, asst. to bd. mem., 1981-82; planner, cons. community programs. Pleasant Hill sponsor Red Cross Youth Vols., 1966-68; chmn. Pleasant Hill City Devel. Com., 1971-76; founding mem., pres. Pleasant Hill Hist. Soc., 1973-82; bd. dirs. Pleasant Hill Bicentennial Commn., 1975-76; chmn. Pleasant Hill Citizens' Forum, 1973, vice chmn., 1976; founding mem. Contra Costa Nurses Community Action Group, Contra Costa Health Forum, 1981-82; founding mem., bd. dirs. Pleasant Hill Arts Council, 1974-76, 78-79, 81-82, service award 1976; community coordinator Adult Health Multiphasic Screening Program, 1974-76; developer awards program Pleasant Hill Beautification Com., 1975-76; consumer rep. Contra Costa Central Dist. council Alameda-Contra Costa Health Systems Agy., 1978-81, sec. governing body, 1981-83, recognition of service award, 1979; vice-chairperson community adv. council Mt. Diablo Hosp. Med. Center, 1979-82, Community Adv. Council rep. to Mt. Diablo Hosp. Planning Com., 1979-82; sec. bd. dirs. Mt. Diablo Edn. Fund., Mt. Diablo Unified Sch. Dist., 1982-83; bd. dirs. Contra Costa Alliance for the Arts, 1982-83; v.p. Pleasant Hill Hist. and Cultural Center, 1979-81. Named Pleasant Hill Citizen of Yr., 1973, lifetime citizen, 1976; 15th ann. appreciation award City of Pleasant Hill, 1976; recipient commendation Calif. State Legislature, 1976. Mem. Calif. Nurses Assn. (dir. 1974-76, service award 1976), AAUW (dir. Pleasant Hill br. 1966-76, 81-83), Pleasant Hill C. of C. (hon. life mem.). Methodist. Club: Commonwealth. Home: 1884 Cannon Dr Walnut Creek CA 94596 Office: 2301 Stanwell Dr Concord CA 94520

YOUNG, SUSAN JEAN, music specialist; b. Chgo., Nov. 9, 1940; d. Walter Lawrence and Grace Helen (Blue) Pennie; B.Mus.Ed. (scholar), Northwestern U., 1962; M.Mus.Ed. (grad. scholar), Am. Conservatory of Music, Chgo., 1974; m. Peter R. Young, Jr., June 23, 1962; children—Laura Jane, Beth Ann. Music specialist Skokie (Ill.) Sch. Dist., 1962-63, Northbrook (Ill.) Sch. Dist., 1974—; pvt. piano tchr., 1963-74; pres. Stevenson High Choral Guild, 1979-81; mem. music com. Long Grove Ch. Mem. Music Educators Nat. Conf., Ill. Music Educators Assn., Ill. Music Tchrs. Assn., Music Tchrs. Nat. Assn., Am. Choral Dirs. Assn., Soc. Am. Musicians, Delta Kappa Gamma, Mu Phi Epsilon. Home: 957 Alden Ln Buffalo Grove IL 60090 Office: 1475 Maple Ave Northbrook IL 60062

YOUNG, VANEICA YVONNE, chemist; b. Topeka, Feb. 18, 1947; d. Jesse Lee and Blanche Beatrice (Hardy) Y.; B.A., U. Kans., 1969; M.S., U. Mo., Kansas City, 1972, Ph.D., 1976; Postdoctoral research asso., vis. asst. prof. Purdue U., West Lafayette, Ind., 1976-78; asst. prof. chemistry Tex. A&M U., College Station, 1978—; cons. NASA, Johnson Space Center, 1980—. NSF summer research fellow, 1970; grantee Petroleum Research Fund, 1979-81, Robert A. Welch Found., 1979—. Mem. Am. Chem. Soc., AAAS, N.Y. Acad. Scis., Soc. Applied Spectroscopy, Microbeam Analysis Soc., Phi Lambda Upsilon. Contbr. articles to profl. jours.

YOUNG, VIRGINIA GARTON (MRS. RAYMOND ARTHUR YOUNG), civic worker; b. Mountain View, Mo., Jan. 16, 1919; d. Charles Clinton and Mattie Belle (Cartwright) Garton; student U. Mo., 1936-38; A.B., So. Mo. State U., 1939; M.L.S., U. Okla., 1940; H.H.D. (hon.), Tarkio Coll., 1978; m. Raymond Arthur Young, June 18, 1940; 1 son, David Bruce. Mem. library staff U. Mo., 1940, 42-44; librarian William Woods Coll., Fulton, Mo., 1941; guest lectr. Columbia U., 1960, 67, Inst. Govt., U. N.C., 1968, Sch. Library Sci., U. Mo., 1971. Del. Internat. Fedn. Library Assns., 1965—; cons. Library Trustee Workshops, U. Colo., 1969; mem. Citizens Com. on Reorgn. Mo. Legislature, 1973—; mem. Mo. Press Bar Commn., 1973—; chmn. Mo. Coordinating Bd. Higher Edn., 1974—; bd. dirs. Friends U. Mo. Library, pres., 1964-66; pres. Columbia LWV, 1943-44, bd. dirs., 1943-44, 68-69; bd. dirs. YWCA, 1953-56, Planned Parenthood, 1970—; mem. adv. com. U.S. Commr. Edn., Library Services br. HEW; mem. def. adv. com. women in services Dept. Def., 1963-65; mem. exec. com. of bd. Nat. Book Com., 1967—; mem. vis. com. Case Western Res. U. Sch. Library Sci., 1969-71; trustee Columbia Pub. Library, 1950-53, 56-59, 62-65, pres., 1957-59, 62-64; pres. Mo. State Library Com., 1956-57; trustee Am. Library in Paris, 1968-73. Recipient Outstanding Alumni award So. Mo. State U., 1965, cert. of Appreciation, Dept. Army, 1966, Disting. Alumni award U. Mo., 1972, Civic award Alpha Kappa Psi, 1973; 50th Anniversary Services to Librarianship award U. Okla. Library Sch., 1980; named Ky. col., Nebr. adm., Ark. traveler. Mem. Am. (trustee citation of merit 1962), Mo. (Meritorious Achievement award 1956, pres. 1967-68) library assns., Am. Library Trustees Assn. (pres. 1959-61, dir. 1962—), Ninety-Niners, Mo. Acad. Squires. Club: Readers. Author: The Trustee of a Small Public Library, 1962, rev. edit., 1976; The Library Trustee: A Practical Guidebook, 1964, rev. edit., 1969, 78; contbr. articles to library periodicals. Home: 10 E Parkway Dr Columbia MO 65201

YOUNG, VIRGINIA SHUMAN, mayor; b. Norfolk, Va., Sept. 16, 1917; d. Irving and Myrtle (Tenbrook) Shuman; student public schs., Ft. Lauderdale, Fla.; m. George Fenwick Young, Mar. 27, 1937; children—George William, Nancy Anne Young Stayman, Catherine Reta Young Moore. Co-owner, George F. Young Bldg. Constrn. Co., Ft. Lauderdale; dir. Landmark Bank. Chmn. bd. trustees Broward County Sch. System, 1953-57, mem. bd. public instrn., 1958-66, chmn. bd., 1961, 65; pres. Fla. Sch. Bds. Assn., 1965; camp dir. Girl Scouts U.S.A., 1945-46; mem. Gov.'s Com. on Aging, 1956, Citizens Tax Council, 1957, Gov.'s Conf. Edn., 1966; vice mayor Ft. Lauderdale, 1971-72, mayor, 1973-82, mayor pro tem, 1982—. Mem. Nat. Sch. Bds. Assn. (legis. com.), Bus. and Profl. Women's Club, LWV, C. of C. (pres. women's div. 1969-71), Delta Kappa Gamma. Methodist. Clubs: Ft. Lauderdale Woman's (pres. 1969-71), Soroptimist. Author: Mangrove Roots of Fort Lauderdale, 1976. Office: PO Box 12450 Fort Lauderdale FL 33302

YOUNGBERG, RUTH MAE, nurse; b. Clearwater, Nebr., Sept. 30, 1921; d. Byron DeForest and Mary Jane (Kletke) Brown; R.N., Lincoln Gen. Hosp. Sch. Nursing, 1943; m. Ira Burnell Youngberg, Sept. 13, 1969; children—Carol Hall Gleason, Mary Hall Hughes, Janet Hall Hays. Office nurse, Lincoln, Nebr., 1947-58; staff nurse Porters Hosp., Denver, 1958-59; head nurse, obstetrical supr. Lincoln Gen. Hosp., 1959-74; maternal child health nurse cons. Nebr. State Health Dept., Lincoln, 1974-77; head nurse labor and delivery Lincoln Gen. Hosp., 1977—. Mem. Nurses Assn. Am. Coll. Obstetricians and Gynecologists (past vice-chmn. Nebr., past membership chmn. Nebr.), Am. Nurse Assn., Nebr. Perinatal Orgn. (dir., pres.), Great Plains Orgn. Perinatal Health Care (past sec.), Lincoln Gen. Hosp. Alumni Assn. Republican. Methodist. Home: 400 S 46th St Lincoln NE 68510 Office: Lincoln Gen Hosp Lincoln NE 68508

YOUNGER, CELIA DAVIS, educator; b. Gretna, Va., Aug. 24, 1939; d. Richard and Mary M. (Younger) Davis; B.S., Va. State U., 1971, M.Ed., 1974; children—Felicia Annette, Terri Eugenia. Program coordinator student union Va. State U., Petersburg, 1971-73; tchr./counselor Jobs Skills Tng., Petersburg, 1971-73; asst. dir. fin. aid Va. State U., 1973-75; adj. faculty bus. adminstrn. J.S. Reynolds Community Coll., Richmond, 1974-75; bus. devel. specialist/procurement officer Va. State OMBE, Petersburg, 1975-79; dir. Learning Resource Center, Georgian Ct. Coll., Lakewood, N.J. and asso. dir. ednl. opportunity fund program, 1978—; adj. faculty bus. adminstrn. Ocean County Coll., Toms River, N.J., 1981—; tchr. Toms River Community Sch., 1981. County commr. Ocean County Commn. on Status of Women, 1980—; chmn. EEO and legis. com. Commn. on Status of Women, 1980—; Central N.J. adv. com. Nat. Council on Alcoholism, 1980—. Recipient Cert. of Appreciation, Ann. Women's Conf., Ocean County, N.J., 1980-81. Mem. N.J. Ednl. Opportunities Fund Profl. Assn., So. Econ. Assn., Assn. Equality and Excellence in Edn., Nat. Assn. Female Execs., N.J. Coll. and Univ. Coalition on Women's Edn. Alpha Kappa Alpha. Baptist. Contbr. articles to profl. jours. Home: 32 Chelsea Rd Jackson NJ 08527 Office: Georgian Court Coll Lakewood NJ 08701

YOUNGS, BETTIE BURRES, educator, author, adminstr.; b. Belmond, Iowa, Mar. 24, 1948; d. Everett H. and Arlene B. Burres; Ed.D., Drake U., 1978; Ph.D., Walden U., 1976; 1 dau., Jennifer Leigh. Program specialist Des Moines Public Schs., 1970-77; internat. ednl. cons. Batten, Batten, Hudson & Swab, 1977-78; adminstr. Iowa Dept. Social Services, 1978-80; adminstr. San Diego State U., 1980—, prof. ednl. adminstrn., 1980—, founder, dir. Internat. Mgmt. and Leadership Inst., 1978—; bd. dirs HED Inst., 1977-80; mem. Nat. Council Adminstrv. Women Edn., 1981—. Recipient Edn. Press award for excellence in ednl. journalism, 1980; named Tchr. of Yr., Iowa Dept. Public Instrn., 1976; Margaret Mann fellow, 1978. Mem. Nat. Assn. Life-Long Learning, NEA, Delta Kappa Gamma, Phi Delta Kappa. Author: Stress Within Youngsters, 1982. Contbr. articles to profl. jours. Home: 6876-33 Caminito Montanoso San Diego CA 92119 Office: Dept Ednl Adminstrn San Diego State Univ San Diego CA 92182

YOUNGWIRTH, JONI CLARICE, mktg. specialist; b. Sioux Falls, S.D., Feb. 12, 1950; d. John Wesley and Clarice Lillian (Stoen) Yttreness; B.S., S.D. State U., 1972; M.S., Boston U., 1977; m. Stephen A. Youngwirth, Apr. 5, 1975. Dir. dietary services New Eng. Deaconess Assn., Concord, Mass., 1975-76; project coordinator New Eng. Deaconess Hosp., Boston, 1978-81, mem. computer applications devel. team, 1981-82; mgr. mktg. services Organizational Dynamics Inc., Burlington, Mass., 1982—; cons. in field. Served with USAF, 1972-75. Mem. Women in Mgmt., Am. Women in Computing, Am. Dietetic Assn., Mass.

Dietetic Assn., LWV (dir. chpt. 1980—), New Eng. Apple Tree Club, Chi Omega. Lutheran. Home: 21 Partridge Rd Lexington MA 02173 Office: 5 Burlington Woods Burlington MA 01803

YOUNKER, DONNA LEE, educator; b. Evanston, Ill., Feb. 7, 1932; d. Fred Lee and Florence (Jett) Y.; B.A., Baylor U., 1952; M.A., So. Meth. U., 1958; Ph.D., U. Tex., 1964. Vis. prof. Purdue U., Lafayette, Ind., 1964; faculty Central State U., Edmond, Okla., 1966—, asso. prof. philosophy of edn., 1966-78, prof., 1978—, mem. faculty senate, 1971-72; tchr. Ind. Sch. Dist., Dallas, 1958-60; lectr. U. Tex., 1962-64, Fellow Philosophy of Edn. Soc.; mem. Southwestern Philosophy of Edn. Soc. (pres. 1971-72), History of Edn. Soc., Am. Ednl. Studies Assn., Am. Ednl. Research Assn., DAR (regent Samuel King chpt. 1980-82), Phi Delta Kappa. Methodist. Home: 1404 Mockingbird Ln Edmond OK 73034

YOUNT, ELOISE ADKINS, nurse; b. Salisbury, Md., June 12, 1943; d. Marion Carlton and Dorothy Mae (Moore) Adkins; Lic. Practical Nurse, Appalachian Sch. Practical Nurses, 1966; R.N. with academic honors, Ky. State U., 1972; m. Eugene Edward Yount, May 19, 1962; children—Eugene Edward, Rhonda Marie. Nurses aide Peninsula Gen. Hosp., Salisbury, Md., 1962; nurses aide, student practical nurse, lic. practical nurse Kings Daus. Meml. Hosp., Frankfort, Ky., 1965-72, relief asst. dir., critical care unit staff nurse, 1972—, head nurse, 1980—, asst. dir. nursing, 1982—; instr. cardiopulmonary resuscitation, inservice tng.; part time nurse Woodford County Hosp., Bendix Westinghouse Air Brake Co.; relief nurse Schenley Distillery. Guard, Aux. Fraternal Order of Police, 1974—. Certified coronary care, trauma and transp. of critically ill. Mem. Am. Assn. Critical Care. Home: Route 9 Jamesway Frankfort KY 40601 Office: Kings' Daughters Dr Frankfort KY 40601

YOUNT, FLORENCE JANE, lawyer; b. Enid, Okla., Dec. 13, 1926; d. William Edward and Florence Evelyn (McCully) Y.; B.A., State U. Iowa, 1948; J.D., S. Tex. Coll. Law, 1958; cert. Parker Sch. Fgn. and Comparative Law, Columbia U., 1976. Admitted to Tex. bar, 1958; atty. Ginther, Warren & Co., Houston, 1959-70; supr. internat. contracts Eastern Hemisphere Petroleum div. Conoco, Inc., N.Y.C., Stamford, Conn., 1970-75; sr. atty. Cities Service Co., Houston, 1975—; adviser to Internat. Law Socs. of three Houston law schs.; bd. dirs. S. Tex. Law Jour., Inc., v.p., 1969, 77, pres., 1970, 78, 79. Bd. dirs. Park Ave. Christian Ch., N.Y.C., 1971-73, First Christian Ch., Houston, 1977; active Vols. of Shelter, N.Y.C., 1973-75; precinct chmn., asso. legal counsel, chmn. rules com. Harris County (Tex.) Republican Party, 1958-68. Recipient Distinguished Alumnus award S. Tex. Coll. Law, 1976; Houston Matrix award, 1978; named One of 100 Top Corporate Women, Bus. Week, 1976, One of Five Outstanding Career Women, Bus. and Profl. Women's Club Houston, 1976. Mem. Am., Tex. (contbg. editor Internat. Law Newsletter), Houston bar assns., S. Tex. Coll. Law Alumni Assn. (dir. 1977-80), Houston World Trade Assn., Zool. Soc. Houston. Mem. Christian Ch. Contbr. articles to law jours. Office: Cities Service Co PO Box 642 Houston TX 77001

YOUSE, GLAD ROBINSON, composer; b. Miami, Okla., Oct. 22, 1898; d. James Fountain and Catherine Elizabeth (Green) Robinson; student Stephens Coll., Columbia, Mo., 1918-20; student composition with Tibor Serly, N.Y.C., 1945-52; D.F.A. (hon.), Baker U., Baldwin, Kans., 1976; m. Clarence E. Youse, May 16, 1920; 1 dau., Madolyn (Mrs. Edmund Page Babcock). Composer-dir. Jenkins Music Conf., Kansas City, Mo., 1948-66; nat. chmn. Sigma Alpha Iota Found., Des Moines, 1949-56; nat. music chmn. Nat. League Am. Pen Women, Washington, 1967-68; trustee Baker U., Baldwin, Kans., 1960-68. Recipient Alumnae Achievement citation Stephens Coll., 1955; Matrix Table award Theta Sigma Phi, 1965; presdl. citation Nat. Fedn. Music Clubs, 1981. Mem. Kans. Authors Club (merit award 1975), ASCAP, Sigma Alpha Iota (hon., Ring of Excellence 1956), Beta Sigma Phi (hon., achievement award 1957). Republican. Methodist. Club: PEO Composer over 200 published songs, choral works; recordings on Golden Crest Records, D/D Record Co. Home and office: 532 E 12th St Baxter Springs KS 66713

YOUSSEF, MARY NAGUIB, statistician; b. Cairo, Oct. 25, 1935; d. Naguib and Fotune (Gorgy) Y.; came to U.S., 1962, naturalized, 1975; B.Sc., Cairo U., 1958; M.A., Columbia U., 1964; M.Sc., Stanford U., 1967; Ph.D., Oreg. State U., 1970; 1 dau., Amany Attia. Asst. instr. Cairo U., 1958-61; mem. tech. staff Inst. Nat. Planning, Cairo, 1963-65; mem. tech. staff Bell Labs., Holmdel, N.J., 1970-76, specialist, 1977-81; asso. prof. Baruch Coll., City U. N.Y., 1981—; sr. engr. Am. Bell Internat., Inc., Holmdel, 1976-77; lectr. in field. Ford Found. fellow, 1962-63, 65-67; NSF grantee, 1967-70. Mem. Am. Statis. Assn., Ops. Research Soc. Am., Sigma Xi. Research in time series analysis and forecasting, traffic theory and its applications, statistics, celestial mechanics. Home: 66 McCarter Ave Fair Haven NJ 07701 Office: Bell Labs Holmdel NJ 07733

YOUTZ, ADELLA CLARK, psychologist, educator; b. Mukwonago, Wis., Sept. 17, 1908; d. Charles Hill and Addie Maria (Merritt) Clark; B.A., Oberlin Coll., 1930; M.A., U. Minn., 1933; Ph.D., Yale U., 1937; m. Richard Pardee Youtz, Sept. 20, 1933; children—Edwin, Carolyn, Kathryn. Oberlin-Shansi teaching fellow, Shansi, China, 1930-32; asst. dir. Reading Clinic, Tchrs. Coll., Columbia U., N.Y.C., 1941-42; adj. instr., 1946-64; asso. prof. psychology Kean Coll. N.J., Union, 1964-67, prof., 1967-79, prof. emeritus, 1979—, adj. prof. grad. program, 1979—; cons. N.J. Bd. Higher Edn., Grad. Adv. Council, 1974-78. Pres. founding bd. trustees Bergen County Mental Health Consultation Center, 1954-56; trustee N.J. Psychol. Trust. Structural reading program for disadvantaged children grantee, 1970-72. Mem. Am. Psychol. Assn., N.J. Psychol. Assn. (sec. 1970-76, pres. 1977-78), N.J. Acad. Psychology (pres. 1979-80), Bergen County Assn. Clin. Psychologists, Phi Beta Kappa, Phi Kappa Phi, Sigma Xi. Unitarian. Author: (with others) College Fields: From Delinquency to Freedom; contbr. articles to profl. jours. Home: 169 Glenwood Ave Leonia NJ 07605 Office: Dept Psychology Kean Coll NJ Morris Ave Union NJ 07083

YOUTZ, CAROL ANN, trust adminstr.; b. Canton, Ohio, June 17, 1953; d. Charles Burton and Florence Nancy (Parks) Youtz; student Baldwin-Wallace Coll., 1971-72; B.S. magna cum laude in Acctg., U. Akron, 1979, postgrad. U. Akron Sch. Law. New accounts counselor The Harter Bank & Trust Co., Canton, Ohio, 1973-75; litigation, corp. and pension paralegal Krugliak, Wilkins, Griffiths & Dougherty Co., Canton, 1975-80; tax and ins. analyst Diebold, Inc., Canton, 1980-81; trust adminstr. Bank One of Akron, N.A., 1981—; mem. Akron Pension Council, 1979-82. Mem. Tuscarawas Philharmonic Orch., 1978-80. Mem. Am. Bar Assn., Akron Pension Council, Beta Alpha Psi, Beta Gamma Sigma, Alpha Sigma Lambda. Mem. United Ch. of Christ. Club: Order of Eastern Star. Home: 1103 17th St NW Canton OH 44703

YU, ANNE RAMONA WING-MUI, psychologist; b. Hong Kong, Apr. 9, 1948; came to U.S., 1968, naturalized, 1974; d. Hing-wan and Sin-wah (Yau) Y.; B.A. with honors in Psychology, Ohio U., 1971; M.A. in Clin. Psychology, So. Ill. U., 1975. Psychologist, Delta Counseling & Guidance Center, Monticello, Ark., 1975-76; psychologist Mid-Nebr. Community Mental Health Center, Grand Island, 1977—; supr. satellite clinic Loup Valley Mental Health Center, Loup City, Nebr., 1977-79; project dir. Protection from Domestic Abuse, 1978-79; pres. Grand Island Task Force on Domestic Violence & Sexual Assault, Inc., 1980-82. Mem. Am. Assn. Marriage & Family Therapy (v.p. Nebr. div. 1981—), AAUW, Am. Psychol. Assn., Asian Am. Psychol. Assn. Home: 1524 Coventry Ln Apt 94 Grand Island NE 68801 Office: 914 Baumann Dr Grand Island NE 68801

YU, CECILIA M. SHEN, physicist; b. Shanghai, China, Jan. 22, 1939; d. J.F. and Zan-Huan (Kang) Shen; B.S. in Physics, Chen Kung U., Taiwan, 1960; M.S. in Physics with high honors, Stevens Inst. Tech., 1968; 1 son, Manfred Yu. Mem. tech. staff RCA David Sarnoff Research Labs., 1976-79; research engring. mgr. Fairchild Camera and Instrument Corp., Mountain View, Calif., 1980-81; program dir. computer sci. and tech. div., very large scale integration research program Telecommunications Scis. Center, SRI Internat., Menlo Park, Calif., 1981—; cons. Shen Assocs. Inc., microelectronics tech. and digital communication systems, 1982—; cons. microelectronics and computer sci. Mem. IEEE, Am. Phys. Inst., Assn. Computing Machinery, Am. Mgmt. Assn. Republican. Roman Catholic. Office: 3790 El Camino Real Suite 336 Palo Alto CA 94306

YU, LINA LAI-LING, physician; b. Hong Kong, Jan. 23, 1941; d. Wing-Kam and Woon-Yu (Tang) Yu; M.B., B.S. with honors, U. Hong Kong, 1965; m. Simon Cheng, May 20, 1967. Asso. dir. Pathology Assos. Med. Lab., Honolulu, 1971-74; co-dir. dept. pathology Westminster (Calif.) Community Hosp., 1974—. Diplomate in clin. and anatomic pathology Am. Bd. Pathology, Am. Bd. Dermatology. Fellow Coll. Am. Pathologists. Office: Westminster Community Hosp 200 Hospital Circle Westminster CA 92683

YU, LINDA, newswoman, television anchorwoman; b. Xian, China, Dec. 1, 1946; B.A. in Journalism, U. So. Calif., 1968; m. Richard K. Baer, June 1982. With Sta. KTLA-TV, Los Angeles, Sta. KABC-TV, Los Angeles; news anchor, reporter Sta. KATU-TV, Portland, Oreg.; gen. assignment reporter Sta. KGO-TV, San Francisco; with Sta. WMAQ-TV, Chgo., 1979—, gen. assignment reporter, weekend anchor, 1979-80, co-anchor Monday-Friday edit. NEWSCENTER5, 4:30 PM, 1980-81, co-anchor, NEWSCENTER5, 10:00 PM, 1981—, spl.: Linda Yu in China, 1980. Recipient Chgo. Emmy award, 1981. Office: care WMAQ-TV Merchandise Mart Chicago IL 60654

YUCHT, SANDRA SMITH, psychiat. social worker; b. N.Y.C., Oct. 24, 1945; d. David and Shirley (Tabach) Smith; B.A. in Sociology, Hunter Coll., 1966; M.S.W., Columbia U., 1970; m. Gerald Yucht, Aug. 14, 1965; children—Lisa, Adam. Dir. social services Smithtown (N.Y.) Gen. Hosp., 1978-79; clin. social worker Queens Children's Psychiat. Center, Bellrose, N.Y., 1975-78; sch. social worker Com. on Handicapped, N.Y.C. Bd. Edn., 1979—; part-time asst. prof. community services SUNY, Farmingdale, 1973-78; cons. South Shore Feminists, 1976-78; clin. dir. Pembroke Therapy Assos., Bellmore, N.Y., 1976-79. Mem. therapy referral com. Women's Liberation Center L.I., Hempstead, 1974-78. N.Y. State Dept. Social Services fellow, 1968-70. Mem. Nat. Assn. Social Workers, Acad. Cert. Social Workers, Soc. Hosp. Social Work Dirs., Am. Hosp. Assn., Columbia U. Alumni Assn. Past v.p. Cancer Care, Massapequa; mem. sisterhood bd. Temple Judea, Massapequa, 1978-79. Home: 26 Pembroke Dr Massapequa NY 11758

YUDAIN, CAROLE GEWIRTZ, free lance writer, photo journalist; b. Bronx, N.Y., May 9; d. Sam I. and Helen (Greenberg) Gewirtz; student Bennington Coll., 1950-53; B.A., Sarah Lawrence Coll., 1972; m. Theodore Yudain, Dec. 28, 1966 (dec. 1970); children by previous marriage—Marc I. Rosenthal. Sales trainee Saks Fifth Ave., N.Y.C., 1952-53; newspaper display advt. asst. Binghamton (N.Y.) Press, 1954-55; fashion copywriter, commentator Fowler, Dick & Walker Dept. Store, Binghamton, N.Y., 1955-56; promotion, publicity writer, TV model, talk show commentator Sta. WNBF-AM-TV, Binghamton, 1956; feature writer Public Relations Asso., Slenderella Internat., Stamford, Conn., 1957; dir. public relations United Fund, Stamford, 1964-66; weekly news columnist Conn. Sunday Herald, 1972-75, Daily Item, 1975-77, Stamford Advocate, 1979; dir. public affairs, news editor United Hosp., Port Chester, N.Y., 1973-74; pres. Carole Yudain Public Relations, 1974-78; dir. public relations Fedn. Jewish Philanthropies, N.Y.C., 1978-79; free lance writer, public relations cons. and photo journalist, Cos Cob, Conn. Mem. Nat. Acad. TV Arts and Scis., Public Relations Soc. Am., Women in Communication, Am. Med. Writers Assn., N.Y. Press Club, Sigma Delta Chi.

YUKIC, ELEANOR CLARKE, retail wine co. exec.; b. Anaheim, Calif., June 10, 1925; d. Courtenay Hargraves and Eleanor O'Connor (Allen) Clarke; B.A., UCLA, 1947, M.A., 1951; postgrad. in edn. U. Calif., Berkeley, 1969—; m. Dec. 28, 1951 (div.); children—Constance, Raymond, Fred. Tchr., Santa Monica (Calif.) High Sch., 1945-50, Berkeley (Calif.) High Sch., 1958-66; tchr., dept. chmn. Soquel (Calif.) High Sch., 1966-67; asst. prof. phys. edn. Calif. State U., San Francisco, 1967-70; exec. dir. Sem Yeta council Camp Fire Girls, 1971-81; treas. Berkeley Wine Cellars, 1981—; teaching asst. U. Oreg., 1950-51; vis. instr. Coll. Holy Names, 1967-69; cons. camping. Recipient gold pin ARC, 1967, Luther Gulick award Camp Fire Girls, 1981. Mem. AAHPER, Am. Camping Assn., Camp Fire Assn. Profls. Democrat. Roman Catholic. Club: Soroptomists. Contbr. articles on camping to mags.; research in group dynamics. Home: 1916 Yolo Ave Berkeley CA 94707 Office: 907 University Ave Berkeley CA 94710

YURA, HELEN, nursing educator; b. Hazleton, Pa., Aug. 1, 1929; d. Michael and Anna (Sokol) Y.; B.S. in Nursing Edn., U. Dayton, 1953; M.S. in Nursing, Cath. U. Am., 1962, Ph.D., 1970. Staff nurse Sacred Heart Hosp., Allentown, Pa., 1950-51, asst. head nurse, 1951, head nurse, 1951, instr. fundamentals of nursing, 1953-60, 62-64; instr. psychiat. mental health nursing Cath. U. Am., Washington, 1964-66, asst. prof. nursing, 1966-70; chmn. dept. nursing St. Joseph Coll., Emmitsburg, Md., 1970-72; cons. nursing edn. Nat. League Nursing, N.Y.C., 1972-73, asst. dir. div. degree programs, 1973-78, nursing project developer, 1979; prof. and grad. program dir. dept. nursing Old Dominion U., Norfolk, Va., 1979—; treas. Tri-State Regional Planning Council on Nursing Edn., 1970-72. Mem. lay adv. bd. Seton Center, Emmitsburg, Md., 1972. Recipient Alumni Achievement award Cath. U. Am., 1978, Spl. Achievement award U. Dayton Alumni Bd. Govs., 1979. Fellow Am. Acad. Nursing; mem. Am. Nurses Assn., Nat. League for Nursing, Assn. for Supervision and Curriculum Devel., Cath. U. Am. Alumni Assn. (sec. nursing chpt. 1968-70), Sigma Theta Tau. Democrat. Mem. Byzantine Cath. Ch. Author: (with M. Walsh) Nursing Process: Assessing, Planning, Implementing and Evaluating, 1978; (with others) Nursing Leadership: Theory and Process, 1981; contbr. articles to nursing jours. Home: 1210 Spotswood Ave Norfolk VA 23507 Office: Nursing Dept Old Dominion Univ Norfolk VA 23508

YUTHAS, LADESSA JOHNSON, educator; b. Platteville, Colo., Oct. 9, 1928; d. James and Mary Christ (Kasbeer) Johnson; B.S. (Pacemaker award 1949), Colo. State U., 1949; M.S., Purdue U., 1954; Ph.D. (Elizabeth Wilson award 1969), U. Colo., 1969; m. Wayne N. Winter, Sept. 1, 1974; children—Lynn, John, Kristi, Susan. Elementary sch. tchr., Colo., 1951-52, 55-56; remedial reading supr., Ind., 1952-55; prof. reading, chmn. reading dept. Met. State Coll., Denver, 1966—; cons. in field. Pres. Broomfield (Colo.) Library Friends, 1967; mem. budget com. City of Broomfield, 1978. Mem. Internat. Reading Assn. (pres. Colo. council 1974; Outstanding Dissertation award Colo. council 1969), Rocky Mountain Reading Specialists (pres. 1978), Nat. Reading Conf., Western Coll. Reading Assn., Colo. Lang. Arts Soc. Methodist. Co-author: Reading and Other College Survival Skills, 1979; contbr. articles to profl. jours. Home: 495 W 4th Ave Dr Broomfield CO 80020 Office: 1006 11th St Denver CO 80204

ZABALAOUI, JUDITH COWAN, fin. planner; b. Gadsden, Ala., Nov. 24, 1937; d. John Gordon and Mary (McKay) Cowan; B.S. in Econs., 1968, Loyola U., New Orleans, M.B.A. in Econs., 1970; m. Nash Sadi Zabalaoui, June 5, 1957; children—Michele Anne, Michael Nash. Instr., Loyola U. of S., New Orleans, 1968-72; controller/bus. mgr. various non-profit orgns., New Orleans, 1972-75; pres. Resource Mgmt., Inc., Metairie, La., 1975—; adj. lectr. Loyola U. of S. Mem. Inst. Cert. Fin. Planners, Internat. Assn. Fin. Planners Inc. Office: 3212 16th St Suite 204 Metairie LA 70002

ZABECKI, CHRISTINE ANN HELLKAMP, indsl. engr.; b. Cin., Mar. 19, 1953; d. Lawrence Edward and Gale Sylvia (Harrison) Hellkamp; B.S., St. Ambrose Coll., 1978; m. David Tadeusz Zabecki, July 29, 1972; 1 son, Konrad Josef. Research lab. technician EPA, Cin., 1972-73; ops. specialist regional enforcement narcotics unit Cin. Police Dept., 1973-74; Realtor, Mel Foster Co., Davenport, Iowa, 1974-75; engring. draftsman Rock Island (Ill.) Arsenal, 1975-78; application specialist Monroe, The Calculator Co., Bettendorf, Iowa, 1978-79; indsl. engr. Plow & Planter Works, John Deere Co., Moline, Ill., 1979—; lectr.; union pres. local R7-72 Nat. Assn. Govt. Employees. 1977-78. Mem. Soc. Mfg. Engrs. Club: Tri-City Toastmistress. Founding editor The Bulldog, Rock Island Arsenal employees newspaper, 1978. Home: 29 Oak Ln Davenport IA 52803 Office: 501 3d Ave Moline IL

ZABEL, NANCY AMALIA, med. assn. exec.; b. Chgo., June 8, 1952; d. William John and Virginia May (Thompson) Suhajda; B.S. cum laude, Carroll Coll., 1974; m. Ronald Alan Zabel, July 21, 1979. Intern in med. tech. Waukesha Meml. Hosp., 1975; med. technologist Meml. Hosp. DuPage County, Elmhurst, Ill., 1975-78; asst. mgr. profl. self-assessment testing program Am. Soc. Clin. Pathologists, Chgo., 1978-79, asst. mgr. Commn. on Assoc. Mems. Activities regional programs, 1979, unit mgr., 1979-81, project mgr., 1981—; mem. adv. council, mem. med. lab. asst. com. DuPage Area Vocat. Authority. Mem. Am. Soc. Clin. Pathologists (assoc.; cert. med. technologist), Career Group, Delta Sigma Nu, Delta Zeta. Club: Homebuilders. Home: 2310 61st Ct Cicero IL 60650 Office: Am Soc Clin Pathologists 2100 W Harrison St Chicago IL 60612

ZACHERT, VIRGINIA, psychologist; b. Jacksonville, Ala., Mar. 1, 1920; d. Rev. R. E. and Cora H. (Massee) Z.; student Norman Jr. Coll., 1937; A.B., Ga. State Woman's Coll. (now Valdosta State Coll.), 1940; M.A., Emory U., 1947; Ph.D., Purdue U., 1949. Statistician, Davison-Paxon Co., Atlanta, 1941-44; research psychologist Mil. Contracts, Auburn Research Found., Ala. Poly. Inst.; indsl. and research psychologist Sturm & O'Brien, cons. engrs., 1958-59; research project dir. Western Design, Biloxi, Miss., 1960-61; self-employed cons. psychologist, Norman Park, Ga., 1961-71, Good Hope, Ga., 1971-77, Augusta, Ga., 1977—; research asso. med. edn. Med. Coll. Ga., Augusta, 1964-66, asso. prof., 1966-70, prof., 1970—, mem. Acad. Council, 1976-79, exec. com., 1979, chmn.-elect, 1982; mem. Ga. Psychology Bd., 1974-79, pres., 1978; adj. prof. McCormick Theol. Sem., 1977-80. Ga. del. White House Conf. on Aging, 1981; exec. com. Sr. Citizens Council, 1981, adv. council, 1982; chmn. Augusta Mayor's Sr. Citizens Adv. Bd., 1982—. Served as aerologist USN, 1944-46, aviation psychologist USAF 1949-54, mem. air tng. command adv. bd. 1967-72. Named Alumna of Yr., Valdosta State Coll., 1980; diplomate Am. Bd. Profl. Psychology. Fellow Am. Psychol. Assn. (com. on profl. practice 1982—); mem. Nat. Soc. Programmed Instruction (nat. sec. 1968, adv. bd. 1969-71), AAUP (pres. med. chpt. 1978-81), Gerontol. Soc. Am., Nat. Council on Aging, New Bordeaux Cottage Assn. (pres. 1981—), Sigma Xi (pres. Med. Coll. Ga. chpt. 1980-81). Baptist. Club: RSVP Augusta (v.p. 1982). Author programmed instruction texts. Home: 1126 Highland Ave Augusta GA 30904 Office: Dept Obstetrics and Gynecology Med Coll GA Augusta GA 30912

ZACHOS, VICTORIA, bus. exec., civic worker; b. Bennington, N.H., July 6, 1929; d. Stephen and Sophia (Bakogiannis) Z.; student Concord (N.H.) Comml. Coll. Vice pres. Associated Enterprises, Inc., Concord. Active Young Republicans 1952-64, sec. N.E. council, 1952-54, chmn. N.H. council, 1954-60, nat. committeewoman 1960-64; mem. Concord Rep. Com., 1964-68; asst. chmn. N.H. Rep. Com., also head Women's div., 1968-72; mem. Rep. Nat. Com., 1972-80, exec. com. 1972-76; N.H. presdl. elector, 1972,76; mem. arrangements com. Rep. Nat. Conv., 1976, 80; mem. Adv. Com. Women in Services, Dept. Def., 1977-80. Choir dir. Holy Trinity Ch., Concord. Home: 82 Warren St Concord NH 03301 Office: 136 N Main St Concord NH 03301

ZACK, SHIRLEY ANN, librarian; b. St. Paul, Nov. 22, 1927; d. Joseph William and Katherine Rose (Katzenberger) Z.; B.B.A., U. Minn., M.A., 1961. Periodicals librarian Mankato (Minn.) State U., 1961-63; law cataloger Law Library, U. Minn., Mpls., 1963-66, sci./bus. cataloger Wilson Library, 1966—, subject authority coordinator, 1978—, mem. faculty, 1966—. Mem. ALA, Assn. Coll. and Research Libraries, Mensa, Internat. Graphoanalysis Soc. (treas. Minn. chpt. 1982—), Beta Phi Mu. Roman Catholic. Clubs: Campus, Faculty Women's. Home: 1756 James Ave Saint Paul MN 55105 Office: Wilson Library U Minn Minneapolis MN 55455

ZACKERY, JACQUELINE PAULINE, ins. rep., employment and manpower cons.; b. Urbana, Ill., Feb. 6, 1950; d. Robert Lee and Julia Ann (Thompson) Z.; B.S., Mankato State Coll., 1973; M.A. in Bus. Mgmt., Central Mich. U., 1981. Asst. to coordinator M-Teps, Concordia Coll., St. Paul, 1972-74; counselor Twin Cities Opportunities Industrialization Center, Mpls., 1974, outreach employment coordinator, 1974-75, adminstrv. asst. II, 1975-76, interim exec. dir., 1977, tng. coordinator, 1976-78; field specialist Opportunities Industrialization Centers Am., Inc., Phila., 1978, project officer, Phila., 1978-81; mgmt. trainee/rep. Equitable Life Assurance Soc. U.S., Atlanta, 1982—; mem. ops. subcom. Manpower Planning and Devel. Com., chairperson Urban Minn. Comprehensive Employment and Tng. Consortium, Mpls., 1976-77. Mem. Am. Mgmt. Assn., Am. Soc. Tng. and Devel., Nat. Assn. Female Execs. Democrat. Roman Catholic. Home: 2039-D Powers Ferry Rd Marietta GA 30067 Office: 100 W Peachtree St Suite 634 Atlanta GA 30303

ZACUR, SUSAN RAWSON, educator; b. Bridgeport, Conn., Jan. 22, 1948; d. Homer Arnold and Harriet Luella (Smith) Rawson; B.A., Simmons Coll., Boston, 1970; M.B.A., U. Md., 1974, D.B.A. (Richard D. Irwin fellow 1976-77), 1979; m. Howard Ardlen Zacur, Aug. 30, 1969. Personnel officer, then personnel specialist Dade County Personnel Dept., Coral Gables, Fla., 1970-73; lectr. organizational mgmt. and indsl. relations U. Md., 1974-76; mem. faculty U. Balt., 1976—, Dean James chair disting. teaching, 1980-81, asso. prof. mgmt., 1980—, dir. women's program mgmt., 1978-81; adj. prof. Johns Hopkins U., 1981—; case adv. SBA, 1979-80; cons. in field. Bd. dirs. YWCA Greater Balt. Area, 1981—. Mem. Acad. Mgmt., Am. Soc. Personnel Adminstrn., Indsl. Relations Research Assn. (chpt. v.p. 1977-80), So. Mgmt. Assn., Female Exec. Network. Club: Johns Hopkins U. Women's. Author articles in field. Office: 1420 N Charles St Baltimore MD 21201

ZAFFOS, JEAN, securities trader; b. Sept. 9, 1929; d. Julius and Yetta (Siegal) Herschkowitz; student N.Y. Inst. Fin., 1963-65; m. Edward Zaffos, Sept. 4, 1948 (dec.); children—Sharon, Steven, Jeffrey. Order clk. Cohen Simonson Rea & Co., 1966; account exec. C.S.R. & Co. (merged into Bruns Nordeman Rea & Co. 1968; now subs. Bache Co.), N.Y.C., 1966—, sr. account exec., 1981—. Mem. Nat. Assn. Securities Dealers, SEC. Jewish. Office: 333 7th Ave New York NY 10001

ZAGORZYCKI, MARIA TERESA, physician; b. Trenton, N.J., Dec. 18, 1953; d. John M. and Janina Zofia (Jaworski) Z.; B.A. in Biochemistry with distinction in all subjects, Cornell U., 1975; M.D., George Washington U., 1979. Intern, UCLA Hosp., 1979-80, resident in ob-gyn., 1980-82, chief resident in ob-gyn., 1982—. Mem. Am. Fertility Soc. (assoc.), Phi Delta Epsilon. Club: Cornell of So. Calif. Office: 10833 Le Conte Ave Los Angeles CA 90024

ZAIDUONDO-GONZALEZ, BELEN, gerontologist, ednl. adminstr.; b. San Juan, P.R., Sept. 29, 1937; d. Roberto Zalduondo and Agustina González; A.D. in Secretarial Sci., Universidad de P.R., 1971; B.B.A., Internat. Inst. of Am., 1974; M.S., Centro Caribeno de Estudios Postgraduados, P.R., 1977, Ph.D., 1982; children—Carmen B. Candelario, Luis Roberto Candelario. Sec., Dept. of Agr., Commonwealth of P.R., 1957-60, adminstrv. sec. Land Authority, 1960-66, adminstrv. sec., Dept. Agr., 1966-68, exec. dir. and asst. to vice pres. Senate of Commonwealth P.R., 1972-77; prof. devel. of individual, chair World U., Hato Rey, P.R., 1977-80; dir. grad. studies Caribbean Center for Advance Studies, Miami, Fla., 1980—, prof., 1980-82; appeared in various TV and radio programs, P.R., 1980-82. Mem. Am. Psychol. Assn., Nat. Assn. of P.R. Women, P.R. Psychol. Assn., Nat. Assn. for Hispanic Aging, Assn. for Gerontology in Higher Edn., Latin Bus. and Profl. Women, Sociedad Interamerican de Psicologia. Mem. Evangelical Ch. Contbr. articles on gerontology to profl. jours. Home: 6526 SW 114th Ave Miami FL 33173 Office: 905 SW 1st St Miami FL 33130 also 960 SE 26 Reparto Metropolitano Rio Piedras PR

ZAIS, EDITH MOREIN, coll. adminstr.; b. Providence, Apr. 8, 1931; d. Samuel Joshua and Sona Morein; A.B., Brown U., 1952; M.A. in Teaching, R.I. Coll., 1964; 6th year diploma edn. U. Conn., 1968; m. Robert S. Zais, Sept. 14, 1952; children—Louis Scott, Roberta Susan. Tchr. English, E. Providence (R.I.) Sr. High Sch., 1964-66; staff writer Willimantic (Conn.) Chronicle, 1966-67; tchr. reading Crestwood Schs., Mantua, Ohio, 1969-70; coordinator learning devel. program Kent (Ohio) State U., 1970—, instr. Exptl. Coll., 1973—; mem. admissions com. Northeastern Ohio Univs. Coll. Medicine, 1979-81; project co-dir. spl. services disadvantaged students Dept. Edn., 1978—. Mem. Nat. Assn. Women Deans, Adminstrs. and Counselors, Internat. Reading Assn., Assn. Children and Adults with Learning Disabilities, Mid-Am. Assn. Ednl. Opportunity Program Personnel, Ohio Assn. Supervision and Curriculum Devel., LWV (chmn. edn. com. Kent chpt. 1976-78), Omicron Delta Kappa. Home: 431 Wilson Ave Kent OH 44240 Office: Kent State U Kent OH 44242

ZAISER, SALLY SOLEMMA VANN (MRS. FOSTER E. ZAISER), retail book co. exec.; b. Birmingham, Ala., Jan. 18, 1917; d. Carl Waldo and Einnan (Herndon) Vann; student Birmingham-So. Coll., 1933-36, Akron Coll. Bus., 1937; m. Foster E. Zaiser, Nov. 11, 1939. Accountant, A. Simionato, San Francisco, 1958-65; head accounting dept. Richard T. Clarke Co., San Francisco, 1966; accountant John Howell-Books, San Francisco, 1967-72, sec., treas., 1972—; sec. Great Eastern Mines, Inc., Albuquerque, 1969-80, dir., 1980—. Braille transcriber for ARC, Kansas City, Mo. 1941-45; vol. worker A.R.C. Hosp. Program, Sao Paulo, Brazil, 1952. Mem. Book Club Calif., Soc. Lit. and the Arts, Calif. Hist. Soc., Theta Upsilon. Republican. Episcopalian. Club: Capitol Hill. Home: 355 Serrano Dr San Francisco CA 94132 Office: 434 Post St San Francisco CA 94102

ZAJICEK, BARBARA JEANNE, health care co. mgr.; b. Peoria, Ill., Jan. 12, 1932; d. Gale Edward and Thelma Beatrice (Drury) Allen; student public schs.; m. Albert F. Zajicek, July 5, 1973; children—Gregg Hahn, Lisa D'Aquila, Dana Hahn. Office supr., then exec. asst. to pres. Larry Smith & Co., Northfield, Ill., 1970-74, 76-77; asst. to pres., leasing agt. Devel. Control Corp., Northfield, 1974-76; bus. mgr. EMSCO, Ltd., Des Plaines, Ill., 1978—; dir., v.p./asst. sec.-treas. Midwest Med. Mgmt., Mem. Emergency Medicine Mgmt. Assn. (v.p.), Nat. Assn. Free-Standing Emergency Centers. Republican. Lutheran. Home: 619 Hillside Rd Glenview IL 60025 Office: 999 E Touhy Ave Suite 145 Des Plaines IL 60018

ZAK, MICHELE WENDER, univ. adminstr.; b. Beckley, W.Va., Apr. 3, 1940; d. Max Harris and Freda (Lewis) Wender; B.A., Ohio State U., 1962, Ph.D., 1973; M.A., UCLA, 1967; m. Laurence Michael Zak, Aug. 31, 1963; children—Peter Andrew, Colin Mark. Social caseworker Los Angeles County Bur. Public Assistance, 1963-67; lectr. English, Ohio State U., 1968-73; asst. EEO coordinator, chief Ohio State Office Women's Affairs, 1974-75; exec. dir. Women's Resource and Policy Devel. Center, Columbus, 1974-76, trustee, 1976—; dir. Office Human Resource Utilization, Kent (Ohio) State U., 1976-82, also co-coordinator women's studies cert. program, asst. prof. English and women's studies; coordinator Affirmative Action planning and rev. U. Calif. System, 1982—; mem. Gov. Ohio's Commn. on Women, 1973-74; mem. edn. com. Ohio Task Force Implementation ERA, 1973-74; cons. in field. Grantee Ohio Dept. Labor, Columbus Found. Needs Assessment Women in Central Ohio, Cleve. Found. Mem. Nat. Coalition Women, MLA, Midwest MLA, Nat. Women's Studies Assn., Am. Assn. Affirmative Action (Ohio coordinator). Author: Women and the Politics of Culture: Studies in the Sexual Economy, 1981; contbr. articles to profl. jours. Office: 2200 University Ave U Calif Berkeley CA 94703

ZALESKI, JEAN, artist; b. Malta; d. John M. and Carolina (Micallef) Busuttil; studied Art Students League, N.Y.C., 1956-59, New Sch. Social Research, 1967-69, Moore Coll. Art, 1970-71, Parsons Sch. Design, 1974-75, Pratt Inst., 1975-76; children—Jeffrey, Philip, Susan. Art dir. Studio 733, Great Neck, N.Y., 1963-67; dir. Naples Art Studio (Italy), 1972-73; corp. sec. Women in Arts, 1974-75, exec. coordinator, 1976-78; adj. lectr. Hofstra U., 1977—, Bklyn. Coll., 1974-75; represented by Alonzo Gallery, N.Y.C.; one-woman shows include: Galleria Stuciv, Florence, Italy, 1976, Adelphi U., 1975, Women in Arts Gallery, N.Y.C., 1975, Il Gabbiano Gallery, Naples, 1973, Wallnuts Gallery, Phila., 1971, Neikrug Gallery, N.Y.C., 1970, Alonzo Gallery, 1979, Va. Center for Creative Arts, Sweet Briar, 1981; group exhbns. include Art: U.S.A., N.Y.C., 1969, Internat. Art Exhbn., Cannes, France, 1969, Frick Mus., Pitts., 1970, NAD, N.Y.C., 1970-71, Phila. Mus. Art, 1971, Am. Women Artists, Palazzo Vecchio, Florence, Italy, 1972, Internat. Women's Arts Festival, Milan Italy (Gold medal), 1973, Bklyn. Mus., 1975, Sweet Briar Coll., 1977, CUNY, 1978, Mus. Hudson Highlands, 1982; represented in permanent collections Easter Seal Human Resource Center, N.Y., Hofstra U., N.Y. Pub. Library, Bklyn. Poly. Inst. Bd. dirs. Visual Dialog mag., Palo Alto, Calif. Mem. Artists Equity, Internat. Assn. Art, Nat. Assn. Women Artists, Nat. Women's Caucus for Art.

ZALITIS, INARA ELGA, dentist; b. Riga, Latvia; came to U.S., 1950, naturalized, 1961; d. Edward and Elvira Lidija (Bendiks) Z.; A.B. in Biology, Boston U., 1965; postgrad. U. Mass., 1965-66; D.D.S., N.Y. U., 1970; m. Janis Cezis, Dec. 18, 1981. Intern in pedodontics Children's Hosp. Med. Center, Boston, 1970-71, resident in pedodontics, 1971-72, mem. vis. staff dental dept., 1976—; pediatric dentist, staff dentist Dimock Community Health Center, Boston, 1972-76; staff dentist Faulkner Hosp., Jamaica Planin, Mass., 1980—; pvt. practice dentistry specializing in pediatric dentistry, Westwood, Mass., 1975-80, West Roxbury, Mass., 1980—; clin. asst. in pedodontics Harvard Sch. Dental Medicine, 1971-72, clin. asst. in dental ecology, 1972-76, mem. admissions com., 1973-75. Active, Girl Scouts U.S.A., 1951-65; asst. leader Laimrota, Boston Latvian Folk Dance Group, 1971-78. Recipient N.Y. U. Alumnae, Inc. award, 1970. Mem. ADA, Am. Acad. Pedodontics, Am. Soc. Dentistry for Children, Women's Dental Soc. Mass. (v.p. 1976-79), Assn. Am. Women Dentists, Mass. Dental Soc. (alt. del. 1980-81), Norfolk County (sec.-treas. 1977-79, v.p. 1979-80, pres. 1980-81), Parkway dental socs., Federation Dentaire Internationale. Latvian Sorority Imeria. Office: 1895 Centre St West Roxbury MA 02132

ZAMBELL, PATRICIA EBENS, educator; b. Rockford, Ill., July 15, 1944; d. John A. and Alvira (Anderson) Ebens; B.S., Ill. Wesleyan U., 1966; M.S., Ill. State U., 1981; m. Robert B. Zambell, June 6, 1964; children—Kimberly Ann, Kirsten Lynn. Actuarial asst. State Farm Assurance Co., Bloomington, Ill., 1965-66; asst. to account mgr. MFA Life Ins. Co., Columbia, Mo., 1967; office mgr. Hawthorne House Inc., Bloomington, Ill., 1973-74; instr. acctg. Ill. State U., Normal, 1981—; cons. Assn. Commerce and Industry, SOAR. Mem. adv. com. Bloomington (Ill.) Bd. Edn., 1976-79, 82—; pres. Bloomington Jr. High Sch. PTA, 1982—. C.P.A., Ill. Mem. Nat. Assn. Accts., Ill. C.P.A. Soc., Am. Acctg. Assn., Am. Inst. C.P.A.s, Acctg. Educators Ill., Beta Gamma Sigma. Office: Dept Acctg Ill State U Normal IL 61761

ZAMBERANO, ANGELA DORA, coll. adminstr.; b. Chgo., Nov. 26, 1949; d. Salvador Martinez Zambrano and Theresa Mary (Dianda) Rios; B.A. in English Lit., Chgo. State U., 1980. Employed in various clerical positions, 1967-78; bilingual coordinator, dir. Latino Service Center, Olive Harvey Coll., Chgo., 1978—. Mem. City of Chgo. Dept. Human Services Interagy. Com., Mex. Community Com., vol. Family Rescue Shelter Recipient Public Service award Latin Am. Student Orgn., 1979, recognition for vol. services Chgo. Public Library. Mem. Nat. Assn. Female Execs., League United Latin Am. Citizens, Kappa Delta Pi, Phi Theta Kappa. Democrat. Office: Olive Harvey Coll 10001 S Woodlawn Ave Chicago IL 60628

ZANDER, JANET ADELE, psychiatrist; b. Miles City, Mont., Feb. 19, 1950; d. Adelbert William and Valborg Constance (Buckneberg) Zander; B.A. summa cum laude, St. Olaf Coll., 1972; M.D., U. Minn., 1976; m. Mark Richard Ellenberger, Sept. 16, 1979. Resident psychiatry U. Minn. Hosp., Mpls., 1976-79, fellow consultation psychiatry U. Minn., Mpls., 1979-80, asst. prof. psychiatry, 1981—; staff psychiatrist St. Paul Ramsey Hosp., St. Paul, Minn., 1980—; Bd. dirs. Concentus Musicus, St. Paul, 1981—. Diplomate Am. Bd. Psychiatry and Neurology. Mem. Am. Psychiat. Assn., Minn. Med. Assn., Ramsey County Med. Soc., Am. Med. Women's Assn., Minn. Psychiat. Soc., Phi Beta Kappa. Democrat. Home: 2092 Fairmount Ave St Paul MN 55105 Office: 640 Jackson St St Paul MN 55101

ZANDERS, CLAUDIA, social worker; b. Beaumont, Tex., Oct. 11, 1939; d. Charles Senters and Ularae Bond; B.A., Trinity U., 1961; M.S.W., Our Lady of the Lake Coll., 1964; m. John Zanders, 1964 (div.); 1 son Anthony. Jr. psychiat. social worker Community Guidance Clinic, Austin, Tex., 1965; jr. psychiat. social worker Child Guidance Clinic, Lackland AFB, San Antonio, Tex., 1966; med. social worker, project social worker Foster Grandparents Project, Bexar County Hosp., San Antonio, Tex., 1966-68; psychiat. social worker Desert Counseling Clinic, China Lake (Calif.) Naval Weapons Base, 1968-70; sr. psychiat. social worker Mental Health Outpatient Services, Santa Cruz County, Calif., 1970-73; social service practitioner adoptions unit Santa Cruz (Calif.) County Social Services, 1974—. Lic. clin. Social Worker, Calif. Mem. Nat. Assn. Social Workers, Acad. Cert. Social Workers. Home: 2100 Quail Hollow Rd Ben Lomond CA 95005 Office: Adoptions Unit Santa Cruz County Social Services PO Box 1320 Santa Cruz CA 95061

ZANDERSON, ANNE LOUISE, constrn., devel. and mgmt. co. exec.; b. Los Angeles, May 16, 1950; d. Raymond Thomas and Elizabeth Helene Blumberg; grad. high sch.; m. J. John Zanderson, May 5, 1973; children—Krista, Sean. Owner, exec. v.p., sec./treas., dir. Zanderson, Inc., San Diego, 1976—; part-owner numerous real estate and devel. related partnerships. Vol., VA Hosp., La Jolla, Calif., 1973, Children's Hosp. and Health Center, San Diego, 1975-77; Confrat. of Christian Doctrine tchr. Good Shepherd Ch., San Diego, 1977-78; tchr., 2d grad coordinator Confrat. Christian Doctrine program St. Gabriel's Ch., Poway, Calif. Mem. Nat. Notary Assn. Republican. Roman Catholic. Home: 16508 Wilderness Rd Poway CA 92064 Office: 10731 Treena St Suite 101 San Diego CA 92131

ZANES, RUTH LEE, mktg. researcher; b. N.Y.C., Feb. 16, 1935; d. Morris Harris and Bertha Clara (Steifel) Bernstein; B.A., Bklyn. Coll., 1956; m. George W. Zanes, June 17, 1970; children—Glenn Weissman, Lee Weissman. Project dir. James M. Vicary Co., 1957-60; dir. mktg. research Gilbert Mktg. Group, N.Y.C., 1960-64; research account exec. Foote Cone & Belding Co., N.Y.C., 1964-66; account research supr. Grey Advt. Co., N.Y.C., 1966-68; mgr. corp. and advt. research Clairol, Inc., N.Y.C., 1968-70; mgr. market research Chesebrough-Pond Corp., Greenwich, Conn., 1970-73; mgr. product research Avon Products, N.Y.C., 1973-74; v.p., then pres. Zanes & Assos., Inc., exec. v.p. The Mktg. Research Workshop, Ft. Lee, N.J., 1974—. Mem. Am. Mktg. Assn., Advt. Women N.Y., Mktg. Research Assn. (dir. N.Y. chpt. 1980-81), N.Y. Profl. and Bus. Women, Nat. Acad. TV Scis. Home: 2200 N Central Rd Fort Lee NJ 07024 Office: 1350 15th St Fort Lee NJ 07024

ZANGHI, NICOLA A., chef, restauranteur; b. N.Y.C., Apr. 6, 1948; d. Antonio J. and Marie (Crisafilli) Zanghi; A.A.S., N.Y.C. Community Coll., 1969. Chef, proprietor Restaurant Zanghi. Roman Catholic. Author 23 cookbooks. Home: 309 West Neck Rd Huntington NY 11743 Office: 50 Forest Ave Glen Cove NY 11542

ZARA, WINIFRED THOMAS, fin. exec.; b. N.Y.C., May 25, 1946; d. Evan Welling and Anne Davis (Robins) Thomas; student Mass. Gen. Hosp. Sch. Nursing, 1964-66, Nat. Sch. Real Estate Fin., Ohio State U., 1979-81; m. Michael Zara, Jr., Dec. 20, 1965; children—Jennifer Robins, Jessica Cogswell. Sales mgr. Manpower Temporary Services, Inc., Stamford, Conn., 1974-76; mortgage broker J. Everett Parker, Inc., Pound Ridge, N.Y., 1976-79; mortgage investment officer Union Trust Co., Stamford, 1979-81; account exec. Mortgage Guaranty Ins. Corp., N.Y.C., 1981—. Mem. L.I. Bd. Realtors, 1981—. Mem. L.I. Assn. Commerce and Industry, Nat. Assn. Female Execs., Mortgage Bankers Assn. Am. Democrat. Office: 1 State Street Plaza New York City NY 10004

ZAREMBER, HELENE RUTH, social worker; b. N.Y.C., Feb. 15, 1934; d. Conrad and Stella (Mankin) Papiere; B.A., Bklyn. Coll., 1955; M.S.W., Columbia U., 1958; postgrad. N.Y. U., 1965-69; m. Irving Zarember, Dec. 25, 1964. Social work supr. East Tremont YM-YWHA, N.Y.C., 1958-61; social work supr. Washington Heights and Inwood YM-YWHA, 1961-62; social worker, field instr. grad. students Mobilization for Youth, N.Y.C., 1962-64; social work supr. Univ. Settlement, N.Y.C., 1964-65; asst. dir. Rhinelander Center of Children's Aid Soc., N.Y.C., 1969-71; dir. Goodhue Complex of Children's Aid Soc., N.Y.C., 1971-79, dir. Lower West Side Center, adminstrv. supr. Community Center and Camping div., 1979—. Mem. Nat. Assn. Social Workers, Acad. Cert. Social Workers, Am. Sociol. Assn., N.Y. State Cert. Social Workers, Alpha Kappa Delta. Home: 405 W 23 St New York NY 10011 Office: 219 Sullivan St New York NY 10012

ZARISKI, BIRDINE ADELSTEIN, govt. ofcl.; b. Lynn, Mass., Sept. 14, 1930; d. Hyman Joseph and Ida (Levine) Adelstein; A.B., Boston U., 1951, J.D., 1954; m. Raphael Zariski, Aug. 15, 1954; children—Daniel Alfred, Adrienne Muriel. Claims examiner VA, Lincoln, Nebr., 1966, rating specialist, 1971-73, legal cons., Washington, 1973-74, chmn. rating bd., Lincoln, 1975—. Active Community Theatre. Mem. Internat. Platform Assn., Am. Fedn. Govt. Employees, Boston U. Law Sch. Alumni Assn., Boston U. Alumni Assn. Home: 2312 Calumet Ct Lincoln NE 68502 Office: 100 Centennial Mall N Lincoln NE 68508

ZASLOW, JACQUELINE GALLER, health orgn. exec.; b. London; came to U.S., 1957, naturalized, 1963; d. Alfred and Doris (Amiel) Galler; Baccalaureate, U. Lausanne, Switzerland, 1948; m. Meyer Zaslow, Dec. 15, 1957. With Cystic Fibrosis Fedn., N.Y.C., 1964-74, nat. govt. relations dir., 1974-75; exec. dir., govt. relations dir. Pediatric Pulmonary Assn., Atlanta, 1974-78; exec. v.p. Childrens Lung Assn., Roswell, Ga., 1980—; cons., exec. sec. Immunology Center Georgetown U., 1975-77. Mem. Coalition for Health Funding. Author: (with Ray F. Goddard) Children and Their Lungs, 1976; chief author, editor Pediatric Pulmonary Digest, 1974—. Home and Office: 150 N Pond Way Roswell GA 30076

ZAWALONKA, FRANCES ELIZABETH FRENCH, broadcasting co. exec.; b. Los Angeles, Sept. 16, 1947; d. William Baxter and Frances Olin (Porter) French; A.A., Glendale (Calif.) Community Coll., 1975; m. George Joseph Zawalonka, Sept. 1, 1968; 1 son, George Joseph. Video tape scheduling coordinator NBC, Burbank, Calif., 1967-72, unit mgr., 1976-81, sr. unit mgr., 1981—; prodn. coordinator KNBC, Burbank, 1972-74, supr. film editing, 1974-75, unit mgr., 1975-76; chief fin. officer, dir. Zawa & Son, Inc., 1980-82. Mem. Am. Women in Radio and TV, NOW, Delta Theta Tau. Republican. Episcopalian. Home: 1534 Ardeevin Ave Glendale CA 91202 Office: 3000 W Alameda St Burbank CA 91523

ZAWISLAK, BARBARA JOAN, communication systems exec.; b. Mpls., Oct. 24, 1939; d. Theodore Raymond and Josephine Dorothy (Traczyk) Z.; Various positions Northwestern Bank, Mpls., 1957-65; clerical coordinator Graco, Inc., Mpls., 1965-70; v.p. Leasing Services, Inc., Mpls., 1970-81; dir. personnel, comptroller M & W Inc., Mpls., 1971—; pres., owner Arklo Distbrs. Inc., Mpls., 1977—; treas. Micro Communication Systems, Inc., Mpls., 1982—; pvt. cons. personnel and fin. Bd. dirs., v.p., librarian, treas. Al-Anon, St. Mary's Rehab. Center; sec., adv. bd. St. Mary's Rehab. Center. Club: Breakfast Club Mpls. Home: Minneapolis MN 55432 Office: Minneapolis MN 55432

ZAYDON, JEMILLE ANN, educator; b. Peckville, Pa., Feb. 21, 1940; d. Joseph and Catherine Ann (Hazzouri) Z.; student Barry Coll. for Women, 1957-59; B.S., Marywood Coll., 1963; M.S. in Edn., Wilkes Coll., 1978; doctoral candidate Temple U. Tchr. St. Hugh Elementary Sch., Coconut Grove, Fla., 1963-64; Allapattah Elementary Sch., Miami, 1964-65, Columbus Elementary Sch., Westfield, N.J., 1965-66; communications instr. Keystone Job Corps, Drums, Pa., 1966-73; vol. instr. Keystone Rehab. Center, Scranton, Pa., 1970-71; curriculum cons. for mentally retarded, Vienna, Austria, 1974; prof. English and reading Lackawanna Jr. Coll., Scranton, 1974—, head dept. English, speech and reading, 1976—, chmn. dept. arts, humanities and social studies, 1977—; communications instr. Lackawanna County Vocat. Tech. Sch., 1974—. Supr. recreation program, Hazleton, Pa., summer 1968; founder, adviser Keystone Kourier, 1967-69. Sec. Fedn. Youth, William W. Scranton, 1963; supr. students Heart Fund campaign, 1968-71; developer program mentally retarded Allied Services for Handicapped Scranton, 1973; Class rep. Marywood Coll. Fund Dr., 1978; active ARC, March of Dimes, Heart Fund, Leukemia and United Fund drives, also Sickle Cell Anemia Found. Bd. dirs. Michael F. Harrity Meml. Fund., 1969-73; mem. exec. bd. Northeastern Pa. Environ. Council, also co-chmn. public edn. and funding. Recipient Staff Mem. of Year award, Job Corps, 1969, Humanitarian award, 1980; Service scholarship, Barry Coll., 1958; Educators award Dade County, 1973, 75. Mem. Nat., Pa. State edn. assns., Beta Lambda Tau, Sigma Tau Delta, Theta Chi Beta (charter pres. 1961-63), Lambda Iota Tau (life). Democrat. Roman Catholic (instr. Confraternity Christian Doctrine 1956-71). Editor Lebanese Am. Jour., 1957-63. Home: 608 N Main Ave Scranton PA 18504

ZEANAH, PAULA LYNN DOYLE, nurse; b. Anderson, S.C., Dec. 20, 1952; d. Robert Hugh and Phyllis Ann (Cliver) Doyle; R.N., Piedmont Hosp., 1973; B.S. in Nursing, Med. Coll. Ga., 1975; M.Sc. in Nursing, U. Va., 1979; m. Charles H. Zeanah, Jr., Nov. 3, 1979; 1 dau., Emily Hunter. Staff nurse pediatric ICU Grady Hosp., Atlanta, 1973-75; pediatric nurse practitioner Dekalb-Grady Clinic, Atlanta, 1976-77; head nurse pediatric clinic Duke U. Med. Center, 1979-80; inservice coordinator Children's Hosp., Stanford, Calif., 1980-81, acting dir. nursing, 1981-82, inservice coordinator, 1982—. Mem. Am. Nurses Assn., Nat. League Nursing, Nat. Assn. Pediatric Nurse Assocs. and Practitioners. Democrat. Office: 520 Willow Rd Palo Alto CA 94304

ZEBB, PATRICIA MARGARET, printed circuit mfg. co. exec.; b. N.Y.C., Jan. 18, 1934; d. Walter L. and Elizabeth (Clark) Yerkes; student public schs.; divorced; children—Patricia, Paul, Tom, Todd. Co-founder Printed Circuit Mfg. Co., Mountain View, Calif., 1968, co-owner, pres., gen. mgr., 1968—; owner, pres., gen. mgr. InnerConn Tech., Inc., 1976—. Mem. exec. bd. Stanford Area council Boy Scouts Am., 1979; bd. dirs. Mountain View United Fund, 1979. Mem. Am. Elec. Plating Assn., Calif. Circuits Assn., Peninsula Profl. Women's Network, Mountain View C. of C., Police Athletic League Mountain View. Clubs: Quota, Order Eastern Star. Address: 327 Moffett Blvd Mountain View CA 94043

ZEBELIAN, JULIEANNE MAY-MIEL, biologist; b. Greenville, Mich., Oct. 24, 1953; d. Clifton Lucas and Kathryn Mary (Daoust) M.; B.S., Alma Coll., 1975; m. William Allen Zebelian, Feb. 19, 1977. Asso. research chemist Gerber Products Co., Fremont, Mich., 1975-77; asst. scientist Warner Lambert/Parke Davis, Rochester, Mich., 1977-81, sr. asst. scientist, 1981—. Mem. NOW, Animal Protection Inst., Anti-Cruelty Soc., AAAS, Am. Soc. Microbiology. Home: 73320 S Fulton St Armada MI 48005 Office: 870 Parkdale St Rochester MI 48063

ZEE, BARBARA JEANNE, see Zajicek Barbara Jeanne.

ZEE, CAROL ANN, systems and energy co. ofcl.; b. Los Angeles, June 24, 1951; d. Zygmund John and Helen (Brasky) Z.; B.A. in Chemistry, Occidental Coll., 1973. Mem. tech. staff TRW Electronics and Def. Sector, TRW Inc., Redondo Beach, Calif., 1974-78, sect. head, project mgr., 1978-80, mem. mgmt. team satellite-to-satellite laser communication system, 1980—. Active local politics and coastal land use planning issues. Mem. Am. Chem. Soc., Soc. Women Engrs., AIAA. Contbr. articles on environ. impact of hazardous waste disposal and synfuel technologies to profl. jours. Home: 432 1st St Manhattan Beach CA 90266 Office: TRW One Space Park MI 2104 Redondo Beach CA 90278

ZEGIOB-DEVEREAUX, LESLIE ELAINE, psychologist; b. Cleve., Oct. 17, 1948; d. Charles George and Elinore Lois (Jones) Z.; student Allegheny Coll., 1966-68; B.A., Am. U., 1971; M.S., U. Ga., 1974, Ph.D., 1976. Asst. prof. dept. psychology Ariz. State U. 1976-78; dir. children's services Dogwood Village, Memphis, 1978; clin. psychologist The Med. Group, Michigan City, Ind., 1978—; cons. Michigan City Head Start; adj. prof. Notre Dame U., 1979. Ariz. State U. Center Family Studies grantee, 1977; cert. psychologist, Ariz., Ind. Mem. Am. Psychol. Assn., Assn. Advancement of Behavior Therapy, Southeastern Psychol. Assn., Ariz. Psychol. Assn., Ind. Cat Soc., Phi Beta Kappa. Contbr. articles to profl. jours. Office: The Med Group 1225 E Coolspring Ave Michigan City IN 46360

ZEHNER, JEAN COLGAN, chemist; b. Donora, Pa., July 12, 1919; d. Howard Oliver and Garnett Farquhar (Colvin) Colgan; A.B., Wilson Coll., 1941; m. Lisle A. Zehner, Jr., Mar. 14, 1941; 1 son, Lisle A. III. Fellow, Mellon Inst. Indsl. Research, Pitts., 1941-58; dir. testing bur. May Dept. Stores, Pitts., 1958-75, v.p. consumer affairs, 1975—; mem. adv. council U.S. Consumer Product Safety Commn.; mem. tech. and consumer affairs coms. Nat. Retail Mchts. Assn. Trustee Wilson Coll., 1970—; bd. dirs. Easter Seal Soc., 1963-79. Named Woman of Yr., Pitts. Advt. Club, 1969. Mem. Pa. C. of C. (dir. 1978—), Am. Chem. Soc., Am. Assn. Textile Technology, Soc. Consumer Affairs Profls., Am. Assn. Textile Chemists and Colorists, Pitts. Advt. Club. Democrat. Presbyterian. Clubs: N.Y. Chemists, 20th Century, Pitts. Coll. Office: 400 5th Ave Pittsburgh PA 15219

ZEITHAMEL, JOYCE MARIE, univ. ofcl.; b. Pensacola, Fla., Sept. 30, 1936; d. Lester F. and Loretta A. (Shebetka) Campbell; dental asst. diploma, U. N.C., Chapel Hill, 1960; divorced; 1 son, Travis. Instr. dental assisting program Kirkwood Community Coll., Cedar Rapids, Iowa, 1967-68; clinic coordinator gen. dentistry Univ. Hosp., Iowa City, 1972-74; dir. info. and referral Johnson County (Iowa), 1974-76; teaching asst. radiology, then supr. and coordinator DAU program Coll. Dentistry, U. Iowa, 1976-77, asst. dir. dental aux. program, 1977—. Grantee, USPHS, 1967-69. Mem. Orgn. Tchrs. of Practice Adminstrn., Am. Dental Assts. Assn. (Juliette A. Southard Scholarship com.), Nat. Assn. Female Execs., Eastern Iowa Execs. Clubs. Republican. Roman Catholic. Author curriculum manuals. Office: S242 DSB Iowa City IA 52242

ZEKMAN, TERRI MARGARET, graphic designer; b. Chgo., Sept. 13, 1950; d. Theodore Nathan and Lois (Bernstein) Z.; B.F.A., Washington U., St. Louis, 1971; postgrad. Art Inst. Chgo., 1974-75; m. Alan Daniels, Apr. 12, 1980. Graphic designer (on retainer) Recycled Paper Products, Chgo., 1970—; apprenticed graphic designer Helmuth, Obata & Kassabaum, St. Louis, 1970-71; graphic designer Container Corp., Chgo., 1971; graphic designer/art dir./photographer Cuerden Advt. Design, Denver, 1971-74; art dir. Darcy, McManus & Masius Advt., Chgo., 1975-76; freelance graphic designer Image Response Design Firm, Goldsmith, Yamasaki & Specht Design, Playboy Enterprises, Chgo., 1976-77; art dir. Garfield Linn Advt., Chgo., 1977-78; graphic designer Keiser Design Group, Van Noy & Co., Los Angeles, 1978-79; owner Graphic Design Studio, Los Angeles, 1979—. Recipient cert. of merit St. Louis Outdoor Poster Contest, 1970, Denver Art Dirs. Club, 1973.

ZELASKO, NANCY FABER, univ. adminstr.; b. N.Y.C., June 4, 1951; d. Robert David and Elaine Margaret (Affleck) Faber; B.S. in Linguistics, Georgetown U., Washington, 1973, M.S. in Sociolinguistics, 1975; m. Franciszek Jozef Zelasko, Nov. 28, 1975. Substitute tchr. D.C. Public Schs., 1973-74, research asst. div. bilingual edn., 1974-76, program specialist, 1976-78, acting adminstrv. officer, 1978-79, project dir. bilingual tng. grant, 1979-80; asst. dir. Georgetown U. Bilingual Edn. Service Center, 1980—; co-chair 12th Ann. Internat. Bilingual Bicultural Edn. Conf., 1983; cons. sch. dists. Recipient outstanding performance rating D.C. Public Schs., 1978-79. Mem. Nat. Assn. Female Execs., TESOL, D.C. Assn. Bilingual Edn. (pres. 1981-83), Nat. Assn. Bilingual Edn. (spl. recognition award 1979-80). Editor NABE News, 1981—. Home: 10917 Orchard St Fairfax VA 22030 Office: Suite 376 3520 Prospect St NW Washington DC 20007

ZELENY, MARJORIE PFEIFFER (MRS. CHARLES ELLINGSON ZELENY), psychologist; b. Balt., Mar. 31, 1924; d. Lloyd Armitage and Mable (Willian) Pfeiffer; B.A., U. Md., 1947; M.S., U. Ill., 1949, postgrad., 1951-54; m. Charles Ellingson Zeleny, Dec. 11, 1950 (dec.); children—Ann Douglas, Charles Timberlake. Vocational counseling psychologist VA, Balt., 1947-48; asst. U. Ill. at Urbana, 1948-50, research asso. Bur. Research, 1952-53; chief psychologist dept. neurology and psychiatry Ohio State U. Coll. Medicine, Columbus, 1950-51; research psychologist, cons., Tucson, Washington, 1954—. Mem. Am., D.C. psychol. assns., A.A.A.S., Soc. for Psychol. Study Social Issues, D.A.R., Mortar Bd., Delta Delta Delta, Sigma Delta Epsilon, Psi Chi, Sigma Tau Epsilon. Roman Catholic. Home: 6825 Wemberly Way McLean VA 22101

ZELEZNIK, PAULINE MARY, chemist; b. Chgo., Jan. 9, 1929; d. Joseph James and Pauline Elizabeth (Drabik) Z.; B.S., Nazareth Coll., 1949; M.S., Marquette U., 1955; Ph.D., U. Notre Dame, 1964. Joined Sisters of St. Joseph, 1951; instr. to prof. chemistry Nazareth (Mich.) Coll., 1954—; pres. cons. assocs. Sci. for Citizens; cons. Women in Sci. Bd. dirs. Borgess Med. Center. NSF grantee, summers; AEC grantee, 1960-64. Mem. Am. Chem. Soc., Mich. Coll. Chemistry Tchrs. Assn., Sigma Xi, Delta Kappa Gamma, Kappa Gamma Pi. Roman Catholic. Home and Office: Nazareth College Nazareth MI 49074

ZELIFF, VIOLA TOMPKINS, emeritus educator, author; b. Newark, Feb. 26, 1896; d. Albert Daniel and Anna Marie (Provost) Tompkins; B.S., Columbia U., 1915, M.A., 1934; Ed.D., N.Y.U., 1946; m. William L. Rhoades, Dec. 20, 1918 (div. 1940); 1 son, Lawrence W.; m. 2d, David E. Zeliff, June 20, 1941. Asst. prof. English, Newark Normal U., 1916-21; writer radio plays Mut. Broadcasting Co., 1925-28; prof. English, dept. head N.J. State Coll., 1932-56, prof. emeritus, 1982—; minister Unity Ch., Boca Raton, Fla., 1960-70; book reviewer Contemporary Life Mag., 1940-50; free lance lectr. Ft. Lauderdale, 1957-81. Recipient Fellowship award Newark High Sch. Alumnae, 1954. Mem. Nat. League Pen Women (pres. Fort Lauderdale), AAUW (pres. 1970), NEA, Ret. Tchrs. N.J., Pi Lambda Theta. Mem. Unity Ch. Clubs: Lake Mohawk Golf (Sparta, N.J.); Fort Lauderdale (Fla.) Carol Ridge Golf. Author: History of Bloomfield, N.J., 1930; Anthology of Poems for Boys, 1951. Home: 2025 SE 17th St Pompano Beach FL 33062

ZELLERS, GWENDOLYN FAYE, educator; b. Independence, Mo., May 18, 1943; d. Franklin James and Gladys Mildred (Dixon) Robinson; A.A., Graceland Coll., 1963, B.A., 1965; postgrad. Calif. State Coll., Hayward, 1966-67; m. Craig Arthur Zellers, June 12, 1966; 1 son, Andrew Joseph. Tchr. elem. schs., Independence, 1965, Castro Valley, Calif., 1966-68, Leon, Iowa, 1968-71, Independence, 1971-76; tchr. Raggedy Ann and Andy Pre-Sch., Marshall, Mo., 1979—, treas. bd., 1981-83. Treas., Ch. Women United, Marshall, 1979. Mem. NEA (sec. Independence chpt. 1975), Am. Bus. Women's Assn., Delta Kappa Gamma, Beta Sigma Phi (v.p. Epsilon Xi chpt. 1980). Club: Welcome Wagon (pres. 1978).

ZEMEL, HELENE LEVEY, assn. exec.; b. N.Y.C., Jan. 3, 1947; d. Theodore Abraham and Sylvia Leah (Bernbach) Levey; B.A. cum laude, Hofstra U., Hempstead, N.Y., 1968; M.A. (teaching fellow), Queens Coll., 1972; m. Leonard S. Zemel, Nov. 27, 1974. Piano instr., concert artist, 1968-77; asst. adminstr. society, group and council activities IEEE, 1977-78, adminstr. conf. activities and publs., 1978—. Mem. Meeting Planners Internat., N.Y. League Bus. and Profl. Women (rec. sec. 1981-82, treas. 1982-83). Democrat. Jewish. Home: 102-40 67th Rd Forest Hills NY 11375 Office: 345 E 47th St 15th Floor New York NY 10017

ZENI, BETTY JOY WAGNER, retail co. exec.; b. Chgo., Mar. 3, 1926; d. Percy E. and Elizabeth Cecelia (McGeeney) Wagner; student U. Chgo., 1942-44; B.A., Vassar Coll., 1947; student U. Zurich, 1946, Katharine Gibbs Sch., 1947-48; m. Ferdinand J. Zeni, Jr., 1974. With Marshall Field & Co., Chgo., 1950—, mem. real estate div., 1950-72, mgr. corp. ins., 1972—, mgr. corporate ins. and property taxes, 1980—. Pres., bd. dirs. Women's Nat. Republican Club Chgo., 1976-78; sec. 9th dist. state central com., 1968-72; alternate del. Rep. Nat. Conv., 1968; mem. adv. bd. Civic Fedn., 1975—, bd. dirs., 1980—; bd. dirs. Lake Shore Condominium Assn., 1975-80; mem. land valuation com. State Street Council. Mem. Vassar Alumnae Assn., Vassar Club Chgo., Katharine Gibbs Alumnae Assn. (past pres.), Risk and Ins. Mgmt. Soc. (dir. Chgo. chpt. 1974-77), Pewter Collectors Club Am., Midwest Pewter Collectors Club, Lambda Alpha. Home: 1440 N Lake Shore Dr Chicago IL 60610 Office: 25 E Washington St Chicago IL 60602

ZENS, MILDRED IRENE LARSEN (MRS. CLARENCE MICHAEL ZENS), librarian, media specialist; b. Racine, Wis., Sept. 14, 1917; d. Lars Anderson and Esther Bolette (Skow) Larsen; student Marquette U., 1936-38; B.A., Lawrence U., 1940; M.A., Catholic U., 1963; postgrad. U. Wis., 1941; m. Clarence Michael Zens, May 24, 1944; children—Michael Louis, Karen Larson. Tchr., librarian, Calumet, Mich., 1940-41, Frank McKee High Sch., Muskegon, Mich., 1941-43; reporter Jour. Times, Racine, 1944; librarian Am. Alumni Council, Washington, 1963-64; Gonzaga Coll. High Sch., Washington, 1964-74, Western High Sch., Washington, 1974-76; staff career resource devel. Staff Devel. Panel, Woodrow Wilson Sch., Washington, 1976—; mem. Middle States Evaluation Commn. on Secondary Schs. Area dir. Girl Scout ann. cookie drive, 1958-59; dir. County Cub Scouts, 1955-56; organizer Friends of the Library, Fairfax City, Va., 1955-57. Mem. Am., D.C. (publicity dir., 1968-71), Catholic (area dir. 1967-72), library assns., D.C. Assn. Sch. Libraries, AAUW, Sch. Libraries Assn., Delta Kappa Gamma. Home: 406 A St SE Washington DC 20003 Office: Woodrow Wilson Sch Chesapeake and Nebraska Sts NW Washington DC 20016

ZERBEST, MARGARET KATHLEEN, microbiologist; b. Clarksburg, W.Va., Mar. 12, 1953; d. Everett William and Norene Edna (Murphy) Z.; B.S., Glenville State Coll., 1975; M.S. (grad. asst.), W.Va. U., Morgantown, 1978. Lab technologist W.Va. U. Hosp. Lab., Morgantown, 1977-78; supr. microbiology lab. United Hosp. Center, Inc., Clarksburg, 1978—; instr. med. lab. tech. dept. allied health Fairmont State Coll., 1978—. Mem. Assn. Women in Sci., Am. Soc. Microbiology (Allegheny br.), Am. Acad. Microbiology, Nat. Registry Microbiologists, Chi Beta Phi. Democrat. Methodist. Home: 132 Anthony St Clarksburg WV 26301 Office: United Hosp Center Lab 3 Hosp Plaza Clarksburg WV 26301

ZETTLE, PAULA RUTH, nurse; b. Youngstown, Ohio, Aug. 9, 1938; d. Paul Vincent and Doris Esther (Snively) Webb; R.N., St. Luke's Hosp. Sch. Nursing, 1959; postgrad. Cuyahoga Community Coll., 1969, St. Joseph's Coll., 1982—; m. Donald Richard Zettle, Oct. 29, 1974; children—Peter, Lisa, Jonathan, Jamie. Nurse, Lakewood (Ohio) Hosp., 1960-61; employee health service nurse Mt. Sinai Hosp., Hillcrest Hosp., Cleve., 1972-78; day supr., patient care coordinator Brentwood Hosp., Cleve., 1978-79, Shaker Med. Center, Cleve., 1979-80; asst. dir. nursing Americana Healthcare, Mayfield Heights, Ohio, 1981; utilization rev. coordinator Kaiser Found., East Side Hosps., Cleve., 1982—; instr. CPR; cons. Leader, Girl Scouts U.S.A., 1968-73; den mother, trainer Boy Scouts Am., 1967-69; active ARC. Mem. St. Luke's Hosp. and Greater Cleve. Gen. Alumni Assn., Nat. League Nursing, Am. Assn. Occupational Health Nurses, Nat. Assn. Quality Assurance Profls. Presbyterian. Home: 993 Professor Rd Lyndhurst OH 44124 Office: 2475 East Blvd Cleveland OH 44120

ZEVIN, SUSAN FAYE, hydrologist; b. Washington, June 20, 1949; d. Albert and Bonnie Ruth (Nathanson) Z.; B.A., U. Pitts., 1971; M.A. with honors (Univ. scholar), U. Tel Aviv, 1974; postgrad. (NOAA scholar) U. Ariz., 1978-79. Hydrologist, Office of Hydrology, U.S. Nat. Weather Service, Silver Spring, Md., 1974-82; dep. dir. U.S. Reference Center for Hydrologic Operational Multipurpose Subprogramme, a program of tech. transfer within World Meteorol. Orgn., Silver Spring Md., 1980—; rapporteur on effectiveness of hydrologic forecasts World Meteorol. Orgn.; public edn. tchr. U.S. Coast Guard Aux. Recipient Outstanding Performance Rating, Nat. Weather Service, 1978. Mem. Am. Geophys. Union, Am. Water Resources Assn. Office: 8060 13th St Silver Spring MD 20910

ZEVON, IRENE ANN, artist; b. Bklyn., Nov. 24, 1918; d. Joe and Minnie (Saslowsky) Zivitofsky; student Tschacbason Sch. Fine Arts, 1950-55; m. John Murray Barton, Mar. 28, 1943 (div. Nov. 1960); 1 son, Leonard; m. 2d, Nahum Tschacbasov, Aug. 30, 1966. Exhibited in one man shows including: Lynn Kottler Galleries, N.Y.C., Mary Buie Mus., Oxford, Miss., Lauren Rogers Library and Mus., Laurel, Miss., Charles Allis Art Library, Milw., Ga. Mus. Art, Athens, Calif. State Library, Sacramento, Columbus (Ga.) Mus. Arts and Crafts, Carnegie Pub. Library, Clarksdale, Miss., Neville Pub. Mus., Green Bay, Wis.; exhibited in group shows including: Stamford Art Mus., Mus. New Britain Inst., Crandall Art Studios, Massillon Mus., Neville Pub. Mus., Kenosha Pub. Mus., Columbia Mus. Art, Nat. Acad. Gallery; represented in permanent collections including: Calif. State Library, Sacramento, Butler Art Inst., Youngstown, Ohio, Dallas Mus. Fine Arts, Library of Congress, Washington, St. Louis Mus. Art, La Jolla (Calif.) Mus. Art, Pensacola (Fla.) Art Center, Wustum Art Mus., Racine, Wis., numerous other coll. and library collections. Mem. Nat. Assn. Women Artists (Marion K. Haldenstein meml. prize 1972).

ZICAFOOSE, BARBARA FRANGO, nurse; b. Alleghany County, Va., Feb. 6, 1949; d. David Ollie and Carol Christine (Bryant) Frango; diploma Chesapeake and Ohio Hosp. Sch. Nursing, 1970; postgrad. Va. Western Community Coll., 1971—; cert. adult nurse practitioner U. Va. Sch. Nursing, Charlottesville, 1979; m. Nelson Dan Zicafoose, Jan. 10, 1970; 1 son, Nelson Dan. Staff nurse Roanoke (Va.) Meml. Hosp., 1970-71, Gill Meml. Eye, Ear, Nose & Throat Hosp., Roanoke, 1971; staff nurse VA Hosp., Salem, Va., 1971-73, charge nurse recovery room, 1973-75 head nurse surg. intensive care, 1975-77, staff nurse intermediate med. ward, 1977—; ward nurse practitioner VA Med. Center, Salem, 1979—. Choir dir., organist, pianist Iron Gate (Va.) Bapt. Ch., 1971-77; pianist, asst. organist, choir dir. Fincastle (Va.) Bapt. Ch., 1977-78, Sunday sch. tchr., pianist, organist, 1979-80; active Troutville (Va.) Bapt. Ch., 1980—. Cert. CPR instr. Mem. Am. Nurses Assn., Va. Nurses Assn., Am. Assn. Critical Care Nurses, Va. Nurse Practitioner Assn. (chmn. 1980—), Nurse Practitioner Profl. Practice Group (chmn.-elect), Kinzie Circle Missionary Group, Women's Internat. Bowling Congress. Home: Route 1 Box 397 Fincastle VA 24090

ZICH, SUE SCHAAB, nursing adminstr.; b. Buffalo, Oct. 18, 1946; d. Milan Harvey and Mary Margaret (Olmsted) Schaab; B.S. in Nursing, Villa Maria Coll., 1968; m. Timothy John Zich, Nov. 25, 1976; children—John Paul Trottman, Scott Francis Trottman. Staff nurse, charge nurse, team leader Children's Hosp., Buffalo, 1968-71; staff nurse plasmapheresis unit Roswell Park Meml. Inst., Buffalo, 1971-72, 73-75; staff devel. coordinator Episcopal Ch. Home, Buffalo, 1975-77; pediatric unit charge nurse Loudoun Meml. Hosp., Leesburg, Va., 1977; nursing instr. No. Va. Mental Health Inst., Falls Church, 1977-78; dir. nursing service Barcroft Inst., Falls Church, Va., 1978—. Troop com. mem., den leader, dist. mem. Prince William Dist. Boy Scouts Am., day camp dir. Cub Scout Camp Tomahawk, 1983. Recipient Key Leader award Prince William dist. Boy Scouts Am., 1982, Den Leader Tng. award, 1982. Mem. Dir. Nurses Group No. Va. (sec.-treas. 1980-81, v.p. 1981-83), Nat. Campers and Hikers Assn., Friends of Nat. Zoo, Smithsonian Assoc., Villa Maria Coll. Alumnae Assn. (life, past. pres. Buffalo chpt.), St. Edmund's Ladies Guild (pres. 1972-73, advisor 1973-74). Roman Catholic. Home: 9709 Evans Ford Rd Manassas VA 22111 Office: 2960 Sleepy Hollow Rd Falls Church VA 22044

ZIEGLER, EILEEN TRACEY, career planner; b. Trenton, N.J., Oct. 22, 1948; d. Arthur J. and Isabelle M. Tracey; B.A., Albertus Magnus Coll., New Haven, 1970; M.A., Rider Coll., Lawrenceville, N.J., 1977; m. Jeffrey W. Ziegler, Sept. 12, 1970; children—Tracey, J. Scott. Grad. asst. Bucks County Community Coll., Newtown, Pa., 1977; job devel. specialist Middlesex County Coll., Edison, N.J., 1977; youth counselor Mercer County Office Tng. and Employment Services, Trenton, 1978-81, employment rep./AA-EEO officer, 1981—. Mem. Am. Personnel and Guidance Assn., Nat. Vocat. Guidance Assn. Office: 640 S Broad St Trenton NJ 08611

ZIFF, RUTH, advt. co. exec.; b. N.Y.C., May 26, 1924; d. Herman and Lena (Medoff) Baron; B.A., Hunter Coll., 1944; M.A. (Acad. scholar), Columbia, 1948; Ph.D., CUNY, 1975; m. Solomon Ziff, Mar. 29, 1942; children—Charles Elliot, Ellen Barbara. Dir. psychol. barometer and link audit pub. attitudes Psychol. Corp., N.Y.C., 1944-49; v.p., mgr. research Benton & Bowles, Inc., N.Y.C., 1950-75; sr. v.p., dir. research and mktg. services Doyle Dane Bernbach Inc., N.Y.C., 1975—. Named Advt. Woman of Yr., Am. Advt. Fedn., 1973. Mem. Advt. Women of N.Y. (dir.), Am. Mktg. Assn. (dir.), Am. Assn. Pub. Opinion Research, Am. Psychol. Assn., Am. Sociol. Assn., Market Research Council, Phi Beta Kappa, Alpha Chi Alpha. Contbr. articles to profl. jours. Office: 437 Madison Ave New York City NY 10022

ZILBERBERG, BARBARA, sch. psychologist; b. Kenya, Sept. 15, 1943; came to U.S., 1950, naturalized, 1957; d. Isidore and Sophie (Werner) Zysman; B.A. cum laude, City U. N.Y., Bklyn. Coll., 1964; M.A., New Sch. for Social Research, 1966; cert. sch. psychologist, Montclair State Coll., 1981; m. Charles Zilberberg, Sept. 2, 1965; 1 dau., Julie Marlene. Intern psychologist Central Islip N.Y. State Hosp., 1965-66; sr. clin. psychologist Kings Park State Hosp., N.Y., 1966-68; psychologist Bonnie Brae Residential Treatment Center, Millington, N.J., 1977-78; sch. psychologist Sayreville (N.J.) Public Schs., 1981—. Bd. dirs. PTA, 1973-82; troop leader Girl Scouts U.S.A., community cons., 1975-79; mem. Friends of Thirteen bd. dirs. sisterhood Temple Emanu-El, Westfield, N.J. Cert. sch. psychologist, N.J. Mem. Am. Psychol. Assn., N.J. Psychol. Assn., N.J. Assn. Sch. Psychologists, Nat. Assn. Sch. Psychologists, Mensa, Psi Chi. Office: 425 Main St Sayreville NJ 08872

ZILCZER, JUDITH KATY, art historian; b. Waterbury, Conn., Nov. 6, 1948; d. Paul and Rose (Merkler) Z.; B.A. with distinction, George Washington U., 1969, M.A., 1971; Ph.D. (Unidel fellow), U. Del., 1975. Teaching fellow George Washington U., Washington, 1970-71; Smithsonian fellow Nat. Collection of Fine Arts, 1973-74; historian Hirshhorn Museum and Sculpture Garden, Smithsonian Instn., Washington, 1974—; asso. professorial lectr. George Washington U.; cons., guest curator Phila. Mus. Art. Penrose Fund postdoctoral research grantee, 1976-77; Smithsonian Instn. fluid research awardee, 1977. Mem. Coll. Art Assn. Am., Nat. Trust for Historic Preservation, Women's Caucus for Art, Assn. Historians of Am. Art. Author: The Noble Buyer: John Quinn, Patron of the Avant-Garde, 1978; Oscar Bluemner: The Hirshhorn Museum and Sculpture Garden Collection, 1979; contbr. articles to profl. jours. Office: Hirshhorn Museum and Sculpture Garden Smithsonian Instn Independence Ave and 8th St Washington DC 20560

ZILE, MAIJA HELENE, biochemist; b. Riga, Latvia, Aug. 3, 1929; came to U.S., 1949, naturalized, 1955; B.S., U. Md., 1954; M.S., U. Wis., Madison, 1956, Ph.D., 1959; m. Zigurds Zole, June 11, 1955 (div. 1980); children—Mara, Anda, Inga. Research asso. Harvard U., 1959-61; project researcher, then asso. scientist biochemistry U. Wis., Madison, 1961-80; asst. prof. nutritional biochemistry Mich. State U., E. Lansing, 1980—. USPHS fellow, 1959; NIH fellow, 1959-61; grantee Nat. Cancer Inst., Dept. Agr., Mich. State U. Mem. Am. Inst. Nutrition, Soc. Exptl. Biology and Medicine, Sigma Xi, Sigma Delta Epsilon. Author papers in field. Office: Dept Food Sci and Human Nutrition Mich State U East Lansing MI 48824

ZILIN, SADYE JOHANNA, lawyer; b. Amsterdam, N.Y.; d. Nikodimas A. and Mary M. (Russell) Z.; B.S. cum laude, SUNY, Albany, 1942; LL.B., J.D., Union U., Albany, 1946; m. David S. MacKay, Aug. 20, 1949; children—James Russell, David Bruce, Marianne R., Robert W. Admitted to N.Y. bar, 1947, since practiced in Albany; individual practice, 1949—; mem. Original Albany County Charter Commn. Mem. Albany County Bar Assn., SUNY Albany Alumni Assn., Albany Law Sch. Alumni Assn. Address: 144 Cardinal Ave Albany NY 12209

ZIMMER, JACQUELINE LEE, clin. psychologist; b. San Diego, Jan. 16, 1941; d. Cletus Lawrence and Lois Eileen (Kirkpatrick) Zimmer; B.A., San Diego State U., 1970, M.S., 1972; Ph.D., Calif. Sch. Profl. Psychology, 1975; m. Douglas Gordon Mitchell, May 2, 1977. Tchr. public schs., Duluth, Minn., Chgo., 1962-69; postdoctoral intern Norfolk (Va.) Community Mental Health Center, 1975-76, asso. dir. adolescent inpatient unit, 1976-77; pvt. practice clin. psychology, Virginia Beach, Va., 1977-78; asst. prof. psychology Baylor U., Waco, Tex., 1978—, dir. Psy.D. program; cons. McLennan County (Tex.) Juvenile Center and Adult Probation. Mem. Am. Psychol. Assn., Tex. Psychol. Assn., McLennan County Psychol. Assn., Calif. Sch. Profl. Psychology Alumni Assn. Roman Catholic. Home: 2016 Charboneau St Waco TX 76710 Office: Dept Psychology Baylor U Waco TX 76798

ZIMMERMAN, ANNE KATHERINE, assn. exec.; b. Helena, Mont., Sept. 1, 1914; d. George and Theresa (Betor) Larson; diploma St. John's unit Sisters of Charity of Leavenworth Sch. Nursing, 1935; L.H.D. (hon.), Loyola U., Chgo., 1975; 1 dau., Nancy Burke; Pvt. duty and staff nurse, 1933-45; exec. dir. Mont Nurses Assn., 1945-47; asso. exec. Calif. Nurses Assn., 1947-54; asst. dir. Am. Nurses Assn., 1951-52; exec. dir. Ill. Nurses Assn., Chgo., 1954—. Mem. various nursing councils and assns. Home: 30 E Elm St Chicago IL 60611 Office: 6 N Michigan Ave Chicago IL 60602

ZIMMERMAN, DONNA MARIE, nurse; b. Matherville, Ill., Feb. 13, 1926; d. Leonard Todd and Violette Pauline (Durney) Dorothy; R.N., Moline (Ill.) Public Hosp., 1947; m. Philip Joseph Zimmerman, Feb. 10, 1952; children—Philip Joseph, Jan Marie, Jay Howard. Surg. staff nurse Moline Public Hosp., 1947-51, St. Luke's Hosp., Davenport, Iowa, 1951; head nurse Mercer County Hosp., Aledo, Ill., 1966-69; office nurse, Aledo, Ill., 1969—. Republican. Methodist. Club: Order Eastern Star. Address: Route 1 Box 150 Aledo IL 62131

ZIMMERMAN, ELIZABETH THAYER, educator; b. Colorado Springs, Colo., Jan. 8, 1907; d. Harry Stanley and Mary Elizabeth (Brown) Thayer; B.A., U. Colo., 1928; m. Austin M. Zimmerman, Dec. 26, 1934; children—Edward Austin, John Jeffrey. Lectr. horticulture, botany, ecology Morton Arboretum, Lisle, Ill., 1956—, instr., 1961—. Rec. sec. Conservation Council Chgo., 1961—; trustee Morton Arboretum, Lisle, Ill., Ill. chpt. Nature Conservancy, 1962—. Recipient Award for Horticulture, 1963, Conservation, 1965; Eloise Payne Luquer medal Garden Club Am., 1971. Mem. Chgo. Hort. Soc. (dir., trustee, mem. exec. com., pres. women's bd., award 1982), Delta Gamma. Home: Brae Burn Farm Barrington Hills PO Algonquin IL 60102

ZIMMERMAN, FRANCES ADDIE, state govt. ofcl.; b. Kansas City, Mo., Oct. 10, 1924; d. Dewey J. and Louise Frances (Wydick) Howell;

Asso. Degree, Park Coll., Parkville, Mo., 1944; student Rockhurst Coll., 1970, U. Mo., Kansas City, 1972, U. Mich., 1976, 77, U. Houston, 1977; m. Eugene R. Zimmerman, Aug. 10, 1945; children—Donald, Nancy Zimmerman Giller, Robert J., Laura. Dir. public relations program, county organizer Am. Cancer Soc., Kansas City, Mo., 1959-60; public relations, Mo. Employment Service, 1962-75; instr., art dir. Regional Tng. Center, U.S. Dept. Labor, Overland Pk., Kans., 1975-80, public relations and employer com. coordinator, Kansas, Mo., 1980—; cons. in field. Pres., Scarritt Sch. PTA, 1950; bd. dirs. Shawnee Mission (Kans.) High Sch., 1960. Mem. Internat. Assn. Personnel (v.p. Mo. 1975, exec. bd. internat. award of merit Mo. 1975), Am. Soc. Trainers (charter mem. orgnl. devel. media div.), Nat. Assn. Female Execs., Nelson Gallery Art, Kansas City C. of C., Urban League Greater Kansas City, Personal Dynamics Assn., Park Coll. Alumni Assn. Art Dirs. Club Kansas City, Nelson Gallery Art Soc. Baptist. Clubs: Kansas City Art Dirs., Overland Park Lioness. Home: 9706 Hayes St Overland Park KS 66212 Office: 911 Walnut St Kansas City MO 64106

ZIMMERMAN, MARLENE JANICE, editor; b. N.Y.C., Jan. 1, 1943; d. Benjamin and Lena (Pavony) Z.; B.A., Bklyn. Coll., 1963, M.A. in English, 1972; M.S. in Ednl. Psychology, N.Y. U., 1977. Tchr., N.Y.C. Bd. Edn., 1963-69, dir. Resource Center, 1969-72, Learning Disabilities Center, 1972-74, Reading Center, 1974-79; conv. dir. N.Y. Mensa, 1977-80, editorial asst. M-phasis, 1978-80; promotion dir. Troupe Theater, N.Y.C., 1978-79; asso. editor Internat. Edit. Jour. Commerce, N.Y.C., 1980—; cons. Manhattan Cable TV, N.Y.C., 1980. Recipient award of Achievement, Am. Mensa, 1979. Mem. Fin. Writers Assn., Am. Film Inst., Women in Communications, Mensa (dir. 1977-82). Contbr. articles on sci. and tech. jours. Home: 160 W 71st St New York NY 10023 Office: 110 Wall St New York NY 10005

ZIMMERMAN, MARY HELEN CAMPION, lawyer; b. St. Louis, July 22, 1901; d. George Henry and Mary (McNamara) Campion; J.D., DePaul U., 1926, L.H.D., 1971; LL.D., Assumption U., Windsor, Ont., Can., 1957; m. George Herbert Zimmerman, July 7, 1926; children—Doris (Mrs. Andrew Bato), Elaine (Mrs. Rankin Peck), Jessie (Mrs. John Daniel Hitchens), Georgia (Mrs. John J. Loftus), Louis. Admitted to Md. bar, 1927, Mich. bar, 1933; practice of law, Balt., 1927-28, Grosse Pointe, Mich. also Detroit, 1933—. Mem. tax com. Detroit Bd. Commerce, 1945-51. Mem. adv. bd. Marygrove Coll., Detroit, 1961-64. Fellow Am. Bar Found.; mem. Women's Assn. Detroit Symphony, League Cath. Women, Cath. Daus. Am., Nat. Assn. Women Lawyers (past pres., editor 75-yr. history), Inter-Am. Bar Assn. (mem. council 1951-63, dir. Found. 1957—), Internat. Bar Assn. (dep. House of Deps., London, 1950, Madrid, 1952), Am. Bar Assn. (resolutions com. 1952-55), Detroit Bar Assn., State Bar Mich. (chmn. com. cooperation with Inter-Am. Bar Assn. 1958-63; trustee State Bar Found. 1960—, pres. 1972-74), Am. Judicature Soc., Women Lawyers Assn. Mich. (past pres.), Federación Internacional de Abogadas, Kappa Beta Pi (editor quarterly 1961-62). Republican. Roman Catholic. Clubs: Pardi (past pres.), Republican Women's (Grosse Pointe); Lawyers (Washington). Home: 125 Kenwood Rd Grosse Pointe Farms MI 48236

ZIMMERMAN, MURIEL LADEN, magazine editor; b. Boston, Nov. 22, 1938; d. Nathan R. and Edna (Droz) Laden; B.S. in Edn., Temple U., Phila., 1959, Ph.D. in English, 1967; m. Everett Zimmerman, Apr. 28, 1963; children—Andrew, Daniel. Instr. English, Temple U., 1963-66; asst. prof. Drexel Inst. Tech., Phila., 1967-68; editor Energy Rev., Santa Barbara, Calif., 1974—; lectr. tech. writing Coll. Engring., U. Calif., Santa Barbara, 1980—. Mem. Phila. Democratic City Com., 1964-68. NDEA fellow, 1960-63. Mem. Soc. Tech. Communication, Calif. Assn. Tchrs. Tech. and Profl. Writing Assn. Tchrs. Tech. Writing, IEEE Profl. Communication Soc. Home: 1822 Prospect Ave Santa Barbara CA 93103 Office: 2074 Alameda Padre Serra Santa Barbara CA 93103

ZIMMERMAN, POLLY (MARY C.) GRIMES, newspaper editor; b. Oshkosh, Wis., Mar. 8, 1925; d. John Joseph and Cecelia Ann (Elkinton) Grimes; student Oshkosh State Tchrs. Coll., 1941-42; B.A. in Comparative Lit., U. Wis., Madison, 1945; m. Orvell Bernhard Zimmerman, Nov. 3, 1945; children—John, Mark, Ellen, Anne, James, Jane, Robert. Ednl. radio writer, performer, producer, 1944-46; free-lance writer/editor, 1946-70; writer The Paper, Oshkosh, 1969-70; writer, asst. women's editor Oshkosh Northwestern, 1971-73, women's editor, 1973-79, Horizons editor, 1979—; public relations cons. Lourdes Acad., Green Bay Diocese, county and mcpl. agys. Mem. ecumenical commn. Catholic Diocese of Green Bay, 1973—; pres.-elect Diocesan Assn. Cath. Women, 1960-72; pres. County Easter Seal Soc., 1960-70, Oshkosh Playground for Handicapped, 1970-77, Curative Workshop Oshkosh, Inc., 1977—; trustee Lourdes Acad., 1974-79; mem. parish adv. bd. and parish council, 1965-70; mem. community arts com. U. Wis., Oshkosh, 1977-79; sec. Lourdes Acad. Found., 1980—. Recipient awards Wis. Press Women, Nat. Mental Health Assn. Mem. Phi Beta Kappa, Phi Kappa Phi, Delta Delta Delta. Republican. Club: Oshkosh Country. Contbr. stories to anthologies and mags. Home: 534 Old Orchard Rd Winneconne WI 54986 Office: 224 State St Oshkosh WI 54901

ZIMMERMAN, SARAH E., immunologist; b. Indpls., Oct. 29, 1937; d. Abraham and Mary (Caplan) Z.; A.B., Ind. U., 1959, M.A., 1961; Ph.D., Wayne State U., Detroit, 1969. Postdoctoral research assoc. in chemistry Ind. U., 1969-71, postdoctoral research assoc. in microbiology Med. Sch., 1971-73, research immunologist in pathology, 1973—. Vol. leader 4-H Club, 1971—. Mem. Am. Assn. Immunologists, Am. Chem. Soc., Am. Soc. Microbiology, Sigma Xi, Sigma Delta Epsilon, Iota Sigma Pi. Clubs: Ind. Arabian Horse, Indpls. Wine Soc. Author articles in field. Office: Riley A-20 Ind U 702 Barnhill Dr Indianapolis IN 46223

ZIMMERMAN, SHIRLEY LEE, social worker, educator; b. Mpls., Nov. 23, 1925; d. Harry and Rose (Abrams) Schwartz; B.A., U. Minn., 1947, M.S.W., 1967, Ph.D., 1977, postdoctoral fellow, 1977-78; m. Peter David Zimmerman, Aug. 3, 1947; children—Michael Reed, Daniel Stephen, Kevin Charles, Julie Deborah. Caseworker, Hennepin County (Minn.) Welfare Dept., 1947-49; cons. child welfare Minn. Dept. Public Welfare, 1967-69; social welfare cons. No. Star Research Inst., 1969-70; social planning cons. Health and Welfare Planning Council, St. Paul, 1969-70; social welfare researcher Interstudy, Mpls., 1970-73; asst. prof., asst. dir. continuing edn. in social work U. Minn., 1970—. Mem. steering com. Minn. Mental Health Planning Council, 1960-64, Mpls. Charter Reform, 1962-63, Minn. Women's Com. on Civil Rights, 1963-64; chmn., organizer Conf. on Income Maintenance, 1969; mem. adv. com. Minn. Bio-Med. Ethics Com.; mem. Gov.'s Task Force on Work and Families. Mem. Nat. Assn. Social Workers, Council Social Work Edn., Am. Public Welfare Assn., Nat. Council Family Relations, Nat. Council Jewish Women (pres. Mpls. section 1961-63), Minn. Social Service Assn., Nat. Conf. Social Welfare, Policy Studies Assn., Phi Kappa Phi. Home: 3843 Glenhurst St Minneapolis MN 55416 Office: 338 Nolte Center U Minn 315 Pillsbury Dr SE Minneapolis MN 55416

ZIMMERMANN, PATRICIA JEANNE, printing and graphics exec., legis. cons.; b. Chgo., Feb. 18, 1940; d. Stanley Marion and Jean (Hallas) Dudek; B.A. in Psychology, No. Ill. U., 1962; postgrad. U. Wis., 1975-79; children—Kimberly Chi, Jacqueline Michele, Bradford William. Research asst. psychology Yale U., 1962-63; dir. govtl. affairs Madison (Wis.) C. of C., 1977-80; owner, operator Printing Plus, Madison, also legis. cons. housing industry in Dane County, 1980—. Vice pres. Eagle Heights Council, 1969; bd. dirs. Dane County LWV, 1972; alderman Madison City Council, 1973-77; program dir. Capitolaires All Girl Drum and Bugle Corps, 1976-78. Recipient cert. of appreciation for service City of Madison, 1977, cert. of recognition Madison Women's Issues Com., 1977. Mem. Nat. Assn. Female Execs. Republican. Roman Catholic. Editor Metropolitan, 1980-82. Home: 6520 Offshore Dr Madison WI 53705 Office: 6820 Odana Rd Madison WI 53719

ZIMMERS, JANET LOUISE SPRINGER, utility co. exec.; b. Aurora, Nebr., Apr. 28, 1944; d. Ralph B. and Eleanor M. (Kraus) Springer; B.S. in Vocat. Home Econs. Edn., U. Nebr., Lincoln, 1966; postgrad. U. Nebr., Omaha, 1972—. Tchr. home econs. Nebraska City (Nebr.) public schs., 1966-67; consumer cons. Peoples Natural Gas Co., Omaha, 1968-73, regional mktg. coordinator, 1973-74, market services analyst, 1974-78, dir. consumer affairs, 1978-80, dir. public affairs, 1980—. Mktg. adviser Jr. Achievement of Omaha, 1976. Mem. Public Relations Soc. Am., Public Utilities Communicators Assn. Republican. Clubs: Omaha Press, Altrusa (pres. 1979-80) (Omaha). Home: 729 N 116th St Omaha NE 68154 Office: Peoples Natural Gas 25 Main Pl Council Bluffs IA 51501

ZINGALE, MARY GENEVIEVE, social worker; b. Bklyn., Oct. 14, 1928; d. Salvatore and Mary (Fornito) Z.; vocat. edn. cert. SUNY, Albany, 1961; B.A. in Social Studies, Coll. St. Rose, Albany, N.Y., 1966; M.S.W., Adelphi U., 1977. Entered Congregation of Religious of Good Shepherd of Angers, 1946; child care worker Euphrasian Residence, N.Y.C., 1950-51; child care worker St. Anne Inst., Albany, 1951-72, trade sewing tchr., 1952-61, tchr. social studies and religion, 1963-72, children's clothing buyer, purchasing agt., adminstr. campus shop, 1951-72, bus. tchr., case aide, 1972-76, social worker, 1976-81, purchasing agt., 1976—, casework supr., 1981—. Mem. Nat. Assn. Social Workers. Roman Catholic. Address: Madonna Heights Burrs Ln Huntington NY 11743

ZINNER, ELIZABETH, social worker; b. N.Y.C., Mar. 27, 1938; d. Abraham and Alice Lee (Cronbach) Uchitelle; B.A., U. Mich., 1960; M.S.W., Harvard U., 1965; M.S.W., Catholic U. Am., 1975; m. June 14, 1961; children—Lisette, Joshua, Noah. Tchr., Newton (Mass.) Public Schs., 1961-63; psychiat. social worker Fairfax (Va.) Public Schs., 1975-76; psychiat. cons. Community Psychiat. Clinic, Wheaton, Md., 1979-81; pvt. practice clin. social work, Bethesda, Md., 1978—; dir. leadership tng. Parents After Childbirth Edn., Inc., Washington, 1975—. Mem. exec. bd. PTA, Bannockburn Sch., Bethesda, 1969-73, chmn. curriculum edn., 1969-70. NIMH research grantee, 1979-80. Mem. Nat. Assn. Social Workers, Acad. Cert. Social Workers. Home and Office: 7111 Laverock Ln Bethesda MD 20817

ZINNES, HARRIET FICH, educator, novelist; b. Hyde Park, Mass.; d. Assir N. and Sara L. (Goldberg) Fich; B.A., Hunter Coll., N.Y.C., 1939; M.A., Bklyn. Coll., 1944; Ph.D., 1953; m. Irving I. Zinnes, Sept. 24, 1943 (dec.); children—Clifford, Alice. Editor publs. div. Raritan (N.J.) Arsenal, 1942-43; asso. editor Harper's Bazaar, 1944-46; tutor Hunter Coll., 1946-49; tutor Queens Coll., Flushing, N.Y., 1949-53, prof. English, 1977—; lectr. Rutgers U., 1961-62; art and lit. critic Weekly Tribune, Geneva, 1968-70; art critic Pictures on Exhibit, 1971—; vis. prof. Am. lit. U. Geneva, 1969; poetry cons. Great Neck (N.Y.) Library, 1973—; author: Book of Ten, 1981; Waiting and Other Poems, 1964; An Eye for an I, 1966; I Wanted to See Something Flying, 1976; Entropisms, 1979; editor: Ezra Pound and the Visual Arts, 1980. Resident fellow MacDowell Colony, 1972-74, 77, Yaddo Found., 1978, 81, Va. Center Creative Arts, 1975-76, 81; grantee Am. Council Learned Socs., 1978, City U. N.Y., 1979, 81. Mem. PEN, Poetry Soc. Am., Acad. Am. Poets, Nat. Book Critics Circle English Grad. Assn. N.Y.U. Home: 9 Cary Rd Great Neck NY 11021 Office: Dept English Queens Coll Flushing NY 11367

ZINS, MARTHA LEE, educator; b. Mankato, Minn., Dec. 14, 1945; d. Hubert Joseph and Rose Marie (Johannes) Z.; B.S. in History, B.A. in English, Mankato State U., 1967; M.L.S., Western Mich. U., Kalamazoo, 1971; postgrad. U. Minn. Tchr. history Worthington (Minn.) High Sch., 1966-67; sch. media specialist Hopkins West Jr. High Sch., Minnetonka, Minn., 1967—; mem. Hopkins Dist. Media Adv. Bd., Affirmative Action Com.; mem. Minn. Gov.'s Task Force Ednl. Policy, 1979-81, Minn. Sex Bias Adv. Com., 1978—, Minn. Title IV ESEA Com., 1978—; adv. mem. Basic Skills Task Force, Washington, 1979. Chmn. Dist. 40B 2A Ind. Republican Com., Minnetonka, 1972-76; del. Hennepin County Ind. Rep. Com., 1972-76. Mem. ALA, NEA (dir. 1976-77), Nat. Women's Polit. Caucus, Minn. Ednl. Media Assn., Minn. Women's Polit. Caucus, Minn. Coalition for Sex Equity in Edn., Public Employees of Minn. (v.p. 1980—), Minn. Edn. Assn. (dir. 1975—, v.p. 1977—bd. dirs. children's fund), Coalition Labor Union Women, Delta Kappa Gamma. Roman Catholic. Home: 155 Gleason Lake Rd Apt 411 Wayzata MN 55391 Office: 3830 Baker Rd Minnetonka MN 55343

ZIOBRO, MARTHA JANE, nuclear co. exec.; b. McKeesport, Pa., Oct. 29, 1954; d. Michael Francis and Stella (Hutsko) Ziobro; A.A., U. Fla., 1974, B.Bldg. Constrn., 1976. Constrn. mgmt. asst. TVA, Hartsville Nuclear Project, 1976-79, asst. laborer supt., 1979—. Sec., Cath. Youth Orgn., 1971. Clearwater chpt. Women in Constrn., scholar, 1972; recipient H.H. Block award dept. bldg. constrn. U. Fla., 1976. Mem. Student Contractors and Builders Assn. (pres. 1976), Nat. Mgmt. Assn. Home: 328 Trina St Gallatin TN 37066 Office: PO Box 2000 Hartsville TN 37074

ZIOLKOWSKI, GLADYS WARNELL, nurse; b. Homerville, Ga., Sept. 10, 1941; d. T. Warren and Beulah Gladys Lyons (Jeffords) Beagle; diploma Orange Meml. Hosp. Sch. Nursing, Orlando, Fla., 1962; m. Robert Raymond Ziolkowski, Sept. 6, 1962; children—Jennifer Warnell, Deborah Denise, Robert Raymond. Staff nurse Pierce County Hosp., Blackshear, Ga., 1962-65, dir. nursing, 1965—. Mem. Am., Ga. nurses' assns., Ga. Soc. Nursing Service Adminstrs., Ga. Adult Educators' Assn., Ga. Assn. Purchasing Agts., Wacona Boosters, Ware County Band Boosters, Ware County Majorettes Mothers' Club, Ga. Dixie Dolls Mothers' Club, Ladies Aux. Pierce County Hosp. (chmn.), Council Catholic Women. Home: 1102 Dover St Waycross GA 31501 Office: PO Box 32 Blackshear GA 31516

ZIPPEL, MARY-ELLA HOLST, religious educator; b. Detroit, Oct. 12, 1934; d. Spencer and Ruth Catherine (McCullough) Holst; B.A., U. Toledo, 1959, M.A., N.Y.U., 1970; m. Bert Zippel, Jan. 18, 1969; children—Patricia Hall, Darcy Hall. Sr. counselor, employment specialist N.Y. Dept. Labor, 1962-75; religious edn. dir. Unitarian Ch. of All Souls, 1976—; mem. Unitarian Universalist Scholarship Com. Bd. mgrs. Soc. for Aging, 1974—; bd. dirs. Yorkville Common Pantry, 1982—. Contbg. editor: Conversations. . . Journal of Women and Religion; contbr. poetry to lit. jours. Home: 150-74 Village Rd Jamaica NY 11432 Office: Unitarian Ch of All Souls 1157 Lexington Ave New York NY 10021

ZIPSNIS, KATE CONGDON, state health adminstr.; b. Pensacola, Fla., June 27, 1943; d. Frederick M. and Irwin Congdon; B.A., Calif. State Coll., Long Beach, 1964; M.P.H., U. Tex., Houston, 1973; m. Steven M. Zipsnis, Mar. 10, 1979; children—Fearn S. Smith, Sarah K. Smith. Coordinator home health program Upjohn Co., Houston, 1971-73; drug abuse counselor Nueces County Mental Health Mental Retardation Center, Corpus Christi, Tex., 1973-75; drug abuse planner Coastal Bend Council Govts., Corpus Christi, 1975-77; planner, program mgr. Ariz. Dept. Health Services, Phoenix, 1977-81, mgr. state cert. of need program, 1981-82, exec. staff to dir. Div. Family Health Services, 1982—; cons. Nat. Inst. Drug Abuse. USPHS fellow, 1965; USPHS trainee, 1973. Mem. Tex. Assn. Drug Abuse Services (dir.), Am. Public Health Assn., Phi Kappa Phi. Home: 8662 E Bonnie Rose Scottsdale AZ 85253 Office: 200 N Curry St Tempe AZ 85281

ZISSIS, CECELIA, univ. dean; b. Lebanon, Ind., Feb. 23, 1919; d. John and Georgia (Antonakous) Z.; B.S., Purdue U., 1949, M.S., 1953; Ph.D., U. Mich., 1962. Producer, dir. Sta. WBAA-FM, West Lafayette, Ind., 1949-50; asst. dean women Purdue U., 1950-55, assoc. dean women, 1957-68, assoc. dean students, 1974—, dir. Splan Plan program, 1970—; mem. adv. bd. Internat. Center. U. Mich. fellow, 1956-57; recipient Helen Schleman Outstanding Woman Faculty award, 1974. Mem. AAUW (nat. dir. 1973-80), Nat. Assn. Women Deans and Counselors, Ind. Assn. Women Deans and Counselors, Am. Personnel and Guidance Assn., Am. Coll. Personnel Assn., Nat. Vocat. Guidance Assn., Mortar Bd., Pi Lambda Theta. Episcopalian. Office: Hovde Hall Purdue U West Lafayette IN 47907

ZIVIC, JANIS MARIE, mgmt. cons.; b. Pitts., July 17, 1942; d. Fritzie and Helen K. Z.; B.S. in Edn., Calif. Coll. Pa., 1964; M.A. in Teaching, U. Pitts., 1967. Tchr., Pitts., 1964-72; manpower placement coordinator Crown-Zellerbach, 1973-74; corp. employment supr., mgr. salaried and profl. recruitment, mgr. profl. and tech. recruitment Castle & Cooke, Inc., San Francisco, 1974-78; asso. Heidrick & Struggles, Inc., San Francisco, 1978-81, v.p., 1981—; owner R. Price, San Francisco, 1978-80; cons. Puerto Rican Women's Center, 1975-78, Cath. Workers House/Teenage Program, 1980—. Mem. Am. Soc. Personnel Adminstrn., Assn. Exec. Recruiting Cons., San Francisco C. of C. (women's council), Peninsula Profl. Women's Network. Clubs: Banker's (San Francisco); Commonwealth; San Francisco Bay. Home: 180 St Germain Ave San Francisco CA 94114 Office: 600 Montgomery St San Francisco CA 94111

ZIVIN, GAIL LYNN, psychologist; b. Chgo., Sept. 17, 1943; d. S. Bernard and Shirley (Fishman) Z.; A.B., Grinnell Coll., 1965; Ph.D. (Woodrow Wilson fellow, Radcliffe Inst. scholar), Harvard U., 1972; m. Craig Lee San Pietro, Aug. 16, 1972. Asst. prof. human learning and devel. U. Pa., Phila., 1970-75; asst. prof. communication U. Pa., 1975-78; asst. prof. psychology Beaver Coll., Glenside, Pa., 1978-80; asst. clin. prof. mental health sci. Hahnemann Med. Coll., Phila., 1977-80; asso. clin. prof. dept. psychiatry and human behavior and dept. family medicine Thomas Jefferson Med. Coll., Phila., 1980—; pvt. practice psychotherapy, Phila., 1978—. Recipient grants Guggenheim Found., Spencer Found., NIMH. Mem. AAUP, Am. Psycho. Assn., Phila. Soc. Clin. Psychologists, Soc. Research in Child Devel., Eastern Psychol. Assn., Pa. Psychol. Assn., Internat. Soc. Human Ethology, Animal Behavior Soc., Nat. Women's Health Network, Women's Health Concerns Com. Phila., Phi Beta Kappa, Phi Delta Kappa, Harvard Club Phila. Jewish. Contbg. editor: The Development of Self-Regulation through Private Speech, 1979; contbr. articles to profl. jours. Office: 404 E Gowen Ave Philadelphia PA 19119 Also dept Psychiatry And Human Behavior Thomas Jefferson U Philadelphia PA 19107

ZIZZO, ALICIA THEODORATOS, concert pianist; b. N.Y.C., Apr. 2, 1945; d. Spiro and Christine (Corda) Theodoratos; B.A., Hofstra U., 1965; postgrad. C.W. Post Coll., 1975, L.I. U., 1976, Mannes Coll. Music, St. John's U. Sch. Law; m. Thomas Edward Zizzo; children—Peter, Claudia. Debut as concert pianist Town Hall, N.Y.C.; performed in major univs. and concert halls of N.Y. including: Avery Fisher Hall, Town Hall, Lincoln Center Library for Performing Arts, Hunter Coll., Hofstra U., Adelphi U., L.I. U.; 1st piano soloist Nassau County Center for Fine Arts, Roslyn, N.Y., 1977, Coe Hall, Oyster Bay, N.Y., 1979; dir. music Portledge Sch., Locust Valley, N.Y., 1980—; lectr. Bd. dirs., dir. programming Friends of Arts; trustee North Shore Preservation Soc. Mem. AAUW, Hofstra U. Alumni Assn., Am. Matthay Assn.

ZOBEL, RYA WEICKERT, fed. judge; b. Zwickau, Germany, Dec. 18, 1931; d. Paul J. K. and Elizabeth Weickert; A.B. cum laude, Radcliffe Coll., 1953; LL.B., Harvard U., 1956; m. Hiller B. Zobel, Nov. 23, 1973; children—Andrea Elizabeth Featherston, David Stephen Featherston, Scott Alexander Featherston; 4 stepchildren. Law clk. to Chief Judge George C. Sweeney, U.S. Dist. Ct., Dist. Mass., 1956-66; asso. firm Hill & Barlow, Boston, 1967-73; asso. firm Goodwin, Procter & Hoar, Boston, 1973-75, partner, 1976-79; judge U.S. Dist. Ct., Dist. Mass., 1979—. Fellow Am. Bar Found., Acad. Matrimonial Lawyers Am. (gov. Mass. chpt. 1978-79); mem. Am. Bar Assn., Mass. Bar Assn., Boston Bar Assn. (council 1973-76). Office: US Dist Ct PO and Courthouse Bldg Boston MA 02109

ZOBLE, ADRIENNE KAPLAN, advt. agy. exec.; b. Newark, July 11, 1940; d. Herman Israel and Ada (Googglass) Kaplan; B.A., Rutgers U., Newark, 1963; m. Jacob Manus Zoble, Aug. 23, 1962; children—Allison Leigh, Jennifer Hope. Sec. media dept., broadcast estimator J. Walter Thompson Co., N.Y.C., 1961-64; asst. buyer, buyer Maxon, Inc., N.Y.C., 1964; media dir. Bruce Friedlich & Co., N.Y.C., 1965-66; media dir. Keyes, Martin & Co., Springfield, N.J., 1966-76; owner Adrienne Zoble Advt., Martinsville, N.J., 1977—; mem. Active Corps Execs., U.S. SBA, 1977—. Mem. LINK (founder, past pres.), N.J. Assn. Women Bus. Owners (founder, past pres. Central N.J.), Raritan Valley C. of C. (trustee, chmn. small bus. council). Office: 380 Foothill Rd Bridgewater NJ 08807

ZOLA, LEONORA KATZ, psychologist; b. Kingston, N.Y., Feb. 28, 1936; d. Felix W. and Beth (Blankfeld) Katz; A.B., Bard Coll., 1957; M.A., Boston U., 1958, Ph.D., 1967; M.P.H., Harvard U., 1981; m. James J. Feeney, Jan. 1, 1976; children—Warren Keith, Amanda Beth. Psychol. cons. Greater Lawrence (Mass.) Mental Health Center, 1969-71; asst. prof. dept. devel. and personality psychology U. Leiden (Netherlands), 1971-72; staff psychologist Childrens Hosp. and Med. Center, Boston, 1972-77; staff psychologist Brighton Allston Mental Health Center, Boston, 1977-80. Bd. mgrs. New England Home for Little Wanderers, Boston, 1978—; chairperson Lexington Com. for Racial Awareness, Lexington Civil Rights Com., 1963-67. NIMH fellow, 1957-58. Mem. Am. Psychol. Assn., Am. Orthopsychiat. Assn., Mass. Psychol. Assn., NOW. Jewish. Home: 4 Moon Hill Rd Lexington MA 02173

ZOLBER, KATHLEEN KEEN (MRS. MELVIN L. ZOLBER), educator; b. Walla Walla, Wash., Dec. 9, 1916; d. Wildie H. and Alice (Johnson) Keen; B.S. in Foods and Nutrition, Walla Walla Coll., 1941; M.A., Wash. State U., 1961; Ph.D., U. Wis., 1968; m. Melvin L. Zolber, Sept. 19, 1937. Dir. food service Walla Walla Coll., 1941-50, mgr. coll store, 1951-59, asst. prof. food and nutrition, 1959-62, asso. prof., 1962-64; asso. prof. nutrition Loma Linda (Calif.) U., 1964-72, prof. nutrition, 1972—, dir. dietetic edn., 1967—, dir. dietetics Med. Center, 1972—; bd. dirs. Nat. Nutrition Consortium, Washington, 1979—. Mead Johnson grantee, 1965-67; recipient Alumna of Year award Walla Walla Coll., 1977; Dolores Nyhus award Calif. Dietetic Assn., 1978; named Outstanding Faculty Lectr., Loma Linda U., 1979. Mem. Am. Dietetic Assn. (chmn. Commn. on Accreditation 1976-79, dir. 1979-81, pres. 1982-83), Am. Public Health Assn., Am. Home Econs. Assn., Am. Mgmt. Assn., AAUP, Soc. Food Service Research, Soc. Personnel Adminstrn., Sigma Xi, Omicron Nu, Delta Omega. Address: Box 981 Loma Linda CA 92354

ZOLOTOW, CHARLOTTE SHAPIRO, editor, author; b. Norfolk, Va., June 26, 1915; d. Louis J. and Ella F. (Bernstein) Shapiro; student

U. Wis., 1933-36; m. Maurice Zolotow, Apr. 14, 1938 (div. 1969); children—Stephen, Ellen. Sr. editor children's book dept. Harper & Row, N.Y.C., 1938-44, sr. editor, 1962—, v.p., asso. pub. jr. books dept., 1976-81, cons., editorial dir. Charlotte Zolotow Books, 1981—; tchr. U. Colo. Writers Conf. on Children's Books, U. Ind. Writers Conf.; also lectr. children's books; author: The Park Book, 1944; Big Brother, 1960; The Sky Was Blue, 1963; The Magic Words, 1952; Indian Indian, 1952; The Bunny Who Found Easter, 1959; In My Garden, 1960; Not a Little Monkey, 1957; The Man with the Purple Eyes, 1961; Mr. Rabbit and the Lovely Present, 1962; The White Marble, 1963; A Rose, a Bridge and a Wild Black Horse, 1964; Someday, 1965; When I Have a Little Girl, 1965; If It Weren't for You, 1966; Big Sister, Little Sister, 1966; All That Sunlight, 1967; When I Have a Son, 1968; My Friend John, 1968; Summer Is, 1968; Some Things Go Together, 1969; The Hating Book, 1969; The New Friend, 1969; River Winding, 1970; Lateef and His World, 1970; Yani and His World, 1970; You and Me, 1971; Wake Up and Goodnight, 1971; William's Doll, 1972; Hold My Hand, 1972; The Beautiful Christmas Tree, 1972; Janey, 1973; My Grandson Lew, 1974; The Summer Night, 1974; The Unfriendly Book, 1975; When the Wind Stops, 1975; May I Visit, 1976; Some One New, 1977; If You Listen, 1980; Say It, 1980 One Step, Two . . ., 1981; The Song, 1982, others. Recipient Harper gold medal for editorial excellence. Mem. Pen Soc., Authors League. Office: Harper and Row 49 E 33d St New York NY 10016

ZONKER, PATRICIA ANN, writer; b. Huntington Park, Calif., Aug. 10; d. Alfred Charles and Mildred Gertrude (Niquette) Mathewson; student Los Angeles City Coll., 1945-47; m. Thomas Edward Zonker, Oct. 14, 1950; children—Laurie Zonker Pevytoe, Jenny Zonker Ashcroft, Daniel, Gregory. Editorial sec. and asst. Western Livestock Jour., Los Angeles, 1947-48; partner, co-operator Aladdin Employment Agy., Southgate, Calif., 1948-55; contbr. numerous articles and short stories to various publs., including Good Housekeeping, 'Teen, The Rotarian, Lady's Circle; author non-fiction book: Murdercycles, 1979; partner Butane Carburetor Service. Mem. PEN Internat., Writers Workshop West (past sec.-treas.), Writers Club of Whittier (sec. 1972-73). TV and radio appearances. Home: 11532 Samoline Ave Downey CA 90241

ZOOK, MARTHA FRANCES HARRIS, nursing adminstr.; b. Topeka, Nov. 15, 1921; d. Dwight Thacher and Helen Muriel (Houston) Harris; R.N., Meriden (Conn.) Hosp. Sch. Nursing, 1947; student U. Kans., 1948-49, Kans. State U., 1960-61, Barton County Community Coll., 1970-73; B.A., Stephens Coll., 1977; postgrad. Ft. Hays State U., 1978-79; m. Paul Warren Zook, July 2, 1948; children—Mark Warren, Mary Elizabeth Zook Hughey. Staff nurse Stormont Hosp., Topeka, 1947-48; staff nurse Watkins Meml. Hosp., Lawrence, Kans., 1948-49; nursing supr. Larned State Hosp., 1949-53, sect. supr., 1956-57, dir. nursing, 1958-61; sect. nurse Sedgewick Sect., 1961-76, clin. instr. nursing edn., 1976-77, dir. nursing edn., 1977—; clinic nurse for podiatrist; sect. supr. Dillon Bldg., Larned, 1957-58; Mem. Am. Nurses Assn., Dist. VII Kans. Nurses Assn., Nat. League Nursing, Kans. League Nursing, Kans. State Bd. Nursing (mental health technicians examination com.), Nat. Assn. Human Service Educators, AAUW. Republican. Roman Catholic. Home: 1109 Johnson St Larned KS 67550 Office: Route 3 Box 89 Larned State Hosp Larned KS 67550

ZOON, KATHRYN EGLOFF, biochemist; b. Yonkers, N.Y., Nov. 6, 1948; d. August R. and Violet T. (Pollock) Egloff; B.S. (N.Y. State Regents fellow), Rensselaer Poly. Inst., 1970; Ph.D. (fellow), Johns Hopkins U., 1975; m. Robert A. Zoon, Aug. 22, 1970; 1 dau., Christine K. Interferon research fellow NIH, Bethesda, Md., 1975-77, staff fellow, 1977-79, sr. staff fellow, 1979-80; sr. staff fellow div. biochem. biophysics Bur. Biologics, FDA, Bethesda, 1980—. Mem. Am. Soc. Microbiology, AAAS. Roman Catholic. Contbr. numerous articles on research in biol. chemistry to sci. jours.; editor Interferon Research, 1980—. Office: Div Biochem Biophysics Bur Biologics Bldg 29 Rm 518 8800 Rockville Pike Bethesda MD 20205

ZORZOLI, ANITA, biochemist; b. N.Y.C., Dec. 27, 1917; A.B., Hunter Coll., 1938; A.M., Columbia U., 1940; Ph.D. in Biology, N.Y.U., 1945. Asst. zoologist Columbia U., 1940-42; asst. instr. biology N.Y.U., 1944-45; research asst. in pathology Washington U. Sch. Medicine, St. Louis, 1945-46, instr. biochemistry, 1946-48, research assoc. pharmacologist, 1948-49, asst. prof. biochemistry, 1948-52; asst. prof. So. Ill. U., 1952-55; assoc. prof. to prof. biology Vassar Coll., Poughkeepsie, N.Y., 1955—, John Guy Vassar prof. biology, 1973—; mem. corp. Marine Biol. Lab., Woods Hole, Mass. Fellow AAAS, Gerontol. Soc. (v.p. 1965-66); mem. Am. Physiol. Soc., Internat. Assn. Gerntology, Am. Aging Assn. Office: Dept of Biology Vassar College Poughkeepsie NY 12601 *

ZUCKER, ISABEL SCHNAPPER (MRS. MYRON ZUCKER), hort. journalist; b. Phila.; d. Henry and Johanna (Neugass) Schnapper; B.S., Cornell U., 1926, postgrad. 1927-28; m. Myron Zucker, Jan. 28, 1929; children—Judith Zucker Clark, Ralph, Jack. Owner flower shops, Great Neck and Little Neck, N.Y., 1926-29, landscape firm, 1929-40; garden editor The Detroit Times, 1941-60; editor Question Box, Flower Grower mag., 1961-62; dir. Nat. Garden Bur., Bloomfield Hills, Mich., 1962-72; columnist indoor plants Horticulture mag., 1977-79; sec., treas., dir. Myron Zucker Engring. Co., Myron Zucker, Inc., both Bloomfield Hills; tchr., counselor Camp Pontiac, Mich. Conservation-Corrections Program, 1954—. Recipient plaque All Am. Selections, 1971; honor plaque award Am. Seed Trade Assn. 1958; named Garden Writer of Year, Am. Assn. Nurserymen, 1964. Fellow Royal Hort. Soc. (Great Britain), Garden Writers Assn. Am. (editor Bull. 1949-69, pres. 1969-71), Am. Hort. Soc. (citation 1967; Hall of Fame 1981); mem. Mich. (medal 1966), Mass. hort. socs., Internat., Am. socs. hort. sci., Internat. Lilac Soc. (dir. 1972-76, award of merit 1975, honors and achievements award 1980). Author: Flowering Shrubs, 1966; Four Seasons of Fun for Youngsters, 1969. Home and Office: 708 W Long Lake Rd Bloomfield Hills MI 48013

ZUCKER, JEAN MAXSON, nurse; b. Dunmore, Pa., Aug. 9, 1925; d. Earl L. and Florence M. (Cromwell) Maxson; R.N., Kings County Hosp. Center, 1948; children—Lawrence F., Pamela J., Diane K. Pvt. duty nurse various locations, N.Y., N.J., 1959-64; indsl. nurse Bendix Corp., Eatontown, N.J., 1955; asst. head nurse Point Pleasant Hosp., N.J., 1964-66; head nurse intensive and coronary care unit VA Hosp., Ft. Howard, Md., 1974-78; clin. nurse USPHS Hosp., Balt., 1978-81; nursing supr. VA Hosp. Center, Ft. Howard, 1981—; tchr. in field. Mem. Am., Md. nurses assns., Am. Assn. Critical Care Nurses. Democrat. Methodist.

ZUCKERBERG, JOAN, clin. psychologist; b. Bklyn., July 22, 1946; d. Bernard and Sally (Malvone) Offerman; B.A. with honors in Psychology, N.Y.U., 1967, cert. in psychoanalysis, 1980; Ph.D., L.I.U., 1972; m. Richard M. Zuckerberg, June 15, 1970; children—Joshua, Benjamin. Pvt. practice psychoanalytic psychotherapy, Bklyn., 1971—; clin. intern Bklyn. Psychiat. Centers, Inc., 1969-71, supr., 1971-77, chief psychologist, 1974-77; staff psychotherapist Whitman Inst. for Psychotherapy, 1972-73, cons. psychodiagnostician Kingsbrook Jewish Med. Center, 1972; cons., attending psychologist Meth. Hosp. Bklyn.; staff psychologist Youth Services Center, 1972-74; clin. supr. L.I.U., Columbia U., N.Y.U., Pratt Inst., Queens Coll., 1972-74; founder Psychol. Consultation Service for Parents and Prospective Parents, 1977—; asst. clin. prof. psychiatry SUNY Downstate Med. Center, Bklyn.; cons. numerous schs., psychiat. programs, 1977—; adj. asst. prof. psychology L.I.U., City U. N.Y., N.Y.U., Nat. Inst. Psychotherapies. Mem. Park Slope Civic Council; mem. Congregation Beth Elohim, Garfield Temple. Cert. dance and art therapist. Mem. N.Y. Soc. Clin. Psychologists, N.Y. State Psychol. Assn., Am. Psychol. Assn., Bklyn. Psychol. Assn. (former dir.), Am. Assn. Marriage and Family Counselors, Psychoanalytic Soc. of Postdoctoral Program of N.Y.U., Nat. Register of Health Service Providers in Psychology, Am. Orthopsychiat. Assn., Ethical Culture Soc. of Bklyn., Phi Beta Kappa. Contbr. articles in field to profl. jours. Home and office: 36 Montgomery Pl Brooklyn NY 11215

ZUCKERMAN, MADELINE MARY, public relations and advt. agy. exec.; b. N.Y.C., Dec. 3, 1947; d. Sterling and Ann (Tunno) Bottenus; B.A. in Communications/Journalism, N.Y.U., 1969; diploma Collegiate Bus. Sch., N.Y.C., 1967; diploma N.Y. Sch. Interior Design, 1970; m. Leonard Zuckerman, Mar. 8, 1970; children—Jennifer, Matthew. Asst. to pres. Worsted div. Burlington Industries, 1965, dir. pub. relations, 1966; v.p., partner Letitia Baldridge Enterprises, Inc., N.Y.C., 1967-75; propr. Madeline Zuckerman Public Relations/Advt., Tustin, Calif., 1977—; lectr., cons., vol. in field. Mem. Women in Communications (past chpt. v.p.), Exec. Women Internat. (past dir.), Public Relations Soc. Am., Greater Irvine Indsl. League, Newport Beach C. of C., Irvine C. of C., Orange County Press Club. Author articles in field. Office: 14751 Plaza Dr Suite E Tustin CA 92680

ZUELOW, MARGO JEANNE, ednl. researcher; b. Eau Claire, Wis., Mar. 8, 1938; d. Ivan Eugene and Alice May (Krause) Chamberlain; divorced; children—Cynthia Jeanne, James Fredrick. Elementary sch. tchr., Minn., Oreg. and Alaska, 1962-74; instr. edn. Kuskokwim Community Coll., U. Alaska, Bethel, 1974-76; grad. teaching fellow U. Oreg., 1976-77; supr. adult edn. Alaska Dept. Edn., Juneau, 1977-78; dean instrn. Kenai Peninsula Community Coll., Soldotna, Alaska, from 1978; now program researcher Rural Edn. div. U. Alaska; adj. prof. Alaska Pacific U. Chmn. statewide adv. com. U. Alaska Telecommunications Consortium. Mem. Kenai C. of C., Phi Delta Kappa (pres. South Central chpt.). Democrat. Club: Soroptomists. Home: 3701 E 20th St Anchorage AK 99508 Office: 3605 Arctic St Suite 420 Anchorage AK

ZUFALL, DOROTHY LUKASIK, educator; b. Passaic, N.J., Apr. 23, 1930; d. George and Mary (Dolinski) Lukasik; B.S. in Biol. Scis. with honors, Rutgers U., Newark, 1952, postgrad. in Genetics, 1954; student Presbyn. Hosp. Sch. Med. Tech., Newark, 1951-52; cert. in sci. edn. Kean State Coll., 1970; M.A. in Edn., Rider Coll., 1975; M.A. in Mgmt., Central Mich. U., 1976. Staff med. technologist Presbyn. Hosp., Newark, 1952-54; supr. med. tech., indsl. lab. Prudential Ins. Co. Am., Newark, 1954-57; edn. coordinator Sch. Med. Tech., Somerset (N.J.) Med. Center, 1970-77, edn. coordinator, 1977-82, dir. ednl. services, 1982—; HEW grantee Allied Health Adminstrn. Tng. Inst., 1977. Vol. in devel./coordination library services Cedar Hill Sch., Basking Ridge, N.J., 1967-69; trustee Somerset County Heart Assn.; mem. Bernards Twp. Bd. Health, 1979-80, v.p. 1981—; treas. Somerset County Hospice, 1981, 82; trustee Somerset & Hunterdon County Heart Assn., Consumer Health Found. N.J. Recipient N.J. Soc. Med. Tech. award, 1975; Alpha Mu Tau grantee, 1970, 73, 76; cert. elem. tchr., biology tchr., counselor, N.J. Mem. Am. Soc. Allied Health Professions, Am. Soc. Health Manpower Edn., Tng., Am. Soc. Med. Technologists, Consumer Health Educators Assn. N.J. Contbr. articles to profl. jours. Home: 297 S Finley Ave Basking Ridge NJ 07920 Office: Dept Edn Somerset Med Center Somerville NJ 08876

ZUKOWSKI, LUCILLE KATHRYN, mathematician, emerita educator; b. Millinocket, Maine, Nov. 2, 1916; d. Percy J. and Winnifred A. (Ball) Pinette; B.A. cum laude, Colby Coll., 1937, M.A., 1971; M.A., Syracuse U., 1943; postgrad. Harvard U., 1946, Bryn Mawr Coll., 1947-48, U. Mich., Ann Arbor, 1954-55; m. Walter H. Zukowski, Dec. 26, 1955; 1 dau., Mary Lucille. Teaching asst. Syracuse U., 1941-43; prof. dept. math. Colby Coll., Waterville, Maine, 1943-44, 45-82, prof. emerita, 1982—, chmn. dept., 1971-82; vis. prof. Robert Coll., Istanbul, Turkey, 1965-66, Iranzamin Coll., Tehran, Iran, 1972-73; prof. NSF Summer Insts., 1958-70; corporator Waterville Savs. Bank, 1980—; chmn. adv. com. Mount Merici Acad., 1979—. NSF Summer Inst. fellow U. Colo., 1953. Mem. Math. Assn. Am., Soc. Indsl. and Applied Math., Phi Beta Kappa, Sigma Xi. Roman Catholic. Office: Colby Coll Waterville ME 04901

ZULBERTI, ANDREA MARIA, real estate investment and mgmt. co. exec.; b. Hong Kong, Sept. 12, 1951; came to U.S., 1969; d. Cassiano R. and Lucia H. (Jorge) Azedo; A.S., Monterey Peninsula Coll., 1971; B.S.B.A., Calif. State U., Hayward, 1973; m. Alan J. Zulberti, July 7, 1973; 1 son, Darren A. Staff auditor Arthur Andersen & Co., C.P.A.'s, San Jose, Calif., 1973-76; jr. fin. acct. Crowley Maritime Corp., San Francisco, 1976-79; dir. investor relations Robert A. McNeil Corp., San Mateo, 1979-81, v.p. investor relations, 1981—; sr. v.p. adminstrn. McNeil Securities Corp., San Mateo, 1981—. Mem. Calif. C.P.A.s Soc., Nat. Assn. Securities Dealers (fin. and ops. prin.), Real Estate Syndication and Securities Inst., Porsche Club Am. Roman Catholic. Club: Crow Canyon Country. Home: 3497 Canfield Dr Danville CA 94526 Office: 2855 Campus Dr San Mateo CA 94403

ZUMWALT, NANCY EILEEN WILLIAMS, nurse, pub. health adminstr.; b. Ferndale, Mich., Aug. 14, 1927; d. Joseph A. and Marcella N. (Wahl) Williams; diploma Highland Park Gen. Hosp. Sch. Nursing, 1948; R.N., B.A., Eastern Ill. U., 1976, M.S. Ed. in Community Counseling, 1980; m. Bruce G. Zumwalt, Jan. 28, 1950; children—Marcy, B. Joseph, Frank, John. Various positions in nursing profession, 1948-77; dir. Iroquois Meml. Hosp. Home Health Agency, Watseka, Ill., 1968-71, dir. nursing Vermilion County Health Dept., Danville, Ill., 1971-74; adminstr. Iroquois County Health Dept., Watseka, 1974-77; instr. health occupations Iroquois Area Career Center, Watseka, 1980—; instr. continuing edn. Kankakee Community Coll., Govs. State U. Mem. regional bd., sec. East Central Ill. Health Service Agy.; mem. exec. bd. Iroquois County Mental Health Center; v.p. Iroquois County Heart Assn. Mem. Iroquois Meml. Hosp. Aux. Methodist. Club: Am. Legion Aux. Home: Rural Route 2 Sheldon IL 60966

ZUNIC, HELEN THERESA, mgmt./career cons.; b. Garden City, N.Y., Jan. 15, 1944; d. Nicholas Joseph and Emily Angelina (Albino) Z.; teaching credential Calif. State U., 1977. Bookkeeper/acct. Bank of Am. Ladish Pacific div. Cerritos Coll., San Diego and Los Angeles, 1961-72; corp. acct. Acapulco Restaurants, Pasadena, 1972-73; with Lynn Carol Employment Agy., Pasadena, 1973-76; ind. ednl. cons./tchr./career counselor, Los Angeles, 1974—; founder, dir. Career Planning Found., Pasadena, 1976-79; asst. v.p. spl. mgmt. tng. programs Security Pacific Nat. Bank, Los Angeles, 1979-80; owner, pres. Life Mgmt. Enterprises, South Pasadena, 1981—; cons. in field. Mem. vocat. adv. com. Arcadia Sch. Dist., 1978—; bd. dirs. New Opportunity Workshop for Handicapped, 1973-75; mem. Mayor's Com. for Employment of Handicapped, San Gabriel Valley, 1974-75; 2d v.p. constn. and by-laws, parliamentarian Calif. Assn. Ednl. Office Employees, 1971-72; hospitality chmn., treas. Ednl. Office Employees of Cerritos area, 1970-72, others. Recipient Spl. Service awards VA Hosp., Long Beach, 1972, Affiliated Coms. on Aging Los Angeles County, 1974. Mem. Am. Soc. Tng. and Devel., Assn. Humanistic Psychology, Entrepreneurs Assn. Am., Am. Personnel and Guidance Assn. Author: College/Career Planning Workbook, 1982; Life/Career Planning Workbook, 1982. Office: 406 Monterey Rd South Pasadena CA 91030

ZWEIGENTHAL, GAIL, editor; b. N.Y.C., Feb. 27, 1944; s. Joseph and Bessie (Lang) Z.; B.A., Tufts U., 1965. Editorial asst. Gourmet Mag., N.Y.C., assoc. editor, sr. editor, now mng. editor. Office: 560 Lexington Ave New York NY 10022

ZWICKL, JUDITH ELLEN, computer cons.; b. Denver, June 13, 1949; d. Arthur Hoober and Julia Lorraine (Koester) Neumann; B.S., Colo. State U., 1971; M.B.A., U. N.H., 1976: m. Ronald Dean Zwickl, June 13, 1970. Service rep. New Eng. Telephone Co., Dover, N.H., 1972-75; account rep. ADP Network Services, Balt., 1977-79, cons. Western div., San Francisco, 1979-80; self-employed cons., 1981—; mem. credit com. Los Alamos Credit Union, 1981—. Mem. Balt. Econ. Soc. (rec. sec. 1978-79). Home: 104 Rover Blvd Los Alamos NM 87544

Who's Who in America

Women Biographees

The following women biographees have sketches appearing in the 42nd Edition of *Who's Who in America.*

Aaron, Betsy
Aaron, Chloe Wellingham
Abbe, Elfriede Martha
Abbott, Berenice
Abbott, Isabella Aiona
Abbott, Jeanne Montague
Abbott, Loretta
Abdellah, Faye Glenn
Abell, Millicent Demmin
Abrahams, Doris Cole
Abrahamson, Shirley Schlanger
Abrams, Ruth I.
Abu-Lughod, Janet Louise
Abzug, Bella Savitzky
Ackerman, Bettye Louise (Mrs. Sam Jaffe)
Ackerman, Helen Page
Adam, Helen
Adams, Algalee Pool
Adams, Alice
Adams, Alice Patricia
Adams, Brooke
Adams, Carolyn Ethel
Adams, Edie
Adams, Eva Bertrand
Adams, Georgia S.
Adams, Harriet Stratemeyer (Carolyn Keene)
Adams, Margaret Bernice
Adams, Phoebe-Lou
Addison, Anne Simone Pomex
Adel, Judith
Adelman, Irma Glicman
Adelsman, H(arriette) Jean
Adler, Freda Schaffer (Mrs. G. O. W. Mueller)
Adrian, Barbara (Mrs. Franklin C. Tramutola)
Adrian, Donna Jean
Affinito, Lilyan Helen
Affleck, Marilyn
Agosta, Karin Engstrom
Ahlers, Eleanor Emily
Ahmad, Sharon Erdkamp
Aiken, Linda Harman
Ainsworth, Mary Dinsmore Salter
Ajzenberg-Selove, Fay
Akiyoshi, Toshiko
Albanese, Licia
Albee, Grace Arnold
Albers, Anni
Albert, Ethel Mary
Alberts, Eunice Dorothy
Albrand, Martha (Mrs. Sydney J. Lamon)
Albright, Lola (Jean)
Albuquerque, Lita
Alcott, Amy Strum
Aldredge, Theoni Vachliotis
Aldrich, Ann
Aldrich, Patricia Anne Richardson
Aldridge, Mary Hennen Dellinger
Alegría, Rosa Luz
Alevizos, Susan Bamberger
Alexander, Denise
Alexander, Jane
Alexander, Judith Ann
Alexander, Lenora Cole
Alexander, Rosemary Elizabeth
Alexander, Shana
Alfin-Slater, Roslyn Berniece
Allan, Virginia Rachel
Allard, Jean
Allen, Alice Catherine Towsley
Allen, Anna Foster
Allen, Ariel Angele
Allen, Betty (Mrs. Ritten Edward Lee, III)
Allen, Catherine Louise
Allen, Frances Elizabeth
Allen, Gina
Allen, Jay Presson
Allen, Lucile
Allen, Maryon Pittman
Allen, Roberta L.
Allen, Sally Lyman
Allen, Sian Barbara
Allyson, June
Alper, Thelma Gorfinkle
Alston, Annie May
Altabe, Joan Augusta Berg
Alter, Eleanor Breitel
Altman, Ellen
Amara, Lucine
Ambrus, Clara Marie
Ameling, Elly
Ames, Louise Bates
Amini, Johari M.
Anagnost, Catherine Cook
Anastasi, Anne (Mrs. John Porter Foley, Jr.)
Ancker-Johnson, Betsy
Anderegg, Karen Klok
Anders, Mariedi
Anderson, Alexandra C.
Anderson, Bette B.
Anderson, Carolyn Jennings
Anderson, Cynthia Lee
Anderson, Donna Kay
Anderson, Edith Helen
Anderson, Grace Merle
Anderson, Loni
Anderson, Lynn (Rene)
Anderson, Marian
Anderson, Mary Jane
Anderson, Shirley Florence Lord
Anderson, Susan Lou
Andrade, Edna
Andreoli, Kathleen Gainor
Andrew, Gwen
Andrews, Evelyn Virginia
Andrews, Julie
Andrews, Lavone D.
Angel, Rifka
Angelou, Maya
Anker, Suzanne Carol
Ann-Margret (Ann-Margret Olsson)
Anspach, Susan
Anthony, Margery Stuart
Antin, Eleanor
Anton, Susan
Antoun, Sister M. Lawreace
Appleby, Joyce Oldham
Appleman, Jean
Archer, Marian Phyllis
Archer, Sara Katherine
Archer, Violet Balestreri
Arden, Eve (Eunice Quedens)
Ardoyno (Dorr), Dolores
Areen, Judith Carol
Arenal, Julie (Mrs. Barry Primus)
Arias, Margot Fonteyn de (Margot Fonteyn)
Armstrong, Anne Legendre (Mrs. Tobin Armstrong)
Armstrong, Jane Botsford
Armstrong, Karan
Arnaz, Lucie Desiree
Arnold, Margaret Long (Mrs. Dexter Otis Arnold)
Arnold, Marilyn
Arnold, Nellye Kathryn
Arpel, Adrien
Arroyo, Martina
Arthur, Beatrice
Arthur, Charthel
Ash, Mary Kay Wagner
Ashel, Joyce Bulifant
Asher, Lila Oliver
Ashley, Elizabeth
Ashley, Merrill
Ashton, Dore
Ashton, Gwynne
Ashton, Sister Mary Madonna
Asprey, Winifred Alice
Astin, Patty Duke (Anna Marie Duke)
Astor, Mrs. Vincent
Atkin, Flora Blumenthal
Attneave, Carolyn (Adams) Lewis
Atwater, Tanya Maria
Atwood, Ann Margaret
Augér, Arleen Joyce
Auld, Isabel George
Austin, Patricia
Austin, Tracy Ann
Autry, Carolyn
Avery, Mary Ellen
Avram, Henriette Davidson
Aycock, Alice
Aydelotte, Myrtle Kitchell
Ayer, Mary Jane
Aylon, Helane
Ayres, Mary Andrews
Azzara, Candy
Babbitt, Natalie Moore
Babcock, Barbara Allen
Babcock, Charlotte Gertrude
Babcock, Hope Madeline
Baber, Alice
Bacall, Lauren (Betty Joan Perske)
Bacall, Teresa Bickle
Bacon, Daisy Sarah
Bacon, Helen Hazard
Bacon, Peggy
Baddeley, Hermione
Baetjer, Anna Medora
Baez, Joan
Bahr, Lauren S.
Bailey, Elizabeth Ellery
Bailey, Exine Margaret Anderson
Bailey, Pamela Giles
Bailey, Pearl (Mae)
Bain, Barbara (Mrs. Martin Landau)
Bain, Helen Pate
Baker, Amy Dee
Baker, Constance Marie
Baker, Diane (Gross)
Baker, Elizabeth Calhoun
Baker, Janet Abbott
Baker, Margery Claire
Baker, Marilyn
Baker, Peggy Laurayne
Baker, Sarah Marinda
Baker-Hall, Deborah
Balakian, Anna
Balakian, Nona Hilda
Baldrige, Letitia
Baldwin, Ruth Workman
Balke, Mary Noël
Ball, Lucille
Ballantine, Morley Cowles (Mrs. Arthur Atwood Ballantine)
Ballard, Kaye
Ballou, Mildred Oralee Tesdahl (Mrs. Philip E. Ballou)
Balthrop, Carmen Arlene
Balukas, Jean
Bancroft, Anne (Mrs. Mel Brooks)
Bandy, Mary Lea
Banks, Virginia
Banning, Elizabeth (Mrs. Charles Perry Davies)
Banning, Margaret Culkin
Baptista, Mildred Gladys
Baranski, Joan Sullivan
Bardwick, Judith Marcia
Barker, Judy
Barker, Lillian Menzies
Barkhorn, Jean Cook (Mrs. Henry C. Barkhorn)
Barnes, Hazel Estella
Barnes, Joanna
Barnet, Ann Birnbaum
Barnett, Ola Wilma
Baron, Carolyn
Barredo, Maniya
Barrie, Barbara Ann
Barritt, Evelyn Ruth Berryman
Barron, Ros
Barrows, Marjorie
Barry, Mary Alice
Bartlett, Jennifer Losch
Bartnoff, Judith
Barton, Babette B.
Barton, Brigid S.
Bass, Barbara DeJong
Bateman, Mildred Mitchell
Bates, Gladys Edgerly
Bateson, Mary Catherine
Batton, Delma-Jane Heck
Bauer, Elaine Louise
Baumrind, Diana
Bausch, Virginia Quinn
Baxter, Anne
Beaird, Betty
Beale, Betty (Mrs. George K. Graeber)
Bean, Joan P.
Beard, Elizabeth Letitia
Beard, Jean Miller
Bearman, Toni Carbo
Beatley, Janice Carson
Beattie, Ann
Beattie, Diana Scott
Beattie, Nora Maureen
Beatty, Patricia Jean
Beaver, Lucile Elizabeth
Beck, Joan Wagner
Beck, Margit
Beck, Marilyn Mohr
Beck, Rosemarie
Beck, Toni
Becker, Eleanor Holden
Beckman, Gail McKnight
Bedelia, Bonnie
Beebe, Mary Livingstone
Beech, Olive Ann Mellor
Beer, Clara Louise Johnson
Beer, Jeanette Mary Ayres
Beers, Charlotte L.
Bégin, Monique
Behrens, Hildegard
Bel Geddes, Barbara
Bel Geddes, Joan
Bell, Carolyn Shaw
Bell, Jane Matlack
Bellamy, Carol
Bellows, Carole Kamin
Belnap, Norma Lee Madsen
Belyea, Helen Reynolds
Bender, Betty Wion
Benerito, Ruth Rogan (Mrs. Frank H. Benerito)
Benglis, Lynda
Benjamin, Lorna Smith
Bennett, Joan
Bennett, Miriam Frances
Benson, Elizabeth Polk
Benson, Lucille
Benson, Lucy Peters Wilson
Benson, Nettie Lee
Bentel, Maria-Luise Ramona Azzarone (Mrs. Frederick R. Bentel)
Bentley, Antoinette Cozell
Bentley, Helen Delich (Mrs. William Roy Bentley)
Berberian, Cathy (Mrs. Luciano Berio)
Beresford-Howe, Constance Elizabeth
Berg, Jean Horton
Berganza, Teresa
Berge, Carol
Bergen, Candice
Bergen, Polly
Berger, Evelyn Miller
Berger, Marilyn
Berger, Patricia Wilson
Bergman, Ingrid
Bergman, Marilyn Keith
Bergson, Maria
Berkman, Lillian
Berman, Ariane R.
Berman, Louise Marguerite
Berman, Mira
Berman, Muriel Mallin
Bernard, Lola Diane
Bernay, Betti
Bernhagen, Lillian Flickinger
Bernheim, Elinor Kridel (Mrs. Leonard H. Bernheim)
Bernikow, Louise
Bernstein, Florence Henderson
Bernstein, Theresa
Berry, Edna Janet
Berry, Mary Frances
Berry, Nancy Michaels
Berwald, Helen Dorothy
Beshar, Christine
Besharah, Margaret Anne
Bettis, Valerie
Betts, Doris June Waugh
Beuerlein, Sister Juliana
Bibbo, Marluce
Bible, Frances Lillian
Bigelow, Jane Elizabeth
Bigelow, Martha Mitchell
Biggy, Mary Virginia
Bigley, Nancy Jane
Billings, Dorothy Baker
Binder, Lucy Simpson
Bingham, Eula
Bingham, Mary Caperton (Mrs. Barry Bingham)
Bird, Agnes Thornton
Bird, Caroline
Bird, Rose Elizabeth
Birk, Sharon Anastasia
Birman, Joan S.
Birnbaum, Sheila L.
Birney, Meredith Baxter
Bishop, Anne
Bishop, Isabel (Mrs. Harold G. Wolff)
Bissell, Jean Galloway
Bisset, Jacqueline
Black, Cathleen Prunty
Black, Emilie Annabelle
Black, Karen
Black, Patricia Carr
Black, Shirley Temple (Mrs. Charles A. Black)
Black, Susan Harrell
Blades, Ann
Blaine, Nell Walden
Blaine, Vivian
Blais, Madeleine Helena
Blake, Judith
Blakely, Florence Ella
Blakely, Susan
Blakley, Ronee
Blalock, Jane
Blandford, Sister Margaret Vincent
Blank, Blanche Davis
Blank, Marion Sue
Blatt, Genevieve
Blaydes, Sophia Boyatzies
Blegen, Judith Eyer
Bley, Carla Borg (Mrs. Michael Mantler)
Bliss, Dorothy Elizabeth
Bliss, Sally Brayley
Bliven, Naomi
Bliznakov, Milka Tcherneva
Block, Amanda Roth
Block, Ruth S.
Bloom, Claire
Bloom, Pauline
Blos, Joan W(insor)
Blos, Joan W.
Bluestein, Venus Weller
Blum, Anna Ottillia
Blum, Barbara Davis
Blumberg, Grace Ganz
Blume, Judy Sussman
Bluth, Elizabeth Jean Catherine
Blutter, Joan Wernick
Blyth, Myrna Greenstein
Boak, Ruth Alice
Bober, Phyllis Pray
Bockman, Marilyn Modern
Boedeker, Alice Vernelle
Bogard, Carole Christine
Boggess, Mildred Morford Andrews
Boggs, Corinne C. (Lindy)
Bohlen, Nina
Bohman, Madeline Amanda
Bohning, Elizabeth Edrop
Bok, Joan Toland
Boland, Janet Lang
Bollinger, Evangeline Grace
Bolsterli, Margaret Jones
Bombeck, Erma Louise (Mrs. William Bombeck)
Bonaventura, Maria Migliorini
Bonazzi, Elaine Claire
Bond, Elaine R.
Bond, Victoria
Bonosaro, Carol Alessandra
Boocock, Sarane Spence
Booker, Sue
Boone, Deborah Ann (Debby)
Boone, Gray Davis
Boosalis, Helen G.
Booth, Shirley
Boozer, Brenda Lynn
Bordallo, Madeleine Mary (Mrs. Ricardo Jerome Bordallo)
Borg, Dorothy
Borgese, Elisabeth Mann
Borgmeyer, Sister Bernard Marie
Boris, Ruthanna
Borland, Kathryn Kilby
Bornholdt, Laura Anna
Borroff, Marie
Bosch, Gulnar Kheirallah
Bothwell, Dorr
Bottel, Helen Alfea
Boulding, Elise Marie
Boultinghouse, Marion Craig Bettinger
Bouquard, Marilyn Lloyd
Bourgeois, Louise
Bourguignon, Erika Eichhorn
Bouthilet, Kirby Otteson
Bovasso, Julia (Julie) Anne
Bowden, Sally Ann
Bowman, Barbara Hyde
Bowman, Barbara Taylor
Bowns, Beverly Henry
Bowser, Betty Ann
Boydston, Jo Ann
Boyle, Barbara Dorman
Boyle, Kay
Boyle, Patricia Jean
Boynton, Sandra Keith
Bozone, Billie Rae
Bracken, Peg
Bradford, Barbara Taylor
Bradley, Patricia Ellen
Bradshaw, Lillian Moore
Brady, Jane Frances
Brady, Sister Mary William
Braver, Rita Lynn
Brazell, Karen Woodard
Brazier, Mary A. B.
Bree, Germaine
Breeskin, Adelyn Dohme
Brennan, Eileen Regina
Brenner, Erma
Brent, Joleene Adalie
Bressel, Ellen Rae
Bretz, (Alma) Linda
Brewer, Wilma Denell
Bricklin, Patricia Ellen
Brico, Antonia
Bridgewater, Dee Dee
Briggs, Shirley Ann
Bright, Margaret
Britain, Radie
Brock, Alice May
Brock, Karena Diane
Brodbeck, May
Broder, Patricia Janis
Brodman, Estelle
Brodsky, Judith Kapstein
Brody, Elaine
Brody, Jane Ellen
Brooks, Ellen Kay
Brooks, Gwendolyn
Brooks, Peggy Jones (Mrs. John Benson Brooks)
Brosseau, Irma Finn
Brothers, Joyce Diane (Mrs. Milton Brothers)
Brott, Lotte
Brown, Ann Catherine
Brown, Billye Jean
Brown, Carolyn Rice
Brown, Dorothy Lavinia
Brown, Elizabeth Ann
Brown, Elsa Clara Lusebrink
Brown, Esther Lucile
Brown, Eve (Schimpf)
Brown, Helen Gurley
Brown, Hermione Kopp
Brown, Marcia
Brown, Myrtle Irene
Brown, Nancy Ann
Brown, Quincalee
Brown, Rowine Hayes
Browne, Leslie
Browne, Rachel
Browning, Norma Lee (Mrs. Russell Joyner Ogg)
Brownlee, Paula Pimlott
Bruce, Lydia
Bruch, Hilde
Bruck, Bella
Brues, Alice Mossie
Bryant, Anita Jane
Bryant, Bertha Estelle
Bryant, Celia Mae Small
Bryant, Margaret M.
Bryant, Ruth Alyne
Buchanan, Angela Marie
Buchanan, Mary Estill
Buchenholz, Jane Jacobs
Buck, Genevieve Carol
Buckler, Beatrice
Buckley, Priscilla Langford
Buckley, Rebecca Hatcher
Bufton, Ruth Hostetler
Buhagiar, Marion
Bujold, Genevieve
Bullock, Mrs. Hugh (Marie Leontine Graves)
Bumbry, Grace
Bundy, Annalee Marshall
Bunim, Mary-Ellis
Bunting, Anne Evelyn (Eve)
Burden, Jean (Prussing)
Burger, Mary Louise
Burke, Lillian Walker
Burke, Mary Thomas
Burke, Yvonne Watson Brathwaite (Mrs. William A. Burke)
Burket, Harriet (Mrs. Francis B. Taussig)
Burnett, Carol
Burnette, Nancy Everitt
Burns, Sister Elizabeth Mary
Burns, Ellen Bree
Burns, Mary Ann Theresa
Burnside, Helen H.
Burr, Helen Gunderson (Mrs. Horace Burr)
Burroughs, Margaret Taylor Goss

Burson, Phyllis S.
Burstyn, Ellen (Edna Rae Gillooly)
Busby, Marjorie Jean (Marjean)
Bush, Beverly
Bush, Dorothy Vredenburgh
Butler, Karla
Butler, Katharine Gorrell
Butler, Margaret Kampschaefer
Butler, Natalie Sturges (Mrs. Benjamin Butler)
Butterfield, Jan Van Alstine (Mrs. Henry T. Hopkins)
Button, Rena Pritsker
Buzzi, Ruth Ann (Mrs. Basil Keko)
Byers, Nina
Byrne, Jane Margaret Burke
Byrne, Margery Eleanor Little (Mrs. Thomas E. Byrne)
Byron, Beverly Butcher
Bysiewicz, Shirley Raissi
Caadwal-Ilott, Pamela
Cagney, Judith Anne
Caine, Lynn
Cajiao Salas, Teresa
Calamar, Gloria
Calderone, Mary Steichen
Caldwell, Eleanor
Caldwell, Sarah
Caldwell, (Janet) Taylor (Mrs. William Robert Prestie)
Calisher, Hortense (Mrs. Curtis Harnack)
Callaham, Betty Elgin
Calland, Diana Baker
Callihan, Dorothy Jeanne
Cameron, Eleanor Frances
Cameron, JoAnna
Campbell, Ann Morgan
Campbell, Gretna
Campbell, Karlyn Kohrs
Campbell, Margaret Amelia
Campbell, Margaret Anne
Campbell, Maria Bouchelle
Campbell, Marion (Mrs. Douglass Campbell)
Campbell, Mona Louise
Camron, Roxanne
Canning, Jessie Marie
Cannon, Dyan
Cannon, Helen Leighton
Cannon, Isabella Walton
Canova, Judy
Cantor, Muriel G.
Cantwell, Mary
Caparn, Rhys (Mrs. Herbert Johannes Steel)
Capers, Charlotte
Capsalis, Barbara Damon
Carbine, Patricia Theresa
Carewe, Sylvia
Carey, Ernestine Gilbreth (Mrs. Charles E. Carey)
Carey, Jane Perry Clark
Cariaga, Marvellee Dyvonne (Moody)
Carlen, Sister Claudia
Carlos, Wendy
Carlson, Natalie Savage
Carlson, Suzanne Olive
Carmichael, Mary Mulloy
Carnahan, Frances Morris
Carner, JoAnne Gunderson
Caroff, Phyllis M.
Caron, Leslie (Leslie Clare Margaret Caron)
Carpenter, Elizabeth Sutherland
Carpenter, Karen Anne
Carpenter, Patricia
Carr, Bernadette Patricia (Carrozza)
Carr, Vikki (Florencia Bisenta de Casillas Martinez Cardona)
Carrier, Estelle Stacy
Carroll, Billy Price
Carroll, Christina
Carroll, Diahann
Carroll, Elisabeth
Carroll, Sister Elizabeth
Carroll, Frances Laverne
Carroll, Gladys Hasty
Carroll, Kathleen Leader
Carroll, Pat
Carroll, Vinnette Justine
Carsey, Marcia Lee Peterson
Carson, Clarice
Carson, Lettie Gay (Mrs. Gerald H. Carson)
Carsten, Mary E.
Carter, Burdellis LaVerne
Carter, Gwendolen Margaret
Carter, Jaine Marie
Carter, Lynda
Carter, Mary Eddie
Carter, Nell
Carter, Rosalynn Smith
Carter, Theresa Howard
Carthy, Margaret
Cartier, Celine Paule
Cartier, Diana
Cartland, Barbara
Cartwright, Hilary Alison
Casals, Rosemary
Casarett, Alison Provoost
Casei, Nedda
Casey, Ethel Laughlin
Casey, Genevieve Mary
Cash, June Carter
Cashin, Bonnie
Caspary, Sister Anita
Cassidy, Claudia
Castagnetta, Grace Sharp

Castle, Marian Johnson
Castleberry, Vivian Lou Anderson (Mrs. Curtis Wales Castleberry)
Castleman, (Esther) Riva
Castro-Klarén, Sara Beatriz
Catlett, Mary Jo
Catto, Isabel Gordon
Caudill, Rebecca (Mrs. James Ayars)
Caughlan, Georgeanne Robertson
Cavallo, Diana
Cazort, Mimi
Cedering, Siv
Cella, Phyllis Ann
Centifanto, Ysolina Mejia
Cesario, Virginia Naill
Chaffee, Suzy
Chamberlain, Betty
Chambers, Anne Cox
Champion, Marge (Marjorie Celeste Belcher)
Chandler, Alice
Chandler, Margaret Kueffner
Channing, Carol
Channing, Rose Marie
Channing, Stockard (Susan Stockard)
Chaplin, Geraldine
Chapman, Janet Carter Goodrich (Mrs. John William Chapman)
Charisse, Cyd (Tula Ellice Finklea)
Charles, Isabel
Charlton, Janet Shields
Charren, Peggy
Chase, Doris Totten
Chase, Lucia
Chase, Sylvia B.
Chase-Riboud, Barbara Dewayne
Chatham, Lois Albro
Chavez, Linda Lou
Chell, Beverly C.
Ch'en, Li-li
Cheney, Frances Neel
Chennault, Anna Chan (Mrs. Claire Lee Chennault)
Cher
Cheshire, Maxine (Mrs. Herbert W. Cheshire)
Chesrown, Melva Anita
Chicago, Judy
Chicorel, Marietta
Child, Julia McWilliams (Mrs. Paul Child)
Childress, Alice
Childs, Lucinda
Chilman, Catherine Earles Street
Chin, Carolyn Sue
Chinoy, Helen Krich
Chiriaeff, Ludmilla Gorny
Chisholm, Margaret Elizabeth Bergman
Chisholm, Shirley Anita St. Hill
Chow, Rita Kathleen
Christensen, Ione Jean
Christian, Betty Jo
Christie, Julie
Christison, Muriel Branham
Christy, Marian
Chryssa
Chung, Constance Yu-hwa
Church, Margaret
Church, Martha Eleanor
Chute, (Beatrice) Joy
Chute, Marchette
Citron, Minna
Claiborne, Liz (Elisabeth)
Claiborne, Mary Lynn
Clark, Alice Thompson
Clark, Anita Louise
Clark, Ann Nolan
Clark, Candy
Clark, Eleanor
Clark, Eloise Elizabeth
Clark, Esther Frances
Clark, Eugenie
Clark, Joan M.
Clark, M(ary) Margaret
Clark, Marguerite Sheridan
Clark, Mary Higgins
Clark, Meredith Kaye Plier (Mrs. Philip C. Clark)
Clark, Peggy
Clark, Petula
Clark, Susan (Nora Goulding)
Clarke, Cordelia Kay Knight Mazuy
Clarke, Irene Fortune
Clarke, Mary Elizabeth
Claster, Jill Nadell
Clauss, Carin Ann
Clayburgh, Jill
Claydon, Sister Margaret
Clayton, Frances Elizabeth
Clayton, Sharon
Cleary, Beverly Atlee (Mrs. Clarence T. Cleary)
Cleaver, Vera Allen
Clement, Hope Elizabeth Anna
Clement, Patricia Morris Worthy
Clevenger, Sarah
Clever, Linda Hawes
Clifford, Geraldine Marie Joncich (Mrs. William F. Clifford)
Clifton, Lucille Thelma
Cline, Marjorie Ann
Clinton, Mariann Hancock
Close, Elizabeth Scheu

Clough, Susan Sebesta
Clubb, Louise George
Clusen, Ruth Chickering
Clymer, Eleanor
Coatsworth, Elizabeth (Mrs. Henry Beston)
Cobb, Jewel Plummer
Cobb, Ruth
Cobb, Virginia Horton
Coburn, Kathleen
Coca, Imogene
Cockrell, Lila May
Codere, Helen Frances
Cogswell, Dorothy McIntosh
Cohen, Lois Ruth Kushner
Cohen, Selma Jeanne
Cohn, Mildred
Coigney, Martha Wadsworth
Coit, Elisabeth
Coit, Margaret Louise
Coker, Elizabeth Boatwright (Mrs. James Lide Coker)
Colahan, Nancy Val
Colbert, Claudette (Lily Chauchoin)
Colby, Ethel
Colby, Joy Hakanson
Colby-Hall, Alice Mary
Colclaser, H. Alberta
Cole, Natalie Maria
Cole, Olivia
Colecchia, Francesca Maria
Coleman, Mary Elisabeth
Coleman, Mary Stallings
Coleman, Winifred E.
Coles, Anna Bailey
Coles, Anna Louise Bailey
Coll, Helen F.
Collett, Joan
Collier, Gaylan Jane
Collings, Sister M. Paulette
Collins, Beulah Stowe
Collins, Cardiss Robertson
Collins, Clella Reeves
Collins, Joan Henrietta
Collins, Judy Marjorie
Collins, Maribeth Wilson
Collins, Martha Layne
Collins, Marva Deloise Nettles
Colon, Doris E.
Colson, Elizabeth Florence
Colter, Jessi (Jennings, Mirriam Joan Johnson)
Colton, Anita Belle (O'Day)
Comden, Betty
Comini, Alessandra
Commire, Anne
Compton, Ann Woodruff
Compton, Norma Haynes
Conant, Mary Placida
Condit, (Eleanor) Louise
Conklin, Marie Eckhardt
Conlin, Roxanne Barton
Conlon, Ellen Catherine
Connell-Tatum, Elizabeth Bishop
Connor, Judith Turner
Connor, Linda
Connors, Dorsey (Mrs. John E. Forbes)
Connors, Jeanne Louise
Conroy, Sarah Booth
Consagra, Sophie Chandler
Conway, Jill Kathryn Ker
Conway, Martha Bell
Conway, Mary Elizabeth
Conwell, Esther Marly
Cook, Ann Jennalie
Cook, Barbara
Cook, Betty (Mary Elizabeth)
Cook, Camille Wright
Cook, Doris Marie
Cook, Frances D.
Cook, Jean Louise
Cook, Ramona Graham
Cooke, Constance Blandy
Cooke, Eileen Delores
Cooley, Nancy Colver (Mrs. Rome G. Arnold, II)
Coolidge, Rita
Cooney, Barbara
Cooney, Joan Ganz
Cooper, Jane
Cooper, Kathleen Marie
Cooper, Louise Field
Cooper, Sandra Macpherson
Cooper, Susan Mary
Copeland, Jo
Copeland, Lila
Copley, Helen Kinney
Coppola, Mary Carmina
Corbett, Gretchen
Corbin, Claire (Mrs. Arnold Corbin)
Corcoran, Barbara Asenath
Corcoran, Eileen Lynch
Cord, Virginia Kirk Tharpe
Cordes, Loverne Christian
Cordis, Maria
Corkle, Francesca Therese
Corley, Ellen
Cormier, Ramona Theresa
Corn, Leslie Joan
Cornelius, Helen Lorene
Corrick, Ann Marjorie
Corry, Martha Lucille
Corsa, Helen Storm
Cory, Eleanor Thayer
Cossotto, Fiorenza
Costa, Mary
Costa-Greenspon, Muriel
Cotrubas, Ileana
Coughlin, Magdalen
Coupe, Irene Fay
Court, Kathryn Diana
Court, Margaret

Courtney, Gladys (Atkins)
Courtney, Jacqueline Dianna
Cousins, Jane Campbell
Cousins, Margaret
Coval, Naomi Miller
Cowen, Donna Ruth
Cowgill, Ursula Moser
Cowles, Fleur Fenton (Mrs. Tom M. Meyer)
Cowles, Milly
Crabb, Barbara Brandriff
Crabtree, Beverly June
Craig, Grace J.
Craig, Nancy Ellen
Crain, Mrs. G.D.
Crane, Barbara Bachmann
Crawford, Cheryl
Crawford, Frances Miriam
Crawford, Olga Elvera Anderson (Mrs. William John Crawford)
Crawford, Susan N. Young
Crawford-Mason, Clare Wootten
Crawley, Judith Rosemary (Mrs. F. Radford Crawley)
Crespin, Regine
Crile, Susan
Crist, Judith (Klein)
Croce, Arlene Louise
Crocker, Diane W.
Crockett, Ethel Stacy
Cromwell, Florence Stevens
Cronin, Bonnie Kathryn Lamb
Crook, Dorothy
Crosby, Elizabeth Caroline
Crosby, Joan Carew
Crosby, Kathryn Grandstaff (Grant)
Cross, Jennifer Mary (Mrs. Ellis M. Gans)
Cross, Lenora Routon
Crow, Elizabeth Smith
Crow, Jane Hanes
Crowley, Dorothy Marie
Crowley, Pat
Cruz-Romo, Gilda
Cuddy, Lucy Hon
Cudjoe, Vera Marie
Culbertson, Janet Lynn
Culbertson, Katheryn Campbell
Cullinan, Elizabeth
Culmer, Marjorie Mehne
Culver, Barbara Green
Culver, Virginia Price
Cummings, Constance
Cummings, Nancy Boucot
Cunningham, Sister Catharine Julie
Cunningham, Dorothy Jane
Cunningham, Julia Woolfolk
Cunningham, Madonna Marie
Cunningham, Marilyn Alice Eneix
Cunningham, Rosemary
Curie, Eve
Currier, Ruth
Curry, Jane Louise
Curry, Nancy Ellen
Curtin, Jane Therese
Curtin, Phyllis
Curtis, Charlotte Murray
Curtis, Doris S. Malkin
Curtis, Marcia
Curtiss, Ursula Reilly (Mrs. John Curtiss, Jr.)
Cusack, Anne Millicent
Cushman, Helen Merle Baker
Cushmore, Carole Lee
Custin, Mildred
Cuthbert, Virginia (Mrs. Philip C. Elliott)
Cutler, Lynn Germain
Czimbalmos, Magdolna Paal
DaCosta, Jacqueline
Dagenais, Camille A.
Dahl, Arlene
Dailey, Irene
Dake, Marcia Allene
Dale, Madeline Houston McWhinney
D'Alessandro, Roseanna Marie
Dalis, Irene
Dalrymple, Jean
Daly, Maggie (Mrs. Arthur Bazlen)
Dames, Joan Foster (Mrs. Urban L. Dames)
Damon, Cathryn
Dandoy, Maxima Antonio
Dandoy, Suzanne Eggleston
Danford, Ardath Anne
Danias, Starr
Daniel, Beth
Daniels, Arlene Kaplan
Daniels, Elizabeth Adams
Daniels, Myra Janco (Mrs. Draper Daniels)
Danilova, Alexandra
Danner, Blythe Katharine (Mrs. Bruce W. Paltrow)
Danner, Patsy (Pat) Ann
Danzig, Sarah H. Palfrey
Darling, Lois MacIntyre (Mrs. Louis Darling)
Daugherty, Fredrica
Davenport, Dona Lee
Davenport, Gwen (Mrs. John Davenport)
Davern, Jeanne Marguerite
Davidovich, Bella
Davidson, Joy Elaine
Davidson, Joyce
Davidson, Rita Charmatz
Davis, Ann Bradford
Davis, Bette Ruth Elizabeth

Davis, Dorothy Salisbury
Davis, Evelyn L.
Davis, Evelyn Y.
Davis, Ginia
Davis, Jacqueline Marie Vincent (Mrs. Louis Reid Davis)
Davis, Joyce Stripling
Davis, Karen Padgett
Davis, Lorraine Jensen
Davis, Lynn Etheridge
Davis, Mattie Belle Edwards
Davis, Victoria (Vicky)
Dawber, Pam
Dawes, Carol J.
Dawidowicz, Lucy S.
Dawson, Mary Ann (Mimi) Weforth
Dawson, Mary Ruth
Day, Doris (Doris von Kappelhoff)
Day, Margaret McVay
Day, Patricia Jean
Day, Wörden
Deal, William Brown
Dean, Frances Childers
Dean, Laura
Dean, Lydia Margaret Carter (Mrs. Halsey Albert Dean)
De Angelo, Ann Marie
Dearing, Audrey Traugott
De Bakey, Lois
Debs, Barbara Knowles
DeBusk, Edith M.
DeCamp, Rosemary Shirley
Décarie, Thérèse Gouin
De Crow, Karen
Decter, Midge
Dederich, Susan Russell
Dee, Ruby
Deffee, Edith Windham
deFord, Sara Whitcraft
De Gaetani, Jan
de Havilland, Olivia Mary
Dehner, Dorothy
de Kooning, Elaine
de Larrocha, Alicia De La Calle
De Lay, Dorothy (Mrs. Edward Newhouse)
Deleeuw, Dianne Margaret
Delson, Elizabeth
DeLuigi, Janice Cecilia Weil Lefton
Delza-Munson, Elizabeth
De Marr, Mary Jean
de Mille, Agnes
Denes, Agnes C.
Deneuve, Catherine (Catherine Dorleac)
Denhof, Miki
Denkhoff, Elizabeth
Denmark, Florence
Dennean, Joan Claire
Dennis, Sandy
Densen-Gerber, Judianne
Denver, Eileen Ann
de Regniers, Beatrice Schenk
Derian, Patricia Murphy
De Rivas, Carmela Foderaro
Derthick, Martha Ann
Desforges, Jane Fay
de Stwolinski, Gail Rounce Boyd
de Tornyay, Rheba
de Varon, Lorna Cooke
DeVore, Margaret Bowen
Dewar, Marion
Dewhurst, Colleen
De Witt, Joyce
De Witt-Morette, Cécile
DeYoung, Karen Jean
DeYoung, Lillian Jeanette
Diamond, Freda
Diamond, Israel
Diamond, Norma Joyce
Diamonstein, Barbaralee Dworkin
DiBerardino, Marie Antoinette
Dick, Nancy E.
Dickerman, Marion
Dickerson, Nancy Hanschman
Dickie, Helen Aird
Dickinson, Alice Braunlich
Dickinson, Angie (Angeline Brown)
Dickinson, Eleanor Creekmore
Dickson, Jennifer Joan
Dickson, Sally Isabelle
Didion, Joan
Diemer, Emma Lou
Dietrich, Marlene (Maria Magdalena von Losch)
Di Franco, Loretta Elizabeth
Dignac, Geny (Bermudez, Eugenia M.)
Dillard, Annie
Diller, Phyllis
Dillon, Diane Claire Sorber
Dillow, Nancy Elizabeth
Dimmick, Carolyn Reaber
DiMuccio, Mary Jo
Dinkins, Carol Eggert
diPrima, Diane
Dispeker, Thea
Dixon, Jeane
Dobbs, Mattiwilda
Doberstein, Audrey K.
Doering, Grace Bernardina (Mrs. John W. McCord)
Doherty, Josephine Kristan
Dolan, Mary Anne
Dole, Elizabeth Hanford
Dollard, Elizabeth
Donahey, Gertrude Walton
Donahue, Elinor

Donnelly, Marian Card
Donnelly, Marjorie Morrison (Mrs. James Ford Donnelly, Jr.)
Donneson, Seena Sand
Donoghue, Mildred Ransdorf
Doran, Ann Lee
Doris Ann (Doris Ann Scharfenberg)
Dorman, Gladys M.
Doro, Marion Elizabeth
Dorsey, Dolores Florence
Dorsey, Rhoda Mary
Douglas, Cathleen Curran Heffernan (Mrs. William O. Douglas)
Douglas, Virginia Isabel Baker
Douvan, Elizabeth
Dow, Dorothy Minerva
Downie, Dana
Downing, Joan Forman
Doyle, Charlotte Lackner (Mrs. James J. Doyle)
Doyle, Katherine Lee Lee
Drabble, Margaret (Mrs. Clive Swift)
Drake (Jurras), Sylvie
Draper, Freda
Dreben, Raya Spiegel
Dresselhaus, Mildred Spiewak
Drew, Elizabeth Heineman
Drew, Katherine Fischer
Drewno, Joanne Meta
Drexler, Rosalyn
Driscoll, Margaret Weyerhaeuser (Mrs. Walter Bridges Driscoll)
Driver, Lottie Elizabeth
Drouin, Marie-Josee
Drucker, Miriam Koontz
Drummond, Sally Hazelet
Dubofsky, Jean Eberhart
Du Bois, Ja'net
Duckert, Audrey Rosalind
Due, Jean Margaret
Duenewald, Doris Annette
Dulany, Elizabeth Gjelsness
Dulles, Eleanor Lansing
Dumas, Rhetaugh Etheldra Graves
Dumovich, Loretta
Dunaway, Faye
Dunbar, Isobel Moira
Dunbar, (Isobel) Moira
Duncan, Cynthia Beryl
Duncan, Irma Wagner
Duncan, Margaret Caroline
Duncan, Sandy
Dunham, Meneve
Dunlap, Connie
Dunlap, Marjorie Snyder
Dunmore, Charlotte Jeanette
Dunn, Helen Ashley
Dunn, Mary Maples
Dunn, Mignon
Dunnahoo, Terry (Mrs. Thomas William Dunnahoo)
Dunnock, Mildred
Dunwiddie, Charlotte
du Pré, Jacqueline
Durieux, Caroline Wogan
Dussault, Nancy Elizabeth
Dusseault, Louise Lucille
Dustan, Harriet Pearson
Duvall, Shelley
Dwan, Lois Smith
Dwyer, Jean Agnes Ferguson
Dwyer, Virginia Alice
Dwyer-Dobbin, Mary Alice
Dyatt, Betty Marie
Dyer, Sister Mary Celestine
Eady, Carol Murphy (Mrs. Karl Ernest Eady)
Earhart, Eileen Magie
Earle, Merie
Earle, Sylvia Alice
Eberhart, Mignon Good
Eberlein, Patricia James
Ebert, Joyce Anne
Eby, Helen Marie
Echelman, Shirley T.
Eckley, Grace Ester
Eckman, Fern Marja
Eddy, Darlene Mathis
Edelman, Judith Hochberg
Edelman, Marian Wright (Mrs. Peter B. Edelman)
Eden, Barbara Jean
Edinger, Lois Virginia
Edmonds, Anne Carey
Edmondson, Jeannette B.
Edmunds, Frances Ravenel
Edwards, Esther G.
Egan, Eileen Mary
Egan, Sylvia
Eglevsky, Marina
Ehlers, Kathryn Hawes (Mrs. James D. Gabler)
Ehrlich, Gertrude
Ehrlich, Susan
Eicher, Joanne Bubolz
Eickhoff, Margaret Kathryn
Eilber, Janet Susan
Einstein, Elizabeth Roboz (Mrs. Hans Albert Einstein)
Eisenberg, Barbara Anne
Eisenstein, Elizabeth Lewisohn
Eisner, Janet Margaret
Eldridge, Marie Delaney
Elias, Rosalind
Elion, Gertrude Belle
Elisar, Patricia Garside
Elizabeth II (Alexandra Mary)
Elks, Hazel Hulbert (Mrs. David Elks)
Ellerbee, Linda

Hibel, Edna (Mrs. Theodore Plotkin)
Hickey, Margaret A.
Hickey, Sister Ruth Cecelia
Hicks, Virginia Sybil Drake
Hieatt, Constance Bartlett
Hieronymus, Clara Booth Wiggins
Hiesinger, Kathryn Bloom
Higgins, Anne Volz
Higgins, Lois Lundell
Higgins, Therese
Hildebrand, Holly Cheryl
Hill, Carol DeChellis
Hill, Kathleen Louise (pen name Kay Hill)
Hill, Pamela
Hiller, Wendy
Hillis, Margaret
Hills, Carla Anderson
Hills, Patricia Gorton Schulze
Hillyer, Kazuko Tatsumura
Hilowitz, Beverley
Hilton, Alice Mary
Hilts, Margarete Louise
Himmelfarb, Gertrude (Mrs. Irving Kristol)
Himms-Hagen, Jean Margaret
Hinderas, Natalie L.
Hinerfeld, Ruth J.
Hinsvark, Inez Genieve
Hinton, S(usan) E(loise)
Hirsch, Roseann Conte
Hite, Shere D.
Hoadley, Irene Braden (Mrs. Edward Hoadley)
Hobson, Laura Zametkin
Hochstadt, Joy
Hodes, Linda
Hodges, Margaret Moore
Hodges, Mary Doris
Hodgman, Joan Elizabeth
Hoeflin, Ruth Merle
Hoffleit, (Ellen) Dorrit
Hoffman, Grace
Hoffman, Lois Wladis
Hogan, Alice Hamilton
Hogan, Ilona Modly
Hogarth, Grace Weston Allen
Holdridge, Barbara
Holgate, Jeanne
Holliday, Barbara Miriam Brooks Gregg
Holliday, Polly Dean
Hollinshead, Ariel Cahill
Holm, Celeste
Holm, Hanya
Holm, Jeanne Marjorie
Holmberg, Ruth Sulzberger
Holmes, Ann Hitchcock
Holmes, Marjorie Rose
Holt, Marjorie Sewell
Holt, Nancy Louise
Holt, Victoria
Homsey, Victorine (Mrs. Samuel E. Homsey)
Hood, Dorothy
Hooper, Edith Ferry
Hooper, Shirley
Hoopes, Janet Louise
Hoover, Helen D. (Mrs. Adrian E. Hoover)
Hopkins, Shirley Knight
Hopper, Grace Brewster Murray
Hopps, Hope Elizabeth Byrne
Horman, Elizabeth
Horn, Carol Ellen
Horn, Karen Nicholson
Hornby, Lesley (Twiggy)
Horne, Marilyn
Horner, B. Elizabeth
Horner, Matina Souretis
Horowitz, Frances Degen
Horsell, Mary Kay
Horstmann, Dorothy Millicent
Houdek, Margaret Anne (Peggy Dunlap Houdek)
Houghton, Katharine
Houlton, Lise Rane
Houlton, Loyce J.
Housser, Yvonne McKague
Hoving, Jane Pickens
Howar, Barbara Dearing
Howard, Hildegarde (Mrs. Henry Anson Wylde)
Howard, Katherine Graham (Mrs. Charles P. Howard)
Howard, Sandy
Howatson, Marianne
Howell, Barbara Thompson
Howes, Barbara
Howland, Beth
Howlett, Carolyn Chance
Howlett, Carolyn Svrluga
Howorth, Lucy Somerville
Hoyt, Mary Finch
Hoyt, Nelly Schargo (Mrs. N. Deming Hoyt)
Hubbard, Elizabeth
Huber, Sister Alberta
Huber, Joan Althaus
Hubley, Faith Elliott
Huddle, Elizabeth Marguerite
Hudson, Harriet Dufresne
Hudson, Mary
Huey, Mary Evelyn Blagg
Hufstedler, Shirley Mount (Mrs. Seth M. Hufstedler)
Huggins, Sara Espe
Hughes, Elinor Lambert
Hughes, Marija Matich
Hughes, Michaela Kelly
Hughes, Sarah Tilghman
Hughes, Sue Margaret
Hull, Suzanne White
Hultgreen, Sara Spears (Sally)
Humphrey, Lucie King
Humphrey, Muriel Fay Buck (Mrs. Hubert Horatio Humphrey)
Humphreys, Mabel Gweneth
Hunnicutt, Virginia Gayle
Hunt, Effie Neva
Hunt, Janet Elaine
Hunter, Barbara Way
Hunter, Celia Margaret
Hunter, Dorian
Hunter, Kim (Janet Cole)
Hunter, Kristin Elaine Eggleston (Mrs. John I. Lattany)
Hunter, Margaret King
Hunter Blair, Pauline Clarke
Hunting, Constance Coulter
Hussey, Ruth
Huston, Beatrice Louise
Huston, Margo
Hutchison, Dorris Jeannette
Hutchison, Kay Bailey
Hutson, Jean Blackwell (Mrs. John O. Hutson)
Hutton, Ann Hawkes
Huxtable, Ada Louise
Hyde, Isabel Emily
Hyde, Mary Morley Crapo (Mrs. Donald F. Hyde)
Hyer, Martha (Mrs. Hal Wallis)
Hylton, Hannelore Menke
Ian, Janis
Ichino, Yoko
Ilchman, Alice Stone
Impellizzeri, Irene Helen
Inez, Colette
Ingpen, Joan Mary Eileen
Ingram, Edith Jacqueline
Ireland, Jill (Jill Dorothy Ireland Bronson)
Irons, Evelyn Christine
Irvine, Louva Elizabeth
Irving, Flora Miller
Irwin, Helen Trathen
Isay, Jane Franzblau
Isham, Sheila Eaton
Istomin, Marta
Istomin, Marta
Itkin, Bella
Ittmann, Marjorie McCullough
Ives, Margaret
Jablonski, Wanda Mary
Jack, Nancy Rayford
Jacker, Corinne Litvin
Jackson, Bettina Adeline Bush (Mrs. Daniel F. Jackson)
Jackson, Denise Suzanne
Jackson, Glenda
Jackson, Hazel Brill
Jackson, Jacqueline Dougan
Jackson, Jacquelyne Johnson
Jackson, Kate
Jackson, Laura (Riding)
Jackson, Mary
Jackson, Ruth Amelia
Jackson, Sarah Jeanette
Jacobi, Eileen M.
Jacobs, Alma Smith
Jacobs, Barbara Beaman
Jacobs, Eleanor Alice
Jacobs, Helen Hull
Jacobs, Jane
Jacobs, Jody (Josephine C. Leason)
Jacobs, Sophia Yarnall
Jacobsen, Josephine Winder Boylan
Jacobson, Leslie Sari
Jacobson, Phyllis Colleen
Jaffe, Jan Paynter
Jaffe, Nora
Jaffe, Rona
Jago, Mary
Jakab, Irene
James, Carolyne Faye
James, Dorothy Buckton
James, Patricia Ann
Jameson, Dorothea
Jamison, Judith
Jancura, Elise Geraldine
Jandt, Elizabeth Carrie
Janeway, Elizabeth Hall
Janning, Mary Bernadette
Jansen, Angela Bing
Jantzen, Alice Catherine
Jaramillo, Mari-Luci
Jarratt, Mary Claiborne
Jarvik, Lissy F.
Jaudon, Valerie
Jedlicka, Judith Ann
Jenness, Phyllis
Jennings, Bojan Hamlin
Jeppson, Gabriella De Ferrari
Jesse, Mary Jane
Jewett, Emelyn Knowland
Jochum, Veronica
Johannesen, Audrey
Johanson, Ann Jeannette
Johanson, Patricia Maureen
Johnson, Betsey Lee
Johnson, Charlotte Buel
Johnson, Diane Lain
Johnson, Harriett
Johnson, Jean Elaine
Johnson, Jerry A.
Johnson, Joan D.
Johnson, Josephine Winslow (Mrs. Grant G. Cannon)
Johnson, Judith Salter
Johnson, Lady Bird (Claudia Alta Taylor) (Mrs. Lyndon Baines Johnson)
Johnson, Margaret Kathleen
Johnson, Marian Willard (Mrs. Dan R. Johnson)
Johnson, Marie-Louise Tully
Johnson, Marilyn P.
Johnson, Mary Elizabeth
Johnson, Norma Holloway
Johnson, Ruth Carter
Johnson, Verdenal Hoag
Johnson-Masters, Virginia E. (Mrs. William H. Masters)
Johnston, Ynez
Johnstone, Rose Mamelak (Mrs. Douglas Johnstone)
Jonasson, Olga
Jones, Bobette LaVelle
Jones, Carolyn
Jones, Christine Massey
Jones, Dorothy Cameron
Jones, Edith Augusta
Jones, Emily Strange
Jones, Frances Follin
Jones, Gwyneth
Jones, Hazel Lucile James
Jones, Helen Hart
Jones, Jennifer
Jones, Kathleen M.
Jones, Lois Mailou (Mrs. V. Pierre-Noel)
Jones, Margaret Eileen Zee
Jones, Mary Ellen
Jones, Muriel Kathleen
Jones, Norma Louise
Jones, Phyllis Edith
Jones, Regina Nickerson
Jones, Shirley
Jones, Shirley B.
Jones, Virginia Lacy (Mrs. E.A. Jones)
Jones. Anne Patricia
Jong, Erica Mann
Jordan, Barbara C.
Jordan, Joye Esch
Jordan, Michelle H.
Jorden, Eleanor Harz
Joseph, Geri M.
Joseph, Marjory L.
Joudry, Patricia
Jourdain, Alice Marie
Judge, Rosemary Ann
Judson, Jeannette Alexander
Jung, Doris
Junz, Helen B.
Jurney, Dorothy Misener
Just, Carolyn Royall
Kachru, Yamuna
Kael, Pauline
Kahane, Melanie
Kahl, Virginia Caroline
Kahler, Elizabeth Sartor
Kahn, Herta Hess (Mrs. Howard Kahn)
Kahn, Jenette Sarah
Kahn, Madeline Gail
Kahn, Susan Beth
Kain, Karen Alexandria
Kaish, Luise
Kalins, Dorothy
Kalisch, Beatrice Jean
Kamali, Norma
Kamar, Astrid Elaine Wennermark
Kaminsky, Alice R.
Kan, Diana Artemis Mann Shu
Kane, Carol
Kane, Katharine Daniels
Kane, Lucile Marie
Kane, Margaret Brassler
Kane, Mary Kay
Kane, Patricia Lanegran
Kanin, Fay
Kanuk, Leslie Lazar
Kaplan, Aline
Kaplan, Bernice Antoville
Kaplan, Helen Singer
Kaplan, Helene Lois
Kaplan, Margaret Lilly
Kaplan, Marilyn Flashenberg
Kaprov, Susan Lee
Karan, Donna (Faske)
Karawina, Erica
Kardas, Barbara Jean
Karl, Jean Edna
Karle, Isabella Lugoski
Karmel, Roberta S.
Karp, Barbara
Karpatkin, Rhoda Hendrick
Karsavina, Jean Faterson
Kassebaum, Nancy Landon
Kassel, Virginia Weltmer
Kaster, Barbara Jeanne
Katz, Dolores Jean
Katz, Hilda
Kaufman, Bel
Kaufman, Jane
Kaufman, Mindy F.
Kay, Herma Hill
Kaye, Evelyn Patricia (Evelyn Patricia Sarson)
Kaye, Nora (Nora Koreff)
Kaye, Sylvia Fine
Kazan, Lainie (Lainie Levine)
Keagy, Ann
Kean, Helen Elizabeth
Kearns, Janet Catherine
Kearse, Amalya Lyle
Keaton, Diane
Keeler, Ruby
Keeton, Kathy
Keith-Spiegel, Patricia Cosette
Keller, Marthe
Kellerman, Sally Claire
Kelley, Helen
Kelley, Kitty
Kelley, Patricia Helen
Kelly, Anne M.
Kelly, Aurel Maxey
Kelly, Dorothy Ann
Kelly, Lucie Stirm Young
Kelsey, Linda
Kendall, Katherine Anne
Kendzierski, Lottie Henryka
Kennan, Elizabeth Topham
Kennedy, Adrienne Lita
Kennedy, Berenice Connor (Mrs. Jefferson Kennedy, Jr.)
Kennedy, Cornelia Groefsema
Kennedy, Frances Midlam (Mrs. Joseph Conrad Kennedy)
Kennedy, Grace Harlan
Kennedy, Rose Fitzgerald (Mrs. Joseph P. Kennedy);
Kennedy, Royal
Kennedy, Ruth Lee
Kennelly, Barbara Bailey
Kent, Linda Gail
Kerbis, Gertrude Lempp
Kern, Edith
Kerr, Deborah
Kerr, Dorothy Marie Burmeister
Kerr, Jean
Kessel, Brina
Kessler, Joan F.
Key, Mary Ritchie
Keyes, Margaret Naumann
Kibre, Pearl
Kibrick, Anne
Kidder, Margot
Kidder, Priscilla
Kilberg, Barbara (Bobbie) Greene
Killam, Eva King
Killebrew, Gwendolyn
Kimball, Vera F.
Kimbrough, Emily (Emily Kimbrough Wrench)
Kimche, Leila Iris
Kimmel, Carol Frances
King, Billie Jean Moffitt
King, Carole
King, Coretta Scott (Mrs. Martin Luther King, Jr.)
King, Imogene Martina
King, Jean Sadako
King, Lyndel Irene Saunders
King, Marian
King, Nina Davis
King, Susan Bennett
King, Willard Fahrenkamp (Mrs. Edmund Ludwig King)
Kinget, G. Marian
Kingston, Maxine Hong
Kinne, Frances Bartlett
Kirby, Emily Baruch
Kirchner, Isabelle Loretta
Kirk, Colleen Jean
Kirkland, Gelsey
Kirkpatrick, Jeane Duane Jordan
Kirschstein, Ruth Lillian
Kirsten, Dorothy
Kitt, Eartha Mae
Kizer, Bernice Lichty
Kizer, Carolyn Ashley
Kizziar, Janet Wright
Klassen, Kathryn Anne
Klaw, Barbara Van Doren
Klein, Joan Dempsey
Klein, Sister M. Rosalie
Klement, Vera
Kliebhan, M(ary) Camille
Klinck, Patricia Ewasco
Klitgaard, Georgina
Kloss, Gene (Mrs. Phillips Kloss, nee Alice Geneva Glasier)
Klotzman, Dorothy Ann
Knapp, Bettina Liebowitz
Knauer, Virginia Harrington Wright (Mrs. Wilhelm F. Knauer)
Knight, Gladys (Gladys Maria)
Knoebel, Betty Lou
Knowles, Alison
Knowles, Lois Nina
Koga, Mary
Kohl, Marguerite C.
Kohler, Charlotte
Kohler, Ruth DeYoung
Kohlhorst, Gail Lewis
Kohlmeyer, Ida Rittenberg
Kohno, Toshiko
Koller, Noemie Benczer (Mrs. Earl L. Koller)
Kollmann, Hilda Hanna
Komarovsky, Mirra (Mrs. Marcus A. Heyman)
Komp, Diane Marilyn
Koner, Pauline
Konigsburg, Elaine Lobl
Konner, Joan Weiner
Konopka, Gisela Peiper (Mrs. Erhardt Paul Konopka)
Kopenhaver, Patricia Ellsworth
Koplovitz, Kay
Kopp, Harriet Green
Korda, Reva (Mrs. William Korda)
Korey, Lois Balk
Korman, Barbara
Korman, Harriet Ruth
Korsyn, Irene Hahne
Koshland, Marian Elliott
Koster, Elaine
Kovacs, Elizabeth Ann
Kovel, Terry Horvitz (Mrs. Ralph Kovel)
Kovitz, Muriel
Krafft, Julia Steven
Kraft, Lisbeth Martha
Krainik, Ardis
Kramer, Binnie Henrietta
Kramer, Jane
Krantz, Judith Tarcher
Krasner, Lee
Kraus, Sister Irene
Kraus, Lili
Kraus, Lorraine Marquardt
Krause, LaVerne Erickson
Kravitch, Phyllis A.
Kravitz, Ellen King
Krementz, Jill
Kreps, Juanita Morris (Mrs. Clifton H. Kreps, Jr.)
Krieger, Dorothy Terrace
Krohn, Albertine
Kromm, Mildred Carolyn
Krukowski, Nancy Harrow (Mrs. Jan Krukowski)
Krupansky, Blanche
Krupsak, Mary Anne
Krupska, Danya (Mrs. Ted Thurston)
Kubiak, Teresa Wojtaszek
Kubler-Ross, Elisabeth
Kuhn, Margaret (Maggie)
Kuhnen, S. Marie
Kullen, Barbara Catoggio
Kulp, Nancy Jane
Kumin, Maxine Winokur
Kundert, Alice E.
Kunin, Madeleine May
Kuntz, Marion Lucile Leathers
Kuskin, Karla
Laartz, Esther Elizabeth
LaBarge, Mary Jane
Lacayo, Carmela Gloria
Lacey, Beatrice Cates
Lach, Alma
Lachman, Marguerite Leanne
Lack, Fredell
Lacy, Edna Balz
Ladd, Cheryl (Cheryl Stoppelmoor)
La Farge, Phyllis
Lafontant, Jewel Stradford
Laing, Gertrude Mary
Laird, E. Ruth
Lamarr, Hedy (born Hedwig Keisler)
Lambert, Eleanor (Mrs. Seymour Berkson)
Lambert, Nadine Murphy
Lammel, Jeanette Osborn
LaMont, Barbara Gibson
Lamont, Rosette Clementine
Lampen, Sister Mary Joel
Lampl, Peggy Ann
Lamport, Felicia (Mrs. Benjamin Kaplan)
Lanchester, Elsa
Landau, Brooksley Elizabeth
Landau, Sybil Harriet
Landers, Ann (Mrs. Esther P. Lederer)
Landsmann, Leanna
Lane, Marilyn Edith
Lane, Nancy
Lane, Rosemary Payne
Lane, Sylvia
Lang, Mabel Louise
Lang, Margo Terzian
Lang, Martha Ann
Lang, Pearl
Langdon, Sue Ane
Lange, Hope
Langford, Anna Riggs
Lanham, Betty Bailey
Lanham, Elizabeth
Lannquist, Beverly Cecelia
Lansbury, Angela Brigid
Lansing, Sherry Lee
Lanyon, Ellen (Mrs. Roland Ginzel)
Lapointe, Renaude Marguerite
Laredo, Ruth
Larkin, June Noble
Larsen, Susan Carol
Larson, Nettabell Girard
Lashof, Joyce R. Cohen
Lasker, Mary (Mrs. Albert D. Lasker)
Lasser, Louise
Laswell, Marcia Lee
Lasswell, Mary Clyde Grayson Lubbock (Mrs. Dudley Winn Smith)
Latham, Jean Lee
Latimer, Allie B.
Lauder, Estee
Laudone, Anita Helene
Lauffer, Alice A.
Laurencelle, Patricia
Laurie, Piper (Rosetta Jacobs)
Lavin, Bernice E.
Lavin, Linda
Lavine, Thelma Zeno
Lawrence, Mary Georgene Wells (Mrs. Harding Lawrence)
Lawrence, Merloyd Ludington
Lawrence, Vera Brodsky
Lawrence, Vicki Ann
Lawry, Sylvia (Mrs. Stanley Englander)
Layman, Emma McCloy (Mrs. James W. Layman)
Leachman, Cloris
Leacock, Eleanor Burke
Lear, Evelyn
Learned, Michael
Leavitt, Joan Kazanjian
Lederer, Edith Madelon
Lederer, Marion Irvine
Lee, Audrey
Lee, Brenda
Lee, Joanna
Lee, Nelle Harper
Leek, Sybil
Leet, Mildred Robbins
Le Gallienne, Eva
Leggett, Roberta Jean (Bobbi)
Le Guin, Ursula Kroeber
Lehiste, Ilse
Lehmann, Phyllis Williams
Lehmann, Ruth Preston Miller
Leiber, Judith Maria
Leichter, Hope Jensen
Leiferman, Silvia Weiner (Mrs. Irwin H. Leiferman)
Leighton, Frances Spatz
Leighton, Gertrude Catherine Kerr
Leland, Joy Hanson
Leland, Sara (Sally Harrington)
L'Engle, Madeleine (Mrs. Hugh Franklin)
Lennon, Sister Mary Isidore
Lenz, Kay
Leon, Tania Justina
Leonard, Joanne
Leopold, Estella Bergere
Lerner, Gerda
Lesh, Janet Rountree
Lessing, Doris (May)
Lester, Virginia Laudano
Leven, Ann Ruth
Leverich, Ivamay (Dennewill)
Levin, Betsy
Levine, Naomi Bronheim
Levine, Ruth Rothenberg
Levine, Suzanne Braun
Levison, Sandra Peltz
Levit, Edithe Judith
Levy, Carol
Levy, Julia Gerwing
Lewicki, Ann Maria
Lewis, Edith Patton
Lewis, Flora
Lewis, Goldy Sarah
Lewis, Helen Phelps Hoyt
Lewis, Jessica Helen (Mrs. Jack D. Myers)
Lewis, Samella Sanders
Lewis, Shari
Lewis, Virginia Elnora
Lewitzky, Bella
Ley, Katherine Louise
Libby, Leona Marshall (Mrs. Willard Libby)
Licht, Jennifer McConnell
Lichtenberg, Margaret Klee
Lightstone, Marilyn
Ligon, Helen Hailey
Lillie, Beatrice (Lady Peel)
Lilly, Doris
Lincoln, J(eannette) Virginia
Lindbergh, Anne Spencer Morrow (Mrs. Charles Augustus Lindbergh)
Linde, Shirley Motter
Linden, Janine M.
Lindfors, Viveca
Lindh, Patricia Sullivan
Lindley, Audra
Lindsay, Vaughnie Jean
Lindt, Gillian
Link, Mae Mills (Mrs. S. Gordden Link)
Link, Marilyn Calmes
Link, Nina Beth
Lippincott, Sarah Lee
Lipscomb-Brown, Edra Evadean
Lipton, Joan Elaine
Lipton, Martha
Liston, Mary Frances
Litman, Roslyn Margolis
Little, Gretchen Dohm
Littman, Lynne
Livingston, Jane Shelton
Livingston, Mollie Parnis
Livingston, Myra Cohn
Lloyd, Kate Rand
Loar, Peggy Ann Wahl
Lobsenz, Amelia
Lochridge, Katherine
Locke, Edith Raymond
Locke, Sondra
Lockhart, Aileene Simpson
Lockhart, June
Loeblich, Helen Nina Tappan
Loeser, Norma Maine
Loewus, Helen Galland
Loggie, Jennifer Mary Hildreth
Lohr, Mary Margaret
Loman-Umbrico, Judith Ann
Long, Beverly Whitaker
Long, Helen Halter
Long, Madeleine J.
Longley, Bernique
Longley, Laura Ann
Loo, Beverly Jane
Lopata, Helena Znaniecka
Lopez, Priscilla
Lorch, Maristella De Panizza (Mrs. Edgar R. Lorch)
Lord, M. G.
Lorde, Audre Geraldin
Loren, Sophia
Loring, Gloria Jean
Lotas, Judith Patton
Lothrop, Kristin Curtis
Lotzkar, Ruth Margaret
Loudon, Dorothy
Love, Nancy
Love, Ruth B.
Love, Shirley
Low, Barbara Wharton
Lowe, Betty Ann
Lowe, Mary Johnson
Lowe, Mildred
Lowell, Juliet

Lowell, Marcia
Lowenstein, Leah Miriam Hiller
Lowrie, Jean Elizabeth
Loy, Myrna
Lubic, Ruth Watson
Lubkin, Gloria Becker
Luce, Clare Boothe
Luckey, Eleanore Braun
Ludwig, Christa
Lund, Sister Candida
Lund, Lois Ann
Lunnon, Betty Sheehan
Lupino, Ida
Lupton, Jeanne Traphagen
Lurie, Alison
Lurie, Nancy Oestreich
Luther, Marylou Jacqueline
Lyall, Katharine C(ulbert)
Lyman, Margaret Morner (Peggy)
Lynch, Beverly Pfeifer
Lynley, Carol Ann
Lynn, Janet (Janet Lynn Nowicki)
Lynn, Loretta Webb (Mrs. Oliver Lynn, Jr.)
Lynn, Naomi Burgos
Lyser, Katharine May
Lystad, Mary Hanemann (Mrs. Robert Lystad)
MacArthur, Gloria
Maccoby, Eleanor Emmons
Macdonald, Cynthia Lee
MacDonald, Flora Isabel
MacDonald, Margaret Mary
Mac Gillivray, Margaret Hilda
Mac Gowan, Mary Eugenia
MacGraw, Ali
Macht, Carol Malisoff
MacInnes, Helen (Mrs. Gilbert Highet)
MacIver, Loren
Mack, Julia Cooper
Mack, Ruth P.
MacKendrick, Lilian
MacKenzie, Gisele
Mac Kimm, Margaret (Mardie) Pontius
Mackler, Tina
MacLaine, Shirley
MacLennan, Beryce W.
MacManus, Yvonne Cristina
MacMinn, Aleene Barnes
MacNeil, Grace M. S. McKittrick (Mrs. Douglas H. MacNeil)
MacRae, Edith Krugelis (Mrs. Duncan MacRae, Jr.)
Mac Rae, Marion Bell
MacRae, Sheila Stephens
Mac Vicar, Margaret Love Agnes
Mac Watters, Virginia
Madgett, Naomi Long
Magafan, Ethel
Mahaffey, Maryann
Mahoney, Sister Colette
Mahoney, Margaret Ellerbe
Makarova, Natalia
Malamud, Phyllis Carole
Malina, Judith
Malis, Louise (Mrs. Louis A. Malis)
Mallett, Jane Dawson
Malone, Rowena James
Mamlok, Ursula
Manchester, Melissa Toni
Mandac, Evelyn Lorenzana
Mandl, Ines
Mandler, Jean Matter
Mandrell, Barbara Ann
Manes, Nella Cellini
Mangel, Margaret Wilson
Manley, Audrey Forbes
Manley, Joan A. Daniels
Mann, Jewell Russell (Mrs. John Henry Clay Mann)
Manning, Karen Nerita
Manoff, Dinah Beth
Mantell, Suzanne
Manton, Ruth McCarthy
March, Beryl Elizabeth
Marchand, Nancy
Marcuccio, Phyllis Rose
Marcus, Ruth Barcan
Marcuse, Judith Rose
Marden, Virginia McAvoy (Mrs. Orison Swett Marden)
Margulis, Lynn Alexander
Marion, Loretta Hunt
Marisol (Marisol Escobar)
Markey, Lucille Parker
Markle, Susan Meyer
Marks, Dorothy Louise Ames (Mrs. Leonard H. Marks)
Marks, Roberta Grace
Markun, Patricia Maloney (Mrs. David Joseph Markun)
Marlatt, Abby Lindsey
Marlowe, Sylvia (Mrs. Leonid Berman)
Marple, Dorothy Jane
Marr, Sally K.
Marriott, Alice Sheets (Mrs. John Willard Marriott)
Marsee, Susanne Irene
Marsh, Florence Gertrude
Marsh, Jean Lyndsey Torren
Marsh, Pamela Olive
Marshall, C. Penny
Marshall, Consuelo Bland
Marshall, Henrietta Harrison
Marshall, Jean McElroy
Marshall, Lois
Marshall, Sarah Catherine Wood (pen name Catherine Marshall)
Marsters, Ann Pierce (Mrs. Stewart S. Battles)
Marston-Scott, Mary Vesta
Martin, Agnes
Martin, Joan Callaham
Martin, Julia Mae
Martin, Lynn Morley
Martin, Marie Young
Martin, Mary
Martin, Susan Katherine
Martindell, Anne Clark
Martinson, Ida Marie
Martyl (Mrs. Alexander Langsdorf, Jr.)
Marx, Anne (Mrs. Frederick E. Marx)
Marx, Gertie Florentine
Masi, Dale A.
Mason, Helen Delaine
Mason, Jimilu
Mason, Marsha
Mason, Pamela Helen
Masters, Bettie Sue Siler
Masterson, Peggy Bell
Matarazzo, Ruth Gadbois
Matheny, Ruth Ann
Mather, Betty Bang
Mather, Katharine
Mathes, Rachel Clarke
Mathews, Carmen Sylva
Mathis, Patricia Ann
Mathis, Sharon Bell
Mattfeld, Jacquelyn Phillips Anderson
Matthews, Burnita Shelton
Matthews, Mary Jean O'Leary
Matthews, Wanda (Lee) Miller
Mauksch, Ingeborg Grosser
Maull, Flora Davis (Mrs. Baldwin Maull)
Maxwell, Carla Lena
Maxwell, Diana Louise
Maxwell, Roberta
Maxwell, Vera Huppe
May, Elaine
May, Gita
Mayne, Lucille Stringer
Mazzo, Kay
Mc Arthur, Janet Ward
Mc Atee, Patricia Anne Rooney
Mc Bride, Patricia
McBurney, Margot B.
Mc Cabe, Cynthia Jaffee
McCaffrey, Anne Inez
Mc Cambridge, Mercedes
Mc Cann, Cecile Nelken
Mc Cann, Frances Veronica
Mc Carn, Grace Hayden
Mc Carthy, Kathryn Agnes
Mc Carthy, Mary
McCarthy, Mary Frances
Mc Carty, Virginia Dill
Mc Clain, Alice
Mc Clanahan, Rue (Eddi-Rue)
McClary, Edith Mae
Mc Clellan, Barbara Lee
Mc Clellan, Carole Keeton
Mc Clellan, Catharine
McClendon, Ernestine Epps
Mc Clendon, Sarah Newcomb
Mc Cluskey, Ellen L.
Mc Cluskey, Judith
Mc Cormack, Elizabeth Jane
McCormack, Patricia Seger
Mc Cormick, Hope Baldwin (Mrs. Brooks McCormick)
Mc Cravey, Mary Alvaretta
McCrudden, Jean Anne
Mc Cue, Carolyn Moore
Mc Cullough, Helen Craig
Mc Cune, Sara Miller (Mrs. George D. McCune)
McCusker, Mary Lauretta
Mc David, Virginia Glenn
Mc Dougall, Pamela Ann
Mc Fadden, Mary Josephine
Mc Farland, Kay Eleanor
Mc Farlane, Karen Elizabeth
Mc Fate, Patricia Ann
Mc Gehee, Nan Elizabeth
Mc Gibbon, Pauline Mills
McGilley, Sister Mary Janet
McGonigal, Pearl
Mc Govern, Maureen Therese
Mc Grath, Lee Parr
Mc Greevy, Susan Brown
McGrew, Elizabeth Anne
Mc Grory, Mary
Mc Guire, Dorothy Hackett
Mc Guire, Marie C.
Mc Hale, Inez Pecore
McHugh, Helen Frances
Mc Ilwaine, Ellen
Mc Intyre, Doris Carter
Mc Intyre, Jane O'Neill Mahady
Mc Intyre, Vonda Neel
McKaig, Dianne L.
Mc Kee, Fran
Mc Kelvey, Jean Trepp
McKelvey, Judith Grant
Mc Kenna, Adrienne Delores
Mc Kenna, Marian Cecilia
McKillop, Lucille
McKown, Roberta Ellen
Mc Laughlin, Ann Dore
Mc Laughlin, Emily
Mc Laughlin, Kathleen
Mc Loughlin, Ellen Veronica
McMaster, Juliet Sylvia
Mc Mullan, Dorothy
Mc Murry, Idanelle Sam
Mc Nair, Barbara
McNamee, Catherine
Mc Neil, Claudia Mae
Mc Nichol, Kristy
Mc Nutt, Dolly Hite
Mc Pherson, Alice Ruth
McPherson, Mary Patterson
McQuary, Joan Susan
Mc Quillan, Margaret Mary
Mc Quown, O. Ruth
Mc Vie, Christine Perfect
McWethy, Patricia Joan
Mc Williams, Margaret Ann
Meade, Julia (Mrs. Oliver Worsham Rudd, Jr.)
Meadow, Lynne (Carolyn) Elizabeth
Meadow, Phyllis Whitcomb
Meadows, Audrey
Meadows, Jayne
Meagher, Cyndi (Cynthia Nash Maza)
Means, Marianne
Meara, Anne
Medina, Kathryn Bach
Medsger, Betty Louise
Meehan, Paula Kent
Meggers, Betty J(ane)
Meldrum, Barbara Ruth Howard
Mellink, Machteld Johanna
Mello, Judy Hendren
Melton, Nancy Lopez
Mengers, Sue
Mensinger, Peggy Boothe
Mentschikoff, Soia
Menzel, Mary Margaret Young
Mercer, Marian
Mercouri, Melina (Maria Amalia)
Mereness, Dorothy Ann
Merivale, Patricia
Meriwether, Lee
Merman, Ethel
Merriam, Eve
Merrill, Dina (Mrs. Cliff Robertson)
Merrill, Jean Fairbanks
Merritt, Doris Honig
Merritt, Evelyn Caroline
Mertins, Christa
Mesrobian, Arpena Sachaklian
Messac, Magali Ernestine Josephine
Messick, Dale
Metz, Mary Clare
Meyer, Helen (Mrs. Abraham J. Meyer)
Meyer, Janet Katherine
Meyer, Kerstin
Meyer, Margaret Eleanor
Meyer, Sandra W.
Meyer, Susan E.
Meyers, Dale (Mrs. Mario Cooper)
Michel, Mary Ann Kedzuf
Michels, Agnes Kirsopp Lake (Mrs. Walter C. Michels)
Michelson, Gertrude Geraldine
Mickiewicz, Ellen Propper
Midler, Bette
Mikulski, Barbara Ann
Mikulsky, Joan Marilyn
Mikus, Eleanore Ann
Milam, Evelyn Louise
Miles, Jeanne Patterson
Miles, Joanna
Miles, Josephine
Miles, Vera
Miles, Virginia
Millar, Margaret Ellis
Millar, Sally Gray
Miller, Angela
Miller, Ann (Lucille Ann Collier)
Miller, Beverly White
Miller, Elizabeth Cavert
Miller, Florence Lowden (Mrs. C. Phillip Miller)
Miller, Harriet Evelyn
Miller, Hope Ridings
Miller, Irma Ganz
Miller, Jacqueline Winslow
Miller, Joan Vita
Miller, Jody
Miller, Joyce Dannen
Miller, Linda B.
Miller, Linda Kay
Miller, Sister Mary Aquin
Miller, Mildred
Miller, Ruby Sills
Mills, Carrol
Mills, Frances Jones
Mills, Margaret Mary Howard
Mills-Fischer Shirley Collum
Milner, Brenda Atkinson Langford
Mink, Patsy Takemoto
Minnelli, Liza
Minnich, Virginia
Minow, Josephine Baskin
Minton, Yvonne Fay
Mirabella, Grace
Mirsky, Jeannette
Mitchell, Andrea Louise
Mitchell, Joan
Mitchell, Joni (Roberta Joan Anderson)
Mitchell, Josephine Margaret (Mrs. Lowell Schoenfeld)
Mitchell, Julia L.
Mitchell, Leona Pearl
Mitchell-Bateman, Mildred
Mitford, Jessica
Model, Lisette
Moffatt, Joyce A.
Moffatt, Katy (Katherine Louella)
Moffo, Anna
Mofford, Rose
Molitor, Sister Margaret Anne
Molloy, Julia Sale
Mommsen, Katharina
Monaghan, Eileen
Mondale, Joan Adams
Monk, Meredith Jane
Monsen, Elaine Ranker
Monson, Karen Ann
Montana, Patsy (Mrs. Paul Edward Rose)
Montgomery, Belinda J.
Montgomery, Elizabeth
Montgomery, Ruth Shick
Moog, Florence Emma
Moon, Marjorie Ruth
Mooneyhan, Esther Louise
Moore, Sister Anne Joachim
Moore, Dorotha (Mrs. Collis P. Moore)
Moore, Dorothy Marie
Moore, Edythe
Moore, Jane Ross
Moore, Joanne Iweita
Moore, Sister Marie
Moore, Mary Tyler
Moore, Melba
Moore, Ruth
Moorhead, Jennelle Vandevort
Moorman, Kay
Moran, Angela Clare
Moran, Juliette M.
Morani, Alma Dea
Morath, Inge
Morawetz, Cathleen Synge
Mordine, Shirley Macaulay
Moreno, Rita
Morgan, Beverly Carver
Morgan, Elizabeth
Morgan, Hazel Nohavec
Morgan, Jane Hale
Morgan, Jaye P.
Morgan, Marabel
Morgan, Norma Gloria
Morgenthau, Ruth Schachter
Morini, Erica
Morris, Joan Clair
Morris, Mary Elizabeth
Morrison, Chloe Anthony (Toni Morrison)
Morrison, Shelley
Morrow, Joyce Knoedler
Morse, Cynthia Brown
Morse, Eugenia Maude
Morton, Margaret Louise
Moss, Karen Canner
Motley, Constance Baker (Mrs. Joel Wilson Motley)
Motto, Anna Lydia (Mrs. John R. Clark)
Mount, Ward
Mountcastle, Katharine Babcock
Mudd, Emily Hartshorne
Mueller, Betty Jeanne
Mueller, Melva L.
Muhlert, Jan Keene
Muir, Gloria Ludwig
Muldaur, Diana Charlton (Mrs. James Mitchell Vickery)
Muldaur, Maria
Mulgrew, Kate
Mullen, Buell (Mrs. J. Bernard Mullen)
Muller, Charlotte Feldman
Muller, Jennifer
Mumford, Emily Hamilton
Munro, Alice
Munzer, Cynthia Brown
Murdoch, (Jean) Iris
Murphey, Vera Edna Randle
Murphy, Anne Marie
Murphy, Betty Jane Southard (Mrs. Cornelius F. Murphy)
Murphy, Diana E.
Murphy, Geraldine Joanne
Murphy, Irene Ellis
Murphy, Janet Gorman
Murphy, Marion Isabel
Murphy, Rosemary
Murray, Anne
Murray, Constance Ann
Murray, Elizabeth
Murray, Florence Kerins
Murray, Joan Elizabeth
Murray, Kathryn Hazel
Murray, Pauli
Murray, Peg
Muse, Martha Twitchell
Musgrave, Thea
Myer, Elizabeth Gallup
Myers, Beverlee Ann Reardan
Myers, Frances
Myers, Sarah Kerr
Myerson, Bess
Narisi, Stella Maria
Narodick, Sally G.
Nash, Katherine Elizabeth
Navratilova, Martina
Neal, Patricia
Neary, Colleen
Neblett, Carol
Nee, Sister Mary Coleman
Nef, Evelyn Stefansson
Neff, Francine Irving (Mrs. Edward John Neff)
Neil, LaVerne
Neilson, Elizabeth Anastasia
Nelson, Dorothy Wright (Mrs. James F. Nelson)
Nelson, Harriet Hilliard
Nelson, Katherine Greacen
Nemeth, Charlan Jeanne
Nemeth, Kathleen Nanette Lucas
Ness, Evaline (Mrs. Arnold A. Bayard)
Nestmann-Hushion, Jacqueline Inez
Nesvold, Betty Anne Krambuhl
Nettleton, Lois
Neuberger, Katherine (Mrs. Harry H. Neuberger)
Neugarten, Bernice Levin
Neustadt, Barbara Mae
Nevelson, Louise
Neville, Emily Cheney
Neville, Phoebe
New, Maria Iandolo
Newell, Barbara Warne
Newhouse, Nancy Riley
Newman, Amy Donna
Newman, Joyce Kligerman
Newman, Laraine
Newman, Muriel Kallis Steinberg
Newman, Rachel
Newman-Gordon, Pauline
Newton-John, Olivia
Nicholas, Nancy
Nichols, Kyra
Nichtern, Claire Joseph (Mrs. Herbert Kallem)
Nickerson, Dorothy
Nickerson, Eileen Tressler
Nickerson, Ruth
Nicks, Stevie
Nida, Jane Bolster (Mrs. Dow Hughes Nida)
Nidetch, Jean
Nies, Helen Wilson
Nilsson, Birgit
Nishitani, Martha
Niska, Maralin
Nixon, Agnes Eckhardt
Nixon, Marni
Nixon, Thelma Catherine Patricia Ryan (Mrs. Richard M. Nixon)
Nochlin, Linda
Nodine-Zeller, Doris Eulalia
Noether, Emiliana Pasca
Noggle, Anne
Nolan, Kathleen
Nolte, Judith Ann
Norman, Jessye
Norris, Carole Veronica
North, Helen Florence
North, Judy
Norton, Andre Alice
Norton, Eunice
Norton-Taylor, Judy
Novak, Barbara
Novak, Kim (Marilyn Novak)
Nover, Naomi (Goll)
Nugent, Nelle
Nurss, Joann Ruth
Nyro, Laura
Oakar, Mary Rose
Oates, Joyce Carol
Obolensky, Marilyn Wall (Mrs. Serge Oblensky)
Obraztsova, Elena
O'Brien, Jeanne Dufour
O'Brien, Margaret (Angela Maxine O'Brien)
O'Brien, Mary Elizabeth
O'Brien, Rosanne P.
O'Connor, Elizabeth
O'Connor, Sister George Aquin (Margaret M.)
O'Connor, Mary Consolata
O'Connor, Sandra Day
Odell, Mary Jane
O'Donnell, Alice Louise
O'Donnell, Sister Miriam Teresa
Oettinger, Katherine Brownell
O'Flaherty, Wendy Doniger
Ogden, Leslie Davis
O'Gorman, Helen Fowler
O'Hair, Madalyn Mays (Mrs. Richard Franklin O'Hair)
O'Hare, Sister Jeanne d'Arc
O'Hern, Jane Susan
O'Keeffe, Georgia
O'Koren, Marie Louise
Okun, Barbara Frank
Olander, Linda Marie Piskorski
Olds, Elizabeth
Olesen, Virginia Lee
Olinsky, Tosca (Mrs. Charles F. Barteau)
Oliphant, Betty
Oliver, Charlotte Elizabeth
Oliver, Edith
Oliver, Mary
Oliver, Mary Wilhelmina
Olivero, Magda
Oliveros, Pauline
Olkowska, Krystyna Maria Nardelli
Oller, Anna Kathryn
Olmsted, Mildred Scott (Mrs. Allen Seymour Olmsted, II)
Olsen, Neva Foster
Olsen, Tillie
Olson, Jane Virginia
Omang, Joanne Brenda
O'Nan, Martha
Onassis, Jacqueline Bouvier Kennedy (Mrs. Aristotle Onassis)
O'Neal, Tatum
O'Neil, Kitty Linn
O'Neill, Jennifer Lee
Oppenheimer, Jane Marion
Ordin, Andrea Sheridan
Ordover, Sondra T.
Orgebin-Crist, Marie-Claire
O'Roark, Sarah Ann (Mrs. Thomas L. O'Roark)
Osborn, June Elaine
Osborn, Mary Jane Merten
Osborn, Stellanova (born Stella Brunt)
Osby, Larissa Geiss
Osfield, Leona Rita
O'Shea, Lynne Edeen
Osmer, Margaret
Osmond, Marie
Oster, Rose Marie Gunhild
Osterwald, Bibi (Margaret Virginia Osterwald)
Ostrander, Nancy
Ostry, Sylvia
Otto, Jean Hammond
Otto, Margaret Amelia
Overstreet, Bonaro Wilkinson
Overton, Jane Vincent Harper
Owen, Lynn Rasmussen
Owens, Rochelle
Owings, Margaret Wentworth
Oxley, Geraldine Motta
Ozick, Cynthia
Ozonoff, Ida (Mrs. Jacob B. Ozonoff)
Pace, Norma
Packer, Katherine Helen
Page, Eleanor
Page, Geraldine
Page, Patti
Page, Ruth
Pagels, Elaine Hiesey
Paglio, Lydia Elizabeth
Painter, Mary Ella
Paley, Grace
Palm, Nancy Jane
Palmer, Alice Eugenia
Palmer, Hazel
Palmer, Irene Sabelberg
Palmer, Lilli
Palmer, Margaret Frances
Palmer, Sandra Jean
Palmeri, Frances Knight
Panaccio, Madeleine
Panov, Valery
Paolucci, Anne
Papalia-Finlay, Diane Ellen
Papas, Irene
Paquette, Sister Gilberte
Parch, Grace Dolores
Parent, Judith Ellen
Paris, Dorothy
Parish, Betty Waldo
Parish, Margaret Cecile
Parker, Ann (Ann Parker Neal)
Parker, Mary Evelyn
Parker, Olivia
Parkins, Barbara
Parkinson, Elizabeth Bliss
Parkinson, Ethelyn Minerva
Parks, Madelyn N.
Parsons, Betty Pierson
Parsons, Estelle
Parsons, Harriet Oettinger
Parton, Dolly Rebecca
Pascasio, Anne
Pate, Martha B. Lucas (Mrs. Maurice Pate)
Patenaude-Yarnell, Joan
Paterson, Katherine Womeldorf
Paterson, Sheena
Patman, Jean Elizabeth
Patrick, Ruth (Mrs. Charles Hodge)
Patten, Bebe Harrison
Patterson, Elizabeth Chambers
Patterson, Mary Marvin Breckinridge (Mrs. Jefferson Patterson)
Pattishall, Beverly Wyckliffe
Pauley, Gay
Pauley, Jane
Paulus, Norma Jean Petersen
Payne, Rose M.
Payton, Carolyn Robertson
Payton-Wright, Pamela
Peacock, Mary Willa
Peale, Ruth Stafford (Mrs. Norman Vincent Peale)
Pearl, Minnie (Sarah Ophelia Colley Cannon)
Pearsall, Marion
Peaslee, Margaret Mae Hermanek
Peck, Ellen
Peck, Maryly VanLeer
Peck, Theresa
Peden, Irene Carswell
Peden, Katherine Graham
Peirce, Carol Marshall
Pellegrini, Anna Maria
Pelswick, Rose
Penalba, Alicia
Pendleton, Barbara Jean
Penniman, Clara
Pentland, Barbara Lally
Pepper, Beverly
Pepperdene, Margaret Williams
Percas de Ponseti, Helena
Peretti, Elsa
Perkins, Jean Ashmead
Perloff, Marjorie Gabrielle
Perrin, Gail
Perrine, Valerie
Perry, Erma Jackson McNeil
Perry, Evelyn Louise
Perry, Jacquelin
Perry, Yvonne Scruggs
Pescow, Donna Gail
Pesmen, Sandra (Mrs. Harold William Pesmen)